BUTTERWC
INSOLVENC
HANDBOOK

Twentieth edition

Editors

GLEN DAVIS QC

MARCUS HAYWOOD

LexisNexis®

Members of the LexisNexis Group worldwide

United Kingdom	RELX (UK) Limited trading as LexisNexis, 1–3 Strand, London WC2N 5JR and 9–10 St Andrew Square, Edinburgh EH2 2AF.
Australia	Reed International Books Australia Pty Ltd trading as LexisNexis, Chatswood, New South Wales
Austria	LexisNexis Verlag ARD Orac GmbH & Co KG, Vienna
Benelux	LexisNexis Benelux, Amsterdam
Canada	LexisNexis Canada, Markham, Ontario
China	LexisNexis China, Beijing and Shanghai
France	LexisNexis SA, Paris
Germany	LexisNexis GmbH, Dusseldorf
Hong Kong	LexisNexis Hong Kong, Hong Kong
India	LexisNexis India, New Delhi
Italy	Giuffrè Editore, Milan
Japan	LexisNexis Japan, Tokyo
Malaysia	Malayan Law Journal Sdn Bhd, Kuala Lumpur
New Zealand	LexisNexis New Zealand Ltd, Wellington
Singapore	LexisNexis Singapore, Singapore
South Africa	LexisNexis, Durban
USA	LexisNexis, Dayton, Ohio

Published by LexisNexis
This is a Butterworths title

A CIP Catalogue record for this book is available from the British Library.

ISBN for this volume: 978 1 4743 0761 1

Printed and bound by CPI Group (UK) Ltd, Croydon, CR0 4YY

Visit LexisNexis at www.lexisnexis.co.uk

PREFACE

This twentieth edition of this Handbook incorporates the changes to the insolvency regimes in England and Wales and in Scotland since the last edition was published in 2017 including the following:

- Amendments brought about by the Insolvency (Miscellaneous Amendments) Regulations 2017 to, amongst other things, the Limited Liability Partnerships Regulations 2001, the Insolvent Partnerships Order 1994, and the Administration of Insolvent Estates of Deceased Persons Order 1986, in order to bring them into line with the insolvency procedures that apply to other entities
- Amendments brought about by the Insolvency Amendment (EU 2015/848) Regulations 2017 to make insolvency legislation compatible with the recast Regulation (EU) 2015/848 on insolvency proceedings
- Amendments to the Directive of the European Parliament and of the Council 2014/59/EU (establishing a framework for the recovery and resolution of credit institutions and investment firms) made by Directive 2017/2399 of 12 December 2017
- Relevant insolvency related provisions of the Risk Transformation Regulations 2017, which concern Insurance Linked Securities businesses
- Relevant insolvency related provisions of the Technical and Further Education Act 2017
- The Alteration of Judicial Titles (Registrar in Bankruptcy of the High Court) Order 2018
- Changes brought about by the Insolvency (England and Wales) and Insolvency (Scotland) (Miscellaneous and Consequential Amendments) Rules 2017 and the Insolvency (England and Wales) Rules 2016 (Consequential Amendments and Savings) Rules 2017.

The book comprises the following Parts:

Part 1—Insolvency Act 1986
Part 2—Transitional Provisions
Part 3—EU and International Materials and Domestic Legislation Implementing EU Directives
Part 4—Company Directors Disqualification Act 1986
Part 5—Bankruptcy (Scotland) Acts 1985, 1993 and 2016
Part 6—Insolvency (England and Wales) Rules 2016
Part 7—Special Insolvency Regimes: England and Wales (relevant primary legislation and statutory instruments)
Part 8—General Insolvency Statutory Instruments: England and Wales
Part 9—Statutory Instruments relating to Corporate Insolvency: England and Wales
Part 10—Statutory Instruments relating to Partnership Insolvency: England and Wales
Part 11—Statutory Instruments relating to Personal Insolvency: England and Wales
Part 12—Statutory Instruments relating to Official Receivers and Insolvency Practitioners: England and Wales
Part 13—Statutory Instruments relating to Cross-Border Insolvency: England and Wales
Part 14—Statutory Instruments relating to Directors Disqualification: England and Wales
Part 15—Insolvency (Scotland) Rules 1986
Part 16—Other Statutory Instruments: Scotland
Part 17—Miscellaneous Acts
Part 18—Miscellaneous Statutory Instruments
Part 19—Practice Directions

This Handbook follows the standard style for Butterworths Handbooks, with amendments made by new legislation incorporated into the text of existing legislation. The notes which follow a provision detail the changes that have been made to the text and list any prospective amendments. In the text:

— an ellipsis (. . .) indicates that text has been repealed or revoked (or is outside the scope of this Handbook);
— square brackets denote text that has been inserted or substituted;

— *italicised* text is prospectively repealed or substituted, or repealed subject to savings.

The statutes reproduced in Parts 1, 4, 5 and 17 incorporate all the amendments which have been made to those statutes to date. Where relevant, the notes reflect the previous state of the legislation.

Part 2 isolates the applicable transitional provisions for England, Wales and Scotland in primary and secondary legislation where these are of particular relevance.

Part 3 includes relevant EU Directives and Regulations, as amended, and where relevant the legislation implementing them in the UK.

Part 6 contains the Insolvency (England and Wales) Rules 2016.

Part 7 collates the relevant primary legislation and statutory instruments relating to special insolvency regimes in England and Wales. These are grouped together in the following sections: Air Traffic, Banks, Building Societies, Contractual Schemes, Energy Companies, Energy Supply Companies, Friendly Societies, Health, Housing, Co-operative and Community Benefit Societies and Credit Unions, Financial Infrastructure Systems, Insurance Companies, Insurers and Insurance Linked Securities, Investment Banks, Open-ended Investment Companies, Postal, Public Private Partnership, Railways, Technical and Further Education and Water Industry.

Parts 8 to 16 contain insolvency-related statutory instruments as they are currently in force, and continue to include the full text of revoked statutory instruments where this is considered likely to be helpful. Parts 15 and 16 contain materials relevant to Scotland.

Part 8 contains general insolvency statutory instruments (which are not included within Part 7) and Part 9 contains statutory instruments relating to corporate insolvency (which are not included within Part 7).

Part 10 contains statutory instruments relating to the insolvency of partnerships: the Insolvent Partnerships Order 1994 (as amended); and the Limited Liability Partnerships Regulations 2001 (as amended).

Part 11 contains statutory instruments relating to personal insolvency.

Part 12 contains statutory instruments relating to Official Receivers and insolvency practitioners.

Part 13 groups together statutory instruments relevant to cross-border insolvency.

Part 14 assembles the statutory instruments relating to the directors disqualification regime.

Part 15 contains the Insolvency (Scotland) Rules 1986, as amended, and Part 16 contains insolvency statutory instruments relating to Scotland.

Parts 17 and 18 contain a selection of other primary and secondary legislation for England and Wales which is of importance for insolvency. Part 17 contains primary legislation, not included within Part 7. Similarly, Part 18 contains other relevant secondary legislation not included within Part 7.

Applicable Practice Directions and Practice Notes are to be found in Part 19.

My colleague in Chambers, Marcus Haywood, continues as the junior editor of the Handbook. I am grateful to the Hon Lord Drummond Young of the Scottish Bench for his invaluable assistance with the selection of Scottish materials for inclusion over these many years. I would also like to thank the editorial team at LexisNexis for all their diligence and assistance in turning this edition around so quickly.

We have done our best to take into account all relevant changes to primary and secondary legislation up to 6 April 2018, and later changes have also been included wherever possible.

In particular, note that this edition includes the Insolvency Practice Direction published on 25 April 2018. The Practice Direction was included at the last possible minute before the Handbook was printed. Consequently, there are no references to it in the index to this edition. Note also, that the Practice Directions that it replaces, have not been removed from this edition.

GLEN DAVIS QC

3–4 South Square
Gray's Inn
12 April 2018

CONTENTS

Preface page v

PART 1 INSOLVENCY ACT 1986

Insolvency Act 1986 .... **[1.1]**
Insolvency Act 1986 Derivation Table .... **[1.601]**
Insolvency Act 1986 Destination Table .... **[1.602]**
Insolvency Act 1986 Comparative Table .... **[1.603]**

PART 2 TRANSITIONAL PROVISIONS

Insolvency Act 2000 (Commencement No 1 and Transitional Provisions) Order 2001, SI 2001/766 .... **[2.1]**
Insolvency Act 2000 (Commencement No 3 and Transitional Provisions) Order 2002, SI 2002/2711 .... **[2.4]**
Enterprise Act 2002, ss 248(3)–(5), 249, 254, 255, 256(2), 261(7)–(10), 266(3)–(5), 268, 270(2), 279–281, Sch 17, para 1, Sch 19 .... **[2.9]**
Insolvency (Amendment) Rules 2003, SI 2003/1730 (Note).......... **[2.23]**
Enterprise Act 2002 (Commencement No 4 and Transitional Provisions and Savings) Order 2003, SI 2003/2093, arts 1–8 .... **[2.24]**
Insolvency (Scotland) Amendment Rules 2003, SI 2003/2111, rr 1, 2, 7 .... **[2.32]**
Insolvency (Amendment) Rules 2004, SI 2004/584 (Note).......... **[2.35]**
Insolvency (Amendment) Rules 2005, SI 2005/527 (Note).......... **[2.36]**
Insolvency Proceedings (Fees) (Amendment) Order 2006, SI 2006/561, arts 1, 3, 6 .... **[2.37]**
Insolvent Partnerships (Amendment) Order 2006, SI 2006/622, arts 1, 2 .... **[2.40]**
Insolvency (Scotland) Amendment Rules 2006, SI 2006/734, rr 1, 2 .... **[2.42]**
Insolvency (Amendment) Rules 2006, SI 2006/1272 (Note).......... **[2.44]**
Insolvency Proceedings (Fees) (Amendment) Order 2007, SI 2007/521, arts 1, 4 .... **[2.45]**
Insolvency Proceedings (Fees) (Amendment) Order 2008, SI 2008/714, arts 1, 3 .... **[2.47]**
Bankruptcy and Diligence etc (Scotland) Act 2007 (Commencement No 3, Savings and Transitionals) Order 2008, SSI 2008/115, arts 1, 2, 5–10, 15 .... **[2.49]**
Insolvency (Amendment) Rules 2008, SI 2008/737 (Note).......... **[2.58]**
Bankruptcy and Diligence etc (Scotland) Act 2007 (Commencement No 4, Savings and Transitionals) Order 2009, SSI 2009/67, arts 1, 2, 5, 6 .... **[2.59]**
Insolvency (Amendment) Rules 2009, SI 2009/642 (Note).......... **[2.63]**
Insolvency Proceedings (Fees) (Amendment) Order 2009, SI 2009/645, arts 1–3, 7 .... **[2.64]**
Companies Act 2006 (Consequential Amendments, Transitional Provisions and Savings) Order 2009, SI 2009/1941, arts 1, 2, 8, 9, 11, Sch 1, para 84 .... **[2.68]**
Insolvency (Amendment) (No 2) Rules 2009, SI 2009/2472 (Note).......... **[2.74]**
Legislative Reform (Insolvency) (Miscellaneous Provisions) Order 2010, SI 2010/18, arts 1, 12 .... **[2.75]**
Insolvency (Amendment) Rules 2010, SI 2010/686 (Note).......... **[2.77]**
Insolvency (Scotland) Amendment Rules 2010, SI 2010/688, rr 1, 2, 4–6 .... **[2.78]**
Insolvency Proceedings (Fees) (Amendment) Order 2010, SI 2010/732, arts 1, 2, 8 .... **[2.83]**
Insolvency (Amendment) (No 2) Rules 2010, SI 2010/734 (Note).......... **[2.86]**
Insolvency (Amendment) Rules 2011, SI 2011/785 (Note).......... **[2.87]**
Bankruptcy and Debt Advice (Scotland) Act 2014 (Commencement No 2, Savings and Transitionals) Order 2014, SSI 2014/261.......... **[2.88]**
Insolvency Amendment (EU 2015/848) Regulations 2017, SI 2017/702.......... **[2.100]**

PART 3 EU AND INTERNATIONAL MATERIALS AND DOMESTIC LEGISLATION IMPLEMENTING EU DIRECTIVES

UNCITRAL Model Law on Cross-Border Insolvency ....**[3.2]**
Directive of the European Parliament and of the Council 2000/12/EC relating to the taking up and pursuit of the business of credit institutions (extract) (Banking Consolidation Directive)..**[3.34]**
Council Regulation 1346/2000/EC on insolvency proceedings (Insolvency Regulation)..**[3.36]**
Insolvency Act 2000, s 14 ....**[3.87]**
Council Directive 2001/17/EC on the reorganisation and winding-up of insurance undertakings (Insurance Reorganisation & Winding-up Directive) .... **[3.88]**
Insurers (Reorganisation and Winding Up) Regulations 2003, SI 2003/1102 (Note)..**[3.123]**
Insurers (Reorganisation and Winding Up) Regulations 2004, SI 2004/353 ....**[3.124]**
Directive of the European Parliament and of the Council 2001/24/EC on the reorganisation and winding up of credit institutions (Credit Institutions Reorganisation & Winding-up Directive) ....**[3.176]**
Credit Institutions (Reorganisation and Winding Up) Regulations 2004, SI 2004/1045 ....**[3.213]**
Council Regulation 2157/2001/EC on the Statute for a European company (SE) (European Company Statute), Preamble (para (20)), Arts 7, 10, 63–66 ...**[3.262]**
Directive of the European Parliament and of the Council 2002/47/EC on financial collateral arrangements (Financial Collateral Arrangements Directive) ....**[3.268]**
Financial Collateral Arrangements (No 2) Regulations 2003, SI 2003/3226 .... **[3.283]**
Cross-Border Insolvency Regulations 2006, SI 2006/1030 ....**[3.302]**
European Parliament and Council Regulation 1082/2006/EC on a European grouping of territorial cooperation (EGTC) (European Grouping of Territorial Cooperation Regulation) ....**[3.329]**
Directive of the European Parliament and of the Council 2008/94/EC on the protection of employees in the event of the insolvency of their employer (Insolvency Directive) .... **[3.340]**
Directive of the European Parliament and of the Council 2009/138/EC on the taking-up and pursuit of the business of Insurance and Reinsurance (Solvency II), recitals 1–3, 105, 117–130, Arts 1–13, 136–143, 160–161, 194, 267–296, 309, 311, 312 ....**[3.361]**
Directive of the European Parliament and of the Council 2014/59/EU.............. **[3.418]**
European Grouping of Territorial Cooperation Regulations 2015, SI 2015/1493, regs 1-2, 6, 8, 10 ....**[3.541]**
Regulation of the European Parliament and of the Council on insolvency proceedings (recast) (2015/848/EU)..**[3.546]**

PART 4 COMPANY DIRECTORS DISQUALIFICATION ACT 1986

Company Directors Disqualification Act 1986 ....**[4.1]**
Company Directors Disqualification Act 1986 Derivation Table ....**[4.58]**
Company Directors Disqualification Act 1986 Destination Table ....**[4.59]**

PART 5 BANKRUPTCY (SCOTLAND) ACTS

Bankruptcy (Scotland) Act 1985 ....**[5.1]**
Bankruptcy (Scotland) Act 1993, ss 9, 10, 12 ....**[5.192]**
Bankruptcy (Scotland) Act 2016 ....**[5.195]**

PART 6 INSOLVENCY RULES

Insolvency Rules 1986, SI 1986/1925 (Note)..**[6.1]**
Insolvency (England and Wales) Rules 2016, SI 2016/1024..**[6.2]**
Insolvency (England and Wales) Rules 2016 (Consequential Amendments and Savings) Rules 2017, SI 2017/369, rr 1, 3..**[6.946]**

PART 7 SPECIAL INSOLVENCY REGIMES—ENGLAND AND WALES

A Air Traffic

Transport Act 2000, ss 26–33, 275, 279, 280, Schs 1–3 .... **[7.1]**

B Banks

Banks (Administration Proceedings) Order 1989, SI 1989/1276 .... **[7.16]**
Banks (Former Authorised Institutions) (Insolvency) Order 2006, SI 2006/3107 .... **[7.21]**
Banking Act 2009, ss 7, 89K, 90–122, 127, 129, 129A, 135–145, 168, 232–236, 263–265 .... **[7.25]**
Banking Act 2009 (Parts 2 and 3 Consequential Amendments) Order 2009, SI 2009/317 .... **[7.84]**
Bank Insolvency (England and Wales) Rules 2009, SI 2009/356 .... **[7.93]**
Bank Administration (England and Wales) Rules 2009, SI 2009/357 .... **[7.386]**

C Building Societies

Building Societies Act 1986, ss 86–92, 125, 126, Schs 15, 15A .... **[7.449]**
Banking Act 2009, ss 130, 158, 259(1) .... **[7.471]**
Building Societies (Insolvency and Special Administration) Order 2009, SI 2009/805, arts 1, 3, 16–18, Schs 1, 2 .... **[7.474]**
Building Society Special Administration (England and Wales) Rules 2010, SI 2010/2580 .... **[7.483]**
Building Society Insolvency (England and Wales) Rules 2010, SI 2010/2581 .... **[7.546]**

D Contractual Schemes

Financial Services and Markets Act 2000, s 235A .... **[7.832]**
Collective Investment in Transferable Securities (Contractual Scheme) Regulations 2013, SI 2013/1388, regs 1, 2, 17, 19, Schs 2–5........................ **[7.833]**

E Energy Companies

Energy Act 2004, ss 110A, 110B, 154–171, 196, 198, Schs 20, 21 .... **[7.849]**
Energy Administration Rules 2005, SI 2005/2483 .... **[7.874]**

F Energy Supply Companies

Energy Act 2011, ss 94–96, 98–102, 120–122 .... **[7.1063]**
Energy Supply Company Administration Rules 2013, SI 2013/1046 .... **[7.1074]**

G Friendly Societies

Friendly Societies Act 1992, ss 1, 19–26, 126, Sch 10 .... **[7.1284]**

H Health

National Health Service Act 2006, ss 25, 33, 35–37, 39, 65A–65D, 65DA, 65F–65O, 277, 278 .... **[7.1298]**
Health and Social Care Act 2012, ss 61–71, 81–100, 128–137, 148–150, 304, 306, 308, 309 .... **[7.1326]**

I Housing

Housing and Planning Act 2016, ss 95–117, 216, 217, Sch 5.......................... **[7.1374]**

J Co-operative and Community Benefit Societies and Credit Unions

Enterprise Act 2002, s 255.. **[7.1402]**
Co-operative and Community Benefit Societies Act 2014, ss 1, 2, 65, 66, 118–126, 134–136, 149, 150, 152–155 .... **[7.1403]**
Co-operative and Community Benefit Societies and Credit Unions (Arrangements, Reconstructions and Administration) Order 2014, SI 2014/229 .... **[7.1425]**

K Financial Infrastructure Systems

Financial Services (Banking Reform) Act 2013, ss 111–128, 144, 147, 148, Schs 6, 7 .... [7.1451]

L Insurance Companies, Insurers and Insurance Linked Securities

Insurance Companies Act 1982, ss 53–59, 95, 96, 96A .... [7.1474]
Insurance Companies (Winding-up) Rules 1985, SI 1985/95 .... [7.1484]
Financial Services and Markets Act 2000, ss 360, 376–379, 426, 428, 430, 431 .... [7.1517]
Financial Services and Markets Act 2000 (Insolvency) (Definition of "Insurer") Order 2001, SI 2001/2634 .... [7.1526]
Financial Services and Markets Act 2000 (Treatment of Assets of Insurers on Winding Up) Regulations 2001, SI 2001/2968 .... [7.1528]
Insurers (Winding Up) Rules 2001, SI 2001/3635 .... [7.1532]
Financial Services and Markets Act 2000 (Administration Orders Relating to Insurers) Order 2002, SI 2002/1242 .... [7.1565]
Insurers (Reorganisation and Winding Up) (Lloyd's) Regulations 2005, SI 2005/1998 .... [7.1570]
Financial Services and Markets Act 2000 (Administration Orders Relating to Insurers) Order 2010, SI 2010/3023 .... [7.1618]
Risk Transformation Regulations 2017, SI 2017/1212, regs 1–3, 12, 13, 42–50, 154, 166–169, 178–185, Schs 2, 3 .... [7.1624]

M Investment Banks

Banking Act 2009, ss 232–236, 259 .... [7.1653]
Investment Bank (Amendment of Definition) Order 2011, SI 2011/239 .... [7.1659]
Investment Bank Special Administration Regulations 2011, SI 2011/245 .... [7.1661]
Investment Bank Special Administration (England and Wales) Rules 2011, SI 2011/1301 .... [7.1711]
Investment Bank (Amendment of Definition) and Special Administration (Amendment) Regulations 2017, SI 2017/443, regs 1, 2, 17 .... [7.2046]

N Open-ended Investment Companies

Financial Services and Markets Act 2000, s 262(1), (2)(h) .... [7.2049]
Open-ended Investment Companies Regulations 2001, SI 2001/1228, regs 1, 2, 31–33C .... [7.2050]

O Postal

Postal Services Act 2011, ss 68–90, 93, Schs 10, 11 .... [7.2058]
Postal Administration Rules 2013, SI 2013/3208 .... [7.2086]

P Public Private Partnership

Greater London Authority Act 1999, ss 210, 220–224, 424, 425, Schs 14, 15 .. [7.2299]
PPP Administration Order Rules 2007, SI 2007/3141 .... [7.2311]

Q Railways

Railways Act 1993, ss 59–65, 83, 151, 154, Schs 6, 7 .... [7.2437]
Railway Administration Order Rules 2001, SI 2001/3352 .... [7.2452]

R Technical and Further Education

Technical and Further Education Act 2017, ss 3–36, 46, 47 .... [7.2580]

S Water Industry

Water Industry Act 1991, ss 23–26, 219, 223, Sch 3 .... [7.2619]
Water Industry (Special Administration) Rules 2009, SI 2009/2477 .... [7.2627]

PART 8 GENERAL INSOLVENCY STATUTORY INSTRUMENTS—ENGLAND AND WALES

Insolvency Proceedings (Monetary Limits) Order 1986, SI 1986/1996 .... **[8.1]**
Insolvency Fees Order 1986, SI 1986/2030 .... **[8.7]**
Insolvency Regulations 1994, SI 1994/2507 .... **[8.22]**
Insolvency Act 1986, Section 72A (Appointed Date) Order 2003, SI 2003/2095 .... **[8.66]**
Insolvency Act 1986 (Prescribed Part) Order 2003, SI 2003/2097 .... **[8.68]**
Insolvency Proceedings (Fees) Order 2004, SI 2004/593 .... **[8.71]**
Insolvency Proceedings (Fees) Order 2016, SI 2016/692 .... **[8.82]**
Alteration of Judicial Titles (Registrar in Bankruptcy of the High Court) Order 2018, SI 2018/130 .... **[8.90]**

PART 9 STATUTORY INSTRUMENTS RELATING TO CORPORATE INSOLVENCY—ENGLAND AND WALES

Financial Markets and Insolvency Regulations 1991, SI 1991/880 .... **[9.1]**
Financial Markets and Insolvency Regulations 1996, SI 1996/1469 .... **[9.14]**
Occupational Pension Schemes (Deficiency on Winding Up Etc) Regulations 1996, SI 1996/3128 .... **[9.22]**
Financial Markets and Insolvency (Settlement Finality) Regulations 1999, SI 1999/2979 .... **[9.40]**
Occupational Pension Schemes (Winding Up Notices and Reports etc) Regulations 2002, SI 2002/459 .... **[9.67]**
Petroleum Licensing (Exploration and Production) (Seaward and Landward Areas) Regulations 2004, SI 2004/352, reg 1, Sch 1, paras 1, 20, Sch 2, paras 1, 38, Sch 3, paras 1, 39, Sch 4, paras 1, 37, Sch 6, paras 1, 36 .... **[9.78]**
Banking Act 2009 (Third Party Compensation Arrangements for Partial Property Transfers) Regulations 2009, SI 2009/319 .... **[9.84]**

PART 10 STATUTORY INSTRUMENTS RELATING TO PARTNERSHIP INSOLVENCY—ENGLAND AND WALES

Insolvent Partnerships Order 1994, SI 1994/2421 .... **[10.1]**
Limited Liability Partnerships Regulations 2001, SI 2001/1090, regs 1, 2, 2A, 4, 5, 10, Schs 2–4, Sch 6, Pts II, III .... **[10.33]**

PART 11 STATUTORY INSTRUMENTS RELATING TO PERSONAL INSOLVENCY—ENGLAND AND WALES

Administration of Insolvent Estates of Deceased Persons Order 1986, SI 1986/1999 .... **[11.1]**
National Health Service Pension Scheme (Additional Voluntary Contributions) Regulations 2000, SI 2000/619, regs 1, 18 .... **[11.11]**
Private Hire Vehicles (London) (Operators' Licences) Regulations 2000, SI 2000/3146, regs 1, 2, 19 .... **[11.13]**
Bankruptcy (Financial Services and Markets Act 2000) Rules 2001, SI 2001/3634 .... **[11.16]**
Occupational and Personal Pension Schemes (Bankruptcy) (No 2) Regulations 2002, SI 2002/836 .... **[11.24]**
National Health Service (Compensation for Premature Retirement) Regulations 2002, SI 2002/1311, regs 1, 13 .... **[11.43]**
Council for Healthcare Regulatory Excellence (Appointment, Procedure etc) Regulations 2008, SI 2008/2927, regs 1, 2 .... **[11.45]**
Education (Student Loans) (Repayment) Regulations 2009, SI 2009/470, regs 1, 80 .... **[11.47]**
Teachers' Pensions Regulations 2010, SI 2010/990, regs 1, 122 .... **[11.49]**
London Insolvency District (County Court at Central London) Order 2014, SI 2014/818 .... **[11.51]**
Teachers (Compensation for Redundancy and Premature Retirement) Regulations 2015, SI 2015/601 .... **[11.53]**

PART 12 STATUTORY INSTRUMENTS RELATING TO OFFICIAL RECEIVERS AND INSOLVENCY PRACTITIONERS—ENGLAND AND WALES

Insolvency Practitioners (Recognised Professional Bodies) Order 1986, SI 1986/1764 .... **[12.1]**
Contracting Out (Functions of the Official Receiver) Order 1995, SI 1995/1386 .... **[12.4]**
Transnational Information and Consultation of Employees Regulations 1999, SI 1999/3323, regs 1, 3 .... **[12.8]**
Financial Services and Markets Act 2000 (Exemption) Order 2001, SI 2001/1201, arts 5, 5A, Schedule, Pt III, para 35 .... **[12.10]**
Financial Services and Markets Act 2000 (Disclosure of Confidential Information) Regulations 2001, SI 2001/2188, regs 1, 5, 10, 10A, 10B, 11, 12, Sch 1, Pt 1, Sch 3 .... **[12.13]**
Insolvency Practitioners and Insolvency Services Account (Fees) Order 2003, SI 2003/3363 .... **[12.23]**
Insolvency Practitioners Regulations 2005, SI 2005/524 .... **[12.30]**
Proceeds of Crime Act 2002 (External Requests and Orders) Order 2005, SI 2005/3181, arts 1–4, 33, 34, 77, 78, 119, 120, 191 .... **[12.49]**
European Union (Recognition of Professional Qualifications) Regulations 2015, SI 2015/2059, regs 1, 4, 8, 34, Sch 1, Pt 1, Sch 3, Pt 1 .... **[12.60]**

PART 13 STATUTORY INSTRUMENTS RELATING TO CROSS-BORDER INSOLVENCY—ENGLAND AND WALES

Co-operation of Insolvency Courts (Designation of Relevant Countries and Territories) Order 1986, SI 1986/2123 .... **[13.1]**
European Economic Interest Grouping Regulations 1989, SI 1989/638, regs 1, 2, 6–8, 18–21, Sch 1, paras 15, 24, 28–37, 40, 43, Sch 4, Pt 1, para 13, Pt 2, paras 26, 27, 31, 37 .... **[13.4]**
Insolvency Act 1986 (Guernsey) Order 1989, SI 1989/2409 .... **[13.16]**
Co-operation of Insolvency Courts (Designation of Relevant Countries) Order 1996, SI 1996/253 .... **[13.19]**
Co-operation of Insolvency Courts (Designation of Relevant Country) Order 1998, SI 1998/2766 .... **[13.22]**

PART 14 STATUTORY INSTRUMENTS RELATING TO DIRECTORS DISQUALIFICATION—ENGLAND AND WALES

Companies (Disqualification Orders) Regulations 1986, SI 1986/2067 .... **[14.1]**
Insolvent Companies (Disqualification of Unfit Directors) Proceedings Rules 1987, SI 1987/2023 .... **[14.7]**
Insolvent Companies (Reports on Conduct of Directors) Rules 1996, SI 1996/1909 .... **[14.18]**
Companies (Disqualification Orders) Regulations 2001, SI 2001/967 .... **[14.25]**
Companies (Disqualification Orders) Regulations 2009, SI 2009/2471 .... **[14.33]**
Insolvent Companies (Reports on Conduct of Directors) (England and Wales) Rules 2016, SI 2016/180 .... **[14.41]**
Compensation Orders (Disqualified Directors) Proceedings (England and Wales) Rules 2016, SI 2016/890 .... **[14.51]**
Disqualified Directors Compensation Orders (Fees) (England and Wales) Order 2016, SI 2016/1047 .... **[14.60]**

PART 15 INSOLVENCY (SCOTLAND) RULES 1986

Insolvency (Scotland) Rules 1986, SI 1986/1915 .... **[15.1]**

PART 16 OTHER STATUTORY INSTRUMENTS—SCOTLAND

Receivers (Scotland) Regulations 1986, SI 1986/1917 .... **[16.1]**
Act of Sederunt (Company Directors Disqualification) 1986, SI 1986/2296 .... **[16.9]**
Act of Sederunt (Sheriff Court Company Insolvency Rules) 1986, SI 1986/2297 .... **[16.12]**
Bankruptcy (Scotland) Act 1993 Commencement and Savings Order 1993, SI 1993/438 .... **[16.55]**
Act of Sederunt (Rules of the Court of Session 1994) 1994, SI 1994/1443, Sch 2, rr 16.1, 16.4, 18.3, 62.90–62.96, 74.1–74.51 .... **[16.60]**
Insolvent Companies (Reports on Conduct of Directors) (Scotland) Rules 1996, SI 1996/1910 .... **[16.126]**
Limited Liability Partnerships (Scotland) Regulations 2001, SSI 2001/128, regs 1–4, 6, Schs 1–3 .... **[16.133]**
Bankruptcy (Financial Services and Markets Act 2000) (Scotland) Rules 2001, SI 2001/3591 .... **[16.141]**
Insurers (Winding Up) (Scotland) Rules 2001, SI 2001/4040 .... **[16.147]**
Energy Administration (Scotland) Rules 2006, SI 2006/772 .... **[16.178]**
Bankruptcy (Scotland) Act 1985 (Low Income, Low Asset Debtors etc) Regulations 2008, SSI 2008/81 (Note) .... **[16.261]**
Bankruptcy (Scotland) Regulations 2008, SSI 2008/82 (Note) .... **[16.262]**
Act of Sederunt (Sheriff Court Bankruptcy Rules) 2008, SSI 2008/119 (Note).. **[16.263]**
Bankruptcy (Certificate for Sequestration) (Scotland) Regulations 2010, SSI 2010/397 (Note) .... **[16.264]**
Investment Bank Special Administration (Scotland) Rules 2011, SI 2011/2262 (Note) .... **[16.265]**
Protected Trust Deeds (Scotland) Regulations 2013, SSI 2013/318 (Note) .... **[16.266]**
Bankruptcy (Scotland) Regulations 2014, SSI 2014/225 (Note) .... **[16.267]**
Bankruptcy (Applications and Decisions) (Scotland) Regulations 2014, SSI 2014/226 (Note) .... **[16.268]**
Bankruptcy Fees (Scotland) Regulations 2014, SSI 2014/227 .... **[16.269]**
Bankruptcy (Money Advice and Deduction from Income etc) (Scotland) Regulations 2014, SSI 2014/296 (Note) .... **[16.284]**
Insolvent Companies (Reports on Conduct of Directors) (Scotland) Rules 2016, SI 2016/185 .... **[16.285]**
Bankruptcy (Applications and Decisions) (Scotland) Regulations 2016, SSI 2016/295 .... **[16.295]**
Act of Sederunt (Sheriff Court Bankruptcy Rules) 2016, SSI 2016/313 .... **[16.322]**
Bankruptcy (Scotland) Regulations 2016, SSI 2016/397 .... **[16.401]**
Protected Trust Deeds (Forms) (Scotland) Regulations 2016, SSI 2016/398 .... **[16.438]**
Disqualified Directors Compensation Orders (Fees) (Scotland) Order 2016, SI 2016/1048 .... **[16.441]**
Scotland Act 1998 (Insolvency Functions) Order 2018, SI 2018/174 .... **[16.446]**

PART 17 MISCELLANEOUS ACTS

Law of Property Act 1925, ss 101, 103–106, 109, 110, 209 .... **[17.1]**
Third Parties (Rights Against Insurers) Act 1930 .... **[17.9]**
Matrimonial Causes Act 1973, ss 39, 55 .... **[17.15]**
Land Compensation Act 1973, ss 33F, 89 .... **[17.17]**
County Courts Act 1984, ss 112A–112AI .... **[17.19]**
Companies Act 1985, ss 458, 746, 747 .... **[17.54]**
Companies Act 1989, ss 154, 155, 155A, 157–167, 169, 170, 170A, 170B, 170C, 172–191, 215, 216 .... **[17.57]**
Environmental Protection Act 1990, ss 78X, 164 .... **[17.99]**
Pension Schemes Act 1993, ss 123–128, 159A, 181(1), 193(1), (2), Sch 4 .... **[17.101]**
Coal Industry Act 1994, ss 29, 36, 59, 65, 68 .... **[17.111]**
Pensions Act 1995, ss 22, 23, 25, 26, 71A, 73, 73A, 73B, 75, 75A, 91–93, 124, 125, 180, 181 .... **[17.116]**
Landlord and Tenant (Covenants) Act 1995, ss 21, 31, 32 .... **[17.133]**
Employment Rights Act 1996, ss 166, 167, 182–189, 243–245 .... **[17.136]**
Housing Act 1996, ss 39–50, 231–233 .... **[17.149]**

Petroleum Act 1998, ss 38A, 38B, 52, 53 ....[17.165]
Welfare Reform and Pensions Act 1999, ss 11–13, 89–91 ....[17.169]
Financial Services and Markets Act 2000, ss 2A, 2AB, 137J–L, 137N, 215, 224, 224ZA, 224A, 355–379, 417, 426, 428, 430, 431, 433 ....[17.175]
Limited Liability Partnerships Act 2000, ss 14, 19 ....[17.218]
Commonhold and Leasehold Reform Act 2002, ss 43–55, 181–183 ....[17.220]
Proceeds of Crime Act 2002, ss 417–422, 426, 427, 430–434, 458, 462 ....[17.236]
Communications Act 2003, ss 124P, 124Q, 411 ....[17.251]
Child Trust Funds Act 2004, ss 1, 4, 27, 30, 31 ....[17.254]
Companies (Audit, Investigations and Community Enterprise) Act 2004, ss 47–50, 65–67 ....[17.259]
Pensions Act 2004, ss 38–58, 120–125, 127–139, 143–145, 191–195, 322, 323, 325 ....[17.266]
Gambling Act 2005, ss 114, 194, Sch 10, para 15, Sch 14, para 15 ....[17.324]
Companies Act 2006, ss 193, 392(3), 754, 993, 1298–1300 ....[17.328]
Banking (Special Provisions) Act 2008 ....[17.335]
Housing and Regeneration Act 2008, ss 143A–169, 324–326 ....[17.355]
Dormant Bank and Building Society Accounts Act 2008, ss 1–11, 30–32 ....[17.384]
Energy Act 2008, ss 56, 110, 112, 113 ....[17.398]
Local Democracy, Economic Development and Construction Act 2009, Sch 1, paras 1(1), (2), (8), 2(1), (8), (9), Sch 5B, paras 1, 9(1)(b) ....[17.402]
Third Parties (Rights against Insurers) Act 2010 ....[17.404]
Charities Act 2011, ss 113, 177–184, 204, 245, 247, 353, 355, 356, 358 ....[17.430]
Pension Schemes Act 2015, ss 26–28, 35, 84(1), (3), (4), 86, 88(1), 89(1)(e), (4)–(6), 90 ....[17.447]
Small Business, Enterprise and Employment Act 2015, ss 144–146, 161, 163(1), (4), 165, Sch 11 ....[17.456]
Regulation and Inspection of Social Care (Wales) Act 2016, s 30 ....[17.463]

PART 18 MISCELLANEOUS STATUTORY INSTRUMENTS

Landfill Tax Regulations 1996, SI 1996/1527, regs 1, 45–47 ....[18.1]
Local Authorities (Contracting Out of Tax Billing, Collection and Enforcement Functions) Order 1996, SI 1996/1880, arts 1, 43, 59 ....[18.5]
Commonhold (Land Registration) Rules 2004, SI 2004/1830, rr 1, 2, 21–23 ....[18.8]
Business Improvement Districts (England) Regulations 2004, SI 2004/2443, reg 1, Sch 4, paras 13(8), (9), 14(5), (6) ....[18.13]
Pension Protection Fund (Multi-employer Schemes) (Modification) Regulations 2005, SI 2005/441, regs 1–72 ....[18.15]
Pension Protection Fund (Entry Rules) Regulations 2005, SI 2005/590, regs 1, 4–13 ....[18.89]
Occupational Pension Schemes (Employer Debt) Regulations 2005, SI 2005/678 ....[18.103]
Community Interest Company Regulations 2005, SI 2005/1788, regs 23, 35 ....[18.137]
Transfer of Undertakings (Protection of Employment) Regulations 2006, SI 2006/246, regs 1–21 ....[18.139]
Occupational Pension Schemes (Fraud Compensation Levy) Regulations 2006, SI 2006/558, regs 1, 2, 7 ....[18.162]
Producer Responsibility Obligations (Packaging Waste) Regulations 2007, SI 2007/871, regs 1, 22A ....[18.165]
Regulated Covered Bonds Regulations 2008, SI 2008/346, reg 1–5, 17, 17A, 24, 27–29, 46, Schedule ....[18.167]
Non-Domestic Rating (Unoccupied Property) (England) Regulations 2008, SI 2008/386, regs 1, 4 ....[18.181]
General Ophthalmic Services Contracts Regulations 2008, SI 2008/1185, regs 1, 4 ....[18.183]
Debt Relief Orders (Designation of Competent Authorities) Regulations 2009, SI 2009/457 ....[18.185]
Overseas Companies Regulations 2009, SI 2009/1801, regs 1, 2, 63(3), (4), (6)(a), 66–74 ....[18.196]
Building Societies (Financial Assistance) Order 2010, SI 2010/1188 ....[18.208]

Electronic Money Regulations 2011, SI 2011/99, regs 1, 22, 24 .... **[18.218]**
Charitable Incorporated Organisations (Insolvency and Dissolution) Regulations 2012, SI 2012/3013 .... **[18.221]**
Legal Aid, Sentencing and Punishment of Offenders Act 2012 (Commencement No 5 and Saving Provision) Order 2013, SI 2013/77.................... **[18.263]**
Financial Services Act 2012 (Transitional Provisions) (Miscellaneous Provisions) Order 2013, SI 2013/442, arts 1, 45–60, 65–68 .... **[18.267]**
Conditional Fee Agreements Order 2013, SI 2013/689 .... **[18.288]**
National College for High Speed Rail (Government) Regulations 2015, SI 2015/1458, regs 1, 2, Sch 1, paras 2, 7(5)–(7).................... **[18.294]**
Care Quality Commission (Membership) Regulations 2015, SI 2015/1479, regs 1–5, Schedule, paras 2–5, 14.................... **[18.297]**
National Health Service (General Medical Services Contracts) Regulations 2015, SI 2015/1862, regs 1, 2, 6(1), (2)(l)–(r), 32(1), Sch 3, para 50(1)(f).................... **[18.303]**
National Health Service (Personal Medical Services Agreements) Regulations 2015, SI 2015/1879, regs 1, 2, 5(1), (2)(l)–(r), 27, Sch 2, para 46(1)(f).................... **[18.308]**
General Medical Council (Constitution of the Medical Practitioners Tribunal Service) Rules Order of Council 2015, SI 2015/1967, r 1, Schedule, para 6(1), (7)–(9).................... **[18.313]**
Legal Aid, Sentencing and Punishment of Offenders Act 2012 (Commencement No 12) Order 2016, SI 2016/345.................... **[18.315]**

PART 19 PRACTICE DIRECTIONS

Practice Direction: Insolvency Proceedings (2014) .... **[19.1]**
Practice Direction: Directors Disqualification Proceedings .... **[19.22]**
Note on listing and criteria for the transfer of work from the registrars to the County Court sitting in Central London .... **[19.31]**
Practice Direction 51P: Pilot for Insolvency Express Trials.................... **[19.32]**
Note on Bankruptcy Petitions–Hearings in Multiple Lists in the Rolls Building.. **[19.37]**
Practice Direction: Insolvency Proceedings (April 2018) .... **[19.38]**

Index *3435*

ALPHABETICAL LIST OF CONTENTS

Act of Sederunt (Company Directors Disqualification) 1986, SI 1986/2296 ....**[16.9]**
Act of Sederunt (Rules of the Court of Session 1994) 1994, SI 1994/1443, Sch 2, rr 16.1, 16.4, 18.3, 62.90–62.96, 74.1–74.51 ....**[16.60]**
Act of Sederunt (Sheriff Court Bankruptcy Rules) 2008, SSI 2008/119 (Note).. **[16.263]**
Act of Sederunt (Sheriff Court Bankruptcy Rules) 2016, SSI 2016/313........... **[16.322]**
Act of Sederunt (Sheriff Court Company Insolvency Rules) 1986, SI 1986/2297 ....**[16.12]**
Administration of Insolvent Estates of Deceased Persons Order 1986, SI 1986/1999 .... **[11.1]**
Alteration of Judicial Titles (Registrar in Bankruptcy of the High Court) Order 2018, SI 2018/130 ....**[8.90]**
Bank Administration (England and Wales) Rules 2009, SI 2009/357 .... **[7.386]**
Bank Insolvency (England and Wales) Rules 2009, SI 2009/356 .... **[7.93]**
Banking Act 2009 (Parts 2 and 3 Consequential Amendments) Order 2009, SI 2009/317 ....**[7.84]**
Banking Act 2009 (Third Party Compensation Arrangements for Partial Property Transfers) Regulations 2009, SI 2009/319 .... **[9.84]**
Banking Act 2009, ss 7, 89K, 90–122, 127, 129, 129A, 135–145, 168, 232–236, 263–265 ....**[7.25]**
Banking Act 2009, ss 130, 158, 259(1) ....**[7.471]**
Banking Act 2009, ss 232–236, 259 .... **[7.1653]**
Banking Consolidation Directive (extract) ....**[3.34]**
Banking (Special Provisions) Act 2008 .... **[17.335]**

Bankruptcy and Debt Advice (Scotland) Act 2014 (Commencement No 2, Savings and Transitionals) Order 2014, SSI 2014/261 .... [2.88]
Bankruptcy and Diligence etc (Scotland) Act 2007 (Commencement No 3, Savings and Transitionals) Order 2008, SSI 2008/115, arts 1, 2, 5–10, 15 .... [2.49]
Bankruptcy and Diligence etc (Scotland) Act 2007 (Commencement No 4, Savings and Transitionals) Order 2009, SSI 2009/67, arts 1, 2, 5, 6 .... [2.59]
Bankruptcy (Applications and Decisions) (Scotland) Regulations 2014, SSI 2014/226 (Note) .... [16.268]
Bankruptcy (Applications and Decisions) (Scotland) Regulations 2016, SSI 2016/295 .... [16.295]
Bankruptcy (Certificate for Sequestration) (Scotland) Regulations 2010, SSI 2010/397 (Note) .... [16.264]
Bankruptcy Fees (Scotland) Regulations 2014, SSI 2014/227 .... [16.269]
Bankruptcy (Financial Services and Markets Act 2000) (Scotland) Rules 2001, SI 2001/3591 .... [16.141]
Bankruptcy (Financial Services and Markets Act 2000) Rules 2001, SI 2001/3634 .... [11.16]
Bankruptcy (Money Advice and Deduction from Income etc) (Scotland) Regulations 2014, SSI 2014/296 (Note) .... [16.284]
Bankruptcy (Scotland) Act 1985 .... [5.1]
Bankruptcy (Scotland) Act 1985 (Low Income, Low Asset Debtors etc) Regulations 2008, SSI 2008/81 (Note) .... [16.261]
Bankruptcy (Scotland) Act 1993 Commencement and Savings Order 1993, SI 1993/438 .... [16.55]
Bankruptcy (Scotland) Act 1993, ss 9, 10, 12 .... [5.192]
Bankruptcy (Scotland) Regulations 2008, SSI 2008/82 (Note) .... [16.262]
Bankruptcy (Scotland) Regulations 2014, SSI 2014/225 (Note) .... [16.267]
Bankruptcy (Scotland) Regulations 2016, SSI 2016/397 .... [16.401]
Banks (Administration Proceedings) Order 1989, SI 1989/1276 .... [7.16]
Banks (Former Authorised Institutions) (Insolvency) Order 2006, SI 2006/3107 .... [7.21]
Building Societies Act 1986, ss 86–92, 125, 126, Schs 15, 15A .... [7.449]
Building Societies (Financial Assistance) Order 2010, SI 2010/1188 .... [18.208]
Building Societies (Insolvency and Special Administration) Order 2009, SI 2009/805, arts 1, 3, 16–18, Schs 1, 2 .... [7.474]
Building Society Insolvency (England and Wales) Rules 2010, SI 2010/2581 .... [7.546]
Building Society Special Administration (England and Wales) Rules 2010, SI 2010/2580 .... [7.483]
Business Improvement Districts (England) Regulations 2004, SI 2004/2443, reg 1, Sch 4, paras 13(8), (9), 14(5), (6) .... [18.13]
Care Quality Commission (Membership) Regulations 2015, SI 2015/1479, regs 1–5, Schedule, paras 2–5, 14 .... [18.297]
Charitable Incorporated Organisations (Insolvency and Dissolution) Regulations 2012, SI 2012/3013 .... [18.221]
Charities Act 2011, ss 113, 177–184, 204, 245, 247, 353, 355, 356, 358 .... [17.430]
Child Trust Funds Act 2004, ss 1, 4, 27, 30, 31 .... [17.254]
Coal Industry Act 1994, ss 29, 36, 59, 65, 68 .... [17.111]
Collective Investment in Transferable Securities (Contractual Scheme) Regulations 2013, SI 2013/1388, regs 1, 2, 17, 19, Schs 2–5 .... [7.833]
Commonhold (Land Registration) Rules 2004, SI 2004/1830, rr 1, 2, 21–23 .... [18.8]
Commonhold and Leasehold Reform Act 2002, ss 43–55, 181–183 .... [17.220]
Communications Act 2003, ss 124P, 124Q, 411 .... [17.251]
Community Interest Company Regulations 2005, SI 2005/1788, regs 23, 35 .... [18.137]
Companies Act 1985, ss 458, 746, 747 .... [17.54]
Companies Act 1989, ss 154, 155, 155A, 157–167, 169, 170, 170A, 170B, 170C, 172–191, 215, 216 .... [17.57]
Companies Act 2006 (Consequential Amendments, Transitional Provisions and Savings) Order 2009, SI 2009/1941, arts 1, 2, 8, 9, 11, Sch 1, para 84 .... [2.68]
Companies Act 2006, ss 193, 392(3), 754, 993, 1298–1300 .... [17.328]
Companies (Audit, Investigations and Community Enterprise) Act 2004, ss 47–50, 65–67 .... [17.259]

Companies (Disqualification Orders) Regulations 1986, SI 1986/2067 .... **[14.1]**
Companies (Disqualification Orders) Regulations 2001, SI 2001/967 .... **[14.25]**
Companies (Disqualification Orders) Regulations 2009, SI 2009/2471 .... **[14.33]**
Company Directors Disqualification Act 1986 .... **[4.1]**
Company Directors Disqualification Act 1986 Derivation Table .... **[4.58]**
Company Directors Disqualification Act 1986 Destination Table .... **[4.59]**
Compensation Orders (Disqualified Directors) Proceedings (England and Wales) Rules 2016, SI 2016/890............... **[14.51]**
Conditional Fee Agreements Order 2013, SI 2013/689 .... **[18.288]**
Contracting Out (Functions of the Official Receiver) Order 1995, SI 1995/1386 .... **[12.4]**
Co-operation of Insolvency Courts (Designation of Relevant Countries and Territories) Order 1986, SI 1986/2123 .... **[13.1]**
Co-operation of Insolvency Courts (Designation of Relevant Countries) Order 1996, SI 1996/253 .... **[13.19]**
Co-operation of Insolvency Courts (Designation of Relevant Country) Order 1998, SI 1998/2766 .... **[13.22]**
Co-operative and Community Benefit Societies Act 2014, ss 1, 2, 65, 66, 118–126, 134–136, 149, 150, 152–155 .... **[7.1403]**
Co-operative and Community Benefit Societies and Credit Unions (Arrangements, Reconstructions and Administration) Order 2014, SI 2014/229 .... **[7.1425]**
Council for Healthcare Regulatory Excellence (Appointment, Procedure etc) Regulations 2008, SI 2008/2927, regs 1, 2 .... **[11.45]**
Council Directive 2001/17/EC on the reorganisation and winding-up of insurance undertakings (Insurance Reorganisation & Winding-up Directive) .... **[3.88]**
Council Regulation 1346/2000/EC on insolvency proceedings .... **[3.36]**
Council Regulation 2157/2001/EC on the Statute for a European company (SE), Preamble (para (20)), Arts 7, 10, 63–66 .... **[3.262]**
County Courts Act 1984, ss 112A–112AI .... **[17.19]**
Credit Institutions Reorganisation and Winding-up Directive............... **[3.176]**
Credit Institutions (Reorganisation and Winding Up) Regulations 2004, SI 2004/1045 .... **[3.213]**
Cross-Border Insolvency Regulations 2006, SI 2006/1030 .... **[3.302]**
Debt Relief Orders (Designation of Competent Authorities) Regulations 2009, SI 2009/457 .... **[18.185]**
Directive of the European Parliament and of the Council 2000/12/EC relating to the taking up and pursuit of the business of credit institutions (extract) ...... **[3.34]**
Directive of the European Parliament and of the Council 2001/24/EC on the reorganisation and winding up of credit institutions .... **[3.176]**
Directive of the European Parliament and of the Council 2002/47/EC on financial collateral arrangements .... **[3.268]**
Directive of the European Parliament and of the Council 2008/94/EC on the protection of employees in the event of the insolvency of their employer ...... **[3.340]**
Directive of the European Parliament and of the Council 2009/138/EC on the taking-up and pursuit of the business of Insurance and Reinsurance (Solvency II), recitals 1–3, 105, 117–130, Arts 1–13, 136–143, 160–161, 194, 267–296, 309, 311, 312 .... **[3.361]**
Directive of the European Parliament and of the Council 2014/59/EU............... **[3.418]**
Disqualified Directors Compensation Orders (Fees) (England and Wales) Order 2016, SI 2016/1047............... **[14.60]**
Disqualified Directors Compensation Orders (Fees) (Scotland) Order 2016, SI 2016/1048............... **[16.441]**
Dormant Bank and Building Society Accounts Act 2008, ss 1–11, 30–32 .... **[17.384]**
Education (Student Loans) (Repayment) Regulations 2009, SI 2009/470, regs 1, 80 .... **[11.47]**
Electronic Money Regulations 2011, SI 2011/99, regs 1, 22, 24 .... **[18.218]**
Employment Rights Act 1996, ss 166, 167, 182–189, 243–245 .... **[17.136]**
Energy Act 2004, ss 110A, 110B, 154–171, 196, 198, Schs 20, 21 .... **[7.849]**
Energy Act 2008, ss 56, 110, 112, 113 .... **[17.398]**
Energy Act 2011, ss 94–96, 98–102, 120–122 .... **[7.1063]**
Energy Administration Rules 2005, SI 2005/2483 .... **[7.874]**

Energy Administration (Scotland) Rules 2006, SI 2006/772 .... [16.178]
Energy Supply Company Administration Rules 2013, SI 2013/1046 .... [7.1074]
Enterprise Act 2002, ss 248(3)–(5), 249, 254, 255, 256(2), 261(7)–(10), 266(3)–(5), 268, 270(2), 279–281, Sch 17, para 1, Sch 19 .... [2.9]
Enterprise Act 2002, s 255 .... [7.1402]
Enterprise Act 2002 (Commencement No 4 and Transitional Provisions and Savings) Order 2003, SI 2003/2093, arts 1–8 .... [2.24]
Environmental Protection Act 1990, ss 78X, 164 .... [17.99]
European Union (Recognition of Professional Qualifications) Regulations 2015, SI 2015/2059, regs 1, 4, 8, 34, Sch 1, Pt 1, Sch 3, Pt 1 ..... [12.60]
European Company Statute, Preamble (para (20)), Arts 7, 10, 63–66 .... [3.262]
European Economic Interest Grouping Regulations 1989, SI 1989/638, regs 1, 2, 6–8, 18–21, Sch 1, paras 15, 24, 28–37, 40, 43, Sch 4, Pt 1, para 13, Pt 2, paras 26, 27, 31, 37 .... [13.4]
European Grouping of Territorial Cooperation Regulation .... [3.329]
European Grouping of Territorial Cooperation Regulations 2015, SI 2015/1493, regs 1-2, 6, 8, 10 .... [3.541]
European Parliament and Council Regulation 1082/2006/EC on a European grouping of territorial cooperation (EGTC) .... [3.329]
Financial Collateral Arrangements Directive .... [3.268]
Financial Collateral Arrangements (No 2) Regulations 2003, SI 2003/3226 .... [3.283]
Financial Markets and Insolvency Regulations 1991, SI 1991/880 .... [9.1]
Financial Markets and Insolvency Regulations 1996, SI 1996/1469 .... [9.14]
Financial Markets and Insolvency (Settlement Finality) Regulations 1999, SI 1999/2979 .... [9.40]
Financial Services Act 2012 (Transitional Provisions) (Miscellaneous Provisions) Order 2013, SI 2013/442, arts 1, 45–60, 65–68 .... [18.267]
Financial Services and Markets Act 2000, ss 2A, 2AB, 137J–L, 137N, 215, 224, 224ZA, 224A, 355–379, 417, 426, 428, 430, 431, 433 .... [17.175]
Financial Services and Markets Act 2000, s 235A .... [7.832]
Financial Services and Markets Act 2000, s 262(1), (2)(h) .... [7.2049]
Financial Services and Markets Act 2000, ss 360, 376–379, 426, 428, 430, 431 .... [7.1517]
Financial Services and Markets Act 2000 (Administration Orders Relating to Insurers) Order 2002, SI 2002/1242 .... [7.1565]
Financial Services and Markets Act 2000 (Administration Orders Relating to Insurers) Order 2010, SI 2010/3023 .... [7.1618]
Financial Services and Markets Act 2000 (Disclosure of Confidential Information) Regulations 2001, SI 2001/2188, regs 1, 5, 10, 10A, 10B, 11, 12, Sch 1, Pt 1, Sch 3 .... [12.13]
Financial Services and Markets Act 2000 (Exemption) Order 2001, SI 2001/1201, arts 5, 5A, Schedule, Pt III, para 35 .... [12.10]
Financial Services and Markets Act 2000 (Insolvency) (Definition of "Insurer") Order 2001, SI 2001/2634 .... [7.1526]
Financial Services and Markets Act 2000 (Treatment of Assets of Insurers on Winding Up) Regulations 2001, SI 2001/2968 .... [7.1528]
Financial Services (Banking Reform) Act 2013, ss 111–128, 144, 147, 148, Schs 6, 7 .... [7.1451]
Friendly Societies Act 1992, ss 1, 19–26, 126, Sch 10 .... [7.1284]
Gambling Act 2005, ss 114, 194, Sch 10, para 15, Sch 14, para 15 .... [17.324]
General Medical Council (Constitution of the Medical Practitioners Tribunal Service) Rules Order of Council 2015, SI 2015/1967, r 1, Schedule, para 6(1), (7)–(9) .... [18.313]
General Ophthalmic Services Contracts Regulations 2008, SI 2008/1185, regs 1, 4 .... [18.183]
Greater London Authority Act 1999, ss 210, 220–224, 424, 425, Schs 14, 15 .. [7.2299]
Health and Social Care Act 2012, ss 61–71, 81–100, 128–137, 148–150, 304, 306, 308, 309 .... [7.1326]
Housing Act 1996, ss 39–50, 231–233 .... [17.149]
Housing and Planning Act 2016, ss 95–117, 216, 217, Sch 5 .... [7.1374]
Housing and Regeneration Act 2008, ss 143A–169, 324–326 .... [17.355]
Insolvency Act 1986 .... [1.1]

Insolvency Act 1986 Comparative Table .... **[1.603]**
Insolvency Act 1986 Derivation Table .... **[1.601]**
Insolvency Act 1986 Destination Table .... **[1.602]**
Insolvency Act 1986 (Guernsey) Order 1989, SI 1989/2409 .... **[13.16]**
Insolvency Act 1986 (Prescribed Part) Order 2003, SI 2003/2097 .... **[8.68]**
Insolvency Act 1986, Section 72A (Appointed Date) Order 2003, SI 2003/2095 .... **[8.66]**
Insolvency Act 2000, s 14 .... **[3.87]**
Insolvency Act 2000 (Commencement No 1 and Transitional Provisions) Order 2001, SI 2001/766 .... **[2.1]**
Insolvency Act 2000 (Commencement No 3 and Transitional Provisions) Order 2002, SI 2002/2711 .... **[2.4]**
Insolvency Amendment (EU 2015/848) Regulations 2017, SI 2017/702 .... **[2.100]**
Insolvency (Amendment) (No 2) Rules 2009, SI 2009/2472 (Note) .... **[2.74]**
Insolvency (Amendment) (No 2) Rules 2010, SI 2010/734 (Note) .... **[2.86]**
Insolvency (Amendment) Rules 2003, SI 2003/1730 (Note) .... **[2.23]**
Insolvency (Amendment) Rules 2004, SI 2004/584 (Note) .... **[2.35]**
Insolvency (Amendment) Rules 2005, SI 2005/527 (Note) .... **[2.36]**
Insolvency (Amendment) Rules 2006, SI 2006/1272 (Note) .... **[2.44]**
Insolvency (Amendment) Rules 2008, SI 2008/737 (Note) .... **[2.58]**
Insolvency (Amendment) Rules 2009, SI 2009/642 (Note) .... **[2.63]**
Insolvency (Amendment) Rules 2010, SI 2010/686 (Note) .... **[2.77]**
Insolvency (Amendment) Rules 2011, SI 2011/785 (Note) .... **[2.87]**
Insolvency Directive .... **[3.340]**
Insolvency (England and Wales) Rules 2016 (Consequential Amendments and Savings) Rules 2017, SI 2017/369, rr 1, 3 .... **[6.946]**
Insolvency (England and Wales) Rules 2016, SI 2016/1024 .... **[6.2]**
Insolvency Fees Order 1986, SI 1986/2030 .... **[8.7]**
Insolvency Practitioners and Insolvency Services Account (Fees) Order 2003, SI 2003/3363 .... **[12.23]**
Insolvency Practitioners (Recognised Professional Bodies) Order 1986, SI 1986/1764 .... **[12.1]**
Insolvency Practitioners Regulations 2005, SI 2005/524 .... **[12.30]**
Insolvency Proceedings (Fees) (Amendment) Order 2006, SI 2006/561, arts 1, 3, 6 .... **[2.37]**
Insolvency Proceedings (Fees) (Amendment) Order 2007, SI 2007/521, arts 1, 4 .... **[2.45]**
Insolvency Proceedings (Fees) (Amendment) Order 2008, SI 2008/714, arts 1, 3 .... **[2.47]**
Insolvency Proceedings (Fees) (Amendment) Order 2009, SI 2009/645, arts 1–3, 7 .... **[2.64]**
Insolvency Proceedings (Fees) (Amendment) Order 2010, SI 2010/732, arts 1, 2, 8 .... **[2.83]**
Insolvency Proceedings (Fees) Order 2004, SI 2004/593 .... **[8.71]**
Insolvency Proceedings (Fees) Order 2016, SI 2016/692 .... **[8.82]**
Insolvency Proceedings (Monetary Limits) Order 1986, SI 1986/1996 .... **[8.1]**
Insolvency Regulation (Council Regulation 1346/2000/EC on insolvency proceedings) .... **[3.36]**
Insolvency Regulations 1994, SI 1994/2507 .... **[8.22]**
Insolvency Rules 1986, SI 1986/1925 (Note) .... **[6.1]**
Insolvency (Scotland) Amendment Rules 2003, SI 2003/2111, rr 1, 2, 7 .... **[2.32]**
Insolvency (Scotland) Amendment Rules 2006, SI 2006/734, rr 1, 2 .... **[2.42]**
Insolvency (Scotland) Amendment Rules 2010, SI 2010/688, rr 1, 2, 4–6 .... **[2.78]**
Insolvency (Scotland) Rules 1986, SI 1986/1915 .... **[15.1]**
Insolvent Companies (Disqualification of Unfit Directors) Proceedings Rules 1987, SI 1987/2023 .... **[14.7]**
Insolvent Companies (Reports on Conduct of Directors) (England and Wales) Rules 2016, SI 2016/180 .... **[14.41]**
Insolvent Companies (Reports on Conduct of Directors) (Scotland) Rules 1996, SI 1996/1910 .... **[16.126]**
Insolvent Companies (Reports on Conduct of Directors) (Scotland) Rules 2016, SI 2016/185 .... **[16.285]**

Insolvent Companies (Reports on Conduct of Directors) Rules 1996, SI 1996/1909 .... **[14.18]**
Insolvent Partnerships (Amendment) Order 2006, SI 2006/622, arts 1, 2 .... **[2.40]**
Insolvent Partnerships Order 1994, SI 1994/2421 .... **[10.1]**
Insurance Companies Act 1982, ss 53–59, 95, 96, 96A .... **[7.1474]**
Insurance Companies (Winding-up) Rules 1985, SI 1985/95 .... **[7.1484]**
Insurance Reorganisation and Winding-up Directive .... **[3.88]**
Insurers (Reorganisation and Winding Up) (Lloyd's) Regulations 2005, SI 2005/1998 .... **[7.1570]**
Insurers (Reorganisation and Winding Up) Regulations 2003, SI 2003/1102 (Note).......... **[3.123]**
Insurers (Reorganisation and Winding Up) Regulations 2004, SI 2004/353 .... **[3.124]**
Insurers (Winding Up) (Scotland) Rules 2001, SI 2001/4040 .... **[16.147]**
Insurers (Winding Up) Rules 2001, SI 2001/3635 .... **[7.1532]**
Investment Bank (Amendment of Definition) and Special Administration (Amendment) Regulations 2017, SI 2017/443, regs 1, 2, 17.......... **[7.2046]**
Investment Bank (Amendment of Definition) Order 2011, SI 2011/239 .... **[7.1659]**
Investment Bank Special Administration (England and Wales) Rules 2011, SI 2011/1301 .... **[7.1711]**
Investment Bank Special Administration (Scotland) Rules 2011, SI 2011/2262 (Note) .... **[16.265]**
Investment Bank Special Administration Regulations 2011, SI 2011/245 .... **[7.1661]**
Land Compensation Act 1973, ss 33F, 89 .... **[17.17]**
Landfill Tax Regulations 1996, SI 1996/1527, regs 1, 45–47 .... **[18.1]**
Landlord and Tenant (Covenants) Act 1995, ss 21, 31, 32 .... **[17.133]**
Law of Property Act 1925, ss 101, 103–106, 109, 110, 209 .... **[17.1]**
Legal Aid, Sentencing and Punishment of Offenders Act 2012 (Commencement No 5 and Saving Provision) Order 2013, SI 2013/77.......... **[18.263]**
Legal Aid, Sentencing and Punishment of Offenders Act 2012 (Commencement No 12) Order 2016, SI 2016/345.......... **[18.315]**
Legislative Reform (Insolvency) (Miscellaneous Provisions) Order 2010, SI 2010/18, arts 1, 12 .... **[2.75]**
Limited Liability Partnerships Act 2000, ss 14, 19 .... **[17.218]**
Limited Liability Partnerships Regulations 2001, SI 2001/1090, regs 1, 2, 2A, 4, 5, 10, Schs 2–4, Sch 6, Pts II, III .... **[10.33]**
Limited Liability Partnerships (Scotland) Regulations 2001, SSI 2001/128, regs 1–4, 6, Schs 1–3 .... **[16.133]**
Local Authorities (Contracting Out of Tax Billing, Collection and Enforcement Functions) Order 1996, SI 1996/1880, arts 1, 43, 59 .... **[18.5]**
Local Democracy, Economic Development and Construction Act 2009, Sch 1, paras 1(1), (2), (8), 2(1), (8), (9), Sch 5B, paras 1, 9(1)(b).......... **[17.402]**
London Insolvency District (County Court at Central London) Order 2014, SI 2014/818 .... **[11.51]**
Matrimonial Causes Act 1973, ss 39, 55 .... **[17.15]**
National College for High Speed Rail (Government) Regulations 2015, SI 2015/1458, regs 1, 2, Sch 1, paras 2, 7(5)–(7).......... **[18.294]**
National Health Service Act 2006, ss 25, 33, 35–37, 39, 65A–65D, 65DA, 65F–65O, 277, 278 .... **[7.1298]**
National Health Service (Compensation for Premature Retirement) Regulations 2002, SI 2002/1311, regs 1, 13 .... **[11.43]**
National Health Service (General Medical Services Contracts) Regulations 2015, SI 2015/1862, regs 1, 2, 6(1), (2)(l)–(r), 32(1), Sch 3, para 50(1)(f).......... **[18.303]**
National Health Service Pension Scheme (Additional Voluntary Contributions) Regulations 2000, SI 2000/619, regs 1, 18 .... **[11.11]**
National Health Service (Personal Medical Services Agreements) Regulations 2015, SI 2015/1879, regs 1, 2, 5(1), (2)(l)–(r), 27, Sch 2, para 46(1)(f).......... **[18.308]**
Non-Domestic Rating (Unoccupied Property) (England) Regulations 2008, SI 2008/386, regs 1, 4 .... **[18.181]**
Note on Bankruptcy Petitions–Hearings in Multiple Lists in the Rolls Building.. **[19.37]**

Note on listing and criteria for the transfer of work from the registrars to the County Court sitting in Central London .... **[19.31]**
Occupational and Personal Pension Schemes (Bankruptcy) (No 2) Regulations 2002, SI 2002/836 .... **[11.24]**
Occupational Pension Schemes (Deficiency on Winding Up Etc) Regulations 1996, SI 1996/3128 .... **[9.22]**
Occupational Pension Schemes (Employer Debt) Regulations 2005, SI 2005/678 .... **[18.103]**
Occupational Pension Schemes (Fraud Compensation Levy) Regulations 2006, SI 2006/558, regs 1, 2, 7 .... **[18.162]**
Occupational Pension Schemes (Winding Up Notices and Reports etc) Regulations 2002, SI 2002/459 .... **[9.67]**
Open-ended Investment Companies Regulations 2001, SI 2001/1228, regs 1, 2, 31–33C .... **[7.2050]**
Overseas Companies Regulations 2009, SI 2009/1801, regs 1, 2, 63(3), (4), (6)(a), 66–74 .... **[18.196]**
Pension Protection Fund (Entry Rules) Regulations 2005, SI 2005/590, regs 1, 4–13 .... **[18.89]**
Pension Protection Fund (Multi-employer Schemes) (Modification) Regulations 2005, SI 2005/441, regs 1–72 .... **[18.15]**
Pension Schemes Act 1993, ss 123–128, 159A, 181(1), 193(1), (2), Sch 4 .... **[17.101]**
Pensions Act 1995, ss 22, 23, 25, 26, 71A, 73, 73A, 73B, 75, 75A, 91–93, 124, 125, 180, 181 .... **[17.116]**
Pensions Act 2004, ss 38–58, 120–125, 127–139, 143–145, 191–195, 322, 323, 325 .... **[17.266]**
Pension Schemes Act 2015, ss 26–28, 35, 84(1), (3), (4), 86, 88(1), 89(1)(e), (4)–(6), 90 .... **[17.447]**
Petroleum Act 1998, ss 38A, 38B, 52, 53 .... **[17.165]**
Petroleum Licensing (Exploration and Production) (Seaward and Landward Areas) Regulations 2004, SI 2004/352, reg 1, Sch 1, paras 1, 20, Sch 2, paras 1, 38, Sch 3, paras 1, 39, Sch 4, paras 1, 37, Sch 6, paras 1, 36 .... **[9.78]**
Postal Administration Rules 2013, SI 2013/3208 .... **[7.2086]**
Postal Services Act 2011, ss 68–90, 93, Schs 10, 11 .... **[7.2058]**
PPP Administration Order Rules 2007, SI 2007/3141 .... **[7.2311]**
Practice Direction 51P: Pilot for Insolvency Express Trials .... **[19.32]**
Practice Direction: Directors Disqualification Proceedings .... **[19.22]**
Practice Direction: Insolvency Proceedings (2014) .... **[19.1]**
Practice Direction: Insolvency Proceedings (April 2018) .... **[19.38]**
Private Hire Vehicles (London) (Operators' Licences) Regulations 2000, SI 2000/3146, regs 1, 2, 19 .... **[11.13]**
Proceeds of Crime Act 2002, ss 417–422, 426, 427, 430–434, 458, 462 .... **[17.236]**
Proceeds of Crime Act 2002 (External Requests and Orders) Order 2005, SI 2005/3181, arts 1–4, 33, 34, 77, 78, 119, 120, 191 .... **[12.49]**
Producer Responsibility Obligations (Packaging Waste) Regulations 2007, SI 2007/871, regs 1, 22A .... **[18.165]**
Protected Trust Deeds (Forms) (Scotland) Regulations 2016, SSI 2016/398 .... **[16.438]**
Protected Trust Deeds (Scotland) Regulations 2013, SSI 2013/318 (Note) .... **[16.266]**
Railway Administration Order Rules 2001, SI 2001/3352 .... **[7.2452]**
Railways Act 1993, ss 59–65, 83, 151, 154, Schs 6, 7 .... **[7.2437]**
Receivers (Scotland) Regulations 1986, SI 1986/1917 .... **[16.1]**
Regulated Covered Bonds Regulations 2008, SI 2008/346, reg 1–5, 17, 17A, 24, 27–29, 46, Schedule .... **[18.167]**
Regulation and Inspection of Social Care (Wales) Act 2016, s 30 .... **[17.463]**
Regulation of the European Parliament and of the Council on insolvency proceedings (recast) (2015/848/EU) .... **[3.546]**
Risk Transformation Regulations 2017, SI 2017/1212, regs 1–3, 12, 13, 42–50, 154, 166–169, 178–185, Schs 2, 3 .... **[7.1624]**
Scotland Act 1998 (Insolvency Functions) Order 2018, SI 2018/174 .... **[16.446]**
Small Business, Enterprise and Employment Act 2015, ss 144–146, 161, 163(1), (4), 165, Sch 11 .... **[17.456]**
Solvency II Directive .... **[3.361]**

Teachers (Compensation for Redundancy and Premature Retirement) Regulations 2015, SI 2015/601 ..... **[11.53]**
Teachers' Pensions Regulations 2010, SI 2010/990, regs 1, 122 ..... **[11.49]**
Third Parties (Rights Against Insurers) Act 1930 ..... **[17.9]**
Third Parties (Rights against Insurers) Act 2010 ..... **[17.404]**
Transfer of Undertakings (Protection of Employment) Regulations 2006, SI 2006/246, regs 1–21 ..... **[18.139]**
Transnational Information and Consultation of Employees Regulations 1999, SI 1999/3323, regs 1, 3 ..... **[12.8]**
Transport Act 2000, ss 26–33, 275, 279, 280, Schs 1–3 ..... **[7.1]**
UNCITRAL Model Law on Cross-Border Insolvency ..... **[3.2]**
Water Industry Act 1991, ss 23–26, 219, 223, Sch 3 ..... **[7.2619]**
Water Industry (Special Administration) Rules 2009, SI 2009/2477 ..... **[7.2627]**
Welfare Reform and Pensions Act 1999, ss 11–13, 89–91 ..... **[17.169]**

Index *3435*

PART 1
INSOLVENCY ACT 1986

INSOLVENCY ACT 1986

(1986 c 45)

ARRANGEMENT OF SECTIONS

THE FIRST GROUP OF PARTS
COMPANY INSOLVENCY; COMPANIES WINDING UP

PART I
COMPANY VOLUNTARY ARRANGEMENTS

The proposal

1 Those who may propose an arrangement . . . [1.1]
1A Moratorium . . . [1.2]
2 Procedure where nominee is not the liquidator or administrator . . . [1.3]
3 Consideration of proposal . . . [1.4]

Consideration and implementation of proposal

4 Decisions of the company and its creditors . . . [1.5]
4A Approval of arrangement . . . [1.6]
5 Effect of approval . . . [1.7]
6 Challenge of decisions . . . [1.8]
6A False representations, etc . . . [1.9]
7 Implementation of proposal . . . [1.10]
7A Prosecution of delinquent officers of company . . . [1.11]
7B Arrangements coming to an end prematurely . . . [1.12]

PART II
ADMINISTRATION

8 Administration . . . [1.13]

PART III
RECEIVERSHIP

CHAPTER I
RECEIVERS AND MANAGERS (ENGLAND AND WALES)

Preliminary and general provisions

28 Extent of this Chapter . . . [1.14]
29 Definitions . . . [1.15]
30 Disqualification of body corporate from acting as receiver . . . [1.16]
31 Disqualification of bankrupt or person in respect of whom a debt relief order is made . . . [1.17]
32 Power for court to appoint official receiver . . . [1.18]

Receivers and managers appointed out of court

33 Time from which appointment is effective . . . [1.19]
34 Liability for invalid appointment . . . [1.20]
35 Application to court for directions . . . [1.21]
36 Court's power to fix remuneration . . . [1.22]
37 Liability for contracts, etc . . . [17.175]
38 Receivership accounts to be delivered to registrar . . . [1.24]

Provisions applicable to every receivership

39 Notification that receiver or manager appointed . . . [1.25]
40 Payment of debts out of assets subject to floating charge . . . [1.26]
41 Enforcement of duty to make returns . . . [1.27]

Administrative receivers: general

42 General powers . . . [1.28]
43 Power to dispose of charged property, etc . . . [1.29]
44 Agency and liability for contracts . . . [1.30]
45 Vacation of office . . . [1.31]

Administrative receivers: ascertainment and investigation of company's affairs

46 Information to be given by administrative receiver . . . [1.32]
47 Statement of affairs to be submitted . . . [1.33]
48 Report by administrative receiver . . . [1.34]

49 Committee of creditors . . . [1.35]

CHAPTER II
RECEIVERS (SCOTLAND)

50 Extent of this Chapter . . . [1.36]
51 Power to appoint receiver . . . [1.37]
52 Circumstances justifying appointment . . . [1.38]
53 Mode of appointment by holder of charge . . . [1.39]
54 Appointment by court . . . [1.40]
55 Powers of receiver . . . [1.41]
56 Precedence among receivers . . . [1.42]
57 Agency and liability of receiver for contracts . . . [1.43]
58 Remuneration of receiver . . . [1.44]
59 Priority of debts . . . [1.45]
60 Distribution of moneys . . . [1.46]
61 Disposal of interest in property . . . [1.47]
62 Cessation of appointment of receiver . . . [1.48]
63 Powers of court . . . [1.49]
64 Notification that receiver appointed . . . [1.50]
65 Information to be given by receiver . . . [1.51]
66 Company's statement of affairs . . . [1.52]
67 Report by receiver . . . [1.53]
68 Committee of creditors . . . [1.54]
69 Enforcement of receiver's duty to make returns, etc . . . [1.55]
70 Interpretation for Chapter II . . . [1.56]
71 Prescription of forms, etc; regulations . . . [1.57]

CHAPTER III
RECEIVERS' POWERS IN GREAT BRITAIN AS A WHOLE

72 Cross-border operation of receivership provisions . . . [1.58]

CHAPTER IV
PROHIBITION OF APPOINTMENT
OF ADMINISTRATIVE RECEIVER

72A Floating charge holder not to appoint administrative receiver . . . [1.59]
72B First exception: capital market . . . [1.60]
72C Second exception: public-private partnership . . . [1.61]
72D Third exception: utilities . . . [1.62]
72DA Exception in respect of urban regeneration projects . . . [1.63]
72E Fourth exception: project finance . . . [1.64]
72F Fifth exception: financial market . . . [1.65]
72G Sixth exception: social landlords . . . [1.66]
72GA Exception in relation to protected railway companies etc . . . [1.67]
72H Sections 72A to 72G: supplementary . . . [1.68]

PART IV
WINDING UP OF COMPANIES REGISTERED
UNDER THE COMPANIES ACTS

CHAPTER I
PRELIMINARY

Introductory

73 Scheme of this Part . . . [1.69]

Contributories

74 Liability as contributories of present and past members . . . [1.70]
75 Directors, etc with unlimited liability . . . [1.71]
76 Liability of past directors and shareholders . . . [1.72]
77 Limited company formerly unlimited . . . [1.73]
78 Unlimited company formerly limited . . . [1.74]
79 Meaning of "contributory" . . . [1.75]
80 Nature of contributory's liability . . . [1.76]
81 Contributories in case of death of a member . . . [1.77]
82 Effect of contributory's bankruptcy . . . [1.78]
83 Companies registered but not formed under the Companies Act 2006 . . . [1.79]

CHAPTER II
VOLUNTARY WINDING UP (INTRODUCTORY AND GENERAL)

Resolutions for, and commencement of, voluntary winding up

84 Circumstances in which company may be wound up voluntarily . . . [1.80]
85 Notice of resolution to wind up . . . [1.81]
86 Commencement of winding up . . . [1.82]

Consequences of resolution to wind up

87 Effect on business and status of company . . . [1.83]
88 Avoidance of share transfers, etc after winding-up resolution . . . [1.84]

Declaration of solvency

89 Statutory declaration of solvency . . . [1.85]
90 Distinction between "members'" and "creditors'" voluntary winding up . . . [1.86]

CHAPTER III
MEMBERS' VOLUNTARY WINDING UP

91 Appointment of liquidator . . . [1.87]
92 Power to fill vacancy in office of liquidator . . . [1.88]
92A Progress report to company (England and Wales) . . . [1.89]
93 General company meeting at each year's end (Scotland) . . . [1.90]
94 Final account prior to dissolution . . . [1.91]
95 Effect of company's insolvency . . . [1.92]
96 Conversion to creditors' voluntary winding up . . . [1.93]

CHAPTER IV
CREDITORS' VOLUNTARY WINDING UP

97 Application of this Chapter . . . [1.94]
98 Meeting of creditors . . . [1.95]
99 Directors to lay statement of affairs before creditors . . . [1.96]
100 Appointment of liquidator . . . [1.97]
101 Appointment of liquidation committee . . . [1.98]
102 Creditors' meeting where winding up converted under s 96 . . . [1.99]
103 Cesser of directors' powers . . . [1.100]
104 Vacancy in office of liquidator . . . [1.101]
104A Progress report to company and creditors (England and Wales) . . . [1.102]
105 Meetings of company and creditors at each year's end (Scotland) . . . [1.103]
106 Final account prior to dissolution . . . [1.104]

CHAPTER V
PROVISIONS APPLYING TO BOTH KINDS OF VOLUNTARY WINDING UP

107 Distribution of company's property . . . [1.105]
108 Appointment or removal of liquidator by the court . . . [1.106]
109 Notice by liquidator of his appointment . . . [1.107]
110 Acceptance of shares, etc, as consideration for sale of company property . . . [1.108]
111 Dissent from arrangement under s 110 . . . [1.109]
112 Reference of questions to court . . . [1.110]
113 Court's power to control proceedings (Scotland) . . . [1.111]
114 No liquidator appointed or nominated by company . . . [1.112]
115 Expenses of voluntary winding up . . . [1.113]
116 Saving for certain rights . . . [1.114]

CHAPTER VI
WINDING UP BY THE COURT

Jurisdiction (England and Wales)

117 High Court and county court jurisdiction . . . [1.115]
118 Proceedings taken in wrong court . . . [1.116]
119 Proceedings in county court; case stated for High Court . . . [1.117]

Jurisdiction (Scotland)

120 Court of Session and sheriff court jurisdiction . . . [1.118]
121 Power to remit winding up to Lord Ordinary . . . [1.119]

Grounds and effect of winding-up petition

122 Circumstances in which company may be wound up by the court . . . [1.120]

123 Definition of inability to pay debts . . . [1.121]
124 Application for winding up . . . [1.122]
124A Petition for winding-up on grounds of public interest . . . [1.123]
124B Petition for winding up of SE . . . [1.124]
124C Petition for winding up of SCE . . . [1.125]
125 Powers of court on hearing of petition . . . [1.126]
126 Power to stay or restrain proceedings against company . . . [1.127]
127 Avoidance of property dispositions, etc . . . [1.128]
128 Avoidance of attachments, etc . . . [1.129]

Commencement of winding up

129 Commencement of winding up by the court . . . [1.130]
130 Consequences of winding-up order . . . [1.131]

Investigation procedures

131 Company's statement of affairs . . . [1.132]
132 Investigation by official receiver . . . [1.133]
133 Public examination of officers . . . [1.134]
134 Enforcement of s 133 . . . [1.135]

Appointment of liquidator

135 Appointment and powers of provisional liquidator . . . [1.136]
136 Functions of official receiver in relation to office of liquidator . . . [1.137]
137 Appointment by Secretary of State . . . [1.138]
138 Appointment of liquidator in Scotland . . . [1.139]
139 Choice of liquidator by creditors and contributories . . . [1.140]
140 Appointment by the court following administration or voluntary arrangement . . . [1.141]

Liquidation committees

141 Liquidation committee (England and Wales) . . . [1.142]
142 Liquidation committee (Scotland) . . . [1.143]

The liquidator's functions

143 General functions in winding up by the court . . . [1.144]
144 Custody of company's property . . . [1.145]
145 Vesting of company property in liquidator . . . [1.146]
146 Final account . . . [1.147]
146A Official receiver's duty to send statement to registrar about other proceedings . . . [1.148]

General powers of court

147 Power to stay or sist winding up . . . [1.149]
148 Settlement of list of contributories and application of assets . . . [1.150]
149 Debts due from contributory to company . . . [1.151]
150 Power to make calls . . . [1.152]
152 Order on contributory to be conclusive evidence . . . [1.153]
153 Power to exclude creditors not proving in time . . . [1.154]
154 Adjustment of rights of contributories . . . [1.155]
155 Inspection of books by creditors, etc . . . [1.156]
156 Payment of expenses of winding up . . . [1.157]
157 Attendance at company meetings (Scotland) . . . [1.158]
158 Power to arrest absconding contributory . . . [1.159]
159 Powers of court to be cumulative . . . [1.160]
160 Delegation of powers to liquidator (England and Wales) . . . [1.161]

Enforcement of, and appeal from, orders

161 Orders for calls on contributories (Scotland) . . . [1.162]
162 Appeals from orders in Scotland . . . [1.163]

CHAPTER VII
LIQUIDATORS

Preliminary

163 Style and title of liquidators . . . [1.164]
164 Corrupt inducement affecting appointment . . . [1.165]

Liquidator's powers and duties

165 Voluntary winding up . . . [1.166]
166 Creditors' voluntary winding up . . . [1.167]

167 Winding up by the court . . . . . [1.168]
168 Supplementary powers (England and Wales) . . . . . [1.169]
169 Supplementary powers (Scotland) . . . . . [1.170]
170 Enforcement of liquidator's duty to make returns, etc . . . . . [1.171]

Removal; vacation of office

171 Removal, etc (voluntary winding up) . . . . . [1.172]
172 Removal, etc (winding up by the court) . . . . . [1.173]

Release of liquidator

173 Release (voluntary winding up) . . . . . [1.174]
174 Release (winding up by the court) . . . . . [1.175]

CHAPTER VIII
PROVISIONS OF GENERAL APPLICATION IN WINDING UP

Preferential debts

175 Preferential debts (general provision) . . . . . [1.176]
176 Preferential charge on goods distrained, etc . . . . . [1.177]

Property subject to floating charge

176ZA Payment of expenses of winding up (England and Wales) . . . . . [1.178]
176ZB Application of proceeds of office-holder claims . . . . . [1.179]
176A Share of assets for unsecured creditors . . . . . [1.180]

Special managers

177 Power to appoint special manager . . . . . [1.181]

Disclaimer (England and Wales only)

178 Power to disclaim onerous property . . . . . [1.182]
179 Disclaimer of leaseholds . . . . . [1.183]
180 Land subject to rentcharge . . . . . [1.184]
181 Powers of court (general) . . . . . [1.185]
182 Powers of court (leaseholds) . . . . . [1.186]

Execution, attachment and the Scottish equivalents

183 Effect of execution or attachment (England and Wales) . . . . . [1.187]
184 Duties of officers charged with execution of writs and other processes (England and Wales) . . . . . [1.188]
185 Effect of diligence (Scotland) . . . . . [1.189]

Miscellaneous matters

186 Rescission of contracts by the court . . . . . [1.190]
187 Power to make over assets to employees . . . . . [1.191]
188 Notification that company is in liquidation . . . . . [1.192]
189 Interest on debts . . . . . [1.193]
190 Documents exempt from stamp duty . . . . . [1.194]
191 Company's books to be evidence . . . . . [1.195]
192 Information as to pending liquidations . . . . . [1.196]
193 Unclaimed dividends (Scotland) . . . . . [1.197]
194 Resolutions passed at adjourned meetings . . . . . [1.198]
195 Court's powers to ascertain wishes of creditors or contributories . . . . . [1.199]
196 Judicial notice of court documents . . . . . [1.200]
197 Commission for receiving evidence . . . . . [1.201]
198 Court order for examination of persons in Scotland . . . . . [1.202]
199 Costs of application for leave to proceed (Scottish companies) . . . . . [1.203]
200 Affidavits etc in United Kingdom and overseas . . . . . [1.204]

CHAPTER IX
DISSOLUTION OF COMPANIES AFTER WINDING UP

201 Dissolution (voluntary winding up) . . . . . [1.205]
202 Early dissolution (England and Wales) . . . . . [1.206]
203 Consequence of notice under s 202 . . . . . [1.207]
204 Early dissolution (Scotland) . . . . . [1.208]
205 Dissolution otherwise than under ss 202–204 . . . . . [1.209]

CHAPTER X
MALPRACTICE BEFORE AND DURING LIQUIDATION; PENALISATION OF COMPANIES AND COMPANY OFFICERS; INVESTIGATIONS AND PROSECUTIONS

Offences of fraud, deception, etc

206 Fraud, etc in anticipation of winding up . . . [1.210]
207 Transactions in fraud of creditors . . . [1.211]
208 Misconduct in course of winding up . . . [1.212]
209 Falsification of company's books . . . [1.213]
210 Material omissions from statement relating to company's affairs . . . [1.214]
211 False representations to creditors. . . . [1.215]

Penalisation of directors and officers

212 Summary remedy against delinquent directors, liquidators, etc . . . [1.216]
213 Fraudulent trading . . . [1.217]
214 Wrongful trading. . . . [1.218]
215 Proceedings under ss 213, 214. . . . [1.219]
216 Restriction on re-use of company names . . . [1.220]
217 Personal liability for debts, following contravention of s 216 . . . [1.221]

Investigation and prosecution of malpractice

218 Prosecution of delinquent officers and members of company . . . [1.222]
219 Obligations arising under s 218 . . . [1.223]

PART V
WINDING UP OF UNREGISTERED COMPANIES

220 Meaning of "unregistered company" . . . [1.224]
221 Winding up of unregistered companies . . . [1.225]
222 Inability to pay debts: unpaid creditor for £750 or more . . . [1.226]
223 Inability to pay debts: debt remaining unsatisfied after action brought . . . [1.227]
224 Inability to pay debts: other cases . . . [1.228]
225 Company incorporated outside Great Britain may be wound up though dissolved . . . [1.229]
226 Contributories in winding up of unregistered company . . . [1.230]
227 Power of court to stay, sist or restrain proceedings . . . [1.231]
228 Actions stayed on winding-up order. . . . [1.232]
229 Provisions of this Part to be cumulative . . . [1.233]

PART VI
MISCELLANEOUS PROVISIONS APPLYING TO COMPANIES WHICH ARE INSOLVENT OR IN LIQUIDATION

Office-holders

230 Holders of office to be qualified insolvency practitioners. . . . [1.234]
231 Appointment to office of two or more persons. . . . [1.235]
232 Validity of office-holder's acts . . . [1.236]

Management by administrators, liquidators, etc

233 Supplies of gas, water, electricity, etc . . . [1.237]
233A Further protection of essential supplies . . . [1.238]
234 Getting in the company's property. . . . [1.239]
235 Duty to co-operate with office-holder . . . [1.240]
236 Inquiry into company's dealings, etc . . . [1.241]
237 Court's enforcement powers under s 236 . . . [1.242]

Adjustment of prior transactions (administration and liquidation)

238 Transactions at an undervalue (England and Wales). . . . [1.243]
239 Preferences (England and Wales) . . . [1.244]
240 "Relevant time" under ss 238, 239 . . . [1.245]
241 Orders under ss 238, 239 . . . [1.246]
242 Gratuitous alienations (Scotland). . . . [1.247]
243 Unfair preferences (Scotland) . . . [1.248]
244 Extortionate credit transactions. . . . [1.249]
245 Avoidance of certain floating charges . . . [1.250]
246 Unenforceability of liens on books, etc . . . [1.251]

Administration: penalisation of directors etc

246ZA Fraudulent trading: administration . . . [1.252]
246ZB Wrongful trading: administration . . . [1.253]

246ZC Proceedings under section 246ZA or 246ZB . . . [1.254]

Power to assign certain causes of action

246ZD Power to assign . . . [1.255]

Decisions by creditors and contributories

246ZE Decisions by creditors and contributories: general . . . [1.256]
246ZF Deemed consent procedure . . . [1.257]
246ZG Power to amend sections 246ZE and 246ZF . . . [1.258]

Remote attendance at meetings

246A Remote attendance at meetings . . . [1.259]

Use of websites

246B Use of websites . . . [1.260]
246C Creditors' ability to opt out of receiving certain notices . . . [1.261]

PART VII
INTERPRETATION FOR FIRST GROUP OF PARTS

247 "Insolvency" and "go into liquidation" . . . [1.262]
248 "Secured creditor", etc . . . [1.263]
248A "Opted-out creditor" . . . [1.264]
249 "Connected" with a company . . . [1.265]
250 "Member" of a company . . . [1.266]
251 Expressions used generally . . . [1.267]

THE SECOND GROUP OF PARTS
INSOLVENCY OF INDIVIDUALS; BANKRUPTCY

PART 7A
DEBT RELIEF ORDERS

Preliminary

251A Debt relief orders . . . [1.268]

Applications for a debt relief order

251B Making of application . . . [1.269]
251C Duty of official receiver to consider and determine application . . . [1.270]
251D Presumptions applicable to the determination of an application . . . [1.271]

Making and effect of debt relief order

251E Making of debt relief orders . . . [1.272]
251F Effect of debt relief order on other debt management arrangements . . . [1.273]
251G Moratorium from qualifying debts . . . [1.274]
251H The moratorium period . . . [1.275]
251I Discharge from qualifying debts . . . [1.276]

Duties of debtor

251J Providing assistance to official receiver etc . . . [1.277]

Objections, investigations and revocation

251K Objections and investigations . . . [1.278]
251L Power of official receiver to revoke or amend a debt relief order . . . [1.279]

Role of the court

251M Powers of court in relation to debt relief orders . . . [1.280]
251N Inquiry into debtor's dealings and property . . . [1.281]

Offences

251O False representations and omissions . . . [1.282]
251P Concealment or falsification of documents . . . [1.283]
251Q Fraudulent disposal of property . . . [1.284]
251R Fraudulent dealing with property obtained on credit . . . [1.285]
251S Obtaining credit or engaging in business . . . [1.286]
251T Offences: supplementary . . . [1.287]

Supplementary

251U Approved intermediaries . . . [1.288]
251V Debt relief restrictions orders and undertakings . . . [1.289]
251W Register of debt relief orders etc . . . [1.290]
251X Interpretation . . . [1.291]

PART VIII
INDIVIDUAL VOLUNTARY ARRANGEMENTS

Moratorium for insolvent debtor

252 Interim order of court . . . . . [1.292]
253 Application for interim order . . . . . [1.293]
254 Effect of application . . . . . [1.294]
255 Cases in which interim order can be made . . . . . [1.295]
256 Nominee's report on debtor's proposal . . . . . [1.296]

Procedure where no interim order made

256A Debtor's proposal and nominee's report . . . . . [1.297]

Creditors' decisions

257 Consideration of debtor's proposal by creditors . . . . . [1.298]

Consideration and implementation of debtor's proposal

258 Approval of debtor's proposal . . . . . [1.299]
259 Report of decisions to court . . . . . [1.300]
260 Effect of approval . . . . . [1.301]
261 Additional effect on undischarged bankrupt . . . . . [1.302]
262 Challenge of creditors' decision . . . . . [1.303]
262A False representations etc . . . . . [1.304]
262B Prosecution of delinquent debtors . . . . . [1.305]
262C Arrangements coming to an end prematurely . . . . . [1.306]
263 Implementation and supervision of approved voluntary arrangement . . . . . [1.307]

Fast-track voluntary arrangement

263A Availability . . . . . [1.308]
263B Decision . . . . . [1.309]
263C Result . . . . . [1.310]
263D Approval of voluntary arrangement . . . . . [1.311]
263E Implementation . . . . . [1.312]
263F Revocation . . . . . [1.313]
263G Offences . . . . . [1.314]

PART IX
BANKRUPTCY

CHAPTER A1
ADJUDICATORS: BANKRUPTCY APPLICATIONS BY DEBTORS AND BANKRUPTCY ORDERS

263H Bankruptcy applications to an adjudicator . . . . . [1.315]
263I Debtors against whom an adjudicator may make a bankruptcy order . . . . . [1.316]
263J Conditions applying to bankruptcy application . . . . . [1.317]
263K Determination of bankruptcy application . . . . . [1.318]
263L Adjudicator's requests for further information . . . . . [1.319]
263M Making of bankruptcy order . . . . . [1.320]
263N Refusal to make a bankruptcy order: review and appeal etc . . . . . [1.321]
263O False representations and omissions . . . . . [1.322]

CHAPTER I
THE COURT: BANKRUPTCY PETITIONS AND BANKRUPTCY ORDERS

Preliminary

264 Who may present a bankruptcy petition . . . . . [1.323]
265 Creditor's petition: debtors against whom the court may make a bankruptcy order . . . . . [1.324]
266 Other preliminary conditions . . . . . [1.325]

Creditor's petition

267 Grounds of creditor's petition . . . . . [1.326]
268 Definition of "inability to pay", etc; the statutory demand . . . . . [1.327]
269 Creditor with security . . . . . [1.328]
270 Expedited petition . . . . . [1.329]
271 Proceedings on creditor's petition . . . . . [1.330]

Debtor's petition

272 Grounds of debtor's petition . . . . . [1.331]
273 Appointment of insolvency practitioner by the court . . . . . [1.332]

274 Action on report of insolvency practitioner . . . [1.333]
274A Debtor who meets conditions for a debt relief order . . . [1.334]
275 Summary administration . . . [1.335]

Other cases for special consideration

276 Default in connection with voluntary arrangement . . . [1.336]
277 Petition based on criminal bankruptcy order . . . [1.337]

CHAPTER IA
COMMENCEMENT AND DURATION OF BANKRUPTCY

278 Commencement and continuance . . . [1.338]
279 Duration . . . [1.339]
280 Discharge by order of the court . . . [1.340]
281 Effect of discharge . . . [1.341]
281A Post-discharge restrictions . . . [1.342]
282 Court's power to annul bankruptcy order . . . [1.343]

CHAPTER II
PROTECTION OF BANKRUPT'S ESTATE
AND INVESTIGATION OF HIS AFFAIRS

283 Definition of bankrupt's estate . . . [1.344]
283A Bankrupt's home ceasing to form part of estate . . . [1.345]
284 Restrictions on dispositions of property . . . [1.346]
285 Restriction on proceedings and remedies . . . [1.347]
286 Power to appoint interim receiver . . . [1.348]
287 Powers of interim receiver . . . [1.349]
288 Statement of affairs . . . [1.350]
289 Investigatory duties of official receiver . . . [1.351]
290 Public examination of bankrupt . . . [1.352]
291 Duties of bankrupt in relation to official receiver . . . [1.353]

CHAPTER III
TRUSTEES IN BANKRUPTCY

Tenure of office as trustee

291A First trustee in bankruptcy . . . [1.354]
292 Appointment of trustees: general provision . . . [1.355]
293 Summoning of meeting to appoint first trustee . . . [1.356]
294 Power of creditors to requisition meeting . . . [1.357]
295 Failure of meeting to appoint trustee . . . [1.358]
296 Appointment of trustee by Secretary of State . . . [1.359]
297 Special cases . . . [1.360]
298 Removal of trustee; vacation of office . . . [1.361]
299 Release of trustee . . . [1.362]
300 Vacancy in office of trustee . . . [1.363]

Control of trustee

301 Creditors' committee . . . [1.364]
302 Exercise by Secretary of State of functions of creditors' committee . . . [1.365]
303 General control of trustee by the court . . . [1.366]
304 Liability of trustee . . . [1.367]

CHAPTER IV
ADMINISTRATION BY TRUSTEE

Preliminary

305 General functions of trustee . . . [1.368]

Acquisition, control and realisation of bankrupt's estate

306 Vesting of bankrupt's estate in trustee . . . [1.369]
306A Property subject to restraint order . . . [1.370]
306AA Property released from detention . . . [1.371]
306B Property in respect of which receivership or administration order is made . . . [1.372]
306BA Property in respect of which realisation order made . . . [1.373]
306C Property subject to certain orders where confiscation order discharged or quashed . . . [1.374]
307 After-acquired property . . . [1.375]
308 Vesting in trustee of certain items of excess value . . . [1.376]

308A Vesting in trustee of certain tenancies . . . . [1.377]
309 Time-limit for notice under s 307 or 308 . . . . [1.378]
310 Income payments orders . . . . [1.379]
310A Income payments agreement . . . . [1.380]
311 Acquisition by trustee of control . . . . [1.381]
312 Obligation to surrender control to trustee . . . . [1.382]
313 Charge on bankrupt's home . . . . [1.383]
313A Low value home: application for sale, possession or charge . . . . [1.384]
314 Powers of trustee . . . . [1.385]

Disclaimer of onerous property

315 Disclaimer (general power) . . . . [1.386]
316 Notice requiring trustee's decision . . . . [1.387]
317 Disclaimer of leaseholds . . . . [1.388]
318 Disclaimer of dwelling house . . . . [1.389]
319 Disclaimer of land subject to rentcharge . . . . [1.390]
320 Court order vesting disclaimed property . . . . [1.391]
321 Order under s 320 in respect of leaseholds . . . . [1.392]

Distribution of bankrupt's estate

322 Proof of debts . . . . [1.393]
323 Mutual credit and set-off . . . . [1.394]
324 Distribution by means of dividend . . . . [1.395]
325 Claims by unsatisfied creditors . . . . [1.396]
326 Distribution of property in specie . . . . [1.397]
327 Distribution in criminal bankruptcy . . . . [1.398]
328 Priority of debts . . . . [1.399]
329 Debts to spouse or civil partner . . . . [1.400]
330 Final distribution . . . . [1.401]
331 Final report . . . . [1.402]
332 Saving for bankrupt's home . . . . [1.403]

Supplemental

333 Duties of bankrupt in relation to trustee . . . . [1.404]
334 Stay of distribution in case of second bankruptcy . . . . [1.405]
335 Adjustment between earlier and later bankruptcy estates . . . . [1.406]

CHAPTER V
EFFECT OF BANKRUPTCY ON CERTAIN RIGHTS, TRANSACTIONS, ETC

Rights under trusts of land

335A Rights under trusts of land . . . . [1.407]

Rights of occupation

336 Rights of occupation etc of bankrupt's spouse or civil partner . . . . [1.408]
337 Rights of occupation of bankrupt . . . . [1.409]
338 Payments in respect of premises occupied by bankrupt . . . . [1.410]

Adjustment of prior transactions, etc

339 Transactions at an undervalue . . . . [1.411]
340 Preferences . . . . [1.412]
341 "Relevant time" under ss 339, 340 . . . . [1.413]
342 Orders under ss 339, 340 . . . . [1.414]
342A Recovery of excessive pension contributions . . . . [1.415]
342B Orders under section 342A . . . . [1.416]
342C Orders under section 342A: supplementary . . . . [1.417]
342D Recovery of excessive contributions in pension-sharing cases . . . . [1.418]
342E Orders under section 339 or 340 in respect of pension-sharing transactions . . . . [1.419]
342F Orders under section 339 or 340 in pension-sharing cases: supplementary . . . . [1.420]
343 Extortionate credit transactions . . . . [1.421]
344 Avoidance of general assignment of book debts . . . . [1.422]
345 Contracts to which bankrupt is a party . . . . [1.423]
346 Enforcement procedures . . . . [1.424]
347 Distress, etc . . . . [1.425]
348 Apprenticeships, etc . . . . [1.426]
349 Unenforceability of liens on books, etc . . . . [1.427]
349A Arbitration agreements to which bankrupt is party . . . . [1.428]

CHAPTER VI
BANKRUPTCY OFFENCES

Preliminary

350 Scheme of this Chapter . . . [1.429]
351 Definitions . . . [1.430]
352 Defence of innocent intention . . . [1.431]

Wrongdoing by the bankrupt before and after bankruptcy

353 Non-disclosure . . . [1.432]
354 Concealment of property . . . [1.433]
355 Concealment of books and papers; falsification . . . [1.434]
356 False statements . . . [1.435]
357 Fraudulent disposal of property . . . [1.436]
358 Absconding . . . [1.437]
359 Fraudulent dealing with property obtained on credit . . . [1.438]
360 Obtaining credit; engaging in business . . . [1.439]
361 Failure to keep proper accounts of business . . . [1.440]
362 Gambling . . . [1.441]

CHAPTER VII
POWERS OF COURT IN BANKRUPTCY

363 General control of court . . . [1.442]
364 Power of arrest . . . [1.443]
365 Seizure of bankrupt's property . . . [1.444]
366 Inquiry into bankrupt's dealings and property . . . [1.445]
367 Court's enforcement powers under s 366 . . . [1.446]
368 Provision corresponding to s 366, where interim receiver appointed . . . [1.447]
369 Order for production of documents by inland revenue . . . [1.448]
370 Power to appoint special manager . . . [1.449]
371 Re-direction of bankrupt's letters, etc . . . [1.450]

PART X
INDIVIDUAL INSOLVENCY: GENERAL PROVISIONS

372 Supplies of gas, water, electricity, etc . . . [1.451]
372A Further protection of essential supplies . . . [1.452]
373 Jurisdiction in relation to insolvent individuals . . . [1.453]
374 Insolvency districts . . . [1.454]
375 Appeals etc from courts exercising insolvency jurisdiction . . . [1.455]
376 Time-limits . . . [1.456]
377 Formal defects . . . [1.457]
378 Exemption from stamp duty . . . [1.458]
379 Annual report . . . [1.459]

Creditors' decisions

379ZA Creditors' decisions: general . . . [1.460]
379ZB Deemed consent procedure . . . [1.461]
379ZC Power to amend sections 379ZA and 379ZB . . . [1.462]

Remote attendance at meetings

379A Remote attendance at meetings . . . [1.463]

Giving of notices etc by office-holders

379B Use of websites . . . [1.464]
379C Creditors' ability to opt out of receiving certain notices . . . [1.465]

PART XI
INTERPRETATION FOR SECOND GROUP OF PARTS

380 Introductory . . . [1.466]
381 "Bankrupt" and associated terminology . . . [1.467]
382 "Bankruptcy debt", "liability", etc . . . [1.468]
383 "Creditor", "security", etc . . . [1.469]
383A "Opted-out creditor" . . . [1.470]
384 "Prescribed" and "the rules" . . . [1.471]
385 Miscellaneous definitions . . . [1.472]

THE THIRD GROUP OF PARTS
MISCELLANEOUS MATTERS BEARING ON BOTH COMPANY AND INDIVIDUAL INSOLVENCY; GENERAL INTERPRETATION; FINAL PROVISIONS

PART XII
PREFERENTIAL DEBTS IN COMPANY AND INDIVIDUAL INSOLVENCY

386 Categories of preferential debts . . . . [1.473]
387 "The relevant date" . . . . [1.474]

PART XIII
INSOLVENCY PRACTITIONERS AND THEIR QUALIFICATION

Restrictions on unqualified persons acting as liquidator, trustee in bankruptcy, etc

388 Meaning of "act as insolvency practitioner" . . . . [1.475]
389 Acting without qualification an offence . . . . [1.476]
389B Official receiver as nominee or supervisor . . . . [1.477]

The requisite qualification, and the means of obtaining it

390 Persons not qualified to act as insolvency practitioners . . . . [1.478]
390A Authorisation . . . . [1.479]
390B Partial authorisation: acting in relation to partnerships . . . . [1.480]
391 Recognised professional bodies . . . . [1.481]
391A Application for recognition as recognised professional body . . . . [1.482]

Regulatory objectives

391B Application of regulatory objectives . . . . [1.483]
391C Meaning of "regulatory functions" and "regulatory objectives" . . . . [1.484]

Oversight of recognised professional bodies

391D Directions . . . . [1.485]
391E Directions: procedure . . . . [1.486]
391F Financial penalty . . . . [1.487]
391G Financial penalty: procedure . . . . [1.488]
391H Appeal against financial penalty . . . . [1.489]
391I Recovery of financial penalties . . . . [1.490]
391J Reprimand . . . . [1.491]
391K Reprimand: procedure . . . . [1.492]

Revocation etc of recognition

391L Revocation of recognition at instigation of Secretary of State . . . . [1.493]
391M Orders under section 391L: procedure . . . . [1.494]
391N Revocation of recognition at request of body . . . . [1.495]

Court sanction of insolvency practitioners in public interest cases

391O Direct sanctions orders . . . . [1.496]
391P Application for, and power to make, direct sanctions order . . . . [1.497]
391Q Direct sanctions order: conditions . . . . [1.498]
391R Direct sanctions direction instead of order . . . . [1.499]

General

391S Power for Secretary of State to obtain information . . . . [1.500]
391T Compliance orders . . . . [1.501]
392 Authorisation by competent authority . . . . [1.502]
393 Grant, refusal and withdrawal of authorisation . . . . [1.503]
394 Notices . . . . [1.504]
395 Right to make representations . . . . [1.505]
396 Reference to Tribunal . . . . [1.506]
397 Action of Tribunal on reference . . . . [1.507]
398 Refusal or withdrawal without reference to Tribunal . . . . [1.508]

PART XIV
PUBLIC ADMINISTRATION (ENGLAND AND WALES)

Adjudicators

398A Appointment etc of adjudicators and assistants . . . . [1.509]

Official Receivers

399 Appointment, etc of official receivers . . . . [1.510]
400 Functions and status of official receivers . . . . [1.511]

401 Deputy official receivers and staff . . . . . [1.512]

The Official Petitioner

402 Official Petitioner . . . . . [1.513]

Insolvency Service finance, accounting and investment

403 Insolvency Services Account . . . . . [1.514]
404 Investment Account . . . . . [1.515]
405 Application of income in Investment Account; adjustment of balances . . . . . [1.516]
406 Interest on money received by liquidators or trustees in bankruptcy and invested. . . . . [1.517]
407 Unclaimed dividends and undistributed balances . . . . . [1.518]
408 Adjustment of balances . . . . . [1.519]
409 Annual financial statement and audit . . . . . [1.520]

Supplementary

410 Extent of this Part . . . . . [1.521]

PART XV
SUBORDINATE LEGISLATION

General insolvency rules

411 Company insolvency rules . . . . . [1.522]
412 Individual insolvency rules (England and Wales) . . . . . [1.523]
413 Insolvency Rules Committee . . . . . [1.524]

Fees orders

414 Fees orders (company insolvency proceedings) . . . . . [1.525]
415 Fees orders (individual insolvency proceedings in England and Wales) . . . . . [1.526]
415A Fees orders (general) . . . . . [1.527]

Specification, increase and reduction of money sums relevant in the operation of this Act

416 Monetary limits (companies winding up) . . . . . [1.528]
417 Money sum in s 222. . . . . . [1.529]
417A Money sums (company moratorium) . . . . . [1.530]
418 Monetary limits (bankruptcy). . . . . . [1.531]

Insolvency practice

419 Regulations for purposes of Part XIII . . . . . [1.532]

Other order-making powers

420 Insolvent partnerships . . . . . [1.533]
421 Insolvent estates of deceased persons . . . . . [1.534]
421A Insolvent estates: joint tenancies . . . . . [1.535]
422 Formerly authorised banks . . . . . [1.536]

PART XVI
PROVISIONS AGAINST DEBT AVOIDANCE
(ENGLAND AND WALES ONLY)

423 Transactions defrauding creditors . . . . . [1.537]
424 Those who may apply for an order under s 423 . . . . . [1.538]
425 Provision which may be made by order under s 423 . . . . . [1.539]

PART XVII
MISCELLANEOUS AND GENERAL

426 Co-operation between courts exercising jurisdiction in relation to insolvency . . . . . [1.540]
426A Disqualification from Parliament (England and Wales and Northern Ireland) . . . . . [1.541]
426B Devolution . . . . . [1.542]
426C Irrelevance of privilege . . . . . [1.543]
427 Disqualification from Parliament (Scotland) . . . . . [1.544]
428 Exemptions from Restrictive Trade Practices Act . . . . . [1.545]
429 Disabilities on revocation of administration order against an individual . . . . . [1.546]
430 Provision introducing Schedule of punishments . . . . . [1.547]
431 Summary proceedings . . . . . [1.548]
432 Offences by bodies corporate . . . . . [1.549]
433 Admissibility in evidence of statements of affairs, etc . . . . . [1.550]
434 Crown application . . . . . [1.551]

PART 17A
SUPPLEMENTARY PROVISIONS

434A Introductory . . . . . [1.552]

434B Representation of corporations at meetings . . . . . [1.553]
434C Legal professional privilege . . . . . [1.554]
434D Enforcement of company's filing obligations. . . . . [1.555]
434E Application of filing obligations to overseas companies . . . . . [1.556]

PART XVIII
INTERPRETATION

435 Meaning of "associate" . . . . . [1.557]
436 Expressions used generally . . . . . [1.558]
436A Proceedings under EU Regulation: modified definition of property . . . . . [1.559]
436B References to things in writing. . . . . [1.560]

PART XIX
FINAL PROVISIONS

437 Transitional provisions, and savings. . . . . [1.561]
438 Repeals . . . . . [1.562]
439 Amendment of enactments . . . . . [1.563]
440 Extent (Scotland) . . . . . [1.564]
441 Extent (Northern Ireland) . . . . . [1.565]
442 Extent (other territories). . . . . [1.566]
443 Commencement . . . . . [1.567]
444 Citation . . . . . [1.568]

SCHEDULES

Schedule A1—Moratorium where directors propose voluntary arrangement
Part I—Introductory . . . . . [1.569]
Part II—Obtaining a moratorium. . . . . [1.570]
Part III—Effects of moratorium . . . . . [1.571]
Part IV—Nominees . . . . . [1.572]
Part V—Consideration and implementation of voluntary arrangement . . . . . [1.573]
Part VI—Miscellaneous . . . . . [1.574]
Schedule B1—Administration . . . . . [1.575]
Schedule 1—Powers of administrator or administrative receiver. . . . . [1.576]
Schedule 2—Powers of a Scottish receiver (additional to those conferred on him by the instrument of charge) . . . . . [1.577]
Schedule 2A—Exceptions to prohibition on appointment of administrative receiver: supplementary provisions . . . . . [1.578]
Schedule 3—Orders in course of winding up pronounced in vacation (Scotland)
Part I—Orders which are to be final. . . . . [1.579]
Part II—Orders which are to take effect until matter disposed of by Inner House. . . . . [1.580]
Schedule 4—Powers of liquidator in a winding up
Part I. . . . . [1.581]
Part II . . . . . [1.582]
Part III. . . . . [1.583]
Schedule 4ZA—Conditions for Making a Debt Relief Order
Part I—Conditions which must be met . . . . . [1.584]
Part II—Other conditions . . . . . [1.585]
Schedule 4ZB—Debt Relief Restrictions Orders and Undertakings . . . . . [1.586]
Schedule 4A—Bankruptcy restrictions order and undertaking . . . . . [1.587]
Schedule 5—Powers of trustee in bankruptcy
Part I. . . . . [1.588]
Part II . . . . . [1.589]
Part III. . . . . [1.590]
Schedule 6—The categories of preferential debts . . . . . [1.591]
Schedule 7—Insolvency practitioners tribunal . . . . . [1.592]
Schedule 8—Provisions capable of inclusion in company insolvency rules. . . . . [1.593]
Schedule 9—Provisions capable of inclusion in individual Insolvency Rules. . . . . [1.594]
Schedule 10—Punishment of offences under this Act . . . . . [1.595]
Schedule 11—Transitional provisions and savings
Part I—Company insolvency and winding up . . . . . [1.596]
Part II—Individual insolvency . . . . . [1.597]
Part III—Transitional effect of Part XVI . . . . . [1.598]
Part IV—Insolvency practitioners . . . . . [1.599]
Part V—General transitional provisions and savings . . . . . [1.600]

An Act to consolidate the enactments relating to company insolvency and winding up (including the winding up of companies that are not insolvent, and of unregistered companies); enactments relating to the insolvency and bankruptcy of individuals; and other enactments bearing on those two subject matters, including the functions and qualification of insolvency practitioners, the public administration of insolvency, the penalisation and redress of malpractice and wrongdoing, and the avoidance of certain transactions at an undervalue

[25 July 1986]

NOTES

Commencement: this Act came into force on 29 December 1986 by virtue of s 443 and the Insolvency Act 1985 (Commencement No 5) Order 1986, SI 1986/1924, art 3.

This Act is extensively applied, with modifications, to various types of business, financial sectors, mutual societies, etc, as follows:

Building societies: in relation to building societies; see the Building Societies Act 1986, ss 90, 90A, Schs 15, 15A at **[7.454]**, **[7.455]**, **[7.464]**,**[7.468]**. For modifications to Sch B1 in relation to building societies see the Building Societies (Insolvency and Special Administration) Order 2009, SI 2009/805, art 3, Sch 1, Pt 3, paras 29, 30 at **[7.475]**, **[7.481]**.

European Economic Interest Groupings: see the European Economic Interest Grouping Regulations 1989, SI 1989/638, reg 19 at **[13.10]**.

Insolvent partnerships: see the Insolvent Partnerships Order 1994, SI 1994/2421 at **[10.1]**.

Scotland: by virtue of the Scotland Act 1998, s 125, Sch 8, para 23, (i) anything directed to be done, or which may be done, to or by the registrar of companies in Scotland by virtue of any of ss 53(1), 54(3), 61(6), 62(5) (so far as relating to the giving of notice), 67(1), 69(2), 84(3), 94(3), 106(3), (5), 112(3), 130(1), 147(3), 170(2) and 172(8), shall, or (as the case may be) may, also be done to or by the Accountant in Bankruptcy, and (ii) anything directed to be done, or which may be done, to or by the registrar of companies in Scotland by virtue of any of sections 89(3), 109(1), 171(5), (6), 173(2)(a) and 192(1), shall, or (as the case may be) shall instead be done to or by the Accountant in Bankruptcy.

See also the Scotland Act 1998 (Insolvency Functions) Order 2018, SI 2018/174 at **[16.446]** which provides that specific insolvency functions relating to reserved matters under Sch 5 to the 1998 Act, that are exercised by a Minister of the Crown in or as regards Scotland, are to be exercisable by both the Scottish Ministers and a Minister of the Crown, and provides for specific insolvency functions within the devolved competence of the Scottish Ministers to be exercised by both the Scottish Ministers and a Minister of the Crown.

Limited liability partnerships: as to the application of this Act to LLPs, see the notes below:

(1) The Limited Liability Partnerships Regulations 2001, SI 2001/1090, reg 5(1) applies Parts I, II, III, IV, VI and VII of the First Group of Parts, and the whole of the Third Group of Parts, to limited liability partnerships (see reg 5(1) at **[10.37]**). For general modifications of this Act in its application to LLPs see reg 5(2) of those Regulations, and for specific modifications see Sch 3 (at **[10.41]**). See also reg 5(3) of, and Sch 4 to, those Regulations (which provide that certain provisions of the First and Third Groups of Parts which are applied to LLPs by reg 5(1) do not apply to Scotland). See also the Companies (Registrar, Languages and Trading Disclosures) Regulations 2006, SI 2006/3429, reg 3(3).

(2) As to the application of this Act in relation to LLPs in Scotland, see also the Limited Liability Partnerships (Scotland) Regulations 2001, SSI 2001/128 at **[16.133]**. Regulation 4(1) of those Regulations (at **[16.136]**) applies the provisions of this Act specified in Sch 2 to those Regulations (at **[16.139]**) to Scotland, subject to the general modifications provided for by reg 4(2), and the specific modifications provided for by Sch 3 (at **[16.140]**).

Open-ended investment companies: where an open-ended investment company is wound up as an unregistered company under Pt V, the provisions of this Act apply for the purposes of the winding up subject to certain modifications; see the Open-Ended Investment Companies Regulations 2001, SI 2001/1228 at **[7.2050]**.

Companies incorporated outside Great Britain: the Enterprise Act 2002, s 254 at **[2.11]** provides that the Secretary of State may by order provide for a provision of this Act to apply (with or without modification) in relation to a company incorporated outside Great Britain. As at 6 April 2014 no orders had been made under that section.

Non-companies: the Enterprise Act 2002, s 255 at **[2.12]** provides that the Treasury may with the concurrence of the Secretary of State by order provide for a company arrangement or administration provision to apply (ie, Pts I, II) in relation to (a) a society registered under the Industrial and Provident Societies Act 1965 (see the Co-operative and Community Benefit Societies and Credit Unions Act 2010 which renames this Act as the Co-operative and Community Benefit Societies and Credit Unions Act 1965); (b) a society registered under the Friendly Societies Act 1974, s 7(1)(b), (c), (d), (e) or (f); (c) a friendly society within the meaning of the Friendly Societies Act 1992; (d) an unregistered friendly society. See the Industrial and Provident Societies and Credit Unions (Arrangements, Reconstructions and Administration) Order 2014, SI 2014/229 at **[7.1425]**, made under the Enterprise Act 2002, s 255.

UK insurers: see the Insurers (Reorganisation and Winding Up) Regulations 2004, SI 2004/353 at **[3.124]**, and the Financial Services and Markets Act 2000 (Administration Orders Relating to Insurers) Order 2010, SI 2010/3023 at **[7.1618]**.

EEA credit institutions: as to the application of this Act to EEA credit institutions or any branch of an EEA credit institution, see the Credit Institutions (Reorganisation and Winding up) Regulations 2004, SI 2004/1045 **[3.213]**.

Former authorised institutions: see the Banks (Former Authorised Institutions) (Insolvency) Order 2006, SI 2006/3107 at **[7.21]** as to the application of Pt II of, and Sch B1 to, this Act, to any company within the meaning of s 735(1) of the Companies Act 1985 (repealed) that (a) has a liability in respect of a deposit which it accepted in accordance with the Banking Act 1979 or Banking Act 1987, but (b) does not have permission under Pt IV of the Financial Services and Markets Act 2000 to accept deposits.

Special administration regimes: see the notes to s 8 of this Act at **[1.13]**; and, with regard to companies which hold a licence under the Electricity Act 1989, s 6(1)(b) or (c) (transmission and distribution licences for electricity) or the Gas Act 1986, s 7 (licensing of gas transporters), see the Energy Act 2004, ss 154–171, Schs 20, 21.

Cross-Border insolvency proceedings: British insolvency law (as defined in Article 2 of the UNCITRAL Model Law as set out in the Cross-Border Insolvency Regulations 2006, SI 2006/1030, Sch 1 at **[3.310]**) shall apply with such modifications as the context requires for the purpose of giving effect to the provisions of the 2006 Regulations; see reg 2 of the 2006 Regulations at **[3.303]**.

European Grouping of Territorial Cooperation: see the European Grouping of Territorial Cooperation Regulations 2015, SI 2015/1493 at **[3.541]**.

Bank insolvency and administration: in respect of bank insolvency and administration, see the Banking Act 2009 at **[7.27]** et seq; see in particular, ss 103, 145 at **[7.39]**, **[7.74]**. As to the application of certain provisions of this Act to particular banks, see the Banking (Special Provisions) Act 2008 at **[17.335]** and the Orders made under it.

Banks in temporary public ownership: see the Banking Act 2009 (Bank Administration) (Modification for Application to Banks in Temporary Public Ownership) Regulations 2009, SI 2009/312, reg 2(1), (3), Schedule.

Authorised banks: in relation to the treatment, holding and issuing of banknotes by the banks who are authorised to issue banknotes in Scotland and Northern Ireland (other than the Bank of England); see the Scottish and Northern Ireland Banknote Regulations 2009, SI 2009/3056, reg 29, Sch 1, Pt 1, para 2.

Postal administration orders: see the Postal Services Act 2011, s 73, Sch 10 at **[7.2063]**, **[7.2082]**.

Investment banks: in respect of the special administration regime for investment banks (as defined in the Banking Act 2009, s 232), see the Investment Bank Special Administration Regulations 2011, SI 2011/245 at **[7.1661]**.

Application to health special administration: see the Health and Social Care Act 2012, s 130 at **[7.1359]**, and regulations made thereunder.

Application to co-ownership schemes: in relation to the winding up of a stand-alone co-ownership scheme or a sub-scheme of an umbrella co-ownership scheme as if it were an unregistered company, see the Collective Investment in Transferable Securities (Contractual Scheme) Regulations 2013, SI 2013/1388, reg 17, Sch 2 at **[7.835]**, **[7.837]**.

Financial market infrastructure companies: see the Financial Services (Banking Reform) Act 2013, Pt 6 (Special Administration for operators of certain infrastructure systems).

Application to societies registered under the Co-operative and Community Benefit Societies Act 2014: see the Co-operative and Community Benefit Societies and Credit Unions (Arrangements, Reconstructions and Administration) Order 2014, SI 2014/229 at **[7.1425]**.

Protected cell companies: see the Risk Transformation Regulations 2017, SI 2017/1212 at **[7.1624]**.

Other bodies etc: this Act is applied (with modifications as appropriate) to various types of other bodies *including* the following: (i) the Friendly Societies Act 1992, ss 23, 52, Sch 10 (application to incorporated and registered friendly societies); (ii) the European Public Limited-Liability Company Regulations 2004, SI 2004/2326 (application to Societas Europaea); (iii) the Companies Act 1989, s 182 (application to certain proceedings begun before the commencement of that section in respect of insolvency proceedings regarding members of recognised investment exchanges and clearing houses and persons to whom market charges have been granted) at **[17.85]**; (iv) the Solicitors' Recognised Bodies Order 1991, SI 1991/2684, arts 2–5, Sch 1 (application to a "recognised body" within the meaning of the Administration of Justice Act 1985, s 9); (v) the Legal Services Act 2007 (Designation as a Licensing Authority) (No 2) Order 2011, SI 2011/2866, art 8, Sch 3 (application to to a body which holds a licence issued by the Law Society which is in force under Part 5 of the Legal Services Act 2007); (vi) the Charities Act 2011 and the Charitable Incorporated Organisations (Insolvency and Dissolution) Regulations 2012, SI 2012/3013 (application to charities and charitable incorporated organisations etc); (vii) the Technical and Further Education Act 2017 (application to technical and further education bodies).

See also the powers to apply this Act in s 420 at **[1.533]** (insolvent partnerships) and s 422 at **[1.536]** (formerly authorised banks).

Miscellaneous:

Registrar of companies: as to the contracting out of certain functions of the registrar of companies in relation to Scotland conferred by or under this Act, see the Contracting Out (Functions in relation to the Registration of Companies) Order 1995, SI 1995/1013, art 4, Sch 2.

Official Receiver: as to the contracting out of functions of the Official Receiver conferred by or under this Act, see the Contracting Out (Functions of the Official Receiver) Order 1995, SI 1995/1386 at **[12.4]**.

Proceeds of crime: if an order for the winding up of a company is made or it passes a resolution for its voluntary winding up, the functions of the liquidator (or any provisional liquidator) are not exercisable in relation to property deemed to be the proceeds of crime; see the Proceeds of Crime Act 2002, Pt 9 at **[17.236]**.

See the Serious Crime Act 2007, ss 27, 29 in relation to the power of the Director of Public Prosecutions, the Director of Revenue and Customs Prosecutions and the Director of the Serious Fraud Office to present a petition to the court for the winding up of a company, partnership (etc) where the company, partnership (etc) has been convicted of an offence under s 25 of that Act (offence of failing to comply with serious crime prevention order) and the Director concerned considers that it would be in the public interest for the company, partnership (etc) to be wound up.

THE FIRST GROUP OF PARTS
COMPANY INSOLVENCY; COMPANIES WINDING UP

NOTES

Application to limited liability partnerships: Pts I–IV, VI, VII of this Group of Parts are applied, with modifications, to limited liability partnerships, by the Limited Liability Partnerships Regulations 2001, SI 2001/1090, reg 5, Sch 4 at **[10.37]**, **[10.42]**.

PART I COMPANY VOLUNTARY ARRANGEMENTS

NOTES

Modification of this Part in relation to building societies: this Part (except s 1A) is applied, with modifications, in respect of the approval of voluntary arrangements in relation to building societies; see the Building Societies Act 1986, s 90A, Sch 15A at **[7.455]**, **[7.468]**.

Application to industrial and provident societies and friendly societies: this Part may be applied, with or without modification, in relation to industrial and provident societies and friendly societies by order of the Treasury, with the concurrence of the Secretary of State; see the Enterprise Act 2002, s 255 at **[2.12]**.

The proposal

[1.1]

1 Those who may propose an arrangement

(1) The directors of a company [(other than one which is in administration or being wound up)] may make a proposal under this Part to the company and to its creditors for a composition in satisfaction of its debts or a scheme of arrangement of its affairs (from here on referred to, in either case, as a "voluntary arrangement").

(2) A proposal under this Part is one which provides for some person ("the nominee") to act in relation to the voluntary arrangement either as trustee or otherwise for the purpose of supervising its implementation; and the nominee must be a person who is qualified to act as an insolvency practitioner [. . . in relation to the voluntary arrangement].

(3) Such a proposal may also be made—
[(a) where the company is in administration, by the administrator,] and
(b) where the company is being wound up, by the liquidator.
[(4) In this Part "company" means—
[(a) a company registered under the Companies Act 2006 in England and Wales or Scotland;]
(b) a company incorporated in an EEA State other than the United Kingdom; or
(c) a company not incorporated in an EEA State but having its centre of main interests in a member State other than Denmark.
(5) In subsection (4), in relation to a company, "centre of main interests" has the same meaning as in [Article 3 of the EU Regulation].
(6) If a company incorporated outside the United Kingdom has a principal place of business in Northern Ireland, no proposal under this Part shall be made in relation to it unless it also has a principal place of business in England and Wales or Scotland (or both in England and Wales or Scotland).]

NOTES

This section derived from the Insolvency Act 1985, s 20.

Sub-s (1): words in square brackets substituted for original words "(other than one for which an administration order is in force, or which is being wound up)" by the Enterprise Act 2002, s 248(3), Sch 17, paras 9, 10(a), subject to savings and transitional provisions (i) in a case where a petition for an administration order has been presented before 15 September 2003 (see the Enterprise Act 2002 (Commencement No 4 and Transitional Provisions and Savings) Order 2003, SI 2003/2093, art 3 at **[2.26]**), and (ii) in relation to special administration regimes (see s 249 of the 2002 Act at **[2.10]**).

Sub-s (2): words in square brackets substituted for original words "in relation to the company" by the Insolvency Act 2000, s 2, Sch 2, Pt I, paras 1, 2, subject to transitional provisions in SI 2002/2711, art 3 at **[2.6]**; words omitted repealed by the Deregulation Act 2015, s 19, Sch 6, Pt 6, para 20(1), (2)(a).

Sub-s (3): para (a) substituted by the Enterprise Act 2002, s 248(3), Sch 17, paras 9, 10(b), subject to savings and transitional provisions as noted to sub-s (1) above, and originally read as follows:

"(a) where an administration order is in force in relation to the company, by the administrator, and".

Sub-s (4): substituted (together with sub-ss (5), (6), for sub-s (4) as originally added by the Insolvency Act 1986 (Amendment) (No 2) Regulations 2002, SI 2002/1240, regs 3, 4) by the Insolvency Act 1986 (Amendment) Regulations 2005, SI 2005/879, regs 2(1), (2), 3, except in relation to a voluntary arrangement under Pt I of this Act or the appointment of an administrator under Pt II of this Act that took effect before 13 April 2005. Sub-s (4) originally read as follows:

"(4) In this Part a reference to a company includes a reference to a company in relation to which a proposal for a voluntary arrangement may be made by virtue of Article 3 of the EC Regulation.".

Sub-s (4)(a) substituted by the Companies Act 2006 (Consequential Amendments, Transitional Provisions and Savings) Order 2009, SI 2009/1941, art 2(1), Sch 1, para 71(1), (2), subject to transitional provisions and savings in art 8, Sch 1, para 84 at **[2.70]**, **[2.73]** and previously read as follows:

"(a) a company within the meaning of section 735(1) of the Companies Act 1985,".

Sub-s (5): substituted as noted to sub-s (4) above; words in square brackets substituted for original words "the EC Regulation and, in the absence of proof to the contrary, is presumed to be the place of its registered office (within the meaning of that Regulation)" by the Insolvency Amendment (EU 2015/848) Regulations 2017, SI 2017/702, regs 2, 3, Schedule, Pt 1, paras 1, 2, except in relation to proceedings opened before 26 June 2017 and subject to savings in reg 4 thereof at **[2.103]**.

Sub-s (6): substituted as noted to sub-s (4) above.

[1.2]

[1A Moratorium

(1) Where the directors of an eligible company intend to make a proposal for a voluntary arrangement, they may take steps to obtain a moratorium for the company.
(2) The provisions of Schedule A1 to this Act have effect with respect to—
(a) companies eligible for a moratorium under this section,
(b) the procedure for obtaining such a moratorium,
(c) the effects of such a moratorium, and
(d) the procedure applicable (in place of sections 2 to 6 and 7) in relation to the approval and implementation of a voluntary arrangement where such a moratorium is or has been in force.]

NOTES

Inserted by the Insolvency Act 2000, s 1, Sch 1, paras 1, 2.

[1.3]

2 Procedure where nominee is not the liquidator or administrator

(1) This section applies where the nominee under section 1 is not the liquidator or administrator of the company [and the directors do not propose to take steps to obtain a moratorium under section 1A for the company].
(2) The nominee shall, within 28 days (or such longer period as the court may allow) after he is given notice of the proposal for a voluntary arrangement, submit a report to the court stating—
(a) [whether, in his opinion, the proposed voluntary arrangement has a reasonable prospect of being approved and implemented,]
[(b) whether, in his opinion, the proposal should be considered by a meeting of the company and by the company's creditors, and
(c) if in his opinion it should, the date on which, and time and place at which, he proposes a meeting of the company should be held.]

(3) For the purposes of enabling the nominee to prepare his report, the person intending to make the proposal shall submit to the nominee—

(a) a document setting out the terms of the proposed voluntary arrangement, and

(b) a statement of the company's affairs containing—

(i) such particulars of its creditors and of its debts and other liabilities and of its assets as may be prescribed, and

(ii) such other information as may be prescribed.

[(4) The court may—

(a) on an application made by the person intending to make the proposal, in a case where the nominee has failed to submit the report required by this section or has died, or

(b) on an application made by that person or the nominee, in a case where it is impracticable or inappropriate for the nominee to continue to act as such,

direct that the nominee be replaced as such by another person qualified to act as an insolvency practitioner . . . in relation to the voluntary arrangement.]

NOTES

This section derived from the Insolvency Act 1985, s 21.

Sub-s (1): words in square brackets added by the Insolvency Act 2000, s 1, Sch 1, paras 1, 3.

Sub-s (2): words in square brackets inserted by the Insolvency Act 2000, s 2, Sch 2, Pt I, paras 1, 3(a), subject to transitional provisions in SI 2002/2711, art 3 at **[2.6]**; paras (b), (c) substituted for paras (aa), (b), by the Small Business, Enterprise and Employment Act 2015, s 126, Sch 9, Pt 1, paras 1, 2, as from 6 April 2017 (in relation to England and Wales and subject to transitional and savings provisions as noted to s 246ZE at **[1.256]**), and as from a day to be appointed (in relation to Scotland). Paras (aa), (b) originally read as follows (with original text numbered as para (aa) by the Insolvency Act 2000, s 2, Sch 2, Pt I, paras 1, 3(a))—

"(aa) whether, in his opinion, meetings of the company and of its creditors should be summoned to consider the proposal, and

(b) if in his opinion such meetings should be summoned, the date on which, and time and place at which, he proposes the meetings should be held.".

Sub-s (4): substituted by the Insolvency Act 2000, s 2, Sch 2, Pt I, paras 1, 3(b), subject to transitional provisions in SI 2002/2711, art 3 at **[2.6]**. Sub-s (4) originally read as follows:

"(4) The court may, on an application made by the person intending to make the proposal, in a case where the nominee has failed to submit the report required by this section, direct that the nominee be replaced as such by another person qualified to act as an insolvency practitioner in relation to the company.";

words omitted from sub-s (4) repealed by the Deregulation Act 2015, s 19, Sch 6, Pt 6, para 20(1), (2)(b).

[1.4]

3 [Consideration of proposal]

(1) Where the nominee under section 1 is not the liquidator or administrator, and it has been reported to the court [under section 2(2) that the proposal should be considered by a meeting of the company and by the company's creditors], the person making the report shall (unless the court otherwise [directs)—

(a) summon a meeting of the company to consider the proposal for the time, date and place proposed in the report, and

(b) seek a decision from the company's creditors as to whether they approve the proposal.]

(2) Where the nominee is the liquidator or administrator, he [shall—

(a) summon a meeting of the company to consider the proposal for such time, date and place as he thinks fit, and

(b) seek a decision from the company's creditors as to whether they approve the proposal.]

[(3) A decision of the company's creditors as to whether they approve the proposal is to be made by a qualifying decision procedure.

(4) Notice of the qualifying decision procedure must be given to every creditor of the company of whose claim and address the person seeking the decision is aware.]

NOTES

This section derived from the Insolvency Act 1985, s 22.

Section heading: words in square brackets substituted for original words "Summoning of meetings" by the Small Business, Enterprise and Employment Act 2015, s 126, Sch 9, Pt 1, paras 1, 3(1), (5), as from 6 April 2017 (in relation to England and Wales and subject to transitional and savings provisions as noted to s 246ZE at **[1.256]**), and as from a day to be appointed (in relation to Scotland).

Sub-s (1): words in first pair of square brackets substituted for original words "that such meetings as are mentioned in section 2(2) should be summoned" and words in second pair of square brackets substituted for original words "directs) summon those meetings for the time, date and place proposed in the report." by the Small Business, Enterprise and Employment Act 2015, s 126, Sch 9, Pt 1, paras 1, 3(1), (2), as from 6 April 2017 (in relation to England and Wales and subject to transitional and savings provisions as noted to s 246ZE at **[1.256]**), and as from a day to be appointed (in relation to Scotland).

Sub-s (2): words in square brackets substituted for original words "shall summon meetings of the company and of its creditors to consider the proposal for such a time, date and place as he thinks fit." by the Small Business, Enterprise and Employment Act 2015, s 126, Sch 9, Pt 1, paras 1, 3(1), (3), as from 6 April 2017 (in relation to England and Wales and subject to transitional and savings provisions as noted to s 246ZE at **[1.256]**), and as from a day to be appointed (in relation to Scotland).

Sub-ss (3), (4): substituted for original sub-s (3) by the Small Business, Enterprise and Employment Act 2015, s 126, Sch 9, Pt 1, paras 1, 3(1), (4), as from 6 April 2017 (in relation to England and Wales and subject to transitional and savings provisions as noted to s 246ZE at **[1.256]**), and as from a day to be appointed (in relation to Scotland). Sub-s (3) originally read as follows—

"(3) The persons to be summoned to a creditors' meeting under this section are every creditor of the company of whose claim and address the person summoning the meeting is aware.".

Consideration and implementation of proposal

[1.5]

4 Decisions of [the company and its creditors]

[(1) This section applies where, under section 3—

(a) a meeting of the company is summoned to consider the proposed voluntary arrangement, and

(b) the company's creditors are asked to decide whether to approve the proposed voluntary arrangement.

(1A) The company and its creditors may approve the proposed voluntary arrangement with or without modifications.]

(2) The modifications may include one conferring the functions proposed to be conferred on the nominee on another person qualified to act as an insolvency practitioner [. . . in relation to the voluntary arrangement].

But they shall not include any modification by virtue of which the proposal ceases to be a proposal such as is mentioned in section 1.

(3) [Neither the company nor its creditors may] approve any proposal or modification which affects the right of a secured creditor of the company to enforce his security, except with the concurrence of the creditor concerned.

(4) Subject as follows, [neither the company nor its creditors may] approve any proposal or modification under which—

(a) any preferential debt of the company is to be paid otherwise than in priority to such of its debts as are not preferential debts, . . .

[(aa) any ordinary preferential debt of the company is to be paid otherwise than in priority to any secondary preferential debts that it may have,]

(b) a preferential creditor of the company is to be paid an amount in respect of [an ordinary preferential debt] that bears to that debt a smaller proportion than is borne to [another ordinary] preferential debt by the amount that is to be paid in respect of that other debt[, or

(c) a preferential creditor of the company is to be paid an amount in respect of a secondary preferential debt that bears to that debt a smaller proportion than is borne to another secondary preferential debt by the amount that is to be paid in respect of that other debt].

However, *the meeting may approve* such a proposal or modification [may be approved] with the concurrence of the preferential creditor concerned

(5) Subject as above, [the meeting of the company and the qualifying decision procedure] shall be conducted in accordance with the rules.

(6) After the conclusion of [the company] meeting in accordance with the rules, the chairman of the meeting shall report the result of the meeting to the court, and, immediately after reporting to the court, shall give notice of the result of the meeting to such persons as may be prescribed.

[(6A) After the company's creditors have decided whether to approve the proposed voluntary arrangement the person who sought the decision must—

(a) report the creditors' decision to the court, and

(b) immediately after reporting to the court, give notice of the creditors' decision to such persons as may be prescribed.]

(7) References in this section to preferential debts[, ordinary preferential debts, secondary preferential debts] and preferential creditors are to be read in accordance with section 386 in Part XII of this Act.

NOTES

This section derived from the Insolvency Act 1985, s 23(1)–(6), (7) (in part).

Section heading: words in square brackets substituted for original word "meetings" by the Small Business, Enterprise and Employment Act 2015, s 126, Sch 9, Pt 1, paras 1, 4(1), (8), as from 6 April 2017 (in relation to England and Wales and subject to transitional and savings provisions as noted to s 246ZE at **[1.256]**), and as from a day to be appointed (in relation to Scotland).

Sub-ss (1), (1A): substituted for original sub-s (1), by the Small Business, Enterprise and Employment Act 2015, s 126, Sch 9, Pt 1, paras 1, 4(1), (2), as from 6 April 2017 (in relation to England and Wales and subject to transitional and savings provisions as noted to s 246ZE at **[1.256]**), and as from a day to be appointed (in relation to Scotland). Sub-s (1) originally read as follows—

"(1) The meetings summoned under section 3 shall decide whether to approve the proposed voluntary arrangement (with or without modifications).".

Sub-s (2): words in square brackets substituted for original words "in relation to the company" by the Insolvency Act 2000, s 2, Sch 2, Pt I, paras 1, 4, subject to transitional provisions in SI 2002/2711, art 3 at **[2.6]**; words omitted repealed by the Deregulation Act 2015, s 19, Sch 6, Pt 6, para 20(1), (2)(c).

Sub-s (3): words in square brackets substituted for original words "A meeting so summoned shall not" by the Small Business, Enterprise and Employment Act 2015, s 126, Sch 9, Pt 1, paras 1, 4(1), (3), as from 6 April 2017 (in relation to England and Wales and subject to transitional and savings provisions as noted to s 246ZE at **[1.256]**), and as from a day to be appointed (in relation to Scotland).

Sub-s (4): words in first pair of square brackets substituted for original words "a meeting so summoned shall not", words in italics are repealed, and words "may be approved" in square brackets inserted, by the Small Business, Enterprise and Employment Act 2015, s 126, Sch 9, Pt 1, paras 1, 4(1), (4), as from 6 April 2017 (in relation to England and Wales and subject to transitional and savings provisions as noted to s 246ZE at **[1.256]**), and as from a day to be appointed (in relation to Scotland); word "or" omitted from para (a) repealed, para (aa) inserted, words in first and second pairs of square brackets in para (b) substituted (for original words "a preferential debt" and "another" respectively) and para (c) (and the preceding word) added, by the Banks and Building Societies (Depositor Preference and Priorities) Order 2014, SI 2014/3486, arts 3, 4(1), (2), except in relation to any insolvency proceedings commenced before 1 January 2015 (see further the note "SI 2014/3486, art 3" below).

Sub-s (5): words in square brackets substituted for original words "each of the meetings" by the Small Business, Enterprise and Employment Act 2015, s 126, Sch 9, Pt 1, paras 1, 4(1), (5), as from 6 April 2017 (in relation to England and Wales and subject to transitional and savings provisions as noted to s 246ZE at **[1.256]**), and as from a day to be appointed (in relation to Scotland).

Sub-s (6): words in square brackets substituted for original word "either" by the Small Business, Enterprise and Employment Act 2015, s 126, Sch 9, Pt 1, paras 1, 4(1), (6), as from 6 April 2017 (in relation to England and Wales and subject to transitional and savings provisions as noted to s 246ZE at **[1.256]**), and as from a day to be appointed (in relation to Scotland).

Sub-s (6A): inserted by the Small Business, Enterprise and Employment Act 2015, s 126, Sch 9, Pt 1, paras 1, 4(1), (7), as from 6 April 2017 (in relation to England and Wales and subject to transitional and savings provisions as noted to s 246ZE at **[1.256]**), and as from a day to be appointed (in relation to Scotland).

Sub-s (7): words in square brackets inserted by SI 2014/3486, arts 3, 4(1), (3), except in relation to any insolvency proceedings commenced before 1 January 2015 (see further the note "SI 2014/3486, art 3" below).

SI 2014/3486, art 3: the Banks and Building Societies (Depositor Preference and Priorities) Order 2014, SI 2014/3486, art 3(2)(b) provides that for the purposes of the 2014 Order, insolvency proceedings commence on (i) the date of presentation of a petition for a winding-up order, bank insolvency order, building society insolvency order, bankruptcy order or award of sequestration; (ii) the date on which an application is made for an administration order, bank administration order or building society administration order; (iii) the date on which notice of appointment of an administrator is given under paragraph 18 or 29 of Schedule B1 to the Insolvency Act 1986; (iv) the date on which a proposal is made by the directors of a company for a company voluntary arrangement under Part 1 of the Insolvency Act 1986 or by an individual debtor for an individual voluntary arrangement under Part 8 of the Insolvency Act 1986; (v) the date on which a resolution for voluntary winding up is passed.

Modification: this section is modified, in relation to a voluntary arrangement proposed under s 1 of this Act in relation to a UK insurer, where that arrangement includes a composition in satisfaction of any insurance debts and a distribution to creditors of some or all of the assets of that insurer in the course of, or with a view to terminating the whole or any part of the business of that insurer, by the Insurers (Reorganisation and Winding Up) Regulations 2004, SI 2004/353, reg 33(1), (2) at **[3.157]**.

[1.6]

[4A Approval of arrangement

(1) This section applies to a decision, under section 4, with respect to the approval of a proposed voluntary arrangement.

(2) The decision has effect if, in accordance with the rules—

(a) it has been taken by [the meeting of the company summoned under section 3 and by the company's creditors pursuant to that section], or

(b) (subject to any order made under subsection (4)) it has been taken by the [company's creditors pursuant to] that section.

(3) If the decision taken by the [company's creditors] differs from that taken by the company meeting, a member of the company may apply to the court.

(4) An application under subsection (3) shall not be made after the end of the period of 28 days beginning with—

(a) the day on which the decision was taken by the [company's creditors], or

(b) where the decision of the company meeting was taken on a later day, that day.

(5) Where a member of a regulated company, within the meaning given by paragraph 44 of Schedule A1, applies to the court under subsection (3), the [appropriate regulator] is entitled to be heard on the application.

[(5A) "The appropriate regulator" means—

(a) where the regulated company is a PRA-regulated company within the meaning of paragraph 44 of Schedule A1, the Financial Conduct Authority and the Prudential Regulation Authority, and

(b) in any other case, the Financial Conduct Authority.]

(6) On an application under subsection (3), the court may—

(a) order the decision of the company meeting to have effect instead of the decision of the [company's creditors], or

(b) make such other order as it thinks fit.]

NOTES

Inserted by the Insolvency Act 2000, s 2, Sch 2, Pt I, paras 1, 5, subject to transitional provisions in SI 2002/2711, art 3 at **[2.6]**.

Sub-s (2): words in square brackets in paras (a), (b) substituted for original words "both meetings summoned under section 3" and "creditors' meeting summoned under" respectively, by the Small Business, Enterprise and Employment Act 2015, s 126, Sch 9, Pt 1, paras 1, 5(1), (2), as from 6 April 2017 (in relation to England and Wales and subject to transitional and savings provisions as noted to s 246ZE at **[1.256]**), and as from a day to be appointed (in relation to Scotland).

Sub-ss (3), (4), (6): words in square brackets substituted for original words "creditors' meeting" by the Small Business, Enterprise and Employment Act 2015, s 126, Sch 9, Pt 1, paras 1, 5, as from 6 April 2017 (in relation to England and Wales and subject to transitional and savings provisions as noted to s 246ZE at **[1.256]**), and as from a day to be appointed (in relation to Scotland).

Sub-s (5): words in square brackets substituted by the Financial Services Act 2012, s 114(1), Sch 18, Pt 2, paras 51, 52(1), (2).

Sub-s (5A): inserted by the Financial Services Act 2012, s 114(1), Sch 18, Pt 2, paras 51, 52(1), (3).

[1.7]

5 Effect of approval

[(1) This section applies where a decision approving a voluntary arrangement has effect under section 4A.]

(2) The . . . voluntary arrangement—

(a) takes effect as if made by the company at the [time the creditors decided to approve the voluntary arrangement], and

[(b) binds every person who in accordance with the rules—

(i) was entitled to vote [in the qualifying decision procedure by which the creditors' decision to approve the voluntary arrangement was made], or

(ii) would have been so entitled if he had had notice of it,

as if he were a party to the voluntary arrangement.]

[(2A) If—

(a) when the arrangement ceases to have effect any amount payable under the arrangement to a person bound by virtue of subsection (2)(b)(ii) has not been paid, and

(b) the arrangement did not come to an end prematurely,

the company shall at that time become liable to pay to that person the amount payable under the arrangement.]

(3) Subject as follows, if the company is being wound up or [is in administration], the court may do one or both of the following, namely—

(a) by order stay or sist all proceedings in the winding up or [provide for the appointment of the administrator to cease to have effect];

(b) give such directions with respect to the conduct of the winding up or the administration as it thinks appropriate for facilitating the implementation of the . . . voluntary arrangement.

(4) The court shall not make an order under subsection (3)(a)—

(a) at any time before the end of the period of 28 days beginning with the first day on which each of the reports required by section 4(6) [and (6A] has been made to the court, or

(b) at any time when an application under the next section or an appeal in respect of such an application is pending, or at any time in the period within which such an appeal may be brought.

[(5) Where the company is in energy administration, the court shall not make an order or give a direction under subsection (3) unless—

(a) the court has given the Secretary of State or the Gas and Electricity Markets Authority a reasonable opportunity of making representations to it about the proposed order or direction; and

(b) the order or direction is consistent with the objective of the energy administration.

(6) In subsection (5) "in energy administration" and "objective of the energy administration" are to be construed in accordance with Schedule B1 to this Act, as applied by Part 1 of Schedule 20 to the Energy Act 2004.]

NOTES

This section derived from the Insolvency Act 1985, s 24.

Sub-s (1): substituted by the Insolvency Act 2000, s 2, Sch 2, Pt I, paras 1, 6(a), subject to transitional provisions in SI 2002/2711, art 3 at **[2.6]**, and originally read as follows:

> "(1) This section has effect where each of the meetings summoned under section 3 approves the proposed voluntary arrangement either with the same modifications or without modifications.".

Sub-s (2): word omitted repealed, and para (b) substituted (together with sub-s (2A)), by the Insolvency Act 2000, ss 2, 15(1), Sch 2, Pt I, paras 1, 6(b), (c), Sch 5, subject to transitional provisions in SI 2002/2711, art 3 at **[2.6]**; words in square brackets in paras (a), (b)(i) substituted for original words "creditors' meeting" and "at that meeting (whether or not he was present or represented at it)" respectively, by the Small Business, Enterprise and Employment Act 2015, s 126, Sch 9, Pt 1, paras 1, 6(1), (2),as from 6 April 2017 (in relation to England and Wales and subject to transitional and savings provisions as noted to s 246ZE at **[1.256]**), and as from a day to be appointed (in relation to Scotland).

Sub-s (2A): substituted as noted to sub-s (2) above, subject to transitional provisions in SI 2002/2711, art 3 at **[2.6]**.

Sub-s (3): first and second words in square brackets substituted by the Enterprise Act 2002, s 248(3), Sch 17, paras 9, 11, subject to savings and transitional provisions (i) in a case where a petition for an administration order has been presented before 15 September 2003 (see the Enterprise Act 2002 (Commencement No 4 and Transitional Provisions and Savings) Order 2003, SI 2003/2093, art 3 at **[2.26]**), and (ii) in relation to special administration regimes (see s 249 of the 2002 Act at **[2.10]**); word omitted from para (b) repealed by the Insolvency Act 2000, ss 2, 15(1), Sch 2, Pt I, paras 1, 6(b), Sch 5, subject to transitional provisions in SI 2002/2711, art 3 at **[2.6]**. Sub-s (3) originally read as follows:

> "(3) Subject as follows, if the company is being wound up or an administration order is in force, the court may do one or both of the following, namely—
>
> (a) by order stay or sist all proceedings in the winding up or discharge the administration order;
>
> (b) give such directions with respect to the conduct of the winding up or the administration as it thinks appropriate for facilitating the implementation of the approved voluntary arrangement.".

Sub-s (4): words in square brackets inserted by the Small Business, Enterprise and Employment Act 2015, s 126, Sch 9, Pt 1, paras 1, 6(1), (3), as from 6 April 2017 (in relation to England and Wales and subject to transitional and savings provisions as noted to s 246ZE at **[1.256]**), and as from a day to be appointed (in relation to Scotland).

Sub-ss (5), (6): added by the Energy Act 2004, s 159(1), Sch 20, Pt 4, para 43.

[1.8]

6 Challenge of decisions

(1) Subject to this section, an application to the court may be made, by any of the persons specified below, on one or both of the following grounds, namely—

(a) that a voluntary arrangement [which has effect under section 4A] unfairly prejudices the interests of a creditor, member or contributory of the company;

(b) that there has been some material irregularity at or in relation to [the meeting of the company, or in relation to the relevant qualifying decision procedure].

[(1A) In this section—

(a) the "relevant qualifying decision procedure" means the qualifying decision procedure in which the company's creditors decide whether to approve a voluntary arrangement;

(b) references to a decision made in the relevant qualifying decision procedure include any other decision made in that qualifying decision procedure.]

(2) The persons who may apply under [subsection (1)] are—

(a) a person entitled, in accordance with the rules, to vote at [the meeting of the company or in the relevant qualifying decision procedure];

[(aa) a person who would have been entitled, in accordance with the rules, to vote [in the relevant qualifying decision procedure] if he had had notice of it]

(b) the nominee or any person who has replaced him under section 2(4) or 4(2); and

(c) if the company is being wound up or [is in administration], the liquidator or administrator.

[(2A) Subject to this section, where a voluntary arrangement in relation to a company in energy administration is approved at the meetings summoned under section 3, an application to the court may be made—

(a) by the Secretary of State, or

(b) with the consent of the Secretary of State, by the Gas and Electricity Markets Authority,

on the ground that the voluntary arrangement is not consistent with the achievement of the objective of the energy administration.]

(3) An application under this section shall not be made

[(a)] after the end of the period of 28 days beginning with the first day on which each of the reports required by section 4(6) [and (6A)] has been made to the court [or

(b) in the case of a person who was not given notice of the [relevant qualifying decision procedure], after the end of the period of 28 days beginning with the day on which he became aware that [the relevant qualifying decision procedure] had taken place,

but (subject to that) an application made by a person within subsection (2)(aa) on the ground that the voluntary arrangement prejudices his interests may be made after the arrangement has ceased to have effect, unless it came to an end prematurely.]

(4) Where on such an application the court is satisfied as to either of the grounds mentioned in subsection (1), it may do [any] of the following, namely—

(a) revoke or suspend [any decision approving the voluntary arrangement which has effect under section 4A] or, in a case falling within subsection (1)(b), any [decision taken by the meeting [of the company, or in the relevant qualifying decision procedure,] which has effect under that section];

(b) give a direction to any person for the summoning of [a further company meeting] to consider any revised proposal the person who made the original proposal may make or, in a case falling within subsection (1)(b) [and relating to the company meeting, a further company] meeting to reconsider the original proposal;

[(c) direct any person—

(i) to seek a decision from the company's creditors (using a qualifying decision procedure) as to whether they approve any revised proposal the person who made the original proposal may make, or

(ii) in a case falling within subsection (1)(b) and relating to the relevant qualifying decision procedure, to seek a decision from the company's creditors (using a qualifying decision procedure) as to whether they approve the original proposal].

(5) Where at any time after giving a direction under subsection (4)(b) [or (c) in relation to] a revised proposal the court is satisfied that the person who made the original proposal does not intend to submit a revised proposal, the court shall revoke the direction and revoke or suspend any [decision approving the voluntary arrangement which has effect under section 4A].

(6) In a case where the court, on an application under this section with respect to any meeting [or relevant qualifying decision procedure]—

(a) gives a direction under subsection (4)(b) [or (c)], or

(b) revokes or suspends an approval under subsection (4)(a) or (5),

the court may give such supplemental directions as it thinks fit and, in particular, directions with respect to things done [under the voluntary arrangement since it took effect].

(7) Except in pursuance of the preceding provisions of this section—

[(a)] [a decision taken] at a [company] meeting summoned under section 3 is not invalidated by any irregularity at or in relation to the meeting[, and

(b) a decision of the company's creditors made in the relevant qualifying decision procedure is not invalidated by any irregularity in relation to the relevant qualifying decision procedure].

[(8) In this section "in energy administration" and "objective of the energy administration" are to be construed in accordance with Schedule B1 to this Act, as applied by Part 1 of Schedule 20 to the Energy Act 2004.]

NOTES

This section derived from the Insolvency Act 1985, s 25.

Sub-s (1): words in square brackets in para (a) substituted for original words "approved at the meetings summoned under section 3" by the Insolvency Act 2000, s 2(a), Sch 2, Pt I, paras 1, 7(1), (2), subject to transitional provisions in SI 2002/2711, art 3 at **[2.6]**; words in square brackets in para (b) substituted for original words "either of the meetings" by the Small Business, Enterprise and Employment Act 2015, s 126, Sch 9, Pt 1, paras 1, 7(1), (2), as from 6 April 2017 (in relation to England and Wales and subject to transitional and savings provisions as noted to s 246ZE at **[1.256]**), and as from a day to be appointed (in relation to Scotland).

Sub-s (1A): inserted by the Small Business, Enterprise and Employment Act 2015, s 126, Sch 9, Pt 1, paras 1, 7(1), (3), as from 6 April 2017 (in relation to England and Wales and subject to transitional and savings provisions as noted to s 246ZE at **[1.256]**), and as from a day to be appointed (in relation to Scotland).

Sub-s (2): words in first pair of square brackets substituted by the Energy Act 2004, s 159(1), Sch 20, Pt 4, para 44(1), (2); para (aa) inserted by the Insolvency Act 2000, s 2, Sch 2, Pt I, paras 1, 7(1), (3), subject to transitional provisions in SI 2002/2711, art 3 at **[2.6]**; words in square brackets in paras (a), (aa) substituted for original words "either of the meetings" and "at the creditors' meeting" respectively, by the Small Business, Enterprise and Employment Act 2015, s 126, Sch 9, Pt 1, paras 1, 7(1), (4), as from 6 April 2017 (in relation to England and Wales and subject to transitional and savings provisions as noted to s 246ZE at **[1.256]**), and as from a day to be appointed (in relation to Scotland); words in square brackets in para (c) substituted for original words "an administration order is in force" by the Enterprise Act 2002, s 248(3), Sch 17, paras 9, 12, subject to savings and transitional provisions (i) in a case where a petition for an administration order has been presented before 15 September 2003 (see the Enterprise Act 2002 (Commencement No 4 and Transitional Provisions and Savings) Order 2003, SI 2003/2093, art 3 at **[2.26]**), and (ii) in relation to special administration regimes (see s 249 of the 2002 Act at **[2.10]**).

Sub-s (2A): inserted by the Energy Act 2004, s 159(1), Sch 20, Pt 4, para 44(1), (3).

Sub-s (3): words "and (6A)" in square brackets inserted, words "relevant qualifying decision procedure" and "the relevant qualifying decision procedure" substituted for original words "creditors' meeting" and "the meeting" respectively, by the Small Business, Enterprise and Employment Act 2015, s 126, Sch 9, Pt 1, paras 1, 7(1), (5), (6), as from 6 April 2017 (in relation to England and Wales and subject to transitional and savings provisions as noted to s 246ZE at **[1.256]**), and as from a day to be appointed (in relation to Scotland); other words in square brackets inserted by the Insolvency Act 2000, s 2, Sch 2, Pt I, paras 1, 7(1), (4), subject to transitional provisions in SI 2002/2711, art 3 at **[2.6]**.

Sub-s (4): word in first pair of square brackets substituted for original words "one or both", words in third (inner) pair of square brackets in sub-para (a) substituted for original words "in question", in sub-para (b) words in first and second pairs of square brackets substituted for original words "further meetings" and ", a further company or (as the case may be) creditors'" respectively, and para (c) is added, by the Small Business, Enterprise and Employment Act 2015, s 126, Sch 9, Pt 1, paras 1, 7(1), (7)–(10), as from 6 April 2017 (in relation to England and Wales and subject to transitional and savings provisions as noted to s 246ZE at **[1.256]**), and as from a day to be appointed (in relation to Scotland); words in first and second (outer) pairs of square brackets in sub-para (a) substituted by the Insolvency Act 2000, s 2, Sch 2, Pt I, paras 1, 7(1), (5), subject to transitional provisions in SI 2002/2711, art 3 at **[2.6]**.

Sub-s (5): words in square brackets substituted for original words "for the summoning of meetings to consider" by the Small Business, Enterprise and Employment Act 2015, s 126, Sch 9, Pt 1, paras 1, 7(1), (11), as from 6 April 2017 (in relation to England and Wales and subject to transitional and savings provisions as noted to s 246ZE at **[1.256]**), and as from a day to be appointed (in relation to Scotland); words in second pair of square brackets substituted for original words "approval given at the previous meetings" by the Insolvency Act 2000, s 2, Sch 2, Pt I, paras 1, 7(1), (6), subject to transitional provisions in SI 2002/2711, art 3 at **[2.6]**.

Sub-s (6): words in first and second pairs of square brackets inserted by the Small Business, Enterprise and Employment Act 2015, s 126, Sch 9, Pt 1, paras 1, 7(1), (12), as from 6 April 2017 (in relation to England and Wales and subject to transitional and savings provisions as noted to s 246ZE at **[1.256]**), and as from a day to be appointed (in relation to Scotland); words in third pair of square brackets substituted by the Insolvency Act 2000, s 2, Sch 2, Pt I, paras 1, 7(1), (7), subject to transitional provisions in SI 2002/2711, art 3 at **[2.6]**.

Sub-s (7): para (a) designated as such, word "company" in square brackets inserted, and para (b) added, by the Small Business, Enterprise and Employment Act 2015, s 126, Sch 9, Pt 1, paras 1, 7(1), (13), as from 6 April 2017 (in relation to England and Wales and subject to transitional and savings provisions as noted to s 246ZE at **[1.256]**), and as from a day to be appointed (in relation to Scotland); words "a decision taken" in square brackets substituted by the Insolvency Act 2000, s 2, Sch 2, Pt I, paras 1, 7(1), (8), subject to transitional provisions in SI 2002/2711, art 3 at **[2.6]**.

Sub-s (8): added by the Energy Act 2004, s 159(1), Sch 20, Pt 4, para 44(1), (5).

[1.9]

[6A False representations, etc

(1) If, for the purpose of obtaining the approval of the members or creditors of a company to a proposal for a voluntary arrangement, a person who is an officer of the company—

(a) makes any false representation, or

(b) fraudulently does, or omits to do, anything,

he commits an offence.

(2) Subsection (1) applies even if the proposal is not approved.

(3) For purposes of this section "officer" includes a shadow director.

(4) A person guilty of an offence under this section is liable to imprisonment or a fine, or both.]

NOTES

Inserted by the Insolvency Act 2000, s 2, Sch 2, Pt I, paras 1, 8, subject to transitional provisions in SI 2002/2711, art 3 at **[2.6]**.

[1.10]

7 Implementation of proposal

(1) This section applies where a voluntary arrangement [has effect under section 4A].

(2) The person who is for the time being carrying out in relation to the voluntary arrangement the functions conferred—

[(a) on the nominee by virtue of the approval [of the voluntary arrangement by the company or its creditors (or both) pursuant to] section 3] or

(b) by virtue of section 2(4) or 4(2) on a person other than the nominee,

shall be known as the supervisor of the voluntary arrangement.

(3) If any of the company's creditors or any other person is dissatisfied by any act, omission or decision of the supervisor, he may apply to the court; and on the application the court may—

(a) confirm, reverse or modify any act or decision of the supervisor,

(b) give him directions, or

(c) make such other order as it thinks fit.

(4) The supervisor—

(a) may apply to the court for directions in relation to any particular matter arising under the voluntary arrangement, and

(b) is included among the persons who may apply to the court for the winding up of the company or for an administration order to be made in relation to it.

(5) The court may, whenever—

(a) it is expedient to appoint a person to carry out the functions of the supervisor, and

(b) it is inexpedient, difficult or impracticable for an appointment to be made without the assistance of the court,

make an order appointing a person who is qualified to act as an insolvency practitioner [. . . in relation to the voluntary arrangement], either in substitution for the existing supervisor or to fill a vacancy.

(6) The power conferred by subsection (5) is exercisable so as to increase the number of persons exercising the functions of supervisor or, where there is more than one person exercising those functions, so as to replace one or more of those persons.

NOTES

This section derived from the Insolvency Act 1985, s 26.

Sub-s (1): words in square brackets substituted for original words "approved by the meetings summoned under section 3 has taken effect" by the Insolvency Act 2000, s 2, Sch 2, Pt I, paras 1, 9(a), subject to transitional provisions in SI 2002/2711, art 3 at **[2.6]**.

Sub-s (2): para (a) substituted by the Insolvency Act 2000, s 2, Sch 2, Pt I, paras 1, 9(b), subject to transitional provisions in SI 2002/2711, art 3 at **[2.6]**, and originally read as follows:

"(a) by virtue of the approval on the nominee, or";

words in square brackets in para (a) substituted for original words "given at one or both of the meetings summoned under" by the Small Business, Enterprise and Employment Act 2015, s 126, Sch 9, Pt 1, paras 1, 8, as from 6 April 2017 (in relation to England and Wales and subject to transitional and savings provisions as noted to s 246ZE at **[1.256]**), and as from a day to be appointed (in relation to Scotland).

Sub-s (5): words in square brackets substituted for original words "in relation to the company" by the Insolvency Act 2000, s 2, Sch 2, Pt I, paras 1, 9(c), subject to transitional provisions in SI 2002/2711, art 3 at **[2.6]**; words omitted repealed by the Deregulation Act 2015, s 19, Sch 6, Pt 6, para 20(1), (2)(d).

[1.11]

[7A Prosecution of delinquent officers of company

(1) This section applies where a moratorium under section 1A has been obtained for a company or the approval of a voluntary arrangement in relation to a company has taken effect under section 4A or paragraph 36 of Schedule A1.

(2) If it appears to the nominee or supervisor that any past or present officer of the company has been guilty of any offence in connection with the moratorium or, as the case may be, voluntary arrangement for which he is criminally liable, the nominee or supervisor shall forthwith—

(a) report the matter to the appropriate authority, and

(b) provide the appropriate authority with such information and give the authority such access to and facilities for inspecting and taking copies of documents (being information or documents in the possession or under the control of the nominee or supervisor and relating to the matter in question) as the authority requires.

In this subsection, "the appropriate authority" means—

(i) in the case of a company registered in England and Wales, the Secretary of State, and

(ii) in the case of a company registered in Scotland, the Lord Advocate.

(3) Where a report is made to the Secretary of State under subsection (2), he may, for the purpose of investigating the matter reported to him and such other matters relating to the affairs of the company as appear to him to require investigation, exercise any of the powers which are exercisable by inspectors appointed under section 431 or 432 of [the Companies Act 1985] to investigate a company's affairs.

(4) For the purpose of such an investigation any obligation imposed on a person by any provision of [the Companies Acts] to produce documents or give information to, or otherwise to assist, inspectors so appointed is to be regarded as an obligation similarly to assist the Secretary of State in his investigation.

(5) An answer given by a person to a question put to him in exercise of the powers conferred by subsection (3) may be used in evidence against him.

(6) However, in criminal proceedings in which that person is charged with an offence to which this subsection applies—

(a) no evidence relating to the answer may be adduced, and

(b) no question relating to it may be asked,

by or on behalf of the prosecution, unless evidence relating to it is adduced, or a question relating to it is asked, in the proceedings by or on behalf of that person.

(7) Subsection (6) applies to any offence other than—

(a) an offence under section 2 or 5 of the Perjury Act 1911 (false statements made on oath otherwise than in judicial proceedings or made otherwise than on oath), or

(b) an offence under section 44(1) or (2) of the Criminal Law (Consolidation) (Scotland) Act 1995 (false statements made on oath or otherwise than on oath).

(8) Where a prosecuting authority institutes criminal proceedings following any report under subsection (2), the nominee or supervisor, and every officer and agent of the company past and present (other than the defendant or defender), shall give the authority all assistance in connection with the prosecution which he is reasonably able to give.

For this purpose—

"agent" includes any banker or solicitor of the company and any person employed by the company as auditor, whether that person is or is not an officer of the company, "prosecuting authority" means the Director of Public Prosecutions, the Lord Advocate or the Secretary of State.

(9) The court may, on the application of the prosecuting authority, direct any person referred to in subsection (8) to comply with that subsection if he has failed to do so.]

NOTES

Inserted, together with s 7B, by the Insolvency Act 2000, s 2, Sch 2, Pt I, paras 1, 10, subject to transitional provisions in SI 2002/2711, art 3 at **[2.6]**.

Sub-s (3): words in square brackets substituted for original words "the Companies Act" by the Companies Act 2006 (Consequential Amendments, Transitional Provisions and Savings) Order 2009, SI 2009/1941, art 2(1), Sch 1, para 71(1), (3)(a), subject to transitional provisions and savings in art 8, Sch 1, para 84 at **[2.70]**, **[2.73]**.

Sub-s (4): words in square brackets substituted for original words "the Companies Act" by SI 2009/1941, art 2(1), Sch 1, para 71(1), (3)(b), subject to transitional provisions and savings in art 8, Sch 1, para 84 at **[2.70]**, **[2.73]**.

[1.12]

[7B Arrangements coming to an end prematurely

For the purposes of this Part, a voluntary arrangement the approval of which has taken effect under section 4A or paragraph 36 of Schedule A1 comes to an end prematurely if, when it ceases to have effect, it has not been fully implemented in respect of all persons bound by the arrangement by virtue of section 5(2)(b)(i) or, as the case may be, paragraph 37(2)(b)(i) of Schedule A1.]

NOTES

Inserted as noted to s 7A at **[1.11]**.

[PART II ADMINISTRATION

NOTES

Application to industrial and provident societies and friendly societies: this Part may be applied, with or without modification, in relation to industrial and provident societies and friendly societies by order of the Treasury, with the concurrence of the Secretary of State; see the Enterprise Act 2002, s 255 at **[2.12]**.

Application to insurers: this Part is modified in relation to insurers, including the making of administration orders in relation to insurers; see the Financial Services and Markets Act 2000 (Administration Orders Relating to Insurers) Order 2010, SI 2010/3023, Schedule at **[7.1623]**.

[1.13]

8 Administration

Schedule B1 to this Act (which makes provision about the administration of companies) shall have effect.]

NOTES

This Part (Pt II (s 8)) substituted for existing Pt II (ss 8–27) by the Enterprise Act 2002, s 248(1), subject to savings and transitional provisions (i) in a case where a petition for an administration order has been presented before 15 September 2003 (see the Enterprise Act 2002 (Commencement No 4 and Transitional Provisions and Savings) Order 2003, SI 2003/2093, art 3 at **[2.26]**), and (ii) in relation to special administration regimes (see s 249 of the 2002 Act at **[2.10]**).

This Part and related notes prior to the substitution by the Enterprise Act 2002 as noted above read as follows:

"PART II
ADMINISTRATION ORDERS

NOTES

Modification of this Part in relation to building societies: this Part is applied with modifications to the making of administration orders in relation to building societies; see the Building Societies Act 1986, s 90A, Sch 15A at **[7.455]**, **[7.468]**.

Application of this Part in relation to financial markets: this Part is applied with modifications in relation to certain proceedings begun before the commencement of the Companies Act 1989, s 182, in respect of insolvency proceedings regarding members of recognised investment exchanges and clearing houses and persons to whom market charges have been granted; see s 182 of the 1989 Act at **[17.85]**.

Modification of this Part in relation to banks: this Part applies in relation to companies which are former authorised institutions within the meaning of the Banking Act 1987 and which are companies within the meaning of the Companies Act 1985, s 735, with modifications in the case of ss 8, 9, 13, 23, 25, 27, by the Banks (Administration Proceedings) Order 1989, SI 1989/1276, art 2, Schedule, at **[7.18]**, **[7.20]**.

Modification of this Part in relation to insurers: this Part applies, with modifications, to insurers; see the Financial Services and Markets Act 2000 (Administration Orders Relating to Insurers) Order 2002, SI 2002/1242, Schedule at **[7.1569]**.

Modification of this Part in relation to water or sewerage undertakers: by the Water Industry Act 1991, ss 23–25, Sch 3 at **[7.2619]–[7.2621]**, **[7.2625]**, this Part applies, with modifications, where a special administration order has been made under ss 23–25 of the 1991 Act in relation to a water or sewerage undertaker holding an appointment under Chapter I (ss 18–26) of Pt II of that Act.

Modification of this Part in relation to railway companies: this Part applies, with modifications, to railway administration orders made under the Railways Act 1993; see s 59(3) of, and Sch 6 to, the 1993 Act at **[7.2437]**, **[7.2448]**. See also the Transport Act 2000, s 215(1), Sch 16, paras 2–7.

Modification of this Part in relation to Public-Private Partnership administration orders: by the Greater London Authority Act 1999, s 220(2), Sch 14 at **[7.2300]**, **[7.2307]**, this Part is applied, with modifications, to PPP administration orders within the meaning of s 220(1) of that Act.

Modification of this Part in relation to air traffic administration orders: this Part is applied, with modifications, to air traffic administration orders, by the Transport Act 2000, s 30, Sch 1 at **[7.5]**, **[7.12]**.

Making etc of administration order

8 Power of court to make order

(1) Subject to this section, if the court—

(a) is satisfied that a company is or is likely to become unable to pay its debts (within the meaning given to that expression by section 123 of this Act), and

(b) considers that the making of an order under this section would be likely to achieve one or more of the purposes mentioned below,

the court may make an administration order in relation to the company.

[(1A) For the purposes of a petition presented by the Financial Services Authority alone or together with any other party, an authorised deposit taker who defaults in an obligation to pay any sum due and payable in respect of a relevant deposit is deemed to be unable to pay its debts as mentioned in subsection (1).

(1B) In subsection (1A)—

(a) "authorised deposit taker" means a person who has permission under Part 4 of the Financial Services and Markets Act 2000 to accept deposits, but excludes a person who has such permission only for the purpose of carrying on another regulated activity in accordance with that permission; and

(b) "relevant deposit" must be read with—

(i) section 22 of the Financial Services and Markets Act 2000,

(ii) any relevant order under that section, and

(iii) Schedule 2 to that Act,

but any restriction on the meaning of deposit which arises from the identity of the person making it is to be disregarded.]

(2) An administration order is an order directing that, during the period for which the order is in force, the affairs, business and property of the company shall be managed by a person ("the administrator") appointed for the purpose by the court.

(3) The purposes for whose achievement an administration order may be made are—

(a) the survival of the company, and the whole or any part of its undertaking, as a going concern;

(b) the approval of a voluntary arrangement under Part I;

[(c) the sanctioning under Part 26 of the Companies Act 2006 of a compromise or arrangement between the company and its creditors or members; and]

(d) a more advantageous realisation of the company's assets than would be effected on a winding up;

and the order shall specify the purpose or purposes for which it is made.

[(4) An administration order shall not be made in relation to a company after it has gone into liquidation.

(5) An administration order shall not be made against a company if—

[(a) it effects or carries out contracts of insurance, but is not—

(i) exempt from the general prohibition, within the meaning of section 19 of the Financial Services and Markets Act 2000, in relation to effecting or carrying out contracts of insurance, or

(ii) an authorised deposit taker within the meaning given by subsection (1B), and effecting or carrying out contracts of insurance in the course of a banking business;]

(b) it continues to have a liability in respect of a deposit which was held by it in accordance with the Banking Act 1979 or the Banking Act 1987[, but is not an authorised deposit taker, within the meaning given by subsection (1B)].

(6) Subsection (5)(a) must be read with—

(a) section 22 of the Financial Services and Markets Act 2000;

(b) any relevant order under that section; and

(c) Schedule 2 to that Act.]

[(7) In this Part a reference to a company includes a reference to a company in relation to which an administration order may be made by virtue of Article 3 of the EC Regulation.]

NOTES

This section derived from the Insolvency Act 1985, s 27.

Sub-ss (1A), (1B): inserted by the Financial Services and Markets Act 2000 (Consequential Amendments and Repeals) Order 2001, SI 2001/3649, art 303.

Sub-s (3): para (c) substituted for original words "(c) the sanctioning under section 425 of the Companies Act of a compromise or arrangement between the company and any such persons as are mentioned in that section; and" by the Companies Act 2006 (Consequential Amendments etc) Order 2008, SI 2008/948, art 3(1)(b), Sch 1, Pt 2, para 101(1), (2), subject to transitional provisions and savings in arts 6, 11, 12 thereof.

Sub-ss (4)–(6): substituted for sub-s (4) by SI 2001/3649, art 304.

Sub-s (5): para (a) substituted, and words in square brackets in para (b) inserted, by the Financial Services and Markets Act 2000 (Consequential Amendments) Order 2002, SI 2002/1555, art 14.

Sub-s (7): added by the Insolvency Act 1986 (Amendment) (No 2) Regulations 2002, SI 2002/1240, regs 3, 5.

9 Application for order

(1) An application to the court for an administration order shall be by petition presented either by the company or the directors, or by a creditor or creditors (including any contingent or prospective creditor or creditors), [or by [a justices' chief executive] in the exercise of the power conferred by section 87A of the Magistrates' Courts Act 1980 (enforcement of fines imposed on companies)] or by all or any of those parties, together or separately.

(2) Where a petition is presented to the court—

(a) notice of the petition shall be given forthwith to any person who has appointed, or is or may be entitled to appoint, an administrative receiver of the company, and to such other persons as may be prescribed, and

(b) the petition shall not be withdrawn except with the leave of the court.

(3) Where the court is satisfied that there is an administrative receiver of the company, the court shall dismiss the petition unless it is also satisfied either—

(a) that the person by whom or on whose behalf the receiver was appointed has consented to the making of the order, or

(b) that, if an administration order were made, any security by virtue of which the receiver was appointed would—

[(i) be void against the administrator to any extent by virtue of the provisions of Part XII of the Companies Act 1985 (registration of company changes),]

[(ii)] be liable to be released or discharged under sections 238 to 240 in Part VI (transactions at an undervalue and preferences),

[(iii)] be avoided under section 245 in that Part (avoidance of floating charges), or

[(iv)] be challengeable under section 242 (gratuitous alienations) or 243 (unfair preferences) in that Part, or under any rule of law in Scotland.

(4) Subject to subsection (3), on hearing a petition the court may dismiss it, or adjourn the hearing conditionally or unconditionally, or make an interim order or any other order that it thinks fit.

(5) Without prejudice to the generality of subsection (4), an interim order under that subsection may restrict the exercise of any powers of the directors or of the company (whether by reference to the consent of the court or of a person qualified to act as an insolvency practitioner in relation to the company, or otherwise).

NOTES

This section derived from the Insolvency Act 1985, s 28.

Sub-s (1): words in first (outer) pair of square brackets inserted by the Criminal Justice Act 1988, s 62(2)(a); words in second (inner) pair of square brackets substituted by the Access to Justice Act 1999, s 90(1), Sch 13, para 133.

Sub-s (3): para (b)(i) inserted and paras (b)(ii)–(iv) renumbered as such by the Companies Act 1989, s 107, Sch 16, para 3, as from a day to be appointed.

10 Effect of application

(1) During the period beginning with the presentation of a petition for an administration order and ending with the making of such an order or the dismissal of the petition—

(a) no resolution may be passed or order made for the winding up of the company;

[(aa) no landlord or other person to whom rent is payable may exercise any right of forfeiture by peaceable re-entry in relation to premises let to the company in respect of a failure by the company to comply with any term or condition of its tenancy of such premises, except with the leave of the court and subject to such terms as the court may impose]

(b) no steps may be taken to enforce any security over the company's property, or to repossess goods in the company's possession under any hire-purchase agreement, except with the leave of the court and subject to such terms as the court may impose; and

(c) no other proceedings and no execution or other legal process may be commenced or continued, and no distress may be levied, against the company or its property except with the leave of the court and subject to such terms as aforesaid.

(2) Nothing in subsection (1) requires the leave of the court—

(a) for the presentation of a petition for the winding up of the company,

(b) for the appointment of an administrative receiver of the company, or

(c) for the carrying out by such a receiver (whenever appointed) of any of his functions.

(3) Where—

(a) a petition for an administration order is presented at a time when there is an administrative receiver of the company, and

(b) the person by or on whose behalf the receiver was appointed has not consented to the making of the order,

the period mentioned in subsection (1) is deemed not to begin unless and until that person so consents.

(4) References in this section and the next to hire-purchase agreements include conditional sale agreements, chattel leasing agreements and retention of title agreements.

(5) In the application of this section and the next to Scotland, references to execution being commenced or continued include references to diligence being carried out or continued, and references to distress being levied shall be omitted.

NOTES

This section derived from the Insolvency Act 1985, s 29.

Sub-s (1): para (aa) inserted by the Insolvency Act 2000, s 9(1), (2).

Default proceedings: nothing in sub-s (1)(c) above, or in ss 11(3), 126, 128, 130, 185 or 285, affects any action taken by an exchange or clearing house for the purpose of its default proceedings; see the Companies Act 1989, s 161(4) at **[17.64]**.

Disapplication: see the Financial Collateral Arrangements (No 2) Regulations 2003, SI 2003/3226, reg 8(3)(a) at **[3.288]**.

11 Effect of order

(1) On the making of an administration order—

(a) any petition for the winding up of the company shall be dismissed, and

(b) any administrative receiver of the company shall vacate office.

(2) Where an administration order has been made, any receiver of part of the company's property shall vacate office on being required to do so by the administrator.

(3) During the period for which an administration order is in force—

(a) no resolution may be passed or order made for the winding up of the company;

(b) no administrative receiver of the company may be appointed;

[(ba) no landlord or other person to whom rent is payable may exercise any right of forfeiture by peaceable re-entry in relation to premises let to the company in respect of a failure by the company to comply with any term or condition of its tenancy of such premises, except with the consent of the administrator or the leave of the court and subject (where the court gives leave) to such terms as the court may impose;]

(c) no other steps may be taken to enforce any security over the company's property, or to repossess goods in the company's possession under any hire-purchase agreement, except with the consent of the administrator or the leave of the court and subject (where the court gives leave) to such terms as the court may impose; and

(d) no other proceedings and no execution or other legal process may be commenced or continued, and no distress may be levied, against the company or its property except with the consent of the administrator or the leave of the court and subject (where the court gives leave) to such terms as aforesaid.

(4) Where at any time an administrative receiver of the company has vacated office under subsection (1)(b), or a receiver of part of the company's property has vacated office under subsection (2)—

(a) his remuneration and any expenses properly incurred by him, and

(b) any indemnity to which he is entitled out of the assets of the company, shall be charged on and (subject to subsection (3) above) paid out of any property of the company which was in his custody or under his control at that time in priority to any security held by the person by or on whose behalf he was appointed.

(5) Neither an administrative receiver who vacates office under subsection (1)(b) nor a receiver who vacates office under subsection (2) is required on or after so vacating office to take any steps for the purpose of complying with any duty imposed on him by section 40 or 59 of this Act (duty to pay preferential creditors).

NOTES

This section derived from the Insolvency Act 1985, s 30.

Sub-s (3): para (ba) inserted by the Insolvency Act 2000, s 9(1), (3).

Default proceedings: see the note to s 10.

Disapplication: see the Financial Collateral Arrangements (No 2) Regulations 2003, SI 2003/3226, reg 8(3)(a), (4) at **[3.288]**.

12 Notification of order

(1) Every invoice, order for goods or business letter which, at a time when an administration order is in force in relation to a company, is issued by or on behalf of the company or the administrator, being a document on or in which the company's name appears, shall also contain the administrator's name and a statement that the affairs, business and property of the company are being managed by the administrator.

(2) If default is made in complying with this section, the company and any of the following persons who without reasonable excuse authorises or permits the default, namely, the administrator and any officer of the company, is liable to a fine.

NOTES

This section derived from the Insolvency Act 1985, s 31.

Administrators

13 Appointment of administrator

(1) The administrator of a company shall be appointed either by the administration order or by an order under the next subsection.

(2) If a vacancy occurs by death, resignation or otherwise in the office of the administrator, the court may by order fill the vacancy.

(3) An application for an order under subsection (2) may be made—

(a) by any continuing administrator of the company; or

(b) where there is no such administrator, by a creditors' committee established under section 26 below; or

(c) where there is no such administrator and no such committee, by the company or the directors or by any creditor or creditors of the company.

NOTES

This section derived from the Insolvency Act 1985, s 32.

14 General powers

(1) The administrator of a company—

(a) may do all such things as may be necessary for the management of the affairs, business and property of the company, and

(b) without prejudice to the generality of paragraph (a), has the powers specified in Schedule 1 to this Act;

and in the application of that Schedule to the administrator of a company the words "he" and "him" refer to the administrator.

(2) The administrator also has power—

(a) to remove any director of the company and to appoint any person to be a director of it, whether to fill a vacancy or otherwise, and

(b) to call any meeting of the members or creditors of the company.

(3) The administrator may apply to the court for directions in relation to any particular matter arising in connection with the carrying out of his functions.

(4) Any power conferred on the company or its officers, whether by this Act or [the Companies Acts] or by [the company's articles], which could be exercised in such a way as to interfere with the exercise by the administrator of his powers is not exercisable except with the consent of the administrator, which may be given either generally or in relation to particular cases.

(5) In exercising his powers the administrator is deemed to act as the company's agent.

(6) A person dealing with the administrator in good faith and for value is not concerned to inquire whether the administrator is acting within his powers.

NOTES

This section derived from the Insolvency Act 1985, s 33.

Sub-s (4): words in square brackets substituted for original words "the Companies Act" and "the memorandum or articles of association" respectively by the Companies Act 2006 (Consequential Amendments, Transitional Provisions and Savings) Order 2009, SI 2009/1941, art 2(1), Sch 1, para 73(1), (2), subject to transitional provisions and savings in art 8, Sch 1, para 84 at **[2.70]**, **[2.73]**.

15 Power to deal with charged property, etc

(1) The administrator of a company may dispose of or otherwise exercise his powers in relation to any property of the company which is subject to a security to which this subsection applies as if the property were not subject to the security.

(2) Where, on an application by the administrator, the court is satisfied that the disposal (with or without other assets) of—

(a) any property of the company subject to a security to which this subsection applies, or

(b) any goods in the possession of the company under a hire-purchase agreement,

would be likely to promote the purpose or one or more of the purposes specified in the administration order, the court may by order authorise the administrator to dispose of the property as if it were not subject to the security or to dispose of the goods as if all rights of the owner under the hire-purchase agreement were vested in the company.

(3) Subsection (1) applies to any security which, as created, was a floating charge; and subsection (2) applies to any other security.

(4) Where property is disposed of under subsection (1), the holder of the security has the same priority in respect of any property of the company directly or indirectly representing the property disposed of as he would have had in respect of the property subject to the security.

(5) It shall be a condition of an order under subsection (2) that—

(a) the net proceeds of the disposal, and

(b) where those proceeds are less than such amount as may be determined by the court to be the net amount which would be realised on a sale of the property or goods in the open market by a willing vendor, such sums as may be required to make good the deficiency,

shall be applied towards discharging the sums secured by the security or payable under the hire-purchase agreement.

(6) Where a condition imposed in pursuance of subsection (5) relates to two or more securities, that condition requires the net proceeds of the disposal and, where paragraph (b) of that subsection applies, the sums mentioned in that paragraph to be applied towards discharging the sums secured by those securities in the order of their priorities.

(7) [A copy] of an order under subsection (2) shall, within 14 days after the making of the order, be sent by the administrator to the registrar of companies.

(8) If the administrator without reasonable excuse fails to comply with subsection (7), he is liable to a fine and, for continued contravention, to a daily default fine.

(9) References in this section to hire-purchase agreements include conditional sale agreements, chattel leasing agreements and retention of title agreements.

NOTES

This section derived from the Insolvency Act 1985, s 34(1)–(8), (12).

Sub-s (7): words in square brackets substituted for original words "An office copy" by the Companies Act 2006 (Consequential Amendments, Transitional Provisions and Savings) Order 2009, SI 2009/1941, art 2(1), Sch 1, para 73(1), (3), subject to transitional provisions and savings in art 8, Sch 1, para 84 at **[2.70]**, **[2.73]**.

Disapplication: see the Financial Collateral Arrangements (No 2) Regulations 2003, SI 2003/3226, reg 8(3)(b) at **[3.288]**.

16 Operation of s 15 in Scotland

(1) Where property is disposed of under section 15 in its application to Scotland, the administrator shall grant to the disponee an appropriate document of transfer or conveyance of the property, and—

(a) that document, or

(b) where any recording, intimation or registration of the document is a legal requirement for completion of title to the property, that recording, intimation or registration,

has the effect of disencumbering the property of or, as the case may be, freeing the property from the security.

(2) Where goods in the possession of the company under a hire-purchase agreement, conditional sale agreement, chattel leasing agreement or retention of title agreement are disposed of under section 15 in its application to Scotland, the disposal has the effect of extinguishing, as against the disponee, all rights of the owner of the goods under the agreement.

NOTES

This section derived from the Insolvency Act 1985, s 34(9), (10).

17 General duties

(1) The administrator of a company shall, on his appointment, take into his custody or under his control all the property to which the company is or appears to be entitled.

(2) The administrator shall manage the affairs, business and property of the company—

(a) at any time before proposals have been approved (with or without modifications) under section 24 below, in accordance with any directions given by the court, and

(b) at any time after proposals have been so approved, in accordance with those proposals as from time to time revised, whether by him or a predecessor of his.

(3) The administrator shall summon a meeting of the company's creditors if—

(a) he is requested, in accordance with the rules, to do so by one-tenth, in value, of the company's creditors, or

(b) he is directed to do so by the court.

NOTES

This section derived from the Insolvency Act 1985, s 35.

18 Discharge or variation of administration order

(1) The administrator of a company may at any time apply to the court for the administration order to be discharged, or to be varied so as to specify an additional purpose.

(2) The administrator shall make an application under this section if—

(a) it appears to him that the purpose or each of the purposes specified in the order either has been achieved or is incapable of achievement; or

(b) he is required to do so by a meeting of the company's creditors summoned for the purpose in accordance with the rules.

(3) On the hearing of an application under this section, the court may by order discharge or vary the administration order and make such consequential provision as it thinks fit, or adjourn the hearing conditionally or unconditionally, or make an interim order or any other order it thinks fit.

(4) Where the administration order is discharged or varied the administrator shall, within 14 days after the making of the order effecting the discharge or variation, send [a copy] of that order to the registrar of companies.

(5) If the administrator without reasonable excuse fails to comply with subsection (4), he is liable to a fine and, for continued contravention, to a daily default fine.

NOTES

This section derived from the Insolvency Act 1985, s 36.

Sub-s (4): words in square brackets substituted for original words "an office copy" by the Companies Act 2006 (Consequential Amendments, Transitional Provisions and Savings) Order 2009, SI 2009/1941, art 2(1), Sch 1, para 73(1), (3), subject to transitional provisions and savings in art 8, Sch 1, para 84 at **[2.70]**, **[2.73]**.

19 Vacation of office

(1) The administrator of a company may at any time be removed from office by order of the court and may, in the prescribed circumstances, resign his office by giving notice of his resignation to the court.

(2) The administrator shall vacate office if—

(a) he ceases to be qualified to act as an insolvency practitioner in relation to the company, or

(b) the administration order is discharged.

(3) Where at any time a person ceases to be administrator, the [following] subsections apply.

(4) His remuneration and any expenses properly incurred by him shall be charged on and paid out of any property of the company which is in his custody or under his control at that time in priority to any security to which section 15(1) then applies.

(5) Any sums payable in respect of debts or liabilities incurred, while he was administrator, under contracts entered into . . . by him or a predecessor of his in the carrying out of his or the predecessor's functions shall be charged on and paid out of any such property as is mentioned in subsection (4) in priority to any charge arising under that subsection.

[(6) Any sums payable in respect of liabilities incurred, while he was administrator, under contracts of employment adopted by him or a predecessor of his in the carrying out of his or the predecessor's functions shall, to the extent that the liabilities are qualifying liabilities, be charged on and paid out of any such property as is mentioned in subsection (4) and enjoy the same priority as any sums to which subsection (5) applies.]

For this purpose, the administrator is not to be taken to have adopted a contract of employment by reason of anything done or omitted to be done within 14 days after his appointment.

[(7) For the purposes of subsection (6), a liability under a contract of employment is a qualifying liability if—

(a) it is a liability to pay a sum by way of wages or salary or contribution to an occupational pension scheme, and

(b) it is in respect of services rendered wholly or partly after the adoption of the contract.

(8) There shall be disregarded for the purposes of subsection (6) so much of any qualifying liability as represents payment in respect of services rendered before the adoption of the contract.

(9) For the purposes of subsections (7) and (8)—

(a) wages or salary payable in respect of a period of holiday or absence from work through sickness or other good cause are deemed to be wages or (as the case may be) salary in respect of services rendered in that period, and

(b) a sum payable in lieu of holiday is deemed to be wages or (as the case may be) salary in respect of services rendered in the period by reference to which the holiday entitlement arose.

(10) . . .]

NOTES

This section derived from the Insolvency Act 1985, s 37(1)–(3).

Sub-s (3): word in square brackets substituted by the Insolvency Act 1994, s 1(1), (2), (7), in relation to contracts of employment adopted on or after 15 March 1994.

Sub-s (5): words omitted repealed by the Insolvency Act 1994, ss 1(1), (3), (7), 5(2), Sch 2, in relation to contracts of employment adopted on or after 15 March 1994.

Sub-s (6): inserted, and the second paragraph of sub-s (5), as originally enacted, became the second paragraph of this subsection by the Insolvency Act 1994, s 1(1), (4), (7), in relation to contracts of employment adopted on or after 15 March 1994.

Sub-ss (7)–(10): added by the Insolvency Act 1994, s 1(1), (6), (7), in relation to contracts of employment adopted on or after 15 March 1994.

Sub-s (10): repealed by the Deregulation Act 2015, s 19, Sch 6, Pt 7, paras 24, 25.

20 Release of administrator

(1) A person who has ceased to be the administrator of a company has his release with effect from the following time, that is to say—

(a) in the case of a person who has died, the time at which notice is given to the court in accordance with the rules that he has ceased to hold office;

(b) in any other case, such time as the court may determine.

(2) Where a person has his release under this section, he is, with effect from the time specified above, discharged from all liability both in respect of acts or omissions of his in the administration and otherwise in relation to his conduct as administrator.

(3) However, nothing in this section prevents the exercise, in relation to a person who has had his release as above, of the court's powers under section 212 in Chapter X of Part IV (summary remedy against delinquent directors, liquidators, etc).

NOTES

This section derived from the Insolvency Act 1985, s 37(4), (5).

Ascertainment and investigation of company's affairs

21 Information to be given by administrator

(1) Where an administration order has been made, the administrator shall—

(a) forthwith send to the company and publish in the prescribed manner a notice of the order, and

(b) within 28 days after the making of the order, unless the court otherwise directs, send such a notice to all creditors of the company (so far as he is aware of their addresses).

(2) Where an administration order has been made, the administrator shall also, within 14 days after the making of the order, send [a copy] of the order to the registrar of companies and to such other persons as may be prescribed.

(3) If the administrator without reasonable excuse fails to comply with this section, he is liable to a fine and, for continued contravention, to a daily default fine.

NOTES

This section derived from the Insolvency Act 1985, s 38.

Sub-s (2): words in square brackets substituted for original words "an office copy" by the Companies Act 2006 (Consequential Amendments, Transitional Provisions and Savings) Order 2009, SI 2009/1941, art 2(1), Sch 1, para 73(1), (3), subject to transitional provisions and savings in art 8, Sch 1, para 84 at **[2.70]**, **[2.73]**.

22 Statement of affairs to be submitted to administrator

(1) Where an administration order has been made, the administrator shall forthwith require some or all of the persons mentioned below to make out and submit to him a statement in the prescribed form as to the affairs of the company.

(2) The statement shall be verified by affidavit by the persons required to submit it and shall show—

(a) particulars of the company's assets, debts and liabilities;

(b) the names and addresses of its creditors;

(c) the securities held by them respectively;

(d) the dates when the securities were respectively given; and

(e) such further or other information as may be prescribed.

(3) The persons referred to in subsection (1) are—

(a) those who are or have been officers of the company;

(b) those who have taken part in the company's formation at any time within one year before the date of the administration order;

(c) those who are in the company's employment or have been in its employment within that year, and are in the administrator's opinion capable of giving the information required;

(d) those who are or have been within that year officers of or in the employment of a company which is, or within that year was, an officer of the company.

In this subsection "employment" includes employment under a contract for services.

(4) Where any persons are required under this section to submit a statement of affairs to the administrator, they shall do so (subject to the next subsection) before the end of the period of 21 days beginning with the day after that on which the prescribed notice of the requirement is given to them by the administrator.

(5) The administrator, if he thinks fit, may—

(a) at any time release a person from an obligation imposed on him under subsection (1) or (2), or

(b) either when giving notice under subsection (4) or subsequently, extend the period so mentioned;

and where the administrator has refused to exercise a power conferred by this subsection, the court, if it thinks fit, may exercise it.

(6) If a person without reasonable excuse fails to comply with any obligation imposed under this section, he is liable to a fine and, for continued contravention, to a daily default fine.

NOTES

This section derived from the Insolvency Act 1985, s 39.

Administrator's proposals

23 Statement of proposals

(1) Where an administration order has been made, the administrator shall, within 3 months (or such longer period as the court may allow) after the making of the order—

(a) send to the registrar of companies and (so far as he is aware of their addresses) to all creditors a statement of his proposals for achieving the purpose or purposes specified in the order, and

(b) lay a copy of the statement before a meeting of the company's creditors summoned for the purpose on not less than 14 days' notice.

(2) The administrator shall also, within 3 months (or such longer period as the court may allow) after the making of the order, either—

(a) send a copy of the statement (so far as he is aware of their addresses) to all members of the company, or

(b) publish in the prescribed manner a notice stating an address to which members of the company should write for copies of the statement to be sent to them free of charge.

(3) If the administrator without reasonable excuse fails to comply with this section, he is liable to a fine and, for continued contravention, to a daily default fine.

NOTES

This section derived from the Insolvency Act 1985, s 40.

24 Consideration of proposals by creditors' meeting

(1) A meeting of creditors summoned under section 23 shall decide whether to approve the administrator's proposals.

(2) The meeting may approve the proposals with modifications, but shall not do so unless the administrator consents to each modification.

(3) Subject as above, the meeting shall be conducted in accordance with the rules.

(4) After the conclusion of the meeting in accordance with the rules, the administrator shall report the result of the meeting to the court and shall give notice of that result to the registrar of companies and to such persons as may be prescribed.

(5) If a report is given to the court under subsection (4) that the meeting has declined to approve the administrator's proposals (with or without modifications), the court may by order discharge the administration order and make such consequential provision as it thinks fit, or adjourn the hearing conditionally or unconditionally, or make an interim order or any other order that it thinks fit.

(6) Where the administration order is discharged, the administrator shall, within 14 days after the making of the order effecting the discharge, send [a copy] of that order to the registrar of companies.

(7) If the administrator without reasonable excuse fails to comply with subsection (6), he is liable to a fine and, for continued contravention, to a daily default fine.

NOTES

This section derived from the Insolvency Act 1985, s 41.

Sub-s (6): words in square brackets substituted by the Companies Act 2006 (Consequential Amendments and Transitional Provisions) Order 2011, SI 2011/1265, art 6(1), (2).

25 Approval of substantial revisions

(1) This section applies where—

(a) proposals have been approved (with or without modifications) under section 24, and

(b) the administrator proposes to make revisions of those proposals which appear to him substantial.

(2) The administrator shall—

(a) send to all creditors of the company (so far as he is aware of their addresses) a statement in the prescribed form of his proposed revisions, and

(b) lay a copy of the statement before a meeting of the company's creditors summoned for the purpose on not less than 14 days' notice; and he shall not make the proposed revisions unless they are approved by the meeting.

(3) The administrator shall also either—

(a) send a copy of the statement (so far as he is aware of their addresses) to all members of the company, or

(b) publish in the prescribed manner a notice stating an address to which members of the company should write for copies of the statement to be sent to them free of charge.

(4) The meeting of creditors may approve the proposed revisions with modifications, but shall not do so unless the administrator consents to each modification.

(5) Subject as above, the meeting shall be conducted in accordance with the rules.

(6) After the conclusion of the meeting in accordance with the rules, the administrator shall give notice of the result of the meeting to the registrar of companies and to such persons as may be prescribed.

NOTES

This section derived from the Insolvency Act 1985, s 42.

Miscellaneous

26 Creditors' committee

(1) Where a meeting of creditors summoned under section 23 has approved the administrator's proposals (with or without modifications), the meeting may, if it thinks fit, establish a committee ("the creditors' committee") to exercise the functions conferred on it by or under this Act.

(2) If such a committee is established, the committee may, on giving not less than 7 days' notice, require the administrator to attend before it at any reasonable time and furnish it with such information relating to the carrying out of his functions as it may reasonably require.

NOTES

This section derived from the Insolvency Act 1985, s 43.

27 Protection of interests of creditors and members

(1) At any time when an administration order is in force, a creditor or member of the company may apply to the court by petition for an order under this section on the ground—

(a) that the company's affairs, business and property are being or have been managed by the administrator in a manner which is unfairly prejudicial to the interests of its creditors or members generally, or of some part of its creditors or members (including at least himself), or

(b) that any actual or proposed act or omission of the administrator is or would be so prejudicial.

(2) On an application for an order under this section the court may, subject as follows, make such order as it thinks fit for giving relief in respect of the matters complained of, or adjourn the hearing conditionally or unconditionally, or make an interim order or any other order that it thinks fit.

(3) An order under this section shall not prejudice or prevent—

(a) the implementation of a voluntary arrangement approved under . . . Part I, or any compromise or arrangement sanctioned under [Part 26 of the Companies Act 2006]; or

(b) where the application for the order was made more than 28 days after the approval of any proposals or revised proposals under section 24 or 25, the implementation of those proposals or revised proposals.

(4) Subject as above, an order under this section may in particular—

(a) regulate the future management by the administrator of the company's affairs, business and property;

(b) require the administrator to refrain from doing or continuing an act complained of by the petitioner, or to do an act which the petitioner has complained he has omitted to do;

(c) require the summoning of a meeting of creditors or members for the purpose of considering such matters as the court may direct;

(d) discharge the administration order and make such consequential provision as the court thinks fit.

(5) Nothing in section 15 or 16 is to be taken as prejudicing applications to the court under this section.

(6) Where the administration order is discharged, the administrator shall, within 14 days after the making of the order effecting the discharge, send [a copy] of that order to the registrar of companies; and if without reasonable excuse he fails to comply with this subsection, he is liable to a fine and, for continued contravention, to a daily default fine.

NOTES

This section derived from the Insolvency Act 1985, ss 34(11), 44.

Sub-s (3): words omitted repealed by the Insolvency Act 2000, ss 1, 15(1), Sch 1, paras 1, 5, Sch 5; words in square brackets substituted for original words "section 425 of the Companies Act" by the Companies Act 2006 (Consequential Amendments etc) Order 2008, SI 2008/948, art 3(1)(b), Sch 1, Pt 2, para 101(1), (3), subject to transitional provisions and savings in arts 6, 11, 12 thereof.

Sub-s (6): words in square brackets substituted for original words "an office copy" by the Companies Act 2006 (Consequential Amendments, Transitional Provisions and Savings) Order 2009, SI 2009/1941, art 2(1), Sch 1, para 73(1), (3), subject to transitional provisions and savings in art 8, Sch 1, para 84 at **[2.70]**, **[2.73]**.

Modification: sub-s (1) is applied, with modifications, for the purposes of the Railway (Licensing of Railway Undertakings) Regulations 2005, by the Railway (Licensing of Railway Undertakings) Regulations 2005, SI 2005/3050, reg 14, Sch 3, Pt 1, para 1(a), Pt 2, para 2.".

PART III RECEIVERSHIP

NOTES

European Economic Interest Groupings: as to the application of this Part of this Act to European Economic Interest Groupings, see the European Economic Interest Grouping Regulations 1989, SI 1989/638, reg 19(1).

CHAPTER I
RECEIVERS AND MANAGERS (ENGLAND AND WALES)

NOTES

Modification of this Chapter in relation to building societies: this Chapter is applied, with modifications, in relation to the appointment of receivers and managers of building societies; see the Building Societies Act 1986, s 90A, Sch 15A at **[7.455]**, **[7.468]**.

Preliminary and general provisions

[1.14]

[28 Extent of this Chapter

(1) In this Chapter "company" means a company registered under the Companies Act 2006 in England and Wales or Scotland.

(2) This Chapter does not apply to receivers appointed under Chapter 2 of this Part (Scotland).]

NOTES

This section as originally enacted derived from the Companies Act 1985, s 488, and the Insolvency Act 1985, s 45(1).

Substituted by the Companies Act 2006 (Consequential Amendments, Transitional Provisions and Savings) Order 2009, SI 2009/1941, art 2(1), Sch 1, para 74(1), (2), subject to transitional provisions and savings in art 8, Sch 1, para 84 at **[2.70]**, **[2.73]**, and previously read as follows:

> **"28 Extent of this Chapter**
> This Chapter does not apply to receivers appointed under Chapter II of this Part (Scotland).".

[1.15]

29 Definitions

(1) It is hereby declared that, except where the context otherwise requires—

(a) any reference in . . . this Act to a receiver or manager of the property of a company, or to a receiver of it, includes a receiver or manager, or (as the case may be) a receiver of part only of that property and a receiver only of the income arising from the property or from part of it; and

(b) any reference in . . . this Act to the appointment of a receiver or manager under powers contained in an instrument includes an appointment made under powers which, by virtue of an enactment, are implied in and have effect as if contained in an instrument.

(2) In this Chapter "administrative receiver" means—

(a) a receiver or manager of the whole (or substantially the whole) of a company's property appointed by or on behalf of the holders of any debentures of the company secured by a charge which, as created, was a floating charge, or by such a charge and one or more other securities; or

(b) a person who would be such a receiver or manager but for the appointment of some other person as the receiver of part of the company's property.

NOTES

This section derived from the Companies Act 1985, s 500, and the Insolvency Act 1985, s 45(2).

Sub-s (1): words "the Companies Act or" omitted from paras (a), (b) repealed by the Companies Act 2006 (Consequential Amendments, Transitional Provisions and Savings) Order 2009, SI 2009/1941, art 2(1), Sch 1, para 74(1), (3), subject to transitional provisions and savings in art 8, Sch 1, para 84 at **[2.70]**, **[2.73]**.

[1.16]

30 Disqualification of body corporate from acting as receiver

A body corporate is not qualified for appointment as receiver of the property of a company, and any body corporate which acts as such a receiver is liable to a fine.

NOTES

This section derived from the Companies Act 1985, s 489.

[1.17]

[31 Disqualification of bankrupt [or person in respect of whom a debt relief order is made]

(1) A person commits an offence if he acts as receiver or manager of the property of a company on behalf of debenture holders while—

(a) he is an undischarged bankrupt,

[(aa) a moratorium period under a debt relief order applies in relation to him,] or

(b) a bankruptcy restrictions order [or a debt relief restrictions order] is in force in respect of him.

(2) A person guilty of an offence under subsection (1) shall be liable to imprisonment, a fine or both.

(3) This section does not apply to a receiver or manager acting under an appointment made by the court.]

NOTES

This section, as originally enacted, derived from the Companies Act 1985, s 490.

Substituted by the Enterprise Act 2002, s 257(3), Sch 21, para 1, subject to transitional provisions in s 256(2) of, and Sch 19 to, that Act at **[2.13]**, **[2.22]**, and originally read as follows:

> **"31 Disqualification of undischarged bankrupt**
> If a person being an undischarged bankrupt acts as receiver or manager of the property of a company on behalf of debenture holders, he is liable to imprisonment or a fine, or both.
> This does not apply to a receiver or a manager acting under an appointment made by the court.".

Section heading: words in square brackets inserted by the Tribunals, Courts and Enforcement Act 2007, s 108(3), Sch 20, Pt 1, paras 1, 2(2).

Sub-s (1): para (aa) and words in square brackets in para (b) inserted by the Tribunals, Courts and Enforcement Act 2007, s 108(3), Sch 20, Pt 1, paras 1, 2(1).

[1.18]
32 Power for court to appoint official receiver
Where application is made to the court to appoint a receiver on behalf of the debenture holders or other creditors of a company which is being wound up by the court, the official receiver may be appointed.

NOTES
This section derived from the Companies Act 1985, s 491.

Receivers and managers appointed out of court

[1.19]
33 Time from which appointment is effective
(1) The appointment of a person as a receiver or manager of a company's property under powers contained in an instrument—
(a) is of no effect unless it is accepted by that person before the end of the business day next following that on which the instrument of appointment is received by him or on his behalf, and
(b) subject to this, is deemed to be made at the time at which the instrument of appointment is so received.
(2) This section applies to the appointment of two or more persons as joint receivers or managers of a company's property under powers contained in an instrument, subject to such modifications as may be prescribed by the rules.

NOTES
This section derived from the Insolvency Act 1985, s 46.

[1.20]
34 Liability for invalid appointment
Where the appointment of a person as the receiver or manager of a company's property under powers contained in an instrument is discovered to be invalid (whether by virtue of the invalidity of the instrument or otherwise), the court may order the person by whom or on whose behalf the appointment was made to indemnify the person appointed against any liability which arises solely by reason of the invalidity of the appointment.

NOTES
This section derived from the Insolvency Act 1985, s 47.

[1.21]
35 Application to court for directions
(1) A receiver or manager of the property of a company appointed under powers contained in an instrument, or the persons by whom or on whose behalf a receiver or manager has been so appointed, may apply to the court for directions in relation to any particular matter arising in connection with the performance of the functions of the receiver or manager.
(2) On such an application, the court may give such directions, or may make such order declaring the rights of persons before the court or otherwise, as it thinks just.

NOTES
This section derived from the Companies Act 1985, s 492(1), (2), and the Insolvency Act 1985, Sch 6, para 16(2).

[1.22]
36 Court's power to fix remuneration
(1) The court may, on an application made by the liquidator of a company, by order fix the amount to be paid by way of remuneration to a person who, under powers contained in an instrument, has been appointed receiver or manager of the company's property.
(2) The court's power under subsection (1), where no previous order has been made with respect thereto under the subsection—
(a) extends to fixing the remuneration for any period before the making of the order or the application for it,
(b) is exercisable notwithstanding that the receiver or manager has died or ceased to act before the making of the order or the application, and
(c) where the receiver or manager has been paid or has retained for his remuneration for any period before the making of the order any amount in excess of that so fixed for that period, extends to requiring him or his personal representatives to account for the excess or such part of it as may be specified in the order.

But the power conferred by paragraph (c) shall not be exercised as respects any period before the making of the application for the order under this section, unless in the court's opinion there are special circumstances making it proper for the power to be exercised.
(3) The court may from time to time on an application made either by the liquidator or by the receiver or manager, vary or amend an order made under subsection (1).

NOTES

This section derived from the Companies Act 1985, s 494.

[1.23]

37 Liability for contracts, etc

(1) A receiver or manager appointed under powers contained in an instrument (other than an administrative receiver) is, to the same extent as if he had been appointed by order of the court—

(a) personally liable on any contract entered into by him in the performance of his functions (except in so far as the contract otherwise provides) and on any contract of employment adopted by him in the performance of those functions, and

(b) entitled in respect of that liability to indemnity out of the assets.

(2) For the purposes of subsection (1)(a), the receiver or manager is not to be taken to have adopted a contract of employment by reason of anything done or omitted to be done within 14 days after his appointment.

(3) Subsection (1) does not limit any right to indemnity which the receiver or manager would have apart from it, nor limit his liability on contracts entered into without authority, nor confer any right to indemnity in respect of that liability.

(4) Where at any time the receiver or manager so appointed vacates office—

(a) his remuneration and any expenses properly incurred by him, and

(b) any indemnity to which he is entitled out of the assets of the company,

shall be charged on and paid out of any property of the company which is in his custody or under his control at that time in priority to any charge or other security held by the person by or on whose behalf he was appointed.

NOTES

This section derived from the Companies Act 1985, s 492(3)–(5), and the Insolvency Act 1985, Sch 6, para 16(3), (4).

[1.24]

38 Receivership accounts to be delivered to registrar

(1) Except in the case of an administrative receiver, every receiver or manager of a company's property who has been appointed under powers contained in an instrument shall deliver to the registrar of companies for registration the requisite accounts of his receipts and payments.

(2) The accounts shall be delivered within one month (or such longer period as the registrar may allow) after the expiration of 12 months from the date of his appointment and of every subsequent period of 6 months, and also within one month after he ceases to act as receiver or manager.

(3) The requisite accounts shall be an abstract in the prescribed form showing—

(a) receipts and payments during the relevant period of 12 or 6 months, or

(b) where the receiver or manager ceases to act, receipts and payments during the period from the end of the period of 12 or 6 months to which the last preceding abstract related (or, if no preceding abstract has been delivered under this section, from the date of his appointment) up to the date of his so ceasing, and the aggregate amount of receipts and payments during all preceding periods since his appointment.

(4) In this section "prescribed" means prescribed by regulations made by statutory instrument by the Secretary of State.

(5) A receiver or manager who makes default in complying with this section is liable to a fine and, for continued contravention, to a daily default fine.

NOTES

This section derived from the Companies Act 1985, s 498, and the Insolvency Act 1985, Sch 6, para 17.

Provisions applicable to every receivership

[1.25]

39 Notification that receiver or manager appointed

[(1) Where a receiver or manager of the property of a company has been appointed—

(a) every invoice, order for goods or services, business letter or order form (whether in hard copy, electronic or any other form) issued by or on behalf of the company or the receiver or manager or the liquidator of the company; and

(b) all the company's websites,

must contain a statement that a receiver or manager has been appointed.]

(2) If default is made in complying with this section, the company and any of the following persons, who knowingly and wilfully authorises or permits the default, namely, any officer of the company, any liquidator of the company and any receiver or manager, is liable to a fine.

NOTES

This section derived from the Companies Act 1985, s 493.

Sub-s (1): substituted by the Companies (Trading Disclosures) (Insolvency) Regulations 2008, SI 2008/1897, reg 2(1).

[1.26]

40 Payment of debts out of assets subject to floating charge

(1) The following applies, in the case of a company, where a receiver is appointed on behalf of the holders of any debentures of the company secured by a charge which, as created, was a floating charge.

(2) If the company is not at the time in course of being wound up, its preferential debts (within the meaning given to that expression by section 386 in Part XII) shall be paid out of the assets coming to the hands of the receiver in priority to any claims for principal or interest in respect of the debentures.

(3) Payments made under this section shall be recouped, as far as may be, out of the assets of the company available for payment of general creditors.

NOTES

This section derived from the Companies Act 1985, s 196 (in part), and the Insolvency Act 1985, Sch 6, para 15(2), (3).

Disapplication: this section is disapplied in respect of regulated covered bonds, by the Regulated Covered Bonds Regulations 2008, SI 2008/346, reg 46, Schedule, Pt 1, para 2(1) at **[18.179]**.

[1.27]

41 Enforcement of duty to make returns

(1) If a receiver or manager of a company's property—

(a) having made default in filing, delivering or making any return, account or other document, or in giving any notice, which a receiver or manager is by law required to file, deliver, make or give, fails to make good the default within 14 days after the service on him of a notice requiring him to do so, or

(b) having been appointed under powers contained in an instrument, has, after being required at any time by the liquidator of the company to do so, failed to render proper accounts of his receipts and payments and to vouch them and pay over to the liquidator the amount properly payable to him,

the court may, on an application made for the purpose, make an order directing the receiver or manager (as the case may be) to make good the default within such time as may be specified in the order.

(2) In the case of the default mentioned in subsection (1)(a), application to the court may be made by any member or creditor of the company or by the registrar of companies; and in the case of the default mentioned in subsection (1)(b), the application shall be made by the liquidator.

In either case the court's order may provide that all costs of and incidental to the application shall be borne by the receiver or manager, as the case may be.

(3) Nothing in this section prejudices the operation of any enactment imposing penalties on receivers in respect of any such default as is mentioned in subsection (1).

NOTES

This section derived from the Companies Act 1985, s 499.

Order to make good the default: as to the making of disqualification orders when an order is made under this section, see the Company Directors Disqualification Act 1986, ss 3, 5 at **[4.4]**, **[4.6]**.

Administrative receivers: general

[1.28]

42 General powers

(1) The powers conferred on the administrative receiver of a company by the debentures by virtue of which he was appointed are deemed to include (except in so far as they are inconsistent with any of the provisions of those debentures) the powers specified in Schedule 1 to this Act.

(2) In the application of Schedule 1 to the administrative receiver of a company—

(a) the words "he" and "him" refer to the administrative receiver, and

(b) references to the property of the company are to the property of which he is or, but for the appointment of some other person as the receiver of part of the company's property, would be the receiver or manager.

(3) A person dealing with the administrative receiver in good faith and for value is not concerned to inquire whether the receiver is acting within his powers.

NOTES

This section derived from the Insolvency Act 1985, s 48.

[1.29]

43 Power to dispose of charged property, etc

(1) Where, on an application by the administrative receiver, the court is satisfied that the disposal (with or without other assets) of any relevant property which is subject to a security would be likely to promote a more advantageous realisation of the company's assets than would otherwise be effected, the court may by order authorise the administrative receiver to dispose of the property as if it were not subject to the security.

(2) Subsection (1) does not apply in the case of any security held by the person by or on whose behalf the administrative receiver was appointed, or of any security to which a security so held has priority.

(3) It shall be a condition of an order under this section that—

(a) the net proceeds of the disposal, and

(b) where those proceeds are less than such amount as may be determined by the court to be the net amount which would be realised on a sale of the property in the open market by a willing vendor, such sums as may be required to make good the deficiency,

shall be applied towards discharging the sums secured by the security.

(4) Where a condition imposed in pursuance of subsection (3) relates to two or more securities, that condition shall require the net proceeds of the disposal and, where paragraph (b) of that subsection applies, the sums mentioned in that paragraph to be applied towards discharging the sums secured by those securities in the order of their priorities.

(5) [A copy] of an order under this section shall, within 14 days of the making of the order, be sent by the administrative receiver to the registrar of companies.
(6) If the administrative receiver without reasonable excuse fails to comply with subsection (5), he is liable to a fine and, for continued contravention, to a daily default fine.
(7) In this section "relevant property", in relation to the administrative receiver, means the property of which he is or, but for the appointment of some other person as the receiver of part of the company's property, would be the receiver or manager.

NOTES

This section derived from the Insolvency Act 1985, s 49.

Sub-s (5): words in square brackets substituted for original words "An office copy" by the Companies Act 2006 (Consequential Amendments, Transitional Provisions and Savings) Order 2009, SI 2009/1941, art 2(1), Sch 1, para 74(1), (4), subject to transitional provisions and savings in art 8, Sch 1, para 84 at **[2.70]**, **[2.73]**.

Disapplication: this section is disapplied in respect of regulated covered bonds, by the Regulated Covered Bonds Regulations 2008, SI 2008/346, reg 46, Schedule, Pt 1, para 2(1) at **[18.179]**.

[1.30]

44 Agency and liability for contracts

(1) The administrative receiver of a company—
 (a) is deemed to be the company's agent, unless and until the company goes into liquidation;
 (b) is personally liable on any contract entered into by him in the carrying out of his functions (except in so far as the contract otherwise provides) and[, to the extent of any qualifying liability,] on any contract of employment adopted by him in the carrying out of those functions; and
 (c) is entitled in respect of that liability to an indemnity out of the assets of the company.
(2) For the purposes of subsection (1)(b) the administrative receiver is not to be taken to have adopted a contract of employment by reason of anything done or omitted to be done within 14 days after his appointment.
[(2A) For the purposes of subsection (1)(b), a liability under a contract of employment is a qualifying liability if—
 (a) it is a liability to pay a sum by way of wages or salary or contribution to an occupational pension scheme,
 (b) it is incurred while the administrative receiver is in office, and
 (c) it is in respect of services rendered wholly or partly after the adoption of the contract.
(2B) Where a sum payable in respect of a liability which is a qualifying liability for the purposes of subsection (1)(b) is payable in respect of services rendered partly before and partly after the adoption of the contract, liability under subsection (1)(b) shall only extend to so much of the sum as is payable in respect of services rendered after the adoption of the contract.
(2C) For the purposes of subsections (2A) and (2B)—
 (a) wages or salary payable in respect of a period of holiday or absence from work through sickness or other good cause are deemed to be wages or (as the case may be) salary in respect of services rendered in that period, and
 (b) a sum payable in lieu of holiday is deemed to be wages or (as the case may be) salary in respect of services rendered in the period by reference to which the holiday entitlement arose.
(2D) . . .]
(3) This section does not limit any right to indemnity which the administrative receiver would have apart from it, nor limit his liability on contracts entered into or adopted without authority, nor confer any right to indemnity in respect of that liability.

NOTES

This section derived from the Insolvency Act 1985, s 50.

Sub-s (1): words in square brackets in para (b) inserted by the Insolvency Act 1994, s 2(1), (2), (4), in relation to contracts of employment adopted on or after 15 March 1994.

Sub-ss (2A)–(2D): inserted by the Insolvency Act 1994, s 2(1), (3), (4), in relation to contracts of employment adopted on or after 15 March 1994.

Sub-s (2D): repealed by the Deregulation Act 2015, s 19, Sch 6, Pt 7, paras 24, 26.

[1.31]

45 Vacation of office

(1) An administrative receiver of a company may at any time be removed from office by order of the court (but not otherwise) and may resign his office by giving notice of his resignation in the prescribed manner to such persons as may be prescribed.
(2) An administrative receiver shall vacate office if he ceases to be qualified to act as an insolvency practitioner in relation to the company.
(3) Where at any time an administrative receiver vacates office—
 (a) his remuneration and any expenses properly incurred by him, and
 (b) any indemnity to which he is entitled out of the assets of the company,
shall be charged on and paid out of any property of the company which is in his custody or under his control at that time in priority to any security held by the person by or on whose behalf he was appointed.
(4) Where an administrative receiver vacates office otherwise than by death, he shall, within 14 days after his vacation of office, send a notice to that effect to the registrar of companies.
(5) If an administrative receiver without reasonable excuse fails to comply with subsection (4), he is liable to a fine *and, for continued contravention, to a daily default fine*.

NOTES

This section derived from the Insolvency Act 1985, s 51.

Sub-s (5): words in italics repealed by the Companies Act 1989, ss 107, 212, Sch 16, para 3, Sch 24, as from a day to be appointed.

Administrative receivers: ascertainment and investigation of company's affairs

[1.32]

46 Information to be given by administrative receiver

(1) Where an administrative receiver is appointed, he shall—

(a) forthwith send to the company and publish in the prescribed manner a notice of his appointment, and

(b) within 28 days after his appointment, unless the court otherwise directs, send such a notice to all the creditors of the company (so far as he is aware of their addresses).

(2) This section and the next do not apply in relation to the appointment of an administrative receiver to act—

(a) with an existing administrative receiver, or

(b) in place of an administrative receiver dying or ceasing to act,

except that, where they apply to an administrative receiver who dies or ceases to act before they have been fully complied with, the references in this section and the next to the administrative receiver include (subject to the next subsection) his successor and any continuing administrative receiver.

(3) If the company is being wound up, this section and the next apply notwithstanding that the administrative receiver and the liquidator are the same person, but with any necessary modifications arising from that fact.

(4) If the administrative receiver without reasonable excuse fails to comply with this section, he is liable to a fine and, for continued contravention, to a daily default fine.

NOTES

This section derived from the Insolvency Act 1985, s 52.

[1.33]

47 Statement of affairs to be submitted

(1) Where an administrative receiver is appointed, he shall forthwith require some or all of the persons mentioned below to make out and submit to him a statement in the prescribed form as to the affairs of the company.

(2) A statement submitted under this section shall be verified by [a statement of truth] by the persons required to submit it and shall show—

(a) particulars of the company's assets, debts and liabilities;

(b) the names and addresses of its creditors;

(c) the securities held by them respectively;

(d) the dates when the securities were respectively given; and

(e) such further or other information as may be prescribed.

(3) The persons referred to in subsection (1) are—

(a) those who are or have been officers of the company;

(b) those who have taken part in the company's formation at any time within one year before the date of the appointment of the administrative receiver;

(c) those who are in the company's employment, or have been in its employment within that year, and are in the administrative receiver's opinion capable of giving the information required;

(d) those who are or have been within that year officers of or in the employment of a company which is, or within that year was, an officer of the company.

In this subsection "employment" includes employment under a contract for services.

(4) Where any persons are required under this section to submit a statement of affairs to the administrative receiver, they shall do so (subject to the next subsection) before the end of the period of 21 days beginning with the day after that on which the prescribed notice of the requirement is given to them by the administrative receiver.

(5) The administrative receiver, if he thinks fit, may—

(a) at any time release a person from an obligation imposed on him under subsection (1) or (2), or

(b) either when giving notice under subsection (4) or subsequently, extend the period so mentioned;

and where the administrative receiver has refused to exercise a power conferred by this subsection, the court, if it thinks fit, may exercise it.

(6) If a person without reasonable excuse fails to comply with any obligation imposed under this section, he is liable to a fine and, for continued contravention, to a daily default fine.

NOTES

This section derived from the Insolvency Act 1985, s 53.

Sub-s (2): words in square brackets substituted by the Legislative Reform (Insolvency) (Miscellaneous Provisions) Order 2010, SI 2010/18, arts 2, 5(1).

[1.34]

48 Report by administrative receiver

(1) Where an administrative receiver is appointed, he shall, within 3 months (or such longer period as the court may allow) after his appointment, send to the registrar of companies, to any trustees for secured creditors of the company and (so far as he is aware of their addresses) to all such creditors[, other than opted-out creditors,] a report as to the following matters, namely—

- (a) the events leading up to his appointment, so far as he is aware of them;
- (b) the disposal or proposed disposal by him of any property of the company and the carrying on or proposed carrying on by him of any business of the company;
- (c) the amounts of principal and interest payable to the debenture holders by whom or on whose behalf he was appointed and the amounts payable to preferential creditors; and
- (d) the amount (if any) likely to be available for the payment of other creditors.

(2) The administrative receiver shall also, within 3 months (or such longer period as the court may allow) after his appointment, either—

- (a) send a copy of the report (so far as he is aware of their addresses) to all unsecured creditors of the company[, other than opted-out creditors,]; or
- (b) publish in the prescribed manner a notice stating an address to which unsecured creditors of the company should write for copies of the report to be sent to them free of charge,

and (in either case), unless the court otherwise directs, lay a copy of the report before a meeting of the company's unsecured creditors summoned for the purpose on not less than 14 days' notice.

(3) The court shall not give a direction under subsection (2) unless—

- *(a) the report states the intention of the administrative receiver to apply for the direction, and*
- *(b) a copy of the report is sent to the persons mentioned in paragraph (a) of that subsection, or a notice is published as mentioned in paragraph (b) of that subsection, not less than 14 days before the hearing of the application.*

(4) Where the company has gone or goes into liquidation, the administrative receiver—

- (a) shall, within 7 days after his compliance with subsection (1) or, if later, the nomination or appointment of the liquidator, send a copy of the report to the liquidator, and
- (b) where he does so within the time limited for compliance with subsection (2), is not required to comply with that subsection.

(5) A report under this section shall include a summary of the statement of affairs made out and submitted to the administrative receiver under section 47 and of his comments (if any) upon it.

(6) Nothing in this section is to be taken as requiring any such report to include any information the disclosure of which would seriously prejudice the carrying out by the administrative receiver of his functions.

(7) Section 46(2) applies for the purposes of this section also.

(8) If the administrative receiver without reasonable excuse fails to comply with this section, he is liable to a fine and, for continued contravention, to a daily default fine.

NOTES

This section derived from the Insolvency Act 1985, s 54.

Words in square brackets in sub-ss (1), (2)(a) inserted, words in italics in sub-s (2) repealed, and sub-s (3) repealed, by the Small Business, Enterprise and Employment Act 2015, s 126, Sch 9, Pt 1, paras 1, 12, as from 6 April 2017 (subject to transitional and savings provisions as noted to s 246ZE at **[1.256]**).

[1.35]

49 Committee of creditors

(1) [Where an administrative receiver has sent or published a report as mentioned in section 48(2) the company's unsecured creditors may, in accordance with the rules], establish a committee ("the creditors' committee") to exercise the functions conferred on it by or under this Act.

(2) If such a committee is established, the committee may, on giving not less than 7 days' notice, require the administrative receiver to attend before it at any reasonable time and furnish it with such information relating to the carrying out by him of his functions as it may reasonably require.

NOTES

This section derived from the Insolvency Act 1985, s 55.

Sub-s (1): words in square brackets substituted for original words "Where a meeting of creditors is summoned under section 48, the meeting may, if it thinks fit" by the Small Business, Enterprise and Employment Act 2015, s 126, Sch 9, Pt 1, paras 1, 13, as from 6 April 2017 (subject to transitional and savings provisions as noted to s 246ZE at **[1.256]**).

CHAPTER II
RECEIVERS (SCOTLAND)

[1.36]

50 Extent of this Chapter

This Chapter extends to Scotland only.

NOTES

This section derived from the Companies Act 1985, s 487.

[1.37]

51 Power to appoint receiver

(1) It is competent under the law of Scotland for the holder of a floating charge over all or any part of the property (including uncalled capital), which may from time to time be comprised in the property and undertaking of an incorporated company (whether [a company registered under the Companies Act 2006] or not):

[(a) which the Court of Session has jurisdiction to wind up; or

(b) where paragraph (a) does not apply, in respect of which a court of a member state other than the United Kingdom has under the EU Regulation jurisdiction to open insolvency proceedings,

to appoint a receiver of such part of the property of the company as is subject to the charge.]

(2) It is competent under the law of Scotland for the court, on the application of the holder of such a floating charge, to appoint a receiver of such part of the property of the company as is subject to the charge.

[(2ZA) But, in relation to a company mentioned in subsection (1)(b), a receiver may be appointed under subsection (1) or (2) only in respect of property situated in Scotland.]

[(2A) Subsections (1) and (2) are subject to section 72A.]

(3) The following are disqualified from being appointed as receiver—

(a) a body corporate;

(b) an undischarged bankrupt; and

[(ba) a person subject to a bankruptcy restrictions order;]

(c) a firm according to the law of Scotland.

(4) A body corporate or a firm according to the law of Scotland which acts as a receiver is liable to a fine.

(5) An undischarged bankrupt [or a person subject to a bankruptcy restrictions order] who so acts is liable to imprisonment or a fine, or both.

(6) In this section, "receiver" includes joint receivers[; and

"bankruptcy restrictions order" means—

(a) a bankruptcy restrictions order made under section [155 of the Bankruptcy (Scotland) Act 2016];

(b) a bankruptcy restrictions undertaking entered into under section 56G of that Act;

(c) a bankruptcy restrictions order made under paragraph 1 of Schedule 4A to this Act; or

(d) a bankruptcy restrictions undertaking entered into under paragraph 7 of that Schedule.

["the EU Regulation" is [Regulation (EU) 2015/848 of the European Parliament and of the Council] on insolvency proceedings;

"court" is to be construed in accordance with [Article 2(6)] of the EU Regulation;

"insolvency proceedings" is to be construed in accordance with [Article 2(4)] of the EU Regulation.]]

NOTES

This section derived from the Companies Act 1985, s 467.

Sub-s (1): words in first pair of square brackets substituted for original words "a company within the meaning of the Companies Act" by the Companies Act 2006 (Consequential Amendments, Transitional Provisions and Savings) Order 2009, SI 2009/1941, art 2(1), Sch 1, para 74(1), (5), subject to transitional provisions and savings in art 8, Sch 1, para 84 at **[2.70]**, **[2.73]**; words in second pair of square brackets substituted by the Insolvency Act 1986 Amendment (Appointment of Receivers) (Scotland) Regulations 2011, SSI 2011/140, reg 2(a).

Sub-s (2ZA): inserted by SSI 2011/140, reg 2(b); repealed by the Public Services Reform (Insolvency) (Scotland) Order 2016, SSI 2016/141, art 2, as from 1 April 2016 (for transitional provisions, see art 14 of the 2016 Order which provides that where a receiver is appointed in respect of a company under this section before 1 April 2016, this section continues to have effect on and after that date as if the amendment made in art 2 had not been made.)

Sub-s (2A): inserted by the Enterprise Act 2002, s 248(3), Sch 17, paras 9, 13, subject to savings and transitional provisions (i) in a case where a petition for an administration order has been presented before 15 September 2003 (see the Enterprise Act 2002 (Commencement No 4 and Transitional Provisions and Savings) Order 2003, SI 2003/2093, art 3 at **[2.26]**), and (ii) in relation to special administration regimes (see s 249 of the 2002 Act at **[2.10]**).

Sub-s (3): para (ba) inserted by the Bankruptcy and Diligence etc (Scotland) Act 2007, s 3(1), (2), subject to transitional provisions and savings in the Bankruptcy and Diligence etc (Scotland) Act 2007 (Commencement No 3, Savings and Transitionals) Order 2008, SSI 2008/115, arts 4–7, 10, 15 at **[2.51]–[2.53]**, **[2.56]**, **[2.57]**.

Sub-s (5): words in square brackets inserted by the Bankruptcy and Diligence etc (Scotland) Act 2007, s 3(1), (3), subject to transitional provisions and savings in SSI 2008/115, arts 4–7, 10, 15 at **[2.51]–[2.53]**, **[2.56]**, **[2.57]**.

Sub-s (6): words in first (outer) pair of square brackets inserted by the Bankruptcy and Diligence etc (Scotland) Act 2007, s 3(1), (4), subject to transitional provisions and savings in SSI 2008/115, arts 4–7, 10, 15 at **[2.51]–[2.53]**, **[2.56]**, **[2.57]**; in definition "bankruptcy restrictions order" words in square brackets in para (a) substituted (for the original words "56A of the Bankruptcy (Scotland) Act 1985 (c 66)") by the Bankruptcy (Scotland) Act 2016 (Consequential Provisions and Modifications) Order 2016, SI 2016/1034, art 7(1), (3), Sch 1, para 4(1), (2), as from 30 November 2016 (except in relation to (i) a sequestration as regards which the petition is presented, or the debtor application is made before that date; or (ii) a trust deed executed before that date); in definition "bankruptcy restrictions order" para (b) repealed by the Bankruptcy and Debt Advice (Scotland) Act 2014, s 56(2), Sch 4, as from 1 April 2015, subject to transitional provisions in SSI 2014/261, arts 4, 12 at **[2.91]**, **[2.99]**; definitions "the EU Regulation", "court", and "insolvency proceedings" inserted by SSI 2011/140, reg 2(c); words in square brackets in definition "the EU Regulation" substituted for original words "the Regulation of the Council of the European Union published as Council Regulation (EC) No 1346/2000", words in square brackets in definition "court" substituted for original words "Article 2(d)" and words in square brackets in definition "insolvency proceedings" substituted for original words "Article 2(a)", by the Insolvency (Regulation (EU) 2015/848) (Miscellaneous Amendments) (Scotland) Regulations 2017, SSI 2017/210, regs 2, 9, as from 26 June 2017, except in relation to proceedings opened before that date.

[1.38]

52 Circumstances justifying appointment

(1) A receiver may be appointed under section 51(1) by the holder of the floating charge on the occurrence of any event which, by the provisions of the instrument creating the charge, entitles the holder of the charge to make that appointment and, in so far as not otherwise provided for by the instrument, on the occurrence of any of the following events, namely—

(a) the expiry of a period of 21 days after the making of a demand for payment of the whole or any part of the principal sum secured by the charge, without payment having been made;

(b) the expiry of a period of 2 months during the whole of which interest due and payable under the charge has been in arrears;

(c) the making of an order or the passing of a resolution to wind up the company;

(d) the appointment of a receiver by virtue of any other floating charge created by the company.

(2) A receiver may be appointed by the court under section 51(2) on the occurrence of any event which, by the provisions of the instrument creating the floating charge, entitles the holder of the charge to make that appointment and, in so far as not otherwise provided for by the instrument on the occurrence of any of the following events, namely—

(a) where the court, on the application of the holder of the charge, pronounces itself satisfied that the position of the holder of the charge is likely to be prejudiced if no such appointment is made;

(b) any of the events referred to in paragraphs (a) to (c) of subsection (1).

NOTES

This section derived from the Companies Act 1985, s 468.

[1.39]

53 Mode of appointment by holder of charge

(1) The appointment of a receiver by the holder of the floating charge under section 51(1) shall be by means of [an instrument subscribed in accordance with the Requirements of Writing (Scotland) Act 1995] ("the instrument of appointment"), a copy (certified in the prescribed manner to be a correct copy) whereof shall be delivered by or on behalf of the person making the appointment to the registrar of companies for registration within 7 days of its execution and shall be accompanied by a notice in the prescribed form.

(2) If any person without reasonable excuse makes default in complying with the requirements of subsection (1), he is liable to a fine *and, for continued contravention, to a daily default fine*.

(3) . . .

[(4) If the receiver is to be appointed by the holders of a series of secured debentures, the instrument of appointment may be executed on behalf of the holders of the floating charge by any person authorised by resolution of the debenture-holders to execute the instrument.]

(5) On receipt of the certified copy of the instrument of appointment in accordance with subsection (1), the registrar shall, on payment of the prescribed fee, enter the particulars of the appointment in the [register].

(6) The appointment of a person as a receiver by an instrument of appointment in accordance with subsection (1)—

(a) is of no effect unless it is accepted by that person before the end of the business day next following that on which the instrument of appointment is received by him or on his behalf, and

(b) subject to paragraph (a), is deemed to be made on the day on and at the time at which the instrument of appointment is so received, as evidence by a written docquet by that person or on his behalf;

and this subsection applies to the appointment of joint receivers subject to such modifications as may be prescribed.

(7) On the appointment of a receiver under this section, the floating charge by virtue of which he was appointed attaches to the property then subject to the charge; and such attachment has effect as if the charge was a fixed security over the property to which it has attached.

NOTES

This section derived from the Companies Act 1985, s 469, and the Insolvency Act 1985, s 56 (in part).

Sub-s (1): words in square brackets substituted by the Requirements of Writing (Scotland) Act 1995, s 14(1), Sch 4, para 58(a).

Sub-s (2): words in italics repealed by the Companies Act 1989, ss 107, 212, Sch 16, para 3, Sch 24, as from a day to be appointed.

Sub-s (3): repealed by the Law Reform (Miscellaneous Provisions) (Scotland) Act 1990, s 74, Sch 8, Pt II, para 35, Sch 9.

Sub-s (4): substituted by the Requirements of Writing (Scotland) Act 1995, s 14(1), Sch 4, para 58(b).

Sub-s (5): word in square brackets substituted by the Companies Act 2006 (Amendment of Part 25) Regulations 2013, SI 2013/600, reg 5, Sch 2, para 2, in relation to charges created on or after 6 April 2013.

Modification in relation to Scotland: see the Note at the beginning of this Act.

Regulations: the Receivers (Scotland) Regulations 1986, SI 1986/1917 at **[16.1]**.

[1.40]

54 Appointment by court

(1) Application for the appointment of a receiver by the court under section 51(2) shall be by petition to the court, which shall be served on the company.

(2) On such an application, the court shall, if it thinks fit, issue an interlocutor making the appointment of the receiver.

(3) A copy (certified by the clerk of the court to be a correct copy) of the court's interlocutor making the appointment shall be delivered by or on behalf of the petitioner to the registrar of companies for registration, accompanied by a notice in the prescribed form within 7 days of the date of the interlocutor or such longer period as the court may allow.

If any person without reasonable excuse makes default in complying with the requirements of this subsection, he is liable to a fine *and, for continued contravention, to a daily default fine*.

(4) On receipt of the certified copy interlocutor in accordance with subsection (3), the registrar shall, on payment of the prescribed fee, enter the particulars of the appointment in the [register].

(5) The receiver is to be regarded as having been appointed on the date of his being appointed by the court.

(6) On the appointment of a receiver under this section, the floating charge by virtue of which he was appointed attaches to the property then subject to the charge; and such attachment has effect as if the charge were a fixed security over the property to which it has attached.

(7) In making rules of court for the purposes of this section, the Court of Session shall have regard to the need for special provision for cases which appear to the court to require to be dealt with as a matter of urgency.

NOTES

This section derived from the Companies Act 1985, s 470.

Sub-s (3): words in italics repealed by the Companies Act 1989, ss 107, 212, Sch 16, para 3, Sch 24, as from a day to be appointed.

Sub-s (4): word in square brackets substituted by the Companies Act 2006 (Amendment of Part 25) Regulations 2013, SI 2013/600, reg 5, Sch 2, para 2, in relation to charges created on or after 6 April 2013.

Modification in relation to Scotland: see the Note at the beginning of this Act.

Regulations: the Receivers (Scotland) Regulations 1986, SI 1986/1917 at **[16.1]**.

[1.41]

55 Powers of receiver

(1) Subject to the next subsection, a receiver has in relation to such part of the property of the company as is attached by the floating charge by virtue of which he was appointed, the powers, if any, given to him by the instrument creating that charge.

(2) In addition, the receiver has under this Chapter the powers as respects that property (in so far as these are not inconsistent with any provision contained in that instrument) which are specified in Schedule 2 to this Act.

(3) Subsections (1) and (2) apply—

(a) subject to the rights of any person who has effectually executed diligence on all or any part of the property of the company prior to the appointment of the receiver, and

(b) subject to the rights of any person who holds over all or any part of the property of the company a fixed security or floating charge having priority over, or ranking pari passu with, the floating charge by virtue of which the receiver was appointed.

(4) A person dealing with a receiver in good faith and for value is not concerned to enquire whether the receiver is acting within his powers.

NOTES

This section derived from the Companies Act 1985, s 471, and the Insolvency Act 1985, s 57.

[1.42]

56 Precedence among receivers

(1) Where there are two or more floating charges subsisting over all or any part of the property of the company, a receiver may be appointed under this Chapter by virtue of each such charge; but a receiver appointed by, or on the application of, the holder of a floating charge having priority of ranking over any other floating charge by virtue of which a receiver has been appointed has the powers given to a receiver by section 55 and Schedule 2 to the exclusion of any other receiver.

(2) Where two or more floating charges rank with one another equally, and two or more receivers have been appointed by virtue of such charges, the receivers so appointed are deemed to have been appointed as joint receivers.

(3) Receivers appointed, or deemed to have been appointed, as joint receivers shall act jointly unless the instrument of appointment or respective instruments of appointment otherwise provide.

(4) Subject to subsection (5) below, the powers of a receiver appointed by, or on the application of, the holder of a floating charge are suspended by, and as from the date of, the appointment of a receiver by, or on the application of, the holder of a floating charge having priority of ranking over that charge to such extent as may be necessary to enable the receiver second mentioned to exercise his powers under section 55 and Schedule 2; and any powers so suspended take effect again when the floating charge having priority of ranking ceases to attach to the property then subject to the charge, whether such cessation is by virtue of section 62(6) or otherwise.

(5) The suspension of the powers of a receiver under subsection (4) does not have the effect of requiring him to release any part of the property (including any letters or documents) of the company from his control until he receives from the receiver superseding him a valid indemnity (subject to the limit of the value of such part of the property of the company as is subject to the charge by virtue of which he was appointed) in respect of any expenses, charges and liabilities he may have incurred in the performance of his functions as receiver.

(6) The suspension of the powers of a receiver under subsection (4) does not cause the floating charge by virtue of which he was appointed to cease to attach to the property to which it attached by virtue of section 53(7) or 54(6).
(7) Nothing in this section prevents the same receiver being appointed by virtue of two or more floating charges.

NOTES

This section derived from the Companies Act 1985, s 472.

[1.43]

57 Agency and liability of receiver for contracts

(1) A receiver is deemed to be the agent of the company in relation to such property of the company as is attached by the floating charge by virtue of which he was appointed.
[(1A) Without prejudice to subsection (1), a receiver is deemed to be the agent of the company in relation to any contract of employment adopted by him in the carrying out of his functions.]
(2) A receiver (including a receiver whose powers are subsequently suspended under section 56) is personally liable on any contract entered into by him in the performance of his functions, except in so far as the contract otherwise provides, and[, to the extent of any qualifying liability,] on any contract of employment adopted by him in the carrying out of those functions.
[(2A) For the purposes of subsection (2), a liability under a contract of employment is a qualifying liability if—
  (a) it is a liability to pay a sum by way of wages or salary or contribution to an occupational pension scheme,
  (b) it is incurred while the receiver is in office, and
  (c) it is in respect of services rendered wholly or partly after the adoption of the contract.
(2B) Where a sum payable in respect of a liability which is a qualifying liability for the purposes of subsection (2) is payable in respect of services rendered partly before and partly after the adoption of the contract, liability under that subsection shall only extend to so much of the sum as is payable in respect of services rendered after the adoption of the contract.
(2C) For the purposes of subsections (2A) and (2B)—
  (a) wages or salary payable in respect of a period of holiday or absence from work through sickness or other good cause are deemed to be wages or (as the case may be) salary in respect of services rendered in that period, and
  (b) a sum payable in lieu of holiday is deemed to be wages or (as the case may be) salary in respect of services rendered in the period by reference to which the holiday entitlement arose.
(2D) . . .]
(3) A receiver who is personally liable by virtue of subsection (2) is entitled to be indemnified out of the property in respect of which he was appointed.
(4) Any contract entered into by or on behalf of the company prior to the appointment of a receiver continues in force (subject to its terms) notwithstanding that appointment, but the receiver does not by virtue only of his appointment incur any personal liability on any such contract.
(5) For the purposes of subsection (2), a receiver is not to be taken to have adopted a contract of employment by reason of anything done or omitted to be done within 14 days after his appointment.
(6) This section does not limit any right to indemnity which the receiver would have apart from it, nor limit his liability on contracts entered into or adopted without authority, nor confer any right to indemnity in respect of that liability.
(7) Any contract entered into by a receiver in the performance of his functions continues in force (subject to its terms) although the powers of the receiver are subsequently suspended under section 56.

NOTES

This section derived from the Companies Act 1985, s 473, and the Insolvency Act 1985, s 58.

Sub-s (1A): inserted by the Insolvency Act 1994, s 3(1), (2), (5), in relation to contracts of employment adopted on or after 15 March 1994.

Sub-s (2): words in square brackets inserted by the Insolvency Act 1994, s 3(1), (3), (5), in relation to contracts of employment adopted on or after 15 March 1994.

Sub-ss (2A)–(2D): inserted by the Insolvency Act 1994, s 3(1), (4), (5), in relation to contracts of employment adopted on or after 15 March 1994. Sub-s (2D) repealed by the Public Services Reform (Insolvency) (Scotland) Order 2016, SSI 2016/141, art 3.

[1.44]

58 Remuneration of receiver

(1) The remuneration to be paid to a receiver is to be determined by agreement between the receiver and the holder of the floating charge by virtue of which he was appointed.
(2) Where the remuneration to be paid to the receiver has not been determined under subsection (1), or where it has been so determined but is disputed by any of the persons mentioned in paragraphs (a) to (d) below, it may be fixed instead by the Auditor of the Court of Session on application made to him by—
  (a) the receiver;
  (b) the holder of any floating charge or fixed security over all or any part of the property of the company;
  (c) the company; or
  (d) the liquidator of the company.

(3) Where the receiver has been paid or has retained for his remuneration for any period before the remuneration has been fixed by the Auditor of the Court of Session under subsection (2) any amount in excess of the remuneration so fixed for that period, the receiver or his personal representatives shall account for the excess.

NOTES

This section derived from the Companies Act 1985, s 474.

[1.45]

59 Priority of debts

(1) Where a receiver is appointed and the company is not at the time of the appointment in course of being wound up, the debts which fall under subsection (2) of this section shall be paid out of any assets coming to the hands of the receiver in priority to any claim for principal or interest by the holder of the floating charge by virtue of which the receiver was appointed.

(2) Debts falling under this subsection are preferential debts (within the meaning given by section 386 in Part XII) which, by the end of a period of 6 months after advertisement by the receiver for claims in the Edinburgh Gazette and in a newspaper circulating in the district where the company carries on business either—

(i) have been intimated to him, or

(ii) have become known to him.

(3) Any payments made under this section shall be recouped as far as may be out of the assets of the company available for payment of ordinary creditors.

NOTES

This section derived from the Companies Act 1985, s 475, and the Insolvency Act 1985, Sch 6, para 20(1), (2).

[1.46]

60 Distribution of moneys

(1) Subject to the next section, and to the rights of any of the following categories of persons (which rights shall, except to the extent otherwise provided in any instrument, have the following order of priority), namely—

(a) the holder of any fixed security which is over property subject to the floating charge and which ranks prior to, or pari passu with, the floating charge;

(b) all persons who have effectually executed diligence on any part of the property of the company which is subject to the charge by virtue of which the receiver was appointed;

(c) creditors in respect of all liabilities, charges and expenses incurred by or on behalf of the receiver;

(d) the receiver in respect of his liabilities, expenses and remuneration, and any indemnity to which he is entitled out of the property of the company; and

(e) the preferential creditors entitled to payment under section 59,

the receiver shall pay moneys received by him to the holder of the floating charge by virtue of which the receiver was appointed in or towards satisfaction of the debt secured by the floating charge.

(2) Any balance of moneys remaining after the provisions of subsection (1) and section 61 below have been satisfied shall be paid in accordance with their respective rights and interests to the following persons, as the case may require—

(a) any other receiver;

(b) the holder of a fixed security which is over property subject to the floating charge;

(c) the company or its liquidator, as the case may be.

(3) Where any question arises as to the person entitled to a payment under this section, or where a receipt or a discharge of a security cannot be obtained in respect of any such payment, the receiver shall consign the amount of such payment in any joint stock bank of issue in Scotland in name of the Accountant of Court for behoof of the person or persons entitled thereto.

NOTES

This section derived from the Companies Act 1985, s 476, and the Insolvency Act 1985, Sch 6, para 21.

[1.47]

61 Disposal of interest in property

(1) Where the receiver sells or disposes, or is desirous of selling or disposing, of any property or interest in property of the company which is subject to the floating charge by virtue of which the receiver was appointed and which is—

(a) subject to any security or interest of, or burden or encumbrance in favour of, a creditor the ranking of which is prior to, or pari passu with, or postponed to the floating charge, or

(b) property or an interest in property affected or attached by effectual diligence executed by any person,

and the receiver is unable to obtain the consent of such creditor or, as the case may be, such person to such a sale or disposal, the receiver may apply to the court for authority to sell or dispose of the property or interest in property free of such security, interest, burden, encumbrance or diligence.

[(1A) For the purposes of subsection (1) above, an inhibition which takes effect after the creation of the floating charge by virtue of which the receiver was appointed is not an effectual diligence.]

[(1B) For the purposes of subsection (1) above, an arrestment is an effectual diligence only where it is executed before the floating charge, by virtue of which the receiver was appointed, attaches to the property comprised in the company's property and undertaking.]

(2) Subject to the next subsection, on such an application the court may, if it thinks fit, authorise the sale or disposal of the property or interest in question free of such security, interest, burden, encumbrance or diligence, and such authorisation may be on such terms or conditions as the court thinks fit.

(3) In the case of an application where a fixed security over the property or interest in question which ranks prior to the floating charge has not been met or provided for in full, the court shall not authorise the sale or disposal of the property or interest in question unless it is satisfied that the sale or disposal would be likely to provide a more advantageous realisation of the company's assets than would otherwise be effected.

(4) It shall be a condition of an authorisation to which subsection (3) applies that—

(a) the net proceeds of the disposal, and

(b) where those proceeds are less than such amount as may be determined by the court to be the net amount which would be realised on a sale of the property or interest in the open market by a willing seller, such sums as may be required to make good the deficiency,

shall be applied towards discharging the sums secured by the fixed security.

(5) Where a condition imposed in pursuance of subsection (4) relates to two or more such fixed securities, that condition shall require the net proceeds of the disposal and, where paragraph (b) of that subsection applies, the sums mentioned in that paragraph to be applied towards discharging the sums secured by those fixed securities in the order of their priorities.

(6) A copy of an authorisation under subsection (2) . . . shall, within 14 days of the granting of the authorisation, be sent by the receiver to the registrar of companies.

(7) If the receiver without reasonable excuse fails to comply with subsection (6), he is liable to a fine and, for continued contravention, to a daily default fine.

(8) Where any sale or disposal is effected in accordance with the authorisation of the court under subsection (2), the receiver shall grant to the purchaser or disponee an appropriate document of transfer or conveyance of the property or interest in question, and that document has the effect, or, where recording, intimation or registration of that document is a legal requirement for completion of title to the property or interest, then that recording, intimation or registration (as the case may be) has the effect, of—

(a) disencumbering the property or interest of the security, interest, burden or encumbrance affecting it, and

(b) freeing the property or interest from the diligence executed upon it.

(9) Nothing in this section prejudices the right of any creditor of the company to rank for his debt in the winding up of the company.

NOTES

This section derived from the Companies Act 1985, s 477, and the Insolvency Act 1985, s 59.

Sub-s (1A): inserted by the Bankruptcy and Diligence etc (Scotland) Act 2007, s 155(1), (2), subject to transitional provisions and savings in the Bankruptcy and Diligence etc (Scotland) Act 2007 (Commencement No 4, Savings and Transitionals) Order 2009, SSI 2009/67, art 6 at **[2.62]**.

Sub-s (1B): inserted by the Bankruptcy and Diligence etc (Scotland) Act 2007, s 226(1), Sch 5, para 14(1), (2), as from a day to be appointed.

Sub-s (6): words "certified by the clerk of the court" (omitted) repealed by the Companies Act 2006 (Consequential Amendments, Transitional Provisions and Savings) Order 2009, SI 2009/1941, art 2(1), Sch 1, para 74(1), (6), subject to transitional provisions and savings in art 8, Sch 1, para 84 at **[2.70]**, **[2.73]**.

Modification in relation to Scotland: see the Note at the beginning of this Act.

[1.48]

62 Cessation of appointment of receiver

(1) A receiver may be removed from office by the court under subsection (3) below and may resign his office by giving notice of his resignation in the prescribed manner to such persons as may be prescribed.

(2) A receiver shall vacate office if he ceases to be qualified to act as an insolvency practitioner in relation to the company.

(3) Subject to the next subsection, a receiver may, on application to the court by the holder of the floating charge by virtue of which he was appointed, be removed by the court on cause shown.

(4) Where at any time a receiver vacates office—

(a) his remuneration and any expenses properly incurred by him, and

(b) any indemnity to which he is entitled out of the property of the company,

shall be paid out of the property of the company which is subject to the floating charge and shall have priority as provided for in section 60(1).

(5) When a receiver ceases to act as such otherwise than by death he shall, and, when a receiver is removed by the court, the holder of the floating charge by virtue of which he was appointed shall, within 14 days of the cessation or removal (as the case may be) give the registrar of companies notice to that effect, and the registrar shall enter the notice in the [register].

If the receiver or the holder of the floating charge (as the case may require) makes default in complying with the requirements of this subsection, he is liable to a fine *and, for continued contravention, to a daily default fine*.

(6) If by the expiry of a period of one month following upon the removal of the receiver or his ceasing to act as such no other receiver has been appointed, the floating charge by virtue of which the receiver was appointed—

(a) thereupon ceases to attach to the property then subject to the charge, and

(b) again subsists as a floating charge;

and for the purposes of calculating the period of one month under this subsection no account shall be taken of any period during which [the company is in administration] under Part II of this Act . . .

NOTES

This section derived from the Companies Act 1985, s 478, and the Insolvency Act 1985, s 60, Sch 6, para 13.

Sub-s (5): word in square brackets substituted by the Companies Act 2006 (Amendment of Part 25) Regulations 2013, SI 2013/600, reg 5, Sch 2, para 2, in relation to charges created on or after 6 April 2013; words in italics repealed by the Companies Act 1989, ss 107, 212, Sch 16, para 3, Sch 24, as from a day to be appointed.

Sub-s (6): words in square brackets substituted for original words "an administration order", and words "is in force" (omitted) repealed, by the Enterprise Act 2002 (Insolvency) Order 2003, SI 2003/2096, arts 4, 6, Schedule, paras 8, 9, except in any case where a petition for an administration order was presented before 15 September 2003.

Modification in relation to Scotland: see the Note at the beginning of this Act.

Regulations: the Receivers (Scotland) Regulations 1986, SI 1986/1917 at **[16.1]**.

[1.49]

63 Powers of court

(1) The court on the application of—

(a) the holder of a floating charge by virtue of which a receiver was appointed, or

(b) a receiver appointed under section 51,

may give directions to the receiver in respect of any matter arising in connection with the performance by him of his functions.

(2) Where the appointment of a person as a receiver by the holder of a floating charge is discovered to be invalid (whether by virtue of the invalidity of the instrument or otherwise), the court may order the holder of the floating charge to indemnify the person appointed against any liability which arises solely by reason of the invalidity of the appointment.

NOTES

This section derived from the Companies Act 1985, s 479, and the Insolvency Act 1985, s 61.

[1.50]

64 Notification that receiver appointed

[(1) Where a receiver has been appointed—

(a) every invoice, order for goods or services, business letter or order form (whether in hard copy, electronic or any other form) issued by or on behalf of the company or the receiver or the liquidator of the company; and

(b) all the company's websites,

must contain a statement that a receiver has been appointed.]

(2) If default is made in complying with the requirements of this section, the company and any of the following persons who knowingly and wilfully authorises or permits the default, namely any officer of the company, any liquidator of the company and any receiver, is liable to a fine.

NOTES

This section derived from the Companies Act 1985, s 480.

Sub-s (1): substituted by the Companies (Trading Disclosures) (Insolvency) Regulations 2008, SI 2008/1897, reg 2(2).

[1.51]

65 Information to be given by receiver

(1) Where a receiver is appointed, he shall—

(a) forthwith send to the company and publish notice of his appointment, and

(b) within 28 days after his appointment, unless the court otherwise directs, send such notice to all the creditors of the company (so far as he is aware of their addresses).

(2) This section and the next do not apply in relation to the appointment of a receiver to act—

(a) with an existing receiver, or

(b) in place of a receiver who has died or ceased to act,

except that, where they apply to a receiver who dies or ceases to act before they have been fully complied with, the references in this section and the next to the receiver include (subject to subsection (3) of this section) his successor and any continuing receiver.

(3) If the company is being wound up, this section and the next apply notwithstanding that the receiver and the liquidator are the same person, but with any necessary modifications arising from that fact.

(4) If a person without reasonable excuse fails to comply with this section, he is liable to a fine and, for continued contravention, to a daily default fine.

NOTES

This section derived from the Companies Act 1985, s 481, and the Insolvency Act 1985, s 62.

Regulations: the Receivers (Scotland) Regulations 1986, SI 1986/1917 at **[16.1]**.

[1.52]

66 Company's statement of affairs

(1) Where a receiver of a company is appointed, the receiver shall forthwith require some or all of the persons mentioned in subsection (3) below to make out and submit to him a statement in the prescribed form as to the affairs of the company.

(2) A statement submitted under this section shall *be verified by affidavit* by the persons required to submit it and shall show—

(a) particulars of the company's assets, debts and liabilities;

(b) the names and addresses of its creditors;

(c) the securities held by them respectively;
(d) the dates when the securities were respectively given; and
(e) such further or other information as may be prescribed.

(3) The persons referred to in subsection (1) are—
(a) those who are or have been officers of the company;
(b) those who have taken part in the company's formation at any time within one year before the date of the appointment of the receiver;
(c) those who are in the company's employment or have been in its employment within that year, and are in the receiver's opinion capable of giving the information required;
(d) those who are or have been within that year officers of or in the employment of a company which is, or within that year was, an officer of the company.

In this subsection "employment" includes employment under a contract for services.

(4) Where any persons are required under this section to submit a statement of affairs to the receiver they shall do so (subject to the next subsection) before the end of the period of 21 days beginning with the day after that on which the prescribed notice of the requirement is given to them by the receiver.

(5) The receiver, if he thinks fit, may—
(a) at any time release a person from an obligation imposed on him under subsection (1) or (2), or
(b) either when giving the notice mentioned in subsection (4) or subsequently extend the period so mentioned,

and where the receiver has refused to exercise a power conferred by this subsection, the court, if it thinks fit, may exercise it.

(6) If a person without reasonable excuse fails to comply with any obligation imposed under this section, he is liable to a fine and, for continued contravention to a daily default fine.

NOTES

This section derived from the Companies Act 1985, s 482, and the Insolvency Act 1985, s 63.

Sub-s (2): for the words in italics there are substituted the words "contain a statutory declaration" by the Public Services Reform (Insolvency) (Scotland) Order 2016, SSI 2016/141, art 4, as from a day to be appointed (being the day that the Small Business, Enterprise and Employment Act 2015, s 122(2) comes into force for all remaining purposes in Scotland). See also the savings note below.

Savings: the Public Services Reform (Insolvency) (Scotland) Order 2016, SSI 2016/141, arts 15, 16 provide as follows (note that the words in square brackets in art 15(1) were substituted and art 16 was inserted, by the Public Services Reform (Corporate Insolvency and Bankruptcy) (Scotland) Order 2017, SSI 2017/209, art 8, and the words in square brackets in art 15(6) were inserted by the Insolvency (Regulation (EU) 2015/848) (Miscellaneous Amendments) (Scotland) Regulations 2017, SSI 2017/210, reg 6, except in relation to proceedings opened before 26 June 2017)—

"15

(1) Where this article applies, subject to article 1(3) the Act continues to have effect on and after the day mentioned in article 1(4) as if the amendments made by articles [4 and 8 to 10] had not been made.

(2) This article applies where, in a receivership, a receiver is appointed in respect of a company under section 51 of the Act before the day mentioned in article 1(4).

(3) This article applies where a company goes into liquidation upon a resolution for voluntary winding up passed before the day mentioned in article 1(4).

(4) This article applies where—
(a) there is an application for the appointment of a provisional liquidator under section 135 of the Act; or
(b) a company goes into liquidation on the making of a winding up order,

on a winding up petition presented before the day mentioned in article 1(4).

(5) This article applies where—
(a) there is an application for the appointment of a provisional liquidator under section 135 of the Act; or
(b) a company goes into liquidation on the making of a winding up order,

on a winding up petition presented on or after the day mentioned in article 1(4) if, at the time the winding up petition is presented, the company is in liquidation upon a resolution for voluntary winding up passed before the day mentioned in article 1(4).

(6) In this article—

"resolution for voluntary winding up" includes a resolution which is deemed to occur by virtue of—
(a) paragraph 83(6)(b) of Schedule B1 of the Act (administration); or
(b) an order made following conversion of administration or a voluntary arrangement into winding up by virtue of Article 37 of Council Regulation (EC) No 1346/2000 on insolvency proceedings [or Article 51 of Regulation (EU) 2015/848 on insolvency proceedings]; and

"winding up petition" includes an administration application under paragraph 12 of Schedule B1 to the Act which the court treats as a winding up petition under paragraph 13(1)(e) of that Schedule.

[16 (1) This article applies where, before the day mentioned in article 1(4)—
(a) there is a members' or creditors' voluntary winding up continuing for more than one year;
(b) the liquidator in that winding up has an obligation under—
(i) section 93 or 105 of the Act to summon a general meeting of the company, either at the end of the first year from the commencement of the winding up, or at the end of any succeeding year; or
(ii) section 105 of the Act to summon a meeting of the creditors, either at the end of the first year from the commencement of the winding up, or at the end of any succeeding year; and
(c) that obligation has not been fulfilled or the meeting has not taken place.

(2) Where this article applies, subject to article 1(3), the Act continues to have effect on and after the day mentioned in article 1(4) as if the amendments made by articles 5, 6 and 7(2) and (3) had not been made in relation to the liquidator's obligations to—
(a) summon the particular meeting;
(b) lay before that meeting an account of the liquidator's acts and dealings, and of the conduct of the winding up, in the preceding year.]".

Regulations: the Receivers (Scotland) Regulations 1986, SI 1986/1917 at **[16.1]**.

[1.53]

67 Report by receiver

(1) Where a receiver is appointed under section 51, he shall within 3 months (or such longer period as the court may allow) after his appointment, send to the registrar of companies, to the holder of the floating charge by virtue of which he was appointed and to any trustees for secured creditors of the company and (so far as he is aware of their addresses) to all such creditors[, other than opted-out creditors,] a report as to the following matters, namely—

(a) the events leading up to his appointment, so far as he is aware of them;

(b) the disposal or proposed disposal by him of any property of the company and the carrying on or proposed carrying on by him of any business of the company;

(c) the amounts of principal and interest payable to the holder of the floating charge by virtue of which he was appointed and the amounts payable to preferential creditors; and

(d) the amount (if any) likely to be available for the payment of other creditors.

(2) The receiver shall also, within 3 months (or such longer period as the court may allow) after his appointment, either—

(a) send a copy of the report (so far as he is aware of their addresses) to all unsecured creditors of the company[, other than opted-out creditors], or

(b) publish in the prescribed manner a notice stating an address to which unsecured creditors of the company should write for copies of the report to be sent to them free of charge,

and (in either case), unless the court otherwise directs, lay a copy of the report before a meeting of the company's unsecured creditors summoned for the purpose on not less than 14 days' notice.

(3) The court shall not give a direction under subsection (2) unless—

(a) the report states the intention of the receiver to apply for the direction, and

(b) a copy of the report is sent to the persons mentioned in paragraph (a) of that subsection, or a notice is published as mentioned in paragraph (b) of that subsection, not less than 14 days before the hearing of the application.

(4) Where the company has gone or goes into liquidation, the receiver—

(a) shall, within 7 days after his compliance with subsection (1) or, if later, the nomination or appointment of the liquidator, send a copy of the report to the liquidator, and

(b) where he does so within the time limited for compliance with subsection (2), is not required to comply with that subsection.

(5) A report under this section shall include a summary of the statement of affairs made out and submitted under section 66 and of his comments (if any) on it.

(6) Nothing in this section shall be taken as requiring any such report to include any information the disclosure of which would seriously prejudice the carrying out by the receiver of his functions.

(7) Section 65(2) applies for the purposes of this section also.

(8) If a person without reasonable excuse fails to comply with this section, he is liable to a fine and, for continued contravention, to a daily default fine.

(9) In this section "secured creditor", in relation to a company, means a creditor of the company who holds in respect of his debt a security over property of the company, and "unsecured creditor" shall be construed accordingly.

NOTES

This section derived from the Companies Act 1985, s 482A, and the Insolvency Act 1985, s 64.

Words in square brackets in sub-ss (1), (2)(a) inserted, words in italics in sub-s (2) repealed, and sub-s (3) repealed, by the Small Business, Enterprise and Employment Act 2015, s 126, Sch 9, Pt 1, paras 1, 14, as from a day to be appointed.

Regulations: the Receivers (Scotland) Regulations 1986, SI 1986/1917 at **[16.1]**.

[1.54]

68 Committee of creditors

(1) *Where a meeting of creditors is summoned under section 67, the meeting may, if it thinks fit,* establish a committee ("the creditors' committee") to exercise the functions conferred on it by or under this Act.

(2) If such a committee is established, the committee may on giving not less than 7 days' notice require the receiver to attend before it at any reasonable time and furnish it with such information relating to the carrying out by him of his functions as it may reasonably require.

NOTES

This section derived from the Companies Act 1985, s 482B, and the Insolvency Act 1985, s 65.

Sub-s (1): for the words in italics there are substituted the words "Where a receiver has sent or published a report as mentioned in section 67(2) the company's unsecured creditors may, in accordance with the rules", by the Small Business, Enterprise and Employment Act 2015, s 126, Sch 9, Pt 1, paras 1, 15, as from a day to be appointed.

[1.55]

69 Enforcement of receiver's duty to make returns, etc

(1) If any receiver—

(a) having made default in filing, delivering or making any return, account or other document, or in giving any notice, which a receiver is by law required to file, deliver, make or give, fails to make good the default within 14 days after the service on him of a notice requiring him to do so; or

(b) has, after being required at any time by the liquidator of the company so to do, failed to render proper accounts of his receipts and payments and to vouch the same and to pay over to the liquidator the amount properly payable to him,

the court may, on an application made for the purpose, make an order directing the receiver to make good the default within such time as may be specified in the order.

(2) In the case of any such default as is mentioned in subsection (1)(a), an application for the purposes of this section may be made by any member or creditor of the company or by the registrar of companies; and, in the case of any such default as is mentioned in subsection (1)(b), the application shall be made by the liquidator; and, in either case, the order may provide that all expenses of and incidental to the application shall be borne by the receiver.

(3) Nothing in this section prejudices the operation of any enactments imposing penalties on receivers in respect of any such default as is mentioned in subsection (1).

NOTES

This section derived from the Companies Act 1985, s 483.

Modification in relation to Scotland: see the Note at the beginning of this Act.

[1.56]

70 Interpretation for Chapter II

(1) In this Chapter, unless the contrary intention appears, the following expressions have the following meanings respectively assigned to them—

"company" means an incorporated company (whether or not [a company registered under the Companies Act 2006]) which the Court of Session has jurisdiction to wind up;

"fixed security", in relation to any property of a company, means any security, other than a floating charge or a charge having the nature of a floating charge, which on the winding up of the company in Scotland would be treated as an effective security over that property, and (without prejudice to that generality) includes a security over that property, being a heritable security within the meaning of the Conveyancing and Feudal Reform (Scotland) Act 1970;

"instrument of appointment" has the meaning given by section 53(1);

"prescribed" means prescribed by regulations made under this Chapter by the Secretary of State;

["prescribed fee" means the fee prescribed by regulations made under this Chapter by the Secretary of State;]

"receiver" means a receiver of such part of the property of the company as is subject to the floating charge by virtue of which he has been appointed under section 51;

["the register" has the meaning given by section 1080 of the Companies Act 2006;]

"secured debenture" means a bond, debenture, debenture stock or other security which, either itself or by reference to any other instrument, creates a floating charge over all or any part of the property of the company, but does not include a security which creates no charge other than a fixed security; and

"series of secured debentures" means two or more secured debentures created as a series by the company in such a manner that the holders thereof are entitled pari passu to the benefit of the floating charge.

(2) Where a floating charge, secured debenture or series of secured debentures has been created by the company, then, except where the context otherwise requires, any reference in this Chapter to the holder of the floating charge shall—

(a) where the floating charge, secured debenture or series of secured debentures provides for a receiver to be appointed by any person or body, be construed as a reference to that person or body;

(b) where, in the case of a series of secured debentures, no such provision has been made therein but—

(i) there are trustees acting for the debenture-holders under and in accordance with a trust deed, be construed as a reference to those trustees, and

(ii) where no such trustees are acting, be construed as a reference to—

(aa) a majority in nominal value of those present or represented by proxy and voting at a meeting of debenture-holders at which the holders of at least one-third in nominal value of the outstanding debentures of the series are present or so represented, or

(bb) where no such meeting is held, the holders of at least one-half in nominal value of the outstanding debentures of the series.

(3) Any reference in this Chapter to a floating charge, secured debenture, series of secured debentures or instrument creating a charge includes, except where the context otherwise requires, a reference to that floating charge, debenture, series of debentures or instrument as varied by any instrument.

(4) References in this Chapter to the instrument by which a floating charge was created are, in the case of a floating charge created by words in a bond or other written acknowledgement, references to the bond or, as the case may be, the other written acknowledgement.

NOTES

This section derived from the Companies Act 1985, ss 462(4), 484, 486 (in part).

Sub-s (1): in definition "company" words in square brackets substituted for original words "a company within the meaning of the Companies Act" by the Companies Act 2006 (Consequential Amendments, Transitional Provisions and Savings) Order 2009, SI 2009/1941, art 2(1), Sch 1, para 74(1), (7), subject to transitional provisions and savings in art 8, Sch 1, para 84 at **[2.70]**, **[2.73]**; definition "register" substituted by the Companies Act 2006 (Amendment of Part 25) Regulations 2013, SI 2013/600, reg 5, Sch 2, para 2, in relation to charges created on or after 6 April 2013; definition "prescribed" repealed, and definition "prescribed fee" inserted, by the Public Services Reform (Corporate Insolvency and Bankruptcy) (Scotland) Order 2017, SSI 2017/209, art 2, as from 1 October 2017 (in so far as they enable the making of (i) rules under s 411 post, or (ii) any other subordinate legislation under this Act), and as from the day appointed for the coming into force, for all remaining purposes, of the Small Business, Enterprise and Employment Act 2015, s 122 in Scotland (otherwise).

[1.57]

71 Prescription of forms, etc; regulations

(1) The notice referred to in section 62(5), and the notice referred to in section 65(1)(a) shall be in such form as may be prescribed.

(2) Any power conferred by this Chapter on the Secretary of State to make regulations is exercisable by statutory instrument; and a statutory instrument made in the exercise of the power so conferred to prescribe a fee is subject to annulment in pursuance of a resolution of either House of Parliament.

NOTES

This section derived from the Companies Act 1985, s 485.

CHAPTER III

RECEIVERS' POWERS IN GREAT BRITAIN AS A WHOLE

[1.58]

72 Cross-border operation of receivership provisions

(1) A receiver appointed under the law of either part of Great Britain in respect of the whole or any part of any property or undertaking of a company and in consequence of the company having created a charge which, as created, was a floating charge may exercise his powers in the other part of Great Britain so far as their exercise is not inconsistent with the law applicable there.

(2) In subsection (1) "receiver" includes a manager and a person who is appointed both receiver and manager.

NOTES

This section derived from the Companies Act 1985, s 724.

[CHAPTER IV

PROHIBITION OF APPOINTMENT OF ADMINISTRATIVE RECEIVER

[1.59]

72A Floating charge holder not to appoint administrative receiver

(1) The holder of a qualifying floating charge in respect of a company's property may not appoint an administrative receiver of the company.

(2) In Scotland, the holder of a qualifying floating charge in respect of a company's property may not appoint or apply to the court for the appointment of a receiver who on appointment would be an administrative receiver of property of the company.

(3) In subsections (1) and (2)—

"holder of a qualifying floating charge in respect of a company's property" has the same meaning as in paragraph 14 of Schedule B1 to this Act, and

"administrative receiver" has the meaning given by section 251.

(4) This section applies—

(a) to a floating charge created on or after a date appointed by the Secretary of State by order made by statutory instrument, and

(b) in spite of any provision of an agreement or instrument which purports to empower a person to appoint an administrative receiver (by whatever name).

(5) An order under subsection (4)(a) may—

(a) make provision which applies generally or only for a specified purpose;

(b) make different provision for different purposes;

(c) make transitional provision.

(6) This section is subject to the exceptions specified in [sections 72B to 72GA].]

NOTES

This Chapter (Ch IV (ss 72A–72H)) inserted by the Enterprise Act 2002, s 250(1).

Sub-s (6): words in square brackets substituted by the Insolvency Act 1986 (Amendment) (Administrative Receivership and Urban Regeneration etc) Order 2003, SI 2003/1832, art 2(a).

Date appointed by the Secretary of State: 15 September 2003; see the Insolvency Act 1986, Section 72A (Appointed Date) Order 2003, SI 2003/2095 at **[8.66]**.

Orders: the Insolvency Act 1986, Section 72A (Appointed Date) Order 2003, SI 2003/2095 at **[8.66]**.

[1.60]

[72B First exception: capital market

(1) Section 72A does not prevent the appointment of an administrative receiver in pursuance of an agreement which is or forms part of a capital market arrangement if—

(a) a party incurs or, when the agreement was entered into was expected to incur, a debt of at least £50 million under the arrangement, and

(b) the arrangement involves the issue of a capital market investment.

(2) In subsection (1)—

"capital market arrangement" means an arrangement of a kind described in paragraph 1 of Schedule 2A, and

"capital market investment" means an investment of a kind described in paragraph 2 or 3 of that Schedule.]

NOTES

Inserted as noted to s 72A at **[1.59]**.

[1.61]

72C Second exception: public-private partnership

(1) Section 72A does not prevent the appointment of an administrative receiver of a project company of a project which—

(a) is a public-private partnership project, and

(b) includes step-in rights.

(2) In this section "public-private partnership project" means a project—

(a) the resources for which are provided partly by one or more public bodies and partly by one or more private persons, or

(b) which is designed wholly or mainly for the purpose of assisting a public body to discharge a function.

(3) In this section—

"step-in rights" has the meaning given by paragraph 6 of Schedule 2A, and

"project company" has the meaning given by paragraph 7 of that Schedule.]

NOTES

Inserted as noted to s 72A at **[1.59]**.

[1.62]

[72D Third exception: utilities

(1) Section 72A does not prevent the appointment of an administrative receiver of a project company of a project which—

(a) is a utility project, and

(b) includes step-in rights.

(2) In this section—

(a) "utility project" means a project designed wholly or mainly for the purpose of a regulated business,

(b) "regulated business" means a business of a kind listed in paragraph 10 of Schedule 2A,

(c) "step-in rights" has the meaning given by paragraph 6 of that Schedule, and

(d) "project company" has the meaning given by paragraph 7 of that Schedule.]

NOTES

Inserted as noted to s 72A at **[1.59]**.

[1.63]

[72DA Exception in respect of urban regeneration projects

(1) Section 72A does not prevent the appointment of an administrative receiver of a project company of a project which—

(a) is designed wholly or mainly to develop land which at the commencement of the project is wholly or partly in a designated disadvantaged area outside Northern Ireland, and

(b) includes step-in rights.

(2) In subsection (1) "develop" means to carry out—

(a) building operations,

(b) any operation for the removal of substances or waste from land and the levelling of the surface of the land, or

(c) engineering operations in connection with the activities mentioned in paragraph (a) or (b).

(3) In this section—

"building" includes any structure or erection, and any part of a building as so defined, but does not include plant and machinery comprised in a building,

"building operations" includes—

(a) demolition of buildings,

(b) filling in of trenches,

(c) rebuilding,

(d) structural alterations of, or additions to, buildings and

(e) other operations normally undertaken by a person carrying on business as a builder,

"designated disadvantaged area" means an area designated as a disadvantaged area under section 92 of the Finance Act 2001,

"engineering operations" includes the formation and laying out of means of access to highways,

"project company" has the meaning given by paragraph 7 of Schedule 2A,

"step-in rights" has the meaning given by paragraph 6 of that Schedule,

"substance" means any natural or artificial substance whether in solid or liquid form or in the form of a gas or vapour, and

"waste" includes any waste materials, spoil, refuse or other matter deposited on land.]

NOTES

Inserted by the Insolvency Act 1986 (Amendment) (Administrative Receivership and Urban Regeneration etc) Order 2003, SI 2003/1832, art 2(b).

[1.64]

[72E Fourth exception: project finance

(1) Section 72A does not prevent the appointment of an administrative receiver of a project company of a project which—

(a) is a financed project, and

(b) includes step-in rights.

(2) In this section—

(a) a project is "financed" if under an agreement relating to the project a project company incurs, or when the agreement is entered into is expected to incur, a debt of at least £50 million for the purposes of carrying out the project,

(b) "project company" has the meaning given by paragraph 7 of Schedule 2A, and

(c) "step-in rights" has the meaning given by paragraph 6 of that Schedule.]

NOTES

Inserted as noted to s 72A at **[1.59]**.

[1.65]

[72F Fifth exception: financial market

Section 72A does not prevent the appointment of an administrative receiver of a company by virtue of—

(a) a market charge within the meaning of section 173 of the Companies Act 1989 (c 40),

(b) a system-charge within the meaning of the Financial Markets and Insolvency Regulations 1996 (SI 1996/1469),

(c) a collateral security charge within the meaning of the Financial Markets and Insolvency (Settlement Finality) Regulations 1999 (SI 1999/2979).]

NOTES

Inserted as noted to s 72A at **[1.59]**.

[1.66]

[72G Sixth exception: [social landlords]

Section 72A does not prevent the appointment of an administrative receiver of a company which is[—

(a) a private registered provider of social housing, or

(b)] registered as a social landlord under Part I of the Housing Act 1996 (c 52) or under [Part 2 of the Housing (Scotland) Act 2010 (asp 17)].]

NOTES

Inserted as noted to s 72A at **[1.59]**.

Section heading: words in square brackets substituted for original words "registered social landlord" by the Housing and Regeneration Act 2008 (Consequential Provisions) Order 2010, SI 2010/866, art 5, Sch 2, para 61(1), (3), subject to transitional provisions in art 6 of, and Sch 3, paras 1, 3, 4 to, that Order.

Words in first pair of square brackets inserted by SI 2010/866, art 5, Sch 2, para 61(1), (2), subject to transitional provisions in art 6 of, and Sch 3, paras 1, 3, 4 to, that Order; words in second pair of square brackets substituted by Housing (Scotland) Act 2010 (Consequential Provisions and Modifications) Order 2012, SI 2012/700, art 4, Schedule, Pt 1, para 3.

[1.67]

[72GA Exception in relation to protected railway companies etc

Section 72A does not prevent the appointment of an administrative receiver of—

(a) a company holding an appointment under Chapter I of Part II of the Water Industry Act 1991,

(b) a protected railway company within the meaning of section 59 of the Railways Act 1993 (including that section as it has effect by virtue of section 19 of the Channel Tunnel Rail Link Act 1996, or

(c) a licence company within the meaning of section 26 of the Transport Act 2000.]

NOTES

Inserted by the Insolvency Act 1986 (Amendment) (Administrative Receivership and Urban Regeneration etc) Order 2003, SI 2003/1832, art 2(c).

[1.68]

[72H Sections 72A to 72G: supplementary

(1) Schedule 2A (which supplements sections 72B to 72G) shall have effect.

(2) The Secretary of State may by order—

(a) insert into this Act provision creating an additional exception to section 72A(1) or (2);

(b) provide for a provision of this Act which creates an exception to section 72A(1) or (2) to cease to have effect;

(c) amend section 72A in consequence of provision made under paragraph (a) or (b);

(d) amend any of sections 72B to 72G;

(e) amend Schedule 2A.

(3) An order under subsection (2) must be made by statutory instrument.

(4) An order under subsection (2) may make—
(a) provision which applies generally or only for a specified purpose;
(b) different provision for different purposes;
(c) consequential or supplementary provision;
(d) transitional provision.
(5) An order under subsection (2)—
(a) in the case of an order under subsection (2)(e), shall be subject to annulment in pursuance of a resolution of either House of Parliament,
(b) in the case of an order under subsection (2)(d) varying the sum specified in section 72B(1)(a) or 72E(2)(a) (whether or not the order also makes consequential or transitional provision), shall be subject to annulment in pursuance of a resolution of either House of Parliament, and
(c) in the case of any other order under subsection (2)(a) to (d), may not be made unless a draft has been laid before and approved by resolution of each House of Parliament.]

NOTES

Inserted as noted to s 72A at **[1.59]**.

PART IV WINDING UP OF COMPANIES REGISTERED UNDER THE COMPANIES ACTS

NOTES

Modification of this Part in relation to building societies: this Part is applied with modifications in relation to the winding up of building societies; see the Building Societies Act 1986, s 90, Sch 15 at **[7.454]**, **[7.464]**.

Application of this Part in relation to financial markets: this Part is applied with modifications in relation to certain proceedings begun before the commencement of the Companies Act 1989, s 182, in respect of insolvency proceedings regarding members of recognised investment exchanges and clearing houses and persons to whom market charges have been granted; see s 182 of the 1989 Act at **[17.85]**.

Modification of this Part in relation to friendly societies: as to the application, with modifications, of this Part to the winding up of incorporated friendly societies under the Friendly Societies Act 1992, s 21(1) or 22(2), see s 23 of, and Sch 10 to, that Act.

CHAPTER I
PRELIMINARY

[Introductory

[1.69]

73 Scheme of this Part

(1) This Part applies to the winding up of a company registered under the Companies Act 2006 in England and Wales or Scotland.
(2) The winding up may be either—
(a) voluntary (see Chapters 2 to 5), or
(b) by the court (see Chapter 6).
(3) This Chapter and Chapters 7 to 10 relate to winding up generally, except where otherwise stated.]

NOTES

This section as originally enacted derived from the Companies Act 1985, s 501.

Substituted together with preceding cross-heading by the Companies Act 2006 (Consequential Amendments, Transitional Provisions and Savings) Order 2009, SI 2009/1941, art 2(1), Sch 1, para 75(1), (2), subject to transitional provisions and savings in art 8, Sch 1, para 84 at **[2.70]**, **[2.73]**, and originally read as follows:

"Modes of winding up

73 Alternative modes of winding up

(1) The winding up of a company, within the meaning given to that expression by section 735 of the Companies Act, may be either voluntary (Chapters II, III, IV and V in this Part) or by the court (Chapter VI).
(2) This Chapter, and Chapters VII to X, relate to winding up generally, except where otherwise stated.".

Contributories

[1.70]

74 Liability as contributories of present and past members

(1) When a company is wound up, every present and past member is liable to contribute to its assets to any amount sufficient for payment of its debts and liabilities, and the expenses of the winding up, and for the adjustment of the rights of the contributories among themselves.
(2) This is subject as follows—
(a) a past member is not liable to contribute if he has ceased to be a member for one year or more before the commencement of the winding up;
(b) a past member is not liable to contribute in respect of any debt or liability of the company contracted after he ceased to be a member;
(c) a past member is not liable to contribute, unless it appears to the court that the existing members are unable to satisfy the contributions required to be made by them . . . ;
(d) in the case of a company limited by shares, no contribution is required from any member exceeding the amount (if any) unpaid on the shares in respect of which he is liable as a present or past member;

(e) nothing in [the Companies Acts] or this Act invalidates any provision contained in a policy of insurance or other contract whereby the liability of individual members on the policy or contract is restricted, or whereby the funds of the company are alone made liable in respect of the policy or contract;

(f) a sum due to any member of the company (in his character of a member) by way of dividends, profits or otherwise is not deemed to be a debt of the company, payable to that member in a case of competition between himself and any other creditor not a member of the company, but any such sum may be taken into account for the purpose of the final adjustment of the rights of the contributories among themselves.

(3) In the case of a company limited by guarantee, no contribution is required from any member exceeding the amount undertaken to be contributed by him to the company's assets in the event of its being wound up; but if it is a company with a share capital, every member of it is liable (in addition to the amount so undertaken to be contributed to the assets), to contribute to the extent of any sums unpaid on shares held by him.

NOTES

This section derived from the Companies Act 1985, s 502.

Sub-s (2): words "in pursuance of the Companies Act and this Act" omitted from para (c) repealed and words in square brackets in para (e) substituted for original words "the Companies Act" by the Companies Act 2006 (Consequential Amendments, Transitional Provisions and Savings) Order 2009, SI 2009/1941, art 2(1), Sch 1, para 75(1), (3), subject to transitional provisions and savings in art 8, Sch 1, para 84 at **[2.70]**, **[2.73]**.

[1.71]

75 Directors, etc with unlimited liability

(1) In the winding up of a limited company, any director or manager (whether past or present) whose liability is under the Companies Act unlimited is liable, in addition to his liability (if any) to contribute as an ordinary member, to make a further contribution as if he were at the commencement of the winding up a member of an unlimited company.

(2) However—

(a) a past director or manager is not liable to make such further contribution if he has ceased to hold office for a year or more before the commencement of the winding up;

(b) a past director or manager is not liable to make such further contribution in respect of any debt or liability of the company contracted after he ceased to hold office;

(c) subject to the company's articles, a director or manager is not liable to make such further contribution unless the court deems it necessary to require that contribution in order to satisfy the company's debts and liabilities, and the expenses of the winding up.

NOTES

This section derived from the Companies Act 1985, s 503.

Repealed by the Companies Act 2006 (Consequential Amendments, Transitional Provisions and Savings) Order 2009, SI 2009/1941, art 2(1), Sch 1, para 75(1), (4), subject to transitional provisions and savings in arts 8, 9, Sch 1, para 84 at **[2.70]**, **[2.71]**, **[2.73]**.

[1.72]

76 Liability of past directors and shareholders

(1) This section applies where a company is being wound up and—

(a) it has under [Chapter 5 of Part 18 of the Companies Act 2006 (acquisition by limited company of its own shares: redemption or purchase by private company out of capital)] made a payment out of capital in respect of the redemption or purchase of any of its own shares (the payment being referred to below as "the relevant payment"), and

(b) the aggregate amount of the company's assets and the amounts paid by way of contribution to its assets (apart from this section) is not sufficient for payment of its debts and liabilities, and the expenses of the winding up.

(2) If the winding up commenced within one year of the date on which the relevant payment was made, then—

(a) the person from whom the shares were redeemed or purchased, and

(b) the directors who signed the [statement] made in accordance with [section 714(1) to (3) of the Companies Act 2006] for purposes of the redemption or purchase (except a director who shows that he had reasonable grounds for forming the opinion set out in the [statement]),

are, so as to enable that insufficiency to be met, liable to contribute to the following extent to the company's assets.

(3) A person from whom any of the shares were redeemed or purchased is liable to contribute an amount not exceeding so much of the relevant payment as was made by the company in respect of his shares; and the directors are jointly and severally liable with that person to contribute that amount.

(4) A person who has contributed any amount to the assets in pursuance of this section may apply to the court for an order directing any other person jointly and severally liable in respect of that amount to pay him such amount as the court thinks just and equitable.

(5) [Section 74 does not apply] in relation to liability accruing by virtue of this section.

(6) . . .

NOTES

This section derived from the Companies Act 1985, s 504.

Sub-s (1): words in square brackets in para (a) substituted for original words "Chapter VII of Part V of the Companies Act (redeemable shares; purchase by a company of its own shares)" by the Companies Act 2006 (Consequential Amendments,

Transitional Provisions and Savings) Order 2009, SI 2009/1941, art 2(1), Sch 1, para 75(1), (5)(a), subject to transitional provisions and savings in art 8, Sch 1, para 84 at **[2.70]**, **[2.73]**.

Sub-s (2): words in first and third pairs of square brackets in para (b) substituted by the Companies Act 2006 (Consequential Amendments and Transitional Provisions) Order 2011, SI 2011/1265, art 6(1), (3); words in second pair of square brackets in para (b) substituted for original words "section 173(3) of the Companies Act" by SI 2009/1941, art 2(1), Sch 1, para 75(1), (5)(b), subject to transitional provisions and savings in art 8, Sch 1, para 84 at **[2.70]**, **[2.73]**.

Sub-s (5): words in square brackets substituted for original words "Sections 74 and 75 do not apply" by SI 2009/1941, art 2(1), Sch 1, para 75(1), (5)(c), subject to transitional provisions and savings in art 8, Sch 1, para 84 at **[2.70]**, **[2.73]**.

Sub-s (6): repealed by SI 2009/1941, art 2(1), Sch 1, para 75(1), (5)(d), subject to transitional provisions and savings in art 8, Sch 1, para 84 at **[2.70]**, **[2.73]**, and originally read as follows:

"(6) This section is deemed included in Chapter VII of Part V of the Companies Act for the purposes of the Secretary of State's power to make regulations under section 179 of that Act.".

[1.73]

77 Limited company formerly unlimited

(1) This section applies in the case of a company being wound up which was at some former time registered as unlimited but has [re-registered as a limited company.]

(2) Notwithstanding section 74(2)(a) above, a past member of the company who was a member of it at the time of re-registration, if the winding up commences within the period of 3 years beginning with the day on which the company was re-registered, is liable to contribute to the assets of the company in respect of debts and liabilities contracted before that time.

(3) If no persons who were members of the company at that time are existing members of it, a person who at that time was a present or past member is liable to contribute as above notwithstanding that the existing members have satisfied the contributions required to be made by them . . .

This applies subject to section 74(2)(a) above and to subsection (2) of this section, but notwithstanding section 74(2)(c).

(4) Notwithstanding section 74(2)(d) and (3), there is no limit on the amount which a person who, at that time, was a past or present member of the company is liable to contribute as above.

NOTES

This section derived from the Companies Act 1985, s 505.

Sub-s (1): words in square brackets substituted by the Companies Act 2006 (Consequential Amendments, Transitional Provisions and Savings) Order 2009, SI 2009/1941, art 2(1), Sch 1, para 75(1), (6)(a), subject to transitional provisions and savings in art 8, Sch 1, para 84 at **[2.70]**, **[2.73]**, and previously read as follows:

"re-registered—

(a) as a public company under section 43 of the Companies Act (or the former corresponding provision, section 5 of the Companies Act 1980), or

(b) as a limited company under section 51 of the Companies Act (or the former corresponding provision, section 44 of the Companies Act 1967).".

Sub-s (3): words "under the Companies Act and this Act" (omitted) repealed by SI 2009/1941, art 2(1), Sch 1, para 75(1), (6)(b), subject to transitional provisions and savings in art 8, Sch 1, para 84 at **[2.70]**, **[2.73]**.

[1.74]

78 Unlimited company formerly limited

(1) This section applies in the case of a company being wound up which was at some former time registered as limited but has been re-registered as unlimited . . .

(2) A person who, at the time when the application for the company to be re-registered was lodged, was a past member of the company and did not after that again become a member of it is not liable to contribute to the assets of the company more than he would have been liable to contribute had the company not been re-registered.

NOTES

This section derived from the Companies Act 1985, s 506.

Sub-s (1): words "under section 49 of the Companies Act (or the former corresponding provision, section 43 of the Companies Act 1967)" (omitted) repealed by the Companies Act 2006 (Consequential Amendments, Transitional Provisions and Savings) Order 2009, SI 2009/1941, art 2(1), Sch 1, para 75(1), (7), subject to transitional provisions and savings in art 8, Sch 1, para 84 at **[2.70]**, **[2.73]**.

[1.75]

79 Meaning of "contributory"

(1) In this Act . . . the expression "contributory" means every person liable to contribute to the assets of a company in the event of its being wound up, and for the purposes of all proceedings for determining, and all proceedings prior to the final determination of, the persons who are to be deemed contributories, includes any person alleged to be a contributory.

(2) The reference in subsection (1) to persons liable to contribute to the assets does not include a person so liable by virtue of a declaration by the court under section 213 (imputed responsibility for company's fraudulent trading) or section 214 (wrongful trading) in Chapter X of this Part.

(3) A reference in a company's articles to a contributory does not (unless the context requires) include a person who is a contributory only by virtue of section 76.

. . .

NOTES

This section derived from the Companies Act 1985, s 507, and the Insolvency Act 1985, Sch 6, para 5.

Sub-s (1): words "and the Companies Act" (omitted) repealed by the Companies Act 2006 (Consequential Amendments, Transitional Provisions and Savings) Order 2009, SI 2009/1941, art 2(1), Sch 1, para 75(1), (8)(a), subject to transitional provisions and savings in art 8, Sch 1, para 84 at **[2.70]**, **[2.73]**.

Sub-s (3): words "This subsection is deemed included in Chapter VII of Part V of the Companies Act for the purposes of the Secretary of State's power to make regulations under section 179 of that Act." (omitted) repealed by SI 2009/1941, art 2(1), Sch 1, para 75(1), (8)(b), subject to transitional provisions and savings in art 8, Sch 1, para 84 at **[2.70]**, **[2.73]**.

[1.76]
80 Nature of contributory's liability

The liability of a contributory creates a debt (in England and Wales in the nature of [an ordinary contract debt]) accruing due from him at the time when his liability commenced, but payable at the times when calls are made for enforcing the liability.

NOTES

This section derived from the Companies Act 1985, s 508.

Words in square brackets substituted for original words "a specialty" by the Companies Act 2006 (Consequential Amendments, Transitional Provisions and Savings) Order 2009, SI 2009/1941, art 2(1), Sch 1, para 75(1), (9), subject to transitional provisions and savings in arts 8, 11, Sch 1, para 84 at **[2.70]**, **[2.72]**, **[2.73]**.

[1.77]
81 Contributories in case of death of a member

(1) If a contributory dies either before or after he has been placed on the list of contributories, his personal representatives, and the heirs and legatees of heritage of his heritable estate in Scotland, are liable in a due course of administration to contribute to the assets of the company in discharge of his liability and are contributories accordingly.

(2) Where the personal representatives are placed on the list of contributories, the heirs or legatees of heritage need not be added, but they may be added as and when the court thinks fit.

(3) If in England and Wales the personal representatives make default in paying any money ordered to be paid by them, proceedings may be taken for administering the estate of the deceased contributory and for compelling payment out of it of the money due.

NOTES

This section derived from the Companies Act 1985, s 509.

[1.78]
82 Effect of contributory's bankruptcy

(1) The following applies if a contributory becomes bankrupt, either before or after he has been placed on the list of contributories.

(2) His trustee in bankruptcy represents him for all purposes of the winding up, and is a contributory accordingly.

(3) The trustee may be called on to admit to proof against the bankrupt's estate, or otherwise allow to be paid out of the bankrupt's assets in due course of law, any money due from the bankrupt in respect of his liability to contribute to the company's assets.

(4) There may be proved against the bankrupt's estate the estimated value of his liability to future calls as well as calls already made.

NOTES

This section derived from the Companies Act 1985, s 510.

[1.79]
83 [Companies registered but not formed under the Companies Act 2006]

(1) The following applies in the event of a company being wound up which [is registered but not formed under the Companies Act 2006.]

(2) Every person is a contributory, in respect of the company's debts and liabilities contracted before registration, who is liable—

(a) to pay, or contribute to the payment of, any debt or liability so contracted, or

(b) to pay, or contribute to the payment of, any sum for the adjustment of the rights of the members among themselves in respect of any such debt or liability, or

(c) to pay, or contribute to the amount of, the expenses of winding up the company, so far as relates to the debts or liabilities above-mentioned.

(3) Every contributory is liable to contribute to the assets of the company, in the course of the winding up, all sums due from him in respect of any such liability.

(4) In the event of the death, bankruptcy or insolvency of any contributory, provisions of this Act, with respect to the personal representatives, to the heirs and legatees of heritage of the heritable estate in Scotland of deceased contributories and to the trustees of bankrupt or insolvent contributories respectively, apply.

NOTES

This section derived from the Companies Act 1985, s 511.

Section heading: words in square brackets substituted for original words "Companies registered under Companies Act, Part XXII, Chapter II" by the Companies Act 2006 (Consequential Amendments, Transitional Provisions and Savings) Order 2009, SI 2009/1941, art 2(1), Sch 1, para 75(1), (10)(a), subject to transitional provisions and savings in art 8, Sch 1, para 84 at **[2.70]**, **[2.73]**.

Sub-s (1): words in square brackets substituted for original words "has been registered under section 680 of the Companies Act (or previous corresponding provisions in the Companies Act 1948 or earlier Acts)" by SI 2009/1941, art 2(1), Sch 1, para 75(1), (10)(b), subject to transitional provisions and savings in art 8, Sch 1, para 84 at **[2.70]**, **[2.73]**.

CHAPTER II
VOLUNTARY WINDING UP (INTRODUCTORY AND GENERAL)

Resolutions for, and commencement of, voluntary winding up

[1.80]
84 Circumstances in which company may be wound up voluntarily

(1) A company may be wound up voluntarily—

(a) when the period (if any) fixed for the duration of the company by the articles expires, or the event (if any) occurs, on the occurrence of which the articles provide that the company is to be dissolved, and the company in general meeting has passed a resolution requiring it to be wound up voluntarily;

(b) if the company resolves by special resolution that it be wound up voluntarily;

(c) . . .

(2) In this Act the expression "a resolution for voluntary winding up" means a resolution passed under [either of the paragraphs] of subsection (1).

[(2A) Before a company passes a resolution for voluntary winding up it must give written notice of the resolution to the holder of any qualifying floating charge to which section 72A applies.

(2B) Where notice is given under subsection (2A) a resolution for voluntary winding up may be passed only—

(a) after the end of the period of five business days beginning with the day on which the notice was given, or

(b) if the person to whom the notice was given has consented in writing to the passing of the resolution.]

[(3) Chapter 3 of Part 3 of the Companies Act 2006 (resolutions affecting a company's constitution) applies to a resolution under paragraph (a) of subsection (1) as well as a special resolution under paragraph (b).]

[(4) This section has effect subject to section 43 of the Commonhold and Leasehold Reform Act 2002.]

NOTES

This section derived from the Companies Act 1985, s 572.

Sub-s (1): para (c) repealed by the Companies Act 2006 (Commencement No 3, Consequential Amendments, Transitional Provisions and Savings) Order 2007, SI 2007/2194, art 10, Sch 4, Pt 3, para 39(1), (2), (5), Sch 5, subject to savings in art 12 thereof and with effect in relation to: (a) written resolutions for which the circulation date (see the Companies Act 2006, s 290) is on or after 1 October 2007; and (b) resolutions passed at a meeting of which notice is given on or after that date. Sub-s (1)(c) previously read as follows:

> "(c) if the company resolves by extraordinary resolution to the effect that it cannot by reason of its liabilities continue its business, and that it is advisable to wind up.".

Sub-s (2): words in square brackets substituted for original words "any of the paragraphs" by SI 2007/2194, art 10(1), (2), Sch 4, Pt 3, para 39(1), (3), (5), with savings and effect as noted to sub-s (1).

Sub-ss (2A), (2B): inserted by the Enterprise Act 2002 (Insolvency) Order 2003, SI 2003/2096, arts 4, 6, Schedule, paras 8, 10, except in any case where a petition for an administration order was presented before 15 September 2003.

Sub-s (3): substituted by SI 2007/2194, art 10(1), (2), Sch 4, Pt 3, para 39(1), (4), (5), with savings and effect as noted to sub-s (1), and previously read as follows:

> "(3) A resolution passed under paragraph (a) of subsection (1), as well as a special resolution under paragraph (b) and an extraordinary resolution under paragraph (c), is subject to section 380 of the Companies Act (copy of resolution to be forwarded to registrar of companies within 15 days).".

Sub-s (4): added by the Commonhold and Leasehold Reform Act 2002, s 68, Sch 5, para 6.

Modification: this section is modified, in relation to a UK credit institution which on or after 5 May 2004 intends to pass a resolution to wind up the institution under sub-s (1)(b) or (c) above, by the Credit Institutions (Reorganisation and Winding up) Regulations 2004, SI 2004/1045, reg 8 at **[3.220]**.

Modification in relation to Scotland: see the Note at the beginning of this Act.

[1.81]
85 Notice of resolution to wind up

(1) When a company has passed a resolution for voluntary winding up, it shall, within 14 days after the passing of the resolution, give notice of the resolution by advertisement in the Gazette.

(2) If default is made in complying with this section, the company and every officer of it who is in default is liable to a fine and, for continued contravention, to a daily default fine.

For purposes of this subsection the liquidator is deemed an officer of the company.

NOTES

This section derived from the Companies Act 1985, s 573.

[1.82]
86 Commencement of winding up

A voluntary winding up is deemed to commence at the time of the passing of the resolution for voluntary winding up.

NOTES

This section derived from the Companies Act 1985, s 574.

Consequences of resolution to wind up

[1.83]

87 Effect on business and status of company

(1) In case of a voluntary winding up, the company shall from the commencement of the winding up cease to carry on its business, except so far as may be required for its beneficial winding up.

(2) However, the corporate state and corporate powers of the company, notwithstanding anything to the contrary in its articles, continue until the company is dissolved.

NOTES

This section derived from the Companies Act 1985, s 575.

[1.84]

88 Avoidance of share transfers, etc after winding-up resolution

Any transfer of shares, not being a transfer made to or with the sanction of the liquidator, and any alteration in the status of the company's members, made after the commencement of a voluntary winding up, is void.

NOTES

This section derived from the Companies Act 1985, s 576.

See further: as to the disapplication of this section in relation to any transfer of shares under a financial collateral arrangement, see the Financial Collateral Arrangements (No 2) Regulations 2003, SI 2003/3226, reg 10(2) at **[3.290]**.

Declaration of solvency

[1.85]

89 Statutory declaration of solvency

(1) Where it is proposed to wind up a company voluntarily, the directors (or, in the case of a company having more than two directors, the majority of them) may at a directors' meeting make a statutory declaration to the effect that they have made a full inquiry into the company's affairs and that, having done so, they have formed the opinion that the company will be able to pay its debts in full, together with interest at the official rate (as defined in section 251), within such period, not exceeding 12 months from the commencement of the winding up, as may be specified in the declaration.

(2) Such a declaration by the directors has no effect for purposes of this Act unless—

(a) it is made within the 5 weeks immediately preceding the date of the passing of the resolution for winding up, or on that date but before the passing of the resolution, and

(b) it embodies a statement of the company's assets and liabilities as at the latest practicable date before the making of the declaration.

(3) The declaration shall be delivered to the registrar of companies before the expiration of 15 days immediately following the date on which the resolution for winding up is passed.

(4) A director making a declaration under this section without having reasonable grounds for the opinion that the company will be able to pay its debts in full, together with interest at the official rate, within the period specified is liable to imprisonment or a fine, or both.

(5) If the company is wound up in pursuance of a resolution passed within 5 weeks after the making of the declaration, and its debts (together with interest at the official rate) are not paid or provided for in full within the period specified, it is to be presumed (unless the contrary is shown) that the director did not have reasonable grounds for his opinion.

(6) If a declaration required by subsection (3) to be delivered to the registrar is not so delivered within the time prescribed by that subsection, the company and every officer in default is liable to a fine and, for continued contravention, to a daily default fine.

NOTES

This section derived from the Companies Act 1985, s 577, and the Insolvency Act 1985, Sch 6, para 35.

Modification in relation to Scotland: see the Note at the beginning of this Act.

[1.86]

90 Distinction between "members'" and "creditors'" voluntary winding up

A winding up in the case of which a directors' statutory declaration under section 89 has been made is a "members' voluntary winding up"; and a winding up in the case of which such a declaration has not been made is a "creditors' voluntary winding up".

NOTES

This section derived from the Companies Act 1985, s 578.

CHAPTER III
MEMBERS' VOLUNTARY WINDING UP

[1.87]

91 Appointment of liquidator

(1) In a members' voluntary winding up, the company in general meeting shall appoint one or more liquidators for the purpose of winding up the company's affairs and distributing its assets.

(2) On the appointment of a liquidator all the powers of the directors cease, except so far as the company in general meeting or the liquidator sanctions their continuance.

NOTES

This section derived from the Companies Act 1985, s 580.

[1.88]

92 Power to fill vacancy in office of liquidator

(1) If a vacancy occurs by death, resignation or otherwise in the office of liquidator appointed by the company, the company in general meeting may, subject to any arrangement with its creditors, fill the vacancy.

(2) For that purpose a general meeting may be convened by any contributory or, if there were more liquidators than one, by the continuing liquidators.

(3) The meeting shall be held in manner provided by this Act or by the articles, or in such manner as may, on application by any contributory or by the continuing liquidators, be determined by the court.

NOTES

This section derived from the Companies Act 1985, s 581.

Meeting shall be held in manner provided by this Act: it is thought that the reference in sub-s (3) above to "this Act" should actually be a reference to the Companies Act 1985.

[1.89]

[92A Progress report to company . . . *(England and Wales)*

(1) Subject to [section 96], [*where the company is registered in England and Wales*], the liquidator must—

- (a) for each prescribed period produce a progress report relating to the prescribed matters; and
- (b) within such period commencing with the end of the period referred to in paragraph (a) as may be prescribed send a copy of the progress report to—
  - (i) the members of the company; and
  - (ii) such other persons as may be prescribed.

(2) A liquidator who fails to comply with this section is liable to a fine.]

NOTES

Inserted by the Legislative Reform (Insolvency) (Miscellaneous Provisions) Order 2010, SI 2010/18, arts 2, 6(1), except in relation to a company in voluntary winding up where the resolution to wind up was passed before 6 April 2010: see art 12(1) of the 2010 Order at **[2.76]**.

Words in italics in the section heading repealed, and second words in italics in sub-s (1) repealed, by the Public Services Reform (Insolvency) (Scotland) Order 2016, SSI 2016/141, art 5(1), as from a day to be appointed (being the day that the Small Business, Enterprise and Employment Act 2015, s 122(2) comes into force for all remaining purposes in Scotland); for savings, see the note to s 66 at **[1.52]**.

Words omitted from the section heading repealed, and words in second pair of square brackets in sub-s (1) substituted by the Small Business, Enterprise and Employment Act 2015, s 136(1), (2).

Words in first pair of square brackets in sub-s (1) substituted for original words "sections 96 and 102" by the Small Business, Enterprise and Employment Act 2015, s 126, Sch 9, Pt 1, paras 1, 16, as from 6 April 2017 (in relation to England and Wales and subject to transitional and savings provisions as noted to s 246ZE at **[1.256]**), and as from a day to be appointed (in relation to Scotland).

[1.90]

93 General company meeting at each year's end [(Scotland)]

(1) Subject to [section 96], in the event of the winding up [of a company registered in Scotland] continuing for more than one year, the liquidator shall summon a general meeting of the company at the end of the first year from the commencement of the winding up, and of each succeeding year, or at the first convenient date within 3 months from the end of the year or such longer period as the Secretary of State may allow.

(2) The liquidator shall lay before the meeting an account of his acts and dealings, and of the conduct of the winding up, during the preceding year.

(3) If the liquidator fails to comply with this section, he is liable to a fine.

NOTES

This section derived from the Companies Act 1985, s 584, and the Insolvency Act 1985, Sch 6, para 36.

Repealed by the Public Services Reform (Insolvency) (Scotland) Order 2016, SSI 2016/141, art 5(2), as from a day to be appointed (being the day that the Small Business, Enterprise and Employment Act 2015, s 122(2) comes into force for all remaining purposes in Scotland); for savings, see the note to s 66 at **[1.52]**.

Section heading: word in square brackets inserted by the Legislative Reform (Insolvency) (Miscellaneous Provisions) Order 2010, SI 2010/18, arts 2, 6(2)(a), except in relation to a company in voluntary winding up where the resolution to wind up was passed before 6 April 2010: see art 12(2) of the 2010 Order at **[2.76]**.

Sub-s (1): words in first pair of square brackets substituted for original words "sections 96 and 102" by the Small Business, Enterprise and Employment Act 2015, s 126, Sch 9, Pt 1, paras 1, 17, as from 6 April 2017 (in relation to England and Wales and subject to transitional and savings provisions as noted to s 246ZE at **[1.256]**), and as from a day to be appointed (in relation to Scotland); words in second pair of square brackets inserted by SI 2010/18, arts 2, 6(2)(b), 12(2), except in relation to a company in voluntary winding up where the resolution to wind up was passed before 6 April 2010: see art 12(2) of the 2010 Order at **[2.76]**.

[1.91]

[94 Final account prior to dissolution

(1) As soon as the company's affairs are fully wound up the liquidator must make up an account of the winding up, showing how it has been conducted and the company's property has been disposed of.

(2) The liquidator must send a copy of the account to the members of the company before the end of the period of 14 days beginning with the day on which the account is made up.

(3) The liquidator must send a copy of the account to the registrar of companies before the end of that period (but not before sending it to the members of the company).

(4) If the liquidator does not comply with subsection (2) the liquidator is liable to a fine.

(5) If the liquidator does not comply with subsection (3) the liquidator is liable to a fine and, for continued contravention, a daily default fine.]

NOTES

Commencement: see note below.

Substituted by the Small Business, Enterprise and Employment Act 2015, s 126, Sch 9, Pt 1, paras 1, 18, as from 6 April 2017 (in relation to England and Wales and subject to transitional and savings provisions as noted to s 246ZE at **[1.256]**), and as from a day to be appointed (in relation to Scotland). The original s 94 reads as follows—

> **"94 Final meeting prior to dissolution**
>
> (1) As soon as the company's affairs are fully wound up, the liquidator shall make up an account of the winding up, showing how it has been conducted and the company's property has been disposed of, and thereupon shall call a general meeting of the company for the purpose of laying before it the account, and giving an explanation of it.
>
> (2) The meeting shall be called by advertisement in the Gazette, specifying its time, place and object and published at least one month before the meeting.
>
> (3) Within one week after the meeting, the liquidator shall send to the registrar of companies a copy of the account, and shall make a return to him of the holding of the meeting and of its date.
>
> (4) If the copy is not sent or the return is not made in accordance with subsection (3), the liquidator is liable to a fine and, for continued contravention, to a daily default fine.
>
> (5) If a quorum is not present at the meeting, the liquidator shall, in lieu of the return mentioned above, make a return that the meeting was duly summoned and that no quorum was present; and upon such a return being made, the provisions of subsection (3) as to the making of the return are deemed complied with.
>
> (6) If the liquidator fails to call a general meeting of the company as required by subsection (1), he is liable to a fine.".

[1.92]

95 Effect of company's insolvency

(1) This section applies where the liquidator is of the opinion that the company will be unable to pay its debts in full (together with interest at the official rate) within the period stated in the directors' declaration under section 89.

[(1A) The liquidator must before the end of the period of 7 days beginning with the day after the day on which the liquidator formed that opinion—

- (a) make out a statement in the prescribed form as to the affairs of the company, and
- (b) send it to the company's creditors.]

(2) [In the case of the winding up of a company registered in Scotland, the liquidator] shall—

- *(a) summon a meeting of creditors for a day not later than the 28th day after the day on which he formed that opinion;*
- *(b) send notices of the creditors' meeting to the creditors by post not less than 7 days before the day on which that meeting is to be held;*
- *(c) cause notice of the creditors' meeting to be advertised once in the Gazette and once at least in 2 newspapers circulating in the relevant locality (that is to say the locality in which the company's principal place of business in Great Britain was situated during the relevant period); and*
- *(d) during the period before the day on which the creditors' meeting is to be held, furnish creditors free of charge with such information concerning the affairs of the company as they may reasonably require;*

and the notice of the creditors' meeting shall state the duty imposed by paragraph (d) above.

[(2A) In the case of the winding up of a company registered in England and Wales, the liquidator—

- *(a) shall summon a meeting of creditors for a day not later than the 28th day after the day on which he formed that opinion;*
- *(b) shall send notices of the creditors' meeting to the creditors . . . not less than 7 days before the day on which that meeting is to be held;*
- *(c) shall cause notice of the creditors' meeting to be advertised once in the Gazette;*
- *(d) may cause notice of the meeting to be advertised in such other manner as he thinks fit; and*
- *(e) shall during the period before the day on which the creditors' meeting is to be held, furnish creditors free of charge with such information concerning the affairs of the company as they may reasonably require;*

and the notice of the creditors' meeting shall state the duty imposed by paragraph (e) above.]

(3) The liquidator shall also—

- *(a) make out a statement in the prescribed form as to the affairs of the company;*
- *(b) lay that statement before the creditors' meeting; and*
- *(c) attend and preside at that meeting.*

(4) The statement as to the affairs of the company . . . shall show—

- (a) particulars of the company's assets, debts and liabilities;
- (b) the names and addresses of the company's creditors;
- (c) the securities held by them respectively;

(d) the dates when the securities were respectively given; and
(e) such further or other information as may be prescribed.

[(4A) The statement as to the affairs of the company shall *be verified by the liquidator*—
(a) in the case of a winding up of a company registered in England and Wales [be verified by the liquidator], by a statement of truth; and
(b) in the case of a winding up of a company registered in Scotland, *by affidavit*.]

[(4B) The company's creditors may in accordance with the rules nominate a person to be liquidator.

(4C) The liquidator must in accordance with the rules seek such a nomination from the company's creditors.]

(5) Where the company's principal place of business in Great Britain was situated in different localities at different times during the relevant period, the duty imposed by subsection (2)(c) applies separately in relation to each of those localities.

(6) Where the company had no place of business in Great Britain during the relevant period, references in subsections (2)(c) and (5) to the company's principal place of business in Great Britain are replaced by references to its registered office.

(7) In this section "the relevant period" means the period of 6 months immediately preceding the day on which were sent the notices summoning the company meeting at which it was resolved that the company be wound up voluntarily.

(8) If the liquidator without reasonable excuse fails to comply with [subsections (1) to (4A)], he is liable to a fine.

NOTES

This section derived from the Insolvency Act 1985, s 83(1)–(6), (9), (10).

Sub-ss (1A), (4B), (4C): inserted by the Small Business, Enterprise and Employment Act 2015, s 126, Sch 9, Pt 1, paras 1, 19(1), (2), (4), as from 6 April 2017 (in relation to England and Wales and subject to transitional and savings provisions as noted to s 246ZE at **[1.256]**), and as from a day to be appointed (in relation to Scotland).

Sub-s (2): repealed by the Small Business, Enterprise and Employment Act 2015, s 126, Sch 9, Pt 1, paras 1, 19(1), (3), as from 6 April 2017 (in relation to England and Wales and subject to transitional and savings provisions as noted to s 246ZE at **[1.256]**), and as from a day to be appointed (in relation to Scotland); words in square brackets substituted for original words "The liquidator" by the Legislative Reform (Insolvency) (Advertising Requirements) Order 2009, SI 2009/864, arts 2, 3(1)(a), 4, except in relation to a company in voluntary winding up where the resolution to wind up was passed before 6 April 2009.

Sub-s (2A): inserted by SI 2009/864, arts 2, 3(1)(b), 4, except in relation to a company in voluntary winding up where the resolution to wind up was passed before 6 April 2009; words "by post" (omitted) repealed in relation to England and Wales by the Legislative Reform (Insolvency) (Miscellaneous Provisions) Order 2010, SI 2010/18, arts 2, 7, except in relation to a company in voluntary winding up where the resolution to wind up was passed before 6 April 2010: see art 12(3) of the 2010 Order at **[2.76]**; repealed by the Small Business, Enterprise and Employment Act 2015, s 126, Sch 9, Pt 1, paras 1, 19(1), (3), as from 6 April 2017 (in relation to England and Wales and subject to transitional and savings provisions as noted to s 246ZE at **[1.256]**), and as from a day to be appointed (in relation to Scotland).

Sub-ss (3), (5)–(7): repealed by the Small Business, Enterprise and Employment Act 2015, s 126, Sch 9, Pt 1, paras 1, 19(1), (3), as from 6 April 2017 (in relation to England and Wales and subject to transitional and savings provisions as noted to s 246ZE at **[1.256]**), and as from a day to be appointed (in relation to Scotland).

Sub-s (4): words omitted repealed by SI 2010/18, arts 2, 5(2)(a).

Sub-s (4A): inserted by SI 2010/18, arts 2, 5(2)(b); first words in italics in repealed, words in square brackets in para (a) inserted, and for the words in italics in para (b) there are substituted the words "contain a statutory declaration by the liquidator", by the Public Services Reform (Insolvency) (Scotland) Order 2016, SSI 2016/141, art 8, as from a day to be appointed (being the day that the Small Business, Enterprise and Employment Act 2015, s 122(2) comes into force for all remaining purposes in Scotland); for savings, see the note to s 66 at **[1.52]**.

Sub-s (8): words in square brackets substituted for original words "this section" by the Small Business, Enterprise and Employment Act 2015, s 126, Sch 9, Pt 1, paras 1, 19(1), (5), as from 6 April 2017 (in relation to England and Wales and subject to transitional and savings provisions as noted to s 246ZE at **[1.256]**), and as from a day to be appointed (in relation to Scotland).

Modification: this section is modified, in relation to the notification to the Financial Conduct Authority and (if the institution is a PRA-authorised person) the Prudential Regulation Authority of the application of this section in the case of a members' voluntary winding up where the liquidator is of the opinion that this section applies, by the Credit Institutions (Reorganisation and Winding up) Regulations 2004, SI 2004/1045, reg 9(4) at **[3.221]**.

[1.93]

[96 Conversion to creditors' voluntary winding up

(1) The winding up becomes a creditors' voluntary winding up as from the day on which—
(a) the company's creditors under section 95 nominate a person to be liquidator, or
(b) the procedure by which the company's creditors were to have made such a nomination concludes without a nomination having been made.

(2) As from that day this Act has effect as if the directors' declaration under section 89 had not been made.

(3) The liquidator in the creditors' voluntary winding up is to be the person nominated by the company's creditors under section 95 or, where no person has been so nominated, the existing liquidator.

(4) In the case of the creditors nominating a person other than the existing liquidator any director, member or creditor of the company may, within 7 days after the date on which the nomination was made by the creditors, apply to the court for an order either—
(a) directing that the existing liquidator is to be liquidator instead of or jointly with the person nominated by the creditors, or
(b) appointing some other person to be liquidator instead of the person nominated by the creditors.

[(4A) The court shall grant an application under subsection (4) made by the holder of a qualifying floating charge in respect of the company's property (within the meaning of paragraph 14 of Schedule B1) unless the court thinks it right to refuse the application because of the particular circumstances of the case.]

(5) The "existing liquidator" is the person who is liquidator immediately before the winding up becomes a creditors' voluntary winding up.]

NOTES

Commencement: see note below.

Substituted by the Small Business, Enterprise and Employment Act 2015, s 126, Sch 9, Pt 1, paras 1, 20(1), as from 6 April 2017 (in relation to England and Wales and subject to transitional and savings provisions as noted to s 246ZE at **[1.256]**), and as from a day to be appointed (in relation to Scotland). The original s 96 reads as follows—

"96 Conversion to creditors' voluntary winding up

As from the day on which the creditors' meeting is held under section 95, this Act has effect as if—

(a) the directors' declaration under section 89 had not been made; and

(b) the creditors' meeting and the company meeting at which it was resolved that the company be wound up voluntarily were the meetings mentioned in section 98 in the next Chapter;

and accordingly the winding up becomes a creditors' voluntary winding up.".

Sub-s (4A): inserted by the Small Business, Enterprise and Employment Act 2015, s 126, Sch 9, Pt 1, paras 1, 20(2), as from 6 April 2017 (in relation to England and Wales and subject to transitional and savings provisions as noted to s 246ZE at **[1.256]**), and as from a day to be appointed (in relation to Scotland).

CHAPTER IV
CREDITORS' VOLUNTARY WINDING UP

[1.94]

97 Application of this Chapter

(1) Subject as follows, this Chapter applies in relation to a creditors' voluntary winding up.

(2) Sections [99 and 100] do not apply where, under section 96 in Chapter III, a members' voluntary winding up has become a creditors' voluntary winding up.

NOTES

This section derived from the Companies Act 1985, s 587, and the Insolvency Act 1985, s 85(1).

Sub-s (1): words in square brackets substituted for original words "98 and 99" by the Small Business, Enterprise and Employment Act 2015, s 126, Sch 9, Pt 1, paras 1, 21, as from 6 April 2017 (in relation to England and Wales and subject to transitional and savings provisions as noted to s 246ZE at **[1.256]**), and as from a day to be appointed (in relation to Scotland).

[1.95]

98 Meeting of creditors

(1) [In the case of the winding up of a company registered in Scotland, the company] shall—

(a) cause a meeting of its creditors to be summoned for a day not later than the 14th day after the day on which there is to be held the company meeting at which the resolution for voluntary winding up is to be proposed;

(b) cause the notices of the creditors' meeting to be sent by post to the creditors not less than 7 days before the day on which that meeting is to be held; and

(c) cause notice of the creditors' meeting to be advertised once in the Gazette and once at least in two newspapers circulating in the relevant locality (that is to say the locality in which the company's principal place of business in Great Britain was situated during the relevant period).

[(1A) In the case of the winding up of a company registered in England and Wales, the company—

(a) shall cause a meeting of its creditors to be summoned for a day not later than the 14th day after the day on which there is to be held the company meeting at which the resolution for voluntary winding up is to be proposed;

(b) shall cause the notices of the creditors' meeting to be sent . . . to the creditors not less than 7 days before the day on which that meeting is to be held;

(c) shall cause notice of the creditors' meeting to be advertised once in the Gazette; and

(d) may cause notice of the meeting to be advertised in such other manner as the directors think fit.]

(2) The notice of the creditors' meeting shall state either—

(a) the name and address of a person qualified to act as an insolvency practitioner in relation to the company who, during the period before the day on which that meeting is to be held, will furnish creditors free of charge with such information concerning the company's affairs as they may reasonably require; or

(b) a place in the relevant locality where, on the two business days falling next before the day on which that meeting is to be held, a list of the names and addresses of the company's creditors will be available for inspection free of charge.

(3) Where the company's principal place of business in Great Britain was situated in different localities at different times during the relevant period, the duties imposed by subsections (1)(c) and (2)(b) above apply separately in relation to each of those localities.

(4) Where the company had no place of business in Great Britain during the relevant period, references in subsections (1)(c) and (3) to the company's principal place of business in Great Britain are replaced by references to its registered office.

(5) In this section "the relevant period" means the period of 6 months immediately preceding the day on which were sent the notices summoning the company meeting at which it was resolved that the company be wound up voluntarily.

(6) If the company without reasonable excuse fails to comply with subsection (1)[, (1A)] or (2), it is guilty of an offence and liable to a fine.

NOTES

This section derived from the Insolvency Act 1985, s 85(2), (3), (6)–(8), (9)(a), (10).

Repealed by the Small Business, Enterprise and Employment Act 2015, s 126, Sch 9, Pt 1, paras 1, 22, as from 6 April 2017 (in relation to England and Wales and subject to transitional and savings provisions as noted to s 246ZE at **[1.256]**), and as from a day to be appointed (in relation to Scotland).

Sub-s (1): words in square brackets substituted for original words "The company" by the Legislative Reform (Insolvency) (Advertising Requirements) Order 2009, SI 2009/864, arts 2, 3(2)(a), 4, except in relation to a company in voluntary winding up where the resolution to wind up was passed before 6 April 2009.

Sub-s (1A): inserted by SI 2009/864, arts 2, 3(2)(b), 4, except in relation to a company in voluntary winding up where the resolution to wind up was passed before 6 April 2009; words "by post" (omitted) repealed in relation to England and Wales by the Legislative Reform (Insolvency) (Miscellaneous Provisions) Order 2010, SI 2010/18, arts 2, 7, except in relation to a company in voluntary winding up where the resolution to wind up was passed before 6 April 2010: see art 12(3) of the 2010 Order at **[2.76]**.

Sub-s (6): figure in square brackets inserted by SI 2009/864, arts 2, 3(2)(c), 4, except in relation to a company in voluntary winding up where the resolution to wind up was passed before 6 April 2009.

[1.96]

99 Directors to lay statement of affairs before creditors

[(1) The directors of the company must, before the end of the period of 7 days beginning with the day after the day on which the company passes a resolution for voluntary winding up—

(a) make out a statement in the prescribed form as to the affairs of the company, and

(b) send the statement to the company's creditors.]

(2) The statement as to the affairs of the company . . . shall show—

(a) particulars of the company's assets, debts and liabilities;

(b) the names and addresses of the company's creditors;

(c) the securities held by them respectively;

(d) the dates when the securities were respectively given; and

(e) such further or other information as may be prescribed.

[(2A) The statement as to the affairs of the company shall *be verified by some or all of the directors*—

(a) in the case of a winding up of a company registered in England and Wales, [be verified by some or all of the directors] by a statement of truth; and

(b) in the case of a winding up of a company registered in Scotland, *by affidavit*.]

[(3) If the directors without reasonable excuse fail to comply with subsection (1), (2) or (2A), they are guilty of an offence and liable to a fine.]

NOTES

This section derived from the Insolvency Act 1985, s 85(4), (5), (9)(b), (c), (10).

Sub-s (1): substituted by the Small Business, Enterprise and Employment Act 2015, s 126, Sch 9, Pt 1, paras 1, 23(1), (2), as from 6 April 2017 (in relation to England and Wales and subject to transitional and savings provisions as noted to s 246ZE at **[1.256]**), and as from a day to be appointed (in relation to Scotland), and originally read as follows—

"(1) The directors of the company shall—

(a) make out a statement in the prescribed form as to the affairs of the company;

(b) cause that statement to be laid before the creditors' meeting under section 98; and

(c) appoint one of their number to preside at that meeting;

and it is the duty of the director so appointed to attend the meeting and preside over it.".

Sub-s (2): words omitted repealed by the Legislative Reform (Insolvency) (Miscellaneous Provisions) Order 2010, SI 2010/18, arts 2, 5(3)(a).

Sub-s (2A): inserted by SI 2010/18, arts 2, 5(3)(b); first words in italics repealed, words in square brackets in para (a) inserted, and for the words in italics in para (b) there are substituted the words "contain a statutory declaration by some or all of the directors", by the Public Services Reform (Insolvency) (Scotland) Order 2016, SSI 2016/141, art 9, as from a day to be appointed (being the day that the Small Business, Enterprise and Employment Act 2015, s 122(2) comes into force for all remaining purposes in Scotland); for savings, see the note to s 66 at **[1.52]**.

Sub-s (3): substituted by the Small Business, Enterprise and Employment Act 2015, s 126, Sch 9, Pt 1, paras 1, 23(1), (3), as from 6 April 2017 (in relation to England and Wales and subject to transitional and savings provisions as noted to s 246ZE at **[1.256]**), and as from a day to be appointed (in relation to Scotland). Sub-s (3) previously read as follows (with words in square brackets substituted by SI 2010/18, arts 2, 5(3)(c))—

"(3) If—

(a) the directors without reasonable excuse fail to comply with subsection (1)[, (2) or (2A)]; or

(b) any director without reasonable excuse fails to comply with subsection (1), so far as requiring him to attend and preside at the creditors' meeting,

the directors are or (as the case may be) the director is guilty of an offence and liable to a fine.".

Unfitness of directors: see the note to s 47 at **[1.33]**.

[1.97]

100 Appointment of liquidator

[(1) The company may nominate a person to be liquidator at the company meeting at which the resolution for voluntary winding up is passed.

(1A) The company's creditors may in accordance with the rules nominate a person to be liquidator.

(1B) The directors of the company must in accordance with the rules seek such a nomination from the company's creditors.]

(2) The liquidator shall be the person nominated by the creditors or, where no person has been so nominated, the person (if any) nominated by the company.

(3) In the case of different persons being nominated, any director, member or creditor of the company may, within 7 days after the date on which the nomination was made by the creditors, apply to the court for an order either—

(a) directing that the person nominated as liquidator by the company shall be liquidator instead of or jointly with the person nominated by the creditors, or

(b) appointing some other person to be liquidator instead of the person nominated by the creditors.

[(4) The court shall grant an application under subsection (3) made by the holder of a qualifying floating charge in respect of the company's property (within the meaning of paragraph 14 of Schedule B1) unless the court thinks it right to refuse the application because of the particular circumstances of the case.]

NOTES

This section derived from the Companies Act 1985, s 589, and the Insolvency Act 1985, Sch 6, para 37(1), (2).

Sub-ss (1), (1A), (1B): substituted for original sub-s (1) by the Small Business, Enterprise and Employment Act 2015, s 126, Sch 9, Pt 1, paras 1, 24, as from 6 April 2017 (in relation to England and Wales and subject to transitional and savings provisions as noted to s 246ZE at **[1.256]**), and as from a day to be appointed (in relation to Scotland). Sub-s (1) originally read as follows—

"(1) The creditors and the company at their respective meetings mentioned in section 98 may nominate a person to be liquidator for the purpose of winding up the company's affairs and distributing its assets.".

Sub-s (4): added by the Enterprise Act 2002, s 248(3), Sch 17, paras 9, 14 (subject to savings in relation to special administration regimes in s 249 of that Act at **[2.10]**), as from a day to be appointed.

Modification: this section is modified, in relation to the notification to the Financial Conduct Authority and (if the institution is a PRA-authorised person) the Prudential Regulation Authority of the appointment of a liquidator, by the Credit Institutions (Reorganisation and Winding up) Regulations 2004, SI 2004/1045, reg 9(3), (5), (5A) at **[3.221]**.

[1.98]

101 Appointment of liquidation committee

[(1) The creditors may in accordance with the rules appoint a committee ("the liquidation committee") of not more than 5 persons to exercise the functions conferred on it by or under this Act.]

(2) If such a committee is appointed, the company may, either at the meeting at which the resolution for voluntary winding up is passed or at any time subsequently in general meeting, appoint such number of persons as they think fit to act as members of the committee, not exceeding 5.

(3) However, the creditors may, if they think fit, [decide] that all or any of the persons so appointed by the company ought not to be members of the liquidation committee; and if the creditors so [decide]—

(a) [those persons] are not then, unless the court otherwise directs, qualified to act as members of the committee; and

(b) on any application to the court under this provision the court may, if it thinks fit, appoint other persons to act as such members in place of [those persons].

(4) In Scotland, the liquidation committee has, in addition to the powers and duties conferred and imposed on it by this Act, such of the powers and duties of commissioners on a bankrupt estate as may be conferred and imposed on liquidation committees by the rules.

NOTES

This section derived from the Companies Act 1985, s 590, and the Insolvency Act 1985, Sch 6, para 38(2)–(4).

Sub-s (1): substituted by the Small Business, Enterprise and Employment Act 2015, s 126, Sch 9, Pt 1, paras 1, 25(1), (2), as from 6 April 2017 (in relation to England and Wales and subject to transitional and savings provisions as noted to s 246ZE at **[1.256]**), and as from a day to be appointed (in relation to Scotland). Sub-s (1) originally read as follows—

"(1) The creditors at the meeting to be held under section 98 or at any subsequent meeting may, if they think fit, appoint a committee ("the liquidation committee") of not more than 5 persons to exercise the functions conferred on it by or under this Act.".

Sub-s (3): word in first and second pairs of square brackets substituted for original word "resolve" and words in square brackets in paras (a), (b) substituted for original words "the persons mentioned in the resolution" by the Small Business, Enterprise and Employment Act 2015, s 126, Sch 9, Pt 1, paras 1, 25(1), (3), as from 6 April 2017 (in relation to England and Wales and subject to transitional and savings provisions as noted to s 246ZE at **[1.256]**), and as from a day to be appointed (in relation to Scotland).

Sub-s (4): repealed by the Public Services Reform (Corporate Insolvency and Bankruptcy) (Scotland) Order 2017, SSI 2017/209, art 3, as from the day appointed for the coming into force, for all remaining purposes, of the Small Business, Enterprise and Employment Act 2015, s 122 in Scotland.

[1.99]

102 Creditors' meeting where winding up converted under s 96

Where, in the case of a winding up which was, under section 96 in Chapter III, converted to a creditors' voluntary winding up, a creditors' meeting is held in accordance with section 95, any appointment made or committee established by that meeting is deemed to have been made or established by a meeting held in accordance with section 98 in this Chapter.

NOTES

This section derived from the Insolvency Act 1985, s 83(7) (in part).

Repealed by the Small Business, Enterprise and Employment Act 2015, s 126, Sch 9, Pt 1, paras 1, 26, as from 6 April 2017 (in relation to England and Wales and subject to transitional and savings provisions as noted to s 246ZE at **[1.256]**), and as from a day to be appointed (in relation to Scotland).

[1.100]

103 Cesser of directors' powers

On the appointment of a liquidator, all the powers of the directors cease, except so far as the liquidation committee (or, if there is no such committee, the creditors) sanction their continuance.

NOTES

This section derived from the Companies Act 1985, s 591, and the Insolvency Act 1985, Sch 6, para 39.

[1.101]

104 Vacancy in office of liquidator

If a vacancy occurs, by death, resignation or otherwise, in the office of a liquidator (other than a liquidator appointed by, or by the direction of, the court), the creditors may fill the vacancy.

NOTES

This section derived from the Companies Act 1985, s 592.

[1.102]

[104A Progress report to company and creditors . . . *(England and Wales)*

(1) *[Where the company is registered in England and Wales]*, the liquidator must—

- (a) for each prescribed period produce a progress report relating to the prescribed matters; and
- (b) within such period commencing with the end of the period referred to in paragraph (a) as may be prescribed send a copy of the progress report to—
  - (i) the members and creditors[, other than opted-out creditors] of the company; and
  - (ii) such other persons as may be prescribed.

(2) A liquidator who fails to comply with this section is liable to a fine.]

NOTES

Inserted by the Legislative Reform (Insolvency) (Miscellaneous Provisions) Order 2010, SI 2010/18, arts 2, 6(3), except in relation to a company in voluntary winding up where the resolution to wind up was passed before 6 April 2010: see art 12(1) of the 2010 Order at **[2.76]**.

Words omitted from the section heading repealed and words in first pair of square brackets in sub-s (1) substituted, by the Small Business, Enterprise and Employment Act 2015, s 136(1), (3).

Words in italics in the section heading repealed, and for the words in italics in sub-s (1) there is substituted "The", by the Public Services Reform (Insolvency) (Scotland) Order 2016, SSI 2016/141, art 6(1), as from a day to be appointed (being the day that the Small Business, Enterprise and Employment Act 2015, s 122(2) comes into force for all remaining purposes in Scotland); for savings, see the note to s 66 at **[1.52]**.

Words in square brackets in sub-s (1)(b)(i) inserted by the Small Business, Enterprise and Employment Act 2015, s 126, Sch 9, Pt 1, paras 1, 27, as from 6 April 2017 (in relation to England and Wales and subject to transitional and savings provisions as noted to s 246ZE at **[1.256]**), and as from a day to be appointed (in relation to Scotland).

[1.103]

105 Meetings of company and creditors at each year's end [(Scotland)]

(1) If the winding up [of a company registered in Scotland] continues for more than one year, the liquidator shall summon a general meeting of the company and a meeting of the creditors at the end of the first year from the commencement of the winding up, and of each succeeding year, or at the first convenient date within 3 months from the end of the year or such longer period as the Secretary of State may allow.

(2) The liquidator shall lay before each of the meetings an account of his acts and dealings and of the conduct of the winding up during the preceding year.

(3) If the liquidator fails to comply with this section, he is liable to a fine.

(4) Where under section 96 a members' voluntary winding up has become a creditors' voluntary winding up, and the [liquidator sends a statement of affairs to the company's creditors under section 95(1A)(b)] 3 months or less before the end of the first year from the commencement of the winding up, the liquidator is not required by this section to summon a meeting of creditors at the end of that year.

NOTES

This section derived from the Companies Act 1985, s 594, and the Insolvency Act 1985, s 83(8).

Repealed by the Public Services Reform (Insolvency) (Scotland) Order 2016, SSI 2016/141, art 6(2), as from a day to be appointed (being the day that the Small Business, Enterprise and Employment Act 2015, s 122(2) comes into force for all remaining purposes in Scotland); for savings, see the note to s 66 at **[1.52]**.

Section heading: word in square brackets inserted by the Legislative Reform (Insolvency) (Miscellaneous Provisions) Order 2010, SI 2010/18, arts 2, 6(4)(a), except in relation to a company in voluntary winding up where the resolution to wind up was passed before 6 April 2010: see art 12(2) of the 2010 Order at **[2.76]**.

Sub-s (1): words in square brackets inserted by SI 2010/18, arts 2, 6(4)(b), except in relation to a company in voluntary winding up where the resolution to wind up was passed before 6 April 2010: see art 12(2) of the 2010 Order at **[2.76]**.

Sub-s (4): words in square brackets substituted for original words "creditors' meeting under section 95 is held", by the Small Business, Enterprise and Employment Act 2015, s 126, Sch 9, Pt 1, paras 1, 28, as from 6 April 2017 (in relation to England and Wales and subject to transitional and savings provisions as noted to s 246ZE at **[1.256]**), and as from a day to be appointed (in relation to Scotland).

[1.104]

[106 Final account prior to dissolution

(1) As soon as the company's affairs are fully wound up the liquidator must make up an account of the winding up, showing how it has been conducted and the company's property has been disposed of.

(2) The liquidator must, before the end of the period of 14 days beginning with the day on which the account is made up—

(a) send a copy of the account to the company's members,

(b) send a copy of the account to the company's creditors (other than opted-out creditors), and

(c) give the company's creditors (other than opted-out creditors) a notice explaining the effect of section 173(2)(e) and how they may object to the liquidator's release.

(3) The liquidator must during the relevant period send to the registrar of companies—

(a) a copy of the account, and

(b) a statement of whether any of the company's creditors objected to the liquidator's release.

(4) The relevant period is the period of 7 days beginning with the day after the last day of the period prescribed by the rules as the period within which the creditors may object to the liquidator's release.

[(4A) Subsection (4B) applies where, immediately before the liquidator sends a copy of the account of the winding up to the registrar under subsection (3), there are EU insolvency proceedings open in respect of the company in one or more other member States.

(4B) The liquidator must send to the registrar, with the copy of the account, a statement—

(a) identifying those proceedings,

(b) identifying the member State liquidator appointed in each of those proceedings, and

(c) indicating, in relation to each of those member State liquidators, whether that member State liquidator consents to the company being dissolved.]

(5) If the liquidator does not comply with subsection (2) the liquidator is liable to a fine.

(6) If the liquidator does not comply with subsection (3) the liquidator is liable to a fine and, for continued contravention, a daily default fine.]

[(7) Subsection (8) applies where, immediately before the liquidator sends a copy of the account of the winding up to the registrar under subsection (3), there are EU insolvency proceedings open in respect of the company in one or more other member States.

(8) The liquidator must send to the registrar, with the copy of the account, a statement—

(a) identifying those proceedings,

(b) identifying the member State liquidator appointed in each of those proceedings, and

(c) indicating, in relation to each of those member State liquidators, whether that member State liquidator consents to the company being dissolved.]

NOTES

Commencement: see note below.

Substituted by the Small Business, Enterprise and Employment Act 2015, s 126, Sch 9, Pt 1, paras 1, 29, as from 6 April 2017 (in relation to England and Wales and subject to transitional and savings provisions as noted to s 246ZE at **[1.256]**), and as from a day to be appointed (in relation to Scotland). This section originally read as follows—

> **"106 Final meeting prior to dissolution**
>
> (1) As soon as the company's affairs are fully wound up, the liquidator shall make up an account of the winding up, showing how it has been conducted and the company's property has been disposed of, and thereupon shall call a general meeting of the company and a meeting of the creditors for the purpose of laying the account before the meetings and giving an explanation of it.
>
> (2) Each such meeting shall be called by advertisement in the Gazette specifying the time, place and object of the meeting, and published at least one month before it.
>
> (3) Within one week after the date of the meetings (or, if they are not held on the same date, after the date on the later one) the liquidator shall send to the registrar of companies a copy of the account, and shall make a return to him of the holding of the meetings and of their dates.
>
> (4) If the copy is not sent or the return is not made in accordance with subsection (3), the liquidator is liable to a fine and, for continued contravention, to a daily default fine.
>
> (5) However, if a quorum is not present at either such meeting, the liquidator shall, in lieu of the return required by subsection (3), make a return that the meeting was duly summoned and that no quorum was present; and upon such return being made the provisions of that subsection as to the making of the return are, in respect of that meeting, deemed complied with.
>
> (6) If the liquidator fails to call a general meeting of the company or a meeting of the creditors as required by this section, he is liable to a fine.".

Sub-ss (4A), (4B): inserted by the Insolvency Amendment (EU 2015/848) Regulations 2017, SI 2017/702, regs 2, 3, Schedule, Pt 1, paras 1, 3, except in relation to proceedings opened before 26 June 2017 and subject to savings in reg 4 thereof at **[2.103]**.

Sub-ss (7), (8): added, in relation to Scotland only, by the Insolvency Amendment (EU 2015/848) Regulations 2017, SI 2017/702, regs 2, 3, Schedule, Pt 4, paras 55, 56, except in relation to proceedings opened before 26 June 2017 and subject to savings in reg 4 thereof at **[2.103]**.

Modification in relation to Scotland: see the Note at the beginning of this Act.

Application to coal mining operations: see further the Coal Industry Act 1994, s 36 at **[17.112]**.

CHAPTER V
PROVISIONS APPLYING TO BOTH KINDS OF VOLUNTARY WINDING UP

[1.105]
107 Distribution of company's property
Subject to the provisions of this Act as to preferential payments, the company's property in a voluntary winding up shall on the winding up be applied in satisfaction of the company's liabilities pari passu and, subject to that application, shall (unless the articles otherwise provide) be distributed among the members according to their rights and interests in the company.

NOTES
This section derived from the Companies Act 1985, s 597.

[1.106]
108 Appointment or removal of liquidator by the court
(1) If from any cause whatever there is no liquidator acting, the court may appoint a liquidator.
(2) The court may, on cause shown, remove a liquidator and appoint another.

NOTES
This section derived from the Companies Act 1985, s 599.

[1.107]
109 Notice by liquidator of his appointment
(1) The liquidator shall, within 14 days after his appointment, publish in the Gazette and deliver to the registrar of companies for registration a notice of his appointment in the form prescribed by statutory instrument made by the Secretary of State.
(2) If the liquidator fails to comply with this section, he is liable to a fine and, for continued contravention, to a daily default fine.

NOTES
This section derived from the Companies Act 1985, s 600.
Modification in relation to Scotland: see the Note at the beginning of this Act.
Orders: the Insolvency (Miscellaneous Amendments) Regulations 2017, SI 2017/1119.

[1.108]
110 Acceptance of shares, etc, as consideration for sale of company property
(1) This section applies, in the case of a company proposed to be, or being, wound up voluntarily, where the whole or part of the company's business or property is proposed to be transferred or sold
[(a)] to another company ("the transferee company"), whether or not the latter is a [company registered under the Companies Act 2006][, or
(b) to a limited liability partnership (the "transferee limited liability partnership")].
(2) With the requisite sanction, the liquidator of the company being, or proposed to be, wound up ("the transferor company") may receive, in compensation or part compensation for the transfer or [sale—
(a) in the case of the transferee company, shares, policies or other like interests in the company for distribution among the members of the transferor company, or
(b) in the case of the transferee limited liability partnership, membership in the limited liability partnership for distribution among the members of the transferor company.]
(3) The sanction requisite under subsection (2) is—
(a) in the case of a members' voluntary winding up, that of a special resolution of the company, conferring either a general authority on the liquidator or an authority in respect of any particular arrangement, and
(b) in the case of a creditors' voluntary winding up, that of either the court or the liquidation committee.
(4) Alternatively to subsection (2), the liquidator may (with that sanction) enter into any other arrangement whereby the members of the transferor [company may—
(a) in the case of the transferee company, in lieu of receiving cash, shares, policies or other like interests (or in addition thereto) participate in the profits of, or receive any other benefit from, the company, or
(b) in the case of the transferee limited liability partnership, in lieu of receiving cash, or membership (or in addition thereto) participate in some other way in the profits of, or receive any other benefit from, the limited liability partnership.]
(5) A sale or arrangement in pursuance of this section is binding on members of the transferor company.
(6) A special resolution is not invalid for purposes of this section by reason that it is passed before or concurrently with a resolution for voluntary winding up or for appointing liquidators; but, if an order is made within a year for winding up the company by the court, the special resolution is not valid unless sanctioned by the court.

NOTES
This section derived from the Companies Act 1985, s 582(1)–(4), (7), 593, and the Insolvency Act 1985, Sch 6, para 40.
Sub-s (1): words in first and third pairs of square brackets inserted, in relation to England and Wales, by the Limited Liability Partnerships Regulations 2001, SI 2001/1090, reg 9, Sch 5, para 15(1), (2), and in relation to Scotland, by the Limited Liability Partnerships (Scotland) Regulations 2001, SSI 2001/128, reg 5, Sch 4, para 1(1), (2); words in second pair of square brackets substituted for original words "company within the meaning of the Companies Act" by the Companies Act 2006 (Consequential

Amendments, Transitional Provisions and Savings) Order 2009, SI 2009/1941, art 2(1), Sch 1, para 75(1), (11), subject to transitional provisions and savings in art 8, Sch 1, para 84 at **[2.70]**, **[2.73]**.

Sub-ss (2), (4): words in square brackets substituted, in relation to England and Wales, by SI 2001/1090, reg 9, Sch 5, para 15(1), (3), (4), and in relation to Scotland, by SSI 2001/128, reg 5, Sch 4, para 1(1), (3), (4).

[1.109]

111 Dissent from arrangement under s 110

(1) This section applies in the case of a voluntary winding up where, for the purposes of section 110(2) or (4), there has been passed a special resolution of the transferor company providing the sanction requisite for the liquidator under that section.

(2) If a member of the transferor company who did not vote in favour of the special resolution expresses his dissent from it in writing, addressed to the liquidator and left at the company's registered office within 7 days after the passing of the resolution, he may require the liquidator either to abstain from carrying the resolution into effect or to purchase his interest at a price to be determined by agreement or by arbitration under this section.

(3) If the liquidator elects to purchase the member's interest, the purchase money must be paid before the company is dissolved and be raised by the liquidator in such manner as may be determined by special resolution.

(4) For purposes of an arbitration under this section, the provisions of the Companies Clauses Consolidation Act 1845 or, in the case of a winding up in Scotland, the Companies Clauses Consolidation (Scotland) Act 1845 with respect to the settlement of disputes by arbitration are incorporated with this Act, and—

(a) in the construction of those provisions this Act is deemed the special Act and "the company" means the transferor company, and

(b) any appointment by the incorporated provisions directed to be made under the hand of the secretary or any two of the directors may be made in writing by the liquidator (or, if there is more than one liquidator, then any two or more of them).

NOTES

This section derived from the Companies Act 1985, s 582(5), (6), (8).

[1.110]

112 Reference of questions to court

(1) The liquidator or any contributory or creditor may apply to the court to determine any question arising in the winding up of a company, or to exercise, as respects the enforcing of calls or any other matter, all or any of the powers which the court might exercise if the company were being wound up by the court.

(2) The court, if satisfied that the determination of the question or the required exercise of power will be just and beneficial, may accede wholly or partially to the application on such terms and conditions as it thinks fit, or may make such other order on the application as it thinks just.

(3) A copy of an order made by virtue of this section staying the proceedings in the winding up shall forthwith be forwarded by the company, or otherwise as may be prescribed, to the registrar of companies, who shall enter it in his records relating to the company.

NOTES

This section derived from the Companies Act 1985, s 602.

Modification in relation to Scotland: see the Note at the beginning of this Act.

[1.111]

113 Court's power to control proceedings (Scotland)

If the court, on the application of the liquidator in the winding up of a company registered in Scotland, so directs, no action or proceeding shall be proceeded with or commenced against the company except by leave of the court and subject to such terms as the court may impose.

NOTES

This section derived from the Companies Act 1985, s 603.

[1.112]

114 No liquidator appointed or nominated by company

(1) This section applies where, in the case of a voluntary winding up, no liquidator has been appointed or nominated by the company.

(2) The powers of the directors shall not be exercised, except with the sanction of the court or (in the case of a creditors' voluntary winding up) so far as may be necessary to secure compliance with sections *98 (creditors' meeting) and* 99 (statement of affairs) [and 100(1B) (nomination of liquidator by creditors)], during the period before the appointment or nomination of a liquidator of the company.

(3) Subsection (2) does not apply in relation to the powers of the directors—

(a) to dispose of perishable goods and other goods the value of which is likely to diminish if they are not immediately disposed of, and

(b) to do all such other things as may be necessary for the protection of the company's assets.

(4) If the directors of the company without reasonable excuse fail to comply with this section, they are liable to a fine.

NOTES

This section derived from the Insolvency Act 1985, s 82.

Sub-s (2): words in italics repealed, and words in square brackets inserted, by the Small Business, Enterprise and Employment Act 2015, s 126, Sch 9, Pt 1, paras 1, 30, as from 6 April 2017 (in relation to England and Wales and subject to transitional and savings provisions as noted to s 246ZE at **[1.256]**), and as from a day to be appointed (in relation to Scotland).

[1.113]

115 Expenses of voluntary winding up

All expenses properly incurred in the winding up, including the remuneration of the liquidator, are payable out of the company's assets in priority to all other claims.

NOTES

This section derived from the Companies Act 1985, s 604.

[1.114]

116 Saving for certain rights

The voluntary winding up of a company does not bar the right of any creditor or contributory to have it wound up by the court; but in the case of an application by a contributory the court must be satisfied that the rights of the contributories will be prejudiced by a voluntary winding up.

NOTES

This section derived from the Companies Act 1985, s 605.

CHAPTER VI
WINDING UP BY THE COURT

Jurisdiction (England and Wales)

[1.115]

117 High Court and county court jurisdiction

(1) The High Court has jurisdiction to wind up any company registered in England and Wales.

(2) Where [in the case of a company registered in England and Wales the amount of its] share capital paid up or credited as paid up does not exceed £120,000, then (subject to this section) the county court . . . has concurrent jurisdiction with the High Court to wind up the company.

[(2A) Despite subsection (2), proceedings for the exercise of the jurisdiction to wind up a company registered in England and Wales may be commenced only in the High Court if the place which has longest been the company's registered office during the 6 months immediately preceding the presentation of the petition for winding up is in the district that is the London insolvency district for the purposes of the second Group of Parts of this Act.]

(3) The money sum for the time being specified in subsection (2) is subject to increase or reduction by order under section 416 in Part XV.

(4) . . .

(5) Every court in England and Wales having winding-up jurisdiction has for the purposes of that jurisdiction all the powers of the High Court; and every prescribed officer of the court shall perform any duties which an officer of the High Court may discharge by order of a judge of that court or otherwise in relation to winding up.

(6) . . .

[(7) This section is subject to Article 3 of [the EU Regulation (jurisdiction under EU Regulation)].]

[(8) The Lord Chief Justice may nominate a judicial office holder (as defined in section 109(4) of the Constitutional Reform Act 2005) to exercise his functions under this section.]

NOTES

This section derived from the Companies Act 1985, s 512, and the Insolvency Act 1985, Sch 6, paras 25, 26.

Sub-s (2): words in square brackets substituted and words omitted repealed by the Crime and Courts Act 2013, s 17(5), Sch 9, Pt 3, para 93(a).

Sub-s (2A): inserted by the High Court and County Courts Jurisdiction Order 1991, SI 1991/724, art 6F, Schedule, Pt I (as amended by SI 2014/821), except in relation to proceedings commenced before 22 April 2014.

Sub-ss (4), (6): repealed by the Crime and Courts Act 2013, s 17(5), Sch 9, Pt 3, para 93(b).

Sub-s (7): added by the Insolvency Act 1986 (Amendment) (No 2) Regulations 2002, SI 2002/1240, regs 3, 6; words in square brackets substituted for original words "the EC Regulation (jurisdiction under EC Regulation)" by the Insolvency Amendment (EU 2015/848) Regulations 2017, SI 2017/702, regs 2, 3, Schedule, Pt 1, paras 1, 4, except in relation to proceedings opened before 26 June 2017 and subject to savings in reg 4 thereof at **[2.103]**.

Sub-s (8): added by the Constitutional Reform Act 2005, s 15(1), Sch 4, Pt 1, paras 185, 186(1), (3).

Disapplication: in relation to the disapplication of sub-ss (2)–(5), and ss 118, 119, 120(3), (5) for the purposes of the European Grouping of Territorial Cooperation Regulations 2007, SI 2007/1949, see SI 2007/1949, regs 2, 7, 10, Schedule, Pt 2, para 6.

Presentation of the petition for winding up: as to the modification of references to "the presentation of the petition for winding up" in this section and s 120 at **[1.118]** for the purposes of the Company Directors Disqualification Act 1986, s 6(3), see s 6(3A) of that Act at **[4.8]**.

Orders: the Civil Courts Order 1983, SI 1983/713 (as amended by various other Orders made under this section).

[1.116]

118 Proceedings taken in wrong court

(1) Nothing in section 117 invalidates a proceeding by reason of its being taken in the wrong court.

(2) The winding up of a company by the court in England and Wales, or any proceedings in the winding up, may be retained in the court in which the proceedings were commenced, although it may not be the court in which they ought to have been commenced.

NOTES

This section derived from the Companies Act 1985, s 513.

Disapplication: see the note to s 117 at **[1.115]**.

[1.117]

119 Proceedings in county court; case stated for High Court

(1) If any question arises in any winding-up proceedings in a county court which all the parties to the proceedings, or which one of them and the judge of the court, desire to have determined in the first instance in the High Court, the judge shall state the facts in the form of a special case for the opinion of the High Court.

(2) Thereupon the special case and the proceedings (or such of them as may be required) shall be transmitted to the High Court for the purposes of the determination.

NOTES

This section derived from the Companies Act 1985, s 514.

Disapplication: see the note to s 117 at **[1.115]**.

Jurisdiction (Scotland)

[1.118]

120 Court of Session and sheriff court jurisdiction

(1) The Court of Session has jurisdiction to wind up any company registered in Scotland.

(2) When the Court of Session is in vacation, the jurisdiction conferred on that court by this section may (subject to the provisions of this Part) be exercised by the judge acting as vacation judge . . .

(3) Where the amount of a company's share capital paid up or credited as paid up does not exceed £120,000, the sheriff court of the sheriffdom in which the company's registered office is situated has concurrent jurisdiction with the Court of Session to wind up the company; but—

(a) the Court of Session may, if it thinks expedient having regard to the amount of the company's assets to do so—

(i) remit to a sheriff court any petition presented to the Court of Session for winding up such a company, or

(ii) require such a petition presented to a sheriff court to be remitted to the Court of Session; and

(b) the Court of Session may require any such petition as above-mentioned presented to one sheriff court to be remitted to another sheriff court; and

(c) in a winding up in the sheriff court the sheriff may submit a stated case for the opinion of the Court of Session on any question of law arising in that winding up.

(4) For purposes of this section, the expression "registered office" means the place which has longest been the company's registered office during the 6 months immediately preceding the presentation of the petition for winding up.

(5) The money sum for the time being specified in subsection (3) is subject to increase or reduction by order under section 416 in Part XV.

[(6) This section is subject to Article 3 of [the EU Regulation (jurisdiction under EU Regulation)].]

NOTES

This section derived from the Companies Act 1985, s 515, and the Insolvency Act 1985, Sch 6, para 25.

Sub-s (2): words omitted repealed by the Court of Session Act 1988, s 52(2), Sch 2, Pt III.

Sub-s (6): added by the Insolvency Act 1986 (Amendment) (No 2) Regulations 2002, SI 2002/1240, regs 3, 7; words in square brackets substituted for original words "the EC Regulation (jurisdiction under EC Regulation)" by the Insolvency Amendment (EU 2015/848) Regulations 2017, SI 2017/702, regs 2, 3, Schedule, Pt 1, paras 1, 5, except in relation to proceedings opened before 26 June 2017 and subject to savings in reg 4 thereof at **[2.103]**.

Disapplication: see the note to s 117 at **[1.115]**.

Presentation of the petition for winding up: see the note to s 117 at **[1.115]**.

Modification: as to the application, with modifications, of this section, to European Economic Interest Groupings, see the European Economic Interest Grouping Regulations 1989, SI 1989/638, reg 19(2).

[1.119]

121 Power to remit winding up to Lord Ordinary

(1) The Court of Session may, by Act of Sederunt, make provision for the taking of proceedings in a winding up before one of the Lords Ordinary; and, where provision is so made, the Lord Ordinary has, for the purposes of the winding up, all the powers and jurisdiction of the court.

(2) However, the Lord Ordinary may report to the Inner House any matter which may arise in the course of a winding up.

NOTES

This section derived from the Companies Act 1985, s 516.

Grounds and effect of winding-up petition

[1.120]

122 Circumstances in which company may be wound up by the court

(1) A company may be wound up by the court if—

(a) the company has by special resolution resolved that the company be wound up by the court,

(b) being a public company which was registered as such on its original incorporation, the company has not been issued with [a trading certificate under section 761 of the Companies Act 2006 (requirement as to minimum share capital)] and more than a year has expired since it was so registered,

(c) it is an old public company, within the meaning of [Schedule 3 to the Companies Act 2006 (Consequential Amendments, Transitional Provisions and Savings) Order 2009],

(d) the company does not commence its business within a year from its incorporation or suspends its business for a whole year,

(e) . . .

(f) the company is unable to pay its debts,

[(fa) at the time at which a moratorium for the company under section 1A comes to an end, no voluntary arrangement approved under Part I has effect in relation to the company]

(g) the court is of the opinion that it is just and equitable that the company should be wound up.

(2) In Scotland, a company which the Court of Session has jurisdiction to wind up may be wound up by the Court if there is subsisting a floating charge over property comprised in the company's property and undertaking, and the court is satisfied that the security of the creditor entitled to the benefit of the floating charge is in jeopardy.

For this purpose a creditor's security is deemed to be in jeopardy if the Court is satisfied that events have occurred or are about to occur which render it unreasonable in the creditor's interests that the company should retain power to dispose of the property which is subject to the floating charge.

NOTES

This section derived from the Companies Act 1985, s 517.

Sub-s (1): words in square brackets in para (b) substituted for original words "a certificate under section 117 of the Companies Act (public company share capital requirements)" by the Companies Act 2006 (Consequential Amendments etc) Order 2008, SI 2008/948, art 3(1)(b), Sch 1, Pt 2, para 102, subject to transitional provisions and savings in arts 6, 12 thereof; words in square brackets in para (c) substituted for original words "the Consequential Provisions Act" by the Companies Act 2006 (Consequential Amendments, Transitional Provisions and Savings) Order 2009, SI 2009/1941, art 2(1), Sch 1, para 75(1), (12), subject to transitional provisions and savings in art 8, Sch 1, para 84 at **[2.70]**, **[2.73]**; para (e) repealed by the Companies Act 2006 (Consequential Amendments and Transitional Provisions) Order 2011, SI 2011/1265, art 6(1), (4); para (fa) inserted by the Insolvency Act 2000, s 1, Sch 1, paras 1, 6.

Disapplication: the European Public Limited-Liability Company Regulations 2004, SI 2004/2326, reg 88, Sch 4, paras 9(b), 11 provide that sub-s (1)(b) of this section does not apply to a converting Societas Europaea.

Modification: in relation to the Lloyd's of London insurance market, sub-s (1) is applied, with modifications, by the Insurers (Reorganisation and Winding Up) (Lloyd's) Regulations 2005, SI 2005/1998, reg 25(3) at **[7.1594]**.

[1.121]

123 Definition of inability to pay debts

(1) A company is deemed unable to pay its debts—

(a) if a creditor (by assignment or otherwise) to whom the company is indebted in a sum exceeding £750 then due has served on the company, by leaving it at the company's registered office, a written demand (in the prescribed form) requiring the company to pay the sum so due and the company has for 3 weeks thereafter neglected to pay the sum or to secure or compound for it to the reasonable satisfaction of the creditor, or

(b) if, in England and Wales, execution or other process issued on a judgment, decree or order of any court in favour of a creditor of the company is returned unsatisfied in whole or in part, or

(c) if, in Scotland, the induciae of a charge for payment on an extract decree, or an extract registered bond, or an extract registered protest, have expired without payment being made, or

(d) if, in Northern Ireland, a certificate of unenforceability has been granted in respect of a judgment against the company, or

(e) if it is proved to the satisfaction of the court that the company is unable to pay its debts as they fall due.

(2) A company is also deemed unable to pay its debts if it is proved to the satisfaction of the court that the value of the company's assets is less than the amount of its liabilities, taking into account its contingent and prospective liabilities.

(3) The money sum for the time being specified in subsection (1)(a) is subject to increase or reduction by order under section 416 in Part XV.

NOTES

This section derived from the Companies Act 1985, s 518, and the Insolvency Act 1985, Sch 6, paras 25, 27.

Special administration orders in relation to water and sewerage undertakers: as to the making of special administration orders in relation to water and sewerage undertakers holding an appointment under Chapter I of Part II of the Water Industry Act 1991, on the ground that the company is unable to pay its debts within the meaning of this section or ss 222–224, see ss 23–25 of that Act at **[7.2619]**–**[7.2621]**, and Sch 3 to that Act at **[7.2625]**.

Railway administration orders: as to the making of railway administration orders, within the meaning of the Railways Act 1993, s 59, on the ground that the company is unable to pay its debts within the meaning of this section or ss 222–224, see s 60(6) of that Act at **[7.2438]**.

[1.122]

124 Application for winding up

(1) Subject to the provisions of this section, an application to the court for the winding up of a company shall be by petition presented either by the company, or the directors, or by any creditor or creditors (including any contingent or prospective creditor or creditors), contributory or contributories[, or by [a member State liquidator appointed in proceedings by virtue of Article 3(1) of the EU Regulation or a temporary administrator (within the meaning of Article 52 of the EU Regulation)]] [or by [the designated officer for a magistrates' court] in the exercise of the power conferred by section 87A of the Magistrates' Courts Act 1980 (enforcement of fines imposed on companies)], or by all or any of those parties, together or separately.

(2) Except as mentioned below, a contributory is not entitled to present a winding-up petition unless either—

- (a) the number of members is reduced below 2, or
- (b) the shares in respect of which he is a contributory, or some of them, either were originally allotted to him, or have been held by him, and registered in his name, for at least 6 months during the 18 months before the commencement of the winding up, or have devolved on him through the death of a former holder.

(3) A person who is liable under section 76 to contribute to a company's assets in the event of its being wound up may petition on either of the grounds set out in section 122(1)(f) and (g), and subsection (2) above does not then apply; but unless the person is a contributory otherwise than under section 76, he may not in his character as contributory petition on any other ground.

. . .

[(3A) A winding-up petition on the ground set out in section 122(1)(fa) may only be presented by one or more creditors.]

(4) A winding-up petition may be presented by the Secretary of State—

- (a) if the ground of the petition is that in section 122(1)(b) or (c), or
- [(b) in a case falling within section 124A [or 124B] below.]

[(4AA) A winding up petition may be presented by the [Financial Conduct Authority] in a case falling within section 124C(1) or (2).]

[(4A) A winding-up petition may be presented by the Regulator of Community Interest Companies in a case falling within section 50 of the Companies (Audit, Investigations and Community Enterprise) Act 2004.]

(5) Where a company is being wound up voluntarily in England and Wales, a winding-up petition may be presented by the official receiver attached to the court as well as by any other person authorised in that behalf under the other provisions of this section; but the court shall not make a winding-up order on the petition unless it is satisfied that the voluntary winding up cannot be continued with due regard to the interests of the creditors or contributories.

NOTES

This section derived from the Companies Act 1985, s 519, and the Insolvency Act 1985, Sch 6, para 28.

Sub-s (1): words in first (outer) pair of square brackets inserted by the Insolvency Act 1986 (Amendment) (No 2) Regulations 2002, SI 2002/1240, regs 3, 8; words in second (inner) pair of square brackets substituted for original words "a liquidator (within the meaning of Article 2(b) of the EC Regulation) appointed in proceedings by virtue of Article 3(1) of the EC Regulation or a temporary administrator (within the meaning of Article 38 of the EC Regulation)" by the Insolvency Amendment (EU 2015/848) Regulations 2017, SI 2017/702, regs 2, 3, Schedule, Pt 1, paras 1, 6, except in relation to proceedings opened before 26 June 2017 and subject to savings in reg 4 thereof at **[2.103]**; words in third (outer) pair of square brackets inserted by the Criminal Justice Act 1988, s 62(2)(b); words in fourth (inner) pair of square brackets substituted by the Courts Act 2003, s 109(1), Sch 8, para 294, subject to transitional provisions in SI 2005/911, arts 2–5.

Sub-s (3): words "This subsection is deemed included in Chapter VII of Part V of the Companies Act (redeemable shares; purchase by a company of its own shares) for the purposes of the Secretary of State's power to make regulations under section 179 of that Act." (omitted) repealed by the Companies Act 2006 (Consequential Amendments, Transitional Provisions and Savings) Order 2009, SI 2009/1941, art 2(1), Sch 1, para 75(1), (13), subject to transitional provisions and savings in art 8, Sch 1, para 84 at **[2.70]**, **[2.73]**.

Sub-s (3A): inserted by the Insolvency Act 2000, s 1, Sch 1, paras 1, 7.

Sub-s (4): para (b) substituted by the Companies Act 1989, s 60(2); words in square brackets therein inserted by the European Public Limited-Liability Company Regulations 2004, SI 2004/2326, reg 73(4)(a).

Sub-s (4AA): inserted by the European Cooperative Society Regulations 2006, SI 2006/2078, reg 33(2); words in square brackets substituted by the Financial Services Act 2012 (Mutual Societies) Order 2013, SI 2013/496, art 2(c), Sch 11, para 2(1), (2)(a).

Sub-s (4A): inserted by the Companies (Audit, Investigations and Community Enterprise) Act 2004, s 50(3).

[1.123]

[124A Petition for winding-up on grounds of public interest

(1) Where it appears to the Secretary of State from—

- (a) any report made or information obtained under Part XIV [(except section 448A)] of the Companies Act 1985 (company investigations, &c),
- [(b) any report made by inspectors under—
  - (i) section 167, 168, 169 or 284 of the Financial Services and Markets Act 2000, or
  - (ii) where the company is an open-ended investment company (within the meaning of that Act), regulations made as a result of section 262(2)(k) of that Act;
- (bb) any information or documents obtained under section 165, 171, 172, 173 or 175 of that Act,]
- (c) any information obtained under section 2 of the Criminal Justice Act 1987 or section 52 of the Criminal Justice (Scotland) Act 1987 (fraud investigations), or

(d) any information obtained under section 83 of the Companies Act 1989 (powers exercisable for purpose of assisting overseas regulatory authorities),

that it is expedient in the public interest that a company should be wound up, he may present a petition for it to be wound up if the court thinks it just and equitable for it to be so.

(2) This section does not apply if the company is already being wound up by the court.]

NOTES

Inserted by the Companies Act 1989, s 60(3).

Sub-s (1): words in square brackets in para (a) inserted by the Companies (Audit, Investigations and Community Enterprise) Act 2004, s 25(1), Sch 2, Pt 3, para 27; paras (b), (bb) substituted for original para (b) by the Financial Services and Markets Act 2000 (Consequential Amendments and Repeals) Order 2001, SI 2001/3649, art 305.

Criminal Justice (Scotland) Act 1987, s 52: repealed by the Criminal Procedure (Consequential Provisions) (Scotland) Act 1995, s 6(1), Sch 5; see now the Criminal Law (Consolidation) (Scotland) Act 1995, s 28.

[1.124]

[124B Petition for winding up of SE

(1) Where—

(a) an SE whose registered office is in Great Britain is not in compliance with Article 7 of Council Regulation (EC) No 2157/2001 on the Statute for a European company (the "EC Regulation") (location of head office and registered office), and

(b) it appears to the Secretary of State that the SE should be wound up, he may present a petition for it to be wound up if the court thinks it is just and equitable for it to be so.

(2) This section does not apply if the SE is already being wound up by the court.

(3) In this section "SE" has the same meaning as in the EC Regulation.]

NOTES

Inserted by the European Public Limited-Liability Company Regulations 2004, SI 2004/2326, reg 73(3).

[1.125]

[124C Petition for winding up of SCE

(1) Where, in the case of an SCE whose registered office is in Great Britain—

(a) there has been such a breach as is mentioned in Article 73(1) of Council Regulation (EC) No 1435/2003 on the Statute for a European Cooperative Society (SCE) (the "European Cooperative Society Regulation") (winding up by the court or other competent authority), and

(b) it appears to the [Financial Conduct Authority] that the SCE should be wound up,

the Authority may present a petition for the SCE to be wound up if the court thinks it is just and equitable for it to be so.

(2) Where, in the case of an SCE whose registered office is in Great Britain—

(a) the SCE is not in compliance with Article 6 of the European Cooperative Society Regulation (location of head office and registered office), and

(b) it appears to the [Financial Conduct Authority] that the SCE should be wound up,

the Authority may present a petition for the SCE to be wound up if the court thinks it is just and equitable for it to be so.

(3) This section does not apply if the SCE is already being wound up by the court.

(4) In this section "SCE" has the same meaning as in the European Cooperative Society Regulation.]

NOTES

Inserted by the European Cooperative Society Regulations 2006, SI 2006/2078, reg 33(1).

Sub-ss (1), (2): words in square brackets substituted by the Financial Services Act 2012 (Mutual Societies) Order 2013, SI 2013/496, art 2(c), Sch 11, para 2(1), (2)(b).

[1.126]

125 Powers of court on hearing of petition

(1) On hearing a winding-up petition the court may dismiss it, or adjourn the hearing conditionally or unconditionally, or make an interim order, or any other order that it thinks fit; but the court shall not refuse to make a winding-up order on the ground only that the company's assets have been mortgaged to an amount equal to or in excess of those assets, or that the company has no assets.

(2) If the petition is presented by members of the company as contributories on the ground that it is just and equitable that the company should be wound up, the court, if it is of opinion—

(a) that the petitioners are entitled to relief either by winding up the company or by some other means, and

(b) that in the absence of any other remedy it would be just and equitable that the company should be wound up,

shall make a winding-up order; but this does not apply if the court is also of the opinion both that some other remedy is available to the petitioners and that they are acting unreasonably in seeking to have the company wound up instead of pursuing that other remedy.

NOTES

This section derived from the Companies Act 1985, s 520.

Modification: this section is modified, in relation to the notification to the Financial Conduct Authority and (if the institution is a PRA-authorised person) the Prudential Regulation Authority of any decision or winding-up order made on or after 5 May 2004, by the Credit Institutions (Reorganisation and Winding up) Regulations 2004, SI 2004/1045, reg 9(1)(b), (5), (5A) at **[3.221]**.

[1.127]

126 Power to stay or restrain proceedings against company

(1) At any time after the presentation of a winding-up petition, and before a winding-up order has been made, the company, or any creditor or contributory, may—

(a) where any action or proceeding against the company is pending in the High Court or Court of Appeal in England and Wales or Northern Ireland, apply to the court in which the action or proceeding is pending for a stay of proceedings therein, and

(b) where any other action or proceeding is pending against the company, apply to the court having jurisdiction to wind up the company to restrain further proceedings in the action or proceeding;

and the court to which application is so made may (as the case may be) stay, sist or restrain the proceedings accordingly on such terms as it thinks fit.

(2) In the case of [a company registered but not formed under the Companies Act 2006], where the application to stay, sist or restrain is by a creditor, this section extends to actions and proceedings against any contributory of the company.

[(3) Subsection (1) applies in relation to any action being taken in respect of the company under Part 1 of Schedule 8 to the Finance (No 2) Act 2015 (enforcement by deduction from accounts) as it applies in relation to any action or proceeding mentioned in paragraph (b) of that subsection.]

NOTES

This section derived from the Companies Act 1985, s 521.

Sub-s (2): words in square brackets substituted for original words "a company registered under section 680 of the Companies Act (pre-1862 companies; companies formed under legislation other than the Companies Acts) or the previous corresponding legislation" by the Companies Act 2006 (Consequential Amendments, Transitional Provisions and Savings) Order 2009, SI 2009/1941, art 2(1), Sch 1, para 75(1), (14), subject to transitional provisions and savings in art 8, Sch 1, para 84 at **[2.70]**, **[2.73]**.

Sub-s (3): added by the Finance (No 2) Act 2015, s 51, Sch 8, Pt 2, paras 26, 27.

Default proceedings: nothing in this section or s 128, 130, 185 or 285 affects any action taken by an exchange or clearing house for the purpose of its default proceedings; see the Companies Act 1989, s 161(4) at **[17.64]**.

[1.128]

127 Avoidance of property dispositions, etc

[(1)] In a winding up by the court, any disposition of the company's property, and any transfer of shares, or alteration in the status of the company's members, made after the commencement of the winding up is, unless the court otherwise orders, void.

[(2) This section has no effect in respect of anything done by an administrator of a company while a winding-up petition is suspended under paragraph 40 of Schedule B1.]

NOTES

This section derived from the Companies Act 1985, s 522.

Sub-s (1): existing provision of this section numbered as such by the Enterprise Act 2002, s 248(3), Sch 17, paras 9, 15, subject to savings and transitional provisions (i) in a case where a petition for an administration order has been presented before 15 September 2003 (see the Enterprise Act 2002 (Commencement No 4 and Transitional Provisions and Savings) Order 2003, SI 2003/2093, art 3 at **[2.26]**), and (ii) in relation to special administration regimes (see s 249 of the 2002 Act at **[2.10]**).

Sub-s (2): added by the Enterprise Act 2002, s 248(3), Sch 17, paras 9, 15, subject to savings and transitional provisions as noted to sub-s (1) above.

Disapplication with regard to market contracts and market charges: see further the Companies Act 1989, ss 164(3)–(6), 175(4)–(7) at **[17.67]**, **[17.78]**.

See further: in relation to winding-up proceedings of a collateral-taker or collateral-provider, the disapplication of this section in relation to any property or security interest subject to a disposition or created or otherwise arising under a financial collateral arrangement, or to prevent a close-out netting provision taking effect in accordance with its terms, see the Financial Collateral Arrangements (No 2) Regulations 2003, SI 2003/3226, reg 10(1) at **[3.290]**.

[1.129]

128 Avoidance of attachments, etc

(1) Where a company registered in England and Wales is being wound up by the court, any attachment, sequestration, distress or execution put in force against the estate or effects of the company after the commencement of the winding up is void.

(2) This section, so far as relates to any estate or effects of the company situated in England and Wales, applies in the case of a company registered in Scotland as it applies in the case of a company registered in England and Wales.

[(3) In subsection (1) "attachment" includes a hold notice or a deduction notice under Part 1 of Schedule 8 to the Finance (No 2) Act 2015 (enforcement by deduction from accounts) and, if subsection (1) has effect in relation to a deduction notice, it also has effect in relation to the hold notice to which the deduction notice relates (whenever the hold notice was given).]

NOTES

This section derived from the Companies Act 1985, s 523.

Sub-s (3): added by the Finance (No 2) Act 2015, s 51, Sch 8, Pt 2, paras 26, 28.

Default proceedings: see the note to s 126 at **[1.127]**.

Commencement of winding up

[1.130]

129 Commencement of winding up by the court

(1) If, before the presentation of a petition for the winding up of a company by the court, a resolution has been passed by the company for voluntary winding up, the winding up of the company is deemed to have commenced at the time of the passing of the resolution; and unless the court, on proof of fraud or mistake, directs otherwise, all proceedings taken in the voluntary winding up are deemed to have been validly taken.

[(1A) Where the court makes a winding-up order by virtue of paragraph 13(1)(e) of Schedule B1, the winding up is deemed to commence on the making of the order.]

(2) In any other case, the winding up of a company by the court is deemed to commence at the time of the presentation of the petition for winding up.

NOTES

This section derived from the Companies Act 1985, s 524.

Sub-s (1A): inserted by the Enterprise Act 2002, s 248(3), Sch 17, paras 9, 16, subject to savings and transitional provisions (i) in a case where a petition for an administration order has been presented before 15 September 2003 (see the Enterprise Act 2002 (Commencement No 4 and Transitional Provisions and Savings) Order 2003, SI 2003/2093, art 3 at **[2.26]**), and (ii) in relation to special administration regimes (see s 249 of the 2002 Act at **[2.10]**).

See further: the Energy Act 2004, s 159(1), Sch 20, Pt 4, para 45 at **[7.854]**, **[7.872]** provides that the reference to Sch B1, para 13(1)(e) to this Act (in sub-s (1A) above) includes a reference to the Energy Act 2004, s 157(1)(e).

[1.131]

130 Consequences of winding-up order

(1) On the making of a winding-up order, a copy of the order must forthwith be forwarded by the company (or otherwise as may be prescribed) to the registrar of companies, who shall enter it in his records relating to the company.

(2) When a winding-up order has been made or a provisional liquidator has been appointed, no action or proceeding shall be proceeded with or commenced against the company or its property, except by leave of the court and subject to such terms as the court may impose.

(3) When an order has been made for winding up a company [registered but not formed under the Companies Act 2006], no action or proceeding shall be commenced or proceeded with against the company or its property or any contributory of the company, in respect of any debt of the company, except by leave of the court, and subject to such terms as the court may impose.

[(3A) In subsections (2) and (3), the reference to an action or proceeding includes action in respect of the company under Part 1 of Schedule 8 to the Finance (No 2) Act 2015 (enforcement by deduction from accounts).]

(4) An order for winding up a company operates in favour of all the creditors and of all contributories of the company as if made on the joint petition of a creditor and of a contributory.

NOTES

This section derived from the Companies Act 1985, s 525, and the Insolvency Act 1985, Sch 6, para 29.

Sub-s (3): words in square brackets substituted for original words "registered under section 680 of the Companies Act" by the Companies Act 2006 (Consequential Amendments, Transitional Provisions and Savings) Order 2009, SI 2009/1941, art 2(1), Sch 1, para 75(1), (15), subject to transitional provisions and savings in art 8, Sch 1, para 84 at **[2.70]**, **[2.73]**.

Sub-s (3A): inserted by the Finance (No 2) Act 2015, s 51, Sch 8, Pt 2, paras 26, 29.

Modification in relation to Scotland: see the Note at the beginning of this Act.

Default proceedings: see the note to s 126 at **[1.127]**.

Investigation procedures

[1.132]

131 Company's statement of affairs

(1) Where the court has made a winding-up order or appointed a provisional liquidator, the official receiver may require some or all of the persons mentioned in subsection (3) below to make out and submit to him a statement in the prescribed form as to the affairs of the company.

(2) The statement . . . shall show—

(a) particulars of the company's assets and liabilities;
(b) the names and addresses of the company's creditors;
(c) the securities held by them respectively;
(d) the dates when the securities were respectively given; and
(e) such further or other information as may be prescribed or as the official receiver may require.

[(2A) The statement shall be verified *by the persons required to submit it*—

(a) in the case of an appointment of a provisional liquidator or a winding up by the court in England and Wales, [be verified by the persons required to submit it] by a statement of truth; and
(b) in the case of an appointment of a provisional liquidator or a winding up by the court in Scotland, *by affidavit*.]

(3) The persons referred to in subsection (1) are—

(a) those who are or have been officers of the company;
(b) those who have taken part in the formation of the company at any time within one year before the relevant date;
(c) those who are in the company's employment, or have been in its employment within that year, and are in the official receiver's opinion capable of giving the information required;

(d) those who are or have been within that year officers of, or in the employment of, a company which is, or within that year was, an officer of the company.

(4) Where any persons are required under this section to submit a statement of affairs to the official receiver, they shall do so (subject to the next subsection) before the end of the period of 21 days beginning with the day after that on which the prescribed notice of the requirement is given to them by the official receiver.

(5) The official receiver, if he thinks fit, may—

(a) at any time release a person from an obligation imposed on him under subsection (1) or (2) above; or

(b) either when giving the notice mentioned in subsection (4) or subsequently, extend the period so mentioned;

and where the official receiver has refused to exercise a power conferred by this subsection, the court, if it thinks fit, may exercise it.

(6) In this section—

"employment" includes employment under a contract for services; and

"the relevant date" means—

(a) in a case where a provisional liquidator is appointed, the date of his appointment; and

(b) in a case where no such appointment is made, the date of the winding-up order.

(7) If a person without reasonable excuse fails to comply with any obligation imposed under this section, he is liable to a fine and, for continued contravention, to a daily default fine.

(8) In the application of this section to Scotland references to the official receiver are to the liquidator or, in a case where a provisional liquidator is appointed, the provisional liquidator.

NOTES

This section derived from the Insolvency Act 1985, s 66.

Sub-s (2): words omitted repealed by the Legislative Reform (Insolvency) (Miscellaneous Provisions) Order 2010, SI 2010/18, arts 2, 5(4)(a).

Sub-s (2A): inserted by SI 2010/18, arts 2, 5(4)(b); first words in italics repealed, words in square brackets in para (a) inserted, and for the words in italics in para (b) there are substituted the words "contain a statutory declaration by the persons required to submit it", by the Public Services Reform (Insolvency) (Scotland) Order 2016, SSI 2016/141, art 10, as from a day to be appointed (being the day that the Small Business, Enterprise and Employment Act 2015, s 122(2) comes into force for all remaining purposes in Scotland); for savings, see the note to s 66 at **[1.52]**.

Unfitness of directors: see the note to s 47 at **[1.33]**.

[1.133]

132 Investigation by official receiver

(1) Where a winding-up order is made by the court in England and Wales, it is the duty of the official receiver to investigate—

(a) if the company has failed, the causes of the failure; and

(b) generally, the promotion, formation, business, dealings and affairs of the company,

and to make such report (if any) to the court as he thinks fit.

(2) The report is, in any proceedings, prima facie evidence of the facts stated in it.

NOTES

This section derived from the Insolvency Act 1985, s 67.

[1.134]

133 Public examination of officers

(1) Where a company is being wound up by the court, the official receiver or, in Scotland, the liquidator may at any time before the dissolution of the company apply to the court for the public examination of any person who—

(a) is or has been an officer of the company; or

(b) has acted as liquidator or administrator of the company or as receiver or manager or, in Scotland, receiver of its property; or

(c) not being a person falling within paragraph (a) or (b), is or has been concerned, or has taken part, in the promotion, formation or management of the company.

(2) Unless the court otherwise orders, the official receiver or, in Scotland, the liquidator shall make an application under subsection (1) if he is requested in accordance with the rules to do so by—

(a) one-half, in value, of the company's creditors; or

(b) three-quarters, in value, of the company's contributories.

(3) On an application under subsection (1), the court shall direct that a public examination of the person to whom the application relates shall be held on a day appointed by the court; and that person shall attend on that day and be publicly examined as to the promotion, formation or management of the company or as to the conduct of its business and affairs, or his conduct or dealings in relation to the company.

(4) The following may take part in the public examination of a person under this section and may question that person concerning the matters mentioned in subsection (3), namely—

(a) the official receiver;

(b) the liquidator of the company;

(c) any person who has been appointed as special manager of the company's property or business;

(d) any creditor of the company who has tendered a proof or, in Scotland, submitted a claim in the winding up;

(e) any contributory of the company.

NOTES

This section derived from the Insolvency Act 1985, s 68(1)–(4).

[1.135]

134 Enforcement of s 133

(1) If a person without reasonable excuse fails at any time to attend his public examination under section 133, he is guilty of a contempt of court and liable to be punished accordingly.

(2) In a case where a person without reasonable excuse fails at any time to attend his examination under section 133 or there are reasonable grounds for believing that a person has absconded, or is about to abscond, with a view to avoiding or delaying his examination under that section, the court may cause a warrant to be issued to a constable or prescribed officer of the court—

(a) for the arrest of that person; and

(b) for the seizure of any books, papers, records, money or goods in that person's possession.

(3) In such a case the court may authorise the person arrested under the warrant to be kept in custody, and anything seized under such a warrant to be held, in accordance with the rules, until such time as the court may order.

NOTES

This section derived from the Insolvency Act 1985, s 68(5), (6).

Appointment of liquidator

[1.136]

135 Appointment and powers of provisional liquidator

(1) Subject to the provisions of this section, the court may, at any time after the presentation of a winding-up petition, appoint a liquidator provisionally.

(2) In England and Wales, the appointment of a provisional liquidator may be made at any time before the making of a winding-up order; and either the official receiver or any other fit person may be appointed.

(3) In Scotland, such an appointment may be made at any time before the first appointment of liquidators.

(4) The provisional liquidator shall carry out such functions as the court may confer on him.

(5) When a liquidator is provisionally appointed by the court, his powers may be limited by the order appointing him.

NOTES

This section derived from the Companies Act 1985, s 532, and the Insolvency Act 1985, s 69(3).

Modification: in relation to the notification to the Financial Conduct Authority and (if the institution is a PRA-authorised person) the Prudential Regulation Authority of the appointment of a provisional liquidator under sub-s (1) of this section on or after 5 May 2004, see the Credit Institutions (Reorganisation and Winding up) Regulations 2004, SI 2004/1045, reg 9(1)(c), (5), (5A) at **[3.221]**.

[1.137]

136 Functions of official receiver in relation to office of liquidator

(1) The following provisions of this section have effect, subject to section 140 below, on a winding-up order being made by the court in England and Wales.

(2) The official receiver, by virtue of his office, becomes the liquidator of the company and continues in office until another person becomes liquidator under the provisions of this Part.

(3) The official receiver is, by virtue of his office, the liquidator during any vacancy.

(4) At any time when he is the liquidator of the company, the official receiver may [in accordance with the rules seek nominations from] the company's creditors and contributories for the purpose of choosing a person to be liquidator of the company in place of the official receiver.

(5) It is the duty of the official receiver—

(a) as soon as practicable in the period of 12 weeks beginning with the day on which the winding-up order was made, to decide whether to exercise his power under subsection (4) *to summon meetings*, and

(b) if in pursuance of paragraph (a) he decides not to exercise that power, to give notice of his decision, before the end of that period, to the court and to the company's creditors and contributories, and

(c) (whether or not he has decided to exercise that power) to exercise his power *to summon meetings* under subsection (4) if he is at any time requested, in accordance with the rules, to do so by one-quarter, in value, of the company's creditors;

and accordingly, where the duty imposed by paragraph (c) arises before the official receiver has performed a duty imposed by paragraph (a) or (b), he is not required to perform the latter duty.

(6) A notice given under subsection (5)(b) to the company's creditors shall contain an explanation of the creditors' power under subsection (5)(c) to require the official receiver to [seek nominations from] the company's creditors and contributories.

NOTES

This section derived from the Insolvency Act 1985, s 70(1)–(3), (4)(a), (5), (6).

Words in square brackets in sub-ss (4), (6) substituted for original words "summon separate meetings of" and "summon meetings of" respectively, and words in italics in sub-s (5) repealed, by the Small Business, Enterprise and Employment Act

2015, s 126, Sch 9, Pt 1, paras 1, 31, as from 6 April 2017 (in relation to England and Wales and subject to transitional and savings provisions as noted to s 246ZE at **[1.256]**), and as from a day to be appointed (in relation to Scotland).

[1.138]

137 Appointment by Secretary of State

(1) In a winding up by the court in England and Wales the official receiver may, at any time when he is the liquidator of the company, apply to the Secretary of State for the appointment of a person as liquidator in his place.

(2) If [nominations are sought from the company's creditors and contributories] in pursuance of a decision under section 136(5)(a), but no person is chosen to be liquidator as a result *of those meetings*, it is the duty of the official receiver to decide whether to refer the need for an appointment to the Secretary of State.

(3) On an application under subsection (1), or a reference made in pursuance of a decision under subsection (2), the Secretary of State shall either make an appointment or decline to make one.

(4) Where a liquidator has been appointed by the Secretary of State under subsection (3), the liquidator shall give notice of his appointment to the company's creditors or, if the court so allows, shall advertise his appointment in accordance with the directions of the court.

(5) In that notice or advertisement the liquidator [must explain the procedure for establishing a liquidation committee under section 141].

NOTES

This section derived from the Insolvency Act 1985, s 70(4)(b), (7)–(9).

Words in square brackets in sub-s (2) substituted for original words "meetings are held", words in italics in sub-s (2) repealed and words in square brackets in sub-s (5) substituted for the following original words, by the Small Business, Enterprise and Employment Act 2015, s 126, Sch 9, Pt 1, paras 1, 32, as from 6 April 2017 (in relation to England and Wales and subject to transitional and savings provisions as noted to s 246ZE at **[1.256]**), and as from a day to be appointed (in relation to Scotland)—

"shall—

(a) state whether he proposes to summon a general meeting of the company's creditors under section 141 below for the purpose of determining (together with any meeting of contributories) whether a liquidation committee should be established under that section, and

(b) if he does not propose to summon such a meeting, set out the power of the company's creditors under that section to require him to summon one.".

[1.139]

138 Appointment of liquidator in Scotland

(1) Where a winding-up order is made by the court in Scotland, a liquidator shall be appointed by the court at the time when the order is made.

(2) The liquidator so appointed (here referred to as "the interim liquidator") continues in office until another person becomes liquidator in his place under this section or the next.

(3) The interim liquidator shall (subject to the next subsection) as soon as practicable in the period of 28 days beginning with the day on which the winding-up order was made or such longer period as the court may allow, *summon separate meetings of* the company's creditors and contributories for the purpose of choosing a person (who may be the person who is the interim liquidator) to be liquidator of the company in place of the interim liquidator.

(4) If it appears to the interim liquidator, in any case where a company is being wound up on grounds including its inability to pay its debts, that it would be inappropriate to *summon under subsection (3) a meeting of the company's contributories, he may summon only a meeting of* the company's creditors for the purpose mentioned in that subsection.

(5) If *one or more meetings are held* in pursuance of this section but no person is appointed or nominated *by the meeting or meetings*, the interim liquidator shall make a report to the court which shall appoint either the interim liquidator or some other person to be liquidator of the company.

(6) A person who becomes liquidator of the company in place of the interim liquidator shall, unless he is appointed by the court, forthwith notify the court of that fact.

NOTES

This section derived from the Companies Act 1985, s 535, and the Insolvency Act 1985, s 71, Sch 6, para 30.

For the words in italics in sub-s (3) there are substituted the words "in accordance with the rules seek nominations from", for the words in italics in sub-s (4) there are substituted the words "seek a nomination from the company's contributories under subsection (3), he may seek a nomination only from", for the first words in italics in sub-s (5) there are substituted the words "a nomination is sought from the company's creditors, or nominations are sought from the company's creditors and contributories,", and for the second words in italics in that subsection there are substituted the words "as a result", by the Small Business, Enterprise and Employment Act 2015, s 126, Sch 9, Pt 1, paras 1, 33, as from day to be appointed.

[1.140]

139 Choice of liquidator [by] creditors and contributories

(1) This section applies where a company is being wound up by the court and [nominations are sought from the company's creditors and contributories] for the purpose of choosing a person to be liquidator of the company.

(2) The creditors and the contributories [may in accordance with the rules] nominate a person to be liquidator.

(3) The liquidator shall be the person nominated by the creditors or, where no person has been so nominated, the person (if any) nominated by the contributories.

(4) In the case of different persons being nominated, any contributory or creditor may, within 7 days after the date on which the nomination was made by the creditors, apply to the court for an order either—

(a) appointing the person nominated as liquidator by the contributories to be a liquidator instead of, or jointly with, the person nominated by the creditors; or

(b) appointing some other person to be liquidator instead of the person nominated by the creditors.

NOTES

This section derived from the Insolvency Act 1985, s 72.

Word in square brackets in section heading substituted for original words "at meetings of", words in square brackets in sub-s (1) substituted for original words "separate meetings of the company's creditors and contributories are summoned", and words in square brackets in sub-s (2) substituted for original words "at their respective meetings may", by the Small Business, Enterprise and Employment Act 2015, s 126, Sch 9, Pt 1, paras 1, 34, as from 6 April 2017 (in relation to England and Wales and subject to transitional and savings provisions as noted to s 246ZE at **[1.256]**), and as from a day to be appointed (in relation to Scotland).

[1.141]

140 Appointment by the court following administration or voluntary arrangement

[(1) Where a winding-up order is made immediately upon the appointment of an administrator ceasing to have effect, the court may appoint as liquidator of the company the person whose appointment as administrator has ceased to have effect.]

(2) Where a winding-up order is made at a time when there is a supervisor of a voluntary arrangement approved in relation to the company under Part I, the court may appoint as liquidator of the company the person who is the supervisor at the time when the winding-up order is made.

(3) Where the court makes an appointment under this section, the official receiver does not become the liquidator as otherwise provided by section 136(2), and [section 136(5)(a) and (b) does not apply].

NOTES

This section derived from the Insolvency Act 1985, s 73.

Sub-s (1): substituted by the Enterprise Act 2002, s 248(3), Sch 17, paras 9, 17, subject to savings and transitional provisions (i) in a case where a petition for an administration order has been presented before 15 September 2003 (see the Enterprise Act 2002 (Commencement No 4 and Transitional Provisions and Savings) Order 2003, SI 2003/2093, art 3 at **[2.26]**), and (ii) in relation to special administration regimes (see s 249 of the 2002 Act at **[2.10]**); the original sub-s (1) read as follows:

"(1) Where a winding-up order is made immediately upon the discharge of an administration order, the court may appoint as liquidator of the company the person who has ceased on the discharge of the administration order to be the administrator of the company.".

Sub-s (3): words in square brackets substituted for original words "he has no duty under section 136(5)(a) or (b) in respect of the summoning of creditors' or contributories' meetings", by the Small Business, Enterprise and Employment Act 2015, s 126, Sch 9, Pt 1, paras 1, 35, as from 6 April 2017 (in relation to England and Wales and subject to transitional and savings provisions as noted to s 246ZE at **[1.256]**), and as from a day to be appointed (in relation to Scotland).

Liquidation committees

[1.142]

141 Liquidation committee (England and Wales)

[(1) This section applies where a winding up order has been made by the court in England and Wales.

(2) If both the company's creditors and the company's contributories decide that a liquidation committee should be established, a liquidation committee is to be established in accordance with the rules.

(3) If only the company's creditors, or only the company's contributories, decide that a liquidation committee should be established, a liquidation committee is to be established in accordance with the rules unless the court orders otherwise.

(3A) A "liquidation committee" is a committee having such functions as are conferred on it by or under this Act.

(3B) The liquidator must seek a decision from the company's creditors and contributories as to whether a liquidation committee should be established if requested, in accordance with the rules, to do so by one-tenth in value of the company's creditors.

(3C) Subsection (3B) does not apply where the liquidator is the official receiver.]

(4) The liquidation committee is not to be able or required to carry out its functions at any time when the official receiver is liquidator; but at any such time its functions are vested in the Secretary of State except to the extent that the rules otherwise provide.

(5) Where there is for the time being no liquidation committee, and the liquidator is a person other than the official receiver, the functions of such a committee are vested in the Secretary of State except to the extent that the rules otherwise provide.

NOTES

This section derived from the Insolvency Act 1985, s 74.

Sub-ss (1)–(3C): substituted for original sub-ss (1)–(3), by the Small Business, Enterprise and Employment Act 2015, s 126, Sch 9, Pt 1, paras 1, 36, as from 6 April 2017 (in relation to England and Wales and subject to transitional and savings provisions as noted to s 246ZE at **[1.256]**). Sub-ss (1)–(3) originally read as follows—

"(1) Where a winding-up order has been made by the court in England and Wales and separate meetings of creditors and contributories have been summoned for the purpose of choosing a person to be liquidator, those meetings may establish a committee ("the liquidation committee") to exercise the functions conferred on it by or under this Act.

(2) The liquidator (not being the official receiver) may at any time, if he thinks fit, summon separate general meetings of the company's creditors and contributories for the purpose of determining whether such a committee should be established and, if it is so determined, of establishing it.

The liquidator (not being the official receiver) shall summon such a meeting if he is requested, in accordance with the rules, to do so by one-tenth, in value, of the company's creditors.

(3) Where meetings are summoned under this section, or for the purpose of choosing a person to be liquidator, and either the meeting of creditors or the meeting of contributories decides that a liquidation committee should be established, but the other meeting does not so decide or decides that a committee should not be established, the committee shall be established in accordance with the rules, unless the court otherwise orders.".

[1.143]

142 Liquidation committee (Scotland)

(1) Where a winding-up order has been made by the court in Scotland and separate meetings of creditors and contributories have been summoned for the purpose of choosing a person to be liquidator or, under section 138(4), only a meeting of creditors has been summoned for that purpose, those meetings or (as the case may be) that meeting may establish a committee ("the liquidation committee") to exercise the functions conferred on it by or under this Act.

(2) The liquidator may at any time, if he thinks fit, summon separate general meetings of the company's creditors and contributories for the purpose of determining whether such a committee should be established and, if it is so determined, of establishing it.

(3) The liquidator, if appointed by the court otherwise than under section 139(4)(a), is required to summon meetings under subsection (2) if he is requested, in accordance with the rules, to do so by one-tenth, in value, of the company's creditors.

[(3A) A "liquidation committee" is a committee having such functions as are conferred on it by or under this Act.]

(4) Where meetings are summoned under this section, or for the purpose of choosing a person to be liquidator, and either the meeting of creditors or the meeting of contributories decides that a liquidation committee should be established, but the other meeting does not so decide or decides that a committee should not be established, the committee shall be established in accordance with the rules, unless the court otherwise orders.

(5) Where in the case of any winding up there is for the time being no liquidation committee, the functions of such a committee are vested in the court except to the extent that the rules otherwise provide.

(6) In addition to the powers and duties conferred and imposed on it by this Act, a liquidation committee has such of the powers and duties of commissioners in a sequestration as may be conferred and imposed on such committees by the rules.

NOTES

This section derived from the Insolvency Act 1985, s 75.

Sub-ss (1)–(4): substituted by the Small Business, Enterprise and Employment Act 2015, s 126, Sch 9, Pt 1, paras 1, 37(1), (2), as from a day to be appointed, as follows—

"(1) This section applies where a winding up order has been made by the court in Scotland.

(2) If both the company's creditors and the company's contributories decide that a liquidation committee should be established, a liquidation committee is to be established in accordance with the rules.

(3) If only the company's creditors, or only the company's contributories, decide that a liquidation committee should be established, a liquidation committee is to be established in accordance with the rules unless the court orders otherwise.

(4) A liquidator appointed by the court other than under section 139(4)(a) must seek a decision from the company's creditors and contributories as to whether a liquidation committee should be established if requested, in accordance with the rules, to do so by one-tenth in value of the company's creditors.".

Sub-s (3A): inserted by the Public Services Reform (Corporate Insolvency and Bankruptcy) (Scotland) Order 2017, SSI 2017/209, art 4(a), as from 1 October 2017 (in so far as it enables the making of (i) rules under s 411 post, or (ii) any other subordinate legislation under this Act), and as from the day appointed for the coming into force, for all remaining purposes, of the Small Business, Enterprise and Employment Act 2015, s 122 in Scotland (otherwise).

Sub-s (6): for the words "in addition to the powers and duties conferred and imposed on it by this Act, a liquidation committee has" there are substituted the words "A "liquidation committee" is a committee having the powers and duties conferred and imposed on it by this Act, and" by the Small Business, Enterprise and Employment Act 2015, s 126, Sch 9, Pt 1, paras 1, 37(1), (3), as from a day to be appointed; repealed by SSI 2017/209, art 4(b), as from the day appointed for the coming into force, for all remaining purposes, of the Small Business, Enterprise and Employment Act 2015, s 122 in Scotland.

The liquidator's functions

[1.144]

143 General functions in winding up by the court

(1) The functions of the liquidator of a company which is being wound up by the court are to secure that the assets of the company are got in, realised and distributed to the company's creditors and, if there is a surplus, to the persons entitled to it.

(2) It is the duty of the liquidator of a company which is being wound up by the court in England and Wales, if he is not the official receiver—

(a) to furnish the official receiver with such information,

(b) to produce to the official receiver, and permit inspection by the official receiver of, such books, papers and other records, and

(c) to give the official receiver such other assistance,

as the official receiver may reasonably require for the purposes of carrying out his functions in relation to the winding up.

NOTES

This section derived from the Insolvency Act 1985, s 69(1), (2).

[1.145]

144 Custody of company's property

(1) When a winding-up order has been made, or where a provisional liquidator has been appointed, the liquidator or the provisional liquidator (as the case may be) shall take into his custody or under his control all the property and things in action to which the company is or appears to be entitled.

(2) In a winding up by the court in Scotland, if and so long as there is no liquidator, all the property of the company is deemed to be in the custody of the court.

NOTES

This section derived from the Companies Act 1985, s 537.

[1.146]

145 Vesting of company property in liquidator

(1) When a company is being wound up by the court, the court may on the application of the liquidator by order direct that all or any part of the property of whatsoever description belonging to the company or held by trustees on its behalf shall vest in the liquidator by his official name; and thereupon the property to which the order relates vests accordingly.

(2) The liquidator may, after giving such indemnity (if any) as the court may direct, bring or defend in his official name any action or other legal proceeding which relates to that property or which it is necessary to bring or defend for the purpose of effectually winding up the company and recovering its property.

NOTES

This section derived from the Companies Act 1985, s 538.

[1.147]

[146 Final account

(1) This section applies where a company is being wound up by the court and the liquidator is not the official receiver.

(2) If it appears to the liquidator that the winding up of the company is for practical purposes complete the liquidator must make up an account of the winding up, showing how it has been conducted and the company's property has been disposed of.

(3) The liquidator must—

(a) send a copy of the account to the company's creditors (other than opted-out creditors), and

(b) give the company's creditors (other than opted-out creditors) a notice explaining the effect of section 174(4)(d) and how they may object to the liquidator's release.

(4) The liquidator must during the relevant period send to the court and the registrar of companies—

(a) a copy of the account, and

(b) a statement of whether any of the company's creditors objected to the liquidator's release.

(5) The relevant period is the period of 7 days beginning with the day after the last day of the period prescribed by the rules as the period within which the creditors may object to the liquidator's release.

[(6) Subsection (7) applies where, immediately before the liquidator sends a copy of the account to the registrar under subsection (4) (or, where the liquidator sends a copy of the account to the court and the registrar on different days, immediately before the liquidator sends the first of those copies) there are EU insolvency proceedings open in respect of the company in one or more other member States.

(7) The liquidator must send to the court and the registrar, with the copy of the account, a statement—

(a) identifying those proceedings,

(b) identifying the member State liquidator appointed in each of those proceedings,

(c) indicating, in relation to each of those member State liquidators, whether that member State liquidator consents to the company being dissolved.]]

NOTES

Commencement: see note below.

Substituted by the Small Business, Enterprise and Employment Act 2015, s 126, Sch 9, Pt 1, paras 1, 38, as from 6 April 2017 (in relation to England and Wales and subject to transitional and savings provisions as noted to s 246ZE at **[1.256]**), and as from a day to be appointed (in relation to Scotland). This section previously read as follows—

"146 Duty to summon final meeting

(1) Subject to the next subsection, if it appears to the liquidator of a company which is being wound by the court that the winding up of the company is for practical purposes complete and the liquidator is not the official receiver, the liquidator shall summon a final general meeting of the company's creditors which—

(a) shall receive the liquidator's report of the winding up, and

(b) shall determine whether the liquidator should have his release under section 174 in Chapter VII of this Part.

(2) The liquidator may, if he thinks fit, give the notice summoning the final general meeting at the same time as giving notice of any final distribution of the company's property but, if summoned for an earlier date, that meeting shall be adjourned (and, if necessary, further adjourned) until a date on which the liquidator is able to report to the meeting that the winding up of the company is for practical purposes complete.

(3) In the carrying out of his functions in the winding up it is the duty of the liquidator to retain sufficient sums from the company's property to cover the expenses of summoning and holding the meeting required by this section.".

Sub-ss (6), (7): added by the Insolvency Amendment (EU 2015/848) Regulations 2017, SI 2017/702, regs 2, 3, Schedule, Pt 1, paras 1, 7, except in relation to proceedings opened before 26 June 2017 and subject to savings in reg 4 thereof at **[2.103]**.

[1.148]

[146A Official receiver's duty to send statement to registrar about other proceedings

(1) This section applies where—

(a) the official receiver sends to the registrar of companies a notice that the winding up of a company by the court is complete, and

(b) immediately before the official receiver sends the notice there are EU insolvency proceedings open in respect of the company in one or more other member States.

(2) The official receiver must send to the registrar, with the notice, a statement—

(a) identifying those proceedings,

(b) identifying the member State liquidator appointed in each of those proceedings, and

(c) indicating, in relation to each of those member State liquidators, whether that member State liquidator consents to the company being dissolved.]

NOTES

Commencement: see note below.

Inserted by the Insolvency Amendment (EU 2015/848) Regulations 2017, SI 2017/702, regs 2, 3, Schedule, Pt 1, paras 1, 8, except in relation to proceedings opened before 26 June 2017 and subject to savings in reg 4 thereof at **[2.103]**.

General powers of court

[1.149]

147 Power to stay or sist winding up

(1) The court may at any time after an order for winding up, on the application either of the liquidator or the official receiver or any creditor or contributory, and on proof to the satisfaction of the court that all proceedings in the winding up ought to be stayed or sisted, make an order staying or sisting the proceedings, either altogether or for a limited time, on such terms and conditions as the court thinks fit.

(2) The court may, before making an order, require the official receiver to furnish to it a report with respect to any facts or matters which are in his opinion relevant to the application.

(3) A copy of every order made under this section shall forthwith be forwarded by the company, or otherwise as may be prescribed, to the registrar of companies, who shall enter it in his records relating to the company.

NOTES

This section derived from the Companies Act 1985, s 549.

Modification in relation to Scotland: see the Note at the beginning of this Act.

Terms and conditions: for the conditions which a court may impose in an order made under this section in the case of the winding up of a building society, see the Building Societies Act 1986, s 90, Sch 15, Pt II, para 24 at **[7.454]**, **[7.465]**.

[1.150]

148 Settlement of list of contributories and application of assets

(1) As soon as may be after making a winding-up order, the court shall settle a list of contributories, with power to rectify the register of members in all cases where rectification is required . . . , and shall cause the company's assets to be collected, and applied in discharge of its liabilities.

(2) If it appears to the court that it will not be necessary to make calls on or adjust the rights of contributories, the court may dispense with the settlement of a list of contributories.

(3) In settling the list, the court shall distinguish between persons who are contributories in their own right and persons who are contributories as being representatives of or liable for the debts of others.

NOTES

This section derived from the Companies Act 1985, s 550.

Sub-s (1): words "in pursuance of the Companies Act or this Act" (omitted) repealed by the Companies Act 2006 (Consequential Amendments, Transitional Provisions and Savings) Order 2009, SI 2009/1941, art 2(1), Sch 1, para 75(1), (16), subject to transitional provisions and savings in art 8, Sch 1, para 84 at **[2.70]**, **[2.73]**.

[1.151]

149 Debts due from contributory to company

(1) The court may, at any time after making a winding-up order, make an order on any contributory for the time being on the list of contributories to pay, in manner directed by the order, any money due from him (or from the estate of the person who he represents) to the company, exclusive of any money payable by him or the estate by virtue of any call . . .

(2) The court in making such an order may—

(a) in the case of an unlimited company, allow to the contributory by way of set-off any money due to him or the estate which he represents from the company on any independent dealing or contract with the company, but not any money due to him as a member of the company in respect of any dividend or profit, and

(b) in the case of a limited company, make to any director or manager whose liability is unlimited or to his estate the like allowance.

(3) In the case of any company, whether limited or unlimited, when all the creditors are paid in full (together with interest at the official rate), any money due on any account whatever to a contributory from the company may be allowed to him by way of set-off against any subsequent call.

NOTES

This section derived from the Companies Act 1985, s 552, and the Insolvency Act 1985, Sch 6, para 32.

Sub-s (1): words "in pursuance of the Companies Act or this Act" (omitted) repealed by the Companies Act 2006 (Consequential Amendments, Transitional Provisions and Savings) Order 2009, SI 2009/1941, art 2(1), Sch 1, para 75(1), (16), subject to transitional provisions and savings in art 8, Sch 1, para 84 at **[2.70]**, **[2.73]**.

[1.152]

150 Power to make calls

(1) The court may, at any time after making a winding-up order, and either before or after it has ascertained the sufficiency of the company's assets, make calls on all or any of the contributories for the time being settled on the list of the contributories to the extent of their liability, for payment of any money which the court considers necessary to satisfy the company's debts and liabilities, and the expenses of winding up, and for the adjustment of the rights of the contributories among themselves, and make an order for payment of any calls so made.

(2) In making a call the court may take into consideration the probability that some of the contributories may partly or wholly fail to pay it.

NOTES

This section derived from the Companies Act 1985, s 553.

151 (*Repealed by the Deregulation Act 2015, s 19, Sch 6, Pt 3, paras 8, 9.*)

[1.153]

152 Order on contributory to be conclusive evidence

(1) An order made by the court on a contributory is conclusive evidence that the money (if any) thereby appearing to be due or ordered to be paid is due, but subject to any right of appeal.

(2) All other pertinent matters stated in the order are to be taken as truly stated as against all persons and in all proceedings except proceedings in Scotland against the heritable estate of a deceased contributory; and in that case the order is only prima facie evidence for the purpose of charging his heritable estate, unless his heirs or legatees of heritage were on the list of contributories at the time of the order being made.

NOTES

This section derived from the Companies Act 1985, s 555.

[1.154]

153 Power to exclude creditors not proving in time

The court may fix a time or times within which creditors are to prove their debts or claims or to be excluded from the benefit of any distribution made before those debts are proved.

NOTES

This section derived from the Companies Act 1985, s 557.

[1.155]

154 Adjustment of rights of contributories

The court shall adjust the rights of the contributories among themselves and distribute any surplus among the persons entitled to it.

NOTES

This section derived from the Companies Act 1985, s 558.

[1.156]

155 Inspection of books by creditors, etc

(1) The court may, at any time after making a winding-up order, make such order for inspection of the company's books and papers by creditors and contributories as the court thinks just; and any books and papers in the company's possession may be inspected by creditors and contributories accordingly, but not further or otherwise.

(2) Nothing in this section excludes or restricts any statutory rights of a government department or person acting under the authority of a government department.

[(3) For the purposes of subsection (2) above, references to a government department shall be construed as including references to any part of the Scottish Administration.]

NOTES

This section derived from the Companies Act 1985, s 559.

Sub-s (3): added by the Scotland Act 1998 (Consequential Modifications) (No 2) Order 1999, SI 1999/1820, art 4, Sch 2, Pt I, para 85.

Disapplication in relation to trust schemes: as to the disapplication of this section in relation to a trust scheme to which the Pensions Act 1995, s 22 applies, see s 26(1) of that Act at **[17.119]**.

[1.157]
156 Payment of expenses of winding up
The court may, in the event of the assets being insufficient to satisfy the liabilities, make an order as to the payment out of the assets of the expenses incurred in the winding up in such order of priority as the court thinks just.

NOTES
This section derived from the Companies Act 1985, s 560.

[1.158]
157 Attendance at company meetings (Scotland)
In the winding up by the court of a company registered in Scotland, the court has power to require the attendance of any officer of the company at any meeting of creditors or of contributories, or of a liquidation committee, for the purpose of giving information as to the trade, dealings, affairs or property of the company.

NOTES
This section derived from the Companies Act 1985, s 562, and the Insolvency Act 1985, Sch 6, para 33.

[1.159]
158 Power to arrest absconding contributory
The court, at any time either before or after making a winding-up order, on proof of probable cause for believing that a contributory is about to quit the United Kingdom or otherwise to abscond or to remove or conceal any of his property for the purpose of evading payment of calls, may cause the contributory to be arrested and his books and papers and moveable personal property to be seized and him and them to be kept safely until such time as the court may order.

NOTES
This section derived from the Companies Act 1985, s 565.

[1.160]
159 Powers of court to be cumulative
Powers conferred [on the court by this Act] are in addition to, and not in restriction of, any existing powers of instituting proceedings against a contributory or debtor of the company, or the estate of any contributory or debtor, for the recovery of any call or other sums.

NOTES
This section derived from the Companies Act 1985, s 566.
Words in square brackets substituted for original words (as amended by SI 2007/2194, art 10(1), (2), Sch 4, Pt 3, para 40, subject to savings in art 12 thereof) "by this Act and [the Companies Acts] on the court" by the Companies Act 2006 (Consequential Amendments, Transitional Provisions and Savings) Order 2009, SI 2009/1941, art 2(1), Sch 1, para 75(1), (17), subject to transitional provisions and savings in art 8, Sch 1, para 84 at **[2.70]**, **[2.73]**.

[1.161]
160 Delegation of powers to liquidator (England and Wales)
(1) Provision may be made by rules for enabling or requiring all or any of the powers and duties conferred and imposed on the court in England and Wales . . . in respect of the following matters—
[(a) the seeking of decisions on any matter from creditors and contributories,]
(b) the settling of lists of contributories and the rectifying of the register of members where required, and the collection and application of the assets,
(c) the payment, delivery, conveyance, surrender or transfer of money, property, books or papers to the liquidator,
(d) the making of calls,
(e) the fixing of a time within which debts and claims must be proved,
to be exercised or performed by the liquidator as an officer of the court, and subject to the court's control.
(2) But the liquidator shall not, without the special leave of the court, rectify the register of members, and shall not make any call without either that special leave or the sanction of the liquidation committee.

NOTES
This section derived from the Companies Act 1985, s 567, and the Insolvency Act 1985, Sch 6, para 34.
Sub-s (1): words "by the Companies Act and this Act" (omitted) repealed by the Companies Act 2006 (Consequential Amendments, Transitional Provisions and Savings) Order 2009, SI 2009/1941, art 2(1), Sch 1, para 75(1), (18), subject to transitional provisions and savings in art 8, Sch 1, para 84 at **[2.70]**, **[2.73]**; para (a) substituted by the Small Business, Enterprise and Employment Act 2015, s 126, Sch 9, Pt 1, paras 1, 39, as from 6 April 2017 (subject to transitional and savings provisions as noted to s 246ZE at **[1.256]**), and originally read as follows—
"(a) the holding and conducting of meetings to ascertain the wishes of creditors and contributories,".

Enforcement of, and appeal from, orders

[1.162]
161 Orders for calls on contributories (Scotland)
(1) In Scotland, where an order, interlocutor or decree has been made for winding up a company by the court, it is competent to the court, on production by the liquidators of a list certified by them of the names of the contributories liable in payment of any calls, and of the amount due by each contributory, and of

the date when that amount became due, to pronounce forthwith a decree against those contributories for payment of the sums so certified to be due, with interest from that date until payment (at 5 per cent. per annum) in the same way and to the same effect as if they had severally consented to registration for execution, on a charge of 6 days, of a legal obligation to pay those calls and interest.
(2) The decree may be extracted immediately, and no suspension of it is competent, except on caution or consignation, unless with special leave of the court.

NOTES

This section derived from the Companies Act 1985, s 569.

[1.163]
162 Appeals from orders in Scotland
(1) Subject to the provisions of this section and to rules of court, an appeal from any order or decision made or given in the winding up of a company by the court in Scotland under this Act lies in the same manner and subject to the same conditions as an appeal from an order or decision of the court in cases within its ordinary jurisdiction.
(2) In regard to orders or judgments pronounced by the judge acting as vacation judge . . . —
- (a) none of the orders specified in Part I of Schedule 3 to this Act are subject to review, reduction, suspension or stay of execution, and
- (b) every other order or judgment (except as mentioned below) may be submitted to review by the Inner House by reclaiming motion enrolled within 14 days from the date of the order or judgment.

(3) However, an order being one of those specified in Part II of that Schedule shall, from the date of the order and notwithstanding that it has been submitted to review as above, be carried out and receive effect until the Inner House have disposed of the matter.
(4) In regard to orders or judgments pronounced in Scotland by a Lord Ordinary before whom proceedings in a winding up are being taken, any such order or judgment may be submitted to review by the Inner House by reclaiming motion enrolled within 14 days from its date; but should it not be so submitted to review during session, the provisions of this section in regard to orders or judgments pronounced by the judge acting as vacation judge apply.
(5) Nothing in this section affects provisions of [the Companies Acts] or this Act in reference to decrees in Scotland for payment of calls in the winding up of companies, whether voluntary or by the court.

NOTES

This section derived from the Companies Act 1985, s 571.

Sub-s (2): words omitted repealed by the Court of Session Act 1988, s 52(2), Sch 2, Pt III.

Sub-s (5): words in square brackets substituted for original words "the Companies Act" by the Companies Act 2006 (Consequential Amendments, Transitional Provisions and Savings) Order 2009, SI 2009/1941, art 2(1), Sch 1, para 75(1), (19), subject to transitional provisions and savings in art 8, Sch 1, para 84 at **[2.70]**, **[2.73]**.

CHAPTER VII
LIQUIDATORS

Preliminary

[1.164]
163 Style and title of liquidators
The liquidator of a company shall be described—
- (a) where a person other than the official receiver is liquidator, by the style of "the liquidator" of the particular company, or
- (b) where the official receiver is liquidator, by the style of "the official receiver and liquidator" of the particular company;

and in neither case shall he be described by an individual name.

NOTES

This section derived from the Insolvency Act 1985, s 94.

[1.165]
164 Corrupt inducement affecting appointment
A person who gives, or agrees or offers to give, to any member or creditor of a company any valuable consideration with a view to securing his own appointment or nomination, or to securing or preventing the appointment or nomination of some person other than himself, as the company's liquidator is liable to a fine.

NOTES

This section derived from the Companies Act 1985, s 635.

Liquidator's powers and duties

[1.166]
165 Voluntary winding up
(1) This section has effect where a company is being wound up voluntarily, but subject to section 166 below in the case of a creditors' voluntary winding up.
[(2) The liquidator may exercise any of the powers specified in Parts 1 to 3 of Schedule 4.]
(4) The liquidator may—

(a) exercise the court's power of settling a list of contributories (which list is prima facie evidence of the liability of the persons named in it to be contributories),

(b) exercise the court's power of making calls,

(c) summon general meetings of the company for the purpose of obtaining its sanction by [special resolution] or for any other purpose he may think fit.

(5) The liquidator shall pay the company's debts and adjust the rights of the contributories among themselves.

(6) Where the liquidator in exercise of the powers conferred on him by this Act disposes of any property of the company to a person who is connected with the company (within the meaning of section 249 in Part VII), he shall, if there is for the time being a liquidation committee, give notice to the committee of that exercise of his powers.

NOTES

This section derived from the Companies Act 1985, ss 539(1)(d), (e), (f), 598, and the Insolvency Act 1985, s 84(1), Sch 6, para 41.

Sub-s (2): substituted (for original sub-ss (2), (3)) by the Small Business, Enterprise and Employment Act 2015, s 120(1), (2).

Sub-s (4): words in square brackets in para (c) substituted for original words "special or extraordinary resolution" by SI 2007/2194, art 10(1), (2), Sch 4, Pt 3, para 41(1)(b), (2), subject to savings in art 12 thereof and with effect in relation to written resolutions for which the circulation date (see the Companies Act 2006, s 290) is on or after 1 October 2007, and to resolutions passed at a meeting of which notice is given on or after that date.

[1.167]

166 Creditors' voluntary winding up

(1) This section applies where, in the case of a creditors' voluntary winding up, a liquidator has been nominated by the company.

[(1A) The exercise by the liquidator of the power specified in paragraph 6 of Schedule 4 to this Act (power to sell any of the company's property) shall not be challengeable on the ground of any prior inhibition.]

(2) The powers conferred on the liquidator by section 165 shall not be exercised, except with the sanction of the court, [before—

(a) the company's creditors under section 100 nominate a person to be liquidator, or

(b) the procedure by which the company's creditors were to have made such a nomination concludes without a nomination having been made.]

(3) Subsection (2) does not apply in relation to the power of the liquidator—

(a) to take into his custody or under his control all the property to which the company is or appears to be entitled;

(b) to dispose of perishable goods and other goods the value of which is likely to diminish if they are not immediately disposed of; and

(c) to do all such other things as may be necessary for the protection of the company's assets.

(4) The liquidator shall attend the creditors' meeting held under section 98 and shall report to the meeting on any exercise by him of his powers (whether or not under this section or under section 112 or 165).

(5) [If the directors fail to comply with—

(a) section 99(1), (2) or (2A), or

(b) section 100(1B),]

the liquidator shall, within 7 days of the relevant day, apply to the court for directions as to the manner in which that default is to be remedied.

(6) "The relevant day" means the day on which the liquidator was nominated by the company or the day on which he first became aware of the default, whichever is the later.

(7) If the liquidator without reasonable excuse fails to comply with this section, he is liable to a fine.

NOTES

This section derived from the Insolvency Act 1985, s 84.

Sub-s (1A): inserted by the Bankruptcy and Diligence etc (Scotland) Act 2007, s 155(1), (3), subject to transitional provisions and savings in the Bankruptcy and Diligence etc (Scotland) Act 2007 (Commencement No 4, Savings and Transitionals) Order 2009, SSI 2009/67, art 6 at **[2.62]**.

Sub-s (2): words in square brackets substituted for original words "during the period before the holding of the creditors' meeting under section 98 in Chapter IV" by the Small Business, Enterprise and Employment Act 2015, s 126, Sch 9, Pt 1, paras 1, 40(1), (2), as from 6 April 2017 (in relation to England and Wales and subject to transitional and savings provisions as noted to s 246ZE at **[1.256]**), and as from a day to be appointed (in relation to Scotland).

Sub-s (4): repealed by the Small Business, Enterprise and Employment Act 2015, s 126, Sch 9, Pt 1, paras 1, 40(1), (3), as from 6 April 2017 (in relation to England and Wales and subject to transitional and savings provisions as noted to s 246ZE at **[1.256]**), and as from a day to be appointed (in relation to Scotland).

Sub-s (5): words in square brackets substituted by the Small Business, Enterprise and Employment Act 2015, s 126, Sch 9, Pt 1, paras 1, 40(1), (4), as from 6 April 2017 (in relation to England and Wales and subject to transitional and savings provisions as noted to s 246ZE at **[1.256]**), and as from a day to be appointed (in relation to Scotland). The words previously read as follows (with figure in square brackets in para (a) inserted by SI 2009/864, arts 2, 3(3), 4 and words in square brackets in para (b) substituted by SI 2010/18, arts 2, 5(5)) —

"If default is made—

(a) by the company in complying with subsection (1)[, (1A)] or (2) of section 98, or

(b) by the directors in complying with subsection (1)[, (2) or (2A)] of section 99,".

[1.168]

167 Winding up by the court

[(1) Where a company is being wound up by the court, the liquidator may exercise any of the powers specified in Parts 1 to 3 of Schedule 4.]

(2) Where the liquidator (not being the official receiver), in exercise of the powers conferred on him by this Act—

(a) disposes of any property of the company to a person who is connected with the company (within the meaning of section 249 in Part VII), or

(b) employs a solicitor to assist him in the carrying out of his functions,

he shall, if there is for the time being a liquidation committee, give notice to the committee of that exercise of his powers.

(3) The exercise by the liquidator in a winding up by the court of the powers conferred by this section is subject to the control of the court, and any creditor or contributory may apply to the court with respect to any exercise or proposed exercise of any of those powers.

NOTES

This section derived from the Companies Act 1985, s 539(1), (2), (2A), (3), and the Insolvency Act 1985, Sch 6, para 31(2), (3).

Sub-s (1): substituted by the Small Business, Enterprise and Employment Act 2015, s 120(1), (3).

[1.169]

168 Supplementary powers (England and Wales)

(1) This section applies in the case of a company which is being wound up by the court in England and Wales.

[(2) The liquidator may seek a decision on any matter from the company's creditors or contributories; and must seek a decision on a matter—

(a) from the company's creditors, if requested to do so by one-tenth in value of the creditors;

(b) from the company's contributories, if requested to do so by one-tenth in value of the contributories.]

(3) The liquidator may apply to the court (in the prescribed manner) for directions in relation to any particular matter arising in the winding up.

(4) Subject to the provisions of this Act, the liquidator shall use his own discretion in the management of the assets and their distribution among the creditors.

(5) If any person is aggrieved by an act or decision of the liquidator, that person may apply to the court; and the court may confirm, reverse or modify the act or decision complained of, and make such order in the case as it thinks just.

[(5A) Where at any time after a winding-up petition has been presented to the court against any person (including an insolvent partnership or other body which may be wound up under Part V of the Act as an unregistered company), whether by virtue of the provisions of the Insolvent Partnerships Order 1994 or not, the attention of the court is drawn to the fact that the person in question is a member of an insolvent partnership, the court may make an order as to the future conduct of the insolvency proceedings and any such order may apply any provisions of that Order with any necessary modifications.

(5B) Any order or directions under subsection (5A) may be made or given on the application of the official receiver, any responsible insolvency practitioner, the trustee of the partnership or any other interested person and may include provisions as to the administration of the joint estate of the partnership, and in particular how it and the separate estate of any member are to be administered.

[(5C) Where the court makes an order for the winding up of an insolvent partnership under—

(a) section 72(1)(a) of the Financial Services Act 1986;

(b) section 92(1)(a) of the Banking Act 1987; or

(c) section 367(3)(a) of the Financial Services and Markets Act 2000,

the court may make an order as to the future conduct of the winding up proceedings, and any such order may apply any provisions of the Insolvent Partnerships Order 1994 with any necessary modifications.]]

NOTES

This section derived from the Companies Act 1985, s 540(3)–(6).

Sub-s (2): substituted by the Small Business, Enterprise and Employment Act 2015, s 126, Sch 9, Pt 1, paras 1, 41, as from 6 April 2017 (subject to transitional and savings provisions as noted to s 246ZE at **[1.256]**), and previously read as follows—

> "(2) The liquidator may summon general meetings of the creditors or contributories for the purpose of ascertaining their wishes; and it is his duty to summon meetings at such times as the creditors or contributories by resolution (either at the meeting appointing the liquidator or otherwise) may direct, or whenever requested in writing to do so by one-tenth in value of the creditors or contributories (as the case may be).".

Sub-ss (5A), (5B): added by the Insolvent Partnerships Order 1994, SI 1994/2421, art 14(1).

Sub-s (5C): added, together with sub-ss (5A), (5B), by the Insolvent Partnerships Order 1994, SI 1994/2421, art 14(1); repealed by the Financial Services and Markets Act 2000 (Consequential Amendments and Repeals) Order 2001, SI 2001/3649, art 306, but subsequently substituted by the Financial Services and Markets Act 2000 (Consequential Amendments) Order 2002, SI 2002/1555, art 15, which further provided that the repeal by SI 2001/3649 is to be treated as if it had not been made.

Financial Services Act 1986; Banking Act 1987: repealed by SI 2001/3649, art 3(1)(c), (d).

[1.170]

169 Supplementary powers (Scotland)

(1) . . .

(2) In a winding up by the court in Scotland, the liquidator has (subject to the rules) the same powers as a trustee on a bankrupt estate.

NOTES

This section derived from the Companies Act 1985, s 539(4), (5), and the Insolvency Act 1985, Sch 6, para 31(4).

Sub-s (1): repealed by the Small Business, Enterprise and Employment Act 2015, s 120(1), (4).

[1.171]

170 Enforcement of liquidator's duty to make returns, etc

(1) If a liquidator who has made any default—

(a) in filing, delivering or making any return, account or other document, or

(b) in giving any notice which he is by law required to file, deliver, make or give,

fails to make good the default within 14 days after the service on him of a notice requiring him to do so, the court has the following powers.

(2) On an application made by any creditor or contributory of the company, or by the registrar of companies, the court may make an order directing the liquidator to make good the default within such time as may be specified in the order.

(3) The court's order may provide that all costs of and incidental to the application shall be borne by the liquidator.

(4) Nothing in this section prejudices the operation of any enactment imposing penalties on a liquidator in respect of any such default as is mentioned above.

NOTES

This section derived from the Companies Act 1985, s 636.

Modification in relation to Scotland: see the Note at the beginning of this Act.

Order to make good the default: as to the making of disqualification orders against liquidators in certain cases where an order is made against them under this section, see the Company Directors Disqualification Act 1986, ss 3, 5 at **[4.4]**, **[4.6]**.

Removal; vacation of office

[1.172]

171 Removal, etc (voluntary winding up)

(1) This section applies with respect to the removal from office and vacation of office of the liquidator of a company which is being wound up voluntarily.

(2) Subject to the next subsection, the liquidator may be removed from office only by an order of the court or—

(a) in the case of a members' voluntary winding up, by a general meeting of the company summoned specially for that purpose, or

(b) in the case of a creditors' voluntary winding up, by a [decision of the company's creditors made by a qualifying decision procedure instigated] specially for that purpose in accordance with the rules.

[(3) Where the liquidator in a members' voluntary winding up was appointed by the court under section 108, a meeting such as is mentioned in subsection (2)(a) shall be summoned only if—

(a) the liquidator thinks fit,

(b) the court so directs, or

(c) the meeting is requested in accordance with the rules by members representing not less than one-half of the total voting rights of all the members having at the date of the request a right to vote at the meeting.

(3A) Where the liquidator in a creditors' voluntary winding up was appointed by the court under section 108, a qualifying decision procedure such as is mentioned in subsection (2)(b) is to be instigated only if—

(a) the liquidator thinks fit,

(b) the court so directs, or

(c) it is requested in accordance with the rules by not less than one-half in value of the company's creditors.]

(4) A liquidator shall vacate office if he ceases to be a person who is qualified to act as an insolvency practitioner in relation to the company.

(5) A liquidator may, in the prescribed circumstances, resign his office by giving notice of his resignation to the registrar of companies.

[(6) In the case of a members' voluntary winding up where the liquidator has produced an account of the winding up under section 94 (final account), the liquidator vacates office as soon as the liquidator has complied with section 94(3) (requirement to send final account to registrar).

(7) In the case of a creditors' voluntary winding up where the liquidator has produced an account of the winding up under section 106 (final account), the liquidator vacates office as soon as the liquidator has complied with section 106(3) (requirement to send final account etc to registrar).]

NOTES

This section derived from the Insolvency Act 1985, s 86.

Sub-s (2): words in square brackets substituted for original words "general meeting of the company's creditors summoned" by the Small Business, Enterprise and Employment Act 2015, s 126, Sch 9, Pt 1, paras 1, 42(1), (2), as from 6 April 2017 (in relation to England and Wales and subject to transitional and savings provisions as noted to s 246ZE at **[1.256]**), and as from a day to be appointed (in relation to Scotland).

Sub-ss (3), (3A): substituted for original sub-s (3) by the Small Business, Enterprise and Employment Act 2015, s 126, Sch 9, Pt 1, paras 1, 42(1), (3), as from 6 April 2017 (in relation to England and Wales and subject to transitional and savings provisions as noted to s 246ZE at **[1.256]**), and as from a day to be appointed (in relation to Scotland). Sub-s (3) originally read as follows—

"(3) Where the liquidator was appointed by the court under section 108 in Chapter V, a meeting such as is mentioned in subsection (2) above shall be summoned for the purpose of replacing him only if he thinks fit or the court so directs or the meeting is requested, in accordance with the rules—

(a) in the case of a members' voluntary winding up, by members representing not less than one-half of the total voting rights of all the members having at the date of the request a right to vote at the meeting, or

(b) in the case of a creditors' voluntary winding up, by not less than one-half, in value, of the company's creditors.".

Sub-ss (6), (7): substituted for original sub-s (6) by the Small Business, Enterprise and Employment Act 2015, s 126, Sch 9, Pt 1, paras 1, 42(1), (4), as from 6 April 2017 (in relation to England and Wales and subject to transitional and savings provisions as noted to s 246ZE at **[1.256]**), and as from a day to be appointed (in relation to Scotland). Sub-s (6) originally read as follows—

"(6) Where—

(a) in the case of a members' voluntary winding up, a final meeting of the company has been held under section 94 in Chapter III, or

(b) in the case of a creditors' voluntary winding up, final meetings of the company and of the creditors have been held under section 106 in Chapter IV,

the liquidator whose report was considered at the meeting or meetings shall vacate office as soon as he has complied with subsection (3) of that section and has given notice to the registrar of companies that the meeting or meetings have been held and of the decisions (if any) of the meeting or meetings.".

Modification in relation to Scotland: see the Note at the beginning of this Act.

[1.173]

172 Removal, etc (winding up by the court)

(1) This section applies with respect to the removal from office and vacation of office of the liquidator of a company which is being wound up by the court, or of a provisional liquidator.

(2) Subject as follows, the liquidator may be removed from office only by an order of the court or by a [decision of the company's creditors made by a qualifying decision procedure instigated] specially for that purpose in accordance with the rules; and a provisional liquidator may be removed from office only by an order of the court.

(3) Where—

(a) the official receiver is liquidator otherwise than in succession under section 136(3) to a person who held office as a result of a nomination by *a meeting of* the company's creditors or contributories, or

(b) the liquidator was appointed by the court otherwise than under section 139(4)(a) or 140(1), or was appointed by the Secretary of State,

[a qualifying decision procedure such as is mentioned in subsection (2) shall be instigated only if the liquidator thinks fit, the court so directs, or it] is requested, in accordance with the rules, by not less than one-quarter, in value, of the creditors.

(4) If appointed by the Secretary of State, the liquidator may be removed from office by a direction of the Secretary of State.

(5) A liquidator or provisional liquidator, not being the official receiver, shall vacate office if he ceases to be a person who is qualified to act as an insolvency practitioner in relation to the company.

(6) A liquidator may, in the prescribed circumstances, resign his office by giving notice of his resignation to the court.

(7) Where an order is made under section 204 (early dissolution in Scotland) for the dissolution of the company, the liquidator shall vacate office when the dissolution of the company takes effect in accordance with that section.

[(8) Where the liquidator has produced an account of the winding up under section 146 (final account), the liquidator vacates office as soon as the liquidator has complied with section 146(4) (requirement to send account etc to registrar and to court).]

[(9) Subsection (10) applies where, immediately before a liquidator gives notice to the court and the registrar under subsection (8) (or, where the liquidator gives notice to the court and the registrar on different days, immediately before the liquidator gives the first of those notices), there are EU insolvency proceedings open in respect of the company in one or more other member States.

(10) The liquidator must send to the court and the registrar, with the notice, a statement—

(a) identifying those proceedings,

(b) identifying the member State liquidator appointed in each of those proceedings, and

(c) indicating, in relation to each of those member State liquidators, whether that member State liquidator consents to the company being dissolved.]

NOTES

This section derived from the Insolvency Act 1985, s 79.

Sub-s (2): words in square brackets substituted for original words "general meeting of the company's creditors summoned" by the Small Business, Enterprise and Employment Act 2015, s 126, Sch 9, Pt 1, paras 1, 43(1), (2), as from 6 April 2017 (in relation to England and Wales and subject to transitional and savings provisions as noted to s 246ZE at **[1.256]**), and as from a day to be appointed (in relation to Scotland).

Sub-s (3): words in italics repealed and words in square brackets substituted for original words "a general meeting of the company's creditors shall be summoned for the purpose of replacing him only if he thinks fit, or the court so directs, or the meeting" by the Small Business, Enterprise and Employment Act 2015, s 126, Sch 9, Pt 1, paras 1, 43(1), (3), as from 6 April 2017 (in relation to England and Wales and subject to transitional and savings provisions as noted to s 246ZE at **[1.256]**), and as from a day to be appointed (in relation to Scotland).

Sub-s (8): substituted by the Small Business, Enterprise and Employment Act 2015, s 126, Sch 9, Pt 1, paras 1, 43(1), (4), as from 6 April 2017 (in relation to England and Wales and subject to transitional and savings provisions as noted to s 246ZE at **[1.256]**), and as from a day to be appointed (in relation to Scotland). Sub-s (8) originally read as follows—

"(8) Where a final meeting has been held under section 146 (liquidator's report on completion of winding up), the liquidator whose report was considered at the meeting shall vacate office as soon as he has given notice to the court and the registrar of companies that the meeting has been held and of the decisions (if any) of the meeting.".

Sub-ss (9), (10): added, in relation to Scotland only, by the Insolvency Amendment (EU 2015/848) Regulations 2017, SI 2017/702, regs 2, 3, Schedule, Pt 4, paras 55, 57, except in relation to proceedings opened before 26 June 2017 and subject to savings in reg 4 thereof at **[2.103]**.

Modification in relation to Scotland: see the Note at the beginning of this Act.

Application to coal mining operations: see further the Coal Industry Act 1994, s 36 at **[17.112]**.

Release of liquidator

[1.174]

173 Release (voluntary winding up)

(1) This section applies with respect to the release of the liquidator of a company which is being wound up voluntarily.

(2) A person who has ceased to be a liquidator shall have his release with effect from the following time, that is to say—

[(a) in the following cases, the time at which notice is given to the registrar of companies in accordance with the rules that the person has ceased to hold office—
(i) the person has been removed from office by a general meeting of the company,
(ii) the person has been removed from office by a decision of the company's creditors and the company's creditors have not decided against his release,
(iii) the person has died;

(b) in the following cases, such time as the Secretary of State may, on the application of the person, determine—
(i) the person has been removed from office by a decision of the company's creditors and the company's creditors have decided against his release,
(ii) the person has been removed from office by the court,
(iii) the person has vacated office under section 171(4);]

(c) in the case of a person who has resigned, such time as may be prescribed;

(d) in the case of a person who has vacated office under subsection [(6)] of section 171, the time at which he vacated office;

[(e) in the case of a person who has vacated office under section 171(7)—
(i) if any of the company's creditors objected to the person's release before the end of the period for so objecting prescribed by the rules, such time as the Secretary of State may, on an application by that person, determine, and
(ii) otherwise, the time at which the person vacated office.]

[(2A) Where the person is removed from office by a decision of the company's creditors, any decision of the company's creditors as to whether the person should have his release must be made by a qualifying decision procedure.]

(3) In the application of subsection (2) to the winding up of a company registered in Scotland, the references to a determination by the Secretary of State as to the time from which a person who has ceased to be liquidator shall have his release are to be read as references to such a determination by the Accountant of Court.

(4) Where a liquidator has his release under subsection (2), he is, with effect from the time specified in that subsection, discharged from all liability both in respect of acts or omissions of his in the winding up and otherwise in relation to his conduct as liquidator.

But nothing in this section prevents the exercise, in relation to a person who has had his release under subsection (2), of the court's powers under section 212 of this Act (summary remedy against delinquent directors, liquidators, etc).

NOTES

This section derived from the Insolvency Act 1985, s 87.

Sub-s (2) is amended as follows:

Paras (a), (b), (e) substituted by the Small Business, Enterprise and Employment Act 2015, s 126, Sch 9, Pt 1, paras 1, 44(1), (2), (4), as from 6 April 2017 (in relation to England and Wales and subject to transitional and savings provisions as noted to s 246ZE at **[1.256]**), and as from a day to be appointed (in relation to Scotland). Paras (a), (b), (e) previously read as follows—

"(a) in the case of a person who has been removed from office by a general meeting of the company or by a general meeting of the company's creditors that has not resolved against his release or who has died, the time at which notice is given to the registrar of companies in accordance with the rules that that person has ceased to hold office;

(b) in the case of a person who has been removed from office by a general meeting of the company's creditors that has resolved against his release, or by the court, or who has vacated office under section 171(4) above, such time as the Secretary of State may, on the application of that person, determine;

(e) in the case of a person who has vacated office under subsection (6)(b) of that section—
(i) if the final meeting of the creditors referred to in that subsection has resolved against that person's release, such time as the Secretary of State may, on an application by that person, determine, and
(ii) if that meeting has not resolved against that person's release, the time at which he vacated office.".

In para (d), figure in square brackets substituted for original figure "(6)(a)" by the Small Business, Enterprise and Employment Act 2015, s 126, Sch 9, Pt 1, paras 1, 44(1), (3), as from 6 April 2017 (in relation to England and Wales and subject to transitional and savings provisions as noted to s 246ZE at **[1.256]**), and as from a day to be appointed (in relation to Scotland).

Sub-s (2A): inserted by the Small Business, Enterprise and Employment Act 2015, s 126, Sch 9, Pt 1, paras 1, 44(1), (5), as from 6 April 2017 (in relation to England and Wales and subject to transitional and savings provisions as noted to s 246ZE at **[1.256]**), and as from a day to be appointed (in relation to Scotland).

Modification in relation to Scotland: see the Note at the beginning of this Act.

[1.175]
174 Release (winding up by the court)

(1) This section applies with respect to the release of the liquidator of a company which is being wound up by the court, or of a provisional liquidator.

(2) Where the official receiver has ceased to be liquidator and a person becomes liquidator in his stead, the official receiver has his release with effect from the following time, that is to say—

(a) in a case where that person was nominated by [the company's] creditors or contributories, or was appointed by the Secretary of State, the time at which the official receiver gives notice to the court that he has been replaced;

(b) in a case where that person is appointed by the court, such time as the court may determine.

(3) If the official receiver while he is a liquidator gives notice to the Secretary of State that the winding up is for practical purposes complete, he has his release with effect from such time as the Secretary of State may determine.

(4) A person other than the official receiver who has ceased to be a liquidator has his release with effect from the following time, that is to say—

[(a) in the following cases, the time at which notice is given to the court in accordance with the rules that the person has ceased to hold office—

(i) the person has been removed from office by a decision of the company's creditors and the company's creditors have not decided against his release,

(ii) the person has died;

(b) in the following cases, such time as the Secretary of State may, on the application of the person, determine—

(i) the person has been removed from office by a decision of the company's creditors and the company's creditors have decided against his release;

(ii) the person has been removed from office by the court or the Secretary of State;

(iii) the person has vacated office under section 172(5) or (7);]

(c) in the case of a person who has resigned, such time as may be prescribed;

(d) in the case of a person who has vacated office under section 172(8)—

[(i) if any of the company's creditors objected to the person's release before the end of the period for so objecting prescribed by the rules, such time as the Secretary of State may, on an application by that person, determine, and

(ii) otherwise, the time at which the person vacated office.]

[(4ZA) Where the person is removed from office by a decision of the company's creditors, any decision of the company's creditors as to whether the person should have his release must be made by a qualifying decision procedure.]

[(4A) Where a winding-up order made by the court in England and Wales is rescinded, the person (whether the official receiver or another person) who is the liquidator of the company at the time the order is rescinded has his release with effect from such time as the court may determine.]

(5) A person who has ceased to hold office as a provisional liquidator has his release with effect from such time as the court may, on an application by him, determine.

(6) Where the official receiver or a liquidator or provisional liquidator has his release under this section, he is, with effect from the time specified in the preceding provisions of this section, discharged from all liability both in respect of acts or omissions of his in the winding up and otherwise in relation to his conduct as liquidator or provisional liquidator.

But nothing in this section prevents the exercise, in relation to a person who has had his release under this section, of the court's powers under section 212 (summary remedy against delinquent directors, liquidators, etc)

(7) In the application of this section to a case where the order for winding up has been made by the court in Scotland, the references to a determination by the Secretary of State as to the time from which a person who has ceased to be liquidator has his release are to such a determination by the Accountant of Court.

NOTES

This section derived from the Insolvency Act 1985, s 80.

Sub-s (2): words in square brackets substituted for original words "a general meeting of" by the Small Business, Enterprise and Employment Act 2015, s 126, Sch 9, Pt 1, paras 1, 45(1), (2), as from 6 April 2017 (in relation to England and Wales and subject to transitional and savings provisions as noted to s 246ZE at **[1.256]**), and as from a day to be appointed (in relation to Scotland).

Sub-s (4) is amended as follows:

Paras (a), (b) substituted by the Small Business, Enterprise and Employment Act 2015, s 126, Sch 9, Pt 1, paras 1, 45(1), (3), as from 6 April 2017 (in relation to England and Wales and subject to transitional and savings provisions as noted to s 246ZE at **[1.256]**), and as from a day to be appointed (in relation to Scotland). Paras (a), (b) originally read as follows—

"(a) in the case of a person who has been removed from office by a general meeting of creditors that has not resolved against his release or who has died, the time at which notice is given to the court in accordance with the rules that that person has ceased to hold office;

(b) in the case of a person who has been removed from office by a general meeting of creditors that has resolved against his release, or by the court or the Secretary of State, or who has vacated office under section 172(5) or (7), such time as the Secretary of State may, on an application by that person, determine;".

Para (d)(i), (ii) substituted by the Small Business, Enterprise and Employment Act 2015, s 126, Sch 9, Pt 1, paras 1, 45(1), (4), as from 6 April 2017 (in relation to England and Wales and subject to transitional and savings provisions as noted to s 246ZE at **[1.256]**), and as from a day to be appointed (in relation to Scotland). Para (d)(i), (ii) originally read as follows—

"(i) if the final meeting referred to in that subsection has resolved against that person's release, such time as the Secretary of State may, on an application by that person, determine, and

(ii) if that meeting has not so resolved, the time at which that person vacated office.".

Sub-s (4ZA): inserted by the Small Business, Enterprise and Employment Act 2015, s 126, Sch 9, Pt 1, paras 1, 45(1), (5),as from 6 April 2017 (in relation to England and Wales and subject to transitional and savings provisions as noted to s 246ZE at **[1.256]**), and as from a day to be appointed (in relation to Scotland).

Sub-s (4A): inserted by the Deregulation Act 2015, s 19, Sch 6, Pt 3, paras 8, 10.

CHAPTER VIII
PROVISIONS OF GENERAL APPLICATION IN WINDING UP

Preferential debts

[1.176]

175 Preferential debts (general provision)

(1) In a winding up the company's preferential debts *(within the meaning given by section 386 in Part XII)* shall be paid in priority to all other debts.

[(1A) Ordinary preferential debts rank equally among themselves after the expenses of the winding up and shall be paid in full, unless the assets are insufficient to meet them, in which case they abate in equal proportions.

(1B) Secondary preferential debts rank equally among themselves after the ordinary preferential debts and shall be paid in full, unless the assets are insufficient to meet them, in which case they abate in equal proportions.]

(2) Preferential debts—

(a) rank equally among themselves after the expenses of the winding up and shall be paid in full, unless the assets are insufficient to meet them, in which case they abate in equal proportions; and

(b) so far as the assets of the company available for payment of general creditors are insufficient to meet them, have priority over the claims of holders of debentures secured by, or holders of, any floating charge created by the company, and shall be paid accordingly out of any property comprised in or subject to that charge.

[(3) In this section "preferential debts", "ordinary preferential debts" and "secondary preferential debts" each has the meaning given in section 386 in Part 12.]

NOTES

This section derived from the Insolvency Act 1985, s 89(1), (2).

Sub-s (1): words in italics repealed by the Banks and Building Societies (Depositor Preference and Priorities) Order 2014, SI 2014/3486, arts 3, 5(1), (2), except in relation to any insolvency proceedings commenced before 1 January 2015 (as to the meaning of this, see further the note "SI 2014/3486, art 3" at **[1.5]**).

Sub-ss (1A), (1B), (3): inserted and added respectively, by SI 2014/3486, arts 3, 5(1), (3), (5), except in relation to any insolvency proceedings commenced before 1 January 2015 (as to the meaning of this, see further the note "SI 2014/3486, art 3" at **[1.5]**).

Sub-s (2): para (a) repealed by SI 2014/3486, arts 3, 5(1), (4), except in relation to any insolvency proceedings commenced before 1 January 2015 (as to the meaning of this, see further the note "SI 2014/3486, art 3" at **[1.5]**).

Transfer to Secretary of State of rights and remedies on employer's insolvency: see further the Employment Rights Act 1996, s 189(2) at **[17.145]**.

See further: in relation to the partial disapplication of this section in the case of a winding up of a UK insurer, see the Insurers (Reorganisation and Winding Up) Regulations 2004, SI 2004/353, regs 20–27 at **[3.143]–[3.150]**. This section is also disapplied in respect of regulated covered bonds, by the Regulated Covered Bonds Regulations 2008, SI 2008/346, reg 46, Schedule, Pt 1, para 2(4) at **[18.179]**.

[1.177]

176 Preferential charge on goods distrained[, etc]

(1) This section applies where a company is being wound up by the court in England and Wales, and is without prejudice to section 128 (avoidance of attachments, etc).

[(2) Subsection (2A) applies where—

(a) any person (whether or not a landlord or person entitled to rent) has distrained upon the goods or effects of the company, or

(b) Her Majesty's Revenue and Customs has been paid any amount from an account of the company under Part 1 of Schedule 8 to the Finance (No 2) Act 2015 (enforcement by deduction from accounts),

in the period of 3 months ending with the date of the winding-up order.

(2A) Where this subsection applies—

(a) in a case within subsection (2)(a), the goods or effects, or the proceeds of their sale, and

(b) in a case within subsection (2)(b), the amount in question,

is charged for the benefit of the company with the preferential debts of the company to the extent that the company's property is for the time being insufficient for meeting those debts.]

(3) Where by virtue of a charge under subsection [(2A)] any person surrenders any goods or effects to a company or makes a payment to a company, that person ranks, in respect of the amount of the proceeds of sale of those goods or effects by the liquidator or (as the case may be) the amount of the payment, as a preferential creditor of the company, except as against so much of the company's property as is available for the payment of preferential creditors by virtue of the surrender or payment.

NOTES

This section derived from the Insolvency Act 1985, s 89(3), (4).

Section heading: word in square brackets inserted by the Finance (No 2) Act 2015, s 51, Sch 8, Pt 2, paras 26, 30(1), (4).

Sub-ss (2), (2A): substituted, for original sub-s (2), by the Finance (No 2) Act 2015, s 51, Sch 8, Pt 2, paras 26, 30(1), (2).

Sub-s (3): reference in square brackets substituted by the Finance (No 2) Act 2015, s 51, Sch 8, Pt 2, paras 26, 30(1), (3).

Transfer to Secretary of State of rights and remedies on employer's insolvency: see further the Employment Rights Act 1996, s 189(2) at **[17.145]**.

[Property subject to floating charge]

NOTES

Cross-heading inserted by the Enterprise Act 2002, s 252.

[1.178]
[176ZA Payment of expenses of winding up (England and Wales)

(1) The expenses of winding up in England and Wales, so far as the assets of the company available for payment of general creditors are insufficient to meet them, have priority over any claims to property comprised in or subject to any floating charge created by the company and shall be paid out of any such property accordingly.

(2) In subsection (1)—
- (a) the reference to assets of the company available for payment of general creditors does not include any amount made available under section 176A(2)(a);
- (b) the reference to claims to property comprised in or subject to a floating charge is to the claims of—
  - (i) the holders of debentures secured by, or holders of, the floating charge, and
  - (ii) any preferential creditors entitled to be paid out of that property in priority to them.

(3) Provision may be made by rules restricting the application of subsection (1), in such circumstances as may be prescribed, to expenses authorised or approved—
- (a) by the holders of debentures secured by, or holders of, the floating charge and by any preferential creditors entitled to be paid in priority to them, or
- (b) by the court.

(4) References in this section to the expenses of the winding up are to all expenses properly incurred in the winding up, including the remuneration of the liquidator.]

NOTES

Inserted by the Companies Act 2006, s 1282(1), subject to transitional provisions and savings in the Companies Act 2006 (Commencement No 5, Transitional Provisions and Savings) Order 2007, SI 2007/3495, arts 9, 12(2) thereof and Sch 4, Pt 1, para 43 thereto which (as substituted by SI 2008/674, art 5, Sch 3, para 6(1), (5)) reads as follows:

"43 Expenses of winding up (s 1282)

(1) The amendment made to the Insolvency Act 1986 by section 1282(1) of the Companies Act 2006 (expenses of winding up) applies—
- (a) to a creditors' voluntary winding up—
  - (i) for which the resolution is passed, or
  - (ii) where commenced as a members' voluntary winding up, for which the conversion to a creditors' voluntary winding up under section 96 of the Insolvency Act 1986 takes effect, or
  - (iii) in respect of which a notice is registered under paragraph 83 of Schedule B1 to the Insolvency Act 1986,

  on or after 6th April 2008;
- (b) to a members' voluntary winding up for which the resolution is passed on or after 6th April 2008;
- (c) to the winding up of a company by the court where the winding-up order is made on or after 6th April 2008, except where the order is made following a resolution for voluntary winding up passed by the company before 6th April 2008.

(2) The amendment made to the Insolvency (Northern Ireland) Order 1989 by section 1282(2) of the Companies Act 2006 (expenses of winding up) applies—
- (a) to a creditors' voluntary winding up—
  - (i) in respect of which the resolution is passed, or
  - (ii) where it commenced as a members' voluntary winding up, for which the conversion to a creditors' voluntary winding up under Article 82 of the Order takes effect, or
  - (iii) in respect of which a notice is registered under paragraph 84 of Schedule B1 to the Order,

  on or after 6th April 2008;
- (b) to a members' voluntary winding up for which the resolution is passed on or after 6th April 2008;
- (c) to the winding up of a company by the court where the winding-up order is made on or after 6th April 2008, except where the order is made following a resolution for voluntary winding up passed by the company before 6th April 2008.".

[1.179]
[176ZB Application of proceeds of office-holder claims

(1) This section applies where—
- (a) there is a floating charge (whether created before or after the coming into force of this section) which relates to property of a company which—
  - (i) is in administration, or
  - (ii) has gone into liquidation; and
- (b) the administrator or the liquidator (referred to in this section as "the office-holder") has—
  - (i) brought a claim under any provision mentioned in subsection (3), or

(ii) made an assignment (or, in Scotland, assignation) in relation to a right of action under any such provision under section 246ZD.

(2) The proceeds of the claim or assignment (or, in Scotland, assignation) are not to be treated as part of the company's net property, that is to say the amount of its property which would be available for satisfaction of claims of holders of debentures secured by, or holders of, any floating charge created by the company.

(3) The provisions are—

(a) section 213 or 246ZA (fraudulent trading);
(b) section 214 or 246ZB (wrongful trading);
(c) section 238 (transactions at an undervalue (England and Wales));
(d) section 239 (preferences (England and Wales));
(e) section 242 (gratuitous alienations (Scotland));
(f) section 243 (unfair preferences (Scotland));
(g) section 244 (extortionate credit transactions).

(4) Subsection (2) does not apply to a company if or in so far as it is disapplied by—

(a) a voluntary arrangement in respect of the company, or
(b) a compromise or arrangement agreed under Part 26 of the Companies Act 2006 (arrangements and reconstructions).]

NOTES

Commencement: 1 October 2015 (in respect of a company which enters administration or goes into liquidation on or after that date).

Inserted by the Small Business, Enterprise and Employment Act 2015, s 119, in respect of a company which enters administration or goes into liquidation on or after 1 October 2015.

Transitional provisions: see the Deregulation Act 2015, the Small Business, Enterprise and Employment Act 2015 and the Insolvency (Amendment) Act (Northern Ireland) 2016 (Consequential Amendments and Transitional Provisions) Regulations 2017, SI 2017/400, reg 14, which provides as follows (note that "the commencement date" is 7 April 2017)—

"(1) Section 176ZB (application of proceeds of office-holder claims) does not apply in relation to any relevant proceedings commenced before the commencement date.

(2) "Relevant proceedings" means—

(a) bank insolvency under Part 2 of the 2009 Act or bank administration under Part 3 of that Act;
(b) building society insolvency under Part 2 of the 2009 Act (as applied by section 90C of the Building Societies Act 1986);
(c) building society special administration under Part 3 of the 2009 Act (as applied by section 90C of the Building Societies Act 1986);
(d) the administration of a building society under Part 2 of the 1986 Act (as applied by section 90A of the Building Societies Act 1986);
(e) special administration, special administration (bank insolvency) or special administration (bank administration) under the Investment Bank Special Administration Regulations 2011; or
(f) the administration of a relevant society (within the meaning given in article 1(2) of the Co-operative and Community Benefit Societies and Credit Unions (Arrangements, Reconstructions and Administration) Order 2014) under Part 2 of the 1986 Act as applied by article 2(2) of that Order.".

[1.180]

[176A Share of assets for unsecured creditors

(1) This section applies where a floating charge relates to property of a company—

(a) which has gone into liquidation,
(b) which is in administration,
(c) of which there is a provisional liquidator, or
(d) of which there is a receiver.

(2) The liquidator, administrator or receiver—

(a) shall make a prescribed part of the company's net property available for the satisfaction of unsecured debts, and
(b) shall not distribute that part to the proprietor of a floating charge except in so far as it exceeds the amount required for the satisfaction of unsecured debts.

(3) Subsection (2) shall not apply to a company if—

(a) the company's net property is less than the prescribed minimum, and
(b) the liquidator, administrator or receiver thinks that the cost of making a distribution to unsecured creditors would be disproportionate to the benefits.

(4) Subsection (2) shall also not apply to a company if or in so far as it is disapplied by—

(a) a voluntary arrangement in respect of the company, or
(b) a compromise or arrangement agreed under [Part 26 of the Companies Act 2006 (arrangements and reconstructions)].

(5) Subsection (2) shall also not apply to a company if—

(a) the liquidator, administrator or receiver applies to the court for an order under this subsection on the ground that the cost of making a distribution to unsecured creditors would be disproportionate to the benefits, and
(b) the court orders that subsection (2) shall not apply.

(6) In subsections (2) and (3) a company's net property is the amount of its property which would, but for this section, be available for satisfaction of claims of holders of debentures secured by, or holders of, any floating charge created by the company.

(7) An order under subsection (2) prescribing part of a company's net property may, in particular, provide for its calculation—

(a) as a percentage of the company's net property, or
(b) as an aggregate of different percentages of different parts of the company's net property.

(8) An order under this section—
(a) must be made by statutory instrument, and
(b) shall be subject to annulment pursuant to a resolution of either House of Parliament.

(9) In this section—
"floating charge" means a charge which is a floating charge on its creation and which is created after the first order under subsection (2)(a) comes into force, and
"prescribed" means prescribed by order by the Secretary of State.

(10) An order under this section may include transitional or incidental provision.]

NOTES

Inserted, together with cross-heading preceding s 176ZA, by the Enterprise Act 2002, s 252.

Sub-s (4): words in square brackets substituted for original words "section 425 of the Companies Act (compromise with creditors and members)" by the Companies Act 2006 (Consequential Amendments etc) Order 2008, SI 2008/948, art 3(1)(b), Sch 1, Pt 2, para 103, subject to transitional provisions and savings in arts 6, 11, 12 thereof.

Prescribed part; prescribed minimum: see the Insolvency Act 1986 (Prescribed Part) Order 2003, SI 2003/2097 at **[8.68]**.

See further: as to the disapplication of this section in relation to any charge created or otherwise arising under a financial collateral arrangement, see the Financial Collateral Arrangements (No 2) Regulations 2003, SI 2003/3226, reg 10(3) at **[3.290]**. This section is also disapplied in respect of regulated covered bonds, by the Regulated Covered Bonds Regulations 2008, SI 2008/346, reg 46, Schedule, Pt 1, para 2(4) at **[18.179]**.

Orders: the Insolvency Act 1986 (Prescribed Part) Order 2003, SI 2003/2097 at **[8.68]**.

Special managers

[1.181]

177 Power to appoint special manager

(1) Where a company has gone into liquidation or a provisional liquidator has been appointed, the court may, on an application under this section, appoint any person to be the special manager of the business or property of the company.

(2) The application may be made by the liquidator or provisional liquidator in any case where it appears to him that the nature of the business or property of the company, or the interests of the company's creditors or contributories or members generally, require the appointment of another person to manage the company's business or property.

(3) The special manager has such powers as may be entrusted to him by the court.

(4) The court's power to entrust powers to the special manager includes power to direct that any provision of this Act that has effect in relation to the provisional liquidator or liquidator of a company shall have the like effect in relation to the special manager for the purposes of the carrying out by him of any of the functions of the provisional liquidator or liquidator.

(5) The special manager shall—
(a) give such security or, in Scotland, caution as may be prescribed;
(b) prepare and keep such accounts as may be prescribed; and
(c) produce those accounts in accordance with the rules to the Secretary of State or to such other persons as may be prescribed.

NOTES

This section derived from the Insolvency Act 1985, s 90.

Disclaimer (England and Wales only)

[1.182]

178 Power to disclaim onerous property

(1) This and the next two sections apply to a company that is being wound up in England and Wales.

(2) Subject as follows, the liquidator may, by the giving of the prescribed notice, disclaim any onerous property and may do so notwithstanding that he has taken possession of it, endeavoured to sell it, or otherwise exercised rights of ownership in relation to it.

(3) The following is onerous property for the purposes of this section—
(a) any unprofitable contract, and
(b) any other property of the company which is unsaleable or not readily saleable or is such that it may give rise to a liability to pay money or perform any other onerous act.

(4) A disclaimer under this section—
(a) operates so as to determine, as from the date of the disclaimer, the rights, interests and liabilities of the company in or in respect of the property disclaimed; but
(b) does not, except so far as is necessary for the purpose of releasing the company from any liability, affect the rights or liabilities of any other person.

(5) A notice of disclaimer shall not be given under this section in respect of any property if—
(a) a person interested in the property has applied in writing to the liquidator or one of his predecessors as liquidator requiring the liquidator or that predecessor to decide whether he will disclaim or not, and
(b) the period of 28 days beginning with the day on which that application was made, or such longer period as the court may allow, has expired without a notice of disclaimer having been given under this section in respect of that property.

(6) Any person sustaining loss or damage in consequence of the operation of a disclaimer under this section is deemed a creditor of the company to the extent of the loss or damage and accordingly may prove for the loss or damage in the winding up.

NOTES

This section derived from the Insolvency Act 1985, s 91(1)–(4), (8).

Disapplication in relation to market contracts: see further the Companies Act 1989, s 164(1) at **[17.67]**.

See further: as to the disapplication of this section, or in Scotland any rule of law having the same effect as this section, in relation to any financial collateral arrangement, where the collateral-provider or collateral-taker under the arrangement is being wound-up, see the Financial Collateral Arrangements (No 2) Regulations 2003, SI 2003/3226, reg 10(4) at **[3.290]**.

[1.183]
179 Disclaimer of leaseholds

(1) The disclaimer under section 178 of any property of a leasehold nature does not take effect unless a copy of the disclaimer has been served (so far as the liquidator is aware of their addresses) on every person claiming under the company as underlessee or mortgagee and either—

(a) no application under section 181 below is made with respect to that property before the end of the period of 14 days beginning with the day on which the last notice served under this subsection was served; or

(b) where such an application has been made, the court directs that the disclaimer shall take effect.

(2) Where the court gives a direction under subsection (1)(b) it may also, instead of or in addition to any order it makes under section 181, make such orders with respect to fixtures, tenant's improvements and other matters arising out of the lease as it thinks fit.

NOTES

This section derived from the Insolvency Act 1985, s 91(5), (6).

[1.184]
180 Land subject to rentcharge

(1) The following applies where, in consequence of the disclaimer under section 178 of any land subject to a rentcharge, that land vests by operation of law in the Crown or any other person (referred to in the next subsection as "the proprietor").

(2) The proprietor and the successors in title of the proprietor are not subject to any personal liability in respect of any sums becoming due under the rentcharge except sums becoming due after the proprietor, or some person claiming under or through the proprietor, has taken possession or control of the land or has entered into occupation of it.

NOTES

This section derived from the Insolvency Act 1985, s 91(7).

[1.185]
181 Powers of court (general)

(1) This section and the next apply where the liquidator has disclaimed property under section 178.

(2) An application under this section may be made to the court by—

(a) any person who claims an interest in the disclaimed property, or

(b) any person who is under any liability in respect of the disclaimed property, not being a liability discharged by the disclaimer.

(3) Subject as follows, the court may on the application make an order, on such terms as it thinks fit, for the vesting of the disclaimed property in, or for its delivery to—

(a) a person entitled to it or a trustee for such a person, or

(b) a person subject to such a liability as is mentioned in subsection (2)(b) or a trustee for such a person.

(4) The court shall not make an order under subsection (3)(b) except where it appears to the court that it would be just to do so for the purpose of compensating the person subject to the liability in respect of the disclaimer.

(5) The effect of any order under this section shall be taken into account in assessing for the purpose of section 178(6) the extent of any loss or damage sustained by any person in consequence of the disclaimer.

(6) An order under this section vesting property in any person need not be completed by conveyance, assignment or transfer.

NOTES

This section derived from the Insolvency Act 1985, s 92(1)–(4), (9), (10).

[1.186]
182 Powers of court (leaseholds)

(1) The court shall not make an order under section 181 vesting property of a leasehold nature in any person claiming under the company as underlessee or mortgagee except on terms making that person—

(a) subject to the same liabilities and obligations as the company was subject to under the lease at the commencement of the winding up, or

(b) if the court thinks fit, subject to the same liabilities and obligations as that person would be subject to if the lease had been assigned to him at the commencement of the winding up.

(2) For the purposes of an order under section 181 relating to only part of any property comprised in a lease, the requirements of subsection (1) apply as if the lease comprised only the property to which the order relates.

(3) Where subsection (1) applies and no person claiming under the company as underlessee or mortgagee is willing to accept an order under section 181 on the terms required by virtue of that subsection, the court may, by order under that section, vest the company's estate or interest in the property in any person who is liable (whether personally or in a representative capacity, and whether alone or jointly with the company) to perform the lessee's covenants in the lease.

The court may vest that estate and interest in such a person freed and discharged from all estates, incumbrances and interests created by the company.

(4) Where subsection (1) applies and a person claiming under the company as underlessee or mortgagee declines to accept an order under section 181, that person is excluded from all interest in the property.

NOTES

This section derived from the Insolvency Act 1985, s 92(5)–(8).

Execution, attachment and the Scottish equivalents

[1.187]

183 Effect of execution or attachment (England and Wales)

(1) Where a creditor has issued execution against the goods or land of a company or has attached any debt due to it, and the company is subsequently wound up, he is not entitled to retain the benefit of the execution or attachment against the liquidator unless he has completed the execution or attachment before the commencement of the winding up.

(2) However—

(a) if a creditor has had notice of a meeting having been called at which a resolution for voluntary winding up is to be proposed, the date on which he had notice is substituted, for the purpose of subsection (1), for the date of commencement of the winding up;

(b) a person who purchases in good faith under a sale by the [enforcement officer or other officer charged with the execution of the writ] any goods of a company on which execution has been levied in all cases acquires a good title to them against the liquidator; and

(c) the rights conferred by subsection (1) on the liquidator may be set aside by the court in favour of the creditor to such extent and subject to such terms as the court thinks fit.

(3) For purposes of this Act—

(a) an execution against goods is completed by seizure and sale, or by the making of a charging order under section 1 of the Charging Orders Act 1979;

(b) an attachment of a debt is completed by receipt of the debt; and

(c) an execution against land is completed by seizure, by the appointment of a receiver, or by the making of a charging order under section 1 of the Act above-mentioned.

(4) In this section, "goods" includes all chattels personal; and ["enforcement officer" means an individual who is authorised to act as an enforcement officer under the Courts Act 2003].

[(4A) For the purposes of this section, Her Majesty's Revenue and Customs is to be regarded as having attached a debt due to a company if it has taken action under Part 1 of Schedule 8 to the Finance (No 2) Act 2015 (enforcement by deduction for accounts) as a result of which an amount standing to the credit of an account held by the company is—

(a) subject to arrangements made under paragraph 6(3) of that Schedule, or

(b) the subject of a deduction notice under paragraph 13 of that Schedule.]

(5) This section does not apply in the case of a winding up in Scotland.

NOTES

This section derived from the Companies Act 1985, s 621.

Sub-ss (2), (4): words in square brackets substituted by the Courts Act 2003, s 109(1), Sch 8, para 295.

Sub-s (4A): inserted by the Finance (No 2) Act 2015, s 51, Sch 8, Pt 2, paras 26, 31.

[1.188]

184 Duties of [officers charged with execution of writs and other processes] (England and Wales)

(1) The following applies where a company's goods are taken in execution and, before their sale or the completion of the execution (by the receipt or recovery of the full amount of the levy), notice is served on the [enforcement officer, or other officer, charged with execution of the writ or other process,] that a provisional liquidator has been appointed or that a winding-up order has been made, or that a resolution for voluntary winding up has been passed.

(2) The [enforcement officer or other officer] shall, on being so required, deliver the goods and any money seized or received in part satisfaction of the execution to the liquidator; but the costs of execution are a first charge on the goods or money so delivered, and the liquidator may sell the goods, or a sufficient part of them, for the purpose of satisfying the charge.

(3) If under an execution in respect of a judgment for a sum exceeding [£500] a company's goods are sold or money is paid in order to avoid sale, the [enforcement officer or other officer] shall deduct the costs of the execution from the proceeds of sale or the money paid and retain the balance for 14 days.

(4) If within that time notice is served on the [enforcement officer or other officer] of a petition for the winding up of the company having been presented, or of a meeting having been called at which there is to be proposed a resolution for voluntary winding up, and an order is made or a resolution passed (as the case may be), the [enforcement officer or other officer] shall pay the balance to the liquidator, who is entitled to retain it as against the execution creditor.

(5) The rights conferred by this section on the liquidator may be set aside by the court in favour of the creditor to such extent and subject to such terms as the court thinks fit.

(6) In this section, "goods" includes all chattels personal; and ["enforcement officer" means an individual who is authorised to act as an enforcement officer under the Courts Act 2003].

(7) The money sum for the time being specified in subsection (3) is subject to increase or reduction by order under section 416 in Part XV.
(8) This section does not apply in the case of a winding up in Scotland.

NOTES

This section derived from the Companies Act 1985, s 622, and the Insolvency Act 1985, Sch 6, para 25.

Section heading, sub-ss (1), (2), (4), (6): words in square brackets substituted by the Courts Act 2003, s 109(1), Sch 8, para 296.

Sub-s (3): amount in first pair of square brackets increased from £250 by the Insolvency Proceedings (Monetary Limits) Order 1986, SI 1986/1996, art 2, Schedule, Pt I, except in relation to any case where the goods are sold or payment to avoid sale is made before 29 December 1986; words in second pair of square brackets substituted by the Courts Act 2003, s 109(1), Sch 8, para 296(1), (3).

[1.189]
185 Effect of diligence (Scotland)

(1) In the winding up of a company registered in Scotland, the following provisions of the Bankruptcy (Scotland) Act [2016—

(a) subsections (3) to (10) of section 23A (effect of sequestration on land attachment) and section 24 (effect of sequestration on diligence generally); and
(b) subsections (6), (7), (10) and (11) of section 109 (management and realisation of estate),]

apply, so far as consistent with this Act, in like manner as they apply in the sequestration of a debtor's estate, with the substitutions specified below and with any other necessary modifications.
(2) The substitutions to be made in those sections of the Act of [2016] are as follows—

(a) for references to the debtor, substitute references to the company;
(b) for references to the sequestration, substitute references to the winding up;
(c) for references to the date of sequestration, substitute references to the commencement of the winding up of the company; and
(d) for references to the . . . trustee, substitute references to the liquidator.

(3) In this section, "the commencement of the winding up of the company" means, where it is being wound up by the court, the day on which the winding-up order is made.
(4) This section, so far as relating to any estate or effects of the company situated in Scotland, applies in the case of a company registered in England and Wales as in the case of one registered in Scotland.

NOTES

This section derived from the Companies Act 1985, s 623, and the Bankruptcy (Scotland) Act 1985, Sch 7, para 21.

Sub-s (1): words in square brackets substituted by the Bankruptcy (Scotland) Act 2016 (Consequential Provisions and Modifications) Order 2016, SI 2016/1034, art 7(1), (3), Sch 1, para 4(1), (3)(a), as from 30 November 2016 (except in relation to (i) a sequestration as regards which the petition is presented, or the debtor application is made before that date; or (ii) a trust deed executed before that date). The original words read as follows (with words in square brackets inserted by the Bankruptcy and Diligence etc (Scotland) Act 2007, s 226(1), Sch 5, para 14(1), (3), as from a day to be appointed)—

"1985—

(a) subsections (1) to (6)[, (8A) to (8F) and (10)] of section 37 (effect of sequestration on diligence); and
(b) subsections (3), (4), (7) and (8) of section 39 (realisation of estate),".

Sub-s (2): year "2016" in square brackets substituted (for the original year "1985") by SI 2016/1034, art 7(1), (3), Sch 1, para 4(1), (3)(b), as from 30 November 2016 (except in relation to (i) a sequestration as regards which the petition is presented, or the debtor application is made before that date; or (ii) a trust deed executed before that date); word "permanent" omitted from para (d) repealed by the Bankruptcy and Diligence etc (Scotland) Act 2007, s 226(2), Sch 6, Pt 1, subject to transitional provisions and savings in the Bankruptcy and Diligence etc (Scotland) Act 2007 (Commencement No 3, Savings and Transitionals) Order 2008, SSI 2008/115, arts 4–7, 10, 15 at **[2.51]–[2.53]**, **[2.56]**, **[2.57]**.

Default proceedings: see the note to s 126 at **[1.127]**.

Miscellaneous matters

[1.190]
186 Rescission of contracts by the court

(1) The court may, on the application of a person who is, as against the liquidator, entitled to the benefit or subject to the burden of a contract made with the company, make an order rescinding the contract on such terms as to payment by or to either party of damages for the non-performance of the contract, or otherwise as the court thinks just.
(2) Any damages payable under the order to such a person may be proved by him as a debt in the winding up.

NOTES

This section derived from the Companies Act 1985, s 619(4).

Disapplication in relation to market contracts: see further the Companies Act 1989, s 164(1) at **[17.67]**.

[1.191]
187 Power to make over assets to employees

(1) On the winding up of a company (whether by the court or voluntarily), the liquidator may, subject to the following provisions of this section, make any payment which the company has, before the commencement of the winding up, decided to make under [section 247 of the Companies Act 2006] (power to provide for employees or former employees on cessation or transfer of business).
[(2) The liquidator may, after the winding up has commenced, make any such provision as is mentioned in section 247(1) if—

(a) the company's liabilities have been fully satisfied and provision has been made for the expenses of the winding up,
(b) the exercise of the power has been sanctioned by a resolution of the company, and
(c) any requirements of the company's [articles] as to the exercise of the power conferred by section 247(1) are complied with.]

(3) Any payment which may be made by a company under this section (that is, a payment after the commencement of its winding up) may be made out of the company's assets which are available to the members on the winding up.

(4) On a winding up by the court, the exercise by the liquidator of his powers under this section is subject to the court's control, and any creditor or contributory may apply to the court with respect to any exercise or proposed exercise of the power.

(5) Subsections (1) and (2) above have effect notwithstanding anything in any rule of law or in section 107 of this Act (property of company after satisfaction of liabilities to be distributed among members).

NOTES

This section derived from the Companies Act 1985, s 659, and the Insolvency Act 1985, Sch 6, para 48.

Sub-s (1): words in square brackets substituted for original words "section 719 of the Companies Act" by the Companies Act 2006 (Commencement No 3, Consequential Amendments, Transitional Provisions and Savings) Order 2007, SI 2007/2194, art 10(1), (2), Sch 4, Pt 3, para 42(1), (2), subject to savings in art 12 thereof.

Sub-s (2): substituted by SI 2007/2194, art 10(1), (2), Sch 4, Pt 3, para 42(1), (3), subject to savings in art 12 thereof, and originally read as follows:

> "(2) The power which a company may exercise by virtue only of that section may be exercised by the liquidator after the winding up has commenced if, after the company's liabilities have been fully satisfied and provision has been made for the expenses of the winding up, the exercise of that power has been sanctioned by such a resolution of the company as would be required of the company itself by section 719(3) before that commencement, if paragraph (b) of that subsection were omitted and any other requirement applicable to its exercise by the company had been met.";

word in square brackets in para (c) substituted for original words "memorandum or articles" by the Companies Act 2006 (Consequential Amendments, Transitional Provisions and Savings) Order 2009, SI 2009/1941, art 2(1), Sch 1, para 75(1), (20), subject to transitional provisions and savings in art 8, Sch 1, para 84 at **[2.70]**, **[2.73]**.

[1.192]

188 Notification that company is in liquidation

[(1) When a company is being wound up, whether by the court or voluntarily—
(a) every invoice, order for goods [or services], business letter or order form (whether in hard copy, electronic or any other form) issued by or on behalf of the company, or a liquidator of the company or a receiver or manager of the company's property, . . . and
(b) all the company's websites,

must contain a statement that the company is being wound up.]

(2) If default is made in complying with this section, the company and any of the following persons who knowingly and wilfully authorises or permits the default, namely, any officer of the company, any liquidator of the company and any receiver or manager, is liable to a fine.

NOTES

This section derived from the Companies Act 1985, s 637.

Sub-s (1): substituted by the Companies (Registrar, Languages and Trading Disclosures) Regulations 2006, SI 2006/3429, reg 7(1); words in square brackets inserted and words omitted repealed by the Companies (Trading Disclosures) (Insolvency) Regulations 2008, SI 2008/1897, reg 5(1).

[1.193]

189 Interest on debts

(1) In a winding up interest is payable in accordance with this section on any debt proved in the winding up, including so much of any such debt as represents interest on the remainder.

(2) Any surplus remaining after the payment of the debts proved in a winding up shall, before being applied for any other purpose, be applied in paying interest on those debts in respect of the periods during which they have been outstanding since the company went into liquidation.

(3) All interest under this section ranks equally, whether or not the debts on which it is payable rank equally.

(4) The rate of interest payable under this section in respect of any debt ("the official rate" for the purposes of any provision of this Act in which that expression is used) is whichever is the greater of—
(a) the rate specified in section 17 of the Judgments Act 1838 on the day on which the company went into liquidation, and
(b) the rate applicable to that debt apart from the winding up.

(5) In the application of this section to Scotland—
(a) references to a debt proved in a winding up have effect as references to a claim accepted in a winding up, and
(b) the reference to section 17 of the Judgments Act 1838 has effect as a reference to the rules.

NOTES

This section derived from the Insolvency Act 1985, s 93.

[1.194]
190 Documents exempt from stamp duty

(1) In the case of a winding up by the court, or of a creditors' voluntary winding up, the following has effect as regards exemption from duties chargeable under the enactments relating to stamp duties.

(2) If the company is registered in England and Wales, the following documents are exempt from stamp duty—

(a) every assurance relating solely to freehold or leasehold property, or to any estate, right or interest in, any real or personal property, which forms part of the company's assets and which, after the execution of the assurance, either at law or in equity, is or remains part of those assets, and

(b) every writ, order, certificate, or other instrument or writing relating solely to the property of any company which is being wound up as mentioned in subsection (1), or to any proceeding under such a winding up.

"Assurance" here includes deed, conveyance, assignment and surrender.

(3) If the company is registered in Scotland, the following documents are exempt from stamp duty—

(a) every conveyance relating solely to property which forms part of the company's assets and which, after the execution of the conveyance, is or remains the company's property for the benefit of its creditors,

(b) any articles of roup or sale, submission and every other instrument and writing whatsoever relating solely to the company's property, and

(c) every deed or writing forming part of the proceedings in the winding up.

"Conveyance" here includes assignation, instrument, discharge, writing and deed.

NOTES

This section derived from the Companies Act 1985, s 638.

[1.195]
191 Company's books to be evidence

Where a company is being wound up, all books and papers of the company and of the liquidators are, as between the contributories of the company, prima facie evidence of the truth of all matters purporting to be recorded in them.

NOTES

This section derived from the Companies Act 1985, s 639.

[1.196]
192 Information as to pending liquidations

(1) If the winding up of a company is not concluded within one year after its commencement, the liquidator shall, at such intervals as may be prescribed, until the winding up is concluded, send to the registrar of companies a statement in the prescribed form and containing the prescribed particulars with respect to the proceedings in, and position of, the liquidation.

(2) If a liquidator fails to comply with this section, he is liable to a fine and, for continued contravention, to a daily default fine.

NOTES

This section derived from the Companies Act 1985, s 641.

Modification in relation to Scotland: see the Note at the beginning of this Act.

[1.197]
193 Unclaimed dividends (Scotland)

(1) The following applies where a company registered in Scotland has been wound up, and is about to be dissolved.

(2) The liquidator shall lodge in an appropriate bank or institution as defined in section [228(1) of the Bankruptcy (Scotland) Act 2016] (not being a bank or institution in or of which the liquidator is acting partner, manager, agent or cashier) in the name of the Accountant of Court the whole unclaimed dividends and unapplied or undistributable balances, and the deposit receipts shall be transmitted to the Accountant of Court.

(3) The provisions of section [150 of the Bankruptcy (Scotland) Act 2016] (so far as consistent with this Act and [the Companies Acts]) apply with any necessary modifications to sums lodged in a bank or institution under this section as they apply to sums deposited under section [148] of the Act first mentioned.

NOTES

This section derived from the Companies Act 1985, s 643, and the Bankruptcy (Scotland) Act 1985, Sch 7, para 22.

Sub-s (2): words in square brackets substituted (for the original words "73(1) of the Bankruptcy (Scotland) Act 1985") by the Bankruptcy (Scotland) Act 2016 (Consequential Provisions and Modifications) Order 2016, SI 2016/1034, art 7(1), (3), Sch 1, para 4(1), (4)(a), as from 30 November 2016 (except in relation to (i) a sequestration as regards which the petition is presented, or the debtor application is made before that date; or (ii) a trust deed executed before that date).

Sub-s (3): words in first pair of square brackets substituted (for the original words "58 of the Bankruptcy (Scotland) Act 1985"), and figure in final pair of square brackets substituted (for the original figure "57"), by SI 2016/1034, art 7(1), (3), Sch 1, para 4(1), (4)(b), as from 30 November 2016 (except in relation to (i) a sequestration as regards which the petition is presented, or the debtor application is made before that date; or (ii) a trust deed executed before that date); words in second pair of square brackets substituted for original words "the Companies Act" by the Companies Act 2006 (Consequential Amendments,

Transitional Provisions and Savings) Order 2009, SI 2009/1941, art 2(1), Sch 1, para 75(1), (21), subject to transitional provisions and savings in art 8, Sch 1, para 84 at **[2.70]**, **[2.73]**.

[1.198]

194 Resolutions passed at adjourned meetings

Where a resolution is passed at an adjourned meeting of a company's creditors or contributories, the resolution is treated for all purposes as having been passed on the date on which it was in fact passed, and not as having been passed on any earlier date.

NOTES

This section derived from the Companies Act 1985, s 644.

Repealed by the Small Business, Enterprise and Employment Act 2015, s 126, Sch 9, Pt 1, paras 1, 46, as from 6 April 2017 (in relation to England and Wales and subject to transitional and savings provisions as noted to s 246ZE at **[1.256]**), and as from a day to be appointed (in relation to Scotland).

[1.199]

195 [Court's powers] to ascertain wishes of creditors or contributories

(1) The court may—

(a) as to all matters relating to the winding up of a company, have regard to the wishes of the creditors or contributories (as proved to it by any sufficient evidence), and

(b) if it thinks fit, for the purpose of ascertaining those wishes, direct [qualifying decision procedures to be instigated or the deemed consent procedure to be used in accordance with any directions given by the court, and appoint a person to report the result to the court].

(2) In the case of creditors, regard shall be had to the value of each creditor's debt.

(3) In the case of contributories, regard shall be had to the number of votes conferred on each contributory . . .

NOTES

This section derived from the Companies Act 1985, s 645.

Section heading: words in square brackets substituted for original word "Meetings" by the Small Business, Enterprise and Employment Act 2015, s 126, Sch 9, Pt 1, paras 1, 47(1), (3), as from 6 April 2017 (in relation to England and Wales and subject to transitional and savings provisions as noted to s 246ZE at **[1.256]**), and as from a day to be appointed (in relation to Scotland).

Sub-s (1): words in square brackets substituted for original words "meetings of the creditors or contributories to be called, held and conducted in such manner as the court directs, and appoint a person to act as chairman of any such meeting and report the result of it to the court" by the Small Business, Enterprise and Employment Act 2015, s 126, Sch 9, Pt 1, paras 1, 47(1), (2), as from 6 April 2017 (in relation to England and Wales and subject to transitional and savings provisions as noted to s 246ZE at **[1.256]**), and as from a day to be appointed (in relation to Scotland).

Sub-s (3): words "by the Companies Act or the articles" (omitted) repealed by the Companies Act 2006 (Consequential Amendments, Transitional Provisions and Savings) Order 2009, SI 2009/1941, art 2(1), Sch 1, para 75(1), (22), subject to transitional provisions and savings in art 8, Sch 1, para 84 at **[2.70]**, **[2.73]**.

[1.200]

196 Judicial notice of court documents

In all proceedings under this Part, all courts, judges and persons judicially acting, and all officers, judicial or ministerial, of any court, or employed in enforcing the process of any court shall take judicial notice—

(a) of the signature of any officer of the High Court or of [the county court] in England and Wales, or of the Court of Session or a sheriff court in Scotland, or of the High Court in Northern Ireland, and also

(b) of the official seal or stamp of the several offices of the High Court in England and Wales or Northern Ireland, or of the Court of Session, appended to or impressed on any document made, issued or signed under the provisions of this Act or [the Companies Acts], or any official copy of such a document.

NOTES

This section derived from the Companies Act 1985, s 646.

In para (a) words in square brackets substituted by the Crime and Courts Act 2013, s 17(5), Sch 9, Pt 3, para 52(1)(b), (2); in para (b) words in square brackets substituted for original words "the Companies Act" by the Companies Act 2006 (Consequential Amendments, Transitional Provisions and Savings) Order 2009, SI 2009/1941, art 2(1), Sch 1, para 75(1), (23), subject to transitional provisions and savings in art 8, Sch 1, para 84 at **[2.70]**, **[2.73]**.

[1.201]

197 Commission for receiving evidence

(1) When a company is wound up in England and Wales or in Scotland, the court may refer the whole or any part of the examination of witnesses—

(a) to [the] county court in England and Wales, or

(b) to the sheriff principal for a specified sheriffdom in Scotland, or

(c) to the High Court in Northern Ireland or a specified Northern Ireland County Court,

("specified" meaning specified in the order of the winding-up court).

(2) Any person exercising jurisdiction as a judge of the court to which the reference is made (or, in Scotland, the sheriff principal to whom it is made) shall then, by virtue of this section, be a commissioner for the purpose of taking the evidence of those witnesses.

(3) The judge or sheriff principal has in the matter referred the same power of summoning and examining witnesses, of requiring the production and delivery of documents, of punishing defaults by witnesses, and of allowing costs and expenses to witnesses, as the court which made the winding-up order.

These powers are in addition to any which the judge or sheriff principal might lawfully exercise apart from this section.

(4) The examination so taken shall be returned or reported to that court which made the order in such manner as the court requests.

(5) This section extends to Northern Ireland.

NOTES

This section derived from the Companies Act 1985, s 647.

Sub-s (1): word in square brackets substituted by the Crime and Courts Act 2013, s 17(5), Sch 9, Pt 3, para 93(c).

[1.202]

198 Court order for examination of persons in Scotland

(1) The court may direct the examination in Scotland of any person for the time being in Scotland (whether a contributory of the company or not), in regard to the trade, dealings, affairs or property of any company in course of being wound up, or of any person being a contributory of the company, so far as the company may be interested by reason of his being a contributory.

(2) The order or commission to take the examination shall be directed to the sheriff principal of the sheriffdom in which the person to be examined is residing or happens to be for the time; and the sheriff principal shall summon the person to appear before him at a time and place to be specified in the summons for examination on oath as a witness or as a haver, and to produce any books or papers called for which are in his possession or power.

(3) The sheriff principal may take the examination either orally or on written interrogatories, and shall report the same in writing in the usual form to the court, and shall transmit with the report the books and papers produced, if the originals are required and specified by the order or commission, or otherwise copies or extracts authenticated by the sheriff.

(4) If a person so summoned fails to appear at the time and place specified, or refuses to be examined or to make the production required, the sheriff principal shall proceed against him as a witness or haver duly cited; and failing to appear or refusing to give evidence or make production may be proceeded against by the law of Scotland.

(5) The sheriff principal is entitled to such fees, and the witness is entitled to such allowances, as sheriffs principal when acting as commissioners under appointment from the Court of Session and as witnesses and havers are entitled to in the like cases according to the law and practice of Scotland.

(6) If any objection is stated to the sheriff principal by the witness, either on the ground of his incompetency as a witness, or as to the production required, or on any other ground, the sheriff principal may, if he thinks fit, report the objection to the court, and suspend the examination of the witness until it has been disposed of by the court.

NOTES

This section derived from the Companies Act 1985, s 648.

[1.203]

199 Costs of application for leave to proceed (Scottish companies)

Where a petition or application for leave to proceed with an action or proceeding against a company which is being wound up in Scotland is unopposed and is granted by the court, the costs of the petition or application shall, unless the court otherwise directs, be added to the amount of the petitioner's or applicant's claim against the company.

NOTES

This section derived from the Companies Act 1985, s 649.

[1.204]

200 Affidavits etc in United Kingdom and overseas

(1) An affidavit required to be sworn under or for the purposes of this Part may be sworn in the United Kingdom, or elsewhere in Her Majesty's dominions, before any court, judge or person lawfully authorised to take and receive affidavits, or before any of Her Majesty's consuls or vice-consuls in any place outside Her dominions.

(2) All courts, judges, justices, commissioners and persons acting judicially shall take judicial notice of the seal or stamp or signature (as the case may be) of any such court, judge, person, consul or vice-consul attached, appended or subscribed to any such affidavit, or to any other document to be used for the purposes of this Part.

NOTES

This section derived from the Companies Act 1985, s 650.

CHAPTER IX
DISSOLUTION OF COMPANIES AFTER WINDING UP

[1.205]
201 Dissolution (voluntary winding up)

(1) This section applies, in the case of a company wound up voluntarily, where the liquidator has sent to the registrar of companies his final account *and return* under section 94 (members' voluntary) or [his final account and statement under] section 106 (creditors' voluntary).

(2) The registrar on receiving the account[, or the account and statement] [and any statement under section 106(4B),] shall forthwith register [it or] them; and on the expiration of 3 months from the registration of [the account] the company is deemed to be dissolved [(except where subsection (2A) applies)].

[(2A) This subsection applies where a statement sent to the registrar under section 106(4B) indicates that a member State liquidator does not consent to the company being dissolved.

(2B) Where subsection (2A) applies, the company is deemed to be dissolved at the end of the period of 3 months beginning with the date (if any) recorded in the register as the date on which the registrar was notified that—

(a) all proceedings identified in the statement sent under section 106(4B) were closed, or
(b) every member State liquidator appointed in those proceedings consented to the company being dissolved.]

(3) However, the court may, on the application of the liquidator or any other person who appears to the court to be interested, make an order deferring the date at which the dissolution of the company is to take effect for such time as the court thinks fit.

(4) It is the duty of the person on whose application an order of the court under this section is made within 7 days after the making of the order to deliver to the registrar [a copy] of the order for registration; and if that person fails to do so he is liable to a fine and, for continued contravention, to a daily default fine.

NOTES

This section derived from the Companies Act 1985, ss 585(5), (6), 595(6), (7).

Sub-s (1): words in italics repealed, and words in square brackets inserted, by the Small Business, Enterprise and Employment Act 2015, s 126, Sch 9, Pt 1, paras 1, 48(1), (2), as from 6 April 2017 (in relation to England and Wales and subject to transitional and savings provisions as noted to s 246ZE at **[1.256]**), and as from a day to be appointed (in relation to Scotland).

Sub-s (2): words in first and fourth pairs of square brackets substituted for original words "and return" and "the return" respectively, and words in third pair of square brackets inserted, by the Small Business, Enterprise and Employment Act 2015, s 126, Sch 9, Pt 1, paras 1, 48(1), (3), as from 6 April 2017 (in relation to England and Wales and subject to transitional and savings provisions as noted to s 246ZE at **[1.256]**), and as from a day to be appointed (in relation to Scotland); words in second and fifth pairs of square brackets inserted by the Insolvency Amendment (EU 2015/848) Regulations 2017, SI 2017/702, regs 2, 3, Schedule, Pt 1, paras 1, 9(1), (2), except in relation to proceedings opened before 26 June 2017 and subject to savings in reg 4 thereof at **[2.103]**.

Sub-s (2) is amended in relation to Scotland only by SI 2017/702, regs 2, 3, Schedule, Pt 4, paras 55, 58(1), as from 26 June 2017, except in relation to proceedings opened before that date, as follows: after "the account and return" there is inserted "and any statement under section 106(8)", and at the end the words "(except where subsection (2A) applies)" are added.

Sub-ss (2A), (2B): inserted by SI 2017/702, regs 2, 3, Schedule, Pt 1, paras 1, 9(1), (3), except in relation to proceedings opened before 26 June 2017 and subject to savings in reg 4 thereof at **[2.103]**.

In relation to Scotland only, sub-ss (2A), (2B) are inserted by SI 2017/702, regs 2, 3, Schedule, Pt 4, paras 55, 58(2), except in relation to proceedings opened before 26 June 2017 and subject to savings in reg 4 thereof at **[2.103]**, as follows:

"(2A) This subsection applies where a statement sent to the registrar under section 106(8) indicates that a member State liquidator does not consent to the company being dissolved.

(2B) Where subsection (2A) applies, the company is deemed to be dissolved on the expiration of 3 months from the date (if any) recorded in the register as the date on which the registrar was notified that—

(a) all proceedings identified in the statement sent under section 106(8) were closed, or
(b) every member State liquidator appointed in those proceedings consented to the company being dissolved.".

Sub-s (4): words in square brackets substituted by the Companies (Registrar, Languages and Trading Disclosures) Regulations 2006, SI 2006/3429, reg 3(1)(d), subject to savings in reg 3(3) thereof.

[1.206]
202 Early dissolution (England and Wales)

(1) This section applies where an order for the winding up of a company has been made by the court in England and Wales.

(2) The official receiver, if—

(a) he is the liquidator of the company, and
(b) it appears to him—
 (i) that the realisable assets of the company are insufficient to cover the expenses of the winding up, and
 (ii) that the affairs of the company do not require any further investigation,

may at any time apply to the registrar of companies for the early dissolution of the company.

[(2A) Subsection (2B) applies where, immediately before the official receiver makes an application under subsection (2), there are EU insolvency proceedings open in respect of the company in one or more other member States.

(2B) The official receiver must send to the registrar, with the application, a statement—

(a) identifying those proceedings,

(b) identifying the member State liquidator appointed in each of those proceedings, and
(c) indicating, in relation to each of those member State liquidators, whether that member State liquidator consents to the company being dissolved.]

(3) Before making [an application under subsection (2)], the official receiver shall give not less than 28 days' notice of his intention to do so to the company's creditors[, other than opted-out creditors,] and contributories and, if there is an administrative receiver of the company, to that receiver.

(4) With the giving of that notice the official receiver ceases (subject to any directions under the next section) to be required to perform any duties imposed on him in relation to the company, its creditors or contributories by virtue of any provision of this Act, apart from a duty to make an application under subsection (2) [and send any statement under subsection (2B)].

(5) On the receipt of the official receiver's application under subsection (2) [and any statement under subsection (2B)] the registrar shall forthwith register it [or them] and, at the end of the period of 3 months beginning with the day of the registration of the application, the company shall be dissolved [(except where subsection (6) applies)].

[(6) This subsection applies where a statement under subsection (2B) indicates that a member State liquidator does not consent to the company being dissolved.

(7) Where subsection (6) applies, the company is deemed to be dissolved at the end of the period of 3 months beginning with the date (if any) recorded in the register as the date on which the registrar was notified that—

(a) all proceedings identified in the statement under subsection (2B) were closed, or
(b) every member State liquidator appointed in those proceedings consented to the company being dissolved.]

[(8)] However, the Secretary of State may, on the application of the official receiver or any other person who appears to the Secretary of State to be interested, give directions under section 203 at any time before the end of [the period in subsection (5) or (7)].

NOTES

This section derived from the Insolvency Act 1985, s 76(1)–(3), (6).

Sub-ss (2A), (2B): inserted by the Insolvency Amendment (EU 2015/848) Regulations 2017, SI 2017/702, regs 2, 3, Schedule, Pt 1, paras 1, 10(1), (2), except in relation to proceedings opened before 26 June 2017 and subject to savings in reg 4 thereof at **[2.103]**.

Sub-s (3): words in first pair of square brackets substituted for original words "that application" by SI 2017/702, regs 2, 3, Schedule, Pt 1, paras 1, 10(1), (3), except in relation to proceedings opened before 26 June 2017 and subject to savings in reg 4 thereof at **[2.103]**; words in second pair of quare brackets inserted by the Small Business, Enterprise and Employment Act 2015, s 126, Sch 9, Pt 1, paras 1, 49, as from 6 April 2017 (subject to transitional and savings provisions as noted to s 246ZE at **[1.256]**).

Sub-s (4): words in square brackets substituted for original words "of this section" by SI 2017/702, regs 2, 3, Schedule, Pt 1, paras 1, 10(1), (4), except in relation to proceedings opened before 26 June 2017 and subject to savings in reg 4 thereof at **[2.103]**.

Sub-s (5): words in square brackets inserted by SI 2017/702, regs 2, 3, Schedule, Pt 1, paras 1, 10(1), (5)(a), except in relation to proceedings opened before 26 June 2017 and subject to savings in reg 4 thereof at **[2.103]**.

Sub-ss (6), (7): added by SI 2017/702, regs 2, 3, Schedule, Pt 1, paras 1, 10(1), (5)(b), except in relation to proceedings opened before 26 June 2017 and subject to savings in reg 4 thereof at **[2.103]**.

Sub-s (8): words originally forming the second sentence of sub-s (5) designated as sub-s (8), and words in square brackets substituted for original words "that period", by SI 2017/702, regs 2, 3, Schedule, Pt 1, paras 1, 10(1), (6), (7), except in relation to proceedings opened before 26 June 2017 and subject to savings in reg 4 thereof at **[2.103]**.

[1.207]

203 Consequence of notice under s 202

(1) Where a notice has been given under section 202(3), the official receiver or any creditor or contributory of the company, or the administrative receiver of the company (if there is one) may apply to the Secretary of State for directions under this section.

(2) The grounds on which that application may be made are—

(a) that the realisable assets of the company are sufficient to cover the expenses of the winding up;
(b) that the affairs of the company do require further investigation; or
(c) that for any other reason the early dissolution of the company is inappropriate.

(3) Directions under this section—

(a) are directions making such provision as the Secretary of State thinks fit for enabling the winding up of the company to proceed as if no notice had been given under section 202(3), and
(b) may, in the case of an application under [section 202(8)], include a direction deferring the date at which the dissolution of the company is to take effect for such period as the Secretary of State thinks fit.

(4) An appeal to the court lies from any decision of the Secretary of State on an application for directions under this section.

(5) It is the duty of the person on whose application any directions are given under this section, or in whose favour an appeal with respect to an application for such directions is determined, within 7 days after the giving of the directions or the determination of the appeal, to deliver to the registrar of companies for registration such a copy of the directions or determination as is prescribed.

(6) If a person without reasonable excuse fails to deliver a copy as required by subsection (5), he is liable to a fine and, for continued contravention, to a daily default fine.

NOTES

This section derived from the Insolvency Act 1985, s 76(4), (5), (7)–(10).

Sub-s (3): words in square brackets substituted for original words "section 202(5)" by the Insolvency Amendment (EU 2015/848) Regulations 2017, SI 2017/702, regs 2, 3, Schedule, Pt 1, paras 1, 11, except in relation to proceedings opened before 26 June 2017 and subject to savings in reg 4 thereof at **[2.103]**.

[1.208]

204 Early dissolution (Scotland)

(1) This section applies where a winding-up order has been made by the court in Scotland.

(2) If after a *meeting or meetings* under section 138 (appointment of liquidator in Scotland) it appears to the liquidator that the realisable assets of the company are insufficient to cover the expenses of the winding up, *he may apply* to the court for an order that the company be dissolved.

(3) Where the liquidator makes that application, if the court is satisfied that the realisable assets of the company are insufficient to cover the expenses of the winding up and it appears to the court appropriate to do so, the court shall make an order that the company be dissolved in accordance with this section.

(4) A copy of the order shall within 14 days from its date be forwarded by the liquidator to the registrar of companies, who shall forthwith register it; and, at the end of the period of 3 months beginning with the day of the registration of the order, the company shall be dissolved.

[(4A) Subsection (4B) applies where immediately before the liquidator makes an application under subsection (2), there are EU insolvency proceedings open in respect of the company in one or more other member States.

(4B) The liquidator must send to the registrar with the copy of the order forwarded under subsection (4) a statement—

- (a) identifying those proceedings,
- (b) identifying the member State liquidator appointed in each of those proceedings, and
- (c) indicating, in relation to each of those member State liquidators, whether that member State liquidator consents to the company being dissolved.

(4C) The registrar must forthwith register a statement received under subsection (4B).

(4D) Subsection (4E) applies where—

- (a) the court makes an order under subsection (3) that the company be dissolved in accordance with this section, but
- (b) a statement under subsection (4B) indicates that a member State liquidator does not consent to the company being dissolved.

(4E) The company is deemed to be dissolved at the end of the period of 3 months beginning with the date (if any) recorded in the register as the date on which the registrar was notified that—

- (a) all proceedings identified in the statement under subsection (4B) were closed, or
- (b) every member State liquidator appointed in those proceedings consented to the company being dissolved.]

(5) The court may, on an application by any person who appears to the court to have an interest, order that the date at which the dissolution of the company is to take effect shall be deferred for such period as the court thinks fit.

(6) It is the duty of the person on whose application an order is made under subsection (5), within 7 days after the making of the order, to deliver to the registrar of companies such a copy of the order as is prescribed.

(7) If the liquidator without reasonable excuse fails to comply with the requirements of subsection (4), he is liable to a fine and, for continued contravention, to a daily default fine.

(8) If a person without reasonable excuse fails to deliver a copy as required by subsection (6), he is liable to a fine and, for continued contravention, to a daily default fine.

NOTES

This section derived from the Insolvency Act 1985, s 77.

Sub-s (2): for the first words in italics there are substituted the words "liquidator has been appointed" by the Small Business, Enterprise and Employment Act 2015, s 126, Sch 9, Pt 1, paras 1, 50, as from a day to be appointed. For the second words in italics there are substituted the words "the liquidator may at any time apply" by the Public Services Reform (Insolvency) (Scotland) Order 2016, SSI 2016/141, art 11, as from a day to be appointed (being the day that the Small Business, Enterprise and Employment Act 2015, s 122(2) comes into force for all remaining purposes in Scotland).

Sub-ss (4A)–(4E): inserted in relation to Scotland only, by the Insolvency Amendment (EU 2015/848) Regulations 2017, SI 2017/702, regs 2, 3, Schedule, Pt 4, paras 55, 59, except in relation to proceedings opened before 26 June 2017 and subject to savings in reg 4 thereof at **[2.103]**.

[1.209]

205 Dissolution otherwise than under ss 202–204

(1) This section applies where the registrar of companies receives—

- [(a) a final account and statement sent under section 146(4) (final account);]
- (b) a notice from the official receiver that the winding up of a company by the court is complete.

(2) The registrar shall, on receipt of [the final account and statement or] the notice [and any statement under section 146(7) or 146A(2)], forthwith register [them or] it; and, subject as follows, at the end of the period of 3 months beginning with the day of the registration *of the notice*, the company shall be dissolved.

[(2A) Subsection (2B) applies where a statement sent to the registrar under section 146(7) or 146A(2) indicates that a member State liquidator does not consent to the company being dissolved.

(2B) The company is not dissolved at the end of the period mentioned in subsection (2) but is instead dissolved at the end of the period of 3 months beginning with the date (if any) recorded in the register as the date on which the registrar was notified that—

- (a) all proceedings identified in the statement under section 146(7) or 146A(2) were closed, or

(b) every member State liquidator appointed in those proceedings consented to the company being dissolved.]

(3) The Secretary of State may, on the application of the official receiver or any other person who appears to the Secretary of State to be interested, give a direction deferring the date at which the dissolution of the company is to take effect for such period as the Secretary of State thinks fit.

(4) An appeal to the court lies from any decision of the Secretary of State on an application for a direction under subsection (3).

(5) Subsection (3) does not apply in a case where the winding-up order was made by the court in Scotland, but in such a case the court may, on an application by any person appearing to the court to have an interest, order that the date at which the dissolution of the company is to take effect shall be deferred for such period as the court thinks fit.

(6) It is the duty of the person—

(a) on whose application a direction is given under subsection (3);

(b) in whose favour an appeal with respect to an application for such a direction is determined; or

(c) on whose application an order is made under subsection (5),

within 7 days after the giving of the direction, the determination of the appeal or the making of the order, to deliver to the registrar for registration such a copy of the direction, determination or order as is prescribed.

(7) If a person without reasonable excuse fails to deliver a copy as required by subsection (6), he is liable to a fine and, for continued contravention, to a daily default fine.

NOTES

This section derived from the Insolvency Act 1985, s 81.

Sub-s (1): para (a) substituted by the Small Business, Enterprise and Employment Act 2015, s 126, Sch 9, Pt 1, paras 1, 51(1), (2), as from 6 April 2017 (in relation to England and Wales and subject to transitional and savings provisions as noted to s 246ZE at **[1.256]**), and as from a day to be appointed (in relation to Scotland). Para (a) originally read as follows—

"(a) a notice served for the purposes of section 172(8) (final meeting of creditors and vacation of office by liquidator), or".

Sub-s (2): words in first and third pairs of square brackets inserted, and words in italics repealed, by the Small Business, Enterprise and Employment Act 2015, s 126, Sch 9, Pt 1, paras 1, 51(1), (3), as from 6 April 2017 (in relation to England and Wales and subject to transitional and savings provisions as noted to s 246ZE at **[1.256]**), and as from a day to be appointed (in relation to Scotland); words in second and fourth pairs of square brackets inserted by the Insolvency Amendment (EU 2015/848) Regulations 2017, SI 2017/702, regs 2, 3, Schedule, Pt 1, paras 1, 12(1), (2), except in relation to proceedings opened before 26 June 2017 and subject to savings in reg 4 thereof at **[2.103]**.

In relation to Scotland only, in sub-s (2) the words "on receipt of the notice, forthwith register it" are substituted by the words "on receipt of the notice and any statement sent under section 172(10), forthwith register it or them", by SI 2017/702, regs 2, 3, Schedule, Pt 4, paras 55, 60(1), except in relation to proceedings opened before 26 June 2017 and subject to savings in reg 4 thereof at **[2.103]**.

Sub-ss (2A), (2B): inserted by SI 2017/702, regs 2, 3, Schedule, Pt 1, paras 1, 12(1), (3), except in relation to proceedings opened before 26 June 2017 and subject to savings in reg 4 thereof at **[2.103]**.In relation to Scotland only, sub-ss (2A), (2B) are inserted by SI 2017/702, regs 2, 3, Schedule, Pt 4, paras 55, 60(2), except in relation to proceedings opened before 26 June 2017 and subject to savings in reg 4 thereof at **[2.103]**, as follows:

"(2A) Subsection (2B) applies where a statement sent to the registrar under section 172(10) indicates that a member State liquidator does not consent to the company being dissolved.

(2B) The company is not dissolved at the end of the period mentioned in subsection (2) but is instead dissolved at the end of the period of 3 months beginning with the date (if any) recorded in the register as the date on which the registrar was notified that—

(a) all proceedings identified in the statement under section 172(10) were closed, or

(b) every member State liquidator appointed in those proceedings consented to the company being dissolved.".

CHAPTER X

MALPRACTICE BEFORE AND DURING LIQUIDATION; PENALISATION OF COMPANIES AND COMPANY OFFICERS; INVESTIGATIONS AND PROSECUTIONS

Offences of fraud, deception, etc

[1.210]

206 Fraud, etc in anticipation of winding up

(1) When a company is ordered to be wound up by the court, or passes a resolution for voluntary winding up, any person, being a past or present officer of the company, is deemed to have committed an offence if, within the 12 months immediately preceding the commencement of the winding up, he has—

(a) concealed any part of the company's property to the value of [£500] or more, or concealed any debt due to or from the company, or

(b) fraudulently removed any part of the company's property to the value of [£500] or more, or

(c) concealed, destroyed, mutilated or falsified any book or paper affecting or relating to the company's property or affairs, or

(d) made any false entry in any book or paper affecting or relating to the company's property or affairs, or

(e) fraudulently parted with, altered or made any omission in any document affecting or relating to the company's property or affairs, or

(f) pawned, pledged or disposed of any property of the company which has been obtained on credit and has not been paid for (unless the pawning, pledging or disposal was in the ordinary way of the company's business).

(2) Such a person is deemed to have committed an offence if within the period above mentioned he has been privy to the doing by others of any of the things mentioned in paragraphs (c), (d) and (e) of subsection (1); and he commits an offence if, at any time after the commencement of the winding up, he does any of the things mentioned in paragraphs (a) to (f) of that subsection, or is privy to the doing by others of any of the things mentioned in paragraphs (c) to (e) of it.

(3) For purposes of this section, "officer" includes a shadow director.

(4) It is a defence—

(a) for a person charged under paragraph (a) or (f) of subsection (1) (or under subsection (2) in respect of the things mentioned in either of those two paragraphs) to prove that he had no intent to defraud, and

(b) for a person charged under paragraph (c) or (d) of subsection (1) (or under subsection (2) in respect of the things mentioned in either of those two paragraphs) to prove that he had no intent to conceal the state of affairs of the company or to defeat the law.

(5) Where a person pawns, pledges or disposes of any property in circumstances which amount to an offence under subsection (1)(f), every person who takes in pawn or pledge, or otherwise receives, the property knowing it to be pawned, pledged or disposed of in such circumstances, is guilty of an offence.

(6) A person guilty of an offence under this section is liable to imprisonment or a fine, or both.

(7) The money sums specified in paragraphs (a) and (b) of subsection (1) are subject to increase or reduction by order under section 416 in Part XV.

NOTES

This section derived from the Companies Act 1985, s 624, and the Insolvency Act 1985, Sch 6, para 25.

Sub-s (1): amounts in square brackets in sub-paras (a), (b) increased from £120 by the Insolvency Proceedings (Monetary Limits) Order 1986, SI 1986/1996, art 2(1), Schedule, Pt I.

[1.211]

207 Transactions in fraud of creditors

(1) When a company is ordered to be wound up by the court or passes a resolution for voluntary winding up, a person is deemed to have committed an offence if he, being at the time an officer of the company—

(a) has made or caused to be made any gift or transfer of, or charge on, or has caused or connived at the levying of any execution against, the company's property, or

(b) has concealed or removed any part of the company's property since, or within 2 months before, the date of any unsatisfied judgment or order for the payment of money obtained against the company.

(2) A person is not guilty of an offence under this section—

(a) by reason of conduct constituting an offence under subsection (1)(a) which occurred more than 5 years before the commencement of the winding up, or

(b) if he proves that, at the time of the conduct constituting the offence, he had no intent to defraud the company's creditors.

(3) A person guilty of an offence under this section is liable to imprisonment or a fine, or both.

NOTES

This section derived from the Companies Act 1985, s 625, and the Insolvency Act 1985, Sch 6, para 42.

[1.212]

208 Misconduct in course of winding up

(1) When a company is being wound up, whether by the court or voluntarily, any person, being a past or present officer of the company, commits an offence if he—

(a) does not to the best of his knowledge and belief fully and truly discover to the liquidator all the company's property, and how and to whom and for what consideration and when the company disposed of any part of that property (except such part as has been disposed of in the ordinary way of the company's business), or

(b) does not deliver up to the liquidator (or as he directs) all such part of the company's property as is in his custody or under his control, and which he is required by law to deliver up, or

(c) does not deliver up to the liquidator (or as he directs) all books and papers in his custody or under his control belonging to the company and which he is required by law to deliver up, or

(d) knowing or believing that a false debt has been proved by any person in the winding up, fails to inform the liquidator as soon as practicable, or

(e) after the commencement of the winding up, prevents the production of any book or paper affecting or relating to the company's property or affairs.

(2) Such a person commits an offence if after the commencement of the winding up he attempts to account for any part of the company's property by fictitious losses or expenses; and he is deemed to have committed that offence if he has so attempted [in connection with any qualifying decision procedure or deemed consent procedure] of the company's creditors within the 12 months immediately preceding the commencement of the winding up.

(3) For purposes of this section, "officer" includes a shadow director.

(4) It is a defence—

(a) for a person charged under paragraph (a), (b) or (c) of subsection (1) to prove that he had no intent to defraud, and

(b) for a person charged under paragraph (e) of that subsection to prove that he had no intent to conceal the state of affairs of the company or to defeat the law.

(5) A person guilty of an offence under this section is liable to imprisonment or a fine, or both.

NOTES

This section derived from the Companies Act 1985, s 626, and the Insolvency Act 1985, Sch 6, para 43.

Sub-s (2): words in square brackets substituted for original words "at any meeting" by the Small Business, Enterprise and Employment Act 2015, s 126, Sch 9, Pt 1, paras 1, 52, as from 6 April 2017 (in relation to England and Wales and subject to transitional and savings provisions as noted to s 246ZE at **[1.256]**), and as from a day to be appointed (in relation to Scotland).

[1.213]

209 Falsification of company's books

(1) When a company is being wound up, an officer or contributory of the company commits an offence if he destroys, mutilates, alters or falsifies any books, papers or securities, or makes or is privy to the making of any false or fraudulent entry in any register, book of account or document belonging to the company with intent to defraud or deceive any person.

(2) A person guilty of an offence under this section is liable to imprisonment or a fine, or both.

NOTES

This section derived from the Companies Act 1985, s 627.

[1.214]

210 Material omissions from statement relating to company's affairs

(1) When a company is being wound up, whether by the court or voluntarily, any person, being a past or present officer of the company, commits an offence if he makes any material omission in any statement relating to the company's affairs.

(2) When a company has been ordered to be wound up by the court, or has passed a resolution for voluntary winding up, any such person is deemed to have committed that offence if, prior to the winding up, he has made any material omission in any such statement.

(3) For purposes of this section, "officer" includes a shadow director.

(4) It is a defence for a person charged under this section to prove that he had no intent to defraud.

(5) A person guilty of an offence under this section is liable to imprisonment or a fine, or both.

NOTES

This section derived from the Companies Act 1985, s 628.

[1.215]

211 False representations to creditors

(1) When a company is being wound up, whether by the court or voluntarily, any person, being a past or present officer of the company—

(a) commits an offence if he makes any false representation or commits any other fraud for the purpose of obtaining the consent of the company's creditors or any of them to an agreement with reference to the company's affairs or to the winding up, and

(b) is deemed to have committed that offence if, prior to the winding up, he has made any false representation, or committed any other fraud, for that purpose.

(2) For purposes of this section, "officer" includes a shadow director.

(3) A person guilty of an offence under this section is liable to imprisonment or a fine, or both.

NOTES

This section derived from the Companies Act 1985, s 629.

Penalisation of directors and officers

[1.216]

212 Summary remedy against delinquent directors, liquidators, etc

(1) This section applies if in the course of the winding up of a company it appears that a person who—

(a) is or has been an officer of the company,

(b) has acted as liquidator . . . or administrative receiver of the company, or

(c) not being a person falling within paragraph (a) or (b), is or has been concerned, or has taken part, in the promotion, formation or management of the company,

has misapplied or retained, or become accountable for, any money or other property of the company, or been guilty of any misfeasance or breach of any fiduciary or other duty in relation to the company.

(2) The reference in subsection (1) to any misfeasance or breach of any fiduciary or other duty in relation to the company includes, in the case of a person who has acted as liquidator . . . of the company, any misfeasance or breach of any fiduciary or other duty in connection with the carrying out of his functions as liquidator . . . of the company.

(3) The court may, on the application of the official receiver or the liquidator, or of any creditor or contributory, examine into the conduct of the person falling within subsection (1) and compel him—

(a) to repay, restore or account for the money or property or any part of it, with interest at such rate as the court thinks just, or

(b) to contribute such sum to the company's assets by way of compensation in respect of the misfeasance or breach of fiduciary or other duty as the court thinks just.

(4) The power to make an application under subsection (3) in relation to a person who has acted as liquidator . . . of the company is not exercisable, except with the leave of the court, after [he] has had his release.

(5) The power of a contributory to make an application under subsection (3) is not exercisable except with the leave of the court, but is exercisable notwithstanding that he will not benefit from any order the court may make on the application.

NOTES

This section derived from the Insolvency Act 1985, s 19.

Sub-s (1): word ", administrator" (omitted) repealed by the Enterprise Act 2002, ss 248(3), 278(2), Sch 17, paras 9, 18(a), Sch 26, subject to savings and transitional provisions (i) in a case where a petition for an administration order has been presented before 15 September 2003 (see the Enterprise Act 2002 (Commencement No 4 and Transitional Provisions and Savings) Order 2003, SI 2003/2093, art 3 at **[2.26]**), and (ii) in relation to special administration regimes (see s 249 of the 2002 Act at **[2.10]**).

Sub-s (2): words "or administrator" omitted in each place, repealed by the Enterprise Act 2002, ss 248(3), 278(2), Sch 17, paras 9, 18(b), Sch 26, subject to savings and transitional provisions as noted to sub-s (1) above.

Sub-s (4): words "or administrator" (omitted) repealed and word in square brackets substituted for original words "that person", by the Enterprise Act 2002, ss 248(3), 278(2), Sch 17, paras 9, 18(c), Sch 26, subject to savings and transitional provisions as noted to sub-s (1) above.

[1.217]
213 Fraudulent trading

(1) If in the course of the winding up of a company it appears that any business of the company has been carried on with intent to defraud creditors of the company or creditors of any other person, or for any fraudulent purpose, the following has effect.
(2) The court, on the application of the liquidator may declare that any persons who were knowingly parties to the carrying on of the business in the manner above-mentioned are to be liable to make such contributions (if any) to the company's assets as the court thinks proper.

NOTES

This section derived from the Companies Act 1985, s 630(1), (2), and the Insolvency Act 1985, Sch 6, para 6(1).

[1.218]
214 Wrongful trading

(1) Subject to subsection (3) below, if in the course of the winding up of a company it appears that subsection (2) of this section applies in relation to a person who is or has been a director of the company, the court, on the application of the liquidator, may declare that that person is to be liable to make such contribution (if any) to the company's assets as the court thinks proper.
(2) This subsection applies in relation to a person if—
 (a) the company has gone into insolvent liquidation,
 (b) at some time before the commencement of the winding up of the company, that person knew or ought to have concluded that there was no reasonable prospect that the company would avoid going into insolvent liquidation [or entering insolvent administration], and
 (c) that person was a director of the company at that time; but the court shall not make a declaration under this section in any case where the time mentioned in paragraph (b) above was before 28th April 1986.
(3) The court shall not make a declaration under this section with respect to any person if it is satisfied that after the condition specified in subsection (2)(b) was first satisfied in relation to him that person took every step with a view to minimising the potential loss to the company's creditors as ([on the assumption that he had knowledge of the matter mentioned in subsection (2)(b)]) he ought to have taken.
(4) For the purposes of subsections (2) and (3), the facts which a director of a company ought to know or ascertain, the conclusions which he ought to reach and the steps which he ought to take are those which would be known or ascertained, or reached or taken, by a reasonably diligent person having both—
 (a) the general knowledge, skill and experience that may reasonably be expected of a person carrying out the same functions as are carried out by that director in relation to the company, and
 (b) the general knowledge, skill and experience that that director has.
(5) The reference in subsection (4) to the functions carried out in relation to a company by a director of the company includes any functions which he does not carry out but which have been entrusted to him.
(6) For the purposes of this section a company goes into insolvent liquidation if it goes into liquidation at a time when its assets are insufficient for the payment of its debts and other liabilities and the expenses of the winding up.
[(6A) For the purposes of this section a company enters insolvent administration if it enters administration at a time when its assets are insufficient for the payment of its debts and other liabilities and the expenses of the administration.]
(7) In this section "director" includes a shadow director.
(8) This section is without prejudice to section 213.

NOTES

This section derived from the Insolvency Act 1985, ss 12(9), 15(1)–(5), (7), Sch 9, para 4.

Sub-s (2): in para (b) words in square brackets inserted by the Small Business, Enterprise and Employment Act 2015, s 117(1), (3)(a), in respect of the carrying on of any business of the company on or after 1 October 2015.

Sub-s (3): words in square brackets substituted for original words "assuming him to have known that there was no reasonable prospect that the company would avoid going into insolvent liquidation", by the Small Business, Enterprise and Employment Act 2015, s 117(1), (3)(b), in respect of the carrying on of any business of the company on or after 1 October 2015.

Sub-s (6A): inserted by the Small Business, Enterprise and Employment Act 2015, s 117(1), (3)(c), in respect of the carrying on of any business of the company on or after 1 October 2015.

Disapplication: this section is disapplied, in respect of certain specified persons while Northern Rock is wholly owned by the Treasury, by the Northern Rock plc Transfer Order 2008, SI 2008/432, art 17, Schedule, para 3(a); in respect of certain specified persons while Bradford & Bingley is wholly owned by the Treasury, by the Bradford & Bingley plc Transfer of Securities and Property etc Order 2008, SI 2008/2546, art 13(1), Sch 1, para 3(a); and in respect of certain specified persons while Deposits Management (Heritable) is wholly owned by the Treasury, by the Heritable Bank plc Transfer of Certain Rights and Liabilities Order 2008, SI 2008/2644, art 26, Sch 2, para 3(a).

[1.219]
215 Proceedings under ss 213, 214

(1) On the hearing of an application under section 213 or 214, the liquidator may himself give evidence or call witnesses.

(2) Where under either section the court makes a declaration, it may give such further directions as it thinks proper for giving effect to the declaration; and in particular, the court may—

- (a) provide for the liability of any person under the declaration to be a charge on any debt or obligation due from the company to him, or on any mortgage or charge or any interest in a mortgage or charge on assets of the company held by or vested in him, or any person on his behalf, or any person claiming as assignee from or through the person liable or any person acting on his behalf, and
- (b) from time to time make such further order as may be necessary for enforcing any charge imposed under this subsection.

(3) For the purposes of subsection (2), "assignee"—

- (a) includes a person to whom or in whose favour, by the directions of the person made liable, the debt, obligation, mortgage or charge was created, issued or transferred or the interest created, but
- (b) does not include an assignee for valuable consideration (not including consideration by way of marriage [or the formation of a civil partnership]) given in good faith and without notice of any of the matters on the ground of which the declaration is made.

(4) Where the court makes a declaration under either section in relation to a person who is a creditor of the company, it may direct that the whole or any part of any debt owed by the company to that person and any interest thereon shall rank in priority after all other debts owed by the company and after any interest on those debts.

(5) Sections 213 and 214 have effect notwithstanding that the person concerned may be criminally liable in respect of matters on the ground of which the declaration under the section is to be made.

NOTES

This section derived from the Companies Act 1985, s 630(3)–(6), and the Insolvency Act 1985, s 15(6), Sch 6, para 6(2), (3).

Sub-s (3): words in square brackets inserted by the Civil Partnership Act 2004, s 261(1), Sch 27, para 112.

[1.220]
216 Restriction on re-use of company names

(1) This section applies to a person where a company ("the liquidating company") has gone into insolvent liquidation on or after the appointed day and he was a director or shadow director of the company at any time in the period of 12 months ending with the day before it went into liquidation.

(2) For the purposes of this section, a name is a prohibited name in relation to such a person if—

- (a) it is a name by which the liquidating company was known at any time in that period of 12 months, or
- (b) it is a name which is so similar to a name falling within paragraph (a) as to suggest an association with that company.

(3) Except with leave of the court or in such circumstances as may be prescribed, a person to whom this section applies shall not at any time in the period of 5 years beginning with the day on which the liquidating company went into liquidation—

- (a) be a director of any other company that is known by a prohibited name, or
- (b) in any way, whether directly or indirectly, be concerned or take part in the promotion, formation or management of any such company, or
- (c) in any way, whether directly or indirectly, be concerned or take part in the carrying on of a business carried on (otherwise than by a company) under a prohibited name.

(4) If a person acts in contravention of this section, he is liable to imprisonment or a fine, or both.

(5) In subsection (3) "the court" means any court having jurisdiction to wind up companies; and on an application for leave under that subsection, the Secretary of State or the official receiver may appear and call the attention of the court to any matters which seem to him to be relevant.

(6) References in this section, in relation to any time, to a name by which a company is known are to the name of the company at that time or to any name under which the company carries on business at that time.

(7) For the purposes of this section a company goes into insolvent liquidation if it goes into liquidation at a time when its assets are insufficient for the payment of its debts and other liabilities and the expenses of the winding up.

(8) In this section "company" includes a company which may be wound up under Part V of this Act.

NOTES

This section derived from the Insolvency Act 1985, s 17, Sch 9, para 5.

[1.221]
217 Personal liability for debts, following contravention of s 216

(1) A person is personally responsible for all the relevant debts of a company if at any time—

(a) in contravention of section 216, he is involved in the management of the company, or
(b) as a person who is involved in the management of the company, he acts or is willing to act on instructions given (without the leave of the court) by a person whom he knows at that time to be in contravention in relation to the company of section 216.

(2) Where a person is personally responsible under this section for the relevant debts of a company, he is jointly and severally liable in respect of those debts with the company and any other person who, whether under this section or otherwise, is so liable.

(3) For the purposes of this section the relevant debts of a company are—
(a) in relation to a person who is personally responsible under paragraph (a) of subsection (1), such debts and other liabilities of the company as are incurred at a time when that person was involved in the management of the company, and
(b) in relation to a person who is personally responsible under paragraph (b) of that subsection, such debts and other liabilities of the company as are incurred at a time when that person was acting or was willing to act on instructions given as mentioned in that paragraph.

(4) For the purposes of this section, a person is involved in the management of a company if he is a director of the company or if he is concerned, whether directly or indirectly, or takes part, in the management of the company.

(5) For the purposes of this section a person who, as a person involved in the management of a company, has at any time acted on instructions given (without the leave of the court) by a person whom he knew at that time to be in contravention in relation to the company of section 216 is presumed, unless the contrary is shown, to have been willing at any time thereafter to act on any instructions given by that person.

(6) In this section "company" includes a company which may be wound up under Part V.

NOTES

This section derived from the Insolvency Act 1985, s 18(1) (in part), (2)–(6).

Investigation and prosecution of malpractice

[1.222]

218 Prosecution of delinquent officers and members of company

(1) If it appears to the court in the course of a winding up by the court that any past or present officer, or any member, of the company has been guilty of any offence in relation to the company for which he is criminally liable, the court may (either on the application of a person interested in the winding up or of its own motion) direct the liquidator to refer the matter—
[(a) in the case of a winding up in England and Wales, to the Secretary of State, and
(b) in the case of a winding up in Scotland, to the Lord Advocate.]

(2) . . .

(3) If in the case of a winding up by the court in England and Wales it appears to the liquidator, not being the official receiver, that any past or present officer of the company, or any member of it, has been guilty of an offence in relation to the company for which he is criminally liable, the liquidator shall report the matter to the official receiver.

(4) If it appears to the liquidator in the course of a voluntary winding up that any past or present officer of the company, or any member of it, has been guilty of an offence in relation to the company for which he is criminally liable, he shall [forthwith report the matter—
(a) in the case of a winding up in England and Wales, to the Secretary of State, and
(b) in the case of a winding up in Scotland, to the Lord Advocate,
and shall furnish to the Secretary of State or (as the case may be) the Lord Advocate] such information and give to him such access to and facilities for inspecting and taking copies of documents (being information or documents in the possession or under the control of the liquidator and relating to the matter in question) as [the Secretary of State or (as the case may be) the Lord Advocate] requires.

[(5) Where a report is made to the Secretary of State under subsection (4) he may, for the purpose of investigating the matter reported to him and such other matters relating to the affairs of the company as appear to him to require investigation, exercise any of the powers which are exercisable by inspectors appointed under section 431 or 432 of [the Companies Act 1985] to investigate a company's affairs.]

(6) If it appears to the court in the course of a voluntary winding up that—
(a) any past or present officer of the company, or any member of it, has been guilty as above-mentioned, and
(b) no report with respect to the matter has been made by the liquidator . . . under subsection (4),
the court may (on the application of any person interested in the winding up or of its own motion) direct the liquidator to make such a report.

On a report being made accordingly, this section has effect as though the report had been made in pursuance of subsection (4).

NOTES

This section derived from the Companies Act 1985, s 632, and the Insolvency Act 1985, Sch 6, para 44.

Sub-ss (1), (4): words in square brackets substituted by the Insolvency Act 2000, s 10(1), (2), (4).

Sub-s (2): repealed by the Insolvency Act 2000, ss 10(1), (3), 15(1), Sch 5.

Sub-s (5): substituted by the Insolvency Act 2000, s 10(1), (5); words in square brackets substituted for original words "the Companies Act" by the Companies Act 2006 (Consequential Amendments, Transitional Provisions and Savings) Order 2009, SI 2009/1941, art 2(1), Sch 1, para 75(1), (24), subject to transitional provisions and savings in art 8, Sch 1, para 84 at **[2.70]**, **[2.73]**.

Sub-s (6): words omitted repealed by the Insolvency Act 2000, ss 10(1), (6), 15(1), Sch 5.

[1.223]

219 Obligations arising under s 218

(1) For the purpose of an investigation by the Secretary of State [in consequence of a report made to him under section 218(4)], any obligation imposed on a person by any provision of [the Companies Act 1985] to produce documents or give information to, or otherwise to assist, inspectors appointed as mentioned in [section 218(5)] is to be regarded as an obligation similarly to assist the Secretary of State in his investigation.

(2) An answer given by a person to a question put to him in exercise of the powers conferred by section 218(5) may be used in evidence against him.

[(2A) However, in criminal proceedings in which that person is charged with an offence to which this subsection applies—

- (a) no evidence relating to the answer may be adduced, and
- (b) no question relating to it may be asked,

by or on behalf of the prosecution, unless evidence relating to it is adduced, or a question relating to it is asked, in the proceedings by or on behalf of that person.

(2B) Subsection (2A) applies to any offence other than—

- (a) an offence under section 2 or 5 of the Perjury Act 1911 (false statements made on oath otherwise than in judicial proceedings or made otherwise than on oath), or
- (b) an offence under section 44(1) or (2) of the Criminal Law (Consolidation) (Scotland) Act 1995 (false statements made on oath or otherwise than on oath).]

(3) Where criminal proceedings are instituted by [the Director of Public Prosecutions, the Lord Advocate] or the Secretary of State following any report or reference under section 218, it is the duty of the liquidator and every officer and agent of the company past and present (other than the defendant or defender) to give to [the Director of Public Prosecutions, the Lord Advocate] or the Secretary of State (as the case may be) all assistance in connection with the prosecution which he is reasonably able to give.

For this purpose "agent" includes any banker or solicitor of the company and any person employed by the company as auditor, whether that person is or is not an officer of the company.

(4) If a person fails or neglects to give assistance in the manner required by subsection (3), the court may, on the application of the [Director of Public Prosecutions, the Lord Advocate] or the Secretary of State (as the case may be) direct the person to comply with that subsection; and if the application is made with respect to a liquidator, the court may (unless it appears that the failure or neglect to comply was due to the liquidator not having in his hands sufficient assets of the company to enable him to do so) direct that the costs shall be borne by the liquidator personally.

NOTES

This section derived from the Companies Act 1985, s 633.

Sub-s (1): words in first and third pairs of square brackets substituted by the Insolvency Act 2000, s 10(1), (7); words in second pair of square brackets substituted for original words "the Companies Act" by the Companies Act 2006 (Consequential Amendments, Transitional Provisions and Savings) Order 2009, SI 2009/1941, art 2(1), Sch 1, para 75(1), (24), subject to transitional provisions and savings in art 8, Sch 1, para 84 at **[2.70]**, **[2.73]**.

Sub-ss (3), (4): words in square brackets substituted by the Insolvency Act 2000, s 10(1), (7).

Sub-ss (2A), (2B): inserted by the Insolvency Act 2000, s 11.

PART V WINDING UP OF UNREGISTERED COMPANIES

NOTES

Application of this Part in relation to agricultural marketing boards: an agricultural marketing scheme may provide for the winding up of the board and, for that purpose, may apply this Part of the Act with certain modifications; see the Agricultural Marketing Act 1958, s 3(3), Sch 2, para 4.

Application of this Part in relation to friendly societies: for the purposes of the Friendly Societies Act 1992, s 52 (application to court in relation to regulation of friendly societies' business), this Part is applied in relation to the winding up of registered friendly societies; see s 52(9) of the 1992 Act.

Application of this Part in relation to financial markets: this Part is applied with modifications in relation to certain proceedings begun before the commencement of the Companies Act 1989, s 182, in respect of insolvency proceedings regarding members of recognised investment exchanges and clearing houses and persons to whom market charges have been granted; see s 182 of the 1989 Act at **[17.85]**.

Application of this Part in relation to the winding up of an open-ended investment company: see the Open-Ended Investment Companies Regulations 2001, SI 2001/1228, reg 31 at **[7.2052]**.

[1.224]

[220 Meaning of "unregistered company"

For the purposes of this Part "unregistered company" includes any association and any company, with the exception of a company registered under the Companies Act 2006 in any part of the United Kingdom.]

NOTES

Substituted by the Companies Act 2006 (Consequential Amendments, Transitional Provisions and Savings) Order 2009, SI 2009/1941, art 2(1), Sch 1, para 76(1), (2), subject to transitional provisions and savings in art 8, Sch 1, para 84 at **[2.70]**, **[2.73]**. Prior to this substitution, s 220 and the notes relating thereto, read as follows:

"220 Meaning of "unregistered company"

(1) For the purposes of this Part, the expression "unregistered company" includes *any trustee savings bank certified under the enactments relating to such banks*, any association and any company, with the following exceptions—

- (a) . . . ,
- (b) a company registered in any part of the United Kingdom under the Joint Stock Companies Acts or under the legislation (past or present) relating to companies in Great Britain.

(2) On such day as the Treasury appoints by order under section 4(3) of the Trustee Savings Banks Act 1985, the words in subsection (1) from "any trustee" to "banks" cease to have effect and are hereby repealed.

NOTES

This section derived from the Companies Act 1985, s 665.

Sub-s (1): words in italics formerly in the Companies Act 1985, s 665(1), and an additional word "and" following the word "banks" which is not reproduced, were repealed by the Trustee Savings Banks Act 1985, ss 4(3), 7(3), Sch 4. The repeal of those words was brought into force on 21 July 1986 by virtue of the Trustee Savings Banks Act 1985 (Appointed Day) (No 4) Order 1986, SI 1986/1223 (made under s 4(3) of that Act). It is thought, therefore, that, as construed in accordance with s 437, Sch 11, para 27 post, the words specified in sub-s (1) above, by virtue of sub-s (2) above, have ceased to have effect and are thus repealed; para (a) repealed by the Transport and Works Act 1992, ss 65(1)(f), 68(1), Sch 4, Pt I.".

[1.225]

221 Winding up of unregistered companies

(1) Subject to the provisions of this Part, any unregistered company may be wound up under this Act; and all the provisions of this Act . . . about winding up apply to an unregistered company with the exceptions and additions mentioned in the following subsections.

(2) If an unregistered company has a principal place of business situated in Northern Ireland, it shall not be wound up under this Part unless it has a principal place of business situated in England and Wales or Scotland, or in both England and Wales and Scotland.

(3) For the purpose of determining a court's winding-up jurisdiction, an unregistered company is deemed—

- (a) to be registered in England and Wales or Scotland, according as its principal place of business is situated in England and Wales or Scotland, or
- (b) if it has a principal place of business situated in both countries, to be registered in both countries;

and the principal place of business situated in that part of Great Britain in which proceedings are being instituted is, for all purposes of the winding up, deemed to be the registered office of the company.

(4) No unregistered company shall be wound up under this Act voluntarily[, except in accordance with the [EU Regulation]].

(5) The circumstances in which an unregistered company may be wound up are as follows—

- (a) if the company is dissolved, or has ceased to carry on business, or is carrying on business only for the purpose of winding up its affairs;
- (b) if the company is unable to pay its debts;
- (c) if the court is of opinion that it is just and equitable that the company should be wound up.

(6) A petition for winding up a trustee savings bank may be presented by the Trustee Savings Banks Central Board or by a commissioner appointed under section 35 of the Trustee Savings Banks Act 1981 as well as by any person authorised under Part IV of this Act to present a petition for the winding up of a company.

On such day as the Treasury appoints by order under section 4(3) of the Trustee Savings Banks Act 1985, this subsection ceases to have effect and is hereby repealed.

(7) In Scotland, an unregistered company which the Court of Session has jurisdiction to wind up may be wound up by the court if there is subsisting a floating charge over property comprised in the company's property and undertaking, and the court is satisfied that the security of the creditor entitled to the benefit of the floating charge is in jeopardy. For this purpose a creditor's security is deemed to be in jeopardy if the court is satisfied that events have occurred or are about to occur which render it unreasonable in the creditor's interests that the company should retain power to dispose of the property which is subject to the floating charge.

NOTES

This section derived from the Companies Act 1985, s 666.

Sub-s (1): words "and the Companies Act" (omitted) repealed by the Companies Act 2006 (Consequential Amendments, Transitional Provisions and Savings) Order 2009, SI 2009/1941, art 2(1), Sch 1, para 76(1), (3), subject to transitional provisions and savings in art 8, Sch 1, para 84 at **[2.70]**, **[2.73]**.

Sub-s (4): words in first (outer) pair of square brackets added by the Insolvency Act 1986 (Amendment) (No 2) Regulations 2002, SI 2002/1240, regs 3, 9; words in second (inner) pair of square brackets substituted for original words "EC Regulation" by the Insolvency Amendment (EU 2015/848) Regulations 2017, SI 2017/702, regs 2, 3, Schedule, Pt 1, paras 1, 13, except in relation to proceedings opened before 26 June 2017 and subject to savings in reg 4 thereof at **[2.103]**.

Sub-s (6): the Companies Act 1985, s 666(6), from which sub-s (6) above was principally derived, was repealed by the Trustee Savings Banks Act 1985, ss 4(3), 7(3), Sch 4, as from 21 July 1986 by virtue of the Trustee Savings Banks Act 1985 (Appointed Day) (No 4) Order 1986, SI 1986/1223 (made under s 4(3) of that Act). It is thought, therefore, that, as construed in accordance with s 437, Sch 11, para 27, sub-s (6) above has ceased to have effect and is thus repealed.

Application: in relation to the Lloyd's of London insurance market, sub-ss (1), (5) are applied by the Insurers (Reorganisation and Winding Up) (Lloyd's) Regulations 2005, SI 2005/1998, reg 29 at **[7.1598]**; in relation to the application of sub-s (1), with modifications, for the purposes of the European Grouping of Territorial Cooperation Regulations 2007, SI 2007/1949, see SI 2007/1949, regs 2, 7, 10, Schedule, Pt 2, para 7.

[1.226]

222 Inability to pay debts: unpaid creditor for £750 or more

(1) An unregistered company is deemed (for the purposes of section 221) unable to pay its debts if there is a creditor, by assignment or otherwise, to whom the company is indebted in a sum exceeding £750 then due and—

(a) the creditor has served on the company, by leaving at its principal place of business, or by delivering to the secretary or some director, manager or principal officer of the company, or by otherwise serving in such manner as the court may approve or direct, a written demand in the prescribed form requiring the company to pay the sum due, and

(b) the company has for 3 weeks after the service of the demand neglected to pay the sum or to secure or compound for it to the creditor's satisfaction.

(2) The money sum for the time being specified in subsection (1) is subject to increase or reduction by regulations under section 417 in Part XV; but no increase in the sum so specified affects any case in which the winding-up petition was presented before the coming into force of the increase.

NOTES

This section derived from the Companies Act 1985, s 667, and the Insolvency Act 1985, Sch 6, para 50.

[1.227]

223 Inability to pay debts: debt remaining unsatisfied after action brought

An unregistered company is deemed (for the purposes of section 221) unable to pay its debts if an action or other proceeding has been instituted against any member for any debt or demand due, or claimed to be due, from the company, or from him in his character of member, and—

(a) notice in writing of the institution of the action or proceeding has been served on the company by leaving it at the company's principal place of business (or by delivering it to the secretary, or some director, manager or principal officer of the company, or by otherwise serving it in such manner as the court may approve or direct), and

(b) the company has not within 3 weeks after service of the notice paid, secured or compounded for the debt or demand, or procured the action or proceeding to be stayed or sisted, or indemnified the defendant or defender to his reasonable satisfaction against the action or proceeding, and against all costs, damages and expenses to be incurred by him because of it.

NOTES

This section derived from the Companies Act 1985, s 668, and the Insolvency Act 1985, Sch 6, para 51.

[1.228]

224 Inability to pay debts: other cases

(1) An unregistered company is deemed (for purposes of section 221) unable to pay its debts—

(a) if in England and Wales execution or other process issued on a judgment, decree or order obtained in any court in favour of a creditor against the company, or any member of it as such, or any person authorised to be sued as nominal defendant on behalf of the company, is returned unsatisfied;

(b) if in Scotland the induciae of a charge for payment on an extract decree, or an extract registered bond, or an extract registered protest, have expired without payment being made;

(c) if in Northern Ireland a certificate of unenforceability has been granted in respect of any judgment, decree or order obtained as mentioned in paragraph (a);

(d) it is otherwise proved to the satisfaction of the court that the company is unable to pay its debts as they fall due.

(2) An unregistered company is also deemed unable to pay its debts if it is proved to the satisfaction of the court that the value of the company's assets is less than the amount of its liabilities, taking into account its contingent and prospective liabilities.

NOTES

This section derived from the Companies Act 1985, s 669, and the Insolvency Act 1985, Sch 6, para 52.

[1.229]

225 [Company incorporated outside Great Britain] may be wound up though dissolved

[(1)] Where a company incorporated outside Great Britain which has been carrying on business in Great Britain ceases to carry on business in Great Britain, it may be wound up as an unregistered company under this Act, notwithstanding that it has been dissolved or otherwise ceased to exist as a company under or by virtue of the laws of the country under which it was incorporated.

[(2) This section is subject to the [EU Regulation].]

NOTES

This section derived from the Companies Act 1985, s 670.

Section heading: words in square brackets substituted for original words "Oversea company" by the Companies Act 2006 (Consequential Amendments, Transitional Provisions and Savings) Order 2009, SI 2009/1941, art 2(1), Sch 1, para 76(1), (4), subject to transitional provisions and savings in art 8, Sch 1, para 84 at **[2.70]**, **[2.73]**.

Sub-s (1): numbered as such by the Insolvency Act 1986 (Amendment) (No 2) Regulations 2002, SI 2002/1240, regs 3, 10.

Sub-s (2): added by SI 2002/1240, regs 3, 10; words in square brackets substituted for original words "EC Regulation" by the Insolvency Amendment (EU 2015/848) Regulations 2017, SI 2017/702, regs 2, 3, Schedule, Pt 1, paras 1, 14, except in relation to proceedings opened before 26 June 2017 and subject to savings in reg 4 thereof at **[2.103]**.

[1.230]

226 Contributories in winding up of unregistered company

(1) In the event of an unregistered company being wound up, every person is deemed a contributory who is liable to pay or contribute to the payment of any debt or liability of the company, or to pay or contribute to the payment of any sum for the adjustment of the rights of members among themselves, or to pay or contribute to the payment of the expenses of winding up the company.

(2) Every contributory is liable to contribute to the company's assets all sums due from him in respect of any such liability as is mentioned above.

(3) In the case of an unregistered company engaged in or formed for working mines within the stannaries, a past member is not liable to contribute to the assets if he has ceased to be a member for 2 years or more either before the mine ceased to be worked or before the date of the winding-up order.

(4) . . .

NOTES

This section derived from the Companies Act 1985, s 671.

Sub-s (4): repealed by the Companies Act 2006 (Consequential Amendments, Transitional Provisions and Savings) Order 2009, SI 2009/1941, art 2(1), Sch 1, para 76(1), (5), subject to transitional provisions and savings in art 8, Sch 1, para 84 at **[2.70]**, **[2.73]**, and originally read as follows:

> "(4) In the event of the death, bankruptcy or insolvency of any contributory, the provisions of this Act with respect to the personal representatives, to the heirs and legatees of heritage of the heritable estate in Scotland of deceased contributories, and to the trustees of bankrupt or insolvent contributories, respectively apply.".

[1.231]

227 Power of court to stay, sist or restrain proceedings

The provisions of this Part with respect to staying, sisting or restraining actions and proceedings against a company at any time after the presentation of a petition for winding up and before the making of a winding-up order extend, in the case of an unregistered company, where the application to stay, sist or restrain is presented by a creditor, to actions and proceedings against any contributory of the company.

NOTES

This section derived from the Companies Act 1985, s 672.

[1.232]

228 Actions stayed on winding-up order

Where an order has been made for winding up an unregistered company, no action or proceeding shall be proceeded with or commenced against any contributory of the company in respect of any debt of the company, except by leave of the court, and subject to such terms as the court may impose.

NOTES

This section derived from the Companies Act 1985, s 673.

[1.233]

229 Provisions of this Part to be cumulative

(1) The provisions of this Part with respect to unregistered companies are in addition to and not in restriction of any provisions in Part IV with respect to winding up companies by the court; and the court or liquidator may exercise any powers or do any act in the case of unregistered companies which might be exercised or done by it or him in winding up [companies registered under the Companies Act 2006 in England and Wales or Scotland].

(2) . . .

NOTES

This section derived from the Companies Act 1985, s 674.

Sub-s (1): words in square brackets substituted for original words "companies formed and registered under the Companies Act" by the Companies Act 2006 (Consequential Amendments, Transitional Provisions and Savings) Order 2009, SI 2009/1941, art 2(1), Sch 1, para 76(1), (6)(a), subject to transitional provisions and savings in art 8, Sch 1, para 84 at **[2.70]**, **[2.73]**.

Sub-s (2): repealed by SI 2009/1941, art 2(1), Sch 1, para 76(1), (6)(b), subject to transitional provisions and savings in art 8, Sch 1, para 84 at **[2.70]**, **[2.73]**, and previously read as follows:

> "(2) However, an unregistered company is not, except in the event of its being wound up, deemed to be a company under the Companies Act, and then only to the extent provided by this Part of this Act.".

PART VI MISCELLANEOUS PROVISIONS APPLYING TO COMPANIES WHICH ARE INSOLVENT OR IN LIQUIDATION

NOTES

Modification of this Part in relation to building societies: this Part is applied with modifications in relation to the winding up, etc, of building societies; see the Building Societies Act 1986, ss 90, 90A, Schs 15, 15A at **[7.454]**, **[7.455]**, **[7.464]**, **[7.468]**.

Modification of this Part in relation to friendly societies: as to the application, with modifications, of this Part to the winding up of incorporated friendly societies by virtue of the Friendly Societies Act 1992, s 21(1) or 22(2), see s 23 of, and Sch 10 to, the 1992 Act.

Office-holders

[1.234]

230 Holders of office to be qualified insolvency practitioners

(1) . . .

(2) Where an administrative receiver of a company is appointed, he must be a person who is so qualified.

(3) Where a company goes into liquidation, the liquidator must be a person who is so qualified.

(4) Where a provisional liquidator is appointed, he must be a person who is so qualified.

(5) Subsections (3) and (4) are without prejudice to any enactment under which the official receiver is to be, or may be, liquidator or provisional liquidator.

NOTES

This section derived from the Insolvency Act 1985, ss 95(1), (2), 96(1).

Sub-s (1): repealed by the Enterprise Act 2002, ss 248(3), 287(2), Sch 17, paras 9, 19, Sch 26, subject to savings and transitional provisions (i) in a case where a petition for an administration order has been presented before 15 September 2003 (see the Enterprise Act 2002 (Commencement No 4 and Transitional Provisions and Savings) Order 2003, SI 2003/2093, art 3 at **[2.26]**), and (ii) in relation to special administration regimes (see s 249 of the 2002 Act at **[2.10]**), and originally read as follows:

"(1) Where an administration order is made in relation to a company, the administrator must be a person who is qualified to act as an insolvency practitioner in relation to the company.".

[1.235]

231 Appointment to office of two or more persons

(1) This section applies if an appointment or nomination of any person to the office of . . . administrative receiver, liquidator or provisional liquidator—

(a) relates to more than one person, or

(b) has the effect that the office is to be held by more than one person.

(2) The appointment or nomination shall declare whether any act required or authorised under any enactment to be done by the . . . administrative receiver, liquidator or provisional liquidator is to be done by all or any one or more of the persons for the time being holding the office in question.

NOTES

This section derived from the Insolvency Act 1985, ss 95(1), (2), 96(2).

Sub-ss (1), (2): word "administrator," (omitted) repealed by the Enterprise Act 2002, ss 248(3), 278(2), Sch 17, paras 9, 20, Sch 26, subject to savings and transitional provisions (i) in a case where a petition for an administration order has been presented before 15 September 2003 (see the Enterprise Act 2002 (Commencement No 4 and Transitional Provisions and Savings) Order 2003, SI 2003/2093, art 3 at **[2.26]**), and (ii) in relation to special administration regimes (see s 249 of the 2002 Act at **[2.10]**).

[1.236]

232 Validity of office-holder's acts

The acts of an individual as . . . administrative receiver, liquidator or provisional liquidator of a company are valid notwithstanding any defect in his appointment, nomination or qualifications.

NOTES

This section derived from the Insolvency Act 1985, ss 95(1), (2), 96(3).

Word "administrator," (omitted) repealed by the Enterprise Act 2002, ss 248(3), 278(2), Sch 17, paras 9, 21, Sch 26, subject to savings and transitional provisions (i) in a case where a petition for an administration order has been presented before 15 September 2003 (see the Enterprise Act 2002 (Commencement No 4 and Transitional Provisions and Savings) Order 2003, SI 2003/2093, art 3 at **[2.26]**), and (ii) in relation to special administration regimes (see s 249 of the 2002 Act at **[2.10]**).

Management by administrators, liquidators, etc

[1.237]

233 Supplies of gas, water, electricity, etc

(1) This section applies in the case of a company where—

[(a) the company enters administration,] or

(b) an administrative receiver is appointed, or

[(ba) a moratorium under section 1A is in force, or]

(c) a voluntary arrangement [approved under Part I], has taken effect, or

(d) the company goes into liquidation, or

(e) a provisional liquidator is appointed;

and "the office-holder" means the administrator, the administrative receiver, [the nominee,] the supervisor of the voluntary arrangement, the liquidator or the provisional liquidator, as the case may be.

(2) If a request is made by or with the concurrence of the office-holder for the giving, after the effective date, of any of the supplies mentioned in the next subsection, the supplier—

(a) may make it a condition of the giving of the supply that the office-holder personally guarantees the payment of any charges in respect of the supply, but

(b) shall not make it a condition of the giving of the supply, or do anything which has the effect of making it a condition of the giving of the supply, that any outstanding charges in respect of a supply given to the company before the effective date are paid.

(3) The supplies referred to in subsection (2) are—

[(a) a supply of gas by a gas supplier within the meaning of Part I of the Gas Act 1986;]

[(aa) a supply of gas by a person within paragraph 1 of Schedule 2A to the Gas Act 1986 (supply by landlords etc);]

[(b) a supply of electricity by an electricity supplier within the meaning of Part I of the Electricity Act 1989;]

[(ba) a supply of electricity by a class of person within Class A (small suppliers) or Class B (resale) of Schedule 4 to the Electricity (Class Exemptions from the Requirement for a Licence) Order 2001 (SI 2001/3270);]

(c) a supply of water by [a water undertaker] or, in Scotland, [Scottish Water],

[(ca) a supply of water by a water supply licensee within the meaning of the Water Industry Act 1991;

(cb) a supply of water by a water services provider within the meaning of the Water Services etc (Scotland) Act 2005;

(cc) a supply of water by a person who has an interest in the premises to which the supply is given;]

[(d) a supply of communications services by a provider of a public electronic communications service.]

[(e) a supply of communications services by a person who carries on a business which includes giving such supplies;

(f) a supply of goods or services mentioned in subsection (3A) by a person who carries on a business which includes giving such supplies, where the supply is for the purpose of enabling or facilitating anything to be done by electronic means.]

[(3A) The goods and services referred to in subsection (3)(f) are—

(a) point of sale terminals;

(b) computer hardware and software;

(c) information, advice and technical assistance in connection with the use of information technology;

(d) data storage and processing;

(e) website hosting.]

(4) "The effective date" for the purposes of this section is whichever is applicable of the following dates—

[(a) the date on which the company entered administration,]

(b) the date on which the administrative receiver was appointed (or, if he was appointed in succession to another administrative receiver, the date on which the first of his predecessors was appointed),

[(ba) the date on which the moratorium came into force,]

(c) the date on which the voluntary arrangement [took effect],

(d) the date on which the company went into liquidation,

(e) the date on which the provisional liquidator was appointed.

(5) The following applies to expressions used in subsection (3)—

(a)–(c) . . .

(d) "communications services" do not include electronic communications services to the extent that they are used to broadcast or otherwise transmit programme services (within the meaning of the Communications Act 2003).]

NOTES

This section derived from the Insolvency Act 1985, ss 95, 97.

Sub-s (1): para (a) substituted by the Enterprise Act 2002, s 248(3), Sch 17, paras 9, 22(a), subject to savings and transitional provisions (i) in a case where a petition for an administration order has been presented before 15 September 2003 (see the Enterprise Act 2002 (Commencement No 4 and Transitional Provisions and Savings) Order 2003, SI 2003/2093, art 3 at **[2.26]**), and (ii) in relation to special administration regimes (see s 249 of the 2002 Act at **[2.10]**), and originally read as follows:

"(a) an administration order is made in relation to the company, or";

para (ba) and final words in square brackets inserted, and second words in square brackets substituted, by the Insolvency Act 2000, s 1, Sch 1, paras 1, 8(1), (2).

Sub-s (3): para (a) substituted by the Gas Act 1995, s 16(1), Sch 4, para 14(1); para (b) substituted by the Utilities Act 2000, s 108, Sch 6, para 47(1), (2)(a); words in first pair of square brackets in para (c) substituted by the Water Act 1989, s 190(1), Sch 25, para 78(1) and words in second pair of square brackets substituted by the Water Industry (Scotland) Act 2002 (Consequential Modifications) Order 2004, SI 2004/1822, art 2, Schedule, Pt I, para 14(a); paras (aa), (ba), (ca)–(cc) inserted and paras (e), (f) added, by the Insolvency (Protection of Essential Supplies) Order 2015, SI 2015/989, art 2(1), (2); para (d) substituted by the Communications Act 2003, s 406(1), Sch 17, para 82(1), (2)(a), for the purpose of enabling network and service functions and spectrum functions to be carried out during the transitional period by the Director General of Telecommunications and the Secretary of State respectively (see further s 408 of, and Sch 18 to, the 2003 Act and the Communications Act 2003 (Commencement No 1) Order 2003, SI 2003/1900); the original para (d) read as follows:

"(d) a supply of telecommunication services by a public telecommunications operator.".

Sub-s (3A): inserted by SI 2015/989, art 2(1), (3).

Sub-s (4): para (a) substituted by the Enterprise Act 2002, s 248(3), Sch 17, paras 9, 22(b), subject to savings and transitional provisions as noted to sub-s (1) above, and originally read as follows:

"(a) the date on which the administration order was made";

para (ba) inserted, and words in square brackets substituted by the Insolvency Act 2000, s 1, Sch 1, paras 1, 8(1), (3).

Sub-s (5): para (a) repealed by the Gas Act 1995, ss 16(1), 17(5), Sch 4, para 14(2), Sch 6; para (b) repealed by the Utilities Act 2000, s 108, Sch 6, para 47(1), (2)(b), Sch 8; para (c) repealed by SI 2004/1822, art 2, Schedule, Pt I, para 14(b); para (d) substituted by the Communications Act 2003, s 406(1), Sch 17, para 82(1), (2)(b), for the purpose of enabling network and service functions and spectrum functions to be carried out during the transitional period by the Director General of

Telecommunications and the Secretary of State respectively (see further s 408 of, and Sch 18 to, the 2003 Act and the Communications Act 2003 (Commencement No 1) Order 2003, SI 2003/1900); the existing para (d), as amended by the Broadcasting Act 1990, s 203(1), Sch 20, para 43, read as follows:

> "(d) "telecommunication services" and "public telecommunications operator" mean the same as in the Telecommunications Act 1984, except that the former does not include [local delivery services within the meaning of Part II of the Broadcasting Act 1990.".

Modification: until the Water Act 2014, s 1 comes into force, sub-s (3)(ca) above is to be read as if for the words "water supply licensee" there were substituted the words "licensed water supplier", by virtue of SI 2015/989, art 2(1), (4).

[1.238]

[233A Further protection of essential supplies

(1) An insolvency-related term of a contract for the supply of essential goods or services to a company ceases to have effect if—

(a) the company enters administration, or

(b) a voluntary arrangement approved under Part 1 takes effect in relation to the company.

(2) An insolvency-related term of a contract does not cease to have effect by virtue of subsection (1) to the extent that—

(a) it provides for the contract or the supply to terminate, or any other thing to take place, because the company becomes subject to an insolvency procedure other than administration or a voluntary arrangement;

(b) it entitles a supplier to terminate the contract or the supply, or do any other thing, because the company becomes subject to an insolvency procedure other than administration or a voluntary arrangement; or

(c) it entitles a supplier to terminate the contract or the supply because of an event that occurs, or may occur, after the company enters administration or the voluntary arrangement takes effect.

(3) Where an insolvency-related term of a contract ceases to have effect under this section the supplier may—

(a) terminate the contract, if the condition in subsection (4) is met;

(b) terminate the supply, if the condition in subsection (5) is met.

(4) The condition in this subsection is that—

(a) the insolvency office-holder consents to the termination of the contract,

(b) the court grants permission for the termination of the contract, or

(c) any charges in respect of the supply that are incurred after the company entered administration or the voluntary arrangement took effect are not paid within the period of 28 days beginning with the day on which payment is due.

The court may grant permission under paragraph (b) only if satisfied that the continuation of the contract would cause the supplier hardship.

(5) The condition in this subsection is that—

(a) the supplier gives written notice to the insolvency office-holder that the supply will be terminated unless the office-holder personally guarantees the payment of any charges in respect of the continuation of the supply after the company entered administration or the voluntary arrangement took effect, and

(b) the insolvency office-holder does not give that guarantee within the period of 14 days beginning with the day the notice is received.

(6) For the purposes of securing that the interests of suppliers are protected, where—

(a) an insolvency-related term of a contract (the "original term") ceases to have effect by virtue of subsection (1), and

(b) the company subsequently enters administration, or a voluntary arrangement subsequently has effect in relation to it,

the contract is treated for the purposes of subsections (1) to (5) as if, immediately before the subsequent administration is entered into or the subsequent voluntary arrangement takes effect, it included an insolvency-related term identical to the original term.

(7) A contract for the supply of essential goods or services is a contract for a supply mentioned in section 233(3).

(8) An insolvency-related term of a contract for the supply of essential goods or services to a company is a provision of the contract under which—

(a) the contract or the supply would terminate, or any other thing would take place, because the company enters administration or the voluntary arrangement takes effect,

(b) the supplier would be entitled to terminate the contract or the supply, or to do any other thing, because the company enters administration or the voluntary arrangement takes effect, or

(c) the supplier would be entitled to terminate the contract or the supply because of an event that occurred before the company enters administration or the voluntary arrangement takes effect.

(9) In this section "insolvency office-holder" means—

(a) in a case where a company enters administration, the administrator;

(b) in a case where a voluntary arrangement under Part 1 takes effect in relation to a company, the supervisor of the voluntary arrangement.

(10) Subsection (1) does not have effect in relation to a contract entered into before 1st October 2015.]

NOTES

Commencement: 1 October 2015.

Inserted by the Insolvency (Protection of Essential Supplies) Order 2015, SI 2015/989, art 4.

[1.239]

234 Getting in the company's property

(1) This section applies in the case of a company where—

[(a) the company enters administration,] or

(b) an administrative receiver is appointed, or

(c) the company goes into liquidation, or

(d) a provisional liquidator is appointed;

and "the office-holder" means the administrator, the administrative receiver, the liquidator or the provisional liquidator, as the case may be.

(2) Where any person has in his possession or control any property, books, papers or records to which the company appears to be entitled, the court may require that person forthwith (or within such period as the court may direct) to pay, deliver, convey, surrender or transfer the property, books, papers or records to the office-holder.

(3) Where the office-holder—

(a) seizes or disposes of any property which is not property of the company, and

(b) at the time of seizure or disposal believes, and has reasonable grounds for believing, that he is entitled (whether in pursuance of an order of the court or otherwise) to seize or dispose of that property,

the next subsection has effect.

(4) In that case the office-holder—

(a) is not liable to any person in respect of any loss or damage resulting from the seizure or disposal except in so far as that loss or damage is caused by the office-holder's own negligence, and

(b) has a lien on the property, or the proceeds of its sale, for such expenses as were incurred in connection with the seizure or disposal.

NOTES

This section derived from the Insolvency Act 1985, ss 95(1), (2), 100(1), (2), (6).

Sub-s (1): para (a) substituted by the Enterprise Act 2002, s 248(3), Sch 17, paras 9, 23, subject to savings and transitional provisions (i) in a case where a petition for an administration order has been presented before 15 September 2003 (see the Enterprise Act 2002 (Commencement No 4 and Transitional Provisions and Savings) Order 2003, SI 2003/2093, art 3 at **[2.26]**), and (ii) in relation to special administration regimes (see s 249 of the 2002 Act at **[2.10]**) and originally read as follows:

"(a) an administration order is made in relation to the company, or".

Unfitness of directors: see the note to s 47 at **[1.33]**.

[1.240]

235 Duty to co-operate with office-holder

(1) This section applies as does section 234; and it also applies, in the case of a company in respect of which a winding-up order has been made by the court in England and Wales, as if references to the office-holder included the official receiver, whether or not he is the liquidator.

(2) Each of the persons mentioned in the next subsection shall—

(a) give to the office-holder such information concerning the company and its promotion, formation, business, dealings, affairs or property as the office-holder may at any time after the effective date reasonably require, and

(b) attend on the office-holder at such times as the latter may reasonably require.

(3) The persons referred to above are—

(a) those who are or have at any time been officers of the company,

(b) those who have taken part in the formation of the company at any time within one year before the effective date,

(c) those who are in the employment of the company, or have been in its employment (including employment under a contract for services) within that year, and are in the office-holder's opinion capable of giving information which he requires,

(d) those who are, or have within that year been, officers of, or in the employment (including employment under a contract for services) of, another company which is, or within that year was, an officer of the company in question, and

(e) in the case of a company being wound up by the court, any person who has acted as administrator, administrative receiver or liquidator of the company.

(4) For the purposes of subsections (2) and (3), "the effective date" is whichever is applicable of the following dates—

[(a) the date on which the company entered administration,]

(b) the date on which the administrative receiver was appointed or, if he was appointed in succession to another administrative receiver, the date on which the first of his predecessors was appointed,

(c) the date on which the provisional liquidator was appointed, and

(d) the date on which the company went into liquidation.

(5) If a person without reasonable excuse fails to comply with any obligation imposed by this section, he is liable to a fine and, for continued contravention, to a daily default fine.

NOTES

This section derived from the Insolvency Act 1985, ss 95(1), (2), 99.

Sub-s (4): para (a) substituted by the Enterprise Act 2002, s 248(3), Sch 17, paras 9, 24, subject to savings and transitional provisions (i) in a case where a petition for an administration order has been presented before 15 September 2003 (see the Enterprise Act 2002 (Commencement No 4 and Transitional Provisions and Savings) Order 2003, SI 2003/2093, art 3 at **[2.26]**), and (ii) in relation to special administration regimes (see s 249 of the 2002 Act at **[2.10]**), and originally read as follows:

"(a) the date on which the administration order was made,".

Unfitness of directors: see the note to s 47 at **[1.33]**.

[1.241]

236 Inquiry into company's dealings, etc

(1) This section applies as does section 234; and it also applies in the case of a company in respect of which a winding-up order has been made by the court in England and Wales as if references to the office-holder included the official receiver, whether or not he is the liquidator.

(2) The court may, on the application of the office-holder, summon to appear before it—

(a) any officer of the company,

(b) any person known or suspected to have in his possession any property of the company or supposed to be indebted to the company, or

(c) any person whom the court thinks capable of giving information concerning the promotion, formation, business, dealings, affairs or property of the company.

(3) The court may require any such person as is mentioned in subsection (2)(a) to (c) to submit [to the court] an account of his dealings with the company or to produce any books, papers or other records in his possession or under his control relating to the company or the matters mentioned in paragraph (c) of the subsection.

[(3A) An account submitted to the court under subsection (3) must be contained in—

(a) a witness statement verified by a statement of truth (in England and Wales), and

(b) an affidavit (in Scotland).]

(4) The following applies in a case where—

(a) a person without reasonable excuse fails to appear before the court when he is summoned to do so under this section, or

(b) there are reasonable grounds for believing that a person has absconded, or is about to abscond, with a view to avoiding his appearance before the court under this section.

(5) The court may, for the purpose of bringing that person and anything in his possession before the court, cause a warrant to be issued to a constable or prescribed officer of the court—

(a) for the arrest of that person, and

(b) for the seizure of any books, papers, records, money or goods in that person's possession.

(6) The court may authorise a person arrested under such a warrant to be kept in custody, and anything seized under such a warrant to be held, in accordance with the rules, until that person is brought before the court under the warrant or until such other time as the court may order.

NOTES

This section derived from the Insolvency Act 1985, ss 95(1), (2), 100(1), (2), (6).

Sub-s (3): words in square brackets substituted by the Legislative Reform (Insolvency) (Miscellaneous Provisions) Order 2010, SI 2010/18, arts 2, 5(6)(a).

Sub-s (3A): inserted by SI 2010/18, arts 2, 5(6)(b).

[1.242]

237 Court's enforcement powers under s 236

(1) If it appears to the court, on consideration of any evidence obtained under section 236 or this section, that any person has in his possession any property of the company, the court may, on the application of the office-holder, order that person to deliver the whole or any part of the property to the officer-holder at such time, in such manner and on such terms as the court thinks fit.

(2) If it appears to the court, on consideration of any evidence so obtained, that any person is indebted to the company, the court may, on the application of the office-holder, order that person to pay to the office-holder, at such time and in such manner as the court may direct, the whole or any part of the amount due, whether in full discharge of the debt or otherwise, as the court thinks fit.

(3) The court may, if it thinks fit, order that any person who if within the jurisdiction of the court would be liable to be summoned to appear before it under section 236 or this section shall be examined in any part of the United Kingdom where he may for the time being be, or in a place outside the United Kingdom.

(4) Any person who appears or is brought before the court under section 236 or this section may be examined on oath, either orally or (except in Scotland) by interrogatories, concerning the company or the matters mentioned in section 236(2)(c).

NOTES

This section derived from the Insolvency Act 1985, s 100(3)–(5), (7).

Adjustment of prior transactions (administration and liquidation)

[1.243]

238 Transactions at an undervalue (England and Wales)

(1) This section applies in the case of a company where—

[(a) the company enters administration,] or

(b) the company goes into liquidation;

and "the office-holder" means the administrator or the liquidator, as the case may be.

(2) Where the company has at a relevant time (defined in section 240) entered into a transaction with any person at an undervalue, the office-holder may apply to the court for an order under this section.

(3) Subject as follows, the court shall, on such an application, make such order as it thinks fit for restoring the position to what it would have been if the company had not entered into that transaction.

(4) For the purposes of this section and section 241, a company enters into a transaction with a person at an undervalue if—

- (a) the company makes a gift to that person or otherwise enters into a transaction with that person on terms that provide for the company to receive no consideration, or
- (b) the company enters into a transaction with that person for a consideration the value of which, in money or money's worth, is significantly less than the value, in money or money's worth, of the consideration provided by the company.

(5) The court shall not make an order under this section in respect of a transaction at an undervalue if it is satisfied—

- (a) that the company which entered into the transaction did so in good faith and for the purpose of carrying on its business, and
- (b) that at the time it did so there were reasonable grounds for believing that the transaction would benefit the company.

NOTES

This section derived from the Insolvency Act 1985, ss 95(1)(a), (b), 100(1) (in part), (2), (3).

Sub-s (1): para (a) substituted by the Enterprise Act 2002, s 248(3), Sch 17, paras 9, 25, subject to savings and transitional provisions (i) in a case where a petition for an administration order has been presented before 15 September 2003 (see the Enterprise Act 2002 (Commencement No 4 and Transitional Provisions and Savings) Order 2003, SI 2003/2093, art 3 at **[2.26]**), and (ii) in relation to special administration regimes (see s 249 of the 2002 Act at **[2.10]**), and originally read as follows:

"(a) an administration order is made in relation to the company,".

Make such order as it thinks fit: see further the Proceeds of Crime Act 2002, s 427 at **[17.243]**.

Unfitness of directors: see the note to s 127 at **[1.128]**.

[1.244]

239 Preferences (England and Wales)

(1) This section applies as does section 238.

(2) Where the company has at a relevant time (defined in the next section) given a preference to any person, the office-holder may apply to the court for an order under this section.

(3) Subject as follows, the court shall, on such an application, make such order as it thinks fit for restoring the position to what it would have been if the company had not given that preference.

(4) For the purposes of this section and section 241, a company gives a preference to a person if—

- (a) that person is one of the company's creditors or a surety or guarantor for any of the company's debts or other liabilities, and
- (b) the company does anything or suffers anything to be done which (in either case) has the effect of putting that person into a position which, in the event of the company going into insolvent liquidation, will be better than the position he would have been in if that thing had not been done.

(5) The court shall not make an order under this section in respect of a preference given to any person unless the company which gave the preference was influenced in deciding to give it by a desire to produce in relation to that person the effect mentioned in subsection (4)(b).

(6) A company which has given a preference to a person connected with the company (otherwise than by reason only of being its employee) at the time the preference was given is presumed, unless the contrary is shown, to have been influenced in deciding to give it by such a desire as is mentioned in subsection (5).

(7) The fact that something has been done in pursuance of the order of a court does not, without more, prevent the doing or suffering of that thing from constituting the giving of a preference.

NOTES

This section derived from the Insolvency Act 1985, ss 95(1)(a), (b), 100(1) (in part), (4)–(7), (11).

Make such order as it thinks fit: see further the Proceeds of Crime Act 2002, s 427 at **[17.243]**.

[1.245]

240 "Relevant time" under ss 238, 239

(1) Subject to the next subsection, the time at which a company enters into a transaction at an undervalue or gives a preference is a relevant time if the transaction is entered into, or the preference given—

- (a) in the case of a transaction at an undervalue or of a preference which is given to a person who is connected with the company (otherwise than by reason only of being its employee), at a time in the period of 2 years ending with the onset of insolvency (which expression is defined below),
- (b) in the case of a preference which is not such a transaction and is not so given, at a time in the period of 6 months ending with the onset of insolvency, . . .
- [(c) in either case, at a time between the making of an administration application in respect of the company and the making of an administration order on that application, and

(d) in either case, at a time between the filing with the court of a copy of notice of intention to appoint an administrator under paragraph 14 or 22 of Schedule B1 and the making of an appointment under that paragraph].

(2) Where a company enters into a transaction at an undervalue or gives a preference at a time mentioned in subsection (1)(a) or (b), that time is not a relevant time for the purposes of section 238 or 239 unless the company—

(a) is at that time unable to pay its debts within the meaning of section 123 in Chapter VI of Part IV, or

(b) becomes unable to pay its debts within the meaning of that section in consequence of the transaction or preference;

but the requirements of this subsection are presumed to be satisfied, unless the contrary is shown, in relation to any transaction at an undervalue which is entered into by a company with a person who is connected with the company.

(3) For the purposes of subsection (1), the onset of insolvency is—

[(a) in a case where section 238 or 239 applies by reason of an administrator of a company being appointed by administration order, the date on which the administration application is made,

(b) in a case where section 238 or 239 applies by reason of an administrator of a company being appointed under paragraph 14 or 22 of Schedule B1 following filing with the court of a copy of a notice of intention to appoint under that paragraph, the date on which the copy of the notice is filed,

(c) in a case where section 238 or 239 applies by reason of an administrator of a company being appointed otherwise than as mentioned in paragraph (a) or (b), the date on which the appointment takes effect,

(d) in a case where section 238 or 239 applies by reason of a company going into liquidation either following conversion of administration into winding up by virtue of [Article 51 of the EU Regulation] or at the time when the appointment of an administrator ceases to have effect, the date on which the company entered administration (or, if relevant, the date on which the application for the administration order was made or a copy of the notice of intention to appoint was filed), and

(e) in a case where section 238 or 239 applies by reason of a company going into liquidation at any other time, the date of the commencement of the winding up.]

NOTES

This section derived from the Insolvency Act 1985, s 100(8)–(11).

Sub-s (1): in para (b) word "and" repealed, and paras (c), (d) substituted for original para (c), by the Enterprise Act 2002, ss 248(3), 278(2), Sch 17, paras 9, 26, Sch 26, subject to savings and transitional provisions (i) in a case where a petition for an administration order has been presented before 15 September 2003 (see the Enterprise Act 2002 (Commencement No 4 and Transitional Provisions and Savings) Order 2003, SI 2003/2093, art 3 at **[2.26]**), and (ii) in relation to special administration regimes (see s 249 of the 2002 Act at **[2.10]**). Original para (c) read as follows:

> "(c) in either case, at a time between the presentation of a petition for the making of an administration order in relation to the company and the making of such an order on that petition.".

Sub-s (3): paras (a)–(e) substituted for existing paras (a), (aa), (b) (as inserted in the case of para (aa) by the Insolvency Act 1986 (Amendment) (No 2) Regulations 2002, SI 2002/1240, regs 3, 11) by the Enterprise Act 2002, s 248(3), Sch 17, paras 9, 26(1), (4), subject to savings and transitional provisions as noted to sub-s (1) above. Paras (a), (aa), (b) read as follows:

> "(a) in a case where section 238 or 239 applies by reason of the making of an administration order or of a company going into liquidation immediately upon the discharge of an administration order, the date of the presentation of the petition on which the administration order was made,
>
> [(aa) in a case where section 238 or 239 applies by reason of a company going into liquidation following conversion of administration into winding up by virtue of Article 37 of the EC Regulation, the date of the presentation of the petition on which the administration order was made,] and
>
> (b) in a case where the section applies by reason of a company going into liquidation at any other time, the date of the commencement of the winding up.";

words in square brackets in para (d) substituted for original words "Article 37 of the EC Regulation" by the Insolvency Amendment (EU 2015/848) Regulations 2017, SI 2017/702, regs 2, 3, Schedule, Pt 1, paras 1, 15, except in relation to proceedings opened before 26 June 2017 and subject to savings in reg 4 thereof at **[2.103]**.

Unfitness of directors: see the note to s 127 at **[1.128]**.

[1.246]

241 Orders under ss 238, 239

(1) Without prejudice to the generality of sections 238(3) and 239(3), an order under either of those sections with respect to a transaction or preference entered into or given by a company may (subject to the next subsection)—

(a) require any property transferred as part of the transaction, or in connection with the giving of the preference, to be vested in the company,

(b) require any property to be so vested if it represents in any person's hands the application either of the proceeds of sale of property so transferred or of money so transferred,

(c) release or discharge (in whole or in part) any security given by the company,

(d) require any person to pay, in respect of benefits received by him from the company, such sums to the office-holder as the court may direct,

(e) provide for any surety or guarantor whose obligations to any person were released or discharged (in whole or in part) under the transaction, or by the giving of the preference, to be under such new or revived obligations to that person as the court thinks appropriate,

(f) provide for security to be provided for the discharge of any obligation imposed by or arising under the order, for such an obligation to be charged on any property and for the security or charge to have the same priority as a security or charge released or discharged (in whole or in part) under the transaction or by the giving of the preference, and

(g) provide for the extent to which any person whose property is vested by the order in the company, or on whom obligations are imposed by the order, is to be able to prove in the winding up of the company for debts or other liabilities which arose from, or were released or discharged (in whole or in part) under or by, the transaction or the giving of the preference.

(2) An order under section 238 or 239 may affect the property of, or impose any obligation on, any person whether or not he is the person with whom the company in question entered into the transaction or (as the case may be) the person to whom the preference was given; but such an order—

(a) shall not prejudice any interest in property which was acquired from a person other than the company and was acquired [in good faith and for value], or prejudice any interest deriving from such an interest, and

(b) shall not require a person who received a benefit from the transaction or preference [in good faith and for value] to pay a sum to the office-holder, except where that person was a party to the transaction or the payment is to be in respect of a preference given to that person at a time when he was a creditor of the company.

[(2A) Where a person has acquired an interest in property from a person other than the company in question, or has received a benefit from the transaction or preference, and at the time of that acquisition or receipt—

(a) he had notice of the relevant surrounding circumstances and of the relevant proceedings, or

(b) he was connected with, or was an associate of, either the company in question or the person with whom that company entered into the transaction or to whom that company gave the preference,

then, unless the contrary is shown, it shall be presumed for the purposes of paragraph (a) or (as the case may be) paragraph (b) of subsection (2) that the interest was acquired or the benefit was received otherwise than in good faith.]

[(3) For the purposes of subsection (2A)(a), the relevant surrounding circumstances are (as the case may require)—

(a) the fact that the company in question entered into the transaction at an undervalue; or

(b) the circumstances which amounted to the giving of the preference by the company in question;

and subsections (3A) to (3C) have effect to determine whether, for those purposes, a person has notice of the relevant proceedings.

[(3A) Where section 238 or 239 applies by reason of a company's entering administration, a person has notice of the relevant proceedings if he has notice that—

(a) an administration application has been made,

(b) an administration order has been made,

(c) a copy of a notice of intention to appoint an administrator under paragraph 14 or 22 of Schedule B1 has been filed, or

(d) notice of the appointment of an administrator has been filed under paragraph 18 or 29 of that Schedule.]

[(3B) Where section 238 or 239 applies by reason of a company's going into liquidation at the time when the appointment of an administrator of the company ceases to have effect, a person has notice of the relevant proceedings if he has notice that—

(a) an administration application has been made,

(b) an administration order has been made,

(c) a copy of a notice of intention to appoint an administrator under paragraph 14 or 22 of Schedule B1 has been filed,

(d) notice of the appointment of an administrator has been filed under paragraph 18 or 29 of that Schedule, or

(e) the company has gone into liquidation.]

(3C) In a case where section 238 or 239 applies by reason of the company in question going into liquidation at any other time, a person has notice of the relevant proceedings if he has notice—

(a) where the company goes into liquidation on the making of a winding-up order, of the fact that the petition on which the winding-up order is made has been presented or of the fact that the company has gone into liquidation;

(b) in any other case, of the fact that the company has gone into liquidation.]

(4) The provisions of sections 238 to 241 apply without prejudice to the availability of any other remedy, even in relation to a transaction or preference which the company had no power to enter into or give.

NOTES

This section derived from the Insolvency Act 1985, ss 95(1), 102.

Sub-s (2): in paras (a), (b), words in square brackets substituted by the Insolvency (No 2) Act 1994, s 1(1), in relation to interests acquired and benefits received after 26 July 1994.

Sub-s (2A): inserted by s 1(2) of the 1994 Act, in relation to interests acquired and benefits received after 26 July 1994.

Sub-s (3): substituted, together with sub-ss (3A)–(3C), for sub-s (3) as originally enacted, by s 1(3) of the 1994 Act, in relation to interests acquired and benefits received after 26 July 1994.

Sub-s (3A): substituted, together with sub-ss (3), (3B), (3C), for sub-s (3) as originally enacted, by s 1(3) of the 1994 Act, in relation to interests acquired and benefits received after 26 July 1994; further substituted by the Enterprise Act 2002, s 248(3), Sch 17, paras 9, 27(1), (2), subject to savings and transitional provisions (i) in a case where a petition for an administration order has been presented before 15 September 2003 (see the Enterprise Act 2002 (Commencement No 4 and Transitional Provisions and Savings) Order 2003, SI 2003/2093, art 3 at **[2.26]**), and (ii) in relation to special administration regimes (see s 249 of the 2002 Act at **[2.10]**). Sub-s (3A) originally read as follows:

"(3A) In a case where section 238 or 239 applies by reason of the making of an administration order, a person has notice of the relevant proceedings if he has notice—

(a) of the fact that the petition on which the administration order is made has been presented; or

(b) of the fact that the administration order has been made.".

Sub-s (3B): substituted together with sub-ss (3), (3A), (3C), for sub-s (3) as originally enacted, by s 1(3) of the 1994 Act, in relation to interests acquired and benefits received after 26 July 1994; further substituted by the Enterprise Act 2002, s 248(3), Sch 17, paras 9, 27(1), (3), subject to savings and transitional provisions as noted to sub-s (3A) above. Sub-s (3B) originally read as follows:

"(3B) In a case where section 238 or 239 applies by reason of the company in question going into liquidation immediately upon the discharge of an administration order, a person has notice of the relevant proceedings if he has notice—

(a) of the fact that the petition on which the administration order is made has been presented;

(b) of the fact that the administration order has been made; or

(c) of the fact that the company has gone into liquidation.".

Sub-s (3C): substituted, together with sub-ss (3), (3A), (3B), for sub-s (3) as originally enacted, by s 1(3) of the 1994 Act, in relation to interests acquired and benefits received after 26 July 1994.

[1.247]

242 Gratuitous alienations (Scotland)

(1) Where this subsection applies and—

(a) the winding up of a company has commenced, an alienation by the company is challengeable by—

(i) any creditor who is a creditor by virtue of a debt incurred on or before the date of such commencement, or

(ii) the liquidator;

(b) [a company enters administration], an alienation by the company is challengeable by the administrator.

(2) Subsection (1) applies where—

(a) by the alienation, whether before or after 1st April 1986 (the coming into force of section 75 of the Bankruptcy (Scotland) Act 1985), any part of the company's property is transferred or any claim or right of the company is discharged or renounced, and

(b) the alienation takes place on a relevant day.

(3) For the purposes of subsection (2)(b), the day on which an alienation takes place is the day on which it becomes completely effectual; and in that subsection "relevant day" means, if the alienation has the effect of favouring—

(a) a person who is an associate (within the meaning of the Bankruptcy (Scotland) Act [2016]) of the company, a day not earlier than 5 years before the date on which—

(i) the winding up of the company commences, or

(ii) as the case may be, [the company enters administration]; or

(b) any other person, a day not earlier than 2 years before that date.

(4) On a challenge being brought under subsection (1), the court shall grant decree of reduction or for such restoration of property to the company's assets or other redress as may be appropriate; but the court shall not grant such a decree if the person seeking to uphold the alienation establishes—

(a) that immediately, or at any other time, after the alienation the company's assets were greater than its liabilities, or

(b) that the alienation was made for adequate consideration, or

(c) that the alienation—

(i) was a birthday, Christmas or other conventional gift, or

(ii) was a gift made, for a charitable purpose, to a person who is not an associate of the company,

which, having regard to all the circumstances, it was reasonable for the company to make:

Provided that this subsection is without prejudice to any right or interest acquired in good faith and for value from or through the transferee in the alienation.

(5) In subsection (4) above, "charitable purpose" means any charitable, benevolent or philanthropic purpose, whether or not it is charitable within the meaning of any rule of law.

(6) For the purposes of the foregoing provisions of this section, an alienation in implementation of a prior obligation is deemed to be one for which there was no consideration or no adequate consideration to the extent that the prior obligation was undertaken for no consideration or no adequate consideration.

(7) A liquidator and an administrator have the same right as a creditor has under any rule of law to challenge an alienation of a company made for no consideration or no adequate consideration.

(8) This section applies to Scotland only.

NOTES

This section derived from the Companies Act 1985, s 615A, and the Bankruptcy (Scotland) Act 1985, Sch 7, para 20.

Sub-s (1): words in square brackets substituted for original words "an administration order is in force in relation to a company" by the Enterprise Act 2002, s 248(3), Sch 17, paras 9, 28(1), (2), subject to savings and transitional provisions (i) in a case where a petition for an administration order has been presented before 15 September 2003 (see the Enterprise Act 2002 (Commencement No 4 and Transitional Provisions and Savings) Order 2003, SI 2003/2093, art 3 at **[2.26]**), and (ii) in relation to special administration regimes (see s 249 of the 2002 Act at **[2.10]**).

Sub-s (3): year "2016" in square brackets substituted (for the original year "1985") by the Bankruptcy (Scotland) Act 2016 (Consequential Provisions and Modifications) Order 2016, SI 2016/1034, art 7(1), (3), Sch 1, para 4(1), (5), as from 30 November 2016 (except in relation to (i) a sequestration as regards which the petition is presented, or the debtor application is made before that date; or (ii) a trust deed executed before that date); words in square brackets substituted for original words "the administration order is made" by the Enterprise Act 2002, s 248(3), Sch 17, paras 9, 28(1), (3), subject to savings as noted to sub-s (1) above.

The court shall grant decree: see further the Proceeds of Crime Act 2002, s 427 at **[17.243]**.

[1.248]

243 Unfair preferences (Scotland)

(1) Subject to subsection (2) below, subsection (4) below applies to a transaction entered into by a company, whether before or after 1st April 1986, which has the effect of creating a preference in favour of a creditor to the prejudice of the general body of creditors, being a preference created not earlier than 6 months before the commencement of the winding up of the company or [the company enters administration].

(2) Subsection (4) below does not apply to any of the following transactions—

- (a) a transaction in the ordinary course of trade or business;
- (b) a payment in cash for a debt which when it was paid had become payable, unless the transaction was collusive with the purpose of prejudicing the general body of creditors;
- (c) a transaction whereby the parties to it undertake reciprocal obligations (whether the performance by the parties of their respective obligations occurs at the same time or at different times) unless the transaction was collusive as aforesaid;
- (d) the granting of a mandate by a company authorising an arrestee to pay over the arrested funds or part thereof to the arrester where—
  - (i) there has been a decree for payment or a warrant for summary diligence, and
  - (ii) the decree or warrant has been preceded by an arrestment on the dependence of the action or followed by an arrestment in execution.

(3) For the purposes of subsection (1) above, the day on which a preference was created is the day on which the preference became completely effectual.

(4) A transaction to which this subsection applies is challengeable by—

- (a) in the case of a winding up—
  - (i) any creditor who is a creditor by virtue of a debt incurred on or before the date of commencement of the winding up, or
  - (ii) the liquidator; and
- (b) [where the company has entered administration], the administrator.

(5) On a challenge being brought under subsection (4) above, the court, if satisfied that the transaction challenged is a transaction to which this section applies, shall grant decree of reduction or for such restoration of property to the company's assets or other redress as may be appropriate:

Provided that this subsection is without prejudice to any right or interest acquired in good faith and for value from or through the creditor in whose favour the preference was created.

(6) A liquidator and an administrator have the same right as a creditor has under any rule of law to challenge a preference created by a debtor.

(7) This section applies to Scotland only.

NOTES

This section derived from the Companies Act 1985, s 615B, and the Bankruptcy (Scotland) Act 1985, Sch 7, para 20.

Sub-s (1): words in square brackets substituted for original words "the making of an administration order in relation to the company" by the Enterprise Act 2002, s 248(3), Sch 17, paras 9, 29(1), (2), subject to savings and transitional provisions (i) in a case where a petition for an administration order has been presented before 15 September 2003 (see the Enterprise Act 2002 (Commencement No 4 and Transitional Provisions and Savings) Order 2003, SI 2003/2093, art 3 at **[2.26]**), and (ii) in relation to special administration regimes (see s 249 of the 2002 Act at **[2.10]**).

Sub-s (4): words in square brackets substituted for original words "in the case of an administration order" by the Enterprise Act 2002, s 248(3), Sch 17, paras 9, 29(1), (3), subject to savings as noted to sub-s (1) above.

The court shall grant decree: see further the Proceeds of Crime Act 2002, s 427 at **[17.243]**.

[1.249]

244 Extortionate credit transactions

(1) This section applies as does section 238, and where the company is, or has been, a party to a transaction for, or involving, the provision of credit to the company.

(2) The court may, on the application of the office-holder, make an order with respect to the transaction if the transaction is or was extortionate and was entered into in the period of 3 years ending with [the day on which the company entered administration or went into liquidation].

(3) For the purposes of this section a transaction is extortionate if, having regard to the risk accepted by the person providing the credit—

- (a) the terms of it are or were such as to require grossly exorbitant payments to be made (whether unconditionally or in certain contingencies) in respect of the provision of the credit, or
- (b) it otherwise grossly contravened ordinary principles of fair dealing;

and it shall be presumed, unless the contrary is proved, that a transaction with respect to which an application is made under this section is or, as the case may be, was extortionate.

(4) An order under this section with respect to any transaction may contain such one or more of the following as the court thinks fit, that is to say—

- (a) provision setting aside the whole or part of any obligation created by the transaction,
- (b) provision otherwise varying the terms of the transaction or varying the terms on which any security for the purposes of the transaction is held,
- (c) provision requiring any person who is or was a party to the transaction to pay to the office-holder any sums paid to that person, by virtue of the transaction, by the company,

(d) provision requiring any person to surrender to the office-holder any property held by him as security for the purposes of the transaction,

(e) provision directing accounts to be taken between any persons.

(5) The powers conferred by this section are exercisable in relation to any transaction concurrently with any powers exercisable in relation to that transaction as a transaction at an undervalue or under section 242 (gratuitous alienations in Scotland).

NOTES

This section derived from the Insolvency Act 1985, ss 95(1)(a), (b), 103.

Sub-s (2): words in square brackets substituted for original words "the day on which the administration order was made or (as the case may be) the company went into liquidation" by the Enterprise Act 2002, s 248(3), Sch 17, paras 9, 30, subject to savings and transitional provisions (i) in a case where a petition for an administration order has been presented before 15 September 2003 (see the Enterprise Act 2002 (Commencement No 4 and Transitional Provisions and Savings) Order 2003, SI 2003/2093, art 3 at **[2.26]**), and (ii) in relation to special administration regimes (see s 249 of the 2002 Act at **[2.10]**).

[1.250]

245 Avoidance of certain floating charges

(1) This section applies as does section 238, but applies to Scotland as well as to England and Wales.

(2) Subject as follows, a floating charge on the company's undertaking or property created at a relevant time is invalid except to the extent of the aggregate of—

(a) the value of so much of the consideration for the creation of the charge as consists of money paid, or goods or services supplied, to the company at the same time as, or after, the creation of the charge,

(b) the value of so much of that consideration as consists of the discharge or reduction, at the same time as, or after, the creation of the charge, of any debt of the company, and

(c) the amount of such interest (if any) as is payable on the amount falling within paragraph (a) or (b) in pursuance of any agreement under which the money was so paid, the goods or services were so supplied or the debt was so discharged or reduced.

(3) Subject to the next subsection, the time at which a floating charge is created by a company is a relevant time for the purposes of this section if the charge is created—

(a) in the case of a charge which is created in favour of a person who is connected with the company, at a time in the period of 2 years ending with the onset of insolvency,

(b) in the case of a charge which is created in favour of any other person, at a time in the period of 12 months ending with the onset of insolvency, . . .

[(c) in either case, at a time between the making of an administration application in respect of the company and the making of an administration order on that application, or

(d) in either case, at a time between the filing with the court of a copy of notice of intention to appoint an administrator under paragraph 14 or 22 of Schedule B1 and the making of an appointment under that paragraph.]

(4) Where a company creates a floating charge at a time mentioned in subsection (3)(b) and the person in favour of whom the charge is created is not connected with the company, that time is not a relevant time for the purposes of this section unless the company—

(a) is at that time unable to pay its debts within the meaning of section 123 in Chapter VI of Part IV, or

(b) becomes unable to pay its debts within the meaning of that section in consequence of the transaction under which the charge is created.

(5) For the purposes of subsection (3), the onset of insolvency is—

[(a) in a case where this section applies by reason of an administrator of a company being appointed by administration order, the date on which the administration application is made,

(b) in a case where this section applies by reason of an administrator of a company being appointed under paragraph 14 or 22 of Schedule B1 following filing with the court of a copy of notice of intention to appoint under that paragraph, the date on which the copy of the notice is filed,

(c) in a case where this section applies by reason of an administrator of a company being appointed otherwise than as mentioned in paragraph (a) or (b), the date on which the appointment takes effect, and

(d) in a case where this section applies by reason of a company going into liquidation, the date of the commencement of the winding up.]

(6) For the purposes of subsection (2)(a) the value of any goods or services supplied by way of consideration for a floating charge is the amount in money which at the time they were supplied could reasonably have been expected to be obtained for supplying the goods or services in the ordinary course of business and on the same terms (apart from the consideration) as those on which they were supplied to the company.

NOTES

This section derived from the Insolvency Act 1985, ss 95(1)(a), (b), 104.

Sub-s (3): in para (b) word "or" repealed, and paras (c), (d) substituted for original para (c), by the Enterprise Act 2002, ss 248(3), 278(2), Sch 17, paras 9, 31(1)–(3), Sch 26, subject to savings and transitional provisions (i) in a case where a petition for an administration order has been presented before 15 September 2003 (see the Enterprise Act 2002 (Commencement No 4 and Transitional Provisions and Savings) Order 2003, SI 2003/2093, art 3 at **[2.26]**), and (ii) in relation to special administration regimes (see s 249 of the 2002 Act at **[2.10]**). Original para (c) read as follows:

"(c) in either case, at a time between the presentation of a petition for the making of an administration order in relation to the company and the making of such an order on that petition.".

Sub-s (5): paras (a)–(d) substituted for original paras (a), (b), by the Enterprise Act 2002, ss 248(3), 278(2), Sch 17, paras 9,

31(1), (4), Sch 26, subject to savings as noted to sub-s (3) above. Original paras (a), (b) read as follows:

"(a) in a case where this section applies by reason of the making of an administration order, the date of the presentation of the petition on which the order was made, and

(b) in a case where this section applies by reason of a company going into liquidation, the date of the commencement of the winding up.".

See further: as to the disapplication of this section in relation to any charge created or otherwise arising under a security financial collateral arrangement: the Financial Collateral Arrangements (No 2) Regulations 2003, SI 2003/3226, reg 10(5) at **[3.290]**.

[1.251]

246 Unenforceability of liens on books, etc

(1) This section applies in the case of a company where—

[(a) the company enters administration,] or

(b) the company goes into liquidation, or

(c) a provisional liquidator is appointed;

and "the office-holder" means the administrator, the liquidator or the provisional liquidator, as the case may be.

(2) Subject as follows, a lien or other right to retain possession of any of the books, papers or other records of the company is unenforceable to the extent that its enforcement would deny possession of any books, papers or other records to the office-holder.

(3) This does not apply to a lien on documents which give a title to property and are held as such.

NOTES

This section derived from the Insolvency Act 1985, ss 95(1)(a), (b), (2), 105.

Sub-s (1): para (a) substituted by the Enterprise Act 2002, s 248(3), Sch 17, paras 9, 32, subject to savings and transitional provisions (i) in a case where a petition for an administration order has been presented before 15 September 2003 (see the Enterprise Act 2002 (Commencement No 4 and Transitional Provisions and Savings) Order 2003, SI 2003/2093, art 3 at **[2.26]**), and (ii) in relation to special administration regimes (see s 249 of the 2002 Act at **[2.10]**), and originally read as follows:

"(a) an administration order is made in relation to the company,".

[Administration: penalisation of directors etc

[1.252]

246ZA Fraudulent trading: administration

(1) If while a company is in administration it appears that any business of the company has been carried on with intent to defraud creditors of the company or creditors of any other person, or for any fraudulent purpose, the following has effect.

(2) The court, on the application of the administrator, may declare that any persons who were knowingly parties to the carrying on of the business in the manner mentioned in subsection (1) are to be liable to make such contributions (if any) to the company's assets as the court thinks proper.]

NOTES

Commencement: 1 October 2015 (in respect of the carrying on of any business of the company on or after that date).

Inserted, together with the preceding cross-heading and ss 246ZB, 246ZC, by the Small Business, Enterprise and Employment Act 2015, s 117(1), (2), in respect of the carrying on of any business of the company on or after 1 October 2015.

Transitional provisions: see the Deregulation Act 2015, the Small Business, Enterprise and Employment Act 2015 and the Insolvency (Amendment) Act (Northern Ireland) 2016 (Consequential Amendments and Transitional Provisions) Regulations 2017, SI 2017/400, reg 15, which provides as follows (note that "the commencement date" is 7 April 2017)—

"(1) Sections 246ZA to 246ZC (administration: penalisation of directors etc) do not apply in relation to—

(a) any relevant proceedings commenced before the commencement date; or

(b) the administration of a building society under Part 2 of the 1986 Act (as applied by section 90A of the Building Societies Act 1986) commenced before the commencement date.

(2) *(Not relevant.)*

(3) "Relevant proceedings" means—

(a) bank administration under Part 3 of the 2009 Act; or

(b) building society special administration under Part 3 of the 2009 Act (as applied by section 90C of the Building Societies Act 1986).".

[1.253]

[246ZB Wrongful trading: administration

(1) Subject to subsection (3), if while a company is in administration it appears that subsection (2) applies in relation to a person who is or has been a director of the company, the court, on the application of the administrator, may declare that that person is to be liable to make such contribution (if any) to the company's assets as the court thinks proper.

(2) This subsection applies in relation to a person if—

(a) the company has entered insolvent administration,

(b) at some time before the company entered administration, that person knew or ought to have concluded that there was no reasonable prospect that the company would avoid entering insolvent administration or going into insolvent liquidation, and

(c) the person was a director of the company at that time.

(3) The court must not make a declaration under this section with respect to any person if it is satisfied that, after the condition specified in subsection (2)(b) was first satisfied in relation to the person, the person took every step with a view to minimising the potential loss to the company's creditors as (on the assumption that the person had knowledge of the matter mentioned in subsection (2)(b)) the person ought to have taken.

(4) For the purposes of subsections (2) and (3), the facts which a director of a company ought to know or ascertain, the conclusions which the director ought to reach and the steps which the director ought to take are those which would be known or ascertained, or reached or taken, by a reasonably diligent person having both—

(a) the general knowledge, skill and experience that may reasonably be expected of a person carrying out the same functions as are carried out by that director in relation to the company, and

(b) the general knowledge, skill and experience that that director has.

(5) The reference in subsection (4) to the functions carried out in relation to a company by a director of the company includes any functions which the director does not carry out but which have been entrusted to the director.

(6) For the purposes of this section—

(a) a company enters insolvent administration if it enters administration at a time when its assets are insufficient for the payment of its debts and other liabilities and the expenses of the administration;

(b) a company goes into insolvent liquidation if it goes into liquidation at a time when its assets are insufficient for the payment of its debts and other liabilities and the expenses of the winding up.

(7) In this section "director" includes shadow director.

(8) This section is without prejudice to section 246ZA.]

NOTES

Commencement: 1 October 2015 (in respect of the carrying on of any business of the company on or after that date).

Inserted as noted to s 246ZA at **[1.252]**.

Transitional provisions: see the note to s 246ZA at **[1.252]**.

[1.254]

[246ZC Proceedings under section 246ZA or 246ZB

Section 215 applies for the purposes of an application under section 246ZA or 246ZB as it applies for the purposes of an application under section 213 but as if the reference in subsection (1) of section 215 to the liquidator was a reference to the administrator.]

NOTES

Commencement: 1 October 2015 (in respect of the carrying on of any business of the company on or after that date).

Inserted as noted to s 246ZA at **[1.252]**.

Transitional provisions: see the note to s 246ZA at **[1.252]**.

[Power to assign certain causes of action

[1.255]

246ZD Power to assign

(1) This section applies in the case of a company where—

(a) the company enters administration, or

(b) the company goes into liquidation;

and "the office-holder" means the administrator or the liquidator, as the case may be.

(2) The office-holder may assign a right of action (including the proceeds of an action) arising under any of the following—

(a) section 213 or 246ZA (fraudulent trading);

(b) section 214 or 246ZB (wrongful trading);

(c) section 238 (transactions at an undervalue (England and Wales));

(d) section 239 (preferences (England and Wales));

(e) section 242 (gratuitous alienations (Scotland));

(f) section 243 (unfair preferences (Scotland));

(g) section 244 (extortionate credit transactions).]

NOTES

Commencement: 1 October 2015 (in respect of a company which enters administration or goes into liquidation on or after that date).

Inserted, together with preceding cross-heading, by the Small Business, Enterprise and Employment Act 2015, s 118, in respect of a company which enters administration or goes into liquidation on or after 1 October 2015.

Transitional provisions: see the Deregulation Act 2015, the Small Business, Enterprise and Employment Act 2015 and the Insolvency (Amendment) Act (Northern Ireland) 2016 (Consequential Amendments and Transitional Provisions) Regulations 2017, SI 2017/400, reg 16, which provides as follows—

"(1) Section 246ZD (power to assign certain causes of action) does not apply in relation to any relevant proceedings commenced before the commencement date.

(2) "Relevant proceedings" means—

(a) any proceedings of a kind specified in regulation 14(2)(a) to (e); or

(b) the winding up of a relevant scheme (within the meaning given in regulation 17(1)(a) of the Collective Investment in Transferable Securities (Contractual Scheme) Regulations 2013).".

Note for the purposes of reg 16 above that "the commencement date" is 7 April 2017. Note also that proceedings of a kind specified in reg 14(2)(a) to (e) are as follows: (a) bank insolvency under Part 2 of the 2009 Act or bank administration under

Part 3 of that Act; (b) building society insolvency under Part 2 of the 2009 Act (as applied by section 90C of the Building Societies Act 1986); (c) building society special administration under Part 3 of the 2009 Act (as applied by section 90C of the Building Societies Act 1986); (d) the administration of a building society under Part 2 of the 1986 Act (as applied by section 90A of the Building Societies Act 1986); and (e) special administration, special administration (bank insolvency) or special administration (bank administration) under the Investment Bank Special Administration Regulations 2011.

[Decisions by creditors and contributories

[1.256]

246ZE Decisions by creditors and contributories: general

(1) This section applies where, for the purposes of this Group of Parts, a person ("P") seeks a decision about any matter from a company's creditors or contributories.

(2) The decision may be made by any qualifying decision procedure P thinks fit, except that it may not be made by a creditors' meeting or (as the case may be) a contributories' meeting unless subsection (3) applies.

(3) This subsection applies if at least the minimum number of creditors or (as the case may be) contributories make a request to P in writing that the decision be made by a creditors' meeting or (as the case may be) a contributories' meeting.

(4) If subsection (3) applies P must summon a creditors' meeting or (as the case may be) a contributories' meeting.

(5) Subsection (2) is subject to any provision of this Act, the rules or any other legislation, or any order of the court—

(a) requiring a decision to be made, or prohibiting a decision from being made, by a particular qualifying decision procedure (other than a creditors' meeting or a contributories' meeting);

(b) permitting or requiring a decision to be made by a creditors' meeting or a contributories' meeting.

(6) Section 246ZF provides that in certain cases the deemed consent procedure may be used instead of a qualifying decision procedure.

(7) For the purposes of subsection (3) the "minimum number" of creditors or contributories is any of the following—

(a) 10% in value of the creditors or contributories;

(b) 10% in number of the creditors or contributories;

(c) 10 creditors or contributories.

(8) The references in subsection (7) to creditors are to creditors of any class, even where a decision is sought only from creditors of a particular class.

(9) In this section references to a meeting are to a meeting where the creditors or (as the case may be) contributories are invited to be present together at the same place (whether or not it is possible to attend the meeting without being present at that place).

(10) Except as provided by subsection (8), references in this section to creditors include creditors of a particular class.

(11) In this Group of Parts "qualifying decision procedure" means a procedure prescribed or authorised under paragraph 8A of Schedule 8.]

NOTES

Commencement: see the note below.

Inserted, together with the preceding heading and ss 236ZF, 246ZG, by the Small Business, Enterprise and Employment Act 2015, s 122(1), (2), as from 26 May 2015 (for the purposes of enabling the exercise of any power to make provision by regulations, rules or order made by statutory instrument or to prepare and issue guidance), as from 6 April 2017 (in relation to England and Wales and subject to transitional and savings provisions as noted below), and as from a day to be appointed (otherwise).

Transitional and savings provisions: the Small Business, Enterprise and Employment Act 2015 (Commencement No 6 and Transitional and Savings Provisions) Regulations 2016, SI 2016/1020, reg 5 provides as follows (with word omitted revoked and words in square brackets substituted by the Small Business, Enterprise and Employment Act 2015 (Commencement No 6 and Transitional and Savings Provisions) Regulations (Amendment) Regulations 2017, SI 2017/363, regs 2, 3)—

"**5 Transitional and saving provision**

(1) This regulation applies where on or after 6th April 2017—

(a) a creditors' or contributories' meeting is to be held as a result of a notice issued before that date in relation to a meeting for which provision is made by the Insolvency Rules 1986 or the 1986 Act;

(b) a meeting is to be held as a result of a requisition by a creditor or contributory made before that date;

(c) a meeting is to be held as a result of a statement made under paragraph 52(1)(b) of Schedule B1 to the 1986 Act and a request made before that date which obliges the administrator to summon an initial creditors' meeting;

(d) a . . . meeting is required by [sections 93 or 105] of the 1986 Act in the winding up of a company where the resolution to wind up was passed before 6th April 2010; or

(e) a meeting is to be held under section 94, 106, 146 or 331 of the 1986 Act as a result of—

(i) a final report to creditors sent under rule 4.49D of the Insolvency Rules 1986 (final report to creditors in liquidation),

(ii) a final report to creditors and bankrupt sent under rule 6.78B of the Insolvency Rules 1986 (final report to creditors and bankrupt), or

(iii) a meeting being called under section 94 of the 1986 Act (final meeting prior to dissolution).

(2) Where such a meeting is to be held, the 1986 Act applies without the amendments made by—

(a) section 122 of the 2015 Act;

(b) section 123 of the 2015 Act; and

(c) section 126 and Schedule 9 to the 2015 Act, insofar as those amendments relate to the abolition of requirements to hold meetings.".

[1.257]

[246ZF Deemed consent procedure

(1) The deemed consent procedure may be used instead of a qualifying decision procedure where a company's creditors or contributories are to make a decision about any matter, unless—

(a) a decision about the matter is required by virtue of this Act, the rules, or any other legislation to be made by a qualifying decision procedure, or

(b) the court orders that a decision about the matter is to be made by a qualifying decision procedure.

(2) If the rules provide for a company's creditors or contributories to make a decision about the remuneration of any person, they must provide that the decision is to be made by a qualifying decision procedure.

(3) The deemed consent procedure is that the relevant creditors (other than opted-out creditors) or (as the case may be) the relevant contributories are given notice of—

(a) the matter about which they are to make a decision,

(b) the decision that the person giving the notice proposes should be made (the "proposed decision"),

(c) the effect of subsections (4) and (5), and

(d) the procedure for objecting to the proposed decision.

(4) If less than the appropriate number of relevant creditors or (as the case may be) relevant contributories object to the proposed decision in accordance with the procedure set out in the notice, the creditors or (as the case may be) the contributories are to be treated as having made the proposed decision.

(5) Otherwise—

(a) the creditors or (as the case may be) the contributories are to be treated as not having made a decision about the matter in question, and

(b) if a decision about that matter is again sought from the creditors or (as the case may be) the contributories, it must be sought using a qualifying decision procedure.

(6) For the purposes of subsection (4) the "appropriate number" of relevant creditors or relevant contributories is 10% in value of those creditors or contributories.

(7) "Relevant creditors" means the creditors who, if the decision were to be made by a qualifying decision procedure, would be entitled to vote in the procedure.

(8) "Relevant contributories" means the contributories who, if the decision were to be made by a qualifying decision procedure, would be entitled to vote in the procedure.

(9) In this section references to creditors include creditors of a particular class.

(10) The rules may make further provision about the deemed consent procedure.]

NOTES

Commencement: see s 246ZE at **[1.256]**.
Inserted as noted to s 246ZE at **[1.256]**.

[1.258]

[246ZG Power to amend sections 246ZE and 246ZF

(1) The Secretary of State may by regulations amend section 246ZE so as to change the definition of—

(a) the minimum number of creditors;

(b) the minimum number of contributories.

(2) The Secretary of State may by regulations amend section 246ZF so as to change the definition of—

(a) the appropriate number of relevant creditors;

(b) the appropriate number of relevant contributories.

(3) Regulations under this section may define the minimum number or the appropriate number by reference to any one or more of—

(a) a proportion in value,

(b) a proportion in number,

(c) an absolute number,

and the definition may include alternative, cumulative or relative requirements.

(4) Regulations under subsection (1) may define the minimum number of creditors or contributories by reference to all creditors or contributories, or by reference to creditors or contributories of a particular description.

(5) Regulations under this section may make provision that will result in section 246ZE or 246ZF having different definitions for different cases, including—

(a) for creditors and for contributories,

(b) for different kinds of decisions.

(6) Regulations under this section may make transitional provision.

(7) The power of the Secretary of State to make regulations under this section is exercisable by statutory instrument.

(8) A statutory instrument containing regulations under this section may not be made unless a draft of the instrument has been laid before, and approved by a resolution of, each House of Parliament.]

NOTES

Commencement: see s 246ZE at **[1.256]**.
Inserted as noted to s 246ZE at **[1.256]**.

[Remote attendance at meetings

[1.259]

246A Remote attendance at meetings

(1) Subject to subsection (2), this section [applies to any meeting of the members of a company summoned by the office-holder under this Act or the rules, other than a meeting of the members of the company in a members' voluntary winding up.]

(2) This section does not apply where—

(a) a company is being wound up in Scotland, or

(b) a receiver is appointed under section 51 in Chapter 2 of Part 3.

(3) Where the person summoning a meeting ("the convener") considers it appropriate, the meeting may be conducted and held in such a way that persons who are not present together at the same place may attend it.

(4) Where a meeting is conducted and held in the manner referred to in subsection (3), a person attends the meeting if that person is able to exercise any rights which that person may have to speak and vote at the meeting.

(5) For the purposes of this section—

(a) a person is able to exercise the right to speak at a meeting when that person is in a position to communicate to all those attending the meeting, during the meeting, any information or opinions which that person has on the business of the meeting; and

(b) a person is able to exercise the right to vote at a meeting when—

(i) that person is able to vote, during the meeting, on resolutions put to the vote at the meeting, and

(ii) that person's vote can be taken into account in determining whether or not such resolutions are passed at the same time as the votes of all the other persons attending the meeting.

(6) The convener of a meeting which is to be conducted and held in the manner referred to in subsection (3) shall make whatever arrangements the convener considers appropriate to—

(a) enable those attending the meeting to exercise their rights to speak or vote, and

(b) ensure the identification of those attending the meeting and the security of any electronic means used to enable attendance.

(7) Where in the reasonable opinion of the convener—

(a) a meeting will be attended by persons who will not be present together at the same place, and

(b) it is unnecessary or inexpedient to specify a place for the meeting,

any requirement under this Act or the rules to specify a place for the meeting may be satisfied by specifying the arrangements the convener proposes to enable persons to exercise their rights to speak or vote.

(8) In making the arrangements referred to in subsection (6) and in forming the opinion referred to in subsection (7)(b), the convener must have regard to the legitimate interests of the [members] and others attending the meeting in the efficient despatch of the business of the meeting.

(9) If—

(a) the notice of a meeting does not specify a place for the meeting,

(b) the convener is requested in accordance with the rules to specify a place for the meeting, and

(c) that request is [made] by members representing not less than ten percent of the total voting rights of all the members having at the date of the request a right to vote at the meeting,

it shall be the duty of the convener to specify a place for the meeting.

(10) In this section, "the office-holder", in relation to a company, means—

(a) its liquidator, provisional liquidator, administrator, [receiver (appointed under section 51)] or administrative receiver, or

(b) where a voluntary arrangement in relation to the company is proposed or has taken effect under Part 1, the nominee or the supervisor of the voluntary arrangement.]

NOTES

Inserted, together with s 246B and associated cross-headings by the Legislative Reform (Insolvency) (Miscellaneous Provisions) Order 2010, SI 2010/18, arts 2, 3(1).

Sub-s (1): words in square brackets substituted for the following original words, by the Small Business, Enterprise and Employment Act 2015, s 126, Sch 9, Pt 1, paras 1, 54(1), (2), as from 6 April 2017 (in relation to England and Wales and subject to transitional and savings provisions as noted to s 246ZE at **[1.256]**), and as from a day to be appointed (in relation to Scotland)—

"applies to—

(a) any meeting of the creditors of a company summoned under this Act or the rules, or

(b) any meeting of the members or contributories of a company summoned by the office-holder under this Act or the rules, other than a meeting of the members of a company in a members' voluntary winding up.".

Sub-s (2): repealed by the Public Services Reform (Corporate Insolvency and Bankruptcy) (Scotland) Order 2017, SSI 2017/209, art 5(a), as from the day appointed for the coming into force, for all remaining purposes, of the Small Business, Enterprise and Employment Act 2015, s 122 in Scotland.

Sub-s (8): word in square brackets substituted for original words "creditors, members or contributories" by the Small Business, Enterprise and Employment Act 2015, s 126, Sch 9, Pt 1, paras 1, 54(1), (3), as from 6 April 2017 (in relation to England and Wales and subject to transitional and savings provisions as noted to s 246ZE at **[1.256]**), and as from a day to be appointed (in relation to Scotland).

Sub-s (9): word in square brackets in para (c) substituted for the following original words, by the Small Business, Enterprise and Employment Act 2015, s 126, Sch 9, Pt 1, paras 1, 54(1), (4), as from 6 April 2017 (in relation to England and Wales and subject to transitional and savings provisions as noted to s 246ZE at **[1.256]**), and as from a day to be appointed (in relation to Scotland)—

"made—

(i) in the case of a meeting of creditors or contributories, by not less than ten percent in value of the creditors or contributories, or

(ii) in the case of a meeting of members,".

Sub-s (10): words in square brackets inserted by SSI 2017/209, art 5(b), as from 1 October 2017 (in so far as enabling the making of (i) rules under s 411 post, or (ii) any other subordinate legislation under this Act), and as from the day appointed for the coming into force, for all remaining purposes, of the Small Business, Enterprise and Employment Act 2015, s 122 in Scotland (otherwise).

[Use of websites

NOTES

The above heading is substituted (by the new heading "Giving of notices etc by office-holders") by the Small Business, Enterprise and Employment Act 2015, s 124(1), (2), as from 6 April 2017 (in relation to England and Wales and subject to transitional and savings provisions as noted to s 246ZE at **[1.256]**), and as from a day to be appointed (in relation to Scotland).

[1.260]

246B Use of websites

(1) Subject to subsection (2), where any provision of this Act or the rules requires the office-holder to give, deliver, furnish or send a notice or other document or information to any person, that requirement is satisfied by making the notice, document or information available on a website—

(a) in accordance with the rules, and

(b) in such circumstances as may be prescribed.

(2) This section does not apply where—

(a) a company is being wound up in Scotland, or

(b) a receiver is appointed under section 51 in Chapter 2 of Part 3.

(3) In this section, "the office-holder" means—

(a) the liquidator, provisional liquidator, administrator, [receiver (appointed under section 51),] or administrative receiver of a company, or

(b) where a voluntary arrangement in relation to a company is proposed or has taken effect under Part 1, the nominee or the supervisor of the voluntary arrangement.]

NOTES

Inserted as noted to s 246A at **[1.259]**.

Sub-s (2) repealed, and words in square brackets in sub-s (3) inserted, by the Public Services Reform (Insolvency) (Scotland) Order 2016, SSI 2016/141, art 12, as from a day to be appointed (being the day that the Small Business, Enterprise and Employment Act 2015, s 122(2) comes into force for all remaining purposes in Scotland).

[1.261]

[246C Creditors' ability to opt out of receiving certain notices

(1) Any provision of the rules which requires an office-holder of a company to give a notice to creditors of the company does not apply, in circumstances prescribed by the rules, in relation to opted-out creditors.

(2) Subsection (1)—

(a) does not apply in relation to a notice of a distribution or proposed distribution to creditors;

(b) is subject to any order of the court requiring a notice to be given to all creditors (or all creditors of a particular category).

(3) Except as provided by the rules, a creditor may participate and vote in a qualifying decision procedure or a deemed consent procedure even though, by virtue of being an opted-out creditor, the creditor does not receive notice of it.

(4) In this section—

"give" includes deliver, furnish or send;

"notice" includes any document or information in any other form;

"office-holder", in relation to a company, means—

(a) a liquidator, provisional liquidator, administrator or administrative receiver of the company,

(b) a receiver appointed under section 51 in relation to any property of the company, or

(c) the supervisor of a voluntary arrangement which has taken effect under Part 1 in relation to the company.]

NOTES

Commencement: see note below.

Inserted by the Small Business, Enterprise and Employment Act 2015, s 124(1), (3), as from 6 April 2017 (in relation to England and Wales and subject to transitional and savings provisions as noted to s 246ZE at **[1.256]**), and as from a day to be appointed (in relation to Scotland).

PART VII INTERPRETATION FOR FIRST GROUP OF PARTS

NOTES

Modification of this Part in relation to building societies: this Part is applied with modifications in relation to the winding up, etc, of building societies; see the Building Societies Act 1986, ss 90, 90A, Schs 15, 15A at **[7.454]**, **[7.455]**, **[7.464]**, **[7.468]**.

Modification of this Part in relation to friendly societies: as to the application, with modifications, of this Part to the winding up of incorporated friendly societies by virtue of the Friendly Societies Act 1992, s 21(1) or 22(2), see s 23 of, and Sch 10 to, the 1992 Act.

[1.262]

247 "Insolvency" and "go into liquidation"

(1) In this Group of Parts, except in so far as the context otherwise requires, "insolvency", in relation to a company, includes the approval of a voluntary arrangement under Part I, [or the appointment of an administrator or an administrative receiver].

(2) For the purposes of any provision in this Group of Parts, a company goes into liquidation if it passes a resolution for voluntary winding up or an order for its winding up is made by the court at a time when it has not already gone into liquidation by passing such a resolution.

[(3) The reference to a resolution for voluntary winding up in subsection (2) includes a reference to a resolution which is deemed to occur by virtue of—

(a) paragraph 83(6)(b) of Schedule B1, or

(b) an order made following conversion of administration or a voluntary arrangement into winding up by virtue of [Article 51 of the EU Regulation].]

NOTES

This section derived from the Insolvency Act 1985, s 108(3) (in part), (4).

Sub-s (1): words in square brackets substituted for original words "the making of an administration order or the appointment of an administrative receiver" by the Enterprise Act 2002, s 248(3), Sch 17, paras 9, 33(1), (2), subject to savings and transitional provisions (i) in a case where a petition for an administration order has been presented before 15 September 2003 (see the Enterprise Act 2002 (Commencement No 4 and Transitional Provisions and Savings) Order 2003, SI 2003/2093, art 3 at **[2.26]**), and (ii) in relation to special administration regimes (see s 249 of the 2002 Act at **[2.10]**).

Sub-s (3): added by the Insolvency Act 1986 (Amendment) (No 2) Regulations 2002, SI 2002/1240, regs 3, 12; further substituted by the Enterprise Act 2002, s 248(3), Sch 17, paras 9, 33(1), (3), subject to savings as noted to sub-s (1) above; words in square brackets in para (b) substituted for original words "Article 37 of the EC Regulation" by the Insolvency Amendment (EU 2015/848) Regulations 2017, SI 2017/702, regs 2, 3, Schedule, Pt 1, paras 1, 16, except in relation to proceedings opened before 26 June 2017 and subject to savings in reg 4 thereof at **[2.103]**.

[1.263]

248 "Secured creditor", etc

In this Group of Parts, except in so far as the context otherwise requires—

(a) "secured creditor", in relation to a company, means a creditor of the company who holds in respect of his debt a security over property of the company, and "unsecured creditor" is to be read accordingly; and

(b) "security" means—

(i) in relation to England and Wales, any mortgage, charge, lien or other security, and

(ii) in relation to Scotland, any security (whether heritable or moveable), any floating charge and any right of lien or preference and any right of retention (other than a right of compensation or set off).

NOTES

This section derived from the Insolvency Act 1985, s 108(3) (in part).

[1.264]

[248A "Opted-out creditor"

(1) For the purposes of this Group of Parts "opted-out creditor", in relation to an office-holder of a company, means a person who—

(a) is a creditor of the company, and

(b) in accordance with the rules has elected (or is deemed to have elected) to be (and not to cease to be) an opted-out creditor in relation to the office-holder.

(2) In this section, "office-holder", in relation to a company, means—

(a) a liquidator, provisional liquidator, administrator or administrative receiver of the company,

(b) a receiver appointed under section 51 in relation to any property of the company, or

(c) the supervisor of a voluntary arrangement which has taken effect under Part 1 in relation to the company.]

NOTES

Commencement: see note below.

Inserted by the Small Business, Enterprise and Employment Act 2015, s 124(1), (4), as from 6 April 2017 (in relation to England and Wales and subject to transitional and savings provisions as noted to s 246ZE at **[1.256]**), and as from a day to be appointed (in relation to Scotland).

[1.265]

249 "Connected" with a company

For the purposes of any provision in this Group of Parts, a person is connected with a company if—

(a) he is a director or shadow director of the company or an associate of such a director or shadow director, or

(b) he is an associate of the company;

and "associate" has the meaning given by section 435 in Part XVIII of this Act.

NOTES

This section derived from the Insolvency Act 1985, s 108(5).

Application: this section and s 435 apply for the purposes of the Pensions Act 1995, s 23(3)(b) at **[17.117]**, and ss 27, 28, 40, as they apply for the purposes of this Act: see s 123(1), (3) of the 1995 Act.

Disapplication: this section is disapplied, in respect of certain specified persons while Northern Rock is wholly owned by the Treasury, by the Northern Rock plc Transfer Order 2008, SI 2008/432, art 17, Schedule, para 3(b); in respect of certain specified persons while Bradford & Bingley is wholly owned by the Treasury, by the Bradford & Bingley plc Transfer of Securities and Property etc Order 2008, SI 2008/2546, art 13(1), Sch 1, para 3(b); and in respect of certain specified persons while Deposits Management (Heritable) is wholly owned by the Treasury, see the Heritable Bank plc Transfer of Certain Rights and Liabilities Order 2008, SI 2008/2644, art 26, Sch 2, para 3(b).

[1.266]
250 "Member" of a company
For the purposes of any provision in this Group of Parts, a person who is not a member of a company but to whom shares in the company have been transferred, or transmitted by operation of law, is to be regarded as a member of the company, and references to a member or members are to be read accordingly.

NOTES

This section derived from the Insolvency Act 1985, s 108(6).

[1.267]
251 Expressions used generally
In this Group of Parts, except in so far as the context otherwise requires—

"administrative receiver" means—

(a) an administrative receiver as defined by section 29(2) in Chapter I of Part III, or
(b) a receiver appointed under section 51 in Chapter II of that Part in a case where the whole (or substantially the whole) of the company's property is attached by the floating charge;

["agent" does not include a person's counsel acting as such;]

["books and papers" and "books or papers" includes accounts, deeds, writing and documents;]

"business day" means any day other than a Saturday, a Sunday, Christmas Day, Good Friday or a day which is a bank holiday in any part of Great Britain;

"chattel leasing agreement" means an agreement for the bailment or, in Scotland, the hiring of goods which is capable of subsisting for more than 3 months; "contributory" has the meaning given by section 79;

["the court", in relation to a company, means a court having jurisdiction to wind up the company;]

["deemed consent procedure" means the deemed consent procedure provided for by section 246ZF;]

"director" includes any person occupying the position of director, by whatever name called;

["document" includes summons, notice, order and other legal process, and registers;]

["EU insolvency proceedings" means insolvency proceedings as defined in Article 2(4) of the EU Regulation;]

"floating charge" means a charge which, as created, was a floating charge and includes a floating charge within section 462 of the Companies Act (Scottish floating charges);

["the Gazette" means—

(a) as respects companies registered in England and Wales, the London Gazette;
(b) as respects companies registered in Scotland, the Edinburgh Gazette;]

. . .

["member State liquidator" means a person falling within the definition of "insolvency practitioner" in Article 2(5) of the EU Regulation appointed in insolvency proceedings listed in Annex A to the EU Regulation;]

["officer", in relation to a body corporate, includes a director, manager or secretary;]

"the official rate", in relation to interest, means the rate payable under section 189(4);

"prescribed" means prescribed by the rules;

["qualifying decision procedure" has the meaning given by section 246ZE(11);]

"receiver", in the expression "receiver or manager", does not include a receiver appointed under section 51 in Chapter II of Part III;

"retention of title agreement" means an agreement for the sale of goods to a company, being an agreement—

(a) which does not constitute a charge on the goods, but
(b) under which, if the seller is not paid and the company is wound up, the seller will have priority over all other creditors of the company as respects the goods or any property representing the goods;

"the rules" means rules under section 411 in Part XV; and

"shadow director", in relation to a company, means a person in accordance with whose directions or instructions the directors of the company are accustomed to act[, but so that a person is not deemed a shadow director by reason only that the directors act—

(a) on advice given by that person in a professional capacity;
(b) in accordance with instructions, a direction, guidance or advice given by that person in the exercise of a function conferred by or under an enactment (within the meaning given by section 1293 of the Companies Act 2006);
(c) in accordance with guidance or advice given by that person in that person's capacity as a Minister of the Crown (within the meaning of the Ministers of the Crown Act 1975)].

[Any expression (other than one defined above in this section)—

(a) for whose interpretation provision is made by Part 26 of the Companies Act, or
(b) that is defined for the purposes of the Companies Acts,

has the same meaning in this Group of Parts.]

NOTES

This section derived from the Insolvency Act 1985, s 108(3) (in part).

Definitions "deemed consent procedure" and "qualifying decision procedure" inserted by the Small Business, Enterprise and Employment Act 2015, s 122(1), (4), as from 6 April 2017 (in relation to England and Wales and subject to transitional and savings provisions as noted to s 246ZE at **[1.256]**), and as from a day to be appointed (in relation to Scotland).

Definitions "agent", "books and papers", "the court", "document", "the Gazette" and "officer" inserted and definition "office copy" repealed by the Companies Act 2006 (Consequential Amendments, Transitional Provisions and Savings) Order 2009, SI 2009/1941, art 2(1), Sch 1, para 77(1)–(3), subject to transitional provisions and savings in art 8, Sch 1, para 84 at **[2.70]**, **[2.73]**. The definition "office copy" originally read as follows:

""office copy", in relation to Scotland, means a copy certified by the clerk of court;".

Definitions "EU insolvency proceedings" and "member State liquidator" inserted by the Insolvency Amendment (EU 2015/848) Regulations 2017, SI 2017/702, regs 2, 3, Schedule, Pt 1, paras 1, 17, except in relation to proceedings opened before 26 June 2017 and subject to savings in reg 4 thereof at **[2.103]**.

Words in square brackets in definition "shadow director" substituted by the Small Business, Enterprise and Employment Act 2015, s 90(1).

Words in final pair of square brackets substituted by the Companies Act 2006 (Commencement No 3, Consequential Amendments, Transitional Provisions and Savings) Order 2007, SI 2007/2194, art 10(1), (2), Sch 4, Pt 3, para 43, subject to savings in art 12 thereof, and repealed by SI 2009/1941, art 2(1), Sch 1, para 77(1), (4), subject to transitional provisions and savings in art 8, Sch 1, para 84 at **[2.70]**, **[2.73]**.

THE SECOND GROUP OF PARTS
INSOLVENCY OF INDIVIDUALS; BANKRUPTCY

NOTES

Modification in relation to the administration of insolvent estates of deceased persons: this Group of Parts and the Third Group of Parts are modified in their application to the administration of insolvent estates of deceased persons by the Administration of Insolvent Estates of Deceased Persons Order 1986, SI 1986/1999, arts 3, 5, Schs, 1, 2 at **[11.3]**, **[11.5]**, **[11.6]**, **[11.9]**.

[PART 7A DEBT RELIEF ORDERS

Preliminary

[1.268]

[251A Debt relief orders

(1) An individual who is unable to pay his debts may apply for an order under this Part ("a debt relief order") to be made in respect of his qualifying debts.

(2) In this Part "qualifying debt" means (subject to subsection (3)) a debt which—

(a) is for a liquidated sum payable either immediately or at some certain future time; and

(b) is not an excluded debt.

(3) A debt is not a qualifying debt to the extent that it is secured.

(4) In this Part "excluded debt" means a debt of any description prescribed for the purposes of this subsection.]

NOTES

Part 7A (ss 251A–251X) inserted by the Tribunals, Courts and Enforcement Act 2007, s 108(1), Sch 17.

[Applications for a debt relief order

[1.269]

251B Making of application

(1) An application for a debt relief order must be made to the official receiver through an approved intermediary.

(2) The application must include—

(a) a list of the debts to which the debtor is subject at the date of the application, specifying the amount of each debt (including any interest, penalty or other sum that has become payable in relation to that debt on or before that date) and the creditor to whom it is owed;

(b) details of any security held in respect of any of those debts; and

(c) such other information about the debtor's affairs (including his creditors, debts and liabilities and his income and assets) as may be prescribed.

(3) The rules may make further provision as to—

(a) the form of an application for a debt relief order;

(b) the manner in which an application is to be made; and

(c) information and documents to be supplied in support of an application.

(4) For the purposes of this Part an application is not to be regarded as having been made until—

(a) the application has been submitted to the official receiver; and

(b) any fee required in connection with the application by an order under section 415 has been paid to such person as the order may specify.]

NOTES

Inserted as noted to s 251A at **[1.268]**.

[1.270]

[251C Duty of official receiver to consider and determine application

(1) This section applies where an application for a debt relief order is made.

(2) The official receiver may stay consideration of the application until he has received answers to any queries raised with the debtor in relation to anything connected with the application.

(3) The official receiver must determine the application by—

(a) deciding whether to refuse the application;

(b) if he does not refuse it, by making a debt relief order in relation to the specified debts he is satisfied were qualifying debts of the debtor at the application date;

but he may only refuse the application if he is authorised or required to do so by any of the following provisions of this section.

(4) The official receiver may refuse the application if he considers that—

(a) the application does not meet all the requirements imposed by or under section 251B;

(b) any queries raised with the debtor have not been answered to the satisfaction of the official receiver within such time as he may specify when they are raised;

(c) the debtor has made any false representation or omission in making the application or on supplying any information or documents in support of it.

(5) The official receiver must refuse the application if he is not satisfied that—

(a) the debtor is an individual who is unable to pay his debts;

(b) at least one of the specified debts was a qualifying debt of the debtor at the application date;

(c) each of the conditions set out in Part 1 of Schedule 4ZA is met.

(6) The official receiver may refuse the application if he is not satisfied that each condition specified in Part 2 of Schedule 4ZA is met.

(7) If the official receiver refuses an application he must give reasons for his refusal to the debtor in the prescribed manner.

(8) In this section "specified debt" means a debt specified in the application.]

NOTES

Inserted as noted to s 251A at **[1.268]**.

[1.271]

[251D Presumptions applicable to the determination of an application

(1) The following presumptions are to apply to the determination of an application for a debt relief order.

(2) The official receiver must presume that the debtor is an individual who is unable to pay his debts at the determination date if—

(a) that appears to the official receiver to be the case at the application date from the information supplied in the application and he has no reason to believe that the information supplied is incomplete or inaccurate; and

(b) he has no reason to believe that, by virtue of a change in the debtor's financial circumstances since the application date, the debtor may be able to pay his debts.

(3) The official receiver must presume that a specified debt (of the amount specified in the application and owed to the creditor so specified) is a qualifying debt at the application date if—

(a) that appears to him to be the case from the information supplied in the application; and

(b) he has no reason to believe that the information supplied is incomplete or inaccurate.

(4) The official receiver must presume that the condition specified in paragraph 1 of Schedule 4ZA is met if—

(a) that appears to him to be the case from the information supplied in the application;

(b) any prescribed verification checks relating to the condition have been made; and

(c) he has no reason to believe that the information supplied is incomplete or inaccurate.

(5) The official receiver must presume that any other condition specified in Part 1 or 2 of Schedule 4ZA is met if—

(a) that appears to him to have been the case as at the application date from the information supplied in the application and he has no reason to believe that the information supplied is incomplete or inaccurate;

(b) any prescribed verification checks relating to the condition have been made; and

(c) he has no reason to believe that, by virtue of a change in circumstances since the application date, the condition may no longer be met.

(6) References in this section to information supplied in the application include information supplied to the official receiver in support of the application.

(7) In this section "specified debt" means a debt specified in the application.]

NOTES

Inserted as noted to s 251A at **[1.268]**.

[Making and effect of debt relief order

[1.272]

251E Making of debt relief orders

(1) This section applies where the official receiver makes a debt relief order on determining an application under section 251C

(2) The order must be made in the prescribed form.

(3) The order must include a list of the debts which the official receiver is satisfied were qualifying debts of the debtor at the application date, specifying the amount of the debt at that time and the creditor to whom it was then owed.

(4) The official receiver must—

(a) give a copy of the order to the debtor; and

(b) make an entry for the order in the register containing the prescribed information about the order or the debtor.

(5) The rules may make provision as to other steps to be taken by the official receiver or the debtor on the making of the order.

(6) Those steps may include in particular notifying each creditor to whom a qualifying debt specified in the order is owed of—

(a) the making of the order and its effect,

(b) the grounds on which a creditor may object under section 251K, and

(c) any other prescribed information.

(7) In this Part the date on which an entry relating to the making of a debt relief order is first made in the register is referred to as "the effective date".]

NOTES

Inserted as noted to s 251A at **[1.268]**.

[1.273]

[251F Effect of debt relief order on other debt management arrangements

(1) This section applies if—

(a) a debt relief order is made, and

(b) immediately before the order is made, other debt management arrangements are in force in respect of the debtor.

(2) The other debt management arrangements cease to be in force when the debt relief order is made.

(3) In this section "other debt management arrangements" means—

(a) an administration order under Part 6 of the County Courts Act 1984;

(b) an enforcement restriction order under Part 6A of that Act;

(c) a debt repayment plan arranged in accordance with a debt management scheme that is approved under Chapter 4 of Part 5 of the Tribunals, Courts and Enforcement Act 2007.]

NOTES

Inserted as noted to s 251A at **[1.268]**.

[1.274]

[251G Moratorium from qualifying debts

(1) A moratorium commences on the effective date for a debt relief order in relation to each qualifying debt specified in the order ("a specified qualifying debt").

(2) During the moratorium, the creditor to whom a specified qualifying debt is owed—

(a) has no remedy in respect of the debt, and

(b) may not—

(i) commence a creditor's petition in respect of the debt, or

(ii) otherwise commence any action or other legal proceedings against the debtor for the debt,

except with the permission of the court and on such terms as the court may impose.

(3) If on the effective date a creditor to whom a specified qualifying debt is owed has any such petition, action or other proceeding as mentioned in subsection (2)(b) pending in any court, the court may—

(a) stay the proceedings on the petition, action or other proceedings (as the case may be), or

(b) allow them to continue on such terms as the court thinks fit.

(4) In subsection (2)(a) and (b) references to the debt include a reference to any interest, penalty or other sum that becomes payable in relation to that debt after the application date.

(5) Nothing in this section affects the right of a secured creditor of the debtor to enforce his security.]

NOTES

Inserted as noted to s 251A at **[1.268]**.

[1.275]

[251H The moratorium period

(1) The moratorium relating to the qualifying debts specified in a debt relief order continues for the period of one year beginning with the effective date for the order, unless—

(a) the moratorium terminates early; or

(b) the moratorium period is extended by the official receiver under this section or by the court under section 251M.

(2) The official receiver may only extend the moratorium period for the purpose of—

(a) carrying out or completing an investigation under section 251K;

(b) taking any action he considers necessary (whether as a result of an investigation or otherwise) in relation to the order; or

(c) in a case where he has decided to revoke the order, providing the debtor with the opportunity to make arrangements for making payments towards his debts.

(3) The official receiver may not extend the moratorium period for the purpose mentioned in subsection (2)(a) without the permission of the court.

(4) The official receiver may not extend the moratorium period beyond the end of the period of three months beginning after the end of the initial period of one year mentioned in subsection (1).
(5) The moratorium period may be extended more than once, but any extension (whether by the official receiver or by the court) must be made before the moratorium would otherwise end.
(6) References in this Part to a moratorium terminating early are to its terminating before the end of what would otherwise be the moratorium period, whether on the revocation of the order or by virtue of any other enactment.]

NOTES

Inserted as noted to s 251A at **[1.268]**.

[1.276]
[251I Discharge from qualifying debts

(1) Subject as follows, at the end of the moratorium applicable to a debt relief order the debtor is discharged from all the qualifying debts specified in the order (including all interest, penalties and other sums which may have become payable in relation to those debts since the application date).
(2) Subsection (1) does not apply if the moratorium terminates early.
(3) Subsection (1) does not apply in relation to any qualifying debt which the debtor incurred in respect of any fraud or fraudulent breach of trust to which the debtor was a party.
(4) The discharge of the debtor under subsection (1) does not release any other person from—
(a) any liability (whether as partner or co-trustee of the debtor or otherwise) from which the debtor is released by the discharge; or
(b) any liability as surety for the debtor or as a person in the nature of such a surety.
(5) If the order is revoked by the court under section 251M after the end of the moratorium period, the qualifying debts specified in the order shall (so far as practicable) be treated as though subsection (1) had never applied to them.]

NOTES

Inserted as noted to s 251A at **[1.268]**.

[Duties of debtor

[1.277]
251J Providing assistance to official receiver etc

(1) The duties in this section apply to a debtor at any time after the making of an application by him for a debt relief order.
(2) The debtor must—
(a) give to the official receiver such information as to his affairs,
(b) attend on the official receiver at such times, and
(c) do all such other things,
as the official receiver may reasonably require for the purpose of carrying out his functions in relation to the application or, as the case may be, the debt relief order made as a result of the application.
(3) The debtor must notify the official receiver as soon as reasonably practicable if he becomes aware of—
(a) any error in, or omission from, the information supplied to the official receiver in, or in support of, the application;
(b) any change in his circumstances between the application date and the determination date that would affect (or would have affected) the determination of the application.
(4) The duties under subsections (2) and (3) apply after (as well as before) the determination of the application, for as long as the official receiver is able to exercise functions of the kind mentioned in subsection (2).
(5) If a debt relief order is made as a result of the application, the debtor must notify the official receiver as soon as reasonably practicable if—
(a) there is an increase in his income during the moratorium period applicable to the order;
(b) he acquires any property or any property is devolved upon him during that period;
(c) he becomes aware of any error in or omission from any information supplied by him to the official receiver after the determination date.
(6) A notification under subsection (3) or (5) must give the prescribed particulars (if any) of the matter being notified.]

NOTES

Inserted as noted to s 251A at **[1.268]**.

[Objections, investigations and revocation

[1.278]
251K Objections and investigations

(1) Any person specified in a debt relief order as a creditor to whom a specified qualifying debt is owed may object to—
(a) the making of the order;
(b) the inclusion of the debt in the list of the debtor's qualifying debts; or
(c) the details of the debt specified in the order.
(2) An objection under subsection (1) must be—
(a) made during the moratorium period relating to the order and within the prescribed period for objections;

(b) made to the official receiver in the prescribed manner;
(c) based on a prescribed ground;
(d) supported by any information and documents as may be prescribed;

and the prescribed period mentioned in paragraph (a) must not be less than 28 days after the creditor in question has been notified of the making of the order.

(3) The official receiver must consider every objection made to him under this section.

(4) The official receiver may—

(a) as part of his consideration of an objection, or
(b) on his own initiative,

carry out an investigation of any matter that appears to the official receiver to be relevant to the making of any decision mentioned in subsection (5) in relation to a debt relief order or the debtor.

(5) The decisions to which an investigation may be directed are—

(a) whether the order should be revoked or amended under section 251L;
(b) whether an application should be made to the court under section 251M; or
(c) whether any other steps should be taken in relation to the debtor.

(6) The power to carry out an investigation under this section is exercisable after (as well as during) the moratorium relating to the order.

(7) The official receiver may require any person to give him such information and assistance as he may reasonably require in connection with an investigation under this section.

(8) Subject to anything prescribed in the rules as to the procedure to be followed in carrying out an investigation under this section, an investigation may be carried out by the official receiver in such manner as he thinks fit.]

NOTES

Inserted as noted to s 251A at **[1.268]**.

[1.279]

[251L Power of official receiver to revoke or amend a debt relief order

(1) The official receiver may revoke or amend a debt relief order during the applicable moratorium period in the circumstances provided for by this section.

(2) The official receiver may revoke the order on the ground that—

(a) any information supplied to him by the debtor—
  (i) in, or in support of, the application, or
  (ii) after the determination date,
  was incomplete, incorrect or otherwise misleading;
(b) the debtor has failed to comply with a duty under section 251J;
(c) a bankruptcy order has been made in relation to the debtor; or
(d) the debtor has made a proposal under Part 8 (or has notified the official receiver of his intention to do so).

(3) The official receiver may revoke the order on the ground that he should not have been satisfied—

(a) that the debts specified in the order were qualifying debts of the debtor as at the application date;
(b) that the conditions specified in Part 1 of Schedule 4ZA were met;
(c) that the conditions specified in Part 2 of that Schedule were met or that any failure to meet such a condition did not prevent his making the order.

(4) The official receiver may revoke the order on the ground that either or both of the conditions in paragraphs 7 and 8 of Schedule 4ZA (monthly surplus income and property) are not met at any time after the order was made.

For this purpose those paragraphs are to be read as if references to the determination date were references to the time in question.

(5) Where the official receiver decides to revoke the order, he may revoke it either—

(a) with immediate effect, or
(b) with effect from such date (not more than three months after the date of the decision) as he may specify.

(6) In considering when the revocation should take effect the official receiver must consider (in the light of the grounds on which the decision to revoke was made and all the other circumstances of the case) whether the debtor ought to be given the opportunity to make arrangements for making payments towards his debts.

(7) If the order has been revoked with effect from a specified date the official receiver may, if he thinks it appropriate to do so at any time before that date, revoke the order with immediate effect.

(8) The official receiver may amend a debt relief order for the purpose of correcting an error in or omission from anything specified in the order.

(9) But subsection (8) does not permit the official receiver to add any debts that were not specified in the application for the debt relief order to the list of qualifying debts.

(10) The rules may make further provision as to the procedure to be followed by the official receiver in the exercise of his powers under this section.]

NOTES

Inserted as noted to s 251A at **[1.268]**.

[Role of the court

[1.280]
251M Powers of court in relation to debt relief orders

(1) Any person may make an application to the court if he is dissatisfied by any act, omission or decision of the official receiver in connection with a debt relief order or an application for such an order.
(2) The official receiver may make an application to the court for directions or an order in relation to any matter arising in connection with a debt relief order or an application for such an order.
(3) The matters referred to in subsection (2) include, among other things, matters relating to the debtor's compliance with any duty arising under section 251J.
(4) An application under this section may, subject to anything in the rules, be made at any time.
(5) The court may extend the moratorium period applicable to a debt relief order for the purposes of determining an application under this section.
(6) On an application under this section the court may dismiss the application or do one or more of the following—

- (a) quash the whole or part of any act or decision of the official receiver;
- (b) give the official receiver directions (including a direction that he reconsider any matter in relation to which his act or decision has been quashed under paragraph (a));
- (c) make an order for the enforcement of any obligation on the debtor arising by virtue of a duty under section 251J;
- (d) extend the moratorium period applicable to the debt relief order;
- (e) make an order revoking or amending the debt relief order;
- (f) make an order under section 251N; or
- (g) make such other order as the court thinks fit.

(7) An order under subsection (6)(e) for the revocation of a debt relief order—

- (a) may be made during the moratorium period applicable to the debt relief order or at any time after that period has ended;
- (b) may be made on the court's own motion if the court has made a bankruptcy order in relation to the debtor during that period;
- (c) may provide for the revocation of the order to take effect on such terms and at such a time as the court may specify.

(8) An order under subsection (6)(e) for the amendment of a debt relief order may not add any debts that were not specified in the application for the debt relief order to the list of qualifying debts.]

NOTES

Inserted as noted to s 251A at **[1.268]**.

[1.281]
[251N Inquiry into debtor's dealings and property

(1) An order under this section may be made by the court on the application of the official receiver.
(2) An order under this section is an order summoning any of the following persons to appear before the court—

- (a) the debtor;
- (b) the debtor's spouse or former spouse or the debtor's civil partner or former civil partner;
- (c) any person appearing to the court to be able to give information or assistance concerning the debtor or his dealings, affairs and property.

(3) The court may require a person falling within subsection (2)(c)—

- (a) to provide a written account of his dealings with the debtor; or
- (b) to produce any documents in his possession or under his control relating to the debtor or to the debtor's dealings, affairs or property.

(4) Subsection (5) applies where a person fails without reasonable excuse to appear before the court when he is summoned to do so by an order under this section.
(5) The court may cause a warrant to be issued to a constable or prescribed officer of the court—

- (a) for the arrest of that person, and
- (b) for the seizure of any records or other documents in that person's possession.

(6) The court may authorise a person arrested under such a warrant to be kept in custody, and anything seized under such a warrant to be held, in accordance with the rules, until that person is brought before the court under the warrant or until such other time as the court may order.]

NOTES

Inserted as noted to s 251A at **[1.268]**.

[Offences

[1.282]
251O False representations and omissions

(1) A person who makes an application for a debt relief order is guilty of an offence if he knowingly or recklessly makes any false representation or omission in making the application or providing any information or documents to the official receiver in support of the application.
(2) A person who makes an application for a debt relief order is guilty of an offence if—

- (a) he intentionally fails to comply with a duty under section 251J(3) in connection with the application; or

(b) he knowingly or recklessly makes any false representation or omission in providing any information to the official receiver in connection with such a duty or otherwise in connection with the application.

(3) It is immaterial for the purposes of an offence under subsection (1) or (2) whether or not a debt relief order is made as a result of the application.

(4) A person in respect of whom a debt relief order is made is guilty of an offence if—

(a) he intentionally fails to comply with a duty under section 251J(5) in connection with the order; or

(b) he knowingly or recklessly makes any false representation or omission in providing information to the official receiver in connection with such a duty or otherwise in connection with the performance by the official receiver of functions in relation to the order.

(5) It is immaterial for the purposes of an offence under subsection (4)—

(a) whether the offence is committed during or after the moratorium period; and

(b) whether or not the order is revoked after the conduct constituting the offence takes place.]

NOTES

Inserted as noted to s 251A at **[1.268]**.

[1.283]

[251P Concealment or falsification of documents

(1) A person in respect of whom a debt relief order is made is guilty of an offence if, during the moratorium period in relation to that order—

(a) he does not provide, at the request of the official receiver, all his books, papers and other records of which he has possession or control and which relate to his affairs;

(b) he prevents the production to the official receiver of any books, papers or other records relating to his affairs;

(c) he conceals, destroys, mutilates or falsifies, or causes or permits the concealment, destruction, mutilation or falsification of, any books, papers or other records relating his affairs;

(d) he makes, or causes or permits the making of, any false entries in any book, document or record relating to his affairs; or

(e) he disposes of, or alters or makes any omission in, or causes or permits the disposal, altering or making of any omission in, any book, document or record relating to his affairs.

(2) A person in respect of whom a debt relief order is made is guilty of an offence if—

(a) he did anything falling within paragraphs (c) to (e) of subsection (1) during the period of 12 months ending with the application date; or

(b) he did anything falling within paragraphs (b) to (e) of subsection (1) after that date but before the effective date.

(3) A person is not guilty of an offence under this section if he proves that, in respect of the conduct constituting the offence, he had no intent to defraud or to conceal the state of his affairs.

(4) In its application to a trading record subsection (2)(a) has effect as if the reference to 12 months were a reference to two years.

(5) In subsection (4) "trading record" means a book, document or record which shows or explains the transactions or financial position of a person's business, including—

(a) a periodic record of cash paid and received,

(b) a statement of periodic stock-taking, and

(c) except in the case of goods sold by way of retail trade, a record of goods sold and purchased which identifies the buyer and seller or enables them to be identified.

(6) It is immaterial for the purposes of an offence under this section whether or not the debt relief order in question is revoked after the conduct constituting the offence takes place (but no offence is committed under this section by virtue of conduct occurring after the order is revoked).]

NOTES

Inserted as noted to s 251A at **[1.268]**.

[1.284]

[251Q Fraudulent disposal of property

(1) A person in respect of whom a debt relief order is made is guilty of an offence if he made or caused to be made any gift or transfer of his property during the period between—

(a) the start of the period of two years ending with the application date; and

(b) the end of the moratorium period.

(2) The reference in subsection (1) to making a transfer of any property includes causing or conniving at the levying of any execution against that property.

(3) A person is not guilty of an offence under this section if he proves that, in respect of the conduct constituting the offence, he had no intent to defraud or to conceal the state of his affairs.

(4) For the purposes of subsection (3) a person is to be taken to have proved that he had no such intent if—

(a) sufficient evidence is adduced to raise an issue as to whether he had such intent; and

(b) the contrary is not proved beyond reasonable doubt.

(5) It is immaterial for the purposes of this section whether or not the debt relief order in question is revoked after the conduct constituting an offence takes place (but no offence is committed by virtue of conduct occurring after the order is revoked).]

NOTES
Inserted as noted to s 251A at **[1.268]**.

[1.285]
[251R Fraudulent dealing with property obtained on credit
(1) A person in respect of whom a debt relief order is made is guilty of an offence if during the relevant period he disposed of any property which he had obtained on credit and, at the time he disposed of it, had not paid for it.
(2) Any other person is guilty of an offence if during the relevant period he acquired or received property from a person in respect of whom a debt relief order was made (the "debtor") knowing or believing—
(a) that the debtor owed money in respect of the property, and
(b) that the debtor did not intend, or was unlikely to be able, to pay the money he so owed.
(3) In subsections (1) and (2) "relevant period" means the period between—
(a) the start of the period of two years ending with the application date; and
(b) the determination date.
(4) A person is not guilty of an offence under subsection (1) or (2) if the disposal, acquisition or receipt of the property was in the ordinary course of a business carried on by the debtor at the time of the disposal, acquisition or receipt.
(5) In determining for the purposes of subsection (4) whether any property is disposed of, acquired or received in the ordinary course of a business carried on by the debtor, regard may be had, in particular, to the price paid for the property.
(6) A person is not guilty of an offence under subsection (1) if he proves that, in respect of the conduct constituting the offence, he had no intent to defraud or to conceal the state of his affairs.
(7) In this section references to disposing of property include pawning or pledging it; and references to acquiring or receiving property shall be read accordingly.
(8) It is immaterial for the purposes of this section whether or not the debt relief order in question is revoked after the conduct constituting an offence takes place (but no offence is committed by virtue of conduct occurring after the order is revoked).]

NOTES
Inserted as noted to s 251A at **[1.268]**.

[1.286]
[251S Obtaining credit or engaging in business
(1) A person in respect of whom a debt relief order is made is guilty of an offence if, during the relevant period—
(a) he obtains credit (either alone or jointly with any other person) without giving the person from whom he obtains the credit the relevant information about his status; or
(b) he engages directly or indirectly in any business under a name other than that in which the order was made without disclosing to all persons with whom he enters into any business transaction the name in which the order was made.
(2) For the purposes of subsection (1)(a) the relevant information about a person's status is the information that—
(a) a moratorium is in force in relation to the debt relief order,
(b) a debt relief restrictions order is in force in respect of him, or
(c) both a moratorium and a debt relief restrictions order is in force,
as the case may be.
(3) In subsection (1) "relevant period" means—
(a) the moratorium period relating to the debt relief order, or
(b) the period for which a debt relief restrictions order is in force in respect of the person in respect of whom the debt relief order is made,
as the case may be.
(4) Subsection (1)(a) does not apply if the amount of the credit is less than the prescribed amount (if any).
(5) The reference in subsection (1)(a) to a person obtaining credit includes the following cases—
(a) where goods are bailed to him under a hire-purchase agreement, or agreed to be sold to him under a conditional sale agreement;
(b) where he is paid in advance (in money or otherwise) for the supply of goods or services.]

NOTES
Inserted as noted to s 251A at **[1.268]**.

[1.287]
[251T Offences: supplementary
(1) Proceedings for an offence under this Part may only be instituted by the Secretary of State or by or with the consent of the Director of Public Prosecutions.
(2) It is not a defence in proceedings for an offence under this Part that anything relied on, in whole or in part, as constituting the offence was done outside England and Wales.
(3) A person guilty of an offence under this Part is liable to imprisonment or a fine, or both (but see section 430).]

NOTES

Inserted as noted to s 251A at **[1.268]**.

[Supplementary

[1.288]

251U Approved intermediaries

(1) In this Part "approved intermediary" means an individual for the time being approved by a competent authority to act as an intermediary between a person wishing to make an application for a debt relief order and the official receiver.

(2) In this section "competent authority" means a person or body for the time being designated by the Secretary of State for the purposes of granting approvals under this section.

(3) Designation as a competent authority may be limited so as to permit the authority only to approve persons of a particular description.

(4) The Secretary of State may by regulations make provision as to—

(a) the procedure for designating persons or bodies as competent authorities;

(b) descriptions of individuals who are ineligible to be approved under this section;

(c) the procedure for granting approvals under this section;

(d) the withdrawal of designations or approvals under this section;

and provision made under paragraph (a) or (c) may include provision requiring the payment of fees.

(5) The rules may make provision about the activities to be carried out by an approved intermediary in connection with an application for a debt relief order, which may in particular include—

(a) assisting the debtor in making the application;

(b) checking that the application has been properly completed;

(c) sending the application to the official receiver.

(6) The rules may also make provision about other activities to be carried out by approved intermediaries.

(7) An approved intermediary may not charge a debtor any fee in connection with an application for a debt relief order.

(8) An approved intermediary is not liable to any person in damages for anything done or omitted to be done when acting (or purporting to act) as an approved intermediary in connection with a particular application by a debtor for a debt relief order.

(9) Subsection (8) does not apply if the act or omission was in bad faith.

(10) Regulations under subsection (4) shall be made by statutory instrument subject to annulment in pursuance of a resolution of either House of Parliament.]

NOTES

Inserted as noted to s 251A at **[1.268]**.

[1.289]

[251V Debt relief restrictions orders and undertakings

Schedule 4ZB (which makes provision about debt relief restrictions orders and debt relief restrictions undertakings) has effect.]

NOTES

Inserted as noted to s 251A at **[1.268]**.

[1.290]

[251W Register of debt relief orders etc

The Secretary of State must maintain a register of matters relating to—

(a) debt relief orders;

(b) debt relief restrictions orders; and

(c) debt relief restrictions undertakings.]

NOTES

Inserted as noted to s 251A at **[1.268]**.

[1.291]

[251X Interpretation

(1) In this Part—

"the application date", in relation to a debt relief order or an application for a debt relief order, means the date on which the application for the order is made to the official receiver;

"approved intermediary" has the meaning given in section 251U(1);

"debt relief order" means an order made by the official receiver under this Part;

"debtor" means—

(a) in relation to an application for a debt relief order, the applicant; and

(b) in relation to a debt relief order, the person in relation to whom the order is made;

"debt relief restrictions order" and "debt relief restrictions undertaking" means an order made, or an undertaking accepted, under Schedule 4ZB;

"the determination date", in relation to a debt relief order or an application for a debt relief order, means the date on which the application for the order is determined by the official receiver;

"the effective date" has the meaning given in section 251E(7);

"excluded debt" is to be construed in accordance with section 251A;
"moratorium" and "moratorium period" are to be construed in accordance with sections 251G and 251H;
"qualifying debt", in relation to a debtor, has the meaning given in section 251A(2);
"the register" means the register maintained under section 251W;
"specified qualifying debt" has the meaning given in section 251G(1).

(2) In this Part references to a creditor specified in a debt relief order as the person to whom a qualifying debt is owed by the debtor include a reference to any person to whom the right to claim the whole or any part of the debt has passed, by assignment or operation of law, after the date of the application for the order.]

NOTES

Inserted as noted to s 251A at **[1.268]**.

PART VIII INDIVIDUAL VOLUNTARY ARRANGEMENTS

Moratorium for insolvent debtor

[1.292]

252 Interim order of court

(1) In the circumstances specified below, the court may in the case of a debtor (being an individual) make an interim order under this section.

(2) An interim order has the effect that, during the period for which it is in force—

(a) no bankruptcy petition relating to the debtor may be presented or proceeded with,

[(aa) no landlord or other person to whom rent is payable may exercise any right of forfeiture by peaceable re-entry in relation to premises let to the debtor in respect of a failure by the debtor to comply with any term or condition of his tenancy of such premises, except with the leave of the court] and

(b) no other proceedings, and no execution or other legal process, may be commenced or continued [and no distress may be levied] against the debtor or his property except with the leave of the court.

NOTES

This section derived from the Insolvency Act 1985, s 112(1) (in part), (3).

Sub-s (2): para (aa) and words in square brackets in para (b) inserted by the Insolvency Act 2000, s 3, Sch 3, paras 1, 2, subject to transitional provisions in SI 2002/2711, art 4 at **[2.7]**.

[1.293]

253 Application for interim order

(1) Application to the court for an interim order may be made where the debtor intends to make a proposal [under this Part, that is, a proposal] to his creditors for a composition in satisfaction of his debts or a scheme of arrangement of his affairs (from here on referred to, in either case, as a "voluntary arrangement").

(2) The proposal must provide for some person ("the nominee") to act in relation to the voluntary arrangement either as trustee or otherwise for the purpose of supervising its implementation [and the nominee must be a person who is qualified to act as an insolvency practitioner, or authorised to act as nominee, in relation to the voluntary arrangement].

(3) Subject as follows, the application may be made—

(a) if the debtor is an undischarged bankrupt, by the debtor, the trustee of his estate, or the official receiver, and

(b) in any other case, by the debtor.

(4) An application shall not be made under subsection (3)(a) unless the debtor has given notice of [the proposal] to the official receiver and, if there is one, the trustee of his estate.

(5) An application shall not be made while a bankruptcy petition presented by the debtor is pending, if the court has, under section 273 below, appointed an insolvency practitioner to inquire into the debtor's affairs and report.

NOTES

This section derived from the Insolvency Act 1985, ss 110, 111(1), (2), (3) (in part).

Sub-ss (1), (2): words in square brackets inserted by the Insolvency Act 2000, s 3, Sch 3, paras 1, 3(a), (b), subject to transitional provisions in SI 2002/2711, art 4 at **[2.7]**.

Sub-s (4): words in square brackets substituted for original words "his proposal (that is, the proposal to his creditors for a voluntary arrangement)" by the Insolvency Act 2000, s 3, Sch 3, paras 1, 3(c), subject to transitional provisions in SI 2002/2711, art 4 at **[2.7]**.

Sub-s (5): repealed by the Enterprise and Regulatory Reform Act 2013, s 71(3), Sch 19, paras 1, 2, in relation to a petition for a bankruptcy order presented to the court by a debtor on or after 6 April 2016.

[1.294]

254 Effect of application

(1) At any time when an application under section 253 for an interim order is pending,

[(a) no landlord or other person to whom rent is payable may exercise any right of forfeiture by peaceable re-entry in relation to premises let to the debtor in respect of a failure by the debtor to comply with any term or condition of his tenancy of such premises, except with the leave of the court, and (b)] the court may [forbid the levying of any distress on the debtor's property or its subsequent sale, or both, and] stay any action, execution or other legal process against the property or person of the debtor.

(2) Any court in which proceedings are pending against an individual may, on proof that an application under that section has been made in respect of that individual, either stay the proceedings or allow them to continue on such terms as it thinks fit.

NOTES

This section derived from the Insolvency Act 1985, s 111(4), (5).

Sub-s (1): para (a) and subsequent reference to para (b) inserted, and in para (b) (as so numbered) words in square brackets inserted, by the Insolvency Act 2000, s 3, Sch 3, paras 1, 4, subject to transitional provisions in SI 2002/2711, art 4 at **[2.7]**.

[1.295]

255 Cases in which interim order can be made

(1) The court shall not make an interim order on an application under section 253 unless it is satisfied—

(a) that the debtor intends to make [a proposal under this Part];

(b) that on the day of the making of the application the debtor was an undischarged bankrupt or was able to [make a bankruptcy application];

(c) that no previous application has been made by the debtor for an interim order in the period of 12 months ending with that day; and

(d) that the nominee under the debtor's proposal . . . is willing to act in relation to the proposal.

(2) The court may make an order if it thinks that it would be appropriate to do so for the purpose of facilitating the consideration and implementation of the debtor's proposal.

(3) Where the debtor is an undischarged bankrupt, the interim order may contain provision as to the conduct of the bankruptcy, and the administration of the bankrupt's estate, during the period for which the order is in force.

(4) Subject as follows, the provision contained in an interim order by virtue of subsection (3) may include provision staying proceedings in the bankruptcy or modifying any provision in this Group of Parts, and any provision of the rules in their application to the debtor's bankruptcy.

(5) An interim order shall not, in relation to a bankrupt, make provision relaxing or removing any of the requirements of provisions in this Group of Parts, or of the rules, unless the court is satisfied that that provision is unlikely to result in any significant diminution in, or in the value of, the debtor's estate for the purposes of the bankruptcy.

(6) Subject to the following provisions of this Part, and interim order made on an application under section 253 ceases to have effect at the end of the period of 14 days beginning with the day after the making of the order.

NOTES

This section derived from the Insolvency Act 1985, s 112.

Sub-s (1): words in square brackets in para (a) substituted for original words "such a proposal as is mentioned in that section", and words "to his creditors is a person who is for the time being qualified to act as an insolvency practitioner in relation to the debtor, and" (omitted) repealed from para (d) by the Insolvency Act 2000, ss 3, 15(1), Sch 3, paras 1, 5, Sch 5, subject to transitional provisions in SI 2002/2711, art 4 at **[2.7]**; words in square brackets in para (b) substituted for original words "petition for his own bankruptcy" by the Enterprise and Regulatory Reform Act 2013, s 71(3), Sch 19, paras 1, 3, in relation to a petition for a bankruptcy order presented to the court by a debtor on or after 6 April 2016.

[1.296]

256 Nominee's report on debtor's proposal

(1) Where an interim order has been made on an application under section 253, the nominee shall, before the order ceases to have effect, submit a report to the court stating—

(a) [whether, in his opinion, the voluntary arrangement which the debtor is proposing has a reasonable prospect of being approved and implemented, [and]

(aa)] whether, in his opinion, [the debtor's creditors should] consider the debtor's proposal, *and*

(b) if in his opinion such a meeting should be summoned, the date on which, and time and place at which, he proposes the meeting should be held.

(2) For the purpose of enabling the nominee to prepare his report the debtor shall submit to the nominee—

(a) a document setting out the terms of the voluntary arrangement which the debtor is proposing, and

(b) a statement of his affairs containing—

(i) such particulars of his creditors and of his debts and other liabilities and of his assets as may be prescribed, and

(ii) such other information as may be prescribed.

[(3) The court may—

(a) on an application made by the debtor in a case where the nominee has failed to submit the report required by this section or has died, or

(b) on an application made by the debtor or the nominee in a case where it is impracticable or inappropriate for the nominee to continue to act as such,

direct that the nominee shall be replaced as such by another person qualified to act as an insolvency practitioner, or authorised to act as nominee, in relation to the voluntary arrangement.

(3A) The court may, on an application made by the debtor in a case where the nominee has failed to submit the report required by this section, direct that the interim order shall continue, or (if it has ceased to have effect) be renewed, for such further period as the court may specify in the direction.]

(4) The court may, on the application of the nominee, extend the period for which the interim order has effect so as to enable the nominee to have more time to prepare his report.
(5) If the court is satisfied on receiving the nominee's report that [the debtor's creditors should] consider the debtor's proposal, the court shall direct that the period for which the interim order has effect shall be extended, for such further period as it may specify in the direction, for the purpose of enabling the debtor's proposal to be considered by his creditors in accordance with the following provisions of this Part.
(6) The court may discharge the interim order if it is satisfied, on the application of the nominee—
(a) that the debtor has failed to comply with his obligations under subsection (2), or
(b) that for any other reason it would be inappropriate for [the debtor's creditors] to consider the debtor's proposal.

NOTES

This section derived from the Insolvency Act 1985, s 113.

Sub-s (1): in para (a) words in first (outer) pair of square brackets and subsequent reference to para (aa) inserted by the Insolvency Act 2000, s 3, Sch 3, paras 1, 6(a), subject to transitional provisions in SI 2002/2711, art 4 at **[2.7]**; word in second pair of square brackets in para (a) inserted, words in square brackets in para (aa) substituted for original words "a meeting of the debtor's creditors should be summoned to", and para (b) repealed together with word preceding it, by the Small Business, Enterprise and Employment Act 2015, s 126, Sch 9, Pt 2, paras 60, 61(1)–(4), as from 6 April 2017 (subject to transitional and savings provisions as noted to s 246ZE at **[1.256]**).

Sub-s (3): substituted, together with sub-s (3A) for original sub-s (3) by the Insolvency Act 2000, s 3, Sch 3, paras 1, 6(b), subject to transitional provisions in SI 2002/2711, art 4 at **[2.7]**. Sub-s (3) originally read as follows:

"(3) The court may, on an application made by the debtor in a case where the nominee has failed to submit the report required by this section, do one or both of the following, namely—
(a) direct that the nominee shall be replaced as such by another person qualified to act as an insolvency practitioner in relation to the debtor;
(b) direct that the interim order shall continue, or (if it has ceased to have effect) be renewed, for such further period as the court may specify in the direction.".

Sub-s (3A): substituted, together with sub-s (3), for original sub-s (3), by the Insolvency Act 2000, s 3, Sch 3, paras 1, 6(b), subject to transitional provisions in SI 2002/2711, art 4 at **[2.7]**.

Sub-s (5): words in square brackets substituted for original words "a meeting of the debtor's creditors should be summoned to" by the Small Business, Enterprise and Employment Act 2015, s 126, Sch 9, Pt 2, paras 60, 61(1), (5), as from 6 April 2017 (subject to transitional and savings provisions as noted to s 246ZE at **[1.256]**).

Sub-s (6): words in square brackets substituted for original words "a meeting of the debtor's creditors to be summoned" by the Small Business, Enterprise and Employment Act 2015, s 126, Sch 9, Pt 2, paras 60, 61(1), (6), as from 6 April 2017 (subject to transitional and savings provisions as noted to s 246ZE at **[1.256]**).

[Procedure where no interim order made

[1.297]
256A Debtor's proposal and nominee's report

(1) This section applies where a debtor (being an individual)—
(a) intends to make a proposal under this Part (but an interim order has not been made in relation to the proposal and no application for such an order is pending), and
(b) if he is an undischarged bankrupt, has given notice of the proposal to the official receiver and, if there is one, the trustee of his estate,

unless a bankruptcy petition presented by the debtor is pending and the court has, under section 273, appointed an insolvency practitioner to inquire into the debtor's affairs and report.

(2) For the purpose of enabling the nominee to prepare a report [under subsection (3)], the debtor shall submit to the nominee—
(a) a document setting out the terms of the voluntary arrangement which the debtor is proposing, and
(b) a statement of his affairs containing—
(i) such particulars of his creditors and of his debts and other liabilities and of his assets as may be prescribed, and
(ii) such other information as may be prescribed.

(3) If the nominee is of the opinion that the debtor is an undischarged bankrupt, or is able to [make a bankruptcy application], the nominee shall, within 14 days (or such longer period as the court may allow) after receiving the document and statement mentioned in subsection (2), submit a [report to the debtor's creditors] stating—
(a) whether, in his opinion, the voluntary arrangement which the debtor is proposing has a reasonable prospect of being approved and implemented, [and]
(b) whether, in his opinion, [the debtor's creditors should] consider the debtor's proposal, *and*
(c) if in his opinion such a meeting should be summoned, the date on which, and time and place at which, he proposes the meeting should be held.

(4) The court may—
(a) on an application made by the debtor in a case where the nominee has failed to submit the report required by this section or has died, or
(b) on an application made by the debtor or the nominee in a case where it is impracticable or inappropriate for the nominee to continue to act as such,

direct that the nominee shall be replaced as such by another person qualified to act as an insolvency practitioner, or authorised to act as nominee, in relation to the voluntary arrangement.

(5) The court may, on an application made by the nominee, extend the period within which the nominee is to submit his report.]

NOTES

Inserted, together with preceding cross-heading, by the Insolvency Act 2000, s 3, Sch 3, paras 1, 7, subject to transitional provisions in SI 2002/2711, art 4 at **[2.7]**.

Sub-s (1): words in italics repealed by the Enterprise and Regulatory Reform Act 2013, s 71(3), Sch 19, paras 1, 4(1), (2), in relation to a petition for a bankruptcy order presented to the court by a debtor on or after 6 April 2016.

Sub-s (2): words in square brackets substituted for original words "to the court" in relation to England and Wales by the Legislative Reform (Insolvency) (Miscellaneous Provisions) Order 2010, SI 2010/18, arts 2, 8(1)(a), subject to transitional provisions in art 12(4) thereof at **[2.76]**.

Sub-s (3): words in first pair of square brackets substituted for original words "petition for his own bankruptcy" by the Enterprise and Regulatory Reform Act 2013, s 71(3), Sch 19, paras 1, 4(1), (3), in relation to a petition for a bankruptcy order presented to the court by a debtor on or after 6 April 2016; words in second pair of square brackets substituted for the words "report to the court" in relation to England and Wales by SI 2010/18, arts 2, 8(1)(b), subject to transitional provisions in art 12(4) thereof at **[2.76]**; word in square brackets in para (a) inserted, words in square brackets in para (b) substituted for original words "a meeting of the debtor's creditors should be summoned to" and para (c) repealed together with word preceding it, by the Small Business, Enterprise and Employment Act 2015, s 126, Sch 9, Pt 2, paras 60, 62, as from 6 April 2017 (subject to transitional and savings provisions as noted to s 246ZE at **[1.256]**).

[Creditors' [decisions]]

NOTES

Cross-heading inserted by the Insolvency Act 2000, s 3, Sch 3, paras 1, 7, subject to transitional provisions in SI 2002/2711, art 4 at **[2.7]**; word in square brackets substituted for original word "meeting". by the Small Business, Enterprise and Employment Act 2015, s 126, Sch 9, Pt 2, paras 60, 63, as from 6 April 2017 (subject to transitional and savings provisions as noted to s 246ZE at **[1.256]**).

[1.298]

257 [Consideration of debtor's proposal by creditors]

[(1) This section applies where it has been reported to the court under section 256 or to the debtor's creditors under section 256A that the debtor's creditors should consider the debtor's proposal.

(2) The nominee (or the nominee's replacement under section 256(3) or 256A(4)) must seek a decision from the debtor's creditors as to whether they approve the proposed voluntary arrangement (unless, in the case of a report to which section 256 applies, the court otherwise directs).

(2A) The decision is to be made by a creditors' decision procedure.

(2B) Notice of the creditors' decision procedure must be given to every creditor of the debtor of whose claim and address the nominee (or the nominee's replacement) is aware.]

(3) For this purpose the creditors of a debtor who is an undischarged bankrupt include—

- (a) every person who is a creditor of the bankrupt in respect of a bankruptcy debt, and
- (b) every person who would be such a creditor if the bankruptcy had commenced on the day on which notice of the [creditors' decision procedure] is given.

NOTES

This section derived from the Insolvency Act 1985, s 114(1) (in part), (2), (3).

Section heading: words in square brackets substituted for original words "Summoning of creditors' meeting" by the Small Business, Enterprise and Employment Act 2015, s 126, Sch 9, Pt 2, paras 60, 64(1), (4), as from 6 April 2017 (subject to transitional and savings provisions as noted to s 246ZE at **[1.256]**).

Sub-ss (1)–(2B): substituted for sub-ss (1), (2), by the Small Business, Enterprise and Employment Act 2015, s 126, Sch 9, Pt 2, paras 60, 64(1), (2), as from 6 April 2017 (subject to transitional and savings provisions as noted to s 246ZE at **[1.256]**). Sub-ss (1), (2) previously read as follows (with sub–s (1) substituted by SI 2010/18, arts 2, 8(2), subject to transitional provisions in art 12(4) thereof)—

> "[(1) Where it has been reported to the court under section 256 or to the debtor's creditors under section 256A that a meeting of debtor's creditors should be summoned, the nominee (or the nominee's replacement under section 256(3) or 256A(4)) shall summon that meeting for the time, date and place proposed in the nominee's report unless, in the case of a report to which section 256 applies, the court otherwise directs.]
>
> (2) The persons to be summoned to the meeting are every creditor of the debtor of whose claim and address the person summoning the meeting is aware.".

Sub-s (3): words in square brackets substituted for original word "meeting" by the Small Business, Enterprise and Employment Act 2015, s 126, Sch 9, Pt 2, paras 60, 64(1), (3), as from 6 April 2017 (subject to transitional and savings provisions as noted to s 246ZE at **[1.256]**).

Consideration and implementation of debtor's proposal

[1.299]

258 [Approval of debtor's proposal]

[(1) This section applies where under section 257 the debtor's creditors are asked to decide whether to approve the proposed voluntary arrangement.]

(2) The [creditors] may approve the proposed voluntary arrangement with [or without] modifications, but shall not do so [approve it with modifications] unless the debtor consents to each modification.

(3) The modifications subject to which the proposed voluntary arrangement may be approved may include one conferring the functions proposed to be conferred on the nominee on another person qualified to act as an insolvency practitioner [or authorised to act as nominee, in relation to the voluntary arrangement].

But they shall not include any modification by virtue of which the proposal ceases to be a proposal [under this Part].

(4) The [creditors] shall not approve any proposal or modification which affects the right of a secured creditor of the debtor to enforce his security, except with the concurrence of the creditor concerned.

(5) Subject as follows, the [creditors] shall not approve any proposal or modification under which—

(a) any preferential debt of the debtor is to be paid otherwise than in priority to such of his debts as are not preferential debts, . . .

[(aa) any ordinary preferential debt of the debtor is to be paid otherwise than in priority to any secondary preferential debts that the debtor may have,]

(b) a preferential creditor of the debtor is to be paid an amount in respect of [an ordinary preferential debt] that bears to that debt a smaller proportion than is borne to [another ordinary] preferential debt by the amount that is to be paid in respect of that other debt[; or

(c) a preferential creditor of the debtor is to be paid an amount in respect of a secondary preferential debt that bears to that debt a smaller proportion than is borne to another secondary preferential debt by the amount that is to be paid in respect of that other debt.]

However, the meeting may approve such a proposal or modification with the concurrence of the preferential creditor concerned.

(6) Subject as above, the meeting shall be conducted in accordance with the rules.

(7) In this section "preferential debt"[, "ordinary preferential debt" and "secondary preferential debt" each has] the meaning given by section 386 in Part XII; and "preferential creditor" is to be construed accordingly.

NOTES

This section derived from the Insolvency Act 1985, s 115(1)–(6), (9).

Section heading: words in square brackets substituted for original words "Decisions of creditors' meeting", by the Small Business, Enterprise and Employment Act 2015, s 126, Sch 9, Pt 2, paras 60, 65(1), (6), as from 6 April 2017 (subject to transitional and savings provisions as noted to s 246ZE at **[1.256]**).

Sub-s (1): substituted by the Small Business, Enterprise and Employment Act 2015, s 126, Sch 9, Pt 2, paras 60, 65(1), (2), as from 6 April 2017 (subject to transitional and savings provisions as noted to s 246ZE at **[1.256]**), and previously read as follows—

"(1) A creditors' meeting summoned under section 257 shall decide whether to approve the proposed voluntary arrangement.",

Sub-s (2):word in first pair of square brackets substituted for original word "meeting" and words in second and third pairs of square brackets inserted, by the Small Business, Enterprise and Employment Act 2015, s 126, Sch 9, Pt 2, paras 60, 65(1), (3), (4), as from 6 April 2017 (subject to transitional and savings provisions as noted to s 246ZE at **[1.256]**).

Sub-s (3): first words in square brackets substituted for original words "in relation to the debtor" and second words in square brackets substituted for original words "such as is mentioned in section 253", by the Insolvency Act 2000, s 3, Sch 3, paras 1, 9, subject to transitional provisions in SI 2002/2711, art 4 at **[2.7]**.

Sub-s (4): word in square brackets substituted for original word "meeting" by the Small Business, Enterprise and Employment Act 2015, s 126, Sch 9, Pt 2, paras 60, 65(1), (3), as from 6 April 2017 (subject to transitional and savings provisions as noted to s 246ZE at **[1.256]**).

Sub-s (5): word in first pair of square brackets substituted for original word "meeting" by the Small Business, Enterprise and Employment Act 2015, s 126, Sch 9, Pt 2, paras 60, 65(1), (3), as from 6 April 2017 (subject to transitional and savings provisions as noted to s 246ZE at **[1.256]**); word "or" omitted from para (a) repealed, para (aa) inserted, words in first and second pairs of square brackets in para (b) substituted (for original words "a preferential debt" and "another" respectively) and para (c) (and the preceding word) added, by the Banks and Building Societies (Depositor Preference and Priorities) Order 2014, SI 2014/3486, arts 3, 6(1), (2), except in relation to any insolvency proceedings commenced before 1 January 2015 (as to the meaning of this, see further the note "SI 2014/3486, art 3" at **[1.5]**).

Sub-s (6): repealed by the Small Business, Enterprise and Employment Act 2015, s 126, Sch 9, Pt 2, paras 60, 65(1), (5), as from 6 April 2017 (subject to transitional and savings provisions as noted to s 246ZE at **[1.256]**).

Sub-s (7): words in square brackets substituted for original word "has" by SI 2014/3486, arts 3, 6(1), (3), except in relation to any insolvency proceedings commenced before 1 January 2015 (as to the meaning of this, see further the note "SI 2014/3486, art 3" at **[1.5]**).

Modification: in relation to the Lloyd's of London insurance market, this section is applied, with modifications, by the Insurers (Reorganisation and Winding Up) Regulations 2004, SI 2004/353, regs 32, 33 at **[3.156]**, **[3.157]** (as modified by the Insurers (Reorganisation and Winding Up) (Lloyd's) Regulations 2005, SI 2005/1998, regs 32, 40(1)–(4), (11) at **[7.1601]**, **[7.1609]**).

[1.300]

259 Report of decisions to court

[(1) When pursuant to section 257 the debtor's creditors have decided whether to approve the debtor's proposal (with or without modifications), the nominee (or the nominee's replacement under section 256(3) or 256A(4)) must—

(a) give notice of the creditors' decision to such persons as may be prescribed, and

(b) where the creditors considered the debtor's proposal pursuant to a report to the court under section 256(1)(aa), report the creditors' decision to the court.]

(2) If the report is that the [creditors have] declined (with or without modifications) to approve the [voluntary arrangement proposed under section 256], the court may discharge any interim order which is in force in relation to the debtor.

NOTES

This section derived from the Insolvency Act 1985, s 115(7), (8).

Sub-s (1): substituted by the Small Business, Enterprise and Employment Act 2015, s 126, Sch 9, Pt 2, paras 60, 66(1), (2), as from 6 April 2017 (subject to transitional and savings provisions as noted to s 246ZE at **[1.256]**). Sub-s (1) (as substituted by the Legislative Reform (Insolvency) (Miscellaneous Provisions) Order 2010, SI 2010/18, arts 2, 8(3)(a), subject to transitional provisions in art 12(4) thereof) previously read as follows—

"[(1) After the conclusion in accordance with the rules of the meeting summoned under section 257, the chairman of the meeting shall—
(a) give notice of the result of the meeting to such persons as may be prescribed, and
(b) where the meeting was summoned under section 257 pursuant to a report to the court under section 256(1)(aa), report the result of it to the court.]".

Sub-s (2): words in first pair of square brackets substituted for original words "meeting has" by the Small Business, Enterprise and Employment Act 2015, s 126, Sch 9, Pt 2, paras 60, 66(1), (3), as from 6 April 2017 (subject to transitional and savings provisions as noted to s 246ZE at **[1.256]**); words in second pair of square brackets substituted for original words "debtor's proposal" by SI 2010/18, arts 2, 8(3)(b), subject to transitional provisions in art 12(4) thereof at **[2.76]**.

[1.301]
260 Effect of approval

(1) This section has effect where [pursuant to section 257 the debtor's creditors decide to approve] the proposed voluntary arrangement (with or without modifications).
(2) The approved arrangement—
(a) takes effect as if made by the debtor [at the time the creditors decided to approve the proposal], and
[(b) binds every person who in accordance with the rules—
(i) was entitled to vote [in the creditors' decision procedure by which the decision to approve the proposal was made], or
(ii) would have been so entitled if he had had notice of it, as if he were a party to the arrangement.
(2A) If—
(a) when the arrangement ceases to have effect any amount payable under the arrangement to a person bound by virtue of subsection (2)(b)(ii) has not been paid, and
(b) the arrangement did not come to an end prematurely,
the debtor shall at that time become liable to pay to that person the amount payable under the arrangement.]
(3) The Deeds of Arrangement Act 1914 does not apply to the approved voluntary arrangement.
(4) Any interim order in force in relation to the debtor immediately before the end of the period of 28 days beginning with the day on which the report with respect to the creditors' [decision] was made to the court under section 259 ceases to have effect at the end of that period.

This subsection applies except to such extent as the court may direct for the purposes of any application under section 262 below.
(5) Where proceedings on a bankruptcy petition have been stayed by an interim order which ceases to have effect under subsection (4), the petition is deemed, unless the court otherwise orders, to have been dismissed.

NOTES

This section derived from the Insolvency Act 1985, s 116(1)–(3), (6), (7).

Sub-s (1): words in square brackets substituted for original words "the meeting summoned under section 257 approves" by the Small Business, Enterprise and Employment Act 2015, s 126, Sch 9, Pt 2, paras 60, 67(1), (2), as from 6 April 2017 (subject to transitional and savings provisions as noted to s 246ZE at **[1.256]**).

Sub-s (2): words in square brackets in para (a) substituted for original words "at the meeting" and words in square brackets in para (b)(i) substituted for original words "at the meeting (whether or not he was present or represented at it)" by the Small Business, Enterprise and Employment Act 2015, s 126, Sch 9, Pt 2, paras 60, 67(1), (3), as from 6 April 2017 (subject to transitional and savings provisions as noted to s 246ZE at **[1.256]**);
para (b) substituted, together with sub-s (2A), by the Insolvency Act 2000, s 3, Sch 3, paras 1, 10, subject to transitional provisions in SI 2002/2711, art 4 at **[2.7]**. Para (b) originally read as follows:

"(b) binds every person who in accordance with the rules had notice of, and was entitled to vote at, the meeting (whether or not he was present or represented at it) as if he were a party to the arrangement.".

Sub-s (2A): substituted, together with sub-s (2)(b), for sub-s (2)(b) as originally enacted, by the Insolvency Act 2000, s 3, Sch 3, paras 1, 10, subject to transitional provisions in SI 2002/2711, art 4 at **[2.7]**.

Sub-s (3): repealed by the Deregulation Act 2015, s 19, Sch 6, Pt 1, paras 2(1), (11)(a), 3, except in relation to a deed of arrangement registered under the Deeds of Arrangement Act 1914, s 5 before 1 October 2015, if, immediately before that date, the estate of the debtor who executed the deed of arrangement has not been finally wound up.

Sub-s (4): word in square brackets substituted for original word "meeting" by the Small Business, Enterprise and Employment Act 2015, s 126, Sch 9, Pt 2, paras 60, 67(1), (4), as from 6 April 2017 (subject to transitional and savings provisions as noted to s 246ZE at **[1.256]**).

[1.302]
[261 Additional effect on undischarged bankrupt

(1) This section applies where—
(a) [pursuant to section 257 the debtor's creditors decide to approve] the proposed voluntary arrangement (with or without modifications), and
(b) the debtor is an undischarged bankrupt.
(2) Where this section applies the court shall annul the bankruptcy order on an application made—
(a) by the bankrupt, or
(b) where the bankrupt has not made an application within the prescribed period, by the official receiver.
(3) An application under subsection (2) may not be made—
(a) during the period specified in section 262(3)(a) during which the [creditors' decision] can be challenged by application under section 262,

(b) while an application under that section is pending, or
(c) while an appeal in respect of an application under that section is pending or may be brought.

(4) Where this section applies the court may give such directions about the conduct of the bankruptcy and the administration of the bankrupt's estate as it thinks appropriate for facilitating the implementation of the approved voluntary arrangement.]

NOTES

Substituted by the Enterprise Act 2002, s 264(1), Sch 22, para 1.

Sub-s (1): words in square brackets substituted for original words "the creditors' meeting summoned under section 257 approves", by the Small Business, Enterprise and Employment Act 2015, s 126, Sch 9, Pt 2, paras 60, 68(1), (2), as from 6 April 2017 (subject to transitional and savings provisions as noted to s 246ZE at **[1.256]**).

Sub-s (3): words in square brackets substituted for original words "decision of the creditors' meeting", by the Small Business, Enterprise and Employment Act 2015, s 126, Sch 9, Pt 2, paras 60, 68(1), (3), as from 6 April 2017 (subject to transitional and savings provisions as noted to s 246ZE at **[1.256]**).

[1.303]
262 Challenge of [creditors'] decision

(1) Subject to this section, an application to the court may be made, by any of the persons specified below, on one or both of the following grounds, namely—

(a) that a voluntary arrangement approved by [a decision of the debtor's creditors pursuant to] section 257 unfairly prejudices the interests of a creditor of the debtor;
(b) that there has been some material irregularity [in relation to a creditors' decision procedure instigated under that section].

(2) The persons who may apply under this section are—

(a) the debtor;
[(b) a person who—
(i) was entitled, in accordance with the rules, to vote [in the creditors' decision procedure], or
(ii) would have been so entitled if he had had notice of it;]
(c) the nominee (or his replacement under section [256(3), 256A(4)] or 258(3)); and
(d) if the debtor is an undischarged bankrupt, the trustee of his estate or the official receiver.

(3) An application under this section shall not be made—

[(a)] after the end of the period of 28 days beginning with the day on which [the creditors decided whether to approve the proposed voluntary arrangement or, where a report was required to be made to the court under section 259(1)(b), the day on which the report was made], [or
(b) in the case of a person who was not given notice of the [creditors' decision procedure], after the end of the period of 28 days beginning with the day on which he became aware that [a decision as to whether to approve the proposed voluntary arrangement had been made],

but (subject to that) an application made by a person within subsection (2)(b)(ii) on the ground that the arrangement prejudices his interests may be made after the arrangement has ceased to have effect, unless it has come to an end prematurely].

(4) Where on an application under this section the court is satisfied as to either of the grounds mentioned in subsection (1), it may do one or both of the following, namely—

(a) revoke or suspend any approval given by [a decision of the debtor's creditors];
[(b) direct any person to seek a decision from the debtor's creditors (using a creditors' decision procedure) as to whether they approve—
(i) any revised proposal the debtor may make, or
(ii) in a case falling within subsection (1)(b), the debtor's original proposal.]

(5) Where at any time after giving a direction under subsection (4)(b) [in relation to] a revised proposal the court is satisfied that the debtor does not intend to submit such a proposal, the court shall revoke the direction and revoke or suspend any approval [previously given by the debtor's creditors].

(6) Where the court gives a direction under subsection (4)(b), it may also give a direction continuing or, as the case may require, renewing, for such period as may be specified in the direction, the effect in relation to the debtor of any interim order.

(7) In any case where the court, on an application made under this section with respect to a creditors' [decision], gives a direction under subsection (4)(b) or revokes or suspends an approval under subsection (4)(a) or (5), the court may give such supplemental directions as it thinks fit and, in particular, directions with respect to—

(a) things done since the [decision] under any voluntary arrangement approved by the [decision], and
(b) such things done since the [decision] as could not have been done if an interim order had been in force in relation to the debtor when they were done.

(8) Except in pursuance of the preceding provisions of this section, [the approval of a voluntary arrangement by a decision of the debtor's creditors pursuant to section 257 is not invalidated by any irregularity in relation to the creditors' decision procedure by which the decision was made].

NOTES

This section derived from the Insolvency Act 1985, s 117.

Section heading: word in square brackets substituted for original word "meeting's", by the Small Business, Enterprise and Employment Act 2015, s 126, Sch 9, Pt 2, paras 60, 69(1), (11), as from 6 April 2017 (subject to transitional and savings provisions as noted to s 246ZE at **[1.256]**).

Sub-s (1): words in square brackets in paras (a), (b) substituted for original words "a creditors' meeting summoned under" and "at or in relation to such a meeting" respectively, by the Small Business, Enterprise and Employment Act 2015, s 126, Sch 9, Pt 2, paras 60, 69(1)–(3), as from 6 April 2017 (subject to transitional and savings provisions as noted to s 246ZE at **[1.256]**).

Sub-s (2): para (b) substituted and words in square brackets in para (c) substituted for original reference "256(3)(a)" by the Insolvency Act 2000, s 3, Sch 3, paras 1, 11(1), subject to transitional provisions in SI 2002/2711, art 4 at **[2.7]**. Para (b) originally read as follows:

"(b) a person entitled, in accordance with the rules, to vote at the creditors' meeting;";

words in square brackets in para (b)(i) substituted for original words "at the creditors' meeting" by the Small Business, Enterprise and Employment Act 2015, s 126, Sch 9, Pt 2, paras 60, 69(1), (4), as from 6 April 2017 (subject to transitional and savings provisions as noted to s 246ZE at **[1.256]**).

Sub-s (3): para (a) numbered as such, and para (b), the word "or" immediately preceding it, and subsequent proviso inserted, by the Insolvency Act 2000, s 3, Sch 3, paras 1, 11(2), subject to transitional provisions in SI 2002/2711, art 4 at **[2.7]**; words in square brackets in para (a) substituted by the Small Business, Enterprise and Employment Act 2015, s 134; words in first and second pairs of square brackets in para (b) substituted for original words "creditors' meeting" and "the meeting had taken place" respectively, by the Small Business, Enterprise and Employment Act 2015, s 126, Sch 9, Pt 2, paras 60, 69(1), (5), as from 6 April 2017 (subject to transitional and savings provisions as noted to s 246ZE at **[1.256]**).

Sub-s (4): words in square brackets in para (a) substituted for original words "the meeting" and para (b) substituted, by the Small Business, Enterprise and Employment Act 2015, s 126, Sch 9, Pt 2, paras 60, 69(1), (6), (7), as from 6 April 2017 (subject to transitional and savings provisions as noted to s 246ZE at **[1.256]**). Para (b) originally read as follows—

"(b) give a direction to any person for the summoning of a further meeting of the debtor's creditors to consider any revised proposal he may make or, in a case falling within subsection (1)(b), to reconsider his original proposal.".

Sub-s (5): words in first and second pairs of square brackets substituted for original words "for the summoning of a meeting to consider" and "given at the previous meeting" respectively, by the Small Business, Enterprise and Employment Act 2015, s 126, Sch 9, Pt 2, paras 60, 69(1), (8), as from 6 April 2017 (subject to transitional and savings provisions as noted to s 246ZE at **[1.256]**).

Sub-s (7): word "decision" in square brackets in each place it appears substituted for original word "meeting", by the Small Business, Enterprise and Employment Act 2015, s 126, Sch 9, Pt 2, paras 60, 69(1), (9), as from 6 April 2017 (subject to transitional and savings provisions as noted to s 246ZE at **[1.256]**).

Sub-s (8): words in square brackets substituted for original words "an approval given at a creditors' meeting summoned under section 257 is not invalidated by any irregularity at or in relation to the meeting" by the Small Business, Enterprise and Employment Act 2015, s 126, Sch 9, Pt 2, paras 60, 69(1), (10), as from 6 April 2017 (subject to transitional and savings provisions as noted to s 246ZE at **[1.256]**).

[1.304]

[262A False representations etc

(1) If for the purpose of obtaining the approval of his creditors to a proposal for a voluntary arrangement, the debtor—

(a) makes any false representation, or

(b) fraudulently does, or omits to do, anything,

he commits an offence.

(2) Subsection (1) applies even if the proposal is not approved.

(3) A person guilty of an offence under this section is liable to imprisonment or a fine, or both.]

NOTES

Inserted, together with ss 262B, 262C, by the Insolvency Act 2000, s 3, Sch 3, paras 1, 12, subject to transitional provisions in SI 2002/2711, art 4 at **[2.7]**.

[1.305]

[262B Prosecution of delinquent debtors

(1) This section applies where a voluntary arrangement approved by a [decision of the debtor's creditors pursuant to] section 257 has taken effect.

(2) If it appears to the nominee or supervisor that the debtor has been guilty of any offence in connection with the arrangement for which he is criminally liable, he shall forthwith—

(a) report the matter to the Secretary of State, and

(b) provide the Secretary of State with such information and give the Secretary of State such access to and facilities for inspecting and taking copies of documents (being information or documents in his possession or under his control and relating to the matter in question) as the Secretary of State requires.

(3) Where a prosecuting authority institutes criminal proceedings following any report under subsection (2), the nominee or, as the case may be, supervisor shall give the authority all assistance in connection with the prosecution which he is reasonably able to give.

For this purpose, "prosecuting authority" means the Director of Public Prosecutions or the Secretary of State.

(4) The court may, on the application of the prosecuting authority, direct a nominee or supervisor to comply with subsection (3) if he has failed to do so.]

NOTES

Inserted as noted to s 262A at **[1.304]**.

Sub-s (1): words in square brackets substituted for original words "creditors' meeting summoned under" by the Small Business, Enterprise and Employment Act 2015, s 126, Sch 9, Pt 2, paras 60, 70, as from 6 April 2017 (subject to transitional and savings provisions as noted to s 246ZE at **[1.256]**).

[1.306]
[262C Arrangements coming to an end prematurely
For the purposes of this Part, a voluntary arrangement approved by a [decision of the debtor's creditors pursuant to] section 257 comes to an end prematurely if, when it ceases to have effect, it has not been fully implemented in respect of all persons bound by the arrangement by virtue of section 260(2)(b)(i).]

NOTES

Inserted as noted to s 262A at **[1.304]**.

Words in square brackets substituted for original words "creditors' meeting summoned under" by the Small Business, Enterprise and Employment Act 2015, s 126, Sch 9, Pt 2, paras 60, 71, as from 6 April 2017 (subject to transitional and savings provisions as noted to s 246ZE at **[1.256]**).

[1.307]
263 Implementation and supervision of approved voluntary arrangement
(1) This section applies where a voluntary arrangement approved by a [decision of the debtor's creditors pursuant to] section 257 has taken effect.
(2) The person who is for the time being carrying out, in relation to the voluntary arrangement, the functions conferred by virtue of the approval on the nominee (or his replacement under section [256(3), 256A(4)] or 258(3)) shall be known as the supervisor of the voluntary arrangement.
(3) If the debtor, any of his creditors or any other person is dissatisfied by any act, omission or decision of the supervisor, he may apply to the court; and on such an application the court may—
 (a) confirm, reverse or modify any act or decision of the supervisor,
 (b) give him directions, or
 (c) make such other order as it thinks fit.
(4) The supervisor may apply to the court for directions in relation to any particular matter arising under the voluntary arrangement.
(5) The court may, whenever—
 (a) it is expedient to appoint a person to carry out the functions of the supervisor, and
 (b) it is inexpedient, difficult or impracticable for an appointment to be made without the assistance of the court,
make an order appointing a person who is qualified to act as an insolvency practitioner [or authorised to act as supervisor, in relation to the voluntary arrangement], either in substitution for the existing supervisor or to fill a vacancy.

This is without prejudice to section 41(2) of the Trustee Act 1925 (power of court to appoint trustees of deeds of arrangement).
(6) The power conferred by subsection (5) is exercisable so as to increase the number of persons exercising the functions of the supervisor or, where there is more than one person exercising those functions, so as to replace one or more of those persons.

NOTES

This section derived from the Insolvency Act 1985, s 118.

Sub-s (1): words in square brackets substituted for original words "creditors' meeting summoned under", by the Small Business, Enterprise and Employment Act 2015, s 126, Sch 9, Pt 2, paras 60, 72, as from 6 April 2017 (subject to transitional and savings provisions as noted to s 246ZE at **[1.256]**).

Sub-s (2): words in square brackets substituted for original reference "256(3)(a)" by the Insolvency Act 2000, s 3, Sch 3, paras 1, 13(a), subject to transitional provisions in SI 2002/2711, art 4 at **[2.7]**.

Sub-s (5): words in square brackets substituted for original words "in relation to the debtor" by the Insolvency Act 2000, s 3, Sch 3, paras 1, 13(b), subject to transitional provisions in SI 2002/2711, art 4 at **[2.7]**; words in italics repealed by the Deregulation Act 2015, s 19, Sch 6, Pt 1, paras 2(1), (11)(b), 3, except in relation to a deed of arrangement registered under the Deeds of Arrangement Act 1914, s 5 before 1 October 2015, if, immediately before that date, the estate of the debtor who executed the deed of arrangement has not been finally wound up.

[Fast-track voluntary arrangement

[1.308]
263A Availability
Section 263B applies where an individual debtor intends to make a proposal to his creditors for a voluntary arrangement and—
 (a) the debtor is an undischarged bankrupt,
 (b) the official receiver is specified in the proposal as the nominee in relation to the voluntary arrangement, and
 (c) no interim order is applied for under section 253.]

NOTES

Inserted, together with preceding cross-heading and ss 263B–263G, by the Enterprise Act 2002, s 264(1), Sch 22, para 2.

Repealed, together with preceding cross-heading and ss 263B–263G, by the Small Business, Enterprise and Employment Act 2015, s 135(1), (4), except in relation to a case where a debtor has submitted the document and statement mentioned in s 263B(1) to the official receiver before 26 May 2015.

[1.309]
[263B Decision
(1) The debtor may submit to the official receiver—
 (a) a document setting out the terms of the voluntary arrangement which the debtor is proposing, and

(b) a statement of his affairs containing such particulars as may be prescribed of his creditors, debts, other liabilities and assets and such other information as may be prescribed.

(2) If the official receiver thinks that the voluntary arrangement proposed has a reasonable prospect of being approved and implemented, he may make arrangements for inviting creditors to decide whether to approve it.

(3) For the purposes of subsection (2) a person is a "creditor" only if—

(a) he is a creditor of the debtor in respect of a bankruptcy debt, and

(b) the official receiver is aware of his claim and his address.

(4) Arrangements made under subsection (2)—

(a) must include the provision to each creditor of a copy of the proposed voluntary arrangement,

(b) must include the provision to each creditor of information about the criteria by reference to which the official receiver will determine whether the creditors approve or reject the proposed voluntary arrangement, and

(c) may not include an opportunity for modifications to the proposed voluntary arrangement to be suggested or made.

(5) Where a debtor submits documents to the official receiver under subsection (1) no application under section 253 for an interim order may be made in respect of the debtor until the official receiver has—

(a) made arrangements as described in subsection (2), or

(b) informed the debtor that he does not intend to make arrangements (whether because he does not think the voluntary arrangement has a reasonable prospect of being approved and implemented or because he declines to act).]

NOTES

Inserted and repealed as noted to s 263A at **[1.308]**.

[1.310]

[263C Result

As soon as is reasonably practicable after the implementation of arrangements under section 263B(2) the official receiver shall [notify the Secretary of State] whether the proposed voluntary arrangement has been approved or rejected.]

NOTES

Inserted and repealed as noted to s 263A at **[1.308]**.

Words in square brackets substituted for original words "report to the court" by the Legislative Reform (Insolvency) (Miscellaneous Provisions) Order 2010, SI 2010/18, arts 2, 9(1), subject to transitional provisions in art 12(4) thereof at **[2.76]**.

[1.311]

[263D Approval of voluntary arrangement

(1) This section applies where the official receiver [notifies the Secretary of State] under section 263C that a proposed voluntary arrangement has been approved.

(2) The voluntary arrangement—

(a) takes effect,

(b) binds the debtor, and

(c) binds every person who was entitled to participate in the arrangements made under section 263B(2).

(3) The court shall annul the bankruptcy order in respect of the debtor on an application made by the official receiver.

(4) An application under subsection (3) may not be made—

(a) during the period specified in section 263F(3) during which the voluntary arrangement can be challenged by application under section 263F(2),

(b) while an application under that section is pending, or

(c) while an appeal in respect of an application under that section is pending or may be brought.

(5) The court may give such directions about the conduct of the bankruptcy and the administration of the bankrupt's estate as it thinks appropriate for facilitating the implementation of the approved voluntary arrangement.

(6) The Deeds of Arrangement Act 1914 (c 47) does not apply to the voluntary arrangement.

(7) A reference in this Act or another enactment to a voluntary arrangement approved under this Part includes a reference to a voluntary arrangement which has effect by virtue of this section.]

NOTES

Inserted and repealed as noted to s 263A at **[1.308]**.

Sub-s (1): words in square brackets substituted for original words "reports to the court" by the Legislative Reform (Insolvency) (Miscellaneous Provisions) Order 2010, SI 2010/18, arts 2, 9(2), subject to transitional provisions in art 12(4) thereof at **[2.76]**.

Sub-s (6): repealed by the Deregulation Act 2015, s 19, Sch 6, Pt 1, paras 2(1), (11)(c), 3, except in relation to a deed of arrangement registered under the Deeds of Arrangement Act 1914, s 5 before 1 October 2015, if, immediately before that date, the estate of the debtor who executed the deed of arrangement has not been finally wound up.

[1.312]

[263E Implementation

Section 263 shall apply to a voluntary arrangement which has effect by virtue of section 263D(2) as it applies to a voluntary arrangement approved by a creditors' meeting.]

NOTES

Inserted and repealed as noted to s 263A at **[1.308]**.

[1.313]

[263F Revocation

(1) The court may make an order revoking a voluntary arrangement which has effect by virtue of section 263D(2) on the ground—

(a) that it unfairly prejudices the interests of a creditor of the debtor, or

(b) that a material irregularity occurred in relation to the arrangements made under section 263B(2).

(2) An order under subsection (1) may be made only on the application of—

(a) the debtor,

(b) a person who was entitled to participate in the arrangements made under section 263B(2),

(c) the trustee of the bankrupt's estate, or

(d) the official receiver.

(3) An application under subsection (2) may not be made after the end of the period of 28 days beginning with the date on which the official receiver [notifies the Secretary of State] under section 263C.

(4) But a creditor who was not made aware of the arrangements under section 263B(2) at the time when they were made may make an application under subsection (2) during the period of 28 days beginning with the date on which he becomes aware of the voluntary arrangement.]

NOTES

Inserted and repealed as noted to s 263A at **[1.308]**.

Sub-s (3): words in square brackets substituted for original words "makes his report to the court" by the Legislative Reform (Insolvency) (Miscellaneous Provisions) Order 2010, SI 2010/18, arts 2, 9(3), subject to transitional provisions in art 12(4) thereof at **[2.76]**.

[1.314]

[263G Offences

(1) Section 262A shall have effect in relation to obtaining approval to a proposal for a voluntary arrangement under section 263D.

(2) Section 262B shall have effect in relation to a voluntary arrangement which has effect by virtue of section 263D(2) (for which purposes the words "by a creditors' meeting summoned under section 257" shall be disregarded).]

NOTES

Inserted and repealed as noted to s 263A at **[1.308]**.

PART IX BANKRUPTCY

NOTES

Application of this Part in relation to financial markets: this Part is applied with modifications in relation to certain proceedings begun before the commencement of the Companies Act 1989, s 182, in respect of insolvency proceedings regarding members of recognised investment exchanges and clearing houses and persons to whom market charges have been granted; see s 182 of the 1989 Act at **[17.85]**.

Effect of freezing orders under the International Criminal Court Act 2001: where a person is adjudged bankrupt in England and Wales, property subject to a freezing order, or an order having like effect in Scotland, made before an order adjudging him bankrupt and proceeds of property realised by virtue of the International Criminal Court Act 2001, Sch 6, para 5(2) in the hands of a receiver appointed under that paragraph is excluded from a bankrupt's estate for the purposes of this Part of this Act; see s 38 of, and Sch 6, para 9(1) to, the 2001 Act. See also Sch 6, para 9(2)(b), (c), (4).

Effect of restraint orders: where, if at the time a person is adjudged bankrupt in England and Wales under this Act, a restraint order has been made or a receiver or administrator has been appointed in respect of any of his property which is subject also to criminal confiscation legislation, that property is excluded from his estate for the purposes of the bankruptcy and first goes to satisfy the confiscation order; see the Proceeds of Crime Act 2002, s 417 at **[17.236]**. See also, however, s 418 of that Act at **[17.237]**.

[CHAPTER A1
ADJUDICATORS: BANKRUPTCY APPLICATIONS BY DEBTORS AND BANKRUPTCY ORDERS

[1.315]

263H Bankruptcy applications to an adjudicator

(1) An individual may make an application to an adjudicator in accordance with this Chapter for a bankruptcy order to be made against him or her.

(2) An individual may make a bankruptcy application only on the ground that the individual is unable to pay his or her debts.]

NOTES

Commencement: 6 April 2016.

Ss 263H–263O (Ch A1) inserted by the Enterprise and Regulatory Reform Act 2013, s 71(2), Sch 18.

[1.316]

[263I Debtors against whom an adjudicator may make a bankruptcy order

(1) An adjudicator has jurisdiction to determine a bankruptcy application only if—

(a) the centre of the debtor's main interests is in England and Wales, or

(b) the centre of the debtor's main interests is not in a member state of the European Union which has adopted the [EU Regulation], but the test in subsection (2) is met.

(2) The test is that—

(a) the debtor is domiciled in England and Wales, or

(b) at any time in the period of three years ending with the day on which the application is made to the adjudicator, the debtor—

(i) has been ordinarily resident, or has had a place of residence, in England and Wales, or

(ii) has carried on business in England and Wales.

(3) The reference in subsection (2) to the debtor carrying on business includes—

(a) the carrying on of business by a firm or partnership of which the debtor is a member, and

(b) the carrying on of business by an agent or manager for the debtor or for such a firm or partnership.

(4) In this section, references to the centre of the debtor's main interests have the same meaning as in Article 3 of the [EU Regulation].]

NOTES

Commencement: 6 April 2016.

Inserted as noted to s 263H at **[1.315]**.

Words in square brackets in sub-ss (1)(b), (4) substituted for original words "EC Regulation" by the Insolvency Amendment (EU 2015/848) Regulations 2017, SI 2017/702, regs 2, 3, Schedule, Pt 1, paras 1, 18, except in relation to proceedings opened before 26 June 2017 and subject to savings in reg 4 thereof at **[2.103]**.

[1.317]

[263J Conditions applying to bankruptcy application

(1) A bankruptcy application must include—

(a) such particulars of the debtor's creditors, debts and other liabilities, and assets, as may be prescribed, and

(b) such other information as may be prescribed.

(2) A bankruptcy application is not to be regarded as having been made unless any fee or deposit required in connection with the application by an order under section 415 has been paid to such person, and within such period, as may be prescribed.

(3) A bankruptcy application may not be withdrawn.

(4) A debtor must notify the adjudicator if, at any time before a bankruptcy order is made against the debtor or the adjudicator refuses to make such an order—

(a) the debtor becomes able to pay his or her debts, or

(b) a bankruptcy petition has been presented to the court in relation to the debtor.]

NOTES

Commencement: 6 April 2016.

Inserted as noted to s 263H at **[1.315]**.

[1.318]

[263K Determination of bankruptcy application

(1) After receiving a bankruptcy application, an adjudicator must determine whether the following requirements are met—

(a) the adjudicator had jurisdiction under section 263I to determine the application on the date the application was made,

(b) the debtor is unable to pay his or her debts at the date of the determination,

(c) no bankruptcy petition is pending in relation to the debtor at the date of the determination, and

(d) no bankruptcy order has been made in respect of any of the debts which are the subject of the application at the date of the determination.

(2) If the adjudicator is satisfied that each of the requirements in subsection (1) are met, the adjudicator must make a bankruptcy order against the debtor.

(3) If the adjudicator is not so satisfied, the adjudicator must refuse to make a bankruptcy order against the debtor.

(4) The adjudicator must make a bankruptcy order against the debtor or refuse to make such an order before the end of the prescribed period ("the determination period").]

NOTES

Commencement: 6 April 2016.

Inserted as noted to s 263H at **[1.315]**.

[1.319]

[263L Adjudicator's requests for further information

(1) An adjudicator may at any time during the determination period request from the debtor information that the adjudicator considers necessary for the purpose of determining whether a bankruptcy order must be made.

(2) The adjudicator may specify a date before which information requested under subsection (1) must be provided; but that date must not be after the end of the determination period.

(3) If the rules so prescribe, a request under subsection (1) may include a request for information to be given orally.
(4) The rules may make provision enabling or requiring an adjudicator to request information from persons of a prescribed description in prescribed circumstances.]

NOTES

Commencement: 6 April 2016.
Inserted as noted to s 263H at **[1.315]**.

[1.320]
[263M Making of bankruptcy order
(1) This section applies where an adjudicator makes a bankruptcy order as a result of a bankruptcy application.
(2) The order must be made in the prescribed form.
(3) The adjudicator must—
(a) give a copy of the order to the debtor, and
(b) give notice of the order to persons of such description as may be prescribed.]

NOTES

Commencement: 6 April 2016.
Inserted as noted to s 263H at **[1.315]**.

[1.321]
[263N Refusal to make a bankruptcy order: review and appeal etc
(1) Where an adjudicator refuses to make a bankruptcy order on a bankruptcy application, the adjudicator must give notice to the debtor—
(a) giving the reasons for the refusal, and
(b) explaining the effect of subsections (2) to (5).
(2) If requested by the debtor before the end of the prescribed period, the adjudicator must review the information which was available to the adjudicator when the determination that resulted in the refusal was made.
(3) Following a review under subsection (2) the adjudicator must—
(a) confirm the refusal to make a bankruptcy order, or
(b) make a bankruptcy order against the debtor.
(4) Where the adjudicator confirms a refusal under subsection (3), the adjudicator must give notice to the debtor—
(a) giving the reasons for the confirmation, and
(b) explaining the effect of subsection (5).
(5) If the refusal is confirmed under subsection (3), the debtor may appeal against the refusal to the court before the end of the prescribed period.]

NOTES

Commencement: 6 April 2016.
Inserted as noted to s 263H at **[1.315]**.

[1.322]
[263O False representations and omissions
(1) It is an offence knowingly or recklessly to make any false representation or omission in—
(a) making a bankruptcy application to an adjudicator, or
(b) providing any information to an adjudicator in connection with a bankruptcy application.
(2) It is an offence knowingly or recklessly to fail to notify an adjudicator of a matter in accordance with a requirement imposed by or under this Part.
(3) It is immaterial for the purposes of an offence under this section whether or not a bankruptcy order is made as a result of the application.
(4) It is not a defence in proceedings for an offence under this section that anything relied on, in whole or in part, as constituting the offence was done outside England and Wales.
(5) Proceedings for an offence under this section may only be instituted—
(a) by the Secretary of State, or
(b) by or with the consent of the Director of Public Prosecutions.]

NOTES

Commencement: 6 April 2016.
Inserted as noted to s 263H at **[1.315]**.

CHAPTER I

[THE COURT: BANKRUPTCY PETITIONS AND BANKRUPTCY ORDERS]

Preliminary

[1.323]
264 Who may present a bankruptcy petition
(1) A petition for a bankruptcy order to be made against an individual may be presented to the court in accordance with the following provisions of this Part—
(a) by one of the individual's creditors or jointly by more than one of them,

(b) *by the individual himself,*
[(ba) by a temporary administrator (within the meaning of [Article 52 of the EU Regulation]),
[(bb) by an insolvency practitioner (within the meaning of Article 2(5) of the EU Regulation) appointed in proceedings by virtue of Article 3(1) of the EU Regulation,]]
(c) by the supervisor of, or any person (other than the individual) who is for the time being bound by, a voluntary arrangement proposed by the individual and approved under Part VIII, *or*
(d) *where a criminal bankruptcy order has been made against the individual, by the Official Petitioner or by any person specified in the order in pursuance of section 39(3)(b) of the Powers of Criminal Courts Act 1973.*

(2) Subject to those provisions, the court may make a bankruptcy order on any such petition.

NOTES

This section derived from the Insolvency Act 1985, s 119(1).

Chapter heading: words in square brackets substituted for original words "Bankruptcy Petitions; Bankruptcy Orders", by the Enterprise and Regulatory Reform Act 2013, s 71(3), Sch 19, paras 1, 5, in respect of a petition for a bankruptcy order presented to the court by a debtor on or after 6 April 2016.

Sub-s (1): para (b) repealed by the Enterprise and Regulatory Reform Act 2013, s 71(3), Sch 19, paras 1, 6, in relation to a petition for a bankruptcy order presented to the court by a debtor on or after 6 April 2016; paras (ba), (bb) inserted by the Insolvency Act 1986 (Amendment) (No 2) Regulations 2002, SI 2002/1240, regs 3, 13; para (d) and word immediately preceding it repealed by the Criminal Justice Act 1988, s 170(2), Sch 16, as from a day to be appointed. In para (ba) words in square brackets substituted for original words "Article 38 of the EC Regulation" and para (bb) substituted, by the Insolvency Amendment (EU 2015/848) Regulations 2017, SI 2017/702, regs 2, 3, Schedule, Pt 1, paras 1, 19, except in relation to proceedings opened before 26 June 2017 and subject to savings in reg 4 thereof at **[2.103]**. Para (bb) originally read as follows—

> "(bb) by a liquidator (within the meaning of Article 2(b) of the EC Regulation) appointed in proceedings by virtue of Article 3(1) of the EC Regulation,".

Powers of Criminal Courts Act 1973, s 39: repealed by the Criminal Justice Act 1988, s 170(2), Sch 16, as from a day to be appointed.

[1.324]

[265 Creditor's petition: debtors against whom the court may make a bankruptcy order

(1) A bankruptcy petition may be presented to the court under section 264(1)(a) only if—
(a) the centre of the debtor's main interests is in England and Wales, or
(b) the centre of the debtor's main interests is not in a member state of the European Union which has adopted the [EU Regulation], but the test in subsection (2) is met.

(2) The test is that—
(a) the debtor is domiciled in England and Wales, or
(b) at any time in the period of three years ending with the day on which the petition is presented, the debtor—
(i) has been ordinarily resident, or has had a place of residence, in England and Wales, or
(ii) has carried on business in England and Wales.

(3) The reference in subsection (2) to the debtor carrying on business includes—
(a) the carrying on of business by a firm or partnership of which the debtor is a member, and
(b) the carrying on of business by an agent or manager for the debtor or for such a firm or partnership.

(4) In this section, references to the centre of the debtor's main interests have the same meaning as in Article 3 of the [EU Regulation].]

NOTES

Commencement: 6 April 2016 (in relation to a petition for a bankruptcy order presented to the court by a debtor on or after that date).

Substituted by the Enterprise and Regulatory Reform Act 2013, s 71(3), Sch 19, paras 1, 7, in relation to a petition for a bankruptcy order presented to the court by a debtor on or after 6 April 2016. This section previously read as follows (with sub-s (3) added by the Insolvency Act 1986 (Amendment) (No 2) Regulations 2002, SI 2002/1240, regs 3, 14)—

> **"265 Conditions to be satisfied in respect of debtor**
>
> (1) A bankruptcy petition shall not be presented to the court under section 264(1)(a) or (b) unless the debtor—
> (a) is domiciled in England and Wales,
> (b) is personally present in England and Wales on the day on which the petition is presented, or
> (c) at any time in the period of 3 years ending with that day—
> (i) has been ordinarily resident, or has had a place of residence, in England and Wales, or
> (ii) has carried on business in England and Wales.
>
> (2) The reference in subsection (1)(c) to an individual carrying on business includes—
> (a) the carrying on of business by a firm or partnership of which the individual is a member, and
> (b) the carrying on of business by an agent or manager for the individual or for such a firm or partnership.
>
> [(3) This section is subject to Article 3 of the EC Regulation.]".

Sub-ss (1)(b), (4): words in square brackets substituted for original words "EC Regulation" by the Insolvency Amendment (EU 2015/848) Regulations 2017, SI 2017/702, regs 2, 3, Schedule, Pt 1, paras 1, 20, except in relation to proceedings opened before 26 June 2017 and subject to savings in reg 4 thereof at **[2.103]**.

[1.325]
266 Other preliminary conditions

(1) Where a bankruptcy petition relating to an individual is presented by a person who is entitled to present a petition under two or more paragraphs of section 264(1), the petition is to be treated for the purposes of this Part as a petition under such one of those paragraphs as may be specified in the petition.
(2) A bankruptcy petition shall not be withdrawn without the leave of the court.
(3) The court has a general power, if it appears to it appropriate to do so on the grounds that there has been a contravention of the rules or for any other reason, to dismiss a bankruptcy petition or to stay proceedings on such a petition; and, where it stays proceedings on a petition, it may do so on such terms and conditions as it thinks fit.
(4) Without prejudice to subsection (3), where a petition under section 264(1)(a), (b) or (c) in respect of an individual is pending at a time when a criminal bankruptcy order is made against him, or is presented after such an order has been so made, the court may on the application of the Official Petitioner dismiss the petition if it appears to it appropriate to do so.

NOTES

This section derived from the Insolvency Act 1985, s 119(4)–(7).

Sub-s (4): repealed by the Criminal Justice Act 1988, s 170(2), Sch 16, as from a day to be appointed; figure ", (b)" repealed by the Enterprise and Regulatory Reform Act 2013, s 71(3), Sch 19, paras 1, 8, in relation to a petition for a bankruptcy order presented to the court by a debtor on or after 6 April 2016.

Creditor's petition

[1.326]
267 Grounds of creditor's petition

(1) A creditor's petition must be in respect of one or more debts owed by the debtor, and the petitioning creditor or each of the petitioning creditors must be a person to whom the debt or (as the case may be) at least one of the debts is owed.
(2) Subject to the next three sections, a creditor's petition may be presented to the court in respect of a debt or debts only if, at the time the petition is presented—
- (a) the amount of the debt, or the aggregate amount of the debts, is equal to or exceeds the bankruptcy level,
- (b) the debt, or each of the debts, is for a liquidated sum payable to the petitioning creditor, or one or more of the petitioning creditors, either immediately or at some certain, future time, and is unsecured,
- (c) the debt, or each of the debts, is a debt which the debtor appears either to be unable to pay or to have no reasonable prospect of being able to pay, and
- (d) there is no outstanding application to set aside a statutory demand served (under section 268 below) in respect of the debt or any of the debts.

(3) A debt is not to be regarded for the purposes of subsection (2) as a debt for a liquidated sum by reason only that the amount of the debt is specified in a criminal bankruptcy order.
(4) "The bankruptcy level" is [£5,000]; but the Secretary of State may by order in a statutory instrument substitute any amount specified in the order for that amount or (as the case may be) for the amount which by virtue of such an order is for the time being the amount of the bankruptcy level.
(5) An order shall not be made under subsection (4) unless a draft of it has been laid before, and approved by a resolution of, each House of Parliament.

NOTES

This section derived from the Insolvency Act 1985, s 120(1), (2), (7)–(9).

Sub-s (3): repealed by the Criminal Justice Act 1988, s 170(2), Sch 16, as from a day to be appointed.

Sub-s (4): sum in square brackets substituted for original sum "£750" by the Insolvency Act 1986 (Amendment) Order 2015, SI 2015/922, arts 2, 3, in relation to petitions presented on or after 1 October 2015.

[1.327]
268 Definition of "inability to pay", etc; the statutory demand

(1) For the purposes of section 267(2)(c), the debtor appears to be unable to pay a debt if, but only if, the debt is payable immediately and either—
- (a) the petitioning creditor to whom the debt is owed has served on the debtor a demand (known as "the statutory demand") in the prescribed form requiring him to pay the debt or to secure or compound for it to the satisfaction of the creditor, at least 3 weeks have elapsed since the demand was served and the demand has been neither complied with nor set aside in accordance with the rules, or
- (b) execution or other process issued in respect of the debt on a judgment or order of any court in favour of the petitioning creditor, or one or more of the petitioning creditors to whom the debt is owed, has been returned unsatisfied in whole or in part.

(2) For the purposes of section 267(2)(c) the debtor appears to have no reasonable prospect of being able to pay a debt if, but only if, the debt is not immediately payable and—
- (a) the petitioning creditor to whom it is owed has served on the debtor a demand (also known as "the statutory demand") in the prescribed form requiring him to establish to the satisfaction of the creditor that there is a reasonable prospect that the debtor will be able to pay the debt when it falls due,
- (b) at least 3 weeks have elapsed since the demand was served, and
- (c) the demand has been neither complied with nor set aside in accordance with the rules.

NOTES

This section derived from the Insolvency Act 1985, s 120(3), (4).

[1.328]

269 Creditor with security

(1) A debt which is the debt, or one of the debts, in respect of which a creditor's petition is presented need not be unsecured if either—

(a) the petition contains a statement by the person having the right to enforce the security that he is willing, in the event of a bankruptcy order being made, to give up his security for the benefit of all the bankrupt's creditors, or

(b) the petition is expressed not to be made in respect of the secured part of the debt and contains a statement by that person of the estimated value at the date of the petition of the security for the secured part of the debt.

(2) In a case falling within subsection (1)(b) the secured and unsecured parts of the debt are to be treated for the purposes of sections 267 and 270 as separate debts.

NOTES

This section derived from the Insolvency Act 1985, s 120(5).

[1.329]

270 Expedited petition

In the case of a creditor's petition presented wholly or partly in respect of a debt which is the subject of a statutory demand under section 268, the petition may be presented before the end of the 3-week period there mentioned if there is a serious possibility that the debtor's property or the value of any of his property will be significantly diminished during that period and the petition contains a statement to that effect.

NOTES

This section derived from the Insolvency Act 1985, s 120(6).

[1.330]

271 Proceedings on creditor's petition

(1) The court shall not make a bankruptcy order on a creditor's petition unless it is satisfied that the debt, or one of the debts, in respect of which the petition was presented is either—

(a) a debt which, having been payable at the date of the petition or having since become payable, has been neither paid nor secured or compounded for, or

(b) a debt which the debtor has no reasonable prospect of being able to pay when it falls due.

(2) In a case in which the petition contains such a statement as is required by section 270, the court shall not make a bankruptcy order until at least 3 weeks have elapsed since the service of any statutory demand under section 268.

(3) The court may dismiss the petition if it is satisfied that the debtor is able to pay all his debts or is satisfied—

(a) that the debtor has made an offer to secure or compound for a debt in respect of which the petition is presented,

(b) that the acceptance of that offer would have required the dismissal of the petition, and

(c) that the offer has been unreasonably refused;

and, in determining for the purposes of this subsection whether the debtor is able to pay all his debts, the court shall take into account his contingent and prospective liabilities.

(4) In determining for the purposes of this section what constitutes a reasonable prospect that a debtor will be able to pay a debt when it falls due, it is to be assumed that the prospect given by the facts and other matters known to the creditor at the time he entered into the transaction resulting in the debt was a reasonable prospect.

(5) Nothing in sections 267 to 271 prejudices the power of the court, in accordance with the rules, to authorise a creditor's petition to be amended by the omission of any creditor or debt and to be proceeded with as if things done for the purposes of those sections had been done only by or in relation to the remaining creditors or debts.

NOTES

This section derived from the Insolvency Act 1985, s 121.

Debtor's petition

[1.331]

272 Grounds of debtor's petition

(1) A debtor's petition may be presented to the court only on the grounds that the debtor is unable to pay his debts.

(2) The petition shall be accompanied by a statement of the debtor's affairs containing—

(a) such particulars of the debtor's creditors and of his debts and other liabilities and of his assets as may be prescribed, and

(b) such other information as may be prescribed.

NOTES

This section derived from the Insolvency Act 1985, s 122.

Repealed, together with preceding cross-heading and s 273, by the Enterprise and Regulatory Reform Act 2013, s 71(3), Sch 19, paras 1, 9(1), in respect of a petition for a bankruptcy order presented to the court by a debtor on or after 6 April 2016, and subject to art 4 of the Enterprise and Regulatory Reform Act 2013 (Commencement No 9 and Saving Provisions) Order 2016, SI 2016/191, which provides as follows—

"4

The repeals of sections 272 and 273 of the Insolvency Act 1986 brought into force by paragraph 9 of Schedule 19 to the Act do not have effect in respect of the application of—

(a) paragraphs 6 and 7 of Part 2 of Schedule 1 (provisions of the Act applying with relevant modifications to the administration in bankruptcy of insolvent estates of deceased persons dying before presentation of a bankruptcy petition) to the Administration of Insolvent Estates of Deceased Persons Order 1986; and

(b) paragraph 5 of Schedule 7 (provisions of the Act which apply with modifications for the purposes of article 11 where joint bankruptcy petition presented by individual members without winding up partnership as unregistered company) to the Insolvent Partnerships Order 1994.".

[1.332]

273 Appointment of insolvency practitioner by the court

(1) Subject to the next section, on the hearing of a debtor's petition the court shall not make a bankruptcy order if it appears to the court—

(a) that if a bankruptcy order were made the aggregate amount of the bankruptcy debts, so far as unsecured, would be less than the small bankruptcies level,

(b) that if a bankruptcy order were made, the value of the bankrupt's estate would be equal to or more than the minimum amount,

(c) that within the period of 5 years ending with the presentation of the petition the debtor has neither been adjudged bankrupt nor made a composition with his creditors in satisfaction of his debts or a scheme of arrangement of his affairs, and

(d) that it would be appropriate to appoint a person to prepare a report under section 274.

"The minimum amount" and "the small bankruptcies level" mean such amounts as may for the time being be prescribed for the purposes of this section.

(2) Where on the hearing of the petition, it appears to the court as mentioned in subsection (1), the court shall appoint a person who is qualified to act as an insolvency practitioner in relation to the debtor—

(a) to prepare a report under the next section, and

(b) subject to section 258(3) in Part VIII, to act in relation to any voluntary arrangement to which the report relates either as trustee or otherwise for the purpose of supervising its implementation.

NOTES

This section derived from the Insolvency Act 1985, s 123(1), (2), (8).

Repealed as noted to s 272 at **[1.331]**.

See further: the Insolvency Proceedings (Monetary Limits) Order 1986, SI 1986/1996, art 3, Schedule, Pt II at **[8.3]**, **[8.6]** which specifies £40,000 and £4,000 as the prescribed sums for sub-s (1)(a) and (b) respectively. As to the fee payable to an insolvency practitioner appointed under this section, see the Insolvency Proceedings (Fees) Order 2004, SI 2004/593, art 5 at **[8.75]**.

[1.333]

274 Action on report of insolvency practitioner

(1) A person appointed under section 273 shall inquire into the debtor's affairs and, within such period as the court may direct, shall submit a report to the court stating whether the debtor is willing, for the purposes of Part VIII, to make a proposal for a voluntary arrangement.

(2) A report which states that the debtor is willing as above mentioned shall also state—

(a) whether, in the opinion of the person making the report, a meeting of the debtor's creditors should be summoned to consider the proposal, and

(b) if in that person's opinion such a meeting should be summoned, the date on which, and time and place at which, he proposes the meeting should be held.

(3) On considering a report under this section the court may—

(a) without any application, make an interim order under section 252, if it thinks that it is appropriate to do so for the purpose of facilitating the consideration and implementation of the debtor's proposal, or

(b) if it thinks it would be inappropriate to make such an order, make a bankruptcy order.

(4) An interim order made by virtue of this section ceases to have effect at the end of such period as the court may specify for the purpose of enabling the debtor's proposal to be considered by his creditors in accordance with the applicable provisions of Part VIII.

(5) Where it has been reported to the court under this section that a meeting of the debtor's creditors should be summoned, the person making the report shall, unless the court otherwise directs, summon that meeting for the time, date and place proposed in his report.

The meeting is then deemed to have been summoned under section 257 in Part VIII, and subsections (2) and (3) of that section, and sections 258 to 263 apply accordingly.

NOTES

This section derived from the Insolvency Act 1985, ss 111(3) (in part), 112(1) (in part), (7)(b), 114(1) (in part), 123(3)–(5).

Repealed by the Enterprise and Regulatory Reform Act 2013, s 71(3), Sch 19, paras 1, 9(1), in respect of a petition for a bankruptcy order presented to the court by a debtor on or after 6 April 2016.

[1.334]
[274A Debtor who meets conditions for a debt relief order
(1) This section applies where, on the hearing of a debtor's petition—
- *(a) it appears to the court that a debt relief order would be made in relation to the debtor if, instead of presenting the petition, he had made an application under Part 7A; and*
- *(b) the court does not appoint an insolvency practitioner under section 273.*

(2) If the court thinks it would be in the debtor's interests to apply for a debt relief order instead of proceeding on the petition, the court may refer the debtor to an approved intermediary (within the meaning of Part 7A) for the purposes of making an application for a debt relief order.
(3) Where a reference is made under subsection (2) the court shall stay proceedings on the petition on such terms and conditions as it thinks fit; but if following the reference a debt relief order is made in relation to the debtor the court shall dismiss the petition.]

NOTES
Inserted by the Tribunals, Courts and Enforcement Act 2007, s 108(3), Sch 20, Pt 1, paras 1, 3.
Repealed by the Enterprise and Regulatory Reform Act 2013, s 71(3), Sch 19, paras 1, 9(1), in respect of a petition for a bankruptcy order presented to the court by a debtor on or after 6 April 2016.

[1.335]
275 Summary administration
(1) Where on the hearing of a debtor's petition the court makes a bankruptcy order and the case is as specified in the next subsection, the court shall, if it appears to it appropriate to do so, issue a certificate for the summary administration of the bankrupt's estate.
(2) That case is where it appears to the court—
- *(a) that if a bankruptcy order were made the aggregate amount of the bankruptcy debts so far as unsecured would be less than the small bankruptcies level (within the meaning given by section 273), and*
- *(b) that within the period of 5 years ending with the presentation of the petition the debtor has neither been adjudged bankrupt nor made a composition with his creditors in satisfaction of his debts or a scheme of arrangement of his affairs,*

whether the bankruptcy order is made because it does not appear to the court as mentioned in section 273(1)(b) or (d), or it is made because the court thinks it would be inappropriate to make an interim order under section 252.
(3) The court may at any time revoke a certificate issued under this section if it appears to it that, on any grounds existing at the time the certificate was issued, the certificate ought not to have been issued.

NOTES
This section derived from the Insolvency Act 1985, s 123(6), (7).
Repealed by the Enterprise Act 2002, ss 269, 278(2), Sch 23, paras 1, 2, Sch 26, subject to savings and transitional provisions in relation to existing bankruptcies in England and Wales where a certificate of summary administration is in force on 1 April 2004 (see the Enterprise Act 2002 (Commencement No 4 and Transitional Provisions and Savings) Order 2003, SI 2003/2093, art 8 at **[2.31]**).

Other cases for special consideration

[1.336]
276 Default in connection with voluntary arrangement
(1) The court shall not make a bankruptcy order on a petition under section 264(1)(c) (supervisor of, or person bound by, voluntary arrangement proposed and approved) unless it is satisfied—
- (a) that the debtor has failed to comply with his obligations under the voluntary arrangement, or
- (b) that information which was false or misleading in any material particular or which contained material omissions—
  - (i) was contained in any statement of affairs or other document supplied by the debtor under Part VIII to any person, or
  - (ii) was otherwise made available by the debtor to his creditors [in connection with a creditors' decision procedure instigated] under that Part, or
- (c) that the debtor has failed to do all such things as may for the purposes of the voluntary arrangement have been reasonably required of him by the supervisor of the arrangement.

(2) Where a bankruptcy order is made on a petition under section 264(1)(c), any expenses properly incurred as expenses of the administration of the voluntary arrangement in question shall be a first charge on the bankrupt's estate.

NOTES
This section derived from the Insolvency Act 1985, s 124.
Sub-s (1):words in square brackets substituted for original words "at or in connection with a meeting summoned" by the Small Business, Enterprise and Employment Act 2015, s 126, Sch 9, Pt 2, paras 60, 73, as from 6 April 2017 (subject to transitional and savings provisions as noted to s 246ZE at **[1.256]**).

[1.337]
277 Petition based on criminal bankruptcy order
(1) Subject to section 266(3), the court shall make a bankruptcy order on a petition under section 264(1)(d) on production of a copy of the criminal bankruptcy order on which the petition is based.
This does not apply if it appears to the court that the criminal bankruptcy order has been rescinded on appeal.

(2) Subject to the provisions of this Part, the fact that an appeal is pending against any conviction by virtue of which a criminal bankruptcy order was made does not affect any proceedings on a petition under section 264(1)(d) based on that order.

(3) For the purposes of this section, an appeal against a conviction is pending—

(a) in any case, until the expiration of the period of 28 days beginning with the date of conviction;

(b) if notice of appeal to the Court of Appeal is given during that period and during that period the appellant notifies the official receiver of it, until the determination of the appeal and thereafter for so long as an appeal to the [Supreme Court] is pending within the meaning of [subsection (4).

(4) For the purposes of subsection (3)(b) an appeal to the Supreme Court shall be treated as pending until any application for leave to appeal is disposed of and, if leave to appeal is granted, until the appeal is disposed of; and for the purposes of this subsection an application for leave to appeal shall be treated as disposed of at the expiration of the time within which it may be made, if it is not made within that time.]

NOTES

This section derived from the Insolvency Act 1985, s 125.

Repealed by the Criminal Justice Act 1988, s 170(2), Sch 16, as from a day to be appointed.

Sub-s (3): words in first pair of square brackets substituted, and words in second pair of square brackets substituted together with new sub-s (4) for words originally in sub-s (3), by the Constitutional Reform Act 2005, s 40(4), Sch 9, Pt 1, para 44.

Sub-s (4): substituted as noted to sub-s (3) above.

[CHAPTER 1A
COMMENCEMENT AND DURATION OF BANKRUPTCY]

NOTES

Chapter heading: substituted for original words "Commencement and duration of bankruptcy; discharge" (which originally formed part of Ch I), by the Enterprise and Regulatory Reform Act 2013, s 71(3), Sch 19, paras 1, 10, in respect of a petition for a bankruptcy order presented to the court by a debtor on or after 6 April 2016.

[1.338]

278 Commencement and continuance

The bankruptcy of an individual against whom a bankruptcy order has been made—

(a) commences with the day on which the order is made, and

(b) continues until the individual is discharged under . . . this Chapter.

NOTES

This section derived from the Insolvency Act 1985, s 126(1).

Words "the following provisions of" omitted from para (b) repealed by the Enterprise and Regulatory Reform Act 2013, s 71(3), Sch 19, paras 1, 11, in relation to a petition for a bankruptcy order presented to the court by a debtor on or after 6 April 2016.

[1.339]

[279 Duration

(1) A bankrupt is discharged from bankruptcy at the end of the period of one year beginning with the date on which the bankruptcy commences.

(2) . . .

(3) On the application of the official receiver or the trustee of a bankrupt's estate, the court may order that the period specified in subsection (1) shall cease to run until—

(a) the end of a specified period, or

(b) the fulfilment of a specified condition.

(4) The court may make an order under subsection (3) only if satisfied that the bankrupt has failed or is failing to comply with an obligation under this Part.

(5) In subsection (3)(b) "condition" includes a condition requiring that the court be satisfied of something.

(6) In the case of an individual who is [made] bankrupt on a petition under section 264(1)(d)—

(a) subsections (1) to (5) shall not apply, and

(b) the bankrupt is discharged from bankruptcy by an order of the court under section 280.

(7) This section is without prejudice to any power of the court to annul a bankruptcy order.]

NOTES

This section, as originally enacted, derived from the Insolvency Act 1985, s 126(2)–(5).

Substituted by the Enterprise Act 2002, s 256(1), subject to transitional provisions in s 256(2) of, and Sch 19 to, that Act at **[2.13]**, **[2.22]**, and originally read as follows:

"279 Duration

(1) Subject as follows, a bankrupt is discharged from bankruptcy—

(a) in the case of an individual who was adjudged bankrupt on a petition under section 264(1)(d) or who had been an undischarged bankrupt at any time in the period of 15 years ending with the commencement of the bankruptcy, by an order of the court under the section next following, and

(b) in any other case, by the expiration of the relevant period under this section.

(2) That period is as follows—

(a) where a certificate for the summary administration of the bankrupt's estate has been issued and is not revoked before the bankrupt's discharge, the period of 2 years beginning with the commencement of the bankruptcy, and

(b) in any other case, the period of 3 years beginning with the commencement of the bankruptcy.

(3) Where the court is satisfied on the application of the official receiver that an undischarged bankrupt in relation to whom subsection (1)(b) applies has failed or is failing to comply with any of his obligations under this Part, the court may order that the relevant period under this section shall cease to run for such period, or until the fulfilment of such conditions (including a condition requiring the court to be satisfied as to any matter), as may be specified in the order.

(4) This section is without prejudice to any power of the court to annul a bankruptcy order.".

Sub-s (2): repealed by the Enterprise and Regulatory Reform Act 2013, s 73, Sch 21, Pt 3, para 5, with effect in relation to bankruptcy orders made on or after 1 October 2013; sub-s (2) previously read as follows:

"(2) If before the end of that period the official receiver files with the court a notice stating that investigation of the conduct and affairs of the bankrupt under section 289 is unnecessary or concluded, the bankrupt is discharged when the notice is filed.".

Sub-s (6): word in square brackets substituted for original word "adjudged" by the Enterprise and Regulatory Reform Act 2013, s 71(3), Sch 19, paras 1, 12, in respect of a petition for a bankruptcy order presented to the court by a debtor on or after 6 April 2016.

[1.340]

280 Discharge by order of the court

(1) An application for an order of the court discharging an individual from bankruptcy in a case falling within [section 279(6)] may be made by the bankrupt at any time after the end of the period of 5 years beginning with the [date on which the bankruptcy commences].

(2) On an application under this section the court may—

(a) refuse to discharge the bankrupt from bankruptcy,

(b) make an order discharging him absolutely, or

(c) make an order discharging him subject to such conditions with respect to any income which may subsequently become due to him, or with respect to property devolving upon him, or acquired by him, after his discharge, as may be specified in the order.

(3) The court may provide for an order falling within subsection (2)(b) or (c) to have immediate effect or to have its effect suspended for such period, or until the fulfilment of such conditions (including a condition requiring the court to be satisfied as to any matter), as may be specified in the order.

NOTES

This section derived from the Insolvency Act 1985, s 127.

Sub-s (1): words in first pair of square brackets substituted for original words "section 279(1)(a)" and words in second pair of square brackets substituted for original words "commencement of the bankruptcy" by the Enterprise Act 2002, s 269, Sch 23, paras 1, 3, subject to transitional provisions in s 256(2) of, and Sch 19 to, that Act at **[2.13]**, **[2.22]**.

Effect of a freezing order under the International Criminal Court Act 2001: where a person has been adjudged bankrupt in England and Wales, the powers conferred on a receiver appointed under the International Criminal Court Act 2001, Sch 6, para 5 shall not be exercised in relation to property which is to be applied for the benefit of creditors of the bankrupt by virtue of a condition imposed under sub-s (2)(c) of this section; see s 38 of, and Sch 6, para 9(2)(c) to the 2001 Act.

[1.341]

281 Effect of discharge

(1) Subject as follows, where a bankrupt is discharged, the discharge releases him from all the bankruptcy debts, but has no effect—

(a) on the functions (so far as they remain to be carried out) of the trustee of his estate, or

(b) on the operation, for the purposes of the carrying out of those functions, of the provisions of this Part;

and, in particular, discharge does not affect the right of any creditor of the bankrupt to prove in the bankruptcy for any debt from which the bankrupt is released.

(2) Discharge does not affect the right of any secured creditor of the bankrupt to enforce his security for the payment of a debt from which the bankrupt is released.

(3) Discharge does not release the bankrupt from any bankruptcy debt which he incurred in respect of, or forbearance in respect of which was secured by means of, any fraud or fraudulent breach of trust to which he was a party.

(4) Discharge does not release the bankrupt from any liability in respect of a fine imposed for an offence or from any liability under a recognisance except, in the case of a penalty imposed for an offence under an enactment relating to the public revenue or of a recognisance, with the consent of the Treasury.

[(4A) In subsection (4) the reference to a fine [imposed for an offence] includes a reference to[—

(a) a charge ordered to be paid under section 21A of the Prosecution of Offences Act 1985 (criminal courts charge), whether on conviction or otherwise;

(b)] a confiscation order under Part 2, 3 or 4 of the Proceeds of Crime Act 2002.]

(5) Discharge does not, except to such extent and on such conditions as the court may direct, release the bankrupt from any bankruptcy debt which—

(a) consists in a liability to pay damages for negligence, nuisance or breach of a statutory, contractual or other duty, [or to pay damages by virtue of Part I of the Consumer Protection Act 1987, being in either case] damages in respect of personal injuries to any person, or

(b) arises under any order made in family proceedings [or under a *maintenance assessment* made under the Child Support Act 1991] . . .

(6) Discharge does not release the bankrupt from such other bankruptcy debts, not being debts provable in his bankruptcy, as are prescribed.

(7) Discharge does not release any person other than the bankrupt from any liability (whether as partner or co-trustee of the bankrupt or otherwise) from which the bankrupt is released by the discharge, or from any liability as surety for the bankrupt or as a person in the nature of such a surety.
(8) In this section—

["family proceedings" means—

(a) family proceedings within the meaning of the Magistrates' Courts Act 1980 and any proceedings which would be such proceedings but for section 65(1)(ii) of that Act (proceedings for variation of order for periodical payments); and
(b) family proceedings within the meaning of Part V of the Matrimonial and Family Proceedings Act 1984.]

"fine" means the same as in the Magistrates' Courts Act 1980; and

"personal injuries" includes death and any disease or other impairment of a person's physical or mental condition.

NOTES

This section derived from the Insolvency Act 1985, s 128.

Sub-s (4A): inserted by the Proceeds of Crime Act 2002, s 456, Sch 11, paras 1, 16(1), (2); words in square brackets inserted by the Criminal Justice and Courts Act 2015, s 54(3), Sch 12, para 6.

Sub-s (5): words in square brackets in para (a) substituted by the Consumer Protection Act 1987, s 48, Sch 4, para 12; words in square brackets in para (b) inserted by the Child Support Act 1991, s 58(13), Sch 5, para 7, and for the words in italics therein there are substituted the words "maintenance calculation" by the Child Support, Pensions and Social Security Act 2000, s 26, Sch 3, para 6, as from 3 March 2003 for certain purposes (see SI 2003/192, arts 3, 8, Schedule) and as from a day to be appointed for remaining purposes; words omitted repealed by the Children Act 1989, ss 92(11), 108(7) Sch 11, Pt II, para 11(1), Sch 15.

Sub-s (8): definition "family proceedings" substituted for original definitions "domestic proceedings" and "family proceedings" by the Children Act 1989, s 92(11), Sch 11, Pt II, para 11(2).

Modification: the reference to a fine in sub-s (4) is modified to include a reference to a confiscation order made under (i) the Criminal Justice (Scotland) Act 1987, see s 45(4) of that Act; (ii) the Criminal Justice Act 1988, see s 170(1) of, and Sch 15, para 110 to, that Act; (iii) the Drug Trafficking Act 1994, see s 65(3) of that Act.

[1.342]
[281A Post-discharge restrictions
Schedule 4A to this Act (bankruptcy restrictions order and bankruptcy restrictions undertaking) shall have effect.]

NOTES

Inserted by the Enterprise Act 2002, s 257(1), subject to transitional provisions in s 256(2) of, and Sch 19 to, that Act at **[2.13]**, **[2.22]**.

Bankruptcy restrictions order: where a court is considering whether or not a bankruptcy restrictions order should be made pursuant to this section and Sch 4A at **[1.587]**, it shall not take into account any conduct of the bankrupt before 1 April 2004; see the Enterprise Act 2002 (Commencement No 4 and Transitional Provisions and Savings) Order 2003, SI 2003/2093, art 7 at **[2.30]**.

[1.343]
282 Court's power to annul bankruptcy order
(1) The court may annul a bankruptcy order if it at any time appears to the court—

(a) that, on the grounds existing at the time the order was made, the order ought not to have been made, or
(b) that, to the extent required by the rules, the bankruptcy debts and the expenses of the bankruptcy have all, since the making of the order, been either paid or secured for to the satisfaction of the court.

(2) The court may annul a bankruptcy order made against an individual on a petition under paragraph (a), (b) or (c) of section 264(1) [or on a bankruptcy application] if it at any time appears to the court, on an application by the Official Petitioner—

(a) that the petition was pending [or the application was ongoing] at a time when a criminal bankruptcy order was made against the individual or was presented after such an order was so made, and
(b) no appeal is pending (within the meaning of section 277) against the individual's conviction of any offence by virtue of which the criminal bankruptcy order was made;

and the court shall annul a bankruptcy order made on a petition under section 264(1)(d) if it at any time appears to the court that the criminal bankruptcy order on which the petition was based has been rescinded in consequence of an appeal.
(3) The court may annul a bankruptcy order whether or not the bankrupt has been discharged from the bankruptcy.
(4) Where the court annuls a bankruptcy order (whether under this section or under section 261 *[or 263D]* in Part VIII)—

(a) any sale or other disposition of property, payment made or other thing duly done, under any provision in this Group of Parts, by or under the authority of the official receiver or a trustee of the bankrupt's estate or by the court is valid, but
(b) if any of the bankrupt's estate is then vested, under any such provision, in such a trustee, it shall vest in such person as the court may appoint or, in default of any such appointment, revert to the bankrupt on such terms (if any) as the court may direct;

and the court may include in its order such supplemental provisions as may be authorised by the rules.
(5) . . .

NOTES

This section derived from the Insolvency Act 1985, s 129.

Sub-s (2): repealed by the Criminal Justice Act 1988, s 170(2), Sch 16, as from a day to be appointed; figure ", (b)" repealed, and words in square brackets inserted, by the Enterprise and Regulatory Reform Act 2013, s 71(3), Sch 19, paras 1, 13, in relation to a petition for a bankruptcy order presented to the court by a debtor on or after 6 April 2016.

Sub-s (4): words in square brackets inserted by the Enterprise Act 2002, s 269, Sch 23, paras 1, 4(a) and repealed by the Small Business, Enterprise and Employment Act 2015, s 135(2)(a), (4), except in relation to a case where a debtor has submitted the document and statement mentioned in s 263B(1) to the official receiver before 26 May 2015.

Sub-s (5): repealed by the Enterprise Act 2002, ss 269, 278(2), Sch 23, paras 1, 4(b), Sch 26, subject to transitional provisions in s 256(2) of, and Sch 19 to, that Act at **[2.13]**, **[2.22]**, and previously read as follows:

"(5) In determining for the purposes of section 279 whether a person was an undischarged bankrupt at any time, any time when he was a bankrupt by virtue of an order that was subsequently annulled is to be disregarded.".

CHAPTER II
PROTECTION OF BANKRUPT'S ESTATE AND INVESTIGATION OF HIS AFFAIRS

[1.344]

283 Definition of bankrupt's estate

(1) Subject as follows, a bankrupt's estate for the purposes of any of this Group of Parts comprises—

(a) all property belonging to or vested in the bankrupt at the commencement of the bankruptcy, and

(b) any property which by virtue of any of the following provisions of this Part is comprised in that estate or is treated as falling within the preceding paragraph.

(2) Subsection (1) does not apply to—

(a) such tools, books, vehicles and other items of equipment as are necessary to the bankrupt for use personally by him in his employment, business or vocation;

(b) such clothing, bedding, furniture, household equipment and provisions as are necessary for satisfying the basic domestic needs of the bankrupt and his family.

This subsection is subject to section 308 in Chapter IV (certain excluded property reclaimable by trustee).

(3) Subsection (1) does not apply to—

(a) property held by the bankrupt on trust for any other person, or

(b) the right of nomination to a vacant ecclesiastical benefice.

[(3A) Subject to section 308A in Chapter IV, subsection (1) does not apply to—

(a) a tenancy which is an assured tenancy or an assured agricultural occupancy, within the meaning of Part I of the Housing Act 1988, and the terms of which inhibit an assignment as mentioned in section 127(5) of the Rent Act 1977, or

(b) a protected tenancy, within the meaning of the Rent Act 1977, in respect of which, by virtue of any provision of Part IX of that Act, no premium can lawfully be required as a condition of assignment, or

(c) a tenancy of a dwelling-house by virtue of which the bankrupt is, within the meaning of the Rent (Agriculture) Act 1976, a protected occupier of the dwelling-house, and the terms of which inhibit an assignment as mentioned in section 127(5) of the Rent Act 1977, or

(d) a secure tenancy, within the meaning of Part IV of the Housing Act 1985, which is not capable of being assigned, except in the cases mentioned in section 91(3) of that Act.]

(4) References in any of this Group of Parts to property, in relation to a bankrupt, include references to any power exercisable by him over or in respect of property except in so far as the power is exercisable over or in respect of property not for the time being comprised in the bankrupt's estate and—

(a) is so exercisable at a time after either the official receiver has had his release in respect of that estate under section 299(2) in Chapter III or a [the trustee of that estate has vacated office under section 298(8)], or

(b) cannot be so exercised for the benefit of the bankrupt;

and a power exercisable over or in respect of property is deemed for the purposes of any of this Group of Parts to vest in the person entitled to exercise it at the time of the transaction or event by virtue of which it is exercisable by that person (whether or not it becomes so exercisable at that time).

(5) For the purposes of any such provision in this Group of Parts, property comprised in a bankrupt's estate is so comprised subject to the rights of any person other than the bankrupt (whether as a secured creditor of the bankrupt or otherwise) in relation thereto, but disregarding—

(a) any rights in relation to which a statement such as is required by section 269(1)(a) was made in the petition on which the bankrupt was [made] bankrupt, and

(b) any rights which have been otherwise given up in accordance with the rules.

(6) This section has effect subject to the provisions of any enactment not contained in this Act under which any property is to be excluded from a bankrupt's estate.

NOTES

This section derived from the Insolvency Act 1985, s 130.

Sub-s (3A): inserted by the Housing Act 1988, s 117(1).

Sub-s (4): words in square brackets substituted for original words "meeting summoned by the trustee of that estate under section 331 in Chapter IV has been held" by the Small Business, Enterprise and Employment Act 2015, s 126, Sch 9, Pt 2, paras 60, 74, as from 6 April 2017 (subject to transitional and savings provisions as noted to s 246ZE at **[1.256]**).

Sub-s (5): word in square brackets in para (a) substituted for original word "adjudged" by the Enterprise and Regulatory Reform Act 2013, s 71(3), Sch 19, paras 1, 14, in respect of a petition for a bankruptcy order presented to the court by a debtor on or after 6 April 2016.

[1.345]

[283A Bankrupt's home ceasing to form part of estate

(1) This section applies where property comprised in the bankrupt's estate consists of an interest in a dwelling-house which at the date of the bankruptcy was the sole or principal residence of—

(a) the bankrupt,

(b) the bankrupt's spouse [or civil partner], or

(c) a former spouse [or former civil partner] of the bankrupt.

(2) At the end of the period of three years beginning with the date of the bankruptcy the interest mentioned in subsection (1) shall—

(a) cease to be comprised in the bankrupt's estate, and

(b) vest in the bankrupt (without conveyance, assignment or transfer).

(3) Subsection (2) shall not apply if during the period mentioned in that subsection—

(a) the trustee realises the interest mentioned in subsection (1),

(b) the trustee applies for an order for sale in respect of the dwelling-house,

(c) the trustee applies for an order for possession of the dwelling-house,

(d) the trustee applies for an order under section 313 in Chapter IV in respect of that interest, or

(e) the trustee and the bankrupt agree that the bankrupt shall incur a specified liability to his estate (with or without the addition of interest from the date of the agreement) in consideration of which the interest mentioned in subsection (1) shall cease to form part of the estate.

(4) Where an application of a kind described in subsection (3)(b) to (d) is made during the period mentioned in subsection (2) and is dismissed, unless the court orders otherwise the interest to which the application relates shall on the dismissal of the application—

(a) cease to be comprised in the bankrupt's estate, and

(b) vest in the bankrupt (without conveyance, assignment or transfer).

(5) If the bankrupt does not inform the trustee or the official receiver of his interest in a property before the end of the period of three months beginning with the date of the bankruptcy, the period of three years mentioned in subsection (2)—

(a) shall not begin with the date of the bankruptcy, but

(b) shall begin with the date on which the trustee or official receiver becomes aware of the bankrupt's interest.

(6) The court may substitute for the period of three years mentioned in subsection (2) a longer period—

(a) in prescribed circumstances, and

(b) in such other circumstances as the court thinks appropriate.

(7) The rules may make provision for this section to have effect with the substitution of a shorter period for the period of three years mentioned in subsection (2) in specified circumstances (which may be described by reference to action to be taken by a trustee in bankruptcy).

(8) The rules may also, in particular, make provision—

(a) requiring or enabling the trustee of a bankrupt's estate to give notice that this section applies or does not apply;

(b) about the effect of a notice under paragraph (a);

(c) requiring the trustee of a bankrupt's estate to make an application to the Chief Land Registrar.

(9) Rules under subsection (8)(b) may, in particular—

(a) disapply this section;

(b) enable a court to disapply this section;

(c) make provision in consequence of a disapplication of this section;

(d) enable a court to make provision in consequence of a disapplication of this section;

(e) make provision (which may include provision conferring jurisdiction on a court or tribunal) about compensation.]

NOTES

Inserted by the Enterprise Act 2002, s 261(1), subject to transitional provisions in s 261(7)–(10) of that Act at **[2.14]**.

Sub-s (1): words in square brackets inserted by the Civil Partnership Act 2004, s 261(1), Sch 27, para 113.

[1.346]

284 Restrictions on dispositions of property

(1) Where a person is [made] bankrupt, any disposition of property made by that person in the period to which this section applies is void except to the extent that it is or was made with the consent of the court, or is or was subsequently ratified by the court.

(2) Subsection (1) applies to a payment (whether in cash or otherwise) as it applies to a disposition of property and, accordingly, where any payment is void by virtue of that subsection, the person paid shall hold the sum paid for the bankrupt as part of his estate.

(3) This section applies to the period beginning with the day of the [making of the bankruptcy application or (as the case may be) the presentation of the bankruptcy petition] and ending with the vesting, under Chapter IV of this Part, of the bankrupt's estate in a trustee.

(4) The preceding provisions of this section do not give a remedy against any person—

(a) in respect of any property or payment which he received before the commencement of the bankruptcy in good faith, for value and without notice that the [bankruptcy application had been made or (as the case may be) that the bankruptcy] petition had been presented, or

(b) in respect of any interest in property which derives from an interest in respect of which there is, by virtue of this subsection, no remedy.

(5) Where after the commencement of his bankruptcy the bankrupt has incurred a debt to a banker or other person by reason of the making of a payment which is void under this section, that debt is deemed for the purposes of any of this Group of Parts to have been incurred before the commencement of the bankruptcy unless—

(a) that banker or person had notice of the bankruptcy before the debt was incurred, or

(b) it is not reasonably practicable for the amount of the payment to be recovered from the person to whom it was made.

(6) A disposition of property is void under this section notwithstanding that the property is not or, as the case may be, would not be comprised in the bankrupt's estate; but nothing in this section affects any disposition made by a person of property held by him on trust for any other person.

NOTES

This section derived from the Insolvency Act 1985, s 131.

Sub-s (1): word in square brackets substituted for original word "adjudged" by the Enterprise and Regulatory Reform Act 2013, s 71(3), Sch 19, paras 1, 15(1), (2), in respect of a petition for a bankruptcy order presented to the court by a debtor on or after 6 April 2016.

Sub-s (3): words in square brackets substituted for original words "presentation of the petition for the bankruptcy order" by the Enterprise and Regulatory Reform Act 2013, s 71(3), Sch 19, paras 1, 15(1), (3), in respect of a petition for a bankruptcy order presented to the court by a debtor on or after 6 April 2016.

Sub-s (4): words in square brackets inserted by the Enterprise and Regulatory Reform Act 2013, s 71(3), Sch 19, paras 1, 15(1), (4), in respect of a petition for a bankruptcy order presented to the court by a debtor on or after 6 April 2016.

Disapplication with regard to market contracts and market charges: see the note to s 127 at **[1.128]**.

[1.347]

285 Restriction on proceedings and remedies

(1) At any time when [proceedings on a bankruptcy application are ongoing or] proceedings on a bankruptcy petition are pending or an individual has been [made] bankrupt the court may stay any action, execution or other legal process against the property or person of the debtor or, as the case may be, of the bankrupt.

(2) Any court in which proceedings are pending against any individual may, on proof that [a bankruptcy application has been made or] a bankruptcy petition has been presented in respect of that individual or that he is an undischarged bankrupt, either stay the proceedings or allow them to continue on such terms as it thinks fit.

(3) After the making of a bankruptcy order no person who is a creditor of the bankrupt in respect of a debt provable in the bankruptcy shall—

(a) have any remedy against the property or person of the bankrupt in respect of that debt, or

(b) before the discharge of the bankrupt, commence any action or other legal proceedings against the bankrupt except with the leave of the court and on such terms as the court may impose.

This is subject to sections 346 (enforcement procedures) and 347 (limited right to distress).

(4) Subject as follows, subsection (3) does not affect the right of a secured creditor of the bankrupt to enforce his security.

(5) Where any goods of an undischarged bankrupt are held by any person by way of pledge, pawn or other security, the official receiver may, after giving notice in writing of his intention to do so, inspect the goods.

Where such a notice has been given to any person, that person is not entitled, without leave of the court, to realise his security unless he has given the trustee of the bankrupt's estate a reasonable opportunity of inspecting the goods and of exercising the bankrupt's right of redemption.

(6) References in this section to the property or goods of the bankrupt are to any of his property or goods, whether or not comprised in his estate.

NOTES

This section derived from the Insolvency Act 1985, s 132.

Sub-s (1): words in first pair of square brackets inserted and word in second pair of square brackets substituted for original word "adjudged", by the Enterprise and Regulatory Reform Act 2013, s 71(3), Sch 19, paras 1, 16(1), (2), in respect of a petition for a bankruptcy order presented to the court by a debtor on or after 6 April 2016.

Sub-s (2): words in square brackets inserted by the Enterprise and Regulatory Reform Act 2013, s 71(3), Sch 19, paras 1, 16(1), (3), in respect of a petition for a bankruptcy order presented to the court by a debtor on or after 6 April 2016.

Default proceedings: see the note to s 126 at **[1.127]**.

[1.348]

286 Power to appoint interim receiver

(1) The court may, if it is shown to be necessary for the protection of the debtor's property, at any time after the presentation of a bankruptcy petition and before making a bankruptcy order, appoint the official receiver [or an insolvency practitioner] to be interim receiver of the debtor's property.

(2) Where the court has, on a debtor's petition, appointed an insolvency practitioner under section 273 and it is shown to the court as mentioned in subsection (1) of this section, the court may, without making a bankruptcy order, appoint that practitioner, instead of the official receiver, to be interim receiver of the debtor's property.

(3) The court may by an order appointing any person to be an interim receiver direct that his powers shall be limited or restricted in any respect; but, save as so directed, an interim receiver has, in relation to the debtor's property, all the rights, powers, duties and immunities [given by] the next section.

(4) An order of the court appointing any person to be an interim receiver shall require that person to take immediate possession of the debtor's property or, as the case may be, the part of it to which his powers as interim receiver are limited.

(5) Where an interim receiver has been appointed, the debtor shall give him such inventory of his property and such other information, and shall attend on the interim receiver at such times, as the latter may for the purpose of carrying out his functions under this section reasonably require.
(6) Where an interim receiver is appointed, section 285(3) applies for the period between the appointment and the making of a bankruptcy order on the petition, or the dismissal of the petition, as if the appointment were the making of such an order.
(7) A person ceases to be interim receiver of a debtor's property if the bankruptcy petition relating to the debtor is dismissed, if a bankruptcy order is made on the petition or if the court by order otherwise terminates the appointment.
(8) References in this section to the debtor's property are to all his property, whether or not it would be comprised in his estate if he were [made] bankrupt.

NOTES

This section derived from the Insolvency Act 1985, s 133.

Sub-s (1): words in square brackets inserted by the Deregulation Act 2015, s 19, Sch 6, Pt 5, paras 12, 13(1).

Sub-s (2): repealed by the Enterprise and Regulatory Reform Act 2013, s 71(3), Sch 19, paras 1, 17(1), (2), in respect of a petition for a bankruptcy order presented to the court by a debtor on or after 6 April 2016.

Sub-s (3): words in square brackets substituted for original words "of a receiver and manager under" by the Small Business, Enterprise and Employment Act 2015, s 133(2), Sch 10, paras 1, 2, as from 6 April 2017 (subject to transitional and savings provisions as noted to s 246ZE at **[1.256]**).

Sub-s (8): word in square brackets substituted for original word "adjudged" by the Enterprise and Regulatory Reform Act 2013, s 71(3), Sch 19, paras 1, 17(1), (3), in respect of a petition for a bankruptcy order presented to the court by a debtor on or after 6 April 2016.

Effect of a freezing order under the International Criminal Court Act 2001: the powers conferred by virtue of this Act on an interim receiver appointed under this section do not apply to property for the time being subject to a freezing order; see the International Criminal Court Act 2001, s 38, Sch 6, para 9(4).

Effect of restraint orders: the powers conferred on an interim receiver appointed under this section do not apply to property for the time being subject to a restraint order made under the Proceeds of Crime Act 2002, ss 41, 120 or 190; see s 417(4) of that Act at **[17.236]**.

[1.349]
287 [Powers of interim receiver]

(1) [An interim receiver appointed under section 286] is the receiver and (subject to section 370 (special manager)) the manager of the [debtor's property] and is under a duty to act as such.
(2) The function of [an interim] receiver while acting as receiver or manager of the [debtor's property] under this section is to protect [the property]; and for this purpose—
- (a) he has the same powers as if he were a receiver or manager appointed by the High Court, and
- (b) he is entitled to sell or otherwise dispose of any perishable goods comprised in [the property] and any other goods so comprised the value of which is likely to diminish if they are not disposed of.

(3) [An interim] receiver while acting as receiver or manager [of the debtor's property] under this section—
- (a) shall take all such steps as he thinks fit for protecting [the debtor's property,]
- [(b) is not required to do anything that involves his incurring expenditure, except in pursuance of directions given by—
  - (i) the Secretary of State, where the official receiver is the interim receiver, or
  - (ii) the court, in any other case,]
- (c) may, if he thinks fit (and shall, if so directed by the court) at any time [seek a decision on a matter from] the [debtor's] creditors.

(4) Where—
- [(a) an interim receiver acting as receiver or manager of the debtor's property under this section seizes or disposes of any property which is not the debtor's property, and]
- (b) at the time of the seizure or disposal the [interim receiver] believes, and has reasonable grounds for believing, that he is entitled (whether in pursuance of an order of the court or otherwise) to seize or dispose of that property,

the [interim receiver is] not to be liable to any person in respect of any loss or damage resulting from the seizure or disposal except in so far as that loss or damage is caused by his negligence; and he has a lien on the property, or the proceeds of its sale, for such of the expenses of the [interim receivership] as were incurred in connection with the seizure or disposal.
(5) This section does not apply where by virtue of section 297 (appointment of trustee; special cases) the bankrupt's estate vests in a trustee immediately on the making of the bankruptcy order.

NOTES

This section derived from the Insolvency Act 1985, s 134.

Section heading: words in square brackets substituted for original words "Receivership pending appointment of trustee" by the Small Business, Enterprise and Employment Act 2015, s 133(2), Sch 10, paras 1, 3(1), (2), as from 6 April 2017 (subject to transitional and savings provisions as noted to s 246ZE at **[1.256]**).

Sub-s (1): words in first and second pairs of square brackets substituted for original words "Between the making of a bankruptcy order and the time at which the bankrupt's estate vests in a trustee under Chapter IV of this Part, the official receiver" and "bankrupt's estate" respectively, by the Small Business, Enterprise and Employment Act 2015, s 133(2), Sch 10, paras 1, 3(1), (3), as from 6 April 2017 (subject to transitional and savings provisions as noted to s 246ZE at **[1.256]**).

Sub-s (2): words in square brackets in each place substituted by the Small Business, Enterprise and Employment Act 2015, s 133(2), Sch 10, paras 1, 3(1), (4), as from 6 April 2017 (subject to transitional and savings provisions as noted to s 246ZE at **[1.256]**), and sub-s (2) originally read as follows—

"(2) The function of the official receiver while acting as receiver or manager of the bankrupt's estate under this section is to protect the estate; and for this purpose—

(a) he has the same powers as if he were a receiver or manager appointed by the High Court, and

(b) he is entitled to sell or otherwise dispose of any perishable goods comprised in the estate and any other goods so comprised the value of which is likely to diminish if they are not disposed of.".

Sub-s (3): words in first and second pairs of square brackets substituted for original words "The official" and "of the estate" respectively, words in square brackets in para (a) substituted for original words "any property which may be claimed for the estate by the trustee of that estate," words in first and second pairs of square brackets substituted for original words "summon a general meeting of" and "bankrupt's" respectively, and para (b) substituted, by the Small Business, Enterprise and Employment Act 2015, ss 126, 133(2), Sch 9, Pt 2, paras 60, 75, Sch 10, paras 1, 3(1), (5), as from 6 April 2017 (subject to transitional and savings provisions as noted to s 246ZE at **[1.256]**). Para (b) originally read as follows—

"(b) is not, except in pursuance of directions given by the Secretary of State, required to do anything that involves his incurring expenditure,".

Sub-s (4): para (a) and other words in square brackets substituted by the Small Business, Enterprise and Employment Act 2015, s 133(2), Sch 10, paras 1, 3(1), (6), as from 6 April 2017 (subject to transitional and savings provisions as noted to s 246ZE at **[1.256]**). Sub-s (4) originally read as follows—

"(4) Where—

(a) the official receiver acting as receiver or manager of the estate under this section seizes or disposes of any property which is not comprised in the estate, and

(b) at the time of the seizure or disposal the official receiver believes, and has reasonable grounds for believing, that he is entitled (whether in pursuance of an order of the court or otherwise) to seize or dispose of that property,

the official receiver is not to be liable to any person in respect of any loss or damage resulting from the seizure or disposal except in so far as that loss or damage is caused by his negligence; and he has a lien on the property, or the proceeds of its sale, for such of the expenses of the bankruptcy as were incurred in connection with the seizure or disposal.".

Sub-s (5): repealed by the Small Business, Enterprise and Employment Act 2015, s 133(2), Sch 10, paras 1, 3(1), (7), as from 6 April 2017 (subject to transitional and savings provisions as noted to s 246ZE at **[1.256]**).

[1.350]

288 Statement of affairs

(1) Where a bankruptcy order has been made otherwise than on a [bankruptcy application], [the official receiver may at any time before the discharge of the bankrupt require the bankrupt to submit to the official receiver a statement of affairs].

(2) The statement of affairs shall contain—

(a) such particulars of the bankrupt's creditors and of his debts and other liabilities and of his assets as may be prescribed, and

(b) such other information as may be prescribed.

[(2A) Where a bankrupt is required under subsection (1) to submit a statement of affairs to the official receiver, the bankrupt shall do so (subject to subsection (3)) before the end of the period of 21 days beginning with the day after that on which the prescribed notice of the requirement is given to the bankrupt by the official receiver.]

(3) The official receiver may, if he thinks fit—

(a) release [a bankrupt from an obligation imposed on the bankrupt] under subsection (1), or

[(b) either when giving the notice mentioned in subsection (2A) or subsequently, extend the period mentioned in that subsection,]

and where the official receiver has refused to exercise a power conferred by this section, the court, if it thinks fit, may exercise it.

(4) A bankrupt who—

(a) without reasonable excuse fails to comply with [an obligation imposed under] this section, or

(b) without reasonable excuse submits a statement of affairs that does not comply with the prescribed requirements,

is guilty of a contempt of court and liable to be punished accordingly (in addition to any other punishment to which he may be subject).

NOTES

This section derived from the Insolvency Act 1985, s 135.

Sub-s (1): words in first pair of square brackets substituted for original words "debtor's petition", by the Enterprise and Regulatory Reform Act 2013, s 71(3), Sch 19, paras 1, 18, in respect of a petition for a bankruptcy order presented to the court by a debtor on or after 6 April 2016; words in second pair of square brackets substituted for original words "the bankrupt shall submit a statement of his affairs to the official receiver before the end of the period of 21 days beginning with the commencement of the bankruptcy", by the Deregulation Act 2015, s 19, Sch 6, Pt 5, paras 12, 15(1), (2), in relation to cases where a bankruptcy order is made on or after 6 April 2017 and the bankrupt is required to submit a statement of affairs.

Sub-s (2A): inserted by the Deregulation Act 2015, s 19, Sch 6, Pt 5, paras 12, 15(1), (3), in relation to cases where a bankruptcy order is made on or after 6 April 2017 and the bankrupt is required to submit a statement of affairs.

Sub-s (3): words in square brackets in para (a) substituted for original words "the bankrupt from his duty" and para (b) substituted, by the Deregulation Act 2015, s 19, Sch 6, Pt 5, paras 12, 15(1), (4), (5), in relation to cases where a bankruptcy order is made on or after 6 April 2017 and the bankrupt is required to submit a statement of affairs. Para (b) originally read as follows—

"(b) extend the period specified in that subsection;".

Sub-s (4): words in square brackets in para (a) substituted for original words "the obligation imposed by", by the Deregulation Act 2015, s 19, Sch 6, Pt 5, paras 12, 15(1), (6), in relation to cases where a bankruptcy order is made on or after 6 April 2017 and the bankrupt is required to submit a statement of affairs.

[1.351]
[289 Investigatory duties of official receiver

(1) The official receiver shall—

(a) investigate the conduct and affairs of each bankrupt (including his conduct and affairs before the making of the bankruptcy order), and

(b) make such report (if any) to the court as the official receiver thinks fit.

(2) Subsection (1) shall not apply to a case in which the official receiver thinks an investigation under that subsection unnecessary.

(3) Where a bankrupt makes an application for discharge under section 280—

(a) the official receiver shall make a report to the court about such matters as may be prescribed, and

(b) the court shall consider the report before determining the application.

(4) A report by the official receiver under this section shall in any proceedings be prima facie evidence of the facts stated in it.]

NOTES

This section, as originally enacted, derived from the Insolvency Act 1985, s 136.

Substituted by the Enterprise Act 2002, s 258, subject to transitional provisions in s 256(2) of, and Sch 19 to, that Act at **[2.13]**, **[2.22]**, and originally read as follows:

"289 Investigatory duties of official receiver

(1) Subject to subsection (5) below, it is the duty of the official receiver to investigate the conduct and affairs of every bankrupt and to make such report (if any) to the court as he thinks fit.

(2) Where an application is made by the bankrupt under section 280 for his discharge from bankruptcy, it is the duty of the official receiver to make a report to the court with respect to the prescribed matters; and the court shall consider that report before determining what order (if any) to make under that section.

(3) A report by the official receiver under this section shall, in any proceedings, be prima facie evidence of the facts stated in it.

(4) In subsection (1) the reference to the conduct and affairs of a bankrupt includes his conduct and affairs before the making of the order by which he was adjudged bankrupt.

(5) Where a certificate for the summary administration of the bankrupt's estate is for the time being in force, the official receiver shall carry out an investigation under subsection (1) only if he thinks fit.".

[1.352]
290 Public examination of bankrupt

(1) Where a bankruptcy order has been made, the official receiver may at any time before the discharge of the bankrupt apply to the court for the public examination of the bankrupt.

(2) Unless the court otherwise orders, the official receiver shall make an application under subsection (1) if notice requiring him to do so is given to him, in accordance with the rules, by one of the bankrupt's creditors with the concurrence of not less than one-half, in value, of those creditors (including the creditor giving notice).

(3) On an application under subsection (1), the court shall direct that a public examination of the bankrupt shall be held on a day appointed by the court; and the bankrupt shall attend on that day and be publicly examined as to his affairs, dealings and property.

(4) The following may take part in the public examination of the bankrupt and may question him concerning his affairs, dealings and property and the causes of his failure, namely—

(a) the official receiver and, in the case of an individual [made] bankrupt on a petition under section 264(1)(d), the Official Petitioner,

(b) the trustee of the bankrupt's estate, if his appointment has taken effect,

(c) any person who has been appointed as special manager of the bankrupt's estate or business,

(d) any creditor of the bankrupt who has tendered a proof in the bankruptcy.

(5) If a bankrupt without reasonable excuse fails at any time to attend his public examination under this section he is guilty of a contempt of court and liable to be punished accordingly (in addition to any other punishment to which he may be subject).

NOTES

This section derived from the Insolvency Act 1985, s 137.

Sub-s (4): word in square brackets in para (a) substituted for original word "adjudged" by the Enterprise and Regulatory Reform Act 2013, s 71(3), Sch 19, paras 1, 19, in respect of a petition for a bankruptcy order presented to the court by a debtor on or after 6 April 2016.

[1.353]
291 Duties of bankrupt in relation to official receiver

(1) Where a bankruptcy order has been made, the bankrupt is under a duty—

(a) to deliver possession of his estate to the official receiver, and

(b) to deliver up to the official receiver all books, papers and other records of which he has possession or control and which relate to his estate and affairs (including any which would be privileged from disclosure in any proceedings).

(2) In the case of any part of the bankrupt's estate which consists of things possession of which cannot be delivered to the official receiver, and in the case of any property that may be claimed for the bankrupt's estate by the trustee, it is the bankrupt's duty to do all such things as may reasonably be required by the official receiver for the protection of those things or that property.

(3) Subsections (1) and (2) do not apply where by virtue of section 297 below the bankrupt's estate vests in a trustee immediately on the making of the bankruptcy order.

[(4) The bankrupt shall give the official receiver such inventory of his estate and such other information, and shall attend on the official receiver at such times, as the official receiver may reasonably require—

(a) for a purpose of this Chapter, or

(b) in connection with the making of a bankruptcy restrictions order.]

(5) Subsection (4) applies to a bankrupt after his discharge.

(6) If the bankrupt without reasonable excuse fails to comply with any obligation imposed by this section, he is guilty of a contempt of court and liable to be punished accordingly (in addition to any other punishment to which he may be subject).

NOTES

This section derived from the Insolvency Act 1985, s 138.

Sub-ss (1)–(3): repealed by the Small Business, Enterprise and Employment Act 2015, s 133(2), Sch 10, paras 1, 4, as from 6 April 2017 (subject to transitional and savings provisions as noted to s 246ZE at **[1.256]**).

Sub-s (4): substituted by the Enterprise Act 2002, s 269, Sch 23, paras 1, 5, subject to transitional provisions in s 256(2) of, and Sch 19 to, that Act at **[2.13]**, **[2.22]**, and originally read as follows:

> "(4) The bankrupt shall give the official receiver such inventory of his estate and such other information, and shall attend on the official receiver at such times, as the official receiver may for any of the purposes of this Chapter reasonably require.".

CHAPTER III
TRUSTEES IN BANKRUPTCY

Tenure of office as trustee

[1.354]

[291A First trustee in bankruptcy

(1) On the making of a bankruptcy order the official receiver becomes trustee of the bankrupt's estate, unless the court appoints another person under subsection (2).

(2) If when the order is made there is a supervisor of a voluntary arrangement approved in relation to the bankrupt under Part 8, the court may on making the order appoint the supervisor of the arrangement as the trustee.

(3) Where a person becomes trustee of a bankrupt's estate under this section, the person must give notice of that fact to the bankrupt's creditors (or, if the court so allows, advertise it in accordance with the court's directions).

(4) A notice or advertisement given by a trustee appointed under subsection (2) must explain the procedure for establishing a creditors' committee under section 301.]

NOTES

Commencement: 6 April 2017 (subject to transitional and savings provisions as noted to s 246ZE at **[1.256]**).

Inserted by the Small Business, Enterprise and Employment Act 2015, s 133(1).

[1.355]

292 [Appointment of trustees: general provision]

[(1) This section applies to any appointment of a person (other than the official receiver) as trustee of a bankrupt's estate.]

(2) No person may be appointed as trustee of a bankrupt's estate unless he is, at the time of the appointment, qualified to act as an insolvency practitioner in relation to the bankrupt.

(3) Any power to appoint a person as trustee of a bankrupt's estate includes power to appoint two or more persons as joint trustees; but such an appointment must make provision as to the circumstances in which the trustees must act together and the circumstances in which one or more of them may act for the others.

(4) The appointment of any person as trustee takes effect only if that person accepts the appointment in accordance with the rules. Subject to this, the appointment of any person as trustee takes effect at the time specified in his certificate of appointment.

(5) This section is without prejudice to the provisions of this Chapter under which the official receiver is, in certain circumstances, to be trustee of the estate.

NOTES

This section derived from the Insolvency Act 1985, s 139.

Section heading: words in square brackets substituted for original words "Power to make appointments" by the Small Business, Enterprise and Employment Act 2015, s 133(2), Sch 10, paras 1, 5(1), (2), as from 6 April 2017 (subject to transitional and savings provisions as noted to s 246ZE at **[1.256]**).

Sub-s (1): substituted by the Small Business, Enterprise and Employment Act 2015, s 133(2), Sch 10, paras 1, 5(1), (3), as from 6 April 2017 (subject to transitional and savings provisions as noted to s 246ZE at **[1.256]**). Sub-s (1) previously read as follows (with words omitted repealed by the Enterprise Act 2002, ss 269, 278(2), Sch 23, paras 1, 6, Sch 26, subject to savings and transitional provisions)—

> "(1) The power to appoint a person as trustee of a bankrupt's estate (whether the first such trustee or a trustee appointed to fill any vacancy) is exercisable—
>
> (a) . . . by a general meeting of the bankrupt's creditors;
>
> (b) under section 295(2), 296(2) or 300(6) below in this Chapter, by the Secretary of State; or
>
> (c) under section 297, by the court.".

Sub-s (5): repealed by the Small Business, Enterprise and Employment Act 2015, s 133(2), Sch 10, paras 1, 5(1), (4), as from 6 April 2017 (subject to transitional and savings provisions as noted to s 246ZE at **[1.256]**).

[1.356]
293 Summoning of meeting to appoint first trustee
(1) Where a bankruptcy order has been made . . . it is the duty of the official receiver, as soon as practicable in the period of 12 weeks beginning with the day on which the order was made, to decide whether to summon a general meeting of the bankrupt's creditors for the purpose of appointing a trustee of the bankrupt's estate.
This section does not apply where the bankruptcy order was made on a petition under section 264(1)(d) (criminal bankruptcy); and it is subject to the provision made in sections 294(3) and 297(6) below.
(2) Subject to the next section, if the official receiver decides not to summon such a meeting, he shall, before the end of the period of 12 weeks above mentioned, give notice of his decision to the [prescribed person] and to every creditor of the bankrupt who is known to the official receiver or is identified in the bankrupt's statement of affairs.
(3) As from the giving to the [prescribed person] of a notice under subsection (2), the official receiver is the trustee of the bankrupt's estate.

NOTES
This section derived from the Insolvency Act 1985, s 140.
Repealed by the Small Business, Enterprise and Employment Act 2015, s 133(2), Sch 10, paras 1, 6, as from 6 April 2017 (subject to transitional and savings provisions as noted to s 246ZE at **[1.256]**).
Sub-s (1): words "and no certificate for the summary administration of the bankrupt's estate has been issued," (omitted) repealed by the Enterprise Act 2002, ss 269, 278(2), Sch 23, paras 1, 7, Sch 26, subject to savings and transitional provisions in relation to existing bankruptcies in England and Wales where a certificate of summary administration is in force on 1 April 2004 (see the Enterprise Act 2002 (Commencement No 4 and Transitional Provisions and Savings) Order 2003, SI 2003/2093, art 8 at **[2.31]**); words from "This section does not" to "sections 294(3) and 297(6) below" repealed by the Criminal Justice Act 1988, s 170(2), Sch 16, as from a day to be appointed.
Sub-ss (2), (3): words in square brackets substituted for original word "court", by the Enterprise and Regulatory Reform Act 2013, s 71(3), Sch 19, paras 1, 20, in respect of a petition for a bankruptcy order presented to the court by a debtor on or after 6 April 2016.

[1.357]
294 Power of creditors to requisition meeting
(1) Where in the case of any bankruptcy—
(a) the official receiver has not yet summoned, or has decided not to summon, a general meeting of the bankrupt's creditors for the purpose of appointing the trustee, . . .
(b) . . .
any creditor of the bankrupt may request the official receiver to summon such a meeting for that purpose.
(2) If such a request appears to the official receiver to be made with the concurrence of not less than one-quarter, in value, of the bankrupt's creditors (including the creditor making the request), it is the duty of the official receiver to summon the requested meeting.
(3) Accordingly, where the duty imposed by subsection (2) has arisen, the official receiver is required neither to reach a decision for the purposes of section 293(1) nor (if he has reached one) to serve any notice under section 293(2).

NOTES
This section derived from the Insolvency Act 1985, s 141.
Repealed by the Small Business, Enterprise and Employment Act 2015, s 133(2), Sch 10, paras 1, 6, as from 6 April 2017 (subject to transitional and savings provisions as noted to s 246ZE at **[1.256]**).
Sub-s (1): word "and" omitted from para (a), and para (b) repealed by the Enterprise Act 2002, ss 269, 278(2), Sch 23, paras 1, 8, Sch 26, subject to savings and transitional provisions in relation to existing bankruptcies in England and Wales where a certificate of summary administration is in force on 1 April 2004 (see the Enterprise Act 2002 (Commencement No 4 and Transitional Provisions and Savings) Order 2003, SI 2003/2093, art 8 at **[2.31]**). Para (b) originally read as follows:
"(b) a certificate for the summary administration of the estate is not for the time being in force,".

[1.358]
295 Failure of meeting to appoint trustee
(1) If a meeting summoned under section 293 or 294 is held but no appointment of a person as trustee is made, it is the duty of the official receiver to decide whether to refer the need for an appointment to the Secretary of State.
(2) On a reference made in pursuance of that decision, the Secretary of State shall either make an appointment or decline to make one.
(3) If—
(a) the official receiver decides not to refer the need for an appointment to the Secretary of State, or
(b) on such a reference the Secretary of State declines to make an appointment,
the official receiver shall give notice of his decision or, as the case may be, of the Secretary of State's decision to the [prescribed person].
(4) As from the giving of notice under subsection (3) in a case in which no notice has been given under section 293(2), the official receiver shall be trustee of the bankrupt's estate.

NOTES
This section derived from the Insolvency Act 1985, s 142.

Repealed by the Small Business, Enterprise and Employment Act 2015, s 133(2), Sch 10, paras 1, 6, as from 6 April 2017 (subject to transitional and savings provisions as noted to s 246ZE at **[1.256]**).

Sub-s (3): words in square brackets substituted for original word "court", by the Enterprise and Regulatory Reform Act 2013, s 71(3), Sch 19, paras 1, 21, in respect of a petition for a bankruptcy order presented to the court by a debtor on or after 6 April 2016.

[1.359]

296 Appointment of trustee by Secretary of State

(1) At any time when the official receiver is the trustee of a bankrupt's estate by virtue of any provision of this Chapter *(other than section 297(1) below)* he may apply to the Secretary of State for the appointment of a person as trustee instead of the official receiver.

(2) On an application under subsection (1) the Secretary of State shall either make an appointment or decline to make one.

(3) Such an application may be made notwithstanding that the Secretary of State has declined to make an appointment either on a previous application under subsection (1) *or on a reference under section 295* or under section 300(4) below.

(4) Where the trustee of a bankrupt's estate has been appointed by the Secretary of State (whether under this section or otherwise), the trustee shall give notice to the bankrupt's creditors of his appointment or, if the court so allows, shall advertise his appointment in accordance with the court's directions.

(5) In that notice or advertisement the trustee shall [explain the procedure for establishing a creditors' committee under section 301.]

NOTES

This section derived from the Insolvency Act 1985, s 143.

Sub-ss (1), (3): words in italics repealed by the Small Business, Enterprise and Employment Act 2015, s 133(2), Sch 10, paras 1, 7, as from 6 April 2017 (subject to transitional and savings provisions as noted to s 246ZE at **[1.256]**).

Sub-s (5): words in square brackets substituted for original paras (a), (b), by the Small Business, Enterprise and Employment Act 2015, s 126, Sch 9, Pt 2, paras 60, 76, as from 6 April 2017 (subject to transitional and savings provisions as noted to s 246ZE at **[1.256]**). Paras (a), (b) originally read as follows—

"(a) state whether he proposes to summon a general meeting of the bankrupt's creditors for the purposes of establishing a creditor's committee under section 301, and

(b) if he does not propose to summon such a meeting, set out the power of the creditors under this Part to require him to summon one.".

[1.360]

297 Special cases

(1) Where a bankruptcy order is made on a petition under section 264(1)(d) (criminal bankruptcy), the official receiver shall be trustee of the bankrupt's estate.

(2), (3) . . .

(4) . . .

(5) Where a bankruptcy order is made (whether or not on a petition under section 264(1)(c)) at a time when there is a supervisor of a voluntary arrangement approved in relation to the bankrupt under Part VIII, the court, if it thinks fit, may on making the order appoint the supervisor of the arrangement as trustee.

(6) Where an appointment is made under subsection . . . *(5) of this section, the official receiver is not under the duty imposed by section 293(1) (to decide whether or not to summon a meeting of creditors).*

(7) Where the trustee of a bankrupt's estate has been appointed by the court, the trustee shall give notice to the bankrupt's creditors of his appointment or, if the court so allows, shall advertise his appointment in accordance with the directions of the court.

(8) In that notice or advertisement he shall—

(a) state whether he proposes to summon a general meeting of the bankrupt's creditors for the purpose of establishing a creditor's committee under section 301 below, and

(b) if he does not propose to summon such a meeting, set out the power of the creditors under this Part to require him to summon one.

NOTES

This section derived from the Insolvency Act 1985, s 144.

Repealed by the Small Business, Enterprise and Employment Act 2015, s 133(2), Sch 10, paras 1, 8, as from 6 April 2017 (subject to transitional and savings provisions as noted to s 246ZE at **[1.256]**).

Sub-s (1): repealed by the Criminal Justice Act 1988, s 170(2), Sch 16, as from a day to be appointed.

Sub-ss (2), (3): repealed by the Enterprise Act 2002, ss 269, 278(2), Sch 23, paras 1, 9(a), Sch 26, subject to savings and transitional provisions in relation to existing bankruptcies in England and Wales where a certificate of summary administration is in force on 1 April 2004 (see the Enterprise Act 2002 (Commencement No 4 and Transitional Provisions and Savings) Order 2003, SI 2003/2093, art 8 at **[2.31]**). Sub-ss (2), (3) originally read as follows:

"(2) Subject to the next subsection, where the court issues a certificate for the summary administration of a bankrupt's estate, the official receiver shall, as from the issue of that certificate, be the trustee.

(3) Where such a certificate is issued or is in force, the court may, if it thinks fit, appoint a person other than the official receiver as trustee.".

Sub-s (4): repealed by the Enterprise and Regulatory Reform Act 2013, s 71(3), Sch 19, paras 1, 22(1), (2), in respect of a petition for a bankruptcy order presented to the court by a debtor on or after 6 April 2016, and previously (as amended by the Enterprise Act 2002, ss 269, 278(2), Sch 23, paras 1, 9(b), Sch 26) read as follows:

"(4) Where a bankruptcy order is made in a case in which an insolvency practitioner's report has been submitted to the court under section 274 . . . , the court, if it thinks fit, may on making the order appoint the person who made the report as trustee.".

Sub-s (6): words "(4) or" (omitted) repealed by the Enterprise and Regulatory Reform Act 2013, s 71(3), Sch 19, paras 1, 22(1), (3), in respect of a petition for a bankruptcy order presented to the court by a debtor on or after 6 April 2016.

[1.361]

298 Removal of trustee; vacation of office

(1) Subject as follows, the trustee of a bankrupt's estate may be removed from office only by an order of the court or by a [decision of the bankrupt's creditors made by a creditors' decision procedure instigated] specially for that purpose in accordance with the rules.

(2) Where the official receiver is trustee by virtue of section 297(1), he shall not be removed from office under this section.

(3) . . .

(4) Where the official receiver is trustee by virtue of [section 291A(1)] or a trustee is appointed by the Secretary of State or (otherwise than under [section 291A(2)]) by the court, a [creditors' decision procedure may be instigated] for the purpose of [removing] the trustee only if—

(a) the trustee thinks fit, or

(b) the court so directs, or

(c) . . . one of the bankrupt's creditors [so requests] with the concurrence of not less than one-quarter, in value, of the creditors (including the creditor making the request).

[(4A) Where the bankrupt's creditors decide to remove a trustee, they may in accordance with the rules appoint another person as trustee in his place.

(4B) Where the decision to remove a trustee is made under subsection (4), the decision does not take effect until the bankrupt's creditors appoint another person as trustee in his place.]

(5) If the trustee was appointed by the Secretary of State, he may be removed by a direction of the Secretary of State.

(6) The trustee (not being the official receiver) shall vacate office if he ceases to be a person who is for the time being qualified to act as an insolvency practitioner in relation to the bankrupt.

(7) The trustee may, in the prescribed circumstances, resign his office by giving notice of his resignation to the [prescribed person].

(8) The trustee shall vacate office on giving notice to the [prescribed person] that [the trustee has given notice under section 331(2)].

[(8A) A notice under subsection (8)—

(a) must not be given before the end of the period prescribed by the rules as the period within which the bankrupt's creditors may object to the trustee's release, and

(b) must state whether any of the bankrupt's creditors objected to the trustee's release.]

(9) The trustee shall vacate office if the bankruptcy order is annulled.

NOTES

This section derived from the Insolvency Act 1985, s 145.

Sub-s (1): words in square brackets substituted for original words "general meeting of the bankrupt's creditors summoned" by the Small Business, Enterprise and Employment Act 2015, s 126, Sch 9, Pt 2, paras 60, 77(1), (2), as from 6 April 2017 (subject to transitional and savings provisions as noted to s 246ZE at **[1.256]**).

Sub-s (2): repealed by the Small Business, Enterprise and Employment Act 2015, s 133(2), Sch 10, paras 1, 9(1), (2), as from 6 April 2017 (subject to transitional and savings provisions as noted to s 246ZE at **[1.256]**).

Sub-s (3): repealed by the Enterprise Act 2002, ss 269, 278(2), Sch 23, paras 1, 10, Sch 26, subject to savings and transitional provisions in relation to existing bankruptcies in England and Wales where a certificate of summary administration is in force on 1 April 2004 (see the Enterprise Act 2002 (Commencement No 4 and Transitional Provisions and Savings) Order 2003, SI 2003/2093, art 8 at **[2.31]**). Sub-s (3) originally read as follows:

"(3) A general meeting of the bankrupt's creditors shall not be held for the purpose of removing the trustee at any time when a certificate for the summary administration of the estate is in force.".

Sub-s (4): words in square brackets substituted or inserted and words omitted repealed by the Small Business, Enterprise and Employment Act 2015, ss 126, 133(2), Sch 9, Pt 2, paras 60, 77(1), (3), Sch 10, paras 1, 9(1), (3), as from 6 April 2017 (subject to transitional and savings provisions as noted to s 246ZE at **[1.256]**). Prior to these amendments, sub-s (4) read as follows—

"(4) Where the official receiver is trustee by virtue of section 293(3) or 295(4) or a trustee is appointed by the Secretary of State or (otherwise than under section 297(5)) by the court, a general meeting of the bankrupt's creditors shall be summoned for the purpose of replacing the trustee only if—

(a) the trustee thinks fit, or

(b) the court so directs, or

(c) the meeting is requested by one of the bankrupt's creditors with the concurrence of not less than one-quarter, in value, of the creditors (including the creditor making the request).".

Sub-ss (4A), (4B): inserted by the Small Business, Enterprise and Employment Act 2015, s 126, Sch 9, Pt 2, paras 60, 77(1), (4), as from 6 April 2017 (subject to transitional and savings provisions as noted to s 246ZE at **[1.256]**).

Sub-ss (7), (8): words "prescribed person" in square brackets substituted for original word "court", by the Enterprise and Regulatory Reform Act 2013, s 71(3), Sch 19, paras 1, 23, in respect of a petition for a bankruptcy order presented to the court by a debtor on or after 6 April 2016; words in second pair of square brackets in sub-s (8) substituted for original words "a final meeting has been held under section 331 in Chapter IV and of the decision (if any) of that meeting", by the Small Business, Enterprise and Employment Act 2015, s 126, Sch 9, Pt 2, paras 60, 77(1), (5), as from 6 April 2017 (subject to transitional and savings provisions as noted to s 246ZE at **[1.256]**).

Sub-s (8A): inserted by the Small Business, Enterprise and Employment Act 2015, s 126, Sch 9, Pt 2, paras 60, 77(1), (6), as from 6 April 2017 (subject to transitional and savings provisions as noted to s 246ZE at **[1.256]**).

[1.362]

299 Release of trustee

(1) Where the official receiver has ceased to be the trustee of a bankrupt's estate and a person is appointed in his stead, the official receiver shall have his release with effect from the following time, that is to say—

(a) where that person is appointed by . . . the bankrupt's creditors or by the Secretary of State, the time at which the official receiver gives notice [under this paragraph to the prescribed person] that he has been replaced, and

(b) where that person is appointed by the court, such time as the court may determine.

(2) If the official receiver while he is the trustee gives notice to the Secretary of State that the administration of the bankrupt's estate in accordance with Chapter IV of this Part is for practical purposes complete, he shall have his release with effect from such time as the Secretary of State may determine.

(3) A person other than the official receiver who has ceased to be the trustee shall have his release with effect from the following time, that is to say—

(a) in the [following cases], the time at which notice is given to the [prescribed person] in accordance with the rules that that person has ceased to hold office;[—

(i) the person has been removed from office by a decision of the bankrupt's creditors and the creditors have not decided against his release,

(ii) the person has died;]

[(b) in the following cases, such time as the Secretary of State may, on an application by the person, determine—

(i) the person has been removed from office by a decision of the bankrupt's creditors and the creditors have decided against his release,

(ii) the person has been removed from office by the court or by the Secretary of State,

(iii) the person has vacated office under section 298(6);]

(c) in the case of a person who has resigned, such time as may be prescribed;

(d) in the case of a person who has vacated office under section 298(8)—

[(i) if any of the bankrupt's creditors objected to the person's release before the end of the period for so objecting prescribed by the rules, such time as the Secretary of State may, on an application by that person, determine, and

(ii) otherwise, the time at which the person vacated office.]

[(3A) Where the person is removed from office by a decision of the bankrupt's creditors, any decision of the bankrupt's creditors as to whether the person should have his release must be made by a creditors' decision procedure.]

(4) Where a bankruptcy order is annulled, the trustee at the time of the annulment has his release with effect from such time as the court may determine.

(5) Where the official receiver or the trustee has his release under this section, he shall, with effect from the time specified in the preceding provisions of this section, be discharged from all liability both in respect of acts or omissions of his in the administration of the estate and otherwise in relation to his conduct as trustee.

But nothing in this section prevents the exercise, in relation to a person who has had his release under this section, of the court's powers under section 304.

NOTES

This section derived from the Insolvency Act 1985, s 146.

Sub-s (1): words "a general meeting of" omitted from para (a) repealed by the Small Business, Enterprise and Employment Act 2015, s 126, Sch 9, Pt 2, paras 60, 78(1), (2), as from 6 April 2017 (subject to transitional and savings provisions as noted to s 246ZE at **[1.256]**); words in square brackets in para (a) substituted for original words "to the court" by the Enterprise and Regulatory Reform Act 2013, s 71(3), Sch 19, paras 1, 24(1), (2), in respect of a petition for a bankruptcy order presented to the court by a debtor on or after 6 April 2016.

Sub-s (3): words in first pair of square brackets in para (a) substituted for original words "case of a person who has been removed from office by a general meeting of the bankrupt's creditors that has not resolved against his release or who has died", words in third pair of square brackets in para (a) inserted and para (b) substituted, by the Small Business, Enterprise and Employment Act 2015, s 126, Sch 9, Pt 2, paras 60, 78(1), (3), (4), as from 6 April 2017 (subject to transitional and savings provisions as noted to s 246ZE at **[1.256]**). Para (b) originally read as follows—

"(b) in the case of a person who has been removed from office by a general meeting of the bankrupt's creditors that has resolved against his release, or by the court, or by the Secretary of State, or who has vacated office under section 298(6), such time as the Secretary of State may, on an application by that person, determine;";

words in second pair of square brackets in para (a) substituted for original word "court" by the Enterprise and Regulatory Reform Act 2013, s 71(3), Sch 19, paras 1, 24(1), (3), in respect of a petition for a bankruptcy order presented to the court by a debtor on or after 6 April 2016;

para (d)(i), (ii) substituted by the Small Business, Enterprise and Employment Act 2015, s 126, Sch 9, Pt 2, paras 60, 78(1), (5), as from 6 April 2017 (subject to transitional and savings provisions as noted to s 246ZE at **[1.256]**). Para (d)(i), (ii)originally read as follows—

"(i) if the final meeting referred to in that subsection has resolved against that person's release, such time as the Secretary of State may, on an application by that person, determine; and

(ii) if that meeting has not so resolved, the time at which the person vacated office.".

Sub-s (3A): inserted by the Small Business, Enterprise and Employment Act 2015, s 126, Sch 9, Pt 2, paras 60, 78(1), (6), as from 6 April 2017 (subject to transitional and savings provisions as noted to s 246ZE at **[1.256]**).

[1.363]
300 Vacancy in office of trustee

(1) This section applies where the appointment of any person as trustee of a bankrupt's estate fails to take effect or, such an appointment having taken effect, there is otherwise a vacancy in the office of trustee.

(2) The official receiver shall be trustee until the vacancy is filled.

[(3) The official receiver may ask the bankrupt's creditors to appoint a person as trustee, and must do so if so requested by not less than one tenth in value of the bankrupt's creditors.

(3A) If the official receiver makes such a request the bankrupt's creditors may in accordance with the rules appoint a person as trustee.]

(4) If at the end of the period of 28 days beginning with the day on which the vacancy first came to the official receiver's attention he has not [asked, and is not proposing to ask, the bankrupt's creditors to appoint a person as trustee], he shall refer the need for an appointment to the Secretary of State.

(5) . . .

(6) On a reference to the Secretary of State under subsection (4) . . . the Secretary of State shall either make an appointment or decline to make one.

(7) If on a reference under subsection (4) . . . no appointment is made, the official receiver shall continue to be trustee of the bankrupt's estate, but without prejudice to his power to make a further reference.

(8) References in this section to a vacancy include a case where it is necessary, in relation to any property which is or may be comprised in a bankrupt's estate, to revive the trusteeship of that estate after the [vacation of office by the trustee under section 298(8)] or the giving by the official receiver of notice under section 299(2).

NOTES

This section derived from the Insolvency Act 1985, s 147.

Sub-ss (3), (3A): substituted for original sub-s (3) by the Small Business, Enterprise and Employment Act 2015, s 126, Sch 9, Pt 2, paras 60, 79(1), (2), as from 6 April 2017 (subject to transitional and savings provisions as noted to s 246ZE at **[1.256]**). Sub-s (3) originally read as follows—

"(3) The official receiver may summon a general meeting of the bankrupt's creditors for the purpose of filling the vacancy and shall summon such a meeting if required to do so in pursuance of section 314(7) (creditors' requisition).".

Sub-s (4): words in square brackets substituted for original words "summoned, and is not proposing to summon, a general meeting of creditors for the purpose of filling the vacancy" by the Small Business, Enterprise and Employment Act 2015, s 126, Sch 9, Pt 2, paras 60, 79(1), (3), as from 6 April 2017 (subject to transitional and savings provisions as noted to s 246ZE at **[1.256]**).

Sub-s (5): repealed by the Enterprise Act 2002, ss 269, 278(2), Sch 23, paras 1, 11(a), Sch 26, subject to savings and transitional provisions in relation to existing bankruptcies in England and Wales where a certificate of summary administration is in force on 1 April 2004 (see the Enterprise Act 2002 (Commencement No 4 and Transitional Provisions and Savings) Order 2003, SI 2003/2093, art 8 at **[2.31]**). Sub-s (5) originally read as follows:

"(5) Where a certificate for the summary administration of the estate is for the time being in force—
(a) the official receiver may refer the need to fill any vacancy to the court or, if the vacancy arises because a person appointed by the Secretary of State has ceased to hold office, to the court or the Secretary of State, and
(b) subsections (3) and (4) of this section do not apply.".

Sub-ss (6), (7): words "or (5)" (omitted) repealed by the Enterprise Act 2002, ss 269, 278(2), Sch 23, paras 1, 11(b), Sch 26, subject to savings and transitional provisions as noted to sub-s (5) above.

Sub-s (8): words in square brackets substituted for original words "holding of a final meeting summoned under section 331" by the Small Business, Enterprise and Employment Act 2015, s 126, Sch 9, Pt 2, paras 60, 79(1), (4), as from 6 April 2017 (subject to transitional and savings provisions as noted to s 246ZE at **[1.256]**).

Control of trustee

[1.364]
301 Creditors' committee

(1) Subject as follows, a [bankrupt's creditors] may, in accordance with the rules, establish a committee (known as "the creditors' committee") to exercise the functions conferred on it by or under this Act.

(2) [The] bankrupt's creditors shall not establish such a committee, or confer any functions on such a committee, at any time when the official receiver is the trustee of the bankrupt's estate, except in connection with [the appointment] of a person to be trustee instead of the official receiver.

NOTES

This section derived from the Insolvency Act 1985, s 148.

Sub-s (1): words in square brackets substituted for original words "general meeting of a bankrupt's creditors (whether summoned under the preceding provisions of this Chapter or otherwise)" by the Small Business, Enterprise and Employment Act 2015, s 126, Sch 9, Pt 2, paras 60, 80(1), (2), as from 6 April 2017 (subject to transitional and savings provisions as noted to s 246ZE at **[1.256]**).

Sub-s (2): words in first and second pairs of square brackets substituted for original words "A general meeting of the" and "an appointment made by that meeting" respectively, by the Small Business, Enterprise and Employment Act 2015, s 126, Sch 9, Pt 2, paras 60, 80(1), (3), as from 6 April 2017 (subject to transitional and savings provisions as noted to s 246ZE at **[1.256]**).

[1.365]

302 Exercise by Secretary of State of functions of creditors' committee

(1) The creditors' committee is not to be able or required to carry out its functions at any time when the official receiver is trustee of the bankrupt's estate; but at any such time the functions of the committee under this Act shall be vested in the Secretary of State, except to the extent that the rules otherwise provide.

(2) Where in the case of any bankruptcy there is for the time being no creditors' committee and the trustee of the bankrupt's estate is a person other than the official receiver, the functions of such a committee shall be vested in the Secretary of State, except to the extent that the rules otherwise provide.

NOTES

This section derived from the Insolvency Act 1985, s 149.

[1.366]

303 General control of trustee by the court

(1) If a bankrupt or any of his creditors or any other person is dissatisfied by any act, omission or decision of a trustee of the bankrupt's estate, he may apply to the court; and on such an application the court may confirm, reverse or modify any act or decision of the trustee, may give him directions or may make such other order as it thinks fit.

(2) The trustee of a bankrupt's estate may apply to the court for directions in relation to any particular matter arising under the bankruptcy.

[(2A) Where at any time after a bankruptcy petition has been presented to the court against any person, whether under the provisions of the Insolvent Partnerships Order 1994 or not, the attention of the court is drawn to the fact that the person in question is a member of an insolvent partnership, the court may make an order as to the future conduct of the insolvency proceedings and any such order may apply any provisions of that Order with any necessary modifications.

(2B) Where a bankruptcy petition has been presented against more than one individual in the circumstances mentioned in subsection (2A) above, the court may give such directions for consolidating the proceedings, or any of them, as it thinks just.

(2C) Any order or directions under subsection (2A) or (2B) may be made or given on the application of the official receiver, any responsible insolvency practitioner, the trustee of the partnership or any other interested person and may include provisions as to the administration of the joint estate of the partnership, and in particular how it and the separate estate of any member are to be administered.]

NOTES

This section derived from the Insolvency Act 1985, s 150.

Sub-ss (2A)–(2C): added by the Insolvent Partnerships Order 1994, SI 1994/2421, art 14(2).

[1.367]

304 Liability of trustee

(1) Where on an application under this section the court is satisfied—

- (a) that the trustee of a bankrupt's estate has misapplied or retained, or become accountable for, any money or other property comprised in the bankrupt's estate, or
- (b) that a bankrupt's estate has suffered any loss in consequence of any misfeasance or breach of fiduciary or other duty by a trustee of the estate in the carrying out of his functions,

the court may order the trustee, for the benefit of the estate, to repay, restore or account for money or other property (together with interest at such rate as the court thinks just) or, as the case may require, to pay such sum by way of compensation in respect of the misfeasance or breach of fiduciary or other duty as the court thinks just.

This is without prejudice to any liability arising apart from this section.

(2) An application under this section may be made by the official receiver, the Secretary of State, a creditor of the bankrupt or (whether or not there is, or is likely to be, a surplus for the purposes of section 330(5) (final distribution)) the bankrupt himself.

But the leave of the court is required for the making of an application if it is to be made by the bankrupt or if it is to be made after the trustee has had his release under section 299.

(3) Where—

- (a) the trustee seizes or disposes of any property which is not comprised in the bankrupt's estate, and
- (b) at the time of the seizure or disposal the trustee believes, and has reasonable grounds for believing, that he is entitled (whether in pursuance of an order of the court or otherwise) to seize or dispose of that property,

the trustee is not liable to any person (whether under this section or otherwise) in respect of any loss or damage resulting from the seizure or disposal except in so far as that loss or damage is caused by the negligence of the trustee; and he has a lien on the property, or the proceeds of its sale, for such of the expenses of the bankruptcy as were incurred in connection with the seizure or disposal.

NOTES

This section derived from the Insolvency Act 1985, s 151.

CHAPTER IV
ADMINISTRATION BY TRUSTEE

Preliminary

[1.368]
305 General functions of trustee

(1) This Chapter applies in relation to any bankruptcy where either—
 (a) the appointment of a person as trustee of a bankrupt's estate takes effect, or
 (b) the official receiver becomes trustee of a bankrupt's estate.

(2) The function of the trustee is to get in, realise and distribute the bankrupt's estate in accordance with the following provisions of this Chapter; and in the carrying out of that function and in the management of the bankrupt's estate the trustee is entitled, subject to those provisions, to use his own discretion.

(3) It is the duty of the trustee, if he is not the official receiver—
 (a) to furnish the official receiver with such information,
 (b) to produce to the official receiver, and permit inspection by the official receiver of, such books, papers and other records, and
 (c) to give the official receiver such other assistance,

as the official receiver may reasonably require for the purpose of enabling him to carry out his functions in relation to the bankruptcy.

(4) The official name of the trustee shall be "the trustee of the estate of . . . ., a bankrupt" (inserting the name of the bankrupt); be he may be referred to as "the trustee in bankruptcy" of the particular bankrupt.

NOTES

This section derived from the Insolvency Act 1985, s 152.

Acquisition, control and realisation of bankrupt's estate

[1.369]
306 Vesting of bankrupt's estate in trustee

(1) The bankrupt's estate shall vest in the trustee immediately on his appointment taking effect or, in the case of the official receiver, on his becoming trustee.

(2) Where any property which is, or is to be, comprised in the bankrupt's estate vests in the trustee (whether under this section or under any other provision of this Part), it shall so vest without any conveyance, assignment or transfer.

NOTES

This section derived from the Insolvency Act 1985, s 153.

[1.370]
[306A Property subject to restraint order

(1) This section applies where—
 (a) property is excluded from the bankrupt's estate by virtue of section 417(2)(a) of the Proceeds of Crime Act 2002 (property subject to a restraint order),
 (b) an order under [section 50, 67A, 128, 131A, 198 or 215A] of that Act has not been made in respect of the property, . . .
 (c) the restraint order is discharged[; and
 (d) immediately after the discharge of the restraint order the property is not detained under or by virtue of section 44A, 47J, 122A, 127J, 193A or 195J of that Act.]

[(2) The property vests in the trustee as part of the bankrupt's estate.]

(3) But subsection (2) does not apply to the proceeds of property realised by a management receiver under section 49(2)(d) or 197(2)(d) of that Act (realisation of property to meet receiver's remuneration and expenses).]

NOTES

Inserted, together with ss 306B, 306C, by the Proceeds of Crime Act 2002, s 456, Sch 11, paras 1, 16(1), (3).

Sub-s (1): words in square brackets in para (b) substituted, word omitted from para (b) repealed, and para (d) and word "and" immediately preceding it added, by the Policing and Crime Act 2009, s 112(1), (2), Sch 7, Pt 6, paras 53, 54(1), (2)(a), (b), Sch 8, Pt 4.

Sub-s (2): substituted by the Policing and Crime Act 2009, s 112(1), Sch 7, Pt 6, paras 53, 54(1), (2)(c).

[1.371]
[306AA Property released from detention

(1) This section applies where—
 (a) property is excluded from the bankrupt's estate by virtue of section 417(2)(b) of the Proceeds of Crime Act 2002 (property detained under certain provisions),
 (b) no order is in force in respect of the property under section 41, 50, 120, 128, 190 or 198 of that Act, and
 (c) the property is released.

(2) The property vests in the trustee as part of the bankrupt's estate.]

NOTES

Commencement: 1 June 2015.

Inserted by the Policing and Crime Act 2009, s 112(1), Sch 7, Pt 6, paras 53, 55.

[1.372]

[306B Property in respect of which receivership or administration order is made

(1) This section applies where—

(a) property is excluded from the bankrupt's estate by virtue of section [section 417(2)(c)] of the Proceeds of Crime Act 2002 (property in respect of which an order for the appointment of a receiver or administrator under certain provisions of that Act is in force),

(b) a confiscation order is made under section 6, 92 or 156 of that Act,

(c) the amount payable under the confiscation order is fully paid, and

(d) any of the property remains in the hands of the receiver or administrator (as the case may be).

(2) The property vests in the trustee as part of the bankrupt's estate.]

NOTES

Inserted as noted to s 306A at **[1.370]**.

Sub-s (1): words in square brackets in para (a) substituted by the Policing and Crime Act 2009, s 112(1), Sch 7, Pt 6, paras 53, 56.

[1.373]

[306BA Property in respect of which realisation order made

(1) This section applies where—

(a) property is excluded from the bankrupt's estate by virtue of section 417(2)(d) of the Proceeds of Crime Act 2002 (property in respect of which an order has been made authorising realisation of the property by an appropriate officer),

(b) a confiscation order is made under section 6, 92 or 156 of that Act,

(c) the amount payable under the confiscation order is fully paid, and

(d) any of the property remains in the hands of the appropriate officer.

(2) The property vests in the trustee as part of the bankrupt's estate.]

NOTES

Commencement: 1 June 2015.

Inserted by the Policing and Crime Act 2009, s 112(1), Sch 7, Pt 6, paras 53, 57.

[1.374]

[306C Property subject to certain orders where confiscation order discharged or quashed

(1) This section applies where—

(a) property is excluded from the bankrupt's estate by virtue of section 417(2)(a), (b), (c) or (d) of the Proceeds of Crime Act 2002 (property [excluded from bankrupt's estate]),

(b) a confiscation order is made under section 6, 92 or 156 of that Act, and

(c) the confiscation order is discharged under section 30, 114 or 180 of that Act (as the case may be) or quashed under that Act or in pursuance of any enactment relating to appeals against conviction or sentence.

[(2) Any such property vests in the trustee as part of the bankrupt's estate if it is in the hands of—

(a) a receiver appointed under Part 2 or 4 of that Act,

(b) an administrator appointed under Part 3 of that Act,

(c) an appropriate officer (within the meaning of section 41A, 120A or 190A of that Act).]

(3) But subsection (2) does not apply to the proceeds of property realised by a management receiver under section 49(2)(d) or 197(2)(d) of that Act (realisation of property to meet receiver's remuneration and expenses).]

NOTES

Inserted as noted to s 306A at **[1.370]**.

Sub-s (1): words in square brackets substituted by the Policing and Crime Act 2009, s 112(1), Sch 7, Pt 6, paras 53, 58(1), (2).

Sub-s (2): substituted by the Policing and Crime Act 2009, s 112(1), Sch 7, Pt 6, paras 53, 58(1), (3).

[1.375]

307 After-acquired property

(1) Subject to this section and section 309, the trustee may by notice in writing claim for the bankrupt's estate any property which has been acquired by, or has devolved upon, the bankrupt since the commencement of the bankruptcy.

(2) A notice under this section shall not served in respect of—

(a) any property falling within subsection (2) or (3) of section 283 in Chapter II,

[(aa) any property vesting in the bankrupt by virtue of section 283A in Chapter II,]

(b) any property which by virtue of any other enactment is excluded from the bankrupt's estate, or

(c) without prejudice to section 280(2)(c) (order of court on application for discharge), any property which is acquired by or, devolves upon, the bankrupt after his discharge.

(3) [Subject to subsections (4) and (4A)], upon the service on the bankrupt of a notice under this section the property to which the notice relates shall vest in the trustee as part of the bankrupt's estate; and the trustee's title to that property has relation back to the time at which the property was acquired by, or devolved upon, the bankrupt.

(4) Where, whether before or after service [on the bankrupt] of a notice under this section—

(a) a person acquires property in good faith, for value and without notice of the bankruptcy, . . .

(b) . . .

the trustee is not in respect of that property . . . entitled by virtue of this section to any remedy against that person . . . , or any person whose title to any property derives from that person . . . .

[(4A) Where a banker enters into a transaction before service on the banker of a notice under this section (and whether before or after service on the bankrupt of a notice under this section) the trustee is not in respect of that transaction entitled by virtue of this section to any remedy against the banker. This subsection applies whether or not the banker has notice of the bankruptcy.]

(5) References in this section to property do not include any property which, as part of the bankrupt's income, may be the subject of an income payments order under section 310.

NOTES

This section derived from the Insolvency Act 1985, s 154(1)–(4), (7).

Sub-s (2): para (aa) inserted by the Enterprise Act 2002, s 261(4), subject to transitional provisions in s 261(7)–(10) of that Act at **[2.14]**.

Sub-s (3): words in square brackets substituted by the Deregulation Act 2015, s 19, Sch 6, Pt 5, paras 12, 16(1), (2).

Sub-s (4): words in square brackets inserted and words omitted repealed, by the Deregulation Act 2015, s 19, Sch 6, Pt 5, paras 12, 16(1), (3).

Sub-s (4A): inserted by the Deregulation Act 2015, s 19, Sch 6, Pt 5, paras 12, 16(1), (4).

Effect of a freezing order under the International Criminal Court Act 2001: where a person has been adjudged bankrupt in England and Wales, the powers conferred on a receiver appointed under the International Criminal Court Act 2001, Sch 6, para 5 shall not be exercised in relation to property in respect of which his trustee in bankruptcy may, without permission of court, serve a notice under this section or ss 308, 308A at **[1.376]**, **[1.377]**; see s 38, Sch 6, para 9(2)(b) of the 2001 Act.

[1.376]

308 Vesting in trustee of certain items of excess value

(1) Subject to [section 309], where—

(a) property is excluded by virtue of section 283(2) (tools of trade, household effects, etc.) from the bankrupt's estate, and

(b) it appears to the trustee that the realisable value of the whole or any part of that property exceeds the cost of a reasonable replacement for that property or that part of it,

the trustee may by notice in writing claim that property or, as the case may be, that part of it for the bankrupt's estate.

(2) Upon the service on the bankrupt of a notice under this section, the property to which the notice relates vests in the trustee as part of the bankrupt's estate; and, except against a purchaser in good faith, for value and without notice of the bankruptcy, the trustee's title to that property has relation back to the commencement of the bankruptcy.

(3) The trustee shall apply funds comprised in the estate to the purchase by or on behalf of the bankrupt of a reasonable replacement for any property vested in the trustee under this section; and the duty imposed by this subsection has priority over the obligation of the trustee to distribute the estate.

(4) For the purposes of this section property is a reasonable replacement for other property if it is reasonably adequate for meeting the needs met by the other property.

NOTES

This section derived from the Insolvency Act 1985, s 155(1), (2), (4), (5).

Sub-s (1): words in square brackets substituted by the Housing Act 1988, s 140(1), Sch 17, para 73.

Effect of a freezing order under the International Criminal Court Act 2001: see the note to s 307 at **[1.375]**.

[1.377]

[308A Vesting in trustee of certain tenancies

Upon the service on the bankrupt by the trustee of a notice in writing under this section, any tenancy—

(a) which is excluded by virtue of section 283(3A) from the bankrupt's estate, and

(b) to which the notice relates,

vests in the trustee as part of the bankrupt's estate; and, except against a purchaser in good faith, for value and without notice of the bankruptcy, the trustee's title to that tenancy has relation back to the commencement of the bankruptcy.]

NOTES

Inserted by the Housing Act 1988, s 117(2).

Effect of a freezing order under the International Criminal Court Act 2001: see the note to s 307 at **[1.375]**.

[1.378]

309 Time-limit for notice under s 307 or 308

(1) Except with the leave of the court, a notice shall not be served—

(a) under section 307, after the end of the period of 42 days beginning with the day on which it first came to the knowledge of the trustee that the property in question had been acquired by, or had devolved upon, the bankrupt;

(b) under section 308 [or section 308A], after the end of the period of 42 days beginning with the day on which the property [or tenancy] in question first came to the knowledge of the trustee.

(2) For the purposes of this section—

(a) anything which comes to the knowledge of the trustee is deemed in relation to any successor of his as trustee to have come to the knowledge of the successor at the same time; and

(b) anything which comes (otherwise than under paragraph (a)) to the knowledge of a person before he is the trustee is deemed to come to his knowledge on his appointment taking effect or, in the case of the official receiver, on his becoming trustee.

NOTES

This section derived from the Insolvency Act 1985, ss 154(5), (6), 155(3).

Sub-s (1): words in square brackets inserted by the Housing Act 1988, s 117(3).

[1.379]

310 Income payments orders

(1) The court may, . . . make an order ("an income payments order") claiming for the bankrupt's estate so much of the income of the bankrupt during the period for which the order is in force as may be specified in the order.

[(1A) An income payments order may be made only on an application instituted—

(a) by the trustee, and

(b) before the discharge of the bankrupt.]

(2) The court shall not make an income payments order the effect of which would be to reduce the income of the bankrupt [when taken together with any payments to which subsection (8) applies] below what appears to the court to be necessary for meeting the reasonable domestic needs of the bankrupt and his family.

(3) An income payments order shall, in respect of any payment of income to which it is to apply, either—

(a) require the bankrupt to pay the trustee an amount equal to so much of that payment as is claimed by the order, or

(b) require the person making the payment to pay so much of it as is so claimed to the trustee, instead of to the bankrupt.

(4) Where the court makes an income payments order it may, if it thinks fit, discharge or vary any attachment of earnings order that is for the time being in force to secure payments by the bankrupt.

(5) Sums received by the trustee under an income payments order form part of the bankrupt's estate.

[(6) An income payments order must specify the period during which it is to have effect; and that period—

(a) may end after the discharge of the bankrupt, but

(b) may not end after the period of three years beginning with the date on which the order is made.

(6A) An income payments order may (subject to subsection (6)(b)) be varied on the application of the trustee or the bankrupt (whether before or after discharge).]

(7) For the purposes of this section the income of the bankrupt comprises every payment in the nature of income which is from time to time made to him or to which he from time to time becomes entitled, including any payment in respect of the carrying on of any business or in respect of any office or employment [and [(despite anything in section 11 or 12 of the Welfare Reform and Pensions Act 1999)] any payment under a pension scheme but excluding any payment to which subsection (8) applies.

(8) This subsection applies to—

(a) payments by way of guaranteed minimum pension; . . .

(b) . . .

(9) In this section, "guaranteed minimum pension" [has] the same meaning as in the Pension Schemes Act 1993.]

NOTES

This section derived from the Insolvency Act 1985, s 156.

Sub-s (1): words "on the application of the trustee," repealed by the Enterprise Act 2002, ss 259(1), (2), 278(2), Sch 26, subject to transitional provisions in s 256(2) of, and Sch 19 to, that Act at **[2.13]**, **[2.22]**.

Sub-s (1A): inserted by the Enterprise Act 2002, s 259(1), (3), subject to transitional provisions as noted to sub-s (1) above.

Sub-s (2): words in square brackets inserted by the Pensions Act 1995, s 122, Sch 3, para 15(a).

Sub-ss (6), (6A): substituted for original sub-s (6) by the Enterprise Act 2002, s 259(1), (4), subject to transitional provisions as noted to sub-s (1) above. Sub-s (6) originally read as follows:

"(6) An income payments order shall not be made after the discharge of the bankrupt, and if made before, shall not have effect after his discharge except—

(a) in the case of a discharge under section 279(1)(a) (order of court), by virtue of a condition imposed by the court under section 280(2)(c) (income, etc. after discharge), or

(b) in the case of a discharge under section 279(1)(b) (expiration of relevant period), by virtue of a provision of the order requiring it to continue in force for a period ending after the discharge but no later than 3 years after the making of the order.".

Sub-s (7): words in first (outer) pair of square brackets inserted, together with sub-ss (8), (9), by the Pensions Act 1995, s 122, Sch 3, para 15(b); words in second (inner) pair of square brackets inserted by the Welfare Reform and Pensions Act 1999, s 18, Sch 2, para 2.

Sub-s (8): inserted as noted to sub-s (7) above; para (b) and word immediately preceding it omitted by Pensions Act 2008 (Abolition of Protected Rights) (Consequential Amendments) (No 2) Order 2011, SI 2011/1730, art 3(1), (2), as amended by Pensions Act 2008 (Abolition of Protected Rights) (Consequential Amendments) (No 2) (Amendment) Order 2012, SI 2012/709, art 2(1), (2).

Sub-s (9): inserted as noted to sub-s (7) above; word in square brackets substituted by SI 2011/1730, art 3(1), (3), as amended by SI 2012/709, art 2(1), (2).

[1.380]

[310A Income payments agreement

(1) In this section "income payments agreement" means a written agreement between a bankrupt and his trustee or between a bankrupt and the official receiver which provides—

(a) that the bankrupt is to pay to the trustee or the official receiver an amount equal to a specified part or proportion of the bankrupt's income for a specified period, or
(b) that a third person is to pay to the trustee or the official receiver a specified proportion of money due to the bankrupt by way of income for a specified period.

(2) A provision of an income payments agreement of a kind specified in subsection (1)(a) or (b) may be enforced as if it were a provision of an income payments order.

(3) While an income payments agreement is in force the court may, on the application of the bankrupt, his trustee or the official receiver, discharge or vary an attachment of earnings order that is for the time being in force to secure payments by the bankrupt.

(4) The following provisions of section 310 shall apply to an income payments agreement as they apply to an income payments order—
(a) subsection (5) (receipts to form part of estate), and
(b) subsections (7) to (9) (meaning of income).

(5) An income payments agreement must specify the period during which it is to have effect; and that period—
(a) may end after the discharge of the bankrupt, but
(b) may not end after the period of three years beginning with the date on which the agreement is made.

(6) An income payments agreement may (subject to subsection (5)(b)) be varied—
(a) by written agreement between the parties, or
(b) by the court on an application made by the bankrupt, the trustee or the official receiver.

(7) The court—
(a) may not vary an income payments agreement so as to include provision of a kind which could not be included in an income payments order, and
(b) shall grant an application to vary an income payments agreement if and to the extent that the court thinks variation necessary to avoid the effect mentioned in section 310(2).]

NOTES

Inserted by the Enterprise Act 2002, s 260, subject to transitional provisions in s 256(2) of, and Sch 19 to, that Act at **[2.13]**, **[2.22]**.

[1.381]
311 Acquisition by trustee of control

(1) The trustee shall take possession of all books, papers and other records which relate to the bankrupt's estate or affairs and which belong to him or are in his possession or under his control (including any which would be privileged from disclosure in any proceedings).

(2) In relation to, and for the purpose of acquiring or retaining possession of, the bankrupt's estate, the trustee is in the same position as if he were a receiver of property appointed by the High Court; and the court may, on his application, enforce such acquisition or retention accordingly.

(3) Where any part of the bankrupt's estate consists of stock or shares in a company, shares in a ship or any other property transferable in the books of a company, office or person, the trustee may exercise the right to transfer the property to the same extent as the bankrupt might have exercised it if he had not become bankrupt.

(4) Where any part of the estate consists of things in action, they are deemed to have been assigned to the trustee; but notice of the deemed assignment need not be given except in so far as it is necessary, in a case where the deemed assignment is from the bankrupt himself, for protecting the priority of the trustee.

(5) Where any goods comprised in the estate are held by any person by way of pledge, pawn or other security and no notice has been served in respect of those goods by the official receiver under subsection (5) of section 285 (restriction on realising security), the trustee may serve such a notice in respect of the goods; and whether or not a notice has been served under this subsection or that subsection, the trustee may, if he thinks fit, exercise the bankrupt's right of redemption in respect of any such goods.

(6) A notice served by the trustee under subsection (5) has the same effect as a notice served by the official receiver under section 285(5).

NOTES

This section derived from the Insolvency Act 1985, s 157.

[1.382]
312 Obligation to surrender control to trustee

(1) The bankrupt shall deliver up to the trustee possession of any property, books, papers or other records of which he has possession or control and of which the trustee is required to take possession.

This is without prejudice to the general duties of the bankrupt under section 333 in this Chapter.

(2) If any of the following is in possession of any property, books, papers or other records of which the trustee is required to take possession, namely—
(a) the official receiver,
(b) a person who has ceased to be trustee of the bankrupt's estate, or
(c) a person who has been the supervisor of a voluntary arrangement approved in relation to the bankrupt under Part VIII,

the official receiver or, as the case may be, that person shall deliver up possession of the property, books, papers or records to the trustee.

(3) Any banker or agent of the bankrupt or any other person who holds any property to the account of, or for, the bankrupt shall pay or deliver to the trustee all property in his possession or under his control which forms part of the bankrupt's estate and which he is not by law entitled to retain as against the bankrupt or trustee.

(4) If any person without reasonable excuse fails to comply with any obligation imposed by this section, he is guilty of a contempt of court and liable to be punished accordingly (in addition to any other punishment to which he may be subject).

NOTES

This section derived from the Insolvency Act 1985, s 158.

[1.383]

313 Charge on bankrupt's home

(1) Where any property consisting of an interest in a dwelling house which is occupied by the bankrupt or by his spouse or former spouse [or by his civil partner or former civil partner] is comprised in the bankrupt's estate and the trustee is, for any reason, unable for the time being to realise that property, the trustee may apply to the court for an order imposing a charge on the property for the benefit of the bankrupt's estate.

(2) If on an application under this section the court imposes a charge on any property, the benefit of that charge shall be comprised in the bankrupt's estate and is enforceable[, up to the charged value from time to time,] for the payment of any amount which is payable otherwise than to the bankrupt out of the estate and of interest on that amount at the prescribed rate.

[(2A) In subsection (2) the charged value means—

(a) the amount specified in the charging order as the value of the bankrupt's interest in the property at the date of the order, plus

(b) interest on that amount from the date of the charging order at the prescribed rate.

(2B) In determining the value of an interest for the purposes of this section the court shall disregard any matter which it is required to disregard by the rules.]

(3) An order under this section made in respect of property vested in the trustee shall provide, in accordance with the rules, for the property to cease to be comprised in the bankrupt's estate and, subject to the charge (and any prior charge), to vest in the bankrupt.

(4) [Subsection (1), (2), (4), (5) and (6) of] section 3 of the Charging Orders Act 1979 (supplemental provisions with respect to charging orders) have effect in relation to orders under this section as in relation to charging orders under that Act.

[(5) But an order under section 3(5) of that Act may not vary a charged value.]

NOTES

This section derived from the Insolvency Act 1985, s 159.

Sub-s (1): words in square brackets inserted by the Civil Partnership Act 2004, s 261(1), Sch 27, para 114.

Sub-s (2): words in square brackets substituted for original words "up to the value from time to time of the property secured," by the Enterprise Act 2002, s 261(2)(a), subject to transitional provisions in s 261(7)–(10) of that Act at **[2.14]**.

Sub-ss (2A), (2B): inserted by the Enterprise Act 2002, s 261(2)(b), subject to transitional provisions in s 261(7)–(10) of that Act at **[2.14]**.

Sub-s (4): words in square brackets substituted by the Tribunals, Courts and Enforcement Act 2007, s 93(5), subject to savings in s 93(6) thereof.

Sub-s (5): added by the Enterprise Act 2002, s 261(2)(c), subject to transitional provisions in s 261(7)–(10) of that Act at **[2.14]**.

[1.384]

[313A Low value home: application for sale, possession or charge

(1) This section applies where—

(a) property comprised in the bankrupt's estate consists of an interest in a dwelling-house which at the date of the bankruptcy was the sole or principal residence of—

(i) the bankrupt,

(ii) the bankrupt's spouse [or civil partner], or

(iii) a former spouse [or former civil partner] of the bankrupt, and

(b) the trustee applies for an order for the sale of the property, for an order for possession of the property or for an order under section 313 in respect of the property.

(2) The court shall dismiss the application if the value of the interest is below the amount prescribed for the purposes of this subsection.

(3) In determining the value of an interest for the purposes of this section the court shall disregard any matter which it is required to disregard by the order which prescribes the amount for the purposes of subsection (2).]

NOTES

Inserted by the Enterprise Act 2002, s 261(3), subject to transitional provisions in s 261(7)–(10) of that Act at **[2.14]**.

Sub-s (1): words in square brackets inserted by the Civil Partnership Act 2004, s 261(1), Sch 27, para 115.

See further: the Insolvency Proceedings (Monetary Limits) Order 1986, SI 1986/1996, art 3, Schedule, Pt II at **[8.3]**, **[8.6]** which specifies £1,000 as the prescribed amount for the purposes of sub-s (2).

[1.385]

314 Powers of trustee

[(1) The trustee may exercise any of the powers specified in Parts 1 and 2 of Schedule 5.]

(2) . . . The trustee may appoint the bankrupt—

(a) to superintend the management of his estate or any part of it,

(b) to carry on his business (if any) for the benefit of his creditors, or

(c) in any other respect to assist in administering the estate in such manner and on such terms as the trustee may direct.

(3) . . .

(4) . . .

(5) Part III of Schedule 5 to this Act has effect with respect to the things which the trustee is able to do for the purposes of, or in connection with, the exercise of any of his powers under any of this Group of Parts.

(6) Where the trustee (not being the official receiver) in exercise of the powers conferred on him by any provision in this Group of Parts—

(a) disposes of any property comprised in the bankrupt's estate to an associate of the bankrupt, or

(b) employs a solicitor,

he shall, if there is for the time being a creditors' committee, give notice to the committee of that exercise of his powers.

(7) Without prejudice to the generality of subsection (5) and Part III of Schedule 5, the trustee may, if he thinks fit, at any time [seek a decision on a matter from] the bankrupt's creditors.

Subject to the preceding provisions in this Group of Parts, he shall [seek a decision on a matter] if he is requested to do so by a creditor of the bankrupt and the request is made with the concurrence of not less than one-tenth, in value, of the bankrupt's creditors (including the creditor making the request).

(8) Nothing in this Act is to be construed as restricting the capacity of the trustee to exercise any of his powers outside England and Wales.

NOTES

This section derived from the Insolvency Act 1985, s 160.

Sub-s (1): substituted by the Small Business, Enterprise and Employment Act 2015, s 121(1), (2)(a).

Sub-s (2): words omitted repealed by the Small Business, Enterprise and Employment Act 2015, s 121(1), (2)(b).

Sub-ss (3), (4): repealed by the Small Business, Enterprise and Employment Act 2015, s 121(1), (2)(c).

Sub-s (7): words in first and second pairs of square brackets substituted for original words "summon a general meeting of" and "summon such a meeting" respectively, by the Small Business, Enterprise and Employment Act 2015, s 126, Sch 9, Pt 2, paras 60, 81, as from 6 April 2017 (subject to transitional and savings provisions as noted to s 246ZE at **[1.256]**).

Disclaimer of onerous property

[1.386]

315 Disclaimer (general power)

(1) Subject as follows, the trustee may, by the giving of the prescribed notice, disclaim any onerous property and may do so notwithstanding that he has taken possession of it, endeavoured to sell it or otherwise exercised rights of ownership in relation to it.

(2) The following is onerous property for the purposes of this section, that is to say—

(a) any unprofitable contract, and

(b) any other property comprised in the bankrupt's estate which is unsaleable or not readily saleable, or is such that it may give rise to a liability to pay money or perform any other onerous act.

(3) A disclaimer under this section—

(a) operates so as to determine, as from the date of the disclaimer, the rights, interests and liabilities of the bankrupt and his estate in or in respect of the property disclaimed, and

(b) discharges the trustee from all personal liability in respect of that property as from the commencement of his trusteeship,

but does not, except so far as is necessary for the purpose of releasing the bankrupt, the bankrupt's estate and the trustee from any liability, affect the rights or liabilities of any other person.

(4) A notice of disclaimer shall not be given under this section in respect of any property that has been claimed for the estate under section 307 (after-acquired property) or 308 (personal property of bankrupt exceeding reasonable replacement value) [or 308A], except with the leave of the court.

(5) Any person sustaining loss or damage in consequence of the operation of a disclaimer under this section is deemed to be a creditor of the bankrupt to the extent of the loss or damage and accordingly may prove for the loss or damage as a bankruptcy debt.

NOTES

This section derived from the Insolvency Act 1985, s 161(1)–(4), (10).

Sub-s (4): words in square brackets inserted by the Housing Act 1988, s 117(4).

Disapplication in relation to market contracts: see the note to s 178 at **[1.182]**.

Power to disclaim property: with regard to tenancies, see further the Landlord and Tenant (Covenants) Act 1995, s 21 at **[17.133]**.

[1.387]

316 Notice requiring trustee's decision

(1) Notice of disclaimer shall not be given under section 315 in respect of any property if—

(a) a person interested in the property has applied in writing to the trustee or one of his predecessors as trustee requiring the trustee or that predecessor to decide whether he will disclaim or not, and

(b) the period of 28 days beginning with the day on which that application was made has expired without a notice of disclaimer having been given under section 315 in respect of that property.

(2) The trustee is deemed to have adopted any contract which by virtue of this section he is not entitled to disclaim.

NOTES

This section derived from the Insolvency Act 1985, s 161(5).

[1.388]

317 Disclaimer of leaseholds

(1) The disclaimer of any property of a leasehold nature does not take effect unless a copy of the disclaimer has been served (so far as the trustee is aware of their addresses) on every person claiming under the bankrupt as underlessee or mortgagee and either—

(a) no application under section 320 below is made with respect to the property before the end of the period of 14 days beginning with the day on which the last notice served under this subsection was served, or

(b) where such an application has been made, the court directs that the disclaimer is to take effect.

(2) Where the court gives a direction under subsection (1)(b) it may also, instead of or in addition to any order it makes under section 320, make such orders with respect to fixtures, tenant's improvements and other matters arising out of the lease as it thinks fit.

NOTES

This section derived from the Insolvency Act 1985, s 161(6), (7).

[1.389]

318 Disclaimer of dwelling house

Without prejudice to section 317, the disclaimer of any property in a dwelling house does not take effect unless a copy of the disclaimer has been served (so far as the trustee is aware of their addresses) on every person in occupation of or claiming a right to occupy the dwelling house and either—

(a) no application under section 320 is made with respect to the property before the end of the period of 14 days beginning with the day on which the last notice served under this section was served, or

(b) where such an application has been made, the court directs that the disclaimer is to take effect.

NOTES

This section derived from the Insolvency Act 1985, s 161(8).

[1.390]

319 Disclaimer of land subject to rentcharge

(1) The following applies where, in consequence of the disclaimer under section 315 of any land subject to a rentcharge, that land vests by operation of law in the Crown or any other person (referred to in the next subsection as "the proprietor").

(2) The proprietor, and the successors in title of the proprietor, are not subject to any personal liability in respect of any sums becoming due under the rentcharge, except sums becoming due after the proprietor, or some person claiming under or through the proprietor, has taken possession or control of the land or has entered into occupation of it.

NOTES

This section derived from the Insolvency Act 1985, s 161(9).

[1.391]

320 Court order vesting disclaimed property

(1) This section and the next apply where the trustee has disclaimed property under section 315.

(2) An application may be made to the court under this section by—

(a) any person who claims an interest in the disclaimed property,

(b) any person who is under any liability in respect of the disclaimed property, not being a liability discharged by the disclaimer, or

(c) where the disclaimed property is property in a dwelling-house, any person who at the time when the [bankruptcy application was made or (as the case may be) the] bankruptcy petition was presented was in occupation of or entitled to occupy the dwelling house.

(3) Subject as follows in this section and the next, the court may, on an application under this section, make an order on such terms as it thinks fit for the vesting of the disclaimed property in, or for its delivery to—

(a) a person entitled to it or a trustee for such a person,

(b) a person subject to such a liability as is mentioned in subsection (2)(b) or a trustee for such a person, or

(c) where the disclaimed property is property in a dwelling-house, any person who at the time when the [bankruptcy application was made or (as the case may be) the] bankruptcy petition was presented was in occupation of or entitled to occupy the dwelling house.

(4) The court shall not make an order by virtue of subsection (3)(b) except where it appears to the court that it would be just to do so for the purpose of compensating the person subject to the liability in respect of the disclaimer.

(5) The effect of any order under this section shall be taken into account in assessing for the purposes of section 315(5) the extent of any loss or damage sustained by any person in consequence of the disclaimer.
(6) An order under this section vesting property in any person need not be completed by any conveyance, assignment or transfer.

NOTES

This section derived from the Insolvency Act 1985, s 162(1)–(4), (9), (10).

Sub-ss (2), (3): words in square brackets inserted by the Enterprise and Regulatory Reform Act 2013, s 71(3), Sch 19, paras 1, 25, in respect of a petition for a bankruptcy order presented to the court by a debtor on or after 6 April 2016.

[1.392]
321 Order under s 320 in respect of leaseholds

(1) The court shall not make an order under section 320 vesting property of a leasehold nature in any person, except on terms making that person—
- (a) subject to the same liabilities and obligations as the bankrupt was subject to under the lease on the day the [bankruptcy application was made or (as the case may be) the] bankruptcy petition was presented, or
- (b) if the court thinks fit, subject to the same liabilities and obligations as that person would be subject to if the lease had been assigned to him on that day.

(2) For the purposes of an order under section 320 relating to only part of any property comprised in a lease, the requirements of subsection (1) apply as if the lease comprised only the property to which the order relates.
(3) Where subsection (1) applies and no person is willing to accept an order under section 320 on the terms required by that subsection, the court may (by order under section 320) vest the estate or interest of the bankrupt in the property in any person who is liable (whether personally or in a representative capacity and whether alone or jointly with the bankrupt) to perform the lessee's covenants in the lease.
The court may by virtue of this subsection vest that estate and interest in such a person freed and discharged from all estates, incumbrances and interests created by the bankrupt.
(4) Where subsection (1) applies and a person declines to accept any order under section 320, that person shall be excluded from all interest in the property.

NOTES

This section derived from the Insolvency Act 1985, s 162(5)–(8).

Sub-s (1): words in square brackets inserted by the Enterprise and Regulatory Reform Act 2013, s 71(3), Sch 19, paras 1, 26, in respect of a petition for a bankruptcy order presented to the court by a debtor on or after 6 April 2016.

Distribution of bankrupt's estate

[1.393]
322 Proof of debts

(1) Subject to this section and the next, the proof of any bankruptcy debt by a secured or unsecured creditor of the bankrupt and the admission or rejection of any proof shall take place in accordance with the rules.
(2) Where a bankruptcy debt bears interest, that interest is provable as part of the debt except in so far as it is payable in respect of any period after the commencement of the bankruptcy.
(3) The trustee shall estimate the value of any bankruptcy debt which, by reason of its being subject to any contingency or contingencies or for any other reason, does not bear a certain value.
(4) Where the value of a bankruptcy debt is estimated by the trustee under subsection (3) or, by virtue of section 303 in Chapter III, by the court, the amount provable in the bankruptcy in respect of the debt is the amount of the estimate.

NOTES

This section derived from the Insolvency Act 1985, s 163.

[1.394]
323 Mutual credit and set-off

(1) This section applies where before the commencement of the bankruptcy there have been mutual credits, mutual debts or other mutual dealings between the bankrupt and any creditor of the bankrupt proving or claiming to prove for a bankruptcy debt.
(2) An account shall be taken of what is due from each party to the other in respect of the mutual dealings and the sums due from one party shall be set off against the sums due from the other.
(3) Sums due from the bankrupt to another party shall not be included in the account taken under subsection (2) if that other party had notice at the time they became due that [proceedings on a bankruptcy application relating to the bankrupt were ongoing or that] a bankruptcy petition relating to the bankrupt was pending.
(4) Only the balance (if any) of the account taken under subsection (2) is provable as a bankruptcy debt or, as the case may be, to be paid to the trustee as part of the bankrupt's estate.

NOTES

This section derived from the Insolvency Act 1985, s 164.

Sub-s (3): words in square brackets inserted by the Enterprise and Regulatory Reform Act 2013, s 71(3), Sch 19, paras 1, 27, in respect of a petition for a bankruptcy order presented to the court by a debtor on or after 6 April 2016.

Default proceedings: as to the taking account under this section of the net sum payable by, or to, a defaulter on the completion of default proceedings, see the Companies Act 1989, s 163 at **[17.66]**.

[1.395]

324 Distribution by means of dividend

(1) Whenever the trustee has sufficient funds in hand for the purpose he shall, subject to the retention of such sums as may be necessary for the expenses of the bankruptcy, declare and distribute dividends among the creditors in respect of the bankruptcy debts which they have respectively proved.

(2) The trustee shall give notice of his intention to declare and distribute a dividend.

(3) Where the trustee has declared a dividend, he shall give notice of the dividend and of how it is proposed to distribute it; and a notice given under this subsection shall contain the prescribed particulars of the bankrupt's estate.

(4) In the calculation and distribution of a dividend the trustee shall make provision—

(a) for any bankruptcy debts which appear to him to be due to persons who, by reason of the distance of their place of residence, may not have had sufficient time to tender and establish their proofs,

(b) for any bankruptcy debts which are the subject of claims which have not yet been determined, and

(c) for disputed proofs and claims.

NOTES

This section derived from the Insolvency Act 1985, s 165(1)–(4).

[1.396]

325 Claims by unsatisfied creditors

(1) A creditor who has not proved his debt before the declaration of any dividend is not entitled to disturb, by reason that he has not participated in it, the distribution of that dividend or any other dividend declared before his debt was proved, but—

(a) when he has proved that debt he is entitled to be paid, out of any money for the time being available for the payment of any further dividend, any dividend or dividends which he has failed to receive; and

(b) any dividend or dividends payable under paragraph (a) shall be paid before that money is applied to the payment of any such further dividend.

(2) No action lies against the trustee for a dividend, but if the trustee refuses to pay a dividend the court may, if it thinks fit, order him to pay it and also to pay, out of his own money—

(a) interest on the dividend, at the rate for the time being specified in section 17 of the Judgments Act 1838, from the time it was withheld, and

(b) the costs of the proceedings in which the order to pay is made.

NOTES

This section derived from the Insolvency Act 1985, s 165(5), (6).

[1.397]

326 Distribution of property in specie

(1) Without prejudice to sections 315 to 319 (disclaimer), the trustee may, with the permission of the creditors' committee, divide in its existing form amongst the bankrupt's creditors, according to its estimated value, any property which from its peculiar nature or other special circumstances cannot be readily or advantageously sold.

(2) A permission given for the purposes of subsection (1) shall not be a general permission but shall relate to a particular proposed exercise of the power in question; and a person dealing with the trustee in good faith and for value is not to be concerned to enquire whether any permission required by subsection (1) has been given.

(3) Where the trustee has done anything without the permission required by subsection (1), the court or the creditors' committee may, for the purpose of enabling him to meet his expenses out of the bankrupt's estate, ratify what the trustee has done.

But the committee shall not do so unless it is satisfied that the trustee acted in a case of urgency and has sought its ratification without undue delay.

NOTES

This section derived from the Insolvency Act 1985, s 165(7), (8).

[1.398]

327 Distribution in criminal bankruptcy

Where the bankruptcy order was made on a petition under section 264(1)(d) (criminal bankruptcy), no distribution shall be made under sections 324 to 326 so long as an appeal is pending (within the meaning of section 277) against the bankrupt's conviction of any offence by virtue of which the criminal bankruptcy order on which the petition was based was made.

NOTES

This section derived from the Insolvency Act 1985, s 165(9).

Repealed by the Criminal Justice Act 1988, s 170(2), Sch 16, as from a day to be appointed.

[1.399]
328 Priority of debts
(1) In the distribution of the bankrupt's estate, his preferential debts . . . shall be paid in priority to other debts.
[(1A) Ordinary preferential debts rank equally among themselves after the expenses of the bankruptcy and shall be paid in full, unless the bankrupt's estate is insufficient to meet them, in which case they abate in equal proportions between themselves.
(1B) Secondary preferential debts rank equally among themselves after the ordinary preferential debts and shall be paid in full, unless the bankrupt's estate is insufficient to meet them, in which case they abate in equal proportions between themselves.]
(2) Preferential debts rank equally between themselves after the expenses of the bankruptcy and shall be paid in full unless the bankrupt's estate is insufficient for meeting them, in which case they abate in equal proportions between themselves.
(3) Debts which are neither preferential debts nor debts to which the next section applies also rank equally between themselves and, after the preferential debts, shall be paid in full unless the bankrupt's estate is insufficient for meeting them, in which case they abate in equal proportions between themselves.
(4) Any surplus remaining after the payment of the debts that are preferential or rank equally under subsection (3) shall be applied in paying interest on those debts in respect of the periods during which they have been outstanding since the commencement of the bankruptcy; and interest on preferential debts ranks equally with interest on debts other than preferential debts.
(5) The rate of interest payable under subsection (4) in respect of any debt is whichever is the greater of the following—

(a) the rate specified in section 17 of the Judgments Act 1838 at the commencement of the bankruptcy, and
(b) the rate applicable to that debt apart from the bankruptcy.

(6) This section and the next are without prejudice to any provision of this Act or any other Act under which the payment of any debt or the making of any other payment is, in the event of bankruptcy, to have a particular priority or to be postponed.
[(7) In this section "preferential debts", "ordinary preferential debts" and "secondary preferential debts" each has the meaning given in section 386 in Part 12.]

NOTES
This section derived from the Insolvency Act 1985, s 166(1)–(5), (7).
Transfer to Secretary of State of rights and remedies on employer's insolvency: see the note to s 175 at **[1.176]**.
Sub-s (1): words "(within the meaning given by section 386 in Part XII)" (omitted) repealed by the Banks and Building Societies (Depositor Preference and Priorities) Order 2014, SI 2014/3486, arts 3, 7(1), (2), except in relation to any insolvency proceedings commenced before 1 January 2015 (as to the meaning of this, see further the note "SI 2014/3486, art 3" at **[1.5]**).
Sub-s (2): repealed by SI 2014/3486, arts 3, 7(1), (4), except in relation to any insolvency proceedings commenced before 1 January 2015 (as to the meaning of this, see further the note "SI 2014/3486, art 3" at **[1.5]**).
Sub-ss (1A), (1B), (7): inserted by SI 2014/3486, arts 3, 7(1), (3), (5), except in relation to any insolvency proceedings commenced before 1 January 2015 (as to the meaning of this, see further the note "SI 2014/3486, art 3" at **[1.5]**).

[1.400]
329 Debts to spouse [or civil partner]
(1) This section applies to bankruptcy debts owed in respect of credit provided by a person who (whether or not the bankrupt's spouse [or civil partner] at the time the credit was provided) was the bankrupt's spouse [or civil partner] at the commencement of the bankruptcy.
(2) Such debts—

(a) rank in priority after the debts and interest required to be paid in pursuance of section 328(3) and (4), and
(b) are payable with interest at the rate specified in section 328(5) in respect of the period during which they have been outstanding since the commencement of the bankruptcy;

and the interest payable under paragraph (b) has the same priority as the debts on which it is payable.

NOTES
This section derived from the Insolvency Act 1985, s 166(6).
Section heading: words in square brackets inserted by virtue of the Civil Partnership Act 2004, s 261(1), Sch 27, para 116.
Sub-s (1): words in square brackets inserted by the Civil Partnership Act 2004, s 261(1), Sch 27, para 116.
Transfer to Secretary of State of rights and remedies on employer's insolvency: see the note to s 175 at **[1.176]**.

[1.401]
330 Final distribution
(1) When the trustee has realised all the bankrupt's estate or so much of it as can, in the trustee's opinion, be realised without needlessly protracting the trusteeship, he shall give notice in the prescribed manner either—

(a) of his intention to declare a final dividend, or
(b) that no dividend, or further dividend, will be declared.

[(1A) A notice under subsection (1)(b) need not be given to opted-out creditors.]
(2) The notice under subsection (1) shall contain the prescribed particulars and shall require claims against the bankrupt's estate to be established by a date ("the final date") specified in the notice.
(3) The court may, on the application of any person, postpone the final date.
(4) After the final date, the trustee shall—

(a) defray any outstanding expenses of the bankruptcy out of the bankrupt's estate, and
(b) if he intends to declare a final dividend, declare and distribute that dividend without regard to the claim of any person in respect of a debt not already proved in the bankruptcy.

(5) If a surplus remains after payment in full and with interest of all the bankrupt's creditors and the payment of the expenses of the bankruptcy, the bankrupt is entitled to the surplus.

[(6) Subsection (5) is subject to [Article 49 of the EU Regulation (assets remaining in the secondary compulsory proceedings)]].

NOTES

This section derived from the Insolvency Act 1985, s 167.

Sub-s (1A): inserted by the Small Business, Enterprise and Employment Act 2015, s 126, Sch 9, Pt 2, paras 60, 82, as from 6 April 2017 (subject to transitional and savings provisions as noted to s 246ZE at **[1.256]**).

Sub-s (6): added by the Insolvency Act 1986 (Amendment) (No 2) Regulations 2002, SI 2002/1240, regs 3, 15; words in square brackets substituted for original words "Article 35 of the EC Regulation (surplus in secondary proceedings to be transferred to main proceedings)" by the Insolvency Amendment (EU 2015/848) Regulations 2017, SI 2017/702, regs 2, 3, Schedule, Pt 1, paras 1, 21, except in relation to proceedings opened before 26 June 2017 and subject to savings in reg 4 thereof at **[2.103]**.

[1.402]

331 Final [report]

(1) Subject as follows in this section and the next, this section applies where—
(a) it appears to the trustee that the administration of the bankrupt's estate in accordance with this Chapter is for practical purposes complete, and
(b) the trustee is not the official receiver.

[(2) The trustee must give the bankrupt's creditors (other than opted-out creditors) notice that it appears to the trustee that the administration of the bankrupt's estate is for practical purposes complete.

(2A) The notice must—
(a) be accompanied by a report of the trustee's administration of the bankrupt's estate;
(b) explain the effect of section 299(3)(d) and how the creditors may object to the trustee's release.]

(3) The trustee may, if he thinks fit, give the notice summoning the final general meeting at the same time as giving notice under section 330(1); but, if summoned for an earlier date, that meeting shall be adjourned (and, if necessary, further adjourned) until a date on which the trustee is able to report to the meeting that the administration of the bankrupt's estate is for practical purposes complete.

(4) In the administration of the estate it is the trustee's duty to retain sufficient sums from the estate to cover the expenses of summoning and holding the meeting required by this section.

NOTES

This section derived from the Insolvency Act 1985, s 168(1), (2), (4).

Section heading: words in square brackets substituted for original word "meeting" by the Small Business, Enterprise and Employment Act 2015, s 126, Sch 9, Pt 2, paras 60, 83(1), (4), as from 6 April 2017 (subject to transitional and savings provisions as noted to s 246ZE at **[1.256]**).

Sub-ss (2), (2A): substituted for original sub-s (2) by the Small Business, Enterprise and Employment Act 2015, s 126, Sch 9, Pt 2, paras 60, 83(1), (2), as from 6 April 2017 (subject to transitional and savings provisions as noted to s 246ZE at **[1.256]**). Sub-s (2) originally read as follows—

"(2) The trustee shall summon a final general meeting of the bankrupt's creditors which—
(a) shall receive the trustee's report of his administration of the bankrupt's estate, and
(b) shall determine whether the trustee should have his release under section 299 in Chapter III.".

Sub-ss (3), (4): repealed by the Small Business, Enterprise and Employment Act 2015, s 126, Sch 9, Pt 2, paras 60, 83(1), (3), as from 6 April 2017 (subject to transitional and savings provisions as noted to s 246ZE at **[1.256]**).

[1.403]

332 Saving for bankrupt's home

(1) This section applies where—
(a) there is comprised in the bankrupt's estate property consisting of an interest in a dwelling house which is occupied by the bankrupt or by his spouse or former spouse [or by his civil partner or former civil partner], and
(b) the trustee has been unable for any reason to realise that property.

(2) The trustee shall not [give notice under section 331(2)] unless either—
(a) the court has made an order under section 313 imposing a charge on that property for the benefit of the bankrupt's estate, or
(b) the court has declined, on an application under that section, to make such an order, or
(c) the Secretary of State has issued a certificate to the trustee stating that it would be inappropriate or inexpedient for such an application to be made in the case in question.

NOTES

This section derived from the Insolvency Act 1985, s 168(3).

Sub-s (1): words in square brackets inserted by the Civil Partnership Act 2004, s 261(1), Sch 27, para 117.

Sub-s (2): words in square brackets substituted for original words "summon a meeting under section 331" by the Small Business, Enterprise and Employment Act 2015, s 126, Sch 9, Pt 2, paras 60, 84, as from 6 April 2017 (subject to transitional and savings provisions as noted to s 246ZE at **[1.256]**).

Supplemental

[1.404]

333 Duties of bankrupt in relation to trustee

(1) The bankrupt shall—

(a) give to the trustee such information as to his affairs,

(b) attend on the trustee at such times, and

(c) do all such other things,

as the trustee may for the purposes of carrying out his functions under any of this Group of Parts reasonably require.

(2) Where at any time after the commencement of the bankruptcy any property is acquired by, or devolves upon, the bankrupt or there is an increase of the bankrupt's income, the bankrupt shall, within the prescribed period, give the trustee notice of the property or, as the case may be, of the increase.

(3) Subsection (1) applies to a bankrupt after his discharge.

(4) If the bankrupt without reasonable excuse fails to comply with any obligation imposed by this section, he is guilty of a contempt of court and liable to be punished accordingly (in addition to any other punishment to which he may be subject).

NOTES

This section derived from the Insolvency Act 1985, s 169.

[1.405]

334 Stay of distribution in case of second bankruptcy

(1) This section and the next apply where a bankruptcy order is made against an undischarged bankrupt; and in both sections—

(a) "the later bankruptcy" means the bankruptcy arising from that order,

(b) "the earlier bankruptcy" means the bankruptcy (or, as the case may be, most recent bankruptcy) from which the bankrupt has not been discharged at the commencement of the later bankruptcy, and

(c) "the existing trustee" means the trustee (if any) of the bankrupt's estate for the purposes of the earlier bankruptcy.

(2) Where the existing trustee has been given the prescribed notice of the [making of the application or (as the case may be) the] presentation of the petition for the later bankruptcy, any distribution or other disposition by him of anything to which the next subsection applies, if made after the giving of the notice, is void except to the extent that it was made with the consent of the court or is or was subsequently ratified by the court.

This is without prejudice to section 284 (restrictions on dispositions of property following bankruptcy order).

(3) This subsection applies to—

(a) any property which is vested in the existing trustee under section 307(3) (after-acquired property);

(b) any money paid to the existing trustee in pursuance of an income payments order under section 310; and

(c) any property or money which is, or in the hands of the existing trustee represents, the proceeds of sale or application of property or money falling within paragraph (a) or (b) of this subsection.

NOTES

This section derived from the Insolvency Act 1985, s 170(1)–(3).

Sub-s (2): words in square brackets inserted by the Enterprise and Regulatory Reform Act 2013, s 71(3), Sch 19, paras 1, 28, in relation to a petition for a bankruptcy order presented to the court by a debtor on or after 6 April 2016.

[1.406]

335 Adjustment between earlier and later bankruptcy estates

(1) With effect from the commencement of the later bankruptcy anything to which section 334(3) applies which, immediately before the commencement of that bankruptcy, is comprised in the bankrupt's estate for the purposes of the earlier bankruptcy is to be treated as comprised in the bankrupt's estate for the purposes of the later bankruptcy and, until there is a trustee of that estate, is to be dealt with by the existing trustee in accordance with the rules.

(2) Any sums which in pursuance of an income payments order under section 310 are payable after the commencement of the later bankruptcy to the existing trustee shall form part of the bankrupt's estate for the purposes of the later bankruptcy; and the court may give such consequential directions for the modification of the order as it thinks fit.

(3) Anything comprised in a bankrupt's estate by virtue of subsection (1) or (2) is so comprised subject to a first charge in favour of the existing trustee for any bankruptcy expenses incurred by him in relation thereto.

(4) Except as provided above and in section 334, property which is, or by virtue of section 308 (personal property of bankrupt exceeding reasonable replacement value) [or section 308A (vesting in trustee of certain tenancies)] is capable of being, comprised in the bankrupt's estate for the purposes of the earlier bankruptcy, or of any bankruptcy prior to it, shall not be comprised in his estate for the purposes of the later bankruptcy.

(5) The creditors of the bankrupt in the earlier bankruptcy and the creditors of the bankrupt in any bankruptcy prior to the earlier one, are not to be creditors of his in the later bankruptcy in respect of the same debts; but the existing trustee may prove in the later bankruptcy for—

(a) the unsatisfied balance of the debts (including any debt under this subsection) provable against the bankrupt's estate in the earlier bankruptcy;
(b) any interest payable on that balance; and
(c) any unpaid expenses of the earlier bankruptcy.

(6) Any amount provable under subsection (5) ranks in priority after all the other debts provable in the later bankruptcy and after interest on those debts and, accordingly, shall not be paid unless those debts and that interest have first been paid in full.

NOTES

This section derived from the Insolvency Act 1985, s 170(4)–(9).

Sub-s (4): words in square brackets inserted by the Housing Act 1988, s 140, Sch 17, Pt I, para 74.

CHAPTER V
EFFECT OF BANKRUPTCY ON CERTAIN RIGHTS, TRANSACTIONS, ETC

[Rights under trusts of land

[1.407]

335A Rights under trusts of land

(1) Any application by a trustee of a bankrupt's estate under section 14 of the Trusts of Land and Appointment of Trustees Act 1996 (powers of court in relation to trusts of land) for an order under that section for the sale of land shall be made to the court having jurisdiction in relation to the bankruptcy.

(2) On such an application the court shall make such order as it thinks just and reasonable having regard to—
(a) the interests of the bankrupt's creditors;
(b) where the application is made in respect of land which includes a dwelling house which is or has been the home of the bankrupt or the [bankrupt's spouse or civil partner or former spouse or former civil partner]—
(i) the conduct of the [spouse, civil partner, former spouse or former civil partner], so far as contributing to the bankruptcy,
(ii) the needs and financial resources of the [spouse, civil partner, former spouse or former civil partner] and
(iii) the needs of any children; and
(c) all the circumstances of the case other than the needs of the bankrupt.

(3) Where such an application is made after the end of the period of one year beginning with the first vesting under Chapter IV of this Part of the bankrupt's estate in a trustee, the court shall assume, unless the circumstances of the case are exceptional, that the interests of the bankrupt's creditors outweigh all other considerations.

(4) The powers conferred on the court by this section are exercisable on an application whether it is made before or after the commencement of this section.]

NOTES

Inserted, together with preceding cross-heading, by the Trusts of Land and Appointment of Trustees Act 1996, s 25(1), Sch 3, para 23, subject to savings in s 25(4), (5) thereof.

Sub-s (2): words in square brackets substituted by the Civil Partnership Act 2004, s 261(1), Sch 27, para 118.

Rights of occupation

[1.408]

336 Rights of occupation etc of bankrupt's spouse [or civil partner]

(1) Nothing occurring in the initial period of the bankruptcy (that is to say, the period beginning with the day of the [making of the bankruptcy application or (as the case may be) the presentation of the bankruptcy petition] and ending with the vesting of the bankrupt's estate in a trustee) is to be taken as having given rise to any [[home rights] under Part IV of the Family Law Act 1996] in relation to a dwelling house comprised in the bankrupt's estate.

(2) Where [a spouse's or civil partner's home rights] [under the Act of 1996] are a charge on the estate or interest of the other spouse [or civil partner], or of trustees for the other spouse [or civil partner], and the other spouse [or civil partner] is [made] bankrupt—
(a) the charge continues to subsist notwithstanding the bankruptcy and, subject to the provisions of that Act, binds the trustee of the bankrupt's estate and persons deriving title under that trustee, and
(b) any application for an order [under section 33 of that Act] shall be made to the court having jurisdiction in relation to the bankruptcy.

(3) . . .

(4) On such an application as is mentioned in subsection (2) . . . the court shall make such order under [section 33 of the Act of 1996] . . . as it thinks just and reasonable having regard to—
(a) the interests of the bankrupt's creditors,
(b) the conduct of the spouse or former spouse [or civil partner or former civil partner], so far as contributing to the bankruptcy,
(c) the needs and financial resources of the spouse or former spouse [or civil partner or former civil partner],
(d) the needs of any children, and
(e) all the circumstances of the case other than the needs of the bankrupt.

(5) Where such an application is made after the end of the period of one year beginning with the first vesting under Chapter IV of this Part of the bankrupt's estate in a trustee, the court shall assume, unless the circumstances of the case are exceptional, that the interests of the bankrupt's creditors outweigh all other considerations.

NOTES

This section derived from the Insolvency Act 1985, s 171.

Section heading: words in square brackets inserted by the Civil Partnership Act 2004, s 82, Sch 9, Pt 2, para 21(1), (5), subject to transitional provisions in Sch 9, Pt 3 thereto.

Sub-s (1): words in first pair of square brackets substituted for original words "presentation of the petition for the bankruptcy order", by the Enterprise and Regulatory Reform Act 2013, s 71(3), Sch 19, paras 1, 29(1), (2), in respect of a petition for a bankruptcy order presented to the court by a debtor on or after 6 April 2016; words in second (outer) pair of square brackets substituted by the Family Law Act 1996, s 66(1), Sch 8, para 57(2); words in third (inner) pair of square brackets substituted by the Civil Partnership Act 2004, s 82, Sch 9, Pt 2, para 21(1), (2), subject to transitional provisions in Sch 9, Pt 3 thereto.

Sub-s (2): words in first, third, fourth and fifth pairs of square brackets inserted by the Civil Partnership Act 2004, s 82, Sch 9, Pt 2, para 21(1), (3), subject to transitional provisions in Sch 9, Pt 3 thereto; words in second and final pairs of square brackets substituted by the Family Law Act 1996, s 66(1), Sch 8, para 57(3); word in sixth pair of square brackets substituted for original word "adjudged" by the Enterprise and Regulatory Reform Act 2013, s 71(3), Sch 19, paras 1, 29(1), (3), in respect of a petition for a bankruptcy order presented to the court by a debtor on or after 6 April 2016.

Sub-s (3): repealed by the Trusts of Land and Appointment of Trustees Act 1996, s 25(2), Sch 4, subject to savings in s 25(4), (5) thereof.

Sub-s (4): words omitted repealed by the Trusts of Land and Appointment of Trustees Act 1996, s 25(2), Sch 4, subject to savings in s 25(4), (5) thereof; words in first pair of square brackets substituted by the Family Law Act 1996, s 66(1), Sch 8, para 57(1), (4); words in second and third pairs of square brackets inserted by the Civil Partnership Act 2004, s 82, Sch 9, Pt 2, para 21(1), (4), subject to transitional provisions in Sch 9, Pt 3 thereto.

[1.409]

337 Rights of occupation of bankrupt

(1) This section applies where—

(a) a person who is entitled to occupy a dwelling house by virtue of a beneficial estate or interest is [made] bankrupt, and

(b) any persons under the age of 18 with whom that person had at some time occupied that dwelling house had their home with that person at the time when the [bankruptcy application was made or (as the case may be) the] bankruptcy petition was presented and at the commencement of the bankruptcy.

(2) Whether or not the bankrupt's [spouse or civil partner (if any) has home rights] [under Part IV of the Family Law Act 1996]—

(a) the bankrupt has the following rights as against the trustee of his estate—

(i) if in occupation, a right not to be evicted or excluded from the dwelling house or any part of it, except with the leave of the court,

(ii) if not in occupation, a right with the leave of the court to enter into and occupy the dwelling house, and

(b) the bankrupt's rights are a charge, having the like priority as an equitable interest created immediately before the commencement of the bankruptcy, on so much of his estate or interest in the dwelling house as vests in the trustee.

[(3) The Act of 1996 has effect, with the necessary modifications, as if—

(a) the rights conferred by paragraph (a) of subsection (2) were [home rights] under that Act,

(b) any application for such leave as is mentioned in that paragraph were an application for an order under section 33 of that Act, and

(c) any charge under paragraph (b) of that subsection on the estate or interest of the trustee were a charge under that Act on the estate or interest of a spouse [or civil partner].]

(4) Any application for leave such as is mentioned in subsection (2)(a) or otherwise by virtue of this section for an order under [section 33 of the Act of 1996] shall be made to the court having jurisdiction in relation to the bankruptcy.

(5) On such an application the court shall make such order under [section 33 of the Act of 1996] as it thinks just and reasonable having regard to the interests of the creditors, to the bankrupt's financial resources, to the needs of the children and to all the circumstances of the case other than the needs of the bankrupt.

(6) Where such an application is made after the end of the period of one year beginning with the vesting (under Chapter IV of this Part) of the bankrupt's estate in a trustee, the court shall assume, unless the circumstances of the case are exceptional, that the interests of the bankrupt's creditors outweigh all other considerations.

NOTES

This section derived from the Insolvency Act 1985, s 172.

Sub-s (1): word in square brackets in para (a) substituted for original word "adjudged", and words in square brackets in para (b) inserted, by the Enterprise and Regulatory Reform Act 2013, s 71(3), Sch 19, paras 1, 30, in respect of a petition for a bankruptcy order presented to the court by a debtor on or after 6 April 2016.

Sub-s (2): words in first pair of square brackets substituted by the Civil Partnership Act 2004, s 82, Sch 9, Pt 2, para 22(1), (2), subject to transitional provisions in Sch 9, Pt 3 thereto; words in second pair of square brackets substituted by the Family Law Act 1996, s 66(1), Sch 8, para 58(1), (2).

Sub-s (3): substituted by the Family Law Act 1996, s 66(1), Sch 8, para 58(1), (3); words in square brackets in para (a) substituted, and words in square brackets in para (c) inserted by the Civil Partnership Act 2004, s 82, Sch 9, Pt 2, para 22(1), (3), subject to transitional provisions in Sch 9, Pt 3 thereto.

Sub-ss (4), (5): words in square brackets substituted by the Family Law Act 1996, s 66(1), Sch 8, para 58(1), (4).

[1.410]

338 Payments in respect of premises occupied by bankrupt

Where any premises comprised in a bankrupt's estate are occupied by him (whether by virtue of the preceding section or otherwise) on condition that he makes payments towards satisfying any liability arising under a mortgage of the premises or otherwise towards the outgoings of the premises, the bankrupt does not, by virtue of those payments, acquire any interest in the premises.

NOTES

This section derived from the Insolvency Act 1985, s 173.

Adjustment of prior transactions, etc

[1.411]

339 Transactions at an undervalue

(1) Subject as follows in this section and sections 341 and 342, where an individual is [made] bankrupt and he has at a relevant time (defined in section 341) entered into a transaction with any person at an undervalue, the trustee of the bankrupt's estate may apply to the court for an order under this section.

(2) The court shall, on such an application, make such order as it thinks fit for restoring the position to what it would have been if that individual had not entered into that transaction.

(3) For the purposes of this section and sections 341 and 342, an individual enters into a transaction with a person at an undervalue if—

- (a) he makes a gift to that person or he otherwise enters into a transaction with that person on terms that provide for him to receive no consideration,
- (b) he enters into a transaction with that person in consideration of marriage [or the formation of a civil partnership], or
- (c) he enters into a transaction with that person for a consideration the value of which, in money or money's worth, is significantly less than the value, in money or money's worth, of the consideration provided by the individual.

NOTES

This section derived from the Insolvency Act 1985, s 174(1) (in part), (2).

Sub-s (1): word in square brackets substituted for original word "adjudged" by the Enterprise and Regulatory Reform Act 2013, s 71(3), Sch 19, paras 1, 31, in respect of a petition for a bankruptcy order presented to the court by a debtor on or after 6 April 2016.

Sub-s (3): words in square brackets inserted by the Civil Partnership Act 2004, s 261(1), Sch 27, para 119.

Settlements made in compliance with property adjustment orders: see further the Matrimonial Causes Act 1973, s 39 at **[17.15]**.

Market contracts: as to the limitations on orders made under this section with regard to adjusting prior transactions in relation to market contracts, and certain other transactions relating to default proceedings, see the Companies Act 1989, s 165(1)(a) at **[17.68]**.

Tainted gifts: no order under this section or s 340 or 423 of this Act at **[1.412]**, **[1.537]** is to be made where a bankrupt has made a "tainted gift"; see the Proceeds of Crime Act 2002, s 419 at **[17.238]**.

[1.412]

340 Preferences

(1) Subject as follows in this and the next two sections, where an individual is [made] bankrupt and he has at a relevant time (defined in section 341) given a preference to any person, the trustee of the bankrupt's estate may apply to the court for an order under this section.

(2) The court shall, on such an application, make such order as it thinks fit for restoring the position to what it would have been if that individual had not given that preference.

(3) For the purposes of this and the next two sections, an individual gives a preference to a person if—

- (a) that person is one of the individual's creditors or a surety or guarantor for any of his debts or other liabilities, and
- (b) the individual does anything or suffers anything to be done which (in either case) has the effect of putting that person into a position which, in the event of the individual's bankruptcy, will be better than the position he would have been in if that thing had not been done.

(4) The court shall not make an order under this section in respect of a preference given to any person unless the individual who gave the preference was influenced in deciding to give it by a desire to produce in relation to that person the effect mentioned in subsection (3)(b) above.

(5) An individual who has given a preference to a person who, at the time the preference was given, was an associate of his (otherwise than by reason only of being his employee) is presumed, unless the contrary is shown, to have been influenced in deciding to give it by such a desire as is mentioned in subsection (4).

(6) The fact that something has been done in pursuance of the order of a court does not, without more, prevent the doing or suffering of that thing from constituting the giving of a preference.

NOTES

This section derived from the Insolvency Act 1985, s 174(1) (in part), (3)–(6), (12) (in part).

Sub-s (1): word in square brackets substituted for original word "adjudged" by the Enterprise and Regulatory Reform Act 2013, s 71(3), Sch 19, paras 1, 32, in respect of a petition for a bankruptcy order presented to the court by a debtor on or after 6 April 2016.

Market contracts: as to the limitations on orders made under this section with regard to adjusting prior transactions in relation to market contracts, and certain other transactions relating to default proceedings, see the Companies Act 1989, s 165(1)(a) at **[17.68]**.

Tainted gifts: see the note to s 339 at **[1.411]**.

[1.413]

341 "Relevant time" under ss 339, 340

(1) Subject as follows, the time at which an individual enters into a transaction at an undervalue or gives a preference is a relevant time if the transaction is entered into or the preference given—

(a) in the case of a transaction at an undervalue, at a time in the period of 5 years ending with the day of the [making of the bankruptcy application as a result of which, or (as the case may be) the presentation of the bankruptcy petition on which, the individual is made] bankrupt,

(b) in the case of a preference which is not a transaction at an undervalue and is given to a person who is an associate of the individual (otherwise than by reason only of being his employee), at a time in the period of 2 years ending with that day, and

(c) in any other case of a preference which is not a transaction at an undervalue, at a time in the period of 6 months ending with that day.

(2) Where an individual enters into a transaction at an undervalue or gives a preference at a time mentioned in paragraph (a), (b) or (c) of subsection (1) (not being, in the case of a transaction at an undervalue, a time less than 2 years before the end of the period mentioned in paragraph (a)), that time is not a relevant time for the purposes of sections 339 and 340 unless the individual—

(a) is insolvent at that time, or

(b) becomes insolvent in consequence of the transaction or preference;

but the requirements of this subsection are presumed to be satisfied, unless the contrary is shown, in relation to any transaction at an undervalue which is entered into by an individual with a person who is an associate of his (otherwise than by reason only of being his employee).

(3) For the purposes of subsection (2), an individual is insolvent if—

(a) he is unable to pay his debts as they fall due, or

(b) the value of his assets is less than the amount of his liabilities, taking into account his contingent and prospective liabilities.

(4) A transaction entered into or preference given by a person who is subsequently adjudged bankrupt on a petition under section 264(1)(d) (criminal bankruptcy) is to be treated as having been entered into or given at a relevant time for the purposes of sections 339 and 340 if it was entered into or given at any time on or after the date specified for the purposes of this subsection in the criminal bankruptcy order on which the petition was based.

(5) No order shall be made under section 339 or 340 by virtue of subsection (4) of this section where an appeal is pending (within the meaning of section 277) against the individual's conviction of any offence by virtue of which the criminal bankruptcy order was made.

NOTES

This section derived from the Insolvency Act 1985, s 174(7)–(11), (12) (in part).

Sub-s (1): words in square brackets in para (a) substituted for original words "presentation of the bankruptcy petition on which the individual is adjudged" by the Enterprise and Regulatory Reform Act 2013, s 71(3), Sch 19, paras 1, 33, in respect of a petition for a bankruptcy order presented to the court by a debtor on or after 6 April 2016.

Sub-ss (4), (5): repealed by the Criminal Justice Act 1988, s 170(2), Sch 16, as from a day to be appointed.

[1.414]

342 Orders under ss 339, 340

(1) Without prejudice to the generality of section 339(2) or 340(2), an order under either of those sections with respect to a transaction or preference entered into or given by an individual who is subsequently [made] bankrupt may (subject as follows)—

(a) require any property transferred as part of the transaction, or in connection with the giving of the preference, to be vested in the trustee of the bankrupt's estate as part of that estate;

(b) require any property to be so vested if it represents in any person's hands the application either of the proceeds of sale of property so transferred or of money so transferred;

(c) release or discharge (in whole or in part) any security given by the individual;

(d) require any person to pay, in respect of benefits received by him from the individual, such sums to the trustee of his estate as the court may direct;

(e) provide for any surety or guarantor whose obligations to any person were released or discharged (in whole or in part) under the transaction or by the giving of the preference to be under such new or revived obligations to that person as the court thinks appropriate;

(f) provide for security to be provided for the discharge of any obligation imposed by or arising under the order, for such an obligation to be charged on any property and for the security or charge to have the same priority as a security or charge released or discharged (in whole or in part) under the transaction or by the giving of the preference; and

(g) provide for the extent to which any person whose property is vested by the order in the trustee of the bankrupt's estate, or on whom obligations are imposed by the order, is to be able to prove in the bankruptcy for debts or other liabilities which arose from, or were released or discharged (in whole or in part) under or by, the transaction or the giving of the preference.

(2) An order under section 339 or 340 may affect the property of, or impose any obligation on, any person whether or not he is the person with whom the individual in question entered into the transaction or, as the case may be, the person to whom the preference was given; but such an order—

(a) shall not prejudice any interest in property which was acquired from a person other than that individual and was acquired [in good faith and for value], or prejudice any interest deriving from such an interest, and

(b) shall not require a person who received a benefit from the transaction or preference [in good faith and for value] to pay a sum to the trustee of the bankrupt's estate, except where he was a party to the transaction or the payment is to be in respect of a preference given to that person at a time when he was a creditor of that individual.

[(2A) Where a person has acquired an interest in property from a person other than the individual in question, or has received a benefit from the transaction or preference, and at the time of that acquisition or receipt—

(a) he had notice of the relevant surrounding circumstances and of the relevant proceedings, or

(b) he was an associate of, or was connected with, either the individual in question or the person with whom that individual entered into the transaction or to whom that individual gave the preference,

then, unless the contrary is shown, it shall be presumed for the purposes of paragraph (a) or (as the case may be) paragraph (b) of subsection (2) that the interest was acquired or the benefit was received otherwise than in good faith.]

(3) Any sums required to be paid to the trustee in accordance with an order under section 339 or 340 shall be comprised in the bankrupt's estate.

[(4) For the purposes of subsection (2A)(a), the relevant surrounding circumstances are (as the case may require)—

(a) the fact that the individual in question entered into the transaction at an undervalue; or

(b) the circumstances which amounted to the giving of the preference by the individual in question.

(5) For the purposes of subsection (2A)(a), a person has notice of the relevant proceedings if he has notice—

[(a) of the fact that the bankruptcy application as a result of which, or (as the case may be) the bankruptcy petition on which, the individual in question is made bankrupt has been made or presented; or]

(b) of the fact that the individual in question has been [made] bankrupt.

(6) Section 249 in Part VII of this Act shall apply for the purposes of subsection (2A)(b) as it applies for the purposes of the first Group of Parts.]

NOTES

This section as originally enacted derived from the Insolvency Act 1985, s 175.

Sub-s (1): word in square brackets substituted for original word "adjudged" by the Enterprise and Regulatory Reform Act 2013, s 71(3), Sch 19, paras 1, 34(1), (2), in respect of a petition for a bankruptcy order presented to the court by a debtor on or after 6 April 2016.

Sub-s (2): words in square brackets substituted by the Insolvency (No 2) Act 1994, s 2(1), in relation to interests acquired and benefits received after 26 July 1994.

Sub-s (2A): inserted by the Insolvency (No 2) Act 1994, s 2(2), in relation to interests acquired and benefits received after 26 July 1994.

Sub-ss (4), (6): substituted, together with sub-s (5), for original sub-s (4), by the Insolvency (No 2) Act 1994, s 2(3), in relation to interests acquired and benefits received after 26 July 1994.

Sub-s (5): substituted as noted above; para (a) further substituted and word in square brackets in para (b) substituted for original word "adjudged", by the Enterprise and Regulatory Reform Act 2013, s 71(3), Sch 19, paras 1, 34(1), (3), in respect of a petition for a bankruptcy order presented to the court by a debtor on or after 6 April 2016. Para (a) previously read as follows:

"(a) of the fact that the petition on which the individual in question is adjudged bankrupt has been presented; or".

[1.415]

[342A Recovery of excessive pension contributions

(1) Where an individual who is [made] bankrupt—

(a) has rights under an approved pension arrangement, or

(b) has excluded rights under an unapproved pension arrangement,

the trustee of the bankrupt's estate may apply to the court for an order under this section.

(2) If the court is satisfied—

(a) that the rights under the arrangement are to any extent, and whether directly or indirectly, the fruits of relevant contributions, and

(b) that the making of any of the relevant contributions ("the excessive contributions") has unfairly prejudiced the individual's creditors,

the court may make such order as it thinks fit for restoring the position to what it would have been had the excessive contributions not been made.

(3) Subsection (4) applies where the court is satisfied that the value of the rights under the arrangement is, as a result of rights of the individual under the arrangement or any other pension arrangement having at any time become subject to a debit under section 29(1)(a) of the Welfare Reform and Pensions Act 1999 (debits giving effect to pension-sharing), less than it would otherwise have been.

(4) Where this subsection applies—

(a) any relevant contributions which were represented by the rights which became subject to the debit shall, for the purposes of subsection (2), be taken to be contributions of which the rights under the arrangement are the fruits, and

(b) where the relevant contributions represented by the rights under the arrangement (including those so represented by virtue of paragraph (a)) are not all excessive contributions, relevant contributions which are represented by the rights under the arrangement otherwise than by virtue of paragraph (a) shall be treated as excessive contributions before any which are so represented by virtue of that paragraph.

(5) In subsections (2) to (4) "relevant contributions" means contributions to the arrangement or any other pension arrangement—

(a) which the individual has at any time made on his own behalf, or
(b) which have at any time been made on his behalf.

(6) The court shall, in determining whether it is satisfied under subsection (2)(b), consider in particular—

(a) whether any of the contributions were made for the purpose of putting assets beyond the reach of the individual's creditors or any of them, and
(b) whether the total amount of any contributions—
  (i) made by or on behalf of the individual to pension arrangements, and
  (ii) represented (whether directly or indirectly) by rights under approved pension arrangements or excluded rights under unapproved pension arrangements,

is an amount which is excessive in view of the individual's circumstances when those contributions were made.

(7) For the purposes of this section and sections 342B and 342C ("the recovery provisions"), rights of an individual under an unapproved pension arrangement are excluded rights if they are rights which are excluded from his estate by virtue of regulations under section 12 of the Welfare Reform and Pensions Act 1999.

(8) In the recovery provisions—

"approved pension arrangement" has the same meaning as in section 11 of the Welfare Reform and Pensions Act 1999;

"unapproved pension arrangement" has the same meaning as in section 12 of that Act.]

NOTES

Substituted (for section as originally inserted by the Pensions Act 1995, s 95(1)) by the Welfare Reform and Pensions Act 1999, s 15.

Sub-s (1): word in square brackets substituted for original word "adjudged", by the Enterprise and Regulatory Reform Act 2013, s 71(3), Sch 19, paras 1, 35, in respect of a petition for a bankruptcy order presented to the court by a debtor on or after 6 April 2016.

[1.416]

[342B Orders under section 342A

(1) Without prejudice to the generality of section 342A(2), an order under section 342A may include provision—

(a) requiring the person responsible for the arrangement to pay an amount to the individual's trustee in bankruptcy,
(b) adjusting the liabilities of the arrangement in respect of the individual,
(c) adjusting any liabilities of the arrangement in respect of any other person that derive, directly or indirectly, from rights of the individual under the arrangement,
(d) for the recovery by the person responsible for the arrangement (whether by deduction from any amount which that person is ordered to pay or otherwise) of costs incurred by that person in complying in the bankrupt's case with any requirement under section 342C(1) or in giving effect to the order.

(2) In subsection (1), references to adjusting the liabilities of the arrangement in respect of a person include (in particular) reducing the amount of any benefit or future benefit to which that person is entitled under the arrangement.

(3) In subsection (1)(c), the reference to liabilities of the arrangement does not include liabilities in respect of a person which result from giving effect to an order or provision falling within section 28(1) of the Welfare Reform and Pensions Act 1999 (pension sharing orders and agreements).

(4) The maximum amount which the person responsible for an arrangement may be required to pay by an order under section 342A is the lesser of—

(a) the amount of the excessive contributions, and
(b) the value of the individual's rights under the arrangement (if the arrangement is an approved pension arrangement) or of his excluded rights under the arrangement (if the arrangement is an unapproved pension arrangement).

(5) An order under section 342A which requires the person responsible for an arrangement to pay an amount ("the restoration amount") to the individual's trustee in bankruptcy must provide for the liabilities of the arrangement to be correspondingly reduced.

(6) For the purposes of subsection (5), liabilities are correspondingly reduced if the difference between—

(a) the amount of the liabilities immediately before the reduction, and
(b) the amount of the liabilities immediately after the reduction,

is equal to the restoration amount.

(7) An order under section 342A in respect of an arrangement—

(a) shall be binding on the person responsible for the arrangement, and
(b) overrides provisions of the arrangement to the extent that they conflict with the provisions of the order.]

NOTES

Substituted (for section as originally inserted by the Pensions Act 1995, s 95(1)) by the Welfare Reform and Pensions Act 1999, s 15.

[1.417]

[342C Orders under section 342A: supplementary

(1) The person responsible for—
  (a) an approved pension arrangement under which a bankrupt has rights,
  (b) an unapproved pension arrangement under which a bankrupt has excluded rights, or
  (c) a pension arrangement under which a bankrupt has at any time had rights,

shall, on the bankrupt's trustee in bankruptcy making a written request, provide the trustee with such information about the arrangement and rights as the trustee may reasonably require for, or in connection with, the making of applications under section 342A.

(2) Nothing in—
  (a) any provision of section 159 of the Pension Schemes Act 1993 or section 91 of the Pensions Act 1995 (which prevent assignment and the making of orders that restrain a person from receiving anything which he is prevented from assigning),
  (b) any provision of any enactment (whether passed or made before or after the passing of the Welfare Reform and Pensions Act 1999) corresponding to any of the provisions mentioned in paragraph (a), or
  (c) any provision of the arrangement in question corresponding to any of those provisions,

applies to a court exercising its powers under section 342A.

(3) Where any sum is required by an order under section 342A to be paid to the trustee in bankruptcy, that sum shall be comprised in the bankrupt's estate.

(4) Regulations may, for the purposes of the recovery provisions, make provision about the calculation and verification of—
  (a) any such value as is mentioned in section 342B(4)(b);
  (b) any such amounts as are mentioned in section 342B(6)(a) and (b).

(5) The power conferred by subsection (4) includes power to provide for calculation or verification—
  (a) in such manner as may, in the particular case, be approved by a prescribed person; or
  [(b) in accordance with guidance from time to time prepared by a prescribed person.]

(6) References in the recovery provisions to the person responsible for a pension arrangement are to—
  (a) the trustees, managers or provider of the arrangement, or
  (b) the person having functions in relation to the arrangement corresponding to those of a trustee, manager or provider.

(7) In this section and sections 342A and 342B—
  "prescribed" means prescribed by regulations;
  "the recovery provisions" means this section and sections 342A and 342B;
  "regulations" means regulations made by the Secretary of State.

(8) Regulations under the recovery provisions may—
  (a) make different provision for different cases;
  (b) contain such incidental, supplemental and transitional provisions as appear to the Secretary of State necessary or expedient.

(9) Regulations under the recovery provisions shall be made by statutory instrument subject to annulment in pursuance of a resolution of either House of Parliament.]

NOTES

Substituted (for section as originally inserted by the Pensions Act 1995, s 95(1)) by the Welfare Reform and Pensions Act 1999, s 15.

Sub-s (5): para (b) substituted by the Pensions Act 2007, s 17, Sch 5, para 3.

Regulations: the Occupational and Personal Pension Schemes (Bankruptcy) (No 2) Regulations 2002, SI 2002/836.

[1.418]

[342D Recovery of excessive contributions in pension-sharing cases

(1) For the purposes of sections 339, 341 and 342, a pension-sharing transaction shall be taken—
  (a) to be a transaction, entered into by the transferor with the transferee, by which the appropriate amount is transferred by the transferor to the transferee; and
  (b) to be capable of being a transaction entered into at an undervalue only so far as it is a transfer of so much of the appropriate amount as is recoverable.

(2) For the purposes of sections 340 to 342, a pension-sharing transaction shall be taken—
  (a) to be something (namely a transfer of the appropriate amount to the transferee) done by the transferor; and
  (b) to be capable of being a preference given to the transferee only so far as it is a transfer of so much of the appropriate amount as is recoverable.

(3) If on an application under section 339 or 340 any question arises as to whether, or the extent to which, the appropriate amount in the case of a pension-sharing transaction is recoverable, the question shall be determined in accordance with subsections (4) to (8).

(4) The court shall first determine the extent (if any) to which the transferor's rights under the shared arrangement at the time of the transaction appear to have been (whether directly or indirectly) the fruits of contributions ("personal contributions")—
  (a) which the transferor has at any time made on his own behalf, or
  (b) which have at any time been made on the transferor's behalf,

to the shared arrangement or any other pension arrangement.

(5) Where it appears that those rights were to any extent the fruits of personal contributions, the court shall then determine the extent (if any) to which those rights appear to have been the fruits of personal contributions whose making has unfairly prejudiced the transferor's creditors ("the unfair contributions").

(6) If it appears to the court that the extent to which those rights were the fruits of the unfair contributions is such that the transfer of the appropriate amount could have been made out of rights under the shared arrangement which were not the fruits of the unfair contributions, then the appropriate amount is not recoverable.

(7) If it appears to the court that the transfer could not have been wholly so made, then the appropriate amount is recoverable to the extent to which it appears to the court that the transfer could not have been so made.

(8) In making the determination mentioned in subsection (5) the court shall consider in particular—

(a) whether any of the personal contributions were made for the purpose of putting assets beyond the reach of the transferor's creditors or any of them, and

(b) whether the total amount of any personal contributions represented, at the time the pension-sharing transaction was made, by rights under pension arrangements is an amount which is excessive in view of the transferor's circumstances when those contributions were made.

(9) In this section and sections 342E and 342F—

"appropriate amount", in relation to a pension-sharing transaction, means the appropriate amount in relation to that transaction for the purposes of section 29(1) of the Welfare Reform and Pensions Act 1999 (creation of pension credits and debits);

"pension-sharing transaction" means an order or provision falling within section 28(1) of the Welfare Reform and Pensions Act 1999 (orders and agreements which activate pension-sharing);

"shared arrangement", in relation to a pension-sharing transaction, means the pension arrangement to which the transaction relates;

"transferee", in relation to a pension-sharing transaction, means the person for whose benefit the transaction is made;

"transferor", in relation to a pension-sharing transaction, means the person to whose rights the transaction relates.]

NOTES

Inserted, together with ss 342E, 342F, by the Welfare Reform and Pensions Act 1999, s 84(1), Sch 12, Pt II, paras 70, 71.

[1.419]

[342E Orders under section 339 or 340 in respect of pension-sharing transactions

(1) This section and section 342F apply if the court is making an order under section 339 or 340 in a case where—

(a) the transaction or preference is, or is any part of, a pension-sharing transaction, and

(b) the transferee has rights under a pension arrangement ("the destination arrangement", which may be the shared arrangement or any other pension arrangement) that are derived, directly or indirectly, from the pension-sharing transaction.

(2) Without prejudice to the generality of section 339(2) or 340(2), or of section 342, the order may include provision—

(a) requiring the person responsible for the destination arrangement to pay an amount to the transferor's trustee in bankruptcy,

(b) adjusting the liabilities of the destination arrangement in respect of the transferee,

(c) adjusting any liabilities of the destination arrangement in respect of any other person that derive, directly or indirectly, from rights of the transferee under the destination arrangement,

(d) for the recovery by the person responsible for the destination arrangement (whether by deduction from any amount which that person is ordered to pay or otherwise) of costs incurred by that person in complying in the transferor's case with any requirement under section 342F(1) or in giving effect to the order,

(e) for the recovery, from the transferor's trustee in bankruptcy, by the person responsible for a pension arrangement, of costs incurred by that person in complying in the transferor's case with any requirement under section 342F(2) or (3).

(3) In subsection (2), references to adjusting the liabilities of the destination arrangement in respect of a person include (in particular) reducing the amount of any benefit or future benefit to which that person is entitled under the arrangement.

(4) The maximum amount which the person responsible for the destination arrangement may be required to pay by the order is the smallest of—

(a) so much of the appropriate amount as, in accordance with section 342D, is recoverable,

(b) so much (if any) of the amount of the unfair contributions (within the meaning given by section 342D(5)) as is not recoverable by way of an order under section 342A containing provision such as is mentioned in section 342B(1)(a), and

(c) the value of the transferee's rights under the destination arrangement so far as they are derived, directly or indirectly, from the pension-sharing transaction.

(5) If the order requires the person responsible for the destination arrangement to pay an amount ("the restoration amount") to the transferor's trustee in bankruptcy it must provide for the liabilities of the arrangement to be correspondingly reduced.

(6) For the purposes of subsection (5), liabilities are correspondingly reduced if the difference between—

(a) the amount of the liabilities immediately before the reduction, and

(b) the amount of the liabilities immediately after the reduction, is equal to the restoration amount.

(7) The order—

(a) shall be binding on the person responsible for the destination arrangement, and

(b) overrides provisions of the destination arrangement to the extent that they conflict with the provisions of the order.]

NOTES

Inserted as noted to s 342D at **[1.418]**.

[1.420]

[342F Orders under section 339 or 340 in pension-sharing cases: supplementary

(1) On the transferor's trustee in bankruptcy making a written request to the person responsible for the destination arrangement, that person shall provide the trustee with such information about—

(a) the arrangement,

(b) the transferee's rights under it, and

(c) where the destination arrangement is the shared arrangement, the transferor's rights under it,

as the trustee may reasonably require for, or in connection with, the making of applications under sections 339 and 340.

(2) Where the shared arrangement is not the destination arrangement, the person responsible for the shared arrangement shall, on the transferor's trustee in bankruptcy making a written request to that person, provide the trustee with such information about—

(a) the arrangement, and

(b) the transferor's rights under it,

as the trustee may reasonably require for, or in connection with, the making of applications under sections 339 and 340.

(3) On the transferor's trustee in bankruptcy making a written request to the person responsible for any intermediate arrangement, that person shall provide the trustee with such information about—

(a) the arrangement, and

(b) the transferee's rights under it,

as the trustee may reasonably require for, or in connection with, the making of applications under sections 339 and 340.

(4) In subsection (3) "intermediate arrangement" means a pension arrangement, other than the shared arrangement or the destination arrangement, in relation to which the following conditions are fulfilled—

(a) there was a time when the transferee had rights under the arrangement that were derived (directly or indirectly) from the pension-sharing transaction, and

(b) the transferee's rights under the destination arrangement (so far as derived from the pension-sharing transaction) are to any extent derived (directly or indirectly) from the rights mentioned in paragraph (a).

(5) Nothing in—

(a) any provision of section 159 of the Pension Schemes Act 1993 or section 91 of the Pensions Act 1995 (which prevent assignment and the making of orders which restrain a person from receiving anything which he is prevented from assigning),

(b) any provision of any enactment (whether passed or made before or after the passing of the Welfare Reform and Pensions Act 1999) corresponding to any of the provisions mentioned in paragraph (a), or

(c) any provision of the destination arrangement corresponding to any of those provisions,

applies to a court exercising its powers under section 339 or 340.

(6) Regulations may, for the purposes of sections 339 to 342, sections 342D and 342E and this section, make provision about the calculation and verification of—

(a) any such value as is mentioned in section 342E(4)(c);

(b) any such amounts as are mentioned in section 342E(6)(a) and (b).

(7) The power conferred by subsection (6) includes power to provide for calculation or verification—

(a) in such manner as may, in the particular case, be approved by a prescribed person; or

[(b) in accordance with guidance from time to time prepared by a prescribed person.]

(8) In section 342E and this section, references to the person responsible for a pension arrangement are to—

(a) the trustees, managers or provider of the arrangement, or

(b) the person having functions in relation to the arrangement corresponding to those of a trustee, manager or provider.

(9) In this section—

"prescribed" means prescribed by regulations;

"regulations" means regulations made by the Secretary of State.

(10) Regulations under this section may—

(a) make different provision for different cases;

(b) contain such incidental, supplemental and transitional provisions as appear to the Secretary of State necessary or expedient.

(11) Regulations under this section shall be made by statutory instrument subject to annulment in pursuance of a resolution of either House of Parliament.]

NOTES

Inserted as noted to s 342D at **[1.418]**.

Sub-s (7): para (b) substituted by the Pensions Act 2007, s 17, Sch 5, para 4.

Regulations: the Occupational and Personal Pension Schemes (Bankruptcy) (No 2) Regulations 2002, SI 2002/836.

[1.421]

343 Extortionate credit transactions

(1) This section applies where a person is [made] bankrupt who is or has been a party to a transaction for, or involving, the provision to him of credit.

(2) The court may, on the application of the trustee of the bankrupt's estate, make an order with respect to the transaction if the transaction is or was extortionate and was not entered into more than 3 years before the commencement of the bankruptcy.

(3) For the purposes of this section a transaction is extortionate if, having regard to the risk accepted by the person providing the credit—

(a) the terms of it are or were such as to require grossly exorbitant payments to be made (whether unconditionally or in certain contingencies) in respect of the provision of the credit, or

(b) it otherwise grossly contravened ordinary principles of fair dealing;

and it shall be presumed, unless the contrary is proved, that a transaction with respect to which an application is made under this section is or, as the case may be, was extortionate.

(4) An order under this section with respect to any transaction may contain such one or more of the following as the court thinks fit, that is to say—

(a) provision setting aside the whole or part of any obligation created by the transaction;

(b) provision otherwise varying the terms of the transaction or varying the terms on which any security for the purposes of the transaction is held;

(c) provision requiring any person who is or was party to the transaction to pay to the trustee any sums paid to that person, by virtue of the transaction, by the bankrupt;

(d) provision requiring any person to surrender to the trustee any property held by him as security for the purposes of the transaction;

(e) provision directing accounts to be taken between any persons.

(5) Any sums or property required to be paid or surrendered to the trustee in accordance with an order under this section shall be comprised in the bankrupt's estate.

(6) *Neither the trustee of a bankrupt's estate nor an undischarged bankrupt is entitled to make an application under section 139(1)(a) of the Consumer Credit Act 1974 (re-opening of extortionate credit agreements) for any agreement by which credit is or has been provided to the bankrupt to be re-opened.*

But the powers conferred by this section are exercisable in relation to any transaction concurrently with any powers exercisable under this Act in relation to that transaction as a transaction at an undervalue.

NOTES

This section derived from the Insolvency Act 1985, s 176.

Sub-s (1): word in square brackets substituted for original word "adjudged" by the Enterprise and Regulatory Reform Act 2013, s 71(3), Sch 19, paras 1, 36, in respect of a petition for a bankruptcy order presented to the court by a debtor on or after 6 April 2016.

Sub-s (6): words in italics repealed by the Consumer Credit Act 2006, s 70, Sch 4, as from 6 April 2007, subject to transitional provisions and savings in Sch 3, para 15(1), (5)(g) to the 2006 Act, which provides as follows:

"15.

(1) The repeal by this Act of sections 137 to 140 of the 1974 Act shall not affect the court's power to reopen an existing agreement under those sections as set out in this paragraph.

(5) The repeal or revocation by this Act of the following provisions has no effect in relation to existing agreements so far as they may be reopened as set out in this paragraph—

(g) in section 343(6) of the Insolvency Act 1986 (c 45), the words from the beginning to "But";".

[1.422]

344 Avoidance of general assignment of book debts

(1) The following applies where a person engaged in any business makes a general assignment to another person of his existing or future book debts, or any class of them, and is subsequently [made] bankrupt.

(2) The assignment is void against the trustee of the bankrupt's estate as regards book debts which were not paid before the [making of the bankruptcy application or (as the case may be) the] presentation of the bankruptcy petition, unless the assignment has been registered under the Bills of Sale Act 1878.

(3) For the purposes of subsections (1) and (2)—

(a) "assignment" includes an assignment by way of security or charge on book debts, and

(b) "general assignment" does not include—

(i) an assignment of book debts due at the date of the assignment from specified debtors or of debts becoming due under specified contracts, or

(ii) an assignment of book debts included either in a transfer of a business made in good faith and for value or in an assignment of assets for the benefit of creditors generally.

(4) For the purposes of registration under the Act of 1878 an assignment of book debts is to be treated as if it were a bill of sale given otherwise than by way of security for the payment of a sum of money; and the provisions of that Act with respect to the registration of bills of sale apply accordingly with such necessary modifications as may be made by rules under that Act.

NOTES

This section derived from the Insolvency Act 1985, s 177.

Sub-s (1): word in square brackets substituted for original word "adjudged" by the Enterprise and Regulatory Reform Act 2013, s 71(3), Sch 19, paras 1, 37(1), (2), in respect of a petition for a bankruptcy order presented to the court by a debtor on or after 6 April 2016.

Sub-s (2): words in square brackets inserted by the Enterprise and Regulatory Reform Act 2013, s 71(3), Sch 19, paras 1, 37(1), (3), in respect of a petition for a bankruptcy order presented to the court by a debtor on or after 6 April 2016.

[1.423]
345 Contracts to which bankrupt is a party
(1) The following applies where a contract has been made with a person who is subsequently [made] bankrupt.
(2) The court may, on the application of any other party to the contract, make an order discharging obligations under the contract on such terms as to payment by the applicant or the bankrupt of damages for non-performance or otherwise as appear to the court to be equitable.
(3) Any damages payable by the bankrupt by virtue of an order of the court under this section are provable as a bankruptcy debt.
(4) Where an undischarged bankrupt is a contractor in respect of any contract jointly with any person, that person may sue or be sued in respect of the contract without the joinder of the bankrupt.

NOTES

This section derived from the Insolvency Act 1985, s 178.

Sub-s (1): word in square brackets substituted for original word "adjudged" by the Enterprise and Regulatory Reform Act 2013, s 71(3), Sch 19, paras 1, 38, in respect of a petition for a bankruptcy order presented to the court by a debtor on or after 6 April 2016.

Disapplication in relation to market contracts: see the note to s 178 at **[1.182]**.

[1.424]
346 Enforcement procedures
(1) Subject to section 285 in Chapter II (restrictions on proceedings and remedies) and to the following provisions of this section, where the creditor of any person who is [made] bankrupt has, before the commencement of the bankruptcy—
(a) issued execution against the goods or land of that person, or
(b) attached a debt due to that person from another person,
that creditor is not entitled, as against the official receiver or trustee of the bankrupt's estate, to retain the benefit of the execution or attachment, or any sums paid to avoid it, unless the execution or attachment was completed, or the sums were paid, before the commencement of the bankruptcy.
[(1A) For the purposes of this section, Her Majesty's Revenue and Customs is to be regarded as having attached a debt due to a person if it has taken action under Part 1 of Schedule 8 to the Finance (No 2) Act 2015 (enforcement by deduction from accounts) as a result of which an amount standing to the credit of an account held by that person is—
(a) subject to arrangements made under paragraph 6(3) of that Schedule, or
(b) the subject of a deduction notice under paragraph 13 of that Schedule.]
(2) Subject as follows, where any goods of a person have been taken in execution, then, if before the completion of the execution notice is given to the [enforcement officer] or other officer charged with the execution that that person has been [made] bankrupt—
(a) the [enforcement officer] or other officer shall on request deliver to the official receiver or trustee of the bankrupt's estate the goods and any money seized or recovered in part satisfaction of the execution, but
(b) the costs of the execution are a first charge on the goods or money so delivered and the official receiver or trustee may sell the goods or a sufficient part of them for the purpose of satisfying the charge.
(3) Subject to subsection (6) below, where—
(a) under an execution in respect of a judgment for a sum exceeding such sum as may be prescribed for the purposes of this subsection, the goods of any person are sold or money is paid in order to avoid a sale, and
(b) before the end of the period of 14 days beginning with the day of the sale or payment the [enforcement officer] or other officer charged with the execution is given notice that a [bankruptcy application has been made or a] bankruptcy petition has been presented in relation to that person, and
(c) a bankruptcy order is or has been made [as a result of that application or] on that petition,
the balance of the proceeds of sale or money paid, after deducting the costs of execution, shall (in priority to the claim of the execution creditor) be comprised in the bankrupt's estate.
(4) Accordingly, in the case of an execution in respect of a judgment for a sum exceeding the sum prescribed for the purposes of subsection (3), the [enforcement officer] or other officer charged with the execution—
(a) shall not dispose of the balance mentioned in subsection (3) at any time within the period of 14 days so mentioned or while [proceedings on a bankruptcy application are ongoing or (as the case may be)] there is pending a bankruptcy petition of which he has been given notice under that subsection, and
(b) shall pay that balance, where by virtue of that subsection it is comprised in the bankrupt's estate, to the official receiver or (if there is one) to the trustee of that estate.
(5) For the purposes of this section—
(a) an execution against goods is completed by seizure and sale or by the making of a charging order under section 1 of the Charging Orders Act 1979;
(b) an execution against land is completed by seizure, by the appointment of a receiver or by the making of a charging order under that section;
(c) an attachment of a debt is completed by the receipt of the debt.
(6) The rights conferred by subsections (1) to (3) on the official receiver or the trustee may, to such extent and on such terms as it thinks fit, be set aside by the court in favour of the creditor who has issued the execution or attached the debt.

(7) Nothing in this section entitles the trustee of a bankrupt's estate to claim goods from a person who has acquired them in good faith under a sale by [an enforcement officer] or other officer charged with an execution.

(8) Neither subsection (2) nor subsection (3) applies in relation to any execution against property which has been acquired by or has devolved upon the bankrupt since the commencement of the bankruptcy, unless, at the time the execution is issued or before it is completed—

(a) the property has been or is claimed for the bankrupt's estate under section 307 (after-acquired property), and

(b) a copy of the notice given under that section has been or is served on the [enforcement officer] or other officer charged with the execution.

[(9) In this section "enforcement officer" means an individual who is authorised to act as an enforcement officer under the Courts Act 2003.]

NOTES

This section derived from the Insolvency Act 1985, s 179.

Sub-s (1): word in square brackets substituted for original word "adjudged" by the Enterprise and Regulatory Reform Act 2013, s 71(3), Sch 19, paras 1, 39(1), (2), in respect of a petition for a bankruptcy order presented to the court by a debtor on or after 6 April 2016.

Sub-s (1A): inserted by the Finance (No 2) Act 2015, s 51, Sch 8, Pt 2, paras 26, 32.

Sub-s (2): words in first and third pairs of square brackets substituted by the Courts Act 2003, s 109(1), Sch 8, para 297(1), (2); word in second pair of square brackets substituted for original word "adjudged" by the Enterprise and Regulatory Reform Act 2013, s 71(3), Sch 19, paras 1, 39(1), (2), in respect of a petition for a bankruptcy order presented to the court by a debtor on or after 6 April 2016.

Sub-s (3): words in first pair of square brackets in para (b) substituted by the Courts Act 2003, s 109(1), Sch 8, para 297(1), (2); words in second pair of square brackets in para (b) and words in square brackets in para (c) inserted by the Enterprise and Regulatory Reform Act 2013, s 71(3), Sch 19, paras 1, 39(1), (3), in respect of a petition for a bankruptcy order presented to the court by a debtor on or after 6 April 2016.

Sub-s (4): words in first pair of square brackets substituted by the Courts Act 2003, s 109(1), Sch 8, para 297(1), (2); words in square brackets in para (a) inserted by the Enterprise and Regulatory Reform Act 2013, s 71(3), Sch 19, paras 1, 39(1), (4), in respect of a petition for a bankruptcy order presented to the court by a debtor on or after 6 April 2016.

Sub-ss (7), (8): words in square brackets substituted by the Courts Act 2003, s 109(1), Sch 8, para 297(1)–(3).

Sub-s (9): added by the Courts Act 2003, s 109(1), Sch 8, para 297(1), (4).

See further: the Insolvency Proceedings (Monetary Limits) Order 1986, SI 1986/1996, art 3, Schedule, Pt II at **[8.3]**, **[8.6]** which specifies £1,000 as the prescribed sum.

[1.425]

347 Distress, etc

(1) [CRAR (the power of commercial rent arrears recovery under section 72(1) of the Tribunals, Courts and Enforcement Act 2007) is exercisable where the tenant is an undischarged bankrupt] (subject to [sections 252(2)(b) and 254(1) above and] subsection (5) below) against goods and effects comprised in the bankrupt's estate, but only for 6 months' rent accrued due before the commencement of the bankruptcy.

(2) [Where CRAR has been exercised to recover rent from] an individual to whom [a bankruptcy application or] a bankruptcy petition relates and a bankruptcy order is subsequently made [as a result of that application or] on that petition, any amount recovered by way of [CRAR] which—

(a) is in excess of the amount which by virtue of subsection (1) would have been recoverable after the commencement of the bankruptcy, or

(b) is in respect of rent for a period or part of a period after [goods were taken control of under CRAR],

shall be held for the bankrupt as part of his estate.

[(3) Subsection (3A) applies where—

(a) any person (whether or not a landlord or person entitled to rent) has distrained upon the goods or effects of an individual who is adjudged bankrupt before the end of the period of 3 months beginning with the distraint, or

(b) Her Majesty's Revenue and Customs has been paid any amount from an account of an individual under Part 1 of Schedule 8 to the Finance (No 2) Act 2015 (enforcement by deduction from accounts) and the individual is adjudged bankrupt before the end of the period of 3 months beginning with the payment.

(3A) Where this subsection applies—

(a) in a case within subsection (3)(a), the goods or effects, or the proceeds of their sale, and

(b) in a case within subsection (3)(b), the amount in question,

is charged for the benefit of the bankrupt's estate with the preferential debts of the bankrupt to the extent that the bankrupt's estate is for the time being insufficient for meeting them.]

(4) Where by virtue of any charge under subsection [(3A)] any person surrenders any goods or effects to the trustee of a bankrupt's estate or makes a payment to such a trustee, that person ranks, in respect of the amount of the proceeds of the sale of those goods or effects by the trustee or, as the case may be, the amount of the payment, as a preferential creditor of the bankrupt, except as against so much of the bankrupt's estate as is available for the payment of preferential creditors by virtue of the surrender or payment.

(5) [CRAR is not exercisable at any time after the discharge of a bankrupt against] any goods or effects comprised in the bankrupt's estate.

(6) . . .

(7) . . .

But this subsection is without prejudice to the liability of the landlord.

(8) [Subject to sections 252(2)(b) and 254(1) above] nothing in this Group of Parts affects any right to distrain otherwise than for rent; and any such right is at any time exercisable without restriction against property comprised in a bankrupt's estate, even if that right is expressed by any enactment to be exercisable in like manner as a right to distrain for rent.
(9) Any right to distrain against property comprised in a bankrupt's estate is exercisable notwithstanding that the property has vested in the trustee.
(10) The provisions of this section are without prejudice to a landlord's right in a bankruptcy to prove for any bankruptcy debt in respect of rent.
[(11) . . .]

NOTES

This section derived from the Insolvency Act 1985, s 180.

Sub-s (1): words in first pair of square brackets substituted by the Tribunals, Courts and Enforcement Act 2007, s 86, Sch 14, para 44(1), (2); words in second pair of square brackets inserted by the Insolvency Act 2000, s 3, Sch 3, paras 1, 14(a), subject to transitional provisions in SI 2002/2711, art 4 at **[2.7]**.

Sub-s (2): words in first and fourth pairs of square brackets and words in square brackets in para (b) substituted, by the Tribunals, Courts and Enforcement Act 2007, s 86, Sch 14, para 44(1), (3); words in second and third pairs of square brackets inserted by the Enterprise and Regulatory Reform Act 2013, s 71(3), Sch 19, paras 1, 40(1), (2), in respect of a petition for a bankruptcy order presented to the court by a debtor on or after 6 April 2016.

Sub-ss (3), (3A): substituted, for original sub-s (3), by the Finance (No 2) Act 2015, s 51, Sch 8, Pt 2, paras 26, 33(1)(a).

Sub-s (4): reference in square brackets substituted by the Finance (No 2) Act 2015, s 51, Sch 8, Pt 2, paras 26, 33(1)(b).

Sub-s (5): words in square brackets substituted by the Tribunals, Courts and Enforcement Act 2007, s 86, Sch 14, para 44(1), (4).

Sub-ss (6), (7): repealed by the Tribunals, Courts and Enforcement Act 2007, ss 86, 146, Sch 14, para 44(1), (5), Sch 23, Pt 4.

Sub-s (8): words in square brackets inserted by the Insolvency Act 2000, s 3, Sch 3, paras 1, 14(b), subject to transitional provisions in SI 2002/2711, art 4 at **[2.7]**.

Sub-s (11): added by the Courts Act 2003, s 109(1), Sch 8, para 298(1), (4); repealed by the Tribunals, Courts and Enforcement Act 2007, ss 86, 146, Sch 14, para 44(1), (6), Sch 23, Pt 4.

[1.426]
348 Apprenticeships, etc
(1) This section applies where—
  (a) a bankruptcy order is made in respect of an individual to whom another individual was an apprentice or articled clerk at the time when the [application for the order was made or (as the case may be) the petition for the order] was presented, and
  (b) the bankrupt or the apprentice or clerk gives notice to the trustee terminating the apprenticeship or articles.

(2) Subject to subsection (6) below, the indenture of apprenticeship or, as the case may be, the articles of agreement shall be discharged with effect from the commencement of the bankruptcy.
(3) If any money has been paid by or on behalf of the apprentice or clerk to the bankrupt as a fee, the trustee may, on an application made by or on behalf of the apprentice or clerk, pay such sum to the apprentice or clerk as the trustee thinks reasonable, having regard to—
  (a) the amount of the fee,
  (b) the proportion of the period in respect of which the fee was paid that has been served by the apprentice or clerk before the commencement of the bankruptcy, and
  (c) the other circumstances of the case.

(4) The power of the trustee to make a payment under subsection (3) has priority over his obligation to distribute the bankrupt's estate.
(5) Instead of making a payment under subsection (3), the trustee may, if it appears to him expedient to do so on an application made by or on behalf of the apprentice or clerk, transfer the indenture or articles to a person other than the bankrupt.
(6) Where a transfer is made under subsection (5), subsection (2) has effect only as between the apprentice or clerk and the bankrupt.

NOTES

This section derived from the Insolvency Act 1985, s 181.

Sub-s (1): words in square brackets in para (a) substituted for original words "petition on which the order was made" by the Enterprise and Regulatory Reform Act 2013, s 71(3), Sch 19, paras 1, 41, in respect of a petition for a bankruptcy order presented to the court by a debtor on or after 6 April 2016.

Transfer to Secretary of State of rights and remedies on employer's insolvency: see the note to s 175 at **[1.176]**.

[1.427]
349 Unenforceability of liens on books, etc
(1) Subject as follows, a lien or other right to retain possession of any of the books, papers or other records of a bankrupt is unenforceable to the extent that its enforcement would deny possession of any books, papers or other records to the official receiver or the trustee of the bankrupt's estate.
(2) Subsection (1) does not apply to a lien on documents which give a title to property and are held as such.

NOTES

This section derived from the Insolvency Act 1985, s 182.

[1.428]

[349A Arbitration agreements to which bankrupt is party

(1) This section applies where a bankrupt had become party to a contract containing an arbitration agreement before the commencement of his bankruptcy.

(2) If the trustee in bankruptcy adopts the contract, the arbitration agreement is enforceable by or against the trustee in relation to matters arising from or connected with the contract.

(3) If the trustee in bankruptcy does not adopt the contract and a matter to which the arbitration agreement applies requires to be determined in connection with or for the purposes of the bankruptcy proceedings—

(a) the trustee with the consent of the creditors' committee, or

(b) any other party to the agreement,

may apply to the court which may, if it thinks fit in all the circumstances of the case, order that the matter be referred to arbitration in accordance with the arbitration agreement.

(4) In this section—

"arbitration agreement" has the same meaning as in Part I of the Arbitration Act 1996; and

"the court" means the court which has jurisdiction in the bankruptcy proceedings.]

NOTES

Inserted by the Arbitration Act 1996, s 107(1), Sch 3, para 46.

CHAPTER VI
BANKRUPTCY OFFENCES

Preliminary

[1.429]

350 Scheme of this Chapter

(1) Subject to section 360(3) below, this Chapter applies[—

(a) where an adjudicator has made a bankruptcy order as a result of a bankruptcy application, or

(b)] where the court has made a bankruptcy order on a bankruptcy petition.

(2) This Chapter applies whether or not the bankruptcy order is annulled, but proceedings for an offence under this Chapter shall not be instituted after the annulment.

(3) Without prejudice to his liability in respect of a subsequent bankruptcy, the bankrupt is not guilty of an offence under this Chapter in respect of anything done after his discharge; but nothing in this Group of Parts prevents the institution of proceedings against a discharged bankrupt for an offence committed before his discharge.

[(3A) Subsection (3) is without prejudice to any provision of this Chapter which applies to a person in respect of whom a bankruptcy restrictions order is in force.]

(4) It is not a defence in proceedings for an offence under this Chapter that anything relied on, in whole or in part, as constituting that offence was done outside England and Wales.

(5) Proceedings for an offence under this Chapter or under the rules shall not be instituted except by the Secretary of State or by or with the consent of the Director of Public Prosecutions.

(6) A person guilty of an offence under this Chapter is liable to imprisonment or a fine, or both.

NOTES

This section derived from the Insolvency Act 1985, ss 183(1)–(3), (5), (6), 192 (in part).

Sub-s (1): words in square brackets inserted by the Enterprise and Regulatory Reform Act 2013, s 71(3), Sch 19, paras 1, 42, in respect of a petition for a bankruptcy order presented to the court by a debtor on or after 6 April 2016.

Sub-s (3A): inserted by the Enterprise Act 2002, s 257(3), Sch 21, para 2, subject to transitional provisions in s 256(2) of, and Sch 19 to, that Act at **[2.13]**, **[2.22]**.

[1.430]

351 Definitions

In the following provisions of this Chapter—

(a) references to property comprised in the bankrupt's estate or to property possession of which is required to be delivered up to the official receiver or the trustee of the bankrupt's estate include any property which would be such property if a notice in respect of it were given under section 307 (after-acquired property)[, section 308] (personal property and effects of bankrupt having more than replacement value) [or section 308A (vesting in trustee of certain tenancies)];

(b) "the initial period" means the period between the [making of the bankruptcy application or (as the case may be) the] presentation of the bankruptcy petition and the commencement of the bankruptcy; *and*

(c) a reference to a number of months or years before petition is to that period ending with the presentation of the bankruptcy petition.

NOTES

This section derived from the Insolvency Act 1985, ss 184(3), (4)(a), (5), 185(2)(a), (d), (3)(b), 186(2)(c), 187(2)(b), (3)(a), 188(1), (2), 190(1), 191(1).

Words in first pair of square brackets in para (a) substituted, and words in second pair of square brackets in para (a) inserted, by the Housing Act 1988, s 140, Sch 17, Pt I, para 75; words in square brackets in para (b) inserted, and para (c) and word immediately preceding it repealed, by the Enterprise and Regulatory Reform Act 2013, s 71(3), Sch 19, paras 1, 43, in respect of a petition for a bankruptcy order presented to the court by a debtor on or after 6 April 2016.

[1.431]

352 Defence of innocent intention

Where in the case of an offence under any provision of this Chapter it is stated that this section applies, a person is not guilty of the offence if he proves that, at the time of the conduct constituting the offence, he had no intent to defraud or to conceal the state of his affairs.

NOTES

This section derived from the Insolvency Act 1985, s 183(4).

Wrongdoing by the bankrupt before and after bankruptcy

[1.432]

353 Non-disclosure

(1) The bankrupt is guilty of an offence if—

(a) he does not to the best of his knowledge and belief disclose all the property comprised in his estate to the official receiver or the trustee, or

(b) he does not inform the official receiver or the trustee of any disposal of any property which but for the disposal would be so comprised, stating how, when, to whom and for what consideration the property was disposed of.

(2) Subsection (1)(b) does not apply to any disposal in the ordinary course of a business carried on by the bankrupt or to any payment of the ordinary expenses of the bankrupt or his family.

(3) Section 352 applies to this offence.

NOTES

This section derived from the Insolvency Act 1985, ss 183(4), 184(1).

[1.433]

354 Concealment of property

(1) The bankrupt is guilty of an offence if—

(a) he does not deliver up possession to the official receiver or trustee, or as the official receiver or trustee may direct, of such part of the property comprised in his estate as is in his possession or under his control and possession of which he is required by law so to deliver up,

(b) he conceals any debt due to or from him or conceals any property the value of which is not less than the prescribed amount and possession of which he is required to deliver up to the official receiver or trustee, or

(c) in the 12 months before [the making of the bankruptcy application or (as the case may be) the presentation of the bankruptcy] petition, or in the initial period, he did anything which would have been an offence under paragraph (b) above if the bankruptcy order had been made immediately before he did it.

Section 352 applies to this offence.

(2) The bankrupt is guilty of an offence if he removes, or in the initial period removed, any property the value of which was not less than the prescribed amount and possession of which he has or would have been required to deliver up to the official receiver or the trustee.

Section 352 applies to this offence.

(3) The bankrupt is guilty of an offence if he without reasonable excuse fails, on being required to do so by the official receiver[, the trustee] or the court—

(a) to account for the loss of any substantial part of his property incurred in the 12 months before [the making of the bankruptcy application or (as the case may be) the presentation of the bankruptcy] petition or in the initial period, or

(b) to give a satisfactory explanation of the manner in which such a loss was incurred.

NOTES

This section derived from the Insolvency Act 1985, ss 183(4), 184(2)–(4).

Sub-s (1): words in square brackets inserted by the Enterprise and Regulatory Reform Act 2013, s 71(3), Sch 19, paras 1, 44(1), (2), in respect of a petition for a bankruptcy order presented to the court by a debtor on or after 6 April 2016.

Sub-s (3): words in first pair of square brackets inserted by the Enterprise Act 2002, s 269, Sch 23, paras 1, 12, subject to transitional provisions in s 256(2) of, and Sch 19 to, that Act at **[2.13]**, **[2.22]**; words in square brackets in para (a) inserted by the Enterprise and Regulatory Reform Act 2013, s 71(3), Sch 19, paras 1, 44(1), (3), in respect of a petition for a bankruptcy order presented to the court by a debtor on or after 6 April 2016.

Prescribed amount: see the Insolvency Proceedings (Monetary Limits) Order 1986, SI 1986/1996, art 3, Schedule, Pt II at **[8.3]**, **[8.6]** which specifies £1,000 as the prescribed amount for the purposes of sub-ss (1), (2).

[1.434]

355 Concealment of books and papers; falsification

(1) The bankrupt is guilty of an offence if he does not deliver up possession to the official receiver or the trustee, or as the official receiver or trustee may direct, of all books, papers and other records of which he has possession or control and which relate to his estate or his affairs.

Section 352 applies to this offence.

(2) The bankrupt is guilty of an offence if—

(a) he prevents, or in the initial period prevented, the production of any books, papers or records relating to his estate or affairs;

(b) he conceals, destroys, mutilates or falsifies, or causes or permits the concealment, destruction, mutilation or falsification of, any books, papers or other records relating to his estate or affairs;

(c) he makes, or causes or permits the making of, any false entries in any book, document or record relating to his estate or affairs; or

(d) in the 12 months before [the making of the bankruptcy application or (as the case may be) the presentation of the bankruptcy] petition, or in the initial period, he did anything which would have been an offence under paragraph (b) or (c) above if the bankruptcy order had been made before he did it.

Section 352 applies to this offence.

(3) The bankrupt is guilty of an offence if—

(a) he disposes of, or alters or makes any omission in, or causes or permits the disposal, altering or making of any omission in, any book, document or record relating to his estate or affairs, or

(b) in the 12 months before [the making of the bankruptcy application or (as the case may be) the presentation of the bankruptcy] petition, or in the initial period, he did anything which would have been an offence under paragraph (a) if the bankruptcy order had been made before he did it.

Section 352 applies to this offence.

[(4) In their application to a trading record subsections (2)(d) and (3)(b) shall have effect as if the reference to 12 months were a reference to two years.

(5) In subsection (4) "trading record" means a book, document or record which shows or explains the transactions or financial position of a person's business, including—

(a) a periodic record of cash paid and received,

(b) a statement of periodic stock-taking, and

(c) except in the case of goods sold by way of retail trade, a record of goods sold and purchased which identifies the buyer and seller or enables them to be identified.]

NOTES

This section derived from the Insolvency Act 1985, ss 183(4), 185.

Sub-ss (2), (3): words in square brackets inserted by the Enterprise and Regulatory Reform Act 2013, s 71(3), Sch 19, paras 1, 45, in respect of a petition for a bankruptcy order presented to the court by a debtor on or after 6 April 2016.

Sub-ss (4), (5): added by the Enterprise Act 2002, s 269, Sch 23, paras 1, 13, subject to transitional provisions in s 256(2) of, and Sch 19 to, that Act at **[2.13]**, **[2.22]**.

[1.435]

356 False statements

(1) The bankrupt is guilty of an offence if he makes or has made any material omission in any statement made under any provision in this Group of Parts and relating to his affairs.

Section 352 applies to this offence.

(2) The bankrupt is guilty of an offence if—

(a) knowing or believing that a false debt has been proved by any person under the bankruptcy, he fails to inform the trustee as soon as practicable; or

(b) he attempts to account for any part of his property by fictitious losses or expenses; or

(c) [in connection with any creditors' decision procedure or deemed consent procedure] in the 12 months before [the making of the bankruptcy application or (as the case may be) the presentation of the bankruptcy] petition or (whether or not [in connection with such a procedure]) at any time in the initial period, he did anything which would have been an offence under paragraph (b) if the bankruptcy order had been made before he did it; or

(d) he is, or at any time has been, guilty of any false representation or other fraud for the purpose of obtaining the consent of his creditors, or any of them, to an agreement with reference to his affairs or to his bankruptcy.

NOTES

This section derived from the Insolvency Act 1985, ss 183(4), 186.

Sub-s (2): words in first and third pairs of square brackets substituted for original words "at any meeting of his creditors" and "at such a meeting" respectively, by the Small Business, Enterprise and Employment Act 2015, s 126, Sch 9, Pt 2, paras 60, 85, as from 6 April 2017 (subject to transitional and savings provisions as noted to s 246ZE at **[1.256]**); words in second pair of square brackets inserted by the Enterprise and Regulatory Reform Act 2013, s 71(3), Sch 19, paras 1, 46, in respect of a petition for a bankruptcy order presented to the court by a debtor on or after 6 April 2016.

[1.436]

357 Fraudulent disposal of property

(1) The bankrupt is guilty of an offence if he makes or causes to be made, or has in the period of 5 years ending with the commencement of the bankruptcy made or caused to be made, any gift or transfer of, or any charge on, his property.

Section 352 applies to this offence.

(2) The reference to making a transfer of or charge on any property includes causing or conniving at the levying of any execution against that property.

(3) The bankrupt is guilty of an offence if he conceals or removes, or has at any time before the commencement of the bankruptcy concealed or removed, any part of his property after, or within 2 months before, the date on which a judgment or order for the payment of money has been obtained against him, being a judgment or order which was not satisfied before the commencement of the bankruptcy.

Section 352 applies to this offence.

NOTES

This section derived from the Insolvency Act 1985, ss 183(4), 187(1), (3)(b).

[1.437]

358 Absconding

The bankrupt is guilty of an offence if—

(a) he leaves, or attempts or makes preparations to leave, England and Wales with any property the value of which is not less than the prescribed amount and possession of which he is required to deliver up to the official receiver or the trustee, or

(b) in the 6 months before [the making of the bankruptcy application or (as the case may be) the presentation of the bankruptcy] petition, or in the initial period, he did anything which would have been an offence under paragraph (a) if the bankruptcy order had been made immediately before he did it.

Section 352 applies to this offence.

NOTES

This section derived from the Insolvency Act 1985, ss 183(4), 187(2).

Words in square brackets in para (b) inserted by the Enterprise and Regulatory Reform Act 2013, s 71(3), Sch 19, paras 1, 47, in respect of a petition for a bankruptcy order presented to the court by a debtor on or after 6 April 2016.

Prescribed amount: see the Insolvency Proceedings (Monetary Limits) Order 1986, SI 1986/1996, art 3, Schedule, Pt II at **[8.3]**, **[8.6]** which specifies £1,000 as the prescribed amount for the purposes of this section.

[1.438]

359 Fraudulent dealing with property obtained on credit

(1) The bankrupt is guilty of an offence if, in the 12 months before [the making of the bankruptcy application or (as the case may be) the presentation of the bankruptcy] petition, or in the initial period, he disposed of any property which he had obtained on credit and, at the time he disposed of it, had not paid for.

Section 352 applies to this offence.

(2) A person is guilty of an offence if, in the 12 months before [the making of the bankruptcy application or (as the case may be) the presentation of the bankruptcy] petition or in the initial period, he acquired or received property from the bankrupt knowing or believing—

(a) that the bankrupt owed money in respect of the property, and

(b) that the bankrupt did not intend, or was unlikely to be able, to pay the money he so owed.

(3) A person is not guilty of an offence under subsection (1) or (2) if the disposal, acquisition or receipt of the property was in the ordinary course of a business carried on by the bankrupt at the time of the disposal, acquisition or receipt.

(4) In determining for the purposes of this section whether any property is disposed of, acquired or received in the ordinary course of a business carried on by the bankrupt, regard may be had, in particular, to the price paid for the property.

(5) In this section references to disposing of property include pawning or pledging it; and references to acquiring or receiving property shall be read accordingly.

NOTES

This section derived from the Insolvency Act 1985, ss 183(4), 188.

Sub-ss (1), (2): words in square brackets inserted by the Enterprise and Regulatory Reform Act 2013, s 71(3), Sch 19, paras 1, 48, in respect of a petition for a bankruptcy order presented to the court by a debtor on or after 6 April 2016.

[1.439]

360 Obtaining credit; engaging in business

(1) The bankrupt is guilty of an offence if—

(a) either alone or jointly with any other person, he obtains credit to the extent of the prescribed amount or more without giving the person from whom he obtains it the relevant information about his status; or

(b) he engages (whether directly or indirectly) in any business under a name other than that in which he was [made] bankrupt without disclosing to all persons with whom he enters into any business transaction the name in which he was so [made].

(2) The reference to the bankrupt obtaining credit includes the following cases—

(a) where goods are bailed to him under a hire-purchase agreement, or agreed to be sold to him under a conditional sale agreement, and

(b) where he is paid in advance (whether in money or otherwise) for the supply of goods or services.

(3) A person whose estate has been sequestrated in Scotland, or who has been adjudged bankrupt in Northern Ireland, is guilty of an offence if, before his discharge, he does anything in England and Wales which would be an offence under subsection (1) if he were an undischarged bankrupt and the sequestration of his estate or the adjudication in Northern Ireland were an adjudication under this Part.

(4) For the purposes of subsection (1)(a), the relevant information about the status of the person in question is the information that he is an undischarged bankrupt or, as the case may be, that his estate has been sequestrated in Scotland and that he has not been discharged.

[(5) This section applies to the bankrupt after discharge while a bankruptcy restrictions order is in force in respect of him.

(6) For the purposes of subsection (1)(a) as it applies by virtue of subsection (5), the relevant information about the status of the person in question is the information that a bankruptcy restrictions order is in force in respect of him.]

NOTES

This section derived from the Insolvency Act 1985, s 189.

Sub-s (1): word in square brackets in both places in para (b) substituted for original word "adjudged" by the Enterprise and Regulatory Reform Act 2013, s 71(3), Sch 19, paras 1, 49, in respect of a petition for a bankruptcy order presented to the court by a debtor on or after 6 April 2016.

Sub-ss (5), (6): added by the Enterprise Act 2002, s 257(3), Sch 21, para 3, subject to transitional provisions in s 256(2) of, and Sch 19 to, that Act at **[2.13]**, **[2.22]**.

Prescribed amount: see the Insolvency Proceedings (Monetary Limits) Order 1986, SI 1986/1996, art 3, Schedule, Pt II at **[8.3]**, **[8.6]** which specifies £500 as the prescribed amount for the purposes of sub-s (1).

[1.440]

361 Failure to keep proper accounts of business

(1) Where the bankrupt has been engaged in any business for any of the period of 2 years before petition, he is guilty of an offence if he—

(a) has not kept proper accounting records throughout that period and throughout any part of the initial period in which he was so engaged, or

(b) has not preserved all the accounting records which he has kept.

(2) The bankrupt is not guilty of an offence under subsection (1)—

(a) if his unsecured liabilities at the commencement of the bankruptcy did not exceed the prescribed amount, or

(b) if he proves that in the circumstances in which he carried on business the omission was honest and excusable.

(3) For the purposes of this section a person is deemed not to have kept proper accounting records if he has not kept such records as are necessary to show or explain his transactions and financial position in his business, including—

(a) records containing entries from day to day, in sufficient detail, of all cash paid and received,

(b) where the business involved dealings in goods, statements of annual stock-takings, and

(c) except in the case of goods sold by way of retail trade to the actual customer, records of all goods sold and purchased showing the buyers and sellers in sufficient detail to enable the goods and the buyers and sellers to be identified.

(4) In relation to any such records as are mentioned in subsection (3), subsections (2)(d) and (3)(b) of section 355 apply with the substitution of 2 years for 12 months.

NOTES

This section derived from the Insolvency Act 1985, s 190.

Repealed by the Enterprise Act 2002, ss 263(a), 278(2), Sch 26, subject to transitional provisions in s 256(2) of, and Sch 19 to, that Act at **[2.13]**, **[2.22]**.

[1.441]

362 Gambling

(1) The bankrupt is guilty of an offence if he has—

(a) in the 2 years before petition, materially contributed to, or increased the extent of, his insolvency by gambling or by rash and hazardous speculations, or

(b) in the initial period, lost any part of his property by gambling or by rash and hazardous speculations.

(2) In determining for the purposes of this section whether any speculations were rash and hazardous, the financial position of the bankrupt at the time when he entered into them shall be taken into consideration.

NOTES

This section derived from the Insolvency Act 1985, s 191.

Repealed by the Enterprise Act 2002, ss 263(b), 278(2), Sch 26, subject to transitional provisions in s 256(2) of, and Sch 19 to, that Act at **[2.13]**, **[2.22]**.

CHAPTER VII
POWERS OF COURT IN BANKRUPTCY

[1.442]

363 General control of court

(1) Every bankruptcy is under the general control of the court and, subject to the provisions in this Group of Parts, the court has full power to decide all questions of priorities and all other questions, whether of law or fact, arising in any bankruptcy.

(2) Without prejudice to any other provision in this Group of Parts, an undischarged bankrupt or a discharged bankrupt whose estate is still being administered under Chapter IV of this Part shall do all such things as he may be directed to do by the court for the purposes of his bankruptcy or, as the case may be, the administration of that estate.

(3) The official receiver or the trustee of a bankrupt's estate may at any time apply to the court for a direction under subsection (2).

(4) If any person without reasonable excuse fails to comply with any obligation imposed on him by subsection (2), he is guilty of a contempt of court and liable to be punished accordingly (in addition to any other punishment to which he may be subject).

NOTES

This section derived from the Insolvency Act 1985, s 193.

[1.443]

364 Power of arrest

(1) In the cases specified in the next subsection the court may cause a warrant to be issued to a constable or prescribed officer of the court—

(a) for the arrest of a debtor to whom a [bankruptcy application or a] bankruptcy petition relates or of an undischarged bankrupt, or of a discharged bankrupt whose estate is still being administered under Chapter IV of this Part, and

(b) for the seizure of any books, papers, records, money or goods in the possession of a person arrested under the warrant,

and may authorise a person arrested under such a warrant to be kept in custody, and anything seized under such a warrant to be held, in accordance with the rules, until such time as the court may order.

(2) The powers conferred by subsection (1) are exercisable in relation to a debtor or undischarged or discharged bankrupt if, at any time after the [making of the bankruptcy application or the] presentation of the bankruptcy petition relating to him or the making of the bankruptcy order against him, it appears to the court—

(a) that there are reasonable grounds for believing that he has absconded, or is about to abscond, with a view to avoiding or delaying the payment of any of his debts or his appearance to a bankruptcy petition or to avoiding, delaying or disrupting any proceedings in bankruptcy against him or any examination of his affairs, or

(b) that he is about to remove his goods with a view to preventing or delaying possession being taken of them by the official receiver or the trustee of his estate, or

(c) that there are reasonable grounds for believing that he has concealed or destroyed, or is about to conceal or destroy, any of his goods or any books, papers or records which might be of use to his creditors in the course of his bankruptcy or in connection with the administration of his estate, or

(d) that he has, without the leave of the official receiver or the trustee of his estate, removed any goods in his possession which exceed in value such sum as may be prescribed for the purposes of this paragraph, or

(e) that he has failed, without reasonable excuse, to attend any examination ordered by the court.

NOTES

This section derived from the Insolvency Act 1985, s 194.

Sub-ss (1), (2): words in square brackets inserted by the Enterprise and Regulatory Reform Act 2013, s 71(3), Sch 19, paras 1, 50, in respect of a petition for a bankruptcy order presented to the court by a debtor on or after 6 April 2016.

Prescribed amount: see the Insolvency Proceedings (Monetary Limits) Order 1986, SI 1986/1996, art 3, Schedule, Pt II at **[8.3]**, **[8.6]** which specifies £1,000 as the prescribed amount for the purposes of sub-s (2)(d).

[1.444]

365 Seizure of bankrupt's property

(1) At any time after a bankruptcy order has been made, the court may, on the application of the official receiver or the trustee of the bankrupt's estate, issue a warrant authorising the person to whom it is directed to seize any property comprised in the bankrupt's estate which is, or any books, papers or records relating to the bankrupt's estate or affairs which are, in the possession or under the control of the bankrupt or any other person who is required to deliver the property, books, papers or records to the official receiver or trustee.

(2) Any person executing a warrant under this section may, for the purpose of seizing any property comprised in the bankrupt's estate or any books, papers or records relating to the bankrupt's estate or affairs, break open any premises where the bankrupt or anything that may be seized under the warrant is or is believed to be and any receptacle of the bankrupt which contains or is believed to contain anything that may be so seized.

(3) If, after a bankruptcy order has been made, the court is satisfied that any property comprised in the bankrupt's estate is, or any books, papers or records relating to the bankrupt's estate or affairs are, concealed in any premises not belonging to him, it may issue a warrant authorising any constable or prescribed officer of the court to search those premises for the property, books, papers or records.

(4) A warrant under subsection (3) shall not be executed except in the prescribed manner and in accordance with its terms.

NOTES

This section derived from the Insolvency Act 1985, s 195.

[1.445]

366 Inquiry into bankrupt's dealings and property

(1) At any time after a bankruptcy order has been made the court may, on the application of the official receiver or the trustee of the bankrupt's estate, summon to appear before it—

(a) the bankrupt or the bankrupt's spouse or former spouse [or civil partner or former civil partner],

(b) any person known or believed to have any property comprised in the bankrupt's estate in his possession or to be indebted to the bankrupt,
(c) any person appearing to the court to be able to give information concerning the bankrupt or the bankrupt's dealings, affairs or property.

The court may require any such person as is mentioned in paragraph (b) or (c) to submit [a witness statement verified by a statement of truth] to the court containing an account of his dealings with the bankrupt or to produce any documents in his possession or under his control relating to the bankrupt or the bankrupt's dealings, affairs or property.

(2) Without prejudice to section 364, the following applies in a case where—
(a) a person without reasonable excuse fails to appear before the court when he is summoned to do so under this section, or
(b) there are reasonable grounds for believing that a person has absconded, or is about to abscond, with a view to avoiding his appearance before the court under this section.

(3) The court may, for the purpose of bringing that person and anything in his possession before the court, cause a warrant to be issued to a constable or prescribed officer of the court—
(a) for the arrest of that person, and
(b) for the seizure of any books, papers, records, money or goods in that person's possession.

(4) The court may authorise a person arrested under such a warrant to be kept in custody, and anything seized under such a warrant to be held, in accordance with the rules, until that person is brought before the court under the warrant or until such other time as the court may order.

NOTES

This section derived from the Insolvency Act 1985, s 196(1), (2).

Sub-s (1): words in square brackets in para (a) inserted by the Civil Partnership Act 2004, s 261(1), Sch 27, para 120; words in second pair of square brackets substituted for the words "an affidavit" by the Legislative Reform (Insolvency) (Miscellaneous Provisions) Order 2010, SI 2010/18, arts 2, 5(7).

[1.446]

367 Court's enforcement powers under s 366

(1) If it appears to the court, on consideration of any evidence obtained under section 366 or this section, that any person has in his possession any property comprised in the bankrupt's estate, the court may, on the application of the official receiver or the trustee of the bankrupt's estate, order that person to deliver the whole or any part of the property to the official receiver or the trustee at such time, in such manner and on such terms as the court thinks fit.

(2) If it appears to the court, on consideration of any evidence obtained under section 366 or this section, that any person is indebted to the bankrupt, the court may, on the application of the official receiver or the trustee of the bankrupt's estate, order that person to pay to the official receiver or trustee, at such time and in such manner as the court may direct, the whole or part of the amount due, whether in full discharge of the debt or otherwise as the court thinks fit.

(3) The court may, if it thinks fit, order that any person who if within the jurisdiction of the court would be liable to be summoned to appear before it under section 366 shall be examined in any part of the United Kingdom where he may be for the time being, or in any place outside the United Kingdom.

(4) Any person who appears or is brought before the court under section 366 or this section may be examined on oath, either orally or by interrogatories, concerning the bankrupt or the bankrupt's dealings, affairs and property.

NOTES

This section derived from the Insolvency Act 1985, s 196(3)–(6).

[1.447]

368 Provision corresponding to s 366, where interim receiver appointed

Sections 366 and 367 apply where an interim receiver has been appointed under section 286 as they apply where a bankruptcy order has been made, as if—
(a) references to the official receiver or the trustee were to the interim receiver, and
(b) references to the bankrupt and to his estate were (respectively) to the debtor and his property.

NOTES

This section derived from the Insolvency Act 1985, s 196(7).

[1.448]

369 Order for production of documents by inland revenue

(1) For the purposes of an examination under section 290 (public examination of bankrupt) or proceedings under sections 366 to 368, the court may, on the application of the official receiver or the trustee of the bankrupt's estate, order an inland revenue official to produce to the court—
(a) any return, account or accounts submitted (whether before or after the commencement of the bankruptcy) by the bankrupt to any inland revenue official,
(b) any assessment or determination made (whether before or after the commencement of the bankruptcy) in relation to the bankrupt by any inland revenue official, or
(c) any correspondence (whether before or after the commencement of the bankruptcy) between the bankrupt and any inland revenue official.

(2) Where the court has made an order under subsection (1) for the purposes of any examination or proceedings, the court may, at any time after the document to which the order relates is produced to it, by order authorise the disclosure of the document, or of any part of its contents, to the official receiver, the trustee of the bankrupt's estate or the bankrupt's creditors.

(3) The court shall not address an order under subsection (1) to an inland revenue official unless it is satisfied that that official is dealing, or has dealt, with the affairs of the bankrupt.

(4) Where any document to which an order under subsection (1) relates is not in the possession of the official to whom the order is addressed, it is the duty of that official to take all reasonable steps to secure possession of it and, if he fails to do so, to report the reasons for his failure to the court.

(5) Where any document to which an order under subsection (1) relates is in the possession of an inland revenue official other than the one to whom the order is addressed, it is the duty of the official in possession of the document, at the request of the official to whom the order is addressed, to deliver it to the official making the request.

(6) In this section "inland revenue official" means any inspector or collector of taxes appointed by the Commissioners of Inland Revenue or any person appointed by the Commissioners to serve in any other capacity.

(7) This section does not apply for the purposes of an examination under sections 366 and 367 which takes place by virtue of section 368 (interim receiver).

NOTES

This section derived from the Insolvency Act 1985, s 197.

[1.449]

370 Power to appoint special manager

(1) The court may, on an application under this section, appoint any person to be the special manager—

(a) of a bankrupt's estate, or

(b) of the business of an undischarged bankrupt, or

(c) of the property or business of a debtor in whose case [an interim receiver has been appointed] under section 286.

(2) An application under this section may be made by the [interim receiver] or the trustee of the bankrupt's estate in any case where it appears to the [interim receiver] or trustee that the nature of the estate, property or business, or the interests of the creditors generally, require the appointment of another person to manage the estate, property or business.

(3) A special manager appointed under this section has such powers as may be entrusted to him by the court.

(4) The power of the court under subsection (3) to entrust powers to a special manager includes power to direct that any provision in this Group of Parts that has effect in relation to the official receiver, interim receiver or trustee shall have the like effect in relation to the special manager for the purposes of the carrying out by the special manager of any of the functions of the official receiver, interim receiver or trustee.

(5) A special manager appointed under this section shall—

(a) give such security as may be prescribed,

(b) prepare and keep such accounts as may be prescribed, and

(c) produce those accounts in accordance with the rules to the Secretary of State or to such other persons as may be prescribed.

NOTES

This section derived from the Insolvency Act 1985, s 198.

Sub-s (1): words in square brackets in para (c) substituted by the Deregulation Act 2015, s 19, Sch 6, Pt 5, paras 12, 14(1), (2).

Sub-s (2): words in square brackets substituted by the Deregulation Act 2015, s 19, Sch 6, Pt 5, paras 12, 14(1), (3).

[1.450]

371 Re-direction of bankrupt's letters, etc

(1) Where a bankruptcy order has been made, the court may from time to time, on the application of the official receiver or the trustee of the bankrupt's estate, order [a postal operator (within the meaning of [Part 3 of the Postal Services Act 2011])] to re-direct and send or deliver to the official receiver or trustee or otherwise any postal packet (within the meaning of [that Act]) which would otherwise be sent or delivered by [the operator concerned] to the bankrupt at such place or places as may be specified in the order.

(2) An order under this section has effect for such period, not exceeding 3 months, as may be specified in the order.

NOTES

This section derived from the Insolvency Act 1985, s 199.

Sub-s (1): words in first (outer), third and fourth pairs of square brackets substituted by the Postal Services Act 2000, s 127(4), Sch 8, Pt II, para 20; words in second (inner) pair of square brackets substituted by the Postal Services Act 2011, s 91(1), (2), Sch 12, Pt 3, paras 124, 125.

PART X INDIVIDUAL INSOLVENCY: GENERAL PROVISIONS

[1.451]

372 Supplies of gas, water, electricity, etc

(1) This section applies where on any day ("the relevant day")—

(a) a bankruptcy order is made against an individual or an interim receiver of an individual's property is appointed, or

(b) a voluntary arrangement proposed by an individual is approved under Part VIII, *or*

(c) a deed of arrangement is made for the benefit of an individual's creditors;

and in this section "the office-holder" means the official receiver, the trustee in bankruptcy, the interim receiver [or the supervisor of the voluntary arrangement], as the case may be.

(2) If a request falling within the next subsection is made for the giving after the relevant day of any of the supplies mentioned in subsection (4), the supplier—

(a) may make it a condition of the giving of the supply that the office-holder personally guarantees the payment of any charges in respect of the supply, but

(b) shall not make it a condition of the giving of the supply, or do anything which has the effect of making it a condition of the giving of the supply, that any outstanding charges in respect of a supply given to the individual before the relevant day are paid.

(3) A request falls within this subsection if it is made—

(a) by or with the concurrence of the office-holder, and

(b) for the purposes of any business which is or has been carried on by the individual, by a firm or partnership of which the individual is or was a member, or by an agent or manager for the individual or for such a firm or partnership.

(4) The supplies referred to in subsection (2) are—

[(a) a supply of gas by a gas supplier within the meaning of Part I of the Gas Act 1986;]

[(aa) a supply of gas by a person within paragraph 1 of Schedule 2A to the Gas Act 1986 (supply by landlords etc);]

[(b) a supply of electricity by an electricity supplier within the meaning of Part I of the Electricity Act 1989;]

[(ba) a supply of electricity by a class of person within Class A (small suppliers) or Class B (resale) of Schedule 4 to the Electricity (Class Exemptions from the Requirement for a Licence) Order 2001 (SI 2001/3270);]

(c) a supply of water by [a water undertaker],

[(ca) a supply of water by a water supply licensee within the meaning of the Water Industry Act 1991;

(cb) a supply of water by a person who has an interest in the premises to which the supply is given;]

[(d) a supply of communications services by a provider of a public electronic communications service.]

[(e) a supply of communications services by a person who carries on a business which includes giving such supplies;

(f) a supply of goods or services mentioned in subsection (4A) by a person who carries on a business which includes giving such supplies, where the supply is for the purpose of enabling or facilitating anything to be done by electronic means.]

[(4A) The goods and services referred to in subsection (4)(f) are—

(a) point of sale terminals;

(b) computer hardware and software;

(c) information, advice and technical assistance in connection with the use of information technology;

(d) data storage and processing;

(e) website hosting.]

(5) The following applies to expressions used in subsection (4)—

(a), (b) . . .

[(c) "communications services" do not include electronic communications services to the extent that they are used to broadcast or otherwise transmit programme services (within the meaning of the Communications Act 2003).]

NOTES

This section derived from the Insolvency Act 1985, s 200.

Sub-s (1): para (c) and word preceding it repealed and words in square brackets substituted for original words ", the supervisor of the voluntary arrangement or the trustee under the deed of arrangement", by the Deregulation Act 2015, s 19, Sch 6, Pt 1, paras 2(1), (11)(d), 3, except in relation to a deed of arrangement registered under the Deeds of Arrangement Act 1914, s 5 before 1 October 2015, if, immediately before that date, the estate of the debtor who executed the deed of arrangement has not been finally wound up.

Sub-s (4): para (a) substituted by the Gas Act 1995, s 16(1), Sch 4, para 14(3); para (b) substituted by the Utilities Act 2000, s 108, Sch 6, Pt III, para 47(1), (3)(a); words in square brackets in para (c) substituted by the Water Act 1989, s 190(1), Sch 25, para 78(1); paras (aa), (ba), (ca), (cb) inserted and paras (e), (f) added, by the Insolvency (Protection of Essential Supplies) Order 2015, SI 2015/989, art 3(1), (2); para (d) substituted by the Communications Act 2003, s 406(1), Sch 17, para 82(1), (3)(a), for the purpose of enabling network and service functions and spectrum functions to be carried out during the transitional period by the Director General of Telecommunications and the Secretary of State respectively (see further s 408 of, and Sch 18 to, the 2003 Act and the Communications Act 2003 (Commencement No 1) Order 2003, SI 2003/1900); the original para (d) read as follows:

"(d) a supply of telecommunication services by a public telecommunications operator.".

Sub-s (4A): inserted by SI 2015/989, art 3(1), (3).

Sub-s (5): para (a) repealed by the Gas Act 1995, ss 16(1), 17(5), Sch 4, para 14(4), Sch 6; para (b) repealed by the Utilities Act 2000, s 108, Sch 6, Pt III, para 47(1), (3)(b), Sch 8; para (c) substituted by the Communications Act 2003, s 406(1), Sch 17, para 82(1), (3)(b), for the purpose noted to sub-s (4) above; the original para (c), as amended by the Broadcasting Act 1990, s 203(1), Sch 20, para 43, read as follows:

"(c) "telecommunication services" and "public telecommunications operator" mean the same as in the Telecommunications Act 1984, except that the former does not include [local delivery services within the meaning of Part II of the Broadcasting Act 1990].".

Modification: Until the Water Act 2014, s 1 comes into force, sub-s (4)(ca) above is to be read as if for the words "water supply licensee" there were substituted the words "licensed water supplier", by virtue of SI 2015/989, art 3(1), (4).

[1.452]
[372A Further protection of essential supplies

(1) An insolvency-related term of a contract for the supply of essential goods or services to an individual ceases to have effect if—

(a) a voluntary arrangement proposed by the individual is approved under Part 8, and
(b) the supply is for the purpose of a business which is or has been carried on by the individual, by a firm or partnership of which the individual is or was a member, or by an agent or manager for the individual or for such a firm or partnership.

(2) An insolvency-related term of a contract does not cease to have effect by virtue of subsection (1) to the extent that—

(a) it provides for the contract or the supply to terminate, or any other thing to take place, because the individual becomes subject to an insolvency procedure other than a voluntary arrangement;
(b) it entitles a supplier to terminate the contract or the supply, or do any other thing, because the individual becomes subject to an insolvency procedure other than a voluntary arrangement; or
(c) it entitles a supplier to terminate the contract or the supply because of an event that occurs, or may occur, after the voluntary arrangement proposed by the individual is approved.

(3) Where an insolvency-related term of a contract ceases to have effect under this section the supplier may—

(a) terminate the contract, if the condition in subsection (4) is met;
(b) terminate the supply, if the condition in subsection (5) is met.

(4) The condition in this subsection is that—

(a) the supervisor of the voluntary arrangement consents to the termination of the contract,
(b) the court grants permission for the termination of the contract, or
(c) any charges in respect of the supply that are incurred after the voluntary arrangement is approved are not paid within the period of 28 days beginning with the day on which payment is due.

The court may grant permission under paragraph (b) only if satisfied that the continuation of the contract would cause the supplier hardship.

(5) The condition in this subsection is that—

(a) the supplier gives written notice to the supervisor of the voluntary arrangement that the supply will be terminated unless the supervisor personally guarantees the payment of any charges in respect of the continuation of the supply after the arrangement was approved, and
(b) the supervisor does not give that guarantee within the period of 14 days beginning with the day the notice is received.

(6) For the purposes of securing that the interests of suppliers are protected, where—

(a) an insolvency-related term of a contract (the "original term") ceases to have effect by virtue of subsection (1), and
(b) a subsequent voluntary arrangement proposed by the individual is approved,

the contract is treated for the purposes of subsections (1) to (5) as if, immediately before the subsequent voluntary arrangement proposed by the individual is approved, it included an insolvency-related term identical to the original term.

(7) A contract for the supply of essential goods or services is a contract for a supply mentioned in section 372(4).

(8) An insolvency-related term of a contract for the supply of essential goods or services to an individual is a provision of the contract under which—

(a) the contract or the supply would terminate, or any other thing would take place, because the voluntary arrangement proposed by the individual is approved,
(b) the supplier would be entitled to terminate the contract or the supply, or to do any other thing, because the voluntary arrangement proposed by the individual is approved, or
(c) the supplier would be entitled to terminate the contract or the supply because of an event that occurred before the voluntary arrangement proposed by the individual is approved.

(9) Subsection (1) does not have effect in relation to a contract entered into before 1st October 2015.]

NOTES

Commencement: 1 October 2015.

Inserted by the Insolvency (Protection of Essential Supplies) Order 2015, SI 2015/989, art 5.

[1.453]
373 Jurisdiction in relation to insolvent individuals

(1) The High Court and the [county court] have jurisdiction throughout England and Wales for the purposes of the Parts in this Group.

(2) For the purposes of those Parts, [the county court] has, in addition to its ordinary jurisdiction, all the powers and jurisdiction of the High Court; and the orders of the court may be enforced accordingly in the prescribed manner.

(3) Jurisdiction for the purposes of those Parts is exercised—

(a) by the High Court [or the [county court]] in relation to the proceedings which, in accordance with the rules, are allocated to the London insolvency district, and

(b) by [the] county court in relation to the proceedings which are so allocated to [any other insolvency district].

(4) Subsection (3) is without prejudice to the transfer of proceedings from one court to another in the manner prescribed by the rules; and nothing in that subsection invalidates any proceedings on the grounds that they were initiated or continued in the wrong court.

NOTES

This section derived from the Insolvency Act 1985, s 201.

Sub-s (1): words in square brackets substituted by the Crime and Courts Act 2013, s 17(5), Sch 9, Pt 3, para 93(d).

Sub-s (2): words in square brackets substituted by the Crime and Courts Act 2013, s 17(5), Sch 9, Pt 3, para 52(1)(b), (2).

Sub-s (3): words in first (outer) pair of square brackets in para (a) inserted by the London Insolvency District (Central London County Court) Order 2011, SI 2011/761, art 5, subject to savings in art 9 thereof; words in second (inner) pair of square brackets in para (a) and words in square brackets in para (b) substituted by the Crime and Courts Act 2013, s 17(5), Sch 9, Pt 3, para 93(e), (f).

[1.454]

374 Insolvency districts

(1) The Lord Chancellor may[, with the concurrence of the Lord Chief Justice,] by order designate the areas which are for the time being to be comprised, for the purposes of the Parts in this Group, in the London insolvency district and the insolvency district[, or districts, of the county court.]

(2) An order under this section may contain such incidental, supplemental and transitional provisions as may appear to the Lord Chancellor [and the Lord Chief Justice] necessary or expedient.

(3) An order under this section shall be made by statutory instrument and, after being made, shall be laid before each House of Parliament.

(4) Subject to any order under this section—

(a) the district which, immediately before the appointed day, is the London bankruptcy district becomes, on that day, the London insolvency district;

(b) any district which immediately before that day is the bankruptcy district of a county court becomes, on that day, the insolvency district of that court, and

(c) any county court which immediately before that day is excluded from having jurisdiction in bankruptcy is excluded, on and after that day, from having jurisdiction for the purposes of the Parts in this Group.

[(5) The Lord Chief Justice may nominate a judicial office holder (as defined in section 109(4) of the Constitutional Reform Act 2005) to exercise his functions under this section.]

NOTES

This section derived from the Insolvency Act 1985, s 202.

Sub-s (1): words in first pair of square brackets inserted by the Constitutional Reform Act 2005, s 15(1), Sch 4, Pt 1, paras 185, 187(1), (2); words in second pair of square brackets substituted by the Crime and Courts Act 2013, s 17(5), Sch 9, Pt 3, para 93(g).

Sub-s (2): words in square brackets inserted by the Constitutional Reform Act 2005, s 15(1), Sch 4, Pt 1, paras 185, 187(1), (3).

Sub-s (5): added by the Constitutional Reform Act 2005, s 15(1), Sch 4, Pt 1, paras 185, 187(1), (4).

Orders: the London Insolvency District (County Court at Central London) Order 2014, SI 2014/818 at **[11.51]**; by virtue of sub-s (4)(b), (c) above and s 437, Sch 11, para 23, the Civil Courts Order 1983, SI 1983/713, as amended, has effect as if made under this section.

[1.455]

375 Appeals etc from courts exercising insolvency jurisdiction

(1) Every court having jurisdiction for the purposes of the Parts in this Group may review, rescind or vary any order made by it in the exercise of that jurisdiction.

(2) An appeal from a decision made in the exercise of jurisdiction for the purposes of those Parts by [the county court] or by [an Insolvency and Companies Court Judge] lies to a single judge of the High Court; and an appeal from a decision of that judge on such an appeal lies . . . to the Court of Appeal.

(3) [The county court] is not, in the exercise of its jurisdiction for the purposes of those Parts, to be subject to be restrained by the order of any other court, and no appeal lies from its decision in the exercise of that jurisdiction except as provided by this section.

NOTES

This section derived from the Insolvency Act 1985, s 203.

Sub-s (2): words in first pair of square brackets substituted by the Crime and Courts Act 2013, s 17(5), Sch 9, Pt 3, para 52(1)(b), (2); words in second pair of square brackets substituted by the Alteration of Judicial Titles (Registrar in Bankruptcy of the High Court) Order 2018, SI 2018/130, art 3, Schedule, para 7(a); words omitted repealed by the Access to Justice Act 1999, s 106, Sch 15, Pt III.

Sub-s (3): words in square brackets substituted by the Crime and Courts Act 2013, s 17(5), Sch 9, Pt 3, para 52(1)(a), (2).

[1.456]
376 Time-limits
Where by any provision in this Group of Parts or by the rules the time for doing anything [(including anything in relation to a bankruptcy application)] is limited, the court may extend the time, either before or after it has expired, on such terms, if any, as it thinks fit.

NOTES
This section derived from the Insolvency Act 1985, s 204.
Words in square brackets inserted by the Enterprise and Regulatory Reform Act 2013, s 71(3), Sch 19, paras 1, 51, in respect of a petition for a bankruptcy order presented to the court by a debtor on or after 6 April 2016.

[1.457]
377 Formal defects
The acts of a person as the trustee of a bankrupt's estate or as a special manager, and the acts of the creditors' committee established for any bankruptcy, are valid notwithstanding any defect in the appointment, election or qualifications of the trustee or manager or, as the case may be, of any member of the committee.

NOTES
This section derived from the Insolvency Act 1985, s 205.

[1.458]
378 Exemption from stamp duty
Stamp duty shall not be charged on—
(a) any document, being a deed, conveyance, assignment, surrender, admission or other assurance relating solely to property which is comprised in a bankrupt's estate and which, after the execution of that document, is or remains at law or in equity the property of the bankrupt or of the trustee of that estate,
(b) any writ, order, certificate or other instrument relating solely to the property of a bankrupt or to any bankruptcy proceedings.

NOTES
This section derived from the Insolvency Act 1985, s 206.

[1.459]
379 Annual report
As soon as practicable after the end of 1986 and each subsequent calendar year, the Secretary of State shall prepare and lay before each House of Parliament a report about the operation during that year of so much of this Act as is comprised in this Group of Parts*, and about proceedings in the course of that year under the Deeds of Arrangement Act 1914*.

NOTES
This section derived from the Insolvency Act 1985, s 210.
Words in italics repealed by the Deregulation Act 2015, s 19, Sch 6, Pt 1, paras 2(1), (11)(e), 3, except in relation to a deed of arrangement registered under the Deeds of Arrangement Act 1914, s 5 before 1 October 2015, if, immediately before that date, the estate of the debtor who executed the deed of arrangement has not been finally wound up.

[Creditors' decisions

[1.460]
379ZA Creditors' decisions: general
(1) This section applies where, for the purposes of this Group of Parts, a person ("P") seeks a decision from an individual's creditors about any matter.
(2) The decision may be made by any creditors' decision procedure P thinks fit, except that it may not be made by a creditors' meeting unless subsection (3) applies.
(3) This subsection applies if at least the minimum number of creditors request in writing that the decision be made by a creditors' meeting.
(4) If subsection (3) applies, P must summon a creditors' meeting.
(5) Subsection (2) is subject to any provision of this Act, the rules or any other legislation, or any order of the court—
(a) requiring a decision to be made, or prohibiting a decision from being made, by a particular creditors' decision procedure (other than a creditors' meeting);
(b) permitting or requiring a decision to be made by a creditors' meeting.
(6) Section 379ZB provides that in certain cases the deemed consent procedure may be used instead of a creditors' decision procedure.
(7) For the purposes of subsection (3) the "minimum number" of creditors is any of the following—
(a) 10% in value of the creditors;
(b) 10% in number of the creditors;
(c) 10 creditors.
(8) The references in subsection (7) to creditors are to creditors of any class, even where a decision is sought only from creditors of a particular class.
(9) In this section references to a meeting are to a meeting where the creditors are invited to be present together at the same place (whether or not it is possible to attend the meeting without being present at that place).

(10) Except as provided by subsection (8), references in this section to creditors include creditors of a particular class.
(11) In this Group of Parts "creditors' decision procedure" means a procedure prescribed or authorised under paragraph 11A of Schedule 9.]

NOTES

Commencement: 6 April 2017 (subject to transitional and savings provisions as noted to s 246ZE at **[1.256]**).
Inserted, together with preceding heading and ss 379ZB, 379ZC, by the Small Business, Enterprise and Employment Act 2015, s 123(1), (2).

[1.461]
[379ZB Deemed consent procedure

(1) The deemed consent procedure may be used instead of a creditors' decision procedure where an individual's creditors are to make a decision about any matter, unless—
(a) a decision about the matter is required by virtue of this Act, the rules or any other legislation to be made by a creditors' decision procedure, or
(b) the court orders that a decision about the matter is to be made by a creditors' decision procedure.
(2) If the rules provide for an individual's creditors to make a decision about the remuneration of any person, they must provide that the decision is to be made by a creditors' decision procedure.
(3) The deemed consent procedure is that the relevant creditors (other than opted-out creditors) are given notice of—
(a) the matter about which the creditors are to make a decision,
(b) the decision the person giving the notice proposes should be made (the "proposed decision"),
(c) the effect of subsections (4) and (5), and
(d) the procedure for objecting to the proposed decision.
(4) If less than the appropriate number of relevant creditors object to the proposed decision in accordance with the procedure set out in the notice, the creditors are to be treated as having made the proposed decision.
(5) Otherwise—
(a) the creditors are to be treated as not having made a decision about the matter in question, and
(b) if a decision about that matter is again sought from the creditors, it must be sought using a creditors' decision procedure.
(6) For the purposes of subsection (4) the "appropriate number" of relevant creditors is 10% in value of those creditors.
(7) "Relevant creditors" means the creditors who, if the decision were to be made by a creditors' decision procedure, would be entitled to vote in the procedure.
(8) In this section references to creditors include creditors of a particular class.
(9) The rules may make further provision about the deemed consent procedure.]

NOTES

Commencement: 6 April 2017 (subject to transitional and savings provisions as noted to s 246ZE at **[1.256]**).
Inserted as noted to s 379ZA at **[1.460]**.

[1.462]
[379ZC Power to amend sections 379ZA and 379ZB

(1) The Secretary of State may by regulations amend section 379ZA so as to change the definition of the minimum number of creditors.
(2) The Secretary of State may by regulations amend section 379ZB so as to change the definition of the appropriate number of relevant creditors.
(3) Regulations under this section may define the minimum number or the appropriate number by reference to any one or more of—
(a) a proportion in value,
(b) a proportion in number,
(c) an absolute number,
and the definition may include alternative, cumulative or relative requirements.
(4) Regulations under subsection (1) may define the minimum number of creditors by reference to all creditors, or by reference to creditors of a particular description.
(5) Regulations under this section may make provision that will result in section 379ZA or 379ZB having different definitions for different cases, including for different kinds of decisions.
(6) Regulations under this section may make transitional provision.
(7) The power of the Secretary of State to make regulations under this section is exercisable by statutory instrument.
(8) A statutory instrument containing regulations under this section may not be made unless a draft of the instrument has been laid before, and approved by a resolution of, each House of Parliament.]

NOTES

Commencement: 6 April 2017 (subject to transitional and savings provisions as noted to s 246ZE at **[1.256]**).
Inserted as noted to s 379ZA at **[1.460]**.

[Remote attendance at meetings

[1.463]
379A Remote attendance at meetings

(1) Where—

(a) a bankruptcy order is made against an individual or an interim receiver of an individual's property is appointed, or

(b) a voluntary arrangement in relation to an individual is proposed or is approved under Part 8,

this section applies to any meeting of the individual's creditors summoned under this Act or the rules.

(2) Where the person summoning a meeting ("the convener") considers it appropriate, the meeting may be conducted and held in such a way that persons who are not present together at the same place may attend it.

(3) Where a meeting is conducted and held in the manner referred to in subsection (2), a person attends the meeting if that person is able to exercise any rights which that person may have to speak and vote at the meeting.

(4) For the purposes of this section—

(a) a person exercises the right to speak at a meeting when that person is in a position to communicate to all those attending the meeting, during the meeting, any information or opinions which that person has on the business of the meeting; and

(b) a person exercises the right to vote at a meeting when—

(i) that person is able to vote, during the meeting, on resolutions put to the vote at the meeting, and

(ii) that person's vote can be taken into account in determining whether or not such resolutions are passed at the same time as the votes of all the other persons attending the meeting.

(5) The convener of a meeting which is to be conducted and held in the manner referred to in subsection (2) may make whatever arrangements the convener considers appropriate to—

(a) enable those attending the meeting to exercise their rights to speak or vote, and

(b) ensure the identification of those attending the meeting and the security of any electronic means used to enable attendance.

(6) Where in the reasonable opinion of the convener—

(a) a meeting will be attended by persons who will not be present together at the same place, and

(b) it is unnecessary or inexpedient to specify a place for the meeting,

any requirement under this Act or the rules to specify a place for the meeting may be satisfied by specifying the arrangements the convener proposes to enable persons to exercise their rights to speak or vote.

(7) In making the arrangements referred to in subsection (5) and in forming the opinion referred to in subsection (6)(b), the convener must have regard to the legitimate interests of the creditors and others attending the meeting in the efficient despatch of the business of the meeting.

(8) If—

(a) the notice of a meeting does not specify a place for the meeting,

(b) the convener is requested in accordance with the rules to specify a place for the meeting, and

(c) that request is made by not less than ten percent in value of the creditors,

it shall be the duty of the convener to specify a place for the meeting.]

NOTES

Inserted, together with s 379B and associated cross-headings, by the Legislative Reform (Insolvency) (Miscellaneous Provisions) Order 2010, SI 2010/18, arts 2, 3(2).

Repealed, together with preceding cross-heading, by the Small Business, Enterprise and Employment Act 2015, s 126, Sch 9, Pt 2, paras 60, 88, as from 6 April 2017 (subject to transitional and savings provisions as noted to s 246ZE at **[1.256]**).

[[Giving of notices etc by office-holders]

NOTES

Cross-heading above substituted for original words "Use of websites", by the Small Business, Enterprise and Employment Act 2015, s 125(1), (2), as from 6 April 2017 (subject to transitional and savings provisions as noted to s 246ZE at **[1.256]**).

[1.464]

379B Use of websites

(1) This section applies where—

(a) a bankruptcy order is made against an individual or an interim receiver of an individual's property is appointed, or

(b) a voluntary arrangement in relation to an individual is proposed or is approved under Part 8,

and "the office-holder" means the official receiver, the trustee in bankruptcy, the interim receiver, the nominee or the supervisor of the voluntary arrangement, as the case may be.

(2) Where any provision of this Act or the rules requires the office-holder to give, deliver, furnish or send a notice or other document or information to any person, that requirement is satisfied by making the notice, document or information available on a website—

(a) in accordance with the rules, and

(b) in such circumstances as may be prescribed.]

NOTES

Inserted as noted to s 379A at **[1.463]**.

[1.465]

[379C Creditors' ability to opt out of receiving certain notices

(1) Any provision of the rules which requires an office-holder to give a notice to creditors of an individual does not apply, in circumstances prescribed by the rules, in relation to opted-out creditors.

(2) Subsection (1)—

(a) does not apply in relation to a notice of a distribution or proposed distribution to creditors;
(b) is subject to any order of the court requiring a notice to be given to all creditors (or all creditors of a particular category).

(3) Except as provided by the rules, a creditor may participate and vote in a qualifying decision procedure or a deemed consent procedure even though, by virtue of being an opted-out creditor, the creditor does not receive notice of it.

(4) In this section—

"give" includes deliver, furnish or send;

"notice" includes any document or information in any other form;

"office-holder", in relation to an individual, means—

(a) where a bankruptcy order is made against the individual, the official receiver or the trustee in bankruptcy;
(b) where an interim receiver of the individual's property is appointed, the interim receiver;
(c) the supervisor of a voluntary arrangement approved under Part 8 in relation to the individual.]

NOTES

Commencement: 6 April 2017 (subject to transitional and savings provisions as noted to s 246ZE at **[1.256]**).

Inserted by the Small Business, Enterprise and Employment Act 2015, s 125(1), (3).

PART XI INTERPRETATION FOR SECOND GROUP OF PARTS

[1.466]

380 Introductory

The next five sections have effect for the interpretation of the provisions of this Act which are comprised in this Group of Parts; and where a definition is provided for a particular expression, it applies except so far as the context otherwise requires.

[1.467]

381 "Bankrupt" and associated terminology

(1) "Bankrupt" means an individual who has been [made] bankrupt and, in relation to a bankruptcy order, it means the individual [made] bankrupt by that order.

[(1A) Bankruptcy application" means an application to an adjudicator for a bankruptcy order.]

(2) "Bankruptcy order" means an order [making] an individual bankrupt.

(3) "Bankruptcy petition" means a petition to the court for a bankruptcy order.

NOTES

This section derived from the Insolvency Act 1985, s 211(1) (in part).

Sub-s (1): word in square brackets in both places substituted for original word "adjudged" by the Enterprise and Regulatory Reform Act 2013, s 71(3), Sch 19, paras 1, 52(1), (2), in respect of a petition for a bankruptcy order presented to the court by a debtor on or after 6 April 2016.

Sub-s (1A): inserted by the Enterprise and Regulatory Reform Act 2013, s 71(3), Sch 19, paras 1, 52(1), (3), in respect of a petition for a bankruptcy order presented to the court by a debtor on or after 6 April 2016.

Sub-s (2): word in square brackets substituted for original word "adjudging", by the Enterprise and Regulatory Reform Act 2013, s 71(3), Sch 19, paras 1, 52(1), (4), in respect of a petition for a bankruptcy order presented to the court by a debtor on or after 6 April 2016.

[1.468]

382 "Bankruptcy debt"[, "liability"], etc

(1) "Bankruptcy debt", in relation to a bankrupt, means (subject to the next subsection) any of the following—

(a) any debt or liability to which he is subject at the commencement of the bankruptcy,
(b) any debt or liability to which he may become subject after the commencement of the bankruptcy (including after his discharge from bankruptcy) by reason of any obligation incurred before the commencement of the bankruptcy,
(c) any amount specified in pursuance of section 39(3)(c) of the Powers of Criminal Courts Act 1973 in any criminal bankruptcy order made against him before the commencement of the bankruptcy, and
(d) any interest provable as mentioned in section 322(2) in Chapter IV of Part IX.

(2) In determining for the purposes of any provision in this Group of Parts whether any liability in tort is a bankruptcy debt, the bankrupt is deemed to become subject to that liability by reason of an obligation incurred at the time when the cause of action accrued.

(3) For the purposes of references in this Group of Parts to a debt or liability, it is immaterial whether the debt or liability is present or future, whether it is certain or contingent or whether its amount is fixed or liquidated, or is capable of being ascertained by fixed rules or as a matter of opinion; and references in this Group of Parts to owing a debt are to be read accordingly.

(4) In this Group of Parts, except in so far as the context otherwise requires, "liability" means (subject to subsection (3) above) a liability to pay money or money's worth, including any liability under an enactment, any liability for breach of trust, any liability in contract, tort or bailment and any liability arising out of an obligation to make restitution.

[(5) Liability under the Child Support Act 1991 to pay child support maintenance to any person is not a debt or liability for the purposes of Part 8.]

NOTES

This section derived from the Insolvency Act 1985, s 211(1) (in part), (2), (3).

Section heading: word in square brackets inserted by the Welfare Reform Act 2012, s 142(2).

Sub-s (1): para (c) repealed by the Criminal Justice Act 1988, s 170(2), Sch 16, as from a day to be appointed.

Sub-s (5): inserted by the Welfare Reform Act 2012, s 142(1).

Powers of Criminal Courts Act 1973, s 39: repealed by the Criminal Justice Act 1988, s 170(2), Sch 16, as from a day to be appointed.

[1.469]

383 "Creditor", "security", etc

(1) "Creditor"—

(a) in relation to a bankrupt, means a person to whom any of the bankruptcy debts is owed *(being, in the case of an amount falling within paragraph (c) of the definition in section 382(1) of "bankruptcy debt", the person in respect of whom that amount is specified in the criminal bankruptcy order in question)*, and

(b) in relation to an individual to whom a [bankruptcy application or] bankruptcy petition relates, means a person who would be a creditor in the bankruptcy if a bankruptcy order were made on that [application or] petition.

(2) Subject to the next two subsections and any provision of the rules requiring a creditor to give up his security for the purposes of proving a debt, a debt is secured for the purposes of this Group of Parts to the extent that the person to whom the debt is owed holds any security for the debt (whether a mortgage, charge, lien or other security) over any property of the person by whom the debt is owed.

(3) Where a statement such as is mentioned in section 269(1)(a) in Chapter I of Part IX has been made by a secured creditor for the purposes of any bankruptcy petition and a bankruptcy order is subsequently made on that petition, the creditor is deemed for the purposes of the Parts in this Group to have given up the security specified in the statement.

(4) In subsection (2) the reference to a security does not include a lien on books, papers or other records, except to the extent that they consist of documents which give a title to property and are held as such.

NOTES

This section derived from the Insolvency Act 1985, s 211(1) (in part), (5)–(7).

Sub-s (1): words in italics in para (a) repealed by the Criminal Justice Act 1988, s 170(2), Sch 16, as from a day to be appointed; words in square brackets in para (b) inserted by the Enterprise and Regulatory Reform Act 2013, s 71(3), Sch 19, paras 1, 53, in respect of a petition for a bankruptcy order presented to the court by a debtor on or after 6 April 2016.

[1.470]

[383A "Opted-out creditor"

(1) For the purposes of this Group of Parts "opted-out creditor" in relation to an office-holder for an individual means a person who—

(a) is a creditor of the individual, and

(b) in accordance with the rules has elected (or is deemed to have elected) to be (and not to cease to be) an opted-out creditor in relation to the office-holder.

(2) In this section, "office-holder", in relation to an individual, means—

(a) where a bankruptcy order is made against the individual, the official receiver or the trustee in bankruptcy;

(b) where an interim receiver of the individual's property is appointed, the interim receiver;

(c) the supervisor of a voluntary arrangement approved under Part 8 in relation to the individual.]

NOTES

Commencement: 6 April 2017 (subject to transitional and savings provisions as noted to s 246ZE at **[1.256]**).

Inserted by the Small Business, Enterprise and Employment Act 2015, s 125(1), (4).

[1.471]

384 "Prescribed" and "the rules"

(1) Subject to the next subsection [and sections 342C(7) and 342F(9) in Chapter V of Part IX], "prescribed" means prescribed by the rules; and "the rules" means rules made under section 412 in Part XV.

(2) References in this Group of Parts to the amount prescribed for the purposes of any of the following provisions—

[section 251S(4);]

. . .

[section 313A;]
section 346(3);
section 354(1) and (2);
section 358;
section 360(1);
section 361(2); . . .
section 364(2)(d),
[paragraphs 6 to 8 of Schedule 4ZA,]

and references in those provisions to the prescribed amount are to be read in accordance with section 418 in Part XV and orders made under that section.

NOTES

This section derived from the Insolvency Act 1985, ss 209(1) (in part), 211(1) (in part).

Sub-s (1): words in square brackets inserted by the Welfare Reform and Pensions Act 1999, s 84(1), Sch 12, Pt II, paras 70, 72.

Sub-s (2): first words omitted repealed by the Enterprise and Regulatory Reform Act 2013, s 71(3), Sch 19, paras 1, 54; words in first and third pairs of square brackets inserted and second word omitted repealed by the Tribunals, Courts and Enforcement Act 2007, s 108(3), Sch 20, Pt 1, paras 1, 4; words in second pair of square brackets inserted by the Enterprise Act 2002, s 261(5), subject to transitional provisions in s 261(7)–(10) of that Act at **[2.14]**.

[1.472]

385 Miscellaneous definitions

(1) The following definitions have effect—

["adjudicator" means a person appointed by the Secretary of State under section 398A;]

"the court", in relation to any matter, means the court to which, in accordance with section 373 in Part X and the rules, proceedings with respect to that matter are allocated or transferred;

["creditors' decision procedure" has the meaning given by section 379ZA(11);]

"creditor's petition" means a bankruptcy petition under section 264(1)(a);

"criminal bankruptcy order" means an order under section 39(1) of the Powers of Criminal Courts Act 1973;

"debt" is to be construed in accordance with section 382(3);

"the debtor"—

[(za) in relation to a debt relief order or an application for such an order, has the same meaning as in Part 7A,]

(a) in relation to a proposal for the purposes of Part VIII, means the individual making or intending to make that proposal, and

(b) in relation to a [bankruptcy application or a] bankruptcy petition, means the individual to whom the [application or] petition relates;

"debtor's petition" means a bankruptcy petition presented by the debtor himself under section 264(1)(b);

["debt relief order" means an order made by the official receiver under Part 7A;]

["deemed consent procedure" means the deemed consent procedure provided for by section 379ZB;]

["determination period" has the meaning given in section 263K(4);]

"dwelling house" includes any building or part of a building which is occupied as a dwelling and any yard, garden, garage or outhouse belonging to the dwelling house and occupied with it;

"estate", in relation to a bankrupt is to be construed in accordance with section 283 in Chapter II of Part IX;

"family", in relation to a bankrupt, means the persons (if any) who are living with him and are dependent on him;

["insolvency administration order" means an order for the administration in bankruptcy of the insolvent estate of a deceased debtor (being an individual at the date of his death);

"insolvency administration petition" means a petition for an insolvency administration order;

"the Rules" means the [Insolvency (England and Wales) Rules 2016].]

"secured" and related expressions are to be construed in accordance with section 383; and

"the trustee", in relation to a bankruptcy and the bankrupt, means the trustee of the bankrupt's estate.

(2) References in this Group of Parts to a person's affairs include his business, if any.

NOTES

This section derived from the Insolvency Act 1985, s 211(1) (in part), (4).

Sub-s (1): definitions "adjudicator" and "determination period" inserted, words in square brackets in para (b) of the definition "the debtor" inserted and definition "debtor's petition" repealed, by the Enterprise and Regulatory Reform Act 2013, s 71(3), Sch 19, paras 1, 55, in respect of a petition for a bankruptcy order presented to the court by a debtor on or after 6 April 2016; definitions "creditors' decision procedure" and "deemed consent procedure" inserted by the Small Business, Enterprise and Employment Act 2015, s 123(1), (4), as from 6 April 2017 (subject to transitional and savings provisions as noted to s 246ZE at **[1.256]**); definition "criminal bankruptcy order" repealed by the Criminal Justice Act 1988, s 170(2), Sch 16, as from a day to be appointed; in definition "the debtor", para (za) inserted and definition "debt relief order" inserted by the Tribunals, Courts and Enforcement Act 2007, s 108(3), Sch 20, Pt 1, paras 1, 5; definitions "insolvency administration order", "insolvency administration petition" and "the Rules" inserted by the Administration of Insolvent Estates of Deceased Persons Order 1986, SI 1986/1999, art 6; words in square brackets in definition "the Rules" substituted by the Insolvency (England and Wales) Rules 2016 (Consequential Amendments and Savings) Rules 2017, SI 2017/369, r 2(1), Sch 1, para 3.

Powers of Criminal Courts Act 1973, s 39: repealed by the Criminal Justice Act 1988, s 170(2), Sch 16, as from a day to be appointed.

THE THIRD GROUP OF PARTS
MISCELLANEOUS MATTERS BEARING ON BOTH COMPANY AND INDIVIDUAL INSOLVENCY; GENERAL INTERPRETATION; FINAL PROVISIONS

NOTES

Modification in relation to the administration of insolvent estates of deceased persons: this Group of Parts is modified in its application to the administration of insolvent estates of deceased persons, by the Administration of Insolvent Estates of Deceased Persons Order 1986, SI 1986/1999, arts 3, 5, Schs 1, 2 at **[11.3]**, **[11.5]**, **[11.6]**, **[11.9]**.

Application to limited liability partnerships: this Group of Parts is applied, with modifications, to limited liability partnerships, by the Limited Liability Partnerships Regulations 2001, SI 2001/1090, reg 5, Sch 4 at **[10.37]**, **[10.42]**.

PART XII PREFERENTIAL DEBTS IN COMPANY AND INDIVIDUAL INSOLVENCY

NOTES

Modification of this Part in relation to building societies: this Part is applied, with modifications, in relation to the winding up, etc, of building societies; see the Building Societies Act 1986, ss 90, 90A, Schs 15, 15A at **[7.454]**, **[7.455]**, **[7.464]**, **[7.468]**.

Friendly societies: as to the application, with modifications, of this Part of this Act to the winding up of incorporated friendly societies by virtue of the Friendly Societies Act 1992, s 21(1) or 22(2), see s 23 of, and Sch 10 to, the 1992 Act.

[1.473]

386 Categories of preferential debts

(1) A reference in this Act to the preferential debts of a company or an individual is to the debts listed in Schedule 6 to this Act [(contributions to occupational pension schemes; remuneration, &c. of employees; levies on coal and steel production)][; debts owed to the Financial Services Compensation Scheme][; deposits covered by Financial Services Compensation Scheme][; other deposits]; and references to preferential creditors are to be read accordingly.

[(1A) A reference in this Act to the "ordinary preferential debts" of a company or an individual is to the preferential debts listed in any of paragraphs 8 to 15B of Schedule 6 to this Act.

(1B) A reference in this Act to the "secondary preferential debts" of a company or an individual is to the preferential debts listed in paragraph 15BA or 15BB of Schedule 6 to this Act.]

(2) In [Schedule 6] "the debtor" means the company or the individual concerned.

(3) Schedule 6 is to be read with [Schedule 4 to the Pension Schemes Act 1993] (occupational pension scheme contributions).

NOTES

This section derived from the Companies Act 1985, ss 196(2), 475(1), and the Insolvency Act 1985, ss 23(7), 89(1), 108(3), 115(9), 166(1), Sch 4, Pt II, para 1(1), Sch 6, para 15(3).

Sub-s (1): words in first pair of square brackets substituted by the Enterprise Act 2002, s 251(3), subject to transitional provisions in relation to the abolition of preferential status for Crown debts in cases which were started before 15 September 2003 (see the Enterprise Act 2002 (Commencement No 4 and Transitional Provisions and Savings) Order 2003, SI 2003/2093, art 4 at **[2.27]**); words in second pair of square brackets inserted by the Deposit Guarantee Scheme Regulations 2015, SI 2015/486, reg 14(1), (2); words in third pair of square brackets inserted by the Financial Services (Banking Reform) Act 2013, s 13(2); words in fourth pair of square brackets inserted by the Banks and Building Societies (Depositor Preference and Priorities) Order 2014, SI 2014/3486, arts 3, 8(1), (2), except in relation to any insolvency proceedings commenced before 1 January 2015 (as to the meaning of this, see further the note "SI 2014/3486, art 3" at **[1.5]**).

Sub-s (1), as amended by the Finance Act 1991, s 7, Sch 2, para 21A, the Finance Act 1993, ss 36(1), 41, the Finance Act 1994, s 64, Sch 7, Pt III, para 7(2), the Finance Act 1995, s 17, the Finance Act 1996, s 60, Sch 5, Pt III, para 12(1), the Finance Act 2000, s 30(2), Sch 7, para 3(1)(a), the Finance Act 2001, s 27, Sch 5, para 17(1)(a), and by the Insolvency (ECSC Levy Debts) Regulations 1987, SI 1987/2093, reg 2, previously read as follows:

> "(1) A reference in this Act to the preferential debts of a company or an individual is to the debts listed in Schedule 6 to this Act (money owed to the Inland Revenue for income tax deducted at source; VAT, [insurance premium tax,] [landfill tax,] [climate change levy,] [aggregates levy,] car tax, betting and gaming duties[, beer duty][, lottery duty][, air passenger duty]; social security and pension scheme contributions; remuneration etc of employees[; levies on coal and steel production]); and references to preferential creditors are to be read accordingly.".

Sub-ss (1A), (1B): inserted by SI 2014/3486, arts 3, 8(1), (3), except in relation to any insolvency proceedings commenced before 1 January 2015 (as to the meaning of this, see further the note "SI 2014/3486, art 3" at **[1.5]**).

Sub-s (2): words in square brackets substituted (for the original words "that Schedule") by SI 2014/3486, arts 3, 8(1), (4), except in relation to any insolvency proceedings commenced before 1 January 2015 (as to the meaning of this, see further the note "SI 2014/3486, art 3" at **[1.5]**).

Sub-s (3): words in square brackets substituted by the Pension Schemes Act 1993, s 190, Sch 8, para 18.

[1.474]

387 "The relevant date"

(1) This section explains references in Schedule 6 to the relevant date (being the date which determines the existence and amount of a preferential debt).

(2) For the purposes of section 4 in Part I ([consideration of] company voluntary arrangement), the relevant date in relation to a company which is not being wound up is—

[(a) if the company is in administration, the date on which it entered administration, and

(b) if the company is not in administration, the date on which the voluntary arrangement takes effect.]

[(2A) For the purposes of paragraph 31 of Schedule A1 ([consideration of] company voluntary arrangement where a moratorium under section 1A is in force), the relevant date in relation to a company is the date of filing.]

(3) In relation to a company which is being wound up, the following applies—

(a) if the winding up is by the court, and the winding-up order was made immediately upon the discharge of an administration order, the relevant date is [the date on which the company entered administration];

[(aa) if the winding up is by the court and the winding-up order was made following conversion of administration into winding up by virtue of [Article 51 of the EU Regulation], the relevant date is [the date on which the company entered administration];

(ab) if the company is deemed to have passed a resolution for voluntary winding up by virtue of an order following conversion of administration into winding up under [Article 51 of the EU Regulation], the relevant date is [the date on which the company entered administration];]

(b) if the case does not fall within paragraph (a)[, (aa) or (ab)] and the company—
(i) is being wound up by the court, and
(ii) had not commenced to be wound up voluntarily before the date of the making of the winding-up order,
the relevant date is the date of the appointment (or first appointment) of a provisional liquidator or, if no such appointment has been made, the date of the winding-up order;
[(ba) if the case does not fall within paragraph (a), (aa), (ab) or (b) and the company is being wound up following administration pursuant to paragraph 83 of Schedule B1, the relevant date is the date on which the company entered administration;]
(c) if the case does not fall within either [paragraph (a), (aa), (ab), (b) or (ba)], the relevant date is the date of the passing of the resolution for the winding up of the company.

[(3A) In relation to a company which is in administration (and to which no other provision of this section applies) the relevant date is the date on which the company enters administration.]

(4) In relation to a company in receivership (where section 40 or, as the case may be, section 59 applies), the relevant date is—
(a) in England and Wales, the date of the appointment of the receiver by debenture-holders, and
(b) in Scotland, the date of the appointment of the receiver under section 53(6) or (as the case may be) 54(5).

(5) For the purposes of section 258 in Part VIII (individual voluntary arrangements), the relevant date is, in relation to a debtor who is not an undischarged bankrupt—
[(a) where an interim order has been made under section 252 with respect to his proposal, the date of that order, and
(b) in any other case, the date on which the voluntary arrangement takes effect.]

(6) In relation to a bankrupt, the following applies—
(a) where at the time the bankruptcy order was made there was an interim receiver appointed under section 286, the relevant date is the date on which the interim receiver was first appointed after [the making of the bankruptcy application or (as the case may be)] the presentation of the bankruptcy petition;
(b) otherwise, the relevant date is the date of the making of the bankruptcy order.

NOTES

This section derived from the Companies Act 1985, ss 196(2)–(4), 475(3), (4), and the Insolvency Act 1985, ss 23(8), 115(10), Sch 4, Pt II, para 1(2), (3), Sch 6, paras 5(4), 20(3).

Sub-s (2): paras (a), (b) substituted by the Enterprise Act 2002, s 248(3), Sch 17, paras 9, 34(1), (2), subject to savings and transitional provisions (i) in a case where a petition for an administration order has been presented before 15 September 2003 (see the Enterprise Act 2002 (Commencement No 4 and Transitional Provisions and Savings) Order 2003, SI 2003/2093, art 3 at **[2.26]**), and (ii) in relation to special administration regimes (see s 249 of the 2002 Act at **[2.10]**); words in square brackets substituted for original words "meetings to consider" by the Small Business, Enterprise and Employment Act 2015, s 126, Sch 9, Pt 1, paras 1, 55, as from 6 April 2017 (in relation to England and Wales and subject to transitional and savings provisions as noted to s 246ZE at **[1.256]**), and as from a day to be appointed (in relation to Scotland).

Sub-s (2A): inserted by the Insolvency Act 2000, s 1, Sch 1, paras 1, 9; words in square brackets substituted for original words "meetings to consider" by the Small Business, Enterprise and Employment Act 2015, s 126, Sch 9, Pt 1, paras 1, 55, as from 6 April 2017 (in relation to England and Wales and subject to transitional and savings provisions as noted to s 246ZE at **[1.256]**), and as from a day to be appointed (in relation to Scotland).

Sub-s (3): paras (aa), (ab) and words in square brackets in para (b) inserted by the Insolvency Act 1986 (Amendment) (No 2) Regulations 2002, SI 2002/1240, regs 3, 16; words in square brackets in para (a), and words in second pair of square brackets in paras (aa), (ab) substituted for original words "the date of the making of the administration order", para (ba) inserted, and words in square brackets in para (c) substituted for words "paragraph (a), (aa), (ab) or (b)" (as previously substituted for original words "paragraph (a) or (b)" by SI 2002/1240, regs 3, 16(c)), by the Enterprise Act 2002, s 248(3), Sch 17, paras 9, 34(1), (3), subject to savings as noted to sub-s (2) above; words in first pair of square brackets in paras (aa), (ab) substituted for original words "Article 37 of the EC Regulation" by the Insolvency Amendment (EU 2015/848) Regulations 2017, SI 2017/702, regs 2, 3, Schedule, Pt 1, paras 1, 22, except in relation to proceedings opened before 26 June 2017 and subject to savings in reg 4 thereof at **[2.103]**.

Sub-s (3A): inserted by the Enterprise Act 2002, s 248(3), Sch 17, paras 9, 34(1), (4), subject to savings as noted to sub-s (2) above.

Sub-s (5): words in square brackets substituted by the Insolvency Act 2000, s 3, Sch 3, paras 1, 15, for original words "the date of the interim order made under section 252 with respect to his proposal", subject to transitional provisions in SI 2002/2711, art 4 at **[2.7]**.

Sub-s (6): words in square brackets in para (a) inserted by the Enterprise and Regulatory Reform Act 2013, s 71(3), Sch 19, paras 1, 56, in respect of a petition for a bankruptcy order presented to the court by a debtor on or after 6 April 2016.

PART XIII INSOLVENCY PRACTITIONERS AND THEIR QUALIFICATION

NOTES

Modification of this Part in relation to building societies: this Part is applied, with modifications, in relation to the winding up, etc, of building societies; see the Building Societies Act 1986, ss 90, 90A, Schs 15, 15A at **[7.454]**, **[7.455]**, **[7.464]**, **[7.468]**.

Friendly societies: as to the application, with modifications, of this Part of this Act to the winding up of incorporated friendly societies by virtue of the Friendly Societies Act 1992, s 21(1) or 22(2), see s 23 of, and Sch 10 to, the 1992 Act.

Restrictions on unqualified persons acting as liquidator, trustee in bankruptcy, etc

[1.475]

388 Meaning of "act as insolvency practitioner"

(1) A person acts as an insolvency practitioner in relation to a company by acting—

(a) as its liquidator, provisional liquidator, administrator or administrative receiver, or
[(b) where a voluntary arrangement in relation to the company is proposed or approved under Part I, as nominee or supervisor].

(2) A person acts as an insolvency practitioner in relation to an individual by acting—
(a) as his trustee in bankruptcy or interim receiver of his property or as [trustee (or interim trustee)] in the sequestration of his estate; or
(b) as trustee under a deed which is *a deed of arrangement made for the benefit of his creditors or*, in Scotland, a trust deed for his creditors; or
[(c) where a voluntary arrangement in relation to the individual is proposed or approved under Part VIII, as nominee or supervisor]
(d) in the case of a deceased individual to the administration of whose estate this section applies by virtue of an order under section 421 (application of provisions of this Act to insolvent estates of deceased persons), as administrator of that estate.

[(2A) A person acts as an insolvency practitioner in relation to an insolvent partnership by acting—
(a) as its liquidator, provisional liquidator or administrator, or
(b) as trustee of the partnership under article 11 of the Insolvent Partnerships Order 1994, or
[(c) where a voluntary arrangement in relation to the insolvent partnership is proposed or approved under Part I of the Act, as nominee or supervisor].]

[(2B) In relation to a voluntary arrangement proposed under Part I or VIII, a person acts as nominee if he performs any of the functions conferred on nominees under the Part in question.]

(3) References in this section to an individual include, except in so far as the context otherwise requires, references . . . to any debtor within the meaning of the Bankruptcy (Scotland) Act [2016].

(4) In this section—
"administrative receiver" has the meaning given by section 251 in Part VII;
["company" means—
(a) a company registered under the Companies Act 2006 in England and Wales or Scotland, or
(b) a company that may be wound up under Part 5 of this Act (unregistered companies)]; and
["sequestration" means sequestration under the Bankruptcy (Scotland) Act 2016].

[(5) Nothing in this section applies to anything done by—
(a) the official receiver; or
(b) the Accountant in Bankruptcy (within the meaning of the Bankruptcy (Scotland) Act [2016]).]

[(6) Nothing in this section applies to anything done (whether in the United Kingdom or elsewhere) in relation to insolvency proceedings under the [EU Regulation] in a member State other than the United Kingdom.]

NOTES

This section derived from the Insolvency Act 1985, s 1(2)–(6).

Sub-s (1): para (b) substituted by the Insolvency Act 2000, s 4(1), (2)(a), subject to transitional provisions in SI 2002/2711, art 5 at **[2.8]**, and originally read as follows:

"(b) as supervisor of a voluntary arrangement approved by it under Part I.".

Sub-s (2): words in square brackets in para (a) substituted (for the original words "permanent or interim trustee") by the Bankruptcy (Scotland) Act 2016 (Consequential Provisions and Modifications) Order 2016, SI 2016/1034, art 7(1), (3), Sch 1, para 4(1), (6)(a), as from 30 November 2016 (except in relation to (i) a sequestration as regards which the petition is presented, or the debtor application is made before that date; or (ii) a trust deed executed before that date); words in italics in para (b) repealed by the Deregulation Act 2015, s 19, Sch 6, Pt 1, paras 2(1), (11)(f), 3, except in relation to a deed of arrangement registered under the Deeds of Arrangement Act 1914, s 5 before 1 October 2015, if, immediately before that date, the estate of the debtor who executed the deed of arrangement has not been finally wound up; para (c) substituted by the Insolvency Act 2000, s 4(1), (2)(b), subject to transitional provisions in SI 2002/2711, art 5 at **[2.8]**, and originally read as follows:

"(c) as supervisor of a voluntary arrangement proposed by him and approved under Part VIII; or".

Sub-s (2A): inserted by the Insolvent Partnerships Order 1994, SI 1994/2421, art 15(1); para (c) substituted by the Insolvent Partnerships (Amendment) (No 2) Order 2002, SI 2002/2708, art 3, subject to transitional provisions in art 11(1), (3) of that Order (see the note to the Insolvent Partnerships Order 1994, SI 1994/2421, art 4 at **[10.4]**).

Sub-s (2B): inserted by the Insolvency Act 2000, s 4(1), (2)(c), subject to transitional provisions in SI 2002/2711, art 5 at **[2.8]**.

Sub-s (3): words omitted repealed by SI 1994/2421, art 15(2); year "2016" in square brackets substituted (for the original year "1985") by SI 2016/1034, art 7(1), (3), Sch 1, para 4(1), (6)(b), as from 30 November 2016 (except in relation to (i) a sequestration as regards which the petition is presented, or the debtor application is made before that date; or (ii) a trust deed executed before that date).

Sub-s (4): definition "company" substituted by the Companies Act 2006 (Consequential Amendments, Transitional Provisions and Savings) Order 2009, SI 2009/1941, art 2(1), Sch 1, para 78(1), (2), subject to transitional provisions and savings in art 8, Sch 1, para 84 at **[2.70]**, **[2.73]**, and originally read as follows:

""company" means a company within the meaning given by section 735(1) of the Companies Act or a company which may be wound up under Part V of this Act (unregistered companies);";

definition "sequestration" substituted (for the original definitions "interim trustee" and "permanent trustee") by SI 2016/1034, art 7(1), (3), Sch 1, para 4(1), (6)(c), as from 30 November 2016 (except in relation to (i) a sequestration as regards which the petition is presented, or the debtor application is made before that date; or (ii) a trust deed executed before that date); the original definitions read as follows—

""interim trustee" and "permanent trustee" mean the same as in the Bankruptcy (Scotland) Act 1985.".

Sub-s (5): substituted by the Bankruptcy (Scotland) Act 1993, s 11(1), subject to s 12(6) of that Act at **[5.194]** and the Bankruptcy (Scotland) Act 1993 Commencement and Savings Order 1993, SI 1993/438, art 4 at **[16.58]**; year "2016" in square brackets substituted (for the original year "1985") by SI 2016/1034, art 7(1), (3), Sch 1, para 4(1), (6)(d), as from 30 November 2016 (except in relation to (i) a sequestration as regards which the petition is presented, or the debtor application is made before that date; or (ii) a trust deed executed before that date).

Sub-s (6): added by the Insolvency Act 1986 (Amendment) (No 2) Regulations 2002, SI 2002/1240, regs 3, 17; words in square brackets substituted for original words "EC Regulation" by the Insolvency Amendment (EU 2015/848) Regulations 2017, SI 2017/702, regs 2, 3, Schedule, Pt 1, paras 1, 23, except in relation to proceedings opened before 26 June 2017 and subject to savings in reg 4 thereof at **[2.103]**.

Property subject to a forfeiture or restraint order: as to the liability and expenses of insolvency practitioners dealing with property that is subject to a forfeiture or restraint order under the Terrorism Act 2000, see s 23(9) of, and Sch 4, Pt IV, para 51 to, that Act.

Disapplication: this section is disapplied in relation to anything done by a foreign representative, under or by virtue of and in relation to relief granted or coordination provided, under the Cross-Border Insolvency Regulations 2006, SI 2006/1030, by the Cross-Border Insolvency Regulations 2006, SI 2006/1030, reg 8 at **[3.309]**.

[1.476]
389 Acting without qualification an offence

(1) A person who acts as an insolvency practitioner in relation to a company or an individual at a time when he is not qualified to do so is liable to imprisonment or a fine, or to both.

[(1A) . . .]

(2) This section does not apply to the official receiver [or the Accountant in Bankruptcy (within the meaning of the Bankruptcy (Scotland) Act [2016])].

NOTES

This section derived from the Insolvency Act 1985, s 1(1).

Sub-s (1A): inserted by the Insolvency Act 2000, s 4(1), (3); repealed by the Deregulation Act 2015, s 19, Sch 6, Pt 6, paras 17, 18.

Sub-s (2): words in first (outer) pair of square brackets added by the Bankruptcy (Scotland) Act 1993, s 11(2); year "2016" in second (inner) pair of square brackets substituted (for the original year "1985") by the Bankruptcy (Scotland) Act 2016 (Consequential Provisions and Modifications) Order 2016, SI 2016/1034, art 7(1), (3), Sch 1, para 4(1), (7), as from 30 November 2016 (except in relation to (i) a sequestration as regards which the petition is presented, or the debtor application is made before that date; or (ii) a trust deed executed before that date).

389A *(Inserted by the Insolvency Act 2000, s 4(1), (4), and repealed by the Deregulation Act 2015, s 19, Sch 6, Pt 6, paras 17, 19.)*

[1.477]
[389B Official receiver as nominee or supervisor

(1) The official receiver is authorised to act as nominee or supervisor in relation to a voluntary arrangement approved under Part VIII provided that the debtor is an undischarged bankrupt when the arrangement is proposed.

(2) The Secretary of State may by order repeal the proviso in subsection (1).

(3) An order under subsection (2)—

(a) must be made by statutory instrument, and

(b) shall be subject to annulment in pursuance of a resolution of either House of Parliament.]

NOTES

Inserted by the Enterprise Act 2002, s 264(1), Sch 22, para 3.

The requisite qualification, and the means of obtaining it

[1.478]
390 Persons not qualified to act as insolvency practitioners

(1) A person who is not an individual is not qualified to act as an insolvency practitioner.

[(2) A person is not qualified to act as an insolvency practitioner at any time unless at that time the person is appropriately authorised under section 390A.]

(3) A person is not qualified to act as an insolvency practitioner in relation to another person at any time unless—

(a) there is in force at that time security or, in Scotland, caution for the proper performance of his functions, and

(b) that security or caution meets the prescribed requirements with respect to his so acting in relation to that other person[; or

(c) he holds an authorisation granted by the Department of Enterprise, Trade and Investment for Northern Ireland under Article 352 of the Insolvency (Northern Ireland) Order 1989.]

(4) A person is not qualified to act as an insolvency practitioner at any time if at that time—

(a) he has been [made] bankrupt [under this Act or the Insolvency (Northern Ireland) Order 1989] or sequestration of his estate has been awarded and (in either case) he has not been discharged,

[(aa) a moratorium period under a debt relief order [under this Act or the Insolvency (Northern Ireland) Order 1989] applies in relation of him,]

[(b) he is subject to a disqualification order made or a disqualification undertaking accepted under the Company Directors Disqualification Act 1986 or the Company Directors Disqualification (Northern Ireland) Order 2002,]

(c) he is a patient within the meaning of . . . [section 329(1) of the Mental Health (Care and Treatment) (Scotland) Act 2003] [or has had a guardian appointed to him under the Adults with Incapacity (Scotland) Act 2000 (asp 4)][, or

(d) he lacks capacity (within the meaning of the Mental Capacity Act 2005) to act as an insolvency practitioner].

[(5) A person is not qualified to act as an insolvency practitioner while there is in force in respect of that person—

(a) a bankruptcy restrictions order under this Act, the Bankruptcy (Scotland) Act 1985 [or the Bankruptcy (Scotland) Act 2016] or the Insolvency (Northern Ireland) Order 1989, or

(b) a debt relief restrictions order under this Act or that Order.]

NOTES

This section derived from the Insolvency Act 1985, ss 2, 3(1).

Sub-s (2): substituted by the Deregulation Act 2015, s 17(1), (2).

Sub-s (4): word in first pair of square brackets in para (a) substituted for original word "adjudged" by the Enterprise and Regulatory Reform Act 2013, s 71(3), Sch 19, paras 1, 58, in respect of a petition for a bankruptcy order presented to the court by a debtor on or after 6 April 2016; para (aa) inserted by the Tribunals, Courts and Enforcement Act 2007, s 108(3), Sch 20, Pt 1, paras 1, 6(1), (2); words in second pair of square brackets in para (a) and words in square brackets in para (aa) inserted by the Small Business, Enterprise and Employment Act 2015, s 115(a), in relation to an individual in respect of whom a bankruptcy restrictions order or a debt relief restrictions order is made or granted on or after 1 October 2015; para (b) substituted by the Companies Act 2006 (Consequential Amendments, Transitional Provisions and Savings) Order 2009, SI 2009/1941, art 2(1), Sch 1, para 78(1), (4), subject to transitional provisions and savings in art 8, Sch 1, para 84 at **[2.70]**, **[2.73]**, and previously (as amended by the Insolvency Act 2000, s 8, Sch 4, Pt II, para 16(1), (2), SI 2004/1941, art 3, Schedule, paras 1, 3 and the Mental Capacity Act 2005, s 67(1), (2), Sch 6, para 31(1), (3)(a), Sch 7), read as follows:

"(b) he is subject to a disqualification order made [or a disqualification undertaking accepted] under the Company Directors Disqualification Act 1986 [or to a disqualification order made under Part II of the Companies (Northern Ireland) Order 1989] [or to a disqualification undertaking accepted under the Company Directors Disqualification (Northern Ireland) Order 2002], . . . ";

words in first pair of square brackets in para (c) substituted in relation to England and Wales by the Mental Health (Care and Treatment) (Scotland) Act 2003 (Consequential Provisions) Order 2005, SI 2005/2078, art 15, Sch 1, para 3(1), (3) and in relation to Scotland by the Mental Health (Care and Treatment) (Scotland) Act 2003 (Modification of Enactments) Order 2005, SSI 2005/465, art 2, Sch 1, para 18(1), (3); words in second pair of square brackets in para (c) inserted by the Adults with Incapacity (Scotland) Act 2000, s 88(2), Sch 5, para 18; words omitted from para (c) repealed, and para (d) and the word immediately preceding it inserted by the Mental Capacity Act 2005, s 67(1), (2), Sch 6, para 31(1), (3)(b), (c), Sch 7.

Sub-s (5): substituted by the Small Business, Enterprise and Employment Act 2015, s 115(b), in relation to an individual in respect of whom a bankruptcy restrictions order or a debt relief restrictions order is made or granted on or after 1 October 2015. Previously, sub-s (5) (as added by the Enterprise Act 2002, s 257(3), Sch 21, para 4, with words in square brackets inserted by the Tribunals, Courts and Enforcement Act 2007, s 108(3), Sch 20, Pt 1, paras 1, 6(1), (3)) read as follows—

"[(5) A person is not qualified to act as an insolvency practitioner while a bankruptcy restrictions order [or a debt relief restrictions order] is in force in respect of him.]".

Words in square brackets in sub-s (5) inserted by the Bankruptcy (Scotland) Act 2016 (Consequential Provisions and Modifications) Order 2016, SI 2016/1034, art 7(1), (3), Sch 1, para 4(1), (8), as from 30 November 2016 (except in relation to (i) a sequestration as regards which the petition is presented, or the debtor application is made before that date; or (ii) a trust deed executed before that date).

Regulations: the Insolvency Practitioners Regulations 2005, SI 2005/524 at **[12.30]**.

[1.479]

[390A Authorisation

(1) In this Part—

"partial authorisation" means authorisation to act as an insolvency practitioner—

(a) only in relation to companies, or

(b) only in relation to individuals;

"full authorisation" means authorisation to act as an insolvency practitioner in relation to companies, individuals and insolvent partnerships;

"partially authorised" and "fully authorised" are to be construed accordingly.

(2) A person is fully authorised under this section to act as an insolvency practitioner—

(a) by virtue of being a member of a professional body recognised under section 391(1) and being permitted to act as an insolvency practitioner for all purposes by or under the rules of that body, or

(b) by holding an authorisation granted by the Department of Enterprise, Trade and Investment in Northern Ireland under Article 352 of the Insolvency (Northern Ireland) Order 1989.

(3) A person is partially authorised under this section to act as an insolvency practitioner—

(a) by virtue of being a member of a professional body recognised under section 391(1) and being permitted to act as an insolvency practitioner in relation only to companies or only to individuals by or under the rules of that body, or

(b) by virtue of being a member of a professional body recognised under section 391(2) and being permitted to act as an insolvency practitioner by or under the rules of that body.]

NOTES

Commencement: 1 October 2015.

Inserted, together with s 390B, by Deregulation Act 2015, s 17(1), (3).

Transitional provisions: see the Deregulation Act 2015, Sch 6, Pt 6, para 23 (as amended by the Deregulation Act 2015 (Commencement No 3 and Transitional and Saving Provisions) Order 2015, SI 2015/1732, art 8) which provides as follows—

"23.

(1) For the purposes of this paragraph—

the "commencement date" is [1 October 2015 (the date on which paragraph 21 of this Schedule came into force)];

the "transitional period" is the period of 1 year beginning with the commencement date.

(2) Where, immediately before the commencement date, a person holds an authorisation granted under section 393 of the Insolvency Act 1986, section 393(3A) to (6) of that Act together with, for the purposes of this sub-paragraph, paragraphs (a) and (b) of section 393(2) of that Act (which are repealed by paragraph 21) continue to have effect in relation to the person and the authorisation during the transitional period.

(3) During the transitional period, a person to whom sub-paragraph (2) applies is to be treated for the purposes of Part 13 of the Insolvency Act 1986 as fully authorised under section 390A of that Act (as inserted by section 17(3) of this Act) to act as an insolvency practitioner unless and until the person's authorisation is (by virtue of sub-paragraph (2)) withdrawn.

(4) Where, immediately before the commencement date, a person has applied under section 392 of the Insolvency Act 1986 for authorisation to act as an insolvency practitioner and the application has not been granted, refused or withdrawn, sections 392(4) to (7) and 393(1) and (2) of that Act (which are repealed by paragraph 21) continue to have effect in relation to the person and the application during the transitional period.

(5) Where, during the transitional period, an authorisation is (by virtue of sub-paragraph (4)) granted under section 393 of the Insolvency Act 1986, sub-paragraphs (2) and (3) above apply as if—

(a) the authorisation had been granted immediately before the commencement date;

(b) in sub-paragraph (2), the reference to section 393(3A) to (6) were a reference to section 393(4) to (6).

(6) For the purposes of sub-paragraphs (2) and (4), sections 394 to 398 of, and Schedule 7 to, the Insolvency Act 1986 (which are repealed by paragraph 21) continue to have effect during the transitional period.".

[1.480]

[390B Partial authorisation: acting in relation to partnerships

(1) A person who is partially authorised to act as an insolvency practitioner in relation to companies may nonetheless not accept an appointment to act in relation to a company if at the time of the appointment the person is aware that the company—

(a) is or was a member of a partnership, and

(b) has outstanding liabilities in relation to the partnership.

(2) A person who is partially authorised to act as an insolvency practitioner in relation to individuals may nonetheless not accept an appointment to act in relation to an individual if at the time of the appointment the person is aware that the individual—

(a) is or was a member of a partnership other than a Scottish partnership, and

(b) has outstanding liabilities in relation to the partnership.

(3) Subject to subsection (9), a person who is partially authorised to act as an insolvency practitioner in relation to companies may nonetheless not continue to act in relation to a company if the person becomes aware that the company—

(a) is or was a member of a partnership, and

(b) has outstanding liabilities in relation to the partnership,

unless the person is granted permission to continue to act by the court.

(4) Subject to subsection (9), a person who is partially authorised to act as an insolvency practitioner in relation to individuals may nonetheless not continue to act in relation to an individual if the person becomes aware that the individual—

(a) is or was a member of a partnership other than a Scottish partnership, and

(b) has outstanding liabilities in relation to the partnership,

unless the person is granted permission to continue to act by the court.

(5) The court may grant a person permission to continue to act for the purposes of subsection (3) or (4) if it is satisfied that the person is competent to do so.

(6) A person who is partially authorised and becomes aware as mentioned in subsection (3) or (4) may alternatively apply to the court for an order (a "replacement order") appointing in his or her place a person who is fully authorised to act as an insolvency practitioner in relation to the company or (as the case may be) the individual.

(7) A person may apply to the court for permission to continue to act or for a replacement order under—

(a) where acting in relation to a company, this section or, if it applies, section 168(5B) (member of insolvent partnership: England and Wales);

(b) where acting in relation to an individual, this section or, if it applies, section 303(2C) (member of insolvent partnership: England and Wales).

(8) A person who acts as an insolvency practitioner in contravention of any of subsections (1) to (4) is guilty of an offence under section 389 (acting without qualification).

(9) A person does not contravene subsection (3) or (4) by continuing to act as an insolvency practitioner during the permitted period if, within the period of 7 business days beginning with the day after the day on which the person becomes aware as mentioned in the subsection, the person—

(a) applies to the court for permission to continue to act, or

(b) applies to the court for a replacement order.

(10) For the purposes of subsection (9)—

"business day" means any day other than a Saturday, a Sunday, Christmas Day, Good Friday or a day which is a bank holiday in any part of Great Britain;

"permitted period" means the period beginning with the day on which the person became aware as mentioned in subsection (3) or (4) and ending on the earlier of—

(a) the expiry of the period of 6 weeks beginning with the day on which the person applies to the court as mentioned in subsection (9)(a) or (b), and

(b) the day on which the court disposes of the application (by granting or refusing it);

"replacement order" has the meaning given by subsection (6).]

NOTES

Commencement: 1 October 2015.

Inserted as noted to s 390A at **[1.479]**.

[1.481]
[391 Recognised professional bodies

(1) The Secretary of State may by order, if satisfied that a body meets the requirements of subsection (4), declare the body to be a recognised professional body which is capable of providing its insolvency specialist members with full authorisation or partial authorisation.

(2) The Secretary of State may by order, if satisfied that a body meets the requirements of subsection (4), declare the body to be a recognised professional body which is capable of providing its insolvency specialist members with partial authorisation only of the kind specified in the order (as to which, see section 390A(1)).

(3) Section 391A makes provision about the making by a body of an application to the Secretary of State for an order under this section.

(4) The requirements are that—

(a) the body regulates (or is going to regulate) the practice of a profession,

(b) the body has rules which it is going to maintain and enforce for securing that its insolvency specialist members—

(i) are fit and proper persons to act as insolvency practitioners, and

(ii) meet acceptable requirements as to education and practical training and experience, and

(c) the body's rules and practices for or in connection with authorising persons to act as insolvency practitioners, and its rules and practices for or in connection with regulating persons acting as such, are designed to ensure that the regulatory objectives are met (as to which, see section 391C).

(5) An order of the Secretary of State under this section has effect from such date as is specified in the order.

(6) An order under this section may be revoked by an order under section 391L or 391N (and see section 415A(1)(b)).

(7) In this Part—

(a) references to members of a recognised professional body are to persons who, whether members of that body or not, are subject to its rules in the practice of the profession in question;

(b) references to insolvency specialist members of a professional body are to members who are permitted by or under the rules of the body to act as insolvency practitioners.

(8) A reference in this Part to a recognised professional body is to a body recognised under this section (and see sections 391L(6) and 391N(5)).]

NOTES

Commencement: 1 October 2015.

Substituted, together with s 391A for the original s 391, by the Small Business, Enterprise and Employment Act 2015, s 137(1), as from 1 October 2015 (and immediately after the Deregulation Act 2015, s 17 comes into force (see further the note below)).

This section was also substituted by the Deregulation Act 2015, s 17(1), (4). The Deregulation Act 2015 (Commencement No 3 and Transitional and Saving Provisions) Order 2015, SI 2015/1732 brought s 17 into force on 1 October 2015. See, however, the Small Business, Enterprise and Employment Act 2015 (Commencement No 2 and Transitional Provisions) Regulations 2015, SI 2015/1689, reg 3 which provides that the Small Business, Enterprise and Employment Act 2015, s 137 comes into force immediately after the coming into force of the Deregulation Act 2015, s 17.

Note that the Small Business, Enterprise and Employment Act 2015, s 137(2) provides that an Order made under sub-ss (1) or (2) before 1 October 2015 is, on that date, to be treated as if it were made under sub-ss (1) or (2) as substituted by s 137(1) of the 2015 Act.

Orders: the Insolvency Practitioners (Recognised Professional Bodies) Order 1986, SI 1986/1764 at **[12.1]**

[1.482]
[391A Application for recognition as recognised professional body

(1) An application for an order under section 391(1) or (2) must—

(a) be made to the Secretary of State in such form and manner as the Secretary of State may require,

(b) be accompanied by such information as the Secretary of State may require, and

(c) be supplemented by such additional information as the Secretary of State may require at any time between receiving the application and determining it.

(2) The requirements which may be imposed under subsection (1) may differ as between different applications.

(3) The Secretary of State may require information provided under this section to be in such form, and verified in such manner, as the Secretary of State may specify.

(4) An application for an order under section 391(1) or (2) must be accompanied by—

(a) a copy of the applicant's rules,

(b) a copy of the applicant's policies and practices, and

(c) a copy of any guidance issued by the applicant in writing.

(5) The reference in subsection (4)(c) to guidance issued by the applicant is a reference to guidance or recommendations which are—

(a) issued or made by it which will apply to its insolvency specialist members or to persons seeking to become such members,

(b) relevant for the purposes of this Part, and

(c) intended to have continuing effect,

including guidance or recommendations relating to the admission or expulsion of members.

(6) The Secretary of State may refuse an application for an order under section 391(1) or (2) if the Secretary of State considers that recognition of the body concerned is unnecessary having regard to the existence of one or more other bodies which have been or are likely to be recognised under section 391.
(7) Subsection (8) applies where the Secretary of State refuses an application for an order under section 391(1) or (2); and it applies regardless of whether the application is refused on the ground mentioned in subsection (6), because the Secretary of State is not satisfied as mentioned in section 391(1) or (2) or because a fee has not been paid (see section 415A(1)(b)).
(8) The Secretary of State must give the applicant a written notice of the Secretary of State's decision; and the notice must set out the reasons for refusing the application.]

NOTES

Commencement: 1 October 2015.
Substituted as noted to s 391 at **[1.481]**.

[Regulatory objectives

[1.483]
391B Application of regulatory objectives
(1) In discharging regulatory functions, a recognised professional body must, so far as is reasonably practicable, act in a way—
(a) which is compatible with the regulatory objectives, and
(b) which the body considers most appropriate for the purpose of meeting those objectives.
(2) In discharging functions under this Part, the Secretary of State must have regard to the regulatory objectives.]

NOTES

Commencement: 1 October 2015.
Inserted, together with the preceding heading and s 391C, by the Small Business, Enterprise and Employment Act 2015, s 138(1).

[1.484]
[391C Meaning of "regulatory functions" and "regulatory objectives"
(1) This section has effect for the purposes of this Part.
(2) "Regulatory functions", in relation to a recognised professional body, means any functions the body has—
(a) under or in relation to its arrangements for or in connection with—
(i) authorising persons to act as insolvency practitioners, or
(ii) regulating persons acting as insolvency practitioners, or
(b) in connection with the making or alteration of those arrangements.
(3) "Regulatory objectives" means the objectives of—
(a) having a system of regulating persons acting as insolvency practitioners that—
(i) secures fair treatment for persons affected by their acts and omissions,
(ii) reflects the regulatory principles, and
(iii) ensures consistent outcomes,
(b) encouraging an independent and competitive insolvency-practitioner profession whose members—
(i) provide high quality services at a cost to the recipient which is fair and reasonable,
(ii) act transparently and with integrity, and
(iii) consider the interests of all creditors in any particular case,
(c) promoting the maximisation of the value of returns to creditors and promptness in making those returns, and
(d) protecting and promoting the public interest.
(4) In subsection (3)(a), "regulatory principles" means—
(a) the principles that regulatory activities should be transparent, accountable, proportionate, consistent and targeted only at cases in which action is needed, and
(b) any other principle appearing to the body concerned (in the case of the duty under section 391B(1)), or to the Secretary of State (in the case of the duty under section 391B(2)), to lead to best regulatory practice.]

NOTES

Commencement: 1 October 2015.
Inserted as noted to s 391B at **[1.483]**.

[Oversight of recognised professional bodies

[1.485]
391D Directions
(1) This section applies if the Secretary of State is satisfied that an act or omission of a recognised professional body (or a series of such acts or omissions) in discharging one or more of its regulatory functions has had, or is likely to have, an adverse impact on the achievement of one or more of the regulatory objectives.
(2) The Secretary of State may, if in all the circumstances of the case satisfied that it is appropriate to do so, direct the body to take such steps as the Secretary of State considers will counter the adverse impact, mitigate its effect or prevent its occurrence or recurrence.
(3) A direction under this section may require a recognised professional body—

(a) to take only such steps as it has power to take under its regulatory arrangements;
(b) to take steps with a view to the modification of any part of its regulatory arrangements.

(4) A direction under this section may require a recognised professional body—
(a) to take steps with a view to the institution of, or otherwise in respect of, specific regulatory proceedings;
(b) to take steps in respect of all, or a specified class of, such proceedings.

(5) For the purposes of this section, a direction to take steps includes a direction which requires a recognised professional body to refrain from taking a particular course of action.

(6) In this section "regulatory arrangements", in relation to a recognised professional body, means the arrangements that the body has for or in connection with—
(a) authorising persons to act as insolvency practitioners, or
(b) regulating persons acting as insolvency practitioners.]

NOTES

Commencement: 1 October 2015.

Inserted, together with the preceding heading and ss 391D–391K, by the Small Business, Enterprise and Employment Act 2015, s 139(1).

[1.486]

[391E Directions: procedure

(1) Before giving a recognised professional body a direction under section 391D, the Secretary of State must give the body a notice accompanied by a draft of the proposed direction.

(2) The notice under subsection (1) must—
(a) state that the Secretary of State proposes to give the body a direction in the form of the accompanying draft,
(b) specify why the Secretary of State has reached the conclusions mentioned in section 391D(1) and (2), and
(c) specify a period within which the body may make written representations with respect to the proposal.

(3) The period specified under subsection (2)(c)—
(a) must begin with the date on which the notice is given to the body, and
(b) must not be less than 28 days.

(4) On the expiry of that period, the Secretary of State must decide whether to give the body the proposed direction.

(5) The Secretary of State must give notice of that decision to the body.

(6) Where the Secretary of State decides to give the proposed direction, the notice under subsection (5) must—
(a) contain the direction,
(b) state the time at which the direction is to take effect, and
(c) specify the Secretary of State's reasons for the decision to give the direction.

(7) Where the Secretary of State decides to give the proposed direction, the Secretary of State must publish the notice under subsection (5); but this subsection does not apply to a direction to take any step with a view to the institution of, or otherwise in respect of, regulatory proceedings against an individual.

(8) The Secretary of State may revoke a direction under section 391D; and, where doing so, the Secretary of State—
(a) must give the body to which the direction was given notice of the revocation, and
(b) must publish the notice and, if the notice under subsection (5) was published under subsection (7), must do so (if possible) in the same manner as that in which that notice was published.]

NOTES

Commencement: 1 October 2015.

Inserted as noted to s 391D at **[1.485]**.

[1.487]

[391F Financial penalty

(1) This section applies if the Secretary of State is satisfied—
(a) that a recognised professional body has failed to comply with a requirement to which this section applies, and
(b) that, in all the circumstances of the case, it is appropriate to impose a financial penalty on the body.

(2) This section applies to a requirement imposed on the recognised professional body—
(a) by a direction given under section 391D, or
(b) by a provision of this Act or of subordinate legislation under this Act.

(3) The Secretary of State may impose a financial penalty, in respect of the failure, of such amount as the Secretary of State considers appropriate.

(4) In deciding what amount is appropriate, the Secretary of State—
(a) must have regard to the nature of the requirement which has not been complied with, and
(b) must not take into account the Secretary of State's costs in discharging functions under this Part.

(5) A financial penalty under this section is payable to the Secretary of State; and sums received by the Secretary of State in respect of a financial penalty under this section (including by way of interest) are to be paid into the Consolidated Fund.

(6) In sections 391G to 391I, "penalty" means a financial penalty under this section.]

NOTES

Commencement: 1 October 2015.

Inserted as noted to s 391D at **[1.485]**.

[1.488]

[391G Financial penalty: procedure

(1) Before imposing a penalty on a recognised professional body, the Secretary of State must give notice to the body—

(a) stating that the Secretary of State proposes to impose a penalty and the amount of the proposed penalty,

(b) specifying the requirement in question,

(c) stating why the Secretary of State is satisfied as mentioned in section 391F(1), and

(d) specifying a period within which the body may make written representations with respect to the proposal.

(2) The period specified under subsection (1)(d)—

(a) must begin with the date on which the notice is given to the body, and

(b) must not be less than 28 days.

(3) On the expiry of that period, the Secretary of State must decide—

(a) whether to impose a penalty, and

(b) whether the penalty should be the amount stated in the notice or a reduced amount.

(4) The Secretary of State must give notice of the decision to the body.

(5) Where the Secretary of State decides to impose a penalty, the notice under subsection (4) must—

(a) state that the Secretary of State has imposed a penalty on the body and its amount,

(b) specify the requirement in question and state—

(i) why it appears to the Secretary of State that the requirement has not been complied with, or

(ii) where, by that time, the requirement has been complied with, why it appeared to the Secretary of State when giving the notice under subsection (1) that the requirement had not been complied with, and

(c) specify a time by which the penalty is required to be paid.

(6) The time specified under subsection (5)(c) must be at least three months after the date on which the notice under subsection (4) is given to the body.

(7) Where the Secretary of State decides to impose a penalty, the Secretary of State must publish the notice under subsection (4).

(8) The Secretary of State may rescind or reduce a penalty imposed on a recognised professional body; and, where doing so, the Secretary of State—

(a) must give the body notice that the penalty has been rescinded or reduced to the amount stated in the notice, and

(b) must publish the notice; and it must (if possible) be published in the same manner as that in which the notice under subsection (4) was published.]

NOTES

Commencement: 1 October 2015.

Inserted as noted to s 391D at **[1.485]**.

[1.489]

[391H Appeal against financial penalty

(1) A recognised professional body on which a penalty is imposed may appeal to the court on one or more of the appeal grounds.

(2) The appeal grounds are—

(a) that the imposition of the penalty was not within the Secretary of State's power under section 391F;

(b) that the requirement in respect of which the penalty was imposed had been complied with before the notice under section 391G(1) was given;

(c) that the requirements of section 391G have not been complied with in relation to the imposition of the penalty and the interests of the body have been substantially prejudiced as a result;

(d) that the amount of the penalty is unreasonable;

(e) that it was unreasonable of the Secretary of State to require the penalty imposed to be paid by the time specified in the notice under section 391G(5)(c).

(3) An appeal under this section must be made within the period of three months beginning with the day on which the notice under section 391G(4) in respect of the penalty is given to the body.

(4) On an appeal under this section the court may—

(a) quash the penalty,

(b) substitute a penalty of such lesser amount as the court considers appropriate, or

(c) in the case of the appeal ground in subsection (2)(e), substitute for the time imposed by the Secretary of State a different time.

(5) Where the court substitutes a penalty of a lesser amount, it may require the payment of interest on the substituted penalty from such time, and at such rate, as it considers just and equitable.

(6) Where the court substitutes a later time for the time specified in the notice under section 391G(5)(c), it may require the payment of interest on the penalty from the substituted time at such rate as it considers just and equitable.

(7) Where the court dismisses the appeal, it may require the payment of interest on the penalty from the time specified in the notice under section 391G(5)(c) at such rate as it considers just and equitable.
(8) In this section, "the court" means the High Court or, in Scotland, the Court of Session.]

NOTES

Commencement: 1 October 2015.
Inserted as noted to s 391D at **[1.485]**.

[1.490]
[391I Recovery of financial penalties

(1) If the whole or part of a penalty is not paid by the time by which it is required to be paid, the unpaid balance from time to time carries interest at the rate for the time being specified in section 17 of the Judgments Act 1838 (but this is subject to any requirement imposed by the court under section 391H(5), (6) or (7)).
(2) If an appeal is made under section 391H in relation to a penalty, the penalty is not required to be paid until the appeal has been determined or withdrawn.
(3) Subsection (4) applies where the whole or part of a penalty has not been paid by the time it is required to be paid and—
  (a) no appeal relating to the penalty has been made under section 391H during the period within which an appeal may be made under that section, or
  (b) an appeal has been made under that section and determined or withdrawn.
(4) The Secretary of State may recover from the recognised professional body in question, as a debt due to the Secretary of State, any of the penalty and any interest which has not been paid.]

NOTES

Commencement: 1 October 2015.
Inserted as noted to s 391D at **[1.485]**.

[1.491]
[391J Reprimand

(1) This section applies if the Secretary of State is satisfied that an act or omission of a recognised professional body (or a series of such acts or omissions) in discharging one or more of its regulatory functions has had, or is likely to have, an adverse impact on the achievement of one or more of the regulatory objectives.
(2) The Secretary of State may, if in all the circumstances of the case satisfied that it is appropriate to do so, publish a statement reprimanding the body for the act or omission (or series of acts or omissions).]

NOTES

Commencement: 1 October 2015.
Inserted as noted to s 391D at **[1.485]**.

[1.492]
[391K Reprimand: procedure

(1) If the Secretary of State proposes to publish a statement under section 391J in respect of a recognised professional body, it must give the body a notice—
  (a) stating that the Secretary of State proposes to publish such a statement and setting out the terms of the proposed statement,
  (b) specifying the acts or omissions to which the proposed statement relates, and
  (c) specifying a period within which the body may make written representations with respect to the proposal.
(2) The period specified under subsection (1)(c)—
  (a) must begin with the date on which the notice is given to the body, and
  (b) must not be less than 28 days.
(3) On the expiry of that period, the Secretary of State must decide whether to publish the statement.
(4) The Secretary of State may vary the proposed statement; but before doing so, the Secretary of State must give the body notice—
  (a) setting out the proposed variation and the reasons for it, and
  (b) specifying a period within which the body may make written representations with respect to the proposed variation.
(5) The period specified under subsection (4)(b)—
  (a) must begin with the date on which the notice is given to the body, and
  (b) must not be less than 28 days.
(6) On the expiry of that period, the Secretary of State must decide whether to publish the statement as varied.]

NOTES

Commencement: 1 October 2015.
Inserted as noted to s 391D at **[1.485]**.

[Revocation etc of recognition

[1.493]

391L Revocation of recognition at instigation of Secretary of State

(1) An order under section 391(1) or (2) in relation to a recognised professional body may be revoked by the Secretary of State by order if the Secretary of State is satisfied that—

(a) an act or omission of the body (or a series of such acts or omissions) in discharging one or more of its regulatory functions has had, or is likely to have, an adverse impact on the achievement of one or more of the regulatory objectives, and

(b) it is appropriate in all the circumstances of the case to revoke the body's recognition under section 391.

(2) If the condition set out in subsection (3) is met, an order under section 391(1) in relation to a recognised professional body may be revoked by the Secretary of State by an order which also declares the body concerned to be a recognised professional body which is capable of providing its insolvency specialist members with partial authorisation only of the kind specified in the order (see section 390A(1)).

(3) The condition is that the Secretary of State is satisfied—

(a) as mentioned in subsection (1)(a), and

(b) that it is appropriate in all the circumstances of the case for the body to be declared to be a recognised professional body which is capable of providing its insolvency specialist members with partial authorisation only of the kind specified in the order.

(4) In this Part—

(a) an order under subsection (1) is referred to as a "revocation order";

(b) an order under subsection (2) is referred to as a "partial revocation order".

(5) A revocation order or partial revocation order—

(a) has effect from such date as is specified in the order, and

(b) may make provision for members of the body in question to continue to be treated as fully or partially authorised (as the case may be) to act as insolvency practitioners for a specified period after the order takes effect.

(6) A partial revocation order has effect as if it were an order made under section 391(2).]

NOTES

Commencement: 1 October 2015.

Inserted, together with the preceding heading and ss 391M, 391N, by the Small Business, Enterprise and Employment Act 2015, s 140(1).

[1.494]

[391M Orders under section 391L: procedure

(1) Before making a revocation order or partial revocation order in relation to a recognised professional body, the Secretary of State must give notice to the body—

(a) stating that the Secretary of State proposes to make the order and the terms of the proposed order,

(b) specifying the Secretary of State's reasons for proposing to make the order, and

(c) specifying a period within which the body, members of the body or other persons likely to be affected by the proposal may make written representations with respect to it.

(2) Where the Secretary of State gives a notice under subsection (1), the Secretary of State must publish the notice on the same day.

(3) The period specified under subsection (1)(c)—

(a) must begin with the date on which the notice is given to the body, and

(b) must not be less than 28 days.

(4) On the expiry of that period, the Secretary of State must decide whether to make the revocation order or (as the case may be) partial revocation order in relation to the body.

(5) The Secretary of State must give notice of the decision to the body.

(6) Where the Secretary of State decides to make the order, the notice under subsection (5) must specify—

(a) when the order is to take effect, and

(b) the Secretary of State's reasons for making the order.

(7) A notice under subsection (5) must be published; and it must (if possible) be published in the same manner as that in which the notice under subsection (1) was published.]

NOTES

Commencement: 1 October 2015.

Inserted as noted to s 391L at **[1.493]**.

[1.495]

[391N Revocation of recognition at request of body

(1) An order under section 391(1) or (2) in relation to a recognised professional body may be revoked by the Secretary of State by order if—

(a) the body has requested that an order be made under this subsection, and

(b) the Secretary of State is satisfied that it is appropriate in all the circumstances of the case to revoke the body's recognition under section 391.

(2) An order under section 391(1) in relation to a recognised professional body may be revoked by the Secretary of State by an order which also declares the body concerned to be a recognised professional body which is capable of providing its insolvency specialist members with partial authorisation only of the kind specified in the order (see section 390A(1)) if—

(a) the body has requested that an order be made under this subsection, and
(b) the Secretary of State is satisfied that it is appropriate in all the circumstances of the case for the body to be declared to be a recognised professional body which is capable of providing its insolvency specialist members with partial authorisation only of the kind specified in the order.

(3) Where the Secretary of State decides to make an order under this section the Secretary of State must publish a notice specifying—
(a) when the order is to take effect, and
(b) the Secretary of State's reasons for making the order.

(4) An order under this section—
(a) has effect from such date as is specified in the order, and
(b) may make provision for members of the body in question to continue to be treated as fully or partially authorised (as the case may be) to act as insolvency practitioners for a specified period after the order takes effect.

(5) An order under subsection (2) has effect as if it were an order made under section 391(2).]

NOTES

Commencement: 1 October 2015.

Inserted as noted to s 391L at **[1.493]**.

Orders: the Insolvency Practitioners (Recognised Professional Bodies) (Revocation of Recognition) Order 2015, SI 2015/2067; the Insolvency Practitioners (Recognised Professional Bodies) (Revocation of Recognition) Order 2016, SI 2016/403.

[Court sanction of insolvency practitioners in public interest cases

[1.496]
391O Direct sanctions orders

(1) For the purposes of this Part a "direct sanctions order" is an order made by the court against a person who is acting as an insolvency practitioner which—
(a) declares that the person is no longer authorised (whether fully or partially) to act as an insolvency practitioner;
(b) declares that the person is no longer fully authorised to act as an insolvency practitioner but remains partially authorised to act as such either in relation to companies or individuals, as specified in the order;
(c) declares that the person's authorisation to act as an insolvency practitioner is suspended for the period specified in the order or until such time as the requirements so specified are complied with;
(d) requires the person to comply with such other requirements as may be specified in the order while acting as an insolvency practitioner;
(e) requires the person to make such contribution as may be specified in the order to one or more creditors of a company, individual or insolvent partnership in relation to which the person is acting or has acted as an insolvency practitioner.

(2) Where the court makes a direct sanctions order, the relevant recognised professional body must take all necessary steps to give effect to the order.

(3) A direct sanctions order must not be made against a person whose authorisation to act as an insolvency practitioner was granted by the Department of Enterprise, Trade and Investment in Northern Ireland (see section 390A(2)(b)).

(4) A direct sanctions order must not specify a contribution as mentioned in subsection (1)(e) which is more than the remuneration that the person has received or will receive in respect of acting as an insolvency practitioner in the case.

(5) In this section and section 391P—
"the court" means the High Court or, in Scotland, the Court of Session;
"relevant recognised professional body", in relation to a person who is acting as an insolvency practitioner, means the recognised professional body by virtue of which the person is authorised so to act.]

NOTES

Commencement: 1 October 2015.

Inserted, together with the preceding heading and ss 391P–391R, by the Small Business, Enterprise and Employment Act 2015, s 141. Note that ss 391O–391R apply in respect of conduct of an individual acting as an insolvency practitioner where that conduct occurs on or after 1 October 2015 notwithstanding the date of the individual's authorisation to act as an insolvency or appointment as office holder in a particular insolvency.

[1.497]
[391P Application for, and power to make, direct sanctions order

(1) The Secretary of State may apply to the court for a direct sanctions order to be made against a person if it appears to the Secretary of State that it would be in the public interest for the order to be made.

(2) The Secretary of State must send a copy of the application to the relevant recognised professional body.

(3) The court may make a direct sanctions order against a person where, on an application under this section, the court is satisfied that condition 1 and at least one of conditions 2, 3, 4 and 5 are met in relation to the person.

(4) The conditions are set out in section 391Q.

(5) In deciding whether to make a direct sanctions order against a person the court must have regard to the extent to which—

(a) the relevant recognised professional body has taken action against the person in respect of the failure mentioned in condition 1, and

(b) that action is sufficient to address the failure.]

NOTES

Commencement: 1 October 2015.

Inserted as noted to s 391O at **[1.496]**.

[1.498]

[391Q Direct sanctions order: conditions

(1) Condition 1 is that the person, in acting as an insolvency practitioner or in connection with any appointment as such, has failed to comply with—

(a) a requirement imposed by the rules of the relevant recognised professional body;

(b) any standards, or code of ethics, for the insolvency-practitioner profession adopted from time to time by the relevant recognised professional body.

(2) Condition 2 is that the person—

(a) is not a fit and proper person to act as an insolvency practitioner;

(b) is a fit and proper person to act as an insolvency practitioner only in relation to companies, but the person's authorisation is not so limited; or

(c) is a fit and proper person to act as an insolvency practitioner only in relation to individuals, but the person's authorisation is not so limited.

(3) Condition 3 is that it is appropriate for the person's authorisation to act as an insolvency practitioner to be suspended for a period or until one or more requirements are complied with.

(4) Condition 4 is that it is appropriate to impose other restrictions on the person acting as an insolvency practitioner.

(5) Condition 5 is that loss has been suffered as a result of the failure mentioned in condition 1 by one or more creditors of a company, individual or insolvent partnership in relation to which the person is acting or has acted as an insolvency practitioner.

(6) In this section "relevant recognised professional body" has the same meaning as in section 391O.]

NOTES

Commencement: 1 October 2015.

Inserted as noted to s 391O at **[1.496]**.

[1.499]

[391R Direct sanctions direction instead of order

(1) The Secretary of State may give a direction (a "direct sanctions direction") in relation to a person acting as an insolvency practitioner to the relevant recognised professional body (instead of applying, or continuing with an application, for a direct sanctions order against the person) if the Secretary of State is satisfied that—

(a) condition 1 and at least one of conditions 2, 3, 4 and 5 are met in relation to the person (see section 391Q), and

(b) it is in the public interest for the direction to be given.

(2) But the Secretary of State may not give a direct sanctions direction in relation to a person without that person's consent.

(3) A direct sanctions direction may require the relevant recognised professional body to take all necessary steps to secure that—

(a) the person is no longer authorised (whether fully or partially) to act as an insolvency practitioner;

(b) the person is no longer fully authorised to act as an insolvency practitioner but remains partially authorised to act as such either in relation to companies or individuals, as specified in the direction;

(c) the person's authorisation to act as an insolvency practitioner is suspended for the period specified in the direction or until such time as the requirements so specified are complied with;

(d) the person must comply with such other requirements as may be specified in the direction while acting as an insolvency practitioner;

(e) the person makes such contribution as may be specified in the direction to one or more creditors of a company, individual or insolvent partnership in relation to which the person is acting or has acted as an insolvency practitioner.

(4) A direct sanctions direction must not be given in relation to a person whose authorisation to act as an insolvency practitioner was granted by the Department of Enterprise, Trade and Investment in Northern Ireland (see section 390A(2)(b)).

(5) A direct sanctions direction must not specify a contribution as mentioned in subsection (3)(e) which is more than the remuneration that the person has received or will receive in respect of acting as an insolvency practitioner in the case.

(6) In this section "relevant recognised professional body" has the same meaning as in section 391O.]

NOTES

Commencement: 1 October 2015.

Inserted as noted to s 391O at **[1.496]**.

[General

[1.500]

391S Power for Secretary of State to obtain information

(1) A person mentioned in subsection (2) must give the Secretary of State such information as the Secretary of State may by notice in writing require for the exercise of the Secretary of State's functions under this Part.

(2) Those persons are—

(a) a recognised professional body;

(b) any individual who is or has been authorised under section 390A to act as an insolvency practitioner;

(c) any person who is connected to such an individual.

(3) A person is connected to an individual who is or has been authorised to act as an insolvency practitioner if, at any time during the authorisation—

(a) the person was an employee of the individual;

(b) the person acted on behalf of the individual in any other way;

(c) the person employed the individual;

(d) the person was a fellow employee of the individual's employer;

(e) in a case where the individual was employed by a firm, partnership or company, the person was a member of the firm or partnership or (as the case may be) a director of the company.

(4) In imposing a requirement under subsection (1) the Secretary of State may specify—

(a) the time period within which the information in question is to be given, and

(b) the manner in which it is to be verified.]

NOTES

Commencement: 1 October 2015.

Inserted, together with the preceding heading, by the Small Business, Enterprise and Employment Act 2015, s 142.

[1.501]

[391T Compliance orders

(1) If at any time it appears to the Secretary of State that—

(a) a recognised professional body has failed to comply with a requirement imposed on it by or by virtue of this Part, or

(b) any other person has failed to comply with a requirement imposed on the person by virtue of section 391S,

the Secretary of State may make an application to the court.

(2) If, on an application under this section, the court decides that the body or other person has failed to comply with the requirement in question, it may order the body or person to take such steps as the court considers will secure that the requirement is complied with.

(3) In this section, "the court" means the High Court or, in Scotland, the Court of Session.]

NOTES

Commencement: 1 October 2015.

Inserted by the Small Business, Enterprise and Employment Act 2015, s 143.

[1.502]

392 Authorisation by competent authority

(1) Application may be made to a competent authority for authorisation to act as an insolvency practitioner.

(2) The competent authorities for this purpose are—

(a) in relation to a case of any description specified in directions given by the Secretary of State, the body or person so specified in relation to cases of that description, and

(b) in relation to a case not falling within paragraph (a), the Secretary of State.

(3) The application—

(a) shall be made in such manner as the competent authority may direct,

(b) shall contain or be accompanied by such information as that authority may reasonably require for the purpose of determining the application, and

(c) shall be accompanied by the prescribed fee;

and the authority may direct that notice of the making of the application shall be published in such manner as may be specified in the direction.

(4) At any time after receiving the application and before determining it the authority may require the applicant to furnish additional information.

(5) Directions and requirements given or imposed under subsection (3) or (4) may differ as between different applications.

(6) Any information to be furnished to the competent authority under this section shall, if it so requires, be in such form or verified in such manner as it may specify.

(7) An application may be withdrawn before it is granted or refused.

(8) Any sums received under this section by a competent authority other than the Secretary of State may be retained by the authority; and any sums so received by the Secretary of State shall be paid into the Consolidated Fund.

[(9) Subsection (3)(c) shall not have effect in respect of an application made to the Secretary of State (but this subsection is without prejudice to section 415A).]

NOTES

This section derived from the Insolvency Act 1985, ss 4, 11 (in part).

Repealed by the Deregulation Act 2015, s 19, Sch 6, Pt 6, paras 17, 21, as from 1 October 2015.

Sub-s (9): added by the Enterprise Act 2002, s 270(3).

Transitional provisions: see the note relating to the Deregulation Act 2015, Sch 6, Pt 6, para 23 at **[1.479]**.

Regulations: the Insolvency Practitioners Regulations 2005, SI 2005/524 at **[12.30]**.

[1.503]

393 Grant, refusal and withdrawal of authorisation

(1) The competent authority may, on an application duly made in accordance with section 392 and after being furnished with all such information as it may require under that section, grant or refuse the application.

(2) The authority shall grant the application if it appears to it from the information furnished by the applicant and having regard to such other information, if any, as it may have—

- *(a) that the applicant is a fit and proper person to act as an insolvency practitioner, and*
- *(b) that the applicant meets the prescribed requirements with respect to education and practical training and experience.*

[(3) An authorisation granted under this section, if not previously withdrawn, continues in force for one year.

(3A) But where an authorisation is granted under this section the competent authority must, before its expiry (and without a further application made in accordance with section 392) grant a further authorisation under this section taking effect immediately after the expiry of the previous authorisation, unless it appears to the authority that the subject of the authorisation no longer complies with subsection (2)(a) and (b).]

(4) An authorisation [granted under this section] may be withdrawn by the competent authority if it appears to it—

- *(a) that the holder of the authorisation is no longer a fit and proper person to act as an insolvency practitioner, or*
- *(b) without prejudice to paragraph (a), that the holder—*
  - *(i) has failed to comply with any provision of this Part or of any regulations made under this Part or Part XV, or*
  - *(ii) in purported compliance with any such provision, has furnished the competent authority with false, inaccurate or misleading information.*

(5) An authorisation granted under this section may be withdrawn by the competent authority at the request or with the consent of the holder of the authorisation.

[(6) Where an authorisation granted under this section is withdrawn—

- *(a) subsection (3A) does not require a further authorisation to be granted, or*
- *(b) if a further authorisation has already been granted at the time of the withdrawal, the further authorisation is also withdrawn.]*

NOTES

This section derived from the Insolvency Act 1985, s 5.

Repealed by the Deregulation Act 2015, s 19, Sch 6, Pt 6, paras 17, 21, as from 1 October 2015.

Sub-ss (3), (3A): substituted for original sub-s (3) by the Provision of Services (Insolvency Practitioners) Regulations 2009, SI 2009/3081, regs 2(1), (4)(a), 5, except in relation to an application for authorisation to act as an insolvency practitioner under this section made or granted before 28 December 2009. Original sub-s (3) read as follows:

"(3) An authorisation granted under this section, if not previously withdrawn, continues in force for such period not exceeding the prescribed maximum as may be specified in the authorisation.".

Sub-s (4): words in square brackets substituted for original words "so granted" by SI 2009/3081, regs 2(1), (4)(b), 5, except in relation to an application for authorisation to act as an insolvency practitioner under this section made or granted before 28 December 2009.

Sub-s (6): added by SI 2009/3081, regs 2(1), (4)(c), 5, except in relation to an application for authorisation to act as an insolvency practitioner under this section made or granted before 28 December 2009.

Transitional provisions: see the note relating to the Deregulation Act 2015, Sch 6, Pt 6, para 23 at **[1.479]**.

Regulations: the Insolvency Practitioners Regulations 2005, SI 2005/524 at **[12.30]**.

[1.504]

394 Notices

(1) Where a competent authority grants an authorisation under section 393, it shall give written notice of that fact to the applicant, specifying the date on which the authorisation takes effect.

(2) Where the authority proposes to refuse an application, or to withdraw an authorisation under section 393(4), it shall give the applicant or holder of the authorisation written notice of its intention to do so, setting out particulars of the grounds on which it proposes to act.

(3) In the case of a proposed withdrawal the notice shall state the date on which it is proposed that the withdrawal should take effect.

(4) A notice under subsection (2) shall give particulars of the rights exercisable under the next two sections by a person on whom the notice is served.

NOTES

This section derived from the Insolvency Act 1985, s 6.

Repealed by the Deregulation Act 2015, s 19, Sch 6, Pt 6, paras 17, 21, as from 1 October 2015.

Transitional provisions: see the note relating to the Deregulation Act 2015, Sch 6, Pt 6, para 23 at **[1.479]**.

[1.505]

395 Right to make representations

(1) A person on whom a notice is served under section 394(2) may within 14 days after the date of service make written representations to the competent authority.

(2) The competent authority shall have regard to any representations so made in determining whether to refuse the application or withdraw the authorisation, as the case may be.

NOTES

This section derived from the Insolvency Act 1985, s 7.

Repealed by the Deregulation Act 2015, s 19, Sch 6, Pt 6, paras 17, 21, as from 1 October 2015.

Transitional provisions: see the note relating to the Deregulation Act 2015, Sch 6, Pt 6, para 23 at **[1.479]**.

[1.506]

396 Reference to Tribunal

(1) The Insolvency Practitioners Tribunal ("the Tribunal") continues in being; and the provisions of Schedule 7 apply to it.

(2) Where a person is served with a notice under section 394(2), he may—

- *(a) at any time within 28 days after the date of service of the notice, or*
- *(b) at any time after the making by him of representations under section 395 and before the end of the period of 28 days after the date of the service on him of a notice by the competent authority that the authority does not propose to alter its decision in consequence of the representations,*

give written notice to the authority requiring the case to be referred to the Tribunal.

(3) Where a requirement is made under subsection (2), then, unless the competent authority—

- *(a) has decided or decides to grant the application or, as the case may be, not to withdraw the authorisation, and*
- *(b) within 7 days after the date of the making of the requirement, gives written notice of that decision to the person by whom the requirement was made,*

it shall refer the case to the Tribunal.

NOTES

This section derived from the Insolvency Act 1985, ss 8(1), (2), (6), 11 (in part).

Repealed by the Deregulation Act 2015, s 19, Sch 6, Pt 6, paras 17, 21, as from 1 October 2015.

Transitional provisions: see the note relating to the Deregulation Act 2015, Sch 6, Pt 6, para 23 at **[1.479]**.

[1.507]

397 Action of Tribunal on reference

(1) On a reference under section 396 the Tribunal shall—

- *(a) investigate the case, and*
- *(b) make a report to the competent authority stating what would in their opinion be the appropriate decision in the matter and the reasons for that opinion,*

and it is the duty of the competent authority to decide the matter accordingly.

(2) The Tribunal shall send a copy of the report to the applicant or, as the case may be, the holder of the authorisation; and the competent authority shall serve him with a written notice of the decision made by it in accordance with the report.

(3) The competent authority may, if he thinks fit, publish the report of the Tribunal.

NOTES

This section derived from the Insolvency Act 1985, s 8(3)–(5).

Repealed by the Deregulation Act 2015, s 19, Sch 6, Pt 6, paras 17, 21, as from 1 October 2015.

Transitional provisions: see the note relating to the Deregulation Act 2015, Sch 6, Pt 6, para 23 at **[1.479]**.

[1.508]

398 Refusal or withdrawal without reference to Tribunal

Where in the case of any proposed refusal or withdrawal of an authorisation either—

- *(a) the period mentioned in section 396(2)(a) has expired without the making of any requirement under that subsection or of any representations under section 395, or*
- *(b) the competent authority has given a notice such as is mentioned in section 396(2)(b) and the period so mentioned has expired without the making of any such requirement,*

the competent authority may give written notice of the refusal or withdrawal to the person concerned in accordance with the proposal in the notice given under section 394(2).

NOTES

This section derived from the Insolvency Act 1985, s 9.

Repealed by the Deregulation Act 2015, s 19, Sch 6, Pt 6, paras 17, 21, as from 1 October 2015.

Transitional provisions: see the note relating to the Deregulation Act 2015, Sch 6, Pt 6, para 23 at **[1.479]**.

PART XIV PUBLIC ADMINISTRATION (ENGLAND AND WALES)

[Adjudicators

[1.509]

398A Appointment etc of adjudicators and assistants

(1) The Secretary of State may appoint persons to the office of adjudicator.

(2) A person appointed under subsection (1)—

(a) is to be paid out of money provided by Parliament such salary as the Secretary of State may direct,

(b) holds office on such other terms and conditions as the Secretary of State may direct, and

(c) may be removed from office by a direction of the Secretary of State.

(3) A person who is authorised to act as an official receiver may not be appointed under subsection (1).

(4) The Secretary of State may appoint officers of the Secretary of State's department to assist adjudicators in the carrying out of their functions.]

NOTES

Commencement: 6 April 2016.

Inserted, together with preceding cross-heading, by the Enterprise and Regulatory Reform Act 2013, s 71(1).

Official Receivers

[1.510]

399 Appointment, etc of official receivers

(1) For the purposes of this Act the official receiver, in relation to any bankruptcy[, winding up[, individual voluntary arrangement, debt relief order or application for such an order]], is any person who by virtue of the following provisions of this section or section 401 below is authorised to act as the official receiver in relation to that bankruptcy[, winding up[, individual voluntary arrangement, debt relief order or application for such an order]].

(2) The Secretary of State may (subject to the approval of the Treasury as to numbers) appoint persons to the office of official receiver, and a person appointed to that office (whether under this section or section 70 of the Bankruptcy Act 1914)—

(a) shall be paid out of money provided by Parliament such salary as the Secretary of State may with the concurrence of the Treasury direct,

(b) shall hold office on such other terms and conditions as the Secretary of State may with the concurrence of the Treasury direct, and

(c) may be removed from office by a direction of the Secretary of State.

(3) Where a person holds the office of official receiver, the Secretary of State shall from time to time attach him either to the High Court or to [the county court]

(4) Subject to any directions under subsection (6) below, an official receiver attached to a particular court is the person authorised to act as the official receiver in relation to every bankruptcy[, winding up[, individual voluntary arrangement, debt relief order or application for such an order]] falling within the jurisdiction of that court.

(5) The Secretary of State shall ensure that there is, at all times, at least one official receiver attached to the High Court and at least one attached to [the county court]; but he may attach the same official receiver to [both] courts.

(6) The Secretary of State may give directions with respect to the disposal of the business of official receivers, and such directions may, in particular—

(a) authorise an official receiver attached to one court to act as the official receiver in relation to any case or description of cases falling within the jurisdiction of [the other] court;

(b) provide, where there is more than one official receiver authorised to act as the official receiver in relation to cases falling within the jurisdiction of any court, for the distribution of their business between or among themselves.

(7) A person who at the coming into force of section 222 of the Insolvency Act 1985 (replaced by this section) is an official receiver attached to a court shall continue in office after the coming into force of that section as an official receiver attached to that court under this section.

NOTES

This section derived from the Insolvency Act 1985, s 222.

Sub-s (1): words in first (outer) and third (outer) pairs of square brackets substituted by the Enterprise Act 2002, s 269, Sch 23, paras 1, 14(a); words in second (inner) and fourth (inner) pairs of square brackets substituted by the Tribunals, Courts and Enforcement Act 2007, s 108(3), Sch 20, Pt 1, paras 1, 7(1), (2).

Sub-s (3): words in square brackets substituted by the Crime and Courts Act 2013, s 17(5), Sch 9, Pt 3, para 93(h).

Sub-s (4): words in first (outer) pair of square brackets substituted by the Enterprise Act 2002, s 269, Sch 23, paras 1, 14(b); words in second (inner) pair of square brackets substituted by the Tribunals, Courts and Enforcement Act 2007, s 108(3), Sch 20, Pt 1, paras 1, 7(1), (3).

Sub-s (5): words in square brackets substituted by the Crime and Courts Act 2013, s 17(5), Sch 9, Pt 3, para 93(i).

Sub-s (6): words in square brackets substituted by the Crime and Courts Act 2013, s 17(5), Sch 9, Pt 3, para 93(j).

Bankruptcy Act 1914, s 70: repealed by the Insolvency Act 1985, s 235(3), Sch 10.

Insolvency Act 1985, s 222: repealed by s 428 of, and Sch 12 to, this Act.

[1.511]

400 Functions and status of official receivers

(1) In addition to any functions conferred on him by this Act, a person holding the office of official receiver shall carry out such other functions as may from time to time be conferred on him by the Secretary of State.

(2) In the exercise of the functions of his office a person holding the office of official receiver shall act under the general directions of the Secretary of State and shall also be an officer of the court in relation to which he exercises those functions.

(3) Any property vested in his official capacity in a person holding the office of official receiver shall, on his dying, ceasing to hold office or being otherwise succeeded in relation to the bankruptcy or winding up in question by another official receiver, vest in his successor without any conveyance, assignment or transfer.

NOTES

This section derived from the Insolvency Act 1985, s 223.

Functions of the Official Receiver: provision is made for certain functions of the Official Receiver conferred by or under this Act to be contracted out by the Contracting Out (Functions of the Official Receiver) Order 1995, SI 1995/1386 (made under the Deregulation and Contracting Out Act 1994, s 69). See also, in connection with the functions of the Official Receiver attached to any court, ss 69 and 74 of the 1994 Act.

[1.512]

401 Deputy official receivers and staff

(1) The Secretary of State may, if he thinks it expedient to do so in order to facilitate the disposal of the business of the official receiver attached to any court, appoint an officer of his department to act as deputy to that official receiver.

(2) Subject to any directions given by the Secretary of State under section 399 or 400, a person appointed to act as deputy to an official receiver has, on such conditions and for such period as may be specified in the terms of his appointment, the same status and functions as the official receiver to whom he is appointed deputy.

Accordingly, references in this Act (except section 399(1) to (5)) to an official receiver include a person appointed to act as his deputy.

(3) An appointment made under subsection (1) may be terminated at any time by the Secretary of State.

(4) The Secretary of State may, subject to the approval of the Treasury as to numbers and remuneration and as to the other terms and conditions of the appointments, appoint officers of his department to assist official receivers in the carrying out of their functions.

NOTES

This section derived from the Insolvency Act 1985, s 224.

The Official Petitioner

[1.513]

402 Official Petitioner

(1) There continues to be an officer known as the Official Petitioner for the purpose of discharging, in relation to cases in which a criminal bankruptcy order is made, the functions assigned to him by or under this Act; and the Director of Public Prosecutions continues, by virtue of his office, to be the Official Petitioner.

(2) The functions of the Official Petitioner include the following—

- *(a) to consider whether, in a case in which a criminal bankruptcy order is made, it is in the public interest that he should himself present a petition under section 264(1)(d) of this Act;*
- *(b) to present such a petition in any case where he determines that it is in the public interest for him to do so;*
- *(c) to make payments, in such cases as he may determine, towards expenses incurred by other persons in connection with proceedings in pursuance of such a petition; and*
- *(d) to exercise, so far as he considers it in the public interest to do so, any of the powers conferred on him by or under this Act.*

(3) Any functions of the Official Petitioner may be discharged on his behalf by any person acting with his authority.

(4) Neither the Official Petitioner nor any person acting with his authority is liable to any action or proceeding in respect of anything done or omitted to be done in the discharge, or purported discharge, of the functions of the Official Petitioner.

(5) In this section "criminal bankruptcy order" means an order under section 39(1) of the Powers of Criminal Courts Act 1973.

NOTES

This section derived from the Insolvency Act 1985, s 225.

Repealed by the Criminal Justice Act 1988, s 170(2), Sch 16, as from a day to be appointed.

Powers of Criminal Courts Act 1973, s 39: repealed by the Criminal Justice Act 1988, s 170(2), Sch 16, as from a day to be appointed.

Insolvency Service finance, accounting and investment

[1.514]

403 Insolvency Services Account

(1) All money received by the Secretary of State in respect of proceedings under this Act as it applies to England and Wales shall be paid into the Insolvency Services Account kept by the Secretary of State with the Bank of England; and all payments out of money standing to the credit of the Secretary of State in that account shall be made by the Bank of England in such manner as he may direct.

(2) Whenever the cash balance standing to the credit of the Insolvency Services Account is in excess of the amount which in the opinion of the Secretary of State is required for the time being to answer demands in respect of bankrupts' estates or companies' estates, the Secretary of State shall—

(a) notify the excess to the National Debt Commissioners, and

(b) pay into the Insolvency Services Investment Account ("the Investment Account") kept by the Commissioners with the Bank of England the whole or any part of the excess as the Commissioners may require for investment in accordance with the following provisions of this Part.

(3) Whenever any part of the money so invested is, in the opinion of the Secretary of State, required to answer any demand in respect of bankrupt's estates or companies' estates, he shall notify to the National Debt Commissioners the amount so required and the Commissioners—

(a) shall thereupon repay to the Secretary of State such sum as may be required to the credit of the Insolvency Services Account, and

(b) for that purpose may direct the sale of such part of the securities in which the money has been invested as may be necessary.

NOTES

This section derived from the Insolvency Services (Accounting and Investment) Act 1970, s 1, the Insolvency Act 1976, s 3, and the Insolvency Act 1985, Sch 8, para 28.

[1.515]

404 Investment Account

Any money standing to the credit of the Investment Account (including any money received by the National Debt Commissioners by way of interest on or proceeds of any investment under this section) may be invested by the Commissioners, in accordance with such directions as may be given by the Treasury, in any manner for the time being specified in Part II of Schedule 1 to the Trustee Investments Act 1961.

NOTES

This section derived from the Insolvency Services (Accounting and Investment) Act 1970, s 2.

[1.516]

405 Application of income in Investment Account; adjustment of balances

(1) Where the annual account to be kept by the National Debt Commissioners under section 409 below shows that in the year for which it is made up the gross amount of the interest accrued from the securities standing to the credit of the Investment Account exceeded the aggregate of—

(a) a sum, to be determined by the Treasury, to provide against the depreciation in the value of the securities, and

(b) the sums paid into the Insolvency Services Account in pursuance of the next section together with the sums paid in pursuance of that section to the Commissioners of Inland Revenue,

the National Debt Commissioners shall, within 3 months after the account is laid before Parliament, cause the amount of the excess to be paid out of the Investment Account into the Consolidated Fund in such manner as may from time to time be agreed between the Treasury and the Commissioners.

(2) Where the said annual account shows that in the year for which it is made up the gross amount of interest accrued from the securities standing to the credit of the Investment Account was less than the aggregate mentioned in subsection (1), an amount equal to the deficiency shall, at such times as the Treasury direct, be paid out of the Consolidated Fund into the Investment Account.

(3) If the Investment Account is insufficient to meet its liabilities the Treasury may, on being informed of the insufficiency by the National Debt Commissioners, issue the amount of the deficiency out of the Consolidated Fund and the Treasury shall certify the deficiency to Parliament.

NOTES

This section derived from the Insolvency Services (Accounting and Investment) Act 1970, s 3, and the Insolvency Act 1976, Sch 2, para 5.

Repealed by the Enterprise Act 2002, ss 272(1), 278(2), Sch 26, and reproduced for reference.

[1.517]

406 [Interest on money received by liquidators or trustees in bankruptcy and invested]

Where under rules made by virtue of paragraph 16 of Schedule 8 to this Act (investment of money received by company liquidators) [or paragraph 21 of Schedule 9 to this Act (investment of money received by trustee in bankruptcy) a company or a bankrupt's estate] has become entitled to any sum by way of interest, the Secretary of State shall certify that sum and the amount of tax payable on it to the National Debt Commissioners; and the Commissioners shall pay, out of the Investment Account—

(a) into the Insolvency Services Account, the sum so certified less the amount of tax so certified, and

(b) to the Commissioners of Inland Revenue, the amount of tax so certified.

NOTES

This section derived from the Insolvency Services (Accounting and Investment) Act 1970, s 4, the Insolvency Act 1976, Sch 2, para 6, and the Insolvency Act 1985, Sch 8, para 17.

Words in square brackets substituted by the Insolvency Act 2000, s 13(2).

[1.518]

407 Unclaimed dividends and undistributed balances

(1) The Secretary of State shall from time to time pay into the Consolidated Fund out of the Insolvency Services Account so much of the sums standing to the credit of that Account as represents—

(a) dividends which were declared before such date as the Treasury may from time to time determine and have not been claimed, and

(b) balances ascertained before that date which are too small to be divided among the persons entitled to them.

(2) For the purposes of this section the sums standing to the credit of the Insolvency Services Account are deemed to include any sums paid out of that Account and represented by any sums or securities standing to the credit of the Investment Account.

(3) The Secretary of State may require the National Debt Commissioners to pay out of the Investment Account into the Insolvency Services Account the whole or part of any sum which he is required to pay out of that account under subsection (1); and the Commissioners may direct the sale of such securities standing to the credit of the Investment Account as may be necessary for that purpose.

NOTES

This section derived from the Insolvency Services (Accounting and Investment) Act 1970, s 5, and the Insolvency Act 1976, Sch 2, para 7.

[1.519]

[408 Adjustment of balances

(1) The Treasury may direct the payment out of the Consolidated Fund of sums into—

(a) the Insolvency Services Account;

(b) the Investment Account.

(2) The Treasury shall certify to the House of Commons the reason for any payment under subsection (1).

(3) The Secretary of State may pay sums out of the Insolvency Services Account into the Consolidated Fund.

(4) The National Debt Commissioners may pay sums out of the Investment Account into the Consolidated Fund.]

NOTES

Substituted by the Enterprise Act 2002, s 272(2).

[1.520]

409 Annual financial statement and audit

(1) The National Debt Commissioners shall for each year ending on 31st March prepare a statement of the sums credited and debited to the Investment Account in such form and manner as the Treasury may direct and shall transmit it to the Comptroller and Auditor General before the end of November next following the year.

(2) The Secretary of State shall for each year ending 31st March prepare a statement of the sums received or paid by him under section 403 above in such form and manner as the Treasury may direct and shall transmit each statement to the Comptroller and Auditor General before the end of November next following the year.

(3) Every such statement shall include such additional information as the Treasury may direct.

(4) The Comptroller and Auditor General shall examine, certify and report on every such statement and shall lay copies of it, and of his report, before Parliament.

NOTES

This section derived from the Insolvency Services (Accounting and Investment) Act 1970, s 7, and the Insolvency Act 1976, Sch 2, para 9.

Supplementary

[1.521]

410 Extent of this Part

This Part of this Act extends to England and Wales only.

NOTES

This section derived from the Insolvency Services (Accounting and Investment) Act 1970, s 9(3), the Insolvency Act 1976, s 14(6), and the Insolvency Act 1985, s 236(3)(i).

PART XV SUBORDINATE LEGISLATION

General insolvency rules

[1.522]

411 Company insolvency rules

(1) Rules may be made—

(a) in relation to England and Wales, by the Lord Chancellor with the concurrence of the Secretary of State [and, in the case of rules that affect court procedure, with the concurrence of the Lord Chief Justice], or

(b) in relation to Scotland, by the Secretary of State,

for the purpose of giving effect to Parts I to VII of this Act [or the [EU Regulation]].

[(1A) Rules may also be made for the purpose of giving effect to Part 2 of the Banking Act 2009 (bank insolvency orders); and rules for that purpose shall be made—

(a) in relation to England and Wales, by the Lord Chancellor with the concurrence of—

(i) the Treasury, and

(ii) in the case of rules that affect court procedure, the Lord Chief Justice, or

(b) in relation to Scotland, by the Treasury.]

[(1B) Rules may also be made for the purpose of giving effect to Part 3 of the Banking Act 2009 (bank administration); and rules for that purpose shall be made—

(a) in relation to England and Wales, by the Lord Chancellor with the concurrence of—

(i) the Treasury, and

(ii) in the case of rules that affect court procedure, the Lord Chief Justice, or

(b) in relation to Scotland, by the Treasury.]

(2) Without prejudice to the generality of subsection (1), [(1A)] [or (1B)] or to any provision of those Parts by virtue of which rules under this section may be made with respect to any matter, rules under this section may contain—

(a) any such provision as is specified in Schedule 8 to this Act or corresponds to provision contained immediately before the coming into force of section 106 of the Insolvency Act 1985 in rules made, or having effect as if made, under section 663(1) or (2) of [the Companies Act 1985] (old winding-up rules), and

(b) such incidental, supplemental and transitional provisions as may appear to the Lord Chancellor or, as the case may be, the Secretary of State [or the Treasury] necessary or expedient.

[(2A) For the purposes of subsection (2), a reference in Schedule 8 to this Act to doing anything under or for the purposes of a provision of this Act includes a reference to doing anything under or for the purposes of the [EU Regulation] (in so far as the provision of this Act relates to a matter to which the [EU Regulation] applies).

(2B) Rules under this section for the purpose of giving effect to the [EU Regulation] may not create an offence of a kind referred to in paragraph 1(1)(d) of Schedule 2 to the European Communities Act 1972.]

[(2C) For the purposes of subsection (2), a reference in Schedule 8 to this Act to doing anything under or for the purposes of a provision of this Act includes a reference to doing anything under or for the purposes of Part 2 of the Banking Act 2009.]

[(2D) For the purposes of subsection (2), a reference in Schedule 8 to this Act to doing anything under or for the purposes of a provision of this Act includes a reference to doing anything under or for the purposes of Part 3 of the Banking Act 2009.]

(3) In Schedule 8 to this Act "liquidator" includes a provisional liquidator [or bank liquidator] [or administrator]; and references above in this section to Parts I to VII of this Act [or Part 2 [or 3] of the Banking Act 2009] are to be read as including [the Companies Acts] so far as relating to, and to matters connected with or arising out of, the insolvency or winding up of companies.

[(3A) In this section references to Part 2 or 3 of the Banking Act 2009 include references to those Parts as applied to building societies (see section 90C of the Building Societies Act 1986).]

(4) Rules under this section shall be made by statutory instrument subject to annulment in pursuance of a resolution of either House of Parliament.

(5) Regulations made by the Secretary of State [or the Treasury] under a power conferred by rules under this section shall be made by statutory instrument and, after being made, shall be laid before each House of Parliament.

(6) Nothing in this section prejudices any power to make rules of court.

[(7) The Lord Chief Justice may nominate a judicial office holder (as defined in section 109(4) of the Constitutional Reform Act 2005) to exercise his functions under this section.]

NOTES

This section derived from the Insolvency Act 1985, s 106.

Sub-s (1): words in first pair of square brackets inserted by the Constitutional Reform Act 2005, s 15(1), Sch 4, Pt 1, paras 185, 188(1), (2); words in second (outer) pair of square brackets inserted by the Insolvency Act 1986 (Amendment) Regulations 2002, SI 2002/1037, regs 2, 3(1); words in third (inner) pair of square brackets substituted for original words "EC Regulation" by the Insolvency Amendment (EU 2015/848) Regulations 2017, SI 2017/702, regs 2, 3, Schedule, Pt 1, paras 1, 24, except in relation to proceedings opened before 26 June 2017 and subject to savings in reg 4 thereof at **[2.103]**.

Sub-ss (1A), (1B): inserted by the Banking Act 2009, ss 125(1), (2), 160(1), (2).

Sub-s (2): words in first and second pairs of square brackets inserted by the Banking Act 2009, ss 125(1), (3), 160(1), (3); words in square brackets in para (a) substituted for original words "the Companies Act" by the Companies Act 2006 (Consequential Amendments, Transitional Provisions and Savings) Order 2009, SI 2009/1941, art 2(1), Sch 1, para 79, subject to transitional provisions and savings in art 8, Sch 1, para 84 at **[2.70]**, **[2.73]**.

Sub-ss (2A), (2B): inserted by SI 2002/1037, regs 2, 3(2); words in square brackets substituted for original words "EC Regulation" by SI 2017/702, regs 2, 3, Schedule, Pt 1, paras 1, 24, except in relation to proceedings opened before 26 June 2017 and subject to savings in reg 4 thereof at **[2.103]**.

Sub-ss (2C), (2D): inserted by the Banking Act 2009, ss 125(1), (4), 160(1), (4).

Sub-s (3): words in first, second, third (outer) and fourth (inner) pairs of square brackets inserted by the Banking Act 2009, ss 125(1), (5), 160(1), (5); words in fifth pair of square brackets substituted for original words "the Companies Act" by the Companies Act 2006 (Commencement No 3, Consequential Amendments, Transitional Provisions and Savings) Order 2007, SI 2007/2194, art 10(1), (2), Sch 4, Pt 3, para 44, subject to savings in art 12 thereof.

Sub-s (3A): inserted by the Building Societies (Insolvency and Special Administration) Order 2009, SI 2009/805, art 13.

Sub-s (5): words in square brackets inserted by the Banking Act 2009, s 125(1), (6).

Sub-s (7): added by the Constitutional Reform Act 2005, s 15(1), Sch 4, Pt 1, paras 185, 188(1), (3).

Extension of the application of the rules: rules may be made under this section for the purposes of the Building Societies Act 1986, with respect to the winding up, etc, of building societies; see s 90A of, and Sch 15A, Pt I, para 4(1) to, the 1986 Act at **[7.455]**, **[7.468]**.

Rules made under this section apply for the purposes of a petition for a special administration order under the Water Industry Act 1991; see ss 23(3), 24(3) of, and Sch 3, Pt II, para 11(4) to, the 1991 Act at **[7.2619]**, **[7.2620]**, **[7.2626]**.

Rules may be made under this section for the purposes of the Friendly Societies Act 1992, with respect to the winding up of incorporated friendly societies; see s 23 of, and Sch 10, Pt IV, para 69(1)(a) to, the 1992 Act.

Rules may be made under this section for the purposes of the Railways Act 1993, with respect to giving effect to the railway administration order provisions of the 1993 Act (ie ss 59–65 of, and Schs 6, 7 to, that Act); see s 59(5) thereof at **[7.2437]**.

Rules may be made under this section for the purposes of the Health and Social Care Act 2012, with respect to giving effect to the health special administration provisions of the 2012 Act (ie ss 128–133); see s 130(9) thereof at **[7.1359]**.

Company directors disqualification: this section and ss 414, 420, 422 and 434 are applied by the Company Directors Disqualification Act 1986, s 21(2), (3) at **[4.39]** for the purposes of certain provisions of that Act.

Rules: the Insurance Companies (Winding-up) Rules 1985, SI 1985/95 (revoked by SI 2001/3635 and reproduced for reference at **[7.1484]**); the Insolvency (Scotland) Rules 1986, SI 1986/1915 at **[15.1]**; the Companies (Unfair Prejudice Applications) Proceedings Rules 1986, SI 1986/2000 (revoked by SI 2009/2469); the Insolvent Companies (Disqualification of Unfit Directors) Proceedings Rules 1987, SI 1987/2023 at **[14.7]**; the Insolvent Companies (Reports on Conduct of Directors) Rules 1996, SI 1996/1909 at **[14.18]**; the Insolvent Companies (Reports on Conduct of Directors) (Scotland) Rules 1996, SI 1996/1910 at **[16.126]**; the Railway Administration Order Rules 2001, SI 2001/3352 at **[7.2452]**; the Insurers (Winding up) Rules 2001, SI 2001/3635 at **[7.1532]**; the Insurers (Winding up) (Scotland) Rules 2001, SI 2001/4040 at **[16.147]**; the Insolvency (Scotland) Amendment Rules 2003, SI 2003/2111 at **[2.32]**; the Energy Administration Rules 2005, SI 2005/2483 at **[7.874]**; the PPP Administration Order Rules 2007, SI 2007/3141 at **[7.2311]**; the Bank Administration (Scotland) Rules 2009, SI 2009/350; the Bank Insolvency (Scotland) Rules 2009, SI 2009/351; the Bank Insolvency (England and Wales) Rules 2009, SI 2009/356 at **[7.93]**; the Bank Administration (England and Wales) Rules 2009, SI 2009/357 at **[7.386]**; the Building Society Special Administration (Scotland) Rules 2009, SI 2009/806; the Companies (Unfair Prejudice Applications) Proceedings Rules 2009, SI 2009/2469; the Water Industry (Special Administration) Rules 2009, SI 2009/2477 at **[7.2627]**; the Building Society Special Administration (England and Wales) Rules 2010, SI 2010/2580 at **[7.483]**; the Building Society Insolvency (England and Wales) Rules 2010, SI 2010/2581 at **[7.546]**; the Building Society Insolvency (Scotland) Rules 2010, SI 2010/2584; the Investment Bank Special Administration (England and Wales) Rules 2011, SI 2011/1301 at **[7.1711]**; the Investment Bank Special Administration (Scotland) Rules 2011, SI 2011/2262; the Energy Supply Company Administration Rules 2013, SI 2013/1046 at **[7.1074]**; the Energy Supply Company Administration (Scotland) Rules 2013, SI 2013/1047; the Postal Administration Rules 2013, SI 2013/3208 at **[7.2086]**; the Insolvent Companies (Reports on Conduct of Directors) (England and Wales) Rules 2016, SI 2016/180 at **[14.41]**; the Insolvent Companies (Reports on Conduct of Directors) (Scotland) Rules 2016, SI 2016/185 at **[16.285]**; the Compensation Orders (Disqualified Directors) Proceedings (England and Wales) Rules 2016, SI 2016/890 at **[14.51]**; the Insolvency (England and Wales) Rules 2016, SI 2016/1024 at **[6.2]**.

Regulations: the Insolvency Regulations 1994, SI 1994/2507 at **[8.22]**.

[1.523]

412 Individual insolvency rules (England and Wales)

(1) The Lord Chancellor may, with the concurrence of the Secretary of State [and, in the case of rules that affect court procedure, with the concurrence of the Lord Chief Justice], make rules for the purpose of giving effect to [Parts 7A to 11] of this Act [or the [EU Regulation]].

(2) Without prejudice to the generality of subsection (1), or to any provision of those Parts by virtue of which rules under this section may be made with respect to any matter, rules under this section may contain—

- (a) any such provision as is specified in Schedule 9 to this Act or corresponds to provision contained immediately before the appointed day in rules made under section 132 of the Bankruptcy Act 1914; and
- (b) such incidental, supplemental and transitional provisions as may appear to the Lord Chancellor necessary or expedient.

[(2A) For the purposes of subsection (2), a reference in Schedule 9 to this Act to doing anything under or for the purposes of a provision of this Act includes a reference to doing anything under or for the purposes of the [EU Regulation] (in so far as the provision of this Act relates to a matter to which the [EU Regulation] applies).

(2B) Rules under this section for the purpose of giving effect to the [EU Regulation] may not create an offence of a kind referred to in paragraph 1(1)(d) of Schedule 2 to the European Communities Act 1972.]

(3) Rules under this section shall be made by statutory instrument subject to annulment in pursuance of a resolution of either House of Parliament.

(4) Regulations made by the Secretary of State under a power conferred by rules under this section shall be made by statutory instrument and, after being made, shall be laid before each House of Parliament.

(5) Nothing in this section prejudices any power to make rules of court.

[(6) The Lord Chief Justice may nominate a judicial office holder (as defined in section 109(4) of the Constitutional Reform Act 2005) to exercise his functions under this section.]

NOTES

This section derived from the Insolvency Act 1985, s 207.

Sub-s (1): words in first pair of square brackets inserted by the Constitutional Reform Act 2005, s 15(1), Sch 4, Pt 1, paras 185, 189(1), (2); words in second pair of square brackets substituted by the Tribunals, Courts and Enforcement Act 2007, s 108(3), Sch 20, Pt 1, paras 1, 8; words in third (outer) pair of square brackets inserted by the Insolvency Act 1986 (Amendment) Regulations 2002, SI 2002/1037, regs 2, 3(3); words in fourth (inner) pair of square brackets substituted for original words "EC Regulation" by the Insolvency Amendment (EU 2015/848) Regulations 2017, SI 2017/702, regs 2, 3, Schedule, Pt 1, paras 1, 25, except in relation to proceedings opened before 26 June 2017 and subject to savings in reg 4 thereof at **[2.103]**.

Sub-ss (2A), (2B): inserted by SI 2002/1037, regs 2, 3(4); words in square brackets substituted for original words "EC Regulation" by SI 2017/702, regs 2, 3, Schedule, Pt 1, paras 1, 25, except in relation to proceedings opened before 26 June 2017 and subject to savings in reg 4 thereof at **[2.103]**.

Sub-s (6): added by the Constitutional Reform Act 2005, s 15(1), Sch 4, Pt 1, paras 185, 189(1), (3).

Extension of the application of the rules: by the Land Charges Act 1972, s 16(2), the power to make rules under this section includes power to make rules as respects the registration and re-registration of a bankruptcy petition under s 5 of that Act, and a bankruptcy order under s 6 of that Act, as if the registration and re-registration were required by Pts VIII–XI of this Act.

Rules: the Bankruptcy (Financial Services and Markets Act 2000) Rules 2001, SI 2001/3634 at **[11.16]**; the Insolvency (England and Wales) Rules 2016, SI 2016/1024 at **[6.2]**.

Regulations: the Insolvency Regulations 1994, SI 1994/2507 at **[8.22]**.

Bankruptcy Act 1914, s 132: repealed by the Insolvency Act 1985, s 235(3), Sch 10, Pt III.

[1.524]

413 Insolvency Rules Committee

(1) The committee established under section 10 of the Insolvency Act 1976 (advisory committee on bankruptcy and winding-up rules) continues to exist for the purpose of being consulted under this section.

(2) The Lord Chancellor shall consult the committee before making any rules under section 411 or 412 [other than rules which contain a statement that the only provision made by the rules is provision applying rules made under section 411, with or without modifications, for the purposes of provision made by [any of sections 23 to 26 of the Water Industry Act 1991 or Schedule 3 to that Act]] [or by any of sections 59 to 65 of, or Schedule 6 or 7 to, the Railways Act 1993].

(3) Subject to the next subsection, the committee shall consist of—

(a) a judge of the High Court attached to the Chancery Division;

(b) a circuit judge;

(c) [an Insolvency and Companies Court Judge];

[(d) a district judge;]

(e) a practising barrister;

(f) a practising solicitor; and

(g) a practising accountant;

and the appointment of any person as a member of the committee shall be made [in accordance with subsection (3A) or (3B)].

[(3A) The Lord Chief Justice must appoint the persons referred to in paragraphs (a) to (d) of subsection (3), after consulting the Lord Chancellor.

(3B) The Lord Chancellor must appoint the persons referred to in paragraphs (e) to (g) of subsection (3), after consulting the Lord Chief Justice.]

(4) The Lord Chancellor may appoint as additional members of the committee any persons appearing to him to have qualifications or experience that would be of value to the committee in considering any matter with which it is concerned.

[(5) The Lord Chief Justice may nominate a judicial office holder (as defined in section 109(4) of the Constitutional Reform Act 2005) to exercise his functions under this section.]

NOTES

This section derived from the Insolvency Act 1985, s 226.

Sub-s (2): words in first (outer) pair of square brackets inserted by the Water Act 1989, s 190(1), Sch 25, para 78(2); words in second (inner) pair of square brackets substituted by the Water Consolidation (Consequential Provisions) Act 1991, s 2(1), Sch 1, para 46; words in third pair of square brackets added by the Railways Act 1993, s 152, Sch 12, para 25.

Sub-s (3): words in square brackets in para (c) substituted by the Alteration of Judicial Titles (Registrar in Bankruptcy of the High Court) Order 2018, SI 2018/130, art 3, Schedule, para 7(b); para (d) substituted by the Crime and Courts Act 2013, s 17(5), Sch 9, Pt 3, para 93(k); final words in square brackets substituted by the Constitutional Reform Act 2005, s 15(1), Sch 4, Pt 1, paras 185, 190(1), (2).

Sub-ss (3A), (3B): inserted by the Constitutional Reform Act 2005, s 15(1), Sch 4, Pt 1, paras 185, 190(1), (3).

Sub-s (5): added by the Constitutional Reform Act 2005, s 15(1), Sch 4, Pt 1, paras 185, 190(1), (4).

See further: in relation to the disapplication of sub-s (2) above, to the first set of rules which is made in reliance on the Banking Act 2009, ss 125, 160, see the Banking Act 2009, ss 125(8), 160(6); in relation to the disapplication of sub-s (2) above, to the first set of rules made in relation to building society insolvency or building society special administration, see the Building Societies (Insolvency and Special Administration) Order 2009, SI 2009/805, art 16.

Fees orders

[1.525]

414 Fees orders (company insolvency proceedings)

(1) There shall be paid in respect of—

(a) proceedings under any of Parts I to VII of this Act, and

(b) the performance by the official receiver or the Secretary of State of functions under those Parts,

such fees as the competent authority may with the sanction of the Treasury by order direct.

(2) That authority is—

(a) in relation to England and Wales, the Lord Chancellor, and

(b) in relation to Scotland, the Secretary of State.

(3) The Treasury may by order direct by whom and in what manner the fees are to be collected and accounted for.

(4) The Lord Chancellor may, with the sanction of the Treasury, by order provide for sums to be deposited, by such persons, in such manner and in such circumstances as may be specified in the order, by way of security for fees payable by virtue of this section.

(5) An order under this section may contain such incidental, supplemental and transitional provisions as may appear to the Lord Chancellor, the Secretary of State or (as the case may be) the Treasury necessary or expedient.

(6) An order under this section shall be made by statutory instrument and, after being made, shall be laid before each House of Parliament.

(7) Fees payable by virtue of this section shall be paid into the Consolidated Fund.

(8) References in subsection (1) to Parts I to VII of this Act are to be read as including [the Companies Acts] so far as relating to, and to matters connected with or arising out of, the insolvency or winding up of companies.

[(8A) This section applies in relation to Part 2 of the Banking Act 2009 (bank insolvency) as in relation to Parts I to VII of this Act.]

[(8B) This section applies in relation to Part 3 of the Banking Act 2009 (bank administration) as in relation to Parts I to VII of this Act.]

[(8C) In subsections (8A) and (8B) the reference to Parts 2 and 3 of the Banking Act 2009 include references to those Parts as applied to building societies (see section 90C of the Building Societies Act 1986).]

(9) . . .

NOTES

This section derived from the Insolvency Act 1985, ss 106(5), 107.

Sub-s (8): words in square brackets substituted for original words "the Companies Act" by the Companies Act 2006 (Commencement No 3, Consequential Amendments, Transitional Provisions and Savings) Order 2007, SI 2007/2194, art 10(1), (2), Sch 4, Pt 3, para 44, subject to savings in art 12 thereof.

Sub-s (8A): inserted by the Banking Act 2009, s 126.

Sub-s (8B): inserted by the Banking Act 2009, s 161.

Sub-s (8C): inserted by the Building Societies (Insolvency and Special Administration) Order 2009, SI 2009/805, art 14.

Sub-s (9): repealed by the Courts Reform (Scotland) Act 2014 (Consequential Provisions) Order 2015, SSI 2015/150, art 2, Schedule, para 4.

Extension of the application of orders: an order made by a competent authority under this section may make provision for fees to be payable in respect of proceedings under the applicable winding up legislation (as defined in the Friendly Societies Act 1992, s 23(3)) and the performance by the official receiver or the Secretary of State of functions under this section; see s 23(2) of, and Sch 10, Pt IV, para 69(2) to, the 1992 Act.

An order made by a competent authority under this section may make provision for fees to be payable in respect of proceedings for the winding up of a building society and the performance by the official receiver or the Secretary of State of functions under this section; see the Building Societies Act 1986, s 90A, Sch 15A, Pt I, para 4(2) at **[7.455]**, **[7.468]**.

Company directors disqualification: see the note to s 411 at **[1.522]**.

Orders: the Insolvency Fees Order 1986, SI 1986/2030 (revoked by SI 2004/593 and reproduced for reference at **[8.7]**); the Insolvency Proceedings (Fees) Order 2004, SI 2004/593 at **[8.71]**; the Civil Proceedings Fees Order 2008, SI 2008/1053; the Courts and Tribunals Fee Remissions Order 2013, SI 2013/2302; the Insolvency Proceedings (Fees) Order 2016, SI 2016/692 at **[8.82]**; the Disqualified Directors Compensation Orders (Fees) (England and Wales) Order 2016, SI 2016/1047 at **[14.60]**; the Disqualified Directors Compensation Orders (Fees) (Scotland) Order 2016, SI 2016/1048 at **[16.445]**.

[1.526]

415 Fees orders (individual insolvency proceedings in England and Wales)

(1) There shall be paid in respect of—

[(za) the costs of persons acting as approved intermediaries under Part 7A,]

(a) proceedings under [Parts 7A to 11] of this Act, . . .

(b) the performance by the official receiver or the Secretary of State of functions under those Parts, [and

(c) the performance by an adjudicator of functions under Part 9 of this Act,]

such fees as the Lord Chancellor may with the sanction of the Treasury by order direct.

[(1A) An order under subsection (1) may make different provision for different purposes, including by reference to the manner or form in which proceedings are commenced.]

(2) The Treasury may by order direct by whom and in what manner the fees are to be collected and accounted for.

(3) The Lord Chancellor may, with the sanction of the Treasury, by order provide for sums to be deposited, by such persons, in such manner and in such circumstances as may be specified in the order, by way of security for—

(a) fees payable by virtue of this section, and

(b) fees payable to any person who has prepared an insolvency practitioner's report under section 274 in Chapter I of Part IX.

(4) An order under this section may contain such incidental, supplemental and transitional provisions as may appear to the Lord Chancellor or, as the case may be, the Treasury, necessary or expedient.

(5) An order under this section shall be made by statutory instrument and, after being made, shall be laid before each House of Parliament.

(6) Fees payable by virtue of this section shall be paid into the Consolidated Fund.

(7) Nothing in this section prejudices any power to make rules of court.

NOTES

This section derived from the Insolvency Act 1985, ss 207(5), 208(1)–(3), (5).

Sub-s (1): para (za) inserted and words in square brackets in para (a) substituted by the Tribunals, Courts and Enforcement Act 2007, s 108(3), Sch 20, Pt 1, paras 1, 9; word "and" omitted from para (a) repealed, and para (c) and word immediately preceding it inserted, by the Enterprise and Regulatory Reform Act 2013, s 71(3), Sch 19, paras 1, 59(1), (2), in respect of a petition for a bankruptcy order presented to the court by a debtor on or after 6 April 2016.

Sub-s (1A): inserted by the Enterprise and Regulatory Reform Act 2013, s 71(3), Sch 19, paras 1, 59(1), (3), in respect of a petition for a bankruptcy order presented to the court by a debtor on or after 6 April 2016.

Orders: the Insolvency Fees Order 1986, SI 1986/2030 (revoked by SI 2004/593 and reproduced for reference at **[8.7]**); the Insolvency Proceedings (Fees) Order 2004, SI 2004/593 at **[8.71]**; the Civil Proceedings Fees Order 2008, SI 2008/1053; the Insolvency Proceedings (Fees) Order 2016, SI 2016/692 at **[8.82]**.

[1.527]
[415A Fees orders (general)

[(A1) The Secretary of State—
 (a) may by order require a person or body to pay a fee in connection with the grant or maintenance of a designation of that person or body as a competent authority under section 251U, and
 (b) may refuse to grant, or may withdraw, any such designation where a fee is not paid.]

(1) The Secretary of State—
 (a) may by order require a body to pay a fee in connection with the grant or maintenance of recognition of the body under section 391 [or (2)], and
 (b) may refuse recognition, or revoke an order of recognition under section 391(1) by a further order, where a fee is not paid.

[(1A) Fees under subsection (1) may vary according to whether the body is recognised under section 391(1) (body providing full and partial authorisation) or under section 391(2) (body providing partial authorisation).]

[(1B) In setting under subsection (1) the amount of a fee in connection with maintenance of recognition, the matters to which the Secretary of State may have regard include, in particular, the costs of the Secretary of State in connection with any functions under sections 391D, 391E, 391J, 391K and 391N.]

(2) The Secretary of State—
 (a) may by order require a person to pay a fee in connection with the grant or maintenance of authorisation of the person under section 393, and
 (b) may disregard an application or withdraw an authorisation where a fee is not paid.

(3) The Secretary of State may by order require the payment of fees in respect of—
 (a) the operation of the Insolvency Services Account;
 (b) payments into and out of that Account.

(4) The following provisions of section 414 apply to fees under this section as they apply to fees under that section—
 (a) subsection (3) (manner of payment),
 (b) subsection (5) (additional provision),
 (c) subsection (6) (statutory instrument),
 (d) subsection (7) (payment into Consolidated Fund), and
 (e) subsection (9) (saving for rules of court).

[(5) Section 391M applies for the purposes of an order under subsection (1)(b) as it applies for the purposes of a revocation order made under section 391L.]]

NOTES

Inserted by the Enterprise Act 2002, s 270(1).

Sub-s (A1): inserted by the Tribunals, Courts and Enforcement Act 2007, s 108(3), Sch 20, Pt 1, paras 1, 10.

Sub-s (1): words in square brackets inserted by the Deregulation Act 2015, s 17(1), (5)(a).

Sub-s (1A): inserted by the Deregulation Act 2015, s 17(1), (5)(b).

Sub-ss (1B), (5): inserted and added respectively by the Small Business, Enterprise and Employment Act 2015, ss 139(2), 140(2).

Sub-s (2): repealed by the Deregulation Act 2015, s 19, Sch 6, Pt 6, para 22(1), (5). Note that where immediately before 1 October 2015 an individual has applied for authorisation under s 392 of this Act or holds an authorisation granted under s 393, this repeal is to have no effect for the transitional period (ie, the period of one year beginning 1 October 2015).

Orders: the Insolvency Practitioners and Insolvency Services Account (Fees) Order 2003, SI 2003/3363 at **[12.23]**; the Provision of Services (Insolvency Practitioners) Regulations 2009, SI 2009/3081.

Specification, increase and reduction of money sums relevant in the operation of this Act

[1.528]
416 Monetary limits (companies winding up)

(1) The Secretary of State may by order in a statutory instrument increase or reduce any of the money sums for the time being specified in the following provisions in the first Group of Parts—

section 117(2) (amount of company's share capital determining whether county court has jurisdiction to wind it up);

section 120(3) (the equivalent as respects sheriff court jurisdiction in Scotland);

section 123(1)(a) (minimum debt for service of demand on company by unpaid creditor);

section 184(3) (minimum value of judgment, affecting sheriff's duties on levying execution);

section 206(1)(a) and (b) (minimum value of company property concealed or fraudulently removed, affecting criminal liability of company's officer).

(2) An order under this section may contain such transitional provisions as may appear to the Secretary of State necessary or expedient.
(3) No order under this section increasing or reducing any of the money sums for the time being specified in section 117(2), 120(3) or 123(1)(a) shall be made unless a draft of the order has been laid before and approved by a resolution of each House of Parliament.
(4) A statutory instrument containing an order under this section, other than an order to which subsection (3) applies, is subject to annulment in pursuance of a resolution of either House of Parliament.

NOTES

This section derived from the Companies Act 1985, s 664, and the Insolvency Act 1985, Sch 6, para 49.

Extension of application of orders: any sum specified by an order made under this section applies in the case of the winding up of an incorporated friendly society; see the Friendly Societies Act 1992, s 23, Sch 10, Pt I, para 5.

Any sum specified by an order made under this section applies in the case of the winding up, etc, of a building society; see the Building Societies Act 1986, ss 90, 90A, Sch 15, Pt I, para 5, Sch 15A, Pt I, para 5 at **[7.454]**, **[7.455]**, **[7.464]**, **[7.468]**.

Orders: the Insolvency Proceedings (Monetary Limits) Order 1986, SI 1986/1996 at **[8.1]**.

[1.529]

417 Money sum in s 222

The Secretary of State may by regulations in a statutory instrument increase or reduce the money sum for the time being specified in section 222(1) (minimum debt for service of demand on unregistered company by unpaid creditor); but such regulations shall not be made unless a draft of the statutory instrument containing them has been approved by resolution of each House of Parliament.

NOTES

This section derived from the Companies Act 1985, s 667(2) (in part).

[1.530]

[417A Money sums (company moratorium)

(1) The Secretary of State may by order increase or reduce any of the money sums for the time being specified in the following provisions of Schedule A1 to this Act—

paragraph 17(1) (maximum amount of credit which company may obtain without disclosure of moratorium);

paragraph 41(4) (minimum value of company property concealed or fraudulently removed, affecting criminal liability of company's officer).

(2) An order under this section may contain such transitional provisions as may appear to the Secretary of State necessary or expedient.
(3) An order under this section shall be made by statutory instrument subject to annulment in pursuance of a resolution of either House of Parliament.]

NOTES

Inserted by the Insolvency Act 2000, s 1, Sch 1, paras 1, 10.

[1.531]

418 Monetary limits (bankruptcy)

(1) The Secretary of State may by order prescribe amounts for the purposes of the following provisions in the second Group of Parts—

[section 251S(4) (maximum amount of credit which a person in respect of whom a debt relief order is made may obtain without disclosure of his status);]

section 273 (minimum value of debtor's estate determining whether immediate bankruptcy order should be made; small bankruptcies level);

[section 313A (value of property below which application for sale, possession or charge to be dismissed);]

section 346(3) (minimum amount of judgment, determining whether amount recovered on sale of debtor's goods is to be treated as part of his estate in bankruptcy);

section 354(1) and (2) (minimum amount of concealed debt, or value of property concealed or removed, determining criminal liability under the section);

section 358 (minimum value of property taken by a bankrupt out of England and Wales, determining his criminal liability);

section 360(1) (maximum amount of credit which bankrupt may obtain without disclosure of his status);

section 361(2) (exemption of bankrupt from criminal liability for failure to keep proper accounts, if unsecured debts not more than the prescribed minimum);

section 364(2)(d) (minimum value of goods removed by the bankrupt, determining his liability to arrest);

[paragraphs 6 to 8 of Schedule 4ZA (maximum amount of a person's debts monthly surplus income and property for purposes of obtaining a debt relief order);]

and references in the second Group of Parts to the amount prescribed for the purposes of any of those provisions, and references in those provisions to the prescribed amount, are to be construed accordingly.
(2) An order under this section may contain such transitional provisions as may appear to the Secretary of State necessary or expedient.
(3) An order under this section shall be made by statutory instrument subject to annulment in pursuance of a resolution of either House of Parliament.

NOTES

This section derived from the Insolvency Act 1985, s 209(1) (in part), (2), (3).

Sub-s (1): words in first and third pairs of square brackets inserted by the Tribunals, Courts and Enforcement Act 2007, s 108(3), Sch 20, Pt 1, paras 1, 11; words in second pair of square brackets inserted by the Enterprise Act 2002, s 261(6), subject to transitional provisions in s 261(7)–(10) of that Act at **[2.14]**.

Orders: the Insolvency Proceedings (Monetary Limits) Order 1986, SI 1986/1996 at **[8.1]**.

Insolvency practice

[1.532]

419 Regulations for purposes of Part XIII

(1) The Secretary of State may make regulations for the purpose of giving effect to Part XIII of this Act; and "prescribed" in that Part means prescribed by regulations made by the Secretary of State.

(2) Without prejudice to the generality of subsection (1) or to any provision of that Part by virtue of which regulations may be made with respect to any matter, regulations under this section may contain—

- (a) provision as to the matters to be taken into account in determining whether a person is a fit and proper person to act as an insolvency practitioner;
- (b) provision prohibiting a person from so acting in prescribed cases, being cases in which a conflict of interest will or may arise;
- (c) provision imposing requirements with respect to—
  - (i) the preparation and keeping by a person who acts as an insolvency practitioner of prescribed books, accounts and other records, and
  - (ii) the production of those books, accounts and records to prescribed persons;
- (d) provision conferring power on prescribed persons—
  - (i) to require any person who acts or has acted as an insolvency practitioner to answer any inquiry in relation to a case in which he is so acting or has so acted, and
  - (ii) to apply to a court to examine such a person or any other person on oath concerning such a case;
- (e) provision making non-compliance with any of the regulations a criminal offence; and
- (f) such incidental, supplemental and transitional provisions as may appear to the Secretary of State necessary or expedient.

(3) Any power conferred by Part XIII or this Part to make regulations, rules or orders is exercisable by statutory instrument subject to annulment by resolution of either House of Parliament.

(4) Any rule or regulation under Part XIII or this Part may make different provision with respect to different cases or descriptions of cases, including different provision for different areas.

[(5) In making regulations under this section, the Secretary of State must have regard to the regulatory objectives (as defined by section 391C(3)).]

NOTES

This section derived from the Insolvency Act 1985, ss 10, 11 (in part).

Sub-s (5): added by the Small Business, Enterprise and Employment Act 2015, s 138(2).

Regulations: the Insolvency Practitioners Regulations 2005, SI 2005/524 at **[12.30]**.

Other order-making powers

[1.533]

420 Insolvent partnerships

(1) The Lord Chancellor may, by order made with the concurrence of the Secretary of State [and the Lord Chief Justice], provide that such provisions of this Act as may be specified in the order shall apply in relation to insolvent partnerships with such modifications as may be so specified.

[(1A) An order under this section may make provision in relation to the [EU Regulation].

(1B) But provision made by virtue of this section in relation to the [EU Regulation] may not create an offence of a kind referred to in paragraph 1(1)(d) of Schedule 2 to the European Communities Act 1972.]

(2) An order under this section may make different provision for different cases and may contain such incidental, supplemental and transitional provisions as may appear to the Lord Chancellor [and the Lord Chief Justice] necessary or expedient.

(3) An order under this section shall be made by statutory instrument subject to annulment in pursuance of a resolution of either House of Parliament.

[(4) The Lord Chief Justice may nominate a judicial office holder (as defined in section 109(4) of the Constitutional Reform Act 2005) to exercise his functions under this section.]

NOTES

This section derived from the Insolvency Act 1985, s 227.

Sub-ss (1), (2): words in square brackets inserted by the Constitutional Reform Act 2005, s 15(1), Sch 4, Pt 1, paras 185, 191(1)–(3).

Sub-ss (1A), (1B): inserted by the Insolvency Act 1986 (Amendment) Regulations 2002, SI 2002/1037, regs 2, 3(5); words in square brackets substituted for original words "EC Regulation" by the Insolvency Amendment (EU 2015/848) Regulations 2017, SI 2017/702, regs 2, 3, Schedule, Pt 1, paras 1, 26, except in relation to proceedings opened before 26 June 2017 and subject to savings in reg 4 thereof at **[2.103]**.

Sub-s (4): added by the Constitutional Reform Act 2005, s 15(1), Sch 4, Pt 1, paras 185, 191(1), (4).

Provisions of this Act: the reference in sub-s (1) to "provisions of this Act" includes the Proceeds of Crime Act 2002, s 311(1)–(3): see s 311(6) of that Act.

Company directors disqualification: see the note to s 411 at **[1.522]**.

Orders: the Insolvent Partnerships Order 1994, SI 1994/2421 at **[10.1]**.

[1.534]

421 Insolvent estates of deceased persons

(1) The Lord Chancellor may, by order made with the concurrence of the Secretary of State [and the Lord Chief Justice], provide that such provisions of this Act as may be specified in the order shall apply [in relation] to the administration of the insolvent estates of deceased persons with such modifications as may be so specified.

[(1A) An order under this section may make provision in relation to the [EU Regulation].

(1B) But provision made by virtue of this section in relation to the [EU Regulation] may not create an offence of a kind referred to in paragraph 1(1)(d) of Schedule 2 to the European Communities Act 1972.]

(2) An order under this section may make different provision for different cases and may contain such incidental, supplemental and transitional provisions as may appear to the Lord Chancellor [and the Lord Chief Justice] necessary or expedient.

(3) An order under this section shall be made by statutory instrument subject to annulment in pursuance of a resolution of either House of Parliament.

(4) For the purposes of this section the estate of a deceased person is insolvent if, when realised, it will be insufficient to meet in full all the debts and other liabilities to which it is subject.

[(5) The Lord Chief Justice may nominate a judicial office holder (as defined in section 109(4) of the Constitutional Reform Act 2005) to exercise his functions under this section.]

NOTES

This section derived from the Insolvency Act 1985, s 228.

Sub-s (1): words in first pair of square brackets inserted by the Constitutional Reform Act 2005, s 15(1), Sch 4, Pt 1, paras 185, 192(1), (2); words in second pair of square brackets inserted by the Insolvency Act 2000, s 12(2).

Sub-ss (1A), (1B): inserted by the Insolvency Act 1986 (Amendment) Regulations 2002, SI 2002/1037, regs 2, 3(6); words in square brackets substituted for original words "EC Regulation" by the Insolvency Amendment (EU 2015/848) Regulations 2017, SI 2017/702, regs 2, 3, Schedule, Pt 1, paras 1, 27, except in relation to proceedings opened before 26 June 2017 and subject to savings in reg 4 thereof at **[2.103]**.

Sub-s (2): words in square brackets inserted by the Constitutional Reform Act 2005, s 15(1), Sch 4, Pt 1, paras 185, 192(1), (3).

Sub-s (5): added by the Constitutional Reform Act 2005, s 15(1), Sch 4, Pt 1, paras 185, 192(1), (4).

Provisions of this Act: the reference in sub-s (1) to "provisions of this Act" includes the Proceeds of Crime Act 2002, s 311(1)–(3): see s 311(6) of that Act.

Insolvency of employer: in the case of an employee who claims that his employer is liable to pay to him an employer's payment and the employer is insolvent in accordance with this section, the employee may apply to the Secretary of State for a payment under the Employment Rights Act 1996, s 166(6)(a) at **[17.136]**.

Orders: the Administration of Insolvent Estates of Deceased Persons Order 1986, SI 1986/1999 at **[11.1]**; the Administration of Insolvent Estates of Deceased Persons (Amendment) Order 2002, SI 2002/1309.

[1.535]

[421A Insolvent estates: joint tenancies

(1) This section applies where—

(a) an insolvency administration order has been made in respect of the insolvent estate of a deceased person,

(b) the petition for the order was presented after the commencement of this section and within the period of five years beginning with the day on which he died, and

(c) immediately before his death he was beneficially entitled to an interest in any property as joint tenant.

(2) For the purpose of securing that debts and other liabilities to which the estate is subject are met, the court may, on an application by the trustee appointed pursuant to the insolvency administration order, make an order under this section requiring the survivor to pay to the trustee an amount not exceeding the value lost to the estate.

(3) In determining whether to make an order under this section, and the terms of such an order, the court must have regard to all the circumstances of the case, including the interests of the deceased's creditors and of the survivor; but, unless the circumstances are exceptional, the court must assume that the interests of the deceased's creditors outweigh all other considerations.

(4) The order may be made on such terms and conditions as the court thinks fit.

(5) Any sums required to be paid to the trustee in accordance with an order under this section shall be comprised in the estate.

(6) The modifications of this Act which may be made by an order under section 421 include any modifications which are necessary or expedient in consequence of this section.

(7) In this section, "survivor" means the person who, immediately before the death, was beneficially entitled as joint tenant with the deceased or, if the person who was so entitled dies after the making of the insolvency administration order, his personal representatives.

(8) If there is more than one survivor—

(a) an order under this section may be made against all or any of them, but

(b) no survivor shall be required to pay more than so much of the value lost to the estate as is properly attributable to him.

(9) In this section—

"insolvency administration order" has the same meaning as in any order under section 421 having effect for the time being,

"value lost to the estate" means the amount which, if paid to the trustee, would in the court's opinion restore the position to what it would have been if the deceased had been [made] bankrupt immediately before his death.]

NOTES

Inserted by the Insolvency Act 2000, s 12(1).

Sub-s (9): word in square brackets in definition "value lost to the estate" substituted for original word "adjudged" by the Enterprise and Regulatory Reform Act 2013, s 71(3), Sch 19, paras 1, 60, in respect of a petition for a bankruptcy order presented to the court by a debtor on or after 6 April 2016.

[1.536]
422 [Formerly authorised banks]

[(1) The Secretary of State may by order made with the concurrence of the Treasury and after consultation with the [Financial Conduct Authority and the Prudential Regulation Authority] provide that specified provisions in the first Group of Parts shall apply with specified modifications in relation to any person who—

(a) has a liability in respect of a deposit which he accepted in accordance with the Banking Act 1979 (c 37) or 1987 (c 22), but

(b) does not have permission under [Part 4A] of the Financial Services and Markets Act 2000 (c 8) (regulated activities) to accept deposits.

(1A) Subsection (1)(b) shall be construed in accordance with—

(a) section 22 of the Financial Services and Markets Act 2000 (classes of regulated activity and categories of investment),

(b) any relevant order under that section, and

(c) Schedule 2 to that Act (regulated activities).]

[(1A) . . .]

(2) An order under this section may make different provision for different cases and may contain such incidental, supplemental and transitional provisions as may appear to the Secretary of State necessary or expedient.

(3) An order under this section shall be made by statutory instrument subject to annulment in pursuance of a resolution of either House of Parliament.

NOTES

This section derived from the Insolvency Act 1985, s 229.

Section heading: substituted by the Financial Services and Markets Act 2000 (Consequential Amendments) Order 2002, SI 2002/1555, art 16(1), (2).

Sub-s (1): substituted, together with (first) sub-s (1A), for existing sub-s (1), by the Enterprise Act 2002, s 248(3), Sch 17, paras 9, 35, subject to savings and transitional provisions (i) in a case where a petition for an administration order has been presented before 15 September 2003 (see the Enterprise Act 2002 (Commencement No 4 and Transitional Provisions and Savings) Order 2003, SI 2003/2093, art 3 at **[2.26]**), and (ii) in relation to special administration regimes (see s 249 of the 2002 Act at **[2.10]**); words in square brackets substituted by the Financial Services Act 2012, s 114(1), Sch 18, Pt 2, paras 51, 53. Sub-s (1), as amended by the Banking Act 1987, s 108(1), Sch 6, para 25(2), the Bank of England Act 1998, s 23(1), Sch 5, para 37, the Financial Services and Markets Act 2000 (Consequential Amendments and Repeals) Order 2001, SI 2001/3649, art 307, and SI 2002/1555, art 16(1), (3), previously read as follows:

"(1) The Secretary of State may, by order made with the concurrence of the Treasury and after consultation with the [Financial Services Authority], provide that such provisions in the first Group of Parts as may be specified in the order shall apply in relation to [any person [(other than an authorised deposit taker)] who continues to have a liability in respect of a deposit which was held by him in accordance with the Banking Act 1979 or the Banking Act 1987] with such modifications as may be so specified.".

First sub-s (1A): substituted, together with sub-s (1), for existing sub-s (1), by the Enterprise Act 2002, s 248(3), Sch 17, paras 9, 35, subject to savings as noted to sub-s (1) above.

Second sub-s (1A): inserted by SI 2002/1555, art 16(1), (4); repealed by the Enterprise Act 2002 (Insolvency) Order 2003, SI 2003/2096, arts 4, 6, Schedule, paras 8, 11, except in any case where a petition for an administration order was presented before 15 September 2003, and originally read as follows:

"(1A) For the purposes of subsection (1), "authorised deposit taker" has the meaning given in section 8(1B).".

Company directors disqualification: see the note to s 411 at **[1.522]**.

Banking Act 1987: repealed by SI 2001/3649, art 3(1)(d).

Orders: the Banks (Administration Proceedings) Order 1989, SI 1989/1276 (revoked by SI 2006/3107 and reproduced for reference at **[7.16]**); the Banks (Former Authorised Institutions) (Insolvency) Order 2006, SI 2006/3107 at **[7.21]**.

PART XVI PROVISIONS AGAINST DEBT AVOIDANCE (ENGLAND AND WALES ONLY)

[1.537]
423 Transactions defrauding creditors

(1) This section relates to transactions entered into at an undervalue; and a person enters into such a transaction with another person if—

(a) he makes a gift to the other person or he otherwise enters into a transaction with the other on terms that provide for him to receive no consideration;

(b) he enters into a transaction with the other in consideration of marriage [or the formation of a civil partnership]; or

(c) he enters into a transaction with the other for a consideration the value of which, in money or money's worth, is significantly less than the value, in money or money's worth, of the consideration provided by himself.

(2) Where a person has entered into such a transaction, the court may, if satisfied under the next subsection, make such order as it thinks fit for—

(a) restoring the position to what it would have been if the transaction had not been entered into, and
(b) protecting the interests of persons who are victims of the transaction.

(3) In the case of a person entering into such a transaction, an order shall only be made if the court is satisfied that it was entered into by him for the purpose—
(a) of putting assets beyond the reach of a person who is making, or may at some time make, a claim against him, or
(b) of otherwise prejudicing the interests of such a person in relation to the claim which he is making or may make.

(4) In this section "the court" means the High Court or—
(a) if the person entering into the transaction is an individual, any other court which would have jurisdiction in relation to a bankruptcy petition relating to him;
(b) if that person is a body capable of being wound up under Part IV or V of this Act, any other court having jurisdiction to wind it up.

(5) In relation to a transaction at an undervalue, references here and below to a victim of the transaction are to a person who is, or is capable of being, prejudiced by it; and in the following two sections the person entering into the transaction is referred to as "the debtor".

NOTES

This section derived from the Insolvency Act 1985, s 212(1), (3), (7) (in part).

Sub-s (1): words in square brackets inserted by the Civil Partnership Act 2004, s 261(1), Sch 27, para 121.

Make such order as it thinks fit: see further the Proceeds of Crime Act 2002, s 427 at **[17.243]**.

Tainted gifts: see the note to s 339 at **[1.411]**.

Market contracts: as to limitations on orders made under this section, with regard to adjusting prior transactions in relation to market contracts and certain other transactions relating to default proceedings, see the Companies Act 1989, s 165(1)(c) at **[17.68]**.

[1.538]

424 Those who may apply for an order under s 423

(1) An application for an order under section 423 shall not be made in relation to a transaction except—
(a) in a case where the debtor has been [made] bankrupt or is a body corporate which is being wound up or [is in administration], by the official receiver, by the trustee of the bankrupt's estate or the liquidator or administrator of the body corporate or (with the leave of the court) by a victim of the transaction;
(b) in a case where a victim of the transaction is bound by a voluntary arrangement approved under Part I or Part VIII of this Act, by the supervisor of the voluntary arrangement or by any person who (whether or not so bound) is such a victim; or
(c) in any other case, by a victim of the transaction.

(2) An application made under any of the paragraphs of subsection (1) is to be treated as made on behalf of every victim of the transaction.

NOTES

This section derived from the Insolvency Act 1985, s 212(2).

Sub-s (1): word in first pair of square brackets in para (a) substituted for original word "adjudged" by the Enterprise and Regulatory Reform Act 2013, s 71(3), Sch 19, paras 1, 61, in respect of a petition for a bankruptcy order presented to the court by a debtor on or after 6 April 2016; words in second pair of square brackets in para (a) substituted for words "in relation to which an administration order is in force" by the Enterprise Act 2002, s 248(3), Sch 17, paras 9, 36, subject to savings and transitional provisions (i) in a case where a petition for an administration order has been presented before 15 September 2003 (see the Enterprise Act 2002 (Commencement No 4 and Transitional Provisions and Savings) Order 2003, SI 2003/2093, art 3 at **[2.26]**), and (ii) in relation to special administration regimes (see s 249 of the 2002 Act at **[2.10]**).

[1.539]

425 Provision which may be made by order under s 423

(1) Without prejudice to the generality of section 423, an order made under that section with respect to a transaction may (subject as follows)—
(a) require any property transferred as part of the transaction to be vested in any person, either absolutely or for the benefit of all the persons on whose behalf the application for the order is treated as made;
(b) require any property to be so vested if it represents, in any person's hands, the application either of the proceeds of sale of property so transferred or of money so transferred;
(c) release or discharge (in whole or in part) any security given by the debtor;
(d) require any person to pay to any other person in respect of benefits received from the debtor such sums as the court may direct;
(e) provide for any surety or guarantor whose obligations to any person were released or discharged (in whole or in part) under the transaction to be under such new or revived obligations as the court thinks appropriate;
(f) provide for security to be provided for the discharge of any obligation imposed by or arising under the order, for such an obligation to be charged on any property and for such security or charge to have the same priority as a security or charge released or discharged (in whole or in part) under the transaction.

(2) An order under section 423 may affect the property of, or impose any obligation on, any person whether or not he is the person with whom the debtor entered into the transaction; but such an order—

(a) shall not prejudice any interest in property which was acquired from a person other than the debtor and was acquired in good faith, for value and without notice of the relevant circumstances, or prejudice any interest deriving from such an interest, and
(b) shall not require a person who received a benefit from the transaction in good faith, for value and without notice of the relevant circumstances to pay any sum unless he was a party to the transaction.

(3) For the purposes of this section the relevant circumstances in relation to a transaction are the circumstances by virtue of which an order under section 423 may be made in respect of the transaction.
(4) In this section "security" means any mortgage, charge, lien or other security.

NOTES

This section derived from the Insolvency Act 1985, s 212(4)–(6), (7) (in part).

PART XVII MISCELLANEOUS AND GENERAL

[1.540]

426 Co-operation between courts exercising jurisdiction in relation to insolvency

(1) An order made by a court in any part of the United Kingdom in the exercise of jurisdiction in relation to insolvency law shall be enforced in any other part of the United Kingdom as if it were made by a court exercising the corresponding jurisdiction in that other part.
(2) However, without prejudice to the following provisions of this section, nothing in subsection (1) requires a court in any part of the United Kingdom to enforce, in relation to property situated in that part, any order made by a court in any other part of the United Kingdom.
(3) The Secretary of State, with the concurrence in relation to property situated in England and Wales of the Lord Chancellor, may by order make provision for securing that a trustee or assignee under the insolvency law of any part of the United Kingdom has, with such modifications as may be specified in the order, the same rights in relation to any property situated in another part of the United Kingdom as he would have in the corresponding circumstances if he were a trustee or assignee under the insolvency law of that other part.
(4) The courts having jurisdiction in relation to insolvency law in any part of the United Kingdom shall assist the courts having the corresponding jurisdiction in any other part of the United Kingdom or any relevant country or territory.
(5) For the purposes of subsection (4) a request made to a court in any part of the United Kingdom by a court in any other part of the United Kingdom or in a relevant country or territory is authority for the court to which the request is made to apply, in relation to any matters specified in the request, the insolvency law which is applicable by either court in relation to comparable matters falling within its jurisdiction.

In exercising its discretion under this subsection, a court shall have regard in particular to the rules of private international law.
(6) Where a person who is a trustee or assignee under the insolvency law of any part of the United Kingdom claims property situated in any other part of the United Kingdom (whether by virtue of an order under subsection (3) or otherwise), the submission of that claim to the court exercising jurisdiction in relation to insolvency law in that other part shall be treated in the same manner as a request made by a court for the purpose of subsection (4).
(7) Section 38 of the Criminal Law Act 1977 (execution of warrant of arrest throughout the United Kingdom) applies to a warrant which, in exercise of any jurisdiction in relation to insolvency law, is issued in any part of the United Kingdom for the arrest of a person as it applies to a warrant issued in that part of the United Kingdom for the arrest of a person charged with an offence.
(8) Without prejudice to any power to make rules of court, any power to make provision by subordinate legislation for the purpose of giving effect in relation to companies or individuals to the insolvency law of any part of the United Kingdom includes power to make provisions for the purpose of giving effect in that part to any provision made by or under the preceding provisions of this section.
(9) An order under subsection (3) shall be made by statutory instrument subject to annulment in pursuance of a resolution of either House of Parliament.
(10) In this section "insolvency law" means—
(a) in relation to England and Wales, provision [extending to England and Wales and] made by or under this Act or sections [1A,] 6 to 10, [12 to 15], 19(c) and 20 (with Schedule 1) of the Company Directors Disqualification Act 1986 [and sections 1 to 17 of that Act as they apply for the purposes of those provisions of that Act];
(b) in relation to Scotland, provision extending to Scotland and made by or under this Act, sections [1A,] 6 to 10, [12 to 15], 19(c) and 20 (with Schedule 1) of the Company Directors Disqualification Act 1986 [and sections 1 to 17 of that Act as they apply for the purposes of those provisions of that Act], Part XVIII of the Companies Act or the Bankruptcy (Scotland) Act [2016];
(c) in relation to Northern Ireland, provision made by or under [the Insolvency (Northern Ireland) Order 1989] [or the Company Directors Disqualification (Northern Ireland) Order 2002];
(d) in relation to any relevant country or territory, so much of the law of that country or territory as corresponds to provisions falling within any of the foregoing paragraphs;

and references in this subsection to any enactment include, in relation to any time before the coming into force of that enactment the corresponding enactment in force at that time.
(11) In this section "relevant country or territory" means—
(a) any of the Channel Islands or the Isle of Man, or

(b) any country or territory designated for the purposes of this section by the Secretary of State by order made by statutory instrument.

[(12) In the application of this section to Northern Ireland—

(a) for any reference to the Secretary of State there is substituted a reference to the Department of Economic Development in Northern Ireland;

(b) in subsection (3) for the words "another part of the United Kingdom" and the words "that other part" there are substituted the words "Northern Ireland";

(c) for subsection (9) there is substituted the following subsection—

"(9) An order made under subsection (3) by the Department of Economic Development in Northern Ireland shall be a statutory rule for the purposes of the Statutory Rules (Northern Ireland) Order 1979 and shall be subject to negative resolution within the meaning of section 41(6) of the Interpretation Act (Northern Ireland) 1954.".]

[(13) Section 129 of the Banking Act 2009 provides for provisions of that Act about bank insolvency to be "insolvency law" for the purposes of this section.]

[(14) Section 165 of the Banking Act 2009 provides for provisions of that Act about bank administration to be "insolvency law" for the purposes of this section.]

NOTES

This section derived from the Insolvency Act 1985, s 213.

Sub-s (10): words in square brackets in paras (a), (b) inserted or substituted by the Insolvency Act 2000, s 8, Sch 4, Pt II, para 16(1), (3); year "2016" in square brackets in para (b) substituted (for the original year "1985") by the Bankruptcy (Scotland) Act 2016 (Consequential Provisions and Modifications) Order 2016, SI 2016/1034, art 7(1), (3), Sch 1, para 4(1), (9), as from 30 November 2016 (except in relation to (i) a sequestration as regards which the petition is presented, or the debtor application is made before that date; or (ii) a trust deed executed before that date); words in first pair of square brackets in para (c) substituted by the Insolvency (Northern Ireland) Order 1989, SI 1989/2405 (NI 19), art 381(2), Sch 9, Pt II, para 41(a); words in second pair of square brackets in para (c) added by the Companies (Northern Ireland) Order 1989, SI 1989/2404, arts 25(2), 36, Sch 4, Pt I, para 1, and substituted for the words "or Part II of the Companies (Northern Ireland) Order 1989" by the Company Directors Disqualification (Northern Ireland) Order 2002, SI 2002/3150 (NI 4), art 26(2), Sch 3, para 2, subject to transitional provisions in the Company Directors Disqualification (2002 Order) (Transitional Provisions) Order (Northern Ireland) 2003, SR 2003/346, arts 3–6.

Sub-s (12): added by SI 1989/2405, art 381(2), Sch 9, Pt II, para 41(b).

Sub-ss (13), (14): added by the Banking Act 2009, ss 129, 165.

Insolvency law: references to insolvency law in this section include, in relation to a part of the UK, provisions made by or under the Companies Act 1989, Pt VII, and, in relation to a relevant country or territory, so much of the law of that country or territory as corresponds to any such provisions; see the Companies Act 1989, s 183(1) at **[17.87]**. See also, as to insolvency proceedings in other jurisdictions, s 183(2), (3) thereof.

See further, the Insolvency Act 2000, s 14, which enables the Secretary of State to give effect to the United Nations Commission on International Trade Law model law on cross-border insolvency by secondary legislation and provides that any such secondary legislation may include amendments to this section.

Criminal Law Act 1977, s 38: repealed by the Criminal Justice and Public Order Act 1994, s 168(3), Sch 11.

Orders: the Co-operation of Insolvency Courts (Designation of Relevant Countries and Territories) Order 1986, SI 1986/2123 at **[13.1]**; the Co-operation of Insolvency Courts (Designation of Relevant Countries) Order 1996, SI 1996/253 at **[13.19]**; the Co-operation of Insolvency Courts (Designation of Relevant Country) Order 1998, SI 1998/2766 at **[13.22]**.

[1.541]

[426A Disqualification from Parliament [(England and Wales and Northern Ireland)]

(1) A person in respect of whom a bankruptcy restrictions order [or a debt relief restrictions order] has effect shall be disqualified—

(a) from membership of the House of Commons,

(b) from sitting or voting in the House of Lords, and

(c) from sitting or voting in a committee of the House of Lords or a joint committee of both Houses.

(2) If a member of the House of Commons becomes disqualified under this section, his seat shall be vacated.

(3) If a person who is disqualified under this section is returned as a member of the House of Commons, his return shall be void.

(4) No writ of summons shall be issued to a member of the House of Lords who is disqualified under this section.

(5) If a court makes a bankruptcy restrictions order or interim order[, or a debt relief restrictions order or an interim debt relief restrictions order,] in respect of a member of the House of Commons or the House of Lords the court shall notify the Speaker of that House.

(6) If the Secretary of State accepts a bankruptcy restrictions undertaking [or a debt relief restrictions undertaking] made by a member of the House of Commons or the House of Lords, the Secretary of State shall notify the Speaker of that House.

[(7) If the Department of Enterprise, Trade and Investment for Northern Ireland accepts a bankruptcy restrictions undertaking made by a member of the House of Commons or the House of Lords under Schedule 2A to the Insolvency (Northern Ireland) Order 1989, the Department shall notify the Speaker of that House.

(8) In this section a reference to a bankruptcy restrictions order or an interim order includes a reference to a bankruptcy restrictions order or an interim order made under Schedule 2A to the Insolvency (Northern Ireland) Order 1989.]]

NOTES

Inserted, together with ss 426B, 426C, by the Enterprise Act 2002, s 266(1).

Heading: words in square brackets substituted by the Insolvency Act 1986 (Disqualification from Parliament) Order 2012, SI 2012/1544, arts 2, 3(a).

Sub-ss (1), (5), (6): words in square brackets inserted by the Tribunals, Courts and Enforcement Act 2007, s 108(3), Sch 20, Pt 1, paras 1, 12.

Sub-ss (7), (8): added by SI 2012/1544, arts 2, 3(b).

[1.542]
[426B Devolution

(1) If a court [in England and Wales] makes a bankruptcy restrictions order or interim order in respect of a member of the Scottish Parliament, the Northern Ireland Assembly or the National Assembly for Wales, [or makes a debt relief restrictions order or interim debt relief restrictions order in respect of such a member,] the court shall notify the presiding officer of that body.

[(1A) If the High Court in Northern Ireland makes a bankruptcy restrictions order or interim order under Schedule 2A to the Insolvency (Northern Ireland) Order 1989 in respect of a member of the Scottish Parliament or the National Assembly for Wales, the Court shall notify the presiding officer of that body.]

(2) If the Secretary of State accepts a bankruptcy restrictions undertaking [or a debt relief restrictions undertaking] made by a member of the Scottish Parliament, the Northern Ireland Assembly or the National Assembly for Wales, the Secretary of State shall notify the presiding officer of that body.

[(3) If the Department of Enterprise, Trade and Investment for Northern Ireland accepts a bankruptcy restrictions undertaking made by a member of the Scottish Parliament or the National Assembly for Wales under Schedule 2A to the Insolvency (Northern Ireland) Order 1989, the Department shall notify the presiding officer of that body.]]

NOTES

Inserted as noted to s 426A at **[1.541]**.

Sub-s (1): words in first pair of square brackets inserted by the Insolvency Act 1986 (Disqualification from Parliament) Order 2012, SI 2012/1544, arts 2, 4(a); words in second pair of square brackets inserted by the Tribunals, Courts and Enforcement Act 2007, s 108(3), Sch 20, Pt 1, paras 1, 13(1), (2).

Sub-ss (1A), (3): inserted by SI 2012/1544, arts 2, 4(b), (c).

Sub-s (2): words in square brackets inserted by the Tribunals, Courts and Enforcement Act 2007, s 108(3), Sch 20, Pt 1, paras 1, 13(1), (3).

[1.543]
[426C Irrelevance of privilege

(1) An enactment about insolvency applies in relation to a member of the House of Commons or the House of Lords irrespective of any Parliamentary privilege.

(2) In this section "enactment" includes a provision made by or under—
  (a) an Act of the Scottish Parliament, or
  (b) Northern Ireland legislation.]

NOTES

Inserted as noted to s 426A at **[1.541]**.

[1.544]
427 [Disqualification from Parliament (Scotland . . .)]

(1) Where . . . a court in Scotland awards sequestration of an individual's estate, the individual is disqualified—
  (a) for sitting or voting in the House of Lords,
  (b) for being elected to, or sitting or voting in, the House of Commons, and
  (c) for sitting or voting in a committee of either House.

(2) Where an individual is disqualified under this section, the disqualification ceases—
  (a) except where [the award is recalled] or reduced without the individual having been first discharged, on the discharge of the individual, and
  (b) in the excepted case, on the . . . recall or reduction, as the case may be.

(3) No writ of summons shall be issued to any lord of Parliament who is for the time being disqualified under this section for sitting and voting in the House of Lords.

(4) Where a member of the House of Commons who is disqualified under this section continues to be so disqualified until the end of the period of 6 months beginning with the day of the . . . award, his seat shall be vacated at the end of that period.

(5) A court which makes an . . . award such as is mentioned in subsection (1) in relation to any lord of Parliament or member of the House of Commons shall forthwith certify the . . . award to the Speaker of the House of Lords or, as the case may be, to the Speaker of the House of Commons.

(6) Where a court has certified an . . . award to the Speaker of the House of Commons under subsection (5), then immediately after it becomes apparent which of the following certificates is applicable, the court shall certify to the Speaker of the House of Commons—
  (a) that the period of 6 months beginning with the day of the . . . award has expired without the . . . award having been . . . recalled or reduced, or
  (b) that the . . . award has been . . . recalled or reduced before the end of that period.

[(6A) Subsections (4) to (6) have effect in relation to a member of the Scottish Parliament but as if—
  (a) references to the House of Commons were to the Parliament and references to the Speaker were to the Presiding Officer, and

(b) in subsection (4), for "under this section" there were substituted "under section 15(1)(b) of the Scotland Act 1998 by virtue of this section".]

[(6B) Subsections (4) to (6) have effect in relation to a member of the National Assembly for Wales but as if—

(a) references to the House of Commons were to the Assembly and references to the Speaker were to the presiding officer, and

(b) in subsection (4), for "under this section" there were substituted "under [section 16(2) of the Government of Wales Act 2006] by virtue of this section".]

[(6C) [Subsections (4) to (6) have effect in relation to a member of the Northern Ireland Assembly but as if—]

(a) references to the House of Commons were to the Assembly and references to the Speaker were to the Presiding Officer; and

(b) in subsection (4), for "under this section" there were substituted "under section 36(4) of the Northern Ireland Act 1998 by virtue of this section".]

(7) . . .

NOTES

This section derived from the Insolvency Act 1985, s 214.

Section heading: substituted by the Enterprise Act 2002, s 266(1); words omitted repealed by the Insolvency Act 1986 (Disqualification from Parliament) Order 2012, SI 2012/1544, arts 2, 5(a).

Sub-s (1): words omitted repealed by SI 2012/1544, arts 2, 5(b).

Sub-s (2): words in square brackets substituted and word omitted repealed by SI 2012/1544, arts 2, 5(c).

Sub-ss (4)–(6): words omitted repealed by SI 2012/1544, arts 2, 5(d)–(f).

Sub-s (6A): inserted by the Scotland Act 1998, s 125(1), Sch 8, para 23(1), (6).

Sub-s (6B): inserted by the Government of Wales Act 1998, s 125, Sch 12, para 24; words in square brackets substituted by the Government of Wales Act 2006, s 160(1), Sch 10, para 18.

Sub-s (6C): inserted by the Northern Ireland Act 1998, s 99, Sch 13, para 6; words in square brackets substituted by SI 2012/1544, arts 2, 5(g).

Sub-s (7): repealed by the Enterprise Act 2002, ss 266(2)(b), 278(2), Sch 26.

[1.545]
428 Exemptions from Restrictive Trade Practices Act

(1), (2) . . .

(3) In this section "insolvency services" means the services of persons acting as insolvency practitioners or carrying out under the law of Northern Ireland functions corresponding to those mentioned in section 388(1) or (2) in Part XIII, in their capacity as such . . .

NOTES

This section derived from the Insolvency Act 1985, s 217(1)–(3).

Sub-ss (1), (2): repealed by the Competition Act 1998 (Transitional, Consequential and Supplemental Provisions) Order 2000, SI 2000/311, art 19.

Sub-s (3): words omitted repealed by SI 2000/311, art 19.

[1.546]
429 Disabilities on revocation of administration order against an individual

(1) The following applies where a person fails to make any payment which he is required to make by virtue of an administration order under Part VI of the County Courts Act 1984.

(2) The court which is administering that person's estate under the order may, if it thinks fit—

(a) revoke the administration order, and

(b) make an order directing that this section and section 12 of the Company Directors Disqualification Act 1986 shall apply to the person for such period, [not exceeding one year], as may be specified in the order.

(3) *A person* to whom this section so applies shall not—

(a) either alone or jointly with another person, obtain credit to the extent of the amount prescribed for the purposes of section 360(1)(a) or more, or

(b) enter into any transaction in the course of or for the purposes of any business in which he is directly or indirectly engaged,

without disclosing to the person from whom he obtains the credit, or (as the case may be) with whom the transaction is entered into, the fact that this section applies to him.

(4) The reference in subsection (3) to *a person* obtaining credit includes—

(a) a case where goods are bailed or hired to him under a hire-purchase agreement or agreed to be sold to him under a conditional sale agreement, and

(b) a case where he is paid in advance (whether in money or otherwise) for the supply of goods or services.

(5) A *person* who contravenes this section is guilty of an offence and liable to imprisonment or a fine, or both.

NOTES

This section derived from the Insolvency Act 1985, s 221(1), (3)–(5).

Sub-s (1): substituted, together with sub-s (2), by new sub-ss (1), (2), (2A), by the Tribunals, Courts and Enforcement Act 2007, s 106(2), Sch 16, para 3(1), (2), as from a day to be appointed, as follows:

"(1) This section applies if [the county court] revokes an administration order made in respect of an individual ("the debtor") on one of the relevant grounds.

(2) The court may, at the time it revokes the administration order, make an order directing that this section and section 12 of the Company Directors Disqualification Act 1986 shall apply to the debtor for such period, not exceeding one year, as may be specified in the order.

(2A) Each of the following is a relevant ground—

(a) the debtor had failed to make two payments (whether consecutive or not) required by the order;

(b) at the time the order was made—

(i) the total amount of the debtor's qualifying debts was more than the prescribed maximum for the purposes of Part 6 of the 1984 Act, but

(ii) because of information provided, or not provided, by the debtor, that amount was thought to be less than, or the same as, the prescribed maximum.".

In sub-s (1) (as substituted): words in square brackets substituted by the Crime and Courts Act 2013, s 17(5), Sch 9, Pt 3, para 52(1)(b), (2).

Sub-s (2): substituted, as from a day to be appointed, as noted to sub-s (1) above; words in square brackets substituted by the Enterprise Act 2002, s 269, Sch 23, paras 1, 15.

Sub-ss (3), (4): for the words in italics in both places they appear, there are substituted the words "an individual" by the Tribunals, Courts and Enforcement Act 2007, s 106(2), Sch 16, para 3(1), (3), (4), as from a day to be appointed.

Sub-s (5): for the word in italics there is substituted the word "individual" by the Tribunals, Courts and Enforcement Act 2007, s 106(2), Sch 16, para 3(1), (5), as from a day to be appointed.

[1.547]

430 Provision introducing Schedule of punishments

(1) Schedule 10 to this Act has effect with respect to the way in which offences under this Act are punishable on conviction.

(2) In relation to an offence under a provision of this Act specified in the first column of the Schedule (the general nature of the offence being described in the second column), the third column shows whether the offence is punishable on conviction on indictment, or on summary conviction, or either in the one way or the other.

(3) The fourth column of the Schedule shows, in relation to an offence, the maximum punishment by way of fine or imprisonment under this Act which may be imposed on a person convicted of the offence in the way specified in relation to it in the third column (that is to say, on indictment or summarily), a reference to a period of years or months being to a term of imprisonment of that duration.

(4) The fifth column shows (in relation to an offence for which there is an entry in that column) that a person convicted of the offence after continued contravention is liable to a daily default fine; that is to say, he is liable on a second or subsequent conviction of the offence to the fine specified in that column for each day on which the contravention is continued (instead of the penalty specified for the offence in the fourth column of the Schedule).

(5) For the purpose of any enactment in this Act whereby an officer of a company who is in default is liable to a fine or penalty, the expression "officer who is in default" means any officer of the company who knowingly and wilfully authorises or permits the default, refusal or contravention mentioned in the enactment.

NOTES

This section derived from the Companies Act 1985, s 730.

[1.548]

431 Summary proceedings

(1) Summary proceedings for any offence under any of Parts I to VII of this Act may (without prejudice to any jurisdiction exercisable apart from this subsection) be taken against a body corporate at any place at which the body has a place of business, and against any other person at any place at which he is for the time being.

(2) Notwithstanding anything in section 127(1) of the Magistrates' Courts Act 1980, an information relating to such an offence which is triable by a magistrates' court in England and Wales may be so tried if it is laid at any time within 3 years after the commission of the offence and within 12 months after the date on which evidence sufficient in the opinion of the Director of Public Prosecutions or the Secretary of State (as the case may be) to justify the proceedings comes to his knowledge.

(3) Summary proceedings in Scotland for such an offence shall not be commenced after the expiration of 3 years from the commission of the offence.

Subject to this (and notwithstanding anything in [section 136 of the Criminal Procedure (Scotland) Act 1995]), such proceedings may (in Scotland) be commenced at any time within 12 months after the date on which evidence sufficient in the Lord Advocate's opinion to justify the proceedings came to his knowledge or, where such evidence was reported to him by the Secretary of State, within 12 months after the date on which it came to the knowledge of the latter; and subsection (3) of that section applies for the purpose of this subsection as it applies for the purpose of that section.

(4) For purposes of this section, a certificate of the Director of Public Prosecutions, the Lord Advocate or the Secretary of State (as the case may be) as to the date on which such evidence as is referred to above came to his knowledge is conclusive evidence.

NOTES

This section derived from the Companies Act 1985, s 731, and the Insolvency Act 1985, s 108(1).

Sub-s (3): words in square brackets substituted by the Criminal Procedure (Consequential Provisions) (Scotland) Act 1995, s 5, Sch 4, para 61.

[1.549]
432 Offences by bodies corporate
(1) This section applies to offences under this Act other than those excepted by subsection (4).
(2) Where a body corporate is guilty of an offence to which this section applies and the offence is proved to have been committed with the consent or connivance of, or to be attributable to any neglect on the part of, any director, manager, secretary or other similar officer of the body corporate or any person who was purporting to act in any such capacity he, as well as the body corporate, is guilty of the offence and liable to be proceeded against and punished accordingly.
(3) Where the affairs of a body corporate are managed by its members, subsection (2) applies in relation to the acts and defaults of a member in connection with his functions of management as if he were a director of the body corporate.
(4) The offences excepted from this section are those under sections 30, 39, 51, 53, 54, 62, 64, 66, 85, 89, 164, 188, 201, 206, 207, 208, 209, 210 and 211 [and those under paragraphs 16(2), 17(3)(a), 18(3)(a), 19(3)(a), 22(1) and 23(1)(a) of Schedule A1].

NOTES
This section derived from the Insolvency Act 1985, s 230.
Sub-s (4): words in square brackets inserted by the Insolvency Act 2000, s 1, Sch 1, paras 1, 11.

[1.550]
433 Admissibility in evidence of statements of affairs, etc
[(1)] In any proceedings (whether or not under this Act)—
(a) a statement of affairs prepared for the purposes of any provision of this Act which is derived from the Insolvency Act 1985,
[(aa) a statement made in pursuance of a requirement imposed by or under Part 2 of the Banking Act 2009 (bank insolvency),]
[(ab) a statement made in pursuance of a requirement imposed by or under Part 3 of that Act (bank administration),] and
(b) any other statement made in pursuance of a requirement imposed by or under any such provision or by or under rules made under this Act,

may be used in evidence against any person making or concurring in making the statement.
[(2) However, in criminal proceedings in which any such person is charged with an offence to which this subsection applies—
(a) no evidence relating to the statement may be adduced, and
(b) no question relating to it may be asked,

by or on behalf of the prosecution, unless evidence relating to it is adduced, or a question relating to it is asked, in the proceedings by or on behalf of that person.
(3) Subsection (2) applies to any offence other than—
(a) an offence under section 22(6), 47(6), 48(8), 66(6), 67(8), 95(8), *98(6),* [99(3)], 131(7), 192(2), 208(1)(a) or (d) or (2), 210, 235(5), 353(1), 354(1)(b) or (3) or 356(1) or (2)(a) or (b) or paragraph 4(3)(a) of Schedule 7;
(b) an offence which is—
  (i) created by rules made under this Act, and
  (ii) designated for the purposes of this subsection by such rules or by regulations made by the Secretary of State;
(c) an offence which is—
  (i) created by regulations made under any such rules, and
  (ii) designated for the purposes of this subsection by such regulations;
(d) an offence under section 1, 2 or 5 of the Perjury Act 1911 (false statements made on oath or made otherwise than on oath); or
(e) an offence under section 44(1) or (2) of the Criminal Law (Consolidation) (Scotland) Act 1995 (false statements made on oath or otherwise than on oath).

(4) Regulations under subsection (3)(b)(ii) shall be made by statutory instrument and, after being made, shall be laid before each House of Parliament.]

NOTES
This section derived from the Insolvency Act 1985, s 231.
Existing provision renumbered as sub-s (1) and sub-ss (2)–(4) added by the Youth Justice and Criminal Evidence Act 1999, s 59, Sch 3, para 7.
Sub-s (1): paras (aa), (ab) inserted by the Banking Act 2009, ss 128, 162.
Sub-s (3): figure in italics repealed, and figure in square brackets substituted for original figure "99(3)(a)," by the Small Business, Enterprise and Employment Act 2015, s 126, Sch 9, Pt 1, paras 1, 56, as from 6 April 2017 (in relation to England and Wales and subject to transitional and savings provisions as noted to s 246ZE at **[1.256]**), and as from a day to be appointed (in relation to Scotland).
Insolvency Act 1985: that Act was mostly repealed by the combined effect of s 438 of, and Sch 12 to, this Act and the Company Directors Disqualification Act 1986, s 23(2), Sch 4.

[1.551]
434 Crown application
For the avoidance of doubt it is hereby declared that provisions of this Act which derive from the Insolvency Act 1985 bind the Crown so far as affecting or relating to the following matters, namely—
(a) remedies against, or against the property of, companies or individuals;
(b) priorities of debts;

(c) transactions at an undervalue or preferences;
(d) voluntary arrangements approved under Part I or Part VIII, and
(e) discharge from bankruptcy.

NOTES

This section derived from the Insolvency Act 1985, s 234.

Company directors disqualification: see the note to s 411 at **[1.522]**.

Insolvency Act 1985: that Act was mostly repealed by the combined effect of s 438 of, and Sch 12 to, this Act and the Company Directors Disqualification Act 1986, s 23(2), Sch 4.

[PART 17A SUPPLEMENTARY PROVISIONS

[1.552]
434A Introductory

The provisions of this Part have effect for the purposes of—
(a) the First Group of Parts, and
(b) sections 411, 413, 414, 416 and 417 in Part 15.]

NOTES

Part 17A (ss 434A–434C) inserted by the Companies Act 2006 (Consequential Amendments etc) Order 2008, SI 2008/948, art 3(1)(b), Sch 1, Pt 2, para 105.

[1.553]
[434B Representation of corporations [in decision procedures and] at meetings

(1) If a corporation is a creditor or debenture-holder, it may by resolution of its directors or other governing body authorise a person or persons to act as its representative or representatives—
[(a) in a qualifying decision procedure, held in pursuance of this Act or of rules made under it, by which a decision is sought from the creditors of a company, or]
(b) at any meeting of a company held in pursuance of the provisions contained in a debenture or trust deed.

(2) Where the corporation authorises only one person, that person is entitled to exercise the same powers on behalf of the corporation as the corporation could exercise if it were an individual creditor or debenture-holder.

(3) Where the corporation authorises more than one person, any one of them is entitled to exercise the same powers on behalf of the corporation as the corporation could exercise if it were an individual creditor or debenture-holder.

(4) Where the corporation authorises more than one person and more than one of them purport to exercise a power under subsection (3)—
(a) if they purport to exercise the power in the same way, the power is treated as exercised in that way;
(b) if they do not purport to exercise the power in the same way, the power is treated as not exercised.]

NOTES

Inserted as noted to s 434A at **[1.552]**.

Words in square brackets in section heading inserted, and sub-s (1)(a) substituted, by the Small Business, Enterprise and Employment Act 2015, s 126, Sch 9, Pt 1, paras 1, 57, as from 6 April 2017 (in relation to England and Wales and subject to transitional and savings provisions as noted to s 246ZE at **[1.256]**), and as from a day to be appointed (in relation to Scotland). Sub-s (1)(a) previously read as follows—

"(a) at any meeting of the creditors of a company held in pursuance of this Act or of rules made under it, or".

[1.554]
[434C Legal professional privilege

In proceedings against a person for an offence under this Act nothing in this Act is to be taken to require any person to disclose any information that he is entitled to refuse to disclose on grounds of legal professional privilege (in Scotland, confidentiality of communications).]

NOTES

Inserted as noted to s 434A at **[1.552]**.

[1.555]
[434D Enforcement of company's filing obligations

(1) This section applies where a company has made default in complying with any obligation under this Act—
(a) to deliver a document to the registrar, or
(b) to give notice to the registrar of any matter.

(2) The registrar, or any member or creditor of the company, may give notice to the company requiring it to comply with the obligation.

(3) If the company fails to make good the default within 14 days after service of the notice, the registrar, or any member or creditor of the company, may apply to the court for an order directing the company, and any specified officer of it, to make good the default within a specified time.

(4) The court's order may provide that all costs (in Scotland, expenses) of or incidental to the application are to be borne by the company or by any officers of it responsible for the default.

(5) This section does not affect the operation of any enactment imposing penalties on a company or its officers in respect of any such default.]

NOTES

Inserted, together with s 434E, by the Companies Act 2006 (Consequential Amendments, Transitional Provisions and Savings) Order 2009, SI 2009/1941, art 2(1), Sch 1, para 81, subject to transitional provisions and savings in art 8, Sch 1, para 84 at **[2.70]**, **[2.73]**.

[1.556]
[434E Application of filing obligations to overseas companies

The provisions of this Act requiring documents to be forwarded or delivered to, or filed with, the registrar of companies apply in relation to an overseas company that is required to register particulars under section 1046 of the Companies Act 2006 as they apply in relation to a company registered under that Act in England and Wales or Scotland.]

NOTES

Inserted as noted to s 434D at **[1.555]**.

PART XVIII INTERPRETATION

NOTES

Modification of this Part in relation to building societies: this Part is applied, with modifications, in relation to the winding up, etc, of building societies; see the Building Societies Act 1986, s 90A, Sch 15A at **[7.455]**, **[7.468]**.

[1.557]
435 Meaning of "associate"

(1) For the purposes of this Act any question whether a person is an associate of another person is to be determined in accordance with the following provisions of this section (any provision that a person is an associate of another person being taken to mean that they are associates of each other).

[(2) A person is an associate of an individual if that person is—
 (a) the individual's husband or wife or civil partner,
 (b) a relative of—
  (i) the individual, or
  (ii) the individual's husband or wife or civil partner, or
 (c) the husband or wife or civil partner of a relative of—
  (i) the individual, or
  (ii) the individual's husband or wife or civil partner.]

(3) A person is an associate of any person with whom he is in partnership, and of the husband or wife [or civil partner] or a relative of any individual with whom he is in partnership; and a Scottish firm is an associate of any person who is a member of the firm.

(4) A person is an associate of any person whom he employs or by whom he is employed.

(5) A person in his capacity as trustee of a trust other than—
 (a) a trust arising under any of the second Group of Parts or the Bankruptcy (Scotland) Act [2016], or
 (b) a pension scheme or an employees' share scheme . . . ,

is an associate of another person if the beneficiaries of the trust include, or the terms of the trust confer a power that may be exercised for the benefit of, that other person or an associate of that other person.

(6) A company is an associate of another company—
 (a) if the same person has control of both, or a person has control of one and persons who are his associates, or he and persons who are his associates, have control of the other, or
 (b) if a group of two or more persons has control of each company, and the groups either consist of the same persons or could be regarded as consisting of the same persons by treating (in one or more cases) a member of either group as replaced by a person of whom he is an associate.

(7) A company is an associate of another person if that person has control of it or if that person and persons who are his associates together have control of it.

(8) For the purposes of this section a person is a relative of an individual if he is that individual's brother, sister, uncle, aunt, nephew, niece, lineal ancestor or lineal descendant, treating—
 (a) any relationship of the half blood as a relationship of the whole blood and the stepchild or adopted child of any person as his child, and
 (b) an illegitimate child as the legitimate child of his mother and reputed father;

and references in this section to a husband or wife include a former husband or wife and a reputed husband or wife [and references to a civil partner include a former civil partner] [and a reputed civil partner].

(9) For the purposes of this section any director or other officer of a company is to be treated as employed by that company.

(10) For the purposes of this section a person is to be taken as having control of a company if—
 (a) the directors of the company or of another company which has control of it (or any of them) are accustomed to act in accordance with his directions or instructions, or
 (b) he is entitled to exercise, or control the exercise of, one third or more of the voting power at any general meeting of the company or of another company which has control of it;

and where two or more persons together satisfy either of the above conditions, they are to be taken as having control of the company.

(11) In this section "company" includes any body corporate (whether incorporated in Great Britain or elsewhere); and references to directors and other officers of a company and to voting power at any general meeting of a company have effect with any necessary modifications.

NOTES

This section derived from the Insolvency Act 1985, s 233.

Sub-s (2): substituted by the Civil Partnership Act 2004, s 261(1), Sch 27, para 122(1), (2).

Sub-s (3): words in square brackets inserted by the Civil Partnership Act 2004, s 261(1), Sch 27, para 122(1), (3).

Sub-s (5): year "2016" in square brackets substituted (for the original year "1985") by the Bankruptcy (Scotland) Act 2016 (Consequential Provisions and Modifications) Order 2016, SI 2016/1034, art 7(1), (3), Sch 1, para 4(1), (10), as from 30 November 2016 (except in relation to (i) a sequestration as regards which the petition is presented, or the debtor application is made before that date; or (ii) a trust deed executed before that date); words "(within the meaning of the Companies Act)" omitted from para (b) repealed by the Companies Act 2006 (Consequential Amendments, Transitional Provisions and Savings) Order 2009, SI 2009/1941, art 2(1), Sch 1, para 82(1), (2), subject to transitional provisions and savings in art 8, Sch 1, para 84 at **[2.70]**, **[2.73]**.

Sub-s (8): words in first pair of square brackets inserted by the Civil Partnership Act 2004, s 261(1), Sch 27, para 122(1), (4); words in second pair of square brackets inserted by the Civil Partnership Act 2004 (Overseas Relationships and Consequential, etc Amendments) Order 2005, SI 2005/3129, art 4(4), Sch 4, para 8.

Application: this section and s 249 apply for the purposes of the Pensions Act 1995, ss 23(3)(b), at **[17.117]**, and ss 27, 28, 40, as they apply for the purposes of this Act: see s 123(1), (3) of the 1995 Act.

[1.558]

436 Expressions used generally

[(1)] In this Act, except in so far as the context otherwise requires (and subject to Parts VII and XI)—

"the appointed day" means the day on which this Act comes into force under section 443;

"associate" has the meaning given by section 435;

["body corporate" includes a body incorporated outside Great Britain, but does not include—

(a) a corporation sole, or

(b) a partnership that, whether or not a legal person, is not regarded as a body corporate under the law by which it is governed;]

"business" includes a trade or profession;

. . .

["the Companies Acts" means the Companies Acts (as defined in section 2 of the Companies Act 2006) as they have effect in Great Britain;]

"conditional sale agreement" and "hire-purchase agreement" have the same meanings as in the Consumer Credit Act 1974;

["distress" includes use of the procedure in Schedule 12 to the Tribunals, Courts and Enforcement Act 2007, and references to levying distress, seizing goods and related expressions shall be construed accordingly;]

["the EC Regulation" means Council Regulation (EC) No 1346/2000;]

["EEA State" means a state that is a Contracting Party to the Agreement on the European Economic Area signed at Oporto on 2nd May 1992 as adjusted by the Protocol signed at Brussels on 17th March 1993;]

["employees' share scheme" means a scheme for encouraging or facilitating the holding of shares in or debentures of a company by or for the benefit of—

(a) the bona fide employees or former employees of—

(i) the company,

(ii) any subsidiary of the company, or

(iii) the company's holding company or any subsidiary of the company's holding company, or

(b) the spouses, civil partners, surviving spouses, surviving civil partners, or minor children or step-children of such employees or former employees];

["the EU Regulation" means Regulation (EU) 2015/848 of the European Parliament and of the Council of 20 May 2015 on insolvency proceedings;]

"modifications" includes additions, alterations and omissions and cognate expressions shall be construed accordingly;

"property" includes money, goods, things in action, land and every description of property wherever situated and also obligations and every description of interest, whether present or future or vested or contingent, arising out of, or incidental to, property;

"records" includes computer records and other non-documentary records;

"subordinate legislation" has the same meaning as in the Interpretation Act 1978; and

"transaction" includes a gift, agreement or arrangement, and references to entering into a transaction shall be construed accordingly.

[(2) The following expressions have the same meaning in this Act as in the Companies Acts—

"articles", in relation to a company (see section 18 of the Companies Act 2006);

"debenture" (see section 738 of that Act);

"holding company" (see sections 1159 and 1160 of, and Schedule 6 to, that Act);

"the Joint Stock Companies Acts" (see section 1171 of that Act);

"overseas company" (see section 1044 of that Act);

"paid up" (see section 583 of that Act);

"private company" and "public company" (see section 4 of that Act);

"registrar of companies" (see section 1060 of that Act);

"share" (see section 540 of that Act);

"subsidiary" (see sections 1159 and 1160 of, and Schedule 6 to, that Act).]

NOTES

This section derived from the Insolvency Act 1985, s 232 (in part).

Sub-s (1): existing provision numbered as sub-s (1), definitions "body corporate" and "employees' share scheme" inserted, and definition ""the Companies Act" means the Companies Act 1985;" (omitted) repealed by the Companies Act 2006 (Consequential Amendments, Transitional Provisions and Savings) Order 2009, SI 2009/1941, art 2(1), Sch 1, para 82(1), (3)(a)–(d), subject to transitional provisions and savings in art 8, Sch 1, para 84 at **[2.70]**, **[2.73]**; definition "the Companies Acts" inserted by the Companies Act 2006 (Commencement No 3, Consequential Amendments, Transitional Provisions and Savings) Order 2007, SI 2007/2194, art 10(1), (2), Sch 4, Pt 3, para 45, subject to savings in art 12 thereof; definition "distress" inserted by the Tribunals, Courts and Enforcement Act 2007, s 62(3), Sch 13, para 85; definition "the EC Regulation" inserted by the Insolvency Act 1986 (Amendment) Regulations 2002, SI 2002/1037, regs 2, 4 and repealed by the Insolvency Amendment (EU 2015/848) Regulations 2017, SI 2017/702, regs 2, 3, Schedule, Pt 1, paras 1, 28(a), except in relation to proceedings opened before 26 June 2017 and subject to savings in reg 4 thereof at **[2.103]**; definition "EEA State" inserted by the Insolvency Act 1986 (Amendment) Regulations 2005, SI 2005/879, regs 2(1), (3), 3, except in relation to a voluntary arrangement under Pt I of this Act or the appointment of an administrator under Pt II of this Act that took effect before 13 April 2005; definition "the EU Regulation" inserted by SI 2017/702, regs 2, 3, Schedule, Pt 1, paras 1, 28(b), except in relation to proceedings opened before 26 June 2017 and subject to savings in reg 4 thereof at **[2.103]**.

Sub-s (2): added by SI 2009/1941, art 2(1), Sch 1, para 82(1), (3)(e), subject to transitional provisions and savings in art 8, Sch 1, para 84 at **[2.70]**, **[2.73]**.

[1.559]

[436A Proceedings under [EU Regulation]: modified definition of property

In the application of this Act to proceedings by virtue of Article 3 of the [EU Regulation], a reference to property is a reference to property which may be dealt with in the proceedings.]

NOTES

Inserted by the Insolvency Act 1986 (Amendment) (No 2) Regulations 2002, SI 2002/1240, regs 3, 18.

Words in square brackets substituted for original words "EC Regulation" by the Insolvency Amendment (EU 2015/848) Regulations 2017, SI 2017/702, regs 2, 3, Schedule, Pt 1, paras 1, 29, except in relation to proceedings opened before 26 June 2017 and subject to savings in reg 4 thereof at **[2.103]**.

[1.560]

[436B References to things in writing

(1) A reference in this Act to a thing in writing includes that thing in electronic form.

(2) Subsection (1) does not apply to the following provisions—

(a) section 53 (mode of appointment by holder of charge),

(b) section 67(2) (report by receiver),

(c) section 70(4) (reference to instrument creating a charge),

(d) section 111(2) (dissent from arrangement under s 110),

(e) in the case of a winding up of a company registered in Scotland, section 111(4),

(f) section 123(1) (definition of inability to pay debts),

(g) section 198(3) (duties of sheriff principal as regards examination),

(h) section 222(1) (inability to pay debts: unpaid creditor for £750 or more), and

(i) section 223 (inability to pay debts: debt remaining unsatisfied after action brought).]

NOTES

Inserted by the Legislative Reform (Insolvency) (Miscellaneous Provisions) Order 2010, SI 2010/18, arts 2, 4(1).

Sub-s (2): paras (b), (e) repealed by the Public Services Reform (Insolvency) (Scotland) Order 2016, SSI 2016/141, art 13, as from a day to be appointed (being the day that the Small Business, Enterprise and Employment Act 2015, s 122(2) comes into force for all remaining purposes in Scotland).

PART XIX FINAL PROVISIONS

[1.561]

437 Transitional provisions, and savings

The transitional provisions and savings set out in Schedule 11 to this Act shall have effect, the Schedule comprising the following Parts—

Part I: company insolvency and winding up (matters arising before appointed day, and continuance of proceedings in certain cases as before that day);

Part II: individual insolvency (matters so arising, and continuance of bankruptcy proceedings in certain cases as before that day);

Part III: transactions entered into before the appointed day and capable of being affected by orders of the court under Part XVI of this Act;

Part IV: insolvency practitioners acting as such before the appointed day; and

Part V: general transitional provisions and savings required consequentially on, and in connection with, the repeal and replacement by this Act and the Company Directors Disqualification Act 1986 of provisions of [the Companies Act 1985], the greater part of the Insolvency Act 1985 and other enactments.

NOTES

Words in square brackets substituted for original words "the Companies Act" by the Companies Act 2006 (Consequential Amendments, Transitional Provisions and Savings) Order 2009, SI 2009/1941, art 2(1), Sch 1, para 83, subject to transitional provisions and savings in art 8, Sch 1, para 84 at **[2.70]**, **[2.73]**.

Insolvency Act 1985: that Act was mostly repealed by the combined effect of s 438 of, and Sch 12 to, this Act and the Company Directors Disqualification Act 1986, s 23(2), Sch 4.

[1.562]
438 Repeals
The enactments specified in the second column of Schedule 12 to this Act are repealed to the extent specified in the third column of that Schedule.

[1.563]
439 Amendment of enactments
(1) The Companies Act is amended as shown in Parts I and II of Schedule 13 to this Act, being amendments consequential on this Act and the Company Directors Disqualification Act 1986.
(2) The enactments specified in the first column of Schedule 14 to this Act (being enactments which refer, or otherwise relate, to those which are repealed and replaced by this Act or the Company Directors Disqualification Act 1986) are amended as shown in the second column of that Schedule.
(3) The Lord Chancellor may by order make such consequential modifications of any provision contained in any subordinate legislation made before the appointed day and such transitional provisions in connection with those modifications as appear to him necessary or expedient in respect of—
(a) any reference in that subordinate legislation to the Bankruptcy Act 1914;
(b) any reference in that subordinate legislation to any enactment repealed by Part III or IV of Schedule 10 to the Insolvency Act 1985; or
(c) any reference in that subordinate legislation to any matter provided for under the Act of 1914 or under any enactment so repealed.
(4) An order under this section shall be made by statutory instrument subject to annulment in pursuance of a resolution of either House of Parliament.

NOTES
Bankruptcy Act 1914: repealed by the Insolvency Act 1985, s 235(3), Sch 10, Pts III, IV.
Insolvency Act 1985, Sch 10, Pts III, IV: repealed by s 438 of, and Sch 12 to, this Act.
Orders: the Insolvency (Amendment of Subordinate Legislation) Order 1986, SI 1986/2001.

[1.564]
440 Extent (Scotland)
(1) Subject to the next subsection, provisions of this Act contained in the first Group of Parts extend to Scotland except where otherwise stated.
(2) The following provisions of this Act do not extend to Scotland—
(a) In the first Group of Parts—
section 43;
sections 238 to 241; and
section 246;
(b) the second Group of Parts;
(c) in the third Group of Parts—
sections 399 to 402,
sections 412, 413, 415, [415A(3),] 418, 420 and 421,
sections 423 to 425, and
section 429(1) and (2); and
(d) in the Schedules—
Parts II and III of Schedule 11; and
Schedules 12 and 14 so far as they repeal or amend enactments which extend to England and Wales only.

NOTES
This section derived from the Insolvency Act 1985, s 236(3).
Sub-s (2): reference in square brackets inserted by the Enterprise Act 2002, s 270(4); for the words in italics there are substituted the words "section 429(1) to (2A)" by the Tribunals, Courts and Enforcement Act 2007, s 106(2), Sch 16, para 4, as from a day to be appointed.

[1.565]
441 Extent (Northern Ireland)
(1) The following provisions of this Act extend to Northern Ireland—
(a) sections 197, 426, [426A, 426B,] 427 and 428; and
(b) so much of section 439 and Schedule 14 as relates to enactments which extend to Northern Ireland.
(2) Subject as above, and to any provision expressly relating to companies incorporated elsewhere than in Great Britain, nothing in this Act extends to Northern Ireland or applies to or in relation to companies registered or incorporated in Northern Ireland.

NOTES
This section derived from the Companies Act 1985, s 745, and the Insolvency Act 1985, s 236(4).
Sub-s (1): figures in square brackets inserted by the Insolvency Act 1986 (Disqualification from Parliament) Order 2012, SI 2012/1544, arts 2, 6.

[1.566]
442 Extent (other territories)
Her Majesty may, by Order in Council, direct that such of the provisions of this Act as are specified in the Order, being provisions formerly contained in the Insolvency Act 1985, shall extend to any of the Channel Islands or any colony with such modifications as may be so specified.

NOTES
This section derived from the Insolvency Act 1985, s 236(5).
Orders: the Insolvency Act 1986 (Guernsey) Order 1989, SI 1989/2409.

[1.567]
443 Commencement
This Act comes into force on the day appointed under section 236(2) of the Insolvency Act 1985 for the coming into force of Part III of that Act (individual insolvency and bankruptcy), immediately after that Part of that Act comes into force for England and Wales.

NOTES
See the note "Commencement" at the beginning of this Act.

[1.568]
444 Citation
This Act may be cited as the Insolvency Act 1986.

SCHEDULES

[SCHEDULE A1
MORATORIUM WHERE DIRECTORS PROPOSE VOLUNTARY ARRANGEMENT

Section 1A

PART I
INTRODUCTORY

Interpretation

[1.569]
1. In this Schedule—
"the beginning of the moratorium" has the meaning given by paragraph 8(1),
"the date of filing" means the date on which the documents for the time being referred to in paragraph 7(1) are filed or lodged with the court,
"hire-purchase agreement" includes a conditional sale agreement, a chattel leasing agreement and a retention of title agreement,
"market contract" and "market charge" have the meanings given by Part VII of the Companies Act 1989,
. . .
"moratorium" means a moratorium under section 1A,
"the nominee" includes any person for the time being carrying out the functions of a nominee under this Schedule,
. . .
"the settlement finality regulations" means the Financial Markets and Insolvency (Settlement Finality) Regulations 1999,
"system-charge" has the meaning given by the Financial Markets and Insolvency Regulations 1996.

Eligible companies

2. (1) A company is eligible for a moratorium if it meets the requirements of paragraph 3, unless—
(a) it is excluded from being eligible by virtue of paragraph 4, or
(b) it falls within sub-paragraph (2).

(2) A company falls within this sub-paragraph if—
[(a) it effects or carries out contracts of insurance, but is not exempt from the general prohibition, within the meaning of section 19 of the Financial Services and Markets Act 2000, in relation to that activity,
(b) it has permission under Part IV of that Act to accept deposits,
(bb) it has a liability in respect of a deposit which it accepted in accordance with the Banking Act 1979 (c 37) or 1987 (c 22),]
(c) it is a party to a market contract . . . or any of its property is subject to a market charge . . . or a system-charge, or
(d) it is a participant (within the meaning of the settlement finality regulations) or any of its property is subject to a collateral security charge (within the meaning of those regulations).

[(3) Paragraphs (a), (b) and (bb) of sub-paragraph (2) must be read with—
(a) section 22 of the Financial Services and Markets Act 2000;
(b) any relevant order under that section; and
(c) Schedule 2 to that Act.]

3. (1) A company meets the requirements of this paragraph if the qualifying conditions are met—

(a) in the year ending with the date of filing, or
(b) in the financial year of the company which ended last before that date.

(2) For the purposes of sub-paragraph (1)—
(a) the qualifying conditions are met by a company in a period if, in that period, it satisfies two or more of the requirements for being a small company specified for the time being in [section 382(3) of the Companies Act 2006], and
(b) a company's financial year is to be determined in accordance with that Act.

(3) [Section 382(4), (5) and (6)] of that Act apply for the purposes of this paragraph as they apply for the purposes of that section.

[(4) A company does not meet the requirements of this paragraph if it is a [parent company] of a group of companies which does not qualify as a small group or a medium-sized group [in relation to] the financial year of the company which ended last before the date of filing.

[(5) For the purposes of sub-paragraph (4)—
(a) "group" has the same meaning as in Part 15 of the Companies Act 2006 (see section 474(1) of that Act); and
(b) a group qualifies as small in relation to a financial year if it so qualifies under section 383(2) to (7) of that Act, and qualifies as medium-sized in relation to a financial year if it so qualifies under section 466(2) to (7) of that Act.]]

[(6) Expressions used in this paragraph that are defined expressions in Part 15 of the Companies Act 2006 (accounts and reports) have the same meaning in this paragraph as in that Part.]

4. (1) A company is excluded from being eligible for a moratorium if, on the date of filing—
[(a) the company is in administration,]
(b) the company is being wound up,
(c) there is an administrative receiver of the company,
(d) a voluntary arrangement has effect in relation to the company,
(e) there is a provisional liquidator of the company,
(f) a moratorium has been in force for the company at any time during the period of 12 months ending with the date of filing and—
(i) no voluntary arrangement had effect at the time at which the moratorium came to an end, or
(ii) a voluntary arrangement which had effect at any time in that period has come to an end prematurely,
[(fa) an administrator appointed under paragraph 22 of Schedule B1 has held office in the period of 12 months ending with the date of filing,] or
(g) a voluntary arrangement in relation to the company which had effect in pursuance of a proposal under section 1(3) has come to an end prematurely and, during the period of 12 months ending with the date of filing, an order under section 5(3)(a) has been made.

(2) Sub-paragraph (1)(b) does not apply to a company which, by reason of a winding-up order made after the date of filing, is treated as being wound up on that date.

[Capital market arrangement

4A. A company is also excluded from being eligible for a moratorium if, on the date of filing, it is a party to an agreement which is or forms part of a capital market arrangement under which—
(i) a party has incurred, or when the agreement was entered into was expected to incur, a debt of at least £10 million under the arrangement, and
(ii) the arrangement involves the issue of a capital market investment.

Public private partnership

4B. A company is also excluded from being eligible for a moratorium if, on the date of filing, it is a project company of a project which—
(i) is a public-private partnership project, and
(ii) includes step-in rights.

Liability under an arrangement

4C. (1) A company is also excluded from being eligible for a moratorium if, on the date of filing, it has incurred a liability under an agreement of £10 million or more.

(2) Where the liability in sub-paragraph (1) is a contingent liability under or by virtue of a guarantee or an indemnity or security provided on behalf of another person, the amount of that liability is the full amount of the liability in relation to which the guarantee, indemnity or security is provided.

(3) In this paragraph—
(a) the reference to "liability" includes a present or future liability whether, in either case, it is certain or contingent,
(b) the reference to "liability" includes a reference to a liability to be paid wholly or partly in foreign currency (in which case the sterling equivalent shall be calculated as at the time when the liability is incurred).

Interpretation of capital market arrangement

4D. (1) For the purposes of paragraph 4A an arrangement is a capital market arrangement if—

(a) it involves a grant of security to a person holding it as trustee for a person who holds a capital market investment issued by a party to the arrangement, or
(b) at least one party guarantees the performance of obligations of another party, or
(c) at least one party provides security in respect of the performance of obligations of another party, or
(d) the arrangement involves an investment of a kind described in articles 83 to 85 of the Financial Services and Markets Act 2000 (Regulated Activities) Order 2001 (SI 2001/544) (options, futures and contracts for differences).

(2) For the purposes of sub-paragraph (1)—
(a) a reference to holding as trustee includes a reference to holding as nominee or agent,
(b) a reference to holding for a person who holds a capital market investment includes a reference to holding for a number of persons at least one of whom holds a capital market investment, and
(c) a person holds a capital market investment if he has a legal or beneficial interest in it.

(3) In paragraph 4A, 4C, 4J and this paragraph—
"agreement" includes an agreement or undertaking effected by—
(a) contract,
(b) deed, or
(c) any other instrument intended to have effect in accordance with the law of England and Wales, Scotland or another jurisdiction, and
"party" to an arrangement includes a party to an agreement which—
(a) forms part of the arrangement,
(b) provides for the raising of finance as part of the arrangement, or
(c) is necessary for the purposes of implementing the arrangement.

Capital market investment

4E. (1) For the purposes of paragraphs 4A and 4D, an investment is a capital market investment if—
(a) it is within article 77 [or 77A] of the Financial Services and Markets Act 2000 (Regulated Activities) Order 2001 (SI 2001/544) (debt instruments) and
(b) it is rated, listed or traded or designed to be rated, listed or traded.

(2) In sub-paragraph (1)—
"listed" means admitted to the official list within the meaning given by section 103(1) of the Financial Services and Markets Act 2000 (c 8) (interpretation),
"rated" means rated for the purposes of investment by an internationally recognised rating agency,
"traded" means admitted to trading on a market established under the rules of a recognised investment exchange or on a foreign market.

(3) In sub-paragraph (2)—
"foreign market" has the same meaning as "relevant market" in article 67(2) of the Financial Services and Markets Act 2000 (Financial Promotion) Order 2001 (SI 2001/1335) (foreign markets),
"recognised investment exchange" has the meaning given by section 285 of the Financial Services and Markets Act 2000 (recognised investment exchange).

4F. (1) For the purposes of paragraphs 4A and 4D an investment is also a capital market investment if it consists of a bond or commercial paper issued to one or more of the following—
(a) an investment professional within the meaning of article 19(5) of the Financial Services and Markets Act 2000 (Financial Promotion) Order 2001,
(b) a person who is, when the agreement mentioned in paragraph 4A is entered into, a certified high net worth individual in relation to a communication within the meaning of article 48(2) of that order,
(c) a person to whom article 49(2) of that order applies (high net worth company, &c),
(d) a person who is, when the agreement mentioned in paragraph 4A is entered into, a certified sophisticated investor in relation to a communication within the meaning of article 50(1) of that order, and
(e) a person in a State other than the United Kingdom who under the law of that State is not prohibited from investing in bonds or commercial paper.

(2) For the purposes of sub-paragraph (1)—
(a) in applying article 19(5) of the Financial Services and Markets Act 2000 (Financial Promotion) Order 2001 for the purposes of sub-paragraph (1)(a)—
(i) in article 19(5)(b), ignore the words after "exempt person",
(ii) in article 19(5)(c)(i), for the words from "the controlled activity" to the end substitute "a controlled activity", and
(iii) in article 19(5)(e) ignore the words from "where the communication" to the end, and
(b) in applying article 49(2) of that order for the purposes of sub-paragraph (1)(c), ignore article 49(2)(e).

(3) In sub-paragraph (1)—
"bond" shall be construed in accordance with article 77 of the Financial Services and Markets Act 2000 (Regulated Activities) Order 2001 (SI 2001/544)[, and includes any instrument falling within article 77A of that Order], and
"commercial paper" has the meaning given by article 9(3) of that order.

Debt

4G. The debt of at least £10 million referred to in paragraph 4A—

(a) may be incurred at any time during the life of the capital market arrangement, and
(b) may be expressed wholly or partly in a foreign currency (in which case the sterling equivalent shall be calculated as at the time when the arrangement is entered into).

Interpretation of project company

4H. (1) For the purposes of paragraph 4B a company is a "project company" of a project if—
(a) it holds property for the purpose of the project,
(b) it has sole or principal responsibility under an agreement for carrying out all or part of the project,
(c) it is one of a number of companies which together carry out the project,
(d) it has the purpose of supplying finance to enable the project to be carried out, or
(e) it is the holding company of a company within any of paragraphs (a) to (d).

(2) But a company is not a "project company" of a project if—
(a) it performs a function within sub-paragraph (1)(a) to (d) or is within sub-paragraph (1)(e), but
(b) it also performs a function which is not—
(i) within sub-paragraph (1)(a) to (d),
(ii) related to a function within sub-paragraph (1)(a) to (d), or
(iii) related to the project.

(3) For the purposes of this paragraph a company carries out all or part of a project whether or not it acts wholly or partly through agents.

Public-private partnership project

4I. (1) In paragraph 4B "public-private partnership project" means a project—
(a) the resources for which are provided partly by one or more public bodies and partly by one or more private persons, or
(b) which is designed wholly or mainly for the purpose of assisting a public body to discharge a function.

(2) In sub-paragraph (1) "resources" includes—
(a) funds (including payment for the provision of services or facilities),
(b) assets,
(c) professional skill,
(d) the grant of a concession or franchise, and
(e) any other commercial resource.

(3) In sub-paragraph (1) "public body" means—
(a) a body which exercises public functions,
(b) a body specified for the purposes of this paragraph by the Secretary of State, and
(c) a body within a class specified for the purposes of this paragraph by the Secretary of State.

(4) A specification under sub-paragraph (3) may be—
(a) general, or
(b) for the purpose of the application of paragraph 4B to a specified case.

Step-in rights

4J. (1) For the purposes of paragraph 4B a project has "step-in rights" if a person who provides finance in connection with the project has a conditional entitlement under an agreement to—
(i) assume sole or principal responsibility under an agreement for carrying out all or part of the project, or
(ii) make arrangements for carrying out all or part of the project.

(2) In sub-paragraph (1) a reference to the provision of finance includes a reference to the provision of an indemnity.

"Person"

4K. For the purposes of paragraphs 4A to 4J, a reference to a person includes a reference to a partnership or another unincorporated group of persons.]

5. The Secretary of State may by regulations modify the qualifications for eligibility of a company for a moratorium.]

NOTES

Schedule inserted by the Insolvency Act 2000, s 1, Sch 1, paras 1, 4.

Para 1: definitions omitted repealed by the Financial Services and Markets Act 2000 (Consequential Amendments) Order 2002, SI 2002/1555, art 28(1), (2).

Para 2: sub-para (2)(a), (b), (bb) substituted for original sub-para (2)(a), (b), words omitted from sub-para (2)(c) repealed and sub-para (3) added, by SI 2002/1555, arts 28(1), (3), 29.

Para 3: words in square brackets in sub-para (2) substituted for original words "section 247(3) of the Companies Act 1985" and words in square brackets in sub-para (3) substituted for original words "Subsections (4), (5) and (6) of section 247" by the Companies Act 2006 (Consequential Amendments etc) Order 2008, SI 2008/948, art 3(1)(b), Sch 1, Pt 2, para 99(1)–(3), (6), in relation to periods, or parts of periods, falling on or after 6 April 2008, and subject to transitional provisions and savings in arts 6, 11,12 thereof; sub-paras (4), (5) added by the Insolvency Act 1986 (Amendment) (No 3) Regulations 2002, SI 2002/1990, reg 3(1), (2); words in square brackets in sub-para (4) substituted for original words "holding company" and "in respect of" respectively, and sub-para (5) substituted by SI 2008/948, art 3(1)(b), Sch 1, Pt 2, para 99(1), (4)–(6), in relation to periods, or parts of periods, falling on or after 6 April 2008, and subject to transitional provisions and savings in arts 6, 11,12 thereof. Sub-para (5) previously read as follows:

> "(5) For the purposes of sub-paragraph (4) "group" has the meaning given by section 262 of the Companies Act 1985 (c 6) (definitions for Part VII) and a group qualifies as small or medium-sized if it qualifies as such under section 249 of the Companies Act 1985 (qualification of group as small or medium-sized).";

sub-para (6) added by the Companies Act 2006 (Consequential Amendments, Transitional Provisions and Savings) Order 2009, SI 2009/1941, art 2(1), Sch 1, para 71(1), (4)(a), subject to transitional provisions and savings in art 8, Sch 1, para 84 at **[2.70]**, **[2.73]**.

Para 4: sub-para (1)(a) substituted and sub-para (1)(fa) inserted by the Enterprise Act 2002, s 248(3), Sch 17, paras 9, 37(1), (2), subject to savings and transitional provisions (i) in a case where a petition for an administration order has been presented before 15 September 2003 (see the Enterprise Act 2002 (Commencement No 4 and Transitional Provisions and Savings) Order 2003, SI 2003/2093, art 3 at **[2.26]**), and (ii) in relation to special administration regimes (see s 249 of the 2002 Act at **[2.10]**). Sub-para (1)(a) originally read as follows:

> "(a) an administration order is in force in relation to the company,".

Paras 4A–4K: inserted by SI 2002/1990, reg 3(1), (3).

Para 4E: words in square brackets inserted by the Financial Services and Markets Act 2000 (Regulated Activities) (Amendment) Order 2010, SI 2010/86, art 4, Schedule, para 1(a).

Para 4F: words in square brackets inserted by SI 2010/86, art 4, Schedule, para 1(b); a reference to commercial paper includes a reference to uncertificated units of an eligible debt security where the issue of units corresponds, in accordance with the current terms of issue of the security, to the issue of commercial paper within the meaning of art 9(3) of the Financial Services and Markets Act 2000 (Regulated Activities) Order 2001, SI 2001/544; see the Uncertificated Securities (Amendment) (Eligible Debt Securities) Regulations 2003, SI 2003/1633, reg 15(1), Sch 2, para 7.

Banking Act 1987, Insurance Companies Act 1982: repealed by the Financial Services and Markets Act 2000 (Consequential Amendments and Repeals) Order 2001, SI 2001/3649, art 3(1)(b), (d).

[PART II
OBTAINING A MORATORIUM

Nominee's statement

[1.570]

6. (1) Where the directors of a company wish to obtain a moratorium, they shall submit to the nominee—

(a) a document setting out the terms of the proposed voluntary arrangement,

(b) a statement of the company's affairs containing—

(i) such particulars of its creditors and of its debts and other liabilities and of its assets as may be prescribed, and

(ii) such other information as may be prescribed, and

(c) any other information necessary to enable the nominee to comply with sub-paragraph (2) which he requests from them.

(2) The nominee shall submit to the directors a statement in the prescribed form indicating whether or not, in his opinion—

(a) the proposed voluntary arrangement has a reasonable prospect of being approved and implemented,

(b) the company is likely to have sufficient funds available to it during the proposed moratorium to enable it to carry on its business, and

[(c) the proposed voluntary arrangement should be considered by a meeting of the company and by the company's creditors.]

(3) In forming his opinion on the matters mentioned in sub-paragraph (2), the nominee is entitled to rely on the information submitted to him under sub-paragraph (1) unless he has reason to doubt its accuracy.

(4) The reference in sub-paragraph (2)(b) to the company's business is to that business as the company proposes to carry it on during the moratorium.

Documents to be submitted to court

7. (1) To obtain a moratorium the directors of a company must file (in Scotland, lodge) with the court—

(a) a document setting out the terms of the proposed voluntary arrangement,

(b) a statement of the company's affairs containing—

(i) such particulars of its creditors and of its debts and other liabilities and of its assets as may be prescribed, and

(ii) such other information as may be prescribed,

(c) a statement that the company is eligible for a moratorium,

(d) a statement from the nominee that he has given his consent to act, and

(e) a statement from the nominee that, in his opinion—

(i) the proposed voluntary arrangement has a reasonable prospect of being approved and implemented,

(ii) the company is likely to have sufficient funds available to it during the proposed moratorium to enable it to carry on its business, and

[(iii) the proposed voluntary arrangement should be considered by a meeting of the company and by the company's creditors.]

(2) Each of the statements mentioned in sub-paragraph (1)(b) to (e), except so far as it contains the particulars referred to in paragraph (b)(i), must be in the prescribed form.

(3) The reference in sub-paragraph (1)(e)(ii) to the company's business is to that business as the company proposes to carry it on during the moratorium.

(4) The Secretary of State may by regulations modify the requirements of this paragraph as to the documents required to be filed (in Scotland, lodged) with the court in order to obtain a moratorium.

Duration of moratorium

8. (1) A moratorium comes into force when the documents for the time being referred to in paragraph 7(1) are filed or lodged with the court and references in this Schedule to "the beginning of the moratorium" shall be construed accordingly.

[(2) A moratorium ends with the later of—

(a) the day on which the company meeting summoned under paragraph 29 is first held, and

(b) the day on which the company's creditors decide whether to approve the proposed voluntary arrangement,

unless it is extended under paragraph 32; but this is subject to the rest of this paragraph.

(3) In this paragraph the "initial period" means the period of 28 days beginning with the day on which the moratorium comes into force.

(3A) If the company meeting has not first met before the end of the initial period the moratorium ends at the end of that period, unless before the end of that period it is extended under paragraph 32.

(3B) If the company's creditors have not decided whether to approve the proposed voluntary arrangement before the end of the initial period the moratorium ends at the end of that period, unless before the end of that period—

(a) the moratorium is extended under paragraph 32, or

(b) a meeting of the company's creditors is summoned in accordance with section 246ZE.

(3C) Where sub-paragraph (3B)(b) applies, the moratorium ends with the day on which the meeting of the company's creditors is first held, unless it is extended under paragraph 32.

(4) The moratorium ends at the end of the initial period if the nominee has not before the end of that period—

(a) summoned a meeting of the company, and

(b) sought a decision from the company's creditors,

as required by paragraph 29(1).]

(5) If the moratorium is extended (or further extended) under paragraph 32, it ends at the end of the day to which it is extended (or further extended).

(6) Sub-paragraphs (2) to (5) do not apply if the moratorium comes to an end before the time concerned by virtue of—

(a) paragraph 25(4) (effect of withdrawal by nominee of consent to act),

(b) an order under paragraph 26(3), 27(3) or 40 (challenge of actions of nominee or directors), or

[(c) a decision of one or both of—

(i) the meeting of the company summoned under paragraph 29, or

(ii) the company's creditors.]

(7) If the moratorium has not previously come to an end in accordance with sub-paragraphs (2) to (6), it ends at the end of the day on which a decision under paragraph 31 to approve a voluntary arrangement takes effect under paragraph 36.

(8) The Secretary of State may by order increase or reduce the period for the time being specified in sub-paragraph (3).

Notification of beginning of moratorium

9. (1) When a moratorium comes into force, the directors shall notify the nominee of that fact forthwith.

(2) If the directors without reasonable excuse fail to comply with sub-paragraph (1), each of them is liable to imprisonment or a fine, or both.

10. (1) When a moratorium comes into force, the nominee shall, in accordance with the rules—

(a) advertise that fact forthwith, and

(b) notify the registrar of companies, the company and any petitioning creditor of the company of whose claim he is aware of that fact.

(2) In sub-paragraph (1)(b), "petitioning creditor" means a creditor by whom a winding-up petition has been presented before the beginning of the moratorium, as long as the petition has not been dismissed or withdrawn.

(3) If the nominee without reasonable excuse fails to comply with sub-paragraph (1)(a) or (b), he is liable to a fine.

Notification of end of moratorium

11. (1) When a moratorium comes to an end, the nominee shall, in accordance with the rules—

(a) advertise that fact forthwith, and

(b) notify the court, the registrar of companies, the company and any creditor of the company of whose claim he is aware of that fact.

(2) If the nominee without reasonable excuse fails to comply with sub-paragraph (1)(a) or (b), he is liable to a fine.]

NOTES

Inserted by the Insolvency Act 2000, s 1, Sch 1, paras 1, 4, as from 1 January 2003.

Para 6: sub-para (2)(c) substituted by the Small Business, Enterprise and Employment Act 2015, s 126, Sch 9, Pt 1, paras 1, 9(1), (2), as from 6 April 2017 (in relation to England and Wales and subject to transitional and savings provisions as noted to s 246ZE at **[1.256]**), and as from a day to be appointed (in relation to Scotland). Sub-para (2)(c) originally read as follows—

"(c) meetings of the company and its creditors should be summoned to consider the proposed voluntary arrangement.".

Para 7: sub-para (1)(e)(iii) substituted by the Small Business, Enterprise and Employment Act 2015, s 126, Sch 9, Pt 1, paras 1, 9(1), (3), as from 6 April 2017 (in relation to England and Wales and subject to transitional and savings provisions as noted to s 246ZE at **[1.256]**), and as from a day to be appointed (in relation to Scotland). Sub-para (1)(e)(iii) originally read as follows—

"(iii) meetings of the company and its creditors should be summoned to consider the proposed voluntary arrangement.".

Para 8 is amended as follows:

Sub-paras (2), (3), (3A)–(3C), (4) substituted for original sub-paras (2), (3), (4), by the Small Business, Enterprise and Employment Act 2015, s 126, Sch 9, Pt 1, paras 1, 9(1), (4), as from 6 April 2017 (in relation to England and Wales and subject to transitional and savings provisions as noted to s 246ZE at **[1.256]**), and as from a day to be appointed (in relation to Scotland). Sub-paras (2), (3), (4), originally read as follows—

"(2) A moratorium ends at the end of the day on which the meetings summoned under paragraph 29(1) are first held (or, if the meetings are held on different days, the later of those days), unless it is extended under paragraph 32.

(3) If either of those meetings has not first met before the end of the period of 28 days beginning with the day on which the moratorium comes into force, the moratorium ends at the end of the day on which those meetings were to be held (or, if those meetings were summoned to be held on different days, the later of those days), unless it is extended under paragraph 32.

(4) If the nominee fails to summon either meeting within the period required by paragraph 29(1), the moratorium ends at the end of the last day of that period.".

Sub-para (6)(c) substituted by the Small Business, Enterprise and Employment Act 2015, s 126, Sch 9, Pt 1, paras 1, 9(1), (5), as from 6 April 2017 (in relation to England and Wales and subject to transitional and savings provisions as noted to s 246ZE at **[1.256]**), and as from a day to be appointed (in relation to Scotland). Sub-para (6)(c) previously read as follows—

"(c) a decision of one or both of the meetings summoned under paragraph 29.".

[PART III
EFFECTS OF MORATORIUM

Effect on creditors, etc

[1.571]

12. (1) During the period for which a moratorium is in force for a company—

(a) no petition may be presented for the winding up of the company,

(b) no meeting of the company may be called or requisitioned except with the consent of the nominee or the leave of the court and subject (where the court gives leave) to such terms as the court may impose,

(c) no resolution may be passed or order made for the winding up of the company,

[(d) no administration application may be made in respect of the company,

(da) no administrator of the company may be appointed under paragraph 14 or 22 of Schedule B1,]

(e) no administrative receiver of the company may be appointed,

(f) no landlord or other person to whom rent is payable may exercise any right of forfeiture by peaceable re-entry in relation to premises let to the company in respect of a failure by the company to comply with any term or condition of its tenancy of such premises, except with the leave of the court and subject to such terms as the court may impose,

(g) no other steps may be taken to enforce any security over the company's property, or to repossess goods in the company's possession under any hire-purchase agreement, except with the leave of the court and subject to such terms as the court may impose, and

(h) no other proceedings and no execution or other legal process may be commenced or continued, and no distress may be levied, against the company or its property except with the leave of the court and subject to such terms as the court may impose.

(2) Where a petition, other than an excepted petition, for the winding up of the company has been presented before the beginning of the moratorium, section 127 shall not apply in relation to any disposition of property, transfer of shares or alteration in status made during the moratorium or at a time mentioned in paragraph 37(5)(a).

(3) In the application of sub-paragraph (1)(h) to Scotland, the reference to execution being commenced or continued includes a reference to diligence being carried out or continued, and the reference to distress being levied is omitted.

(4) paragraph (a) of sub-paragraph (1) does not apply to an excepted petition and, where such a petition has been presented before the beginning of the moratorium or is presented during the moratorium, paragraphs (b) and (c) of that sub-paragraph do not apply in relation to proceedings on the petition.

(5) For the purposes of this paragraph, "excepted petition" means a petition under—

(a) section 124A [or 124B] of this Act,

(b) section 72 of the Financial Services Act 1986 on the ground mentioned in subsection (1)(b) of that section, or
(c) section 92 of the Banking Act 1987 on the ground mentioned in subsection (1)(b) of that section.
[(d) section 367 of the Financial Services and Markets Act 2000 on the ground mentioned in subsection (3)(b) of that section].

13. (1) This paragraph applies where there is an uncrystallised floating charge on the property of a company for which a moratorium is in force.

(2) If the conditions for the holder of the charge to give a notice having the effect mentioned in sub-paragraph (4) are met at any time, the notice may not be given at that time but may instead be given as soon as practicable after the moratorium has come to an end.

(3) If any other event occurs at any time which (apart from this sub-paragraph) would have the effect mentioned in sub-paragraph (4), then—
(a) the event shall not have the effect in question at that time, but
(b) if notice of the event is given to the company by the holder of the charge as soon as is practicable after the moratorium has come to an end, the event is to be treated as if it had occurred when the notice was given.

(4) The effect referred to in sub-paragraphs (2) and (3) is—
(a) causing the crystallisation of the floating charge, or
(b) causing the imposition, by virtue of provision in the instrument creating the charge, of any restriction on the disposal of any property of the company.

(5) Application may not be made for leave under paragraph 12(1)(g) or (h) with a view to obtaining—
(a) the crystallisation of the floating charge, or
(b) the imposition, by virtue of provision in the instrument creating the charge, of any restriction on the disposal of any property of the company.

14. Security granted by a company at a time when a moratorium is in force in relation to the company may only be enforced if, at that time, there were reasonable grounds for believing that it would benefit the company.

Effect on company

15. (1) Paragraphs 16 to 23 apply in relation to a company for which a moratorium is in force.

(2) The fact that a company enters into a transaction in contravention of any of paragraphs 16 to 22 does not—
(a) make the transaction void, or
(b) make it to any extent unenforceable against the company.

Company invoices, etc

16. [(1) Every invoice, order for goods or services, business letter or order form (whether in hard copy, electronic or any other form) issued by or on behalf of the company, and all the company's websites, must also contain the nominee's name and a statement that the moratorium is in force for the company.]

(2) If default is made in complying with sub-paragraph (1), the company and (subject to sub-paragraph (3)) any officer of the company is liable to a fine.

(3) An officer of the company is only liable under sub-paragraph (2) if, without reasonable excuse, he authorises or permits the default.

Obtaining credit during moratorium

17. (1) The company may not obtain credit to the extent of £250 or more from a person who has not been informed that a moratorium is in force in relation to the company.

(2) The reference to the company obtaining credit includes the following cases—
(a) where goods are bailed (in Scotland, hired) to the company under a hire-purchase agreement, or agreed to be sold to the company under a conditional sale agreement, and
(b) where the company is paid in advance (whether in money or otherwise) for the supply of goods or services.

(3) Where the company obtains credit in contravention of sub-paragraph (1)—
(a) the company is liable to a fine, and
(b) if any officer of the company knowingly and wilfully authorised or permitted the contravention, he is liable to imprisonment or a fine, or both.

(4) The money sum specified in sub-paragraph (1) is subject to increase or reduction by order under section 417A in Part XV.

Disposals and payments

18. (1) Subject to sub-paragraph (2), the company may only dispose of any of its property if—
(a) there are reasonable grounds for believing that the disposal will benefit the company, and
(b) the disposal is approved by the committee established under paragraph 35(1) or, where there is no such committee, by the nominee.

(2) Sub-paragraph (1) does not apply to a disposal made in the ordinary way of the company's business.

(3) If the company makes a disposal in contravention of sub-paragraph (1) otherwise than in pursuance of an order of the court—

(a) the company is liable to a fine, and

(b) if any officer of the company authorised or permitted the contravention, without reasonable excuse, he is liable to imprisonment or a fine, or both.

19. (1) Subject to sub-paragraph (2), the company may only make any payment in respect of any debt or other liability of the company in existence before the beginning of the moratorium if—

(a) there are reasonable grounds for believing that the payment will benefit the company, and

(b) the payment is approved by the committee established under paragraph 35(1) or, where there is no such committee, by the nominee.

(2) Sub-paragraph (1) does not apply to a payment required by paragraph 20(6).

(3) If the company makes a payment in contravention of sub-paragraph (1) otherwise than in pursuance of an order of the court—

(a) the company is liable to a fine, and

(b) if any officer of the company authorised or permitted the contravention, without reasonable excuse, he is liable to imprisonment or a fine, or both.

Disposal of charged property, etc

20. (1) This paragraph applies where—

(a) any property of the company is subject to a security, or

(b) any goods are in the possession of the company under a hire-purchase agreement.

(2) If the holder of the security consents, or the court gives leave, the company may dispose of the property as if it were not subject to the security.

(3) If the owner of the goods consents, or the court gives leave, the company may dispose of the goods as if all rights of the owner under the hire-purchase agreement were vested in the company.

(4) Where property subject to a security which, as created, was a floating charge is disposed of under sub-paragraph (2), the holder of the security has the same priority in respect of any property of the company directly or indirectly representing the property disposed of as he would have had in respect of the property subject to the security.

(5) Sub-paragraph (6) applies to the disposal under sub-paragraph (2) or (as the case may be) sub-paragraph (3) of—

(a) any property subject to a security other than a security which, as created, was a floating charge, or

(b) any goods in the possession of the company under a hire-purchase agreement.

(6) It shall be a condition of any consent or leave under sub-paragraph (2) or (as the case may be) sub-paragraph (3) that—

(a) the net proceeds of the disposal, and

(b) where those proceeds are less than such amount as may be agreed, or determined by the court, to be the net amount which would be realised on a sale of the property or goods in the open market by a willing vendor, such sums as may be required to make good the deficiency,

shall be applied towards discharging the sums secured by the security or payable under the hire-purchase agreement.

(7) Where a condition imposed in pursuance of sub-paragraph (6) relates to two or more securities, that condition requires—

(a) the net proceeds of the disposal, and

(b) where paragraph (b) of sub-paragraph (6) applies, the sums mentioned in that paragraph,

to be applied towards discharging the sums secured by those securities in the order of their priorities.

(8) Where the court gives leave for a disposal under sub-paragraph (2) or (3), the directors shall, within 14 days after leave is given, send [a copy] of the order giving leave to the registrar of companies.

(9) If the directors without reasonable excuse fail to comply with sub-paragraph (8), they are liable to a fine.

21. (1) Where property is disposed of under paragraph 20 in its application to Scotland, the company shall grant to the disponee an appropriate document of transfer or conveyance of the property, and

(a) that document, or

(b) where any recording, intimation or registration of the document is a legal requirement for completion of title to the property, that recording, intimation or registration,

has the effect of disencumbering the property of, or (as the case may be) freeing the property from, the security.

(2) Where goods in the possession of the company under a hire-purchase agreement are disposed of under paragraph 20 in its application to Scotland, the disposal has the effect of extinguishing, as against the disponee, all rights of the owner of the goods under the agreement.

22. (1) If the company—

(a) without any consent or leave under paragraph 20, disposes of any of its property which is subject to a security otherwise than in accordance with the terms of the security,

(b) without any consent or leave under paragraph 20, disposes of any goods in the possession of the company under a hire-purchase agreement otherwise than in accordance with the terms of the agreement, or

(c) fails to comply with any requirement imposed by paragraph 20 or 21, it is liable to a fine.

(2) If any officer of the company, without reasonable excuse, authorises or permits any such disposal or failure to comply, he is liable to imprisonment or a fine, or both.

Market contracts, etc

23. (1) If the company enters into any transaction to which this paragraph applies—

(a) the company is liable to a fine, and

(b) if any officer of the company, without reasonable excuse, authorised or permitted the company to enter into the transaction, he is liable to imprisonment or a fine, or both.

(2) A company enters into a transaction to which this paragraph applies if it—

(a) enters into a market contract, a money market contract . . . ,

(b) gives a transfer order,

(c) grants a market charge . . . or a system-charge, or

(d) provides any collateral security.

(3) The fact that a company enters into a transaction in contravention of this paragraph does not—

(a) make the transaction void, or

(b) make it to any extent unenforceable by or against the company.

(4) Where during the moratorium a company enters into a transaction to which this paragraph applies, nothing done by or in pursuance of the transaction is to be treated as done in contravention of paragraphs 12(1)(g), 14 or 16 to 22.

(5) Paragraph 20 does not apply in relation to any property which is subject to a market charge, . . . a system-charge or a collateral security charge.

(6) In this paragraph, "transfer order", "collateral security" and "collateral security charge" have the same meanings as in the settlement finality regulations.]

NOTES

Inserted as noted to Pt I of this Schedule at **[1.569]**.

Para 12: sub-para (1)(d), (da) substituted for original sub-para (1)(d) by the Enterprise Act 2002, s 248(3), Sch 17, paras 9, 37(1), (3), subject to savings and transitional provisions (i) in a case where a petition for an administration order has been presented before 15 September 2003 (see the Enterprise Act 2002 (Commencement No 4 and Transitional Provisions and Savings) Order 2003, SI 2003/2093, art 3 at **[2.26]**), and (ii) in relation to special administration regimes (see s 249 of the 2002 Act at **[2.10]**). Sub-para (1)(d) originally read as follows:

"(d) no petition for an administration order in relation to the company may be presented,";

words in square brackets in sub-para (5)(a) inserted by the European Public Limited-Liability Company Regulations 2004, SI 2004/2326, reg 73(4)(b); sub-para (5)(d) added by the Financial Services and Markets Act 2000 (Consequential Amendments) Order 2002, SI 2002/1555, art 30.

Para 16: sub-para (1) substituted by the Companies (Trading Disclosures) (Insolvency) Regulations 2008, SI 2008/1897, reg 3(1).

Para 20: words in square brackets in sub-para (8) substituted for original words "an office copy" by the Companies Act 2006 (Consequential Amendments, Transitional Provisions and Savings) Order 2009, SI 2009/1941, art 2(1), Sch 1, para 71(1), (4)(b), subject to transitional provisions and savings in art 8, Sch 1, para 84 at **[2.70]**, **[2.73]**.

Para 23: words omitted from sub-paras (2), (5) repealed by SI 2002/1555, art 28(1), (4).

See further: as to the disapplication of paras 12(1)(g), 20 in relation to any security interest created or otherwise arising under a financial collateral arrangement, see the Financial Collateral Arrangements (No 2) Regulations 2003, SI 2003/3226, reg 8(5) at **[3.288]**.

Banking Act 1987, Financial Services Act 1986: repealed by the Financial Services and Markets Act 2000 (Consequential Amendments and Repeals) Order 2001, SI 2001/3649, art 3(1)(c), (d).

[PART IV
NOMINEES

Monitoring of company's activities

[1.572]

24. (1) During a moratorium, the nominee shall monitor the company's affairs for the purpose of forming an opinion as to whether—

(a) the proposed voluntary arrangement or, if he has received notice of proposed modifications under paragraph 31(7), the proposed arrangement with those modifications has a reasonable prospect of being approved and implemented, and

(b) the company is likely to have sufficient funds available to it during the remainder of the moratorium to enable it to continue to carry on its business.

(2) The directors shall submit to the nominee any information necessary to enable him to comply with sub-paragraph (1) which he requests from them.

(3) In forming his opinion on the matters mentioned in sub-paragraph (1), the nominee is entitled to rely on the information submitted to him under sub-paragraph (2) unless he has reason to doubt its accuracy.

(4) The reference in sub-paragraph (1)(b) to the company's business is to that business as the company proposes to carry it on during the remainder of the moratorium.

Withdrawal of consent to act

25. (1) The nominee may only withdraw his consent to act in the circumstances mentioned in this paragraph.

(2) The nominee must withdraw his consent to act if, at any time during a moratorium—

(a) he forms the opinion that—

(i) the proposed voluntary arrangement or, if he has received notice of proposed modifications under paragraph 31(7), the proposed arrangement with those modifications no longer has a reasonable prospect of being approved or implemented, or

(ii) the company will not have sufficient funds available to it during the remainder of the moratorium to enable it to continue to carry on its business,

(b) he becomes aware that, on the date of filing, the company was not eligible for a moratorium, or

(c) the directors fail to comply with their duty under paragraph 24(2).

(3) The reference in sub-paragraph (2)(a)(ii) to the company's business is to that business as the company proposes to carry it on during the remainder of the moratorium.

(4) If the nominee withdraws his consent to act, the moratorium comes to an end.

(5) If the nominee withdraws his consent to act he must, in accordance with the rules, notify the court, the registrar of companies, the company and any creditor of the company of whose claim he is aware of his withdrawal and the reason for it.

(6) If the nominee without reasonable excuse fails to comply with sub-paragraph (5), he is liable to a fine.

Challenge of nominee's actions, etc

26. (1) If any creditor, director or member of the company, or any other person affected by a moratorium, is dissatisfied by any act, omission or decision of the nominee during the moratorium, he may apply to the court.

(2) An application under sub-paragraph (1) may be made during the moratorium or after it has ended.

(3) On an application under sub-paragraph (1) the court may—

(a) confirm, reverse or modify any act or decision of the nominee,

(b) give him directions, or

(c) make such other order as it thinks fit.

(4) An order under sub-paragraph (3) may (among other things) bring the moratorium to an end and make such consequential provision as the court thinks fit.

27. (1) Where there are reasonable grounds for believing that—

(a) as a result of any act, omission or decision of the nominee during the moratorium, the company has suffered loss, but

(b) the company does not intend to pursue any claim it may have against the nominee, any creditor of the company may apply to the court.

(2) An application under sub-paragraph (1) may be made during the moratorium or after it has ended.

(3) On an application under sub-paragraph (1) the court may—

(a) order the company to pursue any claim against the nominee,

(b) authorise any creditor to pursue such a claim in the name of the company, or

(c) make such other order with respect to such a claim as it thinks fit,

unless the court is satisfied that the act, omission or decision of the nominee was in all the circumstances reasonable.

(4) An order under sub-paragraph (3) may (among other things)—

(a) impose conditions on any authority given to pursue a claim,

(b) direct the company to assist in the pursuit of a claim,

(c) make directions with respect to the distribution of anything received as a result of the pursuit of a claim,

(d) bring the moratorium to an end and make such consequential provision as the court thinks fit.

(5) On an application under sub-paragraph (1) the court shall have regard to the interests of the members and creditors of the company generally.

Replacement of nominee by court

28. (1) The court may—

(a) on an application made by the directors in a case where the nominee has failed to comply with any duty imposed on him under this Schedule or has died, or

(b) on an application made by the directors or the nominee in a case where it is impracticable or inappropriate for the nominee to continue to act as such,

direct that the nominee be replaced as such by another person qualified to act as an insolvency practitioner . . . , in relation to the voluntary arrangement.

(2) A person may only be appointed as a replacement nominee under this paragraph if he submits to the court a statement indicating his consent to act.]

NOTES

Inserted as noted to Pt I of this Schedule at **[1.569]**.

Para 28: words omitted repealed by the Deregulation Act 2015, s 19, Sch 6, Pt 6, para 20(1), (2)(e)(i).

[PART V
CONSIDERATION AND IMPLEMENTATION OF VOLUNTARY ARRANGEMENT

[Duty to summon company meeting and seek creditors' decision]

[1.573]
29. (1) Where a moratorium is in force, the nominee [shall—
(a) summon a meeting of the company to consider the proposed voluntary arrangement for such a time, date (within the period of time for the time being specified in paragraph 8(3)) and place as he thinks fit, and
(b) seek a decision from the company's creditors as to whether they approve the proposed voluntary arrangement.]

[(2) The decision of the company's creditors is to be made by a qualifying decision procedure.

(3) Notice of the qualifying decision procedure must be given to every creditor of the company of whose claim the nominee is aware.]

Conduct of [company meeting and qualifying decision procedure]

30. (1) Subject to the provisions of paragraphs 31 to 35, the [company meeting summoned under paragraph 29 and the qualifying decision procedure instigated under that paragraph] shall be conducted in accordance with the rules.

(2) [The company meeting summoned under paragraph 29] may resolve that it be adjourned (or further adjourned).

(3) After the conclusion of [the company] meeting in accordance with the rules, the chairman of the meeting shall report the result of the meeting to the court, and, immediately after reporting to the court, shall give notice of the result of the meeting to such persons as may be prescribed.

[(4) After the company's creditors have decided whether to approve the proposed voluntary arrangement the nominee must—
(a) report the decision to the court, and
(b) immediately after reporting to the court, give notice of the decision to such persons as may be prescribed.]

Approval of voluntary arrangement

31. [(1) This paragraph applies where under paragraph 29—
(a) a meeting of the company is summoned to consider the proposed voluntary arrangement, and
(b) the nominee seeks a decision from the company's creditors as to whether they approve the proposed voluntary arrangement.

(1A) The company and its creditors may approve the proposed voluntary arrangement with or without modifications.]

(2) The modifications may include one conferring the functions proposed to be conferred on the nominee on another person qualified to act as an insolvency practitioner . . . in relation to the voluntary arrangement.

(3) The modifications shall not include one by virtue of which the proposal ceases to be a proposal such as is mentioned in section 1.

(4) [Neither the company nor its creditors may] approve any proposal or modification which affects the right of a secured creditor of the company to enforce his security, except with the concurrence of the creditor concerned.

(5) Subject to sub-paragraph (6), [neither the company nor its creditors may] approve any proposal or modification under which—
(a) any preferential debt of the company is to be paid otherwise than in priority to such of its debts as are not preferential debts, . . .
[(aa) any ordinary preferential debt of the company is to be paid otherwise than in priority to any secondary preferential debts that it may have,]
(b) a preferential creditor of the company is to be paid an amount in respect of [an ordinary preferential debt] that bears to that debt a smaller proportion than is borne to [another ordinary] preferential debt by the amount that is to be paid in respect of that other debt[, or
(c) a preferential creditor of the company is to be paid an amount in respect of a secondary preferential debt that bears to that debt a smaller proportion than is borne to another secondary preferential debt by the amount that is to be paid in respect of that other debt].

(6) [Such a proposal or modification may be approved] with the concurrence of the preferential creditor concerned.

(7) The directors of the company may, before the beginning of the [relevant period], give notice to the nominee of any modifications of the proposal for which the directors intend to seek the approval of [the company and its creditors].

[(7A) The "relevant period" is—
(a) in relation to the company, the period of seven days ending with the company meeting summoned under paragraph 29 being held;
(b) in relation to the company's creditors, the period of 14 days ending with the end of the period mentioned in paragraph 8(3).

(7B) Where under sub-paragraph (7) the nominee is given notice of proposed modifications, the nominee must seek a decision from the company's creditors (using a qualifying decision procedure) as to whether the proposed voluntary arrangement should be approved with those modifications.]

(8) References in this paragraph to preferential debts[, ordinary preferential debts, secondary preferential debts] and preferential creditors are to be read in accordance with section 386 in Part XII of this Act.

Extension of moratorium

32. (1) Subject to sub-paragraph (2), a [company] meeting summoned under paragraph 29 which resolves that it be adjourned (or further adjourned) may resolve that the moratorium be extended (or further extended), with or without conditions.

[(1A) Subject to sub-paragraph (2) the company's creditors may, by a qualifying decision procedure, decide to extend (or further extend) the moratorium, with or without conditions.]

[(2) The moratorium may not be extended (or further extended) to a day later than the end of the period of two months beginning with the day after the last day of the period mentioned in paragraph 8(3).]

(3) [Where] it is proposed to extend (or further extend) the moratorium, before a decision is taken with respect to that proposal, the nominee shall inform the meeting [of the company or (as the case may be) inform the company's creditors]—

(a) of what he has done in order to comply with his duty under paragraph 24 and the cost of his actions for the company, and

(b) of what he intends to do to continue to comply with that duty if the moratorium is extended (or further extended) and the expected cost of his actions for the company.

(4) Where, in accordance with sub-paragraph (3)(b), the nominee informs a meeting [of the company or informs the company's creditors,] of the expected cost of his intended actions, the meeting shall resolve[, or (as the case may be) the creditors by a qualifying decision procedure shall decide,] whether or not to approve that expected cost.

(5) If a decision not to approve the expected cost of the nominee's intended actions has effect under paragraph 36, the moratorium comes to an end.

(6) A meeting [of the company may resolve, and the creditors by a qualifying decision procedure may decide,] that a moratorium which has been extended (or further extended) be brought to an end before the end of the period of the extension (or further extension).

(7) The Secretary of State may by order increase or reduce the period for the time being specified in sub-paragraph (2).

33. (1) The conditions which may be imposed when a moratorium is extended (or further extended) include a requirement that the nominee be replaced as such by another person qualified to act as an insolvency practitioner . . . in relation to the voluntary arrangement.

(2) A person may only be appointed as a replacement nominee by virtue of sub-paragraph (1) if he submits to the court a statement indicating his consent to act.

(3) [Where] it is proposed to appoint a replacement nominee as a condition of extending (or further extending) the moratorium—

(a) the duty imposed by paragraph 32(3)(b) on the nominee shall instead be imposed on the person proposed as the replacement nominee, and

(b) paragraphs 32(4) and (5) and 36(1)(e) apply as if the references to the nominee were to that person.

34. (1) If a decision to extend, or further extend, the moratorium takes effect under paragraph 36, the nominee shall, in accordance with the rules, notify the registrar of companies and the court.

(2) If the moratorium is extended, or further extended, by virtue of an order under paragraph 36(5), the nominee shall, in accordance with the rules, send [a copy] of the order to the registrar of companies.

(3) If the nominee without reasonable excuse fails to comply with this paragraph, he is liable to a fine.

Moratorium committee

35. [(1) This paragraph applies where in accordance with paragraph 32 a meeting of the company resolves, or the company's creditors decide, that the moratorium be extended (or further extended).

(1A) The meeting may resolve, and the company's creditors may by a qualifying decision procedure decide, that a committee be established to exercise the functions conferred on it by the meeting or (as the case may be) by the company's creditors.

(2) The meeting may resolve that such a committee be established only if—

(a) the nominee consents, and

(b) the meeting approves an estimate of the expenses to be incurred by the committee in the exercise of the proposed functions.

(2A) A decision of the company's creditors that such a committee be established is to be taken as made only if—

(a) the nominee consents, and

(b) the creditors by a qualifying decision procedure approve an estimate of the expenses to be incurred by the committee in the exercise of the proposed functions.]

(3) Any expenses, not exceeding the amount of the estimate, incurred by the committee in the exercise of its functions shall be reimbursed by the nominee.

(4) The committee shall cease to exist when the moratorium comes to an end.

Effectiveness of decisions

36. (1) Sub-paragraph (2) applies to references to one of the following decisions having effect, that is, a decision, under paragraph 31, 32 or 35, with respect to—

(a) the approval of a proposed voluntary arrangement,
(b) the extension (or further extension) of a moratorium,
(c) the bringing of a moratorium to an end,
(d) the establishment of a committee, or
(e) the approval of the expected cost of a nominee's intended actions.

(2) The decision has effect if, in accordance with the rules—

(a) it has been taken by [the meeting of the company summoned under paragraph 29 and by the company's creditors], or
(b) (subject to any order made under sub-paragraph (5)) it has been taken by the [company's creditors].

(3) If a decision taken by the [company's creditors] under any of paragraphs 31, 32 or 35 with respect to any of the matters mentioned in sub-paragraph (1) differs from one so taken by the company meeting with respect to that matter, a member of the company may apply to the court.

(4) An application under sub-paragraph (3) shall not be made after the end of the period of 28 days beginning with—

(a) the day on which the decision was taken by the [company's creditors], or
(b) where the decision of the company meeting was taken on a later day, that day.

(5) On an application under sub-paragraph (3), the court may—

(a) order the decision of the company meeting to have effect instead of the decision of the [company's creditors], or
(b) make such other order as it thinks fit.

Effect of approval of voluntary arrangement

37. (1) This paragraph applies where a decision approving a voluntary arrangement has effect under paragraph 36.

(2) The approved voluntary arrangement—

(a) takes effect as if made by the company at the [time the creditors decided to approve the voluntary arrangement], and
(b) binds every person who in accordance with the rules—
    (i) was entitled to vote [in the qualifying decision procedure by which the creditors' decision to approve the voluntary arrangement was made], or
    (ii) would have been so entitled if he had had notice of it,

as if he were a party to the voluntary arrangement.

(3) If—

(a) when the arrangement ceases to have effect any amount payable under the arrangement to a person bound by virtue of sub-paragraph (2)(b)(ii) has not been paid, and
(b) the arrangement did not come to an end prematurely,

the company shall at that time become liable to pay to that person the amount payable under the arrangement.

(4) Where a petition for the winding up of the company, other than an excepted petition within the meaning of paragraph 12, was presented before the beginning of the moratorium, the court shall dismiss the petition.

(5) The court shall not dismiss a petition under sub-paragraph (4)—

(a) at any time before the end of the period of 28 days beginning with the first day on which each of the reports *of the meetings* required by paragraph 30(3) [and (4)] has been made to the court, or
(b) at any time when an application under paragraph 38 or an appeal in respect of such an application is pending, or at any time in the period within which such an appeal may be brought.

Challenge of decisions

38. (1) Subject to the following provisions of this paragraph, any of the persons mentioned in sub-paragraph (2) may apply to the court on one or both of the following grounds—

(a) that a voluntary arrangement [which has taken effect under paragraph 37] unfairly prejudices the interests of a creditor, member or contributory of the company,
(b) that there has been some material irregularity at or in relation to [the meeting of the company summoned under paragraph 29, or in relation to the relevant qualifying decision procedure].

[(1A) In this paragraph—

(a) the "relevant qualifying decision procedure" means the qualifying decision procedure in which the creditors decided whether to approve the voluntary arrangement;
(b) references to a decision made in the relevant qualifying decision procedure include any other decision made in that qualifying decision procedure.]

(2) The persons who may apply under this paragraph are—

(a) a person entitled, in accordance with the rules, to vote at [the meeting of the company or in the relevant qualifying decision procedure],

(b) a person who would have been entitled, in accordance with the rules, to vote [in the relevant qualifying decision procedure] if he had had notice of it, and
(c) the nominee.

(3) An application under this paragraph shall not be made—
(a) after the end of the period of 28 days beginning with the first day on which each of the reports required by paragraph 30(3) [and (4)] has been made to the court, or
(b) in the case of a person who was not given notice of the [relevant qualifying decision procedure], after the end of the period of 28 days beginning with the day on which he became aware that [the relevant qualifying decision procedure] had taken place,

but (subject to that) an application made by a person within sub-paragraph (2)(b) on the ground that the arrangement prejudices his interests may be made after the arrangement has ceased to have effect, unless it came to an end prematurely.

(4) Where on an application under this paragraph the court is satisfied as to either of the grounds mentioned in sub-paragraph (1), it may do any of the following—
(a) revoke or suspend—
(i) any decision approving the voluntary arrangement which has effect under paragraph 36, or
(ii) in a case falling within sub-paragraph (1)(b), any decision taken by the meeting [of the company, or in the relevant qualifying decision procedure,] which has effect under that paragraph,
(b) give a direction to any person—
(i) for the summoning of [a further company meeting] to consider any revised proposal for a voluntary arrangement which the directors may make, or
(ii) in a case falling within sub-paragraph (1)(b) [and relating to the company meeting], for the summoning of a further company . . . meeting to reconsider the original proposal,
[(c) direct any person—
(i) to seek a decision from the company's creditors (using a qualifying decision procedure) as to whether they approve any revised proposal for a voluntary arrangement which the directors may make, or
(ii) in a case falling within sub-paragraph (1)(b) and relating to the relevant qualifying decision procedure, to seek a decision from the company's creditors (using a qualifying decision procedure) as to whether they approve the original proposal].

(5) Where at any time after giving a direction under sub-paragraph (4)(b)(i) [or (c)(i)] the court is satisfied that the directors do not intend to submit a revised proposal, the court shall revoke the direction and revoke or suspend any decision approving the voluntary arrangement which has effect under paragraph 36.

(6) Where the court gives a direction under sub-paragraph (4)(b) [or (c)], it may also give a direction continuing or, as the case may require, renewing, for such period as may be specified in the direction, the effect of the moratorium.

(7) Sub-paragraph (8) applies in a case where the court, on an application under this paragraph—
(a) gives a direction under sub-paragraph (4)(b) [or (c)], or
(b) revokes or suspends a decision under sub-paragraph (4)(a) or (5).

(8) In such a case, the court may give such supplemental directions as it thinks fit and, in particular, directions with respect to—
(a) things done under the voluntary arrangement since it took effect, and
(b) such things done since that time as could not have been done if a moratorium had been in force in relation to the company when they were done.

(9) Except in pursuance of the preceding provisions of this paragraph—
[(a)] a decision taken at a [company] meeting summoned under paragraph 29 is not invalidated by any irregularity at or in relation to the meeting[, and
(b) a decision of the company's creditors made in the relevant qualifying decision procedure is not invalidated by any irregularity in relation to the relevant qualifying decision procedure].

Implementation of voluntary arrangement

39. (1) This paragraph applies where a voluntary arrangement [has taken effect under paragraph 37].

(2) The person who is for the time being carrying out in relation to the voluntary arrangement the functions conferred—
(a) by virtue of the approval of the arrangement, on the nominee, or
(b) by virtue of paragraph 31(2), on a person other than the nominee,

shall be known as the supervisor of the voluntary arrangement.

(3) If any of the company's creditors or any other person is dissatisfied by any act, omission or decision of the supervisor, he may apply to the court.

(4) On an application under sub-paragraph (3) the court may—
(a) confirm, reverse or modify any act or decision of the supervisor,
(b) give him directions, or
(c) make such other order as it thinks fit.

(5) The supervisor—
(a) may apply to the court for directions in relation to any particular matter arising under the voluntary arrangement, and

(b) is included among the persons who may apply to the court for the winding up of the company or for an administration order to be made in relation to it.

(6) The court may, whenever—

(a) it is expedient to appoint a person to carry out the functions of the supervisor, and

(b) it is inexpedient, difficult or impracticable for an appointment to be made without the assistance of the court,

make an order appointing a person who is qualified to act as an insolvency practitioner . . . in relation to the voluntary arrangement, either in substitution for the existing supervisor or to fill a vacancy.

(7) The power conferred by sub-paragraph (6) is exercisable so as to increase the number of persons exercising the functions of supervisor or, where there is more than one person exercising those functions, so as to replace one or more of those persons.

NOTES

Inserted as noted to Pt I of this Schedule at **[1.569]**.

Para 29 is amended as follows:

The heading preceding para 29 is substituted (for original heading "Summoning of meetings") by the Small Business, Enterprise and Employment Act 2015, s 126, Sch 9, Pt 1, paras 1, 9(1), (6), as from 6 April 2017 (in relation to England and Wales and subject to transitional and savings provisions as noted to s 246ZE at **[1.256]**), and as from a day to be appointed (in relation to Scotland).

Words in square brackets in sub-para (1) substituted for original words "shall summon meetings of the company and its creditors for such a time, date (within the period for the time being specified in paragraph 8(3)) and place as he thinks fit." by the Small Business, Enterprise and Employment Act 2015, s 126, Sch 9, Pt 1, paras 1, 9(1), (7), as from 6 April 2017 (in relation to England and Wales and subject to transitional and savings provisions as noted to s 246ZE at **[1.256]**), and as from a day to be appointed (in relation to Scotland).

Sub-paras (2), (3) substituted for original sub-para (2) by the Small Business, Enterprise and Employment Act 2015, s 126, Sch 9, Pt 1, paras 1, 9(1), (8), as from 6 April 2017 (in relation to England and Wales and subject to transitional and savings provisions as noted to s 246ZE at **[1.256]**), and as from a day to be appointed (in relation to Scotland). Sub-para (2) originally read as follows—

"(2) The persons to be summoned to a creditors' meeting under this paragraph are every creditor of the company of whose claim the nominee is aware.".

Para 30: words in square brackets in the preceding heading substituted for original word "meetings", words in square brackets in sub-para (1) substituted for original words "meetings summoned under paragraph 29", words in square brackets in sub-para (2) substituted for original words "A meeting so summoned", words in square brackets in sub-para (3) substituted for original word "either", and sub-para (4) added, by the Small Business, Enterprise and Employment Act 2015, s 126, Sch 9, Pt 1, paras 1, 9(1), (9)–(13), as from 6 April 2017 (in relation to England and Wales and subject to transitional and savings provisions as noted to s 246ZE at **[1.256]**), and as from a day to be appointed (in relation to Scotland).

Para 31 is amended as follows:

Sub-paras (1), (1A) substituted for original sub-para (1) by the Small Business, Enterprise and Employment Act 2015, s 126, Sch 9, Pt 1, paras 1, 9(1), (14), as from 6 April 2017 (in relation to England and Wales and subject to transitional and savings provisions as noted to s 246ZE at **[1.256]**), and as from a day to be appointed (in relation to Scotland). Sub-para (1) originally read as follows—

"(1) The meetings summoned under paragraph 29 shall decide whether to approve the proposed voluntary arrangement (with or without modifications)."

Words omitted from sub-para (2) repealed by the Deregulation Act 2015, s 19, Sch 6, Pt 6, para 20(1), (2)(e)(ii).

Words in square brackets in sub-para (4) substituted for original words "A meeting summoned under paragraph 29 shall not", words in first pair of square brackets in sub-para (5) substituted for original words "a meeting so summoned shall not", words in square brackets in sub-para (6) substituted for original words "The meeting may approve such a proposal or modification" and words in first and second pairs of square brackets in sub-para (7) substituted for original words "period of seven days which ends with the meetings (or either of them) summoned under paragraph 29 being held" and "those meetings" respectively, by the Small Business, Enterprise and Employment Act 2015, s 126, Sch 9, Pt 1, paras 1, 9(1), (15)–(18), as from 6 April 2017 (in relation to England and Wales and subject to transitional and savings provisions as noted to s 246ZE at **[1.256]**), and as from a day to be appointed (in relation to Scotland).

The word "or" at the end of sub-para (5)(a) was repealed, sub-para (5)(aa) was inserted, the words in the first pair of square brackets in sub-para (5)(b) were substituted (for the original words "a preferential debt"), the words in the second pair of square brackets in sub-para (5)(b) were substituted (for the original word "another"), and sub-para (5)(c) (and the preceding word) was added, by the Banks and Building Societies (Depositor Preference and Priorities) Order 2014, SI 2014/3486, arts 3, 9(1), (2), except in relation to any insolvency proceedings commenced before 1 January 2015 (as to the meaning of this, see further the note "SI 2014/3486, art 3" at **[1.5]**).

Sub-paras (7A), (7B) inserted by the Small Business, Enterprise and Employment Act 2015, s 126, Sch 9, Pt 1, paras 1, 9(1), (19), as from 6 April 2017 (in relation to England and Wales and subject to transitional and savings provisions as noted to s 246ZE at **[1.256]**), and as from a day to be appointed (in relation to Scotland).

The words in square brackets in sub-para (8) were inserted by SI 2014/3486, arts 3, 9(1), (3), except in relation to any insolvency proceedings commenced before 1 January 2015 (as to the meaning of this, see further the note "SI 2014/3486, art 3" at **[1.5]**).

Para 32: all words in square brackets substituted or inserted by the Small Business, Enterprise and Employment Act 2015, s 126, Sch 9, Pt 1, paras 1, 9(1), (20)–(25), as from 6 April 2017 (in relation to England and Wales and subject to transitional and savings provisions as noted to s 246ZE at **[1.256]**), and as from a day to be appointed (in relation to Scotland). Para 32 originally read as follows—

"**32.** (1) Subject to sub-paragraph (2), a meeting summoned under paragraph 29 which resolves that it be adjourned (or further adjourned) may resolve that the moratorium be extended (or further extended), with or without conditions.

(2) The moratorium may not be extended (or further extended) to a day later than the end of the period of two months which begins—

(a) where both meetings summoned under paragraph 29 are first held on the same day, with that day,

(b) in any other case, with the day on which the later of those meetings is first held.

(3) At any meeting where it is proposed to extend (or further extend) the moratorium, before a decision is taken with respect to that proposal, the nominee shall inform the meeting—

(a) of what he has done in order to comply with his duty under paragraph 24 and the cost of his actions for the company, and

(b) of what he intends to do to continue to comply with that duty if the moratorium is extended (or further extended) and the expected cost of his actions for the company.

(4) Where, in accordance with sub-paragraph (3)(b), the nominee informs a meeting of the expected cost of his intended actions, the meeting shall resolve whether or not to approve that expected cost.

(5) If a decision not to approve the expected cost of the nominee's intended actions has effect under paragraph 36, the moratorium comes to an end.

(6) A meeting may resolve that a moratorium which has been extended (or further extended) be brought to an end before the end of the period of the extension (or further extension).

(7) The Secretary of State may by order increase or reduce the period for the time being specified in sub-paragraph (2).".

Para 33: words omitted from sub-para (1) repealed by the Deregulation Act 2015, s 19, Sch 6, Pt 7, para 20(1), (2)(e)(iii); word in square brackets in sub-para (3) substituted for original words "At any meeting where", by the Small Business, Enterprise and Employment Act 2015, s 126, Sch 9, Pt 1, paras 1, 9(1), (26), as from 6 April 2017 (in relation to England and Wales and subject to transitional and savings provisions as noted to s 246ZE at **[1.256]**), and as from a day to be appointed (in relation to Scotland).

Para 34: words in square brackets in sub-para (2) substituted by the Companies Act 2006 (Consequential Amendments, Transitional Provisions and Savings) Order 2009, SI 2009/1941, art 2(1), Sch 1, para 71(1), (4)(b), subject to transitional provisions and savings in art 8, Sch 1, para 84 at **[2.70]**, **[2.73]**.

Para 35: sub-paras (1), (1A), (2), (2A) substituted for original sub-paras (1), (2), by the Small Business, Enterprise and Employment Act 2015, s 126, Sch 9, Pt 1, paras 1, 9(1), (27), as from 6 April 2017 (in relation to England and Wales and subject to transitional and savings provisions as noted to s 246ZE at **[1.256]**), and as from a day to be appointed (in relation to Scotland). Sub-paras (1), (2) originally read as follows—

"(1) A meeting summoned under paragraph 29 which resolves that the moratorium be extended (or further extended) may, with the consent of the nominee, resolve that a committee be established to exercise the functions conferred on it by the meeting.

(2) The meeting may not so resolve unless it has approved an estimate of the expenses to be incurred by the committee in the exercise of the proposed functions.".

Para 36: words in square brackets in sub-para (2)(a) substituted for original words "both meetings summoned under paragraph 29", words in square brackets in sub-para (2)(b) substituted for original words "creditors' meeting summoned under that paragraph" and words in square brackets in sub-paras (3), (4)(a) and (5)(a) substituted for original words "creditors' meeting", by the Small Business, Enterprise and Employment Act 2015, s 126, Sch 9, Pt 1, paras 1, 9(1), (28), (29), as from 6 April 2017 (in relation to England and Wales and subject to transitional and savings provisions as noted to s 246ZE at **[1.256]**), and as from a day to be appointed (in relation to Scotland).

Para 37: words in square brackets in sub-paras (2)(a), (2)(b) substituted for original words "creditors' meeting" and "at that meeting (whether or not he was present or represented at it)" respectively, words in italics in sub-para (5)(a) repealed, and words in square brackets in sub-para (5)(a) inserted, by the Small Business, Enterprise and Employment Act 2015, s 126, Sch 9, Pt 1, paras 1, 9(1), (30), (31), as from 6 April 2017 (in relation to England and Wales and subject to transitional and savings provisions as noted to s 246ZE at **[1.256]**), and as from a day to be appointed (in relation to Scotland).

Para 38: all words in square brackets substituted or inserted, and words omitted repealed, by the Small Business, Enterprise and Employment Act 2015, s 126, Sch 9, Pt 1, paras 1, 9(1), (32)–(42), as from 6 April 2017 (in relation to England and Wales and subject to transitional and savings provisions as noted to s 246ZE at **[1.256]**), and as from a day to be appointed (in relation to Scotland). Para 38 originally read as follows:

"**38.** (1) Subject to the following provisions of this paragraph, any of the persons mentioned in sub-paragraph (2) may apply to the court on one or both of the following grounds—

(a) that a voluntary arrangement approved at one or both of the meetings summoned under paragraph 29 and which has taken effect unfairly prejudices the interests of a creditor, member or contributory of the company,

(b) that there has been some material irregularity at or in relation to either of those meetings.

(2) The persons who may apply under this paragraph are—

(a) a person entitled, in accordance with the rules, to vote at either of the meetings,

(b) a person who would have been entitled, in accordance with the rules, to vote at the creditors' meeting if he had had notice of it, and

(c) the nominee.

(3) An application under this paragraph shall not be made—

(a) after the end of the period of 28 days beginning with the first day on which each of the reports required by paragraph 30(3) has been made to the court, or

(b) in the case of a person who was not given notice of the creditors' meeting, after the end of the period of 28 days beginning with the day on which he became aware that the meeting had taken place,

but (subject to that) an application made by a person within sub-paragraph (2)(b) on the ground that the arrangement prejudices his interests may be made after the arrangement has ceased to have effect, unless it came to an end prematurely.

(4) Where on an application under this paragraph the court is satisfied as to either of the grounds mentioned in sub-paragraph (1), it may do any of the following—

(a) revoke or suspend—

(i) any decision approving the voluntary arrangement which has effect under paragraph 36, or

(ii) in a case falling within sub-paragraph (1)(b), any decision taken by the meeting in question which has effect under that paragraph,

(b) give a direction to any person—

(i) for the summoning of further meetings to consider any revised proposal for a voluntary arrangement which the directors may make, or

(ii) in a case falling within sub-paragraph (1)(b), for the summoning of a further company or (as the case may be) creditors' meeting to reconsider the original proposal.

(5) Where at any time after giving a direction under sub-paragraph (4)(b)(i) the court is satisfied that the directors do not intend to submit a revised proposal, the court shall revoke the direction and revoke or suspend any decision approving the voluntary arrangement which has effect under paragraph 36.

(6) Where the court gives a direction under sub-paragraph (4)(b), it may also give a direction continuing or, as the case may require, renewing, for such period as may be specified in the direction, the effect of the moratorium.

(7) Sub-paragraph (8) applies in a case where the court, on an application under this paragraph—

(a) gives a direction under sub-paragraph (4)(b), or

(b) revokes or suspends a decision under sub-paragraph (4)(a) or (5).

(8) In such a case, the court may give such supplemental directions as it thinks fit and, in particular, directions with respect to—

(a) things done under the voluntary arrangement since it took effect, and

(b) such things done since that time as could not have been done if a moratorium had been in force in relation to the company when they were done.

(9) Except in pursuance of the preceding provisions of this paragraph a decision taken at a meeting summoned under paragraph 29 is not invalidated by any irregularity at or in relation to the meeting.".

Para 39: words in square brackets in sub-para (1) substituted for original words "approved by one or both of the meetings summoned under paragraph 29 has taken effect", by the Small Business, Enterprise and Employment Act 2015, s 126, Sch 9, Pt 1, paras 1, 9(1), (43), as from 6 April 2017 (in relation to England and Wales and subject to transitional and savings provisions as noted to s 246ZE at **[1.256]**), and as from a day to be appointed (in relation to Scotland); words omitted from sub-para (6) repealed by the Deregulation Act 2015, s 19, Sch 6, Pt 7, para 20(1), (2)(e)(iv).

[PART VI
MISCELLANEOUS

Challenge of directors' actions

[1.574]

40. (1) This paragraph applies in relation to acts or omissions of the directors of a company during a moratorium.

(2) A creditor or member of the company may apply to the court for an order under this paragraph on the ground—

(a) that the company's affairs, business and property are being or have been managed by the directors in a manner which is unfairly prejudicial to the interests of its creditors or members generally, or of some part of its creditors or members (including at least the petitioner), or

(b) that any actual or proposed act or omission of the directors is or would be so prejudicial.

(3) An application for an order under this paragraph may be made during or after the moratorium.

(4) On an application for an order under this paragraph the court may—

(a) make such order as it thinks fit for giving relief in respect of the matters complained of,

(b) adjourn the hearing conditionally or unconditionally, or

(c) make an interim order or any other order that it thinks fit.

(5) An order under this paragraph may in particular—

(a) regulate the management by the directors of the company's affairs, business and property during the remainder of the moratorium,

(b) require the directors to refrain from doing or continuing an act complained of by the petitioner, or to do an act which the petitioner has complained they have omitted to do,

(c) require the summoning of a meeting of *creditors or* members for the purpose of considering such matters as the court may direct,

[(ca) require a decision of the company's creditors to be sought (using a qualifying decision procedure) on such matters as the court may direct,]

(d) bring the moratorium to an end and make such consequential provision as the court thinks fit.

(6) In making an order under this paragraph the court shall have regard to the need to safeguard the interests of persons who have dealt with the company in good faith and for value.

[(7) Sub-paragraph (8) applies where—

[(a) the appointment of an administrator has effect in relation to the company and that appointment was in pursuance of—

(i) an administration application made, or

(ii) a notice of intention to appoint filed,

before the moratorium came into force, or]

(b) the company is being wound up in pursuance of a petition presented before the moratorium came into force.

(8) No application for an order under this paragraph may be made by a creditor or member of the company; but such an application may be made instead by the administrator or (as the case may be) the liquidator.]

Offences

41. (1) This paragraph applies where a moratorium has been obtained for a company.

(2) If, within the period of 12 months ending with the day on which the moratorium came into force, a person who was at the time an officer of the company—

(a) did any of the things mentioned in paragraphs (a) to (f) of sub-paragraph (4), or

(b) was privy to the doing by others of any of the things mentioned in paragraphs (c), (d) and (e) of that sub-paragraph,

he is to be treated as having committed an offence at that time.

(3) If, at any time during the moratorium, a person who is an officer of the company—

(a) does any of the things mentioned in paragraphs (a) to (f) of sub-paragraph (4), or

(b) is privy to the doing by others of any of the things mentioned in paragraphs (c), (d) and (e) of that sub-paragraph,

he commits an offence.

(4) Those things are—

(a) concealing any part of the company's property to the value of £500 or more, or concealing any debt due to or from the company, or

(b) fraudulently removing any part of the company's property to the value of £500 or more, or

(c) concealing, destroying, mutilating or falsifying any book or paper affecting or relating to the company's property or affairs, or

(d) making any false entry in any book or paper affecting or relating to the company's property or affairs, or

(e) fraudulently parting with, altering or making any omission in any document affecting or relating to the company's property or affairs, or

(f) pawning, pledging or disposing of any property of the company which has been obtained on credit and has not been paid for (unless the pawning, pledging or disposal was in the ordinary way of the company's business).

(5) For the purposes of this paragraph, "officer" includes a shadow director.

(6) It is a defence—

(a) for a person charged under sub-paragraph (2) or (3) in respect of the things mentioned in paragraph (a) or (f) of sub-paragraph (4) to prove that he had no intent to defraud, and

(b) for a person charged under sub-paragraph (2) or (3) in respect of the things mentioned in paragraph (c) or (d) of sub-paragraph (4) to prove that he had no intent to conceal the state of affairs of the company or to defeat the law.

(7) Where a person pawns, pledges or disposes of any property of a company in circumstances which amount to an offence under sub-paragraph (2) or (3), every person who takes in pawn or pledge, or otherwise receives, the property knowing it to be pawned, pledged or disposed of in circumstances which—

(a) would, if a moratorium were obtained for the company within the period of 12 months beginning with the day on which the pawning, pledging or disposal took place, amount to an offence under sub-paragraph (2), or

(b) amount to an offence under sub-paragraph (3),

commits an offence.

(8) A person guilty of an offence under this paragraph is liable to imprisonment or a fine, or both.

(9) The money sums specified in paragraphs (a) and (b) of sub-paragraph (4) are subject to increase or reduction by order under section 417A in Part XV.

42. (1) If, for the purpose of obtaining a moratorium, or an extension of a moratorium, for a company, a person who is an officer of the company—

(a) makes any false representation, or

(b) fraudulently does, or omits to do, anything,

he commits an offence.

(2) Sub-paragraph (1) applies even if no moratorium or extension is obtained.

(3) For the purposes of this paragraph, "officer" includes a shadow director.

(4) A person guilty of an offence under this paragraph is liable to imprisonment or a fine, or both.

Void provisions in floating charge documents

43. (1) A provision in an instrument creating a floating charge is void if it provides for—

(a) obtaining a moratorium, or

(b) anything done with a view to obtaining a moratorium (including any preliminary decision or investigation),

to be an event causing the floating charge to crystallise or causing restrictions which would not otherwise apply to be imposed on the disposal of property by the company or a ground for the appointment of a receiver.

(2) In sub-paragraph (1), "receiver" includes a manager and a person who is appointed both receiver and manager.

Functions of the [Financial Conduct Authority and Prudential Regulation Authority]

44. (1) This Schedule has effect in relation to a moratorium for a regulated company with the modifications in sub-paragraphs (2) to (16) below.

(2) Any notice or other document required by virtue of this Schedule to be sent to a creditor of a regulated company must also be sent to the [appropriate regulator].

(3) The [appropriate regulator] is entitled to be heard on any application to the court for leave under paragraph 20(2) or 20(3) (disposal of charged property, etc).

(4) Where paragraph 26(1) (challenge of nominee's actions, etc) applies, the persons who may apply to the court include the [appropriate regulator].

(5) If a person other than [a regulator] applies to the court under that paragraph, [the appropriate regulator] is entitled to be heard on the application.

(6) Where paragraph 27(1) (challenge of nominee's actions, etc) applies, the persons who may apply to the court include the [appropriate regulator].

(7) If a person other than [a regulator] applies to the court under that paragraph, [the appropriate regulator] is entitled to be heard on the application.

[(8) The appropriate regulator must be given notice of any qualifying decision procedure by which a decision of the company's creditors is sought for the purposes of this Schedule.

(8A) The appropriate regulator, or a person appointed by the appropriate regulator, may in the way provided for by the rules participate in (but not vote in) any qualifying decision procedure by which a decision of the company's creditors is sought for the purposes of this Schedule.]

(9) A person appointed for the purpose by the [appropriate regulator] is entitled to attend and participate in (but not to vote at)—

(a) *any creditors' meeting summoned under that paragraph,*
(b) any meeting of a committee established under paragraph 35 (moratorium committee).

(10) The [appropriate regulator] is entitled to be heard on any application under paragraph 36(3) (effectiveness of decisions).

(11) Where paragraph 38(1) (challenge of decisions) applies, the persons who may apply to the court include the [appropriate regulator].

(12) If a person other than [a regulator] applies to the court under that paragraph, [the appropriate regulator] is entitled to be heard on the application.

(13) Where paragraph 39(3) (implementation of voluntary arrangement) applies, the persons who may apply to the court include the [appropriate regulator].

(14) If a person other than [a regulator] applies to the court under that paragraph, [the appropriate regulator] is entitled to be heard on the application.

(15) Where paragraph 40(2) (challenge of directors' actions) applies, the persons who may apply to the court include the [appropriate regulator].

(16) If a person other than [a regulator] applies to the court under that paragraph, [the appropriate regulator] is entitled to be heard on the application.

[(16A) If either regulator makes an application to the court under any of the provisions mentioned in sub-paragraphs (5), (7), (12), (14) or (16) in relation to a PRA-regulated company, the other regulator is entitled to be heard on the application.]

(17) This paragraph does not prejudice any right the [appropriate regulator] has (apart from this paragraph) as a creditor of a regulated company.

[(17A) "The appropriate regulator" means—

(a) for the purposes of sub-paragraphs (2) to (8) and (10) to (17)—
 (i) where the regulated company is a PRA-regulated company, each of the Financial Conduct Authority and the Prudential Regulation Authority, and
 (ii) in any other case, the Financial Conduct Authority;
(b) for the purposes of [sub-paragraphs (8A) and] (9)—
 (i) where the regulated company is a PRA-regulated company, the Financial Conduct Authority or the Prudential Regulation Authority, and
 (ii) in any other case, the Financial Conduct Authority.]

(18) In this paragraph—

["PRA-authorised person" has the meaning given by section 2B(5) of the Financial Services and Markets Act 2000;

"PRA-regulated activity" has the meaning given by section 22A of the Financial Services and Markets Act 2000;

"PRA-regulated company" means a regulated company which—
 (a) is, or has been, a PRA-authorised person,
 (b) is, or has been, an appointed representative within the meaning given by section 39 of the Financial Services and Markets Act 2000, whose principal (or one of whose principals) is, or was, a PRA-authorised person, or
 (c) is carrying on, or has carried on, a PRA-regulated activity in contravention of the general prohibition;]

"regulated company" means a company which—
 (a) is, or has been, an authorised person within the meaning given by section 31 of the Financial Services and Markets Act 2000,
 (b) is, or has been, an appointed representative within the meaning given by section 39 of that Act, or
 (c) is carrying on, or has carried on, a regulated activity, within the meaning given by section 22 of that Act, in contravention of the general prohibition within the meaning given by section 19 of that Act.

["regulator" means the Financial Conduct Authority or the Prudential Regulation Authority.]

Subordinate legislation

45. (1) Regulations or an order made by the Secretary of State under this Schedule may make different provision for different cases.

(2) Regulations so made may make such consequential, incidental, supplemental and transitional provision as may appear to the Secretary of State necessary or expedient.

(3) Any power of the Secretary of State to make regulations under this Schedule may be exercised by amending or repealing any enactment contained in this Act (including one contained in this Schedule) or contained in the Company Directors Disqualification Act 1986.

(4) Regulations (except regulations under paragraph 5) or an order made by the Secretary of State under this Schedule shall be made by statutory instrument subject to annulment in pursuance of a resolution of either House of Parliament.

(5) Regulations under paragraph 5 of this Schedule are to be made by statutory instrument and shall only be made if a draft containing the regulations has been laid before and approved by resolution of each House of Parliament.]

NOTES

Inserted as noted to Pt I of this Schedule at **[1.569]**.

Para 40: words in italics in sub-para (5)(c) repealed, and sub-para (5)(ca) inserted, by the Small Business, Enterprise and Employment Act 2015, s 126, Sch 9, Pt 1, paras 1, 9(1), (44), as from 6 April 2017 (in relation to England and Wales and subject to transitional and savings provisions as noted to s 246ZE at **[1.256]**), and as from a day to be appointed (in relation to Scotland); sub-paras (7), (8) substituted for original sub-para (7) by the Enterprise Act 2002, s 248(3), Sch 17, paras 9, 37(1), (4), subject to savings and transitional provisions (i) in a case where a petition for an administration order has been presented before 15 September 2003 (see the Enterprise Act 2002 (Commencement No 4 and Transitional Provisions and Savings) Order 2003, SI 2003/2093, art 3 at **[2.26]**), and (ii) in relation to special administration regimes (see s 249 of the 2002 Act at **[2.10]**). Sub-para (7) originally read as follows:

> "(7) In relation to any time when an administration order is in force in relation to the company, or the company is being wound up, in pursuance of a petition presented before the moratorium came into force, no application for an order under this paragraph may be made by a creditor or member of the company; but such an application may be made instead by the administrator or (as the case may be) liquidator.";

sub-para (7)(a) substituted by the Enterprise Act 2002 (Insolvency) Order 2004, SI 2004/2312, art 2.

Para 44 is amended as follows:

Sub-paras (8), (8A) substituted for original sub-para (8) by the Small Business, Enterprise and Employment Act 2015, s 126, Sch 9, Pt 1, paras 1, 9(1), (45), as from 6 April 2017 (in relation to England and Wales and subject to transitional and savings provisions as noted to s 246ZE at **[1.256]**), and as from a day to be appointed (in relation to Scotland). Sub-s (8) previously read as follows—

> "(8) The persons to be summoned to a creditors' meeting under paragraph 29 include the [appropriate regulator].".

Sub-para (9)(a) is repealed, and words in square brackets in sub-para (17A)(b) substituted for original word "sub-paragraph" by the Small Business, Enterprise and Employment Act 2015, s 126, Sch 9, Pt 1, paras 1, 9(1), (46), (47), as from 6 April 2017 (in relation to England and Wales and subject to transitional and savings provisions as noted to s 246ZE at **[1.256]**), and as from a day to be appointed (in relation to Scotland).

All other amendments to para 44 (including the preceding heading) were made by the Financial Services Act 2012, s 114(1), Sch 18, Pt 2, paras 51, 54.

[SCHEDULE B1
ADMINISTRATION

Section 8

[1.575]

Arrangement of Schedule

Nature of administration	Paragraphs 1 to 9
Appointment of administrator by court	Paragraphs 10 to 13
Appointment of administrator by holder of floating charge	Paragraphs 14 to 21
Appointment of administrator by company or directors	Paragraphs 22 to 34
Administration application: special cases	Paragraphs 35 to 39
Effect of administration	Paragraphs 40 to 45
Process of administration	Paragraphs 46 to 58
Functions of administrator	Paragraphs 59 to 75
Ending administration	Paragraphs 76 to 86
Replacing administrator	Paragraphs 87 to 99
General	Paragraphs 100 to 116

NATURE OF ADMINISTRATION

Administration

1. (1) For the purposes of this Act "administrator" of a company means a person appointed under this Schedule to manage the company's affairs, business and property.

(2) For the purposes of this Act—

(a) a company is "in administration" while the appointment of an administrator of the company has effect,

(b) a company "enters administration" when the appointment of an administrator takes effect,

(c) a company ceases to be in administration when the appointment of an administrator of the company ceases to have effect in accordance with this Schedule, and

(d) a company does not cease to be in administration merely because an administrator vacates office (by reason of resignation, death or otherwise) or is removed from office.

2. A person may be appointed as administrator of a company—

(a) by administration order of the court under paragraph 10,
(b) by the holder of a floating charge under paragraph 14, or
(c) by the company or its directors under paragraph 22.

Purpose of administration

3. (1) The administrator of a company must perform his functions with the objective of—
(a) rescuing the company as a going concern, or
(b) achieving a better result for the company's creditors as a whole than would be likely if the company were wound up (without first being in administration), or
(c) realising property in order to make a distribution to one or more secured or preferential creditors.

(2) Subject to sub-paragraph (4), the administrator of a company must perform his functions in the interests of the company's creditors as a whole.

(3) The administrator must perform his functions with the objective specified in sub-paragraph (1)(a) unless he thinks either—
(a) that it is not reasonably practicable to achieve that objective, or
(b) that the objective specified in sub-paragraph (1)(b) would achieve a better result for the company's creditors as a whole.

(4) The administrator may perform his functions with the objective specified in sub-paragraph (1)(c) only if—
(a) he thinks that it is not reasonably practicable to achieve either of the objectives specified in sub-paragraph (1)(a) and (b), and
(b) he does not unnecessarily harm the interests of the creditors of the company as a whole.

4. The administrator of a company must perform his functions as quickly and efficiently as is reasonably practicable.

Status of administrator

5. An administrator is an officer of the court (whether or not he is appointed by the court).

General restrictions

6. A person may be appointed as administrator of a company only if he is qualified to act as an insolvency practitioner in relation to the company.

7. A person may not be appointed as administrator of a company which is in administration (subject to the provisions of paragraphs 90 to 97 and 100 to 103 about replacement and additional administrators).

8. (1) A person may not be appointed as administrator of a company which is in liquidation by virtue of—
(a) a resolution for voluntary winding up, or
(b) a winding-up order.

(2) Sub-paragraph (1)(a) is subject to paragraph 38.

(3) Sub-paragraph (1)(b) is subject to paragraphs 37 and 38.

9. (1) A person may not be appointed as administrator of a company which—
(a) has a liability in respect of a deposit which it accepted in accordance with the Banking Act 1979 (c 37) or 1987 (c 22), but
(b) is not an authorised deposit taker.

(2) A person may not be appointed as administrator of a company which effects or carries out contracts of insurance.

(3) But sub-paragraph (2) does not apply to a company which—
(a) is exempt from the general prohibition in relation to effecting or carrying out contracts of insurance, or
(b) is an authorised deposit taker effecting or carrying out contracts of insurance in the course of a banking business.

(4) In this paragraph—
"authorised deposit taker" means a person with permission under Part IV of the Financial Services and Markets Act 2000 (c 8) to accept deposits, and
"the general prohibition" has the meaning given by section 19 of that Act.

(5) This paragraph shall be construed in accordance with—
(a) section 22 of the Financial Services and Markets Act 2000 (classes of regulated activity and categories of investment),
(b) any relevant order under that section, and
(c) Schedule 2 to that Act (regulated activities).

APPOINTMENT OF ADMINISTRATOR BY COURT

Administration order

10. An administration order is an order appointing a person as the administrator of a company.

Conditions for making order

11. The court may make an administration order in relation to a company only if satisfied—
(a) that the company is or is likely to become unable to pay its debts, and
(b) that the administration order is reasonably likely to achieve the purpose of administration.

Administration application

12. (1) An application to the court for an administration order in respect of a company (an "administration application") may be made only by—
(a) the company,
(b) the directors of the company,
(c) one or more creditors of the company,
(d) the [designated officer] for a magistrates' court in the exercise of the power conferred by section 87A of the Magistrates' Courts Act 1980 (c 43) (fine imposed on company), or
(e) a combination of persons listed in paragraphs (a) to (d).

(2) As soon as is reasonably practicable after the making of an administration application the applicant shall notify—
(a) any person who has appointed an administrative receiver of the company,
(b) any person who is or may be entitled to appoint an administrative receiver of the company,
(c) any person who is or may be entitled to appoint an administrator of the company under paragraph 14, and
(d) such other persons as may be prescribed.

(3) An administration application may not be withdrawn without the permission of the court.

(4) In sub-paragraph (1) "creditor" includes a contingent creditor and a prospective creditor.

[(5) Sub-paragraph (1) is without prejudice to section 7(4)(b).]

Powers of court

13. (1) On hearing an administration application the court may—
(a) make the administration order sought;
(b) dismiss the application;
(c) adjourn the hearing conditionally or unconditionally;
(d) make an interim order;
(e) treat the application as a winding-up petition and make any order which the court could make under section 125;
(f) make any other order which the court thinks appropriate.

(2) An appointment of an administrator by administration order takes effect—
(a) at a time appointed by the order, or
(b) where no time is appointed by the order, when the order is made.

(3) An interim order under sub-paragraph (1)(d) may, in particular—
(a) restrict the exercise of a power of the directors or the company;
(b) make provision conferring a discretion on the court or on a person qualified to act as an insolvency practitioner in relation to the company.

(4) This paragraph is subject to paragraph 39.

APPOINTMENT OF ADMINISTRATOR BY HOLDER OF FLOATING CHARGE

Power to appoint

14. (1) The holder of a qualifying floating charge in respect of a company's property may appoint an administrator of the company.

(2) For the purposes of sub-paragraph (1) a floating charge qualifies if created by an instrument which—
(a) states that this paragraph applies to the floating charge,
(b) purports to empower the holder of the floating charge to appoint an administrator of the company,
(c) purports to empower the holder of the floating charge to make an appointment which would be the appointment of an administrative receiver within the meaning given by section 29(2), or
(d) purports to empower the holder of a floating charge in Scotland to appoint a receiver who on appointment would be an administrative receiver.

(3) For the purposes of sub-paragraph (1) a person is the holder of a qualifying floating charge in respect of a company's property if he holds one or more debentures of the company secured—
(a) by a qualifying floating charge which relates to the whole or substantially the whole of the company's property,
(b) by a number of qualifying floating charges which together relate to the whole or substantially the whole of the company's property, or
(c) by charges and other forms of security which together relate to the whole or substantially the whole of the company's property and at least one of which is a qualifying floating charge.

Restrictions on power to appoint

15. (1) A person may not appoint an administrator under paragraph 14 unless—

(a) he has given at least two business days' written notice to the holder of any prior floating charge which satisfies paragraph 14(2), or
(b) the holder of any prior floating charge which satisfies paragraph 14(2) has consented in writing to the making of the appointment.

(2) One floating charge is prior to another for the purposes of this paragraph if—
(a) it was created first, or
(b) it is to be treated as having priority in accordance with an agreement to which the holder of each floating charge was party.

(3) Sub-paragraph (2) shall have effect in relation to Scotland as if the following were substituted for paragraph (a)—

"(a) it has priority of ranking in accordance with section 464(4)(b) of the Companies Act 1985 (c 6),

16. An administrator may not be appointed under paragraph 14 while a floating charge on which the appointment relies is not enforceable.

17. An administrator of a company may not be appointed under paragraph 14 if—
(a) a provisional liquidator of the company has been appointed under section 135, or
(b) an administrative receiver of the company is in office.

Notice of appointment

18. (1) A person who appoints an administrator of a company under paragraph 14 shall file with the court—
(a) a notice of appointment, and
(b) such other documents as may be prescribed.

(2) The notice of appointment must include a statutory declaration by or on behalf of the person who makes the appointment—
(a) that the person is the holder of a qualifying floating charge in respect of the company's property,
(b) that each floating charge relied on in making the appointment is (or was) enforceable on the date of the appointment, and
(c) that the appointment is in accordance with this Schedule.

(3) The notice of appointment must identify the administrator and must be accompanied by a statement by the administrator—
(a) that he consents to the appointment,
(b) that in his opinion the purpose of administration is reasonably likely to be achieved, and
(c) giving such other information and opinions as may be prescribed.

(4) For the purpose of a statement under sub-paragraph (3) an administrator may rely on information supplied by directors of the company (unless he has reason to doubt its accuracy).

(5) The notice of appointment and any document accompanying it must be in the prescribed form.

(6) A statutory declaration under sub-paragraph (2) must be made during the prescribed period.

(7) A person commits an offence if in a statutory declaration under sub-paragraph (2) he makes a statement—
(a) which is false, and
(b) which he does not reasonably believe to be true.

Commencement of appointment

19. The appointment of an administrator under paragraph 14 takes effect when the requirements of paragraph 18 are satisfied.

20. A person who appoints an administrator under paragraph 14—
(a) shall notify the administrator and such other persons as may be prescribed as soon as is reasonably practicable after the requirements of paragraph 18 are satisfied, and
(b) commits an offence if he fails without reasonable excuse to comply with paragraph (a).

Invalid appointment: indemnity

21. (1) This paragraph applies where—
(a) a person purports to appoint an administrator under paragraph 14, and
(b) the appointment is discovered to be invalid.

(2) The court may order the person who purported to make the appointment to indemnify the person appointed against liability which arises solely by reason of the appointment's invalidity.

APPOINTMENT OF ADMINISTRATOR BY COMPANY OR DIRECTORS

Power to appoint

22. (1) A company may appoint an administrator.

(2) The directors of a company may appoint an administrator.

Restrictions on power to appoint

23. (1) This paragraph applies where an administrator of a company is appointed—
(a) under paragraph 22, or

(b) on an administration application made by the company or its directors.

(2) An administrator of the company may not be appointed under paragraph 22 during the period of 12 months beginning with the date on which the appointment referred to in sub-paragraph (1) ceases to have effect.

24. (1) If a moratorium for a company under Schedule A1 ends on a date when no voluntary arrangement is in force in respect of the company, this paragraph applies for the period of 12 months beginning with that date.

(2) This paragraph also applies for the period of 12 months beginning with the date on which a voluntary arrangement in respect of a company ends if—

(a) the arrangement was made during a moratorium for the company under Schedule A1, and

(b) the arrangement ends prematurely (within the meaning of section 7B).

(3) While this paragraph applies, an administrator of the company may not be appointed under paragraph 22.

25. An administrator of a company may not be appointed under paragraph 22 if—

(a) a petition for the winding up of the company has been presented and is not yet disposed of,

(b) an administration application has been made and is not yet disposed of, or

(c) an administrative receiver of the company is in office.

[25A. (1) Paragraph 25(a) does not prevent the appointment of an administrator of a company if the petition for the winding up of the company was presented after the person proposing to make the appointment filed the notice of intention to appoint with the court under paragraph 27.

(2) But sub-paragraph (1) does not apply if the petition was presented under a provision mentioned in paragraph 42(4).]

Notice of intention to appoint

26. (1) A person who proposes to make an appointment under paragraph 22 shall give at least five business days' written notice to—

(a) any person who is or may be entitled to appoint an administrative receiver of the company, and

(b) any person who is or may be entitled to appoint an administrator of the company under paragraph 14.

(2) A person who [gives notice of intention to appoint under sub-paragraph (1)] shall also give such notice as may be prescribed to such other persons as may be prescribed.

(3) A notice under this paragraph must—

(a) identify the proposed administrator, and

(b) be in the prescribed form.

27. (1) A person who gives notice of intention to appoint under paragraph 26 shall file with the court as soon as is reasonably practicable a copy of—

(a) the notice, and

(b) any document accompanying it.

(2) The copy filed under sub-paragraph (1) must be accompanied by a statutory declaration made by or on behalf of the person who proposes to make the appointment—

(a) that the company is or is likely to become unable to pay its debts,

(b) that the company is not in liquidation, and

(c) that, so far as the person making the statement is able to ascertain, the appointment is not prevented by paragraphs 23 to 25, and

(d) to such additional effect, and giving such information, as may be prescribed.

(3) A statutory declaration under sub-paragraph (2) must—

(a) be in the prescribed form, and

(b) be made during the prescribed period.

(4) A person commits an offence if in a statutory declaration under sub-paragraph (2) he makes a statement—

(a) which is false, and

(b) which he does not reasonably believe to be true.

28. (1) An appointment may not be made under paragraph 22 unless the person who makes the appointment has complied with any requirement of paragraphs 26 and 27 and—

(a) the period of notice specified in paragraph 26(1) has expired, or

(b) each person to whom notice has been given under paragraph 26(1) has consented in writing to the making of the appointment.

(2) An appointment may not be made under paragraph 22 after the period of ten business days beginning with the date on which the notice of intention to appoint is filed under paragraph 27(1).

Notice of appointment

29. (1) A person who appoints an administrator of a company under paragraph 22 shall file with the court—

(a) a notice of appointment, and

(b) such other documents as may be prescribed.

(2) The notice of appointment must include a statutory declaration by or on behalf of the person who makes the appointment—

(a) that the person is entitled to make an appointment under paragraph 22,

(b) that the appointment is in accordance with this Schedule, and

(c) that, so far as the person making the statement is able to ascertain, the statements made and information given in the statutory declaration filed with the notice of intention to appoint remain accurate.

(3) The notice of appointment must identify the administrator and must be accompanied by a statement by the administrator—

(a) that he consents to the appointment,

(b) that in his opinion the purpose of administration is reasonably likely to be achieved, and

(c) giving such other information and opinions as may be prescribed.

(4) For the purpose of a statement under sub-paragraph (3) an administrator may rely on information supplied by directors of the company (unless he has reason to doubt its accuracy).

(5) The notice of appointment and any document accompanying it must be in the prescribed form.

(6) A statutory declaration under sub-paragraph (2) must be made during the prescribed period.

(7) A person commits an offence if in a statutory declaration under sub-paragraph (2) he makes a statement—

(a) which is false, and

(b) which he does not reasonably believe to be true.

30. In a case in which no person is entitled to notice of intention to appoint under paragraph 26(1) (and paragraph 28 therefore does not apply)—

(a) the statutory declaration accompanying the notice of appointment must include the statements and information required under paragraph 27(2), and

(b) paragraph 29(2)(c) shall not apply.

Commencement of appointment

31. The appointment of an administrator under paragraph 22 takes effect when the requirements of paragraph 29 are satisfied.

32. A person who appoints an administrator under paragraph 22—

(a) shall notify the administrator and such other persons as may be prescribed as soon as is reasonably practicable after the requirements of paragraph 29 are satisfied, and

(b) commits an offence if he fails without reasonable excuse to comply with paragraph (a).

33. If before the requirements of paragraph 29 are satisfied the company enters administration by virtue of an administration order or an appointment under paragraph 14—

(a) the appointment under paragraph 22 shall not take effect, and

(b) paragraph 32 shall not apply.

Invalid appointment: indemnity

34. (1) This paragraph applies where—

(a) a person purports to appoint an administrator under paragraph 22, and

(b) the appointment is discovered to be invalid.

(2) The court may order the person who purported to make the appointment to indemnify the person appointed against liability which arises solely by reason of the appointment's invalidity.

ADMINISTRATION APPLICATION—SPECIAL CASES

Application by holder of floating charge

35. (1) This paragraph applies where an administration application in respect of a company—

(a) is made by the holder of a qualifying floating charge in respect of the company's property, and

(b) includes a statement that the application is made in reliance on this paragraph.

(2) The court may make an administration order—

(a) whether or not satisfied that the company is or is likely to become unable to pay its debts, but

(b) only if satisfied that the applicant could appoint an administrator under paragraph 14.

Intervention by holder of floating charge

36. (1) This paragraph applies where—

(a) an administration application in respect of a company is made by a person who is not the holder of a qualifying floating charge in respect of the company's property, and

(b) the holder of a qualifying floating charge in respect of the company's property applies to the court to have a specified person appointed as administrator (and not the person specified by the administration applicant).

(2) The court shall grant an application under sub-paragraph (1)(b) unless the court thinks it right to refuse the application because of the particular circumstances of the case.

Application where company in liquidation

37. (1) This paragraph applies where the holder of a qualifying floating charge in respect of a company's property could appoint an administrator under paragraph 14 but for paragraph 8(1)(b).

(2) The holder of the qualifying floating charge may make an administration application.

(3) If the court makes an administration order on hearing an application made by virtue of sub-paragraph (2)—

(a) the court shall discharge the winding-up order,
(b) the court shall make provision for such matters as may be prescribed,
(c) the court may make other consequential provision,
(d) the court shall specify which of the powers under this Schedule are to be exercisable by the administrator, and
(e) this Schedule shall have effect with such modifications as the court may specify.

38. (1) The liquidator of a company may make an administration application.

(2) If the court makes an administration order on hearing an application made by virtue of sub-paragraph (1)—

(a) the court shall discharge any winding-up order in respect of the company,
(b) the court shall make provision for such matters as may be prescribed,
(c) the court may make other consequential provision,
(d) the court shall specify which of the powers under this Schedule are to be exercisable by the administrator, and
(e) this Schedule shall have effect with such modifications as the court may specify.

Effect of administrative receivership

39. (1) Where there is an administrative receiver of a company the court must dismiss an administration application in respect of the company unless—

(a) the person by or on behalf of whom the receiver was appointed consents to the making of the administration order,
(b) the court thinks that the security by virtue of which the receiver was appointed would be liable to be released or discharged under sections 238 to 240 (transaction at undervalue and preference) if an administration order were made,
(c) the court thinks that the security by virtue of which the receiver was appointed would be avoided under section 245 (avoidance of floating charge) if an administration order were made, or
(d) the court thinks that the security by virtue of which the receiver was appointed would be challengeable under section 242 (gratuitous alienations) or 243 (unfair preferences) or under any rule of law in Scotland.

(2) Sub-paragraph (1) applies whether the administrative receiver is appointed before or after the making of the administration application.

EFFECT OF ADMINISTRATION

Dismissal of pending winding-up petition

40. (1) A petition for the winding up of a company—

(a) shall be dismissed on the making of an administration order in respect of the company, and
(b) shall be suspended while the company is in administration following an appointment under paragraph 14.

(2) Sub-paragraph (1)(b) does not apply to a petition presented under—

(a) section 124A (public interest),
[(aa) section 124B (SEs),] or
(b) section 367 of the Financial Services and Markets Act 2000 (c 8) (petition by [Financial Conduct Authority or Prudential Regulation Authority]).

(3) Where an administrator becomes aware that a petition was presented under a provision referred to in sub-paragraph (2) before his appointment, he shall apply to the court for directions under paragraph 63.

Dismissal of administrative or other receiver

41. (1) When an administration order takes effect in respect of a company any administrative receiver of the company shall vacate office.

(2) Where a company is in administration, any receiver of part of the company's property shall vacate office if the administrator requires him to.

(3) Where an administrative receiver or receiver vacates office under sub-paragraph (1) or (2)—

(a) his remuneration shall be charged on and paid out of any property of the company which was in his custody or under his control immediately before he vacated office, and
(b) he need not take any further steps under section 40 or 59.

(4) In the application of sub-paragraph (3)(a)—

(a) "remuneration" includes expenses properly incurred and any indemnity to which the administrative receiver or receiver is entitled out of the assets of the company,
(b) the charge imposed takes priority over security held by the person by whom or on whose behalf the administrative receiver or receiver was appointed, and
(c) the provision for payment is subject to paragraph 43.

Moratorium on insolvency proceedings

42. (1) This paragraph applies to a company in administration.

(2) No resolution may be passed for the winding up of the company.

(3) No order may be made for the winding up of the company.

(4) Sub-paragraph (3) does not apply to an order made on a petition presented under—

(a) section 124A (public interest),

[(aa) section 124B (SEs),] or

(b) section 367 of the Financial Services and Markets Act 2000 (c 8) (petition by [Financial Conduct Authority or Prudential Regulation Authority]).

(5) If a petition presented under a provision referred to in sub-paragraph (4) comes to the attention of the administrator, he shall apply to the court for directions under paragraph 63.

Moratorium on other legal process

43. (1) This paragraph applies to a company in administration.

(2) No step may be taken to enforce security over the company's property except—

(a) with the consent of the administrator, or

(b) with the permission of the court.

(3) No step may be taken to repossess goods in the company's possession under a hire-purchase agreement except—

(a) with the consent of the administrator, or

(b) with the permission of the court.

(4) A landlord may not exercise a right of forfeiture by peaceable re-entry in relation to premises let to the company except—

(a) with the consent of the administrator, or

(b) with the permission of the court.

(5) In Scotland, a landlord may not exercise a right of irritancy in relation to premises let to the company except—

(a) with the consent of the administrator, or

(b) with the permission of the court.

(6) No legal process (including legal proceedings, execution, distress and diligence) may be instituted or continued against the company or property of the company except—

(a) with the consent of the administrator, or

(b) with the permission of the court.

[(6A) An administrative receiver of the company may not be appointed.]

(7) Where the court gives permission for a transaction under this paragraph it may impose a condition on or a requirement in connection with the transaction.

(8) In this paragraph "landlord" includes a person to whom rent is payable.

Interim moratorium

44. (1) This paragraph applies where an administration application in respect of a company has been made and—

(a) the application has not yet been granted or dismissed, or

(b) the application has been granted but the administration order has not yet taken effect.

(2) This paragraph also applies from the time when a copy of notice of intention to appoint an administrator under paragraph 14 is filed with the court until—

(a) the appointment of the administrator takes effect, or

(b) the period of five business days beginning with the date of filing expires without an administrator having been appointed.

(3) Sub-paragraph (2) has effect in relation to a notice of intention to appoint only if it is in the prescribed form.

(4) This paragraph also applies from the time when a copy of notice of intention to appoint an administrator is filed with the court under paragraph 27(1) until—

(a) the appointment of the administrator takes effect, or

(b) the period specified in paragraph 28(2) expires without an administrator having been appointed.

(5) The provisions of paragraphs 42 and 43 shall apply (ignoring any reference to the consent of the administrator).

(6) If there is an administrative receiver of the company when the administration application is made, the provisions of paragraphs 42 and 43 shall not begin to apply by virtue of this paragraph until the person by or on behalf of whom the receiver was appointed consents to the making of the administration order.

(7) This paragraph does not prevent or require the permission of the court for—

(a) the presentation of a petition for the winding up of the company under a provision mentioned in paragraph 42(4),

(b) the appointment of an administrator under paragraph 14,

(c) the appointment of an administrative receiver of the company, or

(d) the carrying out by an administrative receiver (whenever appointed) of his functions.

Publicity

[**45.** (1) While a company is in administration, every business document issued by or on behalf of the company or the administrator, and all the company's websites, must state—

(a) the name of the administrator, and
(b) that the affairs, business and property of the company are being managed by the administrator.

(2) Any of the following persons commits an offence if without reasonable excuse the person authorises or permits a contravention of sub-paragraph (1)—

(a) the administrator,
(b) an officer of the company, and
(c) the company.

(3) In sub-paragraph (1) "business document" means—

(a) an invoice,
(b) an order for goods or services,
(c) a business letter, and
(d) an order form,

whether in hard copy, electronic or any other form.]

PROCESS OF ADMINISTRATION

Announcement of administrator's appointment

46. (1) This paragraph applies where a person becomes the administrator of a company.

(2) As soon as is reasonably practicable the administrator shall—

(a) send a notice of his appointment to the company, and
(b) publish a notice of his appointment in the prescribed manner.

(3) As soon as is reasonably practicable the administrator shall—

(a) obtain a list of the company's creditors, and
(b) send a notice of his appointment to each creditor of whose claim and address he is aware.

(4) The administrator shall send a notice of his appointment to the registrar of companies before the end of the period of 7 days beginning with the date specified in sub-paragraph (6).

(5) The administrator shall send a notice of his appointment to such persons as may be prescribed before the end of the prescribed period beginning with the date specified in sub-paragraph (6).

(6) The date for the purpose of sub-paragraphs (4) and (5) is—

(a) in the case of an administrator appointed by administration order, the date of the order,
(b) in the case of an administrator appointed under paragraph 14, the date on which he receives notice under paragraph 20, and
(c) in the case of an administrator appointed under paragraph 22, the date on which he receives notice under paragraph 32.

(7) The court may direct that sub-paragraph (3)(b) or (5)—

(a) shall not apply, or
(b) shall apply with the substitution of a different period.

(8) A notice under this paragraph must—

(a) contain the prescribed information, and
(b) be in the prescribed form.

(9) An administrator commits an offence if he fails without reasonable excuse to comply with a requirement of this paragraph.

Statement of company's affairs

47. (1) As soon as is reasonably practicable after appointment the administrator of a company shall by notice in the prescribed form require one or more relevant persons to provide the administrator with a statement of the affairs of the company.

(2) The statement must—

(a) be verified by a statement of truth in accordance with Civil Procedure Rules,
(b) be in the prescribed form,
(c) give particulars of the company's property, debts and liabilities,
(d) give the names and addresses of the company's creditors,
(e) specify the security held by each creditor,
(f) give the date on which each security was granted, and
(g) contain such other information as may be prescribed.

(3) In sub-paragraph (1) "relevant person" means—

(a) a person who is or has been an officer of the company,
(b) a person who took part in the formation of the company during the period of one year ending with the date on which the company enters administration,
(c) a person employed by the company during that period, and
(d) a person who is or has been during that period an officer or employee of a company which is or has been during that year an officer of the company.

(4) For the purpose of sub-paragraph (3) a reference to employment is a reference to employment through a contract of employment or a contract for services.

(5) In Scotland, a statement of affairs under sub-paragraph (1) must be a statutory declaration made in accordance with the Statutory Declarations Act 1835 (c 62) (and sub-paragraph (2)(a) shall not apply).

48. (1) A person required to submit a statement of affairs must do so before the end of the period of 11 days beginning with the day on which he receives notice of the requirement.

(2) The administrator may—

(a) revoke a requirement under paragraph 47(1), or

(b) extend the period specified in sub-paragraph (1) (whether before or after expiry).

(3) If the administrator refuses a request to act under sub-paragraph (2)—

(a) the person whose request is refused may apply to the court, and

(b) the court may take action of a kind specified in sub-paragraph (2).

(4) A person commits an offence if he fails without reasonable excuse to comply with a requirement under paragraph 47(1).

Administrator's proposals

49. (1) The administrator of a company shall make a statement setting out proposals for achieving the purpose of administration.

(2) A statement under sub-paragraph (1) must, in particular—

(a) deal with such matters as may be prescribed, and

(b) where applicable, explain why the administrator thinks that the objective mentioned in paragraph 3(1)(a) or (b) cannot be achieved.

(3) Proposals under this paragraph may include—

(a) a proposal for a voluntary arrangement under Part I of this Act (although this paragraph is without prejudice to section 4(3));

(b) a proposal for a compromise or arrangement to be sanctioned under [Part 26 of the Companies Act 2006 (arrangements and reconstructions)].

(4) The administrator shall send a copy of the statement of his proposals—

(a) to the registrar of companies,

(b) to every creditor of the company[, other than an opted-out creditor,] of whose claim and address he is aware, and

(c) to every member of the company of whose address he is aware.

(5) The administrator shall comply with sub-paragraph (4)—

(a) as soon as is reasonably practicable after the company enters administration, and

(b) in any event, before the end of the period of eight weeks beginning with the day on which the company enters administration.

(6) The administrator shall be taken to comply with sub-paragraph (4)(c) if he publishes in the prescribed manner a notice undertaking to provide a copy of the statement of proposals free of charge to any member of the company who applies in writing to a specified address.

(7) An administrator commits an offence if he fails without reasonable excuse to comply with sub-paragraph (5).

(8) A period specified in this paragraph may be varied in accordance with paragraph 107.

Creditors' meeting

***50.** (1) In this Schedule "creditors' meeting" means a meeting of creditors of a company summoned by the administrator—*

(a) in the prescribed manner, and

(b) giving the prescribed period of notice to every creditor of the company of whose claim and address he is aware.

(2) A period prescribed under sub-paragraph (1)(b) may be varied in accordance with paragraph 107.

(3) A creditors' meeting shall be conducted in accordance with the rules.

[Consideration of administrator's proposals by creditors]

51. [(1) The administrator must seek a decision from the company's creditors as to whether they approve the proposals set out in the statement made under paragraph 49(1).

(2) The initial decision date for that decision must be within the period of 10 weeks beginning with the day on which the company enters administration.

(3) The "initial decision date" for that decision—

(a) if the decision is initially sought using the deemed consent procedure, is the date on which a decision will be made if the creditors by that procedure approve the proposals, and

(b) if the decision is initially sought using a qualifying decision procedure, is the date on or before which a decision will be made if it is made by that qualifying decision procedure (assuming that date does not change after the procedure is instigated).]

(4) A period specified in this paragraph may be varied in accordance with paragraph 107.

(5) An administrator commits an offence if he fails without reasonable excuse to comply with a requirement of this paragraph.

52. (1) Paragraph 51(1) shall not apply where the statement of proposals states that the administrator thinks—

(a) that the company has sufficient property to enable each creditor of the company to be paid in full,
(b) that the company has insufficient property to enable a distribution to be made to unsecured creditors other than by virtue of section 176A(2)(a), or
(c) that neither of the objectives specified in paragraph 3(1)(a) and (b) can be achieved.

(2) But the administrator shall [seek a decision from the company's creditors as to whether they approve the proposals set out in the statement made under paragraph 49(1) if requested to do so]—
(a) by creditors of the company whose debts amount to at least 10% of the total debts of the company,
(b) in the prescribed manner, and
(c) in the prescribed period.

[(3) Where a decision is sought by virtue of sub-paragraph (2) the initial decision date (as defined in paragraph 51(3)) must be within the prescribed period.]

(4) The period prescribed under sub-paragraph (3) may be varied in accordance with paragraph 107.

[Creditors' decision]

53. [(1) The company's creditors may approve the administrator's proposals—
(a) without modification, or
(b) with modification to which the administrator consents.]

(2) [The] administrator shall as soon as is reasonably practicable report any decision taken [by the company's creditors] to—
(a) the court,
(b) the registrar of companies, and
(c) such other persons as may be prescribed.

(3) An administrator commits an offence if he fails without reasonable excuse to comply with sub-paragraph (2).

Revision of administrator's proposals

54. (1) This paragraph applies where—
(a) an administrator's proposals have been approved (with or without modification) [by the company's creditors],
(b) the administrator proposes a revision to the proposals, and
(c) the administrator thinks that the proposed revision is substantial.

(2) The administrator shall—
(a) summon a creditors' meeting,
(b) send a statement in the prescribed form of the proposed revision *with the notice of the meeting sent* to each creditor [who is not an opted-out creditor],
(c) send a copy of the statement, within the prescribed period, to each member of the company of whose address he is aware, and
[(d) seek a decision from the company's creditors as to whether they approve the proposed revision.]

(3) The administrator shall be taken to have complied with sub-paragraph (2)(c) if he publishes a notice undertaking to provide a copy of the statement free of charge to any member of the company who applies in writing to a specified address.

(4) A notice under sub-paragraph (3) must be published—
(a) in the prescribed manner, and
(b) within the prescribed period.

[(5) The company's creditors may approve the proposed revision—
(a) without modification, or
(b) with modification to which the administrator consents.]

(6) [The] administrator shall as soon as is reasonably practicable report any decision taken [by the company's creditors] to—
(a) the court,
(b) the registrar of companies, and
(c) such other persons as may be prescribed.

(7) An administrator commits an offence if he fails without reasonable excuse to comply with sub-paragraph (6).

Failure to obtain approval of administrator's proposals

55. [(1) This paragraph applies where an administrator—
(a) reports to the court under paragraph 53 that a company's creditors have failed to approve the administrator's proposals, or
(b) reports to the court under paragraph 54 that a company's creditors have failed to approve a revision of the administrator's proposals.]

(2) The court may—
(a) provide that the appointment of an administrator shall cease to have effect from a specified time;
(b) adjourn the hearing conditionally or unconditionally;
(c) make an interim order;
(d) make an order on a petition for winding up suspended by virtue of paragraph 40(1)(b);

(e) make any other order (including an order making consequential provision) that the court thinks appropriate.

Further creditors' [decisions]

56. (1) The administrator of a company shall [seek a decision from the company's creditors on a matter] if—

(a) it is requested in the prescribed manner by creditors of the company whose debts amount to at least 10% of the total debts of the company, or

(b) he is directed by the court to [do so].

(2) An administrator commits an offence if he fails without reasonable excuse to [seek a decision from the company's creditors on a matter] as required by this paragraph.

Creditors' committee

57. (1) [The company's creditors may, in accordance with the rules,] establish a creditors' committee.

(2) A creditors' committee shall carry out functions conferred on it by or under this Act.

(3) A creditors' committee may require the administrator—

(a) to attend on the committee at any reasonable time of which he is given at least seven days' notice, and

(b) to provide the committee with information about the exercise of his functions.

Correspondence instead of creditors' meeting

58. *(1) Anything which is required or permitted by or under this Schedule to be done at a creditors' meeting may be done by correspondence between the administrator and creditors—*

(a) in accordance with the rules, and

(b) subject to any prescribed condition.

(2) A reference in this Schedule to anything done at a creditors' meeting includes a reference to anything done in the course of correspondence in reliance on sub-paragraph (1).

(3) A requirement to hold a creditors' meeting is satisfied by conducting correspondence in accordance with this paragraph.

FUNCTIONS OF ADMINISTRATOR

General powers

59. (1) The administrator of a company may do anything necessary or expedient for the management of the affairs, business and property of the company.

(2) A provision of this Schedule which expressly permits the administrator to do a specified thing is without prejudice to the generality of sub-paragraph (1).

(3) A person who deals with the administrator of a company in good faith and for value need not inquire whether the administrator is acting within his powers.

60. [(1)] The administrator of a company has the powers specified in Schedule 1 to this Act.

[(2) But the power to sell, hire out or otherwise dispose of property is subject to any regulations that may be made under paragraph 60A.]

[60A. (1) The Secretary of State may by regulations make provision for—

(a) prohibiting, or

(b) imposing requirements or conditions in relation to,

the disposal, hiring out or sale of property of a company by the administrator to a connected person in circumstances specified in the regulations.

(2) Regulations under this paragraph may in particular require the approval of, or provide for the imposition of requirements or conditions by—

(a) creditors of the company,

(b) the court, or

(c) a person of a description specified in the regulations.

(3) In sub-paragraph (1), "connected person", in relation to a company, means—

(a) a relevant person in relation to the company, or

(b) a company connected with the company.

(4) For the purposes of sub-paragraph (3)—

(a) "relevant person", in relation to a company, means—

(i) a director or other officer, or shadow director, of the company;

(ii) a non-employee associate of such a person;

(iii) a non-employee associate of the company;

(b) a company is connected with another if any relevant person of one is or has been a relevant person of the other.

(5) In sub-paragraph (4), "non-employee associate" of a person means a person who is an associate of that person otherwise than by virtue of employing or being employed by that person.

(6) Subsection (10) of section 435 (extended definition of company) applies for the purposes of sub-paragraphs (3) to (5) as it applies for the purposes of that section.

(7) Regulations under this paragraph may—

(a) make different provision for different purposes;
(b) make incidental, consequential, supplemental and transitional provision.

(8) Regulations under this paragraph are to be made by statutory instrument.

(9) Regulations under this paragraph may not be made unless a draft of the statutory instrument containing the regulations has been laid before Parliament and approved by a resolution of each House of Parliament.

(10) This paragraph expires at the end of the period of 5 years beginning with the day on which it comes into force unless the power conferred by it is exercised during that period.]

61. The administrator of a company—
(a) may remove a director of the company, and
(b) may appoint a director of the company (whether or not to fill a vacancy).

62. The administrator of a company [may—
(a) call a meeting of members of the company;
(b) seek a decision on any matter from the company's creditors.]

63. The administrator of a company may apply to the court for directions in connection with his functions.

64. (1) A company in administration or an officer of a company in administration may not exercise a management power without the consent of the administrator.

(2) For the purpose of sub-paragraph (1)—
(a) "management power" means a power which could be exercised so as to interfere with the exercise of the administrator's powers,
(b) it is immaterial whether the power is conferred by an enactment or an instrument, and
(c) consent may be general or specific.

Distribution

65. (1) The administrator of a company may make a distribution to a creditor of the company.

(2) Section 175 shall apply in relation to a distribution under this paragraph as it applies in relation to a winding up.

(3) A payment may not be made by way of distribution under this paragraph to a creditor of the company who is neither secured nor preferential [unless—
(a) the distribution is made by virtue of section 176A(2)(a), or
(b)] the court gives permission.

66. The administrator of a company may make a payment otherwise than in accordance with paragraph 65 or paragraph 13 of Schedule 1 if he thinks it likely to assist achievement of the purpose of administration.

General duties

67. The administrator of a company shall on his appointment take custody or control of all the property to which he thinks the company is entitled.

68. (1) Subject to sub-paragraph (2), the administrator of a company shall manage its affairs, business and property in accordance with—
(a) any proposals approved under paragraph 53,
(b) any revision of those proposals which is made by him and which he does not consider substantial, and
(c) any revision of those proposals approved under paragraph 54.

(2) If the court gives directions to the administrator of a company in connection with any aspect of his management of the company's affairs, business or property, the administrator shall comply with the directions.

(3) The court may give directions under sub-paragraph (2) only if—
(a) no proposals have been approved under paragraph 53,
(b) the directions are consistent with any proposals or revision approved under paragraph 53 or 54,
(c) the court thinks the directions are required in order to reflect a change in circumstances since the approval of proposals or a revision under paragraph 53 or 54, or
(d) the court thinks the directions are desirable because of a misunderstanding about proposals or a revision approved under paragraph 53 or 54.

Administrator as agent of company

69. In exercising his functions under this Schedule the administrator of a company acts as its agent.

Charged property: floating charge

70. (1) The administrator of a company may dispose of or take action relating to property which is subject to a floating charge as if it were not subject to the charge.

(2) Where property is disposed of in reliance on sub-paragraph (1) the holder of the floating charge shall have the same priority in respect of acquired property as he had in respect of the property disposed of.

(3) In sub-paragraph (2) "acquired property" means property of the company which directly or indirectly represents the property disposed of.

Charged property: non-floating charge

71. (1) The court may by order enable the administrator of a company to dispose of property which is subject to a security (other than a floating charge) as if it were not subject to the security.

(2) An order under sub-paragraph (1) may be made only—

(a) on the application of the administrator, and

(b) where the court thinks that disposal of the property would be likely to promote the purpose of administration in respect of the company.

(3) An order under this paragraph is subject to the condition that there be applied towards discharging the sums secured by the security—

(a) the net proceeds of disposal of the property, and

(b) any additional money required to be added to the net proceeds so as to produce the amount determined by the court as the net amount which would be realised on a sale of the property at market value.

(4) If an order under this paragraph relates to more than one security, application of money under sub-paragraph (3) shall be in the order of the priorities of the securities.

(5) An administrator who makes a successful application for an order under this paragraph shall send a copy of the order to the registrar of companies before the end of the period of 14 days starting with the date of the order.

(6) An administrator commits an offence if he fails to comply with sub-paragraph (5) without reasonable excuse.

Hire-purchase property

72. (1) The court may by order enable the administrator of a company to dispose of goods which are in the possession of the company under a hire-purchase agreement as if all the rights of the owner under the agreement were vested in the company.

(2) An order under sub-paragraph (1) may be made only—

(a) on the application of the administrator, and

(b) where the court thinks that disposal of the goods would be likely to promote the purpose of administration in respect of the company.

(3) An order under this paragraph is subject to the condition that there be applied towards discharging the sums payable under the hire-purchase agreement—

(a) the net proceeds of disposal of the goods, and

(b) any additional money required to be added to the net proceeds so as to produce the amount determined by the court as the net amount which would be realised on a sale of the goods at market value.

(4) An administrator who makes a successful application for an order under this paragraph shall send a copy of the order to the registrar of companies before the end of the period of 14 days starting with the date of the order.

(5) An administrator commits an offence if he fails without reasonable excuse to comply with sub-paragraph (4).

Protection for secured or preferential creditor

73. (1) An administrator's statement of proposals under paragraph 49 may not include any action which—

(a) affects the right of a secured creditor of the company to enforce his security,

(b) would result in a preferential debt of the company being paid otherwise than in priority to its non-preferential debts, . . .

[(bb) would result in an ordinary preferential debt of the company being paid otherwise than in priority to any secondary preferential debts that it may have,]

(c) would result in one preferential creditor of the company being paid a smaller proportion of [an ordinary preferential debt] than another[, or

(d) would result in one preferential creditor of the company being paid a smaller proportion of a secondary preferential debt than another].

(2) Sub-paragraph (1) does not apply to—

(a) action to which the relevant creditor consents,

(b) a proposal for a voluntary arrangement under Part I of this Act (although this sub-paragraph is without prejudice to section 4(3)), . . .

(c) a proposal for a compromise or arrangement to be sanctioned under [Part 26 of the Companies Act 2006 (arrangements and reconstructions)]; [or

(d) a proposal for a cross-border merger within the meaning of regulation 2 of the Companies (Cross-Border Mergers) Regulations 2007].

(3) The reference to a statement of proposals in sub-paragraph (1) includes a reference to a statement as revised or modified.

Challenge to administrator's conduct of company

74. (1) A creditor or member of a company in administration may apply to the court claiming that—

(a) the administrator is acting or has acted so as unfairly to harm the interests of the applicant (whether alone or in common with some or all other members or creditors), or
(b) the administrator proposes to act in a way which would unfairly harm the interests of the applicant (whether alone or in common with some or all other members or creditors).

(2) A creditor or member of a company in administration may apply to the court claiming that the administrator is not performing his functions as quickly or as efficiently as is reasonably practicable.

(3) The court may—
(a) grant relief;
(b) dismiss the application;
(c) adjourn the hearing conditionally or unconditionally;
(d) make an interim order;
(e) make any other order it thinks appropriate.

(4) In particular, an order under this paragraph may—
(a) regulate the administrator's exercise of his functions;
(b) require the administrator to do or not do a specified thing;
[(c) require a decision of the company's creditors to be sought on a matter;]
(d) provide for the appointment of an administrator to cease to have effect;
(e) make consequential provision.

(5) An order may be made on a claim under sub-paragraph (1) whether or not the action complained of—
(a) is within the administrator's powers under this Schedule;
(b) was taken in reliance on an order under paragraph 71 or 72.

(6) An order may not be made under this paragraph if it would impede or prevent the implementation of—
(a) a voluntary arrangement approved under Part I,
(b) a compromise or arrangement sanctioned under [Part 26 of the Companies Act 2006 (arrangements and reconstructions)], . . .
[(ba) a cross-border merger within the meaning of regulation 2 of the Companies (Cross-Border Mergers) Regulations 2007, or].
(c) proposals or a revision approved under paragraph 53 or 54 more than 28 days before the day on which the application for the order under this paragraph is made.

Misfeasance

75. (1) The court may examine the conduct of a person who—
(a) is or purports to be the administrator of a company, or
(b) has been or has purported to be the administrator of a company.

(2) An examination under this paragraph may be held only on the application of—
(a) the official receiver,
(b) the administrator of the company,
(c) the liquidator of the company,
(d) a creditor of the company, or
(e) a contributory of the company.

(3) An application under sub-paragraph (2) must allege that the administrator—
(a) has misapplied or retained money or other property of the company,
(b) has become accountable for money or other property of the company,
(c) has breached a fiduciary or other duty in relation to the company, or
(d) has been guilty of misfeasance.

(4) On an examination under this paragraph into a person's conduct the court may order him—
(a) to repay, restore or account for money or property;
(b) to pay interest;
(c) to contribute a sum to the company's property by way of compensation for breach of duty or misfeasance.

(5) In sub-paragraph (3) "administrator" includes a person who purports or has purported to be a company's administrator.

(6) An application under sub-paragraph (2) may be made in respect of an administrator who has been discharged under paragraph 98 only with the permission of the court.

ENDING ADMINISTRATION

Automatic end of administration

76. (1) The appointment of an administrator shall cease to have effect at the end of the period of one year beginning with the date on which it takes effect.

(2) But—
(a) on the application of an administrator the court may by order extend his term of office for a specified period, and
(b) an administrator's term of office may be extended for a specified period not exceeding [one year] by consent.

77. (1) An order of the court under paragraph 76—

(a) may be made in respect of an administrator whose term of office has already been extended by order or by consent, but
(b) may not be made after the expiry of the administrator's term of office.

(2) Where an order is made under paragraph 76 the administrator shall as soon as is reasonably practicable notify the registrar of companies.

(3) An administrator who fails without reasonable excuse to comply with sub-paragraph (2) commits an offence.

78. (1) In paragraph 76(2)(b) "consent" means consent of—
(a) each secured creditor of the company, and
[(b) if the company has unsecured debts, the unsecured creditors of the company.]

(2) But where the administrator has made a statement under paragraph 52(1)(b) "consent" means—
(a) consent of each secured creditor of the company, or
(b) if the administrator thinks that a distribution may be made to preferential creditors, consent of—
(i) each secured creditor of the company, and
[(ii) the preferential creditors of the company.]

[(2A) Whether the company's unsecured creditors or preferential creditors consent is to be determined by the administrator seeking a decision from those creditors as to whether they consent.]

(3) Consent for the purposes of paragraph 76(2)(b) may be—
(a) written, or
(b) signified at a creditors' meeting.

(4) An administrator's term of office—
(a) may be extended by consent only once,
(b) may not be extended by consent after extension by order of the court, and
(c) may not be extended by consent after expiry.

(5) Where an administrator's term of office is extended by consent he shall as soon as is reasonably practicable—
(a) file notice of the extension with the court, and
(b) notify the registrar of companies.

(6) An administrator who fails without reasonable excuse to comply with sub-paragraph (5) commits an offence.

Court ending administration on application of administrator

79. (1) On the application of the administrator of a company the court may provide for the appointment of an administrator of the company to cease to have effect from a specified time.

(2) The administrator of a company shall make an application under this paragraph if—
(a) he thinks the purpose of administration cannot be achieved in relation to the company,
(b) he thinks the company should not have entered administration, or
(c) [the company's creditors decide that he must] make an application under this paragraph.

(3) The administrator of a company shall make an application under this paragraph if—
(a) the administration is pursuant to an administration order, and
(b) the administrator thinks that the purpose of administration has been sufficiently achieved in relation to the company.

(4) On an application under this paragraph the court may—
(a) adjourn the hearing conditionally or unconditionally;
(b) dismiss the application;
(c) make an interim order;
(d) make any order it thinks appropriate (whether in addition to, in consequence of or instead of the order applied for).

Termination of administration where objective achieved

80. (1) This paragraph applies where an administrator of a company is appointed under paragraph 14 or 22.

(2) If the administrator thinks that the purpose of administration has been sufficiently achieved in relation to the company he may file a notice in the prescribed form—
(a) with the court, and
(b) with the registrar of companies.

(3) The administrator's appointment shall cease to have effect when the requirements of sub-paragraph (2) are satisfied.

(4) Where the administrator files a notice he shall within the prescribed period send a copy to every creditor of the company[, other than an opted-out creditor,] of whose claim and address he is aware.

(5) The rules may provide that the administrator is taken to have complied with sub-paragraph (4) if before the end of the prescribed period he publishes in the prescribed manner a notice undertaking to provide a copy of the notice under sub-paragraph (2) to any creditor of the company who applies in writing to a specified address.

(6) An administrator who fails without reasonable excuse to comply with sub-paragraph (4) commits an offence.

Court ending administration on application of creditor

81. (1) On the application of a creditor of a company the court may provide for the appointment of an administrator of the company to cease to have effect at a specified time.

(2) An application under this paragraph must allege an improper motive—

(a) in the case of an administrator appointed by administration order, on the part of the applicant for the order, or

(b) in any other case, on the part of the person who appointed the administrator.

(3) On an application under this paragraph the court may—

(a) adjourn the hearing conditionally or unconditionally;

(b) dismiss the application;

(c) make an interim order;

(d) make any order it thinks appropriate (whether in addition to, in consequence of or instead of the order applied for).

Public interest winding-up

82. (1) This paragraph applies where a winding-up order is made for the winding up of a company in administration on a petition presented under—

(a) section 124A (public interest),

[(aa) section 124B (SEs),] or

(b) section 367 of the Financial Services and Markets Act 2000 (c 8) (petition by [Financial Conduct Authority or Prudential Regulation Authority]).

(2) This paragraph also applies where a provisional liquidator of a company in administration is appointed following the presentation of a petition under any of the provisions listed in sub-paragraph (1).

(3) The court shall order—

(a) that the appointment of the administrator shall cease to have effect, or

(b) that the appointment of the administrator shall continue to have effect.

(4) If the court makes an order under sub-paragraph (3)(b) it may also—

(a) specify which of the powers under this Schedule are to be exercisable by the administrator, and

(b) order that this Schedule shall have effect in relation to the administrator with specified modifications.

Moving from administration to creditors' voluntary liquidation

83. (1) This paragraph applies in England and Wales where the administrator of a company thinks—

(a) that the total amount which each secured creditor of the company is likely to receive has been paid to him or set aside for him, and

(b) that a distribution will be made to unsecured creditors of the company (if there are any [which is not a distribution by virtue of section 176A(2)(a)]).

(2) This paragraph applies in Scotland where the administrator of a company thinks—

(a) that each secured creditor of the company will receive payment in respect of his debt, and

(b) that a distribution will be made to unsecured creditors (if there are any [which is not a distribution by virtue of section 176A(2)(a)]).

(3) The administrator may send to the registrar of companies a notice that this paragraph applies.

(4) On receipt of a notice under sub-paragraph (3) the registrar shall register it.

(5) If an administrator sends a notice under sub-paragraph (3) he shall as soon as is reasonably practicable—

(a) file a copy of the notice with the court, and

(b) send a copy of the notice to each creditor[, other than an opted-out creditor,] of whose claim and address he is aware.

(6) On the registration of a notice under sub-paragraph (3)—

(a) the appointment of an administrator in respect of the company shall cease to have effect, and

(b) the company shall be wound up as if a resolution for voluntary winding up under section 84 were passed on the day on which the notice is registered.

(7) The liquidator for the purposes of the winding up shall be—

(a) a person nominated by the creditors of the company in the prescribed manner and within the prescribed period, or

(b) if no person is nominated under paragraph (a), the administrator.

(8) In the application of Part IV to a winding up by virtue of this paragraph—

(a) section 85 shall not apply,

(b) section 86 shall apply as if the reference to the time of the passing of the resolution for voluntary winding up were a reference to the beginning of the date of registration of the notice under sub-paragraph (3),

(c) section 89 does not apply,

(d) sections *98,* 99 and 100 shall not apply,

(e) section 129 shall apply as if the reference to the time of the passing of the resolution for voluntary winding up were a reference to the beginning of the date of registration of the notice under sub-paragraph (3), and

(f) any creditors' committee which is in existence immediately before the company ceases to be in administration shall continue in existence after that time as if appointed as a liquidation committee under section 101.

Moving from administration to dissolution

84. (1) If the administrator of a company thinks that the company has no property which might permit a distribution to its creditors, he shall send a notice to that effect to the registrar of companies.

[(1A) Sub-paragraph (1B) applies where, immediately before the administrator sends the notice, there are EU insolvency proceedings open in respect of the company in one or more other member States.

(1B) The administrator must send to the registrar, with the notice, a statement—
- (a) identifying those proceedings,
- (b) identifying the member State liquidator appointed in each of those proceedings, and
- (c) indicating, in relation to each of those member State liquidators, whether that member State liquidator consents to the company being dissolved.]

(2) The court may on the application of the administrator of a company disapply sub-paragraph (1) in respect of the company.

(3) On receipt of a notice under sub-paragraph (1) [and any statement under sub-paragraph (1B)] the registrar shall register it [or them].

(4) On the registration of a notice in respect of a company under sub-paragraph (1) the appointment of an administrator of the company shall cease to have effect.

(5) If an administrator sends a notice under sub-paragraph (1) he shall as soon as is reasonably practicable—
- (a) file a copy of the notice with the court, and
- (b) send a copy of the notice to each creditor[, other than an opted-out creditor,] of whose claim and address he is aware.

(6) At the end of the period of three months beginning with the date of registration of a notice in respect of a company under sub-paragraph (1) the company is deemed to be dissolved [(except where sub-paragraph (6A) applies)].

[(6A) This sub-paragraph applies where a statement under sub-paragraph (1B) indicates that a member State liquidator does not consent to the company being dissolved.

(6B) Where sub-paragraph (6A) applies, the company is deemed to be dissolved at the end of the period of three months beginning with the date (if any) recorded in the register as the date on which the registrar was notified that—
- (a) all proceedings identified in the statement under sub-paragraph (1B) were closed, or
- (b) every member State liquidator appointed in those proceedings consented to the company being dissolved.]

(7) On an application in respect of a company by the administrator or another interested person the court may—
- (a) extend the period specified in sub-paragraph (6) [or (6B)],
- (b) suspend that period, or
- (c) disapply sub-paragraph (6) [or (6B)].

(8) Where an order is made under sub-paragraph (7) in respect of a company the administrator shall as soon as is reasonably practicable notify the registrar of companies.

(9) An administrator commits an offence if he fails without reasonable excuse to comply with sub-paragraph (5).

Discharge of administration order where administration ends

85. (1) This paragraph applies where—
- (a) the court makes an order under this Schedule providing for the appointment of an administrator of a company to cease to have effect, and
- (b) the administrator was appointed by administration order.

(2) The court shall discharge the administration order.

Notice to Companies Registrar where administration ends

86. (1) This paragraph applies where the court makes an order under this Schedule providing for the appointment of an administrator to cease to have effect.

(2) The administrator shall send a copy of the order to the registrar of companies within the period of 14 days beginning with the date of the order.

(3) An administrator who fails without reasonable excuse to comply with sub-paragraph (2) commits an offence.

REPLACING ADMINISTRATOR

Resignation of administrator

87. (1) An administrator may resign only in prescribed circumstances.

(2) Where an administrator may resign he may do so only—
- (a) in the case of an administrator appointed by administration order, by notice in writing to the court,
- (b) in the case of an administrator appointed under paragraph 14, by notice in writing to the [holder of the floating charge by virtue of which the appointment was made],
- (c) in the case of an administrator appointed under paragraph 22(1), by notice in writing to the company, or

(d) in the case of an administrator appointed under paragraph 22(2), by notice in writing to the directors of the company.

Removal of administrator from office

88. The court may by order remove an administrator from office.

Administrator ceasing to be qualified

89. (1) The administrator of a company shall vacate office if he ceases to be qualified to act as an insolvency practitioner in relation to the company.

(2) Where an administrator vacates office by virtue of sub-paragraph (1) he shall give notice in writing—

(a) in the case of an administrator appointed by administration order, to the court,

(b) in the case of an administrator appointed under paragraph 14, to the [holder of the floating charge by virtue of which the appointment was made],

(c) in the case of an administrator appointed under paragraph 22(1), to the company, or

(d) in the case of an administrator appointed under paragraph 22(2), to the directors of the company.

(3) An administrator who fails without reasonable excuse to comply with sub-paragraph (2) commits an offence.

Supplying vacancy in office of administrator

90. Paragraphs 91 to 95 apply where an administrator—

(a) dies,

(b) resigns,

(c) is removed from office under paragraph 88, or

(d) vacates office under paragraph 89.

91. (1) Where the administrator was appointed by administration order, the court may replace the administrator on an application under this sub-paragraph made by—

(a) a creditors' committee of the company,

(b) the company,

(c) the directors of the company,

(d) one or more creditors of the company, or

(e) where more than one person was appointed to act jointly or concurrently as the administrator, any of those persons who remains in office.

(2) But an application may be made in reliance on sub-paragraph (1)(b) to (d) only where—

(a) there is no creditors' committee of the company,

(b) the court is satisfied that the creditors' committee or a remaining administrator is not taking reasonable steps to make a replacement, or

(c) the court is satisfied that for another reason it is right for the application to be made.

92. Where the administrator was appointed under paragraph 14 the holder of the floating charge by virtue of which the appointment was made may replace the administrator.

93. (1) Where the administrator was appointed under paragraph 22(1) by the company it may replace the administrator.

(2) A replacement under this paragraph may be made only—

(a) with the consent of each person who is the holder of a qualifying floating charge in respect of the company's property, or

(b) where consent is withheld, with the permission of the court.

94. (1) Where the administrator was appointed under paragraph 22(2) the directors of the company may replace the administrator.

(2) A replacement under this paragraph may be made only—

(a) with the consent of each person who is the holder of a qualifying floating charge in respect of the company's property, or

(b) where consent is withheld, with the permission of the court.

95. The court may replace an administrator on the application of a person listed in paragraph 91(1) if the court—

(a) is satisfied that a person who is entitled to replace the administrator under any of paragraphs 92 to 94 is not taking reasonable steps to make a replacement, or

(b) that for another reason it is right for the court to make the replacement.

Substitution of administrator: competing floating charge-holder

96. (1) This paragraph applies where an administrator of a company is appointed under paragraph 14 by the holder of a qualifying floating charge in respect of the company's property.

(2) The holder of a prior qualifying floating charge in respect of the company's property may apply to the court for the administrator to be replaced by an administrator nominated by the holder of the prior floating charge.

(3) One floating charge is prior to another for the purposes of this paragraph if—

(a) it was created first, or

(b) it is to be treated as having priority in accordance with an agreement to which the holder of each floating charge was party.

(4) Sub-paragraph (3) shall have effect in relation to Scotland as if the following were substituted for paragraph (a)—

"(a) it has priority of ranking in accordance with section 464(4)(b) of the Companies Act 1985 (c 6),".

Substitution of administrator appointed by company or directors: creditors' [decision]

97. (1) This paragraph applies where—

(a) an administrator of a company is appointed by a company or directors under paragraph 22, and

(b) there is no holder of a qualifying floating charge in respect of the company's property.

[(2) The administrator may be replaced by a decision of the creditors made by a qualifying decision procedure.

(3) The decision has effect only if, before the decision is made, the new administrator has consented to act in writing.]

Vacation of office: discharge from liability

98. (1) Where a person ceases to be the administrator of a company (whether because he vacates office by reason of resignation, death or otherwise, because he is removed from office or because his appointment ceases to have effect) he is discharged from liability in respect of any action of his as administrator.

(2) The discharge provided by sub-paragraph (1) takes effect—

(a) in the case of an administrator who dies, on the filing with the court of notice of his death,

(b) in the case of an administrator appointed under paragraph 14 or 22 [who has not made a statement under paragraph 52(1)(b)], at a time appointed by resolution of the creditors' committee or, if there is no committee, by [decision] of the creditors,

[(ba) in the case of an administrator appointed under paragraph 14 or 22 who has made a statement under paragraph 52(1)(b), at a time decided by the relevant creditors,] or

(c) in any case, at a time specified by the court.

(3) [For the purposes of sub-paragraph (2)(ba), the "relevant creditors" of a company are—]

(a) each secured creditor of the company, or

(b) if the administrator has made a distribution to preferential creditors or thinks that a distribution may be made to preferential creditors—

(i) each secured creditor of the company, and

[(ii) the preferential creditors of the company.]

[(3A) In a case where the administrator is removed from office, a decision of the creditors for the purposes of sub-paragraph (2)(b), or of the preferential creditors for the purposes of sub-paragraph (2)(ba), must be made by a qualifying decision procedure.]

(4) Discharge—

(a) applies to liability accrued before the discharge takes effect, and

(b) does not prevent the exercise of the court's powers under paragraph 75.

Vacation of office: charges and liabilities

99. (1) This paragraph applies where a person ceases to be the administrator of a company (whether because he vacates office by reason of resignation, death or otherwise, because he is removed from office or because his appointment ceases to have effect).

(2) In this paragraph—

"the former administrator" means the person referred to in sub-paragraph (1), and

"cessation" means the time when he ceases to be the company's administrator.

(3) The former administrator's remuneration and expenses shall be—

(a) charged on and payable out of property of which he had custody or control immediately before cessation, and

(b) payable in priority to any security to which paragraph 70 applies.

(4) A sum payable in respect of a debt or liability arising out of a contract entered into by the former administrator or a predecessor before cessation shall be—

(a) charged on and payable out of property of which the former administrator had custody or control immediately before cessation, and

(b) payable in priority to any charge arising under sub-paragraph (3).

(5) Sub-paragraph (4) shall apply to a liability arising under a contract of employment which was adopted by the former administrator or a predecessor before cessation; and for that purpose—

(a) action taken within the period of 14 days after an administrator's appointment shall not be taken to amount or contribute to the adoption of a contract,

(b) no account shall be taken of a liability which arises, or in so far as it arises, by reference to anything which is done or which occurs before the adoption of the contract of employment, and

(c) no account shall be taken of a liability to make a payment other than wages or salary.

(6) In sub-paragraph (5)(c) "wages or salary" includes—

(a) a sum payable in respect of a period of holiday (for which purpose the sum shall be treated as relating to the period by reference to which the entitlement to holiday accrued),

(b) a sum payable in respect of a period of absence through illness or other good cause,
(c) a sum payable in lieu of holiday,
(d) . . . and
(e) a contribution to an occupational pension scheme.

GENERAL

Joint and concurrent administrators

100. (1) In this Schedule—
(a) a reference to the appointment of an administrator of a company includes a reference to the appointment of a number of persons to act jointly or concurrently as the administrator of a company, and
(b) a reference to the appointment of a person as administrator of a company includes a reference to the appointment of a person as one of a number of persons to act jointly or concurrently as the administrator of a company.

(2) The appointment of a number of persons to act as administrator of a company must specify—
(a) which functions (if any) are to be exercised by the persons appointed acting jointly, and
(b) which functions (if any) are to be exercised by any or all of the persons appointed.

101. (1) This paragraph applies where two or more persons are appointed to act jointly as the administrator of a company.

(2) A reference to the administrator of the company is a reference to those persons acting jointly.

(3) But a reference to the administrator of a company in paragraphs 87 to 99 of this Schedule is a reference to any or all of the persons appointed to act jointly.

(4) Where an offence of omission is committed by the administrator, each of the persons appointed to act jointly—
(a) commits the offence, and
(b) may be proceeded against and punished individually.

(5) The reference in paragraph 45(1)(a) to the name of the administrator is a reference to the name of each of the persons appointed to act jointly.

(6) Where persons are appointed to act jointly in respect of only some of the functions of the administrator of a company, this paragraph applies only in relation to those functions.

102. (1) This paragraph applies where two or more persons are appointed to act concurrently as the administrator of a company.

(2) A reference to the administrator of a company in this Schedule is a reference to any of the persons appointed (or any combination of them).

103. (1) Where a company is in administration, a person may be appointed to act as administrator jointly or concurrently with the person or persons acting as the administrator of the company.

(2) Where a company entered administration by administration order, an appointment under sub-paragraph (1) must be made by the court on the application of—
(a) a person or group listed in paragraph 12(1)(a) to (e), or
(b) the person or persons acting as the administrator of the company.

(3) Where a company entered administration by virtue of an appointment under paragraph 14, an appointment under sub-paragraph (1) must be made by—
(a) the holder of the floating charge by virtue of which the appointment was made, or
(b) the court on the application of the person or persons acting as the administrator of the company.

(4) Where a company entered administration by virtue of an appointment under paragraph 22(1), an appointment under sub-paragraph (1) above must be made either by the court on the application of the person or persons acting as the administrator of the company or—
(a) by the company, and
(b) with the consent of each person who is the holder of a qualifying floating charge in respect of the company's property or, where consent is withheld, with the permission of the court.

(5) Where a company entered administration by virtue of an appointment under paragraph 22(2), an appointment under sub-paragraph (1) must be made either by the court on the application of the person or persons acting as the administrator of the company or—
(a) by the directors of the company, and
(b) with the consent of each person who is the holder of a qualifying floating charge in respect of the company's property or, where consent is withheld, with the permission of the court.

(6) An appointment under sub-paragraph (1) may be made only with the consent of the person or persons acting as the administrator of the company.

Presumption of validity

104. An act of the administrator of a company is valid in spite of a defect in his appointment or qualification.

Majority decision of directors

105. A reference in this Schedule to something done by the directors of a company includes a reference to the same thing done by a majority of the directors of a company.

Penalties

106. (1) A person who is guilty of an offence under this Schedule is liable to a fine (in accordance with section 430 and Schedule 10).

(2) A person who is guilty of an offence under any of the following paragraphs of this Schedule is liable to a daily default fine (in accordance with section 430 and Schedule 10)—

(a) paragraph 20,
(b) paragraph 32,
(c) paragraph 46,
(d) paragraph 48,
(e) paragraph 49,
(f) paragraph 51,
(g) paragraph 53,
(h) paragraph 54,
(i) paragraph 56,
(j) paragraph 71,
(k) paragraph 72,
(l) paragraph 77,
(m) paragraph 78,
(n) paragraph 80,
(o) paragraph 84,
(p) paragraph 86, and
(q) paragraph 89.

Extension of time limit

107. (1) Where a provision of this Schedule provides that a period may be varied in accordance with this paragraph, the period may be varied in respect of a company—

(a) by the court, and
(b) on the application of the administrator.

(2) A time period may be extended in respect of a company under this paragraph—

(a) more than once, and
(b) after expiry.

108. (1) A period specified in paragraph 49(5), *50(1)(b)* or 51(2) may be varied in respect of a company by the administrator with consent.

(2) In sub-paragraph (1) "consent" means consent of—

(a) each secured creditor of the company, and
[(b) if the company has unsecured debts, the unsecured creditors of the company.]

(3) But where the administrator has made a statement under paragraph 52(1)(b) "consent" means—

(a) consent of each secured creditor of the company, or
(b) if the administrator thinks that a distribution may be made to preferential creditors, consent of—
    (i) each secured creditor of the company, and
    [(ii) the preferential creditors of the company.]

[(3A) Whether the company's unsecured creditors or preferential creditors consent is to be determined by the administrator seeking a decision from those creditors as to whether they consent.]

(4) Consent for the purposes of sub-paragraph (1) may be—

(a) written, or
(b) signified at a creditors' meeting.

(5) The power to extend under sub-paragraph (1)—

(a) may be exercised in respect of a period only once,
(b) may not be used to extend a period by more than 28 days,
(c) may not be used to extend a period which has been extended by the court, and
(d) may not be used to extend a period after expiry.

109. Where a period is extended under paragraph 107 or 108, a reference to the period shall be taken as a reference to the period as extended.

Amendment of provision about time

110. (1) The Secretary of State may by order amend a provision of this Schedule which—

(a) requires anything to be done within a specified period of time,
(b) prevents anything from being done after a specified time, or
(c) requires a specified minimum period of notice to be given.

(2) An order under this paragraph—

(a) must be made by statutory instrument, and
(b) shall be subject to annulment in pursuance of a resolution of either House of Parliament.

Interpretation

111. (1) In this Schedule—

"administrative receiver" has the meaning given by section 251,

"administrator" has the meaning given by paragraph 1 and, where the context requires, includes a reference to a former administrator,

. . .

"correspondence" includes correspondence by telephonic or other electronic means,
"creditors' meeting" has the meaning given by paragraph 50,
"enters administration" has the meaning given by paragraph 1,
"floating charge" means a charge which is a floating charge on its creation,
"in administration" has the meaning given by paragraph 1,
"hire-purchase agreement" includes a conditional sale agreement, a chattel leasing agreement and a retention of title agreement,
"holder of a qualifying floating charge" in respect of a company's property has the meaning given by paragraph 14,
"market value" means the amount which would be realised on a sale of property in the open market by a willing vendor,
"the purpose of administration" means an objective specified in paragraph 3, and
"unable to pay its debts" has the meaning given by section 123.

[(1A) In this Schedule, "company" means—
- [(a) a company registered under the Companies Act 2006 in England and Wales or Scotland,]
- (b) a company incorporated in an EEA State other than the United Kingdom, or
- (c) a company not incorporated in an EEA State but having its centre of main interests in a member State other than Denmark.

(1B) In sub-paragraph (1A), in relation to a company, "centre of main interests" has the same meaning as in [Article 3 of the EU Regulation].]

(2) . . .

(3) In this Schedule a reference to action includes a reference to inaction.

[Non-UK companies

111A. A company incorporated outside the United Kingdom that has a principal place of business in Northern Ireland may not enter administration under this Schedule unless it also has a principal place of business in England and Wales or Scotland (or both in England and Wales and in Scotland).]

Scotland

112. In the application of this Schedule to Scotland—
- (a) a reference to filing with the court is a reference to lodging in court, and
- (b) a reference to a charge is a reference to a right in security.

113. Where property in Scotland is disposed of under paragraph 70 or 71, the administrator shall grant to the disponee an appropriate document of transfer or conveyance of the property, and—
- (a) that document, or
- (b) recording, intimation or registration of that document (where recording, intimation or registration of the document is a legal requirement for completion of title to the property),

has the effect of disencumbering the property of or, as the case may be, freeing the property from, the security.

114. In Scotland, where goods in the possession of a company under a hire-purchase agreement are disposed of under paragraph 72, the disposal has the effect of extinguishing as against the disponee all rights of the owner of the goods under the agreement.

115. (1) In Scotland, the administrator of a company may make, in or towards the satisfaction of the debt secured by the floating charge, a payment to the holder of a floating charge which has attached to the property subject to the charge.

[(1A) In Scotland, sub-paragraph (1B) applies in connection with the giving by the court of permission as provided for in paragraph 65(3)(b).

(1B) On the giving by the court of such permission, any floating charge granted by the company shall, unless it has already so attached, attach to the property which is subject to the charge.]

(2) In Scotland, where the administrator thinks that the company has insufficient property to enable a distribution to be made to unsecured creditors other than by virtue of section 176A(2)(a), he may file a notice to that effect with the registrar of companies.

(3) On delivery of the notice to the registrar of companies, any floating charge granted by the company shall, unless it has already so attached, attach to the property which is subject to the charge . . .

[(4) Attachment of a floating charge under sub-paragraph (1B) or (3) has effect as if the charge is a fixed security over the property to which it has attached.]

116. In Scotland, the administrator in making any payment in accordance with paragraph 115 shall make such payment subject to the rights of any of the following categories of persons (which rights shall, except to the extent provided in any instrument, have the following order of priority)—
- (a) the holder of any fixed security which is over property subject to the floating charge and which ranks prior to, or pari passu with, the floating charge,
- (b) creditors in respect of all liabilities and expenses incurred by or on behalf of the administrator,
- (c) the administrator in respect of his liabilities, expenses and remuneration and any indemnity to which he is entitled out of the property of the company,
- (d) the preferential creditors entitled to payment in accordance with paragraph 65,

(e) the holder of the floating charge in accordance with the priority of that charge in relation to any other floating charge which has attached, and

(f) the holder of a fixed security, other than one referred to in paragraph (a), which is over property subject to the floating charge.]

NOTES

Inserted by the Enterprise Act 2002, s 248(2), Sch 16.

Para 12: words in square brackets in sub-para (1)(d) substituted by the Courts Act 2003, s 109(1), Sch 8, para 299; sub-para (5) added by the Enterprise Act 2002 (Insolvency) Order 2003, SI 2003/2096, arts 2(1), (2), 6, except in relation to any case where a petition for an administration order was presented before 15 September 2003.

Para 25A: inserted by the Deregulation Act 2015, s 19, Sch 6, Pt 2, paras 4, 5.

Para 26: words in square brackets in sub-para (2) substituted by the Deregulation Act 2015, s 19, Sch 6, Pt 2, paras 4, 6.

Para 40: sub-para (2)(aa) inserted by the European Public Limited-Liability Company Regulations 2004, SI 2004/2326, reg 73(4)(c); words in square brackets in sub-para (2)(b) substituted by the Financial Services Act 2012, s 114(1), Sch 18, Pt 2, paras 51, 55(1), (2).

Para 42: sub-para (4)(aa) inserted by SI 2004/2326, reg 73(4)(c); words in square brackets in sub-para (4)(b) substituted by the Financial Services Act 2012, s 114(1), Sch 18, Pt 2, paras 51, 55(1), (3).

Para 43: sub-para (6A) inserted by SI 2003/2096, art 2(1), (3), except in relation to any case where a petition for an administration order was presented before 15 September 2003.

Para 45: substituted by the Companies (Trading Disclosures) (Insolvency) Regulations 2008, SI 2008/1897, reg 4(1).

Para 49: words in square brackets in sub-para (3)(b) substituted by the Companies Act 2006 (Consequential Amendments etc) Order 2008, SI 2008/948, art 3(1), Sch 1, Pt 2, para 100(a); words in square brackets in sub-para (4)(b) inserted by the Small Business, Enterprise and Employment Act 2015, s 126, Sch 9, Pt 1, paras 1, 10(1), (2), as from 6 April 2017 (in relation to England and Wales and subject to transitional and savings provisions as noted to s 246ZE at **[1.256]**), and as from a day to be appointed (in relation to Scotland).

Para 50: repealed by the Small Business, Enterprise and Employment Act 2015, s 126, Sch 9, Pt 1, paras 1, 10(1), (3), as from 6 April 2017 (in relation to England and Wales and subject to transitional and savings provisions as noted to s 246ZE at **[1.256]**), and as from a day to be appointed (in relation to Scotland).

Para 51: the heading preceding this paragraph is substituted (for the original words "Requirement for initial creditors' meeting") and sub-paras (1)–(3) are substituted, by the Small Business, Enterprise and Employment Act 2015, s 126, Sch 9, Pt 1, paras 1, 10(1), (4), (5), as from 6 April 2017 (in relation to England and Wales and subject to transitional and savings provisions as noted to s 246ZE at **[1.256]**), and as from a day to be appointed (in relation to Scotland). Sub-paras (1)–(3) originally read as follows—

"(1) Each copy of an administrator's statement of proposals sent to a creditor under paragraph 49(4)(b) must be accompanied by an invitation to a creditors' meeting (an "initial creditors' meeting").

(2) The date set for an initial creditors' meeting must be—

(a) as soon as is reasonably practicable after the company enters administration, and

(b) in any event, within the period of ten weeks beginning with the date on which the company enters administration.

(3) An administrator shall present a copy of his statement of proposals to an initial creditors' meeting.".

Para 52: words in square brackets in sub-para (2) substituted for original words "summon an initial creditors' meeting if it is requested" and sub-para (3) is substituted, by the Small Business, Enterprise and Employment Act 2015, s 126, Sch 9, Pt 1, paras 1, 10(1), (6), (7), as from 6 April 2017 (in relation to England and Wales and subject to transitional and savings provisions as noted to s 246ZE at **[1.256]**), and as from a day to be appointed (in relation to Scotland). Sub-para (3) originally read as follows—

"(3) A meeting requested under sub-paragraph (2) must be summoned for a date in the prescribed period.".

Para 53: the heading preceding this paragraph is substituted (for the original words "Business and result of initial creditors' meeting", sub-para (1) is substituted, the word in the first pair of square brackets in sub-para (2) is substituted for the original words "After the conclusion of an initial creditors' meeting the" and the words in the second pair of square brackets in that sub-para are inserted, by the Small Business, Enterprise and Employment Act 2015, s 126, Sch 9, Pt 1, paras 1, 10(1), (8)–(10), as from 6 April 2017 (in relation to England and Wales and subject to transitional and savings provisions as noted to s 246ZE at **[1.256]**), and as from a day to be appointed (in relation to Scotland). Sub-para (1) originally read as follows—

"(1) An initial creditors' meeting to which an administrator's proposals are presented shall consider them and may—

(a) approve them without modification, or

(b) approve them with modification to which the administrator consents.".

Para 54 is amended by the Small Business, Enterprise and Employment Act 2015, s 126, Sch 9, Pt 1, paras 1, 10(1), (11)–(16), as from 6 April 2017 (in relation to England and Wales and subject to transitional and savings provisions as noted to s 246ZE at **[1.256]**), and as from a day to be appointed (in relation to Scotland), as follows:

Words in square brackets in sub-para (1)(a) substituted for original words "at an initial creditors' meeting", sub-para (2)(a) and the words in italics in sub-para (2)(b) are repealed, words in square brackets in sub-para (2)(b) inserted, and sub-para (2)(d) substituted. Sub-para (2)(d) originally read as follows—

"(d) present a copy of the statement to the meeting.".

Sub-para (5) is substituted and originally read as follows—

"(5) A creditors' meeting to which a proposed revision is presented shall consider it and may—

(a) approve it without modification, or

(b) approve it with modification to which the administrator consents.".

In sub-para (6), words in first pair of square brackets substituted for original words "After the conclusion of a creditors' meeting the", and words in second pair of square brackets inserted.

Para 55: sub-para (1) substituted by the Small Business, Enterprise and Employment Act 2015, s 126, Sch 9, Pt 1, paras 1, 10(1), (17), as from 6 April 2017 (in relation to England and Wales and subject to transitional and savings provisions as noted to s 246ZE at **[1.256]**), and as from a day to be appointed (in relation to Scotland), and originally read as follows—

"(1) This paragraph applies where an administrator reports to the court that—

(a) an initial creditors' meeting has failed to approve the administrator's proposals presented to it, or

(b) a creditors' meeting has failed to approve a revision of the administrator's proposals presented to it.".

Para 56: word in square brackets in the heading preceding this paragraph substituted for original word "meetings", words in square brackets in sub-para (1) in both places substituted for original words "summon a creditors' meeting" and words in square brackets in sub-para (2) substituted for original words "summon a creditors' meeting", by the Small Business, Enterprise and Employment Act 2015, s 126, Sch 9, Pt 1, paras 1, 10(1), (18)–(20), as from 6 April 2017 (in relation to England and Wales and subject to transitional and savings provisions as noted to s 246ZE at **[1.256]**), and as from a day to be appointed (in relation to Scotland).

Para 57: words in square brackets in sub-para (1) substituted for original words "A creditors' meeting may" by the Small Business, Enterprise and Employment Act 2015, s 126, Sch 9, Pt 1, paras 1, 10(1), (21), as from 6 April 2017 (in relation to England and Wales and subject to transitional and savings provisions as noted to s 246ZE at **[1.256]**), and as from a day to be appointed (in relation to Scotland).

Para 58: repealed by the Small Business, Enterprise and Employment Act 2015, s 126, Sch 9, Pt 1, paras 1, 10(1), (22), as from 6 April 2017 (in relation to England and Wales and subject to transitional and savings provisions as noted to s 246ZE at **[1.256]**), and as from a day to be appointed (in relation to Scotland).

Para 60: sub-para (1) numbered as such, and sub-para (2) added, by the Small Business, Enterprise and Employment Act 2015, s 129(1)–(3).

Para 60A: inserted by the Small Business, Enterprise and Employment Act 2015, s 129(1), (4).

Para 62: words in square brackets substituted for original words "may call a meeting of members or creditors of the company." by the Small Business, Enterprise and Employment Act 2015, s 126, Sch 9, Pt 1, paras 1, 10(1), (23), as from 6 April 2017 (in relation to England and Wales and subject to transitional and savings provisions as noted to s 246ZE at **[1.256]**), and as from a day to be appointed (in relation to Scotland).

Para 65: words in square brackets substituted by the Small Business, Enterprise and Employment Act 2015, s 128(1), (2).

Para 73: the word "or" omitted from sub-para (1)(b) was repealed, sub-para (1)(bb) was inserted, the words in square brackets in sub-para (1)(c) were substituted (for the original words "his debt"), and sub-para (1)(d) (and the preceding word) was added, by the Banks and Building Societies (Depositor Preference and Priorities) Order 2014, SI 2014/3486, arts 3, 10, as from 1 January 2015, except in relation to any insolvency proceedings commenced before that date; word omitted from sub-para (2)(b) repealed, and sub-para (2)(d) (and the word immediately preceding it) added, by the Companies (Cross-Border Mergers) Regulations 2007, SI 2007/2974, reg 65(1)–(3); words in square brackets in sub-para (2)(c) substituted by SI 2008/948, art 3(1), Sch 1, Pt 2, para 100(a).

Para 74: word omitted from sub-para (6)(b) repealed, and sub-para (6)(ba) added, by SI 2007/2974, reg 65(1), (4), (5); words in square brackets in sub-para (6)(b) substituted by SI 2008/948, art 3(1), Sch 1, Pt 2, para 100(b); sub-para (4)(c) substituted by the Small Business, Enterprise and Employment Act 2015, s 126, Sch 9, Pt 1, paras 1, 10(1), (24), as from 6 April 2017 (in relation to England and Wales and subject to transitional and savings provisions as noted to s 246ZE at **[1.256]**), and as from a day to be appointed (in relation to Scotland) and originally read as follows—

"(c) require a creditors' meeting to be held for a specified purpose;".

Para 76: words in square brackets substituted by the Small Business, Enterprise and Employment Act 2015, s 127.

Para 78 is amended as follows:

Sub-para (1)(b) substituted by the Small Business, Enterprise and Employment Act 2015, s 126, Sch 9, Pt 1, paras 1, 10(1), (25), as from 6 April 2017 (in relation to England and Wales and subject to transitional and savings provisions as noted to s 246ZE at **[1.256]**), and as from a day to be appointed (in relation to Scotland) and originally read as follows—

"(b) if the company has unsecured debts, creditors whose debts amount to more than 50% of the company's unsecured debts, disregarding debts of any creditor who does not respond to an invitation to give or withhold consent.".

Sub-para (2)(b)(ii) substituted by the Small Business, Enterprise and Employment Act 2015, s 126, Sch 9, Pt 1, paras 1, 10(1), (26), as from 6 April 2017 (in relation to England and Wales and subject to transitional and savings provisions as noted to s 246ZE at **[1.256]**), and as from a day to be appointed (in relation to Scotland) and originally read as follows—

"(ii) preferential creditors whose debts amount to more than 50% of the preferential debts of the company, disregarding debts of any creditor who does not respond to an invitation to give or withhold consent.".

Sub-para (2A) inserted, and sub-para (3) repealed, by the Small Business, Enterprise and Employment Act 2015, s 126, Sch 9, Pt 1, paras 1, 10(1), (27), (28), as from 6 April 2017 (in relation to England and Wales and subject to transitional and savings provisions as noted to s 246ZE at **[1.256]**), and as from a day to be appointed (in relation to Scotland)

Para 79: words in square brackets in sub-para (2)(c) substituted for original words "a creditors' meeting requires him to" by the Small Business, Enterprise and Employment Act 2015, s 126, Sch 9, Pt 1, paras 1, 10(1), (29), as from 6 April 2017 (in relation to England and Wales and subject to transitional and savings provisions as noted to s 246ZE at **[1.256]**), and as from a day to be appointed (in relation to Scotland).

Para 80: words in square brackets in sub-para (4) inserted by the Small Business, Enterprise and Employment Act 2015, s 126, Sch 9, Pt 1, paras 1, 10(1), (30), as from 6 April 2017 (in relation to England and Wales and subject to transitional and savings provisions as noted to s 246ZE at **[1.256]**), and as from a day to be appointed (in relation to Scotland).

Para 82: sub-para (1)(aa) inserted by SI 2004/2326, reg 73(4)(c); words in square brackets in sub-para (1)(b) substituted by the Financial Services Act 2012, s 114(1), Sch 18, Pt 2, paras 51, 55(1), (4).

Para 83: words in square brackets in sub-paras (1)(b) and (2)(b) inserted by the Small Business, Enterprise and Employment Act 2015, s 128(1), (3); words in square brackets in sub-para (5)(b) inserted, and figure "98," in italics in sub-para (8)(d) repealed, by s 126 of, and Sch 9, Pt 1, paras 1, 10(1), (31), (32) to, the 2015 Act, as from 6 April 2017 (in relation to England and Wales and subject to transitional and savings provisions as noted to s 246ZE at **[1.256]**), and as from a day to be appointed (in relation to Scotland).

Para 84: sub-paras (1A), (1B), (6A), (6B) inserted and words in square brackets in sub-paras (3), (6), (7) inserted by the Insolvency Amendment (EU 2015/848) Regulations 2017, SI 2017/702, regs 2, 3, Schedule, Pt 1, paras 1, 30, except in relation to proceedings opened before 26 June 2017 and subject to savings in reg 4 thereof at **[2.103]**; words in square brackets in sub-para (5)(b) inserted by the Small Business, Enterprise and Employment Act 2015, s 126, Sch 9, Pt 1, paras 1, 10(1), (33), as from 6 April 2017 (in relation to England and Wales and subject to transitional and savings provisions as noted to s 246ZE at **[1.256]**), and as from a day to be appointed (in relation to Scotland).

Paras 87, 89: words in square brackets in sub-para (2)(b) substituted by SI 2003/2096, arts 2(1), (4), (5), 6, except in relation to any case where a petition for an administration order was presented before 15 September 2003.

Para 97: word in square brackets in the preceding heading substituted for original word "meeting", and sub-paras (2), (3) substituted, by the Small Business, Enterprise and Employment Act 2015, s 126, Sch 9, Pt 1, paras 1, 10(1), (34), (35), as from 6 April 2017 (in relation to England and Wales and subject to transitional and savings provisions as noted to s 246ZE at **[1.256]**), and as from a day to be appointed (in relation to Scotland). Sub-paras (2), (3) originally read as follows—

"(2) A creditors' meeting may replace the administrator.

(3) A creditors' meeting may act under sub-paragraph (2) only if the new administrator's written consent to act is presented to the meeting before the replacement is made.".

Para 98 is amended as follows:

Words in first pair of square brackets in sub-para (2)(b) inserted, sub-para (2)(ba) inserted, words in square brackets in sub-para (3) substituted, by the Deregulation Act 2015, s 19, Sch 6, Pt 2, paras 4, 7.

Words in second pair of square brackets in sub-para (2)(b) substituted for original word "resolution", sub-para (3)(b)(ii) substituted and sub-para (3A) inserted, by the Small Business, Enterprise and Employment Act 2015, s 126, Sch 9, Pt 1, paras 1, 10(1), (36)–(38), as from 6 April 2017 (in relation to England and Wales and subject to transitional and savings provisions as noted to s 246ZE at **[1.256]**), and as from a day to be appointed (in relation to Scotland). Sub-para (3)(b)(ii) (as amended by the Deregulation Act 2015, s 19, Sch 6, Pt 2, paras 4, 7) previously read as follows—

"(ii) preferential creditors whose debts amount to more than 50% of the preferential debts of the company, disregarding debts of any creditor who does not respond to an invitation to [decide on the time of discharge].".

Para 99: words omitted from sub-para (6)(d) repealed by the Deregulation Act 2015, s 19, Sch 6, Pt 7, paras 24, 27.

Para 108 is amended as follows:

Figure ", 50(1)(b)" in italics in sub-para (1) repealed, sub-para (2)(b) substituted by the Small Business, Enterprise and Employment Act 2015, s 126, Sch 9, Pt 1, paras 1, 10(1), (39), (40), as from 6 April 2017 (in relation to England and Wales and subject to transitional and savings provisions as noted to s 246ZE at **[1.256]**), and as from a day to be appointed (in relation to Scotland). Sub-para (2)(b) originally read as follows—

"(b) if the company has unsecured debts, creditors whose debts amount to more than 50% of the company's unsecured debts, disregarding debts of any creditor who does not respond to an invitation to give or withhold consent.".

Sub-para (3)(b)(ii) substituted by the Small Business, Enterprise and Employment Act 2015, s 126, Sch 9, Pt 1, paras 1, 10(1), (41), as from 6 April 2017 (in relation to England and Wales and subject to transitional and savings provisions as noted to s 246ZE at **[1.256]**), and as from a day to be appointed (in relation to Scotland), and originally read as follows—

"(ii) preferential creditors whose debts amount to more than 50% of the total preferential debts of the company, disregarding debts of any creditor who does not respond to an invitation to give or withhold consent.".

Sub-para (3A) inserted, and sub-para (4) repealed, by the Small Business, Enterprise and Employment Act 2015, s 126, Sch 9, Pt 1, paras 1, 10(1), (42), (43), as from 6 April 2017 (in relation to England and Wales and subject to transitional and savings provisions as noted to s 246ZE at **[1.256]**), and as from a day to be appointed (in relation to Scotland).

Para 111 is amended as follows:

Definition omitted from sub-para (1) repealed, and sub-paras (1A), (1B) inserted, by the Insolvency Act 1986 (Amendment) Regulations 2005, SI 2005/879, reg 2(1), (4)(a), (b), except in relation to the appointment of an administrator under Part II that took effect before 13 April 2005.

Definitions in italics in sub-para (1) repealed by the Small Business, Enterprise and Employment Act 2015, s 126, Sch 9, Pt 1, paras 1, 10(1), (44), as from 6 April 2017 (in relation to England and Wales and subject to transitional and savings provisions as noted to s 246ZE at **[1.256]**), and as from a day to be appointed (in relation to Scotland).

Sub-para (1A)(a) substituted by the Companies Act 2006 (Consequential Amendments, Transitional Provisions and Savings) Order 2009, SI 2009/1941, art 2(1), Sch 1, para 72.

Words in square brackets in sub-para (1B) substituted for original words "the EC Regulation and, in the absence of proof to the contrary, is presumed to be the place of its registered office (within the meaning of that Regulation)" by SI 2017/702, regs 2, 3, Schedule, Pt 1, paras 1, 31, except in relation to proceedings opened before 26 June 2017 and subject to savings in reg 4 thereof at **[2.103]**.

Sub-para (2) repealed by the Legislative Reform (Insolvency) (Miscellaneous Provisions) Order 2010, SI 2010/18, arts 2, 4(2).

Para 111A: inserted by SI 2005/879, reg 2(1), (4)(c), except in relation to the appointment of an administrator under Part II that took effect before 13 April 2005.

Para 115: sub-paras (1A), (1B) inserted, words omitted from sub-para (3) repealed, and sub-para (4) added, by the Small Business, Enterprise and Employment Act 2015, s 130.

SCHEDULE 1
POWERS OF ADMINISTRATOR OR ADMINISTRATIVE RECEIVER

Sections 14, 42

[1.576]

1. Power to take possession of, collect and get in the property of the company and, for that purpose, to take such proceedings as may seem to him expedient.

2. Power to sell or otherwise dispose of the property of the company by public auction or private contract or, in Scotland, to sell, . . . hire out or otherwise dispose of the property of the company by public roup or private bargain.

3. Power to raise or borrow money and grant security therefor over the property of the company.

4. Power to appoint a solicitor or accountant or other professionally qualified person to assist him in the performance of his functions.

5. Power to bring or defend any action or other legal proceedings in the name and on behalf of the company.

6. Power to refer to arbitration any question affecting the company.

7. Power to effect and maintain insurances in respect of the business and property of the company.

8. Power to use the company's seal.

9. Power to do all acts and to execute in the name and on behalf of the company any deed, receipt or other document.

10. Power to draw, accept, make and endorse any bill of exchange or promissory note in the name and on behalf of the company.

11. Power to appoint any agent to do any business which he is unable to do himself or which can more conveniently be done by an agent and power to employ and dismiss employees.

12. Power to do all such things (including the carrying out of works) as may be necessary for the realisation of the property of the company.

13. Power to make any payment which is necessary or incidental to the performance of his functions.

14. Power to carry on the business of the company.

15. Power to establish subsidiaries of the company.

16. Power to transfer to subsidiaries of the company the whole or any part of the business and property of the company.

17. Power to grant or accept a surrender of a lease or tenancy of any of the property of the company, and to take a lease or tenancy of any property required or convenient for the business of the company.

18. Power to make any arrangement or compromise on behalf of the company.

19. Power to call up any uncalled capital of the company.

20. Power to rank and claim in the bankruptcy, insolvency, sequestration or liquidation of any person indebted to the company and to receive dividends, and to accede to trust deeds for the creditors of any such person.

21. Power to present or defend a petition for the winding up of the company.

22. Power to change the situation of the company's registered office.

23. Power to do all other things incidental to the exercise of the foregoing powers.

NOTES

This Schedule derived from the Insolvency Act 1985, Sch 3.

Para 2: word omitted repealed by the Abolition of Feudal Tenure etc (Scotland) Act 2000, s 76(2), Sch 13, Pt I.

SCHEDULE 2
POWERS OF A SCOTTISH RECEIVER (ADDITIONAL TO THOSE CONFERRED ON HIM BY THE INSTRUMENT OF CHARGE)

Section 55

[1.577]

1. Power to take possession of, collect and get in the property from the company or a liquidator thereof or any other person, and for that purpose, to take such proceedings as may seem to him expedient.

2. Power to sell, . . . hire out or otherwise dispose of the property by public roup or private bargain and with or without advertisement.

3. Power to raise or borrow money and grant security therefor over the property.

4. Power to appoint a solicitor or accountant or other professionally qualified person to assist him in the performance of his functions.

5. Power to bring or defend any action or other legal proceedings in the name and on behalf of the company.

6. Power to refer to arbitration all questions affecting the company.

7. Power to effect and maintain insurances in respect of the business and property of the company.

8. Power to use the company's seal.

9. Power to do all acts and to execute in the name and on behalf of the company any deed, receipt or other document.

10. Power to draw, accept, make and endorse any bill of exchange or promissory note in the name and on behalf of the company.

11. Power to appoint any agent to do any business which he is unable to do himself or which can more conveniently be done by an agent, and power to employ and dismiss employees.

12. Power to do all such things (including the carrying out of works), as may be necessary for the realisation of the property.

13. Power to make any payment which is necessary or incidental to the performance of his functions.

14. Power to carry on the business of the company or any part of it.

15. Power to grant or accept a surrender of a lease or tenancy of any of the property, and to take a lease or tenancy of any property required or convenient for the business of the company.

16. Power to make any arrangement or compromise on behalf of the company.

17. Power to call up any uncalled capital of the company.

18. Power to establish subsidiaries of the company.

19. Power to transfer to subsidiaries of the company the business of the company or any part of it and any of the property.

20. Power to rank and claim in the bankruptcy, insolvency, sequestration or liquidation of any person or company indebted to the company and to receive dividends, and to accede to trust deeds for creditors of any such person.

21. Power to present or defend a petition for the winding up of the company.

22. Power to change the situation of the company's registered office.

23. Power to do all other things incidental to the exercise of the powers mentioned in section 55(1) of this Act or above in this Schedule.

NOTES

This Schedule derived from the Companies Act 1985, s 471(1), and the Insolvency Act 1985, s 57.

Para 2: word omitted repealed by the Abolition of Feudal Tenure etc (Scotland) Act 2000, s 76(2), Sch 13, Pt I.

[SCHEDULE 2A
EXCEPTIONS TO PROHIBITION ON APPOINTMENT OF ADMINISTRATIVE RECEIVER: SUPPLEMENTARY PROVISIONS

Section 72H(1)

Capital market arrangement

[1.578]

1. (1) For the purposes of section 72B an arrangement is a capital market arrangement if—

(a) it involves a grant of security to a person holding it as trustee for a person who holds a capital market investment issued by a party to the arrangement, or

[(aa) it involves a grant of security to—

(i) a party to the arrangement who issues a capital market investment, or

(ii) a person who holds the security as trustee for a party to the arrangement in connection with the issue of a capital market investment, or

(ab) it involves a grant of security to a person who holds the security as trustee for a party to the arrangement who agrees to provide finance to another party, or]

(b) at least one party guarantees the performance of obligations of another party, or

(c) at least one party provides security in respect of the performance of obligations of another party, or

(d) the arrangement involves an investment of a kind described in articles 83 to 85 of the Financial Services and Markets Act 2000 (Regulated Activities) Order 2001 (SI 2001/544) (options, futures and contracts for differences).

(2) For the purposes of sub-paragraph (1)—

(a) a reference to holding as trustee includes a reference to holding as nominee or agent,

(b) a reference to holding for a person who holds a capital market investment includes a reference to holding for a number of persons at least one of whom holds a capital market investment, and

(c) a person holds a capital market investment if he has a legal or beneficial interest in it[; and

(d) the reference to the provision of finance includes the provision of an indemnity.]

(3) In section 72B(1) and this paragraph "party" to an arrangement includes a party to an agreement which—

(a) forms part of the arrangement,

(b) provides for the raising of finance as part of the arrangement, or

(c) is necessary for the purposes of implementing the arrangement.

Capital market investment

2. (1) For the purposes of section 72B an investment is a capital market investment if it—

(a) is within article 77 [or 77A] of the Financial Services and Markets Act 2000 (Regulated Activities) Order 2001 (SI 2001/544) (debt instruments), and

(b) is rated, listed or traded or designed to be rated, listed or traded.

(2) In sub-paragraph (1)—

"rated" means rated for the purposes of investment by an internationally recognised rating agency,

"listed" means admitted to the official list within the meaning given by section 103(1) of the Financial Services and Markets Act 2000 (c 8) (interpretation), and

"traded" means admitted to trading on a market established under the rules of a recognised investment exchange or on a foreign market.

(3) In sub-paragraph (2)—

"recognised investment exchange" has the meaning given by section 285 of the Financial Services and Markets Act 2000 (recognised investment exchange), and

"foreign market" has the same meaning as "relevant market" in article 67(2) of the Financial Services and Markets Act 2000 (Financial Promotion) Order 2001 (SI 2001/1335) (foreign markets).

3. (1) An investment is also a capital market investment for the purposes of section 72B if it consists of a bond or commercial paper issued to one or more of the following—

(a) an investment professional within the meaning of article 19(5) of the Financial Services and Markets Act 2000 (Financial Promotion) Order 2001,

(b) a person who is, when the agreement mentioned in section 72B(1) is entered into, a certified high net worth individual in relation to a communication within the meaning of article 48(2) of that order,

(c) a person to whom article 49(2) of that order applies (high net worth company, &c),

(d) a person who is, when the agreement mentioned in section 72B(1) is entered into, a certified sophisticated investor in relation to a communication within the meaning of article 50(1) of that order, and

(e) a person in a State other than the United Kingdom who under the law of that State is not prohibited from investing in bonds or commercial paper.

(2) In sub-paragraph (1)—

"bond" shall be construed in accordance with article 77 of the Financial Services and Markets Act 2000 (Regulated Activities) Order 2001 (SI 2001/544)[, and includes any instrument falling within article 77A of that Order], and

"commercial paper" has the meaning given by article 9(3) of that order.

(3) For the purposes of sub-paragraph (1)—

(a) in applying article 19(5) of the Financial Promotion Order for the purposes of sub-paragraph (1)(a)—

(i) in article 19(5)(b), ignore the words after "exempt person",

(ii) in article 19(5)(c)(i), for the words from "the controlled activity" to the end substitute "a controlled activity", and

(iii) in article 19(5)(e) ignore the words from "where the communication" to the end, and

(b) in applying article 49(2) of that order for the purposes of sub-paragraph (1)(c), ignore article 49(2)(e).

"Agreement"

4. For the purposes of sections 72B and 72E and this Schedule "agreement" includes an agreement or undertaking effected by—

(a) contract,

(b) deed, or

(c) any other instrument intended to have effect in accordance with the law of England and Wales, Scotland or another jurisdiction.

Debt

5. The debt of at least £50 million referred to in section 72B(1)(a) or 72E(2)(a)—

(a) may be incurred at any time during the life of the capital market arrangement or financed project, and

(b) may be expressed wholly or partly in foreign currency (in which case the sterling equivalent shall be calculated as at the time when the arrangement is entered into or the project begins).

Step-in rights

6. (1) For the purposes of sections 72C to 72E a project has "step-in rights" if a person who provides finance in connection with the project has a conditional entitlement under an agreement to—

(a) assume sole or principal responsibility under an agreement for carrying out all or part of the project, or

(b) make arrangements for carrying out all or part of the project.

(2) In sub-paragraph (1) a reference to the provision of finance includes a reference to the provision of an indemnity.

Project company

7. (1) For the purposes of sections 72C to 72E a company is a "project company" of a project if—

(a) it holds property for the purpose of the project,

(b) it has sole or principal responsibility under an agreement for carrying out all or part of the project,

(c) it is one of a number of companies which together carry out the project,

(d) it has the purpose of supplying finance to enable the project to be carried out, or

(e) it is the holding company of a company within any of paragraphs (a) to (d).

(2) But a company is not a "project company" of a project if—

(a) it performs a function within sub-paragraph (1)(a) to (d) or is within sub-paragraph (1)(e), but

(b) it also performs a function which is not—

(i) within sub-paragraph (1)(a) to (d),

(ii) related to a function within sub-paragraph (1)(a) to (d), or

(iii) related to the project.

(3) For the purposes of this paragraph a company carries out all or part of a project whether or not it acts wholly or partly through agents.

"Resources"

8. In section 72C "resources" includes—
(a) funds (including payment for the provision of services or facilities),
(b) assets,
(c) professional skill,
(d) the grant of a concession or franchise, and
(e) any other commercial resource.

"Public body"

9. (1) In section 72C "public body" means—
(a) a body which exercises public functions,
(b) a body specified for the purposes of this paragraph by the Secretary of State, and
(c) a body within a class specified for the purposes of this paragraph by the Secretary of State.

(2) A specification under sub-paragraph (1) may be—
(a) general, or
(b) for the purpose of the application of section 72C to a specified case.

Regulated business

10. (1) For the purposes of section 72D a business is regulated if it is carried on—
(a) . . .
(b) in reliance on a licence under section 7[, 7A or 7B] of the Gas Act 1986 (c 44) (transport and supply of gas),
(c) in reliance on a licence granted by virtue of section 41C of that Act (power to prescribe additional licensable activity),
(d) in reliance on a licence under section 6 of the Electricity Act 1989 (c 29) (supply of electricity),
(e) by a water undertaker,
(f) by a sewerage undertaker,
(g) by a universal service provider within the meaning [of Part 3 of the Postal Services Act 2011],
[(h) by a Post Office company within the meaning of Part 1 of that Act,]
(i) . . .
(j) in reliance on a licence under section 8 of the Railways Act 1993 (c 43) (railway services),
(k) in reliance on a licence exemption under section 7 of that Act (subject to sub-paragraph (2) below),
(l) by the operator of a system of transport which is deemed to be a railway for a purpose of Part I of that Act by virtue of section 81(2) of that Act (tramways, &c), . . .
(m) by the operator of a vehicle carried on flanged wheels along a system within paragraph (l) [or
[(n) in reliance on a European licence granted pursuant to—
(i) a provision contained in any instrument made for the purpose of implementing Council Directive 1995/18/EC dated 19th June 1995 on the licensing of railway undertakings or Chapter III of Directive 2012/34/EU of the European Parliament and of the Council of 21st November 2012 establishing a single European railway area (recast), or
(ii) any action taken by an EEA State for that purpose.]]

(2) Sub-paragraph (1)(k) does not apply to the operator of a railway asset on a railway unless on some part of the railway there is a permitted line speed exceeding 40 kilometres per hour.

[(2A) For the purposes of section 72D a business is also regulated to the extent that it consists in the provision of a public electronic communications network or a public electronic communications service.]

[(2B) In sub-paragraph (1)(n), an "EEA State" means a member State, Norway, Iceland or Liechtenstein.]

"Person"

11. A reference to a person in this Schedule includes a reference to a partnership or another unincorporated group of persons.]

NOTES

Inserted by the Enterprise Act 2002, s 250(2), Sch 18.

Para 1: sub-para (1)(aa), (ab), sub-para (2)(d) and word immediately preceding it inserted by the Insolvency Act 1986 (Amendment) (Administrative Receivership and Capital Market Arrangements) Order 2003, SI 2003/1468, arts 2, 3.

Para 2: words in square brackets inserted by the Financial Services and Markets Act 2000 (Regulated Activities) (Amendment) Order 2010, SI 2010/86, art 4, Schedule, para 2(a).

Para 3: words in square brackets inserted by SI 2010/86, art 4, Schedule, para 2(b); a reference to commercial paper includes a reference to uncertificated units of an eligible debt security where the issue of units corresponds, in accordance with the current terms of issue of the security, to the issue of commercial paper within the meaning of art 9(3) of the Financial Services and Markets Act 2000 (Regulated Activities) Order 2001, SI 2001/544; see the Uncertificated Securities (Amendment) (Eligible Debt Securities) Regulations 2003, SI 2003/1633, reg 15(1), Sch 2, para 7.

Para 10: sub-para (1)(a) repealed and sub-para (2A) added by the Communications Act 2003, s 406(1), (7), Sch 17, para 82(1), (4), Sch 19; words in square brackets in sub-para (1)(b) substituted by the Electricity and Gas (Smart Meters Licensable Activity) Order 2012, SI 2012/2400, art 29; words in square brackets in sub-para (1)(g) substituted, sub-para (1)(h) substituted and sub-para (1)(i) repealed by the Postal Services Act 2011, s 91(1), (2), Sch 12, Pt 3, paras 124, 126; word omitted from sub-para (1)(l) repealed, sub-para (1)(n) and word immediately preceding it inserted, and sub-para (2B) inserted by the

Railway (Licensing of Railway Undertakings) Regulations 2005, SI 2005/3050, reg 3, Sch 1, Pt 1, para 2; sub-para (1)(n) substituted by the Railways (Access, Management and Licensing of Railway Undertakings) Regulations 2016, SI 2016/645, reg 2(2), Sch 1, para 2.

SCHEDULE 3
ORDERS IN COURSE OF WINDING UP PRONOUNCED IN VACATION (SCOTLAND)

Section 162

PART I
ORDERS WHICH ARE TO BE FINAL

[1.579]
Orders under section 153, as to the time for proving debts and claims.

Orders under section 195 as to meetings for ascertaining wishes of creditors or contributories.

Orders under section 198, as to the examination of witnesses in regard to the property or affairs of a company.

NOTES

This Part derived from the Companies Act 1985, Sch 16.

PART II
ORDERS WHICH ARE TO TAKE EFFECT UNTIL MATTER DISPOSED OF BY INNER HOUSE

[1.580]
Orders under section 126(1), 130(2) or (3), 147, 227 or 228, restraining or permitting the commencement or the continuance of legal proceedings.

Orders under section 135(5), limiting the powers of provisional liquidators.

Orders under section 108, appointing a liquidator to fill a vacancy.

. . .

Orders under section 158, as to the arrest and detention of an absconding contributory and his property.

NOTES

This Part derived from the Companies Act 1985, Sch 16.

Words omitted repealed by the Small Business, Enterprise and Employment Act 2015, s 120(1), (5).

SCHEDULE 4
POWERS OF LIQUIDATOR IN A WINDING UP

Sections 165, 167

PART I

. . .

[1.581]
1. Power to pay any class of creditors in full.

2. Power to make any compromise or arrangement with creditors or persons claiming to be creditors, or having or alleging themselves to have any claim (present or future, certain or contingent, ascertained or sounding only in damages) against the company, or whereby the company may be rendered liable.

3. [. . .] power to compromise, on such terms as may be agreed—

(a) all calls and liabilities to calls, all debts and liabilities capable of resulting in debts, and all claims (present or future, certain or contingent, ascertained or sounding only in damages) subsisting or supposed to subsist between the company and a contributory or alleged contributory or other debtor or person apprehending liability to the company, and

(b) all questions in any way relating to or affecting the assets or the winding up of the company,

and take any security for the discharge of any such call, debt, liability or claim and give a complete discharge in respect of it.

[**3A.** Power to bring legal proceedings under section 213, 214, 238, 239, 242, 243 or 423.]

NOTES

This Part derived from the Companies Act 1985, ss 539(1)(d)–(f), 598(2).

Part heading: words omitted repealed by the Small Business, Enterprise and Employment Act 2015, s 121(1), (6)(c).

Para 3: words omitted from square brackets inserted by the Legislative Reform (Insolvency) (Miscellaneous Provisions) Order 2010, SI 2010/18, arts 2, 10(1) and repealed by the Small Business, Enterprise and Employment Act 2015, s 121(1), (6)(a).

Para 3A: inserted by the Enterprise Act 2002, s 253, subject to transitional provisions in relation to proceedings of a kind mentioned in para 3A which were commenced before 15 September 2003 (see the Enterprise Act 2002 (Commencement No 4 and Transitional Provisions and Savings) Order 2003, SI 2003/2093, art 5 at **[2.28]**).

Modification: this Schedule is applied, with modifications, in respect of bank administration and applications for bank administration, by the Bank Administration (Scotland) Rules 2009, SI 2009/350, rr 39–42 and in respect of building society special administration and applications for special administration, by the Building Society Special Administration (Scotland) Rules 2009, SI 2009/806, rr 38–41.

PART II

. . .

[1.582]

4. Power to bring or defend any action or other legal proceeding in the name and on behalf of the company.

5. Power to carry on the business of the company so far as may be necessary for its beneficial winding up.

NOTES

This Part derived from the Companies Act 1985, ss 539(1)(a), (b), 598(2).

Part heading: words omitted repealed by the Small Business, Enterprise and Employment Act 2015, s 121(1), (6)(c).

Modification: see the note to Pt I of this Schedule at **[1.581]**.

PART III

. . .

[1.583]

6. Power to sell any of the company's property by public auction or private contract with power to transfer the whole of it to any person or to sell the same in parcels.

[6A. . . .]

7. Power to do all acts and execute, in the name and on behalf of the company, all deeds, receipts and other documents and for that purpose to use, when necessary, the company's seal.

8. Power to prove, rank and claim in the bankruptcy, insolvency or sequestration of any contributory for any balance against his estate, and to receive dividends in the bankruptcy, insolvency or sequestration in respect of that balance, as a separate debt due from the bankrupt or insolvent, and rateably with the other separate creditors.

9. Power to draw, accept, make and indorse any bill of exchange or promissory note in the name and on behalf of the company, with the same effect with respect to the company's liability as if the bill or note had been drawn, accepted, made or indorsed by or on behalf of the company in the course of its business.

10. Power to raise on the security of the assets of the company any money requisite.

11. Power to take out in his official name letters of administration to any deceased contributory, and to do in his official name any other act necessary for obtaining payment of any money due from a contributory or his estate which cannot conveniently be done in the name of the company.

In all such cases the money due is deemed, for the purpose of enabling the liquidator to take out the letters of administration or recover the money, to be due to the liquidator himself.

12. Power to appoint an agent to do any business which the liquidator is unable to do himself.

13. Power to do all such other things as may be necessary for winding up the company's affairs and distributing its assets.

NOTES

This Part derived from the Companies Act 1985, ss 539(2), 598(2).

Part heading: words omitted repealed by the Small Business, Enterprise and Employment Act 2015, s 121(1), (6)(c).

Para 6A: inserted in relation to England and Wales by the Legislative Reform (Insolvency) (Miscellaneous Provisions) Order 2010, SI 2010/18, arts 2, 10(2), and repealed by the Small Business, Enterprise and Employment Act 2015, s 121(1), (6)(b).

Modification: see the note to Pt I of this Schedule at **[1.581]**.

[SCHEDULE 4ZA
CONDITIONS FOR MAKING A DEBT RELIEF ORDER

PART 1
CONDITIONS WHICH MUST BE MET

Connection with England and Wales

[1.584]

1. (1) The debtor—

(a) is domiciled in England and Wales on the application date; or

(b) at any time during the period of three years ending with that date—

(i) was ordinarily resident, or had a place of residence, in England and Wales; or

(ii) carried on business in England and Wales.

(2) The reference in sub-paragraph (1)(b)(ii) to the debtor carrying on business includes—

(a) the carrying on of business by a firm or partnership of which he is a member;
(b) the carrying on of business by an agent or manager for him or for such a firm or partnership.

Debtor's previous insolvency history

2. The debtor is not, on the determination date—
(a) an undischarged bankrupt;
(b) subject to an interim order or voluntary arrangement under Part 8; or
(c) subject to a bankruptcy restrictions order or a debt relief restrictions order.

[**3.** A bankruptcy application under Part 9—
(a) has not been made before the determination date; or
(b) has been so made, but proceedings on the application have been finally disposed of before that date.]

4. A creditor's petition for the debtor's bankruptcy under Part 9—
(a) has not been presented against the debtor at any time before the determination date;
(b) has been so presented, but proceedings on the petition have been finally disposed of before that date; or
(c) has been so presented and proceedings in relation to the petition remain before the court at that date, but the person who presented the petition has consented to the making of an application for a debt relief order.

5. A debt relief order has not been made in relation to the debtor in the period of six years ending with the determination date.

Limit on debtor's overall indebtedness

6. (1) The total amount of the debtor's debts on the determination date, other than unliquidated debts and excluded debts, does not exceed the prescribed amount.

(2) For this purpose an unliquidated debt is a debt that is not for a liquidated sum payable to a creditor either immediately or at some future certain time.

Limit on debtor's monthly surplus income

7. (1) The debtor's monthly surplus income (if any) on the determination date does not exceed the prescribed amount.

(2) For this purpose "monthly surplus income" is the amount by which a person's monthly income exceeds the amount necessary for the reasonable domestic needs of himself and his family.

(3) The rules may—
(a) make provision as to how the debtor's monthly surplus income is to be determined;
(b) provide that particular descriptions of income are to be excluded for the purposes of this paragraph.

Limit on value of debtor's property

8. (1) The total value of the debtor's property on the determination date does not exceed the prescribed amount.

(2) The rules may—
(a) make provision as to how the value of a person's property is to be determined;
(b) provide that particular descriptions of property are to be excluded for the purposes of this paragraph.]

NOTES

Schedule inserted by the Tribunals, Courts and Enforcement Act 2007, s 108(2), Sch 18.

Para 3: substituted by the Enterprise and Regulatory Reform Act 2013, s 71(3), Sch 19, paras 1, 62, in respect of a petition for a bankruptcy order presented to the court by a debtor on or after 6 April 2016, and previously read as follows—

"**3.** A debtor's petition for the debtor's bankruptcy under Part 9—
(a) has not been presented by the debtor before the determination date;
(b) has been so presented, but proceedings on the petition have been finally disposed of before that date; or
(c) has been so presented and proceedings in relation to the petition remain before the court at that date, but the court has referred the debtor under section 274A(2) for the purposes of making an application for a debt relief order.".

[PART 2
OTHER CONDITIONS

[1.585]

9. (1) The debtor has not entered into a transaction with any person at an undervalue during the period between—
(a) the start of the period of two years ending with the application date; and
(b) the determination date.

(2) For this purpose a debtor enters into a transaction with a person at an undervalue if—
(a) he makes a gift to that person or he otherwise enters into a transaction with that person on terms that provide for him to receive no consideration;
(b) he enters into a transaction with that person in consideration of marriage or the formation of a civil partnership; or

(c) he enters into a transaction with that person for a consideration the value of which, in money or money's worth, is significantly less than the value, in money or money's worth, of the consideration provided by the individual.

10. (1) The debtor has not given a preference to any person during the period between—
(a) the start of the period of two years ending with the application date; and
(b) the determination date.

(2) For this purpose a debtor gives a preference to a person if—
(a) that person is one of the debtor's creditors to whom a qualifying debt is owed or is a surety or guarantor for any such debt, and
(b) the debtor does anything or suffers anything to be done which (in either case) has the effect of putting that person into a position which, in the event that a debt relief order is made in relation to the debtor, will be better than the position he would have been in if that thing had not been done.]

NOTES
Inserted as noted to Pt 1 at **[1.584]**.

[SCHEDULE 4ZB
DEBT RELIEF RESTRICTIONS ORDERS AND UNDERTAKINGS

Debt relief restrictions order

[1.586]
1. (1) A debt relief restrictions order may be made by the court in relation to a person in respect of whom a debt relief order has been made.

(2) An order may be made only on the application of—
(a) the Secretary of State, or
(b) the official receiver acting on a direction of the Secretary of State.

Grounds for making order

2. (1) The court shall grant an application for a debt relief restrictions order if it thinks it appropriate to do so having regard to the conduct of the debtor (whether before or after the making of the debt relief order).

(2) The court shall, in particular, take into account any of the following kinds of behaviour on the part of the debtor—
(a) failing to keep records which account for a loss of property by the debtor, or by a business carried on by him, where the loss occurred in the period beginning two years before the application date for the debt relief order and ending with the date of the application for the debt relief restrictions order;
(b) failing to produce records of that kind on demand by the official receiver;
(c) entering into a transaction at an undervalue in the period beginning two years before the application date for the debt relief order and ending with the date of the determination of that application;
(d) giving a preference in the period beginning two years before the application date for the debt relief order and ending with the date of the determination of that application;
(e) making an excessive pension contribution;
(f) a failure to supply goods or services that were wholly or partly paid for;
(g) trading at a time, before the date of the determination of the application for the debt relief order, when the debtor knew or ought to have known that he was himself to be unable to pay his debts;
(h) incurring, before the date of the determination of the application for the debt relief order, a debt which the debtor had no reasonable expectation of being able to pay;
(i) failing to account satisfactorily to the court or the official receiver for a loss of property or for an insufficiency of property to meet his debts;
(j) carrying on any gambling, rash and hazardous speculation or unreasonable extravagance which may have materially contributed to or increased the extent of his inability to pay his debts before the application date for the debt relief order or which took place between that date and the date of the determination of the application for the debt relief order;
(k) neglect of business affairs of a kind which may have materially contributed to or increased the extent of his inability to pay his debts;
(l) fraud or fraudulent breach of trust;
(m) failing to co-operate with the official receiver.

(3) The court shall also, in particular, consider whether the debtor was an undischarged bankrupt at some time during the period of six years ending with the date of the application for the debt relief order.

(4) For the purposes of sub-paragraph (2)—
"excessive pension contribution" shall be construed in accordance with section 342A;
"preference" shall be construed in accordance with paragraph 10(2) of Schedule 4ZA;
"undervalue" shall be construed in accordance with paragraph 9(2) of that Schedule.

Timing of application for order

3. An application for a debt relief restrictions order in respect of a debtor may be made—
(a) at any time during the moratorium period relating to the debt relief order in question, or

(b) after the end of that period, but only with the permission of the court.

Duration of order

4. (1) A debt relief restrictions order—
(a) comes into force when it is made, and
(b) ceases to have effect at the end of a date specified in the order.

(2) The date specified in a debt relief restrictions order under sub-paragraph (1)(b) must not be—
(a) before the end of the period of two years beginning with the date on which the order is made, or
(b) after the end of the period of 15 years beginning with that date.

Interim debt relief restrictions order

5. (1) This paragraph applies at any time between—
(a) the institution of an application for a debt relief restrictions order, and
(b) the determination of the application.

(2) The court may make an interim debt relief restrictions order if the court thinks that—
(a) there are prima facie grounds to suggest that the application for the debt relief restrictions order will be successful, and
(b) it is in the public interest to make an interim debt relief restrictions order.

(3) An interim debt relief restrictions order may only be made on the application of—
(a) the Secretary of State, or
(b) the official receiver acting on a direction of the Secretary of State.

(4) An interim debt relief restrictions order—
(a) has the same effect as a debt relief restrictions order, and
(b) comes into force when it is made.

(5) An interim debt relief restrictions order ceases to have effect—
(a) on the determination of the application for the debt relief restrictions order,
(b) on the acceptance of a debt relief restrictions undertaking made by the debtor, or
(c) if the court discharges the interim debt relief restrictions order on the application of the person who applied for it or of the debtor.

6. (1) This paragraph applies to a case in which both an interim debt relief restrictions order and a debt relief restrictions order are made.

(2) Paragraph 4(2) has effect in relation to the debt relief restrictions order as if a reference to the date of that order were a reference to the date of the interim debt relief restrictions order.

Debt relief restrictions undertaking

7. (1) A debtor may offer a debt relief restrictions undertaking to the Secretary of State.

(2) In determining whether to accept a debt relief restrictions undertaking the Secretary of State shall have regard to the matters specified in paragraph 2(2) and (3).

8. A reference in an enactment to a person in respect of whom a debt relief restrictions order has effect (or who is "the subject of" a debt relief restrictions order) includes a reference to a person in respect of whom a debt relief restrictions undertaking has effect.

9. (1) A debt relief restrictions undertaking—
(a) comes into force on being accepted by the Secretary of State, and
(b) ceases to have effect at the end of a date specified in the undertaking.

(2) The date specified under sub-paragraph (1)(b) must not be—
(a) before the end of the period of two years beginning with the date on which the undertaking is accepted, or
(b) after the end of the period of 15 years beginning with that date.

(3) On an application by the debtor the court may—
(a) annul a debt relief restrictions undertaking;
(b) provide for a debt relief restrictions undertaking to cease to have effect before the date specified under sub-paragraph (1)(b).

Effect of revocation of debt relief order

10. Unless the court directs otherwise, the revocation at any time of a debt relief order does not—
(a) affect the validity of any debt relief restrictions order, interim debt relief restrictions order or debt relief restrictions undertaking which is in force in respect of the debtor;
(b) prevent the determination of any application for a debt relief restrictions order, or an interim debt relief restrictions order, in relation to the debtor that was instituted before that time;
(c) prevent the acceptance of a debt relief restrictions undertaking that was offered before that time; or
(d) prevent the institution of an application for a debt relief restrictions order or interim debt relief restrictions order in respect of the debtor, or the offer or acceptance of a debt relief restrictions undertaking by the debtor, after that time.]

NOTES

Inserted by the Tribunals, Courts and Enforcement Act 2007, s 108(2), Sch 19.

See further: the Tribunals, Courts and Enforcement Act 2007 (Transitional Provision) Order 2009, SI 2009/450, art 2, provides that where a court is considering whether or not a debt relief restrictions order should be made in relation to a debtor under this Schedule it shall not take into account any conduct of the debtor before 6 April 2009.

[SCHEDULE 4A
BANKRUPTCY RESTRICTIONS ORDER AND UNDERTAKING

Bankruptcy restrictions order

[1.587]

1. (1) A bankruptcy restrictions order may be made by the court.

(2) An order may be made only on the application of—

(a) the Secretary of State, or

(b) the official receiver acting on a direction of the Secretary of State.

Grounds for making order

2. (1) The court shall grant an application for a bankruptcy restrictions order if it thinks it appropriate having regard to the conduct of the bankrupt (whether before or after the making of the bankruptcy order).

(2) The court shall, in particular, take into account any of the following kinds of behaviour on the part of the bankrupt—

(a) failing to keep records which account for a loss of property by the bankrupt, or by a business carried on by him, where the loss occurred in the period beginning 2 years before [the making of the bankruptcy application or (as the case may be) the presentation of the bankruptcy petition and ending with the date of the application for the bankruptcy restrictions order];

(b) failing to produce records of that kind on demand by the official receiver or the trustee;

(c) entering into a transaction at an undervalue;

(d) giving a preference;

(e) making an excessive pension contribution;

(f) a failure to supply goods or services which were wholly or partly paid for which gave rise to a claim provable in the bankruptcy;

(g) trading at a time before commencement of the bankruptcy when the bankrupt knew or ought to have known that he was himself to be unable to pay his debts;

(h) incurring, before commencement of the bankruptcy, a debt which the bankrupt had no reasonable expectation of being able to pay;

(i) failing to account satisfactorily to the court, the official receiver or the trustee for a loss of property or for an insufficiency of property to meet bankruptcy debts;

(j) carrying on any gambling, rash and hazardous speculation or unreasonable extravagance which may have materially contributed to or increased the extent of the bankruptcy or which took place between [the making of the bankruptcy application or (as the case may be) the presentation of the bankruptcy petition] and commencement of the bankruptcy;

(k) neglect of business affairs of a kind which may have materially contributed to or increased the extent of the bankruptcy;

(l) fraud or fraudulent breach of trust;

(m) failing to cooperate with the official receiver or the trustee.

(3) The court shall also, in particular, consider whether the bankrupt was an undischarged bankrupt at some time during the period of six years ending with the date of the bankruptcy to which the application relates.

(4) For the purpose of sub-paragraph (2)—

"before petition" shall be construed in accordance with section 351(c),

"excessive pension contribution" shall be construed in accordance with section 342A,

"preference" shall be construed in accordance with section 340, and

"undervalue" shall be construed in accordance with section 339.

Timing of application for order

3. (1) An application for a bankruptcy restrictions order in respect of a bankrupt must be made—

(a) before the end of the period of one year beginning with the date on which the bankruptcy commences, or

(b) with the permission of the court.

(2) The period specified in sub-paragraph (1)(a) shall cease to run in respect of a bankrupt while the period set for his discharge is suspended under section 279(3).

Duration of order

4. (1) A bankruptcy restrictions order—

(a) shall come into force when it is made, and

(b) shall cease to have effect at the end of a date specified in the order.

(2) The date specified in a bankruptcy restrictions order under sub-paragraph (1)(b) must not be—

(a) before the end of the period of two years beginning with the date on which the order is made, or

(b) after the end of the period of 15 years beginning with that date.

Interim bankruptcy restrictions order

5. (1) This paragraph applies at any time between—
(a) the institution of an application for a bankruptcy restrictions order, and
(b) the determination of the application.

(2) The court may make an interim bankruptcy restrictions order if the court thinks that—
(a) there are prima facie grounds to suggest that the application for the bankruptcy restrictions order will be successful, and
(b) it is in the public interest to make an interim order.

(3) An interim order may be made only on the application of—
(a) the Secretary of State, or
(b) the official receiver acting on a direction of the Secretary of State.

(4) An interim order—
(a) shall have the same effect as a bankruptcy restrictions order, and
(b) shall come into force when it is made.

(5) An interim order shall cease to have effect—
(a) on the determination of the application for the bankruptcy restrictions order,
(b) on the acceptance of a bankruptcy restrictions undertaking made by the bankrupt, or
(c) if the court discharges the interim order on the application of the person who applied for it or of the bankrupt.

6. (1) This paragraph applies to a case in which both an interim bankruptcy restrictions order and a bankruptcy restrictions order are made.

(2) Paragraph 4(2) shall have effect in relation to the bankruptcy restrictions order as if a reference to the date of that order were a reference to the date of the interim order.

Bankruptcy restrictions undertaking

7. (1) A bankrupt may offer a bankruptcy restrictions undertaking to the Secretary of State.

(2) In determining whether to accept a bankruptcy restrictions undertaking the Secretary of State shall have regard to the matters specified in paragraph 2(2) and (3).

8. A reference in an enactment to a person in respect of whom a bankruptcy restrictions order has effect (or who is "the subject of" a bankruptcy restrictions order) includes a reference to a person in respect of whom a bankruptcy restrictions undertaking has effect.

9. (1) A bankruptcy restrictions undertaking—
(a) shall come into force on being accepted by the Secretary of State, and
(b) shall cease to have effect at the end of a date specified in the undertaking.

(2) The date specified under sub-paragraph (1)(b) must not be—
(a) before the end of the period of two years beginning with the date on which the undertaking is accepted, or
(b) after the end of the period of 15 years beginning with that date.

(3) On an application by the bankrupt the court may—
(a) annul a bankruptcy restrictions undertaking;
(b) provide for a bankruptcy restrictions undertaking to cease to have effect before the date specified under sub-paragraph (1)(b).

Effect of annulment of bankruptcy order

10. Where a bankruptcy order is annulled under section 282(1)(a) or (2)—
(a) any bankruptcy restrictions order, interim order or undertaking which is in force in respect of the bankrupt shall be annulled,
(b) no new bankruptcy restrictions order or interim order may be made in respect of the bankrupt, and
(c) no new bankruptcy restrictions undertaking by the bankrupt may be accepted.

11. Where a bankruptcy order is annulled under section 261 . . . or 282(1)(b)—
(a) the annulment shall not affect any bankruptcy restrictions order, interim order or undertaking in respect of the bankrupt,
(b) the court may make a bankruptcy restrictions order in relation to the bankrupt on an application instituted before the annulment,
(c) the Secretary of State may accept a bankruptcy restrictions undertaking offered before the annulment, and
(d) an application for a bankruptcy restrictions order or interim order in respect of the bankrupt may not be instituted after the annulment.

Registration

12. The Secretary of State shall maintain a register of—
(a) bankruptcy restrictions orders,
(b) interim bankruptcy restrictions orders, and
(c) bankruptcy restrictions undertakings.]

NOTES

Inserted by the Enterprise Act 2002, s 257(2), Sch 20, subject to transitional provisions in s 256(2) of, and Sch 19 to, that Act at **[2.13]**, **[2.22]**.

Para 2: words in square brackets in sub-para (2)(a) substituted for original words "petition and ending with the date of the application", words in square brackets in sub-para (2)(j) substituted for original words "presentation of the petition" and in sub-para (4) definition "before petition" repealed, by the Enterprise and Regulatory Reform Act 2013, s 71(3), Sch 19, paras 1, 63, in respect of a petition for a bankruptcy order presented to the court by a debtor on or after 6 April 2016.

Para 11: reference to ", 263D" (omitted) repealed by the Small Business, Enterprise and Employment Act 2015, s 135(2)(b), (4), except in relation to a case where a debtor has submitted the document and statement mentioned in s 263B(1) to the official receiver before 26 May 2015.

Bankruptcy restrictions order: where a court is considering whether or not a bankruptcy restrictions order should be made pursuant to this Schedule and section 281A at **[1.342]**, it shall not take into account any conduct of the bankrupt before 1 April 2004; see the Enterprise Act 2002 (Commencement No 4 and Transitional Provisions and Savings) Order 2003, SI 2003/2093, art 7 at **[2.30]**.

SCHEDULE 5
POWERS OF TRUSTEE IN BANKRUPTCY

Section 314

PART I

. . .

[1.588]

1. Power to carry on any business of the bankrupt so far as may be necessary for winding it up beneficially and so far as the trustee is able to do so without contravening any requirement imposed by or under any enactment.

2. Power to bring, institute or defend any action or legal proceedings relating to the property comprised in the bankrupt's estate.

[**2A.** Power to bring legal proceedings under section 339, 340 or 423.]

3. Power to accept as the consideration for the sale of any property comprised in the bankrupt's estate a sum of money payable at a future time subject to such stipulations as to security or otherwise as the creditors' committee or the court thinks fit.

4. Power to mortgage or pledge any part of the property comprised in the bankrupt's estate for the purpose of raising money for the payment of his debts.

5. Power, where any right, option or other power forms part of the bankrupt's estate, to make payments or incur liabilities with a view to obtaining, for the benefit of the creditors, any property which is the subject of the right, option or power.

6. . . .

7. Power to make such compromise or other arrangement as may be thought expedient with creditors, or persons claiming to be creditors, in respect of bankruptcy debts.

8. Power to make such compromise or other arrangement as may be thought expedient with respect to any claim arising out of or incidental to the bankrupt's estate made or capable of being made on the trustee by any person . . .

NOTES

This Part derived from the Insolvency Act 1985, s 160(2).

Part heading: words omitted repealed by the Small Business, Enterprise and Employment Act 2015, s 121(1), (3).

Para 2A: inserted by the Enterprise Act 2002, s 262, subject to transitional provisions in relation to proceedings of a kind mentioned in para 2A which were commenced before 15 September 2003 (see the Enterprise Act 2002 (Commencement No 4 and Transitional Provisions and Savings) Order 2003, SI 2003/2093, art 6 at **[2.29]**).

Para 6: repealed in relation to England and Wales by the Legislative Reform (Insolvency) (Miscellaneous Provisions) Order 2010, SI 2010/18, arts 2, 11(1)(a), subject to transitional provisions in art 12(5) thereof at **[2.76]**, and previously read as follows:

"Power to refer to arbitration, or compromise on such terms as may be agreed on, any debts, claims or liabilities subsisting or supposed to subsist between the bankrupt and any person who may have incurred any liability to the bankrupt.".

Para 8: words "or by the trustee on any person" (omitted) repealed in relation to England and Wales by SI 2010/18, arts 2, 11(1)(b), subject to transitional provisions in art 12(5) thereof at **[2.76]**.

PART II

. . .

[1.589]

9. Power to sell any part of the property for the time being comprised in the bankrupt's estate, including the goodwill and book debts of any business.

[**9A.** Power to refer to arbitration, or compromise on such terms as may be agreed, any debts, claims or liabilities subsisting or supposed to subsist between the bankrupt and any person who may have incurred any liability to the bankrupt.

9B. Power to make such compromise or other arrangement as may be thought expedient with respect to any claim arising out of or incidental to the bankrupt's estate made or capable of being made by the trustee on any person.]

10. Power to give receipts for any money received by him, being receipts which effectually discharge the person paying the money from all responsibility in respect of its application.

11. Power to prove, rank, claim and draw a dividend in respect of such debts due to the bankrupt as are comprised in his estate.

12. Power to exercise in relation to any property comprised in the bankrupt's estate any powers the capacity to exercise which is vested in him under Parts VIII to XI of this Act.

13. Power to deal with any property comprised in the estate to which the bankrupt is beneficially entitled as tenant in tail in the same manner as the bankrupt might have dealt with it.

NOTES

This Part derived from the Insolvency Act 1985, s 160(1).

Part heading: words omitted repealed by the Small Business, Enterprise and Employment Act 2015, s 121(1), (3).

Paras 9A, 9B: inserted in relation to England and Wales by the Legislative Reform (Insolvency) (Miscellaneous Provisions) Order 2010, SI 2010/18, arts 2, 11(2), subject to transitional provisions in art 12(5) thereof at **[2.76]**.

PART III

. . .

[1.590]

14. For the purposes of, or in connection with, the exercise of any of his powers under Parts VIII to XI of this Act, the trustee may, by his official name—

(a) hold property of every description,
(b) make contracts,
(c) sue and be sued,
(d) enter into engagements binding on himself and, in respect of the bankrupt's estate, on his successors in office,
(e) employ an agent,
(f) execute any power of attorney, deed or other instrument;

and he may do any other act which is necessary or expedient for the purposes of or in connection with the exercise of those powers.

NOTES

This Part derived from the Insolvency Act 1985, s 160(6).

Part heading: words omitted repealed by the Small Business, Enterprise and Employment Act 2015, s 121(1), (3).

SCHEDULE 6
THE CATEGORIES OF PREFERENTIAL DEBTS

Section 386

[1.591]

1–7. . . .

Category 4: Contributions to occupational pension schemes, etc

8. Any sum which is owed by the debtor and is a sum to which [Schedule 4 to the Pension Schemes Act 1993] applies (contributions to occupational pension schemes and state scheme premiums).

Category 5: Remuneration, etc, of employees

9. So much of any amount which—

(a) is owed by the debtor to a person who is or has been an employee of the debtor, and
(b) is payable by way of remuneration in respect of the whole or any part of the period of 4 months next before the relevant date,

as does not exceed so much as may be prescribed by order made by the Secretary of State.

10. An amount owed by way of accrued holiday remuneration, in respect of any period of employment before the relevant date, to a person whose employment by the debtor has been terminated, whether before, on or after that date.

11. So much of any sum owed in respect of money advanced for the purpose as has been applied for the payment of a debt which, if it had not been paid, would have been a debt falling within paragraph 9 or 10.

12. So much of any amount which—

(a) is ordered (whether before or after the relevant date) to be paid by the debtor under the Reserve Forces (Safeguard of Employment) Act 1985, and

(b) is so ordered in respect of a default made by the debtor before that date in the discharge of his obligations under that Act,

as does not exceed such amount as may be prescribed by order made by the Secretary of State.

Interpretation for Category 5

13. (1) For the purposes of paragraphs 9 to 12, a sum is payable by the debtor to a person by way of remuneration in respect of any period if—

(a) it is paid as wages or salary (whether payable for time or for piece work or earned wholly or partly by way of commission) in respect of services rendered to the debtor in that period, or

(b) it is an amount falling within the following sub-paragraph and is payable by the debtor in respect of that period.

[(2) An amount falls within this sub-paragraph if it is—

(a) a guarantee payment under Part III of the Employment Rights Act 1996 (employee without work to do);

(b) any payment for time off under section 53 (time off to look for work or arrange training) or section 56 (time off for ante-natal care) of that Act or under section 169 of the Trade Union and Labour Relations (Consolidation) Act 1992 (time off for carrying out trade union duties etc);

(c) remuneration on suspension on medical grounds, or on maternity grounds, under Part VII of the Employment Rights Act 1996; or

(d) remuneration under a protective award under section 189 of the Trade Union and Labour Relations (Consolidation) Act 1992 (redundancy dismissal with compensation).]

14. (1) This paragraph relates to a case in which a person's employment has been terminated by or in consequence of his employer going into liquidation or being [made] bankrupt or (his employer being a company not in liquidation) by or in consequence of—

(a) a receiver being appointed as mentioned in section 40 of this Act (debenture-holders secured by floating charge), or

(b) the appointment of a receiver under section 53(6) or 54(5) of this Act (Scottish company with property subject to floating charge), or

(c) the taking of possession by debenture-holders (so secured), as mentioned in [section 754 of the Companies Act 2006].

(2) For the purposes of paragraphs 9 to 12, holiday remuneration is deemed to have accrued to that person in respect of any period of employment if, by virtue of his contract of employment or of any enactment that remuneration would have accrued in respect of that period if his employment had continued until he became entitled to be allowed the holiday.

(3) The reference in sub-paragraph (2) to any enactment includes an order or direction made under an enactment.

15. Without prejudice to paragraphs 13 and 14—

(a) any remuneration payable by the debtor to a person in respect of a period of holiday or of absence from work through sickness or other good cause is deemed to be wages or (as the case may be) salary in respect of services rendered to the debtor in that period . . .

(b) . . .

[Category 6: Levies on coal and steel production

15A. Any sums due at the relevant date from the debtor in respect of:

(a) the levies on the production of coal and steel referred to in Articles 49 and 50 of the ECSC Treaty, or

(b) any surcharge for delay provided for in Article 50(3) of that Treaty and Article 6 of Decision 3/52 of the High Authority of the Coal and Steel Community.]

[Category 6A: Debts owed to the Financial Services Compensation Scheme

15AA. Any debt owed by the debtor to the scheme manager of the Financial Services Compensation Scheme under section 215(2A) of the Financial Services and Markets Act 2000.]

[Category 7: Deposits covered by Financial Services Compensation Scheme

15B. So much of any amount owed at the relevant date by the debtor in respect of an eligible deposit as does not exceed the compensation that would be payable in respect of the deposit under the Financial Services Compensation Scheme to the person or persons to whom the amount is owed.

[Category 8: Other deposits

[15BA. So much of any amount owed at the relevant date by the debtor to one or more eligible persons in respect of an eligible deposit as exceeds any compensation that would be payable in respect of the deposit under the Financial Services Compensation Scheme to that person or those persons.

15BB. An amount owed at the relevant date by the debtor to one or more eligible persons in respect of a deposit that—

(a) was made through a non-EEA branch of a credit institution authorised by the competent authority of an EEA state, and

(b) would have been an eligible deposit if it had been made through an EEA branch of that credit institution.]

Interpretation for [Categories 6A, 7 and 8]

15C. [(A1) In paragraph 15AA "the scheme manager" has the meaning given in section 212(1) of the Financial Services and Markets Act 2000.]

(1) In [paragraphs 15B to 15BB] "eligible deposit" means a deposit in respect of which the person, or any of the persons, to whom it is owed would be eligible for compensation under the Financial Services Compensation Scheme.

(2) For [the purposes of those paragraphs and this paragraph] a "deposit" means rights of the kind described in—

- (a) paragraph 22 of Schedule 2 to the Financial Services and Markets Act 2000 (deposits), or
- (b) section 1(2)(b) of the Dormant Bank and Building Society Accounts Act 2008 (balances transferred under that Act to authorised reclaim fund).

[(3) In paragraphs 15BA and 15BB, "eligible person" means—

- (a) an individual, or
- (b) a micro-enterprise, a small enterprise or a medium-sized enterprise, each of those terms having the meaning given in Article 2.1(107) of Directive 2014/59/EU of 15th May 2014 establishing a framework for the recovery and resolution of credit institutions and investment firms.

(4) In paragraph 15BB—

- (a) "credit institution" has the meaning given in Article 4.1(1) of the capital requirements regulation;
- (b) "EEA branch" means a branch, as defined in Article 4.1(17) of the capital requirements regulation, which is established in an EEA state;
- (c) "non-EEA branch" means a branch, as so defined, which is established in a country which is not an EEA state;

and for this purpose "the capital requirements regulation" means Regulation (EU) No 575/2013 of the European Parliament and of the Council of 26th June 2013 on prudential requirements for credit institutions and investment firms and amending Regulation (EU) No 648/2012.]]

Orders

16. An order under paragraph 9 or 12—

- (a) may contain such transitional provisions as may appear to the Secretary of State necessary or expedient;
- (b) shall be made by statutory instrument subject to annulment in pursuance of a resolution of either House of Parliament.

NOTES

This Schedule derived from the Insolvency Act 1985, Sch 4, Pt I, Pt II, paras 2–4.

Paras 1–7: repealed by the Enterprise Act 2002, ss 251(1), 278(2), Sch 26, subject to transitional provisions in relation to the abolition of preferential status for Crown debts in cases which were started before 15 September 2003 (see the Enterprise Act 2002 (Commencement No 4 and Transitional Provisions and Savings) Order 2003, SI 2003/2093, art 4 at **[2.27]**).

Para 8: words in square brackets substituted by the Pension Schemes Act 1993, s 190, Sch 8, para 18.

Para 13: sub-para (2) substituted by the Employment Rights Act 1996, s 240, Sch 1, para 29.

Para 14: word in square brackets in sub-para (1) substituted for original word "adjudged", by the Enterprise and Regulatory Reform Act 2013, s 71(3), Sch 19, paras 1, 64, in respect of a petition for a bankruptcy order presented to the court by a debtor on or after 6 April 2016; words in square brackets in sub-para (1)(c) substituted by the Companies Act 2006 (Consequential Amendments etc) Order 2008, SI 2008/948, art 3(1)(b), Sch 1, Pt 2, para 104.

Para 15: sub-para (b) (and the preceding word) repealed by the Deregulation Act 2015, s 19, Sch 6, Pt 7, paras 24, 28.

Para 15A: inserted by the Insolvency (ECSC Levy Debts) Regulations 1987, SI 1987/2093, reg 2(1), (3).

Para 15AA: inserted by the Deposit Guarantee Scheme Regulations 2015, SI 2015/486, reg 14(1), (3)(a).

Para 15B: inserted, together with para 15C, by the Financial Services (Banking Reform) Act 2013, s 13(1).

Paras 15BA, 15BB: inserted by the Banks and Building Societies (Depositor Preference and Priorities) Order 2014, SI 2014/3486, arts 3, 11(1), (2), except in relation to any insolvency proceedings commenced before 1 January 2015 (as to the meaning of this, see further the note "SI 2014/3486, art 3" at **[1.5]**).

Para 15C: inserted as noted to para 15B above; the words in square brackets in the heading preceding para 15C were substituted, and sub-para (A1) was inserted, by SI 2015/486, reg 14(1), (3)(b), (c); the words in square brackets in sub-para (1) were substituted (for the original words "paragraph 15B"), the words in square brackets in sub-para (2) were substituted (for the original words "this purpose"), and sub-paras (3), (4) were added, by SI 2014/3486, arts 3, 11(1), (3), (4), except in relation to any insolvency proceedings commenced before 1 January 2015 (as to the meaning of this, see further the note "SI 2014/3486, art 3" at **[1.5]**).

Transfer to Secretary of State of rights and remedies on employer's insolvency: see the note to s 175 at **[1.176]**.

Orders: the Insolvency Proceedings (Monetary Limits) Order 1986, SI 1986/1996 at **[8.1]**.

SCHEDULE 7
INSOLVENCY PRACTITIONERS TRIBUNAL

Section 396

Panels of members

[1.592]

1. (1) The Secretary of State shall draw up and from time to time revise—

- *(a) a panel of persons who—*
  - *[[(i) satisfy the judicial-appointment eligibility condition on a 5-year basis;]*
  - *(ii) are advocates or solicitors in Scotland of at least [5] years' standing],*

and are nominated for the purpose by the Lord Chancellor or the Lord President of the Court of Session, and

(b) a panel of persons who are experienced in insolvency matters;

and the members of the Tribunal shall be selected from those panels in accordance with this Schedule.

(2) The power to revise the panels includes power to terminate a person's membership of either of them, and is accordingly to that extent subject to [section 7 of the Tribunals and Inquiries Act 1992] (which makes it necessary to obtain the concurrence of the Lord Chancellor and the Lord President of the Court of Session to dismissals in certain cases).

Remuneration of members

***2.** The Secretary of State may out of money provided by Parliament pay to members of the Tribunal such remuneration as he may with the approval of the Treasury determine; and such expenses of the Tribunal as the Secretary of State and the Treasury may approve shall be defrayed by the Secretary of State out of money so provided.*

Sittings of Tribunal

***3.** (1) For the purposes of carrying out their functions in relation to any cases referred to them, the Tribunal may sit either as a single tribunal or in two or more divisions.*

(2) The functions of the Tribunal in relation to any case referred to them shall be exercised by three members consisting of—

(a) a chairman selected by the Secretary of State from the panel drawn up under paragraph 1(1)(a) above, and

(b) two other members selected by the Secretary of State from the panel drawn up under paragraph 1(1)(b).

Procedure of Tribunal

***4.** (1) Any investigation by the Tribunal shall be so conducted as to afford a reasonable opportunity for representations to be made to the Tribunal by or on behalf of the person whose case is the subject of the investigation.*

(2) For the purposes of any such investigation, the Tribunal—

(a) may by summons require any person to attend, at such time and place as is specified in the summons, to give evidence or to produce any books, papers and other records in his possession or under his control which the Tribunal consider it necessary for the purposes of the investigation to examine, and

(b) may take evidence on oath, and for the purpose administer oaths, or may, instead of administering an oath, require the person examined to make and subscribe a declaration of the truth of the matter respecting which he is examined;

but no person shall be required, in obedience to such a summons, to go more than ten miles from his place of residence, unless the necessary expenses of his attendance are paid or tendered to him.

(3) Every person who—

(a) without reasonable excuse fails to attend in obedience to a summons issued under this paragraph, or refuses to give evidence, or

(b) intentionally alters, suppresses, conceals or destroys or refuses to produce any document which he may be required to produce for the purpose of an investigation by the Tribunal,

is liable to a fine.

(4) Subject to the provisions of this paragraph, the Secretary of State may make rules for regulating the procedure on any investigation by the Tribunal.

(5) In their application to Scotland, sub-paragraphs (2) and (3) above have effect as if for any reference to a summons there were substituted a reference to a notice in writing.

NOTES

This Schedule derived from the Insolvency Act 1985, Sch 1.

Repealed by the Deregulation Act 2015, s 19, Sch 6, Pt 6, paras 17, 21, as from 1 October 2015. For transitional provisions, see the note relating to the Deregulation Act 2015, Sch 6, Pt 6, para 23 at **[1.479]**.

Para 1: words in first (outer) pair of square brackets in sub-para (1)(a) substituted by the Courts and Legal Services Act 1990, s 71(2), Sch 10, para 67; sub-para (1)(a)(i) substituted, and in sub-para (1)(a)(ii) number in square brackets substituted for original number "7" by the Tribunals, Courts and Enforcement Act 2007, s 50(6), Sch 10, Pt 1, para 19, subject to transitional provisions in SI 2008/1653, arts 3, 4. Sub-para (1)(a)(i) previously read as follows:

"(i) have a 7 year general qualification, within the meaning of section 71 of the Courts and Legal Services Act 1990;";

words in square brackets in sub-para (2) substituted by the Tribunals and Inquiries Act 1992, s 18(1), Sch 3, para 19.

SCHEDULE 8
PROVISIONS CAPABLE OF INCLUSION IN COMPANY INSOLVENCY RULES

Section 411

Courts

[1.593]

1. Provision for supplementing, in relation to the insolvency or winding up of companies, any provision made by or under section 117 of this Act (jurisdiction in relation to winding up).

2. [(1)] Provision for regulating the practice and procedure of any court exercising jurisdiction for the purposes of Parts I to VII of this Act or [the Companies Acts] so far as relating to, and to matters connected with or arising out of, the insolvency or winding up of companies, being any provision that could be made by rules of court.

[(2) Rules made by virtue of this paragraph about the consequence of failure to comply with practice or procedure may, in particular, include provision about the termination of administration.]

Notices, etc

3. Provision requiring notice of any proceedings in connection with or arising out of the insolvency or winding up of a company to be given or published in the manner prescribed by the rules.

4. Provision with respect to the form, manner of serving, contents and proof of any petition, application, order, notice, statement or other document required to be presented, made, given, published or prepared under any enactment or subordinate legislation relating to, or to matters connected with or arising out of, the insolvency or winding up of companies.

5. Provision specifying the persons to whom any notice is to be given.

[**5A.** Provision for enabling a creditor of a company to elect to be, or to cease to be, an opted-out creditor in relation to an office-holder of the company (within the meaning of section 248A), including, in particular, provision—

(a) for requiring an office-holder to provide information to creditors about how they may elect to be, or cease to be, opted-out creditors;

(b) for deeming an election to be, or cease to be, an opted-out creditor in relation to a particular office-holder of a company to be such an election also in relation to any other office-holder of the company.]

Registration of voluntary arrangements

6. Provision for the registration of voluntary arrangements approved under Part I of this Act, including provision for the keeping and inspection of a register.

Provisional liquidator

7. Provision as to the manner in which a provisional liquidator appointed under section 135 is to carry out his functions.

Conduct of insolvency

8. Provision with respect to the certification of any person as, and as to the proof that a person is, the liquidator, administrator or administrative receiver of a company.

[**8A.** (1) Provision about the making of decisions by creditors and contributories, including provision—

(a) prescribing particular procedures by which creditors and contributories may make decisions;

(b) authorising the use of other procedures for creditors and contributories to make decisions, if those procedures comply with prescribed requirements.

(2) Provision under sub-paragraph (1) may in particular include provision about—

(a) how creditors and contributories may request that a creditors' meeting or a contributories' meeting be held,

(b) the rights of creditors, contributories and others to be given notice of, and participate in, procedures,

(c) creditors' and contributories' rights to vote in procedures,

(d) the period within which any right to participate or vote is to be exercised,

(e) the proportion of creditors or contributories that must vote for a proposal for it to be approved,

(f) how the value of any debt or contribution should be determined,

(g) the time at which decisions taken by a procedure are to be treated as having been made.]

9. The following provision with respect to meetings of a company's creditors, contributories or members—

(a) provision as to the manner of summoning a meeting (including provision as to how any power to require a meeting is to be exercised, provision as to the manner of determining the value of any debt or contribution for the purposes of any such power and provision making the exercise of any such power subject to the deposit of a sum sufficient to cover the expenses likely to be incurred in summoning and holding a meeting);

(b) provision specifying the time and place at which a meeting may be held and the period of notice required for a meeting;

(c) provision as to the procedure to be followed at a meeting (including the manner in which decisions may be reached by a meeting and the manner in which the value of any vote at a meeting is to be determined);

(d) provision for requiring a person who is or has been an officer of the company to attend a meeting;

(e) provision creating, in the prescribed circumstances, a presumption that a meeting has been duly summoned and held;

(f) provision as to the manner of proving the decisions of a meeting.

[9A. Provision about how a company's creditors may nominate a person to be liquidator, including in the case of a voluntary winding up provision conferring functions on the directors of the company.]

10. (1) Provision as to the [establishment,] functions, membership and proceedings of a committee [provided for by] [section 49, 68, 101, 141 or 142 of, or paragraph 57 of Schedule B1 to, this Act].

(2) The following provision with respect to the establishment of a committee under section 101, 141 or 142 of this Act, that is to say—

(a) provision for resolving differences between *a meeting of* the company's creditors and *a meeting of* its contributories or members;

(b) provision authorising the establishment of the committee without [seeking a decision from] contributories in a case where a company is being wound up on grounds including its inability to pay its debts; and

(c) provision modifying the requirements of this Act with respect to the establishment of the committee in a case where a winding-up order has been made immediately upon the discharge of an administration order.

11. Provision as to the manner in which any requirement that may be imposed on a person under any of Parts I to VII of this Act by the official receiver, the liquidator, administrator or administrative receiver of a company or a special manager appointed under section 177 is to be so imposed.

12. Provision as to the debts that may be proved in a winding up, as to the manner and conditions of proving a debt and as to the manner and expenses of establishing the value of any debt or security.

13. Provision with respect to the manner of the distribution of the property of a company that is being wound up, including provision with respect to unclaimed funds and dividends.

[13A. Provision for a creditor who has not proved a small debt to be treated as having done so for purposes relating to the distribution of a company's property (and for provisions of, or contained in legislation made under, this Act to apply accordingly).]

14. Provision which, with or without modifications, applies in relation to the winding up of companies any enactment contained in Parts VIII to XI of this Act or in the Bankruptcy (Scotland) Act [2016].

[14A. Provision about the application of section 176A of this Act which may include, in particular—

(a) provision enabling a receiver to institute winding up proceedings;

(b) provision requiring a receiver to institute winding up proceedings.]

[Administration

14B. Provision which—

(a) applies in relation to administration, with or without modifications, a provision of Parts IV to VII of this Act, or

(b) serves a purpose in relation to administration similar to a purpose that may be served by the rules in relation to winding up by virtue of a provision of this Schedule.]

Financial provisions

15. Provision as to the amount, or manner of determining the amount, payable to the liquidator, administrator or administrative receiver of a company or a special manager appointed under section 177, by way of remuneration for the carrying out of functions in connection with or arising out of the insolvency or winding up of a company.

16. Provision with respect to the manner in which moneys received by the liquidator of a company in the course of carrying out his functions as such are to be invested or otherwise handled and with respect to the payment of interest on sums which, in pursuance of rules made by virtue of this paragraph, have been paid into the Insolvency Services Account.

[16A. Provision enabling the Secretary of State to set the rate of interest paid on sums which have been paid into the Insolvency Services Account.]

17. Provision as to the fees, costs, charges and other expenses that may be treated as the expenses of a winding up.

18. Provision as to the fees, costs, charges and other expenses that may be treated as properly incurred by the administrator or administrative receiver of a company.

19. Provision as to the fees, costs, charges and other expenses that may be incurred for any of the purposes of Part I of this Act or in the administration of any voluntary arrangement approved under that Part.

Information and records

20. Provision requiring registrars and other officers of courts having jurisdiction in England and Wales in relation to, or to matters connected with or arising out of, the insolvency or winding up of companies—

(a) to keep books and other records with respect to the exercise of that jurisdiction, and

(b) to make returns to the Secretary of State of the business of those courts.

21. Provision requiring a creditor, member or contributory, or such a committee as is mentioned in paragraph 10 above, to be supplied (on payment in prescribed cases of the prescribed fee) with such information and with copies of such documents as may be prescribed.

22. Provision as to the manner in which public examinations under sections 133 and 134 of this Act and proceedings under sections 236 and 237 are to be conducted, as to the circumstances in which records of such examinations or proceedings are to be made available to prescribed persons and as to the costs of such examinations and proceedings.

23. Provision imposing requirements with respect to—

(a) the preparation and keeping by the liquidator, administrator or administrative receiver of a company, or by the supervisor of a voluntary arrangement approved under Part I of this Act, of prescribed books, accounts and other records;

(b) the production of those books, accounts and records for inspection by prescribed persons;

(c) the auditing of accounts kept by the liquidator, administrator or administrative receiver of a company, or the supervisor of such a voluntary arrangement; and

(d) the issue by the administrator or administrative receiver of a company of such a certificate as is mentioned in section 22(3)(b) of the Value Added Tax Act 1983 (refund of tax in cases of bad debts) and the supply of copies of the certificate to creditors of the company.

24. Provision requiring the person who is the supervisor of a voluntary arrangement approved under Part I, when it appears to him that the voluntary arrangement has been fully implemented and that nothing remains to be done by him under the arrangement—

(a) to give notice of that fact to persons bound by the voluntary arrangement, and

(b) to report to those persons on the carrying out of the functions conferred on the supervisor of the arrangement.

25. Provision as to the manner in which the liquidator of a company is to act in relation to the books, papers and other records of the company, including provision authorising their disposal.

26. Provision imposing requirements in connection with the carrying out of functions under section [7A] of the Company Directors Disqualification Act 1986 (including, in particular, requirements with respect to the making of periodic returns).

General

27. Provision conferring power on the Secretary of State [or the Treasury] to make regulations with respect to so much of any matter that may be provided for in the rules as relates to the carrying out of the functions of the liquidator, administrator or administrative receiver of a company.

28. Provision conferring a discretion on the court.

29. Provision conferring power on the court to make orders for the purpose of securing compliance with obligations imposed by or under [section 47, 66, 131, 143(2) or 235 of, or paragraph 47 of Schedule B1 to, this Act] or section 7(4) of the Company Directors Disqualification Act 1986.

30. Provision making non-compliance with any of the rules a criminal offence.

31. Provision making different provision for different cases or descriptions of cases, including different provisions for different areas.

NOTES

This Schedule derived from the Insolvency Act 1985, Sch 5.

Para 2: sub-para (1) numbered as such and sub-para (2) added by the Enterprise Act 2002, s 248(3), Sch 17, paras 9, 38(1), (2), subject to savings and transitional provisions (i) in a case where a petition for an administration order has been presented before 15 September 2003 (see the Enterprise Act 2002 (Commencement No 4 and Transitional Provisions and Savings) Order 2003, SI 2003/2093, art 3 at **[2.26]**), and (ii) in relation to special administration regimes (see s 249 of the 2002 Act at **[2.10]**); words in square brackets in sub-para (1) substituted for original words "the Companies Act" by the Companies Act 2006 (Commencement No 3, Consequential Amendments, Transitional Provisions and Savings) Order 2007, SI 2007/2194, art 10(1), (2), Sch 4, Pt 3, para 44, subject to savings in art 12 thereof.

Para 5A: inserted by the Small Business, Enterprise and Employment Act 2015, s 124(1), (5), as from 6 April 2017 (in relation to England and Wales and subject to transitional and savings provisions as noted to s 246ZE at **[1.256]**), and as from a day to be appointed (in relation to Scotland).

Para 8A: inserted by the Small Business, Enterprise and Employment Act 2015, s 122(1), (3), as from 6 April 2017 (in relation to England and Wales and subject to transitional and savings provisions as noted to s 246ZE at **[1.256]**), and as from a day to be appointed (in relation to Scotland).

Para 9A: inserted by the Small Business, Enterprise and Employment Act 2015, s 126, Sch 9, Pt 1, paras 1, 58, as from 6 April 2017 (in relation to England and Wales and subject to transitional and savings provisions as noted to s 246ZE at **[1.256]**), and as from a day to be appointed (in relation to Scotland).

Para 10: word in first pair of square brackets in sub-para (1) inserted, words in second pair of square brackets in sub-para (1) substituted for original words "established under", words in italics in sub-para (2)(a) repealed, and words in square brackets in sub-para (2)(b) substituted for original words "a meeting of", by the Small Business, Enterprise and Employment Act 2015, s 126, Sch 9, Pt 1, paras 1, 59, as from 6 April 2017 (in relation to England and Wales and subject to transitional and savings provisions as noted to s 246ZE at **[1.256]**), and as from a day to be appointed (in relation to Scotland); words in third pair of square brackets in sub-para (1) substituted for original words "section 26, 49, 68, 101, 141 or 142 of this Act" by the Enterprise Act 2002, s 248(3), Sch 17, paras 9, 38(1), (3), subject to savings as noted to para 2 above.

Para 13A: inserted by the Small Business, Enterprise and Employment Act 2015, s 131.

Para 14: year "2016" in square brackets substituted (for the original year "1985") by the Bankruptcy (Scotland) Act 2016 (Consequential Provisions and Modifications) Order 2016, SI 2016/1034, art 7(1), (3), Sch 1, para 4(1), (11), as from 30 November 2016 (except in relation to (i) a sequestration as regards which the petition is presented, or the debtor application is made before that date; or (ii) a trust deed executed before that date).

Paras 14A, 14B: inserted by the Enterprise Act 2002, s 248(3), Sch 17, paras 9, 38(1), (4), (5), subject to savings as noted to para 2 above.

Para 16A: inserted by the Enterprise Act 2002, s 271(1).

Para 26: figure in square brackets substituted by the Enterprise and Regulatory Reform Act 2013 (Consequential Amendments) (Bankruptcy) and the Small Business, Enterprise and Employment Act 2015 (Consequential Amendments) Regulations 2016, SI 2016/481, reg 3.

Para 27: words in square brackets inserted by the Banking Act 2009, s 125(7).

Para 29: words in square brackets substituted for original words "section 22, 47, 66, 131, 143(2) or 235 of this Act" by the Enterprise Act 2002, s 248(3), Sch 17, paras 9, 38(1), (6), subject to savings as noted to para 2 above.

Value Added Tax Act 1983, s 22(3)(b): repealed by the Finance Act 1990, ss 11(9), 132, Sch 19, Pt III.

Regulations: the Insolvency Regulations 1994, SI 1994/2507 at **[8.22]**.

SCHEDULE 9
PROVISIONS CAPABLE OF INCLUSION IN INDIVIDUAL INSOLVENCY RULES

Section 412

Courts

[1.594]

1. Provision with respect to the arrangement and disposition of the business under [Parts 7A to 11] of this Act of courts having jurisdiction for the purpose of those Parts, including provision for the allocation of proceedings under those Parts to particular courts and for the transfer of such proceedings from one court to another.

2. Provision for enabling [an Insolvency and Companies Court Judge] . . . to exercise such of the jurisdiction conferred for those purposes on the High Court . . . as may be prescribed.

3. Provision for regulating the practice and procedure of any court exercising jurisdiction for the purposes of those Parts, being any provision that could be made by rules of court.

4. Provision conferring rights of audience, in courts exercising jurisdiction for the purposes of those Parts, on the official receiver and on solicitors.

[Adjudicators

4A. Provision for regulating the practice and procedure of adjudicators in the discharge of functions for the purposes of Part 9 of this Act.

4B. Provision about the form and content of a bankruptcy application (including an application for a review of an adjudicator's determination).]

[Appeals against determinations by adjudicators

4C. Provision about the making and determining of appeals to the court against a determination by an adjudicator, including provision—

(a) enabling the court to make a bankruptcy order on such an appeal, and
(b) about where such appeals lie.]

Notices, etc

5. Provision requiring notice of any proceedings under [Parts 7A to 11] of this Act or of any matter relating to or arising out of a proposal under Part VIII or a bankruptcy to be given or published in the prescribed manner.

6. Provision with respect to the form, manner of serving, contents and proof of any petition, application, order, notice, statement or other document required to be presented, made, given, published or prepared under any enactment contained in [Parts 7A to 11] or subordinate legislation under those Parts or Part XV (including provision requiring prescribed matters to be verified by affidavit).

7. Provision specifying the persons to whom any notice under Parts VIII to XI is to be given.

[Debt relief orders

7A. Provision as to the manner in which the official receiver is to carry out his functions under Part 7A.

[**7A.** Provision for enabling a creditor of an individual to elect to be, or to cease to be, an opted-out creditor in relation to an office-holder for the individual (within the meaning of section 383A), including, in particular, provision—

(a) for requiring an office-holder to provide information to creditors about how they may elect to be, or cease to be, opted-out creditors;
(b) for deeming an election to be, or cease to be, an opted-out creditor in relation to a particular office-holder for an individual to be such an election also in relation to any other office-holder for the individual.]

7B. Provision as to the manner in which any requirement that may be imposed by the official receiver on a person under Part 7A is to take effect.

7C. Provision modifying the application of Part 7A in relation to an individual who has died at a time when a moratorium period under a debt relief order applies in relation to him.

Debt relief restrictions orders and undertakings

7D. Provision about debt relief restrictions orders, interim orders and undertakings, including provision about evidence.

Register of debt relief orders and debt relief restrictions orders etc

7E. Provision about the register required to be maintained by section 251W and the information to be contained in it, including provision—

(a) enabling the amalgamation of the register with another register;
(b) enabling inspection of the register by the public.]

Registration of voluntary arrangements

8. Provision for the registration of voluntary arrangements approved under Part VIII of this Act, including provision for the keeping and inspection of a register.

[Official receiver acting on voluntary arrangement

8A. Provision about the official receiver acting as nominee or supervisor in relation to a voluntary arrangement under Part VIII of this Act, including—

(a) provision requiring the official receiver to act in specified circumstances;
(b) provision about remuneration;
(c) provision prescribing terms or conditions to be treated as forming part of a voluntary arrangement in relation to which the official receiver acts as nominee or supervisor;
(d) provision enabling those terms or conditions to be varied or excluded, in specified circumstances or subject to specified conditions, by express provision in an arrangement.]

Interim receiver

9. Provision as to the manner in which an interim receiver appointed under section 286 is to carry out his functions, including any such provision as is specified in relation to the trustee of a bankrupt's estate in paragraph 21 or 27 below.

Receiver or manager

10. Provision as to the manner in which the official receiver is to carry out his functions as receiver or manager of a bankrupt's estate under section 287, including any such provision as is specified in relation to the trustee of a bankrupt's estate in paragraph 21 or 27 below.

Administration of individual insolvency

11. Provision with respect to the certification of the appointment of any person as trustee of a bankrupt's estate and as to the proof of that appointment.

[11A. (1) Provision about the making of decisions by creditors, including provision—

(a) prescribing particular procedures by which creditors may make decisions;
(b) authorising the use of other procedures for creditors to make decisions, if those procedures comply with prescribed requirements.

(2) Provision under sub-paragraph (1) may in particular include provision about—

(a) how creditors may request that a creditors' meeting be held,
(b) the rights of creditors and others to be given notice of, and participate in, procedures,
(c) creditors' rights to vote in procedures,
(d) the period within which any right to participate or vote is to be exercised,
(e) the proportion of creditors that must vote for a proposal for it to be approved,
(f) how the value of any debt should be determined,
(g) the time at which decisions taken by a procedure are to be treated as having been made.]

12. The following provision with respect to meetings of creditors—

(a) provision as to the manner of summoning a meeting (including provision as to how any power to require a meeting is to be exercised, provision as to the manner of determining the value of any debt for the purposes of any such power and provision making the exercise of any such power subject to the deposit of a sum sufficient to cover the expenses likely to be incurred in summoning and holding a meeting);
(b) provision specifying the time and place at which a meeting may be held and the period of notice required for a meeting;
(c) provision as to the procedure to be followed at such a meeting (including the manner in which decisions may be reached by a meeting and the manner in which the value of any vote at a meeting is to be determined);
(d) provision for requiring a bankrupt or debtor to attend a meeting;
(e) provision creating, in the prescribed circumstances, a presumption that a meeting has been duly summoned and held; and
(f) provision as to the manner of proving the decisions of a meeting.

[12A. Provision about how a bankrupt's creditors may appoint a person as trustee.]

13. Provision as to the [establishment,] functions, membership and proceedings of a creditors' committee [provided for by] section 301.

14. Provision as to the manner in which any requirement that may be imposed on a person under Parts VIII to XI of this Act by the official receiver, the trustee of a bankrupt's estate or a special manager appointed under section 370 is to be so imposed and, in the case of any requirement imposed under section 305(3) (information etc to be given by the trustee to the official receiver), provision conferring power on the court to make orders for the purpose of securing compliance with that requirement.

15. Provision as to the manner in which any requirement imposed by virtue of section 310(3) (compliance with income payments order) is to take effect.

16. Provision as to the terms and conditions that may be included in a charge under section 313 (dwelling house forming part of bankrupt's estate).

17. Provision as to the debts that may be proved in any bankruptcy, as to the manner and conditions of proving a debt and as to the manner and expenses of establishing the value of any debt or security.

18. Provision with respect to the manner of the distribution of a bankrupt's estate, including provision with respect to unclaimed funds and dividends.

[18A. Provision for a creditor who has not proved a small debt to be treated as having done so for purposes relating to the distribution of a bankrupt's estate (and for provisions of, or contained in legislation made under, this Act to apply accordingly).]

19. Provision modifying the application of Parts VIII to XI of this Act in relation to a debtor or bankrupt who has died.

Financial provisions

20. Provision as to the amount, or manner of determining the amount, payable to an interim receiver, the trustee of a bankrupt's estate or a special manager appointed under section 370 by way of remuneration for the performance of functions in connection with or arising out of the bankruptcy of any person.

21. Provision with respect to the manner in which moneys received by the trustee of a bankrupt's estate in the course of carrying out his functions as such are to be [invested or otherwise handled and with respect to the payment of interest on sums which, in pursuance of rules made by virtue of this paragraph, have been paid into the Insolvency Services Account].

[21A. Provision enabling the Secretary of State to set the rate of interest paid on sums which have been paid into the Insolvency Services Account.]

22. Provision as to the fees, costs, charges and other expenses that may be treated as the expenses of a bankruptcy.

23. Provision as to the fees, costs, charges and other expenses that may be incurred for any of the purposes of Part VIII of this Act or in the administration of any voluntary arrangement approved under that Part.

Information and records

24. Provision requiring registrars and other officers of courts having jurisdiction for the purposes of Parts VIII to XI—

(a) to keep books and other records with respect to the exercise of that jurisdiction *and of jurisdiction under the Deeds of Arrangement Act 1914*, and

(b) to make returns to the Secretary of State of the business of those courts.

[24A. Provision requiring adjudicators—

(a) to keep files and other records relating to bankruptcy applications and bankruptcies resulting from bankruptcy applications,

(b) to make files and records available for inspection by persons of a prescribed description, and

(c) to provide files and records, or copies of them, to persons of a prescribed description.]

24B. Provision requiring an adjudicator to make returns to the Secretary of State of the adjudicator's business under Part 9 of this Act.

24C. Provision requiring official receivers—

(a) to keep files and other records relating to bankruptcy applications and bankruptcies resulting from bankruptcy applications, and

(b) to make files and records available for inspection by persons of a prescribed description.

24D. Provision requiring a person to whom notice is given under section 293(2), 295(3), 298(7) or (8) or section 299(1)(a) or (3)(a)—

(a) to keep files and other records of notices given under the section in question, and

(b) to make files and records available for inspection by persons of a prescribed description.]

25. Provision requiring a creditor or a committee established under section 301 to be supplied (on payment in prescribed cases of the prescribed fee) with such information and with copies of such documents as may be prescribed.

26. Provision as to the manner in which public examinations under section 290 and proceedings under sections 366 to 368 are to be conducted, as to the circumstances in which records of such examinations and proceedings are to be made available to prescribed persons and as to the costs of such examinations and proceedings.

27. Provision imposing requirements with respect to—
- (a) the preparation and keeping by the trustee of a bankrupt's estate, or the supervisor of a voluntary arrangement approved under Part VIII, of prescribed books, accounts and other records;
- (b) the production of those books, accounts and records for inspection by prescribed persons; and
- (c) the auditing of accounts kept by the trustee of a bankrupt's estate or the supervisor of such a voluntary arrangement.

28. Provision requiring the person who is the supervisor of a voluntary arrangement approved under Part VIII, when it appears to him that the voluntary arrangement has been fully implemented and that nothing remains to be done by him under it—
- (a) to give notice of that fact to persons bound by the voluntary arrangement, and
- (b) to report to those persons on the carrying out of the functions conferred on the supervisor of it.

29. Provision as to the manner in which the trustee of a bankrupt's estate is to act in relation to the books, papers and other records of the bankrupt, including provision authorising their disposal.

[Bankruptcy restrictions orders and undertakings

29A. Provision about bankruptcy restrictions orders, interim orders and undertakings, including—
- (a) provision about evidence;
- (b) provision enabling the amalgamation of the register mentioned in paragraph 12 of Schedule 4A with another register;
- (c) provision enabling inspection of that register by the public.]

General

30. Provision conferring power on the Secretary of State to make regulations with respect to so much of any matter that may be provided for in the rules as relates to the carrying out of the functions of an interim receiver appointed under section 286 . . .

31. Provision conferring a discretion on the court.

32. Provision making non-compliance with any of the rules a criminal offence.

33. Provision making different provision for different cases, including different provision for different areas.

NOTES

This Schedule derived from the Insolvency Act 1985, Sch 7.

Paras 1, 5, 6: words in square brackets substituted by the Tribunals, Courts and Enforcement Act 2007, s 108(3), Sch 20, Pt 1, paras 1, 14(1)–(4).

Para 2: words in square brackets substituted by the Alteration of Judicial Titles (Registrar in Bankruptcy of the High Court) Order 2018, SI 2018/130, art 3, Schedule, para 7(c); words omitted repealed by the Crime and Courts Act 2013, s 17(5), Sch 9, Pt 3, para 93(l).

Paras 4A, 4B, 4C: inserted by the Enterprise and Regulatory Reform Act 2013, s 71(3), Sch 19, paras 1, 65(1)–(3), in respect of a petition for a bankruptcy order presented to the court by a debtor on or after 6 April 2016.

Paras 7A–7E: inserted by the Tribunals, Courts and Enforcement Act 2007, s 108(3), Sch 20, Pt 1, paras 1, 14(1), (5).

Second para 7A: inserted by the Small Business, Enterprise and Employment Act 2015, s 125(1), (5), as from 6 April 2017 (subject to transitional and savings provisions as noted to s 246ZE at **[1.256]**).

Para 8A: inserted by the Enterprise Act 2002, s 269, Sch 23, paras 1, 16(1), (2).

Para 10: repealed by the Small Business, Enterprise and Employment Act 2015, s 133(2), Sch 10, paras 1, 10, as from 6 April 2017 (subject to transitional and savings provisions as noted to s 246ZE at **[1.256]**).

Para 11A: inserted by the Small Business, Enterprise and Employment Act 2015, s 123(1), (3), as from 6 April 2017 (subject to transitional and savings provisions as noted to s 246ZE at **[1.256]**).

Para 12A: inserted by the Small Business, Enterprise and Employment Act 2015, s 126, Sch 9, Pt 2, paras 60, 86, as from 6 April 2017 (subject to transitional and savings provisions as noted to s 246ZE at **[1.256]**).

Para 13: word in first pair of square brackets inserted and words in second pair of square brackets substituted for original words "established under", by the Small Business, Enterprise and Employment Act 2015, s 126, Sch 9, Pt 2, paras 60, 87, as from 6 April 2017 (subject to transitional and savings provisions as noted to s 246ZE at **[1.256]**).

Para 18A: inserted by the Small Business, Enterprise and Employment Act 2015, s 132.

Para 21: words in square brackets substituted by the Insolvency Act 2000, s 13(1).

Para 21A: inserted by the Enterprise Act 2002, s 271(2).

Para 24: words in italics repealed by the Deregulation Act 2015, s 19, Sch 6, Pt 1, paras 2(1), (11)(g), 3, except in relation to a deed of arrangement registered under the Deeds of Arrangement Act 1914, s 5 before 1 October 2015, if, immediately before that date, the estate of the debtor who executed the deed of arrangement has not been finally wound up.

Paras 24A–24D: inserted by the Enterprise and Regulatory Reform Act 2013, s 71(3), Sch 19, paras 1, 65(1), (4), in respect of a petition for a bankruptcy order presented to the court by a debtor on or after 6 April 2016.

Para 29A: inserted by the Enterprise Act 2002, s 269, Sch 23, paras 1, 16(1), (3).

Para 30: words ", of the official receiver while acting as a receiver or manager under section 287 or of a trustee of a bankrupt's estate" (omitted) repealed by the Small Business, Enterprise and Employment Act 2015, s 133(2), Sch 10, paras 1, 11, as from 6 April 2017 (subject to transitional and savings provisions as noted to s 246ZE at **[1.256]**).

Regulations: the Insolvency Regulations 1994, SI 1994/2507 at **[8.22]**.

SCHEDULE 10
PUNISHMENT OF OFFENCES UNDER THIS ACT

Section 430

[1.595]

. . .

Section (Section of Act creating offence)	General nature of offence	Mode of prosecution	Punishment	Daily default fine (where applicable)
[6A(1)	False representation or fraud for purpose of obtaining members' or creditors' approval of proposed voluntary arrangement.	1. On indictment. 2. Summary.	7 years or a fine, or both. 6 months or the statutory maximum, or both.]	
. . .	. . .	. . .	. . .	
. . .	. . .	. . .	. . .	. . .
. . .	. . .	. . .	. . .	. . .
. . .	. . .	. . .	. . .	. . .
. . .	. . .	. . .	. . .	. . .
. . .	. . .	. . .	. . .	. . .
. . .	. . .	. . .	. . .	. . .
. . .	. . .	. . .	. . .	. . .
30	Body corporate acting as receiver.	1. On indictment. 2. Summary.	A fine. The statutory maximum.	
31	. . . bankrupt [or person in respect of whom a debt relief order is made] acting as receiver or manager.	1. On indictment. 2. Summary.	2 years or a fine, or both. 6 months or the statutory maximum, or both.	
38(5)	Receiver failing to deliver accounts to registrar.	Summary.	One-fifth of the statutory maximum.	One-fiftieth of the statutory maximum.
39(2)	Company and others failing to state in correspondence that receiver appointed.	Summary.	One-fifth of the statutory maximum.	
43(6)	Administrative receiver failing to file [copy] of order permitting disposal of charged property.	Summary.	One-fifth of the statutory maximum.	One-fiftieth of the statutory maximum.
45(5)	Administrative receiver failing to file notice of vacation of office.	Summary.	One-fifth of the statutory maximum.	*One-fiftieth of the statutory maximum.*

Section (Section of Act creating offence)	General nature of offence	Mode of prosecution	Punishment	Daily default fine (where applicable)
46(4)	Administrative receiver failing to give notice of his appointment.	Summary.	One-fifth of the statutory maximum.	One-fiftieth of the statutory maximum.
47(6)	Failure to comply with provisions relating to statement of affairs, where administrative receiver appointed.	1. On indictment. 2. Summary.	A fine. The statutory maximum.	One-tenth of the statutory maximum.
48(8)	Administrative receiver failing to comply with requirements as to his report.	Summary.	One-fifth of the statutory maximum.	One-fiftieth of the statutory maximum.
51(4)	Body corporate or Scottish firm acting as receiver.	1. On indictment. 2. Summary.	A fine. The statutory maximum.	
51(5)	Undischarged bankrupt acting as receiver (Scotland).	1. On indictment. 2. Summary.	2 years or a fine, or both. 6 months or the statutory maximum, or both.	
53(2)	Failing to deliver to registrar copy of instrument of appointment of receiver.	Summary.	One-fifth of the statutory maximum.	*One-fiftieth of the statutory maximum.*
54(3)	Failing to deliver to registrar the court's interlocutor appointing receiver.	Summary.	One-fifth of the statutory maximum.	*One-fiftieth of the statutory maximum.*
61(7)	Receiver failing to send to registrar certified copy of court order authorising disposal of charged property.	Summary.	One-fifth of the statutory maximum.	One-fiftieth of the statutory maximum.
62(5)	Failing to give notice to registrar of cessation or removal of receiver.	Summary.	One-fifth of the statutory maximum.	*One-fiftieth of the statutory maximum.*
64(2)	Company and others failing to state on correspondence etc that receiver appointed.	Summary.	One-fifth of the statutory maximum.	
65(4)	Receiver failing to send or publish notice of his appointment.	Summary.	One-fifth of the statutory maximum.	One-fiftieth of the statutory maximum.
66(6)	Failing to comply with provisions concerning statement of affairs, where receiver appointed.	1. On indictment. 2. Summary.	A fine. The statutory maximum.	One-tenth of the statutory maximum.
67(8)	Receiver failing to comply with requirements as to his report.	Summary.	One-fifth of the statutory maximum.	One-fiftieth of the statutory maximum.

Section (Section of Act creating offence)	General nature of offence	Mode of prosecution	Punishment	Daily default fine (where applicable)
85(2)	Company failing to give notice in Gazette of resolution for voluntary winding up.	Summary.	One-fifth of the statutory maximum.	One-fiftieth of the statutory maximum.
89(4)	Director making statutory declaration of company's solvency without reasonable grounds for his opinion.	1. On indictment. 2. Summary.	2 years or a fine, or both. 6 months or the statutory maximum, or both.	
89(6)	Declaration under section 89 not delivered to registrar within prescribed time.	Summary.	One-fifth of the statutory maximum.	One-fiftieth of the statutory maximum.
[92A(2)	Liquidator failing to send progress report to members . . .	Summary	Level 3 on the standard scale]	
93(3)	*Liquidator failing to summon general meeting of company at each year's end.*	*Summary.*	*One-fifth of the statutory maximum.*	
94(4)	*Liquidator failing to send to registrar a copy of account of winding up and return of final meeting.*	*Summary.*	*One-fifth of the statutory maximum.*	*One-fiftieth of the statutory maximum.*
94(6)	*Liquidator failing to call final meeting.*	*Summary.*	*One-fifth of the statutory maximum.*	
95(8)	Liquidator failing to comply with [s 95(1) to (4A)], where company insolvent.	Summary.	The statutory maximum.	
98(6)	*Company failing to comply with s. 98 in respect of summoning and giving notice of creditors' meeting.*	*1. On indictment.* *2. Summary.*	*A fine.* *The statutory maximum.*	
99(3)	Directors failing to [send statement in prescribed form to creditors].	1. On indictment. 2. Summary.	A fine. The statutory maximum.	
[104A(2)	Liquidator failing to send progress report to members and creditors . . .	Summary	Level 3 on the standard scale]	
105(3)	*Liquidator failing to summon company general meeting and creditors' meeting at each year's end.*	*Summary.*	*One-fifth of the statutory maximum.*	
106(4)	*Liquidator failing to send to registrar account of winding up and return of final meetings.*	*Summary.*	*One-fifth of the statutory maximum.*	*One-fiftieth of the statutory maximum.*
106(6)	*Liquidator failing to call final meeting of company or creditors.*	*Summary.*	*One-fifth of the statutory maximum.*	

Section (Section of Act creating offence)	General nature of offence	Mode of prosecution	Punishment	Daily default fine (where applicable)
109(2)	Liquidator failing to publish notice of his appointment.	Summary.	One-fifth of the statutory maximum.	One-fiftieth of the statutory maximum.
114(4)	Directors exercising powers in breach of s 114, where no liquidator.	Summary.	The statutory maximum.	
131(7)	Failing to comply with requirements as to statement of affairs, where liquidator appointed.	1. On indictment. 2. Summary.	A fine. The statutory maximum.	One-tenth of the statutory maximum.
164	Giving, offering etc. corrupt inducement affecting appointment of liquidator.	1. On indictment. 2. Summary.	A fine. The statutory maximum.	
166(7)	Liquidator failing to comply with requirements of s 166 in creditors' voluntary winding up.	Summary.	The statutory maximum.	
188(2)	Default in compliance with s 188 as to notification that company being wound up.	Summary.	One-fifth of the statutory maximum.	
192(2)	Liquidator failing to notify registrar as to progress of winding up.	Summary.	One-fifth of the statutory maximum.	One-fiftieth of the statutory maximum.
201(4)	Failing to deliver to registrar [copy] of court order deferring dissolution.	Summary.	One-fifth of the statutory maximum.	One-fiftieth of the statutory maximum.
203(6)	Failing to deliver to registrar copy of directions or result of appeal under s 203.	Summary.	One-fifth of the statutory maximum.	One-fiftieth of the statutory maximum.
204(7)	Liquidator failing to deliver to registrar copy of court order for early dissolution.	Summary.	One-fifth of the statutory maximum.	One-fiftieth of the statutory maximum.
204(8)	Failing to deliver to registrar copy of court order deferring early dissolution.	Summary.	One-fifth of the statutory maximum.	One-fiftieth of the statutory maximum.
205(7)	Failing to deliver to registrar copy of Secretary of State's directions or court order deferring dissolution.	Summary.	One-fifth of the statutory maximum.	One-fiftieth of the statutory maximum.
206(1)	Fraud etc. in anticipation of winding up.	1. On indictment. 2. Summary.	7 years or a fine, or both. 6 months or the statutory maximum, or both.	

Section (Section of Act creating offence)	General nature of offence	Mode of prosecution	Punishment	Daily default fine (where applicable)
206(2)	Privity to fraud in anticipation of winding up; fraud, or privity to fraud, after commencement of winding up.	1. On indictment. 2. Summary.	7 years or a fine, or both. 6 months or the statutory maximum, or both.	
206(5)	Knowingly taking in pawn or pledge, or otherwise receiving, company property.	1. On indictment. 2. Summary.	7 years or a fine, or both. 6 months or the statutory maximum, or both.	
207	Officer of company entering into transaction in fraud of company's creditors.	1. On indictment. 2. Summary.	2 years or a fine, or both. 6 months or the statutory maximum, or both.	
208	Officer of company misconducting himself in course of winding up.	1. On indictment. 2. Summary.	7 years or a fine, or both. 6 months or the statutory maximum, or both.	
209	Officer or contributory destroying, falsifying, etc company's books.	1. On indictment. 2. Summary	7 years or a fine, or both. 6 months or the statutory maximum, or both.	
210	Officer of company making material omission from statement relating to company's affairs.	1. On indictment. 2. Summary.	7 years or a fine, or both. 6 months or the statutory maximum, or both.	
211	False representation or fraud for purpose of obtaining creditors' consent to an agreement in connection with winding up.	1. On indictment. 2. Summary.	7 years or a fine, or both. 6 months or the statutory maximum, or both.	
216(4)	Contravening restrictions on re-use of name of company in insolvent liquidation.	1. On indictment. 2. Summary.	2 years or a fine, or both. 6 months or the statutory maximum, or both.	
235(5)	Failing to co-operate with office-holder.	1. On indictment. 2. Summary.	A fine. The statutory maximum.	One-tenth of the statutory maximum.
[251O(1)	False representations or omissions in making an application for a debt relief order.	1. On indictment 2. Summary	7 years or a fine, or both. 12 months or the statutory maximum, or both.	

Section (Section of Act creating offence)	General nature of offence	Mode of prosecution	Punishment	Daily default fine (where applicable)
251O(2)(a)	Failing to comply with duty in connection with an application for a debt relief order.	1. On indictment 2. Summary	2 years or a fine, or both. 12 months or the statutory maximum, or both.	
251O(2)(b)	False representations or omissions in connection with duty in relation to an application for a debt relief order.	1. On indictment 2. Summary	7 years or a fine, or both. 12 months or the statutory maximum, or both.	
251O(4)(a)	Failing to comply with duty in connection with a debt relief order.	1. On indictment 2. Summary	2 years or a fine, or both. 12 months or the statutory maximum, or both.	
251O(4)(b)	False representations or omissions in connection with a duty in relation to a debt relief order.	1. On indictment 2. Summary	7 years or a fine, or both. 12 months or the statutory maximum, or both.	
251P(1)	Failing to deliver books, records and papers to official receiver, concealing or destroying them or making false entries in them by person in respect of whom a debt relief order is made.	1. On indictment 2. Summary	7 years or a fine, or both. 12 months or the statutory maximum, or both.	
251P(2)	Person in respect of whom debt relief order is made doing anything falling within paragraphs (c) to (e) of section 251P(1) during the period of 12 months ending with the application date or doing anything falling within paragraphs (b) to (e) of section 251P(1) after that date but before the effective date.	1. On indictment 2. Summary	7 years or a fine, or both. 12 months or the statutory maximum, or both.	
251Q(1)	Fraudulent disposal of property by person in respect of whom a debt relief order is made.	1. On indictment 2. Summary	2 years or a fine, or both. 12 months or the statutory maximum, or both.	
251R(1)	Disposal of property that is not paid for by person in respect of whom a debt relief order is made.	1. On indictment 2. Summary	7 years or a fine, or both. 12 months or the statutory maximum, or both.	

Section (Section of Act creating offence)	General nature of offence	Mode of prosecution	Punishment	Daily default fine (where applicable)
251R(2)	Obtaining property in respect of which money is owed by a person in respect of whom a debt relief order is made.	1. On indictment 2. Summary	7 years or a fine, or both. 12 months or the statutory maximum, or both.	
251S(1)	Person in respect of whom a debt relief order is made obtaining credit or engaging in business without disclosing his status or name.	1. On indictment 2. Summary	2 years or a fine, or both. 12 months or the statutory maximum, or both.]	
[262A(1)	False representation or fraud for purpose of obtaining creditors' approval of proposed voluntary arrangement.	1. On indictment. 2. Summary.	7 years or a fine, or both. 6 months or the statutory maximum, or both.]	
[263O	False representations or omissions in connection with a bankruptcy application.	1. On indictment. 2. Summary.	7 years or a fine, or both. 12 months or the statutory maximum, or both.]	
353(1)	Bankrupt failing to disclose property or disposals to official receiver or trustee.	1. On indictment. 2. Summary.	7 years or a fine, or both. 6 months or the statutory maximum, or both.	
354(1)	Bankrupt failing to deliver property to, or concealing property from, official receiver or trustee.	1. On indictment 2. Summary.	7 years or a fine, or both. 6 months or the statutory maximum, or both.	
354(2)	Bankrupt removing property which he is required to deliver to official receiver or trustee.	1. On indictment. 2. Summary.	7 years or a fine, or both. 6 months or the statutory maximum, or both.	
354(3)	Bankrupt failing to account for loss of substantial part of property.	1 On indictment. 2. Summary.	2 years or a fine, or both. 6 months or the statutory maximum, or both.	
355(1)	Bankrupt failing to deliver books, papers and records to official receiver or trustee.	1. On indictment. 2. Summary.	7 years or a fine, or both. 6 months or the statutory maximum, or both.	

Section (Section of Act creating offence)	General nature of offence	Mode of prosecution	Punishment	Daily default fine (where applicable)
355(2)	Bankrupt concealing, destroying etc books, papers or records, or making false entries in them.	1. On indictment. 2. Summary.	7 years or a fine, or both. 6 months or the statutory maximum, or both.	
355(3)	Bankrupt disposing of, or altering, books, papers or records relating to his estate or affairs.	1. On indictment. 2. Summary.	7 years or a fine, or both. 6 months or the statutory maximum, or both.	
356(1)	Bankrupt making material omission in statement relating to his affairs.	1. On indictment. 2. Summary.	7 years or a fine, or both. 6 months or the statutory maximum, or both.	
356(2)	Bankrupt making false statement, or failing to inform trustee, where false debt proved.	1. On indictment. 2. Summary.	7 years or a fine, or both. 6 months or the statutory maximum, or both.	
357	Bankrupt fraudulently disposing of property.	1. On indictment 2. Summary.	2 years or a fine, or both. 6 months or the statutory maximum, or both.	
358	Bankrupt absconding with property he is required to deliver to official receiver or trustee.	1. On indictment. 2. Summary.	2 years or a fine, or both. 6 months or the statutory maximum, or both.	
359(1)	Bankrupt disposing of property obtained on credit and not paid for.	1. On indictment. 2. Summary.	7 years or a fine, or both. 6 months or the statutory maximum, or both.	
359(2)	Obtaining property in respect of which money is owed by a bankrupt.	1. On indictment. 2. Summary.	7 years or a fine, or both. 6 months or the statutory maximum, or both.	
360(1)	Bankrupt obtaining credit or engaging in business without disclosing his status or name in which he was made bankrupt.	1. On indictment. 2. Summary.	2 years or a fine, or both. 6 months or the statutory maximum, or both.	

Section (Section of Act creating offence)	General nature of offence	Mode of prosecution	Punishment	Daily default fine (where applicable)
360(3)	Person made bankrupt in Scotland or Northern Ireland obtaining credit, etc in England and Wales.	1. On indictment. 2. Summary.	2 years or a fine, or both. 6 months or the statutory maximum, or both.	
. . .	. . .	. . . . . .	. . .	
. . .	. . .	. . . . . .	. . . . . .	
389	Acting as insolvency practitioner when not qualified.	1. On indictment. 2. Summary.	2 years or a fine, or both. 6 months or the statutory maximum or both.	
429(5)	Contravening s 429 in respect of disabilities imposed by county court on revocation of administration order.	1. On indictment. 2. Summary.	2 years or a fine, or both. 6 months or the statutory maximum, or both.	
[Sch A1, para 9(2)	Directors failing to notify nominee of beginning of moratorium.	1. On indictment. 2. Summary.	2 years or a fine, or both. 6 months or the statutory maximum, or both.	
Sch A1, para 10(3)	Nominee failing to advertise or notify beginning of moratorium.	Summary.	One-fifth of the statutory maximum.	
Sch A1, para 11(2)	Nominee failing to advertise or notify end of moratorium.	Summary.	One-fifth of the statutory maximum.	
Sch A1, para 16(2)	Company and officers failing to state in correspondence etc that moratorium in force.	Summary.	One-fifth of the statutory maximum.	
Sch A1, para 17(3)(a)	Company obtaining credit without disclosing existence of moratorium.	1. On indictment. 2. Summary.	A fine. The statutory maximum.	
Sch A1, para 17(3)(b)	Obtaining credit for company without disclosing existence of moratorium.	1. On indictment. 2. Summary.	2 years or a fine, or both. 6 months or the statutory maximum, or both.	
Sch A1, para 18(3)(a)	Company disposing of property otherwise than in ordinary way of business.	1. On indictment. 2. Summary.	A fine. The statutory maximum.	

Section (Section of Act creating offence)	General nature of offence	Mode of prosecution	Punishment	Daily default fine (where applicable)
Sch A1, para 18(3)(b)	Authorising or permitting disposal of company property.	1. On indictment. 2. Summary.	2 years or a fine, or both. 6 months or the statutory maximum, or both.	
Sch A1, para 19(3)(a)	Company making payments in respect of liabilities existing before beginning of moratorium.	1. On indictment. 2. Summary.	A fine. The statutory maximum.	
Sch A1, para 19(3)(b)	Authorising or permitting such a payment.	1. On indictment. 2. Summary.	2 years or a fine, or both. 6 months or the statutory maximum, or both.	
Sch A1, para 20(9)	Directors failing to send to registrar [copy] of court order permitting disposal of charged property.	Summary.	One-fifth of the statutory maximum.	
Sch A1, para 22(1)	Company disposing of charged property.	1. On indictment. 2. Summary.	A fine. The statutory maximum.	
Sch A1, para 22(2)	Authorising or permitting such a disposal.	1. On indictment. 2. Summary.	2 years or a fine, or both. 6 months or the statutory maximum, or both.	
Sch A1, para 23(1)(a)	Company entering into market contract, etc.	1. On indictment. 2. Summary.	A fine. The statutory maximum.	
Sch A1, para 23(1)(b)	Authorising or permitting company to do so.	1. On indictment. 2. Summary.	2 years or a fine, or both. 6 months or the statutory maximum, or both.	
Sch A1, para 25(6)	Nominee failing to give notice of withdrawal of consent to act.	Summary.	One-fifth of the statutory maximum.	
Sch A1, para 34(3)	Nominee failing to give notice of extension of moratorium.	Summary.	One-fifth of the statutory maximum.	
Sch A1, para 41(2)	Fraud or privity to fraud in anticipation of moratorium.	1. On indictment. 2. Summary.	7 years or a fine, or both. 6 months or the statutory maximum, or both.	
Sch A1, para 41(3)	Fraud or privity to fraud during moratorium.	1. On indictment.	7 years or a fine, or both.	

Section (Section of Act creating offence)	General nature of offence	Mode of prosecution	Punishment	Daily default fine (where applicable)
		2. Summary.	6 months or the statutory maximum, or both.	
Sch A1, para 41(7)	Knowingly taking in pawn or pledge, or otherwise receiving, company property.	1. On indictment. 2. Summary.	7 years or a fine, or both. 6 months or the statutory maximum, or both.	
Sch A1, para 42(1)	False representation or fraud for purpose of obtaining or extending moratorium.	1. On indictment. 2. Summary.	7 years or a fine, or both. 6 months or the statutory maximum, or both.]	
[Sch B1, para 18(7)	Making false statement in statutory declaration where administrator appointed by holder of floating charge.	1. On indictment. 2. Summary.	2 years, or a fine or both. 6 months, or the statutory maximum or both.	
Sch B1, para 20	Holder of floating charge failing to notify administrator or others of commencement of appointment.	1. On indictment. 2. Summary.	2 years, or a fine or both. 6 months, or the statutory maximum or both.	One-tenth of the statutory maximum.
Sch B1, para 27(4)	Making false statement in statutory declaration where appointment of administrator proposed by company or directors.	1. On indictment. 2. Summary.	2 years, or a fine or both. 6 months, or the statutory maximum or both.	
Sch B1, para 29(7)	Making false statement in statutory declaration where administrator appointed by company or directors.	1. On indictment. 2. Summary.	2 years, or a fine or both. 6 months, or the statutory maximum or both.	
Sch B1, para 32	Company or directors failing to notify administrator or others of commencement of appointment.	1. On indictment. 2. Summary.	2 years, or a fine or both. 6 months, or the statutory maximum or both.	One-tenth of the statutory maximum.
Sch B1, para 45(2)	Administrator, company or officer failing to state in business document that administrator appointed.	Summary.	One-fifth of the statutory maximum.	
Sch B1, para 46(9)	Administrator failing to give notice of his appointment.	Summary.	One-fifth of the statutory maximum.	One-fiftieth of the statutory maximum.
Sch B1, para 48(4)	Failing to comply with provisions about statement of affairs where administrator appointed.	1. On indictment. 2. Summary.	A fine. The statutory maximum.	One-tenth of the statutory maximum.

Section (Section of Act creating offence)	General nature of offence	Mode of prosecution	Punishment	Daily default fine (where applicable)
Sch B1, para 49(7)	Administrator failing to send out statement of his proposals.	Summary.	One-fifth of the statutory maximum.	One-fiftieth of the statutory maximum.
Sch B1, para 51(5)	Administrator failing to [seek creditors' decision].	Summary.	One-fifth of the statutory maximum.	One-fiftieth of the statutory maximum.
Sch B1, para 53(3)	Administrator failing to report decision taken [by creditors].	Summary.	One-fifth of the statutory maximum.	One-fiftieth of the statutory maximum.
Sch B1, para 54(7)	Administrator failing to report [creditors' decision on] revised proposal.	Summary.	One-fifth of the statutory maximum.	One-fiftieth of the statutory maximum.
Sch B1, para 56(2)	Administrator failing to [seek creditors' decision].	Summary.	One-fifth of the statutory maximum.	One-fiftieth of the statutory maximum.
Sch B1, para 71(6)	Administrator failing to file court order enabling disposal of charged property.	Summary.	One-fifth of the statutory maximum.	One-fiftieth of the statutory maximum.
Sch B1, para 72(5)	Administrator failing to file court order enabling disposal of hire-purchase property.	Summary.	One-fifth of the statutory maximum.	One-fiftieth of the statutory maximum.
Sch B1, para 77(3)	Administrator failing to notify Registrar of Companies of automatic end of administration.	Summary.	One-fifth of the statutory maximum.	One-fiftieth of the statutory maximum.
Sch B1, para 78(6)	Administrator failing to give notice of extension by consent of term of office.	Summary.	One-fifth of the statutory maximum.	One-fiftieth of the statutory maximum.
Sch B1, para 80(6)	Administrator failing to give notice of termination of administration where objective achieved.	Summary.	One-fifth of the statutory maximum.	One-fiftieth of the statutory maximum.
Sch B1, para 84(9)	Administrator failing to comply with provisions where company moves to dissolution.	Summary.	One-fifth of the statutory maximum.	One-fiftieth of the statutory maximum.
Sch B1, para 86(3)	Administrator failing to notify Registrar of Companies where court terminates administration.	Summary.	One-fifth of the statutory maximum.	One-fiftieth of the statutory maximum.
Sch B1, para 89(3)	Administrator failing to give notice on ceasing to be qualified.	Summary.	One-fifth of the statutory maximum.	One-fiftieth of the statutory maximum.
. . .	. . .	. . .	. . .	. . .]

NOTES

The Note to this Schedule repealed by the Statute Law (Repeals) Act 1993.

Entry relating to s 6A inserted by the Insolvency Act 2000, s 2, Sch 2, paras 1, 12, (subject to transitional provisions in SI 2002/2711, art 3 at **[2.6]**).

Entries relating to ss 12(2), 15(8), 18(5), 21(3), 22(6), 23(3), 24(7), 27(6) (omitted) repealed and entries relating to Sch B1 inserted by the Enterprise Act 2002, ss 248(3), 278(2), Sch 17, paras 9, 39, Sch 26, subject to savings and transitional provisions (i) in a case where a petition for an administration order has been presented before 15 September 2003 (see SI 2003/2093, art 3 at **[2.26]**), and (ii) in relation to special administration regimes (see s 249 of the 2002 Act at **[2.10]**). Entries omitted originally read as follows:

"12(2)	Company and others failing to state in correspondence etc that administrator appointed.	Summary.	One-fifth of the statutory maximum.
15(8)	Failure of administrator to register office copy of court order permitting disposal of charged property.	Summary.	One-fifth of the statutory maximum.
18(5)	Failure of administrator to register office copy of court order varying or discharging administration order.	Summary.	One-fifth of the statutory maximum.
21(3)	Administrator failing to register administration order and give notice of appointment.	Summary.	One-fifth of the statutory maximum.
22(6)	Failure to comply with provisions relating to statement of affairs, where administrator appointed.	1. On indictment. 2. Summary.	A fine. The statutory maximum.
23(3)	Administrator failing to send out, register and lay before creditors statement of his proposals.	Summary.	One-fifth of the statutory maximum.
24(7)	Administrator failing to file court order discharging administration order under s 24.	Summary.	One-fifth of the statutory maximum.
27(6)	Administrator failing to file court order discharging administration order under s 27.	Summary.	One-fifth of the statutory maximum.".

In entry relating to s 31, word omitted repealed by the Enterprise Act 2002, ss 269, 278(2), Sch 23, paras 1, 17(a), Sch 26, and words in square brackets inserted by the Tribunals, Courts and Enforcement Act 2007, s 108(3), Sch 20, Pt 1, paras 1, 15(1), (2).

In entries relating to ss 43(6), 201(4), and Sch A1, para 20(9), word in square brackets substituted for original words "office copy" by the Companies Act 2006 (Consequential Amendments, Transitional Provisions and Savings) Order 2009, SI 2009/1941, art 2(1), Sch 1, para 80, subject to transitional provisions and savings in art 8, Sch 1, para 84 at **[2.70]**, **[2.73]**.

Entries in italics in column 5 relating to ss 45(5), 53(2), 54(3), 62(5) repealed by the Companies Act 1989, s 212, Sch 24, as from a day to be appointed.

Entries relating to ss 92A(2), 104A(2) inserted by the Legislative Reform (Insolvency) (Miscellaneous Provisions) Order 2010, SI 2010/18, arts 2, 6(5), except in relation to a company in voluntary winding up where the resolution to wind up was passed before 6 April 2010: see r 12(1) of the 2010 Order at **[2.76]**; words omitted from those entries repealed by the Small Business, Enterprise and Employment Act 2015, s 136(1), (4).

Entries relation to ss 93(3), 105(3) repealed by the Public Services Reform (Insolvency) (Scotland) Order 2016, SSI 2016/141, arts 5(3), 6(3), as from a day to be appointed (being the day that the Small Business, Enterprise and Employment Act 2015, s 122(2) comes into force for all remaining purposes in Scotland); for savings, see the note to s 66 at **[1.52]**.

Entries relating to ss 94(4), 94(5), 106(5), 106(6) substituted by the Small Business, Enterprise and Employment Act 2015, s 126, Sch 9, Pt 1, paras 1, 53(1), (2), (6), as from 6 April 2017 (in relation to England and Wales and subject to transitional and savings provisions as noted to s 246ZE at **[1.256]**), and as from a day to be appointed (in relation to Scotland)., as follows—

"94(4)	Liquidator failing to send to company members a copy of account of winding up	Summary	Level 3 on the standard scale	
94(5)		Summary	Level 3 on the standard scale	One tenth of level 3 on the standard scale.
106(5)	Liquidator failing to send to company members and creditors a copy of account of winding up	Summary	Level 3 on the standard scale	
106(6)	Liquidator failing to send to registrar a copy of account of winding up	Summary	Level 3 on the standard scale	One tenth of level 3 on the standard scale."

Words in square brackets in the entry relating to s 95(8) substituted for original reference to "s 95", entry relating to s 98(6) repealed, and words in square brackets in the entry relating to s 99(3) substituted for original words "attend and lay statement in prescribed form before creditors' meeting", by the Small Business, Enterprise and Employment Act 2015, s 126, Sch 9, Pt 1, paras 1, 53(1), (3)–(5), as from 6 April 2017 (in relation to England and Wales and subject to transitional and savings provisions as noted to s 246ZE at **[1.256]**), and as from a day to be appointed (in relation to Scotland).

Entries relating to ss 251O–251S inserted by the Tribunals, Courts and Enforcement Act 2007, s 108(3), Sch 20, Pt 1, paras 1, 15(1), (3), subject to para 15(4) thereof which provides that in the application of those entries in relation to offences committed before the commencement of the Criminal Justice Act 2003, s 154(1), the references in the fourth column to "12 months" are to be read as references to "6 months".

Entry relating to s 262A(1) inserted by the Insolvency Act 2000, s 3, Sch 3, paras 1, 16 (subject to transitional provisions in SI 2002/2711, art 4 at **[2.7]**).

Entry relating to s 263O inserted by the Enterprise and Regulatory Reform Act 2013, s 71(3), Sch 19, paras 1, 66, in respect of a petition for a bankruptcy order presented to the court by a debtor on or after 6 April 2016. Note that in relation to an offence committed before the commencement of the Criminal Justice Act 2003, s 154(1) (limit on magistrates' court powers to impose imprisonment), the reference in the fourth column to "12 months" is to be read as a reference to "6 months"; as at 6 April 2016, s 154(1) had not been brought into force.

Entries relating to ss 361, 362 (omitted) repealed by the Enterprise Act 2002, ss 269, 278(2), Sch 23, paras 1, 17(b), Sch 26.

Entries relating to Sch A1 inserted by the Insolvency Act 2000, s 1, Sch 1, paras 1, 12.

Words in square brackets in the entry relating to Sch B1, para 51(5) substituted for original words "arrange initial creditors' meeting", words in square brackets in the entry relating to Sch B1, para 53(3) substituted for original words "at initial creditors' meeting", words in square brackets in the entry relating to Sch B1, para 54(7) substituted for original words "decision taken at creditors' meeting summoned to consider", and words in square brackets in the entry relating to Sch B1, para 56(2) substituted for original words "summon creditors' meeting", by the Small Business, Enterprise and Employment Act 2015, s 126, Sch 9, Pt 1, paras 1, 11, as from 6 April 2017 (in relation to England and Wales and subject to transitional and savings provisions as noted to s 246ZE at **[1.256]**), and as from a day to be appointed (in relation to Scotland).

Entry relating to Sch 7, para 4(3) (omitted) repealed by the Deregulation Act 2015, s 19, Sch 6, Pt 6, para 22(1), (5).

SCHEDULE 11
TRANSITIONAL PROVISIONS AND SAVINGS

Section 437

PART I
COMPANY INSOLVENCY AND WINDING UP

Administration orders

[1.596]

1. (1) Where any right to appoint an administrative receiver of a company is conferred by any debentures or floating charge created before the appointed day, the conditions precedent to the exercise of that right are deemed to include the presentation of a petition applying for an administration order to be made in relation to the company.

(2) "Administrative receiver" here has the meaning assigned by section 251.

Receivers and managers (England and Wales)

2. (1) In relation to any receiver or manager of a company's property who was appointed before the appointed day, the new law does not apply; and the relevant provisions of the former law continue to have effect.

(2) "The new law" here means Chapter I of Part III, and Part VI, of this Act; and "the former law" means [the Companies Act 1985] and so much of this Act as replaces provisions of that Act (without the amendments in paragraphs 15 to 17 of Schedule 6 to the Insolvency Act 1985, or the associated repeals made by that Act), and any provision of the Insolvency Act 1985 which was in force before the appointed day.

(3) This paragraph is without prejudice to the power conferred by this Act under which rules under section 411 may make transitional provision in connection with the coming into force of those rules; and such provision may apply those rules in relation to the receiver or manager of a company's property notwithstanding that he was appointed before the coming into force of the rules or section 411.

Receivers (Scotland)

3. (1) In relation to any receiver appointed under section 467 of [the Companies Act 1985] before the appointed day, the new law does not apply and the relevant provisions of the former law continue to have effect.

(2) "The new law" here means Chapter II of Part III, and Part VI, of this Act; and "the former law" means [the Companies Act 1985] and so much of this Act as replaces provisions of that Act (without the amendments in paragraphs 18 to 22 of Schedule 6 to the Insolvency Act 1985 or the associated repeals made by that Act), and any provision of the Insolvency Act 1985 which was in force before the appointed day.

(3) This paragraph is without prejudice to the power conferred by this Act under which rules under section 411 may make transitional provision in connection with the coming into force of those rules; and such provision may apply those rules in relation to a receiver appointed under section 467 notwithstanding that he was appointed before the coming into force of the rules or section 411.

Winding up already in progress

4. (1) In relation to any winding up which has commenced, or is treated as having commenced, before the appointed day, the new law does not apply, and the former law continues to have effect, subject to the following paragraphs.

(2) "The new law" here means any provisions in the first Group of Parts of this Act which replace sections 66 to 87 and 89 to 105 of the Insolvency Act 1985; and "the former law" means Parts XX and XXI of [the Companies Act 1985] (without the amendments in paragraphs 23 to 52 of Schedule 6 to the Insolvency Act 1985, or the associated repeals made by that Act).

Statement of affairs

5. (1) Where a winding up by the court in England and Wales has commenced, or is treated as having commenced, before the appointed day, the official receiver or (on appeal from a refusal by him) the court may, at any time on or after that day—

(a) release a person from an obligation imposed on him by or under section 528 of [the Companies Act 1985] (statement of affairs), or

(b) extend the period specified in subsection (6) of that section.

(2) Accordingly, on and after the appointed day, section 528(6) has effect in relation to a winding up to which this paragraph applies with the omission of the words from "or within" onwards.

Provisions relating to liquidator

6. (1) This paragraph applies as regards the liquidator in the case of a winding up by the court in England and Wales commenced, or treated as having commenced, before the appointed day.

(2) The official receiver may, at any time when he is liquidator of the company, apply to the Secretary of State for the appointment of a liquidator in his (the official receiver's) place; and on any such application the Secretary of State shall either make an appointment or decline to make one.

(3) Where immediately before the appointed day the liquidator of the company has not made an application under section 545 of [the Companies Act 1985] (release of liquidators), then—

(a) except where the Secretary of State otherwise directs, sections 146(1) and (2) and 172(8) of this Act apply, and section 545 does not apply, in relation to any liquidator of that company who holds office on or at any time after the appointed day and is not the official receiver;

(b) section 146(3) applies in relation to the carrying out at any time after that day by any liquidator of the company of any of his functions; and

(c) a liquidator in relation to whom section 172(8) has effect by virtue of this paragraph has his release with effect from the time specified in section 174(4)(d) of this Act.

(4) Subsection (6) of section 174 of this Act has effect for the purposes of sub-paragraph (3)(c) above as it has for the purposes of that section, but as if the reference to section 212 were to section 631 of [the Companies Act 1985].

(5) The liquidator may employ a solicitor to assist him in the carrying out of his functions without the permission of the committee of inspection; but if he does so employ a solicitor he shall inform the committee of inspection that he has done so.

Winding up under supervision of the court

7. The repeals in Part II of Schedule 10 to the Insolvency Act 1985 of references (in [the Companies Act 1985] and elsewhere) to a winding up under the supervision of the court do not affect the operation of the enactments in which the references are contained in relation to any case in which an order under section 606 of [the Companies Act 1985] (power to order winding up under supervision) was made before the appointed day.

Saving for power to make rules

8. (1) Paragraphs 4 to 7 are without prejudice to the power conferred by this Act under which rules made under section 411 may make transitional provision in connection with the coming into force of those rules.

(2) Such provision may apply those rules in relation to a winding up notwithstanding that the winding up commenced, or is treated as having commenced, before the coming into force of the rules or section 411.

Setting aside of preferences and other transactions

9. (1) Where a provision in Part VI of this Act applies in relation to a winding up or in relation to a case in which an administration order has been made, a preference given, floating charge created or other transaction entered into before the appointed day shall not be set aside under that provision except to the extent that it could have been set aside under the law in force immediately before that day, assuming for this purpose that any relevant administration order had been a winding-up order.

(2) The references above to setting aside a preference, floating charge or other transaction include the making of an order which varies or reverses any effect of a preference, floating charge or other transaction.

NOTES

This Part derived from the Insolvency Act 1985, Sch 9, paras 6–10.

Paras 2–7: words in square brackets substituted for original words "the Companies Act" by the Companies Act 2006 (Consequential Amendments, Transitional Provisions and Savings) Order 2009, SI 2009/1941, art 2(1), Sch 1, para 83, subject to transitional provisions and savings in art 8, Sch 1, para 84 at **[2.70]**, **[2.73]**.

Insolvency Act 1985: that Act was mostly repealed by the combined effect of s 438 of, and Sch 12 to, this Act and the Company Directors Disqualification Act 1986, s 23(2), Sch 4.

PART II
INDIVIDUAL INSOLVENCY

Bankruptcy (general)

[1.597]
10. (1) Subject to the following provisions of this Part of this Schedule, so much of this Act as replaces Part III of the Insolvency Act 1985 does not apply in relation to any case in which a petition in bankruptcy was presented, or a receiving order or adjudication in bankruptcy was made, before the appointed day.

(2) In relation to any such case as is mentioned above, the enactments specified in Schedule 8 to that Act, so far as they relate to bankruptcy, and those specified in Parts III and IV of Schedule 10 to that Act, so far as they so relate, have effect without the amendments and repeals specified in those Schedules.

(3) Where any subordinate legislation made under an enactment referred to in sub-paragraph (2) is in force immediately before the appointed day, that subordinate legislation continues to have effect on and after that day in relation to any such case as is mentioned in sub-paragraph (1).

11. (1) In relation to any such case as is mentioned in paragraph 10(1) the references in any enactment or subordinate legislation to a petition, order or other matter which is provided for under the Bankruptcy Act 1914 and corresponds to a petition, order or other matter provided for under provisions of this Act replacing Part III of the Insolvency Act 1985 continue on and after the appointed day to have effect as references to the petition, order or matter provided for by the Act of 1914; but otherwise those references have effect on and after that day as references to the petition, order or matter provided for by those provisions of this Act.

(2) Without prejudice to sub-paragraph (1), in determining for the purposes of section 279 of this Act (period of bankruptcy) or paragraph 13 below whether any person was an undischarged bankrupt at a time before the appointed day, an adjudication in bankruptcy and an annulment of a bankruptcy under the Act of 1914 are to be taken into account in the same way, respectively, as a bankruptcy order under the provisions of this Act replacing Part III of the Insolvency Act 1985 and the annulment under section 282 of this Act of such an order.

12. Transactions entered into before the appointed day have effect on and after that day as if references to acts of bankruptcy in the provisions for giving effect to those transactions continued to be references to acts of bankruptcy within the meaning of the Bankruptcy Act 1914, but as if such acts included failure to comply with a statutory demand served under section 268 of this Act.

Discharge from old bankruptcy

13. (1) Where a person—
- (a) was adjudged bankrupt before the appointed day or is adjudged bankrupt on or after that day on a petition presented before that day, and
- (b) that person was not an undischarged bankrupt at any time in the period of 15 years ending with the adjudication,

that person is deemed (if not previously discharged) to be discharged from his bankruptcy for the purposes of the Bankruptcy Act 1914 at the end of the discharge period.

(2) Subject to sub-paragraph (3) below, the discharge period for the purposes of this paragraph is—
- (a) in the case of a person adjudged bankrupt before the appointed day, the period of 3 years beginning with that day, and
- (b) in the case of a person who is adjudged bankrupt on or after that day on a petition presented before that day, the period of 3 years beginning with the date of the adjudication.

(3) Where the court exercising jurisdiction in relation to a bankruptcy to which this paragraph applies is satisfied, on the application of the official receiver, that the bankrupt has failed, or is failing, to comply with any of his obligations under the Bankruptcy Act 1914, any rules made under that Act or any such rules as are mentioned in paragraph 19(1) below, the court may order that the discharge period shall cease to run for such period, or until the fulfilment of such conditions (including a condition requiring the court to be satisfied as to any matter) as may be specified in the order.

Provisions relating to trustee

14. (1) This paragraph applies as regards the trustee in the case of a person adjudged bankrupt before the appointed day, or adjudged bankrupt on or after that day on a petition presented before that day.

(2) The official receiver may at any time when he is the trustee of the bankrupt's estate apply to the Secretary of State for the appointment of a person as trustee instead of the official receiver; and on any such application the Secretary of State shall either make an appointment or decline to make one.

(3) Where on the appointed day the trustee of a bankrupt's estate has not made an application under section 93 of the Bankruptcy Act 1914 (release of trustee), then—
- (a) except where the Secretary of State otherwise directs, sections 298(8), 304 and 331(1) to (3) of this Act apply, and section 93 of the Act of 1914 does not apply, in relation to any trustee of the bankrupt's estate who holds office on or at any time after the appointed day and is not the official receiver;
- (b) section 331(4) of this Act applies in relation to the carrying out at any time on or after the appointed day by the trustee of the bankrupt's estate of any of his functions; and
- (c) a trustee in relation to whom section 298(8) of this Act has effect by virtue of this paragraph has his release with effect from the time specified in section 299(3)(d).

(4) Subsection (5) of section 299 has effect for the purposes of sub-paragraph (3)(c) as it has for the purposes of that section.

(5) In the application of subsection (3) of section 331 in relation to a case by virtue of this paragraph, the reference in that subsection to section 330(1) has effect as a reference to section 67 of the Bankruptcy Act 1914.

(6) The trustee of the bankrupt's estate may employ a solicitor to assist him in the carrying out of his functions without the permission of the committee of inspection; but if he does so employ a solicitor, he shall inform the committee of inspection that he has done so.

Copyright

15. Where a person who is adjudged bankrupt on a petition presented on or after the appointed day is liable, by virtue of a transaction entered into before that day, to pay royalties or a share of the profits to any person in respect of any copyright or interest in copyright comprised in the bankrupt's estate, section 60 of the Bankruptcy Act 1914 (limitation on trustee's powers in relation to copyright) applies in relation to the trustee of that estate as it applies in relation to a trustee in bankruptcy under the Act of 1914.

Second bankruptcy

16. (1) Sections 334 and 335 of this Act apply with the following modifications where the earlier bankruptcy (within the meaning of section 334) is a bankruptcy in relation to which the Act of 1914 applies instead of the second Group of Parts in this Act, that is to say—

(a) references to property vested in the existing trustee under section 307(3) of this Act have effect as references to such property vested in that trustee as was acquired by or devolved on the bankrupt after the commencement (within the meaning of the Act of 1914) of the earlier bankruptcy; and

(b) references to an order under section 310 of this Act have effect as references to an order under section 51 of the Act of 1914.

(2) Section 39 of the Act of 1914 (second bankruptcy) does not apply where a person who is an undischarged bankrupt under that Act is adjudged bankrupt under this Act.

Setting aside of preferences and other transactions

17. (1) A preference given, assignment made or other transaction entered into before the appointed day shall not be set aside under any of sections 339 to 344 of this Act except to the extent that it could have been set aside under the law in force immediately before that day.

(2) References in sub-paragraph (1) to setting aside a preference, assignment or other transaction include the making of any order which varies or reverses any effect of a preference, assignment or other transaction.

Bankruptcy offences

18. (1) Where a bankruptcy order is made under this Act on or after the appointed day, a person is not guilty of an offence under Chapter VI of Part IX in respect of anything done before that day; but, notwithstanding the repeal by the Insolvency Act 1985 of the Bankruptcy Act 1914, is guilty of an offence under the Act of 1914 in respect of anything done before the appointed day which would have been an offence under that Act if the making of the bankruptcy order had been the making of a receiving order under that Act.

(2) Subsection (5) of section 350 of this Act applies (instead of sections 157(2), 158(2), 161 and 165 of the Act of 1914) in relation to proceedings for an offence under that Act which are instituted (whether by virtue of sub-paragraph (1) or otherwise) after the appointed day.

Power to make rules

19. (1) The preceding provisions of this Part of this Schedule are without prejudice to the power conferred by this Act under which rules under section 412 may make transitional provision in connection with the coming into force of those rules; and such provision may apply those rules in relation to a bankruptcy notwithstanding that it arose from a petition presented before either the coming into force of the rules or the appointed day.

(2) Rules under section 412 may provide for such notices served before the appointed day as may be prescribed to be treated for the purposes of this Act as statutory demands served under section 268.

NOTES

This Part derived from the Insolvency Act 1985, Sch 9, paras 11–22.

Insolvency Act 1985: that Act was mostly repealed by the combined effect of s 438 of, and Sch 12 to, this Act and the Company Directors Disqualification Act 1986, s 23(2), Sch 4.

Bankruptcy Act 1914: repealed by the Insolvency Act 1985, s 235(3), Sch 10, Pts III, IV.

PART III
TRANSITIONAL EFFECT OF PART XVI

[1.598]

20. (1) A transaction entered into before the appointed day shall not be set aside under Part XVI of this Act except to the extent that it could have been set aside under the law in force immediately before that day.

(2) References above to setting aside a transaction include the making of any order which varies or reverses any effect of a transaction.

NOTES

This Part derived from the Insolvency Act 1985, Sch 9, para 24.

PART IV
INSOLVENCY PRACTITIONERS

[1.599]

21. Where an individual began to act as an insolvency practitioner in relation to any person before the appointed day, nothing in section 390(2) or (3) prevents that individual from being qualified to act as an insolvency practitioner in relation to that person.

NOTES

This Part derived from the Insolvency Act 1985, Sch 9, para 1.

PART V
GENERAL TRANSITIONAL PROVISIONS AND SAVINGS

Interpretation for this Part

[1.600]

22. In this Part of this Schedule, "the former enactments" means so much of [the Companies Act 1985] as is repealed and replaced by this Act, the Insolvency Act 1985 and the other enactments repealed by this Act.

General saving for past acts and events

23. So far as anything done or treated as done under or for the purposes of any provision of the former enactments could have been done under or for the purposes of the corresponding provision of this Act, it is not invalidated by the repeal of that provision but has effect as if done under or for the purposes of the corresponding provision; and any order, regulation, rule or other instrument made or having effect under any provision of the former enactments shall, insofar as its effect is preserved by this paragraph, be treated for all purposes as made and having effect under the corresponding provision.

Periods of time

24. Where any period of time specified in a provision of the former enactments is current immediately before the appointed day, this Act has effect as if the corresponding provision had been in force when the period began to run; and (without prejudice to the foregoing) any period of time so specified and current is deemed for the purposes of this Act—

(a) to run from the date or event from which it was running immediately before the appointed day, and

(b) to expire (subject to any provision of this Act for its extension) whenever it would have expired if this Act had not been passed;

and any rights, priorities, liabilities, reliefs, obligations, requirements, powers, duties or exemptions dependent on the beginning, duration or end of such a period as above mentioned shall be under this Act as they were or would have been under the former enactments.

Internal cross-references in this Act

25. Where in any provision of this Act there is a reference to another such provision, and the first-mentioned provision operates, or is capable of operating, in relation to things done or omitted, or events occurring or not occurring, in the past (including in particular past acts of compliance with any enactment, failures of compliance, contraventions, offences and convictions of offences), the reference to the other provision is to be read as including a reference to the corresponding provision of the former enactments.

Punishment of offences

26. (1) Offences committed before the appointed day under any provision of the former enactments may, notwithstanding any repeal by this Act, be prosecuted and punished after that day as if this Act had not passed.

(2) A contravention of any provision of the former enactments committed before the appointed day shall not be visited with any severer punishment under or by virtue of this Act than would have been applicable under that provision at the time of the contravention; but where an offence for the continuance of which a penalty was provided has been committed under any provision of the former enactments, proceedings may be taken under this Act in respect of the continuance of the offence on and after the appointed day in the like manner as if the offence had been committed under the corresponding provision of this Act.

References elsewhere to the former enactments

27. (1) A reference in any enactment, instrument or document (whether express or implied, and in whatever phraseology) to a provision of the former enactments (including the corresponding provision of any yet earlier enactment) is to be read, where necessary to retain for the enactment, instrument or document the same force and effect as it would have had but for the passing of this Act, as, or as including, a reference to the corresponding provision by which it is replaced in this Act.

(2) The generality of the preceding sub-paragraph is not affected by any specific conversion of references made by this Act, nor by the inclusion in any provision of this Act of a reference (whether express or implied, and in whatever phraseology) to the provision of the former enactments corresponding to that provision, or to a provision of the former enactments which is replaced by a corresponding provision of this Act.

Saving for power to repeal provisions in section 51

28. The Secretary of State may by order in a statutory instrument repeal subsections (3) to (5) of section 51 of this Act and the entries in Schedule 10 relating to subsections (4) and (5) of that section.

Saving for Interpretation Act 1978 ss 16, 17

29. Nothing in this Schedule is to be taken as prejudicing sections 16 and 17 of the Interpretation Act 1978 (savings from, and effect of, repeals); and for the purposes of section 17(2) of that Act (construction of references to enactments repealed and replaced, etc), so much of section 18 of the Insolvency Act 1985 as is replaced by a provision of this Act is deemed to have been repealed by this Act and not by the Company Directors Disqualification Act 1986.

NOTES

Para 22: words in square brackets substituted for original words "the Companies Act" by the Companies Act 2006 (Consequential Amendments, Transitional Provisions and Savings) Order 2009, SI 2009/1941, art 2(1), Sch 1, para 83, subject to transitional provisions and savings in art 8, Sch 1, para 84 at **[2.70]**, **[2.73]**.

Insolvency Act 1985: that Act was mostly repealed by the combined effect of s 438 of, and Sch 12 to, this Act and the Company Directors Disqualification Act 1986, s 23(2), Sch 4.

SCHEDULES 12–14

(*Sch 12 contains repeals only; Sch 13 contains amendments to the Companies Act 1985 and Sch 14 contains consequential amendments of other enactments. In so far as Schs 13 and 14 are still in force, the amendments they make have been incorporated into the relevant legislation at the appropriate place in this work.*)

DERIVATION TABLE

[1.601]
Note: The following abbreviations are used in this Table—

"INS 1970" = Insolvency Services (Accounting and Investment) Act 1970 (c 8)

"INS 1976" = Insolvency Act 1976 (c 60)

"CA" = Companies Act 1985 (c 6)

"IA" = Insolvency Act 1985 (c 65)

"B(Sc)" = Bankruptcy (Scotland) Act 1985 (c 66)

Provision	Derivation
1	IA s 20
2	IA s 21
3	IA s 22
4	IA s 23(1)–(6), (7) (part)
5	IA s 24
6	IA s 25
7	IA s 26
8	IA s 27
9	IA s 28
10	IA s 29
11	IA s 30
12	IA s 31
13	IA s 32
14	IA s 33
15	IA s 34(1)–(8), (12)
16	IA s 34(9), (10)
17	IA s 35
18	IA s 36
19	IA s 37(1)–(3)
20	IA s 37(4), (5)
21	IA s 38
22	IA s 39
23	IA s 40
24	IA s 41
25	IA s 42
26	IA s 43
27	IA ss 34(11), 44
28	CA s 488; IA s 45(1)
29	CA s 500; IA s 45(2)
30	CA s 489
31	CA s 490
32	CA s 491
33	IA s 46
34	IA s 47
35	CA s 492(1), (2); IA Sch 6 para 16(2)
36	CA s 494
37	CA s 492(3); IA Sch 6 para 16(3), (4)
38	CA s 498; IA Sch 6 para 17
39	CA s 493
40	CA s 196 (part); IA Sch 6 para 15(2), (3)
41	CA s 499
42	IA s 48
43	IA s 49
44	IA s 50
45	IA s 51
46	IA s 52
47	IA s 53
48	IA s 54
49	IA s 55
50	CA s 487
51	CA s 467
52	CA s 468
53	CA s 469; IA s 56 (part)
54	CA s 470
55	CA s 471; IA s 57
56	CA s 472
57	CA s 473; IA s 58
58	CA s 474
59	CA s 475; IA Sch 6 para 20(2)
60	CA s 476; IA Sch 6 para 21
61	CA s 477; IA s 59
62	CA s 478; IA s 60, Sch 6 para 13
63	CA s 479; IA s 61
64	CA s 480
65	CA s 481; IA s 62
66	CA s 482; IA s 63
67	CA s 482A; IA s 64
68	CA s 482B; IA s 65
69	CA s 483
70	CA ss 462(4), 484, 486 (part)
71	CA s 485
72	CA s 724
73	CA s 501
74	CA s 502
75	CA s 503
76	CA s 504

Provision	Derivation
77	CA s 505
78	CA s 506
79	CA s 507; IA Sch 6 para 5
80	CA s 508
81	CA s 509
82	CA s 510
83	CA s 511
84	CA s 572
85	CA s 573
86	CA s 574
87	CA s 575
88	CA s 576
89	CA s 577; IA Sch 6 para 35
90	CA s 578
91	CA s 580
92	CA s 581
93	CA s 584; IA Sch 6 para 36
94	CA s 585(1)–(4), (7)
95	IA s 83(1)–(6), (9), (10)
96	IA s 83(7) (part)
97	CA s 587; IA s 85(1)
98	IA s 85(2), (3), (6)–(8), (9)(a), (10)
99	IA s 85(4), (5), (9)(b), (c), (10)
100	CA s 589; IA Sch 6 para 37(1), (2)
101	CA s 590; IA Sch 6 para 38(2)–(4)
102	IA s 83(7) (part)
103	CA s 591; IA Sch 6 para 39
104	CA s 592
105	CA s 594; IA s 83(8)
106	CA s 595(1)–(5), (8)
107	CA s 597
108	CA s 599
109	CA s 600
110	CA ss 582(1)–(4), (7), 593; IA Sch 6 para 40
111	CA s 582(5), (6), (8)
112	CA s 602
113	CA s 603
114	IA s 82
115	CA s 604
116	CA s 605
117	CA s 512; IA Sch 6 paras 25, 26
118	CA s 513
119	CA s 514
120	CA s 515; IA Sch 6 para 25

Provision	Derivation
121	CA s 516
122	CA s 517
123	CA s 518; IA Sch 6 paras 25, 27
124	CA s 519; IA Sch 6 para 28
125	CA s 520
126	CA s 521
127	CA s 522
128	CA s 523
129	CA s 524
130	CA s 525; IA Sch 6 para 29
131	IA s 66
132	IA s 67
133	IA s 68(1)–(4)
134	IA s 68(5), (6)
135	CA s 532; IA s 69(3)
136	IA s 70(1)–(3), 4(a), (5), (6)
137	IA s 70(4)(b), (7)–(9)
138	CA s 535; IA s 71, Sch 6 para 30
139	IA s 72
140	IA s 73
141	IA s 74
142	IA s 75
143	IA s 69(1), (2)
144	CA s 537
145	CA s 538
146	IA s 78
147	CA s 549
148	CA s 550
149	CA s 522; IA Sch 6 para 32
150	CA s 553
151	CA s 554
152	CA s 555
153	CA s 557
154	CA s 558
155	CA s 559
156	CA s 560
157	CA s 562; IA Sch 6 para 33
158	CA s 565
159	CA s 566
160	CA s 567; IA Sch 6 para 34
161	CA s 569
162	CA s 571
163	IA s 94
164	CA s 635

Provision	Derivation
165	CA ss 539(1)(d), (e), (f), 598; IA s 84(1), Sch 6 para 41
166	IA s 84
167	CA s 539(1), (2), (2A), (3); IA Sch 6 para 31(2), (3)
168	CA s 540(3)–(6)
169	CA s 539(4), (5); IA Sch 6 para 31(4)
170	CA s 636
171	IA s 86
172	IA s 79
173	IA s 87
174	IA s 80
175	IA s 89(1), (2)
176	IA s 89(3), (4)
177	IA s 90
178	IA s 91(1)–(4), (8)
179	IA s 91(5), (6)
180	IA s 91(7)
181	IA s 92(1)–(4), (9), (10)
182	IA s 92(5)–(8)
183	CA s 621
184	CA s 622; IA Sch 6 para 25
185	CA s 623; B(Sc) Sch 7 para 21
186	CA s 619(4)
187	CA s 659; IA Sch 6 para 48
188	CA s 637
189	IA s 93
190	CA s 638
191	CA s 639
192	CA s 641
193	CA s 643; B(Sc) Sch 7 para 22
194	CA s 644
195	CA s 645
196	CA s 646
197	CA s 647
198	CA s 648
199	CA s 649
200	CA s 650
201	CA ss 585(5), (6), 595(6), (7)
202	IA s 76(1)–(3), (6)
203	IA s 76(4), (5), (7)–(10)
204	IA s 77
205	IA s 81
206	CA s 624; IA Sch 6 para 25
207	CA s 625; IA Sch 6 para 42
208	CA s 626; IA Sch 6 para 43
209	CA s 627
210	CA s 628
211	CA s 629
212	IA s 19
213	CA s 630(1), (2); IA Sch 6 para 6(1)
214	IA ss 12(9), 15(1)–(5), (7), Sch 9 para 4
215	CA s 630(3)–(6); IA s 15(6), Sch 6 para 6(2), (3)
216	IA s 17, Sch 9 para 5
217	IA s 18(1) (part), (2)–(6)
218	CA s 632, IA Sch 6 para 44
219	CA s 633
220	CA s 665
221	CA s 666
222	CA s 667; IA Sch 6 para 50
223	CA s 668; IA Sch 6 para 51
224	CA s 669; IA Sch 6 para 52
225	CA s 670
226	CA s 671
227	CA s 672
228	CA s 673
229	CA s 674
230	IA ss 95(1), (2), 96(1)
231	IA ss 95(1), (2), 96(2)
232	IA ss 95(1), (2), 96(3)
233	IA ss 95, 97
234	IA ss 95(1), (2), 98
235	IA ss 95(1), (2), 99
236	IA ss 95(1), (2), 100(1), (2), (6)
237	IA s 100(3)–(5), (7)
238	IA ss 95(1)(a), (b), 101(1) (part)–(3)
239	IA ss 95(1)(a), (b), 101(1) (part), (4)–(7), (11)
240	IA s 101(8)–(11)
241	IA ss 95(1), 102
242	CA s 615A; B(Sc) Sch 7 para 20
243	CA s 615B; B(Sc) Sch 7 para 20
244	IA ss 95(1)(a), (b), 103
245	IA ss 95(1)(a), (b), 104
246	IA ss 95(1)(a), (b), (2), 105
247	IA s 108(3) (part), (4)

Provision	Derivation
248	IA s 108(3) (part)
249	IA s 108(5)
250	IA s 108(6)
251	IA s 108(3) (part)
252	IA s 112(1) (part), (3)
253	IA ss 110, 111(1), (2), (3) (part)
254	IA s 111(4), (5)
255	IA s 112(1) (part), (2), (4)–(7)(a)
256	IA s 113
257	IA s 114(1) (part), (2), (3)
258	IA s 115(1)–(6), (9), (10)
259	IA s 115(7), (8)
260	IA s 116(1)–(3), (6), (7)
261	IA s 116(4), (5)
262	IA s 117
263	IA s 118
264	IA s 119(1)
265	IA s 119(2), (3)
266	IA s 119(4)–(7)
267	IA s 120(1), (2), (7)–(9)
268	IA s 120(3), (4)
269	IA s 120(5)
270	IA s 120(6)
271	IA s 121
272	IA s 122
273	IA s 123(1), (2), (8)
274	IA ss 111(3) (part), 112(1) (part), (7)(b), 114(1) (part), 123(3)–(5)
275	IA s 123(6), (7)
276	IA s 124
277	IA s 125
278	IA s 126(1)
279	IA s 126(2)–(5)
280	IA s 127
281	IA s 128
282	IA s 129
283	IA s 130
284	IA s 131
285	IA s 132
286	IA s 133
287	IA s 134
288	IA s 135
289	IA s 136
290	IA s 137
291	IA s 138
292	IA s 139
293	IA s 140
294	IA s 141
295	IA s 142

Provision	Derivation
296	IA s 143
297	IA s 144
298	IA s 145
299	IA s 146
300	IA s 147
301	IA s 148
302	IA s 149
303	IA s 150
304	IA s 151
305	IA s 152
306	IA s 153
307	IA s 154(1)–(4), (7)
308	IA s 155(1), (2), (4), (5)
309	IA ss 154(5), (6), 155(3)
311	IA s 157
312	IA s 158
313	IA s 159
314	IA s 160
315	IA s 161(1)–(4), (10)
316	IA s 161(5)
317	IA s 161(6), (7)
318	IA s 161(8)
319	IA s 161(9)
320	IA s 162(1)–(4), (9), (10)
321	IA s 162(5)–(8)
322	IA s 163
323	IA s 164
324	IA s 165(1)–(4)
325	IA s 165(5), (6)
326	IA s 165(7), (8)
327	IA s 165(9)
328	IA s 166(1)–(5), (7)
329	IA s 166(6)
330	IA s 167
331	IA s 168(1), (2), (4)
332	IA s 168(3)
333	IA s 169
334	IA s 170(1)–(3)
335	IA s 170(4) (9)
336	IA s 171
337	IA s 172
338	IA s 173
339	IA s 174(1) (part), (2)
340	IA s 174(1) (part), (3)–(6), (12) (part)
341	IA s 174(7)–(11), (12) (part)
342	IA s 175
343	IA s 176
344	IA s 177
345	IA s 178

Provision	Derivation
346	IA s 179
347	IA s 180
348	IA s 181
349	IA s 182
350	IA ss 183(1)–(3), (5), (6), 192
351	IA ss 184(5), 187(3)(a)
352	IA s 183(4)
353	IA ss 183(4), 184(1)
354	IA ss 183(4), 184(2)–(4)
355	IA ss 183(4), 185
356	IA ss 183(4), 186
357	IA ss 183(4), 187(1)(3)(b)
358	IA ss 183(4), 187(2)
359	IA ss 183(4), 188
360	IA s 189
361	IA s 190
362	IA s 191
363	IA s 193
364	IA s 194
365	IA s 195
366	IA s 196(1), (2)
367	IA s 196(3)–(6)
368	IA s 196(7)
369	IA s 197
370	IA s 198
371	IA s 199
372	IA s 200
373	IA s 201
374	IA s 202
375	IA s 203
376	IA s 204
377	IA s 205
378	IA s 206
379	IA s 210
380	—
381	IA s 211(1) (part)
382	IA s 211(1) (part), (2), (3)
383	IA s 211(1) (part), (5)–(7)
384	IA ss 209(1) (part), 211(1) (part)
385	IA s 211(1) (part), (4)
386	CA ss 196(2), 475(1); IA ss 23(7), 89(1), 108(3), 115(9), 166(1), Sch 4 para 1(1), Sch 6 para 15(3)
387	CA ss 196(2)–(4), 475(3), (4); IA ss 23(8), 115(10), Sch 4, Pt II para 1(2), (3), Sch 6 paras 15(4), 20(3)
388	IA s 1(2)–(6)
389	IA s 1(1)
390	IA ss 2, 3(1)
391	IA s 3(2)–(5)
392	IA ss 4, 11 (part)
393	IA s 5
394	IA s 6
395	IA s 7
396	IA ss 8(1), (2), (6), 11 (part)
397	IA s 8(3)–(5)
398	IA s 9
399	IA s 222
400	IA s 223
401	IA s 224
402	IA s 225
403	INS 1970 s 1; INS 1976 s 3; IA Sch 8 para 28
404	INS 1970 s 2
405	INS 1970 s 3; INS 1976 Sch 2 para 5
406	INS 1970 s 4; INS 1976 Sch 2 para 6; IA Sch 8 para 17
407	INS 1970 s 5; INS 1976 Sch 2 para 7
408	INS 1970 s 6; INS 1976 Sch 2 para 8
409	INS 1970 s 7; INS 1976 Sch 2 para 9
410	INS 1970 s 9(3); INS 1976 s 14(6); IA s 236(3)(i)
411	IA s 106
412	IA s 207
413	IA s 226
414	IA ss 106(5), 107
415	IA ss 207(5), 208(1)–(3), (5)
416	CA s 664; IA Sch 6 para 49
417	CA s 667(2) (part)
418	IA s 209(1) (part), (2), (3)
419	IA ss 10, 11 (part)
420	IA s 227
421	IA s 228
422	IA s 229
423	IA s 212(1), (3), (7) (part)
424	IA s 212(2)
425	IA s 212(4)–(6), (7) (part)
426	IA s 213
427	IA s 214
428	IA s 217(1)–(3)
429	IA s 221(1), (3)–(5)
430	CA s 730; IA passim
431	CA s 731; IA s 108(1)
432	IA s 230
433	IA s 231

Provision	Derivation
434	IA s 234
435	IA s 233
436	IA s 232 (part)
437	—
438	—
439	—
440	IA s 236(3)
441	CA s 745; IA s 236(4)
442	IA s 236(5)
443	—
444	—
Sch 1	IA Sch 3
Sch 2	CA s 471(1); IA s 57
Sch 3	CA Sch 16
Sch 4	
Sch 4 Pt I	CA ss 539((1)(d)–(f), 598(1)
Sch 4 Pt II	CA ss 539(1)(a), (b), 598(2)
Sch 4 Pt III	CA ss 539(2), 598(2)
Sch 5	
Sch 5 Pt I	IA s 160(2)
Sch 5 Pt II	IA s 160(1)
Sch 5 Pt III	IA s 160(6)
Sch 6	IA Sch 4 Pt I, Pt II paras 2–4
Sch 7	IA Sch 1
Sch 8	IA Sch 5

Provision	Derivation
Sch 9	IA Sch 7
Sch 10	CA and IA passim
Sch 11	
Sch 11 para 1	IA Sch 9 para 6
Sch 11 para 2	IA Sch 9 para 7
Sch 11 para 3	IA Sch 9 para 8
Sch 11 para 4	IA Sch 9 para 9(1)
Sch 11 para 5	IA Sch 9 para 9(2)
Sch 11 para 6	IA Sch 9 para 9(3)–(5), (8)
Sch 11 para 7	IA Sch 9 para 9(6)
Sch 11 para 8	IA Sch 9 para 9(7)
Sch 11 para 9	IA Sch 9 para 10
Sch 11 para 10	IA Sch 9 para 11
Sch 11 para 11	IA Sch 9 para 12
Sch 11 para 12	IA Sch 9 para 13
Sch 11 para 13	IA Sch 9 para 14
Sch 11 para 14	IA Sch 9 paras 15, 16, 17
Sch 11 para 15	IA Sch 9 para 18
Sch 11 para 16	IA Sch 9 para 19
Sch 11 para 17	IA Sch 9 para 20
Sch 11 para 18	IA Sch 9 para 21
Sch 11 para 19	IA Sch 9 para 22
Sch 11 para 20	IA Sch 9 para 24
Sch 11 para 21	IA Sch 9 para 1
Sch 11 paras 22–28	—
Schs 12–14	—

DESTINATION TABLE

[1.602]
This table shows in column (1) the enactments repealed by the Insolvency Act 1986, s 438, Sch 12 (and, in certain cases where indicated by an asterisk *, provisions repealed by the Company Directors Disqualification Act 1986, s 23(2), Sch 4, although for the bulk of those provisions see the destination table to that Act), and in column (2) the provisions of the former Act corresponding to the repealed provisions.

In certain cases the enactment in column (1), although having a corresponding provision in column (2), is not, or is not wholly, repealed, as it is still required or partly required for the purposes of other legislation.

It will be observed that many of the provisions repealed by the Insolvency Act 1986 consolidate provisions formerly in the Insolvency Act 1985, which itself repealed and replaced directly, or was otherwise comparable to, older legislation. To facilitate cross reference from pre-1985 legislation through to the provisions of the 1986 Act, a comparative table delineating the destination of those provisions repealed by the 1985 Act follows this destination table. The two tables may then be used in conjunction with each other.

(1) **Insolvency Services (Accounting and Investment) Act 1970 (c 8)**	(2) **Insolvency Act 1986 (c 45)**
s 1	s 403
s 2	s 404
s 3	s 405
s 4	s 406
s 5	s 407
s 6	s 408
s 7	s 409
s 8	Spent
s 9(1), (2), (4)	Unnecessary
s 9(3)	s 410
Sch 1	Rep, 1976 c 60, s 14(4), Sch 3
Sch 2	Spent

(1) **Insolvency Act 1976 (c 60)**	(2) **Insolvency Act 1986 (c 45)**
s 3(1), (2), (6)	Unnecessary
s 3(3), (4), (5)	s 403(1), (2), (3)
s 14(6)†	s 410
Sch 2, para 5†	s 405(1)
Sch 2, para 6†	s 406
Sch 2, para 7†	s 407
Sch 2, para 8†	s 408
Sch 2, para 9†	s 409

(1) **Companies Act 1985 (c 6)**	(2) **Insolvency Act 1986 (c 45)**
s 196(1), (2), (5)†	s 40
s 196(2)†	s 386(1)–(3)
s 196(3)†	s 387(4)(a)
ss 462(4), 484, 486 (part)	s 70
s 467	s 51
s 468	s 52
s 469	s 53
s 470	s 54
s 471	s 55
s 472	s 56
s 473	s 57
s 474	s 58
s 475	s 59
s 476	s 60
s 477	s 61
s 478	s 62
s 479	s 63
s 480	s 64
s 481	s 65
s 482	s 66
s 482A	s 67
s 482B	s 68
s 483	s 69
s 485	s 71
s 488	s 28
s 489	s 30
s 490	s 31
s 491	s 32
s 492(1), (2)	s 35
s 492(3)	s 37(1), (3)
s 492(4), (5)	s 37(2), (4)
s 493	s 39
s 494	s 36
ss 495, 496, 497	Rep, 1985 c 65, s 235(3), Sch 10, Pt II
s 498	s 38(1)–(3), (5)
s 499	s 41
s 500	s 29(1)
s 501	s 73

(1) Companies Act 1985 (c 6)	(2) Insolvency Act 1986 (c 45)
s 502	s 74
s 503	s 75
s 504	s 76
s 505	s 77
s 506	s 78
s 507	s 79
s 508	s 80
s 509	s 81
s 510	s 82
s 511	s 83
s 512	s 117
s 513	s 118
s 514	s 119
s 515	s 120
s 516	s 121
s 517	s 122
s 518	s 123
s 519(1)–(3), (7)	s 124(1)–(3), (5)
s 519(4), (6)	s 124(4)
s 519(5)	Rep, 1985 c 65, s 235(3), Sch 10, Pt II
s 520	s 125
s 521	s 126
s 522	s 127
s 523	s 128
s 524	s 129
s 525	s 130
ss 526–531	Rep, 1985 c 65, s 235(3), Sch 10, Pt II
s 532	s 135
ss 533, 534, 536	Rep, 1985 c 65, s 235(3), Sch 10, Pt II
s 535	s 138(1)
s 537	s 144
s 538	s 145
s 539(1), (2)	s 167(1)
s 539(1)(a), (b)	Sch 4, Pt II
s 539(1)(d)–(f)	Sch 4, Pt I
s 539(2)	Sch 4, Pt III
s 539(2A), (3)	s 167(2), (3)
s 540(1), (2)	Rep, 1985 c 65, s 235(3), Sch 10, Pt II
s 540(3)–(6)	s 168(2)–(5)
ss 541–548	Rep, 1985 c 65, s 235(3), Sch 10, Pts I, II
s 549	s 147
s 550	s 148
s 551	Rep, 1985 c 65, s 235(3), Sch 10, Pt II
s 552	s 149
s 553	s 150
s 554	s 151
s 555	s 152
s 556	Rep, 1985 c 65, s 235(3), Sch 10, Pt II
s 557	s 153
s 558	s 154
s 559	s 155
s 560	s 156
s 561	Rep, 1985 c 65, s 235(3), Sch 10, Pt II
s 562	s 157
ss 563, 564	Rep, 1985 c 65, s 235(3), Sch 10, Pt II
s 565	s 158
s 566	s 159
s 567	s 160
s 568	Rep, 1985 c 65, s 235(3), Sch 10, Pt II
s 569	s 161
s 570	Rep, 1985 c 65, s 235(3), Sch 10, Pt IV
s 571	s 162
s 572	s 84
s 573	s 85
s 574	s 86
s 575	s 87
s 576	s 88
s 577	s 89
s 578	s 90
s 579	Unnecessary
s 580	s 91
s 581	s 92
s 582(1), (2)	s 110(1)–(3)
s 582(3), (4)	s 110(4), (5)
s 582(5), (6)	s 111(2), (3)
s 582(7)	s 110(6)
s 582(8)	s 111(4)
s 583	Rep, 1985 c 65, s 235(3), Sch 10, Pt II
s 584	s 93
s 585(1), (2), (4), (7)	s 94(1), (2), (5), (6)
s 585(3)	s 94(3), (4)

(1) Companies Act 1985 (c 6)	(2) Insolvency Act 1986 (c 45)
s 585(5)	s 201(2), (3)
s 585(6)	s 201(4)
s 586	Rep, 1985 c 65, s 235(3), Sch 10, Pt II
s 587	s 97
s 588	Rep, 1985 c 65, s 235(3), Sch 10, Pt II
s 589	s 100
s 590(1)–(3)	s 101
ss 590(4), 591(1)	Rep, 1985 c 65, s 235(3), Sch 10, Pt II
s 591(2)	s 103
s 592	s 104
s 593	s 110
s 594	s 105(1)–(3)
s 595(1)–(5)	s 106(1)–(5)
s 595(6), (7)	s 201(3), (4)
s 595(8)	s 106(6)
s 596	Unnecessary
s 597	s 107
s 598	s 165(2)–(6), Sch 4, Pt III
s 599	s 108
s 600	s 109
s 601	Rep, 1985 c 65, s 235(3), Sch 10, Pt II
s 602	s 112
s 603	s 113
s 604	s 115
s 605	s 116
ss 606–615	Rep, 1985 c 65, s 235(3), Sch 10, Pt II
s 615A	s 242
s 615B	s 243
ss 616–618, 619(1)–(3), (5)–(8)	Rep, 1985 c 65, s 235(3), Sch 10, Pt II
s 619(4)	s 186
s 620	Rep, 1985 c 65, s 235(3), Sch 10, Pt II
s 621	s 183
s 622	s 184
s 623	s 185
s 624	s 206
s 625	s 207
s 626	s 208
s 627	s 209
s 628	s 210
s 629	s 211
s 630(1), (2)	s 213(1), (2)
s 630(3)–(5), (5A), (6)	s 215(1)–(6)
s 631	Rep, 1985 c 65, s 235(3), Sch 10, Pt II
s 632	s 218
s 633	s 219
s 634	Rep, 1985 c 65, s 235(3), Sch 10, Pt I
s 635	s 164
s 636	s 170
s 637	s 188
s 638	s 190
s 639	s 191
s 640	Rep, 1985 c 65, s 235(3), Sch 10, Pt II
s 641	s 192
s 642	Rep, 1985 c 65, s 235(3), Sch 10, Pt II
s 643	s 193
s 644	s 194
s 645	s 195
s 646	s 196
s 647	s 197
s 648	s 198
s 649	s 199
s 650	s 200
s 659	s 187
ss 660–663	Rep, 1985 c 65, s 235(3), Sch 10, Pt II
s 664	s 416
s 665	s 220
s 666	s 221
s 667(1)	s 222(1)
s 667(2)	ss 222(2), 417
s 668	s 223
s 669	s 224
s 670	s 225
s 671	s 226
s 672	s 227
s 673	s 228
s 674	s 229
ss 709(4), 710(4)	—
s 724	s 72
s 730[†]	s 430

(1) Companies Act 1985 (c 6)	(2) Insolvency Act 1986 (c 45)
s 731†	s 431
s 741(1), (2)†	s 251
s 745†	s 441
Sch 16	Sch 3
Sch 16 (pt)	—

(1) Companies Consolidation (Consequential Provisions) Act 1985 (c 9)	(2) Insolvency Act 1986 (c 45)
Sch 2 (pt)†	s 403(1)

(1) Insolvency Act 1985 (c 65)	(2) Insolvency Act 1986 (c 45)
s 1(1)	s 389(1)
s 1(2)–(4)	s 388(1)–(3)
s 1(5)	s 388(1), (4)
s 1(6)	ss 388(5), 389(2)
s 2	s 390
s 3(1)	s 390(2)
s 3(2)	s 391(1), (4)
s 3(3), (5)	s 391(2), (3)
s 3(4)	s 391(5)
s 4	s 392(3)–(8)
s 5	s 393
s 6	s 394
s 7	s 395
s 8(1), (2)	s 396(2), (3)
s 8(3)–(5)	s 397(1)–(3)
s 8(6)	s 396(1)
s 9	s 398
s 10	s 419
s 11	ss 392(2), 396(1), 419(1)
s 12(9)*	s 214(7)
s 15(1)–(5)	s 214(1)–(5)
s 15(6)	ss 214(8), 215(5)
s 15(7)	s 214(6)
s 17	s 216
s 18*	s 217
s 19	s 212
s 20	s 1
s 21	s 2
s 22	s 3
s 23(1)–(7)	s 4
s 23(7)	ss 4, 386(1), (3)
s 23(8)	s 387(2)
s 24	s 5
s 25	s 6
s 26	s 7
s 27	s 8
s 28	s 9
s 29	s 10
s 30	s 11
s 31	s 12
s 32	s 13
s 33	s 14
s 34(1)–(8)	s 15(1)–(8)
s 34(9), (10)	s 16
s 34(11)	s 27(5)
s 34(12)	s 15(9)
s 35	s 17
s 36	s 18
s 37(1)–(3)	s 19
s 37(4), (5)	s 20
s 38	s 21
s 39	s 22
s 40	s 23
s 41	s 24
s 42	s 25
s 43	s 26
s 44(1)–(4)	s 27(1)–(4)
s 44(5)–(6)	s 27(6)
s 45(1)	s 28
s 45(2)	s 29(2)
s 46	s 33
s 47	s 34
s 48	s 42
s 49	s 43
s 50	s 44
s 51	s 45
s 52	s 46
s 53	s 47
s 54	s 48
s 55	s 49
s 56	s 53
s 57	s 55
s 58	s 57
s 59	s 61
s 60	s 62
s 61	s 63
s 62	s 65
s 63	s 66
s 64	s 67
s 65	s 68
s 66	s 131
s 67	s 132

(1) Insolvency Act 1985 (c 65)	(2) Insolvency Act 1986 (c 45)
s 68(1)–(4)	s 133
s 68(5), (6)	s 134
s 69(1), (2)	s 143(1), (2)
s 69(3)	s 135(4)
s 70(1)–(3), (5), (6)	s 136(1)–(3), (5), (6)
s 70(4)(a)	s 136(4)
s 70(4)(b)	s 137(1)
s 70(7), (8)	s 137(2), (3)
s 70(9)	s 137(4), (5)
s 71	s 138(2)–(6)
s 72	s 139
s 73	s 140
s 74	s 141
s 75	Scottish
s 76(1)	s 202(1), (2)
s 76(2), (3), (6)	s 202(3), (4), (5)
s 76(4), (5), (7)–(10)	s 203
s 77	s 204
s 78	s 146
s 79	s 172
s 80	s 174
s 81	s 205
s 82	s 114
s 83(1)–(6), (9), (10)	s 95(1)–(6), (7), (8)
s 83(7)	ss 96, 102, 105(4)
s 83(8)	s 105(4)
s 84	ss 165(1), 166
s 85(1)	s 97
s 85(2), (3)	s 98(1), (2)
s 85(4), (5)	s 99(1), (2)
s 85(6), (7), (8)	s 98(3), (4), (5)
s 85(9)(a)	s 98(6)
s 85(9)(b), (c)	s 99(3)
s 85(10)	ss 98(6), 99(3)
s 86	s 171
s 87	s 173
s 88	Spent
s 89(1), (2)	ss 175, 386
s 89(3)	s 176(1), (2)
s 89(4)	s 176(3)
s 90	s 177
s 91(1)	s 178(1), (2)
s 91(2)–(4)	s 178(3)–(5)
s 91(5), (6)	s 179(1), (2)
s 91(7)	s 180
s 91(8)	s 178(6)
s 92(1)–(4)	s 181(1)–(4)
s 92(5)–(8)	s 182(1)–(4)
s 92(9), (10)	s 181(5), (6)
s 93	s 189

(1) Insolvency Act 1985 (c 65)	(2) Insolvency Act 1986 (c 45)
s 94	s 163
s 95(1)	ss 230(1), (2), 231, 232, 233(1), 234(1), 235(1), 236(1), 238(1), 239(1), 241, 244(1), 245(1), 246(1)
s 95(2)	ss 230(3), (4), 231, 233(1), 234(1), 235(1), 236(1), 246(1)
s 95(3)	s 233(1)
s 96(1)	s 230(1), (2), (5)
s 96(2)	ss 230(3), (4), 231
s 96(3)	s 232
s 97(1), (3), (4)	s 233(2), (4), (5)
s 97(2)	s 233(3), (5)
s 98(1)	s 234(2)
s 98(2)	s 234(3), (4)
s 99(1), (2)	s 235(2), (3)
s 99(3)	s 235(3), (4)
s 99(4)(a)	s 235(3)
s 99(4)(b)	s 235(1)
s 99(5)	s 235(5)
s 100(1)	s 236(2), (3)
s 100(2)	s 236(4)–(6)
s 100(3)	s 237(4)
s 100(4), (5), (7)	s 237(1)–(3)
s 100(6)	s 236(1)
s 101(1)	ss 238(2), (3), 239(2), (3)
s 101(2), (3)	s 238(4), (5)
s 101(4)–(7)	s 239(4)–(7)
s 101(8)	s 240(1)
s 101(9), (10)	s 240(2), (3)
s 101(11)	ss 239(6), 240(1)
s 102	s 241
s 103	s 244
s 104	s 245(2)–(6)
s 105	s 246(2), (3)
s 106(1)	s 411(1), (3)
s 106(2)	s 411(2), (3)
s 106(3), (4)	s 411(4), (5)
s 106(5)	ss 411(6), 414(9)
s 107(1)	s 414(1), (2), (3), (8)
s 107(2)–(5)	s 414(4)–(7)
s 107(6)	s 414(9)
s 108(1)	s 431
s 108(3)	ss 247(1), 248, 251 386(1), (3)
s 108(4)	s 247(2)
s 108(5)	s 249

(1) Insolvency Act 1985 (c 65)	(2) Insolvency Act 1986 (c 45)
s 108(6)	s 250
s 109	Unnecessary
s 110	s 253(1), (2)
s 111(1)	s 253(1), (3)
s 111(2)	s 253(4)
s 111(3)	ss 253(5), 274(3)
s 111(4), (5)	s 254
s 112(1)	ss 252(1), 255(2), 274(3)
s 112(2)	s 255(1)
s 112(3)	s 252(2)
s 112(4)–(6)	s 255(3)–(5)
s 112(7)(a)	s 255(6)
s 112(7)(b)	s 274(4)
s 113(1), (2)	s 256(1)
s 113(3)–(7)	s 256(2)–(6)
s 114(1)	ss 257(1), 274(5)
s 114(2), (3)	s 257(2), (3)
s 115(1)–(6)	s 258(1)–(6)
s 115(7), (8)	s 259
s 115(9)	ss 258(7), 386(1), (3)
s 115(10)(a)	s 387(5)
s 115(10)(b)	—
s 116(1)–(3), (6), (7)	s 260(1)–(3), (4), (5)
s 116(4), (5)	s 261
s 117	s 262
s 118	s 263
s 119(1)	s 264
s 119(2), (3)	s 265
s 119(4)–(7)	s 266
s 120(1), (2), (7)–(9)	s 267(1), (2), (3)–(5)
s 120(3), (4)	s 268
s 120(5)	s 269
s 120(6)	s 270
s 121	s 271
s 122	s 272
s 123(1), (8)	s 273(1)
s 123(2)	s 273(2)
s 123(3), (4), (5)	s 274(1), (2), (3)
s 123(6)	s 275(1), (2)
s 123(7)	ss 274(4), 275(3)
s 124	s 276
s 125	s 277
s 126(1)	s 278
s 126(2)–(5)	s 279
s 127	s 280
s 128	s 281
s 129	s 282
s 130	s 283
s 131	s 284

(1) Insolvency Act 1985 (c 65)	(2) Insolvency Act 1986 (c 45)
s 132	s 285
s 133	s 286
s 134	s 287
s 135	s 288
s 136	s 289
s 137	s 290
s 138	s 291
s 139	s 292
s 140	s 293
s 141	s 294
s 142	s 295
s 143	s 296
s 144	s 297
s 145	s 298
s 146	s 299
s 147	s 300
s 148	s 301
s 149	s 302
s 150	s 303
s 151	s 304
s 152	s 305
s 153	s 306
s 154(1)–(4), (7)	s 307(1)–(4), (5)
s 154(5), (6)	s 309(1), (2)
s 155(1), (2), (4), (5)	s 308(1)–(4)
s 155(3)	s 309(1), (2)
s 156	s 310
s 157	s 311
s 158	s 312
s 159	s 313
s 160(1)	s 314(1), Sch 5, Pt II
s 160(2)	s 314(1), Sch 5, Pt I
s 160(3)–(5), (7)–(9)	s 314(2)–(4), (6)–(8)
s 160(6)	s 314(5), Sch 5, Pt III
s 161(1)–(4), (10)	s 315(1), (4), (5)
s 161(5)	s 316
s 161(6), (7)	s 317
s 161(8)	s 318
s 161(9)	s 319
s 162(1)–(4), (9), (10)	s 320(1)–(6)
s 162(5)–(8)	s 321
s 163	s 322
s 164	s 323
s 165(1)–(4)	s 324
s 165(5), (6)	s 325
s 165(7)	s 326(1)
s 165(8)	s 326(2), (3)
s 165(9)	s 327

(1) **Insolvency Act 1985 (c 65)**	(2) **Insolvency Act 1986 (c 45)**
s 166(1)	ss 328(1), 386(1), (3)
s 166(2)–(5), (7)	s 328(2)–(5), (6)
s 166(6)	s 329
s 167	s 330
s 168(1)	s 331(1), (2)
s 168(2), (4)	s 331(3), (4)
s 168(3)	s 332
s 169	s 333
s 170(1)–(3)	s 334
s 170(4)–(9)	s 335
s 171	s 336
s 172	s 337
s 173	s 338
s 174(1)	ss 339(1), (2), 340(1), (2)
s 174(2)	s 339(3)
s 174(3), (4), (6)	s 340(3), (4), (6)
s 174(5)	s 340(5)
s 174(7)	s 341(1)
s 174(8)	s 341(2)
s 174(9)–(11)	s 341(3)–(5)
s 174(12)	ss 340(5), 341(1), (2)
s 175	s 342
s 176	s 343
s 177	s 344
s 178	s 345
s 179	s 346
s 180	s 347
s 181	s 348
s 182	s 349
s 183(1)–(3)	s 350(1)–(3)
s 183(4)	ss 352, 353(3), 354(1), (2), 355, 356, 357(1), (3), 358, 359
s 183(5), (6)	s 350(4), (5)
s 184(1)	s 353(1), (2)
s 184(2)	s 354(1)
s 184(3)	ss 351(b), (c), 354(2)
s 184(4)	ss 351(b), (c), 354(3)
s 184(5)	s 351(a)
s 185	s 355
s 185(2)(a), (d)	s 351(b), (c)
s 185(3)(b)	s 351(b), (c)
s 186	s 356
s 186(2)(c)	s 351(b), (c)
s 187(1)	s 357(1), (3)
s 187(2)	ss 351(b), (c), 358
s 187(3)(a)	s 351(a)
s 187(3)(b)	s 357(2)
s 188	s 359

(1) **Insolvency Act 1985 (c 65)**	(2) **Insolvency Act 1986 (c 45)**
s 188(1), (2)	s 351(b), (c)
s 189	s 360
s 190	s 361
s 190(1)	s 351(b), (c)
s 191	s 362
s 191(1)	s 351(b), (c)
s 192	s 350(6)
s 193	s 363
s 194	s 364
s 195	s 365
s 196(1)	s 366(1)
s 196(2)	s 366(2)–(4)
s 196(3)	s 367(4)
s 196(4)–(6)	s 367(1)–(3)
s 196(7)	s 368
s 197	s 369
s 198	s 370
s 199	s 371
s 200	s 372
s 201	s 373
s 202	s 374
s 203	s 375
s 204	s 376
s 205	s 377
s 206	s 378
s 207	s 412
s 207(5)	s 415(7)
s 208	s 415(1)–(6)
s 209	s 418
s 209(1)	s 384(2)
s 210	s 379
s 211(1)	ss 381, 382(1), (4), 383(1), 384(1), 385(1)
s 211(2), (3)	s 382(2), (3)
s 211(4)	s 385(2)
s 211(5)–(7)	s 383(2)–(4)
s 212(1)	s 423(2), (3), (5)
s 212(2)	ss 423(5), 424
s 212(3)	s 423(1)
s 212(4)–(6)	s 425(1)–(3)
s 212(7)	ss 423(4), 425(7)
s 213	s 426
s 214	s 427
s 216	Spent
s 217	s 428
s 221	s 429
s 222	s 399
s 223	s 400
s 224	s 401

(1) Insolvency Act 1985 (c 65)	(2) Insolvency Act 1986 (c 45)
s 225	s 402
s 226	s 413
s 227	s 420
s 228	s 421
s 229	s 422
s 230	s 432
s 231	s 433
s 232	s 436
s 233	s 435
s 234	s 434
s 235(2)–(5)	Unnecessary
s 236(1), (2)	Unnecessary
s 236(3)	s 440
s 236(4)	s 441
s 236(5)	s 442
Sch 1	Sch 7
Sch 3	Sch 1
Sch 4, Pt I	Sch 6
Sch 4, Pt II, para 1(1)	s 386(2)
Sch 4, Pt II, para 1(2), (3)	s 387(3), (6)
Sch 4, Pt II, para 2	Sch 6, para 3
Sch 4, Pt II, para 3	Sch 6, paras 13–15
Sch 4, Pt II, para 4	Sch 6, para 16
Sch 5	Sch 8
Sch 6 (pt)	See under enactments affected
Sch 7	Sch 9
Sch 8, para 17†	s 406
Sch 8, para 28†	s 403(1)
Sch 9 (pt)	Sch 11
Sch 10	Spent

† Not repealed

* See notes to this table above

(1) Bankruptcy (Scotland) Act 1986 (c 66)	(2) Insolvency Act 1986 (c 45)
Sch 7 (pt)	s 185(1)–(3) Remainder unnecessary

(1) Gas Act 1986 (c 44)	(2) Insolvency Act 1986 (c 45)
Sch 7, para 31	ss 233(3), 372(4)

COMPARATIVE TABLE

[1.603]
This table shows in column (1) certain enactments within the scope of this work which were repealed by the Insolvency Act 1985, and in column (2) those provisions of that Act which replaced (generally with amendments) or were otherwise comparable with the provisions in column (1). The table does not list every enactment repealed by the 1985 Act; in particular provisions which are not reproduced in any form are omitted.

(1) **Law of Property Act 1925 (c 20)**	(2) **Insolvency Act 1985 (c 65)**
s 172	s 212

(1) **Social Security Act 1975 (c 14)**	(2) **Insolvency Act 1985 (c 65)**
s 153(1), (2), Sch 18	s 89(1), Sch 4, Pt I, para 3(1), Pt II, para 1(2)

(1) **Insolvency Act 1976 (c 60)**	(2) **Insolvency Act 1985 (c 65)**
s 2	Sch 5, paras 2, 3
s 10	s 226

(1) **Employment Protection (Consolidation) Act 1978 (c 44)**	(2) **Insolvency Act 1985 (c 65)**
s 121	Sch 4, Pt II, para 3(1), (2)

(1) **Employment Act 1980 (c 42)**	(2) **Insolvency Act 1985 (c 65)**
Sch 1, para 15	Sch 4, Pt II, para 3(2)(c)

(1) **Social Security and Housing Benefits Act 1982 (c 24)**	(2) **Insolvency Act 1985 (c 65)**
Sch 2, para 12	Sch 4, Pt II, para 3(2)(d)

(1) **Companies Act 1985 (c 6)**	(2) **Insolvency Act 1985 (c 65)**
s 300	s 12
ss 495–497	ss 52–54
s 501(1)(c)	See s 88
s 519(5)	Sch 5, para 2
ss 526, 527	s 222
s 528	s 66
s 529(2)	Sch 5, para 21
s 529(4)	s 231
s 530	s 67
s 531	cf s 70
s 533(1)–(6)	ss 70, 72
s 533(7)	s 94
s 534(b)	s 69(2)
s 536(1)	s 79(2), (6)
s 536(2)	Sch 5, para 15
s 536(4), (5)	s 96(2), (3)
s 541	Sch 5, para 23(a), (b)
s 542	Sch 5, para 16

(1) **Companies Act 1985 (c 6)**	(2) **Insolvency Act 1985 (c 65)**
s 543	Sch 5, para 23(c)
s 545	s 80
s 546	s 74(1)–(4)
s 547	Sch 5, para 10
s 548	s 74(5)
s 551	s 98(1)
s 556	s 90, Sch 5, para 15
s 561	s 100
s 563	s 68
s 564	Sch 5, para 22
s 565*	s 100(2)
s 568	s 81
s 570	s 213
s 580(1)*	Sch 5, para 15
ss 583, 586	s 83
s 588	s 85
s 590(4)	Sch 5, para 10
s 591(1)	Sch 5, para 15
s 598(5)	s 96(2)
s 601	cf ss 24, 25
ss 606–610	See s 88
s 611	Sch 5, para 12
s 612	Sch 5, para 14
s 614	s 89
ss 615, 616	ss 101, 102
s 617	s 104
ss 618, 619(1)–(3), (5)–(8), 620	ss 91, 92
s 631	s 19
s 640	Sch 5, para 25
s 642	Sch 5, para 13
s 660	Sch 5, para 16
s 661	s 224(4)
s 662	Sch 5, para 20
s 663(1)	s 106(1)
s 663(3)	s 231
s 663(4)	s 107(1)
s 663(5)	ss 106(3), 107(4)
s 663(6)	s 107(5)
ss 665*, 666(7)	cf s 227
Sch 12, Pt II	s 12
Sch 17	Sch 5, para 10
Sch 18	See s 88
Sch 19	Sch 4
Sch 20, Pt I	ss 91, 92

* Repealed in part

PART 2
TRANSITIONAL PROVISIONS

INSOLVENCY ACT 2000 (COMMENCEMENT NO 1 AND TRANSITIONAL PROVISIONS) ORDER 2001

(SI 2001/766 (C 27))

NOTES

Made: 1 March 2001.
Authority: Insolvency Act 2000, s 16(1), (3).
Commencement: 1 March 2001.

[2.1]

1 Citation and interpretation

(1) This Order may be cited as the Insolvency Act 2000 (Commencement No 1 and Transitional Provisions) Order 2001.

(2) In this Order, except where contrary provision is made, references to sections and Schedules are references to sections of, and Schedules to, the Insolvency Act 2000.

(3) In this Order—

"administration order" has the same meaning in this Order as it has in section 8(2) of the Insolvency Act 1986;

"appointed day" means the day appointed for the coming into force of the provisions of the Insolvency Act 2000 referred to in article 2;

"official receiver" has the same meaning in this Order as it has in section 399(1) of the Insolvency Act 1986.

[2.2]

2 Appointed day

(1) Subject to article 3, the day appointed for the coming into force of—

(a) sections 5, 6, 7, 8 (Disqualification of company directors etc) and Schedule 4,

(b) sections 9 (Administration orders), 10 (Investigation and prosecution of malpractice), 11 (Restriction on use of answers obtained under compulsion), 12 (Insolvent estates of deceased persons) and 13 (Bankruptcy: interest on sums held in Insolvency Services Account),

(c) section 15(1) (Repeals) and the entries relating to:—

(i) sections 218(2) and 218(6)(b) of the Insolvency Act 1986,

(ii) sections 9(1) and 22(4) of the Company Directors Disqualification Act 1986 and

(iii) section 78 of the Companies Act 1989 contained in Schedule 5,

is 2nd April 2001.

[2.3]

3 Transitional provisions

(1) In a case where a petition for an administration order has been presented before the appointed day the amendments made to sections 10(1) and 11(3) of the Insolvency Act 1986 by section 9 shall not apply and sections 10(1) and 11(3) of the Insolvency Act 1986 as they have effect immediately before the appointed day shall continue to have effect.

(2) In a case where a person subject to a disqualification order under the Company Directors Disqualification Act 1986, made on the application of the Secretary of State, the official receiver or the liquidator, has applied for leave of the court under section 17 of that Act before the appointed day, the amendments made to section 17 of the Company Directors Disqualification Act 1986 by paragraph 12(1) in Part I of Schedule 4 shall not apply and section 17(2) of the Company Directors Disqualification Act 1986 as it has effect immediately before the appointed day shall continue to have effect.

(3) In a case where a person is subject to a disqualification order under Part II of the Companies (Northern Ireland) Order 1989 made before the appointed day the following amendments shall not apply—

(a) the insertion of section 12A into the Company Directors Disqualification Act 1986 by section 7(1),

(b) the insertion of "or 12A" into section 13 of the Company Directors Disqualification Act 1986 by paragraph 8(b) of Schedule 4,

(c) the insertion of "or in contravention of section 12A" into section 14(1) of the Company Directors Disqualification Act 1986 by paragraph 9 of Schedule 4,

(d) the insertion of "or 12A" into section 15(1) of the Company Directors Disqualification Act 1986 by paragraph 10(2)(a) of Schedule 4,

(e) the insertion of "or a disqualification order under Part II of the Companies (Northern Ireland) Order 1989" into section 15(1)(b) of the Company Directors Disqualification Act 1986 by paragraph 10(2)(b) of Schedule 4, and

(f) the insertion of "or a disqualification order under Part II of the Companies (Northern Ireland) Order 1989" into section 15(5) of the Company Directors Disqualification Act 1986 by paragraph 10(3) of Schedule 4.

(4) Where—

(a) a court has directed a liquidator to refer a matter under section 218(1) of the Insolvency Act 1986,

(b) a liquidator has reported a matter under section 218(4) of the Insolvency Act 1986, or

(c) a court has directed a liquidator to make a report under section 218(6) of the Insolvency Act 1986,

before the appointed day, the amendments and repeals, as the case may be, made to section 218 of the Insolvency Act 1986 by section 10 and Schedule 5 shall not apply and section 218 of the Insolvency Act 1986 as it has effect immediately before the appointed day shall continue to have effect.

(5) The provisions of this article are without prejudice to the operation of sections 16 and 17 of the Interpretation Act 1978 (saving from, and effect of, repeals) as they are applied by section 23 of that Act.

INSOLVENCY ACT 2000 (COMMENCEMENT NO 3 AND TRANSITIONAL PROVISIONS) ORDER 2002

(SI 2002/2711 (C 83))

NOTES

Made: 29 October 2002.
Authority: Insolvency Act 2000, s 16(1), (3).
Commencement: 29 October 2002.

[2.4]
1 Citation and interpretation

(1) This Order may be cited as the Insolvency Act 2000 (Commencement No 3 and Transitional Provisions) Order 2002.

(2) In this Order, except where contrary provision is made, references to sections and Schedules are references to sections of, and Schedules to, the Insolvency Act 2000.

(3) In this Order—

"appointed day" means the day appointed for the coming into force of the provisions of the Insolvency Act 2000 referred to in article 2;

"the Act" means the Insolvency Act 1986;

"the Insolvency Rules" means the Insolvency Rules 1986; and

"the Insolvency (Scotland) Rules" means the Insolvency (Scotland) Rules 1986.

[2.5]
2

Subject to articles 3, 4 and 5, 1st January 2003 is the day appointed for the coming into force of the whole of the Insolvency Act 2000 in so far as it is not already in force.

[2.6]
3 Transitional provisions

(1) In a case where—

(a) a proposal is made by the directors of a company and before the appointed day the intended nominee has endorsed a copy of the written notice of the proposal under Rule 1.4(3) of the Insolvency Rules, or, in Scotland, under Rule 1.4(3) of the Insolvency (Scotland) Rules;

(b) a proposal is made by the liquidator or the administrator (acting as nominee) and before the appointed day the liquidator or administrator (as the case may be) has sent out a notice summoning the meetings under section 3 of the Act as required by Rule 1.11 of the Insolvency Rules, or, in Scotland, by Rule 1.11 of the Insolvency (Scotland) Rules; or

(c) a proposal is made by the liquidator or the administrator of a company (not acting as the nominee) and before the appointed day the intended nominee has endorsed a copy of the written notice of the proposal under Rule 1.12(2) of the Insolvency Rules, or, in Scotland, Rule 1.12(2) of the Insolvency (Scotland) Rules,

the amendments made to the Act by Part I of Schedule 2 and the repeal made by section 15(1) and Schedule 5 in respect of section 5(2) and (3) of the Act shall not apply and the provisions of the Act as they have effect immediately before the appointed day shall continue to have effect.

(2) The provisions of paragraph (1) shall—

(a) apply in relation to building societies as they apply in relation to companies; and

(b) in their application to building societies, have effect with the substitution for "company" of "building society".

(3) In this article "proposal" has the same meaning as it has in section 1(2) of the Act.

[2.7]
4

(1) In a case where a proposal is made by a debtor and before the appointed day the intended nominee has endorsed a copy of the written notice of the proposal under Rule 5.4(3) of the Insolvency Rules the amendments made to the Act by section 3 and Schedule 3 and the repeal made by section 15(1) and Schedule 5 in respect of section 255(1)(d) of the Act shall not apply and the provisions of the Act as they have effect immediately before the appointed day shall continue to have effect.

(2) In this article, "proposal" has the same meaning as it has in section 253 of the Act.

[2.8]
5

(1) The amendments made by section 4(1) and 4(2) to section 388 of the Act shall not apply in any case where—

(a) a person acts as a nominee (within the meaning of section 1(2) of the Act) and that case falls within paragraph (1) of article 3; or

(b) a person acts as a nominee (within the meaning of section 253(2) of the Act) and that case falls within paragraph (1) of article 4,

and in such cases section 388 of the Act as it has effect immediately before the appointed day shall continue to have effect.

ENTERPRISE ACT 2002

(2002 c 40)

ARRANGEMENT OF SECTIONS

PART 10
INSOLVENCY

Companies, etc

248 Replacement of Part II of Insolvency Act 1986 . . . . [2.9]
249 Special administration regimes . . . . [2.10]
254 Application of insolvency law to foreign company . . . . [2.11]
255 Application of law about company arrangement or administration to non-company . . . . [2.12]

Individuals

256 Duration of bankruptcy . . . . [2.13]
261 Bankrupt's home . . . . [2.14]
266 Disqualification from office: Parliament . . . . [2.15]
268 Disqualification from office: general . . . . [2.16]

Money

270 Fees . . . . [2.17]

PART 11
SUPPLEMENTARY

279 Commencement . . . . [2.18]
280 Extent . . . . [2.19]
281 Short title . . . . [2.20]

SCHEDULES

Schedule 17—Administration: minor and consequential amendments . . . . [2.21]
Schedule 19—Duration of bankruptcy: transitional provisions . . . . [2.22]

Establish and provide for the functions of the Office of Fair Trading, the Competition Appeal Tribunal and the Competition Service; to make provision about mergers and market structures and conduct; to amend the constitution and functions of the Competition Commission; to create an offence for those entering into certain anti-competitive agreements; to provide for the disqualification of directors of companies engaging in certain anti-competitive practices; to make other provision about competition law; to amend the law relating to the protection of the collective interests of consumers; to make further provision about the disclosure of information obtained under competition and consumer legislation; to amend the Insolvency Act 1986 and make other provision about insolvency; and for connected purposes

[7 November 2002]

1–247 (*(Pts 1–9) outside the scope of this work.*)

PART 10
INSOLVENCY

Companies, etc

[2.9]
248 Replacement of Part II of Insolvency Act 1986

(1), (2) (*Substitute the Insolvency Act 1986, Pt II at* **[1.13]** *and insert Sch B1 into that Act at* **[1.575]**.)

(3) Schedule 17 (minor and consequential amendments relating to administration) shall have effect.

(4) The Secretary of State may by order amend an enactment in consequence of this section.

(5) An order under subsection (4)—

(a) must be made by statutory instrument, and

(b) shall be subject to annulment in pursuance of a resolution of either House of Parliament.

NOTES

Orders: the Enterprise Act 2002 (Insolvency) Order 2003, SI 2003/2096.

[2.10]

249 Special administration regimes

(1) Section 248 shall have no effect in relation to—

(a) *a company holding an appointment under Chapter I of Part II of the Water Industry Act 1991 (c 56) (water and sewerage undertakers),*

[(aa) *a qualifying [water supply licensee] within the meaning of subsection (6) of section 23 of the Water Industry Act 1991 (meaning and effect of special administration order) [or a qualifying sewerage licensee within the meaning of subsection (8) of that section],]*

(b) a protected railway company within the meaning of section 59 of the Railways Act 1993 (c 43) (railway administration order) (including that section as it has effect by virtue of section 19 of the Channel Tunnel Rail Link Act 1996 (c 61) (administration)),

(c) a licence company within the meaning of section 26 of the Transport Act 2000 (c 38) (air traffic services),

(d) a public-private partnership company within the meaning of section 210 of the Greater London Authority Act 1999 (c 29) (public-private partnership agreement), or

(e) a building society within the meaning of section 119 of the Building Societies Act 1986 (c 53) (interpretation).

(2) A reference in an Act listed in subsection (1) to a provision of Part II of the Insolvency Act 1986 (or to a provision which has effect in relation to a provision of that Part of that Act) shall, in so far as it relates to a company or society listed in subsection (1), continue to have effect as if it referred to Part II as it had effect immediately before the coming into force of section 248.

(3) But the effect of subsection (2) in respect of a particular class of company or society may be modified by order of—

(a) the Treasury, in the case of building societies, or

(b) the Secretary of State, in any other case.

(4) An order under subsection (3) may make consequential amendment of an enactment.

(5) An order under subsection (3)—

(a) must be made by statutory instrument, and

(b) may not be made unless a draft has been laid before and approved by resolution of each House of Parliament.

(6) An amendment of the Insolvency Act 1986 (c 45) made by this Act is without prejudice to any power conferred by Part VII of the Companies Act 1989 (c 40) (financial markets) to modify the law of insolvency.

NOTES

Sub-s (1): para (aa) inserted by the Water Act 2003, s 101(1), Sch 8, para 55(1), (3), and repealed, together with para (a), by the Flood and Water Management Act 2010, s 34, Sch 5, para 6(3), as from a day to be appointed; in para (aa) words in first pair of square brackets substituted and words in second pair of square brackets inserted, by the Water Act 2014, s 56, Sch 7, paras 128, 130.

250–253 (*S 250(1) inserts the Insolvency Act 1986, ss 72A–72H at* **[1.59]**–**[1.68]**; *s 250(2) introduces Sch 18 to this Act; s 251 repeals the Insolvency Act 1986, Sch 6, paras 1, 2, 3–5C, 6, 7, amends s 386 of that Act at* **[1.473]**, *and repeals the Bankruptcy (Scotland) Act 1985, Sch 3, paras 1–3; s 252 inserts the Insolvency Act 1986, s 176A at* **[1.180]**; *s 253 inserts the Insolvency Act 1986, Sch 4, Pt I, para 3A at* **[1.581]**.)

[2.11]

254 Application of insolvency law to foreign company

(1) The Secretary of State may by order provide for a provision of the Insolvency Act 1986 to apply (with or without modification) in relation to a company incorporated outside Great Britain.

(2) An order under this section—

(a) may make provision generally or for a specified purpose only,

(b) may make different provision for different purposes, and

(c) may make transitional, consequential or incidental provision.

(3) An order under this section—

(a) must be made by statutory instrument, and

(b) shall be subject to annulment in pursuance of a resolution of either House of Parliament.

[2.12]

255 Application of law about company arrangement or administration to non-company

(1) The Treasury may with the concurrence of the Secretary of State by order provide for a company arrangement or administration provision to apply (with or without modification) in relation to—

(a) . . .

(b) a society registered under section 7(1)(b), (c), (d), (e) or (f) of the Friendly Societies Act 1974 (c 46),

(c) a friendly society within the meaning of the Friendly Societies Act 1992 (c 40), or

(d) an unregistered friendly society.

(2) In subsection (1) "company arrangement or administration provision" means—

(a) a provision of Part I of the Insolvency Act 1986 (company voluntary arrangements),

(b) a provision of Part II of that Act (administration), and
(c) [Part 26 of the Companies Act 2006] (compromise or arrangement with creditors).

(3) An order under this section may not provide for a company arrangement or administration provision to apply in relation to a society which is[—
(a) a private registered provider of social housing, or
(b)] registered as a social landlord under Part I of the Housing Act 1996 (c 52) or under [Part 2 of the Housing (Scotland) Act 2010 (asp 17)].

(4) An order under this section—
(a) may make provision generally or for a specified purpose only,
(b) may make different provision for different purposes, and
(c) may make transitional, consequential or incidental provision.

(5) Provision by virtue of subsection (4)(c) may, in particular—
(a) apply an enactment (with or without modification);
(b) amend an enactment.

(6) An order under this section—
(a) must be made by statutory instrument, and
(b) shall be subject to annulment in pursuance of a resolution of either House of Parliament.

NOTES

Sub-s (1): para (a) repealed by the Co-operative and Community Benefit Societies Act 2014, s 151(4), Sch 7.

Sub-s (2): words in square brackets substituted for original words "section 425 of the Companies Act 1985 (c 6)" by the Companies Act 2006 (Consequential Amendments etc) Order 2008, SI 2008/948, art 3(1)(b), Sch 1, Pt 2, para 225, subject to transitional provisions in arts 6, 11, 12 thereof.

Sub-s (3): words in first pair of square brackets inserted by the Housing and Regeneration Act 2008 (Consequential Provisions) Order 2010, SI 2010/866, art 5, Sch 2, Pt 2, para 119, subject to transitional provisions in art 6 of, and Sch 3, paras 1, 3, 4 to, that Order; words in second pair of square brackets substituted by the Housing (Scotland) Act 2010 (Consequential Provisions and Modifications) Order 2012, SI 2012/700, art 4, Schedule, Pt 1, para 6.

Orders: the Co-operative and Community Benefit Societies and Credit Unions (Arrangements, Reconstructions and Administration) Order 2014, SI 2014/229 at **[7.1425]**.

Individuals

[2.13]
256 Duration of bankruptcy

(1) (*Substitutes the Insolvency Act 1986, s 279 at* **[1.339]**.)

(2) Schedule 19 (which makes transitional provision in relation to this section)—
(a) shall have effect, and
(b) is without prejudice to the generality of section 276.

257–260 (*S 257(1) inserts the Insolvency Act 1986, s 281A at* **[1.342]**; *s 257(2) introduces Sch 20 to this Act; s 257(3) introduces Sch 21 to this Act; s 258 substitutes the Insolvency Act 1986, s 289 at* **[1.351]**; *s 259 amends the Insolvency Act 1986, s 310 at* **[1.379]**; *s 260 inserts the Insolvency Act 1986, s 310A at* **[1.380]**.)

[2.14]
261 Bankrupt's home

(1)–(6) (*Insert the Insolvency Act 1986, ss 283A, 313A at* **[1.345]**, **[1.384]**, *and amend ss 307(2), 313, 384(2), 418(1) of that Act at* **[1.375]**, **[1.383]**, **[1.471]**, **[1.531]**.)

(7) In subsection (8)—
(a) "pre-commencement bankrupt" means an individual who is adjudged bankrupt on a petition presented before subsection (1) above comes into force, and
(b) "the transitional period" is the period of three years beginning with the date on which subsection (1) above comes into force.

(8) If a pre-commencement bankrupt's estate includes an interest in a dwelling-house which at the date of the bankruptcy was the sole or principal residence of him, his spouse or a former spouse of his, at the end of the transitional period that interest shall—
(a) cease to be comprised in the estate, and
(b) vest in the bankrupt (without conveyance, assignment or transfer).

(9) But subsection (8) shall not apply if before or during the transitional period—
(a) any of the events mentioned in section 283A(3) of the Insolvency Act 1986 (c 45) (inserted by subsection (1) above) occurs in relation to the interest or the dwelling-house, or
(b) the trustee obtains any order of a court, or makes any agreement with the bankrupt, in respect of the interest or the dwelling-house.

(10) Subsections 283A(4) to (9) of that Act shall have effect, with any necessary modifications, in relation to the provision made by subsections (7) to (9) above; in particular—
(a) a reference to the period mentioned in section 283A(2) shall be construed as a reference to the transitional period,
(b) in the application of section 283A(5) a reference to the date of the bankruptcy shall be construed as a reference to the date on which subsection (1) above comes into force, and
(c) a reference to the rules is a reference to rules made under section 412 of the Insolvency Act 1986 (for which purpose this section shall be treated as forming part of Parts VIII to XI of that Act).

262–265 (*S 262 inserts the Insolvency Act 1986, Sch 5, Pt I, para 2A at* **[1.588]**; *s 263 repeals the Insolvency Act 1986, ss 361, 362; s 264(1) introduces Sch 22 to this Act, s 264(2)–(4) repealed by the Small Business, Enterprise and Employment Act 2015, s 135(3)(a); s 265 repealed by the Courts Act 2003, s 109(3), Sch 10.*)

[2.15]
266 Disqualification from office: Parliament

(1), (2) (*Insert the Insolvency Act 1986, ss 426A–426C at* **[1.541]–[1.543]** *and amend s 427 of that Act at* **[1.544]**.)

(3) The Secretary of State may by order—
- (a) provide for section 426A or 426B of that Act (as inserted by subsection (1) above) to have effect in relation to orders made or undertakings accepted in Scotland or Northern Ireland under a system which appears to the Secretary of State to be equivalent to the system operating under Schedule 4A to that Act (as inserted by section 257 of this Act);
- (b) make consequential amendment of section 426A or 426B of that Act (as inserted by subsection (1) above);
- (c) make other consequential amendment of an enactment.

(4) An order under this section may make transitional, consequential or incidental provision.

(5) An order under this section—
- (a) must be made by statutory instrument, and
- (b) may not be made unless a draft has been laid before and approved by resolution of each House of Parliament.

NOTES

Orders: the Insolvency Act 1986 (Disqualification from Parliament) Order 2012, SI 2012/1544.

267 (*Outside the scope of this work.*)

[2.16]
268 Disqualification from office: general

(1) The Secretary of State may make an order under this section in relation to a disqualification provision.

(2) A "disqualification provision" is a provision which disqualifies (whether permanently or temporarily and whether absolutely or conditionally) a bankrupt or a class of bankrupts from—
- (a) being elected or appointed to an office or position,
- (b) holding an office or position, or
- (c) becoming or remaining a member of a body or group.

(3) In subsection (2) the reference to a provision which disqualifies a person conditionally includes a reference to a provision which enables him to be dismissed.

(4) An order under subsection (1) may repeal or revoke the disqualification provision.

(5) An order under subsection (1) may amend, or modify the effect of, the disqualification provision—
- (a) so as to reduce the class of bankrupts to whom the disqualification provision applies;
- (b) so as to extend the disqualification provision to some or all individuals who are subject to a bankruptcy restrictions regime;
- (c) so that the disqualification provision applies only to some or all individuals who are subject to a bankruptcy restrictions regime;
- (d) so as to make the application of the disqualification provision wholly or partly subject to the discretion of a specified person, body or group.

(6) An order by virtue of subsection (5)(d) may provide for a discretion to be subject to—
- (a) the approval of a specified person or body;
- (b) appeal to a specified person or body.

(7) An order by virtue of subsection (5)(d) . . . may provide for a discretion to be subject to appeal to a specified court or tribunal[; but any such order must—
- (a) if it relates to England and Wales, be made with the concurrence of the Lord Chief Justice of England and Wales;
- (b) if it relates to Northern Ireland, be made with the concurrence of the Lord Chief Justice of Northern Ireland].

(8) The Secretary of State may specify himself for the purposes of subsection (5)(d) or (6)(a) or (b).

(9) In this section "bankrupt" means an individual—
- [(a) who has been made bankrupt (under Part 9 of the Insolvency Act 1986),
- (aa) who has been adjudged bankrupt by a court in Northern Ireland,]
- (b) whose estate has been sequestrated by a court in Scotland, or
- (c) who has made an agreement with creditors of his for a composition of debts, for a scheme of arrangement of affairs, for the grant of a trust deed or for some other kind of settlement or arrangement.

(10) In this section "bankruptcy restrictions regime" means an order or undertaking—
- (a) under Schedule 4A to the Insolvency Act 1986 (c 45) (bankruptcy restrictions orders), or
- (b) under any system operating in Scotland or Northern Ireland which appears to the Secretary of State to be equivalent to the system operating under that Schedule.

(11) In this section—

"body" includes Parliament and any other legislative body, and

"provision" means—

(a) a provision made by an Act of Parliament passed before or in the same Session as this Act, and

(b) a provision made, before or in the same Session as this Act, under an Act of Parliament.

(12) An order under this section—

(a) may make provision generally or for a specified purpose only,

(b) may make different provision for different purposes, and

(c) may make transitional, consequential or incidental provision.

(13) An order under this section—

(a) must be made by statutory instrument, and

(b) may not be made unless a draft has been laid before and approved by resolution of each House of Parliament.

(14) A reference in this section to the Secretary of State shall be treated as a reference to the National Assembly for Wales in so far as it relates to a disqualification provision which—

(a) is made by the National Assembly for Wales, or

(b) relates to a function of the National Assembly.

(15) Provision made by virtue of subsection (7) is subject to any order of the Lord Chancellor under section 56(1) of the Access to Justice Act 1999 (c 22) (appeals: jurisdiction).

[(16) The Lord Chief Justice may nominate a judicial office holder (as defined in section 109(4) of the Constitutional Reform Act 2005) to exercise his functions under subsection (7).

(17) The Lord Chief Justice of Northern Ireland may nominate any of the following to exercise his functions under subsection (7)—

(a) the holder of one of the offices listed in Schedule 1 to the Justice (Northern Ireland) Act 2002;

(b) a Lord Justice of Appeal (as defined in section 88 of that Act).]

NOTES

Sub-s (7): words omitted repealed, and words in square brackets inserted, by the Constitutional Reform Act 2005, ss 15(1), 146, Sch 4, Pt 1, paras 304, 305(1), (2), Sch 18, Pt 2.

Sub-s (9): paras (a), (aa) substituted, for original para (a), by the Enterprise and Regulatory Reform Act 2013 (Consequential Amendments) (Bankruptcy) and the Small Business, Enterprise and Employment Act 2015 (Consequential Amendments) Regulations 2016, SI 2016/481, reg 2(1), Sch 1, Pt 1, para 16.

Sub-ss (16), (17): added by the Constitutional Reform Act 2005, s 15(1), Sch 4, Pt 1, paras 304, 305(1), (3).

Orders: the Enterprise Act 2002 (Disqualification from Office: General) Order 2006, SI 2006/1722.

269 (*Introduces Sch 23 to this Act.*)

Money

[2.17]
270 Fees

(1) (*Inserts the Insolvency Act 1986, s 415A at* **[1.527]**.)

(2) An order made by virtue of subsection (1) may relate to the maintenance of recognition or authorisation granted before this section comes into force.

(3) . . .

(4) (*Amends the Insolvency Act 1986, s 440(2) at* **[1.564]**.)

NOTES

Sub-s (3): repealed by the Deregulation Act 2015, s 19, Sch 6, Pt 6, para 22(1), (13).

271, 272 (*S 271 inserts the Insolvency Act 1986, Sch 8, para 16A, Sch 9, para 21A at* **[1.593]**, **[1.594]**; *s 272 repeals the Insolvency Act 1986, s 405 and substitutes s 408 of that Act at* **[1.519]**.)

PART 11
SUPPLEMENTARY

273–278 (*Outside the scope of this work.*)

[2.18]
279 Commencement

The preceding provisions of this Act shall come into force on such day as the Secretary of State may by order made by statutory instrument appoint; and different days may be appointed for different purposes.

NOTES

Orders: the commencement order relevant to the provisions reproduced in this work is the Enterprise Act 2002 (Commencement No 4 and Transitional Provisions and Savings) Order 2003, SI 2003/2093 at **[2.24]**, as amended by SI 2003/2332, SI 2003/3340.

[2.19]
280 Extent

(1) Sections 256 to 265, 267, 269 and 272 extend only to England and Wales.

(2) Sections 204, 248 to 255 and 270 extend only to England and Wales and Scotland (but subsection (3) of section 415A as inserted by section 270 extends only to England and Wales).

(3) Any other modifications by this Act of an enactment have the same extent as the enactment being modified.

(4) Otherwise, this Act extends to England and Wales, Scotland and Northern Ireland.

[2.20]
281 Short title
This Act may be cited as the Enterprise Act 2002.

SCHEDULES
SCHEDULES 1–16

(*Schs 1–16 outside the scope of this work.*)

SCHEDULE 17
ADMINISTRATION: MINOR AND CONSEQUENTIAL AMENDMENTS

Section 248

General

[2.21]
1. In any instrument made before section 248(1) to (3) of this Act comes into force—
(a) a reference to the making of an administration order shall be treated as including a reference to the appointment of an administrator under paragraph 14 or 22 of Schedule B1 to the Insolvency Act 1986 (c 45) (inserted by section 248(2) of this Act), and
(b) a reference to making an application for an administration order by petition shall be treated as including a reference to making an administration application under that Schedule, appointing an administrator under paragraph 14 or 22 of that Schedule or giving notice under paragraph 15 or 26 of that Schedule.

2–59. (*Contain minor and consequential amendments relating to administration (in so far as these are relevant to this work they have been incorporated at the appropriate place).*)

SCHEDULE 18

(*Sch 18 inserts the Insolvency Act 1986, Sch 2A at* **[1.578]**.)

SCHEDULE 19
DURATION OF BANKRUPTCY: TRANSITIONAL PROVISIONS

Section 256

Introduction

[2.22]
1. This Schedule applies to an individual who immediately before commencement—
(a) has been adjudged bankrupt, and
(b) has not been discharged from the bankruptcy.

2. In this Schedule—
"commencement" means the date appointed under section 279 for the commencement of section 256, and
"pre-commencement bankrupt" means an individual to whom this Schedule applies.

Neither old law nor new law to apply

3. Section 279 of the Insolvency Act 1986 (c 45) (bankruptcy: discharge) shall not apply to a pre-commencement bankrupt (whether in its pre-commencement or its post-commencement form).

General rule for discharge from pre-commencement bankruptcy

4. (1) A pre-commencement bankrupt is[, subject to sub-paragraphs (2) and (3),] discharged from bankruptcy at whichever is the earlier of—
(a) the end of the period of one year beginning with commencement, and
(b) the end of the relevant period applicable to the bankrupt under section 279(1)(b) of the Insolvency Act 1986 (duration of bankruptcy) as it had effect immediately before commencement.

(2) An order made under section 279(3) of that Act before commencement—
(a) shall continue to have effect in respect of the pre-commencement bankrupt after commencement, and
(b) may be varied or revoked after commencement by an order under section 279(3) as substituted by section 256 of this Act.

(3) Section 279(3) to (5) of that Act as substituted by section 256 of this Act shall have effect after commencement in relation to the period mentioned in sub-paragraph (1)(a) or (b) above.

Second-time bankruptcy

5. (1) This paragraph applies to a pre-commencement bankrupt who was an undischarged bankrupt at some time during the period of 15 years ending with the day before the date on which the pre-commencement bankruptcy commenced.

(2) The pre-commencement bankrupt shall not be discharged from bankruptcy in accordance with paragraph 4 above.

(3) An order made before commencement under section 280(2)(b) or (c) of the Insolvency Act 1986 (c 45) (discharge by order of the court) shall continue to have effect after commencement (including any provision made by the court by virtue of section 280(3)).

(4) A pre-commencement bankrupt to whom this paragraph applies (and in respect of whom no order is in force under section 280(2)(b) or (c) on commencement) is discharged—

(a) at the end of the period of five years beginning with commencement, or

(b) at such earlier time as the court may order on an application under section 280 of the Insolvency Act 1986 (discharge by order) heard after commencement.

(5) Section 279(3) to (5) of the Insolvency Act 1986 as substituted by section 256 of this Act shall have effect after commencement in relation to the period mentioned in sub-paragraph (4)(a) above.

(6) A bankruptcy annulled under section 282 shall be ignored for the purpose of sub-paragraph (1).

Criminal bankruptcy

6. A pre-commencement bankrupt who was adjudged bankrupt on a petition under section 264(1)(d) of the Insolvency Act 1986 (criminal bankruptcy)—

(a) shall not be discharged from bankruptcy in accordance with paragraph 4 above, but

(b) may be discharged from bankruptcy by an order of the court under section 280 of that Act.

Income payments order

7. (1) This paragraph applies where—

(a) a pre-commencement bankrupt is discharged by virtue of paragraph 4(1)(a), and

(b) an income payments order is in force in respect of him immediately before his discharge.

(2) If the income payments order specifies a date after which it is not to have effect, it shall continue in force until that date (and then lapse).

(3) But the court may on the application of the pre-commencement bankrupt—

(a) vary the income payments order;

(b) provide for the income payments order to cease to have effect before the date referred to in sub-paragraph (2).

Bankruptcy restrictions order or undertaking

8. A provision of this Schedule which provides for an individual to be discharged from bankruptcy is subject to—

(a) any bankruptcy restrictions order (or interim order) which may be made in relation to that individual, and

(b) any bankruptcy restrictions undertaking entered into by that individual.

NOTES

Commencement: 1 April 2004 (paras 1–7); to be appointed (otherwise).

Para 4: words in square brackets in sub-para (1) inserted by the Enterprise Act 2002 (Insolvency) Order 2003, SI 2003/2096, art 3.

SCHEDULES 20–26

(*Sch 20 inserts the Insolvency Act 1986, Sch 4A at* **[1.587]***; Sch 21 substitutes the Insolvency Act 1986, s 31 at* **[1.17]***, and amends ss 350, 360, 390 of that Act at* **[1.429]**, **[1.439]**, **[1.478]** *and the Company Directors Disqualification Act 1986, s 11 at* **[4.24]***; Sch 22 substitutes the Insolvency Act 1986, s 261 at* **[1.302]***, and inserts ss 263A–263G, 389B of that Act at* **[1.308]**–**[1.314]**, **[1.477]***; Sch 23 contains minor and consequential amendments relating to individual insolvency which have been incorporated at the appropriate place; Sch 24 (transitional and transitory provisions) is outside the scope of this work; Sch 25 contains minor and consequential amendments and Sch 26 contains repeals and revocations (in so far as these are relevant to this work, they have been incorporated at the appropriate place).*)

INSOLVENCY (AMENDMENT) RULES 2003 (NOTE)

(SI 2003/1730)

[2.23]

NOTES

Made: 8 August 2003.

Authority: Insolvency Act 1986, ss 411, 412.

Commencement: 15 September 2003 (in part), 1 April 2004 (remainder).

These Rules are revoked by the Insolvency (England and Wales) Rules 2016, SI 2016/1024, r 2, Sch 1. They amended the Insolvency Rules 1986, SI 1986/1925 and set out transitional provisions relating to those amendments. The 1986 Rules are also revoked by SI 2016/1024, r 2, Sch 1, as from 6 April 2017 and subject to transitional provisions in Sch 2 thereto at **[6.935]**; they have been omitted from the current edition due to reasons of space and can be found in the 18th edition of this Handbook. Accordingly, these 2003 Rules can also be found in the 18th edition.

ENTERPRISE ACT 2002 (COMMENCEMENT NO 4 AND TRANSITIONAL PROVISIONS AND SAVINGS) ORDER 2003

(SI 2003/2093 (C 85))

NOTES

Made: 8 August 2003.
Authority: Enterprise Act 2002, ss 276(2), 279.
Commencement: 8 August 2003.

ARRANGEMENT OF ARTICLES

1 Citation and interpretation ....[2.24]
2 Appointed days ....[2.25]
3 Administration—transitional provisions ....[2.26]
4 Abolition of Crown preference—transitional provisions ....[2.27]
5 Liquidator's powers....................[2.28]
6 Powers of trustee in bankruptcy....................[2.29]
7 Bankruptcy restrictions orders....................[2.30]
8 Transitional provisions—old summary cases ....[2.31]

[2.24]
1 Citation and interpretation

(1) This Order may be cited as the Enterprise Act 2002 (Commencement No 4 and Transitional Provisions and Savings) Order 2003.

(2) In this Order, except where otherwise stated, references to sections and Schedules are references to sections of, and Schedules to, the Enterprise Act 2002.

(3) In this Order references to sequestration are references to sequestration within the meaning of the Bankruptcy (Scotland) Act 1985.

(4) Except in relation to sequestration, expressions used in this Order which are used in the Insolvency Act 1986 shall have the same meaning as in that Act.

(5) In articles 4, 5 and 6 references to provisions of, and procedures under, the Insolvency Act 1986 include references to those provisions and procedures as they are applied by or under the provisions of any enactment.

[2.25]
2 Appointed days

(1) Subject as set out in this Order, the day appointed for the coming into force of the provisions in Schedule 1 to this Order is 15th September 2003 (hereafter referred to as "the first commencement date").

(2) Subject as set out in this Order, the day appointed for the coming into force of the provisions in Schedule 2 to this Order is 1st April 2004 (hereafter referred to as "the second commencement date").

[2.26]
3 Administration—transitional provisions

(1) In this article "the former administration provisions" means the law relating to administration under Part II of the Insolvency Act 1986 and section 62(2)(a) of the Criminal Justice Act 1988 without the amendments and repeals made by the provisions of the Enterprise Act 2002 mentioned in paragraph (2).

(2) In a case where a petition for an administration order has been presented before the first commencement date—

(a) section 248 and Schedules 16 and 17; and
(b) section 278(2) and Schedule 26 as respects the repeals relating to sections 212, 230(1), 231, 232, 240(1) and 245(3) of the Insolvency Act 1986, the entries in Schedule 10 to the Insolvency Act 1986 in respect of sections 12(2), 15(8), 18(5), 21(3), 22(6), 23(3), 24(7) and 27(6) of that Act and section 62(2)(a) of the Criminal Justice Act 1988,

shall have no effect.

(3) The former administration provisions shall continue to apply insofar as is necessary to give effect to—

(a) the Insolvent Partnerships Order 1994;
(b) regulation 5 of the Limited Liability Partnerships Regulations 2001; and
(c) the Financial Services and Markets Act 2000 (Administration Orders relating to Insurers) Order 2002.

[2.27]
4 Abolition of Crown preference—transitional provisions

(1) This article applies to a case where before the first commencement date—

(a) a petition for an administration order pursuant to Part II of the Insolvency Act 1986 is presented;
(b) a voluntary arrangement under Part I of the Insolvency Act 1986 has effect;
(c) a receiver is appointed under the terms of a charge (which when created was a floating charge) in relation to the property of a company subject to the charge;
(d) a petition for a winding-up order is presented;
(e) a resolution for the winding up of the company is passed;
(f) a petition for a bankruptcy order (or, in Scotland, for sequestration) is presented; or
(g) a voluntary arrangement pursuant to Part VIII of the Insolvency Act 1986 has effect.

[(1A) This article also applies to a case where—
(a) an administration order under Part II of the Insolvency Act 1986 is made on a petition presented prior to the first commencement date;
(b) that order is discharged; and
(c) immediately on the discharge of that order—
(i) a winding-up order is made in respect of the company in question; or
(ii) a resolution for the winding up of the company is passed, on or after the first commencement date.

(1B) This article also applies to a case where—
(a) a winding-up order is made on a petition presented prior to the first commencement date; and
(b) the company in question enters administration by virtue of an order made under paragraphs 37 or 38 of Schedule B1 to the Insolvency Act 1986.

(1C) This article also applies to a case where—
(a) a resolution for the winding up of a company is passed before the first commencement date; and
(b) the company enters administration by virtue of an order made under paragraph 38 of Schedule B1 to the Insolvency Act 1986.

(1D) This article also applies to a case where—
(a) a receiver is appointed before the first commencement date in respect of a company;
(b) the receiver vacates office; and
(c) the company in respect of which the receiver is appointed enters administration within the meaning of paragraph 1(2)(b) of Schedule B1 to the Insolvency Act 1986 during the period that the receiver is in office or immediately after the end of that period.]

(2) This article also applies to a case where proposals for a voluntary arrangement under Part I of the Insolvency Act 1986 are made (whether before or after the first commencement date) by—
(a) a liquidator in a winding up where the winding-up petition is presented or, as the case may be, the resolution for winding up is passed, before the first commencement date; or
(b) an administrator appointed in relation to an administration under Part II of the Insolvency Act 1986 where the administration order is made on a petition which is presented before the first commencement date.

(3) This article also applies to a case in which a proposal for a voluntary arrangement under Part VIII of the Insolvency Act 1986 is made (whether before or after the first commencement date) by a person who was adjudged bankrupt on a petition which was presented before the first commencement date.

(4) In a case to which this article applies—
(a) the provisions of section 251; and
(b) the provisions of section 278(2) and Schedule 26 as respects the repeals relating to paragraphs 1 to 3 and 8 to 8C in Schedule 3 to the Bankruptcy (Scotland) Act 1985, paragraphs 1 to 7 of Schedule 6 to the Insolvency Act 1986, the table in paragraph 32 of Schedule 29 to the Income and Corporation Taxes Act 1988, paragraphs 21A and 22 of Schedule 2 to the Finance Act 1991, paragraph 73 of Schedule 2 to the Social Security (Consequential Provisions) Act 1992, sections 36(1) to (3) of the Finance Act 1993, paragraphs 13(1) and 13(2) of Schedule 6 and paragraph 7(2) of Schedule 7 to the Finance Act 1994, paragraph 8 of Schedule 14 to the Value Added Tax Act 1994, section 17 of the Finance Act 1995, paragraphs 12(1) and 12(2) of Schedule 5 to the Finance Act 1996, sections 166(7)(a), 183(3)(a) and 189(4) of the Employment Rights Act 1996, paragraph 6 of Schedule 2 to the Finance Act 1997, paragraphs 2 and 3 of Schedule 7 to the Finance Act 2000 and paragraphs 17(1) and (2) and 18 of Schedule 5 to the Finance Act 2001,

shall not have effect.

NOTES

Paras (1A)–(1D): inserted by the Enterprise Act 2002 (Transitional Provisions) (Insolvency) Order 2003, SI 2003/2332, art 2.

[2.28]
5 Liquidator's powers

The insertion of paragraph 3A into Schedule 4 of the Insolvency Act 1986 by section 253 (Liquidator's powers) shall have no effect in relation to any proceedings of a kind mentioned in paragraph 3A which were commenced prior to the first commencement date.

[2.29]
6 Powers of trustee in bankruptcy

The insertion of paragraph 2A into Schedule 5 of the Insolvency Act 1986 by section 262 (Powers of Trustee) shall have no effect in relation to any proceedings of a kind mentioned in paragraph 2A which were commenced prior to the first commencement date.

[2.30]
7 Bankruptcy restrictions orders

Where a court is considering whether or not a bankruptcy restrictions order should be made pursuant to the provisions of section 281A and Schedule 4A to the Insolvency Act 1986, it shall not take into account any conduct of the bankrupt before the second commencement date.

[2.31]
8 Transitional provisions—old summary cases

(1) This article applies to a bankruptcy (other than one where the bankrupt has received his discharge) where a certificate of summary administration under section 275 of the Insolvency Act 1986 is in force on the second commencement date.

(2) In a case to which this article applies sections 275, 292(1), 293(1), 294(1), 297, 298(3), 300(5), 300(6) and 300(7) of the Insolvency Act 1986 shall continue to have effect.

(3) Where on or after the second commencement date the court revokes a certificate of summary administration under section 275(3) of the Insolvency Act 1986 as it has effect by virtue of paragraph (2), the relevant period for the purposes of paragraph 4(1)(b) of Schedule 19 shall be the period specified in section 279(1)(b) of the Insolvency Act 1986 as it had effect immediately prior to the second commencement date.

SCHEDULES 1 AND 2

(Schs 1, 2 set out the provisions brought into force by this Order; the effect of the commencement of those provisions which are relevant to this work is noted at the appropriate place.)

INSOLVENCY (SCOTLAND) AMENDMENT RULES 2003

(SI 2003/2111 (S 9))

NOTES

Made: 8 August 2003.
Authority: Insolvency Act 1986, s 411.
Commencement: 15 September 2003.

[2.32]
1 Citation and commencement

(1) The Rules may be cited as the Insolvency (Scotland) Amendment Rules 2003 and shall come into force on 15th September 2003.

(2) References in these Rules to "the commencement date" are to the date referred to in paragraph (1) above.

[2.33]
2 Interpretation

(1) In these Rules—
- (a) references to the "principal Rules" are to the Insolvency (Scotland) Rules 1986 and a Rule referred to by number alone means the Rule so numbered in the principal Rules; and
- (b) references to paragraphs, except where the context otherwise requires, are to paragraphs of Schedule B1 to the Insolvency Act 1986.

(2) These Rules shall be construed as one with the principal Rules.

3–6 *(R 3 introduces Sch 1, Pt 1 (Substitution of the Insolvency (Scotland) Rules 1986, SI 1986/1915, Pt 2); r 4 amends SI 1986/1915, Sch 4 at* **[15.348]***; r 5 introduces Sch 1, Pt 2 (Forms) and amends SI 1986/1915, Sch 5 at* **[15.349]***; r 6 introduces Sch 2 (Consequential amendments to SI 1986/1915, incorporated at the appropriate place in this work).)*

[2.34]
7 Transitional and savings provisions

(1) Rules 3 to 6 of these Rules shall not apply, and Part 2 of, and Forms 2.1 (Scot) to 2.13 (Scot) set out in Schedule 5 to, the principal Rules as they had effect immediately before the coming into force of these Rules shall continue to have effect in relation to the administration of a company in respect of which the petition for an administration order was presented to the court before the commencement date.

(2) Rules 3 to 6 of these Rules shall not apply and Part 2 of, and Forms 2.1 (Scot) to 2.13 (Scot) set out in Schedule 5 to, the principal Rules as they had effect immediately before the coming into force of these Rules shall continue to have effect for the purposes of—
- (a) section 249(2) of the Enterprise Act 2002; and
- (b) the Financial Services and Markets Act 2000 (Administration Orders relating to Insurers) Order 2002.

SCHEDULES

(Sch 1, Pt 1 substitutes the Insolvency (Scotland) Rules 1986, SI 1986/1915, Pt 2 at **[15.70]***, Sch 1, Pt 2 substitutes forms in SI 1986/1915, Sch 5 at* **[15.349]***; Sch 2, Pt 1 makes various amendments to SI 1986/1915 (incorporated at the appropriate place in this work), and Sch 2, Pt 2 sets out substituted Form 4.7 (Scot) in SI 1986/1915, Sch 5 at* **[15.349]***.)*

INSOLVENCY (AMENDMENT) RULES 2004 (NOTE)

(SI 2004/584)

[2.35]

NOTES

Made: 3 March 2004.

Authority: Insolvency Act 1986, ss 411, 412.

Commencement: 1 April 2004.

These Rules are revoked by the Insolvency (England and Wales) Rules 2016, SI 2016/1024, r 2, Sch 1. They amended the Insolvency Rules 1986, SI 1986/1925 and set out transitional provisions relating to those amendments. The 1986 Rules are also revoked by SI 2016/1024, r 2, Sch 1, as from 6 April 2017 and subject to transitional provisions in Sch 2 thereto at **[6.935]**; they have been omitted from the current edition due to reasons of space and can be found in the 18th edition of this Handbook. Accordingly, these 2004 Rules can also be found in the 18th edition.

INSOLVENCY (AMENDMENT) RULES 2005 (NOTE)

(SI 2005/527)

[2.36]

NOTES

Made: 8 March 2005.

Authority: Insolvency Act 1986, ss 411, 412.

Commencement: 1 April 2005.

These Rules are revoked by the Insolvency (England and Wales) Rules 2016, SI 2016/1024, r 2, Sch 1. They amended the Insolvency Rules 1986, SI 1986/1925 and set out transitional provisions relating to those amendments. The 1986 Rules are also revoked by SI 2016/1024, r 2, Sch 1, as from 6 April 2017 and subject to transitional provisions in Sch 2 thereto at **[6.935]**; they have been omitted from the current edition due to reasons of space and can be found in the 18th edition of this Handbook. Accordingly, these 2005 Rules can also be found in the 18th edition.

INSOLVENCY PROCEEDINGS (FEES) (AMENDMENT) ORDER 2006

(SI 2006/561)

NOTES

Made: 2 March 2006.

Authority: Bankruptcy Act 1914, s 133; Companies Act 1985, s 663(4); Insolvency Act 1986, ss 414, 415.

Commencement: 1 April 2006.

This Order is revoked (as from 21 July 2016) by the Insolvency Proceedings (Fees) Order 2016, SI 2016/692, art 6, Sch 2, subject to transitional provisions and savings in art 7 thereof at **[8.88]**.

[2.37]

1 Citation and commencement

This Order may be cited as the Insolvency Proceedings (Fees) (Amendment) Order 2006 and shall come into force on 1st April 2006 ("the commencement date").

NOTES

Revoked as noted at the beginning of this Order.

2 (Amends the Insolvency Proceedings (Fees) Order 2004, SI 2004/593, arts 6, 7, Sch 2 at **[8.76]**, **[8.77]**, **[8.81]***.)*

[2.38]

3 Amendments to the continuing application of the Insolvency Fees Order 1986

(1) Article 3 of, and the entry in Schedule 1 to the principal Order, revoking the Insolvency Fees Order 1986 ("the 1986 Order") to the extent set out in that Schedule, shall be read subject to paragraphs (2) and (3).

Part 2 Transitional Provisions

(2) In relation to a winding up to which the 1986 Order continues to apply by virtue of the provisions of the principal Order referred to in paragraph (1), paragraphs (iii) to (viii) shown in relation to Fee No 10 in Part 1 of the Schedule to the 1986 Order shall cease to have effect in relation to any payments into the Insolvency Services Account made on or after the commencement date.

(3) In relation to a bankruptcy to which the 1986 Order continues to apply by virtue of the provisions of the principal Order referred to in paragraph (1), paragraphs (c) to (h) shown in relation to Fee No 13 in Part 2 of the Schedule to the 1986 Order shall cease to have effect in relation to any payments into the Insolvency Services Account made on or after the commencement date.

NOTES

Revoked as noted at the beginning of this Order.

Revoked by the Insolvency Proceedings (Fees) (Amendment) Order 2007, SI 2007/521, art 3(c), except in relation to any fee or percentage due or payable before 1 April 2007; see art 4(1), (10) thereof at **[2.46]**.

4, 5 *(Amend the Companies (Department of Trade and Industry) Fees Order 1985, SI 1985/1784, Schedule and the Bankruptcy Fees Order 1984, SI 1984/880, Schedule; revoked by the Insolvency Proceedings (Fees) (Amendment) Order 2007, SI 2007/521, art 3(c), except in relation to any fee or percentage due or payable before 1 April 2007; see art 4(1), (10) thereof at* **[2.46]**.)

[2.39]

6 Transitional provisions

(1) The amendments made by article 2(2)(a), (b) and (c) of this Order, increasing the fees prescribed by article 6 of the principal Order, shall only apply to petitions presented on or after the commencement date.

(2) The amendment made by article 2(3) of this Order, reducing the fee prescribed by article 7(1) of the principal Order, shall only apply to notifications sent to the official receiver on or after the commencement date.

(3) The amendment in respect of fee IVA1 made by Article 2(4) shall apply to a voluntary arrangement under Part VIII of the Insolvency Act 1986 in respect of which information required to be submitted to the Secretary of State by virtue of Part 5 of the Insolvency Rules 1986 is first submitted in relation to that arrangement on or after the commencement date.

NOTES

Revoked as noted at the beginning of this Order.

INSOLVENT PARTNERSHIPS (AMENDMENT) ORDER 2006

(SI 2006/622)

NOTES

Made: 7 March 2006.
Authority: Insolvency Act 1986, s 420.
Commencement: 6 April 2006.

[2.40]

1 Citation, commencement and interpretation

(1) This Order may be cited as the Insolvent Partnerships (Amendment) Order 2006 and shall come into force on 6th April 2006 ("the commencement date").

(2) In this Order—

"the Act" means the Insolvency Act 1986; and

"the 1994 Order" means the Insolvent Partnerships Order 1994.

[2.41]

2 Transitional provisions

The amendments to the 1994 Order set out in this Order do not apply to any insolvency proceedings in relation to an insolvent partnership commenced before the commencement date.

3–10 (*Amend the Insolvent Partnerships Order 1994, SI 1994/2421, arts 8, 10, Schs 2–6, 9 at* **[10.8]**, **[10.10]**, **[10.21]**–**[10.27]**, **[10.31]**.)

SCHEDULE

(*The Schedule amends the Insolvent Partnerships Order 1994, SI 1994/2421, Sch 9 at* **[10.31]**.)

INSOLVENCY (SCOTLAND) AMENDMENT RULES 2006

(SI 2006/734 (S 6))

NOTES

Made: 13 March 2006.
Authority: Insolvency Act 1986, s 411.
Commencement: 6 April 2006.

[2.42]
1 Citation, commencement and interpretation

(1) These Rules may be cited as the Insolvency (Scotland) Amendment Rules 2006 and shall come into force on 6th April 2006 ("the commencement date").

(2) In these Rules "the 1986 Rules" means the Insolvency (Scotland) Rules 1986 and references to numbered Rules are to the Rules so numbered in the 1986 Rules.

[2.43]
2 Transitional provision

(1) The provisions of Rules 5 to 8 and 10 of these Rules shall not apply, and the provisions of the 1986 Rules shall continue to apply without the amendments made by those Rules, in any case where a company has entered administration before the commencement date.

(2) The provisions of Rule 14 of these Rules apply in any case where a company entered into administration on or after 15th September 2003 other than a case where the company entered into administration by virtue of a petition presented before that date.

(3) The provisions of Rule 15 of these Rules apply in any case where an insolvency practitioner is appointed on or after the commencement date.

3–15 (*R 3 introduces amendments to the Insolvency (Scotland) Rules 1986, SI 1986/1915; r 4 introduces the Schedule which substitutes Forms 2.4B (Scot)–2.10B (Scot), Form 2.12B (Scot) and amends Form 2.13B (Scot) in SI 1986/1915, Sch 5 at* **[15.349]***; rr 5–15 amend SI 1986/1915, rr 2.2, 2.25, 2.30, 2.41, 2.57, 2.58, 4.6, 7.34 at* **[15.71]**, **[15.94]**, **[15.108]**, **[15.144]**, **[15.162]**, **[15.163]**, **[15.190]**, **[15.342]**, *substitute rr 2.39, 2.39A, for original r 2.39, at* **[15.139]**, **[15.140]**, *and insert rr 2.41A, 7.35 at* **[15.145]**, **[15.343]**.)

SCHEDULE

(*The Schedule sets out substituted Forms 2.4B (Scot)–2.10B (Scot), Form 2.12B (Scot) and amendments to Form 2.13B (Scot) in SI 1986/1915, Sch 5 at* **[15.349]**.)

INSOLVENCY (AMENDMENT) RULES 2006 (NOTE)

(SI 2006/1272)

[2.44]

NOTES

Made: 9 May 2006.
Authority: Insolvency Act 1986, s 411.
Commencement: 1 June 2006.
These Rules are revoked by the Insolvency (England and Wales) Rules 2016, SI 2016/1024, r 2, Sch 1. They amended the Insolvency Rules 1986, SI 1986/1925 and set out transitional provisions relating to those amendments. The 1986 Rules are also revoked by SI 2016/1024, r 2, Sch 1, as from 6 April 2017 and subject to transitional provisions in Sch 2 thereto at **[6.935]**; they have been omitted from the current edition due to reasons of space and can be found in the 18th edition of this Handbook. Accordingly, these 2006 Rules can also be found in the 18th edition.

INSOLVENCY PROCEEDINGS (FEES) (AMENDMENT) ORDER 2007

(SI 2007/521)

NOTES

Made: 20 February 2007.
Authority: Bankruptcy Act 1914, s 133; Companies Act 1985, s 663(4); Insolvency Act 1986, ss 414, 415.
Commencement: 1 April 2007.
This Order is revoked (as from 21 July 2016) by the Insolvency Proceedings (Fees) Order 2016, SI 2016/692, art 6, Sch 2, subject to transitional provisions and savings in art 7 thereof at **[8.88]**.

[2.45]
1 Citation and commencement

This Order may be cited as the Insolvency Proceedings (Fees) (Amendment) Order 2007 and shall come into force on 1st April 2007 ("the commencement date").

NOTES

Revoked as noted at the beginning of this Order.

2, 3 (Art 2 amends the Insolvency Proceedings (Fees) Order 2004, SI 2004/593, arts 5–8, Sch 2 at **[8.75]–[8.78]**, **[8.81]***; art 3 introduces the Schedule to this Order, amends the Insolvency Proceedings (Fees) Order 2004, SI 2004/593, Sch 1 at* **[8.80]***, and revokes the Insolvency Proceedings (Fees) (Amendment) Order 2006, SI 2006/561, arts 3–5 at* **[2.38]***.)*

[2.46]
4 Transitional provisions

(1) The amendments made by articles 2 and 3 of this Order shall apply as set out below.

(2) The amendment made by article 2(2) shall only apply to reports submitted to the court in respect of debtors' petitions presented on or after the commencement date.

(3) The amendments made by sub-paragraphs (a), (b) and (c) of article 2(3), increasing the fees prescribed by article 6 of the principal Order, shall only apply to petitions presented on or after the commencement date.

(4) The amendment made by article 2(4), reducing the fee prescribed by article 7(1) of the principal Order, shall only apply to notifications sent to the official receiver on or after the commencement date.

(5) The amendment made by article 2(5), describing the level to which the official receiver's administration fee B1 is to be reduced where proposals made by a bankrupt for an individual voluntary arrangement are approved by the bankrupt's creditors, shall only apply to those cases in which the bankruptcy order relating to the bankrupt was made on or after the commencement date.

(6) The amendment made by article 2(6) to the definition of "the bankruptcy ceiling" shall only apply in respect of bankruptcy orders made on or after the commencement date.

(7) The amendment made by article 2(7)(a), reducing the fee designated as fee IVA1, shall only apply to a voluntary arrangement under Part VIII of the Insolvency Act 1986 in respect of which information required to be submitted to the Secretary of State by virtue of Part 5 of the Insolvency Rules 1986 is first submitted in relation to that arrangement on or after the commencement date.

(8) The amendment made by article 2(7)(b) shall only apply in respect of bankruptcy orders made on or after the commencement date.

(9) The amendment made by article 2(7)(c) shall only apply in respect of winding-up orders made on or after the commencement date.

(10) The revocations made by article 3 take effect save as respects any fee or percentage due or payable before the commencement date under the Orders or entries referred to.

NOTES

Revoked as noted at the beginning of this Order.

SCHEDULE

(Schedule revokes the Bankruptcy Fees Order 1984, SI 1984/880, the Companies (Department of Trade and Industry) Fees Order 1985, SI 1985/1784 and the Insolvency (Fees) Order 1986, SI 1986/2030 (also in relation to any case where a winding-up or bankruptcy order was made under the Insolvency Act 1986 before 1 April 2004) at **[8.7]** *et seq.)*

INSOLVENCY PROCEEDINGS (FEES) (AMENDMENT) ORDER 2008

(SI 2008/714)

NOTES

Made: 10 March 2008.
Authority: Insolvency Act 1986, ss 414, 415.
Commencement: 6 April 2008.
This Order is revoked (as from 21 July 2016) by the Insolvency Proceedings (Fees) Order 2016, SI 2016/692, art 6, Sch 2, subject to transitional provisions and savings in art 7 thereof at **[8.88]**.

[2.47]
1 Citation and commencement

This Order may be cited as the Insolvency Proceedings (Fees) (Amendment) Order 2008 and shall come into force on 6th April 2008 ("the commencement date").

NOTES

Revoked as noted at the beginning of this Order.

2 (*Amends the Insolvency Proceedings (Fees) Order 2004, SI 2004/593, art 5, Sch 2 at* **[8.75]**, **[8.81]**.)

[2.48]

3 Transitional provisions

(1) The amendments made by article 2 of this Order shall apply as set out below.

(2) The amendment made by article 2(2) shall only apply to reports submitted to the court in respect of debtors' petitions presented on or after the commencement date.

(3) The amendments made by article 2(3), increasing the fees prescribed by article 6 of the principal Order, shall only apply to petitions presented on or after the commencement date.

(4) The amendments made by article 2(4)(a) and (c) shall not affect any liability to pay a fee in excess of £80,000 which has arisen prior to the commencement date.

(5) The amendment made by article 2(4)(b) shall only apply in respect of winding up orders made on or after the commencement date.

NOTES

Revoked as noted at the beginning of this Order.

BANKRUPTCY AND DILIGENCE ETC (SCOTLAND) ACT 2007 (COMMENCEMENT NO 3, SAVINGS AND TRANSITIONALS) ORDER 2008

(SSI 2008/115 (C 10))

NOTES

Made: 12 March 2008.

Authority: Bankruptcy and Diligence etc (Scotland) Act 2007, ss 224(2), 227(3), (4).

ARRANGEMENT OF ARTICLES

1 Citation . . . . . [2.49]

2 Interpretation . . . . . [2.50]

5 Sequestrations—petitions presented before 1st April 2008 . . . . . [2.51]

6 Trust deeds—trust deeds granted before 1st April 2008 . . . . . [2.52]

7 Transitional arrangements—bankruptcy restrictions orders, debt advice and information packages in bankruptcy and definition of apparent insolvency . . . . . [2.53]

8, 9 . . . . . [2.54], [2.55]

10 Diligence on the dependence, summary warrants, time to pay—proceedings before 1st April 2008 . . . . . [2.56]

15 . . . . . [2.57]

[2.49]

1 Citation

This Order may be cited as the Bankruptcy and Diligence etc (Scotland) Act 2007 (Commencement No 3, Savings and Transitionals) Order 2008.

[2.50]

2 Interpretation

In this Order—

"the Act" means the Bankruptcy and Diligence etc (Scotland) Act 2007;

"the 1985 Act" means the Bankruptcy (Scotland) Act 1985;

"the 1987 Act" means the Debtors (Scotland) Act 1987; and

"the 2002 Act" means the Debt Arrangement and Attachment (Scotland) Act 2002.

3, 4 (*Art 3 sets out the provisions brought into force by this Order; the effect of the commencement of those provisions which are relevant to this work is noted at the appropriate place; art 4 revoked by the Bankruptcy and Diligence etc (Scotland) Act 2007 (Commencement No 7 and Transitionals) Order 2011, SSI 2011/31, art 5(a)*).

[2.51]

5 Sequestrations—petitions presented before 1st April 2008

(1) Nothing in any provision brought into force by this Order[, except for section 7 of the Act,] has effect as regards any sequestration in respect of which the petition is presented before 1st April 2008.

(2) The 1985 Act[, except for sections 2(3)(a) and 24(2)(d)], as in force immediately before 1st April 2008 continues to apply and have effect in relation to any sequestration in respect of which the petition is presented before that date.

NOTES

Paras (1), (2): words in square brackets inserted by the Bankruptcy and Diligence etc (Scotland) Act 2007 (Commencement No 9 and Savings Amendment) Order 2014, SSI 2014/173, art 3(1), (2).

[2.52]

6 Trust deeds—trust deeds granted before 1st April 2008

(1) Nothing in any provision brought into force by this Order has effect as regards any trust deed granted before 1st April 2008.

(2) Sections 1A(1)(a) and 59 of, and Schedule 5 to, the 1985 Act, as in force immediately before 1st April 2008, continue to apply and have effect in relation to any trust deed granted before that date.

[(3) This article does not save any residence requirement to be repealed by section 7 or 20 of the Act.]

NOTES

Para (3): inserted by the Bankruptcy and Diligence etc (Scotland) Act 2007 (Commencement No 9 and Savings Amendment) Order 2014, SSI 2014/173, art 3(1), (3).

[2.53]

7 Transitional arrangements—bankruptcy restrictions orders, debt advice and information packages in bankruptcy and definition of apparent insolvency

Where a sheriff is considering whether to make a bankruptcy restrictions order or interim bankruptcy restrictions order, or the Accountant in Bankruptcy is determining whether to accept a bankruptcy restrictions undertaking pursuant to section 56A, 56F or 56G, respectively, of the 1985 Act, neither the sheriff nor the Accountant in Bankruptcy is to take into account any conduct of the debtor before 1st April 2008.

[2.54]

8

Section 5(2D) of the 1985 Act (creditor to provide debt advice and information package) has no effect in relation to a petition by a creditor presented before 22nd April 2008.

[2.55]

9

Notwithstanding the repeal of section 7(1)(c)(iii) of the 1985 Act by Part 1 of Schedule 6 to the Act the apparent insolvency of a debtor may still be constituted by 14 days elapsing without payment following an attachment (or an attempt to attach) or the seizure of moveable property in pursuance of a summary warrant for the recovery of rates or taxes, where the attachment (or attempt to attach) or seizure occurred before 1st April 2008.

[2.56]

10 Diligence on the dependence, summary warrants, time to pay—proceedings before 1st April 2008

(1) Nothing in any provision brought into force by this Order, except sections 15K and 15L of the 1987 Act (inserted by section 169 of the Act) and section 95A of the 1987 Act (inserted by section 170 of the Act), has effect as regards any diligence on the dependence of an action for which a warrant is applied for before 1st April 2008.

(2) Nothing in any provision brought into force by this Order has effect as regards—
- (a) any diligence which is—
  - (i) authorised by a summary warrant granted before 1st April 2008; and
  - (ii) executed before 1st July 2008; and
- (b) any application for a time to pay direction or a time to pay order made before 1st April 2008.

11–14 (*Outside the scope of this work.*)

[2.57]

15

Notwithstanding any requirement to serve a charge for payment by or under any provision of the Act commenced by this Order, such a requirement shall not prevent execution of the diligence to which that requirement relates before 15th April 2008 (or where the person on whom the charge is to be served is outside the United Kingdom, before 29th April 2008).

SCHEDULES 1–3

(*Schs 1–3 set out the provisions brought into force by this Order; the effect of the commencement of those provisions which are relevant to this work is noted at the appropriate place.*)

INSOLVENCY (AMENDMENT) RULES 2008 (NOTE)

(SI 2008/737)

[2.58]

NOTES

Made: 13 March 2008.

Authority: Insolvency Act 1986, s 411.

Commencement: 6 April 2008.

These Rules are revoked by the Insolvency (England and Wales) Rules 2016, SI 2016/1024, r 2, Sch 1. They amended the Insolvency Rules 1986, SI 1986/1925 and set out transitional provisions relating to those amendments. The 1986 Rules are also revoked by SI 2016/1024, r 2, Sch 1, as from 6 April 2017 and subject to transitional provisions in Sch 2 thereto at **[6.935]**; they have been omitted from the current edition due to reasons of space and can be found in the 18th edition of this Handbook. Accordingly, these 2008 Rules can also be found in the 18th edition.

BANKRUPTCY AND DILIGENCE ETC (SCOTLAND) ACT 2007 (COMMENCEMENT NO 4, SAVINGS AND TRANSITIONALS) ORDER 2009

(SSI 2009/67 (C 4))

NOTES

Made: 23 February 2009.

Authority: Bankruptcy and Diligence etc (Scotland) Act 2007, ss 224(2), 227(3), (4).

[2.59]

1 Citation

This Order may be cited as the Bankruptcy and Diligence etc (Scotland) Act 2007 (Commencement No 4, Savings and Transitionals) Order 2009.

[2.60]

2 Interpretation

In this Order—

"the Act" means the Bankruptcy and Diligence etc (Scotland) Act 2007; and

"the 1987 Act" means the Debtors (Scotland) Act 1987.

3, 4 (*Art 3 sets out the provisions brought into force by this Order; the effect of the commencement of those provisions which are relevant to this work is noted at the appropriate place; art 4 revoked by the Bankruptcy and Diligence etc (Scotland) Act 2007 (Commencement No 7 and Transitionals) Order 2011, SSI 2011/31, art 5(b).*)

[2.61]

5 Transitional modification of the Act—references to the Registers of Inhibitions

(1) Any reference to "the Register of Inhibitions" in, or having effect by virtue of, any provision of the Act commenced by this Order is to be read as a reference to the Register of Inhibitions and Adjudications.

(2) This article ceases to have effect on the day to be appointed for the coming into force of section 80 of the Act (renaming of the Register of Inhibitions and Adjudications).

[2.62]

6 Inhibition and arrestment—execution before 22nd April 2009

Nothing in any provision brought into force by this Order has effect as regards an inhibition or arrestment executed before 22nd April 2009, unless—

(a) the inhibition was on the dependence of an action and it converts to an inhibition in execution on or after 22nd April 2009; or

(b) the arrestment was on the dependence of an action and the creditor obtains a final decree in that action (within the meaning of Part 3A of the 1987 Act) on or after 22nd April 2009.

7 (*Outside the scope of this work.*)

SCHEDULES 1 AND 2

(*Schs 1, 2 set out the provisions brought into force by this Order; the effect of the commencement of those provisions which are relevant to this work is noted at the appropriate place.*)

Part 2 Transitional Provisions

INSOLVENCY (AMENDMENT) RULES 2009 (NOTE)

(SI 2009/642)

[2.63]

NOTES

Made: 10 March 2009.

Authority: Insolvency Act 1986, ss 411, 412.

Commencement: 6 April 2009.

These Rules are revoked by the Insolvency (England and Wales) Rules 2016, SI 2016/1024, r 2, Sch 1. They amended the Insolvency Rules 1986, SI 1986/1925 and set out transitional provisions relating to those amendments. The 1986 Rules are also revoked by SI 2016/1024, r 2, Sch 1, as from 6 April 2017 and subject to transitional provisions in Sch 2 thereto at **[6.935]**; they have been omitted from the current edition due to reasons of space and can be found in the 18th edition of this Handbook. Accordingly, these 2009 Rules can also be found in the 18th edition.

INSOLVENCY PROCEEDINGS (FEES) (AMENDMENT) ORDER 2009

(SI 2009/645)

NOTES

Made: 12 March 2009.

Authority: Bankruptcy Act 1914, s 133; Companies Act 1985, s 663(4); Insolvency Act 1986, ss 414(1), (5), 415(1), (4).

Commencement: 6 April 2009.

This Order is revoked (as from 21 July 2016) by the Insolvency Proceedings (Fees) Order 2016, SI 2016/692, art 6, Sch 2, subject to transitional provisions and savings in art 7 thereof at **[8.88]**.

[2.64]

1 Citation and commencement and interpretation

This Order may be cited as the Insolvency Proceedings (Fees) (Amendment) Order 2009 and comes into force on 6th April 2009.

NOTES

Revoked as noted at the beginning of this Order.

[2.65]

2

In this Order, "the principal Order" means the Insolvency Proceedings (Fees) Order 2004.

NOTES

Revoked as noted at the beginning of this Order.

[2.66]

3 Amendments to the Insolvency Proceedings (Fees) Order 2004

Subject to article 7 of this Order, the principal Order is amended as set out in articles 4 to 6 of this Order.

NOTES

Revoked as noted at the beginning of this Order.

4–6 *(Art 4 amends the Insolvency Proceedings (Fees) Order 2004, SI 2004/593, arts 4–7 at* **[8.74]–[8.77]***; art 5 revoked by the Insolvency Proceedings (Fees) (Amendment) Order 2010, SI 2010/732; art 6 amends Sch 2 thereto at* **[8.81]**.)

[2.67]

7 Transitional provisions

(1) The amendments made by this Order shall apply as follows.

(2) The amendment made by article 4(1)(c) to article 4(4) of the principal Order increasing the fee with respect to the purchase of government securities and introducing a fee for the sale of government securities by a trustee in bankruptcy under the Bankruptcy Act 1914 or a liquidator in a winding up under the provisions of the Companies Act 1985, shall only apply where the request to purchase or sell is made on or after 6th April 2009 and, in the case of a sale, only where the request to purchase the securities which are to be sold was also made after on or after 6th April 2009.

(3) The amendment made by article 4(2) to article 5 of the principal Order shall only apply to reports submitted to the court in respect of debtor's petitions presented on or after 6th April 2009.

(4) The amendments made by article 4(3), increasing the amounts of appropriate deposit prescribed by article 6 of the principal Order, shall only apply to petitions presented on or after 6th April 2009.

(5) The amendment made by article 4(4), increasing the amount of security deposit prescribed by article 7(1) of the principal Order, shall only apply to notifications sent to the official receiver on or after 6th April 2009.

(6) The amendment made by article 6(2) to fee IVA1 shall only apply to a voluntary arrangement under Part 8 of the Insolvency Act 1986 in respect of which information required to be submitted to the Secretary of State by virtue of Part 5 of the Insolvency Rules 1986 is first submitted in relation to that arrangement on or after 6th April 2009.

(7) The amendment made by article 6(6) to fee INV1, increasing the fee for the purchase of government securities and introducing a fee for the sale of government securities, shall only apply where the request to purchase or sell is made on or after 6th April 2009 and, in the case of a sale, only where the request to purchase the securities which are to be sold was also made on or after 6th April 2009.

NOTES

Revoked as noted at the beginning of this Order.

COMPANIES ACT 2006 (CONSEQUENTIAL AMENDMENTS, TRANSITIONAL PROVISIONS AND SAVINGS) ORDER 2009

(SI 2009/1941)

NOTES

Made: 21 July 2009.

Authority: European Communities Act 1972, s 2(2); Companies Act 2006, ss 657, 1088, 1292, 1294, 1296(1), 1300(2); Charities Act 2006, s 75(4), (5).

Commencement: 1 October 2009.

ARRANGEMENT OF ARTICLES

1 Citation and commencement . . . . [2.68]
2 Consequential amendments, repeals and revocations . . . . [2.69]
8 Amendments of insolvency legislation . . . . [2.70]
9 Saving for unlimited liabilities of directors etc . . . . [2.71]
11 Saving for provisions relating to nature of liability of member or contributory . . . . [2.72]

SCHEDULES

Schedule 1—Consequential amendments . . . . [2.73]

Introductory

[2.68]

1 Citation and commencement

(1) This Order may be cited as the Companies Act 2006 (Consequential Amendments, Transitional Provisions and Savings) Order 2009.

(2) The provisions of this Order come into force on 1st October 2009.

Consequential amendments

[2.69]

2 Consequential amendments, repeals and revocations

(1) Schedule 1 to this Order contains consequential amendments.

(2) Schedule 2 to this Order contains other consequential repeals and revocations.

3, 4 (*Outside the scope of this work.*)

Transitional provisions

5–7 (*Outside the scope of this work.*)

[2.70]

8 Amendments of insolvency legislation

(1) The amendments by this Order of the Insolvency Act 1986 ("the 1986 Act") and the Insolvency (Northern Ireland) Order 1989 ("the 1989 Order") apply as follows.

(2) They apply where, in a company voluntary arrangement, a moratorium comes into force in relation to a company on or after 1st October 2009.

(3) They apply where a company enters administration on or after 1st October 2009, except where—
- (a) it enters administration by virtue of an administration order under paragraph 10 of Schedule B1 to the 1986 Act (or paragraph 11 of Schedule B1 to the 1989 Order) on an application made before 1st October 2009,
- (b) the administration is immediately preceded by a voluntary liquidation in respect of which the resolution to wind up was passed before 1st October 2009, or
- (c) the administration is immediately preceded by a liquidation on the making of a winding-up order on a petition which was presented before 1st October 2009.

(4) They apply where, in a receivership, a receiver or manager is appointed in respect of a company on or after 1st October 2009.

(5) They apply where a company goes into liquidation upon the passing on or after 1st October 2009 of a resolution to wind up.

(6) They apply where a company goes into voluntary liquidation under paragraph 83 of Schedule B1 to the 1986 Act (or paragraph 84 of Schedule B1 to the 1989 Order), except where the preceding administration—

(a) commenced before 1st October 2009, or

(b) is an administration which commenced by virtue of an administration order under paragraph 10 of Schedule B1 to the 1986 Act (or paragraph 11 of Schedule B1 to the 1989 Order) on an application which was made before 1st October 2009.

(7) They apply where a company goes into liquidation on the making of a winding-up order on a petition presented on or after 1st October 2009, except where the liquidation is immediately preceded by—

(a) an administration under paragraph 10 of Schedule B1 to the 1986 Act (or paragraph 11 of Schedule B1 to the 1989 Order) where the administration order was made on an application made before 1st October 2009,

(b) an administration in respect of which the appointment of an administrator under paragraph 14 or 22 of Schedule B1 to the 1986 Act (or paragraph 15 or 23 of Schedule B1 to the 1989 Order) took effect before 1st October 2009, or

(c) a voluntary liquidation in respect of which the resolution to wind up was passed before 1st October 2009.

Savings

[2.71]

9 Saving for unlimited liabilities of directors etc

The repeal of the provisions relating to unlimited liability of directors and others, that is—

(a) sections 306 and 307 of the Companies Act 1985 and section 75 of the Insolvency Act 1986, or

(b) Articles 314 and 315 of the Companies (Northern Ireland) Order 1986 and Article 62 of the Insolvency (Northern Ireland) Order 1989,

does not affect the operation of those provisions in relation to liabilities arising before 1st October 2009 or in connection with the holding of an office to which a person was appointed before that date on the understanding that their liability would be unlimited.

10 (*Outside the scope of this work.*)

[2.72]

11 Saving for provisions relating to nature of liability of member or contributory

(1) The new provisions as to the nature of a member's or contributory's liability apply to liabilities arising on or after 1st October 2009 and the old provisions continue to apply to liabilities arising before that date.

(2) The new provisions are section 33(2) of the Companies Act 2006 and (in England and Wales) section 80 of the Insolvency Act 1986 as amended by this Order.

(3) The old provisions are—

(a) in England and Wales, section 14(2) of the Companies Act 1985 and section 80 of the Insolvency Act 1986 as it has effect before that amendment;

(b) in Northern Ireland, Articles 4(d)(ii) and 15(c) of the Limitation (Northern Ireland) Order 1989.

(4) For the purposes of this article a liability is treated as arising when the limitation period starts to run for the purposes of the Limitation Act 1980 or the Limitation (Northern Ireland) Order 1989.

12, 13 (*Outside the scope of this work.*)

SCHEDULE 1
CONSEQUENTIAL AMENDMENTS

Article 2(1)

[2.73]

1–83. . . .

84. Nothing in the amendments of the Insolvency Act 1986 made by this Schedule is to be read as qualifying the generality of section 441(2) of that Act (which provides that, with certain exceptions, nothing in the Act extends to Northern Ireland or applies to or in relation to companies registered or incorporated in Northern Ireland).

85–270. . . .

NOTES

Paras 1–70, 85–270: contain amendments which in so far as relevant to this work have been incorporated at the appropriate place.

Paras 71–83: amend the Insolvency Act 1986 at **[1.1]** et seq and the amendments have been incorporated at the appropriate places in the 1986 Act.

SCHEDULES 2 AND 3

(Sch 2 contains repeals and revocations which in so far as relevant to this work have been incorporated at the appropriate place; Sch 3 outside the scope of this work.)

INSOLVENCY (AMENDMENT) (NO 2) RULES 2009 (NOTE)

(SI 2009/2472)

[2.74]

NOTES

Made: 8 September 2009.

Authority: Insolvency Act 1986, ss 411, 412.

Commencement: 1 October 2009.

These Rules are revoked by the Insolvency (England and Wales) Rules 2016, SI 2016/1024, r 2, Sch 1. They amended the Insolvency Rules 1986, SI 1986/1925 and set out transitional provisions relating to those amendments. The 1986 Rules are also revoked by SI 2016/1024, r 2, Sch 1, as from 6 April 2017 and subject to transitional provisions in Sch 2 thereto at **[6.935]**; they have been omitted from the current edition due to reasons of space and can be found in the 18th edition of this Handbook. Accordingly, these 2009 Rules can also be found in the 18th edition.

LEGISLATIVE REFORM (INSOLVENCY) (MISCELLANEOUS PROVISIONS) ORDER 2010

(SI 2010/18)

NOTES

Made: 6 January 2010.

Authority: Legislative and Regulatory Reform Act 2006, s 1.

Commencement: 6 April 2010.

[2.75]

1 Citation, commencement and extent

(1) This Order may be cited as the Legislative Reform (Insolvency) (Miscellaneous Provisions) Order 2010 and comes into force on 6th April 2010.

(2) Subject to paragraph (3), this Order extends to England and Wales and to Scotland.

(3) Articles 3(2), 5(7), 7, 8, 9, 10(2) and 11 do not extend to Scotland.

2–11 *(Art 2 introduces amendments to the Insolvency Act 1986; arts 3–11 amend the 1986 Act as follows: art 3 inserts ss 246A, 246B, 379A, 379B at* **[1.259]**, **[1.260]**, **[1.463]**, **[1.464]**, *art 4 inserts s 436B at* **[1.560]** *and amends Sch B1 at* **[1.575]**, *art 5 amends ss 47, 95, 99, 131, 166, 236, 366 at* **[1.33]**, **[1.92]**, **[1.96]**, **[1.132]**, **[1.167]**, **[1.241]**, **[1.445]**, *art 6 inserts ss 92A, 104A at* **[1.89]**, **[1.102]** *and amends ss 93, 105, Sch 10 at* **[1.90]**, **[1.103]**, **[1.595]**, *art 7 amends ss 95, 98 at* **[1.92]**, **[1.95]**, *art 8 amends ss 256A, 257, 259 at* **[1.297]**, **[1.298]**, **[1.300]**, *art 9 amends ss 263C, 263D, 263F at* **[1.310]**, **[1.311]**, **[1.313]**, *art 10 amends Sch 4, Pts 1, 3 at* **[1.581]**, **[1.583]**, *art 11 amends Sch 5, Pts 1, 2 at* **[1.588]**, **[1.589]**.)

Transitional provisions

[2.76]

12 Transitional provisions

(1) Sections 92A and 104A of the Insolvency Act 1986 ("the 1986 Act") inserted by article 6 do not apply in respect of a company in voluntary winding up where the resolution to wind up was passed before 6th April 2010.

(2) The amendments to sections 93 and 105 of the 1986 Act made by article 6 do not apply in respect of a company in voluntary winding up where the resolution to wind up was passed before 6th April 2010.

(3) The amendments to sections 95 and 98 of the 1986 Act made by article 7 do not apply in respect of a company in voluntary winding up where the resolution to wind up was passed before 6th April 2010.

(4) Where a person agrees before 6th April 2010 to act as nominee in respect of a proposal for a voluntary arrangement under Part 8 of the 1986 Act by a debtor for a composition in satisfaction of his debts or for a scheme of arrangement of his affairs to a nominee under section 256A or 263B of the 1986 Act, the provisions of the 1986 Act relevant to a proposal under those sections as they were prior to the amendments made by this Order shall continue to apply to it.

(5) The amendments made to Schedules 4 and 5 to the 1986 Act by articles 10 and 11 respectively do not apply in respect of any proceedings under the 1986 Act where—

(a) in the case of a company in voluntary winding up, the resolution to wind up was passed before 6th April 2010;

(b) in the case of a company in voluntary winding up pursuant to paragraph 83 of Schedule B1 to the 1986 Act, the preceding administration commenced before 6th April 2010;

(c) in the case of a company in winding up following an order for the conversion of administration or a voluntary arrangement into winding up by virtue of article 37 of Council Regulation (EC) No 1346/2000 on insolvency proceedings, the order for conversion was made before 6th April 2010;
(d) in the case of a company being wound up by the court, the winding-up order was made before 6th April 2010;
(e) in the case of a bankruptcy, the debtor was adjudged bankrupt before 6th April 2010; and
(f) in the case of a bankruptcy following an order for the conversion of a voluntary arrangement into a bankruptcy by virtue of article 37 of Council Regulation (EC) No 1346/2000, the order for conversion was made before 6th April 2010.

INSOLVENCY (AMENDMENT) RULES 2010 (NOTE)

(SI 2010/686)

[2.77]

NOTES

Made: 3 March 2010.
Authority: Insolvency Act 1986, s 413.
Commencement: 6 April 2010.

These Rules are revoked by the Insolvency (England and Wales) Rules 2016, SI 2016/1024, r 2, Sch 1. They amended the Insolvency Rules 1986, SI 1986/1925 and set out transitional provisions relating to those amendments. The 1986 Rules are also revoked by SI 2016/1024, r 2, Sch 1, as from 6 April 2017 and subject to transitional provisions in Sch 2 thereto at **[6.935]**; they have been omitted from the current edition due to reasons of space and can be found in the 18th edition of this Handbook. Accordingly, these 2010 Rules can also be found in the 18th edition.

INSOLVENCY (SCOTLAND) AMENDMENT RULES 2010

(SI 2010/688 (S 2))

NOTES

Made: 9 March 2010.
Authority: Insolvency Act 1986, s 411.
Commencement: 6 April 2010.

[2.78]

1 Citation, commencement and interpretation

These Rules may be cited as the Insolvency (Scotland) Amendment Rules 2010 and come into force on 6th April 2010.

[2.79]

2

In these Rules "the principal Rules" means the Insolvency (Scotland) Rules 1986.

3 (*Introduces amendments to the Insolvency (Scotland) Rules 1986, SI 1986/1915 at* **[15.1]** *et seq.*)

[2.80]

4 Transitional provisions—general

(1) The amendments to the principal Rules by these Rules apply as provided by paragraphs (2) and (3), except where Rules 5 and 6 provide differently.

(2) They apply where a person agrees to act as nominee in respect of a proposal for a company voluntary arrangement on or after 6th April 2010.

(3) They apply where a company enters administration on or after 6th April 2010, except where—
(a) it enters administration by virtue of an administration order under paragraph 10 of Schedule B1 to the Insolvency Act 1986 on an application made before 6th April 2010;
(b) the administration is immediately preceded by a voluntary liquidation in respect of which the resolution to wind up was passed before 6th April 2010; or
(c) the administration is immediately preceded by a liquidation on the making of a winding-up order on a petition which was presented before 6th April 2010.

[2.81]

5 Revocations and amendments relating to new provisions in the Act

The amendments made by the following paragraphs of Schedule 1 to these Rules apply on and after 6th April 2010 in all cases, namely paragraphs 2, 3, 4, 22, 27 (in so far as that paragraph inserts new Rules 1.16C to 1.16E), 68 (in so far as that paragraph inserts new Rules 2.25B to 2.25E), 70 (in so far as that paragraph inserts a new Rule 2.26B), 83, 85, 92, 94 and 114.

[2.82]
6 Amendments relating to preparation of proposals for voluntary arrangements

The amendments made by paragraphs 5, 11 and 15 of Schedule 1 to these Rules apply where a copy of the proposal for a company voluntary arrangement is delivered to the intended nominee on or after 6th April 2010.

SCHEDULES

(Sch 1 amends the Insolvency (Scotland) Rules 1986, SI 1986/1915 at **[15.1]** *et seq and the amendments have been incorporated at the appropriate places in the 1986 Rules; Sch 2 contains a new form for insertion in the 1986 Rules as noted to Sch 5 at* **[15.349]**.)

INSOLVENCY PROCEEDINGS (FEES) (AMENDMENT) ORDER 2010

(SI 2010/732)

NOTES

Made: 8 March 2010.

Authority: Insolvency Act 1986, ss 414, 415.

Commencement: 6 April 2010.

This Order is revoked (as from 21 July 2016) by the Insolvency Proceedings (Fees) Order 2016, SI 2016/692, art 6, Sch 2, subject to transitional provisions and savings in art 7 thereof at **[8.88]**.

[2.83]
1 Citation, commencement and interpretation

This Order may be cited as the Insolvency Proceedings (Fees) (Amendment) Order 2010 and comes into force on 6th April 2010.

NOTES

Revoked as noted at the beginning of this Order.

[2.84]
2

In this Order, "the principal Order" means the Insolvency Proceedings (Fees) Order 2004.

NOTES

Revoked as noted at the beginning of this Order.

3–7 (Amend the Insolvency Proceedings (Fees) Order 2004, SI 2004/593, arts 5, 6, Sch 2 at **[8.75]**, **[8.76]**, **[8.81]** *and revoke the Insolvency Proceedings (Fees) (Amendment) Order 2009, SI 2009/645, art 5.)*

[2.85]
8 Transitional provisions

(1) The amendments and revocations made by this Order apply as follows.

(2) The amendment made by article 4 to article 5 of the principal Order applies only to reports submitted to the court in respect of debtor's petitions presented on or after 6th April 2010.

(3) The amendments made by article 5 to article 6 of the principal Order apply only to petitions presented on or after 6th April 2010.

(4) The amendments made by article 6(2), (3) and (4) to Schedule 2 to the principal Order apply only in respect of bankruptcy and winding-up orders made on or after 6th April 2010.

(5) The revocations made by article 7(1) to Schedule 2 to the principal Order have effect only in respect of bankruptcy and winding-up orders made on or after 6th April 2010.

(6) The revocation made by article 7(2) to the Insolvency Proceedings (Fees) (Amendment) Order 2009 has effect only in respect of bankruptcy and winding-up orders made on or after 6th April 2010.

NOTES

Revoked as noted at the beginning of this Order.

INSOLVENCY (AMENDMENT) (NO 2) RULES 2010 (NOTE)

(SI 2010/734)

[2.86]

NOTES

Made: 10 March 2010.

Authority: Insolvency Act 1986, ss 411, 412.

Commencement: 6 April 2010.

These Rules are revoked by the Insolvency (England and Wales) Rules 2016, SI 2016/1024, r 2, Sch 1. They amended the Insolvency Rules 1986, SI 1986/1925 and set out transitional provisions relating to those amendments. The 1986 Rules are also revoked by SI 2016/1024, r 2, Sch 1, as from 6 April 2017 and subject to transitional provisions in Sch 2 thereto at **[6.935]**; they have been omitted from the current edition due to reasons of space and can be found in the 18th edition of this Handbook. Accordingly, these 2010 Rules can also be found in the 18th edition.

INSOLVENCY (AMENDMENT) RULES 2011 (NOTE)

(SI 2011/785)

[2.87]

NOTES

Made: 14 March 2011.

Authority: Insolvency Act 1986, s 412.

Commencement: 6 April 2011.

These Rules are revoked by the Insolvency (England and Wales) Rules 2016, SI 2016/1024, r 2, Sch 1. They amended the Insolvency Rules 1986, SI 1986/1925 and set out transitional provisions relating to those amendments. The 1986 Rules are also revoked by SI 2016/1024, r 2, Sch 1, as from 6 April 2017 and subject to transitional provisions in Sch 2 thereto at **[6.935]**; they have been omitted from the current edition due to reasons of space and can be found in the 18th edition of this Handbook. Accordingly, these 2011 Rules can also be found in the 18th edition.

BANKRUPTCY AND DEBT ADVICE (SCOTLAND) ACT 2014 (COMMENCEMENT NO 2, SAVINGS AND TRANSITIONALS) ORDER 2014

(SSI 2014/261 (C 23))

NOTES

Made: 29 September 2014.

Authority: Bankruptcy and Debt Advice (Scotland) Act 2014, s 57(2), (3).

Commencement: 1 April 2015.

ARRANGEMENT OF ARTICLES

1 Citation and commencement . . . [2.88]
2 Interpretation . . . [2.89]
3 Day appointed . . . [2.90]

Savings and transitional arrangements

4 Sequestration before 1st April 2015 . . . [2.91]
5 Money advice . . . [2.92]
6 Common financial tool . . . [2.93]
7 Moratorium on diligence . . . [2.94]
8 Recall of sequestration . . . [2.95]
9 Applications for trustee directions . . . [2.96]
10 Review of decisions by Accountant in Bankruptcy . . . [2.97]
11 Power of trustee in relation to debtor's family home . . . [2.98]
12 Trust deeds granted before 1st April 2015 . . . [2.99]

[2.88]

1 Citation and commencement

This Order may be cited as the Bankruptcy and Debt Advice (Scotland) Act 2014 (Commencement No 2, Savings and Transitionals) Order 2014 and comes into force on 1st April 2015.

NOTES

Commencement: 1 April 2015.

[2.89]
2 Interpretation

(1) In this Order—

"the Act" means the Bankruptcy and Debt Advice (Scotland) Act 2014; and

"the 1985 Act" means the Bankruptcy (Scotland) Act 1985.

(2) This Order is to be construed in accordance with section 73 (interpretation) of the 1985 Act.

NOTES

Commencement: 1 April 2015.

[2.90]
3 Day appointed

The day appointed for the coming into force of the Act, insofar as not already in force, is 1st April 2015, except in respect of section 27 (recall of sequestration by Accountant in Bankruptcy) for the purpose of inserting section 17G(7) into the 1985 Act.

NOTES

Commencement: 1 April 2015.

Savings and transitional arrangements

[2.91]
4 Sequestration before 1st April 2015

(1) Except as mentioned in paragraph (3) and article 6, nothing brought into force by this Order has effect as regards any sequestration in respect of which—

(a) the petition is presented before 1st April 2015; or

(b) a debtor application [is] made before that date.

(2) The 1985 Act, as in force immediately before 1st April 2015, continues to apply and have effect in relation to any such sequestration.

(3) This article does not apply as regards the following provisions of the Act—

(a) section 8 (moratorium on diligence),

(b) section 12 (concurrent proceedings: recall),

(c) section 20 (unclaimed dividends and unapplied balances),

(d) section 22 (register of insolvencies),

(e) section 24 (abolition of Edinburgh Gazette requirements),

(f) section 25 (directions),

(g) sections 26(1)(a), (2) and (3) and 27 (recall of sequestration),

(h) section 34 (conversion of trust deed into sequestration),

(i) sections 38 to 43 (review of decisions made by Accountant in Bankruptcy),

(j) section 48 (renewal of inhibition period),

(k) section 49 (division and sale of family home),

(l) section 50 (effect of debtor discharge), and

(m) in schedule 3—

(i) paragraph 3(a) (moratorium on diligence and register of insolvencies),

(ii) paragraphs 12 and 13 (expiry of inhibitory effect sequestration: recall),

(iii) paragraphs 25 and 26 (review by Accountant in Bankruptcy of adjudication of claims),

(iv) paragraph 31 (unclaimed dividends and unapplied balances), and

(v) paragraph 35(b), (c) and (e) (definitions of "common financial tool", "DAS register", "debtor contribution order" and "debtor's contribution").

(4) For the purposes of paragraph (1) the bankruptcy restrictions undertaking of a debtor is treated as sequestration of that debtor.

NOTES

Commencement: 1 April 2015.

Para (1): word in square brackets substituted by the Bankruptcy and Debt Advice (Scotland) Act 2014 (Commencement No 2, Savings and Transitionals) Amendment Order 2015, SSI 2015/54, art 2.

[2.92]
5 Money advice

(1) A debtor application signed by the debtor before 1st April 2015 may be made on or after that date notwithstanding that the debtor has not obtained money advice in accordance with section 5C of the 1985 Act.

(2) To that extent it is to be treated as an incomplete application under section 11A(1) of the 1985 Act.

NOTES

Commencement: 1 April 2015.

[2.93]
6 Common financial tool

(1) This article applies to sequestrations to which article 4(1)(a) or (b) applies, unless they meet the conditions under section 5A of the 1985 Act (low income, low asset debtors).

(2) Where an application is made on or after 1st April 2015 for variation of—

(a) an income payment order, under section 32(4) of the 1985 Act; or

(b) an income payment agreement, under section 32(4G)(b) of that Act on a change in the debtor's circumstances,

the sheriff must have regard to the common financial tool.

(3) Where on or after 1st April 2015 a trustee is considering entering into a written agreement to vary an income payment agreement under section 32(4G)(a) of the 1985 Act on a change in the debtor's circumstances, the trustee must have regard to the common financial tool.

(4) In so applying the common financial tool, it is modified as follows—

(a) regulations made under section 5D of the 1985 Act (assessment of debtor's contribution) apply as if for any reference to variation or removal under section 32F of the 1985 Act there were substituted a reference to variation or recall under section 32(4) of the 1985 Act; and

(b) any provision of those regulations in pursuance of section 5D(3) to (6) of the 1985 Act (assessment of debtor's contribution) does not apply.

(5) For the avoidance of doubt this article does not prevent a sheriff or trustee having regard to other factors, including the amount initially determined by the order or provided for in the agreement (or any extant variation of either).

(6) The introduction of the common financial tool is not itself a change in the debtor's circumstances for the purposes of this article (or section 32(4) of the 1985 Act).

NOTES

Commencement: 1 April 2015.

[2.94]

7 Moratorium on diligence

Notice received by the Accountant in Bankruptcy on or after 1st April 2015 which is—

(a) in accordance with section 4A(1) or 4B(1) of the 1985 Act (notice of intention to apply for sequestration, protected trust deed for debt payment programme); and

(b) in the form required under the 1985 Act from that date,

has effect as if given on 1st April 2015 notwithstanding that it was given before that date.

NOTES

Commencement: 1 April 2015.

[2.95]

8 Recall of sequestration

Section 24(1) (replacement of Edinburgh Gazette recall requirement) of the Act does not apply to a petition for recall of sequestration presented before 1st April 2015.

NOTES

Commencement: 1 April 2015.

[2.96]

9 Applications for trustee directions

Section 25 of the Act (application for trustee directions) does not apply to any application to the sheriff for directions made before 1st April 2015 (and any appeal from any such direction).

NOTES

Commencement: 1 April 2015.

[2.97]

10 Review of decisions by Accountant in Bankruptcy

(1) The amendments in sections 38 to 42 of the Act (review of decisions by the Accountant in Bankruptcy) relevant to review by the Accountant in Bankruptcy of the following decisions of the Accountant in Bankruptcy do not apply—

(a) to a determination notified before 1st April 2015 under section 13A(10)(b) (certificate of interim trustee discharge), or where notice is sent before that date under section 13B(4)(a)(iii) or (b) (discharge of Accountant in Bankruptcy as interim trustee), of the 1985 Act,

(b) to a direction given under section 18(1) (direction for interim preservation of estate) of the 1985 Act before 1st April 2015,

(c) to a refusal to award sequestration under section 15(3A) (debtor application) of the 1985 Act before 1st April 2015,

(d) where notice is sent before 1st April 2015 under section 26A(3) (discharge of Accountant in Bankruptcy as trustee) of the 1985 Act,

(e) to a determination notified before 1st April 2015 under section 27(3)(b) (certificate of original trustee's discharge) of the 1985 Act,

(f) to claims accepted or rejected in a list sent before 1st April 2015, or notification given before that date, under section 49(2A) or (4) respectively (adjudication of claims) of the 1985 Act, or

(g) to a determination notified before 1st April 2015 under section 57(3)(b) (certificate of trustee discharge), or where notice is sent before that date under section 58A(4)(b) (discharge of Accountant in Bankruptcy as trustee), of the 1985 Act.

(2) Sections 38 to 42 of the Act do not apply to any decision by the Accountant in Bankruptcy which is subject to court proceedings by way of appeal or review before 1st April 2015.

NOTES
Commencement: 1 April 2015.

[2.98]
11 Power of trustee in relation to debtor's family home

Section 49 of the Act (procedure on power of trustee in relation to debtor's family home) does not apply to any court proceedings commenced before 1st April 2015 (and any appeal in respect of those proceedings).

NOTES
Commencement: 1 April 2015.

[2.99]
12 Trust deeds granted before 1st April 2015

(1) Nothing brought into force by this Order except section 8 (moratorium on diligence) has effect as regards any trust deed granted before 1st April 2015.

(2) The 1985 Act as in force immediately before 1st April 2015, continues to apply and have effect in relation to any such trust deed.

NOTES
Commencement: 1 April 2015.

INSOLVENCY AMENDMENT (EU 2015/848) REGULATIONS 2017

(SI 2017/702)

NOTES
Made: 21 June 2017.
Authority: European Communities Act 1972, s 2(2).
Commencement: 26 June 2017.

[2.100]
1 Citation and Commencement

These Regulations may be cited as the Insolvency Amendment (EU 2015/848) Regulations 2017 and come into force on 26th June 2017.

NOTES
Commencement: 26 June 2017.

[2.101]
2 Amendments and extent

(1) The Schedule has effect.

(2) Any provision of these Regulations amending or applying an enactment has the same extent as the enactment amended or applied, except that—

(a) the amendments made to the Insolvency Act 1986 by paragraphs 3, 7, 9, and 12, of the Schedule extend to England and Wales only; and

(b) the amendments to that Act made by Part 4 of that Schedule apply to Scotland only.

NOTES
Commencement: 26 June 2017.

[2.102]
3 Temporal application

(1) These Regulations do not apply to proceedings opened before 26 June 2017.

(2) The time at which proceedings are opened is to be determined in accordance with Article 2(8) of Regulation (EU) 2015/848 of the European Parliament and of the Council.

NOTES
Commencement: 26 June 2017.

[2.103]
4 Saving

The Insolvency Act 1986 as it applies to the instruments listed in regulation 4(2) of the Deregulation Act 2015 and Small Business, Enterprise and Employment Act 2015 (Consequential Amendments) (Savings) Regulations 2017 continues to apply to those instruments without the amendments made to the Insolvency Act 1986 by Parts 1 and 4 of the Schedule.

NOTES

Commencement: 26 June 2017.

Note: the instruments listed in the Deregulation Act 2015 and Small Business, Enterprise and Employment Act 2015 (Consequential Amendments) (Savings) Regulations 2017, SI 2017/540, reg 4(2) are as follows:

(a) the Railway Administration Order Rules 2001, SI 2001/3352 at **[7.2452]**;
(b) the Limited Liability Partnerships Regulations 2001, SI 2001/1090 at**[10.33]**;
(c) the Energy Act 2004 at **[7.849]**;
(d) the Energy Administration Rules 2005, SI 2005/2483 at **[7.874]**;
(e) the PPP Administration Order Rules 2007, SI 2007/3141 at **[7.2311]**;
(f) the Water Industry (Special Administration) Rules 2009, SI 2009/2477 at **[7.2627]**;
(g) the Energy Act 2011 at **[7.1063]**;
(h) the Charitable Incorporated Organisations (Insolvency and Dissolution) Regulations 2012, SI 2012/3013 at **[18.221]**;
(i) the Energy Supply Company Administration Rules 2013, SI 2013/1046 at **[7.1074]**; and
(j) the Postal Administration Rules 2013, SI 2013/3208 at **[7.2086]**.

SCHEDULE

(*The Schedule amends various pieces of insolvency legislation for England and Wales, Scotland and Northern Ireland to make it compatible with the recast of the Regulation (EU) 2015/848 of the European Parliament and of the Council of 20 May 2015 on insolvency proceedings "the EIR". The EIR replaces Council Regulation (EC) No 1346/2000 on insolvency proceedings.*)

PART 3
EU AND INTERNATIONAL MATERIALS AND DOMESTIC LEGISLATION IMPLEMENTING EU DIRECTIVES

UNITED NATIONS COMMISSION ON INTERNATIONAL TRADE LAW (UNCITRAL) MODEL LAW ON CROSS-BORDER INSOLVENCY

NOTES

Adopted by UNCITRAL on 30 May 1997.

Legislation based on the UNCITRAL Model Law on Cross-Border Insolvency has, at the time of going to press, been adopted in 43 states in a total of 45 jurisdictions. An up to date list of the states which have implemented the Model Law can be found on the UNCITRAL website at www.uncitral.org.

The Cross-Border Insolvency Regulations 2006, SI 2006/1030 at **[3.302]** et seq, give effect to the Model Law in Great Britain.

The Practice Guide on Cross-Border Insolvency Cooperation, adopted by UNCITRAL on 1 July 2009, is not reproduced in this work due to its size. It provides information for insolvency practitioners and judges on practical aspects of cooperation and communication in cross-border insolvency cases. The information is based upon a description of collected experience and practice, focusing on the use and negotiation of cross-border agreements. It provides an analysis of more than 39 agreements, ranging from written agreements approved by courts to oral arrangement between parties to the proceedings, that have been entered into over the last decade or so. The Practice Guide is not intended to be prescriptive, but rather to illustrate how the resolution of issues and conflicts that might arise in cross-border insolvency cases could be facilitated by cross-border cooperation, in particular the use of such agreements, tailored to meet the specific needs of each case and the particular requirements of applicable law. The Practice Guide includes a number of sample clauses to illustrate how different issues have been, or might be, addressed — they are not intended to serve as model provisions for direct incorporation into a cross-border agreement. It also includes summaries of the cases in which the cross-border agreements that form the basis of the analysis were used.

The 'UNCITRAL Model Law on Cross-Border Insolvency: the Judicial Perspective' is also not reproduced in this work. The text was finalised and adopted by UNCITRAL on 1 July 2011. The text discusses the UNCITRAL Model Law on Cross-Border Insolvency from a judge's perspective. It provides assistance for judges with respect to questions arising under the Model Law. It was prepared through consultation principally with judges but also with insolvency practitioners and other experts, in much the same manner as the Practice Guide was developed. The text makes references to decisions given in a number of jurisdictions. However, no attempt is made to critique the decisions, beyond pointing out issues that a judge may want to consider should a similar case come before him or her.

The *Guide to Enactment and Interpretation of the UNCITRAL Model Law on Cross-Border Insolvency* is also not reproduced in this work. The text of the *Guide* was adopted by UNCITRAL on 18 July 2013. It provides further guidance as to the enactment and interpretation of the Model Law. The text of the *Guide* is available on the UNCITRAL website at www.uncitral.org/pdf/english/texts/insolven/1997-Model-Law-Insol-2013-Guide-Enactment-e.pdf.

PART ONE

[3.1]

Preamble

The purpose of this Law is to provide effective mechanisms for dealing with cases of cross-border insolvency so as to promote the objectives of:

(a) Cooperation between the courts and other competent authorities of this State and foreign States involved in cases of cross-border insolvency;

(b) Greater legal certainty for trade and investment;

(c) Fair and efficient administration of cross-border insolvencies that protects the interests of all creditors and other interested persons, including the debtor;

(d) Protection and maximization of the value of the debtor's assets; and

(e) Facilitation of the rescue of financially troubled businesses, thereby protecting investment and preserving employment.

CHAPTER I GENERAL PROVISIONS

[3.2]

Article 1

Scope of application

1. This Law applies where:

(a) Assistance is sought in this State by a foreign court or a foreign representative in connection with a foreign proceeding; or

(b) Assistance is sought in a foreign State in connection with a proceeding under *[identify laws of the enacting State relating to insolvency]*; or

(c) A foreign proceeding and a proceeding under *[identify laws of the enacting State relating to insolvency]* in respect of the same debtor are taking place concurrently; or

(d) Creditors or other interested persons in a foreign State have an interest in requesting the commencement of, or participating in, a proceeding under *[identify laws of the enacting State relating to insolvency]*.

2. This Law does not apply to a proceeding concerning *[designate any types of entities, such as banks or insurance companies, that are subject to a special insolvency regime in this State and that this State wishes to exclude from this Law]*.

[3.3]
Article 2
Definitions

For the purposes of this Law:

(a) "Foreign proceeding" means a collective judicial or administrative proceeding in a foreign State, including an interim proceeding, pursuant to a law relating to insolvency in which proceeding the assets and affairs of the debtor are subject to control or supervision by a foreign court, for the purpose of reorganization or liquidation;

(b) "Foreign main proceeding" means a foreign proceeding taking place in the State where the debtor has the centre of its main interests;

(c) "Foreign non-main proceeding" means a foreign proceeding, other than a foreign main proceeding, taking place in a State where the debtor has an establishment within the meaning of subparagraph (f) of this article;

(d) "Foreign representative" means a person or body, including one appointed on an interim basis, authorized in a foreign proceeding to administer the reorganization or the liquidation of the debtor's assets or affairs or to act as a representative of the foreign proceeding;

(e) "Foreign court" means a judicial or other authority competent to control or supervise a foreign proceeding;

(f) "Establishment" means any place of operations where the debtor carries out a non-transitory economic activity with human means and goods or services.

[3.4]
Article 3
International obligations of this State

To the extent that this Law conflicts with an obligation of this State arising out of any treaty or other form of agreement to which it is a party with one or more other States, the requirements of the treaty or agreement prevail.

[3.5]
Article 4
Competent court or authority[1]

The functions referred to in this Law relating to recognition of foreign proceedings and cooperation with foreign courts shall be performed by *[specify the court, courts, authority or authorities competent to perform those functions in the enacting State]*.

NOTES

1 A State where certain functions relating to insolvency proceedings have been conferred upon government-appointed officials or bodies might wish to include in article 4 or elsewhere in chapter I the following provision:
"Nothing in this Law affects the provisions in force in this State governing the authority of *[insert the title of the government-appointed person or body]*.".

[3.6]
Article 5
Authorization of *[insert the title of the person or body administering reorganization or liquidation under the law of the enacting State]* to act in a foreign State

A *[insert the title of the person or body administering a reorganization or liquidation under the law of the enacting State]* is authorized to act in a foreign State on behalf of a proceeding under *[identify laws of the enacting State relating to insolvency]*, as permitted by the applicable foreign law.

[3.7]
Article 6
Public policy exception

Nothing in this Law prevents the court from refusing to take an action governed by this Law if the action would be manifestly contrary to the public policy of this State.

[3.8]
Article 7
Additional assistance under other laws

Nothing in this Law limits the power of a court or a *[insert the title of the person or body administering a reorganization or liquidation under the law of the enacting State]* to provide additional assistance to a foreign representative under other laws of this State.

[3.9]
Article 8
Interpretation

In the interpretation of this Law, regard is to be had to its international origin and to the need to promote uniformity in its application and the observance of good faith.

CHAPTER II ACCESS OF FOREIGN REPRESENTATIVES AND CREDITORS TO COURTS IN THIS STATE

[3.10]
Article 9
Right of direct access
A foreign representative is entitled to apply directly to a court in this State.

[3.11]
Article 10
Limited jurisdiction
The sole fact that an application pursuant to this Law is made to a court in this State by a foreign representative does not subject the foreign representative or the foreign assets and affairs of the debtor to the jurisdiction of the courts of this State for any purpose other than the application.

[3.12]
Article 11
Application by a foreign representative to commence a proceeding under *[identify laws of the enacting State relating to insolvency]*
A foreign representative is entitled to apply to commence a proceeding under *[identify laws of the enacting State relating to insolvency]* if the conditions for commencing such a proceeding are otherwise met.

[3.13]
Article 12
Participation of a foreign representative in a proceeding under *[identify laws of the enacting State relating to insolvency]*
Upon recognition of a foreign proceeding, the foreign representative is entitled to participate in a proceeding regarding the debtor under *[identify laws of the enacting State relating to insolvency]*.

[3.14]
Article 13
Access of foreign creditors to a proceeding under *[identify laws of the enacting State relating to insolvency]*
1. Subject to paragraph 2 of this article, foreign creditors have the same rights regarding the commencement of, and participation in, a proceeding under *[identify laws of the enacting State relating to insolvency]* as creditors in this State.
2. Paragraph 1 of this article does not affect the ranking of claims in a proceeding under *[identify laws of the enacting State relating to insolvency]*, except that the claims of foreign creditors shall not be ranked lower than *[identify the class of general non-preference claims, while providing that a foreign claim is to be ranked lower than the general non-preference claims if an equivalent local claim (eg claim for a penalty or deferred-payment claim) has a rank lower than the general non-preference claims]*. [1]

NOTES

[1] The enacting State may wish to consider the following alternative wording to replace paragraph 2 of article 13(2):

"2. Paragraph 1 of this article does not affect the ranking of claims in a proceeding under *[identify laws of the enacting State relating to insolvency]* or the exclusion of foreign tax and social security claims from such a proceeding. Nevertheless, the claims of foreign creditors other than those concerning tax and social security obligations shall not be ranked lower than *[identify the class of general non-preference claims, while providing that a foreign claim is to be ranked lower than the general non-preference claims if an equivalent local claim (eg claim for a penalty or deferred-payment claim) has a rank lower than the general non-preference claims]*.".

[3.15]
Article 14
Notification to foreign creditors of a proceeding under *[identify laws of the enacting State relating to insolvency]*
1. Whenever under *[identify laws of the enacting State relating to insolvency]* notification is to be given to creditors in this State, such notification shall also be given to the known creditors that do not have addresses in this State. The court may order that appropriate steps be taken with a view to notifying any creditor whose address is not yet known.
2. Such notification shall be made to the foreign creditors individually, unless the court considers that, under the circumstances, some other form of notification would be more appropriate. No letters rogatory or other, similar formality is required.
3. When a notification of commencement of a proceeding is to be given to foreign creditors, the notification shall:
   (a) Indicate a reasonable time period for filing claims and specify the place for their filing;
   (b) Indicate whether secured creditors need to file their secured claims; and
   (c) Contain any other information required to be included in such a notification to creditors pursuant to the law of this State and the orders of the court.

CHAPTER III RECOGNITION OF A FOREIGN PROCEEDING AND RELIEF

[3.16]
Article 15
Application for recognition of a foreign proceeding

1. A foreign representative may apply to the court for recognition of the foreign proceeding in which the foreign representative has been appointed.
2. An application for recognition shall be accompanied by:
   (a) A certified copy of the decision commencing the foreign proceeding and appointing the foreign representative; or
   (b) A certificate from the foreign court affirming the existence of the foreign proceeding and of the appointment of the foreign representative; or
   (c) In the absence of evidence referred to in subparagraphs (a) and (b), any other evidence acceptable to the court of the existence of the foreign proceeding and of the appointment of the foreign representative.
3. An application for recognition shall also be accompanied by a statement identifying all foreign proceedings in respect of the debtor that are known to the foreign representative.
4. The court may require a translation of documents supplied in support of the application for recognition into an official language of this State.

[3.17]
Article 16
Presumptions concerning recognition

1. If the decision or certificate referred to in paragraph 2 of article 15 indicates that the foreign proceeding is a proceeding within the meaning of subparagraph (a) of article 2 and that the foreign representative is a person or body within the meaning of subparagraph (d) of article 2, the court is entitled to so presume.
2. The court is entitled to presume that documents submitted in support of the application for recognition are authentic, whether or not they have been legalized.
3. In the absence of proof to the contrary, the debtor's registered office, or habitual residence in the case of an individual, is presumed to be the centre of the debtor's main interests.

[3.18]
Article 17
Decision to recognize a foreign proceeding

1. Subject to article 6, a foreign proceeding shall be recognized if:
   (a) The foreign proceeding is a proceeding within the meaning of subparagraph (a) of article 2;
   (b) The foreign representative applying for recognition is a person or body within the meaning of subparagraph (d) of article 2;
   (c) The application meets the requirements of paragraph 2 of article 15; and
   (d) The application has been submitted to the court referred to in article 4.
2. The foreign proceeding shall be recognized:
   (a) As a foreign main proceeding if it is taking place in the State where the debtor has the centre of its main interests; or
   (b) As a foreign non-main proceeding if the debtor has an establishment within the meaning of subparagraph (f) of article 2 in the foreign State.
3. An application for recognition of a foreign proceeding shall be decided upon at the earliest possible time.
4. The provisions of articles 15, 16, 17 and 18 do not prevent modification or termination of recognition if it is shown that the grounds for granting it were fully or partially lacking or have ceased to exist.

[3.19]
Article 18
Subsequent information

From the time of filing the application for recognition of the foreign proceeding, the foreign representative shall inform the court promptly of:
   (a) Any substantial change in the status of the recognized foreign proceeding or the status of the foreign representative's appointment; and
   (b) Any other foreign proceeding regarding the same debtor that becomes known to the foreign representative.

[3.20]
Article 19
Relief that may be granted upon application for recognition of a foreign proceeding

1. From the time of filing an application for recognition until the application is decided upon, the court may, at the request of the foreign representative, where relief is urgently needed to protect the assets of the debtor or the interests of the creditors, grant relief of a provisional nature, including:
   (a) Staying execution against the debtor's assets;
   (b) Entrusting the administration or realization of all or part of the debtor's assets located in this State to the foreign representative or another person designated by the court, in order to protect and preserve the value of assets that, by their nature or because of other circumstances, are perishable, susceptible to devaluation or otherwise in jeopardy;
   (c) Any relief mentioned in paragraph 1(c), (d) and (g) of article 21.
2. *[Insert provisions (or refer to provisions in force in the enacting State) relating to notice.]*

3. Unless extended under paragraph 1(f) of article 21, the relief granted under this article terminates when the application for recognition is decided upon.
4. The court may refuse to grant relief under this article if such relief would interfere with the administration of a foreign main proceeding.

[3.21]
Article 20
Effects of recognition of a foreign main proceeding
1. Upon recognition of a foreign proceeding that is a foreign main proceeding,
 (a) Commencement or continuation of individual actions or individual proceedings concerning the debtor's assets, rights, obligations or liabilities is stayed;
 (b) Execution against the debtor's assets is stayed; and
 (c) The right to transfer, encumber or otherwise dispose of any assets of the debtor is suspended.
2. The scope, and the modification or termination, of the stay and suspension referred to in paragraph 1 of this article are subject to *[refer to any provisions of law of the enacting State relating to insolvency that apply to exceptions, limitations, modifications or termination in respect of the stay and suspension referred to in paragraph 1 of this article]*.
3. Paragraph 1(a) of this article does not affect the right to commence individual actions or proceedings to the extent necessary to preserve a claim against the debtor.
4. Paragraph 1 of this article does not affect the right to request the commencement of a proceeding under *[identify laws of the enacting State relating to insolvency]* or the right to file claims in such a proceeding.

[3.22]
Article 21
Relief that may be granted upon recognition of a foreign proceeding
1. Upon recognition of a foreign proceeding, whether main or non-main, where necessary to protect the assets of the debtor or the interests of the creditors, the court may, at the request of the foreign representative, grant any appropriate relief, including:
 (a) Staying the commencement or continuation of individual actions or individual proceedings concerning the debtor's assets, rights, obligations or liabilities, to the extent they have not been stayed under paragraph 1(a) of article 20;
 (b) Staying execution against the debtor's assets to the extent it has not been stayed under paragraph 1(b) of article 20;
 (c) Suspending the right to transfer, encumber or otherwise dispose of any assets of the debtor to the extent this right has not been suspended under paragraph 1(c) of article 20;
 (d) Providing for the examination of witnesses, the taking of evidence or the delivery of information concerning the debtor's assets, affairs, rights, obligations or liabilities;
 (e) Entrusting the administration or realization of all or part of the debtor's assets located in this State to the foreign representative or another person designated by the court;
 (f) Extending relief granted under paragraph 1 of article 19;
 (g) Granting any additional relief that may be available to *[insert the title of a person or body administering a reorganization or liquidation under the law of the enacting State]* under the laws of this State.
2. Upon recognition of a foreign proceeding, whether main or non-main, the court may, at the request of the foreign representative, entrust the distribution of all or part of the debtor's assets located in this State to the foreign representative or another person designated by the court, provided that the court is satisfied that the interests of creditors in this State are adequately protected.
3. In granting relief under this article to a representative of a foreign non-main proceeding, the court must be satisfied that the relief relates to assets that, under the law of this State, should be administered in the foreign non-main proceeding or concerns information required in that proceeding.

[3.23]
Article 22
Protection of creditors and other interested persons
1. In granting or denying relief under article 19 or 21, or in modifying or terminating relief under paragraph 3 of this article, the court must be satisfied that the interests of the creditors and other interested persons, including the debtor, are adequately protected.
2. The court may subject relief granted under article 19 or 21 to conditions it considers appropriate.
3. The court may, at the request of the foreign representative or a person affected by relief granted under article 19 or 21, or at its own motion, modify or terminate such relief.

[3.24]
Article 23
Actions to avoid acts detrimental to creditors
1. Upon recognition of a foreign proceeding, the foreign representative has standing to initiate *[refer to the types of actions to avoid or otherwise render ineffective acts detrimental to creditors that are available in this State to a person or body administering a reorganization or liquidation]*.
2. When the foreign proceeding is a foreign non-main proceeding, the court must be satisfied that the action relates to assets that, under the law of this State, should be administered in the foreign non-main proceeding.

[3.25]
Article 24
Intervention by a foreign representative in proceedings in this State
Upon recognition of a foreign proceeding, the foreign representative may, provided the requirements of the law of this State are met, intervene in any proceedings in which the debtor is a party.

CHAPTER IV COOPERATION WITH FOREIGN COURTS AND FOREIGN REPRESENTATIVES

[3.26]
Article 25
Cooperation and direct communication between a court of this State and foreign courts or foreign representatives
1. In matters referred to in article 1, the court shall cooperate to the maximum extent possible with foreign courts or foreign representatives, either directly or through a *[insert the title of a person or body administering a reorganization or liquidation under the law of the enacting State]*.
2. The court is entitled to communicate directly with, or to request information or assistance directly from, foreign courts or foreign representatives.

[3.27]
Article 26
Cooperation and direct communication between the *[insert the title of a person or body administering a reorganization or liquidation under the law of the enacting State]* and foreign courts or foreign representatives
1. In matters referred to in article 1, a *[insert the title of a person or body administering a reorganization or liquidation under the law of the enacting State]* shall, in the exercise of its functions and subject to the supervision of the court, cooperate to the maximum extent possible with foreign courts or foreign representatives.
2. The *[insert the title of a person or body administering a reorganization or liquidation under the law of the enacting State]* is entitled, in the exercise of its functions and subject to the supervision of the court, to communicate directly with foreign courts or foreign representatives.

[3.28]
Article 27
Forms of cooperation
Cooperation referred to in articles 25 and 26 may be implemented by any appropriate means, including:
(a) Appointment of a person or body to act at the direction of the court;
(b) Communication of information by any means considered appropriate by the court;
(c) Coordination of the administration and supervision of the debtor's assets and affairs;
(d) Approval or implementation by courts of agreements concerning the coordination of proceedings;
(e) Coordination of concurrent proceedings regarding the same debtor;
(f) [The enacting State may wish to list additional forms or examples of cooperation].

CHAPTER V CONCURRENT PROCEEDINGS

[3.29]
Article 28
Commencement of a proceeding under *[identify laws of the enacting State relating to insolvency]* after recognition of a foreign main proceeding
After recognition of a foreign main proceeding, a proceeding under *[identify laws of the enacting State relating to insolvency]* may be commenced only if the debtor has assets in this State; the effects of that proceeding shall be restricted to the assets of the debtor that are located in this State and, to the extent necessary to implement cooperation and coordination under articles 25, 26 and 27, to other assets of the debtor that, under the law of this State, should be administered in that proceeding.

[3.30]
Article 29
Coordination of a proceeding under *[identify laws of the enacting State relating to insolvency]* and a foreign proceeding
Where a foreign proceeding and a proceeding under *[identify laws of the enacting State relating to insolvency]* are taking place concurrently regarding the same debtor, the court shall seek cooperation and coordination under articles 25, 26 and 27, and the following shall apply:
(a) When the proceeding in this State is taking place at the time the application for recognition of the foreign proceeding is filed,
  (i) Any relief granted under article 19 or 21 must be consistent with the proceeding in this State; and
  (ii) If the foreign proceeding is recognized in this State as a foreign main proceeding, article 20 does not apply;
(b) When the proceeding in this State commences after recognition, or after the filing of the application for recognition, of the foreign proceeding,
  (i) Any relief in effect under article 19 or 21 shall be reviewed by the court and shall be modified or terminated if inconsistent with the proceeding in this State; and

(ii) If the foreign proceeding is a foreign main proceeding, the stay and suspension referred to in paragraph 1 of article 20 shall be modified or terminated pursuant to paragraph 2 of article 20 if inconsistent with the proceeding in this State;

(c) In granting, extending or modifying relief granted to a representative of a foreign non-main proceeding, the court must be satisfied that the relief relates to assets that, under the law of this State, should be administered in the foreign non-main proceeding or concerns information required in that proceeding.

[3.31]
Article 30
Coordination of more than one foreign proceeding

In matters referred to in article 1, in respect of more than one foreign proceeding regarding the same debtor, the court shall seek cooperation and coordination under articles 25, 26 and 27, and the following shall apply:

(a) Any relief granted under article 19 or 21 to a representative of a foreign non-main proceeding after recognition of a foreign main proceeding must be consistent with the foreign main proceeding;

(b) If a foreign main proceeding is recognized after recognition, or after the filing of an application for recognition, of a foreign non-main proceeding, any relief in effect under article 19 or 21 shall be reviewed by the court and shall be modified or terminated if inconsistent with the foreign main proceeding;

(c) If, after recognition of a foreign non-main proceeding, another foreign non-main proceeding is recognized, the court shall grant, modify or terminate relief for the purpose of facilitating coordination of the proceedings.

[3.32]
Article 31
Presumption of insolvency based on recognition of a foreign main proceeding

In the absence of evidence to the contrary, recognition of a foreign main proceeding is, for the purpose of commencing a proceeding under *[identify laws of the enacting State relating to insolvency]*, proof that the debtor is insolvent.

[3.33]
Article 32
Rule of payment in concurrent proceedings

Without prejudice to secured claims or rights in rem, a creditor who has received part payment in respect of its claim in a proceeding pursuant to a law relating to insolvency in a foreign State may not receive a payment for the same claim in a proceeding under *[identify laws of the enacting State relating to insolvency]* regarding the same debtor, so long as the payment to the other creditors of the same class is proportionately less than the payment the creditor has already received.

(Part Two (Guide to Enactment of the Model Law) outside the scope of this work.)

DIRECTIVE OF THE EUROPEAN PARLIAMENT AND OF THE COUNCIL

(2000/12/EC)

of 20 March 2000

relating to the taking up and pursuit of the business of credit institutions

NOTES

Date of publication in OJ: OJ L126, 26.5.2000, p 1.

Note: this Directive was repealed by European Parliament and Council Directive 2006/48/EC, Art 158(1), as from 20 July 2006, subject to transitional provisions. Articles 1, 2 only are reproduced due to their relevance in construing Council Directive 2001/24/EC at **[3.176]**.

TITLE I DEFINITIONS AND SCOPE

[3.34]
Article 1
Definitions

For the purpose of this Directive—

[1. "Credit institution" shall mean—

(a) an undertaking whose business is to receive deposits or other repayable funds from the public and to grant credits for its own account; or

(b) an electronic money institution within the meaning of Directive 2000/46/EC of the European Parliament and of the Council of 18 September 2000 on the taking up, pursuit and prudential supervision of the business of electronic money institutions.[1]]

Part 3 EU & International Materials

For the purposes of applying the supervision on a consolidated basis, shall be considered as a credit institution, a credit institution according to the first paragraph and any private or public undertaking which corresponds to the definition in the first paragraph and which has been authorised in a third country.

For the purposes of applying the supervision and control of large exposures, shall be considered as a credit institution, a credit institution according to the first paragraph, including branches of a credit institution in third countries and any private or public undertaking, including its branches, which corresponds to the definition in the first paragraph and which has been authorised in a third country;

2. "authorisation" shall mean an instrument issued in any form by the authorities by which the right to carry on the business of a credit institution is granted;

3. "branch" shall mean a place of business which forms a legally dependent part of a credit institution and which carries out directly all or some of the transactions inherent in the business of credit institutions; any number of places of business set up in the same Member State by a credit institution with headquarters in another Member State shall be regarded as a single branch;

4. "competent authorities" shall mean the national authorities which are empowered by law or regulation to supervise credit institutions;

5. "financial institution" shall mean an undertaking other than a credit institution, the principal activity of which is to acquire holdings or to carry on one or more of the activities listed in points 2 to 12 of Annex I;

6. "home Member State" shall mean the Member State in which a credit institution has been authorised in accordance with Articles 4 to 11;

7. "host Member State" shall mean the Member State in which a credit institution has a branch or in which it provides services;

8. "control" shall mean the relationship between a parent undertaking and a subsidiary, as defined in Article 1 of Directive 83/349/EEC, or a similar relationship between any natural or legal person and an undertaking;

[9. "participation for the purposes of supervision on a consolidated basis and for the purposes of points 15 and 16 of Article 34(2)" shall mean participation within the meaning of the first sentence of Article 17 of Directive 78/660/EEC, or the ownership, direct or indirect, of 20% or more of the voting rights or capital of an undertaking;]

10. "qualifying holding" shall mean a direct or indirect holding in an undertaking which represents 10% or more of the capital or of the voting rights or which makes it possible to exercise a significant influence over the management of the undertaking in which a holding subsists;

11. "initial capital" shall mean capital as defined in Article 34(2)(1) and (2);

12. "parent undertaking" shall mean a parent undertaking as defined in Articles 1 and 2 of Directive 83/349/EEC.

It shall, for the purposes of supervision on a consolidated basis and control of large exposures, mean a parent undertaking within the meaning of Article 1(1) of Directive 83/349/EEC and any undertaking which, in the opinion of the competent authorities, effectively exercises a dominant influence over another undertaking;

13. "subsidiary" shall mean a subsidiary or undertaking as defined in Articles 1 and 2 of Directive 83/349/EEC.

It shall, for the purposes of supervision on a consolidated basis and control of large exposures, mean a subsidiary undertaking within the meaning of Article 1(1) of Directive 83/349/EEC and any undertaking over which, in the opinion of the competent authorities, a parent undertaking effectively exercises a dominant influence.

All subsidiaries of subsidiary undertakings shall also be considered subsidiaries of the undertaking that is their original parent;

14. "Zone A" shall comprise all the Member States and all other countries which are full members of the Organisation for Economic Cooperation and Development (OECD) and those countries which have concluded special lending arrangements with the International Monetary Fund (IMF) associated with the Fund's general arrangements to borrow (GAB). Any country which reschedules its external sovereign debt is, however, precluded from Zone A for a period of five years;

15. "Zone B" shall comprise all countries not in Zone A;

16. "Zone A credit institutions" shall mean all credit institutions authorised in the Member States, in accordance with Article 4, including their branches in third countries, and all private and public undertakings covered by the definitions in point 1, first subparagraph and authorised in other Zone A countries, including their branches;

17. "Zone B credit institutions" shall mean all private and public undertakings authorised outside Zone A covered by the definition in point 1, first subparagraph, including their branches within the Community;

18. "non-bank sector" shall mean all borrowers other than credit institutions as defined in points 16 and 17, central governments and central banks, regional governments and local authorities, the European Communities, the European Investment Bank (EIB) and multilateral development banks as defined in point 19;

[19. "multilateral development banks" shall mean the International Bank for Reconstruction and Development, the International Finance Corporation, the Inter-American Development Bank, the Asian Development Bank, the African Development Bank, the Council of Europe Resettlement Fund, the Nordic Investment Bank, the Caribbean Development Bank, the European Bank for Reconstruction and Development, the European Investment Fund, the Inter-American Investment Corporation and the Multilateral Investment Guarantee Agency;]

20. ""full-risk", "medium-risk", "medium/low-risk" and "low-risk" off-balance-sheet items" shall mean the items described in Article 43(2) and listed in Annex II;

[21. "financial holding company" shall mean a financial institution, the subsidiary undertakings of which are either exclusively or mainly credit institutions or financial institutions, at least one of such subsidiaries being a credit institution, and which is not a mixed financial holding company within the meaning of Directive 2002/87/EC of the European Parliament and of the Council of 16 December 2002 on the supplementary supervision of credit institutions, insurance undertakings and investment firms in a financial conglomerate;[2]

22. "mixed-activity holding company" shall mean a parent undertaking, other than a financial holding company or a credit institution or a mixed financial holding company within the meaning of Directive 2002/87/EC, the subsidiaries of which include at least one credit institution;]

23. "ancillary banking services undertaking" shall mean an undertaking the principal activity of which consists in owning or managing property, managing data-processing services, or any other similar activity which is ancillary to the principal activity of one or more credit institutions;

24. "exposures" for the purpose of applying Articles 48, 49 and 50 shall mean the assets and off-balance-sheet items referred to in Article 43 and in Annexes II and IV thereto, without application of the weightings or degrees of risk there provided for; the risks referred to in Annex IV must be calculated in accordance with one of the methods set out in Annex III, without application of the weightings for counterparty risk; all elements entirely covered by own funds may, with the agreement of the competent authorities, be excluded from the definition of exposures provided that such own funds are not included in the calculation of the solvency ratio or of other monitoring ratios provided for in this Directive and in other Community acts; exposures shall not include—

— *in the case of foreign exchange transactions, exposures incurred in the ordinary course of settlement during the 48 hours following payment, or*

— *in the case of transactions for the purchase or sale of securities, exposures incurred in the ordinary course of settlement during the five working days following payment or delivery of the securities, whichever is the earlier;*

25. "group of connected clients" shall mean—

— *two or more natural or legal persons who, unless it is shown otherwise, constitute a single risk because one of them, directly or indirectly, has control over the other or others or*

— *two or more natural or legal persons between whom there is no relationship of control as defined in the first indent but who are to be regarded as constituting a single risk because they are so interconnected that, if one of them were to experience financial problems, the other or all of the others would be likely to encounter repayment difficulties;*

26. "close links" shall mean a situation in which two or more natural or legal persons are linked by—

(a) participation, which shall mean the ownership, direct or by way of control, of 20% or more of the voting rights or capital of an undertaking, or

(b) control, which shall mean the relationship between a parent undertaking and a subsidiary, in all the cases referred to in Article 1(1) and (2) of Directive 83/349/EEC, or a similar relationship between any natural or

legal person and an undertaking; any subsidiary undertaking of a subsidiary undertaking shall also be considered a subsidiary of the parent undertaking which is at the head of those undertakings.

A situation in which two or more natural or legal persons are permanently linked to one and the same person by a control relationship shall also be regarded as constituting a close link between such persons;

27. "recognised exchanges" shall mean exchanges recognised by the competent authorities which—

(i) function regularly,

(ii) have rules, issued or approved by the appropriate authorities of the home country of the exchange, which define the conditions for the operation of the exchange, the conditions of access to the exchange as well as the conditions that must be satisfied by a contract before it can effectively be dealt on the exchange,

(iii) have a clearing mechanism that provides for contracts listed in Annex IV to be subject to daily margin requirements providing an appropriate protection in the opinion of the competent authorities.

NOTES

Repealed as noted at the beginning of this Directive.

Para 1: words in square brackets substituted by European Parliament and Council Directive 2000/28/EC, Art 1(1).

Paras 9, 21, 22: substituted by European Parliament and Council Directive 2002/87/EC, Art 29(1).

Para 19: substituted by Commission Directive 2004/69/EC, Art 1.

1 OJ L275, 27.10.2000, p 39.

2 OJ L35, 11.2.2003.

[3.35]
Article 2
Scope

1, 2. . . .

3. This Directive shall not apply to—

— *the central banks of Member States,*

— *post office giro institutions,*

— *in Belgium, the "Institut de Réescompte et de Garantie/Herdiscontering-en Waarborginstituut",*

[— *in Denmark, the "Dansk Eksportfinansieringsfond", the "Danmarks Skibskreditfond", the "Dansk Landbrugs Realkreditfond", and the "KommuneKredit",]*

— *in Germany, the "Kreditanstalt für Wiederaufbau", undertakings which are recognised under the "Wohnungsgemeinnützigkeitsgesetz" as bodies of State housing policy and are not mainly engaged in banking transactions, and undertakings recognised under that law as non-profit housing undertakings,*

[— *in Greece, the "Ταμείο Παρακαταθηκών και Δανείων" (Tamio Parakatathikon kai Danion),]*

— *in Spain, the "Instituto de Crédito Oficial",*

— *in France, the "Caisse des dépôts et consignations",*

— *in Ireland, credit unions and the friendly societies,*

— *in Italy, the "Cassa depositi e prestiti",*

— *in the Netherlands, the "Netherlandse Investeringsbank voor Ontwikkelingslanden NV", the "NV Noordelijke Ontwikkelingsmaatschappij", the "NV Industriebank Limburgs Instituut voor Ontwikkeling en Financiering" and the "Overijsselse Ontwikkelingsmaatschappij NV",*

— *in Austria, undertakings recognised as housing associations in the public interest and the "Österreichische Kontrollbank AG",*

— *in Portugal, "Caixas Económicas" existing on 1 January 1986 with the exception of those incorporated as limited companies and of the "Caixa Económica Montepio Geral",*

[— *in Finland, the "Teollisen yhteistyön rahasto Oy/Fonden för industriellt samarbete AB", and the "Finnvera Oyj/Finnvera Abp",]*

— *in Sweden, the "Svenska Skeppshypotekskassan",*

— *in the United Kingdom, the National Savings Bank, the Commonwealth Development Finance Company Ltd, the Agricultural Mortgage Corporation Ltd, the Scottish Agricultural Securities Corporation Ltd, the Crown Agents for overseas governments and administrations, credit unions and municipal banks,*

[— *in Latvia, the "krâjaizdevu sabiedrîbas", undertakings that are recognised under the "krâjaizdevu sabiedrîbu likums" as cooperative undertakings rendering financial services solely to their members,*

— *in Lithuania, the "kredito unijos" other than the "Centrinë kredito unija",*

— *in Hungary, the "Magyar Fejlesztési Bank Rt." and the "Magyar Export-Import Bank Rt.",*

— *in Poland, the "Spódzielcze Kasy Oszczêdnoœciowo-Kreditowe" and the "Bank Gospodarstwa Krajowego"].*

4–6. . . .

NOTES

Repealed as noted at the beginning of this Directive.

Paras 1–2, 4–6: outside the scope of this work.

Para 3: words in first, second and third pairs of square brackets substituted by Commission Directive 2006/29/EC, Arts 1–3; words in fourth pair of square brackets added by AA5.

COUNCIL REGULATION

(1346/2000/EC)

of 29 May 2000

on insolvency proceedings

[3.36]

NOTES

Date of publication in OJ: OJ L160, 30.06.2000, p 1.

This Regulation came into force on 31 May 2002; see Art 47 at **[3.83]**.

This Regulation is repealed by European Parliament and Council Regulation 2015/848/EU, Art 91, with effect from 26 June 2017; see Art 92 thereof at **[3.636]**.

THE COUNCIL OF THE EUROPEAN UNION,

Having regard to the Treaty establishing the European Community, and in particular Articles 61(c) and 67(1) thereof,

Having regard to the initiative of the Federal Republic of Germany and the Republic of Finland,

Having regard to the opinion of the European Parliament,[1]

Having regard to the opinion of the Economic and Social Committee,[2]

Whereas:

(1) The European Union has set out the aim of establishing an area of freedom, security and justice.

(2) The proper functioning of the internal market requires that cross-border insolvency proceedings should operate efficiently and effectively and this Regulation needs to be adopted in order to achieve this objective which comes within the scope of judicial cooperation in civil matters within the meaning of Article 65 of the Treaty.

(3) The activities of undertakings have more and more cross-border effects and are therefore increasingly being regulated by Community law. While the insolvency of such undertakings also affects the proper functioning of the internal market, there is a need for a Community act requiring coordination of the measures to be taken regarding an insolvent debtor's assets.

(4) It is necessary for the proper functioning of the internal market to avoid incentives for the parties to transfer assets or judicial proceedings from one Member State to another, seeking to obtain a more favourable legal position (forum shopping).

(5) These objectives cannot be achieved to a sufficient degree at national level and action at Community level is therefore justified.

(6) In accordance with the principle of proportionality this Regulation should be confined to provisions governing jurisdiction for opening insolvency proceedings and judgments which are delivered directly on the basis of the insolvency proceedings and are closely connected with such proceedings. In addition, this Regulation should contain provisions regarding the recognition of those judgments and the applicable law which also satisfy that principle.

(7) Insolvency proceedings relating to the winding-up of insolvent companies or other legal persons, judicial arrangements, compositions and analogous proceedings are excluded from the scope of the 1968 Brussels Convention on Jurisdiction and the Enforcement of Judgments in Civil and Commercial Matters,[3] *as amended by the Conventions on Accession to this Convention.*[4]

(8) In order to achieve the aim of improving the efficiency and effectiveness of insolvency proceedings having cross-border effects, it is necessary, and appropriate, that the provisions on jurisdiction, recognition and applicable law in this area should be contained in a Community law measure which is binding and directly applicable in Member States.

(9) This Regulation should apply to insolvency proceedings, whether the debtor is a natural person or a legal person, a trader or an individual. The insolvency proceedings to which this Regulation applies are listed in the Annexes. Insolvency proceedings concerning insurance undertakings, credit institutions, investment undertakings holding funds or securities for third parties and collective investment undertakings should be excluded from the scope of this Regulation. Such undertakings should not be covered by this Regulation since they are subject to special arrangements and, to some extent, the national supervisory authorities have extremely wide-ranging powers of intervention.

(10) Insolvency proceedings do not necessarily involve the intervention of a judicial authority; the expression "court" in this Regulation should be given a broad meaning and include a person or body empowered by national law to open insolvency proceedings. In order for this Regulation to apply, proceedings (comprising acts and formalities set down in law) should not only have to comply with the provisions of this Regulation, but they should also be officially recognised and legally effective in the Member State in which the insolvency proceedings are opened and should be collective insolvency proceedings which entail the partial or total divestment of the debtor and the appointment of a liquidator.

(11) This Regulation acknowledges the fact that as a result of widely differing substantive laws it is not practical to introduce insolvency proceedings with universal scope in the entire Community. The application without exception of the law of the State of opening of proceedings would, against this background, frequently lead to difficulties. This applies, for example, to the widely differing laws on security interests to be found in the Community. Furthermore, the preferential rights enjoyed by some creditors in the insolvency proceedings are, in some cases, completely different. This Regulation should take account of this in two different ways. On the one hand, provision should be made for special rules on applicable law in the case of particularly significant rights and legal relationships (eg rights in rem and contracts of employment). On the other hand, national proceedings covering only assets situated in the State of opening should also be allowed alongside main insolvency proceedings with universal scope.

(12) This Regulation enables the main insolvency proceedings to be opened in the Member State where the debtor has the centre of his main interests. These proceedings have universal scope and aim at encompassing all the debtor's assets. To protect the diversity of interests, this Regulation permits secondary proceedings to be opened to run in parallel with the main proceedings. Secondary proceedings may be opened in the Member State where the debtor has an establishment. The effects of secondary proceedings are limited to the assets located in that State. Mandatory rules of coordination with the main proceedings satisfy the need for unity in the Community.

(13) The "centre of main interests" should correspond to the place where the debtor conducts the administration of his interests on a regular basis and is therefore ascertainable by third parties.

(14) This Regulation applies only to proceedings where the centre of the debtor's main interests is located in the Community.

(15) The rules of jurisdiction set out in this Regulation establish only international jurisdiction, that is to say, they designate the Member State the courts of which may open insolvency proceedings. Territorial jurisdiction within that Member State must be established by the national law of the Member State concerned.

(16) The court having jurisdiction to open the main insolvency proceedings should be enabled to order provisional and protective measures from the time of the request to open proceedings. Preservation measures both prior to and after the commencement of the insolvency proceedings are very important to guarantee the effectiveness of the insolvency proceedings. In that connection this Regulation should afford different possibilities. On the one hand, the court competent for the main insolvency proceedings should be able also to order provisional protective measures covering assets situated in the territory of other Member States. On the other hand, a liquidator temporarily appointed prior to the opening of the main insolvency proceedings should be able, in the Member States in which an establishment belonging to the debtor is to be found, to apply for the preservation measures which are possible under the law of those States.

(17) Prior to the opening of the main insolvency proceedings, the right to request the opening of

insolvency proceedings in the Member State where the debtor has an establishment should be limited to local creditors and creditors of the local establishment or to cases where main proceedings cannot be opened under the law of the Member State where the debtor has the centre of his main interest. The reason for this restriction is that cases where territorial insolvency proceedings are requested before the main insolvency proceedings are intended to be limited to what is absolutely necessary. If the main insolvency proceedings are opened, the territorial proceedings become secondary.

(18) Following the opening of the main insolvency proceedings, the right to request the opening of insolvency proceedings in a Member State where the debtor has an establishment is not restricted by this Regulation. The liquidator in the main proceedings or any other person empowered under the national law of that Member State may request the opening of secondary insolvency proceedings.

(19) Secondary insolvency proceedings may serve different purposes, besides the protection of local interests. Cases may arise where the estate of the debtor is too complex to administer as a unit or where differences in the legal systems concerned are so great that difficulties may arise from the extension of effects deriving from the law of the State of the opening to the other States where the assets are located. For this reason the liquidator in the main proceedings may request the opening of secondary proceedings when the efficient administration of the estate so requires.

(20) Main insolvency proceedings and secondary proceedings can, however, contribute to the effective realisation of the total assets only if all the concurrent proceedings pending are coordinated. The main condition here is that the various liquidators must cooperate closely, in particular by exchanging a sufficient amount of information. In order to ensure the dominant role of the main insolvency proceedings, the liquidator in such proceedings should be given several possibilities for intervening in secondary insolvency proceedings which are pending at the same time. For example, he should be able to propose a restructuring plan or composition or apply for realisation of the assets in the secondary insolvency proceedings to be suspended.

(21) Every creditor, who has his habitual residence, domicile or registered office in the Community, should have the right to lodge his claims in each of the insolvency proceedings pending in the Community relating to the debtor's assets. This should also apply to tax authorities and social insurance institutions. However, in order to ensure equal treatment of creditors, the distribution of proceeds must be coordinated. Every creditor should be able to keep what he has received in the course of insolvency proceedings but should be entitled only to participate in the distribution of total assets in other proceedings if creditors with the same standing have obtained the same proportion of their claims.

(22) This Regulation should provide for immediate recognition of judgments concerning the opening, conduct and closure of insolvency proceedings which come within its scope and of judgments handed down in direct connection with such insolvency proceedings. Automatic recognition should therefore mean that the effects attributed to the proceedings by the law of the State in which the proceedings were opened extend to all other Member States. Recognition of judgments delivered by the courts of the Member States should be based on the principle of mutual trust. To that end, grounds for non-recognition should be reduced to the minimum necessary. This is also the basis on which any dispute should be resolved where the courts of two Member States both claim competence to open the main insolvency proceedings. The decision of the first court to open proceedings should be recognised in the other Member States without those Member States having the power to scrutinise the court's decision.

(23) This Regulation should set out, for the matters covered by it, uniform rules on conflict of laws which replace, within their scope of application, national rules of private international law. Unless otherwise stated, the law of the Member State of the opening of the proceedings should be applicable (lex concursus). This rule on conflict of laws should be valid both for the main proceedings and for local proceedings; the lex concursus determines all the effects of the insolvency proceedings, both procedural and substantive, on the persons and legal relations concerned. It governs all the conditions for the opening, conduct and closure of the insolvency proceedings.

(24) Automatic recognition of insolvency proceedings to which the law of the opening State normally applies may interfere with the rules under which transactions are carried out in other Member States. To protect legitimate expectations and the certainty of transactions in Member States other than that in which proceedings are opened, provisions should be made for a number of exceptions to the general rule.

(25) There is a particular need for a special reference diverging from the law of the opening State in the case of rights in rem, since these are of considerable importance for the granting of credit. The basis, validity and extent of such a right in rem should therefore normally be determined according to the lex situs and not be affected by the opening of insolvency proceedings. The proprietor of the right in rem should therefore be able to continue to assert his right to segregation or separate settlement of the collateral security. Where assets are subject to rights in rem under the lex situs in one Member State but the main proceedings are being carried out in another Member State, the liquidator in the main proceedings should be able to request the opening of secondary proceedings in the jurisdiction where the rights in rem arise if the debtor has an establishment there. If a secondary proceeding is not opened, the surplus on sale of the asset covered by rights in rem must be paid to the liquidator in the main proceedings.

(26) If a set-off is not permitted under the law of the opening State, a creditor should nevertheless be entitled to the set-off if it is possible under the law applicable to the claim of the insolvent debtor. In this way, set-off will acquire a kind of guarantee function based on legal provisions on which the creditor concerned can rely at the time when the claim arises.

(27) There is also a need for special protection in the case of payment systems and financial markets. This applies for example to the position-closing agreements and netting agreements to be found in such systems as well as to the sale of securities and to the guarantees provided for such transactions as

governed in particular by Directive 98/26/EC of the European Parliament and of the Council of 19 May 1998 on settlement finality in payment and securities settlement systems.[5] *For such transactions, the only law which is material should thus be that applicable to the system or market concerned. This provision is intended to prevent the possibility of mechanisms for the payment and settlement of transactions provided for in the payment and set-off systems or on the regulated financial markets of the Member States being altered in the case of insolvency of a business partner. Directive 98/26/EC contains special provisions which should take precedence over the general rules in this Regulation.*

(28) In order to protect employees and jobs, the effects of insolvency proceedings on the continuation or termination of employment and on the rights and obligations of all parties to such employment must be determined by the law applicable to the agreement in accordance with the general rules on conflict of law. Any other insolvency-law questions, such as whether the employees' claims are protected by preferential rights and what status such preferential rights may have, should be determined by the law of the opening State.

(29) For business considerations, the main content of the decision opening the proceedings should be published in the other Member States at the request of the liquidator. If there is an establishment in the Member State concerned, there may be a requirement that publication is compulsory. In neither case, however, should publication be a prior condition for recognition of the foreign proceedings.

(30) It may be the case that some of the persons concerned are not in fact aware that proceedings have been opened and act in good faith in a way that conflicts with the new situation. In order to protect such persons who make a payment to the debtor because they are unaware that foreign proceedings have been opened when they should in fact have made the payment to the foreign liquidator, it should be provided that such a payment is to have a debt-discharging effect.

(31) This Regulation should include Annexes relating to the organisation of insolvency proceedings. As these Annexes relate exclusively to the legislation of Member States, there are specific and substantiated reasons for the Council to reserve the right to amend these Annexes in order to take account of any amendments to the domestic law of the Member States.

(32) The United Kingdom and Ireland, in accordance with Article 3 of the Protocol on the position of the United Kingdom and Ireland annexed to the Treaty on European Union and the Treaty establishing the European Community, have given notice of their wish to take part in the adoption and application of this Regulation.

(33) Denmark, in accordance with Articles 1 and 2 of the Protocol on the position of Denmark annexed to the Treaty on European Union and the Treaty establishing the European Community, is not participating in the adoption of this Regulation, and is therefore not bound by it nor subject to its application,

NOTES

1 Opinion delivered on 2 March 2000 (not yet published in the Official Journal).

2 Opinion delivered on 26 January 2000 (not yet published in the Official Journal).

3 OJ L299, 31.12.1972, p 32.

4 OJ L204, 2.8.1975, p 28; OJ L304, 30.10.1978, p 1; OJ L388, 31.12.1982, p 1; OJ L285, 3.10.1989, p 1; OJ C15, 15.1.1997, p 1.

5 OJ L166, 11.6.1998, p 45.

HAS ADOPTED THIS REGULATION—

CHAPTER I GENERAL PROVISIONS

[3.37]
Article 1
Scope

1. This Regulation shall apply to collective insolvency proceedings which entail the partial or total divestment of a debtor and the appointment of a liquidator.

2. This Regulation shall not apply to insolvency proceedings concerning insurance undertakings, credit institutions, investment undertakings which provide services involving the holding of funds or securities for third parties, or to collective investment undertakings.

NOTES

Repealed as noted at the beginning of this Regulation.

[3.38]
Article 2
Definitions

For the purposes of this Regulation—

(a) "insolvency proceedings" shall mean the collective proceedings referred to in Article 1(1). These proceedings are listed in Annex A;

(b) "liquidator" shall mean any person or body whose function is to administer or liquidate assets of which the debtor has been divested or to supervise the administration of his affairs. Those persons and bodies are listed in Annex C;

(c) *"winding-up proceedings" shall mean insolvency proceedings within the meaning of point (a) involving realising the assets of the debtor, including where the proceedings have been closed by a composition or other measure terminating the insolvency, or closed by reason of the insufficiency of the assets. Those proceedings are listed in Annex B;*

(d) *"court" shall mean the judicial body or any other competent body of a Member State empowered to open insolvency proceedings or to take decisions in the course of such proceedings;*

(e) *"judgment" in relation to the opening of insolvency proceedings or the appointment of a liquidator shall include the decision of any court empowered to open such proceedings or to appoint a liquidator;*

(f) *"the time of the opening of proceedings" shall mean the time at which the judgment opening proceedings becomes effective, whether it is a final judgment or not;*

(g) *"the Member State in which assets are situated" shall mean, in the case of:*
- *tangible property, the Member State within the territory of which the property is situated,*
- *property and rights ownership of or entitlement to which must be entered in a public register, the Member State under the authority of which the register is kept,*
- *claims, the Member State within the territory of which the third party required to meet them has the centre of his main interests, as determined in Article 3(1);*

(h) *"establishment" shall mean any place of operations where the debtor carries out a non-transitory economic activity with human means and goods.*

NOTES

Repealed as noted at the beginning of this Regulation.

[3.39]
Article 3
International jurisdiction

1. The courts of the Member State within the territory of which the centre of a debtor's main interests is situated shall have jurisdiction to open insolvency proceedings. In the case of a company or legal person, the place of the registered office shall be presumed to be the centre of its main interests in the absence of proof to the contrary.

2. Where the centre of a debtor's main interests is situated within the territory of a Member State, the courts of another Member State shall have jurisdiction to open insolvency proceedings against that debtor only if he possesses an establishment within the territory of that other Member State. The effects of those proceedings shall be restricted to the assets of the debtor situated in the territory of the latter Member State.

3. Where insolvency proceedings have been opened under paragraph 1, any proceedings opened subsequently under paragraph 2 shall be secondary proceedings. These latter proceedings must be winding-up proceedings.

4. Territorial insolvency proceedings referred to in paragraph 2 may be opened prior to the opening of main insolvency proceedings in accordance with paragraph 1 only:

(a) *where insolvency proceedings under paragraph 1 cannot be opened because of the conditions laid down by the law of the Member State within the territory of which the centre of the debtor's main interests is situated; or*

(b) *where the opening of territorial insolvency proceedings is requested by a creditor who has his domicile, habitual residence or registered office in the Member State within the territory of which the establishment is situated, or whose claim arises from the operation of that establishment.*

NOTES

Repealed as noted at the beginning of this Regulation.

[3.40]
Article 4
Law applicable

1. Save as otherwise provided in this Regulation, the law applicable to insolvency proceedings and their effects shall be that of the Member State within the territory of which such proceedings are opened, hereafter referred to as the "State of the opening of proceedings".

2. The law of the State of the opening of proceedings shall determine the conditions for the opening of those proceedings, their conduct and their closure. It shall determine in particular:

(a) *against which debtors insolvency proceedings may be brought on account of their capacity;*

(b) *the assets which form part of the estate and the treatment of assets acquired by or devolving on the debtor after the opening of the insolvency proceedings;*

(c) *the respective powers of the debtor and the liquidator;*

(d) *the conditions under which set-offs may be invoked;*

(e) *the effects of insolvency proceedings on current contracts to which the debtor is party;*

(f) *the effects of the insolvency proceedings on proceedings brought by individual creditors, with the exception of lawsuits pending;*

(g) *the claims which are to be lodged against the debtor's estate and the treatment of claims arising after the opening of insolvency proceedings;*

(h) *the rules governing the lodging, verification and admission of claims;*

(i) *the rules governing the distribution of proceeds from the realisation of assets, the ranking of claims and the rights of creditors who have obtained partial satisfaction after the opening of insolvency proceedings by virtue of a right in rem or through a set-off;*
(j) *the conditions for and the effects of closure of insolvency proceedings, in particular by composition;*
(k) *creditors' rights after the closure of insolvency proceedings;*
(l) *who is to bear the costs and expenses incurred in the insolvency proceedings;*
(m) *the rules relating to the voidness, voidability or unenforceability of legal acts detrimental to all the creditors.*

NOTES

Repealed as noted at the beginning of this Regulation.

[3.41]
Article 5
Third parties' rights in rem

1. The opening of insolvency proceedings shall not affect the rights in rem of creditors or third parties in respect of tangible or intangible, moveable or immoveable assets—both specific assets and collections of indefinite assets as a whole which change from time to time—belonging to the debtor which are situated within the territory of another Member State at the time of the opening of proceedings.
2. The rights referred to in paragraph 1 shall in particular mean:
(a) *the right to dispose of assets or have them disposed of and to obtain satisfaction from the proceeds of or income from those assets, in particular by virtue of a lien or a mortgage;*
(b) *the exclusive right to have a claim met, in particular a right guaranteed by a lien in respect of the claim or by assignment of the claim by way of a guarantee;*
(c) *the right to demand the assets from, and/or to require restitution by, anyone having possession or use of them contrary to the wishes of the party so entitled;*
(d) *a right in rem to the beneficial use of assets.*

3. The right, recorded in a public register and enforceable against third parties, under which a right in rem within the meaning of paragraph 1 may be obtained, shall be considered a right in rem.
4. Paragraph 1 shall not preclude actions for voidness, voidability or unenforceability as referred to in Article 4(2)(m).

NOTES

Repealed as noted at the beginning of this Regulation.

[3.42]
Article 6
Set-off

1. The opening of insolvency proceedings shall not affect the right of creditors to demand the set-off of their claims against the claims of the debtor, where such a set-off is permitted by the law applicable to the insolvent debtor's claim.
2. Paragraph 1 shall not preclude actions for voidness, voidability or unenforceability as referred to in Article 4(2)(m).

NOTES

Repealed as noted at the beginning of this Regulation.

[3.43]
Article 7
Reservation of title

1. The opening of insolvency proceedings against the purchaser of an asset shall not affect the seller's rights based on a reservation of title where at the time of the opening of proceedings the asset is situated within the territory of a Member State other than the State of opening of proceedings.
2. The opening of insolvency proceedings against the seller of an asset, after delivery of the asset, shall not constitute grounds for rescinding or terminating the sale and shall not prevent the purchaser from acquiring title where at the time of the opening of proceedings the asset sold is situated within the territory of a Member State other than the State of the opening of proceedings.
3. Paragraphs 1 and 2 shall not preclude actions for voidness, voidability or unenforceability as referred to in Article 4(2)(m).

NOTES

Repealed as noted at the beginning of this Regulation.

[3.44]
Article 8
Contracts relating to immoveable property

The effects of insolvency proceedings on a contract conferring the right to acquire or make use of immoveable property shall be governed solely by the law of the Member State within the territory of which the immoveable property is situated.

NOTES

Repealed as noted at the beginning of this Regulation.

[3.45]
Article 9
Payment systems and financial markets
1. Without prejudice to Article 5, the effects of insolvency proceedings on the rights and obligations of the parties to a payment or settlement system or to a financial market shall be governed solely by the law of the Member State applicable to that system or market.
2. Paragraph 1 shall not preclude any action for voidness, voidability or unenforceability which may be taken to set aside payments or transactions under the law applicable to the relevant payment system or financial market.

NOTES
Repealed as noted at the beginning of this Regulation.

[3.46]
Article 10
Contracts of employment
The effects of insolvency proceedings on employment contracts and relationships shall be governed solely by the law of the Member State applicable to the contract of employment.

NOTES
Repealed as noted at the beginning of this Regulation.

[3.47]
Article 11
Effects on rights subject to registration
The effects of insolvency proceedings on the rights of the debtor in immoveable property, a ship or an aircraft subject to registration in a public register shall be determined by the law of the Member State under the authority of which the register is kept.

NOTES
Repealed as noted at the beginning of this Regulation.

[3.48]
Article 12
Community patents and trade marks
For the purposes of this Regulation, a Community patent, a Community trade mark or any other similar right established by Community law may be included only in the proceedings referred to in Article 3(1).

NOTES
Repealed as noted at the beginning of this Regulation.

[3.49]
Article 13
Detrimental acts
Article 4(2)(m) shall not apply where the person who benefited from an act detrimental to all the creditors provides proof that:
— *the said act is subject to the law of a Member State other than that of the State of the opening of proceedings, and*
— *that law does not allow any means of challenging that act in the relevant case.*

NOTES
Repealed as noted at the beginning of this Regulation.

[3.50]
Article 14
Protection of third-party purchasers
Where, by an act concluded after the opening of insolvency proceedings, the debtor disposes, for consideration, of:
— *an immoveable asset, or*
— *a ship or an aircraft subject to registration in a public register, or*
— *securities whose existence presupposes registration in a register laid down by law,*
the validity of that act shall be governed by the law of the State within the territory of which the immoveable asset is situated or under the authority of which the register is kept.

NOTES
Repealed as noted at the beginning of this Regulation.

[3.51]
Article 15
Effects of insolvency proceedings on lawsuits pending
The effects of insolvency proceedings on a lawsuit pending concerning an asset or a right of which the debtor has been divested shall be governed solely by the law of the Member State in which that lawsuit is pending.

NOTES

Repealed as noted at the beginning of this Regulation.

CHAPTER II RECOGNITION OF INSOLVENCY PROCEEDINGS

[3.52]
Article 16
Principle

1. Any judgment opening insolvency proceedings handed down by a court of a Member State which has jurisdiction pursuant to Article 3 shall be recognised in all the other Member States from the time that it becomes effective in the State of the opening of proceedings.

This rule shall also apply where, on account of his capacity, insolvency proceedings cannot be brought against the debtor in other Member States.

2. Recognition of the proceedings referred to in Article 3(1) shall not preclude the opening of the proceedings referred to in Article 3(2) by a court in another Member State. The latter proceedings shall be secondary insolvency proceedings within the meaning of Chapter III.

NOTES

Repealed as noted at the beginning of this Regulation.

[3.53]
Article 17
Effects of recognition

1. The judgment opening the proceedings referred to in Article 3(1) shall, with no further formalities, produce the same effects in any other Member State as under this law of the State of the opening of proceedings, unless this Regulation provides otherwise and as long as no proceedings referred to in Article 3(2) are opened in that other Member State.

2. The effects of the proceedings referred to in Article 3(2) may not be challenged in other Member States. Any restriction of the creditors' rights, in particular a stay or discharge, shall produce effects vis-à-vis assets situated within the territory of another Member State only in the case of those creditors who have given their consent.

NOTES

Repealed as noted at the beginning of this Regulation.

[3.54]
Article 18
Powers of the liquidator

1. The liquidator appointed by a court which has jurisdiction pursuant to Article 3(1) may exercise all the powers conferred on him by the law of the State of the opening of proceedings in another Member State, as long as no other insolvency proceedings have been opened there nor any preservation measure to the contrary has been taken there further to a request for the opening of insolvency proceedings in that State. He may in particular remove the debtor's assets from the territory of the Member State in which they are situated, subject to Articles 5 and 7.

2. The liquidator appointed by a court which has jurisdiction pursuant to Article 3(2) may in any other Member State claim through the courts or out of court that moveable property was removed from the territory of the State of the opening of proceedings to the territory of that other Member State after the opening of the insolvency proceedings. He may also bring any action to set aside which is in the interests of the creditors.

3. In exercising his powers, the liquidator shall comply with the law of the Member State within the territory of which he intends to take action, in particular with regard to procedures for the realisation of assets. Those powers may not include coercive measures or the right to rule on legal proceedings or disputes.

NOTES

Repealed as noted at the beginning of this Regulation.

[3.55]
Article 19
Proof of the liquidator's appointment

The liquidator's appointment shall be evidenced by a certified copy of the original decision appointing him or by any other certificate issued by the court which has jurisdiction.

A translation into the official language or one of the official languages of the Member State within the territory of which he intends to act may be required. No legalisation or other similar formality shall be required.

NOTES

Repealed as noted at the beginning of this Regulation.

[3.56]
Article 20
Return and imputation

1. A creditor who, after the opening of the proceedings referred to in Article 3(1) obtains by any means, in particular through enforcement, total or partial satisfaction of his claim on the assets belonging to the debtor situated within the territory of another Member State, shall return what he has obtained to the liquidator, subject to Articles 5 and 7.

2. In order to ensure equal treatment of creditors a creditor who has, in the course of insolvency proceedings, obtained a dividend on his claim shall share in distributions made in other proceedings only where creditors of the same ranking or category have, in those other proceedings, obtained an equivalent dividend.

NOTES

Repealed as noted at the beginning of this Regulation.

[3.57]
Article 21
Publication

1. The liquidator may request that notice of the judgment opening insolvency proceedings and, where appropriate, the decision appointing him, be published in any other Member State in accordance with the publication procedures provided for in that State. Such publication shall also specify the liquidator appointed and whether the jurisdiction rule applied is that pursuant to Article 3(1) or Article 3(2).

2. However, any Member State within the territory of which the debtor has an establishment may require mandatory publication. In such cases, the liquidator or any authority empowered to that effect in the Member State where the proceedings referred to in Article 3(1) are opened shall take all necessary measures to ensure such publication.

NOTES

Repealed as noted at the beginning of this Regulation.

[3.58]
Article 22
Registration in a public register

1. The liquidator may request that the judgment opening the proceedings referred to in Article 3(1) be registered in the land register, the trade register and any other public register kept in the other Member States.

2. However, any Member State may require mandatory registration. In such cases, the liquidator or any authority empowered to that effect in the Member State where the proceedings referred to in Article 3(1) have been opened shall take all necessary measures to ensure such registration.

NOTES

Repealed as noted at the beginning of this Regulation.

[3.59]
Article 23
Costs

The costs of the publication and registration provided for in Articles 21 and 22 shall be regarded as costs and expenses incurred in the proceedings.

NOTES

Repealed as noted at the beginning of this Regulation.

[3.60]
Article 24
Honouring of an obligation to a debtor

1. Where an obligation has been honoured in a Member State for the benefit of a debtor who is subject to insolvency proceedings opened in another Member State, when it should have been honoured for the benefit of the liquidator in those proceedings, the person honouring the obligation shall be deemed to have discharged it if he was unaware of the opening of proceedings.

2. Where such an obligation is honoured before the publication provided for in Article 21 has been effected, the person honouring the obligation shall be presumed, in the absence of proof to the contrary, to have been unaware of the opening of insolvency proceedings; where the obligation is honoured after such publication has been effected, the person honouring the obligation shall be presumed, in the absence of proof to the contrary, to have been aware of the opening of proceedings.

NOTES

Repealed as noted at the beginning of this Regulation.

[3.61]
Article 25
Recognition and enforceability of other judgments
1. Judgments handed down by a court whose judgment concerning the opening of proceedings is recognised in accordance with Article 16 and which concern the course and closure of insolvency proceedings, and compositions approved by that court shall also be recognised with no further formalities. Such judgments shall be enforced in accordance with Articles 31 to 51, with the exception of Article 34(2), of the Brussels Convention on Jurisdiction and the Enforcement of Judgments in Civil and Commercial Matters, as amended by the Conventions of Accession to this Convention.

The first subparagraph shall also apply to judgments deriving directly from the insolvency proceedings and which are closely linked with them, even if they were handed down by another court.

The first subparagraph shall also apply to judgments relating to preservation measures taken after the request for the opening of insolvency proceedings.

2. The recognition and enforcement of judgments other than those referred to in paragraph 1 shall be governed by the Convention referred to in paragraph 1, provided that that Convention is applicable.

3. The Member States shall not be obliged to recognise or enforce a judgment referred to in paragraph 1 which might result in a limitation of personal freedom or postal secrecy.

NOTES

Repealed as noted at the beginning of this Regulation.

[3.62]
Article 26
Public policy
Any Member State may refuse to recognise insolvency proceedings opened in another Member State or to enforce a judgment handed down in the context of such proceedings where the effects of such recognition or enforcement would be manifestly contrary to that State's public policy, in particular its fundamental principles or the constitutional rights and liberties of the individual.[1]

NOTES

Repealed as noted at the beginning of this Regulation.

[1] Note the Declaration by Portugal concerning the application of Articles 26 and 37 (OJ C183, 30.6.2000, p 1).

CHAPTER III SECONDARY INSOLVENCY PROCEEDINGS

[3.63]
Article 27
Opening of proceedings
The opening of the proceedings referred to in Article 3(1) by a court of a Member State and which is recognised in another Member State (main proceedings) shall permit the opening in that other Member State, a court of which has jurisdiction pursuant to Article 3(2), of secondary insolvency proceedings without the debtor's insolvency being examined in that other State. These latter proceedings must be among the proceedings listed in Annex B. Their effects shall be restricted to the assets of the debtor situated within the territory of that other Member State.

NOTES

Repealed as noted at the beginning of this Regulation.

[3.64]
Article 28
Applicable law
Save as otherwise provided in this Regulation, the law applicable to secondary proceedings shall be that of the Member State within the territory of which the secondary proceedings are opened.

NOTES

Repealed as noted at the beginning of this Regulation.

[3.65]
Article 29
Right to request the opening of proceedings
The opening of secondary proceedings may be requested by:
(a) the liquidator in the main proceedings;
(b) any other person or authority empowered to request the opening of insolvency proceedings under the law of the Member State within the territory of which the opening of secondary proceedings is requested.

NOTES

Repealed as noted at the beginning of this Regulation.

[3.66]
Article 30
Advance payment of costs and expenses
Where the law of the Member State in which the opening of secondary proceedings is requested requires that the debtor's assets be sufficient to cover in whole or in part the costs and expenses of the proceedings, the court may, when it receives such a request, require the applicant to make an advance payment of costs or to provide appropriate security.

NOTES
Repealed as noted at the beginning of this Regulation.

[3.67]
Article 31
Duty to cooperate and communicate information
1. Subject to the rules restricting the communication of information, the liquidator in the main proceedings and the liquidators in the secondary proceedings shall be duty bound to communicate information to each other. They shall immediately communicate any information which may be relevant to the other proceedings, in particular the progress made in lodging and verifying claims and all measures aimed at terminating the proceedings.
2. Subject to the rules applicable to each of the proceedings, the liquidator in the main proceedings and the liquidators in the secondary proceedings shall be duty bound to cooperate with each other.
3. The liquidator in the secondary proceedings shall give the liquidator in the main proceedings an early opportunity of submitting proposals on the liquidation or use of the assets in the secondary proceedings.

NOTES
Repealed as noted at the beginning of this Regulation.

[3.68]
Article 32
Exercise of creditors' rights
1. Any creditor may lodge his claim in the main proceedings and in any secondary proceedings.
2. The liquidators in the main and any secondary proceedings shall lodge in other proceedings claims which have already been lodged in the proceedings for which they were appointed, provided that the interests of creditors in the latter proceedings are served thereby, subject to the right of creditors to oppose that or to withdraw the lodgement of their claims where the law applicable so provides.
3. The liquidator in the main or secondary proceedings shall be empowered to participate in other proceedings on the same basis as a creditor, in particular by attending creditors' meetings.

NOTES
Repealed as noted at the beginning of this Regulation.

[3.69]
Article 33
Stay of liquidation
1. The court, which opened the secondary proceedings, shall stay the process of liquidation in whole or in part on receipt of a request from the liquidator in the main proceedings, provided that in that event it may require the liquidator in the main proceedings to take any suitable measure to guarantee the interests of the creditors in the secondary proceedings and of individual classes of creditors. Such a request from the liquidator may be rejected only if it is manifestly of no interest to the creditors in the main proceedings. Such a stay of the process of liquidation may be ordered for up to three months. It may be continued or renewed for similar periods.
2. The court referred to in paragraph 1 shall terminate the stay of the process of liquidation:
— *at the request of the liquidator in the main proceedings,*
— *of its own motion, at the request of a creditor or at the request of the liquidator in the secondary proceedings if that measure no longer appears justified, in particular, by the interests of creditors in the main proceedings or in the secondary proceedings.*

NOTES
Repealed as noted at the beginning of this Regulation.

[3.70]
Article 34
Measures ending secondary insolvency proceedings
1. Where the law applicable to secondary proceedings allows for such proceedings to be closed without liquidation by a rescue plan, a composition or a comparable measure, the liquidator in the main proceedings shall be empowered to propose such a measure himself.
Closure of the secondary proceedings by a measure referred to in the first subparagraph shall not become final without the consent of the liquidator in the main proceedings; failing his agreement, however, it may become final if the financial interests of the creditors in the main proceedings are not affected by the measure proposed.

2. Any restriction of creditors' rights arising from a measure referred to in paragraph 1 which is proposed in secondary proceedings, such as a stay of payment or discharge of debt, may not have effect in respect of the debtor's assets not covered by those proceedings without the consent of all the creditors having an interest.

3. During a stay of the process of liquidation ordered pursuant to Article 33, only the liquidator in the main proceedings or the debtor, with the former's consent, may propose measures laid down in paragraph 1 of this Article in the secondary proceedings; no other proposal for such a measure shall be put to the vote or approved.

NOTES

Repealed as noted at the beginning of this Regulation.

[3.71]
Article 35
Assets remaining in the secondary proceedings

If by the liquidation of assets in the secondary proceedings it is possible to meet all claims allowed under those proceedings, the liquidator appointed in those proceedings shall immediately transfer any assets remaining to the liquidator in the main proceedings.

NOTES

Repealed as noted at the beginning of this Regulation.

[3.72]
Article 36
Subsequent opening of the main proceedings

Where the proceedings referred to in Article 3(1) are opened following the opening of the proceedings referred to in Article 3(2) in another Member State, Articles 31 to 35 shall apply to those opened first, in so far as the progress of those proceedings so permits.

NOTES

Repealed as noted at the beginning of this Regulation.

[3.73]
Article 37
Conversion of earlier proceedings

The liquidator in the main proceedings may request that proceedings listed in Annex A previously opened in another Member State be converted into winding-up proceedings if this proves to be in the interests of the creditors in the main proceedings.

The court with jurisdiction under Article 3(2) shall order conversion into one of the proceedings listed in Annex B.[1]

NOTES

Repealed as noted at the beginning of this Regulation.

[1] Note the Declaration by Portugal concerning the application of Articles 26 and 37 (OJ C183, 30.6.2000, p 1).

[3.74]
Article 38
Preservation measures

Where the court of a Member State which has jurisdiction pursuant to Article 3(1) appoints a temporary administrator in order to ensure the preservation of the debtor's assets, that temporary administrator shall be empowered to request any measures to secure and preserve any of the debtor's assets situated in another Member State, provided for under the law of that State, for the period between the request for the opening of insolvency proceedings and the judgment opening the proceedings.

NOTES

Repealed as noted at the beginning of this Regulation.

CHAPTER IV PROVISION OF INFORMATION FOR CREDITORS AND LODGEMENT OF THEIR CLAIMS

[3.75]
Article 39
Right to lodge claims

Any creditor who has his habitual residence, domicile or registered office in a Member State other than the State of the opening of proceedings, including the tax authorities and social security authorities of Member States, shall have the right to lodge claims in the insolvency proceedings in writing.

NOTES

Repealed as noted at the beginning of this Regulation.

[3.76]
Article 40
Duty to inform creditors
1. As soon as insolvency proceedings are opened in a Member State, the court of that State having jurisdiction or the liquidator appointed by it shall immediately inform known creditors who have their habitual residences, domiciles or registered offices in the other Member States.
2. That information, provided by an individual notice, shall in particular include time limits, the penalties laid down in regard to those time limits, the body or authority empowered to accept the lodgement of claims and the other measures laid down. Such notice shall also indicate whether creditors whose claims are preferential or secured in rem need lodge their claims.

NOTES
Repealed as noted at the beginning of this Regulation.

[3.77]
Article 41
Content of the lodgement of a claim
A creditor shall send copies of supporting documents, if any, and shall indicate the nature of the claim, the date on which it arose and its amount, as well as whether he alleges preference, security in rem or a reservation of title in respect of the claim and what assets are covered by the guarantee he is invoking.

NOTES
Repealed as noted at the beginning of this Regulation.

[3.78]
Article 42
Languages
1. The information provided for in Article 40 shall be provided in the official language or one of the official languages of the State of the opening of proceedings. For that purpose a form shall be used bearing the heading "Invitation to lodge a claim. Time limits to be observed" in all the official languages of the institutions of the European Union.
2. Any creditor who has his habitual residence, domicile or registered office in a Member State other than the State of the opening of proceedings may lodge his claim in the official language or one of the official languages of that other State. In that event, however, the lodgement of his claim shall bear the heading "Lodgement of claim" in the official language or one of the official languages of the State of the opening of proceedings. In addition, he may be required to provide a translation into the official language or one of the official languages of the State of the opening of proceedings.

NOTES
Repealed as noted at the beginning of this Regulation.

CHAPTER V TRANSITIONAL AND FINAL PROVISIONS

[3.79]
Article 43
Applicability in time
The provisions of this Regulation shall apply only to insolvency proceedings opened after its entry into force. Acts done by a debtor before the entry into force of this Regulation shall continue to be governed by the law which was applicable to them at the time they were done.

NOTES
Repealed as noted at the beginning of this Regulation.

[3.80]
Article 44
Relationship to Conventions
1. After its entry into force, this Regulation replaces, in respect of the matters referred to therein, in the relations between Member States, the Conventions concluded between two or more Member States, in particular:

- *(a) the Convention between Belgium and France on Jurisdiction and the Validity and Enforcement of Judgments, Arbitration Awards and Authentic Instruments, signed at Paris on 8 July 1899;*
- *(b) the Convention between Belgium and Austria on Bankruptcy, Winding-up, Arrangements, Compositions and Suspension of Payments (with Additional Protocol of 13 June 1973), signed at Brussels on 16 July 1969;*
- *(c) the Convention between Belgium and the Netherlands on Territorial Jurisdiction, Bankruptcy and the Validity and Enforcement of Judgments, Arbitration Awards and Authentic Instruments, signed at Brussels on 28 March 1925;*
- *(d) the Treaty between Germany and Austria on Bankruptcy, Winding-up, Arrangements and Compositions, signed at Vienna on 25 May 1979;*
- *(e) the Convention between France and Austria on Jurisdiction, Recognition and Enforcement of Judgments on Bankruptcy, signed at Vienna on 27 February 1979;*
- *(f) the Convention between France and Italy on the Enforcement of Judgments in Civil and Commercial Matters, signed at Rome on 3 June 1930;*

(g) the Convention between Italy and Austria on Bankruptcy, Winding-up, Arrangements and Compositions, signed at Rome on 12 July 1977;

(h) the Convention between the Kingdom of the Netherlands and the Federal Republic of Germany on the Mutual Recognition and Enforcement of Judgments and other Enforceable Instruments in Civil and Commercial Matters, signed at The Hague on 30 August 1962;

(i) the Convention between the United Kingdom and the Kingdom of Belgium providing for the Reciprocal Enforcement of Judgments in Civil and Commercial Matters, with Protocol, signed at Brussels on 2 May 1934;

(j) the Convention between Denmark, Finland, Norway, Sweden and Iceland on Bankruptcy, signed at Copenhagen on 7 November 1933;

(k) the European Convention on Certain International Aspects of Bankruptcy, signed at Istanbul on 5 June 1990;

[(l) the Convention between the Federative People's Republic of Yugoslavia and the Kingdom of Greece on the Mutual Recognition and Enforcement of Judgments, signed at Athens on 18 June 1959;

(m) the Agreement between the Federative People's Republic of Yugoslavia and the Republic of Austria on the Mutual Recognition and Enforcement of Arbitral Awards and Arbitral Settlements in Commercial Matters, signed at Belgrade on 18 March 1960;

(n) the Convention between the Federative People's Republic of Yugoslavia and the Republic of Italy on Mutual Judicial Cooperation in Civil and Administrative Matters, signed at Rome on 3 December 1960;

(o) the Agreement between the Socialist Federative Republic of Yugoslavia and the Kingdom of Belgium on Judicial Cooperation in Civil and Commercial Matters, signed at Belgrade on 24 September 1971;

(p) the Convention between the Governments of Yugoslavia and France on the Recognition and Enforcement of Judgments in Civil and Commercial Matters, signed at Paris on 18 May 1971;

(q) the Agreement between the Czechoslovak Socialist Republic and the Hellenic Republic on Legal Aid in Civil and Criminal Matters, signed at Athens on 22 October 1980, still in force between the Czech Republic and Greece;

(r) the Agreement between the Czechoslovak Socialist Republic and the Republic of Cyprus on Legal Aid in Civil and Criminal Matters, signed at Nicosia on 23 April 1982, still in force between the Czech Republic and Cyprus;

(s) the Treaty between the Government of the Czechoslovak Socialist Republic and the Government of the Republic of France on Legal Aid and the Recognition and Enforcement of Judgments in Civil, Family and Commercial Matters, signed at Paris on 10 May 1984, still in force between the Czech Republic and France;

(t) the Treaty between the Czechoslovak Socialist Republic and the Italian Republic on Legal Aid in Civil and Criminal Matters, signed at Prague on 6 December 1985, still in force between the Czech Republic and Italy; signed at Tallinn on 27 November 1998;

(w) the Agreement between the Republic of Lithuania and the Republic of Poland on Legal Assistance and Legal Relations in Civil, Family, Labour and Criminal Matters, signed in Warsaw on 26 January 1993.]

[(x) the Convention between Socialist Republic of Romania and the Hellenic Republic on legal assistance in civil and criminal matters and its Protocol, signed at Bucharest on 19 October 1972;

(y) the Convention between Socialist Republic of Romania and the French Republic on legal assistance in civil and commercial matters, signed at Paris on 5 November 1974;

(z) the Agreement between the People's Republic of Bulgaria and the Hellenic Republic on Legal Assistance in Civil and Criminal Matters, signed at Athens on 10 April 1976;

(aa) the Agreement between the People's Republic of Bulgaria and the Republic of Cyprus on Legal Assistance in Civil and Criminal Matters, signed at Nicosia on 29 April 1983;

(ab) the Agreement between the Government of the People's Republic of Bulgaria and the Government of the French Republic on Mutual Legal Assistance in Civil Matters, signed at Sofia on 18 January 1989;

(ac) the Treaty between Romania and the Czech Republic on judicial assistance in civil matters, signed at Bucharest on 11 July 1994;

(ad) the Treaty between Romania and Poland on legal assistance and legal relations in civil cases, signed at Bucharest on 15 May 1999.]

2. The Conventions referred to in paragraph 1 shall continue to have effect with regard to proceedings opened before the entry into force of this Regulation.

3. This Regulation shall not apply:

(a) in any Member State, to the extent that it is irreconcilable with the obligations arising in relation to bankruptcy from a convention concluded by that State with one or more third countries before the entry into force of this Regulation;

(b) in the United Kingdom of Great Britain and Northern Ireland, to the extent that is irreconcilable with the obligations arising in relation to bankruptcy and the winding-up of insolvent companies from any arrangements with the Commonwealth existing at the time this Regulation enters into force.

NOTES

Repealed as noted at the beginning of this Regulation.

Para 1: sub-paras (l)–(w) added by AA5; sub-paras (x)–(ad) added by Council Regulation 1791/2006/EC, Art 1, Annex, Pt 11.

[3.81]
Article 45
Amendment of the Annexes
The Council, acting by qualified majority on the initiative of one of its members or on a proposal from the Commission, may amend the Annexes.

NOTES
Repealed as noted at the beginning of this Regulation.

[3.82]
Article 46
Reports
No later than 1 June 2012, and every five years thereafter, the Commission shall present to the European Parliament, the Council and the Economic and Social Committee a report on the application of this Regulation. The report shall be accompanied if need be by a proposal for adaptation of this Regulation.

NOTES
Repealed as noted at the beginning of this Regulation.

[3.83]
Article 47
Entry into force
This Regulation shall enter into force on 31 May 2002.
This Regulation shall be binding in its entirety and directly applicable in the Member States in accordance with the Treaty establishing the European Community.

NOTES
Repealed as noted at the beginning of this Regulation.

[ANNEX A
INSOLVENCY PROCEEDINGS REFERRED TO IN ARTICLE 2(A)

[3.84]
BELGIQUE/BELGIË
— *Het faillissement/La faillite,*
— *De gerechtelijke reorganisatie door een collectief akkoord/La réorganisation judiciaire par accord collectif,*
— *De gerechtelijke reorganisatie door overdracht onder gerechtelijk gezag/La réorganisation judiciaire par transfert sous autorité de justice,*
— *De collectieve schuldenregeling/Le règlement collectif de dettes,*
— *De vrijwillige vereffening/La liquidation volontaire,*
— *De gerechtelijke vereffening/La liquidation judiciaire,*
— *De voorlopige ontneming van beheer, bepaald in artikel 8 van de faillissementswet/Le dessaisissement provisoire, visé à l'article 8 de la loi sur les faillites,*

БЪЛГАРИЯ
— *Производство по несъстоятелност,*

ČESKÁ REPUBLIKA
— *Konkurs,*
— *Reorganizace,*
— *Oddlužení,*

DEUTSCHLAND
— *Das Konkursverfahren,*
— *Das gerichtliche Vergleichsverfahren,*
— *Das Gesamtvollstreckungsverfahren,*
— *Das Insolvenzverfahren,*

EESTI
— *Pankrotimenetlus,*

ÉIRE/IRELAND
— *Compulsory winding-up by the court,*
— *Bankruptcy,*
— *The administration in bankruptcy of the estate of persons dying insolvent,*
— *Winding-up in bankruptcy of partnerships,*
— *Creditors' voluntary winding-up (with confirmation of a court),*
— *Arrangements under the control of the court which involve the vesting of all or part of the property of the debtor in the Official Assignee for realisation and distribution,*
— *Company examinership,*
— *Debt Relief Notice,*
— *Debt Settlement Arrangement,*
— *Personal Insolvency Arrangement,*

ΕΛΛΑΔΑ

— Η πτώχευση,
— Η ειδική εκκαθάριση εν λειτουργία,
— Σχέδιο αναδιοργάνωσης,
— Απλοποιημένη διαδικασία επί πτωχεύσεων μικρού αντικειμένου,

ESPAÑA

— *Concurso,*

FRANCE

— *Sauvegarde,*
— *Redressement judiciaire,*
— *Liquidation judiciaire,*

HRVATSKA

— *Stečajni postupak,*

ITALIA

— *Fallimento,*
— *Concordato preventivo,*
— *Liquidazione coatta amministrativa,*
— *Amministrazione straordinaria,*

ΚΥΠΡΟΣ

— Υποχρεωτική εκκαθάριση από το Δικαστήριο,
— Εκούσια εκκαθάριση από μέλη,
— Εκούσια εκκαθάριση από πιστωτές,
— Εκκαθάριση με την εποπτεία του Δικαστηρίου,
— Διάταγμα Παραλαβής και πτώχευσης κατόπιν Δικαστικού Διατάγματος,
— Διαχείριση της περιουσίας προσώπων που απεβίωσαν αφερέγγυα,

LATVIJA

— *Tiesiskās aizsardzības process,*
— *Juridiskās personas maksātnespējas process,*
— *Fiziskās personas maksātnespējas process,*

LIETUVA

— *Įmonės restruktūrizavimo byla,*
— *Įmonės bankroto byla,*
— *Įmonės bankroto procesas ne teismo tvarka,*
— *Fizinio asmens bankroto byla,*

LUXEMBOURG

— *Faillite,*
— *Gestion contrôlée,*
— *Concordat préventif de faillite (par abandon d'actif),*
— *Régime spécial de liquidation du notariat,*
— *Procédure de règlement collectif des dettes dans le cadre du surendettement,*

MAGYARORSZÁG

— *Csődeljárás,*
— *Felszámolási eljárás,*

MALTA

— *Xoljiment,*
— *Amministrazzjoni,*
— *Stralċ volontarju mill-membri jew mill-kredituri,*
— *Stralċ mill-Qorti,*
— *Falliment f'każ ta' negozjant,*

NEDERLAND

— *Het faillissement,*
— *De surséance van betaling,*
— *De schuldsaneringsregeling natuurlijke personen,*

ÖSTERREICH

— *Das Konkursverfahren (Insolvenzverfahren),*
— *Das Sanierungsverfahren ohne Eigenverwaltung (Insolvenzverfahren),*
— *Das Sanierungsverfahren mit Eigenverwaltung (Insolvenzverfahren),*
— *Das Schuldenregulierungsverfahren,*
— *Das Abschöpfungsverfahren,*
— *Das Ausgleichsverfahren,*

POLSKA

— *Postępowanie naprawcze,*
— *Upadłość obejmująca likwidację,*
— *Upadłość z możliwością zawarcia układu,*

— *Upadłość,*
— *Przyspieszone postępowanie układowe,*
— *Postępowanie układowe,*
— *Postępowanie sanacyjne*

PORTUGAL
— *Processo de insolvência,*
— *Processo especial de revitalização,*

ROMÂNIA
— *Procedura insolvenţei,*
— *Reorganizarea judiciară,*
— *Procedura falimentului,*

SLOVENIJA
— *Stečajni postopek,*
— *Skrajšani stečajni postopek,*
— *Postopek prisilne poravnave,*
— *Prisilna poravnava v stečaju,*

SLOVENSKO
— *Konkurzné konanie,*
— *Reštrukturalizačné konanie,*
— *Oddlženie*

SUOMI/FINLAND
— *Konkurssi/konkurs,*
— *Yrityssaneeraus/företagssanering,*

SVERIGE
— *Konkurs,*
— *Företagsrekonstruktion,*

UNITED KINGDOM
— *Winding-up by or subject to the supervision of the court,*
— *Creditors' voluntary winding-up (with confirmation by the court),*
— *Administration, including appointments made by filing prescribed documents with the court,*
— *Voluntary arrangements under insolvency legislation,*
— *Bankruptcy or sequestration.]*

NOTES

Repealed as noted at the beginning of this Regulation.

Substituted by Council Implementing Regulation 2016/1792/EU, Art 1, Annex.

[ANNEX B
WINDING-UP PROCEEDINGS REFERRED TO IN ARTICLE 2(C)

[3.85]
BELGIQUE/BELGIË
— *Het faillissement/La faillite,*
— *De vrijwillige vereffening/La liquidation volontaire,*
— *De gerechtelijke vereffening/La liquidation judiciaire,*
— *De gerechtelijke reorganisatie door overdracht onder gerechtelijk gezag/La réorganisation judiciaire par transfert sous autorité de justice,*

БЪЛГАРИЯ
— *Производство по несъстоятелност,*

ČESKÁ REPUBLIKA
— *Konkurs,*

DEUTSCHLAND
— *Das Konkursverfahren,*
— *Das Gesamtvollstreckungsverfahren,*
— *Das Insolvenzverfahren,*

EESTI
— *Pankrotimenetlus,*

ÉIRE/IRELAND
— *Compulsory winding-up,*
— *Bankruptcy,*
— *The administration in bankruptcy of the estate of persons dying insolvent,*
— *Winding-up in bankruptcy of partnerships,*
— *Creditors' voluntary winding-up (with confirmation of a court),*
— *Arrangements under the control of the court which involve the vesting of all or part of the property of the debtor in the Official Assignee for realisation and distribution,*

ΕΛΛΑΔΑ
— Η πτώχευση,
— Η ειδική εκκαθάριση,
— *Απλοποιημένη* διαδικασία *επί* πτωχεύσεων *μικρού* αντικειμένου,

ESPAÑA
— *Concurso,*

FRANCE
— *Liquidation judiciaire,*

HRVATSKA
— *Stečajni postupak,*

ITALIA
— *Fallimento,*
— *Concordato preventivo,*
— *Liquidazione coatta amministrativa,*
— *Amministrazione straordinaria,*

ΚΥΠΡΟΣ
— Υποχρεωτική εκκαθάριση από το Δικαστήριο,
— Εκκαθάριση *με* την εποπτεία του Δικαστηρίου,
— Εκούσια εκκαθάριση από πιστωτές, *με* επιβεβαίωση του Δικαστηρίου,
— Πτώχευση,
— Διαχείριση της περιουσίας προσώπων που απεβίωσαν αφερέγγυα,

LATVIJA
— *Juridiskās personas maksātnespējas process,*
— *Fiziskās personas maksātnespējas process,*

LIETUVA
— *Įmonės bankroto byla,*
— *Įmonės bankroto procesas ne teismo tvarka,*

LUXEMBOURG
— *Faillite,*
— *Régime spécial de liquidation du notariat,*
— *Liquidation judiciaire dans le cadre du surendettement,*

MAGYARORSZÁG
— *Felszámolási eljárás,*

MALTA
— *Stralċ volontarju,*
— *Stralċ mill-Qorti,*
— *Falliment inkluż il-ħruġ ta' mandat ta' qbid mill-Kuratur f'każ ta' negozjant fallut,*

NEDERLAND
— *Het faillissement,*
— *De schuldsaneringsregeling natuurlijke personen,*

ÖSTERREICH
— *Das Konkursverfahren (Insolvenzverfahren),*

POLSKA
— *Upadłość obejmująca likwidację,*
— *Upadłość,*

PORTUGAL
— *Processo de insolvência,*

ROMÂNIA
— *Procedura falimentului,*

SLOVENIJA
— *Stečajni postopek,*
— *Skrajšani stečajni postopek,*

SLOVENSKO
— *Konkurzné konanie,*

SUOMI/FINLAND
— *Konkurssi/konkurs,*

SVERIGE
— *Konkurs,*

UNITED KINGDOM

— *Winding-up by or subject to the supervision of the court,*
— *Winding-up through administration, including appointments made by filing prescribed documents with the court,*
— *Creditors' voluntary winding-up (with confirmation by the court),*
— *Bankruptcy or sequestration.]*

NOTES

Repealed as noted at the beginning of this Regulation.
Substituted by Council Implementing Regulation 2016/1792/EU, Art 1, Annex.

[ANNEX C
LIQUIDATORS REFERRED TO IN ARTICLE 2(B)

[3.86]

BELGIQUE/BELGIË
— *De curator/Le curateur,*
— *De gedelegeerd rechter/Le juge-délégué,*
— *De gerechtsmandataris/Le mandataire de justice,*
— *De schuldbemiddelaar/Le médiateur de dettes,*
— *De vereffenaar/Le liquidateur,*
— *De voorlopige bewindvoerder/L'administrateur provisoire,*

БЪЛГАРИЯ
— *Назначен предварително временен синдик,*
— *Временен синдик,*
— *(Постоянен) синдик,*
— *Служебен синдик,*

ČESKÁ REPUBLIKA
— *Insolvenční správce,*
— *Předběžný insolvenční správce,*
— *Oddělený insolvenční správce,*
— *Zvláštní insolvenční správce,*
— *Zástupce insolvenčního správce,*

DEUTSCHLAND
— *Konkursverwalter,*
— *Vergleichsverwalter,*
— *Sachwalter (nach der Vergleichsordnung),*
— *Verwalter,*
— *Insolvenzverwalter,*
— *Sachwalter (nach der Insolvenzordnung),*
— *Treuhänder,*
— *Vorläufiger Insolvenzverwalter,*

EESTI
— *Pankrotihaldur,*
— *Ajutine pankrotihaldur,*
— *Usaldusisik,*

ÉIRE/IRELAND
— *Liquidator,*
— *Official Assignee,*
— *Trustee in bankruptcy,*
— *Provisional Liquidator,*
— *Examiner,*
— *Personal Insolvency Practitioner,*
— *Insolvency Service,*

ΕΛΛΑΔΑ
— Ο σύνδικος,
— Ο εισηγητής,
— Η επιτροπή των πιστωτών,
— Ο ειδικός εκκαθαριστής,

ESPAÑA
— *Administradores concursales,*

FRANCE
— *Mandataire judiciaire,*
— *Liquidateur,*
— *Administrateur judiciaire,*
— *Commissaire à l'exécution du plan,*

HRVATSKA
— *Stečajni upravitelj,*

— *Privremeni stečajni upravitelj,*
— *Stečajni povjerenik,*
— *Povjerenik,*

ITALIA
— *Curatore,*
— *Commissario giudiziale,*
— *Commissario straordinario,*
— *Commissario liquidatore,*
— *Liquidatore giudiziale,*

ΚΥΠΡΟΣ
— Εκκαθαριστής και Προσωρινός Εκκαθαριστής,
— Επίσημος Παραλήπτης,
— Διαχειριστής της Πτώχευσης,

LATVIJA
— *Maksātnespējas procesa administrators,*

LIETUVA
— *Bankroto administratorius,*
— *Restruktūrizavimo administratorius,*

LUXEMBOURG
— *Le curateur,*
— *Le commissaire,*
— *Le liquidateur,*
— *Le conseil de gérance de la section d'assainissement du notariat,*
— *Le liquidateur dans le cadre du surendettement,*

MAGYARORSZÁG
— *Vagyonfelügyelő,*
— *Felszámoló,*

MALTA
— *Amministratur Provižorju,*
— *Riċevitur Uffiċjali,*
— *Stralċjarju,*
— *Manager Speċjali,*
— *Kuraturi f'każ ta' proċeduri ta' falliment,*

NEDERLAND
— *De curator in het faillissement,*
— *De bewindvoerder in de surséance van betaling,*
— *De bewindvoerder in de schuldsaneringsregeling natuurlijke personen,*

ÖSTERREICH
— *Masseverwalter,*
— *Sanierungsverwalter,*
— *Ausgleichsverwalter,*
— *Besonderer Verwalter,*
— *Einstweiliger Verwalter,*
— *Sachwalter,*
— *Treuhänder,*
— *Insolvenzgericht,*
— *Konkursgericht,*

POLSKA
— *Syndyk,*
— *Nadzorca sądowy,*
— *Zarządca,*
— *Nadzorca układu,*
— *Tymczasowy nadzorca sądowy,*
— *Tymczasowy zarządca,*
— *Zarządca przymusowy,*

PORTUGAL
— *Administrador da insolvência,*
— *Administrador judicial provisório,*

ROMÂNIA
— *Practician în insolvenţă,*
— *Administrator judiciar,*
— *Lichidator,*

SLOVENIJA
— *Upravitelj prisilne poravnave,*

— *Stečajni upravitelj,*
— *Sodišče, pristojno za postopek prisilne poravnave,*
— *Sodišče, pristojno za stečajni postopek,*

SLOVENSKO
— *Predbežný správca,*
— *Správca,*

SUOMI/FINLAND
— *Pesänhoitaja/boförvaltare,*
— *Selvittäjä/utredare,*

SVERIGE
— *Förvaltare,*
— *Rekonstruktör,*

UNITED KINGDOM
— *Liquidator,*
— *Supervisor of a voluntary arrangement,*
— *Administrator,*
— *Official Receiver,*
— *Trustee,*
— *Provisional Liquidator,*
— *Judicial factor.]*

NOTES

Repealed as noted at the beginning of this Regulation.
Substituted by Council Implementing Regulation 2016/1792/EU, Art 1, Annex.

INSOLVENCY ACT 2000

(2000 c 39)

An Act to amend the law about insolvency; to amend the Company Directors Disqualification Act 1986; and for connected purposes.

[30 November 2000]

1–13 (*Ss 1–3, 7, 8 outside the scope of this work; ss 4–6, 9–13 contain amendments which in so far as relevant to this work have been incorporated at the appropriate place.*)

[3.87]
14 Model law on cross-border insolvency

(1) The Secretary of State may by regulations make any provision which he considers necessary or expedient for the purpose of giving effect, with or without modifications, to the model law on cross-border insolvency.

(2) In particular, the regulations may—
- (a) apply any provision of insolvency law in relation to foreign proceedings (whether begun before or after the regulations come into force),
- (b) modify the application of insolvency law (whether in relation to foreign proceedings or otherwise),
- (c) amend any provision of section 426 of the Insolvency Act 1986 (co-operation between courts),

and may apply or, as the case may be, modify the application of insolvency law in relation to the Crown.

(3) The regulations may make different provision for different purposes and may make—
- (a) any supplementary, incidental or consequential provision, or
- (b) any transitory, transitional or saving provision,

which the Secretary of State considers necessary or expedient.

(4) In this section—

"foreign proceedings" has the same meaning as in the model law on cross-border insolvency,

"insolvency law" has the same meaning as in section 426(10)(a) and (b) of the Insolvency Act 1986,

"the model law on cross-border insolvency" means the model law contained in Annex I of the report of the 30th session of UNCITRAL.

(5) Regulations under this section are to be made by statutory instrument and may only be made if a draft has been laid before and approved by resolution of each House of Parliament.

(6) Making regulations under this section requires the agreement—
- (a) if they extend to England and Wales, of the Lord Chancellor,
- (b) if they extend to Scotland, of the Scottish Ministers.

NOTES

Regulations: the Cross-Border Insolvency Regulations 2006, SI 2006/1030 at **[3.302]**.

15–18 (*S 15 contains amendments which in so far as relevant to this work have been incorporated at the appropriate place; ss 16–18 outside the scope of this work.*)

SCHEDULES 1–5

(Schs 1–5 contain amendments and repeals which in so far as relevant to this work have been incorporated at the appropriate place.)

COUNCIL DIRECTIVE

(2001/17/EC)

of 19 March 2001

on the reorganisation and winding-up of insurance undertakings

[3.88]

NOTES

Date of publication in OJ: OJ L110, 20.4.2001, p 28.

This Directive was implemented in the UK by the Insurers (Reorganisation and Winding Up) Regulations 2003, SI 2003/1102 (noted at **[3.123]**). These Regulations were revoked and replaced by the Insurers (Reorganisation and Winding Up) Regulations 2004, SI 2004/353, reg 53(1), subject to transitional provisions in reg 53(2), (3) thereof at **[3.175]**.

This Directive is repealed by European Parliament and Council Directive 2009/138/EC on the taking-up and pursuit of the business of Insurance and Reinsurance (Solvency II) at **[3.361]** et seq, with effect from 1 January 2016 (see Art 310 thereof (as amended)) and is reproduced for reference.

THE EUROPEAN PARLIAMENT AND THE COUNCIL OF THE EUROPEAN UNION,

Having regard to the Treaty establishing the European Community, and in particular Articles 47(2) and 55 thereof,

Having regard to the proposal from the Commission,[1]

Having regard to the opinion of the Economic and Social Committee,[2]

Acting in accordance with the procedure laid down in Article 251 of the Treaty,[3]

Whereas:

(1) First Council Directive 73/239/EEC of 24 July 1973 on the coordination of laws, regulations and administrative provisions relating to the taking up and pursuit of the business of direct insurance other than life assurance,[4] *as supplemented by Directive 92/49/EEC,*[5] *and the First Council Directive 79/267/EEC of 5 March 1979 on the coordination of laws, regulations and administrative provisions relating to the taking up and pursuit of the business of direct life assurance,*[6] *as supplemented by Directive 92/96/EEC,*[7] *provide for a single authorisation of the insurance undertakings granted by the home Member State supervisory authority. This single authorisation allows the insurance undertaking to carry out its activities in the Community by means of establishment or free provision of services without any further authorisation by the host Member State and under the sole prudential supervision of the home Member State supervisory authorities.*

(2) The insurance directives providing a single authorisation with a Community scope for the insurance undertakings do not contain coordination rules in the event of winding-up proceedings. Insurance undertakings as well as other financial institutions are expressly excluded from the scope of Council Regulation (EC) No 1346/2000 of 29 May 2000 on insolvency proceedings.[8] *It is in the interest of the proper functioning of the internal market and of the protection of creditors that coordinated rules are established at Community level for winding-up proceedings in respect of insurance undertakings.*

(3) Coordination rules should also be established to ensure that the reorganisation measures, adopted by the competent authority of a Member State in order to preserve or restore the financial soundness of an insurance undertaking and to prevent as much as possible a winding-up situation, produce full effects throughout the Community. The reorganisation measures covered by this Directive are those affecting pre-existing rights of parties other than the insurance undertaking itself. The measures provided for in Article 20 of Directive 73/239/EEC and Article 24 of Directive 79/267/EEC should be included within the scope of this Directive provided that they comply with the conditions contained in the definition of reorganisation measures.

(4) This Directive has a Community scope which affects insurance undertakings as defined in Directives 73/239/EEC and 79/267/EEC which have their head office in the Community, Community branches of insurance undertakings which have their head office in third countries and creditors resident in the Community. This Directive should not regulate the effects of the reorganisation measures and winding-up proceedings vis-à-vis third countries.

(5) This Directive should concern winding-up proceedings whether or not they are founded on insolvency and whether they are voluntary or compulsory. It should apply to collective proceedings as defined by the home Member State's legislation in accordance with Article 9 involving the realisation of the assets of an insurance undertaking and the distribution of their proceeds. Winding-up proceedings which, without being founded on insolvency, involve for the payment of insurance claims a priority order in accordance with Article 10 should also be included in the scope of this Directive. Claims by the employees of an insurance undertaking arising from employment contracts and employment relationships should be capable of being subrogated to a national wage guarantee scheme; such subrogated claims should benefit from the treatment determined by the home Member State's law (lex concursus) according

Part 3 EU & International Materials

to the principles of this Directive. The provisions of this Directive should apply to the different cases of winding-up proceedings as appropriate.

(6) The adoption of reorganisation measures does not preclude the opening of winding-up proceedings. Winding-up proceedings may be opened in the absence of, or following, the adoption of reorganisation measures and they may terminate with composition or other analogous measures, including reorganisation measures.

(7) The definition of branch, in accordance with existing insolvency principles, should take account of the single legal personality of the insurance undertaking. The home Member State's legislation should determine the way in which the assets and liabilities held by independent persons who have a permanent authority to act as agent for an insurance undertaking should be treated in the winding-up of an insurance undertaking.

(8) A distinction should be made between the competent authorities for the purposes of reorganisation measures and winding-up proceedings and the supervisory authorities of the insurance undertakings. The competent authorities may be administrative or judicial authorities depending on the Member State's legislation. This Directive does not purport to harmonise national legislation concerning the allocation of competences between such authorities.

(9) This Directive does not seek to harmonise national legislation concerning reorganisation measures and winding-up proceedings but aims at ensuring mutual recognition of Member States' reorganisation measures and winding-up legislation concerning insurance undertakings as well as the necessary cooperation. Such mutual recognition is implemented in this Directive through the principles of unity, universality, coordination, publicity, equivalent treatment and protection of insurance creditors.

(10) Only the competent authorities of the home Member State should be empowered to take decisions on winding-up proceedings concerning insurance undertakings (principle of unity). These proceedings should produce their effects throughout the Community and should be recognised by all Member States. All the assets and liabilities of the insurance undertaking should, as a general rule, be taken into consideration in the winding-up proceedings (principle of universality).

(11) The home Member State's law should govern the winding-up decision concerning an insurance undertaking, the winding-up proceedings themselves and their effects, both substantive and procedural, on the persons and legal relations concerned, except where this Directive provides otherwise. Therefore all the conditions for the opening, conduct and closure of winding-up proceedings should in general be governed by the home Member State's law. In order to facilitate its application this Directive should include a non-exhaustive list of aspects which, in particular, are subject to the general rule of the home Member State's legislation.

(12) The supervisory authorities of the home Member State and those of all the other Member States should be informed as a matter of urgency of the opening of winding-up proceedings (principle of coordination).

(13) It is of utmost importance that insured persons, policy-holders, beneficiaries and any injured party having a direct right of action against the insurance undertaking on a claim arising from insurance operations be protected in winding-up proceedings. Such protection should not include claims which arise not from obligations under insurance contracts or insurance operations but from civil liability caused by an agent in negotiations for which, according to the law applicable to the insurance contract or operation, the agent himself is not responsible under such insurance contract or operation. In order to achieve this objective Member States should ensure special treatment for insurance creditors according to one of two optional methods provided for in this Directive. Member States may choose between granting insurance claims absolute precedence over any other claim with respect to assets representing the technical provisions or granting insurance claims a special rank which may only be preceded by claims on salaries, social security, taxes and rights in rem over the whole assets of the insurance undertaking. Neither of the two methods provided for in this Directive impedes a Member State from establishing a ranking between different categories of insurance claims.

(14) This Directive should ensure an appropriate balance between the protection of insurance creditors and other privileged creditors protected by the Member State's legislation and not harmonise the different systems of privileged creditors existing in the Member States.

(15) The two optional methods for treatment of insurance claims are considered substantially equivalent. The first method ensures the affectation of assets representing the technical provisions to insurance claims, the second method ensures insurance claims a position in the ranking of creditors which not only affects the assets representing the technical provisions but all the assets of the insurance undertaking.

(16) Member States which, in order to protect insurance creditors, opt for the method of granting insurance claims absolute precedence with respect to the assets representing the technical provisions should require their insurance undertakings to establish and keep up to date a special register of such assets. Such a register is a useful instrument for identifying the assets affected to such claims.

(17) In order to strengthen equivalence between both methods of treatment of insurance claims, this Directive should oblige the Member States which apply the method set out in Article 10(1)(b) to require every insurance undertaking to represent, at any moment and independently of a possible winding-up, claims, which according to that method may have precedence over insurance claims and which are registered in the insurance undertaking's accounts, by assets allowed by the insurance directives in force to represent the technical provisions.

(18) The home Member State should be able to provide that, where the rights of insurance creditors

have been subrogated to a guarantee scheme established in such home Member State, claims by that scheme should not benefit from the treatment of insurance claims under this Directive.

(19) The opening of winding-up proceedings should involve the withdrawal of the authorisation to conduct business granted to the insurance undertaking unless such authorisation has previously been withdrawn.

(20) The decision to open winding-up proceedings, which may produce effects throughout the Community according to the principle of universality, should have appropriate publicity within the Community. In order to protect interested parties, the decision should be published in accordance with the home Member State's procedures and in the Official Journal of the European Communities and, further, by any other means decided by the other Member States' supervisory authorities within their respective territories. In addition to publication of the decision, known creditors who are resident in the Community should be individually informed of the decision and this information should contain at least the elements specified in this Directive. Liquidators should also keep creditors regularly informed of the progress of the winding-up proceedings.

(21) Creditors should have the right to lodge claims or to submit written observations in winding-up proceedings. Claims by creditors resident in a Member State other than the home Member State should be treated in the same way as equivalent claims in the home Member State without any discrimination on the grounds of nationality or residence (principle of equivalent treatment).

(22) This Directive should apply to reorganisation measures adopted by a competent authority of a Member State principles which are similar mutatis mutandis to those provided for in winding-up proceedings. The publication of such reorganisation measures should be limited to the case in which an appeal in the home Member State is possible by parties other than the insurance undertaking itself. When reorganisation measures affect exclusively the rights of shareholders, members or employees of the insurance undertaking considered in those capacities, the competent authorities should determine the manner in which the parties affected should be informed in accordance with relevant legislation.

(23) This Directive provides for coordinated rules to determine the law applicable to reorganisation measures and winding-up proceedings of insurance undertakings. This Directive does not seek to establish rules of private international law determining the law applicable to contracts and other legal relations. In particular, this Directive does not seek to govern the applicable rules on the existence of a contract, the rights and obligations of parties and the evaluation of debts.

(24) The general rule of this Directive, according to which reorganisation measures and the winding-up proceedings are governed by the law of the home Member State, should have a series of exceptions in order to protect legitimate expectations and the certainty of certain transactions in Member States other than the home Member State. Such exceptions should concern the effects of such reorganisation measures or winding-up proceedings on certain contracts and rights, third parties' rights in rem, reservations of title, set-off, regulated markets, detrimental acts, third party purchasers and lawsuits pending.

(25) The exception concerning the effects of reorganisation measures and winding-up proceedings on certain contracts and rights provided for in Article 19 should be limited to the effects specified therein and should not include any other issues related to reorganisation measures and winding-up proceedings such as the lodging, verification, admission and ranking of claims regarding such contracts and rights, which should be governed by the home Member State's legislation.

(26) The effects of reorganisation measures or winding-up proceedings on a lawsuit pending should be governed by the law of the Member States in which the lawsuit is pending concerning an asset or a right of which the insurance undertaking has been divested as an exception to the application of the law of the home Member State. The effects of such measures and proceedings on individual enforcement actions arising from these lawsuits should be governed by the home Member State's legislation, according to the general rule of this Directive.

(27) All persons required to receive or divulge information connected with the procedures of communication provided for in this Directive should be bound by professional secrecy in the same manner as that established in Article 16 of Directive 92/49/EEC and Article 15 of Directive 92/96/EEC, with the exception of any judicial authority to which specific national legislation applies.

(28) For the sole purpose of applying the provisions of this Directive to reorganisation measures and winding-up proceedings concerning branches situated in the Community of an insurance undertaking whose head office is located in a third country the home Member State should be defined as the Member State in which the branch is located and the supervisory authorities and competent authorities as the authorities of that Member State.

(29) Where there are branches in more than one Member State of an insurance undertaking whose head office is located outside the Community, each branch should be treated independently with regard to the application of this Directive. In that case the competent authorities, supervisory authorities, administrators and liquidators should endeavour to coordinate their actions,

NOTES

Repealed as noted at the beginning of this Directive.

1 OJ C71, 19.3.1987, p 5, and OJ C253, 6.10.1989, p 3.

2 OJ C319, 30.11.1987, p 10.

3 Opinion of the European Parliament of 15 March 1989 (OJ C96, 17.4.1989, p 99), confirmed on 27 October 1999, Council Common Position of 9 October 2000 (OJ C344, 1.12.2000, p 23) and Decision of the European Parliament of 15 February 2001.

[4] OJ L228, 16.8.1973, p 3. Directive as last amended by European Parliament and Council Directive 95/26/EC (OJ L168, 18.7.1995, p 7).

[5] Council Directive 92/49/EEC of 18 June 1992 on the coordination of laws, regulations and administrative provisions relating to direct insurance other than life assurance and amending Directives 73/239/EEC and 88/357/EEC (third non-life insurance directive) (OJ L228, 11.8.1992, p 1).

[6] OJ L63, 13.3.1979, p 1. Directive as last amended by Directive 95/26/EC.

[7] Council Directive 92/96/EEC of 10 November 1992 on the coordination of laws, regulations and administrative provisions relating to direct life assurance and amending Directives 79/267/EEC and 90/619/EEC (third life assurance directive) (OJ L360, 9.12.1992, p 1).

[8] OJ L160, 30.6.2000, p 1.

HAVE ADOPTED THIS DIRECTIVE—

TITLE I SCOPE AND DEFINITIONS

[3.89]
Article 1
Scope

1. This Directive applies to reorganisation measures and winding-up proceedings concerning insurance undertakings.

2. This Directive also applies, to the extent provided for in Article 30, to reorganisation measures and winding-up proceedings concerning branches in the territory of the Community of insurance undertakings having their head office outside the Community.

NOTES

Repealed as noted at the beginning of this Directive.

[3.90]
Article 2
Definitions

For the purpose of this Directive—

(a) "insurance undertaking" means an undertaking which has received official authorisation in accordance with Article 6 of Directive 73/239/EEC or Article 6 of Directive 79/267/EEC;

(b) "branch" means any permanent presence of an insurance undertaking in the territory of a Member State other than the home Member State which carries out insurance business;

(c) "reorganisation measures" means measures involving any intervention by administrative bodies or judicial authorities which are intended to preserve or restore the financial situation of an insurance undertaking and which affect pre-existing rights of parties other than the insurance undertaking itself, including but not limited to measures involving the possibility of a suspension of payments, suspension of enforcement measures or reduction of claims;

(d) "winding-up proceedings" means collective proceedings involving realising the assets of an insurance undertaking and distributing the proceeds among the creditors, shareholders or members as appropriate, which necessarily involve any intervention by the administrative or the judicial authorities of a Member State, including where the collective proceedings are terminated by a composition or other analogous measure, whether or not they are founded on insolvency or are voluntary or compulsory;

(e) "home Member State" means the Member State in which an insurance undertaking has been authorised in accordance with Article 6 of Directive 73/239/EEC or Article 6 of Directive 79/267/EEC;

(f) "host Member State" means the Member State other than the home Member State in which an insurance undertaking has a branch;

(g) "competent authorities" means the administrative or judicial authorities of the Member States which are competent for the purposes of the reorganisation measures or the winding-up proceedings;

(h) "supervisory authorities" means the competent authorities within the meaning of Article 1(k) of Directive 92/49/EEC and of Article 1(l) of Directive 92/96/EEC;

(i) "administrator" means any person or body appointed by the competent authorities for the purpose of administering reorganisation measures;

(j) "liquidator" means any person or body appointed by the competent authorities or by the governing bodies of an insurance undertaking, as appropriate, for the purpose of administering winding-up proceedings;

(k) "insurance claims" means any amount which is owed by an insurance undertaking to insured persons, policy holders, beneficiaries or to any injured party having direct right of action against the insurance undertaking and which arises from an insurance contract or from any operation provided for in Article 1(2) and (3), of Directive 79/267/EEC in direct insurance business, including amounts set aside for the aforementioned persons, when some elements of the debt are not yet known. The premiums owed by an insurance undertaking as a result of the non-conclusion or cancellation of these insurance contracts and operations in accordance with the law applicable to such contracts or operations before the opening of the winding-up proceedings shall also be considered insurance claims.

NOTES

Repealed as noted at the beginning of this Directive.

TITLE II REORGANISATION MEASURES

[3.91]
Article 3
Scope
This Title applies to the reorganisation measures defined in Article 2(c).

NOTES
Repealed as noted at the beginning of this Directive.

[3.92]
Article 4
Adoption of reorganisation measures—applicable law
1. Only the competent authorities of the home Member State shall be entitled to decide on the reorganisation measures with respect to an insurance undertaking, including its branches in other Member States. The reorganisation measures shall not preclude the opening of winding-up proceedings by the home Member State.
2. The reorganisation measures shall be governed by the laws, regulations and procedures applicable in the home Member State, unless otherwise provided in Articles 19 to 26.
3. The reorganisation measures shall be fully effective throughout the Community in accordance with the legislation of the home Member State without any further formalities, including against third parties in other Member States, even if the legislation of those other Member States does not provide for such reorganisation measures or alternatively makes their implementation subject to conditions which are not fulfilled.
4. The reorganisation measures shall be effective throughout the Community once they become effective in the Member State where they have been taken.

NOTES
Repealed as noted at the beginning of this Directive.

[3.93]
Article 5
Information to the supervisory authorities
The competent authorities of the home Member State shall inform as a matter of urgency the home Member State's supervisory authorities of their decision on any reorganisation measure, where possible before the adoption of such a measure and failing that immediately thereafter. The supervisory authorities of the home Member State shall inform as a matter of urgency the supervisory authorities of all other Member States of the decision to adopt reorganisation measures including the possible practical effects of such measures.

NOTES
Repealed as noted at the beginning of this Directive.

[3.94]
Article 6
Publication
1. Where an appeal is possible in the home Member State against a reorganisation measure, the competent authorities of the home Member State, the administrator or any person entitled to do so in the home Member State shall make public its decision on a reorganisation measure in accordance with the publication procedures provided for in the home Member State and, furthermore, publish in the Official Journal of the European Communities at the earliest opportunity an extract from the document establishing the reorganisation measure. The supervisory authorities of all the other Member States which have been informed of the decision on a reorganisation measure pursuant to Article 5 may ensure the publication of such decision within their territory in the manner they consider appropriate.
2. The publications provided for in paragraph 1 shall also specify the competent authority of the home Member State, the applicable law as provided in Article 4(2) and the administrator appointed, if any. They shall be carried out in the official language or in one of the official languages of the Member State in which the information is published.
3. The reorganisation measures shall apply regardless of the provisions concerning publication set out in paragraphs 1 and 2 and shall be fully effective as against creditors, unless the competent authorities of the home Member State or the law of that State provide otherwise.
4. When reorganisation measures affect exclusively the rights of shareholders, members or employees of an insurance undertaking, considered in those capacities, this Article shall not apply unless the law applicable to these reorganisation measures provides otherwise. The competent authorities shall determine the manner in which the interested parties affected by such reorganisation measures shall be informed in accordance with the relevant legislation.

NOTES
Repealed as noted at the beginning of this Directive.

[3.95]
Article 7
Information to known creditors—right to lodge claims
1. Where the legislation of the home Member State requires lodgement of a claim with a view to its recognition or provides for compulsory notification of a reorganisation measure to creditors who have their normal place of residence, domicile or head office in that State, the competent authorities of the home Member State or the administrator shall also inform known creditors who have their normal place of residence, domicile or head office in another Member State, in accordance with the procedures laid down in Articles 15 and 17(1).
2. Where the legislation of the home Member State provides for the right of creditors who have their normal place of residence, domicile or head office in that State to lodge claims or to submit observations concerning their claims, creditors who have their normal place of residence, domicile or head office in another Member State shall have the same right to lodge claims or submit observations in accordance with the procedures laid down in Articles 16 and 17(2).

NOTES
Repealed as noted at the beginning of this Directive.

TITLE III WINDING-UP PROCEEDINGS

[3.96]
Article 8
Opening of winding-up proceedings—information to the supervisory authorities
1. Only the competent authorities of the home Member State shall be entitled to take a decision concerning the opening of winding-up proceedings with regard to an insurance undertaking, including its branches in other Member States. This decision may be taken in the absence, or following the adoption, of reorganisation measures.
2. A decision adopted according to the home Member State's legislation concerning the opening of winding-up proceedings of an insurance undertaking, including its branches in other Member States, shall be recognised without further formality within the territory of all other Member States and shall be effective there as soon as the decision is effective in the Member State in which the proceedings are opened.
3. The supervisory authorities of the home Member State shall be informed as a matter of urgency of the decision to open winding-up proceedings, if possible before the proceedings are opened and failing that immediately thereafter. The supervisory authorities of the home Member State shall inform as a matter of urgency the supervisory authorities of all other Member States of the decision to open winding-up proceedings including the possible practical effects of such proceedings.

NOTES
Repealed as noted at the beginning of this Directive.

[3.97]
Article 9
Applicable law
1. The decision to open winding-up proceedings with regard to an insurance undertaking, the winding-up proceedings and their effects shall be governed by the laws, regulations and administrative provisions applicable in its home Member State unless otherwise provided in Articles 19 to 26.
2. The law of the home Member State shall determine in particular—
- *(a) the assets which form part of the estate and the treatment of assets acquired by, or devolving on, the insurance undertaking after the opening of the winding-up proceedings;*
- *(b) the respective powers of the insurance undertaking and the liquidator;*
- *(c) the conditions under which set-off may be invoked;*
- *(d) the effects of the winding-up proceedings on current contracts to which the insurance undertaking is party;*
- *(e) the effects of the winding-up proceedings on proceedings brought by individual creditors, with the exception of lawsuits pending as provided for in Article 26;*
- *(f) the claims which are to be lodged against the insurance undertaking's estate and the treatment of claims arising after the opening of winding-up proceedings;*
- *(g) the rules governing the lodging, verification and admission of claims;*
- *(h) the rules governing the distribution of proceeds from the realisation of assets, the ranking of claims, and the rights of creditors who have obtained partial satisfaction after the opening of winding-up proceedings by virtue of a right in rem or through a set-off;*
- *(i) the conditions for and the effects of closure of winding-up proceedings, in particular by composition;*
- *(j) creditors' rights after the closure of winding-up proceedings;*
- *(k) who is to bear the cost and expenses incurred in the winding-up proceedings;*
- *(l) the rules relating to the voidness, voidability or unenforceability of legal acts detrimental to all the creditors.*

NOTES
Repealed as noted at the beginning of this Directive.

[3.98]
Article 10
Treatment of insurance claims
1. Member States shall ensure that insurance claims take precedence over other claims on the insurance undertaking according to one or both of the following methods—
- *(a) insurance claims shall, with respect to assets representing the technical provisions, take absolute precedence over any other claim on the insurance undertaking;*
- *(b) insurance claims shall, with respect to the whole of the insurance undertaking's assets, take precedence over any other claim on the insurance undertaking with the only possible exception of—*
  - *(i) claims by employees arising from employment contracts and employment relationships,*
  - *(ii) claims by public bodies on taxes,*
  - *(iii) claims by social security systems,*
  - *(iv) claims on assets subject to rights in rem.*

2. Without prejudice to paragraph 1, Member States may provide that the whole or a part of the expenses arising from the winding-up procedure, as defined by their national legislation, shall take precedence over insurance claims.
3. Member States which have opted for the method provided for in paragraph 1(a) shall require that insurance undertakings establish and keep up to date a special register in line with the provisions set out in the Annex.

NOTES
Repealed as noted at the beginning of this Directive.

[3.99]
Article 11
Subrogation to a guarantee scheme
The home Member State may provide that, where the rights of insurance creditors have been subrogated to a guarantee scheme established in that Member State, claims by that scheme shall not benefit from the provisions of Article 10(1).

NOTES
Repealed as noted at the beginning of this Directive.

[3.100]
Article 12
Representation of preferential claims by assets
By way of derogation from Article 18 of Directive 73/239/EEC and Article 21 of Directive 79/267/EEC, Member States which apply the method set out in Article 10(1)(b) of this Directive shall require every insurance undertaking to represent, at any moment and independently from a possible winding-up, the claims which may take precedence over insurance claims pursuant to Article 10(1)(b) and which are registered in the insurance undertaking's accounts, by assets mentioned in Article 21 of Directive 92/49/EEC and Article 21 of Directive 92/96/EEC.

NOTES
Repealed as noted at the beginning of this Directive.

[3.101]
Article 13
Withdrawal of the authorisation
1. Where the opening of winding-up proceedings is decided in respect of an insurance undertaking, the authorisation of the insurance undertaking shall be withdrawn, except to the extent necessary for the purposes of paragraph 2, in accordance with the procedure laid down in Article 22 of Directive 73/239/EEC and Article 26 of Directive 79/267/EEC, if the authorisation has not been previously withdrawn.
2. The withdrawal of authorisation pursuant to paragraph 1 shall not prevent the liquidator or any other person entrusted by the competent authorities from carrying on some of the insurance undertakings' activities in so far as that is necessary or appropriate for the purposes of winding-up. The home Member State may provide that such activities shall be carried on with the consent and under the supervision of the supervisory authorities of the home Member State.

NOTES
Repealed as noted at the beginning of this Directive.

[3.102]
Article 14
Publication
1. The competent authority, the liquidator or any person appointed for that purpose by the competent authority shall publish the decision to open winding-up proceedings in accordance with the publication procedures provided for in the home Member State and also publish an extract from the winding-up

decision in the Official Journal of the European Communities. The supervisory authorities of all the other Member States which have been informed of the decision to open winding-up proceedings in accordance with Article 8(3) may ensure the publication of such decision within their territories in the manner they consider appropriate.

2. The publication of the decision to open winding-up proceedings provided for in paragraph 1 shall also specify the competent authority of the home Member State, the applicable law and the liquidator appointed. It shall be in the official language or in one of the official languages of the Member State in which the information is published.

NOTES

Repealed as noted at the beginning of this Directive.

[3.103]
Article 15
Information to known creditors

1. When winding-up proceedings are opened, the competent authorities of the home Member State, the liquidator or any person appointed for that purpose by the competent authorities shall without delay individually inform by written notice each known creditor who has his normal place of residence, domicile or head office in another Member State thereof.

2. The notice referred to in paragraph 1 shall in particular deal with time limits, the penalties laid down with regard to those time limits, the body or authority empowered to accept the lodgement of claims or observations relating to claims and the other measures laid down. The notice shall also indicate whether creditors whose claims are preferential or secured in rem need to lodge their claims. In the case of insurance claims, the notice shall further indicate the general effects of the winding-up proceedings on the insurance contracts, in particular, the date on which the insurance contracts or the operations will cease to produce effects and the rights and duties of insured persons with regard to the contract or operation.

NOTES

Repealed as noted at the beginning of this Directive.

[3.104]
Article 16
Right to lodge claims

1. Any creditor who has his normal place of residence, domicile or head office in a Member State other than the home Member State, including Member States' public authorities, shall have the right to lodge claims or to submit written observations relating to claims.

2. The claims of all creditors who have their normal place of residence, domicile or head office in a Member State other than the home Member State, including the aforementioned authorities, shall be treated in the same way and accorded the same ranking as claims of an equivalent nature lodgeable by creditors who have their normal place of residence, domicile or head office in the home Member State.

3. Except in cases where the law of the home Member State allows otherwise, a creditor shall send copies of supporting documents, if any, and shall indicate the nature of the claim, the date on which it arose and the amount, whether he alleges preference, security in rem or reservation of title in respect of the claim and what assets are covered by his security. The precedence granted to insurance claims by Article 10 need not be indicated.

NOTES

Repealed as noted at the beginning of this Directive.

[3.105]
Article 17
Languages and form

1. The information in the notice referred to in Article 15 shall be provided in the official language or one of the official languages of the home Member State. For that purpose a form shall be used bearing the heading "Invitation to lodge a claim; time limits to be observed" or, where the law of the home Member State provides for the submission of observations relating to claims, "Invitation to submit observations relating to a claim; time limits to be observed", in all the official languages of the European Union.

However, where a known creditor is a holder of an insurance claim, the information in the notice referred to in Article 15 shall be provided in the official language or one of the official languages of the Member State in which the creditor has his normal place of residence, domicile or head office.

2. Any creditor who has his normal place of residence, domicile or head office in a Member State other than the home Member State may lodge his claim or submit observations relating to his claim in the official language or one of the official languages of that other Member State. However, in that event the lodgement of his claim or the submission of observations on his claim, as appropriate, shall bear the heading "Lodgement of claim" or "Submission of observations relating to claims", as appropriate, in the official language or one of the official languages of the home Member State.

NOTES

Repealed as noted at the beginning of this Directive.

[3.106]
Article 18
Regular information to the creditors
1. Liquidators shall keep creditors regularly informed, in an appropriate manner, in particular regarding the progress of the winding-up.
2. The supervisory authorities of the Member States may request information on developments in the winding-up procedure from the supervisory authorities of the home Member State.

NOTES
Repealed as noted at the beginning of this Directive.

TITLE IV PROVISIONS COMMON TO REORGANISATION MEASURES AND WINDING-UP PROCEEDINGS

[3.107]
Article 19
Effects on certain contracts and rights
By way of derogation from Articles 4 and 9, the effects of the opening of reorganisation measures or of winding-up proceedings on the contracts and rights specified below shall be governed by the following rules—
- *(a) employment contracts and employment relationships shall be governed solely by the law of the Member State applicable to the employment contract or employment relationship;*
- *(b) a contract conferring the right to make use of or acquire immovable property shall be governed solely by the law of the Member State in whose territory the immovable property is situated;*
- *(c) rights of the insurance undertaking with respect to immovable property, a ship or an aircraft subject to registration in a public register shall be governed by the law of the Member State under whose authority the register is kept.*

NOTES
Repealed as noted at the beginning of this Directive.

[3.108]
Article 20
Third parties' rights in rem
1. The opening of reorganisation measures or winding-up proceedings shall not affect the rights in rem of creditors or third parties in respect of tangible or intangible, movable or immovable assets—both specific assets and collections of indefinite assets as a whole which change from time to time—belonging to the insurance undertaking which are situated within the territory of another Member State at the time of the opening of such measures or proceedings.
2. The rights referred to in paragraph 1 shall in particular mean—
- *(a) the right to dispose of assets or have them disposed of and to obtain satisfaction from the proceeds of or income from those assets, in particular by virtue of a lien or a mortgage;*
- *(b) the exclusive right to have a claim met, in particular a right guaranteed by a lien in respect of the claim or by assignment of the claim by way of a guarantee;*
- *(c) the right to demand the assets from, and/or to require restitution by, anyone having possession or use of them contrary to the wishes of the party so entitled;*
- *(d) a right in rem to the beneficial use of assets.*

3. The right, recorded in a public register and enforceable against third parties, under which a right in rem within the meaning of paragraph 1 may be obtained, shall be considered a right in rem.
4. Paragraph 1 shall not preclude actions for voidness, voidability or unenforceability referred to in Article 9(2)(l).

NOTES
Repealed as noted at the beginning of this Directive.

[3.109]
Article 21
Reservation of title
1. The opening of reorganisation measures or winding-up proceedings against an insurance undertaking purchasing an asset shall not affect the seller's rights based on a reservation of title where at the time of the opening of such measures or proceedings the asset is situated within the territory of a Member State other than the State in which such measures or proceedings were opened.
2. The opening of reorganisation measures or winding-up proceedings against an insurance undertaking selling an asset, after delivery of the asset, shall not constitute grounds for rescinding or terminating the sale and shall not prevent the purchaser from acquiring title where at the time of the opening of such measures or proceedings the asset sold is situated within the territory of a Member State other than the State in which such measures or proceedings were opened.
3. Paragraphs 1 and 2 shall not preclude actions for voidness, voidability or unenforceability referred to in Article 9(2)(l).

NOTES
Repealed as noted at the beginning of this Directive.

[3.110]
Article 22
Set-off
1. The opening of reorganisation measures or winding-up proceedings shall not affect the right of creditors to demand the set-off of their claims against the claims of the insurance undertaking, where such a set-off is permitted by the law applicable to the insurance undertaking's claim.
2. Paragraph 1 shall not preclude actions for voidness, voidability or unenforceability referred to in Article 9(2)(l).

NOTES
Repealed as noted at the beginning of this Directive.

[3.111]
Article 23
Regulated markets
1. Without prejudice to Article 20 the effects of a reorganisation measure or the opening of winding-up proceedings on the rights and obligations of the parties to a regulated market shall be governed solely by the law applicable to that market.
2. Paragraph 1 shall not preclude any action for voidness, voidability, or unenforceability referred to in Article 9(2)(l) which may be taken to set aside payments or transactions under the law applicable to that market.

NOTES
Repealed as noted at the beginning of this Directive.

[3.112]
Article 24
Detrimental acts
Article 9(2)(l) shall not apply, where a person who has benefited from a legal act detrimental to all the creditors provides proof that—
- *(a) the said act is subject to the law of a Member State other than the home Member State, and*
- *(b) that law does not allow any means of challenging that act in the relevant case.*

NOTES
Repealed as noted at the beginning of this Directive.

[3.113]
Article 25
Protection of third-party purchasers
Where, by an act concluded after the adoption of a reorganisation measure or the opening of winding-up proceedings, an insurance undertaking disposes, for a consideration, of—
- *(a) an immovable asset,*
- *(b) a ship or an aircraft subject to registration in a public register, or*
- *(c) transferable or other securities whose existence or transfer presupposes entry in a register or account laid down by law or which are placed in a central deposit system governed by the law of a Member State,*

the validity of that act shall be governed by the law of the Member State within whose territory the immovable asset is situated or under whose authority the register, account or system is kept.

NOTES
Repealed as noted at the beginning of this Directive.

[3.114]
Article 26
Lawsuits pending
The effects of reorganisation measures or winding-up proceedings on a pending lawsuit concerning an asset or a right of which the insurance undertaking has been divested shall be governed solely by the law of the Member State in which the lawsuit is pending.

NOTES
Repealed as noted at the beginning of this Directive.

[3.115]
Article 27
Administrators and liquidators
1. The administrator's or liquidator's appointment shall be evidenced by a certified copy of the original decision appointing him or by any other certificate issued by the competent authorities of the home Member State.
A translation into the official language or one of the official languages of the Member State within the territory of which the administrator or liquidator wishes to act may be required. No legalisation or other similar formality shall be required.

2. Administrators and liquidators shall be entitled to exercise within the territory of all the Member States all the powers which they are entitled to exercise within the territory of the home Member State. Persons to assist or, where appropriate, represent administrators and liquidators may be appointed, according to the home Member State's legislation, in the course of the reorganisation measure or winding-up proceedings, in particular in host Member States and, specifically, in order to help overcome any difficulties encountered by creditors in the host Member State.

3. In exercising his powers according to the home Member State's legislation, an administrator or liquidator shall comply with the law of the Member States within whose territory he wishes to take action, in particular with regard to procedures for the realisation of assets and the informing of employees. Those powers may not include the use of force or the right to rule on legal proceedings or disputes.

NOTES

Repealed as noted at the beginning of this Directive.

[3.116]

Article 28

Registration in a public register

1. The administrator, liquidator or any other authority or person duly empowered in the home Member State may request that a reorganisation measure or the decision to open winding-up proceedings be registered in the land register, the trade register and any other public register kept in the other Member States.

However, if a Member State prescribes mandatory registration, the authority or person referred to in subparagraph 1 shall take all the measures necessary to ensure such registration.

2. The costs of registration shall be regarded as costs and expenses incurred in the proceedings.

NOTES

Repealed as noted at the beginning of this Directive.

[3.117]

Article 29

Professional secrecy

All persons required to receive or divulge information in connection with the procedures of communication laid down in Articles 5, 8 and 30 shall be bound by professional secrecy, in the same manner as laid down in Article 16 of Directive 92/49/EEC and Article 15 of Directive 92/96/EEC, with the exception of any judicial authorities to which existing national provisions apply.

NOTES

Repealed as noted at the beginning of this Directive.

[3.118]

Article 30

Branches of third country insurance undertakings

1. Notwithstanding the definitions laid down in Article 2(e), (f) and (g) and for the purpose of applying the provisions of this Directive to the reorganisation measures and winding-up proceedings concerning a branch situated in a Member State of an insurance undertaking whose head office is located outside the Community—

- *(a) "home Member State" means the Member State in which the branch has been granted authorisation according to Article 23 of Directive 73/239/EEC and Article 27 of Directive 79/267/EEC, and*
- *(b) "supervisory authorities" and "competent authorities" mean such authorities of the Member State in which the branch was authorised.*

2. When an insurance undertaking whose head office is outside the Community has branches established in more than one Member State, each branch shall be treated independently with regard to the application of this Directive. The competent authorities and the supervisory authorities of these Member States shall endeavour to coordinate their actions. Any administrators or liquidators shall likewise endeavour to coordinate their actions.

NOTES

Repealed as noted at the beginning of this Directive.

[3.119]

Article 31

Implementation of this Directive

1. Member States shall bring into force the laws, regulations and administrative provisions necessary to comply with this Directive before 20 April 2003. They shall forthwith inform the Commission thereof.

When Member States adopt these measures, they shall contain a reference to this Directive or shall be accompanied by such reference on the occasion of their official publication. The methods of making such reference shall be laid down by Member States.

2. National provisions adopted in application of this Directive shall apply only to reorganisation measures or winding-up proceedings adopted or opened after the date referred to in paragraph 1. Reorganisation measures adopted or winding-up proceedings opened before that date shall continue to be governed by the law that was applicable to them at the time of adoption or opening.

3. Member States shall communicate to the Commission the text of the main provisions of domestic law which they adopt in the field governed by this Directive.

NOTES

Repealed as noted at the beginning of this Directive.

[3.120]
Article 32
Entry into force
This Directive shall enter into force on the day of its publication in the Official Journal of the European Communities.

NOTES

Repealed as noted at the beginning of this Directive.

[3.121]
Article 33
Addressees
This Directive is addressed to the Member States.

NOTES

Repealed as noted at the beginning of this Directive.

ANNEX

SPECIAL REGISTER REFERRED TO IN ARTICLE 10(3)

[3.122]
1. Every insurance undertaking must keep at its head office a special register of the assets used to cover the technical provisions calculated and invested in accordance with the home Member State's rules.

2. Where an insurance undertaking transacts both non-life and life business, it must keep at its head office separate registers for each type of business. However, where a Member State authorises insurance undertakings to cover life and the risks listed in points 1 and 2 of Annex A to Directive 73/239/EEC, it may provide that those insurance undertakings must keep a single register for the whole of their activities.

3. The total value of the assets entered, valued in accordance with the rules applicable in the home Member State, must at no time be less than the value of the technical provisions.

4. Where an asset entered in the register is subject to a right in rem in favour of a creditor or a third party, with the result that part of the value of the asset is not available for the purpose of covering commitments, that fact is recorded in the register and the amount not available is not included in the total value referred to in point 3.

5. Where an asset employed to cover technical provisions is subject to a right in rem in favour of a creditor or a third party, without meeting the conditions of point 4, or where such an asset is subject to a reservation of title in favour of a creditor or of a third party or where a creditor has a right to demand the set-off of his claim against the claim of the insurance undertaking, the treatment of such asset in case of the winding-up of the insurance undertaking with respect to the method provided for in Article 10(1)(a) shall be determined by the legislation of the home Member State except where Articles 20, 21 or 22 apply to that asset.

6. The composition of the assets entered in the register in accordance with points 1 to 5, at the time when winding-up proceedings are opened, must not thereafter be changed and no alteration other than the correction of purely clerical errors must be made in the registers, except with the authorisation of the competent authority.

7. Notwithstanding point 6, the liquidators must add to the said assets the yield therefrom and the value of the pure premiums received in respect of the class of business concerned between the opening of the winding-up proceedings and the time of payment of the insurance claims or until any transfer of portfolio is effected.

8. If the product of the realisation of assets is less than their estimated value in the registers, the liquidators must be required to justify this to the home Member States' competent authorities.

9. The supervisory authorities of the Member States must take appropriate measures to ensure full application by the insurance undertakings of the provisions of this Annex.

NOTES

Repealed as noted at the beginning of this Directive.

INSURERS (REORGANISATION AND WINDING UP) REGULATIONS 2003 (NOTE)

(SI 2003/1102)

[3.123]

NOTES

Made: 14 April 2003.

Authority: European Communities Act 1972, s 2(2).

Commencement: 20 April 2003.

These Regulations were revoked and replaced by the Insurers (Reorganisation and Winding Up) Regulations 2004, SI 2004/353, reg 53(1), as from 18 February 2004, subject to transitional provisions in reg 53(2), (3) thereof at **[3.175]**. They have been omitted from the current edition due to reasons of space and can be found in the 18th edition of this Handbook.

INSURERS (REORGANISATION AND WINDING UP) REGULATIONS 2004

(SI 2004/353)

NOTES

Made: 12 February 2004.

Authority: European Communities Act 1972, s 2(2).

Commencement: 18 February 2004.

ARRANGEMENT OF REGULATIONS

PART I
GENERAL

1 Citation and Commencement . . . [3.124]
2 Interpretation . . . [3.125]
3 Scope . . . [3.126]

PART II
INSOLVENCY MEASURES AND PROCEEDINGS:
JURISDICTION IN RELATION TO INSURERS

4 Prohibition against winding up etc EEA insurers in the United Kingdom . . . [3.127]
5 Schemes of arrangement: EEA insurers . . . [3.128]
6 Reorganisation measures and winding up proceedings in respect of EEA insurers effective in the United Kingdom . . . [3.129]
7 Confirmation by the court of a creditors' voluntary winding up . . . [3.130]

PART III
MODIFICATIONS OF THE LAW OF INSOLVENCY:
NOTIFICATION AND PUBLICATION

8 Modifications of the law of insolvency . . . [3.131]
9 Notification of relevant decision to the FCA and, if the insurer is a PRA-authorised person, the PRA . . . [3.132]
10 Notification of relevant decision to EEA regulators . . . [3.133]
11 Publication of voluntary arrangement, administration order, winding up order or scheme of arrangement . . . [3.134]
12 Notification to creditors: winding up proceedings . . . [3.135]
13 Submission of claims by EEA creditors . . . [3.136]
14 Reports to creditors . . . [3.137]
15 Service of notices and documents . . . [3.138]
16 Disclosure of confidential information received from an EEA regulator . . . [3.139]

PART IV
PRIORITY OF PAYMENT OF INSURANCE
CLAIMS IN WINDING UP ETC

17 Interpretation of this Part . . . [3.140]
18 Application of regulations 19 to 27 . . . [3.141]
19 Application of this Part: certain assets excluded from insolvent estate of UK insurer . . . [3.142]
20 Preferential debts: disapplication of section 175 of the 1986 Act or Article 149 of the 1989 Order . . . [3.143]
21 Preferential debts: long term insurers and general insurers . . . [3.144]
22 Composite insurers: preferential debts attributable to long term and general business . . . [3.145]
23 Preferential debts: long term business of a non-transferring composite insurer . . . [3.146]
24 Preferential debts: general business of a composite insurer . . . [3.147]

25 Insufficiency of long term business assets and general business assets . . . . [3.148]
26 Composite insurers: excess of long term business assets and general business assets . . . . [3.149]
27 Composite insurers: application of other assets . . . . [3.150]
28 Composite insurers: proof of debts . . . . [3.151]
28A Composite insurers: seeking decisions from creditors . . . . [3.152]
29 Composite insurers: general meetings of creditors . . . . [3.153]
30 Composite insurers: apportionment of costs payable out of the assets . . . . [3.154]
31 Summary remedy against liquidators . . . . [3.155]
32 Priority of subrogated claims by the Financial Services Compensation Scheme . . . . [3.156]
33 Voluntary arrangements: treatment of insurance debts . . . . [3.157]

PART V
REORGANISATION OR WINDING UP OF UK INSURERS:
RECOGNITION OF EEA RIGHTS

34 Application of this Part. . . . . [3.158]
35 Application of this Part: certain assets excluded from insolvent estate of UK insurer . . . . [3.159]
36 Interpretation of this Part. . . . . [3.160]
37 EEA rights: applicable law in the winding up of a UK insurer . . . . [3.161]
38 Employment contracts and relationships . . . . [3.162]
39 Contracts in connection with immovable property . . . . [3.163]
40 Registrable rights . . . . [3.164]
41 Third parties' rights in rem. . . . . [3.165]
42 Reservation of title agreements etc . . . . [3.166]
43 Creditors' rights to set off . . . . [3.167]
44 Regulated markets. . . . . [3.168]
45 Detrimental acts pursuant to the law of an EEA State . . . . [3.169]
46 Protection of third party purchasers. . . . . [3.170]
47 Lawsuits pending . . . . [3.171]

PART VI
THIRD COUNTRY INSURERS

48 Interpretation of this Part. . . . . [3.172]
49 Application of these Regulations to a third country insurer . . . . [3.173]
50 Disclosure of confidential information: third country insurers. [3.174]

PART VII
REVOCATION AND AMENDMENTS

53 Revocation and Transitional . . . . [3.175]

PART I
GENERAL

[3.124]
1 Citation and Commencement

These Regulations may be cited as the Insurers (Reorganisation and Winding Up) Regulations 2004, and come into force on 18th February 2004.

[3.125]
2 Interpretation

(1) In these Regulations—

. . .

"the 1986 Act" means the Insolvency Act 1986;

"the 2000 Act" means the Financial Services and Markets Act 2000;

["the 2006 Act" means the Companies Act 2006;]

"the 1989 Order" means the Insolvency (Northern Ireland) Order 1989;

"administrator" has the meaning given by paragraph 13 of Schedule B1[, or by paragraph 14 of Schedule B1 to the 1989 Order];

. . .

. . .

"branch", in relation to an EEA or UK insurer has the meaning given by [Article 268(1)(b) of the Solvency 2 Directive];

"claim" means a claim submitted by a creditor of a UK insurer in the course of—

(a) a winding up,

(b) an administration, or

(c) a voluntary arrangement,

with a view to recovering his debt in whole or in part, and includes a proof of debt, within the meaning of Rule 4.73(4) of the Insolvency Rules, Rule 4.079(4) of the Insolvency Rules

(Northern Ireland) or in Scotland a claim made in accordance with rule 4.15 of the Insolvency (Scotland) Rules;

. . .

"creditors' voluntary winding up" has the meaning given by section 90 of the 1986 Act or Article 76 of the 1989 Order;

"debt"—

(a) in England and Wales and Northern Ireland—

(i) in relation to a winding up or administration of a UK insurer, has the meaning given by Rule 13.12 of the Insolvency Rules or Article 5 of the 1989 Order, and

(ii) in a case where a voluntary arrangement has effect, in relation to a UK insurer, means a debt which would constitute a debt in relation to the winding up of that insurer, except that references in paragraph (1) of Rule 13.12 or paragraph (1) of Article 5 of the 1989 Order to the date on which the company goes into liquidation are to be read as references to the date on which the voluntary arrangement has effect;

(b) in Scotland—

(i) in relation to a winding up of a UK insurer, shall be interpreted in accordance with Schedule 1 to the Bankruptcy (Scotland) Act 1985 as applied by Chapter 5 of Part 4 of the Insolvency (Scotland) Rules, and

(ii) in a case where a voluntary arrangement has effect in relation to a UK insurer, means a debt which would constitute a debt in relation to the winding up of that insurer, except that references in Chapter 5 of Part 4 of the Insolvency (Scotland) Rules to the date of commencement of winding up are to be read as references to the date on which the voluntary arrangement has effect;

"directive reorganisation measure" means a reorganisation measure as defined in [Article 268(1)(c) of the Solvency 2 Directive] which was adopted or imposed on or after 20th April 2003;

"directive winding up proceedings" means winding up proceedings as defined in [Article 268(1)(d) of the Solvency 2 Directive] which were opened on or after 20th April 2003;

"EEA creditor" means a creditor of a UK insurer who—

(a) in the case of an individual, is ordinarily resident in an EEA State, and

(b) in the case of a body corporate or unincorporated association of persons, has its head office in an EEA State;

["EEA insurer" means an insurance undertaking, other than a UK insurer, pursuing the activity of direct insurance (within the meaning of the Solvency 2 Directive) which has received authorisation under Article 14 or Article 162 of the Solvency 2 Directive from its home state regulator;]

["EEA regulator" means a supervisory authority (within the meaning of Article 13(10) of the Solvency 2 Directive) of an EEA State;]

["EEA State" has the meaning given by Schedule 1 to the Interpretation Act 1978;]

["the FCA" means the Financial Conduct Authority;]

. . .

["home state regulator", in relation to an EEA insurer, means the EEA regulator—

(a) in the EEA State in which its head office is located; or

(b) if it is a branch of a third-country insurance undertaking (within the meaning of Article 13(3) of the Solvency 2 Directive), the EEA State in which the branch was granted authorisation in accordance with Articles 145 to 149 of the Solvency 2 Directive;]

"the Insolvency Rules" means the Insolvency Rules 1986;

"the Insolvency Rules (Northern Ireland)" means the Insolvency Rules (Northern Ireland) 1991;

"the Insolvency (Scotland) Rules" means the Insolvency (Scotland) Rules 1986;

"insurance claim" means any claim in relation to an insurance debt;

"insurance creditor" means a person who has an insurance claim against a UK insurer (whether or not he has claims other than insurance claims against that insurer);

"insurance debt" means a debt to which a UK insurer is, or may become liable, pursuant to a contract of insurance, to a policyholder or to any person who has a direct right of action against that insurer, and includes any premium paid in connection with a contract of insurance (whether or not that contract was concluded) which the insurer is liable to refund;

. . .

"officer", in relation to a company, has the meaning given by [section 1173(1) of the Companies Act 2006];

"official language" means a language specified in Article 1 of Council Regulation No 1 of 15th April 1958 determining the languages to be used by the European Economic Community (Regulation 1/58/EEC), most recently amended by paragraph (a) of Part XVIII of Annex I to the Act of Accession 1994 (194 N);

"policyholder" has the meaning given by the Financial Services and Markets Act 2000 (Meaning of "Policy" and "Policyholder") Order 2001;

["the PRA" means the Prudential Regulation Authority;]

["PRA-authorised person" has the meaning given in section 2B of the 2000 Act;]

["registered society" means a society, other than a society registered as a credit union, which is—

(a) a registered society within the meaning given by section 1(1) of the Co-operative and Community Benefit Societies Act 2014; or

(b) a society registered or deemed to be registered under the Industrial and Provident Societies Act (Northern Ireland) 1969;]

. . .

"Schedule B1" means Schedule B1 to the 1986 Act as inserted by section 248 of the Enterprise Act 2002[, unless specified otherwise];

["section 899 compromise or arrangement" means a compromise or arrangement sanctioned by the court in relation to a UK insurer under section 899 of the 2006 Act but does not include a compromise or arrangement falling within section 900 (powers of court to facilitate reconstruction or amalgamation) or Part 27 (mergers and divisions of public companies) of that Act;]

["the Solvency 2 Directive" means Directive 2009/138/EC of the European Parliament and of the Council of 25 November 2009 on the taking-up and pursuit of the business of Insurance and Reinsurance (Solvency II);]

. . .

"supervisor" has the meaning given by section 7 of the 1986 Act or Article 20 of the 1989 Order;

. . .

"UK insurer" means a person who has permission under [Part 4A] of the 2000 Act to effect or carry out contracts of insurance, but does not include a person who, in accordance with that permission, carries on that activity exclusively in relation to reinsurance contracts;

"voluntary arrangement" means a voluntary arrangement which has effect in relation to a UK insurer in accordance with section 4A of the 1986 Act or Article 17A of the 1989 Order; and

"winding up" means—

(a) winding up by the court, or

(b) a creditors' voluntary winding up.

(2) In paragraph (1)—

(a) for the purposes of the definition of "directive reorganisation measure", a reorganisation measure is adopted or imposed at the time when it is treated as adopted or imposed by the law of the relevant EEA State; and

(b) for the purposes of the definition of "directive winding up proceedings", winding up proceedings are opened at the time when they are treated as opened by the law of the relevant EEA State,

and in this paragraph "relevant EEA State" means the EEA State under the law of which the reorganisation is adopted or imposed, or the winding up proceedings are opened, as the case may be.

(3) In these Regulations, references to the general law of insolvency of the United Kingdom include references to every provision made by or under the 1986 Act or the 1989 Order; and in relation to friendly societies or to [registered societies] references to the law of insolvency or to any provision of the 1986 Act or the 1989 Order are to that law as modified by the Friendly Societies Act 1992 or by [the Co-operative and Community Benefit Societies Act 2014] or the Industrial and Provident Societies Act (Northern Ireland) 1969 (as the case may be).

(4) References in these Regulations to a "contract of insurance" must be read with—

(a) section 22 of the 2000 Act;

(b) any relevant order made under that section; and

(c) Schedule 2 to that Act,

but for the purposes of these Regulations a contract of insurance does not include a reinsurance contract.

(5) Functions imposed or falling on the [FCA or the PRA] by or under these Regulations shall be deemed to be functions under the 2000 Act.

NOTES

Para (1): words in square brackets in definitions "administrator" and "Schedule B1" inserted by the Insurers (Reorganisation and Winding Up) (Amendment) Regulations 2007, SI 2007/851, reg 2(1), (2); definition "the Authority" revoked, definitions "the FCA", "the PRA" and "PRA-authorised person" inserted, and in definition "UK insurer", words in square brackets substituted by the Financial Services Act 2012 (Consequential Amendments and Transitional Provisions) Order 2013, SI 2013/472, arts 3, 4, Sch 2, para 88(a); definition "EEA State" substituted by the Financial Services (EEA State) Regulations 2007, SI 2007/108, reg 8; definitions "the 1985 Act", "Article 418 compromise or arrangement", "the Companies Order" and "section 425 or Article 418 compromise or arrangement" (omitted) revoked, definition "the 2006 Act" inserted, words in square brackets in definition "officer" substituted, and definition "section 899 compromise or arrangement" substituted (for original definition "section 425 compromise or arrangement"), by the Companies Act 2006 (Consequential Amendments and Transitional Provisions) Order 2011, SI 2011/1265, art 23(1), (2); definitions "the first non-life insurance directive", "life insurance directive", "the reorganisation and winding-up directive" and "the third non-life insurance directive" (omitted) revoked, definition "the Solvency 2 Directive" inserted, words in square brackets in definitions "branch", "directive reorganisation measure" and "directive winding up proceedings" substituted, and definitions "EEA insurer", "EEA regulator" and "home state regulator" substituted, by the Solvency 2 Regulations 2015, SI 2015/575, reg 60, Sch 2, paras 17(1), (2); definition "registered society" inserted by the Co-operative and Community Benefit Societies and Credit Unions Act 2010 (Consequential Amendments) Regulations 2014, SI 2014/1815, reg 2, Schedule, para 12(1), (2)(a).

Para (3): words in square brackets substituted by SI 2014/1815, reg 2, Schedule, para 12(1), (2)(b).

Para (5): words in square brackets substituted by SI 2013/472, art 3, Sch 2, para 88(b).

Note that the Insolvency Rules 1986, SI 1986/1925 are revoked and replaced (as from 6 April 2017 and subject to transitional provisions) by the Insolvency (England and Wales) Rules 2016, SI 2016/1024 at **[6.2]**.

[3.126]

3 Scope

For the purposes of these Regulations, neither the Society of Lloyd's nor the persons specified in section 316(1) of the 2000 Act are UK insurers.

PART II
INSOLVENCY MEASURES AND PROCEEDINGS: JURISDICTION IN RELATION TO INSURERS

[3.127]

4 Prohibition against winding up etc EEA insurers in the United Kingdom

(1) On or after the relevant date a court in the United Kingdom may not, in relation to an EEA insurer or any branch of an EEA insurer—

(a) make a winding up order pursuant to section 221 of the 1986 Act or Article 185 of the 1989 Order;

(b) appoint a provisional liquidator;

(c) make an administration order.

(2) Paragraph (1)(a) does not prevent—

(a) the court from making a winding up order after the relevant date in relation to an EEA insurer if—

(i) a provisional liquidator was appointed in relation to that insurer before the relevant date, and

(ii) that appointment continues in force until immediately before that winding up order is made;

(b) the winding up of an EEA insurer after the relevant date pursuant to a winding up order which was made, and has not been discharged, before that date.

(3) Paragraph (1)(b) does not prevent a provisional liquidator of an EEA insurer appointed before the relevant date from acting in relation to that insurer after that date.

(4) Paragraph (1)(c) does not prevent an administrator appointed before the relevant date from acting after that date in a case in which the administration order under which he or his predecessor was appointed remains in force after that date.

(5) An administrator may not, in relation to an EEA insurer, be appointed under paragraphs 14 or 22 of Schedule B1 [or paragraph 15 or 23 of Schedule B1 to the 1989 Order.]

(6) A proposed voluntary arrangement shall not have effect in relation to an EEA insurer if a decision, under section 4 of the 1986 Act or Article 17 of the 1989 Order, with respect to the approval of that arrangement was made after the relevant date.

(7) Section 377 of the 2000 Act (reducing the value of contracts instead of winding up) does not apply in relation to an EEA insurer.

[(8) An order under section 254 of the Enterprise Act 2002 (application of insolvency law to a foreign company) or under Article 9 of the Insolvency (Northern Ireland) Order 2005 (application of insolvency law to company incorporated outside Northern Ireland) may not provide for any of the following provisions of the 1986 Act or of the 1989 Order to apply in relation to an EEA insurer—

(a) Part I of the 1986 Act or Part II of the 1989 Order (company voluntary arrangements);

(b) Part II of the 1986 Act or Part III of the 1989 Order (administration);

(c) Chapter VI of Part IV of the 1986 Act (winding up by the Court) or Chapter VI of Part V of the 1989 Order (winding up by the High Court).]

(9) In this regulation and regulation 5, "relevant date" means 20th April 2003.

NOTES

Para (5): words in square brackets inserted by the Insurers (Reorganisation and Winding Up) (Amendment) Regulations 2007, SI 2007/851, reg 2(1), (3).

Para (8): substituted by SI 2007/851, reg 2(1), (4).

[3.128]

5 Schemes of arrangement: EEA insurers

(1) For the purposes of [section 895(2)(b) of the 2006 Act], an EEA insurer or a branch of an EEA insurer is to be treated as a company liable to be wound up under the 1986 Act or the 1989 Order if it would be liable to be wound up under that Act or Order but for the prohibition in regulation 4(1)(a).

(2) But a court may not make a relevant order under [section 899 of the 2006 Act] in relation to an EEA insurer which is subject to a directive reorganisation measure or directive winding up proceedings, or a branch of an EEA insurer which is subject to such a measure or proceedings unless the conditions set out in paragraph (3) are satisfied.

(3) Those conditions are—

(a) the person proposing [the section 899 compromise or arrangement] ("the proposal") has given—

(i) the administrator or liquidator, and

(ii) the relevant competent authority,

reasonable notice of the details of that proposal; and

(b) no person notified in accordance with sub-paragraph (a) has objected to the proposal.

(4) Nothing in this regulation invalidates a compromise or arrangement which was sanctioned by the court by an order made before the relevant date.

(5) For the purposes of paragraph (2), a relevant order means an order sanctioning [a section 899 compromise or arrangement] which—

(a) is intended to enable the insurer, and the whole or any part of its undertaking, to survive as a going concern and which affects the rights of persons other than the insurer or its contributories; or

(b) includes among its purposes a realisation of some or all of the assets of the EEA insurer to which the order relates and the distribution of the proceeds to creditors, with a view to terminating the whole or any part of the business of that insurer.

(6) For the purposes of this regulation—

(a) "administrator" means an administrator, as defined by [Article 268(1)(e) of the Solvency 2 Directive], who is appointed in relation to the EEA insurer in relation to which the proposal is made;

(b) "liquidator" means a liquidator, as defined by [Article 268(1)(f) of the Solvency 2 Directive], who is appointed in relation to the EEA insurer in relation to which the proposal is made;

(c) "competent authority" means the competent authority, as defined by [Article 268(1)(a) of the Solvency 2 Directive], which is competent for the purposes of the directive reorganisation measure or directive winding up proceedings mentioned in paragraph (2).

NOTES

Paras (1)–(3), (5): words in square brackets substituted by the Companies Act 2006 (Consequential Amendments and Transitional Provisions) Order 2011, SI 2011/1265, art 23(1), (3).

Para (6): words in square brackets in sub-paras (a)–(c) substituted by the Solvency 2 Regulations 2015, SI 2015/575, reg 60, Sch 2, paras 17(1), (3).

[3.129]

6 Reorganisation measures and winding up proceedings in respect of EEA insurers effective in the United Kingdom

(1) An EEA insolvency measure has effect in the United Kingdom in relation to—

(a) any branch of an EEA insurer,

(b) any property or other assets of that insurer,

(c) any debt or liability of that insurer

as if it were part of the general law of insolvency of the United Kingdom.

(2) Subject to paragraph (4)—

(a) a competent officer who satisfies the condition mentioned in paragraph (3); or

(b) a qualifying agent appointed by a competent officer who satisfies the condition mentioned in paragraph (3),

may exercise in the United Kingdom, in relation to the EEA insurer which is subject to an EEA insolvency measure, any function which, pursuant to that measure, he is entitled to exercise in relation to that insurer in the relevant EEA State.

(3) The condition mentioned in paragraph (2) is that the appointment of the competent officer is evidenced—

(a) by a certified copy of the order or decision by a judicial or administrative authority in the relevant EEA State by or under which the competent officer was appointed; or

(b) by any other certificate issued by the judicial or administrative authority which has jurisdiction in relation to the EEA insolvency measure,

and accompanied by a certified translation of that order, decision or certificate (as the case may be).

(4) In exercising functions of the kind mentioned in paragraph (2), the competent officer or qualifying agent—

(a) may not take any action which would constitute an unlawful use of force in the part of the United Kingdom in which he is exercising those functions;

(b) may not rule on any dispute arising from a matter falling within Part V of these Regulations which is justiciable by a court in the part of the United Kingdom in which he is exercising those functions; and

(c) notwithstanding the way in which functions may be exercised in the relevant EEA State, must act in accordance with relevant laws or rules as to procedure which have effect in the part of the United Kingdom in which he is exercising those functions.

(5) For the purposes of paragraph (4)(c), "relevant laws or rules as to procedure" mean—

(a) requirements as to consultation with or notification of employees of an EEA insurer;

(b) law and procedures relevant to the realisation of assets;

(c) where the competent officer is bringing or defending legal proceedings in the name of, or on behalf of, an EEA insurer, the relevant rules of court.

(6) In this regulation—

"competent officer" means a person appointed under or in connection with an EEA insolvency measure for the purpose of administering that measure;

"qualifying agent" means an agent validly appointed (whether in the United Kingdom or elsewhere) by a competent officer in accordance with the relevant law in the relevant EEA State;

"EEA insolvency measure" means, as the case may be, a directive reorganisation measure or directive winding up proceedings which has effect in relation to an EEA insurer by virtue of the law of the relevant EEA State;

"relevant EEA State", in relation to an EEA insurer, means the EEA State in which that insurer has been authorised in accordance with [Article 14 or Article 162 of the Solvency 2 Directive].

NOTES

Para (6): in definition "relevant EEA State" words in square brackets substituted by the Solvency 2 Regulations 2015, SI 2015/575, reg 60, Sch 2, paras 17(1), (4).

[3.130]

7 Confirmation by the court of a creditors' voluntary winding up

(1) Rule 7.62 of the Insolvency Rules or Rule 7.56 of the Insolvency Rules (Northern Ireland) applies in relation to a UK insurer with the modification specified in paragraph (2) or (3).

(2) In Rule 7.62 paragraph (1), after the words
"the Insurers (Reorganisation and Winding Up) Regulations 2003" insert the words "or the Insurers (Reorganisation and Winding Up) Regulations 2004".

In Rule 7.56 of the Insolvency Rules (Northern Ireland) paragraph (1), after the words "the Insurers (Reorganisation and Winding Up) Regulations 2003" insert the words "or the Insurers (Reorganisation and Winding Up) Regulations 2004".

PART III
MODIFICATIONS OF THE LAW OF INSOLVENCY: NOTIFICATION AND PUBLICATION

[3.131]

8 Modifications of the law of insolvency

The general law of insolvency has effect in relation to UK insurers subject to the provisions of this Part.

[3.132]

9 Notification of relevant decision to the [FCA and, if the insurer is a PRA-authorised person, the PRA]

(1) Where on or after [3rd March 2004] the court makes a decision, order or appointment of any of the following kinds—

(a) an administration order under paragraph 13 of Schedule B1[, or paragraph 14 of Schedule B1 to the 1989 Order];

(b) a winding up order under section 125 of the 1986 Act or Article 105 of the 1989 Order;

(c) the appointment of a provisional liquidator under section 135(1) of the 1986 Act or Article 115(1) of the 1989 Order;

(d) an interim order under paragraph 13(1)(d) of Schedule B1 [or paragraph 14(1)(d) of Schedule B1 to the 1989 Order];

(e) a decision to reduce the value of one or more of the insurer's contracts, in accordance with section 377 of the 2000 Act,

it must immediately inform the [FCA and, if the insurer is a PRA-authorised person, the PRA], or cause the [FCA and, if the insurer is a PRA-authorised person, the PRA] to be informed of the decision, order or appointment which has been made.

(2) Where a decision with respect to the approval of a voluntary arrangement has effect, and the arrangement which is the subject of that decision is a qualifying arrangement, the supervisor must forthwith inform the [FCA and, if the insurer is a PRA-authorised person, the PRA] of the arrangement.

(3) Where a liquidator is appointed as mentioned in section 100 of the 1986 Act, paragraph 83 of Schedule B1[, paragraph 84 of Schedule B1 to the 1989 Order] or Article 86 of the 1989 Order (appointment of liquidator in a creditors' voluntary winding up), the liquidator must inform the [FCA and, if the insurer is a PRA-authorised person, the PRA] forthwith of his appointment.

(4) Where in the case of a members' voluntary winding up, section 95 of the 1986 Act (effect of company's insolvency) or Article 81 of the 1989 Order applies, the liquidator must inform the [FCA and, if the insurer is a PRA-authorised person, the PRA] forthwith that he is of that opinion.

[(6) Paragraphs (1), (2) and (3) do not require the FCA to be informed in any case where the FCA was represented at all hearings in connection with the application in relation to which the decision, order or appointment is made.

(6A) Paragraphs (1), (2) and (3) do not require the PRA to be informed in any case where the PRA was represented at all hearings in connection with the application in relation to which the decision, order or appointment is made.]

(7) For the purposes of paragraph (2), a "qualifying arrangement" means a voluntary arrangement which—

(a) varies the rights of creditors as against the insurer and is intended to enable the insurer, and the whole or any part of its undertaking, to survive as a going concern; or

(b) includes a realisation of some or all of the assets of the insurer and distribution of the proceeds to creditors, with a view to terminating the whole or any part of the business of that insurer.

(8) An administrator, supervisor or liquidator who fails without reasonable excuse to comply with paragraph (2), (3), or (4) (as the case may be) commits an offence and is liable on summary conviction to a fine not exceeding level 3 on the standard scale.

NOTES

In the regulation heading and paras (1)–(4) words "FCA and, if the insurer is a PRA-authorised person, the PRA" in square brackets substituted by the Financial Services Act 2012 (Consequential Amendments and Transitional Provisions) Order 2013, SI 2013/472, art 3, Sch 2, para 88(c).

Para (1): words in first pair of square brackets substituted by the Insurers (Reorganisation and Winding Up) (Amendment) Regulations 2004, SI 2004/546, reg 2(1), (2); words in square brackets in paras (a), (d) inserted by the Insurers (Reorganisation and Winding Up) (Amendment) Regulations 2007, SI 2007/851, reg 2(1), (5).

Para (3): words in first pair of square brackets inserted by SI 2007/851, reg 2(1), (6); words in second pair of square brackets substituted by SI 2013/472, art 3, Sch 2, para 88(c).

Paras (6), (6A): substituted by SI 2013/472, art 3, Sch 2, para 88(d).

Modification: in relation to the Lloyd's of London insurance market, this regulation is applied, with modifications, by the Insurers (Reorganisation and Winding Up) (Lloyd's) Regulations 2005, SI 2005/1998, regs 32, 33 at **[7.1601]**, **[7.1602]**.

[3.133]

10 Notification of relevant decision to EEA regulators

(1) Where [the FCA or the PRA] is informed of a decision, order or appointment in accordance with regulation 9, [that authority] must as soon as is practicable inform the EEA regulators in every EEA State—

(a) that the decision, order or appointment has been made; and

(b) in general terms, of the possible effect of a decision, order or appointment of that kind on—

(i) the business of an insurer, and

(ii) the rights of policyholders under contracts of insurance effected and carried out by an insurer.

(2) Where [the FCA or the PRA] has been represented at all hearings in connection with the application in relation to which the decision, order or appointment has been made, [that authority] must inform the EEA regulators in every EEA State of the matters mentioned in paragraph (1) as soon as is practicable after that decision, order or appointment has been made.

NOTES

Words in square brackets substituted by the Financial Services Act 2012 (Consequential Amendments and Transitional Provisions) Order 2013, SI 2013/472, art 3, Sch 2, para 88(e).

Modification: in relation to the Lloyd's of London insurance market, this regulation is applied, with modifications, by the Insurers (Reorganisation and Winding Up) (Lloyd's) Regulations 2005, SI 2005/1998, regs 32, 34 at **[7.1601]**, **[7.1603]**.

[3.134]

11 Publication of voluntary arrangement, administration order, winding up order or scheme of arrangement

(1) This regulation applies where a qualifying decision has effect, or a qualifying order or qualifying appointment is made, in relation to a UK insurer on or after 20th April 2003.

(2) For the purposes of this regulation—

(a) a qualifying decision means a decision with respect to the approval of a proposed voluntary arrangement, in accordance with section 4A of the 1986 Act or Article 17A of the 1989 Order;

(b) a qualifying order means—

(i) an administration order under paragraph 13 of Schedule B1 [or under paragraph 14 of Schedule B1 to the 1989 Order],

(ii) an order appointing a provisional liquidator in accordance with section 135 of the 1986 Act or Article 115 of the 1989 Order, or

(iii) a winding up order made by the court under Part IV of the 1986 Act or Part V of the 1989 Order.

(c) a qualifying appointment means the appointment of a liquidator as mentioned in section 100 of the 1986 Act or Article 86 of the 1989 Order (appointment of liquidator in a creditors' voluntary winding up).

(3) Subject to paragraph (8), as soon as is reasonably practicable after a qualifying decision has effect, or a qualifying order or a qualifying appointment has been made, the relevant officer must publish, or cause to be published, in the Official Journal of the European Communities the information mentioned in paragraph (4) and (if applicable) paragraphs (5), (6) or (7).

(4) That information is—

(a) a summary of the terms of the qualifying decision or qualifying appointment or the provisions of the qualifying order (as the case may be);

(b) the identity of the relevant officer; and

(c) the statutory provisions in accordance with which the qualifying decision has effect or the qualifying order or appointment has been made or takes effect.

(5) In the case of a qualifying appointment falling within paragraph (2)(c), that information includes the court to which an application under section 112 of the 1986 Act (reference of questions to the court) or Article 98 of the 1989 Order (reference of questions to the High Court) may be made.

(6) In the case of a qualifying decision, that information includes the court to which an application under section 6 of the 1986 Act or Article 19 of the 1989 Order (challenge of decisions) may be made.

(7) Paragraph (3) does not apply where a qualifying decision or qualifying order falling within paragraph (2)(b)(i) affects the interests only of the members, or any class of members, or employees of the insurer (in their capacity as members or employees).

(8) This regulation is without prejudice to any requirement to publish information imposed upon a relevant officer under any provision of the general law of insolvency.

(9) A relevant officer who fails to comply with paragraph (3) of this regulation commits an offence and is liable on summary conviction to a fine not exceeding level 3 on the standard scale.

(10) A qualifying decision, qualifying order or qualifying appointment is not invalid or ineffective if the relevant official fails to comply with paragraph (3) of this regulation.

(11) In this regulation, "relevant officer" means—

(a) in the case of a voluntary arrangement, the supervisor;
(b) in the case of an administration order or the appointment of an administrator, the administrator;
(c) in the case of a creditors' voluntary winding up, the liquidator;
(d) in the case of winding up order, the liquidator;
(e) in the case of an order appointing a provisional liquidator, the provisional liquidator.

NOTES

Para (2): words in square brackets in sub-para (b) inserted by the Insurers (Reorganisation and Winding Up) (Amendment) Regulations 2007, SI 2007/851, reg 2(1), (7).

Modification: in relation to the Lloyd's of London insurance market, this regulation is applied, with modifications, by the Insurers (Reorganisation and Winding Up) (Lloyd's) Regulations 2005, SI 2005/1998, regs 32, 35 at **[7.1601]**, **[7.1604]**.

[3.135]

12 Notification to creditors: winding up proceedings

(1) When a relevant order or appointment is made, or a relevant decision is taken, in relation to a UK insurer on or after 20th April 2003, the appointed officer must as soon as is reasonably practicable—

(a) notify all known creditors of that insurer in writing of—
  (i) the matters mentioned in paragraph (4), and
  (ii) the matters mentioned in paragraph (5); and
(b) notify all known insurance creditors of that insurer in writing of the matters mentioned in paragraph 6,

in any case.

(2) The appointed officer may comply with the requirement in paragraph (1)(a)(i) and the requirement in paragraph (1)(a)(ii) by separate notifications.

(3) For the purposes of this regulation—

(a) "relevant order" means—
  (i) an administration order made under section 8 of the 1986 Act before 15th September 2003, or made on or after that date under paragraph 13 of Schedule B1 in the prescribed circumstances [or under paragraph 14 of Schedule B1 to the 1989 Order in the prescribed circumstances],
  (ii) a winding up order under section 125 of the 1986 Act (powers of the court on hearing a petition) or Article 105 of the 1989 Order (powers of High Court on hearing of petition),
  (iii) the appointment of a liquidator in accordance with section 138 of the 1986 Act (appointment of a liquidator in Scotland), and
  (iv) an order appointing a provisional liquidator in accordance with section 135 of that Act or Article 115 of the 1989 Order;
(b) "relevant appointment" means the appointment of a liquidator as mentioned in section 100 of the 1986 Act or Article 86 of the 1989 Order (appointment of liquidator in a creditors' voluntary winding up); and
(c) "relevant decision" means a decision as a result of which a qualifying voluntary arrangement has effect.

(4) The matters which must be notified to all known creditors in accordance with paragraph (1)(a)(i) are as follows—

(a) that a relevant order or appointment has been made, or a relevant decision taken, in relation to the UK insurer; and
(b) the date from which that order, appointment or decision has effect.

(5) The matters which must be notified to all known creditors in accordance with paragraph (1)(a)(ii) are as follows—

(a) if applicable, the date by which a creditor must submit his claim in writing;
(b) the matters which must be stated in a creditor's claim;
(c) details of any category of debt in relation to which a claim is not required;
(d) the person to whom any such claim or any observations on a claim must be submitted; and
(e) the consequences of any failure to submit a claim by any specified deadline.

(6) The matters which must be notified to all known insurance creditors, in accordance with paragraph (1)(b), are as follows—

(a) the effect which the relevant order, appointment or decision will, or is likely, to have on the kind of contract of insurance under, or in connection with, which that creditor's insurance claim against the insurer is founded; and
(b) the date from which any variation (resulting from the relevant order or relevant decision) to the risks covered by, or the sums recoverable under, that contract has effect.

(7) Subject to paragraph (8), where a creditor is notified in accordance with paragraph (1)(a)(ii), the notification must be headed with the words "Invitation to lodge a claim: time limits to be observed", and that heading must be given in—

(a) the official language, or one of the official languages, of the EEA State in which that creditor is ordinarily resident; or
(b) every official language.

(8) Where a creditor notified in accordance with paragraph (1) is—

(a) an insurance creditor; and

(b) ordinarily resident in an EEA State,

the notification must be given in the official language, or one of the official languages, of that EEA State.

(9) The obligation under paragraph (1)(a)(ii) may be discharged by sending a form of proof in accordance with Rule 4.74 of the Insolvency Rules, Rule 4.080 of the Insolvency Rules (Northern Ireland) or Rule 4.15(2) of the Insolvency (Scotland) Rules as applicable in cases where any of those rules applies, provided that the form of proof complies with paragraph (7) or (8) (whichever is applicable).

[(10) The prescribed circumstances are where the administrator includes in the statement required under Rule 2.3 of the Insolvency Rules or under Rule 2.003 of the Insolvency Rules (Northern Ireland) a statement to the effect that the objective set out in paragraph 3(1)(a) of Schedule B1 or in paragraph 4(1)(a) of Schedule B1 to the 1989 Order is not reasonably likely to be achieved.]

(11) Where, after the appointment of an administrator, the administrator concludes that it is not reasonably practicable to achieve the objective specified in paragraph 3(1)(a) of Schedule B1 [or in paragraph 4(1)(a) of Schedule B1 to the 1989 Order], he shall inform the court [, the FCA and, if the insurer is a PRA-authorised person, the PRA] in writing of that conclusion and upon so doing the order by which he was appointed shall be a relevant order for the purposes of this regulation and the obligation under paragraph (1) shall apply as from the date on which he so informs the court [, the FCA and, if the insurer is a PRA-authorised person, the PRA].

(12) An appointed officer commits an offence if he fails without reasonable excuse to comply with an applicable requirement under this regulation, and is liable on summary conviction to a fine not exceeding level 3 on the standard scale.

(13) For the purposes of this regulation—

(a) "appointed officer" means—

(i) in the case of a relevant order falling within paragraph (3)(a)(i) or a relevant appointment falling within paragraph (3)(b)(i), the administrator,

(ii) in the case of a relevant order falling within paragraph (3)(a)(ii) or (iii) or a relevant appointment falling within paragraph (3)(b)(ii), the liquidator,

(iii) in the case of a relevant order falling within paragraph (3)(a)(iv), the provisional liquidator, or

(iv) in the case of a relevant decision, the supervisor; and

(b) a creditor is a "known" creditor if the appointed officer is aware, or should reasonably be aware of—

(i) his identity,

(ii) his claim or potential claim, and

(iii) a recent address where he is likely to receive a communication.

(14) For the purposes of paragraph (3), and of regulations 13 and 14, a voluntary arrangement is a qualifying voluntary arrangement if its purposes include a realisation of some or all of the assets of the UK insurer to which the order relates and a distribution of the proceeds to creditors, with a view to terminating the whole or any part of the business of that insurer.

NOTES

Para (3): words in square brackets in sub-para (a) inserted by the Insurers (Reorganisation and Winding Up) (Amendment) Regulations 2007, SI 2007/851, reg 2(1), (8).

Para (10): substituted by SI 2007/851, reg 2(1), (9).

Para (11): words in first pair of square brackets inserted by SI 2007/851, reg 2(1), (8), (10); words in second and third pairs of square brackets substituted by the Financial Services Act 2012 (Consequential Amendments and Transitional Provisions) Order 2013, SI 2013/472, art 3, Sch 2, para 88(f).

Modification: in relation to the Lloyd's of London insurance market, this regulation is applied, with modifications, by the Insurers (Reorganisation and Winding Up) (Lloyd's) Regulations 2005, SI 2005/1998, regs 32, 36 at **[7.1601]**, **[7.1605]**.

[3.136]

13 Submission of claims by EEA creditors

(1) An EEA creditor who on or after 20th April 2003 submits a claim or observations relating to his claim in any relevant proceedings (irrespective of when those proceedings were commenced or had effect) may do so in his domestic language, provided that the requirements in paragraphs (3) and (4) are complied with.

(2) For the purposes of this regulation, "relevant proceedings" means—

(a) a winding up;

(b) a qualifying voluntary arrangement;

(c) administration.

(3) Where an EEA creditor submits a claim in his domestic language, the document must be headed with the words "Lodgement of claim" (in English).

(4) Where an EEA creditor submits observations on his claim (otherwise than in the document by which he submits his claim), the observations must be headed with the words "Submission of observations relating to claims" (in English).

(5) Paragraph (3) does not apply where an EEA creditor submits his claim using—

(a) in the case of a winding up, a form of proof supplied by the liquidator in accordance with Rule 4.74 of the Insolvency Rules, Rule 4.080 of the Insolvency Rules (Northern Ireland) or rule 4.15(2) of the Insolvency (Scotland) Rules as the case may be;

(b) in the case of a qualifying voluntary arrangement, a form approved by the court for that purpose.

(6) In this regulation—

(a) "domestic language", in relation to an EEA creditor, means the official language, or one of the official languages, of the EEA State in which he is ordinarily resident or, if the creditor is not an individual, in which the creditor's head office is located; and

(b) "qualifying voluntary arrangement" has the meaning given by regulation 12(12).

NOTES

Modification: in relation to the Lloyd's of London insurance market, this regulation is applied, with modifications, by the Insurers (Reorganisation and Winding Up) (Lloyd's) Regulations 2005, SI 2005/1998, regs 32, 37 at **[7.1601]**, **[7.1606]**.

[3.137]

14 Reports to creditors

(1) This regulation applies where, on or after 20th April 2003—

(a) a liquidator is appointed in accordance with section 100 of the 1986 Act or Article 86 of the 1989 Order (creditors' voluntary winding up: appointment of liquidator) or, on or after 15th September 2003, paragraph 83 of Schedule B1 [or paragraph 84 of Schedule B1 to the 1989 Order] (moving from administration to creditors' voluntary liquidation);

(b) a winding up order is made by the court;

(c) a provisional liquidator is appointed; or

(d) [an administrator is appointed under paragraph 13 of Schedule B1] [or under paragraph 14 of Schedule B1 to the 1989 Order].

(2) The liquidator or provisional liquidator (as the case may be) must send to every known creditor a report once in every 12 months beginning with the date when his appointment has effect.

(3) The requirement in paragraph (2) does not apply where a liquidator or provisional liquidator is required by order of the court to send a report to creditors at intervals which are more frequent than those required by this regulation.

(4) This regulation is without prejudice to any requirement to send a report to creditors, imposed by the court on the liquidator or provisional liquidator, which is supplementary to the requirements of this regulation.

(5) A liquidator or provisional liquidator commits an offence if he fails without reasonable excuse to comply with an applicable requirement under this regulation, and is liable on summary conviction to a fine not exceeding level 3 on the standard scale.

(6) For the purposes of this regulation—

(a) "known creditor" means—

(i) a creditor who is known to the liquidator or provisional liquidator, and

(ii) in a case falling within paragraph (1)(b) or (c), a creditor who is specified in the insurer's statement of affairs (within the meaning of section 131 of the 1986 Act or Article 111 of the 1989 Order); and

(b) "report" means a written report setting out the position generally as regards the progress of the winding up or provisional liquidation (as the case may be).

NOTES

Para (1): words in square brackets in sub-para (a) and words in second pair of square brackets in sub-para (d) inserted by the Insurers (Reorganisation and Winding Up) (Amendment) Regulations 2007, SI 2007/851, reg 2(1), (11); words in first pair of square brackets in sub-para (d) substituted by the Insurers (Reorganisation and Winding Up) (Amendment) Regulations 2004, SI 2004/546, reg 2(1), (3).

Modification: in relation to the Lloyd's of London insurance market, this regulation is applied, with modifications, by the Insurers (Reorganisation and Winding Up) (Lloyd's) Regulations 2005, SI 2005/1998, regs 32, 38 at **[7.1601]**, **[7.1607]**.

[3.138]

15 Service of notices and documents

(1) This regulation applies to any notification, report or other document which is required to be sent to a creditor of a UK insurer by a provision of this Part ("a relevant notification").

(2) A relevant notification may be sent to a creditor by either of the following methods—

(a) posting it to the proper address of the creditor;

(b) transmitting it electronically, in accordance with paragraph (4).

(3) For the purposes of paragraph (2)(a), the proper address of a creditor is any current address provided by that creditor as an address for service of a relevant notification or, if no such address is provided—

(a) the last known address of that creditor (whether his residence or a place where he carries on business);

(b) in the case of a body corporate, the address of its registered or principal office; or

(c) in the case of an unincorporated association, the address of its principal office.

(4) A relevant notification may be transmitted electronically only if it is sent to—

(a) an electronic address notified to the relevant officer by the creditor for this purpose; or

(b) if no such address has been notified, an electronic address at which the relevant officer reasonably believes the creditor will receive the notification.

(5) Any requirement in this part to send a relevant notification to a creditor shall also be treated as satisfied if—

(a) the creditor has agreed with—

(i) the UK insurer which is liable under the creditor's claim, or

(ii) the relevant officer,

that information which is required to be sent to him (whether pursuant to a statutory or contractual obligation, or otherwise) may instead be accessed by him on a web site;

(b) the agreement applies to the relevant notification in question;

(c) the creditor is notified of—

(i) the publication of the relevant notification on a web site,

(ii) the address of that web site,

(iii) the place on that web site where the relevant notification may be accessed, and how it may be accessed; and

(d) the relevant notification is published on that web site throughout a period of at least one month beginning with the date on which the creditor is notified in accordance with sub-paragraph (c):

(6) Where, in a case in which paragraph (5) is relied on for compliance with a requirement of regulation 12 or 14—

(a) a relevant notification is published for a part, but not all, of the period mentioned in paragraph (5)(d); but

(b) the failure to publish it throughout that period is wholly attributable to circumstances which it would not be reasonable to have expected the relevant officer to prevent or avoid,

no offence is committed under regulation 12(10) or regulation 14(5) (as the case may be) by reason of that failure.

(7) In this regulation—

(a) "electronic address" includes any number or address used for the purposes of receiving electronic communications;

(b) "electronic communication" means an electronic communication within the meaning of the Electronic Communications Act 2000 the processing of which on receipt is intended to produce writing; and

(c) "relevant officer" means (as the case may be) an administrator, liquidator, provisional liquidator or supervisor who is required to send a relevant notification to a creditor by a provision of this Part.

NOTES

Modification: in relation to the Lloyd's of London insurance market, this regulation is applied, with modifications, by the Insurers (Reorganisation and Winding Up) (Lloyd's) Regulations 2005, SI 2005/1998, regs 32, 39 at **[7.1601]**, **[7.1608]**.

[3.139]

16 Disclosure of confidential information received from an EEA regulator

(1) This regulation applies to information ("insolvency information") which—

(a) relates to the business or affairs of any other person; and

(b) is supplied to the [FCA or the PRA] by an EEA regulator acting in accordance with Articles 5, 8 or 30 of the reorganisation and winding up directive.

(2) Subject to paragraphs (3) and (4), sections 348, 349 and 352 of the 2000 Act apply in relation to insolvency information in the same way as they apply in relation to confidential information within the meaning of section 348(2) of the 2000 Act.

(3) Insolvency information is not subject to the restrictions on disclosure imposed by section 348(1) of the 2000 Act (as it applies by virtue of paragraph (2)) if it satisfies any of the criteria set out in section 348(4) of the 2000 Act.

(4) The Disclosure Regulations apply in relation to insolvency information as they apply in relation to single market directive information (within the meaning of those Regulations).

(5) In this regulation, "the Disclosure Regulations" means the Financial Services and Markets Act 2000 (Disclosure of Confidential Information) Regulations 2001.

NOTES

Para (1): words in square brackets substituted by the Financial Services Act 2012 (Consequential Amendments and Transitional Provisions) Order 2013, SI 2013/472, art 3, Sch 2, para 88(g).

PART IV
PRIORITY OF PAYMENT OF INSURANCE CLAIMS IN WINDING UP ETC

[3.140]

17 Interpretation of this Part

(1) For the purposes of this Part—

"composite insurer" means a UK insurer who is authorised to carry on both general business and long term business, in accordance with [Article 73(2) of the Solvency 2 Directive];

"floating charge" has the meaning given by section 251 of the 1986 Act or paragraph (1) of Article 5 of the 1989 Order;

"general business" means the business of effecting or carrying out a contract of general insurance;

"general business assets" means the assets of a composite insurer which are, or should properly be, apportioned to that insurer's general business, in accordance with the requirements of [Article 73(5) of the Solvency 2 Directive] (separate management of long term and general business of a composite insurer);

"general business liabilities" means the debts of a composite insurer which are attributable to the general business carried on by that insurer;

"general insurer" means a UK insurer who carries on exclusively general business;

"long term business" means the business of effecting or carrying out a contract of long term insurance;

"long term business assets" means the assets of a composite insurer which are, or should properly be, apportioned to that insurer's long term business, in accordance with the requirements of [Article 73(5) of the Solvency 2 Directive] (separate management of long term and general business of a composite insurer);

"long term business liabilities" means the debts of a composite insurer which are attributable to the long term business carried on by that insurer;

"long term insurer" means a UK insurer who—

(a) carries on long term business exclusively, or

(b) carries on long term business and permitted general business;

"non-transferring composite insurer" means a composite insurer the long term business of which has not been, and is not to be, transferred as a going concern to a person who may lawfully carry out those contracts, in accordance with section 376(2) of the 2000 Act;

"other assets" means any assets of a composite insurer which are not long term business assets or general business assets;

"other business", in relation to a composite insurer, means such of the business (if any) of the insurer as is not long term business or general business;

"permitted general business" means the business of effecting or carrying out a contract of general insurance where the risk insured against relates to either accident or sickness;

"preferential debt" means a debt falling into any of categories 4 or 5 of the debts listed in Schedule 6 to the 1986 Act or Schedule 4 to the 1989 Order, that is—

(a) contributions to occupational pension schemes, etc, and

(b) remuneration etc of employees;

"society" means—

(a) a friendly society incorporated under the Friendly Societies Act 1992,

(b) a society which is a friendly society within the meaning of section 7(1)(a) of the Friendly Societies Act 1974, and registered within the meaning of that Act, or

[(c) a registered society.]

(2) In this Part, references to assets include a reference to proceeds where an asset has been realised, and any other sums representing assets.

(3) References in paragraph (1) to a contract of long term or of general insurance must be read with—

(a) section 22 of the 2000 Act;

(b) any relevant order made under that section; and

(c) Schedule 2 to that Act.

NOTES

Para (1): in definitions "composite insurer", "general business assets" and "long term business assets", words in square brackets substituted by the Solvency 2 Regulations 2015, SI 2015/575, reg 60, Sch 2, paras 17(1), (5); in definition "society" sub-para (c) substituted by the Co-operative and Community Benefit Societies and Credit Unions Act 2010 (Consequential Amendments) Regulations 2014, SI 2014/1815, reg 2, Schedule, para 12(1), (3).

Modification: in relation to the Lloyd's of London insurance market, this regulation is applied, with modifications, by the Insurers (Reorganisation and Winding Up) (Lloyd's) Regulations 2005, SI 2005/1998, regs 32, 40(1)–(4), 43 at **[7.1601]**, **[7.1609]**, **[7.1612]**.

[3.141]

18 Application of regulations 19 to 27

(1) Subject to paragraph (2), regulations 19 to 27 apply in the winding up of a UK insurer where—

(a) in the case of a winding up by the court, the winding up order is made on or after 20th April 2003; or

(b) in the case of a creditors' voluntary winding up, the liquidator is appointed, as mentioned in section 100 of the 1986 Act, paragraph 83 of Schedule B1[, paragraph 84 of Schedule B1 to the 1989 Order] or Article 86 of the 1989 Order, on or after 20th April 2003.

(2) Where a [relevant compromise or arrangement] is in place,

(a) no winding up proceedings may be opened without the permission of the court, and

(b) the permission of the court is to be granted only if required by the exceptional circumstances of the case.

(3) For the purposes of paragraph (2), winding up proceedings include proceedings for a winding up order or for a creditors' voluntary liquidation with confirmation by the court.

(4) Regulations 20 to 27 do not apply to a winding up falling within paragraph (1) where, in relation to a UK insurer—

(a) an administration order was made before 20th April 2003, and that order is not discharged until the commencement date; or

(b) a provisional liquidator was appointed before 20th April 2003, and that appointment is not discharged until the commencement date.

(5) For purposes of this regulation, "the commencement date" means the date when a UK insurer goes into liquidation within the meaning given by section 247(2) of the 1986 Act or Article 6(2) of the 1989 Order.

[(6) In paragraph (2) "relevant compromise or arrangement" means—

(a) a section 899 compromise or arrangement, or

(b) a compromise or arrangement sanctioned by the court in relation to a UK insurer before 6th April 2008 under—
(i) section 425 of the Companies Act 1985 (excluding a compromise or arrangement falling within section 427 or 427A of that Act), or
(ii) Article 418 of the Companies (Northern Ireland) Order 1986 (excluding a compromise or arrangement falling within Article 420 or 420A of that Order).]

NOTES

Para (1): words in square brackets in sub-para (b) inserted by the Insurers (Reorganisation and Winding Up) (Amendment) Regulations 2007, SI 2007/851, reg 2(1), (12).

Para (2): words in square brackets substituted by the Companies Act 2006 (Consequential Amendments and Transitional Provisions) Order 2011, SI 2011/1265, art 23(1), (4)(a).

Para (6): added by SI 2011/1265, art 23(1), (4)(b).

Modification: in relation to the Lloyd's of London insurance market, this regulation is applied, with modifications, by the Insurers (Reorganisation and Winding Up) (Lloyd's) Regulations 2005, SI 2005/1998, regs 32, 40(1)–(4), 43 at **[7.1601]**, **[7.1609]**, **[7.1612]**.

[3.142]

19 Application of this Part: [certain assets excluded from insolvent estate of UK insurer]

(1) For the purposes of this Part, the insolvent estate of a UK insurer shall not include any assets which at the commencement date are subject to [a relevant compromise or arrangement].

(2) In this regulation—
(a) "assets" has the same meaning as "property" in section 436 of the 1986 Act or Article 2(2) of the 1989 Order;
(b) "commencement date" has the meaning given in [regulation 18(5)];
(c) "insolvent estate"—
(i) in England, Wales and Northern Ireland has the meaning given by Rule 13.8 of the Insolvency Rules or Rule 0.2 of the Insolvency Rules (Northern Ireland), and
(ii) in Scotland means the company's assets;
[(d) "relevant compromise or arrangement" means—
(i) a compromise or arrangement sanctioned by the court in relation to a UK insurer before 20th April 2003 under—
(aa) section 425 of the Companies Act 1985 (excluding a compromise or arrangement falling within section 427 or 427A of that Act), or
(bb) Article 418 of the Companies (Northern Ireland) Order 1986 (excluding a compromise or arrangement falling within Article 420 or 420A of that Order); or
(ii) any subsequent compromise or arrangement sanctioned by the court to amend or replace a compromise or arrangement of a kind mentioned in paragraph (i) which is—
(aa) itself of a kind mentioned in sub-paragraph (aa) or (bb) of paragraph (i) (whether sanctioned before, on or after 20th April 2003), or
(bb) a section 899 compromise or arrangement.]

NOTES

Regulation heading: words in square brackets substituted by the Companies Act 2006 (Consequential Amendments and Transitional Provisions) Order 2011, SI 2011/1265, art 23(1), (5).

Para (1): words in square brackets substituted by SI 2011/1265, art 23(1), (6)(a).

Para (2): words in square brackets in sub-para (b) substituted by the Insurers (Reorganisation and Winding Up) (Lloyd's) Regulations 2005, SI 2005/1998, reg 49; sub-para (d) substituted by SI 2011/1265, art 23(1), (6)(b).

Modification: in relation to the Lloyd's of London insurance market, this regulation is applied, with modifications, by the Insurers (Reorganisation and Winding Up) (Lloyd's) Regulations 2005, SI 2005/1998, regs 32, 40(1)–(4), 43 at **[7.1601]**, **[7.1609]**, **[7.1612]**.

[3.143]

20 Preferential debts: disapplication of section 175 of the 1986 Act or Article 149 of the 1989 Order

Except to the extent that they are applied by regulation 27, section 175 of the 1986 Act or Article 149 of the 1989 Order (preferential debts (general provision)) does not apply in the case of a winding up of a UK insurer, and instead the provisions of regulations 21 to 26 have effect.

NOTES

Modification: in relation to the Lloyd's of London insurance market, this regulation is applied, with modifications, by the Insurers (Reorganisation and Winding Up) (Lloyd's) Regulations 2005, SI 2005/1998, regs 32, 40(1)–(5), 43 at **[7.1601]**, **[7.1609]**, **[7.1612]**.

[3.144]

21 Preferential debts: long term insurers and general insurers

(1) This regulation applies in the case of a winding up of—
(a) a long term insurer;
(b) a general insurer;
(c) a composite insurer, where the long term business of that insurer has been or is to be transferred as a going concern to a person who may lawfully carry out the contracts in that long term business in accordance with section 376(2) of the 2000 Act.

(2) Subject to paragraph (3), the debts of the insurer must be paid in the following order of priority—

(a) preferential debts;

(b) insurance debts;

(c) all other debts.

(3) Preferential debts rank equally among themselves [after the expenses of the winding up] and must be paid in full, unless the assets are insufficient to meet them, in which case they abate in equal proportions.

(4) Insurance debts rank equally among themselves and must be paid in full, unless the assets available after the payment of preferential debts are insufficient to meet them, in which case they abate in equal proportions.

(5) Subject to paragraph (6), so far as the assets of the insurer available for the payment of unsecured creditors are insufficient to meet the preferential debts, those debts (and only those debts) have priority over the claims of holders of debentures secured by, or holders of, any floating charge created by the insurer, and must be paid accordingly out of any property comprised in or subject to that charge.

(6) The order of priority specified in paragraph (2)(a) and (b) applies for the purposes of any payment made in accordance with paragraph (5).

(7) Section 176A of the 1986 Act [and Article 150A of the 1989 Order] [have] effect with regard to an insurer so that insurance debts must be paid out of the prescribed part in priority to all other unsecured debts.

NOTES

Para (3): words in square brackets inserted by the Insurers (Reorganisation and Winding Up) (Amendment) Regulations 2004, SI 2004/546, reg 2(1), (4).

Para (7): words in first pair of square brackets inserted and word in second pair of square brackets substituted by the Insurers (Reorganisation and Winding Up) (Amendment) Regulations 2007, SI 2007/851, reg 2(1), (13).

Modification: in relation to the Lloyd's of London insurance market, this regulation is applied, with modifications, by the Insurers (Reorganisation and Winding Up) (Lloyd's) Regulations 2005, SI 2005/1998, regs 32, 40(1)–(4), (6), 43 at **[7.1601]**, **[7.1609]**, **[7.1612]**.

[3.145]

22 Composite insurers: preferential debts attributable to long term and general business

(1) This regulation applies in the case of the winding up of a non-transferring composite insurer.

(2) Subject to the payment of costs in accordance with regulation 30, the long term business assets and the general business assets must be applied separately in accordance with paragraphs (3) and (4).

(3) Subject to paragraph (6), the long term business assets must be applied in discharge of the long term business preferential debts in the order of priority specified in regulation 23(1).

(4) Subject to paragraph (8), the general business assets must be applied in discharge of the general business preferential debts in the order of priority specified in regulation 24(1).

(5) Paragraph (6) applies where the value of the long term business assets exceeds the long term business preferential debts and the general business assets are insufficient to meet the general business preferential debts.

(6) Those long term business assets which represent the excess must be applied in discharge of the outstanding general business preferential debts of the insurer, in accordance with the order of priority specified in regulation 24(1).

(7) Paragraph (8) applies where the value of the general business assets exceeds the general business preferential debts, and the long term business assets are insufficient to meet the long term business preferential debts.

(8) Those general business assets which represent the excess must be applied in discharge of the outstanding long term business preferential debts of the insurer, in accordance with the order of priority specified in regulation 23(1).

(9) For the purposes of this regulation and regulations 23 and 24—

"long term business preferential debts" means those debts mentioned in regulation 23(1) and, unless the court orders otherwise, any expenses of the winding up which are apportioned to the long term business assets in accordance with regulation 30;

"general business preferential debts" means those debts mentioned in regulation 24(1) and, unless the court orders otherwise, any expenses of the winding up which are apportioned to the general business assets in accordance with regulation 30.

(10) For the purposes of paragraphs (6) and (8)—

"outstanding long term business preferential debts" means those long term business preferential debts, if any, which remain unpaid, either in whole or in part, after the application of the long term business assets, in accordance with paragraph (3);

"outstanding general business preferential debts" means those general business preferential debts, if any, which remain unpaid, either in whole or in part, after the application of the general business assets, in accordance with paragraph (3).

NOTES

Modification: in relation to the Lloyd's of London insurance market, this regulation is applied, with modifications, by the Insurers (Reorganisation and Winding Up) (Lloyd's) Regulations 2005, SI 2005/1998, regs 32, 40(1)–(4), 43 at **[7.1601]**, **[7.1609]**, **[7.1612]**.

[3.146]

23 Preferential debts: long term business of a non-transferring composite insurer

(1) For the purpose of compliance with the requirement in regulation 22(3), the long term business assets of a non-transferring composite insurer must be applied in discharge of the following debts and in the following order of priority—

(a) relevant preferential debts;
(b) long term insurance debts.

(2) Relevant preferential debts rank equally among themselves, unless the long term business assets, any available general business assets and other assets (if any) applied in accordance with regulation 24 are insufficient to meet them, in which case they abate in equal proportions.

(3) Long term insurance debts rank equally among themselves, unless the long term business assets available after the payment of relevant preferential debts and any available general business assets and other assets (if any) applied in accordance with regulation 25 are insufficient to meet them, in which case they abate in equal proportions.

(4) So far as the long term business assets, and any available general business assets, which are available for the payment of unsecured creditors are insufficient to meet the relevant preferential debts, those debts (and only those debts) have priority over the claims of holders of debentures secured by, or holders of, any floating charge created by the insurer over any of its long term business assets, and must be paid accordingly out of any property comprised in or subject to that charge.

(5) The order of priority specified in paragraph (1) applies for the purposes of any payment made in accordance with paragraph (4).

(6) For the purposes of this regulation—

"available general business assets" means those general business assets which must be applied in discharge of the insurer's outstanding long term business preferential debts, in accordance with regulation 22(8);

"long term insurance debt" means an insurance debt which is attributable to the long term business of the insurer;

"relevant preferential debt" means a preferential debt which is attributable to the long term business of the insurer.

NOTES

Modification: in relation to the Lloyd's of London insurance market, this regulation is applied, with modifications, by the Insurers (Reorganisation and Winding Up) (Lloyd's) Regulations 2005, SI 2005/1998, regs 32, 40(1)–(4), 43 at **[7.1601]**, **[7.1609]**, **[7.1612]**.

[3.147]

24 Preferential debts: general business of a composite insurer

(1) For the purpose of compliance with the requirement in regulation 22(4), the long term business assets of a non-transferring composite insurer must be applied in discharge of the following debts and in the following order of priority—

(a) relevant preferential debts;
(b) general insurance debts.

(2) Relevant preferential debts rank equally among themselves, unless the general business assets, any available long term business assets, and other assets (if any) applied in accordance with regulation 25 are insufficient to meet them, in which case they abate in equal proportions.

(3) General insurance debts rank equally among themselves, unless the general business assets available after the payment of relevant preferential debts, any available long term business assets, and other assets (if any) applied in accordance with regulation 26 are insufficient to meet them, in which case they abate in equal proportions.

(4) So far as the other business assets and available long term assets of the insurer which are available for the payment of unsecured creditors are insufficient to meet relevant preferential debts, those debts (and only those debts) have priority over the claims of holders of debentures secured by, or holders of, any floating charge created by the insurer, and must be paid accordingly out of any property comprised in or subject to that charge.

(5) The order of priority specified in paragraph (1) applies for the purposes of any payment made in accordance with paragraph (4).

(6) For the purposes of this regulation—

"available long term business assets" means those long term business assets which must be applied in discharge of the insurer's outstanding general business preferential debts, in accordance with regulation 22(6);

"general insurance debt" means an insurance debt which is attributable to the general business of the insurer;

"relevant preferential debt" means a preferential debt which is attributable to the general business of the insurer.

NOTES

Modification: in relation to the Lloyd's of London insurance market, this regulation is applied, with modifications, by the Insurers (Reorganisation and Winding Up) (Lloyd's) Regulations 2005, SI 2005/1998, regs 32, 40(1)–(4), 43 at **[7.1601]**, **[7.1609]**, **[7.1612]**.

[3.148]
25 Insufficiency of long term business assets and general business assets

(1) This regulation applies in the case of the winding up of a non-transferring composite insurer where the long term business assets and the general business assets, applied in accordance with regulation 22, are insufficient to meet in full the preferential debts and insurance debts.

(2) In a case in which this regulation applies, the other assets (if any) of the insurer must be applied in the following order of priority—

(a) outstanding preferential debts;
(b) unattributed preferential debts;
(c) outstanding insurance debts;
(d) all other debts.

(3) So far as the long term business assets, and any available general business assets, which are available for the payment of unsecured creditors are insufficient to meet the outstanding preferential debts and the unattributed preferential debts, those debts (and only those debts) have priority over the claims of holders of debentures secured by, or holders of, any floating charge created by the insurer over any of its other assets, and must be paid accordingly out of any property comprised in or subject to that charge.

(4) For the purposes of this regulation—

"outstanding insurance debt" means any insurance debt, or any part of an insurance debt, which was not discharged by the application of the long term business assets and the general business assets in accordance with regulation 22;

"outstanding preferential debt" means any preferential debt attributable either to the long term business or the general business of the insurer which was not discharged by the application of the long term business assets and the general business assets in accordance with regulation 23;

"unattributed preferential debt" means a preferential debt which is not attributable to either the long term business or the general business of the insurer.

NOTES

Modification: in relation to the Lloyd's of London insurance market, this regulation is applied, with modifications, by the Insurers (Reorganisation and Winding Up) (Lloyd's) Regulations 2005, SI 2005/1998, regs 32, 40(1)–(4), 43 at **[7.1601]**, **[7.1609]**, **[7.1612]**.

[3.149]
26 Composite insurers: excess of long term business assets and general business assets

(1) This regulation applies in the case of the winding up of a non-transferring composite insurer where the value of the long term business assets and the general business assets, applied in accordance with regulation 22, exceeds the value of the sum of the long term business preferential debts and the general business preferential debts.

(2) In a case to which this regulation applies, long term business assets or general business assets which have not been applied in discharge of long term business preferential debts or general business preferential debts must be applied in accordance with regulation 27.

(3) In this regulation, "long term business preferential debts" and "general business preferential debts" have the same meaning as in regulation 22.

NOTES

Modification: in relation to the Lloyd's of London insurance market, this regulation is applied, with modifications, by the Insurers (Reorganisation and Winding Up) (Lloyd's) Regulations 2005, SI 2005/1998, regs 32, 40(1)–(4), 43 at **[7.1601]**, **[7.1609]**, **[7.1612]**.

[3.150]
27 Composite insurers: application of other assets

(1) This regulation applies in the case of the winding up of a non-transferring composite insurer where regulation 25 does not apply.

(2) The other assets of the insurer, together with any outstanding business assets, must be paid in discharge of the following debts in accordance with section 175 of the 1986 Act or Article 149 of the 1989 Order—

(a) unattributed preferential debts;
(b) all other debts.

(3) In this regulation—

"unattributed preferential debt" has the same meaning as in regulation 25;

"outstanding business assets" means assets of the kind mentioned in regulation 26(2).

NOTES

Modification: in relation to the Lloyd's of London insurance market, this regulation is applied, with modifications, by the Insurers (Reorganisation and Winding Up) (Lloyd's) Regulations 2005, SI 2005/1998, regs 32, 40(1)–(4), (7), 43 at **[7.1601]**, **[7.1609]**, **[7.1612]**.

[3.151]
28 Composite insurers: proof of debts

(1) This regulation applies in the case of the winding up of a non-transferring composite insurer in compliance with the requirement in regulation 23(2).

(2) The liquidator may in relation to the insurer's long term business assets and its general business assets fix different days on or before which the creditors of the company who are required to prove their debts or claims are to prove their debts or claims, and he may fix one of those days without at the same time fixing the other.

(3) In submitting a proof of any debt a creditor may claim the whole or any part of such debt as is attributable to the company's long term business or to its general business, or he may make no such attribution.

(4) When he admits any debt, in whole or in part, the liquidator must state in writing how much of what he admits is attributable to the company's long term business, how much is attributable to the company's general business, and how much is attributable to its other business (if any).

(5) Paragraph (2) does not apply in Scotland.

NOTES

Modification: in relation to the Lloyd's of London insurance market, this regulation is applied, with modifications, by the Insurers (Reorganisation and Winding Up) (Lloyd's) Regulations 2005, SI 2005/1998, regs 32, 40(1)–(4), 43 at **[7.1601]**, **[7.1609]**, **[7.1612]**.

[3.152]

[28A Composite insurers: seeking decisions from creditors

(1) This regulation applies in the same circumstances as regulation 28, but only if the non-transferring composite insurer is—

(a) a company registered in England and Wales;

(b) a registered society within the meaning given by section 1(1) of the Co-operative and Community Benefit Societies Act 2014 which the courts in England and Wales have jurisdiction to wind up; or

(c) a friendly society within the meaning of section 7(1)(a) of the Friendly Societies Act 1974, which is registered within the meaning of that Act and is being wound up by the High Court under the Insolvency Act 1986.

(2) The creditors from whom the liquidator is to seek a decision about any matter in relation to the winding up are to be—

(a) in relation to the long term business assets of that insurer, only those who are creditors in respect of long term business liabilities, and

(b) in relation to the general business assets of that insurer, only those who are creditors in respect of general business liabilities.]

NOTES

Commencement: 13 March 2018.

Inserted by the Small Business, Enterprise and Employment Act 2015 (Consequential Amendments, Savings and Transitional Provisions) Regulations 2018, SI 2018/208, reg 9(1), (2), as from 13 March 2018 (for transitional provisions, see the note below).

Transitional provisions: the Small Business, Enterprise and Employment Act 2015 (Consequential Amendments, Savings and Transitional Provisions) Regulations 2018, SI 2018/208, regs 16, 20 provide as follows—

"16 Interpretation of Part 4

In this Part—

"the 1986 Act" means the Insolvency Act 1986;

"the 2000 Act" means the Financial Services and Markets Act 2000;

"the 2009 Act" means the Banking Act 2009; and

"relevant meeting" means a meeting of creditors which is to be held on or after the date on which Parts 2 and 3 of these Regulations come into force, and was—

(a) called, summoned or otherwise required before 6th April 2017 under a provision of the 1986 Act or the Insolvency Rules 1986;

(b) requisitioned by a creditor before 6th April 2017 under a provision of the 1986 Act or the Insolvency Rules 1986; or

(c) called or summoned under section 106, 146 or 331 of the 1986 Act as a result of—

(i) a final report to creditors sent before 6th April 2017 under rule 4.49D of the Insolvency Rules 1986 (final report to creditors in liquidation);

(ii) a final report to creditors and bankrupt sent before that date under rule 6.78B of those Rules (final report to creditors and bankrupt).

20 Transitional provision for regulation 9

(1) Where a relevant meeting is to be held in proceedings for the winding up by the court or a creditors' voluntary winding up of a non-transferring composite insurer (within the meaning given in regulation 17(1) of the Insurers (Reorganisation and Winding Up) Regulations 2004), those Regulations apply in relation to the meeting without the amendments made by regulation 9(2) and (3).

(2) Where a relevant meeting is to be held in proceedings relating to a proposal for a company voluntary arrangement made under Part 1 of the 1986 Act in respect of a UK insurer (within the meaning given in regulation 2(1) of the Insurers (Reorganisation and Winding Up) Regulations 2004), those Regulations apply in relation to the meeting without the amendments made by regulation 9(4)."

[3.153]
29 Composite insurers: general meetings of creditors

(1) This regulation applies in the same circumstances as regulation 28[, but only if the non-transferring composite insurer is a company registered in Scotland or Northern Ireland or a society other than a society of a kind to which regulation 28A applies].

(2) The creditors mentioned in section 168(2) of the 1986 Act [(as applied in relation to such a society)], Article 143(2) of the 1989 Order or rule 4.13 of the Insolvency (Scotland) Rules (power of liquidator to summon general meetings of creditors) are to be—

(a) in relation to the long term business assets of that insurer, only those who are creditors in respect of long term business liabilities; and

(b) in relation to the general business assets of that insurer, only those who are creditors in respect of general business liabilities,

and, accordingly, any general meetings of creditors summoned for the purposes of that section, Article or rule are to be separate general meetings of creditors in respect of long term business liabilities and general business liabilities.

NOTES

Paras (1), (2): words in square brackets inserted by the Small Business, Enterprise and Employment Act 2015 (Consequential Amendments, Savings and Transitional Provisions) Regulations 2018, SI 2018/208, reg 9(1), (3), as from 13 March 2018 and subject to transitional provisions as noted to reg 28A at **[3.152]**.

Modification: in relation to the Lloyd's of London insurance market, this regulation is applied, with modifications, by the Insurers (Reorganisation and Winding Up) (Lloyd's) Regulations 2005, SI 2005/1998, regs 32, 40(1)–(4), (8), 43 at **[7.1601]**, **[7.1609]**, **[7.1612]**.

[3.154]
30 Composite insurers: apportionment of costs payable out of the assets

(1) In the case of the winding up of a non-transferring composite insurer, Rule 4.218 of the Insolvency Rules or Rule 4.228 of the Insolvency Rules (Northern Ireland) (general rules as to priority) or rule 4.67 (order of priority of expenses of liquidation) of the Insolvency (Scotland) Rules applies separately to long-term business assets and to the general business assets of that insurer.

(2) But where any fee, expense, cost, charge, or remuneration does not relate exclusively to the long-term business assets or to the general business assets of that insurer, the liquidator must apportion it amongst those assets in such manner as he shall determine.

NOTES

Modification: in relation to the Lloyd's of London insurance market, this regulation is applied, with modifications, by the Insurers (Reorganisation and Winding Up) (Lloyd's) Regulations 2005, SI 2005/1998, regs 32, 40(1)–(4), (9), 43 at **[7.1601]**, **[7.1609]**, **[7.1612]**.

[3.155]
31 Summary remedy against liquidators

Section 212 of the 1986 Act or Article 176 of the 1989 Order (summary remedy against delinquent directors, liquidators etc) applies in relation to a liquidator who is required to comply with regulations 21 to 27, as it applies in relation to a liquidator who is required to comply with section 175 of the 1986 Act or Article 149 of the 1989 Order.

NOTES

Modification: in relation to the Lloyd's of London insurance market, this regulation is applied, with modifications, by the Insurers (Reorganisation and Winding Up) (Lloyd's) Regulations 2005, SI 2005/1998, regs 32, 40(1)–(4), (10), 43 at **[7.1601]**, **[7.1609]**, **[7.1612]**.

[3.156]
32 Priority of subrogated claims by the Financial Services Compensation Scheme

(1) This regulation applies where an insurance creditor has assigned a relevant right to the scheme manager ("a relevant assignment").

(2) For the purposes of regulations 21, 23 and 24, where the scheme manager proves for an insurance debt in the winding up of a UK insurer pursuant to a relevant assignment, that debt must be paid to the scheme manager in the same order of priority as any other insurance debt.

(3) In this regulation—

"relevant right" means any direct right of action against a UK insurer under a contract of insurance, including the right to prove for a debt under that contract in a winding up of that insurer;

"scheme manager" has the meaning given by section 212(1) of the 2000 Act.

NOTES

Modification: in relation to the Lloyd's of London insurance market, this regulation is applied, with modifications, by the Insurers (Reorganisation and Winding Up) (Lloyd's) Regulations 2005, SI 2005/1998, regs 32, 40(1)–(4), 43 at **[7.1601]**, **[7.1609]**, **[7.1612]**.

[3.157]

33 Voluntary arrangements: treatment of insurance debts

(1) The modifications made by paragraph (2) apply where a voluntary arrangement is proposed under section 1 of the 1986 Act or Article 14 of the 1989 Order in relation to a UK insurer, and that arrangement includes—

(a) a composition in satisfaction of any insurance debts; and

(b) a distribution to creditors of some or all of the assets of that insurer in the course of, or with a view to, terminating the whole or any part of the business of that insurer.

(2) Section 4 of the 1986 Act (decisions of meetings) has effect as if—

(a) after subsection (4) there were inserted—

"[(4ZA) In relation to a company registered in England and Wales, neither the company nor its creditors may approve any proposal or modification under which any insurance debt of the company is to be paid otherwise than in priority to such of its debts as are not insurance debts or preferential debts.]

(4A) [In relation to a company registered in Scotland, a meeting summoned under section 3] and taking place on or after 20th April 2003 shall not approve any proposal or modification under which any insurance debt of the company is to be paid otherwise than in priority to such of its debts as are not insurance debts or preferential debts.

(4B) Paragraph (4A) does not apply where—

(a) a winding up order made before 20th April 2003 is in force; or

(b) a relevant insolvency appointment made before 20th April 2003 has effect,

in relation to the company.";

(b) for subsection (7) there were substituted—

"(7) References in this section to preferential debts mean debts falling into any of categories 4 and 5 of the debts listed in Schedule 6 to this Act; and references to preferential creditors are to be construed accordingly."; and

(c) after subsection (7) as so substituted there were inserted—

"(8) For the purposes of this section—

(a) "insurance debt" has the meaning it has in the Insurers (Reorganisation and Winding up) Regulations 2004; and

(b) "relevant insolvency measure" means—

(i) the appointment of a provisional liquidator, or

(ii) the appointment of an administrator,

where an effect of the appointment will be, or is intended to be, a realisation of some or all of the assets of the insurer and the distribution of the proceeds to creditors, with a view to terminating the whole or any part of the business of that insurer.".

(3) Article 17 of the 1989 Order (decisions of meetings) has effect as if—

(a) after paragraph (4) there were inserted—

"(4A) A meeting so summoned and taking place on or after 20th April 2003 shall not approve any proposal or modification under which any insurance debt of the company is to be paid otherwise than in priority to such of its debts as are not insurance debts or preferential debts.

(4B) Paragraph (4A) does not apply where—

(a) a winding up order made before 20th April 2003 is in force; or

(b) a relevant insolvency appointment made before 20th April 2003 has effect, in relation to the company.";

(b) for paragraph (7) there were substituted—

"(7) References in this Article to preferential debts mean debts falling into any of categories 4 and 5 of the debts listed in Schedule 4 to this Order, and references to preferential creditors are to be construed accordingly."; and

(c) after paragraph (7) as so substituted there were inserted—

"(8) For the purposes of this section—

(a) "insurance debt" has the meaning it has in the Insurers (Reorganisation and Winding Up) Regulations 2004 and

(b) "relevant insolvency measure" means—

(i) the appointment of a provisional liquidator, or

(ii) the appointment of an administrator,

where an effect of the appointment will be, or is intended to be, a realisation of some or all of the assets of the insurer and the distribution of the proceeds to creditors, with a view to terminating the whole or any part of the business of that insurer.".

NOTES

Para (2): in s 4 of the 1986 Act as set out, sub-s (4ZA) inserted and words in square brackets in sub-s (4A) substituted for original words "A meeting so summoned", by the Small Business, Enterprise and Employment Act 2015 (Consequential Amendments, Savings and Transitional Provisions) Regulations 2018, SI 2018/208, reg 9(1), (4), as from 13 March 2018 and subject to transitional provisions as noted to reg 28A at **[3.152]**.

Modification: in relation to the Lloyd's of London insurance market, this regulation is applied, with modifications, by the Insurers (Reorganisation and Winding Up) (Lloyd's) Regulations 2005, SI 2005/1998, regs 32, 40(1)–(4), (11), 43 at **[7.1601]**, **[7.1609]**, **[7.1612]**.

PART V
REORGANISATION OR WINDING UP OF UK INSURERS: RECOGNITION OF EEA RIGHTS

[3.158]

34 Application of this Part

(1) This Part applies—

(a) where a decision with respect to the approval of a proposed voluntary arrangement having a qualifying purpose is made under section 4A of the 1986 Act or Article 17A of the 1989 Order on or after 20th April 2003 in relation to a UK insurer;

(b) where an administration order made under section 8 of the 1986 Act on or after 20th April 2003 or, on or after 15th September 2003, made under paragraph 13 of Schedule B1 [or under paragraph 14 of Schedule B1 to the 1989 Order] is in force in relation to a UK insurer;

(c) where on or after 20th April 2003 the court reduces the value of one or more of the contracts of a UK insurer under section 377 of the 2000 Act or section 24(5) of the Friendly Societies Act 1992;

(d) where a UK insurer is subject to a relevant winding up;

(e) where a provisional liquidator is appointed in relation to a UK insurer on or after 20th April 2003.

(2) For the purposes of paragraph (1)(a), a voluntary arrangement has a qualifying purpose if it—

(a) varies the rights of the creditors as against the insurer and is intended to enable the insurer, and the whole or any part of its undertaking, to survive as a going concern; or

(b) includes a realisation of some or all of the assets of the insurer to which it relates and the distribution of the proceeds to creditors, with a view to terminating the whole or any part of the business of that insurer.

(3) For the purposes of paragraph (1)(d), a winding up is a relevant winding up if—

(a) in the case of a winding up by the court, the winding up order is made on or after 20th April 2003; or

(b) in the case of a creditors' voluntary winding up, the liquidator is appointed in accordance with section 100 of the 1986 Act, paragraph 83 of Schedule B1[, paragraph 84 of Schedule B1 to the 1989 Order] or Article 86 of the 1989 Order on or after 20th April 2003.

NOTES

Para (1): words in square brackets in sub-para (b) inserted by the Insurers (Reorganisation and Winding Up) (Amendment) Regulations 2007, SI 2007/851, reg 2(1), (14).

Para (3): words in square brackets in sub-para (b) inserted by SI 2007/851, reg 2(1), (15).

Modification: in relation to the Lloyd's of London insurance market, this regulation is applied, with modifications, by the Insurers (Reorganisation and Winding Up) (Lloyd's) Regulations 2005, SI 2005/1998, regs 45, 47 at **[7.1614]**, **[7.1616]**.

[3.159]

35 Application of this Part: [certain assets excluded from insolvent estate of UK insurer]

(1) For the purposes of this Part, the insolvent estate of a UK insurer shall not include any assets which at the commencement date are subject to [a relevant compromise or arrangement].

(2) In this regulation—

(a) "assets" has the same meaning as "property" in section 436 of the 1986 Act or Article 2(2) of the 1989 Order;

(b) "commencement date" has the meaning given in regulation 18(4);

(c) "insolvent estate" in England and Wales and Northern Ireland has the meaning given by Rule 13.8 of the Insolvency Rules or Rule 0.2 of the Insolvency Rules (Northern Ireland) and in Scotland means the company's assets;

[(d) "relevant compromise or arrangement" means—

(i) a compromise or arrangement sanctioned by the court in relation to a UK insurer before 20th April 2003 under—

(aa) section 425 of the Companies Act 1985 (excluding a compromise or arrangement falling within section 427 or 427A of that Act), or

(bb) Article 418 of the Companies (Northern Ireland) Order 1986 (excluding a compromise or arrangement falling within Article 420 or 420A of that Order); or

(ii) any subsequent compromise or arrangement sanctioned by the court to amend or replace a compromise or arrangement of a kind mentioned in paragraph (i) which is—

(aa) itself of a kind mentioned in sub-paragraph (aa) or (bb) of paragraph (i) (whether sanctioned before, on or after 20th April 2003), or

(bb) a section 899 compromise or arrangement.]

NOTES

Regulation heading: words in square brackets substituted by the Companies Act 2006 (Consequential Amendments and Transitional Provisions) Order 2011, SI 2011/1265, art 23(1), (7).

Para (1): words in square brackets substituted by SI 2011/1265, art 23(1), (8)(a).

Para (2): sub-para (d) substituted by SI 2011/1265, art 23(1), (8)(b).

Modification: in relation to the Lloyd's of London insurance market, this regulation is applied, with modifications, by the Insurers (Reorganisation and Winding Up) (Lloyd's) Regulations 2005, SI 2005/1998, regs 45, 46(1), (2), 47 at **[7.1614]–[7.1616]**.

[3.160]

36 Interpretation of this Part

(1) For the purposes of this Part—

(a) "affected insurer" means a UK insurer which is the subject of a relevant reorganisation or a relevant winding up;

(b) "relevant reorganisation or a relevant winding up" means any voluntary arrangement, administration order, winding up, or order referred to in regulation 34(1)(d) to which this Part applies; and

(c) "relevant time" means the date of the opening of a relevant reorganisation or a relevant winding up.

(2) In this Part, references to the opening of a relevant reorganisation or a relevant winding up mean—

(a) in the case of winding up proceedings—

(i) in the case of a winding up by the court, the date on which the winding up order is made, or

(ii) in the case of a creditors' voluntary winding up, the date on which the liquidator is appointed in accordance with section 100 of the 1986 Act, paragraph 83 of Schedule B1 or Article 86 of the 1989 Order [or paragraph 84 of Schedule B1 to the 1989 Order];

(b) in the case of a voluntary arrangement, the date when a decision with respect to that voluntary arrangement has effect in accordance with section 4A(2) of the 1986 Act or Article 17A(2) of the 1989 Order;

(c) in a case where an administration order under paragraph 13 of Schedule B1 [or under paragraph 14 of Schedule B1 to the 1989 Order] is in force, the date of the making of that order;

(d) in a case where an administrator is appointed under paragraphs 14 or 22 of Schedule B1 [or under paragraph 15 or 23 of Schedule B1 to the 1989 Order,] the date on which that appointment takes effect;

(e) in a case where the court reduces the value of one or more of the contracts of a UK insurer under section 377 of the 2000 Act or section 24(5) of the Friendly Societies Act 1992, the date the court exercises that power; and

(f) in a case where a provisional liquidator has been appointed, the date of that appointment,

and references to the time of an opening must be construed accordingly.

NOTES

Para (2): words in square brackets inserted by the Insurers (Reorganisation and Winding Up) (Amendment) Regulations 2007, SI 2007/851, reg 2(1), (16).

Modification: in relation to the Lloyd's of London insurance market, this regulation is applied, with modifications, by the Insurers (Reorganisation and Winding Up) (Lloyd's) Regulations 2005, SI 2005/1998, regs 45, 46(1), (3), 47 at **[7.1614]–[7.1616]**.

[3.161]

37 EEA rights: applicable law in the winding up of a UK insurer

(1) This regulation is subject to the provisions of regulations 38 to 47.

(2) In a relevant winding up, the matters mentioned in paragraph (3) in particular are to be determined in accordance with the general law of insolvency of the United Kingdom.

(3) Those matters are—

(a) the assets which form part of the estate of the affected insurer;

(b) the treatment of assets acquired by, or devolving on, the affected insurer after the opening of the relevant winding up;

(c) the respective powers of the affected insurer and the liquidator or provisional liquidator;

(d) the conditions under which set-off may be revoked;

(e) the effects of the relevant winding up on current contracts to which the affected insurer is a party;

(f) the effects of the relevant winding up on proceedings brought by creditors;

(g) the claims which are to be lodged against the estate of the affected insurer;

(h) the treatment of claims against the affected insurer arising after the opening of the relevant winding up;

(i) the rules governing—

(i) the lodging, verification and admission of claims,

(ii) the distribution of proceeds from the realisation of assets,

(iii) the ranking of claims,

(iv) the rights of creditors who have obtained partial satisfaction after the opening of the relevant winding up by virtue of a right in rem or through set-off;

(j) the conditions for and the effects of the closure of the relevant winding up, in particular by composition;

(k) the rights of creditors after the closure of the relevant winding up;

(l) who is to bear the cost and expenses incurred in the relevant winding up;

(m) the rules relating to the voidness, voidability or unenforceability of legal acts detrimental to all the creditors.

(4) In this regulation, "relevant winding up" has the meaning given by regulation 34(3).

NOTES

Modification: in relation to the Lloyd's of London insurance market, this regulation is applied, with modifications, by the Insurers (Reorganisation and Winding Up) (Lloyd's) Regulations 2005, SI 2005/1998, regs 45, 46(1), (4), 47 at **[7.1614]–[7.1616]**.

[3.162]

38 Employment contracts and relationships

(1) The effects of a relevant reorganisation or a relevant winding up on any EEA employment contract and any EEA employment relationship are to be determined in accordance with the law of the EEA State to which that contract or that relationship is subject.

(2) In this regulation, an employment contract is an EEA employment contract, and an employment relationship is an EEA employment relationship, if it is subject to the law of an EEA State.

NOTES

Modification: in relation to the Lloyd's of London insurance market, this regulation is applied, with modifications, by the Insurers (Reorganisation and Winding Up) (Lloyd's) Regulations 2005, SI 2005/1998, regs 45, 47 at **[7.1614]**, **[7.1616]**.

[3.163]

39 Contracts in connection with immovable property

The effects of a relevant reorganisation or a relevant winding up on a contract conferring the right to make use of or acquire immovable property situated within the territory of an EEA State are to be determined in accordance with the law of that State.

NOTES

Modification: in relation to the Lloyd's of London insurance market, this regulation is applied, with modifications, by the Insurers (Reorganisation and Winding Up) (Lloyd's) Regulations 2005, SI 2005/1998, regs 45, 47 at **[7.1614]**, **[7.1616]**.

[3.164]

40 Registrable rights

The effects of a relevant reorganisation or a relevant winding up on rights of the affected insurer with respect to—

(a) immovable property,
(b) a ship, or
(c) an aircraft

which is subject to registration in a public register kept under the authority of an EEA State are to be determined in accordance with the law of that State.

NOTES

Modification: in relation to the Lloyd's of London insurance market, this regulation is applied, with modifications, by the Insurers (Reorganisation and Winding Up) (Lloyd's) Regulations 2005, SI 2005/1998, regs 45, 47 at **[7.1614]**, **[7.1616]**.

[3.165]

41 Third parties' rights in rem

(1) A relevant reorganisation or a relevant winding up shall not affect the rights in rem of creditors or third parties in respect of tangible or intangible, movable or immovable assets (including both specific assets and collections of indefinite assets as a whole which change from time to time) belonging to the affected insurer which are situated within the territory of an EEA State at the relevant time.

(2) The rights in rem referred to in paragraph (1) shall in particular include—

(a) the right to dispose of the assets in question or have them disposed of and to obtain satisfaction from the proceeds of or the income from those assets, in particular by virtue of a lien or a mortgage;
(b) the exclusive right to have a claim met out of the assets in question, in particular a right guaranteed by a lien in respect of the claim or by assignment of the claim by way of guarantee;
(c) the right to demand the assets in question from, or to require restitution by, any person having possession or use of them contrary to the wishes of the party otherwise entitled to the assets;
(d) a right in rem to the beneficial use of assets.

(3) A right, recorded in a public register and enforceable against third parties, under which a right in rem within the meaning of paragraph (1) may be obtained, is also to be treated as a right in rem for the purposes of this regulation.

(4) Paragraph (1) does not preclude actions for voidness, voidability or unenforceability of legal acts detrimental to creditors under the general law of insolvency of the United Kingdom, as referred to in regulation 37(3)(m).

NOTES

Modification: in relation to the Lloyd's of London insurance market, this regulation is applied, with modifications, by the Insurers (Reorganisation and Winding Up) (Lloyd's) Regulations 2005, SI 2005/1998, regs 45, 47 at **[7.1614]**, **[7.1616]**.

[3.166]
42 Reservation of title agreements etc

(1) The opening of a relevant reorganisation or a relevant winding up in relation to an insurer purchasing an asset shall not affect the seller's rights based on a reservation of title where at the time of that opening the asset is situated within the territory of an EEA State.

(2) The opening of a relevant reorganisation or a relevant winding up in relation to an insurer selling an asset, after delivery of the asset, shall not constitute grounds for rescinding or terminating the sale and shall not prevent the purchaser from acquiring title where at the time of that opening the asset sold is situated within the territory of an EEA State.

(3) Paragraphs (1) and (2) do not preclude actions for voidness, voidability or unenforceability of legal acts detrimental to creditors under the general law of insolvency of the United Kingdom, as referred to in regulation 37(3)(m).

NOTES

Modification: in relation to the Lloyd's of London insurance market, this regulation is applied, with modifications, by the Insurers (Reorganisation and Winding Up) (Lloyd's) Regulations 2005, SI 2005/1998, regs 45, 46(1), (5), 47 at **[7.1614]–[7.1616]**.

[3.167]
43 Creditors' rights to set off

(1) A relevant reorganisation or a relevant winding up shall not affect the right of creditors to demand the set-off of their claims against the claims of the affected insurer, where such a set-off is permitted by the applicable EEA law.

(2) In paragraph (1), "applicable EEA law" means the law of the EEA State which is applicable to the claim of the affected insurer.

(3) Paragraph (1) does not preclude actions for voidness, voidability or unenforceability of legal acts detrimental to creditors under the general law of insolvency of the United Kingdom, as referred to in regulation 37(3)(m).

NOTES

Modification: in relation to the Lloyd's of London insurance market, this regulation is applied, with modifications, by the Insurers (Reorganisation and Winding Up) (Lloyd's) Regulations 2005, SI 2005/1998, regs 45, 47 at **[7.1614]**, **[7.1616]**.

[3.168]
44 Regulated markets

(1) Without prejudice to regulation 40, the effects of a relevant reorganisation measure or winding up on the rights and obligations of the parties to a regulated market operating in an EEA State must be determined in accordance with the law applicable to that market.

(2) Paragraph (1) does not preclude actions for voidness, voidability or unenforceability of legal acts detrimental to creditors under the general law of insolvency of the United Kingdom, as referred to in regulation 37(3)(m).

(3) For the purposes of this regulation, "regulated market" has the meaning given by [Article [4.1.21] of Directive [2014/65/EU] of the European Parliament and of the Council of [15 May 2014] on markets in financial instruments].

NOTES

Para (3): words in first (outer) pair of square brackets substituted by the Financial Services and Markets Act 2000 (Markets in Financial Instruments) Regulations 2007, SI 2007/126, reg 3(6), Sch 6, Pt 2, para 17; other words in square brackets substituted by the Financial Services and Markets Act 2000 (Markets in Financial Instruments) Regulations 2017, SI 2017/701, reg 50(4), Sch 5, para 4.

Modification: in relation to the Lloyd's of London insurance market, this regulation is applied, with modifications, by the Insurers (Reorganisation and Winding Up) (Lloyd's) Regulations 2005, SI 2005/1998, regs 45, 47 at **[7.1614]**, **[7.1616]**.

[3.169]
45 Detrimental acts pursuant to the law of an EEA State

(1) In a relevant reorganisation or a relevant winding up, the rules relating to detrimental transactions shall not apply where a person who has benefited from a legal act detrimental to all the creditors provides proof that—

(a) the said act is subject to the law of an EEA State; and
(b) that law does not allow any means of challenging that act in the relevant case.

(2) For the purposes of paragraph (1), "the rules relating to detrimental transactions" means any provisions of the general law of insolvency relating to the voidness, voidability or unenforceability of legal acts detrimental to all the creditors, as referred to in regulation 37(3)(m).

NOTES

Modification: in relation to the Lloyd's of London insurance market, this regulation is applied, with modifications, by the Insurers (Reorganisation and Winding Up) (Lloyd's) Regulations 2005, SI 2005/1998, regs 45, 47 at **[7.1614]**, **[7.1616]**.

[3.170]
46 Protection of third party purchasers

(1) This regulation applies where, by an act concluded after the opening of a relevant reorganisation or a relevant winding up, an affected insurer disposes for a consideration of—
(a) an immovable asset situated within the territory of an EEA State;
(b) a ship or an aircraft subject to registration in a public register kept under the authority of an EEA State; or
(c) securities whose existence or transfer presupposes entry into a register or account laid down by the law of an EEA State or which are placed in a central deposit system governed by the law of an EEA State.

(2) The validity of that act is to be determined in accordance with the law of the EEA State within whose territory the immovable asset is situated or under whose authority the register, account or system is kept, as the case may be.

NOTES

Modification: in relation to the Lloyd's of London insurance market, this regulation is applied, with modifications, by the Insurers (Reorganisation and Winding Up) (Lloyd's) Regulations 2005, SI 2005/1998, regs 45, 47 at **[7.1614]**, **[7.1616]**.

[3.171]
47 Lawsuits pending

(1) The effects of a relevant reorganisation or a relevant winding up on a relevant lawsuit pending in an EEA State shall be determined solely in accordance with the law of that EEA State.

(2) In paragraph (1), "relevant lawsuit" means a lawsuit concerning an asset or right of which the affected insurer has been divested.

NOTES

Modification: in relation to the Lloyd's of London insurance market, this regulation is applied, with modifications, by the Insurers (Reorganisation and Winding Up) (Lloyd's) Regulations 2005, SI 2005/1998, regs 45, 47 at **[7.1614]**, **[7.1616]**.

PART VI
THIRD COUNTRY INSURERS

[3.172]
48 Interpretation of this Part

(1) In this Part—
(a) "relevant measure", in relation to a third country insurer, means
(i) a winding up;
(ii) an administration order made under paragraph 13 of Schedule B1 [or under paragraph 14 of Schedule B1 to the 1989 Order]; or
(iii) a decision of the court to reduce the value of one or more of the insurer's contracts, in accordance with section 377 of the 2000 Act;
(b) "third country insurer" means a person—
(i) who has permission under the 2000 Act to effect or carry out contracts of insurance; and
(ii) whose head office is not in the United Kingdom or an EEA State.

(2) In paragraph (1), the definition of "third country insurer" must be read with—
(a) section 22 of the 2000 Act;
(b) any relevant order made under that section; and
(c) Schedule 2 to that Act.

NOTES

Para (1): words in square brackets in sub-para (a) inserted by the Insurers (Reorganisation and Winding Up) (Amendment) Regulations 2007, SI 2007/851, reg 2(1), (17).

[3.173]
49 Application of these Regulations to a third country insurer

Parts III, IV and V of these Regulations apply where a third country insurer is subject to a relevant measure, as if references in those Parts to a UK insurer included a reference to a third country insurer.

[3.174]
50 Disclosure of confidential information: third country insurers

(1) This regulation applies to information ("insolvency practitioner information") which—
(a) relates to the business or other affairs of any person; and
(b) is information of a kind mentioned in paragraph (2).

(2) Information falls within paragraph (1)(b) if it is supplied to—
(a) the [FCA or the PRA] by an EEA regulator; or
(b) an insolvency practitioner by an EEA administrator or liquidator,
in accordance with or pursuant to [Article 296 of the Solvency 2 Directive].

(3) Subject to paragraphs (4), (5) and (6), sections 348, 349 and 352 of the 2000 Act apply in relation to insolvency practitioner information in the same way as they apply in relation to confidential information within the meaning of section 348(2) of that Act.

(4) For the purposes of this regulation, sections 348, 349 and 352 of the 2000 Act and the Disclosure Regulations have effect as if the primary recipients specified in subsection (5) of section 348 of the 2000 Act included an insolvency practitioner.

(5) Insolvency practitioner information is not subject to the restrictions on disclosure imposed by section 348(1) of the 2000 Act (as it applies by virtue of paragraph (3)) if it satisfies any of the criteria set out in section 348(4) of the 2000 Act.

(6) The Disclosure Regulations apply in relation to insolvency practitioner information as they apply in relation to single market directive information (within the meaning of those Regulations).

(7) In this regulation—

"the Disclosure Regulations" means the Financial Services and Markets Act 2000 (Disclosure of Confidential Information) Regulations 2001;

"EEA administrator" and "EEA liquidator" mean respectively an administrator or liquidator within the meaning of [Title IV of the Solvency 2 Directive];

"insolvency practitioner" means an insolvency practitioner, within the meaning of section 388 of the 1986 Act or Article 3 of the 1989 Order, who is appointed or acts in relation to a third country insurer.

NOTES

Para (2): words in square brackets in sub-para (a) substituted by the Financial Services Act 2012 (Consequential Amendments and Transitional Provisions) Order 2013, SI 2013/472, art 3, Sch 2, para 88(h); words in second pair of square brackets substituted by the Solvency 2 Regulations 2015, SI 2015/575, reg 60, Sch 2, paras 17(1), (6)(a).

Para (7): in definition ""EEA administrator" and "EEA liquidator"" words in square brackets substituted by SI 2015/575, reg 60, Sch 2, paras 17(1), (6)(b).

PART VII
REVOCATION AND AMENDMENTS

51, 52 *(Reg 51 amends the Insurers (Winding Up) Rules 2001, SI 2001/3635, r 24 at* **[7.1555]** *and the Insurers (Winding Up) (Scotland) Rules 2001, SI 2001/4040, r 23 at* **[16.169]**; *reg 52 amends the Financial Services and Markets Act 2000 (Administration Orders Relating to Insurers) Order 2002, SI 2002/1242, reg 3 at* **[7.1566]** *and is revoked by the Financial Services and Markets Act 2000 (Administration Orders Relating to Insurers) Order 2010, SI 2010/3023, art 5, except where the appointment of an administrator takes effect before 1 February 2011: see art 6 of the 2010 Order at* **[7.1622]**.)

[3.175]

53 Revocation and Transitional

(1) Except as provided in this regulation, the Insurers (Reorganisation and Winding Up) Regulations 2003 are revoked.

(2) Subject to (3), the provisions of Parts III and IV shall continue in force in respect of decisions orders or appointments referred to therein and made before the coming into force of these Regulations.

(3) Where an administrator has been appointed in respect of a UK insurer on or after 15th September 2003, he shall be treated as being so appointed on the date these regulations come into force.

DIRECTIVE OF THE EUROPEAN PARLIAMENT AND OF THE COUNCIL

(2001/24/EC)

of 4 April 2001

on the reorganisation and winding up of credit institutions

[3.176]

NOTES

Date of publication in OJ: OJ L125, 5.5.2001, p 15.

This Directive has been implemented in the UK with effect from 5 May 2004 by the Credit Institutions (Reorganisation and Winding up) Regulations 2004, SI 2004/1045 at **[3.213]**.

THE EUROPEAN PARLIAMENT AND THE COUNCIL OF THE EUROPEAN UNION,

Having regard to the Treaty establishing the European Community, and in particular Article 47(2) thereof,

Having regard to the proposal from the Commission,[1]

Having regard to the opinion of the Economic and Social Committee,[2]

Having regard to the opinion of the European Monetary Institute,[3]

Acting in accordance with the procedure laid down in Article 251 of the Treaty,[4]

Whereas—

(1) In accordance with the objectives of the Treaty, the harmonious and balanced development of economic activities throughout the Community should be promoted through the elimination of any obstacles to the freedom of establishment and the freedom to provide services within the Community.

(2) At the same time as those obstacles are eliminated, consideration should be given to the situation which might arise if a credit institution runs into difficulties, particularly where that institution has branches in other Member States.

(3) This Directive forms part of the Community legislative framework set up by Directive 2000/12/EC of the European Parliament and of the Council of 20 March 2000 relating to the taking up and pursuit of the business of credit institutions.[5] It follows therefrom that, while they are in operation, a credit institution and its branches form a single entity subject to the supervision of the competent authorities of the State where authorisation valid throughout the Community was granted.

(4) It would be particularly undesirable to relinquish such unity between an institution and its branches where it is necessary to adopt reorganisation measures or open winding-up proceedings.

(5) The adoption of Directive 94/19/EC of the European Parliament and of the Council of 30 May 1994 on deposit-guarantee schemes,[6] which introduced the principle of compulsory membership by credit institutions of a guarantee scheme in their home Member State, brings out even more clearly the need for mutual recognition of reorganisation measures and winding-up proceedings.

(6) The administrative or judicial authorities of the home Member State must have sole power to decide upon and to implement the reorganisation measures provided for in the law and practices in force in that Member State. Owing to the difficulty of harmonising Member States' laws and practices, it is necessary to establish mutual recognition by the Member States of the measures taken by each of them to restore to viability the credit institutions which it has authorised.

(7) It is essential to guarantee that the reorganisation measures adopted by the administrative or judicial authorities of the home Member State and the measures adopted by persons or bodies appointed by those authorities to administer those reorganisation measures, including measures involving the possibility of a suspension of payments, suspension of enforcement measures or reduction of claims and any other measure which could affect third parties' existing rights, are effective in all Member States.

(8) Certain measures, in particular those affecting the functioning of the internal structure of credit institutions or managers' or shareholders' rights, need not be covered by this Directive to be effective in Member States insofar as, pursuant to the rules of private international law, the applicable law is that of the home State.

(9) Certain measures, in particular those connected with the continued fulfilment of conditions of authorisation, are already the subject of mutual recognition pursuant to Directive 2000/12/EC insofar as they do not affect the rights of third parties existing before their adoption.

(10) Persons participating in the operation of the internal structures of credit institutions as well as managers and shareholders of such institutions, considered in those capacities, are not to be regarded as third parties for the purposes of this Directive.

(11) It is necessary to notify third parties of the implementation of reorganisation measures in Member States where branches are situated when such measures could hinder the exercise of some of their rights.

(12) The principle of equal treatment between creditors, as regards the opportunities open to them to take action, requires the administrative or judicial authorities of the home Member State to adopt such measures as are necessary for the creditors in the host Member State to be able to exercise their rights to take action within the time limit laid down.

(13) There must be some coordination of the role of the administrative or judicial authorities in reorganisation measures and winding-up proceedings for branches of credit institutions having head offices outside the Community and situated in different Member States.

(14) In the absence of reorganisation measures, or in the event of such measures failing, the credit institutions in difficulty must be wound up. Provision should be made in such cases for mutual recognition of winding-up proceedings and of their effects in the Community.

(15) The important role played by the competent authorities of the home Member State before winding-up proceedings are opened may continue during the process of winding up so that these proceedings can be properly carried out.

(16) Equal treatment of creditors requires that the credit institution is wound up according to the principles of unity and universality, which require the administrative or judicial authorities of the home Member State to have sole jurisdiction and their decisions to be recognised and to be capable of producing in all the other Member States, without any formality, the effects ascribed to them by the law of the home Member State, except where this Directive provides otherwise.

(17) The exemption concerning the effects of reorganisation measures and winding-up proceedings on certain contracts and rights is limited to those effects and does not cover other questions concerning reorganisation measures and winding-up proceedings such as the lodging, verification, admission and ranking of claims concerning those contracts and rights and the rules governing the distribution of the proceeds of the realisation of the assets, which are governed by the law of the home Member State.

(18) Voluntary winding up is possible when a credit institution is solvent. The administrative or judicial authorities of the home Member State may nevertheless, where appropriate, decide on a reorganisation measure or winding-up proceedings, even after voluntary winding up has commenced.

(19) Withdrawal of authorisation to pursue the business of banking is one of the consequences which winding up a credit institution necessarily entails. Withdrawal should not, however, prevent certain activities of the institution from continuing insofar as is necessary or appropriate for the purposes of winding up. Such a continuation of activity may nonetheless be made subject by the home Member State

to the consent of, and supervision by, its competent authorities.

(20) Provision of information to known creditors on an individual basis is as essential as publication to enable them, where necessary, to lodge their claims or submit observations relating to their claims within the prescribed time limits. This should take place without discrimination against creditors domiciled in a Member State other than the home Member State, based on their place of residence or the nature of their claims. Creditors must be kept regularly informed in an appropriate manner throughout winding-up proceedings.

(21) For the sole purpose of applying the provisions of this Directive to reorganisation measures and winding-up proceedings involving branches located in the Community of a credit institution of which the head office is situated in a third country, the definitions of "home Member State", "competent authorities" and "administrative or judicial authorities" should be those of the Member State in which the branch is located.

(22) Where a credit institution which has its head office outside the Community possesses branches in more than one Member State, each branch should receive individual treatment in regard to the application of this Directive. In such a case, the administrative or judicial authorities and the competent authorities as well as the administrators and liquidators should endeavour to coordinate their activities.

(23) Although it is important to follow the principle that the law of the home Member State determines all the effects of reorganisation measures or winding-up proceedings, both procedural and substantive, it is also necessary to bear in mind that those effects may conflict with the rules normally applicable in the context of the economic and financial activity of the credit institution in question and its branches in other Member States. In some cases reference to the law of another Member State represents an unavoidable qualification of the principle that the law of the home Member State is to apply.

(24) That qualification is especially necessary to protect employees having a contract of employment with a credit institution, ensure the security of transactions in respect of certain types of property and protect the integrity of regulated markets functioning in accordance with the law of a Member State on which financial instruments are traded.

(25) Transactions carried out in the framework of a payment and settlement system are covered by Directive 98/26/EC of the European Parliament and of the Council of 19 May 1998 on settlement finality in payment and securities settlement systems.[7]

(26) The adoption of this Directive does not call into question the provisions of Directive 98/26/EC according to which insolvency proceedings must not have any effect on the enforceability of orders validly entered into a system, or on collateral provided for a system.

(27) Some reorganisation measures or winding-up proceedings involve the appointment of a person to administer them. The recognition of his appointment and his powers in all other Member States is therefore an essential factor in the implementation of decisions taken in the home Member State. However, the limits within which he may exercise his powers when he acts outside the home Member State should be specified.

(28) Creditors who have entered into contracts with a credit institution before a reorganisation measure is adopted or winding-up proceedings are opened should be protected against provisions relating to voidness, voidability or unenforceability laid down in the law of the home Member State, where the beneficiary of the transaction produces evidence that in the law applicable to that transaction there is no available means of contesting the act concerned in the case in point.

(29) The confidence of third-party purchasers in the content of the registers or accounts regarding certain assets entered in those registers or accounts and by extension of the purchasers of immovable property should be safeguarded, even after winding-up proceedings have been opened or a reorganisation measure adopted. The only means of safeguarding that confidence is to make the validity of the purchase subject to the law of the place where the immovable asset is situated or of the State under whose authority the register or account is kept.

(30) The effects of reorganisation measures or winding-up proceedings on a lawsuit pending are governed by the law of the Member State in which the lawsuit is pending, by way of exception to the application of the lex concursus. The effects of those measures and procedures on individual enforcement actions arising from such lawsuits are governed by the legislation of the home Member State, in accordance with the general rule established by this Directive.

(31) Provision should be made for the administrative or judicial authorities in the home Member State to notify immediately the competent authorities of the host Member State of the adoption of any reorganisation measure or the opening of any winding-up proceedings, if possible before the adoption of the measure or the opening of the proceedings, or, if not, immediately afterwards.

(32) Professional secrecy as defined in Article 30 of Directive 2000/12/EC is an essential factor in all information or consultation procedures. For that reason it should be respected by all the administrative authorities taking part in such procedures, whereas the judicial authorities remain, in this respect, subject to the national provisions relating to them,

NOTES

1 OJ C356, 31.12.85, p 55 and OJ C36, 8.2.88, p 1.

2 OJ C263, 20.10.86, p 13.

3 OJ C332, 30.10.98, p 13.

4 Opinion of the European Parliament of 13 March 1987 (OJ C99, 13.4.87, p 211), confirmed on 2 December 1993

(OJ C342, 20.12.93, p 30), Council Common Position of 17 July 2000 (OJ C300, 20.10.2000, p 13) and Decision of the European Parliament of 16 January 2001 (not yet published in the Official Journal). Council Decision of 12 March 2001.

5 OJ L126, 26.5.2000, p 1.

6 OJ L135, 31.5.94, p 5.

7 OJ L166, 11.6.98, p 45.

HAVE ADOPTED THIS DIRECTIVE—

TITLE I SCOPE AND DEFINITIONS

[3.177]
Article 1
Scope

1. This Directive shall apply to credit institutions and their branches set up in Member States other than those in which they have their head offices, as defined in points (1) and (3) of Article 1 of Directive 2000/12/EC, subject to the conditions and exemptions laid down in Article 2(3) of that Directive.
2. The provisions of this Directive concerning the branches of a credit institution having a head office outside the Community shall apply only where that institution has branches in at least two Member States of the Community.
[3. This Directive shall also apply to investment firms as defined in point (2) of Article 4(1) of Regulation (EU) No 575/2013 of the European Parliament and of the Council and their branches located in Member States other than those in which they have their head offices.
4. In the event of application of the resolution tools and exercise of the resolution powers provided for in Directive 2014/59/EU of the European Parliament and of the Council, this Directive shall also apply to the financial institutions, firms and parent undertakings falling within the scope of Directive 2014/59/EU.
5. Articles 4 and 7 of this Directive shall not apply where Article 83 of Directive 2014/59/EU applies.
6. Article 33 of this Directive shall not apply where Article 84 of Directive 2014/59/EU applies.]

NOTES

Paras 3–6: added by European Parliament and Council Directive 2014/59/EU, Art 117(1).

[3.178]
[Article 2
Definitions

For the purposes of this Directive—

— "home Member State" shall mean a home Member State as defined in Article 4(1)(43) of Regulation (EU) No 575/2013;
— "host Member State" shall mean a host Member State as defined in Article 4(1)(44) of Regulation (EU) No 575/2013;
— "branch" shall mean a branch as defined in Article 4(1)(17) of Regulation (EU) No 575/2013;
— "competent authority" shall mean a competent authority as defined in Article 4(1)(40) of Regulation (EU) No 575/2013 or a resolution authority within the meaning of Article 2(1)(18) of Directive 2014/59/EU in respect of reorganisation measures taken pursuant to that Directive;
— "administrator" shall mean any person or body appointed by the administrative or judicial authorities whose task is to administer reorganisation measures;
— "administrative or judicial authorities" shall mean such administrative or judicial authorities of the Member States as are competent for the purposes of reorganisation measures or winding-up proceedings;
— "reorganisation measures" shall mean measures which are intended to preserve or restore the financial situation of a credit institution or an investment firm as defined in Article 4(1), point (2) of Regulation (EU) No 575/2013 and which could affect third parties' pre-existing rights, including measures involving the possibility of a suspension of payments, suspension of enforcement measures or reduction of claims; those measures include the application of the resolution tools and the exercise of resolution powers provided for in Directive 2014/59/EU;
— "liquidator" shall mean any person or body appointed by the administrative or judicial authorities whose task is to administer winding-up proceedings;
— "winding-up proceedings" shall mean collective proceedings opened and monitored by the administrative or judicial authorities of a Member State with the aim of realising assets under the supervision of those authorities, including where the proceedings are terminated by a composition or other, similar measure;
— "regulated market" shall mean a regulated market as defined in Article 4(1), point (21) of Directive 2014/65/EU of the European Parliament and of the Council;
— "instrument" shall mean a financial instrument as defined in Article 4(1), point (50)(b) of Regulation (EU) No 575/2013.]

NOTES

Substituted by European Parliament and Council Directive 2014/59/EU, Art 117(2).

TITLE II REORGANISATION MEASURES

A

Credit institutions having their head offices within the Community

[3.179]
Article 3
Adoption of reorganisation measures—applicable law

1. The administrative or judicial authorities of the home Member State shall alone be empowered to decide on the implementation of one or more reorganisation measures in a credit institution, including branches established in other Member States.

2. The reorganisation measures shall be applied in accordance with the laws, regulations and procedures applicable in the home Member State, unless otherwise provided in this Directive.

They shall be fully effective in accordance with the legislation of that Member State throughout the Community without any further formalities, including as against third parties in other Member States, even where the rules of the host Member State applicable to them do not provide for such measures or make their implementation subject to conditions which are not fulfilled.

The reorganisation measures shall be effective throughout the Community once they become effective in the Member State where they have been taken.

[3.180]
Article 4
Information for the competent authorities of the host Member State

The administrative or judicial authorities of the home Member State shall without delay inform, by any available means, the competent authorities of the host Member State of their decision to adopt any reorganisation measure, including the practical effects which such a measure may have, if possible before it is adopted or otherwise immediately thereafter. Information shall be communicated by the competent authorities of the home Member State.

[3.181]
Article 5
Information for the supervisory authorities of the home Member State

Where the administrative or judicial authorities of the host Member State deem it necessary to implement within their territory one or more reorganisation measures, they shall inform the competent authorities of the home Member State accordingly. Information shall be communicated by the host Member State's competent authorities.

[3.182]
Article 6
Publication

1. Where implementation of the reorganisation measures decided on pursuant to Article 3(1) and (2) is likely to affect the rights of third parties in a host Member State and where an appeal may be brought in the home Member State against the decision ordering the measure, the administrative or judicial authorities of the home Member State, the administrator or any person empowered to do so in the home Member State shall publish an extract from the decision in the *Official Journal of the European Communities* and in two national newspapers in each host Member State, in order in particular to facilitate the exercise of the right of appeal in good time.

2. The extract from the decision provided for in paragraph 1 shall be forwarded at the earliest opportunity, by the most appropriate route, to the Office for Official Publications of the European Communities and to the two national newspapers in each host Member State.

3. The Office for Official Publications of the European Communities shall publish the extract at the latest within twelve days of its dispatch.

4. The extract from the decision to be published shall specify, in the official language or languages of the Member States concerned, in particular the purpose and legal basis of the decision taken, the time limits for lodging appeals, specifically a clearly understandable indication of the date of expiry of the time limits, and the full address of the authorities or court competent to hear an appeal.

5. The reorganisation measures shall apply irrespective of the measures prescribed in paragraphs 1 to 3 and shall be fully effective as against creditors, unless the administrative or judicial authorities of the home Member State or the law of that State governing such measures provide otherwise.

[3.183]
Article 7
Duty to inform known creditors and right to lodge claims

1. Where the legislation of the home Member State requires lodgement of a claim with a view to its recognition or provides for compulsory notification of the measure to creditors who have their domiciles, normal places of residence or head offices in that State, the administrative or judicial authorities of the home Member State or the administrator shall also inform known creditors who have their domiciles, normal places of residence or head offices in other Member States, in accordance with the procedures laid down in Articles 14 and 17(1).

2. Where the legislation of the home Member State provides for the right of creditors who have their domiciles, normal places of residence or head offices in that State to lodge claims or to submit observations concerning their claims, creditors who have their domiciles, normal places of residence or head offices in other Member States shall also have that right in accordance with the procedures laid down in Article 16 and Article 17(2).

B

Credit institutions having their head offices outside the Community

[3.184]
Article 8
Branches of third-country credit institutions
1. The administrative or judicial authorities of the host Member State of a branch of a credit institution having its head office outside the Community shall without delay inform, by any available means, the competent authorities of the other host Member States in which the institution has set up branches which are included on the list referred to in Article 11 of Directive 2000/12/EC and published each year in the *Official Journal of the European Communities*, of their decision to adopt any reorganisation measure, including the practical effects which that measure may have, if possible before it is adopted or otherwise immediately thereafter. Information shall be communicated by the competent authorities of the host Member State whose administrative or judicial authorities decide to apply the measure.
2. The administrative or judicial authorities referred to in paragraph 1 shall endeavour to coordinate their actions.

TITLE III WINDING-UP PROCEEDINGS

A

Credit institutions having their head offices within the Community

[3.185]
Article 9
Opening of winding-up proceedings—Information to be communicated to other competent authorities
1. The administrative or judicial authorities of the home Member State which are responsible for winding up shall alone be empowered to decide on the opening of winding-up proceedings concerning a credit institution, including branches established in other Member States. A decision to open winding-up proceedings taken by the administrative or judicial authority of the home Member State shall be recognised, without further formality, within the territory of all other Member States and shall be effective there when the decision is effective in the Member State in which the proceedings are opened.
2. The administrative or judicial authorities of the home Member State shall without delay inform, by any available means, the competent authorities of the host Member State of their decision to open winding-up proceedings, including the practical effects which such proceedings may have, if possible before they open or otherwise immediately thereafter. Information shall be communicated by the competent authorities of the home Member State.

[3.186]
Article 10
Law applicable
1. A credit institution shall be wound up in accordance with the laws, regulations and procedures applicable in its home Member State insofar as this Directive does not provide otherwise.
2. The law of the home Member State shall determine in particular—
- (a) the goods subject to administration and the treatment of goods acquired by the credit institution after the opening of winding-up proceedings;
- (b) the respective powers of the credit institution and the liquidator;
- (c) the conditions under which set-offs may be invoked;
- (d) the effects of winding-up proceedings on current contracts to which the credit institution is party;
- (e) the effects of winding-up proceedings on proceedings brought by individual creditors, with the exception of lawsuits pending, as provided for in Article 32;
- (f) the claims which are to be lodged against the credit institution and the treatment of claims arising after the opening of winding-up proceedings;
- (g) the rules governing the lodging, verification and admission of claims;
- (h) the rules governing the distribution of the proceeds of the realisation of assets, the ranking of claims and the rights of creditors who have obtained partial satisfaction after the opening of insolvency proceedings by virtue of a right *in re* or through a set-off;
- (i) the conditions for, and the effects of, the closure of insolvency proceedings, in particular by composition;
- (j) creditors' rights after the closure of winding-up proceedings;
- (k) who is to bear the costs and expenses incurred in the winding-up proceedings;
- (l) the rules relating to the voidness, voidability or unenforceability of legal acts detrimental to all the creditors.

[3.187]
Article 11
Consultation of competent authorities before voluntary winding up

1. The competent authorities of the home Member State shall be consulted in the most appropriate form before any voluntary winding-up decision is taken by the governing bodies of a credit institution.
2. The voluntary winding up of a credit institution shall not preclude the adoption of a reorganisation measure or the opening of winding-up proceedings.

[3.188]
Article 12
Withdrawal of a credit institution's authorisation

1. Where the opening of winding-up proceedings is decided on in respect of a credit institution in the absence, or following the failure, of reorganisation measures, the authorisation of the institution shall be withdrawn in accordance with, in particular, the procedure laid down in Article 22(9) of Directive 2000/12/EC.
2. The withdrawal of authorisation provided for in paragraph 1 shall not prevent the person or persons entrusted with the winding up from carrying on some of the credit institution's activities insofar as that is necessary or appropriate for the purposes of winding up.

The home Member State may provide that such activities shall be carried on with the consent, and under the supervision, of the competent authorities of that Member State.

[3.189]
Article 13
Publication

The liquidators or any administrative or judicial authority shall announce the decision to open winding-up proceedings through publication of an extract from the winding-up decision in the *Official Journal of the European Communities* and at least two national newspapers in each of the host Member States.

[3.190]
Article 14
Provision of information to known creditors

1. When winding-up proceedings are opened, the administrative or judicial authority of the home Member State or the liquidator shall without delay individually inform known creditors who have their domiciles, normal places of residence or head offices in other Member States, except in cases where the legislation of the home State does not require lodgement of the claim with a view to its recognition.
2. That information, provided by the dispatch of a notice, shall in particular deal with time limits, the penalties laid down in regard to those time limits, the body or authority empowered to accept the lodgement of claims or observations relating to claims and the other measures laid down. Such a notice shall also indicate whether creditors whose claims are preferential or secured *in re* need lodge their claims.

[3.191]
Article 15
Honouring of obligations

Where an obligation has been honoured for the benefit of a credit institution which is not a legal person and which is the subject of winding-up proceedings opened in another Member State, when it should have been honoured for the benefit of the liquidator in those proceedings, the person honouring the obligation shall be deemed to have discharged it if he was unaware of the opening of proceedings. Where such an obligation is honoured before the publication provided for in Article 13 has been effected, the person honouring the obligation shall be presumed, in the absence of proof to the contrary, to have been unaware of the opening of winding-up proceedings; where the obligation is honoured after the publication provided for in Article 13 has been effected, the person honouring the obligation shall be presumed, in the absence of proof to the contrary, to have been aware of the opening of proceedings.

[3.192]
Article 16
Right to lodge claims

1. Any creditor who has his domicile, normal place of residence or head office in a Member State other than the home Member State, including Member States' public authorities, shall have the right to lodge claims or to submit written observations relating to claims.
2. The claims of all creditors whose domiciles, normal places of residence or head offices are in Member States other than the home Member State shall be treated in the same way and accorded the same ranking as claims of an equivalent nature which may be lodged by creditors having their domiciles, normal places of residence, or head offices in the home Member State.
3. Except in cases where the law of the home Member State provides for the submission of observations relating to claims, a creditor shall send copies of supporting documents, if any, and shall indicate the nature of the claim, the date on which it arose and its amount, as well as whether he alleges preference, security *in re* or reservation of title in respect of the claim and what assets are covered by his security.

[3.193]
Article 17
Languages
1. The information provided for in Articles 13 and 14 shall be provided in the official language or one of the official languages of the home Member State. For that purpose a form shall be used bearing, in all the official languages of the European Union, the heading "Invitation to lodge a claim. Time limits to be observed" or, where the law of the home Member State provides for the submission of observations relating to claims, the heading "Invitation to submit observations relating to a claim. Time limits to be observed".
2. Any creditor who has his domicile, normal place of residence or head office in a Member State other than the home Member State may lodge his claim or submit observations relating to his claim in the official language or one of the official languages of that other Member State. In that event, however, the lodgement of his claim or the submission of observations on his claim shall bear the heading "Lodgement of claim" or "Submission of observations relating to claims" in the official language or one of the official languages of the home Member State. In addition, he may be required to provide a translation into that language of the lodgement of claim or submission of observations relating to claims.

[3.194]
Article 18
Regular provision of information to creditors
Liquidators shall keep creditors regularly informed, in an appropriate manner, particularly with regard to progress in the winding up.

B
Credit institutions the head offices of which are outside the Community

[3.195]
Article 19
Branches of third-country credit institutions
1. The administrative or judicial authorities of the host Member State of the branch of a credit institution the head office of which is outside the Community shall without delay inform, by any available means, the competent authorities of the other host Member States in which the credit institution has set up branches on the list referred to in Article 11 of Directive 2000/12/EC and published each year in the *Official Journal of the European Communities*, of their decision to open winding-up proceedings, including the practical effects which these proceedings may have, if possible before they open or otherwise immediately thereafter. Information shall be communicated by the competent authorities of the first above-mentioned host Member State.
2. Administrative or judicial authorities which decide to open proceedings to wind up a branch of a credit institution the head office of which is outside the Community shall inform the competent authorities of the other host Member States that winding-up proceedings have been opened and authorisation withdrawn.

Information shall be communicated by the competent authorities in the host Member State which has decided to open the proceedings.
3. The administrative or judicial authorities referred to in paragraph 1 shall endeavour to coordinate their actions.

Any liquidators shall likewise endeavour to coordinate their actions.

TITLE IV PROVISIONS COMMON TO REORGANISATION MEASURES AND WINDING-UP PROCEEDINGS

[3.196]
Article 20
Effects on certain contracts and rights
The effects of a reorganisation measure or the opening of winding-up proceedings on—
- (a) employment contracts and relationships shall be governed solely by the law of the Member State applicable to the employment contract;
- (b) a contract conferring the right to make use of or acquire immovable property shall be governed solely by the law of the Member State within the territory of which the immovable property is situated. That law shall determine whether property is movable or immovable;
- (c) rights in respect of immovable property, a ship or an aircraft subject to registration in a public register shall be governed solely by the law of the Member State under the authority of which the register is kept.

[3.197]
Article 21
Third parties' rights in re
1. The adoption of reorganisation measures or the opening of winding-up proceedings shall not affect the rights *in re* of creditors or third parties in respect of tangible or intangible, movable or immovable assets—both specific assets and collections of indefinite assets as a whole which change from time to time—belonging to the credit institution which are situated within the territory of another Member State at the time of the adoption of such measures or the opening of such proceedings.
2. The rights referred to in paragraph 1 shall in particular mean—

(a) the right to dispose of assets or have them disposed of and to obtain satisfaction from the proceeds of or income from those assets, in particular by virtue of a lien or a mortgage;
(b) the exclusive right to have a claim met, in particular a right guaranteed by a lien in respect of the claim or by assignment of the claim by way of a guarantee;
(c) the right to demand the assets from, and/or to require restitution by, anyone having possession or use of them contrary to the wishes of the party so entitled;
(d) a right *in re* to the beneficial use of assets.

3. The right, recorded in a public register and enforceable against third parties, under which a right *in re* within the meaning of paragraph 1 may be obtained, shall be considered a right *in re*.
4. Paragraph 1 shall not preclude the actions for voidness, voidability or unenforceability laid down in Article 10(2)(l).

[3.198]
Article 22
Reservation of title

1. The adoption of reorganisation measures or the opening of winding-up proceedings concerning a credit institution purchasing an asset shall not affect the seller's rights based on a reservation of title where at the time of the adoption of such measures or opening of such proceedings the asset is situated within the territory of a Member State other than the State in which the said measures were adopted or the said proceedings were opened.
2. The adoption of reorganisation measures or the opening of winding-up proceedings concerning a credit institution selling an asset, after delivery of the asset, shall not constitute grounds for rescinding or terminating the sale and shall not prevent the purchaser from acquiring title where at the time of the adoption of such measures or the opening of such proceedings the asset sold is situated within the territory of a Member State other than the State in which such measures were adopted or such proceedings were opened.
3. Paragraphs 1 and 2 shall not preclude the actions for voidness, voidability or unenforceability laid down in Article 10(2)(l).

[3.199]
Article 23
Set-off

1. The adoption of reorganisation measures or the opening of winding-up proceedings shall not affect the right of creditors to demand the set-off of their claims against the claims of the credit institution, where such a set-off is permitted by the law applicable to the credit institution's claim.
2. Paragraph 1 shall not preclude the actions for voidness, voidability or unenforceability laid down in Article 10(2)(l).

[3.200]
Article 24
Lex rei sitae

The enforcement of proprietary rights in instruments or other rights in such instruments the existence or transfer of which presupposes their recording in a register, an account or a centralised deposit system held or located in a Member State shall be governed by the law of the Member State where the register, account, or centralised deposit system in which those rights are recorded is held or located.

[3.201]
[Article 25
Netting agreements

Without prejudice to Articles 68 and 71 of Directive 2014/59/EU, netting agreements shall be governed solely by the law of the contract which governs such agreements.]

NOTES

Substituted by European Parliament and Council Directive 2014/59/EU, Art 117(3).

[3.202]
[Article 26
Repurchase agreements

Without prejudice to Articles 68 and 71 of Directive 2014/59/EU and Article 24 of this Directive, repurchase agreements shall be governed solely by the law of the contract which governs such agreements.]

NOTES

Substituted by European Parliament and Council Directive 2014/59/EU, Art 117(4).

[3.203]
Article 27
Regulated markets

Without prejudice to Article 24, transactions carried out in the context of a regulated market shall be governed solely by the law of the contract which governs such transactions.

[3.204]
Article 28
Proof of liquidators' appointment

1. The administrator or liquidator's appointment shall be evidenced by a certified copy of the original decision appointing him or by any other certificate issued by the administrative or judicial authority of the home Member State.

A translation into the official language or one of the official languages of the Member State within the territory of which the administrator or liquidator wishes to act may be required. No legalisation or other similar formality shall be required.

2. Administrators and liquidators shall be entitled to exercise within the territory of all the Member States all the powers which they are entitled to exercise within the territory of the home Member State. They may also appoint persons to assist or, where appropriate, represent them in the course of the reorganisation measure or winding-up proceedings, in particular in host Member States and, specifically, in order to help overcome any difficulties encountered by creditors in the host Member State.

3. In exercising his powers, an administrator or liquidator shall comply with the law of the Member States within the territory of which he wishes to take action, in particular with regard to procedures for the realisation of assets and the provision of information to employees. Those powers may not include the use of force or the right to rule on legal proceedings or disputes.

[3.205]
Article 29
Registration in a public register

1. The administrator, liquidator or any administrative or judicial authority of the home Member State may request that a reorganisation measure or the decision to open winding-up proceedings be registered in the land register, the trade register and any other public register kept in the other Member States. A Member State may, however, prescribe mandatory registration. In that event, the person or authority referred to in the preceding subparagraph shall take all the measures necessary to ensure such registration.

2. The costs of registration shall be regarded as costs and expenses incurred in the proceedings.

[3.206]
Article 30
Detrimental acts

1. Article 10 shall not apply as regards the rules relating to the voidness, voidability or unenforceability of legal acts detrimental to the creditors as a whole, where the beneficiary of these acts provides proof that—

— the act detrimental to the creditors as a whole is subject to the law of a Member State other than the home Member State, and
— that law does not allow any means of challenging that act in the case in point.

2. Where a reorganisation measure decided on by a judicial authority provides for rules relating to the voidness, voidability or unenforceability of legal acts detrimental to the creditors as a whole performed before adoption of the measure, Article 3(2) shall not apply in the cases provided for in paragraph 1 of this Article.

[3.207]
Article 31
Protection of third parties

Where, by an act concluded after the adoption of a reorganisation measure or the opening of winding-up proceedings, a credit institution disposes, for consideration, of—

— an immovable asset,
— a ship or an aircraft subject to registration in a public register, or
— instruments or rights in such instruments the existence or transfer of which presupposes their being recorded in a register, an account or a centralised deposit system held or located in a Member State,

the validity of that act shall be governed by the law of the Member State within the territory of which the immovable asset is situated or under the authority of which that register, account or deposit system is kept.

[3.208]
Article 32
Lawsuits pending

The effects of reorganisation measures or winding-up proceedings on a pending lawsuit concerning an asset or a right of which the credit institution has been divested shall be governed solely by the law of the Member State in which the lawsuit is pending.

[3.209]
Article 33
Professional secrecy

All persons required to receive or divulge information in connection with the information or consultation procedures laid down in Articles 4, 5, 8, 9, 11 and 19 shall be bound by professional secrecy, in accordance with the rules and conditions laid down in Article 30 of Directive 2000/12/EC, with the exception of any judicial authorities to which existing national provisions apply.

TITLE V FINAL PROVISIONS

[3.210]
Article 34
Implementation

1. Member States shall bring into force the laws, regulations and administrative provisions necessary to comply with this Directive on 5 May 2004. They shall forthwith inform the Commission thereof.

National provisions adopted in application of this Directive shall apply only to reorganisation measures or winding-up proceedings adopted or opened after the date referred to in the first subparagraph. Measures adopted or proceedings opened before that date shall continue to be governed by the law that was applicable to them at the time of adoption or opening.

2. When Member States adopt these measures, they shall contain a reference to this Directive or shall be accompanied by such reference on the occasion of their official publication. The methods of making such reference shall be laid down by Member States.

3. Member States shall communicate to the Commission the texts of the main provisions of national law which they adopt in the field governed by this Directive.

[3.211]
Article 35
Entry into force

This Directive shall enter into force on the date of its publication.

[3.212]
Article 36
Addressees

This Directive is addressed to the Member States.

CREDIT INSTITUTIONS (REORGANISATION AND WINDING UP) REGULATIONS 2004

(SI 2004/1045)

NOTES

Made: 1 April 2004.

Authority: European Communities Act 1972, s 2(2).

Commencement: 5 May 2004.

Modifications: these Regulations are applied, with modifications, in so far as they relate to bank insolvency or administration under the Banking Act 2009, Pts 2, 3, by the Banking Act 2009 (Parts 2 and 3 Consequential Amendments) Order 2009, SI 2009/317, art 3, Schedule at **[7.86]**, **[7.92]**. The Regulations are also applied, with such modifications as the context requires for the purpose of the restructuring of Northern Rock plc, by the Northern Rock plc Transfer Order 2009, SI 2009/3226, art 8, Sch 2.

ARRANGEMENT OF REGULATIONS

PART 1
GENERAL

1 Citation and commencement . . . . . [3.213]
2 Interpretation . . . . . [3.214]

PART 2
INSOLVENCY MEASURES AND PROCEEDINGS:
JURISDICTION IN RELATION TO CREDIT INSTITUTIONS

3 Prohibition against winding up etc EEA credit institutions in the United Kingdom . . . . . [3.215]
4 Schemes of arrangement . . . . . [3.216]
5 Reorganisation measures and winding-up proceedings in respect of EEA credit institutions effective in the United Kingdom . . . . . [3.217]
6 Confirmation by the court of a creditors' voluntary winding up . . . . . [3.218]

PART 3
MODIFICATIONS OF THE LAW OF INSOLVENCY:
NOTIFICATION AND PUBLICATION

7 Modifications of the law of insolvency . . . . . [3.219]
8 Consultation of the FCA and, if the institution is a PRA-authorised person, the PRA prior to a voluntary winding up . . . . . [3.220]
9 Notification of relevant decision to the FCA and, if the institution is a PRA-authorised person, the PRA . . . . . [3.221]
10 Notification to EEA regulators . . . . . [3.222]
11 Withdrawal of authorisation . . . . . [3.223]
12 Publication of voluntary arrangement, administration order, winding-up order or scheme of arrangement . . . . . [3.224]
13 Honouring of certain obligations . . . . . [3.225]

14 Notification to creditors: winding-up proceedings . . . . [3.226]
15 Submission of claims by EEA creditors . . . . [3.227]
16 Reports to creditors . . . . [3.228]
17 Service of notices and documents . . . . [3.229]
18 Disclosure of confidential information received from an EEA regulator . . . . [3.230]

PART 4
REORGANISATION OR WINDING UP OF UK CREDIT INSTITUTIONS: RECOGNITION OF EEA RIGHTS

19 Application of this Part . . . . [3.231]
20 Application of this Part: certain assets excluded from insolvent estate of UK credit institution . . . . [3.232]
21 Interpretation of this Part . . . . [3.233]
22 EEA rights: applicable law in the winding up of a UK credit institution . . . . [3.234]
23 Employment contracts and relationships . . . . [3.235]
24 Contracts in connection with immovable property . . . . [3.236]
25 Registrable rights . . . . [3.237]
26 Third parties' rights in rem . . . . [3.238]
27 Reservation of title agreements etc . . . . [3.239]
28 Creditors' rights to set off . . . . [3.240]
29 Regulated markets . . . . [3.241]
30 Detrimental acts pursuant to the law of an EEA State . . . . [3.242]
31 Protection of third party purchasers . . . . [3.243]
32 Lawsuits pending . . . . [3.244]
33 Lex rei sitae . . . . [3.245]
34 Netting agreements . . . . [3.246]
35 Repurchase agreements . . . . [3.247]

PART 5
THIRD COUNTRY CREDIT INSTITUTIONS

36 Interpretation of this Part . . . . [3.248]
37 Application of these Regulations to a third country credit institution . . . . [3.249]
38 Disclosure of confidential information: third country credit institution . . . . [3.250]

PART 6
APPLICATION TO INVESTMENT FIRMS

39 Interpretation of this Part . . . . [3.251]
40 Application to UK investment firms . . . . [3.252]
41 Application to EEA investment firms . . . . [3.253]
42 Withdrawal of authorisation . . . . [3.254]
43 Reorganisation measures and winding-up proceedings in respect of EEA investment firms effective in the United Kingdom . . . . [3.255]

PART 7
APPLICATION TO GROUP COMPANIES

44 Interpretation of this Part . . . . [3.256]
45 Application to UK group companies . . . . [3.257]
46 Application to EEA group companies . . . . [3.258]
47 Reorganisation measures and winding-up proceedings in respect of EEA group companies effective in the United Kingdom . . . . [3.259]

PART 8
APPLICATION TO THIRD COUNTRY INVESTMENT FIRMS

48 Interpretation of this Part . . . . [3.260]
49 Application to third country investment firms . . . . [3.261]

PART 1
GENERAL

[3.213]
1 Citation and commencement

These Regulations may be cited as the Credit Institutions (Reorganisation and Winding up) Regulations 2004, and come into force on 5th May 2004.

[3.214]
2 Interpretation

(1) In these Regulations—

. . .

"the 1986 Act" means the Insolvency Act 1986;

"the 2000 Act" means the Financial Services and Markets Act 2000;
["the 2006 Act" means the Companies Act 2006;]
"the 1989 Order" means the Insolvency (Northern Ireland) Order 1989;
"administrator" has the meaning given by paragraph 13 of Schedule B1 to the 1986 Act[, paragraph 14 of Schedule B1 to the 1989 Order,] section 8(2) of the 1986 Act [or Article 21(2) of the 1989 Order] as the case may be;

. . .

. . .

. . .

"branch", in relation to an EEA or UK credit institution has the meaning given by [Article 4(1)(17) of the capital requirements regulation];
["capital requirements directive" means Directive 2013/36/EU of the European Parliament and of the Council of 26 June 2013 relating to the activity of credit institutions and the prudential supervision of credit institutions and investment firms, amending Directive 2002/87/EC and repealing Directives 2006/48/EC and 2006/49/EC;
"capital requirements regulation" means Regulation (EU) No 575/2013 of the European Parliament and of the Council of 26 June 2013 on prudential requirements for credit institutions and investment firms and amending Regulation (EU) No 648/2012;]
"claim" means a claim submitted by a creditor of a UK credit institution in the course of—

(a) a winding up,
(b) an administration, or
(c) a voluntary arrangement,

with a view to recovering his debt in whole or in part, and includes a proof, within the meaning of rule 2.72 of the Insolvency Rules, or a proof of debt within the meaning of rule 4.73(4) of the Insolvency Rules or Rule 4.079(4) of the Insolvency Rules (Northern Ireland), as the case may be, or in Scotland a claim made in accordance with rule 4.15 of the Insolvency (Scotland) Rules;

. . .

"creditors' voluntary winding up" has the meaning given by section 90 of the 1986 Act or Article 76 of the 1989 Order as the case may be;
"debt"—

(a) in relation to a winding up or administration of a UK credit institution, has the meaning given by rule 13.12 of the Insolvency Rules or Article 5(1) of the 1989 Order except that where the credit institution is not a company, references in rule 13.12 or Article 5(1) to a company are to be read as references to the credit institution, and
(b) in a case where a voluntary arrangement has effect, in relation to a UK credit institution, means a debt which would constitute a debt in relation to the winding up of that credit institution, except that references in paragraph (1) of rule 13.12 or paragraph (1) of Article 5 of the 1989 Order to the date on which the company goes into liquidation are to be read as references to the date on which the voluntary arrangement has effect;
(c) in Scotland—
    (i) in relation to the winding up of a UK credit institution, shall be interpreted in accordance with Schedule 1 of the Bankruptcy (Scotland) Act 1985 as applied by Chapter 5 of Part 4 of the Insolvency (Scotland) Rules; and
    (ii) in a case where a voluntary arrangement has effect in relation to a UK credit institution, means a debt which would constitute a debt in relation to the winding up of that credit institution, except that references in Chapter 5 of Part 4 of the Insolvency (Scotland) Rules to the date of commencement of winding up are to be read as references to the date on which the voluntary arrangement has effect;

["directive reorganisation measure" means a reorganisation measure as defined in Article 2 of the reorganisation and winding up directive which was adopted or imposed on or after the 5th May 2004, or any other measure to be given effect in or under the law of the United Kingdom pursuant to Article 66 of the recovery and resolution directive;]
"directive winding-up proceedings" means winding-up proceedings as defined in Article 2 of the reorganisation and winding up directive which were opened on or after the 5th May 2004;
"Disclosure Regulations" means the Financial Services and Markets Act 2000 (Disclosure of Confidential Information) Regulations 2001;
["EEA credit institution" means an EEA undertaking, other than a UK credit institution, of the kind mentioned in Article 4(1)(1) and 4(1)(17) of the capital requirements regulation and subject to the exclusion of the undertakings referred to in Article 2(5)(2) to (23) of the capital requirements directive;]
"EEA creditor" means a creditor of a UK credit institution who—

(a) in the case of an individual, is ordinarily resident in an EEA State; and
(b) in the case of a body corporate or unincorporated association of persons, has its head office in an EEA State;

["EEA regulator" means—

(a) a competent authority (within the meaning given by point (40) of Article 4(1) of the capital requirements regulation) established in an EEA State; or
(b) the resolution authority (within the meaning given by point (18) of Article 2(1) of the recovery and resolution directive) established in an EEA State;]

["EEA State" has the meaning given by Schedule 1 to the Interpretation Act 1978;]
["the FCA" means the Financial Conduct Authority;]

"home state regulator", in relation to an EEA credit institution, means the relevant EEA regulator in the EEA State where its head office is located;

"the Insolvency Rules" means the Insolvency Rules 1986;

"the Insolvency Rules (Northern Ireland)" means the Insolvency Rules (Northern Ireland) 1991;

"the Insolvency (Scotland) Rules" means the Insolvency (Scotland) Rules 1986;

"liquidator", except for the purposes of regulation 4, includes any person or body appointed by the administrative or judicial authorities whose task is to administer winding-up proceedings in respect of a UK credit institution which is not a body corporate;

"officer", in relation to a company, has the meaning given by [section 1173(1) of the Companies Act 2006];

"official language" means a language specified in Article 1 of Council Regulation No 1 of 15 April 1958 determining the languages to be used by the European Economic Community (Regulation 1/58/EEC), most recently amended by paragraph (a) of Part XVIII of Annex I to the Act of Accession 1994 (194 N);

["the PRA" means the Prudential Regulation Authority;]

["PRA-authorised person" has the meaning given in section 2B of the 2000 Act;]

["recovery and resolution directive" means Directive 2014/59/EU of the European Parliament and of the Council of 15th May 2014 establishing a framework for the recovery and resolution of credit institutions and investment firms;]

["the reorganisation and winding up directive" means Directive 2001/24/EC of the European Parliament and of the Council of 4th April 2001 on the reorganisation and winding up of credit institutions as amended by Article 117 of the recovery and resolution directive;]

["section 899 compromise or arrangement" means a compromise or arrangement sanctioned by the court in relation to a UK credit institution under section 899 of the 2006 Act but does not include a compromise or arrangement falling within section 900 (powers of court to facilitate reconstruction or amalgamation) or Part 27 (mergers and divisions of public companies) of that Act;]

["stabilisation instrument" means any of the following—

(a) a "mandatory reduction instrument" made under section 6B of the Banking Act 2009;
(b) a "resolution instrument" made under section 12A of the Banking Act 2009;
(c) a "share transfer instrument" as defined in section 15 of the Banking Act 2009;
(d) a "share transfer order" as defined in section 16 of the Banking Act 2009;
(e) a "property transfer instrument" as defined in section 33 of the Banking Act 2009; or
(f) a "third country instrument" made under section 89H of the Banking Act 2009;]

"supervisor" has the meaning given by section 7 of the 1986 Act or Article 20 of the 1989 Order as the case may be;

"UK credit institution" means an undertaking whose head office is in the United Kingdom with permission under Part 4 of the 2000 Act to accept deposits or to issue electronic money as the case may be but does not include—

(a) an undertaking which also has permission under Part 4 of the 2000 Act to effect or carry out contracts of insurance; or
(b) a credit union within the meaning of section 1 of the Credit Unions Act 1979;

"voluntary arrangement" means a voluntary arrangement which has effect in relation to a UK credit institution in accordance with section 4A of the 1986 Act or Article 17A of the 1989 Order as the case may be; and

"winding up" means—

(a) winding up by the court, or
(b) a creditors' voluntary winding up.

(2) In paragraph (1)—

(a) for the purposes of the definition of "directive reorganisation measure", a reorganisation measure is adopted at the time when it is treated as adopted or imposed by the law of the relevant EEA State; and
(b) for the purposes of the definition of "directive winding-up proceedings", winding-up proceedings are opened at the time when they are treated as opened by the law of the relevant EEA State,

and in this paragraph "relevant EEA State" means the EEA State under the law of which the reorganisation is adopted or imposed, or the winding-up proceedings are opened, as the case may be.

(3) In these Regulations, references to the law of insolvency of the United Kingdom include references to every provision made by or under the 1986 Act or the 1989 Order as the case may be; and in relation to partnerships, limited liability partnerships or building societies, references to the law of insolvency or to any provision of the 1986 Act or the 1989 Order are to that law as modified by the Insolvent Partnerships Order 1994, the Insolvent Partnerships Order (Northern Ireland) 1995, the Limited Liability Partnerships Regulations 2001[, the Limited Liability Partnerships Regulations (Northern Ireland) 2004] or the Building Societies Act 1986 (as the case may be).

(4) References in these Regulations to "accepting deposits" and a "contract of insurance" must be read with—

(a) section 22 of the 2000 Act;
(b) any relevant order made under that section; and
(c) Schedule 2 to that Act.

(5) For the purposes of the 2000 Act, functions imposed or falling on the [FCA or the PRA] under these Regulations shall be deemed to be functions under the 2000 Act.

NOTES

Para (1): definitions "the 1985 Act", "Article 418 compromise or arrangement" and "the Companies Order" revoked, definition "the 2006 Act" inserted, words in square brackets in definition "officer" substituted, and definition "section 899 compromise or arrangement" substituted for original definition "section 425 compromise or arrangement" by the Companies Act 2006 (Consequential Amendments and Transitional Provisions) Order 2011, SI 2011/1265, art 24(1), (2); in definition "administrator", words in first pair of square brackets substituted and words in second pair of square brackets inserted by the Credit Institutions (Reorganisation and Winding Up) (Amendment) Regulations 2007, SI 2007/830, reg 2(1), (2); definition "the Authority" revoked, and definitions "the FCA", "the PRA" and "PRA-authorised person" inserted by the Financial Services Act 2012 (Consequential Amendments and Transitional Provisions) Order 2013, SI 2013/472, art 3, Sch 2, para 91(a); definition "banking consolidation directive" revoked, words in square brackets in definition "branch" substituted, definition "EEA credit institution" substituted, and definitions "capital requirements directive" and "capital requirements regulation" inserted, by the Capital Requirements Regulations 2013, SI 2013/3115, reg 46(1), Sch 2, Pt 3, para 63(1), (2)(a)–(d); definitions "directive reorganisation measure", "EEA regulator" and "the reorganisation and winding up directive" substituted, and definitions "recovery and resolution directive" and "stabilisation instrument" inserted, by the Bank Recovery and Resolution (No 2) Order 2014, SI 2014/3348, art 226, Sch 3, Pt 3, para 10(1), (2); definition "EEA State" substituted by the Financial Services (EEA State) Regulations 2007, SI 2007/108, reg 9; words in square brackets in definition "banking consolidation directive" inserted by the Electronic Money Regulations 2011, SI 2011/99, reg 79, Sch 4, Pt 2, para 16.

Para (3): words in square brackets inserted by SI 2007/830, reg 2(1), (3).

Para (5): words in square brackets substituted by SI 2013/472, art 3, Sch 2, para 91(b).

Note that the Insolvency Rules 1986, SI 1986/1925 are revoked and replaced (as from 6 April 2017 and subject to transitional provisions) by the Insolvency (England and Wales) Rules 2016, SI 2016/1024 at **[6.2]**.

PART 2
INSOLVENCY MEASURES AND PROCEEDINGS: JURISDICTION IN RELATION TO CREDIT INSTITUTIONS

[3.215]

3 Prohibition against winding up etc EEA credit institutions in the United Kingdom

(1) On or after the relevant date a court in the United Kingdom may not, in relation to an EEA credit institution or any branch of an EEA credit institution—

- (a) make a winding-up order pursuant to section 221 of the 1986 Act or Article 185 of the 1989 Order;
- (b) appoint a provisional liquidator;
- (c) make an administration order.

(2) Paragraph (1)(a) does not prevent—

- (a) the court from making a winding-up order on or after the relevant date in relation to an EEA credit institution if—
  - (i) a provisional liquidator was appointed in relation to that credit institution before the relevant date, and
  - (ii) that appointment continues in force until immediately before that winding-up order is made;
- (b) the winding up of an EEA credit institution on or after the relevant date pursuant to a winding-up order which was made, and has not been discharged, before that date.

(3) Paragraph (1)(b) does not prevent a provisional liquidator of an EEA credit institution appointed before the relevant date from acting in relation to that credit institution on or after that date.

(4) Paragraph (1)(c) does not prevent an administrator appointed before the relevant date from acting on or after that date in a case in which the administration order under which he or his predecessor was appointed remains in force after that date.

(5) On or after the relevant date, an administrator may not, in relation to an EEA credit institution, be appointed under paragraphs 14 or 22 of Schedule B1 [to] the 1986 Act [or paragraphs 15 or 23 of Schedule B1 to the 1989 Order].

(6) A proposed voluntary arrangement shall not have effect in relation to an EEA credit institution if a decision under section 4 of the 1986 Act or Article 17 of the 1989 Order with respect to the approval of that arrangement was taken on or after the relevant date.

[(7) An order under section 254 of the Enterprise Act 2002 (application of insolvency law to a foreign company) or under Article 9 of the Insolvency (Northern Ireland) Order 2005 (application of insolvency law to company incorporated outside Northern Ireland) may not provide for any of the following provisions of the 1986 Act or of the 1989 Order to apply in relation to an incorporated EEA credit institution—

- (a) Part 1 of the 1986 Act or Part 2 of the 1989 Order (company voluntary arrangements);
- (b) Part 2 of the 1986 Act or Part 3 of the 1989 Order (administration);
- (c) Chapter 4 of Part 4 of the 1986 Act or chapter 4 of Part 5 of the 1989 Order (creditors' voluntary winding up);
- (d) Chapter 6 of Part 4 of the 1986 Act (winding up by the Court).]

[(7A) A stabilisation instrument shall not be made in respect of an EEA credit institution.]

(8) In this regulation and regulation 4, "relevant date" means the 5th May 2004.

NOTES

Para (5): word in first pair of square brackets substituted and words in second pair of square brackets inserted by the Credit Institutions (Reorganisation and Winding Up) (Amendment) Regulations 2007, SI 2007/830, reg 2(1), (4).

Para (7): substituted by SI 2007/830, reg 2(1), (5).

Para (7A): inserted by the Bank Recovery and Resolution (No 2) Order 2014, SI 2014/3348, art 226, Sch 3, Pt 3, para 10(1), (3).

[3.216]

4 Schemes of arrangement

(1) For the purposes of [section 895(2)(b) of the 2006 Act], an EEA credit institution or a branch of an EEA credit institution is to be treated as a company liable to be wound up under the 1986 Act or the 1989 Order if it would be liable to be wound up under that Act or Order but for the prohibition in regulation 3(1)(a).

(2) But a court may not make a relevant order under [section 899 of the 2006 Act] in relation to an EEA credit institution which is subject to a directive reorganisation measure or directive winding-up proceedings, or a branch of an EEA credit institution which is subject to such a measure or proceedings, unless the conditions set out in paragraph (3) are satisfied.

(3) Those conditions are—

(a) the person proposing [the section 899 compromise or arrangement] ("the proposal") has given—

(i) the administrator or liquidator, and

(ii) the relevant administrative or judicial authority,

reasonable notice of the details of that proposal; and

(b) no person notified in accordance with sub-paragraph (a) has objected to the proposal.

(4) Nothing in this regulation invalidates a compromise or arrangement which was sanctioned by the court by an order made before the relevant date.

(5) For the purposes of paragraph (2), a relevant order means an order sanctioning [a section 899 compromise or arrangement] which—

(a) is intended to enable the credit institution, and the whole or any part of its undertaking, to survive as a going concern and which affects the rights of persons other than the credit institution or its contributories; or

(b) includes among its purposes a realisation of some or all of the assets of the EEA credit institution to which the order relates and the distribution of the proceeds to creditors, with a view to terminating the whole or any part of the business of that credit institution.

(6) For the purposes of this regulation—

(a) "administrator" means an administrator, as defined by Article 2 of the reorganisation and winding up directive, who is appointed in relation to the EEA credit institution in relation to which the proposal is made;

(b) "liquidator" means a liquidator, as defined by Article 2 of the reorganisation and winding up directive, who is appointed in relation to the EEA credit institution in relation to which the proposal is made;

(c) "administrative or judicial authority" means the administrative or judicial authority, as defined by Article 2 of the reorganisation and winding up directive, which is competent for the purposes of the directive reorganisation measure or directive winding-up proceedings mentioned in paragraph (2).

NOTES

Paras (1)–(3), (5): words in square brackets substituted by the Companies Act 2006 (Consequential Amendments and Transitional Provisions) Order 2011, SI 2011/1265, art 24(1), (3).

[3.217]

5 Reorganisation measures and winding-up proceedings in respect of EEA credit institutions effective in the United Kingdom

(1) An EEA insolvency measure has effect in the United Kingdom in relation to—

(a) any branch of an EEA credit institution,

(b) any property or other assets of that credit institution,

(c) any debt or liability of that credit institution,

as if it were part of the general law of insolvency of the United Kingdom.

(2) Subject to paragraph (4)—

(a) a competent officer who satisfies the condition mentioned in paragraph (3); or

(b) a qualifying agent appointed by a competent officer who satisfies the condition mentioned in paragraph (3),

may exercise in the United Kingdom, in relation to the EEA credit institution which is subject to an EEA insolvency measure, any function which, pursuant to that measure, he is entitled to exercise in relation to that credit institution in the relevant EEA State.

(3) The condition mentioned in paragraph (2) is that the appointment of the competent officer is evidenced—

(a) by a certified copy of the order or decision by a judicial or administrative authority in the relevant EEA State by or under which the competent officer was appointed; or

(b) by any other certificate issued by the judicial or administrative authority which has jurisdiction in relation to the EEA insolvency measure,

and accompanied by a certified translation of that order, decision or certificate (as the case may be).

(4) In exercising the functions of the kind mentioned in paragraph (2), the competent officer or qualifying agent—

(a) may not take any action which would constitute an unlawful use of force in the part of the United Kingdom in which he is exercising those functions;

(b) may not rule on any dispute arising from a matter falling within Part 4 of these Regulations which is justiciable by a court in the part of the United Kingdom in which he is exercising those functions; and

(c) notwithstanding the way in which functions may be exercised in the relevant EEA State, must act in accordance with relevant laws or rules as to procedure which have effect in the part of the United Kingdom in which he is exercising those functions.

(5) For the purposes of paragraph (4)(c), "relevant laws or rules as to procedure" means—

(a) requirements as to consultation with or notification of employees of an EEA credit institution;

(b) law and procedures relevant to the realisation of assets;

(c) where the competent officer is bringing or defending legal proceedings in the name of, or on behalf of an EEA credit institution, the relevant rules of court.

(6) In this regulation—

"competent officer" means a person appointed under or in connection with an EEA insolvency measure for the purpose of administering that measure;

"qualifying agent" means an agent validly appointed (whether in the United Kingdom or elsewhere) by a competent officer in accordance with the relevant law in the relevant EEA State;

"EEA insolvency measure" means, as the case may be, a directive reorganisation measure or directive winding-up proceedings which have effect in relation to an EEA credit institution by virtue of the law of the relevant EEA State;

"relevant EEA State", in relation to an EEA credit institution, means the EEA State in which that credit institution has been authorised in accordance with [Article 8 of the capital requirements directive].

NOTES

Para (6): words in square brackets in definition "relevant EEA State" substituted by the Capital Requirements Regulations 2013, SI 2013/3115, reg 46(1), Sch 2, Pt 3, para 63(1), (3).

[3.218]

6 Confirmation by the court of a creditors' voluntary winding up

(1) Rule 7.62 of the Insolvency Rules or Rule 7.56 of the Insolvency Rules (Northern Ireland) applies in relation to a UK credit institution with the modification specified in paragraph (2) or (3).

(2) For the purposes of this regulation, rule 7.62 has effect as if there were substituted for paragraph (1)—

"(1) Where a UK credit institution (within the meaning of the Credit Institutions (Reorganisation and Winding up) Regulations 2004) has passed a resolution for voluntary winding up, and no declaration under section 89 has been made, the liquidator may apply to court for an order confirming the creditors' voluntary winding up for the purposes of Articles 10 and 28 of directive 2001/24/EC of the European Parliament and of the Council of 4 April 2001 on the reorganisation and winding up of credit institutions.".

(3) For the purposes of this regulation, Rule 7.56 of the Insolvency Rules (Northern Ireland) has effect as if there were substituted for paragraph (1)—

"(1) Where a UK credit institution (within the meaning of the Credit Institutions (Reorganisation and Winding up) Regulations 2004) has passed a resolution for voluntary winding up, and no declaration under Article 75 has been made, the liquidator may apply to court for an order confirming the creditors' voluntary winding up for the purposes of Articles 10 and 28 of directive 2001/24/EC of the European Parliament and of the Council of 4 April 2001 on the reorganisation and winding up of credit institutions.".

PART 3
MODIFICATIONS OF THE LAW OF INSOLVENCY: NOTIFICATION AND PUBLICATION

[3.219]

7 Modifications of the law of insolvency

The general law of insolvency has effect in relation to UK credit institutions subject to the provisions of this Part.

[3.220]

8 Consultation of the [FCA and, if the institution is a PRA-authorised person, the PRA] prior to a voluntary winding up

(1) Where, on or after 5th May 2004, a UK credit institution ("the institution") intends to pass a resolution to wind up the institution under paragraph (b) or (c) of section 84(1) of the 1986 Act or sub-paragraph (b) or (c) of Article 70(1) of the 1989 Order, the institution must give written notice of the resolution to the [FCA and, if the institution is a PRA-authorised person, the PRA] before it passes the resolution.

(2) Where notice is given under paragraph (1), the resolution may be passed only after the end of the period of five business days beginning with the day on which the notice was given.

NOTES

Para (1): words in square brackets substituted by the Financial Services Act 2012 (Consequential Amendments and Transitional Provisions) Order 2013, SI 2013/472, art 3, Sch 2, para 91(c), subject to a transitional provision; see SI 2013/472, art 3, Sch 2, para 92(a) which provides that where, before 1 April 2013, notice was given to the Financial Services Authority for the purposes of this regulation, and the resolution was not passed, the notice is to be treated as if it had also been given to the Prudential Regulation Authority.

[3.221]

9 Notification of relevant decision to the [FCA and, if the institution is a PRA-authorised person, the PRA]

(1) Where on or after 5th May 2004 the court makes a decision, order or appointment of any of the following kinds—

(a) an administration order under paragraph 13 of Schedule B1 to the 1986 Act[, paragraph 14 of Schedule B1 to the 1989 Order,] section 8(1) of the 1986 Act [or Article 21(1) of the 1989 Order];

(b) a winding-up order under section 125 of the 1986 Act or Article 105 of the 1989 Order;

(c) the appointment of a provisional liquidator under section 135(1) of the 1986 Act or Article 115(1) of the 1989 Order;

(d) the appointment of an administrator in an interim order under paragraph 13(1)(d) of Schedule B1 to the 1986 Act[, paragraph 14(1)(d) of Schedule B1 to the 1989 Order, section 9(4) of the 1986 Act] or Article 22(4) of the 1989 Order,

it must immediately inform the [FCA and, if the institution is a PRA-authorised person, the PRA], or cause the [FCA and, if the institution is a PRA-authorised person, the PRA] to be informed, of the order or appointment which has been made.

(2) Where a decision with respect to the approval of a voluntary arrangement has effect, and the arrangement which is the subject of that decision is a qualifying arrangement, the supervisor must forthwith inform the [FCA and, if the institution is a PRA-authorised person, the PRA] of the arrangement which has been approved.

(3) Where a liquidator is appointed as mentioned in section 100 of the 1986 Act, paragraph 83 of Schedule B1 to the 1986 Act[, paragraph 84 of Schedule B1 to the 1989 Order] or Article 86 of the 1989 Order (appointment of liquidator in a creditors' voluntary winding up), the liquidator must inform the [FCA and, if the institution is a PRA-authorised person, the PRA] forthwith of his appointment.

(4) Where in the case of a members' voluntary winding up, section 95 of the 1986 Act (effect of company's insolvency) or Article 81 of the 1989 Order applies, the liquidator must inform the [FCA and, if the institution is a PRA-authorised person, the PRA] forthwith that he is of that opinion.

[(5) Paragraphs (1), (2) and (3) do not require the FCA to be informed in any case where the FCA was represented at all hearings in connection with the application in relation to which the decision, order or appointment is made.

(5A) Paragraphs (1), (2) and (3) do not require the PRA to be informed in any case where the PRA was represented at all hearings in connection with the application in relation to which the decision, order or appointment is made.]

(6) For the purposes of paragraph (2), a "qualifying arrangement" means a voluntary arrangement which—

(a) varies the rights of creditors as against the credit institution and is intended to enable the credit institution, and the whole or any part of its undertaking, to survive as a going concern; or

(b) includes a realisation of some or all of the assets of the credit institution, with a view to terminating the whole or any part of the business of that credit institution.

(7) A supervisor, administrator or liquidator who fails without reasonable excuse to comply with paragraph (2), (3), or (4) (as the case may be) commits an offence and is liable on summary conviction to a fine not exceeding level 3 on the standard scale.

NOTES

Regulation heading, paras (1), (2), (4): words "FCA and, if the institution is a PRA-authorised person, the PRA" in square brackets substituted by the Financial Services Act 2012 (Consequential Amendments and Transitional Provisions) Order 2013, SI 2013/472, art 3, Sch 2, para 91(d), subject to a transitional provision; see SI 2013/472, art 3, Sch 2, para 92(b) which provides that any obligation to inform the Prudential Regulation Authority, or to cause the Prudential Regulation Authority to be informed, which arose under this regulation before 1 April 2013, is to be treated as satisfied if the information was given to the Financial Services Authority.

Para (1): words in first pair of square brackets in sub-para (a) substituted, and words in second pair of square brackets in sub-para (a) and words in square brackets in sub-para (d) inserted by the Credit Institutions (Reorganisation and Winding Up) (Amendment) Regulations 2007, SI 2007/830, reg 2(1), (6).

Para (3): words in first pair of square brackets inserted by SI 2007/830, reg 2(1), (7); words in second pair of square brackets substituted by SI 2013/472, art 3, Sch 2, para 91(d), subject to a transitional provision; see SI 2013/472, art 3, Sch 2, para 92(b) which provides that any obligation to inform the Prudential Regulation Authority, or to cause the Prudential Regulation Authority to be informed, which arose under this regulation before 1 April 2013, is to be treated as satisfied if the information was given to the Financial Services Authority.

Paras (5), (5A): substituted by SI 2013/472, art 3, Sch 2, para 91(e), subject to a transitional provision; see SI 2013/472, art 3, Sch 2, para 92(b) which provides that any obligation to inform the Prudential Regulation Authority, or to cause the Prudential Regulation Authority to be informed, which arose under this regulation before 1 April 2013, is to be treated as satisfied if the information was given to the Financial Services Authority.

[3.222]

10 Notification to EEA regulators

(1) Where [the FCA or the PRA] is informed of a decision, order or appointment in accordance with regulation 9, [that authority] must as soon as is practicable inform the relevant person—

(a) that the decision, order or appointment has been made; and

(b) in general terms, of the possible effect of a decision, order or appointment of that kind on the business of a credit institution.

(2) Where [the FCA or the PRA] has been represented at all hearings in connection with the application in relation to which the decision, order or appointment has been made, [that authority] must inform the relevant person of the matters mentioned in paragraph (1) as soon as is practicable after that decision, order or appointment has been made.

(3) Where, on or after 5th May 2004, it appears to [the Bank of England [(acting otherwise than in its capacity as the Prudential Regulation Authority)],] the [FCA or the PRA] that a directive reorganisation measure should be adopted in relation to or imposed on an EEA credit institution which has a branch in the United Kingdom, it will inform the home state regulator as soon as is practicable.

(4) In this regulation, the "relevant person" means the EEA regulator of any EEA State in which the UK credit institution has a branch.

NOTES

Paras (1), (2): words in square brackets substituted by the Financial Services Act 2012 (Consequential Amendments and Transitional Provisions) Order 2013, SI 2013/472, art 3, Sch 2, para 91(f).

Para (3): words in first (outer) pair of square brackets inserted by the Bank Recovery and Resolution (No 2) Order 2014, SI 2014/3348, art 226, Sch 3, Pt 3, para 10(1), (4); words in second (inner) pair of square brackets inserted by the Bank of England and Financial Services (Consequential Amendments) Regulations 2017, SI 2017/80, reg 2, Schedule, para 26; words in third pair of square brackets substituted by SI 2013/472, art 3, Sch 2, para 91(g).

[3.223]

11 Withdrawal of authorisation

(1) For the purposes of this regulation—

(a) a qualifying decision means a decision with respect to the approval of a voluntary arrangement where the voluntary arrangement includes a realisation of some or all of the assets of the credit institution with a view to terminating the whole or any part of the business of that credit institution;

(b) a qualifying order means—

(i) a winding-up order under section 125 of the 1986 Act or Article 105 of the 1989 Order; or

(ii) an administration order under paragraph 13 of Schedule B1 to the 1986 Act [or paragraph 14 of Schedule B1 to the 1989 Order] in the prescribed circumstances;

(c) a qualifying appointment means—

(i) the appointment of a provisional liquidator under section 135(1) of the 1986 Act or Article 115(1) of the 1989 Order; or

(ii) the appointment of a liquidator as mentioned in section 100 of the 1986 Act, Article 86 of the 1989 Order (appointment of liquidator in a creditors' voluntary winding up) or paragraph 83 of Schedule B1 to the 1986 Act [or paragraph 84 of Schedule B1 to the 1989 Order] (moving from administration to creditors' voluntary liquidation).

(2) The prescribed circumstances are where, after the appointment of an administrator, the administrator concludes that it is not reasonably practicable to achieve the objective specified in paragraph 3(1)(a) of Schedule B1 to the 1986 Act [or paragraph 4(1)(a) of Schedule B1 to the 1989 Order].

(3) When [the FCA or the PRA] is informed of a qualifying decision, qualifying order or qualifying appointment, [that authority] will as soon as reasonably practicable exercise its power under [section 55J] of the 2000 Act to vary or to cancel the UK credit institution's permission under Part 4 of that Act to accept deposits or to issue electronic money as the case may be.

NOTES

Para (1): words in square brackets in sub-paras (b), (c) inserted by the Credit Institutions (Reorganisation and Winding Up) (Amendment) Regulations 2007, SI 2007/830, reg 2(1), (8).

Para (2): words in square brackets inserted by SI 2007/830, reg 2(1), (9).

Para (3): words in square brackets substituted by the Financial Services Act 2012 (Consequential Amendments and Transitional Provisions) Order 2013, SI 2013/472, art 3, Sch 2, para 91(h), subject to a transitional provision; see SI 2013/472, art 3, Sch 2, para 92(c) which provides regulation 11(3) applies in addition to the circumstances specified in that provision, where the Financial Services Authority, before 1 April 2013, was informed of a qualifying decision, qualifying order or qualifying appointment, and did not exercise its power under section 45 of the Financial Services and Markets Act 2000 to vary or to cancel the UK credit institution's permission under Part 4 of that Act to accept deposits or to issue electronic money as the case may be.

[3.224]

12 Publication of voluntary arrangement, administration order, winding-up order or scheme of arrangement

(1) This regulation applies where a qualifying decision is approved, or a qualifying order or qualifying appointment is made, in relation to a UK credit institution on or after 5th May 2004.

(2) For the purposes of this regulation—

(a) a qualifying decision means a decision with respect to the approval of a proposed voluntary arrangement, in accordance with section 4A of the 1986 Act or Article 17A of the 1989 Order;

(b) a qualifying order means—

(i) an administration order under paragraph 13 of Schedule B1 to the 1986 Act[, paragraph 14 of Schedule B1 to the 1989 Order,] section 8(1) of the 1986 Act [or Article 21(1) of the 1989 Order],

(ii) an order appointing a provisional liquidator in accordance with section 135 of that Act or Article 115 of that Order, or

(iii) a winding-up order made by the court under Part 4 of that Act or Part V of the 1989 Order;

(c) a qualifying appointment means the appointment of a liquidator as mentioned in section 100 of the 1986 Act or Article 86 of the 1989 Order (appointment of liquidator in a creditors' voluntary winding up).

(3) Subject to paragraph (7), as soon as is reasonably practicable after a qualifying decision has effect or a qualifying order or a qualifying appointment has been made, the relevant officer must publish, or cause to be published, in the Official Journal of the European Communities and in 2 national newspapers in each EEA State in which the UK credit institution has a branch the information mentioned in paragraph (4) and (if applicable) paragraphs (5) or (6).

(4) That information is—

(a) a summary of the terms of the qualifying decision, qualifying appointment or the provisions of the qualifying order (as the case may be);

(b) the identity of the relevant officer;

(c) the statutory provisions in accordance with which the qualifying decision has effect or the qualifying order or appointment has been made or takes effect.

(5) In the case of a qualifying appointment, that information includes the court to which an application under section 112 of the 1986 Act (reference of questions to the court) . . . or Article 98 of the 1989 Order (reference of questions to the High Court) may be made.

(6) In the case of a qualifying decision, that information includes the court to which an application under section 6 of the 1986 Act or Article 19 of the 1989 Order (challenge of decisions) may be made.

(7) Paragraph (3) does not apply where a qualifying decision or qualifying order falling within paragraph (2)(b)(i) affects the interests only of the members, or any class of members, or employees of the credit institution (in their capacity as members or employees).

(8) This regulation is without prejudice to any requirement to publish information imposed upon a relevant officer under any provision of the general law of insolvency.

(9) A relevant officer who fails to comply with paragraph (3) of this regulation commits an offence and is liable on summary conviction to a fine not exceeding level 3 on the standard scale.

(10) A qualifying decision, qualifying order or qualifying appointment is not invalid or ineffective if the relevant official fails to comply with paragraph (3) of this regulation.

(11) In this regulation, "relevant officer" means—

(a) in the case of a voluntary arrangement, the supervisor;

(b) in the case of an administration order, the administrator;

(c) in the case of a creditors' voluntary winding up, the liquidator;

(d) in the case of winding-up order, the liquidator; or

(e) in the case of an order appointing a provisional liquidator, the provisional liquidator.

(12) The information to be published in accordance with paragraph (3) of this regulation shall be—

(a) in the case of the Official Journal of the European Communities, in the official language or languages of each EEA State in which the UK credit institution has a branch;

(b) in the case of the national newspapers of each EEA State in which the UK credit institution has a branch, in the official language or languages of that EEA State.

NOTES

Para (2): words in first pair of square brackets substituted and words in second pair of square brackets inserted by the Credit Institutions (Reorganisation and Winding Up) (Amendment) Regulations 2007, SI 2007/830, reg 2(1), (10).

Para (5): words omitted revoked by SI 2007/830, reg 2(1), (11).

[3.225]

13 Honouring of certain obligations

(1) This regulation applies where, on or after 5th May 2004, a relevant obligation has been honoured for the benefit of a relevant credit institution by a relevant person.

(2) Where a person has honoured a relevant obligation for the benefit of a relevant credit institution, he shall be deemed to have discharged that obligation if he was unaware of the winding up of that credit institution.

(3) For the purposes of this regulation—

(a) a relevant obligation is an obligation which, after the commencement of the winding up of a relevant credit institution, should have been honoured for the benefit of the liquidator of that credit institution;

(b) a relevant credit institution is a UK credit institution which—

(i) is not a body corporate; and

(ii) is the subject of a winding up;

(c) a relevant person is a person who at the time the obligation is honoured—

(i) is in the territory of an EEA State; and
(ii) is unaware of the winding up of the relevant credit institution.

(4) For the purposes of paragraph (3)(c)(ii) of this regulation—
(a) a relevant person shall be presumed, in the absence of evidence to the contrary, to have been unaware of the winding up of a relevant credit institution where the relevant obligation was honoured before date of the publication provided for in regulation 12 in relation to that winding up;
(b) a relevant person shall be presumed, in the absence of evidence to the contrary, to have been aware of the winding up of the relevant credit institution where the relevant obligation was honoured on or after the date of the publication provided for in regulation 12 in relation to that winding up.

[3.226]
14 Notification to creditors: winding-up proceedings

(1) When a relevant order or appointment is made, or a relevant decision is taken, in relation to a UK credit institution on or after 5th May 2004, the appointed officer must, as soon as is reasonably practicable, notify in writing all known creditors of that credit institution—
(a) of the matters mentioned in paragraph (4); and
(b) of the matters mentioned in paragraph (5).

(2) The appointed officer may comply with the requirement in paragraphs (1)(a) and the requirement in paragraph (1)(b) by separate notifications.

(3) For the purposes of this regulation—
(a) "relevant order" means—
(i) an administration order under paragraph 13 of Schedule B1 to the 1986 Act [or paragraph 14 of Schedule B1 to the 1989 Order] in the prescribed circumstances or an administration order made for the purposes set out in section 8(3)(b) or (d) of the 1986 Act [or Article 21(3) (b) or (d) of the 1989 Order], as the case may be,
(ii) a winding-up order under section 125 of the 1986 Act (powers of the court on hearing a petition) or Article 105 of the 1989 Order (powers of High Court on hearing of petition),
(iii) the appointment of a liquidator in accordance with section 138 of the 1986 Act (appointment of a liquidator in Scotland), or
(iv) an order appointing a provisional liquidator in accordance with section 135 of that Act or Article 115 of the 1989 Order;
(b) a "relevant appointment" means the appointment of a liquidator as mentioned in section 100 of the 1986 Act or Article 86 of the 1989 Order (appointment of liquidator in a creditors' voluntary winding up); and
(c) a "relevant decision" means a decision as a result of which a qualifying voluntary arrangement has effect.

(4) The matters which must be notified to all known creditors in accordance with paragraph (1)(a) are as follows—
(a) that a relevant order or appointment has been made, or a relevant decision taken, in relation to the UK credit institution; and
(b) the date from which that order, appointment or decision has effect.

(5) The matters which must be notified to all known creditors in accordance with paragraph (1)(b) are as follows—
(a) if applicable, the date by which a creditor must submit his claim in writing;
(b) the matters which must be stated in a creditor's claim;
(c) details of any category of debt in relation to which a claim is not required;
(d) the person to whom any such claim or any observations on a claim must be submitted; and
(e) the consequences of any failure to submit a claim by any specified deadline.

(6) Where a creditor is notified in accordance with paragraph (1)(b), the notification must be headed with the words "Invitation to lodge a claim. Time limits to be observed", and that heading must be given in every official language.

(7) The obligation under paragraph (1)(b) may be discharged by sending a form of proof in accordance with rule 4.74 of the Insolvency Rules, Rule 4.080 of the Insolvency Rules (Northern Ireland) or Rule 4.15(2) of the (Insolvency) Scotland Rules as applicable in cases where any of those rules applies, provided that the form of proof complies with paragraph (6).

[(8) The prescribed circumstances are where the administrator includes in the statement required under Rule 2.3 of the Insolvency Rules or under Rule 2.003 of the Insolvency Rules (Northern Ireland) a statement to the effect that the objective set out in paragraph 3(1)(a) of Schedule B1 to the 1986 Act or in paragraph 4(1)(a) of Schedule B1 to the 1989 Order is not reasonably likely to be achieved.]

(9) Where, after the appointment of an administrator, the administrator concludes that it is not reasonably practicable to achieve the objective specified in paragraph 3(1)(a) of Schedule B1 to the 1986 Act [or paragraph 4(1)(a) of Schedule B1 to the 1989 Order], he shall inform the court[, the FCA and, if the institution is a PRA-authorised person, the PRA] in writing of that conclusion and upon so doing the order by which he was appointed shall be a relevant order for the purposes of this regulation and the obligation under paragraph (1) shall apply as from the date on which he so informs the court[, the FCA and, if the institution is a PRA-authorised person, the PRA].

(10) An appointed officer commits an offence if he fails without reasonable excuse to comply with a requirement under paragraph (1) of this regulation, and is liable on summary conviction to a fine not exceeding level 3 on the standard scale.

(11) For the purposes of this regulation—

(a) "appointed officer" means—

(i) in the case of a relevant order falling within paragraph (3)(a)(i), the administrator,

(ii) in the case of a relevant order falling within paragraph (3)(a)(ii) or (iii) or a relevant appointment falling within paragraph (3)(b), the liquidator,

(iii) in the case of a relevant order falling within paragraph (3)(a)(iv), the provisional liquidator, or

(iv) in the case of a relevant decision, the supervisor; and

(b) a creditor is a "known" creditor if the appointed officer is aware of—

(i) his identity,

(ii) his claim or potential claim, and

(iii) a recent address where he is likely to receive a communication.

(12) For the purposes of paragraph (3), a voluntary arrangement is a qualifying voluntary arrangement if its purposes include a realisation of some or all of the assets of the UK credit institution to which the order relates with a view to terminating the whole or any part of the business of that credit institution.

NOTES

Para (3): words in square brackets inserted by the Credit Institutions (Reorganisation and Winding Up) (Amendment) Regulations 2007, SI 2007/830, reg 2(1), (12)(a).

Para (8): substituted by SI 2007/830, reg 2(1), (12)(b).

Para (9): words in first pair of square brackets inserted by SI 2007/830, reg 2(1), (12)(c); words in second and third pairs of square brackets substituted by the Financial Services Act 2012 (Consequential Amendments and Transitional Provisions) Order 2013, SI 2013/472, art 3, Sch 2, para 91(i), subject to a transitional provision; see SI 2013/472, art 3, Sch 2, para 92(d) which provides that any obligation to inform the Authority which arose under regulation 14(9) before 1 April 2013 is to be treated as satisfied if the information was given to the Financial Service Authority, and the obligation under regulation 14(1) shall apply as from the date on which the court and the Financial Services Authority were informed.

[3.227]
15 Submission of claims by EEA creditors

(1) An EEA creditor who, on or after 5th May 2004, submits a claim or observations relating to his claim in any relevant proceedings (irrespective of when those proceedings were commenced or had effect) may do so in his domestic language, provided that the requirements in paragraphs (3) and (4) are complied with.

(2) For the purposes of this regulation, "relevant proceedings" means—

(a) a winding up;

(b) a qualifying voluntary arrangement; or

(c) administration.

(3) Where an EEA creditor submits a claim in his domestic language, the document must be headed with the words "Lodgement of claim" (in English).

(4) Where an EEA creditor submits observations on his claim (otherwise than in the document by which he submits his claim), the observations must be headed with the words "Submission of observations relating to claims" (in English).

(5) Paragraph (3) does not apply where an EEA creditor submits his claim using—

(a) in the case of a winding up, a form of proof supplied by the liquidator in accordance with rule 4.74 of the Insolvency Rules, Rule 4.080 of the Insolvency Rules (Northern Ireland) or rule 4.15(2) of the Insolvency (Scotland) Rules;

(b) in the case of a qualifying voluntary arrangement, a form approved by the court for that purpose.

(6) In this regulation—

(a) "domestic language", in relation to an EEA creditor, means the official language, or one of the official languages, of the EEA State in which he is ordinarily resident or, if the creditor is not an individual, in which the creditor's head office is located; and

(b) "qualifying voluntary arrangement" means a voluntary arrangement whose purposes include a realisation of some or all of the assets of the UK credit institution to which the order relates with a view to terminating the whole or any part of the business of that credit institution.

[3.228]
16 Reports to creditors

(1) This regulation applies where, on or after 5th May 2004—

(a) a liquidator is appointed in accordance with section 100 of the 1986 Act, Article 86 of [the 1989 Order] (creditors' voluntary winding up: appointment of liquidator) or paragraph 83 of Schedule B1 to the 1986 Act [or paragraph 84 of Schedule B1 to the 1989 Order] (moving from administration to creditors' voluntary liquidation);

(b) a winding-up order is made by the court;

(c) a provisional liquidator is appointed; or

[(d) an administrator is appointed under paragraph 13 of Schedule B1 to the 1986 Act or paragraph 14 of Schedule B1 to the 1989 Order].

(2) The liquidator, provisional liquidator or administrator (as the case may be) must send a report to every known creditor once in every 12 months beginning with the date when his appointment has effect.

(3) The requirement in paragraph (2) does not apply where a liquidator, provisional liquidator or administrator is required by order of the court to send a report to creditors at intervals which are more frequent than those required by this regulation.

(4) This regulation is without prejudice to any requirement to send a report to creditors, imposed by the court on the liquidator, provisional liquidator or administrator, which is supplementary to the requirements of this regulation.

(5) A liquidator, provisional liquidator or administrator commits an offence if he fails without reasonable excuse to comply with an applicable requirement under this regulation, and is liable on summary conviction to a fine not exceeding level 3 on the standard scale.

(6) For the purposes of this regulation—

(a) "known creditor" means—

(i) a creditor who is known to the liquidator, provisional liquidator or administrator, and

(ii) in a case falling within paragraph (1)(b) or (c), a creditor who is specified in the credit institution's statement of affairs (within the meaning of section 131 of the 1986 Act or Article 111 of the 1989 Order);

(b) "report" means a written report setting out the position generally as regards the progress of the winding up, provisional liquidation or administration (as the case may be).

NOTES

Para (1): words in first pair of square brackets in sub-para (a), and sub-para (d) substituted, and words in second pair of square brackets in sub-para (a) inserted by the Credit Institutions (Reorganisation and Winding Up) (Amendment) Regulations 2007, SI 2007/830, reg 2(1), (13).

[3.229]

17 Service of notices and documents

(1) This regulation applies to any notification, report or other document which is required to be sent to a creditor of a UK credit institution by a provision of this Part ("a relevant notification").

(2) A relevant notification may be sent to a creditor by one of the following methods—

(a) by posting it to the proper address of the creditor;

(b) by transmitting it electronically, in accordance with paragraph (4).

(3) For the purposes of paragraph (2)(a), the proper address of a creditor is any current address provided by that person as an address for service of a relevant notification and, if no such address is provided—

(a) the last known address of that creditor (whether his residence or a place where he carries on business);

(b) in the case of a body corporate, the address of its registered or principal office; or

(c) in the case of an unincorporated association, the address of its principal office.

(4) A relevant notification may be transmitted electronically only if it is sent to—

(a) an electronic address notified to the relevant officer by the creditor for this purpose; or

(b) if no such address has been notified, to an electronic address at which the relevant officer reasonably believes the creditor will receive the notification.

(5) Any requirement in this Part to send a relevant notification to a creditor shall also be treated as satisfied if the conditions set out in paragraph (6) are satisfied.

(6) The conditions of this paragraph are satisfied in the case of a relevant notification if—

(a) the creditor has agreed with—

(i) the UK credit institution which is liable under the creditor's claim, or

(ii) the relevant officer,

that information which is required to be sent to him (whether pursuant to a statutory or contractual obligation, or otherwise) may instead be accessed by him on a web site;

(b) the agreement applies to the relevant notification in question;

(c) the creditor is notified of—

(i) the publication of the relevant notification on a web site,

(ii) the address of that web site,

(iii) the place on that web site where the relevant notification may be accessed, and how it may be accessed; and

(d) the relevant notification is published on that web site throughout a period of at least one month beginning with the date on which the creditor is notified in accordance with sub-paragraph (c).

(7) Where, in a case in which paragraph (5) is relied on for compliance with a requirement of regulation 14 or 16—

(a) a relevant notification is published for a part, but not all, of the period mentioned in paragraph (6)(d) but

(b) the failure to publish it throughout that period is wholly attributable to circumstances which it would not be reasonable to have expected the relevant officer to prevent or avoid,

no offence is committed under regulation 14(10) or regulation 16(5) (as the case may be) by reason of that failure.

(8) In this regulation—

(a) "electronic address" includes any number or address used for the purposes of receiving electronic communications which are sent electronically;

(b) "electronic communication" means an electronic communication within the meaning of the Electronic Communications Act 2000 the processing of which on receipt is intended to produce writing; and

(c) "relevant officer" means (as the case may be) an administrator, liquidator, provisional liquidator or supervisor who is required to send a relevant notification to a creditor by a provision of this Part.

[3.230]

18 Disclosure of confidential information received from an EEA regulator

(1) This regulation applies to information ("insolvency information") which—

(a) relates to the business or affairs of any other person; and

(b) is supplied to the [FCA or the PRA] by an EEA regulator acting in accordance with Articles 4, 5, 9, or 11 of the reorganisation and winding up directive.

(2) Subject to paragraphs [(3), (4) and (5)], sections 348, 349 and 352 of the 2000 Act apply in relation to insolvency information as they apply in relation to confidential information within the meaning of section 348(2) of the 2000 Act.

(3) Insolvency information is not subject to the restrictions on disclosure imposed by section 348(1) of the 2000 Act (as it applies by virtue of paragraph (2)) if it satisfies any of the criteria set out in section 348(4) of the 2000 Act.

(4) The Disclosure Regulations apply in relation to insolvency information as they apply in relation to single market . . . information (within the meaning of those Regulations).

[(5) The sections of the 2000 Act specified in paragraph (2) apply with the modifications set out in section 89L of the Banking Act 2009 where that section applies.]

NOTES

Para (1): words in square brackets in sub-para (b) substituted by the Financial Services Act 2012 (Consequential Amendments and Transitional Provisions) Order 2013, SI 2013/472, art 3, Sch 2, para 91(j).

Para (2): words in square brackets substituted by the Bank Recovery and Resolution (No 2) Order 2014, SI 2014/3348, art 226, Sch 3, Pt 3, para 10(1), (5)(a).

Para (4): word omitted revoked by SI 2014/3348, art 226, Sch 3, Pt 3, para 10(1), (5)(b).

Para (5): added by SI 2014/3348, art 226, Sch 3, Pt 3, para 10(1), (5)(c).

PART 4
REORGANISATION OR WINDING UP OF UK CREDIT INSTITUTIONS: RECOGNITION OF EEA RIGHTS

[3.231]

19 Application of this Part

(1) This Part applies as follows—

(a) where a decision with respect to the approval of a proposed voluntary arrangement having a qualifying purpose is made under section 4A of the 1986 Act or Article 17A of the 1989 Order on or after 5th May 2004 in relation to a UK credit institution;

(b) where an administration order made under paragraph 13 of Schedule B1 to the 1986 Act[, paragraph 14 of Schedule B1 to the 1989 Order,] section 8(1) of the 1986 Act [or Article 21(1) of the 1989 Order] on or after 5th May 2004 is in force in relation to a UK credit institution;

(c) where a UK credit institution is subject to a relevant winding up; . . .

(d) where a provisional liquidator is appointed in relation to a UK credit institution on or after 5th May 2004 [or

(e) where a stabilisation instrument is made in respect of a UK credit institution].

(2) For the purposes of paragraph (1)(a), a voluntary arrangement has a qualifying purpose if it—

(a) varies the rights of the creditors as against the credit institution and is intended to enable the credit institution, and the whole or any part of its undertaking, to survive as a going concern; or

(b) includes a realisation of some or all of the assets of the credit institution to which the compromise or arrangement relates, with a view to terminating the whole or any part of the business of that credit institution.

(3) For the purposes of paragraph (1)(c), a winding up is a relevant winding up if—

(a) in the case of a winding up by the court, the winding-up order is made on or after 5th May 2004; or

(b) in the case of a creditors' voluntary winding up, the liquidator is appointed in accordance with section 100 of the 1986 Act, Article 86 of the 1989 Order or paragraph 83 of Schedule B1 to the 1986 Act [or paragraph 84 of Schedule B1 to the 1989 Order] on or after 5th May 2004.

NOTES

Para (1): in sub-para (b), words in first pair of square brackets substituted and words in second pair of square brackets inserted by the Credit Institutions (Reorganisation and Winding Up) (Amendment) Regulations 2007, SI 2007/830, reg 2(1), (14); word omitted from sub-para (c) revoked, and sub-para (e) and word immediately preceding it added, by the Bank Recovery and Resolution (No 2) Order 2014, SI 2014/3348, art 226, Sch 3, Pt 3, para 10(1), (6).

Para (3): words in square brackets inserted by SI 2007/830, reg 2(1), (15).

[3.232]
20 Application of this Part: [certain assets excluded from insolvent estate of UK credit institution]

(1) For the purposes of this Part, the insolvent estate of a UK credit institution shall not include any assets which at the commencement date are subject to [a relevant compromise or arrangement].

(2) In this regulation—

(a) "assets" has the same meaning as "property" in section 436 of the 1986 Act or Article 2(2) of the 1989 Order;

(b) "commencement date" means the date when a UK credit institution goes into liquidation within the meaning given by section 247(2) of the 1986 Act or Article 6(2) of the 1989 Order;

(c) "insolvent estate" has the meaning given by rule 13.8 of the Insolvency Rules or Rule 0.2 of the Insolvency Rules (Northern Ireland) and in Scotland means the company's assets;

[(d) "relevant compromise or arrangement" means—

(i) a compromise or arrangement sanctioned by the court before 5th May 2004 under—

(aa) section 425 of the Companies Act 1985 (excluding a compromise or arrangement falling within section 427 or 427A of that Act), or

(bb) Article 418 of the Companies (Northern Ireland) Order 1986 (excluding a compromise or arrangement falling within Article 420 or 420A of that Order); or

(ii) any subsequent compromise or arrangement sanctioned by the court to amend or replace a compromise or arrangement of a kind mentioned in paragraph (i) which is—

(aa) itself of a kind mentioned in sub-paragraph (aa) or (bb) of paragraph (i) (whether sanctioned before, on or after 5th May 2004), or

(bb) a section 899 compromise or arrangement.]

NOTES

Regulation heading: words in square brackets substituted by the Companies Act 2006 (Consequential Amendments and Transitional Provisions) Order 2011, SI 2011/1265, art 24(1), (4).

Para (1): words in square brackets substituted by SI 2011/1265, art 24(1), (5)(a).

Para (2): sub-para (d) substituted by SI 2011/1265, art 24(1), (5)(b).

[3.233]
21 Interpretation of this Part

(1) For the purposes of this Part—

(a) "affected credit institution" means a UK credit institution which is the subject of a relevant reorganisation or winding up;

(b) "relevant reorganisation" or "relevant winding up" means any voluntary arrangement, administration, winding up, [making of a stabilisation instrument] or order referred to in regulation 19(1) to which this Part applies; and

(c) "relevant time" means the date of the opening of a relevant reorganisation or a relevant winding up.

(2) In this Part, references to the opening of a relevant reorganisation or a relevant winding up mean—

(a) in the case of winding-up proceedings—

(i) in the case of a winding up by the court, the date on which the winding-up order is made, or

(ii) in the case of a creditors' voluntary winding up, the date on which the liquidator is appointed in accordance with section 100 of the 1986 Act, Article 86 of the 1989 Order or paragraph 83 of Schedule B1 to the 1986 Act [or paragraph 84 of Schedule B1 to the 1989 Order];

(b) in the case of a voluntary arrangement, the date when a decision with respect to the approval of that voluntary arrangement has effect in accordance with section 4A(2) of the 1986 Act or Article 17A(2) of the 1989 Order;

(c) in a case where an administration order under paragraph 13 of Schedule B1 to the 1986 Act[, paragraph 14 of Schedule B1 to the 1989 Order,] section 8(1) of the 1986 Act [or Article 21(1) of the 1989 Order] is in force, the date of the making of that order; . . .

(d) in a case where a provisional liquidator has been appointed, the date of that appointment, [and

(e) in a case where a stabilisation instrument is made, the date on which that instrument is made,]

and references to the time of an opening must be construed accordingly.

NOTES

Para (1): words in square brackets in sub-para (b) inserted by the Bank Recovery and Resolution (No 2) Order 2014, SI 2014/3348, art 226, Sch 3, Pt 3, para 10(1), (7)(a).

Para (2): words in square brackets in sub-para (a) and words in second pair of square brackets in sub-para (c) inserted, and words in first pair of square brackets in sub-para (c) substituted by the Credit Institutions (Reorganisation and Winding Up) (Amendment) Regulations 2007, SI 2007/830, reg 2(1), (16); word omitted from sub-para (c) revoked, and sub-para (e) and word immediately preceding it added by SI 2014/3348, art 226, Sch 3, Pt 3, para 10(1), (7)(b), (c).

[3.234]
22 EEA rights: applicable law in the winding up of a UK credit institution

(1) This regulation is subject to the provisions of regulations 23 to 35.

(2) In a relevant winding up, the matters mentioned in paragraph (3) are to be determined in accordance with the general law of insolvency of the United Kingdom.

(3) Those matters are—

(a) the assets which form part of the estate of the affected credit institution;
(b) the treatment of assets acquired by the affected credit institution after the opening of the relevant winding up;
(c) the respective powers of the affected credit institution and the liquidator or provisional liquidator;
(d) the conditions under which set-off may be invoked;
(e) the effects of the relevant winding up on current contracts to which the affected credit institution is a party;
(f) the effects of the relevant winding up on proceedings brought by creditors;
(g) the claims which are to be lodged against the estate of the affected credit institution;
(h) the treatment of claims against the affected credit institution arising after the opening of the relevant winding up;
(i) the rules governing—
 (i) the lodging, verification and admission of claims,
 (ii) the distribution of proceeds from the realisation of assets,
 (iii) the ranking of claims,
 (iv) the rights of creditors who have obtained partial satisfaction after the opening of the relevant winding up by virtue of a right in rem or through set-off;
(j) the conditions for and the effects of the closure of the relevant winding up, in particular by composition;
(k) the rights of creditors after the closure of the relevant winding up;
(l) who is to bear the cost and expenses incurred in the relevant winding up;
(m) the rules relating to the voidness, voidability or unenforceability of legal acts detrimental to all the creditors.

[3.235]
23 Employment contracts and relationships

(1) The effects of a relevant reorganisation or a relevant winding up on EEA employment contracts and EEA employment relationships are to be determined in accordance with the law of the EEA State to which that contract or that relationship is subject.

(2) In this regulation, an employment contract is an EEA employment contract, and an employment relationship is an EEA employment relationship if it is subject to the law of an EEA State.

[3.236]
24 Contracts in connection with immovable property

(1) The effects of a relevant reorganisation or a relevant winding up on a contract conferring the right to make use of or acquire immovable property situated within the territory of an EEA State shall be determined in accordance with the law of that State.

(2) The law of the EEA State in whose territory the property is situated shall determine whether the property is movable or immovable.

[3.237]
25 Registrable rights

The effects of a relevant reorganisation or a relevant winding up on rights of the affected UK credit institution with respect to—
(a) immovable property,
(b) a ship, or
(c) an aircraft
which is subject to registration in a public register kept under the authority of an EEA State are to be determined in accordance with the law of that State.

[3.238]
26 Third parties' rights in rem

(1) A relevant reorganisation or a relevant winding up shall not affect the rights in rem of creditors or third parties in respect of tangible or intangible, movable or immovable assets (including both specific assets and collections of indefinite assets as a whole which change from time to time) belonging to the affected credit institution which are situated within the territory of an EEA State at the relevant time.

(2) The rights in rem referred to in paragraph (1) shall mean—
(a) the right to dispose of assets or have them disposed of and to obtain satisfaction from the proceeds of or the income from those assets, in particular by virtue of a lien or a mortgage;
(b) the exclusive right to have a claim met, in particular a right guaranteed by a lien in respect of the claim or by assignment of the claim by way of guarantee;
(c) the right to demand the assets from, or to require restitution by, any person having possession or use of them contrary to the wishes of the party so entitled;
(d) a right in rem to the beneficial use of assets.

(3) A right, recorded in a public register and enforceable against third parties, under which a right in rem within the meaning of paragraph (1) may be obtained, is also to be treated as a right in rem for the purposes of this regulation.

(4) Paragraph (1) does not preclude actions for voidness, voidability or unenforceability of legal acts detrimental to creditors under the general law of insolvency of the United Kingdom.

[3.239]
27 Reservation of title agreements etc

(1) The adoption of a relevant reorganisation or opening of a relevant winding up in relation to a credit institution purchasing an asset shall not affect the seller's rights based on a reservation of title where at the time of that adoption or opening the asset is situated within the territory of an EEA State.

(2) The adoption of a relevant reorganisation or opening of a relevant winding up in relation to a credit institution selling an asset, after delivery of the asset, shall not constitute grounds for rescinding or terminating the sale and shall not prevent the purchaser from acquiring title where at the time of that adoption or opening the asset sold is situated within the territory of an EEA State.

(3) Paragraphs (1) and (2) do not preclude actions for voidness, voidability or unenforceability of legal acts detrimental to creditors under the general law of insolvency of the United Kingdom.

[3.240]
28 Creditors' rights to set off

(1) A relevant reorganisation or a relevant winding up shall not affect the right of creditors to demand the set-off of their claims against the claims of the affected credit institution, where such a set-off is permitted by the law applicable to the affected credit institution's claim.

(2) Paragraph (1) does not preclude actions for voidness, voidability or unenforceability of legal acts detrimental to creditors under the general law of insolvency of the United Kingdom.

[3.241]
29 Regulated markets

(1) Subject to regulation 33, the effects of a relevant reorganisation or winding up on transactions carried out in the context of a regulated market operating in an EEA State must be determined in accordance with the law applicable to those transactions.

[(2) For the purposes of this regulation "regulated market" has the meaning given by point (21) of Article 4(1) of Directive 2014/65/EU of the European Parliament and of the Council on markets in financial instruments.]

NOTES

Para (2): substituted by the Bank Recovery and Resolution (No 2) Order 2014, SI 2014/3348, art 226, Sch 3, Pt 3, para 10(1), (8).

[3.242]
30 Detrimental acts pursuant to the law of an EEA State

(1) In a relevant reorganisation or a relevant winding up, the rules relating to detrimental transactions shall not apply where a person who has benefited from a legal act detrimental to all the creditors provides proof that—

(a) the said act is subject to the law of an EEA State; and
(b) that law does not allow any means of challenging that act in the relevant case.

(2) For the purposes of paragraph (1), "the rules relating to detrimental transactions" means any provision of the general law of insolvency relating to the voidness, voidability or unenforceability of legal acts detrimental to all the creditors.

[3.243]
31 Protection of third party purchasers

(1) This regulation applies where, by an act concluded after the adoption of a relevant reorganisation or opening of a relevant winding up, an affected credit institution disposes for a consideration of—

(a) an immovable asset situated within the territory of an EEA State;
(b) a ship or an aircraft subject to registration in a public register kept under the authority of an EEA State;
(c) relevant instruments or rights in relevant instruments whose existence or transfer presupposes entry into a register or account laid down by the law of an EEA State or which are placed in a central deposit system governed by the law of an EEA State.

(2) The validity of that act is to be determined in accordance with the law of the EEA State within whose territory the immoveable asset is situated or under whose authority the register, account or system is kept, as the case may be.

(3) In this regulation, "relevant instruments" means the instruments referred to in [Section C of Annex I to Directive [2014/65/EU] of the European Parliament and of the Council of [15 May 2014] on markets in financial instruments].

NOTES

Para (3): words in first (outer) pair of square brackets substituted by the Financial Services and Markets Act 2000 (Markets in Financial Instruments) Regulations 2007, SI 2007/126, reg 3(6), Sch 6, Pt 2, para 18(1), (3); words in second and third (inner) pairs of square brackets substituted by the Financial Services and Markets Act 2000 (Markets in Financial Instruments) Regulations 2017, SI 2017/701, reg 50(4), Sch 5, para 5.

[3.244]
32 Lawsuits pending

(1) The effects of a relevant reorganisation or a relevant winding up on a relevant lawsuit pending in an EEA State shall be determined solely in accordance with the law of that EEA State.

(2) In paragraph (1), "relevant lawsuit" means a lawsuit concerning an asset or right of which the affected credit institution has been divested.

[3.245]
33 Lex rei sitae

(1) The effects of a relevant reorganisation or a relevant winding up on the enforcement of a relevant proprietary right shall be determined by the law of the relevant EEA State.

(2) In this regulation—

"relevant proprietary right" means proprietary rights in relevant instruments or other rights in relevant instruments the existence or transfer of which is recorded in a register, an account or a centralised deposit system held or located in an EEA state;

"relevant EEA State" means the Member State where the register, account or centralised deposit system in which the relevant proprietary right is recorded is held or located;

"relevant instrument" has the meaning given by regulation 31(3).

[3.246]
[34 Netting agreements

(1) The effects of a relevant reorganisation or a relevant winding up on a netting agreement shall be determined in accordance with the law applicable to that agreement.

(2) Nothing in paragraph (1) affects the application of—

(a) section 48Z of the Banking Act 2009;
(b) section 70C of the Banking Act 2009;
(c) Articles 68 and 71 of the recovery and resolution directive or the law of any EEA State (other than the United Kingdom) transposing these provisions; or
(d) any instrument made under the provisions referred to in sub-paragraph (a) or (b).]

NOTES

Commencement: 10 January 2015.
Substituted by the Bank Recovery and Resolution (No 2) Order 2014, SI 2014/3348, art 226, Sch 3, Pt 3, para 10(1), (9).

[3.247]
[35 Repurchase agreements

(1) Subject to regulation 33, the effects of a relevant reorganisation or a relevant winding up on a repurchase agreement shall be determined in accordance with the law applicable to that agreement.

(2) Nothing in paragraph (1) affects the application of—

(a) section 48Z of the Banking Act 2009;
(b) section 70C of the Banking Act 2009;
(c) Articles 68 and 71 of the recovery and resolution directive or the law of any EEA State (other than the United Kingdom) transposing these provisions; or
(d) any instrument made under the provisions referred to in sub-paragraph (a) or (b).]

NOTES

Commencement: 10 January 2015.
Substituted by the Bank Recovery and Resolution (No 2) Order 2014, SI 2014/3348, art 226, Sch 3, Pt 3, para 10(1), (10).

PART 5
THIRD COUNTRY CREDIT INSTITUTIONS

[3.248]
36 Interpretation of this Part

(1) In this Part—

(a) "relevant measure", in relation to a third country credit institution, means—
   (i) a winding up;
   (ii) a provisional liquidation; . . .
   (iii) an administration order made under paragraph 13 of Schedule B1 to the 1986 Act[, paragraph 14 of Schedule B1 to the 1989 Order,] section 8(1) of the 1986 Act [or Article 21(1) of the 1989 Order] as the case may be [or
   (iv) the making of a stabilisation instrument].
(b) "third country credit institution" means a person—
   (i) who has permission under the 2000 Act to accept deposits or to issue electronic money as the case may be; and
   (ii) whose head office is not in the United Kingdom or an EEA State.

(2) In paragraph (1), the definition of "third country credit institution" must be read with—

(a) section 22 of the 2000 Act;
(b) any relevant order made under that section; and
(c) Schedule 2 to that Act.

NOTES

Para (1): word omitted from sub-para (a)(ii) revoked, and sub-para (a)(iv) and word immediately preceding it added, by the Bank Recovery and Resolution (No 2) Order 2014, SI 2014/3348, art 226, Sch 3, Pt 3, para 10(1), (11); in sub-para (a)(iii) words in first pair of square brackets substituted and words in second pair of square brackets inserted by the Credit Institutions (Reorganisation and Winding Up) (Amendment) Regulations 2007, SI 2007/830, reg 2(1), (17).

[3.249]
37 Application of these Regulations to a third country credit institution

Regulations 9 and 10 apply where a third country credit institution is subject to a relevant measure, as if references in those regulations to a UK credit institution included a reference to a third country credit institution.

[3.250]
38 Disclosure of confidential information: third country credit institution

(1) This regulation applies to information ("insolvency practitioner information") which—
(a) relates to the business or other affairs of any person; and
(b) is information of a kind mentioned in paragraph (2).

(2) Information falls within paragraph (1)(b) if it is supplied to—
(a) the [FCA or the PRA] by an EEA regulator; or
(b) an insolvency practitioner by an EEA administrator or liquidator,
in accordance with or pursuant to Articles 8 or 19 of the reorganisation and winding up directive.

(3) Subject to paragraphs [(4), (5), (6) and (8)], sections 348, 349 and 352 of the 2000 Act apply in relation to insolvency practitioner information in the same way as they apply in relation to confidential information within the meaning of section 348(2) of that Act.

(4) For the purposes of this regulation, sections 348, 349 and 352 of the 2000 Act and the Disclosure Regulations have effect as if the primary recipients specified in subsection (5) of section 348 of the 2000 Act included an insolvency practitioner.

(5) Insolvency practitioner information is not subject to the restrictions on disclosure imposed by section 348(1) of the 2000 Act (as it applies by virtue of paragraph (2)) if it satisfies any of the criteria set out in section 348(4) of the 2000 Act.

(6) The Disclosure Regulations apply in relation to insolvency practitioner information as they apply in relation to single market . . . information (within the meaning of those Regulations).

(7) In this regulation—
"EEA administrator" and "EEA liquidator" mean an administrator or liquidator of a third country credit institution as the case may be within the meaning of the reorganisation and winding up directive;
"insolvency practitioner" means an insolvency practitioner, within the meaning of section 388 of the 1986 Act or Article 3 of the 1989 Order, who is appointed or acts in relation to a third country credit institution.

[(8) The sections of the 2000 Act specified in paragraph (3) apply with the additional modifications set out in section 89L of the Banking Act 2009 where that section applies.]

NOTES

Para (2): words in square brackets in sub-para (a) substituted by the Financial Services Act 2012 (Consequential Amendments and Transitional Provisions) Order 2013, SI 2013/472, art 3, Sch 2, para 91(k).

Para (3): words in square brackets substituted by the Bank Recovery and Resolution (No 2) Order 2014, SI 2014/3348, art 226, Sch 3, Pt 3, para 10(1), (12)(a).

Para (6): word omitted revoked by SI 2014/3348, art 226, Sch 3, Pt 3, para 10(1), (12)(b).

Para (8): added by SI 2014/3348, art 226, Sch 3, Pt 3, para 10(1), (12)(c).

[PART 6
APPLICATION TO INVESTMENT FIRMS

[3.251]
39 Interpretation of this Part

In this Part—
(a) "EEA investment firm" means an investment firm as defined in point (2) of Article 4(1) of the capital requirements regulation whose head office is in an EEA State other than the United Kingdom; and
(b) "UK investment firm" means an investment firm as defined in subsections (1) and (2)(a) of section 258A of the Banking Act 2009.]

NOTES

Commencement: 10 January 2015.

Parts 6–8 (regs 39–49) inserted by the Bank Recovery and Resolution (No 2) Order 2014, SI 2014/3348, art 226, Sch 3, Pt 3, para 10(1), (13).

[3.252]
[40 Application to UK investment firms

These Regulations apply to UK investment firms as if such firms were UK credit institutions, subject to the modifications set out in this Part.]

NOTES

Commencement: 10 January 2015.

Inserted as noted to reg 39 at **[3.251]**.

[3.253]
[41 Application to EEA investment firms

These Regulations apply to EEA investment firms as if such firms were EEA credit institutions, subject to the modifications set out in this Part.]

NOTES

Commencement: 10 January 2015.
Inserted as noted to reg 39 at **[3.251]**.

[3.254]
[42 Withdrawal of authorisation

Paragraph (3) of regulation 11 (withdrawal of authorisation) applies to UK investment firms as if the reference in that paragraph to section 55J of the 2000 Act included a reference to any other power of the FCA or PRA under that Act to vary or cancel any permission of a body or firm.]

NOTES

Commencement: 10 January 2015.
Inserted as noted to reg 39 at **[3.251]**.

[3.255]
[43 Reorganisation measures and winding-up proceedings in respect of EEA investment firms effective in the United Kingdom

Regulation 5 (reorganisation measures and winding-up proceedings in respect of EEA credit institutions effective in the United Kingdom) applies to EEA investment firms as if, in paragraph (6), the phrase "relevant EEA State" meant the EEA State under the law of which the reorganisation is adopted or imposed, or the winding-up proceedings are opened, as the case may be.]

NOTES

Commencement: 10 January 2015.
Inserted as noted to reg 39 at **[3.251]**.

[PART 7
APPLICATION TO GROUP COMPANIES

[3.256]
44 Interpretation of this Part

In this Part—

(a) "EEA group company" means—
  (i) a financial institution as defined in point (26) of Article 4(1) of the capital requirements regulation,
  (ii) a parent undertaking as defined in point (15)(a) of Article 4(1) of the capital requirements regulation, or
  (iii) any other firm within the scope of Article 1(1) of the recovery and resolution directive,
  the head office of which is in an EEA State other than the United Kingdom and which is not otherwise subject to these Regulations; and
(b) "UK group company" means—
  (i) a financial institution as defined in point (26) of Article 4(1) of the capital requirements regulation that is authorised by the PRA or FCA,
  (ii) a parent undertaking as defined in Article 4(1)(15)(a) of the capital requirements regulation, or
  (iii) any other firm within the scope of Article 1(1) of the recovery and resolution directive,
  the head office of which is in the United Kingdom and which is not otherwise subject to these Regulations.]

NOTES

Commencement: 10 January 2015.
Inserted as noted to reg 39 at **[3.251]**.

[3.257]
[45 Application to UK group companies

These Regulations apply to UK group companies with respect to which a stabilisation instrument has been made, as if they were UK credit institutions.]

NOTES

Commencement: 10 January 2015.
Inserted as noted to reg 39 at **[3.251]**.

[3.258]
[46 Application to EEA group companies

These Regulations apply to EEA group companies with respect to which one or more of the resolution tools or resolution powers provided for in the recovery and resolution directive have been applied, as if they were EEA credit institutions, subject to the modifications set out in this Part.]

NOTES

Commencement: 10 January 2015.
Inserted as noted to reg 39 at **[3.251]**.

[3.259]
[47 Reorganisation measures and winding-up proceedings in respect of EEA group companies effective in the United Kingdom

Regulation 5 (reorganisation measures and winding-up proceedings in respect of EEA group companies effective in the United Kingdom) applies to EEA group companies as if, in paragraph (6), the phrase "relevant EEA State" meant the EEA State under the law of which the reorganisation is adopted or imposed, or the winding-up proceedings are opened, as the case may be.]

NOTES

Commencement: 10 January 2015.
Inserted as noted to reg 39 at **[3.251]**.

[PART 8
APPLICATION TO THIRD COUNTRY INVESTMENT FIRMS

[3.260]
48 Interpretation of this Part

In this Part "third country investment firm" means an investment firm as defined in point (2) of Article 4(1) of the capital requirements regulation whose head office is not in an EEA State.]

NOTES

Commencement: 10 January 2015.
Inserted as noted to reg 39 at **[3.251]**.

[3.261]
[49 Application to third country investment firms

Part 5 of these Regulations applies to third country investment firms as if such firms were third country credit institutions (within the meaning given by regulation 36(1)(b) (interpretation of Part 5)).]

NOTES

Commencement: 10 January 2015.
Inserted as noted to reg 39 at **[3.251]**.

COUNCIL REGULATION

(2157/2001/EC)

of 8 October 2001

on the Statute for a European company (SE)

NOTES

Date of publication in OJ: OJ L294, 10.11.2001, p 1.
Only those provisions of the Regulation relevant to this work are reproduced here. Provisions not reproduced are not annotated.

THE COUNCIL OF THE EUROPEAN UNION,

Whereas:

. . .

(20) This Regulation does not cover other areas of law such as taxation, competition, intellectual property or insolvency. The provisions of the Member States' law and of Community law are therefore applicable in the above areas and in other areas not covered by this Regulation.

. . .

HAS ADOPTED THIS REGULATION:

TITLE I GENERAL PROVISIONS

[3.262]
Article 7
The registered office of an SE shall be located within the Community, in the same Member State as its head office. A Member State may in addition impose on SEs registered in its territory the obligation of locating their head office and their registered office in the same place.

[3.263]
Article 10
Subject to this Regulation, an SE shall be treated in every Member State as if it were a public limited-liability company formed in accordance with the law of the Member State in which it has its registered office.

TITLE V WINDING UP, LIQUIDATION, INSOLVENCY AND CESSATION OF PAYMENTS

[3.264]
Article 63
As regards winding up, liquidation, insolvency, cessation of payments and similar procedures, an SE shall be governed by the legal provisions which would apply to a public limited-liability company formed in accordance with the law of the Member State in which its registered office is situated, including provisions relating to decision-making by the general meeting.

[3.265]
Article 64
1. When an SE no longer complies with the requirement laid down in Article 7, the Member State in which the SE's registered office is situated shall take appropriate measures to oblige the SE to regularise its position within a specified period either—
 (a) by re-establishing its head office in the Member State in which its registered office is situated or
 (b) by transferring the registered office by means of the procedure laid down in Article 8.
2. The Member State in which the SE's registered office is situated shall put in place the measures necessary to ensure that an SE which fails to regularise its position in accordance with paragraph 1 is liquidated.
3. The Member State in which the SE's registered office is situated shall set up a judicial remedy with regard to any established infringement of Article 7. That remedy shall have a suspensory effect on the procedures laid down in paragraphs 1 and 2.
4. Where it is established on the initiative of either the authorities or any interested party that an SE has its head office within the territory of a Member State in breach of Article 7, the authorities of that Member State shall immediately inform the Member State in which the SE's registered office is situated.

[3.266]
Article 65
Without prejudice to provisions of national law requiring additional publication, the initiation and termination of winding up, liquidation, insolvency or cessation of payment procedures and any decision to continue operating shall be publicised in accordance with Article 13.

[3.267]
Article 66
1. An SE may be converted into a public limited-liability company governed by the law of the Member State in which its registered office is situated. No decision on conversion may be taken before two years have elapsed since its registration or before the first two sets of annual accounts have been approved.
2. The conversion of an SE into a public limited-liability company shall not result in the winding up of the company or in the creation of a new legal person.
3. The management or administrative organ of the SE shall draw up draft terms of conversion and a report explaining and justifying the legal and economic aspects of the conversion and indicating the implications of the adoption of the public limited-liability company for the shareholders and for the employees.
4. The draft terms of conversion shall be publicised in the manner laid down in each Member State's law in accordance with Article 3 of Directive 68/151/EEC at least one month before the general meeting called to decide thereon.
5. Before the general meeting referred to in paragraph 6, one or more independent experts appointed or approved, in accordance with the national provisions adopted in implementation of Article 10 of Directive 78/855/EEC, by a judicial or administrative authority in the Member State to which the SE being converted into a public limited-liability company is subject shall certify that the company has assets at least equivalent to its capital.
6. The general meeting of the SE shall approve the draft terms of conversion together with the statutes of the public limited-liability company. The decision of the general meeting shall be passed as laid down in the provisions of national law adopted in implementation of Article 7 of Directive 78/855/EEC.

DIRECTIVE OF THE EUROPEAN PARLIAMENT AND OF THE COUNCIL

(2002/47/EC)
of 6 June 2002

on financial collateral arrangements

[3.268]

NOTES

Date of publication in OJ: OJ L168, 27.6.02, p 43.

This Directive has been implemented in the UK with effect from 26 December 2003 by the Financial Collateral Arrangements (No 2) Regulations 2003, SI 2003/3226 at **[3.283]**.

THE EUROPEAN PARLIAMENT AND THE COUNCIL OF THE EUROPEAN UNION,

Having regard to the Treaty establishing the European Community, and in particular Article 95 thereof,

Having regard to the proposal from the Commission,[1]

Having regard to the opinion of the European Central Bank,[2]

Having regard to the opinion of the Economic and Social Committee,[3]

Acting in accordance with the procedure laid down in Article 251 of the Treaty,[4]

Whereas:

(1) Directive 98/26/EC of the European Parliament and of the Council of 19 May 1998 on settlement finality in payment and securities settlement systems[5] constituted a milestone in establishing a sound legal framework for payment and securities settlement systems. Implementation of that Directive has demonstrated the importance of limiting systemic risk inherent in such systems stemming from the different influence of several jurisdictions, and the benefits of common rules in relation to collateral constituted to such systems.

(2) In its communication of 11 May 1999 to the European Parliament and to the Council on financial services: implementing the framework for financial markets: action plan, the Commission undertook, after consultation with market experts and national authorities, to work on further proposals for legislative action on collateral urging further progress in the field of collateral, beyond Directive 98/26/EC.

(3) A Community regime should be created for the provision of securities and cash as collateral under both security interest and title transfer structures including repurchase agreements (repos). This will contribute to the integration and cost-efficiency of the financial market as well as to the stability of the financial system in the Community, thereby supporting the freedom to provide services and the free movement of capital in the single market in financial services. This Directive focuses on bilateral financial collateral arrangements.

(4) This Directive is adopted in a European legal context which consists in particular of the said Directive 98/ 26/EC as well as Directive 2001/24/EC of the European Parliament and of the Council of 4 April 2001 on the reorganisation and winding up of credit institutions,[6] Directive 2001/17/EC of the European Parliament and of the Council of 19 March 2001 on the reorganisation and winding-up of insurance undertakings[7] and Council Regulation (EC) No 1346/2000 of 29 May 2000 on insolvency proceedings.[8] This Directive is in line with the general pattern of these previous legal acts and is not opposed to it. Indeed, this Directive complements these existing legal acts by dealing with further issues and going beyond them in connection with particular matters already dealt with by these legal acts.

(5) In order to improve the legal certainty of financial collateral arrangements, Member States should ensure that certain provisions of insolvency law do not apply to such arrangements, in particular, those that would inhibit the effective realisation of financial collateral or cast doubt on the validity of current techniques such as bilateral close-out netting, the provision of additional collateral in the form of top-up collateral and substitution of collateral.

(6) This Directive does not address rights which any person may have in respect of assets provided as financial collateral, and which arise otherwise than under the terms of the financial collateral arrangement and otherwise than on the basis of any legal provision or rule of law arising by reason of the commencement or continuation of winding-up proceedings or reorganisation measures, such as restitution arising from mistake, error or lack of capacity.

(7) The principle in Directive 98/26/EC, whereby the law applicable to book entry securities provided as collateral is the law of the jurisdiction where the relevant register, account or centralised deposit system is located, should be extended in order to create legal certainty regarding the use of such securities held in a cross-border context and used as financial collateral under the scope of this Directive.

(8) The *lex rei sitae* rule, according to which the applicable law for determining whether a financial collateral arrangement is properly perfected and therefore good against third parties is the law of the country where the financial collateral is located, is currently recognised by all Member States. Without affecting the application of this Directive to directly-held securities, the location of book entry securities provided as financial collateral and held through one or more intermediaries should be determined. If the collateral taker has a valid and effective collateral arrangement according to the governing law of the country in which the relevant account is maintained, then the validity against any competing title or interest and the enforceability of the collateral should be governed solely by the law of that country, thus preventing legal uncertainty as a result of other unforeseen legislation.

[(9) In order to limit the administrative burdens for parties using financial collateral under the scope of this Directive, the only perfection requirement regarding parties which national law may impose in respect of financial collateral should be that the financial collateral is under the control of the collateral taker or of a person acting on the collateral taker's behalf while not excluding collateral techniques where the collateral provider is allowed to substitute collateral or to withdraw excess collateral. This Directive should not prohibit Member States from requiring that a credit claim be delivered by means of inclusion in a list of claims.]

(10) For the same reasons, the creation, validity, perfection, enforceability or admissibility in evidence of a financial collateral arrangement, or the provision of financial collateral under a financial collateral arrangement, should not be made dependent on the performance of any formal act such as the execution of any document in a specific form or in a particular manner, the making of any filing with an official or public body or registration in a public register, advertisement in a newspaper or journal, in an official register or publication or in any other matter, notification to a public officer or the provision of evidence in a particular form as to the date of execution of a document or instrument, the amount of the relevant financial obligations or any other matter. This Directive must however provide a balance between market efficiency and the safety of the parties to the arrangement and third parties, thereby avoiding *inter alia* the risk of fraud. This balance should be achieved through the scope of this Directive covering only those financial collateral arrangements which provide for some form of dispossession, ie the provision of the financial collateral, and where the provision of the financial collateral can be evidenced in writing or in a durable medium, ensuring thereby the traceability of that collateral. For the purpose of this Directive, acts required under the law of a Member State as conditions for transferring or creating a security interest on financial instruments, other than book entry securities, such as endorsement in the case of instruments to order, or recording on the issuer's register in the case of registered instruments, should not be considered as formal acts.

(11) Moreover, this Directive should protect only financial collateral arrangements which can be evidenced. Such evidence can be given in writing or in any other legally enforceable manner provided by the law which is applicable to the financial collateral arrangement.

(12) The simplification of the use of financial collateral through the limitation of administrative burdens promotes the efficiency of the cross-border operations of the European Central Bank and the national central banks of Member States participating in the economic and monetary union, necessary for the implementation of the common monetary policy. Furthermore, the provision of limited protection of financial collateral arrangements from some rules of insolvency law in addition supports the wider aspect of the common monetary policy, where the participants in the money market balance the overall amount of liquidity in the market among themselves, by cross-border transactions backed by collateral.

(13) This Directive seeks to protect the validity of financial collateral arrangements which are based upon the transfer of the full ownership of the financial collateral, such as by eliminating the so-called re-characterisation of such financial collateral arrangements (including repurchase agreements) as security interests.

(14) The enforceability of bilateral close-out netting should be protected, not only as an enforcement mechanism for title transfer financial collateral arrangements including repurchase agreements but more widely, where close-out netting forms part of a financial collateral arrangement. Sound risk management practices commonly used in the financial market should be protected by enabling participants to manage and reduce their credit exposures arising from all kinds of financial transactions on a net basis, where the credit exposure is calculated by combining the estimated current exposures under all outstanding transactions with a counterparty, setting off reciprocal items to produce a single aggregated amount that is compared with the current value of the collateral.

(15) This Directive should be without prejudice to any restrictions or requirements under national law on bringing into account claims, on obligations to set-off, or on netting, for example relating to their reciprocity or the fact that they have been concluded prior to when the collateral taker knew or ought to have known of the commencement (or of any mandatory legal act leading to the commencement) of winding-up proceedings or reorganisation measures in respect of the collateral provider.

(16) The sound market practice favoured by regulators whereby participants in the financial market use top-up financial collateral arrangements to manage and limit their credit risk to each other by mark-to-market calculations of the current market value of the credit exposure and the value of the financial collateral and accordingly ask for top-up financial collateral or return the surplus of financial collateral should be protected against certain automatic avoidance rules. The same applies to the possibility of substituting for assets provided as financial collateral other assets of the same value. The intention is merely that the provision of top-up or substitution financial collateral cannot be questioned on the sole basis that the relevant financial obligations existed before that financial collateral was provided, or that the financial collateral was provided during a prescribed period. However, this does not prejudice the possibility of questioning under national law the financial collateral arrangement and the provision of financial collateral as part of the initial provision, top-up or substitution of financial collateral, for example where this has been intentionally done to the detriment of the other creditors (this covers *inter alia* actions based on fraud or similar avoidance rules which may apply in a prescribed period).

(17) This Directive provides for rapid and non-formalistic enforcement procedures in order to safeguard financial stability and limit contagion effects in case of a default of a party to a financial collateral arrangement. However, this Directive balances the latter objectives with the protection of the collateral provider and third-parties by explicitly confirming the possibility for Member States to keep or introduce in their national legislation an *a posteriori* control which the Courts can exercise in relation to the realisation or valuation of financial collateral and the calculation of the relevant financial obligations.

Such control should allow for the judicial authorities to verify that the realisation or valuation has been conducted in a commercially reasonable manner.

(18) It should be possible to provide cash as collateral under both title transfer and secured structures respectively protected by the recognition of netting or by the pledge of cash collateral. Cash refers only to money which is represented by a credit to an account, or similar claims on repayment of money (such as money market deposits), thus explicitly excluding banknotes.

(19) This Directive provides for a right of use in case of security financial collateral arrangements, which increases liquidity in the financial market stemming from such reuse of pledged securities. This reuse however should be without prejudice to national legislation about separation of assets and unfair treatment of creditors.

[(20) This Directive does not prejudice the operation or effect of the contractual terms of financial instruments or credit claims provided as financial collateral, such as rights, obligations or other conditions contained in the terms of issue of such instruments, or any other rights, obligations or other conditions which apply between the issuers and holders of such instruments or between the debtor and the creditor of such credit claims.]

(21) This Act complies with the fundamental rights and follows the principles laid down in particular in the Charter of Fundamental Rights of the European Union.

(22) Since the objective of the proposed action, namely to create a minimum regime relating to the use of financial collateral, cannot be sufficiently achieved by the Member States and can therefore, by reason of the scale and effects of the action, be better achieved at Community level, the Community may adopt measures, in accordance with the principle of subsidiarity as set out in Article 5 of the Treaty. In accordance with the principle of proportionality, as set out in that Article, this Directive does not go beyond what is necessary in order to achieve that objective,

[(23) This Directive does not affect the rights of Member States to impose rules to ensure the effectiveness of financial collateral arrangements in relation to third parties as regards credit claims,]

NOTES

Recitals 9, 20: substituted by European Parliament and Council Directive 2009/44/EC, Art 2(1), (2).
Recital 23: added by European Parliament and Council Directive 2009/44/EC, Art 2(3).

1 OJ C180 E, 26.6.2001, p 312.

2 OJ C196, 12.7.2001, p 10.

3 OJ C48, 21.2.2002, p 1.

4 Opinion of the European Parliament of 13 December 2001, Council Common Position of 5 March 2002 and Decision of the European Parliament of 15 May 2002.

5 OJ L166, 11.6.1998, p 45.

6 OJ L125, 5.5.2001, p 15.

7 OJ L110, 20.4.2001, p 28.

8 OJ L160, 30.6.2000, p 1.

HAVE ADOPTED THIS DIRECTIVE:

[3.269]
Article 1
Subject matter and scope

1. This Directive lays down a Community regime applicable to financial collateral arrangements which satisfy the requirements set out in paragraphs 2 and 5 and to financial collateral in accordance with the conditions set out in paragraphs 4 and 5.

2. The collateral taker and the collateral provider must each belong to one of the following categories:
   (a) a public authority (excluding publicly guaranteed undertakings unless they fall under points (b) to (e)) including:
      (i) public sector bodies of Member States charged with or intervening in the management of public debt, and
      (ii) public sector bodies of Member States authorised to hold accounts for customers;
   [(b) a central bank, the European Central Bank, the Bank for International Settlements, a multilateral development bank as referred to in Annex VI, Part 1, Section 4 of Directive 2006/48/EC of the European Parliament and of the Council of 14 June 2006 relating to the taking up and pursuit of the business of credit institutions (recast),[1] the International Monetary Fund and the European Investment Bank;]
   (c) a financial institution subject to prudential supervision including:
      [(i) a credit institution as defined in Article 4(1) of Directive 2006/48/EC, including the institutions listed in Article 2 of that Directive;
      (ii) an investment firm as defined in Article 4(1)(1) of Directive 2004/39/EC of the European Parliament and of the Council of 21 April 2004 on markets in financial instruments;[2]
      (iii) a financial institution as defined in Article 4(5) of Directive 2006/48/EC;
      (iv) an insurance undertaking as defined in Article 1(a) of Council Directive 92/49/EEC of 18 June 1992 on the coordination of laws, regulations and administrative provisions relating to direct insurance other than life insurance (third non-life insurance Directive)[3] and an assurance undertaking as defined in Article 1(1)(a) of Directive 2002/83/EC of the European Parliament and of the Council of 5 November 2002 concerning life assurance;[4]]

(v) an undertaking for collective investment in transferable securities (UCITS) as defined in Article 1(2) of Council Directive 85/611/EEC of 20 December 1985 on the coordination of laws, regulations and administrative provisions relating to undertakings for collective investment in transferable securities (UCITS),[5]

(vi) a management company as defined in Article 1a(2) of Directive 85/611/EEC;

(d) a central counterparty, settlement agent or clearing house, as defined respectively in Article 2(c), (d) and (e) of Directive 98/26/EC, including similar institutions regulated under national law acting in the futures, options and derivatives markets to the extent not covered by that Directive, and a person, other than a natural person, who acts in a trust or representative capacity on behalf of any one or more persons that includes any bondholders or holders of other forms of securitised debt or any institution as defined in points (a) to (d);

(e) a person other than a natural person, including unincorporated firms and partnerships, provided that the other party is an institution as defined in points (a) to (d).

If they make use of this option Member States shall inform the Commission which shall inform the other Member States thereof.

3. Member States may exclude from the scope of this Directive financial collateral arrangements where one of the parties is a person mentioned in paragraph 2(e).

4.

[(a) The financial collateral to be provided shall consist of cash, financial instruments or credit claims.]

(b) Member States may exclude from the scope of this Directive financial collateral consisting of the collateral provider's own shares, shares in affiliated undertakings within the meaning of seventh Council Directive 83/349/EEC of 13 June 1983 on consolidated accounts[6], and shares in undertakings whose exclusive purpose is to own means of production that are essential for the collateral provider's business or to own real property.

[(c) Member States may exclude from the scope of this Directive credit claims where the debtor is a consumer as defined in Article 3(a) of Directive 2008/48/EC of the European Parliament and of the Council of 23 April 2008 on credit agreements for consumers[7] or a micro or small enterprise as defined in Article 1 and Article 2(2) and (3) of the Annex to Commission Recommendation 2003/361/EC of 6 May 2003 concerning the definition of micro, small and medium-sized enterprises,[8] save where the collateral taker or the collateral provider of such credit claims is one of the institutions referred under Article 1(2)(b) of this Directive.]

5. This Directive applies to financial collateral once it has been provided and if that provision can be evidenced in writing.

The evidencing of the provision of financial collateral must allow for the identification of the financial collateral to which it applies. For this purpose, it is sufficient to prove that the book entry securities collateral has been credited to, or forms a credit in, the relevant account and that the cash collateral has been credited to, or forms a credit in, a designated account. [For credit claims, the inclusion in a list of claims submitted in writing, or in a legally equivalent manner, to the collateral taker is sufficient to identify the credit claim and to evidence the provision of the claim provided as financial collateral between the parties.]

[Without prejudice to the second subparagraph, Member States may provide that the inclusion in a list of claims submitted in writing, or in a legally equivalent manner, to the collateral taker is also sufficient to identify the credit claim and to evidence the provision of the claim provided as financial collateral against the debtor or third parties.]

This Directive applies to financial collateral arrangements if that arrangement can be evidenced in writing or in a legally equivalent manner.

[6. Articles 4 to 7 of this Directive shall not apply to any restriction on the enforcement of financial collateral arrangements or any restriction on the effect of a security financial collateral arrangement, any close out netting or set-off provision that is imposed by virtue of Title IV, Chapter V or VI of Directive 2014/59/EU of the European Parliament and of the Council,[9] or to any such restriction that is imposed by virtue of similar powers in the law of a Member State to facilitate the orderly resolution of any entity referred to in points (c)(iv) and (d) of paragraph 2 which is subject to safeguards at least equivalent to those set out in Title IV, Chapter VII of Directive 2014/59/EU.]

NOTES

Para 2: sub-paras (b), (c)(i)–(iv) substituted by European Parliament and Council Directive 2009/44/EC, Art 2(4)(a), (b).

Para 4: sub-para (a) substituted and sub-para (c) added by European Parliament and Council Directive 2009/44/EC, Art 2(4)(c), (d).

Para 5: words in square brackets inserted by European Parliament and Council Directive 2009/44/EC, Art 2(4)(e), (f).

Para 6: added by European Parliament and Council Directive 2014/59/EU, Article 118(1).

1 OJ L177, 30.6.2006, p 1.

2 OJ L145, 30.4.2004, p. 1.

3 OJ L228, 11.8.1992, p 1.

4 OJ L345, 19.12.2002, p 1.

5 OJ L375, 31.12.1985, p 3.

6 OJ L193, 18.7.1983, p 1.

7 OJ L133, 22.5.2008, p 66.

8 OJ L124, 20.5.2003, p 36.

9 Directive 2014/59/EU of the European Parliament and of the Council of 15 May 2014 establishing a framework for the recovery and resolution of credit institutions and investment firms and amending Council Directive 82/891/EEC and

Directives 2001/24/EC, 2002/47/EC, 2004/25/EC, 2005/56/EC, 2007/36/EC, 2011/35/EU, 2012/30/EU and 2013/36/EU, and Regulations (EU) No 1093/2010 and (EU) No 648/2012, of the European Parliament and of the Council (OJ L173, 12.6.2014, p 190).

[3.270]
Article 2
Definitions

1. For the purpose of this Directive:
(a) financial collateral arrangement means a title transfer financial collateral arrangement or a security financial collateral arrangement whether or not these are covered by a master agreement or general terms and conditions;
[(b) title transfer financial collateral arrangement means an arrangement, including repurchase agreements, under which a collateral provider transfers full ownership of, or full entitlement to, financial collateral to a collateral taker forth purpose of securing or otherwise covering the performance of relevant financial obligations;
(c) security financial collateral arrangement means an arrangement under which a collateral provider provides financial collateral by way of security to or in favour of a collateral taker, anywhere the full or qualified ownership of, or full entitlement to, the financial collateral remains with the collateral provider when the security right is established;]
(d) cash means money credited to an account in any currency, or similar claims for the repayment of money, such as money market deposits;
(e) financial instruments means shares in companies and other securities equivalent to shares in companies and bonds and other forms of debt instruments if these are negotiable on the capital market, and any other securities which are normally dealt in and which give the right to acquire any such shares, bonds or other securities by subscription, purchase or exchange or which give rise to a cash settlement (excluding instruments of payment), including units in collective investment undertakings, money market instruments and claims relating to or rights in or in respect of any of the foregoing;
(f) relevant financial obligations means the obligations which are secured by a financial collateral arrangement and which give a right to cash settlement and/or delivery of financial instruments.
Relevant financial obligations may consist of or include:
(i) present or future, actual or contingent or prospective obligations (including such obligations arising under a master agreement or similar arrangement);
(ii) obligations owed to the collateral taker by a person other than the collateral provider; or
(iii) obligations of a specified class or kind arising from time to time;
(g) book entry securities collateral means financial collateral provided under a financial collateral arrangement which consists of financial instruments, title to which is evidenced by entries in a register or account maintained by or on behalf of an intermediary;
(h) relevant account means in relation to book entry securities collateral which is subject to a financial collateral arrangement, the register or account which may be maintained by the collateral taker i which the entries are made by which that book entry securities collateral is provided to the collateral taker;
(i) equivalent collateral:
(i) in relation to cash, means a payment of the same amount and in the same currency;
(ii) in relation to financial instruments, means financial instruments of the same issuer or debtor, forming part of the same issue or class and of the same nominal amount, currency and description or, where a financial collateral arrangement provides for the transfer of other assets following the occurrence of any event relating to or affecting any financial instruments provided as financial collateral, those other assets;
(j) winding-up proceedings means collective proceedings involving realisation of the assets and distribution of the proceeds among the creditors, shareholders or members as appropriate, which involve any intervention by administrative or judicial authorities, including where the collective proceedings are terminated by a composition or other analogous measure, whether or not they are founded on insolvency or are voluntary or compulsory;
(k) reorganisation measures means measures which involve any intervention by administrative or judicial authorities which are intended to preserve or restore the financial situation and which affect pre-existing rights of third-parties, including but not limited to measures involving a suspension of payments, suspension of enforcement measures or reduction of claims;
(l) enforcement event means an event of default or any similar event as agreed between the parties on the occurrence of which, under the terms of a financial collateral arrangement or by operation of law, the collateral taker is entitled to realise or appropriate financial collateral or a close-out netting provision comes into effect;
(m) right of use means the right of the collateral taker to use and dispose of financial collateral provided under a security financial collateral arrangement as the owner of it in accordance with the terms of the security financial collateral arrangement;
(n) close-out netting provision means a provision of a financial collateral arrangement, or of an arrangement of which a financial collateral arrangement forms part, or, in the absence of any such provision, any statutory rule by which, on the occurrence of an enforcement event, whether through the operation of netting or set-off or otherwise:
(i) the obligations of the parties are accelerated so as to be immediately due and expressed as an obligation to pay an amount representing their estimated current value, or are terminated and replaced by an obligation to pay such an amount; and/or

(ii) an account is taken of what is due from each party to the other in respect of such obligations, and a net sum equal to the balance of the account is payable by the party from whom the larger amount is due to the other party.

[(o) credit claims means pecuniary claims arising out of an agreement whereby a credit institution, as defined in Article 4(1) of Directive 2006/48/EC, including the institutions listed in Article 2 of that Directive, grants credit in the form of a loan.]

2. References in this Directive to financial collateral being provided, or to the provision of financial collateral, are to the financial collateral being delivered, transferred, held, registered or otherwise designated so as to be in the possession or under the control of the collateral taker or of a person acting on the collateral taker's behalf. [Any right of substitution, right to withdraw excess financial collateral in favour of the collateral provider or, in the case of credit claims, right to collect the proceeds thereof until further notice, shall not prejudice the financial collateral having been provided to the collateral taker as mentioned in this Directive.]

3. References in this Directive to writing include recording by electronic means and any other durable medium.

NOTES

Para 1: sub-paras (b), (c) substituted and sub-para (o) added by European Parliament and Council Directive 2009/44/EC, Art 2(5)(a).

Para 2: words in square brackets inserted by European Parliament and Council Directive 2009/44/EC, Art 2(5)(b).

[3.271]
Article 3
Formal requirements

1. Member States shall not require that the creation, validity, perfection, enforceability or admissibility in evidence of a financial collateral arrangement or the provision of financial collateral under a financial collateral arrangement be dependent on the performance of any formal act.

[Without prejudice to Article 1(5), when credit claims are provided as financial collateral, Member States shall not require that the creation, validity, perfection, priority, enforceability or admissibility in evidence of such financial collateral be dependent on the performance of any formal act such as the registration or the notification of the debtor of the credit claim provided as collateral. However, Member States may require the performance of a formal act, such as registration or notification, for purposes of perfection, priority, enforceability or admissibility in evidence against the debtor or third parties.

By 30 June 2014, the Commission shall report to the European Parliament and to the Council on whether this paragraph continues to be appropriate.]

2. Paragraph 1 is without prejudice to the application of this Directive to financial collateral only once it has been provided and if that provision can be evidenced in writing and where the financial collateral arrangement can be evidenced in writing or in a legally equivalent manner.

[3. Without prejudice to Council Directive 93/13/EEC of 5 April 1993 on unfair terms in consumer contracts[1] and national provisions concerning unfair contract terms, Member States shall ensure that debtors of the credit claims may validly waive, in writing or in a legally equivalent manner:

(i) their rights of set-off vis-à-vis the creditors of the credit claim and vis-à-vis persons to whom the creditor assigned, pledged or otherwise mobilised the credit claim as collateral; and

(ii) their rights arising from banking secrecy rules that would otherwise prevent or restrict the ability of the creditor of the credit claim to provide information on the credit claim or the debtor for the purposes of using the credit claim as collateral.]

NOTES

Para 1: words in square brackets added by European Parliament and Council Directive 2009/44/EC, Art 2(6)(a).

Para 3: added by European Parliament and Council Directive 2009/44/EC, Art 2(6)(b).

[1] OJ L95, 21.4.1993, p 29.

[3.272]
Article 4
Enforcement of financial collateral arrangements

1. Member States shall ensure that on the occurrence of an enforcement event, the collateral taker shall be able to realise in the following manners, any financial collateral provided under, and subject to the terms agreed in, a security financial collateral arrangement:

(a) financial instruments by sale or appropriation and by setting off their value against, or applying their value in discharge of, the relevant financial obligations;

(b) cash by setting off the amount against or applying it in discharge of the relevant financial obligations;

[(c) credit claims, by sale or appropriation and by setting off their value against, or applying their value in discharge of, the relevant financial obligations.]

2. Appropriation is possible only if:

(a) this has been agreed by the parties in the security financial collateral arrangement; and

[(b) the parties have agreed in the security financial collateral arrangement on the valuation of the financial instruments and the credit claims.]

3. . . .

4. The manners of realising the financial collateral referred to in paragraph 1 shall, subject to the terms agreed in the security financial collateral arrangement, be without any requirement to the effect that:

(a) prior notice of the intention to realise must have been given;

(b) the terms of the realisation be approved by any court, public officer or other person;
(c) the realisation be conducted by public auction or in any other prescribed manner; or
(d) any additional time period must have elapsed.

5. Member States shall ensure that a financial collateral arrangement can take effect in accordance with its terms notwithstanding the commencement or continuation of winding-up proceedings or reorganisation measures in respect of the collateral provider or collateral taker.

6. This Article and Articles 5, 6 and 7 shall be without prejudice to any requirements under national law to the effect that the realisation or valuation of financial collateral and the calculation of the relevant financial obligations must be conducted in a commercially reasonable manner.

NOTES

Para 1: sub-para (c) added by European Parliament and Council Directive 2009/44/EC, Art 2(7)(a).
Para 2: para (b) substituted by European Parliament and Council Directive 2009/44/EC, Art 2(7)(b).
Para 3: repealed by European Parliament and Council Directive 2009/44/EC, Art 2(7)(c).

[3.273]
Article 5
Right of use of financial collateral under security financial collateral arrangements

1. If and to the extent that the terms of a security financial collateral arrangement so provide, Member States shall ensure that the collateral taker is entitled to exercise a right of use in relation to financial collateral provided under the security financial collateral arrangement.

2. Where a collateral taker exercises a right of use, he thereby incurs an obligation to transfer equivalent collateral to replace the original financial collateral at the latest on the due date for the performance of the relevant financial obligations covered by the security financial collateral arrangement.

Alternatively, the collateral taker shall, on the due date for the performance of the relevant financial obligations, either transfer equivalent collateral, or, if and to the extent that the terms of a security financial collateral arrangement so provide, set off the value of the equivalent collateral against or apply it in discharge of the relevant financial obligations.

3. The equivalent collateral transferred in discharge of an obligation as described in paragraph 2, first subparagraph, shall be subject to the same security financial collateral agreement to which the original financial collateral was subject and shall be treated as having been provided under the security financial collateral arrangement at the same time as the original financial collateral was first provided.

4. Member States shall ensure that the use of financial collateral by the collateral taker according to this Article does not render invalid or unenforceable the rights of the collateral taker under the security financial collateral arrangement in relation to the financial collateral transferred by the collateral taker in discharge of an obligation as described in paragraph 2, first subparagraph.

5. If an enforcement event occurs while an obligation as described in paragraph 2 first subparagraph remains outstanding, the obligation may be the subject of a close-out netting provision.

[6. This Article shall not apply to credit claims.]

NOTES

Para 6: added by European Parliament and Council Directive 2009/44/EC, Art 2(8).

[3.274]
Article 6
Recognition of title transfer financial collateral arrangements

1. Member States shall ensure that a title transfer financial collateral arrangement can take effect in accordance with its terms.

2. If an enforcement event occurs while any obligation of the collateral taker to transfer equivalent collateral under a title transfer financial collateral arrangement remains outstanding, the obligation may be the subject of a close-out netting provision.

[3.275]
Article 7
Recognition of close-out netting provisions

1. Member States shall ensure that a close-out netting provision can take effect in accordance with its terms:
(a) notwithstanding the commencement or continuation of winding-up proceedings or reorganisation measures in respect of the collateral provider and/or the collateral taker; and/or
(b) notwithstanding any purported assignment, judicial or other attachment or other disposition of or in respect of such rights.

2. Member States shall ensure that the operation of a close-out netting provision may not be subject to any of the requirements that are mentioned in Article 4(4), unless otherwise agreed by the parties.

[3.276]
Article 8
Certain insolvency provisions disapplied

1. Member States shall ensure that a financial collateral arrangement, as well as the provision of financial collateral under such arrangement, may not be declared invalid or void or be reversed on the sole basis that the financial collateral arrangement has come into existence, or the financial collateral has been provided:
(a) on the day of the commencement of winding-up proceedings or reorganisation measures, but prior to the order or decree making that commencement; or

(b) in a prescribed period prior to, and defined by reference to, the commencement of such proceedings or measures or by reference to the making of any order or decree or the taking of any other action or occurrence of any other event in the course of such proceedings or measures.

2. Member States shall ensure that where a financial collateral arrangement or a relevant financial obligation has come into existence, or financial collateral has been provided on the day of, but after the moment of the commencement of, winding-up proceedings or reorganisation measures, it shall be legally enforceable and binding on third parties if the collateral taker can prove that he was not aware, nor should have been aware, of the commencement of such proceedings or measures.

3. Where a financial collateral arrangement contains:

(a) an obligation to provide financial collateral or additional financial collateral in order to take account of changes in the value of the financial collateral or in the amount of the relevant financial obligations, or

(b) a right to withdraw financial collateral on providing, by way of substitution or exchange, financial collateral of substantially the same value,

Member States shall ensure that the provision of financial collateral, additional financial collateral or substitute or replacement financial collateral under such an obligation or right shall not be treated as invalid or reversed or declared void on the sole basis that:

(i) such provision was made on the day of the commencement of winding-up proceedings or reorganisation measures, but prior to the order or decree making that commencement or in a prescribed period prior to, and defined by reference to, the commencement of winding-up proceedings or reorganisation measures or by reference to the making of any order or decree or the taking of any other action or occurrence of any other event in the course of such proceedings or measures; and/or

(ii) the relevant financial obligations were incurred prior to the date of the provision of the financial collateral, additional financial collateral or substitute or replacement financial collateral.

4. Without prejudice to paragraphs 1, 2 and 3, this Directive leaves unaffected the general rules of national insolvency law in relation to the violence of transactions entered into during the prescribed period referred to in paragraph 1(b) and in paragraph 3(i).

[3.277]
Article 9
Conflict of laws

1. Any question with respect to any of the matters specified in paragraph 2 arising in relation to book entry securities collateral shall be governed by the law of the country in which the relevant account is maintained. The reference to the law of a country is a reference to its domestic law, disregarding any rule under which, in deciding the relevant question, reference should be made to the law of another country.

2. The matters referred to in paragraph 1 are:

(a) the legal nature and proprietary effects of book entry securities collateral;

(b) the requirements for perfecting a financial collateral arrangement relating to book entry securities collateral and the provision of book entry securities collateral under such an arrangement, and more generally the completion of the steps necessary to render such an arrangement and provision effective against third parties;

(c) whether a person's title to or interest in such book entry securities collateral is overridden by or subordinated to a competing title or interest, or a good faith acquisition has occurred;

(d) the steps required for the realisation of book entry securities collateral following the occurrence of an enforcement event.

[3.278]
[Article 9a
Directives 2008/48/EC and 2014/59/EU

This Directive shall be without prejudice to Directives 2008/48/EC and 2014/59/EU.]

NOTES

Inserted by European Parliament and Council Directive 2009/44/EC, Art 2(9).
Substituted by European Parliament and Council Directive 2014/59/EU, Article 118(2).

[3.279]
Article 10
Report by the Commission

Not later than 27 December 2006, the Commission shall present a report to the European Parliament and the Council on the application of this Directive, in particular on the application of Article 1(3), Article 4(3) and Article 5, accompanied where appropriate by proposals for its revision.

[3.280]
Article 11
Implementation

Member States shall bring into force the laws, regulations and administrative provisions necessary to comply with this Directive by 27 December 2003 at the latest. They shall forthwith inform the Commission thereof.

When Member States adopt those provisions, they shall contain a reference to this Directive or be accompanied by such reference on the occasion of their official publication. Member States shall determine how such reference is to be made.

[3.281]
Article 12
Entry into force
This Directive shall enter into force on the day of its publication in the *Official Journal of the European Communities.*

[3.282]
Article 13
Addressees
This Directive is addressed to the Member States.

FINANCIAL COLLATERAL ARRANGEMENTS (NO 2) REGULATIONS 2003

(SI 2003/3226)

NOTES

Made: 10 December 2003.

Authority: European Communities Act 1972, s 2(2).

Commencement: 11 December 2003 (regulation 2); 26 December 2003 (remainder).

Modification: these Regulations are applied, with modifications, in so far as they relate to bank insolvency or administration under the Banking Act 2009, Pts 2, 3, by the Banking Act 2009 (Parts 2 and 3 Consequential Amendments) Order 2009, SI 2009/317, art 3, Schedule at **[7.86]**, **[7.92]**.

ARRANGEMENT OF REGULATIONS

PART 1
GENERAL

1 Citation and commencement . . . [3.283]
3 Interpretation . . . [3.284]

PART 2
MODIFICATION OF LAW REQUIRING FORMALITIES

4 Certain legislation requiring formalities not to apply to financial collateral arrangements . . . [3.285]
6 No additional formalities required for creation of a right in security over book entry securities collateral in Scotland . . . [3.286]
6A Certain legislation affecting overseas companies not to apply to financial collateral arrangements . . . [3.287]

PART 3
MODIFICATION OF INSOLVENCY LAW

8 Certain legislation restricting enforcement of security not to apply to financial collateral arrangements . . . [3.288]
9 Certain Northern Ireland legislation restricting enforcement of security not to apply to financial collateral arrangements . . . [3.289]
10 Certain insolvency legislation on avoidance of contracts and floating charges not to apply to financial collateral arrangements . . . [3.290]
11 Certain Northern Ireland insolvency legislation on avoidance of contracts and floating charges not to apply to financial collateral arrangements . . . [3.291]
12 Close-out netting provisions to take effect in accordance with their terms . . . [3.292]
13 Financial collateral arrangements to be enforceable where collateral-taker not aware of commencement of winding-up proceedings or reorganisation measures . . . [3.293]
14 Modification of the Insolvency Rules 1986 and the Insolvency Rules (Northern Ireland) 1991 . . . [3.294]
15 Modification of the Insolvency (Scotland) Rules 1986 . . . [3.295]
15A Insolvency proceedings in other jurisdictions . . . [3.296]

PART 4
RIGHT OF USE AND APPROPRIATION

16 Right of use under a security financial collateral arrangement . . . [3.297]
17 No requirement to apply to court to appropriate financial collateral under a security financial collateral arrangement . . . [3.298]
18 Duty to value collateral and account for any difference in value on appropriation . . . [3.299]
18A Restrictions on enforcement of financial collateral arrangements, etc . . . [3.300]

PART 5
CONFLICT OF LAWS

19 Standard test regarding the applicable law to book entry securities financial collateral arrangements . . . [3.301]

PART 1
GENERAL

[3.283]
1 Citation and commencement

(1) These Regulations may be cited as the Financial Collateral Arrangements (No 2) Regulations 2003.

(2) Regulation 2 shall come into force on 11th December 2003 and all other Regulations thereof shall come into force on 26th December 2003.

2 (*Revokes the Financial Collateral Arrangements Regulations 2003, SI 2003/3112.*)

[3.284]
3 Interpretation

[(1)] In these Regulations—

"book entry securities collateral" means financial collateral subject to a financial collateral arrangement which consists of financial instruments, title to which is evidenced by entries in a register or account maintained by or on behalf of an intermediary;

"cash" means money in any currency, credited to an account, or a similar claim for repayment of money and includes money market deposits and sums due or payable to, or received between the parties in connection with the operation of a financial collateral arrangement or a close-out netting provision;

"close-out netting provision" means a term of a financial collateral arrangement, or of an arrangement of which a financial collateral arrangement forms part, or any legislative provision under which on the occurrence of an enforcement event, whether through the operation of netting or set-off or otherwise—

(a) the obligations of the parties are accelerated to become immediately due and expressed as an obligation to pay an amount representing the original obligation's estimated current value or replacement cost, or are terminated and replaced by an obligation to pay such an amount; or

(b) an account is taken of what is due from each party to the other in respect of such obligations and a net sum equal to the balance of the account is payable by the party from whom the larger amount is due to the other party;

["credit claims" means pecuniary claims which arise out of an agreement whereby a credit institution, as defined in Article 4(1)(1) of Regulation (EU) 575/2013 of the European Parliament and of the Council of 26 June 2013, and including the institutions listed in Article 2(5)(2) to (23) of Directive 2013/36/EU of the European Parliament and of the Council of 26 June 2013, grants credit in the form of a loan;]

. . .

"equivalent financial collateral" means—

(a) in relation to cash, a payment of the same amount and in the same currency;

(b) in relation to financial instruments, financial instruments of the same issuer or debtor, forming part of the same issue or class and of the same nominal amount, currency and description or, where the financial collateral arrangement provides for the transfer of other assets following the occurrence of any event relating to or affecting any financial instruments provided as financial collateral, those other assets;

and includes the original financial collateral provided under the arrangement;

"financial collateral arrangement" means a title transfer financial collateral arrangement or a security financial collateral arrangement, whether or not these are covered by a master agreement or general terms and conditions;

"financial collateral" means either [cash, financial instruments or credit claims];

"financial instruments" means—

(a) shares in companies and other securities equivalent to shares in companies;

(b) bonds and other forms of instruments giving rise to or acknowledging indebtedness if these are tradeable on the capital market; and

(c) any other securities which are normally dealt in and which give the right to acquire any such shares, bonds, instruments or other securities by subscription, purchase or exchange or which give rise to a cash settlement (excluding instruments of payment);

and includes units of a collective investment scheme within the meaning of the Financial Services and Markets Act 2000, eligible debt securities within the meaning of the Uncertificated Securities Regulations 2001, money market instruments, claims relating to or rights in or in respect of any of the financial instruments included in this definition and any rights, privileges or benefits attached to or arising from any such financial instruments;

"intermediary" means a person that maintains registers or accounts to which financial instruments may be credited or debited, for others or both for others and for its own account but does not include—

(a) a person who acts as a registrar or transfer agent for the issuer of financial instruments; or

(b) a person who maintains registers or accounts in the capacity of operator of a system for the holding and transfer of financial instruments on records of the issuer or other records which constitute the primary record of entitlement to financial instruments as against the issuer;

"non-natural person" means any corporate body, unincorporated firm, partnership or body with legal personality except an individual, including any such entity constituted under the law of a country or territory outside the United Kingdom or any such entity constituted under international law;

["recovery and resolution directive" means Directive 2014/59/EU of the European Parliament and of the Council of 15th May 2014 establishing a framework for the recovery and resolution of credit institutions and investment firms;]

"relevant account" means, in relation to book entry securities collateral which is subject to a financial collateral arrangement, the register or account, which may be maintained by the collateral-taker, in which entries are made, by which that book entry securities collateral is transferred or designated so as to be in the possession or under the control of the collateral-taker or a person acting on its behalf;

"relevant financial obligations" means the obligations which are secured or otherwise covered by a financial collateral arrangement, and such obligations may consist of or include—

(a) present or future, actual or contingent or prospective obligations (including such obligations arising under a master agreement or similar arrangement);
(b) obligations owed to the collateral-taker by a person other than the collateral-provider;
(c) obligations of a specified class or kind arising from time to time;

"reorganisation measures" means—

(a) administration within the meaning of the Insolvency Act 1986 or the Insolvency (Northern Ireland) Order 1989;
(b) a company voluntary arrangement within the meaning of that Act or that Order;
(c) administration of a partnership within the meaning of that Act or that Order or, in the case of a Scottish partnership, [a protected trust deed within the meaning of] the Bankruptcy (Scotland) Act 1985;
(d) a partnership voluntary arrangement within the meaning of the Insolvency Act 1986 or the Insolvency (Northern Ireland) Order 1989 or, in the case of a Scottish partnership, [a protected trust deed within the meaning of] the Bankruptcy (Scotland) Act 1985; and
(e) the making of an interim order on an administration application;

"security financial collateral arrangement" means an agreement or arrangement, evidenced in writing, where—

(a) the purpose of the agreement or arrangement is to secure the relevant financial obligations owed to the collateral-taker;
(b) the collateral-provider creates or there arises a security interest in financial collateral to secure those obligations;
(c) the financial collateral is delivered, transferred, held, registered or otherwise designated so as to be in the possession or under the control of the collateral-taker or a person acting on its behalf; any right of the collateral-provider to substitute [financial collateral of the same or greater value] or withdraw excess financial collateral [or to collect the proceeds of credit claims until further notice] shall not prevent the financial collateral being in the possession or under the control of the collateral-taker; and
(d) the collateral-provider and the collateral-taker are both non-natural persons;

"security interest" means any legal or equitable interest or any right in security, other than a title transfer financial collateral arrangement, created or otherwise arising by way of security including—

(a) a pledge;
(b) a mortgage;
(c) a fixed charge;
(d) a charge created as a floating charge where the financial collateral charged is delivered, transferred, held, registered or otherwise designated so as to be in the possession or under the control of the collateral-taker or a person acting on its behalf; any right of the collateral-provider to substitute [financial collateral of the same or greater value] or withdraw excess financial collateral [or to collect the proceeds of credit claims until further notice] shall not prevent the financial collateral being in the possession or under the control of the collateral-taker; or
(e) a lien;

"title transfer financial collateral arrangement" means an agreement or arrangement, including a repurchase agreement, evidenced in writing, where—

(a) the purpose of the agreement or arrangement is to secure or otherwise cover the relevant financial obligations owed to the collateral-taker;
(b) the collateral-provider transfers legal and beneficial ownership in financial collateral to a collateral-taker on terms that when the relevant financial obligations are discharged the collateral-taker must transfer legal and beneficial ownership of equivalent financial collateral to the collateral-provider; and
(c) the collateral-provider and the collateral-taker are both non-natural persons;

["winding-up proceedings" means—

(a) winding up by the court or voluntary winding up within the meaning of the Insolvency Act 1986 or the Insolvency (Northern Ireland) Order 1989;
(b) sequestration of a Scottish partnership under the Bankruptcy (Scotland) Act 1985;
(c) bank insolvency within the meaning of the Banking Act 2009.]

[(1A) For the purpose of these Regulations—

(a) "enforcement event" means an event of default, or (subject to sub-paragraph (b)) any similar event as agreed between the parties, on the occurrence of which, under the terms of a financial collateral agreement or by operation of law, the collateral taker is entitled to realise or appropriate financial collateral or a close-out netting provision comes into effect;

(b) a crisis management measure or crisis prevention measure taken in relation to an entity under the recovery and resolution directive shall not be considered to be an enforcement event pursuant to an agreement between the parties if the substantive obligations provided for in that agreement (including payment and delivery obligations and provision of collateral) continue to be performed; and

(c) for the purposes of sub-paragraph (b) "crisis prevention measure" and "crisis management measure" have the meaning given in section 48Z of the Banking Act 2009.]

[(2) For the purposes of these Regulations "possession" of financial collateral in the form of cash or financial instruments includes the case where financial collateral has been credited to an account in the name of the collateral-taker or a person acting on his behalf (whether or not the collateral-taker, or person acting on his behalf, has credited the financial collateral to an account in the name of the collateral-provider on his, or that person's, books) provided that any rights the collateral-provider may have in relation to that financial collateral are limited to the right to substitute financial collateral of the same or greater value or to withdraw excess financial collateral.]

NOTES

Para (1): numbered as such by the Financial Markets and Insolvency (Settlement Finality and Financial Collateral Arrangements) (Amendment) Regulations 2010, SI 2010/2993, reg 4(1), (2)(a), and is amended as follows—

Definition "credit claims" originally inserted by SI 2010/2993, reg 4(1), (2)(b)(i); substituted by the Capital Requirements Regulations 2013, SI 2013/3115, reg 46(1), Sch 2, Pt 3, para 61.

Definition "enforcement event" (omitted) revoked, and definition "recovery and resolution directive" inserted, by the Bank Recovery and Resolution (No 2) Order 2014, SI 2014/3348, art 226, Sch 3, Pt 3, para 9(1), (2)(a).

Words in square brackets in the definition "financial collateral" substituted by SI 2010/2993, reg 4(1), (2)(b)(ii).

Words in square brackets in the definition "reorganisation measures" inserted by SI 2010/2993, reg 4(1), (2)(b)(iii).

In the definitions "security financial collateral arrangement" and "security interest" the words "financial collateral of the same or greater value" were substituted, and the other words in square brackets were inserted, by SI 2010/2993, reg 4(1), (2)(b)(iv).

Definition "winding up proceedings" substituted by SI 2010/2993, reg 4(1), (2)(b)(v).

Para (1A): inserted by SI 2014/3348, art 226, Sch 3, Pt 3, para 9(1), (2)(b).

Para (2): added by SI 2010/2993, reg 4(1), (2)(c).

PART 2
MODIFICATION OF LAW REQUIRING FORMALITIES

[3.285]

4 Certain legislation requiring formalities not to apply to financial collateral arrangements

(1) Section 4 of the Statute of Frauds 1677 (no action on a third party's promise unless in writing and signed) shall not apply (if it would otherwise do so) in relation to a financial collateral arrangement.

(2) Section 53(1)(c) of the Law of Property Act 1925 (disposition of equitable interest to be in writing and signed) shall not apply (if it would otherwise do so) in relation to a financial collateral arrangement.

(3) Section 136 of the Law of Property Act 1925 (legal assignments of things in action) shall not apply (if it would otherwise do so) in relation to a financial collateral arrangement, to the extent that the section requires an assignment to be signed by the assignor or a person authorised on its behalf, in order to be effectual in law.

(4) [[Sections 859A] (charges created by a company) and [859H] (consequence of failure to register charges created by a company) of the Companies Act 2006] shall not apply [(if they would otherwise do so)] in relation to a security financial collateral arrangement or any charge created or otherwise arising under a security financial collateral arrangement [or, in Scotland, to relation to any charge created or arising under a financial collateral arrangement].

(5) Section 4 of the Industrial and Provident Societies Act 1967 (filing of information relating to charges) shall not apply (if it would otherwise do so) in relation to a . . . financial collateral arrangement or any charge created or otherwise arising under a . . . financial collateral arrangement.

NOTES

Para (4): words in first (outer) and fourth pairs of square brackets substituted by the Financial Collateral Arrangements (No 2) Regulations 2003 (Amendment) Regulations 2009, SI 2009/2462, reg 2(1), (2); words in second and third (inner) pairs of square brackets substituted by the Companies Act 2006 (Amendment of Part 25) Regulations 2013, SI 2013/600, reg 5, Sch 2, para 4, in relation to charges created on or after 6 April 2013; words in fifth pair of square brackets inserted by the Financial Markets and Insolvency (Settlement Finality and Financial Collateral Arrangements) (Amendment) Regulations 2010, SI 2010/2993, reg 4(1), (3)(a).

Para (5): words omitted revoked by SI 2010/2993, reg 4(1), (3)(b).

Industrial and Provident Societies Act 1967: repealed by the Co-operative and Community Benefit Societies Act 2014.

5 *(Revoked by the Companies Act 2006 (Amendment of Part 25) Regulations 2013, SI 2013/600, reg 5, Sch 2, para 4, in relation to charges created on or after 6 April 2013.)*

[3.286]

6 No additional formalities required for creation of a right in security over book entry securities collateral in Scotland

(1) Where under the law of Scotland an act is required as a condition for transferring, creating or enforcing a right in security over any book entry securities collateral, that requirement shall not apply (if it would otherwise do so).

(2) For the purposes of paragraph (1) an "act"—

(a) is any act other than an entry on a register or account maintained by or on behalf of an intermediary which evidences title to the book entry securities collateral;

(b) includes the entering of the collateral-taker's name in a company's register of members.

[3.287]

[6A Certain legislation affecting overseas companies not to apply to financial collateral arrangements

Any provision about registration of charges made by regulations under section 1052 of the Companies Act 2006 (overseas companies) does not apply (if it would otherwise do so) in relation to a security financial collateral arrangement or any charge created or otherwise arising under a security financial collateral arrangement [or, in Scotland, to any charge created or arising under a financial collateral arrangement].]

NOTES

Inserted by the Financial Collateral Arrangements (No 2) Regulations 2003 (Amendment) Regulations 2009, SI 2009/2462, reg 2(1), (4).

Words in square brackets inserted by the Financial Markets and Insolvency (Settlement Finality and Financial Collateral Arrangements) (Amendment) Regulations 2010, SI 2010/2993, reg 4(1), (5).

7 (*Revoked by the Financial Collateral Arrangements (No 2) Regulations 2003 (Amendment) Regulations 2009, SI 2009/2462, reg 2(1), (5).*)

PART 3
MODIFICATION OF INSOLVENCY LAW

[3.288]

8 Certain legislation restricting enforcement of security not to apply to financial collateral arrangements

(1) The following provisions of Schedule B1 to the Insolvency Act 1986 (administration) shall not apply to any security interest created or otherwise arising under a financial collateral arrangement—

(a) paragraph 43(2) (restriction on enforcement of security or repossession of goods) including that provision as applied by paragraph 44 (interim moratorium); . . .

[(aa) paragraph 65(2) (distribution);]

(b) paragraphs 70 and 71 (power of administrator to deal with charged property); [and]

[(c) paragraph 99(3) and (4) (administrator's remuneration, expenses and liabilities).]

(2) Paragraph 41(2) of Schedule B1 to the Insolvency Act 1986 (receiver to vacate office when so required by administrator) shall not apply to a receiver appointed under a charge created or otherwise arising under a financial collateral arrangement.

(3) The following provisions of the Insolvency Act 1986 (administration) shall not apply in relation to any security interest created or otherwise arising under a financial collateral arrangement—

(a) sections 10(1)(b) and 11(3)(c) (restriction on enforcement of security while petition for administration order pending or order in force); and

(b) section 15(1) and 15(2) (power of administrator to deal with charged property) [and]

[(c) section 19(4) and 19(5) (administrator's remuneration, expenses and liabilities).]

(4) Section 11(2) of the Insolvency Act 1986 (receiver to vacate office when so required by administrator) shall not apply to a receiver appointed under a charge created or otherwise arising under a financial collateral arrangement.

(5) Paragraph 20 and sub-paragraph 12(1)(g) of Schedule A1 to the Insolvency Act 1986 (Effect of moratorium on creditors) shall not apply (if it would otherwise do so) to any security interest created or otherwise arising under a financial collateral arrangement.

NOTES

Para (1): word omitted from sub-para (a) revoked and words in square brackets inserted by the Financial Markets and Insolvency (Settlement Finality and Financial Collateral Arrangements) (Amendment) Regulations 2010, SI 2010/2993, reg 4(1), (6)(a)–(d).

Para (3): words in square brackets inserted by SI 2010/2993, reg 4(1), (6)(e).

[3.289]

9 Certain Northern Ireland legislation restricting enforcement of security not to apply to financial collateral arrangements

(1) The following provisions of the Insolvency (Northern Ireland) Order 1989 (administration) shall not apply to any security interest created or otherwise arising under a financial collateral arrangement—

(a) Article 23(1)(b) and Article 24(3)(c) (restriction on enforcement of security while petition for administration order pending or order in force); . . .

(b) Article 28(1) and (2) (power of administrator to deal with charged property);

[(c) Article 31(4) and (5) (administrator's remuneration, expenses and liabilities); and

(d) Paragraphs 44(2), 45 (restriction on enforcement of security), 66(2) (distribution), 71, 72 (power of administrator to deal with charged property), 100(3) and (4) (administrator's remuneration, expenses and liabilities) of Schedule B1 to the Order.]

(2) Article 24(2) of that Order (receiver to vacate office at request of administrator) shall not apply to a receiver appointed under a charge created or otherwise arising under a financial collateral arrangement.

NOTES

Para (1): word omitted from sub-para (a) revoked and sub-paras (c), (d) added by the Financial Markets and Insolvency (Settlement Finality and Financial Collateral Arrangements) (Amendment) Regulations 2010, SI 2010/2993, reg 4(1), (7).

[3.290]

10 Certain insolvency legislation on avoidance of contracts and floating charges not to apply to financial collateral arrangements

(1) In relation to winding-up proceedings of a collateral-taker or collateral-provider, section 127 of the Insolvency Act 1986 (avoidance of property dispositions, etc) shall not apply (if it would otherwise do so)—

(a) to any property or security interest subject to a disposition or created or otherwise arising under a financial collateral arrangement; or

(b) to prevent a close-out netting provision taking effect in accordance with its terms.

(2) Section 88 of the Insolvency Act 1986 (avoidance of share transfers, etc after winding-up resolution) shall not apply (if it would otherwise do so) to any transfer of shares under a financial collateral arrangement.

[(2A) Sections 40 (or in Scotland, sections 59, 60(1)(e)) and 175 of the Insolvency Act 1986 (preferential debts) shall not apply to any debt which is secured by a charge created or otherwise arising under a financial collateral arrangement.

(2B) Section 176ZA of the Insolvency Act 1986 (expenses of winding up) shall not apply in relation to any claim to any property which is subject to a disposition or created or otherwise arising under a financial collateral arrangement.]

(3) Section 176A of the Insolvency Act 1986 (share of assets for unsecured creditors) shall not apply (if it would otherwise do so) to any charge created or otherwise arising under a financial collateral arrangement.

(4) Section 178 of the Insolvency Act 1986 (power to disclaim onerous property) or, in Scotland, any rule of law having the same effect as that section, shall not apply where the collateral-provider or collateral-taker under the arrangement is [subject to winding-up proceedings], to any financial collateral arrangement.

(5) Section 245 of the Insolvency Act 1986 (avoidance of certain floating charges) shall not apply (if it would otherwise do so) to any charge created or otherwise arising under a security financial collateral arrangement.

(6) [Section 754 of the Companies Act 2006 (priorities where debentures secured by floating charge) [(including that section as applied or modified by any enactment made under the Banking Act 2009)]] shall not apply (if it would otherwise do so) to any charge created or otherwise arising under a financial collateral arrangement.

NOTES

Paras (2A), (2B): inserted by the Financial Markets and Insolvency (Settlement Finality and Financial Collateral Arrangements) (Amendment) Regulations 2010, SI 2010/2993, reg 4(1), (8)(a).

Para (4): words in square brackets substituted by SI 2010/2993, reg 4(1), (8)(b).

Para (6): words in first (outer) pair of square brackets substituted by the Financial Collateral Arrangements (No 2) Regulations 2003 (Amendment) Regulations 2009, SI 2009/2462, reg 2(1), (6); words in second (inner) pair of square brackets inserted by SI 2010/2993, reg 4(1), (8)(c).

[3.291]

11 Certain Northern Ireland insolvency legislation on avoidance of contracts and floating charges not to apply to financial collateral arrangements

(1) In relation to winding-up proceedings of a collateral-provider or collateral-taker, Article 107 of the Insolvency (Northern Ireland) Order 1989 (avoidance of property dispositions effected after commencement of winding up) shall not apply (if it would otherwise do so)—

(a) to any property or security interest subject to a disposition or created or otherwise arising under a financial collateral arrangement; or

(b) to prevent a close-out netting provision taking effect in accordance with its terms.

[(1A) Article 50 of that Order (payment of debts out of assets subject to floating charge) shall not apply (if it would otherwise do so), to any charge created or otherwise arising under a financial collateral arrangement.]

(2) Article 74 of that Order (avoidance of share transfers, etc after winding-up resolution) shall not apply (if it would otherwise do so) to any transfer of shares under a financial collateral arrangement.

[(2A) Articles 149 of that Order (preferential debts) and 150ZA (expenses of winding up) shall not apply (if they would otherwise do so) to any charge created or otherwise arising under a financial collateral arrangement.]

(3) Article 152 of that Order (power to disclaim onerous property) shall not apply where the collateral-provider or collateral-taker under the arrangement is being wound-up, to any financial collateral arrangement.

(4) Article 207 of that Order (avoidance of certain floating charges) shall not apply (if it would otherwise do so) to any charge created or otherwise arising under a security financial collateral arrangement.

(5) . . .

NOTES

Paras (1A), (2A): inserted by the Financial Markets and Insolvency (Settlement Finality and Financial Collateral Arrangements) (Amendment) Regulations 2010, SI 2010/2993, reg 4(1), (9).

Para (5): revoked by the Financial Collateral Arrangements (No 2) Regulations 2003 (Amendment) Regulations 2009, SI 2009/2462, reg 2(1), (7).

[3.292]

12 Close-out netting provisions to take effect in accordance with their terms

(1) A close-out netting provision shall, subject to paragraph (2), take effect in accordance with its terms notwithstanding that the collateral-provider or collateral-taker under the arrangement is subject to winding-up proceedings or reorganisation measures.

(2) Paragraph (1) shall not apply if at the time that a party to a financial collateral arrangement entered into such an arrangement or that the relevant financial obligations came into existence—

(a) that party was aware or should have been aware that winding up proceedings or re-organisation measures had commenced in relation to the other party;

[(aa) in Scotland, that party had notice that a meeting of creditors of the other party had been summoned under section 98 of the Insolvency Act 1986;

(ab) in England and Wales, that party had notice that a statement as to the affairs of the other party had been sent to the other party's creditors under section 99(1) of that Act(c);

(ac) that party had notice that a meeting of creditors of the other party had been summoned under Article 84 of the Insolvency (Northern Ireland) Order 1989;]

(b) that party had notice . . . that a petition for the winding-up of [or, in Scotland, a petition for winding-up proceedings in relation to] the other party was pending;

(c) that party had notice that an application for an administration order was pending or that any person had given notice of an intention to appoint an administrator; or

(d) that party had notice that an application for an administration order was pending or that any person had given notice of an intention to appoint an administrator and liquidation of the other party to the financial collateral arrangement was immediately preceded by an administration of that party.

(3) For the purposes of paragraph (2)—

(a) winding-up proceedings commence on the making of a winding-up order [or, in the case of a Scottish partnership, the award of sequestration] by the court; and

(b) reorganisation measures commence on the appointment of an administrator, whether by a court or otherwise [or, in the case of a Scottish partnership, when a protected trust deed is entered into].

(4) Rules 2.85(4)(a) and (c) and 4.90(3)(b) of the Insolvency Rules 1986 (mutual credit and set-off)[, or in Scotland, any rule of law with the same or similar effect to the effect of these Rules] shall not apply to a close-out netting provision unless sub-paragraph (2)(a) applies.

[(5) Nothing in this regulation prevents the Bank of England imposing a restriction on the effect of a close out netting provision in the exercise of its powers under Part 1 of the Banking Act 2009.]

NOTES

Para (2): sub-para (aa)–(ac) were inserted, and the words "that a meeting of creditors of the other party had been summoned under section 98 of the Insolvency Act 1986, or Article 84 of the Companies (Northern Ireland) Order 1989 or" omitted from sub-para (b) were revoked, by the Small Business, Enterprise and Employment Act 2015 (Consequential Amendments, Savings and Transitional Provisions) Regulations 2018, SI 2018/208, reg 8, as from 13 March 2018 (for transitional provisions, see the note below).

Para (5): added by the Bank Recovery and Resolution (No 2) Order 2014, SI 2014/3348, art 226, Sch 3, Pt 3, para 9(1), (3).

All other words in square brackets in this regulation were inserted by the Financial Markets and Insolvency (Settlement Finality and Financial Collateral Arrangements) (Amendment) Regulations 2010, SI 2010/2993, reg 4(1), (10).

Transitional provisions: the Small Business, Enterprise and Employment Act 2015 (Consequential Amendments, Savings and Transitional Provisions) Regulations 2018, SI 2018/208, regs 16, 19 provide as follows—

"16 Interpretation of Part 4

In this Part—

"the 1986 Act" means the Insolvency Act 1986;

"the 2000 Act" means the Financial Services and Markets Act 2000;

"the 2009 Act" means the Banking Act 2009; and

"relevant meeting" means a meeting of creditors which is to be held on or after the date on which Parts 2 and 3 of these Regulations come into force, and was—

(a) called, summoned or otherwise required before 6th April 2017 under a provision of the 1986 Act or the Insolvency Rules 1986;

(b) requisitioned by a creditor before 6th April 2017 under a provision of the 1986 Act or the Insolvency Rules 1986; or

(c) called or summoned under section 106, 146 or 331 of the 1986 Act as a result of—

(i) a final report to creditors sent before 6th April 2017 under rule 4.49D of the Insolvency Rules 1986 (final report to creditors in liquidation);

(ii) a final report to creditors and bankrupt sent before that date under rule 6.78B of those Rules (final report to creditors and bankrupt).

19 Transitional provision for regulation 8

(1) Paragraph (2) applies where a relevant meeting is to be held in winding up proceedings or in relation to reorganisation measures commenced in England and Wales in respect of the collateral-provider or collateral-taker under—

(a) a financial collateral arrangement; or

(b) an arrangement of which a financial collateral arrangement forms part.

(2) Regulation 12 of the Financial Collateral Arrangements (No 2) Regulations 2003 applies in relation to the meeting without the amendments made by regulation 8.

(3) In this regulation—

(a) the reference to the commencement of winding up proceedings or reorganisation measures is to be construed in accordance with regulation 12(3) of those Regulations;

(b) "financial collateral arrangement" has the same meaning as in those Regulations;

(c) "reorganisation measures" means—

(i) administration under Schedule B1 to the 1986 Act;

(ii) administration of a partnership under Schedule B1 to the 1986 Act (as applied to insolvent partnerships under section 420 of that Act);

(iii) a proposal for a company voluntary arrangement under Part 1 of the 1986 Act (company voluntary arrangements);

(iv) a proposal for a partnership voluntary arrangement under Part 1 of the 1986 Act (as applied to insolvent partnerships under section 420 of that Act); or

(v) the making of an interim order on an administration application (within the meaning given in paragraph 12 of Schedule B1 to the 1986 Act, including that paragraph as applied to insolvent partnerships); and

(d) "winding up proceedings" means—

(i) voluntary winding up or winding up by the court under Part 4 of the 1986 Act; or

(ii) bank insolvency under Part 2 of the 2009 Act.".

[3.293]

13 Financial collateral arrangements to be enforceable where collateral-taker not aware of commencement of winding-up proceedings or reorganisation measures

(1) Where any of the events specified in paragraph (2) occur on the day of, but after the moment of commencement of, winding-up proceedings or reorganisation measures those events, arrangements and obligations shall be legally enforceable and binding on third parties if the collateral-taker can show that he was not aware, nor should have been aware, of the commencement of such proceedings or measures.

(2) The events referred to in paragraph (1) are—

(a) a financial collateral arrangement coming into existence;

(b) a relevant financial obligation secured by a financial collateral arrangement coming into existence; or

(c) the delivery, transfer, holding, registering or other designation of financial collateral so as to be in the possession or under the control of the collateral-taker.

(3) For the purposes of paragraph (1)—

(a) the commencement of winding-up proceedings means the making of a winding-up order [or, in the case of a Scottish partnership, the award of sequestration] by the court; and

(b) commencement of reorganisation measures means the appointment of an administrator, whether by a court or otherwise [or, in the case of a Scottish partnership, the date of registration of a protected trust deed].

NOTES

Para (3): words in square brackets inserted by the Financial Markets and Insolvency (Settlement Finality and Financial Collateral Arrangements) (Amendment) Regulations 2010, SI 2010/2993, reg 4(1), (11).

[3.294]

14 Modification of the Insolvency Rules 1986 and the Insolvency Rules (Northern Ireland) 1991

Where the collateral-provider or the collateral-taker under a financial collateral arrangement goes into liquidation or administration and the arrangement or a close out netting provision provides for, or the mechanism provided under the arrangement permits, either—

(a) the debt owed by the party in liquidation or administration under the arrangement, to be assessed or paid in a currency other than sterling; or

(b) the debt to be converted into sterling at a rate other than the official exchange rate prevailing on the date when that party went into liquidation or administration;

then rule 4.91 (liquidation), or rule 2.86 (administration) of the Insolvency Rules 1986 (debt in foreign currency), or rule 4.097 of the Insolvency Rules (Northern Ireland) 1991 (liquidation, debt in foreign currency), as appropriate, shall not apply unless the arrangement provides for an unreasonable exchange rate or the collateral-taker uses the mechanism provided under the arrangement to impose an unreasonable exchange rate in which case the appropriate rule shall apply.

[3.295]

15 Modification of the Insolvency (Scotland) Rules 1986

Where the collateral-provider or the collateral-taker under a financial collateral arrangement goes into liquidation [or administration] or, in the case of a partnership, sequestration and the arrangement provides for, or the mechanism provided under the arrangement permits, either—

(a) the debt owed by the party in liquidation or sequestration under the arrangement, to be assessed or paid in a currency other than sterling; or

(b) the debt to be converted into sterling at a rate other than the official exchange rate prevailing on the date when that party went into liquidation or sequestration;

then rules 4.16 and 4.17 of the Insolvency (Scotland) Rules 1986 and [the provisions of the Bankruptcy (Scotland) Act 1985 referred to in those rules and such rules and provisions as applied by rule 2.41 of the Insolvency (Scotland) Rules 1986], as appropriate, shall not apply unless the arrangement provides for an unreasonable exchange rate or the collateral-taker uses the mechanism provided under the arrangement to impose an unreasonable exchange rate in which case the appropriate rule shall apply.

NOTES

Words in first pair of square brackets inserted and words in second pair of square brackets substituted by the Financial Markets and Insolvency (Settlement Finality and Financial Collateral Arrangements) (Amendment) Regulations 2010, SI 2010/2993, reg 4(1), (12).

[3.296]

[15A Insolvency proceedings in other jurisdictions

(1) The references to insolvency law in section 426 of the Insolvency Act 1986 (co-operation between courts exercising jurisdiction in relation to insolvency) include, in relation to a part of the United Kingdom, this Part of these Regulations and, in relation to a relevant country or territory within the meaning of that section, so much of the law of that country or territory as corresponds to this Part.

(2) A court shall not, in pursuance of that section or any other enactment or rule of law, recognise or give effect to—

(a) any order of a court exercising jurisdiction in relation to insolvency law in a country or territory outside the United Kingdom, or

(b) any act of a person appointed in such a country or territory to discharge any functions under insolvency law,

in so far as the making of the order or the doing of the act would be prohibited by this Part in the case of a court in England and Wales or Scotland, the High Court in Northern Ireland or a relevant office holder.

(3) Paragraph (2) does not affect the recognition of a judgment required to be recognised or enforced under or by virtue of the Civil Jurisdiction and Judgments Act 1982 or Council Regulation (EC) No 44/2001 of 22nd December 2000 on jurisdiction and the recognition and enforcement of judgments in civil and commercial matters, as amended from time to time and as applied by the Agreement made on 19th October 2005 between the European Community and the Kingdom of Denmark on jurisdiction and the recognition and enforcement of judgments in civil and commercial matters.]

NOTES

Inserted by the Financial Markets and Insolvency (Settlement Finality and Financial Collateral Arrangements) (Amendment) Regulations 2010, SI 2010/2993, reg 4(1), (13).

PART 4
RIGHT OF USE AND APPROPRIATION

[3.297]

16 Right of use under a security financial collateral arrangement

(1) If a security financial collateral arrangement provides for the collateral-taker to use and dispose of any financial collateral provided under the arrangement, as if it were the owner of it, the collateral-taker may do so in accordance with the terms of the arrangement.

(2) If a collateral-taker exercises such a right of use, it is obliged to replace the original financial collateral by transferring equivalent financial collateral on or before the due date for the performance of the relevant financial obligations covered by the arrangement or, if the arrangement so provides, it may set off the value of the equivalent financial collateral against or apply it in discharge of the relevant financial obligations in accordance with the terms of the arrangement.

(3) The equivalent financial collateral which is transferred in discharge of an obligation as described in paragraph (2), shall be subject to the same terms of the security financial collateral arrangement as the original financial collateral was subject to and shall be treated as having been provided under the security financial collateral arrangement at the same time as the original financial collateral was first provided.

[(3A) In Scotland, paragraphs (1) and (3) apply to title transfer financial collateral arrangements as they apply to security financial collateral arrangements.]

(4) If a collateral-taker has an outstanding obligation to replace the original financial collateral with equivalent financial collateral when an enforcement event occurs, that obligation may be the subject of a close-out netting provision.

[(5) This regulation does not apply in relation to credit claims.]

NOTES

Para (3A): inserted by the Financial Markets and Insolvency (Settlement Finality and Financial Collateral Arrangements) (Amendment) Regulations 2010, SI 2010/2993, reg 4(1), (14)(a).

Para (5): added by SI 2010/2993, reg 4(1), (14)(b).

[3.298]

[17 Appropriation of financial collateral under a security financial collateral arrangement

(1) Where a security interest is created or arises under a security financial collateral arrangement on terms that include a power for the collateral-taker to appropriate the financial collateral, the collateral-taker may exercise that power in accordance with the terms of the security financial collateral arrangement, without any order for foreclosure from the courts (and whether or not the remedy of foreclosure would be available).

(2) Upon the exercise by the collateral-taker of the power to appropriate the financial collateral, the equity of redemption of the collateral-provider shall be extinguished and all legal and beneficial interest of the collateral-provider in the financial collateral shall vest in the collateral taker.]

NOTES

Substituted by the Financial Markets and Insolvency (Settlement Finality and Financial Collateral Arrangements) (Amendment) Regulations 2010, SI 2010/2993, reg 4(1), (15).

[3.299]

18 Duty to value collateral and account for any difference in value on appropriation

(1) Where a collateral-taker exercises a power contained in a security financial collateral arrangement to appropriate the financial collateral the collateral-taker must value the financial collateral in accordance with the terms of the arrangement and in any event in a commercially reasonable manner.

(2) Where a collateral-taker exercises such a power and the value of the financial collateral appropriated differs from the amount of the relevant financial obligations, then as the case may be, either—

(a) the collateral-taker must account to the collateral-provider for the amount by which the value of the financial collateral exceeds the relevant financial obligations; or

(b) the collateral-provider will remain liable to the collateral-taker for any amount whereby the value of the financial collateral is less than the relevant financial obligations.

[3.300]

[18A Restrictions on enforcement of financial collateral arrangements, etc

(1) Nothing in regulations 16 and 17 prevents the Bank of England imposing a restriction—

(a) on the enforcement of financial collateral arrangements, or

(b) on the effect of a security financial collateral arrangement, close out netting provision or set-off arrangement,

in the exercise of its powers under Part 1 of the Banking Act 2009.

(2) For the purpose of paragraph (1) "set-off arrangement" has the meaning given in Article 2.1(99) of the recovery and resolution directive.]

NOTES

Commencement: 10 January 2015.

Inserted by the Bank Recovery and Resolution (No 2) Order 2014, SI 2014/3348, art 226, Sch 3, Pt 3, para 9(1), (4).

PART 5
CONFLICT OF LAWS

[3.301]

19 Standard test regarding the applicable law to book entry securities financial collateral arrangements

(1) This regulation applies to financial collateral arrangements where book entry securities collateral is used as collateral under the arrangement and are held through one or more intermediaries.

(2) Any question relating to the matters specified in paragraph (4) of this regulation which arises in relation to book entry securities collateral which is provided under a financial collateral arrangement shall be governed by the domestic law of the country in which the relevant account is maintained.

(3) For the purposes of paragraph (2) "domestic law" excludes any rule under which, in deciding the relevant question, reference should be made to the law of another country.

(4) The matters referred to in paragraph (2) are—

(a) the legal nature and proprietary effects of book entry securities collateral;

(b) the requirements for perfecting a financial collateral arrangement relating to book entry securities collateral and the transfer or passing of control or possession of book entry securities collateral under such an arrangement;

(c) the requirements for rendering a financial collateral arrangement which relates to book entry securities collateral effective against third parties;

(d) whether a person's title to or interest in such book entry securities collateral is overridden by or subordinated to a competing title or interest; and

(e) the steps required for the realisation of book entry securities collateral following the occurrence of any enforcement event.

CROSS-BORDER INSOLVENCY REGULATIONS 2006

(SI 2006/1030)

NOTES

Made: 3 April 2006.

Authority: Insolvency Act 2000, s 14.

Commencement: 4 April 2006 (see reg 1(1) at **[3.302]**).

Disapplication: these Regulations are disapplied, in respect of regulated covered bonds, by the Regulated Covered Bonds Regulations 2008, SI 2008/346, reg 46, Schedule, Pt 2, para 11 at **[18.180]**.

ARRANGEMENT OF REGULATIONS

1 Citation, commencement and interpretation . . . [3.302]
2 UNCITRAL Model Law to have force of law . . . [3.303]
3 Modification of British insolvency law . . . [3.304]
4 Procedural matters in England and Wales . . . [3.305]
5 Procedural matters in Scotland . . . [3.306]
6 Notices delivered to the registrar of companies . . . [3.307]
7 Co-operation between courts exercising jurisdiction in relation to cross-border insolvency . . . [3.308]
8 Disapplication of section 388 of the Insolvency Act 1986 . . . [3.309]

SCHEDULES

Schedule 1—UNCITRAL Model Law on Cross-Border Insolvency . . . [3.310]
Schedule 2—Procedural Matters in England and Wales
Part 1—Introductory Provisions . . . [3.311]
Part 2—Applications to Court for Recognition of Foreign Proceedings . . . [3.312]
Part 3—Applications for Relief Under the Model Law . . . [3.313]
Part 4—Replacement of Foreign Representative . . . [3.314]
Part 5—Reviews of Court Orders . . . [3.315]
Part 6—Court Procedure and Practice with Regard to Principal Applications and Orders . . . [3.316]
Part 7—Applications to the Chief Land Registrar . . . [3.317]
Part 8—Misfeasance . . . [3.318]
Part 9—General Provision as to Court Procedure and Practice . . . [3.319]
Part 10—Costs and Detailed Assessment . . . [3.320]
Part 11—Appeals in Proceedings Under these Regulations . . . [3.321]
Part 12—General . . . [3.322]
Schedule 3—Procedural Matters in Scotland
Part 1—Interpretation . . . [3.323]
Part 2—The Foreign Representative . . . [3.324]
Part 3—Court Procedure and Practice . . . [3.325]
Part 3—General . . . [3.326]
Schedule 4—Notices Delivered to the Registrar of Companies . . . [3.327]
Schedule 5—Forms . . . [3.328]

[3.302]

1 Citation, commencement and interpretation

(1) These Regulations may be cited as the Cross-Border Insolvency Regulations 2006 and shall come into force on the day after the day on which they are made.

(2) In these Regulations "the UNCITRAL Model Law" means the Model Law on cross-border insolvency as adopted by the United Nations Commission on International Trade Law on 30th May 1997.

[(3) In these Regulations "overseas company" has the meaning given by section 1044 of the Companies Act 2006 and "establishment", in relation to such a company, has the same meaning as in the Overseas Companies Regulations 2009.]

NOTES

Para (3): inserted by the Companies Act 2006 (Consequential Amendments, Transitional Provisions and Savings) Order 2009, SI 2009/1941, art 2(1), Sch 1, para 264(1), (2).

[3.303]

2 UNCITRAL Model Law to have force of law

(1) The UNCITRAL Model Law shall have the force of law in Great Britain in the form set out in Schedule 1 to these Regulations (which contains the UNCITRAL Model Law with certain modifications to adapt it for application in Great Britain).

(2) Without prejudice to any practice of the courts as to the matters which may be considered apart from this paragraph, the following documents may be considered in ascertaining the meaning or effect of any provision of the UNCITRAL Model Law as set out in Schedule 1 to these Regulations—

(a) the UNCITRAL Model Law;

(b) any documents of the United Nations Commission on International Trade Law and its working group relating to the preparation of the UNCITRAL Model Law; and
(c) the Guide to Enactment of the UNCITRAL Model Law (UNCITRAL document A/CN 9/442) prepared at the request of the United Nations Commission on International Trade Law made in May 1997.

[3.304]
3 Modification of British insolvency law

(1) British insolvency law (as defined in article 2 of the UNCITRAL Model Law as set out in Schedule 1 to these Regulations) and Part 3 of the Insolvency Act 1986 shall apply with such modifications as the context requires for the purpose of giving effect to the provisions of these Regulations.

(2) In the case of any conflict between any provision of British insolvency law or of Part 3 of the Insolvency Act 1986 and the provisions of these Regulations, the latter shall prevail.

[3.305]
4 Procedural matters in England and Wales

Schedule 2 to these Regulations (which makes provision about procedural matters in England and Wales in connection with the application of the UNCITRAL Model Law as set out in Schedule 1 to these Regulations) shall have effect.

[3.306]
5 Procedural matters in Scotland

Schedule 3 to these Regulations (which makes provision about procedural matters in Scotland in connection with the application of the UNCITRAL Model Law as set out in Schedule 1 to these Regulations) shall have effect.

[3.307]
6 Notices delivered to the registrar of companies

Schedule 4 to these Regulations (which makes provision about notices delivered to the registrar of companies under these Regulations) shall have effect.

[3.308]
7 Co-operation between courts exercising jurisdiction in relation to cross-border insolvency

(1) An order made by a court in either part of Great Britain in the exercise of jurisdiction in relation to the subject matter of these Regulations shall be enforced in the other part of Great Britain as if it were made by a court exercising the corresponding jurisdiction in that other part.

(2) However, nothing in paragraph (1) requires a court in either part of Great Britain to enforce, in relation to property situated in that part, any order made by a court in the other part of Great Britain.

(3) The courts having jurisdiction in relation to the subject matter of these Regulations in either part of Great Britain shall assist the courts having the corresponding jurisdiction in the other part of Great Britain.

[3.309]
8 Disapplication of section 388 of the Insolvency Act 1986

Nothing in section 388 of the Insolvency Act 1986 applies to anything done by a foreign representative—
(a) under or by virtue of these Regulations;
(b) in relation to relief granted or cooperation or coordination provided under these Regulations.

SCHEDULES

SCHEDULE 1
UNCITRAL MODEL LAW ON CROSS-BORDER INSOLVENCY

Regulation 2(1)

CHAPTER I GENERAL PROVISIONS

Article 1
Scope of Application

[3.310]
1. This Law applies where—
(a) assistance is sought in Great Britain by a foreign court or a foreign representative in connection with a foreign proceeding; or
(b) assistance is sought in a foreign State in connection with a proceeding under British insolvency law; or
(c) a foreign proceeding and a proceeding under British insolvency law in respect of the same debtor are taking place concurrently; or
(d) creditors or other interested persons in a foreign State have an interest in requesting the commencement of, or participating in, a proceeding under British insolvency law.

2. This Law does not apply to a proceeding concerning—

(a) a company holding an appointment under Chapter 1 of Part 2 of the Water Industry Act 1991 (water and sewage undertakers) or a qualifying [water supply licensee] within the meaning of section 23(6) of that Act (meaning and effect of special administration order);
(b) Scottish Water established under section 20 of the Water Industry (Scotland) Act 2002 (Scottish Water);
(c) a protected railway company within the meaning of section 59 of the Railways Act 1993 (railway administration order) (including that section as it has effect by virtue of section 19 of the Channel Tunnel Rail Link Act 1996 (administration));
(d) a licence company within the meaning of section 26 of the Transport Act 2000 (air traffic services);
(e) a public private partnership company within the meaning of section 210 of the Greater London Authority Act 1999 (public-private partnership agreement);
(f) a protected energy company within the meaning of section 154(5) of the Energy Act 2004 (energy administration orders);
(g) a building society within the meaning of section 119 of the Building Societies Act 1986 (interpretation);
(h) a UK credit institution or an EEA credit institution or any branch of either such institution as those expressions are defined by regulation 2 of the Credit Institutions (Reorganisation and Winding Up) Regulations 2004 (interpretation);
(i) a third country credit institution within the meaning of regulation 36 of the Credit Institutions (Reorganisation and Winding Up) Regulations 2004 (interpretation of this Part);
(j) a person who has permission under or by virtue of Parts 4 or 19 of the Financial Services and Markets Act 2000 to effect or carry out contracts of insurance;
(k) an EEA insurer within the meaning of regulation 2 of the Insurers (Reorganisation and Winding Up) Regulations 2004 (interpretation);
(l) a person (other than one included in paragraph 2(j)) pursuing the activity of reinsurance who has received authorisation for that activity from a competent authority within an EEA State; or
(m) any of the Concessionaires within the meaning of section 1 of the Channel Tunnel Act 1987.

3. In paragraph 2 of this article—
(a) in sub-paragraph (j) the reference to "contracts of insurance" must be construed in accordance with—
(i) section 22 of the Financial Services and Markets Act 2000 (classes of regulated activity and categories of investment);
(ii) any relevant order under that section; and
(iii) Schedule 2 to that Act (regulated activities);
(b) in sub-paragraph (1) "EEA State" means a State, other than the United Kingdom, which is a contracting party to the agreement on the European Economic Area signed at Oporto on 2 May 1992.

4. The court shall not grant any relief, or modify any relief already granted, or provide any co-operation or coordination, under or by virtue of any of the provisions of this Law if and to the extent that such relief or modified relief or cooperation or coordination would—
(a) be prohibited under or by virtue of—
(i) Part 7 of the Companies Act 1989;
(ii) Part 3 of the Financial Markets and Insolvency (Settlement Finality) Regulations 1999; or
(iii) Part 3 of the Financial Collateral Arrangements (No 2) Regulations 2003;
in the case of a proceeding under British insolvency law; or
(b) interfere with or be inconsistent with any rights of a collateral taker under Part 4 of the Financial Collateral Arrangements (No 2) Regulations 2003 which could be exercised in the case of such a proceeding.

5. Where a foreign proceeding regarding a debtor who is an insured in accordance with the provisions of the [Third Parties (Rights against Insurers) Act 2010] is recognised under this Law, any stay and suspension referred to in article 20(1) and any relief granted by the court under article 19 or 21 shall not apply to or affect—
(a) any transfer of rights of the debtor under that Act; or
(b) any claim, action, cause or proceeding by a third party against an insurer under or in respect of rights of the debtor transferred under that Act.

6. Any suspension under this Law of the right to transfer, encumber or otherwise dispose of any of the debtor's assets—
(a) is subject to section 26 of the Land Registration Act 2002 where owner's powers are exercised in relation to a registered estate or registered charge;
(b) is subject to section 52 of the Land Registration Act 2002, where the powers referred to in that section are exercised by the proprietor of a registered charge; and
(c) in any other case, shall not bind a purchaser of a legal estate in good faith for money or money's worth unless the purchaser has express notice of the suspension.

7. In paragraph 6—
(a) "owner's powers" means the powers described in section 23 of the Land Registration Act 2002 and "registered charge" and "registered estate" have the same meaning as in section 132(1) of that Act; and

(b) "legal estate" and "purchaser" have the same meaning as in section 17 of the Land Charges Act 1972.

Article 2
Definitions

For the purposes of this Law—

(a) "British insolvency law" means—
  (i) in relation to England and Wales, provision extending to England and Wales and made by or under the Insolvency Act 1986 (with the exception of Part 3 of that Act) or by or under that Act as extended or applied by or under any other enactment (excluding these Regulations); and
  (ii) in relation to Scotland, provision extending to Scotland and made by or under the Insolvency Act 1986 (with the exception of Part 3 of that Act), the Bankruptcy (Scotland) Act 1985 or by or under those Acts as extended or applied by or under any other enactment (excluding these Regulations);

(b) "British insolvency officeholder" means—
  (i) the official receiver within the meaning of section 399 of the Insolvency Act 1986 when acting as liquidator, provisional liquidator, trustee, interim receiver or nominee or supervisor of a voluntary arrangement;
  (ii) a person acting as an insolvency practitioner within the meaning of section 388 of that Act but shall not include a person acting as an administrative receiver; and
  (iii) the Accountant in Bankruptcy within the meaning of section 1 of the Bankruptcy (Scotland) Act 1985 when acting as interim or permanent trustee;

(c) "the court" except as otherwise provided in articles 14(4) and 23(6)(b), means in relation to any matter the court which in accordance with the provisions of article 4 of this Law has jurisdiction in relation to that matter;

[(d) "the EU Insolvency Regulation" means Regulation (EU) 2015/848 of the European Parliament and of the Council of 20 May 2015;]

(e) "establishment" means any place of operations where the debtor carries out a non-transitory economic activity with human means and assets or services;

(f) "foreign court" means a judicial or other authority competent to control or supervise a foreign proceeding;

(g) "foreign main proceeding" means a foreign proceeding taking place in the State where the debtor has the centre of its main interests;

(h) "foreign non-main proceeding" means a foreign proceeding, other than a foreign main proceeding, taking place in a State where the debtor has an establishment within the meaning of sub-paragraph (e) of this article;

(i) "foreign proceeding" means a collective judicial or administrative proceeding in a foreign State, including an interim proceeding, pursuant to a law relating to insolvency in which proceeding the assets and affairs of the debtor are subject to control or supervision by a foreign court, for the purpose of reorganisation or liquidation;

(j) "foreign representative" means a person or body, including one appointed on an interim basis, authorised in a foreign proceeding to administer the reorganisation or the liquidation of the debtor's assets or affairs or to act as a representative of the foreign proceeding;

(k) "hire-purchase agreement" includes a conditional sale agreement, a chattel leasing agreement and a retention of title agreement;

(l) "section 426 request" means a request for assistance in accordance with section 426 of the Insolvency Act 1986 made to a court in any part of the United Kingdom;

(m) "secured creditor" in relation to a debtor, means a creditor of the debtor who holds in respect of his debt a security over property of the debtor;

(n) "security" means—
  (i) in relation to England and Wales, any mortgage, charge, lien or other security; and
  (ii) in relation to Scotland, any security (whether heritable or moveable), any floating charge and any right of lien or preference and any right of retention (other than a right of compensation or set off);

(o) in the application of Articles 20 and 23 to Scotland, "an individual" means any debtor within the meaning of the Bankruptcy (Scotland) Act 1985;

(p) in the application of this Law to Scotland, references howsoever expressed to—
  (i) "filing" an application or claim are to be construed as references to lodging an application or submitting a claim respectively;
  (ii) "relief" and "standing" are to be construed as references to "remedy" and "title and interest" respectively; and
  (iii) a "stay" are to be construed as references to restraint, except in relation to continuation of actions or proceedings when they shall be construed as a reference to sist; and

(q) references to the law of Great Britain include a reference to the law of either part of Great Britain (including its rules of private international law).

Article 3
International Obligations of Great Britain Under the [EU Insolvency Regulation]

To the extent that this Law conflicts with an obligation of the United Kingdom under the [EU Insolvency Regulation], the requirements of the [EU Insolvency Regulation] prevail.

Article 4
Competent Court

1. The functions referred to in this Law relating to recognition of foreign proceedings and cooperation with foreign courts shall be performed by the High Court and assigned to the Chancery Division, as regards England and Wales and the Court of Session as regards Scotland.

2. Subject to paragraph 1 of this article, the court in either part of Great Britain shall have jurisdiction in relation to the functions referred to in that paragraph if—

(a) the debtor has—
  (i) a place of business; or
  (ii) in the case of an individual, a place of residence; or
  (iii) assets,

  situated in that part of Great Britain; or

(b) the court in that part of Great Britain considers for any other reason that it is the appropriate forum to consider the question or provide the assistance requested.

3. In considering whether it is the appropriate forum to hear an application for recognition of a foreign proceeding in relation to a debtor, the court shall take into account the location of any court in which a proceeding under British insolvency law is taking place in relation to the debtor and the likely location of any future proceedings under British insolvency law in relation to the debtor.

Article 5
Authorisation of British Insolvency Officeholders to Act in a Foreign State

A British insolvency officeholder is authorised to act in a foreign State on behalf of a proceeding under British insolvency law, as permitted by the applicable foreign law.

Article 6
Public Policy Exception

Nothing in this Law prevents the court from refusing to take an action governed by this Law if the action would be manifestly contrary to the public policy of Great Britain or any part of it.

Article 7
Additional Assistance under other Laws

Nothing in this Law limits the power of a court or a British insolvency officeholder to provide additional assistance to a foreign representative under other laws of Great Britain.

Article 8
Interpretation

In the interpretation of this Law, regard is to be had to its international origin and to the need to promote uniformity in its application and the observance of good faith.

CHAPTER II ACCESS OF FOREIGN REPRESENTATIVES AND CREDITORS TO COURTS IN GREAT BRITAIN

Article 9
Right of Direct Access

A foreign representative is entitled to apply directly to a court in Great Britain.

Article 10
Limited Jurisdiction

The sole fact that an application pursuant to this Law is made to a court in Great Britain by a foreign representative does not subject the foreign representative or the foreign assets and affairs of the debtor to the jurisdiction of the courts of Great Britain or any part of it for any purpose other than the application.

Article 11

Application by a Foreign Representative to Commence a Proceeding under British Insolvency Law

A foreign representative appointed in a foreign main proceeding or foreign non-main proceeding is entitled to apply to commence a proceeding under British insolvency law if the conditions for commencing such a proceeding are otherwise met.

Article 12

Participation of a Foreign Representative in a Proceeding under British Insolvency Law

Upon recognition of a foreign proceeding, the foreign representative is entitled to participate in a proceeding regarding the debtor under British insolvency law.

Article 13

Access of Foreign Creditors to a Proceeding under British Insolvency Law

1. Subject to paragraph 2 of this article, foreign creditors have the same rights regarding the commencement of, and participation in, a proceeding under British insolvency law as creditors in Great Britain.

2. Paragraph 1 of this article does not affect the ranking of claims in a proceeding under British insolvency law, except that the claim of a foreign creditor shall not be given a lower priority than that of general unsecured claims solely because the holder of such a claim is a foreign creditor.

3. A claim may not be challenged solely on the grounds that it is a claim by a foreign tax or social security authority but such a claim may be challenged—
- (a) on the ground that it is in whole or in part a penalty, or
- (b) on any other ground that a claim might be rejected in a proceeding under British insolvency law.

Article 14

Notification to Foreign Creditors of a Proceeding under British Insolvency Law

1. Whenever under British insolvency law notification is to be given to creditors in Great Britain, such notification shall also be given to the known creditors that do not have addresses in Great Britain. The court may order that appropriate steps be taken with a view to notifying any creditor whose address is not yet known.

2. Such notification shall be made to the foreign creditors individually, unless—
- (a) the court considers that under the circumstances some other form of notification would be more appropriate; or
- (b) the notification to creditors in Great Britain is to be by advertisement only, in which case the notification to the known foreign creditors may be by advertisement in such foreign newspapers as the British insolvency officeholder considers most appropriate for ensuring that the content of the notification comes to the notice of the known foreign creditors.

3. When notification of a right to file a claim is to be given to foreign creditors, the notification shall—
- (a) indicate a reasonable time period for filing claims and specify the place for their filing;
- (b) indicate whether secured creditors need to file their secured claims; and
- (c) contain any other information required to be included in such a notification to creditors pursuant to the law of Great Britain and the orders of the court.

4. In this article "the court" means the court which has jurisdiction in relation to the particular proceeding under British insolvency law under which notification is to be given to creditors.

CHAPTER III RECOGNITION OF A FOREIGN PROCEEDING AND RELIEF

Article 15

Application for Recognition of a Foreign Proceeding

1. A foreign representative may apply to the court for recognition of the foreign proceeding in which the foreign representative has been appointed.

2. An application for recognition shall be accompanied by—
- (a) a certified copy of the decision commencing the foreign proceeding and appointing the foreign representative; or
- (b) a certificate from the foreign court affirming the existence of the foreign proceeding and of the appointment of the foreign representative; or
- (c) in the absence of evidence referred to in sub-paragraphs (a) and (b), any other evidence acceptable to the court of the existence of the foreign proceeding and of the appointment of the foreign representative.

3. An application for recognition shall also be accompanied by a statement identifying all foreign proceedings, proceedings under British insolvency law and section 426 requests in respect of the debtor that are known to the foreign representative.

4. The foreign representative shall provide the court with a translation into English of documents supplied in support of the application for recognition.

Article 16
Presumptions Concerning Recognition

1. If the decision or certificate referred to in paragraph 2 of article 15 indicates that the foreign proceeding is a proceeding within the meaning of sub-paragraph (i) of article 2 and that the foreign representative is a person or body within the meaning of sub-paragraph (j) of article 2, the court is entitled to so presume.

2. The court is entitled to presume that documents submitted in support of the application for recognition are authentic, whether or not they have been legalised.

3. In the absence of proof to the contrary, the debtor's registered office, or habitual residence in the case of an individual, is presumed to be the centre of the debtor's main interests.

Article 17
Decision to Recognise a Foreign Proceeding

1. Subject to article 6, a foreign proceeding shall be recognised if—
(a) it is a foreign proceeding within the meaning of sub-paragraph (i) of article 2;
(b) the foreign representative applying for recognition is a person or body within the meaning of sub-paragraph (j) of article 2;
(c) the application meets the requirements of paragraphs 2 and 3 of article 15; and
(d) the application has been submitted to the court referred to in article 4.

2. The foreign proceeding shall be recognised—
(a) as a foreign main proceeding if it is taking place in the State where the debtor has the centre of its main interests; or
(b) as a foreign non-main proceeding if the debtor has an establishment within the meaning of sub-paragraph (e) of article 2 in the foreign State.

3. An application for recognition of a foreign proceeding shall be decided upon at the earliest possible time.

4. The provisions of articles 15 to 16, this article and article 18 do not prevent modification or termination of recognition if it is shown that the grounds for granting it were fully or partially lacking or have fully or partially ceased to exist and in such a case, the court may, on the application of the foreign representative or a person affected by recognition, or of its own motion, modify or terminate recognition, either altogether or for a limited time, on such terms and conditions as the court thinks fit.

Article 18
Subsequent Information

From the time of filing the application for recognition of the foreign proceeding, the foreign representative shall inform the court promptly of—
(a) any substantial change in the status of the recognised foreign proceeding or the status of the foreign representative's appointment; and
(b) any other foreign proceeding, proceeding under British insolvency law or section 426 request regarding the same debtor that becomes known to the foreign representative.

Article 19
Relief that may be Granted upon Application for Recognition of a Foreign Proceeding

1. From the time of filing an application for recognition until the application is decided upon, the court may, at the request of the foreign representative, where relief is urgently needed to protect the assets of the debtor or the interests of the creditors, grant relief of a provisional nature, including—
(a) staying execution against the debtor's assets;
(b) entrusting the administration or realisation of all or part of the debtor's assets located in Great Britain to the foreign representative or another person designated by the court, in order to protect and preserve the value of assets that, by their nature or because of other circumstances, are perishable, susceptible to devaluation or otherwise in jeopardy; and
(c) any relief mentioned in paragraph 1 (c), (d) or (g) of article 21.

2. Unless extended under paragraph 1(f) of article 21, the relief granted under this article terminates when the application for recognition is decided upon.

3. The court may refuse to grant relief under this article if such relief would interfere with the administration of a foreign main proceeding.

Article 20

Effects of Recognition of a Foreign Main Proceeding

1. Upon recognition of a foreign proceeding that is a foreign main proceeding, subject to paragraph 2 of this article—

(a) commencement or continuation of individual actions or individual proceedings concerning the debtor's assets, rights, obligations or liabilities is stayed;

(b) execution against the debtor's assets is stayed; and

(c) the right to transfer, encumber or otherwise dispose of any assets of the debtor is suspended.

2. The stay and suspension referred to in paragraph 1 of this article shall be—

(a) the same in scope and effect as if the debtor, in the case of an individual, had been adjudged bankrupt under the Insolvency Act 1986 or had his estate sequestrated under the Bankruptcy (Scotland) Act 1985, or, in the case of a debtor other than an individual, had been made the subject of a winding-up order under the Insolvency Act 1986; and

(b) subject to the same powers of the court and the same prohibitions, limitations, exceptions and conditions as would apply under the law of Great Britain in such a case,

and the provisions of paragraph 1 of this article shall be interpreted accordingly.

3. Without prejudice to paragraph 2 of this article, the stay and suspension referred to in paragraph 1 of this article, in particular, does not affect any right—

(a) to take any steps to enforce security over the debtor's property;

(b) to take any steps to repossess goods in the debtor's possession under a hire-purchase agreement;

(c) exercisable under or by virtue of or in connection with the provisions referred to in article 1(4); or

(d) of a creditor to set off its claim against a claim of the debtor,

being a right which would have been exercisable if the debtor, in the case of an individual, had been adjudged bankrupt under the Insolvency Act 1986 or had his estate sequestrated under the Bankruptcy (Scotland) Act 1985, or, in the case of a debtor other than an individual, had been made the subject of a winding-up order under the Insolvency Act 1986.

4. Paragraph 1(a) of this article does not affect the right to—

(a) commence individual actions or proceedings to the extent necessary to preserve a claim against the debtor; or

(b) commence or continue any criminal proceedings or any action or proceedings by a person or body having regulatory, supervisory or investigative functions of a public nature, being an action or proceedings brought in the exercise of those functions.

5. Paragraph 1 of this article does not affect the right to request or otherwise initiate the commencement of a proceeding under British insolvency law or the right to file claims in such a proceeding.

6. In addition to and without prejudice to any powers of the court under or by virtue of paragraph 2 of this article, the court may, on the application of the foreign representative or a person affected by the stay and suspension referred to in paragraph 1 of this article, or of its own motion, modify or terminate such stay and suspension or any part of it, either altogether or for a limited time, on such terms and conditions as the court thinks fit.

Article 21

Relief that may be Granted upon Recognition of a Foreign Proceeding

1. Upon recognition of a foreign proceeding, whether main or non-main, where necessary to protect the assets of the debtor or the interests of the creditors, the court may, at the request of the foreign representative, grant any appropriate relief, including—

(a) staying the commencement or continuation of individual actions or individual proceedings concerning the debtor's assets, rights, obligations or liabilities, to the extent they have not been stayed under paragraph 1(a) of article 20;

(b) staying execution against the debtor's assets to the extent it has not been stayed under paragraph 1(b) of article 20;

(c) suspending the right to transfer, encumber or otherwise dispose of any assets of the debtor to the extent this right has not been suspended under paragraph 1(c) of article 20;

(d) providing for the examination of witnesses, the taking of evidence or the delivery of information concerning the debtor's assets, affairs, rights, obligations or liabilities;

(e) entrusting the administration or realisation of all or part of the debtor's assets located in Great Britain to the foreign representative or another person designated by the court;

(f) extending relief granted under paragraph 1 of article 19; and

(g) granting any additional relief that may be available to a British insolvency officeholder under the law of Great Britain, including any relief provided under paragraph 43 of Schedule B1 to the Insolvency Act 1986.

2. Upon recognition of a foreign proceeding, whether main or non-main, the court may, at the request of the foreign representative, entrust the distribution of all or part of the debtor's assets located in Great Britain to the foreign representative or another person designated by the court, provided that the court is satisfied that the interests of creditors in Great Britain are adequately protected.

3. In granting relief under this article to a representative of a foreign non-main proceeding, the court must be satisfied that the relief relates to assets that, under the law of Great Britain, should be administered in the foreign non-main proceeding or concerns information required in that proceeding.

4. No stay under paragraph 1(a) of this article shall affect the right to commence or continue any criminal proceedings or any action or proceedings by a person or body having regulatory, supervisory or investigative functions of a public nature, being an action or proceedings brought in the exercise of those functions.

Article 22
Protection of Creditors and other Interested Persons

1. In granting or denying relief under article 19 or 21, or in modifying or terminating relief under paragraph 3 of this article or paragraph 6 of article 20, the court must be satisfied that the interests of the creditors (including any secured creditors or parties to hire-purchase agreements) and other interested persons, including if appropriate the debtor, are adequately protected.

2. The court may subject relief granted under article 19 or 21 to conditions it considers appropriate, including the provision by the foreign representative of security or caution for the proper performance of his functions.

3. The court may, at the request of the foreign representative or a person affected by relief granted under article 19 or 21, or of its own motion, modify or terminate such relief.

Article 23
Actions to Avoid Acts Detrimental to Creditors

1. Subject to paragraphs 6 and 9 of this article, upon recognition of a foreign proceeding, the foreign representative has standing to make an application to the court for an order under or in connection with sections 238, 239, 242, 243, 244, 245, 339, 340, 342A, 343, and 423 of the Insolvency Act 1986 and sections 34, 35, 36, 36A and 61 of the Bankruptcy (Scotland) Act 1985.

2. Where the foreign representative makes such an application ("an article 23 application"), the sections referred to in paragraph 1 of this article and sections 240, 241, 341, 342, 342B to 342F, 424 and 425 of the Insolvency Act 1986 and sections 36B and 36C of the Bankruptcy (Scotland) Act 1985 shall apply—
(a) whether or not the debtor, in the case of an individual, has been adjudged bankrupt or had his estate sequestrated, or, in the case of a debtor other than an individual, is being wound up or is in administration, under British insolvency law; and
(b) with the modifications set out in paragraph 3 of this article.

3. The modifications referred to in paragraph 2 of this article are as follows—
(a) for the purposes of sections 241(2A)(a) and 342(2A)(a) of the Insolvency Act 1986, a person has notice of the relevant proceedings if he has notice of the opening of the relevant foreign proceeding;
(b) for the purposes of sections 240(1) and 245(3) of that Act, the onset of insolvency shall be the date of the opening of the relevant foreign proceeding;
(c) the periods referred to in sections 244(2), 341(1)(a) to (c) and 343(2) of that Act shall be periods ending with the date of the opening of the relevant foreign proceeding;
(d) for the purposes of sections 242(3)(a), (3)(b) and 243(1) of that Act, the date on which the winding up of the company commences or it enters administration shall be the date of the opening of the relevant foreign proceeding; and
(e) for the purposes of sections 34(3)(a), (3)(b), 35(1)(c), 36(1)(a) and (1)(b) and 61(2) of the Bankruptcy (Scotland) Act 1985, the date of sequestration or granting of the trust deed shall be the date of the opening of the relevant foreign proceeding.

4. For the purposes of paragraph 3 of this article, the date of the opening of the foreign proceeding shall be determined in accordance with the law of the State in which the foreign proceeding is taking place, including any rule of law by virtue of which the foreign proceeding is deemed to have opened at an earlier time.

5. When the foreign proceeding is a foreign non-main proceeding, the court must be satisfied that the article 23 application relates to assets that, under the law of Great Britain, should be administered in the foreign non-main proceeding.

6. At any time when a proceeding under British insolvency law is taking place regarding the debtor—
(a) the foreign representative shall not make an article 23 application except with the permission of—

(i) in the case of a proceeding under British insolvency law taking place in England and Wales, the High Court; or
(ii) in the case of a proceeding under British insolvency law taking place in Scotland, the Court of Session; and

(b) references to "the court" in paragraphs 1, 5 and 7 of this article are references to the court in which that proceeding is taking place.

7. On making an order on an article 23 application, the court may give such directions regarding the distribution of any proceeds of the claim by the foreign representative, as it thinks fit to ensure that the interests of creditors in Great Britain are adequately protected.

8. Nothing in this article affects the right of a British insolvency officeholder to make an application under or in connection with any of the provisions referred to in paragraph 1 of this article.

9. Nothing in paragraph 1 of this article shall apply in respect of any preference given, floating charge created, alienation, assignment or relevant contributions (within the meaning of section 342A(5) of the Insolvency Act 1986) made or other transaction entered into before the date on which this Law comes into force.

Article 24
Intervention by a Foreign Representative in Proceedings in Great Britain

Upon recognition of a foreign proceeding, the foreign representative may, provided the requirements of the law of Great Britain are met, intervene in any proceedings in which the debtor is a party.

CHAPTER IV COOPERATION WITH FOREIGN COURTS AND FOREIGN REPRESENTATIVES

Article 25
Cooperation and Direct Communication between a Court of Great Britain and Foreign Courts or Foreign Representatives

1. In matters referred to in paragraph 1 of article 1, the court may cooperate to the maximum extent possible with foreign courts or foreign representatives, either directly or through a British insolvency officeholder.

2. The court is entitled to communicate directly with, or to request information or assistance directly from, foreign courts or foreign representatives.

Article 26
Cooperation and Direct Communication between the British Insolvency Officeholder and Foreign Courts or Foreign Representatives

1. In matters referred to in paragraph 1 of article 1, a British insolvency officeholder shall to the extent consistent with his other duties under the law of Great Britain, in the exercise of his functions and subject to the supervision of the court, cooperate to the maximum extent possible with foreign courts or foreign representatives.

2. The British insolvency officeholder is entitled, in the exercise of his functions and subject to the supervision of the court, to communicate directly with foreign courts or foreign representatives.

Article 27
Forms of Cooperation

Cooperation referred to in articles 25 and 26 may be implemented by any appropriate means, including—
(a) appointment of a person to act at the direction of the court;
(b) communication of information by any means considered appropriate by the court;
(c) coordination of the administration and supervision of the debtor's assets and affairs;
(d) approval or implementation by courts of agreements concerning the coordination of proceedings;
(e) coordination of concurrent proceedings regarding the same debtor.

CHAPTER V CONCURRENT PROCEEDINGS

Article 28
Commencement of a Proceeding Under British Insolvency Law after Recognition of a Foreign Main Proceeding

After recognition of a foreign main proceeding, the effects of a proceeding under British insolvency law in relation to the same debtor shall, insofar as the assets of that debtor are concerned, be restricted to assets that are located in Great Britain and, to the extent necessary to implement cooperation and coordination under articles 25, 26 and 27, to other assets of the debtor that, under the law of Great Britain, should be administered in that proceeding.

Article 29

Coordination of a Proceeding Under British Insolvency Law and a Foreign Proceeding

Where a foreign proceeding and a proceeding under British insolvency law are taking place concurrently regarding the same debtor, the court may seek cooperation and coordination under articles 25, 26 and 27, and the following shall apply—

(a) when the proceeding in Great Britain is taking place at the time the application for recognition of the foreign proceeding is filed—

(i) any relief granted under article 19 or 21 must be consistent with the proceeding in Great Britain; and

(ii) if the foreign proceeding is recognised in Great Britain as a foreign main proceeding, article 20 does not apply;

(b) when the proceeding in Great Britain commences after the filing of the application for recognition of the foreign proceeding—

(i) any relief in effect under article 19 or 21 shall be reviewed by the court and shall be modified or terminated if inconsistent with the proceeding in Great Britain;

(ii) if the foreign proceeding is a foreign main proceeding, the stay and suspension referred to in paragraph 1 of article 20 shall be modified or terminated pursuant to paragraph 6 of article 20, if inconsistent with the proceeding in Great Britain; and

(iii) any proceedings brought by the foreign representative by virtue of paragraph 1 of article 23 before the proceeding in Great Britain commenced shall be reviewed by the court and the court may give such directions as it thinks fit regarding the continuance of those proceedings; and

(c) in granting, extending or modifying relief granted to a representative of a foreign non-main proceeding, the court must be satisfied that the relief relates to assets that, under the law of Great Britain, should be administered in the foreign non-main proceeding or concerns information required in that proceeding.

Article 30

Coordination of more than one Foreign Proceeding

In matters referred to in paragraph 1 of article 1, in respect of more than one foreign proceeding regarding the same debtor, the court may seek cooperation and coordination under articles 25, 26 and 27, and the following shall apply—

(a) any relief granted under article 19 or 21 to a representative of a foreign non-main proceeding after recognition of a foreign main proceeding must be consistent with the foreign main proceeding;

(b) if a foreign main proceeding is recognised after the filing of an application for recognition of a foreign non-main proceeding, any relief in effect under article 19 or 21 shall be reviewed by the court and shall be modified or terminated if inconsistent with the foreign main proceeding; and

(c) if, after recognition of a foreign non-main proceeding, another foreign non-main proceeding is recognised, the court shall grant, modify or terminate relief for the purpose of facilitating coordination of the proceedings.

Article 31

Presumption of Insolvency Based on Recognition of a Foreign Main Proceeding

In the absence of evidence to the contrary, recognition of a foreign main proceeding is, for the purpose of commencing a proceeding under British insolvency law, proof that the debtor is unable to pay its debts or, in relation to Scotland, is apparently insolvent within the meaning given to those expressions under British insolvency law.

Article 32

Rule of Payment in Concurrent Proceedings

Without prejudice to secured claims or rights in rem, a creditor who has received part payment in respect of its claim in a proceeding pursuant to a law relating to insolvency in a foreign State may not receive a payment for the same claim in a proceeding under British insolvency law regarding the same debtor, so long as the payment to the other creditors of the same class is proportionately less than the payment the creditor has already received.

NOTES

Art 1: words in square brackets in para 2(a) substituted by the Water Act 2014 (Consequential Amendments etc) Order 2017, SI 2017/506, art 24; words in square brackets in para 5 substituted for original words "Third Parties (Rights against Insurers) Act 1930" by the Third Parties (Rights against Insurers) Act 2010, s 20(1), Sch 2, para 4, as from 1 August 2016, subject to transitional provisions and savings in s 20(2) of, and Sch 3, para 3 to, the 2010 Act at **[17.425]**, **[17.429]**.

Art 2: para (d) substituted by the Insolvency Amendment (EU 2015/848) Regulations 2017, SI 2017/702, regs 2, 3, Schedule, Pt 6, para 94(1), (2), as from 26 June 2017, except in relation to proceedings opened before that date, and previously read as follows:

"(d) "the EC Insolvency Regulation" means Council Regulation (EC) No 1346/2000 of 29 May 2000 on Insolvency Proceedings;".

Art 3: words in square brackets substituted by the Insolvency (Miscellaneous Amendments) Regulations 2017, SI 2017/1119, reg 2, Sch 5, para 1(1), (2).

SCHEDULE 2
PROCEDURAL MATTERS IN ENGLAND AND WALES

Regulation 4

PART 1
INTRODUCTORY PROVISIONS

[3.311]

1 Interpretation

(1) In this Schedule—

"the 1986 Act" means the Insolvency Act 1986;

"article 21 relief application" means an application to the court by a foreign representative under article 21(1) or (2) of the Model Law for relief;

"business day" means any day other than a Saturday, a Sunday, Christmas Day, Good Friday or a day which is a bank holiday in England and Wales under or by virtue of the Banking and Financial Dealings Act 1971;

"CPR" means the Civil Procedure Rules 1998 and "CPR" followed by a Part or rule by number means the Part or rule with that number in those Rules;

"enforcement officer" means an individual who is authorised to act as an enforcement officer under the Courts Act 2003;

"file in court" and "file with the court" means deliver to the court for filing;

"the Gazette" means the London Gazette;

"interim relief application" means an application to the court by a foreign representative under article 19 of the Model Law for interim relief;

"main proceedings" means proceedings opened in accordance with Article 3(1) of the [EU Insolvency Regulation] and falling within the definition of insolvency proceedings in [Article 2(4)] of the [EU Insolvency Regulation];

["member State liquidator" means a person falling within the definition of "insolvency practitioner" in Article 2(5) of the EU Insolvency Regulation appointed in proceedings to which the Regulation applies in a member State other than the United Kingdom;]

"the Model Law" means the UNCITRAL Model Law as set out in Schedule 1 to these Regulations;

"modification or termination order" means an order by the court pursuant to its powers under the Model Law modifying or terminating recognition of a foreign proceeding, the stay and suspension referred to in article 20(1) or any part of it or any relief granted under article 19 or 21 of the Model Law;

"originating application" means an application to the court which is not an application in pending proceedings before the court;

"ordinary application" means any application to the court other than an originating application;

"practice direction" means a direction as to the practice and procedure of any court within the scope of the CPR;

"recognition application" means an application to the court by a foreign representative in accordance with article 15 of the Model Law for an order recognising the foreign proceeding in which he has been appointed;

"recognition order" means an order by the court recognising a proceeding the subject of a recognition application as a foreign main proceeding or foreign non-main proceeding, as appropriate;

["relevant company" means a company that is—

(a) registered under the Companies Act 2006,

(b) subject to a requirement imposed by regulations under section 1043 of that Act 2006 (unregistered UK companies) to deliver any documents to the registrar of companies, or

(c) subject to a requirement imposed by regulations under section 1046 of that Act (overseas companies) to deliver any documents to the registrar of companies;]

"review application" means an application to the court for a modification or termination order;

"the Rules" means the [Insolvency (England and Wales) Rules 2016] and "Rule" followed by a number means the rule with that number in those Rules;

"secondary proceedings" means proceedings opened in accordance with [Articles 3(2) and 3(3) of the EU Insolvency Regulation] and falling within the definition of [insolvency proceedings in Article 2(4) of the EU Insolvency Regulation];

"territorial proceedings" means proceedings opened in accordance with [Articles 3(2) and 3(4) of the EU Insolvency Regulation] and falling within the definition of insolvency proceedings in [Article 2(4) of the EU Insolvency Regulation].

(2) Expressions defined in the Model Law have the same meaning when used in this Schedule.

(3) In proceedings under these Regulations, "Registrar" means—

(a) [an Insolvency and Companies Court Judge]; and

(b) where the proceedings are in a district registry, the district judge.

(4) References to the "venue" for any proceedings or attendance before the court, are to the time, date and place for the proceedings or attendance.

(5) References in this Schedule to ex parte hearings shall be construed as references to hearings without notice being served on any other party, and references to applications made ex parte as references to applications made without notice being served on any other party; and other references which include the expression "ex parte" shall be similarly construed.

[(6) References in this Schedule to a debtor who is of interest to the Financial Conduct Authority are references to a debtor who—

(a) is, or has been, an authorised person within the meaning of the Financial Services and Markets Act 2000;
(b) is, or has been, an appointed representative within the meaning of section 39 of the Financial Services and Markets Act 2000; or
(c) is carrying on, or has carried on, a regulated activity in contravention of the general prohibition.

(6A) References in this Schedule to a debtor who is of interest to the Prudential Regulation Authority are references to a debtor who—

(a) is, or has been, a PRA-authorised person within the meaning of the Financial Services and Markets Act 2000; or
(b) is carrying on, or has carried on, a PRA-regulated activity within the meaning of the Financial Services and Markets Act 2000 in contravention of the general prohibition.]

(7) In [sub-paragraphs (6) and (6A)] "the general prohibition" has the meaning given by section 19 of the Financial Services and Markets Act 2000 and the reference to a "regulated activity" must be construed in accordance with—

(a) section 22 of that Act (classes of regulated activity and categories of investment);
(b) any relevant order under that section; and
(c) Schedule 2 to that Act (regulated activities).

(8) References in this Schedule to a numbered form are to the form that bears that number in Schedule 5.

NOTES

Para 1: in sub-para (1), definition "relevant company" substituted by the Companies Act 2006 (Consequential Amendments, Transitional Provisions and Savings) Order 2009, SI 2009/1941, art 2(1), Sch 1, para 264(1), (3)(a); words in square brackets in definition "the Rules" substituted by the Insolvency (England and Wales) Rules 2016 (Consequential Amendments and Savings) Rules 2017, SI 2017/369, r 2(2), Sch 2, para 1 (and note that the same amendment is made by the Insolvency (England and Wales) and Insolvency (Scotland) (Miscellaneous and Consequential Amendments) Rules 2017, SI 2017/1115, rr 20, 21);

in the definition of "main proceedings" words in first and third pairs of square brackets substituted for original words "EC Insolvency Regulation" and words in second pair of square brackets substituted for original words "Article 2(a)" and definition "member state liquidator" substituted, by the Insolvency Amendment (EU 2015/848) Regulations 2017, SI 2017/702, regs 2, 3, Schedule, Pt 6, para 94(1), (3), as from 26 June 2017, except in relation to proceedings opened before that date. The definition "member state liquidator" previously read as follows:

"member State liquidator" means a person falling within the definition of liquidator in Article 2(b) of the EC Insolvency Regulation appointed in proceedings to which it applies in a member State other than the United Kingdom;";

words in square brackets in definitions "secondary proceedings" and "territorial proceedings" substituted by the Insolvency (Miscellaneous Amendments) Regulations 2017, SI 2017/1119, reg 2, Sch 5, para 1(1), (3)(a), (b);

words in square brackets in sub-para (3)(a) substituted by the Alteration of Judicial Titles (Registrar in Bankruptcy of the High Court) Order 2018, SI 2018/130, art 3, Schedule, para 12(1)(d); sub-paras (6), (6A) substituted and words in square brackets in sub-para (7) substituted by the Financial Services Act 2012 (Consequential Amendments and Transitional Provisions) Order 2013, SI 2013/472, art 3, Sch 2, para 116(a)(i).

PART 2
APPLICATIONS TO COURT FOR RECOGNITION OF FOREIGN PROCEEDINGS

[3.312]

2 Affidavit in support of recognition application

A recognition application shall be in Form ML1 and shall be supported by an affidavit sworn by the foreign representative complying with paragraph 4.

3 Form and content of application

The application shall state the following matters—

(a) the name of the applicant and his address for service within England and Wales;
(b) the name of the debtor in respect of which the foreign proceeding is taking place;
(c) the name or names in which the debtor carries on business in the country where the foreign proceeding is taking place and in this country, if other than the name given under sub-paragraph (b);
(d) the principal or last known place of business of the debtor in Great Britain (if any) and, in the case of an individual, his usual or last known place of residence in Great Britain (if any);
(e) any registered number allocated to the debtor under [the Companies Act 2006];
(f) brief particulars of the foreign proceeding in respect of which recognition is applied for, including the country in which it is taking place and the nature of the proceeding;
(g) that the foreign proceeding is a proceeding within the meaning of article 2(i) of the Model Law;
(h) that the applicant is a foreign representative within the meaning of article 2(j) of the Model Law;
(i) the address of the debtor's centre of main interests and, if different, the address of its registered office or habitual residence, as appropriate; and

(j) if the debtor does not have its centre of main interests in the country where the foreign proceeding is taking place, whether the debtor has an establishment within the meaning of article 2(e) of the Model Law in that country, and if so, its address.

4 Contents of affidavit in support

(1) There shall be attached to the application an affidavit in support which shall contain or have exhibited to it—

(a) the evidence and statement required under article 15(2) and (3) respectively of the Model Law;
(b) any other evidence which in the opinion of the applicant will assist the court in deciding whether the proceeding the subject of the application is a foreign proceeding within the meaning of article 2(i) of the Model Law and whether the applicant is a foreign representative within the meaning of article 2(j) of the Model Law;
(c) evidence that the debtor has its centre of main interests or an establishment, as the case may be, within the country where the foreign proceeding is taking place; and
(d) any other matters which in the opinion of the applicant will assist the court in deciding whether to make a recognition order.

(2) The affidavit shall state whether, in the opinion of the applicant, the [EU Insolvency Regulation] applies to any of the proceedings identified in accordance with article 15(3) of the Model Law and, if so, whether those proceedings are main proceedings, secondary proceedings or territorial proceedings.

(3) The affidavit shall also have exhibited to it the translations required under article 15(4) of the Model Law and a translation in English of any other document exhibited to the affidavit which is in a language other than English.

(4) All translations referred to in sub-paragraph (3) must be certified by the translator as a correct translation.

5 The hearing and powers of court

(1) On hearing a recognition application the court may in addition to its powers under the Model Law to make a recognition order—

(a) dismiss the application;
(b) adjourn the hearing conditionally or unconditionally;
(c) make any other order which the court thinks appropriate.

(2) If the court makes a recognition order, it shall be in Form ML2.

6 Notification of subsequent information

(1) The foreign representative shall set out any subsequent information required to be given to the court under article 18 of the Model Law in a statement which he shall attach to Form ML3 and file with the court.

(2) The statement shall include—

(a) details of the information required to be given under article 18 of the Model Law; and
(b) in the case of any proceedings required to be notified to the court under that article, a statement as to whether, in the opinion of the foreign representative, any of those proceedings are main proceedings, secondary proceedings or territorial proceedings under the [EU Insolvency Regulation].

(3) The foreign representative shall send a copy of the Form ML3 and attached statement filed with the court to the following—

(a) the debtor; and
(b) those persons referred to in paragraph 26(3).

NOTES

Para 3: words in square brackets in sub-para (e) substituted by the Companies Act 2006 (Consequential Amendments, Transitional Provisions and Savings) Order 2009, SI 2009/1941, art 2(1), Sch 1, para 264(1), (3)(b).

Paras 4, 6: words in square brackets substituted by the Insolvency (Miscellaneous Amendments) Regulations 2017, SI 2017/1119, reg 2, Sch 5, para 1(1), (3)(c), (d).

PART 3
APPLICATIONS FOR RELIEF UNDER THE MODEL LAW

[3.313]

7 Application for interim relief—affidavit in support

(1) An interim relief application must be supported by an affidavit sworn by the foreign representative stating—

(a) the grounds on which it is proposed that the interim relief applied for should be granted;
(b) details of any proceeding under British insolvency law taking place in relation to the debtor;
(c) whether, to the foreign representative's knowledge, an administrative receiver or receiver or manager of the debtor's property is acting in relation to the debtor;
(d) an estimate of the value of the assets of the debtor in England and Wales in respect of which relief is applied for;
(e) whether, to the best of the knowledge and belief of the foreign representative, the interests of the debtor's creditors (including any secured creditors or parties to hire-purchase agreements) and any other interested parties, including if appropriate the debtor, will be adequately protected;

(f) whether, to the best of the foreign representative's knowledge and belief, the grant of any of the relief applied for would interfere with the administration of a foreign main proceeding; and
(g) all other matters that in the opinion of the foreign representative will assist the court in deciding whether or not it is appropriate to grant the relief applied for.

8 Service of interim relief application not required

Unless the court otherwise directs, it shall not be necessary to serve the interim relief application on, or give notice of it to, any person.

9 The hearing and powers of court

On hearing an interim relief application the court may in addition to its powers under the Model Law to make an order granting interim relief under article 19 of the Model Law—
(a) dismiss the application;
(b) adjourn the hearing conditionally or unconditionally;
(c) make any other order which the court thinks appropriate.

10 Application for relief under article 21 of the Model Law—affidavit in support

An article 21 relief application must be supported by an affidavit sworn by the foreign representative stating—
(a) the grounds on which it is proposed that the relief applied for should be granted;
(b) an estimate of the value of the assets of the debtor in England and Wales in respect of which relief is applied for;
(c) in the case of an application by a foreign representative who is or believes that he is a representative of a foreign non-main proceeding, the reasons why the applicant believes that the relief relates to assets that, under the law of Great Britain, should be administered in the foreign non-main proceeding or concerns information required in that proceeding;
(d) whether, to the best of the knowledge and belief of the foreign representative, the interests of the debtor's creditors (including any secured creditors or parties to hire-purchase agreements) and any other interested parties, including if appropriate the debtor, will be adequately protected; and
(e) all other matters that in the opinion of the foreign representative will assist the court in deciding whether or not it is appropriate to grant the relief applied for.

11 The hearing and powers of court

On hearing an article 21 relief application the court may in addition to its powers under the Model Law to make an order granting relief under article 21 of the Model Law—
(a) dismiss the application;
(b) adjourn the hearing conditionally or unconditionally;
(c) make any other order which the court thinks appropriate.

PART 4
REPLACEMENT OF FOREIGN REPRESENTATIVE

[3.314]

12 Application for confirmation of status of replacement foreign representative

(1) This paragraph applies where following the making of a recognition order the foreign representative dies or for any other reason ceases to be the foreign representative in the foreign proceeding in relation to the debtor.

(2) In this paragraph "the former foreign representative" shall mean the foreign representative referred to in sub-paragraph (1).

(3) If a person has succeeded the former foreign representative or is otherwise holding office as foreign representative in the foreign proceeding in relation to the debtor, that person may apply to the court for an order confirming his status as replacement foreign representative for the purpose of proceedings under these Regulations.

13 Contents of application and affidavit in support

(1) An application under paragraph 12(3) shall in addition to the matters required to be stated by paragraph 19(2) state the following matters—
(a) the name of the replacement foreign representative and his address for service within England and Wales;
(b) details of the circumstances in which the former foreign representative ceased to be foreign representative in the foreign proceeding in relation to the debtor (including the date on which he ceased to be the foreign representative);
(c) details of his own appointment as replacement foreign representative in the foreign proceeding (including the date of that appointment).

(2) The application shall be accompanied by an affidavit in support sworn by the applicant which shall contain or have attached to it—
(a) a certificate from the foreign court affirming—
  (i) the cessation of the appointment of the former foreign representative as foreign representative; and
  (ii) the appointment of the applicant as the foreign representative in the foreign proceeding; or
(b) in the absence of such a certificate, any other evidence acceptable to the court of the matters referred to in paragraph (a); and

(c) a translation in English of any document exhibited to the affidavit which is in a language other than English.

(3) All translations referred to in paragraph (c) must be certified by the translator as a correct translation.

14 The hearing and powers of court

(1) On hearing an application under paragraph 12(3) the court may—

(a) make an order confirming the status of the replacement foreign representative as foreign representative for the purpose of proceedings under these Regulations;
(b) dismiss the application;
(c) adjourn the hearing conditionally or unconditionally;
(d) make an interim order;
(e) make any other order which the court thinks appropriate, including in particular an order making such provision as the court thinks fit with respect to matters arising in connection with the replacement of the foreign representative.

(2) If the court dismisses the application, it may also if it thinks fit make an order terminating recognition of the foreign proceeding and—

(a) such an order may include such provision as the court thinks fit with respect to matters arising in connection with the termination; and
(b) paragraph 15 shall not apply to such an order.

PART 5
REVIEWS OF COURT ORDERS

[3.315]

15 Reviews of court orders—where court makes order of its own motion

(1) The court shall not of its own motion make a modification or termination order unless the foreign representative and the debtor have either—

(a) had an opportunity of being heard on the question; or
(b) consented in writing to such an order.

(2) Where the foreign representative or the debtor desires to be heard on the question of such an order, the court shall give all relevant parties notice of a venue at which the question will be considered and may give directions as to the issues on which it requires evidence.

(3) For the purposes of sub-paragraph (2), all relevant parties means the foreign representative, the debtor and any other person who appears to the court to have an interest justifying his being given notice of the hearing.

(4) If the court makes a modification or termination order, the order may include such provision as the court thinks fit with respect to matters arising in connection with the modification or termination.

16 Review application—affidavit in support

A review application must be supported by an affidavit sworn by the applicant stating—

(a) the grounds on which it is proposed that the relief applied for should be granted;
(b) whether, to the best of the knowledge and belief of the applicant, the interests of the debtor's creditors (including any secured creditors or parties to hire-purchase agreements) and any other interested parties, including if appropriate the debtor, will be adequately protected; and
(c) all other matters that in the opinion of the applicant will assist the court in deciding whether or not it is appropriate to grant the relief applied for.

17 Hearing of review application and powers of the court

On hearing a review application, the court may in addition to its powers under the Model Law to make a modification or termination order—

(a) dismiss the application;
(b) adjourn the hearing conditionally or unconditionally;
(c) make an interim order;
(c) make any other order which the court thinks appropriate, including an order making such provision as the court thinks fit with respect to matters arising in connection with the modification or termination.

PART 6
COURT PROCEDURE AND PRACTICE WITH REGARD TO PRINCIPAL APPLICATIONS AND ORDERS

[3.316]

18 Preliminary and interpretation

(1) This Part applies to—

(a) any of the following applications made to the court under these Regulations—
   (i) a recognition application;
   (ii) an article 21 relief application;
   (iii) an application under paragraph 12(3) for an order confirming the status of a replacement foreign representative;
   (iv) a review application; and
(b) any of the following orders made by the court under these Regulations—

(i) a recognition order;
(ii) an order granting interim relief under article 19 of the Model Law;
(iii) an order granting relief under article 21 of the Model Law;
(iv) an order confirming the status of a replacement foreign representative; and
(v) a modification or termination order.

19 Form and contents of application

(1) Subject to sub-paragraph (4) every application to which this Part applies shall be an ordinary application and shall be in Form ML5.

(2) Each application shall be in writing and shall state—
(a) the names of the parties;
(b) the nature of the relief or order applied for or the directions sought from the court;
(c) the names and addresses of the persons (if any) on whom it is intended to serve the application;
(d) the names and addresses of all those persons on whom these Regulations require the application to be served (so far as known to the applicant); and
(e) the applicant's address for service.

(3) The application must be signed by the applicant if he is acting in person, or, when he is not so acting, by or on behalf of his solicitor.

(4) This paragraph does not apply to a recognition application.

20 Filing of application

(1) The application (and all supporting documents) shall be filed with the court, with a sufficient number of copies for service and use as provided by paragraph 21(2).

(2) Each of the copies filed shall have applied to it the seal of the court and be issued to the applicant; and on each copy there shall be endorsed the date and time of filing.

(3) The court shall fix a venue for the hearing of the application and this also shall be endorsed on each copy of the application issued under sub-paragraph (2).

21 Service of the application

(1) In sub-paragraph (2), references to the application are to a sealed copy of the application issued by the court together with any affidavit in support of it and any documents exhibited to the affidavit.

(2) Unless the court otherwise directs, the application shall be served on the following persons, unless they are the applicant—
(a) on the foreign representative;
(b) on the debtor;
(c) if a British insolvency officeholder is acting in relation to the debtor, on him;
(d) if any person has been appointed an administrative receiver of the debtor or, to the knowledge of the foreign representative, as a receiver or manager of the property of the debtor in England and Wales, on him;
(e) if a member State liquidator has been appointed in main proceedings in relation to the debtor, on him;
(f) if to the knowledge of the foreign representative a foreign representative has been appointed in any other foreign proceeding regarding the debtor, on him;
(g) if there is pending in England and Wales a petition for the winding up or bankruptcy of the debtor, on the petitioner;
(h) on any person who to the knowledge of the foreign representative is or may be entitled to appoint an administrator of the debtor under paragraph 14 of Schedule B1 to the 1986 Act (appointment of administrator by holder of qualifying floating charge); . . .
[(i) if the debtor is a debtor who is of interest to the Financial Conduct Authority, on that Authority; and
(j) if the debtor is a debtor who is of interest to the Prudential Regulation Authority, on that Authority.]

22 Manner in which service to be effected

(1) Service of the application in accordance with paragraph 21(2) shall be effected by the applicant, or his solicitor, or by a person instructed by him or his solicitor, not less than 5 business days before the date fixed for the hearing.

(2) Service shall be effected by delivering the documents to a person's proper address or in such other manner as the court may direct.

(3) A person's proper address is any which he has previously notified as his address for service within England and Wales; but if he has not notified any such address or if for any reason service at such address is not practicable, service may be effected as follows—
(a) (subject to sub-paragraph (4)) in the case of a company incorporated in England and Wales, by delivery to its registered office;
(b) in the case of any other person, by delivery to his usual or last known address or principal place of business in Great Britain.

(4) If delivery to a company's registered office is not practicable, service may be effected by delivery to its last known principal place of business in Great Britain.

(5) Delivery of documents to any place or address may be made by leaving them there or sending them by first class post in accordance with the provisions of paragraphs 70 and 75(1).

23 Proof of service

(1) Service of the application shall be verified by an affidavit of service in Form ML6, specifying the date on which, and the manner in which, service was effected.

(2) The affidavit of service, with a sealed copy of the application exhibited to it, shall be filed with the court as soon as reasonably practicable after service, and in any event not less than 1 business day before the hearing of the application.

24 In case of urgency

Where the case is one of urgency, the court may (without prejudice to its general power to extend or abridge time limits)—

(a) hear the application immediately, either with or without notice to, or the attendance of, other parties; or

(b) authorise a shorter period of service than that provided for by paragraph 22(1),

and any such application may be heard on terms providing for the filing or service of documents, or the carrying out of other formalities, as the court thinks fit.

25 The hearing

(1) At the hearing of the application, the applicant and any of the following persons (not being the applicant) may appear or be represented—

(a) the foreign representative;

(b) the debtor and, in the case of any debtor other than an individual, any one or more directors or other officers of the debtor, including—

[(i) where applicable, any person specified in particulars registered under section 1046 of the Companies Act 2006 (overseas companies) as authorised to represent the debtor;]

(ii) in the case of a debtor which is a partnership, any person who is an officer of the partnership within the meaning of article 2 of the Insolvent Partnerships Order 1994;

(c) if a British insolvency officeholder is acting in relation to the debtor, that person;

(d) if any person has been appointed an administrative receiver of the debtor or as a receiver or manager of the property of the debtor in England and Wales, that person;

(e) if a member State liquidator has been appointed in main proceedings in relation to the debtor, that person;

(f) if a foreign representative has been appointed in any other foreign proceeding regarding the debtor, that person;

(g) any person who has presented a petition for the winding up or bankruptcy of the debtor in England and Wales;

(h) any person who is or may be entitled to appoint an administrator of the debtor under paragraph 14 of Schedule B1 to the 1986 Act (appointment of administrator by holder of qualifying floating charge);

[(i) if the debtor is a debtor who is of interest to the Financial Conduct Authority, that Authority;

(ia) if the debtor is a debtor who is of interest to the Prudential Regulation Authority, that Authority; and]

(j) with the permission of the court, any other person who appears to have an interest justifying his appearance.

26 Notification and advertisement of order

(1) If the court makes any of the orders referred to in paragraph 18(1)(b), it shall as soon as reasonably practicable send two sealed copies of the order to the foreign representative.

(2) The foreign representative shall send a sealed copy of the order as soon as reasonably practicable to the debtor.

(3) The foreign representative shall, as soon as reasonably practicable after the date of the order give notice of the making of the order—

(a) if a British insolvency officeholder is acting in relation to the debtor, to him;

(b) if any person has been appointed an administrative receiver of the debtor or, to the knowledge of the foreign representative, as a receiver or manager of the property of the debtor, to him;

(c) if a member State liquidator has been appointed in main proceedings in relation to the debtor, to him;

(d) if to his knowledge a foreign representative has been appointed in any other foreign proceeding regarding the debtor, that person;

(e) if there is pending in England and Wales a petition for the winding up or bankruptcy of the debtor, to the petitioner;

(f) to any person who to his knowledge is or may be entitled to appoint an administrator of the debtor under paragraph 14 of Schedule B1 to the 1986 Act (appointment of administrator by holder of qualifying floating charge);

[(g) if the debtor is a debtor who is of interest to the Financial Conduct Authority, to that Authority;

(ga) if the debtor is a debtor who is of interest to the Prudential Regulation Authority, to that Authority;]

(h) to such other persons as the court may direct.

(4) In the case of an order recognising a foreign proceeding in relation to the debtor as a foreign main proceeding, or an order under article 19 or 21 of the Model Law staying execution, distress or other legal process against the debtor's assets, the foreign representative shall also, as soon as reasonably practicable after the date of the order give notice of the making of the order—

(a) to any enforcement officer or other officer who to his knowledge is charged with an execution or other legal process against the debtor or its property; and

(b) to any person who to his knowledge is distraining against the debtor or its property.

(5) In the application of sub-paragraphs (3) and (4) the references to property shall be taken as references to property situated within England and Wales.

(6) Where the debtor is a relevant company, the foreign representative shall send notice of the making of the order to the registrar of companies before the end of the period of 5 business days beginning with the date of the order. The notice to the registrar of companies shall be in Form ML7.

(7) The foreign representative shall advertise the making of the following orders once in the Gazette and once in such newspaper as he thinks most appropriate for ensuring that the making of the order comes to the notice of the debtor's creditors—

(a) a recognition order;

(b) an order confirming the status of a replacement foreign representative; and

(c) a modification or termination order which modifies or terminates recognition of a foreign proceeding,

and the advertisement shall be in Form ML8.

27 Adjournment of hearing; directions

(1) This paragraph applies in any case where the court exercises its power to adjourn the hearing of the application.

(2) The court may at any time give such directions as it thinks fit as to—

(a) service or notice of the application on or to any person, whether in connection with the venue of a resumed hearing or for any other purpose;

(b) the procedure on the application;

(c) the manner in which any evidence is to be adduced at a resumed hearing and in particular as to—

(i) the taking of evidence wholly or in part by affidavit or orally;

(ii) the cross-examination on the hearing in court or in chambers, of any deponents to affidavits;

(d) the matters to be dealt with in evidence.

NOTES

Para 21: in sub-para (2) word omitted revoked, and paras (i), (j) substituted by the Financial Services Act 2012 (Consequential Amendments and Transitional Provisions) Order 2013, SI 2013/472, art 3, Sch 2, para 116(a)(ii).

Para 25: sub-para (1)(b)(i) substituted by the Companies Act 2006 (Consequential Amendments, Transitional Provisions and Savings) Order 2009, SI 2009/1941, art 2(1), Sch 1, para 264(1), (3)(c); sub-para (1)(i), (ia) substituted by SI 2013/472, art 3, Sch 2, para 116(a)(iii).

Para 26: sub-para (3)(g), (ga) substituted by SI 2013/472, art 3, Sch 2, para 116(a)(iv).

PART 7
APPLICATIONS TO THE CHIEF LAND REGISTRAR

[3.317]

28 Applications to Chief Land Registrar following court orders

(1) Where the court makes any order in proceedings under these Regulations which is capable of giving rise to an application or applications under the Land Registration Act 2002, the foreign representative shall, as soon as reasonably practicable after the making of the order or at the appropriate time, make the appropriate application or applications to the Chief Land Registrar.

(2) In sub-paragraph (1) an appropriate application is—

(a) in any case where—

(i) a recognition order in respect of a foreign main proceeding or an order suspending the right to transfer, encumber or otherwise dispose of any assets of the debtor is made, and

(ii) the debtor is the registered proprietor of a registered estate or registered charge and holds it for his sole benefit,

an application under section 43 of the Land Registration Act 2002 for a restriction of the kind referred to in sub-paragraph (3) to be entered in the relevant registered title; and

(b) in any other case, an application under the Land Registration Act 2002 for such an entry in the register as shall be necessary to reflect the effect of the court order under these Regulations.

(3) The restriction referred to in sub-paragraph (2)(a) is a restriction to the effect that no disposition of the registered estate or registered charge (as appropriate) by the registered proprietor of that estate or charge is to be completed by registration within the meaning of section 27 of the Land Registration Act 2002 except under a further order of the court.

PART 8
MISFEASANCE

[3.318]

29 Misfeasance by foreign representative

(1) The court may examine the conduct of a person who—

(a) is or purports to be the foreign representative in relation to a debtor; or

(b) has been or has purported to be the foreign representative in relation to a debtor.

(2) An examination under this paragraph may be held only on the application of—
(a) a British insolvency officeholder acting in relation to the debtor;
(b) a creditor of the debtor; or
(c) with the permission of the court, any other person who appears to have an interest justifying an application.

(3) An application under sub-paragraph (2) must allege that the foreign representative—
(a) has misapplied or retained money or other property of the debtor;
(b) has become accountable for money or other property of the debtor;
(c) has breached a fiduciary or other duty in relation to the debtor; or
(d) has been guilty of misfeasance.

(4) On an examination under this paragraph into a person's conduct the court may order him—
(a) to repay, restore or account for money or property;
(b) to pay interest;
(c) to contribute a sum to the debtor's property by way of compensation for breach of duty or misfeasance.

(4) In sub-paragraph (3) "foreign representative" includes a person who purports or has purported to be a foreign representative in relation to a debtor.

PART 9
GENERAL PROVISION AS TO COURT PROCEDURE AND PRACTICE

[3.319]
30 Principal court rules and practice to apply with modifications

(1) The CPR and the practice and procedure of the High Court (including any practice direction) shall apply to proceedings under these Regulations in the High Court with such modifications as may be necessary for the purpose of giving effect to the provisions of these Regulations and in the case of any conflict between any provision of the CPR and the provisions of these Regulations, the latter shall prevail.

(2) All proceedings under these Regulations shall be allocated to the multi-track for which CPR Part 29 (the multi-track) makes provision, and accordingly those provisions of the CPR which provide for allocation questionnaires and track allocation shall not apply.

31 Applications other than the principal applications—preliminary

Paragraphs 32 to 37 of this Part apply to any application made to the court under these Regulations, except any of the applications referred to in paragraph 18(1)(a).

32 Form and contents of application

(1) Every application shall be in the form appropriate to the application concerned. Forms ML4 and ML5 shall be used for an originating application and an ordinary application respectively under these Regulations.

(2) Each application shall be in writing and shall state—
(a) the names of the parties;
(b) the nature of the relief or order applied for or the directions sought from the court;
(c) the names and addresses of the persons (if any) on whom it is intended to serve the application or that no person is intended to be served;
(d) where these Regulations require that notice of the application is to be given to specified persons, the names and addresses of all those persons (so far as known to the applicant); and
(e) the applicant's address for service.

(3) An originating application shall set out the grounds on which the applicant claims to be entitled to the relief or order sought.

(4) The application must be signed by the applicant if he is acting in person or, when he is not so acting, by or on behalf of his solicitor.

33 Filing and service of application

(1) The application shall be filed in court, accompanied by one copy and a number of additional copies equal to the number of persons who are to be served with the application.

(2) Subject as follows in this paragraph and in paragraph 34, or unless the court otherwise orders, upon the presentation of the documents mentioned in sub-paragraph (1), the court shall fix a venue for the application to be heard.

(3) Unless the court otherwise directs, the applicant shall serve a sealed copy of the application, endorsed with the venue of the hearing, on the respondent named in the application (or on each respondent if more than one).

(4) The court may give any of the following directions—
(a) that the application be served upon persons other than those specified by the relevant provision of these Regulations;
(b) that the giving of notice to any person may be dispensed with;
(c) that notice be given in some way other than that specified in sub-paragraph (3).

(5) Subject to sub-paragraph (6), the application must be served at least 10 business days before the date fixed for the hearing.

(6) Where the case is one of urgency, the court may (without prejudice to its general power to extend or abridge time limits)—

(a) hear the application immediately, either with or without notice to, or the attendance of, other parties; or

(b) authorise a shorter period of service than that provided for by sub-paragraph (5);

and any such application may be heard on terms providing for the filing or service of documents, or the carrying out of other formalities, as the court thinks fit.

34 Other hearings *ex parte*

(1) Where the relevant provisions of these Regulations do not require service of the application on, or notice of it to be given to, any person, the court may hear the application *ex parte*.

(2) Where the application is properly made *ex parte*, the court may hear it forthwith, without fixing a venue as required by paragraph 33(2).

(3) Alternatively, the court may fix a venue for the application to be heard, in which case paragraph 33 applies (so far as relevant).

35 Use of affidavit evidence

(1) In any proceedings evidence may be given by affidavit unless the court otherwise directs; but the court may, on the application of any party, order the attendance for cross-examination of the person making the affidavit.

(2) Where, after such an order has been made, the person in question does not attend, his affidavit shall not be used in evidence without the permission of the court.

36 Filing and service of affidavits

(1) Unless the court otherwise allows—

(a) if the applicant intends to rely at the first hearing on affidavit evidence, he shall file the affidavit or affidavits (if more than one) in court and serve a copy or copies on the respondent, not less than 10 business days before the date fixed for the hearing; and

(b) where a respondent to an application intends to oppose it and to rely for that purpose on affidavit evidence, he shall file the affidavit or affidavits (if more than one) in court and serve a copy or copies on the applicant, not less than 5 business days before the date fixed for the hearing.

(2) Any affidavit may be sworn by the applicant or by the respondent or by some other person possessing direct knowledge of the subject matter of the application.

37 Adjournment of hearings; directions

The court may adjourn the hearing of an application on such terms (if any) as it thinks fit and in the case of such an adjournment paragraph 27(2) shall apply.

38 Transfer of proceedings within the High Court

(1) The High Court may, having regard to the criteria in CPR rule 30.3(2), order proceedings in the Royal Courts of Justice or a district registry, or any part of such proceedings (such as an application made in the proceedings), to be transferred—

(a) from the Royal Courts of Justice to a district registry; or

(b) from a district registry to the Royal Courts of Justice or to another district registry.

(2) The High Court may order proceedings before a district registry for the detailed assessment of costs to be transferred to another district registry if it is satisfied that the proceedings could be more conveniently or fairly taken in that other district registry.

(3) An application for an order under sub-paragraph (1) or (2) must, if the claim is proceeding in a district registry, be made to that registry.

(4) A transfer of proceedings under this paragraph may be ordered—

(a) by the court of its own motion; or

(b) on the application of a person appearing to the court to have an interest in the proceedings.

(5) Where the court orders proceedings to be transferred, the court from which they are to be transferred must give notice of the transfer to all the parties.

(6) An order made before the transfer of the proceedings shall not be affected by the order to transfer.

39 Transfer of proceedings—actions to avoid acts detrimental to creditors

(1) If—

(a) in accordance with article 23(6) of the Model Law, the court grants a foreign representative permission to make an application in accordance with paragraph 1 of that article; and

(b) the relevant proceedings under British insolvency law taking place regarding the debtor are taking place in the county court,

the court may also order those proceedings to be transferred to the High Court.

(2) Where the court makes an order transferring proceedings under sub-paragraph (1)—

(a) it shall send sealed copies of the order to the county court from which the proceedings are to be transferred, and to the official receivers attached to that court and the High Court respectively; and

(b) the county court shall send the file of the proceedings to the High Court.

(3) Following compliance with this paragraph, if the official receiver attached to the court to which the proceedings are transferred is not already, by virtue of directions given by the Secretary of State under section 399(6)(a) of the 1986 Act, the official receiver in relation to those proceedings, he becomes, in relation to those proceedings, the official receiver in place of the official receiver attached to the other court concerned.

40 Shorthand writers

(1) The judge may in writing nominate one or more persons to be official shorthand writers to the court.

(2) The court may, at any time in the course of proceedings under these Regulations, appoint a shorthand writer to take down the evidence of a person examined in pursuance of a court order under article 19 or 21 of the Model Law.

(3) The remuneration of a shorthand writer appointed in proceedings under these Regulations shall be paid by the party at whose instance the appointment was made or otherwise as the court may direct.

(4) Any question arising as to the rates of remuneration payable under this paragraph shall be determined by the court in its discretion.

41 Enforcement procedures

In any proceedings under these Regulations, orders of the court may be enforced in the same manner as a judgment to the same effect.

42 Title of proceedings

(1) Every proceeding under these Regulations shall, with any necessary additions, be intituled "IN THE MATTER OF . . . (naming the debtor to which the proceedings relate) AND IN THE MATTER OF THE CROSS-BORDER INSOLVENCY REGULATIONS 2006".

(2) Sub-paragraph (1) shall not apply in respect of any form prescribed under these Regulations.

43 Court records

The court shall keep records of all proceedings under these Regulations, and shall cause to be entered in the records the taking of any step in the proceedings, and such decisions of the court in relation thereto, as the court thinks fit.

44 Inspection of records

(1) Subject as follows, the court's records of proceedings under these Regulations shall be open to inspection by any person.

(2) If in the case of a person applying to inspect the records the Registrar is not satisfied as to the propriety of the purpose for which inspection is required, he may refuse to allow it. That person may then apply forthwith and *ex parte* to the judge, who may refuse the inspection or allow it on such terms as he thinks fit.

(3) The decision of the judge under sub-paragraph (2) is final.

45 File of court proceedings

(1) In respect of all proceedings under these Regulations, the court shall open and maintain a file for each case; and (subject to directions of the Registrar) all documents relating to such proceedings shall be placed on the relevant file.

(2) No proceedings under these Regulations shall be filed in the Central Office of the High Court.

46 Right to inspect the file

(1) In the case of any proceedings under these Regulations, the following have the right, at all reasonable times, to inspect the court's file of the proceedings—

- (a) the Secretary of State;
- (b) the person who is the foreign representative in relation to the proceedings;
- (c) if a foreign representative has been appointed in any other foreign proceeding regarding the debtor to which the proceedings under these Regulations relate, that person;
- (d) if a British insolvency officeholder is acting in relation to the debtor to which the proceedings under these Regulations relate, that person;
- (e) any person stating himself in writing to be a creditor of the debtor to which the proceedings under these Regulations relate;
- (f) if a member State liquidator has been appointed in relation to the debtor to which the proceedings under these Regulations relate, that person; and
- (g) the debtor to which the proceedings under these Regulations relate, or, if that debtor is a company, corporation or partnership, every person who is, or at any time has been—
  - (i) a director or officer of the debtor;
  - (ii) a member of the debtor; or
  - [(iii) where applicable, any person specified in particulars registered under section 1046 of the Companies Act 2006 (overseas companies) as authorised to represent the debtor.]

(2) The right of inspection conferred as above on any person may be exercised on his behalf by a person properly authorised by him.

(3) Any person may, by leave of the court, inspect the file.

(4) The right of inspection conferred by this paragraph is not exercisable in the case of documents, or parts of documents, as to which the court directs (either generally or specially) that they are not to be made open to inspection without the court's permission.

An application for a direction of the court under this sub-paragraph may be made by the foreign representative or by any party appearing to the court to have an interest.

(5) If, for the purpose of powers conferred by the 1986 Act or the Rules, the Secretary of State or the official receiver wishes to inspect the file of any proceedings under these Regulations, and requests the transmission of the file, the court shall comply with such request (unless the file is for the time being in use for the court's purposes).

(6) Paragraph 44(2) and (3) apply in respect of the court's file of any proceedings under these Regulations as they apply in respect of court records.

(7) Where these Regulations confer a right for any person to inspect documents on the court's file of proceedings, the right includes that of taking copies of those documents on payment of the fee chargeable under any order made under section 92 of the Courts Act 2003.

47 Copies of court orders

(1) In any proceedings under these Regulations, any person who under paragraph 46 has a right to inspect documents on the court file also has the right to require the foreign representative in relation to those proceedings to furnish him with a copy of any court order in the proceedings.

(2) Sub-paragraph (1) does not apply if a copy of the court order has been served on that person or notice of the making of the order has been given to that person under other provisions of these Regulations.

48 Filing of Gazette notices and advertisements

(1) In any court in which proceedings under these Regulations are pending, an officer of the court shall file a copy of every issue of the Gazette which contains an advertisement relating to those proceedings.

(2) Where there appears in a newspaper an advertisement relating to proceedings under these Regulations pending in any court, the person inserting the advertisement shall file a copy of it in that court.

The copy of the advertisement shall be accompanied by, or have endorsed on it, such particulars as are necessary to identify the proceedings and the date of the advertisement's appearance.

(3) An officer of any court in which proceedings under these Regulations are pending shall from time to time file a memorandum giving the dates of, and other particulars relating to, any notice published in the Gazette, and any newspaper advertisements, which relate to proceedings so pending.

The officer's memorandum is prima facie evidence that any notice or advertisement mentioned in it was duly inserted in the issue of the newspaper or the Gazette which is specified in the memorandum.

49 Persons incapable of managing their affairs—introductory

(1) Paragraphs 50 to 52 apply where in proceedings under these Regulations it appears to the court that a person affected by the proceedings is one who is incapable of managing and administering his property and affairs either—

(a) by reason of mental disorder within the meaning of the Mental Health Act 1983; or
(b) due to physical affliction or disability.

(2) The person concerned is referred to as "the incapacitated person".

50 Appointment of another person to act

(1) The court may appoint such person as it thinks fit to appear for, represent or act for the incapacitated person.

(2) The appointment may be made either generally or for the purpose of any particular application or proceeding, or for the exercise of particular rights or powers which the incapacitated person might have exercised but for his incapacity.

(3) The court may make the appointment either of its own motion or on application by—

(a) a person who has been appointed by a court in the United Kingdom or elsewhere to manage the affairs of, or to represent, the incapacitated person; or
(b) any relative or friend of the incapacitated person who appears to the court to be a proper person to make the application; or
(c) in any case where the incapacitated person is the debtor, the foreign representative.

(4) Application under sub-paragraph (3) may be made *ex parte*; but the court may require such notice of the application as it thinks necessary to be given to the person alleged to be incapacitated, or any other person, and may adjourn the hearing of the application to enable the notice to be given.

51 Affidavit in support of application

An application under paragraph 50(3) shall be supported by an affidavit of a registered medical practitioner as to the mental or physical condition of the incapacitated person.

52 Service of notices following appointment

Any notice served on, or sent to, a person appointed under paragraph 50 has the same effect as if it had been served on, or given to, the incapacitated person.

53 Rights of audience

Rights of audience in proceedings under these Regulations are the same as obtain in proceedings under British insolvency law.

54 Right of attendance

(1) Subject as follows, in proceedings under these Regulations, any person stating himself in writing, in records kept by the court for that purpose, to be a creditor of the debtor to which the proceedings relate, is entitled at his own cost, to attend in court or in chambers at any stage of the proceedings.

(2) Attendance may be by the person himself, or his solicitor.

(3) A person so entitled may request the court in writing to give him notice of any step in the proceedings; and, subject to his paying the costs involved and keeping the court informed as to his address, the court shall comply with the request.

(4) If the court is satisfied that the exercise by a person of his rights under this paragraph has given rise to costs for the estate of the debtor which would not otherwise have been incurred and ought not, in the circumstances, to fall on that estate, it may direct that the costs be paid by the person concerned, to an amount specified.

The rights of that person under this paragraph shall be in abeyance so long as those costs are not paid.

(5) The court may appoint one or more persons to represent the creditors of the debtor to have the rights conferred by this paragraph, instead of the rights being exercised by any or all of them individually.

If two or more persons are appointed under this paragraph to represent the same interest, they must (if at all) instruct the same solicitor.

55 Right of attendance for member State liquidator

For the purposes of paragraph 54(1), a member State liquidator appointed in relation to a debtor subject to proceedings under these Regulations shall be deemed to be a creditor.

56 British insolvency officeholder's solicitor

Where in any proceedings the attendance of the British insolvency officeholder's solicitor is required, whether in court or in chambers, the British insolvency officeholder himself need not attend, unless directed by the court.

57 Formal defects

No proceedings under these Regulations shall be invalidated by any formal defect or by any irregularity, unless the court before which objection is made considers that substantial injustice has been caused by the defect or irregularity, and that the injustice cannot be remedied by any order of the court.

58 Restriction on concurrent proceedings and remedies

Where in proceedings under these Regulations the court makes an order staying any action, execution or other legal process against the property of a debtor, service of the order may be effected by sending a sealed copy of the order to whatever is the address for service of the claimant or other party having the carriage of the proceedings to be stayed.

59 Affidavits

(1) Where in proceedings under these Regulations, an affidavit is made by any British insolvency officeholder acting in relation to the debtor, he shall state the capacity in which he makes it, the position which he holds and the address at which he works.

(2) Any officer of the court duly authorised in that behalf, may take affidavits and declarations.

(3) Subject to sub-paragraph (4), where these Regulations provide for the use of an affidavit, a witness statement verified by a statement of truth may be used as an alternative.

(4) Sub-paragraph (3) does not apply to paragraphs 4 (affidavit in support of recognition application), 7 (affidavit in support of interim relief application), 10 (affidavit in support of article 21 relief application), 13 (affidavit in support of application regarding status of replacement foreign representative) and 16 (affidavit in support of review application).

60 Security in court

(1) Where security has to be given to the court (otherwise than in relation to costs), it may be given by guarantee, bond or the payment of money into court.

(2) A person proposing to give a bond as security shall give notice to the party in whose favour the security is required, and to the court, naming those who are to be sureties to the bond.

(3) The court shall forthwith give notice to the parties concerned of a venue for the execution of the bond and the making of any objection to the sureties.

(4) The sureties shall make an affidavit of their sufficiency (unless dispensed with by the party in whose favour the security is required) and shall, if required by the court, attend the court to be cross-examined.

61 Further information and disclosure

(1) Any party to proceedings under these Regulations may apply to the court for an order—

- (a) that any other party—
  - (i) clarify any matter which is in dispute in the proceedings; or
  - (ii) give additional information in relation to any such matter,

  in accordance with CPR Part 18 (further information); or
- (b) to obtain disclosure from any other party in accordance with CPR Part 31 (disclosure and inspection of documents).

(2) An application under this paragraph may be made without notice being served on any other party.

62 Office copies of documents

(1) Any person who has under these Regulations the right to inspect the court file of proceedings may require the court to provide him with an office copy of any document from the file.

(2) A person's right under this paragraph may be exercised on his behalf by his solicitor.

(3) An office copy provided by the court under this paragraph shall be in such form as the Registrar thinks appropriate, and shall bear the court's seal.

63 "The court"

(1) Anything to be done in proceedings under these Regulations by, to or before the court may be done by, to or before a judge of the High Court or a Registrar.

(2) Where these Regulations require or permit the court to perform an act of a formal or administrative character, that act may be performed by a court officer.

NOTES

Para 46: sub-para (1)(g)(iii) substituted by the Companies Act 2006 (Consequential Amendments, Transitional Provisions and Savings) Order 2009, SI 2009/1941, art 2(1), Sch 1, para 264(1), (3)(d).

PART 10
COSTS AND DETAILED ASSESSMENT

[3.320]

64 Requirement to assess costs by the detailed procedure

In any proceedings before the court, the court may order costs to be decided by detailed assessment.

65 Costs of officers charged with execution of writs or other process

(1) Where by virtue of article 20 of the Model Law or a court order under article 19 or 21 of the Model Law an enforcement officer, or other officer, charged with execution of the writ or other process—

(a) is required to deliver up goods or money; or

(b) has deducted costs from the proceeds of an execution or money paid to him,

the foreign representative may require in writing that the amount of the enforcement officer's or other officer's bill of costs be decided by detailed assessment.

(2) Where such a requirement is made, if the enforcement officer or other officer does not commence detailed assessment proceedings within 3 months of the requirement under sub-paragraph (1), or within such further time as the court, on application, may permit, any claim by the enforcement officer or other officer in respect of his costs is forfeited by such failure to commence proceedings.

(3) Where, in the case of a deduction of costs by the enforcement officer or other officer, any amount deducted is disallowed at the conclusion of the detailed assessment proceedings, the enforcement officer or other officer shall forthwith pay a sum equal to that disallowed to the foreign representative for the benefit of the debtor.

66 Final costs certificate

(1) A final costs certificate of the costs officer is final and conclusive as to all matters which have not been objected to in the manner provided for under the rules of the court.

(2) Where it is proved to the satisfaction of a costs officer that a final costs certificate has been lost or destroyed, he may issue a duplicate.

PART 11
APPEALS IN PROCEEDINGS UNDER THESE REGULATIONS

[3.321]

67 Appeals from court orders

(1) An appeal from a decision of a Registrar of the High Court in proceedings under these Regulations lies to a single judge of the High Court; and an appeal from a decision of that judge on such an appeal lies, with the permission of the Court of Appeal, to the Court of Appeal.

(2) An appeal from a decision of a judge of the High Court in proceedings under these Regulations which is not a decision on an appeal made to him under sub-paragraph (1) lies, with the permission of that judge or the Court of Appeal, to the Court of Appeal.

68 Procedure on appeals

(1) Subject as follows, CPR Part 52 (appeals to the Court of Appeal) and its practice direction apply to appeals in proceedings under these Regulations.

(2) The provisions of Part 4 of the practice direction on Insolvency Proceedings supporting CPR Part 49 relating to first appeals (as defined in that Part) apply in relation to any appeal to a single judge of the High Court under paragraph 67, with any necessary modifications.

(3) In proceedings under these Regulations, the procedure under CPR Part 52 is by ordinary application and not by appeal notice.

PART 12
GENERAL

[3.322]
69 Notices

(1) All notices required or authorised by or under these Regulations to be given must be in writing, unless it is otherwise provided, or the court allows the notice to be given in some other way.

(2) Where in proceedings under these Regulations a notice is required to be sent or given by any person, the sending or giving of it may be proved by means of a certificate by that person that he posted the notice, or instructed another person (naming him) to do so.

(3) A certificate under this paragraph may be endorsed on a copy or specimen of the notice to which it relates.

70 "Give notice" etc

(1) A reference in these Regulations to giving notice, or to delivering, sending or serving any document, means that the notice or document may be sent by post.

(2) Subject to paragraph 75, any form of post may be used.

(3) Personal service of a document is permissible in all cases.

(4) Notice of the venue fixed for an application may be given by service of the sealed copy of the application under paragraph 33(3).

71 Notice, etc to solicitors

Where in proceedings under these Regulations a notice or other document is required or authorised to be given to a person, it may, if he has indicated that his solicitor is authorised to accept service on his behalf, be given instead to the solicitor.

72 Notice to joint British insolvency officeholders

Where two or more persons are acting jointly as the British insolvency officeholder in proceedings under British insolvency law, delivery of a document to one of them is to be treated as delivery to them all.

73 Forms for use in proceedings under these Regulations

(1) The forms contained in Schedule 5 to these Regulations shall be used in, and in connection with, proceedings under these Regulations.

(2) The forms shall be used with such variations, if any, as the circumstances may require.

74 Time limits

(1) The provisions of CPR Rule 2.8 (time) apply, as regards computation of time, to anything required or authorised to be done by these Regulations.

(2) The provisions of CPR rule 3.1(2)(a) (the court's general powers of management) apply so as to enable the court to extend or shorten the time for compliance with anything required or authorised to be done by these Regulations.

75 Service by post

(1) For a document to be properly served by post, it must be contained in an envelope addressed to the person on whom service is to be effected, and pre-paid for first class post.

(2) A document to be served by post may be sent to the last known address of the person to be served.

(3) Where first class post is used, the document is treated as served on the second business day after the date of posting, unless the contrary is shown.

(4) The date of posting is presumed, unless the contrary is shown, to be the date shown in the post-mark on the envelope in which the document is contained.

76 General provisions as to service and notice

Subject to paragraphs 22, 75 and 77, CPR Part 6 (service of documents) applies as regards any matter relating to the service of documents and the giving of notice in proceedings under these Regulations.

77 Service outside the jurisdiction

(1) Sections III and IV of CPR Part 6 (service out of the jurisdiction and service of process of foreign court) do not apply in proceedings under these Regulations.

(2) Where for the purposes of proceedings under these Regulations any process or order of the court, or other document, is required to be served on a person who is not in England and Wales, the court may order service to be effected within such time, on such person, at such place and in such manner as it thinks fit, and may also require such proof of service as it thinks fit.

(3) An application under this paragraph shall be supported by an affidavit stating—

(a) the grounds on which the application is made; and

(b) in what place or country the person to be served is, or probably may be found.

78 False claim of status as creditor

(1) Rule 12.18 (false claim of status as creditor, etc) shall apply with any necessary modifications in any case where a person falsely claims the status of a creditor of a debtor, with the intention of obtaining a sight of documents whether on the court's file or in the hands of the foreign representative or other person, which he has not under these Regulations any right to inspect.

(2) Rule 21.21 and Schedule 5 of the Rules shall apply to an offence under Rule 12.18 as applied by sub-paragraph (1) as they apply to an offence under Rule 12.18.

79 The Gazette

(1) A copy of the Gazette containing any notice required by these Regulations to be gazetted is evidence of any fact stated in the notice.

(2) In the case of an order of the court notice of which is required by these Regulations to be gazetted, a copy of the Gazette containing the notice may in any proceedings be produced as conclusive evidence that the order was made on the date specified in the notice.

SCHEDULE 3
PROCEDURAL MATTERS IN SCOTLAND

Regulation 5

PART 1
INTERPRETATION

[3.323]

1 Interpretation

(1) In this Schedule—

"the 1986 Act" means the Insolvency Act 1986;

"article 21 remedy application" means an application to the court by a foreign representative under article 21(1) or (2) of the Model Law for remedy;

"business day" means any day other than a Saturday, a Sunday, Christmas Day, Good Friday or a day which is a bank holiday in Scotland under or by virtue of the Banking and Financial Dealings Act 1971;

"the Gazette" means the Edinburgh Gazette;

"main proceedings" means proceedings opened in accordance with Article 3(1) of the [EU Insolvency Regulation] and falling within the definition of insolvency proceedings in [Article 2(4)] of the [EU Insolvency Regulation];

["member State liquidator" means a person falling within the definition of "insolvency practitioner" in Article 2(5) of the EU Insolvency Regulation appointed in proceedings to which the Regulation applies in a member State other than the United Kingdom;]

"the Model Law" means the UNCITRAL Model Law as set out in Schedule 1 to these Regulations;

"modification or termination order" means an order by the court pursuant to its powers under the Model Law modifying or terminating recognition of a foreign proceeding, the sist, restraint or suspension referred to in article 20(1) or any part of it or any remedy granted under article 19 or 21 of the Model Law;

"recognition application" means an application to the court by a foreign representative in accordance with article 15 of the Model Law for an order recognising the foreign proceeding in which he has been appointed;

"recognition order" means an order by the court recognising a proceeding the subject of a recognition application as a foreign main proceeding or foreign non-main proceeding, as appropriate;

["relevant company" means a company that is—

(a) registered under the Companies Act 2006,

(b) subject to a requirement imposed by regulations under section 1043 of that Act (unregistered UK companies) to deliver any documents to the registrar of companies, or

(c) subject to a requirement imposed by regulations under section 1046 of that Act (overseas companies) to deliver any documents to the registrar of companies;]

"review application" means an application to the court for a modification or termination order.

(2) Expressions defined in the Model Law have the same meaning when used in this Schedule.

[(3) References in this Schedule to a debtor who is of interest to the Financial Conduct Authority are references to a debtor who—

(a) is, or has been, an authorised person within the meaning of the Financial Services and Markets Act 2000;

(b) is, or has been, an appointed representative within the meaning of section 39 of the Financial Services and Markets Act 2000; or

(c) is carrying on, or has carried on, a regulated activity in contravention of the general prohibition.

(3A) References in this Schedule to a debtor who is of interest to the Prudential Regulation Authority are references to a debtor who—

(a) is, or has been, a PRA-authorised person within the meaning of the Financial Services and Markets Act 2000; or

(b) is carrying on, or has carried on, a PRA-regulated activity within the meaning of the Financial Services and Markets Act 2000 in contravention of the general prohibition.]

(4) In [sub-paragraphs (3) and (3A)] "the general prohibition" has the meaning given by section 19 of the Financial Services and Markets Act 2000 and the reference to a "regulated activity" must be construed in accordance with—

(a) section 22 of that Act (classes of regulated activity and categories of investment);

(b) any relevant order under that section; and

(c) Schedule 2 to that Act (regulated activities).

(5) References in this Schedule to a numbered form are to the form that bears that number in Schedule 5.

NOTES

Para 1: in sub-para (1) definition "relevant company" substituted by the Companies Act 2006 (Consequential Amendments, Transitional Provisions and Savings) Order 2009, SI 2009/1941, art 2(1), Sch 1, para 264(1), (4)(a); sub-paras (3), (3A) substituted and words in square brackets in sub-para (4) substituted by the Financial Services Act 2012 (Consequential Amendments and Transitional Provisions) Order 2013, SI 2013/472, art 3, Sch 2, para 116(b)(i).

In sub-para (1) in the definition of "main proceedings" words in first and third pairs of square brackets substituted for original words "EC Insolvency Regulation" and words in second pair of square brackets substituted for original words "Article 2(a)" and definition "member state liquidator" substituted, by the Insolvency Amendment (EU 2015/848) Regulations 2017, SI 2017/702, regs 2, 3, Schedule, Pt 6, para 94(1), (4), as from 26 June 2017, except in relation to proceedings opened before that date. The definition "member state liquidator" previously read as follows:

""member State liquidator" means a person falling within the definition of liquidator in Article 2(b) of the EC Insolvency Regulation appointed in proceedings to which it applies in a member State other than the United Kingdom;".

PART 2
THE FOREIGN REPRESENTATIVE

[3.324]

2 Application for confirmation of status of replacement foreign representative

(1) This paragraph applies where following the making of a recognition order the foreign representative dies or for any other reason ceases to be the foreign representative in the foreign proceedings in relation to the debtor.

(2) In this paragraph "the former foreign representative" means the foreign representative referred to in sub-paragraph (1).

(3) If a person has succeeded the former foreign representative or is otherwise holding office as foreign representative in the foreign proceeding in relation to the debtor, that person may apply to the court for an order confirming his status as replacement foreign representative for the purpose of proceedings under these Regulations.

(4) If the court dismisses an application under sub-paragraph (3) then it may also, if it thinks fit, make an order terminating recognition of the foreign proceeding and—

(a) such an order may include such provision as the court thinks fit with respect to matters arising in connection with the termination; and

(b) paragraph 5 shall not apply to such an order.

3 Misfeasance by a foreign representative

(1) The court may examine the conduct of a person who—

(a) is or purports to be the foreign representative in relation to a debtor, or

(b) has been or has purported to be the foreign representative in relation to a debtor.

(2) An examination under this paragraph may be held only on the application of—

(a) a British insolvency officeholder acting in relation to the debtor,

(b) a creditor of the debtor, or

(c) with the permission of the court, any other person who appears to have an interest justifying an application.

(3) An application under sub-paragraph (2) must allege that the foreign representative—

(a) has misapplied or retained money or other property of the debtor,

(b) has become accountable for money or other property of the debtor,

(c) has breached a fiduciary duty or other duty in relation to the debtor, or

(d) has been guilty of misfeasance.

(4) On an examination under this paragraph into a person's conduct the court may order him—

(a) to repay, restore or account for money or property;

(b) to pay interest;

(c) to contribute a sum to the debtor's property by way of compensation for breach of duty or misfeasance.

(5) In sub-paragraph (3), "foreign representative" includes a person who purports or has purported to be a foreign representative in relation to a debtor.

PART 3
COURT PROCEDURE AND PRACTICE

[3.325]

4 Preliminary and interpretation

(1) This Part applies to—

(a) any of the following applications made to the court under these Regulations—

(i) a recognition application;
(ii) an article 21 remedy application;
(iii) an application under paragraph 2(3) for an order confirming the status of a replacement foreign representative;
(iv) a review application; and

(b) any of the following orders made by the court under these Regulations—
(i) a recognition order;
(ii) an order granting interim remedy under article 19 of the Model Law;
(iii) an order granting remedy under article 21 of the Model Law;
(iv) an order confirming the status of a replacement foreign representative; or
(v) a modification or termination order.

5 Reviews of court orders—where court makes order of its own motion

(1) The court shall not of its own motion make a modification or termination order unless the foreign representative and the debtor have either—

(a) had an opportunity of being heard on the question, or
(b) consented in writing to such an order.

(2) If the court makes a modification or termination order, the order may include such provision as the court thinks fit with respect to matters arising in connection with the modification or termination.

6 The hearing

(1) At the hearing of the application, the applicant and any of the following persons (not being the applicant) may appear or be represented—

(a) the foreign representative;
(b) the debtor and, in the case of any debtor other than an individual, any one or more directors or other officers of the debtor, including—
[(i) where applicable, any person specified in particulars registered under section 1046 of the Companies Act 2006 (overseas companies) as authorised to represent the debtor;]
(ii) in the case of a debtor which is a partnership, any person who is a member of the partnership;
(c) if a British insolvency officeholder is acting in relation to the debtor, that person;
(d) if any person has been appointed an administrative receiver of the debtor or as a receiver or manager of the property of the debtor, that person;
(e) if a member State liquidator has been appointed in main proceedings in relation to the debtor, that person;
(f) if a foreign representative has been appointed in any other foreign proceeding regarding the debtor, that person;
(g) any person who has presented a petition for the winding up or sequestration of the debtor in Scotland;
(h) any person who is or may be entitled to appoint an administrator of the debtor under paragraph 14 of Schedule B1 to the 1986 Act (appointment of administrator by holder of qualifying floating charge);
[(i) if the debtor is a debtor who is of interest to the Financial Conduct Authority, that Authority;
(ia) if the debtor is a debtor who is of interest to the Prudential Regulation Authority, that Authority; and]
(j) with the permission of the court, any other person who appears to have an interest justifying his appearance.

7 Notification and advertisement of order

(1) This paragraph applies where the court makes any of the orders referred to in paragraph 4(1)(b).

(2) The foreign representative shall send a certified copy of the interlocutor as soon as reasonably practicable to the debtor.

(3) The foreign representative shall, as soon as reasonably practicable after the date of the order, give notice of the making of the order—

(a) if a British insolvency officeholder is acting in relation to the debtor, to him;
(b) if any person has been appointed an administrative receiver of the debtor or, to the knowledge of the foreign representative, as a receiver or manager of the property of the debtor, to him;
(c) if a member State liquidator has been appointed in main proceedings in relation to the debtor, to him;
(d) if to his knowledge a foreign representative has been appointed in any other foreign proceeding regarding the debtor, that person;
(e) if there is pending in Scotland a petition for the winding up or sequestration of the debtor, to the petitioner;
(f) to any person who to his knowledge is or may be entitled to appoint an administrator of the debtor under paragraph 14 of Schedule B1 to the 1986 Act (appointment of administrator by holder of qualifying floating charge);
[(g) if the debtor is a debtor who is of interest to the Financial Conduct Authority, to that Authority;
(ga) if the debtor is a debtor who is of interest to the Prudential Regulation Authority, to that Authority; and]
(h) to such persons as the court may direct.

(4) Where the debtor is a relevant company, the foreign representative shall send notice of the making of the order to the registrar of companies before the end of the period of 5 business days beginning with the date of the order. The notice to the registrar of companies shall be in Form ML7.

(5) The foreign representative shall advertise the making of the following orders once in the Gazette and once in such newspaper as he thinks most appropriate for ensuring that the making of the order comes to the notice of the debtor's creditors—

(a) a recognition order,
(b) an order confirming the status of a replacement foreign representative, and
(c) a modification or termination order which modifies or terminates recognition of a foreign proceeding,

and the advertisement shall be in Form ML8.

8 Registration of court order

(1) Where the court makes a recognition order in respect of a foreign main proceeding or an order suspending the right to transfer, encumber or otherwise dispose of any assets of the debtor being heritable property, the clerk of the court shall send forthwith a certified copy of the order to the keeper of the register of inhibitions and adjudications for recording in that register.

(2) Recording under sub-paragraph (1) or (3) shall have the effect as from the date of the order of an inhibition and of a citation in an adjudication of the debtor's heritable estate at the instance of the foreign representative.

(3) Where the court makes a modification or termination order, the clerk of the court shall send forthwith a certified copy of the order to the keeper of the register of inhibitions and adjudications for recording in that register.

(4) The effect mentioned in sub-paragraph (2) shall expire—

(a) on the recording of a modification or termination order under sub-paragraph (3); or
(b) subject to sub-paragraph (5), if the effect has not expired by virtue of paragraph (a), at the end of the period of 3 years beginning with the date of the order.

(5) The foreign representative may, if recognition of the foreign proceeding has not been modified or terminated by the court pursuant to its powers under the Model Law, before the end of the period of 3 years mentioned in sub-paragraph (4)(b), send a memorandum in a form prescribed by the Court of Session by act of sederunt to the keeper of the register of inhibitions and adjudications for recording in that register, and such recording shall renew the effect mentioned in sub-paragraph (2); and thereafter the said effect shall continue to be preserved only if such memorandum is so recorded before the expiry of every subsequent period of 3 years.

9 Right to inspect court process

(1) In the case of any proceedings under these Regulations, the following have the right, at all reasonable times, to inspect the court process of the proceedings—

(a) the Secretary of State;
(b) the person who is the foreign representative in relation to the proceedings;
(c) if a foreign representative has been appointed in any other foreign proceeding regarding the debtor, that person;
(d) if a British insolvency officeholder is acting in relation to the debtor, that person;
(e) any person stating himself in writing to be a creditor of the debtor to which the proceedings under these Regulations relate;
(f) if a member State liquidator has been appointed in relation to a debtor which is subject to proceedings under these Regulations, that person; and
(g) the debtor to which the proceedings under these Regulations relate, or, if that debtor is a company, corporation or partnership, every person who is, or at any time has been—
    (i) a director or officer of the debtor,
    (ii) a member of the debtor, or
    [(iii) where applicable, any person specified in particulars registered under section 1046 of the Companies Act 2006 (overseas companies) as authorised to represent the debtor;]

(2) The right of inspection conferred as above on any person may be exercised on his behalf by a person properly authorised by him.

10 Copies of court orders

(1) In any proceedings under these Regulations, any person who under paragraph 9 has a right to inspect documents in the court process also has the right to require the foreign representative in relation to those proceedings to furnish him with a copy of any court order in the proceedings.

(2) Sub-paragraph (1) does not apply if a copy of the court order has been served on that person or notice of the making of the order has been given to that person under other provisions of these Regulations.

11 Transfer of proceedings—actions to avoid acts detrimental to creditors

If, in accordance with article 23(6) of the Model Law, the court grants a foreign representative permission to make an application in accordance with paragraph (1) of that article, it may also order the relevant proceedings under British insolvency law taking place regarding the debtor to be transferred to the Court of Session if those proceedings are taking place in Scotland and are not already in that court.

NOTES

Para 6: sub-para (1)(b)(i) substituted by the Companies Act 2006 (Consequential Amendments, Transitional Provisions and Savings) Order 2009, SI 2009/1941, art 2(1), Sch 1, para 264(1), (4)(b); sub-paras (1)(i), (ia) substituted by the Financial Services Act 2012 (Consequential Amendments and Transitional Provisions) Order 2013, SI 2013/472, art 3, Sch 2, para 116(b)(ii).

Para 7: sub-paras (7)(g), (ga) substituted by the Financial Services Act 2012 (Consequential Amendments and Transitional Provisions) Order 2013, SI 2013/472, art 3, Sch 2, para 116(b)(iii).

Para 9: sub-para (1)(g)(iii) substituted by SI 2009/1941, art 2(1), Sch 1, para 264(1), (4)(c).

PART 3
GENERAL

[3.326]
12 Giving of notices, etc

(1) All notices required or authorised by or under these Regulations to be given, sent or delivered must be in writing, unless it is otherwise provided, or the court allows the notice to be sent or given in some other way.

(2) Any reference in these Regulations to giving, sending or delivering a notice or any such document means, without prejudice to any other way and unless it is otherwise provided, that the notice or document may be sent by post, and that, subject to paragraph 13, any form of post may be used. Personal service of the notice or document is permissible in all cases.

(3) Where under these Regulations a notice or other document is required or authorised to be given, sent or delivered by a person ("the sender") to another ("the recipient"), it may be given, sent or delivered by any person duly authorised by the sender to do so to any person duly authorised by the recipient to receive or accept it.

(4) Where two or more persons are acting jointly as the British insolvency officeholder in proceedings under British insolvency law, the giving, sending or delivering of a notice or document to one of them is to be treated as the giving, sending or delivering of a notice or document to each or all.

13 Sending by post

(1) For a document to be properly sent by post, it must be contained in an envelope addressed to the person to whom it is to be sent, and pre-paid for either first or second class post.

(2) Any document to be sent by post may be sent to the last known address of the person to whom the document is to be sent.

(3) Where first class post is used, the document is to be deemed to be received on the second business day after the date of posting, unless the contrary is shown.

(4) Where second class post is used, the document is to be deemed to be received on the fourth business day after the date of posting, unless the contrary is shown.

14 Certificate of giving notice, etc

(1) Where in any proceedings under these Regulations a notice or document is required to be given, sent or delivered by any person, the date of giving, sending or delivery of it may be proved by means of a certificate by that person that he gave, posted or otherwise sent or delivered the notice or document on the date stated in the certificate, or that he instructed another person (naming him) to do so.

(2) A certificate under this paragraph may be endorsed on a copy of the notice to which it relates.

(3) A certificate purporting to be signed by or on behalf of the person mentioned in sub-paragraph (1) shall be deemed, unless the contrary is shown, to be sufficient evidence of the matters stated therein.

15 Forms for use in proceedings under these Regulations

(1) Forms ML7 and ML8 contained in Schedule 5 to these Regulations shall be used in, and in connection with, proceedings under these Regulations.

(2) The forms shall be used with such variations, if any, as the circumstances may require.

SCHEDULE 4
NOTICES DELIVERED TO THE REGISTRAR OF COMPANIES

Regulation 6

[3.327]
1 Interpretation

(1) In this Schedule—

. . .

"electronic communication" means the same as in the Electronic Communications Act 2000;

"Model Law notice" means a notice delivered to the registrar of companies under paragraph 26(6) of Schedule 2 or paragraph 7(4) of Schedule 3.

(2) Expressions defined in the Model Law or Schedule 2 or 3, as appropriate, have the same meaning when used in this Schedule.

(3) References in this Schedule to delivering a notice include sending, forwarding, producing or giving it.

2 Functions of the registrar of companies

(1) Where a Model Law notice is delivered to the registrar of companies in respect of a relevant company, the registrar shall enter a note in the register relating to that company.

(2) The note referred to in sub-paragraph (1) shall contain the following particulars, in each case as stated in the notice delivered to the registrar—

- (a) brief details of the court order made;
- (b) the date of the court order; and
- (c) the name and address for service of the person who is the foreign representative in relation to the company.

3 . . .

4 Delivery to registrar of notices

(1) Electronic communications may be used for the delivery of any Model Law notice, provided that such delivery is in such form and manner as is directed by the registrar.

(2) Where the Model Law notice is required to be signed, it shall instead be authenticated in such manner as is directed by the registrar.

(3) If a Model Law notice is delivered to the registrar which does not comply with the requirements of these Regulations, he may serve on the person by whom the notice was delivered (or, if there are two or more such persons, on any of them) a notice (a non-compliance notice) indicating the respect in which the Model Law notice does not comply.

(4) Where the registrar serves a non-compliance notice, then, unless a replacement Model Law notice—

- (a) is delivered to him within 14 days after the service of the non-compliance notice, and
- (b) complies with the requirements of these Regulations or is not rejected by him for failure to comply with those requirements,

the original Model Law notice shall be deemed not to have been delivered to him.

5 Enforcement of foreign representative's duty to give notice to registrar

(1) If a foreign representative, having made default in complying with paragraph 26(6) of Schedule 2 or paragraph 7(4) of Schedule 3 fails to make good the default within 14 days after the service of a notice on the foreign representative requiring him to do so, the court may, on an application made to it by any creditor, member, director or other officer of the debtor or by the registrar of companies, make an order directing the foreign representative to make good the default within such time as may be specified in the order.

(2) The court's order may provide that all costs of and incidental to the application shall be borne by the foreign representative.

6 Rectification of the register under court order

(1) The registrar shall remove from the register any note, or part of a note—

- (a) that relates to or is derived from a court order that the court has declared to be invalid or ineffective, or
- (b) that the court declares to be factually inaccurate or derived from something that is factually inaccurate or forged,

and that the court directs should be removed from the register.

(2) The court order must specify what is to be removed from the register and indicate where on the register it is and the registrar shall carry out his duty under sub-paragraph (1) within a reasonable time of receipt by him of the relevant court order.

NOTES

Para 1: definition "the 1985 Act" omitted from sub-para (1) revoked by the Companies Act 2006 (Consequential Amendments, Transitional Provisions and Savings) Order 2009, SI 2009/1941, art 2(1), Sch 1, para 264(1), (5)(a).

Para 3: revoked by SI 2009/1941, art 2(1), Sch 1, para 264(1), (5)(b).

SCHEDULE 5
FORMS

Sch 2, para 73 and Sch 3, para 15

[3.328]

NOTES

The forms themselves are not reproduced in this work, but their numbers and descriptions are listed below.

FORM NO	*TITLE*
ML1	Recognition application
ML2	Recognition order
ML3	Statement of subsequent information
ML4	Originating application
ML5	Ordinary application
ML6	Affidavit of service of application under the Cross-Border Insolvency Regulations 2006

FORM NO	TITLE
ML7	Notice to registrar of companies of order under the Cross-Border Insolvency Regulations 2006
ML8	Notice of order under the Cross-Border Insolvency Regulations 2006 (for newspaper and London or Edinburgh Gazette)

NOTES

Forms ML1, ML7: amended by the Companies Act 2006 (Consequential Amendments, Transitional Provisions and Savings) Order 2009, SI 2009/1941, art 2(1), Sch 1, para 264(1), (6).

Form ML6: amended by the Financial Services Act 2012 (Consequential Amendments and Transitional Provisions) Order 2013, SI 2013/472, art 3, Sch 2, para 116(c).

EUROPEAN PARLIAMENT AND COUNCIL REGULATION

(1082/2006/EC)

of 5 July 2006

on a European grouping of territorial cooperation (EGTC)

[3.329]

NOTES

Date of publication in OJ: OJ L210, 31.07.2006, p 19.

This Regulation came into force on 1 August 2006; see Art 18 at **[3.339]**.

THE EUROPEAN PARLIAMENT AND THE COUNCIL OF THE EUROPEAN UNION,

Having regard to the Treaty establishing the European Community, and in particular the third subparagraph of Article 159 thereof,

Having regard to the proposal from the Commission,

Having regard to the opinion of the European Economic and Social Committee,[1]

Having regard to the opinion of the Committee of the Regions,[2]

Acting in accordance with the procedure laid down in Article 251 of the Treaty,[3]

Whereas:

(1) The third subparagraph of Article 159 of the Treaty provides for specific actions to be decided upon outside the Funds which are the subject of the first subparagraph of that Article, in order to achieve the objective of social and economic cohesion envisaged by the Treaty. The harmonious development of the entire Community territory and greater economic, social and territorial cohesion imply the strengthening of territorial cooperation. To this end it is appropriate to adopt the measures necessary to improve the implementation conditions for actions of territorial cooperation.

(2) Measures are necessary to reduce the significant difficulties encountered by Member States and, in particular, by regional and local authorities in implementing and managing actions of territorial cooperation within the framework of differing national laws and procedures.

(3) Taking into account notably the increase in the number of land and maritime borders in the Community following its enlargement, it is necessary to facilitate the reinforcement of territorial cooperation in the Community.

(4) The existing instruments, such as the European economic interest grouping, have proven ill-adapted to organising structured cooperation under the INTERREG initiative during the 2000–2006 programming period.

(5) The Council of Europe acquis provides different opportunities and frameworks within which regional and local authorities can cooperate across borders. This instrument is not intended to circumvent those frameworks or provide a set of specific common rules which would uniformly govern all such arrangements throughout the Community.

(6) Council Regulation (EC) No 1083/2006 of 11 July 2006 laying down general provisions on the European Regional Development Fund, the European Social Fund and the Cohesion Fund[4] increases the means in support of European territorial cooperation.

(7) It is likewise necessary to facilitate and follow up the implementation of territorial cooperation actions without a financial contribution from the Community.

(8) In order to overcome the obstacles hindering territorial cooperation, it is necessary to institute a cooperation instrument at Community level for the creation of cooperative groupings in Community territory, invested with legal personality, called "European groupings of territorial cooperation" (EGTC). Recourse to an EGTC should be optional.

(9) It is appropriate for an EGTC to be given the capacity to act on behalf of its members, and notably the regional and local authorities of which it is composed.

(10) The tasks and competencies of an EGTC are to be set out in a convention.

(11) An EGTC should be able to act, either for the purpose of implementing territorial cooperation

programmes or projects co-financed by the Community, notably under the Structural Funds in conformity with Regulation (EC) No 1083/2006 and Regulation (EC) No 1080/2006 of the European Parliament and of the Council of 5 July 2006 on the European Regional Development Fund,[5] or for the purpose of carrying out actions of territorial cooperation which are at the sole initiative of the Member States and their regional and local authorities with or without a financial contribution from the Community.

(12) It should be specified that the financial responsibility of regional and local authorities, as well as that of Member States, with regard to the management of both Community funds and national funds, is not affected by the formation of an EGTC.

(13) It should be specified that the powers exercised by regional and local authorities as public authorities, notably police and regulatory powers, cannot be the subject of a convention.

(14) It is necessary for an EGTC to establish its statutes and equip itself with its own organs, as well as rules for its budget and for the exercise of its financial responsibility.

(15) The conditions for territorial cooperation should be created in accordance with the subsidiarity principle enshrined in Article 5 of the Treaty. In accordance with the principle of proportionality, as set out in that Article, this Regulation does not go beyond what is necessary in order to achieve its objectives, recourse to an EGTC being optional, in accordance with the constitutional system of each Member State.

(16) The third subparagraph of Article 159 of the Treaty does not allow the inclusion of entities from third countries in legislation based on that provision. The adoption of a Community measure allowing the creation of an EGTC should not, however, exclude the possibility of entities from third countries participating in an EGTC formed in accordance with this Regulation where the legislation of a third country or agreements between Member States and third countries so allow,

NOTES

1 OJ C255, 14.10.2005, p 76.

2 OJ C71, 22.3.2005, p 46.

3 Opinion of the European Parliament of 6 July 2005 (not yet published in the Official Journal), Council Common Position of 12 June 2006 (not yet published in the Official Journal) and Position of the European Parliament of 4 July 2006 (not yet published in the Official Journal).

4 See page 25 of this Official Journal.

5 See page 1 of this Official Journal.

HAVE ADOPTED THIS REGULATION—

[3.330]
Article 1
Nature of an EGTC

[1. A European grouping of territorial cooperation ("EGTC") may be established on Union territory under the conditions and subject to the arrangements provided for by this Regulation.

2. The objective of an EGTC shall be to facilitate and promote, in particular, territorial cooperation, including one or more of the cross-border, transnational and interregional strands of cooperation, between its members as set out in Article 3(1), with the aim of strengthening Union economic, social and territorial cohesion.]

3. An EGTC shall have legal personality.

4. An EGTC shall have in each Member State the most extensive legal capacity accorded to legal persons under that Member State's national law. It may, in particular, acquire or dispose of movable and immovable property and employ staff and may be a party to legal proceedings.

[5. The registered office of an EGTC shall be located in a Member State under whose law at least one of the EGTC's members is established.]

NOTES

Paras 1, 2: substituted by European Parliament and Council Regulation 1302/2013/EU, Art 1(1)(a), subject to transitional provisions in Art 2 thereof as noted below, and originally read as follows:

> "1. A European grouping of territorial cooperation, hereinafter referred to as "EGTC", may be established on Community territory under the conditions and subject to the arrangements provided for by this Regulation.
>
> 2. The objective of an EGTC shall be to facilitate and promote cross-border, transnational and/or interregional cooperation, hereinafter referred to as "territorial cooperation", between its members as set out in Article 3(1), with the exclusive aim of strengthening economic and social cohesion.".

Para 5: added by European Parliament and Council Regulation 1302/2013/EU, Art 1(1)(b), subject to transitional provisions in Art 2 thereof as noted below.

Transitional provisions: European Parliament and Council Regulation 1302/2013/EU, Art 2 provides as follows:

> **"Article 2 Transitional provisions**
>
> 1. EGTCs established before 21 December 2013 shall not be obliged to align their convention and statutes with the provisions of Regulation (EC) No 1082/2006 as amended by this Regulation.
>
> 2. In the case of EGTCs, for which a procedure under Article 4 of Regulation (EC) No 1082/2006 was started before 22 June 2014 and for which only the registration or publication under Article 5 of Regulation (EC) No 1082/2006 is outstanding, the convention and the statutes shall be registered or published, or both, in accordance with the provisions of Regulation (EC) No 1082/2006 before its amendment by this Regulation.
>
> 3. EGTCs for which a procedure under Article 4 of Regulation (EC) No 1082/2006 was started more than six months before 22 June 2014 shall be approved in accordance with the provisions of Regulation (EC) No 1082/2006 before its amendment by this Regulation.

4. EGTCs other than those under paragraphs 2 and 3 of this Article for which a procedure under Article 4 of Regulation (EC) No 1082/2006 was started before 22 June 2014 shall be approved in accordance with the provisions of Regulation (EC) No 1082/2006 as amended by this Regulation.

5. Member States shall submit to the Commission the necessary amendments to the national provisions adopted in accordance with Article 16(1) of Regulation (EC) No 1082/2006 as amended by this Regulation no later than 22 June 2014.".

[3.331]
Article 2
Applicable law

[1. The acts of the organs of an EGTC shall be governed by the following:

(a) this Regulation;

(b) the convention referred to in Article 8, where it is expressly authorised under this Regulation to do so; and

(c) in the case of matters not, or only partly, regulated under this Regulation, the national law of the Member State where the EGTC has its registered office.

Where it is necessary to determine the applicable law under Union law or private international law, an EGTC shall be considered to be an entity of the Member State where it has its registered office.]

[1A. The activities of an EGTC relating to carrying out tasks, referred to in Article 7(2) and (3), inside the Union shall be governed by applicable Union law and national law as specified in the convention referred to in Article 8.

The activities of an EGTC that are co-financed from the Union budget shall comply with the requirements set out in applicable Union law and the national law relating to the application of that Union law.]

2. Where a Member State comprises several territorial entities which have their own rules of applicable law, the reference to the law applicable under paragraph 1(c) shall include the law of those entities, taking into account the constitutional structure of the Member State concerned.

NOTES

Para 1: substituted by European Parliament and Council Regulation 1302/2013/EU, Art 1(2)(a), subject to transitional provisions in Art 2 thereof, as noted to Art 1 at **[3.330]**, and originally read as follows—

"1. An EGTC shall be governed by the following:

(a) this Regulation;

(b) where expressly authorised by this Regulation, the provisions of the convention and the statutes referred to in Articles 8 and 9;

(c) in the case of matters not, or only partly, regulated by this Regulation, the laws of the Member State where the EGTC has its registered office.

Where it is necessary under Community or international private law to establish the choice of law which governs an EGTC's acts, an EGTC shall be treated as an entity of the Member State where it has its registered office.".

Para 1A: inserted by European Parliament and Council Regulation 1302/2013/EU, Art 1(2)(b), subject to transitional provisions in Art 2 thereof, as noted to Art 1 at **[3.330]**.

[3.332]
Article 3
Composition of an EGTC

[1. The following entities may become members of an EGTC:

(a) Member States or authorities at national level;

(b) regional authorities;

(c) local authorities;

(d) public undertakings within the meaning of point (b) of Article 2(1) of Directive 2004/17/EC of the European Parliament and of the Council[1] or bodies governed by public law within the meaning of the second subparagraph of Article 1(9) of Directive 2004/18/EC of the European Parliament and of the Council;[2]

(e) undertakings entrusted with operations of services of general economic interest in compliance with applicable Union and national law;

(f) national, regional or local authorities, or bodies or public undertakings, equivalent to those referred to under points (d) and (e), from third countries, subject to the conditions laid down in Article 3a.]

Associations consisting of bodies belonging to one or more of these categories may also be members.

[2. An EGTC shall be made up of members located on the territory of at least two Member States, except as provided for in Article 3a(2) and (5).]

NOTES

Para 1: first sub-paragraph in square brackets substituted, together with associated footnotes, by European Parliament and Council Regulation 1302/2013/EU, Art 1(3)(a), subject to transitional provisions in Art 2 thereof, as noted to Art 1 at **[3.330]**, and originally read as follows—

"1. An EGTC shall be made up of members, within the limits of their competences under national law, belonging to one or more of the following categories:

(a) Member States;

(b) regional authorities;

(c) local authorities;

(d) bodies governed by public law within the meaning of the second subparagraph of Article 1(9) of Directive 2004/18/EC of the European Parliament and of the Council of 31 March 2004 on the coordination of procedures for the award of public works contracts, public supply contracts and public service contracts.".

Para 2: substituted by European Parliament and Council Regulation 1302/2013/EU, Art 1(3)(b), subject to transitional provisions in Art 2 thereof, as noted to Art 1 at **[3.330]**, and originally read as follows—

"2. An EGTC shall be made up of members located on the territory of at least two Member States.".

[1] Directive 2004/17/EC of the European Parliament and of the Council of 31 March 2004 coordinating the procurement procedures of entities operating in the water, energy, transport and postal services sectors (OJ L134, 30.4.2004, p 1).

[2] Directive 2004/18/EC of the European Parliament and of the Council of 31 March 2004 on the coordination of procedures for the award of public works contracts, public supply contracts and public service contracts (OJ L134, 30.4.2004, p 114).

[3.333]
[Article 3a
Accession of members from third countries or overseas countries or territories (OCTs)

1. In accordance with Article 4(3a), an EGTC may be made up of members located on the territory of at least two Member States and of one or more third countries neighbouring at least one of those Member States, including its outermost regions, where those Member States and third countries jointly carry out territorial cooperation actions or implement programmes supported by the Union.

For the purposes of this Regulation, a third country or an OCT shall be considered to be neighbouring a Member State, including its outermost regions, where the third country or the OCT and that Member State share a common land border or where both the third country or OCT and the Member State are eligible under a joint maritime cross-border or transnational programme under the European territorial cooperation goal, or are eligible under another cross-border, sea-crossing or sea-basin cooperation programme, including where they are separated by international waters.

2. An EGTC may be made up of members located on the territory of only one Member State and of one or more third countries neighbouring that Member State, including its outermost regions, where the Member State concerned considers that EGTC to be consistent with the scope of its territorial cooperation in the context of cross-border or transnational cooperation or bilateral relations with the third countries concerned.

3. For the purposes of paragraphs 1 and 2, third countries neighbouring a Member State, including its outermost regions, include maritime borders between the countries concerned.

4. In accordance with Article 4a and subject to the conditions set out in paragraph 1 of this Article, an EGTC may also be made up of members located on the territory of at least two Member States, including their outermost regions, and of one or more OCTs, with or without members from one or more third countries.

5. In accordance with Article 4a and subject to the conditions set out in paragraph 2 of this Article, an EGTC may also be made up of members located on the territory of only one Member State, including its outermost regions, and of one or more OCTs, with or without members from one or more third countries.

6. An EGTC shall not be set up only between members from a Member State and one or more OCTs linked to that same Member State.]

NOTES

Inserted by European Parliament and Council Regulation 1302/2013/EU, Art 1(4), subject to transitional provisions in Art 2 thereof, as noted to Art 1 at **[3.330]**.

(Arts 4–11 outside the scope of this work.)

[3.334]
Article 12
Liquidation, insolvency, cessation of payments and liability

1. As regards liquidation, insolvency, cessation of payments and similar procedures, an EGTC shall be governed by the laws of the Member State where it has its registered office, unless otherwise provided in paragraphs 2 and 3.

[An EGTC shall be liable for all its debts.]

[2. Without prejudice to paragraph 3, to the extent that the assets of an EGTC are insufficient to meet its liabilities, its members shall be liable for its debts irrespective of the nature of those debts, each member's share being fixed in proportion to its financial contribution. The arrangements for financial contributions shall be fixed in the statutes.

The EGTC's members may provide in the statutes that they are to be liable, after they have ceased to be members of an EGTC, for obligations arising out of activities of the EGTC during their membership.

2A. If the liability of at least one member of an EGTC from a Member State is limited as a result of the national law under which it is established, the other members may also limit their liability in the convention where national law implementing this Regulation enables them to do so.

The name of an EGTC whose members have limited liability shall include the word 'limited'.

The requirements for the publication of the convention, statutes and accounts of an EGTC whose members have limited liability shall be at least equal to those required for other legal entities with limited liability under the laws of the Member State where that EGTC has its registered office.

In the case of an EGTC whose members have limited liability, any Member State concerned may require that the EGTC take out appropriate insurance or that it be subject to a guarantee provided by a bank or other financial institution established in a Member State or that it be covered by a facility provided as a guarantee by a public entity or by a Member State to cover the risks specific to the activities of the EGTC.]

3. Without prejudice to the financial responsibility of Member States in relation to any funding from the Structural and/or Cohesion Funds provided to an EGTC, no financial liability shall arise for Member States on account of this Regulation in relation to an EGTC of which they are not a member.

NOTES

Para 1: words in square brackets added by European Parliament and Council Regulation 1302/2013/EU, Art 1(13)(a), subject to transitional provisions in Art 2 thereof, as noted to Art 1 at **[3.330]**.

Paras 2, 2A: substituted, for the original para 2, by European Parliament and Council Regulation 1302/2013/EU, Art 1(13)(b), subject to transitional provisions in Art 2 thereof, as noted to Art 1 at **[3.330]**. Para 2 originally read as follows—

"2. An EGTC shall be liable for its debts whatever their nature.

To the extent that the assets of an EGTC are insufficient to meet its liabilities, its members shall be liable for the EGTC's debts whatever their nature, each member's share being fixed in proportion to its contribution, unless the national law under which a member is formed excludes or limits the liability of that member. The arrangements for contributions shall be fixed in the statutes.

If the liability of at least one member of an EGTC is limited as a result of the national law under which it is formed, the other members may also limit their liability in the statutes.

The members may provide in the statutes that they will be liable, after they have ceased to be members of an EGTC, for obligations arising out of activities of the EGTC during their membership.

The name of an EGTC whose members have limited liability shall include the word "limited".

Publication of the convention, statutes and accounts of an EGTC whose members have limited liability shall be at least equal to that required for other kinds of legal entity whose members have limited liability, formed under the laws of the Member State where that EGTC has its registered office.

A Member State may prohibit the registration on its territory of an EGTC whose members have limited liability.".

[3.335]
Article 13
Public interest

Where an EGTC carries out any activity in contravention of a Member State's provisions on public policy, public security, public health or public morality, or in contravention of the public interest of a Member State, a competent body of that Member State may prohibit that activity on its territory or require those members which have been formed under its law to withdraw from the EGTC unless the EGTC ceases the activity in question.

Such prohibitions shall not constitute a means of arbitrary or disguised restriction on territorial cooperation between the EGTC's members. Review of the competent body's decision by a judicial authority shall be possible.

[3.336]
Article 14
Dissolution

1. Notwithstanding the provisions on dissolution contained in the convention, on an application by any competent authority with a legitimate interest, the competent court or authority of the Member State where an EGTC has its registered office shall order the EGTC to be wound up if it finds that the EGTC no longer complies with the requirements laid down in Articles 1(2) or 7 or, in particular, that the EGTC is acting outside the confines of the tasks laid down in Article 7. The competent court or authority shall inform all the Member States under whose law the members have been formed of any application to dissolve an EGTC.

2. The competent court or authority may allow the EGTC time to rectify the situation. If the EGTC fails to do so within the time allowed, the competent court or authority shall order it to be wound up.

[3.337]
Article 15
Jurisdiction

1. Third parties who consider themselves wronged by the acts or omissions of an EGTC shall be entitled to pursue their claims by judicial process.

2. [Except where otherwise provided for in this Regulation, Union law on jurisdiction shall apply to disputes involving an EGTC. In any case which is not provided for in such Union law, the competent courts for the resolution of disputes shall be the courts of the Member State where the EGTC has its registered office.]

The competent courts for the resolution of disputes under Article 4(3) or (6) or under Article 13 shall be the courts of the Member State whose decision is challenged.

3. Nothing in this Regulation shall deprive citizens from exercising their national constitutional rights of appeal against public bodies which are members of an EGTC in respect of:

(a) administrative decisions in respect of activities which are being carried out by the EGTC;
(b) access to services in their own language; and
(c) access to information.

In these cases the competent courts shall be those of the Member State under whose constitution the rights of appeal arise.

NOTES

Para 2: words in square brackets substituted by European Parliament and Council Regulation 1302/2013/EU, Art 1(14), subject to transitional provisions in Art 2 thereof, as noted to Art 1 at **[3.330]**, and originally read as follows—

"Except where otherwise provided for in this Regulation, Community legislation on jurisdiction shall apply to disputes involving an EGTC. In any case which is not provided for in such Community legislation, the competent courts for the resolution of disputes shall be the courts of the Member State where the EGTC has its registered office.".

[3.338]
Article 16
Final provisions

[1. Member States shall adopt provisions to ensure the effective application of this Regulation, including with regard to the determination of the competent authorities responsible for the approval procedure, in accordance with their legal and administrative arrangements.

Where required under the terms of a Member State's national law, that Member State may establish a comprehensive list of the tasks which the members of an EGTC within the meaning of Article 3(1) established under its laws already have, as far as territorial cooperation within that Member State is concerned.

The Member State shall submit to the Commission any provisions adopted under this Article, as well as any amendments thereof. The Commission shall transmit those provisions to the other Member States and the Committee of the Regions.]

[1A. The provisions referred to in paragraph 1 insofar as they concern a Member State to which an OCT is linked shall, taking into account the relationship of the Member State with that OCT, also ensure the effective application of this Regulation with regard to that OCT, neighbouring other Member States or outermost regions of those Member States.]

2. Member States may provide for the payment of fees in connection with the registration of the convention and statutes. Those fees may not, however, exceed the administrative cost thereof.

NOTES

Para 1: substituted by European Parliament and Council Regulation 1302/2013/EU, Art 1(15)(a), subject to transitional provisions in Art 2 thereof, as noted to Art 1 at **[3.330]**, and originally read as follows—

"1. Member States shall make such provisions as are appropriate to ensure the effective application of this Regulation.

Where required under the terms of that Member State's national law, a Member State may establish a comprehensive list of the tasks which the members of an EGTC within the meaning of Article 3(1) formed under its laws already have, as far as territorial cooperation within that Member State is concerned.

The Member State shall inform the Commission and the other Member States accordingly of any provisions adopted under this Article.".

Para 1A: inserted by European Parliament and Council Regulation 1302/2013/EU, Art 1(15)(b), subject to transitional provisions in Art 2 thereof, as noted to Art 1 at **[3.330]**.

(Arts 17, 17a outside the scope of this work.)

[3.339]
Article 18
Entry into force

This Regulation shall enter into force on the day following its publication in the Official Journal of the European Union.

It shall apply by 1 August 2007, with the exception of Article 16, which shall apply from 1 August 2006.

This Regulation shall be binding in its entirety and directly applicable in all Member States.

DIRECTIVE OF THE EUROPEAN PARLIAMENT AND OF THE COUNCIL

(2008/94/EC)
of 22 October 2008

on the protection of employees in the event of the insolvency of their employer

(Codified version) Text with EEA relevance

[3.340]

NOTES

Date of publication in OJ: OJ L283, 28.10.2008, p 36.

THE EUROPEAN PARLIAMENT AND THE COUNCIL OF THE EUROPEAN UNION,

Having regard to the Treaty establishing the European Community, and in particular Article 137(2) thereof,

Having regard to the proposal from the Commission,
Having regard to the opinion of the European Economic and Social Committee,[1]
After consultation of the Committee of the Regions,
Acting in accordance with the procedure laid down in Article 251 of the Treaty,[2]
Whereas:

(1) Council Directive 80/987/EEC of 20 October 1980 on the protection of employees in the event of the insolvency of their employer[3] has been substantially amended several times.[4] In the interests of clarity and rationality the said Directive should be codified.

(2) The Community Charter of Fundamental Social Rights for Workers adopted on 9 December 1989 states, in point 7, that the completion of the internal market must lead to an improvement in the living and working conditions of workers in the Community and that this improvement must cover, where necessary, the development of certain aspects of employment regulations such as procedures for collective redundancies and those regarding bankruptcies.

(3) It is necessary to provide for the protection of employees in the event of the insolvency of their employer and to ensure a minimum degree of protection, in particular in order to guarantee payment of their outstanding claims, while taking account of the need for balanced economic and social development in the Community. To this end, the Member States should establish a body which guarantees payment of the outstanding claims of the employees concerned.

(4) In order to ensure equitable protection for the employees concerned, the state of insolvency should be defined in the light of the legislative trends in the Member States and that concept should also include insolvency proceedings other than liquidation. In this context, Member States should, in order to determine the liability of the guarantee institution, be able to lay down that where an insolvency situation results in several insolvency proceedings, the situation is to be treated as a single insolvency procedure.

(5) It should be ensured that the employees referred to in Council Directive 97/81/EC of 15 December 1997 concerning the Framework Agreement on part-time work concluded by UNICE, CEEP and the ETUC,[5] Council Directive 1999/70/EC of 28 June 1999 concerning the framework agreement on fixed-term work concluded by the ETUC, UNICE and CEEP[6] and Council Directive 91/383/EEC of 25 June 1991 supplementing the measures to encourage improvements in the safety and health at work of workers with a fixed-duration employment relationship or a temporary employment relationship[7] are not excluded from the scope of this Directive.

(6) In order to ensure legal certainty for employees in the event of insolvency of undertakings pursuing their activities in a number of Member States, and to strengthen employees' rights in line with the established case-law of the Court of Justice of the European Communities, provisions should be laid down which expressly state which institution is responsible for meeting pay claims in these cases and establish as the aim of cooperation between the competent administrative authorities of the Member States the early settlement of employees' outstanding claims. Furthermore it is necessary to ensure that the relevant arrangements are properly implemented by making provision for collaboration between the competent administrative authorities in the Member States.

(7) Member States may set limitations on the responsibility of the guarantee institutions. Those limitations must be compatible with the social objective of the Directive and may take into account the different levels of claims.

(8) In order to make it easier to identify insolvency proceedings, in particular in situations with a cross-border dimension, provision should be made for the Member States to notify the Commission and the other Member States about the types of insolvency proceedings which give rise to intervention by the guarantee institution.

(9) Since the objective of the action to be taken cannot be sufficiently achieved by the Member States and can therefore be better achieved at Community level, the Community may adopt measures, in accordance with the principle of subsidiarity as set out in Article 5 of the Treaty. In accordance with the principle of proportionality, as set out in that Article, this Directive does not go beyond what is necessary in order to achieve that objective.

(10) The Commission should submit to the European Parliament and the Council a report on the implementation and application of this Directive in particular as regards the new forms of employment emerging in the Member States.

(11) This Directive should be without prejudice to the obligations of the Member States relating to the time-limits for transposition into national law and application of the Directives set out in Annex I, Part C,

NOTES

1 OJ C161, 13.7.2007, p 75.

2 Opinion of the European Parliament of 19 June 2007 (OJ C146 E, 12.6.2008, p 71) and Council Decision of 25 September 2008.

3 OJ L283, 28.10.1980, p 23.

4 See Annex I, Parts A and B.

5 OJ L14, 20.1.1998, p 9.

6 OJ L175, 10.7.1999, p 43.

7 OJ L206, 29.7.1991, p 19.

HAVE ADOPTED THIS DIRECTIVE:

CHAPTER I SCOPE AND DEFINITIONS

[3.341]
Article 1
1. This Directive shall apply to employees' claims arising from contracts of employment or employment relationships and existing against employers who are in a state of insolvency within the meaning of Article 2(1).
2. Member States may, by way of exception, exclude claims by certain categories of employee from the scope of this Directive, by virtue of the existence of other forms of guarantee if it is established that these offer the persons concerned a degree of protection equivalent to that resulting from this Directive.
[3. Where such provision already applies in their national legislation, Member States may continue to exclude domestic servants employed by a natural person from the scope of this Directive.]

NOTES
Para 3: substituted by European Parliament and Council Directive 2015/1794/EU, Art 1.

[3.342]
Article 2
1. For the purposes of this Directive, an employer shall be deemed to be in a state of insolvency where a request has been made for the opening of collective proceedings based on insolvency of the employer, as provided for under the laws, regulations and administrative provisions of a Member State, and involving the partial or total divestment of the employer's assets and the appointment of a liquidator or a person performing a similar task, and the authority which is competent pursuant to the said provisions has:
(a) either decided to open the proceedings; or
(b) established that the employer's undertaking or business has been definitively closed down and that the available assets are insufficient to warrant the opening of the proceedings.
2. This Directive is without prejudice to national law as regards the definition of the terms "employee", "employer", "pay", "right conferring immediate entitlement" and "right conferring prospective entitlement".
However, the Member States may not exclude from the scope of this Directive:
(a) part-time employees within the meaning of Directive 97/81/EC;
(b) employees with a fixed-term contract within the meaning of Directive 1999/70/EC;
(c) employees with a temporary employment relationship within the meaning of Article 1(2) of Directive 91/383/EEC.
3. Member States may not set a minimum duration for the contract of employment or the employment relationship in order for employees to qualify for claims under this Directive.
4. This Directive does not prevent Member States from extending employee protection to other situations of insolvency, for example where payments have been de facto stopped on a permanent basis, established by proceedings different from those mentioned in paragraph 1 as provided for under national law.
Such procedures shall not however create a guarantee obligation for the institutions of the other Member States in the cases referred to in Chapter IV.

CHAPTER II PROVISIONS CONCERNING GUARANTEE INSTITUTIONS

[3.343]
Article 3
Member States shall take the measures necessary to ensure that guarantee institutions guarantee, subject to Article 4, payment of employees' outstanding claims resulting from contracts of employment or employment relationships, including, where provided for by national law, severance pay on termination of employment relationships.
The claims taken over by the guarantee institution shall be the outstanding pay claims relating to a period prior to and/or, as applicable, after a given date determined by the Member States.

[3.344]
Article 4
1. Member States shall have the option to limit the liability of the guarantee institutions referred to in Article 3.
2. If Member States exercise the option referred to in paragraph 1, they shall specify the length of the period for which outstanding claims are to be met by the guarantee institution. However, this may not be shorter than a period covering the remuneration of the last three months of the employment relationship prior to and/or after the date referred to in the second paragraph of Article 3.
Member States may include this minimum period of three months in a reference period with a duration of not less than six months.
Member States having a reference period of not less than 18 months may limit the period for which outstanding claims are met by the guarantee institution to eight weeks. In this case, those periods which are most favourable to the employee shall be used for the calculation of the minimum period.
3. Member States may set ceilings on the payments made by the guarantee institution. These ceilings must not fall below a level which is socially compatible with the social objective of this Directive.
If Member States exercise this option, they shall inform the Commission of the methods used to set the ceiling.

[3.345]
Article 5
Member States shall lay down detailed rules for the organisation, financing and operation of the guarantee institutions, complying with the following principles in particular:
(a) the assets of the institutions must be independent of the employers' operating capital and be inaccessible to proceedings for insolvency;
(b) employers must contribute to financing, unless it is fully covered by the public authorities;
(c) the institutions' liabilities must not depend on whether or not obligations to contribute to financing have been fulfilled.

CHAPTER III PROVISIONS CONCERNING SOCIAL SECURITY

[3.346]
Article 6
Member States may stipulate that Articles 3, 4 and 5 shall not apply to contributions due under national statutory social security schemes or under supplementary occupational or inter-occupational pension schemes outside the national statutory social security schemes.

[3.347]
Article 7
Member States shall take the measures necessary to ensure that non-payment of compulsory contributions due from the employer, before the onset of his insolvency, to their insurance institutions under national statutory social security schemes does not adversely affect employees' benefit entitlement in respect of these insurance institutions in so far as the employees' contributions have been deducted at source from the remuneration paid.

[3.348]
Article 8
Member States shall ensure that the necessary measures are taken to protect the interests of employees and of persons having already left the employer's undertaking or business at the date of the onset of the employer's insolvency in respect of rights conferring on them immediate or prospective entitlement to old-age benefits, including survivors' benefits, under supplementary occupational or inter-occupational pension schemes outside the national statutory social security schemes.

CHAPTER IV PROVISIONS CONCERNING TRANSNATIONAL SITUATIONS

[3.349]
Article 9
1. If an undertaking with activities in the territories of at least two Member States is in a state of insolvency within the meaning of Article 2(l), the institution responsible for meeting employees' outstanding claims shall be that in the Member State in whose territory they work or habitually work.
2. The extent of employees' rights shall be determined by the law governing the competent guarantee institution.
3. Member States shall take the measures necessary to ensure that, in the cases referred to in paragraph 1 of this Article, decisions taken in the context of insolvency proceedings referred to in Article 2(1), which have been requested in another Member State, are taken into account when determining the employer's state of insolvency within the meaning of this Directive.

[3.350]
Article 10
1. For the purposes of implementing Article 9, Member States shall make provision for the sharing of relevant information between their competent administrative authorities and/or the guarantee institutions mentioned in the first paragraph of Article 3, making it possible in particular to inform the guarantee institution responsible for meeting the employees' outstanding claims.
2. Member States shall notify the Commission and the other Member States of the contact details of their competent administrative authorities and/or guarantee institutions. The Commission shall make that information publicly accessible.

CHAPTER V GENERAL AND FINAL PROVISIONS

[3.351]
Article 11
This Directive shall not affect the option of Member States to apply or introduce laws, regulations or administrative provisions which are more favourable to employees.

Implementation of this Directive shall not under any circumstances be sufficient grounds for a regression in relation to the current situation in the Member States and in relation to the general level of protection of employees in the area covered by it.

[3.352]
Article 12
This Directive shall not affect the option of Member States:
(a) to take the measures necessary to avoid abuses;

(b) to refuse or reduce the liability referred to in the first paragraph of Article 3 or the guarantee obligation referred to in Article 7 if it appears that fulfilment of the obligation is unjustifiable because of the existence of special links between the employee and the employer and of common interests resulting in collusion between them;

(c) to refuse or reduce the liability referred to in the first paragraph of Article 3 or the guarantee obligation referred to in Article 7 in cases where the employee, on his or her own or together with his or her close relatives, was the owner of an essential part of the employer's undertaking or business and had a considerable influence on its activities.

[3.353]
Article 13
Member States shall notify the Commission and the other Member States of the types of national insolvency proceedings falling within the scope of this Directive, and of any amendments relating thereto.

The Commission shall publish these communications in the *Official Journal of the European Union*.

[3.354]
Article 14
Member States shall communicate to the Commission the text of the laws, regulations and administrative provisions which they adopt in the field covered by this Directive.

[3.355]
Article 15
By 8 October 2010 at the latest, the Commission shall submit to the European Parliament and to the Council a report on the implementation and application in the Member States of Articles 1 to 4, 9 and 10, Article 11, second paragraph, Article 12, point (c), and Articles 13 and 14.

[3.356]
Article 16
Directive 80/987/EEC, as amended by the acts listed in Annex I, is repealed, without prejudice to the obligations of the Member States relating to the time-limits for transposition into national law and application of the Directives set out in Annex I, Part C.

References to the repealed Directive shall be construed as references to this Directive and shall be read in accordance with the correlation table in Annex II.

[3.357]
Article 17
This Directive shall enter into force on the 20th day following its publication in the *Official Journal of the European Union*.

[3.358]
Article 18
This Directive is addressed to the Member States.

ANNEX I

PART A REPEALED DIRECTIVE WITH ITS SUCCESSIVE AMENDMENTS

(referred to in Article 16)

[3.359]

Council Directive 80/987/EEC	(OJ L283, 28.10.1980, p 23).
Council Directive 87/164/EEC	(OJ L66, 11.3.1987, p 11).
Directive 2002/74/EC of the European Parliament and of the Council	(OJ L270, 8.10.2002, p 10).

PART B NON-REPEALED AMENDING ACT

(referred to in Article 16)

1994 Act of Accession

PART C TIME-LIMITS FOR TRANSPOSITION INTO NATIONAL LAW AND APPLICATION

(referred to in Article 16)

Directive	*Time-limit for transposition*	*Date of application*
80/987/EEC	23 October 1983	
87/164/EEC		1 January 1986
2002/74/EC	7 October 2005	

ANNEX II
CORRELATION TABLE

[3.360]

Directive 80/987/EEC	*This Directive*
Article 1	Article 1
Article 2	Article 2
Article 3	Article 3
Article 4	Article 4
Article 5	Article 5
Article 6	Article 6
Article 7	Article 7
Article 8	Article 8
Article 8a	Article 9
Article 8b	Article 10
Article 9	Article 11
Article 10	Article 12
Article 10a	Article 13
Article 11(1)	—
Article 11(2)	Article 14
Article 12	—
—	Article 15
—	Article 16
—	Article 17
Article 13	Article 18
—	Annex I
—	Annex II

EUROPEAN PARLIAMENT AND COUNCIL DIRECTIVE

(2009/138/EC)

of 25 November 2009

on the taking-up and pursuit of the business of Insurance and Reinsurance (Solvency II)

(recast)

(Text with EEA relevance)

NOTES

Date of publication in OJ: OJ L335, 17.12.2009, p 1.

The Solvency II Directive is implemented in the UK, in part, by the Solvency 2 Regulations 2015, SI 2015/575, the provisions of which fall outside the scope of this work. The remainder of the Solvency II Directive is implemented by the Financial Services and Markets Act 2000 (FSMA), and by rules and individually binding requirements imposed by the Prudential Regulation Authority (PRA) and the Financial Conduct Authority (FCA) under the FSMA. Relevant provisions of the FSMA which implement the Solvency II Directive are included in Part 17 of this work at **[17.177]** et seq.

THE EUROPEAN PARLIAMENT AND THE COUNCIL OF THE EUROPEAN UNION,

Having regard to the Treaty establishing the European Community, and in particular Article 47(2) and Article 55 thereof,

Having regard to the proposal from the Commission,

Having regard to the opinion of the European Economic and Social Committee,[1]

After consulting the Committee of the Regions,

Acting in accordance with the procedure laid down in Article 251 of the Treaty,[2]

Whereas:

(1) A number of substantial changes are to be made to First Council Directive 73/239/EEC of 24 July 1973 on the coordination of laws, regulations and administrative provisions relating to the taking-up and pursuit of the business of direct insurance other than life assurance;[3] Council Directive 78/473/EEC of 30 May 1978 on the coordination of laws, regulations and administrative provisions relating to Community co-insurance;[4] Council Directive 87/344/EEC of 22 June 1987 on the coordination of laws, regulations and administrative provisions relating to legal expenses insurance;[5] Second Council Directive 88/357/EEC of 22 June 1988 on the coordination of laws, regulations and administrative provisions

relating to direct insurance other than life assurance and laying down provisions to facilitate the effective exercise of freedom to provide services;[6] Council Directive 92/49/EEC of 18 June 1992 on the coordination of laws, regulations and administrative provisions relating to direct insurance other than life assurance (third non-life insurance Directive);[7] Directive 98/78/EC of the European Parliament and of the Council of 27 October 1998 on the supplementary supervision of insurance undertakings in an insurance group[8] Directive 2001/17/EC of the European Parliament and of the Council of 19 March 2001 on the reorganisation and winding-up of insurance undertakings;[9] Directive 2002/83/EC of the European Parliament and of the Council of 5 November 2002 concerning life assurance;[10] and Directive 2005/68/EC of the European Parliament and of the Council of 16 November 2005 on reinsurance.[11] In the interests of clarity those Directives should be recast.

(2) In order to facilitate the taking-up and pursuit of the activities of insurance and reinsurance, it is necessary to eliminate the most serious differences between the laws of the Member States as regards the rules to which insurance and reinsurance undertakings are subject. A legal framework should therefore be provided for insurance and reinsurance undertakings to conduct insurance business throughout the internal market thus making it easier for insurance and reinsurance undertakings with head offices in the Community to cover risks and commitments situated therein.

(3) It is in the interests of the proper functioning of the internal market that coordinated rules be established relating to the supervision of insurance groups and, with a view to the protection of creditors, to the reorganisation and winding-up proceedings in respect of insurance undertakings.

(4)–(104) (*Outside the scope of this work*)

(105) All policy holders and beneficiaries should receive equal treatment regardless of their nationality or place of residence. For this purpose, each Member State should ensure that all measures taken by a supervisory authority on the basis of that supervisory authority's national mandate are not regarded as contrary to the interests of that Member State or of policy holders and beneficiaries in that Member State. In all situations of settling of claims and winding-up, assets should be distributed on an equitable basis to all relevant policy holders, regardless of their nationality or place of residence.

(106)–(116) (*Outside the scope of this work*)

(117) Since national legislation concerning reorganisation measures and winding-up proceedings is not harmonised, it is appropriate, in the framework of the internal market, to ensure the mutual recognition of reorganisation measures and winding-up legislation of the Member States concerning insurance undertakings, as well as the necessary cooperation, taking into account the need for unity, universality, coordination and publicity for such measures and the equivalent treatment and protection of insurance creditors.

(118) It should be ensured that reorganisation measures which were adopted by the competent authority of a Member State in order to preserve or restore the financial soundness of an insurance undertaking and to prevent as far as possible a winding-up situation, produce full effects throughout the Community. However, the effects of any such reorganisation measures as well as winding-up proceedings vis-à-vis third countries should not be affected.

(119) A distinction should be made between the competent authorities for the purposes of reorganisation measures and winding-up proceedings and the supervisory authorities of the insurance undertakings.

(120) The definition of a branch for insolvency purposes, should, in accordance with existing insolvency principles, take account of the single legal personality of the insurance undertaking. However, the legislation of the home Member State should determine the manner in which the assets and liabilities held by independent persons who have a permanent authority to act as agent for an insurance undertaking are to be treated in the winding-up of that insurance undertaking.

(121) Conditions should be laid down under which winding-up proceedings which, without being founded on insolvency, involve a priority order for the payment of insurance claims, fall within the scope of this Directive. Claims by the employees of an insurance undertaking arising from employment contracts and employment relationships should be capable of being subrogated to a national wage guarantee scheme. Such subrogated claims should benefit from the treatment determined by the law of the home Member State (lex concursus).

(122) Reorganisation measures do not preclude the opening of winding-up proceedings. Winding-up proceedings should therefore be able to be opened in the absence of, or following, the adoption of reorganisation measures and they may terminate with composition or other analogous measures, including reorganisation measures.

(123) Only the competent authorities of the home Member State should be empowered to take decisions on winding-up proceedings concerning insurance undertakings. The decisions should produce their effects throughout the Community and should be recognised by all Member States. The decisions should be published in accordance with the procedures of the home Member State and in the Official Journal of the European Union. Information should also be made available to known creditors who are resident in the Community, who should have the right to lodge claims and submit observations.

(124) All the assets and liabilities of the insurance undertaking should be taken into consideration in the winding-up proceedings.

(125) All the conditions for the opening, conduct and closure of winding-up proceedings should be governed by the law of the home Member State.

(126) In order to ensure coordinated action amongst the Member States the supervisory authorities of

the home Member State and those of all the other Member States should be informed as a matter of urgency of the opening of winding-up proceedings.

(127) It is of utmost importance that insured persons, policy holders, beneficiaries and any injured party having a direct right of action against the insurance undertaking on a claim arising from insurance operations be protected in winding-up proceedings, it being understood that such protection does not include claims which arise not from obligations under insurance contracts or insurance operations but from civil liability caused by an agent in negotiations for which, according to the law applicable to the insurance contract or operation, the agent is not responsible under such insurance contract or operation. In order to achieve that objective, Member States should be provided with a choice between equivalent methods to ensure special treatment for insurance creditors, none of those methods impeding a Member State from establishing a ranking between different categories of insurance claim. Furthermore, an appropriate balance should be ensured between the protection of insurance creditors and other privileged creditors protected under the legislation of the Member State concerned.

(128) The opening of winding-up proceedings should involve the withdrawal of the authorisation to conduct business granted to the insurance undertaking unless this has already occurred.

(129) Creditors should have the right to lodge claims or to submit written observations in winding-up proceedings. Claims by creditors resident in a Member State other than the home Member State should be treated in the same way as equivalent claims in the home Member State without discrimination on grounds of nationality or residence.

(130) In order to protect legitimate expectations and the certainty of certain transactions in Member States other than the home Member State, it is necessary to determine the law applicable to the effects of reorganisation measures and winding-up proceedings on pending lawsuits and on individual enforcement actions arising from lawsuits.

(131)–(142) (*Outside the scope of this work*)

NOTES

[1] OJ C224, 30.8.2008, p 11.

[2] Opinion of the European Parliament of 22 April 2009 (not yet published in the Official Journal) and Council Decision of 10 November 2009.

[3] OJ L228, 16.8.1973, p 3.

[4] OJ L151, 7.6.1978, p 25.

[5] OJ L185, 4.7.1987, p 77.

[6] OJ L172, 4.7.1988, p 1.

[7] OJ L228, 11.8.1992, p 1.

[8] OJ L330, 5.12.1998, p 1.

[9] OJ L110, 20.4.2001, p 28.

[10] OJ L345, 19.12.2002, p 1.

[11] OJ L323, 9.12.2005, p 1.

HAVE ADOPTED THIS DIRECTIVE:

TITLE I GENERAL RULES ON THE TAKING-UP AND PURSUIT OF DIRECT INSURANCE AND REINSURANCE ACTIVITIES

CHAPTER I SUBJECT MATTER, SCOPE AND DEFINITIONS

SECTION 1
SUBJECT MATTER AND SCOPE

[3.361]
Article 1
Subject matter

This Directive lays down rules concerning the following:

(1) the taking-up and pursuit, within the Community, of the self-employed activities of direct insurance and reinsurance;
(2) the supervision of insurance and reinsurance groups;
(3) the reorganisation and winding-up of direct insurance undertakings.

[3.362]
Article 2
Scope

1. This Directive shall apply to direct life and non-life insurance undertakings which are established in the territory of a Member State or which wish to become established there.

It shall also apply to reinsurance undertakings which conduct only reinsurance activities and which are established in the territory of a Member State or which wish to become established there with the exception of Title IV.

2. In regard to non-life insurance, this Directive shall apply to activities of the classes set out in Part A of Annex I. For the purposes of the first subparagraph of paragraph 1, non-life insurance shall include the activity which consists of assistance provided for persons who get into difficulties while travelling, while

away from their home or their habitual residence. It shall comprise an undertaking, against prior payment of a premium, to make aid immediately available to the beneficiary under an assistance contract where that person is in difficulties following the occurrence of a chance event, in the cases and under the conditions set out in the contract.

The aid may comprise the provision of benefits in cash or in kind. The provision of benefits in kind may also be effected by means of the staff and equipment of the person providing them.

The assistance activity shall not cover servicing, maintenance, after-sales service or the mere indication or provision of aid as an intermediary.

3. In regard to life insurance, this Directive shall apply:

(a) to the following life insurance activities where they are on a contractual basis:
- (i) life insurance which comprises assurance on survival to a stipulated age only, assurance on death only, assurance on survival to a stipulated age or on earlier death, life assurance with return of premiums, marriage assurance, birth assurance;
- (ii) annuities;
- (iii) supplementary insurance underwritten in addition to life insurance, in particular, insurance against personal injury including incapacity for employment, insurance against death resulting from an accident and insurance against disability resulting from an accident or sickness;
- (iv) types of permanent health insurance not subject to cancellation currently existing in Ireland and the United Kingdom;

(b) to the following operations, where they are on a contractual basis, in so far as they are subject to supervision by the authorities responsible for the supervision of private insurance:
- (i) operations whereby associations of subscribers are set up with a view to capitalising their contributions jointly and subsequently distributing the assets thus accumulated among the survivors or among the beneficiaries of the deceased (tontines);
- (ii) capital redemption operations based on actuarial calculation whereby, in return for single or periodic payments agreed in advance, commitments of specified duration and amount are undertaken;
- (iii) management of group pension funds, comprising the management of investments, and in particular the assets representing the reserves of bodies that effect payments on death or survival or in the event of discontinuance or curtailment of activity;
- (iv) the operations referred to in point (iii) where they are accompanied by insurance covering either conservation of capital or payment of a minimum interest;
- (v) the operations carried out by life insurance undertakings such as those referred to in Chapter 1, Title 4 of Book IV of the French 'Code des assurances';

(c) to operations relating to the length of human life which are prescribed by or provided for in social insurance legislation, in so far as they are effected or managed by life insurance undertakings at their own risk in accordance with the laws of a Member State.

SECTION 2
EXCLUSIONS FROM SCOPE

Subsection 1
General

[3.363]
Article 3
Statutory systems

Without prejudice to Article 2(3)(c), this Directive shall not apply to insurance forming part of a statutory system of social security.

[3.364]
Article 4
Exclusion from scope due to size

1. Without prejudice to Article 3 and Articles 5 to 10, this Directive shall not apply to an insurance undertaking which fulfils all the following conditions:

(a) the undertaking's annual gross written premium income does not exceed EUR 5 million;

(b) the total of the undertaking's technical provisions, gross of the amounts recoverable from reinsurance contracts and special purpose vehicles, as referred to in Article 76, does not exceed EUR 25 million;

(c) where the undertaking belongs to a group, the total of the technical provisions of the group defined as gross of the amounts recoverable from reinsurance contracts and special purpose vehicles does not exceed EUR 25 million;

(d) the business of the undertaking does not include insurance or reinsurance activities covering liability, credit and suretyship insurance risks, unless they constitute ancillary risks within the meaning of Article 16(1);

(e) the business of the undertaking does not include reinsurance operations exceeding EUR 0,5 million of its gross written premium income or EUR 2,5 million of its technical provisions gross of the amounts recoverable from reinsurance contracts and special purpose vehicles, or more than 10% of its gross written premium income or more than 10% of its technical provisions gross of the amounts recoverable from reinsurance contracts and special purpose vehicles.

Part 3 EU & International Materials

2. If any of the amounts set out in paragraph 1 is exceeded for three consecutive years this Directive shall apply as from the fourth year.
3. By way of derogation from paragraph 1, this Directive shall apply to all undertakings seeking authorisation to pursue insurance and reinsurance activities of which the annual gross written premium income or technical provisions gross of the amounts recoverable from reinsurance contracts and special purpose vehicles are expected to exceed any of the amounts set out in paragraph 1 within the following five years.
4. This Directive shall cease to apply to those insurance undertakings for which the supervisory authority has verified that all of the following conditions are met:
(a) none of the thresholds set out in paragraph 1 has been exceeded for the three previous consecutive years; and
(b) none of the thresholds set out in paragraph 1 is expected to be exceeded during the following five years.

For as long as the insurance undertaking concerned pursues activities in accordance with Articles 145 to 149, paragraph 1 of this Article shall not apply.
5. Paragraphs 1 and 4 shall not prevent any undertaking from applying for authorisation or continuing to be authorised under this Directive.

Subsection 2
Non-life

[3.365]
Article 5
Operations
In regard to non-life insurance, this Directive shall not apply to the following operations:
(1) capital redemption operations, as defined by the law in each Member State;
(2) operations of provident and mutual benefit institutions whose benefits vary according to the resources available and in which the contributions of the members are determined on a flat-rate basis;
(3) operations carried out by organisations not having a legal personality with the purpose of providing mutual cover for their members without there being any payment of premiums or constitution of technical reserves; or
(4) export credit insurance operations for the account of or guaranteed by the State, or where the State is the insurer.

[3.366]
Article 6
Assistance
1. This Directive shall not apply to an assistance activity which fulfils all the following conditions:
(a) the assistance is provided in the event of an accident or breakdown involving a road vehicle when the accident or breakdown occurs in the territory of the Member State of the undertaking providing cover;
(b) the liability for the assistance is limited to the following operations:
(i) an on-the-spot breakdown service for which the undertaking providing cover uses, in most circumstances, its own staff and equipment;
(ii) the conveyance of the vehicle to the nearest or the most appropriate location at which repairs may be carried out and the possible accompaniment, normally by the same means of assistance, of the driver and passengers to the nearest location from where they may continue their journey by other means; and
(iii) where provided for by the home Member State of the undertaking providing cover, the conveyance of the vehicle, possibly accompanied by the driver and passengers, to their home, point of departure or original destination within the same State; and
(c) the assistance is not carried out by an undertaking subject to this Directive.
2. In the cases referred to in points (i) and (ii) of paragraph 1(b), the condition that the accident or breakdown must have happened in the territory of the Member State of the undertaking providing cover shall not apply where the beneficiary is a member of the body providing cover and the breakdown service or conveyance of the vehicle is provided simply on presentation of a membership card, without any additional premium being paid, by a similar body in the country concerned on the basis of a reciprocal agreement, or, in the case of Ireland and the United Kingdom, where the assistance operations are provided by a single body operating in both States.
3. This Directive shall not apply in the case of operations referred to in point (iii) of paragraph 1(b), where the accident or the breakdown has occurred in the territory of Ireland or, in the case of the United Kingdom, in the territory of Northern Ireland and the vehicle, possibly accompanied by the driver and passengers, is conveyed to their home, point of departure or original destination within either territory.
4. This Directive shall not apply to assistance operations carried out by the Automobile Club of the Grand Duchy of Luxembourg where the accident or the breakdown of a road vehicle has occurred outside the territory of the Grand Duchy of Luxembourg and the assistance consists in conveying the vehicle which has been involved in that accident or breakdown, possibly accompanied by the driver and passengers, to their home.

[3.367]
Article 7
Mutual undertakings

This Directive shall not apply to mutual undertakings which pursue non-life insurance activities and which have concluded with other mutual undertakings an agreement which provides for the full reinsurance of the insurance policies issued by them or under which the accepting undertaking is to meet the liabilities arising under such policies in the place of the ceding undertaking. In such a case the accepting undertaking shall be subject to the rules of this Directive.

[3.368]
Article 8
Institutions

This Directive shall not apply to the following institutions which pursue non-life insurance activities unless their statutes or the applicable law are amended as regards capacity:

(1) in Denmark, Falck Danmark;
(2) in Germany, the following semi-public institutions:
  (a) Postbeamtenkrankenkasse,
  (b) Krankenversorgung der Bundesbahnbeamten;
(3) in Ireland, the Voluntary Health Insurance Board;
(4) in Spain, the Consorcio de Compensación de Seguros.

Subsection 3
Life

[3.369]
Article 9
Operations and activities

In regard to life insurance, this Directive shall not apply to the following operations and activities:

(1) operations of provident and mutual-benefit institutions whose benefits vary according to the resources available and which require each of their members to contribute at the appropriate flat rate;
(2) operations carried out by organisations, other than undertakings referred to in Article 2, whose object is to provide benefits for employed or self-employed persons belonging to an undertaking or group of undertakings, or a trade or group of trades, in the event of death or survival or of discontinuance or curtailment of activity, whether or not the commitments arising from such operations are fully covered at all times by mathematical provisions;
(3) the pension activities of pension insurance undertakings prescribed in the Employees Pension Act (TyEL) and other related Finnish legislation provided that:
  (a) pension insurance companies which already under Finnish law are obliged to have separate accounting and management systems for their pension activities, as from 1 January 1995, set up separate legal entities for pursuing those activities; and
  (b) the Finnish authorities allow, in a non-discriminatory manner, all nationals and companies of Member States to perform according to Finnish legislation the activities specified in Article 2 related to *that* exemption whether by means of ownership or participation in an existing insurance company or group or by means of creation or participation of new insurance companies or groups, including pension insurance companies.

[3.370]
Article 10
Organisations, undertakings and institutions

In regard to life insurance, this Directive shall not apply to the following organisations, undertakings and institutions:

(1) organisations which undertake to provide benefits solely in the event of death, where the amount of such benefits does not exceed the average funeral costs for a single death or where the benefits are provided in kind;
(2) the 'Versorgungsverband deutscher Wirtschaftsorganisationen' in Germany, unless its statutes are amended as regards the scope of its capacity;
(3) the 'Consorcio de Compensación de Seguros' in Spain, unless its statutes are amended as regards the scope of its activities or capacity.

Subsection 4
Reinsurance

[3.371]
Article 11
Reinsurance

In regard to reinsurance, this Directive shall not apply to the activity of reinsurance conducted or fully guaranteed by the government of a Member State when that government is acting, for reasons of substantial public interest, in the capacity of reinsurer of last resort, including in circumstances where such a role is required by a situation in the market in which it is not feasible to obtain adequate commercial cover.

[3.372]
Article 12
Reinsurance undertakings closing their activity

1. Reinsurance undertakings which by 10 December 2007 ceased to conduct new reinsurance contracts and exclusively administer their existing portfolio in order to terminate their activity shall not be subject to this Directive.

2. Member States shall draw up a list of the reinsurance undertakings concerned and communicate that list to all the other Member States.

SECTION 3
DEFINITIONS

[3.373]
Article 13
Definitions

For the purposes of this Directive, the following definitions shall apply:

(1) 'insurance undertaking' means a direct life or non-life insurance undertaking which has received authorisation in accordance with Article 14;

(2) 'captive insurance undertaking' means an insurance undertaking, owned either by a financial undertaking other than an insurance or reinsurance undertaking or a group of insurance or reinsurance undertakings within the meaning of Article 212(1)(c) or by a non-financial undertaking, the purpose of which is to provide insurance cover exclusively for the risks of the undertaking or undertakings to which it belongs or of an undertaking or undertakings of the group of which it is a member;

(3) 'third-country insurance undertaking' means an undertaking which would require authorisation as an insurance undertaking in accordance with Article 14 if its head office were situated in the Community;

(4) 'reinsurance undertaking' means an undertaking which has received authorisation in accordance with Article 14 to pursue reinsurance activities;

(5) 'captive reinsurance undertaking' means a reinsurance undertaking, owned either by a financial undertaking other than an insurance or reinsurance undertaking or a group of insurance or reinsurance undertakings within the meaning of Article 212(1)(c) or by a non-financial undertaking, the purpose of which is to provide reinsurance cover exclusively for the risks of the undertaking or undertakings to which it belongs or of an undertaking or undertakings of the group of which it is a member;

(6) 'third-country reinsurance undertaking' means an undertaking which would require authorisation as a reinsurance undertaking in accordance with Article 14 if its head office were situated in the Community;

[(7) 'reinsurance' means one of the following:

(a) the activity consisting in accepting risks ceded by an insurance undertaking or third-country insurance undertaking, or by another reinsurance undertaking or third-country reinsurance undertaking;

(b) in the case of the association of underwriters known as Lloyd's, the activity consisting in accepting risks, ceded by any member of Lloyd's, by an insurance or reinsurance undertaking other than the association of underwriters known as Lloyd's; or

(c) the provision of cover by a reinsurance undertaking to an institution that falls within the scope of Directive (EU) 2016/2341 of the European Parliament and of the Council.[1]]

(8) 'home Member State' means any of the following:

(a) for non-life insurance, the Member State in which the head office of the insurance undertaking covering the risk is situated;

(b) for life insurance, the Member State in which the head office of the insurance undertaking covering the commitment is situated; or

(c) for reinsurance, the Member State in which the head office of the reinsurance undertaking is situated;

(9) 'host Member State' means the Member State, other than the home Member State, in which an insurance or a reinsurance undertaking has a branch or provides services; for life and non-life insurance, the Member State of the provisions of services means, respectively, the Member State of the commitment or the Member State in which the risk is situated, where that commitment or risk is covered by an insurance undertaking or a branch situated in another Member State;

(10) 'supervisory authority' means the national authority or the national authorities empowered by law or regulation to supervise insurance or reinsurance undertakings;

(11) 'branch' means an agency or a branch of an insurance or reinsurance undertaking which is located in the territory of a Member State other than the home Member State;

(12) 'establishment' of an undertaking means its head office or any of its branches;

(13) 'Member State in which the risk is situated' means any of the following:

(a) the Member State in which the property is situated, where the insurance relates either to buildings or to buildings and their contents, in so far as the contents are covered by the same insurance policy;

(b) the Member State of registration, where the insurance relates to vehicles of any type;

(c) the Member State where the policy holder took out the policy in the case of policies of a duration of four months or less covering travel or holiday risks, whatever the class concerned;

(d) in all cases not explicitly covered by points (a), (b) or (c), the Member State in which either of the following is situated:
   (i) the habitual residence of the policy holder; or
   (ii) if the policy holder is a legal person, that policy holder's establishment to which the contract relates;

(14) 'Member State of the commitment' means the Member State in which either of the following is situated:
   (a) the habitual residence of the policy holder;
   (b) if the policy holder is a legal person, that policy holder's establishment, to which the contract relates;

(15) 'parent undertaking' means a parent undertaking within the meaning of Article 1 of Directive 83/349/EEC;

(16) 'subsidiary undertaking' means any subsidiary undertaking within the meaning of Article 1 of Directive 83/349/EEC, including subsidiaries thereof;

(17) 'close links' means a situation in which two or more natural or legal persons are linked by control or participation, or a situation in which two or more natural or legal persons are permanently linked to one and the same person by a control relationship;

(18) 'control' means the relationship between a parent undertaking and a subsidiary undertaking, as set out in Article 1 of Directive 83/349/EEC, or a similar relationship between any natural or legal person and an undertaking;

(19) 'intra-group transaction' means any transaction by which an insurance or reinsurance undertaking relies, either directly or indirectly, on other undertakings within the same group or on any natural or legal person linked to the undertakings within that group by close links, for the fulfilment of an obligation, whether or not contractual, and whether or not for payment;

(20) 'participation' means the ownership, direct or by way of control, of 20% or more of the voting rights or capital of an undertaking;

(21) 'qualifying holding' means a direct or indirect holding in an undertaking which represents 10% or more of the capital or of the voting rights or which makes it possible to exercise a significant influence over the management of that undertaking;

(22) 'regulated market' means either of the following:
   (a) in the case of a market situated in a Member State, a regulated market as defined in Article 4(1)(14) of Directive 2004/39/EC; or
   (b) in the case of a market situated in a third country, a financial market which fulfils the following conditions:
      (i) it is recognised by the home Member State of the insurance undertaking and fulfils requirements comparable to those laid down in Directive 2004/39/EC; and
      (ii) the financial instruments dealt in on that market are of a quality comparable to that of the instruments dealt in on the regulated market or markets of the home Member State;

(23) 'national bureau' means a national insurers' bureau as defined in Article 1(3) of Directive 72/166/EEC;

(24) 'national guarantee fund' means the body referred to in Article 1(4) of Directive 84/5/EEC;

(25) 'financial undertaking' means any of the following entities:
   (a) a credit institution, a financial institution or an ancillary banking services undertaking within the meaning of Article 4(1), (5) and (21) of Directive 2006/48/EC respectively;
   (b) an insurance undertaking, or a reinsurance undertaking or an insurance holding company within the meaning of Article 212(1)(f);
   (c) an investment firm or a financial institution within the meaning of Article 4(1)(1) of Directive 2004/39/EC; or
   (d) a mixed financial holding company within the meaning of Article 2(15) of Directive 2002/87/EC

(26) 'special purpose vehicle' means any undertaking, whether incorporated or not, other than an existing insurance or reinsurance undertaking, which assumes risks from insurance or reinsurance undertakings and which fully funds its exposure to such risks through the proceeds of a debt issuance or any other financing mechanism where the repayment rights of the providers of such debt or financing mechanism are subordinated to the reinsurance obligations of such an undertaking;

(27) 'large risks' means:
   (a) risks classified under classes 4, 5, 6, 7, 11 and 12 in Part A of Annex I;
   (b) risks classified under classes 14 and 15 in Part A of Annex I, where the policy holder is engaged professionally in an industrial or commercial activity or in one of the liberal professions and the risks relate to such activity;
   (c) risks classified under classes 3, 8, 9, 10, 13 and 16 in Part A of Annex I in so far as the policy holder exceeds the limits of at least two of the following criteria:
      (i) a balance-sheet total of EUR 6,2 million;
      (ii) a net turnover, within the meaning of Fourth Council Directive 78/660/EEC of 25 July 1978 based on Article 54(3)(g) of the Treaty on the annual accounts of certain types of companies,[2] of EUR 12,8 million;
      (iii) an average number of 250 employees during the financial year.

If the policy holder belongs to a group of undertakings for which consolidated accounts within the meaning of Directive 83/349/EEC are drawn up, the criteria set out in point (c) of the first subparagraph shall be applied on the basis of the consolidated accounts.

Member States may add to the category referred to in point (c) of the first subparagraph the risks insured by professional associations, joint ventures or temporary groupings;

(28) 'outsourcing' means an arrangement of any form between an insurance or reinsurance undertaking and a service provider, whether a supervised entity or not, by which that service provider performs a process, a service or an activity, whether directly or by sub-outsourcing, which would otherwise be performed by the insurance or reinsurance undertaking itself;

(29) 'function', within a system of governance, means an internal capacity to undertake practical tasks; a system of governance includes the risk-management function, the compliance function, the internal audit function and the actuarial function;

(30) 'underwriting risk' means the risk of loss or of adverse change in the value of insurance liabilities, due to inadequate pricing and provisioning assumptions;

(31) 'market risk' means the risk of loss or of adverse change in the financial situation resulting, directly or indirectly, from fluctuations in the level and in the volatility of market prices of assets, liabilities and financial instruments;

(32) 'credit risk' means the risk of loss or of adverse change in the financial situation, resulting from fluctuations in the credit standing of issuers of securities, counterparties and any debtors to which insurance and reinsurance undertakings are exposed, in the form of counterparty default risk, or spread risk, or market risk concentrations;

[(32a) "qualifying central counterparty" means a central counterparty that has been either authorised in accordance with Article 14 of Regulation (EU) No 648/2012 of the European Parliament and of the Council[3] or recognised in accordance with Article 25 of that Regulation;]

(33) 'operational risk' means the risk of loss arising from inadequate or failed internal processes, personnel or systems, or from external events;

(34) 'liquidity risk' means the risk that insurance and reinsurance undertakings are unable to realise investments and other assets in order to settle their financial obligations when they fall due;

(35) 'concentration risk' means all risk exposures with a loss potential which is large enough to threaten the solvency or the financial position of insurance and reinsurance undertakings;

(36) 'risk-mitigation techniques' means all techniques which enable insurance and reinsurance undertakings to transfer part or all of their risks to another party;

(37) 'diversification effects' means the reduction in the risk exposure of insurance and reinsurance undertakings and groups related to the diversification of their business, resulting from the fact that the adverse outcome from one risk can be offset by a more favourable outcome from another risk, where those risks are not fully correlated;

(38) 'probability distribution forecast' means a mathematical function that assigns to an exhaustive set of mutually exclusive future events a probability of realisation;

(39) 'risk measure' means a mathematical function which assigns a monetary amount to a given probability distribution forecast and increases monotonically with the level of risk exposure underlying that probability distribution forecast.

[(40) "external credit assessment institution" or "ECAI" means a credit rating agency that is registered or certified in accordance with Regulation (EC) No 1060/2009 of the European Parliament and of the Council[4] or a central bank issuing credit ratings which are exempt from the application of that Regulation.]

NOTES

Para 7: substituted by European Parliament and Council Directive 2016/2341/EU, Art 63.

Paras 32a, 40: inserted and added respectively by European Parliament and Council Directive 2014/51/EU, Art 2(1).

1 Directive (EU) 2016/2341 of 14 December 2016 on the activities and supervision of institutions for occupational retirement provision (IORPs) (OJ L354, 23.12.2016, p. 37).

2 OJ L222, 14.8.1978, p 11.

3 Regulation (EU) No 648/2012 of the European Parliament and of the Council of 4 July 2012 on OTC derivatives, central counterparties and trade repositories (OJ L201, 27.7.2012, p. 1).

4 Regulation (EC) No 1060/2009 of the European Parliament and of the Council of 16 September 2009 on credit rating agencies (OJ L302, 17.11.2009, p. 1).

(Arts 14–135 (Chs II–VI) outside the scope of this work.)

CHAPTER VII INSURANCE AND REINSURANCE UNDERTAKINGS IN DIFFICULTY OR IN AN IRREGULAR SITUATION

[3.374]

Article 136

Identification and notification of deteriorating financial conditions by the insurance and reinsurance undertaking

Insurance and reinsurance undertakings shall have procedures in place to identify deteriorating financial conditions and shall immediately notify the supervisory authorities when such deterioration occurs.

[3.375]
Article 137
Non-Compliance with technical provisions

Where an insurance or reinsurance undertaking does not comply with Chapter VI, Section 2, the supervisory authorities of its home Member State may prohibit the free disposal of its assets after having communicated their intentions to the supervisory authorities of the host Member States. The supervisory authorities of the home Member State shall designate the assets to be covered by such measures.

[3.376]
Article 138
Non-Compliance with the Solvency Capital Requirement

1. Insurance and reinsurance undertakings shall immediately inform the supervisory authority as soon as they observe that the Solvency Capital Requirement is no longer complied with, or where there is a risk of non-compliance in the following three months.

2. Within two months from the observation of non-compliance with the Solvency Capital Requirement the insurance or reinsurance undertaking concerned shall submit a realistic recovery plan for approval by the supervisory authority.

3. The supervisory authority shall require the insurance or reinsurance undertaking concerned to take the necessary measures to achieve, within six months from the observation of non-compliance with the Solvency Capital Requirement, the re-establishment of the level of eligible own funds covering the Solvency Capital Requirement or the reduction of its risk profile to ensure compliance with the Solvency Capital Requirement.

The supervisory authority may, if appropriate, extend that period by three months.

[4. In the event of exceptional adverse situations affecting insurance and reinsurance undertakings representing a significant share of the market or of the affected lines of business, as declared by EIOPA, and where appropriate after consulting the ESRB, the supervisory authority may extend, for affected undertakings, the period set out in the second subparagraph of paragraph 3 by a maximum period of seven years, taking into account all relevant factors including the average duration of the technical provisions.

Without prejudice to the powers of EIOPA under Article 18 of Regulation (EU) No 1094/2010, for the purposes of this paragraph EIOPA shall, following a request by the supervisory authority concerned, declare the existence of exceptional adverse situations. The supervisory authority concerned may make a request if insurance or reinsurance undertakings representing a significant share of the market or of the affected lines of business are unlikely to meet one of the requirements set out in paragraph 3. Exceptional adverse situations exist where the financial situation of insurance or reinsurance undertakings representing a significant share of the market or of the affected lines of business are seriously or adversely affected by one or more of the following conditions:

(a) a fall in financial markets which is unforeseen, sharp and steep;
(b) a persistent low interest rate environment;
(c) a high-impact catastrophic event.

EIOPA shall, in cooperation with the supervisory authority concerned, assess on a regular basis whether the conditions referred to in the second subparagraph still apply. EIOPA shall, in cooperation with the supervisory authority concerned, declare when an exceptional adverse situation has ceased to exist.

The insurance or reinsurance undertaking concerned shall, every three months, submit a progress report to its supervisory authority setting out the measures taken and the progress made to re-establish the level of eligible own funds covering the Solvency Capital Requirement or to reduce the risk profile to ensure compliance with the Solvency Capital Requirement.

The extension referred to in the first subparagraph shall be withdrawn where that progress report shows that there was no significant progress in achieving the re-establishment of the level of eligible own funds covering the Solvency Capital Requirement or the reduction of the risk profile to ensure compliance with the Solvency Capital Requirement between the date of the observation of non-compliance of the Solvency Capital Requirement and the date of the submission of the progress report.]

5. In exceptional circumstances, where the supervisory authority is of the opinion that the financial situation of the undertaking concerned will deteriorate further, it may also restrict or prohibit the free disposal of the assets of that undertaking. That supervisory authority shall inform the supervisory authorities of the host Member States of any measures it has taken. Those authorities shall, at the request of the supervisory authority of the home Member State, take the same measures. The supervisory authority of the home Member State shall designate the assets to be covered by such measures.

NOTES

Para 4: substituted by European Parliament and Council Directive 2014/51/EU, Art 2(36).

[3.377]
Article 139
Non-Compliance with the Minimum Capital Requirement

1. Insurance and reinsurance undertakings shall inform the supervisory authority immediately where they observe that the Minimum Capital Requirement is no longer complied with or where there is a risk of non-compliance in the following three months.

2. Within one month from the observation of non-compliance with the Minimum Capital Requirement, the insurance or reinsurance undertaking concerned shall submit, for approval by the supervisory authority, a short-term realistic finance scheme to restore, within three months of that observation, the eligible basic own funds, at least to the level of the Minimum Capital Requirement or to reduce its risk profile to ensure compliance with the Minimum Capital Requirement.

3. The supervisory authority of the home Member State may also restrict or prohibit the free disposal of the assets of the insurance or reinsurance undertaking. It shall inform the supervisory authorities of the host Member States accordingly. At the request of the supervisory authority of the home Member State, those authorities shall, take the same measures. The supervisory authority of the home Member State shall designate the assets to be covered by such measures.

[3.378]
Article 140
Prohibition of free disposal of assets located within the territory of a Member State
Member States shall take the measures necessary to be able, in accordance with national law, to prohibit the free disposal of assets located within their territory at the request, in the cases provided for in Articles 137 to 139 and Article 144(2) of the undertaking's home Member State, which shall designate the assets to be covered by such measures.

[3.379]
Article 141
Supervisory powers in deteriorating financial conditions
Notwithstanding Articles 138 and 139, where the solvency position of the undertaking continues to deteriorate, the supervisory authorities shall have the power to take all measures necessary to safeguard the interests of policy holders in the case of insurance contracts, or the obligations arising out of reinsurance contracts.

Those measures shall be proportionate and thus reflect the level and duration of the deterioration of the solvency position of the insurance or reinsurance undertaking concerned.

[3.380]
Article 142
Recovery plan and finance scheme
1. The recovery plan referred to in Article 138(2) and the finance scheme referred to in Article 139(2) shall, at least include particulars or evidence concerning the following:
- (a) estimates of management expenses, in particular current general expenses and commissions;
- (b) estimates of income and expenditure in respect of direct business, reinsurance acceptances and reinsurance cessions;
- (c) a forecast balance sheet;
- (d) estimates of the financial resources intended to cover the technical provisions and the Solvency Capital Requirement and the Minimum Capital Requirement;
- (e) the overall reinsurance policy.

2. Where the supervisory authorities have required a recovery plan referred to in Article 138(2) or a finance scheme referred to in Article 139(2) in accordance with paragraph 1 of this Article, they shall refrain from issuing a certificate in accordance with Article 39 for as long as they consider that the rights of the policy holders, or the contractual obligations of the reinsurance undertaking are threatened.

[3.381]
[Article 143
Delegated acts and regulatory technical standards concerning Article 138(4)
1. The Commission shall adopt delegated acts in accordance with Article 301a supplementing the types of exceptional adverse situations and specifying the factors and criteria to be taken into account by EIOPA in declaring the existence of exceptional adverse situations and by supervisory authorities in determining the extension to recovery period in accordance with Article 138(4).
2. In order to ensure consistent harmonisation in relation to Article 138(2), Article 139(2) and Article 141, EIOPA shall, subject to Article 301b, develop draft regulatory technical standards to specify the recovery plan referred to in Article 138(2), and the finance scheme referred to in Article 139(2) and with respect to Article 141, taking due care to avoid pro-cyclical effects.
Power is delegated to the Commission to adopt the regulatory technical standards referred to in the first subparagraph in accordance with Articles 10 to 14 of Regulation (EU) No 1094/2010.]

NOTES
Substituted by European Parliament and Council Directive 2014/51/EU, Art 2(37).

(*Art 144 outside the scope of this work.*)

CHAPTER VIII RIGHT OF ESTABLISHMENT AND FREEDOM TO PROVIDE SERVICES

(*Arts 145–159 (Sections 1–4) outside the scope of this work.*)

SECTION 5
TREATMENT OF CONTRACTS OF BRANCHES IN WINDING-UP PROCEEDINGS

[3.382]
Article 160
Winding-up of insurance undertakings
Where an insurance undertaking is wound up, commitments arising out of contracts underwritten through a branch or under the freedom to provide services shall be met in the same way as those arising out of the

other insurance contracts of that undertaking, without distinction as to nationality as far as the persons insured and the beneficiaries are concerned.

[3.383]
Article 161
Winding-up of reinsurance undertakings
Where a reinsurance undertaking is wound up, commitments arising out of contracts underwritten through a branch or under the freedom to provide services shall be met in the same way as those arising out of the other reinsurance contracts of that undertaking.

(Arts 162–177 (Chs IX–X) outside the scope of this work.)

TITLE II SPECIFIC PROVISIONS FOR INSURANCE AND REINSURANCE

(Arts 178–186 (Ch I) outside the scope of this work.)

CHAPTER II PROVISIONS SPECIFIC TO NON-LIFE INSURANCE

(Arts 187–189 (Section 1) outside the scope of this work.)

SECTION 2
COMMUNITY CO-INSURANCE

(Arts 190–193 outside the scope of this work.)

[3.384]
Article 194
Treatment of co-insurance contracts in winding-up proceedings
In the event of an insurance undertaking being wound up, liabilities arising from participation in Community co-insurance contracts shall be met in the same way as those arising under the other insurance contracts of that undertaking without distinction as to the nationality of the insured and of the beneficiaries.

(Arts 195, 196, Arts 197–207 (Sections 3–6), Arts 208–211 (Chs IX, X), Arts 212–266 (Title III) outside the scope of this work.)

TITLE IV REORGANISATION AND WINDING-UP OF INSURANCE UNDERTAKINGS

CHAPTER I SCOPE AND DEFINITIONS

[3.385]
Article 267
Scope of this Title
This Title shall apply to reorganisation measures and winding-up proceedings concerning the following:
- (a) insurance undertakings;
- (b) branches situated in the territory of the Community of third-country insurance undertakings.

[3.386]
Article 268
Definitions
1. For the purpose of this Title the following definitions shall apply:
   - (a) 'competent authorities' means the administrative or judicial authorities of the Member States which are competent for the purposes of the reorganisation measures or the winding-up proceedings;
   - (b) 'branch' means a permanent presence of an insurance undertaking in the territory of a Member State other than the home Member State which pursues insurance activities;
   - (c) 'reorganisation measures' means measures involving any intervention by the competent authorities which are intended to preserve or restore the financial situation of an insurance undertaking and which affect pre-existing rights of parties other than the insurance undertaking itself, including but not limited to measures involving the possibility of a suspension of payments, suspension of enforcement measures or reduction of claims;
   - (d) 'winding-up proceedings' means collective proceedings involving the realisation of the assets of an insurance undertaking and the distribution of the proceeds among the creditors, shareholders or members as appropriate, which necessarily involve any intervention by the competent authorities, including where the collective proceedings are terminated by a composition or other analogous measure, whether or not they are founded on insolvency or are voluntary or compulsory;
   - (e) 'administrator' means a person or body appointed by the competent authorities for the purpose of administering reorganisation measures;

(f) 'liquidator' means a person or body appointed by the competent authorities or by the governing bodies of an insurance undertaking for the purpose of administering winding-up proceedings;
(g) 'insurance claim' means an amount which is owed by an insurance undertaking to insured persons, policy holders, beneficiaries or to any injured party having direct right of action against the insurance undertaking and which arises from an insurance contract or from any operation provided for in Article 2(3)(b) and (c) in direct insurance business, including an amount set aside for those persons, when some elements of the debt are not yet known.

The premium owed by an insurance undertaking as a result of the non-conclusion or cancellation of an insurance contract or operation referred to in point (g) of the first subparagraph in accordance with the law applicable to such a contract or operation before the opening of the winding-up proceedings shall also be considered an insurance claim.

2. For the purpose of applying this Title to reorganisation measures and winding-up proceedings concerning a branch situated in a Member State of a third-country insurance undertaking the following definitions shall apply:
(a) 'home Member State' means the Member State in which the branch was granted authorisation in accordance with Articles 145 to 149;
(b) 'supervisory authorities' means the supervisory authorities of the home Member State;
(c) 'competent authorities' means the competent authorities of the home Member State.

CHAPTER II REORGANISATION MEASURES

[3.387]
Article 269
Adoption of reorganisation measures applicable law

1. Only the competent authorities of the home Member State shall be entitled to decide on the reorganisation measures with respect to an insurance undertaking, including its branches.
2. The reorganisation measures shall not preclude the opening of winding-up proceedings by the home Member State.
3. The reorganisation measures shall be governed by the laws, regulations and procedures applicable in the home Member State, unless otherwise provided in Articles 285 to 292.
4. Reorganisation measures taken in accordance with the legislation of the home Member State shall be fully effective throughout the Community without any further formalities, including against third parties in other Member States, even where the legislation of those other Member States does not provide for such reorganisation measures or alternatively makes their implementation subject to conditions which are not fulfilled.
5. The reorganisation measures shall be effective throughout the Community once they become effective in the home Member State.

[3.388]
Article 270
Information to the supervisory authorities

The competent authorities of the home Member State shall inform as a matter or urgency the supervisory authorities of that Member State of their decision on any reorganisation measure, where possible before the adoption of such a measure and failing that immediately thereafter.

The supervisory authorities of the home Member State shall inform as a matter of urgency the supervisory authorities of all other Member States of the decision to adopt reorganisation measures including the possible practical effects of such measures.

[3.389]
Article 271
Publication of decisions on reorganisation measures

1. Where an appeal is possible in the home Member State against a reorganisation measure, the competent authorities of the home Member State, the administrator or any person entitled to do so in the home Member State shall make public the decision on a reorganisation measure in accordance with the publication procedures provided for in the home Member State and, furthermore, publish in the *Official Journal of the European Union* at the earliest opportunity an extract from the document establishing the reorganisation measure.

The supervisory authorities of the other Member States which have been informed of the decision on a reorganisation measure pursuant to Article 270 may ensure the publication of such decision within their territory in the manner they consider appropriate.

2. The publications provided for in paragraph 1 shall specify the competent authority of the home Member State, the applicable law as provided in Article 269(3) and the administrator appointed, if any. They shall be made in the official language or in one of the official languages of the Member State in which the information is published.
3. The reorganisation measures shall apply regardless of the provisions concerning publication set out in paragraphs 1 and 2 and shall be fully effective as against creditors, unless the competent authorities of the home Member State or the law of that Member State provide otherwise.
4. Where reorganisation measures affect exclusively the rights of shareholders, members or employees of an insurance undertaking, considered in those capacities, paragraphs 1, 2 and 3 shall not apply unless the law applicable to the reorganisation measures provides otherwise.

The competent authorities shall determine the manner in which the parties referred to in the first subparagraph are to be informed in accordance with the applicable law.

[3.390]
Article 272
Information to known creditors right to lodge claims

1. Where the law of the home Member State requires a claim to be lodged in order for it to be recognised or provides for compulsory notification of a reorganisation measure to creditors whose habitual residence, domicile or head office is situated in that Member State, the competent authorities of the home Member State or the administrator shall also inform known creditors whose habitual residence, domicile or head office is situated in another Member State, in accordance with Article 281 and Article 283(1).

2. Where the law of the home Member State provides for the right of creditors whose habitual residence, domicile or head office is situated in that Member State to lodge claims or to submit observations concerning their claims, creditors whose habitual residence, domicile or head office is situated in another Member State shall have the same right in accordance with Article 282 and Article 283(2).

CHAPTER III WINDING-UP PROCEEDINGS

[3.391]
Article 273
Opening of winding-up proceedings information to the supervisory authorities

1. Only the competent authorities of the home Member State shall be entitled to take a decision concerning the opening of winding-up proceedings with regard to an insurance undertaking, including its branches in other Member States. This decision may be taken in the absence, or following the adoption, of reorganisation measures.

2. A decision concerning the opening of winding-up proceedings of an insurance undertaking, including its branches in other Member States, adopted in accordance with the legislation of the home Member State shall be recognised without further formality throughout the Community and shall be effective there as soon as the decision is effective in the Member State in which the proceedings are opened.

3. The competent authorities of the home Member State shall inform as a matter of urgency the supervisory authorities of that Member State of the decision to open winding-up proceedings, where possible before the proceedings are opened and failing that immediately thereafter.

The supervisory authorities of the home Member State shall inform as a matter of urgency the supervisory authorities of all other Member States of the decision to open winding-up proceedings including the possible practical effects of such proceedings.

[3.392]
Article 274
Applicable law

1. The decision to open winding-up proceedings with regard to an insurance undertaking, the winding-up proceedings and their effects shall be governed by the law applicable in the home Member State unless otherwise provided in Articles 285 to 292.

2. The law of the home Member State shall determine at least the following:

(a) the assets which form part of the estate and the treatment of assets acquired by, or devolving to, the insurance undertaking after the opening of the winding-up proceedings;
(b) the respective powers of the insurance undertaking and the liquidator;
(c) the conditions under which set-off may be invoked;
(d) the effects of the winding-up proceedings on current contracts to which the insurance undertaking is party;
(e) the effects of the winding-up proceedings on proceedings brought by individual creditors, with the exception of lawsuits pending referred to in Article 292;
(f) the claims which are to be lodged against the estate of the insurance undertaking and the treatment of claims arising after the opening of winding-up proceedings;
(g) the rules governing the lodging, verification and admission of claims;
(h) the rules governing the distribution of proceeds from the realisation of assets, the ranking of claims, and the rights of creditors who have obtained partial satisfaction after the opening of winding-up proceedings by virtue of a right in rem or through a set-off;
(i) the conditions for and the effects of closure of winding-up proceedings, in particular by composition;
(j) rights of the creditors after the closure of winding-up proceedings;
(k) the party who is to bear the cost and expenses incurred in the winding-up proceedings; and
(l) the rules relating to the nullity, voidability or unenforceability of legal acts detrimental to all the creditors.

[3.393]
Article 275
Treatment of insurance claims

1. Member States shall ensure that insurance claims take precedence over other claims against the insurance undertaking in one or both of the following ways:

(a) with regard to assets representing the technical provisions, insurance claims shall take absolute precedence over any other claim on the insurance undertaking; or

(b) with regard to the whole of the assets of the insurance undertaking, insurance claims shall take precedence over any other claim on the insurance undertaking with the only possible exception of the following:
   (i) claims by employees arising from employment contracts and employment relationships;
   (ii) claims by public bodies on taxes;
   (iii) claims by social security systems;
   (iv) claims on assets subject to rights in rem.

2. Without prejudice to paragraph 1, Member States may provide that the whole or part of the expenses arising from the winding-up procedure, as determined by their national law, shall take precedence over insurance claims.

3. Member States which have chosen the option provided for in paragraph 1(a) shall require insurance undertakings to establish and keep up to date a special register in accordance with Article 276.

[3.394]
Article 276
Special register

1. Every insurance undertaking shall keep at its head office a special register of the assets used to cover the technical provisions calculated and invested in accordance with the law of the home Member State.

2. Where an insurance undertaking carries on both life and non-life insurance activities, it shall keep at its head office separate registers for each type of business.

However, where a Member State authorises insurance undertakings to cover life and the risks listed in classes 1 and 2 of Part A of Annex I, it may provide that those insurance undertakings must keep a single register for the whole of their activities.

3. The total value of the assets entered, valued in accordance with the law applicable in the home Member State, shall at no time be less than the value of the technical provisions.

4. Where an asset entered in the register is subject to a right in rem in favour of a creditor or a third party, with the result that part of the value of the asset is not available for the purpose of covering commitments, that fact shall be recorded in the register and the amount not available shall not be included in the total value referred to in paragraph 3.

5. The treatment of an asset in the case of the winding-up of the insurance undertaking with respect to the option provided for in Article 275(1)(a) shall be determined by the legislation of the home Member State, except where Articles 286, 287 or 288 apply to that asset where:
(a) the asset used to cover technical provisions is subject to a right in rem in favour of a creditor or a third party, without meeting the conditions set out in paragraph 4;
(b) such an asset is subject to a reservation of title in favour of a creditor or of a third party; or
(c) a creditor has a right to demand the set-off of his claim against the claim of the insurance undertaking.

6. Once winding-up proceedings have been opened, the composition of the assets entered in the register in accordance with paragraphs 1 to 5 shall not be changed and no alteration other than the correction of purely clerical errors shall be made in the registers, except with the authorisation of the competent authority.

However, the liquidators shall add to those assets the yield therefrom and the value of the pure premiums received in respect of the class of insurance concerned between the opening of the winding-up proceedings and the time of payment of the insurance claims or until any transfer of portfolio is effected.

7. Where the product of the realisation of assets is less than their estimated value in the registers, the liquidators shall justify this to the supervisory authorities of the home Member States.

[3.395]
Article 277
Subrogation to a guarantee scheme

The home Member State may provide that, where the rights of insurance creditors have been subrogated to a guarantee scheme established in that Member State, claims by that scheme shall not benefit from the provisions of Article 275(1).

[3.396]
Article 278
Representation of preferential claims by assets

Member States which choose the option set out in Article 275(1)(b) shall require every insurance undertaking to ensure that the claims which may take precedence over insurance claims pursuant to Article 275(1)(b) and which are registered in the insurance undertaking's accounts are represented, at any moment and independently of a possible winding-up, by assets.

[3.397]
Article 279
Withdrawal of the authorisation

1. Where the opening of winding-up proceedings is decided in respect of an insurance undertaking, the authorisation of that undertaking shall be withdrawn in accordance with the procedure laid down in Article 144, except to the extent necessary for the purposes of paragraph 2.

2. The withdrawal of authorisation pursuant to paragraph 1 shall not prevent the liquidator or any other person appointed by the competent authorities from pursuing some of the activities of the insurance undertaking in so far as that is necessary or appropriate for the purposes of winding-up.

The home Member State may provide that such activities shall be pursued with the consent and under the supervision of the supervisory authorities of that Member State.

[3.398]
Article 280
Publication of decisions on winding-up proceedings

1. The competent authority, the liquidator or any person appointed for that purpose by the competent authority shall publish the decision to open winding-up proceedings in accordance with the publication procedures provided for in the home Member State and also publish an extract from the winding-up decision in the *Official Journal of the European Union*.

The supervisory authorities of all other Member States which have been informed of the decision to open winding-up proceedings in accordance with Article 273(3) may ensure the publication of such decision within their territories in the manner they consider appropriate.

2. The publication referred to in paragraph 1 shall specify the competent authority of the home Member State, the applicable law and the liquidator appointed. It shall be in the official language or in one of the official languages of the Member State in which the information is published.

[3.399]
Article 281
Information to known creditors

1. When winding-up proceedings are opened, the competent authorities of the home Member State, the liquidator or any person appointed for that purpose by the competent authorities shall without delay individually inform by written notice each known creditor whose habitual residence, domicile or head office is situated in another Member State.

2. The notice referred to in paragraph 1 shall cover time-limits, the sanctions laid down with regard to those time-limits, the body or authority empowered to accept the lodging of claims or observations relating to claims and any other measures.

The notice shall also indicate whether creditors whose claims are preferential or secured in rem need to lodge their claims.

In the case of insurance claims, the notice shall further indicate the general effects of the winding-up proceedings on the insurance contracts, in particular, the date on which the insurance contracts or the operations will cease to produce effects and the rights and duties of insured persons with regard to the contract or operation.

[3.400]
Article 282
Right to lodge claims

1. Any creditor, including public authorities of Member States, whose habitual residence, domicile or head office is situated in a Member State other than the home Member State shall have the right to lodge claims or to submit written observations relating to claims.

2. The claims of all creditors referred to in paragraph 1 shall be treated in the same way and given the same ranking as claims of an equivalent nature which may be lodged by creditors whose habitual residence, domicile or head office is situated in the home Member State. Competent authorities shall therefore operate without discrimination at Community level.

3. Except in cases where the law of the home Member State otherwise allows, a creditor shall send to the competent authority copies of any supporting documents and shall indicate the following:

(a) the nature and the amount of the claim;
(b) the date on which the claim arose;
(c) whether he alleges preference, security in rem or reservation of title in respect of the claim;
(d) where appropriate, what assets are covered by his security.

The precedence granted to insurance claims by Article 275 need not be indicated.

[3.401]
Article 283
Languages and form

1. The information in the notice referred to in Article 281(1) shall be provided in the official language or one of the official languages of the home Member State.

For that purpose a form shall be used bearing either of the following headings in all the official languages of the European Union:

(a) 'Invitation to lodge a claim; time-limits to be observed'; or
(b) where the law of the home Member State provides for the submission of observations relating to claims, 'Invitation to submit observations relating to a claim; time-limits to be observed'.

However, where a known creditor is the holder of an insurance claim, the information in the notice referred to in Article 281(1) shall be provided in the official language or one of the official languages of the Member State in which the habitual residence, domicile or head office of the creditor is situated.

2. Creditors whose habitual residence, domicile or head office is situated in a Member State other than the home Member State may lodge their claims or submit observations relating to claims in the official language or one of the official languages of that other Member State.

However, in that case, the lodging of their claims or the submission of observations on their claims, as appropriate, shall bear the heading 'Lodgement of claim' or 'Submission of observations relating to claims', as appropriate, in the official language or in one of the official languages of the home Member State.

[3.402]
Article 284
Regular information to the creditors

1. Liquidators shall, in an appropriate manner, keep creditors regularly informed on the progress of the winding-up.

2. The supervisory authorities of the Member States may request information on developments in the winding-up procedure from the supervisory authorities of the home Member State.

CHAPTER IV COMMON PROVISIONS

[3.403]
Article 285
Effects on certain contracts and rights

By way of derogation from Articles 269 and 274, the effects of the opening of reorganisation measures or of winding-up proceedings shall be governed as follows:

(a) in regard to employment contracts and employment relationships, exclusively by the law of the Member State applicable to the employment contract or employment relationship;

(b) in regard to contracts conferring the right to make use of or acquire immovable property, exclusively by the law of the Member State where the immovable property is situated; and

(c) in regard to rights of the insurance undertaking with respect to immovable property, a ship or an aircraft subject to registration in a public register, exclusively by the law of the Member State under the authority of which the register is kept.

[3.404]
Article 286
Rights in rem of third parties

1. The opening of reorganisation measures or winding-up proceedings shall not affect the rights in rem of creditors or third parties in respect of tangible or intangible, movable or immovable assets — both specific assets and collections of indefinite assets as a whole which change from time to time — which belong to the insurance undertaking and which are situated within the territory of another Member State at the time of the opening of such measures or proceedings.

2. The rights referred to in paragraph 1 shall include at least:

(a) the right to dispose of assets or have them disposed of and to obtain satisfaction from the proceeds of or income from those assets, in particular by virtue of a lien or a mortgage;

(b) the exclusive right to have a claim met, in particular a right guaranteed by a lien in respect of the claim or by assignment of the claim by way of a guarantee;

(c) the right to demand the assets from or to require restitution by anyone having possession or use of them contrary to the wishes of the party so entitled;

(d) a right to the beneficial use of assets.

3. The right, recorded in a public register and enforceable against third parties, under which a right in rem within the meaning of paragraph 1 may be obtained, shall be considered to be a right in rem.

4. Paragraph 1 shall not preclude actions for nullity, voidability or unenforceability referred to in Article 274(2)(l).

[3.405]
Article 287
Reservation of title

1. The opening of reorganisation measures or winding-up proceedings against an insurance undertaking purchasing an asset shall not affect the rights of a seller which are based on a reservation of title where at the time of the opening of such measures or proceedings the asset is situated within the territory of a Member State other than that in which such measures or proceedings were opened.

2. The opening, after delivery of the asset, of reorganisation measures or winding-up proceedings against an insurance undertaking which is selling an asset shall not constitute grounds for rescinding or terminating the sale and shall not prevent the purchaser from acquiring title where at the time of the opening of such measures or proceedings the asset sold is situated within the territory of a Member State other than that in which such measures or proceedings were opened.

3. Paragraphs 1 and 2 shall not preclude actions for nullity, voidability or unenforceability referred to in Article 274(2)(l).

[3.406]
Article 288
Set-off

1. The opening of reorganisation measures or winding-up proceedings shall not affect the right of creditors to demand the set-off of their claims against the claims of the insurance undertaking, where such a set-off is permitted by the law applicable to the claim of the insurance undertaking.

2. Paragraph 1 shall not preclude actions for nullity, voidability or unenforceability referred to in Article 274(2)(l).

[3.407]
Article 289
Regulated markets

1. Without prejudice to Article 286 the effects of a reorganisation measure or the opening of winding-up proceedings on the rights and obligations of the parties to a regulated market shall be governed solely by the law applicable to that market.

2. Paragraph 1 shall not preclude actions for nullity, voidability, or unenforceability referred to in Article 274(2)(l) which may be taken to set aside payments or transactions under the law applicable to that market.

[3.408]
Article 290
Detrimental acts
Article 274(2)(l) shall not apply where a person who has benefited from a legal act which is detrimental to all the creditors provides proof of that act being subject to the law of a Member State other than the home Member State, and proof that that law does not allow any means of challenging that act in the relevant case.

[3.409]
Article 291
Protection of third-party purchasers
The following law shall be applicable where, by an act concluded after the adoption of a reorganisation measure or the opening of winding-up proceedings, an insurance undertaking disposes, for consideration, of any of the following:

(a) in regard to immovable assets, the law of the Member State where the immovable property is situated;
(b) in regard to ships or aircraft subject to registration in a public register, the law of the Member State under the authority of which the register is kept;
(c) in regard to transferable or other securities, the existence or transfer of which presupposes entry in a register or account laid down by law or which are placed in a central deposit system governed by the law of a Member State, the law of the Member State under the authority of which the register, account or system is kept.

[3.410]
Article 292
Lawsuits pending
The effects of reorganisation measures or winding-up proceedings on a pending lawsuit concerning an asset or a right of which the insurance undertaking has been divested shall be governed solely by the law of the Member State in which the lawsuit is pending.

[3.411]
Article 293
Administrators and liquidators
1. The appointment of the administrator or the liquidator shall be evidenced by a certified copy of the original decision of appointment or by any other certificate issued by the competent authorities of the home Member State.

The Member State in which the administrator or liquidator wishes to act may require a translation into the official language or one of the official languages of that Member State. No formal authentication of that translation or other similar formality shall be required.

2. Administrators and liquidators shall be entitled to exercise within the territory of all the Member States all the powers which they are entitled to exercise within the territory of the home Member State.

Persons to assist or represent administrators and liquidators may be appointed, in accordance with the law of the home Member State, in the course of the reorganisation measure or winding-up proceedings, in particular in host Member States and, specifically, in order to help overcome any difficulties encountered by creditors in that State.

3. In exercising their powers according to the law of the home Member State, administrators or liquidators shall comply with the law of the Member States within which they wish to take action, in particular with regard to procedures for the realisation of assets and the informing of employees.

Those powers shall not include the use of force or the right to rule on legal proceedings or disputes.

[3.412]
Article 294
Registration in a public register
1. The administrator, liquidator or any other authority or person duly empowered in the home Member State may request that a reorganisation measure or the decision to open winding-up proceedings be registered in any relevant public register kept in the other Member States.

However, where a Member State provides for mandatory registration, the authority or person referred to in the first subparagraph shall take all the measures necessary to ensure such registration.

2. The costs of registration shall be regarded as costs and expenses incurred in the proceedings.

[3.413]
Article 295
Professional secrecy
All persons required to receive or divulge information in connection with the procedures laid down in Articles 270, 273 and 296 shall be bound by the provisions on professional secrecy, as laid down in Articles 64 to 69, with the exception of any judicial authorities to which existing national provisions apply.

[3.414]
Article 296
Treatment of branches of third-country insurance undertakings
Where a third-country insurance undertaking has branches established in more than one Member State, each branch shall be treated independently with regard to the application of this Title.

The competent authorities and the supervisory authorities of those Member States shall endeavour to coordinate their actions.

Any administrators or liquidators shall likewise endeavour to coordinate their actions.

(*Arts 297–304 (Title V) outside the scope of this work.*)

TITLE VI TRANSITIONAL AND FINAL PROVISIONS

(*Arts 305–308e (Ch I) outside the scope of this work.*)

CHAPTER II FINAL PROVISIONS

[3.415]
Article 309
Transposition
1. Member States shall bring into force the laws, regulations and administrative provisions necessary to comply with Articles 4, 10, 13, 14, 18, 23, 26–32, 34–49, 51–55, 67, 68, 71, 72, 74–85, 87–91, 93–96, 98, 100–110, 112, 113, 115–126, 128, 129, 131–134, 136–142, 144, 146, 148, 162–167, 172, 173, 178, 185, 190, 192, 210–233, 235–240, 243–258, 260–263, 265, 266, 303 and 304 and Annexes III and IV by [31 March 2015].

When they are adopted by Member States, those measures shall contain a reference to this Directive or shall be accompanied by such a reference on the occasion of their official publication. They shall also include a statement that references in existing laws, regulations and administrative provisions to the directives repealed by this Directive shall be construed as references to this Directive. Member States shall determine how such reference is to be made and how that statement is to be formulated.

[The laws, regulations and administrative provisions referred to in the first subparagraph shall apply from [1 January 2016].]

2. Member States shall communicate to the Commission the text of the main provisions of national law which they adopt in the field covered by this Directive.

NOTES

Para 1: dates in first and third (inner) pairs of square brackets substituted by European Parliament and Council Directive 2013/58/EU, Art 1(1); words in second (outer) pair of square brackets inserted by European Parliament and Council Directive 2012/23/EU, Art 1(b).

Article 310 (*Art 310 (as amended by European Parliament and Council Directive 2013/58/EU, Art 1(2)) repeals Directives 64/225/EEC, 73/239/EEC, 73/240/EEC, 76/580/EEC, 78/473/EEC, 84/641/EEC, 87/344/EEC, 88/357/EEC, 92/49/EEC, 98/78/EC, 2001/17/EC, 2002/83/EC and 2005/68/EC, with effect from 1 January 2016.*)

[3.416]
Article 311
Entry into force
This Directive shall enter into force on the 20th day following its publication in the Official Journal of the European Union.

Articles 1–3, 5–9, 11, 12, 15–17, 19–22, 24, 25, 33, 56–66, 69, 70, 73, 143, 145, 147, 149–161, 168–171, 174–177, 179–184, 186–189, 191, 193–209, 267–300, 302, 305–308 and Annexes I and II, V, VI and VII shall apply from [1 January 2016].

NOTES

Words in square brackets substituted by European Parliament and Council Directive 2013/58/EU, Art 1(3).

[3.417]
Article 312
Addressees
This Directive is addressed to the Member States.

(*Annexes I–VII outside the scope of this work.*)

DIRECTIVE OF THE EUROPEAN PARLIAMENT AND OF THE COUNCIL

(2014/59/EU)

of 15 May 2014

establishing a framework for the recovery and resolution of credit institutions and investment firms and amending Council Directive 82/891/EEC, and Directives 2001/24/EC, 2002/47/EC, 2004/25/EC, 2005/56/EC, 2007/36/EC, 2011/35/EU, 2012/30/EU and 2013/36/EU, and Regulations (EU) No 1093/2010 and (EU) No 648/2012, of the European Parliament and of the Council

(Text with EEA relevance)

[3.418]

NOTES

Date of publication in OJ: OJ L173, 12.6.2014, p 190.

THE EUROPEAN PARLIAMENT AND THE COUNCIL OF THE EUROPEAN UNION,

Having regard to the Treaty on the Functioning of the European Union, and in particular Article 114 thereof,

Having regard to the proposal from the European Commission,

After transmission of the draft legislative act to the national parliaments,

Having regard to the opinion of the European Central Bank,[1]

Having regard to the opinion of the European Economic and Social Committee,[2]

Acting in accordance with the ordinary legislative procedure,[3]

Whereas:

(1) The financial crisis has shown that there is a significant lack of adequate tools at Union level to deal effectively with unsound or failing credit institutions and investment firms ('institutions'). Such tools are needed, in particular, to prevent insolvency or, when insolvency occurs, to minimise negative repercussions by preserving the systemically important functions of the institution concerned. During the crisis, those challenges were a major factor that forced Member States to save institutions using taxpayers' money. The objective of a credible recovery and resolution framework is to obviate the need for such action to the greatest extent possible.

(2) The financial crisis was of systemic dimension in the sense that it affected the access to funding of a large proportion of credit institutions. To avoid failure, with consequences for the overall economy, such a crisis necessitates measures aiming to secure access to funding under equivalent conditions for all credit institutions that are otherwise solvent. Such measures involve liquidity support from central banks and guarantees from Member States for securities issued by solvent credit institutions.

(3) Union financial markets are highly integrated and interconnected with many institutions operating extensively beyond national borders. The failure of a cross-border institution is likely to affect the stability of financial markets in the different Member States in which it operates. The inability of Member States to seize control of a failing institution and resolve it in a way that effectively prevents broader systemic damage can undermine Member State' mutual trust and the credibility of the internal market in the field of financial services. The stability of financial markets is, therefore, an essential condition for the establishment and functioning of the internal market.

(4) There is currently no harmonisation of the procedures for resolving institutions at Union level. Some Member States apply to institutions the same procedures that they apply to other insolvent enterprises, which in certain cases have been adapted for institutions. There are considerable substantial and procedural differences between the laws, regulations and administrative provisions which govern the insolvency of institutions in the Member States. In addition, the financial crisis has exposed the fact that general corporate insolvency procedures may not always be appropriate for institutions as they may not always ensure sufficient speed of intervention, the continuation of the critical functions of institutions and the preservation of financial stability.

(5) A regime is therefore needed to provide authorities with a credible set of tools to intervene sufficiently early and quickly in an unsound or failing institution so as to ensure the continuity of the institution's critical financial and economic functions, while minimising the impact of an institution's failure on the economy and financial system. The regime should ensure that shareholders bear losses first and that creditors bear losses after shareholders, provided that no creditor incurs greater losses than it would have incurred if the institution had been wound up under normal insolvency proceedings in accordance with the no creditor worse off principle as specified in this Directive. New powers should enable authorities, for example, to maintain uninterrupted access to deposits and payment transactions, sell viable portions of the institution where appropriate, and apportion losses in a manner that is fair and predictable. Those objectives should help avoid destabilising financial markets and minimise the costs for taxpayers.

(6) The ongoing review of the regulatory framework, in particular the strengthening of capital and liquidity buffers and better tools for macro-prudential policies, should reduce the likelihood of future crises and enhance the resilience of institutions to economic stress, whether caused by systemic disturbances or

by events specific to the individual institution. It is not possible, however, to devise a regulatory and supervisory framework that can prevent those institutions from ever getting into difficulties. Member States should therefore be prepared and have adequate recovery and resolution tools to handle situations involving both systemic crises and failures of individual institutions. Such tools should include mechanisms that allow authorities to deal effectively with institutions that are failing or likely to fail.

(7) The exercise of such powers and the measures taken should take into account the circumstances in which the failure occurs. If the problem arises in an individual institution and the rest of the financial system is not affected, authorities should be able to exercise their resolution powers without much concern for contagion effects. In a fragile environment, on the other hand, greater care should be exercised to avoid destabilising financial markets.

(8) Resolution of an institution which maintains it as a going concern may, as a last resort, involve government financial stabilisation tools, including temporary public ownership. It is therefore essential to structure the resolution powers and the financing arrangements for resolution in such a way that taxpayers are the beneficiaries of any surplus that may result from the restructuring of an institution that is put back on a safe footing by the authorities. Responsibility and assumption of risk should be accompanied by reward.

(9) Some Member States have already enacted legislative changes that introduce mechanisms to resolve failing institutions; others have indicated their intention to introduce such mechanisms if they are not adopted at Union level. The absence of common conditions, powers and processes for the resolution of institutions is likely to constitute a barrier to the smooth operation of the internal market and hinder cooperation between national authorities when dealing with failing cross-border groups of institutions. This is particularly true where different approaches mean that national authorities do not have the same level of control or the same ability to resolve institutions. Those differences in resolution regimes may affect the funding costs of institutions differently across Member States and potentially create competitive distortions between institutions. Effective resolution regimes in all Member States are necessary to ensure that institutions cannot be restricted in the exercise of the internal market rights of establishment by the financial capacity of their home Member State to manage their failure.

(10) Those obstacles should be eliminated and rules should be adopted in order to ensure that the internal market provisions are not undermined. To that end, rules governing the resolution of institutions should be made subject to common minimum harmonisation rules.

(11) In order to ensure consistency with existing Union legislation in the area of financial services as well as the greatest possible level of financial stability across the spectrum of institutions, the resolution regime should apply to institutions subject to the prudential requirements laid down in Regulation (EU) No 575/2013 of the European Parliament and of the Council[4] and Directive 2013/36/EU of the European Parliament and of the Council.[5] The regime should also apply to financial holding companies, mixed financial holding companies provided for in Directive 2002/87/EC of the European Parliament and of the Council,[6] mixed-activity holding companies and financial institutions, when the latter are subsidiaries of an institution or of a financial holding company, a mixed financial holding company or a mixed-activity holding company and are covered by the supervision of the parent undertaking on a consolidated basis. The crisis has demonstrated that the insolvency of an entity affiliated to a group can rapidly impact the solvency of the whole group and, thus, even have its own systemic implications. Authorities should therefore possess effective means of action with respect to those entities in order to prevent contagion and produce a consistent resolution scheme for the group as a whole, as the insolvency of an entity affiliated to a group could rapidly impact the solvency of the whole group.

(12) To ensure consistency in the regulatory framework, central counterparties, as defined in Regulation (EU) No 648/2012 of the European Parliament and of the Council[7] and central securities depositories as defined in Regulation of the European Parliament and of the Council on improving securities settlement in the European Union and on central securities depositories (CSDs) and amending Directive 98/26/EC could be covered by a separate legislative initiative establishing a recovery and resolution framework for those entities.

(13) The use of resolution tools and powers provided for in this Directive may disrupt the rights of shareholders and creditors. In particular, the power of the authorities to transfer the shares or all or part of the assets of an institution to a private purchaser without the consent of shareholders affects the property rights of shareholders. In addition, the power to decide which liabilities to transfer out of a failing institution based upon the objectives of ensuring the continuity of services and avoiding adverse effects on financial stability may affect the equal treatment of creditors. Accordingly, resolution action should be taken only where necessary in the public interest and any interference with rights of shareholders and creditors which results from resolution action should be compatible with the Charter of Fundamental Rights of the European Union (the Charter). In particular, where creditors within the same class are treated differently in the context of resolution action, such distinctions should be justified in the public interest and proportionate to the risks being addressed and should be neither directly nor indirectly discriminatory on the grounds of nationality.

(14) Authorities should take into account the nature of an institution's business, shareholding structure, legal form, risk profile, size, legal status and interconnectedness to other institutions or to the financial system in general, the scope and complexity of its activities, whether it is a member of an institutional protection scheme or other cooperative mutual solidarity systems, whether it exercises any investment services or activities and whether its failure and subsequent winding up under normal insolvency proceedings would be likely to have a significant negative effect on financial markets, on other institutions, on funding conditions, or on the wider economy in the context of recovery and resolution plans and when using the different powers and tools at their disposal, making sure that the regime is

applied in an appropriate and proportionate way and that the administrative burden relating to the recovery and resolution plan preparation obligations is minimised. Whereas the contents and information specified in this Directive and in Annexes A, B and C establish a minimum standard for institutions with evident systemic relevance, authorities are permitted to apply different or significantly reduced recovery and resolution planning and information requirements on an institution-specific basis, and at a lower frequency for updates than one year. For a small institution of little interconnectedness and complexity, a recovery plan could be reduced to some basic information on its structure, triggers for recovery actions and recovery options. If an institution could be permitted to go insolvent, then the resolution plan could be reduced. Further, the regime should be applied so that the stability of financial markets is not jeopardised. In particular, in situations characterised by broader problems or even doubts about the resilience of many institutions, it is essential that authorities consider the risk of contagion from the actions taken in relation to any individual institution.

(15) In order to ensure the required speed of action, to guarantee independence from economic actors and to avoid conflicts of interest, Member States should appoint public administrative authorities or authorities entrusted with public administrative powers to perform the functions and tasks in relation to resolution pursuant to this Directive. Member States should ensure that appropriate resources are allocated to those resolution authorities. The designation of public authorities should not exclude delegation under the responsibility of a resolution authority. However, it is not necessary to prescribe the type of authority or authorities that Member States should appoint as a resolution authority. While harmonisation of that aspect may facilitate coordination, it would considerably interfere with the constitutional and administrative systems of Member States. A sufficient degree of coordination can still be achieved with a less intrusive requirement: all the national authorities involved in the resolution of institutions should be represented in resolution colleges, where coordination at cross-border or Union level should take place. Member States should therefore be free to choose which authorities should be responsible for applying the resolution tools and exercising the powers laid down in this Directive. Where a Member State designates the authority responsible for the prudential supervision of institutions (competent authority) as a resolution authority, adequate structural arrangements should be put in place to separate the supervisory and resolution functions. That separation should not prevent the resolution function from having access to any information available to the supervisory function.

(16) In light of the consequences that the failure of an institution may have on the financial system and the economy of a Member State as well as the possible need to use public funds to resolve a crisis, the Ministries of Finance or other relevant ministries in the Member States should be closely involved, at an early stage, in the process of crisis management and resolution.

(17) Effective resolution of institutions or group entities operating across the Union requires cooperation among competent authorities and resolution authorities within supervisory and resolution colleges at all the stages covered by this Directive, from the preparation of recovery and resolution plans to the actual resolution of an institution. In the event of disagreement between national authorities on decisions to be taken in accordance with this Directive with regard to institutions, the European Supervisory Authority (European Banking Authority) ('EBA'), established by Regulation (EU) No 1093/2010 of the European Parliament and of the Council[8] should, where specified in this Directive, as a last resort, play a mediation role. In certain cases, this Directive provides for binding mediation by EBA in accordance with Article 19 of Regulation (EU) No 1093/2010. Such binding mediation does not prevent non-binding mediation in accordance with Article 31 of Regulation (EU) No 1093/2010 in other cases.

(18) In the resolution of institutions or groups operating across the Union, the decisions taken should also aim to preserve financial stability and minimise economic and social effects in the Member States where the institution or group operates.

(19) In order to deal in an efficient manner with failing institutions, authorities should have the power to impose preparatory and preventative measures.

(20) Given the extension of EBA's responsibilities and tasks as laid down in this Directive, the European Parliament, the Council and the Commission should ensure that adequate human and financial resources are made available without delay. For that purpose, the procedure for the establishment, implementation and control of its budget as referred to in Articles 63 and 64 of Regulation (EU) No 1093/2010 should take due account of those tasks. The European Parliament and the Council should ensure that the best standards of efficiency are met.

(21) It is essential that institutions prepare and regularly update recovery plans that set out measures to be taken by those institutions for the restoration of their financial position following a significant deterioration. Such plans should be detailed and based on realistic assumptions applicable in a range of robust and severe scenarios. The requirement to prepare a recovery plan should, however, be applied proportionately, reflecting the systemic importance of the institution or the group and its interconnectedness, including through mutual guarantee schemes. Accordingly, the required content should take into account the nature of the institution's sources of funding, including mutually guaranteed funding or liabilities, and the degree to which group support would be credibly available. Institutions should be required to submit their plans to competent authorities for a complete assessment, including whether the plans are comprehensive and could feasibly restore an institution's viability, in a timely manner, even in periods of severe financial stress.

(22) Recovery plans should include possible measures which could be taken by the management of the institution where the conditions for early intervention are met.

(23) In determining whether a private sector action could prevent the failure of an institution within

a reasonable timeframe, the relevant authority should take into account the effectiveness of early intervention measures undertaken within the timeframe predetermined by the competent authority. In the case of group recovery plans, the potential impact of the recovery measures on all the Member States where the group operates should be taken into account while drawing up the plans.

(24) Where an institution does not present an adequate recovery plan, competent authorities should be empowered to require that institution to take measures necessary to redress the material deficiencies of the plan. That requirement may affect the freedom to conduct a business as guaranteed by Article 16 of the Charter. The limitation of that fundamental right is however necessary to meet the objectives of financial stability. More specifically, such a limitation is necessary in order to strengthen the business of institutions and avoid institutions growing excessively or taking excessive risks without being able to tackle setbacks and losses and to restore their capital base. The limitation is proportionate because it permits preventative action to the extent that it is necessary to address the deficiencies and therefore complies with Article 52 of the Charter.

(25) Resolution planning is an essential component of effective resolution. Authorities should have all the information necessary in order to identify and ensure the continuance of critical functions. The content of a resolution plan should, however, be proportionate to the systemic importance of the institution or group.

(26) Because of the institution's privileged knowledge of its own functioning and any problems arising from it, resolution plans should be drawn up by resolution authorities on the basis of, inter alia, the information provided by the institutions concerned.

(27) In order to comply with the principle of proportionality and to avoid excessive administrative burden, the possibility for competent authorities and, where relevant, resolution authorities, to waive the requirements relating to the preparation of the recovery and resolution plans on a case-by-case basis should be allowed in the limited cases specified in this Directive. Such cases comprise institutions affiliated to a central body and wholly or partially exempt from prudential requirements in national law in accordance with Article 21 of Directive 2013/36/EU and institutions which belong to an institutional protection scheme in accordance with Article 113(7) of Regulation (EU) No 575/2013. In each case the granting of a waiver should be subject to the conditions specified in this Directive.

(28) Having regard to the capital structure of institutions affiliated to a central body, for the purposes of this Directive, those institutions should not be obliged to each draw up separate recovery or resolution plans solely on the grounds that the central body to which they are affiliated is under the direct supervision of the European Central Bank.

(29) Resolution authorities, on the basis of the assessment of resolvability by the relevant resolution authorities, should have the power to require changes to the structure and organisation of institutions directly or indirectly through the competent authority, to take measures which are necessary and proportionate to reduce or remove material impediments to the application of resolution tools and ensure the resolvability of the entities concerned. Due to the potentially systemic nature of all institutions, it is crucial, in order to maintain financial stability, that authorities have the possibility to resolve any institution. In order to respect the right to conduct business laid down in Article 16 of the Charter, the authorities' discretion should be limited to what is necessary in order to simplify the structure and operations of the institution solely to improve its resolvability. In addition, any measure imposed for such purposes should be consistent with Union law. Measures should be neither directly nor indirectly discriminatory on the grounds of nationality, and should be justified by the overriding reason of being conducted in the public interest in financial stability. Furthermore, action should not go beyond the minimum necessary to attain the objectives sought. When determining the measures to be taken, resolution authorities should take into account the warnings and recommendations of the European Systemic Risk Board established by Regulation (EU) No 1092/2010 of the European Parliament and of the Council.[9]

(30) Measures proposed to address or remove impediments to the resolvability of an institution or a group should not prevent institutions from exercising the right of establishment conferred on them by the Treaty on the Functioning of the European Union ('TFEU).

(31) Recovery and resolution plans should not assume access to extraordinary public financial support or expose taxpayers to the risk of loss.

(32) The group treatment for recovery and resolution planning provided for in this Directive should apply to all groups of institutions supervised on a consolidated basis, including groups whose undertakings are linked by a relationship within the meaning of Article 22(7) of Directive 2013/34/EU of the European Parliament and of the Council.[10] The recovery and resolution plans should take into account the financial, technical and business structure of the relevant group. If individual recovery and resolution plans for institutions that are a part of a group are prepared, the relevant authorities should aim to achieve, to the extent possible, consistency with recovery and resolution plans for the rest of the group.

(33) It should be the general rule that the group recovery and resolution plans are prepared for the group as a whole and identify measures in relation to a parent institution as well as all individual subsidiaries that are part of a group. The relevant authorities, acting within the resolution college, should make every effort to reach a joint decision on the assessment and adoption of those plans. However, in specific cases where an individual recovery or resolution plan has been drawn up, the scope of the group recovery plan assessed by the consolidating supervisor or the group resolution plan decided by the group-level resolution authority should not cover those group entities for which the individual plans have been assessed or prepared by the relevant authorities.

(34) In the case of group resolution plans, the potential impact of the resolution measures in all the Member States where the group operates should be specifically taken into account in the drawing up of

group resolution plans. The resolution authorities of the Member States where the group has subsidiaries should be involved in the drawing up of the plan.

(35) Recovery and resolution plans should include procedures for informing and consulting employee representatives throughout the recovery and resolution processes where appropriate. Where applicable, collective agreements, or other arrangements provided for by social partners, as well as national and Union law on the involvement of trade unions and workers' representatives in company restructuring processes, should be complied with in that regard.

(36) Given the sensitivity of the information contained in them, confidential information in the recovery and resolution plans should be subject to the confidentiality provisions as laid down in this Directive.

(37) The competent authorities should transmit the recovery plans and any changes thereto to the relevant resolution authorities, and the latter should transmit the resolution plans and any changes thereto to the former, in order to permanently keep every relevant resolution authority fully informed.

(38) The provision of financial support from one entity of a cross-border group to another entity of the same group is currently restricted by a number of provisions laid down in national law in some Member States. Those provisions are designed to protect the creditors and shareholders of each entity. Those provisions, however, do not take into account the interdependency of the entities of the same group. It is, therefore, appropriate to set out under which conditions financial support may be transferred among entities of a cross-border group of institutions with a view to ensuring the financial stability of the group as a whole without jeopardising the liquidity or solvency of the group entity providing the support. Financial support between group entities should be voluntary and should be subject to appropriate safeguards. It is appropriate that the exercise of the right of establishment is not directly or indirectly made conditional by Member States to the existence of an agreement to provide financial support. The provisions regarding intra-group financial support in this Directive do not affect contractual or statutory liability arrangements between institutions which protect the participating institutions through cross-guarantees and equivalent arrangements. Where a competent authority restricts or prohibits intragroup financial support and where the group recovery plan makes reference to intragroup financial support, such a prohibition or restriction should be considered to be a material change for the purpose of reviewing the recovery plan.

(39) During the recovery and early intervention phases laid down in this Directive, shareholders should retain full responsibility and control of the institution except when a temporary administrator has been appointed by the competent authority. They should no longer retain such a responsibility once the institution has been put under resolution.

(40) In order to preserve financial stability, it is important that competent authorities are able to remedy the deterioration of an institution's financial and economic situation before that institution reaches a point at which authorities have no other alternative than to resolve it. To that end, competent authorities should be granted early intervention powers, including the power to appoint a temporary administrator, either to replace or to temporarily work with the management body and senior management of an institution. The task of the temporary administrator should be to exercise any powers conferred on it with a view to promoting solutions to redress the financial situation of the institution. The appointment of the temporary administrator should not unduly interfere with rights of the shareholders or owners or procedural obligations established under Union or national company law and should respect international obligations of the Union or Member States, relating to investment protection. The early intervention powers should include those already provided for in Directive 2013/36/EU for circumstances other than those considered to be early intervention as well as other situations considered to be necessary to restore the financial soundness of an institution.

(41) The resolution framework should provide for timely entry into resolution before a financial institution is balance-sheet insolvent and before all equity has been fully wiped out. Resolution should be initiated when a competent authority, after consulting a resolution authority, determines that an institution is failing or likely to fail and alternative measures as specified in this Directive would prevent such a failure within a reasonable timeframe. Exceptionally, Member States may provide that, in addition to the competent authority, the determination that the institution is failing or likely to fail can be made also by the resolution authority, after consulting the competent authority. The fact that an institution does not meet the requirements for authorisation should not justify per-se the entry into resolution, especially if the institution is still or likely to still be viable. An institution should be considered to be failing or likely to fail when it infringes or is likely in the near future to infringe the requirements for continuing authorisation, when the assets of the institution are or are likely in the near future to be less than its liabilities, when the institution is or is likely in the near future to be unable to pay its debts as they fall due, or when the institution requires extraordinary public financial support except in the particular circumstances laid down in this Directive. The need for emergency liquidity assistance from a central bank should not, per se, be a condition that sufficiently demonstrates that an institution is or will be, in the near future, unable to pay its liabilities as they fall due.

If that facility were guaranteed by a State, an institution accessing such a facility would be subject to the State aid framework. In order to preserve financial stability, in particular in the case of a systemic liquidity shortage, State guarantees on liquidity facilities provided by central banks or State guarantees of newly issued liabilities to remedy a serious disturbance in the economy of a Member State should not trigger the resolution framework provided that a number of conditions are met. In particular, the State guarantee measures should be approved under the State aid framework and should not be part of a larger aid package, and the use of the guarantee measures should be strictly limited in time. Member States guarantees for equity claims should be prohibited. When providing a guarantee for newly issued liabilities other than equity, a Member State should ensure that the guarantee is sufficiently remunerated by the institution. Furthermore, the provision of extraordinary public financial support should not trigger resolution where, as a precautionary measure, a Member State takes an equity stake in an institution, including an institution which is publicly owned, which complies with its capital requirements. This may be the case, for example, where an institution is required to raise new capital due to the outcome of a scenario-based stress test or of the equivalent exercise conducted by macroprudential authorities which includes a requirement that is set to maintain financial stability in the context of a systemic crisis, but the institution is unable to raise capital privately in markets. An institution should not be considered to be failing or likely to fail solely on the basis that extraordinary public financial support was provided before the entry into force of this Directive. Finally, access to liquidity facilities including emergency liquidity assistance by central banks may constitute State aid pursuant to the State aid framework.

(42) In the event of resolution of a group with cross-border activity, any resolution action should take into account the potential impact of the resolution in all the Member States where the institution or the group operates.

(43) The powers of resolution authorities should also apply to holding companies where both the holding company is failing or likely to fail and a subsidiary institution, whether in the Union or in a third country, is failing or likely to fail. In addition, notwithstanding the fact that a holding company might not be failing or likely to fail, the powers of resolution authorities should apply to the holding company where one or more subsidiary institutions meet the conditions for resolution, or a third-country institution meets the conditions for resolution in that third country and the application of the resolution tools and powers in relation to the holding company is necessary for the resolution of one or more of its subsidiaries or for the resolution of the group as a whole.

(44) Where an institution is failing or likely to fail, national resolution authorities should have at their disposal a minimum harmonised set of resolution tools and powers. Their exercise should be subject to common conditions, objectives, and general principles. Once the resolution authority has taken the decision to put the institution under resolution, normal insolvency proceedings should be excluded except if they need to be combined with the use of the resolution tools and at the initiative of the resolution authority. Member States should be able to confer on the resolution authorities powers and tools in addition to those conferred on them under this Directive. The use of those additional tools and powers, however, should be consistent with the resolution principles and objectives as laid down in this Directive. In particular, the use of such tools or powers should not impinge on the effective resolution of cross-border groups.

(45) In order to avoid moral hazard, any failing institution should be able to exit the market, irrespective of its size and interconnectedness, without causing systemic disruption. A failing institution should in principle be liquidated under normal insolvency proceedings. However, liquidation under normal insolvency proceedings might jeopardise financial stability, interrupt the provision of critical functions, and affect the protection of depositors. In such a case it is highly likely that there would be a public interest in placing the institution under resolution and applying resolution tools rather than resorting to normal insolvency proceedings. The objectives of resolution should therefore be to ensure the continuity of critical functions, to avoid adverse effects on financial stability, to protect public funds by minimising reliance on extraordinary public financial support to failing institutions and to protect covered depositors, investors, client funds and client assets.

(46) The winding up of a failing institution through normal insolvency proceedings should always be considered before resolution tools are applied. A failing institution should be maintained through the use of resolution tools as a going concern with the use, to the extent possible, of private funds. That may be achieved either through sale to or merger with a private sector purchaser, or after having written down the liabilities of the institution, or after having converted its debt to equity, in order to effect a recapitalisation.

(47) When applying resolutions tools and exercising resolution powers, resolution authorities should take all appropriate measures to ensure that resolution action is taken in accordance with principles including that shareholders and creditors bear an appropriate share of the losses, that the management should in principle be replaced, that the costs of the resolution of the institution are minimised and that creditors of the same class are treated in an equitable manner. In particular, where creditors within the same class are treated differently in the context of resolution action, such distinctions should be justified in the public interest and should be neither directly nor indirectly discriminatory on the grounds of nationality. When the use of the resolution tools involves the granting of State aid, interventions should have to be assessed in accordance with the relevant State aid provisions. State aid may be involved, inter alia, where resolution funds or deposit guarantee funds intervene to assist in the resolution of failing institutions.

(48) When applying resolution tools and exercising resolution powers, resolution authorities should inform and consult employee representatives where appropriate. Where applicable, collective agreements, or other arrangements provided for by social partners, should be fully taken into account in that regard.

(49) The limitations on the rights of shareholders and creditors should be in accordance with Article 52 of the Charter. The resolution tools should therefore be applied only to those institutions that are failing or likely to fail, and only when it is necessary to pursue the objective of financial stability in the general interest. In particular, resolution tools should be applied where the institution cannot be wound up under normal insolvency proceedings without destabilising the financial system and the measures are necessary in order to ensure the rapid transfer and continuation of systemically important functions and where there is no reasonable prospect for any alternative private solution, including any increase of capital by the existing shareholders or by any third party sufficient to restore the full viability of the institution. In addition, when applying resolutions tools and exercising resolution powers, the principle of

proportionality and the particularities of the legal form of an institution should be taken into account.

(50) Interference with property rights should not be disproportionate. Affected shareholders and creditors should not incur greater losses than those which they would have incurred if the institution had been wound up at the time that the resolution decision is taken. In the event of a partial transfer of assets of an institution under resolution to a private purchaser or to a bridge bank, the residual part of the institution under resolution should be wound up under normal insolvency proceedings. In order to protect shareholders and creditors who are left in the winding up proceedings of the institution, they should be entitled to receive in payment of, or compensation for, their claims in the winding up proceedings not less than what it is estimated they would have recovered if the whole institution had been wound up under normal insolvency proceedings.

(51) For the purpose of protecting the right of shareholders and creditors, clear obligations should be laid down concerning the valuation of the assets and liabilities of the institution under resolution and, where required under this Directive, valuation of the treatment that shareholders and creditors would have received if the institution had been wound up under normal insolvency proceedings. It should be possible to commence a valuation already in the early intervention phase. Before any resolution action is taken, a fair and realistic valuation of the assets and liabilities of the institution should be carried out. Such a valuation should be subject to a right of appeal only together with the resolution decision. In addition, where required under this Directive, an *ex-post* comparison between the treatment that shareholders and creditors have actually been afforded and the treatment they would have received under normal insolvency proceedings should be carried out after resolution tools have been applied. If it is determined that shareholders and creditors have received, in payment of, or compensation for, their claims, the equivalent of less than the amount that they would have received under normal insolvency proceedings, they should be entitled to the payment of the difference where required under this Directive. As opposed to the valuation prior to the resolution action, it should be possible to challenge that comparison separately from the resolution decision. Member States should be free to decide on the procedure as to how to pay any difference of treatment that has been determined to shareholders and creditors. That difference, if any, should be paid by the financial arrangements established in accordance with this Directive.

(52) It is important that losses be recognised upon failure of the institution. The valuation of assets and liabilities of failing institutions should be based on fair, prudent and realistic assumptions at the moment when the resolution tools are applied. The value of liabilities should not, however, be affected in the valuation by the institution's financial state. It should be possible, for reasons of urgency, that the resolution authorities make a rapid valuation of the assets or the liabilities of a failing institution. That valuation should be provisional and should apply until an independent valuation is carried out. EBA's binding technical standards relating to valuation methodology should establish a framework of principles to be used in conducting such valuations and should allow different specific methodologies to be applied by resolution authorities and independent valuers, as appropriate.

(53) Rapid and coordinated action is necessary to sustain market confidence and minimise contagion. Once an institution is deemed to be failing or likely to fail and there is no reasonable prospect that any alternative private sector or supervisory action would prevent the failure of the institution within a reasonable timeframe, resolution authorities should not delay in taking appropriate and coordinated resolution action in the public interest. The circumstances under which the failure of an institution may occur, and in particular taking account of the possible urgency of the situation, should allow resolution authorities to take resolution action without imposing an obligation to first use the early intervention powers.

(54) When taking resolution actions, resolution authorities should take into account and follow the measures provided for in the resolution plans unless resolution authorities assess, taking into account circumstances of the case, that resolution objectives will be achieved more effectively by taking actions which are not provided for in the resolution plans.

(55) Save as expressly specified in this Directive, the resolution tools should be applied before any public sector injection of capital or equivalent extraordinary public financial support to an institution. This, however, should not impede the use of funds from the deposit guarantee schemes or resolution funds in order to absorb losses that would have otherwise been suffered by covered depositors or discretionarily excluded creditors. In that respect, the use of extraordinary public financial support, resolution funds or deposit guarantee schemes to assist in the resolution of failing institutions should comply with the relevant State aid provisions.

(56) Problems in financial markets in the Union arising from system-wide events could have adverse effects on the Union economy and citizens of the Union. Therefore, resolution tools should be designed and suitable to counter a broad set of largely unpredictable scenarios, taking into account that there could be a difference between a single institution in a crisis and a broader systemic banking crisis.

(57) When the Commission undertakes State aid assessment under Article 107 TFEU of the government stabilisation tools referred to in this Directive, it should separately assess whether the notified government stabilisation tools do not infringe any intrinsically linked provisions of Union law, including those relating to the minimum loss absorption requirement of 8% contained in this Directive, as well as whether there is a very extraordinary situation of a systemic crisis justifying resorting to those tools under this Directive while ensuring the level playing field in the internal market. In accordance with Articles 107 and 108 TFEU, that assessment should be made before any government stabilisation tools may be used.

(58) The application of government stabilisation tools should be fiscally neutral in the medium term.

(59) The resolution tools should include the sale of the business or shares of the institution under resolution, the setting up of a bridge institution, the separation of the performing assets from the impaired

or under-performing assets of the failing institution, and the bail-in of the shareholders and creditors of the failing institution.

(60) Where the resolution tools have been used to transfer the systemically important services or viable business of an institution to a sound entity such as a private sector purchaser or bridge institution, the residual part of the institution should be liquidated within an appropriate time frame having regard to any need for the failing institution to provide services or support to enable the purchaser or bridge institution to carry out the activities or services acquired by virtue of that transfer.

(61) The sale of business tool should enable authorities to effect a sale of the institution or parts of its business to one or more purchasers without the consent of shareholders. When applying the sale of business tool, authorities should make arrangements for the marketing of that institution or part of its business in an open, transparent and non-discriminatory process, while aiming to maximise, as far as possible, the sale price. Where, for reasons of urgency, such a process is impossible, authorities should take steps to redress detrimental effects on competition and on the internal market.

(62) Any net proceeds from the transfer of assets or liabilities of the institution under resolution when applying the sale of business tool should benefit the institution left in the winding up proceedings. Any net proceeds from the transfer of shares or other instruments of ownership issued by the institution under resolution when applying the sale of business tool should benefit the owners of those shares or other instruments of ownership. Proceeds should be calculated net of the costs arisen from the failure of the institution and from the resolution process.

(63) In order to perform the sale of business in a timely manner and protect financial stability, the assessment of the buyer of a qualifying holding should be carried out in a timely manner that does not delay the application of the sale of business tool in accordance with this Directive by way of derogation from the time-limits and procedures laid down in Directive 2013/36/EU and Directive 2014/65/EU of the European Parliament and of the Council.[11]

(64) Information concerning the marketing of a failing institution and the negotiations with potential acquirers prior to the application of the sale-of-business tool is likely to be of systemic importance. In order to ensure financial stability, it is important that the disclosure to the public of such information required by Regulation (EU) No 596/2014 of the European Parliament and of the Council[12] may be delayed for the time necessary to plan and structure the resolution of the institution in accordance with delays permitted under the market abuse regime.

(65) As an institution which is wholly or partially owned by one or more public authorities or controlled by the resolution authority, a bridge institution would have as its main purpose ensuring that essential financial services continue to be provided to the clients of the failing institution and that essential financial activities continue to be performed. The bridge institution should be operated as a viable going concern and be put back on the market when conditions are appropriate and within the period laid down in this Directive or wound up if not viable.

(66) The asset separation tool should enable authorities to transfer assets, rights or liabilities of an institution under resolution to a separate vehicle. That tool should be used only in conjunction with other tools to prevent an undue competitive advantage for the failing institution.

(67) An effective resolution regime should minimise the costs of the resolution of a failing institution borne by the taxpayers. It should ensure that systemic institutions can be resolved without jeopardising financial stability. The bail-in tool achieves that objective by ensuring that shareholders and creditors of the failing institution suffer appropriate losses and bear an appropriate part of the costs arising from the failure of the institution. The bail-in tool will therefore give shareholders and creditors of institutions a stronger incentive to monitor the health of an institution during normal circumstances and meets the Financial Stability Board recommendation that statutory debt-write down and conversion powers be included in a framework for resolution, as an additional option in conjunction with other resolution tools.

(68) In order to ensure that resolution authorities have the necessary flexibility to allocate losses to creditors in a range of circumstances, it is appropriate that those authorities be able to apply the bail-in tool both where the objective is to resolve the failing institution as a going concern if there is a realistic prospect that the institution's viability may be restored, and where systemically important services are transferred to a bridge institution and the residual part of the institution ceases to operate and is wound up.

(69) Where the bail-in tool is applied with the objective of restoring the capital of the failing institution to enable it to continue to operate as a going concern, the resolution through bail-in should be accompanied by replacement of management, except where retention of management is appropriate and necessary for the achievement of the resolution objectives, and a subsequent restructuring of the institution and its activities in a way that addresses the reasons for its failure. That restructuring should be achieved through the implementation of a business reorganisation plan. Where applicable, such plans should be compatible with the restructuring plan that the institution is required to submit to the Commission under the State aid framework. In particular, in addition to measures aiming to restore the long-term viability of the institution, the plan should include measures limiting the aid to the minimum burden sharing, and measures limiting distortions of competition.

(70) It is not appropriate to apply the bail-in tool to claims in so far as they are secured, collateralised or otherwise guaranteed. However, in order to ensure that the bail-in tool is effective and achieves its objectives, it is desirable that it can be applied to as wide a range of the unsecured liabilities of a failing institution as possible. Nevertheless, it is appropriate to exclude certain kinds of unsecured liability from the scope of application of the bail-in tool. In order to protect holders of covered deposits, the bail-in tool should not apply to those deposits that are protected under Directive 2014/49/EU of the European Parliament and of the Council.[13] In order to ensure continuity of critical functions, the bail-in tool should

not apply to certain liabilities to employees of the failing institution or to commercial claims that relate to goods and services critical to the daily functioning of the institution. In order to honour pension entitlements and pension amounts owed or owing to pension trusts and pension trustees, the bail-in tool should not apply to the failing institution's liabilities to a pension scheme. However, the bail-in tool would apply to liabilities for pension benefits attributable to variable remuneration which do not arise from collective bargaining agreements, as well as to the variable component of the remuneration of material risk takers. To reduce risk of systemic contagion, the bail-in tool should not apply to liabilities arising from a participation in payment systems which have a remaining maturity of less than seven days, or liabilities to institutions, excluding entities that are part of the same group, with an original maturity of less than seven days.

(71) As the protection of covered depositors is one of the most important objectives of resolution, covered deposits should not be subject to the exercise of the bail-in tool. The deposit guarantee scheme should, however, contribute to funding the resolution process by absorbing losses to the extent of the net losses that it would have had to suffer after compensating depositors in normal insolvency proceedings. The exercise of the bail-in powers would ensure that depositors continue to have access to their deposits up to at least the coverage level which is the main reason why the deposit guarantee schemes have been established. Not providing for the involvement of those schemes in such cases would constitute an unfair advantage with respect to the rest of creditors which would be subject to the exercise of the powers by the resolution authority.

(72) Resolution authorities should be able to exclude or partially exclude liabilities in a number of circumstances including where it is not possible to bail-in such liabilities within a reasonable timeframe, the exclusion is strictly necessary and is proportionate to achieving the continuity of critical functions and core business lines or the application of the bail-in tool to liabilities would cause a destruction in value such that losses borne by other creditors would be higher than if those liabilities were not excluded from bail-in. Resolution authorities should be able to exclude or partially exclude liabilities where necessary to avoid the spreading of contagion and financial instability which may cause serious disturbance to the economy of a Member State. When carrying out those assessments, resolution authorities should give consideration to the consequences of a potential bail-in of liabilities stemming from eligible deposits held by natural persons and micro, small and medium-sized enterprises above the coverage level provided for in Directive 2014/49/EU.

(73) Where those exclusions are applied, the level of write down or conversion of other eligible liabilities may be increased to take account of such exclusions subject to the 'no creditor worse off than under normal insolvency proceedings' principle being respected. Where the losses cannot be passed to other creditors, the resolution financing arrangement may make a contribution to the institution under resolution subject to a number of strict conditions including the requirement that losses totalling not less than 8% of total liabilities including own funds have already been absorbed, and the funding provided by the resolution fund is limited to the lower of 5% of total liabilities including own funds or the means available to the resolution fund and the amount that can be raised through *ex-post* contributions within three years.

(74) In extraordinary circumstances, where liabilities have been excluded and the resolution fund has been used to contribute to bail-in in lieu of those liabilities to the extent of the permissible cap, the resolution authority should be able to seek funding from alternative financing sources.

(75) The minimum amount of contribution to loss absorption and recapitalisation of 8% of total liabilities including own funds or, where applicable, of 20% of risk-weighted assets should be calculated based on the valuation for the purposes of resolution in accordance with this Directive. Historical losses which have already been absorbed by shareholders through a reduction in own funds prior to such a valuation should not be included in those percentages.

(76) Nothing in this Directive should require Member States to finance resolution financing arrangements by means from their general budget.

(77) Except where otherwise specified in this Directive, resolution authorities should apply the bail-in tool in a way that respects the *pari passu* treatment of creditors and the statutory ranking of claims under the applicable insolvency law. Losses should first be absorbed by regulatory capital instruments and should be allocated to shareholders either through the cancellation or transfer of shares or through severe dilution. Where those instruments are not sufficient, subordinated debt should be converted or written down. Senior liabilities should be converted or written down if the subordinate classes have been converted or written down entirely.

(78) Where there are exemptions of liabilities such as for payment and settlement systems, employee or trade creditors, or preferential ranking such as for deposits of natural persons and micro, small and medium-sized enterprises, they should apply in third countries as well as in the Union. To ensure the ability to write down or convert liabilities when appropriate in third countries, recognition of that possibility should be included in the contractual provisions governed by the law of the third countries, especially for those liabilities ranking at a lower level within the hierarchy of creditors. Such contractual terms should not be required for liabilities exempted from bail-in for deposits of natural persons and micro, small and medium-sized enterprises or where the law of the third country or a binding agreement concluded with that third country allow the resolution authority of the Member State to exercise its write down or conversion powers.

(79) To avoid institutions structuring their liabilities in a manner that impedes the effectiveness of the bail-in tool it is appropriate to establish that the institutions meet at all times a minimum requirement for own funds and eligible liabilities expressed as a percentage of the total liabilities and own funds of the

institution. Resolution authorities should be able to require, on a case-by-case basis, that that percentage is wholly or partially composed of own funds or of a specific type of liabilities.

(80) This Directive adopts a 'top down' approach to the determination of the minimum requirement for own funds and eligible liabilities (MREL) within a group. The approach further recognises that resolution action is applied at the level of the individual legal person, and that it is imperative that loss-absorbing capacity is located in, or accessible to, the legal person within the group in which losses occur. To that end, resolution authorities should ensure that loss-absorbing capacity within a group is distributed across the group in accordance with the level of risk in its constituent legal persons. The minimum requirement necessary for each individual subsidiary should be separately assessed. Furthermore, resolution authorities should ensure that all capital and liabilities which are counted towards the consolidated minimum requirement are located in entities where losses are liable to occur, or are otherwise available to absorb losses. This Directive should allow for a multiple-point-of-entry or a single-point-of-entry resolution. The MREL should reflect the resolution strategy which is appropriate to a group in accordance with the resolution plan. In particular, the MREL should be required at the appropriate level in the group in order to reflect a multiple-point-of-entry approach or single-point-of-entry-approach contained in the resolution plan while keeping in mind that there could be circumstances where an approach different from that contained in the plan is used as it would allow, for instance, reaching the resolution objectives more efficiently. Against that background, regardless of whether a group has chosen the single-point-of-entry or the multiple-point-of entry approach, all institutions and other legal persons in the group where required by the resolution authorities should, at all times, have a robust MREL so as to avoid the risk of contagion or a bank run.

(81) Member States should ensure that Additional Tier 1 and Tier 2 capital instruments fully absorb losses at the point of non-viability of the issuing institution. Accordingly, resolution authorities should be required to write down those instruments in full, or to convert them to Common Equity Tier 1 instruments, at the point of non-viability and before any resolution action is taken. For that purpose, the point of non-viability should be understood as the point at which the relevant authority determines that the institution meets the conditions for resolution or the point at which the authority decides that the institution would cease to be viable if those capital instruments were not written down or converted. The fact that the instruments are to be written down or converted by authorities in the circumstances required by this Directive should be recognised in the terms governing the instrument, and in any prospectus or offering documents published or provided in connection with the instruments.

(82) In order to allow for effective resolution outcomes, it should be possible to apply the bail-in tool before 1 January 2016.

(83) Resolution authorities should be able to apply the bail-in tool only partially where an assessment of the potential impact on the stability of the financial system in the Member States concerned and in the rest of the Union demonstrates that its full application would be contrary to the overall public interests of the Member State or the Union as a whole.

(84) Resolution authorities should have all the necessary legal powers that, in different combinations, may be exercised when applying the resolution tools. They should include the power to transfer shares in, or assets, rights or liabilities of, a failing institution to another entity such as another institution or a bridge institution, the power to write down or cancel shares, or write down or convert liabilities of a failing institution, the power to replace the management and the power to impose a temporary moratorium on the payment of claims. Supplementary powers are needed, including the power to require continuity of essential services from other parts of a group.

(85) It is not necessary to prescribe the exact means through which the resolution authorities should intervene in the failing institution. Resolution authorities should have the choice between taking control through a direct intervention in the institution or through executive order. They should decide according to the circumstances of the case. It does not appear necessary for efficient cooperation between Member States to impose a single model at this stage.

(86) The resolution framework should include procedural requirements to ensure that resolution actions are properly notified and, subject to the limited exceptions laid down in this Directive, made public. However, as information obtained by resolution authorities and their professional advisers during the resolution process is likely to be sensitive, before the resolution decision is made public, that information should be subject to an effective confidentiality regime. The fact that information on the contents and details of recovery and resolution plans and the result of any assessment of those plans may have far-reaching effects, in particular on the undertakings concerned, must be taken into account. Any information provided in respect of a decision before it is taken, be it on whether the conditions for resolution are satisfied, on the use of a specific tool or of any action during the proceedings, must be presumed to have effects on the public and private interests concerned by the action. However, information that the resolution authority is examining a specific institution could be enough for there to be negative effects on that institution. It is therefore necessary to ensure that there are appropriate mechanisms for maintaining the confidentiality of such information, such as the content and details of recovery and resolution plans and the result of any assessment carried out in that context.

(87) Resolution authorities should have ancillary powers to ensure the effectiveness of the transfer of shares or debt instruments and assets, rights and liabilities. Subject to the safeguards specified in this Directive, those powers should include the power to remove third parties rights from the transferred instruments or assets and the power to enforce contracts and to provide for the continuity of arrangements vis-à-vis the recipient of the transferred assets and shares. However, the rights of employees to terminate a contract of employment should not be affected. The right of a party to terminate a contract with an institution under resolution, or a group entity thereof, for reasons other than the resolution of the failing

institution should not be affected either. Resolution authorities should have the ancillary power to require the residual institution that is being wound up under normal insolvency proceedings to provide services that are necessary to enable the institution to which assets or shares have been transferred by virtue of the application of the sale of business tool or the bridge institution tool to operate its business.

(88) In accordance with Article 47 of the Charter, the parties concerned have a right to due process and to an effective remedy against the measures affecting them. Therefore, the decisions taken by the resolution authorities should be subject to a right of appeal.

(89) Crisis management measures taken by national resolution authorities may require complex economic assessments and a large margin of discretion. The national resolution authorities are specifically equipped with the expertise needed for making those assessments and for determining the appropriate use of the margin of discretion. Therefore, it is important to ensure that the complex economic assessments made by national resolution authorities in that context are used as a basis by national courts when reviewing the crisis management measures concerned. However, the complex nature of those assessments should not prevent national courts from examining whether the evidence relied on by the resolution authority is factually accurate, reliable and consistent, whether that evidence contains all relevant information which should be taken into account in order to assess a complex situation and whether it is capable of substantiating the conclusions drawn therefrom.

(90) Since this Directive aims to cover situations of extreme urgency, and since the suspension of any decision of the resolution authorities might impede the continuity of critical functions, it is necessary to provide that the lodging of any appeal should not result in automatic suspension of the effects of the challenged decision and that the decision of the resolution authority should be immediately enforceable with a presumption that its suspension would be against the public interest.

(91) In addition, where necessary in order to protect third parties who have acquired assets, rights and liabilities of the institution under resolution in good faith by virtue of the exercise of the resolution powers by the authorities and to ensure the stability of the financial markets, a right of appeal should not affect any subsequent administrative act or transaction concluded on the basis of an annulled decision. In such cases, remedies for a wrongful decision should therefore be limited to the award of compensation for the damages suffered by the affected persons.

(92) Given that crisis management measures may be required to be taken urgently due to serious financial stability risks in the Member State and the Union, any procedure under national law relating to the application for *ex-ante* judicial approval of a crisis management measure and the court's consideration of such an application should be swift. Given the requirement for a crisis management measure to be taken urgently, the court should give its decision within 24 hours and Member States should ensure that the relevant authority can take its decision immediately after the court has given its approval. This is without prejudice to the right that interested parties might have in making an application to the court to set aside the decision for a limited period after the resolution authority has taken the crisis management measure.

(93) It is in the interest of an efficient resolution, and in order to avoid conflicts of jurisdiction, that no normal insolvency proceedings for the failing institution be opened or continued whilst the resolution authority is exercising its resolution powers or applying the resolution tools, except at the initiative of, or with the consent of, the resolution authority. It is useful and necessary to suspend, for a limited period, certain contractual obligations so that the resolution authority has time to put into practice the resolution tools. This should not, however, apply to obligations in relation to systems designated under Directive 98/26/EC of the European Parliament and of the Council,[14] central counterparties and central banks. Directive 98/26/EC reduces the risk associated with participation in payment and securities settlement systems, in particular by reducing disruption in the event of the insolvency of a participant in such a system. To ensure that those protections apply appropriately in crisis situations, whilst maintaining appropriate certainty for operators of payment and securities systems and other market participants, this Directive provides that a crisis prevention measure or a crisis management measure should not, per se, be deemed to be insolvency proceedings within the meaning of Directive 98/26/EC, provided that the substantive obligations under the contract continue to be performed. However, nothing in this Directive prejudices the operation of a system designated under Directive 98/26/EC or the right to collateral security guaranteed by Article 9 of Directive 98/26/EC.

(94) In order to ensure that resolution authorities, when transferring assets and liabilities to a private sector purchaser or bridge institution, have an adequate period to identify contracts that need to be transferred, it might be appropriate to impose proportionate restrictions on counterparties' rights to close out, accelerate or otherwise terminate financial contracts before the transfer is made. Such a restriction would be necessary to allow authorities to obtain a true picture of the balance sheet of the failing institution, without the changes in value and scope that extensive exercise of termination rights would entail. In order to interfere with the contractual rights of counterparties to the minimum extent necessary, the restriction on termination rights should apply only in relation to the crisis prevention measure or crisis management measure, including the occurrence of any event directly linked to the application of such a measure, and rights to terminate arising from any other default, including failure to pay or deliver margin, should remain.

(95) In order to preserve legitimate capital market arrangements in the event of a transfer of some, but not all, of the assets, rights and liabilities of a failing institution, it is appropriate to include safeguards to prevent the splitting of linked liabilities, rights and contracts, as appropriate. Such a restriction on selected practices in relation to linked contracts should extend to contracts with the same counterparty covered by security arrangements, title transfer financial collateral arrangements, set-off arrangements, close out netting agreements, and structured finance arrangements. Where the safeguard applies, resolution authorities should be bound to transfer all linked contracts within a protected arrangement, or leave them

all with the residual failing institution. Those safeguards should ensure that the regulatory capital treatment of exposures covered by a netting agreement for the purposes of Directive 2013/36/EU is not affected.

(96) While ensuring that resolution authorities have the same tools and powers at their disposal will facilitate coordinated action in the event of a failure of a cross-border group, further action appears necessary to promote cooperation and prevent fragmented national responses. Resolution authorities should be required to consult each other and cooperate in resolution colleges when resolving group entities with a view to agreeing a group resolution scheme. Resolution colleges should be established around the core of the existing supervisory colleges through the inclusion of resolution authorities and the involvement of competent ministries, central banks, EBA and, where appropriate, authorities responsible for the deposit guarantee schemes. In the event of a crisis, the resolution college should provide a forum for the exchange of information and the coordination of resolution actions.

(97) Resolution of cross-border groups should strike the balance between the need, on the one hand, for procedures that take into account the urgency of the situation and allow for efficient, fair and timely solutions for the group as a whole and, on the other, the necessity to protect financial stability in all the Member States where the group operates. The different resolution authorities should share their views in the resolution college. Resolution actions proposed by the group-level resolution authority should be prepared and discussed amongst different resolution authorities in the context of the group resolution plans. Resolution colleges should incorporate the views of the resolution authorities of all the Member States in which the group is active, in order to facilitate swift and joint decisions wherever possible. Resolution actions by the group-level resolution authority should always take into account their impact on the financial stability in the Member States where the group operates. This should be ensured by the possibility for the resolution authorities of the Member State in which a subsidiary is established to object to the decisions of the group-level resolution authority, not only on appropriateness of resolution actions and measures but also on ground of the need to protect financial stability in that Member State.

(98) The resolution college should not be a decision-making body, but a platform facilitating decision-making by national authorities. The joint decisions should be taken by the national authorities concerned.

(99) The production of a group resolution scheme should facilitate coordinated resolution that is more likely to deliver the best result for all institutions of a group. The group-level resolution authority should propose the group resolution scheme and submit it to the resolution college. National resolution authorities that disagree with the scheme or decide to take independent resolution action should explain the reasons for their disagreement and notify those reasons, together with details of any independent resolution action they intend to take, to the group-level resolution authority and other resolution authorities covered by the group resolution scheme. Any national authority that decides to depart from the group resolution scheme should duly consider the potential impact on financial stability in the Member States where the other resolution authorities are located and the potential effects on other parts of the group.

(100) As part of a group resolution scheme, authorities should be invited to apply the same tool to legal persons meeting the conditions for resolution. The group-level resolution authorities should have the power to apply the bridge institution tool at group level (which may involve, where appropriate, burden sharing arrangements) to stabilise a group as a whole. Ownership of subsidiaries could be transferred to the bridge bank with a view to onward sale, either as a package or individually, when market conditions are appropriate. In addition, the group-level resolution authority should have the power to apply the bail-in tool at parent level.

(101) Effective resolution of internationally active institutions and groups requires cooperation between the Union, Member States and third-country resolution authorities. Cooperation will be facilitated if the resolution regimes of third countries are based on common principles and approaches that are being developed by the Financial Stability Board and the G20. For that purpose EBA should be empowered to develop and enter into non-binding framework cooperation arrangements with authorities of third countries in accordance with Article 33 of Regulation (EU) No 1093/2010 and national authorities should be permitted to conclude bilateral arrangements in line with EBA framework arrangements. The development of those arrangements between national authorities responsible for managing the failure of global firms should be a means to ensure effective planning, decision-making and coordination in respect of international groups. In general, there should be reciprocity in those arrangements. National resolution authorities, as part of the European resolution college, where applicable, should recognise and enforce third-country resolution proceedings in the circumstances laid down in this Directive.

(102) Cooperation should take place both with regard to subsidiaries of Union or third-country groups and with regard to branches of Union or third-country institutions. Subsidiaries of third-country groups are enterprises established in the Union and therefore are fully subject to Union law, including the resolution tools laid down in this Directive. It is necessary, however, that Member States retain the right to act in relation to branches of institutions having their head office in third countries, when the recognition and application of third-country resolution proceedings relating to a branch would endanger financial stability in the Union or when Union depositors would not receive equal treatment with third-country depositors. In those circumstances, and in the other circumstances as laid down in this Directive, Member States should have the right, after consulting the national resolution authorities, to refuse recognition of third-country resolution proceedings with regard to Union branches of third-country institutions.

(103) There are circumstances when the effectiveness of the resolution tools applied may depend on the availability of short-term funding for an institution or a bridge institution, the provision of guarantees to potential purchasers, or the provision of capital to the bridge institution. Notwithstanding the role of central banks in providing liquidity to the financial system even in times of stress, it is important that Member States set up financing arrangements to avoid that the funds needed for such purposes come from

the national budgets. It should be the financial industry, as a whole, that finances the stabilisation of the financial system.

(104) As a general rule, Member States should establish their national financing arrangements through funds controlled by resolution authorities to be used for the purposes as laid down in this Directive. However, a strictly framed exception should be provided to allow Member States to establish their national financing arrangements through mandatory contributions from institutions which are authorised in their territories and which are not held through funds controlled by their resolution authorities provided that certain conditions are met.

(105) As a principle, contributions should be collected from the industry prior to and independently of any operation of resolution. When prior funding is insufficient to cover the losses or costs incurred by the use of the financing arrangements, additional contributions should be collected to bear the additional cost or loss.

(106) In order to reach a critical mass and to avoid pro-cyclical effects which would arise if financing arrangements had to rely solely on *ex-post* contributions in a systemic crisis, it is indispensable that the *ex-ante* available financial means of the national financing arrangements amount at least to a certain minimum target level.

(107) In order to ensure a fair calculation of contributions and provide incentives to operate under a less risky model, contributions to national financing arrangements should take account of the degree of credit, liquidity and market risk incurred by the institutions.

(108) Ensuring effective resolution of failing institutions within the Union is an essential element in the completion of the internal market. The failure of such institutions has an effect not only on the financial stability of the markets where it directly operates but also on the whole Union financial market. With the completion of the internal market in financial services, the interplay between the different national financial systems is reinforced. Institutions operate outside their Member State of establishment and are interrelated through the interbank and other markets which, in essence, are pan-European. Ensuring effective financing of the resolution of those institutions across Member States is not only in the best interests of the Member States in which they operate but also of all the Member States in general as a means of ensuring a level competitive playing field and improving the functioning of the internal financial market. Setting up a European system of financing arrangements should ensure that all institutions that operate in the Union are subject to equally effective resolution financing arrangements and contribute to the stability of the internal market.

(109) In order to build up the resilience of that European system of financing arrangements, and in accordance with the objective requiring that financing should come primarily from the shareholders and creditors of the institution under resolution and then from industry rather than from public budgets, financing arrangements may make a request to borrow from other financing arrangements in the case of need. Likewise they should have the power to grant loans to other arrangements that are in need. Such lending should be strictly voluntary. The decision to lend to other arrangements should be made by the lending financing arrangement, but due to potential fiscal implications, Member States should be able to require consultation or the consent of the competent ministry.

(110) While financing arrangements are set up at national level, they should be mutualised in the context of group resolution, provided that an agreement is found between national authorities on the resolution of the institution. Deposits covered by deposit guarantee schemes should not bear any losses in the resolution process. When a resolution action ensures that depositors continue to have access to their deposits, deposit guarantee schemes to which an institution under resolution is affiliated should be required to make a contribution not greater than the amount of losses that they would have had to bear if the institution had been wound up under normal insolvency proceedings.

(111) While covered deposits are protected from losses in resolution, other eligible deposits are potentially available for loss absorbency purposes. In order to provide a certain level of protection for natural persons and micro, small and medium-sized enterprises holding eligible deposits above the level of covered deposits, such deposits should have a higher priority ranking over the claims of ordinary unsecured, non-preferred creditors under the national law governing normal insolvency proceedings. The claim of the deposit guarantee scheme should have an even higher ranking under such national law than the aforementioned categories of eligible deposits. Harmonisation of national insolvency law in that area is necessary in order to minimise exposure of the resolution funds of Member States under the no creditor worse off principle as specified in this Directive.

(112) Where deposits are transferred to another institution in the context of the resolution of a institution, depositors should not be insured beyond the coverage level provided for in Directive 2014/49/EU. Therefore, claims with regard to deposits remaining in the institution under resolution should be limited to the difference between the funds transferred and the coverage level provided for in Directive 2014/49/EU. Where transferred deposits are superior to the coverage level, the depositor should have no claim against the deposit guarantee scheme with regard to deposits remaining in the institution under resolution.

(113) The setting up of financing arrangements establishing the European system of financing arrangements laid down in this Directive should ensure coordination of the use of funds available at national level for resolution.

(114) The power to adopt acts in accordance with Article 290 TFEU should be delegated to the Commission in order to specify the criteria for defining 'critical functions' and 'core business lines' for the purposes of this Directive; the circumstances when exclusion of liabilities from the write down or conversion requirements under this Directive is necessary; the classes of arrangement for which

Member States should ensure appropriate protection in partial transfers; the manner in which institutions' contributions to resolution financing arrangements should be adjusted in proportion to their risk profile; the registration, accounting, reporting obligations and other obligations intended to ensure that the *ex-ante* contributions are effectively paid; and the circumstances in which and conditions subject to which an institution may be temporarily exempted from paying *ex-post* contributions. It is of particular importance that the Commission carry out appropriate consultations during its preparatory work, including at expert level. The Commission, when preparing and drawing up delegated acts, should ensure a simultaneous, timely and appropriate transmission of relevant documents to the European Parliament and to the Council.

(115) Where provided for in this Directive, it is appropriate that EBA promote convergence of the practices of national authorities through guidelines in accordance with Article 16 of Regulation (EU) No 1093/2010. In areas not covered by regulatory or implementing technical standards, EBA is able to issue guidelines and recommendations on the application of Union law under its own initiative.

(116) The European Parliament and the Council should have three months from the date of notification to object to a delegated act. It should be possible for the European Parliament and the Council to inform the other institutions of their intention not to raise objections.

(117) Technical standards in financial services should facilitate consistent harmonisation and adequate protection of depositors, investors and consumers across the Union. As a body with highly specialised expertise, it would be efficient and appropriate, where provided for in this Directive, to entrust EBA with the development of draft regulatory and implementing technical standards which do not involve policy choices, for submission to the Commission.

(118) The Commission should, where provided for in this Directive, adopt draft regulatory technical standards developed by EBA by means of delegated acts pursuant to Article 290 TFEU, in accordance with Articles 10 to 14 of Regulation (EU) No 1093/2010. The Commission should, where provided for in this Directive, adopt draft implementing technical standards developed by EBA by means of implementing acts pursuant to Article 291 TFEU, in accordance with Article 15 of Regulation (EU) No 1093/2010.

(119) Directive 2001/24/EC of the European Parliament and of the Council[15] provides for the mutual recognition and enforcement in all Member States of decisions concerning the reorganisation or winding up of institutions having branches in Member States other than those in which they have their head offices. That directive ensures that all assets and liabilities of the institution, regardless of the country in which they are situated, are dealt with in a single process in the home Member State and that creditors in the host Member States are treated in the same way as creditors in the home Member State. In order to achieve an effective resolution, Directive 2001/24/EC should apply in the event of use of the resolution tools both when those instruments are applied to institutions and when they are applied to other entities covered by the resolution regime. Directive 2001/24/EC should therefore be amended accordingly.

(120) Union company law directives contain mandatory rules for the protection of shareholders and creditors of institutions which fall within the scope of those directives. In a situation where resolution authorities need to act rapidly, those rules may hinder effective action and use of resolution tools and powers by resolution authorities and appropriate derogations should be included in this Directive. In order to guarantee the maximum degree of legal certainty for stakeholders, the derogations should be clearly and narrowly defined, and they should only be used in the public interest and when resolution triggers are met. The use of resolution tools presupposes that the resolution objectives and the conditions for resolution laid down in this Directive are met.

(121) Directive 2012/30/EU of the European Parliament and of the Council[16] contains rules on shareholders' rights to decide on capital increases and reductions, on their right to participate in any new share issue for cash consideration, on creditor protection in the event of capital reduction and the convening of shareholders' meeting in the event of serious loss of capital. Those rules may hinder the rapid action by resolution authorities and appropriate derogations from them should be provided for.

(122) Directive 2011/35/EU of the European Parliament and of the Council[17] lays down rules, inter alia, on the approval of mergers by the general meeting of each of the merging companies, on the requirements concerning the draft terms of merger, management report and expert report, and on creditor protection. Council Directive 82/891/EEC[18] contains similar rules on the division of public limited liability companies. Directive 2005/56/EC of the European Parliament and of the Council[19] provides for corresponding rules concerning cross-border mergers of limited liability companies. Appropriate derogations from those directives should be provided in order to allow a rapid action by resolution authorities.

(123) Directive 2004/25/EC of the European Parliament and of the Council[20] sets out an obligation to launch a mandatory takeover bid on all shares of the company for the equitable price, as defined in that directive, if a shareholder acquires, directly or indirectly and alone or in concert with others, a certain percentage of shares of that company, which gives it control of that company and is defined by national law. The purpose of the mandatory bid rule is to protect minority shareholders in the case of change of control. However, the prospect of such a costly obligation might deter possible investors in the affected institution, thereby making it difficult for resolution authorities to make use of all their resolution powers. Appropriate derogations should be provided from the mandatory bid rule, to the extent necessary for the use of the resolution powers, while after the resolution period the mandatory bid rule should be applied to any shareholder acquiring control in the affected institution.

(124) Directive 2007/36/EC of the European Parliament and of the Council,[21] provides for procedural shareholders' rights relating to general meetings. Directive 2007/36/EC provides, inter alia, for a minimum notice period for general meetings and the contents of the notice of general meeting. Those rules may hinder rapid action by resolution authorities and appropriate derogations from the directive should be provided for. Prior to resolution there may be a need for a rapid increase of capital when the institution

does not meet or is likely not to fulfil the requirements of Regulation (EU) No 575/2013 and Directive 2013/36/EU and an increase of capital is likely to restore the financial situation and avoid a situation where the threshold conditions for resolution are met. In such situations a possibility for convening a general meeting at short notice should be permitted. However, the shareholders should retain the decision making power on the increase and on the shortening of the notice period for the general meetings. Appropriate derogations from Directive 2007/36/EC should be provided for the establishment of that mechanism.

(125) In order to ensure that resolution authorities are represented in the European System of Financial Supervision established by Regulation (EU) No 1092/2010, Regulation (EU) No 1093/2010, Regulation (EU) No 1094/2010 of the European Parliament and of the Council[22] and Regulation (EU) No 1095/2010 of the European Parliament and of the Council,[23] and to ensure that EBA has the expertise necessary to carry out the tasks laid down in this Directive, Regulation (EU) No 1093/2010 should be amended in order to include national resolution authorities as defined in this Directive in the concept of competent authorities established by that Regulation. Such assimilation between resolution authorities and competent authorities pursuant to Regulation (EU) No 1093/2010 is consistent with the functions attributed to EBA pursuant to Article 25 of Regulation (EC) No 1093/2010 to contribute and participate actively in the development and coordination of recovery and resolution plans and to aim at the facilitation of the resolution of failing institutions and in particular cross-border groups.

(126) In order to ensure compliance by institutions, those who effectively control their business and their management body with the obligations deriving from this Directive and to ensure that they are subject to similar treatment across the Union, Member States should be required to provide for administrative sanctions and other administrative measures which are effective, proportionate and dissuasive. Therefore, administrative sanctions and other administrative measures laid down by Member States should satisfy certain essential requirements in relation to addressees, criteria to be taken into account when applying a sanction or other administrative measure, publication of sanctions or other administrative measures, key penalising powers and levels of administrative fines. Subject to strict professional secrecy, EBA should maintain a central database of all administrative sanctions and information on the appeals reported to it by competent authorities and resolution authorities.

(127) This Directive refers to both administrative sanctions and other administrative measures in order to cover all actions applied after an infringement is committed, and which are intended to prevent further infringements, irrespective of their qualification as a sanction or another administrative measure under national law.

(128) Even though nothing prevents Member States from laying down rules for administrative sanctions as well as criminal sanctions for the same infringements, Member States should not be required to lay down rules for administrative sanctions for infringements of this Directive which are subject to national criminal law. In accordance with national law, Member States are not obliged to impose both administrative and criminal sanctions for the same offence, but they can do so if their national law so permits. However, the maintenance of criminal sanctions rather than administrative sanctions or other administrative measures for infringements of this Directive should not reduce or otherwise affect the ability of resolution authorities and competent authorities to cooperate, access and exchange information in a timely way with resolution authorities and competent authorities in other Member States for the purposes of this Directive, including after any referral of the relevant infringements to the competent judicial authorities for prosecution.

(129) In accordance with the Joint Political Declaration of Member States and the Commission of 28 September 2011 on explanatory documents,[24] Member States have undertaken to accompany, in justified cases, the notification of their transposition measures with one or more documents explaining the relationship between the components of a directive and the corresponding parts of national transposition instruments. With regard to this Directive, the legislator considers the transmission of such documents to be justified.

(130) This Directive respects the fundamental rights and observes the rights, freedoms and principles recognised in particular by the Charter, and, in particular, the right to property, the right to an effective remedy and to a fair trial and the right of defence.

(131) Since the objective of this Directive, namely the harmonisation of the rules and processes for the resolution of institutions, cannot be sufficiently achieved by the Member States, but can rather, by reason of the effects of a failure of any institution in the whole Union, be better achieved at Union level, the Union may adopt measures, in accordance with the principle of subsidiarity as set out in Article 5 of the Treaty on European Union. In accordance with the principle of proportionality, as set out in that Article, this Directive does not go beyond what is necessary in order to achieve that objective.

(132) When taking decisions or actions under this Directive, competent authorities and resolution authorities should always have due regard to the impact of their decisions and actions on financial stability in other Member States and on the economic situation in other Member States and should give consideration to the significance of any subsidiary or branch for the financial sector and the economy of the Member State where such a subsidiary or branch is established or located, even in cases where the subsidiary or branch concerned is of lesser importance for the consolidated group.

(133) The Commission will review the general application of this Directive and, in particular, consider, in light of the arrangements taken under any act of Union law establishing a resolution mechanism covering more than one Member State, the exercise of EBA's powers under this Directive to mediate between a resolution authority in a Member State participating in the mechanism and a resolution authority in a Member State not participating therein,

NOTES

1 OJ C39, 12.2.2013, p 1.

2 OJ C44, 15.2.2013, p 68.

3 Position of the European Parliament of 15 April 2014 (not yet published in the Official Journal) and the decision of the Council of 6 May 2014.

4 Regulation (EU) No 575/2013 of the European Parliament and of the Council of 26 June 2013 on prudential requirements for credit institutions and investment firms and amending Regulation (EU) No 648/2012 (OJ L176, 27.6.2013, p 1).

5 Directive 2013/36/EU of the European Parliament and of the Council of 26 June 2013 on access to the activity of credit institutions and the prudential supervision of credit institutions and investment firms, amending Directive 2002/87/EC and repealing Directives 2006/48/EC and 2006/49/EC (OJ L176, 27.6.2013, p 338).

6 Directive 2002/87/EC of the European Parliament and of the Council of 16 December 2002 on the supplementary supervision of credit institutions, insurance undertakings and investment firms in a financial conglomerate and amending Council Directives 73/239/EEC, 79/267/EEC, 92/49/EEC, 92/96/EEC, 93/6/EEC and 93/22/EEC, and Directives 98/78/EC and 2000/12/EC of the European Parliament and of the Council (OJ L35, 11.2.2003, p 1).

7 Regulation (EU) No 648/2012 of the European Parliament and of the Council of 4 July 2012 on OTC derivatives, central counterparties and trade repositories (OJ L201, 7.2.2012, p 1).

8 Regulation (EU) No 1093/2010 of the European Parliament and of the Council of 24 November 2010 establishing a European Supervisory Authority (European Banking Authority), amending Decision No 716/2009/EC and repealing Commission Decision 2009/78/EC (OJ L331, 15.12.2010, p 12).

9 Regulation (EU) No 1092/2010 of the European Parliament and of the Council of 24 November 2010 on European Union macro-prudential oversight of the financial system and establishing a European Systemic Risk Board (OJ L331, 15.12.2010, p 1).

10 Directive 2013/34/EU of the European Parliament and of the Council of 26 June 2013 on the annual financial statements, consolidated financial statements and related reports of certain types of undertakings, amending Directive 2006/43/EC of the European Parliament and of the Council and repealing Council Directives 78/660/EEC and 83/349/EEC (OJ L182, 29.6.2013, p 19).

11 Directive 2014/65/EU of 15 May 2014 of the European Parliament and of the Council on markets in financial instruments and amending Directive 2002/92/EC and Directive 2011/61/EU (see page 349 of this Official Journal).

12 Regulation (EU) No 596/2014 of the European Parliament and of the Council of 16 April 2014 on market abuse (market abuse regulation) and repealing Directive 2003/6/EC of the European Parliament and of the Council and Commission Directives 2003/124/EC, 2003/125/EC and 2004/72/EC (See page 1 of this Official Journal).

13 Directive 2014/49/EU of the European Parliament and of the Council of 16 April 2014 on Deposit Guarantee Schemes (see page 149 of this Official Journal).

14 Directive 98/26/EC of the European Parliament and of the Council of 19 May 1998 on settlement finality in payment and securities settlement systems (OJ L166, 11.6.1998, p 45).

15 Directive 2001/24/EC of the European Parliament and of the Council of 4 April 2001 on the reorganisation and winding-up of credit institutions (OJ L125, 5.5.2001, p 15).

16 Directive 2012/30/EU of the European Parliament and of the Council of 25 October 2012 on coordination of safeguards which, for the protection of the interests of members and others, are required by Member States of companies within the meaning of the second paragraph of Article 54 of the Treaty on the Functioning of the European Union, in respect of the formation of public limited liability companies and the maintenance and alteration of their capital, with a view to making such safeguards equivalent (OJ L315, 14.11.2012, p 74).

17 Directive 2011/35/EU of the European Parliament and of the Council of 5 April 2011 concerning mergers of public limited liability companies (OJ L110, 29.4.2011, p 1).

18 Sixth Council Directive 82/891/EEC of 17 December 1982 based on Article 54(3)(g) of the Treaty, concerning the division of public limited liability companies (OJ L378, 31.12.1982, p 47).

19 Directive 2005/56/EC of the European Parliament and of the Council of 26 October 2005 on cross-border mergers of limited liability companies (OJ L310, 25.11.2005, p 1).

20 Directive 2004/25/EC of the European Parliament and of the Council of 21 April 2004 on takeover bids (OJ L142, 30.4.2004, p 12).

21 Directive 2007/36/EC of the European Parliament and of the Council of 11 July 2007 on the exercise of certain rights of shareholders in listed companies (OJ L184, 14.7.2007, p 17).

22 Regulation (EU) No 1094/2010 of the European Parliament and of the Council of 24 November 2010 establishing a European Supervisory Authority (European Investment and Occupational Pensions Authority), amending Decision No 716/2009/EC and repealing Commission Decision 2009/79/EC (OJ L331, 15.12.2010, p 48).

23 Regulation (EU) No 1095/2010 of the European Parliament and of the Council of 24 November 2010 establishing a European Supervisory Authority (European Securities and Markets Authority), amending Decision No 716/2009/EC and repealing Commission Decision 2009/77/EC (OJ L331, 15.12.2010, p 84).

24 OJ C369, 17.12.2011, p 14.

HAVE ADOPTED THIS DIRECTIVE:

TITLE I SCOPE, DEFINITIONS AND AUTHORITIES

[3.419]
Article 1
Subject matter and scope

1. This Directive lays down rules and procedures relating to the recovery and resolution of the following entities:

(a) institutions that are established in the Union;

(b) financial institutions that are established in the Union when the financial institution is a subsidiary of a credit institution or investment firm, or of a company referred to in point (c) or (d), and is covered by the supervision of the parent undertaking on a consolidated basis in accordance with Articles 6 to 17 of Regulation (EU) No 575/2013;
(c) financial holding companies, mixed financial holding companies and mixed-activity holding companies that are established in the Union;
(d) parent financial holding companies in a Member State, Union parent financial holding companies, parent mixed financial holding companies in a Member State, Union parent mixed financial holding companies;
(e) branches of institutions that are established outside the Union in accordance with the specific conditions laid down in this Directive.

When establishing and applying the requirements under this Directive and when using the different tools at their disposal in relation to an entity referred to in the first subparagraph, and subject to specific provisions, resolution authorities and competent authorities shall take account of the nature of its business, its shareholding structure, its legal form, its risk profile, size and legal status, its interconnectedness to other institutions or to the financial system in general, the scope and the complexity of its activities, its membership of an institutional protection scheme (IPS) that meets the requirements of Article 113(7) of Regulation (EU) No 575/2013 or other cooperative mutual solidarity systems as referred to in Article 113(6) of that Regulation and whether it exercises any investment services or activities as defined in point (2) of Article 4(1) of Directive 2014/65/EU.

2. Member States may adopt or maintain rules that are stricter or additional to those laid down in this Directive and in the delegated and implementing acts adopted on the basis of this Directive, provided that they are of general application and do not conflict with this Directive and with the delegated and implementing acts adopted on its basis.

[3.420]
Article 2
Definitions

1. For the purposes of this Directive the following definitions apply:
(1) 'resolution' means the application of a resolution tool or a tool referred to in Article 37(9) in order to achieve one or more of the resolution objectives referred to in Article 31(2);
(2) 'credit institution' means a credit institution as defined in point (1) of Article 4(1) of Regulation (EU) No 575/2013, not including the entities referred to in Article 2(5) of Directive 2013/36/EU;
(3) 'investment firm' means an investment firm as defined in point (2) of Article 4(1) of Regulation (EU) No 575/2013 that is subject to the initial capital requirement laid down in Article 28(2) of Directive 2013/36/EU;
(4) 'financial institution' means a financial institution as defined in point (26) of Article 4(1) of Regulation (EU) No 575/2013;
(5) 'subsidiary' means a subsidiary as defined in point (16) of Article 4(1) of Regulation (EU) No 575/2013;
(6) 'parent undertaking' means a parent undertaking as defined in point (15)(a) of Article 4(1) of Regulation (EU) No 575/2013;
(7) 'consolidated basis' means the basis of the consolidated situation as defined in point (47) of Article 4(1) of Regulation (EU) No 575/2013;
(8) 'institutional protection scheme' or 'IPS' means an arrangement that meets the requirements laid down in Article 113(7) of Regulation (EU) No 575/2013;
(9) 'financial holding company' means a financial holding company as defined in point (20) of Article 4(1) of Regulation (EU) No 575/2013;
(10) 'mixed financial holding company' means a mixed financial holding company as defined in point (21) of Article 4(1) of Regulation (EU) No 575/2013;
(11) 'mixed-activity holding company' means a mixed-activity holding company as defined in point (22) of Article 4(1) of Regulation (EU) No 575/2013;
(12) 'parent financial holding company in a Member State' means a parent financial holding company in a Member State as defined in point (30) of Article 4(1) of Regulation (EU) No 575/2013;
(13) 'Union parent financial holding company' means an EU parent financial holding company as defined in point (31) of Article 4(1) of Regulation (EU) No 575/2013;
(14) 'parent mixed financial holding company in a Member State' means a parent mixed financial holding company in a Member State as defined in point (32) of Article 4(1)of Regulation (EU) No 575/2013;
(15) 'Union parent mixed financial holding company' means an EU parent mixed financial holding company as defined in point (33) of Article 4(1) of Regulation (EU) No 575/2013;
(16) 'resolution objectives' means the resolution objectives referred to in Article 31(2);
(17) 'branch' means a branch as defined in point (17) of Article 4(1) of Regulation (EU) No 575/2013;
(18) 'resolution authority' means an authority designated by a Member State in accordance with Article 3;
(19) 'resolution tool' means a resolution tool referred to in Article 37(3);
(20) 'resolution power' means a power referred to in Articles 63 to 72;
(21) 'competent authority' means a competent authority as defined in point (40) of Article 4(1) of Regulation (EU) No 575/2013 including the European Central Bank with regard to specific tasks conferred on it by Council Regulation (EU) No 1024/2013;[1]

(22) 'competent ministries' means finance ministries or other ministries of the Member States which are responsible for economic, financial and budgetary decisions at the national level according to national competencies and which have been designated in accordance with Article 3(5);
(23) 'institution' means a credit institution or an investment firm;
(24) 'management body' means a management body as defined in point (7) of Article 3(1) of Directive 2013/36/EU;
(25) 'senior management' means senior management as defined in point (9) of Article 3(1) of Directive 2013/36/EU;
(26) 'group' means a parent undertaking and its subsidiaries;
(27) 'cross-border group' means a group having group entities established in more than one Member State;
(28) 'extraordinary public financial support' means State aid within the meaning of Article 107(1) TFEU, or any other public financial support at supra-national level, which, if provided for at national level, would constitute State aid, that is provided in order to preserve or restore the viability, liquidity or solvency of an institution or entity referred to in point (b), (c) or (d) of Article 1(1) or of a group of which such an institution or entity forms part;
(29) 'emergency liquidity assistance' means the provision by a central bank of central bank money, or any other assistance that may lead to an increase in central bank money, to a solvent financial institution, or group of solvent financial institutions, that is facing temporary liquidity problems, without such an operation being part of monetary policy;
(30) 'systemic crisis' means a disruption in the financial system with the potential to have serious negative consequences for the internal market and the real economy. All types of financial intermediaries, markets and infrastructure may be potentially systemically important to some degree;
(31) 'group entity' means a legal person that is part of a group;
(32) 'recovery plan' means a recovery plan drawn up and maintained by an institution in accordance with Article 5;
(33) 'group recovery plan' means a group recovery plan drawn up and maintained in accordance with Article 7;
(34) 'significant branch' means a branch that would be considered to be significant in a host Member State in accordance with Article 51(1) of Directive 2013/36/EU;
(35) 'critical functions' means activities, services or operations the discontinuance of which is likely in one or more Member States, to lead to the disruption of services that are essential to the real economy or to disrupt financial stability due to the size, market share, external and internal interconnectedness, complexity or cross-border activities of an institution or group, with particular regard to the substitutability of those activities, services or operations;
(36) 'core business lines' means business lines and associated services which represent material sources of revenue, profit or franchise value for an institution or for a group of which an institution forms part;
(37) 'consolidating supervisor' means consolidating supervisor as defined in point (41) of Article 4(1) of Regulation (EU) No 575/2013;
(38) 'own funds' means own funds as defined in point (118) of Article 4(1) of Regulation (EU) No 575/2013;
(39) 'conditions for resolution' means the conditions referred to in Article 32(1);
(40) 'resolution action' means the decision to place an institution or entity referred to in point (b), (c) or (d) of Article 1(1) under resolution pursuant to Article 32 or 33, the application of a resolution tool, or the exercise of one or more resolution powers;
(41) 'resolution plan' means a resolution plan for an institution drawn up in accordance with Article 10;
(42) 'group resolution' means either of the following:
  (a) the taking of resolution action at the level of a parent undertaking or of an institution subject to consolidated supervision, or
  (b) the coordination of the application of resolution tools and the exercise of resolution powers by resolution authorities in relation to group entities that meet the conditions for resolution;
(43) 'group resolution plan' means a plan for group resolution drawn up in accordance with Articles 12 and 13;
(44) 'group-level resolution authority' means the resolution authority in the Member State in which the consolidating supervisor is situated;
(45) 'group resolution scheme' means a plan drawn up for the purposes of group resolution in accordance with Article 91;
(46) 'resolution college' means a college established in accordance with Article 88 to carry out the tasks referred to in Article 88(1);
(47) 'normal insolvency proceedings' means collective insolvency proceedings which entail the partial or total divestment of a debtor and the appointment of a liquidator or an administrator normally applicable to institutions under national law and either specific to those institutions or generally applicable to any natural or legal person;
[(48) 'debt instruments':
  (i) for the purpose of points (g) and (j) of Article 63(1), means bonds and other forms of transferable debt, instruments creating or acknowledging a debt, and instruments giving rights to acquire debt instruments; and

(ii) for the purpose of Article 108, means bonds and other forms of transferable debt and instruments creating or acknowledging a debt;]

(49) 'parent institution in a Member State' means a parent institution in a Member State as defined in point (28) of Article 4(1) of Regulation (EU) No 575/2013;

(50) 'Union parent institution' means an EU parent institution as defined in point (29) of Article 4(1) of Regulation (EU) No 575/2013;

(51) 'own funds requirements' means the requirements laid down in Articles 92 to 98 of Regulation (EU) No 575/2013;

(52) 'supervisory college' means a college of supervisors established in accordance with Article 116 of Directive 2013/36/EU;

(53) 'Union State aid framework' means the framework established by Articles 107, 108 and 109 TFEU and regulations and all Union acts, including guidelines, communications and notices, made or adopted pursuant to Article 108(4) or Article 109 TFEU;

(54) 'winding up' means the realisation of assets of an institution or entity referred to in point (b), (c) or (d) of Article 1(1);

(55) 'asset separation tool' means the mechanism for effecting a transfer by a resolution authority of assets, rights or liabilities of an institution under resolution to an asset management vehicle in accordance with Article 42;

(56) 'asset management vehicle' means a legal person that meets the requirements laid down in Article 42(2);

(57) 'bail-in tool' means the mechanism for effecting the exercise by a resolution authority of the write-down and conversion powers in relation to liabilities of an institution under resolution in accordance with Article 43;

(58) 'sale of business tool' means the mechanism for effecting a transfer by a resolution authority of shares or other instruments of ownership issued by an institution under resolution, or assets, rights or liabilities, of an institution under resolution to a purchaser that is not a bridge institution, in accordance with Article 38;

(59) 'bridge institution' means a legal person that meets the requirements laid down in Article 40(2);

(60) 'bridge institution tool' means the mechanism for transferring shares or other instruments of ownership issued by an institution under resolution or assets, rights or liabilities of an institution under resolution to a bridge institution, in accordance with Article 40;

(61) 'instruments of ownership' means shares, other instruments that confer ownership, instruments that are convertible into or give the right to acquire shares or other instruments of ownership, and instruments representing interests in shares or other instruments of ownership;

(62) 'shareholders' means shareholders or holders of other instruments of ownership;

(63) 'transfer powers' means the powers specified in point (c) or (d) of Article 63(1) to transfer shares, other instruments of ownership, debt instruments, assets, rights or liabilities, or any combination of those items from an institution under resolution to a recipient;

(64) 'central counterparty' means a CCP as defined in point (1) of Article 2 of Regulation (EU) No 648/2012;

(65) 'derivative', means a derivative as defined in point (5) of Article 2 of Regulation (EU) No 648/2012;

(66) 'write-down and conversion powers' means the powers referred to in Article 59(2) and in points (e) to (i) of Article 63(1);

(67) 'secured liability' means a liability where the right of the creditor to payment or other form of performance is secured by a charge, pledge or lien, or collateral arrangements including liabilities arising from repurchase transactions and other title transfer collateral arrangements;

(68) 'Common Equity Tier 1 instruments' means capital instruments that meet the conditions laid down in Article 28(1) to (4), Article 29(1) to (5) or Article 31(1) of Regulation (EU) No 575/2013;

(69) 'Additional Tier 1 instruments' means capital instruments that meet the conditions laid down in Article 52(1) of Regulation (EU) No 575/2013;

(70) 'aggregate amount' means the aggregate amount by which the resolution authority has assessed that eligible liabilities are to be written down or converted, in accordance with Article 46(1);

(71) 'eligible liabilities' means the liabilities and capital instruments that do not qualify as Common Equity Tier 1, Additional Tier 1 or Tier 2 instruments of an institution or entity referred to in point (b), (c) or (d) of Article 1(1) that are not excluded from the scope of the bail-in tool by virtue of Article 44(2);

(72) 'deposit guarantee scheme' means a deposit guarantee scheme introduced and officially recognised by a Member State pursuant to Article 4 of Directive 2014/49/EU;

(73) 'Tier 2 instruments' means capital instruments or subordinated loans that meet the conditions laid down in Article 63 of Regulation (EU) No 575/2013;

(74) 'relevant capital instruments' for the purposes of Section 5 of Chapter IV of Title IV and Chapter V of Title IV, means Additional Tier 1 instruments and Tier 2 instruments;

(75) 'conversion rate' means the factor that determines the number of shares or other instruments of ownership into which a liability of a specific class will be converted, by reference either to a single instrument of the class in question or to a specified unit of value of a debt claim;

(76) 'affected creditor' means a creditor whose claim relates to a liability that is reduced or converted to shares or other instruments of ownership by the exercise of the write down or conversion power pursuant to the use of the bail-in tool;

(77) 'affected holder' means a holder of instruments of ownership whose instruments of ownership are cancelled by means of the power referred to in point (h) of Article 63(1);

(78) 'appropriate authority' means authority of the Member State identified in accordance with Article 61 that is responsible under the national law of that State for making the determinations referred to in Article 59(3);

(79) 'relevant parent institution' means a parent institution in a Member State, a Union parent institution, a financial holding company, a mixed financial holding company, a mixed-activity holding company, a parent financial holding company in a Member State, a Union parent financial holding company, a parent mixed financial holding company in a Member State, or a Union parent mixed financial holding company, in relation to which the bail-in tool is applied;

(80) 'recipient' means the entity to which shares, other instruments of ownership, debt instruments, assets, rights or liabilities, or any combination of those items are transferred from an institution under resolution;

(81) 'business day' means a day other than a Saturday, a Sunday or a public holiday in the Member State concerned;

(82) 'termination right' means a right to terminate a contract, a right to accelerate, close out, set-off or net obligations or any similar provision that suspends, modifies or extinguishes an obligation of a party to the contract or a provision that prevents an obligation under the contract from arising that would otherwise arise;

(83) 'institution under resolution' means an institution, a financial institution, a financial holding company, a mixed financial holding company, a mixed-activity holding company, a parent financial holding company in a Member State, a Union parent financial holding company, a parent mixed financial holding company in a Member State, or a Union parent mixed financial holding company, in respect of which a resolution action is taken;

(84) 'Union subsidiary' means an institution which is established in a Member State and which is a subsidiary of a third-country institution or a third-country parent undertaking;

(85) 'Union parent undertaking' means a Union parent institution, a Union parent financial holding company or a Union parent mixed financial holding company;

(86) 'third-country institution' means an entity, the head office of which is established in a third country, that would, if it were established within the Union, be covered by the definition of an institution;

(87) 'third-country parent undertaking' means a parent undertaking, a parent financial holding company or a parent mixed financial holding company, established in a third country;

(88) 'third-country resolution proceedings' means an action under the law of a third country to manage the failure of a third-country institution or a third-country parent undertaking that is comparable, in terms of objectives and anticipated results, to resolution actions under this Directive;

(89) 'Union branch' means a branch located in a Member State of a third-country institution;

(90) 'relevant third-country authority' means a third-country authority responsible for carrying out functions comparable to those of resolution authorities or competent authorities pursuant to this Directive;

(91) 'group financing arrangement' means the financing arrangement or arrangements of the Member State of the group-level resolution authority;

(92) 'back-to-back transaction' means a transaction entered into between two group entities for the purpose of transferring, in whole or in part, the risk generated by another transaction entered into between one of those group entities and a third party;

(93) 'intra-group guarantee' means a contract by which one group entity guarantees the obligations of another group entity to a third party;

(94) 'covered deposits' means covered deposits as defined in point (5) of Article 2(1) of Directive 2014/49/EU;

(95) 'eligible deposits' means eligible deposits as defined in point (4) of Article 2(1) of Directive 2014/49/EU;

(96) 'covered bond' means an instrument as referred to in Article 52(4) of Directive 2009/65/EC of the European Parliament and of the Council;[2]

(97) 'title transfer financial collateral arrangement' means a title transfer financial collateral arrangement as defined in point (b) of Article 2(1) of Directive 2002/47/EC of the European Parliament and of the Council;[3]

(98) 'netting arrangement' means an arrangement under which a number of claims or obligations can be converted into a single net claim, including close-out netting arrangements under which, on the occurrence of an enforcement event (however or wherever defined) the obligations of the parties are accelerated so as to become immediately due or are terminated, and in either case are converted into or replaced by a single net claim, including 'close-out netting provisions' as defined in point (n)(i) of Article 2(1) of Directive 2002/47/EC and 'netting' as defined in point (k) of Article 2 of Directive 98/26/EC;

(99) 'set-off arrangement' means an arrangement under which two or more claims or obligations owed between the institution under resolution and a counterparty can be set off against each other;

(100) 'financial contracts' includes the following contracts and agreements:

- (a) securities contracts, including:
  - (i) contracts for the purchase, sale or loan of a security, a group or index of securities;
  - (ii) options on a security or group or index of securities;
  - (iii) repurchase or reverse repurchase transactions on any such security, group or index;
- (b) commodities contracts, including:

(i) contracts for the purchase, sale or loan of a commodity or group or index of commodities for future delivery;
(ii) options on a commodity or group or index of commodities;
(iii) repurchase or reverse repurchase transactions on any such commodity, group or index;

(c) futures and forwards contracts, including contracts (other than a commodities contract) for the purchase, sale or transfer of a commodity or property of any other description, service, right or interest for a specified price at a future date;
(d) swap agreements, including:
(i) swaps and options relating to interest rates; spot or other foreign exchange agreements; currency; an equity index or equity; a debt index or debt; commodity indexes or commodities; weather; emissions or inflation;
(ii) total return, credit spread or credit swaps;
(iii) any agreements or transactions that are similar to an agreement referred to in point (i) or (ii) which is the subject of recurrent dealing in the swaps or derivatives markets;

(e) inter-bank borrowing agreements where the term of the borrowing is three months or less;
(f) master agreements for any of the contracts or agreements referred to in points (a) to (e);

(101) 'crisis prevention measure' means the exercise of powers to direct removal of deficiencies or impediments to recoverability under Article 6(6), the exercise of powers to address or remove impediments to resolvability under Article 17 or 18, the application of an early intervention measure under Article 27, the appointment of a temporary administrator under Article 29 or the exercise of the write down or conversion powers under Article 59;
(102) 'crisis management measure' means a resolution action or the appointment of a special manager under Article 35 or a person under Article 51(2) or under Article 72(1);
(103) 'recovery capacity' means the capability of an institution to restore its financial position following a significant deterioration;
(104) 'depositor' means a depositor as defined in point (6) of Article 2(1) of Directive 2014/49/EU;
(105) 'investor' means an investor within the meaning of point (4) of Article 1 of Directive 97/9/EC of the European Parliament and of the Council;[4]
(106) 'designated national macroprudential authority' means the authority entrusted with the conduct of macroprudential policy referred to in Recommendation B1 of the Recommendation of the European Systemic Risk Board of 22 December 2011 on the macroprudential mandate of national authorities (ESRB/2011/3);
(107) 'micro, small and medium-sized enterprises' means micro, small and medium-sized enterprises as defined with regard to the annual turnover criterion referred to in Article 2(1) of the Annex to Commission Recommendation 2003/361/EC;[5]
(108) 'regulated market' means a regulated market as defined in point (21) of Article 4(1) of Directive 2014/65/EU.

2. The Commission shall be empowered to adopt delegated acts in accordance with Article 115 in order to specify the criteria for the determination of the activities, services and operations referred to in point (35) of the first subparagraph as regards the definition of 'critical functions' and the criteria for the determination of the business lines and associated services referred to in point (36) of the first subparagraph as regards the definition of 'core business lines'.

NOTES

Point (48): substituted by European Parliament and Council Directive 2017/2399/EU, Art 1(1).

1 Council Regulation (EU) No 1024/2013 of 15 October 2013 conferring specific tasks on the European Central Bank concerning policies relating to the prudential supervision of credit institutions (OJ L287, 29.10.2013, p 63).

2 Directive 2009/65/EC of the European Parliament and of the Council of 13 July 2009 on the coordination of laws, regulations and administrative provisions relating to undertakings for collective investment in transferable securities (UCITS) (OJ L302, 17.11.2009, p 32).

3 Directive 2002/47/EC of the European Parliament and of the Council of 6 June 2002 on financial collateral arrangements (OJ L168, 27.6.2002, p 43).

4 Directive 97/9/EC of the European Parliament and of the Council of 3 March 1997 on investor-compensation schemes (OJ L84, 26.3.1997, p 22).

5 Commission Recommendation 2003/361/EC of 6 May 2003 concerning the definition of micro, small and medium-sized enterprises (OJ L124, 20.5.2003, p 36).

[3.421]
Article 3
Designation of authorities responsible for resolution

1. Each Member State shall designate one or, exceptionally, more resolution authorities that are empowered to apply the resolution tools and exercise the resolution powers.
2. The resolution authority shall be a public administrative authority or authorities entrusted with public administrative powers.
3. Resolution authorities may be national central banks, competent ministries or other public administrative authorities or authorities entrusted with public administrative powers. Member States may exceptionally provide for the resolution authority to be the competent authorities for supervision for the purposes of Regulation (EU) No 575/2013 and Directive 2013/36/EU. Adequate structural arrangements shall be in place to ensure operational independence and avoid conflicts of interest between the functions of supervision pursuant to Regulation (EU) No 575/2013 and Directive 2013/36/EU or the other functions

of the relevant authority and the functions of resolution authorities pursuant to this Directive, without prejudice to the exchange of information and cooperation obligations as required by paragraph 4. In particular, Member States shall ensure that, within the competent authorities, national central banks, competent ministries or other authorities there is operational independence between the resolution function and the supervisory or other functions of the relevant authority.

The staff involved in carrying out the functions of the resolution authority pursuant to this Directive shall be structurally separated from, and subject to, separate reporting lines from the staff involved in carrying out the tasks pursuant to Regulation (EU) No 575/2013 and Directive 2013/36/EU or with regard to the other functions of the relevant authority.

For the purposes of this paragraph, the Member States or the resolution authority shall adopt and make public any necessary relevant internal rules including rules regarding professional secrecy and information exchanges between the different functional areas.

4. Member States shall require that authorities exercising supervision and resolution functions and persons exercising those functions on their behalf cooperate closely in the preparation, planning and application of resolution decisions, both where the resolution authority and the competent authority are separate entities and where the functions are carried out in the same entity.

5. Each Member State shall designate a single ministry which is responsible for exercising the functions of the competent ministry under this Directive.

6. Where the resolution authority in a Member State is not the competent ministry it shall inform the competent ministry of the decisions pursuant to this Directive and, unless otherwise laid down in national law, have its approval before implementing decisions that have a direct fiscal impact or systemic implications.

7. Decisions taken by competent authorities, resolution authorities and EBA in accordance with this Directive shall take into account the potential impact of the decision in all the Member States where the institution or the group operate and minimise the negative effects on financial stability and negative economic and social effects in those Member States. Decisions of EBA are subject to Article 38 of Regulation (EU) No 1093/2010.

8. Member States shall ensure that each resolution authority has the expertise, resources and operational capacity to apply resolution actions, and is able to exercise their powers with the speed and flexibility that are necessary to achieve the resolution objectives.

9. EBA, in cooperation with competent authorities and resolution authorities, shall develop the required expertise, resources and operational capacity and shall monitor the implementation of paragraph 8, including through periodical peer reviews.

10. Where, in accordance with paragraph 1, a Member State designates more than one authority to apply the resolution tools and exercise the resolution powers, it shall provide a fully reasoned notification to EBA and the Commission for doing so and shall allocate functions and responsibilities clearly between those authorities, ensure adequate coordination between them and designate a single authority as a contact authority for the purposes of cooperation and coordination with the relevant authorities of other Member States.

11. Member States shall inform EBA of the national authority or authorities designated as resolution authorities and the contact authority and, where relevant, their specific functions and responsibilities. EBA shall publish the list of those resolution authorities and contact authorities.

12. Without prejudice to Article 85, Member States may limit the liability of the resolution authority, the competent authority and their respective staff in accordance with national law for acts and omissions in the course of discharging their functions under this Directive.

TITLE II PREPARATION

CHAPTER I RECOVERY AND RESOLUTION PLANNING

SECTION 1
GENERAL PROVISIONS

[3.422]
Article 4
Simplified obligations for certain institutions

1. Having regard to the impact that the failure of the institution could have, due to the nature of its business, its shareholding structure, its legal form, its risk profile, size and legal status, its interconnectedness to other institutions or to the financial system in general, the scope and the complexity of its activities, its membership of an IPS or other cooperative mutual solidarity systems as referred to in Article 113(7) of Regulation (EU) No 575/2013 and any exercise of investment services or activities as defined in point (2) of Article 4(1) of Directive 2014/65/EU, and whether its failure and subsequent winding up under normal insolvency proceedings would be likely to have a significant negative effect on financial markets, on other institutions, on funding conditions, or on the wider economy, Member States shall ensure that competent and resolution authorities determine:

(a) the contents and details of recovery and resolution plans provided for in Articles 5 to 12;

(b) the date by which the first recovery and resolution plans are to be drawn up and the frequency for updating recovery and resolution plans which may be lower than that provided for in Article 5(2), Article 7(5), Article 10(6) and Article 13(3);

(c) the contents and details of the information required from institutions as provided for in Article 5(5), Article 11(1) and Article 12(2) and in Sections A and B of the Annex;

(d) the level of detail for the assessment of resolvability provided for in Articles 15 and 16, and Section C of the Annex.

2. Competent authorities and, where relevant, resolution authorities shall make the assessment referred to in paragraph 1 after consulting, where appropriate, the national macroprudential authority.
3. Member States shall ensure that where simplified obligations are applied the competent authorities and, where relevant, resolution authorities can impose full, unsimplified obligations at any time.
4. Member States shall ensure that the application of simplified obligations shall not, per se, affect the competent authority's and, where relevant, the resolution authority's powers to take a crisis prevention measure or a crisis management measure.
5. EBA shall, by 3 July 2015, issue guidelines in accordance with Article 16 of Regulation (EU) No 1093/2010 to specify the criteria referred to in paragraph 1, for assessing, in accordance with that paragraph, the impact of an institution's failure on financial markets, on other institutions and on funding conditions.
6. Taking into account, where appropriate, experience acquired in the application of the guidelines referred to in paragraph 5, EBA shall develop draft regulatory technical standards to specify the criteria referred to in paragraph 1, for assessing, in accordance with that paragraph, the impact of an institution's failure on financial markets, on other institutions and on funding conditions.
EBA shall submit those draft regulatory technical standards to the Commission by 3 July 2017.
Power is conferred on the Commission to adopt the regulatory technical standards referred to in the first subparagraph in accordance with Articles 10 to 14 of Regulation (EU) No 1093/2010.
7. Competent authorities and resolution authorities shall inform EBA of the way they have applied paragraphs 1, 8, 9 and 10 to institutions in their jurisdiction. EBA shall submit a report to the European Parliament, to the Council and to the Commission by 31 December 2017 on the implementation of paragraphs 1, 8, 9 and 10. In particular, that report shall identify any divergences regarding the implementation at national level of paragraphs 1, 8,9 and 10.
8. Subject to paragraphs 9 and 10, Member States shall ensure that competent authorities and, where relevant, resolution authorities may waive the application of:
(a) the requirements of Sections 2 and 3 of this Chapter to institutions affiliated to a central body and wholly or partially exempted from prudential requirements in national law in accordance with Article 10 of Regulation (EU) No 575/2013;
(b) the requirements of Section 2 to institutions which are members of an IPS.
9. Where a waiver pursuant to paragraph 8 is granted, Member States shall:
(a) apply the requirements of Sections 2 and 3 of this Chapter on a consolidated basis to the central body and institutions affiliated to it within the meaning of Article 10 of Regulation (EU) No 575/2013;
(b) require the IPS to fulfil the requirements of Section 2 in cooperation with each of its waived members.
For that purpose, any reference in Sections 2 and 3 of this Chapter to a group shall include a central body and institutions affiliated to it within the meaning of Article 10 of Regulation (EU) No 575/2013 and their subsidiaries, and any reference to parent undertakings or institutions that are subject to consolidated supervision pursuant to Article 111 of Directive 2013/36/EU shall include the central body.
10. Institutions subject to direct supervision by the European Central Bank pursuant to Article 6(4) of Regulation (EU) No 1024/2013 or constituting a significant share in the financial system of a Member State shall draw up their own recovery plans in accordance with Section 2 of this Chapter and shall be the subject of individual resolution plans in accordance with Section 3.
For the purposes of this paragraph, the operations of an institution shall be considered to constitute a significant share of that Member State's financial system if any of the following conditions are met:
(a) the total value of its assets exceeds EUR 30 000 000 000; or
(b) the ratio of its total assets over the GDP of the Member State of establishment exceeds 20%, unless the total value of its assets is below EUR 5 000 000 000.
11. EBA shall develop draft implementing technical standards to specify uniform formats, templates and definitions for the identification and transmission of information by competent authorities and resolution authorities to EBA for the purposes of paragraph 7, subject to the principle of proportionality.
EBA shall submit those draft implementing technical standards to the Commission by 3 July 2015.
Power is conferred on the Commission to adopt the implementing technical standards referred to in the first subparagraph in accordance with Article 15 of Regulation (EU) No 1093/2010.

SECTION 2
RECOVERY PLANNING

[3.423]
Article 5
Recovery plans
1. Member States shall ensure that each institution, that is not part of a group subject to consolidated supervision pursuant to Articles 111 and 112 of Directive 2013/36/EU, draws up and maintains a recovery plan providing for measures to be taken by the institution to restore its financial position following a significant deterioration of its financial situation. Recovery plans shall be considered to be a governance arrangement within the meaning of Article 74 of Directive 2013/36/EU.
2. Competent authorities shall ensure that the institutions update their recovery plans at least annually or after a change to the legal or organisational structure of the institution, its business or its financial situation, which could have a material effect on, or necessitates a change to, the recovery plan. Competent authorities may require institutions to update their recovery plans more frequently.
3. Recovery plans shall not assume any access to or receipt of extraordinary public financial support.

4. Recovery plans shall include, where applicable, an analysis of how and when an institution may apply, in the conditions addressed by the plan, for the use of central bank facilities and identify those assets which would be expected to qualify as collateral.
5. Without prejudice to Article 4, Member States shall ensure that the recovery plans include the information listed in Section A of the Annex. Member States may require that additional information is included in the recovery plans.
Recovery plans shall also include possible measures which could be taken by the institution where the conditions for early intervention under Article 27 are met.
6. Member States shall require that recovery plans include appropriate conditions and procedures to ensure the timely implementation of recovery actions as well as a wide range of recovery options. Member States shall require that recovery plans contemplate a range of scenarios of severe macroeconomic and financial stress relevant to the institution's specific conditions including system-wide events and stress specific to individual legal persons and to groups.
7. EBA, in close cooperation with the European Systemic Risk Board (ESRB), shall, by 3 July 2015, issue guidelines in accordance with Article 16 of Regulation (EU) No 1093/2010 to specify further the range of scenarios to be used for the purposes of paragraph 6 of this Article.
8. Member States may provide that competent authorities have the power to require an institution to maintain detailed records of financial contracts to which the institution concerned is a party.
9. The management body of the institution referred to in paragraph 1 shall assess and approve the recovery plan before submitting it to the competent authority.
10. EBA shall develop draft regulatory technical standards further specifying, without prejudice to Article 4, the information to be contained in the recovery plan referred to in paragraph 5 of this Article.
EBA shall submit those draft regulatory technical standards to the Commission by 3 July 2015.
Power is delegated to the Commission to adopt the regulatory technical standards referred to in the first subparagraph in accordance with Articles 10 to 14 of Regulation (EU) No 1093/2010.

[3.424]
Article 6
Assessment of recovery plans

1. Member States shall require institutions that are required to draw up recovery plans under Article 5(1) and Article 7(1) to submit those recovery plans to the competent authority for review. Member States shall require institutions to demonstrate to the satisfaction of the competent authority that those plans meet the criteria of paragraph 2.
2. The competent authorities shall, within six months of the submission of each plan, and after consulting the competent authorities of the Member States where significant branches are located insofar as is relevant to that branch, review it and assess the extent to which it satisfies the requirements laid down in Article 5 and the following criteria:
   (a) the implementation of the arrangements proposed in the plan is reasonably likely to maintain or restore the viability and financial position of the institution or of the group, taking into account the preparatory measures that the institution has taken or has planned to take;
   (b) the plan and specific options within the plan are reasonably likely to be implemented quickly and effectively in situations of financial stress and avoiding to the maximum extent possible any significant adverse effect on the financial system, including in scenarios which would lead other institutions to implement recovery plans within the same period.
3. When assessing the appropriateness of the recovery plans, the competent authority shall take into consideration the appropriateness of the institution's capital and funding structure to the level of complexity of the organisational structure and the risk profile of the institution.
4. The competent authority shall provide the recovery plan to the resolution authority. The resolution authority may examine the recovery plan with a view to identifying any actions in the recovery plan which may adversely impact the resolvability of the institution and make recommendations to the competent authority with regard to those matters.
5. Where the competent authority assesses that there are material deficiencies in the recovery plan, or material impediments to its implementation, it shall notify the institution or the parent undertaking of the group of its assessment and require the institution to submit, within two months, extendable with the authorities' approval by one month, a revised plan demonstrating how those deficiencies or impediments are addressed.
Before requiring an institution to resubmit a recovery plan the competent authority shall give the institution the opportunity to state its opinion on that requirement.
Where the competent authority does not consider the deficiencies and impediments to have been adequately addressed by the revised plan, it may direct the institution to make specific changes to the plan.
6. If the institution fails to submit a revised recovery plan, or if the competent authority determines that the revised recovery plan does not adequately remedy the deficiencies or potential impediments identified in its original assessment, and it is not possible to adequately remedy the deficiencies or impediments through a direction to make specific changes to the plan, the competent authority shall require the institution to identify within a reasonable timeframe changes it can make to its business in order to address the deficiencies in or impediments to the implementation of the recovery plan.
If the institution fails to identify such changes within the timeframe set by the competent authority, or if the competent authority assesses that the actions proposed by the institution would not adequately address the deficiencies or impediments, the competent authority may direct the institution to take any measures it considers to be necessary and proportionate, taking into account the seriousness of the deficiencies and impediments and the effect of the measures on the institution's business.

The competent authority may, without prejudice to Article 104 of Directive 2013/36/EU, direct the institution to:

(a) reduce the risk profile of the institution, including liquidity risk;
(b) enable timely recapitalisation measures;
(c) review the institution's strategy and structure;
(d) make changes to the funding strategy so as to improve the resilience of the core business lines and critical functions;
(e) make changes to the governance structure of the institution.

The list of measures referred to in this paragraph does not preclude Member States from authorising competent authorities to take additional measures under national law.

7. When the competent authority requires an institution to take measures according to paragraph 6, its decision on the measures shall be reasoned and proportionate.

The decision shall be notified in writing to the institution and subject to a right of appeal.

8. EBA shall develop draft regulatory technical standards specifying the minimum criteria that the competent authority is to assess for the purposes of the assessment of paragraph 2 of this Article and of Article 8(1).

EBA shall submit those draft regulatory technical standards to the Commission by 3 July 2015.

Power is delegated to the Commission to adopt the regulatory technical standards referred to in the first subparagraph in accordance with Articles 10 to 14 of Regulation (EU) No 1093/2010.

[3.425]
Article 7
Group recovery plans

1. Member States shall ensure that Union parent undertakings draw up and submit to the consolidating supervisor a group recovery plan. Group recovery plans shall consist of a recovery plan for the group headed by the Union parent undertaking as a whole. The group recovery plan shall identify measures that may be required to be implemented at the level of the Union parent undertaking and each individual subsidiary.

2. In accordance with Article 8, competent authorities may require subsidiaries to draw up and submit recovery plans on an individual basis.

3. The consolidating supervisor shall, provided that the confidentiality requirements laid down in this Directive are in place, transmit the group recovery plans to:

(a) the relevant competent authorities referred to in Articles 115 and 116 of Directive 2013/36/EU;
(b) the competent authorities of the Member States where significant branches are located insofar as is relevant to that branch;
(c) the group-level resolution authority; and
(d) the resolution authorities of subsidiaries.

4. The group recovery plan shall aim to achieve the stabilisation of the group as a whole, or any institution of the group, when it is in a situation of stress so as to address or remove the causes of the distress and restore the financial position of the group or the institution in question, at the same time taking into account the financial position of other group entities.

The group recovery plan shall include arrangements to ensure the coordination and consistency of measures to be taken at the level of the Union parent undertaking, at the level of the entities referred to in points (c) and (d) of Article 1(1) as well as measures to be taken at the level of subsidiaries and, where applicable, in accordance with Directive 2013/36/EU at the level of significant branches.

5. The group recovery plan, and any plan drawn up for an individual subsidiary, shall include the elements specified in Article 5. Those plans shall include, where applicable, arrangements for intra-group financial support adopted pursuant to an agreement for intra-group financial support that has been concluded in accordance with Chapter III.

6. Group recovery plans shall include a range of recovery options setting out actions to address those scenarios provided for in Article 5(6).

For each of the scenarios, the group recovery plan shall identify whether there are obstacles to the implementation of recovery measures within the group, including at the level of individual entities covered by the plan, and whether there are substantial practical or legal impediments to the prompt transfer of own funds or the repayment of liabilities or assets within the group.

7. The management body of the entity drawing up the group recovery plan pursuant to paragraph 1 shall assess and approve the group recovery plan before submitting it to the consolidating supervisor.

[3.426]
Article 8
Assessment of group recovery plans

1. The consolidating supervisor shall, together with the competent authorities of subsidiaries, after consulting the competent authorities referred to in Article 116 of Directive 2013/36/EU and with the competent authorities of significant branches insofar as is relevant to the significant branch, review the group recovery plan and assess the extent to which it satisfies the requirements and criteria laid down in Articles 6 and 7. That assessment shall be made in accordance with the procedure established in Article 6 and with this Article and shall take into account the potential impact of the recovery measures on financial stability in all the Member States where the group operates.

2. The consolidating supervisor and the competent authorities of subsidiaries shall endeavour to reach a joint decision on:

(a) the review and assessment of the group recovery plan;
(b) whether a recovery plan on an individual basis shall be drawn up for institutions that are part of the group; and

(c) the application of the measures referred to in Article 6(5) and (6).

The parties shall endeavour to reach a joint decision within four months of the date of the transmission by the consolidating supervisor of the group recovery plan in accordance with Article 7(3).

EBA may, at the request of a competent authority, assist the competent authorities in reaching a joint decision in accordance with Article 31(c) of Regulation (EU) No 1093/2010.

3. In the absence of a joint decision between the competent authorities, within four months of the date of transmission, on the review and assessment of the group recovery plan or on any measures the Union parent undertaking is required to take in accordance with Article 6(5) and (6), the consolidating supervisor shall make its own decision with regard to those matters. The consolidating supervisor shall make its decision having taken into account the views and reservations of the other competent authorities expressed during the four-month period. The consolidating supervisor shall notify the decision to the Union parent undertaking and to the other competent authorities.

If, at the end of that four-month period, any of the competent authorities referred to in paragraph 2 has referred a matter mentioned in paragraph 7 to EBA in accordance with Article 19 of Regulation (EU) No 1093/2010, the consolidating supervisor shall defer its decision and await any decision that EBA may take in accordance with Article 19(3) of that Regulation, and shall take its decision in accordance with the decision of EBA. The four-month period shall be deemed to be the conciliation period within the meaning of the Regulation. EBA shall take its decision within one month. The matter shall not be referred to EBA after the end of the four-month period or after a joint decision has been reached. In the absence of an EBA decision within one month, the decision of the consolidating supervisor shall apply.

4. In the absence of a joint decision between the competent authorities within four months of the date of transmission on:

(a) whether a recovery plan on an individual basis is to be drawn up for the institutions under its jurisdiction; or

(b) the application at subsidiary level of the measures referred to in Article 6(5) and (6);

each competent authority shall make its own decision on that matter.

If, at the end of the four-month period, any of the competent authorities concerned has referred a matter mentioned in paragraph 7 to EBA in accordance with Article 19 of Regulation (EU) No 1093/2010, the competent authority of the subsidiary shall defer its decision and await any decision that EBA may take in accordance with Article 19(3) of that Regulation, and shall take its decision in accordance with the decision of EBA. The four-month period shall be deemed to be the conciliation period within the meaning of that Regulation. EBA shall take its decision within one month. The matter shall not be referred to EBA after the end of the four-month period or after a joint decision has been reached. In the absence of an EBA decision within one month, the decision of the competent authority responsible for the subsidiary at an individual level shall apply.

5. The other competent authorities which do not disagree under paragraph 4 may reach a joint decision on a group recovery plan covering group entities under their jurisdictions.

6. The joint decision referred to in paragraph 2 or 5 and the decisions taken by the competent authorities in the absence of a joint decision referred to in paragraphs 3 and 4 shall be recognised as conclusive and applied by the competent authorities in the Member States concerned.

7. Upon request of a competent authority in accordance with paragraph 3 or 4, EBA may only assist the competent authorities in reaching an agreement in accordance with Article 19(3) of Regulation (EU) No 1093/2010 in relation to the assessment of recovery plans and implementation of the measures of point (a), (b) and (d) of Article 6(6).

[3.427]
Article 9
Recovery Plan Indicators

1. For the purpose of Articles 5 to 8, competent authorities shall require that each recovery plan includes a framework of indicators established by the institution which identifies the points at which appropriate actions referred to in the plan may be taken. Such indicators shall be agreed by competent authorities when making the assessment of recovery plans in accordance with Articles 6 and 8. The indicators may be of a qualitative or quantitative nature relating to the institution's financial position and shall be capable of being monitored easily. Competent authorities shall ensure that institutions put in place appropriate arrangements for the regular monitoring of the indicators.

Notwithstanding the first subparagraph, an institution may:

(a) take action under its recovery plan where the relevant indicator has not been met, but where the management body of the institution considers it to be appropriate in the circumstances; or

(b) refrain from taking such an action where the management body of the institution does not consider it to be appropriate in the circumstances of the situation.

A decision to take an action referred to in the recovery plan or a decision to refrain from taking such an action shall be notified to the competent authority without delay.

2. EBA shall, by 3 July 2015, issue guidelines in accordance with Article 16 of Regulation (EU) No 1093/2010 to specify the minimum list of qualitative and quantitative indicators as referred to in paragraph 1.

SECTION 3
RESOLUTION PLANNING

[3.428]
Article 10
Resolution plans

1. The resolution authority, after consulting the competent authority and after consulting the resolution authorities of the jurisdictions in which any significant branches are located insofar as is relevant to the significant branch shall draw up a resolution plan for each institution that is not part of a group subject to consolidated supervision pursuant to Articles 111 and 112 of Directive 2013/36/EU. The resolution plan shall provide for the resolution actions which the resolution authority may take where the institution meets the conditions for resolution. Information referred to paragraph 7(a) shall be disclosed to the institution concerned.

2. When drawing up the resolution plan, the resolution authority shall identify any material impediments to resolvability and, where necessary and proportionate, outline relevant actions for how those impediments could be addressed, according to Chapter II of this Title.

3. The resolution plan shall take into consideration relevant scenarios including that the event of failure may be idiosyncratic or may occur at a time of broader financial instability or system wide events. The resolution plan shall not assume any of the following:

(a) any extraordinary public financial support besides the use of the financing arrangements established in accordance with Article 100;

(b) any central bank emergency liquidity assistance; or

(c) any central bank liquidity assistance provided under non-standard collateralisation, tenor and interest rate terms.

4. The resolution plan shall include an analysis of how and when an institution may apply, in the conditions addressed by the plan, for the use of central bank facilities and shall identify those assets which would be expected to qualify as collateral.

5. Resolution authorities may require institutions to assist them in the drawing up and updating of the plans.

6. Resolution plans shall be reviewed, and where appropriate updated, at least annually and after any material changes to the legal or organisational structure of the institution or to its business or its financial position that could have a material effect on the effectiveness of the plan or otherwise necessitates a revision of the resolution plan.

For the purpose of the revision or update of the resolution plans referred to in the first subparagraph, the institutions and the competent authorities shall promptly communicate to the resolution authorities any change that necessitates such a revision or update.

7. Without prejudice to Article 4, the resolution plan shall set out options for applying the resolution tools and resolution powers referred to in Title IV to the institution. It shall include, quantified whenever appropriate and possible:

(a) a summary of the key elements of the plan;

(b) a summary of the material changes to the institution that have occurred after the latest resolution information was filed;

(c) a demonstration of how critical functions and core business lines could be legally and economically separated, to the extent necessary, from other functions so as to ensure continuity upon the failure of the institution;

(d) an estimation of the timeframe for executing each material aspect of the plan;

(e) a detailed description of the assessment of resolvability carried out in accordance with paragraph 2 of this Article and with Article 15;

(f) a description of any measures required pursuant to Article 17 to address or remove impediments to resolvability identified as a result of the assessment carried out in accordance with Article 15;

(g) a description of the processes for determining the value and marketability of the critical functions, core business lines and assets of the institution;

(h) a detailed description of the arrangements for ensuring that the information required pursuant to Article 11 is up to date and at the disposal of the resolution authorities at all times;

(i) an explanation by the resolution authority as to how the resolution options could be financed without the assumption of any of the following:

  (i) any extraordinary public financial support besides the use of the financing arrangements established in accordance with Article 100;

  (ii) any central bank emergency liquidity assistance; or

  (iii) any central bank liquidity assistance provided under non-standard collateralisation, tenor and interest rate terms;

(j) a detailed description of the different resolution strategies that could be applied according to the different possible scenarios and the applicable timescales;

(k) a description of critical interdependencies;

(l) a description of options for preserving access to payments and clearing services and other infrastructures and, an assessment of the portability of client positions;

(m) an analysis of the impact of the plan on the employees of the institution, including an assessment of any associated costs, and a description of envisaged procedures to consult staff during the resolution process, taking into account national systems for dialogue with social partners where applicable;

(n) a plan for communicating with the media and the public;

(o) the minimum requirement for own funds and eligible liabilities required pursuant to Article 45(1) and a deadline to reach that level, where applicable;

(p) where applicable, the minimum requirement for own funds and contractual bail-in instruments pursuant to Article 45(1), and a deadline to reach that level, where applicable;
(q) a description of essential operations and systems for maintaining the continuous functioning of the institution's operational processes;
(r) where applicable, any opinion expressed by the institution in relation to the resolution plan.

8. Member States shall ensure that resolution authorities have the power to require an institution and an entity referred to in point (b), (c) or (d) of Article 1(1) to maintain detailed records of financial contracts to which it is a party. The resolution authority may specify a time-limit within which the institution or entity referred to in point (b), (c) or (d) of Article 1(1) is to be capable of producing those records. The same time-limit shall apply to all institutions and all entities referred to in point (b), (c) and (d) of Article 1(1) under its jurisdiction. The resolution authority may decide to set different time-limits for different types of financial contracts as referred to in Article 2(100). This paragraph shall not affect the information gathering powers of the competent authority.

9. EBA, after consulting the ESRB, shall develop draft regulatory technical standards further specifying the contents of the resolution plan.

EBA shall submit those draft regulatory technical standards to the Commission by 3 July 2015.

Power is delegated to the Commission to adopt the regulatory technical standards referred to in the first subparagraph in accordance with Articles 10 to 14 of Regulation (EU) No 1093/2010.

[3.429]
Article 11
Information for the purpose of resolution plans and cooperation from the institution

1. Member States shall ensure that resolution authorities have the power to require institutions to:
(a) cooperate as much as necessary in the drawing up of resolution plans;
(b) provide them, either directly or through the competent authority, with all of the information necessary to draw up and implement resolution plans.

In particular the resolution authorities shall have the power to require, among other information, the information and analysis specified in Section B of the Annex.

2. Competent authorities in the relevant Member States shall cooperate with resolution authorities in order to verify whether some or all of the information referred to in paragraph 1 is already available. Where such information is available, competent authorities shall provide that information to the resolution authorities.

3. EBA shall develop draft implementing technical standards to specify procedures and a minimum set of standard forms and templates for the provision of information under this Article.

EBA shall submit those draft implementing technical standards to the Commission by 3 July 2015.

Power is conferred on the Commission to adopt the implementing technical standards referred to in the first subparagraph in accordance with Article 15 of Regulation (EU) No 1093/2010.

[3.430]
Article 12
Group resolution plans

1. Member States shall ensure that group-level resolution authorities, together with the resolution authorities of subsidiaries and after consulting the resolution authorities of significant branches insofar as is relevant to the significant branch, draw up group resolution plans. Group resolution plans shall include a plan for resolution of the group headed by the Union parent undertaking as a whole, either through resolution at the level of the Union parent undertaking or through break up and resolution of the subsidiaries. The group resolution plan shall identify measures for the resolution of:
(a) the Union parent undertaking;
(b) the subsidiaries that are part of the group and that are located in the Union;
(c) the entities referred to in points (c) and (d) of Article 1(1); and
(d) subject to Title VI, the subsidiaries that are part of the group and that are located outside the Union.

2. The group resolution plan shall be drawn up on the basis of the information provided pursuant to Article 11.

3. The group resolution plan shall:
(a) set out the resolution actions to be taken in relation to group entities, both through resolution actions in respect of the entities referred to in points (b), (c) and (d) of Article 1(1), the parent undertaking and subsidiary institutions and through coordinated resolution actions in respect of subsidiary institutions, in the scenarios provided for in Article 10(3);
(b) examine the extent to which the resolution tools and powers could be applied and exercised in a coordinated way to group entities established in the Union, including measures to facilitate the purchase by a third party of the group as a whole, or separate business lines or activities that are delivered by a number of group entities, or particular group entities, and identify any potential impediments to a coordinated resolution;
(c) where a group includes entities incorporated in third countries, identify appropriate arrangements for cooperation and coordination with the relevant authorities of those third countries and the implications for resolution within the Union;
(d) identify measures, including the legal and economic separation of particular functions or business lines, that are necessary to facilitate group resolution when the conditions for resolution are met;
(e) set out any additional actions, not referred to in this Directive, which the group-level resolution authority intends to take in relation to the resolution of the group;

(f) identify how the group resolution actions could be financed and, where the financing arrangement would be required, set out principles for sharing responsibility for that financing between sources of funding in different Member States. The plan shall not assume any of the following:
  (i) any extraordinary public financial support besides the use of the financing arrangements established in accordance with Article 100;
  (ii) any central bank emergency liquidity assistance; or
  (iii) any central bank liquidity assistance provided under non-standard collateralisation, tenor and interest rate terms.

Those principles shall be set out on the basis of equitable and balanced criteria and shall take into account, in particular Article 107(5) and the impact on financial stability in all Member States concerned.

4. The assessment of the resolvability of the group under Article 16 shall be carried out at the same time as the drawing up and updating of the group resolution plan in accordance with this Article. A detailed description of the assessment of resolvability carried out in accordance with Article 16 shall be included in the group resolution plan.

5. The group resolution plan shall not have a disproportionate impact on any Member State.

6. EBA shall, after consulting the ESRB, develop draft regulatory technical standards specifying the contents of group resolution plans, by taking into account the diversity of business models of groups in the internal market.

EBA shall submit those draft regulatory technical standards to the Commission by 3 July 2015.

Power is delegated to the Commission to adopt the regulatory technical standards referred to in the first subparagraph in accordance with Articles 10 to 14 of Regulation (EU) No 1093/2010.

[3.431]
Article 13
Requirement and procedure for group resolution plans

1. Union parent undertakings shall submit the information that may be required in accordance with Article 11 to the group-level resolution authority. That information shall concern the Union parent undertaking and to the extent required each of the group entities including entities referred to in points (c) and (d) of Article 1(1).

The group-level resolution authority shall, provided that the confidentiality requirements laid down in this Directive are in place, transmit the information provided in accordance with this paragraph to:
(a) EBA;
(b) the resolution authorities of subsidiaries;
(c) the resolution authorities of the jurisdictions in which significant branches are located insofar as is relevant to the significant branch;
(d) the relevant competent authorities referred to in Articles 115 and 116 of Directive 2013/36/EU; and
(e) the resolution authorities of the Member States where the entities referred to in points (c) and (d) of Article 1(1) are established.

The information provided by the group-level resolution authority to the resolution authorities and competent authorities of subsidiaries, resolution authorities of the jurisdiction in which any significant branches are located, and to the relevant competent authorities referred to in Articles 115 and 116 of Directive 2013/36/EU, shall include at a minimum all information that is relevant to the subsidiary or significant branch. The information provided to EBA shall include all information that is relevant to the role of EBA in relation the group resolution plans. In the case of information relating to third-country subsidiaries, the group-level resolution authority shall not be obliged to transmit that information without the consent of the relevant third-country supervisory authority or resolution authority.

2. Member States shall ensure that group-level resolution authorities, acting jointly with the resolution authorities referred to in the second subparagraph of paragraph 1 of this Article, in resolution colleges and after consulting the relevant competent authorities, including the competent authorities of the jurisdictions of Member States in which any significant branches are located, draw up and maintain group resolution plans. Group-level resolution authorities may, at their discretion, and subject to them meeting the confidentiality requirements laid down in Article 98 of this Directive, involve in the drawing up and maintenance of group resolution plans third-country resolution authorities of jurisdictions in which the group has established subsidiaries or financial holding companies or significant branches as referred to in Article 51 of Directive 2013/36/EU.

3. Member States shall ensure that group resolution plans are reviewed, and where appropriate updated, at least annually, and after any change to the legal or organisational structure, to the business or to the financial position of the group including any group entity, that could have a material effect on or require a change to the plan.

4. The adoption of the group resolution plan shall take the form of a joint decision of the group-level resolution authority and the resolution authorities of subsidiaries.

Those resolution authorities shall make a joint decision within four months of the date of the transmission by the group-level resolution authority of the information referred to in the second subparagraph of paragraph 1.

EBA may, at the request of a resolution authority, assist the resolution authorities in reaching a joint decision in accordance with Article 31(c) of Regulation (EU) No 1093/2010.

5. In the absence of a joint decision between the resolution authorities within four months, the group-level resolution authority shall make its own decision on the group resolution plan. The decision shall be fully reasoned and shall take into account the views and reservations of other resolution authorities. The decision shall be provided to the Union parent undertaking by the group-level resolution authority.

Subject to paragraph 9 of this Article, if, at the end of the four-month period, any resolution authority has referred the matter to EBA in accordance with Article 19 of Regulation (EU) No 1093/2010, the group-level resolution authority shall defer its decision and await any decision that EBA may take in accordance with Article 19(3) of that Regulation, and shall take its decision in accordance with the decision of EBA. The four-month period shall be deemed to be the conciliation period within the meaning of that Regulation. EBA shall take its decision within one month. The matter shall not be referred to EBA after the end of the four-month period or after a joint decision has been reached. In the absence of an EBA decision within one month, the decision of the group-level resolution authority shall apply.

6. In the absence of a joint decision between the resolution authorities within four months, each resolution authority responsible for a subsidiary shall make its own decision and shall draw up and maintain a resolution plan for the entities under its jurisdiction. Each of the individual decisions shall be fully reasoned, shall set out the reasons disagreement with the proposed group resolution plan and shall take into account the views and reservations of the other competent authorities and resolution authorities. Each resolution authority shall notify its decision to the other members of the resolution college.

Subject to paragraph 9 of this Article, if, at the end of the four-month period, any resolution authority has referred the matter to EBA in accordance with Article 19 of Regulation (EU) No 1093/2010, the resolution authority concerned shall defer its decision and await any decision that EBA may take in accordance with Article 19(3) of that Regulation, and shall take its decision in accordance with the decision of EBA. The four-month period shall be deemed to be the conciliation period within the meaning of that Regulation. EBA shall take its decision within one month. The matter shall not be referred to EBA after the end of the four-month period or after a joint decision has been reached. In the absence of an EBA decision within one month, the decision of the resolution authority of the subsidiary shall apply.

7. The other resolution authorities which do not disagree under paragraph 6 may reach a joint decision on a group resolution plan covering group entities under their jurisdictions.

8. The joint decisions referred to in paragraphs 4 and 7 and the decisions taken by the resolution authorities in the absence of a joint decision referred to in paragraphs 5 and 6 shall be recognised as conclusive and applied by the other resolution authorities concerned.

9. In accordance with paragraphs 5 and 6 of this Article, upon request of a resolution authority, EBA may assist the resolution authorities in reaching an agreement in accordance with Article 19(3) of Regulation (EU) No 1093/2010 unless any resolution authority concerned assesses that the subject matter under disagreement may in any way impinge on its Member States' fiscal responsibilities.

10. Where joint decisions are taken pursuant to paragraphs 4 and 7 and where a resolution authority assesses under paragraph 9 that the subject matter of a disagreement regarding group resolution plans impinges on the fiscal responsibilities of its Member State, the group-level resolution authority shall initiate a reassessment of the group resolution plan, including the minimum requirement for own funds and eligible liabilities.

[3.432]
Article 14
Transmission of resolution plans to the competent authorities

1. The resolution authority shall transmit the resolution plans and any changes thereto to the relevant competent authorities.

2. The group-level resolution authority shall transmit group resolution plans and any changes thereto to the relevant competent authorities.

CHAPTER II RESOLVABILITY

[3.433]
Article 15
Assessment of resolvability for institutions

1. Member States shall ensure that, after the resolution authority has consulted the competent authority and the resolution authorities of the jurisdictions in which significant branches are located insofar as is relevant to the significant branch, it assesses the extent to which an institution which is not part of a group is resolvable without the assumption of any of the following:

(a) any extraordinary public financial support besides the use of the financing arrangements established in accordance with Article 100;
(b) any central bank emergency liquidity assistance;
(c) any central bank liquidity assistance provided under non-standard collateralisation, tenor and interest rate terms.

An institution shall be deemed to be resolvable if it is feasible and credible for the resolution authority to either liquidate it under normal insolvency proceedings or to resolve it by applying the different resolution tools and powers to the institution while avoiding to the maximum extent possible any significant adverse effect on the financial system, including in circumstances of broader financial instability or system-wide events, of the Member State in which the institution is established, or other Member States or the Union and with a view to ensuring the continuity of critical functions carried out by the institution. The resolution authorities shall notify EBA in a timely manner whenever an institution is deemed not to be resolvable.

2. For the purposes of the assessment of resolvability referred to in paragraph 1, the resolution authority shall, as a minimum, examine the matters specified in Section C of the Annex.

3. The resolvability assessment under this Article shall be made by the resolution authority at the same time as and for the purposes of the drawing up and updating of the resolution plan in accordance with Article 10.

4. EBA, after consulting the ESRB, shall develop draft regulatory technical standards to specify the matters and criteria for the assessment of the resolvability of institutions or groups provided for in paragraph 2 of this Article and in Article 16.
EBA shall submit those draft regulatory technical standards to the Commission by 3 July 2015.
Power is conferred on the Commission to adopt the draft regulatory technical standards referred to in the first subparagraph in accordance with Articles 10 to 14 of Regulation (EU) No 1093/2010.

[3.434]
Article 16
Assessment of resolvability for groups
1. Member States shall ensure that group-level resolution authorities, together with the resolution authorities of subsidiaries, after consulting the consolidating supervisor and the competent authorities of such subsidiaries, and the resolution authorities of the jurisdictions in which significant branches are located insofar as is relevant to the significant branch, assess the extent to which groups are resolvable without the assumption of any of the following:
(a) any extraordinary public financial support besides the use of the financing arrangements established in accordance with Article 100;
(b) any central bank emergency liquidity assistance;
(c) any central bank liquidity assistance provided under non-standard collateralisation, tenor and interest rate terms.
A group shall be deemed to be resolvable if it is feasible and credible for the resolution authorities to either wind up group entities under normal insolvency proceedings or to resolve group entities by applying resolution tools and powers to group entities while avoiding to the maximum extent possible any significant adverse effect on the financial system, including in circumstances of broader financial instability or system wide events, of the Member States in which group entities are established, or other Member States or the Union and with a view to ensuring the continuity of critical functions carried out by the group entities, where they can be easily separated in a timely manner or by other means. Group-level resolution authorities shall notify EBA in a timely manner whenever a group is deemed not to be resolvable.
The assessment of group resolvability shall be taken into consideration by the resolution colleges referred to in Article 88.
2. For the purposes of the assessment of group resolvability, resolution authorities shall, as a minimum, examine the matters specified in Section C of the Annex.
3. The assessment of group resolvability under this Article shall be made at the same time as, and for the purposes of drawing up and updating of the group resolution plans in accordance with Article 12. The assessment shall be made under the decision-making procedure laid down in Article 13.

[3.435]
Article 17
Powers to address or remove impediments to resolvability
1. Member States shall ensure that when, pursuant to an assessment of resolvability for an institution carried out in accordance with Articles 15 and 16, a resolution authority after consulting the competent authority determines that there are substantive impediments to the resolvability of that institution, the resolution authority shall notify in writing that determination to the institution concerned, to the competent authority and to the resolution authorities of the jurisdictions in which significant branches are located.
2. The requirement for resolution authorities to draw up resolution plans and for the relevant resolution authorities to reach a joint decision on group resolution plans in Article 10(1) and Article 13(4) respectively shall be suspended following the notification referred to in paragraph 1 of this Article until the measures to remove the substantive impediments to resolvability have been accepted by the resolution authority pursuant to paragraph 3 of this Article or decided pursuant to paragraph 4 of this Article.
3. Within four months of the date of receipt of a notification made in accordance with paragraph 1, the institution shall propose to the resolution authority possible measures to address or remove the substantive impediments identified in the notification. The resolution authority, after consulting the competent authority, shall assess whether those measures effectively address or remove the substantive impediments in question.
4. Where the resolution authority assesses that the measures proposed by an institution in accordance with paragraph 3 do not effectively reduce or remove the impediments in question, it shall, either directly or indirectly through the competent authority, require the institution to take alternative measures that may achieve that objective, and notify in writing those measures to the institution, which shall propose within one month a plan to comply with them.
In identifying alternative measures, the resolution authority shall demonstrate how the measures proposed by the institution would not be able to remove the impediments to resolvability and how the alternative measures proposed are proportionate in removing them. The resolution authority shall take into account the threat to financial stability of those impediments to resolvability and the effect of the measures on the business of the institution, its stability and its ability to contribute to the economy.
5. For the purposes of paragraph 4, resolution authorities shall have the power to take any of the following measures:
(a) require the institution to revise any intragroup financing agreements or review the absence thereof, or draw up service agreements, whether intra-group or with third parties, to cover the provision of critical functions;
(b) require the institution to limit its maximum individual and aggregate exposures;
(c) impose specific or regular additional information requirements relevant for resolution purposes;

(d) require the institution to divest specific assets;
(e) require the institution to limit or cease specific existing or proposed activities;
(f) restrict or prevent the development of new or existing business lines or sale of new or existing products;
(g) require changes to legal or operational structures of the institution or any group entity, either directly or indirectly under its control, so as to reduce complexity in order to ensure that critical functions may be legally and operationally separated from other functions through the application of the resolution tools;
(h) require an institution or a parent undertaking to set up a parent financial holding company in a Member State or a Union parent financial holding company;
(i) require an institution or entity referred to in point (b), (c) or (d) of Article 1(1) to issue eligible liabilities to meet the requirements of Article 45;
(j) require an institution or entity referred to in point(b), (c) or (d) of Article 1(1), to take other steps to meet the minimum requirement for own funds and eligible liabilities under Article 45, including in particular to attempt to renegotiate any eligible liability, additional Tier 1 instrument or Tier 2 instrument it has issued, with a view to ensuring that any decision of the resolution authority to write down or convert that liability or instrument would be effected under the law of the jurisdiction governing that liability or instrument; and
(k) where an institution is the subsidiary of a mixed-activity holding company, requiring that the mixed-activity holding company set up a separate financial holding company to control the institution, if necessary in order to facilitate the resolution of the institution and to avoid the application of the resolution tools and powers referred to in Title IV having an adverse effect on the non-financial part of the group.

6. A decision made pursuant to paragraph 1 or 4 shall meet the following requirements:
(a) it shall be supported by reasons for the assessment or determination in question;
(b) it shall indicate how that assessment or determination complies with the requirement for proportionate application laid down in paragraph 4; and
(c) it shall be subject to a right of appeal.

7. Before identifying any measure referred to in paragraph 4, the resolution authority, after consulting the competent authority and, if appropriate, the designated national macroprudential authority, shall duly consider the potential effect of those measures on the particular institution, on the internal market for financial services, on the financial stability in other Member States and Union as a whole.

8. EBA shall, by 3 July 2015, issue guidelines in accordance with Article 16 of Regulation (EU) No 1093/2010 to specify further details on the measures provided for in paragraph 5 and the circumstances in which each measure may be applied.

[3.436]
Article 18
Powers to address or remove impediments to resolvability: group treatment

1. The group-level resolution authority together with the resolution authorities of subsidiaries, after consulting the supervisory college and the resolution authorities of the jurisdictions in which significant branches are located insofar as is relevant to the significant branch, shall consider the assessment required by Article 16 within the resolution college and shall take all reasonable steps to reach a joint decision on the application of measures identified in accordance with Article 17(4) in relation to all institutions that are part of the group.

2. The group-level resolution authority, in cooperation with the consolidating supervisor and EBA in accordance with Article 25(1) of Regulation (EU) No 1093/2010, shall prepare and submit a report to the Union parent undertaking, to the resolution authorities of subsidiaries, which will provide it to the subsidiaries under their supervision, and to the resolution authorities of jurisdictions in which significant branches are located. The report shall be prepared after consulting the competent authorities, and shall analyse the substantive impediments to the effective application of the resolution tools and the exercising of the resolution powers in relation to the group. The report shall consider the impact on the institution's business model and recommend any proportionate and targeted measures that, in the authority's view, are necessary or appropriate to remove those impediments.

3. Within four months of the date of receipt of the report, the Union parent undertaking may submit observations and propose to the group-level resolution authority alternative measures to remedy the impediments identified in the report.

4. The group-level resolution authority shall communicate any measure proposed by the Union parent undertaking to the consolidating supervisor, EBA, the resolution authorities of the subsidiaries and the resolution authorities of the jurisdictions in which significant branches are located insofar as is relevant to the significant branch. The group-level resolution authorities and the resolution authorities of the subsidiaries, after consulting the competent authorities and the resolution authorities of jurisdictions in which significant branches are located, shall do everything within their power to reach a joint decision within the resolution college regarding the identification of the material impediments, and if necessary, the assessment of the measures proposed by the Union parent undertaking and the measures required by the authorities in order to address or remove the impediments, which shall take into account the potential impact of the measures in all the Member States where the group operates.

5. The joint decision shall be reached within four months of submission of any observations by the Union parent undertaking or at the expiry of the four-month period referred to in paragraph 3, whichever the earlier. It shall be reasoned and set out in a document which shall be provided by the group-level resolution authority to the Union parent undertaking.

EBA may, at the request of a resolution authority, assist the resolution authorities in reaching a joint decision in accordance with Article 31(c) of Regulation (EU) No 1093/2010.

6. In the absence of a joint decision within the period referred to in paragraph 5, the group-level resolution authority shall make its own decision on the appropriate measures to be taken in accordance with Article 17(4) at the group level.

The decision shall be fully reasoned and shall take into account the views and reservations of other resolution authorities. The decision shall be provided to the Union parent undertaking by the group-level resolution authority.

If, at the end of the four-month period, any resolution authority has referred a matter mentioned in paragraph 9 of this Article to EBA in accordance with Article 19 of Regulation (EU) No 1093/2010, the group-level resolution authority shall defer its decision and await any decision that EBA may take in accordance with Article 19(3) of that Regulation, and shall take its decision in accordance with the decision of EBA. The four-month period shall be deemed to be the conciliation period within the meaning of that Regulation. EBA shall take its decision within one month. The matter shall not be referred to EBA after the end of the four-month period or after a joint decision has been reached. In the absence of an EBA decision within one month, the decision of the group-level resolution authority shall apply.

7. In the absence of a joint decision, the resolution authorities of subsidiaries shall make their own decisions on the appropriate measures to be taken by subsidiaries at individual level in accordance with Article 17(4). The decision shall be fully reasoned and shall take into account the views and reservations of the other resolution authorities. The decision shall be provided to the subsidiary concerned and to the group-level resolution authority.

If, at the end of the four-month period, any resolution authority has referred a matter mentioned in paragraph 9 of this Article to EBA in accordance with Article 19 of Regulation (EU) No 1093/2010, the resolution authority of the subsidiary shall defer its decision and await any decision that EBA may take in accordance with Article 19(3) of that Regulation, and shall take its decision in accordance with the decision of EBA. The four-month period shall be deemed to be the conciliation period within the meaning of that Regulation. EBA shall take its decision within one month. The matter shall not be referred to EBA after the end of the four-month period or after a joint decision has been reached. In the absence of an EBA decision within one month, the decision of the resolution authority of the subsidiary shall apply.

8. The joint decision referred to in paragraph 5 and the decisions taken by the resolution authorities in the absence of a joint decision referred to in paragraph 6 shall be recognised as conclusive and applied by the other resolution authorities concerned.

9. In the absence of a joint decision on the taking of any measures referred to in point (g), (h) or (k) of Article 17(5), EBA may, upon the request of a resolution authority in accordance with paragraph 6 or 7 of this Article, assist the resolution authorities in reaching an agreement in accordance with Article 19(3) of Regulation (EU) No 1093/2010.

CHAPTER III INTRA GROUP FINANCIAL SUPPORT

[3.437]
Article 19
Group financial support agreement

1. Member States shall ensure that a parent institution in a Member State, a Union parent institution, or an entity referred to in point (c) or (d) of Article 1(1) and its subsidiaries in other Member States or third countries that are institutions or financial institutions covered by the consolidated supervision of the parent undertaking, may enter into an agreement to provide financial support to any other party to the agreement that meets the conditions for early intervention pursuant to Article 27, provided that the conditions laid down in this Chapter are also met.

2. This Chapter does not apply to intra-group financial arrangements including funding arrangements and the operation of centralised funding arrangements provided that none of the parties to such arrangements meets the conditions for early intervention.

3. A group financial support agreement shall not constitute a prerequisite:
   (a) to provide group financial support to any group entity that experiences financial difficulties if the institution decides to do so, on a case-by-case basis and according to the group policies if it does not represent a risk for the whole group; or
   (b) to operate in a Member State.

4. Member States shall remove any legal impediment in national law to intra-group financial support transactions that are undertaken in accordance with this Chapter, provided that nothing in this Chapter shall prevent Member States from imposing limitations on intra-group transactions in connection with national laws exercising the options provided for in Regulation (EU) No 575/2013, transposing Directive 2013/36/EU or requiring the separation of parts of a group or activities carried on within a group for reasons of financial stability.

5. The group financial support agreement may:
   (a) cover one or more subsidiaries of the group, and may provide for financial support from the parent undertaking to subsidiaries, from subsidiaries to the parent undertaking, between subsidiaries of the group that are party to the agreement, or any combination of those entities;
   (b) provide for financial support in the form of a loan, the provision of guarantees, the provision of assets for use as collateral, or any combination of those forms of financial support, in one or more transactions, including between the beneficiary of the support and a third party.

6. Where, in accordance with the terms of the group financial support agreement, a group entity agrees to provide financial support to another group entity, the agreement may include a reciprocal agreement by the group entity receiving the support to provide financial support to the group entity providing the support.

7. The group financial support agreement shall specify the principles for the calculation of the consideration, for any transaction made under it. Those principles shall include a requirement that the consideration shall be set at the time of the provision of financial support. The agreement, including the principles for calculation of the consideration for the provision of financial support and the other terms of the agreement, shall comply with the following principles:

(a) each party must be acting freely in entering into the agreement;

(b) in entering into the agreement and in determining the consideration for the provision of financial support, each party must be acting in its own best interests which may take account of any direct or any indirect benefit that may accrue to a party as a result of provision of the financial support;

(c) each party providing financial support must have full disclosure of relevant information from any party receiving financial support prior to determination of the consideration for the provision of financial support and prior to any decision to provide financial support;

(d) the consideration for the provision of financial support may take account of information in the possession of the party providing financial support based on it being in the same group as the party receiving financial support and which is not available to the market; and

(e) the principles for the calculation of the consideration for the provision of financial support are not obliged to take account of any anticipated temporary impact on market prices arising from events external to the group.

8. The group financial support agreement may only be concluded if, at the time the proposed agreement is made, in the opinion of their respective competent authorities, none of the parties meets the conditions for early intervention.

9. Member States shall ensure that any right, claim or action arising from the group financial support agreement may be exercised only by the parties to the agreement, with the exclusion of third parties.

[3.438]
Article 20
Review of proposed agreement by competent authorities and mediation

1. The Union parent institution shall submit to the consolidating supervisor an application for authorisation of any proposed group financial support agreement proposed pursuant to Article 19. The application shall contain the text of the proposed agreement and identify the group entities that propose to be parties.

2. The consolidating supervisor shall forward without delay the application to the competent authorities of each subsidiary that proposes to be a party to the agreement, with a view to reaching a joint decision.

3. The consolidating supervisor shall, in accordance with the procedure set out in paragraphs 5 and 6 of this Article, grant the authorisation if the terms of the proposed agreement are consistent with the conditions for financial support set out in Article 23.

4. The consolidating supervisor may, in accordance with the procedure set out in paragraphs 5 and 6 of this Article, prohibit the conclusion of the proposed agreement if it is considered to be inconsistent with the conditions for financial support set out in Article 23.

5. The competent authorities shall do everything within their power to reach a joint decision, taking into account the potential impact, including any fiscal consequences, of the execution of the agreement in all the Member States where the group operates, on whether the terms of the proposed agreement are consistent with the conditions for financial support laid down in Article 23 within four months of the date of receipt of the application by the consolidating supervisor. The joint decision shall be set out in a document containing the fully reasoned decision, which shall be provided to the applicant by the consolidating supervisor.

EBA may at the request of a competent authority assist the competent authorities in reaching an agreement in accordance with Article 31 of Regulation (EU) No 1093/2010.

6. In the absence of a joint decision between the competent authorities within four months, the consolidating supervisor shall make its own decision on the application. The decision shall be set out in a document containing the full reasoning and shall take into account the views and reservations of the other competent authorities expressed during the four-month period. The consolidating supervisor shall notify its decision to the applicant and the other competent authorities.

7. If, at the end of the four-month period, any of the competent authorities concerned has referred the matter to EBA in accordance with Article 19 of Regulation (EU) No 1093/2010, the consolidating supervisor shall defer its decision and await any decision that EBA may take in accordance with Article 19(3) of that Regulation, and shall take its decision in accordance with the decision of EBA. The four-month period shall be deemed to be the conciliation period within the meaning of that Regulation. EBA shall take its decision within one month. The matter shall not be referred to EBA after the end of the four-month period or after a joint decision has been reached.

[3.439]
Article 21
Approval of proposed agreement by shareholders

1. Member States shall require that any proposed agreement that has been authorised by the competent authorities be submitted for approval to the shareholders of every group entity that proposes to enter into the agreement. In such a case, the agreement shall be valid only in respect of those parties whose shareholders have approved the agreement in accordance with paragraph 2.

2. A group financial support agreement shall be valid in respect of a group entity only if its shareholders have authorised the management body of that group entity to make a decision that the group entity shall provide or receive financial support in accordance with the terms of the agreement and in accordance with the conditions laid down in this Chapter and that shareholder authorisation has not been revoked.

3. The management body of each entity that is party to an agreement shall report each year to the shareholders on the performance of the agreement, and on the implementation of any decision taken pursuant to the agreement.

[3.440]
Article 22
Transmission of the group financial support agreements to resolution authorities
Competent authorities shall transmit to the relevant resolution authorities the group financial support agreements they authorised and any changes thereto.

[3.441]
Article 23
Conditions for group financial support
1. Financial support by a group entity in accordance with Article 19 may only be provided if all the following conditions are met:
- (a) there is a reasonable prospect that the support provided significantly redresses the financial difficulties of the group entity receiving the support;
- (b) the provision of financial support has the objective of preserving or restoring the financial stability of the group as a whole or any of the entities of the group and is in the interests of the group entity providing the support;
- (c) the financial support is provided on terms, including consideration in accordance with Article 19(7);
- (d) there is a reasonable prospect, on the basis of the information available to the management body of the group entity providing financial support at the time when the decision to grant financial support is taken, that the consideration for the support will be paid and, if the support is given in the form of a loan, that the loan will be reimbursed, by the group entity receiving the support. If the support is given in the form of a guarantee or any form of security, the same condition shall apply to the liability arising for the recipient if the guarantee or the security is enforced;
- (e) the provision of the financial support would not jeopardise the liquidity or solvency of the group entity providing the support;
- (f) the provision of the financial support would not create a threat to financial stability, in particular in the Member State of the group entity providing support;
- (g) the group entity providing the support complies at the time the support is provided with the requirements of Directive 2013/36/EU relating to capital or liquidity and any requirements imposed pursuant to Article 104(2) of Directive 2013/36/EU and the provision of the financial support shall not cause the group entity to infringe those requirements, unless authorised by the competent authority responsible for the supervision on an individual basis of the entity providing the support;
- (h) the group entity providing the support complies, at the time when the support is provided, with the requirements relating to large exposures laid down in Regulation (EU) No 575/2013 and in Directive 2013/36/EU including any national legislation exercising the options provided therein, and the provision of the financial support shall not cause the group entity to infringe those requirements, unless authorised by the competent authority responsible for the supervision on an individual basis of the group entity providing the support;
- (i) the provision of the financial support would not undermine the resolvability of the group entity providing the support.

2. EBA shall develop draft regulatory technical standards to specify the conditions laid down in points (a), (c), (e) and (i) of paragraph 1.
EBA shall submit those draft regulatory technical standards to the Commission by 3 July 2015.
Power is conferred on the Commission to adopt the regulatory technical standards referred to in the first subparagraph in accordance with Articles 10 to 14 of Regulation (EU) No 1093/2010.
3. EBA shall, by 3 January 2016, issue guidelines in accordance with Article 16 of Regulation (EU) No 1093/2010 to promote convergence in practices to specify the conditions laid down in points (b), (d), (f), (g) and (h) of paragraph 1 of this Article.

[3.442]
Article 24
Decision to provide financial support
The decision to provide group financial support in accordance with the agreement shall be taken by the management body of the group entity providing financial support. That decision shall be reasoned and shall indicate the objective of the proposed financial support. In particular, the decision shall indicate how the provision of the financial support complies with the conditions laid down in Article 23(1). The decision to accept group financial support in accordance with the agreement shall be taken by the management body of the group entity receiving financial support.

[3.443]
Article 25
Right of opposition of competent authorities
1. Before providing support in accordance with a group financial support agreement, the management body of a group entity that intends to provide financial support shall notify:
- (a) its competent authority;
- (b) where different from authorities in points (a) and (c), where applicable, the consolidating supervisor;

Part 3 EU & International Materials

(c) where different from points (a) and (b), the competent authority of the group entity receiving the financial support; and
(d) EBA.

The notification shall include the reasoned decision of the management body in accordance with Article 24 and details of the proposed financial support including a copy of the group financial support agreement.

2. Within five business days from the date of receipt of a complete notification, the competent authority of the group entity providing financial support may agree with the provision of financial support, or may prohibit or restrict it if it assesses that the conditions for group financial support laid down in Article 23 have not been met. A decision of the competent authority to prohibit or restrict the financial support shall be reasoned.

3. The decision of the competent authority to agree, prohibit or restrict the financial support shall be immediately notified to:
(a) the consolidating supervisor;
(b) the competent authority of the group entity receiving the support; and
(c) EBA.

The consolidating supervisor shall immediately inform other members of the supervisory college and the members of the resolution college.

4. Where the consolidating supervisor or the competent authority responsible for the group entity receiving support has objections regarding the decision to prohibit or restrict the financial support, they may within two days refer the matter to EBA and request its assistance in accordance with Article 31 of Regulation (EU) No 1093/2010.

5. If the competent authority does not prohibit or restrict the financial support within the period indicated in paragraph 2, or has agreed before the end of that period to that support, financial support may be provided in accordance with the terms submitted to the competent authority.

6. The decision of the management body of the institution to provide financial support shall be transmitted to:
(a) the competent authority;
(b) where different from authorities in points (a) and (c), and where applicable, the consolidating supervisor;
(c) where different from points (a) and (b), the competent authority of the group entity receiving the financial support; and
(d) EBA.

The consolidating supervisor shall immediately inform the other members of the supervisory college and the members of the resolution college.

7. If the competent authority restricts or prohibits group financing support pursuant to paragraph 2 of this Article and where the group recovery plan in accordance with Article 7(5) makes reference to intra-group financial support, the competent authority of the group entity in relation to whom the support is restricted or prohibited may request the consolidating supervisor to initiate a reassessment of the group recovery plan pursuant to Article 8 or, where a recovery plan is drawn up on an individual basis, request the group entity to submit a revised recovery plan.

[3.444]
Article 26
Disclosure

1. Member States shall ensure that group entities make public whether or not they have entered into a group financial support agreement pursuant to Article 19 and make public a description of the general terms of any such agreement and the names of the group entities that are party to it and update that information at least annually.

Articles 431 to 434 of Regulation (EU) No 575/2013 shall apply.

2. EBA shall develop draft implementing technical standards to specify the form and content of the description referred to in paragraph 1.

EBA shall submit those draft implementing technical standards to the Commission by 3 July 2015.

Power is conferred on the Commission to adopt the draft implementing technical standards referred to in the first subparagraph in accordance with Article 15 of Regulation (EU) No 1093/2010.

TITLE III EARLY INTERVENTION

[3.445]
Article 27
Early intervention measures

1. Where an institution infringes or, due, inter alia, to a rapidly deteriorating financial condition, including deteriorating liquidity situation, increasing level of leverage, non-performing loans or concentration of exposures, as assessed on the basis of a set of triggers, which may include the institution's own funds requirement plus 1,5 percentage points, is likely in the near future to infringe the requirements of Regulation (EU) No 575/2013, Directive 2013/36/EU, Title II of Directive 2014/65/EU or any of Articles 3 to 7, 14 to 17, and 24, 25 and 26 of Regulation (EU) No 600/2014, Member States shall ensure that competent authorities have at their disposal, without prejudice to the measures referred to in Article 104 of Directive 2013/36/EU where applicable, at least the following measures:
(a) require the management body of the institution to implement one or more of the arrangements or measures set out in the recovery plan or in accordance with Article 5(2) to update such a recovery plan when the circumstances that led to the early intervention are different from the

assumptions set out in the initial recovery plan and implement one or more of the arrangements or measures set out in the updated plan within a specific timeframe and in order to ensure that the conditions referred to in the introductory phrase no longer apply;

(b) require the management body of the institution to examine the situation, identify measures to overcome any problems identified and draw up an action programme to overcome those problems and a timetable for its implementation;

(c) require the management body of the institution to convene, or if the management body fails to comply with that requirement convene directly, a meeting of shareholders of the institution, and in both cases set the agenda and require certain decisions to be considered for adoption by the shareholders;

(d) require one or more members of the management body or senior management to be removed or replaced if those persons are found unfit to perform their duties pursuant to Article 13 of Directive 2013/36/EU or Article 9 of Directive 2014/65/EU;

(e) require the management body of the institution to draw up a plan for negotiation on restructuring of debt with some or all of its creditors according to the recovery plan, where applicable;

(f) require changes to the institution's business strategy;

(g) require changes to the legal or operational structures of the institution; and

(h) acquire, including through on-site inspections and provide to the resolution authority, all the information necessary in order to update the resolution plan and prepare for the possible resolution of the institution and for valuation of the assets and liabilities of the institution in accordance with Article 36.

2. Member States shall ensure that the competent authorities shall notify the resolution authorities without delay upon determining that the conditions laid down in paragraph 1 have been met in relation to an institution and that the powers of the resolution authorities include the power to require the institution to contact potential purchasers in order to prepare for the resolution of the institution, subject to the conditions laid down in Article 39(2) and the confidentiality provisions laid down in Article 84.

3. For each of the measures referred to in paragraph 1, competent authorities shall set an appropriate deadline for completion, and to enable the competent authority to evaluate the effectiveness of the measure.

4. EBA shall, by 3 July 2015, issue guidelines in accordance with Article 16 of Regulation (EU) No 1093/2010 to promote the consistent application of the trigger for use of the measures referred to in paragraph 1 of this Article.

5. Taking into account, where appropriate, experience acquired in the application of the guidelines referred to in paragraph 4, EBA may develop draft regulatory technical standards in order to specify a minimum set of triggers for the use of the measures referred to in paragraph 1.

Power is delegated to the Commission to adopt the regulatory technical standards referred to in the first subparagraph in accordance with Articles 10 to 14 of Regulation (EU) No 1093/2010.

[3.446]
Article 28
Removal of senior management and management body

Where there is a significant deterioration in the financial situation of an institution or where there are serious infringements of law, of regulations or of the statutes of the institution, or serious administrative irregularities, and other measures taken in accordance with Article 27 are not sufficient to reverse that deterioration, Member States shall ensure that competent authorities may require the removal of the senior management or management body of the institution, in its entirety or with regard to individuals. The appointment of the new senior management or management body shall be done in accordance with national and Union law and be subject to the approval or consent of the competent authority.

[3.447]
Article 29
Temporary administrator

1. Where replacement of the senior management or management body as referred to in Article 28 is deemed to be insufficient by the competent authority to remedy the situation, Member States shall ensure that competent authorities may appoint one or more temporary administrators to the institution. Competent authorities may, based on what is proportionate in the circumstances, appoint any temporary administrator either to replace the management body of the institution temporarily or to work temporarily with the management body of the institution and the competent authority shall specify its decision at the time of appointment. If the competent authority appoints a temporary administrator to work with the management body of the institution, the competent authority shall further specify at the time of such an appointment the role, duties and powers of the temporary administrator and any requirements for the management body of the institution to consult or to obtain the consent of the temporary administrator prior to taking specific decisions or actions. The competent authority shall be required to make public the appointment of any temporary administrator except where the temporary administrator does not have the power to represent the institution. Member States shall further ensure that any temporary administrator has the qualifications, ability and knowledge required to carry out his or her functions and is free of any conflict of interests.

2. The competent authority shall specify the powers of the temporary administrator at the time of the appointment of the temporary administrator based on what is proportionate in the circumstances. Such powers may include some or all of the powers of the management body of the institution under the statutes of the institution and under national law, including the power to exercise some or all of the administrative functions of the management body of the institution. The powers of the temporary administrator in relation to the institution shall comply with the applicable company law.

3. The role and functions of the temporary administrator shall be specified by competent authority at the time of appointment and may include ascertaining the financial position of the institution, managing the business or part of the business of the institution with a view to preserving or restoring the financial position of the institution and taking measures to restore the sound and prudent management of the business of the institution. The competent authority shall specify any limits on the role and functions of the temporary administrator at the time of appointment.
4. Member States shall ensure that the competent authorities have the exclusive power to appoint and remove any temporary administrator. The competent authority may remove a temporary administrator at any time and for any reason. The competent authority may vary the terms of appointment of a temporary administrator at any time subject to this Article.
5. The competent authority may require that certain acts of a temporary administrator be subject to the prior consent of the competent authority. The competent authority shall specify any such requirements at the time of appointment of a temporary administrator or at the time of any variation of the terms of appointment of a temporary administrator.
In any case, the temporary administrator may exercise the power to convene a general meeting of the shareholders of the institution and to set the agenda of such a meeting only with the prior consent of the competent authority.
6. The competent authority may require that a temporary administrator draws up reports on the financial position of the institution and on the acts performed in the course of its appointment, at intervals set by the competent authority and at the end of his or her mandate.
7. The appointment of a temporary administrator shall not last more than one year. That period may be exceptionally renewed if the conditions for appointing the temporary administrator continue to be met. The competent authority shall be responsible for determining whether conditions are appropriate to maintain a temporary administrator and justifying any such decision to shareholders.
8. Subject to this Article the appointment of a temporary administrator shall not prejudice the rights of the shareholders in accordance with Union or national company law.
9. Member States may limit the liability of any temporary administrator in accordance with national law for acts and omissions in the discharge of his or her duties as temporary administrator in accordance with paragraph 3.
10. A temporary administrator appointed pursuant to this Article shall not be deemed to be a shadow director or a de facto director under national law.

[3.448]
Article 30
Coordination of early intervention measures and appointment of temporary administrator in relation to groups
1. Where the conditions for the imposition of requirements under Article 27 or the appointment of a temporary administrator in accordance with Article 29 are met in relation to a Union parent undertaking, the consolidating supervisor shall notify EBA and consult the other competent authorities within the supervisory college.
2. Following that notification and consultation the consolidating supervisor shall decide whether to apply any of the measures in Article 27 or appoint a temporary administrator under Article 29 in respect of the relevant Union parent undertaking, taking into account the impact of those measures on the group entities in other Member States. The consolidating supervisor shall notify the decision to the other competent authorities within the supervisory college and EBA.
3. Where the conditions for the imposition of requirements under Article 27 or the appointment of a temporary administrator under Article 29 are met in relation to a subsidiary of an Union parent undertaking, the competent authority responsible for the supervision on an individual basis that intends to take a measure in accordance with those Articles shall notify EBA and consult the consolidating supervisor.
On receiving the notification the consolidating supervisor may assess the likely impact of the imposition of requirements under Article 27 or the appointment of a temporary administrator in accordance with Article 29 to the institution in question, on the group or on group entities in other Member States. It shall communicate that assessment to the competent authority within three days.
Following that notification and consultation the competent authority shall decide whether to apply any of the measures in Article 27 or appoint a temporary administrator under Article 29. The decision shall give due consideration to any assessment of the consolidating supervisor. The competent authority shall notify the decision to the consolidating supervisor and other competent authorities within the supervisory college and EBA.
4. Where more than one competent authority intends to appoint a temporary administrator or apply any of the measures in Article 27 to more than one institution in the same group, the consolidating supervisor and the other relevant competent authorities shall consider whether it is more appropriate to appoint the same temporary administrator for all the entities concerned or to coordinate the application of any measures in Article 27 to more than one institution in order to facilitate solutions restoring the financial position of the institution concerned. The assessment shall take the form of a joint decision of the consolidating supervisor and the other relevant competent authorities. The joint decision shall be reached within five days from the date of the notification referred to in paragraph 1. The joint decision shall be reasoned and set out in a document, which shall be provided by the consolidating supervisor to the Union parent undertaking.
EBA may at the request of a competent authority assist the competent authorities in reaching an agreement in accordance with Article 31 of Regulation (EU) No 1093/2010.
In the absence of a joint decision within five days the consolidating supervisor and the competent authorities of subsidiaries may take individual decisions on the appointment of a temporary administrator

to the institutions for which they have responsibility and on the application of any of the measures in Article 27.

5. Where a competent authority concerned does not agree with the decision notified in accordance with paragraph 1 or 3, or in the absence of a joint decision under paragraph 4, the competent authority may refer the matter to EBA in accordance with paragraph 6.

6. EBA may at the request of any competent authority assist the competent authorities that intend to apply one or more of the measures in point (a) of Article 27(1) of this Directive with respect to the points (4), (10), (11) and (19) of Section A of the Annex to this Directive, in point (e) of Article 27(1) of this Directive or in point (g) of Article 27(1) of this Directive in reaching an agreement in accordance with Article 19(3) of Regulation (EU) No 1093/2010.

7. The decision of each competent authority shall be reasoned. The decision shall take into account the views and reservations of the other competent authorities expressed during the consultation period referred to in paragraph 1 or 3 or the five-day period referred to in paragraph 4 as well as the potential impact of the decision on financial stability in the Member States concerned. The decisions shall be provided by the consolidating supervisor to the Union parent undertaking and to the subsidiaries by the respective competent authorities.

In the cases referred to in paragraph 6 of this Article, where, before the end of the consultation period referred to in paragraphs 1 and 3 of this Article or at the end of the five-day period referred to in paragraph 4 of this Article, any of the competent authorities concerned has referred the matter to EBA in accordance with Article 19(3) of Regulation (EU) No 1093/2010, the consolidating supervisor and the other competent authorities shall defer their decisions and await any decision that EBA may take in accordance with Article 19(3) of that Regulation, and shall take their decision in accordance with the decision of EBA. The five-day period shall be deemed to be the conciliation period within the meaning of that Regulation. EBA shall take its decision within three days. The matter shall not be referred to EBA after the end of the five-day period or after a joint decision has been reached.

8. In the absence of a decision by EBA within three days, individual decisions taken in accordance with paragraph 1 or 3, or the third subparagraph of paragraph 4, shall apply.

TITLE IV RESOLUTION

CHAPTER I OBJECTIVES, CONDITIONS AND GENERAL PRINCIPLES

[3.449]
Article 31
Resolution objectives

1. When applying the resolution tools and exercising the resolution powers, resolution authorities shall have regard to the resolution objectives, and choose the tools and powers that best achieve the objectives that are relevant in the circumstances of the case.

2. The resolution objectives referred to in paragraph 1 are:

(a) to ensure the continuity of critical functions;

(b) to avoid a significant adverse effect on the financial system, in particular by preventing contagion, including to market infrastructures, and by maintaining market discipline;

(c) to protect public funds by minimising reliance on extraordinary public financial support;

(d) to protect depositors covered by Directive 2014/49/EU and investors covered by Directive 97/9/EC;

(e) to protect client funds and client assets.

When pursuing the above objectives, the resolution authority shall seek to minimise the cost of resolution and avoid destruction of value unless necessary to achieve the resolution objectives.

3. Subject to different provisions of this Directive, the resolution objectives are of equal significance, and resolution authorities shall balance them as appropriate to the nature and circumstances of each case.

[3.450]
Article 32
Conditions for resolution

1. Member States shall ensure that resolution authorities shall take a resolution action in relation to an institution referred to in point (a) of Article 1(1) only if the resolution authority considers that all of the following conditions are met:

(a) the determination that the institution is failing or is likely to fail has been made by the competent authority, after consulting the resolution authority or,; subject to the conditions laid down in paragraph 2, by the resolution authority after consulting the competent authority;

(b) having regard to timing and other relevant circumstances, there is no reasonable prospect that any alternative private sector measures, including measures by an IPS, or supervisory action, including early intervention measures or the write down or conversion of relevant capital instruments in accordance with Article 59(2) taken in respect of the institution, would prevent the failure of the institution within a reasonable timeframe;

(c) a resolution action is necessary in the public interest pursuant to paragraph 5.

2. Member States may provide that, in addition to the competent authority, the determination that the institution is failing or likely to fail under point (a) of paragraph 1 can be made by the resolution authority, after consulting the competent authority, where resolution authorities under national law have the necessary tools for making such a determination including, in particular, adequate access to the relevant information. The competent authority shall provide the resolution authority with any relevant information that the latter requests in order to perform its assessment without delay.

3. The previous adoption of an early intervention measure according to Article 27 is not a condition for taking a resolution action.

4. For the purposes of point (a) of paragraph 1, an institution shall be deemed to be failing or likely to fail in one or more of the following circumstances:

(a) the institution infringes or there are objective elements to support a determination that the institution will, in the near future, infringe the requirements for continuing authorisation in a way that would justify the withdrawal of the authorisation by the competent authority including but not limited to because the institution has incurred or is likely to incur losses that will deplete all or a significant amount of its own funds;

(b) the assets of the institution are or there are objective elements to support a determination that the assets of the institution will, in the near future, be less than its liabilities;

(c) the institution is or there are objective elements to support a determination that the institution will, in the near future, be unable to pay its debts or other liabilities as they fall due;

(d) extraordinary public financial support is required except when, in order to remedy a serious disturbance in the economy of a Member State and preserve financial stability, the extraordinary public financial support takes any of the following forms:

(i) a State guarantee to back liquidity facilities provided by central banks according to the central banks' conditions;

(ii) a State guarantee of newly issued liabilities; or

(iii) an injection of own funds or purchase of capital instruments at prices and on terms that do not confer an advantage upon the institution, where neither the circumstances referred to in point (a), (b) or (c) of this paragraph nor the circumstances referred to in Article 59(3) are present at the time the public support is granted.

In each of the cases mentioned in points (d)(i), (ii) and (iii) of the first subparagraph, the guarantee or equivalent measures referred to therein shall be confined to solvent institutions and shall be conditional on final approval under the Union State aid framework. Those measures shall be of a precautionary and temporary nature and shall be proportionate to remedy the consequences of the serious disturbance and shall not be used to offset losses that the institution has incurred or is likely to incur in the near future.

Support measures under point (d)(iii) of the first subparagraph shall be limited to injections necessary to address capital shortfall established in the national, Union or SSM-wide stress tests, asset quality reviews or equivalent exercises conducted by the European Central Bank, EBA or national authorities, where applicable, confirmed by the competent authority.

EBA shall, by 3 January 2015, issue guidelines in accordance with Article 16 of Regulation (EU) No 1093/2010 on the type of tests, reviews or exercises referred to above which may lead to such support.

By 31 December 2015, the Commission shall review whether there is a continuing need for allowing the support measures under point (d)(iii) of the first subparagraph and the conditions that need to be met in the case of continuation and report thereon to the European Parliament and to the Council. If appropriate, that report shall be accompanied by a legislative proposal.

5. For the purposes of point (c) of paragraph 1 of this Article, a resolution action shall be treated as in the public interest if it is necessary for the achievement of and is proportionate to one or more of the resolution objectives referred to in Article 31 and winding up of the institution under normal insolvency proceedings would not meet those resolution objectives to the same extent.

6. EBA shall, by 3 July 2015, issue guidelines in accordance with Article 16 of Regulation (EU) No 1093/2010 to promote the convergence of supervisory and resolution practices regarding the interpretation of the different circumstances when an institution shall be considered to be failing or likely to fail.

[3.451]
Article 33
Conditions for resolution with regard to financial institutions and holding companies

1. Member States shall ensure that resolution authorities may take a resolution action in relation to a financial institution referred to in point (b) of Article 1(1), when the conditions laid down in Article 32(1), are met with regard to both the financial institution and with regard to the parent undertaking subject to consolidated supervision.

2. Member States shall ensure that resolution authorities may take a resolution action in relation to an entity referred to in point (c) or (d) of Article 1(1), when the conditions laid down in Article 32(1) are met with regard to both the entity referred to in point (c) or (d) of Article 1(1) and with regard to one or more subsidiaries which are institutions or, where the subsidiary is not established in the Union, the third-country authority has determined that it meets the conditions for resolution under the law of that third country.

3. Where the subsidiary institutions of a mixed-activity holding company are held directly or indirectly by an intermediate financial holding company, Member States shall ensure that resolution actions for the purposes of group resolution are taken in relation to the intermediate financial holding company, and shall not take resolution actions for the purposes of group resolution in relation to the mixed-activity holding company.

4. Subject to paragraph 3 of this Article, notwithstanding the fact that an entity referred to in point (c) or (d) of Article 1(1) does not meet the conditions established in Article 32(1), resolution authorities may take resolution action with regard to an entity referred to in point (c) or (d) of Article 1(1) when one or more of the subsidiaries which are institutions comply with the conditions established in Article 32(1), (4) and (5) and their assets and liabilities are such that their failure threatens an institution or the group as a whole or the insolvency law of the Member State requires that groups be treated as a whole and resolution action with regard to the entity referred to in point (c) or (d) of Article 1(1) is necessary for the resolution of such subsidiaries which are institutions or for the resolution of the group as a whole.

For the purposes of paragraph 2 and of the first subparagraph of this paragraph, when assessing whether the conditions in Article 32(1) are met in respect of one or more subsidiaries which are institutions, the resolution authority of the institution and the resolution authority of the entity referred to in point (c) or (d) of Article 1(1) may by way of joint agreement disregard any intra-group capital or loss transfers between the entities, including the exercise of write down or conversion powers.

[3.452]
Article 34
General principles governing resolution

1. Member States shall ensure that, when applying the resolution tools and exercising the resolution powers, resolution authorities take all appropriate measures to ensure that the resolution action is taken in accordance with the following principles:
   (a) the shareholders of the institution under resolution bear first losses;
   (b) creditors of the institution under resolution bear losses after the shareholders in accordance with the order of priority of their claims under normal insolvency proceedings, save as expressly provided otherwise in this Directive;
   (c) management body and senior management of the institution under resolution are replaced, except in those cases when the retention of the management body and senior management, in whole or in part, as appropriate to the circumstances, is considered to be necessary for the achievement of the resolution objectives;
   (d) management body and senior management of the institution under resolution shall provide all necessary assistance for the achievement of the resolution objectives;
   (e) natural and legal persons are made liable, subject to Member State law, under civil or criminal law for their responsibility for the failure of the institution;
   (f) except where otherwise provided in this Directive, creditors of the same class are treated in an equitable manner;
   (g) no creditor shall incur greater losses than would have been incurred if the institution or entity referred to in point (b), (c) or (d) of Article 1(1) had been wound up under normal insolvency proceedings in accordance with the safeguards in Articles 73 to 75;
   (h) covered deposits are fully protected; and
   (i) resolution action is taken in accordance with the safeguards in this Directive.
2. Where an institution is a group entity resolution authorities shall, without prejudice to Article 31, apply resolution tools and exercise resolution powers in a way that minimises the impact on other group entities and on the group as a whole and minimises the adverse effects on financial stability in the Union and its Member States, in particular, in the countries where the group operates.
3. When applying the resolution tools and exercising the resolution powers, Member States shall ensure that they comply with the Union State aid framework, where applicable.
4. Where the sale of business tool, the bridge institution tool or the asset separation tool is applied to an institution or entity referred to in point (b), (c) or (d) of Article 1(1), that institution or entity shall be considered to be the subject of bankruptcy proceedings or analogous insolvency proceedings for the purposes of Article 5(1) of Council Directive 2001/23/EC.[1]
5. When applying the resolution tools and exercising the resolution powers, resolution authorities shall inform and consult employee representatives where appropriate.
6. Resolution authorities shall apply resolution tools and exercise resolution powers without prejudice to provisions on the representation of employees in management bodies as provided for in national law or practice.

NOTES

[1] Council Directive 2001/23/EC of 12 March 2001 on the approximation of the laws of the Member States relating to the safeguarding of employees' rights in the event of transfers of undertakings, businesses or parts of undertakings or businesses (OJ L82 22.3.2001, p 16).

CHAPTER II SPECIAL MANAGEMENT

[3.453]
Article 35
Special management

1. Member States shall ensure that resolution authorities may appoint a special manager to replace the management body of the institution under resolution. Resolution authorities shall make public the appointment of a special manager. Member States shall further ensure that the special manager has the qualifications, ability and knowledge required to carry out his or her functions.
2. The special manager shall have all the powers of the shareholders and the management body of the institution. However, the special manager may only exercise such powers under the control of the resolution authority.
3. The special manager shall have the statutory duty to take all the measures necessary to promote the resolution objectives referred to in Article 31 and implement resolution actions according to the decision of the resolution authority. Where necessary, that duty shall override any other duty of management in accordance with the statutes of the institution or national law, insofar as they are inconsistent. Those measures may include an increase of capital, reorganisation of the ownership structure of the institution or takeovers by institutions that are financially and organisationally sound in accordance with the resolution tools referred to in Chapter IV.

4. Resolution authorities may set limits to the action of a special manager or require that certain acts of the special manager be subject to the resolution authority's prior consent. The resolution authorities may remove the special manager at any time.
5. Member States shall require that a special manager draw up reports for the appointing resolution authority on the economic and financial situation of the institution and on the acts performed in the conduct of his or her duties, at regular intervals set by the resolution authority and at the beginning and the end of his or her mandate.
6. A special manager shall not be appointed for more than one year. That period may be renewed, on an exceptional basis, if the resolution authority determines that the conditions for appointment of a special manager continue to be met.
7. Where more than one resolution authority intends to appoint a special manager in relation to an entity affiliated to a group, they shall consider whether it is more appropriate to appoint the same special manager for all the entities concerned in order to facilitate solutions redressing the financial soundness of the entities concerned.
8. In the event of insolvency, where national law provides for the appointment of insolvency management, such management may constitute special management as referred to in this Article.

CHAPTER III VALUATION

[3.454]
Article 36
Valuation for the purposes of resolution

1. Before taking resolution action or exercising the power to write down or convert relevant capital instruments resolution authorities shall ensure that a fair, prudent and realistic valuation of the assets and liabilities of the institution or entity referred to in point (b), (c) or (d) of Article 1(1) is carried out by a person independent from any public authority, including the resolution authority, and the institution or entity referred to in point (b), (c) or (d) of Article 1(1). Subject to paragraph 13 of this Article and to Article 85, where all the requirements laid down in this Article are met, the valuation shall be considered to be definitive.
2. Where an independent valuation according to paragraph 1 is not possible, resolution authorities may carry out a provisional valuation of the assets and liabilities of the institution or entity referred to in point (b), (c) or (d) of Article 1(1), in accordance with paragraph 9 of this Article.
3. The objective of the valuation shall be to assess the value of the assets and liabilities of the institution or entity referred to in point (b), (c) or (d) of Article 1(1) that meets the conditions for resolution of Articles 32 and 33.
4. The purposes of the valuation shall be:
   (a) to inform the determination of whether the conditions for resolution or the conditions for the write down or conversion of capital instruments are met;
   (b) if the conditions for resolution are met, to inform the decision on the appropriate resolution action to be taken in respect of the institution or entity referred to in point (b), (c) or (d) of Article 1(1);
   (c) when the power to write down or convert relevant capital instruments is applied, to inform the decision on the extent of the cancellation or dilution of shares or other instruments of ownership, and the extent of the write down or conversion of relevant capital instruments;
   (d) when the bail-in tool is applied, to inform the decision on the extent of the write down or conversion of eligible liabilities;
   (e) when the bridge institution tool or asset separation tool is applied, to inform the decision on the assets, rights, liabilities or shares or other instruments of ownership to be transferred and the decision on the value of any consideration to be paid to the institution under resolution or, as the case may be, to the owners of the shares or other instruments of ownership;
   (f) when the sale of business tool is applied, to inform the decision on the assets, rights, liabilities or shares or other instruments of ownership to be transferred and to inform the resolution authority's understanding of what constitutes commercial terms for the purposes of Article 38;
   (g) in all cases, to ensure that any losses on the assets of the institution or entity referred to in point (b), (c) or (d) of Article 1(1) are fully recognised at the moment the resolution tools are applied or the power to write down or convert relevant capital instruments is exercised.
5. Without prejudice to the Union State aid framework, where applicable, the valuation shall be based on prudent assumptions, including as to rates of default and severity of losses. The valuation shall not assume any potential future provision of extraordinary public financial support or central bank emergency liquidity assistance or any central bank liquidity assistance provided under non-standard collateralisation, tenor and interest rate terms to the institution or entity referred to in point (b), (c) or (d) of Article 1(1) from the point at which resolution action is taken or the power to write down or convert relevant capital instruments is exercised. Furthermore, the valuation shall take account of the fact that, if any resolution tool is applied:
   (a) the resolution authority and any financing arrangement acting pursuant to Article 101 may recover any reasonable expenses properly incurred from the institution under resolution, in accordance with Article 37(7);
   (b) the resolution financing arrangement may charge interest or fees in respect of any loans or guarantees provided to the institution under resolution, in accordance with Article 101.
6. The valuation shall be supplemented by the following information as appearing in the accounting books and records of the institution or entity referred to in point (b), (c) or (d) of Article 1(1):
   (a) an updated balance sheet and a report on the financial position of the institution or entity referred to in point (b), (c) or (d) of Article 1(1);

(b) an analysis and an estimate of the accounting value of the assets;
(c) the list of outstanding on balance sheet and off balance sheet liabilities shown in the books and records of the institution or entity referred to in point (b), (c) or (d) of Article 1(1), with an indication of the respective credits and priority levels under the applicable insolvency law.

7. Where appropriate, to inform the decisions referred to in points (e) and (f) of paragraph 4, the information in point (b) of paragraph 6 may be complemented by an analysis and estimate of the value of the assets and liabilities of the institution or entity referred to in point (b), (c) or (d) of Article 1(1) on a market value basis.

8. The valuation shall indicate the subdivision of the creditors in classes in accordance with their priority levels under the applicable insolvency law and an estimate of the treatment that each class of shareholders and creditors would have been expected to receive, if the institution or entity referred to in point (b), (c) or (d) of Article 1(1) were wound up under normal insolvency proceedings.

That estimate shall not affect the application of the 'no creditor worse off' principle to be carried out under Article 74.

9. Where due to the urgency in the circumstances of the case it is not possible to comply with the requirements in paragraphs 6 and 8 or paragraph 2 applies, a provisional valuation shall be carried out. The provisional valuation shall comply with the requirements in paragraph 3 and in so far as reasonably practicable in the circumstances with the requirements of paragraphs 1, 6 and 8.

The provisional valuation referred to in this paragraph shall include a buffer for additional losses, with appropriate justification.

10. A valuation that does not comply with all the requirements laid down in this Article shall be considered to be provisional until an independent person has carried out a valuation that is fully compliant with all the requirements laid down in this Article. That *ex-post* definitive valuation shall be carried out as soon as practicable. It may be carried out either separately from the valuation referred to in Article 74, or simultaneously with and by the same independent person as that valuation, but shall be distinct from it.

The purposes of the *ex-post* definitive valuation shall be:
(a) to ensure that any losses on the assets of the institution or entity referred to in point (b), (c) or (d) of Article 1(1) are fully recognised in the books of accounts of the institution or entity referred to in point (b), (c) or (d) of Article 1(1);
(b) to inform a decision to write back creditors' claims or to increase the value of the consideration paid, in accordance with paragraph 11.

11. In the event that the *ex-post* definitive valuation's estimate of the net asset value of the institution or entity referred to in point (b), (c) or (d) of Article 1(1) is higher than the provisional valuation's estimate of the net asset value of the institution or entity referred to in point (b), (c) or (d) of Article 1(1), the resolution authority may:
(a) exercise its power to increase the value of the claims of creditors or owners of relevant capital instruments which have been written down under the bail-in tool;
(b) instruct a bridge institution or asset management vehicle to make a further payment of consideration in respect of the assets, rights, liabilities to the institution under resolution, or as the case may be, in respect of the shares or instruments of ownership to the owners of the shares or other instruments of ownership.

12. Notwithstanding paragraph 1, a provisional valuation conducted in accordance with paragraphs 9 and 10 shall be a valid basis for resolution authorities take resolution actions, including taking control of a failing institution or entity referred to in point (b), (c) or (d) of Article 1(1), or to exercise the write down or conversion power of capital instruments.

13. The valuation shall be an integral part of the decision to apply a resolution tool or exercise a resolution power, or the decision to exercise the write down or conversion power of capital instruments. The valuation itself shall not be subject to a separate right of appeal but may be subject to an appeal together with the decision in accordance with Article 85.

14. EBA shall develop draft regulatory technical standards to specify the circumstances in which a person is independent from both the resolution authority and the institution or entity referred to in point (b), (c) or (d) of Article 1(1) for the purposes of paragraph 1of this Article, and for the purposes of Article 74.

15. EBA may develop draft regulatory technical standards to specify the following criteria for the purposes of paragraphs 1, 3 and 9 of this Article, and for the purposes of Article 74:
(a) the methodology for assessing the value of the assets and liabilities of the institution or entity referred to in point (b), (c) or (d) of Article 1(1);
(b) the separation of the valuations under Articles 36 and 74;
(c) the methodology for calculating and including a buffer for additional losses in the provisional valuation.

16. EBA shall submit the draft regulatory technical standards referred to in paragraph 14 to the Commission by 3 July 2015.

Power is delegated to the Commission to adopt the regulatory technical standards referred to in paragraphs 14 and 15 in accordance with Articles 10 to 14 of Regulation (EU) No 1093/2010.

CHAPTER IV RESOLUTION TOOLS

SECTION 1

GENERAL PRINCIPLES

[3.455]
Article 37
General principles of resolution tools

1. Member States shall ensure that resolution authorities have the necessary powers to apply the resolution tools to institutions and to entities referred to in point (b), (c) or (d) of Article 1(1) that meet the applicable conditions for resolution.

2. Where a resolution authority decides to apply a resolution tool to an institution or entity referred to in point (b), (c) or (d) of Article 1(1), and that resolution action would result in losses being borne by creditors or their claims being converted, the resolution authority shall exercise the power to write down and convert capital instruments in accordance with Article 59 immediately before or together with the application of the resolution tool.

3. The resolution tools referred to in paragraph 1 are the following:

(a) the sale of business tool;
(b) the bridge institution tool;
(c) the asset separation tool;
(d) the bail-in tool.

4. Subject to paragraph 5, resolution authorities may apply the resolution tools individually or in any combination.

5. Resolution authorities may apply the asset separation tool only together with another resolution tool.

6. Where only the resolution tools referred to in point (a) or (b) of paragraph 3 of this Article are used, and they are used to transfer only part of the assets, rights or liabilities of the institution under resolution, the residual institution or entity referred to in point (b), (c) or (d) of Article 1(1) from which the assets, rights or liabilities have been transferred, shall be wound up under normal insolvency proceedings. Such winding up shall be done within a reasonable timeframe, having regard to any need for that institution or entity referred to in point (b), (c) or (d) of Article 1(1) to provide services or support pursuant to Article 65 in order to enable the recipient to carry out the activities or services acquired by virtue of that transfer, and any other reason that the continuation of the residual institution or entity referred to in point (b), (c) or (d) of Article 1(1) is necessary to achieve the resolution objectives or comply with the principles referred to in Article 34.

7. The resolution authority and any financing arrangement acting pursuant to Article 101 may recover any reasonable expenses properly incurred in connection with the use of the resolution tools or powers or government financial stabilisation tools in one or more of the following ways:

(a) as a deduction from any consideration paid by a recipient to the institution under resolution or, as the case may be, to the owners of the shares or other instruments of ownership;
(b) from the institution under resolution, as a preferred creditor; or
(c) from any proceeds generated as a result of the termination of the operation of the bridge institution or the asset management vehicle, as a preferred creditor.

8. Member States shall ensure that rules under national insolvency law relating to the voidability or unenforceability of legal acts detrimental to creditors do not apply to transfers of assets, rights or liabilities from an institution under resolution to another entity by virtue of the application of a resolution tool or exercise of a resolution power, or use of a government financial stabilisation tool.

9. Member States may confer upon resolution authorities additional tools and powers exercisable where an institution or entity referred to in point (b), (c) or (d) of Article 1(1) meets the conditions for resolution, provided that:

(a) when applied to a cross-border group, those additional powers do not pose obstacles to effective group resolution; and
(b) they are consistent with the resolution objectives and the general principles governing resolution referred to in Articles 31 and 34.

10. In the very extraordinary situation of a systemic crisis, the resolution authority may seek funding from alternative financing sources through the use of government stabilisation tools provided for in Articles 56 to 58 when the following conditions are met:

(a) a contribution to loss absorption and recapitalisation equal to an amount not less than 8% of total liabilities including own funds of the institution under resolution, measured at the time of resolution action in accordance with the valuation provided for in Article 36, has been made by the shareholders and the holders of other instruments of ownership, the holders of relevant capital instruments and other eligible liabilities through write down, conversion or otherwise;
(b) it shall be conditional on prior and final approval under the Union State aid framework.

SECTION 2

THE SALE OF BUSINESS TOOL

[3.456]
Article 38
The sale of business tool

1. Member States shall ensure that resolution authorities have the power to transfer to a purchaser that is not a bridge institution:

(a) shares or other instruments of ownership issued by an institution under resolution;
(b) all or any assets, rights or liabilities of an institution under resolution;

Subject to paragraphs 8 and 9 of this Article and to Article 85, the transfer referred to in the first subparagraph shall take place without obtaining the consent of the shareholders of the institution under resolution or any third party other than the purchaser, and without complying with any procedural requirements under company or securities law other than those included in Article 39.

2. A transfer made pursuant to paragraph 1 shall be made on commercial terms, having regard to the circumstances, and in accordance with the Union State aid framework.

3. In accordance with paragraph 2 of this Article, resolution authorities shall take all reasonable steps to obtain commercial terms for the transfer that conform with the valuation conducted under Article 36, having regard to the circumstances of the case.

4. Subject to Article 37(7), any consideration paid by the purchaser shall benefit:

(a) the owners of the shares or other instruments of ownership, where the sale of business has been effected by transferring shares or instruments of ownership issued by the institution under resolution from the holders of those shares or instruments to the purchaser;

(b) the institution under resolution, where the sale of business has been effected by transferring some or all of the assets or liabilities of the institution under resolution to the purchaser.

5. When applying the sale of business tool the resolution authority may exercise the transfer power more than once in order to make supplemental transfers of shares or other instruments of ownership issued by an institution under resolution or, as the case may be, assets, rights or liabilities of the institution under resolution.

6. Following an application of the sale of business tool, resolution authorities may, with the consent of the purchaser, exercise the transfer powers in respect of assets, rights or liabilities transferred to the purchaser in order to transfer the assets, rights or liabilities back to the institution under resolution, or the shares or other instruments of ownership back to their original owners, and the institution under resolution or original owners shall be obliged to take back any such assets, rights or liabilities, or shares or other instruments of ownership.

7. A purchaser shall have the appropriate authorisation to carry out the business it acquires when the transfer is made pursuant to paragraph 1. Competent authorities shall ensure that an application for authorisation shall be considered, in conjunction with the transfer, in a timely manner.

8. By way of derogation from Articles 22 to 25 of Directive 2013/36/EU, from the requirement to inform the competent authorities in Article 26 of Directive 2013/36/EU, from Article 10(3), Article 11(1) and (2) and Articles 12 and 13 of Directive 2014/65/EU and from the requirement to give a notice in Article 11(3) of that Directive, where a transfer of shares or other instruments of ownership by virtue of an application of the sale of business tool would result in the acquisition of or increase in a qualifying holding in an institution of a kind referred to in Article 22(1) of Directive 2013/36/EU or Article 11(1) of Directive 2014/65/EU, the competent authority of that institution shall carry out the assessment required under those Articles in a timely manner that does not delay the application of the sale of business tool and prevent the resolution action from achieving the relevant resolution objectives.

9. Member States shall ensure that if the competent authority of that institution has not completed the assessment referred to in paragraph 8 from the date of transfer of shares or other instruments of ownership in the application of the sale of business tool by the resolution authority, the following provisions shall apply:

(a) such a transfer of shares or other instruments of ownership to the acquirer shall have immediate legal effect;

(b) during the assessment period and during any divestment period provided by point (f), the acquirer's voting rights attached to such shares or other instruments of ownership shall be suspended and vested solely in the resolution authority, which shall have no obligation to exercise any such voting rights and which shall have no liability whatsoever for exercising or refraining from exercising any such voting rights;

(c) during the assessment period and during any divestment period provided by point (f), the penalties and other measures for infringing the requirements for acquisitions or disposals of qualifying holdings contemplated by Articles 66, 67 and 68 of Directive 2013/36/EU shall not apply to such a transfer of shares or other instruments of ownership;

(d) promptly upon completion of the assessment by the competent authority, the competent authority shall notify the resolution authority and the acquirer in writing of whether the competent authority approves or, in accordance with Article 22(5) of Directive 2013/36/EU, opposes such a transfer of shares or other instruments of ownership to the acquirer;

(e) if the competent authority approves such a transfer of shares or other instruments of ownership to the acquirer, then the voting rights attached to such shares or other instruments of ownership shall be deemed to be fully vested in the acquirer immediately upon receipt by the resolution authority and the acquirer of such an approval notice from the competent authority;

(f) if the competent authority opposes such a transfer of shares or other instruments of ownership to the acquirer, then:

(i) the voting rights attached to such shares or other instruments of ownership as provided by point (b) shall remain in full force and effect;

(ii) the resolution authority may require the acquirer to divest such shares or other instruments of ownership within a divestment period determined by the resolution authority having taken into account prevailing market conditions; and

(iii) if the acquirer does not complete such a divestment within the divestment period established by the resolution authority, then the competent authority, with the consent of the resolution authority, may impose on the acquirer penalties and other measures for infringing the requirements for acquisitions or disposals of qualifying holdings contemplated by Articles 66, 67, and 68 of Directive 2013/36/EU.

10. Transfers made by virtue of the sale of business tool shall be subject to the safeguards referred to in Chapter VII of Title IV.

11. For the purposes of exercising the rights to provide services or to establish itself in another Member State in accordance with Directive 2013/36/EU or Directive 2014/65/EU, the purchaser shall be considered to be a continuation of the institution under resolution, and may continue to exercise any such right that was exercised by the institution under resolution in respect of the assets, rights or liabilities transferred.

12. Member States shall ensure that the purchaser referred to in paragraph 1 may continue to exercise the rights of membership and access to payment, clearing and settlement systems, stock exchanges, investor compensation schemes and deposit guarantee schemes of the institution under resolution, provided that it meets the membership and participation criteria for participation in such systems.

Notwithstanding the first subparagraph, Member States shall ensure that:

(a) access is not denied on the ground that the purchaser does not possess a rating from a credit rating agency, or that rating is not commensurate to the rating levels required to be granted access to the systems referred to in the first subparagraph;

(b) where the purchaser does not meet the membership or participation criteria for a relevant payment, clearing or settlement system, stock exchange, investor compensation scheme or deposit guarantee scheme, the rights referred to in the first subparagraph are exercised for such a period of time as may be specified by the resolution authority, not exceeding 24 months, renewable on application by the purchaser to the resolution authority.

13. Without prejudice to Chapter VII of Title IV, shareholders or creditors of the institution under resolution and other third parties whose assets, rights or liabilities are not transferred shall not have any rights over or in relation to the assets, rights or liabilities transferred.

[3.457]
Article 39
Sale of business tool: procedural requirements

1. Subject to paragraph 3 of this Article, when applying the sale of business tool to an institution or entity referred to in point (b), (c) or (d) of Article 1(1), a resolution authority shall market, or make arrangements for the marketing of the assets, rights, liabilities, shares or other instruments of ownership of that institution that the authority intends to transfer. Pools of rights, assets, and liabilities may be marketed separately.

2. Without prejudice to the Union State aid framework, where applicable, the marketing referred to in paragraph 1 shall be carried out in accordance with the following criteria:

(a) it shall be as transparent as possible and shall not materially misrepresent the assets, rights, liabilities, shares or other instruments of ownership of that institution that the authority intends to transfer, having regard to the circumstances and in particular the need to maintain financial stability;

(b) it shall not unduly favour or discriminate between potential purchasers;

(c) it shall be free from any conflict of interest;

(d) it shall not confer any unfair advantage on a potential purchaser;

(e) it shall take account of the need to effect a rapid resolution action;

(f) it shall aim at maximising, as far as possible, the sale price for the shares or other instruments of ownership, assets, rights or liabilities involved.

Subject to point (b) of the first subparagraph, the principles referred to in this paragraph shall not prevent the resolution authority from soliciting particular potential purchasers.

Any public disclosure of the marketing of the institution or entity referred to in point (b), (c) or (d) of Article 1(1) of this Directive that would otherwise be required in accordance with Article 17(1) of Regulation (EU) No 596/2014 may be delayed in accordance with Article 17(4) or (5) of that Regulation.

3. The resolution authority may apply the sale of business tool without complying with the requirement to market as laid down in paragraph 1 when it determines that compliance with those requirements would be likely to undermine one or more of the resolution objectives and in particular if the following conditions are met:

(a) it considers that there is a material threat to financial stability arising from or aggravated by the failure or likely failure of the institution under resolution; and

(b) it considers that compliance with those requirements would be likely to undermine the effectiveness of the sale of business tool in addressing that threat or achieving the resolution objective referred to in point (b) of Article 31(2).

4. EBA shall, by 3 July 2015, issue guidelines in accordance with Article 16 of Regulation (EU) No 1093/2010 specifying the factual circumstances amounting to a material threat and the elements relating to the effectiveness of the sale of business tool provided for in points (a) and (b) of paragraph 3.

SECTION 3
THE BRIDGE INSTITUTION TOOL

[3.458]
Article 40
Bridge institution tool

1. In order to give effect to the bridge institution tool and having regard to the need to maintain critical functions in the bridge institution, Member States shall ensure that resolution authorities have the power to transfer to a bridge institution:

(a) shares or other instruments of ownership issued by one or more institutions under resolution;

(b) all or any assets, rights or liabilities of one or more institutions under resolution.

Subject to Article 85, the transfer referred to in the first subparagraph may take place without obtaining the consent of the shareholders of the institutions under resolution or any third party other than the bridge institution, and without complying with any procedural requirements under company or securities law.

2. The bridge institution shall be a legal person that meets all of the following requirements:

(a) it is wholly or partially owned by one or more public authorities which may include the resolution authority or the resolution financing arrangement and is controlled by the resolution authority;

(b) it is created for the purpose of receiving and holding some or all of the shares or other instruments of ownership issued by an institution under resolution or some or all of the assets, rights and liabilities of one or more institutions under resolution with a view to maintaining access to critical functions and selling the institution or entity referred to in point (b), (c) or (d) of Article 1(1).

The application of the bail-in tool for the purpose referred to in point (b) of Article 43(2) shall not interfere with the ability of the resolution authority to control the bridge institution.

3. When applying the bridge institution tool, the resolution authority shall ensure that the total value of liabilities transferred to the bridge institution does not exceed the total value of the rights and assets transferred from the institution under resolution or provided by other sources.

4. Subject to Article 37(7), any consideration paid by the bridge institution shall benefit:

(a) the owners of the shares or instruments of ownership, where the transfer to the bridge institution has been effected by transferring shares or instruments of ownership issued by the institution under resolution from the holders of those shares or instruments to the bridge institution;

(b) the institution under resolution, where the transfer to the bridge institution has been effected by transferring some or all of the assets or liabilities of the institution under resolution to the bridge institution.

5. When applying the bridge institution tool, the resolution authority may exercise the transfer power more than once in order to make supplemental transfers of shares or other instruments of ownership issued by an institution under resolution or, as the case may be, assets, rights or liabilities of the institution under resolution.

6. Following an application of the bridge institution tool, the resolution authority may:

(a) transfer rights, assets or liabilities back from the bridge institution to the institution under resolution, or the shares or other instruments of ownership back to their original owners, and the institution under resolution or original owners shall be obliged to take back any such assets, rights or liabilities, or shares or other instruments of ownership, provided that the conditions laid down in paragraph 7 are met;

(b) transfer, shares or other instruments of ownership, or assets, rights or liabilities from the bridge institution to a third party.

7. Resolution authorities may transfer shares or other instruments of ownership, or assets, rights or liabilities back from the bridge institution in one of the following circumstances:

(a) the possibility that the specific shares or other instruments of ownership, assets, rights or liabilities might be transferred back is stated expressly in the instrument by which the transfer was made;

(b) the specific shares or other instruments of ownership, assets, rights or liabilities do not in fact fall within the classes of, or meet the conditions for transfer of shares or other instruments of ownership, assets, rights or liabilities specified in the instrument by which the transfer was made.

Such a transfer back may be made within any period, and shall comply with any other conditions, stated in that instrument for the relevant purpose.

8. Transfers between the institution under resolution, or the original owners of shares or other instruments of ownership, on the one hand, and the bridge institution on the other, shall be subject to the safeguards referred to in Chapter VII of Title IV.

9. For the purposes of exercising the rights to provide services or to establish itself in another Member State in accordance with Directive 2013/36/EU or Directive 2014/65/EU, a bridge institution shall be considered to be a continuation of the institution under resolution, and may continue to exercise any such right that was exercised by the institution under resolution in respect of the assets, rights or liabilities transferred.

For other purposes, resolution authorities may require that a bridge institution be considered to be a continuation of the institution under resolution, and be able to continue to exercise any right that was exercised by the institution under resolution in respect of the assets, rights or liabilities transferred.

10. Member States shall ensure that the bridge institution may continue to exercise the rights of membership and access to payment, clearing and settlement systems, stock exchanges, investor compensation schemes and deposit guarantee schemes of the institution under resolution, provided that it meets the membership and participation criteria for participation in such systems.

Notwithstanding the first subparagraph, Member States shall ensure that:

(a) access is not denied on the ground that the bridge institution does not possess a rating from a credit rating agency, or that rating is not commensurate to the rating levels required to be granted access to the systems referred to in the first subparagraph;

(b) where the bridge institution does not meet the membership or participation criteria for a relevant payment, clearing or settlement system, stock exchange, investor compensation scheme or deposit guarantee scheme, the rights referred to in the first subparagraph are exercised for such a period of time as may be specified by the resolution authority, not exceeding 24 months, renewable on application by the bridge institution to the resolution authority.

11. Without prejudice to Chapter VII of Title IV, shareholders or creditors of the institution under resolution and other third parties whose assets, rights or liabilities are not transferred to the bridge institution shall not have any rights over or in relation to the assets, rights or liabilities transferred to the bridge institution, its management body or senior management.
12. The objectives of the bridge institution shall not imply any duty or responsibility to shareholders or creditors of the institution under resolution, and the management body or senior management shall have no liability to such shareholders or creditors for acts and omissions in the discharge of their duties unless the act or omission implies gross negligence or serious misconduct in accordance with national law which directly affects rights of such shareholders or creditors.
Member States may further limit the liability of a bridge institution and its management body or senior management in accordance with national law for acts and omissions in the discharge of their duties.

[3.459]
Article 41
Operation of a bridge institution
1. Member States shall ensure that the operation of a bridge institution respects the following requirements:
- (a) the contents of the bridge institution's constitutional documents are approved by the resolution authority;
- (b) subject to the bridge institution's ownership structure, the resolution authority either appoints or approves the bridge institution's management body;
- (c) the resolution authority approves the remuneration of the members of the management body and determines their appropriate responsibilities;
- (d) the resolution authority approves the strategy and risk profile of the bridge institution;
- (e) the bridge institution is authorised in accordance with Directive 2013/36/EU or Directive 2014/65/EU, as applicable, and has the necessary authorisation under the applicable national law to carry out the activities or services that it acquires by virtue of a transfer made pursuant to Article 63 of this Directive;
- (f) the bridge institution complies with the requirements of, and is subject to supervision in accordance with Regulation (EU) No 575/2013 and with Directives 2013/36/EU and Directive 2014/65/EU, as applicable;
- (g) the operation of the bridge institution shall be in accordance with the Union State aid framework and the resolution authority may specify restrictions on its operations accordingly.

Notwithstanding the provisions referred to in points (e) and (f) of the first subparagraph and where necessary to meet the resolution objectives, the bridge institution may be established and authorised without complying with Directive 2013/36/EU or Directive 2014/65/EU for a short period of time at the beginning of its operation. To that end, the resolution authority shall submit a request in that sense to the competent authority. If the competent authority decides to grant such an authorisation, it shall indicate the period for which the bridge institution is waived from complying with the requirements of those Directives.
2. Subject to any restrictions imposed in accordance with Union or national competition rules, the management of the bridge institution shall operate the bridge institution with a view to maintaining access to critical functions and selling the institution or entity referred to in point (b), (c) or (d) of Article 1(1), its assets, rights or liabilities, to one or more private sector purchasers when conditions are appropriate and within the period specified in paragraph 4 of this Article or, where applicable, paragraph 6 of this Article.
3. The resolution authority shall take a decision that the bridge institution is no longer a bridge institution within the meaning of Article 40(2) in any of the following cases, whichever occurs first:
- (a) the bridge institution merges with another entity;
- (b) the bridge institution ceases to meet the requirements of Article 40(2);
- (c) the sale of all or substantially all of the bridge institution's assets, rights or liabilities to a third party;
- (d) the expiry of the period specified in paragraph 5 or, where applicable, paragraph 6;
- (e) the bridge institution's assets are completely wound down and its liabilities are completely discharged.

4. Member States shall ensure, in cases when the resolution authority seeks to sell the bridge institution or its assets, rights or liabilities, that the bridge institution or the relevant assets or liabilities are marketed openly and transparently, and that the sale does not materially misrepresent them or unduly favour or discriminate between potential purchasers.
Any such sale shall be made on commercial terms, having regard to the circumstances and in accordance with the Union State aid framework.
5. If none of the outcomes referred to in points (a), (b), (c) and (e) of paragraph 3 applies, the resolution authority shall terminate the operation of a bridge institution as soon as possible and in any event two years after the date on which the last transfer from an institution under resolution pursuant to the bridge institution tool was made.
6. The resolution authority may extend the period referred to in paragraph 5 for one or more additional one-year periods where such an extension:
- (a) supports the outcomes referred to in point (a), (b), (c) or (e) of paragraph 3; or
- (b) is necessary to ensure the continuity of essential banking or financial services.

7. Any decision of the resolution authority to extend the period referred to in paragraph 5 shall be reasoned and shall contain a detailed assessment of the situation, including of the market conditions and outlook, that justifies the extension.

8. Where the operations of a bridge institution are terminated in the circumstances referred to in point (c) or (d) of paragraph 3, the bridge institution shall be wound up under normal insolvency proceedings.

Subject to Article 37(7), any proceeds generated as a result of the termination of the operation of the bridge institution shall benefit the shareholders of the bridge institution.

9. Where a bridge institution is used for the purpose of transferring assets and liabilities of more than one institution under resolution the obligation referred to in paragraph 8 shall refer to the assets and liabilities transferred from each of the institutions under resolution and not to the bridge institution itself.

SECTION 4
THE ASSET SEPARATION TOOL

[3.460]

Article 42

Asset separation tool

1. In order to give effect to the asset separation tool, Member States shall ensure that resolution authorities have the power to transfer assets, rights or liabilities of an institution under resolution or a bridge institution to one or more asset management vehicles.

Subject to Article 85, the transfer referred to in the first subparagraph may take place without obtaining the consent of the shareholders of the institutions under resolution or any third party other than the bridge institution, and without complying with any procedural requirements under company or securities law.

2. For the purposes of the asset separation tool, an asset management vehicle shall be a legal person that meets all of the following requirements:
   (a) it is wholly or partially owned by one or more public authorities which may include the resolution authority or the resolution financing arrangement and is controlled by the resolution authority;
   (b) it has been created for the purpose of receiving some or all of the assets, rights and liabilities of one or more institutions under resolution or a bridge institution.

3. The asset management vehicle shall manage the assets transferred to it with a view to maximising their value through eventual sale or orderly wind down.

4. Member States shall ensure that the operation of an asset management vehicle respects the following provisions:
   (a) the contents of the asset management vehicle's constitutional documents are approved by the resolution authority;
   (b) subject to the asset management vehicle's ownership structure, the resolution authority either appoints or approves the vehicle's management body;
   (c) the resolution authority approves the remuneration of the members of the management body and determines their appropriate responsibilities;
   (d) the resolution authority approves the strategy and risk profile of the asset management vehicle.

5. Resolution authorities may exercise the power specified in paragraph 1 to transfer assets, rights or liabilities only if:
   (a) the situation of the particular market for those assets is of such a nature that the liquidation of those assets under normal insolvency proceedings could have an adverse effect on one or more financial markets.
   (b) such a transfer is necessary to ensure the proper functioning of the institution under resolution or bridge institution; or
   (c) such a transfer is necessary to maximise liquidation proceeds.

6. When applying the asset separation tool, resolution authorities shall determine the consideration for which assets, rights and liabilities are transferred to the asset management vehicle in accordance with the principles established in Article 36 and in accordance with the Union State aid framework. This paragraph does not prevent the consideration having nominal or negative value.

7. Subject to Article 37(7), any consideration paid by the asset management vehicle in respect of the assets, rights or liabilities acquired directly from the institution under resolution shall benefit the institution under resolution. Consideration may be paid in the form of debt issued by the asset management vehicle.

8. Where the bridge institution tool has been applied, an asset management vehicle may, subsequent to the application of the bridge institution tool, acquire assets, rights or liabilities from the bridge institution.

9. Resolution authorities may transfer assets, rights or liabilities from the institution under resolution to one or more asset management vehicles on more than one occasion and transfer assets, rights or liabilities back from one or more asset management vehicles to the institution under resolution provided that the conditions specified in paragraph 10 are met.

The institution under resolution shall be obliged to take back any such assets, rights or liabilities.

10. Resolution authorities may transfer rights, assets or liabilities back from the asset management vehicle to the institution under resolution in one of the following circumstances:
   (a) the possibility that the specific rights, assets or liabilities might be transferred back is stated expressly in the instrument by which the transfer was made;
   (b) the specific rights, assets or liabilities do not in fact fall within the classes of, or meet the conditions for transfer of, rights, assets or liabilities specified in the instrument by which the transfer was made.

In either of the cases referred in points (a) and (b), the transfer back may be made within any period, and shall comply with any other conditions, stated in that instrument for the relevant purpose.

11. Transfers between the institution under resolution and the asset management vehicle shall be subject to the safeguards for partial property transfers specified in Chapter VII of Title IV.

12. Without prejudice to Chapter VII of Title IV shareholders or creditors of the institution under resolution and other third parties whose assets, rights or liabilities are not transferred to the asset management vehicle shall not have any rights over or in relation to the assets, rights or liabilities transferred to the asset management vehicle or its management body or senior management.

13. The objectives of an asset management vehicle shall not imply any duty or responsibility to shareholders or creditors of the institution under resolution, and the management body or senior management shall have no liability to such shareholders or creditors for acts and omissions in the discharge of their duties unless the act or omission implies gross negligence or serious misconduct in accordance with national law which directly affects rights of such shareholders or creditors.

Member States may further limit the liability of an asset management vehicle and its management body or senior management in accordance with national law for acts and omissions in the discharge of their duties

14. EBA shall, by 3 July 2015, issue guidelines in accordance with Article 16 of Regulation (EU) No 1093/2010 to promote the convergence of supervisory and resolution practices regarding the determination when, in accordance to paragraph 5 of this Article the liquidation of the assets or liabilities under normal insolvency proceeding could have an adverse effect on one or more financial markets.

SECTION 5
THE BAIL-IN TOOL

Subsection 1
Objective and scope of the bail-in tool

[3.461]
Article 43
The bail-in tool

1. In order to give effect to the bail-in tool, Member States shall ensure that resolution authorities have the resolution powers specified in Article 63(1).

2. Member States shall ensure that resolution authorities may apply the bail-in tool to meet the resolution objectives specified in Article 31, in accordance with the resolution principles specified in Article 34 for any of the following purposes:

(a) to recapitalise an institution or an entity referred to in point (b), (c) or (d) of Article 1(1) of this Directive that meets the conditions for resolution to the extent sufficient to restore its ability to comply with the conditions for authorisation (to the extent that those conditions apply to the entity) and to continue to carry out the activities for which it is authorised under Directive 2013/36/EU or Directive 2014/65/EU, where the entity is authorised under those Directives, and to sustain sufficient market confidence in the institution or entity;

(b) to convert to equity or reduce the principal amount of claims or debt instruments that are transferred:

(i) to a bridge institution with a view to providing capital for that bridge institution; or

(ii) under the sale of business tool or the asset separation tool.

3. Member States shall ensure that resolution authorities may apply the bail-in tool for the purpose referred to in point (a) of paragraph 2 of this Article only if there is a reasonable prospect that the application of that tool together with other relevant measures including measures implemented in accordance with the business reorganisation plan required by Article 52 will, in addition to achieving relevant resolution objectives, restore the institution or entity referred to in point (b), (c) or (d) of Article 1(1) in question to financial soundness and long-term viability.

Member States shall ensure that resolution authorities may apply any of the resolution tools referred to in points (a), (b) and (c) of Article 37(3), and the bail-in tool referred to in point (b) of paragraph 2 of this Article, where the conditions laid down in the first subparagraph are not met.

4. Member States shall ensure that resolution authorities may apply the bail-in tool to all institutions or entities referred to in point (b), (c) or (d) of Article 1(1) while respecting in each case the legal form of the institution or entity concerned or may change the legal form.

[3.462]
Article 44
Scope of bail-in tool

1. Member States shall ensure that the bail-in tool may be applied to all liabilities of an institution or entity referred to in point (b), (c) or (d) of Article 1(1) that are not excluded from the scope of that tool pursuant to paragraphs 2 or 3 of this Article.

2. Resolution authorities shall not exercise the write down or conversion powers in relation to the following liabilities whether they are governed by the law of a Member State or of a third country:

(a) covered deposits;

(b) secured liabilities including covered bonds and liabilities in the form of financial instruments used for hedging purposes which form an integral part of the cover pool and which according to national law are secured in a way similar to covered bonds;

(c) any liability that arises by virtue of the holding by the institution or entity referred to in point (b), (c) or (d) of Article 1(1) of this Directive of client assets or client money including client assets or client money held on behalf of UCITS as defined in Article 1(2) of Directive 2009/65/EC or of AIFs as defined in point (a) of Article 4(1) of Directive 2011/61/EU of the European Parliament and of the Council,[1] provided that such a client is protected under the applicable insolvency law;

(d) any liability that arises by virtue of a fiduciary relationship between the institution or entity referred to in point (b), (c) or (d) of Article 1(1) (as fiduciary) and another person (as beneficiary) provided that such a beneficiary is protected under the applicable insolvency or civil law;

(e) liabilities to institutions, excluding entities that are part of the same group, with an original maturity of less than seven days;

(f) liabilities with a remaining maturity of less than seven days, owed to systems or operators of systems designated according to Directive 98/26/EC or their participants and arising from the participation in such a system;

(g) a liability to any one of the following:

(i) an employee, in relation to accrued salary, pension benefits or other fixed remuneration, except for the variable component of remuneration that is not regulated by a collective bargaining agreement;

(ii) a commercial or trade creditor arising from the provision to the institution or entity referred to in point (b), (c) or (d) of Article 1(1) of goods or services that are critical to the daily functioning of its operations, including IT services, utilities and the rental, servicing and upkeep of premises;

(iii) tax and social security authorities, provided that those liabilities are preferred under the applicable law;

(iv) deposit guarantee schemes arising from contributions due in accordance with Directive 2014/49/EU.

Point (g)(i) of the first subparagraph shall not apply to the variable component of the remuneration of material risk takers as identified in Article 92(2) of Directive 2013/36/EU.

Member States shall ensure that all secured assets relating to a covered bond cover pool remain unaffected, segregated and with enough funding. Neither that requirement nor point (b) of the first subparagraph shall prevent resolution authorities, where appropriate, from exercising those powers in relation to any part of a secured liability or a liability for which collateral has been pledged that exceeds the value of the assets, pledge, lien or collateral against which it is secured.

Point (a) of the first subparagraph shall not prevent resolution authorities, where appropriate, from exercising those powers in relation to any amount of a deposit that exceeds the coverage level provided for in Article 6 of Directive 2014/49/EU.

Without prejudice to the large exposure rules in Regulation (EU) No 575/2013 and Directive 2013/36/EU, Member States shall ensure that in order to provide for the resolvability of institutions and groups, resolution authorities limit, in accordance with point (b) of Article 17(5) of this Directive, the extent to which other institutions hold liabilities eligible for a bail-in tool, save for liabilities that are held at entities that are part of the same group.

3. In exceptional circumstances, where the bail-in tool is applied, the resolution authority may exclude or partially exclude certain liabilities from the application of the write-down or conversion powers where:

(a) it is not possible to bail-in that liability within a reasonable time notwithstanding the good faith efforts of the resolution authority;

(b) the exclusion is strictly necessary and is proportionate to achieve the continuity of critical functions and core business lines in a manner that maintains the ability of the institution under resolution to continue key operations, services and transactions;

(c) the exclusion is strictly necessary and proportionate to avoid giving rise to widespread contagion, in particular as regards eligible deposits held by natural persons and micro, small and medium sized enterprises, which would severely disrupt the functioning of financial markets, including of financial market infrastructures, in a manner that could cause a serious disturbance to the economy of a Member State or of the Union; or

(d) the application of the bail-in tool to those liabilities would cause a destruction in value such that the losses borne by other creditors would be higher than if those liabilities were excluded from bail-in.

Where a resolution authority decides to exclude or partially exclude an eligible liability or class of eligible liabilities under this paragraph, the level of write down or conversion applied to other eligible liabilities may be increased to take account of such exclusions, provided that the level of write down and conversion applied to other eligible liabilities complies with the principle in point (g) of Article 34(1).

4. Where a resolution authority decides to exclude or partially exclude an eligible liability or class of eligible liabilities pursuant to this Article, and the losses that would have been borne by those liabilities have not been passed on fully to other creditors, the resolution financing arrangement may make a contribution to the institution under resolution to do one or both of the following:

(a) cover any losses which have not been absorbed by eligible liabilities and restore the net asset value of the institution under resolution to zero in accordance with point (a) of Article 46(1);

(b) purchase shares or other instruments of ownership or capital instruments in the institution under resolution, in order to recapitalise the institution in accordance with point (b) of Article 46(1).

5. The resolution financing arrangement may make a contribution referred to in paragraph 4 only where:

(a) a contribution to loss absorption and recapitalisation equal to an amount not less than 8% of the total liabilities including own funds of the institution under resolution, measured at the time of resolution action in accordance with the valuation provided for in Article 36, has been made by the shareholders and the holders of other instruments of ownership, the holders of relevant capital instruments and other eligible liabilities through write down, conversion or otherwise; and

(b) the contribution of the resolution financing arrangement does not exceed 5% of the total liabilities including own funds of the institution under resolution, measured at the time of resolution action in accordance with the valuation provided for in Article 36.

6. The contribution of the resolution financing arrangement referred to in paragraph 4 may be financed by:

(a) the amount available to the resolution financing arrangement which has been raised through contributions by institutions and Union branches in accordance with Article 100(6) and Article 103;

(b) the amount that can be raised through *ex-post* contributions in accordance with Article 104 within three years; and

(c) where the amounts referred to (a) and (b) of this paragraph are insufficient, amounts raised from alternative financing sources in accordance with Article 105.

7. In extraordinary circumstances, the resolution authority may seek further funding from alternative financing sources after:

(a) the 5% limit specified in paragraph 5(b) has been reached; and

(b) all unsecured, non-preferred liabilities, other than eligible deposits, have been written down or converted in full.

As an alternative or in addition, where the conditions laid down in the first subparagraph are met, the resolution financing arrangement may make a contribution from resources which have been raised through *ex-ante* contributions in accordance with Article 100(6) and Article 103 and which have not yet been used.

8. By way of derogation from paragraph 5 (a), the resolution financing arrangement may also make a contribution as referred to in paragraph 4 provided that:

(a) the contribution to loss absorption and recapitalisation referred to in point (a) of paragraph 5 is equal to an amount not less than 20% of the risk weighted assets of the institution concerned;

(b) the resolution financing arrangement of the Member State concerned has at its disposal, by way of *ex-ante* contributions (not including contributions to a deposit guarantee scheme) raised in accordance with Article 100(6) and Article 103, an amount which is at least equal to 3% of covered deposits of all the credit institutions authorised in the territory of that Member State; and

(c) the institution concerned has assets below EUR 900 billion on a consolidated basis.

9. When exercising the discretions under paragraph 3, resolution authorities shall give due consideration to:

(a) the principle that losses should be borne first by shareholders and next, in general, by creditors of the institution under resolution in order of preference;

(b) the level of loss absorbing capacity that would remain in the institution under resolution if the liability or class of liabilities were excluded; and

(c) the need to maintain adequate resources for resolution financing.

10. Exclusions under paragraph 3 may be applied either to completely exclude a liability from write down or to limit the extent of the write down applied to that liability.

11. The Commission shall be empowered to adopt delegated acts in accordance with Article 115 in order to specify further the circumstances when exclusion is necessary to achieve the objectives specified in paragraph 3 of this Article.

12. Before exercising the discretion to exclude a liability under paragraph 3, the resolution authority shall notify the Commission. Where the exclusion would require a contribution by the resolution financing arrangement or an alternative financing source under paragraphs 4 to 8, the Commission may, within 24 hours of receipt of such a notification, or a longer period with the agreement of the resolution authority, prohibit or require amendments to the proposed exclusion if the requirements of this Article and delegated acts are not met in order to protect the integrity of the internal market. This is without prejudice to the application by the Commission of the Union State aid framework.

NOTES

[1] Directive 2011/61/EU of the European Parliament and of the Council of 8 June 2011 on Alternative Investment Fund Managers and amending Directives 2003/41/EC and 2009/65/EC and Regulations (EC) No 1060/2009 and (EU) No 1095/2010 (OJ L174, 1.7.2011, p 1).

Subsection 2
Minimum requirement for own funds and eligible liabilities

[3.463]
Article 45
Application of the minimum requirement

1. Member States shall ensure that institutions meet, at all times, a minimum requirement for own funds and eligible liabilities. The minimum requirement shall be calculated as the amount of own funds and eligible liabilities expressed as a percentage of the total liabilities and own funds of the institution.

For the purpose of the first subparagraph derivative liabilities shall be included in the total liabilities on the basis that full recognition is given to counterparty netting rights.

2. EBA shall draft technical regulatory standards which specify further the assessment criteria mentioned in points (a) to (f) of paragraph 6 on the basis of which, for each institution, a minimum requirement for own funds and eligible liabilities, including subordinated debt and senior unsecured debt with at least 12 months remaining on their terms that are subject to the bail-in power and those that qualify as own funds, is to be determined.

EBA shall submit those draft regulatory technical standards to the Commission by 3 July 2015.

Power is delegated to the Commission to adopt the regulatory technical standards referred to in the first subparagraph in accordance with Articles 10 to 14 of Regulation (EU) No 1093/2010.

Member States may provide for additional criteria on the basis of which the minimum requirement for own funds and eligible liabilities shall be determined.

3. Notwithstanding paragraph 1, resolution authorities shall exempt mortgage credit institutions financed by covered bonds which, according to national law are not allowed to receive deposits from the obligation to meet, at all times, a minimum requirement for own funds and eligible liabilities, as:

(a) those institutions will be wound-up through national insolvency procedures, or other types of procedure implemented in accordance with Article 38, 40 or 42 of this Directive, provided for those institutions; and

(b) such national insolvency procedures, or other types of procedure, will ensure that creditors of those institutions, including holders of covered bonds where relevant, will bear losses in a way that meets the resolution objectives.

4. Eligible liabilities shall be included in the amount of own funds and eligible liabilities referred to in paragraph 1 only if they satisfy the following conditions:

(a) the instrument is issued and fully paid up;

(b) the liability is not owed to, secured by or guaranteed by the institution itself;

(c) the purchase of the instrument was not funded directly or indirectly by the institution;

(d) the liability has a remaining maturity of at least one year;

(e) the liability does not arise from a derivative;

(f) the liability does not arise from a deposit which benefits from preference in the national insolvency hierarchy in accordance with Article 108.

For the purpose of point (d) where a liability confers upon its owner a right to early reimbursement, the maturity of that liability shall be the first date where such a right arises.

5. Where a liability is governed by the law of a third-country, resolution authorities may require the institution to demonstrate that any decision of a resolution authority to write down or convert that liability would be effective under the law of that third country, having regard to the terms of the contract governing the liability, international agreements on the recognition of resolution proceedings and other relevant matters. If the resolution authority is not satisfied that any decision would be effective under the law of that third country, the liability shall not be counted towards the minimum requirement for own funds and eligible liabilities.

6. The minimum requirement for own funds and eligible liabilities of each institution pursuant to paragraph 1 shall be determined by the resolution authority, after consulting the competent authority, at least on the basis of the following criteria:

(a) the need to ensure that the institution can be resolved by the application of the resolution tools including, where appropriate, the bail-in tool, in a way that meets the resolution objectives;

(b) the need to ensure, in appropriate cases, that the institution has sufficient eligible liabilities to ensure that, if the bail-in tool were to be applied, losses could be absorbed and the Common Equity Tier 1 ratio of the institution could be restored to a level necessary to enable it to continue to comply with the conditions for authorisation and to continue to carry out the activities for which it is authorised under Directive 2013/36/EU or Directive 2014/65/EU and to sustain sufficient market confidence in the institution or entity;

(c) the need to ensure that, if the resolution plan anticipates that certain classes of eligible liabilities might be excluded from bail-in under Article 44(3) or that certain classes of eligible liabilities might be transferred to a recipient in full under a partial transfer, that the institution has sufficient other eligible liabilities to ensure that losses could be absorbed and the Common Equity Tier 1 ratio of the institution could be restored to a level necessary to enable it to continue to comply with the conditions for authorisation and to continue to carry out the activities for which it is authorised under Directive 2013/36/EU or Directive 2014/65/EU;

(d) the size, the business model, the funding model and the risk profile of the institution;

(e) the extent to which the Deposit Guarantee Scheme could contribute to the financing of resolution in accordance with Article 109;

(f) the extent to which the failure of the institution would have adverse effects on financial stability, including, due to its interconnectedness with other institutions or with the rest of the financial system through contagion to other institutions.

7. Institutions shall comply with the minimum requirements laid down in this Article on an individual basis.

A resolution authority may, after consulting a competent authority, decide to apply the minimum requirement laid down in this Article to an entity referred to in point (b), (c) or (d) of Article 1(1).

8. In addition to paragraph 7, Union parent undertakings shall comply with the minimum requirements laid down in this Article on a consolidated basis.

The minimum requirement for own funds and eligible liabilities at consolidated level of an Union parent undertaking shall be determined by the group-level resolution authority, after consulting the consolidating supervisor, in accordance with paragraph 9, at least on the basis of the criteria laid down in paragraph 6 and of whether the third-country subsidiaries of the group are to be resolved separately according to the resolution plan.

9. The group-level resolution authority and the resolution authorities responsible for the subsidiaries on an individual basis shall do everything within their power to reach a joint decision on the level of the minimum requirement applied at the consolidated level.

The joint decision shall be fully reasoned and shall be provided to the Union parent undertaking by the group-level resolution authority.

In the absence of such a joint decision within four months, a decision shall be taken on the consolidated

Part 3 EU & International Materials

minimum requirement by the group-level resolution authority after duly taking into consideration the assessment of subsidiaries performed by the relevant resolution authorities. If, at the end of the four-month period, any of the resolution authorities concerned has referred the matter to EBA in accordance with Article 19 of Regulation (EU) No 1093/2010, the group-level resolution authority shall defer its decision and await any decision that EBA may take in accordance with Article 19(3) of that Regulation, and shall take its decision in accordance with the decision of EBA. The four-month period shall be deemed to be the conciliation period within the meaning of that Regulation. EBA shall take its decision within one month. The matter shall not be referred to EBA after the end of the four-month period or after a joint decision has been reached. In the absence of an EBA decision within one month, the decision of the group-level resolution authority shall apply.

The joint decision and the decision taken by the group-level resolution authority in the absence of a joint decision shall be binding on the resolution authorities in the Member States concerned.

The joint decision and any decision taken in the absence of a joint decision shall be reviewed and where relevant updated on a regular basis.

10. Resolution authorities shall set the minimum requirement to be applied to the group's subsidiaries on an individual basis. Those minimum requirements shall be set at a level appropriate for the subsidiary having regard to:

(a) the criteria listed in paragraph 6, in particular the size, business model and risk profile of the subsidiary, including its own funds; and
(b) the consolidated requirement that has been set for the group under paragraph 9.

The group-level resolution authority and the resolution authorities responsible for subsidiaries on an individual basis shall do everything within their power to reach a joint decision on the level of the minimum requirement to be applied to each respective subsidiary at an individual level.

The joint decision shall be fully reasoned and shall be provided to the subsidiaries and to the Union parent institution by the resolution authority of the subsidiaries and by the group-level resolution authority, respectively.

In the absence of such a joint decision between the resolution authorities within a period of four months the decision shall be taken by the respective resolution authorities of the subsidiaries duly considering the views and reservations expressed by the group-level resolution authority.

If, at the end of the four-month period, the group-level resolution authority has referred the matter to EBA in accordance with Article 19 of Regulation (EU) No 1093/2010, the resolution authorities responsible for the subsidiaries on an individual basis shall defer their decisions and await any decision that EBA may take in accordance with Article 19(3) of that Regulation, and shall take their decisions in accordance with the decision of EBA. The four-month period shall be deemed to be the conciliation period within the meaning of that Regulation. EBA shall take its decision within one month. The matter shall not be referred to EBA after the end of the four-month period or after a joint decision has been reached. The group-level resolution authority shall not refer the matter to EBA for binding mediation where the level set by the resolution authority of the subsidiary is within one percentage point of the consolidated level set under paragraph 9 of this Article.

In the absence of an EBA decision within one month, the decisions of the resolution authorities of the subsidiaries shall apply.

The joint decision and any decisions taken by the resolution authorities of the subsidiaries in the absence of a joint decision shall be binding on the resolution authorities concerned.

The joint decision and any decisions taken in the absence of a joint decision shall be reviewed and where relevant updated on a regular basis.

11. The group-level resolution authority may fully waive the application of the individual minimum requirement to an Union parent institution where:

(a) the Union parent institution complies on a consolidated basis with the minimum requirement set under paragraph 8; and
(b) the competent authority of the Union parent institution has fully waived the application of individual capital requirements to the institution in accordance with Article 7(3) of Regulation (EU) No 575/2013.

12. The resolution authority of a subsidiary may fully waive the application of paragraph 7 to that subsidiary where:

(a) both the subsidiary and its parent undertaking are subject to authorisation and supervision by the same Member State;
(b) the subsidiary is included in the supervision on a consolidated basis of the institution which is the parent undertaking;
(c) the highest level group institution in the Member State of the subsidiary, where different to the Union parent institution, complies on a sub-consolidated basis with the minimum requirement set under paragraph 7;
(d) there is no current or foreseen material practical or legal impediment to the prompt transfer of own funds or repayment of liabilities to the subsidiary by its parent undertaking;
(e) either the parent undertaking satisfies the competent authority regarding the prudent management of the subsidiary and has declared, with the consent of the competent authority, that it guarantees the commitments entered into by the subsidiary, or the risks in the subsidiary are of no significance;
(f) the risk evaluation, measurement and control procedures of the parent undertaking cover the subsidiary;
(g) the parent undertaking holds more than 50% of the voting rights attached to shares in the capital of the subsidiary or has the right to appoint or remove a majority of the members of the management body of the subsidiary; and

(h) the competent authority of the subsidiary has fully waived the application of individual capital requirements to the subsidiary under Article 7(1) of Regulation (EU) No 575/2013.

13. The decisions taken in accordance with this Article may provide that the minimum requirement for own funds and eligible liabilities is partially met at consolidated or individual level through contractual bail-in instruments.

14. To qualify as a contractual bail-in instrument under paragraph 13, the resolution authority shall be satisfied that the instrument:

(a) contains a contractual term providing that, where a resolution authority decides to apply the bail-in tool to that institution, the instrument shall be written down or converted to the extent required before other eligible liabilities are written down or converted; and

(b) is subject to a binding subordination agreement, undertaking or provision under which in the event of normal insolvency proceedings, it ranks below other eligible liabilities and cannot be repaid until other eligible liabilities outstanding at the time have been settled.

15. Resolution authorities, in coordination with competent authorities, shall require and verify that institutions meet the minimum requirement for own funds and eligible liabilities laid down in paragraph 1 and where relevant the requirement laid down in paragraph 13, and shall take any decision pursuant to this Article in parallel with the development and the maintenance of resolution plans.

16. Resolution authorities, in coordination with competent authorities, shall inform EBA of the minimum requirement for own funds and eligible liabilities, and where relevant the requirement laid down in paragraph 13, that have been set for each institution under their jurisdiction.

17. EBA shall develop draft implementing technical standards to specify uniform formats, templates and definitions for the identification and transmission of information by resolution authorities, in coordination with competent authorities, to EBA for the purposes of paragraph 16.

EBA shall submit those draft implementing technical standards to the Commission by 3 July 2015.

Power is conferred on the Commission to adopt the implementing technical standards referred to in the first subparagraph in accordance with Article 15 of Regulation (EU) No 1093/2010.

18. Based on the results of the report referred to in paragraph 19, the Commission shall, if appropriate, submit by 31 December 2016 to the European Parliament and the Council a legislative proposal on the harmonised application of the minimum requirement for own funds and eligible liabilities. That proposal shall include, where appropriate, proposals for the introduction of an appropriate number of minimum levels of the minimum requirement, taking account of the different business models of institutions and groups. The proposal shall include any appropriate adjustments to the parameters of the minimum requirement, and if necessary, appropriate amendments to the application of the minimum requirement to groups.

19. EBA shall submit a report to the Commission by 31 October 2016 on at least the following:

(a) how the minimum requirement for own funds and eligible liabilities has been implemented at national level, and in particular whether there have been divergences in the levels set for comparable institutions across Member States;

(b) how the power to require institutions to meet the minimum requirement through contractual bail-in instruments has been applied across Member States and whether there have been divergences in those approaches;

(c) the identification of business models that reflect the overall risk profiles of the institution;

(d) the appropriate level of the minimum requirement for each of the business models identified under point (c);

(e) whether a range for the level of the minimum requirement of each business model should be established;

(f) the appropriate transitional period for institutions to achieve compliance with any harmonised minimum levels prescribed;

(g) whether the requirements laid down in Article 45 are sufficient to ensure that each institution has adequate loss-absorbing capacity and, if not, which further enhancements are needed in order to ensure that objective;

(h) whether changes to the calculation methodology provided for in this Article are necessary to ensure that the minimum requirement can be used as an appropriate indicator of an institution's loss-absorbing capacity;

(i) whether it is appropriate to base the requirement on total liabilities and own funds and in particular whether it is more appropriate to use the institution's risk-weighted assets as a denominator for the requirement;

(j) whether the approach of this Article on the application of the minimum requirement to groups is appropriate, and in particular whether the approach adequately ensures that loss absorbing capacity in the group is located in, or accessible to, the entities where losses might arise;

(k) whether the conditions for waivers from the minimum requirement are appropriate, and in particular whether such waivers should be available for subsidiaries on a cross-border basis;

(l) whether it is appropriate that resolution authorities may require that the minimum requirement be met through contractual bail-in instruments, and whether further harmonisation of the approach to contractual bail-in instruments is appropriate;

(m) whether the requirements for contractual bail-in instruments laid down in paragraph 14 are appropriate; and

(n) whether it is appropriate for institutions and groups to be required to disclose their minimum requirement for own funds and eligible liabilities, or their level of own funds and eligible liabilities, and if so the frequency and format of such disclosure.

20. The report in paragraph 19 shall cover at least the period from 2 July 2014 until 30 June 2016 and shall take account of at least the following:

(a) the impact of the minimum requirement, and any proposed harmonised levels of the minimum requirement on:
(i) financial markets in general and markets for unsecured debt and derivatives in particular;
(ii) business models and balance sheet structures of institutions, in particular the funding profile and funding strategy of institutions, and the legal and operational structure of groups;
(iii) the profitability of institutions, in particular their cost of funding;
(iv) the migration of exposures to entities which are not subject to prudential supervision;
(v) financial innovation;
(vi) the prevalence of contractual bail-in instruments, and the nature and marketability of such instruments;
(vii) the risk-taking behaviour of institutions;
(viii) the level of asset encumbrance of institutions;
(ix) the actions taken by institutions to comply with minimum requirements, and in particular the extent to which minimum requirements have been met by asset deleveraging, long-term debt issuance and capital raising; and
(x) the level of lending by credit institutions, with a particular focus on lending to micro, small and medium-sized enterprises, local authorities, regional governments and public sector entities and on trade financing, including lending under official export credit insurance schemes;
(b) the interaction of the minimum requirements with the own funds requirements, leverage ratio and the liquidity requirements laid down in Regulation (EU) No 575/2013 and in Directive 2013/36/EU;
(c) the capacity of institutions to independently raise capital or funding from markets in order to meet any proposed harmonised minimum requirements;
(d) consistency with the minimum requirements relating to any international standards developed by international fora.

Subsection 3
Implementation of the bail-in tool

[3.464]
Article 46
Assessment of amount of bail-in

1. Member States shall ensure that, when applying the bail-in tool, resolution authorities assess on the basis of a valuation that complies with Article 36 the aggregate of:
(a) where relevant, the amount by which eligible liabilities must be written down in order to ensure that the net asset value of the institution under resolution is equal to zero; andEN
(b) where relevant, the amount by which eligible liabilities must be converted into shares or other types of capital instruments in order to restore the Common Equity Tier 1 capital ratio of either:
(i) the institution under resolution; or
(ii) the bridge institution.

2. The assessment referred to in paragraph 1 of this Article shall establish the amount by which eligible liabilities need to be written down or converted in order to restore the Common Equity Tier 1 capital ratio of the institution under resolution or where applicable establish the ratio of the bridge institution taking into account any contribution of capital by the resolution financing arrangement pursuant to point (d) of Article 101(1) of this Directive, and to sustain sufficient market confidence in the institution under resolution or the bridge institution and enable it to continue to meet, for at least one year, the conditions for authorisation and to continue to carry out the activities for which it is authorised under Directive 2013/36/EU or Directive 2014/65/EU.

Where resolution authorities intend to use the asset separation tool referred to in Article 42, the amount by which eligible liabilities need to be reduced shall take into account a prudent estimate of the capital needs of the asset management vehicle as appropriate.

3. Where capital has been written down in accordance with Articles 59 to 62 and bail-in has been applied pursuant to Article 43(2) and the level of write-down based on the preliminary valuation according to Article 36 is found to exceed requirements when assessed against the definitive valuation according to Article 36(10), a write-up mechanism may be applied to reimburse creditors and then shareholders to the extent necessary.

4. Resolution authorities shall establish and maintain arrangements to ensure that the assessment and valuation is based on information about the assets and liabilities of the institution under resolution that is as up to date and comprehensive as is reasonably possible.

[3.465]
Article 47
Treatment of shareholders in bail-in or write down or conversion of capital instruments

1. Member States shall ensure that, when applying the bail-in tool in Article 43(2) or the write down or conversion of capital instruments in Article 59, resolution authorities take in respect of shareholders and holders of other instruments of ownership one or both of the following actions:
(a) cancel existing shares or other instruments of ownership or transfer them to bailed-in creditors;
(b) provided that, in accordance to the valuation carried out under Article 36, the institution under resolution has a positive net value, dilute existing shareholders and holders of other instruments of ownership as a result of the conversion into shares or other instruments of ownership of:

(i) relevant capital instruments issued by the institution pursuant to the power referred to in Article 59(2); or
(ii) eligible liabilities issued by the institution under resolution pursuant to the power referred to in point (f) of Article 63(1).

With regard to point (b) of the first subparagraph, the conversion shall be conducted at a rate of conversion that severely dilutes existing holdings of shares or other instruments of ownership.

2. The actions referred to in paragraph 1 shall also be taken in respect of shareholders and holders of other instruments of ownership where the shares or other instruments of ownership in question were issued or conferred in the following circumstances:

(a) pursuant to conversion of debt instruments to shares or other instruments of ownership in accordance with contractual terms of the original debt instruments on the occurrence of an event that preceded or occurred at the same time as the assessment by the resolution authority that the institution or entity referred to in point (b), (c) or (d)of Article 1(1) met the conditions for resolution;
(b) pursuant to the conversion of relevant capital instruments to Common Equity Tier 1 instruments pursuant to Article 60.

3. When considering which action to take in accordance with paragraph 1, resolution authorities shall have regard to:

(a) the valuation carried out in accordance with Article 36;
(b) the amount by which the resolution authority has assessed that Common Equity Tier 1 items must be reduced and relevant capital instruments must be written down or converted pursuant to Article 60(1); and
(c) the aggregate amount assessed by the resolution authority pursuant to Article 46.

4. By way of derogation from Articles 22 to 25 of Directive 2013/36/EU, the requirement to give a notice in Article 26 of Directive 2013/36/EU, Article 10(3), Article 11(1) and(2) and Articles 12 and 13of Directive 2014/65/EU and the requirement to give a notice in Article 11(3) of Directive 2014/65/EU, where the application of the bail-in tool or the conversion of capital instruments would result in the acquisition of or increase in a qualifying holding in an institution as referred to in Article 22(1) of Directive 2013/36/EU or Article 11(1) of Directive 2014/65/EU, competent authorities shall carry out the assessment required under those Articles in a timely manner that does not delay the application of the bail-in tool or the conversion of capital instruments, or prevent resolution action from achieving the relevant resolution objectives.

5. If the competent authority of that institution has not completed the assessment required under paragraph 4 on the date of application of the bail-in tool or the conversion of capital instruments, Article 38(9) shall apply to any acquisition of or increase in a qualifying holding by an acquirer resulting from the application of the bail-in tool or the conversion of capital instruments.

6. EBA shall, by 3 July 2016, issue guidelines, in accordance with Article 16 of Regulation (EU) No 1093/2010, on the circumstances in which each of the actions referred to in paragraph 1 of this Article would be appropriate, having regard to the factors specified in paragraph 3 of this Article.

[3.466]
Article 48
Sequence of write down and conversion

1. Member States shall ensure that, when applying the bail-in tool, resolution authorities exercise the write down and conversion powers, subject to any exclusions under Article 44(2) and (3), meeting the following requirements:

(a) Common Equity Tier 1 items are reduced in accordance with point (a) of Article 60(1);
(b) if, and only if, the total reduction pursuant to point (a) is less than the sum of the amounts referred to in points (b) and (c) of Article 47(3), authorities reduce the principal amount of Additional Tier 1 instruments to the extent required and to the extent of their capacity;
(c) if, and only if, the total reduction pursuant to points (a) and (b) is less than the sum of the amounts referred to in points (b) and (c) of Article 47(3), authorities reduce the principal amount of Tier 2 instruments to the extent required and to the extent of their capacity;
(d) if, and only if, the total reduction of shares or other instruments of ownership and relevant capital instruments pursuant to points (a), (b) and (c) is less than the sum of the amounts referred to in points (b) and (c) of Article 47(3), authorities reduce to the extent required the principal amount of subordinated debt that is not Additional Tier 1 or Tier 2 capital in accordance with the hierarchy of claims in normal insolvency proceedings, in conjunction with the write down pursuant to points (a), (b) and (c) to produce the sum of the amounts referred to in points (b) and (c) of Article 47(3);
(e) if, and only if, the total reduction of shares or other instruments of ownership, relevant capital instruments and eligible liabilities pursuant to points (a) to (d) of this paragraph is less than the sum of the amounts referred to in points (b) and (d) of Article 47(3), authorities reduce to the extent required the principal amount of, or outstanding amount payable in respect of, the rest of eligible liabilities in accordance with the hierarchy of claims in normal insolvency proceedings, including the ranking of deposits provided for in Article 108, pursuant to Article 44, in conjunction with the write down pursuant to points (a), (b), (c) and (d) of this paragraph to produce the sum of the amounts referred to in points (b) and (c) of Article 47(3).

2. When applying the write down or conversion powers, resolution authorities shall allocate the losses represented by the sum of the amounts referred to in points (b) and (c) of Article 47(3) equally between shares or other instruments of ownership and eligible liabilities of the same rank by reducing the principal

Part 3 EU & International Materials

amount of, or outstanding amount payable in respect of, those shares or other instruments of ownership and eligible liabilities to the same extent pro rata to their value except where a different allocation of losses amongst liabilities of the same rank is allowed in the circumstances specified in Article 44(3).

This paragraph shall not prevent liabilities which have been excluded from bail-in in accordance with Article 44(2) and (3) from receiving more favourable treatment than eligible liabilities which are of the same rank in normal insolvency proceedings.

3. Before applying the write down or conversion referred to in point (e) of paragraph 1, resolution authorities shall convert or reduce the principal amount on instruments referred to in points (b), (c) and (d) of paragraph 1 when those instruments contain the following terms and have not already been converted:

(a) terms that provide for the principal amount of the instrument to be reduced on the occurrence of any event that refers to the financial situation, solvency or levels of own funds of the institution or entity referred to in point (b), (c) or (d) of Article 1(1);

(b) terms that provide for the conversion of the instruments to shares or other instruments of ownership on the occurrence of any such event.

4. Where the principal amount of an instrument has been reduced, but not to zero, in accordance with terms of the kind referred to in point (a) of paragraph 3 before the application of the bail-in pursuant to paragraph 1, resolution authorities shall apply the write-down and conversion powers to the residual amount of that principal in accordance with paragraph 1.

5. When deciding on whether liabilities are to be written down or converted into equity, resolution authorities shall not convert one class of liabilities, while a class of liabilities that is subordinated to that class remains substantially unconverted into equity or not written down, unless otherwise permitted under Article 44(2) and (3).

6. For the purposes of this Article, EBA shall, by 3 January 2016, issue guidelines in accordance with Article 16 of Regulation (EU) No 1093/2010 for any interpretation relating to the interrelationship between the provisions of this Directive and those of Regulation (EU) No 575/2013 and Directive 2013/36/EU.

[3.467]
Article 49
Derivatives

1. Member States shall ensure that this Article is complied with when resolution authorities apply the write-down and conversion powers to liabilities arising from derivatives.

2. Resolution authorities shall exercise the write-down and conversion powers in relation to a liability arising from a derivative only upon or after closing-out the derivatives. Upon entry into resolution, resolution authorities shall be empowered to terminate and close out any derivative contract for that purpose.

Where a derivative liability has been excluded from the application of the bail-in tool under Article 44(3), resolution authorities shall not be obliged to terminate or close out the derivative contract.

3. Where derivative transactions are subject to a netting agreement, the resolution authority or an independent valuer shall determine as part of the valuation under Article 36 the liability arising from those transactions on a net basis in accordance with the terms of the agreement.

4. Resolution authorities shall determine the value of liabilities arising from derivatives in accordance with the following:

(a) appropriate methodologies for determining the value of classes of derivatives, including transactions that are subject to netting agreements;

(b) principles for establishing the relevant point in time at which the value of a derivative position should be established; and

(c) appropriate methodologies for comparing the destruction in value that would arise from the close out and bail-in of derivatives with the amount of losses that would be borne by derivatives in a bail-in.

5. EBA, after consulting the European Supervisory Authority (European Securities and Markets Authority) ('ESMA'), established by Regulation (EU) No 1095/2010, shall develop draft regulatory technical standards specifying methodologies and the principles referred to in points (a), (b) and (c) of paragraph 4 on the valuation of liabilities arising from derivatives.

In relation to derivative transactions that are subject to a netting agreement, EBA shall take into account the methodology for close-out set out in the netting agreement.

EBA shall submit those draft regulatory technical standards to the Commission by 3 January 2016.

Power is delegated to the Commission to adopt the regulatory technical standards referred to in the first subparagraph in accordance with Articles 10 to 14 of Regulation (EU) No 1093/2010.

[3.468]
Article 50
Rate of conversion of debt to equity

1. Member States shall ensure that, when resolution authorities exercise the powers specified in Article 59(3) and point (f) of Article 63(1), they may apply a different conversion rate to different classes of capital instruments and liabilities in accordance with one or both of the principles referred to in paragraphs 2 and 3 of this Article.

2. The conversion rate shall represent appropriate compensation to the affected creditor for any loss incurred by virtue of the exercise of the write down and conversion powers.

3. When different conversion rates are applied according to paragraph 1, the conversion rate applicable to liabilities that are considered to be senior under applicable insolvency law shall be higher than the conversion rate applicable to subordinated liabilities.

4. EBA shall, by 3 January 2016, issue guidelines in accordance with Article 16 of Regulation (EU) No 1093/2010 on the setting of conversion rates.
Those guidelines shall indicate, in particular, how affected creditors may be appropriately compensated by means of the conversion rate, and the relative conversion rates that might be appropriate to reflect the priority of senior liabilities under applicable insolvency law.

[3.469]
Article 51
Recovery and reorganisation measures to accompany bail-in
1. Member States shall ensure that, where resolution authorities apply the bail-in tool to recapitalise an institution or entity referred to in point (b), (c) or (d) of Article 1(1) in accordance with point (a) of Article 43(2), arrangements are adopted to ensure that a business reorganisation plan for that institution or entity is drawn up and implemented in accordance with Article 52.
2. The arrangements referred to in paragraph 1 of this Article may include the appointment by the resolution authority of a person or persons appointed in accordance with Article 72(1) with the objective of drawing up and implementing the business reorganisation plan required by Article 52.

[3.470]
Article 52
Business reorganisation plan
1. Member States shall require that, within one month after the application of the bail-in tool to an institution or entity referred to in point (b), (c) or (d) of Article 1(1) in accordance with point (a) of Article 43(2), the management body or the person or persons appointed in accordance with Article 72(1) shall draw up and submit to the resolution authority, a business reorganisation plan that satisfies the requirements of paragraphs 4 and 5 of this Article. Where the Union State aid framework is applicable, Member States shall ensure that such a plan is compatible with the restructuring plan that the institution or entity referred to in point (b), (c) or (d) of Article 1(1) is required to submit to the Commission under that framework.
2. When the bail-in tool in point (a) of Article 43(2) is applied to two or more group entities, the business reorganisation plan shall be prepared by the Union parent institution and cover all of the institutions in the group in accordance with the procedure specified in Articles 7 and 8 and shall be submitted to the group-level resolution authority. The group-level resolution authority shall communicate the plan to other resolution authorities concerned and to EBA.
3. In exceptional circumstances, and if it is necessary for achieving the resolution objectives, the resolution authority may extend the period in paragraph 1 up to a maximum of two months since the application of the bail-in tool. Where the business reorganisation plan is required to be notified within the Union State aid framework, the resolution authority may extend the period in paragraph 1 up to a maximum of two months since the application of the bail-in tool or until the deadline laid down by the Union State aid framework, whichever occurs earlier.
4. A business reorganisation plan shall set out measures aiming to restore the long-term viability of the institution or entity referred to in point (b), (c) or (d) of Article 1(1) or parts of its business within a reasonable timescale. Those measures shall be based on realistic assumptions as to the economic and financial market conditions under which the institution or entity referred to in point (b), (c) or (d) of Article 1(1) will operate.
The business reorganisation plan shall take account, inter alia, of the current state and future prospects of the financial markets, reflecting best-case and worst-case assumptions, including a combination of events allowing the identification of the institution's main vulnerabilities. Assumptions shall be compared with appropriate sector-wide benchmarks.
5. A business reorganisation plan shall include at least the following elements:
   (a) a detailed diagnosis of the factors and problems that caused the institution or entity referred to in point (b), (c) or (d) of Article 1(1) to fail or to be likely to fail, and the circumstances that led to its difficulties;
   (b) a description of the measures aiming to restore the long-term viability of the institution or entity referred to in point (b), (c) or (d) of Article 1(1) that are to be adopted;
   (c) a timetable for the implementation of those measures.
6. Measures aiming to restore the long-term viability of an institution or entity referred to in point (b), (c) or (d) of Article 1(1) may include:
   (a) the reorganisation of the activities of the institution or entity referred to in point (b), (c) or (d) of Article 1(1);
   (b) changes to the operational systems and infrastructure within the institution;
   (c) the withdrawal from loss-making activities;
   (d) the restructuring of existing activities that can be made competitive;
   (e) the sale of assets or of business lines.
7. Within one month of the date of submission of the business reorganisation plan, the relevant resolution authority shall assess the likelihood that the plan, if implemented, will restore the long-term viability of the institution or entity referred to in point (b), (c) or (d) of Article 1(1). The assessment shall be completed in agreement with the relevant competent authority.
If the resolution authority and the competent authority are satisfied that the plan would achieve that objective, the resolution authority shall approve the plan.
8. If the resolution authority is not satisfied that the plan would achieve the objective referred to in paragraph 7, the resolution authority, in agreement with the competent authority, shall notify the management body or the person or persons appointed in accordance with Article 72(1) of its concerns and require the amendment of the plan in a way that addresses those concerns.

9. Within two weeks from the date of receipt of the notification referred to in paragraph 8, the management body or the person or persons appointed in accordance with Article 72(1) shall submit an amended plan to the resolution authority for approval. The resolution authority shall assess the amended plan, and shall notify the management body or the person or persons appointed in accordance with Article 72(1) within one week whether it is satisfied that the plan, as amended, addresses the concerns notified or whether further amendment is required.
10. The management body or the person or persons appointed in accordance with Article 72(1) shall implement the reorganisation plan as agreed by the resolution authority and competent authority, and shall submit a report to the resolution authority at least every six months on progress in the implementation of the plan.
11. The management body or the person or persons appointed in accordance with Article 72(1) shall revise the plan if, in the opinion of the resolution authority with the agreement of the competent authority, it is necessary to achieve the aim referred to in paragraph 4, and shall submit any such revision to the resolution authority for approval.
12. EBA shall develop draft regulatory technical standards to specify further:
(a) the minimum elements that should be included in a business reorganisation plan pursuant to paragraph 5; and
(b) the minimum contents of the reports pursuant to paragraph 10.

EBA shall submit those draft regulatory technical standards to the Commission by 3 January 2016.
Power is delegated to the Commission to adopt the regulatory technical standards referred to in the first subparagraph in accordance with Articles 10 to 14 of Regulation (EU) No 1093/2010.
13. EBA shall, by 3 January 2016, issue guidelines in accordance with Article 16 of Regulation (EU) No 1093/2010 to specify further the minimum criteria that a business reorganisation plan is to fulfil for approval by the resolution authority pursuant to paragraph 7.
14. Taking into account, where appropriate, experience acquired in the application of the guidelines referred to in paragraph 13, EBA may develop draft regulatory technical standards in order to specify further the minimum criteria that a business reorganisation plan is to fulfil for approval by the resolution authority pursuant to paragraph 7.
Power is delegated to the Commission to adopt the regulatory technical standards referred to in the first subparagraph in accordance with Articles 10 to 14 of Regulation (EU) No 1093/2010.

Subsection 4
Bail-in tool: ancillary provisions

[3.471]
Article 53
Effect of bail-in

1. Member States shall ensure that where a resolution authority exercises a power referred to in Article 59(2) and in points (e) to (i) of Article 63(1), the reduction of principal or outstanding amount due, conversion or cancellation takes effect and is immediately binding on the institution under resolution and affected creditors and shareholders.
2. Member States shall ensure that the resolution authority shall have the power to complete or require the completion of all the administrative and procedural tasks necessary to give effect to the exercise of a power referred to in Article 59(2) and in points (e) to (i) of Article 63(1), including:
(a) the amendment of all relevant registers;
(b) the delisting or removal from trading of shares or other instruments of ownership or debt instruments;
(c) the listing or admission to trading of new shares or other instruments of ownership;
(d) the relisting or readmission of any debt instruments which have been written down, without the requirement for the issuing of a prospectus pursuant to Directive 2003/71/EC of the European Parliament and of the Council.[1]
3. Where a resolution authority reduces to zero the principal amount of, or outstanding amount payable in respect of, a liability by means of the power referred to in point (e) of Article 63(1), that liability and any obligations or claims arising in relation to it that are not accrued at the time when the power is exercised shall be treated as discharged for all purposes, and shall not be provable in any subsequent proceedings in relation to the institution under resolution or any successor entity in any subsequent winding up.
4. Where a resolution authority reduces in part, but not in full, the principal amount of, or outstanding amount payable in respect of, a liability by means of the power referred to in point (e) of Article 63(1):
(a) the liability shall be discharged to the extent of the amount reduced;
(b) the relevant instrument or agreement that created the original liability shall continue to apply in relation to the residual principal amount of, or outstanding amount payable in respect of the liability, subject to any modification of the amount of interest payable to reflect the reduction of the principal amount, and any further modification of the terms that the resolution authority might make by means of the power referred to in point (j) of Article 63(1).

NOTES

[1] Directive 2003/71/EC of the European Parliament and of the Council of 4 November 2003 on the prospectus to be published when securities are offered to the public or admitted to trading and amending Directive 2001/34/EC (OJ L345, 31.12.2003, p 64).

[3.472]
Article 54
Removal of procedural impediments to bail-in

1. Without prejudice to point (i) of Article 63(1), Member States shall, where applicable, require institutions and entities referred to in points (b), (c) and (d) of Article 1(1) to maintain at all times a sufficient amount of authorised share capital or of other Common Equity Tier 1 instruments, so that, in the event that the resolution authority exercises the powers referred to in points (e) and (f) of Article 63(1) in relation to an institution or an entity referred to in point (b), (c) or (d) of Article 1(1) or any of its subsidiaries, the institution or entity referred to in point (b), (c) or (d) of Article 1(1) is not prevented from issuing sufficient new shares or other instruments of ownership to ensure that the conversion of liabilities into shares or other instruments of ownership could be carried out effectively.
2. Resolution authorities shall assess whether it is appropriate to impose the requirement laid down in paragraph 1 in the case of a particular institution or entity referred to in point (b), (c) or (d) of Article 1(1) in the context of the development and maintenance of the resolution plan for that institution or group, having regard, in particular, to the resolution actions contemplated in that plan. If the resolution plan provides for the possible application of the bail-in tool, authorities shall verify that the authorised share capital or other Common Equity Tier 1 instruments is sufficient to cover the sum of the amounts referred to in points (b) and (c) of Article 47(3).
3. Member States shall ensure that there are no procedural impediments to the conversion of liabilities to shares or other instruments of ownership existing by virtue of their instruments of incorporation or statutes, including pre-emption rights for shareholders or requirements for the consent of shareholders to an increase in capital.
4. This Article is without prejudice to the amendments to Directives 82/891/EEC, 2004/25/EC, 2005/56/EC, 2007/36/EC, 2011/35/EU and Directive 2012/30/EU set out in Title X of this Directive.

[3.473]
Article 55
Contractual recognition of bail-in

1. Member States shall require institutions and entities referred to in points (b), (c) and (d) of Article 1(1) to include a contractual term by which the creditor or party to the agreement creating the liability recognises that liability may be subject to the write-down and conversion powers and agrees to be bound by any reduction of the principal or outstanding amount due, conversion or cancellation that is effected by the exercise of those powers by a resolution authority, provided that such liability is:
   (a) not excluded under Article 44(2);
   (b) not a deposit referred to in point (a) of Article 108;
   (c) governed by the law of a third country; and
   (d) issued or entered into after the date on which a Member State applies the provisions adopted in order to transpose this Section.

The first subparagraph shall not apply where the resolution authority of a Member State determines that the liabilities or instruments referred to in the first subparagraph can be subject to write down and conversion powers by the resolution authority of a Member State pursuant to the law of the third country or to a binding agreement concluded with that third country.

Member States shall ensure that resolution authorities may require institutions and entities referred to in points (b), (c) and (d) of Article 1(1) to provide authorities with a legal opinion relating to the legal enforceability and effectiveness of such a term.
2. If an institution or entity referred to in point (b), (c) or (d) of Article 1(1) fails to include in the contractual provisions governing a relevant liability a term required in accordance paragraph 1, that failure shall not prevent the resolution authority from exercising the write down and conversion powers in relation to that liability.
3. EBA shall develop draft regulatory technical standards in order to further determine the list of liabilities to which the exclusion in paragraph 1 applies, and the contents of the term required in that paragraph, taking into account banks' different business models.

EBA shall submit those draft regulatory technical standards to the Commission by 3 July 2015.

Power is delegated to the Commission to adopt the regulatory technical standards referred to in the first subparagraph in accordance with Articles 10 to 14 of Regulation (EU) No 1093/2010.

[3.474]
Article 56
Government financial stabilisation tools

1. Member States may provide extraordinary public financial support through additional financial stabilisation tools in accordance with paragraph 3 of this Article, Article 37(10) and with Union State aid framework, for the purpose of participating in the resolution of an institution or an entity referred to in point (b), (c) or (d) of Article 1(1), including by intervening directly in order to avoid its winding up, with a view to meeting the objectives for resolution referred to in Article 31(2) in relation to the Member State or the Union as a whole. Such an action shall be carried out under the leadership of the competent ministry or the government in close cooperation with the resolution authority.
2. In order to give effect to the government financial stabilisation tools, Member States shall ensure that their competent ministries or governments have the relevant resolution powers specified in Articles 63 to 72, and shall ensure that Articles 66, 68, 83 and 117 apply.
3. The government financial stabilisation tools shall be used as a last resort after having assessed and exploited the other resolution tools to the maximum extent practicable whilst maintaining financial stability, as determined by the competent ministry or the government after consulting the resolution authority.

4. When applying the government financial stabilisation tools, Member States shall ensure that their competent ministries or governments and the resolution authority apply the tools only if all the conditions laid down in Article 32(1) as well as one of the following conditions are met:
(a) the competent ministry or government and the resolution authority, after consulting the central bank and the competent authority, determine that the application of the resolution tools would not suffice to avoid a significant adverse effect on the financial system;
(b) the competent ministry or government and the resolution authority determine that the application of the resolution tools would not suffice to protect the public interest, where extraordinary liquidity assistance from the central bank has previously been given to the institution;
(c) in respect of the temporary public ownership tool, the competent ministry or government, after consulting the competent authority and the resolution authority, determines that the application of the resolution tools would not suffice to protect the public interest, where public equity support through the equity support tool has previously been given to the institution.

5. The financial stabilisation tools shall consist of the following:
(a) public equity support tool as referred to in Article 57;
(b) temporary public ownership tool as referred to in Article 58.

[3.475]
Article 57
Public equity support tool

1. Member States may, while complying with national company law, participate in the recapitalisation of an institution or an entity referred to in point (b), (c) or (d) of Article 1(1) of this Directive by providing capital to the latter in exchange for the following instruments, subject to the requirements of Regulation (EU) No 575/2013:
(a) Common Equity Tier 1 instruments;
(b) Additional Tier 1 instruments or Tier 2 instruments.

2. Member States shall ensure, to the extent that their shareholding in an institution or an entity referred to in point (b), (c) or (d) of Article 1(1) permits, that such institutions or entities subject to public equity support tool in accordance with this Article are managed on a commercial and professional basis.

3. Where a Member State provides public equity support tool in accordance with this Article, it shall ensure that its holding in the institution or an entity referred to in point (b), (c) or (d) of Article 1(1) is transferred to the private sector as soon as commercial and financial circumstances allow.

[3.476]
Article 58
Temporary public ownership tool

1. Member States may take an institution or an entity referred to in point (b), (c) or (d) of Article 1(1) into temporary public ownership.

2. For that purpose a Member State may make one or more share transfer orders in which the transferee is:
(a) a nominee of the Member State; or
(b) a company wholly owned by the Member State.

3. Member States shall ensure that institutions or entities referred to in point (b), (c) or (d) of Article 1(1) subject to the temporary public ownership tool in accordance with this Article are managed on a commercial and professional basis and that they are transferred to the private sector as soon as commercial and financial circumstances allow.

CHAPTER V WRITE DOWN OF CAPITAL INSTRUMENTS

[3.477]
Article 59
Requirement to write down or convert capital instruments

1. The power to write down or convert relevant capital instruments may be exercised either:
(a) independently of resolution action; or
(b) in combination with a resolution action, where the conditions for resolution specified in Articles 32 and 33 are met.

2. Member States shall ensure that the resolution authorities have the power to write down or convert relevant capital instruments into shares or other instruments of ownership of institutions and entities referred to in points (b), (c) and (d) of Article 1(1).

3. Member States shall require that resolution authorities exercise the write down or conversion power, in accordance with Article 60 and without delay, in relation to relevant capital instruments issued by an institution or an entity referred to in point (b), (c) or (d) of Article 1(1) when one or more of the following circumstances apply:
(a) where the determination has been made that conditions for resolution specified in Articles 32 and 33 have been met, before any resolution action is taken;
(b) the appropriate authority determines that unless that power is exercised in relation to the relevant capital instruments, the institution or the entity referred to in point (b), (c) or (d) of Article 1(1) will no longer be viable;
(c) in the case of relevant capital instruments issued by a subsidiary and where those capital instruments are recognised for the purposes of meeting own funds requirements on an individual and on a consolidated basis, the appropriate authority of the Member State of the consolidating

supervisor and the appropriate authority of the Member State of the subsidiary make a joint determination taking the form of a joint decision in accordance with Article 92(3) and (4) that unless the write down or conversion power is exercised in relation to those instruments, the group will no longer be viable;

(d) in the case of relevant capital instruments issued at the level of the parent undertaking and where those capital instruments are recognised for the purposes of meeting own funds requirements on an individual basis at the level of the parent undertaking or on a consolidated basis, and the appropriate authority of the Member State of the consolidating supervisor makes a determination that unless the write down or conversion power is exercised in relation to those instruments, the group will no longer be viable;

(e) extraordinary public financial support is required by the institution or the entity referred to in point (b), (c) or (d) of Article 1(1) except in any of the circumstances set out in point (d)(iii) of Article 32(4).

4. For the purposes of paragraph 3, an institution or an entity referred to in point (b), (c) or (d) of Article 1(1) or a group shall be deemed to be no longer viable only if both of the following conditions are met:

(a) the institution or the entity referred to in point (b), (c) or (d) of Article 1(1) or the group is failing or likely to fail;

(b) having regard to timing and other relevant circumstances, there is no reasonable prospect that any action, including alternative private sector measures or supervisory action (including early intervention measures), other than the write down or conversion of capital instruments, independently or in combination with a resolution action, would prevent the failure of the institution or the entity referred to in point (b), (c) or (d) of Article 1(1) or the group within a reasonable timeframe.

5. For the purposes of point (a) of paragraph 4 of this Article, an institution or an entity referred to in point (b), (c) or (d) of Article 1(1) shall be deemed to be failing or likely to fail where one or more of the circumstances set out in Article 32(4) occurs.

6. For the purposes of point (a) of paragraph 4, a group shall be deemed to be failing or likely to fail where the group infringes or there are objective elements to support a determination that the group, in the near future, will infringe its consolidated prudential requirements in a way that would justify action by the competent authority including but not limited to because the group has incurred or is likely to incur losses that will deplete all or a significant amount of its own funds.

7. A relevant capital instrument issued by a subsidiary shall not be written down to a greater extent or converted on worse terms pursuant to point (c) of paragraph 3 than equally ranked capital instruments at the level of the parent undertaking which have been written down or converted.

8. Where an appropriate authority makes a determination referred to in paragraph 3 of this Article, it shall immediately notify the resolution authority responsible for the institution or for the entity referred to in point (b), (c) or (d) of Article 1(1) in question, if different.

9. Before making a determination referred to in point (c) of paragraph 3of this Article in relation to a subsidiary that issues relevant capital instruments that are recognised for the purposes of meeting the own funds requirements on an individual and on a consolidated basis, the appropriate authority shall comply with the notification and consultation requirements laid down in Article 62.

10. Before exercising the power to write down or convert capital instruments, resolution authorities shall ensure that a valuation of the assets and liabilities of the institution or the entity referred to in point (b), (c) or (d) of Article 1(1) is carried out in accordance with Article 36. That valuation shall form the basis of the calculation of the write down to be applied to the relevant capital instruments in order to absorb losses and the level of conversion to be applied to relevant capital instruments in order to recapitalise the institution or the entity referred to in point (b), (c) or (d) of Article 1(1).

[3.478]
Article 60
Provisions governing the write down or conversion of capital instruments

1. When complying with the requirement laid down in Article 59, resolution authorities shall exercise the write down or conversion power in accordance with the priority of claims under normal insolvency proceedings, in a way that produces the following results:

(a) Common Equity Tier 1 items are reduced first in proportion to the losses and to the extent of their capacity and the resolution authority takes one or both of the actions specified in Article 47(1) in respect of holders of Common Equity Tier 1 instruments;

(b) the principal amount of Additional Tier 1 instruments is written down or converted into Common Equity Tier 1 instruments or both, to the extent required to achieve the resolution objectives set out in Article 31 or to the extent of the capacity of the relevant capital instruments, whichever is lower;

(c) the principal amount of Tier 2 instruments is written down or converted into Common Equity Tier 1 instruments or both, to the extent required to achieve the resolution objectives set out in Article 31 or to the extent of the capacity of the relevant capital instruments, whichever is lower.

2. Where the principal amount of a relevant capital instrument is written down:

(a) the reduction of that principal amount shall be permanent, subject to any write up in accordance with the reimbursement mechanism in Article 46(3);

(b) no liability to the holder of the relevant capital instrument shall remain under or in connection with that amount of the instrument, which has been written down, except for any liability already accrued, and any liability for damages that may arise as a result of an appeal challenging the legality of the exercise of the write-down power;

(c) no compensation is paid to any holder of the relevant capital instruments other than in accordance with paragraph 3.

Point (b) shall not prevent the provision of Common Equity Tier 1 instruments to a holder of relevant capital instruments in accordance with paragraph 3.

3. In order to effect a conversion of relevant capital instruments under point (b) of paragraph 1 of this Article, resolution authorities may require institutions and entities referred to in points (b), (c) and (d) of Article 1(1) to issue Common Equity Tier 1 instruments to the holders of the relevant capital instruments. Relevant capital instruments may only be converted where the following conditions are met:

(a) those Common Equity Tier 1 instruments are issued by the institution or the entity referred to in point (b), (c) or (d) of Article 1(1) or by a parent undertaking of the institution or the entity referred to in point (b), (c) or (d) of Article 1(1), with the agreement of the resolution authority of the institution or the entity referred to in points (b), (c) or (d) of Article 1(1) or, where relevant, of the resolution authority of the parent undertaking;

(b) those Common Equity Tier 1 instruments are issued prior to any issuance of shares or other instruments of ownership by that institution or that entity referred to in point (b), (c) or (d) of Article 1(1) for the purposes of provision of own funds by the State or a government entity;

(c) those Common Equity Tier 1 instruments are awarded and transferred without delay following the exercise of the conversion power;

(d) the conversion rate that determines the number of Common Equity Tier 1 instruments that are provided in respect of each relevant capital instrument complies with the principles set out in Article 50 and any guidelines developed by EBA pursuant to Article 50(4).

4. For the purposes of the provision of Common Equity Tier 1 instruments in accordance with paragraph 3, resolution authorities may require institutions and entities referred to in points (b), (c) and (d) of Article 1(1) to maintain at all times the necessary prior authorisation to issue the relevant number of Common Equity Tier 1 instruments.

5. Where an institution meets the conditions for resolution and the resolution authority decides to apply a resolution tool to that institution, the resolution authority shall comply with the requirement laid down in Article 59(3) before applying the resolution tool.

[3.479]
Article 61
Authorities responsible for determination

1. Member States shall ensure that the authorities responsible for making the determinations referred to in Article 59(3) are those set out in this Article.

2. Each Member State shall designate in national law the appropriate authority which shall be responsible for making determinations pursuant to Article 59. The appropriate authority may be the competent authority or the resolution authority, in accordance with Article 32.

3. Where the relevant capital instruments are recognised for the purposes of meeting the own funds requirements in accordance with Article 92 of Regulation (EU) No 575/2013 on an individual basis, the authority responsible for making the determination referred to in Article 59(3) of this Directive shall be the appropriate authority of the Member State where the institution or the entity referred to in point (b), (c) or (d) of Article 1(1) has been authorised in accordance with Title III of Directive 2013/36/EU.

4. Where relevant capital instruments are issued by an institution or an entity referred to in point (b), (c) or (d) of Article 1(1) that is a subsidiary and are recognised for the purposes of meeting the own funds requirements on an individual and on a consolidated basis, the authority responsible for making the determinations referred to in Articles 59(3) shall be the following:

(a) the appropriate authority of the Member State where the institution or the entity referred to in point (b), (c) or (d) of Article 1(1) of this Directive that issued those instruments has been established in accordance with Title III of Directive 2013/36/EU shall be responsible for making the determinations referred to in (b) of Article 59(3) of this Directive;

(b) the appropriate authority of the Member State of the consolidating supervisor and the appropriate authority of the Member State where the institution or the entity referred to in point (b), (c) or (d) of Article 1(1) of this Directive that issued those instruments has been established in accordance with Title III of Directive 2013/36/EU shall be responsible for making the joint determination taking the form of a joint decision referred to in point (c) of Article 59(3) of this Directive.

[3.480]
Article 62
Consolidated application: procedure for determination

1. Member States shall ensure that, before making a determination referred to in point (b), (c), (d) or (e) of Article 59(3) in relation to a subsidiary that issues relevant capital instruments that are recognised for the purposes of meeting the own funds requirements on an individual and a consolidated basis, appropriate authorities comply with the following requirements:

(a) an appropriate authority that is considering whether to make a determination referred to in point (b), (c), (d) or (e) of Article 59(3) notifies, without delay, the consolidating supervisor and, if different, the appropriate authority in the Member State where the consolidating supervisor is located;

(b) an appropriate authority that is considering whether to make a determination referred to in point (c) of Article 59(3) notifies, without delay, the competent authority responsible for each institution or entity referred to in point (b), (c) or (d) of Article 1(1) that has issued the relevant capital instruments in relation to which the write down or conversion power is to be exercised if that determination were made, and, if different, the appropriate authorities in the Member States where those competent authorities and the consolidating supervisor are located.

2. When making a determination referred to in point (c), (d) or (e) of Article 59(3) in the case of an institution or of a group with cross-border activity, the appropriate authorities shall take into account the potential impact of the resolution in all the Member States where the institution or the group operate.

3. An appropriate authority shall accompany a notification made pursuant to paragraph 1 with an explanation of the reasons why it is considering making the determination in question.

4. Where a notification has been made pursuant to paragraph 1, the appropriate authority, after consulting the authorities notified, shall assess the following matters:

(a) whether an alternative measure to the exercise of the write down or conversion power in accordance with Article 59(3) is available;

(b) if such an alternative measure is available, whether it can feasibly be applied;

(c) if such an alternative measure could feasibly be applied, whether there is a realistic prospect that it would address, in an adequate timeframe, the circumstances that would otherwise require a determination referred to in Article 59(3) to be made.

5. For the purposes of paragraph 4 of this Article, alternative measures mean early intervention measures referred to in Article 27 of this Directive, measures referred to in Article 104(1) of Directive 2013/36/EU or a transfer of funds or capital from the parent undertaking.

6. Where, pursuant to paragraph 4, the appropriate authority, after consulting the notified authorities, assesses that one or more alternative measures are available, can feasibly be applied and would deliver the outcome referred to in point (c) of that paragraph, it shall ensure that those measures are applied.

7. Where, in a case referred to in point (a) of paragraph 1, and pursuant to paragraph 4 of this Article, the appropriate authority, after consulting the notified authorities, assesses that no alternative measures are available that would deliver the outcome referred to in point (c) of paragraph 4, the appropriate authority shall decide whether the determination referred to in Article 59(3) under consideration is appropriate.

8. Where an appropriate authority decides to make a determination under point (c) of Article 59(3), it shall immediately notify the appropriate authorities of the Member States in which the affected subsidiaries are located and the determination shall take the form of a joint decision as set out in Article 92(3) and (4). In the absence of a joint decision no determination under point (c) of Article 59(3) shall be made.

9. The resolution authorities of the Member States where each of the affected subsidiaries are located shall promptly implement a decision to write down or convert capital instruments made in accordance with this Article having due regard to the urgency of the circumstances.

CHAPTER VI RESOLUTION POWERS

[3.481]
Article 63
General powers

1. Member States shall ensure that the resolution authorities have all the powers necessary to apply the resolution tools to institutions and to entities referred to in points (b), (c) and (d) of Article 1(1) that meet the applicable conditions for resolution. In particular, the resolution authorities shall have the following resolution powers, which they may exercise individually or in any combination:

(a) the power to require any person to provide any information required for the resolution authority to decide upon and prepare a resolution action, including updates and supplements of information provided in the resolution plans and including requiring information to be provided through on-site inspections;

(b) the power to take control of an institution under resolution and exercise all the rights and powers conferred upon the shareholders, other owners and the management body of the institution under resolution;

(c) the power to transfer shares or other instruments of ownership issued by an institution under resolution;

(d) the power to transfer to another entity, with the consent of that entity, rights, assets or liabilities of an institution under resolution;

(e) the power to reduce, including to reduce to zero, the principal amount of or outstanding amount due in respect of eligible liabilities, of an institution under resolution;

(f) the power to convert eligible liabilities of an institution under resolution into ordinary shares or other instruments of ownership of that institution or entity referred to in point (b), (c) or (d) of Article 1(1), a relevant parent institution or a bridge institution to which assets, rights or liabilities of the institution or the entity referred to in point (b), (c) or (d) of Article 1(1) are transferred;

(g) the power to cancel debt instruments issued by an institution under resolution except for secured liabilities subject to Article 44(2);

(h) the power to reduce, including to reduce to zero, the nominal amount of shares or other instruments of ownership of an institution under resolution and to cancel such shares or other instruments of ownership;

(i) the power to require an institution under resolution or a relevant parent institution to issue new shares or other instruments of ownership or other capital instruments, including preference shares and contingent convertible instruments;

(j) the power to amend or alter the maturity of debt instruments and other eligible liabilities issued by an institution under resolution or amend the amount of interest payable under such instruments and other eligible liabilities, or the date on which the interest becomes payable, including by suspending payment for a temporary period, except for secured liabilities subject to Article 44(2);

(k) the power to close out and terminate financial contracts or derivatives contracts for the purposes of applying Article 49;

(l) the power to remove or replace the management body and senior management of an institution under resolution;

(m) the power to require the competent authority to assess the buyer of a qualifying holding in a timely manner by way of derogation from the time-limits laid down in Article 22 of Directive 2013/36/EU and Article 12 of Directive 2014/65/EU.

2. Member States shall take all necessary measures to ensure that, when applying the resolution tools and exercising the resolution powers, resolution authorities are not subject to any of the following requirements that would otherwise apply by virtue of national law or contract or otherwise:

(a) subject to Article 3(6) and Article 85(1), requirements to obtain approval or consent from any person either public or private, including the shareholders or creditors of the institution under resolution;

(b) prior to the exercise of the power, procedural requirements to notify any person including any requirement to publish any notice or prospectus or to file or register any document with any other authority.

In particular, Member States shall ensure that resolution authorities can exercise the powers under this Article irrespective of any restriction on, or requirement for consent for, transfer of the financial instruments, rights, assets or liabilities in question that might otherwise apply.

Point (b) of the first subparagraph is without prejudice to the requirements laid down in Articles 81 and 83 and any notification requirements under the Union State aid framework.

3. Member States shall ensure that, to the extent that any of the powers listed in paragraph 1 of this Article is not applicable to an entity within the scope of Article 1(1) of this Directive as a result of its specific legal form, resolution authorities shall have powers which are as similar as possible including in terms of their effects.

4. Member States shall ensure that, when resolution authorities exercise the powers pursuant to paragraph 3 the safeguards provided for in this Directive, or safeguards that deliver the same effect, shall be applied to the persons affected, including shareholders, creditors and counterparties.

[3.482]
Article 64
Ancillary powers

1. Member States shall ensure that, when exercising a resolution power, resolution authorities have the power to:

(a) subject to Article 78, provide for a transfer to take effect free from any liability or encumbrance affecting the financial instruments, rights, assets or liabilities transferred; for that purpose, any right of compensation in accordance with this Directive shall not be considered to be a liability or an encumbrance;

(b) remove rights to acquire further shares or other instruments of ownership;

(c) require the relevant authority to discontinue or suspend the admission to trading on a regulated market or the official listing of financial instruments pursuant to Directive 2001/34/EC of the European Parliament and of the Council;[1]

(d) provide for the recipient to be treated as if it were the institution under resolution for the purposes of any rights or obligations of, or actions taken by, the institution under resolution, including, subject to Articles 38 and 40, any rights or obligations relating to participation in a market infrastructure;

(e) require the institution under resolution or the recipient to provide the other with information and assistance; and

(f) cancel or modify the terms of a contract to which the institution under resolution is a party or substitute a recipient as a party.

2. Resolution authorities shall exercise the powers specified in paragraph 1 where it is considered by the resolution authority to be appropriate to help to ensure that a resolution action is effective or to achieve one or more resolution objectives.

3. Member States shall ensure that, when exercising a resolution power, resolution authorities have the power to provide for continuity arrangements necessary to ensure that the resolution action is effective and, where relevant, the business transferred may be operated by the recipient. Such continuity arrangements shall include, in particular:

(a) the continuity of contracts entered into by the institution under resolution, so that the recipient assumes the rights and liabilities of the institution under resolution relating to any financial instrument, right, asset or liability that has been transferred and is substituted for the institution under resolution, expressly or implicitly in all relevant contractual documents;

(b) the substitution of the recipient for the institution under resolution in any legal proceedings relating to any financial instrument, right, asset or liability that has been transferred.

4. The powers in point (d) of paragraph 1 and point (b) of paragraph 3 shall not affect the following:

(a) the right of an employee of the institution under resolution to terminate a contract of employment;

(b) subject to Articles 69, 70 and 71, any right of a party to a contract to exercise rights under the contract, including the right to terminate, where entitled to do so in accordance with the terms of the contract by virtue of an act or omission by the institution under resolution prior to the relevant transfer, or by the recipient after the relevant transfer.

NOTES

[1] Directive 2001/34/EC of the European Parliament and of the Council of 28 May 2001 on the admission of securities to official stock exchange listing and on information to be published on those securities (OJ L184, 6.7.2001, p 1).

[3.483]
Article 65
Power to require the provision of services and facilities

1. Member States shall ensure that resolution authorities have the power to require an institution under resolution, or any of its group entities, to provide any services or facilities that are necessary to enable a recipient to operate effectively the business transferred to it.

The first subparagraph shall apply including where the institution under resolution or relevant group entity has entered into normal insolvency proceedings.

2. Member States shall ensure that their resolution authorities have powers to enforce obligations imposed, pursuant to paragraph 1, on group entities established in their territory by resolution authorities in other Member States.

3. The services and facilities referred to in paragraphs 1 and 2 are restricted to operational services and facilities and do not include any form of financial support.

4. The services and facilities provided in accordance with paragraphs 1 and 2 shall be on the following terms:

(a) where the services and facilities were provided under an agreement to the institution under resolution immediately before the resolution action was taken and for the duration of that agreement, on the same terms;

(b) where there is no agreement or where the agreement has expired, on reasonable terms.

5. EBA shall, by 3 July 2015, issue guidelines in accordance with Article 16 of Regulation (EU) No 1093/2010 to specify the minimum list of services or facilities that are necessary to enable a recipient to effectively operate a business transferred to it.

[3.484]
Article 66
Power to enforce crisis management measures or crisis prevention measures by other Member States

1. Member States shall ensure that, where a transfer of shares, other instruments of ownership, or assets, rights or liabilities includes assets that are located in a Member State other than the State of the resolution authority or rights or liabilities under the law of a Member State other than the State of the resolution authority, the transfer has effect in or under the law of that other Member State.

2. Member States shall provide the resolution authority that has made or intends to make the transfer with all reasonable assistance to ensure that the shares or other instruments of ownership or assets, rights or liabilities are transferred to the recipient in accordance with any applicable requirements of national law.

3. Member States shall ensure that shareholders, creditors and third parties that are affected by the transfer of shares, other instruments of ownership, assets, rights or liabilities referred to in paragraph 1 are not entitled to prevent, challenge, or set aside the transfer under any provision of law of the Member State where the assets are located or of the law governing the shares, other instruments of ownership, rights or liabilities.

4. Where a resolution authority of a Member State (Member State A) exercises the write-down or conversion powers, including in relation to capital instruments in accordance with Article 59, and the eligible liabilities or relevant capital instruments of the institution under resolution include the following:

(a) instruments or liabilities that are governed by the law of a Member State other than the State of the resolution authority that exercised the write down or conversion powers (Member State B);

(b) liabilities owed to creditors located in Member State B.

Member State B shall ensure that the principal amount of those liabilities or instruments is reduced, or liabilities or instruments are converted, in accordance with the exercise of the write-down or conversion powers by the resolution authority of Member State A.

5. Member States shall ensure that creditors that are affected by the exercise of write-down or conversion powers referred to in paragraph 4 are not entitled to challenge the reduction of the principal amount of the instrument or liability or its conversion, as the case may be, under any provision of law of Member State B.

6. Each Member State shall ensure that the following are determined in accordance with the law of the Member State of the resolution authority:

(a) the right for shareholders, creditors and third parties to challenge, by way of appeal pursuant to Article 85, a transfer of shares, other instruments of ownership, assets, rights or liabilities referred to in paragraph 1 of this Article;

(b) the right for creditors to challenge, by way of appeal pursuant to Article 85, the reduction of the principal amount, or the conversion, of an instrument or liability covered by points (a) or (b) of paragraph 4 of this Article;

(c) the safeguards for partial transfers, as referred to in Chapter VII, in relation to assets, rights or liabilities referred to in paragraph 1.

[3.485]
Article 67
Power in respect of assets, rights, liabilities, shares and other instruments of ownership located in third countries

1. Member States shall provide that, in cases in which resolution action involves action taken in respect of assets located in a third country or shares, other instruments of ownership, rights or liabilities governed by the law of a third country, resolution authorities may require that:
   (a) the administrator, receiver or other person exercising control of the institution under resolution and the recipient take all necessary steps to ensure that the transfer, write down, conversion or action becomes effective;
   (b) the administrator, receiver or other person exercising control of the institution under resolution hold the shares, other instruments of ownership, assets or rights or discharge the liabilities on behalf of the recipient until the transfer, write down, conversion or action becomes effective;
   (c) the reasonable expenses of the recipient properly incurred in carrying out any action required under points (a) and (b) of this paragraph are met in any of the ways referred to in Article 37(7).

2. Where the resolution authority assesses that, in spite of all the necessary steps taken by the administrator, receiver or other person in accordance with paragraph 1(a), it is highly unlikely that the transfer, conversion or action will become effective in relation to certain assets located in a third country or certain shares, other instruments of ownership, rights or liabilities under the law of a third country, the resolution authority shall not proceed with the transfer, write down, conversion or action. If it has already ordered the transfer, write down, conversion or action, that order shall be void in relation to the assets, shares, instruments of ownership, rights or liabilities concerned.

[3.486]
Article 68
Exclusion of certain contractual terms in early intervention and resolution

1. A crisis prevention measure or a crisis management measure taken in relation to an entity in accordance with this Directive, including the occurrence of any event directly linked to the application of such a measure, shall not, per se, under a contract entered into by the entity, be deemed to be an enforcement event within the meaning of Directive 2002/47/EC or as insolvency proceedings within the meaning of Directive 98/26/EC provided that the substantive obligations under the contract, including payment and delivery obligations and the provision of collateral, continue to be performed.
In addition, a crisis prevention measure or crisis management measure shall not, per se, be deemed to be an enforcement event or insolvency proceedings under a contract entered into by:
   (a) a subsidiary, the obligations under which are guaranteed or otherwise supported by the parent undertaking or by any group entity; or
   (b) any entity of a group which includes cross-default provisions.

2. Where third country resolution proceedings are recognised pursuant to Article 94, or otherwise where a resolution authority so decides, such proceedings shall for the purposes of this Article constitute a crisis management measure.

3. Provided that the substantive obligations under the contract, including payment and delivery obligations, and provision of collateral, continue to be performed, a crisis prevention measure or a crisis management measure, including the occurrence of any event directly linked to the application of such a measure, shall not, per se, make it possible for anyone to:
   (a) exercise any termination, suspension, modification, netting or set-off rights, including in relation to a contract entered into by:
      (i) a subsidiary, the obligations under which are guaranteed or otherwise supported by a group entity;
      (ii) any group entity which includes cross-default provisions;
   (b) obtain possession, exercise control or enforce any security over any property of the institution or the entity referred to in point (b), (c) or (d) of Article 1(1) concerned or any group entity in relation to a contract which includes cross-default provisions;
   (c) affect any contractual rights of the institution or the entity referred to in point (b), (c) or (d) of Article 1(1) concerned or any group entity in relation to a contract which includes cross-default provisions.

4. This Article shall not affect the right of a person to take an action referred to in paragraph 3 where that right arises by virtue of an event other than the crisis prevention measure, the crisis management measure or the occurrence of any event directly linked to the application of such a measure.

5. A suspension or restriction under Article 69, 70 or 71 shall not constitute non-performance of a contractual obligation for the purposes of paragraphs 1 and 2 of this Article.

6. The provisions contained in this Article shall be considered to be overriding mandatory provisions within the meaning of Article 9 of Regulation (EC) No 593/2008 of the European Parliament and of the Council.[1]

NOTES

[1] Regulation (EC) No 593/2008 of the European Parliament and of the Council of 17 June 2008 on the law applicable to contractual obligations (Rome I) (OJ L177, 4.7.2008, p 6).

[3.487]
Article 69
Power to suspend certain obligations

1. Member States shall ensure that resolution authorities have the power to suspend any payment or delivery obligations pursuant to any contract to which an institution under resolution is a party from the publication of a notice of the suspension in accordance with Article 83(4) until midnight in the Member State of the resolution authority of the institution under resolution at the end of the business day following that publication.
2. When a payment or delivery obligation would have been due during the suspension period the payment or delivery obligation shall be due immediately upon expiry of the suspension period.
3. If an institution under resolution's payment or delivery obligations under a contract are suspended under paragraph 1, the payment or delivery obligations of the institution under resolution's counterparties under that contract shall be suspended for the same period of time.
4. Any suspension under paragraph 1 shall not apply to:
   (a) eligible deposits;
   (b) payment and delivery obligations owed to systems or operators of systems designated for the purposes of Directive 98/26/EC, central counterparties, and central banks;
   (c) eligible claims for the purpose of Directive 97/9/EC.
5. When exercising a power under this Article, resolution authorities shall have regard to the impact the exercise of that power might have on the orderly functioning of financial markets.

[3.488]
Article 70
Power to restrict the enforcement of security interests

1. Member States shall ensure that resolution authorities have the power to restrict secured creditors of an institution under resolution from enforcing security interests in relation to any assets of that institution under resolution from the publication of a notice of the restriction in accordance with Article 83(4) until midnight in the Member State of the resolution authority of the institution under resolution at the end of the business day following that publication.
2. Resolution authorities shall not exercise the power referred to in paragraph 1 in relation to any security interest of systems or operators of systems designated for the purposes of Directive 98/26/EC, central counterparties, and central banks over assets pledged or provided by way of margin or collateral by the institution under resolution.
3. Where Article 80 applies, resolution authorities shall ensure that any restrictions imposed pursuant to the power referred to in paragraph 1 of this Article are consistent for all group entities in relation to which a resolution action is taken.
4. When exercising a power under this Article, resolution authorities shall have regard to the impact the exercise of that power might have on the orderly functioning of financial markets.

[3.489]
Article 71
Power to temporarily suspend termination rights

1. Member States shall ensure that resolution authorities have the power to suspend the termination rights of any party to a contract with an institution under resolution from the publication of the notice pursuant to Article 83(4) until midnight in the Member State of the resolution authority of the institution under resolution at the end of the business day following that publication, provided that the payment and delivery obligations and the provision of collateral continue to be performed.
2. Member States shall ensure that resolution authorities have the power to suspend the termination rights of any party to a contract with a subsidiary of an institution under resolution where:
   (a) the obligations under that contract are guaranteed or are otherwise supported by the institution under resolution;
   (b) the termination rights under that contract are based solely on the insolvency or financial condition of the institution under resolution; and
   (c) in the case of a transfer power that has been or may be exercised in relation to the institution under resolution, either:
      (i) all the assets and liabilities of the subsidiary relating to that contract have been or may be transferred to and assumed by the recipient; or
      (ii) the resolution authority provides in any other way adequate protection for such obligations.

The suspension shall take effect from the publication of the notice pursuant to Article 83(4) until midnight in the Member State where the subsidiary of the institution under resolution is established on the business day following that publication.
3. Any suspension under paragraph 1 or 2 shall not apply to systems or operators of systems designated for the purposes of Directive 98/26/EC, central counterparties, or central banks.
4. A person may exercise a termination right under a contract before the end of the period referred to in paragraph 1 or 2 if that person receives notice from the resolution authority that the rights and liabilities covered by the contract shall not be:
   (a) transferred to another entity; or
   (b) subject to write down or conversion on the application of the bail-in tool in accordance with point (a) of Article 43(2).
5. Where a resolution authority exercises the power specified in paragraph 1 or 2 of this Article to suspend termination rights, and where no notice has been given pursuant to paragraph 4 of this Article, those rights may be exercised on the expiry of the period of suspension, subject to Article 68, as follows:

(a) if the rights and liabilities covered by the contract have been transferred to another entity, a counterparty may exercise termination rights in accordance with the terms of that contract only on the occurrence of any continuing or subsequent enforcement event by the recipient entity;
(b) if the rights and liabilities covered by the contract remain with the institution under resolution and the resolution authority has not applied the bail-in tool in accordance with Article 43(2)(a)to that contract, a counterparty may exercise termination rights in accordance with the terms of that contract on the expiry of a suspension under paragraph 1.

6. When exercising a power under this Article, resolution authorities shall have regard to the impact the exercise of that power might have on the orderly functioning of the financial markets.

7. Competent authorities or resolution authorities may require an institution or an entity referred to in point (b), (c) or (d) of Article 1(1) to maintain detailed records of financial contracts.

Upon the request of a competent authority or a resolution authority, a trade repository shall make the necessary information available to competent authorities or resolution authorities to enable them to fulfil their respective responsibilities and mandates in accordance with Article 81 of Regulation (EU) No 648/2012.

8. EBA shall develop draft regulatory technical standards specifying the following elements for the purposes of paragraph 7:
(a) a minimum set of the information on financial contracts that should be contained in the detailed records; and
(b) the circumstances in which the requirement should be imposed.

EBA shall submit those draft regulatory technical standards to the Commission by 3 July 2015.

Power is delegated to the Commission to adopt the regulatory technical standards referred to in the first subparagraph in accordance with Articles 10 to 14 of Regulation (EU) No 1093/2010.

[3.490]
Article 72
Exercise of the resolution powers

1. Member States shall ensure that, in order to take a resolution action, resolution authorities are able to exercise control over the institution under resolution, so as to:
(a) operate and conduct the activities and services of the institution under resolution with all the powers of its shareholders and management body; and
(b) manage and dispose of the assets and property of the institution under resolution.

The control referred to in the first subparagraph may be exercised directly by the resolution authority or indirectly by a person or persons appointed by the resolution authority. Member States shall ensure that voting rights conferred by shares or other instruments of ownership of the institution under resolution cannot be exercised during the period of resolution.

2. Subject to Article 85(1), Member States shall ensure that resolution authorities are able to take a resolution action through executive order in accordance with national administrative competences and procedures, without exercising control over the institution under resolution.

3. Resolution authorities shall decide in each particular case whether it is appropriate to carry out the resolution action through the means specified in paragraph 1 or in paragraph 2, having regard to the resolution objectives and the general principles governing resolution, the specific circumstances of the institution under resolution in question and the need to facilitate the effective resolution of cross-border groups.

4. Resolution authorities shall not be deemed to be shadow directors or de facto directors under national law.

CHAPTER VII SAFEGUARDS

[3.491]
Article 73
Treatment of shareholders and creditors in the case of partial transfers and application of the bail-in tool

Member States shall ensure that, where one or more resolution tools have been applied and, in particular for the purposes of Article 75:
(a) except where point (b) applies, where resolution authorities transfer only parts of the rights, assets and liabilities of the institution under resolution, the shareholders and those creditors whose claims have not been transferred, receive in satisfaction of their claims at least as much as what they would have received if the institution under resolution had been wound up under normal insolvency proceedings at the time when the decision referred to in Article 82 was taken;
(b) where resolution authorities apply the bail-in tool, the shareholders and creditors whose claims have been written down or converted to equity do not incur greater losses than they would have incurred if the institution under resolution had been wound up under normal insolvency proceedings immediately at the time when the decision referred to in Article 82 was taken.

[3.492]
Article 74
Valuation of difference in treatment

1. For the purposes of assessing whether shareholders and creditors would have received better treatment if the institution under resolution had entered into normal insolvency proceedings, including but not limited to for the purpose of Article 73, Member States shall ensure that a valuation is carried out by an independent person as soon as possible after the resolution action or actions have been effected. That valuation shall be distinct from the valuation carried out under Article 36.

2. The valuation in paragraph 1 shall determine:
   (a) the treatment that shareholders and creditors, or the relevant deposit guarantee schemes, would have received if the institution under resolution with respect to which the resolution action or actions have been effected had entered normal insolvency proceedings at the time when the decision referred to in Article 82 was taken;
   (b) the actual treatment that shareholders and creditors have received, in the resolution of the institution under resolution; and
   (c) if there is any difference between the treatment referred to in point (a) and the treatment referred to in point (b).
3. The valuation shall:
   (a) assume that the institution under resolution with respect to which the resolution action or actions have been effected, would have entered normal insolvency proceedings at the time when the decision referred to in Article 82 was taken;
   (b) assume that the resolution action or actions had not been effected;
   (c) disregard any provision of extraordinary public financial support to the institution under resolution.
4. EBA may develop draft regulatory technical standards specifying the methodology for carrying out the valuation in this Article, in particular the methodology for assessing the treatment that shareholders and creditors would have received if the institution under resolution had entered insolvency proceedings at the time when the decision referred to in Article 82 was taken.

Power is delegated to the Commission to adopt the regulatory technical standards referred to in the first subparagraph in accordance with Articles 10 to 14 of Regulation (EU) No 1093/2010.

[3.493]
Article 75
Safeguard for shareholders and creditors

Member States shall ensure that if the valuation carried out under Article 74 determines that any shareholder or creditor referred to in Article 73, or the deposit guarantee scheme in accordance with Article 109(1), has incurred greater losses than it would have incurred in a winding up under normal insolvency proceedings, it is entitled to the payment of the difference from the resolution financing arrangements.

[3.494]
Article 76
Safeguard for counterparties in partial transfers

1. Member States shall ensure that the protections specified in paragraph 2 apply in the following circumstances:
   (a) a resolution authority transfers some but not all of the assets, rights or liabilities of an institution under resolution to another entity or, in the exercise of a resolution tool, from a bridge institution or asset management vehicle to another person;
   (b) a resolution authority exercises the powers specified in point (f) of Article 64(1).
2. Member States shall ensure appropriate protection of the following arrangements and of the counterparties to the following arrangements:
   (a) security arrangements, under which a person has by way of security an actual or contingent interest in the assets or rights that are subject to transfer, irrespective of whether that interest is secured by specific assets or rights or by way of a floating charge or similar arrangement;
   (b) title transfer financial collateral arrangements under which collateral to secure or cover the performance of specified obligations is provided by a transfer of full ownership of assets from the collateral provider to the collateral taker, on terms providing for the collateral taker to transfer assets if those specified obligations are performed;
   (c) set-off arrangements under which two or more claims or obligations owed between the institution under resolution and a counterparty can be set off against each other;
   (d) netting arrangements;
   (e) covered bonds;
   (f) structured finance arrangements, including securitisations and instruments used for hedging purposes which form an integral part of the cover pool and which according to national law are secured in a way similar to the covered bonds, which involve the granting and holding of security by a party to the arrangement or a trustee, agent or nominee.

The form of protection that is appropriate, for the classes of arrangements specified in points (a) to (f) of this paragraph is further specified in Articles 77 to 80, and shall be subject to the restrictions specified in Articles 68 to 71.

3. The requirement under paragraph 2 applies irrespective of the number of parties involved in the arrangements and of whether the arrangements:
   (a) are created by contract, trusts or other means, or arise automatically by operation of law;
   (b) arise under or are governed in whole or in part by the law of another Member State or of a third country.
4. The Commission shall adopt delegated acts in accordance with Article 115 further specifying the classes of arrangement that fall within the scope of points (a) to (f) of paragraph 2 of this Article.

[3.495]
Article 77
Protection for financial collateral, set off and netting agreements

1. Member States shall ensure that there is appropriate protection for title transfer financial collateral arrangements and set-off and netting arrangements so as to prevent the transfer of some, but not all, of the rights and liabilities that are protected under a title transfer financial collateral arrangement, a set-off arrangement or a netting arrangement between the institution under resolution and another person and the modification or termination of rights and liabilities that are protected under such a title transfer financial collateral arrangement, a set-off arrangement or a netting arrangement through the use of ancillary powers.

For the purposes of the first subparagraph, rights and liabilities are to be treated as protected under such an arrangement if the parties to the arrangement are entitled to set-off or net those rights and liabilities.

2. Notwithstanding paragraph 1, where necessary in order to ensure availability of the covered deposits the resolution authority may:

(a) transfer covered deposits which are part of any of the arrangements mentioned in paragraph 1 without transferring other assets, rights or liabilities that are part of the same arrangement; and

(b) transfer, modify or terminate those assets, rights or liabilities without transferring the covered deposits.

[3.496]
Article 78
Protection for security arrangements

1. Member States shall ensure that there is appropriate protection for liabilities secured under a security arrangement so as to prevent one of the following:

(a) the transfer of assets against which the liability is secured unless that liability and benefit of the security are also transferred;

(b) the transfer of a secured liability unless the benefit of the security are also transferred;

(c) the transfer of the benefit of the security unless the secured liability is also transferred; or

(d) the modification or termination of a security arrangement through the use of ancillary powers, if the effect of that modification or termination is that the liability ceases to be secured.

2. Notwithstanding paragraph 1, where necessary in order to ensure availability of the covered deposits the resolution authority may:

(a) transfer covered deposits which are part of any of the arrangements mentioned in paragraph 1 without transferring other assets, rights or liabilities that are part of the same arrangement; and

(b) transfer, modify or terminate those assets, rights or liabilities without transferring the covered deposits

[3.497]
Article 79
Protection for structured finance arrangements and covered bonds

1. Member States shall ensure that there is appropriate protection for structured finance arrangements including arrangements referred to in points (e) and (f) of Article 76(2) so as to prevent either of the following:

(a) the transfer of some, but not all, of the assets, rights and liabilities which constitute or form part of a structured finance arrangement, including arrangements referred to in points (e) and (f) of Article 76(2), to which the institution under resolution is a party;

(b) the termination or modification through the use of ancillary powers of the assets, rights and liabilities which constitute or form part of a structured finance arrangement, including arrangements referred to in points (e) and (f) of Article 76(2), to which the institution under resolution is a party.

2. Notwithstanding paragraph 1, where necessary in order to ensure availability of the covered deposits the resolution authority may:

(a) transfer covered deposits which are part of any of the arrangements mentioned in paragraph 1 without transferring other assets, rights or liabilities that are part of the same arrangement, and

(b) transfer, modify or terminate those assets, rights or liabilities without transferring the covered deposits.

[3.498]
Article 80
Partial transfers: protection of trading, clearing and settlement systems

1. Member States shall ensure that the application of a resolution tool does not affect the operation of systems and rules of systems covered by Directive 98/26/EC, where the resolution authority:

(a) transfers some but not all of the assets, rights or liabilities of an institution under resolution to another entity; or

(b) uses powers under Article 64 to cancel or amend the terms of a contract to which the institution under resolution is a party or to substitute a recipient as a party.

2. In particular, a transfer, cancellation or amendment as referred to in paragraph 1 of this Article shall not revoke a transfer order in contravention of Article 5 of Directive 98/26/EC; and shall not modify or negate the enforceability of transfer orders and netting as required by Articles 3 and 5 of that Directive, the use of funds, securities or credit facilities as required by Article 4 thereof or protection of collateral security as required by Article 9 thereof.

CHAPTER VIII PROCEDURAL OBLIGATIONS

[3.499]
Article 81
Notification requirements

1. Member States shall require the management body of an institution or any entity referred to in point (b), (c) or (d) of Article 1(1) to notify the competent authority where they consider that the institution or the entity referred to in point (b), (c) or (d) of Article 1(1) is failing or likely to fail, within the meaning specified in Article 32(4).
2. Competent authorities shall inform the relevant resolution authorities of any notifications received under paragraph 1 of this Article, and of any crisis prevention measures, or any actions referred to in Article 104 of Directive 2013/36/EU they require an institution or an entity referred to in point (b), (c) or (d) of Article 1(1) of this Directive to take.
3. Where a competent authority or resolution authority determines that the conditions referred to in points (a) and (b) of Article 32(1) are met in relation to an institution or an entity referred to in point (b), (c) or (d) of Article 1(1), it shall communicate that determination without delay to the following authorities, if different:
   (a) the resolution authority for that institution or entity referred to in point (b), (c) or (d) of Article 1(1);
   (b) the competent authority for that institution or entity referred to in point (b), (c) or (d) of Article 1(1);
   (c) the competent authority of any branch of that institution or entity referred to in point (b), (c) or (d) of Article 1(1);
   (d) the resolution authority of any branch of that institution or entity referred to in point (b), (c) or (d) of Article 1, (1)
   (e) the central bank;
   (f) the deposit guarantee scheme to which a credit institution is affiliated where necessary to enable the functions of the deposit guarantee scheme to be discharged;
   (g) the body in charge of the resolution financing arrangements where necessary to enable the functions of the resolution financing arrangements to be discharged;
   (h) where applicable, the group-level resolution authority;
   (i) the competent ministry;
   (j) where the institution or the entity referred to in point (b), (c) or (d) of Article 1(1) of this Directive is subject to supervision on consolidated basis under Chapter 3 of Title VII of Directive 2013/36/EU, the consolidating supervisor; and
   (k) the ESRB and the designated national macro-prudential authority.
4. Where the transmission of information referred to in paragraphs 3(f) and 3(g) does not guarantee the appropriate level of confidentiality, the competent authority or resolution authority shall establish alternative communication procedures that achieve the same objectives while ensuring the appropriate level of confidentiality.

[3.500]
Article 82
Decision of the resolution authority

1. On receiving a communication from the competent authority pursuant to paragraph 3 of Article 81, or on its own initiative, the resolution authority shall determine, in accordance with Article 32(1) and Article 33, whether the conditions of that paragraph are met in respect of the institution or the entity referred to in point (b), (c) or (d) of Article 1(1) in question.
2. A decision whether or not to take resolution action in relation to an institution or an entity referred to in point (b), (c) or (d) of Article 1(1) shall contain the following information:
   (a) the reasons for that decision, including the determination that the institution meets or does not meet the conditions for resolution;
   (b) the action that the resolution authority intends to take including, where appropriate, the determination to apply for winding up, the appointment of an administrator or any other measure under applicable normal insolvency proceedings or, subject to Article 37(9), under national law.
3. EBA shall develop draft regulatory technical standards in order to specify the procedures and contents relating to the following requirements:
   (a) the notifications referred to in Article 81(1), (2) and (3);
   (b) the notice of suspension referred to in Article 83.

EBA shall submit those draft regulatory technical standards to the Commission by 3 July 2015.

Power is delegated to the Commission to adopt the regulatory technical standards referred to in the first subparagraph in accordance with Articles 10 to 14 of Regulation (EU) No 1093/2010.

[3.501]
Article 83
Procedural obligations of resolution authorities

1. Member States shall ensure that, as soon as reasonably practicable after taking a resolution action, resolution authorities comply with the requirements laid down in paragraphs 2, 3 and 4.
2. The resolution authority shall notify the institution under resolution and the following authorities, if different:
   (a) the competent authority for the institution under resolution;
   (b) the competent authority of any branch of the institution under resolution;
   (c) the central bank;

(d) the deposit guarantee scheme to which the credit institution under resolution is affiliated;
(e) the body in charge of the resolution financing arrangements;
(f) where applicable, the group-level resolution authority;
(g) the competent ministry;
(h) where the institution under resolution is subject to supervision on a consolidated basis under Chapter 3 of Title VII of Directive 2013/36/EU, the consolidating supervisor;
(i) the designated national macroprudential authority and the ESRB;
(j) the Commission, the European Central Bank, ESMA, the European Supervisory Authority (European Investment and Occupational Pensions Authority) ('EIOPA') established by Regulation (EU) No 1094/2010 and EBA;
(k) where the institution under resolution is an institution as defined in Article 2(b) of Directive 98/26/EC, the operators of the systems in which it participates.

3. The notification referred to in paragraph 2 shall include a copy of any order or instrument by which the relevant powers are exercised and indicate the date from which the resolution action or actions are effective.

4. The resolution authority shall publish or ensure the publication of a copy of the order or instrument by which the resolution action is taken, or a notice summarising the effects of the resolution action, and in particular the effects on retail customers and, if applicable, the terms and period of suspension or restriction referred to in Articles 69, 70 and 71, by the following means:
(a) on its official website;
(b) on the website of the competent authority, if different from the resolution authority, and on the website of EBA;
(c) on the website of the institution under resolution;
(d) where the shares, other instruments of ownership or debt instruments of the institution under resolution are admitted to trading on a regulated market, the means used for the disclosure of regulated information concerning the institution under resolution in accordance with Article 21(1) of Directive 2004/109/EC of the European Parliament and of the Council.[1]

5. If the shares, instruments of ownership or debt instruments are not admitted to trading on a regulated market, the resolution authority shall ensure that the documents providing proof of the instruments referred to in paragraph 4 are sent to the shareholders and creditors of the institution under resolution that are known through the registers or databases of the institution under resolution which are available to the resolution authority.

NOTES

[1] Directive 2004/109/EC of the European Parliament and of the Council of 15 December 2004 on the harmonisation of transparency requirements in relation to information about issuers whose securities are admitted to trading on a regulated market and amending Directive 2001/34/EC (OJ L390, 31.12.2004, p 38).

[3.502]
Article 84
Confidentiality

1. The requirements of professional secrecy shall be binding in respect of the following persons:
(a) resolution authorities;
(b) competent authorities and EBA;
(c) competent ministries;
(d) special managers or temporary administrators appointed under this Directive;
(e) potential acquirers that are contacted by the competent authorities or solicited by the resolution authorities, irrespective of whether that contact or solicitation was made as preparation for the use of the sale of business tool, and irrespective of whether the solicitation resulted in an acquisition;
(f) auditors, accountants, legal and professional advisors, valuers and other experts directly or indirectly engaged by the resolution authorities, competent authorities, competent ministries or by the potential acquirers referred to in point (e);
(g) bodies which administer deposit guarantee schemes;
(h) bodies which administer investor compensation schemes;
(i) the body in charge of the resolution financing arrangements;
(j) central banks and other authorities involved in the resolution process;
(k) a bridge institution or an asset management vehicle;
(l) any other persons who provide or have provided services directly or indirectly, permanently or occasionally, to persons referred to in points (a) to (k);
(m) senior management, members of the management body, and employees of the bodies or entities referred to in points (a) to (k) before, during and after their appointment.

2. With a view to ensuring that the confidentiality requirements laid down in paragraphs 1 and 3 are complied with, the persons in points (a), (b), (c), (g), (h), (j) and (k) of paragraph 1 shall ensure that there are internal rules in place, including rules to secure secrecy of information between persons directly involved in the resolution process.

3. Without prejudice to the generality of the requirements under paragraph 1, the persons referred to in that paragraph shall be prohibited from disclosing confidential information received during the course of their professional activities or from a competent authority or resolution authority in connection with its functions under this Directive, to any person or authority unless it is in the exercise of their functions

under this Directive or in summary or collective form such that individual institutions or entities referred to in point (b), (c) or (d) of Article 1(1) cannot be identified or with the express and prior consent of the authority or the institution or the entity referred to in point (b), (c) or (d) of Article 1(1) which provided the information.

Member States shall ensure that no confidential information is disclosed by the persons referred to in paragraph 1 and that the possible effects of disclosing information on the public interest as regards financial, monetary or economic policy, on the commercial interests of natural and legal persons, on the purpose of inspections, on investigations and on audits, are assessed.

The procedure for checking the effects of disclosing information shall include a specific assessment of the effects of any disclosure of the contents and details of recovery and resolution plan as referred to in Articles 5, 7, 10, 11 and 12 and the result of any assessment carried out under Articles 6, 8 and 15.

Any person or entity referred to in paragraph 1 shall be subject to civil liability in the event of an infringement of this Article, in accordance with national law.

4. This Article shall not prevent:

(a) employees and experts of the bodies or entities referred to in points (a) to (j) of paragraph 1 from sharing information among themselves within each body or entity; or

(b) resolution authorities and competent authorities, including their employees and experts, from sharing information with each other and with other Union resolution authorities, other Union competent authorities, competent ministries, central banks, deposit guarantee schemes, investor compensation schemes, authorities responsible for normal insolvency proceedings, authorities responsible for maintaining the stability of the financial system in Member States through the use of macroprudential rules, persons charged with carrying out statutory audits of accounts, EBA, or, subject to Article 98, third-country authorities that carry out equivalent functions to resolution authorities, or, subject to strict confidentiality requirements, to a potential acquirer for the purposes of planning or carrying out a resolution action.

5. Notwithstanding any other provision of this Article, Member States may authorise the exchange of information with any of the following:

(a) subject to strict confidentiality requirements, any other person where necessary for the purposes of planning or carrying out a resolution action;

(b) parliamentary enquiry committees in their Member State, courts of auditors in their Member State and other entities in charge of enquiries in their Member State, under appropriate conditions; andEN

(c) national authorities responsible for overseeing payment systems, the authorities responsible for normal insolvency proceedings, the authorities entrusted with the public duty of supervising other financial sector entities, the authorities responsible for the supervision of financial markets and insurance undertakings and inspectors acting on their behalf, the authorities of Member States responsible for maintaining the stability of the financial system in Member States through the use of macroprudential rules, the authorities responsible for protecting the stability of the financial system, and persons charged carrying out statutory audits;

6. This Article shall be without prejudice to national law concerning the disclosure of information for the purpose of legal proceedings in criminal or civil cases.

7. EBA shall, by 3 July 2015, issue guidelines in accordance with Article 16 of Regulation (EU) No 1093/2010 to specify how information should be provided in summary or collective form for the purposes of paragraph 3.

CHAPTER IX RIGHT OF APPEAL AND EXCLUSION OF OTHER ACTIONS

[3.503]
Article 85
Ex-ante judicial approval and rights to challenge decisions

1. Member States may require that a decision to take a crisis prevention measure or a crisis management measure is subject to *ex-ante* judicial approval, provided that in respect of a decision to take a crisis management measure, according to national law, the procedure relating to the application for approval and the court's consideration are expeditious.

2. Member States shall provide in national law for a right of appeal against a decision to take a crisis prevention measure or a decision to exercise any power, other than a crisis management measure, under this Directive.

3. Member States shall ensure that all persons affected by a decision to take a crisis management measure, have the right to appeal against that decision. Member States shall ensure that the review is expeditious and that national courts use the complex economic assessments of the facts carried out by the resolution authority as a basis for their own assessment.

4. The right to appeal referred to in paragraph 3 shall be subject to the following provisions:

(a) the lodging of an appeal shall not entail any automatic suspension of the effects of the challenged decision;

(b) the decision of the resolution authority shall be immediately enforceable and it shall give rise to a rebuttable presumption that a suspension of its enforcement would be against the public interest.

Where it is necessary to protect the interests of third parties acting in good faith who have acquired shares, other instruments of ownership, assets, rights or liabilities of an institution under resolution by virtue of the use of resolution tools or exercise of resolution powers by a resolution authority, the annulment of a decision of a resolution authority shall not affect any subsequent administrative acts or transactions concluded by the resolution authority concerned which were based on the annulled decision. In that case, remedies for a wrongful decision or action by the resolution authorities shall be limited to compensation for the loss suffered by the applicant as a result of the decision or act.

[3.504]
Article 86
Restrictions on other proceedings

1. Without prejudice to point (b) of Article 82(2), Member States shall ensure with respect to an institution under resolution or an institution or an entity referred to in point (b), (c) or (d) of Article 1(1) in relation to which the conditions for resolution have been determined to be met, that normal insolvency proceedings shall not be commenced except at the initiative of the resolution authority and that a decision placing an institution or an entity referred to in point (b), (c) or (d) of Article 1(1) into normal insolvency proceedings shall be taken only with the consent of the resolution authority.
2. For the purposes of paragraph 1, Member States shall ensure that:
   (a) competent authorities and resolution authorities are notified without delay of any application for the opening of normal insolvency proceedings in relation to an institution or an entity referred to in point (b), (c) or (d) of Article 1(1), irrespective of whether the institution or the entity referred to in point (b), (c) or (d) of Article 1(1) is under resolution or a decision has been made public in accordance with Article 83(4) and (5);
   (b) the application is not determined unless the notifications referred to in point (a) have been made and either of the following occurs:
      (i) the resolution authority has notified the authorities responsible for normal insolvency proceedings that it does not intend to take any resolution action in relation to the institution or the entity referred to in point (b), (c) or (d) of Article 1(1);
      (ii) a period of seven days beginning with the date on which the notifications referred to in point (a) were made has expired.
3. Without prejudice to any restriction on the enforcement of security interests imposed pursuant to Article 70, Member States shall ensure that, if necessary for the effective application of the resolution tools and powers, resolution authorities may request the court to apply a stay for an appropriate period of time in accordance with the objective pursued, on any judicial action or proceeding in which an institution under resolution is or becomes a party.

TITLE V CROSS-BORDER GROUP RESOLUTION

[3.505]
Article 87
General principles regarding decision-making involving more than one Member State

Member States shall ensure that, when making decisions or taking action pursuant to this Directive which may have an impact in one or more other Member States, their authorities have regard to the following general principles:
   (a) the imperatives of efficacy of decision-making and of keeping resolution costs as low as possible when taking resolution action;
   (b) that decisions are made and action is taken in a timely manner and with due urgency when required;
   (c) that resolution authorities, competent authorities and other authorities cooperate with each other to ensure that decisions are made and action is taken in a coordinated and efficient manner;
   (d) that the roles and responsibilities of relevant authorities within each Member State are e defined clearly;
   (e) that due consideration is given to the interests of the Member States where the Union parent undertakings are established, in particular the impact of any decision or action or inaction on the financial stability, fiscal resources, resolution fund, deposit guarantee scheme or investor compensation scheme of those Member States;
   (f) that due consideration is given to the interests of each individual Member State where a subsidiary is established, in particular the impact of any decision or action or inaction on the financial stability, fiscal resources, resolution fund, deposit guarantee scheme or investor compensation scheme of those Member States;
   (g) that due consideration is given to the interests of each Member State where significant branches are located, in particular the impact of any decision or action or inaction on the financial stability of those Member States;
   (h) that due consideration is given to the objectives of balancing the interests of the various Member States involved and of avoiding unfairly prejudicing or unfairly protecting the interests of particular Member States, including avoiding unfair burden allocation across Member States;
   (i) that any obligation under this Directive to consult an authority before any decision or action is taken implies at least that such an obligation to consult that authority on those elements of the proposed decision or action which have or which are likely to have:
      (i) an effect on the Union parent undertaking, the subsidiary or the branch,; and
      (ii) an impact on the stability of the Member State where the Union parent undertaking, the subsidiary or the branch, is established or located;
   (j) that resolution authorities, when taking resolution actions, take into account and follow the resolution plans referred to in Article 13 unless the resolution authorities consider, taking into account the circumstances of the case, that the resolution objectives will be achieved more effectively by taking actions which are not provided for in the resolution plans;
   (k) that the requirement for transparency whenever a proposed decision or action is likely to have implications on the financial stability, fiscal resources, resolution fund, deposit guarantee scheme or investor compensation scheme of any relevant Member State; and

(l) recognition that coordination and cooperation are most likely to achieve a result which lowers the overall cost of resolution.

[3.506]
Article 88
Resolution colleges

1. Group-level resolution authorities shall establish resolution colleges to carry out the tasks referred to in Articles 12, 13, 16, 18, 45, 91 and 92, and, where appropriate, to ensure cooperation and coordination with third-country resolution authorities.

In particular, resolution colleges shall provide a framework for the group-level resolution authority, the other resolution authorities and, where appropriate, competent authorities and consolidating supervisors concerned to perform the following tasks:

(a) exchanging information relevant for the development of group resolution plans, for the application to groups of preparatory and preventative powers and for group resolution;
(b) developing group resolution plans pursuant to Articles 12 and 13;
(c) assessing the resolvability of groups pursuant to Article 16;
(d) exercising powers to address or remove impediments to the resolvability of groups pursuant to Article 18;
(e) deciding on the need to establish a group resolution scheme as referred to in Article 91 or 92;
(f) reaching the agreement on a group resolution scheme proposed in accordance with Article 91 or 92;
(g) coordinating public communication of group resolution strategies and schemes;
(h) coordinating the use of financing arrangements established under Title VII;
(i) setting the minimum requirements for groups at consolidated and subsidiary level under Article 45.

In addition, resolution colleges may be used as a forum to discuss any issues relating to cross-border group resolution.

2. The following shall be members of the resolution college:

(a) the group-level resolution authority;
(b) the resolution authorities of each Member State in which a subsidiary covered by consolidated supervision is established;
(c) the resolution authorities of Member States where a parent undertaking of one or more institutions of the group, that is an entity referred to in point (d) of Article 1(1), are established;
(d) the resolution authorities of Member States in which significant branches are located;
(e) the consolidating supervisor and the competent authorities of the Member States where the resolution authority is a member of the resolution college. Where the competent authority of a Member State is not the Member State's central bank, the competent authority may decide to be accompanied by a representative from the Member State's central bank;
(f) the competent ministries, where the resolution authorities which are members of the resolution college are not the competent ministries;
(g) the authority that is responsible for the deposit guarantee scheme of a Member State, where the resolution authority of that Member State is a member of a resolution college;
(h) EBA, subject to paragraph 4.

3. The resolution authorities of third countries where a parent undertaking or an institution established in the Union has a subsidiary institution or a branch that would be considered to be significant were it located in the Union may, at their request, be invited to participate in the resolution college as observers, provided that they are subject to confidentiality requirements equivalent, in the opinion of the group-level resolution authority, to those established by Article 98.

4. EBA shall contribute to promoting and monitoring the efficient, effective and consistent functioning of resolution colleges, taking into account international standards. EBA shall be invited to attend the meetings of the resolution college for that purpose. EBA shall not have any voting rights to the extent that any voting takes place within the framework of resolution colleges.

5. The group-level resolution authority shall be the chair of the resolution college. In that capacity it shall:

(a) establish written arrangements and procedures for the functioning of the resolution college, after consulting the other members of the resolution college;
(b) coordinate all activities of the resolution college;
(c) convene and chair all its meetings and keep all members of the resolution college fully informed in advance of the organisation of meetings of the resolution college, of the main issues to be discussed and of the items to be considered;
(d) notify the members of the resolution college of any planned meetings so that they can request to participate;
(e) decide which members and observers shall be invited to attend particular meetings of the resolution college, on the basis of specific needs, taking into account the relevance of the issue to be discussed for those members and observers, in particular the potential impact on financial stability in the Member States concerned;
(f) keep all of the members of the college informed, in a timely manner, of the decisions and outcomes of those meetings.

The members participating in the resolution college shall cooperate closely.

Notwithstanding point (e), resolution authorities shall be entitled to participate in resolution college meetings whenever matters subject to joint decision-making or relating to a group entity located in their Member State are on the agenda.

6. Group-level resolution authorities are not obliged to establish a resolution college if other groups or colleges perform the same functions and carry out the same tasks specified in this Article and comply with all the conditions and procedures, including those covering membership and participation in resolution colleges, established in this Article and in Article 90. In such a case, all references to resolution colleges in this Directive shall also be understood as references to those other groups or colleges.
7. EBA shall, taking into account international standards, develop draft regulatory standards in order to specify the operational functioning of the resolution colleges for the performance of the tasks referred to in paragraph 1.
EBA shall submit those draft regulatory technical standards to the Commission by 3 July 2015.
Power is delegated to the Commission to adopt the regulatory standards referred to in the first subparagraph in accordance with Articles 10 to 14 of Regulation (EU) No 1093/2010.

[3.507]
Article 89
European resolution colleges

1. Where a third country institution or third country parent undertaking has Union subsidiaries established in two or more Member States, or two or more Union branches that are regarded as significant by two or more Member States, the resolution authorities of Member States where those Union subsidiaries are established or where those significant branches are located shall establish a European resolution college.
2. The European resolution college shall perform the functions and carry out the tasks specified in Article 88 with respect to the subsidiary institutions and, in so far as those tasks are relevant, to branches.
3. Where the Union subsidiaries are held by, or the significant branches are of, a financial holding company established within the Union in accordance with the third subparagraph of Article 127(3) of Directive 2013/36/EU, the European resolution college shall be chaired by the resolution authority of the Member State where the consolidating supervisor is located for the purposes of consolidated supervision under that Directive.
Where the first subparagraph does not apply, the members of the European resolution college shall nominate and agree the chair.
4. Member States may, by mutual agreement of all the relevant parties, waive the requirement to establish a European resolution college if other groups or colleges, including a resolution college established under Article 88, perform the same functions and carry out the same tasks specified in this Article and comply with all the conditions and procedures, including those covering membership and participation in European resolution colleges, established in this Article and in Article 90. In such a case, all references to European resolution colleges in this Directive shall also be understood as references to those other groups or colleges.
5. Subject to paragraphs 3 and 4 of this Article, the European resolution college shall otherwise function in accordance with Article 88.

[3.508]
Article 90
Information exchange

1. Subject to Article 84, resolution authorities and competent authorities shall provide one another on request with all the information relevant for the exercise of the other authorities' tasks under this Directive.
2. The group-level resolution authority shall coordinate the flow of all relevant information between resolution authorities. In particular, the group-level resolution authority shall provide the resolution authorities in other Member States with all the relevant information in a timely manner with a view to facilitating the exercise of the tasks referred to in points (b) to (i) of the second subparagraph of Article 88(1).
3. Upon a request for information which has been provided by a third-country resolution authority, the resolution authority shall seek the consent of the third-country resolution authority for the onward transmission of that information, save where the third-country resolution authority has already consented to the onward transmission of that information.
Resolution authorities shall not be obliged to transmit information provided from a third-country resolution authority if the third-country resolution authority has not consented to its onward transmission.
4. Resolution authorities shall share information with the competent ministry when it relates to a decision or matter which requires notification, consultation or consent of the competent ministry or which may have implications for public funds.

[3.509]
Article 91
Group resolution involving a subsidiary of the group

1. Where a resolution authority decides that an institution or any entity referred to in point (b), (c) or (d) of Article 1(1) that is a subsidiary in a group meets the conditions referred to in Article 32 or 33, that authority shall notify the following information without delay to the group-level resolution authority, if different, to the consolidating supervisor, and to the members of the resolution college for the group in question:
(a) the decision that the institution or entity referred to in point (b), (c) or (d) of Article 1(1) meets the conditions referred to in Article 32 or 33;
(b) the resolution actions or insolvency measures that the resolution authority considers to be appropriate for that institution or that entity referred to in point (b), (c) or (d) of Article 1(1).

2. On receiving a notification under paragraph 1, the group-level resolution authority, after consulting the other members of the relevant resolution college, shall assess the likely impact of the resolution actions or other measures notified in accordance with point (b) of paragraph 1, on the group and on group entities in other Member States, and, in particular, whether the resolution actions or other measures would make it likely that the conditions for resolution would be satisfied in relation to a group entity in another Member State.

3. If the group-level resolution authority, after consulting the other members of the resolution college, assesses that the resolution actions or other measures notified in accordance with point (b) of paragraph 1, would not make it likely that the conditions laid down in Article 32 or 33 would be satisfied in relation to a group entity in another Member State, the resolution authority responsible for that institution or that entity referred to in point (b), (c) or (d) of Article 1(1) may take the resolution actions or other measures that it notified in accordance with point (b) of paragraph 1 of this Article.

4. If the group-level resolution authority, after consulting the other members of the resolution college, assesses that the resolution actions or other measures notified in accordance with point (b) of paragraph 1 of this Article, would make it likely that the conditions laid down in Article 32 or 33 would be satisfied in relation to a group entity in another Member State, the group-level resolution authority shall, no later than 24 hours after receiving the notification under paragraph 1, propose a group resolution scheme and submit it to the resolution college. That 24-hour period may be extended with the consent of the resolution authority which made the notification referred to in paragraph 1 of this Article.

5. In the absence of an assessment by the group-level resolution authority within 24 hours, or a longer period that has been agreed, after receiving the notification under paragraph 1, the resolution authority which made the notification referred to in paragraph 1 may take the resolution actions or other measures that it notified in accordance with point (b) of that paragraph.

6. A group resolution scheme required under paragraph 4 shall:
   (a) take into account and follow the resolution plans as referred to in Article 13 unless resolution authorities assess, taking into account circumstances of the case, that resolution objectives will be achieved more effectively by taking actions which are not provided for in the resolution plans;
   (b) outline the resolution actions that should be taken by the relevant resolution authorities in relation to the Union parent undertaking or particular group entities with the aim of meeting the resolution objectives and principles referred to in Articles 31 and 34;
   (c) specify how those resolution actions should be coordinated;
   (d) establish a financing plan which takes into account the group resolution plan, principles for sharing responsibility as established in accordance with point (f) of Article 12(3) and the mutualisation as referred to in Article 107.

7. Subject to paragraph 8, the group resolution scheme shall take the form of a joint decision of the group-level resolution authority and the resolution authorities responsible for the subsidiaries that are covered by the group resolution scheme.

EBA may, at the request of a resolution authority, assist the resolution authorities in reaching a joint decision in accordance with Article 31(c) of Regulation (EU) No 1093/2010.

8. If any resolution authority disagrees with or departs from the group resolution scheme proposed by the group-level resolution authority or considers that it needs to take independent resolution actions or measures other than those proposed in the scheme in relation to an institution or an entity referred to in point (b), (c) or (d) of Article 1(1) for reasons of financial stability, it shall set out in detail the reasons for the disagreement or the reasons to depart from the group resolution scheme, notify the group-level resolution authority and the other resolution authorities that are covered by the group resolution scheme of the reasons and inform them about the actions or measures it will take. When setting out the reasons for its disagreement, that resolution authority shall take into consideration the resolution plans as referred to in Article 13, the potential impact on financial stability in the Member States concerned as well as the potential effect of the actions or measures on other parts of the group.

9. The resolution authorities which did not disagree under paragraph 8 may reach a joint decision on a group resolution scheme covering group entities in their Member State.

10. The joint decision referred to in paragraph 7 or 9 and the decisions taken by the resolution authorities in the absence of a joint decision referred to in paragraph 8 shall be recognised as conclusive and applied by the resolution authorities in the Member States concerned.

11. Authorities shall perform all actions under this Article without delay, and with due regard to the urgency of the situation.

12. In any case where a group resolution scheme is not implemented and resolution authorities take resolution actions in relation to any group entity, those resolution authorities shall cooperate closely within the resolution college with a view to achieving a coordinated resolution strategy for all the group entities that are failing or likely to fail.

13. Resolution authorities that take any resolution action in relation to any group entity shall inform the members of the resolution college regularly and fully about those actions or measures and their on-going progress.

[3.510]
Article 92
Group resolution

1. Where a group-level resolution authority decides that a Union parent undertaking for which it is responsible meets the conditions referred to in Article 32 or 33 it shall notify the information referred to in points (a) and (b) of Article 91(1) without delay to the consolidating supervisor, if different, and to the other members of the resolution college of the group in question.

The resolution actions or insolvency measures for the purposes of point (b) of Article 91(1) may include the implementation of a group resolution scheme drawn up in accordance with Article 91(6) in any of the following circumstances:

(a) resolution actions or other measures at parent level notified in accordance with point (b) of Article 91(1) make it likely that the conditions laid down in Article 32 or 33 would be fulfilled in relation to a group entity in another Member State;

(b) resolution actions or other measures at parent level only are not sufficient to stabilise the situation or are not likely to provide an optimum outcome;

(c) one or more subsidiaries meet the conditions referred to in Article 32 or 33 according to a determination by the resolution authorities responsible for those subsidiaries; or

(d) resolution actions or other measures at group level will benefit the subsidiaries of the group in a way which makes a group resolution scheme appropriate.

2. Where the actions proposed by the group-level resolution authority under paragraph 1 do not include a group resolution scheme, the group-level resolution authority shall take its decision after consulting the members of the resolution college.

The decision of the group-level resolution authority shall take into account:

(a) and follow the resolution plans as referred to in Article 13 unless resolution authorities assess, taking into account circumstances of the case, that resolution objectives will be achieved more effectively by taking actions which are not provided for in the resolution plans;

(b) the financial stability of the Member States concerned.

3. Where the actions proposed by the group-level resolution authority under paragraph 1 include a group resolution scheme, the group resolution scheme shall take the form of a joint decision of the group-level resolution authority and the resolution authorities responsible for the subsidiaries that are covered by the group resolution scheme.

EBA may, at the request of a resolution authority, assist the resolution authorities in reaching a joint decision in accordance with Article 31(c) of Regulation (EU) No 1093/2010.

4. If any resolution authority disagrees with or departs from the group resolution scheme proposed by the group-level resolution authority or considers that it needs to take independent resolution actions or measures other than those proposed in the scheme in relation to an institution or entity referred to in point (b), (c) or (d) of Article 1(1) for reasons of financial stability, it shall set out in detail the reasons for the disagreement or the reasons to depart from the group resolution scheme, notify the group-level resolution authority and the other resolution authorities that are covered by the group resolution scheme of the reasons and inform them about the actions or measures it intends to take. When setting out the reasons for its disagreement, that resolution authority shall give consideration to the resolution plans as referred to in Article 13, the potential impact on financial stability in the Member States concerned as well as the potential effect of the actions or measures on other parts of the group.

5. Resolution authorities which did not disagree with the group resolution scheme under the paragraph 4 may reach a joint decision on a group resolution scheme covering group entities in their Member State.

6. The joint decision referred to in paragraph 3 or 5 and the decisions taken by the resolution authorities in the absence of a joint decision referred to in paragraph 4 shall be recognised as conclusive and applied by the resolution authorities in the Member States concerned.

7. Authorities shall perform all actions under this Article without delay, and with due regard to the urgency of the situation.

In any case where a group resolution scheme is not implemented and resolution authorities take resolution action in relation to any group entity, those resolution authorities shall cooperate closely within the resolution college with a view to achieving a coordinated resolution strategy for all affected group entities.

Resolution authorities that take resolution action in relation to any group entity shall inform the members of the resolution college regularly and fully about those actions or measures and their on-going progress.

TITLE VI RELATIONS WITH THIRD COUNTRIES

[3.511]
Article 93
Agreements with third countries

1. In accordance with Article 218 TFEU, the Commission may submit to the Council proposals for the negotiation of agreements with one or more third countries regarding the means of cooperation between the resolution authorities and the relevant third country authorities, inter alia, for the purpose of information sharing in connection with recovery and resolution planning in relation to institutions, financial institutions, parent undertakings and third country institutions, with regard to the following situations:

(a) in cases where a third country parent undertaking has subsidiary institutions or branches where such branches are regarded as significant in two or more Member States;

(b) in cases where a parent undertaking established in a Member State and which has a subsidiary or a significant branch in at least one other Member State has one or more third country subsidiary institutions;

(c) in cases where an institution established in a Member State and which has a parent undertaking, a subsidiary or a significant branch in at least one other Member State has one or more branches in one or more third countries.

2. The agreements referred to in paragraph 1 shall, in particular, seek to ensure the establishment of processes and arrangements between resolution authorities and the relevant third country authorities for cooperation in carrying out some or all of the tasks and exercising some or all of the powers indicated in Article 97.

3. The agreements referred to in paragraph 1 shall not make provision in relation to individual institutions, financial institutions, parent undertakings or third country institutions.
4. Member States may enter into bilateral agreements with a third country regarding the matters referred to in paragraphs 1 and 2 until the entry into force of an agreement referred to in paragraph 1 with the relevant third country to the extent that such bilateral agreements are not inconsistent with this Title.

[3.512]
Article 94
Recognition and enforcement of third-country resolution proceedings
1. This Article shall apply in respect of third-country resolution proceedings unless and until an international agreement as referred to in Article 93(1) enters into force with the relevant third country. It shall also apply following the entry into force of an international agreement as referred to in Article 93(1) with the relevant third country to the extent that recognition and enforcement of third-country resolution proceedings is not governed by that agreement.
2. Where there is a European resolution college established in accordance with Article 89, it shall take a joint decision on whether to recognise, except as provided for in Article 95, third-country resolution proceedings relating to a third-country institution or a parent undertaking that:
(a) has Union subsidiaries established in, or Union branches located in and regarded as significant by, two or more Member States; or
(b) has assets, rights or liabilities located in two or more Member States or are governed by the law of those Member States.

Where the joint decision on the recognition of the third-country resolution proceedings is reached, respective national resolution authorities shall seek the enforcement of the recognised third-country resolution proceedings in accordance with their national law.
3. In the absence of a joint decision between the resolution authorities participating in the European resolution college, or in the absence of a European resolution college, each resolution authority concerned shall make its own decision on whether to recognise and enforce, except as provided for in Article 95, third-country resolution proceedings relating to a third-country institution or a parent undertaking.
The decision shall give due consideration to the interests of each individual Member State where a third-country institution or parent undertaking operates, and in particular to the potential impact of the recognition and enforcement of the third-country resolution proceedings on the other parts of the group and the financial stability in those Member States.
4. Member States shall ensure that resolution authorities are, as a minimum, empowered to do the following:
(a) exercise the resolution powers in relation to the following:
(i) assets of a third-country institution or parent undertaking that are located in their Member State or governed by the law of their Member State;
(ii) rights or liabilities of a third-country institution that are booked by the Union branch in their Member State or governed by the law of their Member State, or where claims in relation to such rights and liabilities are enforceable in their Member State;
(b) perfect, including to require another person to take action to perfect, a transfer of shares or other instruments of ownership in a Union subsidiary established in the designating Member State;
(c) exercise the powers in Article 69, 70 or 71 in relation to the rights of any party to a contract with an entity referred to in paragraph 2 of this Article, where such powers are necessary in order to enforce third-country resolution proceedings; and
(d) render unenforceable any right to terminate, liquidate or accelerate contracts, or affect the contractual rights, of entities referred to in paragraph 2 and other group entities, where such a right arises from resolution action taken in respect of the third-country institution, parent undertaking of such entities or other group entities, whether by the third-country resolution authority itself or otherwise pursuant to legal or regulatory requirements as to resolution arrangements in that country, provided that the substantive obligations under the contract, including payment and delivery obligations, and provision of collateral, continue to be performed.

5. Resolution authorities may take, where necessary in the public interest, resolution action with respect to a parent undertaking where the relevant third-country authority determines that an institution that is incorporated in that third country meets the conditions for resolution under the law of that third country. To that end, Member States shall ensure that resolution authorities are empowered to use any resolution power in respect of that parent undertaking, and Article 68 shall apply.
6. The recognition and enforcement of third-country resolution proceedings shall be without prejudice to any normal insolvency proceedings under national law applicable, where appropriate, in accordance with this Directive.

[3.513]
Article 95
Right to refuse recognition or enforcement of third-country resolution proceedings
The resolution authority, after consulting other resolution authorities, where a European resolution college is established under Article 89, may refuse to recognise or to enforce third-country resolution proceedings pursuant to Article 94(2) if it considers:
(a) that the third-country resolution proceedings would have adverse effects on financial stability in the Member State in which the resolution authority is based or that the proceedings would have adverse effects on financial stability in another Member State;
(b) that independent resolution action under Article 96 in relation to a Union branch is necessary to achieve one or more of the resolution objectives;

(c) that creditors, including in particular depositors located or payable in a Member State, would not receive the same treatment as third-country creditors and depositors with similar legal rights under the third-country home resolution proceedings;
(d) that recognition or enforcement of the third-country resolution proceedings would have material fiscal implications for the Member State; or
(e) that the effects of such recognition or enforcement would be contrary to the national law.

[3.514]
Article 96
Resolution of Union branches

1. Member States shall ensure that resolution authorities have the powers necessary to act in relation to a Union branch that is not subject to any third-country resolution proceedings or that is subject to third-country proceedings and one of the circumstances referred to in Article 95 applies.
Member States shall ensure that Article 68 applies to the exercise of such powers.
2. Member States shall ensure that the powers required in paragraph 1 may be exercised by resolution authorities where the resolution authority considers that action is necessary in the public interest and one or more of the following conditions is met:
(a) the Union branch no longer meets, or is likely not to meet, the conditions imposed by national law for its authorisation and operation within that Member State and there is no prospect that any private sector, supervisory or relevant third-country action would restore the branch to compliance or prevent failure in a reasonable timeframe;
(b) the third-country institution is, in the opinion of the resolution authority, unable or unwilling, or is likely to be unable, to pay its obligations to Union creditors, or obligations that have been created or booked through the branch, as they fall due and the resolution authority is satisfied that no third-country resolution proceedings or insolvency proceedings have been or will be initiated in relation to that third-country institution in a reasonable timeframe;
(c) the relevant third-country authority has initiated third-country resolution proceedings in relation to the third-country institution, or has notified to the resolution authority its intention to initiate such a proceeding.
3. Where a resolution authority takes an independent action in relation to a Union branch, it shall have regard to the resolution objectives and take the action in accordance with the following principles and requirements, insofar as they are relevant:
(a) the principles set out in Article 34;
(b) the requirements relating to the application of the resolution tools in Chapter III of Title IV.

[3.515]
Article 97
Cooperation with third-country authorities

1. This Article shall apply in respect of cooperation with a third country unless and until an international agreement as referred to in Article 93(1) enters into force with the relevant third country. It shall also apply following the entry into force of an international agreement provided for in Article 93(1) with the relevant third country to the extent that the subject matter of this Article is not governed by that agreement.
2. EBA may conclude non-binding framework cooperation arrangements with the following relevant third-country authorities:
(a) in cases where a Union subsidiary is established in two or more Member States, the relevant authorities of the third country where the parent undertaking or a company referred to in points (c) and (d) of Article 1(1) are established;
(b) in cases where a third-country institution operates Union branches in two or more Member States, the relevant authority of the third country where that institution is established;
(c) in cases where a parent undertaking or a company referred to in points (c) and (d) of Article 1(1) established in a Member State with a subsidiary institution or significant branch in another Member State also has one or more third-country subsidiary institutions, the relevant authorities of the third countries where those subsidiary institutions are established;
(d) in cases where an institution with a subsidiary institution or significant branch in another Member State has established one or more branches in one or more third countries, the relevant authorities of the third countries where those branches are located.

The arrangements referred to in this paragraph shall not make provision in relation to specific institutions. They shall not impose legal obligations upon Member States.
3. The framework cooperation agreements referred to in paragraph 2 shall establish processes and arrangements between the participating authorities for sharing information necessary for and cooperation in carrying out some or all or the following tasks and exercising some or all of the following powers in relation to institutions referred to in points (a) to (d) of paragraph 2 or groups including such institutions:
(a) the development of resolution plans in accordance with Articles 10 to 13 and similar requirements under the law of the relevant third countries;
(b) the assessment of the resolvability of such institutions and groups, in accordance with Articles 15 and 16 and similar requirements under the law of the relevant third countries;
(c) the application of powers to address or remove impediments to resolvability pursuant to Articles 17 and 18 and any similar powers under the law of the relevant third countries;
(d) the application of early intervention measures pursuant to Article 27 and similar powers under the law of the relevant third countries;
(e) the application of resolution tools and exercise of resolution powers and similar powers exercisable by the relevant third-country authorities.

4. Competent authorities or resolution authorities, where appropriate, shall conclude non-binding cooperation arrangements in line with EBA framework arrangement with the relevant third-country authorities indicated in paragraph 2.

This Article shall not prevent Member States or their competent authorities from concluding bilateral or multilateral arrangements with third countries, in accordance with Article 33 of Regulation (EU) No 1093/2010.

5. Cooperation arrangements concluded between resolution authorities of Member States and third countries in accordance with this Article may include provisions on the following matters:

(a) the exchange of information necessary for the preparation and maintenance of resolution plans;

(b) consultation and cooperation in the development of resolution plans, including principles for the exercise of powers under Articles 94 and 96 and similar powers under the law of the relevant third countries;

(c) the exchange of information necessary for the application of resolution tools and exercise of resolution powers and similar powers under the law of the relevant third countries;

(d) early warning to or consultation of parties to the cooperation arrangement before taking any significant action under this Directive or relevant third-country law affecting the institution or group to which the arrangement relates;

(e) the coordination of public communication in the case of joint resolution actions;

(f) procedures and arrangements for the exchange of information and cooperation under points (a) to (e), including, where appropriate, through the establishment and operation of crisis management groups.

6. Member States shall notify EBA of any cooperation arrangements that resolution authorities and competent authorities have concluded in accordance with this Article.

[3.516]
Article 98
Exchange of confidential information

1. Member States shall ensure that resolution authorities, competent authorities and competent ministries exchange confidential information, including recovery plans, with relevant third-country authorities only if the following conditions are met:

(a) those third-country authorities are subject to requirements and standards of professional secrecy at least considered to be equivalent, in the opinion of all the authorities concerned, to those imposed by Article 84.

In so far as the exchange of information relates to personal data, the handling and transmission of such personal data to third-country authorities shall be governed by the applicable Union and national data protection law.

(b) the information is necessary for the performance by the relevant third-country authorities of their resolution functions under national law that are comparable to those under this Directive and, subject to point (a) of this paragraph, is not used for any other purposes.

2. Where confidential information originates in another Member State, resolution authorities, competent authorities and competent ministries shall not disclose that information to relevant third-country authorities unless the following conditions are met:

(a) the relevant authority of the Member State where the information originated (the originating authority) agrees to that disclosure;

(b) the information is disclosed only for the purposes permitted by the originating authority.

3. For the purposes of this Article, information is deemed to be confidential if it is subject to confidentiality requirements under Union law.

TITLE VII FINANCING ARRANGEMENTS

[3.517]
Article 99
European system of financing arrangements

A European system of financing arrangements shall be established and shall consist of:

(a) national financing arrangements established in accordance with Article 100;

(b) the borrowing between national financing arrangements as specified in Article 106,

(c) the mutualisation of national financing arrangements in the case of a group resolution as referred to in Article 107.

[3.518]
Article 100
Requirement to establish resolution financing arrangements

1. Member States shall establish one or more financing arrangements for the purpose of ensuring the effective application by the resolution authority of the resolution tools and powers.

Member States shall ensure that the use of the financing arrangements may be triggered by a designated public authority or authority entrusted with public administrative powers.

The financing arrangements shall be used only in accordance with the resolution objectives and the principles set out in Articles 31 and 34.

2. Member States may use the same administrative structure as their financing arrangements for the purposes of their deposit guarantee scheme.

3. Member States shall ensure that the financing arrangements have adequate financial resources.

4. For the purpose of paragraph 3, financing arrangements shall in particular have the power to:

(a) raise *ex-ante* contributions as referred to in Article 103 with a view to reaching the target level specified in Article 102;
(b) raise *ex-post* extraordinary contributions as referred to in Article 104 where the contributions specified in point (a) are insufficient; and
(c) contract borrowings and other forms of support as referred to in Article 105.

5. Save where permitted under paragraph 6, each Member State shall establish its national financing arrangements through a fund, the use of which may be triggered by its resolution authority for the purposes set out in Article 101(1).

6. Notwithstanding paragraph 5 of this Article, a Member State may, for the purpose of fulfilling its obligations under paragraph 1 of this Article, establish its national financing arrangements through mandatory contributions from institutions which are authorised in its territory, which contributions are based on the criteria referred to in Article 103(7) and which are not held through a fund controlled by its resolution authority provided that all of the following conditions are met:
(a) the amount raised by contributions is at least equal to the amount that is required to be raised under Article 102;
(b) the Member State's resolution authority is entitled to an amount that is equal to the amount of such contributions, which the Member State makes immediately available to that resolution authority upon the latter's request, for use exclusively for the purposes set out in Article 101;
(c) the Member State notifies the Commission of its decision to avail itself of the discretion to structure its financing arrangements in accordance with this paragraph;
(d) the Member State notifies the Commission of the amount referred to in point (b) at least annually; and
(e) save as laid down in this paragraph, the financing arrangements comply with Articles 99 to 102, Article 103(1) to (4) and (6) and Articles 104 to 109.

For the purposes of this paragraph, the available financial means to be taken into account in order to reach the target level specified in Article 102 may include mandatory contributions from any scheme of mandatory contributions established by a Member State at any date between 17 June 2010 and 2 July 2014 from institutions in its territory for the purposes of covering the costs relating to systemic risk, failure and resolution of institutions, provided that the Member State complies with this Title. Contributions to deposit guarantee schemes shall not count towards the target level for resolution financing arrangements set out in Article 102.

[3.519]
Article 101
Use of the resolution financing arrangements

1. The financing arrangements established in accordance with Article 100 may be used by the resolution authority only to the extent necessary to ensure the effective application of the resolution tools, for the following purposes:
(a) to guarantee the assets or the liabilities of the institution under resolution, its subsidiaries, a bridge institution or an asset management vehicle;
(b) to make loans to the institution under resolution, its subsidiaries, a bridge institution or an asset management vehicle;
(c) to purchase assets of the institution under resolution;
(d) to make contributions to a bridge institution and an asset management vehicle;
(e) to pay compensation to shareholders or creditors in accordance with Article 75;
(f) to make a contribution to the institution under resolution in lieu of the write down or conversion of liabilities of certain creditors, when the bail-in tool is applied and the resolution authority decides to exclude certain creditors from the scope of bail-in in accordance with Article 44(3) to (8);
(g) to lend to other financing arrangements on a voluntary basis in accordance with Article 106;
(h) to take any combination of the actions referred to in points (a) to (g).

The financing arrangements may be used to take the actions referred to in the first subparagraph also with respect to the purchaser in the context of the sale of business tool.

2. The resolution financing arrangement shall not be used directly to absorb the losses of an institution or an entity referred to in point (b), (c) or (d) of Article 1(1) or to recapitalise such an institution or an entity. In the event that the use of the resolution financing arrangement for the purposes in paragraph 1 of this Article indirectly results in part of the losses of an institution or an entity referred to in point (b), (c) or (d) of Article 1(1) being passed on to the resolution financing arrangement, the principles governing the use of the resolution financing arrangement set out in Article 44 shall apply.

[3.520]
Article 102
Target level

1. Member States shall ensure that, by 31 December 2024, the available financial means of their financing arrangements reach at least 1% of the amount of covered deposits of all the institutions authorised in their territory. Member States may set target levels in excess of that amount.

2. During the initial period of time referred to in paragraph 1, contributions to the financing arrangements raised in accordance with Article 103 shall be spread out in time as evenly as possible until the target level is reached, but with due account of the phase of the business cycle and the impact pro-cyclical contributions may have on the financial position of contributing institutions.

Member States may extend the initial period of time for a maximum of four years if the financing arrangements have made cumulative disbursements in excess of 0.5% of covered deposits of all the institutions authorised in their territory which are guaranteed under Directive 2014/49/EU.

3. If, after the initial period of time referred to in paragraph 1, the available financial means diminish below the target level specified in that paragraph, the regular contributions raised in accordance with Article 103 shall resume until the target level is reached. After the target level has been reached for the first time and where the available financial means have subsequently been reduced to less than two thirds of the target level, those contributions shall be set at a level allowing for reaching the target level within six years.

The regular contribution shall take due account of the phase of the business cycle, and the impact procyclical contributions may have when setting annual contributions in the context of this paragraph.

4. EBA shall submit a report to the Commission by 31 October 2016 with recommendations on the appropriate reference point for setting the target level for resolution financing arrangements, and in particular whether total liabilities constitute a more appropriate basis than covered deposits.

5. Based on the results of the report referred to in paragraph 4, the Commission shall, if appropriate, submit, by 31 December 2016, to the European Parliament and to the Council a legislative proposal on the basis for the target level for resolution financing arrangements.

[3.521]
Article 103
Ex-ante contributions

1. In order to reach the target level specified in Article 102, Member States shall ensure that contributions are raised at least annually from the institutions authorised in their territory including Union branches.

2. The contribution of each institution shall be pro rata to the amount of its liabilities (excluding own funds) less covered deposits, with respect to the aggregate liabilities (excluding own funds) less covered deposits of all the institutions authorised in the territory of the Member State.

Those contributions shall be adjusted in proportion to the risk profile of institutions, in accordance with the criteria adopted under paragraph 7.

3. The available financial means to be taken into account in order to reach the target level specified in Article 102 may include irrevocable payment commitments which are fully backed by collateral of low risk assets unencumbered by any third party rights, at the free disposal and earmarked for the exclusive use by the resolution authorities for the purposes specified in Article 101(1). The share of irrevocable payment commitments shall not exceed 30% of the total amount of contributions raised in accordance with this Article.

4. Member States shall ensure that the obligation to pay the contributions specified in this Article is enforceable under national law, and that due contributions are fully paid.

Member States shall set up appropriate regulatory, accounting, reporting and other obligations to ensure that due contributions are fully paid. Member States shall ensure measures for the proper verification of whether the contributions have been paid correctly. Member States shall ensure measures to prevent evasion, avoidance and abuse.

5. The amounts raised in accordance with this Article shall only be used for the purposes specified in Article 101(1).

6. Subject to Articles 37, 38, 40, 41 and 42, the amounts received from the institution under resolution or the bridge institution, the interest and other earnings on investments and any other earnings may benefit the financing arrangements.

7. The Commission shall be empowered to adopt delegated acts in accordance with Article 115 in order to specify the notion of adjusting contributions in proportion to the risk profile of institutions as referred to in paragraph 2 of this Article, taking into account all of the following:

(a) the risk exposure of the institution, including the importance of its trading activities, its off-balance sheet exposures and its degree of leverage;
(b) the stability and variety of the company's sources of funding and unencumbered highly liquid assets;
(c) the financial condition of the institution;
(d) the probability that the institution enters into resolution;
(e) the extent to which the institution has previously benefited from extraordinary public financial support;
(f) the complexity of the structure of the institution and its resolvability;
(g) the importance of the institution to the stability of the financial system or economy of one or more Member States or of the Union;
(h) the fact that the institution is part of an IPS.

8. The Commission shall be empowered to adopt delegated acts in accordance with Article 115 in order to specify:

(a) the registration, accounting, reporting obligations and other obligations referred to in paragraph 4 intended to ensure that the contributions are in fact paid;
(b) the measures referred to in paragraph 4 to ensure proper verification of whether the contributions have been paid correctly.

[3.522]
Article 104
Extraordinary ex-post contributions

1. Where the available financial means are not sufficient to cover the losses, costs or other expenses incurred by the use of the financing arrangements, Member States shall ensure that extraordinary *ex-post* contributions are raised from the institutions authorised in their territory, in order to cover the additional amounts. Those extraordinary *ex-post* contributions shall be allocated between institutions in accordance with the rules laid down in Article 103(2).

Extraordinary *ex-post* contributions shall not exceed three times the annual amount of contributions determined in accordance with Article 103.

2. Article 103(4) to (8) shall be applicable to the contributions raised under this Article.

3. The resolution authority may defer, in whole or in part, an institution's payment of extraordinary *ex-post* contributions to the resolution financing arrangement if the payment of those contributions would jeopardise the liquidity or solvency of the institution. Such a deferral shall not be granted for a period of longer than six months but may be renewed upon the request of the institution. The contributions deferred pursuant to this paragraph shall be paid when such a payment no longer jeopardises the institution's liquidity or solvency.

4. The Commission shall be empowered to adopt delegated acts in accordance with Article 115 to specify the circumstances and conditions under which the payment of contributions by an institution may be deferred pursuant to paragraph 3 of this Article.

[3.523]
Article 105
Alternative funding means

Member States shall ensure that financing arrangements under their jurisdiction are enabled to contract borrowings or other forms of support from institutions, financial institutions or other third parties in the event that the amounts raised in accordance with Article 103 are not sufficient to cover the losses, costs or other expenses incurred by the use of the financing arrangements, and the extraordinary *ex-post* contributions provided for in Article 104 are not immediately accessible or sufficient.

[3.524]
Article 106
Borrowing between financing arrangements

1. Member States shall ensure that financing arrangements under their jurisdiction may make a request to borrow from all other financing arrangements within the Union, in the event that:
   (a) the amounts raised under Article 103 are not sufficient to cover the losses, costs or other expenses incurred by the use of the financing arrangements;
   (b) the extraordinary *ex-post* contributions provided for in Article 104 are not immediately accessible; and
   (c) the alternative funding means provided for in Article 105 are not immediately accessible on reasonable terms.

2. Member States shall ensure that financing arrangements under their jurisdiction have the power to lend to other financing arrangements within the Union in the circumstances specified in paragraph 1.

3. Following a request under paragraph 1, each of the other financing arrangements in the Union shall decide whether to lend to the financing arrangement which has made the request. Member States may require that that decision is taken after consulting, or with the consent of, the competent ministry or the government. The decision shall be taken with due urgency.

4. The rate of interest, repayment period and other terms and conditions of the loans shall be agreed between the borrowing financing arrangement and the other financing arrangements which have decided to participate. The loan of every participating financing arrangement shall have the same interest rate, repayment period and other terms and conditions, unless all participating financing arrangements agree otherwise.

5. The amount lent by each participating resolution financing arrangement shall be pro rata to the amount of covered deposits in the Member State of that resolution financing arrangement, with respect to the aggregate of covered deposits in the Member States of participating resolution financing arrangements. Those rates of contribution may vary upon agreement of all participating financing arrangements.

6. An outstanding loan to a resolution financing arrangement of another Member State under this Article shall be treated as an asset of the resolution financing arrangement which provided the loan and may be counted towards that financing arrangement's target level.

[3.525]
Article 107
Mutualisation of national financing arrangements in the case of a group resolution

1. Member States shall ensure that, in the case of a group resolution as referred to in Article 91 or Article 92, the national financing arrangement of each institution that is part of a group contributes to the financing of the group resolution in accordance with this Article.

2. For the purposes of paragraph 1, the group-level resolution authority, after consulting the resolution authorities of the institutions that are part of the group, shall propose, if necessary before taking any resolution action, a financing plan as part of the group resolution scheme provided for in Articles 91 and 92.

The financing plan shall be agreed in accordance with the decision-making procedure referred to in Articles 91 and 92.

3. The financing plan shall include:
   (a) a valuation in accordance with Article 36 in respect of the affected group entities;
   (b) the losses to be recognised by each affected group entity at the moment the resolution tools are exercised;
   (c) for each affected group entity, the losses that would be suffered by each class of shareholders and creditors;
   (d) any contribution that deposit guarantee schemes would be required to make in accordance with Article 109(1);

(e) the total contribution by resolution financing arrangements and the purpose and form of the contribution;
(f) the basis for calculating the amount that each of the national financing arrangements of the Member States where affected group entities are located is required to contribute to the financing of the group resolution in order to build up the total contribution referred to in point (e);
(g) the amount that the national financing arrangement of each affected group entity is required to contribute to the financing of the group resolution and the form of those contributions;
(h) the amount of borrowing that the financing arrangements of the Member States where the affected group entities are located, will contract from institutions, financial institutions and other third parties under Article 105;
(i) a timeframe for the use of the financing arrangements of the Member States where the affected group entities are located, which should be capable of being extended where appropriate.

4. The basis for apportioning the contribution referred to in point (e) of paragraph 3 shall be consistent with paragraph 5 of this Article and with the principles set out in the group resolution plan in accordance with point (f) of Article 12(3), unless otherwise agreed in the financing plan.

5. Unless agreed otherwise in the financing plan, the basis for calculating the contribution of each national financing arrangement shall in particular have regard to:
(a) the proportion of the group's risk-weighted assets held at institutions and entities referred to in points (b), (c) and (d) of Article 1(1) established in the Member State of that resolution financing arrangement;
(b) the proportion of the group's assets held at institutions and entities referred to in points (b), (c) and (d) of Article 1(1) established in the Member State of that resolution financing arrangement;
(c) the proportion of the losses, which have given rise to the need for group resolution, which originated in group entities under the supervision of competent authorities in the Member State of that resolution financing arrangement; and
(d) the proportion of the resources of the group financing arrangements which, under the financing plan, are expected to be used to benefit group entities established in the Member State of that resolution financing arrangement directly.

6. Member States shall establish rules and procedures in advance to ensure that each national financing arrangement can effect its contribution to the financing of group resolution immediately without prejudice to paragraph 2.

7. For the purpose of this Article, Member States shall ensure that group financing arrangements are allowed, under the conditions laid down in Article 105, to contract borrowings or other forms of support, from institutions, financial institutions or other third parties.

8. Member States shall ensure that national financing arrangements under their jurisdiction may guarantee any borrowing contracted by the group financing arrangements in accordance with paragraph 7.

9. Member States shall ensure that any proceeds or benefits that arise from the use of the group financing arrangements are allocated to national financing arrangements in accordance with their contributions to the financing of the resolution as established in paragraph 2.

[3.526]
[Article 108
Ranking in insolvency hierarchy

1. Member States shall ensure that in their national laws governing normal insolvency proceedings:
(a) the following have the same priority ranking which is higher than the ranking provided for the claims of ordinary unsecured creditors:
  (i) that part of eligible deposits from natural persons and micro, small and medium-sized enterprises which exceeds the coverage level provided for in Article 6 of Directive 2014/49/EU;
  (ii) deposits that would be eligible deposits from natural persons and micro, small and medium-sized enterprises were they not made through branches located outside the Union of institutions established within the Union;
(b) the following have the same priority ranking which is higher than the ranking provided for under point (a):
  (i) covered deposits;
  (ii) deposit guarantee schemes subrogating to the rights and obligations of covered depositors in insolvency.

2. Member States shall ensure that, for entities referred to in points (a) to (d) of the first subparagraph of Article 1(1), ordinary unsecured claims have, in their national laws governing normal insolvency proceedings, a higher priority ranking than that of unsecured claims resulting from debt instruments that meet the following conditions:
(a) the original contractual maturity of the debt instruments is of at least one year;
(b) the debt instruments contain no embedded derivatives and are not derivatives themselves;
(c) the relevant contractual documentation and, where applicable, the prospectus related to the issuance explicitly refer to the lower ranking under this paragraph.

3. Member States shall ensure that unsecured claims resulting from debt instruments that meet the conditions laid down in points (a), (b) and (c) of paragraph 2 of this Article have a higher priority ranking in their national laws governing normal insolvency proceedings than the priority ranking of claims resulting from instruments referred to in points (a) to (d) of Article 48(1).

4. Without prejudice to paragraphs 5 and 7, Member States shall ensure that their national laws governing normal insolvency proceedings as they were adopted at 31 December 2016 apply to the ranking in normal insolvency proceedings of unsecured claims resulting from debt instruments issued by

Part 3 EU & International Materials

entities referred to in points (a) to (d) of the first subparagraph of Article 1(1) of this Directive prior to the date of entry into force of measures under national law transposing Directive (EU) 2017/2399 of the European Parliament and of the Council[1].

5. Where, after 31 December 2016 and before 28 December 2017, a Member State adopted a national law governing the ranking in normal insolvency proceedings of unsecured claims resulting from debt instruments issued after the date of application of such national law, paragraph 4 of this Article shall not apply to claims resulting from debt instruments issued after the date of application of that national law, provided that all of the following conditions are met:

(a) under that national law, and for entities referred to in points (a) to (d) of the first subparagraph of Article 1(1), ordinary unsecured claims have, in normal insolvency proceedings, a higher priority ranking than that of unsecured claims resulting from debt instruments that meet the following conditions:
   (i) the original contractual maturity of the debt instruments is of at least one year;
   (ii) the debt instruments contain no embedded derivatives and are not derivatives themselves; and
   (iii) the relevant contractual documentation and, where applicable, the prospectus related to the issuance explicitly refer to the lower ranking under the national law;

(b) under that national law, unsecured claims resulting from debt instruments that meet the conditions laid down in point (a) of this subparagraph have, in normal insolvency proceedings, a higher priority ranking than the priority ranking of claims resulting from instruments referred to in points (a) to (d) of Article 48(1).

On the date of entry into force of measures under national law transposing Directive (EU) 2017/2399, the unsecured claims resulting from debt instruments referred to in point (b) of the first subparagraph shall have the same priority ranking as the one referred to in points (a), (b) and (c) of paragraph 2 and in paragraph 3 of this Article.

6. For the purposes of point (b) of paragraph 2 and point (a)(ii) of the first subparagraph of paragraph 5, debt instruments with variable interest derived from a broadly used reference rate and debt instruments not denominated in the domestic currency of the issuer, provided that principal, repayment and interest are denominated in the same currency, shall not be considered to be debt instruments containing embedded derivatives solely because of those features.

7. Member States that, prior to 31 December 2016, adopted a national law governing normal insolvency proceedings whereby ordinary unsecured claims resulting from debt instruments issued by entities referred to in points (a) to (d) of the first subparagraph of Article 1(1) are split into two or more different priority rankings, or whereby the priority ranking of ordinary unsecured claims resulting from such debt instruments is changed in relation to all other ordinary unsecured claims of the same ranking, may provide that debt instruments with the lowest priority ranking among those ordinary unsecured claims have the same ranking as that of claims that meet the conditions of points (a), (b) and (c) of paragraph 2 and of paragraph 3 of this Article.]

NOTES

Substituted by European Parliament and Council Directive 2017/2399/EU, Art 1(2).

This Article (as originally enacted) was implemented in the UK by the Banks and Building Societies (Depositor Preference and Priorities) Order 2014, SI 2014/3486. This Order amends certain domestic legislation, and these amendments have been incorporated at the appropriate places in this work, including the Insolvency Act 1986 at **[1.1]** et seq.

[1] Directive (EU) 2017/2399 of the European Parliament and of the Council of 12 December 2017 amending Directive 2014/59/EU as regards the ranking of unsecured debt instruments in insolvency hierarchy (OJ L345, 27.12.2017, p 96).

[3.527]
Article 109
Use of deposit guarantee schemes in the context of resolution

1. Member States shall ensure that, where the resolution authorities take resolution action, and provided that that action ensures that depositors continue to have access to their deposits, the deposit guarantee scheme to which the institution is affiliated is liable for:

(a) when the bail-in tool is applied, the amount by which covered deposits would have been written down in order to absorb the losses in the institution pursuant to point (a) of Article 46(1), had covered deposits been included within the scope of bail-in and been written down to the same extent as creditors with the same level of priority under the national law governing normal insolvency proceedings; or

(b) when one or more resolution tools other than the bail-in tool is applied, the amount of losses that covered depositors would have suffered, had covered depositors suffered losses in proportion to the losses suffered by creditors with the same level of priority under the national law governing normal insolvency proceedings.

In all cases, the liability of the deposit guarantee scheme shall not be greater than the amount of losses that it would have had to bear had the institution been wound up under normal insolvency proceedings.

When the bail-in tool is applied, the deposit guarantee scheme shall not be required to make any contribution towards the costs of recapitalising the institution or bridge institution pursuant to point (b) of Article 46(1).

Where it is determined by a valuation under Article 74 that the deposit guarantee scheme's contribution to resolution was greater than the net losses it would have incurred had the institution been wound up under normal insolvency proceedings, the deposit guarantee scheme shall be entitled to the payment of the difference from the resolution financing arrangement in accordance with Article 75.

2. Member States shall ensure that the determination of the amount by which the deposit guarantee scheme is liable in accordance with paragraph 1 of this Article complies with the conditions referred to in Article 36.
3. The contribution from the deposit guarantee scheme for the purpose of paragraph 1 shall be made in cash.
4. Where eligible deposits at an institution under resolution are transferred to another entity through the sale of business tool or the bridge institution tool, the depositors have no claim under Directive 2014/49/EU against the deposit guarantee scheme in relation to any part of their deposits at the institution under resolution that are not transferred, provided that the amount of funds transferred is equal to or more than the aggregate coverage level provided for in Article 6 of Directive 2014/49/EU.
5. Notwithstanding paragraphs 1 to 4, if the available financial means of a deposit guarantee scheme are used in accordance therewith and are subsequently reduced to less than two thirds of the target level of the deposit guarantee scheme, the regular contribution to the deposit guarantee scheme shall be set at a level allowing for reaching the target level within six years.
In all cases, the liability of a deposit guarantee scheme shall not be greater than the amount equal to 50% of its target level pursuant to Article 10 of Directive 2014/49/EU. Member States, may, by taking into account the specificities of their national banking sector, set a percentage which is higher than 50%.
In any circumstances, the deposit guarantee scheme's participation under this Directive shall not exceed the losses it would have incurred in a winding up under normal insolvency proceedings.

TITLE VIII PENALTIES

[3.528]
Article 110
Administrative penalties and other administrative measures

1. Without prejudice to the right of Member States to provide for and impose criminal penalties, Member States shall lay down rules on administrative penalties and other administrative measures applicable where the national provisions transposing this Directive have not been complied with, and shall take all measures necessary to ensure that they are implemented. Where Member States decide not to lay down rules for administrative penalties for infringements which are subject to national criminal law they shall communicate to the Commission the relevant criminal law provisions. The administrative penalties and other administrative measures shall be effective, proportionate and dissuasive.
2. Member States shall ensure that, where obligations referred to in the first paragraph apply to institutions, financial institutions and Union parent undertakings, in the event of an infringement, administrative penalties can be applied, subject to the conditions laid down in national law, to the members of the management body, and to other natural persons who under national law are responsible for the infringement.
3. The powers to impose administrative penalties provided for in this Directive shall be attributed to resolution authorities or, where different, to competent authorities, depending on the type of infringement. Resolution authorities and competent authorities shall have all information-gathering and investigatory powers that are necessary for the exercise of their respective functions. In the exercise of their powers to impose penalties, resolution authorities and competent authorities shall cooperate closely to ensure that administrative penalties or other administrative measures produce the desired results and coordinate their action when dealing with cross-border cases.
4. Resolution authorities and competent authorities shall exercise their administrative powers to impose penalties in accordance with this Directive and national law in any of the following ways:
   (a) directly;
   (b) in collaboration with other authorities;
   (c) under their responsibility by delegation to such authorities;
   (d) by application to the competent judicial authorities.

[3.529]
Article 111
Specific provisions

1. Member States shall ensure that their laws, regulations and administrative provisions provide for penalties and other administrative measures at least in respect of the following situations:
   (a) failure to draw up, maintain and update recovery plans and group recovery plans, infringing Article 5 or 7;
   (b) failure to notify an intention to provide group financial support to the competent authority infringing Article 25;
   (c) failure to provide all the information necessary for the development of resolution plans infringing Article 11;
   (d) failure of the management body of an institution or an entity referred to in point (b), (c) or (d) of Article 1(1) to notify the competent authority when the institution or entity referred to in point (b), (c) or (d) of Article 1(1) is failing or likely to fail, infringing Article 81(1).
2. Member States shall ensure that, in the cases referred to in paragraph 1, the administrative penalties and other administrative measures that can be applied include at least the following:
   (a) a public statement which indicates the natural person, institution, financial institution, Union parent undertaking or other legal person responsible and the nature of the infringement;
   (b) an order requiring the natural or legal person responsible to cease the conduct and to desist from a repetition of that conduct;

Part 3 EU & International Materials

(c) a temporary ban against any member of the management body or senior management of the institution or the entity referred to in point (b), (c) or (d) of Article 1(1) or any other natural person, who is held responsible, to exercise functions in institutions or entities referred to in point (b), (c) or (d) of Article 1(1);

(d) in the case of a legal person, administrative fines of up to 10% of the total annual net turnover of that legal person in the preceding business year. Where the legal person is a subsidiary of a parent undertaking, the relevant turnover shall be turnover resulting from the consolidated accounts of the ultimate parent undertaking in the preceding business year;

(e) in the case of a natural person, administrative fines of up to EUR 5 000 000, or in the Member States where the Euro is not the official currency, the corresponding value in the national currency on 2 July 2014;

(f) administrative fines of up to twice the amount of the benefit derived from the infringement where that benefit can be determined.

[3.530]
Article 112
Publication of administrative penalties

1. Member States shall ensure that resolution authorities and competent authorities publish on their official website at least any administrative penalties imposed by them for infringing the national provisions transposing this Directive where such penalties have not been the subject of an appeal or where the right of appeal has been exhausted. Such publication shall be made without undue delay after the natural or legal person is informed of that penalty including information on the type and nature of the infringement and the identity of the natural or legal person on whom the penalty is imposed.

Where Member States permit publication of penalties against which there is an appeal, resolution authorities and competent authorities shall, without undue delay, publish on their official websites information on the status of that appeal and the outcome thereof.

2. Resolution authorities and competent authorities shall publish the penalties imposed by them on an anonymous basis, in a manner which is in accordance with national law, in any of the following circumstances:

(a) where the penalty is imposed on a natural person and publication of personal data is shown to be disproportionate by an obligatory prior assessment of the proportionality of such publication;

(b) where publication would jeopardise the stability of financial markets or an ongoing criminal investigation;

(c) where publication would cause, insofar as it can be determined, disproportionate damage to the institutions or entities referred to in point (b), (c) or (d) of Article 1(1) or natural persons involved.

Alternatively, in such cases, the publication of the data in question may be postponed for a reasonable period of time, if it is foreseeable that the reasons for anonymous publication will cease to exist within that period.

3. Resolution authorities and competent authorities shall ensure that any publication in accordance with this Article shall remain on their official website for a period of at least five years. Personal data contained in the publication shall only be kept on the official website of the resolution authority or the competent authority for the period which is necessary in accordance with applicable data protection rules.

4. By 3 July 2016, EBA shall submit a report to the Commission on the publication of penalties by Member States on an anonymous basis as provided for under paragraph 2 and in particular whether there have been significant divergences between Member States in that respect. That report shall also address any significant divergences in the duration of publication of penalties under national law for Member States for publication of penalties.

[3.531]
Article 113
Maintenance of central database by EBA

1. Subject to the professional secrecy requirements referred to in Article 84, resolution authorities and competent authorities shall inform EBA of all administrative penalties imposed by them under Article 111 and of the status of that appeal and outcome thereof. EBA shall maintain a central database of penalties reported to it solely for the purpose of exchange of information between resolution authorities which shall be accessible to resolution authorities only and shall be updated on the basis of the information provided by resolution authorities. EBA shall maintain a central database of penalties reported to it solely for the purpose of exchange of information between competent authorities which shall be accessible to competent authorities only and shall be updated on the basis of the information provided by competent authorities.

2. EBA shall maintain a webpage with links to each resolution authority's publication of penalties and each competent authority's publication of penalties under Article 112 and indicate the period for which each Member State publishes penalties.

[3.532]
Article 114
Effective application of penalties and exercise of powers to impose penalties by competent authorities and resolution authorities

Member States shall ensure that when determining the type of administrative penalties or other administrative measures and the level of administrative fines, the competent authorities and resolution authorities take into account all relevant circumstances, including where appropriate:

(a) the gravity and the duration of the infringement;

(b) the degree of responsibility of the natural or legal person responsible;
(c) the financial strength of the natural or legal person responsible, for example, as indicated by the total turnover of the responsible legal person or the annual income of the responsible natural person;
(d) the amount of profits gained or losses avoided by the natural or legal person responsible, insofar as they can be determined;
(e) the losses for third parties caused by the infringement, insofar as they can be determined;
(f) the level of cooperation of the natural or legal person responsible with the competent authority and the resolution authority;
(g) previous infringements by the natural or legal person responsible;
(h) any potential systemic consequences of the infringement.

TITLE IX POWERS OF EXECUTION

[3.533]
Article 115
Exercise of the delegation

1. The power to adopt delegated acts is conferred on the Commission subject to the conditions laid down in this Article.
2. The power to adopt delegated acts referred to in the second paragraph of Article 2, Article 44(11), Article 76(4), Article 103(7) and (8) and Article 104(4) shall be conferred on the Commission for an indeterminate period of time from 2 July 2014.
3. The delegation of power referred to in the second paragraph of Article 2, Article 44(11), Article 76(4), Article 103(7) and (8) and Article 104(4) may be revoked at any time by the European Parliament or by the Council. A decision of revocation shall put an end to the delegation of the power specified in that decision. It shall take effect the day following the publication of the decision in the *Official Journal of the European Union* or at a later date specified therein. It shall not affect the validity of any delegated acts already in force.
4. As soon as it adopts a delegated act, the Commission shall notify it simultaneously to the European Parliament and to the Council.
5. A delegated act adopted pursuant to in the second paragraph of Article 2, Article 44(11), Article 76(4), Article 103(7) and (8) or Article 104(4) shall enter into force only if no objection has been expressed either by the European Parliament or the Council within three months of notification of that act to the European Parliament and the Council or if, before the expiry of that period, the European Parliament and the Council have both informed the Commission that they will not object. That period shall be extended by three months at the initiative of the European Parliament or the Council.
6. The Commission shall not adopt delegated acts where the scrutiny time of the European Parliament is reduced through recess to less than five months, including any extension.

Articles 116–126 (Title X)
(*Articles 116, 120, 122, 123 repealed by European Parliament and Council Directive 2017/1132/EU, Art 166, Annex III; Articles 119, 121, 124–126 amend EU legislation outside the scope of this work; Art 117 amends European Parliament and Council Directive 2001/24/EC, Arts 1, 2, 25, 26 at* **[3.177]**, **[3.178]**, **[3.201]** *and* **[3.202]**; *Art 118 amends European Parliament and Council Directive 2002/47/EC, Arts 1, 9a at* **[3.269]**, **[3.278]**.)

TITLE XI FINAL PROVISIONS

[3.534]
Article 127
EBA Resolution Committee

EBA shall create a permanent internal committee pursuant to Article 41 of Regulation (EU) No 1093/2010 for the purpose of preparing EBA decisions to be taken in accordance with Article 44 thereof, including decisions relating to draft regulatory technical standards and draft implementing technical standards, relating to tasks that have been conferred on resolution authorities as provided for in this Directive. In particular, in accordance with Article 38(1) of Regulation (EU) No 1093/2010, EBA shall ensure that no decision referred to in that article impinges in any way on the fiscal responsibilities of Member States. That internal committee shall be composed of the resolution authorities referred to in Article 3 of this Directive.
For the purposes of this Directive, EBA shall cooperate with EIOPA and ESMA within the framework of the Joint Committee of the European Supervisory Authorities established in Article 54 of Regulation (EU) No 1093/2010, of Regulation (EU) No 1094/2010 and of Regulation (EU) No 1095/2010.
For the purposes of this Directive, EBA shall ensure structural separation between the resolution committee and other functions referred to in Regulation (EU) No 1093/2010. The resolution committee shall promote the development and coordination of resolution plans and develop methods for the resolution of failing financial institutions.

[3.535]
Article 128
Cooperation with EBA

The competent and resolution authorities shall cooperate with EBA for the purposes of this Directive in accordance with Regulation (EU) No 1093/2010.
The competent and resolution authorities shall, without delay, provide EBA with all the information

necessary to carry out its duties in accordance with Article 35 of Regulation (EU) No 1093/2010.

[3.536]
Article 129
Review

By 1 June 2018, the Commission shall review the implementation of this Directive and shall submit a report thereon to the European Parliament and to the Council. It shall assess in particular the following:

(a) on the basis of the report from EBA referred to in Article 4(7), the need for any amendments with regard to minimising divergences at national level;

(b) on the basis of the report from EBA referred to in Article 45(19), the need for any amendments with regard to minimising divergences at national level;

(c) the functioning and efficiency of the role conferred on EBA in this Directive, including carrying out of mediation.

Where appropriate, that report shall be accompanied by a legislative proposal.

Notwithstanding the review provided for in the first subparagraph, the Commission shall, by 3 July 2017, specifically review the application of Articles 13, 18 and 45 as regards EBA's powers to conduct binding mediation to take account of future developments in financial services law. That report and any accompanying proposals, as appropriate, shall be forwarded to the European Parliament and to the Council.

[3.537]
Article 130
Transposition

1. Member States shall adopt and publish by 31 December 2014 the laws, regulations and administrative provisions necessary to comply with this Directive. They shall forthwith communicate to the Commission the text of those measures.

Member States shall apply those measures from 1 January 2015.

However, Member States shall apply provisions adopted in order to comply with Section 5 of Chapter IV of Title IV from 1 January 2016 at the latest.

2. When Member States adopt the measures referred to in paragraph 1, they shall contain a reference to this Directive or be accompanied by such a reference on the occasion of their official publication. Member States shall determine how such a reference is to be made.

3. Member States shall communicate to the Commission and to EBA the text of the main provisions of national law which they adopt in the field covered by this Directive.

[3.538]
Article 131
Entry into force

This Directive shall enter into force on the twentieth day following that of its publication in the *Official Journal of the European Union*.

Article 124 shall enter into force on 1 January 2015.

[3.539]
Article 132
Addressees

This Directive is addressed to the Member States.

ANNEX

SECTION A INFORMATION TO BE INCLUDED IN RECOVERY PLANS

[3.540]

The recovery plan shall include the following information:

(1) A summary of the key elements of the plan and a summary of overall recovery capacity;

(2) a summary of the material changes to the institution since the most recently filed recovery plan;

(3) a communication and disclosure plan outlining how the firm intends to manage any potentially negative market reactions;

(4) a range of capital and liquidity actions required to maintain or restore the viability and financial position of the institution;

(5) an estimation of the timeframe for executing each material aspect of the plan;

(6) a detailed description of any material impediment to the effective and timely execution of the plan, including consideration of impact on the rest of the group, customers and counterparties;

(7) identification of critical functions;

(8) a detailed description of the processes for determining the value and marketability of the core business lines, operations and assets of the institution;

(9) a detailed description of how recovery planning is integrated into the corporate governance structure of the institution as well as the policies and procedures governing the approval of the recovery plan and identification of the persons in the organisation responsible for preparing and implementing the plan;

(10) arrangements and measures to conserve or restore the institution's own funds;

(11) arrangements and measures to ensure that the institution has adequate access to contingency funding sources, including potential liquidity sources, an assessment of available collateral and an assessment of the possibility to transfer liquidity across group entities and business lines, to ensure that it can continue to carry out its operations and meet its obligations as they fall due;
(12) arrangements and measures to reduce risk and leverage;
(13) arrangements and measures to restructure liabilities;
(14) arrangements and measures to restructure business lines;
(15) arrangements and measures necessary to maintain continuous access to financial markets infrastructures;
(16) arrangements and measures necessary to maintain the continuous functioning of the institution's operational processes, including infrastructure and IT services;
(17) preparatory arrangements to facilitate the sale of assets or business lines in a timeframe appropriate for the restoration of financial soundness;
(18) other management actions or strategies to restore financial soundness and the anticipated financial effect of those actions or strategies;
(19) preparatory measures that the institution has taken or plans to take in order to facilitate the implementation of the recovery plan, including those necessary to enable the timely recapitalisation of the institution;
(20) a framework of indicators which identifies the points at which appropriate actions referred to in the plan may be taken.

SECTION B INFORMATION THAT RESOLUTION AUTHORITIES MAY REQUEST INSTITUTIONS TO PROVIDE FOR THE PURPOSES OF DRAWING UP AND MAINTAINING RESOLUTION PLANS

Resolution authorities may request institutions to provide for the purposes of drawing up and maintaining resolution plans at least the following information:

(1) a detailed description of the institution's organisational structure including a list of all legal persons;
(2) identification of the direct holders and the percentage of voting and non-voting rights of each legal person;
(3) the location, jurisdiction of incorporation, licensing and key management associated with each legal person;
(4) a mapping of the institution's critical operations and core business lines including material asset holdings and liabilities relating to such operations and business lines, by reference to legal persons;
(5) a detailed description of the components of the institution's and all its legal entities' liabilities, separating, at a minimum by types and amounts of short term and long-term debt, secured, unsecured and subordinated liabilities;
(6) details of those liabilities of the institution that are eligible liabilities;
(7) an identification of the processes needed to determine to whom the institution has pledged collateral, the person that holds the collateral and the jurisdiction in which the collateral is located;
(8) a description of the off balance sheet exposures of the institution and its legal entities, including a mapping to its critical operations and core business lines;
(9) the material hedges of the institution including a mapping to legal persons;
(10) identification of the major or most critical counterparties of the institution as well as an analysis of the impact of the failure of major counterparties in the institution's financial situation;
(11) each system on which the institution conducts a material number or value amount of trades, including a mapping to the institution's legal persons, critical operations and core business lines;
(12) each payment, clearing or settlement system of which the institution is directly or indirectly a member, including a mapping to the institution's legal persons, critical operations and core business lines;
(13) a detailed inventory and description of the key management information systems, including those for risk management, accounting and financial and regulatory reporting used by the institution including a mapping to the institution's legal persons, critical operations and core business lines;
(14) an identification of the owners of the systems identified in point (13), service level agreements related thereto, and any software and systems or licenses, including a mapping to their legal entities, critical operations and core business lines;
(15) an identification and mapping of the legal persons and the interconnections and interdependencies among the different legal persons such as:
- common or shared personnel, facilities and systems;
- capital, funding or liquidity arrangements;
- existing or contingent credit exposures;
- cross guarantee agreements, cross-collateral arrangements, cross-default provisions and cross-affiliate netting arrangements;
- risks transfers and back-to-back trading arrangements; service level agreements;

(16) the competent and resolution authority for each legal person;
(17) the member of the management body responsible for providing the information necessary to prepare the resolution plan of the institution as well as those responsible, if different, for the different legal persons, critical operations and core business lines;

(18) a description of the arrangements that the institution has in place to ensure that, in the event of resolution, the resolution authority will have all the necessary information, as determined by the resolution authority, for applying the resolution tools and powers;
(19) all the agreements entered into by the institutions and their legal entities with third parties the termination of which may be triggered by a decision of the authorities to apply a resolution tool and whether the consequences of termination may affect the application of the resolution tool;
(20) a description of possible liquidity sources for supporting resolution;
(21) information on asset encumbrance, liquid assets, off-balance sheet activities, hedging strategies and booking practices.

SECTION C MATTERS THAT THE RESOLUTION AUTHORITY IS TO CONSIDER WHEN ASSESSING THE RESOLVABILITY OF AN INSTITUTION OR GROUP

When assessing the resolvability of an institution or group, the resolution authority shall consider the following:

When assessing the resolvability of a group, references to an institution shall be deemed to include any institution or entity referred to in point (c) or (d) of Article 1(1) within a group:

(1) the extent to which the institution is able to map core business lines and critical operations to legal persons;
(2) the extent to which legal and corporate structures are aligned with core business lines and critical operations;
(3) the extent to which there are arrangements in place to provide for essential staff, infrastructure, funding, liquidity and capital to support and maintain the core business lines and the critical operations;
(4) the extent to which the service agreements that the institution maintains are fully enforceable in the event of resolution of the institution;
(5) the extent to which the governance structure of the institution is adequate for managing and ensuring compliance with the institution's internal policies with respect to its service level agreements;
(6) the extent to which the institution has a process for transitioning the services provided under service level agreements to third parties in the event of the separation of critical functions or of core business lines;
(7) the extent to which there are contingency plans and measures in place to ensure continuity in access to payment and settlement systems;
(8) the adequacy of the management information systems in ensuring that the resolution authorities are able to gather accurate and complete information regarding the core business lines and critical operations so as to facilitate rapid decision making;
(9) the capacity of the management information systems to provide the information essential for the effective resolution of the institution at all times even under rapidly changing conditions;
(10) the extent to which the institution has tested its management information systems under stress scenarios as defined by the resolution authority;
(11) the extent to which the institution can ensure the continuity of its management information systems both for the affected institution and the new institution in the case that the critical operations and core business lines are separated from the rest of the operations and business lines;
(12) the extent to which the institution has established adequate processes to ensure that it provides the resolution authorities with the information necessary to identify depositors and the amounts covered by the deposit guarantee schemes;
(13) where the group uses intra-group guarantees, the extent to which those guarantees are provided at market conditions and the risk management systems concerning those guarantees are robust;
(14) where the group engages in back-to-back transactions, the extent to which those transactions are performed at market conditions and the risk management systems concerning those transactions practices are robust;
(15) the extent to which the use of intra-group guarantees or back-to-back booking transactions increases contagion across the group;
(16) the extent to which the legal structure of the group inhibits the application of the resolution tools as a result of the number of legal persons, the complexity of the group structure or the difficulty in aligning business lines to group entities;
(17) the amount and type of eligible liabilities of the institution;
(18) where the assessment involves a mixed activity holding company, the extent to which the resolution of group entities that are institutions or financial institutions could have a negative impact on the non-financial part of the group;
(19) the existence and robustness of service level agreements;
(20) whether third-country authorities have the resolution tools necessary to support resolution actions by Union resolution authorities, and the scope for coordinated action between Union and third-country authorities;
(21) the feasibility of using resolution tools in such a way which meets the resolution objectives, given the tools available and the institution's structure;
(22) the extent to which the group structure allows the resolution authority to resolve the whole group or one or more of its group entities without causing a significant direct or indirect adverse effect on the financial system, market confidence or the economy and with a view to maximising the value of the group as a whole;

(23) the arrangements and means through which resolution could be facilitated in the cases of groups that have subsidiaries established in different jurisdictions;
(24) the credibility of using resolution tools in such a way which meets the resolution objectives, given possible impacts on creditors, counterparties, customers and employees and possible actions that third-country authorities may take;
(25) the extent to which the impact of the institution's resolution on the financial system and on financial market's confidence can be adequately evaluated;
(26) the extent to which the resolution of the institution could have a significant direct or indirect adverse effect on the financial system, market confidence or the economy;
(27) the extent to which contagion to other institutions or to the financial markets could be contained through the application of the resolution tools and powers;
(28) the extent to which the resolution of the institution could have a significant effect on the operation of payment and settlement systems.

EUROPEAN GROUPING OF TERRITORIAL COOPERATION REGULATIONS 2015

(SI 2015/1493)

NOTES

Made: 8 July 2015.
Authority: European Communities Act 1972, s 2(2).
Commencement: 31 July 2015.

PART 1
GENERAL

[3.541]
1 Citation and commencement

(1) These Regulations may be cited as the European Grouping of Territorial Cooperation Regulations 2015.
(2) These Regulations come into force on 31st July 2015.

NOTES

Commencement: 31 July 2015.

[3.542]
2 Interpretation

(1) In these Regulations—
"the 2006 Act" means the Companies Act 2006;
"the 1986 Act" means the Insolvency Act 1986;
"the 1989 Order" means the Insolvency (Northern Ireland) Order 1989;
"the EU Regulation" means Regulation (EC) No 1082/2006 of the European Parliament and of the Council as amended by Regulation (EU) 1302/2013 of the European Parliament and of the Council ;
"EGTC" means a European grouping of territorial cooperation formed under the EC Regulation;
"the Insolvency Rules" means—
in the case of a UK EGTC with its registered office in England and Wales, [Insolvency (England and Wales) Rules 2016];
in the case of a UK ECTG with its registered office in Scotland, the Insolvency (Scotland) Rules 1986;
in the case of a UK EGTC with its registered office in Northern Ireland, the Insolvency Rules (Northern Ireland) 1991; and
"UK EGTC" means an EGTC which has a registered office in the United Kingdom.

(2) In any provision of an enactment applied to a UK EGTC by virtue of these Regulations—
"articles" means the statutes and convention of a UK EGTC;
"board of directors" means the assembly of a UK EGTC, and all the directors of a UK EGTC if more than one, and if only one, the director of a UK EGTC;
"company" means a UK EGTC;
"director" or "past director" of a company means, as appropriate, a director or a former director of a UK EGTC, a member or former member of the assembly of a UK EGTC, or any other person who has or has had control of the management of a UK EGTC's business;
"officer" means a director or a member of the assembly of a UK EGTC, or a member of any other organ of the UK EGTC provided for in its statutes or convention;
"registered office" means the office specified in the convention of an EGTC to be its registered office; and
"ordinary resolution", "written resolution" and "general meeting" mean the procedures of a UK EGTC set out in its statutes and convention which most closely correspond to those things as provided for in the 2006 Act.

(3) Any other expressions used in these Regulations that are defined in the 2006 Act, or in relation to insolvency, by the 1986 Act or the 1989 Order have the meaning assigned to them by those provisions.

NOTES

Commencement: 31 July 2015.

Para (1): words in square brackets in definition "the Insolvency Rules" substituted by the Insolvency (England and Wales) Rules 2016 (Consequential Amendments and Savings) Rules 2017, SI 2017/369, r 2(2), Sch 2, para 1.

PART 2
PROVISIONS RELATING TO THE ESTABLISHMENT OF AN EGTC

3–5 (*Outside the scope of this work.*)

[3.543]

6 Proceedings in relation to the winding-up of a UK EGTC (Article 14(1) of the EU Regulation)

(1) The High Court is the competent court for the purpose of ordering the winding-up of a UK EGTC which has its registered office in England and Wales or in Northern Ireland.

(2) The Court of Session will be the competent court for the purposes of ordering the winding-up of a UK EGTC which has its registered office in Scotland.

NOTES

Commencement: 31 July 2015.

7 (*Outside the scope of this work.*)

[3.544]

8 Insolvency and winding up (Article 12(1) of the EU Regulation)

(1) A UK EGTC will be wound-up as an unregistered company—

(a) if its registered office is in England and Wales or in Scotland, under Part 5 of the 1986 Act; or

(b) if its registered office is in Northern Ireland, under Part 6 of the 1989 Order.

(2) The provisions of the 1986 Act or the 1989 Order and the Insolvency Rules apply to a UK EGTC that is being wound up in accordance with paragraph (1), with the modifications set out in Parts 2 and 3 of the Schedule to The European Grouping of Territorial Cooperation Regulations 2007.

NOTES

Commencement: 31 July 2015.

9 (*(Pt 3) Outside the scope of this work.*)

PART 4
SUPPLEMENTAL PROVISIONS RELATING TO THE EFFECTIVE APPLICATION OF THE EU REGULATION

[3.545]

10 Application of the Company Directors Disqualification Act 1986

Where a UK EGTC is wound-up under regulation 9(1)(a) or 9(1)(b) of these regulations, the Company Directors Disqualification Act 1986 or the Company Directors Disqualification (Northern Ireland) Order 2002, as appropriate, applies to the UK EGTC and does so as if the EGTC were a company as defined by section 22(2)(b) of that Act or by article 2(2) of that Order

NOTES

Commencement: 31 July 2015.

11–13 (*Outside the scope of this work.*)

REGULATION OF THE EUROPEAN PARLIAMENT AND OF THE COUNCIL

(2015/848/EU)

of 20 May 2015

on insolvency proceedings

(recast)

NOTES

Date of publication in OJ: OJ L141, 5.6.2015, p 19.

The text of this Regulation is reproduced as corrected by the Corrigendum published in OJ L349, 21.12.2016, p 9.

THE EUROPEAN PARLIAMENT AND THE COUNCIL OF THE EUROPEAN UNION,

Having regard to the Treaty on the Functioning of the European Union, and in particular Article 81 thereof,

Having regard to the proposal from the European Commission,

After transmission of the draft legislative act to the national parliaments,

Having regard to the opinion of the European Economic and Social Committee,[1]

Acting in accordance with the ordinary legislative procedure,[2]

Whereas:

(1) On 12 December 2012, the Commission adopted a report on the application of Council Regulation (EC) No 1346/2000.[3] The report concluded that the Regulation is functioning well in general but that it would be desirable to improve the application of certain of its provisions in order to enhance the effective administration of cross-border insolvency proceedings. Since that Regulation has been amended several times and further amendments are to be made, it should be recast in the interest of clarity.

(2) The Union has set the objective of establishing an area of freedom, security and justice.

(3) The proper functioning of the internal market requires that cross-border insolvency proceedings should operate efficiently and effectively. This Regulation needs to be adopted in order to achieve that objective, which falls within the scope of judicial cooperation in civil matters within the meaning of Article 81 of the Treaty.

(4) The activities of undertakings have more and more cross-border effects and are therefore increasingly being regulated by Union law. The insolvency of such undertakings also affects the proper functioning of the internal market, and there is a need for a Union act requiring coordination of the measures to be taken regarding an insolvent debtor's assets.

(5) It is necessary for the proper functioning of the internal market to avoid incentives for parties to transfer assets or judicial proceedings from one Member State to another, seeking to obtain a more favourable legal position to the detriment of the general body of creditors (forum shopping).

(6) This Regulation should include provisions governing jurisdiction for opening insolvency proceedings and actions which are directly derived from insolvency proceedings and are closely linked with them. This Regulation should also contain provisions regarding the recognition and enforcement of judgments issued in such proceedings, and provisions regarding the law applicable to insolvency proceedings. In addition, this Regulation should lay down rules on the coordination of insolvency proceedings which relate to the same debtor or to several members of the same group of companies.

(7) Bankruptcy, proceedings relating to the winding-up of insolvent companies or other legal persons, judicial arrangements, compositions and analogous proceedings and actions related to such proceedings are excluded from the scope of Regulation (EU) No 1215/2012 of the European Parliament and of the Council.[4] Those proceedings should be covered by this Regulation. The interpretation of this Regulation should as much as possible avoid regulatory loopholes between the two instruments. However, the mere fact that a national procedure is not listed in Annex A to this Regulation should not imply that it is covered by Regulation (EU) No 1215/2012.

(8) In order to achieve the aim of improving the efficiency and effectiveness of insolvency proceedings having cross-border effects, it is necessary, and appropriate, that the provisions on jurisdiction, recognition and applicable law in this area should be contained in a Union measure which is binding and directly applicable in Member States.

(9) This Regulation should apply to insolvency proceedings which meet the conditions set out in it, irrespective of whether the debtor is a natural person or a legal person, a trader or an individual. Those insolvency proceedings are listed exhaustively in Annex A. In respect of the national procedures contained in Annex A, this Regulation should apply without any further examination by the courts of another Member State as to whether the conditions set out in this Regulation are met. National insolvency procedures not listed in Annex A should not be covered by this Regulation.

(10) The scope of this Regulation should extend to proceedings which promote the rescue of economically viable but distressed businesses and which give a second chance to entrepreneurs. It should, in particular, extend to proceedings which provide for restructuring of a debtor at a stage where there is only a likelihood of insolvency, and to proceedings which leave the debtor fully or partially in control of its assets and affairs. It should also extend to proceedings providing for a debt discharge or a debt adjustment in relation to consumers and self-employed persons, for example by reducing the amount to be paid by the debtor or by extending the payment period granted to the debtor. Since such proceedings do not necessarily entail the appointment of an insolvency practitioner, they should be covered by this Regulation if they take place under the control or supervision of a court. In this context, the term 'control' should include situations where the court only intervenes on appeal by a creditor or other interested parties.

(11) This Regulation should also apply to procedures which grant a temporary stay on enforcement actions brought by individual creditors where such actions could adversely affect negotiations and hamper the prospects of a restructuring of the debtor's business. Such procedures should not be detrimental to the general body of creditors and, if no agreement on a restructuring plan can be reached, should be preliminary to other procedures covered by this Regulation.

(12) This Regulation should apply to proceedings the opening of which is subject to publicity in order to allow creditors to become aware of the proceedings and to lodge their claims, thereby ensuring the collective nature of the proceedings, and in order to give creditors the opportunity to challenge the jurisdiction of the court which has opened the proceedings.

(13) Accordingly, insolvency proceedings which are confidential should be excluded from the scope of this Regulation. While such proceedings may play an important role in some Member States, their

confidential nature makes it impossible for a creditor or a court located in another Member State to know that such proceedings have been opened, thereby making it difficult to provide for the recognition of their effects throughout the Union.

(14) The collective proceedings which are covered by this Regulation should include all or a significant part of the creditors to whom a debtor owes all or a substantial proportion of the debtor's outstanding debts provided that the claims of those creditors who are not involved in such proceedings remain unaffected. Proceedings which involve only the financial creditors of a debtor should also be covered. Proceedings which do not include all the creditors of a debtor should be proceedings aimed at rescuing the debtor. Proceedings that lead to a definitive cessation of the debtor's activities or the liquidation of the debtor's assets should include all the debtor's creditors. Moreover, the fact that some insolvency proceedings for natural persons exclude specific categories of claims, such as maintenance claims, from the possibility of a debt-discharge should not mean that such proceedings are not collective.

(15) This Regulation should also apply to proceedings that, under the law of some Member States, are opened and conducted for a certain period of time on an interim or provisional basis before a court issues an order confirming the continuation of the proceedings on a non-interim basis. Although labelled as 'interim', such proceedings should meet all other requirements of this Regulation.

(16) This Regulation should apply to proceedings which are based on laws relating to insolvency. However, proceedings that are based on general company law not designed exclusively for insolvency situations should not be considered to be based on laws relating to insolvency. Similarly, the purpose of adjustment of debt should not include specific proceedings in which debts of a natural person of very low income and very low asset value are written off, provided that this type of proceedings never makes provision for payment to creditors.

(17) This Regulation's scope should extend to proceedings which are triggered by situations in which the debtor faces non-financial difficulties, provided that such difficulties give rise to a real and serious threat to the debtor's actual or future ability to pay its debts as they fall due. The time frame relevant for the determination of such threat may extend to a period of several months or even longer in order to account for cases in which the debtor is faced with non-financial difficulties threatening the status of its business as a going concern and, in the medium term, its liquidity. This may be the case, for example, where the debtor has lost a contract which is of key importance to it.

(18) This Regulation should be without prejudice to the rules on the recovery of State aid from insolvent companies as interpreted by the case-law of the Court of Justice of the European Union.

(19) Insolvency proceedings concerning insurance undertakings, credit institutions, investment firms and other firms, institutions or undertakings covered by Directive 2001/24/EC of the European Parliament and of the Council[5] and collective investment undertakings should be excluded from the scope of this Regulation, as they are all subject to special arrangements and the national supervisory authorities have wide-ranging powers of intervention.

(20) Insolvency proceedings do not necessarily involve the intervention of a judicial authority. Therefore, the term 'court' in this Regulation should, in certain provisions, be given a broad meaning and include a person or body empowered by national law to open insolvency proceedings. In order for this Regulation to apply, proceedings (comprising acts and formalities set down in law) should not only have to comply with the provisions of this Regulation, but they should also be officially recognised and legally effective in the Member State in which the insolvency proceedings are opened.

(21) Insolvency practitioners are defined in this Regulation and listed in Annex B. Insolvency practitioners who are appointed without the involvement of a judicial body should, under national law, be appropriately regulated and authorised to act in insolvency proceedings. The national regulatory framework should provide for proper arrangements to deal with potential conflicts of interest.

(22) This Regulation acknowledges the fact that as a result of widely differing substantive laws it is not practical to introduce insolvency proceedings with universal scope throughout the Union. The application without exception of the law of the State of the opening of proceedings would, against this background, frequently lead to difficulties. This applies, for example, to the widely differing national laws on security interests to be found in the Member States. Furthermore, the preferential rights enjoyed by some creditors in insolvency proceedings are, in some cases, completely different. At the next review of this Regulation, it will be necessary to identify further measures in order to improve the preferential rights of employees at European level. This Regulation should take account of such differing national laws in two different ways. On the one hand, provision should be made for special rules on the applicable law in the case of particularly significant rights and legal relationships (e.g. rights *in rem* and contracts of employment). On the other hand, national proceedings covering only assets situated in the State of the opening of proceedings should also be allowed alongside main insolvency proceedings with universal scope.

(23) This Regulation enables the main insolvency proceedings to be opened in the Member State where the debtor has the centre of its main interests. Those proceedings have universal scope and are aimed at encompassing all the debtor's assets. To protect the diversity of interests, this Regulation permits secondary insolvency proceedings to be opened to run in parallel with the main insolvency proceedings. Secondary insolvency proceedings may be opened in the Member State where the debtor has an establishment. The effects of secondary insolvency proceedings are limited to the assets located in that State. Mandatory rules of coordination with the main insolvency proceedings satisfy the need for unity in the Union.

(24) Where main insolvency proceedings concerning a legal person or company have been opened in a Member State other than that of its registered office, it should be possible to open secondary insolvency

proceedings in the Member State of the registered office, provided that the debtor is carrying out an economic activity with human means and assets in that State, in accordance with the case-law of the Court of Justice of the European Union.

(25) This Regulation applies only to proceedings in respect of a debtor whose centre of main interests is located in the Union.

(26) The rules of jurisdiction set out in this Regulation establish only international jurisdiction, that is to say, they designate the Member State the courts of which may open insolvency proceedings. Territorial jurisdiction within that Member State should be established by the national law of the Member State concerned.

(27) Before opening insolvency proceedings, the competent court should examine of its own motion whether the centre of the debtor's main interests or the debtor's establishment is actually located within its jurisdiction.

(28) When determining whether the centre of the debtor's main interests is ascertainable by third parties, special consideration should be given to the creditors and to their perception as to where a debtor conducts the administration of its interests. This may require, in the event of a shift of centre of main interests, informing creditors of the new location from which the debtor is carrying out its activities in due course, for example by drawing attention to the change of address in commercial correspondence, or by making the new location public through other appropriate means.

(29) This Regulation should contain a number of safeguards aimed at preventing fraudulent or abusive forum shopping.

(30) Accordingly, the presumptions that the registered office, the principal place of business and the habitual residence are the centre of main interests should be rebuttable, and the relevant court of a Member State should carefully assess whether the centre of the debtor's main interests is genuinely located in that Member State. In the case of a company, it should be possible to rebut this presumption where the company's central administration is located in a Member State other than that of its registered office, and where a comprehensive assessment of all the relevant factors establishes, in a manner that is ascertainable by third parties, that the company's actual centre of management and supervision and of the management of its interests is located in that other Member State. In the case of an individual not exercising an independent business or professional activity, it should be possible to rebut this presumption, for example where the major part of the debtor's assets is located outside the Member State of the debtor's habitual residence, or where it can be established that the principal reason for moving was to file for insolvency proceedings in the new jurisdiction and where such filing would materially impair the interests of creditors whose dealings with the debtor took place prior to the relocation.

(31) With the same objective of preventing fraudulent or abusive forum shopping, the presumption that the centre of main interests is at the place of the registered office, at the individual's principal place of business or at the individual's habitual residence should not apply where, respectively, in the case of a company, legal person or individual exercising an independent business or professional activity, the debtor has relocated its registered office or principal place of business to another Member State within the 3-month period prior to the request for opening insolvency proceedings, or, in the case of an individual not exercising an independent business or professional activity, the debtor has relocated his habitual residence to another Member State within the 6-month period prior to the request for opening insolvency proceedings.

(32) In all cases, where the circumstances of the matter give rise to doubts about the court's jurisdiction, the court should require the debtor to submit additional evidence to support its assertions and, where the law applicable to the insolvency proceedings so allows, give the debtor's creditors the opportunity to present their views on the question of jurisdiction.

(33) In the event that the court seised of the request to open insolvency proceedings finds that the centre of main interests is not located on its territory, it should not open main insolvency proceedings.

(34) In addition, any creditor of the debtor should have an effective remedy against the decision to open insolvency proceedings. The consequences of any challenge to the decision to open insolvency proceedings should be governed by national law.

(35) The courts of the Member State within the territory of which insolvency proceedings have been opened should also have jurisdiction for actions which derive directly from the insolvency proceedings and are closely linked with them. Such actions should include avoidance actions against defendants in other Member States and actions concerning obligations that arise in the course of the insolvency proceedings, such as advance payment for costs of the proceedings. In contrast, actions for the performance of the obligations under a contract concluded by the debtor prior to the opening of proceedings do not derive directly from the proceedings. Where such an action is related to another action based on general civil and commercial law, the insolvency practitioner should be able to bring both actions in the courts of the defendant's domicile if he considers it more efficient to bring the action in that forum. This could, for example, be the case where the insolvency practitioner wishes to combine an action for director's liability on the basis of insolvency law with an action based on company law or general tort law.

(36) The court having jurisdiction to open the main insolvency proceedings should be able to order provisional and protective measures as from the time of the request to open proceedings. Preservation measures both prior to and after the commencement of the insolvency proceedings are important to guarantee the effectiveness of the insolvency proceedings. In that connection, this Regulation should provide for various possibilities. On the one hand, the court competent for the main insolvency proceedings should also be able to order provisional and protective measures covering assets situated in

the territory of other Member States. On the other hand, an insolvency practitioner temporarily appointed prior to the opening of the main insolvency proceedings should be able, in the Member States in which an establishment belonging to the debtor is to be found, to apply for the preservation measures which are possible under the law of those Member States.

(37) Prior to the opening of the main insolvency proceedings, the right to request the opening of insolvency proceedings in the Member State where the debtor has an establishment should be limited to local creditors and public authorities, or to cases in which main insolvency proceedings cannot be opened under the law of the Member State where the debtor has the centre of its main interests. The reason for this restriction is that cases in which territorial insolvency proceedings are requested before the main insolvency proceedings are intended to be limited to what is absolutely necessary.

(38) Following the opening of the main insolvency proceedings, this Regulation does not restrict the right to request the opening of insolvency proceedings in a Member State where the debtor has an establishment. The insolvency practitioner in the main insolvency proceedings or any other person empowered under the national law of that Member State may request the opening of secondary insolvency proceedings.

(39) This Regulation should provide for rules to determine the location of the debtor's assets, which should apply when determining which assets belong to the main or secondary insolvency proceedings, or to situations involving third parties' rights *in rem*. In particular, this Regulation should provide that European patents with unitary effect, a Community trade mark or any other similar rights, such as Community plant variety rights or Community designs, should only be included in the main insolvency proceedings.

(40) Secondary insolvency proceedings can serve different purposes, besides the protection of local interests. Cases may arise in which the insolvency estate of the debtor is too complex to administer as a unit, or the differences in the legal systems concerned are so great that difficulties may arise from the extension of effects deriving from the law of the State of the opening of proceedings to the other Member States where the assets are located. For that reason, the insolvency practitioner in the main insolvency proceedings may request the opening of secondary insolvency proceedings where the efficient administration of the insolvency estate so requires.

(41) Secondary insolvency proceedings may also hamper the efficient administration of the insolvency estate. Therefore, this Regulation sets out two specific situations in which the court seised of a request to open secondary insolvency proceedings should be able, at the request of the insolvency practitioner in the main insolvency proceedings, to postpone or refuse the opening of such proceedings.

(42) First, this Regulation confers on the insolvency practitioner in main insolvency proceedings the possibility of giving an undertaking to local creditors that they will be treated as if secondary insolvency proceedings had been opened. That undertaking has to meet a number of conditions set out in this Regulation, in particular that it be approved by a qualified majority of local creditors. Where such an undertaking has been given, the court seised of a request to open secondary insolvency proceedings should be able to refuse that request if it is satisfied that the undertaking adequately protects the general interests of local creditors. When assessing those interests, the court should take into account the fact that the undertaking has been approved by a qualified majority of local creditors.

(43) For the purposes of giving an undertaking to local creditors, the assets and rights located in the Member State where the debtor has an establishment should form a sub-category of the insolvency estate, and, when distributing them or the proceeds resulting from their realisation, the insolvency practitioner in the main insolvency proceedings should respect the priority rights that creditors would have had if secondary insolvency proceedings had been opened in that Member State.

(44) National law should be applicable, as appropriate, in relation to the approval of an undertaking. In particular, where under national law the voting rules for adopting a restructuring plan require the prior approval of creditors' claims, those claims should be deemed to be approved for the purpose of voting on the undertaking. Where there are different procedures for the adoption of restructuring plans under national law, Member States should designate the specific procedure which should be relevant in this context.

(45) Second, this Regulation should provide for the possibility that the court temporarily stays the opening of secondary insolvency proceedings, when a temporary stay of individual enforcement proceedings has been granted in the main insolvency proceedings, in order to preserve the efficiency of the stay granted in the main insolvency proceedings. The court should be able to grant the temporary stay if it is satisfied that suitable measures are in place to protect the general interest of local creditors. In such a case, all creditors that could be affected by the outcome of the negotiations on a restructuring plan should be informed of the negotiations and be allowed to participate in them.

(46) In order to ensure effective protection of local interests, the insolvency practitioner in the main insolvency proceedings should not be able to realise or re-locate, in an abusive manner, assets situated in the Member State where an establishment is located, in particular, with the purpose of frustrating the possibility that such interests can be effectively satisfied if secondary insolvency proceedings are opened subsequently.

(47) This Regulation should not prevent the courts of a Member State in which secondary insolvency proceedings have been opened from sanctioning a debtor's directors for violation of their duties, provided that those courts have jurisdiction to address such disputes under their national law.

(48) Main insolvency proceedings and secondary insolvency proceedings can contribute to the efficient administration of the debtor's insolvency estate or to the effective realisation of the total assets if there is proper cooperation between the actors involved in all the concurrent proceedings. Proper

cooperation implies the various insolvency practitioners and the courts involved cooperating closely, in particular by exchanging a sufficient amount of information. In order to ensure the dominant role of the main insolvency proceedings, the insolvency practitioner in such proceedings should be given several possibilities for intervening in secondary insolvency proceedings which are pending at the same time. In particular, the insolvency practitioner should be able to propose a restructuring plan or composition or apply for a suspension of the realisation of the assets in the secondary insolvency proceedings. When cooperating, insolvency practitioners and courts should take into account best practices for cooperation in cross-border insolvency cases, as set out in principles and guidelines on communication and cooperation adopted by European and international organisations active in the area of insolvency law, and in particular the relevant guidelines prepared by the United Nations Commission on International Trade Law (Uncitral).

(49) In light of such cooperation, insolvency practitioners and courts should be able to enter into agreements and protocols for the purpose of facilitating cross-border cooperation of multiple insolvency proceedings in different Member States concerning the same debtor or members of the same group of companies, where this is compatible with the rules applicable to each of the proceedings. Such agreements and protocols may vary in form, in that they may be written or oral, and in scope, in that they may range from generic to specific, and may be entered into by different parties. Simple generic agreements may emphasise the need for close cooperation between the parties, without addressing specific issues, while more detailed, specific agreements may establish a framework of principles to govern multiple insolvency proceedings and may be approved by the courts involved, where the national law so requires. They may reflect an agreement between the parties to take, or to refrain from taking, certain steps or actions.

(50) Similarly, the courts of different Member States may cooperate by coordinating the appointment of insolvency practitioners. In that context, they may appoint a single insolvency practitioner for several insolvency proceedings concerning the same debtor or for different members of a group of companies, provided that this is compatible with the rules applicable to each of the proceedings, in particular with any requirements concerning the qualification and licensing of the insolvency practitioner.

(51) This Regulation should ensure the efficient administration of insolvency proceedings relating to different companies forming part of a group of companies.

(52) Where insolvency proceedings have been opened for several companies of the same group, there should be proper cooperation between the actors involved in those proceedings. The various insolvency practitioners and the courts involved should therefore be under a similar obligation to cooperate and communicate with each other as those involved in main and secondary insolvency proceedings relating to the same debtor. Cooperation between the insolvency practitioners should not run counter to the interests of the creditors in each of the proceedings, and such cooperation should be aimed at finding a solution that would leverage synergies across the group.

(53) The introduction of rules on the insolvency proceedings of groups of companies should not limit the possibility for a court to open insolvency proceedings for several companies belonging to the same group in a single jurisdiction if the court finds that the centre of main interests of those companies is located in a single Member State. In such cases, the court should also be able to appoint, if appropriate, the same insolvency practitioner in all proceedings concerned, provided that this is not incompatible with the rules applicable to them.

(54) With a view to further improving the coordination of the insolvency proceedings of members of a group of companies, and to allow for a coordinated restructuring of the group, this Regulation should introduce procedural rules on the coordination of the insolvency proceedings of members of a group of companies. Such coordination should strive to ensure the efficiency of the coordination, whilst at the same time respecting each group member's separate legal personality.

(55) An insolvency practitioner appointed in insolvency proceedings opened in relation to a member of a group of companies should be able to request the opening of group coordination proceedings. However, where the law applicable to the insolvency so requires, that insolvency practitioner should obtain the necessary authorisation before making such a request. The request should specify the essential elements of the coordination, in particular an outline of the coordination plan, a proposal as to whom should be appointed as coordinator and an outline of the estimated costs of the coordination.

(56) In order to ensure the voluntary nature of group coordination proceedings, the insolvency practitioners involved should be able to object to their participation in the proceedings within a specified time period. In order to allow the insolvency practitioners involved to take an informed decision on participation in the group coordination proceedings, they should be informed at an early stage of the essential elements of the coordination. However, any insolvency practitioner who initially objects to inclusion in the group coordination proceedings should be able to subsequently request to participate in them. In such a case, the coordinator should take a decision on the admissibility of the request. All insolvency practitioners, including the requesting insolvency practitioner, should be informed of the coordinator's decision and should have the opportunity of challenging that decision before the court which has opened the group coordination proceedings.

(57) Group coordination proceedings should always strive to facilitate the effective administration of the insolvency proceedings of the group members, and to have a generally positive impact for the creditors. This Regulation should therefore ensure that the court with which a request for group coordination proceedings has been filed makes an assessment of those criteria prior to opening group coordination proceedings.

(58) The advantages of group coordination proceedings should not be outweighed by the costs of those proceedings. Therefore, it is necessary to ensure that the costs of the coordination, and the share of those costs that each group member will bear, are adequate, proportionate and reasonable, and are

determined in accordance with the national law of the Member State in which group coordination proceedings have been opened. The insolvency practitioners involved should also have the possibility of controlling those costs from an early stage of the proceedings. Where the national law so requires, controlling costs from an early stage of proceedings could involve the insolvency practitioner seeking the approval of a court or creditors' committee.

(59) Where the coordinator considers that the fulfilment of his or her tasks requires a significant increase in costs compared to the initially estimated costs and, in any case, where the costs exceed 10% of the estimated costs, the coordinator should be authorised by the court which has opened the group coordination proceedings to exceed such costs. Before taking its decision, the court which has opened the group coordination proceedings should give the possibility to the participating insolvency practitioners to be heard before it in order to allow them to communicate their observations on the appropriateness of the coordinator's request.

(60) For members of a group of companies which are not participating in group coordination proceedings, this Regulation should also provide for an alternative mechanism to achieve a coordinated restructuring of the group. An insolvency practitioner appointed in proceedings relating to a member of a group of companies should have standing to request a stay of any measure related to the realisation of the assets in the proceedings opened with respect to other members of the group which are not subject to group coordination proceedings. It should only be possible to request such a stay if a restructuring plan is presented for the members of the group concerned, if the plan is to the benefit of the creditors in the proceedings in respect of which the stay is requested, and if the stay is necessary to ensure that the plan can be properly implemented.

(61) This Regulation should not prevent Member States from establishing national rules which would supplement the rules on cooperation, communication and coordination with regard to the insolvency of members of groups of companies set out in this Regulation, provided that the scope of application of those national rules is limited to the national jurisdiction and that their application would not impair the efficiency of the rules laid down by this Regulation.

(62) The rules on cooperation, communication and coordination in the framework of the insolvency of members of a group of companies provided for in this Regulation should only apply to the extent that proceedings relating to different members of the same group of companies have been opened in more than one Member State.

(63) Any creditor which has its habitual residence, domicile or registered office in the Union should have the right to lodge its claims in each of the insolvency proceedings pending in the Union relating to the debtor's assets. This should also apply to tax authorities and social insurance institutions. This Regulation should not prevent the insolvency practitioner from lodging claims on behalf of certain groups of creditors, for example employees, where the national law so provides. However, in order to ensure the equal treatment of creditors, the distribution of proceeds should be coordinated. Every creditor should be able to keep what it has received in the course of insolvency proceedings, but should be entitled only to participate in the distribution of total assets in other proceedings if creditors with the same standing have obtained the same proportion of their claims.

(64) It is essential that creditors which have their habitual residence, domicile or registered office in the Union be informed about the opening of insolvency proceedings relating to their debtor's assets. In order to ensure a swift transmission of information to creditors, Regulation (EC) No 1393/2007 of the European Parliament and of the Council[6] should not apply where this Regulation refers to the obligation to inform creditors. The use of standard forms available in all official languages of the institutions of the Union should facilitate the task of creditors when lodging claims in proceedings opened in another Member State. The consequences of the incomplete filing of the standard forms should be a matter for national law.

(65) This Regulation should provide for the immediate recognition of judgments concerning the opening, conduct and closure of insolvency proceedings which fall within its scope, and of judgments handed down in direct connection with such insolvency proceedings. Automatic recognition should therefore mean that the effects attributed to the proceedings by the law of the Member State in which the proceedings were opened extend to all other Member States. The recognition of judgments delivered by the courts of the Member States should be based on the principle of mutual trust. To that end, grounds for non-recognition should be reduced to the minimum necessary. This is also the basis on which any dispute should be resolved where the courts of two Member States both claim competence to open the main insolvency proceedings. The decision of the first court to open proceedings should be recognised in the other Member States without those Member States having the power to scrutinise that court's decision.

(66) This Regulation should set out, for the matters covered by it, uniform rules on conflict of laws which replace, within their scope of application, national rules of private international law. Unless otherwise stated, the law of the Member State of the opening of proceedings should be applicable (*lex concursus*). This rule on conflict of laws should be valid both for the main insolvency proceedings and for local proceedings. The *lex concursus* determines all the effects of the insolvency proceedings, both procedural and substantive, on the persons and legal relations concerned. It governs all the conditions for the opening, conduct and closure of the insolvency proceedings.

(67) Automatic recognition of insolvency proceedings to which the law of the State of the opening of proceedings normally applies may interfere with the rules under which transactions are carried out in other Member States. To protect legitimate expectations and the certainty of transactions in Member States other than that in which proceedings are opened, provision should be made for a number of exceptions to the general rule.

(68) There is a particular need for a special reference diverging from the law of the opening State in the case of rights *in rem*, since such rights are of considerable importance for the granting of credit. The basis, validity and extent of rights *in rem* should therefore normally be determined according to the *lex situs* and not be affected by the opening of insolvency proceedings. The proprietor of a right *in rem* should therefore be able to continue to assert its right to segregation or separate settlement of the collateral security. Where assets are subject to rights *in rem* under the *lex situs* in one Member State but the main insolvency proceedings are being carried out in another Member State, the insolvency practitioner in the main insolvency proceedings should be able to request the opening of secondary insolvency proceedings in the jurisdiction where the rights *in rem* arise if the debtor has an establishment there. If secondary insolvency proceedings are not opened, any surplus on the sale of an asset covered by rights *in rem* should be paid to the insolvency practitioner in the main insolvency proceedings.

(69) This Regulation lays down several provisions for a court to order a stay of opening proceedings or a stay of enforcement proceedings. Any such stay should not affect the rights *in rem* of creditors or third parties.

(70) If a set-off of claims is not permitted under the law of the State of the opening of proceedings, a creditor should nevertheless be entitled to the set-off if it is possible under the law applicable to the claim of the insolvent debtor. In this way, set-off would acquire a kind of guarantee function based on legal provisions on which the creditor concerned can rely at the time when the claim arises.

(71) There is also a need for special protection in the case of payment systems and financial markets, for example in relation to the position-closing agreements and netting agreements to be found in such systems, as well as the sale of securities and the guarantees provided for such transactions as governed in particular by Directive 98/26/EC of the European Parliament and of the Council.[7] For such transactions, the only law which is relevant should be that applicable to the system or market concerned. That law is intended to prevent the possibility of mechanisms for the payment and settlement of transactions, and provided for in payment and set-off systems or on the regulated financial markets of the Member States, being altered in the case of insolvency of a business partner. Directive 98/26/EC contains special provisions which should take precedence over the general rules laid down in this Regulation.

(72) In order to protect employees and jobs, the effects of insolvency proceedings on the continuation or termination of employment and on the rights and obligations of all parties to such employment should be determined by the law applicable to the relevant employment agreement, in accordance with the general rules on conflict of laws. Moreover, in cases where the termination of employment contracts requires approval by a court or administrative authority, the Member State in which an establishment of the debtor is located should retain jurisdiction to grant such approval even if no insolvency proceedings have been opened in that Member State. Any other questions relating to the law of insolvency, such as whether the employees' claims are protected by preferential rights and the status such preferential rights may have, should be determined by the law of the Member State in which the insolvency proceedings (main or secondary) have been opened, except in cases where an undertaking to avoid secondary insolvency proceedings has been given in accordance with this Regulation.

(73) The law applicable to the effects of insolvency proceedings on any pending lawsuit or pending arbitral proceedings concerning an asset or right which forms part of the debtor's insolvency estate should be the law of the Member State where the lawsuit is pending or where the arbitration has its seat. However, this rule should not affect national rules on recognition and enforcement of arbitral awards.

(74) In order to take account of the specific procedural rules of court systems in certain Member States flexibility should be provided with regard to certain rules of this Regulation. Accordingly, references in this Regulation to notice being given by a judicial body of a Member State should include, where a Member State's procedural rules so require, an order by that judicial body directing that notice be given.

(75) For business considerations, the main content of the decision opening the proceedings should be published, at the request of the insolvency practitioner, in a Member State other than that of the court which delivered that decision. If there is an establishment in the Member State concerned, such publication should be mandatory. In neither case, however, should publication be a prior condition for recognition of the foreign proceedings.

(76) In order to improve the provision of information to relevant creditors and courts and to prevent the opening of parallel insolvency proceedings, Member States should be required to publish relevant information in cross-border insolvency cases in a publicly accessible electronic register. In order to facilitate access to that information for creditors and courts domiciled or located in other Member States, this Regulation should provide for the interconnection of such insolvency registers via the European e-Justice Portal. Member States should be free to publish relevant information in several registers and it should be possible to interconnect more than one register per Member State.

(77) This Regulation should determine the minimum amount of information to be published in the insolvency registers. Member States should not be precluded from including additional information. Where the debtor is an individual, the insolvency registers should only have to indicate a registration number if the debtor is exercising an independent business or professional activity. That registration number should be understood to be the unique registration number of the debtor's independent business or professional activity published in the trade register, if any.

(78) Information on certain aspects of insolvency proceedings is essential for creditors, such as time limits for lodging claims or for challenging decisions. This Regulation should, however, not require Member States to calculate those time-limits on a case-by-case basis. Member States should be able to fulfil their obligations by adding hyperlinks to the European e-Justice Portal, where self-explanatory information on the criteria for calculating those time-limits is to be provided.

(79) In order to grant sufficient protection to information relating to individuals not exercising an independent business or professional activity, Member States should be able to make access to that information subject to supplementary search criteria such as the debtor's personal identification number, address, date of birth or the district of the competent court, or to make access conditional upon a request to a competent authority or upon the verification of a legitimate interest.

(80) Member States should also be able not to include in their insolvency registers information on individuals not exercising an independent business or professional activity. In such cases, Member States should ensure that the relevant information is given to the creditors by individual notice, and that claims of creditors who have not received the information are not affected by the proceedings.

(81) It may be the case that some of the persons concerned are not aware that insolvency proceedings have been opened, and act in good faith in a way that conflicts with the new circumstances. In order to protect such persons who, unaware that foreign proceedings have been opened, make a payment to the debtor instead of to the foreign insolvency practitioner, provision should be made for such a payment to have a debt-discharging effect.

(82) In order to ensure uniform conditions for the implementation of this Regulation, implementing powers should be conferred on the Commission. Those powers should be exercised in accordance with Regulation (EU) No 182/2011 of the European Parliament and of the Council.[8]

(83) This Regulation respects the fundamental rights and observes the principles recognised in the Charter of Fundamental Rights of the European Union. In particular, this Regulation seeks to promote the application of Articles 8, 17 and 47 concerning, respectively, the protection of personal data, the right to property and the right to an effective remedy and to a fair trial.

(84) Directive 95/46/EC of the European Parliament and of the Council[9] and Regulation (EC) No 45/2001 of the European Parliament and of the Council[10] apply to the processing of personal data within the framework of this Regulation.

(85) This Regulation is without prejudice to Regulation (EEC, Euratom) No 1182/71 of the Council.[11]

(86) Since the objective of this Regulation cannot be sufficiently achieved by the Member States but can rather, by reason of the creation of a legal framework for the proper administration of cross-border insolvency proceedings, be better achieved at Union level, the Union may adopt measures in accordance with the principle of subsidiarity as set out in Article 5 of the Treaty on European Union. In accordance with the principle of proportionality, as set out in that Article, this Regulation does not go beyond what is necessary in order to achieve that objective.

(87) In accordance with Article 3 and Article 4a(1) of Protocol No 21 on the position of the United Kingdom and Ireland in respect of the area of freedom, security and justice, annexed to the Treaty on European Union and the Treaty on the Functioning of the European Union, the United Kingdom and Ireland have notified their wish to take part in the adoption and application of this Regulation.

(88) In accordance with Articles 1 and 2 of Protocol No 22 on the position of Denmark annexed to the Treaty on European Union and the Treaty on the Functioning of the European Union, Denmark is not taking part in the adoption of this Regulation and is not bound by it or subject to its application.

(89) The European Data Protection Supervisor was consulted and delivered an opinion on 27 March 2013[12]

NOTES

1 OJ C271, 19.9.2013, p 55.

2 Position of the European Parliament of 5 February 2014 (not yet published in the Official Journal) and position of the Council at first reading of 12 March 2015 (not yet published in the Official Journal). Position of the European Parliament of 20 May 2015 (not yet published in the Official Journal).

3 Council Regulation (EC) No 1346/2000 of 29 May 2000 on insolvency proceedings (OJ L160, 30.6.2000, p 1).

4 Regulation (EU) No 1215/2012 of the European Parliament and of the Council of 12 December 2012 on jurisdiction and the recognition and enforcement of judgments in civil and commercial matters (OJ L351, 20.12.2012, p 1).

5 Directive 2001/24/EC of the European Parliament and of the Council of 4 April 2001 on the reorganisation and winding-up of credit institutions (OJ L125, 5.5.2001, p 15).

6 Regulation (EC) No 1393/2007 of the European Parliament and of the Council of 13 November 2007 on the service in the Member States of judicial and extrajudicial documents in civil and commercial matters (service of documents), and repealing Council Regulation (EC) No 1348/2000 (OJ L324, 10.12.2007, p 79).

7 Directive 98/26/EC of the European Parliament and of the Council of 19 May 1998 on settlement finality in payment and securities settlement systems (OJ L166, 11.6.1998, p 45).

8 Regulation (EU) No 182/2011 of the European Parliament and of the Council of 16 February 2011 laying down the rules and general principles concerning mechanisms for control by the Member States of the Commission's exercise of implementing powers (OJ L55, 28.2.2011, p 13).

9 Directive 95/46/EC of the European Parliament and of the Council of 24 October 1995 on the protection of individuals with regard to the processing of personal data and on the free movement of such data (OJ L281, 23.11.1995, p 31).

10 Regulation (EC) No 45/2001 of the European Parliament and of the Council of 18 December 2000 on the protection of individuals with regard to the processing of personal data by the Community institutions and bodies and on the free movement of such data (OJ L8, 12.1.2001, p 1).

11 Regulation (EEC, Euratom) No 1182/71 of the Council of 3 June 1971 determining the rules applicable to periods, dates and time limits (OJ L124, 8.6.1971, p 1).

12 OJ C358, 7.12.2013, p 15.

HAS ADOPTED THIS REGULATION:

CHAPTER I GENERAL PROVISIONS

[3.546]
Article 1
Scope

1. This Regulation shall apply to public collective proceedings, including interim proceedings, which are based on laws relating to insolvency and in which, for the purpose of rescue, adjustment of debt, reorganisation or liquidation:
   (a) a debtor is totally or partially divested of its assets and an insolvency practitioner is appointed;
   (b) the assets and affairs of a debtor are subject to control or supervision by a court; or
   (c) a temporary stay of individual enforcement proceedings is granted by a court or by operation of law, in order to allow for negotiations between the debtor and its creditors, provided that the proceedings in which the stay is granted provide for suitable measures to protect the general body of creditors, and, where no agreement is reached, are preliminary to one of the proceedings referred to in point (a) or (b).

Where the proceedings referred to in this paragraph may be commenced in situations where there is only a likelihood of insolvency, their purpose shall be to avoid the debtor's insolvency or the cessation of the debtor's business activities.

The proceedings referred to in this paragraph are listed in Annex A.

2. This Regulation shall not apply to proceedings referred to in paragraph 1 that concern:
   (a) insurance undertakings;
   (b) credit institutions;
   (c) investment firms and other firms, institutions and undertakings to the extent that they are covered by Directive 2001/24/EC; or
   (d) collective investment undertakings.

[3.547]
Article 2
Definitions

For the purposes of this Regulation:
   (1) 'collective proceedings' means proceedings which include all or a significant part of a debtor's creditors, provided that, in the latter case, the proceedings do not affect the claims of creditors which are not involved in them;
   (2) 'collective investment undertakings' means undertakings for collective investment in transferable securities (UCITS) as defined in Directive 2009/65/EC of the European Parliament and of the Council[1] and alternative investment funds (AIFs) as defined in Directive 2011/61/EU of the European Parliament and of the Council;[2]
   (3) 'debtor in possession' means a debtor in respect of which insolvency proceedings have been opened which do not necessarily involve the appointment of an insolvency practitioner or the complete transfer of the rights and duties to administer the debtor's assets to an insolvency practitioner and where, therefore, the debtor remains totally or at least partially in control of its assets and affairs;
   (4) 'insolvency proceedings' means the proceedings listed in Annex A;
   (5) 'insolvency practitioner' means any person or body whose function, including on an interim basis, is to:
      (i) verify and admit claims submitted in insolvency proceedings;
      (ii) represent the collective interest of the creditors;
      (iii) administer, either in full or in part, assets of which the debtor has been divested;
      (iv) liquidate the assets referred to in point (iii); or
      (v) supervise the administration of the debtor's affairs.

   The persons and bodies referred to in the first subparagraph are listed in Annex B;
   (6) 'court' means:
      (i) in points (b) and (c) of Article 1(1), Article 4(2), Articles 5 and 6, Article 21(3), point (j) of Article 24(2), Articles 36 and 39, and Articles 61 to 77, the judicial body of a Member State;
      (ii) in all other articles, the judicial body or any other competent body of a Member State empowered to open insolvency proceedings, to confirm such opening or to take decisions in the course of such proceedings;
   (7) 'judgment opening insolvency proceedings' includes:
      (i) the decision of any court to open insolvency proceedings or to confirm the opening of such proceedings; and
      (ii) the decision of a court to appoint an insolvency practitioner;
   (8) 'the time of the opening of proceedings' means the time at which the judgment opening insolvency proceedings becomes effective, regardless of whether the judgment is final or not;
   (9) 'the Member State in which assets are situated' means, in the case of:
      (i) registered shares in companies other than those referred to in point (ii), the Member State within the territory of which the company having issued the shares has its registered office;
      (ii) financial instruments, the title to which is evidenced by entries in a register or account maintained by or on behalf of an intermediary ('book entry securities'), the Member State in which the register or account in which the entries are made is maintained;

(iii) cash held in accounts with a credit institution, the Member State indicated in the account's IBAN, or, for cash held in accounts with a credit institution which does not have an IBAN, the Member State in which the credit institution holding the account has its central administration or, where the account is held with a branch, agency or other establishment, the Member State in which the branch, agency or other establishment is located;
(iv) property and rights, ownership of or entitlement to which is entered in a public register other than those referred to in point (i), the Member State under the authority of which the register is kept;
(v) European patents, the Member State for which the European patent is granted;
(vi) copyright and related rights, the Member State within the territory of which the owner of such rights has its habitual residence or registered office;
(vii) tangible property, other than that referred to in points (i) to (iv), the Member State within the territory of which the property is situated;
(viii) claims against third parties, other than those relating to assets referred to in point (iii), the Member State within the territory of which the third party required to meet the claims has the centre of its main interests, as determined in accordance with Article 3(1);

(10) 'establishment' means any place of operations where a debtor carries out or has carried out in the 3-month period prior to the request to open main insolvency proceedings a non-transitory economic activity with human means and assets;
(11) 'local creditor' means a creditor whose claims against a debtor arose from or in connection with the operation of an establishment situated in a Member State other than the Member State in which the centre of the debtor's main interests is located;
(12) 'foreign creditor' means a creditor which has its habitual residence, domicile or registered office in a Member State other than the State of the opening of proceedings, including the tax authorities and social security authorities of Member States;
(13) 'group of companies' means a parent undertaking and all its subsidiary undertakings;
(14) 'parent undertaking' means an undertaking which controls, either directly or indirectly, one or more subsidiary undertakings. An undertaking which prepares consolidated financial statements in accordance with Directive 2013/34/EU of the European Parliament and of the Council[3] shall be deemed to be a parent undertaking.

NOTES

1 Directive 2009/65/EC of the European Parliament and of the Council of 13 July 2009 on the coordination of laws, regulations and administrative provisions relating to undertakings for collective investment in transferable securities (UCITS) (OJ L302, 17.11.2009, p 32).

2 Directive 2011/61/EU of the European Parliament and of the Council of 8 June 2011 on Alternative Investment Fund Managers and amending Directives 2003/41/EC and 2009/65/EC and Regulations (EC) No 1060/2009 and (EU) No 1095/2010 (OJ L174, 1.7.2011, p 1).

3 Directive 2013/34/EU of the European Parliament and of the Council of 26 June 2013 on the annual financial statements, consolidated financial statements and related reports of certain types of undertaking, amending Directive 2006/43/EC of the European Parliament and of the Council and repealing Council Directives 78/660/EEC and 83/349/EEC (OJ L182, 29.6.2013, p 19).

[3.548]
Article 3
International jurisdiction

1. The courts of the Member State within the territory of which the centre of the debtor's main interests is situated shall have jurisdiction to open insolvency proceedings ('main insolvency proceedings'). The centre of main interests shall be the place where the debtor conducts the administration of its interests on a regular basis and which is ascertainable by third parties.

In the case of a company or legal person, the place of the registered office shall be presumed to be the centre of its main interests in the absence of proof to the contrary. That presumption shall only apply if the registered office has not been moved to another Member State within the 3-month period prior to the request for the opening of insolvency proceedings.

In the case of an individual exercising an independent business or professional activity, the centre of main interests shall be presumed to be that individual's principal place of business in the absence of proof to the contrary. That presumption shall only apply if the individual's principal place of business has not been moved to another Member State within the 3-month period prior to the request for the opening of insolvency proceedings.

In the case of any other individual, the centre of main interests shall be presumed to be the place of the individual's habitual residence in the absence of proof to the contrary. This presumption shall only apply if the habitual residence has not been moved to another Member State within the 6-month period prior to the request for the opening of insolvency proceedings.

2. Where the centre of the debtor's main interests is situated within the territory of a Member State, the courts of another Member State shall have jurisdiction to open insolvency proceedings against that debtor only if it possesses an establishment within the territory of that other Member State. The effects of those proceedings shall be restricted to the assets of the debtor situated in the territory of the latter Member State.

3. Where insolvency proceedings have been opened in accordance with paragraph 1, any proceedings opened subsequently in accordance with paragraph 2 shall be secondary insolvency proceedings.

4. The territorial insolvency proceedings referred to in paragraph 2 may only be opened prior to the opening of main insolvency proceedings in accordance with paragraph 1 where

(a) insolvency proceedings under paragraph 1 cannot be opened because of the conditions laid down by the law of the Member State within the territory of which the centre of the debtor's main interests is situated; or
(b) the opening of territorial insolvency proceedings is requested by:
  (i) a creditor whose claim arises from or is in connection with the operation of an establishment situated within the territory of the Member State where the opening of territorial proceedings is requested; or
  (ii) a public authority which, under the law of the Member State within the territory of which the establishment is situated, has the right to request the opening of insolvency proceedings.

When main insolvency proceedings are opened, the territorial insolvency proceedings shall become secondary insolvency proceedings.

[3.549]
Article 4
Examination as to jurisdiction
1. A court seised of a request to open insolvency proceedings shall of its own motion examine whether it has jurisdiction pursuant to Article 3. The judgment opening insolvency proceedings shall specify the grounds on which the jurisdiction of the court is based, and, in particular, whether jurisdiction is based on Article 3(1) or (2).
2. Notwithstanding paragraph 1, where insolvency proceedings are opened in accordance with national law without a decision by a court, Member States may entrust the insolvency practitioner appointed in such proceedings to examine whether the Member State in which a request for the opening of proceedings is pending has jurisdiction pursuant to Article 3. Where this is the case, the insolvency practitioner shall specify in the decision opening the proceedings the grounds on which jurisdiction is based and, in particular, whether jurisdiction is based on Article 3(1) or (2).

Article 5
Judicial review of the decision to open main insolvency proceedings
1. The debtor or any creditor may challenge before a court the decision opening main insolvency proceedings on grounds of international jurisdiction.
2. The decision opening main insolvency proceedings may be challenged by parties other than those referred to in paragraph 1 or on grounds other than a lack of international jurisdiction where national law so provides.

[3.550]
Article 6
Jurisdiction for actions deriving directly from insolvency proceedings and closely linked with them
1. The courts of the Member State within the territory of which insolvency proceedings have been opened in accordance with Article 3 shall have jurisdiction for any action which derives directly from the insolvency proceedings and is closely linked with them, such as avoidance actions.
2. Where an action referred to in paragraph 1 is related to an action in civil and commercial matters against the same defendant, the insolvency practitioner may bring both actions before the courts of the Member State within the territory of which the defendant is domiciled, or, where the action is brought against several defendants, before the courts of the Member State within the territory of which any of them is domiciled, provided that those courts have jurisdiction pursuant to Regulation (EU) No 1215/2012.
The first subparagraph shall apply to the debtor in possession, provided that national law allows the debtor in possession to bring actions on behalf of the insolvency estate.
3. For the purpose of paragraph 2, actions are deemed to be related where they are so closely connected that it is expedient to hear and determine them together to avoid the risk of irreconcilable judgments resulting from separate proceedings.

[3.551]
Article 7
Applicable law
1. Save as otherwise provided in this Regulation, the law applicable to insolvency proceedings and their effects shall be that of the Member State within the territory of which such proceedings are opened (the 'State of the opening of proceedings').
2. The law of the State of the opening of proceedings shall determine the conditions for the opening of those proceedings, their conduct and their closure. In particular, it shall determine the following:
(a) the debtors against which insolvency proceedings may be brought on account of their capacity;
(b) the assets which form part of the insolvency estate and the treatment of assets acquired by or devolving on the debtor after the opening of the insolvency proceedings;
(c) the respective powers of the debtor and the insolvency practitioner;
(d) the conditions under which set-offs may be invoked;
(e) the effects of insolvency proceedings on current contracts to which the debtor is party;
(f) the effects of the insolvency proceedings on proceedings brought by individual creditors, with the exception of pending lawsuits;
(g) the claims which are to be lodged against the debtor's insolvency estate and the treatment of claims arising after the opening of insolvency proceedings;
(h) the rules governing the lodging, verification and admission of claims;

(i) the rules governing the distribution of proceeds from the realisation of assets, the ranking of claims and the rights of creditors who have obtained partial satisfaction after the opening of insolvency proceedings by virtue of a right *in rem* or through a set-off;
(j) the conditions for, and the effects of closure of, insolvency proceedings, in particular by composition;
(k) creditors' rights after the closure of insolvency proceedings;
(l) who is to bear the costs and expenses incurred in the insolvency proceedings;
(m) the rules relating to the voidness, voidability or unenforceability of legal acts detrimental to the general body of creditors.

[3.552]
Article 8
Third parties' rights in rem
1. The opening of insolvency proceedings shall not affect the rights *in rem* of creditors or third parties in respect of tangible or intangible, moveable or immoveable assets, both specific assets and collections of indefinite assets as a whole which change from time to time, belonging to the debtor which are situated within the territory of another Member State at the time of the opening of proceedings.
2. The rights referred to in paragraph 1 shall, in particular, mean:
(a) the right to dispose of assets or have them disposed of and to obtain satisfaction from the proceeds of or income from those assets, in particular by virtue of a lien or a mortgage;
(b) the exclusive right to have a claim met, in particular a right guaranteed by a lien in respect of the claim or by assignment of the claim by way of a guarantee;
(c) the right to demand assets from, and/or to require restitution by, anyone having possession or use of them contrary to the wishes of the party so entitled;
(d) a right *in rem* to the beneficial use of assets.
3. The right, recorded in a public register and enforceable against third parties, based on which a right *in rem* within the meaning of paragraph 1 may be obtained shall be considered to be a right *in rem*.
4. Paragraph 1 shall not preclude actions for voidness, voidability or unenforceability as referred to in point (m) of Article 7(2).

[3.553]
Article 9
Set-off
1. The opening of insolvency proceedings shall not affect the right of creditors to demand the set-off of their claims against the claims of a debtor, where such a set-off is permitted by the law applicable to the insolvent debtor's claim.
2. Paragraph 1 shall not preclude actions for voidness, voidability or unenforceability as referred to in point (m) of Article 7(2).

[3.554]
Article 10
Reservation of title
1. The opening of insolvency proceedings against the purchaser of an asset shall not affect sellers' rights that are based on a reservation of title where at the time of the opening of proceedings the asset is situated within the territory of a Member State other than the State of the opening of proceedings.
2. The opening of insolvency proceedings against the seller of an asset, after delivery of the asset, shall not constitute grounds for rescinding or terminating the sale and shall not prevent the purchaser from acquiring title where at the time of the opening of proceedings the asset sold is situated within the territory of a Member State other than the State of the opening of proceedings.
3. Paragraphs 1 and 2 shall not preclude actions for voidness, voidability or unenforceability as referred to in point (m) of Article 7(2).

[3.555]
Article 11
Contracts relating to immoveable property
1. The effects of insolvency proceedings on a contract conferring the right to acquire or make use of immoveable property shall be governed solely by the law of the Member State within the territory of which the immoveable property is situated.
2. The court which opened main insolvency proceedings shall have jurisdiction to approve the termination or modification of the contracts referred to in this Article where:
(a) the law of the Member State applicable to those contracts requires that such a contract may only be terminated or modified with the approval of the court opening insolvency proceedings; and
(b) no insolvency proceedings have been opened in that Member State.

[3.556]
Article 12
Payment systems and financial markets
1. Without prejudice to Article 8, the effects of insolvency proceedings on the rights and obligations of the parties to a payment or settlement system or to a financial market shall be governed solely by the law of the Member State applicable to that system or market.
2. Paragraph 1 shall not preclude any action for voidness, voidability or unenforceability which may be taken to set aside payments or transactions under the law applicable to the relevant payment system or financial market.

[3.557]
Article 13
Contracts of employment
1. The effects of insolvency proceedings on employment contracts and relationships shall be governed solely by the law of the Member State applicable to the contract of employment.
2. The courts of the Member State in which secondary insolvency proceedings may be opened shall retain jurisdiction to approve the termination or modification of the contracts referred to in this Article even if no insolvency proceedings have been opened in that Member State.
The first subparagraph shall also apply to an authority competent under national law to approve the termination or modification of the contracts referred to in this Article.

[3.558]
Article 14
Effects on rights subject to registration
The effects of insolvency proceedings on the rights of a debtor in immoveable property, a ship or an aircraft subject to registration in a public register shall be determined by the law of the Member State under the authority of which the register is kept.

[3.559]
Article 15
European patents with unitary effect and Community trade marks
For the purposes of this Regulation, a European patent with unitary effect, a Community trade mark or any other similar right established by Union law may be included only in the proceedings referred to in Article 3(1).

[3.560]
Article 16
Detrimental acts
Point (m) of Article 7(2) shall not apply where the person who benefited from an act detrimental to all the creditors provides proof that:
(a) the act is subject to the law of a Member State other than that of the State of the opening of proceedings; and
(b) the law of that Member State does not allow any means of challenging that act in the relevant case.

[3.561]
Article 17
Protection of third-party purchasers
Where, by an act concluded after the opening of insolvency proceedings, a debtor disposes, for consideration, of:
(a) an immoveable asset;
(b) a ship or an aircraft subject to registration in a public register; or
(c) securities the existence of which requires registration in a register laid down by law;
the validity of that act shall be governed by the law of the State within the territory of which the immoveable asset is situated or under the authority of which the register is kept.

[3.562]
Article 18
Effects of insolvency proceedings on pending lawsuits or arbitral proceedings
The effects of insolvency proceedings on a pending lawsuit or pending arbitral proceedings concerning an asset or a right which forms part of a debtor's insolvency estate shall be governed solely by the law of the Member State in which that lawsuit is pending or in which the arbitral tribunal has its seat.

CHAPTER II RECOGNITION OF INSOLVENCY PROCEEDINGS

[3.563]
Article 19
Principle
1. Any judgment opening insolvency proceedings handed down by a court of a Member State which has jurisdiction pursuant to Article 3 shall be recognised in all other Member States from the moment that it becomes effective in the State of the opening of proceedings.
The rule laid down in the first subparagraph shall also apply where, on account of a debtor's capacity, insolvency proceedings cannot be brought against that debtor in other Member States.
2. Recognition of the proceedings referred to in Article 3(1) shall not preclude the opening of the proceedings referred to in Article 3(2) by a court in another Member State. The latter proceedings shall be secondary insolvency proceedings within the meaning of Chapter III.

[3.564]
Article 20
Effects of recognition
1. The judgment opening insolvency proceedings as referred to in Article 3(1) shall, with no further formalities, produce the same effects in any other Member State as under the law of the State of the opening of proceedings, unless this Regulation provides otherwise and as long as no proceedings referred to in Article 3(2) are opened in that other Member State.

2. The effects of the proceedings referred to in Article 3(2) may not be challenged in other Member States. Any restriction of creditors' rights, in particular a stay or discharge, shall produce effects vis-à-vis assets situated within the territory of another Member State only in the case of those creditors who have given their consent.

[3.565]
Article 21
Powers of the insolvency practitioner

1. The insolvency practitioner appointed by a court which has jurisdiction pursuant to Article 3(1) may exercise all the powers conferred on it, by the law of the State of the opening of proceedings, in another Member State, as long as no other insolvency proceedings have been opened there and no preservation measure to the contrary has been taken there further to a request for the opening of insolvency proceedings in that State. Subject to Articles 8 and 10, the insolvency practitioner may, in particular, remove the debtor's assets from the territory of the Member State in which they are situated.
2. The insolvency practitioner appointed by a court which has jurisdiction pursuant to Article 3(2) may in any other Member State claim through the courts or out of court that moveable property was removed from the territory of the State of the opening of proceedings to the territory of that other Member State after the opening of the insolvency proceedings. The insolvency practitioner may also bring any action to set aside which is in the interests of the creditors.
3. In exercising its powers, the insolvency practitioner shall comply with the law of the Member State within the territory of which it intends to take action, in particular with regard to procedures for the realisation of assets. Those powers may not include coercive measures, unless ordered by a court of that Member State, or the right to rule on legal proceedings or disputes.

[3.566]
Article 22
Proof of the insolvency practitioner's appointment

The insolvency practitioner's appointment shall be evidenced by a certified copy of the original decision appointing it or by any other certificate issued by the court which has jurisdiction.
A translation into the official language or one of the official languages of the Member State within the territory of which it intends to act may be required. No legalisation or other similar formality shall be required.

[3.567]
Article 23
Return and imputation

1. A creditor which, after the opening of the proceedings referred to in Article 3(1), obtains by any means, in particular through enforcement, total or partial satisfaction of its claim on the assets belonging to a debtor situated within the territory of another Member State, shall return what it has obtained to the insolvency practitioner, subject to Articles 8 and 10.
2. In order to ensure the equal treatment of creditors, a creditor which has, in the course of insolvency proceedings, obtained a dividend on its claim shall share in distributions made in other proceedings only where creditors of the same ranking or category have, in those other proceedings, obtained an equivalent dividend.

[3.568]
Article 24
Establishment of insolvency registers

1. Member States shall establish and maintain in their territory one or several registers in which information concerning insolvency proceedings is published ('insolvency registers'). That information shall be published as soon as possible after the opening of such proceedings.
2. The information referred to in paragraph 1 shall be made publicly available, subject to the conditions laid down in Article 27, and shall include the following ('mandatory information'):
   (a) the date of the opening of insolvency proceedings;
   (b) the court opening insolvency proceedings and the case reference number, if any;
   (c) the type of insolvency proceedings referred to in Annex A that were opened and, where applicable, any relevant subtype of such proceedings opened in accordance with national law;
   (d) whether jurisdiction for opening proceedings is based on Article 3(1), 3(2) or 3(4);
   (e) if the debtor is a company or a legal person, the debtor's name, registration number, registered office or, if different, postal address;
   (f) if the debtor is an individual whether or not exercising an independent business or professional activity, the debtor's name, registration number, if any, and postal address or, where the address is protected, the debtor's place and date of birth;
   (g) the name, postal address or e-mail address of the insolvency practitioner, if any, appointed in the proceedings;
   (h) the time limit for lodging claims, if any, or a reference to the criteria for calculating that time limit;
   (i) the date of closing main insolvency proceedings, if any;
   (j) the court before which and, where applicable, the time limit within which a challenge of the decision opening insolvency proceedings is to be lodged in accordance with Article 5, or a reference to the criteria for calculating that time limit.
3. Paragraph 2 shall not preclude Member States from including documents or additional information in their national insolvency registers, such as directors' disqualifications related to insolvency.

4. Member States shall not be obliged to include in the insolvency registers the information referred to in paragraph 1 of this Article in relation to individuals not exercising an independent business or professional activity, or to make such information publicly available through the system of interconnection of those registers, provided that known foreign creditors are informed, pursuant to Article 54, of the elements referred to under point (j) of paragraph 2 of this Article.
Where a Member State makes use of the possibility referred to in the first subparagraph, the insolvency proceedings shall not affect the claims of foreign creditors who have not received the information referred to in the first subparagraph.
5. The publication of information in the registers under this Regulation shall not have any legal effects other than those set out in national law and in Article 55(6).

[3.569]
Article 25
Interconnection of insolvency registers
1. The Commission shall establish a decentralised system for the interconnection of insolvency registers by means of implementing acts. That system shall be composed of the insolvency registers and the European e-Justice Portal, which shall serve as a central public electronic access point to information in the system. The system shall provide a search service in all the official languages of the institutions of the Union in order to make available the mandatory information and any other documents or information included in the insolvency registers which the Member States choose to make available through the European e-Justice Portal.
2. By means of implementing acts in accordance with the procedure referred to in Article 87, the Commission shall adopt the following by 26 June 2019:
(a) the technical specification defining the methods of communication and information exchange by electronic means on the basis of the established interface specification for the system of interconnection of insolvency registers;
(b) the technical measures ensuring the minimum information technology security standards for communication and distribution of information within the system of interconnection of insolvency registers;
(c) minimum criteria for the search service provided by the European e-Justice Portal based on the information set out in Article 24;
(d) minimum criteria for the presentation of the results of such searches based on the information set out in Article 24;
(e) the means and the technical conditions of availability of services provided by the system of interconnection; and
(f) a glossary containing a basic explanation of the national insolvency proceedings listed in Annex A.

[3.570]
Article 26
Costs of establishing and interconnecting insolvency registers
1. The establishment, maintenance and future development of the system of interconnection of insolvency registers shall be financed from the general budget of the Union.
2. Each Member State shall bear the costs of establishing and adjusting its national insolvency registers to make them interoperable with the European e-Justice Portal, as well as the costs of administering, operating and maintaining those registers. This shall be without prejudice to the possibility to apply for grants to support such activities under the Union's financial programmes.

[3.571]
Article 27
Conditions of access to information via the system of interconnection
1. Member States shall ensure that the mandatory information referred to in points (a) to (j) of Article 24(2) is available free of charge via the system of interconnection of insolvency registers.
2. This Regulation shall not preclude Member States from charging a reasonable fee for access to the documents or additional information referred to in Article 24(3) via the system of interconnection of insolvency registers.
3. Member States may make access to mandatory information concerning individuals who are not exercising an independent business or professional activity, and concerning individuals exercising an independent business or professional activity when the insolvency proceedings are not related to that activity, subject to supplementary search criteria relating to the debtor in addition to the minimum criteria referred to in point (c) of Article 25(2).
4. Member States may require that access to the information referred to in paragraph 3 be made conditional upon a request to the competent authority. Member States may make access conditional upon the verification of the existence of a legitimate interest for accessing such information. The requesting person shall be able to submit the request for information electronically by means of a standard form via the European e-Justice Portal. Where a legitimate interest is required, it shall be permissible for the requesting person to justify his request by electronic copies of relevant documents. The requesting person shall be provided with an answer by the competent authority within 3 working days.
The requesting person shall not be obliged to provide translations of the documents justifying his request, or to bear any costs of translation which the competent authority may incur.

[3.572]
Article 28
Publication in another Member State

1. The insolvency practitioner or the debtor in possession shall request that notice of the judgment opening insolvency proceedings and, where appropriate, the decision appointing the insolvency practitioner be published in any other Member State where an establishment of the debtor is located in accordance with the publication procedures provided for in that Member State. Such publication shall specify, where appropriate, the insolvency practitioner appointed and whether the jurisdiction rule applied is that pursuant to Article 3(1) or (2).
2. The insolvency practitioner or the debtor in possession may request that the information referred to in paragraph 1 be published in any other Member State where the insolvency practitioner or the debtor in possession deems it necessary in accordance with the publication procedures provided for in that Member State.

[3.573]
Article 29
Registration in public registers of another Member State

1. Where the law of a Member State in which an establishment of the debtor is located and this establishment has been entered into a public register of that Member State, or the law of a Member State in which immovable property belonging to the debtor is located, requires information on the opening of insolvency proceedings referred to in Article 28 to be published in the land register, company register or any other public register, the insolvency practitioner or the debtor in possession shall take all the necessary measures to ensure such a registration.
2. The insolvency practitioner or the debtor in possession may request such registration in any other Member State, provided that the law of the Member State where the register is kept allows such registration.

[3.574]
Article 30
Costs

The costs of the publication and registration provided for in Articles 28 and 29 shall be regarded as costs and expenses incurred in the proceedings.

[3.575]
Article 31
Honouring of an obligation to a debtor

1. Where an obligation has been honoured in a Member State for the benefit of a debtor who is subject to insolvency proceedings opened in another Member State, when it should have been honoured for the benefit of the insolvency practitioner in those proceedings, the person honouring the obligation shall be deemed to have discharged it if he was unaware of the opening of the proceedings.
2. Where such an obligation is honoured before the publication provided for in Article 28 has been effected, the person honouring the obligation shall be presumed, in the absence of proof to the contrary, to have been unaware of the opening of insolvency proceedings. Where the obligation is honoured after such publication has been effected, the person honouring the obligation shall be presumed, in the absence of proof to the contrary, to have been aware of the opening of proceedings.

[3.576]
Article 32
Recognition and enforceability of other judgments

1. Judgments handed down by a court whose judgment concerning the opening of proceedings is recognised in accordance with Article 19 and which concern the course and closure of insolvency proceedings, and compositions approved by that court, shall also be recognised with no further formalities. Such judgments shall be enforced in accordance with Articles 39 to 44 and 47 to 57 of Regulation (EU) No 1215/2012.
The first subparagraph shall also apply to judgments deriving directly from the insolvency proceedings and which are closely linked with them, even if they were handed down by another court.
The first subparagraph shall also apply to judgments relating to preservation measures taken after the request for the opening of insolvency proceedings or in connection with it.
2. The recognition and enforcement of judgments other than those referred to in paragraph 1 of this Article shall be governed by Regulation (EU) No 1215/2012 provided that that Regulation is applicable.

[3.577]
Article 33
Public policy

Any Member State may refuse to recognise insolvency proceedings opened in another Member State or to enforce a judgment handed down in the context of such proceedings where the effects of such recognition or enforcement would be manifestly contrary to that State's public policy, in particular its fundamental principles or the constitutional rights and liberties of the individual.

CHAPTER III SECONDARY INSOLVENCY PROCEEDINGS

[3.578]
Article 34
Opening of proceedings

Where main insolvency proceedings have been opened by a court of a Member State and recognised in another Member State, a court of that other Member State which has jurisdiction pursuant to Article 3(2) may open secondary insolvency proceedings in accordance with the provisions set out in this Chapter. Where the main insolvency proceedings required that the debtor be insolvent, the debtor's insolvency shall not be re-examined in the Member State in which secondary insolvency proceedings may be opened. The effects of secondary insolvency proceedings shall be restricted to the assets of the debtor situated within the territory of the Member State in which those proceedings have been opened.

[3.579]
Article 35
Applicable law

Save as otherwise provided for in this Regulation, the law applicable to secondary insolvency proceedings shall be that of the Member State within the territory of which the secondary insolvency proceedings are opened.

[3.580]
Article 36
Right to give an undertaking in order to avoid secondary insolvency proceedings

1. In order to avoid the opening of secondary insolvency proceedings, the insolvency practitioner in the main insolvency proceedings may give a unilateral undertaking (the 'undertaking') in respect of the assets located in the Member State in which secondary insolvency proceedings could be opened, that when distributing those assets or the proceeds received as a result of their realisation, it will comply with the distribution and priority rights under national law that creditors would have if secondary insolvency proceedings were opened in that Member State. The undertaking shall specify the factual assumptions on which it is based, in particular in respect of the value of the assets located in the Member State concerned and the options available to realise such assets.

2. Where an undertaking has been given in accordance with this Article, the law applicable to the distribution of proceeds from the realisation of assets referred to in paragraph 1, to the ranking of creditors' claims, and to the rights of creditors in relation to the assets referred to in paragraph 1 shall be the law of the Member State in which secondary insolvency proceedings could have been opened. The relevant point in time for determining the assets referred to in paragraph 1 shall be the moment at which the undertaking is given.

3. The undertaking shall be made in the official language or one of the official languages of the Member State where secondary insolvency proceedings could have been opened, or, where there are several official languages in that Member State, the official language or one of the official languages of the place in which secondary insolvency proceedings could have been opened.

4. The undertaking shall be made in writing. It shall be subject to any other requirements relating to form and approval requirements as to distributions, if any, of the State of the opening of the main insolvency proceedings.

5. The undertaking shall be approved by the known local creditors. The rules on qualified majority and voting that apply to the adoption of restructuring plans under the law of the Member State where secondary insolvency proceedings could have been opened shall also apply to the approval of the undertaking. Creditors shall be able to participate in the vote by distance means of communication, where national law so permits. The insolvency practitioner shall inform the known local creditors of the undertaking, of the rules and procedures for its approval, and of the approval or rejection of the undertaking.

6. An undertaking given and approved in accordance with this Article shall be binding on the estate. If secondary insolvency proceedings are opened in accordance with Articles 37 and 38, the insolvency practitioner in the main insolvency proceedings shall transfer any assets which it removed from the territory of that Member State after the undertaking was given or, where those assets have already been realised, their proceeds, to the insolvency practitioner in the secondary insolvency proceedings.

7. Where the insolvency practitioner has given an undertaking, it shall inform local creditors about the intended distributions prior to distributing the assets and proceeds referred to in paragraph 1. If that information does not comply with the terms of the undertaking or the applicable law, any local creditor may challenge such distribution before the courts of the Member State in which main insolvency proceedings have been opened in order to obtain a distribution in accordance with the terms of the undertaking and the applicable law. In such cases, no distribution shall take place until the court has taken a decision on the challenge.

8. Local creditors may apply to the courts of the Member State in which main insolvency proceedings have been opened, in order to require the insolvency practitioner in the main insolvency proceedings to take any suitable measures necessary to ensure compliance with the terms of the undertaking available under the law of the State of the opening of main insolvency proceedings.

9. Local creditors may also apply to the courts of the Member State in which secondary insolvency proceedings could have been opened in order to require the court to take provisional or protective measures to ensure compliance by the insolvency practitioner with the terms of the undertaking.

10. The insolvency practitioner shall be liable for any damage caused to local creditors as a result of its non- compliance with the obligations and requirements set out in this Article.

11. For the purpose of this Article, an authority which is established in the Member State where secondary insolvency proceedings could have been opened and which is obliged under Directive 2008/94/EC of the European Parliament and of the Council[1] to guarantee the payment of employees' outstanding claims resulting from contracts of employment or employment relationships shall be considered to be a local creditor, where the national law so provides.

NOTES

1 Directive 2008/94/EC of the European Parliament and of the Council of 22 October 2008 on the protection of employees in the event of the insolvency of their employer (OJ L283, 28.10.2008, p 36).

[3.581]
Article 37
Right to request the opening of secondary insolvency proceedings

1. The opening of secondary insolvency proceedings may be requested by:
   (a) the insolvency practitioner in the main insolvency proceedings;
   (b) any other person or authority empowered to request the opening of insolvency proceedings under the law of the Member State within the territory of which the opening of secondary insolvency proceedings is requested.

2. Where an undertaking has become binding in accordance with Article 36, the request for opening secondary insolvency proceedings shall be lodged within 30 days of having received notice of the approval of the undertaking.

[3.582]
Article 38
Decision to open secondary insolvency proceedings

1. A court seised of a request to open secondary insolvency proceedings shall immediately give notice to the insolvency practitioner or the debtor in possession in the main insolvency proceedings and give it an opportunity to be heard on the request.

2. Where the insolvency practitioner in the main insolvency proceedings has given an undertaking in accordance with Article 36, the court referred to in paragraph 1 of this Article shall, at the request of the insolvency practitioner, not open secondary insolvency proceedings if it is satisfied that the undertaking adequately protects the general interests of local creditors.

3. Where a temporary stay of individual enforcement proceedings has been granted in order to allow for negotiations between the debtor and its creditors, the court, at the request of the insolvency practitioner or the debtor in possession, may stay the opening of secondary insolvency proceedings for a period not exceeding 3 months, provided that suitable measures are in place to protect the interests of local creditors.

The court referred to in paragraph 1 may order protective measures to protect the interests of local creditors by requiring the insolvency practitioner or the debtor in possession not to remove or dispose of any assets which are located in the Member State where its establishment is located unless this is done in the ordinary course of business. The court may also order other measures to protect the interest of local creditors during a stay, unless this is incompatible with the national rules on civil procedure.

The stay of the opening of secondary insolvency proceedings shall be lifted by the court of its own motion or at the request of any creditor if, during the stay, an agreement in the negotiations referred to in the first subparagraph has been concluded.

The stay may be lifted by the court of its own motion or at the request of any creditor if the continuation of the stay is detrimental to the creditor's rights, in particular if the negotiations have been disrupted or it has become evident that they are unlikely to be concluded, or if the insolvency practitioner or the debtor in possession has infringed the prohibition on disposal of its assets or on removal of them from the territory of the Member State where the establishment is located.

4. At the request of the insolvency practitioner in the main insolvency proceedings, the court referred to in paragraph 1 may open a type of insolvency proceedings as listed in Annex A other than the type initially requested, provided that the conditions for opening that type of proceedings under national law are fulfilled and that that type of proceedings is the most appropriate as regards the interests of the local creditors and coherence between the main and secondary insolvency proceedings. The second sentence of Article 34 shall apply.

[3.583]
Article 39
Judicial review of the decision to open secondary insolvency proceedings

The insolvency practitioner in the main insolvency proceedings may challenge the decision to open secondary insolvency proceedings before the courts of the Member State in which secondary insolvency proceedings have been opened on the ground that the court did not comply with the conditions and requirements of Article 38.

[3.584]
Article 40
Advance payment of costs and expenses

Where the law of the Member State in which the opening of secondary insolvency proceedings is requested requires that the debtor's assets be sufficient to cover in whole or in part the costs and expenses of the proceedings, the court may, when it receives such a request, require the applicant to make an advance payment of costs or to provide appropriate security.

[3.585]
Article 41
Cooperation and communication between insolvency practitioners

1. The insolvency practitioner in the main insolvency proceedings and the insolvency practitioner or practitioners in secondary insolvency proceedings concerning the same debtor shall cooperate with each other to the extent such cooperation is not incompatible with the rules applicable to the respective proceedings. Such cooperation may take any form, including the conclusion of agreements or protocols.
2. In implementing the cooperation set out in paragraph 1, the insolvency practitioners shall:
   (a) as soon as possible communicate to each other any information which may be relevant to the other proceedings, in particular any progress made in lodging and verifying claims and all measures aimed at rescuing or restructuring the debtor, or at terminating the proceedings, provided appropriate arrangements are made to protect confidential information;
   (b) explore the possibility of restructuring the debtor and, where such a possibility exists, coordinate the elaboration and implementation of a restructuring plan;
   (c) coordinate the administration of the realisation or use of the debtor's assets and affairs; the insolvency practitioner in the secondary insolvency proceedings shall give the insolvency practitioner in the main insolvency proceedings an early opportunity to submit proposals on the realisation or use of the assets in the secondary insolvency proceedings.
3. Paragraphs 1 and 2 shall apply mutatis mutandis to situations where, in the main or in the secondary insolvency proceedings or in any territorial insolvency proceedings concerning the same debtor and open at the same time, the debtor remains in possession of its assets.

[3.586]
Article 42
Cooperation and communication between courts

1. In order to facilitate the coordination of main, territorial and secondary insolvency proceedings concerning the same debtor, a court before which a request to open insolvency proceedings is pending, or which has opened such proceedings, shall cooperate with any other court before which a request to open insolvency proceedings is pending, or which has opened such proceedings, to the extent that such cooperation is not incompatible with the rules applicable to each of the proceedings. For that purpose, the courts may, where appropriate, appoint an independent person or body acting on its instructions, provided that it is not incompatible with the rules applicable to them.
2. In implementing the cooperation set out in paragraph 1, the courts, or any appointed person or body acting on their behalf, as referred to in paragraph 1, may communicate directly with, or request information or assistance directly from, each other provided that such communication respects the procedural rights of the parties to the proceedings and the confidentiality of information.
3. The cooperation referred to in paragraph 1 may be implemented by any means that the court considers appropriate. It may, in particular, concern:
   (a) coordination in the appointment of the insolvency practitioners;
   (b) communication of information by any means considered appropriate by the court;
   (c) coordination of the administration and supervision of the debtor's assets and affairs;
   (d) coordination of the conduct of hearings;
   (e) coordination in the approval of protocols, where necessary.

[3.587]
Article 43
Cooperation and communication between insolvency practitioners and courts

1. In order to facilitate the coordination of main, territorial and secondary insolvency proceedings opened in respect of the same debtor:
   (a) an insolvency practitioner in main insolvency proceedings shall cooperate and communicate with any court before which a request to open secondary insolvency proceedings is pending or which has opened such proceedings;
   (b) an insolvency practitioner in territorial or secondary insolvency proceedings shall cooperate and communicate with the court before which a request to open main insolvency proceedings is pending or which has opened such proceedings; and
   (c) an insolvency practitioner in territorial or secondary insolvency proceedings shall cooperate and communicate with the court before which a request to open other territorial or secondary insolvency proceedings is pending or which has opened such proceedings;

to the extent that such cooperation and communication are not incompatible with the rules applicable to each of the proceedings and do not entail any conflict of interest.
2. The cooperation referred to in paragraph 1 may be implemented by any appropriate means, such as those set out in Article 42(3).

[3.588]
Article 44
Costs of cooperation and communication

The requirements laid down in Articles 42 and 43 shall not result in courts charging costs to each other for cooperation and communication.

[3.589]
Article 45
Exercise of creditors' rights

1. Any creditor may lodge its claim in the main insolvency proceedings and in any secondary insolvency proceedings.
2. The insolvency practitioners in the main and any secondary insolvency proceedings shall lodge in other proceedings claims which have already been lodged in the proceedings for which they were appointed, provided that the interests of creditors in the latter proceedings are served by doing so, subject to the right of creditors to oppose such lodgement or to withdraw the lodgement of their claims where the law applicable so provides.
3. The insolvency practitioner in the main or secondary insolvency proceedings shall be entitled to participate in other proceedings on the same basis as a creditor, in particular by attending creditors' meetings.

[3.590]
Article 46
Stay of the process of realisation of assets

1. The court which opened the secondary insolvency proceedings shall stay the process of realisation of assets in whole or in part on receipt of a request from the insolvency practitioner in the main insolvency proceedings. In such a case, it may require the insolvency practitioner in the main insolvency proceedings to take any suitable measure to guarantee the interests of the creditors in the secondary insolvency proceedings and of individual classes of creditors. Such a request from the insolvency practitioner may be rejected only if it is manifestly of no interest to the creditors in the main insolvency proceedings. Such a stay of the process of realisation of assets may be ordered for up to 3 months. It may be continued or renewed for similar periods.
2. The court referred to in paragraph 1 shall terminate the stay of the process of realisation of assets:
(a) at the request of the insolvency practitioner in the main insolvency proceedings;
(b) of its own motion, at the request of a creditor or at the request of the insolvency practitioner in the secondary insolvency proceedings if that measure no longer appears justified, in particular, by the interests of creditors in the main insolvency proceedings or in the secondary insolvency proceedings.

[3.591]
Article 47
Power of the insolvency practitioner to propose restructuring plans

1. Where the law of the Member State where secondary insolvency proceedings have been opened allows for such proceedings to be closed without liquidation by a restructuring plan, a composition or a comparable measure, the insolvency practitioner in the main insolvency proceedings shall be empowered to propose such a measure in accordance with the procedure of that Member State.
2. Any restriction of creditors' rights arising from a measure referred to in paragraph 1 which is proposed in secondary insolvency proceedings, such as a stay of payment or discharge of debt, shall have no effect in respect of assets of a debtor that are not covered by those proceedings, without the consent of all the creditors having an interest.

[3.592]
Article 48
Impact of closure of insolvency proceedings

1. Without prejudice to Article 49, the closure of insolvency proceedings shall not prevent the continuation of other insolvency proceedings concerning the same debtor which are still open at that point in time.
2. Where insolvency proceedings concerning a legal person or a company in the Member State of that person's or company's registered office would entail the dissolution of the legal person or of the company, that legal person or company shall not cease to exist until any other insolvency proceedings concerning the same debtor have been closed, or the insolvency practitioner or practitioners in such proceedings have given consent to the dissolution.

[3.593]
Article 49
Assets remaining in the secondary insolvency proceedings

If, by the liquidation of assets in the secondary insolvency proceedings, it is possible to meet all claims allowed under those proceedings, the insolvency practitioner appointed in those proceedings shall immediately transfer any assets remaining to the insolvency practitioner in the main insolvency proceedings.

[3.594]
Article 50
Subsequent opening of the main insolvency proceedings

Where the proceedings referred to in Article 3(1) are opened following the opening of the proceedings referred to in Article 3(2) in another Member State, Articles 41, 45, 46, 47 and 49 shall apply to those opened first, in so far as the progress of those proceedings so permits.

[3.595]
Article 51
Conversion of secondary insolvency proceedings

1. At the request of the insolvency practitioner in the main insolvency proceedings, the court of the Member State in which secondary insolvency proceedings have been opened may order the conversion of the secondary insolvency proceedings into another type of insolvency proceedings listed in Annex A, provided that the conditions for opening that type of proceedings under national law are fulfilled and that that type of proceedings is the most appropriate as regards the interests of the local creditors and coherence between the main and secondary insolvency proceedings.
2. When considering the request referred to in paragraph 1, the court may seek information from the insolvency practitioners involved in both proceedings.

[3.596]
Article 52
Preservation measures

Where the court of a Member State which has jurisdiction pursuant to Article 3(1) appoints a temporary administrator in order to ensure the preservation of a debtor's assets, that temporary administrator shall be empowered to request any measures to secure and preserve any of the debtor's assets situated in another Member State, provided for under the law of that Member State, for the period between the request for the opening of insolvency proceedings and the judgment opening the proceedings.

CHAPTER IV PROVISION OF INFORMATION FOR CREDITORS AND LODGEMENT OF THEIR CLAIMS

[3.597]
Article 53
Right to lodge claims

Any foreign creditor may lodge claims in insolvency proceedings by any means of communication, which are accepted by the law of the State of the opening of proceedings. Representation by a lawyer or another legal professional shall not be mandatory for the sole purpose of lodging of claims.

[3.598]
Article 54
Duty to inform creditors

1. As soon as insolvency proceedings are opened in a Member State, the court of that State having jurisdiction or the insolvency practitioner appointed by that court shall immediately inform the known foreign creditors.
2. The information referred to in paragraph 1, provided by an individual notice, shall in particular include time limits, the penalties laid down with regard to those time limits, the body or authority empowered to accept the lodgement of claims and any other measures laid down. Such notice shall also indicate whether creditors whose claims are preferential or secured *in rem* need to lodge their claims. The notice shall also include a copy of the standard form for lodging of claims referred to in Article 55 or information on where that form is available.
3. The information referred to in paragraphs 1 and 2 of this Article shall be provided using the standard notice form to be established in accordance with Article 88. The form shall be published in the European e-Justice Portal and shall bear the heading 'Notice of insolvency proceedings' in all the official languages of the institutions of the Union. It shall be transmitted in the official language of the State of the opening of proceedings or, if there are several official languages in that Member State, in the official language or one of the official languages of the place where insolvency proceedings have been opened, or in another language which that State has indicated it can accept, in accordance with Article 55(5), if it can be assumed that that language is easier to understand for the foreign creditors.
4. In insolvency proceedings relating to an individual not exercising a business or professional activity, the use of the standard form referred to in this Article shall not be obligatory if creditors are not required to lodge their claims in order to have their claims taken into account in the proceedings.

[3.599]
Article 55
Procedure for lodging claims

1. Any foreign creditor may lodge its claim using the standard claims form to be established in accordance with Article 88. The form shall bear the heading 'Lodgement of claims' in all the official languages of the institutions of the Union.
2. The standard claims form referred to in paragraph 1 shall include the following information:
   (a) the name, postal address, e-mail address, if any, personal identification number, if any, and bank details of the foreign creditor referred to in paragraph 1;
   (b) the amount of the claim, specifying the principal and, where applicable, interest and the date on which it arose and the date on which it became due, if different;
   (c) if interest is claimed, the interest rate, whether the interest is of a legal or contractual nature, the period of time for which the interest is claimed and the capitalised amount of interest;
   (d) if costs incurred in asserting the claim prior to the opening of proceedings are claimed, the amount and the details of those costs;
   (e) the nature of the claim;
   (f) whether any preferential creditor status is claimed and the basis of such a claim;

(g) whether security *in rem* or a reservation of title is alleged in respect of the claim and if so, what assets are covered by the security interest being invoked, the date on which the security was granted and, where the security has been registered, the registration number; and
(h) whether any set-off is claimed and, if so, the amounts of the mutual claims existing on the date when insolvency proceedings were opened, the date on which they arose and the amount net of set-off claimed.

The standard claims form shall be accompanied by copies of any supporting documents.
3. The standard claims form shall indicate that the provision of information concerning the bank details and the personal identification number of the creditor referred to in point (a) of paragraph 2 is not compulsory.
4. When a creditor lodges its claim by means other than the standard form referred to in paragraph 1, the claim shall contain the information referred to in paragraph 2.
5. Claims may be lodged in any official language of the institutions of the Union. The court, the insolvency practitioner or the debtor in possession may require the creditor to provide a translation in the official language of the State of the opening of proceedings or, if there are several official languages in that Member State, in the official language or one of the official languages of the place where insolvency proceedings have been opened, or in another language which that Member State has indicated it can accept. Each Member State shall indicate whether it accepts any official language of the institutions of the Union other than its own for the purpose of the lodging of claims.
6. Claims shall be lodged within the period stipulated by the law of the State of the opening of proceedings. In the case of a foreign creditor, that period shall not be less than 30 days following the publication of the opening of insolvency proceedings in the insolvency register of the State of the opening of proceedings. Where a Member State relies on Article 24(4), that period shall not be less than 30 days following a creditor having been informed pursuant to Article 54.
7. Where the court, the insolvency practitioner or the debtor in possession has doubts in relation to a claim lodged in accordance with this Article, it shall give the creditor the opportunity to provide additional evidence on the existence and the amount of the claim.

CHAPTER V INSOLVENCY PROCEEDINGS OF MEMBERS OF A GROUP OF COMPANIES

SECTION 1 COOPERATION AND COMMUNICATION

[3.600]
Article 56
Cooperation and communication between insolvency practitioners
1. Where insolvency proceedings relate to two or more members of a group of companies, an insolvency practitioner appointed in proceedings concerning a member of the group shall cooperate with any insolvency practitioner appointed in proceedings concerning another member of the same group to the extent that such cooperation is appropriate to facilitate the effective administration of those proceedings, is not incompatible with the rules applicable to such proceedings and does not entail any conflict of interest. That cooperation may take any form, including the conclusion of agreements or protocols.
2. In implementing the cooperation set out in paragraph 1, insolvency practitioners shall:
(a) as soon as possible communicate to each other any information which may be relevant to the other proceedings, provided appropriate arrangements are made to protect confidential information;
(b) consider whether possibilities exist for coordinating the administration and supervision of the affairs of the group members which are subject to insolvency proceedings, and if so, coordinate such administration and supervision;
(c) consider whether possibilities exist for restructuring group members which are subject to insolvency proceedings and, if so, coordinate with regard to the proposal and negotiation of a coordinated restructuring plan.

For the purposes of points (b) and (c), all or some of the insolvency practitioners referred to in paragraph 1 may agree to grant additional powers to an insolvency practitioner appointed in one of the proceedings where such an agreement is permitted by the rules applicable to each of the proceedings. They may also agree on the allocation of certain tasks amongst them, where such allocation of tasks is permitted by the rules applicable to each of the proceedings.

[3.601]
Article 57
Cooperation and communication between courts
1. Where insolvency proceedings relate to two or more members of a group of companies, a court which has opened such proceedings shall cooperate with any other court before which a request to open proceedings concerning another member of the same group is pending or which has opened such proceedings to the extent that such cooperation is appropriate to facilitate the effective administration of the proceedings, is not incompatible with the rules applicable to them and does not entail any conflict of interest. For that purpose, the courts may, where appropriate, appoint an independent person or body to act on its instructions, provided that this is not incompatible with the rules applicable to them.
2. In implementing the cooperation set out in paragraph 1, courts, or any appointed person or body acting on their behalf, as referred to in paragraph 1, may communicate directly with each other, or request information or assistance directly from each other, provided that such communication respects the procedural rights of the parties to the proceedings and the confidentiality of information.

3. The cooperation referred to in paragraph 1 may be implemented by any means that the court considers appropriate. It may, in particular, concern:
(a) coordination in the appointment of insolvency practitioners;
(b) communication of information by any means considered appropriate by the court;
(c) coordination of the administration and supervision of the assets and affairs of the members of the group;
(d) coordination of the conduct of hearings;
(e) coordination in the approval of protocols where necessary.

[3.602]
Article 58
Cooperation and communication between insolvency practitioners and courts
An insolvency practitioner appointed in insolvency proceedings concerning a member of a group of companies:
(a) shall cooperate and communicate with any court before which a request for the opening of proceedings in respect of another member of the same group of companies is pending or which has opened such proceedings; and
(b) may request information from that court concerning the proceedings regarding the other member of the group or request assistance concerning the proceedings in which he has been appointed;
to the extent that such cooperation and communication are appropriate to facilitate the effective administration of the proceedings, do not entail any conflict of interest and are not incompatible with the rules applicable to them.

[3.603]
Article 59
Costs of cooperation and communication in proceedings concerning members of a group of companies
The costs of the cooperation and communication provided for in Articles 56 to 60 incurred by an insolvency practitioner or a court shall be regarded as costs and expenses incurred in the respective proceedings.

[3.604]
Article 60
Powers of the insolvency practitioner in proceedings concerning members of a group of companies
1. An insolvency practitioner appointed in insolvency proceedings opened in respect of a member of a group of companies may, to the extent appropriate to facilitate the effective administration of the proceedings:
(a) be heard in any of the proceedings opened in respect of any other member of the same group;
(b) request a stay of any measure related to the realisation of the assets in the proceedings opened with respect to any other member of the same group, provided that:
(i) a restructuring plan for all or some members of the group for which insolvency proceedings have been opened has been proposed under point (c) of Article 56(2) and presents a reasonable chance of success;
(ii) such a stay is necessary in order to ensure the proper implementation of the restructuring plan;
(iii) the restructuring plan would be to the benefit of the creditors in the proceedings for which the stay is requested; and
(iv) neither the insolvency proceedings in which the insolvency practitioner referred to in paragraph 1 of this Article has been appointed nor the proceedings in respect of which the stay is requested are subject to coordination under Section 2 of this Chapter;
(c) apply for the opening of group coordination proceedings in accordance with Article 61.
2. The court having opened proceedings referred to in point (b) of paragraph 1 shall stay any measure related to the realisation of the assets in the proceedings in whole or in part if it is satisfied that the conditions referred to in point (b) of paragraph 1 are fulfilled.
Before ordering the stay, the court shall hear the insolvency practitioner appointed in the proceedings for which the stay is requested. Such a stay may be ordered for any period, not exceeding 3 months, which the court considers appropriate and which is compatible with the rules applicable to the proceedings.
The court ordering the stay may require the insolvency practitioner referred to in paragraph 1 to take any suitable measure available under national law to guarantee the interests of the creditors in the proceedings.
The court may extend the duration of the stay by such further period or periods as it considers appropriate and which are compatible with the rules applicable to the proceedings, provided that the conditions referred to in points (b)(ii) to (iv) of paragraph 1 continue to be fulfilled and that the total duration of the stay (the initial period together with any such extensions) does not exceed 6 months.

SECTION 2 COORDINATION

SUBSECTION 1
PROCEDURE

[3.605]
Article 61
Request to open group coordination proceedings

1. Group coordination proceedings may be requested before any court having jurisdiction over the insolvency proceedings of a member of the group, by an insolvency practitioner appointed in insolvency proceedings opened in relation to a member of the group.
2. The request referred to in paragraph 1 shall be made in accordance with the conditions provided for by the law applicable to the proceedings in which the insolvency practitioner has been appointed.
3. The request referred to in paragraph 1 shall be accompanied by:
 (a) a proposal as to the person to be nominated as the group coordinator ('the coordinator'), details of his or her eligibility pursuant to Article 71, details of his or her qualifications and his or her written agreement to act as coordinator;
 (b) an outline of the proposed group coordination, and in particular the reasons why the conditions set out in Article 63(1) are fulfilled;
 (c) a list of the insolvency practitioners appointed in relation to the members of the group and, where relevant, the courts and competent authorities involved in the insolvency proceedings of the members of the group;
 (d) an outline of the estimated costs of the proposed group coordination and the estimation of the share of those costs to be paid by each member of the group.

[3.606]
Article 62
Priority rule

Without prejudice to Article 66, where the opening of group coordination proceedings is requested before courts of different Member States, any court other than the court first seised shall decline jurisdiction in favour of that court.

[3.607]
Article 63
Notice by the court seised

1. The court seised of a request to open group coordination proceedings shall give notice as soon as possible of the request for the opening of group coordination proceedings and of the proposed coordinator to the insolvency practitioners appointed in relation to the members of the group as indicated in the request referred to in point (c) of Article 61(3), if it is satisfied that:
 (a) the opening of such proceedings is appropriate to facilitate the effective administration of the insolvency proceedings relating to the different group members;
 (b) no creditor of any group member expected to participate in the proceedings is likely to be financially disadvantaged by the inclusion of that member in such proceedings; and
 (c) the proposed coordinator fulfils the requirements laid down in Article 71.
2. The notice referred to in paragraph 1 of this Article shall list the elements referred to in points (a) to (d) of Article 61(3).
3. The notice referred to in paragraph 1 shall be sent by registered letter, attested by an acknowledgment of receipt.
4. The court seised shall give the insolvency practitioners involved the opportunity to be heard.

[3.608]
Article 64
Objections by insolvency practitioners

1. An insolvency practitioner appointed in respect of any group member may object to:
 (a) the inclusion within group coordination proceedings of the insolvency proceedings in respect of which it has been appointed; or
 (b) the person proposed as a coordinator.
2. Objections pursuant to paragraph 1 of this Article shall be lodged with the court referred to in Article 63 within 30 days of receipt of notice of the request for the opening of group coordination proceedings by the insolvency practitioner referred to in paragraph 1 of this Article.
The objection may be made by means of the standard form established in accordance with Article 88.
3. Prior to taking the decision to participate or not to participate in the coordination in accordance with point (a) of paragraph 1, an insolvency practitioner shall obtain any approval which may be required under the law of the State of the opening of proceedings for which it has been appointed.

[3.609]
Article 65
Consequences of objection to the inclusion in group coordination

1. Where an insolvency practitioner has objected to the inclusion of the proceedings in respect of which it has been appointed in group coordination proceedings, those proceedings shall not be included in the group coordination proceedings.
2. The powers of the court referred to in Article 68 or of the coordinator arising from those proceedings shall have no effect as regards that member, and shall entail no costs for that member.

[3.610]
Article 66
Choice of court for group coordination proceedings

1. Where at least two-thirds of all insolvency practitioners appointed in insolvency proceedings of the members of the group have agreed that a court of another Member State having jurisdiction is the most appropriate court for the opening of group coordination proceedings, that court shall have exclusive jurisdiction.
2. The choice of court shall be made by joint agreement in writing or evidenced in writing. It may be made until such time as group coordination proceedings have been opened in accordance with Article 68.
3. Any court other than the court seised under paragraph 1 shall decline jurisdiction in favour of that court.
4. The request for the opening of group coordination proceedings shall be submitted to the court agreed in accordance with Article 61.

[3.611]
Article 67
Consequences of objections to the proposed coordinator

Where objections to the person proposed as coordinator have been received from an insolvency practitioner which does not also object to the inclusion in the group coordination proceedings of the member in respect of which it has been appointed, the court may refrain from appointing that person and invite the objecting insolvency practitioner to submit a new request in accordance with Article 61(3).

[3.612]
Article 68
Decision to open group coordination proceedings

1. After the period referred to in Article 64(2) has elapsed, the court may open group coordination proceedings where it is satisfied that the conditions of Article 63(1) are met. In such a case, the court shall:
   (a) appoint a coordinator;
   (b) decide on the outline of the coordination; and
   (c) decide on the estimation of costs and the share to be paid by the group members.
2. The decision opening group coordination proceedings shall be brought to the notice of the participating insolvency practitioners and of the coordinator.

[3.613]
Article 69
Subsequent opt-in by insolvency practitioners

1. In accordance with its national law, any insolvency practitioner may request, after the court decision referred to in Article 68, the inclusion of the proceedings in respect of which it has been appointed, where:
   (a) there has been an objection to the inclusion of the insolvency proceedings within the group coordination proceedings; or
   (b) insolvency proceedings with respect to a member of the group have been opened after the court has opened group coordination proceedings.
2. Without prejudice to paragraph 4, the coordinator may accede to such a request, after consulting the insolvency practitioners involved, where
   (a) he or she is satisfied that, taking into account the stage that the group coordination proceedings has reached at the time of the request, the criteria set out in points (a) and (b) of Article 63(1) are met; or
   (b) all insolvency practitioners involved agree, subject to the conditions in their national law.
3. The coordinator shall inform the court and the participating insolvency practitioners of his or her decision pursuant to paragraph 2 and of the reasons on which it is based.
4. Any participating insolvency practitioner or any insolvency practitioner whose request for inclusion in the group coordination proceedings has been rejected may challenge the decision referred to in paragraph 2 in accordance with the procedure set out under the law of the Member State in which the group coordination proceedings have been opened.

[3.614]
Article 70
Recommendations and group coordination plan

1. When conducting their insolvency proceedings, insolvency practitioners shall consider the recommendations of the coordinator and the content of the group coordination plan referred to in Article 72(1).
2. An insolvency practitioner shall not be obliged to follow in whole or in part the coordinator's recommendations or the group coordination plan.

If it does not follow the coordinator's recommendations or the group coordination plan, it shall give reasons for not doing so to the persons or bodies that it is to report to under its national law, and to the coordinator.

SUBSECTION 2
GENERAL PROVISIONS

[3.615]
Article 71
The coordinator

1. The coordinator shall be a person eligible under the law of a Member State to act as an insolvency practitioner.
2. The coordinator shall not be one of the insolvency practitioners appointed to act in respect of any of the group members, and shall have no conflict of interest in respect of the group members, their creditors and the insolvency practitioners appointed in respect of any of the group members.

[3.616]
Article 72
Tasks and rights of the coordinator

1. The coordinator shall:
   (a) identify and outline recommendations for the coordinated conduct of the insolvency proceedings;
   (b) propose a group coordination plan that identifies, describes and recommends a comprehensive set of measures appropriate to an integrated approach to the resolution of the group members' insolvencies. In particular, the plan may contain proposals for:
      (i) the measures to be taken in order to re-establish the economic performance and the financial soundness of the group or any part of it;
      (ii) the settlement of intra-group disputes as regards intra-group transactions and avoidance actions;
      (iii) agreements between the insolvency practitioners of the insolvent group members.
2. The coordinator may also:
   (a) be heard and participate, in particular by attending creditors' meetings, in any of the proceedings opened in respect of any member of the group;
   (b) mediate any dispute arising between two or more insolvency practitioners of group members;
   (c) present and explain his or her group coordination plan to the persons or bodies that he or she is to report to under his or her national law;
   (d) request information from any insolvency practitioner in respect of any member of the group where that information is or might be of use when identifying and outlining strategies and measures in order to coordinate the proceedings; and
   (e) request a stay for a period of up to 6 months of the proceedings opened in respect of any member of the group, provided that such a stay is necessary in order to ensure the proper implementation of the plan and would be to the benefit of the creditors in the proceedings for which the stay is requested; or request the lifting of any existing stay. Such a request shall be made to the court that opened the proceedings for which a stay is requested.
3. The plan referred to in point (b) of paragraph 1 shall not include recommendations as to any consolidation of proceedings or insolvency estates.
4. The coordinator's tasks and rights as defined under this Article shall not extend to any member of the group not participating in group coordination proceedings.
5. The coordinator shall perform his or her duties impartially and with due care.
6. Where the coordinator considers that the fulfilment of his or her tasks requires a significant increase in the costs compared to the cost estimate referred to in point (d) of Article 61(3), and in any case, where the costs exceed 10% of the estimated costs, the coordinator shall:
   (a) inform without delay the participating insolvency practitioners; and
   (b) seek the prior approval of the court opening group coordination proceedings.

[3.617]
Article 73
Languages

1. The coordinator shall communicate with the insolvency practitioner of a participating group member in the language agreed with the insolvency practitioner or, in the absence of an agreement, in the official language or one of the official languages of the institutions of the Union, and of the court which opened the proceedings in respect of that group member.
2. The coordinator shall communicate with a court in the official language applicable to that court.

[3.618]
Article 74
Cooperation between insolvency practitioners and the coordinator

1. Insolvency practitioners appointed in relation to members of a group and the coordinator shall cooperate with each other to the extent that such cooperation is not incompatible with the rules applicable to the respective proceedings.
2. In particular, insolvency practitioners shall communicate any information that is relevant for the coordinator to perform his or her tasks.

[3.619]
Article 75
Revocation of the appointment of the coordinator

The court shall revoke the appointment of the coordinator of its own motion or at the request of the insolvency practitioner of a participating group member where:

(a) the coordinator acts to the detriment of the creditors of a participating group member; or
(b) the coordinator fails to comply with his or her obligations under this Chapter.

[3.620]
Article 76
Debtor in possession
The provisions applicable, under this Chapter, to the insolvency practitioner shall also apply, where appropriate, to the debtor in possession.

[3.621]
Article 77
Costs and distribution
1. The remuneration for the coordinator shall be adequate, proportionate to the tasks fulfilled and reflect reasonable expenses.
2. On having completed his or her tasks, the coordinator shall establish the final statement of costs and the share to be paid by each member, and submit this statement to each participating insolvency practitioner and to the court opening coordination proceedings.
3. In the absence of objections by the insolvency practitioners within 30 days of receipt of the statement referred to in paragraph 2, the costs and the share to be paid by each member shall be deemed to be agreed. The statement shall be submitted to the court opening coordination proceedings for confirmation.
4. In the event of an objection, the court that opened the group coordination proceedings shall, upon the application of the coordinator or any participating insolvency practitioner, decide on the costs and the share to be paid by each member in accordance with the criteria set out in paragraph 1 of this Article, and taking into account the estimation of costs referred to in Article 68(1) and, where applicable, Article 72(6).
5. Any participating insolvency practitioner may challenge the decision referred to in paragraph 4 in accordance with the procedure set out under the law of the Member State where group coordination proceedings have been opened.

CHAPTER VI DATA PROTECTION

[3.622]
Article 78
Data protection
1. National rules implementing Directive 95/46/EC shall apply to the processing of personal data carried out in the Member States pursuant to this Regulation, provided that processing operations referred to in Article 3(2) of Directive 95/46/EC are not concerned.
2. Regulation (EC) No 45/2001 shall apply to the processing of personal data carried out by the Commission pursuant to this Regulation.

[3.623]
Article 79
Responsibilities of Member States regarding the processing of personal data in national insolvency registers
1. Each Member State shall communicate to the Commission the name of the natural or legal person, public authority, agency or any other body designated by national law to exercise the functions of controller in accordance with point (d) of Article 2 of Directive 95/46/EC, with a view to its publication on the European e-Justice Portal.
2. Member States shall ensure that the technical measures for ensuring the security of personal data processed in their national insolvency registers referred to in Article 24 are implemented.
3. Member States shall be responsible for verifying that the controller, designated by national law in accordance with point (d) of Article 2 of Directive 95/46/EC, ensures compliance with the principles of data quality, in particular the accuracy and the updating of data stored in national insolvency registers.
4. Member States shall be responsible, in accordance with Directive 95/46/EC, for the collection and storage of data in national databases and for decisions taken to make such data available in the interconnected register that can be consulted via the European e-Justice Portal.
5. As part of the information that should be provided to data subjects to enable them to exercise their rights, and in particular the right to the erasure of data, Member States shall inform data subjects of the accessibility period set for personal data stored in insolvency registers.

[3.624]
Article 80
Responsibilities of the Commission in connection with the processing of personal data
1. The Commission shall exercise the responsibilities of controller pursuant to Article 2(d) of Regulation (EC) No 45/2001 in accordance with its respective responsibilities defined in this Article.
2. The Commission shall define the necessary policies and apply the necessary technical solutions to fulfil its responsibilities within the scope of the function of controller.
3. The Commission shall implement the technical measures required to ensure the security of personal data while in transit, in particular the confidentiality and integrity of any transmission to and from the European e-Justice Portal.
4. The obligations of the Commission shall not affect the responsibilities of the Member States and other bodies for the content and operation of the interconnected national databases run by them.

[3.625]
Article 81
Information obligations

Without prejudice to the information to be given to data subjects in accordance with Articles 11 and 12 of Regulation (EC) No 45/2001, the Commission shall inform data subjects, by means of publication through the European e-Justice Portal, about its role in the processing of data and the purposes for which those data will be processed.

[3.626]
Article 82
Storage of personal data

As regards information from interconnected national databases, no personal data relating to data subjects shall be stored in the European e-Justice Portal. All such data shall be stored in the national databases operated by the Member States or other bodies.

[3.627]
Article 83
Access to personal data via the European e-Justice Portal

Personal data stored in the national insolvency registers referred to in Article 24 shall be accessible via the European e-Justice Portal for as long as they remain accessible under national law.

CHAPTER VII TRANSITIONAL AND FINAL PROVISIONS

[3.628]
Article 84
Applicability in time

1. The provisions of this Regulation shall apply only to insolvency proceedings opened from 26 June 2017. Acts committed by a debtor before that date shall continue to be governed by the law which was applicable to them at the time they were committed.
2. Notwithstanding Article 91 of this Regulation, Regulation (EC) No 1346/2000 shall continue to apply to insolvency proceedings which fall within the scope of that Regulation and which have been opened before 26 June 2017.

[3.629]
Article 85
Relationship to Conventions

1. This Regulation replaces, in respect of the matters referred to therein, and as regards relations between Member States, the Conventions concluded between two or more Member States, in particular:
(a) the Convention between Belgium and France on Jurisdiction and the Validity and Enforcement of Judgments, Arbitration Awards and Authentic Instruments, signed at Paris on 8 July 1899;
(b) the Convention between Belgium and Austria on Bankruptcy, Winding-up, Arrangements, Compositions and Suspension of Payments (with Additional Protocol of 13 June 1973), signed at Brussels on 16 July 1969;
(c) the Convention between Belgium and the Netherlands on Territorial Jurisdiction, Bankruptcy and the Validity and Enforcement of Judgments, Arbitration Awards and Authentic Instruments, signed at Brussels on 28 March 1925;
(d) the Treaty between Germany and Austria on Bankruptcy, Winding-up, Arrangements and Compositions, signed at Vienna on 25 May 1979;
(e) the Convention between France and Austria on Jurisdiction, Recognition and Enforcement of Judgments on Bankruptcy, signed at Vienna on 27 February 1979;
(f) the Convention between France and Italy on the Enforcement of Judgments in Civil and Commercial Matters, signed at Rome on 3 June 1930;
(g) the Convention between Italy and Austria on Bankruptcy, Winding-up, Arrangements and Compositions, signed at Rome on 12 July 1977;
(h) the Convention between the Kingdom of the Netherlands and the Federal Republic of Germany on the Mutual Recognition and Enforcement of Judgments and other Enforceable Instruments in Civil and Commercial Matters, signed at The Hague on 30 August 1962;
(i) the Convention between the United Kingdom and the Kingdom of Belgium providing for the Reciprocal Enforcement of Judgments in Civil and Commercial Matters, with Protocol, signed at Brussels on 2 May 1934;
(j) the Convention between Denmark, Finland, Norway, Sweden and Iceland on Bankruptcy, signed at Copenhagen on 7 November 1933;
(k) the European Convention on Certain International Aspects of Bankruptcy, signed at Istanbul on 5 June 1990;
(l) the Convention between the Federative People's Republic of Yugoslavia and the Kingdom of Greece on the Mutual Recognition and Enforcement of Judgments, signed at Athens on 18 June 1959;
(m) the Agreement between the Federative People's Republic of Yugoslavia and the Republic of Austria on the Mutual Recognition and Enforcement of Arbitral Awards and Arbitral Settlements in Commercial Matters, signed at Belgrade on 18 March 1960;
(n) the Convention between the Federative People's Republic of Yugoslavia and the Italian Republic on Mutual Judicial Cooperation in Civil and Administrative Matters, signed at Rome on 3 December 1960;

(o) the Agreement between the Socialist Federative Republic of Yugoslavia and the Kingdom of Belgium on Judicial Cooperation in Civil and Commercial Matters, signed at Belgrade on 24 September 1971;

(p) the Convention between the Governments of Yugoslavia and France on the Recognition and Enforcement of Judgments in Civil and Commercial Matters, signed at Paris on 18 May 1971;

(q) the Agreement between the Czechoslovak Socialist Republic and the Hellenic Republic on Legal Aid in Civil and Criminal Matters, signed at Athens on 22 October 1980, still in force between the Czech Republic and Greece;

(r) the Agreement between the Czechoslovak Socialist Republic and the Republic of Cyprus on Legal Aid in Civil and Criminal Matters, signed at Nicosia on 23 April 1982, still in force between the Czech Republic and Cyprus;

(s) the Treaty between the Government of the Czechoslovak Socialist Republic and the Government of the Republic of France on Legal Aid and the Recognition and Enforcement of Judgments in Civil, Family and Commercial Matters, signed at Paris on 10 May 1984, still in force between the Czech Republic and France;

(t) the Treaty between the Czechoslovak Socialist Republic and the Italian Republic on Legal Aid in Civil and Criminal Matters, signed at Prague on 6 December 1985, still in force between the Czech Republic and Italy;

(u) the Agreement between the Republic of Latvia, the Republic of Estonia and the Republic of Lithuania on Legal Assistance and Legal Relationships, signed at Tallinn on 11 November 1992;

(v) the Agreement between Estonia and Poland on Granting Legal Aid and Legal Relations on Civil, Labour and Criminal Matters, signed at Tallinn on 27 November 1998;

(w) the Agreement between the Republic of Lithuania and the Republic of Poland on Legal Assistance and Legal Relations in Civil, Family, Labour and Criminal Matters, signed at Warsaw on 26 January 1993;

(x) the Convention between the Socialist Republic of Romania and the Hellenic Republic on legal assistance in civil and criminal matters and its Protocol, signed at Bucharest on 19 October 1972;

(y) the Convention between the Socialist Republic of Romania and the French Republic on legal assistance in civil and commercial matters, signed at Paris on 5 November 1974;

(z) the Agreement between the People's Republic of Bulgaria and the Hellenic Republic on Legal Assistance in Civil and Criminal Matters, signed at Athens on 10 April 1976;

(aa) the Agreement between the People's Republic of Bulgaria and the Republic of Cyprus on Legal Assistance in Civil and Criminal Matters, signed at Nicosia on 29 April 1983;

(ab) the Agreement between the Government of the People's Republic of Bulgaria and the Government of the French Republic on Mutual Legal Assistance in Civil Matters, signed at Sofia on 18 January 1989;

(ac) the Treaty between Romania and the Czech Republic on judicial assistance in civil matters, signed at Bucharest on 11 July 1994;

(ad) the Treaty between Romania and the Republic of Poland on legal assistance and legal relations in civil cases, signed at Bucharest on 15 May 1999.

2. The Conventions referred to in paragraph 1 shall continue to have effect with regard to proceedings opened before the entry into force of Regulation (EC) No 1346/2000.

3. This Regulation shall not apply:

(a) in any Member State, to the extent that it is irreconcilable with the obligations arising in relation to bankruptcy from a convention concluded by that Member State with one or more third countries before the entry into force of Regulation (EC) No 1346/2000;

(b) in the United Kingdom of Great Britain and Northern Ireland, to the extent that is irreconcilable with the obligations arising in relation to bankruptcy and the winding-up of insolvent companies from any arrangements with the Commonwealth existing at the time Regulation (EC) No 1346/2000 entered into force.

[3.630]
Article 86
Information on national and Union insolvency law

1. The Member States shall provide, within the framework of the European Judicial Network in civil and commercial matters established by Council Decision 2001/470/EC,[1] and with a view to making the information available to the public, a short description of their national legislation and procedures relating to insolvency, in particular relating to the matters listed in Article 7(2).

2. The Member States shall update the information referred to in paragraph 1 regularly.

3. The Commission shall make information concerning this Regulation available to the public.

NOTES

[1] Council Decision 2001/470/EC of 28 May 2001 establishing a European Judicial Network in civil and commercial matters (OJ L 174, 27.6.2001, p. 25).

[3.631]
Article 87
Establishment of the interconnection of registers

The Commission shall adopt implementing acts establishing the interconnection of insolvency registers as referred to in Article 25. Those implementing acts shall be adopted in accordance with the examination procedure referred to in Article 89(3).

[3.632]
Article 88
Establishment and subsequent amendment of standard forms
The Commission shall adopt implementing acts establishing and, where necessary, amending the forms referred to in Article 27(4), Articles 54 and 55 and Article 64(2). Those implementing acts shall be adopted in accordance with the advisory procedure referred to in Article 89(2).

[3.633]
Article 89
Committee procedure
1. The Commission shall be assisted by a committee. That committee shall be a committee within the meaning of Regulation (EU) No 182/2011.
2. Where reference is made to this paragraph, Article 4 of Regulation (EU) No 182/2011 shall apply.
3. Where reference is made to this paragraph, Article 5 of Regulation (EU) No 182/2011 shall apply.

[3.634]
Article 90
Review clause
1. No later than 27 June 2027, and every 5 years thereafter, the Commission shall present to the European Parliament, the Council and the European Economic and Social Committee a report on the application of this Regulation. The report shall be accompanied where necessary by a proposal for adaptation of this Regulation.
2. No later than 27 June 2022, the Commission shall present to the European Parliament, the Council and the European Economic and Social Committee a report on the application of the group coordination proceedings. The report shall be accompanied where necessary by a proposal for adaptation of this Regulation.
3. No later than 1 January 2016, the Commission shall submit to the European Parliament, the Council and the European Economic and Social Committee a study on the cross-border issues in the area of directors' liability and disqualifications.
4. No later than 27 June 2020, the Commission shall submit to the European Parliament, the Council and the European Economic and Social Committee a study on the issue of abusive forum shopping.

[3.635]
Article 91
Repeal
Regulation (EC) No 1346/2000 is repealed.
References to the repealed Regulation shall be construed as references to this Regulation and shall be read in accordance with the correlation table set out in Annex D to this Regulation.

[3.636]
Article 92
Entry into force
This Regulation shall enter into force on the twentieth day following that of its publication in the *Official Journal of the European Union*.
It shall apply from 26 June 2017, with the exception of:
(a) Article 86, which shall apply from 26 June 2016;
(b) Article 24(1), which shall apply from 26 June 2018; and
(c) Article 25, which shall apply from 26 June 2019.
This Regulation shall be binding in its entirety and directly applicable in the Member States in accordance with the Treaties.

[ANNEX A
INSOLVENCY PROCEEDINGS REFERRED TO IN POINT (4) OF ARTICLE 2

[3.637]
BELGIQUE/BELGIË
— Het faillissement/La faillite,
— De gerechtelijke reorganisatie door een collectief akkoord/La réorganisation judiciaire par accord collectif,
— De gerechtelijke reorganisatie door een minnelijk akkoord/La réorganisation judiciaire par accord amiable,
— De gerechtelijke reorganisatie door overdracht onder gerechtelijk gezag/La réorganisation judiciaire par transfert sous autorité de justice,
— De collectieve schuldenregeling/Le règlement collectif de dettes,
— De vrijwillige vereffening/La liquidation volontaire,
— De gerechtelijke vereffening/La liquidation judiciaire,
— De voorlopige ontneming van beheer, bepaald in artikel 8 van de faillissementswet/Le dessaisissement provisoire, visé à l'article 8 de la loi sur les faillites,

БЪЛГАРИЯ
— Производство по несъстоятелност,

ČESKÁ REPUBLIKA
— Konkurs,

— Reorganizace,
— Oddlužení,

DEUTSCHLAND
— Das Konkursverfahren,
— Das gerichtliche Vergleichsverfahren,
— Das Gesamtvollstreckungsverfahren,
— Das Insolvenzverfahren,

EESTI
— Pankrotimenetlus,
— Võlgade ümberkujundamise menetlus,

ÉIRE/IRELAND
— Compulsory winding-up by the court,
— Bankruptcy,
— The administration in bankruptcy of the estate of persons dying insolvent,
— Winding-up in bankruptcy of partnerships,
— Creditors' voluntary winding-up (with confirmation of a court),
— Arrangements under the control of the court which involve the vesting of all or part of the property of the debtor in the Official Assignee for realisation and distribution,
— Examinership,
— Debt Relief Notice,
— Debt Settlement Arrangement,
— Personal Insolvency Arrangement,

ΕΛΛΑΔΑ
— Η πτώχευση,
— Η ειδική εκκαθάριση εν λειτουργία,
— Σχέδιο αναδιοργάνωσης,
— Απλοποιημένη διαδικασία επί πτωχεύσεων μικρού αντικειμένου,
— Διαδικασία Εξυγίανσης,

ESPAÑA
— Concurso,
— Procedimiento de homologación de acuerdos de refinanciación,
— Procedimiento de acuerdos extrajudiciales de pago,
— Procedimiento de negociación pública para la consecución de acuerdos de refinanciación colectivos, acuerdos de refinanciación homologados y propuestas anticipadas de convenio,

FRANCE
— Sauvegarde,
— Sauvegarde accélérée,
— Sauvegarde financière accélérée,
— Redressement judiciaire,
— Liquidation judiciaire,

HRVATSKA
— Stečajni postupak,

ITALIA
— Fallimento,
— Concordato preventivo,
— Liquidazione coatta amministrativa,
— Amministrazione straordinaria,
— Accordi di ristrutturazione,
— Procedure di composizione della crisi da sovraindebitamento del consumatore (accordo o piano),
— Liquidazione dei beni,

ΚΥΠΡΟΣ
— Υποχρεωτική εκκαθάριση από το Δικαστήριο,
— Εκούσια εκκαθάριση από μέλη,
— Εκούσια εκκαθάριση από πιστωτές
— Εκκαθάριση με την εποπτεία του Δικαστηρίου,
— Διάταγμα Παραλαβής και πτώχευσης κατόπιν Δικαστικού Διατάγματος,
— Διαχείριση της περιουσίας προσώπων που απεβίωσαν αφερέγγυα,

LATVIJA
— Tiesiskās aizsardzības process,
— Juridiskās personas maksātnespējas process,
— Fiziskās personas maksātnespējas process,

LIETUVA
— Įmonės restruktūrizavimo byla,
— Įmonės bankroto byla,
— Įmonės bankroto procesas ne teismo tvarka,

— Fizinio asmens bankroto procesas,

LUXEMBOURG
— Faillite,
— Gestion contrôlée,
— Gestion contrôlée,
— Concordat préventif de faillite (par abandon d'actif),
— Régime spécial de liquidation du notariat,
— Procédure de règlement collectif des dettes dans le cadre du surendettement,

MAGYARORSZÁG
— Csődeljárás,
— Felszámolási eljárás,

MALTA
— Xoljiment,
— Amministrazzjoni,
— Stralċ volontarju mill-membri jew mill-kredituri,
— Stralċ mill-Qorti,
— Falliment f'każ ta' kummerċjant,
— Proċedura biex kumpanija tirkupra,

NEDERLAND
— Het faillissement,
— De surséance van betaling,
— De schuldsaneringsregeling natuurlijke personen,

ÖSTERREICH
— Das Konkursverfahren (Insolvenzverfahren),
— Das Sanierungsverfahren ohne Eigenverwaltung (Insolvenzverfahren),
— Das Sanierungsverfahren mit Eigenverwaltung (Insolvenzverfahren),
— Das Schuldenregulierungsverfahren,
— Das Abschöpfungsverfahren,
— Das Ausgleichsverfahren,

POLSKA
— Upadłość,
— Postępowanie o zatwierdzenie układu,
— Przyspieszone postępowanie układowe,
— Postępowanie układowe,
— Postępowanie sanacyjne,

PORTUGAL
— Processo de insolvência,
— Processo especial de revitalização,

ROMÂNIA
— Procedura insolvenței,
— Reorganizarea judiciară,
— Procedura falimentului,
— Concordatul preventiv,

SLOVENIJA
— Postopek preventivnega prestrukturiranja,
— Postopek prisilne poravnave,
— Postopek poenostavljene prisilne poravnave,
— Stečajni postopek: stečajni postopek nad pravno osebo, postopek osebnega stečaja and postopek stečaja zapuščine,

SLOVENSKO
— Konkurzné konanie,
— Reštrukturalizačné konanie,
— Oddlženie,

SUOMI/FINLAND
— Konkurssi/konkurs,
— Yrityssaneeraus/företagssanering,
— Yksityishenkilön velkajärjestely/skuldsanering för privatpersoner,

SVERIGE
— Konkurs,
— Företagsrekonstruktion,
— Skuldsanering,

UNITED KINGDOM
— Winding-up by or subject to the supervision of the court,
— Creditors' voluntary winding-up (with confirmation by the court),

— Administration, including appointments made by filing prescribed documents with the court,
— Voluntary arrangements under insolvency legislation,
— Bankruptcy or sequestration.]

NOTES

Substituted by European Parliament and Council Directive 2017/353/EU, Art 1.

[ANNEX B
INSOLVENCY PRACTITIONERS REFERRED TO IN POINT (5) OF ARTICLE 2

[3.638]

BELGIQUE/BELGIË
— De curator/Le curateur,
— De gedelegeerd rechter/Le juge-délégué,
— De gerechtsmandataris/Le mandataire de justice,
— De schuldbemiddelaar/Le médiateur de dettes,
— De vereffenaar/Le liquidateur,
— De voorlopige bewindvoerder/L'administrateur provisoire,

БЪЛГАРИЯ
— Назначен предварително временен синдик,
— Временен синдик,
— (Постоянен) синдик,
— Служебен синдик,

ČESKÁ REPUBLIKA
— Insolvenční správce,
— Předběžný insolvenční správce,
— Oddělený insolvenční správce,
— Zvláštní insolvenční správce,
— Zástupce insolvenčního správce,

DEUTSCHLAND
— Konkursverwalter,
— Vergleichsverwalter,
— Sachwalter (nach der Vergleichsordnung),
— Verwalter,
— Insolvenzverwalter,
— Sachwalter (nach der Insolvenzordnung),
— Treuhänder,
— Vorläufiger Insolvenzverwalter,
— Vorläufiger Sachwalter,

EESTI
— Pankrotihaldur,
— Ajutine pankrotihaldur,
— Usaldusisik,

ÉIRE/IRELAND
— Liquidator,
— Official Assignee,
— Trustee in bankruptcy,
— Provisional Liquidator,
— Examiner,
— Personal Insolvency Practitioner,
— Insolvency Service,

ΕΛΛΑΔΑ
— Ο σύνδικος,
— Ο εισηγητής,
— Η επιτροπή των πιστωτών,
— Ο ειδικός εκκαθαριστής,

ESPAÑA
— Administrador concursal,
— Mediador concursal,

FRANCE
— Mandataire judiciaire,
— Liquidateur,
— Administrateur judiciaire,
— Commissaire à l'exécution du plan,

HRVATSKA
— Stečajni upravitelj,
— Privremeni stečajni upravitelj,

— Stečajni povjerenik,
— Povjerenik,

ITALIA
— Curatore,
— Commissario giudiziale,
— Commissario straordinario,
— Commissario liquidatore,
— Liquidatore giudiziale,
— Professionista nominato dal Tribunale,
— Organismo di composizione della crisi nella procedura di composizione della crisi da sovraindebitamento del consumatore,
— Liquidatore,

ΚΥΠΡΟΣ
— Εκκαθαριστής και Προσωρινός Εκκαθαριστής,
— Επίσημος Παραλήπτης,
— Διαχειριστής της Πτώχευσης,

LATVIJA
— Maksātnespējas procesa administrators,

LIETUVA
— Bankroto administratorius,
— Restruktūrizavimo administratorius,

LUXEMBOURG
— Le curateur,
— Le commissaire,
— Le liquidateur,
— Le conseil de gérance de la section d'assainissement du notariat,
— Le liquidateur dans le cadre du surendettement,

MAGYARORSZÁG
— Vagyonfelügyelő,
— Felszámoló,

MALTA
— Amministratur Proviżorju,
— Riċevitur Uffiċjali,
— Stralċjarju,
— Manager Speċjali,
— Kuraturi f'każ ta' proċeduri ta' falliment,
— Kontrolur Speċjali,

NEDERLAND
— De curator in het faillissement,
— De bewindvoerder in de surséance van betaling,
— De De bewindvoerder in de schuldsaneringsregeling natuurlijke personen,

ÖSTERREICH
— Masseverwalter,
— Sanierungsverwalter,
— Ausgleichsverwalter,
— Besonderer Verwalter,
— Einstweiliger Verwalter,
— Sachwalter,
— Treuhänder,
— Insolvenzgericht,
— Konkursgericht,

POLSKA
— Syndyk,
— Nadzorca sądowy,
— Zarządca,
— Nadzorca układu,
— Tymczasowy nadzorca sądowy,
— Tymczasowy zarządca,
— Zarządca przymusowy,

PORTUGAL
— Administrador da insolvência,
— Administrador judicial provisório,

ROMÂNIA
— Practician în insolvență,

— Administrator concordatar,
— Administrator judiciar,
— Lichidator judiciar,

SLOVENIJA
— Upravitelj,

SLOVENSKO
— Predbežný správca,
— Správca,

SUOMI/FINLAND
— Pesänhoitaja/boförvaltare,
— Selvittäjä/utredare,

SVERIGE
— Förvaltare,
— Rekonstruktör,

UNITED KINGDOM
— Liquidator,
— Supervisor of a voluntary arrangement,
— Administrator,
— Official Receiver,
— Trustee,
— Provisional Liquidator,
— Interim Receiver,
— Judicial factor.]

NOTES

Substituted by European Parliament and Council Directive 2017/353/EU, Art 1.

ANNEX C
REPEALED REGULATION WITH LIST OF THE SUCCESSIVE AMENDMENTS THERETO

[3.639]

Council Regulation (EC) No 1346/2000

(OJ L 160, 30.6.2000, p. 1)

Council Regulation (EC) No 603/2005

(OJ L 100, 20.4.2005, p. 1)

Council Regulation (EC) No 694/2006

(OJ L 121, 6.5.2006, p. 1)

Council Regulation (EC) No 1791/2006

(OJ L 363, 20.12.2006, p. 1)

Council Regulation (EC) No 681/2007

(OJ L 159, 20.6.2007, p. 1)

Council Regulation (EC) No 788/2008

(OJ L 213, 8.8.2008, p. 1)

Implementing Regulation of the Council (EU) No 210/2010

(OJ L 65, 13.3.2010, p. 1)

Council Implementing Regulation (EU) No 583/2011

(OJ L 160, 18.6.2011, p. 52)

Council Regulation (EU) No 517/2013

(OJ L 158, 10.6.2013, p. 1)

Council Implementing Regulation (EU) No 663/2014

(OJ L 179, 19.6.2014, p. 4)

Act concerning the conditions of accession of the Czech Republic, the Republic of Estonia, the Republic of Cyprus, the Republic of Latvia, the Republic of Lithuania, the Republic of Hungary, the Republic of Malta, the Republic of Poland, the Republic of Slovenia and the Slovak Republic and the adjustments to the Treaties on which the European Union is founded

(OJ L 236, 23.9.2003, p. 33)

ANNEX D
CORRELATION TABLE

[3.640]

Regulation (EC) No 1346/2000	This Regulation
Article 1	Article 1
Article 2, introductory words	Article 2, introductory words
Article 2, point (a)	Article 2, point (4)
Article 2, point (b)	Article 2, point (5)
Article 2, point (c)	—
Article 2, point (d)	Article 2, point (6)
Article 2, point (e)	Article 2, point (7)
Article 2, point (f)	Article 2, point (8)
Article 2, point (g), introductory words	Article 2, point (9), introductory words
Article 2, point (g), first indent	Article 2, point (9)(vii)
Article 2, point (g), second indent	Article 2, point (9)(iv)
Article 2, point (g), third indent	Article 2, point (9)(viii)
Article 2, point (h)	Article 2, point 10
—	Article 2, points (1) to (3) and (11) to (13)
—	Article 2, point (9)(i) to (iii), (v), (vi)
Article 3	Article 3
—	Article 4
—	Article 5
—	Article 6
Article 4	Article 7
Article 5	Article 8
Article 6	Article 9
Article 7	Article 10
Article 8	Article 11(1)
—	Article 11(2)
Article 9	Article 12
Article 10	Article 13(1)
—	Article 13(2)
Article 11	Article 14
Article 12	Article 15
Article 13, first indent	Article 16, point (a)
Article 13, second indent	Article 16, point (b)
Article 14, first indent	Article 17, point (a)
Article 14, second indent	Article 17, point (b)
Article 14, third indent	Article 17, point (c)
Article 15	Article 18
Article 16	Article 19
Article 17	Article 20
Article 18	Article 21
Article 19	Article 22
Article 20	Article 23
—	Article 24
—	Article 25
—	Article 26

Regulation (EC) No 1346/2000	This Regulation
—	Article 27
Article 21(1)	Article 28(2)
Article 21(2)	Article 28(1)
Article 22	Article 29
Article 23	Article 30
Article 24	Article 31
Article 25	Article 32
Article 26	Article 33
Article 27	Article 34
Article 28	Article 35
—	Article 36
Article 29	Article 37(1)
—	Article 37(2)
—	Article 38
—	Article 39
Article 30	Article 40
Article 31	Article 41
—	Article 42
—	Article 43
—	Article 44
Article 32	Article 45
Article 33	Article 46
Article 34(1)	Article 47(1)
Article 34(2)	Article 47(2)
Article 34(3)	—
—	Article 48
Article 35	Article 49
Article 36	Article 50
Article 37	Article 51
Article 38	Article 52
Article 39	Article 53
Article 40	Article 54
Article 41	Article 55
Article 42	—
—	Article 56
—	Article 57
—	Article 58
—	Article 59
—	Article 60
—	Article 61
—	Article 62
—	Article 63
—	Article 64
—	Article 65
—	Article 66
—	Article 67
—	Article 68
—	Article 69

Regulation (EC) No 1346/2000	This Regulation
—	Article 70
—	Article 71
—	Article 72
—	Article 73
—	Article 74
—	Article 75
—	Article 76
—	Article 77
—	Article 78
—	Article 79
—	Article 80
—	Article 81
—	Article 82
—	Article 83
Article 43	Article 84(1)
—	Article 84(2)
Article 44	Article 85
—	Article 86
Article 45	—
—	Article 87
—	Article 88
—	Article 89
Article 46	Article 90(1)
—	Article 90(2) to (4)
—	Article 91
Article 47	Article 92
Annex A	Annex A
Annex B	—
Annex C	Annex B
—	Annex C
—	Annex D

PART 4
COMPANY DIRECTORS DISQUALIFICATION ACT 1986

COMPANY DIRECTORS DISQUALIFICATION ACT 1986

(1986 c 46)

ARRANGEMENT OF SECTIONS

Preliminary

1 Disqualification orders: general . . . [4.1]
1A Disqualification undertakings: general . . . [4.2]

Disqualification for general misconduct in connection with companies

2 Disqualification on conviction of indictable offence . . . [4.3]
3 Disqualification for persistent breaches of companies legislation . . . [4.4]
4 Disqualification for fraud, etc, in winding up . . . [4.5]
5 Disqualification on summary conviction . . . [4.6]
5A Disqualification for certain convictions abroad . . . [4.7]

Disqualification for unfitness

6 Duty of court to disqualify unfit directors of insolvent companies . . . [4.8]
7 Disqualification orders under section 6: applications and acceptance of undertakings . . . [4.9]
7A Office-holder's report on conduct of directors . . . [4.10]
8 Disqualification of director on finding of unfitness . . . [4.11]

Persons instructing unfit directors

8ZA Order disqualifying person instructing unfit director of insolvent company . . . [4.12]
8ZB Application for order under section 8ZA . . . [4.13]
8ZC Disqualification undertaking instead of an order under section 8ZA . . . [4.14]
8ZD Order disqualifying person instructing unfit director: other cases . . . [4.15]
8ZE Disqualification undertaking instead of an order under section 8ZD . . . [4.16]

Further provision about disqualification undertakings

8A Variation etc of disqualification undertaking . . . [4.17]

Disqualification for competition infringements

9A Competition disqualification order . . . [4.18]
9B Competition undertakings . . . [4.19]
9C Competition investigations . . . [4.20]
9D Co-ordination . . . [4.21]
9E Interpretation . . . [4.22]

Other cases of disqualification

10 Participation in wrongful trading . . . [4.23]
11 Undischarged bankrupts . . . [4.24]
12 Failure to pay under county court administration order . . . [4.25]
12C Determining unfitness etc: matters to be taken into account . . . [4.26]

Consequences of contravention

13 Criminal penalties . . . [4.27]
14 Offences by body corporate . . . [4.28]
15 Personal liability for company's debts where person acts while disqualified . . . [4.29]

Compensation orders and undertakings

15A Compensation orders and undertakings . . . [4.30]
15B Amounts payable under compensation orders and undertakings . . . [4.30]
15C Variation and revocation of compensation undertakings . . . [4.30]

Supplementary provisions

16 Application for disqualification order . . . [4.33]
17 Application for leave under an order or undertaking . . . [4.34]
18 Register of disqualification orders and undertakings . . . [4.35]
19 Special savings from repealed enactments . . . [4.36]

Miscellaneous and general

20 Admissibility in evidence of statements . . . [4.37]
20A Legal professional privilege . . . [4.38]
21 Interaction with Insolvency Act 1986 . . . [4.39]
21A Bank insolvency . . . [4.40]
21B Bank administration . . . [4.41]

21C Building society insolvency and special administration . . . [4.42]
22 Interpretation . . . [4.43]
22A Application of Act to building societies . . . [4.44]
22B Application of Act to incorporated friendly societies . . . [4.45]
22C Application of Act to NHS foundation trusts . . . [4.46]
22E Application of Act to registered societies . . . [4.47]
22F Application of Act to charitable incorporated organisations . . . [4.48]
22G Application of Act to further education bodies . . . [4.49]
22H Application of Act to protected cell companies . . . [4.50]
23 Transitional provisions, savings, repeals . . . [4.51]
24 Extent . . . [4.52]
25 Commencement . . . [4.53]
26 Citation . . . [4.54]

SCHEDULES

Schedule 1—Determining Unfitness etc: Matters to be Taken into Account . . . [4.55]
Schedule 2—Savings from Companies Act 1981, ss 93, 94, and Insolvency Act 1985, Sch 9 . . . [4.56]
Schedule 3—Transitional Provisions and Savings . . . [4.57]

An Act to consolidate certain enactments relating to the disqualification of persons from being directors of companies, and from being otherwise concerned with a company's affairs

[25 July 1986]

NOTES

European Economic Interest Groupings: as to the application, with modifications, of ss 1, 2, 4–11, 12(2), 15–17, 20, 22 of, and Sch 1 to, this Act, to European Economic Interest Groupings, see the European Economic Interest Grouping Regulations 1989, SI 1989/638, reg 20.

Insolvent partnerships: as to the application, with modifications, of this Act in relation to insolvent partnerships, see the Insolvent Partnerships Order 1994, SI 1994/2421 at **[10.1]**.

Limited liability partnerships: as to the application, with modifications, of this Act in relation to limited liability partnerships, see the Limited Liability Partnerships Regulations 2001, SI 2001/1090 at **[10.33]**.

Official Receiver: as to the contracting out of certain functions of the Official Receiver conferred by or under this Act, see the Contracting Out (Functions of the Official Receiver) Order 1995, SI 1995/1386 at **[12.4]**.

Preliminary

[4.1]

1 Disqualification orders: general

(1) In the circumstances specified below in this Act a court may, and under [sections 6 and 9A] shall, make against a person a disqualification order, that is to say an order that [for a period specified in the order—

- (a) he shall not be a director of a company, act as receiver of a company's property or in any way, whether directly or indirectly, be concerned or take part in the promotion, formation or management of a company unless (in each case) he has the leave of the court, and
- (b) he shall not act as an insolvency practitioner.]

(2) In each section of this Act which gives to a court power or, as the case may be, imposes on it the duty to make a disqualification order there is specified the maximum (and, in [sections 6 and 8ZA], the minimum) period of disqualification which may or (as the case may be) must be imposed by means of the order [and, unless the court otherwise orders, the period of disqualification so imposed shall begin at the end of the period of 21 days beginning with the date of the order].

(3) Where a disqualification order is made against a person who is already subject to such an order [or to a disqualification undertaking], the periods specified in those orders [or, as the case may be, in the order and the undertaking] shall run concurrently.

(4) A disqualification order may be made on grounds which are or include matters other than criminal convictions, notwithstanding that the person in respect of whom it is to be made may be criminally liable in respect of those matters.

NOTES

This section derived from the Companies Act 1985, s 295(1), (2), (4), and the Insolvency Act 1985, Sch 6, para 1(1)–(3).

Sub-s (1): words in first pair of square brackets substituted by the Enterprise Act 2002, s 204(1), (3); words in second pair of square brackets substituted by the Insolvency Act 2000, s 5(1).

Sub-s (2): words in first pair of square brackets substituted by the Small Business, Enterprise and Employment Act 2015, s 111, Sch 7, Pt 1, paras 1, 2; words in second pair of square brackets added by the Insolvency Act 2000, s 5(2).

Sub-s (3): words in square brackets inserted by the Insolvency Act 2000, s 8, Sch 4, Pt I, paras 1, 2.

[4.2]

[1A Disqualification undertakings: general

(1) In the circumstances specified in sections [5A, 7, 8, 8ZC and 8ZE] the Secretary of State may accept a disqualification undertaking, that is to say an undertaking by any person that, for a period specified in the undertaking, the person—

(a) will not be a director of a company, act as receiver of a company's property or in any way, whether directly or indirectly, be concerned or take part in the promotion, formation or management of a company unless (in each case) he has the leave of a court, and

(b) will not act as an insolvency practitioner.

(2) The maximum period which may be specified in a disqualification undertaking is 15 years; and the minimum period which may be specified in a disqualification undertaking under section 7 [or 8ZC] is two years.

(3) Where a disqualification undertaking by a person who is already subject to such an undertaking or to a disqualification order is accepted, the periods specified in those undertakings or (as the case may be) the undertaking and the order shall run concurrently.

(4) In determining whether to accept a disqualification undertaking by any person, the Secretary of State may take account of matters other than criminal convictions, notwithstanding that the person may be criminally liable in respect of those matters.]

NOTES

Inserted by the Insolvency Act 2000, s 6(1), (2).

Sub-s (1): words in square brackets substituted by the Small Business, Enterprise and Employment Act 2015, s 111, Sch 7, Pt 1, paras 1, 3(1), (2).

Sub-s (2): words in square brackets inserted by the Small Business, Enterprise and Employment Act 2015, s 111, Sch 7, Pt 1, paras 1, 3(1), (3).

Disqualification for general misconduct in connection with companies

[4.3]

2 Disqualification on conviction of indictable offence

(1) The court may make a disqualification order against a person where he is convicted of an indictable offence (whether on indictment or summarily) in connection with the promotion, formation, management[, liquidation or striking off] of a company [with the receivership of a company's property or with his being an administrative receiver of a company].

[(1A) In subsection (1), "company" includes overseas company.]

(2) "The court" for this purpose means—

(a) any court having jurisdiction to wind up the company in relation to which the offence was committed, or

[(aa) in relation to an overseas company not falling within paragraph (a), the High Court or, in Scotland, the Court of Session, or]

(b) the court by or before which the person is convicted of the offence, or

(c) in the case of a summary conviction in England and Wales, any other magistrates' court acting [in the same local justice] area;

and for the purposes of this section the definition of "indictable offence" in Schedule 1 to the Interpretation Act 1978 applies for Scotland as it does for England and Wales.

(3) The maximum period of disqualification under this section is—

(a) where the disqualification order is made by a court of summary jurisdiction, 5 years, and

(b) in any other case, 15 years.

NOTES

This section derived from the Companies Act 1985, ss 295(2), 296.

Sub-s (1): words in first pair of square brackets substituted by the Deregulation and Contracting Out Act 1994, s 39, Sch 11, para 6; words in second pair of square brackets substituted by the Insolvency Act 2000, s 8, Sch 4, Pt I, paras 1, 3.

Sub-s (1A): inserted by the Small Business, Enterprise and Employment Act 2015, s 111, Sch 7, Pt 1, paras 1, 4(1), (2).

Sub-s (2): para (aa) inserted by the Small Business, Enterprise and Employment Act 2015, s 111, Sch 7, Pt 1, paras 1, 4(1), (3); in para (c) words in square brackets substituted by the Courts Act 2003, s 109(1), Sch 8, para 300(a), subject to transitional provisions in SI 2005/911, arts 2–5.

[4.4]

3 Disqualification for persistent breaches of companies legislation

(1) The court may make a disqualification order against a person where it appears to it that he has been persistently in default in relation to provisions of the companies legislation requiring any return, account or other document to be filed with, delivered or sent, or notice of any matter to be given, to the registrar of companies.

(2) On an application to the court for an order to be made under this section, the fact that a person has been persistently in default in relation to such provisions as are mentioned above may (without prejudice to its proof in any other manner) be conclusively proved by showing that in the 5 years ending with the date of the application he has been adjudged guilty (whether or not on the same occasion) of three or more defaults in relation to those provisions.

(3) A person is to be treated under subsection (2) as being adjudged guilty of a default in relation to any provision of that legislation if—

(a) he is convicted (whether on indictment or summarily) of an offence consisting in a contravention of or failure to comply with that provision (whether on his own part or on the part of any company), or

(b) a default order is made against him, that is to say an order under any of the following provisions—

(i) [section 452 of the Companies Act 2006] (order requiring delivery of company accounts),

[(ia) [section 456] of that Act (order requiring preparation of revised accounts),]

(ii) [section 1113 of that Act (enforcement of company's filing obligations)],

(iii) section 41 of the Insolvency Act [1986] (enforcement of receiver's or manager's duty to make returns), or

(iv) section 170 of that Act (corresponding provision for liquidator in winding up),

in respect of any such contravention of or failure to comply with that provision (whether on his own part or on the part of any company).

[(3A) In this section "company" includes overseas company.]

(4) In this section "the court" means[—

(a)] any court having jurisdiction to wind up any of the companies in relation to which the offence or other default has been or is alleged to have been committed[, or

(b) in relation to an overseas company not falling within paragraph (a), the High Court or, in Scotland, the Court of Session.]

[(4A) In this section "the companies legislation" means the Companies Acts and Parts 1 to 7 of the Insolvency Act 1986 (company insolvency and winding up).]

(5) The maximum period of disqualification under this section is 5 years.

NOTES

This section derived from the Companies Act 1985, ss 295(2), 297.

Sub-s (3): para (b)(ia) inserted by the Companies Act 1989, s 23, Sch 10, para 35(1), (2)(b); words in square brackets in para (b)(i) substituted for words "section 242(4) of the Companies Act" and words in square brackets in para (b)(ia) substituted for words "section 245B" by the Companies Act 2006 (Consequential Amendments etc) Order 2008, SI 2008/948, art 3(1)(b), Sch 1, Pt 2, para 106(1), (2)(a), (b), subject to transitional provisions and savings in arts 6, 11, 12 thereof; words in square brackets in para (b)(ii) substituted and date in square brackets in para (b)(iii) inserted by the Companies Act 2006 (Consequential Amendments, Transitional Provisions and Savings) Order 2009, SI 2009/1941, art 2(1), Sch 1, para 85(1), (2)(a).

Sub-s (3A): inserted by the Small Business, Enterprise and Employment Act 2015, s 111, Sch 7, Pt 1, paras 1, 5(1), (2).

Sub-s (4): para (a) designated as such and preceding punctuation inserted, and para (b) and word preceding it inserted, by the Small Business, Enterprise and Employment Act 2015, s 111, Sch 7, Pt 1, paras 1, 5(1), (3).

Sub-s (4A): inserted by SI 2009/1941, art 2(1), Sch 1, para 85(1), (2)(b).

[4.5]

4 Disqualification for fraud, etc, in winding up

(1) The court may make a disqualification order against a person if, in the course of the winding up of a company, it appears that he—

(a) has been guilty of an offence for which he is liable (whether he has been convicted or not) under [section 993 of the Companies Act 2006] (fraudulent trading), or

(b) has otherwise been guilty, while an officer or liquidator of the company [receiver of the company's property or administrative receiver of the company], of any fraud in relation to the company or of any breach of his duty as such officer, liquidator, [receiver or administrative receiver].

(2) In this section "the court" means any court having jurisdiction to wind up any of the companies in relation to which the offence or other default has been or is alleged to have been committed; and "officer" includes a shadow director.

(3) The maximum period of disqualification under this section is 15 years.

NOTES

This section derived from the Companies Act 1985, ss 295(2), 298.

Sub-s (1): words in square brackets in sub-para (a) substituted for original words "section 458 of the Companies Act" by the Companies Act 2006 (Commencement No 3, Consequential Amendments, Transitional Provisions and Savings) Order 2007, SI 2007/2194, art 10(1), (2), Sch 4, Pt 3, para 46, subject to savings in art 12 thereof; words in square brackets in sub-para (b) substituted by the Insolvency Act 2000, s 8, Sch 4, Pt I, paras 1, 4.

[4.6]

5 Disqualification on summary conviction

(1) An offence counting for the purposes of this section is one of which a person is convicted (either on indictment or summarily) in consequence of a contravention of, or failure to comply with, any provision of the companies legislation requiring a return, account or other document to be filed with, delivered or sent, or notice of any matter to be given, to the registrar of companies (whether the contravention or failure is on the person's own part or on the part of any company).

(2) Where a person is convicted of a summary offence counting for those purposes, the court by which he is convicted (or, in England and Wales, any other magistrates' court acting [in the same local justice] area) may make a disqualification order against him if the circumstances specified in the next subsection are present.

(3) Those circumstances are that, during the 5 years ending with the date of the conviction, the person has had made against him, or has been convicted of, in total not less than 3 default orders and offences counting for the purposes of this section; and those offences may include that of which he is convicted as mentioned in subsection (2) and any other offence of which he is convicted on the same occasion.

(4) For the purposes of this section—

(a) the definition of "summary offence" in Schedule 1 to the Interpretation Act 1978 applies for Scotland as for England and Wales, and

(b) "default order" means the same as in section 3(3)(b).

[(4A) In this section "the companies legislation" means the Companies Acts and Parts 1 to 7 of the Insolvency Act 1986 (company insolvency and winding up).]

[(4B) In this section "company" includes overseas company.]

(5) The maximum period of disqualification under this section is 5 years.

NOTES

This section derived from the Companies Act 1985, ss 295(2), 299.

Sub-s (2): words in square brackets substituted by the Courts Act 2003, s 109(1), Sch 8, para 300(b), subject to transitional provisions in SI 2005/911, arts 2–5.

Sub-s (4A): inserted by the Companies Act 2006 (Consequential Amendments, Transitional Provisions and Savings) Order 2009, SI 2009/1941, art 2(1), Sch 1, para 85(1), (3).

Sub-s (4B): inserted by the Small Business, Enterprise and Employment Act 2015, s 111, Sch 7, Pt 1, paras 1, 6.

[4.7]
[5A Disqualification for certain convictions abroad

(1) If it appears to the Secretary of State that it is expedient in the public interest that a disqualification order under this section should be made against a person, the Secretary of State may apply to the court for such an order.

(2) The court may, on an application under subsection (1), make a disqualification order against a person who has been convicted of a relevant foreign offence.

(3) A "relevant foreign offence" is an offence committed outside Great Britain—

(a) in connection with—

(i) the promotion, formation, management, liquidation or striking off of a company (or any similar procedure),

(ii) the receivership of a company's property (or any similar procedure), or

(iii) a person being an administrative receiver of a company (or holding a similar position), and

(b) which corresponds to an indictable offence under the law of England and Wales or (as the case may be) an indictable offence under the law of Scotland.

(4) Where it appears to the Secretary of State that, in the case of a person who has offered to give a disqualification undertaking—

(a) the person has been convicted of a relevant foreign offence, and

(b) it is expedient in the public interest that the Secretary of State should accept the undertaking (instead of applying, or proceeding with an application, for a disqualification order),

the Secretary of State may accept the undertaking.

(5) In this section—

"company" includes an overseas company;

"the court" means the High Court or, in Scotland, the Court of Session.

(6) The maximum period of disqualification under an order under this section is 15 years.]

NOTES

Commencement: 1 October 2015.

Inserted by the Small Business, Enterprise and Employment Act 2015, s 104. Note that sub-ss (2), (4) apply in relation to a conviction of a relevant foreign offence which occurs on or after 1 October 2015 regardless of whether the act or omission which constituted the offence occurred before that date.

Disqualification for unfitness

[4.8]
6 Duty of court to disqualify unfit directors of insolvent companies

(1) The court shall make a disqualification order against a person in any case where, on an application under this section, it is satisfied—

(a) that he is or has been a director of a company which has at any time become insolvent (whether while he was a director or subsequently), and

(b) that his conduct as a director of that company (either taken alone or taken together with his conduct as a director of [one or more other companies or overseas companies]) makes him unfit to be concerned in the management of a company.

[(1A) In this section references to a person's conduct as a director of any company or overseas company include, where that company or overseas company has become insolvent, references to that person's conduct in relation to any matter connected with or arising out of the insolvency.]

(2) For the purposes of this section *and the next*, a company becomes insolvent if—

(a) the company goes into liquidation at a time when its assets are insufficient for the payment of its debts and other liabilities and the expenses of the winding up,

[(b) the company enters administration,]

(c) an administrative receiver of the company is appointed;

and references to a person's conduct as a director of any company or companies include, where that company or any of those companies has become insolvent, that person's conduct in relation to any matter connected with or arising out of the insolvency of that company.

[(2A) For the purposes of this section, an overseas company becomes insolvent if the company enters into insolvency proceedings of any description (including interim proceedings) in any jurisdiction.]

[(3) In this section and section 7(2), "the court" means—

(a) where the company in question is being or has been wound up by the court, that court,

(b) where the company in question is being or has been wound up voluntarily, any court which has or (as the case may be) had jurisdiction to wind it up,

[(c) where neither paragraph (a) nor (b) applies but an administrator or administrative receiver has at any time been appointed in respect of the company in question, any court which has jurisdiction to wind it up.]

(3A) Sections 117 and 120 of the Insolvency Act 1986 (jurisdiction) shall apply for the purposes of subsection (3) as if the references in the definitions of "registered office" to the presentation of the petition for winding up were references—

(a) in a case within paragraph (b) of that subsection, to the passing of the resolution for voluntary winding up,

[(b) in a case within paragraph (c) of that subsection, to the appointment of the administrator or (as the case may be) administrative receiver.]

(3B) Nothing in subsection (3) invalidates any proceedings by reason of their being taken in the wrong court; and proceedings—

(a) for or in connection with a disqualification order under this section, or

(b) in connection with a disqualification undertaking accepted under section 7,

may be retained in the court in which the proceedings were commenced, although it may not be the court in which they ought to have been commenced.

(3C) In this section and section 7, "director" includes a shadow director.]

(4) Under this section the minimum period of disqualification is 2 years, and the maximum period is 15 years.

NOTES

This section derived from the Companies Act 1985, s 295(2), and the Insolvency Act 1985, ss 12(1), (2), (7)–(9), 108(2).

Sub-s (1): words in square brackets in para (b) substituted (for the original words "any other company or companies") by the Small Business, Enterprise and Employment Act 2015, s 106(1), (2)(a), in respect of a person's conduct as a director of an overseas company where that conduct occurs on or after 1 October 2015.

Sub-ss (1A), (2A): inserted by the Small Business, Enterprise and Employment Act 2015, s 106(1), (2)(b), (d), in respect of a person's conduct as a director of an overseas company where that conduct occurs on or after 1 October 2015.

Sub-s (2): words in italics in both places repealed by the Small Business, Enterprise and Employment Act 2015, ss 106(1), (2)(c), 111, Sch 7, Pt 1, paras 1, 7, in respect of a person's conduct as a director of an overseas company where that conduct occurs on or after 1 October 2015; para (b) substituted by the Enterprise Act 2002, s 248(3), Sch 17, paras 40, 41(a), subject to savings and transitional provisions (i) in a case where a petition for an administration order has been presented before 15 September 2003 (see the Enterprise Act 2002 (Commencement No 4 and Transitional Provisions and Savings) Order 2003, SI 2003/2093, art 3 at **[2.26]**), and (ii) in relation to special administration regimes (see s 249 of the 2002 Act at **[2.10]**), and originally read as follows:

> "(b) an administration order is made in relation to the company".

Sub-s (3): substituted (together with sub-ss (3A)–(3C)) for original sub-s (3) by the Insolvency Act 2000, s 8, Sch 4, Pt I, paras 1, 5; para (c) substituted by the Enterprise Act 2002, s 248(3), Sch 17, paras 40, 41(b), subject to savings and transitional provisions as noted to sub-s (2) above, and originally read as follows:

> "(c) where neither of the preceding paragraphs applies but an administration order has at any time been made, or an administrative receiver has at any time been appointed, in relation to the company in question, any court which has jurisdiction to wind it up".

Sub-s (3A): substituted as noted to sub-s (3) above; para (b) substituted by the Enterprise Act 2002, s 248(3), Sch 17, paras 40, 41(c), subject to savings and transitional provisions as noted to sub-s (2) above, and originally read as follows:

> "(b) in a case within paragraph (c) of that subsection, to the making of the administration order or (as the case may be) the appointment of the administrative receiver".

Sub-ss (3B), (3C): substituted as noted to sub-s (3) above.

[4.9]

7 [Disqualification orders under section 6: applications and acceptance of undertakings]

(1) If it appears to the Secretary of State that it is expedient in the public interest that a disqualification order under section 6 should be made against any person, an application for the making of such an order against that person may be made—

(a) by the Secretary of State, or

(b) if the Secretary of State so directs in the case of a person who is or has been a director of a company which is being [or has been] wound up by the court in England and Wales, by the official receiver.

(2) Except with the leave of the court, an application for the making under that section of a disqualification order against any person shall not be made after the end of the period of [3 years] beginning with the day on which the company of which that person is or has been a director became insolvent.

[(2A) If it appears to the Secretary of State that the conditions mentioned in section 6(1) are satisfied as respects any person who has offered to give him a disqualification undertaking, he may accept the undertaking if it appears to him that it is expedient in the public interest that he should do so (instead of applying, or proceeding with an application, for a disqualification order).]

(3) If it appears to the office-holder responsible under this section, that is to say—

(a) in the case of a company which is being wound up by the court in England and Wales, the official receiver,

(b) in the case of a company which is being wound up otherwise, the liquidator,

[(c) in the case of a company which is in administration, the administrator,] or

(d) in the case of a company of which there is an administrative receiver, that receiver,

that the conditions mentioned in section 6(1) are satisfied as respects a person who is or has been a director of that company, the officer-holder shall forthwith report the matter to the Secretary of State.

(4) The Secretary of State or the official receiver may require [any person]—

(a) to furnish him with such information with respect to [that person's or another person's conduct as a director of a company which has at any time become insolvent (whether while the person was a director or subsequently), and]

(b) to produce and permit inspection of such books, papers and other records [as are considered by the Secretary of State or (as the case may be) the official receiver to be relevant to that person's or another person's conduct as such a director],

as the Secretary of State or the official receiver may reasonably require for the purpose of determining whether to exercise, or of exercising, any function of his under this section.

[(5) Subsections (1A) and (2) of section 6 apply for the purposes of this section as they apply for the purposes of that section.]

NOTES

Section heading: substituted (for the previous heading "Disqualification order or undertaking; and reporting provisions") by the Small Business, Enterprise and Employment Act 2015, s 107(1), (4) (for transitional provisions see the note below).

Sub-s (1): words in square brackets inserted by the Insolvency Act 2000, s 8, Sch 4, Pt I, paras 1, 6(a).

Sub-s (2): words in square brackets substituted (for the original words "2 years") by the Small Business, Enterprise and Employment Act 2015, s 108(1). Note that this amendment applies only to an application relating to a company which has become insolvent after 1 October 2015 and, for these purposes, the Insolvency Act 1986, s 6(2) applies (meaning of "becoming insolvent") (see s 108(2), (3) of the 2015 Act).

Sub-s (2A): inserted by the Insolvency Act 2000, s 6(1), (3).

Sub-s (3): repealed by the Small Business, Enterprise and Employment Act 2015, s 107(1), (3), as from 6 April 2016 (for transitional provisions see the note below); para (c) substituted by the Enterprise Act 2002, s 248(3), Sch 17, paras 40, 42, subject to savings and transitional provisions (i) in a case where a petition for an administration order has been presented before 15 September 2003 (see the Enterprise Act 2002 (Commencement No 4 and Transitional Provisions and Savings) Order 2003, SI 2003/2093, art 3 at **[2.26]**), and (ii) in relation to special administration regimes (see s 249 of the 2002 Act at **[2.10]**), and originally read as follows:

"(c) in the case of a company in relation to which an administration order is in force, the administrator,".

Sub-s (4): words in first pair of square brackets substituted (for the original words "the liquidator, administrator or administrative receiver of a company, or the former liquidator, administrator or administrative receiver of a company"), words in second pair of square brackets substituted (for the original words "any person's conduct as a director of the company, and"), and words in third pair of square brackets substituted (for the original words "relevant to that person's conduct as such a director"), by the Deregulation Act 2015, s 19, Sch 6, Pt 4, para 11. Note that the Deregulation Act 2015 (Commencement No 3 and Transitional and Saving Provisions) Order 2015, SI 2015/1732, art 5 provides that these amendments do not have effect in respect of a person who is or has been a director of a company that becomes insolvent (within the meaning of s 6(2) *ante*) before 1 October 2015.

Sub-s (5): added by the Small Business, Enterprise and Employment Act 2015, s 111, Sch 7, Pt 1, paras 1, 8.

Transitional provisions: the Small Business, Enterprise and Employment Act 2015 (Commencement No 4, Transitional and Savings Provisions) Regulations 2016, SI 2016/321, Schedule, Pt 1, paras 1, 2 provide as follows—

1.
"The changes made by section 107 of the Act have no effect in respect of an office-holder reporting on the conduct of a person who is or has been a director of an insolvent company in cases where the insolvency date in respect of that company is before 6th April 2016.

2. "Insolvency date" in paragraph 1 has the meaning given in section 7A(10) of the Company Directors Disqualification Act 1986.".

[4.10]

[7A Office-holder's report on conduct of directors

(1) The office-holder in respect of a company which is insolvent must prepare a report (a "conduct report") about the conduct of each person who was a director of the company—

(a) on the insolvency date, or

(b) at any time during the period of 3 years ending with that date.

(2) For the purposes of this section a company is insolvent if—

(a) the company is in liquidation and at the time it went into liquidation its assets were insufficient for the payment of its debts and other liabilities and the expenses of the winding up,

(b) the company has entered administration, or

(c) an administrative receiver of the company has been appointed;

and subsection (1A) of section 6 applies for the purposes of this section as it applies for the purpose of that section.

(3) A conduct report must, in relation to each person, describe any conduct of the person which may assist the Secretary of State in deciding whether to exercise the power under section 7(1) or (2A) in relation to the person.

(4) The office-holder must send the conduct report to the Secretary of State before the end of—

(a) the period of 3 months beginning with the insolvency date, or

(b) such other longer period as the Secretary of State considers appropriate in the particular circumstances.

(5) If new information comes to the attention of an office-holder, the office-holder must send that information to the Secretary of State as soon as reasonably practicable.

(6) "New information" is information which an office-holder considers should have been included in a conduct report prepared in relation to the company, or would have been so included had it been available before the report was sent.

(7) If there is more than one office-holder in respect of a company at any particular time (because the company is insolvent by virtue of falling within more than one paragraph of subsection (2) at that time), subsection (1) applies only to the first of the office-holders to be appointed.

(8) In the case of a company which is at different times insolvent by virtue of falling within one or more different paragraphs of subsection (2)—

(a) the references in subsection (1) to the insolvency date are to be read as references to the first such date during the period in which the company is insolvent, and

(b) subsection (1) does not apply to an office-holder if at any time during the period in which the company is insolvent a conduct report has already been prepared and sent to the Secretary of State.

(9) The "office-holder" in respect of a company which is insolvent is—

(a) in the case of a company being wound up by the court in England and Wales, the official receiver;

(b) in the case of a company being wound up otherwise, the liquidator;

(c) in the case of a company in administration, the administrator;

(d) in the case of a company of which there is an administrative receiver, the receiver.

(10) The "insolvency date"—

(a) in the case of a company being wound up by the court, means the date on which the court makes the winding-up order (see section 125 of the Insolvency Act 1986);

(b) in the case of a company being wound up by way of a members' voluntary winding up, means the date on which the liquidator forms the opinion that the company will be unable to pay its debts in full (together with interest at the official rate) within the period stated in the directors' declaration of solvency under section 89 of the Insolvency Act 1986;

(c) in the case of a company being wound up by way of a creditors' voluntary winding up where no such declaration under section 89 of that Act has been made, means the date of the passing of the resolution for voluntary winding up;

(d) in the case of a company which has entered administration, means the date the company did so;

(e) in the case of a company in respect of which an administrative receiver has been appointed, means the date of that appointment.

(11) For the purposes of subsection (10)(e), any appointment of an administrative receiver to replace an administrative receiver who has died or vacated office pursuant to section 45 of the Insolvency Act 1986 is to be ignored.

(12) In this section—

"court" has the same meaning as in section 6;

"director" includes a shadow director.]

NOTES

Commencement: 6 April 2016.

Inserted by the Small Business, Enterprise and Employment Act 2015, s 107(1), (2). For transitional provisions see the note to s 7 (relating to SI 2016/321) at **[4.9]**.

[4.11]

8 [Disqualification of director on finding of unfitness]

[(1) If it appears to the Secretary of State . . . that it is expedient in the public interest that a disqualification order should be made against a person who is, or has been, a director or shadow director of a company, he may apply to the court for such an order.

(1A) . . .]

(2) The court may make a disqualification order against a person where, on an application under this section, it is satisfied that his conduct in relation to the company [(either taken alone or taken together with his conduct as a director or shadow director of one or more other companies or overseas companies)] makes him unfit to be concerned in the management of a company.

[(2A) Where it appears to the Secretary of State . . . that, in the case of a person who has offered to give him a disqualification undertaking—

(a) the conduct of the person in relation to a company of which the person is or has been a director or shadow director [(either taken alone or taken together with his conduct as a director or shadow director of one or more other companies or overseas companies)] makes him unfit to be concerned in the management of a company, and

(b) it is expedient in the public interest that he should accept the undertaking (instead of applying, or proceeding with an application, for a disqualification order),

he may accept the undertaking.]

[(2B) Subsection (1A) of section 6 applies for the purposes of this section as it applies for the purposes of that section.]

(3) In this section "the court" means the High Court or, in Scotland, the Court of Session.

(4) The maximum period of disqualification under this section is 15 years.

NOTES

This section derived from the Companies Act 1985, s 295(2), and the Insolvency Act 1985, ss 12(9), 13, 108(2).

Section heading: substituted by the Small Business, Enterprise and Employment Act 2015, s 109(2).

Sub-s (1): substituted, together with sub-s (1A), for original sub-s (1) by the Financial Services and Markets Act 2000 (Consequential Amendments and Repeals) Order 2001, SI 2001/3649, art 39; words omitted repealed by the Small Business, Enterprise and Employment Act 2015, s 109(1)(a).

Sub-s (1A): substituted as noted above, and repealed by the Small Business, Enterprise and Employment Act 2015, s 109(1)(b).

Sub-s (2): words in square brackets inserted by the Small Business, Enterprise and Employment Act 2015, s 106(1), (3)(a), in respect of a person's conduct as a director of an overseas company where that conduct occurs on or after 1 October 2015.

Sub-s (2A): inserted by the Insolvency Act 2000, s 6(1), (4); words omitted repealed by the Small Business, Enterprise and Employment Act 2015, s 109(1)(c); words in square brackets inserted by s 106(1), (3)(b) of the 2015 Act, in respect of a person's conduct as a director of an overseas company where that conduct occurs on or after 1 October 2015.

Sub-s (2B): inserted by the Small Business, Enterprise and Employment Act 2015, s 106(1), (3)(c), in respect of a person's conduct as a director of an overseas company where that conduct occurs on or after 1 October 2015.

[Persons instructing unfit directors

[4.12]

8ZA Order disqualifying person instructing unfit director of insolvent company

(1) The court may make a disqualification order against a person ("P") if, on an application under section 8ZB, it is satisfied—

(a) either—

(i) that a disqualification order under section 6 has been made against a person who is or has been a director (but not a shadow director) of a company, or

(ii) that the Secretary of State has accepted a disqualification undertaking from such a person under section 7(2A), and

(b) that P exercised the requisite amount of influence over the person.

That person is referred to in this section as "the main transgressor".

(2) For the purposes of this section, P exercised the requisite amount of influence over the main transgressor if any of the conduct—

(a) for which the main transgressor is subject to the order made under section 6, or

(b) in relation to which the undertaking was accepted from the main transgressor under section 7(2A),

was the result of the main transgressor acting in accordance with P's directions or instructions.

(3) But P does not exercise the requisite amount of influence over the main transgressor by reason only that the main transgressor acts on advice given by P in a professional capacity.

(4) Under this section the minimum period of disqualification is 2 years and the maximum period is 15 years.

(5) In this section and section 8ZB "the court" has the same meaning as in section 6; and subsection (3B) of section 6 applies in relation to proceedings mentioned in subsection (6) below as it applies in relation to proceedings mentioned in section 6(3B)(a) and (b).

(6) The proceedings are proceedings—

(a) for or in connection with a disqualification order under this section, or

(b) in connection with a disqualification undertaking accepted under section 8ZC.]

NOTES

Commencement: 1 October 2015 (for effect see note below).

Inserted, together with preceding cross-heading and ss 8ZB–8ZE, by the Small Business, Enterprise and Employment Act 2015, s 105, in relation to cases where the main transgressor's conduct (as mentioned in sub-s (2) above) and the exercise by P of the requisite amount of influence (as mentioned in sub-ss (1), (2) above), occur on or after 1 October 2015.

[4.13]

[8ZB Application for order under section 8ZA

(1) If it appears to the Secretary of State that it is expedient in the public interest that a disqualification order should be made against a person under section 8ZA, the Secretary of State may—

(a) make an application to the court for such an order, or

(b) in a case where an application for an order under section 6 against the main transgressor has been made by the official receiver, direct the official receiver to make such an application.

(2) Except with the leave of the court, an application for a disqualification order under section 8ZA must not be made after the end of the period of 3 years beginning with the day on which the company in question became insolvent (within the meaning given by section 6(2)).

(3) Subsection (4) of section 7 applies for the purposes of this section as it applies for the purposes of that section.]

NOTES

Commencement: 1 October 2015 (for effect see note to s 8ZA at **[4.12]**).

Inserted as noted to s 8ZA at **[4.12]**.

[4.14]

[8ZC Disqualification undertaking instead of an order under section 8ZA

(1) If it appears to the Secretary of State that it is expedient in the public interest to do so, the Secretary of State may accept a disqualification undertaking from a person ("P") if—

(a) any of the following is the case—

(i) a disqualification order under section 6 has been made against a person who is or has been a director (but not a shadow director) of a company,

(ii) the Secretary of State has accepted a disqualification undertaking from such a person under section 7(2A), or

(iii) it appears to the Secretary of State that such an undertaking could be accepted from such a person (if one were offered), and

(b) it appears to the Secretary of State that P exercised the requisite amount of influence over the person.

That person is referred to in this section as "the main transgressor".

(2) For the purposes of this section, P exercised the requisite amount of influence over the main transgressor if any of the conduct—

(a) for which the main transgressor is subject to the disqualification order made under section 6,

(b) in relation to which the disqualification undertaking was accepted from the main transgressor under section 7(2A), or

(c) which led the Secretary of State to the conclusion set out in subsection (1)(a)(iii),

was the result of the main transgressor acting in accordance with P's directions or instructions.

(3) But P does not exercise the requisite amount of influence over the main transgressor by reason only that the main transgressor acts on advice given by P in a professional capacity.

(4) Subsection (4) of section 7 applies for the purposes of this section as it applies for the purposes of that section.]

NOTES

Commencement: 1 October 2015 (for effect see note to s 8ZA at **[4.12]**).

Inserted as noted to s 8ZA at **[4.12]**.

[4.15]

[8ZD Order disqualifying person instructing unfit director: other cases

(1) The court may make a disqualification order against a person ("P") if, on an application under this section, it is satisfied—

(a) either—

(i) that a disqualification order under section 8 has been made against a person who is or has been a director (but not a shadow director) of a company, or

(ii) that the Secretary of State has accepted a disqualification undertaking from such a person under section 8(2A), and

(b) that P exercised the requisite amount of influence over the person.

That person is referred to in this section as "the main transgressor".

(2) The Secretary of State may make an application to the court for a disqualification order against P under this section if it appears to the Secretary of State that it is expedient in the public interest for such an order to be made.

(3) For the purposes of this section, P exercised the requisite amount of influence over the main transgressor if any of the conduct—

(a) for which the main transgressor is subject to the order made under section 8, or

(b) in relation to which the undertaking was accepted from the main transgressor under section 8(2A),

was the result of the main transgressor acting in accordance with P's directions or instructions.

(4) But P does not exercise the requisite amount of influence over the main transgressor by reason only that the main transgressor acts on advice given by P in a professional capacity.

(5) Under this section the maximum period of disqualification is 15 years.

(6) In this section "the court" means the High Court or, in Scotland, the Court of Session.]

NOTES

Commencement: 1 October 2015 (for effect see note to s 8ZA at **[4.12]**).

Inserted as noted to s 8ZA at **[4.12]**.

[4.16]

[8ZE Disqualification undertaking instead of an order under section 8ZD

(1) If it appears to the Secretary of State that it is expedient in the public interest to do so, the Secretary of State may accept a disqualification undertaking from a person ("P") if—

(a) any of the following is the case—

(i) a disqualification order under section 8 has been made against a person who is or has been a director (but not a shadow director) of a company,

(ii) the Secretary of State has accepted a disqualification undertaking from such a person under section 8(2A), or

(iii) it appears to the Secretary of State that such an undertaking could be accepted from such a person (if one were offered), and

(b) it appears to the Secretary of State that P exercised the requisite amount of influence over the person.

That person is referred to in this section as "the main transgressor".

(2) For the purposes of this section, P exercised the requisite amount of influence over the main transgressor if any of the conduct—

(a) for which the main transgressor is subject to the disqualification order made under section 8,

(b) in relation to which the disqualification undertaking was accepted from the main transgressor under section 8(2A), or

(c) which led the Secretary of State to the conclusion set out in subsection (1)(a)(iii),

was the result of the main transgressor acting in accordance with P's directions or instructions.

(3) But P does not exercise the requisite amount of influence over the main transgressor by reason only that the main transgressor acts on advice given by P in a professional capacity.]

NOTES

Commencement: 1 October 2015 (for effect see note to s 8ZA at **[4.12]**).

Inserted as noted to s 8ZA at **[4.12]**.

[Further provision about disqualification undertakings]

[4.17]

[8A Variation etc of disqualification undertaking

(1) The court may, on the application of a person who is subject to a disqualification undertaking—

(a) reduce the period for which the undertaking is to be in force, or

(b) provide for it to cease to be in force.

(2) On the hearing of an application under subsection (1), the Secretary of State shall appear and call the attention of the court to any matters which seem to him to be relevant, and may himself give evidence or call witnesses.

[(2A) Subsection (2) does not apply to an application in the case of an undertaking given under section 9B, and in such a case on the hearing of the application whichever of the [Competition and Markets Authority] or a specified regulator (within the meaning of section 9E) accepted the undertaking—

(a) must appear and call the attention of the court to any matters which appear to it or him (as the case may be) to be relevant;

(b) may give evidence or call witnesses.]

[(3) In this section "the court"—

[(za) in the case of an undertaking given under section 8ZC has the same meaning as in section 8ZA;

(zb) in the case of an undertaking given under section 8ZE means the High Court or, in Scotland, the Court of Session;]

(a) in the case of an undertaking given under section 9B means the High Court or (in Scotland) the Court of Session;

(b) in any other case has the same meaning as in section [5A(5),] 7(2) or 8 (as the case may be).]]

NOTES

Cross-heading: inserted by the Small Business, Enterprise and Employment Act 2015, s 111, Sch 7, Pt 1, paras 1, 9.

Inserted by the Insolvency Act 2000, s 6(1), (5).

Sub-s (2A): inserted by the Enterprise Act 2002, s 204(1), (4); words in square brackets substituted by the Enterprise and Regulatory Reform Act 2013 (Competition) (Consequential, Transitional and Saving Provisions) Order 2014, SI 2014/892, art 2, Sch 1, Pt 2, paras 52, 53(a) (for transitional provisions in relation to the abolition of the OFT and the Competition Commission and the continuity of functions, etc, see art 3 of that Order).

Sub-s (3): substituted by the Enterprise Act 2002, s 204(1), (5); paras (za), (zb), and the figure in square brackets in para (b) inserted by the Small Business, Enterprise and Employment Act 2015, s 111, Sch 7, Pt 1, paras 1, 10.

9 *(Repealed by the Small Business, Enterprise and Employment Act 2015, s 106(1), (4).)*

[Disqualification for competition infringements

[4.18]

9A Competition disqualification order

(1) The court must make a disqualification order against a person if the following two conditions are satisfied in relation to him.

(2) The first condition is that an undertaking which is a company of which he is a director commits a breach of competition law.

(3) The second condition is that the court considers that his conduct as a director makes him unfit to be concerned in the management of a company.

(4) An undertaking commits a breach of competition law if it engages in conduct which infringes any of the following—

(a) the Chapter 1 prohibition (within the meaning of the Competition Act 1998) (prohibition on agreements, etc preventing, restricting or distorting competition);

(b) the Chapter 2 prohibition (within the meaning of that Act) (prohibition on abuse of a dominant position);

(c) [Article 101 of the Treaty on the Functioning of the European Union] (prohibition on agreements, etc preventing, restricting or distorting competition);

(d) [Article 102] of that Treaty (prohibition on abuse of a dominant position).

(5) For the purpose of deciding under subsection (3) whether a person is unfit to be concerned in the management of a company the court—

(a) must have regard to whether subsection (6) applies to him;

(b) may have regard to his conduct as a director of a company in connection with any other breach of competition law;

(c) must not have regard to the matters mentioned in Schedule 1.

(6) This subsection applies to a person if as a director of the company—

(a) his conduct contributed to the breach of competition law mentioned in subsection (2);

(b) his conduct did not contribute to the breach but he had reasonable grounds to suspect that the conduct of the undertaking constituted the breach and he took no steps to prevent it;

(c) he did not know but ought to have known that the conduct of the undertaking constituted the breach.

(7) For the purposes of subsection (6)(a) it is immaterial whether the person knew that the conduct of the undertaking constituted the breach.

(8) For the purposes of subsection (4)(a) or (c) references to the conduct of an undertaking are references to its conduct taken with the conduct of one or more other undertakings.

(9) The maximum period of disqualification under this section is 15 years.

(10) An application under this section for a disqualification order may be made by the [Competition and Markets Authority] or by a specified regulator.

(11) Section 60 of the Competition Act 1998 (c 41) (consistent treatment of questions arising under United Kingdom and [EU] law) applies in relation to any question arising by virtue of subsection (4)(a) or (b) above as it applies in relation to any question arising under Part 1 of that Act.]

NOTES

Inserted, together with preceding cross-heading and ss 9B–9E, by the Enterprise Act 2002, s 204(1), (2).

Sub-s (4): words and reference in square brackets substituted by the Treaty of Lisbon (Changes in Terminology) Order 2012, SI 2012/1809, art 3(1), Schedule, Pt 1.

Sub-s (10): words in square brackets substituted by the Enterprise and Regulatory Reform Act 2013 (Competition) (Consequential, Transitional and Saving Provisions) Order 2014, SI 2014/892, art 2, Sch 1, Pt 2, paras 52, 53(b) (for transitional provisions in relation to the abolition of the OFT and the Competition Commission and the continuity of functions, etc, see art 3 of that Order).

Sub-s (11): reference in square brackets substituted by the Treaty of Lisbon (Changes in Terminology) Order 2011, SI 2011/1043, art 6(2)(a).

[4.19]

[9B Competition undertakings

(1) This section applies if—

(a) the [Competition and Markets Authority] or a specified regulator thinks that in relation to any person an undertaking which is a company of which he is a director has committed or is committing a breach of competition law,

(b) the [Competition and Markets Authority] or the specified regulator thinks that the conduct of the person as a director makes him unfit to be concerned in the management of a company, and

(c) the person offers to give the [Competition and Markets Authority] or the specified regulator (as the case may be) a disqualification undertaking.

(2) The [Competition and Markets Authority] or the specified regulator (as the case may be) may accept a disqualification undertaking from the person instead of applying for or proceeding with an application for a disqualification order.

(3) A disqualification undertaking is an undertaking by a person that for the period specified in the undertaking he will not—

(a) be a director of a company;

(b) act as receiver of a company's property;

(c) in any way, whether directly or indirectly, be concerned or take part in the promotion, formation or management of a company;

(d) act as an insolvency practitioner.

(4) But a disqualification undertaking may provide that a prohibition falling within subsection (3)(a) to (c) does not apply if the person obtains the leave of the court.

(5) The maximum period which may be specified in a disqualification undertaking is 15 years.

(6) If a disqualification undertaking is accepted from a person who is already subject to a disqualification undertaking under this Act or to a disqualification order the periods specified in those undertakings or the undertaking and the order (as the case may be) run concurrently.

(7) Subsections (4) to (8) of section 9A apply for the purposes of this section as they apply for the purposes of that section but in the application of subsection (5) of that section the reference to the court must be construed as a reference to the [Competition and Markets Authority] or a specified regulator (as the case may be).]

NOTES

Inserted as noted to s 9A at **[4.18]**.

Sub-ss (1), (2), (7): words in square brackets substituted by the Enterprise and Regulatory Reform Act 2013 (Competition) (Consequential, Transitional and Saving Provisions) Order 2014, SI 2014/892, art 2, Sch 1, Pt 2, paras 52, 53(c) (for transitional provisions in relation to the abolition of the OFT and the Competition Commission and the continuity of functions, etc, see art 3 of that Order).

[4.20]

[9C Competition investigations

(1) If the [Competition and Markets Authority] or a specified regulator has reasonable grounds for suspecting that a breach of competition law has occurred it or he (as the case may be) may carry out an investigation for the purpose of deciding whether to make an application under section 9A for a disqualification order.

(2) For the purposes of such an investigation sections 26 to 30 of the Competition Act 1998 (c 41) apply to the [Competition and Markets Authority] and the specified regulators as they apply to the [Competition and Markets Authority] for the purposes of an investigation under section 25 of that Act.

(3) Subsection (4) applies if as a result of an investigation under this section the [Competition and Markets Authority] or a specified regulator proposes to apply under section 9A for a disqualification order.

(4) Before making the application the [Competition and Markets Authority] or regulator (as the case may be) must—

(a) give notice to the person likely to be affected by the application, and

(b) give that person an opportunity to make representations.]

NOTES

Inserted as noted to s 9A at **[4.18]**.

Words in square brackets substituted by the Enterprise and Regulatory Reform Act 2013 (Competition) (Consequential, Transitional and Saving Provisions) Order 2014, SI 2014/892, art 2, Sch 1, Pt 2, paras 52, 53(d) (for transitional provisions in relation to the abolition of the OFT and the Competition Commission and the continuity of functions, etc, see art 3 of that Order).

[4.21]

[9D Co-ordination

(1) The Secretary of State may make regulations for the purpose of co-ordinating the performance of functions under sections 9A to 9C (relevant functions) which are exercisable concurrently by two or more persons.

(2) Section 54(5) to (7) of the Competition Act 1998 (c 41) applies to regulations made under this section as it applies to regulations made under that section and for that purpose in that section—

(a) references to Part 1 functions must be read as references to relevant functions;

(b) references to a regulator must be read as references to a specified regulator;

[(ba) the reference in subsection (6A)(b) to notice under section 31(1) of the Competition Act 1998 that the regulator proposes to make a decision within the meaning given by section 31(2) of that Act is to be read as notice under section 9C(4) that the specified regulator proposes to apply under section 9A for a disqualification order;]

(c) a competent person also includes any of the specified regulators.

(3) The power to make regulations under this section must be exercised by statutory instrument subject to annulment in pursuance of a resolution of either House of Parliament.

(4) Such a statutory instrument may—

(a) contain such incidental, supplemental, consequential and transitional provision as the Secretary of State thinks appropriate;

(b) make different provision for different cases.]

NOTES

Inserted as noted to s 9A at **[4.18]**.

Sub-s (2): para (ba) inserted by the Enterprise and Regulatory Reform Act 2013 (Competition) (Consequential, Transitional and Saving Provisions) Order 2014, SI 2014/892, art 2, Sch 1, Pt 2, paras 52, 54 (for transitional provisions in relation to the abolition of the OFT and the Competition Commission and the continuity of functions, etc, see art 3 of that Order).

[4.22]

[9E Interpretation

(1) This section applies for the purposes of sections 9A to 9D.

(2) Each of the following is a specified regulator for the purposes of a breach of competition law in relation to a matter in respect of which he or it has a function—

[(a) the Office of Communications;]

(b) the Gas and Electricity Markets Authority;

[(c) the Water Services Regulation Authority;]

(d) [the Office of Rail and Road];

(e) the Civil Aviation Authority[;

(f) Monitor];

[(g) the Payment Systems Regulator established under section 40 of the Financial Services (Banking Reform) Act 2013;

(h) the Financial Conduct Authority.]

(3) The court is the High Court or (in Scotland) the Court of Session.

(4) Conduct includes omission.

(5) Director includes shadow director.]

NOTES

Inserted as noted to s 9A at **[4.18]**.

Sub-s (2): para (a) substituted by the Communications Act 2003, s 406(1), Sch 17, para 83; para (c) substituted by the Water Act 2003, s 101(1), Sch 7, para 25; words in square brackets in para (d) substituted by the Office of Rail Regulation (Change of Name) Regulations 2015, SI 2015/1682, reg 2(2), Schedule, Pt 1, para 4(h); para (f) added by the Health and Social Care Act 2012, s 74(4); paras (g), (h) added by the Financial Services (Banking Reform) Act 2013, ss 67(1), 129, Sch 8, Pt 2, para 8.

Other cases of disqualification

[4.23]

10 Participation in wrongful trading

(1) Where the court makes a declaration under section 213 or 214 of the Insolvency Act [1986] that a person is liable to make a contribution to a company's assets, then, whether or not an application for such an order is made by any person, the court may, if it thinks fit, also make a disqualification order against the person to whom the declaration relates.

(2) The maximum period of disqualification under this section is 15 years.

[(3) In this section "company" includes overseas company.]

NOTES

This section derived from the Companies Act 1985, s 295(2), and the Insolvency Act 1985, ss 16, 108(2).

Sub-s (1): date in square brackets inserted by the Companies Act 2006 (Consequential Amendments, Transitional Provisions and Savings) Order 2009, SI 2009/1941, art 2(1), Sch 1, para 85(1), (6)(a).

Sub-s (3): added by the Small Business, Enterprise and Employment Act 2015, s 111, Sch 7, Pt 1, paras 1, 11.

[4.24]

11 Undischarged bankrupts

[(1) It is an offence for a person to act as director of a company or directly or indirectly to take part in or be concerned in the promotion, formation or management of a company, without the leave of the court, at a time when any of the circumstances mentioned in subsection (2) apply to the person.

(2) The circumstances are—

(a) the person is an undischarged bankrupt—

(i) in England and Wales or Scotland, or

(ii) in Northern Ireland,

(b) a bankruptcy restrictions order or undertaking is in force in respect of the person under—

(i) the Bankruptcy (Scotland) Act 1985 [or 2016] or the Insolvency Act 1986, or

(ii) the Insolvency (Northern Ireland) Order 1989,

(c) a debt relief restrictions order or undertaking is in force in respect of the person under—

(i) the Insolvency Act 1986, or

(ii) the Insolvency (Northern Ireland) Order 1989,

(d) a moratorium period under a debt relief order applies in relation to the person under—

(i) the Insolvency Act 1986, or

(ii) the Insolvency (Northern Ireland) Order 1989.

(2A) In subsection (1) "the court" means—

(a) for the purposes of subsection (2)(a)(i)—

[(i) the court by which the bankruptcy order was made or (if the order was not made by a court) the court to which a debtor may appeal against a refusal to make a bankruptcy order, or]

(ii) in Scotland, the court by which sequestration of the person's estate was awarded or, if awarded other than by the court, the court which would have jurisdiction in respect of sequestration of the person's estate,

(b) for the purposes of subsection (2)(b)(i)—

(i) the court which made the order,

(ii) in Scotland, if the order has been made other than by the court, the court to which the person may appeal against the order, or

(iii) the court to which the person may make an application for annulment of the undertaking,

(c) for the purposes of subsection (2)(c)(i)—

(i) the court which made the order, or

(ii) the court to which the person may make an application for annulment of the undertaking,

(d) for the purposes of subsection (2)(d)(i), the court to which the person would make an application under section 251M(1) of the Insolvency Act 1986 (if the person were dissatisfied as mentioned there),

(e) for the purposes of paragraphs (a)(ii), (b)(ii), (c)(ii) and (d)(ii) of subsection (2), the High Court of Northern Ireland.]

(3) In England and Wales, the leave of the court shall not be given unless notice of intention to apply for it has been served on the official receiver; and it is the latter's duty, if he is of opinion that it is contrary to the public interest that the application should be granted, to attend on the hearing of the application and oppose it.

[(4) In this section "company" includes a company incorporated outside Great Britain that has an established place of business in Great Britain.]

NOTES

This section derived from the Companies Act 1985, s 302.

Sub-ss (1), (2), (2A): substituted (for the original sub-ss (1), (2)) by the Small Business, Enterprise and Employment Act 2015, s 113(1), as from 1 October 2015, in respect of a person where (a) a bankruptcy order, a bankruptcy restrictions order, a debt relief restrictions order, (b) a bankruptcy restrictions undertaking, a debt relief restrictions undertaking, or (c) a moratorium period under a debt relief order, is, as the case may be, made, awarded, accepted, granted or commences on or after that date. Sub-ss (1), (2) and the related notes previously read as follows—

"[(1) It is an offence for a person to act as director of a company or directly or indirectly to take part in or be concerned in the promotion, formation or management of a company, without the leave of the court, at a time when—

(a) he is an undischarged bankrupt,

[(aa) a moratorium period under a debt relief order applies in relation to him,] or

(b) a bankruptcy restrictions order [or a debt relief restrictions order] is in force in respect of him.]

[(2) For this purpose, the court is—

(a) in the case of a person adjudged bankrupt or, in Scotland, whose estate was sequestrated, the court by which the person was adjudged bankrupt or sequestration of the person's estate was awarded,

(b) in the case of a person in respect of whom a court made a debt relief restrictions order (under Schedule 4ZB of the Insolvency Act 1986), the court by which the order was made, and

(c) in the case of any other person, the court to which the person would make an application under section 251M(1) of the Insolvency Act 1986 (if the person were dissatisfied as mentioned there).]

NOTES

Sub-s (1): substituted by the Enterprise Act 2002, s 257(3), Sch 21, para 5, subject to transitional provisions in s 256(2) of, and Sch 19 to, that Act at **[2.13]**, **[2.22]**; para (aa) and words in square brackets in para (b) inserted by the Tribunals, Courts and Enforcement Act 2007, s 108(3), Sch 20, Pt 2, para 16.

Sub-s (2): substituted, in relation to England and Wales, by the Tribunals, Courts and Enforcement Act 2007 (Consequential Amendments) Order 2012, SI 2012/2404, arts 3(1), 4(1), Sch 1, para 1.".

Sub-s (2): words in square brackets in para (b)(i) inserted by the Bankruptcy (Scotland) Act 2016 (Consequential Provisions and Modifications) Order 2016, SI 2016/1034, art 7(1), (3), Sch 1, para 5, as from 30 November 2016 (except in relation to (i) a sequestration as regards which the petition is presented, or the debtor application is made before that date; or (ii) a trust deed executed before that date).

In sub-s (2A), para (a)(i) substituted by the Enterprise and Regulatory Reform Act 2013 (Consequential Amendments) (Bankruptcy) and the Small Business, Enterprise and Employment Act 2015 (Consequential Amendments) Regulations 2016, SI 2016/481, reg 2(1), Sch 1, para 8.

Sub-s (4): added by the Companies Act 2006 (Consequential Amendments, Transitional Provisions and Savings) Order 2009, SI 2009/1941, art 2(1), Sch 1, para 85(1), (7).

[4.25]

12 *Failure to pay under county court administration order*

(1) The following has effect where a court under section 429 of the Insolvency Act revokes an administration order under Part VI of the County Courts Act 1984.

(2) A person to whom *that section applies by virtue of the order under section 429(2)(b)* shall not, except with the leave of the court which made the order, act as director or liquidator of, or directly or indirectly take part or be concerned in the promotion, formation or management of, a company.

NOTES

This section derived from the Insolvency Act 1985, s 221(2).

Section heading: substituted by the words "Disabilities on revocation of administration order" by the Tribunals, Courts and Enforcement Act 2007, s 106, Sch 16, para 5(1), (2), as from a day to be appointed, except in relation to any case in which an administration order was made, or an application for such an order was made, before the day on which s 106 comes into force.

Sub-s (1): repealed by the Tribunals, Courts and Enforcement Act 2007, ss 106(2), 146, Sch 16, para 5(1), (3), Sch 23, Pt 5, as from a day to be appointed, except in relation to any case in which an administration order was made, or an application for such an order was made, before the day on which s 106 comes into force.

Sub-s (2): for the words in italics there are substituted the words "section 429 of the Insolvency Act applies by virtue of an order under subsection (2) of that section" by the Tribunals, Courts and Enforcement Act 2007, s 106, Sch 16, para 5(1), (4), as from a day to be appointed, except in relation to any case in which an administration order was made, or an application for such an order was made, before the day on which s 106 comes into force. Note that the Companies Act 2006 (Consequential Amendments, Transitional Provisions and Savings) Order 2009, SI 2009/1941, art 2(1), Sch 1, para 85(1), (6)(a) provides that "1986" should be inserted after the words "the Insolvency Act" in sub-s (2) of this section (as from 1 October 2009). It is assumed that this amendment should take effect after the substitution noted above comes into force.

12A, 12B *(S 12A inserted by the Insolvency Act 2000, s 7(1) (applies to Northern Ireland only); s 12B inserted by the Insolvency Act 2000 (Company Directors Disqualification Undertakings) Order 2004, SI 2004/1941, art 2(1), (2) (applies to Northern Ireland only).)*

[4.26]

[12C Determining unfitness etc: matters to be taken into account

(1) This section applies where a court must determine—

(a) whether a person's conduct as a director of one or more companies or overseas companies makes the person unfit to be concerned in the management of a company;

(b) whether to exercise any discretion it has to make a disqualification order under any of sections 2 to 4, 5A, 8 or 10;

(c) where the court has decided to make a disqualification order under any of those sections or is required to make an order under section 6, what the period of disqualification should be.

(2) But this section does not apply where the court in question is one mentioned in section 2(2)(b) or (c).

(3) This section also applies where the Secretary of State must determine—

(a) whether a person's conduct as a director of one or more companies or overseas companies makes the person unfit to be concerned in the management of a company;

(b) whether to exercise any discretion the Secretary of State has to accept a disqualification undertaking under section 5A, 7 or 8.

(4) In making any such determination in relation to a person, the court or the Secretary of State must—

(a) in every case, have regard in particular to the matters set out in paragraphs 1 to 4 of Schedule 1;

(b) in a case where the person concerned is or has been a director of a company or overseas company, also have regard in particular to the matters set out in paragraphs 5 to 7 of that Schedule.

(5) In this section "director" includes a shadow director.

(6) Subsection (1A) of section 6 applies for the purposes of this section as it applies for the purposes of that section.

(7) The Secretary of State may by order modify Schedule 1; and such an order may contain such transitional provision as may appear to the Secretary of State to be necessary or expedient.

(8) The power to make an order under this section is exercisable by statutory instrument.

(9) An order under this section may not be made unless a draft of the instrument containing it has been laid before, and approved by a resolution of, each House of Parliament.

NOTES

Commencement: see the note below.

Inserted by the Small Business, Enterprise and Employment Act 2015, s 106(1), (5), as from 26 May 2015 (for the purposes of enabling the exercise of any power to make provision by order made by statutory instrument), and as from 1 October 2015 (otherwise). Save where conduct is considered by a court or by the Secretary of State under s 5A of this Act, this section applies to a person's conduct as a director where that conduct occurs on or after 1 October 2015 (see SI 2015/1689, Schedule, para 3).

Consequences of contravention

[4.27]

13 Criminal penalties

If a person acts in contravention of a disqualification order or [disqualification undertaking or in contravention] of section 12(2)[, 12A or 12B], or is guilty of an offence under section 11, he is liable—

(a) on conviction on indictment, to imprisonment for not more than 2 years or a fine, or both; and

(b) on summary conviction, to imprisonment for not more than 6 months or a fine not exceeding the statutory maximum, or both.

NOTES

This section derived from the Companies Act 1985, ss 295(7), 302(1), Sch 24.

Words in first pair of square brackets inserted by the Insolvency Act 2000, s 8, Sch 4, paras 1, 8(a); words in second pair of square brackets substituted by the Insolvency Act 2000 (Company Directors Disqualification Undertakings) Order 2004, SI 2004/1941, art 2(1), (3), in relation to disqualification undertakings under the Company Directors Disqualification (Northern Ireland) Order 2002, SI 2002/3150, accepted on or after 1 September 2004.

[4.28]

14 Offences by body corporate

(1) Where a body corporate is guilty of an offence of acting in contravention of a disqualification order [or disqualification undertaking or in contravention of section 12A] [or 12B], and it is proved that the offence occurred with the consent or connivance of, or was attributable to any neglect on the part of any director, manager, secretary or other similar officer of the body corporate, or any person who was purporting to act in any such capacity he, as well as the body corporate, is guilty of the offence and liable to be proceeded against and punished accordingly.

(2) Where the affairs of a body corporate are managed by its members, subsection (1) applies in relation to the acts and defaults of a member in connection with his functions of management as if he were a director of the body corporate.

NOTES

This section derived from the Companies Act 1985, s 733(1)–(3), and the Insolvency Act 1985, Sch 6, para 7.

Sub-s (1): words in first pair of square brackets inserted by the Insolvency Act 2000, s 8, Sch 4, Pt I, paras 1, 9; words in second pair of square brackets inserted by the Insolvency Act 2000 (Company Directors Disqualification Undertakings) Order 2004, SI 2004/1941, art 2(1), (4), in relation to disqualification undertakings under the Company Directors Disqualification (Northern Ireland) Order 2002, SI 2002/3150, accepted on or after 1 September 2004.

[4.29]

15 Personal liability for company's debts where person acts while disqualified

(1) A person is personally responsible for all the relevant debts of a company if at any time—

(a) in contravention of a disqualification order or [disqualification undertaking or in contravention] of section 11[, 12A or 12B] of this Act he is involved in the management of the company, or

[(b) as a person who is involved in the management of the company, he acts or is willing to act on instructions given without the leave of the court by a person whom he knows at that time—

(i) to be the subject of a disqualification order made or disqualification undertaking accepted under this Act or under the Company Directors Disqualification (Northern Ireland) Order 2002, or

(ii) to be an undischarged bankrupt.]

(2) Where a person is personally responsible under this section for the relevant debts of a company, he is jointly and severally liable in respect of those debts with the company and any other person who, whether under this section or otherwise, is so liable.

(3) For the purposes of this section the relevant debts of a company are—

(a) in relation to a person who is personally responsible under paragraph (a) of subsection (1), such debts and other liabilities of the company as are incurred at a time when that person was involved in the management of the company, and

(b) in relation to a person who is personally responsible under paragraph (b) of that subsection, such debts and other liabilities of the company as are incurred at a time when that person was acting or was willing to act on instructions given as mentioned in that paragraph.

(4) For the purposes of this section, a person is involved in the management of a company if he is a director of the company or if he is concerned, whether directly or indirectly, or takes part, in the management of the company.

[(5) For the purposes of this section a person who, as a person involved in the management of a company, has at any time acted on instructions given without the leave of the court by a person whom he knew at that time—

(a) to be the subject of a disqualification order made or disqualification undertaking accepted under this Act or under the Company Directors Disqualification (Northern Ireland) Order 2002, or

(b) to be an undischarged bankrupt,

is presumed, unless the contrary is shown, to have been willing at any time thereafter to act on any instructions given by that person.]

NOTES

This section derived from the Insolvency Act 1985, s 18(1)–(6).

Sub-s (1): in para (a), words in first pair of square brackets inserted by the Insolvency Act 2000, s 8, Sch 4, Pt I, paras 1, 10(1), (2) and words in second pair of square brackets substituted by the Insolvency Act 2000 (Company Directors Disqualification Undertakings) Order 2004, SI 2004/1941, art 2(1), (5)(a), in relation to disqualification undertakings under the Company Directors Disqualification (Northern Ireland) Order 2002, SI 2002/3150, accepted on or after 1 September 2004; para (b) substituted by the Companies Act 2006 (Consequential Amendments, Transitional Provisions and Savings) Order 2009, SI 2009/1941, art 2(1), Sch 1, para 85(1), (9)(a).

Sub-s (5): substituted by SI 2009/1941, art 2(1), Sch 1, para 85(1), (9)(b).

[Compensation orders and undertakings

[4.30]

15A Compensation orders and undertakings

(1) The court may make a compensation order against a person on the application of the Secretary of State if it is satisfied that the conditions mentioned in subsection (3) are met.

(2) If it appears to the Secretary of State that the conditions mentioned in subsection (3) are met in respect of a person who has offered to give the Secretary of State a compensation undertaking, the Secretary of State may accept the undertaking instead of applying, or proceeding with an application, for a compensation order.

(3) The conditions are that—

(a) the person is subject to a disqualification order or disqualification undertaking under this Act, and

(b) conduct for which the person is subject to the order or undertaking has caused loss to one or more creditors of an insolvent company of which the person has at any time been a director.

(4) An "insolvent company" is a company that is or has been insolvent and a company becomes insolvent if—

(a) the company goes into liquidation at a time when its assets are insufficient for the payment of its debts and other liabilities and the expenses of the winding up,

(b) the company enters administration, or

(c) an administrative receiver of the company is appointed.

(5) The Secretary of State may apply for a compensation order at any time before the end of the period of two years beginning with the date on which the disqualification order referred to in paragraph (a) of subsection (3) was made, or the disqualification undertaking referred to in that paragraph was accepted.

(6) In the case of a person subject to a disqualification order under section 8ZA or 8ZD, or a disqualification undertaking under section 8ZC or 8ZE, the reference in subsection (3)(b) to conduct is a reference to the conduct of the main transgressor in relation to which the person has exercised the requisite amount of influence.

(7) In this section and sections 15B and 15C "the court" means—

(a) in a case where a disqualification order has been made, the court that made the order,

(b) in any other case, the High Court or, in Scotland, the Court of Session.]

NOTES

Commencement: 1 October 2015 (for effect see note below).

Inserted, together with ss 15B, 15C, by the Small Business, Enterprise and Employment Act 2015, s 110, in respect of a person's conduct (as mentioned in sub-s (3)(b) above) or exercise of the requisite amount of influence (as mentioned in sub-s (6) above), occurring on or after 1 October 2015.

[4.31]

[15B Amounts payable under compensation orders and undertakings

(1) A compensation order is an order requiring the person against whom it is made to pay an amount specified in the order—

(a) to the Secretary of State for the benefit of—

(i) a creditor or creditors specified in the order;

(ii) a class or classes of creditor so specified;

(b) as a contribution to the assets of a company so specified.

(2) A compensation undertaking is an undertaking to pay an amount specified in the undertaking—

(a) to the Secretary of State for the benefit of—

(i) a creditor or creditors specified in the undertaking;

(ii) a class or classes of creditor so specified;

(b) as a contribution to the assets of a company so specified.

(3) When specifying an amount the court (in the case of an order) and the Secretary of State (in the case of an undertaking) must in particular have regard to—

(a) the amount of the loss caused;

(b) the nature of the conduct mentioned in section 15A(3)(b);

(c) whether the person has made any other financial contribution in recompense for the conduct (whether under a statutory provision or otherwise).

(4) An amount payable by virtue of subsection (2) under a compensation undertaking is recoverable as if payable under a court order.

(5) An amount payable under a compensation order or compensation undertaking is provable as a bankruptcy debt.]

NOTES

Commencement: 1 October 2015 (for effect see note to s 15A at **[4.30]**).

Inserted as noted to s 15A at **[4.30]**.

[4.32]

[15C Variation and revocation of compensation undertakings

(1) The court may, on the application of a person who is subject to a compensation undertaking—

(a) reduce the amount payable under the undertaking, or
(b) provide for the undertaking not to have effect.

(2) On the hearing of an application under subsection (1), the Secretary of State must appear and call the attention of the court to any matters which the Secretary of State considers relevant, and may give evidence or call witnesses.]

NOTES

Commencement: 1 October 2015 (for effect see note to s 15A at **[4.30]**).

Inserted as noted to s 15A at **[4.30]**.

Supplementary provisions

[4.33]

16 Application for disqualification order

(1) A person intending to apply for the making of a disqualification order . . . shall give not less than 10 days' notice of his intention to the person against whom the order is sought; and on the hearing of the application the last-mentioned person may appear and himself give evidence or call witnesses.

(2) An application to a court[, other than a court mentioned in section 2(2)(b) or (c),] for the making against any person of a disqualification order under any of sections 2 to [4] may be made by the Secretary of State or the official receiver, or by the liquidator or any past or present member or creditor of any company [or overseas company] in relation to which that person has committed or is alleged to have committed an offence or other default.

(3) On the hearing of any application under this Act made by [a person falling within subsection (4)], the applicant shall appear and call the attention of the court to any matters which seem to him to be relevant, and may himself give evidence or call witnesses.

[(4) The following fall within this subsection—
(a) the Secretary of State;
(b) the official receiver;
(c) the [Competition and Markets Authority];
(d) the liquidator;
(e) a specified regulator (within the meaning of section 9E).]

NOTES

This section derived from the Companies Act 1985, s 295(6), Sch 12, paras 1–3, and the Insolvency Act 1985, s 108(2), Sch 6, para 1(4).

Sub-s (1): words omitted repealed by the Small Business, Enterprise and Employment Act 2015, s 111, Sch 7, Pt 1, paras 1, 12(1), (2).

Sub-s (2): words in first pair of square brackets substituted and words in third pair of square brackets inserted by the Small Business, Enterprise and Employment Act 2015, s 111, Sch 7, Pt 1, paras 1, 12(1), (3); figure in second pair of square brackets substituted by the Insolvency Act 2000, s 8, Sch 4, Pt I, paras 1, 11.

Sub-s (3): words in square brackets substituted by the Enterprise Act 2002, s 204(1), (6).

Sub-s (4): added by the Enterprise Act 2002, s 204(1), (7); words in square brackets in para (c) substituted by the Enterprise and Regulatory Reform Act 2013 (Competition) (Consequential, Transitional and Saving Provisions) Order 2014, SI 2014/892, art 2, Sch 1, Pt 2, paras 52, 53(e) (for transitional provisions in relation to the abolition of the OFT and the Competition Commission and the continuity of functions, etc, see art 3 of that Order).

[4.34]

[17 Application for leave under an order or undertaking

(1) Where a person is subject to a disqualification order made by a court having jurisdiction to wind up companies, any application for leave for the purposes of section 1(1)(a) shall be made to that court.

(2) Where—
(a) a person is subject to a disqualification order made under section 2 by a court other than a court having jurisdiction to wind up companies, or
(b) a person is subject to a disqualification order made under section 5,

any application for leave for the purposes of section 1(1)(a) shall be made to any court which, when the order was made, had jurisdiction to wind up the company (or, if there is more than one such company, any of the companies) to which the offence (or any of the offences) in question related.

(3) Where a person is subject to a disqualification undertaking accepted at any time under section [5A,] 7 or 8, any application for leave for the purposes of section 1A(1)(a) shall be made to any court to which, if the Secretary of State had applied for a disqualification order under the section in question at that time, his application could have been made.

[(3ZA) Where a person is subject to a disqualification undertaking accepted at any time under section 8ZC, any application for leave for the purposes of section 1A(1)(a) must be made to any court to which, if the Secretary of State had applied for a disqualification order under section 8ZA at that time, that application could have been made.

(3ZB) Where a person is subject to a disqualification undertaking accepted at any time under section 8ZE, any application for leave for the purposes of section 1A(1)(a) must be made to the High Court or, in Scotland, the Court of Session.]

[(3A) Where a person is subject to a disqualification undertaking accepted at any time under section 9B any application for leave for the purposes of section 9B(4) must be made to the High Court or (in Scotland) the Court of Session.]

(4) But where a person is subject to two or more disqualification orders or undertakings (or to one or more disqualification orders and to one or more disqualification undertakings), any application for leave for the purposes of section 1(1)(a) [1A(1)(a) or 9B(4)] shall be made to any court to which any such application relating to the latest order to be made, or undertaking to be accepted, could be made.
(5) On the hearing of an application for leave for the purposes of section 1(1)(a) or 1A(1)(a), the Secretary of State shall appear and call the attention of the court to any matters which seem to him to be relevant, and may himself give evidence or call witnesses.
[(6) Subsection (5) does not apply to an application for leave for the purposes of section 1(1)(a) if the application for the disqualification order was made under section 9A.
(7) In such a case and in the case of an application for leave for the purposes of section 9B(4) on the hearing of the application whichever of the [Competition and Markets Authority] or a specified regulator (within the meaning of section 9E) applied for the order or accepted the undertaking (as the case may be)—

(a) must appear and draw the attention of the court to any matters which appear to it or him (as the case may be) to be relevant;
(b) may give evidence or call witnesses.]]

NOTES

This section, as originally enacted, derived from the Companies Act 1985, s 295(6), Sch 12, paras 4, 5, and the Insolvency Act 1985, s 108(2), Sch 6, paras 1(4), 14.

Substituted by the Insolvency Act 2000, s 8, Sch 4, Pt I, paras 1, 12.

Sub-s (3): figure in square brackets inserted by the Small Business, Enterprise and Employment Act 2015, s 111, Sch 7, Pt 1, paras 1, 13(1), (2).

Sub-ss (3ZA), (3ZB): inserted by the Small Business, Enterprise and Employment Act 2015, s 111, Sch 7, Pt 1, paras 1, 13(1), (3).

Sub-s (3A): inserted by the Enterprise Act 2002, s 204(1), (8).

Sub-s (4): words in square brackets substituted by the Enterprise Act 2002, s 204(1), (9).

Sub-s (6): added by the Enterprise Act 2002, s 204(1), (10).

Sub-s (7): added by the Enterprise Act 2002, s 204(1), (10); words in square brackets substituted by the Enterprise and Regulatory Reform Act 2013 (Competition) (Consequential, Transitional and Saving Provisions) Order 2014, SI 2014/892, art 2, Sch 1, Pt 2, paras 52, 53(f) (for transitional provisions in relation to the abolition of the OFT and the Competition Commission and the continuity of functions, etc, see art 3 of that Order).

[4.35]
18 [Register of disqualification orders and undertakings]
(1) The Secretary of State may make regulations requiring officers of courts to furnish him with such particulars as the regulations may specify of cases in which—

(a) a disqualification order is made, or
(b) any action is taken by a court in consequence of which such an order [or a disqualification undertaking] is varied or ceases to be in force, or
(c) leave is granted by a court for a person subject to such an order to do any thing which otherwise the order prohibits him from doing[, or
(d) leave is granted by a court for a person subject to such an undertaking to do anything which otherwise the undertaking prohibits him from doing];

and the regulations may specify the time within which, and the form and manner in which, such particulars are to be furnished.
(2) The Secretary of State shall, from the particulars so furnished, continue to maintain the register of orders, and of cases in which leave has been granted as mentioned in subsection (1)(c) . . .
[(2A) The Secretary of State must include in the register such particulars as he considers appropriate of—

(a) disqualification undertakings accepted by him under section [5A, 7, 8, 8ZC or 8ZE];
(b) disqualification undertakings accepted by the [Competition and Markets Authority] or a specified regulator under section 9B;
(c) cases in which leave has been granted as mentioned in subsection (1)(d).]

(3) When an order [or undertaking] of which entry is made in the register ceases to be in force, the Secretary of State shall delete the entry from the register and all particulars relating to it which have been furnished to him under this section or any previous corresponding provision [and, in the case of a disqualification undertaking, any other particulars he has included in the register].
(4) The register shall be open to inspection on payment of such fee as may be specified by the Secretary of State in regulations.
[(4A) Regulations under this section may extend the preceding provisions of this section, to such extent and with such modifications as may be specified in the regulations, to disqualification orders . . . [or disqualification undertakings made under the Company Directors Disqualification (Northern Ireland) Order 2002].]
(5) Regulations under this section shall be made by statutory instrument subject to annulment in pursuance of a resolution of either House of Parliament.

NOTES

This section derived from the Companies Act 1985, s 301, and the Insolvency Act 1985, s 108(2), Sch 6, para 2.

Section heading: substituted by the Insolvency Act 2000, s 8, Sch 4, Pt I, paras 1, 13(1), (6).

Sub-s (1): words in square brackets in para (b) and para (d) and word immediately preceding it inserted by the Insolvency Act 2000, s 8, Sch 4, Pt I, paras 1, 13(1), (2).

Sub-s (2): words omitted repealed by the Companies Act 2006 (Consequential Amendments, Transitional Provisions and Savings) Order 2009, SI 2009/1941, art 2(1), Sch 1, para 85(1), (10)(a).

Sub-s (2A): inserted by the Insolvency Act 2000, s 8, Sch 4, Pt I, paras 1, 13(1), (3); substituted by the Enterprise Act 2002, s 204(1), (11); words in square brackets in para (a) substituted by the Small Business, Enterprise and Employment Act 2015, s 111, Sch 7, Pt 1, paras 1, 14; words in square brackets in para (b) substituted by the Enterprise and Regulatory Reform Act 2013 (Competition) (Consequential, Transitional and Saving Provisions) Order 2014, SI 2014/892, art 2, Sch 1, Pt 2, paras 52, 53(g) (for transitional provisions in relation to the abolition of the OFT and the Competition Commission and the continuity of functions, etc, see art 3 of that Order).

Sub-s (3): words in square brackets inserted by the Insolvency Act 2000, s 8, Sch 4, Pt I, paras 1, 13(1), (4).

Sub-s (4A): inserted by the Insolvency Act 2000, s 8, Sch 4, Pt I, paras 1, 13(1), (5); words omitted repealed by SI 2009/1941, art 2(1), Sch 1, para 85(1), (10)(b); words in square brackets inserted by the Insolvency Act 2000 (Company Directors Disqualification Undertakings) Order 2004, SI 2004/1941, art 2(1), (6), in relation to disqualification undertakings under the Company Directors Disqualification (Northern Ireland) Order 2002, SI 2002/3150, accepted on or after 1 September 2004.

Regulations: the Companies (Disqualification Orders) Regulations 2001, SI 2001/967 (revoked by SI 2009/2471 and reproduced for reference at **[14.25]**); the Companies (Disqualification Orders) Regulations 2009, SI 2009/2471 at **[14.33]**.

[4.36]

19 Special savings from repealed enactments

Schedule 2 to this Act has effect—

(a) in connection with certain transitional cases arising under sections 93 and 94 of the Companies Act 1981, so as to limit the power to make a disqualification order, or to restrict the duration of an order, by reference to events occurring or things done before those sections came into force,

(b) to preserve orders made under section 28 of the Companies Act 1976 (repealed by the Act of 1981), and

(c) to preclude any applications for a disqualification order under section 6 or 8, where the relevant company went into liquidation before 28th April 1986.

NOTES

This section derived from the Companies Act 1985, s 295(6).

Companies Act 1981, ss 93, 94: repealed by the Companies Consolidation (Consequential Provisions) Act 1985, s 29, Sch 1.

Companies Act 1976, s 28: repealed by the Companies Act 1981, ss 93(5), 119(5), Sch 4.

Miscellaneous and general

[4.37]

20 Admissibility in evidence of statements

[(1)] In any proceedings (whether or not under this Act), any statement made in pursuance of a requirement imposed by or under sections [5A, 6 to 10, 12C, 15 to 15C] or 19(c) of, or Schedule 1 to, this Act, or by or under rules made for the purposes of this Act under the Insolvency Act [1986], may be used in evidence against any person making or concurring in making the statement.

[(2) However, in criminal proceedings in which any such person is charged with an offence to which this subsection applies—

(a) no evidence relating to the statement may be adduced, and

(b) no question relating to it may be asked,

by or on behalf of the prosecution, unless evidence relating to it is adduced, or a question relating to it is asked, in the proceedings by or on behalf of that person.

(3) Subsection (2) applies to any offence other than—

(a) an offence which is—

(i) created by rules made for the purposes of this Act under the Insolvency Act [1986], and

(ii) designated for the purposes of this subsection by such rules or by regulations made by the Secretary of State;

(b) an offence which is—

(i) created by regulations made under any such rules, and

(ii) designated for the purposes of this subsection by such regulations;

(c) an offence under section 5 of the Perjury Act 1911 (false statements made otherwise than on oath); or

(d) an offence under section 44(2) of the Criminal Law (Consolidation) (Scotland) Act 1995 (false statements made otherwise than on oath).

(4) Regulations under subsection (3)(a)(ii) shall be made by statutory instrument and, after being made, shall be laid before each House of Parliament.]

NOTES

This section derived from the Insolvency Act 1985, s 231 (in part).

The existing provision of this section renumbered as sub-s (1) and sub-ss (2)–(4) added by the Youth Justice and Criminal Evidence Act 1999, s 59, Sch 3, para 8.

Sub-s (1): words in first pair of square brackets substituted by the Small Business, Enterprise and Employment Act 2015, s 111, Sch 7, Pt 1, paras 1, 15; date in square brackets inserted by the Companies Act 2006 (Consequential Amendments, Transitional Provisions and Savings) Order 2009, SI 2009/1941, art 2(1), Sch 1, para 85(1), (6)(a).

Sub-s (3): date in square brackets inserted by SI 2009/1941, art 2(1), Sch 1, para 85(1), (6)(a).

[4.38]

[20A Legal professional privilege

In proceedings against a person for an offence under this Act nothing in this Act is to be taken to require any person to disclose any information that he is entitled to refuse to disclose on grounds of legal professional privilege (in Scotland, confidentiality of communications).]

NOTES

Inserted by the Companies Act 2006 (Consequential Amendments etc) Order 2008, SI 2008/948, art 3(1)(b), Sch 1, Pt 2, para 106(1), (3).

[4.39]

21 Interaction with Insolvency Act [1986]

(1) References in this Act to the official receiver, in relation to the winding up of a company or the bankruptcy of an individual, are to any person who, by virtue of section 399 of the Insolvency Act [1986], is authorised to act as the official receiver in relation to that winding up or bankruptcy; and, in accordance with section 401(2) of that Act, references in this Act to an official receiver includes a person appointed as his deputy.

(2) Sections [1A,] [5A, 6 to 10, 12C to 15C], 19(c) and 20 of, and Schedule 1 to, this Act [and sections 1 and 17 of this Act as they apply for the purposes of those provisions] are deemed included in Parts I to VII of the Insolvency Act [1986] for the purposes of the following sections of that Act—

section 411 (power to make insolvency rules);
section 414 (fees orders);
section 420 (orders extending provisions about insolvent companies to insolvent partnerships);
section 422 (modification of such provisions in their application to recognised banks); . . .

. . .

(3) Section 434 of that Act (Crown application) applies to sections [1A,] [5A, 6 to 10, 12C to 15C], 19(c) and 20 of, and Schedule 1 to, this Act [and sections 1 and 17 of this Act as they apply for the purposes of those provisions] as it does to the provisions of that Act which are there mentioned.

[(4) For the purposes of summary proceedings in Scotland, section 431 of that Act applies to summary proceedings for an offence under section 11 or 13 of this Act as it applies to summary proceedings for an offence under Parts I to VII of that Act.]

NOTES

This section derived from the Insolvency Act 1985, ss 106, 107, 108(1), (2), 222(1), 224(2), 227, 229, 234.

Section heading and sub-s (1): date in square brackets inserted by the Companies Act 2006 (Consequential Amendments, Transitional Provisions and Savings) Order 2009, SI 2009/1941, art 2(1), Sch 1, para 85(1), (6)(a).

Sub-s (2): words in first and third pairs of square brackets inserted by the Insolvency Act 2000, s 8, Sch 4, Pt I, paras 1, 14(1), (2); words in second pair of square brackets substituted by the Small Business, Enterprise and Employment Act 2015, s 111, Sch 7, Pt 1, paras 1, 16; date in square brackets inserted by SI 2009/1941, art 2(1), Sch 1, para 85(1), (6)(a); words omitted repealed by the Companies Act 1989, s 212, Sch 24.

Sub-s (3): words in first and third pairs of square brackets inserted by the Insolvency Act 2000, s 8, Sch 4, Pt I, paras 1, 14(1), (3); words in second pair of square brackets substituted by the Small Business, Enterprise and Employment Act 2015, s 111, Sch 7, Pt 1, paras 1, 16.

Sub-s (4): added by the Companies Act 1989, s 208.

Rules: the Insolvent Companies (Disqualification of Unfit Directors) Proceedings Rules 1987, SI 1987/2023 at **[14.7]**; the Insolvent Companies (Reports on Conduct of Directors) Rules 1996, SI 1996/1909 at **[14.18]**; the Insolvent Companies (Reports on Conduct of Directors) (Scotland) Rules 1996, SI 1996/1910 at **[16.126]**; the Insolvent Companies (Reports on Conduct of Directors) (England and Wales) Rules 2016, SI 2016/180 at **[14.41]**; the Insolvent Companies (Reports on Conduct of Directors) (Scotland) Rules 2016, SI 2016/185 at **[16.285]**.

Orders: the Insolvent Partnerships Order 1994, SI 1994/2421 at **[10.1]**.

[4.40]

[21A Bank insolvency

Section 121 of the Banking Act 2009 provides for this Act to apply in relation to bank insolvency as it applies in relation to liquidation.]

NOTES

Inserted by the Banking Act 2009, s 121(4).

[4.41]

[21B Bank administration

Section 155 of the Banking Act 2009 provides for this Act to apply in relation to bank administration as it applies in relation to liquidation.]

NOTES

Inserted by the Banking Act 2009, s 155(4).

[4.42]

[21C Building society insolvency and special administration

Section 90E of the Building Societies Act 1986 provides for this Act to apply in relation to building society insolvency and building society special administration as it applies in relation to liquidation.]

NOTES

Inserted by the Building Societies (Insolvency and Special Administration) Order 2009, SI 2009/805, art 12.

[4.43]

22 Interpretation

(1) This section has effect with respect to the meaning of expressions used in this Act, and applies unless the context otherwise requires.

[(2) "Company" means—
(a) a company registered under the Companies Act 2006 in Great Britain, or
(b) a company that may be wound up under Part 5 of the Insolvency Act 1986 (unregistered companies).]
[(2A) An "overseas company" is a company incorporated or formed outside Great Britain.]
(3) Section 247 in Part VII of the Insolvency Act [1986] (interpretation for the first Group of Parts of that Act) applies as regards references to a company's insolvency and to its going into liquidation; and "administrative receiver" has the meaning given by section 251 of that Act [and references to acting as an insolvency practitioner are to be read in accordance with section 388 of that Act].
(4) "Director" includes any person occupying the position of director, by whatever name called . . .
(5) "Shadow director", in relation to a company, means a person in accordance with whose directions or instructions the directors of the company are accustomed to act[, but so that a person is not deemed a shadow director by reason only that the directors act—
(a) on advice given by that person in a professional capacity;
(b) in accordance with instructions, a direction, guidance or advice given by that person in the exercise of a function conferred by or under an enactment;
(c) in accordance with guidance or advice given by that person in that person's capacity as a Minister of the Crown (within the meaning of the Ministers of the Crown Act 1975)].
[(6) "Body corporate" and "officer" have the same meaning as in the Companies Acts (see section 1173(1) of the Companies Act 2006).]
[(7) "The Companies Acts" has the meaning given by section 2(1) of the Companies Act 2006.]
[(8) Any reference to provisions, or a particular provision, of the Companies Acts or the Insolvency Act 1986 includes the corresponding provisions or provision of corresponding earlier legislation.]
[(9) Subject to the provisions of this section, expressions that are defined for the purposes of the Companies Acts [(see section 1174 of, and Schedule 8 to, the Companies Act 2006)] have the same meaning in this Act.]
[(10) Any reference to acting as receiver—
(a) includes acting as manager or as both receiver and manager, but
(b) does not include acting as administrative receiver;
and "receivership" is to be read accordingly.]

NOTES

This section derived from the Insolvency Act 1985, s 108(1)–(4).

Sub-s (2): substituted by the Companies Act 2006 (Consequential Amendments, Transitional Provisions and Savings) Order 2009, SI 2009/1941, art 2(1), Sch 1, para 85(1), (11)(a).

Sub-s (2A): inserted by the Small Business, Enterprise and Employment Act 2015, s 111, Sch 7, Pt 1, paras 1, 17.

Sub-s (3): date in first pair of square brackets inserted by SI 2009/1941, art 2(1), Sch 1, para 85(1), (6)(a); words in second pair of square brackets added by the Insolvency Act 2000, s 8, Sch 4, Pt I, paras 1, 15(1), (2).

Sub-s (4): words omitted repealed by the Insolvency Act 2000, ss 8, 15(1), Sch 4, Pt I, paras 1, 15(1), (3), Sch 5.

Sub-s (5): words in square brackets substituted by the Small Business, Enterprise and Employment Act 2015, s 90(2).

Sub-ss (6)–(8): substituted by SI 2009/1941, art 2(1), Sch 1, para 85(1), (11)(b)–(d).

Sub-s (9): substituted by SI 2008/948, art 3(1)(b), Sch 1, Pt 2, para 106(1), (4)(c), subject to transitional provisions and savings in arts 6, 11, 12 thereof; words in square brackets inserted by SI 2009/1941, art 2(1), Sch 1, para 85(1), (11)(e). Sub-s (9) originally read as follows:

"(9) Any expression for whose interpretation provision is made by Part XXVI of the Companies Act (and not by subsections (3) to (8) above) is to be construed in accordance with that provision.".

Sub-s (10): added by the Insolvency Act 2000, s 5(3).

[4.44]
[22A Application of Act to building societies
(1) This Act applies to building societies as it applies to companies.
(2) References in this Act to a company, or to a director or an officer of a company include, respectively, references to a building society within the meaning of the Building Societies Act 1986 or to a director or officer, within the meaning of that Act, of a building society.
(3) In relation to a building society the definition of "shadow director" in section 22(5) applies with the substitution of "building society" for "company".
(4) . . .]

NOTES

Inserted by the Companies Act 1989, s 211(3).

Sub-s (4): repealed by the Small Business, Enterprise and Employment Act 2015, s 111, Sch 7, Pt 1, paras 1, 18.

[4.45]
[22B Application of Act to incorporated friendly societies
(1) This Act applies to incorporated friendly societies as it applies to companies.
(2) References in this Act to a company, or to a director or an officer of a company include, respectively, references to an incorporated friendly society within the meaning of the Friendly Societies Act 1992 or to a member of the committee of management or officer, within the meaning of that Act, of an incorporated friendly society.
(3) In relation to an incorporated friendly society every reference to a shadow director shall be omitted.
[(3A) In relation to an incorporated friendly society, this Act applies as if sections 8ZA to 8ZE were omitted.]
(4) . . .]

NOTES

Inserted by the Friendly Societies Act 1992, s 120(1), Sch 21, Pt I, para 8.
Sub-s (3A): inserted by the Small Business, Enterprise and Employment Act 2015, s 111, Sch 7, Pt 1, paras 1, 19(a).
Sub-s (4): repealed by the Small Business, Enterprise and Employment Act 2015, s 111, Sch 7, Pt 1, paras 1, 19(b).

[4.46]
[22C Application of Act to NHS foundation trusts
(1) This Act applies to NHS foundation trusts as it applies to companies within the meaning of this Act.
(2) References in this Act to a company, or to a director or officer of a company, include, respectively, references to an NHS foundation trust or to a director or officer of the trust; but references to shadow directors are omitted.
(3) . . .]

NOTES

Inserted by the Health and Social Care (Community Health and Standards) Act 2003, s 34, Sch 4, paras 67, 68.
Sub-s (3): repealed by the Small Business, Enterprise and Employment Act 2015, s 111, Sch 7, Pt 1, paras 1, 20.

22D *(Inserted by the Companies Act 2006 (Consequential Amendments, Transitional Provisions and Savings) Order 2009, SI 2009/1941, art 2(1), Sch 1, para 85(1), (13); repealed by the Small Business, Enterprise and Employment Act 2015, s 111, Sch 7, Pt 1, paras 1, 21.)*

[4.47]
[22E [Application of Act to registered societies]
[(1) In this section "registered society" has the same meaning as in the Co-operative and Community Benefit Societies Act 2014 ("the 2014 Act").]
(2) This Act applies to registered societies as it applies to companies.
(3) Accordingly, in this Act—
(a) references to a company include a registered society, and
(b) references to a director or an officer of a company include a member of the committee or an officer of a registered society.

In paragraph (b) "committee" and "officer" have the same meaning as in [the 2014 Act: see section 149 of that Act].
(4) As they apply in relation to registered societies, the provisions of this Act have effect with the following modifications—
(a) in section 2(1) (disqualification on conviction of indictable offence), the reference to striking off includes cancellation of the registration of a society under [the 2014 Act];
(b) in section 3 (disqualification for persistent breaches) and section 5 (disqualification on summary conviction), references to the companies legislation shall be read as references to the legislation relating to registered societies;
(c) . . .
(d) references to the registrar shall be read as references to the [Financial Conduct Authority];
(e) references to a shadow director shall be disregarded.
[(f) sections 8ZA to 8ZE are to be disregarded.]
(5) . . .
[(6) "The legislation relating to registered societies" means the Credit Unions Act 1979 and the Co-operative and Community Benefit Societies Act 2014.]

NOTES

Commencement: 6 April 2014.
Inserted by the Co-operative and Community Benefit Societies and Credit Unions Act 2010, s 3.
Section heading: substituted by the Co-operative and Community Benefit Societies Act 2014, s 151(1), Sch 4, Pt 2, para 38(1), (6).
Sub-ss (1), (6): substituted by the Co-operative and Community Benefit Societies Act 2014, s 151(1), Sch 4, Pt 2, para 38(1), (2), (5).
Sub-s (3): words in square brackets substituted by the Co-operative and Community Benefit Societies Act 2014, s 151(1), Sch 4, Pt 2, para 38(1), (3).
Sub-s (4): first and second words in square brackets substituted by the Co-operative and Community Benefit Societies Act 2014, s 151(1), Sch 4, Pt 2, para 38(1), (4); para (c) repealed, and para (f) added, by the Small Business, Enterprise and Employment Act 2015, s 111, Sch 7, Pt 1, paras 1, 22(1), (2); in para (d) words in square brackets substituted by the Financial Services Act 2012 (Mutual Societies) Order 2013, SI 2013/496, art 2(c), Sch 1, para 3.
Sub-s (5): repealed by the Small Business, Enterprise and Employment Act 2015, s 111, Sch 7, Pt 1, paras 1, 22(1), (3).

[4.48]
[22F Application of Act to charitable incorporated organisations
(1) This Act applies to charitable incorporated organisations ("CIOs") as it applies to companies.
(2) Accordingly, in this Act—
(a) references to a company are to be read as including references to a CIO;
(b) references to a director or an officer of a company are to be read as including references to a charity trustee of a CIO; and
(c) any reference to the Insolvency Act 1986 is to be read as including a reference to that Act as it applies to CIOs.
(3) As they apply in relation to CIOs, the provisions of this Act have effect with the following modifications—

(a) in section 2(1), the reference to striking off is to be read as including a reference to dissolution;
(b) in section 4(1)(a), the reference to an offence under section 993 of the Companies Act 2006 is to be read as including a reference to an offence under regulation 60 of the Charitable Incorporated Organisations (General) Regulations 2012(fraudulent trading);
(c) sections 9A to 9E are to be disregarded;
(d) references to any of sections 9A to 9E are to be disregarded;
(e) references to a shadow director are to be disregarded.

(4) . . .

(5) In this section "charity trustees" has the meaning given by section 177 of the Charities Act 2011.]

NOTES

Inserted by the Charitable Incorporated Organisations (Consequential Amendments) Order 2012, SI 2012/3014, art 2.
Sub-s (4): repealed by the Small Business, Enterprise and Employment Act 2015, s 111, Sch 7, Pt 1, paras 1, 23.

[4.49]
[22G Application of Act to further education bodies

(1) This Act applies to further education bodies as it applies to companies.

(2) Accordingly, in this Act—
(a) references to a company are to be read as including references to a further education body;
(b) references to a director or an officer of a company are to be read as including references to a member of a further education body;
(c) any reference to the Insolvency Act 1986 is to be read as including a reference to that Act as it applies to further education bodies.

(3) As they apply in relation to further education bodies, the provisions of this Act have effect with the following modifications—
(a) in section 2(1), the reference to striking off is to be read as including a reference to dissolution;
(b) sections 9A to 9E are to be disregarded;
(c) references to any of sections 9A to 9E are to be disregarded.

(4) In this section—
"further education body" means—
(a) a further education corporation, or
(b) a sixth form college corporation;
"further education corporation" means a body corporate that—
(a) is established under section 15 or 16 of the Further and Higher Education Act 1992, or
(b) has become a further education corporation by virtue of section 33D or 47 of that Act;
"sixth form college corporation" means a body corporate—
(a) designated as a sixth form college corporation under section 33A or 33B of the Further and Higher Education Act 1992, or
(b) established under section 33C of that Act.]

NOTES

Commencement: to be appointed.
Inserted by the Technical and Further Education Act 2017, s 39, as from a day to be appointed.

[4.50]
[22H Application of Act to protected cell companies

(1) In this section—
(a) "protected cell company" means a protected cell company incorporated under Part 4 of the Risk Transformation Regulations 2017 which has its registered office in England and Wales (or Wales) or Scotland; and
(b) a reference to a part of a protected cell company is a reference to the core or a cell of the protected cell company (see regulations 42 and 43 of the Risk Transformation Regulations 2017).

(2) This Act applies to protected cell companies as it applies to companies.

(3) Accordingly, in this Act, references to a company are to be read as including references to a protected cell company.

(4) As they apply in relation to protected cell companies, the provisions of this Act have effect with the following modifications—
(a) references to the administration, insolvency, liquidation or winding up of a company are to be read as references to the administration, insolvency, liquidation or winding up of a part of a protected cell company;
(b) references to striking off are to be read as including references to dissolution;
(c) references to a director of a company which is or has been insolvent are to be read as references to the director of a protected cell company, a part of which is or has been insolvent;
(d) references to a director of a company which is being or has been wound up are to be read as references to the director of a protected cell company, a part of which is being or has been wound up;
(e) references to the court with jurisdiction to wind up a company are to be read as references to the court with jurisdiction to wind up the parts of a protected cell company;
(f) references to the companies legislation are to be read as references to Part 4 of, and Schedules 1 to 3 to, the Risk Transformation Regulations 2017;
(g) references to the Insolvency Act 1986 are to be read as references to that Act as applied by Part 4 of, and Schedules 1 to 3 to, the Risk Transformation Regulations 2017;

(h) references to section 452 and 456 of the Companies Act 2006 are to be read as references to those sections as applied by regulation 163 of the Risk Transformation Regulations 2017;
(i) references to the registrar of companies are to be read as references to the Financial Conduct Authority; and
(j) references to an overseas company include references to a protected cell company incorporated under the Risk Transformation Regulations 2017 which has its registered office in Northern Ireland.

(5) Where two or more parts of a protected cell company are or have been insolvent, then sections 6 to 7A and 8ZA to 8ZC apply in relation to each part separately.
(6) A contribution to the assets of a protected cell company given in accordance with a compensation order under section 15A(1) or a compensation undertaking under section 15A(2) is to be held by the protected cell company on behalf of the part of the protected cell company specified in the order or undertaking.]

NOTES

Commencement: 8 December 2017.
Inserted by the Risk Transformation Regulations 2017, SI 2017/1212, reg 190, Sch 4, Pt 1, para 3.

[4.51]
23 Transitional provisions, savings, repeals
(1) The transitional provisions and savings in Schedule 3 to this Act have effect, and are without prejudice to anything in the Interpretation Act 1978 with regard to the effect of repeals.
(2) The enactments specified in the second column of Schedule 4 to this Act are repealed to the extent specified in the third column of that Schedule.

[4.52]
24 Extent
(1) This Act extends to England and Wales and to Scotland.
[(2) Subsections (1) to (2A) of section 11 also extend to Northern Ireland.]

NOTES

This section derived from the Companies Act 1985, s 745(2), and the Insolvency Act 1985, s 236(4)(a).
Sub-s (2): substituted by the Small Business, Enterprise and Employment Act 2015, s 113(2).

[4.53]
25 Commencement
This Act comes into force simultaneously with the Insolvency Act 1986.

NOTES

The Insolvency Act 1986 came into force on 29 December 1986 by virtue of the Insolvency Act 1985 (Commencement No 5) Order 1986, SI 1986/1924, art 3.

[4.54]
26 Citation
This Act may be cited as the Company Directors Disqualification Act 1986.

SCHEDULES

[SCHEDULE 1
DETERMINING UNFITNESS ETC: MATTERS TO BE TAKEN INTO ACCOUNT

Section 12C

Matters to be taken into account in all cases

[4.55]
1. The extent to which the person was responsible for the causes of any material contravention by a company or overseas company of any applicable legislative or other requirement.

2. Where applicable, the extent to which the person was responsible for the causes of a company or overseas company becoming insolvent.

3. The frequency of conduct of the person which falls within paragraph 1 or 2.

4. The nature and extent of any loss or harm caused, or any potential loss or harm which could have been caused, by the person's conduct in relation to a company or overseas company.

Additional matters to be taken into account where person is or has been a director

5. Any misfeasance or breach of any fiduciary duty by the director in relation to a company or overseas company.

6. Any material breach of any legislative or other obligation of the director which applies as a result of being a director of a company or overseas company.

7. The frequency of conduct of the director which falls within paragraph 5 or 6.

Interpretation

8. Subsections (1A) to (2A) of section 6 apply for the purposes of this Schedule as they apply for the purposes of that section.

9. In this Schedule "director" includes a shadow director.]

NOTES

Commencement: see note below.

This Schedule was substituted by the Small Business, Enterprise and Employment Act 2015, s 106(1), (6), as from 1 October 2015 (note that s 106 also came into force on 26 May 2015 for the purposes of enabling the exercise of any power to make provision by regulations, rules or order made by statutory instrument or to prepare and issue guidance). Note also that save where conduct is considered by a court or by the Secretary of State under s 5A of this Act, this Schedule applies to a person's conduct as a director where that conduct occurs on or after 1 October 2015 (see SI 2015/1689, Schedule, para 3).

Prior to this substitution, Schedule 1 (and the related notes) read as follows—

"SCHEDULE 1
MATTERS FOR DETERMINING UNFITNESS OF DIRECTORS

Section 9

PART I
MATTERS APPLICABLE IN ALL CASES

1. Any misfeasance or breach of any fiduciary or other duty by the director in relation to the company[, including in particular any breach by the director of a duty under Chapter 2 of Part 10 of the Companies Act 2006 (general duties of directors) owed to the company].

2. Any misapplication or retention by the director of, or any conduct by the director giving rise to an obligation to account for, any money or other property of the company.

3. The extent of the director's responsibility for the company entering into any transaction liable to be set aside under Part XVI of the Insolvency Act [1986] (provisions against debt avoidance).

[**4.** The extent of the director's responsibility for any failure by the company to comply with any of the following provisions of the Companies Act 2006—

(a) section 113 (register of members);
(b) section 114 (register to be kept available for inspection);
(c) section 162 (register of directors);
(d) section 165 (register of directors' residential addresses);
(e) section 167 (duty to notify registrar of changes: directors);
(f) section 275 (register of secretaries);
(g) section 276 (duty to notify registrar of changes: secretaries);
(h) section 386 (duty to keep accounting records);
(i) section 388 (where and for how long accounting records to be kept);
(j) section 854 (duty to make annual returns);
(k) section 860 (duty to register charges);
(l) section 878 (duty to register charges: companies registered in Scotland).]

[**5.** The extent of the director's responsibility for any failure by the directors of the company to comply with the following provisions of the Companies Act 2006—

(a) section 394 or 399 (duty to prepare annual accounts);
(b) section 414 or 450 (approval and signature of abbreviated accounts); or
(c) section 433 (name of signatory to be stated in published copy of accounts).]

[**5A.** . . .]

NOTES

This Schedule derived from the Insolvency Act 1985, Sch 2.

Para 1: words in square brackets inserted by the Companies Act 2006 (Consequential Amendments, Transitional Provisions and Savings) Order 2009, SI 2009/1941, art 2(1), Sch 1, para 85(1), (14)(a).

Para 3: date in square brackets inserted by SI 2009/1941, art 2(1), Sch 1, para 85(1), (6)(b).

Paras 4, 4A: substituted, together with para 5 for original paras 4, 5, by the Companies Act 2006 (Consequential Amendments etc) Order 2008, SI 2008/948, art 3(1)(b), Sch 1, Pt 2, para 106(1), (8)(a), (b), subject to transitional provisions and savings in arts 6, 11, 12 thereof; paras 4, 4A further substituted by new para 4 by SI 2009/1941, art 2(1), Sch 1, para 85(1), (14)(b).

Para 5: substituted by SI 2008/948, art 3(1), Sch 1, Pt 2, para 106(1), (8)(b), as noted above.

Para 5A: originally inserted by SI 1996/2827, reg 75, Sch 8, Pt I, para 10; repealed by SI 2009/1941, art 2(1), Sch 1, para 85(1), (14)(c). Note that Sch 1, para 85(1), (14)(c) also includes the words "(but see section 22D(3))" at the end of the sub-paragraph.

PART II
MATTERS APPLICABLE WHERE COMPANY HAS BECOME INSOLVENT

6. The extent of the director's responsibility for the causes of the company becoming insolvent.

7. The extent of the director's responsibility for any failure by the company to supply any goods or services which have been paid for (in whole or in part).

8. The extent of the director's responsibility for the company entering into any transaction or giving any preference, being a transaction or preference—

(a) liable to be set aside under section 127 or sections 238 to 240 of the Insolvency Act [1986], or
(b) challengeable under section 242 or 243 of that Act or under any rule of law in Scotland.

9. The extent of the director's responsibility for any failure by the directors of the company to comply with section 98 of the Insolvency Act [1986] (duty to call creditors' meeting in creditors' voluntary winding up).

10. Any failure by the director to comply with any obligation imposed on him by or under any of the following provisions of the Insolvency Act [1986]—

(a) [paragraph 47 of Schedule B1] (company's statement of affairs in administration);
(b) section 47 (statement of affairs to administrative receiver);
(c) section 66 (statement of affairs in Scottish receivership);
(d) section 99 (directors' duty to attend meeting; statement of affairs in creditors' voluntary winding up);
(e) section 131 (statement of affairs in winding up by the court);
(f) section 234 (duty of any one with company property to deliver it up);
(g) section 235 (duty to co-operate with liquidator, etc).

NOTES

This Schedule derived from the Insolvency Act 1985, Sch 2.

Paras 8, 9: date in square brackets inserted by the Companies Act 2006 (Consequential Amendments, Transitional Provisions and Savings) Order 2009, SI 2009/1941, art 2(1), Sch 1, para 85(1), (6)(b).

Para 10: date in square brackets inserted by SI 2009/1941, art 2(1), Sch 1, para 85(1), (6)(b); words in square brackets in sub-para (a) substituted for original words "section 22", by the Enterprise Act 2002 (Insolvency) Order 2003, SI 2003/2096, arts 4, 6, Schedule, para 12, except in any case where a petition for an administration order was presented before 15 September 2003.

Modification: Pt II of this Schedule is modified in relation to limited liability partnerships by the Limited Liability Partnerships Regulations 2001, SI 2001/1090, regs 4(2), 10, Sch 2, Pt II at **[10.36]**, **[10.38]**, **[10.40]**.".

SCHEDULE 2
SAVINGS FROM COMPANIES ACT 1981 SS 93, 94, AND INSOLVENCY ACT 1985 SCHEDULE 9

Section 19

[4.56]

1. Sections 2 and 4(1)(b) do not apply in relation to anything done before 15th June 1982 by a person in his capacity as liquidator of a company or as receiver or manager of a company's property.

2. Subject to paragraph 1—
(a) section 2 applies in a case where a person is convicted on indictment of an offence which he committed (and, in the case of a continuing offence, has ceased to commit) before 15th June 1982; but in such a case a disqualification order under that section shall not be made for a period in excess of 5 years;
(b) that section does not apply in a case where a person is convicted summarily—
  (i) in England and Wales, if he had consented so to be tried before that date, or
  (ii) in Scotland, if the summary proceedings commenced before that date.

3. Subject to paragraph 1, section 4 applies in relation to an offence committed or other thing done before 15th June 1982; but a disqualification order made on the grounds of such an offence or other thing done shall not be made for a period in excess of 5 years.

4. The powers of a court under section 5 are not exercisable in a case where a person is convicted of an offence which he committed (and, in the case of a continuing offence, had ceased to commit) before 15th June 1982.

5. For purposes of section 3(1) and section 5, no account is to be taken of any offence which was committed, or any default order which was made, before 1st June 1977.

6. An order made under section 28 of the Companies Act 1976 has effect as if made under section 3 of this Act; and an application made before 15th June 1982 for such an order is to be treated as an application for an order under the section last mentioned.

7. Where—
(a) an application is made for a disqualification order under section 6 of this Act by virtue of paragraph (a) of subsection (2) of that section, and
(b) the company in question went into liquidation before 28th April 1986 (the coming into force of the provision replaced by section 6),

the court shall not make an order under that section unless it could have made a disqualification order under section 300 of [the Companies Act 1985] as it had effect immediately before the date specified in sub-paragraph (b) above.

8. An application shall not be made under section 8 of this Act in relation to a report made or information or documents obtained before 28th April 1986.

NOTES

This Schedule derived from the Companies Act 1985, Sch 12, Pt III, and the Insolvency Act 1985, Sch 9, paras 2, 3.

Para 7: words in square brackets substituted by the Companies Act 2006 (Consequential Amendments, Transitional Provisions and Savings) Order 2009, SI 2009/1941, art 2(1), Sch 1, para 85(1), (15).

Companies Act 1976, s 28: repealed by the Companies Act 1981, ss 93(5), 119(5), Sch 4.

Companies Act 1985, s 300: repealed by the Insolvency Act 1985, s 235(3), Sch 10, Pt II.

SCHEDULE 3
TRANSITIONAL PROVISIONS AND SAVINGS

Section 23(1)

[4.57]

1. In this Schedule, "the former enactments" means so much of [the Companies Act 1985], and so much of [the Insolvency Act 1986], as is repealed and replaced by this Act; and "the appointed day" means the day on which this Act comes into force.

2. So far as anything done or treated as done under or for the purposes of any provision of the former enactments could have been done under or for the purposes of the corresponding provision of this Act, it is not invalidated by the repeal of that provision but has effect as if done under or for the purposes of the corresponding provision; and any order, regulation, rule or other instrument made or having effect under any provision of the former enactments shall, insofar as its effect is preserved by this paragraph, be treated for all purposes as made and having effect under the corresponding provision.

3. Where any period of time specified in a provision of the former enactments is current immediately before the appointed day, this Act has effect as if the corresponding provision had been in force when the period began to run; and (without prejudice to the foregoing) any period of time so specified and current is deemed for the purposes of this Act—

(a) to run from the date or event from which it was running immediately before the appointed day, and

(b) to expire (subject to any provision of this Act for its extension) whenever it would have expired if this Act had not been passed;

and any rights, priorities, liabilities, reliefs, obligations, requirements, powers, duties or exemptions dependent on the beginning, duration or end of such a period as above mentioned shall be under this Act as they were or would have been under the former enactments.

4. Where in any provision of this Act there is a reference to another such provision, and the first-mentioned provision operates, or is capable of operating, in relation to things done or omitted, or events occurring or not occurring, in the past (including in particular past acts of compliance with any enactment, failures of compliance, contraventions, offences and convictions of offences) the reference to the other provision is to be read as including a reference to the corresponding provision of the former enactments.

5. Offences committed before the appointed day under any provision of the former enactments may, notwithstanding any repeal by this Act, be prosecuted and punished after that day as if this Act had not passed.

6. A reference in any enactment, instrument or document (whether express or implied, and in whatever phraseology) to a provision of the former enactments (including the corresponding provision of any yet earlier enactment) is to be read, where necessary to retain for the enactment, instrument or document the same force and effect as it would have had but for the passing of this Act, as, or as including, a reference to the corresponding provision by which it is replaced in this Act.

NOTES

Para 1: words in square brackets substituted by the Companies Act 2006 (Consequential Amendments, Transitional Provisions and Savings) Order 2009, SI 2009/1941, art 2(1), Sch 1, para 85(1), (16).

SCHEDULE 4

(*Sch 4 contains repeals only.*)

DERIVATION TABLE

[4.58]
Note: The following abbreviations are used in this Table:—

"CA" = Companies Act 1985 (c 6)

"IA" = Insolvency Act 1985 (c 65)

Provision	Derivation
1	CA s 295(1), (2), (4); IA Sch 6 para 1(1)–(3)
2	CA ss 295(2), 296
3	CA ss 295(2), 297
4	CA ss 295(2), 298
5	CA ss 295(2), 299
6	CA ss 295(2); IA ss 12(1), (2), (7)–(9), 108(2)
7	IA s 12(3)–(6)
8	CA s 295(2); IA ss 12(9), 13, 108(2)
9	IA ss 12(9), 14
10	CA s 295(2); IA ss 16, 108(2)
11	CA s 302
12	IA s 221(2)
13	CA ss 295(7), 302(1), Sch 24; IA s 221(5)
14	CA s 733(1)–(3); IA Sch 6 para 7
15	IA s 18(1) (part), (2)–(6)
16	CA s 295(6) (part), Sch 12 paras 1–3; IA s 108(2), Sch 6 para 1(4)
17	CA s 295(6) (part), Sch 12 paras 4, 5; IA s 108(2), Sch 6 paras 1(4), 14
18	CA s 301; IA s 108(2), Sch 6 para 2
19	CA s 295(6); and see Sch 2
20	IA s 231 (part)
21	IA ss 106, 107, 108(1), (2), 221(1), 224(2), 227, 229, 234
22	IA s 108(1)–(4)
23	—
24	CA s 745(2); IA s 236(4)
25	—
26	—
Sch 1	IA Sch 2
Sch 2	CA Sch 12 Pt III; IA Sch 9 paras 2, 3
Sch 3	—
Sch 4	—

DESTINATION TABLE

[4.59]

This table shows in column (1) the enactments repealed by the Company Directors Disqualification Act 1986, s 23(2), Sch 4 (and, in certain cases where indicated by an asterisk *, provisions repealed by the Insolvency Act 1986, s 438, Sch 12), and in column (2) the provisions of the former Act corresponding to the repealed provisions.

In certain cases the enactment in column (1), although having a corresponding provision in column (2), is not, or is not wholly, repealed, as it is still required, or partly required, for the purposes of other legislation.

(1) **Companies Act 1985 (c 6)**	(2) **Company Directors Disqualification Act 1986 (c 46)**
s 295(1)	s 1(1)
s 295(2)	ss 1(2), (3), 2(3), 3(5), 4(3), 5(5), 6(4), 8(4), 10(2)
s 295(3)	s 22(2)
s 295(4)	s 1(4)
s 295(5)	Unnecessary
s 295(6)	ss 16, 17, 19(a), (b)
s 295(7)	s 13
s 296	s 2
s 297	s 3
s 298	s 4
s 299	s 5
s 301	s 18
s 302(1)	s 13
s 302(1)–(3)	s 11(1)–(3)
s 302(4)	s 22(2)
s 733(1)†	s 14(1), (2)
s 733(2), (3)†	s 14(1), (2)
s 745(2)†	s 24
Sch 12, paras 1–3	s 16(1)–(3)
Sch 12, paras 4, 5	s 17(1), (2)
Sch 12, paras 6–8, 15, 16	Rep, 1985 c 65, s 235(3), Sch 10, Pt II
Sch 12, paras 9–14	Sch 2, paras 1–6
Sch 24 (part)	s 13

(1) **Insolvency Act 1985 (c 65)**	(2) **Company Directors Disqualification Act 1986 (c 46)**
s 12(1), (2)	s 6(1), (4)
s 12(3)–(6)	s 7(1)–(4)
s 12(7)	s 6(2)
s 12(8), (9)	s 6(3)
s 13	s 8
s 14	s 9
s 16	s 10(1)
s 18(1)–(5)	s 15(1)–(5)
s 18(6)	s 22(2)
ss 106, 107, 108(1)*	ss 21, 22ˣ
s 108(2)	ss 6(4), 8(4), 10(2), 16, 17, 18, 21, 22ˣ
s 108(3), (4)*	s 22ˣ
s 221(2)*	s 12(2)
s 221(5)*	s 13

(1) **Insolvency Act 1985 (c 65)**	(2) **Company Directors Disqualification Act 1986 (c 46)**
ss 221(1), 224(2), 227, 229*	s 21
s 231*	s 20
s 234*	s 21
s 236(4)*	s 24
Sch 2	Sch 1
Sch 6, para 1(2), (3)	s 1(1), (3)
Sch 6, para 1(4)	ss 16, 17
Sch 6, para 2	s 18(1)
Sch 6, para 7	s 14
Sch 6, para 14	s 17(1)
Sch 9, paras 2, 3	Sch 2, paras 7, 8

† Not repealed

x See specific derivation note

* See notes to this table above

PART 5
BANKRUPTCY (SCOTLAND) ACTS

BANKRUPTCY (SCOTLAND) ACT 1985

(1985 c 66)

ARRANGEMENT OF SECTIONS

Administration of bankruptcy

1 Accountant in Bankruptcy .... [5.1]
1A Supervisory functions of the Accountant in Bankruptcy .... [5.2]
1B Performance of certain functions of the Accountant in Bankruptcy .... [5.3]
1C Directions .... [5.4]
1D Conduct of proceedings in the sheriff court .... [5.5]
2 Appointment and functions of the trustee in the sequestration .... [5.6]
3 Functions of the trustee .... [5.7]
3A Application to Accountant in Bankruptcy for a direction .... [5.8]
4 Commissioners .... [5.9]

Moratorium on diligence

4A Notice of intention to apply: debtor application etc .... [5.10]
4B Notice of intention to apply: sequestration of estate under section 6 .... [5.11]
4C Moratorium on diligence .... [5.12]
4D Period of moratorium .... [5.13]

Petitions for sequestration

5 Sequestration of the estate of living or deceased debtor .... [5.14]
5A Debtor applications by low income, low asset debtors .... [5.15]
5B Certificate for sequestration .... [5.16]
5C Money advice .... [5.17]
5D Assessment of debtor's contribution .... [5.18]
6 Sequestration of other estates .... [5.19]
6A Petition for sequestration of estate: provision of information .... [5.20]
6B Debtor application: provision of information .... [5.21]
7 Meaning of apparent insolvency .... [5.22]
8 Further provisions relating to presentation of petitions .... [5.23]
8A Further provisions relating to debtor applications .... [5.24]
9 Jurisdiction .... [5.25]
10 Duty to notify existence of concurrent proceedings for sequestration or analogous remedy .... [5.26]
10A Powers in relation to concurrent proceedings for sequestration or analogous remedy .... [5.27]
11 Creditor's oath .... [5.28]

Award of sequestration and appointment and resignation of interim trustee

11A Debtor application: incomplete application .... [5.29]
11B Refusal of debtor application: inappropriate application .... [5.30]
12 When sequestration is awarded .... [5.31]
13 Resignation, removal etc of interim trustee .... [5.32]
13A Termination of interim trustee's functions where not appointed as trustee .... [5.33]
13B Termination of Accountant in Bankruptcy's functions as interim trustee where not appointed as trustee .... [5.34]
14 Registration of warrant or determination of debtor application .... [5.35]
15 Further provisions relating to award of sequestration .... [5.36]
16 Petitions for recall of sequestration .... [5.37]
17 Recall of sequestration by sheriff .... [5.38]
17A Application to Accountant in Bankruptcy for recall of sequestration .... [5.39]
17B Application under section 17A: further procedure .... [5.40]
17C Determination of outlays and remuneration .... [5.41]
17D Recall of sequestration by Accountant in Bankruptcy .... [5.42]
17E Recall where Accountant in Bankruptcy the trustee .... [5.43]
17F Reference to sheriff .... [5.44]
17G Recall of sequestration by Accountant in Bankruptcy: review and appeal .... [5.45]

Initial stages of sequestration

18 Interim preservation of estate .... [5.46]
19 Statement of assets and liabilities etc .... [5.47]
20 Trustee's duties on receipt of list of assets and liabilities .... [5.48]

Statutory meeting of creditors and trustee vote

20A Statutory meeting . . . [5.49]
21 Calling of statutory meeting . . . [5.50]
21A Calling of statutory meeting . . . [5.51]
21B Procedure where no statutory meeting called. . . . [5.52]
22 Submission of claims for voting purposes at statutory meeting . . . [5.53]
23 Proceedings at statutory meeting before trustee vote . . . [5.54]
23A Summary administration . . . [5.55]
24 Trustee vote . . . [5.56]
25 Appointment of replacement trustee. . . . [5.57]
25A Applications to Accountant in Bankruptcy: procedure . . . [5.58]
25B Applications and appeals to sheriff: procedure . . . [5.59]
26 Provisions relating to termination of original trustee's functions . . . [5.60]
26A Accountant in Bankruptcy to account for intromissions . . . [5.61]
27 Discharge of original trustee . . . [5.62]

Replacement of trustee

28 Resignation and death of trustee . . . [5.63]
28A Replacement of trustee acting in more than one sequestration . . . [5.64]
28B Determination etc under section 28A: review . . . [5.65]
29 Removal of trustee and trustee not acting . . . [5.66]

Election, resignation and removal of commissioners

30 Election, resignation and removal of commissioners . . . [5.67]

Vesting of estate in trustee

31 Vesting of estate at date of sequestration . . . [5.68]
31ZA Proceedings under EC Regulation: modified definition of "estate" . . . [5.69]
31A Property subject to restraint order . . . [5.70]
31AA Property released from detention . . . [5.71]
31B Property in respect of which receivership or administration order is made. . . . [5.72]
31BA Property in respect of which realisation order made . . . [5.73]
31C Property subject to certain orders where confiscation order discharged or quashed . . . [5.74]
32 Vesting of estate, and dealings of debtor, after sequestration. . . . [5.75]
32A Debtor contribution order. . . . [5.76]
32B Debtor contribution order: payment period and intervals . . . [5.77]
32C Debtor contribution order: review and appeal . . . [5.78]
32D Effect of debtor contribution order . . . [5.79]
32E Deductions from debtor's earnings and other income . . . [5.80]
32F Variation and removal of debtor contribution order by trustee . . . [5.81]
32G Payment break . . . [5.82]
32H Sections 32F and 32G: review and appeal . . . [5.83]
33 Limitations on vesting . . . [5.84]

Safeguarding of interests of creditors of insolvent persons

34 Gratuitous alienations . . . [5.85]
35 Recalling of order for payment of capital sum on divorce . . . [5.86]
36 Unfair preferences . . . [5.87]
36A Recovery of excessive pension contributions . . . [5.88]
36B Orders under section 36A. . . . [5.89]
36C Orders under section 36A: supplementary . . . [5.90]
36D Recovery of excessive contributions in pension-sharing cases . . . [5.91]
36E Recovery orders . . . [5.92]
36F Recovery orders: supplementary . . . [5.93]

Effect of sequestration on diligence

37 Effect of sequestration on diligence . . . [5.94]

Administration of estate by trustee

38 Taking possession of estate by trustee . . . [5.95]
39 Management and realisation of estate . . . [5.96]
39A Debtor's home ceasing to form part of sequestrated estate. . . . [5.97]
40 Power of trustee in relation to the debtor's family home . . . [5.98]
41 Protection of rights of spouse against arrangements intended to defeat them . . . [5.99]
41A Protection of rights of civil partner against arrangements intended to defeat them . . . [5.100]
42 Contractual powers of trustee . . . [5.101]
43 Money received by trustee . . . [5.102]

43A Debtor's requirement to give account of state of affairs. . . . [5.103]
43B Financial education. . . . [5.104]

Examination of debtor

44 Private examination . . . . [5.105]
45 Public examination. . . . [5.106]
46 Provisions ancillary to sections 44 and 45 . . . . [5.107]
47 Conduct of examination . . . . [5.108]

Submission and adjudication of claims

48 Submission of claims to trustee . . . . [5.109]
49 Adjudication of claims. . . . [5.110]

Entitlement to vote and draw dividend

50 Entitlement to vote and draw dividend . . . . [5.111]

Distribution of debtor's estate

51 Order of priority in distribution . . . . [5.112]
52 Estate to be distributed in respect of accounting periods . . . . [5.113]
53 Procedure after end of accounting period . . . . [5.114]
53A Modification of procedure under section 53 where Accountant in Bankruptcy is trustee . . . . [5.115]

Discharge of debtor

54 Discharge where Accountant in Bankruptcy not the trustee. . . . [5.116]
54A Discharge where Accountant in Bankruptcy the trustee . . . . [5.117]
54B Discharge of debtor: review and appeal . . . . [5.118]
54C Debtor to whom section 5(2ZA) applies: discharge . . . . [5.119]
54D Deferral of discharge where debtor cannot be traced . . . . [5.120]
54E Debtor not traced: new trustee . . . . [5.121]
54F Debtor not traced: subsequent debtor contact . . . . [5.122]
54G Subsequent debtor contact: review and appeal . . . . [5.123]
55 Effect of discharge under section 54, 54A or 54C . . . . [5.124]
55A Discharge under section 54C: conditions . . . . [5.125]
55B Section 55A: sanctions . . . . [5.126]
56 Discharge on composition. . . . [5.127]

Bankruptcy restrictions orders and undertakings

56A Bankruptcy restrictions order. . . . [5.128]
56B Grounds for making order. . . . [5.130]
56C Application of section 67(9) . . . . [5.131]
56D Timing for making an order . . . . [5.132]
56E Duration of order and application for annulment. . . . [5.133]
56F Interim bankruptcy restrictions order. . . . [5.134]
56G Bankruptcy restrictions undertaking . . . . [5.135]
56H Bankruptcy restrictions undertakings: application of section 67(9) . . . . [5.136]
56J Effect of recall of sequestration . . . . [5.137]
56K Effect of discharge on approval of offer of composition . . . . [5.138]

Discharge of trustee

57 Discharge of trustee . . . . [5.139]
58 Unclaimed dividends. . . . [5.140]
58A Discharge of Accountant in Bankruptcy. . . . [5.141]
58B Assets discovered after trustee discharge: appointment of trustee . . . . [5.142]
58C Assets discovered after trustee discharge: notice . . . . [5.143]
58D Assets discovered after trustee discharge: appeal. . . . [5.144]

Voluntary trust deeds for creditors

59 Voluntary trust deeds for creditors . . . . [5.145]
59A Application for conversion to sequestration. . . . [5.146]
59B Contents of affidavit . . . . [5.147]
59C Power of Accountant in Bankruptcy . . . . [5.148]

Miscellaneous and supplementary

60 Liabilities and rights of co-obligants. . . . [5.149]
60A Member State liquidator deemed creditor. . . . [5.150]
60B Trustee's duties concerning notices and copies of documents . . . . [5.151]
61 Extortionate credit transactions. . . . [5.152]
62 Sederunt book and other documents . . . . [5.153]

63 Power of court to cure defects in procedure . . . [5.154]
63A Power of Accountant in Bankruptcy to cure defects in procedure . . . [5.155]
63B Decision under section 63A: review . . . [5.156]
63C Review of decisions by Accountant in Bankruptcy: grounds of appeal . . . [5.157]
64 Debtor to co-operate with trustee . . . [5.158]
65 Arbitration and compromise . . . [5.159]
66 Meetings of creditors and commissioners . . . [5.160]
67 General offences by debtor etc . . . [5.161]
68 Summary proceedings . . . [5.162]
69 Outlays of insolvency practitioner in actings as interim trustee or trustee . . . [5.163]
69A Fees for the Accountant in Bankruptcy . . . [5.164]
70 Supplies by utilities . . . [5.165]
71 Edinburgh Gazette . . . [5.166]
71A Further duty of Accountant in Bankruptcy . . . [5.167]
71B Disqualification provisions: power to make orders . . . [5.168]
71C Regulations: applications to Accountant in Bankruptcy etc . . . [5.169]
72 Regulations . . . [5.170]
72ZA Modification of regulation making powers . . . [5.171]
72A Variation of references to time, money etc . . . [5.172]
73 Interpretation . . . [5.173]
74 Meaning of "associate" . . . [5.174]
75 Amendments, repeals and transitional provisions . . . [5.175]
76 Receipts and expenses . . . [5.176]
77 Crown application . . . [5.177]
78 Short title, commencement and extent . . . [5.178]

SCHEDULES

Schedule A1—Debtor to whom section 5(2ZA) applies: Application of Act. . . . [5.179]
Schedule 1—Determination of amount of creditor's claim. . . . [5.180]
Schedule 2—Adaptation of procedure etc under this Act where permanent trustee not elected . . . [5.181]
Schedule 2A—Modification of duties of permanent trustee in summary administration . . . [5.182]
Schedule 3—Preferred debts
Part I—List of preferred debts. . . . [5.183]
Part II—Interpretation of Part I . . . [5.184]
Schedule 3A—Information to be Included in the Sederunt Book . . . [5.185]
Schedule 4—Discharge on composition . . . [5.186]
Schedule 5—Voluntary trust deeds for creditors. . . . [5.187]
Schedule 6—Meetings of creditors and commissioners
Part I—Meetings of creditors other than the statutory meeting . . . [5.188]
Part II—All meetings of creditors. . . . [5.189]
Part III—Meetings of commissioners. . . . [5.190]
Schedule 7
Part II—Re-enactment of certain provisions of Bankruptcy (Scotland) Act 1913 (c 20). . . . [5.191]

An Act to reform the law of Scotland relating to sequestration and personal insolvency; and for connected purposes

[30 October 1985]

NOTES

Note: this Act is repealed by the Bankruptcy (Scotland) Act 2016, s 234(2), Sch 9, Pt 1, as from 30 November 2016, subject to transitional provisions and savings in s 234(3)–(8) thereof at [5.432] and is reproduced for reference.

Enforcement of insolvency law in other parts of the United Kingdom: see the Insolvency Act 1986, s 426 at **[1.540]**, for provision for co-operation between courts exercising jurisdiction in relation to insolvency.

Modification: certain provisions of this Act are applied, with modifications, in relation to the special administration of an investment bank, by the Investment Bank Special Administration (Scotland) Rules 2011, SI 2011/2262. See in particular rr 66, 127, 132 thereof. As to the application of this Act, with modifications, in relation to a partnership scheme in respect of which an authorisation order has been made under the Financial Services and Markets Act 2000, s 261D(1), see the Collective Investment in Transferable Securities (Contractual Scheme) Regulations 2013, SI 2013/1388, reg 19 at **[7.836]**.

Administration of bankruptcy

[5.1]

[1 Accountant in Bankruptcy

(1) The Accountant in Bankruptcy shall be appointed by the Scottish Ministers.

[(1A) The Accountant in Bankruptcy shall be an officer of the court.]

(2) The Scottish Ministers may appoint a member of the staff of the Accountant in Bankruptcy to be Depute Accountant in Bankruptcy to exercise all of the functions of the Accountant in Bankruptcy at any time when the Accountant in Bankruptcy is unable to do so.]

NOTES

Repealed as noted at the beginning of this Act.

Substituted by the Scotland Act 1998, s 125, Sch 8, para 22; previously substituted, together with ss 1A–1C, for original s 1, by the Bankruptcy (Scotland) Act 1993, s 1(1), subject to s 12(6) thereof, at **[5.194]** and to the Bankruptcy (Scotland) Act 1993 Commencement and Savings Order 1993, SI 1993/438, arts 4, 5, at **[16.58]**, **[16.59]**.

Sub-s (1A): inserted by the Bankruptcy and Diligence etc (Scotland) Act 2007, s 22, subject to transitional provisions and savings in SSI 2008/115, arts 5–7, 10, 15 at **[2.51]–[2.53]**, **[2.56]**, **[2.57]**.

Acts of Sederunt: at the time of going to press no Acts of Sederunt had been made under this section but note the Act of Sederunt (Rules of Court Amendment No 1) (Bankruptcy Forms) 1986, SI 1986/514, made under s 1 of this Act as originally enacted.

[5.2]

[1A Supervisory functions of the Accountant in Bankruptcy

(1) The Accountant in Bankruptcy shall have the following general functions in the administration of sequestration and personal insolvency—

(a) the supervision of the performance by—
  (i) interim trustees (not being the Accountant in Bankruptcy);
  (ii) [trustees (not being the Accountant in Bankruptcy)];
  [(iia) trustees under protected trust deeds;] and
  (iii) commissioners,

of the functions conferred on them by this Act or any other enactment (including an enactment contained in subordinate legislation) or any rule of law and the investigation of any complaints made against them;

[(aa) the determination of debtor applications;]

(b) the maintenance of a register (in this Act referred to as the "register of insolvencies"), in such form as may be prescribed by [regulations made by the Scottish Ministers], which shall contain particulars of—
  [(ai) persons who are the subject of notices under section 4A(1) and 4B(1),]
  (i) estates which have been sequestrated; . . .
  (ii) trust deeds which have been sent to him for registration . . . ;
  [(iia) bankruptcy restrictions orders [and interim bankruptcy restrictions orders];]
  [(iib) orders made under subsection (2) of section 32 of this Act and agreements made under subsection (4B) of that section;] [and
  (iii) the winding up and receivership of business associations which the Court of Session has jurisdiction to wind up][; and
  (iv) any other document as may be specified in regulations made under this subsection or any other enactment.]

(c) the preparation of an annual report which shall be presented to the Secretary of State and the Court of Session and shall contain—
  (i) statistical information relating to the state of all sequestrations [and the winding up and receivership of business associations] of which particulars have been registered in the register of insolvencies during the year to which the report relates;
  (ii) particulars of trust deeds registered as protected trust deeds in that year; and
  (iii) particulars of the performance of the Accountant in Bankruptcy's functions under this Act;

. . .

(d) such other functions as may from time to time be conferred on him by the Secretary of State [and

(e) in this subsection "business association" has the meaning given in Section C2 of Part II of Schedule 5 to the Scotland Act 1998.]

(2) If it appears to the Accountant in Bankruptcy that a person mentioned in paragraph (a) of subsection (1) above has failed without reasonable excuse to perform a duty imposed on him by any provision of this Act or by any other enactment (including an enactment contained in subordinate legislation) or by any rule of law, he shall report the matter to the [sheriff who], after hearing that person on the matter, may remove him from office or censure him or make such other order as the circumstances of the case may require.

(3) Where the Accountant in Bankruptcy has reasonable grounds to suspect that an offence has been committed—

(a) by a person mentioned in paragraph (a) of subsection (1) above in the performance of his functions under this Act or any other enactment (including an enactment contained in subordinate legislation) or any rule of law; or

(b) in relation to a sequestration, by the debtor in respect of his assets, his dealings with them or his conduct in relation to his business or financial affairs; or

(c) in relation to a sequestration, by a person other than the debtor in that person's dealings with the debtor, the interim trustee or the . . . trustee in respect of the debtor's assets, business or financial affairs,

he shall report the matter to the Lord Advocate.

(4) The Accountant in Bankruptcy shall—

(a) make the register of insolvencies, at all reasonable times, available for inspection; and

(b) provide any person, on request, with a certified copy of any entry in the register.

[(5) Regulations under subsection (1)(b) may in particular prescribe circumstances where information need not be included in the register of insolvencies, if in the opinion of the Accountant in Bankruptcy inclusion of the information would be likely to jeopardise the safety or welfare of any person.]]

NOTES

Repealed as noted at the beginning of this Act.

Substituted, together with ss 1, 1B, 1C, for original s 1, by the Bankruptcy (Scotland) Act 1993, s 1(1), subject to s 12(6) thereof, at **[5.194]** and to the Bankruptcy (Scotland) Act 1993 Commencement and Savings Order 1993, SI 1993/438, arts 4, 5, at **[16.58]**, **[16.59]**.

Sub-s (1): words in square brackets in para (a)(ii) substituted for original words "permanent trustees", paras (a)(iia), (aa), (b)(iia) inserted, and words "under paragraph 5(1)(e) of Schedule 5 to this Act" omitted from para (b)(ii) repealed by the Bankruptcy and Diligence etc (Scotland) Act 2007, ss 2(2), 14(1), 23(2), 36, 226(2), Sch 1, paras 1, 2(a), Sch 6, Pt 1, subject to transitional provisions and savings in SSI 2008/115, arts 5–7, 10, 15 at **[2.51]**–**[2.53]**, **[2.56]**, **[2.57]**; words in first pair of square brackets in para (b) substituted for original words "the Court of Session by act of sederunt", para (b)(ai) inserted, words in square brackets in para (b)(iia) substituted for original words "interim bankruptcy restrictions orders and bankruptcy restrictions undertakings" and para (b)(iv) inserted together with word immediately preceding it, by the Bankruptcy and Debt Advice (Scotland) Act 2014, ss 22(a), 56(1), Sch 3, paras 2, 3, subject to transitional provisions and savings in SSI 2014/261, arts 4, 12 at **[2.91]**, **[2.99]**; para (b)(iib) inserted by the Bankruptcy and Diligence etc (Scotland) Act 2007, s 18(5), as from a day to be appointed; words omitted from paras (b)(i), (c) repealed, para (b)(iii) and word immediately preceding it and words in square brackets in paras (c)–(e) inserted by the Scotland Act 1998 (Consequential Modifications) (No 2) Order 1999, SI 1999/1820, art 4, Sch 2, Pt I, para 82(1), (2).

Sub-s (2): words in square brackets substituted for original words "court which" by the Bankruptcy and Diligence etc (Scotland) Act 2007, s 36, Sch 1, paras 1, 2(b), subject to transitional provisions and savings in SSI 2008/115, arts 5–7, 10, 15 at **[2.51]**–**[2.53]**, **[2.56]**, **[2.57]**.

Sub-s (3): word "permanent" omitted from para (c) repealed by the Bankruptcy and Diligence etc (Scotland) Act 2007, s 226(2), Sch 6, Pt 1, subject to transitional provisions and savings in SSI 2008/115, arts 5–7, 10, 15 at **[2.51]**–**[2.53]**, **[2.56]**, **[2.57]**.

Sub-s (5): added by the Bankruptcy and Debt Advice (Scotland) Act 2014, s 22(b), subject to transitional provisions and savings in SSI 2014/261, arts 4, 12 at **[2.91]**, **[2.99]**.

Regulations: the Bankruptcy (Scotland) Regulations 2014, SSI 2014/225 at **[16.267]**.

Acts of Sederunt: the Act of Sederunt (Rules of the Court of Session Amendment) (Register of Insolvencies) 1993, SI 1993/899; the Act of Sederunt (Bankruptcy Rules) 1993, SI 1993/921; the Act of Sederunt (Rules of the Court of Session 1994), SI 1994/1443 at **[16.60]**; the Act of Sederunt (Sheriff Court Bankruptcy Rules) 2008, SSI 2008/119 at **[16.263]**.

[5.3]

[1B Performance of certain functions of the Accountant in Bankruptcy

(1) The functions of the Accountant in Bankruptcy, other than functions conferred by section 1A of this Act, may be carried out on his behalf by any member of his staff authorised by him to do so.

(2) Without prejudice to subsection (1) above, the Accountant in Bankruptcy may appoint on such terms and conditions as he considers appropriate such persons as he considers fit to perform on his behalf any of his functions in respect of the sequestration of the estate of any debtor.

(3) A person appointed under subsection (2) above shall comply with such general or specific directions as the Accountant in Bankruptcy may from time to time give to such person as to the performance of his functions in relation to any sequestration.

(4) The Accountant in Bankruptcy may pay to a person appointed under subsection (2) above such fee as he may consider appropriate.]

NOTES

Repealed as noted at the beginning of this Act.

Substituted, together with ss 1, 1A, 1C, for original s 1, by the Bankruptcy (Scotland) Act 1993, s 1(1), subject to s 12(6) thereof, at **[5.194]** and to the Bankruptcy (Scotland) Act 1993 Commencement and Savings Order 1993, SI 1993/438, arts 4, 5, at **[16.58]**, **[16.59]**.

[5.4]

[1C Directions

(1) The Secretary of State may, after consultation with the Lord President of the Court of Session, give to the Accountant in Bankruptcy general directions as to the performance of his functions under this Act.

(2) Directions under this section may be given in respect of all cases or any class or description of cases, but may not be given in respect of any particular case.

(3) The Accountant in Bankruptcy shall comply with any directions given to him under this section.]

NOTES

Repealed as noted at the beginning of this Act.

Substituted, together with ss 1, 1A, 1B, for original s 1, by the Bankruptcy (Scotland) Act 1993, s 1(1), subject to s 12(6) thereof, at **[5.194]** and to the Bankruptcy (Scotland) Act 1993 Commencement and Savings Order 1993, SI 1993/438, arts 4, 5, at **[16.58]**, **[16.59]**.

[5.5]

[1D Conduct of proceedings in the sheriff court

(1) A person authorised by the Accountant in Bankruptcy may conduct civil proceedings in the sheriff court in relation to a function of the Accountant in Bankruptcy (including the functions listed in section 1A).

(2) In subsection (1), "civil proceedings" are proceedings which are not in respect of an offence.]

NOTES

Commencement: 30 June 2014.

Inserted by the Bankruptcy and Debt Advice (Scotland) Act 2014, s 44.

Repealed as noted at the beginning of this Act.

[5.6]

[2 [Appointment and functions of the trustee in the sequestration]

(1) Where the [sheriff] awards sequestration of the debtor's estate and the petition for the sequestration—

(a) nominates a person to be [the] trustee;

(b) states that the person satisfies the conditions mentioned in subsection (3) below; and

(c) has annexed to it a copy of the undertaking mentioned in subsection (3)(c) below,

the [sheriff] may, if it appears to the [sheriff] that the person satisfies those conditions and if no interim trustee has been appointed in pursuance of subsection (5) below, appoint that person to be [the] trustee in the sequestration.

[(1A) Subject to subsection [(1D)] below, where the Accountant in Bankruptcy awards sequestration of the debtor's estate and the debtor application—

(a) nominates a person to be the trustee;

(b) states that the person satisfies the conditions mentioned in subsection (3) below; and

(c) has annexed to it a copy of the undertaking mentioned in subsection (3)(c) below,

the Accountant in Bankruptcy may, if it appears to him that the person satisfies those conditions, appoint that person to be the trustee in the sequestration.

(1B) Where the Accountant in Bankruptcy awards sequestration of the debtor's estate and does not appoint a person to be the trustee in pursuance of subsection (1A) above, the Accountant in Bankruptcy shall be deemed to be appointed to be the trustee in the sequestration.

(1C) Where—

(a) the debtor application is made by a debtor to whom section 5(2B)(c)(ia) applies; and

(b) the Accountant in Bankruptcy awards sequestration of the debtor's estate,

the Accountant in Bankruptcy shall be deemed to be appointed as trustee in the sequestration.]

[(1D) The Accountant in Bankruptcy is not to make an appointment under subsection (1A) where—

(a) the debtor application is made by a debtor to whom section 5(2ZA) applies, and

(b) the Accountant in Bankruptcy awards sequestration of the debtor's estate.]

(2) Where the [sheriff] awards sequestration of the debtor's estate and—

(a) [he] does not appoint a person to be [the] trustee in pursuance of subsection (1) above; and

(b) no interim trustee has been appointed in pursuance of subsection (5) below,

the [sheriff] shall appoint the Accountant in Bankruptcy to be [the] trustee in the sequestration.

[(2A) Where the sheriff awards sequestration of the debtor's estate and an interim trustee has been appointed in pursuance of subsection (5) below, the sheriff may appoint—

(a) the interim trustee; or

(b) subject to subsection (2B) below, such other person as may be nominated by the petitioner,

to be the trustee in the sequestration.

(2B) A person nominated under subsection (2A)(b) above may be appointed to be the trustee in the sequestration only if—

(a) it appears to the sheriff that the person satisfies the conditions mentioned in subsection (3) below; and

(b) a copy of the undertaking mentioned in subsection (3)(c) below has been lodged with the sheriff.

(2C) Where the sheriff does not appoint a person to be trustee in pursuance of subsection (2A) above, the sheriff shall appoint the Accountant in Bankruptcy to be the trustee in the sequestration.]

(3) The conditions referred to in subsection (1) above are that the person—

(a) . . .

(b) is qualified to act as an insolvency practitioner; and

(c) has given an undertaking, in writing, that he will act [as the trustee].

(4) . . .

(5) Where a petition for sequestration is presented by a creditor or a trustee acting under a trust deed, the [sheriff] may appoint an interim trustee before sequestration is awarded—

(a) if the debtor consents; or

(b) if the trustee acting under the trust deed or any creditor shows cause.

(6) For the purposes of the appointment of an interim trustee under subsection (5) above—

(a) where a person is nominated as mentioned in subsection (1)(a) above and the provisions of that subsection apply, the [sheriff] may appoint that person; and

(b) where such a person is not appointed, the [sheriff] shall appoint the Accountant in Bankruptcy.

[(6A) The interim trustee's general function shall be to safeguard the debtor's estate pending the determination of the petition for sequestration.

(6B) Whether or not the interim trustee is still acting in the sequestration, the interim trustee shall supply the Accountant in Bankruptcy with such information as the Accountant in Bankruptcy considers necessary to enable him to discharge his functions under this Act.]

(7) Where

[(a) a trustee is appointed in a sequestration where the petition was presented by a creditor or the trustee acting under a trust deed; or

(b) an interim trustee is appointed in pursuance of subsection (5) above,

he] shall, as soon as practicable, notify the debtor of his appointment.

[(8) The trustee must at the same time as notifying the debtor under subsection (7)(a) or (b), send to the debtor, for signature by the debtor, a statement of undertakings in the form prescribed.]]

NOTES

Repealed as noted at the beginning of this Act.

Substituted by the Bankruptcy (Scotland) Act 1993, s 2, subject to s 12(6) thereof, at **[5.194]** and to the Bankruptcy (Scotland) Act 1993 Commencement and Savings Order 1993, SI 1993/438, arts 4, 5, at **[16.58]**, **[16.59]**.

Section heading: substituted for original words "Appointment and functions of interim trustee" by the Bankruptcy and Diligence etc (Scotland) Act 2007, s 6(1)(c), subject to transitional provisions and savings in SSI 2008/115, arts 5–7, 10, 15 at **[2.51]–[2.53]**, **[2.56]**, **[2.57]**.

Sub-s (1): words "sheriff" and "the" in square brackets in each place they appear substituted for original words "court" and "interim" respectively by the Bankruptcy and Diligence etc (Scotland) Act 2007, s 36, Sch 1, paras 1, 3(1)–(3), subject to transitional provisions and savings in SSI 2008/115, arts 5–7, 10, 15 at **[2.51]–[2.53]**, **[2.56]**, **[2.57]**.

Sub-ss (1A)–(1C): inserted by the Bankruptcy and Diligence etc (Scotland) Act 2007, s 14(2), subject to transitional provisions and savings in SSI 2008/115, arts 5–7, 10, 15 at **[2.51]–[2.53]**, **[2.56]**, **[2.57]**; figure in square brackets in sub-s (1A) substituted (for original figure "(1C)") and sub-s (1C) repealed by the Bankruptcy and Debt Advice (Scotland) Act 2014, ss 6(a), 56(2), Sch 4 subject to transitional provisions and savings in SSI 2014/261, arts 4, 12 at **[2.91]**, **[2.99]**.

Sub-s (1D): inserted by the Bankruptcy and Debt Advice (Scotland) Act 2014, s 6(b), subject to transitional provisions and savings in SSI 2014/261, arts 4, 12 at **[2.91]**, **[2.99]**.

Sub-s (2): words "sheriff", "he" and "the" in square brackets substituted for original words "court", "it" and "interim" respectively by the Bankruptcy and Diligence etc (Scotland) Act 2007, s 36, Sch 1, paras 1, 3(1), (2), (4), subject to transitional provisions and savings in SSI 2008/115, arts 5–7, 10, 15 at **[2.51]–[2.53]**, **[2.56]**, **[2.57]**.

Sub-ss (2A)–(2C): inserted by the Bankruptcy and Diligence etc (Scotland) Act 2007, s 6(1)(a), subject to transitional provisions and savings in SSI 2008/115, arts 5–7, 10, 15 at **[2.51]–[2.53]**, **[2.56]**, **[2.57]**.

Sub-s (3): para (a) repealed by the Bankruptcy and Diligence etc (Scotland) Act 2007, s 7(1), subject to transitional provisions and savings in SSI 2008/115, arts 5–7, 10, 15 at **[2.51]–[2.53]**, **[2.56]**, **[2.57]**, and previously read as follows:

"(a) resides within the jurisdiction of the Court of Session;";

words in square brackets in para (c) substituted for original para (c)(i), (ii) by the Bankruptcy and Diligence etc (Scotland) Act 2007, s 36, Sch 1, paras 1, 3(1), (5), subject to transitional provisions and savings as noted above, and previously read as follows:

"(i) as interim trustee; and
(ii) where no permanent trustee is elected, as permanent trustee, in the sequestration.".

Sub-s (4): repealed by the Bankruptcy and Diligence etc (Scotland) Act 2007, s 226(2), Sch 6, Pt 1, subject to transitional provisions and savings in SSI 2008/115, arts 5–7, 10, 15 at **[2.51]–[2.53]**, **[2.56]**, **[2.57]**, and previously read as follows:

"(4) The interim trustee's general functions shall be—
(a) to safeguard the debtor's estate pending the appointment of a permanent trustee under this Act;
(b) to ascertain the reasons for the debtor's insolvency and the circumstances surrounding it;
(c) to ascertain the state of the debtor's liabilities and assets;
(d) to administer the sequestration process pending the appointment of a permanent trustee; and
(e) whether or not he is still acting in the sequestration, to supply the Accountant in Bankruptcy with such information as the Accountant in Bankruptcy considers necessary to enable him to discharge his functions under this Act.".

Sub-ss (5), (6): word "sheriff" in square brackets in each place it appears substituted for original word "court" by the Bankruptcy and Diligence etc (Scotland) Act 2007, s 36, Sch 1, paras 1, 3(1), (2), subject to transitional provisions and savings in SSI 2008/115, arts 5–7, 10, 15 at **[2.51]–[2.53]**, **[2.56]**, **[2.57]**.

Sub-ss (6A), (6B): inserted by the Bankruptcy and Diligence etc (Scotland) Act 2007, s 6(1)(b), subject to transitional provisions and savings in SSI 2008/115, arts 5–7, 10, 15 at **[2.51]–[2.53]**, **[2.56]**, **[2.57]**.

Sub-s (7): words in square brackets substituted for original words "the petition for sequestration was presented by a creditor or the trustee acting under a trust deed, the interim trustee" by the Bankruptcy and Diligence etc (Scotland) Act 2007, s 36, Sch 1, paras 1, 3(1), (6), subject to transitional provisions and savings in SSI 2008/115, arts 5–7, 10, 15 at **[2.51]–[2.53]**, **[2.56]**, **[2.57]**.

Sub-s (8): added by the Bankruptcy and Debt Advice (Scotland) Act 2014, s 9(1), subject to transitional provisions and savings in SSI 2014/261, arts 4, 12 at **[2.91]**, **[2.99]**.

Regulations: the Bankruptcy (Scotland) Regulations 2014, SSI 2014/225 at **[16.267]**.

[5.7]

3 [Functions of the trustee]

(1) In every sequestration there shall be a . . . trustee whose general functions shall be—

(a) to recover, manage and realise the debtor's estate, whether situated in Scotland or elsewhere;
(b) to distribute the estate among the debtor's creditors according to their respective entitlements;
(c) to ascertain the reasons for the debtor's insolvency and the circumstances surrounding it;
(d) to ascertain the state of the debtor's liabilities and assets;
(e) to maintain a sederunt book during his term of office for the purpose of providing an accurate record of the sequestration process;
(f) to keep regular accounts of his intromissions with the debtor's estate, such accounts being available for inspection at all reasonable times by the commissioners (if any), the creditors and the debtor; and
(g) whether or not he is still acting in the sequestration, to supply the Accountant in Bankruptcy with such information as the Accountant in Bankruptcy considers necessary to enable him to discharge his functions under this Act.

(2) A . . . trustee in performing his functions under this Act shall have regard to advice offered to him by the commissioners (if any).

(3) If the . . . trustee has reasonable grounds to suspect that an offence has been committed in relation to a sequestration—

(a) by the debtor in respect of his assets, his dealings with them or his conduct in relation to his business or financial affairs; or

(b) by a person other than the debtor in that person's dealings with the debtor, the interim trustee or the . . . trustee in respect of the debtor's assets, business or financial affairs,

he shall report the matter to the Accountant in Bankruptcy.

[(3A) If the trustee has reasonable grounds to believe that any behaviour on the part of the debtor is of a kind that would result in a sheriff granting, under section 56B(1) of this Act, an application for a bankruptcy restrictions order, he shall report the matter to the Accountant in Bankruptcy.]

(4) A report under subsection (3) [or (3A)] above shall be absolutely privileged.

[(5) Paragraph (g) of subsection (1) above and [subsections (3) and (3A)] above shall not apply in any case where the . . . trustee is the Accountant in Bankruptcy.

(6) [Where the Accountant in Bankruptcy is the trustee, the Accountant in Bankruptcy] may apply to the sheriff for directions in relation to any particular matter arising in the sequestration.

(7) Where the debtor, a creditor or any other person having an interest is dissatisfied with any act, omission or decision of the . . . trustee, he may apply to the sheriff and, on such an application being made, the sheriff may confirm, annul or modify any act or decision of the . . . trustee or may give him directions or make such order as he thinks fit.]

[(8) The trustee shall comply with the requirements of subsections (1)(a) to (d) and (2) above only in so far as, in his view, it would be of financial benefit to the estate of the debtor and in the interests of the creditors to do so.]

NOTES

Repealed as noted at the beginning of this Act.

Section heading: substituted for original words "Permanent trustee" by the Bankruptcy and Diligence etc (Scotland) Act 2007, s 6(2), subject to transitional provisions and savings in SSI 2008/115, arts 5–7, 10, 15 at **[2.51]–[2.53]**, **[2.56]**, **[2.57]**.

Sub-ss (1)–(3): word "permanent" omitted in each place repealed by the Bankruptcy and Diligence etc (Scotland) Act 2007, s 226(2), Sch 6, Pt 1, subject to transitional provisions and savings in SSI 2008/115, arts 5–7, 10, 15 at **[2.51]–[2.53]**, **[2.56]**, **[2.57]**.

Sub-s (3A): inserted by the Bankruptcy and Diligence etc (Scotland) Act 2007, s 8(1)(a), subject to transitional provisions and savings in SSI 2008/115, arts 5–7, 10, 15 at **[2.51]–[2.53]**, **[2.56]**, **[2.57]**.

Sub-s (4): words in square brackets inserted by the Bankruptcy and Diligence etc (Scotland) Act 2007, s 8(1)(b), subject to transitional provisions and savings in SSI 2008/115, arts 5–7, 10, 15 at **[2.51]–[2.53]**, **[2.56]**, **[2.57]**.

Sub-s (5): added by the Bankruptcy (Scotland) Act 1993, s 11(3), Sch 1, para 1, subject to s 12(6) thereof, at **[5.194]** and to the Bankruptcy (Scotland) Act 1993 Commencement and Savings Order 1993, SI 1993/438, arts 4, 5, at **[16.58]**, **[16.59]**; words in square brackets substituted for original words "subsection (3)" and word "permanent" (omitted) repealed by the Bankruptcy and Diligence etc (Scotland) Act 2007, ss 8(1)(c), 226(2), Sch 6, Pt 1, subject to transitional provisions and savings in SSI 2008/115, arts 5–7, 10, 15 at **[2.51]–[2.53]**, **[2.56]**, **[2.57]**.

Sub-ss (6), (7): added by the Bankruptcy (Scotland) Act 1993, s 11(3), Sch 1, para 1, subject to s 12(6) thereof, at **[5.194]** and to SI 1993/438, arts 4, 5, at **[16.58]**, **[16.59]**; in sub-s (6) words in square brackets substituted for original words "A trustee", by the Bankruptcy and Debt Advice (Scotland) Act 2014, s 25(1), subject to transitional provisions and savings in SSI 2014/261, arts 9, 12 at **[2.96]**, **[2.99]**; word "permanent" omitted in each place in sub-s (7) repealed by the Bankruptcy and Diligence etc (Scotland) Act 2007, s 226(2), Sch 6, Pt 1, subject to transitional provisions and savings in SSI 2008/115, arts 5–7, 10, 15 at **[2.51]–[2.53]**, **[2.56]**, **[2.57]**.

Sub-s (8): added by the Bankruptcy and Diligence etc (Scotland) Act 2007, s 8(1)(d), subject to transitional provisions and savings in SSI 2008/115, arts 5–7, 10, 15 at **[2.51]–[2.53]**, **[2.56]**, **[2.57]**.

[5.8]

[3A Application to Accountant in Bankruptcy for a direction

(1) This section applies where the Accountant in Bankruptcy is not the trustee.

(2) The trustee may apply to the Accountant in Bankruptcy for a direction in relation to any particular matter arising in the sequestration.

(3) The Accountant in Bankruptcy may, before giving a direction on any particular matter under this section, refer the matter to the sheriff by making an application for a direction in relation to that matter.

(4) The trustee may apply to the Accountant in Bankruptcy for a review of a direction given by the Accountant in Bankruptcy under this section.

(5) An application for a review under subsection (4) may not be made—

(a) by an interim trustee,

(b) after the expiry of the period of 14 days beginning with the day on which notice of the direction by the Accountant in Bankruptcy is given to the trustee, or

(c) in relation to a matter on which the Accountant in Bankruptcy has applied to the sheriff for a direction under subsection (3).

(6) If an application for a review under subsection (4) is made, the Accountant in Bankruptcy must—

(a) take into account any representations made by the trustee, the debtor, any creditor and any other person having an interest before the expiry of the period of 21 days beginning with the day on which the application is made, and

(b) confirm, amend or revoke the direction before the expiry of the period of 28 days beginning with the day on which the application is made.

(7) The trustee may appeal to the sheriff against a decision by the Accountant in Bankruptcy under subsection (6)(b) before the expiry of the period of 14 days beginning with the day of the decision.]

NOTES

Commencement: 1 April 2015.

Inserted by the Bankruptcy and Debt Advice (Scotland) Act 2014, s 25(2), subject to transitional provisions and savings in SSI 2014/261, arts 9, 12 at **[2.96]**, **[2.99]**.

Repealed as noted at the beginning of this Act.

[5.9]

4 Commissioners

In any sequestration . . . commissioners, whose general functions shall be to supervise the intromissions of the . . . trustee with the sequestrated estate and to advise him, may be elected in accordance with section 30 of this Act.

NOTES

Repealed as noted at the beginning of this Act.

Words "(other than one to which Schedule 2 to this Act applies)" and "permanent" omitted in first and second places respectively, repealed by the Bankruptcy and Diligence etc (Scotland) Act 2007, s 226(2), Sch 6, Pt 1, subject to transitional provisions and savings in SSI 2008/115, arts 5–7, 10, 15 at **[2.51]–[2.53]**, **[2.56]**, **[2.57]**.

[Moratorium on diligence

[5.10]

4A Notice of intention to apply: debtor application etc

(1) A person may give written notice to the Accountant in Bankruptcy of the person's intention—

(a) to make a debtor application for sequestration under section 5,

(b) to seek to fulfil the conditions required in order for a trust deed granted by or on behalf of that person to be granted the status of protected trust deed,

(c) to apply for the approval of a debt payment programme in accordance with section 2 of the Debt Arrangement and Attachment (Scotland) Act 2002 (asp 17).

(2) A person may not give a notice if that person has given a notice under subsection (1) in the immediately preceding period of 12 months.

(3) The Accountant in Bankruptcy must, without delay after receipt of a notice under subsection (1), enter in the registers mentioned in subsection (4)—

(a) the name of the person who gave the notice, and

(b) such other information as the Accountant in Bankruptcy considers appropriate in relation to that person.

(4) The registers are—

(a) the register of insolvencies, and

(b) the register of debt payment programmes established and maintained in accordance with section 7 of the Debt Arrangement and Attachment (Scotland) Act 2002 (the "DAS register").]

NOTES

Commencement: 1 April 2015.

Inserted, together with preceding cross-heading and ss 4B–4D, by the Bankruptcy and Debt Advice (Scotland) Act 2014, s 8, subject to transitional provisions and savings in SSI 2014/261, arts 7, 12 at **[2.94]**, **[2.99]**.

Repealed as noted at the beginning of this Act.

[5.11]

[4B Notice of intention to apply: sequestration of estate under section 6

(1) A person may give written notice to the Accountant in Bankruptcy of the person's intention to make a debtor application under section 6.

(2) A person may not give a notice in respect of an estate mentioned in section 6 if any person has given a notice under subsection (1) in respect of the same estate in the immediately preceding period of 12 months.

(3) The Accountant in Bankruptcy must, without delay after receipt of a notice under subsection (1), enter in the register of insolvencies—

(a) the name of the person who is the subject of the notice, and

(b) such other information as the Accountant in Bankruptcy considers appropriate in relation to that person.]

NOTES

Commencement: 1 April 2015.

Inserted as noted to s 4A at **[5.10]**.

Repealed as noted at the beginning of this Act.

[5.12]

[4C Moratorium on diligence

(1) This section applies where a person gives notice to the Accountant in Bankruptcy in accordance with section 4A(1) or 4B(1).

(2) A moratorium on diligence applies in relation to the person who is the subject of the notice for the moratorium period determined in accordance with section 4D.

(3) While a moratorium on diligence applies in relation to the person it is not competent—

(a) to serve a charge for payment in respect of any debt owed by the person,

(b) to commence or execute any diligence to enforce payment of any debt owed by the person,

(c) to found on any debt owed by the person in presenting, or concurring in the presentation of, a petition for sequestration of the person's estate, or

(d) in the case where an arrestment mentioned in subsection (1) of section 73J of the Debtors (Scotland) Act 1987 (c 18) has been granted in respect of funds due to the person, to release funds to the creditor under subsection (2) of that section.

(4) The moratorium period applying in relation to the person is to be disregarded for the purposes of determining the period mentioned in section 73J(3) of the Debtors (Scotland) Act 1987 (c 18).

(5) Despite subsection (3)(b), it is competent to—

(a) auction an article which has been attached in accordance with the Debt Arrangement and Attachment (Scotland) Act 2002 (asp 17) where—

(i) notice has been given to the debtor under section 27(4) of that Act, or

(ii) the article has been removed, or notice of removal has been given, under section 53 of that Act,

(b) implement a decree of furthcoming,

(c) implement a decree or order for sale of a ship (or a share of it) or cargo,

(d) execute an earnings arrestment, a current maintenance arrestment or a conjoined arrestment order which came into effect before the day on which the moratorium period in relation to the person begins.]

NOTES

Commencement: 1 April 2015.

Inserted as noted to s 4A at **[5.10]**.

Repealed as noted at the beginning of this Act.

[5.13]

[4D Period of moratorium

(1) The moratorium period applying in relation to the person is the period which—

(a) begins on the day on which an entry is made in the register of insolvencies under section 4A(3) or 4B(3), and

(b) ends on—

(i) the day which is 6 weeks after that day,

(ii) such earlier day as is mentioned in subsection (2), or

(iii) if subsection (3), (5) or (7) applies, such later day as is determined in accordance with subsection (4), (6) or (8).

(2) The earlier day is the day on which, in relation to the person who is the subject of the moratorium—

(a) an entry is made in the register of insolvencies recording the award of sequestration of the estate,

(b) an entry is made in the register of insolvencies recording that a trust deed granted by the person has been granted or refused protected status,

(c) an entry is made in the DAS register recording the approval of a debt payment programme in accordance with section 2 of the Debt Arrangement and Attachment (Scotland) Act 2002, or

(d) written notice is given to the Accountant in Bankruptcy—

(i) by the person withdrawing the notice given under section 4A(1), or

(ii) by or on behalf of the person withdrawing the notice given under section 4B(1).

(3) This subsection applies if, on the day which is 6 weeks after the day on which the moratorium began under subsection (1)(a)—

(a) a person has made a debtor application for sequestration of the estate of the person who is the subject of the moratorium,

(b) the moratorium has not ended in accordance with subsection (2)(a), and

(c) no decision has been made by the Accountant in Bankruptcy under section 15(3C)(b).

(4) Where subsection (3) applies, the moratorium period ends on—

(a) the day on which an entry is made in the register of insolvencies recording the award of sequestration of the estate,

(b) in the case of refusal to award sequestration—

(i) the day of the expiry of the period applying by virtue of section 15(3B) where no application for review is made under section 15(3A), or

(ii) the day on which a decision is made by the Accountant in Bankruptcy under section 15(3C)(b) where an application for review is made, or

(c) the day on which written notice is given to the Accountant in Bankruptcy—

(i) by the person withdrawing the notice given under section 4A(1), or

(ii) by or on behalf of the person withdrawing the notice given under section 4B(1).

(5) This subsection applies if, on the day which is 6 weeks after the day on which the moratorium began under subsection (1)(a)—

(a) an entry has been made in the register of insolvencies recording an application for a trust deed granted by or on behalf of the person who is the subject of the moratorium to be granted the status of protected trust deed, and

(b) the moratorium has not ended in accordance with subsection (2)(b).

(6) Where subsection (5) applies, the moratorium period ends on—

(a) the day on which an entry is made in the register of insolvencies recording that the trust deed granted by or on behalf of the person has been granted the status of protected trust deed,

(b) where such an entry is not made, the day which is 13 weeks after the day on which the moratorium began under subsection (1)(a), or

(c) the day on which written notice is given to the Accountant in Bankruptcy by the person withdrawing the notice given under section 4A(1).

(7) This subsection applies if, on the day which is 6 weeks after the day on which the moratorium began under subsection (1)(a)—

(a) the person who is the subject of the moratorium has applied for approval of a debt payment programme under section 2 of the Debt Arrangement and Attachment (Scotland) Act 2002,

(b) the moratorium has not ended in accordance with subsection (2)(c), and

(c) the application has not been determined.

(8) Where subsection (7) applies, the moratorium period ends on—

(a) the day on which an entry is made in the DAS register recording the approval of the debt payment programme in accordance with section 2 of the Debt Arrangement and Attachment (Scotland) Act 2002,

(b) in the case of a rejection of a debt payment programme, the day on which an entry is made in the DAS register recording the rejection, or

(c) the day on which written notice is given to the Accountant in Bankruptcy by the person withdrawing the notice given under section 4A(1).]

NOTES

Commencement: 1 April 2015.
Inserted as noted to s 4A at **[5.10]**.
Repealed as noted at the beginning of this Act.

Petitions for sequestration

[5.14]

5 Sequestration of the estate of living or deceased debtor

(1) The estate of a debtor may be sequestrated in accordance with the provisions of this Act.

[[(2) The sequestration of the estate of a living debtor shall be—

(a) by debtor application made by the debtor, if [subsection] [(2ZA) or] (2B) below applies to the debtor; or

(b) on the petition of—

(i) subject to subsection (2D) below, a qualified creditor or qualified creditors, if the debtor is apparently insolvent;

(ii) a temporary administrator;

(iii) a member State liquidator appointed in main proceedings; or

(iv) the trustee acting under a trust deed if, and only if, one or more of the conditions in subsection (2C) below is satisfied.]

[(2ZA) This subsection applies to the debtor where—

(a) the debtor—

(i) has been assessed by the common financial tool as requiring to make no debtor's contribution, or

(ii) has been in receipt of a prescribed payment for a period of at least 6 months ending with the day on which the application is made,

(b) the total amount of the debtor's debts (including interest) at the date the debtor application is made is—

(i) not less than £1500 or such other sum as may be prescribed, and

(ii) no more than £17000 or such other sum as may be prescribed,

(c) the total value of the debtor's assets (leaving out of account any liabilities) on the date the debtor application is made does not exceed £2000 or such other amount as may be prescribed,

(d) the value of a single asset of the debtor does not exceed £1000 or such other amount as may be prescribed,

(e) the debtor does not own land,

(f) within the prescribed period, the debtor has been granted a certificate for sequestration of the debtor's estate in accordance with section 5B,

(g) in the period of 10 years ending on the day before the day on which the debtor application is made or such other period as may be prescribed no award of sequestration has been made against the debtor in pursuance of an application made by the debtor by virtue of this subsection, and

(h) in the period of 5 years ending on the day before the day on which the debtor application is made no award of sequestration has been made against the debtor in pursuance of—

(i) an application made by the debtor other than by virtue of this subsection, or

(ii) a petition.

(2ZB) For the purposes of subsection (2ZA)(c) and (d)—

(a) any property of the debtor is not to be regarded as an asset if, under any provision of this or any other enactment, it would be excluded from vesting in the Accountant in Bankruptcy as trustee,

(b) if the debtor reasonably requires the use of a vehicle, any vehicle owned by the debtor the value of which does not exceed £3000 or such other amount as may be prescribed is not to be regarded as an asset,

(c) any other property of the debtor that is of a prescribed type is not to be regarded as an asset.

(2ZC) For the purposes of subsection (2ZA)(c) and (d), the Scottish Ministers may by regulations make provision about how the value of the debtor's assets is to be determined.

(2ZD) The Scottish Ministers may by regulations modify subsection (2ZA).

(2ZE) Schedule A1 to this Act makes further provision about the application of certain provisions of this Act in relation to a debtor to whom subsection (2ZA) applies.]

(2A) This subsection applies to the debtor if a qualified creditor or qualified creditors concur in the [application].

(2B) This subsection applies to the debtor where—
(a) the total amount of his debts (including interest) at the date [the debtor application is made] is not less than [£3,000 or such sum as may be prescribed];
(b) an award of sequestration has not been made against him in the period of 5 years ending on the day before the date [the debtor application is made]; and
[(ba) the debtor has obtained the advice of a money adviser in accordance with section 5C(1),]
[(bb) the debtor has given a statement of undertakings (including an undertaking to pay to the trustee after the award of sequestration of the debtor's estate an amount determined using the common financial tool),]
(c) the debtor . . . —
(i) is apparently insolvent; *or*
[(ia) is unable to pay his debts and each of the conditions in section 5A of this Act is met;]
[(ib) has, within the prescribed period, been granted a certificate for sequestration of the debtor's estate in accordance with section 5B of this Act,] [or]
(ii) has granted a trust deed [which is not a protected trust deed by reason of the creditors objecting, or not agreeing, in accordance with regulations under paragraph 5 of Schedule 5 to this Act, to the trust deed],
and for the purposes of this paragraph a debtor shall not be apparently insolvent by reason only that he has granted a trust deed or that he has given notice to his creditors as mentioned in paragraph (b) of section 7(1) of this Act.
(2C) The conditions mentioned in subsection [(2)(b)(iv)] above are—
(a) that the debtor has failed to comply—
(i) with any obligation imposed on him under the trust deed with which he could reasonably have complied; or
(ii) with any instruction or requirement reasonably given to or made of him by the trustee for the purposes of the trust deed; or
(b) that the trustee avers in his petition that it would be in the best interests of the creditors that an award of sequestration be made.]
[(2D) No petition may be presented under subsection (2)(b)(i) above unless the qualified creditor has provided, by such time prior to the presentation of the petition as may be prescribed, the debtor with a debt advice and information package.
(2E) In subsection (2D) above, "debt advice and information package" means the debt advice and information package referred to in section 10(5) of the Debt Arrangement and Attachment (Scotland) Act 2002 (asp 17).]
[(2F) In subsection (2B)(c)(ib) above "the prescribed period" means such period, ending immediately before the debtor application is made, as may be prescribed under section 5B(5)(c) of this Act.]
[(3) The sequestration of the estate of a deceased debtor is—
(a) by debtor application made by the executor, or a person entitled to be appointed as executor, on the estate,
(b) on the petition of a qualified creditor, or qualified creditors, of the deceased debtor,
(c) on the petition of a temporary administrator,
(d) on the petition of a member State liquidator appointed in main proceedings, or
(e) on the petition of a trustee acting under a trust deed.]
(4) In this Act "qualified creditor" means a creditor who, at the date of the presentation of the petition [or, as the case may be, the date the debtor application is made], is a creditor of the debtor in respect of liquid or illiquid debts (other than contingent or future debts [or amounts payable under a confiscation order]), whether secured or unsecured, which amount (or of one such debt which amounts) to not less than [£3,000] or such sum as may be prescribed; and "qualified creditors" means creditors who at the said date are creditors of the debtor in respect of such debts as aforesaid amounting in aggregate to not less than [£3,000] or such sum as may be prescribed[; and in the foregoing provisions of this subsection "confiscation order" [means a confiscation order under Part 2, 3 or 4 of the Proceeds of Crime Act 2002]].
[(4A) In this Act, "trust deed" means[—
(a)] a voluntary trust deed granted by or on behalf of the debtor whereby his estate (other than such of his estate as would not, under [any provision of this or any other enactment], vest in the . . . trustee if his estate were sequestrated) is conveyed to the trustee for the benefit of his creditors generally[; and
(b) any other trust deed which would fall within paragraph (a) but for—
(i) the exclusion from the estate conveyed to the trustee of the whole or part of the debtor's dwellinghouse, where a secured creditor holds a security over it; and
(ii) the fact that the debtor's estate is not conveyed to the trustee for the benefit of creditors generally because the secured creditor has, at the debtor's request, agreed before the trust deed is granted not to claim under the trust deed for any of the debt in respect of which the security is held.]
[(4AA) In subsection (4A)(b) above "debtor's dwellinghouse" means a dwellinghouse (including any yard, garden, outbuilding or other pertinents) which, on the day immediately preceding the date the trust deed was granted—
(a) the debtor (whether alone or in common with any other person)—
(i) owned; or
(ii) leased under a long lease (long lease having the same meaning as in section [9(2) of the Land Registration etc (Scotland) Act 2012 (asp 5)]; and
(b) was the sole or main residence of the debtor.

(4AB) For the purposes of subsection (4AA)(b) above, a dwellinghouse may be a sole or main residence irrespective of whether it is used, to any extent, by the debtor for the purposes of any profession, trade or business.]

[(4B) A debtor application shall—

(a) be made to the Accountant in Bankruptcy; *and*

(b) be in such form as may be prescribed.

[(4BA) A debtor application must—

(a) include a declaration by the money adviser who provided the advice referred to in section 5C(1) that such advice has been given, and

(b) specify the name and address of the money adviser.]

(4C) The Scottish Ministers may, by regulations, make provision—

(a) in relation to the procedure to be followed in a debtor application (in so far as not provided for in this Act);

(b) prescribing the form of any document that may be required for the purposes of making a debtor application; and

(c) prescribing the fees and charges which may be levied by the Accountant in Bankruptcy in relation to debtor applications.]

(5) Paragraphs 1(1) and (3), 2(1)(a) and (2) and 6 of Schedule 1 to this Act shall apply in order to ascertain the amount of the debt or debts for the purposes of subsection (4) above as they apply in order to ascertain the amount which a creditor is entitled to claim, but as if for any reference to the date of sequestration there were substituted a reference to the date of presentation of the petition [or, as the case may be, the date the debtor application is made].

(6) The petitioner shall[, on the day the petition for sequestration is presented under this section, send a copy of the petition] to the Accountant in Bankruptcy.

[(6A) In the case of a debtor application, the debtor shall send a statement of assets and liabilities to the Accountant in Bankruptcy along with the application.]

[(6B) In the case of a debtor application, the debtor must send a statement of undertakings to the Accountant in Bankruptcy along with the application.]

(7) Where, after a petition for sequestration has been presented but before the sequestration has been awarded, the debtor dies then—

(a)

(b) if the petitioner is a creditor, the proceedings shall continue in accordance with this Act so far as circumstances will permit.

[(7A) Where, after a debtor application is made but before the sequestration is awarded, the debtor dies, then the application shall fall.]

(8) Where, after a petition for sequestration has been presented under this section but before the sequestration has been awarded, a creditor who—

(a) is the petitioner . . . ; or

(b) has lodged answers to the petition, withdraws or dies, there may be sisted in the place of—

(i) the creditor mentioned in paragraph (a) above, any creditor who was a qualified creditor at the date when the petition was presented and who remains so qualified at the date of the sist;

(ii) the creditor mentioned in paragraph (b) above, any other creditor.

[(8A) Where, after a debtor application is made but before the sequestration is awarded, a creditor who concurs in the application withdraws or dies, any other creditor who was a qualified creditor at the date the debtor application was made and who remains so qualified may notify the Accountant in Bankruptcy that he concurs in the application in place of the creditor who has withdrawn or died.]

[(9) If the debtor—

(a) fails to send to the Accountant in Bankruptcy in accordance with subsection [(6A)] above such statement of assets and liabilities; or

(b) fails to disclose any material fact in [a statement of assets and liabilities sent to the Accountant in Bankruptcy in accordance with subsection (6A)]; or

(c) makes a material misstatement in such statement of assets and liabilities, he shall be guilty of an offence and liable on summary conviction to a fine not exceeding level 5 on the standard scale or to imprisonment for a term not exceeding 3 months or to both such fine and imprisonment.

(10) In any proceedings for an offence under subsection (9) above, it shall be a defence for the accused to show that he had a reasonable excuse for—

(a) failing to send to the Accountant in Bankruptcy in accordance with subsection [(6A)] above such statement of assets and liabilities; or

(b) failing to disclose a material fact; or

(c) making a material misstatement.]

NOTES

Repealed as noted at the beginning of this Act.

Sub-s (2): substituted by the Bankruptcy and Diligence etc (Scotland) Act 2007, s 14(3)(a), subject to transitional provisions and savings in SSI 2008/115, arts 5–7, 10, 15 at **[2.51]–[2.53]**, **[2.56]**, **[2.57]**; first word in square brackets in para (a) substituted by the Home Owner and Debtor Protection (Scotland) Act 2010, s 9(1)(a); second words in square brackets in para (a) inserted by the Bankruptcy and Debt Advice (Scotland) Act 2014, s 5(1)(a), subject to transitional provisions and savings in SSI 2014/261, arts 4, 12 at **[2.91]**, **[2.99]**.

Sub-ss (2ZA)–(2ZE): inserted by the Bankruptcy and Debt Advice (Scotland) Act 2014, s 5(1)(b), subject to transitional provisions and savings in SSI 2014/261, arts 4, 12 at **[2.91]**, **[2.99]**.

Sub-s (2A): substituted, together with sub-ss (2), (2B), (2C), for original sub-s (2) by the Bankruptcy (Scotland) Act 1993, s 3(1), (2), subject to s 12(6) thereof, at **[5.194]** and to SI 1993/438, arts 4, 5, at **[16.58]**, **[16.59]**; word in square brackets substituted for original word "petition" by the Bankruptcy and Diligence etc (Scotland) Act 2007, s 36, Sch 1, paras 1, 4(1), (2), subject to transitional provisions and savings in SSI 2008/115, arts 5–7, 10, 15 at **[2.51]–[2.53]**, **[2.56]**, **[2.57]**; repealed by the Home Owner and Debtor Protection (Scotland) Act 2010, s 9(1)(b), subject to transitional provisions and savings in the Home Owner and Debtor Protection (Scotland) Act 2010 (Transitional and Saving Provisions) Order 2010, SSI 2010/316, art 7(1).

Sub-s (2B): substituted as noted to sub-s (2A) above; words in first pair of square brackets in para (a), and words in square brackets in para (b) substituted for original words "of presentation of the petition", words in second pair of square brackets in para (a) substituted for original sum "£1,500", word "either" omitted from para (c) repealed, sub-para (c)(ia) inserted, and words in square brackets in para (c)(ii) substituted for the following original words, by the Bankruptcy and Diligence etc (Scotland) Act 2007, ss 15(1), 25(a), 36, Sch 1, paras 1, 4(1), (3), subject to transitional provisions and savings in SSI 2008/115, arts 5–7, 10, 15 at **[2.51]–[2.53]**, **[2.56]**, **[2.57]**:

"and the trustee has complied with the requirements of sub-sub-paragraphs (a) to (c) of paragraph 5(1) of Schedule 5 to this Act but has received notification as mentioned in sub-sub-paragraph (d) of that paragraph,";

sub-paras (ba), (bb) inserted, word in square brackets in sub-para (c)(ib) inserted and sub-para (c)(ia) repealed (together with word preceding it) by the Bankruptcy and Debt Advice (Scotland) Act 2014, ss 1(1)(a), 9(2)(a), 56, Sch 3, paras 2, 4(a), Sch 4, subject to transitional provisions and savings in SSI 2014/261, arts 4, 12 at **[2.91]**, **[2.99]**; sub-para (c)(ib) inserted by the Home Owner and Debtor Protection (Scotland) Act 2010, s 9(1)(c).

Sub-s (2C): substituted as noted to sub-s (2A) above; figure in square brackets substituted for original figure "(2)(c)" by the Bankruptcy and Diligence etc (Scotland) Act 2007, s 36, Sch 1, paras 1, 4(1), (4), subject to transitional provisions and savings in SSI 2008/115, arts 5–7, 10, 15 at **[2.51]–[2.53]**, **[2.56]**, **[2.57]**.

Sub-ss (2D), (2E), (4B), (4C), (7A), (8A): inserted by the Bankruptcy and Diligence etc (Scotland) Act 2007, ss 14(3)(b), 26, 36, Sch 1, paras 1, 4(1), (8), (9), subject to transitional provisions and savings in SSI 2008/115, arts 5–7, 10, 15 at **[2.51]–[2.53]**, **[2.56]**, **[2.57]**; in sub-s (4B), para (b) and word immediately preceding it repealed, and sub-s (4C) repealed, by the Bankruptcy and Debt Advice (Scotland) Act 2014, s 56(2), Sch 4, subject to transitional provisions and savings in SSI 2014/261, arts 4, 12 at **[2.91]**, **[2.99]**.

Sub-s (2F): inserted by the Home Owner and Debtor Protection (Scotland) Act 2010, s 9(1)(d).

Sub-s (3): substituted by the Bankruptcy and Debt Advice (Scotland) Act 2014, s 11(1), subject to transitional provisions and savings in SSI 2014/261, arts 4, 12 at **[2.91]**, **[2.99]** and previously read as follows (with paras (ba), (bb) inserted by SI 2003/2109, regs 3, 5(2))—

"(3) The sequestration of the estate of a deceased debtor shall be on the petition of—
(a) an executor or a person entitled to be appointed as executor on the estate;
(b) a qualified creditor or qualified creditors of the deceased debtor;
[(ba) a temporary administrator;
(bb) a member State liquidator appointed in main proceedings;] or
(c) the trustee acting under a trust deed.".

Sub-s (4): words in first pair of square brackets inserted by the Bankruptcy and Diligence etc (Scotland) Act 2007, s 36, Sch 1, paras 1, 4(1), (5), subject to transitional provisions and savings in SSI 2008/115, arts 5–7, 10, 15 at **[2.51]–[2.53]**, **[2.56]**, **[2.57]**; words in second and fifth (outer) pairs of square brackets inserted by the Criminal Justice (Scotland) Act 1987, s 45(5)(a); sums in third and fourth pairs of square brackets substituted (for sum "£1,500" as previously substituted by the Bankruptcy (Scotland) Act 1993, s 3(1), (3)) by the Bankruptcy and Diligence etc (Scotland) Act 2007, s 25(b), subject to transitional provisions and savings in SSI 2008/115, arts 5–7, 10, 15 at **[2.51]–[2.53]**, **[2.56]**, **[2.57]**; words in sixth (inner) pair of square brackets substituted by the Proceeds of Crime Act 2002, s 456, Sch 11, paras 1, 15(1), (2), subject to savings in SSI 2003/210, art 7(1), (2)(b).

Sub-s (4A): inserted by the Bankruptcy (Scotland) Act 1993, s 3(1), (4) subject to s 12(6) thereof, at **[5.194]** and to SI 1993/438, arts 4, 5, at **[16.58]**, **[16.59]**; para (a) numbered as such and para (b) inserted, together with word preceding it, by the Home Owner and Debtor Protection (Scotland) Act 2010, s 10(1), subject to transitional provisions and savings in SSI 2010/316, art 7(2); words in square brackets in para (a) substituted (for original words "section 33(1) of this Act") by the Bankruptcy and Debt Advice (Scotland) Act 2014, s 56(1), Sch 3, paras 2, 4(b), subject to transitional provisions and savings in SSI 2014/261, arts 4, 12 at **[2.91]**, **[2.99]**; word "permanent" (omitted) from para (a) repealed by the Bankruptcy and Diligence etc (Scotland) Act 2007, s 226(2), Sch 6, Pt 1, subject to transitional provisions and savings in SSI 2008/115, arts 5–7, 10, 15 at **[2.51]–[2.53]**, **[2.56]**, **[2.57]**.

Sub-s (4AA): inserted, together with sub-s (4AB), by the Home Owner and Debtor Protection (Scotland) Act 2010, s 10(2), subject to transitional provisions and savings in SSI 2010/316, art 7(2); words in square brackets substituted by the Land Registration etc (Scotland) Act 2012, s 119, Sch 5, para 28(1), (2).

Sub-s (4AB): inserted as noted sub-s (4AA) above.

Sub-s (4BA): inserted by the Bankruptcy and Debt Advice (Scotland) Act 2014, s 1(1)(b), subject to transitional provisions and savings in SSI 2014/261, arts 4, 12 at **[2.91]**, **[2.99]**.

Sub-s (5): words in square brackets inserted by the Bankruptcy and Diligence etc (Scotland) Act 2007, s 36, Sch 1, paras 1, 4(1), (6), subject to transitional provisions and savings in SSI 2008/115, arts 5–7, 10, 15 at **[2.51]–[2.53]**, **[2.56]**, **[2.57]**.

Sub-s (6): words in square brackets substituted by the Bankruptcy (Scotland) Act 1993, s 3(1), (5) subject to s 12(6) thereof, at **[5.194]** and to SI 1993/438, arts 4, 5, at **[16.58]**, **[16.59]**.

Sub-s (6A): inserted by the Bankruptcy (Scotland) Act 1993, s 3(1), (6), subject to s 12(6) thereof, at **[5.194]** and to SI 1993/438, arts 4, 5, at **[16.58]**, **[16.59]**; substituted by the Bankruptcy and Diligence etc (Scotland) Act 2007, s 36, Sch 1, paras 1, 4(1), (7), subject to transitional provisions and savings in SSI 2008/115, arts 5–7, 10, 15 at **[2.51]–[2.53]**, **[2.56]**, **[2.57]**, and previously read as follows:

"(6A) Where the petitioner is the debtor—
(a) he shall lodge with the petition a statement of assets and liabilities; and
(b) he shall, on the day the petition is presented, send to the Accountant in Bankruptcy such statement of assets and liabilities as was lodged in court in pursuance of paragraph (a) above.".

Sub-s (6B): inserted by the Bankruptcy and Debt Advice (Scotland) Act 2014, s 9(2)(b), subject to transitional provisions and savings in SSI 2014/261, arts 4, 12 at **[2.91]**, **[2.99]**.

Sub-s (7): para (a) repealed by the Bankruptcy and Diligence etc (Scotland) Act 2007, s 226(2), Sch 6, Pt 1, subject to transitional provisions and savings in SSI 2008/115, arts 5–7, 10, 15 at **[2.51]–[2.53]**, **[2.56]**, **[2.57]**, and previously read as follows:

"(a) if the petitioner was the debtor, the petition shall fall;".

Sub-s (8): words "or concurs in a petition by the debtor" omitted from para (a) repealed by the Bankruptcy and Diligence etc (Scotland) Act 2007, s 226(2), Sch 6, Pt 1, subject to transitional provisions and savings in SSI 2008/115, arts 5–7, 10, 15 at **[2.51]–[2.53]**, **[2.56]**, **[2.57]**.

Sub-ss (9), (10): added by the Bankruptcy (Scotland) Act 1993, s 3(1), (7) subject to s 12(6) thereof, at **[5.194]** and to SI 1993/438, arts 4, 5, at **[16.58]**, **[16.59]**; figures in square brackets in sub-ss (9)(a), (10(a) substituted for original figure "(6A)(b)" by the Bankruptcy and Diligence etc (Scotland) Act 2007, s 36, Sch 1, paras 1, 4(1), (10), (11), subject to transitional provisions and savings in SSI 2008/115, arts 5–7, 10, 15 at **[2.51]–[2.53]**, **[2.56]**, **[2.57]**; sub-ss (9)(a), (10(a) repealed and words in square brackets in sub-s (9)(b) substituted for original words "such statement of assets and liabilities" by the Bankruptcy and Debt Advice (Scotland) Act 2014, s 45(1), subject to transitional provisions and savings in SSI 2014/261, arts 4, 12 at **[2.91]**, **[2.99]**.

Regulations: the Bankruptcy (Scotland) Regulations 2008, SSI 2008/82 at **[16.262]**; the Bankruptcy (Certificate for Sequestration) (Scotland) Regulations 2010, SSI 2010/397 at **[16.264]**; the Bankruptcy (Scotland) Regulations 2014, SSI 2014/225 at **[16.267]**.

[5.15]

[5A Debtor applications by low income, low asset debtors

(1) The conditions referred to in section 5(2B)(c)(ia) of this Act are as follows.

(2) The debtor's weekly income (if any) on the date the debtor application is made does not exceed £100 or such other amount as may be prescribed.

(3) The debtor does not own any land.

(4) The total value of the debtor's assets (leaving out of account any liabilities) on the date the debtor application is made does not exceed £1000 or such other amount as may be prescribed.

(5) The Scottish Ministers may by regulations—

- *(a) make provision as to how the debtor's weekly income is to be determined;*
- *(b) provide that particular descriptions of income are to be excluded for the purposes of subsection (2) above;*
- *(c) make provision as to how the value of the debtor's assets is to be determined;*
- *(d) provide that particular descriptions of asset are to be excluded for the purposes of subsection (4) above;*
- *(e) make different provision for different classes or description of debtor;*
- *(f) add further conditions which must be met before a debtor application may be made by virtue of section 5(2B)(c)(ia) of this Act; and*
- *(g) where such further conditions are added—*
  - *(i) remove; or*
  - *(ii) otherwise vary,*

  those conditions.]

NOTES

Repealed as noted at the beginning of this Act.

Inserted by the Bankruptcy and Diligence etc (Scotland) Act 2007, s 15(2), subject to transitional provisions and savings in SSI 2008/115, arts 5–7, 10, 15 at **[2.51]–[2.53]**, **[2.56]**, **[2.57]**.

Repealed by the Bankruptcy and Debt Advice (Scotland) Act 2014, s 56(2), Sch 4, subject to transitional provisions and savings in SSI 2014/261, arts 4, 12 at **[2.91]**, **[2.99]**.

Regulations: the Bankruptcy (Scotland) Act 1985 (Low Income, Low Asset Debtors etc) Regulations 2008, SSI 2008/81 at **[16.261]**; the Bankruptcy (Money Advice and Deduction from Income etc) (Scotland) Regulations 2014, SSI 2014/296 at **[16.284]**.

[5.16]

[5B Certificate for sequestration

(1) A certificate for sequestration of a debtor's estate is a certificate granted by [a money adviser] certifying that the debtor is unable to pay debts as they become due.

(2) A certificate may be granted only on the application of the debtor.

(3) [A money adviser] must grant a certificate if, and only if, the debtor can demonstrate that the debtor is unable to pay debts as they become due.

(4) In this section "authorised person" means a person falling within a class prescribed under subsection (5)(a).

(5) The Scottish Ministers may by regulations—

- *(a) prescribe classes of persons authorised to grant a certificate under this section;*
- (b) make provision about certification by [a money adviser], including—
  - (i) the form and manner in which a certification must be made;
  - (ii) the fee, if any, which [a money adviser] is entitled to charge for or in connection with granting a certificate;
- (c) prescribe a period for the purpose of section 5(2B)(c)(ib) of this Act;
- *(d) make different provision for different cases or classes of case.*]

NOTES

Repealed as noted at the beginning of this Act.

Inserted by the Home Owner and Debtor Protection (Scotland) Act 2010, s 9(2).

Words in square brackets in sub-ss (1), (3), (5) substituted for original words "an authorised person" and sub-ss (4), (5)(a), (d) repealed, by the Bankruptcy and Debt Advice (Scotland) Act 2014, s 56, Sch 3, paras 2, 5, Sch 4, subject to transitional provisions and savings in SSI 2014/261, arts 4, 12 at **[2.91]**, **[2.99]**.

Regulations: the Bankruptcy (Certificate for Sequestration) (Scotland) Regulations 2010, SSI 2010/397 at **[16.264]**; the Bankruptcy (Money Advice and Deduction from Income etc) (Scotland) Regulations 2014, SSI 2014/296 at **[16.284]**.

[5.17]
[5C Money advice

(1) An application for the sequestration of a living debtor's estate may not be made unless the debtor has obtained from a money adviser—

(a) advice on the debtor's financial circumstances,
(b) advice on the effect of the proposed sequestration of the debtor's estate,
(c) advice on the preparation of the application, and
(d) advice on such other matters as may be prescribed.

(2) In this Act, "money adviser" means a person who—

(a) is not an associate of the debtor, and
(b) is of a prescribed description or falls within a prescribed class.]

NOTES

Commencement: 1 April 2015.

Inserted by the Bankruptcy and Debt Advice (Scotland) Act 2014, s 1(2), subject to transitional provisions and savings in SSI 2014/261, arts 4, 5, 12 at **[2.91]**, **[2.92]**, **[2.99]**.

Repealed as noted at the beginning of this Act.

Regulations: the Bankruptcy (Money Advice and Deduction from Income etc) (Scotland) Regulations 2014, SSI 2014/296 at **[16.284]**.

[5.18]
[5D Assessment of debtor's contribution

(1) The Scottish Ministers may by regulations specify a method (the "common financial tool") to be used to assess an appropriate amount of a living debtor's income to be paid to a trustee after the sequestration of the debtor's estate (the "debtor's contribution").

(2) Regulations under subsection (1) may in particular—

(a) prescribe a method for assessing a debtor's financial circumstances (including the debtor's assets, income, liabilities and expenditure),
(b) prescribe a method for determining a reasonable amount of expenditure for a debtor after the sequestration of the debtor's estate,
(c) prescribe the proportion of a debtor's income that is to constitute the debtor's contribution,
(d) prescribe that a method determined by another person is to be used (with or without modification in accordance with regulations made under subsection (1)) as the common financial tool.

(3) The common financial tool must ensure that the amount of reasonable expenditure for a debtor is not less than the total amount of any income received by the debtor by way of guaranteed minimum pension (within the meaning of the Pension Schemes Act 1993 (c 48)).

(4) The common financial tool must ensure that an amount is allowed for—

(a) aliment for the debtor,
(b) the debtor's relevant obligations.

(5) The "debtor's relevant obligations" are—

(a) any obligation of aliment owed by the debtor ("obligation of aliment" having the same meaning as in the Family Law (Scotland) Act 1985 (c 37)),
(b) any obligation of the debtor to make a periodical allowance to a former spouse or former civil partner, and
(c) any obligation of the debtor to pay child support maintenance under the Child Support Act 1991 (c 48).

(6) The amount allowed for the debtor's relevant obligations referred to in paragraphs (a) and (b) of subsection (5) need not be sufficient for compliance with a subsisting order or agreement as regards the aliment or periodical allowance.]

NOTES

Commencement: 30 June 2014.

Inserted by the Bankruptcy and Debt Advice (Scotland) Act 2014, s 3(1).

Repealed as noted at the beginning of this Act.

See further: the Bankruptcy and Debt Advice (Scotland) Act 2014 (Commencement No 2, Savings and Transitionals) Order 2014, SSI 2014/261, art 6 at **[2.93]**.

Regulations: the Subordinate Legislation Common Financial Tool etc (Scotland) Regulations 2014, SSI 2014/290.

[5.19]
6 Sequestration of other estates

(1) Subject to subsection (2) below, the estate belonging to or held for or jointly by the members of any of the following entities may be sequestrated—

(a) a trust in respect of debts incurred by it;
(b) a partnership, including a dissolved partnership;
(c) a body corporate or an unincorporated body;
(d) a limited partnership (including a dissolved partnership) within the meaning of the Limited Partnerships Act 1907.

(2) It shall not be competent to sequestrate the estate of any of the following entities—

[(a) a company registered under the Companies Act 2006; or]
[(aa) a limited liability partnership,]

(b) an entity in respect of which an enactment provides, expressly or by implication, that sequestration is incompetent.

(3) The sequestration of a trust estate in respect of debts incurred by the trust shall be—

[(a) by debtor application made by a majority of trustees, with the concurrence of a qualified creditor or qualified creditors; or

(b) on the petition of—

(i) a temporary administrator;

(ii) a member State liquidator appointed in main proceedings; or

(iii) a qualified creditor or qualified creditors, if the trustees as such are apparently insolvent.]

(4) The sequestration of the estate of a partnership shall be—

[(za) by debtor application made by the partnership where the partnership is apparently insolvent,]

[(a) by debtor application made by the partnership with the concurrence of a qualified creditor or qualified creditors; or

(b) on the petition of—

(i) a temporary administrator;

(ii) a member State liquidator appointed in main proceedings;

(iii) a trustee acting under a trust deed; or

(iv) a qualified creditor or qualified creditors, if the partnership is apparently insolvent.]

[(4A) For the purposes of an application under subsection (4)(za), section 7(3)(a) is to be read as if—

(a) the word "either" were omitted, and

(b) the words "or if any of the partners is apparently insolvent for a debt of the partnership" were omitted.]

(5) A petition under [subsection (4)(b)] above may be combined with a petition for the sequestration of the estate of any of the partners as an individual where that individual is apparently insolvent.

(6) The sequestration of the estate of a body corporate or of an unincorporated body shall be—

[(a) by debtor application made by a person authorised to act on behalf of the body, with the concurrence of a qualified creditor or qualified creditors; or

(b) on the petition of—

(i) a temporary administrator;

(ii) a member State liquidator appointed in main proceedings; or

(iii) a qualified creditor or qualified creditors, if the body is apparently insolvent.]

(7) The application of this Act to the sequestration of the estate of a limited partnership shall be subject to such modifications as may be prescribed.

(8) Subsections (6)[, (6A), (8) and (8A)] [(but not (9) or (10))] of section 5 of this Act shall apply for the purposes of this section as they apply for the purposes of that section.

NOTES

Repealed as noted at the beginning of this Act.

Sub-s (2): para (a) substituted by the Companies Act 2006 (Consequential Amendments, Transitional Provisions and Savings) Order 2009, SI 2009/1941, art 2(1), Sch 1, para 60; para (aa) inserted by the Bankruptcy and Debt Advice (Scotland) Act 2014, s 56(1), Sch 3, paras 2, 6(a), subject to transitional provisions and savings in SSI 2014/261, arts 4, 12 at **[2.91]**, **[2.99]**.

Sub-s (3): paras (a), (b) substituted for the following words (as previously amended by the Insolvency (Scotland) Regulations 2003, SI 2003/2109, regs 3, 6(1)) by the Bankruptcy and Diligence etc (Scotland) Act 2007, s 14(4)(a), subject to transitional provisions and savings in SSI 2008/115, arts 5–7, 10, 15 at **[2.51]–[2.53]**, **[2.56]**, **[2.57]**:

"on the petition of—

(a) a majority of the trustees, with the concurrence of a qualified creditor or qualified creditors;

[(aa) a temporary administrator;

(ab) a member State liquidator appointed in main proceedings;] or

(b) a qualified creditor or qualified creditors, if the trustees as such are apparently insolvent.".

Sub-s (4): para (za) inserted by the Bankruptcy and Debt Advice (Scotland) Act 2014, s 56(1), Sch 3, paras 2, 6(b), subject to transitional provisions and savings in SSI 2014/261, arts 4, 12 at **[2.91]**, **[2.99]**; paras (a), (b) substituted for the following words (as previously amended by SI 2003/2109, regs 3, 6(1)) by the Bankruptcy and Diligence etc (Scotland) Act 2007, s 14(4)(b), subject to transitional provisions and savings in SSI 2008/115, arts 5–7, 10, 15 at **[2.51]–[2.53]**, **[2.56]**, **[2.57]**:

"on the petition of—

(a) the partnership, with the concurrence of a qualified creditor or qualified creditors;

[(aa) a temporary administrator;

(ab) a member State liquidator appointed in main proceedings;] or

(b) a qualified creditor or qualified creditors, if the partnership is apparently insolvent.".

Sub-s (4A): inserted by the Bankruptcy and Debt Advice (Scotland) Act 2014, s 56(1), Sch 3, paras 2, 6(c), subject to transitional provisions and savings in SSI 2014/261, arts 4, 12 at **[2.91]**, **[2.99]**.

Sub-s (5): words in square brackets substituted for words "subsection (4)(aa) to (b)" (as previously substituted by SI 2003/2109, regs 3, 6(2)), by the Bankruptcy and Diligence etc (Scotland) Act 2007, s 36, Sch 1, paras 1, 5, subject to transitional provisions and savings in SSI 2008/115, arts 5–7, 10, 15 at **[2.51]–[2.53]**, **[2.56]**, **[2.57]**.

Sub-s (6): paras (a), (b) substituted for the following words (as previously amended by SI 2003/2109, regs 3, 6(1)) by the Bankruptcy and Diligence etc (Scotland) Act 2007, s 14(4)(c), subject to transitional provisions and savings in SSI 2008/115, arts 5–7, 10, 15 at **[2.51]–[2.53]**, **[2.56]**, **[2.57]**:

"on the petition of—

(a) a person authorised to act on behalf of the body, with the concurrence of a qualified creditor or qualified creditors;

[(aa) a temporary administrator;

(ab) a member State liquidator appointed in main proceedings;] or

(b) a qualified creditor or qualified creditors, if the body is apparently insolvent.".

Sub-s (8): words in first pair of square brackets substituted for original words "and (8)" by the Bankruptcy and Diligence etc (Scotland) Act 2007, s 14(4)(d), subject to transitional provisions and savings in SSI 2008/115, arts 5–7, 10, 15 at **[2.51]–[2.53]**, **[2.56]**, **[2.57]**; words in second pair of square brackets inserted by the Bankruptcy and Debt Advice (Scotland) Act 2014, s 56(1), Sch 3, paras 2, 6(d), subject to transitional provisions and savings in SSI 2014/261, arts 4, 12 at **[2.91]**, **[2.99]**.

Regulations: the Bankruptcy (Scotland) Regulations 2008, SSI 2008/82 at **[16.262]**; the Bankruptcy (Scotland) Regulations 2014, SSI 2014/225 at **[16.267]**.

[5.20]

[6A Petition for sequestration of estate: provision of information

(1) A petitioner for sequestration of a debtor's estate shall, insofar as it is within the petitioner's knowledge, state in the petition—

(a) whether or not the debtor's centre of main interests is situated—

(i) in the United Kingdom; or

(ii) in another member State; and

(b) whether or not the debtor possesses an establishment—

(i) in the United Kingdom; or

(ii) in any other member State.

(2) If, to the petitioner's knowledge, there is a member State liquidator appointed in main proceedings in relation to the debtor, the petitioner shall, as soon as reasonably practicable, send a copy of the petition to that member State liquidator.]

NOTES

Inserted by the Insolvency (Scotland) Regulations 2003, SI 2003/2109, regs 3, 7.

Repealed as noted at the beginning of this Act.

[5.21]

[6B Debtor application: provision of information

(1) Where a debtor application[, other than an application under section 5(3)(a),] is made, the debtor shall state in the application—

(a) whether or not the debtor's centre of main interests is situated—

(i) in the United Kingdom; or

(ii) in another member State; and

(b) whether not the debtor possesses an establishment—

(i) in the United Kingdom; or

(ii) in any other member State.

(2) If, to the debtor's knowledge, there is a member State liquidator appointed in main proceedings in relation to the debtor, the debtor shall, as soon as reasonably practicable, send a copy of the debtor application to that member State liquidator.

[(2A) Where a debtor application is made by an executor under section 5(3)(a) the executor must—

(a) state in the application whether or not the debtor's centre of main interests was situated in the United Kingdom or in another member State, and

(b) state in the application whether or not the debtor possessed an establishment in the United Kingdom or in another member State.]]

NOTES

Inserted by the Bankruptcy and Diligence etc (Scotland) Act 2007, s 14(5), subject to transitional provisions and savings in SSI 2008/115, arts 5–7, 10, 15 at **[2.51]–[2.53]**, **[2.56]**, **[2.57]**.

Repealed as noted at the beginning of this Act.

Sub-s (1): words in square brackets inserted by the Bankruptcy and Debt Advice (Scotland) Act 2014, s 11(2)(a), subject to transitional provisions and savings in SSI 2014/261, arts 4, 12 at **[2.91]**, **[2.99]**.

Sub-s (2A): inserted by the Bankruptcy and Debt Advice (Scotland) Act 2014, s 11(2)(b), subject to transitional provisions and savings in SSI 2014/261, arts 4, 12 at **[2.91]**, **[2.99]**.

[5.22]

7 Meaning of apparent insolvency

(1) A debtor's apparent insolvency shall be constituted (or, where he is already apparently insolvent, constituted anew) whenever—

(a) his estate is sequestrated, or he is adjudged bankrupt in England or Wales or Northern Ireland; or

(b) [not being a person whose property is for the time being affected by a restraint order[, detained under or by virtue of a relevant detention power] or subject to a confiscation, or charging, order,] he gives written notice to his creditors that he has ceased to pay his debts in the ordinary course of business; or

[(ba) he becomes subject to main proceedings in a member State other than the United Kingdom;]

[(c) the debtor grants a trust deed,

(ca) following the service on the debtor of a duly executed charge for payment of a debt, the days of charge expire without payment (unless the circumstances are shown to be such as are mentioned in subsection (1A)),

(cb) a decree of adjudication of any part of the debtor's estate is granted, either for payment or in security (unless the circumstances are shown to be such as are mentioned in subsection (1A)), (cc) a debt constituted by a decree or document of debt (as defined in section 10 of the Debt Arrangement and Attachment (Scotland) Act 2002) is being paid by the debtor under a debt payment programme under Part 1 of that Act and the programme is revoked (unless the circumstances are shown to be such as are mentioned in subsection (1A)),]

(d) a creditor of the debtor, in respect of a liquid debt which amounts (or liquid debts which in aggregate amount) to not less than £750 or such sum as may be prescribed, has served on the debtor, by personal service by an officer of court, a demand in the prescribed form requiring him either to pay the debt (or debts) or to find security for its (or their) payment, and within 3 weeks after the date of service of the demand the debtor has not—

(i) complied with the demand; or

(ii) intimated to the creditor, by recorded delivery, that he denies that there is a debt or that the sum claimed by the creditor as the debt is immediately payable.

[In paragraph (d) above, "liquid debt" does not include a sum payable under a confiscation order; and in the foregoing provisions of this subsection—

"charging order" has the meaning assigned . . . [. . . by section 78(2) of the Criminal Justice Act 1988] [or by section 27(2) of the Drug Trafficking Act 1994];

["relevant detention power" means section 44A, 47J, 47K, 47M, 47P, 122A, 127J, 127K, 127M, 127P, 193A, 195J, 195K, 195M or 195P of the Proceeds of Crime Act 2002;]

[. . . and "restraint order" mean a confiscation order or a restraint order made under Part 2, 3 or 4 of the Proceeds of Crime Act 2002].]

[(1A) The circumstances are—

(a) that, at the time of the occurrence, the debtor was able and willing to pay the debtor's debts as they became due, or

(b) that, but for the debtor's property being affected by a restraint order or being subject to a confiscation order or charging order, the debtor would at that time have been able to pay those debts as they became due.]

(2) A debtor's apparent insolvency shall continue, if constituted under—

(a) subsection (1)(a) above, until his discharge; . . .

(b) subsection (1)(b), (c)[, (ca), (cb), (cc)] or (d) above, until he becomes able to pay his debts and pays them as they become due; [or

(c) subsection (1)(ba), [until] main proceedings have ended].

(3) The apparent insolvency of—

(a) a partnership shall be constituted [(or, as the case may be, again constituted)] either in accordance with the foregoing provisions of this section or if any of the partners is apparently insolvent for a debt of the partnership;

(b) an unincorporated body shall be constituted [(or, as the case may be, again constituted)] if a person representing the body is apparently insolvent, or a person holding property of the body in a fiduciary capacity is apparently insolvent, for a debt of the body.

(4) Notwithstanding subsection (2) of section 6 of this Act, the apparent insolvency of an entity such as is mentioned in . . . that subsection may be constituted (or as the case may be constituted anew) under subsection (1) above; and any reference in the foregoing provisions of this section to a debtor shall, except where the context otherwise requires, be construed as including a reference to such an entity.

NOTES

Repealed as noted at the beginning of this Act.

Sub-s (1) is amended as follows:

in para (b), words in first (outer) pair of square brackets inserted by the Criminal Justice (Scotland) Act 1987, s 45(5)(b)(i) and words in second (inner) pair of square brackets inserted by the Policing and Crime Act 2009, s 112(1), Sch 7, Pt 6, paras 46, 47(a);

para (ba) inserted by the Insolvency (Scotland) Regulations 2003, SI 2003/2109, regs 3, 8(1);

paras (c), (ca)–(cc) substituted for original para (c), by the Bankruptcy and Debt Advice (Scotland) Act 2014, s 56(1), Sch 3, paras 2, 7(a), subject to transitional provisions and savings in SSI 2014/261, arts 4, 12 at **[2.91]**, **[2.99]**; para (c) and the notes relating to it previously read as follows—

"(c) any of the following circumstances occurs—

(i) he grants a trust deed;

(ii) following the service on him of a duly executed charge for payment of a debt, the days of charge expire without payment;

(iii) . . .

(iv) a decree of adjudication of any part of his estate is granted, either for payment or in security;

(v) . . .

(vi) . . .

[(vii) . . .]

unless it is shown that at the time when any such circumstance occurred, the debtor was able and willing to pay his debts as they became due [or that but for his property being affected by a restraint order or subject to a confiscation, or charging, order he would be able to do so]; or

NOTES

Para (c)(iii), (v), (vi) repealed by the Bankruptcy and Diligence etc (Scotland) Act 2007, s 226(2), Sch 6, Pt 1, subject to transitional provisions and savings in SSI 2008/115, arts 5–7, 10, 15 at **[2.51]–[2.53]**, **[2.56]**, **[2.57]**; para (c)(iv) repealed by the Bankruptcy and Diligence etc (Scotland) Act 2007, s 226(2), Sch 6, Pt 1, as from a day to be appointed; para (c)(vii) and the word immediately preceding it inserted by the Debt Arrangement Scheme (Scotland) Regulations 2004,

SSI 2004/468, reg 46(b), and repealed by the Debt Arrangement Scheme (Scotland) Amendment Regulations 2013, SSI 2013/225, reg 19(3)(a); words in final pair of square brackets in para (c) inserted by the Criminal Justice (Scotland) Act 1987, s 45(5)(b)(ii).";

words in first (outer) pair of square brackets following para (d) inserted by the Criminal Justice (Scotland) Act 1987, s 45(5)(b)(iii);

in definition "charging order" words omitted repealed by the Drug Trafficking Act 1994, ss 65, 67, Sch 1, para 10(1), (2)(a), Sch 3, words in first pair of square brackets inserted by the Criminal Justice Act 1988, s 170(1), Sch 15, paras 106, 108(a), words in second pair of square brackets inserted by the Drug Trafficking Act 1994, s 65, Sch 1, para 10(2)(a);

definition "relevant detention power" inserted by the Policing and Crime Act 2009, s 112(1), Sch 7, Pt 6, paras 46, 47(b);

definition "confiscation order" and "restraint order" substituted by the Proceeds of Crime Act 2002, s 456, Sch 11, paras 1, 15(1), (3), subject to savings in SSI 2003/210, art 7(1), (2)(b), and words ""confiscation order"" (omitted) repealed by the Bankruptcy and Diligence etc (Scotland) Act 2007, s 226(2), Sch 6, Pt 1, subject to transitional provisions and savings in SSI 2008/115, arts 5–7, 10, 15 at **[2.51]–[2.53]**, **[2.56]**, **[2.57]**.

Sub-s (1A): inserted by the Bankruptcy and Debt Advice (Scotland) Act 2014, s 56(1), Sch 3, paras 2, 7(b), subject to transitional provisions and savings in SSI 2014/261, arts 4, 12 at **[2.91]**, **[2.99]**.

Sub-s (2): word omitted from para (a) repealed, and para (c) and word "or" immediately preceding it added, by the Insolvency (Scotland) Regulations 2003, SI 2003/2109, regs 3, 8(2); word in square brackets in para (c) substituted for original word "when" by the Bankruptcy and Diligence etc (Scotland) Act 2007, s 36, Sch 1, paras 1, 6, subject to transitional provisions and savings in SSI 2008/115, arts 5–7, 10, 15 at **[2.51]–[2.53]**, **[2.56]**, **[2.57]**; words in square brackets in para (b) inserted by the Bankruptcy and Debt Advice (Scotland) Act 2014 (Consequential Provisions) Order 2016, SSI 2016/140, arts 3(1), 4. Note this amendment does not affect the operation of this section in relation to a sequestration where the petition was presented before 1 April 2015, or a debtor application was made before that date.

Sub-s (3): words in square brackets inserted by the Bankruptcy and Debt Advice (Scotland) Act 2014, s 56(1), Sch 3, paras 2, 7(c), subject to transitional provisions and savings in SSI 2014/261, arts 4, 12 at **[2.91]**, **[2.99]**.

Sub-s (4): words "paragraph (a) or (b) of" (omitted) repealed by SSI 2016/140, arts 3(2), 4. Note this amendment does not affect the operation of this section in relation to a sequestration where the petition was presented before 1 April 2015, or a debtor application was made before that date.

Regulations: the Bankruptcy (Scotland) Regulations 2008, SSI 2008/82 at **[16.262]**; the Bankruptcy (Scotland) Regulations 2014, SSI 2014/225 at **[16.267]**.

[5.23]

8 Further provisions relating to presentation of petitions

(1) Subject to subsection (2) below, a petition for the sequestration of a debtor's estate (other than a deceased debtor's estate) may be presented—

[(a) at any time by—

(i) . . .

(ii) a trustee acting under a trust deed;

(iii) a temporary administrator; or

(iv) a member State liquidator appointed in main proceedings;] but

(b) by a qualified creditor or qualified creditors, only if the apparent insolvency founded on in the petition was constituted within 4 months before the petition is presented.

[(2) A petition for the sequestration of the estate of a limited partnership may be presented—

(a) by a qualified creditor or qualified creditors only if the apparent insolvency founded on in the petition was constituted within 4 months (or such other period as may be prescribed) before the date of presentation of the petition, or

(b) at any time by—

(i) a temporary administrator,

(ii) a member State liquidator appointed in main proceedings, or

(iii) a trustee acting under a trust deed.]

(3) A petition for the sequestration of the estate of a deceased debtor may be presented—

[(a) at any time by—

(i) an executor;

(ii) a person entitled to be appointed as executor of the estate;

(iii) a trustee acting under a trust deed;

(iv) a temporary administrator; or

(v) a member State liquidator appointed in main proceedings;]

(b) by a qualified creditor or qualified creditors of the deceased debtor—

(i) in a case where the apparent insolvency of the debtor was constituted within 4 months before his death, at any time;

(ii) in any other case (whether or not apparent insolvency has been constituted), not earlier than 6 months after the debtor's death.

(4) If an executor does not petition for sequestration of the deceased debtor's estate or for the appointment of a judicial factor to administer the estate within a reasonable period after he knew or ought to have known that the estate was absolutely insolvent and likely to remain so, any intromission by him with the estate after the expiry of that period shall be deemed to be an intromission without a title.

(5) The presentation of . . . a petition for sequestration shall bar the effect of any enactment or rule of law relating to the limitation of actions in any part of the United Kingdom.

(6) Where before sequestration is awarded it becomes apparent that a petitioning . . . creditor was ineligible so to petition . . . he shall withdraw, or as the case may be withdraw from, the petition but another creditor may be sisted in his place.

NOTES

Repealed as noted at the beginning of this Act.

Sub-s (1): para (a) substituted by the Insolvency (Scotland) Regulations 2003, SI 2003/2109, regs 3, 9(1); para (a)(i) repealed by the Bankruptcy and Diligence etc (Scotland) Act 2007, s 226(2), Sch 6, Pt 1, subject to transitional provisions and savings in SSI 2008/115, arts 5–7, 10, 15 at **[2.51]–[2.53]**, **[2.56]**, **[2.57]**.

Sub-s (2): substituted by the Bankruptcy and Debt Advice (Scotland) Act 2014, s 46(1), subject to transitional provisions and savings in SSI 2014/261, arts 4, 12 at **[2.91]**, **[2.99]**, and previously read as follows—

> "(2) A petition for the sequestration of the estate of a limited partnership may be presented within such time as may be prescribed.".

Sub-s (3): para (a) substituted by SI 2003/2109, regs 3, 9(2); para (a)(i) repealed by the Bankruptcy and Debt Advice (Scotland) Act 2014, s 56(2), Sch 4, subject to transitional provisions and savings in SSI 2014/261, arts 4, 12 at **[2.91]**, **[2.99]**.

Sub-s (4): repealed by the Bankruptcy and Debt Advice (Scotland) Act 2014, s 56(2), Sch 4, subject to transitional provisions and savings in SSI 2014/261, arts 4, 12 at **[2.91]**, **[2.99]**.

Sub-s (5): words ", or the concurring in," (omitted) repealed by the Bankruptcy and Diligence etc (Scotland) Act 2007, s 226(2), Sch 6, Pt 1, subject to transitional provisions and savings in SSI 2008/115, arts 5–7, 10, 15 at **[2.51]–[2.53]**, **[2.56]**, **[2.57]**.

Sub-s (6): words "or concurring" and "or concur" (omitted) repealed by the Bankruptcy and Diligence etc (Scotland) Act 2007, s 226(2), Sch 6, Pt 1, subject to transitional provisions and savings in SSI 2008/115, arts 5–7, 10, 15 at **[2.51]–[2.53]**, **[2.56]**, **[2.57]**.

Regulations: the Bankruptcy (Scotland) Regulations 2008, SSI 2008/82 at **[16.262]**.

[5.24]

[8A Further provisions relating to debtor applications

(1) Subject to [subsections (2) and (2A)] below, a debtor application may be made at any time.

[(2) A debtor application made in relation to the estate of a limited partnership may be made—

(a) at any time, or

(b) within such time as may be prescribed.]

[(2A) Any intromission by an executor with the deceased debtor's estate after the period mentioned in subsection (2B) is deemed an intromission without a title unless, within that period, the executor—

(a) makes a debtor application under section 5(3)(a), or

(b) petitions for the appointment of a judicial factor to administer the estate.

(2B) The period referred to in subsection (2A) is the period of 12 months following the day on which the executor knew or ought to have known that the estate was absolutely insolvent and likely to remain so.]

(3) The making of, or the concurring in, a debtor application shall bar the effect of any enactment or rule of law relating to the limitation of actions.

(4) Where, before sequestration is awarded, it becomes apparent that a creditor concurring in a debtor application was ineligible to so concur the Accountant in Bankruptcy shall withdraw him from the application but another creditor may concur in the place of the ineligible creditor and that other creditor shall notify the Accountant in Bankruptcy of that fact.]

NOTES

Inserted by the Bankruptcy and Diligence etc (Scotland) Act 2007, s 14(6), subject to transitional provisions and savings in SSI 2008/115, arts 5–7, 10, 15 at **[2.51]–[2.53]**, **[2.56]**, **[2.57]**.

Repealed as noted at the beginning of this Act.

Sub-s (1): words in square brackets substituted for original words "subsection (2)" by the Bankruptcy and Debt Advice (Scotland) Act 2014, s 11(3)(a), subject to transitional provisions and savings in SSI 2014/261, arts 4, 12 at **[2.91]**, **[2.99]**.

Sub-s (2): substituted by the Bankruptcy and Debt Advice (Scotland) Act 2014, s 46(2), subject to transitional provisions and savings in SSI 2014/261, arts 4, 12 at **[2.91]**, **[2.99]**, and previously read as follows—

> "(2) A debtor application made in relation to the estate of a limited partnership may be made within such time as may be prescribed.".

Sub-ss (2A), (2B): inserted by the Bankruptcy and Debt Advice (Scotland) Act 2014, s 11(3)(b), subject to transitional provisions and savings in SSI 2014/261, arts 4, 12 at **[2.91]**, **[2.99]**.

[5.25]

9 Jurisdiction

(1) [Where a petition is presented for the sequestration of an estate,] the [sheriff] shall have jurisdiction in respect of the sequestration of the estate of a living debtor or of a deceased debtor if the debtor had an established place of business in [the sheriffdom], or was habitually resident there, at the relevant time.

[(1A) The Accountant in Bankruptcy may determine a debtor application for the sequestration of the estate of a living [or deceased] debtor if the debtor had an established place of business in Scotland, or was habitually resident there, at the relevant time.]

(2) [Where a petition is presented for the sequestration of an estate,] the [sheriff] shall have jurisdiction in respect of the sequestration of the estate of any entity which may be sequestrated by virtue of section 6 of this Act, if the entity—

(a) had an established place of business in [the sheriffdom] at the relevant time; or

(b) was constituted or formed under Scots law, and at any time carried on business in [the sheriffdom].

[(2A) The Accountant in Bankruptcy may determine a debtor application for the sequestration of the estate of any entity which may be sequestrated by virtue of section 6 of this Act, if the entity—

(a) had an established place of business in Scotland at the relevant time; or

(b) was constituted or formed under Scots law, and at any time carried on business in Scotland.]

(3) Notwithstanding that the partner of a firm, whether alive or deceased, does not fall within subsection (1) above, the [sheriff] shall have jurisdiction in respect of the sequestration of his estate if a petition has been presented for the sequestration of the estate of the firm of which he is, or was at the relevant time before his decease, a partner and the process of that sequestration is still current.

[(3A) Any proceedings under this Act which—

(a) relate to—

(i) a debtor application; or

(ii) the sequestration of a debtor's estate awarded following such an application; and

(b) may be brought before a sheriff,

shall be brought before the sheriff who would, under subsection (1) or (2) above, have had jurisdiction in respect of a petition for sequestration of the debtor's estate.]

(4) . . .

(5) In this section "the relevant time" means at any time in the year immediately preceding the date of presentation of the petition[, the date the debtor application is made] or the date of death, as the case may be.

[(6) This section is subject to Article 3 of the EC Regulation.]

NOTES

Repealed as noted at the beginning of this Act.

Sub-s (1): words in first pair of square brackets inserted and words in second and third pairs of square brackets substituted for original words "Court of Session" and "Scotland" respectively by the Bankruptcy and Diligence etc (Scotland) Act 2007, ss 14(7)(a), 16(1)(a), subject to transitional provisions and savings in SSI 2008/115, arts 5–7, 10, 15 at **[2.51]–[2.53]**, **[2.56]**, **[2.57]**.

Sub-ss (1A), (2A) (3A): inserted by the Bankruptcy and Diligence etc (Scotland) Act 2007, s 14(7)(b), (d), (e), subject to transitional provisions and savings in SSI 2008/115, arts 5–7, 10, 15 at **[2.51]–[2.53]**, **[2.56]**, **[2.57]**; words in square brackets in sub-s (1A) inserted by the Bankruptcy and Debt Advice (Scotland) Act 2014, s 56(1), Sch 3, paras 2, 8, subject to transitional provisions and savings in SSI 2014/261, arts 4, 12 at **[2.91]**, **[2.99]**.

Sub-s (2): words in first pair of square brackets inserted, word in second pair of square brackets substituted for original words "Court of Session" and words in third and fourth pairs of square brackets substituted for original word "Scotland" by the Bankruptcy and Diligence etc (Scotland) Act 2007, ss 14(7)(c), 16(1)(b), subject to transitional provisions and savings in SSI 2008/115, arts 5–7, 10, 15 at **[2.51]–[2.53]**, **[2.56]**, **[2.57]**.

Sub-s (3): word in square brackets substituted for original words "Court of Session" by the Bankruptcy and Diligence etc (Scotland) Act 2007, s 16(1)(c), subject to transitional provisions and savings in SSI 2008/115, arts 5–7, 10, 15 at **[2.51]–[2.53]**, **[2.56]**, **[2.57]**.

Sub-s (4): repealed by the Bankruptcy and Diligence etc (Scotland) Act 2007, s 16(1)(d), subject to transitional provisions and savings in SSI 2008/115, arts 5–7, 10, 15 at **[2.51]–[2.53]**, **[2.56]**, **[2.57]**, and previously read as follows:

"(4) The provisions of this section shall apply to the sheriff as they apply to the Court of Session but as if for the word "Scotland" wherever it occurs there were substituted the words "the sheriffdom" and in subsection (3) after the word "presented" there were inserted the words "in the sheriffdom".".

Sub-s (5): words in square brackets inserted by the Bankruptcy and Diligence etc (Scotland) Act 2007, s 36, Sch 1, paras 1, 7, subject to transitional provisions and savings in SSI 2008/115, arts 5–7, 10, 15 at **[2.51]–[2.53]**, **[2.56]**, **[2.57]**.

Sub-s (6): added by the Insolvency (Scotland) Regulations 2003, SI 2003/2109, regs 3, 10.

[5.26]

[10 Duty to notify existence of concurrent proceedings for sequestration or analogous remedy

(1) If, in the course of sequestration proceedings (referred to in this section and in section 10A of this Act as the "instant proceedings")—

(a) a petitioner for sequestration;

(b) the debtor; or

(c) a creditor concurring in a debtor application,

is, or becomes, aware of any of the circumstances mentioned in subsection (2) below, he shall as soon as possible take the action mentioned in subsection (3) below.

(2) Those circumstances are that, notwithstanding the instant proceedings—

(a) a petition for sequestration of the debtor's estate is before a sheriff or such sequestration has been awarded;

(b) a debtor application has been made in relation to the debtor's estate or sequestration has been awarded by virtue of such an application;

(c) a petition for the appointment of a judicial factor on the debtor's estate is before a court or such a judicial factor has been appointed;

(d) a petition is before a court for the winding up of the debtor under Part IV or V of the Insolvency Act 1986 (c 45) or section 372 of the Financial Services and Markets Act 2000 (c 8); or

(e) an application for an analogous remedy in respect of the debtor's estate is proceeding or such an analogous remedy is in force.

(3) The action referred to in subsection (1) above is—

(a) in a case where the instant proceedings are by petition for sequestration, to notify the sheriff to whom that petition was presented; and

(b) in a case where the instant proceedings are by debtor application, to notify the Accountant in Bankruptcy,

of the circumstance referred to in subsection (2) above.

(4) If a petitioner fails to comply with subsection (1) above, he may be made liable for the expenses of presenting the petition for sequestration.

(5) If a creditor concurring in a debtor application fails to comply with subsection (1) above, he may be made liable for the expenses of making the debtor application.

(6) If a debtor fails to comply with subsection (1) above, he shall be guilty of an offence and liable, on summary conviction, to a fine not exceeding level 5 on the standard scale.
(7) In this section and in section 10A of this Act "analogous remedy" means . . . an individual voluntary arrangement or bankruptcy order under the Insolvency Act 1986 (c 45) or an administration order under section 112 of the County Courts Act 1984 (c 28) in England and Wales or under any enactment having the like effect in Northern Ireland or a remedy analogous to any of the aforesaid remedies, or to sequestration, in any other country (including England, Wales and Northern Ireland).]

NOTES

Repealed as noted at the beginning of this Act.

Substituted, together with s 10A for original s 10, by the Bankruptcy and Diligence etc (Scotland) Act 2007, s 36, Sch 1, paras 1, 8, subject to transitional provisions and savings in SSI 2008/115, arts 5–7, 10, 15 at **[2.51]–[2.53]**, **[2.56]**, **[2.57]**. Prior to this substitution, s 10 and the related notes read as follows:

"10 Concurrent proceedings for sequestration or analogous remedy

(1) If, in the course of sequestration proceedings, the petitioner for sequestration, the debtor or a creditor concurring in the petition (the petition in such proceedings being hereafter in this section referred to as the "instant petition") is, or becomes, aware that—

(a) another petition for sequestration of the debtor's estate is before a court or such sequestration has been awarded; or

(b) a petition for the appointment of a judicial factor on the debtor's estate is before a court or such a judicial factor has been appointed; or

[(c) a petition is before a court for the winding up of the debtor under Part IV or V of the Insolvency Act 1986 [section 372 of the Financial Services and Markets Act 2000];]

(d) an application for an analogous remedy in respect of the debtor's estate is proceeding or such an analogous remedy is in force,

he shall as soon as possible bring that fact to the notice of the court to which the instant petition was presented.

(2) If a petitioner (not being the debtor) or a creditor concurring in the petition fails to comply with subsection (1) above, he may be made liable for the expenses of presenting the petition for sequestration; and, if the debtor fails to comply with subsection (1) above, he shall be guilty of an offence and liable, on summary conviction, to a fine not exceeding level 5 on the standard scale.

(3) Where in the course of sequestration proceedings any of the circumstances mentioned in paragraph (a), (b) or (c) of subsection (1) above exists then—

(a) the court to which the instant petition was presented may, on its own motion or at the instance of the debtor or any creditor or other person having an interest, allow that petition to proceed or may sist or dismiss it; or

(b) without prejudice to paragraph (a) above, the Court of Session may, on its own motion or on application by the debtor or any creditor or other person having an interest, direct the sheriff before whom the instant petition is pending, or the court before which the other petition is pending, to sist or dismiss the instant petition or, as the case may be, the other petition, or may order the petitions to be heard together.

(4) Where in respect of the same estate—

(a) a petition for sequestration is pending before a court; and

(b) an application for an analogous remedy is proceeding or an analogous remedy is in force,

the court, on its own motion or at the instance of the debtor or any creditor or other person having an interest, may allow the petition for sequestration to proceed or may sist or dismiss it.

(5) In this section "analogous remedy" means a bankruptcy order under the Bankruptcy Act 1914 or under the Insolvency Act 1985 or an administration order under section 112 of the County Courts Act 1984 in England and Wales or under any enactment having the like effect in Northern Ireland or a remedy analogous to either of the aforesaid remedies, or to sequestration, in any other country.

NOTES

Repealed as noted at the beginning of this Act.

Sub-s (1): para (c) substituted by the Financial Services Act 1986, s 212(2), Sch 16, para 29; words in square brackets substituted by the Financial Services and Markets Act 2000 (Consequential Amendments and Repeals) Order 2001, SI 2001/3649, art 224.

Bankruptcy Act 1914: whole Act repealed by the Insolvency Act 1985, s 235(3), Sch 10, Pts III, IV, and the Insolvency Act 1986, s 437, Sch 11, Pt II, paras 12, 16(1)(a).

Insolvency Act 1985: largely repealed by the combined effect of the Insolvency Act 1986, s 438, Sch 12, and the Company Directors Disqualification Act 1986, s 23(2), Sch 4.".

Sub-s (7): words "a bankruptcy order under the Bankruptcy Act 1914 (c 59) or" (omitted) repealed by the Bankruptcy and Debt Advice (Scotland) Act 2014, s 56(2), Sch 4, subject to transitional provisions and savings in SSI 2014/261, arts 4, 12 at **[2.91]**, **[2.99]**

[5.27]

[10A Powers in relation to concurrent proceedings for sequestration or analogous remedy

(1) Where, in the course of instant proceedings which are by petition, any of the circumstances mentioned in paragraphs (a) to (d) of section 10(2) of this Act exists, the sheriff to whom the petition in the instant proceedings was presented may, on his own motion or at the instance of the debtor or any creditor or other person having an interest, allow that petition to proceed or may sist or dismiss it.
(2) Without prejudice to subsection (1) above, where, in the course of instant proceedings which are by petition, any of the circumstances mentioned in paragraphs (a), (c) or (d) of section 10(2) of this Act exists, the Court of Session may, on its own motion or on the application of the debtor or any creditor or other person having an interest, direct the sheriff before whom the petition in the instant proceedings is pending, or the sheriff before whom the other petition is pending, to sist or dismiss the petition in the instant proceedings or, as the case may be, the other petition, or may order the petitions to be heard together.

(3) Without prejudice to subsection (1) above, where, in the course of instant proceedings which are by petition, the circumstance mentioned in paragraph (b) of section 10(2) of this Act exists, the sheriff to whom the petition in the instant proceedings was presented may, on his own motion or at the instance of the debtor or any creditor or other person having an interest, direct the Accountant in Bankruptcy to dismiss the debtor application.

[(3A) The Accountant in Bankruptcy must grant a recall of an award of sequestration if—

(a) sequestration has been awarded by virtue of a debtor application, and

(b) the sheriff directs the Accountant in Bankruptcy to dismiss the debtor application.

(3B) The effect of the recall of an award of sequestration is, so far as practicable, to restore the debtor and any other person affected by the sequestration to the position the debtor or, as the case may be, the other person would have been in if the sequestration had not been awarded.

(3C) A recall of an award of sequestration does not—

(a) affect the interruption of prescription caused by—

(i) the presentation of the petition for sequestration,

(ii) the making of the debtor application, or

(iii) the submission of a claim under section 22 or 48,

(b) invalidate any transaction entered into before such recall by the interim trustee, or by the trustee, with a person acting in good faith, or

(c) affect a bankruptcy restrictions order which has not been annulled under section 56J(1)(a).

(3D) Without delay after granting a recall of an award of sequestration under subsection (3A), the Accountant in Bankruptcy must send a certified copy of the decision to the Keeper of the Register of Inhibitions for recording in that register.]

(4) Where, in the course of instant proceedings which are by debtor application, any of the circumstances mentioned in paragraphs (a) to (d) of section 10(2) of this Act exists, the Accountant in Bankruptcy may dismiss the debtor application in the instant proceedings.

(5) Where, in respect of the same estate—

(a) a petition for sequestration is pending before a sheriff; and

(b) an application for an analogous remedy is proceeding or an analogous remedy is in force,

the sheriff, on his own motion or at the instance of the debtor or any creditor or other person having an interest, may allow the petition for sequestration to proceed or may sist or dismiss it.

(6) Where, in respect of the same estate—

(a) a debtor application has been made and has not been determined; and

(b) an application for an analogous remedy is proceeding or an analogous remedy is in force,

the Accountant in Bankruptcy may proceed to determine the application or may dismiss it.]

NOTES

Repealed as noted at the beginning of this Act.

Substituted as noted to s 10 at **[5.26]**.

Sub-ss (3A)–(3D): inserted by the Bankruptcy and Debt Advice (Scotland) Act 2014, s 12, subject to transitional provisions and savings in SSI 2014/261, arts 4, 12 at **[2.91]**, **[2.99]**.

[5.28]

11 Creditor's oath

(1) Every creditor, being a petitioner for sequestration, a creditor who concurs in a [debtor application] or a qualified creditor who becomes sisted under subsection (8)(i) of section 5 of this Act or under that subsection as applied by section 6(8) of this Act, shall produce an oath in the prescribed form made by him or on his behalf.

(2) The oath may be made—

(a) in the United Kingdom, before any person entitled to administer an oath there;

(b) outwith the United Kingdom, before a British diplomatic or consular officer or any person authorised to administer an oath or affirmation under the law of the place where the oath is made.

(3) The identity of the person making the oath and the identity of the person before whom the oath is made and their authority to make and to administer the oath respectively shall be presumed to be correctly stated, and any seal or signature on the oath shall be presumed to be authentic, unless the contrary is established.

(4) If the oath contains any error or has omitted any fact, the [sheriff to whom] the petition for sequestration was presented [or, in the case of a creditor concurring in a debtor application, the Accountant in Bankruptcy] may, at any time before sequestration is awarded, allow another oath to be produced rectifying the original oath; and this section shall apply to the making of that other oath as it applies to the making of the original oath.

(5) Every creditor must produce along with the oath an account or voucher (according to the nature of the debt) which constitutes *prima facie* evidence of the debt; and a petitioning creditor shall in addition produce such evidence as is available to him to show the apparent insolvency of the debtor.

NOTES

Repealed as noted at the beginning of this Act.

Sub-s (1): words in square brackets substituted for original words "petition by a debtor" by the Bankruptcy and Diligence etc (Scotland) Act 2007, s 36, Sch 1, paras 1, 9(a), subject to transitional provisions and savings in SSI 2008/115, arts 5–7, 10, 15 at **[2.51]–[2.53]**, **[2.56]**, **[2.57]**.

Sub-s (4): words in first pair of square brackets substituted for original words "court to which" and words in second pair of square brackets inserted by the Bankruptcy and Diligence etc (Scotland) Act 2007, s 36, Sch 1, paras 1, 9(b), subject to transitional provisions and savings in SSI 2008/115, arts 5–7, 10, 15 at **[2.51]–[2.53]**, **[2.56]**, **[2.57]**.

Regulations: the Bankruptcy (Scotland) Regulations 2008, SSI 2008/82 at **[16.262]**; the Bankruptcy (Scotland) Regulations 2014, SSI 2014/225 at **[16.267]**.

Award of sequestration and appointment and resignation of interim trustee

[5.29]

[11A Debtor application: incomplete application

(1) This section applies where a debtor application is made and the Accountant in Bankruptcy considers that—

- (a) the application is incomplete,
- (b) further information is required in relation to the application,
- (c) further evidence is required to substantiate any fact relevant to the application, or
- (d) any fee or charge applicable to the application is outstanding.

(2) The Accountant in Bankruptcy must specify by notice in writing to the debtor—

- (a) any further information which is to be provided,
- (b) any further evidence which is to be provided, and
- (c) any fee or charge to be paid.

(3) Any information, evidence, fee or charge to be provided or paid under subsection (2) must be provided or paid within 21 days or such longer period as may be specified by the Accountant in Bankruptcy.

(4) The Accountant in Bankruptcy may refuse to award sequestration if, after the expiry of the period referred to in subsection (3), the Accountant in Bankruptcy considers that—

- (a) the application remains incomplete,
- (b) the debtor has provided insufficient information or evidence under subsection (2)(a) or (b), or
- (c) any fee or charge applicable to the application remains outstanding.]

NOTES

Commencement: 1 April 2015.

Inserted, together with s 11B, by the Bankruptcy and Debt Advice (Scotland) Act 2014, s 10, subject to transitional provisions and savings in SSI 2014/261, arts 4, 5, 12 at **[2.91]**, **[2.92]**, **[2.99]**.

Repealed as noted at the beginning of this Act.

[5.30]

[11B Refusal of debtor application: inappropriate application

(1) This section applies where a debtor application is made and the Accountant in Bankruptcy considers that an award of sequestration may not be appropriate in the circumstances of the case.

(2) The Accountant in Bankruptcy must specify by notice in writing to the debtor—

- (a) the reason why the Accountant in Bankruptcy considers the application may not be appropriate, and
- (b) any further information which is to be provided within 21 days or such longer period as may be specified by the Accountant in Bankruptcy.

(3) The Accountant in Bankruptcy may refuse to award sequestration if, after the expiry of the period referred to in subsection (2), the Accountant in Bankruptcy remains of the view that an award of sequestration would be inappropriate in the circumstances of the case.]

NOTES

Commencement: 1 April 2015.

Inserted as noted to s 11A at **[5.29]**.

Repealed as noted at the beginning of this Act.

[5.31]

12 When sequestration is awarded

[(1) Where a [debtor application[, other than an application under section 5(3)(a),] is made [and sections 11A and 11B do not apply], the Accountant in Bankruptcy shall award sequestration forthwith if he is satisfied—

- (a) that the application has been made in accordance with the provisions of this Act and any provisions made under this Act;]
- (b) that [subsection] (2B) of section 5 of this Act applies to the debtor; and
- (c) that the provisions of [subsection] (6A) of that section have been complied with.]

[(1A) . . .]

[(1B) Where a debtor application is made under section 5(3)(a) the Accountant in Bankruptcy must award sequestration forthwith if the Accountant is satisfied—

- (a) that the application has been made in accordance with the provisions of this Act and any provision made under this Act, and
- (b) that the provisions of subsection (6A) of section 5 have been complied with.]

(2) Where a petition for sequestration of a debtor's estate is presented by a creditor or a trustee acting under a trust deed, the [sheriff to whom] the petition is presented shall grant warrant to cite the debtor to appear before [him] on such date as shall be specified in the warrant, being a date not less than 6 nor more than 14 days after the date of citation, to show cause why sequestration should not be awarded.

[(3) Where, on a petition for sequestration presented by a creditor or a trustee acting under a trust deed, the [sheriff] is satisfied—

- (a) that, if the debtor has not appeared, proper citation has been made of the debtor;
- (b) that the petition has been presented in accordance with the provisions of this Act;
- (c) that the provisions of subsection (6) of section 5 of this Act have been complied with;

(d) that, in the case of a petition by a creditor, the requirements of this Act relating to apparent insolvency have been fulfilled; and

[(e) that, in the case of a petition by a trustee—

(i) one or more of the conditions in section 5(2C)(a) applies, or

(ii) the petition includes an averment in accordance with section 5(2C)(b),]

[he] shall, subject to [subsections (3A) to (3C) below], award sequestration forthwith.

(3A) Sequestration shall not be awarded in pursuance of subsection (3) above if—

(a) cause is shown why sequestration cannot competently be awarded; or

(b) the debtor forthwith pays or satisfies, or produces written evidence of the payment or satisfaction of . . . —

(i) the debt in respect of which he became apparently insolvent; and

(ii) any other debt due by him to the petitioner and any creditor concurring in the petition.]

[(3B) Where the sheriff is satisfied that the debtor shall, before the expiry of the period of 42 days beginning with the day on which the debtor appears before the sheriff, pay or satisfy—

(a) the debt in respect of which the debtor became apparently insolvent; and

(b) any other debt due by the debtor to the petitioner and any creditor concurring in the petition,

the sheriff may continue the petition for a period of no more than 42 days.

(3C) Where the sheriff is satisfied—

(a) that a debt payment programme (within the meaning of Part 1 of the Debt Arrangement and Attachment (Scotland) Act 2002 (asp 17)) relating to—

(i) the debt in respect of which the debtor became apparently insolvent; and

(ii) any other debt due by the debtor to the petitioner and any creditor concurring in the petition,

has been applied for and has not yet been approved or rejected; or

(b) that such a debt payment programme will be applied for,

the sheriff may continue the petition for such period as he thinks fit.]

[(4) In this Act "the date of sequestration" means—

(a) where [a debtor application is made], the date on which sequestration is awarded;

(b) where the petition for sequestration is presented by a creditor or a trustee acting under a trust deed [and sequestration is awarded]—

(i) the date on which the [sheriff] grants warrant under subsection (2) above to cite the debtor; or

(ii) where more than one such warrant is granted, the date on which the first such warrant is granted.]

NOTES

Repealed as noted at the beginning of this Act.

Sub-s (1): substituted by the Bankruptcy (Scotland) Act 1993, s 4(1), (2), subject to s 12(6) thereof, at **[5.194]** and to the Bankruptcy (Scotland) Act 1993 Commencement and Savings Order 1993, SI 1993/438, arts 4, 5, at **[16.58]**, **[16.59]**; words in first (outer) pair of square brackets substituted for the following original words:

"a petition for sequestration of his estate is presented by the debtor, unless cause is shown why sequestration cannot competently be awarded, the court shall award sequestration forthwith if it is satisfied—

(a) that the petition has been presented in accordance with the provisions of this Act;";

and word in square brackets in para (c) substituted for original words "subsections (6) and" by the Bankruptcy and Diligence etc (Scotland) Act 2007, ss 14(8), 36, Sch 1, paras 1, 10(a), subject to transitional provisions and savings in SSI 2008/115, arts 5–7, 10, 15 at **[2.51]–[2.53]**, **[2.56]**, **[2.57]**; words in second (inner) and third pairs of square brackets inserted by the Bankruptcy and Debt Advice (Scotland) Act 2014, ss 11(4)(a), 56(1), Sch 3, paras 2, 9(a), subject to transitional provisions and savings in SSI 2014/261, arts 4, 12 at **[2.91]**, **[2.99]**; word in square brackets in para (b) substituted by the Home Owner and Debtor Protection (Scotland) Act 2010, s 9(3).

Sub-s (1A): inserted by the Bankruptcy (Scotland) Act 1993, s 4(1), (3), subject to s 12(6) thereof, at **[5.194]** and to SI 1993/438, arts 4, 5, at **[16.58]**, **[16.59]**; repealed by the Bankruptcy and Diligence etc (Scotland) Act 2007, s 226(2), Sch 6, Pt 1, subject to transitional provisions and savings in SSI 2008/115, arts 5–7, 10, 15 at **[2.51]–[2.53]**, **[2.56]**, **[2.57]**, and previously read as follows:

"(1A) Where a petition is presented as mentioned in subsection (1) above, the Accountant in Bankruptcy may, not later than 7 days after the date on which sequestration is awarded, apply to the court for the grant of a certificate for the summary administration of the sequestration of the debtor's estate.".

Sub-s (1B): inserted by the Bankruptcy and Debt Advice (Scotland) Act 2014, s 11(4)(b), subject to transitional provisions and savings in SSI 2014/261, arts 4, 12 at **[2.91]**, **[2.99]**.

Sub-s (2): words in square brackets substituted for original words "court to which" and "it" respectively by the Bankruptcy and Diligence etc (Scotland) Act 2007, s 36, Sch 1, paras 1, 10(b), subject to transitional provisions and savings in SSI 2008/115, arts 5–7, 10, 15 at **[2.51]–[2.53]**, **[2.56]**, **[2.57]**.

Sub-s (3): substituted, together with sub-s (3A), for original sub-s (3) by the Bankruptcy (Scotland) Act 1993, s 4(1), (4), subject to s 12(6) thereof, at **[5.194]** and to SI 1993/438, arts 4, 5, at **[16.58]**, **[16.59]**; words in square brackets substituted for original words "court", "it" and "subsection (3A)" respectively by the Bankruptcy and Diligence etc (Scotland) Act 2007, ss 27(1), (2), 36, Sch 1, paras 1, 10(c), subject to transitional provisions and savings in SSI 2008/115, arts 5–7, 10, 15 at **[2.51]–[2.53]**, **[2.56]**, **[2.57]**; para (e) substituted by the Bankruptcy and Debt Advice (Scotland) Act 2014, s 47, subject to transitional provisions and savings in SSI 2014/261, arts 4, 12 at **[2.91]**, **[2.99]**, and previously read as follows—

"(e) that, in the case of a petition by a trustee, the averments in his petition as to any of the conditions in subsection (2C) of the said section 5 are true,".

Sub-s (3A): substituted as noted to sub-s (3) above; words ", or gives or shows that there is sufficient security for the payment of" (omitted) repealed by the Bankruptcy and Debt Advice (Scotland) Act 2014, s 56(2), Sch 4, subject to transitional provisions and savings in SSI 2014/261, arts 4, 12 at **[2.91]**, **[2.99]**.

Sub-ss (3B), (3C): inserted by the Bankruptcy and Diligence etc (Scotland) Act 2007, s 27(1), (3), subject to transitional provisions and savings in SSI 2008/115, arts 5–7, 10, 15 at **[2.51]–[2.53]**, **[2.56]**, **[2.57]**.

Sub-s (4): substituted by the Bankruptcy (Scotland) Act 1993, s 4(1), (5), subject to s 12(6) thereof, at **[5.194]** and to SI 1993/438, arts 4, 5, at **[16.58]**, **[16.59]**; words in square brackets in para (a) substituted for original words "the petition for sequestration is presented by the debtor" and word in square brackets in para (b)(i) substituted for original word "court" by the Bankruptcy and Diligence etc (Scotland) Act 2007, s 36, Sch 1, paras 1, 10(d), subject to transitional provisions and savings in SSI 2008/115, arts 5–7, 10, 15 at **[2.51]–[2.53]**, **[2.56]**, **[2.57]**; words in first pair of square brackets in para (b) inserted by the Bankruptcy and Debt Advice (Scotland) Act 2014, s 56(1), Sch 3, paras 2, 9(b), subject to transitional provisions and savings in SSI 2014/261, arts 4, 12 at **[2.91]**, **[2.99]**.

[5.32]

[13 Resignation, removal etc of interim trustee

[(A1) This section applies where an interim trustee is appointed under section 2(5) of this Act and the petition for sequestration has not been determined.]

(1) Where, under section 1A(2) of this Act, the [sheriff] removes from office an interim trustee, the [sheriff] shall, on the application of the Accountant in Bankruptcy, appoint a new interim trustee.

(2) Without prejudice to section 1A(2) of this Act or to subsection (1) above, where the [sheriff] is satisfied that an interim trustee—

(a) is unable to act [for any reason mentioned in subsection (2A) below or] by, under or by virtue of [any other] provision of this Act . . . ; or

(b) has so conducted himself that he should no longer continue to act . . . ,

the [sheriff], on the application of the debtor, a creditor or the Accountant in Bankruptcy, shall remove from office the interim trustee and appoint a new interim trustee.

[(2A) The reasons referred to in subsection (2)(a) above are that the interim trustee—

(a) is incapable within the meaning of section 1(6) of the Adults with Incapacity (Scotland) Act 2000 (asp 4); or

(b) has some other incapacity by virtue of which he is unable to act as interim trustee.]

(3) An interim trustee (not being the Accountant in Bankruptcy) may apply to the [sheriff] for authority to resign office; and if the [sheriff] is satisfied that the grounds mentioned in paragraph (a) or (b) of subsection (2) above apply in relation to the interim trustee, [the sheriff] shall grant the application.

(4) Where, following an application under subsection (3) above, the interim trustee resigns office, the [sheriff] shall appoint a new interim trustee.

(5) Where the interim trustee has died, the [sheriff], on the application of the debtor, a creditor or the Accountant in Bankruptcy, shall appoint a new interim trustee.

(6) No one (other than the Accountant in Bankruptcy) shall act as interim trustee in a sequestration if he would, by virtue of section 24(2) of this Act, be [ineligible to be elected as replacement] trustee in that sequestration; but where an interim trustee is, by virtue of this subsection, prohibited from so acting, he shall forthwith make an application under subsection (3) above.

(7) Subsections (1) and (2) of section 2 of this Act shall apply as regards the appointment of an interim trustee under this section as if for any reference to—

(a) the [sheriff] awarding sequestration of the debtor's estate, there was substituted a reference to the [sheriff] appointing a new interim trustee; and

(b) the petition for sequestration there was substituted a reference to the application under this section for the appointment of a new interim trustee.]

NOTES

Repealed as noted at the beginning of this Act.

Substituted by the Bankruptcy (Scotland) Act 1993, s 11(3), Sch 1, para 2, subject to s 12(6) thereof, at **[5.194]** and to the Bankruptcy (Scotland) Act 1993 Commencement and Savings Order 1993, SI 1993/438, arts 4, 5, at **[16.58]**, **[16.59]**.

Sub-s (A1): inserted by the Bankruptcy and Diligence etc (Scotland) Act 2007, s 36, Sch 1, paras 1, 11(1), (2), subject to transitional provisions and savings in SSI 2008/115, arts 5–7, 10, 15 at **[2.51]–[2.53]**, **[2.56]**, **[2.57]**.

Sub-ss (1), (4), (5), (7): word "sheriff" in square brackets in each place it appears substituted for original word "court" by the Bankruptcy and Diligence etc (Scotland) Act 2007, s 36, Sch 1, paras 1, 11(1), (3), subject to transitional provisions and savings in SSI 2008/115, arts 5–7, 10, 15 at **[2.51]–[2.53]**, **[2.56]**, **[2.57]**.

Sub-s (2): word "sheriff" in first and final pairs of square brackets substituted for original word "court", in para (a), words in square brackets substituted for original words "(whether" and "a" respectively and words "or from any other cause whatsoever)" (omitted) repealed, and words "in the sequestration" omitted from para (b) repealed by the Bankruptcy and Diligence etc (Scotland) Act 2007, ss 9(1)(a), 36, 226(2), Sch 1, paras 1, 11(1), (3), Sch 6, Pt 1, subject to transitional provisions and savings in SSI 2008/115, arts 5–7, 10, 15 at **[2.51]–[2.53]**, **[2.56]**, **[2.57]**.

Sub-s (2A): inserted by the Bankruptcy and Diligence etc (Scotland) Act 2007, s 9(1)(b), subject to transitional provisions and savings in SSI 2008/115, arts 5–7, 10, 15 at **[2.51]–[2.53]**, **[2.56]**, **[2.57]**.

Sub-s (3): word in first and second pairs of square brackets substituted for original word "court" and words in third pair of square brackets substituted for original word "it" by the Bankruptcy and Diligence etc (Scotland) Act 2007, s 36, Sch 1, paras 1, 11(1), (3), (4), subject to transitional provisions and savings in SSI 2008/115, arts 5–7, 10, 15 at **[2.51]–[2.53]**, **[2.56]**, **[2.57]**.

Sub-s (6): words in square brackets substituted for original words "disqualified from acting as permanent" by the Bankruptcy and Diligence etc (Scotland) Act 2007, s 36, Sch 1, paras 1, 11(1), (5), subject to transitional provisions and savings in SSI 2008/115, arts 5–7, 10, 15 at **[2.51]–[2.53]**, **[2.56]**, **[2.57]**.

[5.33]

[13A Termination of interim trustee's functions where not appointed as trustee

(1) This section applies where an interim trustee (not being the Accountant in Bankruptcy) is appointed under section 2(5) of this Act and the sheriff—

(a) awards sequestration and appoints another person as trustee under subsection (2A) or (2C) of section 2 of this Act; or

(b) refuses to award sequestration.

(2) Where the sheriff awards sequestration and appoints another person as trustee, the interim trustee shall hand over to the trustee everything in his possession which relates to the sequestration and shall thereupon cease to act in the sequestration.

(3) The sheriff may make such order in relation to liability for the outlays and remuneration of the interim trustee as may be appropriate.

(4) Within 3 months of the sheriff awarding or, as the case may be, refusing to award sequestration, the interim trustee shall—

(a) submit to the Accountant in Bankruptcy—

(i) his accounts of his intromissions (if any) with the debtor's estate; and

(ii) a claim for outlays reasonably incurred, and for remuneration for work reasonably undertaken, by him; and

(b) send a copy of his accounts and the claim to—

(i) the debtor;

(ii) the petitioner; and

(iii) in a case where sequestration is awarded, the trustee and all creditors known to the interim trustee.

(5) On a submission being made to him under subsection (4)(a) above, the Accountant in Bankruptcy shall—

(a) audit the accounts;

(b) issue a determination fixing the amount of the outlays and remuneration payable to the interim trustee;

(c) send a copy of the determination to—

(i) the interim trustee; and

(ii) the persons mentioned in subsection (4)(b) above; and

(d) where a trustee (not being the Accountant in Bankruptcy) has been appointed in the sequestration, send a copy of the audited accounts and of the determination to the trustee . . .

(6) Where the Accountant in Bankruptcy has been appointed as the trustee in the sequestration, the Accountant in Bankruptcy shall insert a copy of the audited accounts and the determination in the sederunt book.

(7) The interim trustee or any person mentioned in subsection (4)(b) above may, within 14 days after the issuing of the determination under subsection (5)(b) above, appeal to the sheriff against the determination.

(8) On receiving a copy of the Accountant in Bankruptcy's determination sent under subsection (5)(c)(i) above the interim trustee may apply to him for a certificate of discharge.

(9) The interim trustee shall send notice of an application under subsection (8) above to the persons mentioned in subsection (4)(b) above and shall inform them—

(a) that they may make written representations relating to the application to the Accountant in Bankruptcy within the period of 14 days after such notification; and

(b) of the effect mentioned in subsection (16) below.

(10) On the expiry of the period mentioned in subsection (9)(a) above the Accountant in Bankruptcy, after considering any representations duly made to him, shall—

(a) grant or refuse to grant the certificate of discharge; and

(b) notify the persons mentioned in subsection (4)(b) above accordingly.

[(10A) The interim trustee or any person mentioned in subsection (4)(b) may apply to the Accountant in Bankruptcy for a review of a determination under subsection (10).

(10B) An application under subsection (10A) must be made before the expiry of the period of 14 days beginning with the day on which the determination is issued under subsection (10).

(10C) If an application under subsection (10A) is made, the Accountant in Bankruptcy must—

(a) take into account any representations made by an interested person before the expiry of the period of 21 days beginning with the day on which the application is made, and

(b) confirm, amend or revoke the determination under subsection (10) before the expiry of the period of 28 days beginning with the day on which the application is made.]

[(11) The interim trustee or any person mentioned in subsection (4)(b) may appeal to the sheriff against a decision by the Accountant in Bankruptcy under subsection (10C)(b) before the expiry of the period of 14 days beginning with the day of the decision.]

(12) If, following an appeal under subsection (11) above, the sheriff determines that a certificate of discharge which has been refused should be granted he shall order the Accountant in Bankruptcy to grant it.

(13) If, following an appeal under subsection (11) above, the sheriff determines that a certificate of discharge which has been granted should have been refused he shall revoke the certificate.

(14) The sheriff clerk shall send a copy of the decree of the sheriff following an appeal under subsection (11) above to the Accountant in Bankruptcy.

(15) The decision of the sheriff in an appeal under subsection (7) or (11) above shall be final.

(16) The grant of a certificate of discharge under this section by the Accountant in Bankruptcy shall have the effect of discharging the interim trustee from all liability (other than any liability arising from fraud) to the debtor, to the petitioner or to the creditors in respect of any act or omission of the interim trustee in exercising the functions conferred on him by this Act.]

NOTES

Inserted, together with s 13B, by the Bankruptcy and Diligence etc (Scotland) Act 2007, s 10, subject to transitional provisions and savings in SSI 2008/115, arts 5–7, 10, 15 at **[2.51]**–**[2.53]**, **[2.56]**, **[2.57]**.

Repealed as noted at the beginning of this Act.

Words ", who shall insert them in the sederunt book" omitted from sub-s (5)(d), and sub-s (6) repealed by the Bankruptcy and Debt Advice (Scotland) Act 2014, s 56(2), Sch 4, subject to transitional provisions and savings in SSI 2014/261, arts 4, 12 at **[2.91]**, **[2.99]**.

Sub-ss (10A)–(10C): inserted by the Bankruptcy and Debt Advice (Scotland) Act 2014, s 38(1)(a), subject to transitional provisions and savings in SSI 2014/261, arts 10, 12 at **[2.97]**, **[2.99]**.

Sub-s (11): substituted by the Bankruptcy and Debt Advice (Scotland) Act 2014, s 38(1)(b), subject to transitional provisions and savings in SSI 2014/261, arts 10, 12 at **[2.97]**, **[2.99]**, and previously read as follows—

"(11) The interim trustee or any person mentioned in subsection (4)(b) above may, within 14 days after the issuing of the determination under subsection (10) above, appeal therefrom to the sheriff.".

[5.34]

[13B Termination of Accountant in Bankruptcy's functions as interim trustee where not appointed as trustee

(1) This section applies where the Accountant in Bankruptcy is appointed as interim trustee under section 2(5) of this Act and the sheriff—

(a) awards sequestration and appoints another person as trustee under section 2(2A) of this Act; or

(b) refuses to award sequestration.

(2) Where the sheriff awards sequestration and appoints another person as trustee, the Accountant in Bankruptcy shall hand over to the trustee everything in his possession which relates to the sequestration and shall thereupon cease to act in the sequestration.

(3) The sheriff may make such order in relation to liability for the outlays and remuneration of the Accountant in Bankruptcy as may be appropriate.

(4) Within 3 months of the sheriff awarding or, as the case may be, refusing to award sequestration, the Accountant in Bankruptcy shall—

(a) send to the debtor and the petitioner—

(i) his accounts of his intromissions (if any) with the debtor's estate;

(ii) a determination of his fees and outlays calculated in accordance with regulations made under section 69A of this Act; and

(iii) the notice mentioned in subsection (5) below; and

(b) in a case where sequestration is awarded, send a copy of his accounts, the [determination] and the notice to all creditors known to him.

(5) The notice referred to in subsection (4)(a)(iii) above is a notice in writing stating—

(a) that the Accountant in Bankruptcy has commenced procedure under this Act leading to discharge in respect of his actings as interim trustee;

[(aa) that an application for a review may be made under subsection (6A)];

(b) that an appeal may be made to the sheriff under subsection (7) below; and

[(c) that, in the circumstances mentioned in subsection (9), the Accountant in Bankruptcy is discharged from any liability incurred while acting as interim trustee.]

(6) The Accountant in Bankruptcy shall, unless the sheriff refuses to award sequestration, insert a copy of the accounts and the determination in the sederunt book.

[(6A) The debtor, the petitioner or any creditor may apply to the Accountant in Bankruptcy for a review of the discharge of the Accountant in Bankruptcy in respect of the Accountant in Bankruptcy's actings as interim trustee.

(6B) An application under subsection (6A) must be made before the expiry of the period of 14 days beginning with the day on which notice is sent under subsection (4)(a)(iii) or (b).

(6C) If an application for a review under subsection (6A) is made, the Accountant in Bankruptcy must—

(a) take into account any representations made by an interested person before the expiry of the period of 21 days beginning with the day on which the application is made, and

(b) confirm or revoke the discharge before the expiry of the period of 28 days beginning with the day on which the application is made.]

[(7) The debtor, the petitioner or any creditor may appeal to the sheriff against—

(a) the determination of the Accountant in Bankruptcy mentioned in subsection (4)(a)(ii) before the expiry of the period of 14 days beginning with the day on which notice is sent under subsection (4)(a)(iii) or (b),

(b) a decision by the Accountant in Bankruptcy under subsection (6C)(b) before the expiry of the period of 14 days beginning with the day of the decision.

(7A) The sheriff clerk must, following an appeal, send a copy of the decree to the Accountant in Bankruptcy.]

(8) The decision of the sheriff in an appeal under subsection (7) above shall be final.

(9) Where—

(a) the requirements of this section have been complied with; and

(b) no appeal is made to the sheriff under subsection (7) above or such an appeal is made but is refused as regards the discharge of the Accountant in Bankruptcy,

the Accountant in Bankruptcy shall be discharged from all liability (other than any liability arising from fraud) to the debtor, to the petitioner or to the creditors in respect of any act or omission of the Accountant in Bankruptcy in exercising the functions of interim trustee conferred on him by this Act.]

NOTES

Inserted as noted to s 13A at **[5.33]**.

Repealed as noted at the beginning of this Act.

Sub-s (4): word in square brackets in para (b) substituted for original word "claim", by the Bankruptcy and Debt Advice (Scotland) Act 2014, s 56(1), Sch 3, paras 2, 10(a), subject to transitional provisions and savings in SSI 2014/261, arts 4, 12 at **[2.91]**, **[2.99]**.

Sub-s (5): para (aa) inserted and para (c) substituted, by the Bankruptcy and Debt Advice (Scotland) Act 2014, ss 38(2)(a), 56(1), Sch 3, paras 2, 10(b), subject to transitional provisions and savings in SSI 2014/261, arts 4, 10, 12 at **[2.91]**, **[2.97]**, **[2.99]**; para (c) previously read as follows—

"(c) the effect mentioned in subsection (9) below.".

Sub-s (6): repealed by the Bankruptcy and Debt Advice (Scotland) Act 2014, s 56(2), Sch 4, subject to transitional provisions and savings in SSI 2014/261, arts 4, 12 at **[2.91]**, **[2.99]**.

Sub-ss (6A)–(6C): inserted by the Bankruptcy and Debt Advice (Scotland) Act 2014, s 38(2)(c), subject to transitional provisions and savings in SSI 2014/261, arts 10, 12 at **[2.97]**, **[2.99]**.

Sub-ss (7), (7A): substituted for original sub-s (7), by the Bankruptcy and Debt Advice (Scotland) Act 2014, s 38(2)(c), subject to transitional provisions and savings in SSI 2014/261, arts 10, 12 at **[2.97]**, **[2.99]**. Sub-s (7) originally read as follows:

"(7) The debtor, the petitioner and any creditor may, within 14 days after the sending of the notice under subsection (4)(a)(iii) or, as the case may be, subsection (4)(b) above, appeal to the sheriff against—

(a) the determination of the Accountant in Bankruptcy mentioned in subsection (4)(a)(ii) above;

(b) the discharge of the Accountant in Bankruptcy in respect of his actings as interim trustee;

(c) both such determination and discharge,

and the sheriff clerk shall send a copy of the decree of the sheriff to the Accountant in Bankruptcy.".

[5.35]

14 Registration of warrant or determination of debtor application

(1) The [sheriff clerk] shall forthwith after the [sheriff grants warrant under section 12(2)] send—

(a) a certified copy of the [order of the sheriff granting warrant under [that section]] to the keeper of the register of inhibitions . . . for recording in that register; and

(b) a copy of the order to the Accountant in Bankruptcy[. . .

(c) . . .]

[(1A) Where the Accountant in Bankruptcy awards sequestration on a debtor application he shall forthwith after the date of sequestration send a certified copy of his determination of the application to the keeper of the register of inhibitions for recording in that register.]

(2) Recording under subsection (1)(a) [or (1A)] above shall have the effect as from the date of sequestration of an inhibition . . . of the debtor's heritable estate at the instance of the creditors who subsequently have claims in the sequestration accepted under section 49 of this Act.

(3) The effect mentioned in subsection (2) above shall expire—

(a) on the recording under section 15(5)(a) or 17(8)(a) of . . . this Act of a certified copy of an order;

[(aa) on the recording under paragraph 11(4)(a) of Schedule 4 to this Act of a certified copy of a certificate;]

[(ab) on the recording under section 10A(3D), 17D(6) or 17E(8) of a certified copy of a decision;] or

(b) subject to subsection (4) below, if the effect has not expired by virtue of [paragraphs (a) and (aa)] above, at the end of the period of 3 years beginning with the date of sequestration.

[(4) The trustee may, if not discharged, send a memorandum in a form prescribed by the Court of Session by act of sederunt to the Keeper of the Register of Inhibitions for recording in that register before the expiry of—

(a) the period of 3 years mentioned in subsection (3)(b), or

(b) a period for which the effect mentioned in subsection (2) has been renewed by virtue of subsection (4A).

(4A) The recording of a memorandum sent in accordance with subsection (4) renews the effect mentioned in subsection (2) for a period of 3 years beginning with the expiry of—

(a) the period mentioned in subsection (3)(b), or

(b) as the case may be, the period mentioned in subsection (4)(b).

(4B) The trustee may, if appointed or reappointed under section 58B, send a memorandum in a form prescribed by the Court of Session by act of sederunt to the Keeper of the Register of Inhibitions for recording in that register before the expiry of that appointment.

(4C) The recording of a memorandum sent in accordance with subsection (4B) imposes the effect mentioned in subsection (2) for a period of 3 years beginning with the day of notification in accordance with section 58C(1).]

(5) . . .

NOTES

Repealed as noted at the beginning of this Act.

Section heading: substituted for original words "Registration of court order" by the Bankruptcy and Diligence etc (Scotland) Act 2007, s 36, Sch 1, paras 1, 12(1), (6), subject to transitional provisions and savings in SSI 2008/115, arts 5–7, 10, 15 at **[2.51]**–**[2.53]**, **[2.56]**, **[2.57]**.

Sub-s (1): words in first pair of square brackets substituted for original words "clerk of the court", in para (a) words in first pair of square brackets substituted for original words "relevant court order" and words "and adjudications" (omitted) repealed by the Bankruptcy and Diligence etc (Scotland) Act 2007, ss 36, 226(2), Sch 1, paras 1, 12(1), (2), Sch 6, Pt 1, subject to transitional provisions and savings in SSI 2008/115, arts 5–7, 10, 15 at **[2.51]**–**[2.53]**, **[2.56]**, **[2.57]**; words in second pair of square brackets substituted for original words "date of sequestration" and words in second pair of square brackets in para (a) substituted for original words "section 12(2) of this Act" by the Bankruptcy and Debt Advice (Scotland) Act 2014, s 56(1), Sch 3, paras 2, 11, subject to transitional provisions and savings in SSI 2014/261, arts 4, 12 at **[2.91]**, **[2.99]**; para (c) inserted by the Debt Arrangement Scheme (Scotland) Regulations 2004, SSI 2004/468, reg 6, Sch 3, para 1 and repealed by the Debt Arrangement Scheme (Scotland) Amendment Regulations 2013, SSI 2013/225, reg 19(3)(b).

Sub-s (1A): inserted by the Bankruptcy and Diligence etc (Scotland) Act 2007, s 36, Sch 1, paras 1, 12(1), (3), subject to transitional provisions and savings in SSI 2008/115, arts 5–7, 10, 15 at **[2.51]–[2.53]**, **[2.56]**, **[2.57]**.

Sub-s (2): words in square brackets inserted and words "and of a citation in an adjudication" (omitted) repealed by the Bankruptcy and Diligence etc (Scotland) Act 2007, ss 36, 226(2), Sch 1, paras 1, 12(1), (4), Sch 6, Pt 1, subject to transitional provisions and savings in SSI 2008/115, arts 5–7, 10, 15 at **[2.51]–[2.53]**, **[2.56]**, **[2.57]**.

Sub-s (3): words ", or by virtue of paragraph 11 of Schedule 4 to," omitted from para (a) repealed, para (aa) inserted and words in square brackets in para (b) substituted for original words "paragraph (a)" by the Bankruptcy and Diligence etc (Scotland) Act 2007, ss 36, 226(2), Sch 1, paras 1, 12(1), (5), Sch 6, Pt 1, subject to transitional provisions and savings in SSI 2008/115, arts 5–7, 10, 15 at **[2.51]–[2.53]**, **[2.56]**, **[2.57]**; para (aa) repealed and para (ab) inserted by the Bankruptcy and Debt Advice (Scotland) Act 2014, s 56, Sch 3, paras 2, 12, Sch 4, subject to transitional provisions and savings in SSI 2014/261, arts 4, 12 at **[2.91]**, **[2.99]**.

Sub-ss (4), (4A)–(4C): substituted for original sub-s (4) by the Bankruptcy and Debt Advice (Scotland) Act 2014, s 48, subject to transitional provisions and savings in SSI 2014/261, arts 4, 12 at **[2.91]**, **[2.99]**, and sub-s (4) previously read as follows (with words omitted repealed by the Bankruptcy and Diligence etc (Scotland) Act 2007, s 226(2), Sch 6, Pt 1, subject to transitional provisions and savings in SSI 2008/115, arts 5–7, 10, 15 and word in square brackets substituted by the Bankruptcy (Scotland) Act 1993, s 11(3), Sch 1, para 3)—

> "(4) The . . . trustee, if not discharged, [may] before the end of the period of 3 years mentioned in subsection (3)(b) above send a memorandum in a form prescribed by the Court of Session by act of sederunt to the keeper of the register of inhibitions . . . for recording in that register, and such recording shall renew the effect mentioned in subsection (2) above; and thereafter the said effect shall continue to be preserved only if such a memorandum is so recorded before the expiry of every subsequent period of 3 years.".

Sub-s (5): repealed by the Bankruptcy and Diligence etc (Scotland) Act 2007, s 226(2), Sch 6, Pt 1, subject to transitional provisions and savings in SSI 2008/115, arts 5–7, 10, 15 at **[2.51]–[2.53]**, **[2.56]**, **[2.57]**, and previously read as follows:

> "(5) In this section "relevant court order" means, if the petition for sequestration is presented by—
> (a) the debtor, the order of the court awarding sequestration; or
> (b) a creditor or the trustee acting under a trust deed, the order of the court granting warrant under section 12(2) of this Act.".

Acts of Sederunt: Act of Sederunt (Rules of Court Amendment No 1) (Bankruptcy Forms) 1986, SI 1986/514; the Act of Sederunt (Bankruptcy Rules) 1993, SI 1993/921; Act of Sederunt (Rules of the Court of Session 1994), SI 1994/1443 at **[16.60]**; the Act of Sederunt (Sheriff Court Bankruptcy Rules) 2008, SSI 2008/119 at **[16.263]**.

[5.36]

15 Further provisions relating to award of sequestration

(1) . . .

(2) The [sheriff] may at any time after sequestration has been awarded, on application being made to [him and subject to subsection (2A) below], transfer the sequestration . . . to any other sheriff.

[(2A) The debtor may, with leave of the sheriff, appeal to the sheriff principal against a transfer under subsection (2) above.]

(3) Where the [sheriff] makes an order refusing to award sequestration, the petitioner . . . may appeal against the order within 14 days of the date of making of the order.

[(3A) If, following a debtor application, the Accountant in Bankruptcy refuses to award sequestration, the debtor or a creditor concurring in the application may apply to the Accountant in Bankruptcy for a review of the refusal.

(3B) An application under subsection (3A) must be made before the expiry of the period of 14 days beginning with the day on which the Accountant in Bankruptcy refuses to award sequestration.

(3C) If an application under subsection (3A) is made, the Accountant in Bankruptcy must—

(a) take into account any representations made by an interested person before the expiry of the period of 21 days beginning with the day on which the application is made, and

(b) confirm the refusal or award sequestration before the expiry of the period of 28 days beginning with the day on which the application is made.

(3D) If the Accountant in Bankruptcy confirms the refusal to award sequestration under subsection (3C)(b), the debtor or a creditor concurring in the application may, before the expiry of the period of 14 days beginning with the day of that confirmation, appeal to the sheriff.]

(4) Without prejudice to any right to bring an action of reduction of an award of sequestration, such an award shall not be subject to review otherwise than by recall under sections [10A(3A), 16, 17, 17D and 17E] of this Act.

(5) Where a petition for sequestration is presented by a creditor or a trustee acting under a trust deed, the [sheriff clerk] shall—

(a) on the final determination or abandonment of any appeal under subsection (3) above in relation to the petition, or if there is no such appeal on the expiry of the 14 days mentioned in that subsection, send a certified copy of an order refusing to award sequestration to the keeper of the register of inhibitions *and adjudications* for recording in that register;

[(b) forthwith send a copy of the order refusing or awarding sequestration—

(i) to the Accountant in Bankruptcy; and

(ii) where the debtor is taking part in a debt payment programme under Part 1 of the Debt Arrangement and Attachment (Scotland) Act 2002, to the DAS Administrator (as defined in regulation 2(1) of the Debt Arrangement Scheme (Scotland) Regulations 2011).]

(6) . . .

(7) Where sequestration has been awarded, the process of sequestration shall not fall asleep.

(8) Where a debtor learns, whether before or after the date of sequestration, that he may derive benefit from another estate, he shall as soon as practicable after that date inform—

(a) the . . . trustee of that fact; and

(b) the person who is administering that other estate of the sequestration.

(9) If the debtor fails to comply with subsection (8) above, he shall be guilty of an offence and liable, on summary conviction, to a fine not exceeding level 5 on the standard scale.

NOTES

Repealed as noted at the beginning of this Act.

Sub-s (1): repealed by the Bankruptcy and Diligence etc (Scotland) Act 2007, s 16(2)(a), subject to transitional provisions and savings in SSI 2008/115, arts 5–7, 10, 15 at **[2.51]–[2.53]**, **[2.56]**, **[2.57]**, and previously read as follows:

> "(1) Where sequestration has been awarded by the Court of Session, it shall remit the sequestration to such sheriff as in all the circumstances of the case it considers appropriate.".

Sub-s (2): words in first pair of square brackets substituted for original words "Court of Session", words in second pair of square brackets substituted for original word "it", and words "from the sheriff before whom it is depending or to whom it has been remitted" (omitted) repealed by the Bankruptcy and Diligence etc (Scotland) Act 2007, s 16(2)(b), subject to transitional provisions and savings in SSI 2008/115, arts 5–7, 10, 15 at **[2.51]–[2.53]**, **[2.56]**, **[2.57]**.

Sub-s (2A): inserted by the Bankruptcy and Diligence etc (Scotland) Act 2007, ss 16(2)(c), 36, Sch 1, paras 1, 13, subject to transitional provisions and savings in SSI 2008/115, arts 5–7, 10, 15 at **[2.51]–[2.53]**, **[2.56]**, **[2.57]**.

Sub-s (3): word in square brackets substituted for original word "court" and words "or a creditor concurring in the petition for sequestration" (omitted) repealed by the Bankruptcy and Diligence etc (Scotland) Act 2007, ss 16(2)(d), 226(2), Sch 6, Pt 1, subject to transitional provisions and savings in SSI 2008/115, arts 5–7, 10, 15 at **[2.51]–[2.53]**, **[2.56]**, **[2.57]**.

Sub-ss (3A)–(3D): substituted (for sub-s (3A) as inserted by the Bankruptcy and Diligence etc (Scotland) Act 2007, ss 16(2)(c), 36, Sch 1, paras 1, 13, subject to transitional provisions and savings in SSI 2008/115, arts 5–7, 10, 15), by the Bankruptcy and Debt Advice (Scotland) Act 2014, s 39, subject to transitional provisions and savings in SSI 2014/261, arts 10, 12 at **[2.97]**, **[2.99]**. Sub-s (3A) previously read as follows—

> "[(3A) Where the Accountant in Bankruptcy, on determining a debtor application, refuses to award sequestration, the debtor or a creditor concurring in the application may appeal against such a determination within 14 days of it being made to the sheriff.]".

Sub-s (4): words in square brackets substituted for original words "16 and 17" by the Bankruptcy and Debt Advice (Scotland) Act 2014, s 56(1), Sch 3, paras 2, 13, subject to transitional provisions and savings in SSI 2014/261, arts 4, 12 at **[2.91]**, **[2.99]**.

Sub-s (5): words in square brackets substituted for original words "clerk of the court" by the Bankruptcy and Diligence etc (Scotland) Act 2007, s 16(2)(e), subject to transitional provisions and savings in SSI 2008/115, arts 5–7, 10, 15 at **[2.51]–[2.53]**, **[2.56]**, **[2.57]**; words "and adjudications" in para (a) repealed by the Bankruptcy and Diligence etc (Scotland) Act 2007, s 226(2), Sch 6, Pt 1, as from a day to be appointed; para (b) substituted by virtue of the Debt Arrangement Scheme (Scotland) Regulations 2011, SSI 2011/141, reg 6, Sch 2, para 2.

Sub-s (6): repealed by the Home Owner and Debtor Protection (Scotland) Act 2010, s 12, subject to transitional provisions and savings in the Home Owner and Debtor Protection (Scotland) Act 2010 (Transitional and Saving Provisions) Order 2010, SSI 2010/316, art 7(3). Sub-s (6) and related notes previously read as follows:

> "[(6) The . . . trustee shall, as soon as an award of sequestration has been granted, publish in the Edinburgh Gazette a notice—
>
> (a) stating that sequestration of the debtor's estate has been awarded;
>
> (b) inviting the submission of claims to him; and
>
> (c) giving such other information as may be prescribed.]
>
> **NOTES**
>
> Repealed as noted at the beginning of this Act.
>
> Sub-s (6): substituted by the Bankruptcy (Scotland) Act 1993, s 11(3), Sch 1, para 4, subject to s 12(6) thereof, at **[5.194]** and to the Bankruptcy (Scotland) Act 1993 Commencement and Savings Order 1993, SI 1993/438, arts 4, 5, at **[16.58]**, **[16.59]**; word "interim" (omitted) repealed by the Bankruptcy and Diligence etc (Scotland) Act 2007, s 226(2), Sch 6, Pt 1, subject to transitional provisions and savings in SSI 2008/115, arts 5–7, 10, 15 at **[2.51]–[2.53]**, **[2.56]**, **[2.57]**.".

Sub-s (8): words "permanent trustee or, if the permanent trustee has not yet been elected or appointed, the interim" (omitted) repealed by the Bankruptcy and Diligence etc (Scotland) Act 2007, s 226(2), Sch 6, Pt 1, subject to transitional provisions and savings in SSI 2008/115, arts 5–7, 10, 15 at **[2.51]–[2.53]**, **[2.56]**, **[2.57]**.

Regulations: the Bankruptcy (Scotland) Regulations 2008, SSI 2008/82 at **[16.262]**.

[5.37]

16 Petitions for recall of sequestration

(1) A petition for recall of an award of sequestration may be presented to the [sheriff] by—

(a) the debtor, any creditor or any other person having an interest (notwithstanding that he was a petitioner, or concurred in the [debtor application], for the sequestration);

(b) the . . . trustee, or the Accountant in Bankruptcy.

[(1A) A petition for recall of an award of sequestration may not be presented to the sheriff if the only ground is that the debtor has paid or is able to pay the debtor's debts in full.

(1B) Subsection (1A) does not apply where—

(a) sequestration was awarded following a petition of a qualified creditor or qualified creditors, and

(b) a petition for recall of the award of sequestration includes the ground that the debtor was not apparently insolvent.]

(2) The petitioner shall serve upon the debtor, any person who was a petitioner, or concurred in the [debtor application], for the sequestration, the . . . trustee and the Accountant in Bankruptcy, a copy of the petition along with a notice stating that the recipient of the notice may lodge answers to the petition within 14 days of the service of the notice.
[(3) On service of a copy of the petition under subsection (2), the Accountant in Bankruptcy must enter particulars of the petition in the register of insolvencies.]
(4) Subject to [sections 41(1)(b) and 41A(1)(b)] of this Act, a petition under this section may be presented [at any time]—
(a) within 10 weeks after the date of [the award of] sequestration; but
(b) at any time if the petition is presented on any of the grounds mentioned in paragraphs (a) to (c) of section 17(1) of this Act.
(5) Notwithstanding that a petition has been presented under this section, the proceedings in the sequestration shall continue (subject to section 17(6) of this Act) as if that petition had not been presented until the recall is granted.
(6) Where—
(a) a petitioner under this section; or
(b) a person who has lodged answers to the petition,
withdraws or dies, any person entitled to present or, as the case may be, lodge answers to a petition under this section may be sisted in his place.

NOTES

Repealed as noted at the beginning of this Act.

Sub-s (1): words in first pair of square brackets substituted for original words "Court of Session", words in square brackets in para (a) substituted for original word "petition" and words "interim trustee, the permanent" omitted from para (b) repealed by the Bankruptcy and Diligence etc (Scotland) Act 2007, ss 16(3), 36, 226(2), Sch 1, paras 1, 14(a), Sch 6, Pt 1 subject to transitional provisions and savings in SSI 2008/115, arts 5–7, 10, 15 at **[2.51]–[2.53]**, **[2.56]**, **[2.57]**.

Sub-ss (1A), (1B): inserted by the Bankruptcy and Debt Advice (Scotland) Act 2014, s 26(1)(a), subject to transitional provisions and savings in SSI 2014/261, art 12 at **[2.99]**.

Sub-s (2): words in square brackets substituted for original word "petition" and words "interim trustee or permanent" (omitted) repealed by the Bankruptcy and Diligence etc (Scotland) Act 2007, ss 36, 226(2), Sch 1, paras 1, 14(b), Sch 6, Pt 1, subject to transitional provisions and savings in SSI 2008/115, arts 5–7, 10, 15 at **[2.51]–[2.53]**, **[2.56]**, **[2.57]**.

Sub-s (3): substituted by the Bankruptcy and Debt Advice (Scotland) Act 2014, s 24(1), subject to transitional provisions and savings in SSI 2014/261, arts 8, 12 at **[2.95]**, **[2.99]** and originally read as follows—

"(3) At the same time as service is made under subsection (2) above, the petitioner shall publish a notice in the Edinburgh Gazette stating that a petition has been presented under this section and that any person having an interest may lodge answers to the petition within 14 days of the publication of the notice.".

Sub-s (4): words in first pair of square brackets substituted by the Civil Partnership Act 2004, s 261(2), Sch 28, para 31; words in square brackets in para (a) inserted by the Bankruptcy (Scotland) Act 1993, s 11(3), Sch 1, para 5, subject to s 12(6) thereof, at **[5.194]** and to the Bankruptcy (Scotland) Act 1993 Commencement and Savings Order 1993, SI 1993/438, arts 4, 5, at **[16.58]**, **[16.59]**; words in second pair of square brackets inserted and paras (a), (b) repealed, by the Bankruptcy and Debt Advice (Scotland) Act 2014, s 26(1)(b), subject to transitional provisions and savings in SSI 2014/261, arts 4, 12 at **[2.91]**, **[2.99]**

[5.38]

17 [Recall of sequestration by sheriff]

(1) The [sheriff] may recall an award of sequestration if [he] is satisfied that in all the circumstances of the case (including those arising after the date of the award of sequestration) it is appropriate to do so and, without prejudice to the foregoing generality, may recall the award if [he] is satisfied that—
(a) the debtor has paid his debts in full . . . ;
(b) a majority in value of the creditors reside in a country other than Scotland and that it is more appropriate for the debtor's estate to be administered in that other country; or
(c) one or more other awards of sequestration of the estate or analogous remedies (as defined in [section 10(7)] of this Act) have been granted.
(2) Where one or more [other] awards of sequestration of the debtor's estate have been granted, the [sheriff] may, after such intimation as [he] considers necessary, recall an award whether or not the one in respect of which the petition for recall was presented.
[(2A) Where the sheriff intends to recall an award of sequestration on the ground that the debtor has paid the debtor's debts in full, the order recalling the award may not—
(a) be made before the payment in full of the outlays and remuneration of the interim trustee and the trustee,
(b) be subject to any conditions which are to be fulfilled before the order takes effect.]
(3) On [or before] recalling an award of sequestration, the [sheriff]—
(a) shall make provision for the payment of the outlays and remuneration of [any] interim trustee and [the] trustee by directing that such payment shall be made out of the debtor's estate or by requiring any person who was a party to the petition for sequestration [or, as the case may be, the debtor application] to pay the whole or any part of the said outlays and remuneration;
(b) without prejudice to subsection (7) below, may direct that payment of the expenses of a creditor who was a petitioner, or concurred in the [debtor application], for sequestration shall be made out of the debtor's estate;
(c) may make any further order that [he] considers necessary or reasonable in all the circumstances of the case.

(4) Subject to subsection (5) below, the effect of the recall of an award of sequestration shall be, so far as predictable, to restore the debtor and any other person affected by the sequestration to the position he would have been in if the sequestration had not been awarded.

(5) A recall of an award of sequestration shall not—

(a) affect the interruption of prescription caused by the presentation of the petition for sequestration[, the making of the debtor application] or the submission of a claim under section 22 or 48 of this Act;

(b) invalidate any transaction entered into before such recall by the interim trustee or [the] trustee with a person acting in good faith.

[(c) affect a bankruptcy restrictions order which has not been annulled under section 56J(1)(a) of this Act.]

(6) Where the [sheriff] considers that it is inappropriate to recall or to refuse to recall an award of sequestration forthwith, [he] may order that the proceedings in the sequestration shall continue but shall be subject to such conditions as [he] may think fit.

(7) The [sheriff] may make such order in relation to the expenses in a petition for recall as [he] thinks fit.

(8) The [sheriff clerk] shall send—

(a) a certified copy of any order recalling an award of sequestration to the keeper of the register of inhibitions *and adjudications* for recording in that register; and

(b) a copy of any [interim or final] order recalling or refusing to recall an award of sequestration, or of any order under this section 41(1)(b)(ii) [or 41A(1)(b)(ii)] of this Act, to—

(i) the Accountant in Bankruptcy; and

(ii) [if the Accountant in Bankruptcy is not the trustee in the sequestration, the trustee in the sequestration] . . .

NOTES

Repealed as noted at the beginning of this Act.

Section heading: substituted (for original words "Recall of sequestration") by the Bankruptcy and Debt Advice (Scotland) Act 2014, s 26(2), subject to transitional provisions and savings in SSI 2014/261, art 12 at **[2.99]**.

Sub-s (1): words "sheriff" and "he" in square brackets substituted for original words "Court of Session" and "it" respectively, and words in square brackets in para (c) substituted for original words "section 10(5)" by the Bankruptcy and Diligence etc (Scotland) Act 2007, ss 16(4)(a), 36, Sch 1, paras 1, 15(a), subject to transitional provisions and savings in SSI 2008/115, arts 5–7, 10, 15 at **[2.51]–[2.53]**, **[2.56]**, **[2.57]**; words "or has given sufficient security for their payment" omitted from para (a) repealed by the Bankruptcy and Debt Advice (Scotland) Act 2014, s 26(3)(a), subject to transitional provisions and savings in SSI 2014/261, art 12 at **[2.99]**.

Sub-s (2): word "other" in square brackets inserted by the Bankruptcy and Debt Advice (Scotland) Act 2014, s 56(1), Sch 3, paras 2, 14(a), subject to transitional provisions and savings in SSI 2014/261, arts 4, 12 at **[2.91]**, **[2.99]**; words "sheriff" and "he" in square brackets substituted for original words "Court" and "it" respectively by the Bankruptcy and Diligence etc (Scotland) Act 2007, s 16(4)(b), subject to transitional provisions and savings in SSI 2008/115, arts 5–7, 10, 15 at **[2.51]–[2.53]**, **[2.56]**, **[2.57]**.

Sub-s (2A): inserted by the Bankruptcy and Debt Advice (Scotland) Act 2014, s 26(3)(b), subject to transitional provisions and savings in SSI 2014/261, art 12 at **[2.99]**.

Sub-s (3): words "or before" in first pair of square brackets inserted and word in first pair of brackets in para (a) substituted for original word "the", by the Bankruptcy and Debt Advice (Scotland) Act 2014, ss 26(3)(c), 56(1), Sch 3, paras 2, 14(b), subject to transitional provisions and savings in SSI 2014/261, arts 4, 12 at **[2.91]**, **[2.99]**; word in second pair of square brackets substituted for original word "Court", in para (a), word in second pair of square brackets substituted for original word "permanent" and words in third pair of square brackets inserted, and words in square brackets in paras (b), (c) substituted for original words "petition" and "it" respectively by the Bankruptcy and Diligence etc (Scotland) Act 2007, ss 16(4)(c), 36, Sch 1, paras 1, 15(b), (c), subject to transitional provisions and savings in SSI 2008/115, arts 5–7, 10, 15 at **[2.51]–[2.53]**, **[2.56]**, **[2.57]**.

Sub-s (5): words in square brackets in para (a) and the whole of para (c) inserted, and word in square brackets in para (b) substituted for original word "permanent" by the Bankruptcy and Diligence etc (Scotland) Act 2007, s 36, Sch 1, paras 1, 15(d), subject to transitional provisions and savings in SSI 2008/115, arts 5–7, 10, 15 at **[2.51]–[2.53]**, **[2.56]**, **[2.57]**.

Sub-ss (6), (7): words "sheriff" and "he" in square brackets substituted for original words "Court" and "it" respectively by the Bankruptcy and Diligence etc (Scotland) Act 2007, s 16(4)(d), (e), subject to transitional provisions and savings in SSI 2008/115, arts 5–7, 10, 15 at **[2.51]–[2.53]**, **[2.56]**, **[2.57]**.

Sub-s (8): words in first pair of square brackets substituted for original words "clerk of court" and words "and adjudications" in para (a) repealed (as from a day to be appointed) by the Bankruptcy and Diligence etc (Scotland) Act 2007, ss 16(4)(f), 226(2), Sch 6, Pt 1, subject to transitional provisions and savings in SSI 2008/115, arts 5–7, 10, 15 at **[2.51]–[2.53]**, **[2.56]**, **[2.57]**; in para (b) words in first pair of square brackets inserted, words in third pair of square brackets substituted for original words "the trustee (if any)" and words "who shall insert it in the sederunt book" (omitted) repealed, by the Bankruptcy and Debt Advice (Scotland) Act 2014, ss 26(3)(d), 56, Sch 3, paras 2, 14(c), Sch 4, subject to transitional provisions and savings in SSI 2014/261, arts 4, 12 at **[2.91]**, **[2.99]**; words in second pair of square brackets in para (b) inserted by the Civil Partnership Act 2004, s 261(2), Sch 28, para 32.

[5.39]

[17A Application to Accountant in Bankruptcy for recall of sequestration

(1) An application for recall of an award of sequestration may be made to the Accountant in Bankruptcy on the ground that the debtor has paid or is able to pay the debtor's debts in full.

(2) An application may be made by—

(a) the debtor,

(b) any creditor (whether or not a person who was a petitioner for, or concurred in a debtor application for, the sequestration),

(c) the trustee (where the Accountant in Bankruptcy is not the trustee), or

(d) any other person having an interest (whether or not a person who was a petitioner for the sequestration).

(3) The person making an application must, at the same time as applying to the Accountant in Bankruptcy, give to the persons mentioned in subsection (4)—

(a) a copy of the application, and

(b) a notice informing the recipient that the person has a right to make representations to the Accountant in Bankruptcy in relation to the application before the expiry of the period of 21 days beginning with the day on which the notice is given.

(4) The persons are—

(a) the debtor,

(b) any person who was a petitioner for, or concurred in a debtor application for, the sequestration,

(c) the trustee.

(5) Despite an application being made, the proceedings in the sequestration are to continue as if the application had not been made until a recall of an award of sequestration is granted under section 17D(1) (subject to any conditions imposed under section 17D(5)).

(6) Where the applicant withdraws the application or dies, the Accountant in Bankruptcy may continue the application by substituting any person mentioned in subsection (2) for the applicant.]

NOTES

Commencement: 1 April 2015.

Inserted, together with ss 17B–17G, by the Bankruptcy and Debt Advice (Scotland) Act 2014, s 27, subject to transitional provisions and savings in SSI 2014/261, arts 4, 12 at **[2.91]**, **[2.99]**.

Repealed as noted at the beginning of this Act.

[5.40]

[17B Application under section 17A: further procedure

(1) This section applies where an application is made under section 17A.

(2) The trustee must prepare a statement on the debtor's affairs, so far as within the knowledge of the trustee.

(3) The trustee must submit the statement to the Accountant in Bankruptcy—

(a) at the same time as the trustee makes the application under section 17A, or

(b) where the application is made by another person, before the expiry of the period of 21 days beginning with the day on which the notice is given under section 17A(3)(b).

(4) The statement must—

(a) indicate whether the debtor has agreed to—

(i) the interim trustee's claim for outlays reasonably incurred and for remuneration for work reasonably undertaken by the interim trustee (including any outlays and remuneration which are yet to be incurred), and

(ii) the trustee's claim for outlays reasonably incurred and for remuneration for work reasonably undertaken by the trustee (including any outlays and remuneration which are yet to be incurred),

(b) state whether or not the debtor's debts have been paid in full (including the payment of the outlays and remuneration of the interim trustee and the trustee),

(c) where the debtor's debts have not been so paid—

(i) provide details of any debt which has not been paid, and

(ii) indicate whether, in the opinion of the trustee, the debtor's assets are likely to be sufficient to pay the debts in full (including the payment of the outlays and remuneration of the interim trustee and the trustee) before the day which is 8 weeks after the day on which the statement is submitted, and

(d) provide details of any distribution of the debtor's estate.

(5) The trustee must notify every creditor known to the trustee that an application has been made—

(a) where the application is made by the trustee, before the expiry of the period of 7 days beginning with the day on which the application is made,

(b) where the application is made by another person, before the expiry of the period of 7 days beginning with the day on which the notice is given under section 17A(3)(b).

(6) If a creditor has not previously submitted a claim under section 22 or 48, the creditor must, in order to be included in the statement made by the trustee, submit a claim.

(7) A claim must be submitted—

(a) in accordance with section 22(2) and (3), and

(b) before the expiry of the period of 14 days beginning with the day on which notice is given under subsection (5).

(8) If any creditor submits a claim in accordance with subsection (7), the trustee must update and resubmit the statement before the expiry of the period of 7 days beginning with the expiry of the period mentioned in subsection (7)(b).

(9) The trustee must update and resubmit the statement if—

(a) the statement previously submitted did not state in accordance with subsection (4)(b) that the debtor's debts have been paid in full, and

(b) before the day on which the application is determined by the Accountant in Bankruptcy, the trustee is able to make that statement.]

NOTES

Commencement: 1 April 2015.

Inserted as noted to s 17A at **[5.39]**.

Repealed as noted at the beginning of this Act.

[5.41]

[17C Determination of outlays and remuneration

(1) This section applies where—

(a) the Accountant in Bankruptcy receives an application under section 17A, and

(b) the statement submitted by the trustee under section 17B indicates that the amount of the outlays and remuneration of the trustee is not agreed.

(2) The trustee must provide to the Accountant in Bankruptcy—

(a) at the same time as submitting the statement under section 17B—

(i) the trustee's accounts of the trustee's intromissions with the debtor's estate for audit, and

(ii) details of the trustee's claim for outlays reasonably incurred and for remuneration for work reasonably undertaken by the trustee (including any outlays and remuneration which are yet to be incurred), and

(b) such other information in relation to that claim as may be reasonably requested by the Accountant in Bankruptcy.

(3) The Accountant in Bankruptcy must before the expiry of the period of 28 days beginning with the expiry of the period mentioned in section 17B(8) issue a determination fixing the amount of the outlays and the remuneration payable to the trustee.

(4) The Accountant in Bankruptcy may before the expiry of the period mentioned in subsection (3) determine the expenses reasonably incurred by a creditor who was a petitioner or, as the case may be, concurred in a debtor application for sequestration.

(5) Subsections (4) and (5) of section 53 apply to the Accountant in Bankruptcy for the purpose of making a determination in accordance with subsection (3) as they apply to the commissioners or the Accountant in Bankruptcy for the purpose of fixing an amount under that section.]

NOTES

Commencement: 1 April 2015.
Inserted as noted to s 17A at **[5.39]**.
Repealed as noted at the beginning of this Act.

[5.42]

[17D Recall of sequestration by Accountant in Bankruptcy

(1) The Accountant in Bankruptcy may grant a recall of an award of sequestration if—

(a) the trustee has notified the Accountant in Bankruptcy in the statement submitted under section 17B that the debtor's debts have been paid in full (including the payment of the outlays and remuneration of the interim trustee and the trustee), and

(b) the Accountant in Bankruptcy is satisfied that in all the circumstances of the case, it is appropriate to do so.

(2) The Accountant in Bankruptcy may not grant a recall of an award of sequestration after—

(a) where no appeal is made under section 17G(5)(a), the day which is 8 weeks after the day on which the statement was first submitted under section 17B(3), or

(b) where such an appeal is made, such later day which is 14 days after the day on which the appeal is finally determined or abandoned.

(3) The effect of the recall of an award of sequestration is, so far as practicable, to restore the debtor and any other person affected by the sequestration to the position the debtor or, as the case may be, the other person would have been in if the sequestration had not been awarded.

(4) A recall of an award of sequestration is not to—

(a) affect the interruption of prescription caused by—

(i) the presentation of the petition for sequestration,

(ii) the making of the debtor application, or

(iii) the submission of a claim under section 22 or 48,

(b) invalidate any transaction entered into before such recall by the interim trustee, or by the trustee, with a person acting in good faith, or

(c) affect a bankruptcy restrictions order which has not been annulled under section 56J(1)(a).

(5) If the Accountant in Bankruptcy does not grant a recall of an award of sequestration under subsection (1) the sequestration is to continue but is to be subject to such conditions as the Accountant in Bankruptcy thinks fit.

(6) Without delay after granting a recall of an award of sequestration under subsection (1), the Accountant in Bankruptcy must send a certified copy of the decision to the Keeper of the Register of Inhibitions for recording in that register.]

NOTES

Commencement: 1 April 2015.
Inserted as noted to s 17A at **[5.39]**.
Repealed as noted at the beginning of this Act.

[5.43]

[17E Recall where Accountant in Bankruptcy the trustee

(1) This section applies where the Accountant in Bankruptcy—

(a) is the trustee, and

(b) considers that recall of an award of sequestration should be granted on the ground that the debtor has paid or is able to pay the debtor's debts in full (including the payment of the outlays and remuneration of the interim trustee and the trustee).

(2) The Accountant in Bankruptcy must notify the debtor and every creditor known to the Accountant in Bankruptcy that the Accountant in Bankruptcy considers that subsection (1) applies.

(3) If a creditor has not previously submitted a claim under section 22 or 48, the creditor must, in order for the creditor's claim to a dividend out of the debtor's estate to be considered, submit a claim.

(4) A claim must be submitted—

(a) in accordance with section 22(2) and (3), and

(b) before the expiry of the period of 14 days beginning with the day on which notice is given under subsection (2).

(5) Before granting a recall of an award of sequestration the Accountant in Bankruptcy must—

(a) take into account any representations made by an interested person before the expiry of the period of 21 days beginning with the day on which the notice is given under subsection (2), and

(b) make a determination of the Accountant in Bankruptcy's fees and outlays calculated in accordance with regulations made under section 69A.

(6) The Accountant in Bankruptcy may grant a recall of an award of sequestration if the Accountant in Bankruptcy is satisfied that—

(a) the debtor has paid the debtor's debts in full (including the payment of the outlays and remuneration of the interim trustee and the trustee),

(b) those debts were paid in full before the expiry of the period of 8 weeks beginning with the expiry of the period mentioned in subsection (5)(a), and

(c) in all the circumstances of the case, it is appropriate to do so.

(7) Subsections (2) and (3) of section 17D apply in relation to a recall of an award of sequestration granted under subsection (6) as they apply in relation to a recall of an award of sequestration granted under that section.

(8) Without delay after granting a recall of an award of sequestration under subsection (6), the Accountant in Bankruptcy must send a certified copy of the decision to the Keeper of the Register of Inhibitions for recording in that register.]

NOTES

Commencement: 1 April 2015.
Inserted as noted to s 17A at **[5.39]**.
Repealed as noted at the beginning of this Act.

[5.44]
[17F Reference to sheriff

(1) The Accountant in Bankruptcy may, at any time before deciding under section 17D(1) whether to grant an application for recall of an award of sequestration, remit to the sheriff an application made under section 17A.

(2) The Accountant in Bankruptcy may, at any time before deciding under section 17E(6) whether to grant a recall of an award of sequestration, remit the case to the sheriff.

(3) If an application is remitted to the sheriff under subsection (1) or (2), the sheriff may dispose of the application or the case in accordance with section 17 as if it were a petition presented by the Accountant in Bankruptcy under section 16.]

NOTES

Commencement: 1 April 2015.
Inserted as noted to s 17A at **[5.39]**.
Repealed as noted at the beginning of this Act.

[5.45]
[17G Recall of sequestration by Accountant in Bankruptcy: review and appeal

(1) A person mentioned in subsection (2) may apply to the Accountant in Bankruptcy for a review of—

(a) a decision of the Accountant in Bankruptcy under section 17D(1) or 17E(6) to grant or refuse to grant a recall of an award of sequestration,

(b) a determination of the Accountant in Bankruptcy under section 17C(4).

(2) The persons are—

(a) the debtor,

(b) any creditor,

(c) the trustee,

(d) any other person having an interest.

(3) An application under subsection (1) must be made before the expiry of the period of 14 days beginning with the day on which the decision or, as the case may be, the determination or requirement is made.

(4) If an application under subsection (1) is made, the Accountant in Bankruptcy must—

(a) take into account any representations made by an interested person before the expiry of the period of 21 days beginning with the day on which the application is made, and

(b) confirm, amend or revoke the decision, determination or requirement before the expiry of the period of 28 days beginning with the day on which the application is made.

(5) A person mentioned in subsection (2) may, before the expiry of the period of 14 days beginning with the day on which the decision, determination or requirement is made, appeal to the sheriff against—

(a) a determination of the Accountant in Bankruptcy under section 17C(3) or 17E(5)(b),

(b) a decision of the Accountant in Bankruptcy under subsection (4)(b),

(6) Any decision of the sheriff on an appeal relating to a determination of the Accountant in Bankruptcy under section 17C(3) or 17E(5)(b) is final.

(7) In upholding an appeal relating to a decision under section 17C(1) or the sheriff may quash the decision of the Accountant in Bankruptcy and remit the case, together with reasons for the sheriff's decision, to the Accountant in Bankruptcy.]

NOTES

Commencement: 1 April 2015 (sub-ss (1)–(6)); to be appointed (sub-s (7)).

Inserted as noted to s 17A at **[5.39]**.

Repealed as noted at the beginning of this Act.

[Initial stages of sequestration]

NOTES

Cross-heading: substituted for original words "Period between award of sequestration and statutory meeting of creditors" by the Bankruptcy and Diligence etc (Scotland) Act 2007, s 36, Sch 1, paras 1, 16(1), (7), subject to transitional provisions and savings in SSI 2008/115, arts 5–7, 10, 15 at **[2.51]–[2.53]**, **[2.56]**, **[2.57]**.

[5.46]

18 Interim preservation of estate

(1) The interim trustee may[, in pursuance of the function conferred on him by section 2(6A) of this Act,] give general or particular directions to the debtor relating to the management of the debtor's estate.

(2) In exercising the [function] conferred on him by section [2(6A)] of this Act, an interim trustee may—

(a) require the debtor to deliver up to him any money or valuables, or any document relating to the debtor's business or financial affairs, belonging to or in the possession of the debtor or under his control;

(b) place in safe custody anything mentioned in paragraph (a) above;

(c) require the debtor to deliver up to him any perishable goods belonging to the debtor or under his control and may arrange for the sale or disposal of such goods;

(d) make or cause to be made an inventory or valuation of any property belonging to the debtor;

(e) require the debtor to implement any transaction entered into by the debtor;

(f) effect or maintain insurance policies in respect of the business or property of the debtor;

(g) . . .

[(h) carry on any business of the debtor or borrow money in so far as it is necessary for the interim trustee to do so to safeguard the debtor's estate.]

[(2A) Section 43 of this Act applies to an interim trustee as it applies to a trustee.]

(3) The [sheriff], on the application of the interim trustee, may—

(a) . . .

(b) on cause shown, grant a warrant authorising the interim trustee to enter the house where the debtor resides or his business premises and to search for and take possession of anything mentioned in paragraphs (a) and (c) of subsection (2) above, if need be by opening shut and lock-fast places; or

(c) make such other order to safeguard the debtor's estate as [he] thinks appropriate.

[(3A) Where the Accountant in Bankruptcy is the interim trustee, the debtor may apply to the Accountant in Bankruptcy for a review of a direction under subsection (1) on the ground that the direction is unreasonable.

(3B) If an application under subsection (3A) is made, the Accountant in Bankruptcy must—

(a) take into account any representations made by an interested person before the expiry of the period of 21 days beginning with the day on which the application is made, and

(b) confirm, amend or revoke the direction (whether or not substituting a new direction) before the expiry of the period of 28 days beginning with the day on which the application is made.

(3C) The sheriff may, on an application by the debtor made before the expiry of the period of 14 days beginning with the day on which the Accountant in Bankruptcy makes a decision under subsection (3B)(b)—

(a) set aside a direction under subsection (1) or (3B)(b) if the sheriff considers it to be unreasonable, and

(b) in any event, give such directions to the debtor regarding the management of the debtor's estate as the sheriff considers appropriate.

(3D) The debtor must comply with a direction—

(a) under subsection (1) pending a decision by the Accountant in Bankruptcy under subsection (3B)(b),

(b) under subsection (3B)(b) pending the final determination of any appeal (subject to any interim order of the sheriff).]

(4) [Where the Accountant in Bankruptcy is not the interim trustee,] the [sheriff], on an application by the debtor on the grounds that a direction under subsection (1) above is unreasonable, may—

(a) if [he] considers the direction to be unreasonable, set aside the direction; and

(b) in any event, give such directions to the debtor regarding the management of his estate as [he] considers appropriate;

but, subject to any interim order of the [sheriff], the debtor shall comply with the direction appealed against pending the final determination of the appeal.

(5) The debtor shall be guilty of an offence if—

(a) he fails without reasonable excuse to comply with—

(i) a direction under subsection (1)[, (3B)(b), (3C)(b)] or (4)(b) above; or
(ii) a requirement under subsection (2)(a), (c) or (e) above; or
(b) he obstructs the interim trustee where the interim trustee is acting in pursuance of subsection (3)(b) above.

(6) A person convicted of an offence under subsection (5) above shall be liable—
(a) on summary conviction to a fine not exceeding the statutory maximum or—
(i) to imprisonment for a term not exceeding 3 months; or
(ii) if he has previously been convicted of an offence inferring dishonest appropriation of property or an attempt at such appropriation, to imprisonment for a term not exceeding 6 months,

or (in the case of either sub-paragraph) to both such fine and such imprisonment; or
(b) on conviction on indictment to a fine or to imprisonment for a term not exceeding 2 years or to both.

NOTES

Repealed as noted at the beginning of this Act.

Sub-s (1): words in square brackets inserted by the Bankruptcy and Diligence etc (Scotland) Act 2007, s 36, Sch 1, paras 1, 16(1), (2), subject to transitional provisions and savings in SSI 2008/115, arts 5–7, 10, 15 at **[2.51]–[2.53]**, **[2.56]**, **[2.57]**.

Sub-s (2): word in first pair of square brackets substituted for original word "functions", figure in second pair of square brackets substituted for figure "2(4)(a)" (as previously substituted by the Bankruptcy (Scotland) Act 1993, s 11(3), Sch 1, para 6), and para (g) repealed by the Bankruptcy and Diligence etc (Scotland) Act 2007, ss 36, 226(2), Sch 1, paras 1, 16(1), (3), Sch 6, Pt 1, subject to transitional provisions and savings in SSI 2008/115, arts 5–7, 10, 15 at **[2.51]–[2.53]**, **[2.56]**, **[2.57]**. Para (g) previously read as follows:

"(g) close down the debtor's business;";

para (h) inserted by the Bankruptcy (Scotland) Act 1993, s 11(3), Sch 1, para 6, subject to s 12(6) thereof, at **[5.194]** and to the Bankruptcy (Scotland) Act 1993 Commencement and Savings Order 1993, SI 1993/438, arts 4, 5, at **[16.58]**, **[16.59]**.

Sub-s (2A): inserted by the Bankruptcy and Diligence etc (Scotland) Act 2007, s 36, Sch 1, paras 1, 16(1), (4), subject to transitional provisions and savings in SSI 2008/115, arts 5–7, 10, 15 at **[2.51]–[2.53]**, **[2.56]**, **[2.57]**.

Sub-s (3): words "sheriff" and "he" in square brackets substituted for original words "court" and "it" respectively by the Bankruptcy and Diligence etc (Scotland) Act 2007, s 36, Sch 1, paras 1, 16(1), (5), subject to transitional provisions and savings in SSI 2008/115, arts 5–7, 10, 15 at **[2.51]–[2.53]**, **[2.56]**, **[2.57]**; para (a) repealed by the Bankruptcy (Scotland) Act 1993, s 11(4), Sch 2, subject to s 12(6) thereof, at **[5.194]** and to SI 1993/438, arts 4, 5, at **[16.58]**, **[16.59]**.

Sub-ss (3A)–(3D): inserted by the Bankruptcy and Debt Advice (Scotland) Act 2014, s 38(3)(a), subject to transitional provisions and savings in SSI 2014/261, arts 10, 12 at **[2.97]**, **[2.99]**.

Sub-s (4): words in first pair of square brackets inserted by the Bankruptcy and Debt Advice (Scotland) Act 2014, s 38(3)(b), subject to transitional provisions and savings in SSI 2014/261, arts 10, 12 at **[2.97]**, **[2.99]**; words "sheriff" and "he" in square brackets substituted for original words "court" and "it" respectively by the Bankruptcy and Diligence etc (Scotland) Act 2007, s 36, Sch 1, paras 1, 16(1), (6), subject to transitional provisions and savings in SSI 2008/115, arts 5–7, 10, 15 at **[2.51]–[2.53]**, **[2.56]**, **[2.57]**.

Sub-s (5): words in square brackets inserted by the Bankruptcy and Debt Advice (Scotland) Act 2014, s 38(3)(c), subject to transitional provisions and savings in SSI 2014/261, arts 10, 12 at **[2.97]**, **[2.99]**.

[5.47]

[19 Statement of assets and liabilities etc

(1) Where the [debtor has made a debtor application] he shall, not later than 7 days after the appointment of the [trustee under section 2 of this Act] (where he is not the Accountant in Bankruptcy), send to the . . . trustee such statement of assets and liabilities as was [sent to the Accountant in Bankruptcy in pursuance of section 5(6A)] of this Act.

(2) Where the petitioner for sequestration is a creditor or a trustee acting under a trust deed, the debtor shall, not later than 7 days after having been notified by the . . . trustee as mentioned in section [2(7)(a)] of this Act, send to the . . . trustee a statement of assets and liabilities.

(3) If the debtor—
(a) fails to send to the . . . trustee in accordance with subsection (1) or (2) above such statement of assets and liabilities; or
(b) fails to disclose any material fact in [a statement of assets and liabilities sent to the trustee in accordance with subsection (1) or (2)]; or
(c) makes a material misstatement in such statement of assets and liabilities,

he shall be guilty of an offence and liable on summary conviction to a fine not exceeding level 5 on the standard scale or to imprisonment for a term not exceeding 3 months or to both such fine and imprisonment.

(4) In any proceedings for an offence under subsection (3) above, it shall be a defence for the accused to show that he had a reasonable excuse for—
(a) failing to send to the . . . trustee in accordance with subsection (1) or (2) above such statement of assets and liabilities; or
(b) failing to disclose a material fact; or
(c) making a material misstatement.]

NOTES

Repealed as noted at the beginning of this Act.

Substituted by the Bankruptcy (Scotland) Act 1993, s 11(3), Sch 1, para 7, subject to s 12(6) thereof, at **[5.194]** and to the Bankruptcy (Scotland) Act 1993 Commencement and Savings Order 1993, SI 1993/438, arts 4, 5, at **[16.58]**, **[16.59]**.

Sub-s (1): words in first pair of square brackets substituted for original words "petitioner for sequestration is the debtor", words in second pair of square brackets substituted for original words "interim trustee", word "interim" (omitted) repealed, and words in third pair of square brackets substituted for original words "lodged in court in pursuance of section 5(6A)(a)" by the

Bankruptcy and Diligence etc (Scotland) Act 2007, ss 36, 226(2), Sch 1, paras 1, 17(1), (2), Sch 6, Pt 1, subject to transitional provisions and savings in SSI 2008/115, arts 5–7, 10, 15 at **[2.51]–[2.53]**, **[2.56]**, **[2.57]**.

Sub-s (2): word "interim" omitted in both places repealed, and figure in square brackets substituted for original figure "2(7)" by the Bankruptcy and Diligence etc (Scotland) Act 2007, ss 36, 226(2), Sch 1, paras 1, 17(1), (3), Sch 6, Pt 1, subject to transitional provisions and savings in SSI 2008/115, arts 5–7, 10, 15 at **[2.51]–[2.53]**, **[2.56]**, **[2.57]**.

Sub-s (3): word "interim" omitted repealed by the Bankruptcy and Diligence etc (Scotland) Act 2007, s 226(2), Sch 6, Pt 1, subject to transitional provisions and savings in SSI 2008/115, arts 5–7, 10, 15 at **[2.51]–[2.53]**, **[2.56]**, **[2.57]**; para (a) repealed and words in square brackets in para (b) substituted for original words "such statement of assets and liabilities" by the Bankruptcy and Debt Advice (Scotland) Act 2014, s 45(2)(a), subject to transitional provisions and savings in SSI 2014/261, arts 4, 12 at **[2.91]**, **[2.99]**.

Sub-s (4): word "interim" omitted repealed by the Bankruptcy and Diligence etc (Scotland) Act 2007, s 226(2), Sch 6, Pt 1, subject to transitional provisions and savings in SSI 2008/115, arts 5–7, 10, 15 at **[2.51]–[2.53]**, **[2.56]**, **[2.57]**; para (a) repealed by the Bankruptcy and Debt Advice (Scotland) Act 2014, s 45(2)(b), subject to transitional provisions and savings in SSI 2014/261, arts 4, 12 at **[2.91]**, **[2.99]**.

Regulations: the Bankruptcy (Scotland) Regulations 2008, SSI 2008/82 at **[16.262]**; the Bankruptcy (Scotland) Regulations 2014, SSI 2014/225 at **[16.267]**.

[5.48]

20 Trustee's duties on receipt of list of assets and liabilities

[(1) When the . . . trustee has received the statement of assets and liabilities, he shall, as soon as practicable, prepare a statement of the debtor's affairs so far as within the knowledge of the . . . trustee and [if], in his opinion, the debtor's assets are unlikely to be sufficient to pay any dividend whatsoever in respect of the debts mentioned in paragraphs (e) to (h) of section 51(1) of this Act [the trustee is so to indicate in the statement of the debtor's affairs].]

(2) The . . . trustee shall, not later than 4 days before the date fixed for the statutory meeting [or, where the trustee does not intend to hold such a meeting, not later than 60 days after the date on which sequestration is awarded,] send to the Accountant in Bankruptcy—

- (a) [the statement] of assets and liabilities [(unless the statement has already been received by the Accountant in Bankruptcy by virtue of section 5(6A) of this Act)]; and
- (b) [subject to subsection (2A) below,] a copy of the . . . statement of the debtor's affairs; and
- (c) written comments by the . . . trustee indicating what in his opinion are the causes of the insolvency and to what extent the conduct of the debtor may have contributed to the insolvency.

[(2A) The trustee need not send a statement of the debtor's affairs to the Accountant in Bankruptcy in accordance with subsection (2)(b) above if the trustee has sent a copy of the inventory and valuation to the Accountant in Bankruptcy in accordance with section 38(1)(c) of this Act.]

(3) The written comments made under subsection (2)(c) above shall be absolutely privileged.

(4), (5) . . .

[(5A) Subsections (2) and (3) above do not apply in any case where the Accountant in Bankruptcy is the . . . trustee.]

NOTES

Repealed as noted at the beginning of this Act.

Sub-s (1): substituted by the Bankruptcy (Scotland) Act 1993, s 11(3), Sch 1, para 8(1), (2), subject to s 12(6) thereof, at **[5.194]** and to the Bankruptcy (Scotland) Act 1993 Commencement and Savings Order 1993, SI 1993/438, arts 4, 5, at **[16.58]**, **[16.59]**; word "interim" omitted in both places repealed by the Bankruptcy and Diligence etc (Scotland) Act 2007, s 226(2), Sch 6, Pt 1, subject to transitional provisions and savings in SSI 2008/115, arts 5–7, 10, 15 at **[2.51]–[2.53]**, **[2.56]**, **[2.57]**; word in first pair of square brackets substituted for original words "shall indicate in the statement of the debtor's affairs whether" and words in second pair of square brackets inserted, by the Bankruptcy and Debt Advice (Scotland) Act 2014, s 56(1), Sch 3, paras 2, 15, subject to transitional provisions and savings in SSI 2014/261, arts 4, 12 at **[2.91]**, **[2.99]**.

Sub-s (2): word "interim" omitted in first and third places repealed and words in first, third and fourth pairs of square brackets inserted by the Bankruptcy and Diligence etc (Scotland) Act 2007, ss 36, 226(2), Sch 1, paras 1, 18(a), Sch 6, Pt 1, subject to transitional provisions and savings in SSI 2008/115, arts 5–7, 10, 15 at **[2.51]–[2.53]**, **[2.56]**, **[2.57]**; words in second pair of square brackets substituted, and second words omitted repealed, by the Bankruptcy (Scotland) Act 1993, s 11(3), (4), Sch 1, para 8(1), (3), Sch 2, subject to s 12(6) thereof, at **[5.194]** and to SI 1993/438, arts 4, 5, at **[16.58]**, **[16.59]**.

Sub-s (2A): inserted by the Bankruptcy and Diligence etc (Scotland) Act 2007, s 36, Sch 1, paras 1, 18(b), subject to transitional provisions and savings in SSI 2008/115, arts 5–7, 10, 15 at **[2.51]–[2.53]**, **[2.56]**, **[2.57]**.

Sub-ss (4), (5): repealed by the Bankruptcy and Diligence etc (Scotland) Act 2007, s 226(2), Sch 6, Pt 1, subject to transitional provisions and savings in SSI 2008/115, arts 5–7, 10, 15 at **[2.51]–[2.53]**, **[2.56]**, **[2.57]**, and prior to this repeal (as amended by the Civil Partnership Act 2004, s 261(2), Sch 28, para 33) read as follows:

"(4) The interim trustee may request—

- (a) the debtor to appear before him and to give information relating to his assets, his dealings with them or his conduct in relation to his business or financial affairs; or
- (b) the debtor's spouse [or civil partner] or any other person who the interim trustee believes can give such information to give that information,

and if the interim trustee considers it necessary he may apply to the sheriff for an order requiring the debtor, spouse[, civil partner] or other person to appear before the sheriff for private examination.

(5) Subsections (2) to (4) of section 44 and sections 46 and 47 of this Act shall apply, subject to any necessary modifications, in respect of private examination under subsection (4) above as they apply in respect of private examination under the said subsection (2).".

Sub-s (5A): added by the Bankruptcy (Scotland) Act 1993, s 11(3), Sch 1, para 8(1), (4), subject to s 12(6) thereof, at **[5.194]** and to SI 1993/438, arts 4, 5, at **[16.58]**, **[16.59]**; word "interim" (omitted) repealed by the Bankruptcy and Diligence etc (Scotland) Act 2007, s 226(2), Sch 6, Pt 1, subject to transitional provisions and savings in SSI 2008/115, arts 5–7, 10, 15 at **[2.51]–[2.53]**, **[2.56]**, **[2.57]**.

[Statutory meeting of creditors and trustee vote]

NOTES

Cross-heading: substituted for original words "Statutory meeting of creditors and confirmation of permanent trustee" by the Bankruptcy and Diligence etc (Scotland) Act 2007, s 36, Sch 1, paras 1, 19, subject to transitional provisions and savings in SSI 2008/115, arts 5–7, 10, 15 at **[2.51]–[2.53]**, **[2.56]**, **[2.57]**.

[5.49]

[20A Statutory meeting

A meeting of creditors called by the . . . trustee under section . . . 21A of this Act shall, in this Act, be referred to as "the statutory meeting".]

NOTES

Repealed as noted at the beginning of this Act.

Inserted by the Bankruptcy (Scotland) Act 1993, s 11(3), Sch 1, para 9, subject to s 12(6) thereof, at **[5.194]** and to the Bankruptcy (Scotland) Act 1993 Commencement and Savings Order 1993, SI 1993/438, arts 4, 5, at **[16.58]**, **[16.59]**; words "interim" and "21 or" (omitted) repealed by the Bankruptcy and Diligence etc (Scotland) Act 2007, s 226(2), Sch 6, Pt 1, subject to transitional provisions and savings in SSI 2008/115, arts 5–7, 10, 15 at **[2.51]–[2.53]**, **[2.56]**, **[2.57]**.

[5.50]

21 Calling of statutory meeting

(1) [Where the interim trustee is not the Accountant in Bankruptcy he shall call the statutory meeting] to be held within [60 days], or such longer period as the sheriff on cause shown may allow, after the date of the award of sequestration.

[(1A) The statutory meeting shall be held at such time and place as the interim trustee determines.]

(2) Not less than 7 days before the date fixed for the statutory meeting, the interim trustee shall notify—

(a) every creditor known to him; and

(b) the Accountancy in Bankruptcy,

of the date, time and place of the meeting, and shall in the notification to creditors invite the submission of such claims as have not already been submitted and inform them of his duties under section 23(3) and (5) of this Act.

(3) The creditors may continue the statutory meeting to a date not later than 7 days after the end of the period—

(a) of [60 days] mentioned in subsection (1) above; or (as the case may be),

(b) allowed by the sheriff under that subsection.

[(4) This section does not apply in any case where the Accountant in Bankruptcy is the interim trustee.]

NOTES

Repealed as noted at the beginning of this Act.

Repealed by the Bankruptcy and Diligence etc (Scotland) Act 2007, s 11(1), subject to transitional provisions and savings in SSI 2008/115, arts 5–7, 10, 15 at **[2.51]–[2.53]**, **[2.56]**, **[2.57]**.

Sub-s (1): words in first pair of square brackets substituted by the Bankruptcy (Scotland) Act 1993, s 11(3), Sch 1, para 10(1), (2), subject to s 12(6) thereof, at **[5.194]** and to the Bankruptcy (Scotland) Act 1993 Commencement and Savings Order 1993, SI 1993/438, arts 4, 5, at **[16.58]**, **[16.59]**; words in second pair of square brackets substituted by the Bankruptcy (Scotland) Regulations 1985, SI 1985/1925, reg 15 (as inserted by SI 1993/439, reg 5).

Sub-ss (1A), (4): inserted by the Bankruptcy (Scotland) Act 1993, s 11(3), Sch 1, para 10(1), (3), (4), subject to s 12(6) thereof, at **[5.194]** and to SI 1993/438, arts 4, 5, at **[16.58]**, **[16.59]**.

Sub-s (3): words in square brackets in para (a) substituted by SI 1985/1925, reg 15 (as inserted by SI 1993/439, reg 5).

[5.51]

[21A [Calling of statutory meeting]

(1) Subject to subsections (5) and (6) below, . . . the statutory meeting may be held at such time and place as the . . . trustee may determine.

(2) Not later than 60 days after the date [on which sequestration is awarded], or such longer period as the sheriff may on cause shown allow, the . . . trustee shall give notice to every creditor known to him of whether he intends to call the statutory meeting.

(3) A notice given under subsection (2) above shall—

(a) be accompanied by a copy of the . . . trustee's statement of the debtor's affairs; and

(b) where the . . . trustee is notifying his intention not to hold the statutory meeting, inform creditors—

(i) of the effect of subsections (4) and (5) below; . . .

(ii) . . .

(4) Within 7 days of the giving of notice under subsection (2) above, any creditor may request the . . . trustee to call the statutory meeting.

(5) Where a request or requests under subsection (4) above are made by not less than one quarter in value of the debtor's creditors, the . . . trustee shall call the statutory meeting not later than 28 days, or such other period as the sheriff may on cause shown allow, after the giving of notice under subsection (2) above.

(6) Where the . . . trustee gives notice under subsection (2) above that he intends to call the statutory meeting, such meeting shall be called not later than 28 days after the giving of such notice.

(7) Not less than 7 days before the date fixed for the statutory meeting, the . . . trustee shall notify every creditor known to him of the date, time and place of the meeting, and shall in such notice invite the submission of such claims as have not already been submitted and inform them of his duties under section 23(3) of this Act.

(8) The creditors may continue the statutory meeting to a date not later than 7 days after the end of the period mentioned in subsection (6) above or such longer period as the sheriff may on cause shown allow.
(9) . . .]

NOTES

Inserted, together with s 21B, by the Bankruptcy (Scotland) Act 1993, s 5, subject to s 12(6) thereof, at **[5.194]** and to the Bankruptcy (Scotland) Act 1993 Commencement and Savings Order 1993, SI 1993/438, arts 4, 5, at **[16.58]**, **[16.59]**.

Repealed as noted at the beginning of this Act.

Section heading: words substituted for original words "Calling of statutory meeting where interim trustee is Accountant in Bankruptcy" by the Bankruptcy and Diligence etc (Scotland) Act 2007, s 11(2)(b), subject to transitional provisions and savings in SSI 2008/115, arts 5–7, 10, 15 at **[2.51]–[2.53]**, **[2.56]**, **[2.57]**.

Sub-s (1): words "where the interim trustee is the Accountant in Bankruptcy" and "interim" (omitted) repealed by the Bankruptcy and Diligence etc (Scotland) Act 2007, ss 11(2)(a), 226(2), Sch 6, Pt 1, subject to transitional provisions and savings in SSI 2008/115, arts 5–7, 10, 15 at **[2.51]–[2.53]**, **[2.56]**, **[2.57]**.

Sub-s (2): words in square brackets substituted for original words "of the sequestration" and word "interim" repealed by the Bankruptcy and Diligence etc (Scotland) Act 2007, ss 36, 226(2), Sch 1, paras 1, 20, Sch 6, Pt 1, subject to transitional provisions and savings in SSI 2008/115, arts 5–7, 10, 15 at **[2.51]–[2.53]**, **[2.56]**, **[2.57]**.

Sub-s (3): word "interim" omitted in first and second places, and para (b)(ii) and word "and" immediately preceding it repealed by the Bankruptcy and Diligence etc (Scotland) Act 2007, ss 28(1), (2), 226(2), Sch 6, Pt 1, subject to transitional provisions and savings in SSI 2008/115, arts 5–7, 10, 15 at **[2.51]–[2.53]**, **[2.56]**, **[2.57]**. Para (b)(ii) previously read as follows:

"(ii) whether he intends to apply for the grant of a certificate for the summary administration of the sequestration of the debtor's estate.".

Sub-ss (4)–(7): word "interim" omitted in each place repealed by the Bankruptcy and Diligence etc (Scotland) Act 2007, s 226(2), Sch 6, Pt 1, subject to transitional provisions and savings in SSI 2008/115, arts 5–7, 10, 15 at **[2.51]–[2.53]**, **[2.56]**, **[2.57]**.

Sub-s (9): repealed by the Bankruptcy and Diligence etc (Scotland) Act 2007, s 226(2), Sch 6, Pt 1, subject to transitional provisions and savings in SSI 2008/115, arts 5–7, 10, 15 at **[2.51]–[2.53]**, **[2.56]**, **[2.57]**, and previously read as follows:

"(9) This section applies in any case where the Accountant in Bankruptcy is the interim trustee.".

[5.52]
[21B Procedure where no statutory meeting called

(1) Where the . . . trustee does not call the statutory meeting and the period mentioned in section 21A(4) of this Act has expired, he shall—
 (a) forthwith make a report to the [Accountant in Bankruptcy] on the circumstances of the sequestration; . . .
 (b) . . .

[(1A) This section does not apply in any case where the Accountant in Bankruptcy is the trustee.]
(2) . . .]

NOTES

Inserted as noted to s 21A at **[5.51]**.

Repealed as noted at the beginning of this Act.

Sub-s (1): word "interim" omitted in the first place repealed, words in square brackets in para (a) substituted for original word "sheriff", and para (b) and word "and" immediately preceding it repealed by the Bankruptcy and Diligence etc (Scotland) Act 2007, ss 36, 226(2), Sch 1, paras 1, 21(a), Sch 6, Pt 1, subject to transitional provisions and savings in SSI 2008/115, arts 5–7, 10, 15 at **[2.51]–[2.53]**, **[2.56]**, **[2.57]**. Para (b) previously read as follows:

"(b) provide to the sheriff a copy of the interim trustee's statement of the debtor's affairs.".

Sub-s (1A): inserted by the Bankruptcy and Diligence etc (Scotland) Act 2007, ss 36, Sch 1, paras 1, 21(b), subject to transitional provisions and savings in SSI 2008/115, arts 5–7, 10, 15 at **[2.51]–[2.53]**, **[2.56]**, **[2.57]**.

Sub-s (2): repealed by the Bankruptcy and Diligence etc (Scotland) Act 2007, s 226(2), Sch 6, Pt 1, subject to transitional provisions and savings in SSI 2008/115, arts 5–7, 10, 15 at **[2.51]–[2.53]**, **[2.56]**, **[2.57]**, and previously read as follows:

"(2) In the case of a sequestration which falls within subsection (1) above—
 (a) section 25A of this Act shall apply; and
 (b) the interim trustee may apply to the sheriff for the grant of a certificate for the summary administration of the sequestration of the debtor's estate.".

[5.53]
22 Submission of claims for voting purposes at statutory meeting

(1) For the purposes of voting at the statutory meeting, a creditor shall submit a claim in accordance with this section to the . . . trustee at or before the meeting.
(2) A creditor shall submit a claim under this section by producing to the . . . trustee—
 (a) a statement of claim in the prescribed form; and
 (b) an account or voucher (according to the nature of the debt) which constitutes *prima facie* evidence of the debt:

Provided that the . . . trustee may dispense with any requirement under this subsection in respect of any debt or any class of debt.
(3) Where a creditor neither resides nor has a place of business in the United Kingdom, the . . . trustee—
 (a) shall, if he knows where the creditor resides or has a place of business and if no notification has been given to that creditor under section [21A(2)] of this Act, write to him informing him that he may submit a claim under this section;

(b) may allow the creditor to submit an informal claim in writing.

(4) A creditor who has produced a statement of claim in accordance with subsection (2) above may at any time before the statutory meeting produce in place of that statement of claim another such statement of claim specifying a different amount for his claim.

(5) If a creditor produces under this section a statement of claim, account, voucher or other evidence which is false—

(a) the creditor shall be guilty of an offence unless he shows that he neither knew nor had reason to believe that the statement of claim, account, voucher or other evidence was false;

(b) the debtor shall be guilty of an offence if he—

(i) knew or became aware that the statement of claim, account, voucher or other evidence was false; and

(ii) failed as soon as practicable after acquiring such knowledge to report it to the . . . trustee . . .

(6) A creditor may, in such circumstances as may be prescribed, state the amount of his claim in foreign currency.

(7) The . . . trustee shall, on production of any document to him under this section, initial the document and keep a record of it stating the date when it was produced to him, and, if requested by the sender, shall return it (if it is not a statement of claim) to him.

(8) The submission of a claim under this section shall bar the effect of any enactment or rule of law relating to the limitation of actions in any part of the United Kingdom.

(9) Schedule 1 to this Act shall have effect for determining the amount in respect of which a creditor shall be entitled to claim.

(10) A person convicted of an offence under subsection (5) above shall be liable—

(a) on summary conviction to a fine not exceeding the statutory maximum or—

(i) to imprisonment for a term not exceeding 3 months; or

(ii) if he has previously been convicted of an offence inferring dishonest appropriation of property or an attempt at such appropriation, to imprisonment for a term not exceeding 6 months,

or (in the case of either sub-paragraph) to both such fine and such imprisonment; or

(b) on conviction on indictment to a fine or to imprisonment for a term not exceeding 2 years or to both.

NOTES

Repealed as noted at the beginning of this Act.

Sub-ss (1), (2), (7): word "interim" omitted in each place repealed by the Bankruptcy and Diligence etc (Scotland) Act 2007, s 226(2), Sch 6, Pt 1, subject to transitional provisions and savings in SSI 2008/115, arts 5–7, 10, 15 at **[2.51]–[2.53]**, **[2.56]**, **[2.57]**.

Sub-s (3): word "interim" (omitted) repealed and figure in square brackets in para (a) substituted for original figure "21(2)" by the Bankruptcy and Diligence etc (Scotland) Act 2007, ss 36, 226(2), Sch 1, paras 1, 22, Sch 6, Pt 1, subject to transitional provisions and savings in SSI 2008/115, arts 5–7, 10, 15 at **[2.51]–[2.53]**, **[2.56]**, **[2.57]**.

Sub-s (5): words "interim" and "or permanent trustee" omitted respectively from para (b)(ii), repealed by the Bankruptcy and Diligence etc (Scotland) Act 2007, s 226(2), Sch 6, Pt 1, subject to transitional provisions and savings in SSI 2008/115, arts 5–7, 10, 15 at **[2.51]–[2.53]**, **[2.56]**, **[2.57]**.

Regulations: the Bankruptcy (Scotland) Regulations 2008, SSI 2008/82 at **[16.262]**; the Bankruptcy (Scotland) Regulations 2014, SSI 2014/225 at **[16.267]**.

[5.54]

23 [Proceedings at statutory meeting before trustee vote]

(1) At the commencement of the statutory meeting, the chairman shall be the . . . trustee who as chairman shall—

(a) for the purposes of subsection (2) below, accept or reject in whole or in part the claim of each creditor, and, if the amount of a claim is stated in foreign currency, he shall convert that amount into sterling, in such manner as may be prescribed, at the rate of exchange prevailing at the close of business on the date of sequestration;

(b) invite the creditors thereupon to elect one of their number as chairman in his place and shall preside over the election:

Provided that if a chairman is not elected in pursuance of this paragraph, the . . . trustee shall remain the chairman throughout the meeting; and

(c) arrange for a record to be made of the proceedings at the meeting.

(2) The acceptance of a claim in whole or in part under subsection (1) above shall, subject to section 24(3) of this Act, determine the entitlement of a creditor to vote at the statutory meeting.

(3) On the conclusion of the proceedings under subsection (1) above, the . . . trustee—

[(a) shall make available for inspection—

(i) the statement of assets and liabilities; and

(ii) his statement of the debtor's affairs prepared under section 20(1) of this Act;]

(b) shall answer to the best of his ability any questions, and shall consider any representations, put to him by the creditors relating to the debtor's assets, business or financial affairs or his conduct in relation thereto;

[(c) after considering any such representations as are mentioned in paragraph (b), shall, if in the interim trustee's opinion the debtor's assets are unlikely to be sufficient to pay any dividend whatsoever in respect of the debts mentioned in paragraphs (e) to (h) of section 51(1), so indicate;] and [(d) shall determine whether it is necessary to revise his statement of the debtor's affairs and, if he determines that it is necessary to revise the statement, he shall do so either at, or as soon as possible after, the statutory meeting.]

(4) . . .

[(5) Where the . . . trustee has revised his statement of the debtor's affairs, he shall, as soon as possible after the statutory meeting, send a copy of the revised statement to every creditor known to him.]

NOTES

Repealed as noted at the beginning of this Act.

Section heading: words substituted for original words "Proceedings at statutory meeting before election of permanent trustee" by the Bankruptcy and Diligence etc (Scotland) Act 2007, s 11(3), subject to transitional provisions and savings in SSI 2008/115, arts 5–7, 10, 15 at **[2.51]–[2.53]**, **[2.56]**, **[2.57]**.

Sub-s (1): word "interim" omitted in both places repealed by the Bankruptcy and Diligence etc (Scotland) Act 2007, s 226(2), Sch 6, Pt 1, subject to transitional provisions and savings in SSI 2008/115, arts 5–7, 10, 15 at **[2.51]–[2.53]**, **[2.56]**, **[2.57]**.

Sub-s (3): word "interim" (omitted) repealed by the Bankruptcy and Diligence etc (Scotland) Act 2007, s 226(2), Sch 6, Pt 1, subject to transitional provisions and savings in SSI 2008/115, arts 5–7, 10, 15 at **[2.51]–[2.53]**, **[2.56]**, **[2.57]**; paras (a), (d) substituted by the Bankruptcy (Scotland) Act 1993, s 11(3), Sch 1, para 11(1), (2), subject to s 12(6) thereof, at **[5.194]** and to the Bankruptcy (Scotland) Act 1993 Commencement and Savings Order 1993, SI 1993/438, arts 4, 5, at **[16.58]**, **[16.59]**; para (c) substituted by the Bankruptcy and Debt Advice (Scotland) Act 2014, s 56(1), Sch 3, paras 2, 16, subject to transitional provisions and savings in SSI 2014/261, arts 4, 12 at **[2.91]**, **[2.99]**, and previously read as follows—

"(c) shall, after considering any such representations as are mentioned in paragraph (b) above, indicate whether, in his opinion, the debtor's assets are unlikely to be sufficient as mentioned in section 20(1) of this Act;".

Sub-s (4): repealed by the Bankruptcy (Scotland) Act 1993, s 11(4), Sch 2, subject to s 12(6) thereof, at **[5.194]** and to SI 1993/438, arts 4, 5, at **[16.58]**, **[16.59]**.

Sub-s (5): substituted by the Bankruptcy (Scotland) Act 1993, s 11(3), Sch 1, para 11(1), (3), subject to s 12(6) thereof, at **[5.194]** and to SI 1993/438, arts 4, 5, at **[16.58]**, **[16.59]**; word "interim" (omitted) repealed by the Bankruptcy and Diligence etc (Scotland) Act 2007, s 226(2), Sch 6, Pt 1, subject to transitional provisions and savings in SSI 2008/115, arts 5–7, 10, 15 at **[2.51]–[2.53]**, **[2.56]**, **[2.57]**.

Regulations: the Bankruptcy (Scotland) Regulations 2008, SSI 2008/82 at **[16.262]**; the Bankruptcy (Scotland) Regulations 2014, SSI 2014/225 at **[16.267]**.

[5.55]

[23A ***Summary administration***

(1) Where an application is made to the court under this Act for the grant of a certificate for the summary administration of the sequestration of the debtor's estate, the court shall, subject to subsection (9) below, grant such a certificate where it appears to the court that—

(a) the aggregate amount of the debtor's liabilities does not exceed £20,000; and

(b) the aggregate amount of the debtor's assets does not exceed £2,000.

(2) In calculating—

(a) the aggregate amount of the debtor's liabilities under paragraph (a) of subsection (1) above, no account shall be taken of any debt to the extent that a creditor holds a security for that debt; and

(b) the aggregate amount of the debtor's assets under paragraph (b) of that subsection, no account shall be taken of—

(i) any heritable property of his; or

(ii) any property of his which, under section 33(1) of this Act, does not vest in the permanent trustee.

(3) For the purposes of an application under subsection (1) above made by—

(a) the Accountant in Bankruptcy; or

(b) an interim trustee who is not the Accountant in Bankruptcy,

a certificate by the Accountant in Bankruptcy or, as the case may be, the interim trustee as to the aggregate amounts of the debtor's liabilities and assets shall be sufficient evidence of such aggregate amounts.

(4) Where a certificate for the summary administration of the sequestration of the debtor's estate is granted—

(a) in any case where the application for the certificate was made by the Accountant in Bankruptcy, section 25A of this Act; and

(b) in every case, Schedule 2A to this Act (which modifies the duties of the permanent trustee),

shall apply to the sequestration.

(5) The debtor, a creditor, the permanent trustee or the Accountant in Bankruptcy may, at any time, apply to the sheriff to withdraw the certificate for the summary administration of the sequestration of the debtor's estate.

(6) Where an application is made under subsection (5) above by a person who is not the permanent trustee, the applicant shall send a copy of the application to the permanent trustee who shall prepare and present to the sheriff a report on all of the circumstances of the sequestration.

(7) If it appears to the sheriff, on considering an application under subsection (5) above and any report under subsection (6) above, that it is no longer appropriate for the sequestration to be subject to summary administration, he shall withdraw the certificate and the sequestration of the estate shall proceed as if the certificate had not been granted.

(8) The sheriff clerk shall send to the permanent trustee and, where he is not the permanent trustee, the Accountant in Bankruptcy a copy of the sheriff's decision on any application under subsection (5) above.

(9) The court shall not grant an application as mentioned in subsection (1) above—

(a) in any case where the application is made by the Accountant in Bankruptcy and the court has appointed as interim trustee a person who is not the Accountant in Bankruptcy; or

(b) in any other case—

(i) where a person has been elected as permanent trustee, before the sheriff has confirmed the election of that person as permanent trustee; or

(ii) where no such person has been elected, unless the court at the same time appoints the interim trustee as permanent trustee.]

NOTES

Inserted by the Bankruptcy (Scotland) Act 1993, s 6(1), subject to s 12(6) thereof, at **[5.194]** and to the Bankruptcy (Scotland) Act 1993 Commencement and Savings Order 1993, SI 1993/438, arts 4, 5, at **[16.58]**, **[16.59]**.

Repealed as noted at the beginning of this Act.

Repealed by the Bankruptcy and Diligence etc (Scotland) Act 2007, s 28(1), (3), subject to transitional provisions and savings in SSI 2008/115, arts 5–7, 10, 15 at **[2.51]–[2.53]**, **[2.56]**, **[2.57]**.

[5.56]

24 [Trustee vote]

[(1) At the statutory meeting, the creditors shall, at the conclusion of the proceedings under section 23(3) of this Act, proceed to [a vote at which they shall—

(a) confirm the appointment of the trustee appointed under section 2 of this Act (referred to in this section and in sections 25 to 27 of this Act as the "original trustee"); or

(b) elect another person as the trustee in the sequestration (referred to in this section and in sections 13 and 25 to 29 of this Act as the "replacement trustee"),

such a vote being referred to in this Act as a "trustee vote"].]

(2) None of the following persons shall be eligible for election as [replacement] trustee, nor shall anyone who becomes such a person after having been elected as [replacement] trustee be qualified to continue to act as . . . trustee—

(a) the debtor;

(b) a person who is not qualified to act as an insolvency practitioner or who, though qualified to act as an insolvency practitioner, is not qualified to act as such in relation to the debtor;

(c) a person who holds an interest opposed to the general interests of the creditors;

(d) . . .

[(e) a person who has not given an undertaking, in writing, to act as . . . trustee;

(f) the Accountant in Bankruptcy.]

(3) The following persons shall not be entitled to vote in the [trustee vote]—

(a) anyone acquiring a debt due by the debtor, otherwise than by succession, after the date of sequestration;

(b) any creditor to the extent that his debt is a postponed debt.

[(3A) In any case where the Accountant in Bankruptcy is the [original] trustee, if—

(a) no creditor entitled to vote in the [trustee vote] attends the statutory meeting; or

(b) no [replacement] trustee is elected,

the Accountant in Bankruptcy shall forthwith report the proceedings at the statutory meeting to the sheriff and [shall continue to act as the trustee].

(3B) . . .]

(4) [In any case where the Accountant in Bankruptcy is not the [original] trustee,] if no creditor entitled to vote in the [trustee vote] attends the statutory meeting or if no [replacement] trustee is elected, the [original] trustee shall forthwith—

(a) so notify the Accountant in Bankruptcy; and

(b) report the proceedings at the statutory meeting to the sheriff, . . .

[and he shall continue to act as the trustee].

[(4A) . . .]

(5) . . .

NOTES

Repealed as noted at the beginning of this Act.

Section heading: substituted for original words "Election of permanent trustee" by the Bankruptcy and Diligence etc (Scotland) Act 2007, s 11(4)(b), subject to transitional provisions and savings in SSI 2008/115, arts 5–7, 10, 15 at **[2.51]–[2.53]**, **[2.56]**, **[2.57]**.

Sub-s (1): substituted by the Bankruptcy (Scotland) Act 1993, s 11(3), Sch 1, para 12(1), (2), subject to s 12(6) thereof, at **[5.194]** and to the Bankruptcy (Scotland) Act 1993 Commencement and Savings Order 1993, SI 1993/438, arts 4, 5, at **[16.58]**, **[16.59]**; words in square brackets substituted for original words "the election of the permanent trustee" by the Bankruptcy and Diligence etc (Scotland) Act 2007, s 11(4)(a), subject to transitional provisions and savings in SSI 2008/115, arts 5–7, 10, 15 at **[2.51]–[2.53]**, **[2.56]**, **[2.57]**.

Sub-s (2): word in first and second pairs of square brackets substituted for original word "permanent", word "permanent" omitted in both places and para (d) repealed by the Bankruptcy and Diligence etc (Scotland) Act 2007, ss 7(2), 36, 226(2), Sch 1, paras 1, 23(1), (2), Sch 6, Pt 1, subject to transitional provisions and savings in SSI 2008/115, arts 5–7, 10, 15 at **[2.51]–[2.53]**, **[2.56]**, **[2.57]**, and para (d) previously read as follows:

"(d) a person who resides outwith the jurisdiction of the Court of Session.";

paras (e), (f) inserted by the Bankruptcy (Scotland) Act 1993, s 11(3), Sch 1, para 12(1), (3), subject to s 12(6) thereof, at **[5.194]** and to SI 1993/438, arts 4, 5, at **[16.58]**, **[16.59]**.

Sub-s (3): words in square brackets substituted for original words "election of the permanent trustee" by the Bankruptcy and Diligence etc (Scotland) Act 2007, s 36, Sch 1, paras 1, 23(1), (3), subject to transitional provisions and savings in SSI 2008/115, arts 5–7, 10, 15 at **[2.51]–[2.53]**, **[2.56]**, **[2.57]**.

Sub-s (3A): inserted, together with sub-s (3B), by the Bankruptcy (Scotland) Act 1993, s 11(3), Sch 1, para 12(1), (4), (6), subject to s 12(6) thereof, at **[5.194]** and to SI 1993/438, arts 4, 5, at **[16.58]**, **[16.59]**; word in first pair of square brackets substituted for original word "interim", words in second pair of square brackets substituted for original words "election of the permanent trustee", word in third pair of square brackets substituted for original word "permanent", and words in final pair of square brackets substituted for original words "section 25A of this Act shall apply" by the Bankruptcy and Diligence etc (Scotland) Act 2007, s 36, Sch 1, paras 1, 23(1), (4), subject to transitional provisions and savings in SSI 2008/115, arts 5–7, 10, 15 at **[2.51]–[2.53]**, **[2.56]**, **[2.57]**.

Sub-s (3B): inserted as noted to sub-s (3A); repealed by the Bankruptcy and Diligence etc (Scotland) Act 2007, s 28(1), (4), subject to transitional provisions and savings in SSI 2008/115, arts 5–7, 10, 15 at **[2.51]–[2.53]**, **[2.56]**, **[2.57]**, and previously read as follows:

"(3B) Where a report is made in pursuance of subsection (3A) above, the Accountant in Bankruptcy may apply to the sheriff for the grant of a certificate for the summary administration of the sequestration of the debtor's estate.".

Sub-s (4): words in first (outer) pair of square brackets inserted by the Bankruptcy (Scotland) Act 1993, s 11(3), Sch 1, para 12(1), (5), subject to s 12(6) thereof, at **[5.194]** and to SI 1993/438, arts 4, 5, at **[16.58]**, **[16.59]**; word in second (inner) and fifth pairs of square brackets substituted for original word "interim", words in third pair of square brackets substituted for original words "election of the permanent trustee", word in fourth pair of square brackets substituted for original word "permanent", words "who shall thereupon appoint the interim trustee as the permanent trustee" omitted from para (b) repealed and words in final pair of square brackets inserted by the Bankruptcy and Diligence etc (Scotland) Act 2007, ss 36, 226(2), Sch 1, paras 1, 23(1), (5), Sch 6, Pt 1, subject to transitional provisions and savings in SSI 2008/115, arts 5–7, 10, 15 at **[2.51]–[2.53]**, **[2.56]**, **[2.57]**.

Sub-s (4A): inserted by the Bankruptcy (Scotland) Act 1993, s 11(3), Sch 1, para 12(1), (4), (6), subject to s 12(6) thereof, at **[5.194]** and to SI 1993/438, arts 4, 5, at **[16.58]**, **[16.59]**; repealed by the Bankruptcy and Diligence etc (Scotland) Act 2007, s 28(1), (4), subject to transitional provisions and savings in SSI 2008/115, arts 5–7, 10, 15 at **[2.51]–[2.53]**, **[2.56]**, **[2.57]**, and previously read as follows:

"(4A) Where a report is made in pursuance of subsection (4) above, the interim trustee may apply to the sheriff for the grant of a certificate for the summary administration of the sequestration of the debtor's estate.".

Sub-s (5): repealed by the Bankruptcy and Diligence etc (Scotland) Act 2007, s 28(1), (4), subject to transitional provisions and savings in SSI 2008/115, arts 5–7, 10, 15 at **[2.51]–[2.53]**, **[2.56]**, **[2.57]**, and previously read as follows:

"(5) Where subsection (4) above applies, the provisions of this Act shall have effect as regards the sequestration subject to such modifications, and with such further provisions, as are set out in Schedule 2 to this Act.".

[5.57]

[25 Appointment of replacement trustee

(1) This section applies where a replacement trustee is elected by virtue of a trustee vote.

(2) On the election of the replacement trustee, the original trustee must immediately make a report of the proceedings at the statutory meeting—

(a) where the original trustee was not the Accountant in Bankruptcy, to the Accountant in Bankruptcy,

(b) where the original trustee was the Accountant in Bankruptcy, to the sheriff.

(3) The debtor, a creditor, the original trustee, the replacement trustee or the Accountant in Bankruptcy may object to any matter connected with the election—

(a) in the case of an objection by a person other than the Accountant in Bankruptcy, by applying to the Accountant in Bankruptcy, or

(b) in the case of an objection by the Accountant in Bankruptcy, by making a summary application to the sheriff.

(4) An objection under subsection (3) must—

(a) specify the grounds on which the objection is taken, and

(b) be made before the expiry of the period of 4 days beginning with the day of the statutory meeting.

(5) If there is no timeous objection under subsection (3), the Accountant in Bankruptcy must without delay declare the elected person to be the trustee in the sequestration.

(6) No expense in objecting under this section is to fall on the debtor's estate.]

NOTES

Commencement: 1 April 2015.

Repealed as noted at the beginning of this Act.

Substituted, together with ss 25A, 25B for original s 25, by the Bankruptcy and Debt Advice (Scotland) Act 2014, s 28(1), subject to transitional provisions and savings in SSI 2014/261, arts 4, 12 at **[2.91]**, **[2.99]**. Prior to this substitution, s 25 and the notes relating to it read as follows:

"**25 [Appointment of replacement trustee]**

[(A1) This section applies where a replacement trustee is elected by virtue of a trustee vote.]

(1) On the election of the [replacement] trustee—

(a) the [original] trustee shall forthwith make a report of the proceedings at the statutory meeting to the sheriff; and

(b) the debtor, a creditor, the [original] trustee, the [replacement] trustee or the Accountant in Bankruptcy may, within 4 days after the statutory meeting, object to any matter connected with the election; and such objection shall be by summary application to the sheriff, specifying the grounds on which the objection is taken.

(2) If there is no timeous objection under subsection (1)(b) above, the sheriff shall forthwith declare the elected person to be the [trustee in the sequestration]; and the sheriff shall [make an order appointing him as such].

[(2A) . . .]

(3) If there is a timeous objection under subsection (1)(b) above, the sheriff shall forthwith give parties an opportunity to be heard thereon and shall give his decision.

(4) If in his decision under subsection (3) above the sheriff—

(a) rejects the objection, subsection (2) above shall apply as if there had been no timeous objection;

(b) sustains the objection, he shall order the [original] trustee to arrange a new meeting [at which a new trustee vote shall be held]; and sections 23 and 24 of this Act and this section shall apply in relation to such a meeting.

(5) Any declaration, [appointment] or decision of the sheriff under this section shall be final, and no expense in objecting under this section shall fall on the debtor's estate.

(6) . . .

NOTES

Repealed as noted at the beginning of this Act.

Section heading: substituted by the Bankruptcy and Diligence etc (Scotland) Act 2007, s 11(5)(b), subject to transitional provisions and savings in SSI 2008/115, arts 5–7, 10, 15 at **[2.51]–[2.53]**, **[2.56]**, **[2.57]**.

Sub-s (A1): inserted by the Bankruptcy and Diligence etc (Scotland) Act 2007, s 11(5)(a), subject to transitional provisions and savings in SSI 2008/115, as noted above.

Sub-s (1): words in square brackets substituted by the Bankruptcy and Diligence etc (Scotland) Act 2007, s 36, Sch 1, paras 1, 24(1), (2), subject to transitional provisions and savings in SSI 2008/115, as noted above.

Sub-s (2): words in square brackets substituted by the Bankruptcy and Diligence etc (Scotland) Act 2007, s 36, Sch 1, paras 1, 24(1), (3), subject to transitional provisions and savings in SSI 2008/115, as noted above.

Sub-s (2A): inserted by the Bankruptcy (Scotland) Act 1993, s 11(3), Sch 1, para 13(1), (2), subject to s 12(6) thereof, at **[5.194]** and to SI 1993/438, arts 4, 5, at **[16.58]**, **[16.59]**; repealed by the Bankruptcy and Diligence etc (Scotland) Act 2007, s 28(1), (5), subject to transitional provisions and savings in SSI 2008/115, as noted above.

Sub-s (4): words in square brackets in para (b) substituted by the Bankruptcy and Diligence etc (Scotland) Act 2007, s 36, Sch 1, paras 1, 24(1), (4), subject to transitional provisions and savings in SSI 2008/115, as noted above.

Sub-s (5): word in square brackets substituted by the Bankruptcy and Diligence etc (Scotland) Act 2007, s 36, Sch 1, paras 1, 24(1), (5), subject to transitional provisions and savings in SSI 2008/115, as noted above.

Sub-s (6): repealed by the Home Owner and Debtor Protection (Scotland) Act 2010, s 12, subject to transitional provisions and savings in the Home Owner and Debtor Protection (Scotland) Act 2010 (Transitional and Saving Provisions) Order 2010, SSI 2010/316, art 7(3).

Acts of Sederunt: the Act of Sederunt (Bankruptcy Rules) 1993, SI 1993/921.

Regulations: the Bankruptcy (Scotland) Regulations 2008, SSI 2008/82 at **[16.262]**.".

[5.58]

[25A Applications to Accountant in Bankruptcy: procedure

(1) This section applies where an application is made to the Accountant in Bankruptcy under section 25(3)(a).

(2) The Accountant in Bankruptcy must—

- (a) without delay give the original trustee, the replacement trustee, the objector and any other interested person an opportunity to make written submissions on the application, and
- (b) make a decision.

(3) If the Accountant in Bankruptcy decides—

- (a) to reject the objection in the application, the Accountant in Bankruptcy must without delay declare the elected person to be the trustee in the sequestration,
- (b) to sustain the objection in the application, the Accountant in Bankruptcy must order the original trustee to arrange a new meeting at which a new trustee vote must be held.

(4) Sections 23 to 25B apply in relation to a meeting arranged by virtue of subsection (3)(b).

(5) The original trustee, the replacement trustee, the objector and any other interested person may apply to the Accountant in Bankruptcy for a review of a decision under subsection (2)(b).

(6) An application under subsection (5) must be made before the expiry of the period of 14 days beginning with the day on which notice of the decision is given.

(7) If an application for a review under subsection (5) is made, the Accountant in Bankruptcy must—

- (a) take into account any representations made by an interested person before the expiry of the period of 21 days beginning with the day on which the application is made, and
- (b) confirm, amend or revoke the decision before the expiry of the period of 28 days beginning with the day on which the application is made.

(8) The trustee, the objector and any other interested person may by summary application appeal to the sheriff against a decision by the Accountant in Bankruptcy under subsection (7)(b), before the expiry of the period of 14 days beginning with the day of the decision.

(9) No expense in objecting under this section is to fall on the debtor's estate.]

NOTES

Commencement: 1 April 2015.

Repealed as noted at the beginning of this Act.

Substituted, together with ss 25, 25B for original s 25, as noted to s 25 at **[5.57]**. Note that previously a section 25A was inserted by the Bankruptcy (Scotland) Act 1993, s 7 and was repealed by the Bankruptcy and Diligence etc (Scotland) Act 2007, s 226(2), Sch 6, Pt 1, subject to transitional provisions and savings in SSI 2008/115, arts 5–7, 10, 15; it is reproduced here for reference, as follows—

"[25A Appointment of permanent trustee in certain cases

(1) Where this section applies as mentioned in section 21B(2), 23A(4) or 24(3A) of this Act, the court shall appoint as permanent trustee—

- *(a) the Accountant in Bankruptcy; or*
- *(b) such person as may be nominated by the Accountant in Bankruptcy (being a person who is not ineligible for election as permanent trustee under section 24(2) of this Act) if that person consents to the nomination.*

(2) Where this section applies as mentioned in section 28(5) of this Act, if either of the persons mentioned in paragraphs (a) and (b) of subsection (1) above applies to the sheriff for appointment as permanent trustee, the sheriff shall so appoint such person.

(3) Where a person is appointed to be permanent trustee under this section, the provisions of this Act shall apply to the sequestration subject to such modifications, and with such further provisions, as are set out in Schedule 2 to this Act.]

[5.59]
[25B Applications and appeals to sheriff: procedure

(1) This section applies where there is—

(a) an application by the Accountant in Bankruptcy under section 25(3)(b), or

(b) an appeal under section 25A(8).

(2) The sheriff must—

(a) without delay give the parties an opportunity to be heard on the application, and

(b) make a decision.

(3) If the sheriff decides—

(a) to reject an objection to the appointment of an elected person, the sheriff must without delay declare the elected person to be the trustee in the sequestration and make an order appointing the elected person to be the trustee in the sequestration,

(b) to sustain an objection to the appointment of an elected person, the sheriff must order the original trustee to arrange a new meeting at which a new trustee vote must be held.

(4) Sections 23 to 25B apply in relation to a meeting arranged by virtue of subsection (3)(b).

(5) Any declaration, appointment or decision of the sheriff under this section is final.]

NOTES

Commencement: 1 April 2015.

Substituted, together with ss 25, 25A for original s 25, as noted to s 25 at **[5.57]**.

Repealed as noted at the beginning of this Act.

[5.60]
26 [Provisions relating to termination of original trustee's functions]

[(A1) This section applies where a replacement trustee is appointed under section 25 of this Act.]

(1) [The original trustee, shall, on the appointment of the replacement trustee], hand over to him everything in his possession which relates to the sequestration (including [the statement of assets and liabilities, and a copy] of the statement [of the debtor's affairs prepared under section 20(1) (as revised under section 23(3)(d) if so revised)], and of the written comments sent under section 20(2)(c) of this Act) and shall thereupon cease to act in the sequestration.

(2) Within 3 months of the [appointment of the replacement trustee, the original] trustee shall—

(a) submit to the Accountant in Bankruptcy—

(i) his accounts of his intromissions (if any) with the debtor's estate; and

(ii) a claim for outlays reasonably incurred, and for remuneration for work reasonably undertaken, by him; and

(b) send to the [replacement] trustee . . . , a copy of what is submitted to the Accountant in Bankruptcy under paragraph (a) above.

[(2A) Where the original trustee was appointed under section 2(5) of this Act as the interim trustee in the sequestration, his accounts and the claim referred to in subsection (2)(a) above shall include accounts and a claim for the period of his appointment as interim trustee.]

(3) On a submission being made to him under subsection (2) above, the Accountant in Bankruptcy—

(a) shall—

(i) audit the accounts; and

(ii) issue a determination fixing the amount of the outlays and remuneration payable to the [original] trustee; and

(b) shall send a copy of—

(i) the said determination to the [original] trustee . . . ; and

(ii) the [original] trustee's audited accounts and of the said determination to the [replacement] trustee . . . .

(4) The [original] trustee, the [replacement] trustee, the debtor or any creditor may appeal to the sheriff against a determination under subsection (3)(a)(ii) above within 14 days of its issue[; and the decision of the sheriff on such an appeal shall be final].

(5) The [replacement] trustee, on being [appointed], shall make such insertions in the sederunt book as are appropriate to provide a record of the sequestration process before his [appointment], but he shall make no insertion therein relating to the written comments made by the [original] trustee under section 20(2)(c) of this Act.

[(5A) This section does not apply in any case where the Accountant in Bankruptcy is the [original] trustee.]

NOTES

Repealed as noted at the beginning of this Act.

Section heading: substituted for original words "Provisions relating to termination of interim trustee's functions" by the Bankruptcy and Diligence etc (Scotland) Act 2007, s 36, Sch 1, paras 1, 25(1), (10), subject to transitional provisions and savings in SSI 2008/115, arts 5–7, 10, 15 at **[2.51]–[2.53]**, **[2.56]**, **[2.57]**.

Sub-ss (A1), (2A): inserted by the Bankruptcy and Diligence etc (Scotland) Act 2007, s 36, Sch 1, paras 1, 25(1), (2), (5), subject to transitional provisions and savings in SSI 2008/115, arts 5–7, 10, 15 at **[2.51]–[2.53]**, **[2.56]**, **[2.57]**.

Sub-s (1): words in first pair of square brackets substituted for original words "Where the interim trustee does not himself become the permanent trustee, he shall, on confirmation of the permanent trustees in office" by the Bankruptcy and Diligence etc (Scotland) Act 2007, s 36, Sch 1, paras 1, 25(1), (3), subject to transitional provisions and savings in SSI 2008/115, arts 5–7, 10, 15 at **[2.51]–[2.53]**, **[2.56]**, **[2.57]**; words in second pair of square brackets substituted by the Bankruptcy (Scotland) Act 1993, s 11(3), Sch 1, para 14(1), (2), subject to s 12(6) thereof, at **[5.194]** and to the Bankruptcy (Scotland) Act 1993 Commencement and Savings Order 1993, SI 1993/438, arts 4, 5, at **[16.58]**, **[16.59]**; words in third pair of square brackets substituted for original words "prepared under section 23(3)(d)" by the Bankruptcy and Debt Advice (Scotland) Act 2014, s 56(1), Sch 3, paras 2, 17, subject to transitional provisions and savings in SSI 2014/261, arts 4, 12 at **[2.91]**, **[2.99]**.

Sub-s (2): words in first pair of square brackets substituted for original words "confirmation in office of the permanent trustee, the interim", word in second pair of square brackets substituted for original word "permanent", and words "(unless the interim trustee has himself become the permanent trustee)" (omitted) repealed by the Bankruptcy and Diligence etc (Scotland) Act 2007, ss 36, 226(2), Sch 1, paras 1, 25(1), (4), Sch 6, Pt 1, subject to transitional provisions and savings in SSI 2008/115, arts 5–7, 10, 15 at **[2.51]–[2.53]**, **[2.56]**, **[2.57]**.

Sub-s (3): word "original" in square brackets in each place it appears substituted for original word "interim", words "(except where the interim trustee has himself become the permanent trustee)" omitted from para (b)(i) repealed and word "replacement" in square brackets substituted for original word "permanent", by the Bankruptcy and Diligence etc (Scotland) Act 2007, ss 36, 226(2), Sch 1, paras 1, 25(1), (6), Sch 6, Pt 1, subject to transitional provisions and savings in SSI 2008/115, arts 5–7, 10, 15 at **[2.51]–[2.53]**, **[2.56]**, **[2.57]**; words omitted in the final place in para (b) repealed by the Bankruptcy and Debt Advice (Scotland) Act 2014, s 56(2), Sch 4, subject to transitional provisions and savings in SSI 2014/261, arts 4, 12 at **[2.91]**, **[2.99]**.

Sub-s (4): words in first and second pairs of square brackets substituted for original words "interim" and "permanent" respectively by the Bankruptcy and Diligence etc (Scotland) Act 2007, s 36, Sch 1, paras 1, 25(1), (7), subject to transitional provisions and savings in SSI 2008/115, arts 5–7, 10, 15 at **[2.51]–[2.53]**, **[2.56]**, **[2.57]**; words in third pair of square brackets added by the Bankruptcy (Scotland) Act 1993, s 11(3), Sch 1, para 14(1), (3), subject to s 12(6) thereof, at **[5.194]** and to SI 1993/438, arts 4, 5, at **[16.58]**, **[16.59]**.

Sub-s (5): repealed by the Bankruptcy and Debt Advice (Scotland) Act 2014, s 56(2), Sch 4, subject to transitional provisions and savings in SSI 2014/261, arts 4, 12 at **[2.91]**, **[2.99]**; words in square brackets substituted for original words "permanent", "confirmed in office", "confirmation" and "interim" respectively by the Bankruptcy and Diligence etc (Scotland) Act 2007, s 36, Sch 1, paras 1, 25(1), (8), subject to transitional provisions and savings in SSI 2008/115, arts 5–7, 10, 15 at **[2.51]–[2.53]**, **[2.56]**, **[2.57]**.

Sub-s (5A): inserted by the Bankruptcy (Scotland) Act 1993, s 11(3), Sch 1, para 14(1), (4), subject to s 12(6) thereof, at **[5.194]** and to SI 1993/438, arts 4, 5, at **[16.58]**, **[16.59]**; word in square brackets substituted for original word "interim" by the Bankruptcy and Diligence etc (Scotland) Act 2007, s 36, Sch 1, paras 1, 25(1), (9), subject to transitional provisions and savings in SSI 2008/115, arts 5–7, 10, 15 at **[2.51]–[2.53]**, **[2.56]**, **[2.57]**.

[5.61]

[26A Accountant in Bankruptcy to account for intromissions

(1) This section applies in any case where the Accountant in Bankruptcy was the [original] trustee and some other person [is appointed as replacement trustee under section 25 of this Act].

(2) The Accountant in Bankruptcy shall, on [the appointment of the replacement trustee], hand over to the [replacement] trustee everything in his possession which relates to the sequestration and which he obtained in his capacity as [original] trustee (including the statement of assets and liabilities); and thereupon he shall cease to act as . . . trustee.

(3) The Accountant in Bankruptcy shall, not later than 3 months after the [appointment of the replacement] trustee, supply to the [replacement] trustee—
- (a) his accounts of his intromissions (if any) as [original] trustee with the debtor's estate;
- (b) a determination of his fees and outlays calculated in accordance with regulations made under section 69A of this Act; and
- (c) a copy of the notice mentioned in subsection (4)(b) below.

(4) The Accountant in Bankruptcy shall send to the debtor and to all creditors known to him—
- (a) a copy of the determination mentioned in subsection (3)(b) above; and
- (b) a notice in writing stating—
  - (i) that the Accountant in Bankruptcy has commenced the procedure under this Act leading to discharge in respect of his actings as . . . trustee;
  - (ii) that the accounts of his intromissions (if any) with the debtor's estate are available for inspection at such address as the Accountant in Bankruptcy may determine;
  - [(iia) that an application for a review may be made under subsection (4A)];
  - (iii) that an appeal may be made to the sheriff under subsection (5) below; and
  - (iv) the effect of subsection (7) below.

[(4A) The replacement trustee, the debtor or any creditor may apply to the Accountant in Bankruptcy for a review of the discharge of the Accountant in Bankruptcy in respect of the Accountant in Bankruptcy's actings as trustee.

(4B) An application under subsection (4A) must be made before the expiry of the period of 14 days beginning with the day on which notice is sent under subsection (4)(b).

(4C) If an application under subsection (4A) is made, the Accountant in Bankruptcy must—
- (a) take into account any representations made by an interested person before the expiry of the period of 21 days beginning with the day on which the application is made, and
- (b) confirm or revoke the discharge before the expiry of the period of 28 days beginning with the day on which the application is made.]

[(5) The replacement trustee, the debtor or any creditor may appeal to the sheriff against—
- (a) the determination of the Accountant in Bankruptcy mentioned in subsection (3)(b) before the expiry of the period of 14 days beginning with the day on which notice is sent under subsection (4)(b),
- (b) a decision by the Accountant in Bankruptcy under subsection (4C)(b) before the expiry of the period of 14 days beginning with the day on which the decision is made.]

[(6) The decision of the sheriff on an appeal under subsection (5) is final.]

(7) Where—
- (a) the requirements of this section have been complied with; and
- (b) no appeal is made to the sheriff under subsection (5) above or such an appeal is made but is refused as regards the discharge of the Accountant in Bankruptcy,

the Accountant in Bankruptcy shall be discharged from all liability (other than any liability arising from fraud) to the creditors or to the debtor in respect of any act or omission of the Accountant in Bankruptcy in exercising the functions of . . . trustee in the sequestration.

(8) The [replacement] trustee, on being [appointed], shall make such insertions in the sederunt book as are appropriate to provide a record of the sequestration process before his [appointment].]

NOTES

Repealed as noted at the beginning of this Act.

Inserted by the Bankruptcy (Scotland) Act 1993, s 11(3), Sch 1, para 15(1), subject to s 12(6) thereof, at **[5.194]** and to the Bankruptcy (Scotland) Act 1993 Commencement and Savings Order 1993, SI 1993/438, arts 4, 5, at **[16.58]**, **[16.59]**.

Sub-s (1): words in square brackets substituted for original words "interim" and "becomes the permanent trustee" respectively, by the Bankruptcy and Diligence etc (Scotland) Act 2007, s 36, Sch 1, paras 1, 26(1), (2), subject to transitional provisions and savings in SSI 2008/115, arts 5–7, 10, 15 at **[2.51]–[2.53]**, **[2.56]**, **[2.57]**.

Sub-s (2): words in first pair of square brackets substituted for original words "confirmation of the permanent trustee in office", word in second pair of square brackets substituted for original word "permanent", word in third pair of square brackets substituted for original word "interim", and word "interim" (omitted) repealed by the Bankruptcy and Diligence etc (Scotland) Act 2007, ss 36, 226(2), Sch 1, paras 1, 26(1), (3), Sch 6, Pt 1, subject to transitional provisions and savings in SSI 2008/115, arts 5–7, 10, 15 at **[2.51]–[2.53]**, **[2.56]**, **[2.57]**.

Sub-s (3): words in first and second pairs of square brackets substituted for original words "confirmation in office of the permanent" and "permanent" respectively, and word in square brackets in para (a) substituted for original word "interim" by the Bankruptcy and Diligence etc (Scotland) Act 2007, s 36, Sch 1, paras 1, 26(1), (4), subject to transitional provisions and savings in SSI 2008/115, arts 5–7, 10, 15 at **[2.51]–[2.53]**, **[2.56]**, **[2.57]**.

Sub-s (4): word "interim" omitted from para (b)(i) repealed by the Bankruptcy and Diligence etc (Scotland) Act 2007, s 226(2), Sch 6, Pt 1, subject to transitional provisions and savings in SSI 2008/115, arts 5–7, 10, 15 at **[2.51]–[2.53]**, **[2.56]**, **[2.57]**; para (b)(iia) inserted by the Bankruptcy and Debt Advice (Scotland) Act 2014, s 40(1)(a), subject to transitional provisions and savings in SSI 2014/261, arts 10, 12 at **[2.97]**, **[2.99]**.

Sub-ss (4A)–(4C): inserted by the Bankruptcy and Debt Advice (Scotland) Act 2014, s 40(1)(b), subject to transitional provisions and savings in SSI 2014/261, arts 10, 12 at **[2.97]**, **[2.99]**.

Sub-ss (5), (6): substituted by the Bankruptcy and Debt Advice (Scotland) Act 2014, s 40(1)(c), (d), subject to transitional provisions and savings in SSI 2014/261, arts 10, 12 at **[2.97]**, **[2.99]**. Sub-ss (5), (6) previously read as follows (with word in square brackets in sub-s (5) substituted and word omitted from sub-s (5) repealed by the Bankruptcy and Diligence etc (Scotland) Act 2007, ss 36, 226(2), Sch 1, paras 1, 26(1), (5), Sch 6, Pt 1, subject to transitional provisions and savings in SSI 2008/115, arts 5–7, 10, 15)—

"(5) The [replacement] trustee, the debtor and any creditor may appeal to the sheriff against—
(a) the determination of the Accountant in Bankruptcy mentioned in subsection (3)(b) above;
(b) the discharge of the Accountant in Bankruptcy in respect of his actings as . . . trustee; or
(c) both such determination and discharge.

(6) An appeal under subsection (5) above shall be made not more than 14 days after the issue of the notice mentioned in subsection (4)(b) above; and the decision of the sheriff on such an appeal shall be final.".

Sub-s (7): word "interim" (omitted) repealed by the Bankruptcy and Diligence etc (Scotland) Act 2007, s 226(2), Sch 6, Pt 1, subject to transitional provisions and savings in SSI 2008/115, arts 5–7, 10, 15 at **[2.51]–[2.53]**, **[2.56]**, **[2.57]**.

Sub-s (8): words in square brackets substituted for original words "permanent", "confirmed in office" and "confirmation" respectively by the Bankruptcy and Diligence etc (Scotland) Act 2007, s 36, Sch 1, paras 1, 26(1), (6), subject to transitional provisions and savings in SSI 2008/115, arts 5–7, 10, 15 at **[2.51]–[2.53]**, **[2.56]**, **[2.57]**; repealed by the Bankruptcy and Debt Advice (Scotland) Act 2014, s 56(2), Sch 4, subject to transitional provisions and savings in SSI 2014/261, arts 4, 12 at **[2.91]**, **[2.99]**.

[5.62]

27 [Discharge of original trustee]

(1) On receiving a copy of the Accountant in Bankruptcy's determination sent under subsection (3)(b)(i) of section 26 of this Act the [original] trustee may apply to him for a certificate of discharge.

(2) The [original] trustee shall send notice of an application under subsection (1) above to the debtor[, to all creditors known to the original trustee] and to the [replacement] trustee and shall inform the debtor—
(a) that he, the [replacement] trustee or any creditor may make written representations relating to the application to the Accountant in Bankruptcy within a period of 14 days after such notification;
(b) that the audited accounts of his intromissions (if any) with the debtor's estate are available for inspection at the office of the [original] trustee and that a copy of those accounts has been sent to the [replacement] trustee . . . ; and
(c) of the effect mentioned in subsection (5) below.

(3) On the expiry of the period mentioned in subsection (2)(a) above the Accountant in Bankruptcy, after considering any representations duly made to him, shall—
(a) grant or refuse to grant the certificate of discharge; and
(b) notify (in addition to the [original] trustee) the debtor, the [replacement] trustee, and all creditors who have made such representations, accordingly.

[(3A) The original trustee, the replacement trustee, the debtor or any creditor who has made representations may apply to the Accountant in Bankruptcy for a review of a determination under subsection (3).

(3B) An application under subsection (3A) must be made before the expiry of the period of 14 days beginning with the day on which the determination is issued under subsection (3).

(3C) If an application under subsection (3A) is made, the Accountant in Bankruptcy must—
(a) take into account any representations made by an interested person before the expiry of the period of 21 days beginning with the day on which the application is made, and

(b) confirm, amend or revoke the determination under subsection (3) (whether or not granting a certificate of discharge) before the expiry of the period of 28 days beginning with the day on which the application is made.]

(4) The [original] trustee, the [replacement] trustee, the debtor or any creditor who has made representations [by virtue of] subsection (2)(a) above may, within 14 days after the [day of the decision under subsection (3C)(b)], appeal therefrom to the sheriff and if the sheriff determines that a certificate of discharge which has been refused should be granted he shall order the Accountant in Bankruptcy to grant it; and the sheriff clerk shall send a copy of the decree of the sheriff to the Accountant in Bankruptcy.

[(4A) The decision of the sheriff in an appeal under subsection (4) above shall be final.]

(5) The grant of a certificate of discharge under this section by the Accountant in Bankruptcy shall have the effect of discharging the [original] trustee from all liability (other than any liability arising from fraud) to the creditors or to the debtor in respect of any act or omission of the [original] trustee in exercising the functions conferred on him by this Act.

(6) . . .

(7) . . .

[(7A) This section does not apply in any case where the Accountant in Bankruptcy is the [original] trustee.]

NOTES

Repealed as noted at the beginning of this Act.

Section heading: substituted for original words "Discharge of interim trustee" by the Bankruptcy and Diligence etc (Scotland) Act 2007, s 36, Sch 1, paras 1, 27(2), subject to transitional provisions and savings in SSI 2008/115, arts 5–7, 10, 15 at **[2.51]–[2.53]**, **[2.56]**, **[2.57]**.

Sub-ss (1), (5): word in square brackets in each place it appears substituted for original word "interim" by the Bankruptcy and Diligence etc (Scotland) Act 2007, s 36, Sch 1, paras 1, 27(1)(b), subject to transitional provisions and savings in SSI 2008/115, arts 5–7, 10, 15 at **[2.51]–[2.53]**, **[2.56]**, **[2.57]**.

Sub-s (2): words "original" and "replacement" in square brackets in each place they appear substituted for original words "interim" and "permanent" respectively, and words in second pair of square brackets inserted, by the Bankruptcy and Diligence etc (Scotland) Act 2007, s 36, Sch 1, paras 1, 27(1), subject to transitional provisions and savings in SSI 2008/115, arts 5–7, 10, 15 at **[2.51]–[2.53]**, **[2.56]**, **[2.57]**; words "for insertion in the sederunt book" omitted from para (b) repealed by the Bankruptcy and Debt Advice (Scotland) Act 2014, s 56(2), Sch 4, subject to transitional provisions and savings in SSI 2014/261, arts 4, 12 at **[2.91]**, **[2.99]**.

Sub-s (3): words "original" and "replacement" in square brackets substituted for original words "interim" and "permanent" respectively by the Bankruptcy and Diligence etc (Scotland) Act 2007, s 36, Sch 1, paras 1, 27(1)(b), (c), subject to transitional provisions and savings in SSI 2008/115, arts 5–7, 10, 15 at **[2.51]–[2.53]**, **[2.56]**, **[2.57]**.

Sub-ss (3A)–(3C): inserted by the Bankruptcy and Debt Advice (Scotland) Act 2014, s 40(2)(a), subject to transitional provisions and savings in SSI 2014/261, arts 10, 12 at **[2.97]**, **[2.99]**.

Sub-s (4): words "original" and "replacement" in square brackets substituted for original words "interim" and "permanent" respectively by the Bankruptcy and Diligence etc (Scotland) Act 2007, s 36, Sch 1, paras 1, 27(1)(b), (c), subject to transitional provisions and savings in SSI 2008/115, arts 5–7, 10, 15 at **[2.51]–[2.53]**, **[2.56]**, **[2.57]**; words in third and fourth pairs of square brackets substituted for original words "under" and issuing of the determination under subsection (3) above" respectively, by the Bankruptcy and Debt Advice (Scotland) Act 2014, ss 40(2)(b), 56(1), Sch 3, paras 2, 18, subject to transitional provisions and savings in SSI 2014/261, arts 4, 10, 12 at **[2.91]**, **[2.97]**, **[2.99]**.

Sub-s (4A): inserted by the Bankruptcy (Scotland) Act 1993, s 11(3), Sch 1, para 16, subject to s 12(6) thereof, at **[5.194]** and to the Bankruptcy (Scotland) Act 1993 Commencement and Savings Order 1993, SI 1993/438, arts 4, 5, at **[16.58]**, **[16.59]**.

Sub-s (6): repealed by the Bankruptcy and Debt Advice (Scotland) Act 2014, s 56(2), Sch 4, subject to transitional provisions and savings in SSI 2014/261, arts 4, 12 at **[2.91]**, **[2.99]**, and previously read as follows (with word in square brackets substituted by the Bankruptcy and Diligence etc (Scotland) Act 2007, s 36, Sch 1, paras 1, 27(1)(c), subject to transitional provisions and savings in SSI 2008/115, arts 5–7, 10, 15)—

> "(6) Where a certificate of discharge is granted under this section, the [replacement] trustee shall make an appropriate entry in the sederunt book.".

Sub-s (7): repealed by the Bankruptcy and Diligence etc (Scotland) Act 2007, s 226(2), Sch 6, Pt 1, subject to transitional provisions and savings in SSI 2008/115, arts 5–7, 10, 15 at **[2.51]–[2.53]**, **[2.56]**, **[2.57]**, and previously read as follows:

> "(7) Where the interim trustee has died, resigned office or been removed from office, then once the accounts of his intromissions (if any) with the debtor's estate are or have been submitted to and audited by the Accountant in Bankruptcy, the Accountant in Bankruptcy shall issue a determination fixing the amount of the outlays and remuneration payable to the interim trustee and the provisions of subsection (4) of section 26 of this Act and the foregoing provisions of this section shall, subject to any necessary modifications, apply in relation to that interim trustee or, if he has died, to his executor as they apply in relation to an interim trustee receiving a copy of such a determination under subsection (3)(b)(i) of that section.".

Sub-s (7A): added by the Bankruptcy (Scotland) Act 1993, s 11(3), Sch 1, para 16, subject to s 12(6) thereof, at **[5.194]** and to SI 1993/438, arts 4, 5, at **[16.58]**, **[16.59]**; word in square brackets substituted for original word "interim" by the Bankruptcy and Diligence etc (Scotland) Act 2007, s 36, Sch 1, paras 1, 27(1)(b), subject to transitional provisions and savings in SSI 2008/115, arts 5–7, 10, 15 at **[2.51]–[2.53]**, **[2.56]**, **[2.57]**.

[Replacement of trustee]

NOTES

Cross-heading: substituted for original words "Replacement of permanent trustee" by the Bankruptcy and Diligence etc (Scotland) Act 2007, s 36, Sch 1, paras 1, 28(1), (6), subject to transitional provisions and savings in SSI 2008/115, arts 5–7, 10, 15 at **[2.51]–[2.53]**, **[2.56]**, **[2.57]**.

[5.63]

28 [Resignation and death of trustee]

[(1) The . . . trustee may apply to the [Accountant in Bankruptcy] for authority to resign office and, where the [Accountant in Bankruptcy] is satisfied that [the trustee—

(a) is unable to act (whether by, under or by virtue of a provision of this Act or from any other cause whatsoever); or

(b) has so conducted himself that he should no longer continue to act,

the Accountant in Bankruptcy] shall grant the application.

(1A) The [Accountant in Bankruptcy] may make the granting of an application under subsection (1) above subject to the election of a new . . . trustee and to such conditions as he thinks appropriate in all the circumstances of the case.]

(2) Where the [Accountant in Bankruptcy] grants an application under . . . subsection (1) above—

(a) except where paragraph (b) below applies, the commissioners, or if there are no commissioners, the Accountant in Bankruptcy, shall call a meeting of the creditors, to be held not more than 28 days after the . . . trustee has resigned, for the election by them of a new . . . trustee;

(b) if the application has been granted subject to the election of a new . . . trustee, the resigning . . . trustee shall himself call a meeting of the creditors, to be held not more than 28 days after the granting of the application, for the purpose referred to in paragraph (a) above.

(3) Where the commissioners become, or if there are no commissioners the Accountant in Bankruptcy becomes, aware that the . . . trustee has died, they or as the case may be the Accountant in Bankruptcy shall as soon as practicable after becoming so aware call a meeting of creditors for the election by the creditors of a new . . . trustee.

(4) The foregoing provisions of this Act relating to the election [of a replacement trustee and the appointment of that] . . . trustee shall, subject to any necessary modifications, apply in relation to the election and [appointment] of a new . . . trustee in pursuance of subsection (1), [(1A)], (2) or (3) above.

[(5) Where no new trustee is elected in pursuance of subsection (2) or (3) the Accountant in Bankruptcy may appoint as the trustee in the sequestration—

(a) a person who applies to the Accountant in Bankruptcy within the period of 14 days beginning with the day of the meeting arranged under subsection (2) or (3), or

(b) any other person as may be determined by the Accountant in Bankruptcy and who consents to the appointment.

(5A) A person may not be appointed under subsection (5) if the person is ineligible for election as a replacement trustee under section 24(2).

(5B) If, after the expiry of the period mentioned in subsection (5)(a), the Accountant in Bankruptcy determines that no person is to be appointed under subsection (5), the Accountant in Bankruptcy is deemed to be the trustee in the sequestration.]

(6) The new . . . trustee may require—

(a) delivery to him of all documents relating to the sequestration in the possession of the former trustee or his representatives, except the former trustee's accounts of which he shall be entitled to delivery of only a copy;

(b) the former trustee or his representatives to submit the trustee's accounts for audit to the commissioners or, if there are no commissioners, to the Accountant in Bankruptcy, and the commissioners or the Accountant in Bankruptcy shall issue a determination fixing the amount of the outlays and remuneration payable to the trustee or representatives in accordance with section 53 of this Act.

(7) The former trustee or his representatives, the new . . . trustee, the debtor or any creditor may appeal against a determination issued under subsection (6)(b) above within 14 days after it is issued—

(a) where it is a determination of the commissioners, to the Accountant in Bankruptcy; and

(b) where it is a determination of the Accountant in Bankruptcy, to the sheriff; and the determination of the Accountant in Bankruptcy under paragraph (a) above shall be appealable to the sheriff.

[(8) The decision of the sheriff on an appeal under subsection (7) above shall be final.]

NOTES

Repealed as noted at the beginning of this Act.

Section heading: substituted for original words "Resignation and death of permanent trustee" by the Bankruptcy and Diligence etc (Scotland) Act 2007, s 36, Sch 1, paras 1, 28(1), (5), subject to transitional provisions and savings in SSI 2008/115, arts 5–7, 10, 15 at **[2.51]–[2.53]**, **[2.56]**, **[2.57]**.

Sub-s (1): substituted together with sub-s (1A), for original sub-s (1) by the Bankruptcy (Scotland) Act 1993, s 11(3), Sch 1, para 17(1), (2), subject to s 12(6) thereof, at **[5.194]** and to the Bankruptcy (Scotland) Act 1993 Commencement and Savings Order 1993, SI 1993/438, arts 4, 5, at **[16.58]**, **[16.59]**; word "permanent" (omitted) repealed, words in first and second pairs of square brackets substituted for original word "sheriff", and words in third pair of square brackets substituted for original words "either of the grounds mentioned in paragraphs (a) and (b) of section 13(2) of this Act applies to the permanent trustee, he", by the Bankruptcy and Diligence etc (Scotland) Act 2007, ss 9(2), 36, 226(2), Sch 1, paras 1, 28(1), (2), Sch 6, Pt 1, subject to transitional provisions and savings in SSI 2008/115, arts 5–7, 10, 15 at **[2.51]–[2.53]**, **[2.56]**, **[2.57]**.

Sub-s (1A): substituted as noted to sub-s (1); words in square brackets substituted for original word "sheriff" and word "permanent" (omitted) repealed by the Bankruptcy and Diligence etc (Scotland) Act 2007, ss 36, 226(2), Sch 1, paras 1, 28(1), (2), Sch 6, Pt 1, subject to transitional provisions and savings in SSI 2008/115, arts 5–7, 10, 15 at **[2.51]–[2.53]**, **[2.56]**, **[2.57]**.

Sub-s (2): words in square brackets substituted for original word "sheriff" and word "permanent" omitted from each place in paras (a), (b) repealed by the Bankruptcy and Diligence etc (Scotland) Act 2007, ss 36, 226(2), Sch 1, paras 1, 28(1), (2), Sch 6, Pt 1, subject to transitional provisions and savings in SSI 2008/115, arts 5–7, 10, 15 at **[2.51]–[2.53]**, **[2.56]**, **[2.57]**; words omitted in the first place repealed by the Bankruptcy (Scotland) Act 1993, s 11(4), Sch 2, subject to s 12(6) thereof, at **[5.194]** and to SI 1993/438, arts 4, 5, at **[16.58]**, **[16.59]**.

Sub-ss (3), (6), (7): word "permanent" omitted in each place repealed by the Bankruptcy and Diligence etc (Scotland) Act 2007, s 226(2), Sch 6, Pt 1, subject to transitional provisions and savings in SSI 2008/115, arts 5–7, 10, 15 at **[2.51]–[2.53]**, **[2.56]**, **[2.57]**.

Sub-s (4): words in first and second pairs of square brackets substituted for original words "and confirmation in office of the" and "confirmation in office" respectively and word "permanent" omitted in both places repealed, by the Bankruptcy and Diligence etc (Scotland) Act 2007, ss 36, 226(2), Sch 1, paras 1, 28(1), (3), Sch 6, Pt 1, subject to transitional provisions and savings in SSI 2008/115, arts 5–7, 10, 15 at **[2.51]–[2.53]**, **[2.56]**, **[2.57]**; figure in third pair of square brackets inserted by the Bankruptcy (Scotland) Act 1993, s 11(3), Sch 1, para 17(1), (3), subject to s 12(6) thereof, at **[5.194]** and to SI 1993/438, arts 4, 5, at **[16.58]**, **[16.59]**.

Sub-ss (5), (5A), (5B): substituted for sub-s (5), by the Bankruptcy and Debt Advice (Scotland) Act 2014, s 28(2), subject to transitional provisions and savings in SSI 2014/261, arts 4, 12 at **[2.91]**, **[2.99]**. Sub-s (5) (as substituted by the Bankruptcy (Scotland) Act 1993, s 11(3), Sch 1, para 17(1), (4), and amended by the Bankruptcy and Diligence etc (Scotland) Act 2007, ss 36, 226(2), Sch 1, paras 1, 28(1), (4), Sch 6, Pt 1, subject to transitional provisions and savings in SSI 2008/115, arts 5–7, 10, 15) previously read as follows:

"[(5) Where no new . . . trustee is elected in pursuance of subsection (2) or (3) above—

[(a) the Accountant in Bankruptcy; or

(b) such person as may be nominated by the Accountant in Bankruptcy (being a person who is not ineligible for election as replacement trustee under section 24(2) of this Act) if that person consents to the nomination,

may apply to the sheriff for appointment as trustee in the sequestration; and, on such application, the sheriff shall make an order so appointing the Accountant in Bankruptcy or, as the case may be, the person nominated by him].]".

Sub-s (8): added by the Bankruptcy (Scotland) Act 1993, s 11(3), Sch 1, para 17(1), (5), subject to s 12(6) thereof, at **[5.194]** and to SI 1993/438, arts 4, 5, at **[16.58]**, **[16.59]**.

[5.64]

[28A Replacement of trustee acting in more than one sequestration

(1) This section applies where a trustee acting as such in two or more sequestrations—

(a) dies,

(b) ceases to be qualified to continue to act as trustee by virtue of section 24(2), or

(c) becomes subject to the circumstances mentioned in subsection (2).

(2) The circumstances are that—

(a) there is a conflict of interest affecting the trustee, or

(b) there is a change in the personal circumstances of the trustee,

which prevents, or makes it impracticable for, the trustee to carry out the trustee's functions.

(3) The Accountant in Bankruptcy may in a case where subsection (1)(b) or (c) applies, determine that the trustee is removed from office in each sequestration in which the trustee has ceased to be qualified.

(4) The Accountant in Bankruptcy may appoint as the trustee in each sequestration in which the former trustee was acting a person—

(a) determined by the Accountant in Bankruptcy, and

(b) who consents to the appointment.

(5) A person may not be appointed under subsection (4) if the person is ineligible for election as a replacement trustee under section 24(2).

(6) If, in relation to any sequestration, the Accountant in Bankruptcy determines that no person is to be appointed under subsection (4), the Accountant in Bankruptcy is deemed to be the trustee in that sequestration.

(7) A determination or appointment under this section may be made—

(a) on the application of any person having an interest, or

(b) without an application, where the Accountant in Bankruptcy proposes to make a determination or appointment of the Accountant in Bankruptcy's own accord.

(8) The applicant must notify all interested persons where an application is made under subsection (7)(a).

(9) The Accountant in Bankruptcy must notify all interested persons where the Accountant in Bankruptcy proposes to make a determination or appointment by virtue of subsection (7)(b).

(10) A notice under subsection (8) or (9) must inform the recipient that the person has a right to make representations to the Accountant in Bankruptcy in relation to the application or the proposed determination or appointment before the expiry of the period of 14 days beginning with the day on which the notice is given.

(11) Before making a determination or appointment under this section, the Accountant in Bankruptcy must take into account any representations made by an interested person.

(12) The Accountant in Bankruptcy must notify any determination or appointment under this section to—

(a) the former trustee (or in the case where the former trustee has died, the former trustee's representatives),

(b) the debtor,

(c) the trustee appointed under this section (where the trustee appointed is not the Accountant in Bankruptcy),

(d) each sheriff who awarded sequestration or to whom sequestration was transferred under section 15(2) of this Act.

(13) The trustee appointed under this section—

(a) must notify the determination or appointment under this section to every creditor known to the trustee,

(b) may require—

(i) delivery of all documents relating to each sequestration in which the former trustee was acting which are in the possession of the former trustee or the former trustee's representatives (other than the former trustee's accounts),
(ii) delivery of a copy of the former trustee's accounts,
(iii) the former trustee or the former trustee's representatives to submit the trustee's accounts for audit to the commissioners or, if there are no commissioners, to the Accountant in Bankruptcy.

(14) Where the trustee appointed under this section requires submission of the accounts in accordance with subsection (13)(b)(iii), the commissioners or, as the case may be, the Accountant in Bankruptcy must issue a determination fixing the amount of the outlays and remuneration payable to the former trustee or the former trustee's representatives in accordance with section 53.]

NOTES

Commencement: 1 April 2015.

Repealed as noted at the beginning of this Act.

Substituted, together with s 28B for original s 28A, by the Bankruptcy and Debt Advice (Scotland) Act 2014, s 29, subject to transitional provisions and savings in SSI 2014/261, arts 4, 12 at **[2.91]**, **[2.99]**. Section 28A and the notes relating to it previously read as follows—

"**[28A Replacement of trustee acting in more than one sequestration**

(1) This section applies where a trustee acting as such in two or more sequestrations—
(a) dies; or
(b) ceases to be qualified to continue to act as trustee by virtue of section 24(2) of this Act.

(2) The Accountant in Bankruptcy may, by a single petition to the Court of Session, apply—
(a) in a case where subsection (1)(b) above applies, for the removal of the trustee from office in each sequestration in which he has so ceased to be qualified; and
(b) for the appointment of—
(i) the Accountant in Bankruptcy; or
(ii) such person as may be nominated by the Accountant in Bankruptcy (being a person who is not ineligible for election as replacement trustee under section 24(2) of this Act) if that person consents to the nomination,

as the trustee in each sequestration in which the trustee was acting.

(3) The procedure in a petition under subsection (2) above shall be as the Court of Session may, by act of sederunt, prescribe.

(4) An act of sederunt made under subsection (3) above may, in particular, make provision as to the intimation to each sheriff who awarded sequestration or to whom sequestration was transferred under section 15(2) of this Act of the appointment by the Court of Session of a trustee in that sequestration.]

NOTES

Inserted by the Bankruptcy and Diligence etc (Scotland) Act 2007, s 12, subject to transitional provisions and savings in SSI 2008/115, arts 5–7, 10, 15 at **[2.51]–[2.53]**, **[2.56]**, **[2.57]**.".

Repealed as noted at the beginning of this Act.

[5.65]

[28B Determination etc under section 28A: review

(1) The persons mentioned in subsections (12)(a) and (b) and (13)(a) of section 28A may apply to the Accountant in Bankruptcy for a review by the Accountant in Bankruptcy of any determination or appointment under that section.

(2) An application under subsection (1) must be made before the expiry of the period of 14 days beginning with the day on which notice of the determination or appointment is given.

(3) If an application under subsection (1) is made, the Accountant in Bankruptcy must—
(a) take into account any representations made by an interested person before the expiry of the period of 21 days beginning with the day on which the application is made, and
(b) confirm, amend or revoke the determination or appointment before the expiry of the period of 28 days beginning with the day on which the application is made.

(4) The persons mentioned in subsections (12)(a) and (b) and (13)(a) of section 28A may appeal to the sheriff against a decision by the Accountant in Bankruptcy under subsection (3)(b) before the expiry of the period of 14 days beginning with the day of the decision.

(5) The Accountant in Bankruptcy may refer a case to the court for a direction before—
(a) making any determination or appointment under section 28A, or
(b) undertaking any review under this section.

(6) An appeal under subsection (4) and a referral under subsection (5) must be made—
(a) by a single petition to the Court of Session, where the appeal relates to two or more sequestrations and the sequestrations are, by virtue of section 9, in different sheriffdoms, and
(b) in any other case to the sheriff.]

NOTES

Commencement: 1 April 2015.

Substituted as noted to s 28A at **[5.64]**.

Repealed as noted at the beginning of this Act.

[5.66]

29 [Removal of trustee and trustee not acting]

(1) The . . . trustee may be removed from office—

(a) by the creditors (other than any such person as is mentioned in section 24(3) of this Act) at a meeting called for the purpose if they also elect forthwith a new . . . trustee; or
[(b) by order made by the Accountant in Bankruptcy, if the Accountant in Bankruptcy is satisfied that there are reasons to do so on the basis of circumstances other than those mentioned in subsection (9),]

if the sheriff is satisfied that cause has been shown on the basis of circumstances other than those to which subsection (9) below applies.

[(1A) An order removing a trustee in accordance with subsection (1)(b) may be made—
(a) on the application of—
(i) the commissioners, or
(ii) a person representing not less than one quarter in value of the creditors, or
(b) in any other case, where the Accountant in Bankruptcy is satisfied that there are reasons to do so on the basis of circumstances other than those mentioned in subsection (9).]

[(2) The Accountant in Bankruptcy must—
(a) order an application by a person mentioned in subsection (1A)(a) to be served on the trustee,
(b) enter particulars of the application in the register of insolvencies, and
(c) before deciding whether or not to make an order under subsection (1)(b), give the trustee the opportunity to make representations.]

[(3) The Accountant in Bankruptcy may in ordering, or instead of ordering, the removal of the trustee from office under subsection (1)(b), make such further or other order as the Accountant in Bankruptcy thinks fit.

(3A) The trustee, the commissioners or any creditor may apply to the Accountant in Bankruptcy for a review of any decision of the Accountant in Bankruptcy under subsection (1)(b) or (3).

(3B) An application under subsection (3A) must be made before the expiry of the period of 14 days beginning with the day on which the decision is given.

(3C) If an application for a review under subsection (3A) is made, the Accountant in Bankruptcy must—
(a) take into account any representations made by an interested person before the expiry of the period of 21 days beginning with the day on which the application is made, and
(b) confirm, amend or revoke the decision before the expiry of the period of 28 days beginning with the day on which the application is made.]

[(4) The trustee, the commissioners or any creditor may appeal to the sheriff against any decision of the Accountant in Bankruptcy under subsection (3C)(b) before the end of the period of 14 days beginning with the date of the decision.]

(5) If the . . . trustee has been removed from office under subsection (1)(b) above or under section [1A(2)] of this Act or following [a review under subsection (3A) or] an appeal under subsection (4) above, the commissioners or, if there are no commissioners, the Accountant in Bankruptcy shall call a meeting of creditors, to be held not more than 28 days after such removal, for the election by them of a new . . . trustee.

[(6) If the Accountant in Bankruptcy is satisfied that any of the circumstances mentioned in subsection (9) apply, the Accountant in Bankruptcy may—
(a) declare the office of trustee to have become or to be vacant, and
(b) make any necessary order to enable the sequestration of the estate to proceed or to safeguard the estate pending the election of a new trustee.

(6A) The declaration of the office of trustee as vacant and any necessary order in accordance with subsection (6) may be made—
(a) on the application of—
(i) the commissioners,
(ii) the debtor, or
(iii) a creditor, or
(b) in any other case, where the Accountant in Bankruptcy is satisfied that there are reasons to do so on the basis of the circumstances mentioned in subsection (9).

(6B) The Accountant in Bankruptcy must order such intimation of an application by a person mentioned in subsection (6A)(a) as the Accountant in Bankruptcy considers necessary.

(6C) If the Accountant in Bankruptcy makes a declaration under subsection (6A), the commissioners, or if there are no commissioners the Accountant in Bankruptcy, must call a meeting of creditors for the election of a new trustee by the creditors.

(6D) A meeting called under subsection (6C) must be held before the end of the period of 28 days beginning with the date of the declaration under subsection (6A).

(6E) The trustee, the debtor, the commissioners or any creditor may apply to the Accountant in Bankruptcy for a review of any declaration or any order made by the Accountant in Bankruptcy under subsection (6).

(6F) An application under subsection (6E) must be made before the expiry of the period of 14 days beginning with the day on which the declaration is made.

(6G) If an application for a review under subsection (6E) is made, the Accountant in Bankruptcy must—
(a) take into account any representations made by an interested person before the expiry of the period of 21 days beginning with the day on which the application is made, and
(b) confirm, amend or revoke the declaration or order before the expiry of the period of 28 days beginning with the day on which the application is made.

(6H) The trustee, the debtor, the commissioners or any creditor may appeal to the sheriff against any decision of the Accountant in Bankruptcy under subsection (6G)(b) before the end of the period of 14 days beginning with the date of the decision.

(6I) The Accountant in Bankruptcy may refer a case to the sheriff for a direction before—

(a) making any order under subsection (1)(b) or (3),

(b) making any declaration or any order under subsection (6), or

(c) undertaking any review under this section.

(6J) An application for a review under subsection (3A) or (6E) may not be made in relation to a matter on which the Accountant in Bankruptcy has applied to the sheriff for a direction under subsection (6I).]

(7) The foregoing provisions of this Act relating to the election [of a replacement trustee and the appointment of that] . . . trustee shall, subject to any necessary modifications, apply in relation to the election and [appointment] of a new . . . trustee in pursuance of subsection (5) or [(6C)] above.

(8) Subsections (5) to [(8)] of section 28 of this Act shall apply for the purposes of this section as they apply for the purposes of that section.

(9) The circumstances to which this subsection applies are that the . . . trustee—

(a) is unable to act (whether by, under or by virtue of a provision of this Act or from any other cause whatsoever other than death); or

(b) has so conducted himself that he should no longer continue to act in the sequestration.

[(10) This section does not apply in any case where the Accountant in Bankruptcy is the trustee [and is without prejudice to the powers under section 1A(2)].]

NOTES

Repealed as noted at the beginning of this Act.

Section heading: words substituted for original words "Removal of permanent trustee and trustee not acting" by the Bankruptcy and Diligence etc (Scotland) Act 2007, s 36, Sch 1, paras 1, 29(1), (4), subject to transitional provisions and savings in SSI 2008/115, arts 5–7, 10, 15 at **[2.51]–[2.53]**, **[2.56]**, **[2.57]**.

Sub-s (1): word "permanent" omitted in both places repealed by the Bankruptcy and Diligence etc (Scotland) Act 2007, s 226(2), Sch 6, Pt 1, subject to transitional provisions and savings in SSI 2008/115, arts 5–7, 10, 15 at **[2.51]–[2.53]**, **[2.56]**, **[2.57]**; para (b) substituted by the Bankruptcy and Debt Advice (Scotland) Act 2014, s 30(a), subject to transitional provisions and savings in SSI 2014/261, arts 4, 12 at **[2.91]**, **[2.99]** and previously read as follows (with figure in square brackets substituted by the Bankruptcy (Scotland) Act 1993, s 11(3), Sch 1, para 18)—

"(b) without prejudice to section [1A(2)] of this Act, by order of the sheriff, on the application of—

(i) the Accountant in Bankruptcy;

(ii) the commissioners; or

(iii) a person representing not less than one quarter in value of the creditors,".

Sub-s (1A): inserted by the Bankruptcy and Debt Advice (Scotland) Act 2014, s 30(b), subject to transitional provisions and savings in SSI 2014/261, arts 4, 12 at **[2.91]**, **[2.99]**.

Sub-ss (2), (3), (3A), (3B), (3C), (4): substituted for original sub-ss (2), (3), (4), by the Bankruptcy and Debt Advice (Scotland) Act 2014, s 30(c)–(e), subject to transitional provisions and savings in SSI 2014/261, arts 4, 12 at **[2.91]**, **[2.99]**. Sub-ss (2), (3), (4) previously read as follows (with the word "permanent" omitted in each place repealed by the Bankruptcy and Diligence etc (Scotland) Act 2007, s 226(2), Sch 6, Pt 1, subject to transitional provisions and savings in SSI 2008/115, arts 5–7, 10, 15)—

"(2) The sheriff shall order any application under subsection (1)(b) above to be served on the . . . trustee and intimated in the Edinburgh Gazette, and before disposing of the application shall give the . . . trustee an opportunity of being heard.

(3) On an application under subsection (1)(b) above, the sheriff may, in ordering the removal of the . . . trustee from office, make such further order as he thinks fit or may, instead of removing the . . . trustee from office, make such other order as he thinks fit.

(4) The . . . trustee, the Accountant in Bankruptcy, the commissioners or any creditor may appeal against the decision of the sheriff on an application under subsection (1)(b) above within 14 days after the date of that decision.".

Sub-s (5): word "permanent" omitted in each place repealed by the Bankruptcy and Diligence etc (Scotland) Act 2007, s 226(2), Sch 6, Pt 1, subject to transitional provisions and savings in SSI 2008/115, arts 5–7, 10, 15 at **[2.51]–[2.53]**, **[2.56]**, **[2.57]**; figure in first pair of square brackets substituted by the Bankruptcy (Scotland) Act 1993, s 11(3), Sch 1, para 18, subject to s 12(6) thereof, at **[5.194]** and to SI 1993/438, arts 4, 5, at **[16.58]**, **[16.59]**; words in second pair of square brackets inserted by the Bankruptcy and Debt Advice (Scotland) Act 2014, s 30(f), subject to transitional provisions and savings in SSI 2014/261, arts 4, 12 at **[2.91]**, **[2.99]**.

Sub-ss (6), (6A)–(6J): substituted for original sub-s (6) by the Bankruptcy and Debt Advice (Scotland) Act 2014, s 30(g), subject to transitional provisions and savings in SSI 2014/261, arts 4, 12 at **[2.91]**, **[2.99]**. Sub-s (6) previously read as follows (with word "permanent" omitted in each place repealed by the Bankruptcy and Diligence etc (Scotland) Act 2007, s 226(2), Sch 6, Pt 1, subject to transitional provisions and savings in SSI 2008/115, arts 5–7, 10, 15 and figure in square brackets substituted by the Bankruptcy (Scotland) Act 1993, s 11(3), Sch 1, para 18)—

"(6) Without prejudice to section [1A(2)] of this Act, where the sheriff is satisfied of any of the circumstances to which subsection (9) below applies he may, on the application of a commissioner, the debtor, a creditor or the Accountant in Bankruptcy, and after such intimation as the sheriff considers necessary—

(a) declare the office of . . . trustee to have become or to be vacant; and

(b) make any necessary order to enable the sequestration to proceed or to safeguard the estate pending the election of a new . . . trustee;

and thereafter the commissioners or, if there are no commissioners, the Accountant in Bankruptcy shall call a meeting of creditors, to be held not more than 28 days after such declaration, for the election by them of a new . . . trustee.".

Sub-s (7): words in first pair of square brackets substituted for original words "and confirmation in office of the", word in second pair of square brackets substituted for original words "confirmation in office", and word "permanent" omitted in both places repealed by the Bankruptcy and Diligence etc (Scotland) Act 2007, ss 36, 226(2), Sch 1, paras 1, 29(1), (2), Sch 6, Pt 1, subject to transitional provisions and savings in SSI 2008/115, arts 5–7, 10, 15 at **[2.51]–[2.53]**, **[2.56]**, **[2.57]**; figure in final pair of square brackets substituted for original figure "(6)" by the Bankruptcy and Debt Advice (Scotland) Act 2014, s 30(h), subject to transitional provisions and savings in SSI 2014/261, arts 4, 12 at **[2.91]**, **[2.99]**.

Sub-s (8): figure in square brackets substituted for original figure "(7)", by the Bankruptcy and Debt Advice (Scotland) Act 2014, s 56(1), Sch 3, paras 2, 19, subject to transitional provisions and savings in SSI 2014/261, arts 4, 12 at **[2.91]**, **[2.99]**.

Sub-s (9): word "permanent" omitted in each place repealed by the Bankruptcy and Diligence etc (Scotland) Act 2007, s 226(2), Sch 6, Pt 1, subject to transitional provisions and savings in SSI 2008/115, arts 5–7, 10, 15 at **[2.51]–[2.53]**, **[2.56]**, **[2.57]**.

Sub-s (10): added by the Bankruptcy and Diligence etc (Scotland) Act 2007, s 36, Sch 1, paras 1, 29(1), (3), subject to transitional provisions and savings in SSI 2008/115, arts 5–7, 10, 15 at **[2.51]–[2.53]**, **[2.56]**, **[2.57]**; words in square brackets inserted by the Bankruptcy and Debt Advice (Scotland) Act 2014, s 30(i), subject to transitional provisions and savings in SSI 2014/261, arts 4, 12 at **[2.91]**, **[2.99]**.

Election, resignation and removal of commissioners

[5.67]

30 Election, resignation and removal of commissioners

(1) At the statutory meeting or any subsequent meeting of creditors, the creditors (other than any such person as is mentioned in section 24(3) of this Act) may, from among the creditors or their mandatories, elect one or more commissioners (or new or additional commissioners); but not more than 5 commissioners shall hold office in any sequestration at any one time.

(2) None of the following persons shall be eligible for election as a commissioner, nor shall anyone who becomes such a person after having been elected as a commissioner be entitled to continue to act as a commissioner—

(a) any person mentioned in paragraph (a) or (c) of section 24(2) of this Act as not being eligible for election;

(b) a person who is an associate of the debtor or of the . . . trustee.

(3) A commissioner may resign office at any time.

(4) Without prejudice to section [1A(2)] of this Act, a commissioner may be removed from office—

(a) if he is a mandatory of a creditor, by the creditor recalling the mandate and intimating in writing its recall to the . . . trustee;

(b) by the creditors (other than any such person as is mentioned in section 24(3) of this Act) at a meeting called for the purpose;

[(c) by order of the sheriff if the sheriff is satisfied that the commissioner is no longer acting in the interests of the efficient conduct of the sequestration.]

[(5) An order under subsection (4)(c) may be made on the application of—

(a) the Accountant in Bankruptcy,

(b) a person representing not less than one quarter in value of the creditors, or

(c) the trustee.

(6) The sheriff must—

(a) order an application by a person mentioned in subsection (5) to be served on the commissioner,

(b) order that the application is intimated to every creditor who has given a mandate to the commissioner, and

(c) before deciding whether or not to make an order under subsection (4)(c), give the commissioner the opportunity to make representations.

(7) On an application under subsection (4)(c), the sheriff may, in ordering the removal of the commissioner from office, make such further order as the sheriff thinks fit or may, instead of removing the commissioner from office, make such other order as the sheriff thinks fit.

(8) The trustee, the Accountant in Bankruptcy, any commissioner or any creditor may appeal against the decision of the sheriff on an application under subsection (4)(c) within 14 days after the date of that decision.]

NOTES

Repealed as noted at the beginning of this Act.

Sub-s (2): word "permanent" (omitted) repealed by the Bankruptcy and Diligence etc (Scotland) Act 2007, s 226(2), Sch 6, Pt 1, subject to transitional provisions and savings in SSI 2008/115, arts 5–7, 10, 15 at **[2.51]–[2.53]**, **[2.56]**, **[2.57]**.

Sub-s (4): reference in square brackets substituted by the Bankruptcy (Scotland) Act 1993, s 11(3), Sch 1, para 19, subject to s 12(6) thereof, at **[5.194]** and to the Bankruptcy (Scotland) Act 1993 Commencement and Savings Order 1993, SI 1993/438, arts 4, 5, at **[16.58]**, **[16.59]**; word "permanent" omitted from para (a) repealed by the Bankruptcy and Diligence etc (Scotland) Act 2007, s 226(2), Sch 6, Pt 1, subject to transitional provisions and savings in SSI 2008/115, arts 5–7, 10, 15 at **[2.51]–[2.53]**, **[2.56]**, **[2.57]**; para (c) added by the Bankruptcy and Debt Advice (Scotland) Act 2014, s 31(a), subject to transitional provisions and savings in SSI 2014/261, arts 4, 12 at **[2.91]**, **[2.99]**.

Sub-ss (5)–(8): added by the Bankruptcy and Debt Advice (Scotland) Act 2014, s 31(b), subject to transitional provisions and savings in SSI 2014/261, arts 4, 12 at **[2.91]**, **[2.99]**.

[Vesting of estate in trustee]

NOTES

Cross-heading: substituted for original words "Vesting of estate in permanent trustee" by the Bankruptcy and Diligence etc (Scotland) Act 2007, s 36, Sch 1, paras 1, 30(1), (6), subject to transitional provisions and savings in SSI 2008/115, arts 5–7, 10, 15 at **[2.51]–[2.53]**, **[2.56]**, **[2.57]**.

[5.68]

31 Vesting of estate at date of sequestration

(1) Subject to section 33 of this Act [and section 91(3) of the Pensions Act 1995], the whole estate of the debtor shall[, by virtue of the trustee's appointment,] vest [in the trustee] as at the date of sequestration . . . for the benefit of the creditors . . .

(a) . . .

(b) . . .

[(1A) It shall not be competent for—

(a) the trustee; or

(b) any person deriving title from the trustee,

to complete title to any heritable estate in Scotland vested in the trustee by virtue of his appointment before the expiry of the period mentioned in subsection (1B) below.

(1B) That period is the period of 28 days (or such other period as may be prescribed) beginning with the day on which—

(a) the certified copy of the order of the sheriff granting warrant is recorded under subsection (1)(a) of section 14 of this Act; or

(b) the certified copy of the determination of the Accountant in Bankruptcy awarding sequestration is recorded under subsection (1A) of that section,

in the register of inhibitions.]

(2) The exercise by the . . . trustee of any power conferred on him by this Act in respect of any heritable estate vested in him by virtue of [his appointment] shall not be challengeable on the ground of any prior inhibition . . .

(3) Where the debtor has an uncompleted title to any heritable estate in Scotland, the . . . trustee may complete title thereto either in his own name or in the name of the debtor, but completion of title in the name of the debtor shall not validate by accretion any unperfected right in favour of any person other than the . . . trustee.

(4) Any moveable property, in respect of which but for this subsection—

(a) delivery or possession; or

(b) intimation of its assignation,

would be required in order to complete title to it, shall vest in the . . . trustee by virtue of [his appointment] as if at the date of sequestration the . . . trustee had taken delivery or possession of the property or had made intimation of its assignation to him, as the case may be.

(5) Any non-vested contingent interest which the debtor has shall vest in the . . . trustee as if an assignation of that interest had been executed by the debtor and intimation thereof made at the date of sequestration.

[(5A) Any non-vested contingent interest vested in the trustee by virtue of subsection (5) above shall, where it remains so vested in the trustee on the date [which is 4 years after the date of sequestration], be reinvested in the debtor as if an assignation of that interest had been executed by the trustee and intimation thereof made at that date.]

(6) Any person claiming a right to any estate claimed by the . . . trustee may apply to the [sheriff] for the estate to be excluded from such vesting, a copy of the application being served on the . . . trustee; and the [sheriff] shall grant the application if [he] is satisfied that the estate should not be so vested.

(7) Where any successor of a deceased debtor whose estate has been sequestrated has made up title to, or is in possession of, any part of that estate, the [sheriff] may, on the application of the . . . trustee, order the successor to convey such estate to him.

(8) In subsection (1) above[, subject to section 31A of this Act,] the "whole estate of the debtor" means[, subject to subsection (9) below,] [. . .] his whole estate at the date of sequestration, wherever situated, including—

(a) any income or estate vesting in the debtor on that date;

[(aa) any property of the debtor, title to which has not been completed by another person deriving right from the debtor;] and

(b) the capacity to exercise and to take proceedings for exercising, all such powers in, over, or in respect of any property as might have been exercised by the debtor for his own benefit as at, or on, the date of sequestration or might be exercised on a relevant date (within the meaning of section 32(10) of this Act).

[(9) Subject to subsection (10) below, the "whole estate of the debtor" does not include any interest of the debtor as tenant under any of the following tenancies—

(a) a tenancy which is an assured tenancy within the meaning of Part II of the Housing (Scotland) Act 1988, or

(b) a protected tenancy within the meaning of the Rent (Scotland) Act 1984 in respect of which, by virtue of any provision of Part VIII of that Act, no premium can lawfully be required as a condition of the assignation, or

[(c) a Scottish secure tenancy within the meaning of the Housing (Scotland) Act 2001 (asp 10)][, or

(d) a private residential tenancy as defined in the Private Housing (Tenancies) (Scotland) Act 2016.]]

(10) On the date on which the . . . trustee serves notice to that effect on the debtor, the interest of the debtor as tenant under any of the tenancies referred to in subsection (9) above shall form part of his estate and vest in the . . . trustee as if it had vested in him under section 32(6) of this Act.]

NOTES

Repealed as noted at the beginning of this Act.

Sub-s (1): words in first pair of square brackets inserted by the Pensions Act 1995, s 122, Sch 3, para 13; words in second and third pairs of square brackets inserted, words "in the permanent trustee" omitted in the first place repealed and paras (a), (b) together with word "; and" immediately preceding para (a) repealed by the Bankruptcy and Diligence etc (Scotland) Act 2007, s 226(1), (2), Sch 5, para 13(1), (2), Sch 6, Pt 1, subject to transitional provisions and savings in SSI 2008/115, arts 5–7, 10, 15 at **[2.51]–[2.53]**, **[2.56]**, **[2.57]**. Paras (a), (b) previously read as follows:

"(a) the estate shall so vest by virtue of the act and warrant issued on confirmation of the permanent trustee's appointment; and

(b) the act and warrant shall, in respect of the heritable estate in Scotland of the debtor, have the same effect as if a decree of adjudication in implement of sale, as well as a decree of adjudication for payment and in security of debt, subject to no legal reversion, had been pronounced in favour of the permanent trustee.".

Sub-ss (1A), (1B): inserted by the Bankruptcy and Diligence etc (Scotland) Act 2007, s 17(1)(a), subject to transitional provisions and savings in SSI 2008/115, arts 5–7, 10, 15 at **[2.51]–[2.53]**, **[2.56]**, **[2.57]**.

Sub-s (2): word "permanent" (omitted in the first place) repealed, and words in square brackets substituted for original words "the act and warrant" by the Bankruptcy and Diligence etc (Scotland) Act 2007, ss 36, 226(2), Sch 1, paras 1, 30(1), (2), Sch 6, Pt 1, subject to transitional provisions and savings in SSI 2008/115, arts 5–7, 10, 15 at **[2.51]–[2.53]**, **[2.56]**, **[2.57]**; words "(reserving any effect of such inhibition on ranking)" (omitted in the second place) repealed by the Bankruptcy and Diligence etc (Scotland) Act 2007, s 226(2), Sch 6, Pt 1, subject to transitional provisions and savings in the Bankruptcy and Diligence etc (Scotland) Act 2007 (Commencement No 4, Savings and Transitionals) Order 2009, SSI 2009/67, art 6 at **[2.62]**.

Sub-ss (3), (5): word "permanent" omitted in each place repealed by the Bankruptcy and Diligence etc (Scotland) Act 2007, s 226(2), Sch 6, Pt 1, subject to transitional provisions and savings in SSI 2008/115, arts 5–7, 10, 15 at **[2.51]–[2.53]**, **[2.56]**, **[2.57]**.

Sub-s (4): word "permanent" omitted in both places repealed and words in square brackets substituted for original words "the act and warrant" by the Bankruptcy and Diligence etc (Scotland) Act 2007, ss 36, 226(2), Sch 1, paras 1, 30(1), (3), Sch 6, Pt 1, subject to transitional provisions and savings in SSI 2008/115, arts 5–7, 10, 15 at **[2.51]–[2.53]**, **[2.56]**, **[2.57]**.

Sub-s (5A): inserted by the Bankruptcy and Diligence etc (Scotland) Act 2007, s 29, subject to transitional provisions and savings in SSI 2008/115, arts 5–7, 10, 15 at **[2.51]–[2.53]**, **[2.56]**, **[2.57]**; words in square brackets substituted for original words "on which the debtor's discharge becomes effective", by the Bankruptcy and Debt Advice (Scotland) Act 2014, s 16(1), subject to transitional provisions and savings in SSI 2014/261, arts 4, 12 at **[2.91]**, **[2.99]**.

Sub-s (6): word "permanent" omitted in both places repealed, and words "sheriff" and "he" in square brackets substituted for original words "court" and "it" respectively by the Bankruptcy and Diligence etc (Scotland) Act 2007, ss 36, 226(2), Sch 1, paras 1, 30(1), (4), Sch 6, Pt 1, subject to transitional provisions and savings in SSI 2008/115, arts 5–7, 10, 15 at **[2.51]–[2.53]**, **[2.56]**, **[2.57]**.

Sub-s (7): word in square brackets substituted for original word "court" and word "permanent" (omitted) repealed by the Bankruptcy and Diligence etc (Scotland) Act 2007, ss 36, 226(2), Sch 1, paras 1, 30(1), (5), Sch 6, Pt 1, subject to transitional provisions and savings in SSI 2008/115, arts 5–7, 10, 15 at **[2.51]–[2.53]**, **[2.56]**, **[2.57]**.

Sub-s (8): words in first pair of square brackets inserted by the Insolvency (Scotland) Regulations 2003, SI 2003/2109, regs 3, 11; words in second pair of square brackets inserted by the Housing Act 1988, s 118(1); words omitted from third pair of square brackets (as inserted by the Social Security Act 1989, s 22(7), Sch 4, para 23) repealed by the Social Security (Recovery of Benefits) Act 1997, s 33(2), Sch 4; para (aa) inserted by the Bankruptcy and Diligence etc (Scotland) Act 2007, s 17(1)(b), subject to transitional provisions and savings in SSI 2008/115, arts 5–7, 10, 15 at **[2.51]–[2.53]**, **[2.56]**, **[2.57]**.

Sub-s (9): added by the Housing Act 1988, s 118(2); para (c) substituted by the Housing (Scotland) Act 2001, s 112, Sch 10, para 10; para (d) and word preceding it inserted by the Private Housing (Tenancies) (Scotland) Act 2016, s 74, Sch 4, para 3.

Sub-s (10): added by the Housing Act 1988, s 118(2); word "permanent" omitted in both places repealed by the Bankruptcy and Diligence etc (Scotland) Act 2007, s 226(2), Sch 6, Pt 1, subject to transitional provisions and savings in SSI 2008/115, arts 5–7, 10, 15 at **[2.51]–[2.53]**, **[2.56]**, **[2.57]**.

[5.69]

[[31ZA] Proceedings under EC Regulation: modified definition of "estate"

In the application of this Act to insolvency proceedings under the EC Regulation, a reference to "estate" is a reference to estate which may be dealt with in those proceedings.]

NOTES

Repealed as noted at the beginning of this Act.

Inserted (as s 31A) by the Insolvency (Scotland) Regulations 2003, SI 2003/2109, regs 3, 12; renumbered as s 31ZA by the Bankruptcy and Diligence etc (Scotland) Act 2007, s 36, Sch 1, paras 1, 31, subject to transitional provisions and savings in SSI 2008/115, arts 5–7, 10, 15 at **[2.51]–[2.53]**, **[2.56]**, **[2.57]**.

[5.70]

[31A Property subject to restraint order

(1) This section applies where—

(a) property is excluded from the debtor's estate by virtue of section 420(2)(a) of the Proceeds of Crime Act 2002 (property subject to a restraint order),

(b) an order under [section 50, 67A, 128, 131A, 198 or 215A] of that Act has not been made in respect of the property, . . .

(c) the restraint order is discharged, [and

(d) immediately after the discharge of the restraint order the property is not detained under or by virtue of section 44A, 47J, 122A, 127J, 193A or 195J of that Act.]

[(2) The property vests in the trustee as part of the debtor's estate.]

(3) But subsection (2) does not apply to the proceeds of property realised by a management receiver under section 49(2)(d) or 197(2)(d) of that Act (realisation of property to meet receiver's remuneration and expenses).]

NOTES

Repealed as noted at the beginning of this Act.

Inserted, together with ss 31B, 31C, by the Proceeds of Crime Act 2002, s 456, Sch 11, paras 1, 15(1), (4).

Sub-s (1): words in square brackets in para (b) substituted, word omitted from para (b) repealed, and para (d) and word "and" immediately preceding it added by the Policing and Crime Act 2009, s 112(1), (2), Sch 7, Pt 6, paras 46, 48(1), (2), Sch 8, Pt 4.

Sub-s (2): substituted by the Policing and Crime Act 2009, s 112(1), Sch 7, Pt 6, paras 46, 48(1), (3).

[5.71]

[31AA Property released from detention

(1) This section applies where—

(a) property is excluded from the debtor's estate by virtue of section 420(2)(b) of the Proceeds of Crime Act 2002 (property detained under certain provisions),
(b) no order is in force in respect of the property under section 41, 50, 120, 128, 190 or 198 of that Act, and
(c) the property is released.

(2) The property vests in the trustee as part of the debtor's estate.]

NOTES

Commencement: 1 June 2015.

Inserted by the Policing and Crime Act 2009, s 112(1), Sch 7, Pt 6, paras 46, 49.

Repealed as noted at the beginning of this Act.

[5.72]

[31B Property in respect of which receivership or administration order is made

(1) This section applies where—
(a) property is excluded from the debtor's estate by virtue of [section 420(2)(c)] of the Proceeds of Crime Act 2002 (property in respect of which an order for the appointment of a receiver or administrator under certain provisions of that Act is in force), . . .
(b) a confiscation order is made under section 6, 92 or 156 of that Act,
(c) the amount payable under the confiscation order is fully paid, and
(d) any of the property remains in the hands of the receiver or administrator (as the case may be).

(2) The property vests in the . . . trustee as part of the debtor's estate.]

NOTES

Inserted as noted to s 31A at **[5.70]**.

Repealed as noted at the beginning of this Act.

Sub-s (1): words in square brackets in para (a) substituted by the Policing and Crime Act 2009, s 112(1), Sch 7, Pt 6, paras 46, 50; word "and" omitted from para (a) repealed by the Bankruptcy and Diligence etc (Scotland) Act 2007, s 226(2), Sch 6, Pt 1, subject to transitional provisions and savings in SSI 2008/115, arts 5–7, 10, 15 at **[2.51]–[2.53]**, **[2.56]**, **[2.57]**.

Sub-s (2): word "permanent" (omitted) repealed by the Bankruptcy and Diligence etc (Scotland) Act 2007, s 226(2), Sch 6, Pt 1, subject to transitional provisions and savings in SSI 2008/115, arts 5–7, 10, 15 at **[2.51]–[2.53]**, **[2.56]**, **[2.57]**.

[5.73]

[31BA Property in respect of which realisation order made

(1) This section applies where—
(a) property is excluded from the debtor's estate by virtue of section 420(2)(d) of the Proceeds of Crime Act 2002 (property in respect of which an order has been made authorising realisation of the property by an appropriate officer),
(b) a confiscation order is made under section 6, 92 or 156 of that Act,
(c) the amount payable under the confiscation order is fully paid, and
(d) any of the property remains in the hands of the appropriate officer.

(2) The property vests in the trustee as part of the debtor's estate.]

NOTES

Commencement: 1 June 2015.

Inserted by the Policing and Crime Act 2009, s 112(1), Sch 7, Pt 6, paras 46, 51.

Repealed as noted at the beginning of this Act.

[5.74]

[31C Property subject to certain orders where confiscation order discharged or quashed

(1) This section applies where—
(a) property is excluded from the debtor's estate by virtue of section 420(2)(a), (b), (c) or (d) of the Proceeds of Crime Act 2002 (property [excluded from debtor's estate]),
(b) a confiscation order is made under section 6, 92 or 156 of that Act, and
(c) the confiscation order is discharged under section 30, 114 or 180 of that Act (as the case may be) or quashed under that Act or in pursuance of any enactment relating to appeals against conviction or sentence.

[(2) Any such property vests in the trustee as part of the debtor's estate if it is in the hands of—
(a) a receiver appointed under Part 2 or 4 of that Act,
(b) an administrator appointed under Part 3 of that Act,
(c) an appropriate officer (within the meaning of section 41A, 120A or 190A of that Act).]

(3) But subsection (2) does not apply to the proceeds of property realised by a management receiver under section 49(2)(d) or 197(2)(d) of that Act (realisation of property to meet receiver's remuneration and expenses).]

NOTES

Inserted as noted to s 31A at **[5.70]**.

Repealed as noted at the beginning of this Act.

Sub-s (1): words in square brackets in para (a) substituted by the Policing and Crime Act 2009, s 112(1), Sch 7, Pt 6, paras 46, 52(1), (2).

Sub-s (2): substituted by the Policing and Crime Act 2009, s 112(1), Sch 7, Pt 6, paras 46, 52(1), (3).

[5.75]

32 Vesting of estate, and dealings of debtor, after sequestration

(1) Subject to [sections 32A to 32H] below, any income of whatever nature received by the debtor on a relevant date, other than income arising from the estate which is vested in the . . . trustee, shall vest in the debtor.

(2) [Notwithstanding anything in section 11 or 12 of the Welfare Reform and Pensions Act 1999,] the sheriff, on the application of the . . . trustee, may, after having regard to all the circumstances, determine a suitable amount to allow for—

(a) aliment for the debtor; and

(b) the debtor's relevant obligations;

and if the debtor's income is in excess of the total amount so allowed the sheriff shall fix the amount of the excess and order it to be paid to the . . . trustee.

[(2WA) Subject to subsection (4L) below, no application may be made under subsection (2) above after the date on which the debtor's discharge becomes effective.

(2XA) An order made by the sheriff under subsection (2) above shall specify the period during which it has effect and that period—

(a) may end after the date on which the debtor's discharge becomes effective; and

(b) shall end no later than 3 years after the date on which the order is made.

(2YA) An order made by the sheriff under subsection (2) above may provide that a third person is to pay to the trustee a specified proportion of money due to the debtor by way of income.

(2ZA) If the debtor fails to comply with an order made under subsection (2) above, he shall be guilty of an offence and liable on summary conviction to a fine not exceeding level 5 on the standard scale or to imprisonment for a term not exceeding 3 months or to both.]

[(2A) The amount allowed for the purposes specified in paragraphs (a) and (b) of subsection (2) above shall not be less than the total amount of any income received by the debtor—

(a) by way of guaranteed minimum pension; . . .

(b) . . .

"guaranteed minimum pension" [having the same meaning] as in the Pension Schemes Act 1993.]

(3) The debtor's relevant obligations referred to in paragraph (b) of subsection (2) above are—

(a) any obligation of aliment owed by him ("obligation of aliment" having the same meaning as in the Family Law (Scotland) Act 1985);

(b) any obligation of his to make a periodical allowance to a former spouse [or former civil partner];

[(c) any obligation of his to pay child support maintenance under the Child Support Act 1991,]

but any amount allowed under that subsection for the relevant obligations [referred to in paragraphs (a) and (b) above] need not be sufficient for compliance with a subsisting order or agreement as regards such aliment or periodical allowance.

(4) In the event of any change in the debtor's circumstances, the sheriff, on the application of the . . . trustee, the debtor or any other interested person, may vary or recall any order under subsection (2) above.

[(4A) The sheriff clerk shall send a copy of any order made under subsection (2) above (and a copy of any variation or recall of such an order) to the Accountant in Bankruptcy.

(4B) Where no order has been made under subsection (2) above, a debtor may enter into an agreement in writing with the trustee which provides—

(a) that the debtor is to pay to the trustee an amount equal to a specified part or proportion of his income; or

(b) that a third person is to pay to the trustee a specified proportion of money due to the debtor by way of income.

(4C) No agreement under subsection (4B) above may be entered into after the date on which the debtor's discharge becomes effective.

(4D) Subsection (2XA) above applies to agreements entered into under subsection (4B) above as it applies to orders made under subsection (2) above.

(4E) An agreement entered into under subsection (4B) above may, if subsection (4K) below has been complied with, be enforced, subject to subsection (4F) below, as if it were an order made under subsection (2) above.

(4F) Subsection (2ZA) above does not apply to an agreement entered into under subsection (4B) above.

(4G) An agreement entered into under subsection (4B) above may be varied—

(a) by written agreement between the parties; or

(b) by the sheriff, on an application made by the trustee, the debtor or any other interested person.

(4H) The sheriff—

(a) may not vary an agreement entered into under subsection (4B) above so as to include provision of a kind which could not be included in an order made under subsection (2) above; and

(b) shall grant an application to vary such an agreement if and to the extent that the sheriff thinks variation is necessary to determine a suitable amount to allow for the purposes specified in paragraphs (a) and (b) of subsection (2) above, being an amount which shall not be included in the amount to be paid to the trustee.

(4J) Where a third person pays a sum of money to the trustee under subsection (2YA) or (4B)(b) above, that person shall be discharged of any liability to the debtor to the extent of the sum of money so paid.

(4K) The trustee shall (unless he is the Accountant in Bankruptcy) send a copy of any agreement entered into under subsection (4B) above (and a copy of any variation of such an agreement) to the Accountant in Bankruptcy.

(4L) If the debtor fails to comply with an agreement entered into under subsection (4B) above, the sheriff, on the application of the trustee, may make an order under subsection (2) above—

(a) ending on the date on which the agreement would, had the debtor continued to comply with it, have ended; and

(b) on the same terms as the agreement.]

(5) Diligence [(which, for the purposes of this section, includes the making of a deduction from earnings order under the Child Support Act 1991)] in respect of a debt or obligation of which the debtor would be discharged under section 55 of this Act were he discharged under section 54[, 54A or 54C] thereof shall not be competent against income vesting in him under subsection (1) above.

[(5A) Where the trustee knows, or becomes aware, of any estate vested in the trustee under section 31 or this section which comprises funds held by a bank, the trustee must serve a notice on the bank—

(a) informing the bank of the sequestration, and

(b) specifying reasonable detail in order to allow the bank to identify the debtor and the funds held.

(5B) A notice under subsection (5A)—

(a) must be in writing and may be sent—

(i) by first class post or by using a registered or recorded delivery postal service to the bank,

(ii) in some other manner (including by electronic means) which the trustee reasonably considers likely to cause it to be delivered to the bank on the same or next day,

(b) is deemed to have been received the day after it is sent.]

(6) Without prejudice to subsection (1) above, any estate, wherever situated, which—

(a) is acquired by the debtor on a relevant date; and

(b) would have vested in the . . . trustee if it had been part of the debtor's estate on the date of sequestration,

shall vest in the . . . trustee for the benefit of the creditors as at the date of acquisition; and any person who holds any such estate shall, on production to him of a copy of the [order] certified by the sheriff clerk [or, as the case may be, by the Accountant in Bankruptcy appointing the trustee], convey or deliver the estate to the . . . trustee: Provided that—

(i) if such a person has in good faith and without knowledge of the sequestration conveyed the estate to the debtor or to anyone on the instructions of the debtor, he shall incur no liability to the . . . trustee except to account for any proceeds of the conveyance which are in his hands; and

[(ia) the trustee is not entitled by virtue of this subsection to any remedy against a bank in respect of a banking transaction entered into before the receipt by the bank of a notice under subsection (5A) (whether or not the bank is aware of the sequestration),]

(ii) this subsection shall be without prejudice to any right . . . acquired in the estate in good faith and for value.

(7) The debtor shall immediately notify the . . . trustee of any assets acquired by him on a relevant date or of any other substantial change in his financial circumstances; and, if the debtor fails to comply with this subsection, he shall be guilty of an offence and liable on summary conviction to a fine not exceeding level 5 on the standard scale or to imprisonment for a term not exceeding 3 months or to both.

(8) Subject to subsection (9) [and (9C)] below, any dealing of or with the debtor relating to his estate vested in the . . . trustee under [this section or] section 31 of this Act shall be of no effect in a question with the . . . trustee.

(9) Subsection (8) above shall not apply where the person seeking to uphold the dealing establishes—

(a) that the . . . trustee—

(i) which has abandoned to the debtor the property to which the dealing relates;

(ii) has expressly or impliedly authorised the dealing; or

(iii) is otherwise personally barred from challenging the dealing, or

(b) that the dealing is—

(i) the performance of an obligation undertaken before the date of sequestration by a person obliged to the debtor in the obligation;

(ii) the purchase from the debtor of goods for which the purchaser has given value to the debtor or is willing to give value to the . . . trustee; or

(iii) a banking transaction in the ordinary course of business between the banker and the debtor[; or

(iv) one which satisfies the conditions mentioned in subsection (9ZA) below,]

and that the person dealing with the debtor was, at the time when the dealing occurred, unaware of the sequestration and had at that time no reason to believe that the debtor's estate had been sequestrated or was the subject of sequestration proceedings.

[(9ZA) The conditions are that—

(a) the dealing constitutes—

(i) the transfer of incorporeal moveable property; or

(ii) the creation, transfer, variation or extinguishing of a real right in heritable property,

for which the person dealing with the debtor has given adequate consideration to the debtor, or is willing to give adequate consideration to the trustee;

(b) the dealing requires the delivery of a deed; and

(c) the delivery occurs during the period beginning with the date of sequestration and ending on the day which falls 7 days after the day on which—

(i) the certified copy of the order of the sheriff granting warrant is recorded under subsection (1)(a) of section 14 of this Act; or

(ii) the certified copy of the determination of the Accountant in Bankruptcy awarding sequestration is recorded under subsection (1A) of that section,

in the register of inhibitions.]

[(9A) Where the trustee has abandoned to the debtor any heritable property, notice in such form as may be prescribed given to the debtor by the trustee shall be sufficient evidence that the property is vested in the debtor.

(9B) Where the trustee gives notice under subsection (9A) above, he shall, as soon as reasonably practicable after giving the notice, record a certified copy of it in the register of inhibitions.]

[(9C) Subsection (8) does not apply where the dealing is a banking transaction entered into before the receipt by the bank of a notice under subsection (5A) (whether or not the bank is aware of the sequestration).]

(10) In this section "a relevant date" means a date after the date of sequestration and before the date [which is 4 years after the date of sequestration].

[(11) In this section "bank" has the same meaning as "appropriate bank or institution" in section 73(1).]

NOTES

Repealed as noted at the beginning of this Act.

Sub-s (1): words in square brackets substituted (for words "subsections (2) and (4B)" as substituted by the Bankruptcy and Diligence etc (Scotland) Act 2007, ss 18(1), (2)) by the Bankruptcy and Debt Advice (Scotland) Act 2014, s 56(1), Sch 3, paras 2, 20(a), subject to transitional provisions and savings in SSI 2014/261, arts 4, 12 at **[2.91]**, **[2.99]**; word "permanent" (omitted) repealed by the Bankruptcy and Diligence etc (Scotland) Act 2007, s 226(2), Sch 6, Pt 1, subject to transitional provisions and savings in SSI 2008/115, arts 5–7, 10, 15 at **[2.51]–[2.53]**, **[2.56]**, **[2.57]**.

Sub-s (2): words in square brackets inserted by the Welfare Reform and Pensions Act 1999, s 18, Sch 2, para 1; word "permanent" omitted in both places repealed by the Bankruptcy and Diligence etc (Scotland) Act 2007, s 226(2), Sch 6, Pt 1, subject to transitional provisions and savings in SSI 2008/115, arts 5–7, 10, 15 at **[2.51]–[2.53]**, **[2.56]**, **[2.57]**. Repealed, together with sub-ss (2WA)–(2ZA), (2A), (3), (4), (4A)–(4L), by the Bankruptcy and Debt Advice (Scotland) Act 2014, s 56(2), Sch 4, subject to transitional provisions and savings in SSI 2014/261, arts 4, 12 at **[2.91]**, **[2.99]**.

Sub-ss (2WA)–(2ZA): inserted by the Bankruptcy and Diligence etc (Scotland) Act 2007, s 18(1), (3), subject to transitional provisions and savings in SSI 2008/115, arts 5–7, 10, 15 at **[2.51]–[2.53]**, **[2.56]**, **[2.57]**; repealed as noted to sub-s (2) above.

Sub-s (2A): inserted by the Pensions Act 1995, s 122, Sch 3, para 14; words omitted repealed and words in square brackets substituted by the Pensions Act 2008 (Abolition of Protected Rights) (Consequential Amendments) (No 2) Order 2011, SI 2011/1730, art 2; repealed as noted to sub-s (2) above.

Sub-s (3): words in first pair of square brackets inserted by the Civil Partnership Act 2004, s 261(2), Sch 28, para 34; words in second and third pairs of square brackets inserted by the Child Support Act 1991, s 58(13), Sch 5, para 6(1), (2); repealed as noted to sub-s (2) above.

Sub-s (4): word "permanent" (omitted) repealed by the Bankruptcy and Diligence etc (Scotland) Act 2007, s 226(2), Sch 6, Pt 1, subject to transitional provisions and savings in SSI 2008/115, arts 5–7, 10, 15 at **[2.51]–[2.53]**, **[2.56]**, **[2.57]**; repealed as noted to sub-s (2) above.

Sub-ss (4A)–(4L): inserted by the Bankruptcy and Diligence etc (Scotland) Act 2007, s 18(1), (4), subject to transitional provisions and savings in SSI 2008/115, arts 5–7, 10, 15 at **[2.51]–[2.53]**, **[2.56]**, **[2.57]**; repealed as noted to sub-s (2) above.

Sub-s (5): words in first pair of square brackets inserted by the Child Support Act 1991, s 58(13), Sch 5, para 6(1), (2); words in second pair of square brackets inserted by the Bankruptcy and Debt Advice (Scotland) Act 2014, s 56(1), Sch 3, paras 2, 20(b), subject to transitional provisions and savings in SSI 2014/261, arts 4, 12 at **[2.91]**, **[2.99]**.

Sub-ss (5A), (5B): inserted by the Bankruptcy and Debt Advice (Scotland) Act 2014, s 13(a), subject to transitional provisions and savings in SSI 2014/261, arts 4, 12 at **[2.91]**, **[2.99]**.

Sub-s (6): word "permanent" omitted in each place repealed, word in first pair of square brackets substituted for original words "act and warrant" and words in second pair of square brackets substituted for original words "confirming the permanent trustee's appointment" by the Bankruptcy and Diligence etc (Scotland) Act 2007, ss 36, 226(2), Sch 1, paras 1, 32, Sch 6, Pt 1, subject to transitional provisions and savings in SSI 2008/115, arts 5–7, 10, 15 at **[2.51]–[2.53]**, **[2.56]**, **[2.57]**; in the proviso, para (ia) inserted and words "or interest" omitted from para (ii) repealed, by the Bankruptcy and Debt Advice (Scotland) Act 2014, ss 13(b), 56(2), Sch 4, subject to transitional provisions and savings in SSI 2014/261, arts 4, 12 at **[2.91]**, **[2.99]**.

Sub-s (7): word "permanent" (omitted) repealed by the Bankruptcy and Diligence etc (Scotland) Act 2007, s 226(2), Sch 6, Pt 1, subject to transitional provisions and savings in SSI 2008/115, arts 5–7, 10, 15 at **[2.51]–[2.53]**, **[2.56]**, **[2.57]**.

Sub-s (8): words in first pair of square brackets inserted by the Bankruptcy and Debt Advice (Scotland) Act 2014, s 13(c), subject to transitional provisions and savings in SSI 2014/261, arts 4, 12 at **[2.91]**, **[2.99]**; word "permanent" omitted in both places repealed and words in second pair of square brackets inserted by the Bankruptcy and Diligence etc (Scotland) Act 2007, ss 17(2)(a), 226(2), Sch 6, Pt 1, subject to transitional provisions and savings in SSI 2008/115, arts 5–7, 10, 15 at **[2.51]–[2.53]**, **[2.56]**, **[2.57]**.

Sub-s (9): word "permanent" omitted in both places repealed and para (b)(iv) and word immediately preceding it inserted by the Bankruptcy and Diligence etc (Scotland) Act 2007, ss 17(2)(b), 226(2), Sch 6, Pt 1, subject to transitional provisions and savings in SSI 2008/115, arts 5–7, 10, 15 at **[2.51]–[2.53]**, **[2.56]**, **[2.57]**; para (b)(iii) repealed by the Bankruptcy and Debt Advice (Scotland) Act 2014, s 56(2), Sch 4, subject to transitional provisions and savings in SSI 2014/261, arts 4, 12 at **[2.91]**, **[2.99]**.

Sub-ss (9ZA), (9A), (9B): inserted by the Bankruptcy and Diligence etc (Scotland) Act 2007, ss 17(2)(c), 19(1), subject to transitional provisions and savings in SSI 2008/115, arts 5–7, 10, 15 at **[2.51]–[2.53]**, **[2.56]**, **[2.57]**.

Sub-s (9C): inserted by the Bankruptcy and Debt Advice (Scotland) Act 2014, s 13(d), subject to transitional provisions and savings in SSI 2014/261, arts 4, 12 at **[2.91]**, **[2.99]**.

Sub-s (10): words in square brackets substituted for original words "on which the debtor's discharge becomes effective" by the Bankruptcy and Debt Advice (Scotland) Act 2014, s 16(2), subject to transitional provisions and savings in SSI 2014/261, arts 4, 12 at **[2.91]**, **[2.99]**.

Sub-s (11): added by the Bankruptcy and Debt Advice (Scotland) Act 2014, s 13(e), subject to transitional provisions and savings in SSI 2014/261, arts 4, 12 at **[2.91]**, **[2.99]**.

Regulations: the Bankruptcy (Scotland) Regulations 2014, SSI 2014/225 at **[16.267]**.

[5.76]

[32A Debtor contribution order

(1) The Accountant in Bankruptcy must make an order fixing the debtor's contribution (a "debtor contribution order")—

(a) in the case of a debtor application, at the same time as awarding sequestration of the debtor's estate,
(b) in the case of an award of sequestration following a petition under section 5(2)(b), after considering initial proposals for the debtor's contribution provided by the trustee.

(2) In a case referred to in subsection (1)(b), the trustee must send initial proposals for the debtor's contribution before the end of the period of 6 weeks beginning with the date of award of sequestration.

(3) In making a debtor contribution order, the Accountant in Bankruptcy must use the common financial tool to assess the debtor's contribution.

(4) A debtor contribution order may fix the amount of the debtor's contribution as zero.

(5) A debtor contribution order may be made irrespective of sections 11 and 12 of the Welfare Reform and Pensions Act 1999 (c 30).

(6) A debtor contribution order may provide that a third person is to pay to the trustee a specified proportion of money due to the debtor by way of income.

(7) Where a third person pays a sum of money to the trustee in accordance with subsection (6), the third person is discharged from any liability to the debtor to the extent of the sum so paid.

(8) The Accountant in Bankruptcy must, immediately following the making of a debtor contribution order, give written notice of the order to—
(a) the debtor,
(b) the trustee, and
(c) any third person mentioned in the order.

(9) A debtor contribution order must not take effect on a date before the expiry of the period of 14 days beginning with the day of notification of the order.]

NOTES

Commencement: 1 April 2015.

Inserted, together with ss 32B–32H, by the Bankruptcy and Debt Advice (Scotland) Act 2014, s 4, subject to transitional provisions and savings in SSI 2014/261, arts 4, 12 at **[2.91]**, **[2.99]**.

Repealed as noted at the beginning of this Act.

[5.77]

[32B Debtor contribution order: payment period and intervals

(1) A debtor contribution order must contain provision requiring the debtor to pay the debtor's contribution (if not zero)—
(a) during the payment period, and
(b) at regular intervals determined by the person making or varying the order.

(2) In subsection (1)(a), "payment period" means—
(a) the period of 48 months beginning with the date of the first payment,
(b) such shorter period as is determined by the person making or varying the order, or
(c) such longer period as is—
  (i) determined by the trustee where there is a period during which the debtor did not pay an amount required under the debtor contribution order, or
  (ii) agreed by the debtor and the trustee.

(3) The person making or varying the order may determine a shorter period under subsection (2)(b) only if, in the opinion of that person, the value of—
(a) the debtor's contribution during the shorter period, and
(b) any other estate of the debtor taken possession of by the trustee,

would be sufficient to allow a distribution of the debtor's estate to meet in full all of the debts mentioned in section 51.

(4) The Accountant in Bankruptcy must, when making an order under section 32A—
(a) determine the date of the first payment, or
(b) in a case where the debtor's contribution is fixed as zero, determine the date which is to be deemed as the date of the first payment under the order.]

NOTES

Commencement: 1 April 2015.

Inserted as noted to s 32A at **[5.76]**.

Repealed as noted at the beginning of this Act.

[5.78]

[32C Debtor contribution order: review and appeal

(1) The debtor, the trustee or any other interested person may apply to the Accountant in Bankruptcy for a review of a debtor contribution order made by the Accountant in Bankruptcy under section 32A.

(2) An application under subsection (1) must be made before the expiry of the period of 14 days beginning with the day on which the debtor contribution order is made.

(3) If an application under subsection (1) is made, the debtor contribution order is suspended until the determination of that review by the Accountant in Bankruptcy.

(4) If an application for a review under subsection (1) is made, the Accountant in Bankruptcy must—
(a) take into account any representations made by an interested person before the expiry of the period of 21 days beginning with the day on which the application is made, and
(b) confirm, amend or revoke the debtor contribution order before the expiry of the period of 28 days beginning with the day on which the application is made.

(5) The trustee or the debtor may appeal to the sheriff against any decision of the Accountant in Bankruptcy under subsection (4)(b) before the expiry of the period of 14 days beginning with the date of the decision.]

NOTES

Commencement: 1 April 2015.
Inserted as noted to s 32A at **[5.76]**.
Repealed as noted at the beginning of this Act.

[5.79]
[32D Effect of debtor contribution order

(1) The debtor must pay to the trustee any debtor's contribution which is not zero as—
- (a) fixed by the Accountant in Bankruptcy in making the debtor contribution order, or
- (b) varied in accordance with section 32F.

(2) The requirement to pay the debtor's contribution applies irrespective of the debtor's discharge.
(3) If the value of the debtor's estate and income when taken possession of by the trustee is sufficient to allow a distribution of the debtor's estate to meet in full all of the debts mentioned in section 51, any debtor contribution order ceases to have effect.]

NOTES

Commencement: 1 April 2015.
Inserted as noted to s 32A at **[5.76]**.
Repealed as noted at the beginning of this Act.

[5.80]
[32E Deductions from debtor's earnings and other income

(1) Subsections (2) to (6) apply where under a debtor contribution order—
- (a) the debtor is required to pay to the trustee an amount from the debtor's earnings or other income, or
- (b) in accordance with section 32A(6), a third person is required to pay to the trustee money otherwise due to the debtor by way of income.

(2) The debtor must give the person mentioned in subsection (3) an instruction to make—
- (a) deductions of specified amounts from the debtor's earnings or other income, and
- (b) payments to the trustee of the amounts so deducted.

(3) The person mentioned is—
- (a) in the case of an amount to be paid from the debtor's earnings from employment, the person by whom the debtor is employed,
- (b) in the case of an amount to be paid from other earnings or income of the debtor, a third person who is required to pay the earnings or income to the debtor, and
- (c) in the case mentioned in subsection (1)(b), the third person who is required to pay the income to the trustee.

(4) The trustee may give the person mentioned in subsection (3) an instruction of the type mentioned in subsection (2) if—
- (a) the debtor fails to comply with the requirements imposed by that subsection, and
- (b) the debtor fails to pay the debtor's contribution in respect of 2 payment intervals applying by virtue of the debtor contribution order.

(5) A person mentioned in subsection (3) must comply with an instruction provided in accordance with subsection (2) or (4).
(6) Where the person by whom the debtor is employed or another third person pays a sum of money to the trustee in accordance with this section, that person is discharged from any liability to the debtor to the extent of the sum so paid.
(7) The Scottish Ministers may by regulations make provision about instructions to be provided under this section, including in particular—
- (a) the form in which an instruction must be made,
- (b) the manner in which an instruction provided in accordance with subsection (2) or (4) affects the recipient of that instruction, and
- (c) the consequence of any failure of a recipient of an instruction provided in accordance with subsection (2) or (4) to comply with the duty imposed by subsection (5).]

NOTES

Commencement: 30 June 2014 (for the purpose of making regulations); 1 April 2015 (otherwise).
Inserted as noted to s 32A at **[5.76]**.
Repealed as noted at the beginning of this Act.
Regulations: the Bankruptcy (Money Advice and Deduction from Income etc) (Scotland) Regulations 2014, SSI 2014/296 at **[16.284]**.

[5.81]
[32F Variation and removal of debtor contribution order by trustee

(1) The trustee may vary or quash a debtor contribution order—
- (a) on the application of the debtor, following any change in the debtor's circumstances,
- (b) if the trustee considers it to be appropriate, following any change in the debtor's circumstances, or
- (c) if the trustee considers it to be appropriate when—

(i) sending a report to the Accountant in Bankruptcy under section 54(4), or
(ii) granting a discharge under section 54A(2).

(2) In deciding whether to vary or quash a debtor contribution order, the trustee must use the common financial tool to assess the debtor's contribution.

(3) A decision by the trustee under subsection (1)(b) must not take effect on a day before the end of the period of 14 days beginning with the day on which the decision is made.

(4) The trustee must notify in writing the persons mentioned in subsection (5) immediately following—
(a) any variation or quashing of a debtor contribution order,
(b) any refusal of an application.

(5) The persons are—
(a) the debtor,
(b) the Accountant in Bankruptcy (if the trustee is not the Accountant in Bankruptcy),
(c) any third person required to make a payment under the debtor contribution order or under section 32E(5), and
(d) any other interested person.]

NOTES

Commencement: 1 April 2015.
Inserted as noted to s 32A at **[5.76]**.
Repealed as noted at the beginning of this Act.

[5.82]
[32G Payment break

(1) The trustee may, on the application of the debtor, extend the payment period of a debtor contribution order by granting a payment break.

(2) A "payment break" is a period not exceeding 6 months during which payments under the debtor contribution order are deferred.

(3) A debtor may apply for a payment break if—
(a) there has been a reduction of at least 50% in the debtor's disposable income (as determined using the common financial tool) as a result of any of the circumstances mentioned in subsection (4) arising in relation to the debtor, and
(b) the debtor has not previously applied for a payment break in relation to a debtor contribution order applying after the sequestration of the debtor's estate.

(4) The circumstances are—
(a) a period of unemployment or change in employment,
(b) a period of leave from employment because of the birth or adoption of a child or the need to care for a dependant,
(c) a period of illness of the debtor,
(d) a divorce or dissolution of civil partnership,
(e) a separation from a person to whom the debtor is married or is the civil partner,
(f) the death of a person who, along with the debtor, cared for a dependant of the debtor.

(5) An application for a payment break must specify the period during which the debtor wishes payments to be deferred.

(6) If, in the opinion of the trustee, a payment break is fair and reasonable, the trustee may grant a payment break on such conditions and for such period as the trustee thinks fit.

(7) The trustee must notify in writing the grant of a payment break to—
(a) the debtor,
(b) the Accountant in Bankruptcy (if the trustee is not the Accountant in Bankruptcy), and
(c) any third person required to make a payment under the debtor contribution order.

(8) If the trustee decides not to grant a payment break, the trustee must notify the debtor of that decision and of the reasons.

(9) The payment period in a debtor contribution order is deemed to be varied by the addition to the period of any payment break granted under this section.]

NOTES

Commencement: 1 April 2015.
Inserted as noted to s 32A at **[5.76]**.
Repealed as noted at the beginning of this Act.

[5.83]
[32H Sections 32F and 32G: review and appeal

(1) The debtor or any other interested person may apply to the Accountant in Bankruptcy for a review of a decision by the trustee under section 32F or 32G.

(2) An application under subsection (1) must be made before the expiry of the period of 14 days beginning with the day on which the decision is made.

(3) If an application under subsection (1) relates to a decision by the trustee under section 32F(1)(b), the decision is suspended until the determination of that review by the Accountant in Bankruptcy.

(4) If an application for a review under subsection (1) is made, the Accountant in Bankruptcy must—
(a) take into account any representations made by an interested person before the expiry of the period of 21 days beginning with the day on which the application is made, and
(b) confirm, amend or revoke the decision before the expiry of the period of 28 days beginning with the day on which the application is made.

(5) The trustee or the debtor may appeal to the sheriff against any decision of the Accountant in Bankruptcy under subsection (4)(b) before the expiry of the period of 14 days beginning with the date of the decision.]

NOTES

Commencement: 1 April 2015.

Inserted as noted to s 32A at **[5.76]**.

Repealed as noted at the beginning of this Act.

[5.84]

33 Limitations on vesting

(1) The following property of the debtor shall not vest in the . . . trustee—

[(a) any property kept outwith a dwellinghouse in respect of which attachment is, by virtue of section 11(1) of the Debt Arrangement and Attachment (Scotland) Act 2002 (asp 17), incompetent;

(aa) any property kept in a dwellinghouse which is not a non-essential asset for the purposes of Part 3 of that Act;]

(b) property held on trust by the debtor for any other person.

(2) The vesting of a debtor's estate in a . . . trustee shall not affect the right of hypothec of a landlord.

(3) Sections 31 and 32 of this Act are without prejudice to the right of any secured creditor which is preferable to the rights of the . . . trustee.

NOTES

Repealed as noted at the beginning of this Act.

Sub-s (1): word "permanent" (omitted) repealed by the Bankruptcy and Diligence etc (Scotland) Act 2007, s 226(2), Sch 6, Pt 1, subject to transitional provisions and savings in SSI 2008/115, arts 5–7, 10, 15 at **[2.51]–[2.53]**, **[2.56]**, **[2.57]**; paras (a), (aa) substituted for original para (a) by the Debt Arrangement and Attachment (Scotland) Act 2002, s 61, Sch 3, Pt 1, para 15(1), (3).

Sub-ss (2), (3): word "permanent" omitted in each place repealed by the Bankruptcy and Diligence etc (Scotland) Act 2007, s 226(2), Sch 6, Pt 1, subject to transitional provisions and savings in SSI 2008/115, arts 5–7, 10, 15 at **[2.51]–[2.53]**, **[2.56]**, **[2.57]**.

Safeguarding of interests of creditors of insolvent persons

[5.85]

34 Gratuitous alienations

(1) Where this subsection applies, an alienation by a debtor shall be challengeable by—

(a) any creditor who is a creditor by virtue of a debt incurred on or before the date of sequestration, or before the granting of the trust deed or the debtor's death, as the case may be; or

(b) the . . . trustee, the trustee acting under the trust deed or the judicial factor, as the case may be.

(2) Subsection (1) above applies where—

(a) by the alienation, whether before or after the coming into force of this section, any of the debtor's property has been transferred or any claim or right of the debtor has been discharged or renounced; and

(b) any of the following has occurred—

(i) his estate has been sequestrated (other than, in the case of a natural person, after his death); or

(ii) he has granted a trust deed which has become a protected trust deed; or

(iii) he has died and within 12 months after his death, his estate has been sequestrated; or

(iv) he has died and within the said 12 months, a judicial factor has been appointed under section 11A of the Judicial Factors (Scotland) Act 1889 to administer his estate and the estate was absolutely insolvent at the date of death; and

(c) the alienation took place on a relevant day.

(3) For the purposes of paragraph (c) of subsection (2) above, the day on which an alienation took place shall be the day on which the alienation became completely effectual; and in that paragraph "relevant day" means, if the alienation has the effect of favouring—

(a) a person who is an associate of the debtor, a day not earlier than 5 years before the date of sequestration, the granting of the trust deed or the debtor's death, as the case may be; or

(b) any other person, a day not earlier than 2 years before the said date.

(4) On a challenge being brought under subsection (1) above, the court shall grant decree of reduction or for such restoration of property to the debtor's estate or other redress as may be appropriate, but the court shall not grant such a decree if the person seeking to uphold the alienation establishes—

(a) that immediately, or at any other time, after the alienation the debtor's assets were greater than his liabilities; or

(b) that the alienation was made for adequate consideration; or

(c) that the alienation—

(i) was a birthday, Christmas or other conventional gift; or

(ii) was a gift made, for a charitable purpose, to a person who is not an associate of the debtor, which having regard to all the circumstances, it was reasonable for the debtor to make:

Provided that this subsection shall be without prejudice to any right . . . acquired in good faith and for value from or through the transferee in the alienation.

(5) In subsection (4) above, "charitable purpose" means any charitable, benevolent or philanthropic purpose whether or not it is charitable within the meaning of any rule of law.
(6) For the purposes of the foregoing provisions of this section, an alienation in implementation of a prior obligation shall be deemed to be one for which there was no consideration or no adequate consideration to the extent that the prior obligation was undertaken for no consideration or no adequate consideration.
(7) This section is without prejudice to the operation of section 2 of the Married Women's Policies of Assurance (Scotland) Act 1880 (policy of assurance may be effected in trust for spouse, future spouse and children) [including the operation of that section as applied by section 132 of the Civil Partnership Act 2004].
(8) A . . . trustee, the trustee acting under a protected trust deed and a judicial factor appointed under section 11A of the Judicial Factors (Scotland) Act 1889 shall have the same right as a creditor has under any rule of law to challenge an alienation of a debtor made for no consideration or for no adequate consideration.
(9) The . . . trustee shall insert in the sederunt book a copy of any decree under this section affecting the sequestrated estate.

NOTES

Repealed as noted at the beginning of this Act.

Word "permanent" omitted in each place repealed by the Bankruptcy and Diligence etc (Scotland) Act 2007, s 226(2), Sch 6, Pt 1, subject to transitional provisions and savings in SSI 2008/115, arts 5–7, 10, 15 at **[2.51]–[2.53]**, **[2.56]**, **[2.57]**.

Sub-s (4): words "or interest" (omitted) repealed by the Bankruptcy and Debt Advice (Scotland) Act 2014, s 56(2), Sch 4, subject to transitional provisions and savings in SSI 2014/261, arts 4, 12 at **[2.91]**, **[2.99]**.

Sub-s (7): words in square brackets inserted by the Civil Partnership Act 2004, s 261(2), Sch 28, para 35.

Sub-s (9): repealed by the Bankruptcy and Debt Advice (Scotland) Act 2014, s 56(2), Sch 4, subject to transitional provisions and savings in SSI 2014/261, arts 4, 12 at **[2.91]**, **[2.99]**.

[5.86]
35 Recalling of order for payment of capital sum on divorce

(1) This section applies where—
   (a) a court has made an order, whether before or after the coming into force of this section, under section 5 of the Divorce (Scotland) Act 1976 or section 8(2) of the Family Law (Scotland) Act 1985, for the payment by a debtor of a capital sum or [a court has, under the said section 8(2), made an order for the transfer of property by him or made a pension sharing order];
   (b) on the date of the making of the order the debtor was absolutely insolvent or was rendered so by implementation of the order; and
   (c) within 5 years after the making of the order—
      (i) the debtor's estate has been sequestrated other than after his death; or
      (ii) he has granted a trust deed which has (whether or not within the 5 years) become a protected trust deed; or
      (iii) he has died and, within 12 months after his death, his estate has been sequestrated; or
      (iv) he has died and, within the said 12 months, a judicial factor has been appointed under section 11A of the Judicial Factors (Scotland) Act 1889 to administer his estate.

(2) Where this section applies, the court, on an application brought by the . . . trustee, the trustee acting under the trust deed or the judicial factor, may make an order for recall of the order made under the said section 5 or 8(2) and for the repayment to the applicant of the whole or part of any sum already paid, or as the case may be for the return to the applicant of all or part of any property already transferred, under that order, or, where such property has been sold, for payment to the applicant of all or part of the proceeds of sale:

Provided that before making an order under this subsection the court shall have regard to all the circumstances including, without prejudice to the generality of this proviso, the financial, and other, circumstances (in so far as made known to the court) of the person against whom the order would be made.

(3) Where an application is brought under this section in a case where the debtor's estate has been sequestrated, the . . . trustee shall insert a copy of the decree of recall in the sederunt book.

NOTES

Repealed as noted at the beginning of this Act.

Sub-s (1): words in square brackets in para (a) substituted by the Welfare Reform and Pensions Act 1999, s 84, Sch 12, Pt II, paras 67, 68.

Sub-ss (2), (3): word "permanent" omitted in each place repealed by the Bankruptcy and Diligence etc (Scotland) Act 2007, s 226(2), Sch 6, Pt 1, subject to transitional provisions and savings in SSI 2008/115, arts 5–7, 10, 15 at **[2.51]–[2.53]**, **[2.56]**, **[2.57]**.

Sub-s (3): repealed by the Bankruptcy and Debt Advice (Scotland) Act 2014, s 56(2), Sch 4, subject to transitional provisions and savings in SSI 2014/261, arts 4, 12 at **[2.91]**, **[2.99]**.

[5.87]
36 Unfair preferences

(1) Subject to subsection (2) below, subsection (4) below applies to a transaction entered into by a debtor, whether before or after the coming into force of this section, which has the effect of creating a preference in favour of a creditor to the prejudice of the general body of creditors, being a preference created not earlier than 6 months before—

(a) the date of sequestration of the debtor's estate (if, in the case of a natural person, a date within his lifetime); or
(b) the granting by him of a trust deed which has become a protected trust deed; or
(c) his death where, within 12 months after his death—
(i) his estate has been sequestrated, or
(ii) a judicial factor has been appointed under section 11A of the Judicial Factors (Scotland) Act 1889 to administer his estate and his estate was absolutely insolvent at the date of death.

(2) Subsection (4) below shall not apply to any of the following transactions—
(a) a transaction in the ordinary course of trade or business;
(b) a payment in cash for a debt which when it was paid had become payable unless the transaction was collusive with the purpose of prejudicing the general body of creditors;
(c) a transaction whereby the parties thereto undertake reciprocal obligations (whether the performance by the parties of their respective obligations occurs at the same time or at different times) unless the transaction was collusive as aforesaid;
(d) the granting of a mandate by a debtor authorising an arrestee to pay over the arrested funds or part thereof to the arrester where—
(i) there has been a decree for payment or a warrant for summary diligence; and
(ii) the decree or warrant has been preceded by an arrestment on the dependence of the action or followed by an arrestment in execution.

(3) For the purposes of subsection (1) above, the day on which a preference was created shall be the day on which the preference became completely effectual.

(4) A transaction to which this subsection applies shall be challengeable by—
(a) any creditor who is a creditor by virtue of a debt incurred on or before the date of sequestration, the granting of the protected trust deed or the debtor's death, as the case may be; or
(b) the . . . trustee, the trustee acting under the protected trust deed, or the judicial factor, as the case may be.

(5) On a challenge being brought under subsection (4) above, the court, if satisfied that the transaction challenged is a transaction to which this section applies, shall grant decree of reduction or for such restoration of property to the debtor's estate or other redress as may be appropriate.

Provided that this subsection shall be without prejudice to any right . . . acquired in good faith and for value from or through the creditor in whose favour the preference was created.

(6) A . . . trustee, the trustee acting under a protected trust deed and a judicial factor appointed under section 11A of the Judicial Factors (Scotland) Act 1889 shall have the same right as a creditor has under any rule of law to challenge a preference created by a debtor.

(7) The . . . trustee shall insert in the sederunt book a copy of any decree under this section affecting the sequestrated estate.

NOTES

Repealed as noted at the beginning of this Act.

Word "permanent" omitted in each place repealed by the Bankruptcy and Diligence etc (Scotland) Act 2007, s 226(2), Sch 6, Pt 1, subject to transitional provisions and savings in SSI 2008/115, arts 5–7, 10, 15 at **[2.51]–[2.53]**, **[2.56]**, **[2.57]**.

Words "or interest" omitted from sub-s (5), and sub-s (7) repealed by the Bankruptcy and Debt Advice (Scotland) Act 2014, s 56(2), Sch 4, subject to transitional provisions and savings in SSI 2014/261, arts 4, 12 at **[2.91]**, **[2.99]**

[5.88]

[36A Recovery of excessive pension contributions

(1) Where a debtor's estate has been sequestrated and he—
(a) has rights under an approved pension arrangement, or
(b) has excluded rights under an unapproved pension arrangement,

the . . . trustee may apply to the court for an order under this section.

(2) If the court is satisfied—
(a) that the rights under the arrangement are to any extent, and whether directly or indirectly, the fruits of relevant contributions, and
(b) that the making of any of the relevant contributions ("the excessive contributions") has unfairly prejudiced the debtor's creditors,

the court may make such order as it thinks fit for restoring the position to what it would have been had the excessive contributions not been made.

(3) Subsection (4) applies where the court is satisfied that the value of the rights under the arrangement is, as a result of rights of the debtor under the arrangement or any other pension arrangement having at any time become subject to a debit under section 29(1)(a) of the Welfare Reform and Pensions Act 1999 (debits giving effect to pension-sharing), less than it would otherwise have been.

(4) Where this subsection applies—
(a) any relevant contributions which were represented by the rights which became subject to the debit shall, for the purposes of subsection (2), be taken to be contributions of which the rights under the arrangement are the fruits, and
(b) where the relevant contributions represented by the rights under the arrangement (including those so represented by virtue of paragraph (a)) are not all excessive contributions, relevant contributions which are represented by the rights under the arrangement otherwise than by virtue of paragraph (a) shall be treated as excessive contributions before any which are so represented by virtue of that paragraph.

(5) In subsections (2) to (4) "relevant contributions" means contributions to the arrangement or any other pension arrangement—

(a) which the debtor has at any time made on his own behalf, or
(b) which have at any time been made on his behalf.

(6) The court shall, in determining whether it is satisfied under subsection (2)(b), consider in particular—
(a) whether any of the contributions were made for the purpose of putting assets beyond the reach of the debtor's creditors or any of them, and
(b) whether the total amount of any contributions—
(i) made by or on behalf of the debtor to pension arrangements, and
(ii) represented (whether directly or indirectly) by rights under approved pension arrangements or excluded rights under unapproved pensions arrangements,

is an amount which is excessive in view of the debtor's circumstances when those contributions were made.

(7) For the purposes of this section and sections 36B and 36C ("the recovery provisions"), rights of a debtor under an unapproved pension arrangement are excluded rights if they are rights which are excluded from his estate by virtue of regulations under section 12 of the Welfare Reform and Pensions Act 1999.

(8) In the recovery provisions—
"approved pension arrangement" has the same meaning as in section 11 of the Welfare Reform and Pensions Act 1999;
"unapproved pension arrangement" has the same meaning as in section 12 of that Act.]

NOTES

Repealed as noted at the beginning of this Act.

Substituted (for text as inserted by the Pensions Act 1995, s 95(2)) by the Welfare Reform and Pensions Act 1999, s 16.

Sub-s (1): word "permanent" (omitted) repealed by the Bankruptcy and Diligence etc (Scotland) Act 2007, s 226(2), Sch 6, Pt 1, subject to transitional provisions and savings in SSI 2008/115, arts 5–7, 10, 15 at **[2.51]–[2.53]**, **[2.56]**, **[2.57]**.

[5.89]
[36B Orders under section 36A

(1) Without prejudice to the generality of section 36A(2) an order under section 36A may include provision—
(a) requiring the person responsible for the arrangement to pay an amount to the . . . trustee,
(b) adjusting the liabilities of the arrangement in respect of the debtor,
(c) adjusting any liabilities of the arrangement in respect of any other person that derive, directly or indirectly, from rights of the debtor under the arrangement,
(d) for the recovery by the person responsible for the arrangement (whether by deduction from any amount which that person is ordered to pay or otherwise) of costs incurred by that person in complying in the debtor's case with any requirement under section 36C(1) or in giving effect to the order.

(2) In subsection (1), references to adjusting the liabilities of the arrangement in respect of a person include (in particular) reducing the amount of any benefit or future benefit to which that person is entitled under the arrangement.

(3) In subsection (1)(c), the reference to liabilities of the arrangement does not include liabilities in respect of a person which result from giving effect to an order or provision falling within section 28(1) of the Welfare Reform and Pensions Act 1999 (pension sharing orders and agreements).

(4) The maximum amount which the person responsible for an arrangement may be required to pay by an order under section 36A is the lesser of—
(a) the amount of the excessive contributions, and
(b) the value of the debtor's rights under the arrangement (if the arrangement is an approved pension arrangement) or of his excluded rights under the arrangement (if the arrangement is an unapproved pension arrangement).

(5) An order under section 36A which requires the person responsible for an arrangement to pay an amount ("the restoration amount") to the . . . trustee must provide for the liabilities of the arrangement to be correspondingly reduced.

(6) For the purposes of subsection (5), liabilities are correspondingly reduced if the difference between—
(a) the amount of the liabilities immediately before the reduction, and
(b) the amount of the liabilities immediately after the reduction, is equal to the restoration amount.

(7) An order under section 36A in respect of an arrangement—
(a) shall be binding on the person responsible for the arrangement; and
(b) overrides provisions of the arrangement to the extent that they conflict with the provisions of the order.]

NOTES

Repealed as noted at the beginning of this Act.

Substituted (for text as inserted by the Pensions Act 1995, s 95(2)) by the Welfare Reform and Pensions Act 1999, s 16.

Sub-ss (1), (5): word "permanent" omitted in each place repealed by the Bankruptcy and Diligence etc (Scotland) Act 2007, s 226(2), Sch 6, Pt 1, subject to transitional provisions and savings in SSI 2008/115, arts 5–7, 10, 15 at **[2.51]–[2.53]**, **[2.56]**, **[2.57]**.

[5.90]
[36C Orders under section 36A: supplementary

(1) The person responsible for—

(a) an approved pension arrangement under which a debtor has rights,
(b) an unapproved pension arrangement under which a debtor has excluded rights, or
(c) a pension arrangement under which a debtor has at any time had rights,

shall, on the . . . trustee making a written request, provide the . . . trustee with such information about the arrangement and rights as the . . . trustee may reasonably require for, or in connection with, the making of applications under section 36A.

(2) Nothing in—
(a) any provision of section 159 of the Pensions Schemes Act 1993 or section 91 of the Pensions Act 1995 (which prevent assignation and the making of orders that restrain a person from receiving anything which he is prevented from assigning),
(b) any provision of any enactment (whether passed or made before or after the passing of the Welfare Reform and Pensions Act 1999) corresponding to any of the provisions mentioned in paragraph (a), or
(c) any provision of the arrangement in question corresponding to any of those provisions,

applies to a court exercising its powers under section 36A.

(3) Where any sum is required by an order under section 36A to be paid to the . . . trustee, that sum shall be comprised in the debtor's estate.

(4) Regulations may, for the purposes of the recovery provisions, make provision about the calculation and verification of—
(a) any such value as is mentioned in section 36B(4)(b);
(b) any such amounts as are mentioned in section 36B(6)(a) and (b).

(5) The power conferred by subsection (4) includes power to provide for calculation or verification—
(a) in such manner as may, in the particular case, be approved by a prescribed person; or
[(b) in accordance with guidance from time to time prepared by a prescribed person.]

(6) References in the recovery provisions to the person responsible for a pension arrangement are to—
(a) the trustees, managers or provider of the arrangement, or
(b) the person having functions in relation to the arrangement corresponding to those of a trustee, manager or provider.

(7) In this section and sections 36A and 36B—
"the recovery" provisions means this section and sections 36A and 36B;
"regulations" means regulations made by the Secretary of State.

(8) Regulations under the recovery provisions may contain such incidental, supplemental and transitional provisions as appear to the Secretary of State necessary or expedient.]

NOTES

Repealed as noted at the beginning of this Act.

Substituted (for text as inserted by the Pensions Act 1995, s 95(2)) by the Welfare Reform and Pensions Act 1999, s 16.

Sub-ss (1), (3): word "permanent" omitted in each place repealed by the Bankruptcy and Diligence etc (Scotland) Act 2007, s 226(2), Sch 6, Pt 1, subject to transitional provisions and savings in SSI 2008/115, arts 5–7, 10, 15 at **[2.51]**–**[2.53]**, **[2.56]**, **[2.57]**.

Sub-s (5): para (b) substituted by the Pensions Act 2007, s 17, Sch 5, para 1.

Regulations: the Occupational and Personal Pension Schemes (Bankruptcy) (No 2) Regulations 2002, SI 2002/836.

[5.91]

[36D Recovery of excessive contributions in pension-sharing cases

(1) For the purposes of section 34 of this Act, a pension-sharing transaction shall be taken—
(a) to be a transaction, entered into by the transferor with the transferee, by which the appropriate amount is transferred by the transferor to the transferee; and
(b) to be capable of being an alienation challengeable under that section only so far as it is a transfer of so much of the appropriate amount as is recoverable.

(2) For the purposes of section 35 of this Act, a pension-sharing transaction shall be taken—
(a) to be a pension sharing order made by the court under section 8(2) of the Family Law (Scotland) Act 1985; and
(b) to be an order capable of being recalled under that section only so far as it is a payment or transfer of so much of the appropriate amount as is recoverable.

(3) For the purposes of section 36 of this Act, a pension-sharing transaction shall be taken—
(a) to be something (namely a transfer of the appropriate amount to the transferee) done by the transferor; and
(b) to be capable of being an unfair preference given to the transferee only so far as it is a transfer of so much of the appropriate amount as is recoverable.

(4) Where—
(a) an alienation is challenged under section 34;
(b) an application is made under section 35 for the recall of an order made in divorce proceedings; or
(c) a transaction is challenged under section 36,

if any question arises as to whether, or the extent to which, the appropriate amount in the case of a pension-sharing transaction is recoverable, the question shall be determined in accordance with subsections (5) to (9).

(5) The court shall first determine the extent (if any) to which the transferor's rights under the shared arrangement at the time of the transaction appear to have been (whether directly or indirectly) the fruits of contributions ("personal contributions")—
(a) which the transferor has at any time made on his own behalf, or
(b) which have at any time been made on the transferor's behalf,

to the shared arrangement or any other pension arrangement.

(6) Where it appears that those rights were to any extent the fruits of personal contributions, the court shall then determine the extent (if any) to which those rights appear to have been the fruits of personal contributions whose making has unfairly prejudiced the transferor's creditors ("the unfair contributions").

(7) If it appears to the court that the extent to which those rights were the fruits of the unfair contributions is such that the transfer of the appropriate amount could have been made out of rights under the shared arrangement which were not the fruits of the unfair contributions, then the appropriate amount is not recoverable.

(8) If it appears to the court that the transfer could not have been wholly so made, then the appropriate amount is recoverable to the extent to which it appears to the court that the transfer could not have been so made.

(9) In making the determination mentioned in subsection (6) the court shall consider in particular—

(a) whether any of the personal contributions were made for the purpose of putting assets beyond the reach of the transferor's creditors or any of them; and

(b) whether the total amount of any personal contributions represented, at the time the pension sharing arrangement was made, by rights under pension arrangements is an amount which is excessive in view of the transferor's circumstances when those contributions were made.

(10) In this section and sections 36E and 36F—

"appropriate amount", in relation to a pension-sharing transaction, means the appropriate amount in relation to that transaction for the purposes of section 29(1) of the Welfare Reform and Pensions Act 1999 (creation of pension credits and debits);

"pension-sharing transaction" means an order or provision falling within section 28(1) of the Welfare Reform and Pensions Act 1999 (orders and agreements which activate pension-sharing);

"shared arrangement", in relation to a pension-sharing transaction, means the pension arrangement to which the transaction relates;

"transferee", in relation to a pension-sharing transaction, means the person for whose benefit the transaction is made;

"transferor", in relation to a pension-sharing transaction, means the person to whose rights the transaction relates.]

NOTES

Inserted by the Welfare Reform and Pensions Act 1999, s 84, Sch 12, Pt II, paras 67, 69.

Repealed as noted at the beginning of this Act.

[5.92]

[36E Recovery orders

(1) In this section and section 36F of this Act, "recovery order" means—

(a) a decree granted under section 34(4) of this Act;

(b) an order made under section 35(2) of this Act;

(c) a decree granted under section 36(5) of this Act,

in any proceedings to which section 36D of this Act applies.

(2) Without prejudice to the generality of section 34(4), 35(2) or 36(5) a recovery order may include provision—

(a) requiring the person responsible for a pension arrangement in which the transferee has acquired rights derived directly or indirectly from the pension-sharing transaction to pay an amount to the . . . trustee,

(b) adjusting the liabilities of the pension arrangement in respect of the transferee,

(c) adjusting any liabilities of the pension arrangement in respect of any other person that derive, directly or indirectly, from rights of the transferee under the arrangement,

(d) for the recovery by the person responsible for the pension arrangement (whether by deduction from any amount which that person is ordered to pay or otherwise) of costs incurred by that person in complying in the debtor's case with any requirement under section 36F(1) or in giving effect to the order.

(3) In subsection (2), references to adjusting the liabilities of a pension arrangement in respect of a person include (in particular) reducing the amount of any benefit or future benefit to which that person is entitled under the arrangement.

(4) The maximum amount which the person responsible for an arrangement may be required to pay by a recovery order is the smallest of—

(a) so much of the appropriate amount as, in accordance with section 36D of this Act, is recoverable,

(b) so much (if any) of the amount of the unfair contributions (within the meaning given by section 36D(6)) as is not recoverable by way of an order under section 36A of this Act containing provision such as is mentioned in section 36B(1)(a), and

(c) the value of the debtor's rights under the arrangement acquired by the transferee as a consequence of the transfer of the appropriate amount.

(5) A recovery order which requires the person responsible for an arrangement to pay an amount ("the restoration amount") to the . . . trustee must provide for the liabilities of the arrangement to be correspondingly reduced.

(6) For the purposes of subsection (5), liabilities are correspondingly reduced if the difference between—

(a) the amount of the liabilities immediately before the reduction, and

(b) the amount of the liabilities immediately after the reduction,

is equal to the restoration amount.

(7) A recovery order in respect of an arrangement—

(a) shall be binding on the person responsible for the arrangement, and

(b) overrides provisions of the arrangement to the extent that they conflict with the provisions of the order.]

NOTES

Inserted by the Welfare Reform and Pensions Act 1999, s 84, Sch 12, Pt II, paras 67, 69.

Repealed as noted at the beginning of this Act.

Sub-ss (2), (5): word "permanent" omitted in each place repealed by the Bankruptcy and Diligence etc (Scotland) Act 2007, s 226(2), Sch 6, Pt 1, subject to transitional provisions and savings in SSI 2008/115, arts 5–7, 10, 15 at **[2.51]–[2.53]**, **[2.56]**, **[2.57]**.

[5.93]

[36F Recovery orders: supplementary

(1) The person responsible for a pension arrangement under which the transferee has, at any time, acquired rights by virtue of the transfer of the appropriate amount shall, on the . . . trustee making a written request, provide the trustee with such information about the arrangement and the rights under it of the transferor and transferee as the . . . trustee may reasonably require for, or in connection with, the making of an application for a recovery order.

(2) Nothing in—

(a) any provision of section 159 of the Pension Schemes Act 1993 or section 91 of the Pensions Act 1995 (which prevent assignation and the making of orders which restrain a person from receiving anything which he is prevented from assigning),

(b) any provision of any enactment (whether passed or made before or after the passing of the Welfare Reform and Pensions Act 1999) corresponding to any of the provisions mentioned in paragraph (a), or

(c) any provision of the arrangement in question corresponding to any of those provisions,

applies to a court exercising its power to make a recovery order.

(3) Regulations may, for the purposes of the recovery provisions, make provision about the calculation and verification of—

(a) any such value as is mentioned in section 36E(4)(c);

(b) any such amounts as are mentioned in section 36E(6)(a) and (b).

(4) The power conferred by subsection (3) includes power to provide for calculation or verification—

(a) in such manner as may, in the particular case, be approved by a prescribed person; or

[(b) in accordance with guidance from time to time prepared by a prescribed person.]

(5) References in the recovery provisions to the person responsible for a pension arrangement are to—

(a) the trustees, managers or provider of the arrangement, or

(b) the person having functions in relation to the arrangement corresponding to those of a trustee, manager or provider.

(6) In this section—

"prescribed" means prescribed by regulations;

"the recovery provisions" means this section and sections 34, 35, 36 and 36E of this Act;

"regulations" means regulations made by the Secretary of State.

(7) Regulations under the recovery provisions may—

(a) make different provision for different cases;

(b) contain such incidental, supplemental and transitional provisions as appear to the Secretary of State necessary or expedient.

(8) Regulations under the recovery provisions shall be made by statutory instrument subject to annulment in pursuance of a resolution of either House of Parliament.]

NOTES

Inserted by the Welfare Reform and Pensions Act 1999, s 84, Sch 12, Pt II, paras 67, 69.

Repealed as noted at the beginning of this Act.

Sub-s (1): word "permanent" omitted in both places repealed by the Bankruptcy and Diligence etc (Scotland) Act 2007, s 226(2), Sch 6, Pt 1, subject to transitional provisions and savings in SSI 2008/115, arts 5–7, 10, 15 at **[2.51]–[2.53]**, **[2.56]**, **[2.57]**.

Sub-s (4): para (b) substituted by the Pensions Act 2007, s 17, Sch 5, para 2.

Regulations: the Occupational and Personal Pension Schemes (Bankruptcy) (No 2) Regulations 2002, SI 2002/836.

Effect of sequestration on diligence

[5.94]

37 Effect of sequestration on diligence

(1) The order of the [sheriff or, as the case may be, the determination of the debtor application by the Accountant in Bankruptcy] awarding sequestration shall as from the date of sequestration have the effect, in relation to diligence done (whether before or after the date of sequestration) in respect of any part of the debtor's estate, of—

(a) a decree of adjudication of the heritable estate of the debtor for payment of his debts which has been duly recorded in the register of inhibitions and adjudications on that date; and

(b) an arrestment in execution and decree of furthcoming, an arrestment in execution and warrant of sale, and [an attachment],

in favour of the creditors according to their respective entitlements.

(2) [Where an] inhibition on the estate of the debtor . . . takes effect within the period of 60 days before the date of sequestration . . . any relevant right of challenge shall, at the date of sequestration, vest in the . . . trustee as shall any right of the inhibitor to receive payment for the discharge of the inhibition:

Provided that this subsection shall neither entitle the trustee to receive any payment made to the inhibitor before the date of sequestration nor affect the validity of anything done before that date in consideration of such payment.

(3) In subsection (2) above, "any relevant right of challenge" means any right to challenge a deed voluntarily granted by the debtor if it is a right which vested in the inhibitor by virtue of the inhibition.

(4) No arrestment[, money attachment, interim attachment] or [attachment] of the estate of the debtor (including any estate vesting in the . . . trustee under section 32(6) of this Act) executed—

- (a) within the period of 60 days before the date of sequestration and whether or not subsisting at that date; or
- (b) on or after the date of sequestration,

shall be effectual to create a preference for the arrester or [attacher]; and the estate so arrested or [attached][, or any funds released under section 73J(2) of the Debtors (Scotland) Act 1987 (c 18) (automatic release of funds)], or the proceeds of sale thereof, shall be handed over to the . . . trustee.

(5) An arrester or [attacher] whose arrestment[, money attachment, interim attachment] or [attachment] is executed within the said period of 60 days shall be entitled to payment, out of the arrested or [attached] estate or out of the proceeds of the sale thereof, of the expenses incurred—

- (a) in obtaining—
  - [(i) warrant for interim attachment; or
  - (ii)] the extract of the decree or other document on which the arrestment[, money attachment] or [attachment] proceeded;
- (b) in executing the arrestment[, money attachment, interim attachment] or [attachment]; and
- (c) in taking any further action in respect of the diligence.

[(5A) Nothing in subsection (4) or (5) above shall apply to an earnings arrestment, a current maintenance arrestment[, a conjoined arrestment order or a deduction from earnings order under the Child Support Act 1991].]

[(5B) No land attachment of heritable property of the debtor created within the period of six months before the date of sequestration and whether or not subsisting at that date shall be effectual to create a preference for the creditor.

(5C) A creditor who creates a land attachment within the period of six months mentioned in subsection (5B) above shall be entitled to payment, out of the attached land or out of the proceeds of the sale of it, of the expenses incurred—

- (a) in obtaining the extract of the decree, or other document, containing the warrant for land attachment; and
- (b) in—
  - (i) serving the charge for payment;
  - (ii) registering the notice of land attachment;
  - (iii) serving a copy of that notice; and
  - (iv) registering certificate of service of that copy.]

(6) No poinding of the ground in respect of the estate of the debtor (including any estate vesting in the . . . trustee under section 32(6) of this Act) executed within the period of 60 days before the date of sequestration or on or after that date shall be effectual in a question with the . . . trustee, except for the interest on the debt of a secured creditor, being interest for the current half-yearly term and arrears of interest for one year immediately before the commencement of that term.

(7) The foregoing provisions of this section shall apply to the estate of a deceased debtor which—

- (a) has been sequestrated; or
- (b) was absolutely insolvent at the date of death and in respect of which a judicial factor has been appointed under section 11A of the Judicial Factors (Scotland) Act 1889,

within 12 months after his death, but as if for any reference to the date of sequestration and the debtor there were substituted respectively a reference to the date of the deceased's death and to the deceased debtor.

(8) It shall be incompetent on or after the date of sequestration for any creditor *to raise or insist in an adjudication against the estate of a debtor (including any estate vesting in the permanent trustee under section 32(6) of this Act) or* to be confirmed as executor-creditor on the estate.

[(8A) A notice of land attachment registered—

- (a) on or after the date of sequestration against land forming part of the heritable estate of the debtor (including any estate vesting in the trustee by virtue of section 32(6) of this Act); or
- (b) before that date in relation to which, by that date, no land attachment is created,

shall be of no effect.

(8B) Subject to subsections (8C) to (8F) below, it shall not be competent for a creditor to insist in a land attachment—

- (a) created over heritable estate of the debtor before the beginning of the period of six months mentioned in subsection (5B) above; and
- (b) which subsists on the date of sequestration.

(8C) Where, in execution of a warrant for sale, a contract to sell the land has been concluded—

- (a) the trustee shall concur in and ratify the deed implementing that contract; and
- (b) the appointed person shall account for and pay to the trustee any balance of the proceeds of sale which would, but for the sequestration, be due to the debtor after disbursing those proceeds in accordance with section 116 of the Bankruptcy and Diligence etc (Scotland) Act 2007 (asp 3) (disbursement of proceeds of sale of attached land).

(8D) Subsection (8C) above shall not apply where the deed implementing the contract is not registered before the expiry of the period of 28 days beginning with the day on which—

(a) the certified copy of the order of the sheriff granting warrant is recorded under subsection (1)(a) of section 14 of this Act; or

(b) the certified copy of the determination of the Accountant in Bankruptcy awarding sequestration is recorded under subsection (1A) of that section,

in the register of inhibitions.

(8E) Where a decree of foreclosure has been granted but an extract of it has not registered, the creditor may proceed to complete title to the land by so registering that extract provided that the extract is registered before the expiry of the period mentioned in subsection (8D) above.

(8F) The Scottish Ministers may—

(a) prescribe such other period for the period mentioned in subsection (8D) above; and

(b) prescribe different periods for the purposes of that subsection and subsection (8E) above,

as they think fit.]

(9) Where—

(a) a deceased debtor's estate is sequestrated; or

(b) a judicial factor is appointed under section 11A of the Judicial Factors (Scotland) Act 1889 to administer his estate (in a case where the estate is absolutely insolvent),

within 12 months after the debtor's death, no confirmation as executor-creditor on that estate at any time after the debtor's death shall be effectual in a question with the . . . trustee or the judicial factor; but the executor-creditor shall be entitled out of that estate, or out of the proceeds of sale thereof, to the expenses incurred by him in obtaining the confirmation.

[(10) Expressions used in subsections (5B), (5C) and (8A) to (8F) above which are also used in Chapter 2 of Part 4 of the Bankruptcy and Diligence etc (Scotland) Act 2007 (asp 3) have the same meanings in those subsections as they have in that Chapter.]

NOTES

Repealed as noted at the beginning of this Act.

Sub-s (1): words in first pair of square brackets substituted for original word "court", and words in square brackets in para (b) substituted for original words "a completed poinding" by the Bankruptcy and Diligence etc (Scotland) Act 2007, ss 36, 226(1), Sch 1, paras 1, 33, Sch 5, para 13(1), (3)(a), subject to transitional provisions and savings in SSI 2008/115, arts 5–7, 10, 15 at **[2.51]–[2.53]**, **[2.56]**, **[2.57]**; para (a) repealed by the Bankruptcy and Diligence etc (Scotland) Act 2007, s 226(2), Sch 6, Pt 1, as from a day to be appointed.

Sub-s (2): words in first pair of square brackets substituted for original word "No" and words, "which" and "shall be effectual to create a preference for the inhibitor and" (omitted in first and second places) repealed by the Bankruptcy and Diligence etc (Scotland) Act 2007, s 226(1), (2), Sch 5, para 13(1), (3)(b), Sch 6, Pt 1, subject to transitional provisions and savings in the Bankruptcy and Diligence etc (Scotland) Act 2007 (Commencement No 4, Savings and Transitionals) Order 2009, SSI 2009/67, art 6 at **[2.62]**; word "permanent" (omitted in the third place) repealed by s 226(2) of, and Sch 6, Pt 1 to, the 2007 Act, subject to transitional provisions and savings in SSI 2008/115, arts 5–7, 10, 15 at **[2.51]–[2.53]**, **[2.56]**, **[2.57]**.

Sub-s (4): words in first and fifth pairs of square brackets inserted and word "permanent" omitted in both places repealed by the Bankruptcy and Diligence etc (Scotland) Act 2007, s 226(1), (2), Sch 5, para 13(1), (3)(c), Sch 6, Pt 1, subject to transitional provisions and savings in SSI 2008/115, arts 5–7, 10, 15 at **[2.51]–[2.53]**, **[2.56]**, **[2.57]**; words in second, third and fourth pairs of square brackets substituted by the Debt Arrangement and Attachment (Scotland) Act 2002, s 61, Sch 3, Pt 1, para 15(1), (4).

Sub-s (5): words in first, third, fourth, seventh and ninth pairs of square brackets substituted by the Debt Arrangement and Attachment (Scotland) Act 2002, s 61, Sch 3, Pt 1, para 15(1), (4); words in second, fifth, sixth and eighth pairs of square brackets inserted by the Bankruptcy and Diligence etc (Scotland) Act 2007, s 226(1), Sch 5, para 13(1), (3)(d), subject, for certain purposes, to transitional provisions and savings in SSI 2008/115, arts 5–7, 10, 15 at **[2.51]–[2.53]**, **[2.56]**, **[2.57]**.

Sub-s (5A): inserted by the Debtors (Scotland) Act 1987, s 108(1), Sch 6, para 27; words in square brackets substituted by the Child Support Act 1991, s 58(13), Sch 5, para 6(1), (3).

Sub-ss (5B), (5C): inserted by the Bankruptcy and Diligence etc (Scotland) Act 2007, s 226(1), Sch 5, para 13(1), (3)(e), as from a day to be appointed.

Sub-ss (6), (9): word "permanent" omitted in each place repealed by the Bankruptcy and Diligence etc (Scotland) Act 2007, s 226(2), Sch 6, Pt 1, subject to transitional provisions and savings in SSI 2008/115, arts 5–7, 10, 15 at **[2.51]–[2.53]**, **[2.56]**, **[2.57]**.

Sub-s (8): words "to raise or insist in an adjudication against the estate of a debtor (including any estate vesting in the permanent trustee under section 32(6) of this Act) or" repealed by the Bankruptcy and Diligence etc (Scotland) Act 2007, s 226(2), Sch 6, Pt 1, as from a day to be appointed.

Sub-ss (8A)–(8F), (10): inserted by the Bankruptcy and Diligence etc (Scotland) Act 2007, s 226(1), Sch 5, para 13(1), (3)(f), (g), as from 1 April 2008 for the purpose of making regulations or orders, subject to transitional provisions and savings in SSI 2008/115, arts 5–7, 10, 15 at **[2.51]–[2.53]**, **[2.56]**, **[2.57]**, and as from a day to be appointed for remaining purposes.

Companies winding up: sub-ss (1)–(6) of this section, and s 39(3), (4), (7), (8) post, are applied by the Insolvency Act 1986, s 185 (so far as consistent with that Act) at **[1.189]**, in the winding up of a company registered in Scotland in like manner as they apply in the sequestration of a debtor's estate, with the following substitutions, and with any other necessary modifications: for references to "the debtor", "the sequestration", "the date of sequestration" and "the permanent trustee" there are substituted, respectively, references to "the company", "the winding up", "the commencement of the winding up" and "the liquidator".

[Administration of estate by trustee]

NOTES

Cross-heading: substituted for original words "Administration of estate by permanent trustee" by the Bankruptcy and Diligence etc (Scotland) Act 2007, s 36, Sch 1, paras 1, 34(1), (3), subject to transitional provisions and savings in SSI 2008/115, arts 5–7, 10, 15 at **[2.51]–[2.53]**, **[2.56]**, **[2.57]**.

[5.95]

38 [Taking possession of estate by trustee]

(1) The . . . trustee shall—

(a) as soon as may be after his [appointment], for the purpose of recovering the debtor's estate under section 3(1)(a) of this Act, and subject to section 40 of this Act, take possession of the debtor's whole estate so far as vesting in the . . . trustee under sections 31 and 32 of this Act and any document in the debtor's possession or control relating to his assets or his business or financial affairs;

(b) make up and maintain an inventory and valuation of the estate . . . ; and

(c) forthwith thereafter send a copy of any such inventory and valuation to the Accountant in Bankruptcy.

(2) The . . . trustee shall be entitled to have access to all documents relating to the assets or the business or financial affairs of the debtor sent by or on behalf of the debtor to a third party and in that third party's hands and to make copies of any such documents.

(3) If any person obstructs a . . . trustee who is exercising, or attempting to exercise, a power conferred by subsection (2) above, the sheriff, on the application of the . . . trustee, may order that person to cease so to obstruct the . . . trustee.

(4) The . . . trustee may require delivery to him of any title deed or other document of the debtor, notwithstanding that a right of lien is claimed over the title deed or document; but this subsection is without prejudice to any preference of the holder of the lien.

NOTES

Repealed as noted at the beginning of this Act.

Section heading: substituted for original words "Taking possession of estate by permanent trustee" by the Bankruptcy and Diligence etc (Scotland) Act 2007, s 36, Sch 1, paras 1, 34(1), (2), subject to transitional provisions and savings in SSI 2008/115, arts 5–7, 10, 15 at **[2.51]–[2.53]**, **[2.56]**, **[2.57]**.

Sub-s (1): word "permanent" omitted in both places repealed and word in square brackets substituted for original words "confirmation in office" by the Bankruptcy and Diligence etc (Scotland) Act 2007, ss 36, 226(2), Sch 1, paras 1, 34(1), Sch 6, Pt 1, subject to transitional provisions and savings in SSI 2008/115, arts 5–7, 10, 15 at **[2.51]–[2.53]**, **[2.56]**, **[2.57]**; words omitted from para (b) repealed by the Bankruptcy and Debt Advice (Scotland) Act 2014, s 56(2), Sch 4, subject to transitional provisions and savings in SSI 2014/261, arts 4, 12 at **[2.91]**, **[2.99]**

Sub-ss (2)–(4): word "permanent" omitted in each place repealed by the Bankruptcy and Diligence etc (Scotland) Act 2007, s 226(2), Sch 6, Pt 1, subject to transitional provisions and savings in SSI 2008/115, arts 5–7, 10, 15 at **[2.51]–[2.53]**, **[2.56]**, **[2.57]**.

[5.96]

39 Management and realisation of estate

(1) As soon as may be after his [appointment], the . . . trustee shall consult . . . with the Accountant in Bankruptcy concerning the exercise of his functions under section 3(1)(a) of this Act; and, subject to [subsections (1A), (6) and (9)] below, the . . . trustee shall comply with any general or specific directions given to him, as the case may be—

(a) by the creditors;

(b) on the application under this subsection of the commissioners, by the [sheriff]; or

(c) . . . by the Accountant in Bankruptcy,

as to the exercise by him of such functions.

[(1A) Subsection (1) above does not apply in any case where the Accountant in Bankruptcy is the trustee.]

(2) The . . . trustee may . . . do any of the following things . . . —

(a) carry on [or close down] any business of the debtor;

(b) bring, defend or continue any legal proceedings relating to the estate of the debtor;

(c) create a security over any part of the estate;

(d) where any right, option or other power forms part of the debtor's estate, make payments or incur liabilities with a view to obtaining, for the benefit of the creditors, any property which is the subject of the right, option or power;

[(e) borrow money in so far as it is necessary for the trustee to do so to safeguard the debtor's estate;

(f) effect or maintain insurance policies in respect of the business or property of the debtor.]

(3) Any sale of the debtor's estate by the . . . trustee may be by either public sale or private bargain.

(4) The following rules shall apply to the sale of any part of the debtor's heritable estate over which a heritable security is held by a creditor or creditors if the rights of the secured creditor or creditors are preferable to those of the . . . trustee—

(a) the . . . trustee may sell that part only with the concurrence of every such creditor unless he obtains a sufficiently high price to discharge every such security;

(b) subject to paragraph (c) below, the following acts shall be precluded—

(i) the taking of steps by a creditor to enforce his security over that part after the . . . trustee has intimated to the creditor that he intends to sell it;

(ii) the commencement by the . . . trustee of the procedure for the sale of that part after a creditor has intimated to the . . . trustee that he intends to commence the procedure for its sale;

(c) where the . . . trustee or a creditor has given intimation under paragraph (b) above, but has unduly delayed in proceeding with the sale, then, if authorised by the [sheriff] in the case of intimation under—

(i) sub-paragraph (i) of that paragraph, any creditor to whom intimation has been given may enforce his security; or

(ii) sub-paragraph (ii) of that paragraph, the . . . trustee may sell that part.

(5) The function of the . . . trustee under section 3(1)(a) of this Act to realise the debtor's estate shall include the function of selling, with or without recourse against the estate, debts owing to the estate.

(6) The . . . trustee may sell any perishable goods without complying with any directions given to him under subsection (1)(a) or (c) above if the . . . trustee considers that compliance with such directions would adversely affect the sale.

(7) The validity of the title of any purchaser shall not be challengeable on the ground that there has been a failure to comply with a requirement of this section.

(8) It shall be incompetent for the . . . trustee or an associate of his or for any commissioner, to produce any of the debtor's estate in pursuance of this section.

[(9) The trustee—

(a) shall comply with the requirements of subsection (4) of this section; and

(b) may do anything permitted by this section,

only in so far as, in his view, it would be of financial benefit to the estate of the debtor and in the interests of the creditors to do so.]

NOTES

Repealed as noted at the beginning of this Act.

Sub-s (1): word in first pair of square brackets substituted for original words "confirmation in office", word "permanent" omitted in the first and third places repealed, words "with the commissioners or, if there are no commissioners," omitted in the second place repealed, words in second pair of square brackets substituted for original words "subsection (6)", word in square brackets in para (b) substituted for original word "court", and words "if there are no commissioners," omitted from para (c) repealed, by the Bankruptcy and Diligence etc (Scotland) Act 2007, ss 36, 226(2), Sch 1, paras 1, 35(1), (2), Sch 6, Pt 1, subject to transitional provisions and savings in SSI 2008/115, arts 5–7, 10, 15 at **[2.51]–[2.53]**, **[2.56]**, **[2.57]**.

Sub-s (1A): inserted by the Bankruptcy and Diligence etc (Scotland) Act 2007, s 36, Sch 1, paras 1, 35(1), (3), subject to transitional provisions and savings in SSI 2008/115, arts 5–7, 10, 15 at **[2.51]–[2.53]**, **[2.56]**, **[2.57]**.

Sub-s (2): words "permanent", "but if there are commissioners only with the consent of the commissioners, the creditors or the court,", and "if he considers that its doing would be beneficial for the administration of the estate" (omitted in first, second and third places respectively) repealed and words in square brackets in para (a) and paras (e), (f) inserted by the Bankruptcy and Diligence etc (Scotland) Act 2007, ss 36, 226(2), Sch 1, paras 1, 35(1), (4), Sch 6, Pt 1, subject to transitional provisions and savings in SSI 2008/115, arts 5–7, 10, 15 at **[2.51]–[2.53]**, **[2.56]**, **[2.57]**.

Sub-ss (3), (5), (6), (8): word "permanent" omitted in each place repealed by the Bankruptcy and Diligence etc (Scotland) Act 2007, s 226(2), Sch 6, Pt 1, subject to transitional provisions and savings in SSI 2008/115, arts 5–7, 10, 15 at **[2.51]–[2.53]**, **[2.56]**, **[2.57]**.

Sub-s (4): word "permanent" omitted in each place repealed and word in square brackets in para (c) substituted for original word "court" by the Bankruptcy and Diligence etc (Scotland) Act 2007, ss 36, 226(2), Sch 1, paras 1, 35(1), (5), Sch 6, Pt 1, subject to transitional provisions and savings in SSI 2008/115, arts 5–7, 10, 15 at **[2.51]–[2.53]**, **[2.56]**, **[2.57]**.

Sub-s (9): added by the Bankruptcy and Diligence etc (Scotland) Act 2007, s 8(2), subject to transitional provisions and savings in SSI 2008/115, arts 5–7, 10, 15 at **[2.51]–[2.53]**, **[2.56]**, **[2.57]**.

Companies winding up: see the note to s 37 at **[5.94]**.

[5.97]

[39A Debtor's home ceasing to form part of sequestrated estate

(1) This section applies where a debtor's sequestrated estate includes any right or interest in the debtor's family home.

(2) At the end of the period of 3 years beginning with the date of sequestration the right or interest mentioned in subsection (1) above shall—

(a) cease to form part of the debtor's sequestrated estate; and

(b) be reinvested in the debtor (without disposition, conveyance, assignation or other transfer).

(3) Subsection (2) above shall not apply if, during the period mentioned in that subsection—

(a) the trustee disposes of or otherwise realises the right or interest mentioned in subsection (1) above;

(b) the trustee concludes missives for sale of the right or interest;

(c) the trustee sends a memorandum to the keeper of the register of inhibitions under section 14(4) of this Act;

(d) the trustee [completes title in the Land Register of Scotland or, as the case may be, the Register of Sasines] in relation to the right or interest mentioned in subsection (1) above;

(e) the trustee commences proceedings—

(i) to obtain the authority of the sheriff under section 40(1)(b) of this Act to sell or dispose of the right or interest;

(ii) in an action for division and sale of the family home; or

(iii) in an action for the purpose of obtaining vacant possession of the family home;

(f) the trustee and the debtor enter into an agreement such as is mentioned in subsection (5) below;

[(g) the trustee has commenced an action under section 34 of this Act in respect of any right or interest mentioned in subsection (1) above or the trustee has not known about the facts giving rise to a right of action under section 34 of this Act, provided the trustee commences such an action reasonably soon after the trustee becomes aware of such right.]

(4) The Scottish Ministers may, by regulations, modify paragraphs (a) to (f) of subsection (3) above so as to—

(a) add or remove a matter; or

(b) vary any such matter,

referred to in that subsection.

(5) The agreement referred to in subsection (3)(f) above is an agreement that the debtor shall incur a specified liability to his estate (with or without interest from the date of the agreement) in consideration of which the right or interest mentioned in subsection (1) above shall—

(a) cease to form part of the debtor's sequestrated estate; and

(b) be reinvested in the debtor (without disposition, conveyance, assignation or other transfer).

(6) If the debtor does not inform the trustee or the Accountant in Bankruptcy of his right or interest in the family home before the end of the period of 3 months beginning with the date of sequestration, the period of 3 years mentioned in subsection (2) above—

(a) shall not begin with the date of sequestration; but

(b) shall begin with the date on which the trustee . . . becomes aware of the debtor's right or interest.

(7) The sheriff may, on the application of the trustee, substitute for the period of 3 years mentioned in subsection (2) above a longer period—

(a) in prescribed circumstances; and

(b) in such other circumstances as the sheriff thinks appropriate.

(8) The Scottish Ministers may, by regulations—

(a) make provision for this section to have effect with the substitution, in such circumstances as the regulations may prescribe, of a shorter period for the period of 3 years mentioned in subsection (2) above;

(b) prescribe circumstances in which this section does not apply;

(c) prescribe circumstances in which a sheriff may disapply this section;

(d) make provision requiring the trustee to give notice that this section applies or does not apply;

(e) make provision about compensation;

(f) make such provision as they consider necessary or expedient in consequence of regulations made under paragraphs (a) to (e) above.

(9) In this section, "family home" has the same meaning as in section 40 of this Act.]

NOTES

Inserted by the Bankruptcy and Diligence etc (Scotland) Act 2007, s 19(2), subject to transitional provisions and savings in SSI 2008/115, arts 5–7, 10, 15 at **[2.51]**–**[2.53]**, **[2.56]**, **[2.57]**.

Repealed as noted at the beginning of this Act.

Sub-s (3): words in square brackets in para (d) substituted for original words "registers in the Land Register of Scotland or, as the case may be, records in the Register of Sasines a notice of title" by the Bankruptcy and Debt Advice (Scotland) Act 2014, s 56(1), Sch 3, paras 2, 21, subject to transitional provisions and savings in SSI 2014/261, arts 4, 12 at **[2.91]**, **[2.99]**; para (g) inserted by the Bankruptcy (Scotland) Act 1985 (Low Income, Low Asset Debtors etc) Regulations 2008, SSI 2008/81, reg 4 and substituted by the Bankruptcy (Money Advice and Deduction from Income etc) (Scotland) Regulations 2014, SSI 2014/296, reg 9.

Sub-s (6): words "or the Accountant in Bankruptcy" omitted from para (b) repealed by the Bankruptcy and Debt Advice (Scotland) Act 2014, s 56(2), Sch 4, subject to transitional provisions and savings in SSI 2014/261, arts 4, 12 at **[2.91]**, **[2.99]**.

Regulations: the Bankruptcy (Scotland) Act 1985 (Low Income, Low Asset Debtors etc) Regulations 2008, SSI 2008/81 at **[16.261]**; the Bankruptcy (Money Advice and Deduction from Income etc) (Scotland) Regulations 2014, SSI 2014/296 at **[16.284]**.

[5.98]

40 [Power of trustee in relation to the debtor's family home]

(1) Before the . . . trustee [or the trustee acting under the trust deed] sells or disposes of any right or interest in the debtor's family home he shall—

(a) obtain the relevant consent; or

(b) where he is unable to do so, obtain the authority of the [sheriff] in accordance with subsection (2) [or, as the case may be, subsection (3)] below.

(2) Where the . . . trustee [or the trustee acting under the trust deed] requires to obtain the authority of the [sheriff] in terms of subsection (1)(b) above, the [sheriff], after having regard to all the circumstances of the case, including—

(a) the needs and financial resources of the debtor's spouse or former spouse;

[(aa) the needs and financial resources of the debtor's civil partner or former civil partner;]

(b) the needs and financial resources of any child of the family;

(c) the interests of the creditors;

(d) the length of the period during which (whether before or after the relevant date) the family home was used as a residence by any of the persons referred to in [paragraphs (a) to (b)] above,

may refuse to grant the application or may postpone the granting of the application for such period (not exceeding [3 years]) as [he] may consider reasonable in the circumstances or may grant the application subject to such conditions as [he] may prescribe.

(3) Subsection (2) above shall apply—

(a) to an action for division and sale of the debtor's family home; or

(b) to an action for the purpose of obtaining vacant possession of the debtor's family home,

brought by the . . . trustee [or the trustee acting under the trust deed] as it applies to an application under subsection (1)(b) above and, for the purposes of this subsection, any reference in the said subsection (2) to that granting of the application shall be construed as a reference to the granting of decree in the action.

[(3A) Before commencing proceedings to obtain the authority of the sheriff under [subsection (2) or (3)] the trustee, or the trustee acting under the trust deed, must give notice of the proceedings to the local authority in whose area the home is situated.

(3B) Notice under subsection (3A) must be given in such form and manner as may be prescribed by the Scottish Ministers.]

(4) In this section—

(a) "family home" means any property in which, at the relevant date, the debtor had (whether alone or in common with any other person) a right or interest, being property which was occupied at that date as a residence by the debtor and his spouse [or civil partner] or by the debtor's spouse [or civil partner] or former spouse [or civil partner] (in any case with or without a child of the family) or by the debtor with a child of the family;

(b) "child of the family" includes any child or grandchild of either the debtor or his spouse [or civil partner] or former spouse [or civil partner], and any person who has been brought up or accepted by either the debtor or his spouse [or civil partner] or former spouse [or civil partner] as if he or she were a child of the debtor, spouse [or civil partner] or former spouse [or civil partner] whatever the age of such a child, grandchild or person may be;

[(ba) "local authority" means a council constituted under section 2 of the Local Government etc (Scotland) Act 1994 (c 39);]

(c) "relevant consent" means in relation to the sale or disposal of any right or interest in a family home—

(i) in a case where the family home is occupied by the debtor's spouse [or civil partner] or former spouse [or civil partner], the consent of the spouse [or civil partner], or, as the case may be, the former spouse [or civil partner], whether or not the family home is also occupied by the debtor;

(ii) where sub-paragraph (i) above does not apply, in a case where the family home is occupied by the debtor with a child of the family, the consent of the debtor; and

(d) "relevant date" means the day immediately preceding the date of sequestration [or, as the case may be, the day immediately preceding the date the trust deed was granted].

NOTES

Repealed as noted at the beginning of this Act.

Section heading: substituted for original words "Power of permanent trustee in relation to the debtor's family home" by the Bankruptcy and Diligence etc (Scotland) Act 2007, s 36, Sch 1, paras 1, 36(c), subject to transitional provisions and savings in SSI 2008/115, arts 5–7, 10, 15 at **[2.51]–[2.53]**, **[2.56]**, **[2.57]**.

Sub-s (1): word "permanent" (omitted) repealed and word in first pair of square brackets in para (b) substituted for original word "court" by the Bankruptcy and Diligence etc (Scotland) Act 2007, ss 36, 226(2), Sch 1, paras 1, 36(a), Sch 6, Pt 1, subject to transitional provisions and savings in SSI 2008/115, arts 5–7, 10, 15 at **[2.51]–[2.53]**, **[2.56]**, **[2.57]**; words in first pair of square brackets inserted by the Home Owner and Debtor Protection (Scotland) Act 2010, s 11(a); words in second pair of square brackets in para (b) inserted by the Bankruptcy and Debt Advice (Scotland) Act 2014, s 49(a), subject to transitional provisions and savings in SSI 2014/261, arts 4, 12 at **[2.91]**, **[2.99]**.

Sub-s (2): word "permanent" (omitted) repealed, and words "sheriff" and "he" in square brackets substituted for original words "court" and "it" respectively by the Bankruptcy and Diligence etc (Scotland) Act 2007, ss 36, 226(2), Sch 1, paras 1, 36(b), Sch 6, Pt 1, subject to transitional provisions and savings in SSI 2008/115, arts 5–7, 10, 15 at **[2.51]–[2.53]**, **[2.56]**, **[2.57]**; words in first pair of square brackets inserted and words in sixth pair of square brackets substituted by the Home Owner and Debtor Protection (Scotland) Act 2010, s 11(a), (b); para (aa) inserted, and words in square brackets in para (d) substituted by the Civil Partnership Act 2004, s 261(2), Sch 28, para 36(1)–(3).

Sub-s (3): word "permanent" (omitted) repealed by the Bankruptcy and Diligence etc (Scotland) Act 2007, s 226(2), Sch 6, Pt 1, subject to transitional provisions and savings in SSI 2008/115, arts 5–7, 10, 15 at **[2.51]–[2.53]**, **[2.56]**, **[2.57]**; words in square brackets inserted by the Home Owner and Debtor Protection (Scotland) Act 2010, s 11(a).

Sub-ss (3A), (3B): inserted by the Home Owner and Debtor Protection (Scotland) Act 2010, s 11(c); words in square brackets in sub-s (3A) substituted for original words "subsection (1)(b)" by the Bankruptcy and Debt Advice (Scotland) Act 2014, s 49(b), subject to transitional provisions and savings in SSI 2014/261, arts 4, 12 at **[2.91]**, **[2.99]**.

Sub-s (4): words in square brackets in paras (a), (b), (c) inserted by the Civil Partnership Act 2004, s 261(2), Sch 28, para 36(1), (4); para (ba) inserted and words in square brackets in para (d) added by the Home Owner and Debtor Protection (Scotland) Act 2010, s 11(d).

Regulations: the Bankruptcy (Scotland) Regulations 2014, SSI 2014/225 at **[16.267]**.

[5.99]

41 Protection of rights of spouse against arrangements intended to defeat them

(1) If a debtor's sequestrated estate includes a matrimonial home of which the debtor, immediately before the date [the order is made appointing] the . . . trustee (or, if more than one [trustee is appointed] in the sequestration, of the first [order making such an appointment]) was an entitled spouse and the other spouse is a non-entitled spouse—

(a) the . . . trustee shall, where he—

(i) is aware that the entitled spouse is married to the non-entitled spouse; and

(ii) knows where the non-entitled spouse is residing,

inform the non-entitled spouse, within the period of 14 days beginning with that date, of the fact that sequestration of the entitled spouse's estate has been awarded, of the right of petition which exists under section 16 of this Act and of the effect of paragraph (b) below; and

(b) the [sheriff], on the petition under section 16 of this Act of the non-entitled spouse presented either within the period of 40 days beginning with that date or within the period of 10 weeks beginning with the date [of the award] of sequestration may—

(i) under section 17 of this Act recall the sequestration; or

(ii) make such order as [he] thinks appropriate to protect the occupancy rights of the non-entitled spouse;

if [he] is satisfied that the purpose of the petition for sequestration [or, as the case may be, the debtor application] was wholly or mainly to defeat the occupancy rights of the non-entitled spouse.

(2) In subsection (1) above—

"entitled spouse" and "non-entitled spouse" have the same meanings as in section 6 of the Matrimonial Homes (Family Protection) (Scotland) Act 1981;

"matrimonial home" has the meaning assigned by section 22 of that Act as amended by the Law Reform (Miscellaneous Provisions) (Scotland) Act 1985; and

"occupancy rights" has the meaning assigned by section 1(4) of the said Act of 1981.

NOTES

Repealed as noted at the beginning of this Act.

Sub-s (1): amended by the Bankruptcy and Diligence etc (Scotland) Act 2007, ss 36, 226(2), Sch 1, paras 1, 37, Sch 6, Pt 1, subject to transitional provisions and savings in SSI 2008/115, arts 5–7, 10, 15 at **[2.51]–[2.53]**, **[2.56]**, **[2.57]**, as follows:

words in first pair of square brackets substituted for original words "of issue of the act and warrant of", word "permanent" (omitted) repealed, words in second pair of square brackets substituted for original words "such act and warrant is issued" and words in third pair of square brackets substituted for original words "such issue";

word "permanent" omitted from para (a) repealed; and

in para (b) word in first pair of square brackets substituted for original words "Court of Session", words in second and fifth pairs of square brackets inserted and word in third and fourth pairs of square brackets substituted for original word "it".

[5.100]

[41A Protection of rights of civil partner against arrangements intended to defeat them

(1) If a debtor's sequestrated estate includes a family home of which the debtor, immediately before the date [the order is made appointing] the . . . trustee (or, if more than one [trustee is appointed] in the sequestration, of the first [order making such an appointment]) was an entitled partner and the other partner in the civil partnership is a non-entitled partner—

(a) the . . . trustee shall, where he—

(i) is aware that the entitled partner is in civil partnership with the non-entitled partner; and

(ii) knows where the non-entitled partner is residing,

inform the non-entitled partner, within the period of 14 days beginning with that date, of the fact that sequestration of the entitled partner's estate has been awarded, of the right of petition which exists under section 16 of this Act and of the effect of paragraph (b) below; and

(b) the [sheriff], on the petition under section 16 of this Act of the non-entitled partner presented either within the period of 40 days beginning with that date or within the period of 10 weeks beginning with the date [of the award] of sequestration may—

(i) under section 17 of this Act recall the sequestration; or

(ii) make such order as [he] thinks appropriate to protect the occupancy rights of the non-entitled partner,

if [he] is satisfied that the purpose of the petition for sequestration [or, as the case may be, the debtor application] was wholly or mainly to defeat the occupancy rights of the non-entitled partner.

(2) In subsection (1) above—

"entitled partner" and "non-entitled partner" have the same meanings as in section 101 of the Civil Partnership Act 2004;

"family home" has the meaning assigned by section 135 of the 2004 Act; and

"occupancy rights" means the rights conferred by subsection (1) of that section 101.]

NOTES

Inserted by the Civil Partnership Act 2004, s 261(2), Sch 28, para 37.

Repealed as noted at the beginning of this Act.

Sub-s (1): amended by the Bankruptcy and Diligence etc (Scotland) Act 2007, ss 36, 226(2), Sch 1, paras 1, 38, Sch 6, Pt 1, subject to transitional provisions and savings in SSI 2008/115, arts 5–7, 10, 15 at **[2.51]–[2.53]**, **[2.56]**, **[2.57]**, as follows:

words in first pair of square brackets substituted for original words "of issue of the act and warrant of", word "permanent" (omitted) repealed, words in second pair of square brackets substituted for original words "such act and warrant is issued" and words in third pair of square brackets substituted for original words "such issue";

word "permanent" omitted from para (a) repealed; and

in para (b) word in first pair of square brackets substituted for original words "Court of Session", words in second and fifth pairs of square brackets inserted and word in third and fourth pairs of square brackets substituted for original word "it".

[5.101]

42 [Contractual powers of trustee]

(1) Subject to subsections (2) and (3) below, the . . . trustee may adopt any contract entered into by the debtor before the date of sequestration where he considers that its adoption would be beneficial to the administration of the debtor's estate, except where the adoption is precluded by the express or implied terms of the contract, or may refuse to adopt any such contract.

[(2) The trustee must, within 28 days from the receipt by the trustee of a request in writing from any party to a contract entered into by the debtor, adopt or refuse to adopt the contract.

(2A) The period mentioned in subsection (2) may be extended—

(a) in a case where the Accountant in Bankruptcy is the trustee, by the sheriff on the application of the Accountant in Bankruptcy,

(b) in any other case, by the Accountant in Bankruptcy on the application of the trustee.

(2B) The trustee may, before the expiry of the period of 14 days beginning with the day of the decision, apply to the Accountant in Bankruptcy for a review of a decision of the Accountant in Bankruptcy under subsection (2A)(b).

(2C) If an application for a review under subsection (2B) is made, the Accountant in Bankruptcy must—

(a) take into account any representations made by an interested person before the expiry of the period of 21 days beginning with the day on which the application is made, and

(b) confirm, amend or revoke the decision before the expiry of the period of 28 days beginning with the day on which the application is made.

(2D) The trustee may appeal to the sheriff against a decision by the Accountant in Bankruptcy under subsection (2C)(b), before the expiry of the period of 14 days beginning with the day of the decision.

(2E) The Accountant in Bankruptcy may refer a case to the sheriff for a direction before—

(a) making a decision under subsection (2A)(b), or

(b) undertaking any review under this section.

(2F) An application for a review under subsection (2B) may not be made in relation to a matter on which the Accountant in Bankruptcy has applied to the sheriff for a direction under subsection (2E).]

(3) If the . . . trustee does not reply in writing to the request under subsection (2) above within the said period of 28 days or longer period, as the case may be, he shall be deemed to have refused to adopt the contract.

(4) The . . . trustee may enter into any contract where he considers that this would be beneficial for the administration of the debtor's estate.

NOTES

Repealed as noted at the beginning of this Act.

Section heading: substituted for original words "Contractual powers of permanent trustee" by the Bankruptcy and Diligence etc (Scotland) Act 2007, s 36, Sch 1, paras 1, 39(b), subject to transitional provisions and savings in SSI 2008/115, arts 5–7, 10, 15 at **[2.51]–[2.53]**, **[2.56]**, **[2.57]**.

Sub-ss (1), (3), (4): word "permanent" omitted in each place repealed by the Bankruptcy and Diligence etc (Scotland) Act 2007, s 226(2), Sch 6, Pt 1, subject to transitional provisions and savings in SSI 2008/115, arts 5–7, 10, 15 at **[2.51]–[2.53]**, **[2.56]**, **[2.57]**.

Sub-ss (2), (2A)–(2F): substituted for original sub-s (2), by the Bankruptcy and Debt Advice (Scotland) Act 2014, s 32, subject to transitional provisions and savings in SSI 2014/261, arts 4, 12 at **[2.91]**, **[2.99]**. Sub-s (2) previously read as follows (with word "permanent" omitted in both places repealed and word in square brackets substituted for original word "court" by the Bankruptcy and Diligence etc (Scotland) Act 2007, ss 36, 226(2), Sch 1, paras 1, 39(a), Sch 6, Pt 1, subject to transitional provisions and savings in SSI 2008/115, arts 5–7, 10, 15)—

> "(2) The . . . trustee shall, within 28 days from the receipt by him of a request in writing from any party to a contract entered into by the debtor or within such longer period of that receipt as the [sheriff] on application by the . . . trustee may allow, adopt or refuse to adopt the contract.".

[5.102]

43 [Money received by trustee]

(1) Subject to [subsections (1A) and (2)] below, all money received by the . . . trustee in the exercise of his functions shall be deposited by him in the name of the debtor's estate in an [interest-bearing account in an] appropriate bank or institution.

[(1A) In any case where the Accountant in Bankruptcy is the trustee, subject to subsection (2) below, all money received by the Accountant in Bankruptcy in the exercise of his functions as trustee shall be deposited by him in an interest bearing account in the name of the debtor's estate or in the name of the Scottish Ministers in an appropriate bank or institution.]

(2) The . . . trustee may at any time retain in his hands a sum not exceeding £200 or such other sum as may be prescribed.

NOTES

Repealed as noted at the beginning of this Act.

Section heading: words substituted for original words "Money received by permanent trustee" by the Bankruptcy and Diligence etc (Scotland) Act 2007, s 36, Sch 1, paras 1, 40, subject to transitional provisions and savings in SSI 2008/115, arts 5–7, 10, 15 at **[2.51]–[2.53]**, **[2.56]**, **[2.57]**.

Sub-s (1): words in first pair of square brackets substituted for original words "subsection (2)", word "permanent" (omitted) repealed, and words in second pair of square brackets inserted by the Bankruptcy and Diligence etc (Scotland) Act 2007, ss 13(a), 226(2), Sch 6, Pt 1, subject to transitional provisions and savings in SSI 2008/115, arts 5–7, 10, 15 at **[2.51]–[2.53]**, **[2.56]**, **[2.57]**.

Sub-s (1A): inserted by the Bankruptcy and Diligence etc (Scotland) Act 2007, s 13(b), subject to transitional provisions and savings in SSI 2008/115, arts 5–7, 10, 15 at **[2.51]–[2.53]**, **[2.56]**, **[2.57]**.

Sub-s (2): word "permanent" (omitted) repealed by the Bankruptcy and Diligence etc (Scotland) Act 2007, s 226(2), Sch 6, Pt 1, subject to transitional provisions and savings in SSI 2008/115, arts 5–7, 10, 15 at **[2.51]–[2.53]**, **[2.56]**, **[2.57]**.

[5.103]

[43A Debtor's requirement to give account of state of affairs

(1) This section applies to a debtor who—

(a) has not been discharged under this Act; or

[(b) is subject to a debtor contribution order.]

(2) The trustee shall, at the end of—

(a) the period of 6 months beginning with the date of sequestration; and

(b) each subsequent period of 6 months,

require the debtor to give an account in writing, in such form as may be prescribed, of his current state of affairs.]

NOTES

Inserted by the Bankruptcy and Diligence etc (Scotland) Act 2007, s 30, subject to transitional provisions and savings in SSI 2008/115, arts 5–7, 10, 15 at **[2.51]**–**[2.53]**, **[2.56]**, **[2.57]**.

Repealed as noted at the beginning of this Act.

Sub-s (1): para (b) substituted by the Bankruptcy and Debt Advice (Scotland) Act 2014, s 56(1), Sch 3, paras 2, 22, subject to transitional provisions and savings in SSI 2014/261, arts 4, 12 at **[2.91]**, **[2.99]**, and previously read as follows—

"(b) is subject to—
(i) an order made by the sheriff under subsection (2) of section 32 of this Act; or
(ii) an agreement entered into under subsection (4B) of that section.".

Regulations: the Bankruptcy (Scotland) Regulations 2014, SSI 2014/225 at **[16.267]**.

[5.104]

[43B Financial education

(1) The trustee must notify a living debtor that the debtor is required to undertake a prescribed course of financial education (a "financial education course") specified by the trustee if, in the opinion of the trustee—
(a) any of the circumstances mentioned in subsection (2) apply, and
(b) undertaking the course would be appropriate for the debtor.

(2) The circumstances are—
(a) in the period of 5 years ending on the date on which the sequestration of the debtor's estate was awarded—
(i) the debtor's estate was sequestrated,
(ii) the debtor granted a protected trust deed,
(iii) an analogous remedy (within the meaning of section 10(7)) was in force in respect of the debtor, or
(iv) the debtor participated in a debt management programme under which the debtor made regular payments (including in particular a programme approved in accordance with section 2 of the Debt Arrangement and Attachment (Scotland) Act 2002 (asp 17)),
(b) the debtor is subject to, or under investigation with a view to an application being made for, a bankruptcy restrictions order,
(c) the trustee considers that the pattern of the debtor's behaviour, whether before or after the award of sequestration, is such that the debtor would benefit from a financial education course,
(d) the debtor agrees to undertake a financial education course.

(3) The trustee must decide whether to issue a notification under subsection (1)—
(a) before the end of the period of 6 months beginning with the date of award of sequestration, and
(b) in a case where section 54F applies, as soon as reasonably practicable after the trustee ascertains the whereabouts of the debtor or the debtor makes contact with the trustee.

(4) A debtor must not be required to undertake or, as the case may be, complete the financial education course specified by the trustee if, in the opinion of the trustee—
(a) the debtor is unable to participate in the course as a result of the debtor's health (including by reason of disability or physical or mental illness), or
(b) the debtor has completed a financial education course in the period of 5 years ending on the date on which the sequestration of the debtor's estate was awarded.

(5) Regulations under subsection (1) may in particular—
(a) prescribe the content, format and method of delivery of a course,
(b) prescribe different courses for different circumstances,
(c) make provision for particular courses to be specified by a trustee where particular circumstances in subsection (2) apply.]

NOTES

Commencement: 30 June 2014 (for the purpose of making regulations); 1 April 2015 (otherwise).

Inserted by the Bankruptcy and Debt Advice (Scotland) Act 2014, s 2, subject to transitional provisions and savings in SSI 2014/261, arts 4, 12 at **[2.91]**, **[2.99]**.

Repealed as noted at the beginning of this Act.

Regulations: the Bankruptcy (Scotland) Regulations 2014, SSI 2014/225 at **[16.267]**.

Examination of debtor

[5.105]

44 Private examination

(1) The . . . trustee may request—
(a) the debtor to appear before him and to give information relating to his assets, his dealings with them or his conduct in relation to his business or financial affairs; or
(b) the debtor's spouse [or civil partner] or any other person who the . . . trustee believes can give such information (in this Act such spouse[, civil partner] or other person being referred to as a "relevant person"), to give that information,

and, if he considers it necessary, the . . . trustee may apply to the sheriff for an order to be made under subsection (2) below.

(2) Subject to section 46(2) of this Act, on application to him under subsection (1) above the sheriff may make an order requiring the debtor or a relevant person to attend for private examination before him on a date (being not earlier than 8 days nor later than 16 days after the date of the order) and at a time specified in the order.

(3) A person who fails without reasonable excuse to comply with an order made under subsection (2) above shall be guilty of an offence and liable on summary conviction to a fine not exceeding level 5 on the standard scale or to imprisonment for a term not exceeding 3 months or to both.

(4) Where the debtor is an entity whose estate may be sequestrated by virtue of section 6(1) of this Act, the references in this section and in sections 45 to 47 of this Act to the debtor shall be construed, unless the context otherwise requires, as references to a person representing the entity.

NOTES

Repealed as noted at the beginning of this Act.

Sub-s (1): word "permanent" omitted in each place repealed by the Bankruptcy and Diligence etc (Scotland) Act 2007, s 226(2), Sch 6, Pt 1, subject to transitional provisions and savings in SSI 2008/115, arts 5–7, 10, 15 at **[2.51]–[2.53]**, **[2.56]**, **[2.57]**; words in square brackets inserted by the Civil Partnership Act 2004, s 261(2), Sch 28, para 38.

[5.106]

45 Public examination

(1) Not less than 8 weeks before the end of the first accounting period, the . . . trustee—

(a) may; or

(b) if requested to do so by the Accountant in Bankruptcy or the commissioners (if any) or one quarter in value of the creditors, shall,

apply to the sheriff for an order for the public examination before the sheriff of the debtor or of a relevant person relating to the debtor's assets, his dealings with them or his conduct in relation to his business or financial affairs:

Provided that, on cause shown, such application may be made by the . . . trustee at any time.

(2) Subject to section 46(2) of this Act, the sheriff, on an application under subsection (1) above, shall make an order requiring the debtor or relevant person to attend for examination before him in open court on a date (being not earlier than 8 days nor later than 16 days after the date of the order) and at a time specified in the order.

(3) On the sheriff making an order under subsection (2) above, the . . . trustee shall—

(a) [send to the Accountant in Bankruptcy] a notice in such form and containing such particulars as may be prescribed; and

(b) send a copy of the said notice—

(i) to every creditor known to the . . . trustee; and

(ii) where the order is in respect of a relevant person, to the debtor, and inform the creditor and, where applicable, the debtor that he may participate in the examination.

[(3A) The Accountant in Bankruptcy must enter particulars of the notice sent under subsection (3)(a) in the register of insolvencies.]

(4) A person who fails without reasonable excuse to comply with an order made under subsection (2) above shall be guilty of an offence and liable on summary conviction to a fine not exceeding level 5 on the standard scale or to imprisonment for a term not exceeding 3 months or to both.

NOTES

Repealed as noted at the beginning of this Act.

Sub-s (1): word "permanent" omitted in each place repealed by the Bankruptcy and Diligence etc (Scotland) Act 2007, s 226(2), Sch 6, Pt 1, subject to transitional provisions and savings in SSI 2008/115, arts 5–7, 10, 15 at **[2.51]–[2.53]**, **[2.56]**, **[2.57]**.

Sub-s (3): word "permanent" omitted in each place repealed by the Bankruptcy and Diligence etc (Scotland) Act 2007, s 226(2), Sch 6, Pt 1, subject to transitional provisions and savings in SSI 2008/115, arts 5–7, 10, 15 at **[2.51]–[2.53]**, **[2.56]**, **[2.57]**; words in square brackets in para (a) substituted for original words "publish in the Edinburgh Gazette", by the Bankruptcy and Debt Advice (Scotland) Act 2014, s 24(2)(a), subject to transitional provisions and savings in SSI 2014/261, arts 4, 12 at **[2.91]**, **[2.99]**.

Sub-s (3A): inserted by the Bankruptcy and Debt Advice (Scotland) Act 2014, s 24(2)(b), subject to transitional provisions and savings in SSI 2014/261, arts 4, 12 at **[2.91]**, **[2.99]**.

Regulations: the Bankruptcy (Scotland) Regulations 2008, SSI 2008/82 at **[16.262]**; the Bankruptcy (Scotland) Regulations 2014, SSI 2014/225 at **[16.267]**.

[5.107]

46 Provisions ancillary to sections 44 and 45

(1) If the debtor or relevant person is residing—

(a) in Scotland, the sheriff may, on the application of the . . . trustee, grant a warrant which may be executed by a *messenger-at-arms or sheriff officer* anywhere in Scotland; or [to apprehend]

(b) in any other part of the United Kingdom, . . . the sheriff may, on the application of the . . . trustee, [grant a warrant for the arrest of]

. . . the debtor or relevant person and [to] have him taken to the place of the examination:

Provided that a warrant under [this subsection shall not be granted] unless the [sheriff] is satisfied that it is necessary to do so to secure the attendance of the debtor or relevant person at the examination.

(2) If the debtor or a relevant person is for any good reason prevented from attending for examination, the sheriff may, without prejudice to subsection (3) below, grant a commission to take his examination (the commissioner being in this section and section 47 below referred to as an "examining commissioner").

(3) The sheriff or the examining commissioner may at any time adjourn the examination to such day as the sheriff or the examining commissioner may fix.

(4) The sheriff or the examining commissioner may order the debtor or a relevant person to produce for inspection any document in his custody or control relating to the debtor's assets, his dealings with them or his conduct in relation to his business or financial affairs, and to deliver the document or a copy thereof to the . . . trustee for further examination by him.

NOTES

Repealed as noted at the beginning of this Act.

Sub-s (1): in para (a), word "permanent" (omitted) repealed and for the words "messenger-at-arms or sheriff officer" there are substituted the words "judicial officer" (as from a day to be appointed), by the Bankruptcy and Diligence etc (Scotland) Act 2007, ss 36, 226(2), Sch 1, paras 1, 41(a), Sch 6, Pt 1, subject to transitional provisions and savings in SSI 2008/115, arts 5–7, 10, 15 at **[2.51]–[2.53]**, **[2.56]**, **[2.57]**; words in square brackets inserted by the Bankruptcy (Scotland) Act 1993, s 11, Sch 1, para 20, subject to s 12(6) thereof, at **[5.194]** and to SI 1993/438, arts 4, 5, at **[16.58]**, **[16.59]**; in para (b) words "the Court of Session or" and "permanent" omitted in first and second places respectively, repealed by the Bankruptcy and Diligence etc (Scotland) Act 2007, s 226(2), Sch 6, Pt 1, subject to transitional provisions and savings as noted above, words in first pair of square brackets substituted, word omitted in the third place repealed and word in second pair of square brackets inserted by the Bankruptcy (Scotland) Act 1993, s 11(3), (4), Sch 1, para 20, Sch 2, subject to s 12(6) thereof, at **[5.194]** and to SI 1993/438, arts 4, 5, at **[16.58]**, **[16.59]**; and in the proviso, words in first pair of square brackets substituted by the Bankruptcy (Scotland) Act 1993, s 11(3), (4), Sch 1, para 20, Sch 2, subject to s 12(6) thereof, at **[5.194]** and to SI 1993/438, arts 4, 5, at **[16.58]**, **[16.59]**, and word in second pair of square brackets substituted for original word "court" by the Bankruptcy and Diligence etc (Scotland) Act 2007, s 36, Sch 1, paras 1, 41(b), subject to transitional provisions and savings as noted above.

Sub-s (4): word "permanent" (omitted) repealed by the Bankruptcy and Diligence etc (Scotland) Act 2007, s 226(2), Sch 6, Pt 1, subject to transitional provisions and savings in SSI 2008/115, arts 5–7, 10, 15 at **[2.51]–[2.53]**, **[2.56]**, **[2.57]**.

[5.108]

47 Conduct of examination

(1) The examination, whether before the sheriff or an examining commissioner, shall be taken on oath.

(2) At the examination—

- (a) the . . . trustee or a solicitor or counsel acting on his behalf and, in the case of public examination, any creditor may question the debtor or a relevant person; and
- (b) the debtor may question a relevant person,

as to any matter relating to the debtor's assets, his dealings with them or his conduct in relation to his business or financial affairs.

(3) The debtor or a relevant person shall be required to answer any question relating to the debtor's assets, his dealings with them or his conduct in relation to his business or financial affairs and shall not be excused from answering any such question on the ground that the answer may incriminate or tend to incriminate him or on the ground of confidentiality:

Provided that—

- (a) a statement made by the debtor or a relevant person in answer to such a question shall not be admissible in evidence in any subsequent criminal proceedings against the person making the statement, except where the proceedings are in respect of a charge of perjury relating to the statement;
- (b) a person subject to examination shall not be required to disclose any information which he has received from a person who is not called for examination if the information is confidential between them.

(4) [The rules relating to the recording of evidence in ordinary causes specified in the First Schedule to the Sheriff Courts (Scotland) Act 1907] shall apply in relation to the recording of evidence at the examination before the sheriff or the examining commissioner.

(5) The debtor's deposition at the examination shall be subscribed by himself and by the sheriff (or, as the case may be, the examining commissioner) . . .

[(6) The trustee must send a copy of the record of the examination to the Accountant in Bankruptcy.]

(7) A relevant person shall be entitled to fees or allowances in respect of his attendance at the examination as if he were a witness in an ordinary civil cause in the sheriff court:

Provided that, if the sheriff thinks that it is appropriate in all the circumstances, he may disallow or restrict the entitlement to such fees or allowances.

NOTES

Repealed as noted at the beginning of this Act.

Sub-s (2): word "permanent" omitted repealed by the Bankruptcy and Diligence etc (Scotland) Act 2007, s 226(2), Sch 6, Pt 1, subject to transitional provisions and savings in SSI 2008/115, arts 5–7, 10, 15 at **[2.51]–[2.53]**, **[2.56]**, **[2.57]**.

Sub-s (4): words in square brackets substituted by the Act of Sederunt (Bankruptcy) 1986, SI 1986/517, art 5.

Sub-s (5): words "and shall be inserted in the sederunt book" (omitted) repealed by the Bankruptcy and Debt Advice (Scotland) Act 2014, s 56(2), Sch 4, subject to transitional provisions and savings in SSI 2014/261, arts 4, 12 at **[2.91]**, **[2.99]**.

Sub-s (6): substituted by the Bankruptcy and Debt Advice (Scotland) Act 2014, s 56(1), Sch 3, paras 2, 23, subject to transitional provisions and savings in SSI 2014/261, arts 4, 12 at **[2.91]**, **[2.99]**. Sub-s (6) previously read as follows (with word "permanent" omitted repealed by the Bankruptcy and Diligence etc (Scotland) Act 2007, s 226(2), Sch 6, Pt 1, subject to transitional provisions and savings in SSI 2008/115, arts 5–7, 10, 15)—

> "(6) The . . . trustee shall insert a copy of the record of the examination in the sederunt book and send a copy of the record to the Accountant in Bankruptcy.".

Submission and adjudication of claims

[5.109]

48 [Submission of claims to trustee]

(1) Subject to [subsections (1A) and (2)] below and subsections (8) and (9) of section 52 of this Act, a creditor in order to obtain an adjudication as to his entitlement—

(a) to vote at a meeting of creditors other than the statutory meeting; or

(b) (so far as funds are available), to a dividend out of the debtor's estate in respect of any accounting period,

shall submit a claim in accordance with this section to the . . . trustee respectively—

(i) at or before the meeting; or

[(ii) in accordance with subsection (1A).]

[(1A) A creditor must, in order to obtain an adjudication as to the creditor's entitlement (so far as funds are available) to a dividend out of the debtor's estate, submit a claim to the trustee not later than the relevant day.

(1B) The "relevant day", in relation to a creditor, means—

(a) where a notice is given to the creditor under section 21A(2), the day which is 120 days after the day on which the notice is given, or

(b) where no notice is given to the creditor under that section, the day which is 120 days after the day on which the trustee gives notice to that creditor inviting the submission of claims.

(1C) If a creditor submits a claim to the trustee after the relevant day, the trustee may, in respect of any accounting period, provide an adjudication as to the creditor's entitlement (so far as funds are available) to a dividend out of the debtor's estate if—

(a) the claim is submitted not later than 8 weeks before the end of the accounting period, and

(b) there were exceptional circumstances which prevented the claim from being submitted before the relevant day.]

(2) A claim submitted by a creditor—

(a) under section 22 of this Act and accepted in whole or in part by the . . . trustee for the purpose of voting at the statutory meeting; or

(b) under this section [which has not been rejected in whole],

shall be deemed to have been re-submitted for the purpose of obtaining an adjudication as to his entitlement both to vote at any subsequent meeting and (so far as funds are available) to a dividend in respect of an accounting period, or, as the case may be, any subsequent accounting period.

(3) Subsections (2) and (3) of section 22 of this Act shall apply for the purposes of this section but as if in the proviso to subsection (2) [after the word "trustee" there were inserted the words "] with the consent of the commissioners, if any" . . .

(4) A creditor who has submitted a claim under this section (or under section 22 of this Act, a statement of claim which has been deemed re-submitted as mentioned in subsection (2) above) may at any time submit a further claim under this section specifying a different amount for his claim:

Provided that a secured creditor shall not be entitled to produce a further claim specifying a different value for the security at any time after the . . . trustee requires the creditor to discharge, or convey or assign, the security under paragraph 5(2) of Schedule 1 to this Act.

(5) The . . . trustee, for the purpose of satisfying himself as to the validity or amount of a claim submitted by a creditor under this section, may require—

(a) the creditor to produce further evidence; or

(b) any other person who he believes can produce relevant evidence, to produce such evidence,

and, if the creditor or other person refuses or delays to do so, the . . . trustee may apply to the sheriff for an order requiring the creditor or other person to attend for his private examination before the sheriff.

(6) Sections 44(2) and (3) and 47(1) of this Act shall apply, subject to any necessary modifications, to the examination of the creditor or other person as they apply to the examination of a relevant person; and references in this subsection and subsection (5) above to a creditor in a case where the creditor is an entity mentioned in section 6(1) of this Act shall be construed, unless the context otherwise requires, as references to a person representing the entity.

(7) Subsections (5) to (10) of section 22 of this Act shall apply for the purposes of this section but as if—

(a) . . .

[(b) in subsection (7) the words "and keep a record of it stating the date when it was produced to him" were repealed.]

(8) At any private examination under subsection (5) above, a solicitor or counsel may act on behalf of the . . . trustee or he may appear himself.

NOTES

Repealed as noted at the beginning of this Act.

Section heading: substituted for original words "Submission of claims to permanent trustee" by the Bankruptcy and Diligence etc (Scotland) Act 2007, s 36, Sch 1, paras 1, 42(c), subject to transitional provisions and savings in SSI 2008/115, arts 5–7, 10, 15 at **[2.51]–[2.53]**, **[2.56]**, **[2.57]**.

Sub-s (1): word "permanent" omitted repealed by the Bankruptcy and Diligence etc (Scotland) Act 2007, s 226(2), Sch 6, Pt 1, subject to transitional provisions and savings in SSI 2008/115, arts 5–7, 10, 15 at **[2.51]–[2.53]**, **[2.56]**, **[2.57]**; words in square brackets substituted by the Bankruptcy and Debt Advice (Scotland) Act 2014, s 14(a), subject to transitional provisions and savings in SSI 2014/261, arts 4, 12 at **[2.91]**, **[2.99]**.

Sub-ss (1A)–(1C): inserted by the Bankruptcy and Debt Advice (Scotland) Act 2014, s 14(b), subject to transitional provisions and savings in SSI 2014/261, arts 4, 12 at **[2.91]**, **[2.99]**.

Sub-s (2): word "interim" omitted from para (a) repealed, and words in square brackets in para (b) substituted by the Bankruptcy and Diligence etc (Scotland) Act 2007, ss 36, 226(2), Sch 1, paras 1, 42(a), Sch 6, Pt 1, subject to transitional provisions and savings in SSI 2008/115, arts 5–7, 10, 15 at **[2.51]–[2.53]**, **[2.56]**, **[2.57]**.

Sub-s (3): words in square brackets substituted for original words "for the words "interim trustee" there were substituted the words "permanent trustee" and words ", and for any other reference to the interim trustee there were substituted a reference to the permanent trustee" (omitted) repealed by the Bankruptcy and Diligence etc (Scotland) Act 2007, ss 36, 226(2), Sch 1, paras 1, 42(b), Sch 6, Pt 1, subject to transitional provisions and savings in SSI 2008/115, arts 5–7, 10, 15 at **[2.51]–[2.53]**, **[2.56]**, **[2.57]**.

Sub-ss (4), (5), (8): word "permanent" omitted in each place repealed by the Bankruptcy and Diligence etc (Scotland) Act 2007, s 226(2), Sch 6, Pt 1, subject to transitional provisions and savings in SSI 2008/115, arts 5–7, 10, 15 at **[2.51]–[2.53]**, **[2.56]**, **[2.57]**.

Sub-s (7): para (a) repealed by the Bankruptcy and Diligence etc (Scotland) Act 2007, s 226(2), Sch 6, Pt 1, subject to transitional provisions and savings in SSI 2008/115, arts 5–7, 10, 15 at **[2.51]–[2.53]**, **[2.56]**, **[2.57]**; para (b) substituted by the Bankruptcy and Debt Advice (Scotland) Act 2014, s 56(1), Sch 3, paras 2, 24, subject to transitional provisions and savings in SSI 2014/261, arts 4, 12 at **[2.91]**, **[2.99]**, and para (b) previously read as follows (with words omitted repealed by the Bankruptcy and Diligence etc (Scotland) Act 2007, s 226(2), Sch 6, Pt 1, subject to transitional provisions and savings in SSI 2008/115, arts 5–7, 10, 15)—

"(b) in subsection (7) for the words . . . "keep a record of it" there were substituted . . . the words . . . "make an insertion relating thereto in the sederunt book".".

Regulations: the Bankruptcy (Scotland) Regulations 2008, SSI 2008/82 at **[16.262]**.

[5.110]

49 Adjudication of claims

(1) At the commencement of every meeting of creditors (other than the statutory meeting), the . . . trustee shall, for the purposes of section 50 of this Act so far as it relates to voting at that meeting, accept or reject the claim of each creditor.

(2) Where funds are available for payment of a dividend out of the debtor's estate in respect of an accounting period, the . . . trustee for the purpose of determining who is entitled to such a dividend shall, not later than 4 weeks before the end of the period, accept or reject every claim submitted or deemed to have been re-submitted to him under this Act; and shall at the same time make a decision on any matter requiring to be specified under paragraph (a) or (b) of subsection (5) below.

[(2A) On accepting or rejecting, under subsection (2) above, every claim submitted or deemed to have been re-submitted, the trustee shall, as soon as is reasonably practicable, send a list of every claim so accepted or rejected (including the amount of each claim and whether he has accepted or rejected it) to—

(a) the debtor; and
(b) every creditor known to the trustee.]

(3) If the amount of a claim is stated in foreign currency the . . . trustee in adjudicating on the claim under subsection (1) or (2) above shall convert the amount into sterling, in such manner as may be prescribed, at the rate of exchange prevailing at the close of business on the date of sequestration.

(4) Where the . . . trustee rejects a claim, he shall forthwith notify the creditor giving reasons for the rejection.

(5) Where the . . . trustee accepts or rejects a claim, he shall record *in the sederunt book* his decision on the claim specifying—

(a) the amount of the claim accepted by him,
(b) the category of debt, and the value of any security, as decided by him, and
(c) if he is rejecting the claim, his reasons therefor.

[(6) The debtor or any creditor may apply to the Accountant in Bankruptcy for a review of—

(a) the acceptance or rejection of any claim, or
(b) a decision in respect of any matter requiring to be specified under subsection (5)(a) or (b).]

[(6A) The debtor may make an application under subsection (6) only if the debtor satisfies the Accountant in Bankruptcy that the debtor has, or is likely to have, a pecuniary interest in the outcome of the review.

(6B) An application under subsection (6) must be made—

(a) in the case of a review relating to an acceptance or rejection under subsection (1), before the expiry of the period of 14 days beginning with the day of that decision, and
(b) in the case of a review relating to an acceptance or rejection under subsection (2), before the expiry of the period of 28 days beginning with the day of that decision.

(6C) If an application under subsection (6) is made, the Accountant in Bankruptcy must—

(a) take into account any representations made by an interested person before the expiry of the period of 21 days beginning with the day on which the application is made, and
(b) confirm, amend or revoke the decision before the expiry of the period of 28 days beginning with the day on which the application is made.

(6D) The debtor or any creditor may appeal to the sheriff against a decision by the Accountant in Bankruptcy under subsection (6C)(b) before the expiry of the period of 14 days beginning with the day of the decision.

(6E) The debtor may appeal under subsection (6D) only if the debtor satisfies the sheriff that the debtor has, or is likely to have, a pecuniary interest in the outcome of the appeal.]

(7) Any reference in this section to the acceptance or rejection of a claim shall be construed as a reference to the acceptance or rejection of the claim in whole or in part.

NOTES

Repealed as noted at the beginning of this Act.

Word "permanent" omitted in each place repealed by the Bankruptcy and Diligence etc (Scotland) Act 2007, s 226(2), Sch 6, Pt 1, subject to transitional provisions and savings in SSI 2008/115, arts 5–7, 10, 15 at **[2.51]–[2.53]**, **[2.56]**, **[2.57]**.

Sub-s (2A): inserted by the Bankruptcy and Diligence etc (Scotland) Act 2007, ss 8(3), 31(1)(b), subject to transitional provisions and savings in SSI 2008/115, arts 5–7, 10, 15 at **[2.51]–[2.53]**, **[2.56]**, **[2.57]**.

Sub-s (5): words "in the sederunt book" repealed by the Bankruptcy and Debt Advice (Scotland) Act 2014, s 56(2), Sch 4, subject to transitional provisions and savings in SSI 2014/261, arts 4, 12 at **[2.91]**, **[2.99]**.

Sub-s (6): substituted by the Bankruptcy and Debt Advice (Scotland) Act 2014, s 41(a), subject to transitional provisions and savings in SSI 2014/261, arts 10, 12 at **[2.97]**, **[2.99]** and previously read as follows (with words in square brackets inserted and word (omitted) repealed by the Bankruptcy and Diligence etc (Scotland) Act 2007, ss 31(1)(a), 226(2), Sch 6, Pt 1, subject to transitional provisions and savings in SSI 2008/115, arts 5–7, 10, 15)—

"(6) The debtor [(subject to subsection (6A) below)] or any creditor may, if dissatisfied with the acceptance or rejection of any claim (or, in relation to such acceptance or rejection, with a decision in respect of any matter requiring to be specified under subsection (5)(a) or (b) above), appeal therefrom to the sheriff—

(a) if the acceptance or rejection is under subsection (1) above, within 2 weeks of that acceptance or rejection;

(b) if the acceptance or rejection is under subsection (2) above, not later than 2 weeks before the end of the accounting period,

and the . . . trustee shall record the sheriff's decision in the sederunt book.".

Sub-ss (6A)–(6E): substituted (for sub-s (6A) as inserted by the Bankruptcy and Diligence etc (Scotland) Act 2007, ss 8(3), 31(1)(b), subject to transitional provisions and savings in SSI 2008/115, arts 5–7, 10, 15) by the Bankruptcy and Debt Advice (Scotland) Act 2014, s 41(b), subject to transitional provisions and savings in SSI 2014/261, arts 10, 12 at **[2.97]**, **[2.99]**. Sub-s (6A) previously read as follows—

"[(6A) A debtor may appeal under subsection (6) above if, and only if, he satisfies the sheriff that he has, or is likely to have, a pecuniary interest in the outcome of the appeal.]".

Regulations: the Bankruptcy (Scotland) Regulations 2008, SSI 2008/82 at **[16.262]**; the Bankruptcy (Scotland) Regulations 2014, SSI 2014/225 at **[16.267]**.

Entitlement to vote and draw dividend

[5.111]

50 Entitlement to vote and draw dividend

[(1)] A creditor who has had his claim accepted in whole or in part by the . . . trustee or [on review or appeal under] section 49 of this Act shall be entitled—

(a) subject to sections 29(1)(a) and 30(1) and (4)(b) of this Act, in a case where the acceptance is under (or on appeal arising from) subsection (1) of the said section 49, to vote on any matter at the meeting of creditors for the purpose of voting at which the claim is accepted; and

(b) in a case where the acceptance is under (or on appeal arising from) subsection (2) of the said section 49, to payment out of the debtor's estate of a dividend in respect of the accounting period for the purposes of which the claim is accepted; but such entitlement to payment shall arise only in so far as that estate has funds available to make that payment, having regard to section 51 of this Act.

[(2) No vote shall be cast by virtue of a debt more than once on any resolution put to a meeting of creditors.

(3) Where a creditor—

(a) is entitled to vote under this section;

(b) has lodged his claim in one or more sets of other proceedings; and

(c) votes (either in person or by proxy) on a resolution put to the meeting, only the creditor's vote shall be counted.

(4) Where—

(a) a creditor has lodged his claim in more than one set of other proceedings; and

(b) more than one member State liquidator seeks to vote by virtue of that claim, the entitlement to vote by virtue of that claim is exercisable by the member State liquidator in main proceedings, whether or not the creditor has lodged his claim in the main proceedings.

(5) For the purposes of subsections (3) and (4) above, "other proceedings" means main proceedings, secondary proceedings or territorial proceedings in a member State other than the United Kingdom.]

NOTES

Repealed as noted at the beginning of this Act.

Sub-s (1): numbered as such by the Insolvency (Scotland) Regulations 2003, SI 2003/2109, regs 3, 13(a); word "permanent" (omitted) repealed by the Bankruptcy and Diligence etc (Scotland) Act 2007, s 226(2), Sch 6, Pt 1, subject to transitional provisions and savings in SSI 2008/115, arts 5–7, 10, 15 at **[2.51]–[2.53]**, **[2.56]**, **[2.57]**; words in square brackets substituted for original words "on appeal under subsection (6) of" by the Bankruptcy and Debt Advice (Scotland) Act 2014, s 56(1), Sch 3, paras 2, 25, subject to transitional provisions and savings in SSI 2014/261, art 12 at **[2.99]**.

Sub-ss (2)–(5): added by SI 2003/2109, regs 3, 13(b).

Distribution of debtor's estate

[5.112]

51 Order of priority in distribution

(1) The funds of the debtor's estate shall be distributed by the . . . trustee to meet the following debts in the order in which they are mentioned—

(a) the outlays and remuneration of the interim trustee in the administration of the debtor's estate;

(b) the outlays and remuneration of the . . . trustee in the administration of the debtor's estate;

(c) where the debtor is a deceased debtor, deathbed and funeral expenses reasonably incurred and expenses reasonably incurred in administering the deceased's estate;

(d) the expenses reasonably incurred by a creditor who is a petitioner, or concurs in [a debtor application], for sequestration;

[(e) ordinary preferred debts (excluding any interest which has accrued thereon to the date of sequestration);

(ea) secondary preferred debts (excluding any interest which has accrued thereon to the date of sequestration);]

(f) ordinary debts, that is to say a debt which is neither a secured debt nor a debt mentioned in any other paragraph of this subsection;

(g) interest at the rate specified in subsection (7) below on—

(i) the [ordinary] preferred debts;

[(ia) the secondary preferred debts;]

(ii) the ordinary debts,

between the date of sequestration and the date of payment of the debt;

(h) any postponed debt.

[(2) In this Act—

(a) "preferred debt" means a debt listed in Part I of Schedule 3 to this Act,

(b) "ordinary preferred debt" means a debt within any of paragraphs 4 to 6B of Part I of Schedule 3 to this Act,

(c) "secondary preferred debt" means a debt within paragraph 6C or 6D of Part 1 of Schedule 3 to this Act, and

Part II of that Schedule shall have effect for the interpretation of Part I.]

(3) In this Act "postponed debt" means—

(a) a loan made to the debtor, in consideration of a share of the profits in his business, which is postponed under section 3 of the Partnership Act 1890 to the claims of other creditors;

(b) a loan made to the debtor by the debtor's spouse [or civil partner];

(c) a creditor's right to anything vesting in the . . . trustee by virtue of a successful challenge under section 34 of this Act or to the proceeds of sale of such a thing.

(4) Any debt falling within any of paragraphs (c) to (h) of subsection (1) above shall have the same priority as any other debt falling within the same paragraph and, where the funds of the estate are inadequate to enable the debts mentioned in the paragraph to be paid in full, they shall abate in equal proportions.

(5) Any surplus remaining, after all the debts mentioned in this section have been paid in full, shall be made over to the debtor or to his successors or assignees; and in this subsection "surplus" includes any kind of estate but does not include any unclaimed dividend.

[(5A) Subsection (5) above is subject to Article 35 of the EC Regulation (surplus in secondary proceedings to be transferred to main proceedings).]

(6) Nothing in this section shall affect—

(a) the right of a secured creditor which is preferable to the rights of the . . . trustee; or

(b) any preference of the holder of a lien over a title deed or other document which has been delivered to the . . . trustee in accordance with a requirement under section 38(4) of this Act.

(7) The rate of interest referred to in paragraph (g) of subsection (1) above shall be whichever is the greater of—

(a) the prescribed rate at the date of sequestration; and

(b) the rate applicable to that debt apart from the sequestration.

NOTES

Repealed as noted at the beginning of this Act.

Sub-s (1): word "permanent" omitted in both places repealed, and words in square brackets in para (d) substituted for original words "the petition" by the Bankruptcy and Diligence etc (Scotland) Act 2007, ss 36, 226(2), Sch 1, paras 1, 43, Sch 6, Pt 1, subject to transitional provisions and savings in SSI 2008/115, arts 5–7, 10, 15 at **[2.51]–[2.53]**, **[2.56]**, **[2.57]**; paras (e), (ea) substituted for original para (e), word in square brackets in para (g)(i) inserted and para (g)(ia) inserted, by the Banks and Building Societies (Depositor Preference and Priorities) Order 2014, SI 2014/3486, art 28(1), (2)(a), except in relation to any insolvency proceedings commenced before 1 January 2015 (as to the meaning of this, see further the note "SI 2014/3486, art 3" to the Insolvency Act 1986, s 4 at **[1.5]**). Para (e) originally read as follows—

"(e) preferred debts (excluding any interest which has accrued thereon to the date of sequestration);".

Sub-s (2): substituted by SI 2014/3486, art 28(1), (2)(b), except in relation to any insolvency proceedings commenced before 1 January 2015 (as to the meaning of this, see further the note "SI 2014/3486, art 3" to the Insolvency Act 1986, s 4 at **[1.5]**). Sub-s (2) originally read as follows—

"(2) In this Act "preferred debt" means a debt listed in Part I of Schedule 3 to this Act; and Part II of that Schedule shall have effect for the interpretation of the said Part I.".

Sub-s (3): words in square brackets in para (b) inserted by the Civil Partnership Act 2004, s 261(2), Sch 28, para 39; word "permanent" omitted from para (c) repealed by the Bankruptcy and Diligence etc (Scotland) Act 2007, s 226(2), Sch 6, Pt 1, subject to transitional provisions and savings in SSI 2008/115, arts 5–7, 10, 15 at **[2.51]–[2.53]**, **[2.56]**, **[2.57]**.

Sub-s (5A): inserted by the Insolvency (Scotland) Regulations 2003, SI 2003/2109, regs 3, 14.

Sub-s (6): word "permanent" omitted in both places repealed by the Bankruptcy and Diligence etc (Scotland) Act 2007, s 226(2), Sch 6, Pt 1, subject to transitional provisions and savings in SSI 2008/115, arts 5–7, 10, 15 at **[2.51]–[2.53]**, **[2.56]**, **[2.57]**.

Regulations: the Bankruptcy (Scotland) Regulations 2008, SSI 2008/82 at **[16.262]**; the Bankruptcy (Scotland) Regulations 2014, SSI 2014/225 at **[16.267]**.

[5.113]
52 Estate to be distributed in respect of accounting periods
[(1) The . . . trustee shall make up accounts of his intromissions with the debtor's estate in respect of each accounting period.
(2) In this Act "accounting period" shall be construed as follows—
(a) [subject to subsection (2ZA) below,] the first accounting period shall be the period of [12] months [or such shorter period as may be agreed or determined in accordance with subsection (2ZB), either period] beginning with the date [on which sequestration is awarded]; and
(b) any subsequent accounting period shall be the period of [12] months beginning with the end of the last accounting period; except that—
(i) in a case where the Accountant in Bankruptcy is not the . . . trustee, the . . . trustee and the commissioners or, if there are no commissioners, the Accountant in Bankruptcy agree; or
(ii) in a case where the Accountant in Bankruptcy is the . . . trustee, he determines, that the accounting period shall be such other period beginning with the end of the last accounting period as may be agreed or, as the case may be determined, it shall be that other period.
[(2ZA) Where the trustee was appointed under section 2(5) of this Act as interim trustee in the sequestration, the first accounting period shall be the period beginning with the date of his appointment as interim trustee and ending on the date 12 months after the date on which sequestration is awarded [or such shorter period as may be agreed or determined in accordance with subsection (2ZB)].]
[(2ZB) This subsection applies where the trustee considers that the funds of the debtor's estate are sufficient to pay a dividend in accordance with subsection (3) in respect of—
(a) in the case where the trustee is the Accountant in Bankruptcy, a shorter period of not less than 6 months determined by the Accountant in Bankruptcy,
(b) in any other case, a shorter period of not less than 6 months agreed—
(i) between the trustee and the commissioners, or
(ii) if there are no commissioners, between the trustee and the Accountant in Bankruptcy.]
(2A) An agreement or determination under subsection (2)(b)(i) or (ii) above—
(a) may be made in respect of one or more than one accounting period;
(b) may be made before the beginning of the accounting period in relation to which it has effect and, in any event, shall not have effect unless made before the day on which such accounting period would, but for the agreement or determination, have ended;
(c) may provide for different accounting periods to be of different durations,
. . .]
(3) Subject to the following provisions of this section, the . . . trustee shall, if the funds of the debtor's estate are sufficient and after making allowance for future contingencies, pay under section 53(7) of this Act a dividend out of the estate to the creditors in respect of each accounting period.
(4) The . . . trustee may pay—
(a) the debts mentioned in subsection (1)(a) to (d) of section 51 of this Act, other than his own remuneration, at any time;
(b) the preferred debts at any time but only with the consent of the commissioners or, if there are no commissioners, of the Accountant in Bankruptcy.
(5) If the . . . trustee—
(a) is not ready to pay a dividend in respect of an accounting period; or
(b) considers it would be inappropriate to pay such a dividend because the expense of doing so would be disproportionate to the amount of the dividend,
he may, with the consent of the commissioners, or if there are no commissioners of the Accountant in Bankruptcy, postpone such payment to a date not later than the time for payment of a dividend in respect of the next accounting period.
(6) . . .
(7) Where [a review or appeal is made under section 49] of this Act against the acceptance or rejection of a creditor's claim, the . . . trustee shall, at the time of payment of dividends and until the [review or appeal] is determined, set aside an amount which would be sufficient, if the determination in the [review or appeal] were to provide for the claim being accepted in full, to pay a dividend in respect of that claim.
(8) Where a creditor—
(a) has failed to produce evidence in support of his claim earlier than 8 weeks before the end of an accounting period on being required by the . . . trustee to do so under section 48(5) of this Act; and
(b) has given a reason for such failure which is acceptable to the . . . trustee,
the . . . trustee shall set aside, for such time as is reasonable to enable him to produce that evidence or any other evidence that will enable the . . . trustee to be satisfied under the said section 48(5), an amount which would be sufficient, if the claim were accepted in full, to pay a dividend in respect of that claim.
(9) Where a creditor submits a claim to the . . . trustee later than 8 weeks before the end of an accounting period but more than 8 weeks before the end of a subsequent accounting period in respect of which, after making allowance for contingencies, funds are available for the payment of a dividend, the . . . trustee shall, if he accepts the claim in whole or in part, pay to the creditor—
(a) the same dividend or dividends as has or have already been paid to creditors of the same class in respect of any accounting period or periods; and
(b) whatever dividend may be payable to him in respect of the said subsequent accounting period:
Provided that paragraph (a) above shall be without prejudice to any dividend which has already been paid.

[(10) In the declaration of and payment of a dividend, no payments shall be made more than once by virtue of the same debt.
(11) Any dividend paid in respect of a claim should be paid to the creditor.]

NOTES

Repealed as noted at the beginning of this Act.

Sub-s (1): substituted, together with sub-ss (2), (2A), for original sub-ss (1), (2) by the Bankruptcy (Scotland) Act 1993, s 11(3), Sch 1, para 21, subject to s 12(6) thereof, at **[5.194]** and to the Bankruptcy (Scotland) Act 1993 Commencement and Savings Order 1993, SI 1993/438, arts 4, 5, at **[16.58]**, **[16.59]**; word "permanent" (omitted) repealed by the Bankruptcy and Diligence etc (Scotland) Act 2007, s 226(2), Sch 6, Pt 1, subject to transitional provisions and savings in SSI 2008/115, arts 5–7, 10, 15 at **[2.51]**–**[2.53]**, **[2.56]**, **[2.57]**.

Sub-s (2): substituted as noted to sub-s (1); in para (a) words in first pair of square brackets inserted, figure in second pair of square brackets substituted for original figure "6", words in fourth pair of square brackets substituted for original words "of sequestration", in para (b) figure in square brackets substituted for original figure "6", and word "permanent" omitted in each place repealed by the Bankruptcy and Diligence etc (Scotland) Act 2007, ss 36, 226(2), Sch 1, paras 1, 44(1), (2), Sch 6, Pt 1, subject to transitional provisions and savings in SSI 2008/115, arts 5–7, 10, 15 at **[2.51]**–**[2.53]**, **[2.56]**, **[2.57]**, and as from a day to be appointed in relation to the substitution of "12" for "6" as regards company insolvencies; words in third pair of square brackets in para (a) inserted by the Bankruptcy and Debt Advice (Scotland) Act 2014, s 15(a), subject to transitional provisions and savings in SSI 2014/261, arts 4, 12 at **[2.91]**, **[2.99]**.

Sub-s (2ZA): inserted by the Bankruptcy and Diligence etc (Scotland) Act 2007, s 36, Sch 1, paras 1, 44(1), (3), subject to transitional provisions and savings in SSI 2008/115, arts 5–7, 10, 15 at **[2.51]**–**[2.53]**, **[2.56]**, **[2.57]**; words in square brackets added by the Bankruptcy and Debt Advice (Scotland) Act 2014, s 15(b), subject to transitional provisions and savings in SSI 2014/261, arts 4, 12 at **[2.91]**, **[2.99]**.

Sub-s (2ZB): inserted by the Bankruptcy and Debt Advice (Scotland) Act 2014, s 15(c), subject to transitional provisions and savings in SSI 2014/261, arts 4, 12 at **[2.91]**, **[2.99]**.

Sub-s (2A): substituted as noted to sub-s (1); word "permanent" (omitted) repealed by the Bankruptcy and Diligence etc (Scotland) Act 2007, s 226(2), Sch 6, Pt 1, subject to transitional provisions and savings in SSI 2008/115, arts 5–7, 10, 15 at **[2.51]**–**[2.53]**, **[2.56]**, **[2.57]**; words "and shall be recorded in the sederunt book by the trustee" (omitted) repealed by the Bankruptcy and Debt Advice (Scotland) Act 2014, s 56(2), Sch 4, subject to transitional provisions and savings in SSI 2014/261, arts 4, 12 at **[2.91]**, **[2.99]**.

Sub-ss (3)–(5), (7)–(9): word "permanent" omitted in each place repealed by the Bankruptcy and Diligence etc (Scotland) Act 2007, s 226(2), Sch 6, Pt 1, subject to transitional provisions and savings in SSI 2008/115, arts 5–7, 10, 15 at **[2.51]**–**[2.53]**, **[2.56]**, **[2.57]**.

Sub-s (6): repealed by the Bankruptcy (Scotland) Act 1993, s 11(4), Sch 2, subject to s 12(6) thereof, at **[5.194]** and to SI 1993/438, arts 4, 5, at **[16.58]**, **[16.59]**.

Sub-s (7): words in first pair of square brackets substituted for original words "an appeal is taken under section 49(6)(b)" and words in second and third pairs of square brackets substituted for original word "appeal", by the Bankruptcy and Debt Advice (Scotland) Act 2014, s 56(1), Sch 3, paras 2, 26, subject to transitional provisions and savings in SSI 2014/261, art 12 at **[2.99]**.

Sub-ss (10), (11): added by the Insolvency (Scotland) Regulations 2003, SI 2003/2109, regs 3, 15.

[5.114]

53 Procedure after end of accounting period

(1) Within 2 weeks after the end of an accounting period, the . . . trustee shall in respect of that period submit to the commissioners or, if there are no commissioners, to the Accountant in Bankruptcy—

- (a) his accounts of his intromissions with the debtor's estate for audit and, where funds are available after making allowance for contingencies, a scheme of division of the divisible funds; and
- (b) a claim for the outlays reasonably incurred by him and for his remuneration; and, where the said documents are submitted to the commissioners, he shall send a copy of them to the Accountant in Bankruptcy.

[(2) Subject to subsection (2A) below, all accounts in respect of legal services incurred by the . . . trustee shall, before payment thereof by him, be submitted for taxation to the auditor of the court before which the sequestration is pending.

(2A) Where—

- (a) any such account has been agreed between the . . . trustee and the person entitled to payment in respect of that account (in this subsection referred to as "the payee");
- (b) the . . . trustee is not an associate of the payee; and
- (c) the commissioners [or, if there are no commissioners, the Accountant in Bankruptcy, have determined that the account need not] be submitted for taxation,

the . . . trustee may pay such account without submitting it for taxation.]

(3) Within 6 weeks after the end of an accounting period—

- (a) the commissioners or, as the case may be, the Accountant in Bankruptcy . . . —
  - (i) [may] audit the accounts; and
  - (ii) [shall] issue a determination fixing the amount of the outlays and the remuneration payable to the . . . trustee; and
- (b) the . . . trustee shall make the audited accounts, scheme of division and the said determination available for inspection by the debtor and the creditors.

(4) The basis for fixing the amount of the remuneration payable to the . . . trustee may be a commission calculated by reference to the value of the debtor's estate which has been realised by the . . . trustee, but there shall in any event be taken into account—

- (a) the work which, having regard to that value, was reasonably undertaken by him; and
- (b) the extent of his responsibilities in administering the debtor's estate.

(5) In fixing the amount of such remuneration in respect of [any] accounting period, the commissioners or, as the case may be, the Accountant in Bankruptcy may take into account any adjustment which the commissioners or the Accountant in Bankruptcy may wish to make in the amount of the remuneration fixed in respect of any earlier accounting period.

(6) Not later than 8 weeks after the end of an accounting period, the . . . trustee, the debtor [(subject to subsection (6A) below)] or any creditor may appeal against a determination issued under subsection (3)(a)(ii) above—

(a) where it is a determination of the commissioners, to the Accountant in Bankruptcy; and

(b) where it is a determination of the Accountant in Bankruptcy, to the sheriff;

and the determination of the Accountant in Bankruptcy under paragraph (a) above shall be appealable to the sheriff[; and the decision of the sheriff on [an appeal against a determination under paragraph (a) or, as the case may be, an appeal under paragraph (b)] shall be final].

[(6A) A debtor may appeal under subsection [(6)(a) or (b)] above if, and only if, he satisfies the Accountant in Bankruptcy or, as the case may be, the sheriff that he has, or is likely to have, a pecuniary interest in the outcome of the appeal.]

[(6B) Before—

(a) a debtor; or

(b) a creditor,

appeals under subsection (6) above, he must give notice to the trustee of his intention to appeal.]

(7) On the expiry of the period within which an appeal may be taken under subsection (6) above or, if an appeal is so taken, on the final determination of the last such appeal, the . . . trustee shall pay to the creditors their dividends in accordance with the scheme of division.

(8) Any dividend—

(a) allocated to a creditor which is not cashed or uplifted; or

(b) dependent on a claim in respect of which an amount has been set aside under subsection (7) or (8) of section 52 of this Act,

shall be deposited by the . . . trustee in an appropriate bank or institution.

(9) If a creditor's claim is revalued, the . . . trustee may—

(a) in paying any dividend to that creditor, make such adjustment to it as he considers necessary to take account of that revaluation; or

(b) require the creditor to repay to him the whole or part of a dividend already paid to him.

(10) The . . . trustee shall insert in the sederunt book [his] accounts, the scheme of division and the final determination in relation to the . . . trustee's outlays and remuneration.

NOTES

Repealed as noted at the beginning of this Act.

Sub-ss (1), (4), (7)–(9): word "permanent" omitted in each place repealed by the Bankruptcy and Diligence etc (Scotland) Act 2007, s 226(2), Sch 6, Pt 1, subject to transitional provisions and savings in SSI 2008/115, arts 5–7, 10, 15 at **[2.51]–[2.53]**, **[2.56]**, **[2.57]**.

Sub-s (2): substituted together with sub-s (2A) for original sub-s (2) by the Bankruptcy (Scotland) Act 1993, s 11(3), Sch 1, para 22(1), (2), subject to s 12(6) thereof, at **[5.194]** and to the Bankruptcy (Scotland) Act 1993 Commencement and Savings Order 1993, SI 1993/438, arts 4, 5, at **[16.58]**, **[16.59]**; word "permanent" (omitted) repealed by the Bankruptcy and Diligence etc (Scotland) Act 2007, s 226(2), Sch 6, Pt 1, subject to transitional provisions and savings in SSI 2008/115, arts 5–7, 10, 15 at **[2.51]–[2.53]**, **[2.56]**, **[2.57]**.

Sub-s (2A): substituted as noted to sub-s (2); word "permanent" omitted in each place repealed and words in square brackets in para (c) substituted for original words "have not determined that the account should" by the Bankruptcy and Diligence etc (Scotland) Act 2007, ss 36, Sch 1, paras 1, 45(a), 226(2), Sch 6, Pt 1, subject to transitional provisions and savings in SSI 2008/115, arts 5–7, 10, 15 at **[2.51]–[2.53]**, **[2.56]**, **[2.57]**.

Sub-s (3): first words omitted repealed, and words in square brackets inserted, by the Bankruptcy (Scotland) Act 1993, s 11(3), (4), Sch 1, para 22(1), (3), Sch 2, subject to s 12(6) thereof, at **[5.194]** and to SI 1993/438, arts 4, 5, at **[16.58]**, **[16.59]**; word "permanent" omitted in second and third places repealed by the Bankruptcy and Diligence etc (Scotland) Act 2007, s 226(2), Sch 6, Pt 1, subject to transitional provisions and savings in SSI 2008/115, arts 5–7, 10, 15 at **[2.51]–[2.53]**, **[2.56]**, **[2.57]**.

Sub-s (5): word in square brackets substituted by the Bankruptcy (Scotland) Act 1993, s 11(3), Sch 1, para 22(1), (4), subject to s 12(6) thereof, at **[5.194]** and to SI 1993/438, arts 4, 5, at **[16.58]**, **[16.59]**.

Sub-s (6): word "permanent" (omitted) repealed and words in first pair of square brackets inserted by the Bankruptcy and Diligence etc (Scotland) Act 2007, ss 31(2)(a), 226(2), Sch 6, Pt 1, subject to transitional provisions and savings in SSI 2008/115, arts 5–7, 10, 15 at **[2.51]–[2.53]**, **[2.56]**, **[2.57]**; words in second (outer) pair of square brackets added by the Bankruptcy (Scotland) Act 1993, s 11(3), Sch 1, para 22(1), (5); words in third (inner) pair of square brackets substituted for original words "such an appeal", by the Bankruptcy and Debt Advice (Scotland) Act 2014, s 56(1), Sch 3, paras 2, 27(a), subject to transitional provisions and savings in SSI 2014/261, arts 4, 12 at **[2.91]**, **[2.99]**.

Sub-ss (6A), (6B): inserted by the Bankruptcy and Diligence etc (Scotland) Act 2007, ss 31(2)(b), 36, Sch 1, paras 1, 45(b), subject to transitional provisions and savings in SSI 2008/115, arts 5–7, 10, 15 at **[2.51]–[2.53]**, **[2.56]**, **[2.57]**; words in square brackets in sub-s (6A) substituted for original figure "(6)", by the Bankruptcy and Debt Advice (Scotland) Act 2014, s 56(1), Sch 3, paras 2, 27(b), subject to transitional provisions and savings in SSI 2014/261, arts 4, 12 at **[2.91]**, **[2.99]**.

Sub-s (10): word "permanent" omitted in both places repealed and word in square brackets substituted for original words "the audited" by the Bankruptcy and Diligence etc (Scotland) Act 2007, ss 36, 226(2), Sch 1, paras 1, 46(1), (3), Sch 6, Pt 1, subject to transitional provisions and savings in SSI 2008/115, arts 5–7, 10, 15 at **[2.51]–[2.53]**, **[2.56]**, **[2.57]**; repealed by the Bankruptcy and Debt Advice (Scotland) Act 2014, s 56(2), Sch 4, subject to transitional provisions and savings in SSI 2014/261, arts 4, 12 at **[2.91]**, **[2.99]**.

See further, the Bankruptcy (Scotland) Act 1993, s 9, at **[5.192]**.

[5.115]
[53A Modification of procedure under section 53 where Accountant in Bankruptcy is trustee
(1) In any case where the Accountant in Bankruptcy is the trustee, section 53 of this Act shall have effect subject to the following modifications.
(2) For subsections (1) to (7) of that section, there shall be substituted—

"(1) At the end of each accounting period, the Accountant in Bankruptcy shall prepare accounts of his intromissions with the debtor's estate and he shall make a determination of his fees and outlays calculated in accordance with regulations made under section 69A of this Act.
(2) Such accounts and determination shall be available for inspection by the debtor and the creditors not later than 6 weeks after the end of the accounting period to which they relate.
(3) In making a determination as mentioned in subsection (1) above, the Accountant in Bankruptcy may take into account any adjustment which he may wish to make in the amount of his remuneration fixed in respect of any earlier accounting period.
(4) Not later than 8 weeks after the end of an accounting period, the debtor (subject to subsection (5) below) or any creditor may appeal to the sheriff against the determination of the Accountant in Bankruptcy; and the decision of the sheriff on such an appeal shall be final.
(5) A debtor may appeal under subsection (4) above if, and only if, he satisfies the sheriff that he has, or is likely to have, a pecuniary interest in the outcome of the appeal.
(6) Before—
(a) a debtor; or
(b) any creditor,

appeals under subsection (4) above, he must give notice to the Accountant in Bankruptcy of his intention to appeal.
(7) On the expiry of the period within which an appeal may be made under subsection (4) above, the Accountant in Bankruptcy shall pay to the creditors their dividends in accordance with the scheme of division.".

(3) In subsection (10) for the words "the audited" there shall be substituted the word "his".]

NOTES
Inserted by the Bankruptcy and Diligence etc (Scotland) Act 2007, s 36, Sch 1, paras 1, 46, subject to transitional provisions and savings in SSI 2008/115, arts 5–7, 10, 15 at **[2.51]–[2.53]**, **[2.56]**, **[2.57]**.
Repealed as noted at the beginning of this Act.

Discharge of debtor

[5.116]
[54 Discharge where Accountant in Bankruptcy not the trustee
(1) This section applies where the Accountant in Bankruptcy is not the trustee.
(2) The Accountant in Bankruptcy may discharge the debtor at any time after the date which is 12 months after the date on which sequestration is awarded by granting a certificate of discharge in the prescribed form.
(3) Before deciding whether to discharge the debtor under subsection (2), the Accountant in Bankruptcy must—
(a) consider the report provided by the trustee under subsection (4), and
(b) take into account any representations received during the period mentioned in subsection (6)(b).
(4) The trustee must prepare and send a report to the Accountant in Bankruptcy—
(a) without delay after the date which is 10 months after the date on which sequestration is awarded, and
(b) if the debtor is not otherwise discharged, before sending to the Accountant in Bankruptcy the documentation referred to in section 57(1)(b).
(5) The report must include—
(a) information about—
(i) the debtor's assets, liabilities, financial affairs and business affairs,
(ii) the debtor's conduct in relation to those assets, liabilities, financial affairs and business affairs,
(iii) the sequestration, and
(iv) the debtor's conduct in the course of the sequestration,
(b) a statement of whether, in the opinion of the trustee, the debtor has as at the date of the report—
(i) complied with any debtor contribution order,
(ii) co-operated with the trustee in accordance with section 64,
(iii) complied with the statement of undertakings,
(iv) made a full and fair surrender of the debtor's estate,
(v) made a full disclosure of all claims which the debtor is entitled to make against other persons, and
(vi) delivered to the trustee every document under the debtor's control relating to the debtor's estate, business or financial affairs, and
(c) a statement of whether the trustee has, as at the date that the report is sent to the Accountant in Bankruptcy, carried out all of the trustee's functions in accordance with section 3.
(6) The trustee must, at the same time as sending a report to the Accountant in Bankruptcy under this section, give to the debtor and every creditor known to the trustee—
(a) a copy of the report, and

(b) a notice informing the recipient that the person has a right to make representations to the Accountant in Bankruptcy in relation to the report before the expiry of the period of 28 days beginning with the day on which the notice is given.

(7) A discharge under this section must not take effect before the end of the period of 14 days beginning with the day of notification of the decision.]

NOTES

Commencement: 1 April 2015.

Repealed as noted at the beginning of this Act.

Substituted, together with ss 54A, 54B for original s 54, by the Bankruptcy and Debt Advice (Scotland) Act 2014, s 17, subject to transitional provisions and savings in SSI 2014/261, arts 4, 12 at **[2.91]**, **[2.99]**. Section 54 (and the notes relating to it) previously read as follows:

"54 [Automatic discharge of debtor]

(1) Subject to the following provisions of this section, the debtor shall be discharged on the expiry of [1 year] from the date of sequestration.

(2) Every debtor who has been discharged under or by virtue of this section or section 75(4) of this Act may apply to the Accountant in Bankruptcy for a certificate that he has been so discharged; and the Accountant in Bankruptcy, if satisfied of such discharge, shall grant a certificate of discharge in the prescribed form.

(3) The . . . trustee or any creditor may, not later than . . . 9 months after the date of sequestration, apply to the sheriff for a deferment of the debtor's discharge by virtue of subsection (1) above.

(4) On an application being made to him under subsection (3) above, the sheriff shall order—

(a) the applicant to serve the application on the debtor and (if he is not himself the applicant and is not discharged) the . . . trustee; and

(b) the debtor to lodge in court a declaration—

(i) that he has made a full and fair surrender of his estate and a full disclosure of all claims which he is entitled to make against other persons; and

(ii) that he has delivered to the . . . trustee every document under his control relating to his estate or his business or financial affairs;

and, if the debtor fails to lodge such a declaration in court within 14 days of being required to do so, the sheriff shall defer his discharge without a hearing for a period not exceeding 2 years.

(5) If the debtor lodges the declaration in court within the said period of 14 days, the sheriff shall—

(a) fix a date for a hearing not earlier than 28 days after the date of the lodging of the declaration; and

(b) order the applicant to notify the debtor and the . . . trustee or (if he has been discharged) the Accountant in Bankruptcy of the date of the hearing;

and the . . . trustee or (if he has been discharged) the Accountant in Bankruptcy shall, not later than 7 days before the date fixed under paragraph (a) above, lodge in court a report upon the debtor's assets and liabilities, his financial and business affairs and his conduct in relation thereto and upon the sequestration and his conduct in the course of it.

(6) After considering at the hearing any representations made by the applicant, the debtor or any creditor, the sheriff shall make an order either deferring the discharge for such period not exceeding 2 years as he thinks appropriate or dismissing the application:

Provided that the applicant or the debtor may appeal against an order under this subsection within 14 days after it is made.

(7) Where the discharge is deferred under subsection (4) or (6) above, the clerk of the court shall send—

(a) a certified copy of the order of the sheriff deferring discharge to the keeper of the register of inhibitions *and adjudications* for recording in that register; and

(b) a copy of such order to—

(i) the Accountant in Bankruptcy; and

(ii) the . . . trustee (if not discharged) for insertion in the sederunt book.

(8) A debtor whose discharge has been deferred under subsection (4) or (6) above may, at any time thereafter and provided that he lodges in court a declaration as to the matters mentioned in sub-paragraphs (i) and (ii) of paragraph (b) of the said subsection (4), petition the sheriff for his discharge; and subsections (5) to (7) above shall, with any necessary modifications, apply in relation to the proceedings which shall follow the lodging of a declaration under this subsection as they apply in relation to the proceedings which follow the timeous lodging of a declaration under the said paragraph (b).

(9) The . . . trustee or any creditor may, not later than 3 months before the end of a period of deferment, apply to the sheriff for a further deferment of the discharge; and subsections (4) to (8) above and this subsection shall apply in relation to that further deferment.

NOTES

Repealed as noted at the beginning of this Act.

Section heading: substituted for original words "Automatic discharge after 3 years" by the Bankruptcy and Diligence etc (Scotland) Act 2007, s 1(1), (4), subject to transitional provisions and savings in SSI 2008/115, arts 5–7, 10, 15 at **[2.51]–[2.53]**, **[2.56]**, **[2.57]**.

Sub-s (1): words in square brackets substituted for original words "3 years" by the Bankruptcy and Diligence etc (Scotland) Act 2007, s 1(1), (2), subject to transitional provisions and savings in SSI 2008/115, arts 5–7, 10, 15.

Sub-s (3): words "permanent" and "2 years and" (omitted respectively) repealed by the Bankruptcy and Diligence etc (Scotland) Act 2007, ss 1(1), (3), 226(2), Sch 6, Pt 1, subject to transitional provisions and savings in SSI 2008/115, arts 5–7, 10, 15.

Sub-s (4): words "permanent" omitted from para (a) and "interim or permanent" omitted from para (b)(ii) repealed by the Bankruptcy and Diligence etc (Scotland) Act 2007, s 226(2), Sch 6, Pt 1, subject to transitional provisions and savings in SSI 2008/115, arts 5–7, 10, 15.

Sub-ss (5), (9): word "permanent" omitted in each place repealed by the Bankruptcy and Diligence etc (Scotland) Act 2007, s 226(2), Sch 6, Pt 1, subject to transitional provisions and savings in SSI 2008/115, arts 5–7, 10, 15.

Sub-s (7): words "and adjudications" in para (a) repealed as from a day to be appointed and word "permanent" omitted from para (b)(ii) repealed by the Bankruptcy and Diligence etc (Scotland) Act 2007, s 226(2), Sch 6, Pt 1, subject to transitional provisions and savings in SSI 2008/115, arts 5–7, 10, 15.".

Regulations: the Bankruptcy (Scotland) Regulations 2014, SSI 2014/225 at **[16.267]**.

[5.117]

[54A Discharge where Accountant in Bankruptcy the trustee

(1) This section applies where the Accountant in Bankruptcy is the trustee.

(2) The Accountant in Bankruptcy may discharge the debtor at any time after the date which is 12 months after the date on which sequestration is awarded by granting a certificate of discharge in the prescribed form.

(3) The Accountant in Bankruptcy must, as soon as is practicable after the date which is 12 months after the date on which sequestration is awarded—

(a) decide whether to discharge the debtor under subsection (2),

(b) notify the debtor and every creditor known to the Accountant in Bankruptcy of that decision, and

(c) send a report to those persons.

(4) The report must give an account of—

(a) the debtor's assets, liabilities, financial affairs and business affairs,

(b) the debtor's conduct in relation to those assets, liabilities, financial affairs and business affairs,

(c) the sequestration, and

(d) the debtor's conduct in the course of the sequestration, including compliance with the statement of undertakings.

(5) Subsection (6) applies where—

(a) the Accountant in Bankruptcy refuses to discharge the debtor under subsection (2), and

(b) the debtor is not otherwise discharged.

(6) The Accountant in Bankruptcy must, as soon as is practicable after the date which is 12 months after the date of the refusal—

(a) decide whether to discharge or refuse to discharge the debtor under subsection (2),

(b) notify the debtor and every creditor known to the Accountant in Bankruptcy of that decision, and

(c) send a report giving an account of the matters mentioned in subsection (4) to those persons.

(7) A discharge under this section must not take effect before the end of the period of 14 days beginning with the day of notification of the decision.]

NOTES

Commencement: 1 April 2015.

Substituted as noted to s 54 at **[5.116]**.

Repealed as noted at the beginning of this Act.

Regulations: the Bankruptcy (Scotland) Regulations 2014, SSI 2014/225 at **[16.267]**.

[5.118]

[54B Discharge of debtor: review and appeal

(1) The trustee or the debtor may apply to the Accountant in Bankruptcy for a review of a decision under section 54(2) or 54A(2) to refuse to discharge the debtor.

(2) Any creditor may apply to the Accountant in Bankruptcy for a review of a decision under section 54(2) or 54A(2) to discharge the debtor.

(3) An application under subsection (1) or (2) must be made before the end of the period of 14 days beginning with the day of notification of the decision under section 54(2) or, as the case may be, 54A(2).

(4) If an application for a review under subsection (2) is made, the discharge is suspended until the determination of that review by the Accountant in Bankruptcy.

(5) If an application for a review under subsection (1) or (2) is made, the Accountant in Bankruptcy must—

(a) take into account any representations made by an interested person before the expiry of the period of 21 days beginning with the day on which the application is made, and

(b) confirm or revoke the decision before the expiry of the period of 28 days beginning with the day on which the application is made.

(6) The debtor, the trustee or any creditor may appeal to the sheriff against any decision of the Accountant in Bankruptcy under subsection (5)(b) before the end of the period of 14 days beginning with the date of the decision.]

NOTES

Commencement: 1 April 2015.

Substituted as noted to s 54 at **[5.116]**.

Repealed as noted at the beginning of this Act.

[5.119]

[54C Debtor to whom section 5(2ZA) applies: discharge

(1) Where section 5(2ZA) applies to a debtor, the debtor is discharged on the date which is 6 months after the date on which sequestration is awarded.

(2) A debtor may, following a discharge, apply to the Accountant in Bankruptcy for a certificate of discharge in the prescribed form.]

NOTES

Commencement: 1 April 2015.

Inserted by the Bankruptcy and Debt Advice (Scotland) Act 2014, s 7(1), subject to transitional provisions and savings in SSI 2014/261, arts 4, 12 at **[2.91]**, **[2.99]**.

Repealed as noted at the beginning of this Act.

Regulations: the Bankruptcy (Scotland) Regulations 2014, SSI 2014/225 at **[16.267]**.

[5.120]
[54D Deferral of discharge where debtor cannot be traced
(1) Subsection (2) applies where—
(a) the trustee, having made reasonable inquiries, is unable to ascertain the whereabouts of the debtor, and
(b) as a result is unable to carry out the trustee's functions in accordance with section 3.
(2) The trustee must—
(a) notify the debtor by sending to the last known address of the debtor a deferral notice in the prescribed form,
(b) give a deferral notice to every creditor known to the trustee, and
(c) where the trustee is not the Accountant in Bankruptcy, apply in the prescribed form to the Accountant in Bankruptcy for a deferral.
(3) A deferral application under subsection (2)(c) must be made by the trustee—
(a) no earlier than the date which is 8 months after the date on which sequestration is awarded, and
(b) no later than the date which is 10 months after the date on which sequestration is awarded.
(4) After receiving a deferral application, the Accountant in Bankruptcy must—
(a) take into account any representations made by an interested person before the expiry of the period of 14 days beginning with the day on which the application is made, and
(b) if satisfied of the matters mentioned in subsection (5), issue a certificate deferring indefinitely the discharge of the debtor.
(5) The matters are—
(a) that the trustee is unable to ascertain the whereabouts of the debtor, and
(b) it would not be reasonably practicable for the trustee to continue to search for the debtor.
(6) Where the Accountant in Bankruptcy is the trustee and has given a deferral notice in accordance with subsection (2)(b), the Accountant in Bankruptcy must—
(a) take into account any representations made by an interested person before the expiry of the period of 14 days beginning with the day on which the deferral notice is given, and
(b) if satisfied that it would not be reasonably practicable to continue to search for the debtor, issue a certificate deferring indefinitely the discharge of the debtor.
(7) Where a certificate is issued under subsection (4)(b) or (6)(b), the Accountant in Bankruptcy must make an appropriate entry in the register of insolvencies.]

NOTES
Commencement: 1 April 2015.
Inserted, together with ss 54E–54G, by the Bankruptcy and Debt Advice (Scotland) Act 2014, s 19, subject to transitional provisions and savings in SSI 2014/261, arts 4, 12 at **[2.91]**, **[2.99]**.
Repealed as noted at the beginning of this Act.
Regulations: the Bankruptcy (Scotland) Regulations 2014, SSI 2014/225 at **[16.267]**.

[5.121]
[54E Debtor not traced: new trustee
(1) This section applies where a certificate is issued under section 54D(4)(b).
(2) The trustee may apply to the Accountant in Bankruptcy in the prescribed form for authority to resign office.
(3) An application under subsection (2) must include details of every creditor known to the trustee.
(4) An application under subsection (2) may not be made—
(a) if after the certificate is issued the trustee ascertains the whereabouts of the debtor or the debtor makes contact with the trustee,
(b) after the date which is 6 months after the date on which the certificate is awarded.
(5) Where an application is made under subsection (2), the Accountant in Bankruptcy must issue to the trustee who made the application a notice in the prescribed form granting the application.
(6) Where a notice is issued under subsection (5)—
(a) the Accountant in Bankruptcy is deemed to be the trustee,
(b) the Accountant in Bankruptcy must notify every creditor known to the Accountant in Bankruptcy that the Accountant in Bankruptcy is deemed to be the trustee,
(c) the former trustee is not entitled to recover outlays and remuneration payable in accordance with section 53 other than by a claim in the final distribution of the debtor's estate, and
(d) subsections (6) to (8) of section 28 apply in relation to the appointment of the Accountant in Bankruptcy as the new trustee as they apply in relation to the appointment of a new trustee under that section.]

NOTES
Commencement: 1 April 2015.
Inserted as noted to s 54D at **[5.120]**.
Repealed as noted at the beginning of this Act.
Regulations: the Bankruptcy (Scotland) Regulations 2014, SSI 2014/225 at **[16.267]**.

[5.122]
[54F Debtor not traced: subsequent debtor contact
(1) This section applies where—
(a) a certificate is issued under section 54D(4)(b) or (6)(b), and
(b) the trustee ascertains the whereabouts of the debtor or the debtor makes contact with the trustee.

(2) Where the Accountant in Bankruptcy is the trustee, the Accountant in Bankruptcy may discharge the debtor at any time after the date which is 12 months after the date on which—

(a) the whereabouts of the debtor were ascertained, or

(b) the debtor made contact with the trustee.

(3) Where the Accountant in Bankruptcy is not the trustee, the trustee must prepare and send a report to the Accountant in Bankruptcy without delay after the date which is 10 months after the earlier of the date on which—

(a) the whereabouts of the debtor were ascertained by the trustee, or

(b) the debtor made contact with the trustee.

(4) If the trustee sends a report to the Accountant in Bankruptcy under subsection (3)—

(a) the report must include the matters included in a report sent to the Accountant in Bankruptcy in accordance with subsection (5) of section 54, and

(b) subsection (6) of that section applies to the report as it applies to a report sent in accordance with subsection (4) of that section.

(5) After receiving a report under subsection (3), the Accountant in Bankruptcy may discharge the debtor by granting a certificate of discharge in the prescribed form.

(6) Before deciding whether to discharge the debtor under subsection (5), the Accountant in Bankruptcy must—

(a) consider the report prepared by the trustee under subsection (3), and

(b) take into account any representations received during the period mentioned in subsection (6) of section 54 (as applied in accordance with subsection (4)).

(7) A discharge under subsection (2) or (5) must not take effect on a date before the end of the period of 14 days beginning with the day of notification of the decision.

(8) A discharge under subsection (2) or (5) is deemed for the purposes of section 55 to have been given under section 54(2).]

NOTES

Commencement: 1 April 2015.

Inserted as noted to s 54D at **[5.120]**.

Repealed as noted at the beginning of this Act.

[5.123]

[54G Subsequent debtor contact: review and appeal

(1) The debtor may apply to the Accountant in Bankruptcy for a review of a decision under section 54F(2) or (5) to refuse to discharge the debtor.

(2) Any creditor may apply to the Accountant in Bankruptcy for a review of a decision under section 54F(2) or (5) to discharge the debtor.

(3) An application under subsection (1) or (2) must be made before the end of the period of 14 days beginning with the day of notification of the decision under section 54F(2) or, as the case may be, 54F(5).

(4) If an application for a review under subsection (2) is made, the discharge is suspended until the determination of that review by the Accountant in Bankruptcy.

(5) If an application for a review under subsection (1) or (2) is made, the Accountant in Bankruptcy must—

(a) take into account any representations made by an interested person before the expiry of the period of 21 days beginning with the day on which the application is made, and

(b) confirm or revoke the decision before the expiry of the period of 28 days beginning with the day on which the application is made.

(6) The debtor, the trustee or any creditor may appeal to the sheriff against any decision of the Accountant in Bankruptcy under subsection (5)(b) before the end of the period of 14 days beginning with the date of the decision.]

NOTES

Commencement: 1 April 2015.

Inserted as noted to s 54D at **[5.120]**.

Repealed as noted at the beginning of this Act.

[5.124]

55 [Effect of discharge under section 54, 54A or 54C]

(1) Subject to [subsections (2) and (3)] below, on the debtor's discharge under section 54[, 54A or 54C] of this Act, the debtor shall be discharged within the United Kingdom of all debts and obligations contracted by him, or for which he was liable, at the date of sequestration.

(2) The debtor shall not be discharged by virtue of subsection (1) above from—

(a) any liability to pay a fine or other penalty due to the Crown;

[(aa) any liability to pay a fine imposed in a [justice of the peace court (or a district court)];

(ab) any liability under a compensation order within the meaning of section 249 of the Criminal Procedure (Scotland) Act 1995;]

(b) any liability to forfeiture of a sum of money deposited in court under under [section 24(6) of the Criminal Procedure (Scotland) Act 1995 (c 46)];

(c) any liability incurred by reason of fraud or breach of trust;

(d) any obligation to pay aliment or any sum of an alimentary nature under any enactment or rule of law or any periodical allowance payable on divorce by virtue of a court order or under an obligation, not being

(i) aliment or a periodical allowance which could be included in the amount of a creditor's claim under paragraph 2 of Schedule 1 to this Act [or;

(ii) child support maintenance within the meaning of the Child Support Act 1991 which was unpaid in respect of any period before the date of sequestration of—

(aa) any person by whom it was due to be paid; or

(bb) any employer by whom it was, or was due to be, deducted under section 31(5) of that Act.]

(e) the obligation imposed on him by section 64 of this Act.

[[(2A)] In subsection (2)(a) above the reference to a fine or other penalty due to the Crown includes a reference to a confiscation order made under Part 2, 3 or 4 of the Proceeds of Crime Act 2002.]

[(3) The discharge of the debtor under the said section 54[, 54A or 54C] shall not affect any right of a secured creditor—

(a) for a debt in respect of which the debtor has been discharged to enforce his security for payment of the debt and any interest due and payable on the debt until the debt is paid in full; or

(b) for an obligation in respect of which the debtor has been discharged to enforce his security in respect of the obligation.]

[(4) Nothing in this section affects regulations in relation to which section 73B of the Education (Scotland) Act 1980 (c 44) (regulations relating to student loans) applies.]

NOTES

Repealed as noted at the beginning of this Act.

Section heading: words in square brackets substituted for original words "Effect of discharge under section 54" by the Bankruptcy and Debt Advice (Scotland) Act 2014, s 56(1), Sch 3, paras 2, 28, subject to transitional provisions and savings in SSI 2014/261, arts 4, 12 at **[2.91]**, **[2.99]**.

Sub-s (1): words in first pair of square brackets substituted with retrospective effect by the Bankruptcy (Scotland) Act 1993, s 11(3), Sch 1, para 23(1), (2); words in second pair of square brackets inserted by the Bankruptcy and Debt Advice (Scotland) Act 2014, s 56(1), Sch 3, paras 2, 29(a), subject to transitional provisions and savings in SSI 2014/261, arts 4, 12 at **[2.91]**, **[2.99]**.

Sub-s (2): paras (aa), (ab) inserted by the Criminal Procedure (Consequential Provisions) (Scotland) Act 1995, s 5, Sch 4, para 58(4); words in square brackets in para (aa) substituted for original words "district court" and words in square brackets in para (b) substituted for original words "section 1(3) of the Bail etc (Scotland) Act 1980", by the Bankruptcy and Debt Advice (Scotland) Act 2014, s 56(1), Sch 3, paras 2, 29(b), subject to transitional provisions and savings in SSI 2014/261, arts 4, 12 at **[2.91]**, **[2.99]**; words in square brackets in para (d) inserted by the Child Support Act 1991, s 58(13), Sch 5, para 6(1), (4).

Sub-s (2A): originally added as sub-s (3) by the Proceeds of Crime Act 2002, s 456, Sch 11, paras 1, 15(1), (5); renumbered as sub-s (2A) by the Bankruptcy and Diligence etc (Scotland) Act 2007, s 36, Sch 1, paras 1, 47, subject to transitional provisions and savings in SSI 2008/115, arts 5–7, 10, 15 at **[2.51]–[2.53]**, **[2.56]**, **[2.57]**.

Sub-s (3): added with retrospective effect by the Bankruptcy (Scotland) Act 1993, s 11(3), Sch 1, para 23(1), (3); words in square brackets inserted and para (a) repealed by the Bankruptcy and Debt Advice (Scotland) Act 2014, s 56, Sch 3, paras 2, 29(c), Sch 4, subject to transitional provisions and savings in SSI 2014/261, arts 4, 12 at **[2.91]**, **[2.99]**.

Sub-s (4): added by the Bankruptcy and Debt Advice (Scotland) Act 2014, s 50, subject to transitional provisions and savings in SSI 2014/261, arts 4, 12 at **[2.91]**, **[2.99]**.

[5.125]

[55A Discharge under section 54C: conditions

(1) This section applies where a debtor is discharged under section 54C.

(2) During the relevant period the debtor must comply with the condition in subsection (3) before the debtor, either alone or jointly with another person, obtains credit—

(a) to the extent of £2000 (or such other sum as may be prescribed) or more, or

(b) of any amount where, at the time of obtaining credit, the debtor has debts amounting to £1000 (or such other sum as may be prescribed) or more.

(3) The condition is that the debtor must inform the person who is providing credit to the debtor (or, as the case may be, jointly to the debtor and another person) that the debtor is required to comply with the conditions in this section.

(4) During the relevant period, the debtor must not engage (whether directly or indirectly) in a business under a name other than that to which the discharge relates unless the debtor complies with the condition in subsection (5).

(5) The condition is that the debtor must inform any person with whom the debtor enters into any business transaction of the name of the business to which the discharge relates.

(6) In this section, "relevant period" means the period of 6 months beginning with the date of discharge.]

NOTES

Commencement: 1 April 2015.

Inserted, together with s 55B, by the Bankruptcy and Debt Advice (Scotland) Act 2014, s 7(2), subject to transitional provisions and savings in SSI 2014/261, arts 4, 12 at **[2.91]**, **[2.99]**.

Repealed as noted at the beginning of this Act.

[5.126]

[55B Section 55A: sanctions

(1) If a debtor fails to comply with the requirement imposed by subsection (2) or (4) of section 55A, that section applies in relation to the debtor as if the relevant period were the period of 12 months beginning with the date of discharge of the debtor.

(2) If a debtor fails to comply with the requirement imposed by subsection (2) or (4) of section 55A during the period when the section applies in relation to the debtor by virtue of subsection (1), the debtor commits an offence.

(3) A debtor who is guilty of an offence under subsection (2) is liable on summary conviction to—

(a) a fine not exceeding the statutory maximum,

(b) imprisonment for—

(i) a term not exceeding 3 months, or

(ii) a term not exceeding 6 months, if the person has previously been convicted of an offence inferring dishonest appropriation of property or an attempt at such appropriation, or

(c) both such fine and imprisonment.

(4) A debtor who is guilty of an offence under subsection (2) is liable on conviction on indictment to—

(a) a fine,

(b) imprisonment for a term not exceeding 2 years, or

(c) both such fine and imprisonment.]

NOTES

Commencement: 1 April 2015.
Inserted as noted to s 55A at **[5.125]**.
Repealed as noted at the beginning of this Act.

[5.127]

56 Discharge on composition

Schedule 4 to this Act shall have effect in relation to an offer of composition by or on behalf of the debtor to the . . . trustee in respect of his debts and his discharge and the discharge of the . . . trustee where the offer is approved.

NOTES

Repealed as noted at the beginning of this Act.
Repealed by the Bankruptcy and Debt Advice (Scotland) Act 2014, s 18(1), subject to transitional provisions and savings in SSI 2014/261, arts 4, 12 at **[2.91]**, **[2.99]**.
Word "permanent" omitted in both places repealed by the Bankruptcy and Diligence etc (Scotland) Act 2007, s 226(2), Sch 6, Pt 1, subject to transitional provisions and savings in SSI 2008/115, arts 5–7, 10, 15 at **[2.51]–[2.53]**, **[2.56]**, **[2.57]**.

[Bankruptcy restrictions orders and undertakings]

NOTES

Cross-heading inserted by the Bankruptcy and Diligence etc (Scotland) Act 2007, s 2(1), subject to transitional provisions and savings in SSI 2008/115, arts 5–7, 10, 15 at **[2.51]–[2.53]**, **[2.56]**, **[2.57]**.

[5.128]

[56A Bankruptcy restrictions order

(1) Where sequestration of a living debtor's estate is awarded, an order (to be known as a "bankruptcy restrictions order") in respect of the debtor may be made by the—

(a) Accountant in Bankruptcy, or

(b) the sheriff.

(2) A bankruptcy restrictions order may be made by the sheriff only on the application of the Accountant in Bankruptcy.

(3) The Accountant in Bankruptcy must notify the debtor where the Accountant in Bankruptcy proposes to make a bankruptcy restrictions order.

(4) A notice under subsection (3) must inform the debtor that the debtor has a right to make representations to the Accountant in Bankruptcy in relation to the proposed bankruptcy restrictions order.

(5) Before making a bankruptcy restrictions order the Accountant in Bankruptcy must take into account any representations made by the debtor.]

NOTES

Commencement: 1 April 2015.
Repealed as noted at the beginning of this Act.
Inserted, together with preceding cross-heading and ss 56B–56K by the Bankruptcy and Diligence etc (Scotland) Act 2007, s 2(1), subject to transitional provisions and savings in SSI 2008/115, arts 5–7, 10, 15 at **[2.51]–[2.53]**, **[2.56]**, **[2.57]**; substituted by the Bankruptcy and Debt Advice (Scotland) Act 2014, s 33(1), subject to transitional provisions and savings in SSI 2014/261, arts 4, 12 at **[2.91]**, **[2.99]** and previously read as follows—

> **"[56A Bankruptcy restrictions order**
>
> (1) Where sequestration of a living debtor's estate is awarded, an order (known as a "bankruptcy restrictions order") in respect of the debtor may be made by the sheriff.
>
> (2) An order may be made only on the application of the Accountant in Bankruptcy.]".

[5.130]

[56B Grounds for making order

[(1) A bankruptcy restrictions order must be made if the Accountant in Bankruptcy, or as the case may be, the sheriff thinks it appropriate having regard to the conduct of the debtor (whether before or after the date of sequestration).]

(2) The [Accountant in Bankruptcy, or as the case may be, the] sheriff shall, in particular, take into account any of the following kinds of behaviour on the part of the debtor—

(a) failing to keep records which account for a loss of property by the debtor, or by a business carried on by him, where the loss occurred in the period beginning 2 years before the date of presentation of the petition for sequestration or, as the case may be, the date the debtor application was made and ending with the date of the application for a bankruptcy restrictions order;
(b) failing to produce records of that kind on demand by—
  (i) the Accountant in Bankruptcy;
  (ii) the interim trustee; or
  (iii) the trustee;
[(ba) failing to supply accurate information to an authorised person for the purpose of the granting under section 5B of a certificate for sequestration of the debtor's estate,]
(c) making a gratuitous alienation or any other alienation for no consideration or for no adequate consideration which a creditor has, under any rule of law, right to challenge;
(d) creating an unfair preference or any other preference which a creditor has, under any rule of law, right to challenge;
(e) making an excessive pension contribution;
(f) failing to supply goods or services which were wholly or partly paid for which gave rise to a claim submitted by a creditor under section 22 or 48 of this Act;
(g) trading at a time before the date of sequestration when the debtor knew or ought to have known that he was to be unable to meet his debts;
(h) incurring, before the date of sequestration, a debt which the debtor had no reasonable expectation of being able to pay;
(j) failing to account satisfactorily to—
  (i) the sheriff;
  (ii) the Accountant in Bankruptcy;
  (iii) the interim trustee; or
  (iv) the trustee,
  for a loss of property or for an insufficiency of property to meet his debts;
(k) carrying on any gambling, speculation or extravagance which may have materially contributed to or increased the extent of his debts or which took place between the date of presentation of the petition for sequestration or, as the case may be, the date the debtor application was made and the date on which sequestration is awarded;
(l) neglect of business affairs of a kind which may have materially contributed to or increased the extent of his debts;
(m) fraud or breach of trust;
(n) failing to co-operate with—
  (i) the Accountant in Bankruptcy;
  (ii) the interim trustee; or
  (iii) the trustee.

(3) The [Accountant in Bankruptcy, or as the case may be, the] sheriff shall also, in particular, consider whether the debtor—
(a) has previously been sequestrated; and
(b) remained undischarged from that sequestration at any time during the period of 5 years ending with the date of the sequestration to which the application relates.

(4) For the purposes of subsection (2) above—
"excessive pension contribution" shall be construed in accordance with section 36A of this Act; and
"gratuitous alienation" means an alienation challengeable under section 34(1) of this Act.]

NOTES

Inserted as noted to s 56A at **[5.128]**.

Repealed as noted at the beginning of this Act.

Sub-s (1): substituted by the Bankruptcy and Debt Advice (Scotland) Act 2014, s 33(2)(a), subject to transitional provisions and savings in SSI 2014/261, arts 4, 12 at **[2.91]**, **[2.99]**, and previously read as follows—

"(1) The sheriff shall grant an application for a bankruptcy restrictions order if he thinks it appropriate having regard to the conduct of the debtor (whether before or after the date of sequestration).".

Sub-ss (2), (3): words in square brackets in each place they appear inserted by the Bankruptcy and Debt Advice (Scotland) Act 2014, s 33(2)(b), (c), subject to transitional provisions and savings in SSI 2014/261, arts 4, 12 at **[2.91]**, **[2.99]**.

[5.131]
[56C Application of section 67(9)

(1) Where the [Accountant in Bankruptcy, or as the case may be, the] sheriff thinks it appropriate, the [Accountant in Bankruptcy, or as the case may be, the] sheriff may specify in the bankruptcy restrictions order that subsection (9) of section 67 of this Act shall apply to the debtor during the period he is subject to the order as if he were a debtor within the meaning of subsection (10)(a) of that section.

(2) For the purposes of subsection (1) above, section 67(10) of this Act shall have effect as if, for paragraph (c) of that subsection, there were substituted—

"(c) the relevant information about the status of the debtor is the information that—
  (i) he is subject to a bankruptcy restrictions order; or
  (ii) where his estate has been sequestrated and he has not been discharged, that fact.".]

NOTES

Inserted as noted to s 56A at **[5.128]**.

Repealed as noted at the beginning of this Act.

Sub-s (1): words in square brackets inserted by the Bankruptcy and Debt Advice (Scotland) Act 2014, s 33(3), subject to transitional provisions and savings in SSI 2014/261, arts 4, 12 at **[2.91]**, **[2.99]**.

[5.132]

[56D [Timing for making an order]

(1) [The Accountant in Bankruptcy must make, or apply to the sheriff for, a bankruptcy restrictions order], subject to subsection (2) below, within the period beginning with the date of sequestration and ending with the date on which the debtor's discharge becomes effective.

[(2) After the end of the period referred to in subsection (1), the Accountant in Bankruptcy may—

(a) make a bankruptcy restrictions order only with the permission of the sheriff, and

(b) make an application for a bankruptcy restrictions order only with the permission of the sheriff.]]

NOTES

Inserted as noted to s 56A at **[5.128]**.

Repealed as noted at the beginning of this Act.

Section heading: words in square brackets substituted for original words "Timing of application for order" by the Bankruptcy and Debt Advice (Scotland) Act 2014, s 33(4), subject to transitional provisions and savings in SSI 2014/261, arts 4, 12 at **[2.91]**, **[2.99]**.

Sub-s (1): words in square brackets substituted for original words "An application for a bankruptcy restrictions order must be made", by the Bankruptcy and Debt Advice (Scotland) Act 2014, s 33(5)(a), subject to transitional provisions and savings in SSI 2014/261, arts 4, 12 at **[2.91]**, **[2.99]**.

Sub-s (2): substituted by the Bankruptcy and Debt Advice (Scotland) Act 2014, s 33(5)(b), subject to transitional provisions and savings in SSI 2014/261, arts 4, 12 at **[2.91]**, **[2.99]**, and previously read as follows—

"(2) An application may be made after the end of the period referred to in subsection (1) above only with the permission of the sheriff.".

[5.133]

[56E Duration of order and application for annulment

(1) A bankruptcy restrictions order—

(a) shall come into force when it is made; and

(b) shall cease to have effect at the end of the date specified in the order.

[(2) The date specified in a bankruptcy restrictions order under subsection (1)(b)—

(a) in the case of an order made by the Accountant in Bankruptcy—

(i) must not be before the end of the period of 2 years beginning with the date on which the order is made, but

(ii) must be before the end of the period of 5 years beginning with that date, and

(b) in the case of an order made by the sheriff must not be—

(i) before the end of the period of 5 years beginning with the date on which the order is made, or

(ii) after the end of the period of 15 years beginning with that date.]

(3) On an application by the debtor the [person mentioned in subsection (4)] may—

(a) annul a bankruptcy restrictions order; or

(b) vary such an order, including providing for such an order to cease to have effect at the end of a date earlier than the date specified in the order under subsection (1)(b) above.

[(4) The person is—

(a) in the case of a bankruptcy restrictions order made by the Accountant in Bankruptcy, the Accountant in Bankruptcy, and

(b) in the case of a bankruptcy restrictions order made by the sheriff, the sheriff.

(5) If an application under subsection (3) is made to the Accountant in Bankruptcy, the Accountant in Bankruptcy must—

(a) take into account any representations made by an interested person before the expiry of the period of 21 days beginning with the day on which the application is made, and

(b) confirm, amend or revoke the decision before the expiry of the period of 28 days beginning with the day on which the application is made.

(6) The debtor may appeal to the sheriff against any decision of the Accountant in Bankruptcy under subsection (5)(b) before the end of the period of 14 days beginning with the date of the decision.

(7) The sheriff may—

(a) in determining such an appeal, or

(b) otherwise on an application by the Accountant in Bankruptcy,

make an order providing that the debtor may not make another application under subsection (3) for such period as may be specified in the order.]]

NOTES

Inserted as noted to s 56A at **[5.128]**.

Repealed as noted at the beginning of this Act.

Sub-s (2): substituted by the Bankruptcy and Debt Advice (Scotland) Act 2014, s 33(6)(a), subject to transitional provisions and savings in SSI 2014/261, arts 4, 12 at **[2.91]**, **[2.99]**, and previously read as follows—

"(2) The date specified in a bankruptcy restrictions order under subsection (1)(b) above must not be—

(a) before the end of the period of 2 years beginning with the date on which the order is made; or

(b) after the end of the period of 15 years beginning with that date.".

Sub-s (3): words in square brackets substituted for original word "sheriff" by the Bankruptcy and Debt Advice (Scotland) Act 2014, s 33(6)(b), subject to transitional provisions and savings in SSI 2014/261, arts 4, 12 at **[2.91]**, **[2.99]**.

Sub-ss (4)–(7): added by the Bankruptcy and Debt Advice (Scotland) Act 2014, s 33(6)(c), subject to transitional provisions and savings in SSI 2014/261, arts 4, 12 at **[2.91]**, **[2.99]**.

[5.134]

[56F Interim bankruptcy restrictions order

[(1) Subsection (2) applies at any time—

(a) after the Accountant in Bankruptcy notifies the debtor under section 56A(3) that the Accountant in Bankruptcy proposes to make a bankruptcy restrictions order, and

(b) before the Accountant in Bankruptcy decides whether to make the order.

(2) The Accountant in Bankruptcy may make an interim bankruptcy restrictions order if the Accountant in Bankruptcy thinks that—

(a) there are *prima facie* grounds to suggest that a bankruptcy restrictions order will be made, and

(b) it is in the public interest to make an interim bankruptcy restrictions order.

(2A) Subsection (2B) applies at any time between—

(a) the making of an application to the sheriff for a bankruptcy restrictions order, and

(b) the determination of the application.

(2B) The sheriff may, on the application of the Accountant in Bankruptcy, make an interim bankruptcy restrictions order if the sheriff thinks that—

(a) there are *prima facie* grounds to suggest that the application for the bankruptcy restrictions order will be successful, and

(b) it is in the public interest to make an interim bankruptcy restrictions order.]

(3) . . .

(4) An interim order—

(a) shall have the same effect as a bankruptcy restrictions order; and

(b) shall come into force when it is made.

[(5) An interim order ceases to have effect—

(a) in the case of an interim order made by the Accountant in Bankruptcy, on the Accountant in Bankruptcy deciding whether or not to make a bankruptcy restrictions order,

(b) in the case of an interim order made by the sheriff, on the determination of the application for the bankruptcy restrictions order, or

(c) if the sheriff discharges the interim order, on the application of the Accountant in Bankruptcy or of the debtor.]

(6) Where a bankruptcy restrictions order is made in respect of a debtor who is subject to an interim order, section 56E(2) of this Act shall have effect in relation to the bankruptcy restrictions order as if the reference to the date on which the order is made were a reference to the date on which the interim order was made.]

NOTES

Inserted as noted to s 56A at **[5.128]**.

Repealed as noted at the beginning of this Act.

Sub-ss (1), (2), (2A), (2B), (5) were substituted (for original sub-ss (1), (2), (5)) and sub-s (3) was repealed, by the Bankruptcy and Debt Advice (Scotland) Act 2014, s 33(7), subject to transitional provisions and savings in SSI 2014/261, arts 4, 12 at **[2.91]**, **[2.99]**. Sub-ss (1), (2), (3), (5) originally read as follows—

"(1) This section applies at any time between—

(a) the making of an application for a bankruptcy restrictions order; and

(b) the determination of the application.

(2) The sheriff may make an interim bankruptcy restrictions order if he thinks that—

(a) there are prima facie grounds to suggest that the application for the bankruptcy restrictions order will be successful; and

(b) it is in the public interest to make an interim order.

(3) An interim order may be made only on the application of the Accountant in Bankruptcy.

(5) An interim order shall cease to have effect—

(a) on the determination of the application for the bankruptcy restrictions order;

(b) on the acceptance of a bankruptcy restrictions undertaking made by the debtor; or

(c) if the sheriff discharges the interim order on the application of the Accountant in Bankruptcy or of the debtor.".

[5.135]

[56G Bankruptcy restrictions undertaking

(1) A living debtor who is not subject to a bankruptcy restrictions order may offer an undertaking (known as a "bankruptcy restrictions undertaking") to the Accountant in Bankruptcy.

(2) In determining whether to accept a bankruptcy restrictions undertaking, the Accountant in Bankruptcy shall have regard to the matters specified in section 56B(2) and (3) of this Act.

(3) A bankruptcy restrictions undertaking—

(a) shall take effect on being accepted by the Accountant in Bankruptcy; and

(b) shall cease to have effect at the end of the date specified in the undertaking.

(4) The date specified under subsection (3)(b) above must not be—

(a) before the end of the period of 2 years beginning with the date on which the undertaking is accepted; or

(b) after the end of the period of 15 years beginning with that date.

(5) On an application by the debtor the sheriff may—

(a) annul a bankruptcy restrictions undertaking; or
(b) vary such an undertaking, including providing for a bankruptcy restrictions undertaking to cease to have effect at the end of a date earlier than the date specified in the undertaking under subsection (3)(b) above.]

NOTES

Inserted as noted to s 56A at **[5.128]**.

Repealed as noted at the beginning of this Act.

Repealed by the Bankruptcy and Debt Advice (Scotland) Act 2014, s 52, subject to transitional provisions and savings in SSI 2014/261, arts 4, 12 at **[2.91]**, **[2.99]**.

[5.136]

[56H Bankruptcy restrictions undertakings: application of section 67(9)

(1) A debtor may, with the agreement of the Accountant in Bankruptcy, specify in a bankruptcy restrictions undertaking that subsection (9) of section 67 of this Act shall apply to the debtor during the period the undertaking has effect as if he were a debtor within the meaning of subsection (10)(a) of that section.

(2) For the purposes of subsection (1) above, section 67(10) of this Act shall have effect as if, for paragraph (c) of that subsection, there were substituted—

"(c) the relevant information about the status of the debtor is the information that—
(i) he is subject to a bankruptcy restrictions undertaking; or
(ii) where his estate has been sequestrated and he has not been discharged, that fact.".]

NOTES

Inserted as noted to s 56A at **[5.128]**.

Repealed as noted at the beginning of this Act.

Repealed by the Bankruptcy and Debt Advice (Scotland) Act 2014, s 56(2), Sch 4, subject to transitional provisions and savings in SSI 2014/261, arts 4, 12 at **[2.91]**, **[2.99]**.

[5.137]

[56J Effect of recall of sequestration

(1) Where an award of sequestration of a debtor's estate is recalled under section 17(1) of this Act—
(a) the sheriff may annul any bankruptcy restrictions order, [or interim bankruptcy restrictions order] which is in force in respect of the debtor; [and]
(b) no new bankruptcy restrictions order or interim order may be made in respect of the debtor*; and*
(c) no new bankruptcy restrictions undertaking by the debtor may be accepted.

(2) Where the sheriff refuses to annul a bankruptcy restrictions order, [or interim bankruptcy restrictions order] under subsection (1)(a) above the debtor may, no later than 28 days after the date on which the award of sequestration is recalled, appeal to the sheriff principal against such a refusal.

(3) The decision of the sheriff principal on an appeal under subsection (2) above is final.

[(4) Where an award of sequestration of a debtor's estate is recalled under section 17D(1) or 17E(6)—
(a) the Accountant in Bankruptcy may annul any bankruptcy restrictions order or interim bankruptcy restrictions order which is in force in respect of the debtor, and
(b) no new bankruptcy restrictions order or interim bankruptcy restrictions order may be made in respect of the debtor.

(5) Where the Accountant in Bankruptcy refuses to annul a bankruptcy restrictions order or interim bankruptcy restrictions order under subsection (4) the debtor may apply to the Accountant in Bankruptcy for a review of such a refusal.

(6) An application under subsection (5) must be made before the end of the period of 14 days beginning with the day on which the award of sequestration is recalled.

(7) If an application under subsection (5) is made, the Accountant in Bankruptcy must—
(a) take into account any representations made by an interested person before the expiry of the period of 21 days beginning with the day on which the application is made, and
(b) confirm the refusal or annul the order before the expiry of the period of 28 days beginning with the day on which the application is made.

(8) The debtor may appeal to the sheriff against any decision of the Accountant in Bankruptcy under subsection (7)(b) before the end of the period of 14 days beginning with the date of the decision.

(9) The decision of the sheriff on an appeal under subsection (8) is final.]]

NOTES

Inserted as noted to s 56A at **[5.128]**.

Repealed as noted at the beginning of this Act.

Sub-s (1): words in first pair of square brackets in para (a) substituted for original words "interim bankruptcy restrictions order or bankruptcy restrictions undertaking", word "and" in square brackets inserted and para (c), together with word preceding in, repealed by the Bankruptcy and Debt Advice (Scotland) Act 2014, s 56, Sch 3, paras 2, 30(a), Sch 4, subject to transitional provisions and savings in SSI 2014/261, arts 4, 12 at **[2.91]**, **[2.99]**.

Sub-s (2): words in square brackets substituted for original words "interim bankruptcy restrictions order or bankruptcy restrictions undertaking" by the Bankruptcy and Debt Advice (Scotland) Act 2014, s 56(1), Sch 3, paras 2, 30(b), subject to transitional provisions and savings in SSI 2014/261, arts 4, 12 at **[2.91]**, **[2.99]**.

Sub-ss (4)–(9): added by the Bankruptcy and Debt Advice (Scotland) Act 2014, s 33(8), subject to transitional provisions and savings in SSI 2014/261, arts 4, 12 at **[2.91]**, **[2.99]**.

[5.138]

[56K Effect of discharge on approval of offer of composition

(1) This section applies where a certificate of discharge is granted under paragraph 11(1) of Schedule 4 to this Act discharging a debtor.

(2) Subject to sections 56E(3)(a), 56F(5)(c) and 56G(5)(a) of this Act, the debtor shall remain subject to any bankruptcy restrictions order, interim bankruptcy restrictions order or bankruptcy restrictions undertaking which is in force in respect of him.

(3) The sheriff may make a bankruptcy restrictions order in relation to the debtor on an application made before the discharge.

(4) The Accountant in Bankruptcy may accept a bankruptcy restrictions undertaking offered before the discharge.

(5) No application for a bankruptcy restrictions order or interim order may be made in respect of the debtor.]

NOTES

Inserted as noted to s 56A at **[5.128]**.

Repealed as noted at the beginning of this Act.

Repealed by the Bankruptcy and Debt Advice (Scotland) Act 2014, s 18(2), subject to transitional provisions and savings in SSI 2014/261, arts 4, 12 at **[2.91]**, **[2.99]**.

[Discharge of trustee]

NOTES

Cross-heading: substituted for original words "Discharge of permanent trustee" by the Bankruptcy and Diligence etc (Scotland) Act 2007, s 36, Sch 1, paras 1, 48, subject to transitional provisions and savings in SSI 2008/115, arts 5–7, 10, 15 at **[2.51]–[2.53]**, **[2.56]**, **[2.57]**.

[5.139]

57 [Discharge of trustee]

(1) After the . . . trustee has made a final division of the debtor's estate and has inserted his final audited accounts in the sederunt book, he—

[(a) must pay to the Accountant in Bankruptcy any unclaimed dividends and unapplied balances,]

(b) shall thereafter send to the Accountant in Bankruptcy the sederunt book [in the format specified by subsection (1A) and], a copy of the audited accounts . . . ; and

(c) may at the same time as sending the said documents apply to the Accountant in Bankruptcy for a certificate of discharge.

[(1A) The trustee must send an electronic version of the sederunt book in such format as the Accountant in Bankruptcy may from time to time direct.]

[(1B) The Accountant in Bankruptcy must deposit any unclaimed dividends and any unapplied balances paid to the Accountant in Bankruptcy under subsection (1)(a) in an appropriate bank or institution.]

(2) The . . . trustee shall send notice of an application under subsection (1)(c) above to the debtor and to all the creditors known to the . . . trustee and shall inform the debtor and such creditors—

(a) that they may make written representations relating to the application to the Accountant in Bankruptcy within a period of 14 days after such notification;

(b) that the sederunt book is available for inspection [following a request made to the Accountant in Bankruptcy] and contains the audited accounts of, and scheme of division in, the sequestration; and

(c) of the effect mentioned in subsection (5) below.

(3) On the expiry of the period mentioned in subsection (2)(a) above, the Accountant in Bankruptcy, after examining the documents sent to him and considering any representations duly made to him, shall—

(a) grant or refuse to grant the certificate of discharge; and

(b) notify (in addition to the . . . trustee) the debtor and all creditors who have made such representations accordingly.

[(3A) A certificate of discharge granted under subsection (3)—

(a) must take effect after the expiry of the period mentioned in subsection (3C), and

(b) has no effect if an application for review is made under subsection (3B).

(3B) The trustee, the debtor or any creditor who has made representations under subsection (2)(a) may apply to the Accountant in Bankruptcy for a review of a determination under subsection (3).

(3C) An application under subsection (3B) must be made before the expiry of the period of 14 days beginning with the day of the determination.

(3D) If an application for a review under subsection (3B) is made, the Accountant in Bankruptcy must—

(a) take into account any representations made by an interested person before the expiry of the period of 21 days beginning with the day on which the application is made, and

(b) confirm, amend or revoke the determination (whether or not issuing a new certificate of discharge) before the expiry of the period of 28 days beginning with the day on which the application is made.]

(4) The . . . trustee, the debtor or any creditor who has made representations under subsection (2)(a) above, may within 14 days after [a decision by the Accountant in Bankruptcy under subsection (3D)(b)], appeal therefrom to the sheriff and if the sheriff determines that a certificate of discharge which has been refused should be granted he shall order the Accountant in Bankruptcy to grant it; and the sheriff clerk shall send a copy of the decree of the sheriff to the Accountant in Bankruptcy.

[(4A) The decision of the sheriff on an appeal under subsection (4) above shall be final.]

(5) The grant of a certificate of discharge under this section by the Accountant in Bankruptcy shall have the effect of discharging the . . . trustee from all liability (other than any liability arising from fraud) to the creditors or to the debtor in respect of any act or omission of the . . . trustee in exercising the functions conferred on him by this Act including, where he was also the interim trustee, the functions conferred on him as interim trustee.
(6) Where a certificate of discharge is granted under this section, the Accountant in Bankruptcy shall make an appropriate entry in the register of insolvencies and in the sederunt book.
(7) Where the . . . trustee has died, resigned office or been removed from office, the provisions of this section shall, subject to any necessary modifications, apply in relation to that . . . trustee or, if he has died, to his executor as they apply to a . . . trustee who has made a final division of the debtor's estate in accordance with the foregoing provisions of this Act.
[(8) This section does not apply in any case where the Accountant in Bankruptcy is the . . . trustee.]

NOTES

Repealed as noted at the beginning of this Act.

Section heading: substituted for original words "Discharge of permanent trustee" by the Bankruptcy and Diligence etc (Scotland) Act 2007, s 36, Sch 1, paras 1, 49, subject to transitional provisions and savings in SSI 2008/115, arts 5–7, 10, 15 at **[2.51]–[2.53]**, **[2.56]**, **[2.57]**.

Sub-s (1): word "permanent" (omitted) repealed by the Bankruptcy and Diligence etc (Scotland) Act 2007, s 226(2), Sch 6, Pt 1, subject to transitional provisions and savings in SSI 2008/115, arts 5–7, 10, 15 at **[2.51]–[2.53]**, **[2.56]**, **[2.57]**; para (a) substituted, words in square brackets in para (b) inserted and words "and a receipt for the deposit of the unclaimed dividends and unapplied balances" omitted from para (b) repealed, by the Bankruptcy and Debt Advice (Scotland) Act 2014, ss 20(a), 23(1)(a), subject to transitional provisions and savings in SSI 2014/261, arts 4, 12 at **[2.91]**, **[2.99]**. Para (a) previously read as follows:

"(a) shall deposit any unclaimed dividends and any unapplied balances in an appropriate bank or institution;".

Sub-ss (1A), (1B): inserted by the Bankruptcy and Debt Advice (Scotland) Act 2014, ss 20(b), 23(1)(b), subject to transitional provisions and savings in SSI 2014/261, arts 4, 12 at **[2.91]**, **[2.99]**.

Sub-ss (2), (3), (5), (7): word "permanent" omitted in each place repealed by the Bankruptcy and Diligence etc (Scotland) Act 2007, s 226(2), Sch 6, Pt 1, subject to transitional provisions and savings in SSI 2008/115, arts 5–7, 10, 15 at **[2.51]–[2.53]**, **[2.56]**, **[2.57]**; words in square brackets in sub-s (2)(b) substituted for original words "at the office of the Accountant in Bankruptcy" by the Bankruptcy and Debt Advice (Scotland) Act 2014, s 23(1)(c), subject to transitional provisions and savings in SSI 2014/261, arts 4, 12 at **[2.91]**, **[2.99]**.

Sub-ss (3A)–(3D): inserted by the Bankruptcy and Debt Advice (Scotland) Act 2014, s 42(1)(a), subject to transitional provisions and savings in SSI 2014/261, arts 10, 12 at **[2.97]**, **[2.99]**.

Sub-s (4): word "permanent" (omitted) repealed by the Bankruptcy and Diligence etc (Scotland) Act 2007, s 226(2), Sch 6, Pt 1, subject to transitional provisions and savings in SSI 2008/115, arts 5–7, 10, 15 at **[2.51]–[2.53]**, **[2.56]**, **[2.57]**; words in square brackets substituted for original words "the issuing of the determination under subsection (3) above" by the Bankruptcy and Debt Advice (Scotland) Act 2014, s 42(1)(b), subject to transitional provisions and savings in SSI 2014/261, arts 10, 12 at **[2.97]**, **[2.99]**.

Sub-s (4A): inserted by the Bankruptcy (Scotland) Act 1993, s 11(3), Sch 1, para 24, subject to s 12(6) thereof, at **[5.194]** and to the Bankruptcy (Scotland) Act 1993 Commencement and Savings Order 1993, SI 1993/438, arts 4, 5, at **[16.58]**, **[16.59]**.

Sub-s (8): added by the Bankruptcy (Scotland) Act 1993, s 11(3), Sch 1, para 24, subject to s 12(6) thereof, at **[5.194]** and to SI 1993/438, arts 4, 5, at **[16.58]**, **[16.59]**; word "permanent" (omitted) repealed by the Bankruptcy and Diligence etc (Scotland) Act 2007, s 226(2), Sch 6, Pt 1, subject to transitional provisions and savings in SSI 2008/115, arts 5–7, 10, 15 at **[2.51]–[2.53]**, **[2.56]**, **[2.57]**.

[5.140]
58 Unclaimed dividends

(1) Any person, producing evidence of his right, may apply to the Accountant in Bankruptcy to receive a dividend deposited under section [57(1B)] [or 58A(3)] of this Act, if the application is made not later than 7 years after the date of such deposit.
(2) If the Accountant in Bankruptcy is satisfied of the applicant's right to the dividend, he shall authorise the appropriate bank or institution to pay to the applicant the amount of that dividend and of any interest which has accrued thereon.
(3) The Accountant in Bankruptcy shall, at the expiry of 7 years from the date of deposit of any unclaimed dividend or unapplied balance under section [57(1B)] [or 58A(3)] of this Act, hand over the deposit receipt or other voucher relating to such dividend or balance to the Secretary of State, who shall thereupon be entitled to payment of the amount due, principal and interest, from the bank or institution in which the deposit was made.

NOTES

Repealed as noted at the beginning of this Act.

Sub-ss (1), (3): figure in first pair of square brackets substituted for original figure "57(1)(a)" by the Bankruptcy and Debt Advice (Scotland) Act 2014, s 56(1), Sch 3, paras 2, 31, subject to transitional provisions and savings in SSI 2014/261, arts 4, 12 at **[2.91]**, **[2.99]**; words in second pair of square brackets inserted by the Bankruptcy (Scotland) Act 1993, s 11(3), Sch 1, para 25, subject to s 12(6) thereof, at **[5.194]** and to the Bankruptcy (Scotland) Act 1993 Commencement and Savings Order 1993, SI 1993/438, arts 4, 5, at **[16.58]**, **[16.59]**.

Companies winding up: this section is applied, with any necessary modifications, to sums lodged in a bank or institution under the Insolvency Act 1986, s 193, and to sums deposited under the Companies Act 1985, s 430(13) (so far as it is consistent with those Acts); see s 193(3) of the 1986 Act at **[1.197]** and s 430(14) of the 1985 Act.

[5.141]

[58A Discharge of Accountant in Bankruptcy

(1) This section applies where the Accountant in Bankruptcy has acted as the . . . trustee in any sequestration.

(2) . . .

(3) The Accountant in Bankruptcy shall deposit any unclaimed dividends and any unapplied balances in an appropriate bank or institution.

(4) The Accountant in Bankruptcy shall send to the debtor and to all creditors known to him—

(a) a copy of [a determination of the Accountant in Bankruptcy's fees and outlays calculated in accordance with regulations made under section 69A]; and

(b) a notice in writing stating—

(i) that the Accountant in Bankruptcy has commenced the procedure under this Act leading to discharge in respect of his actings as . . . trustee;

(ii) that the sederunt book relating to the sequestration is available for inspection [following a request made to the Accountant in Bankruptcy];

[(iia) that an application for a review may be made under subsection (4A)];

(iii) that an appeal may be made to the sheriff under subsection (5) below; and

(iv) the effect of subsection (7) below.

[(4A) The debtor or any creditor may apply to the Accountant in Bankruptcy for a review of the discharge of the Accountant in Bankruptcy in respect of the Accountant in Bankruptcy's actings as trustee.

(4B) An application under subsection (4A) must be made before the expiry of the period of 14 days beginning with the day on which notice is sent under subsection (4)(b).

(4C) If an application under subsection (4A) is made, the Accountant in Bankruptcy must—

(a) take into account any representations made by an interested person before the expiry of the period of 21 days beginning with the day on which the application is made, and

(b) confirm or revoke the discharge before the expiry of the period of 28 days beginning with the day on which the application is made.]

[(5) The debtor or any creditor may appeal to the sheriff against a decision by the Accountant in Bankruptcy under subsection (4C)(b) before the expiry of the period of 14 days beginning with the day on which the decision is made.]

[(6) The decision of the sheriff on an appeal under subsection (5) is final.]

(7) Where—

(a) the requirements of this section have been complied with; and

(b) no appeal to the sheriff is made under subsection (5) above or such an appeal is made but is refused as regards the discharge of the Accountant in Bankruptcy,

the Accountant in Bankruptcy shall be discharged from all liability (other than any liability arising from fraud) to the creditors or to the debtor in respect of any act or omission of the Accountant in Bankruptcy in exercising the functions of . . . trustee in the sequestration [including, where the Accountant in Bankruptcy was the interim trustee, the functions of the interim trustee].

(8) . . .

(9) . . .]

NOTES

Inserted by the Bankruptcy (Scotland) Act 1993, s 11(3), Sch 1, para 26, subject to s 12(6) thereof, at **[5.194]** and to the Bankruptcy (Scotland) Act 1993 Commencement and Savings Order 1993, SI 1993/438, arts 4, 5, at **[16.58]**, **[16.59]**.

Repealed as noted at the beginning of this Act.

Sub-s (1): word "permanent" (omitted) repealed by the Bankruptcy and Diligence etc (Scotland) Act 2007, s 226(2), Sch 6, Pt 1, subject to transitional provisions and savings in SSI 2008/115, arts 5–7, 10, 15 at **[2.51]**–**[2.53]**, **[2.56]**, **[2.57]**.

Sub-s (2): repealed by the Bankruptcy and Debt Advice (Scotland) Act 2014, s 56(2), Sch 4, subject to transitional provisions and savings in SSI 2014/261, arts 4, 12 at **[2.91]**, **[2.99]**, and previously read as follows—

"(2) After the Accountant in Bankruptcy has made a final division of the debtor's estate, he shall insert in the sederunt book—

(a) his final accounts of his intromissions (if any) with the debtor's estate;

(b) the scheme of division (if any); and

(c) a determination of his fees and outlays calculated in accordance with regulations made under section 69A of this Act.".

Sub-s (4): word "permanent" omitted from para (b)(i) repealed by the Bankruptcy and Diligence etc (Scotland) Act 2007, s 226(2), Sch 6, Pt 1, subject to transitional provisions and savings in SSI 2008/115, arts 5–7, 10, 15 at **[2.51]**–**[2.53]**, **[2.56]**, **[2.57]**; words in square brackets in para (a) substituted for original words "the determination mentioned in subsection (2)(c) above", words in square brackets in para (b)(ii) substituted for original words "at such address as the Accountant in Bankruptcy may determine" and para (b)(iia) inserted, by the Bankruptcy and Debt Advice (Scotland) Act 2014, ss 23(2), 42(2)(a), 56(1), Sch 3, paras 2, 32, subject to transitional provisions and savings in SSI 2014/261, arts 4, 10, 12 at **[2.91]**, **[2.97]**, **[2.99]**.

Sub-ss (4A)–(4C): inserted by the Bankruptcy and Debt Advice (Scotland) Act 2014, s 42(2)(b), subject to transitional provisions and savings in SSI 2014/261, arts 10, 12 at **[2.97]**, **[2.99]**.

Sub-ss (5), (6): substituted by the Bankruptcy and Debt Advice (Scotland) Act 2014, s 42(2)(c), (d), subject to transitional provisions and savings in SSI 2014/261, arts 10, 12 at **[2.97]**, **[2.99]**, and previously read as follows (with word "permanent" (omitted) from sub-s (5)(b) repealed by the Bankruptcy and Diligence etc (Scotland) Act 2007, s 226(2), Sch 6, Pt 1, subject to transitional provisions and savings in SSI 2008/115)—

"(5) The debtor and any creditor may appeal to the sheriff against—

(a) the determination of the Accountant in Bankruptcy mentioned in subsection (2)(c) above;

(b) the discharge of the Accountant in Bankruptcy in respect of his actings as . . . trustee; or

(c) both such determination and discharge.

(6) An appeal under subsection (5) above shall be made not more than 14 days after the issue of the notice mentioned in subsection (4)(b) above; and the decision of the sheriff on such an appeal shall be final.".

Sub-s (7): word "permanent" (omitted) repealed and words in square brackets added by the Bankruptcy and Diligence etc (Scotland) Act 2007, ss 36, 226(2), Sch 1, paras 1, 50, Sch 6, Pt 1, subject to transitional provisions and savings in SSI 2008/115, arts 5–7, 10, 15 at **[2.51]–[2.53]**, **[2.56]**, **[2.57]**.

Sub-s (8): repealed by the Bankruptcy and Debt Advice (Scotland) Act 2014, s 56(2), Sch 4, subject to transitional provisions and savings in SSI 2014/261, arts 4, 12 at **[2.91]**, **[2.99]**, and previously read as follows—

"(8) Where the Accountant in Bankruptcy is discharged from all liability as mentioned in subsection (7) above, he shall make an entry in the sederunt book recording such discharge.".

Sub-s (9): repealed by the Bankruptcy and Diligence etc (Scotland) Act 2007, s 226(2), Sch 6, Pt 1, subject to transitional provisions and savings in SSI 2008/115, arts 5–7, 10, 15 at **[2.51]–[2.53]**, **[2.56]**, **[2.57]**, and previously read as follows:

"(9) Where the Accountant in Bankruptcy—

(a) has acted as both interim trustee and permanent trustee in a sequestration;

(b) has not been discharged under section 26A(7) of this Act,

references in this section to his acting as or exercising the functions of permanent trustee shall be construed as including references to his acting as or exercising the functions of interim trustee; and subsection (7) above shall have effect accordingly.".

[5.142]

[58B Assets discovered after trustee discharge: appointment of trustee

(1) This section applies where, after the trustee's discharge under section 57 or 58A but before the expiry of the period of 5 years from the date of sequestration, the trustee or the Accountant in Bankruptcy becomes aware of any newly identified estate with a value of not less than £1000 (or such other sum as may be prescribed).

(2) In this section, "newly identified estate" means any part of the debtor's estate which—

(a) vested in the trustee in accordance with section 31 or 32, and

(b) was not, before the trustee was discharged, known to the trustee.

(3) The Accountant in Bankruptcy may—

(a) in the case where the trustee was discharged under section 57—

(i) on the application of the trustee who was discharged, reappoint that person as trustee on the debtor's estate, or

(ii) appoint the Accountant in Bankruptcy as trustee on the debtor's estate,

(b) in the case where the Accountant in Bankruptcy was discharged under section 58A, reappoint the Accountant in Bankruptcy as trustee on the debtor's estate.

(4) The Accountant in Bankruptcy may make an appointment or reappointment under subsection (3) only if, in the opinion of the Accountant in Bankruptcy, the value of the newly identified estate is likely to exceed the costs of—

(a) the appointment or reappointment, and

(b) the recovery, management, realisation and distribution of the newly identified estate.

(5) Where the trustee was discharged under section 57 and applies for reappointment under subsection (3)(a)(i), the discharged trustee must provide to the Accountant in Bankruptcy the information mentioned in subsection (8)(a) to (c).

(6) Where the trustee was discharged under section 57 and does not apply for reappointment under subsection (3)(a)(i), the discharged trustee must—

(a) provide to the Accountant in Bankruptcy details of any newly identified estate that the discharged trustee becomes aware of, where that estate has a value which is not less than the value mentioned in subsection (1), and

(b) if requested by the Accountant in Bankruptcy, provide to the Accountant in Bankruptcy the information mentioned in subsection (8)(b) and (c).

(7) Where the Accountant in Bankruptcy was discharged under section 58A, the Accountant in Bankruptcy must record and consider the information mentioned in subsection (8).

(8) The information is—

(a) the estimated value of the newly identified estate,

(b) the reason why the newly identified estate forms part of the debtor's estate,

(c) the reason why the newly identified estate was not recovered,

(d) the estimated outlays and remuneration of the trustee following an appointment or reappointment under subsection (3), and

(e) the likely distribution under section 51 following an appointment or reappointment under subsection (3).

(9) This section is without prejudice to any other right to take action following the discharge of the trustee.]

NOTES

Commencement: 1 April 2015.

Inserted, together with ss 58C, 58D, by the Bankruptcy and Debt Advice (Scotland) Act 2014, s 21, subject to transitional provisions and savings in SSI 2014/261, arts 4, 12 at **[2.91]**, **[2.99]**.

Repealed as noted at the beginning of this Act.

[5.143]

[58C Assets discovered after trustee discharge: notice

(1) The Accountant in Bankruptcy must notify the debtor and any other person the Accountant in Bankruptcy considers to have an interest—

(a) where an application is made under section 58B(3)(a)(i), and
(b) where the Accountant in Bankruptcy proposes to make an appointment or reappointment under section 58B(3)(a)(ii) or (b).

(2) A notice under subsection (1) must inform the recipient that the person has a right to make representations to the Accountant in Bankruptcy in relation to the application or the proposed appointment or reappointment before the expiry of the period of 14 days beginning with the day on which the notice is given.

(3) Before making an appointment or reappointment under section 58B, the Accountant in Bankruptcy must take into account any representations made by an interested person.

(4) If the Accountant in Bankruptcy makes an appointment or reappointment under section 58B, the Accountant in Bankruptcy must as soon as is practicable notify the debtor of the appointment or reappointment.

(5) A notice under subsection (4) must include information in relation to the debtor's duties to co-operate with the trustee under section 64.]

NOTES

Commencement: 1 April 2015.

Inserted as noted to s 58B at **[5.142]**.

Repealed as noted at the beginning of this Act.

[5.144]

[58D Assets discovered after trustee discharge: appeal

Where the Accountant in Bankruptcy makes or refuses to make an order under section 58B, an interested person may, no later than 14 days after the date of the decision, appeal to the sheriff.]

NOTES

Commencement: 1 April 2015.

Inserted as noted to s 58B at **[5.142]**.

Repealed as noted at the beginning of this Act.

Voluntary trust deeds for creditors

[5.145]

59 Voluntary trust deeds for creditors

Schedule 5 to this Act shall have effect in relation to trust deeds executed after the commencement of this section.

NOTES

Repealed as noted at the beginning of this Act.

[5.146]

[59A [Application for conversion to sequestration]

(1) Where a member State liquidator proposes to [apply to the Accountant in Bankruptcy] for the conversion under Article 37 of the EC Regulation (conversion of earlier proceedings) of a protected trust deed into sequestration, an affidavit complying with section 59B of this Act must be prepared and sworn, and [submitted to the Accountant in Bankruptcy in support of the application].

(2) The [application] and the affidavit required under subsection (1) above shall be served upon—
(a) the debtor;
(b) the trustee;
(c) such other person as may be prescribed.]

NOTES

Inserted, together with ss 59B, 59C, by the Insolvency (Scotland) Regulations 2003, SI 2003/2109, regs 3, 16.

Repealed as noted at the beginning of this Act.

Section heading: words in square brackets substituted for original words "Petition for conversion into sequestration" by the Bankruptcy and Debt Advice (Scotland) Act 2014, s 34(1), subject to transitional provisions and savings in SSI 2014/261, art 12 at **[2.99]**.

Sub-s (1): words in first and second pairs of square brackets substituted for original words "petition the sheriff" and "lodged in court in support of the petition" respectively, by the Bankruptcy and Debt Advice (Scotland) Act 2014, s 34(2)(a), subject to transitional provisions and savings in SSI 2014/261, art 12 at **[2.99]**.

Sub-s (2): word in square brackets substituted for original word "petition" by the Bankruptcy and Debt Advice (Scotland) Act 2014, s 34(2)(b), subject to transitional provisions and savings in SSI 2014/261, art 12 at **[2.99]**.

[5.147]

[59B Contents of affidavit

(1) The affidavit shall—
(a) state that main proceedings have been opened in relation to the debtor in a member State other than the United Kingdom;
(b) state that the member State liquidator believes that the conversion of the trust deed into a sequestration would prove to be in the interests of the creditors in the main proceedings;
(c) contain such other information the member State liquidator considers will be of assistance to the [Accountant in Bankruptcy]—
(i) in deciding whether to make an order under section 59C; and
(ii) if the [Accountant in Bankruptcy] were to do so, in considering the need for any consequential provision that would be necessary or desirable; and

(d) contain any other matters as may be prescribed.
(2) An affidavit under this section shall be sworn by, or on behalf of, the member State liquidator.]

NOTES

Inserted as noted to s 59A at **[5.146]**.

Repealed as noted at the beginning of this Act.

Sub-s (1): words in square brackets in para (c) substituted for word "sheriff" (as substituted by the Bankruptcy and Diligence etc (Scotland) Act 2007, s 36, Sch 1, paras 1, 52) by the Bankruptcy and Debt Advice (Scotland) Act 2014, s 34(3), subject to transitional provisions and savings in SSI 2014/261, arts 4, 12 at **[2.91]**, **[2.99]**.

[5.148]
[59C [Power of Accountant in Bankruptcy]

[(1) The Accountant in Bankruptcy may, after considering an application for conversion of a protected trust deed into a sequestration, make such order as the Accountant in Bankruptcy thinks fit.]

(2) If the [Accountant in Bankruptcy] makes an order for conversion into sequestration the order may contain all such consequential provisions as the [Accountant in Bankruptcy] deems necessary or desirable.

[(2A) The provisions of this Act shall apply to an order made by the [Accountant in Bankruptcy] under subsection (1) above as if it was a determination by the Accountant in Bankruptcy of a debtor application under section 12(1) of this Act and in relation to which the member State liquidator was a concurring creditor.]

(3) Where the [Accountant in Bankruptcy] makes an order for conversion into sequestration under subsection (1) above, any expenses properly incurred as expenses of the administration of the trust deed in question shall be a first charge on the debtor's estate.]

NOTES

Inserted as noted to s 59A at **[5.146]**.

Repealed as noted at the beginning of this Act.

Section heading: words in square brackets substituted, for words "Power of sheriff" (as previously substituted by the Bankruptcy and Diligence etc (Scotland) Act 2007, s 36, Sch 1, paras 1, 53(c), subject to transitional provisions and savings in SSI 2008/115, arts 5–7, 10, 15), by the Bankruptcy and Debt Advice (Scotland) Act 2014, s 34(4), subject to transitional provisions and savings in SSI 2014/261, art 12 at **[2.99]**.

Sub-s (1): substituted by the Bankruptcy and Debt Advice (Scotland) Act 2014, s 34(5)(a), subject to transitional provisions and savings in SSI 2014/261, arts 4, 12 at **[2.91]**, **[2.99]**, and previously read as follows (with words in square brackets substituted by the Bankruptcy and Diligence etc (Scotland) Act 2007, s 36, Sch 1, paras 1, 53(a), (b), subject to transitional provisions and savings in SSI 2008/115, arts 5–7, 10, 15)—

"(1) On hearing the petition for conversion of a trust deed into a sequestration the [sheriff] may make such order as [he] thinks fit.".

Sub-s (2A): inserted by the Bankruptcy and Diligence etc (Scotland) Act 2007, s 32, subject to transitional provisions and savings in SSI 2008/115, arts 5–7, 10, 15 at **[2.51]–[2.53]**, **[2.56]**, **[2.57]**; words in square brackets substituted (for original word "sheriff") by the Bankruptcy and Debt Advice (Scotland) Act 2014, s 34(5)(b), subject to transitional provisions and savings in SSI 2014/261, art 12 at **[2.99]**.

Sub-ss (2), (3): words in square brackets in each place substituted (for word "sheriff" as substituted by the Bankruptcy and Diligence etc (Scotland) Act 2007, s 36, Sch 1, paras 1, 53(a), subject to transitional provisions and savings in SSI 2008/115, arts 5–7, 10, 15) by the Bankruptcy and Debt Advice (Scotland) Act 2014, s 34(5)(b), subject to transitional provisions and savings in SSI 2014/261, art 12 at **[2.99]**.

Miscellaneous and supplementary

[5.149]
60 Liabilities and rights of co-obligants

(1) Where a creditor has an obligant (in this section referred to as the "co-obligant") bound to him along with the debtor for the whole or part of the debt, the co-obligant shall not be freed or discharged from his liability for the debt by reason of the discharge of the debtor or by virtue of the creditor's voting or drawing a dividend or assenting to, or not opposing—

(a) the discharge of the debtor; *or*
(b) any composition.

(2) Where—

(a) a creditor has had a claim accepted in whole or in part; and
(b) a co-obligant holds a security over any part of the debtor's estate,

the co-obligant shall account to the . . . trustee so as to put the estate in the same position as if the co-obligant had paid the debt to the creditor and thereafter had had his claim accepted in whole or in part in the sequestration after deduction of the value of the security.

(3) Without prejudice to any right under any rule of law of a co-obligant who has paid the debt, the co-obligant may require and obtain at his own expense from the creditor an assignation of the debt on payment of the amount thereof, and thereafter may in respect of that debt submit a claim, and vote and draw a dividend, if otherwise legally entitled to do so.

(4) In this section a "co-obligant" includes a cautioner.

NOTES

Repealed as noted at the beginning of this Act.

Sub-s (1): para (b) and word "; or" immediately preceding it repealed by the Bankruptcy and Debt Advice (Scotland) Act 2014, s 56(2), Sch 4, subject to transitional provisions and savings in SSI 2014/261, arts 4, 12 at **[2.91]**, **[2.99]**.

Sub-s (2): word "permanent" (omitted) repealed by the Bankruptcy and Diligence etc (Scotland) Act 2007, s 226(2), Sch 6, Pt 1, subject to transitional provisions and savings in SSI 2008/115, arts 5–7, 10, 15 at **[2.51]–[2.53]**, **[2.56]**, **[2.57]**.

[5.150]
[60A Member State liquidator deemed creditor
For the purposes of this Act, and without prejudice to the generality of the right to participate referred to in paragraph 3 of Article 32 of the EC Regulation (exercise of creditors' rights) a member State liquidator appointed in relation to the debtor is deemed to be a creditor in the sum due to creditors in proceedings in relation to which he holds office.]

NOTES
Inserted, together with s 60B, by the Insolvency (Scotland) Regulations 2003, SI 2003/2109, regs 3, 17.
Repealed as noted at the beginning of this Act.

[5.151]
[60B Trustee's duties concerning notices and copies of documents
(1) This section applies where a member State liquidator has been appointed in relation to the debtor.
(2) Where an interim [trustee or a] trustee is obliged to give notice to, or provide a copy of a document (including an order of court) to, the [sheriff] or the Accountant in Bankruptcy, the trustee shall [also] give notice or provide copies, as appropriate, to the member State liquidator.
(3) Subsection (2) above is without prejudice to the generality of the obligations imposed by Article 31 of the EC Regulation (duty to co-operate and communicate information).]

NOTES
Inserted as noted to s 60A at **[5.150]**.
Repealed as noted at the beginning of this Act.
Sub-s (2): words in first pair of square brackets substituted for original words "or a permanent", and word in second pair of square brackets substituted for original word "court" by the Bankruptcy and Diligence etc (Scotland) Act 2007, s 36, Sch 1, paras 1, 54, subject to transitional provisions and savings in SSI 2008/115, arts 5–7, 10, 15 at **[2.51]–[2.53]**, **[2.56]**, **[2.57]**; word in third pair of square brackets inserted by the Bankruptcy and Debt Advice (Scotland) Act 2014, s 56(1), Sch 3, paras 2, 33, subject to transitional provisions and savings in SSI 2014/261, arts 4, 12 at **[2.91]**, **[2.99]**.

[5.152]
61 Extortionate credit transactions
(1) This section applies where the debtor is or has been a party to a transaction for, or involving, the provision to him of credit and his estate is sequestrated.
(2) The [sheriff] may, on the application of the . . . trustee, make an order with respect to the transaction if the transaction is or was extortionate and was not entered into more than three years before the date of sequestration.
(3) For the purposes of this section a transaction is extortionate if, having regard to the risk accepted by the person providing the credit—
(a) the terms of it are or were such as to require grossly exorbitant payments to be made (whether unconditionally or in certain contingencies) in respect of the provision of the credit; or
(b) it otherwise grossly contravened ordinary principles of fair dealing; and it shall be presumed, unless the contrary is proved, that a transaction with respect to which an application is made under this section is, or as the case may be was, extortionate.
(4) An order under this section with respect to any transaction may contain such one or more of the following as the [sheriff] thinks fit—
(a) provision setting aside the whole or part of any obligation created by the transaction;
(b) provision otherwise varying the terms of the transaction or varying the terms on which any security for the purposes of the transaction is held;
(c) provision requiring any person who is a party to the transaction to pay to the . . . trustee any sums paid to that person, by virtue of the transaction, by the debtor;
(d) provision requiring any person to surrender to the . . . trustee any property held by him as security for the purposes of the transaction;
(e) provision directing accounts to be taken between any persons.
(5) Any sums or property required to be paid or surrendered to the . . . trustee in accordance with an order under this section shall vest in the . . . trustee.
(6) . . . the powers conferred by this section shall be exercisable in relation to any transaction concurrently with any powers exercisable under this Act in relation to that transaction as a gratuitous alienation or unfair preference.
(7) In this section "credit" has the same meaning as in the said Act of 1974.

NOTES
Repealed as noted at the beginning of this Act.
Sub-s (2): word in square brackets substituted for original word "court" and word "permanent" (omitted) repealed by the Bankruptcy and Diligence etc (Scotland) Act 2007, ss 36, 226(2), Sch 1, paras 1, 55, Sch 6, Pt 1, subject to transitional provisions and savings in SSI 2008/115, arts 5–7, 10, 15 at **[2.51]–[2.53]**, **[2.56]**, **[2.57]**.
Sub-s (4): word in square brackets substituted for original word "court" and word "permanent" omitted from paras (c), (d) repealed by the Bankruptcy and Diligence etc (Scotland) Act 2007, ss 36, 226(2), Sch 1, paras 1, 55, Sch 6, Pt 1, subject to transitional provisions and savings in SSI 2008/115, arts 5–7, 10, 15 at **[2.51]–[2.53]**, **[2.56]**, **[2.57]**.
Sub-s (5): word "permanent" omitted in both places repealed by the Bankruptcy and Diligence etc (Scotland) Act 2007, s 226(2), Sch 6, Pt 1, subject to transitional provisions and savings in SSI 2008/115, arts 5–7, 10, 15 at **[2.51]–[2.53]**, **[2.56]**, **[2.57]**.

Sub-s (6): words omitted repealed by the Consumer Credit Act 2006, s 70, Sch 4, subject to transitional provisions and savings in Sch 3, para 15(1), (5)(f) thereto.

[5.153]

62 Sederunt book and other documents

(1) Subject to subsection (2) below, whoever by virtue of this Act for the time being holds the sederunt book shall make it available for inspection at all reasonable hours by any interested person.

(2) As regards any case in which the person on whom a duty is imposed by subsection (1) above is the Accountant in Bankruptcy, [the Scottish Ministers may by regulations]—

(a) limit the period for which the duty is so imposed; and

(b) prescribe conditions in accordance with which the duty shall be carried out.

[(2A) The trustee must insert in the sederunt book the information listed in Schedule 3A to this Act.

(2B) The Scottish Ministers may by regulations modify Schedule 3A.]

(3) Any entry in the sederunt book shall be sufficient evidence of the facts stated therein, except where it is founded on by the . . . trustee in his own interest.

(4) Notwithstanding any provision of this Act, the . . . trustee shall not be bound to insert in the sederunt book any document of a confidential nature.

(5) The . . . trustee shall not be bound to exhibit to any person other than a commissioner or the Accountant in Bankruptcy any document in his possession of a confidential nature.

(6) An extract from the register of insolvencies bearing to be signed by the Accountant in Bankruptcy shall be sufficient evidence of the facts stated therein.

NOTES

Repealed as noted at the beginning of this Act.

Words in square brackets in sub-s (2) substituted for original words "Court of Session may by act of sederunt" and sub-ss (2A), (2B) inserted by the Bankruptcy and Debt Advice (Scotland) Act 2014, s 23(3), subject to transitional provisions and savings in SSI 2014/261, arts 4, 12 at **[2.91]**, **[2.99]**.

Sub-ss (3)–(5): word "permanent" omitted in each place repealed by the Bankruptcy and Diligence etc (Scotland) Act 2007, s 226(2), Sch 6, Pt 1, subject to transitional provisions and savings in SSI 2008/115, arts 5–7, 10, 15 at **[2.51]**–**[2.53]**, **[2.56]**, **[2.57]**.

Act of Sederunt: the Act of Sederunt (Rules of Court Amendment No 1) (Bankruptcy Forms) 1986, SI 1986/514; the Act of Sederunt (Rules of the Court of Session 1994), SI 1994/1443 at **[16.60]**; the Act of Sederunt (Sheriff Court Bankruptcy Rules) 2008, SSI 2008/119 at **[16.263]**.

[5.154]

63 [Power of court to cure defects in procedure]

(1) The sheriff may, on the application of any person having an interest—

(a) if there has been a failure to comply with any requirement of this Act or any regulations made under it, make an order waiving any such failure and, so far as practicable, restoring any person prejudiced by the failure to the position he would have been in but for the failure;

(b) if for any reason anything required or authorised to be done in, or in connection with, the sequestration process cannot be done, make such order as may be necessary to enable that thing to be done.

[(1A) An order under subsection (1) may waive a failure to comply with a requirement mentioned in section 63A(1)(a) or (b) only if the failure relates to—

(a) a document to be lodged with the sheriff,

(b) a document issued by the sheriff, or

(c) a time limit specified in relation to proceedings before the sheriff or a document relating to those proceedings.]

(2) The sheriff, in an order under subsection (1) above, may impose such conditions, including conditions as to expenses, as he thinks fit and may—

(a) authorise or dispense with the performance of any act in the sequestration process;

(b) appoint as . . . trustee on the debtor's estate [the Accountant in Bankruptcy or] a person who would be eligible to be elected under section 24 of this Act, whether or not in place of an existing trustee;

(c) extend or waive any time limit specified in or under this Act.

(3) An application under subsection (1) above—

(a) may at any time be remitted by the sheriff to the Court of Session, of his own accord or on an application by any person having an interest;

(b) shall be so remitted, if the Court of Session so directs on an application by any such person,

if the sheriff or the Court of Session, as the case may be, considers that the remit is desirable because of the importance or complexity of the matters raised by the application.

(4) The . . . trustee shall record in the sederunt book the decision of the sheriff or the Court of Session under this section.

NOTES

Repealed as noted at the beginning of this Act.

Section heading: words in square brackets substituted for original words "Power to cure defects in procedure" by the Bankruptcy and Debt Advice (Scotland) Act 2014, s 35(1), subject to transitional provisions and savings in SSI 2014/261, arts 4, 12 at **[2.91]**, **[2.99]**.

Sub-s (1A): inserted by the Bankruptcy and Debt Advice (Scotland) Act 2014, s 35(2)(a), subject to transitional provisions and savings in SSI 2014/261, arts 4, 12 at **[2.91]**, **[2.99]**.

Sub-s (2): word "permanent" (omitted from para (b)) repealed by the Bankruptcy and Diligence etc (Scotland) Act 2007, s 226(2), Sch 6, Pt 1, subject to transitional provisions and savings in SSI 2008/115, arts 5–7, 10, 15 at **[2.51]**–**[2.53]**, **[2.56]**,

[2.57]; words in square brackets in para (b) inserted by the Bankruptcy and Debt Advice (Scotland) Act 2014, s 35(2)(b), subject to transitional provisions and savings in SSI 2014/261, arts 4, 12 at **[2.91]**, **[2.99]**.

Sub-s (4): word "permanent" (omitted) repealed by the Bankruptcy and Diligence etc (Scotland) Act 2007, s 226(2), Sch 6, Pt 1, subject to transitional provisions and savings in SSI 2008/115, arts 5–7, 10, 15 at **[2.51]–[2.53]**, **[2.56]**, **[2.57]**; repealed by the Bankruptcy and Debt Advice (Scotland) Act 2014, s 56(2), Sch 4, subject to transitional provisions and savings in SSI 2014/261, arts 4, 12 at **[2.91]**, **[2.99]**.

[5.155]
[63A Power of Accountant in Bankruptcy to cure defects in procedure

(1) The Accountant in Bankruptcy may make an order—

(a) correcting a clerical or incidental error in a document required by or under this Act, or

(b) waiving a failure to comply with a time limit—

(i) which is specified by or under this Act, and

(ii) for which no provision is made by or under this Act.

(2) An order under subsection (1) may be made—

(a) on the application of any person having an interest, or

(b) without an application if the Accountant in Bankruptcy proposes to correct or waive a matter mentioned in subsection (1).

(3) The applicant must notify all interested persons where an application is made under subsection (2)(a).

(4) The Accountant in Bankruptcy must notify all interested persons where the Accountant in Bankruptcy proposes to make an order by virtue of subsection (2)(b).

(5) A notice under subsection (3) or (4) must inform the recipient that the person has a right to make representations to the Accountant in Bankruptcy in relation to the application or the proposed order before the expiry of the period of 14 days beginning with the day on which the notice is given.

(6) Before making an order under subsection (1), the Accountant in Bankruptcy must take into account any representations made by an interested person.

(7) An order under subsection (1) may—

(a) so far as practicable, restore any person prejudiced by the error or failure to the position that person would have been in but for the error or failure,

(b) impose such conditions, including conditions as to expenses, as the Accountant in Bankruptcy thinks fit.

(8) After making an order which affects a matter which is recorded in the Register of Inhibitions, the Accountant in Bankruptcy must without delay send a certified copy of the order to the Keeper of that register for recording in that register.]

NOTES

Commencement: 1 April 2015.

Inserted, together with s 63B, by the Bankruptcy and Debt Advice (Scotland) Act 2014, s 35(3), subject to transitional provisions and savings in SSI 2014/261, arts 4, 12 at **[2.91]**, **[2.99]**.

Repealed as noted at the beginning of this Act.

[5.156]
[63B Decision under section 63A: review

(1) An interested person may apply to the Accountant in Bankruptcy for a review of a decision of the Accountant in Bankruptcy to make, or refuse to make, an order under section 63A(1).

(2) An application under subsection (1) must be made before the expiry of the period of 14 days beginning with the day of the decision.

(3) If an application under subsection (1) is made, the Accountant in Bankruptcy must—

(a) take into account any representations made by an interested person before the expiry of the period of 21 days beginning with the day on which the application is made, and

(b) confirm, amend or revoke the decision before the expiry of the period of 28 days beginning with the day on which the application is made.

(4) An interested person may appeal to the sheriff against a decision by the Accountant in Bankruptcy under subsection (3)(b) before the expiry of the period of 14 days beginning with the day of the decision.

(5) The decision of the sheriff on an appeal under subsection (4) is final.]

NOTES

Commencement: 1 April 2015.

Inserted as noted to s 63A at **[5.155]**.

Repealed as noted at the beginning of this Act.

[5.157]
[63C Review of decisions by Accountant in Bankruptcy: grounds of appeal

(1) For the avoidance of doubt, an appeal under a provision mentioned in subsection (2) may be made on—

(a) a matter of fact,

(b) a point of law, or

(c) the merits.

(2) The provisions are—

(a) section 3A(7),

(b) section 13A(11),

(c) section 13B(7),

(d) section 15(3D),
(e) section 17G(5),
(f) section 25A(8),
(g) section 26A(5),
(h) section 27(4),
(i) section 28B(4),
(j) section 29(4),
(k) section 29(6H),
(l) section 32C(5),
(m) section 32H(5),
(n) section 42(2D),
(o) section 49(6D),
(p) section 54B(6),
(q) section 54G(6),
(r) section 56J(8),
(s) section 57(4),
(t) section 58A(5),
(u) section 63B(4),
(v) paragraph 3(6) of Schedule 1.]

NOTES

Commencement: 1 April 2015.

Inserted by the Bankruptcy and Debt Advice (Scotland) Act 2014, s 43, subject to transitional provisions and savings in SSI 2014/261, arts 4, 12 at **[2.91]**, **[2.99]**.

Repealed as noted at the beginning of this Act.

[5.158]

64 [Debtor to co-operate with trustee]

(1) The debtor shall take every practicable step, and in particular shall execute any document, which may be necessary to enable the . . . trustee to perform the functions conferred on him by this Act.

(2) If the sheriff, on the application of the . . . trustee, is satisfied that the debtor has failed—

(a) to execute any document in compliance with subsection (1) above, he may authorise the sheriff clerk to do so; and the execution of a document by the sheriff clerk under this paragraph shall have the like force and effect in all respects as if the document had been executed by the debtor;

(b) to comply in any other respect with subsection (1) above, he may order the debtor to do so.

(3) If the debtor fails to comply with an order of the sheriff under subsection (2) above, he shall be guilty of an offence.

(4) In this section "debtor" includes a debtor discharged under this Act.

(5) A person convicted of an offence under subsection (3) above shall be liable—

(a) on summary conviction, to a fine not exceeding the statutory maximum or—

(i) to imprisonment for a term not exceeding 3 months; or

(ii) if he has previously been convicted of an offence inferring dishonest appropriation of property or an attempt at such appropriation, to imprisonment for a term not exceeding 6 months,

or (in the case of either sub-paragraph) to both such fine and such imprisonment; or

(b) on conviction on indictment to a fine or to imprisonment for a term not exceeding 2 years or to both.

NOTES

Repealed as noted at the beginning of this Act.

Section heading: substituted for original words "Debtor to co-operate with permanent trustee" by the Bankruptcy and Diligence etc (Scotland) Act 2007, s 36, Sch 1, paras 1, 56, subject to transitional provisions and savings in SSI 2008/115, arts 5–7, 10, 15 at **[2.51]–[2.53]**, **[2.56]**, **[2.57]**.

Sub-ss (1), (2): word "permanent" omitted in both places repealed by the Bankruptcy and Diligence etc (Scotland) Act 2007, s 226(2), Sch 6, Pt 1, subject to transitional provisions and savings in SSI 2008/115, arts 5–7, 10, 15 at **[2.51]–[2.53]**, **[2.56]**, **[2.57]**.

[5.159]

65 Arbitration and compromise

(1) The . . . trustee may (but if there are commissioners only with the consent of the commissioners, the creditors or the [sheriff])—

(a) refer to arbitration any claim or question of whatever nature which may arise in the course of the sequestration; or

(b) make a compromise with regard to any claim of whatever nature made against or on behalf of the sequestrated estate;

and the decree arbitral or compromise shall be binding on the creditors and the debtor.

(2) Where any claim or question is referred to arbitration under this section, the Accountant in Bankruptcy may vary any time limit in respect of which any procedure under this Act has to be carried out.

(3) The . . . trustee shall insert a copy of the decree arbitral, or record the compromise, in the sederunt book.

NOTES

Repealed as noted at the beginning of this Act.

Sub-s (1): word "permanent" (omitted) repealed and word in square brackets substituted for original word "court" by the Bankruptcy and Diligence etc (Scotland) Act 2007, ss 36, 226(2), Sch 1, paras 1, 57, Sch 6, Pt 1, subject to transitional provisions and savings in SSI 2008/115, arts 5–7, 10, 15 at **[2.51]–[2.53]**, **[2.56]**, **[2.57]**.

Sub-s (3): repealed by the Bankruptcy and Debt Advice (Scotland) Act 2014, s 56(2), Sch 4, subject to transitional provisions and savings in SSI 2014/261, arts 4, 12 at **[2.91]**, **[2.99]**; word "permanent" (omitted) repealed by the Bankruptcy and Diligence etc (Scotland) Act 2007, s 226(2), Sch 6, Pt 1, subject to transitional provisions and savings in SSI 2008/115, arts 5–7, 10, 15 at **[2.51]–[2.53]**, **[2.56]**, **[2.57]**.

[5.160]

66 Meetings of creditors and commissioners

Part I of Schedule 6 to this Act shall have effect in relation to meetings of creditors other than the statutory meeting; Part II of that Schedule shall have effect in relation to all meetings of creditors under this Act; and Part III of that Schedule shall have effect in relation to meetings of commissioners.

NOTES

Repealed as noted at the beginning of this Act.

[5.161]

67 General offences by debtor etc

(1) A debtor who during the relevant period makes a false statement in relation to his assets or his business or financial affairs to any creditor or to any person concerned in the administration of his estate shall be guilty of an offence, unless he shows that he neither knew nor had reason to believe that his statement was false.

(2) A debtor, or other person acting in his interest whether with or without his authority, who during the relevant period destroys, damages, conceals[, disposes of] or removes from Scotland any part of the debtor's estate or any document relating to his assets or his business or financial affairs shall be guilty of an offence, unless the debtor or other person shows that he did not do so with intent to prejudice the creditors.

(3) A debtor who is absent from Scotland and who after the date of sequestration of his estate fails, when required by the court, to come to Scotland for any purpose connected with the administration of his estate, shall be guilty of an offence.

(4) A debtor, or other person acting in his interest whether with or without his authority, who during the relevant period falsifies any document relating to the debtor's assets or his business or financial affairs, shall be guilty of an offence, unless the debtor or other person shows that he had no intention to mislead the . . . trustee, a commissioner or any creditor.

(5) If a debtor whose estate is sequestrated—

(a) knows that a person has falsified any document relating to the debtor's assets or his business or financial affairs; and

(b) fails, within one month of the date of acquiring such knowledge, to report his knowledge to the . . . trustee,

he shall be guilty of an offence.

(6) A person who is absolutely insolvent and who during the relevant period transfers anything to another person for an inadequate consideration or grants any unfair preference to any of his creditors shall be guilty of an offence, unless the transferor or grantor shows that he did not do so with intent to prejudice the creditors.

(7) A debtor who is engaged in trade or business shall be guilty of an offence if at any time in the period of one year ending with the date of sequestration of his estate, he pledges or disposes of, otherwise than in the ordinary course of his trade or business, any property which he has obtained on credit and has not paid for unless he shows that he did not intend to prejudice his creditors.

(8) . . .

(9) If a debtor, either alone or jointly with another person, obtains credit—

[(a) to the extent of [£2000] (or such other sum as may be prescribed) or more; or

(b) of any amount, where, at the time of obtaining credit, the debtor has debts amounting to £1,000 (or such other sum as may be prescribed) or more,]

without giving the person from whom he obtained it the relevant information about his status he shall be guilty of an offence.

[(9A) For the purposes of calculating an amount of—

(a) credit mentioned in subsection (9) above; or

(b) debts mentioned in paragraph (b) of that subsection,

no account shall be taken of any credit obtained or, as the case may be, any liability for charges in respect of—

(i) any of the supplies mentioned in section 70(4) of this Act; and

(ii) any council tax within the meaning of section 99(1) of the Local Government Finance Act 1992 (c 14).]

(10) For the purposes of subsection (9) above—

(a) "debtor" means—

(i) a debtor whose estate has been sequestrated, . . .

(ii) a person who has been adjudged bankrupt in England and Wales or Northern Ireland[; or

(iii) a person subject to a bankruptcy restrictions order, or a bankruptcy restrictions undertaking, made in England or Wales,]

and who, in [the case mentioned in sub-paragraph (i) or (ii) above], has not been discharged;

(b) the reference to the debtor obtaining credit includes a reference to a case where goods are hired to him under a hire-purchase agreement or agreed to be sold to him under a conditional sale agreement; and

[(c) the relevant information about the status of the debtor is the information that—

(i) his estate has been sequestrated and that he has not been discharged;

(ii) he is an undischarged bankrupt in England and Wales or Northern Ireland; or

(iii) he is subject to a bankruptcy restrictions order, or a bankruptcy restrictions undertaking, made in England or Wales,

as the case may be.]

(11) In this section—

(a) "the relevant period" means the period commencing one year immediately before the date of sequestration of the debtor's estate and ending with his discharge;

(b) references to intent to prejudice creditors shall include references to intent to prejudice an individual creditor.

[(11A) A person shall be guilty of an offence under subsection (1), (2), (4), (5), (6) or (7) above if that person does or, as the case may be, fails to do, in any place in England and Wales or Northern Ireland, anything which would, if done or, as the case may be, not done in Scotland, be an offence under the subsection in question.]

(12) A person convicted of any offence under this section shall be liable—

(a) on summary conviction, to a fine not exceeding the statutory maximum or—

(i) to imprisonment for a term not exceeding 3 months; or

(ii) if he has previously been convicted of an offence inferring dishonest appropriation of property or an attempt at such appropriation, to imprisonment for a term not exceeding 6 months,

or (in the case of either sub-paragraph) to both such fine and such imprisonment; or

(b) on conviction on indictment to a fine or—

(i) in the case of an offence under subsection (1), (2), (4) or (7) above to imprisonment for a term not exceeding 5 years,

(ii) in any other case to imprisonment for a term not exceeding 2 years. or (in the case of either sub-paragraph) to both such fine and such imprisonment.

NOTES

Repealed as noted at the beginning of this Act.

Sub-s (2): words in square brackets inserted by the Bankruptcy and Diligence etc (Scotland) Act 2007, s 24(1), (2), subject to transitional provisions and savings in SSI 2008/115, arts 5–7, 10, 15 at **[2.51]–[2.53]**, **[2.56]**, **[2.57]**.

Sub-s (4): word "permanent" (omitted) repealed by the Bankruptcy and Diligence etc (Scotland) Act 2007, s 226(2), Sch 6, Pt 1, subject to transitional provisions and savings in SSI 2008/115, arts 5–7, 10, 15 at **[2.51]–[2.53]**, **[2.56]**, **[2.57]**.

Sub-s (5): words "interim or permanent" omitted from para (b) repealed by the Bankruptcy and Diligence etc (Scotland) Act 2007, s 226(2), Sch 6, Pt 1, subject to transitional provisions and savings in SSI 2008/115, arts 5–7, 10, 15 at **[2.51]–[2.53]**, **[2.56]**, **[2.57]**.

Sub-s (8): repealed by the Bankruptcy and Diligence etc (Scotland) Act 2007, s 24(1), (3), subject to transitional provisions and savings in SSI 2008/115, arts 5–7, 10, 15 at **[2.51]–[2.53]**, **[2.56]**, **[2.57]**, and previously read as follows:

"(8) A debtor who is engaged in trade or business shall be guilty of an offence if at any time in the period of 2 years ending with the date of sequestration, he has failed to keep or preserve such records as are necessary to give a fair view of the state of his assets or his business and financial affairs and to explain his transactions, unless he shows that such failure was neither reckless nor dishonest:

Provided that a debtor shall not be guilty of an offence under this subsection if, at the date of sequestration, his unsecured liabilities did not exceed the prescribed amount; but, for the purposes of this proviso, if at any time the amount of a debt (or part of a debt) over which a security is held exceeds the value of the security, that debt (or part) shall be deemed at that time to be unsecured to the extent of the excess.".

Sub-s (9): paras (a), (b) substituted for original words "to the extent of £100 (or such other sum as may be prescribed) or more" by the Bankruptcy and Diligence etc (Scotland) Act 2007, s 24(1), (4), subject to transitional provisions and savings in SSI 2008/115, arts 5–7, 10, 15 at **[2.51]–[2.53]**, **[2.56]**, **[2.57]**; sum in square brackets in para (a) substituted for previous sum "£500" by the Bankruptcy and Debt Advice (Scotland) Act 2014, s 51, subject to transitional provisions and savings in SSI 2014/261, arts 4, 12 at **[2.91]**, **[2.99]**.

Sub-ss (9A), (11A): inserted by the Bankruptcy and Diligence etc (Scotland) Act 2007, s 24(1), (5), (8), subject to transitional provisions and savings in SSI 2008/115, arts 5–7, 10, 15 at **[2.51]–[2.53]**, **[2.56]**, **[2.57]**.

Sub-s (10): word "or" omitted from para (a)(i) repealed, para (a)(iii) and word immediately preceding it inserted, final words in square brackets in para (a) substituted for original words "either case", and para (c) substituted by the Bankruptcy and Diligence etc (Scotland) Act 2007, s 24(1), (6), (7), subject to transitional provisions and savings in SSI 2008/115, arts 5–7, 10, 15 at **[2.51]–[2.53]**, **[2.56]**, **[2.57]**. Para (c) previously read as follows:

"(c) the relevant information about the status of the debtor is the information that his estate has been sequestrated and that he has not received his discharge or, as the case may be, that he is an undischarged bankrupt in England and Wales or Northern Ireland.".

Regulations: the Bankruptcy (Scotland) Regulations 2008, SSI 2008/82 at **[16.262]**.

[5.162]

68 Summary proceedings

(1) [Subject to subsection 1A below,] summary proceedings for an offence under this Act may be commenced at any time within the period of [12] months after the date on which evidence sufficient in the opinion of the Lord Advocate to justify the proceedings comes to his knowledge.

[(1A) No such proceedings shall be commenced by virtue of this section more than three years after the commission of the offence.]

(2) Subsection (3) of [section 136 of the Criminal Procedure (Scotland) Act 1995] (date of commencement of summary proceedings) shall have effect for the purposes of [this section] as it has effect for the purposes of that section.

(3) For the purposes of subsection (1) above, a certificate of the Lord Advocate as to the date on which the evidence in question came to his knowledge is conclusive evidence of the date on which it did so.

NOTES

Repealed as noted at the beginning of this Act.

Sub-s (1): words in first pair of square brackets inserted and words in the second pair of square brackets substituted by the Bankruptcy (Scotland) Act 1993, s 11(3), Sch 1, para 27(1), (2), subject to s 12(6) thereof, at **[5.194]** and to the Bankruptcy (Scotland) Act 1993 Commencement and Savings Order 1993, SI 1993/438, arts 4, 5, at **[16.58]**, **[16.59]**.

Sub-s (1A): inserted by the Bankruptcy (Scotland) Act 1993, s 11(3), Sch 1, para 27(1), (3), subject to s 12(6) thereof, at **[5.194]** and to SI 1993/438, arts 4, 5, at **[16.58]**, **[16.59]**.

Sub-s (2): words in first pair of square brackets substituted by the Criminal Procedure (Consequential Provisions) (Scotland) Act 1995, s 5, Sch 4, para 58(5); words in second pair of square brackets substituted by the Bankruptcy (Scotland) Act 1993, s 11(3), Sch 1, para 27(1), (4), subject to s 12(6) thereof, at **[5.194]** and to SI 1993/438, arts 4, 5, at **[16.58]**, **[16.59]**.

[5.163]

69 [Outlays of insolvency practitioner in actings as interim trustee or trustee]

The Secretary of State may, by regulations, provide for the premium (or a proportionate part thereof) of any bond of caution or other security required, for the time being, to be given by an insolvency practitioner to be taken into account as part of the outlays of the insolvency practitioner in his actings as an interim trustee or . . . trustee.

NOTES

Repealed as noted at the beginning of this Act.

Section heading: substituted for original words "Outlays of interim and permanent trustee" by the Bankruptcy and Diligence etc (Scotland) Act 2007, s 36, Sch 1, paras 1, 58, subject to transitional provisions and savings in SSI 2008/115, arts 5–7, 10, 15 at **[2.51]**–**[2.53]**, **[2.56]**, **[2.57]**.

Word "permanent" (omitted) repealed by the Bankruptcy and Diligence etc (Scotland) Act 2007, s 226(2), Sch 6, Pt 1, subject to transitional provisions and savings in SSI 2008/115, arts 5–7, 10, 15 at **[2.51]**–**[2.53]**, **[2.56]**, **[2.57]**.

Regulations: the Bankruptcy (Scotland) Regulations 2008, SSI 2008/82 at **[16.262]**; the Bankruptcy (Scotland) Regulations 2014, SSI 2014/225 at **[16.267]**.

[5.164]

[69A Fees for the Accountant in Bankruptcy

The Secretary of State may prescribe—

(a) the fees and outlays to be payable to the Accountant in Bankruptcy in respect of the exercise of any of his functions under this Act [or the Insolvency Act 1986];

(b) the time and manner in which such fees and outlays are to be paid; and

(c) the circumstances, if any, in which the Accountant in Bankruptcy may allow exemption from payment or the remission or modification of payment of any fees or outlays payable or paid to him.]

NOTES

Inserted by the Bankruptcy (Scotland) Act 1993, s 8.

Repealed as noted at the beginning of this Act.

Words in square brackets in para (a) inserted by the Scotland Act 1998 (Consequential Modifications) (No 2) Order 1999, SI 1999/1820, art 4, Sch 2, Pt I, para 82 (1), (3).

Regulations: the Bankruptcy Fees (Scotland) Regulations 1993, SI 1993/486; the Protected Trust Deeds (Scotland) Regulations 2013, SSI 2013/318 at **[16.266]**; the Bankruptcy Fees (Scotland) Regulations 2014, SSI 2014/227 at **[16.269]**; the Bankruptcy Fees (Scotland) Revocation Regulations 2017, SSI 2017/97.

[5.165]

70 Supplies by utilities

(1) This section applies where on any day ("the relevant day")—

(a) sequestration is awarded in a case where [a debtor application was made],

(b) a warrant is granted under section 12(2) of this Act in a case where the petition was presented by a creditor or a trustee acting under a trust deed; or

(c) the debtor grants a trust deed,

and in this section "the office holder" means the interim trustee, the . . . trustee or the trustee acting under a trust deed, as the case may be.

(2) If a request falling within subsection (3) below is made for the giving after the relevant day of any of the supplies mentioned in subsection (4) below, the supplier—

(a) may make it a condition of the giving of the supply that the office holder personally guarantees the payment of any charges in respect of the supply; and

(b) shall not make it a condition of the giving of the supply, or do anything which has the effect of making it a condition of the giving of the supply, that any outstanding charges in respect of a supply given to the debtor before the relevant day are paid.

(3) A request falls within this subsection if it is made—

(a) by or with the concurrence of the office holder; and

(b) for the purposes of any business which is or has been carried on by or on behalf of the debtor.

(4) The supplies referred to in subsection (2) above are—
(a) a supply of gas by [a [gas supplier] within the meaning of Part I of the Gas Act 1986];
(b) a supply of electricity by [[an] [electricity supplier] within the meaning of Part I of the Electricity Act 1989];
(c) a supply of water by [Scottish Water];
[(d) a supply of communications services by a provider of a public electronic communications service.]

[(5) In subsection (4), "communications services" do not include electronic communications services to the extent that they are used to broadcast or otherwise transmit programme services (within the meaning of the Communications Act 2003).]

NOTES

Repealed as noted at the beginning of this Act.

Sub-s (1): words in square brackets in para (a) substituted for original words "the petition was presented by the debtor" and word "permanent" (omitted) repealed by the Bankruptcy and Diligence etc (Scotland) Act 2007, ss 36, 226(2), Sch 1, paras 1, 59, Sch 6, Pt 1, subject to transitional provisions and savings in SSI 2008/115, arts 5–7, 10, 15 at **[2.51]–[2.53]**, **[2.56]**, **[2.57]**.

Sub-s (4): words in first (outer) pair of square brackets in para (a) substituted by the Gas Act 1986, s 67(1), Sch 7, para 32, words in second (inner) pair of square brackets in para (a) substituted by the Gas Act 1995, s 16(1), Sch 4, para 13; in para (b) words in first (outer) pair of square brackets substituted by the Electricity Act 1989, s 112(1), Sch 16, para 32, words in third (inner) pair of square brackets substituted by the Utilities Act 2000, s 108, Sch 6, Pt III, para 46, and preceding word in square brackets consequently amended for grammatical purposes; words in square brackets in para (c) substituted by the Water Industry (Scotland) Act 2002, s 71(2), Sch 7, para 16; para (d) substituted by the Communications Act 2003, s 406(1), Sch 17, para 78(1), (2), for the purpose of enabling network and service functions and spectrum functions to be carried out during the transitional period by the Director General of Telecommunications and the Secretary of State respectively (see further s 408 of, and Sch 18 to, the 2003 Act and the Communications Act 2003 (Commencement No 1) Order 2003, SI 2003/1900); the original para (d) read as follows:

"(d) a supply of telecommunication services (within the meaning of the Telecommunications Act 1984) by a public telecommunications operator (within the meaning of that Act)".

Sub-s (5): substituted by the Communications Act 2003, s 406(1), Sch 17, para 78(1), (3), for the purpose noted to sub-s (4) above; the existing sub-s (5), as amended by the Broadcasting Act 1990, s 203(1), Sch 20, para 41, read as follows:

"(5) In subsection (4) above the reference to telecommunication services does not include a reference to [local delivery services within the meaning of Part II of the Broadcasting Act 1990].".

[5.166]

71 Edinburgh Gazette

The keeper of the Edinburgh Gazette shall, on each day of its publication, send a free copy of it to—
(a) the Accountant in Bankruptcy; and
(b) the petition department of the Court of Session.

NOTES

Repealed as noted at the beginning of this Act.

Repealed by the Bankruptcy and Debt Advice (Scotland) Act 2014, s 24(3), subject to transitional provisions and savings in SSI 2014/261, art 12 at **[2.99]**.

[5.167]

[71A Further duty of Accountant in Bankruptcy

The Accountant in Bankruptcy shall, on receiving any notice under section 109(1) of the Insolvency Act 1986 in relation to a community interest company, forward a copy of that notice to the Regulator of Community Interest Companies.]

NOTES

Inserted by the Companies (Audit, Investigations and Community Enterprise) Act 2004, s 59(2).

Repealed as noted at the beginning of this Act.

[5.168]

[71B Disqualification provisions: power to make orders

(1) The Scottish Ministers may make an order under this section in relation to a disqualification provision.

(2) A "disqualification provision" is a provision made by or under any enactment which disqualifies (whether permanently or temporarily and whether absolutely or conditionally) a relevant debtor or a class of relevant debtors from—
(a) being elected or appointed to an office or position;
(b) holding an office or position; or
(c) becoming or remaining a member of a body or group.

(3) In subsection (2) above, the reference to a provision which disqualifies a person conditionally includes a reference to a provision which enables him to be dismissed.

(4) An order under subsection (1) above may repeal or revoke the disqualification provision.

(5) An order under subsection (1) above may amend, or modify the effect of, the disqualification provision—
(a) so as to reduce the class of relevant debtors to whom the disqualification provision applies;
(b) so as to extend the disqualification provision to some or all individuals who are subject to a bankruptcy restrictions order;

(c) so that the disqualification provision applies only to some or all individuals who are subject to a bankruptcy restrictions order;
(d) so as to make the application of the disqualification provision wholly or partly subject to the discretion of a specified person, body or group.

(6) An order by virtue of subsection (5)(d) above may provide for a discretion to be subject to—
(a) the approval of a specified person or body;
(b) appeal to a specified person, body, court or tribunal.

(7) The Scottish Ministers may be specified for the purposes of subsection (5)(d) or (6)(a) or (b) above.

(8) In this section—
"bankruptcy restrictions order" includes—
(a) a bankruptcy restrictions undertaking;
(b) a bankruptcy restrictions order made under paragraph 1 of Schedule 4A to the Insolvency Act 1986 (c 45); and
(c) a bankruptcy restrictions undertaking entered into under paragraph 7 of that Schedule;
"relevant debtor" means a debtor—
(a) whose estate has been sequestrated;
(b) who has granted (or on whose behalf there has been granted) a trust deed;
(c) who has been adjudged bankrupt by a court in England and Wales or in Northern Ireland; or
(d) who, in England and Wales or in Northern Ireland, has made an agreement with his creditors for a composition in satisfaction of his debts or a scheme of arrangement of his affairs or for some other kind of settlement or arrangement.

(9) An order under this section—
(a) may make provision generally or for a specified purpose only;
(b) may make different provision for different purposes; and
(c) may make transitional, consequential or incidental provision.

(10) An order under this section—
(a) shall be made by statutory instrument; and
(b) shall not be made unless a draft has been laid before and approved by a resolution of the Scottish Parliament.]

NOTES

Inserted by the Bankruptcy and Diligence etc (Scotland) Act 2007, s 5, subject to transitional provisions and savings in SSI 2008/115, arts 5–7, 10, 15 at **[2.51]–[2.53]**, **[2.56]**, **[2.57]**.

Repealed as noted at the beginning of this Act.

Sub-s (8): in definition "bankruptcy restrictions order" para (a) repealed by the Bankruptcy and Debt Advice (Scotland) Act 2014, s 56(2), Sch 4, subject to transitional provisions and savings in SSI 2014/261, arts 4, 12 at **[2.91]**, **[2.99]**.

[5.169]

[71C Regulations: applications to Accountant in Bankruptcy etc

(1) The Scottish Ministers may, by regulations, make provision in relation to the procedure to be followed in relation to—
(a) an application to the Accountant in Bankruptcy under this Act,
(b) an application to the Accountant in Bankruptcy for a review under this Act,
(c) any other decision made by the Accountant in Bankruptcy under this Act.

(2) In this section "decision" includes any appointment, determination, direction, award, acceptance, rejection, adjudication, requirement, declaration, order or valuation made by the Accountant in Bankruptcy.

(3) Regulations under subsection (1) may in particular make provision for or in connection with—
(a) the procedure to be followed by the person making an application,
(b) the form of any report or other document that may be required for the purposes of an application or a decision,
(c) the form of a statement of undertakings that must be given by the debtor when making a debtor application,
(d) time limits applying in relation to the procedure,
(e) the procedure to be followed in connection with the production and recovery of documents relating to an application or a decision,
(f) the procedure to be followed (including provision about those entitled to participate) in determining an application or making a decision, and
(g) the procedure to be followed after an application is determined or a decision is made.

(4) Regulations under subsection (1) may—
(a) include such supplementary, incidental or consequential provision as the Scottish Ministers consider appropriate,
(b) modify any enactment (including this Act).]

NOTES

Commencement: 30 June 2014.

Inserted by the Bankruptcy and Debt Advice (Scotland) Act 2014, s 36.

Repealed as noted at the beginning of this Act.

Regulations: the Bankruptcy (Scotland) Regulations 2014, SSI 2014/225 at **[16.267]**; the Bankruptcy (Applications and Decisions) (Scotland) Regulations 2014, SSI 2014/226 at **[16.268]**; the Common Financial Tool etc (Scotland) Regulations 2014, SSI 2014/290; the Bankruptcy (Money Advice and Deduction from Income etc) (Scotland) Regulations 2014, SSI 2014/296 at **[16.284]**.

[5.170]
72 Regulations
[(1)] [Subject to subsection (2) below,] any power to make regulations under this Act shall be exercisable by statutory instrument subject to annulment in pursuance of a resolution of either House of Parliament . . .
[(1A) Regulations under this Act may make different provision for different cases or classes of case.]
[(2) No regulations such as are mentioned in subsection (3) below may be made unless a draft of the statutory instrument containing the regulations has been laid before, and approved by a resolution of, the Scottish Parliament.
(3) The regulations are—
(a) regulations made under—
(i) subsection (2B)(a) and (4) of section 5;
[(ia) section 5(2ZC),
(ib) section 5(2ZD),]
(ii) section 5A; and
[(iia) section 5B(5);]
[(iib) section 5C(2)(b),
(iic) section 5D(1),
(iid) section 32E(7),]
(iii) section 39A(4),
[(iv) section 71C(1) which contain provisions which add to, replace or omit any part of the text of an Act or an Act of the Scottish Parliament,
(v) paragraph 2(7) of Schedule A1,]
of this Act; and
(b) . . . regulations under paragraph 5 of Schedule 5 to this Act . . .]

NOTES
Repealed as noted at the beginning of this Act.
Existing provision renumbered as sub-s (1), words in square brackets inserted, and sub-ss (2), (3) added by the Bankruptcy and Diligence etc (Scotland) Act 2007, s 35; words omitted from sub-s (1) repealed by the Bankruptcy and Debt Advice (Scotland) Act 2014, s 56(2), Sch 4.
Sub-s (1A): inserted by the Bankruptcy and Debt Advice (Scotland) Act 2014, s 56(1), Sch 3, paras 2, 34(a).
Sub-s (3): sub-para (a)(iia) inserted and words omitted from para (b) repealed by the Home Owner and Debtor Protection (Scotland) Act 2010, s 13(1); sub-para (a)(ii) repealed and sub-para (a)(ia), (ib), (iib), (iic), (iid), (iv), (v) inserted by the Bankruptcy and Debt Advice (Scotland) Act 2014, s 56, Sch 3, paras 2, 34(b), Sch 4, subject to transitional provisions and savings (so far as relating to the repeal of sub-para (a)(ii)) in SSI 2014/261, arts 4, 12 at **[2.91]**, **[2.99]**.
Regulations: the Bankruptcy Fees (Scotland) Regulations 1993, SI 1993/486; the Protected Trust Deeds (Scotland) Regulations 2013, SSI 2013/318 at **[16.266]**; the Bankruptcy (Scotland) Regulations 2014, SSI 2014/225 at **[16.267]**; the Bankruptcy (Applications and Decisions) (Scotland) Regulations 2014, SSI 2014/226 at **[16.268]**; the Bankruptcy Fees (Scotland) Regulations 2014, SSI 2014/227 at **[16.269]**; the Bankruptcy (Money Advice and Deduction from Income etc) (Scotland) Regulations 2014, SSI 2014/296 at **[16.284]**; the Bankruptcy Fees (Scotland) Revocation Regulations 2017, SSI 2017/97.

[5.171]
[72ZA Modification of regulation making powers
Any power in any provision of this Act to make regulations may, insofar as that provision relates to a matter to which the EC Regulation applies, be exercised for the purpose of making provision in consequence of the EC Regulation.]

NOTES
Inserted by the Insolvency (Scotland) Regulations 2003, SI 2003/2109, regs 3, 18.
Repealed as noted at the beginning of this Act.

[5.172]
[72A Variation of references to time, money etc
For any reference in this Act to—
(a) a period of time;
(b) an amount of money; or
(c) a fraction,
there shall be substituted a reference to such other period or, as the case may be, amount or fraction as may be prescribed.]

NOTES
Inserted by the Bankruptcy (Scotland) Act 1993, s 11(3), Sch 1, para 28, subject to s 12(6) thereof, at **[5.194]** and to the Bankruptcy (Scotland) Act 1993 Commencement and Savings Order 1993, SI 1993/438, arts 4, 5, at **[16.58]**, **[16.59]**.
Repealed as noted at the beginning of this Act.
Regulations: the Bankruptcy (Applications and Decisions) (Scotland) Regulations 2014, SSI 2014/226 at **[16.268]**.

[5.173]
73 Interpretation
(1) In this Act, unless the context otherwise requires—
"Accountant in Bankruptcy" shall be construed in accordance with section 1 of this Act;
"accounting period" shall be construed in accordance with section [52(2)] of this Act;

"apparent insolvency" and "apparently insolvent" shall be construed in accordance with section 7 of this Act;

["appropriate bank or institution" means—

(a) the Bank of England;

(b) a person who has permission under Part 4 of the Financial Services and Markets Act 2000 to accept deposits,

(c) an EEA firm of the kind mentioned in paragraph 5(b) of Schedule 3 to that Act which has permission under paragraph 15 of that Schedule (as a result of qualifying for authorisation under paragraph 12 of that Schedule) to accept deposits, or

(d) a person who is exempt from the general prohibition in respect of accepting deposits as a result of an exemption order made under section 38(1) of that Act,

and the expressions in this definition must be read with section 22 of the Financial Services and Markets Act 2000, any relevant order under that section and Schedule 2 to that Act;]

"act and warrant" means an act and warrant issued under section 25(2) of, or paragraph 2(2) of Schedule 2 to, this Act;

"associate" shall be construed in accordance with section 74 of this Act;

["bankruptcy restrictions order" has the meaning given by section 56A(1) of this Act;

"bankruptcy restrictions undertaking" has the meaning given by section 56G(1) of this Act;]

"business" means the carrying on of any activity, whether for profit or not;

["centre of main interests" has the same meaning as in the EC Regulation;]

"commissioner", except in the expression "examining commissioner", shall be construed in accordance with section [4] of this Act;

["common financial tool" has the meaning given by section 5D(1),]

"court" means Court of Session or sheriff;

["creditor" includes a member State liquidator deemed to be a creditor under section 60A of this Act;]

["DAS register" has the meaning given by section 4A(4)(b),]

"date of sequestration" has the meaning assigned by section 12(4) of this Act;

"debtor" includes, without prejudice to the expression's generality, an entity whose estate may be sequestrated by virtue of section 6 of this Act, a deceased debtor or his executor or a person entitled to be appointed as executor to a deceased debtor;

["debtor application" means an application for sequestration made to the Accountant in Bankruptcy under sections 5(2)(a) [or (3)(a)] or 6(3)(a), (4)(a) or (6)(a) of this Act;]

["debtor contribution order" has the meaning given by section 32A(1),]

["debtor's contribution" has the meaning given by section 5D(1),]

["the EC Regulation" means Council Regulation (EC) No 1346/2000 of 29th May 2000 on insolvency proceedings;]

["enactment" includes an Act of the Scottish Parliament and any enactment comprised in subordinate legislation under such an Act;]

["establishment" has the meaning given by Article 2(h) of the EC Regulation;]

"examination" means a public examination under section 45 of this Act or a private examination under section 44 of this Act;

"examining commissioner" shall be construed in accordance with section 46(2) of this Act;

"interim trustee" shall be construed in accordance with section [2(5)] of this Act;

. . .

["main proceedings" means proceedings opened in accordance with Article 3(1) of the EC Regulation and falling within the definition of insolvency proceedings in Article 2(a) of the EC Regulation and—

(a) in relation to England and Wales and Scotland, set out in Annex A to the EC Regulation under the heading "United Kingdom"; and

(b) in relation to another member State, set out in Annex A to the EC Regulation under the heading relating to that member State;]

["member State liquidator" means a person falling within the definition of liquidator in Article 2(b) of the EC Regulation appointed in proceedings to which it applies in a member State other than the United Kingdom;]

["money adviser" has the meaning given by section 5C(2),]

"ordinary debt" shall be construed in accordance with section 51(1)(f) of this Act;

["original trustee" shall be construed in accordance with section 24(1)(a) of this Act;]

. . .

"postponed debt" has the meaning assigned by section 51(3) of this Act;

"preferred debt" has the meaning assigned by section 51(2) of this Act;

"prescribed" means prescribed by regulations made by the Secretary of State;

["protected trust deed" means a trust deed which has been granted protected status in accordance with regulations made under paragraph 5 of Schedule 5 to this Act;]

"qualified creditor" and "qualified creditors" shall be construed in accordance with section 5(4) of this Act;

["qualified to act as an insolvency practitioner" is to be construed in accordance with section 390 of the Insolvency Act 1986,]

Provided that, until the coming into force of that section the expression shall instead mean satisfying such requirements (which, without prejudice to the generality of this definition, may include requirements as to the finding of caution) as may be prescribed for the purposes of this Act;

"register of insolvencies" has the meaning assigned by section [1A(1)(b)] of this Act;

"relevant person" has the meaning assigned by section 44(1)(b) of this Act;

["replacement trustee" shall be construed in accordance with section 24(1)(b) of this Act;]

["secondary proceedings" means proceedings opened in accordance with Articles 3(2) and 3(3) of the EC Regulation and falling within the definition of winding-up proceedings in Article 2(c) of the EC Regulation, and—

(a) in relation to England and Wales and Scotland, set out in Annex B to the EC Regulation under the heading "United Kingdom"; and

(b) in relation to another member State, set out in Annex B to the EC Regulation under the heading relating to that member State;]

"secured creditor" means a creditor who holds a security for his debt over any part of the debtor's estate;

"security" means any security, heritable or moveable, or any right of lien, retention or preference;

"sederunt book" means the sederunt book maintained under section 3(1)(e) of this Act;

["sequestration proceedings" includes a debtor application and analogous expressions shall be construed accordingly;]

. . .

["statement of assets and liabilities" means a document (including a copy of a document) in such form as may be prescribed containing—

(i) a list of the debtor's assets and liabilities;

(ii) a list of his income and expenditure; and

(iii) such other information as may be prescribed;]

["statement of undertakings" means the statement of debtor undertakings sent to the debtor under section 2(8) or, in the case of a debtor application, given by the debtor when making the application,]

. . .

"statutory meeting" has the meaning assigned by [section 20A] of this Act;

["temporary administrator" means a temporary administrator referred to by Article 38 of the EC Regulation;]

["territorial proceedings" means proceedings opened in accordance with Articles 3(2) and 3(4) of the EC Regulation and falling within the definition of insolvency proceedings in Article 2(a) of the EC Regulation, and—

(a) in relation to England and Wales and Scotland, set out in Annex A to the EC Regulation under the heading "United Kingdom"; and

(b) in relation to another member State, set out in Annex A to the EC Regulation under the heading relating to that member State.]

["trust deed" has the meaning assigned by section 5(4A) of this Act;]

["trustee" means trustee in the sequestration;

"trustee vote" shall be construed in accordance with section 24(1) of this Act;] and

"unfair preference" means a preference created as is mentioned in subsection (1) of section 36 of this Act by a transaction to which subsection (4) of that section applies.

(2) Any reference in this Act to a debtor being absolutely insolvent shall be construed as a reference to his liabilities being greater than his assets, and any reference to a debtor's estate being absolutely insolvent shall be construed accordingly.

(3) Any reference in this Act to value of the creditors is, in relation to any matter, a reference to the value of their claims as accepted for the purposes of that matter.

(4) Any reference in this Act to "the creditors" in the context of their giving consent or doing any other thing shall, unless the context otherwise requires, be construed as a reference to the majority in value of such creditors as vote in that context at a meeting of creditors.

(5) Any reference in this Act to any of the following acts by a creditor barring the effect of any enactment or rule of law relating to the limitation of actions in any part of the United Kingdom, namely—

(a) the presentation of a petition for sequestration;

(b) the concurrence in [a debtor application]; and

(c) the submission of a claim, shall be construed as a reference to that Act having the same effect, for the purposes of any such enactment or rule of law, as an effective acknowledgement of the creditor's claim; and any reference in this Act to any such enactment shall not include a reference to an enactment which implements or gives effect to any international agreement or obligation.

[(6) Any reference in this Act, howsoever expressed, to the time when a petition for sequestration is presented shall be construed as a reference to the time when the petition is received by the [sheriff clerk].]

[(6A) Any reference in this Act, howsoever expressed, to the time when a debtor application is made shall be construed as a reference to the time when the application is received by the Accountant in Bankruptcy.]

NOTES

Repealed as noted at the beginning of this Act.

Sub-s (1): words in square brackets in definitions "accounting period", "register of insolvencies" and "statutory meeting" and the whole of the definition "trust deed" substituted, definition "list of interim trustees" repealed, and definition "statement of assets and liabilities" inserted, by the Bankruptcy (Scotland) Act 1993, s 11(3), (4), Sch 1, para 29(1)–(6), subject to s 12(6) thereof, at **[5.194]** and to the Bankruptcy (Scotland) Act 1993 Commencement and Savings Order 1993, SI 1993/438, arts 4, 5, at **[16.58]**, **[16.59]**;

definition "appropriate bank or institution" substituted by the Financial Services and Markets Act 2000 (Consequential Amendments and Repeals) Order 2001, SI 2001/3649, art 225;

definitions "bankruptcy restrictions order", "bankruptcy restrictions undertaking", "debtor application", "enactment", "original trustee", "replacement trustee", "sequestration proceedings", "trustee" and "trustee vote" inserted, figure in square brackets in definition "interim trustee" substituted for original figure "2", and definition "permanent trustee" repealed by the Bankruptcy and Diligence etc (Scotland) Act 2007, ss 36, 226(1), Sch 1, paras 1, 60(1), (2), Sch 6, Pt 1, subject to transitional provisions and savings in SSI 2008/115, arts 5–7, 10, 15 at **[2.51]–[2.53]**, **[2.56]**, **[2.57]**; definition "permanent trustee" previously read as follows:

""permanent trustee" shall be construed in accordance with section 3 of this Act;";

definition "bankruptcy restrictions undertaking" repealed, in definition "commissioner" figure in square brackets substituted for original figure "30(1)", definitions "common financial tool", "DAS register", "debtor contribution order", "debtor's contribution", "money adviser", "statement of undertakings" inserted, words in square brackets in definition "debtor application" inserted, and definition "qualified to act as an insolvency practitioner" substituted, by the Bankruptcy and Debt Advice (Scotland) Act 2014, s 56, Sch 3, paras 2, 35, Sch 4, subject to transitional provisions and savings in SSI 2014/261, arts 4, 12 at **[2.91]**, **[2.99]**;

definitions "centre of main interests", "creditor", "the EC Regulation", "establishment", "main proceedings", "member State liquidator", "secondary proceedings", "temporary administrator" and "territorial proceedings" inserted by the Insolvency (Scotland) Regulations 2003, SI 2003/2109, regs 3, 19; definition "protected trust deed" substituted by the Bankruptcy and Diligence etc (Scotland) Act 2007, s 20(2); definitions "standard scale" and "statutory maximum" repealed by the Statute Law (Repeals) Act 1993.

Sub-s (5): words in square brackets in para (b) substituted for original words "such a petition" by the Bankruptcy and Diligence etc (Scotland) Act 2007, s 36, Sch 1, paras 1, 60(1), (3), subject to transitional provisions and savings in SSI 2008/115, arts 5–7, 10, 15 at **[2.51]–[2.53]**, **[2.56]**, **[2.57]**.

Sub-s (6): added by the Bankruptcy (Scotland) Act 1993, s 11(3), Sch 1, para 29(1), (7), subject to s 12(6) thereof, at **[5.194]** and to SI 1993/438, arts 4, 5, at **[16.58]**, **[16.59]**; words in square brackets substituted for original words "clerk of the court" by the Bankruptcy and Diligence etc (Scotland) Act 2007, s 36, Sch 1, paras 1, 60(1), (4), subject to transitional provisions and savings in SSI 2008/115, arts 5–7, 10, 15 at **[2.51]–[2.53]**, **[2.56]**, **[2.57]**.

Sub-s (6A): inserted by the Bankruptcy and Diligence etc (Scotland) Act 2007, s 36, Sch 1, paras 1, 60(1), (5), subject to transitional provisions and savings in SSI 2008/115, arts 5–7, 10, 15 at **[2.51]–[2.53]**, **[2.56]**, **[2.57]**.

Insolvency Act 1985: largely repealed by the combined effect of the Insolvency Act 1986, s 438, Sch 12, and the Company Directors Disqualification Act 1986, s 23(2), Sch 4.

Regulations: the Bankruptcy Fees (Scotland) Regulations 1993, SI 1993/486; the Bankruptcy (Scotland) Regulations 2008, SSI 2008/82 at **[16.262]**; the Bankruptcy (Scotland) Regulations 2014, SSI 2014/225 at **[16.267]**.

[5.174]

74 Meaning of "associate"

(1) Subject to subsection (7) below, for the purposes of this Act any question whether a person is an associate of another person shall be determined in accordance with the following provisions of this section (any reference, whether in those provisions or in regulations under the said subsection (7), to a person being an associate of another person being taken to be a reference to their being associates of each other).

(2) A person is an associate of an individual if that person is the individual's [husband, wife or civil partner], or is a relative, or the [husband, wife or civil partner] of a relative, of the individual or of the individual's [husband, wife or civil partner].

(3) A person is an associate of any person with whom he is in partnership, [and of any person who is an associate of any person with whom he is in partnership;] and a firm is an associate of any person who is a member of the firm.

(4) For the purposes of this section a person is a relative of an individual if he is that individual's brother, sister, uncle, aunt, nephew, niece, lineal ancestor or lineal descendant treating—

(a) any relationship of the half blood as a relationship of the whole blood and the stepchild or adopted child of any person as his child; *and*

(b) an illegitimate child as the legitimate child of his mother and reputed father,

and references in this section to a [husband, wife or civil partner] include a former [husband, wife or civil partner] and a reputed [husband, wife or civil partner].

(5) A person is an associate of any person whom he employs or by whom he is employed; and for the purposes of this subsection any director or other officer of a company shall be treated as employed by that company.

[(5A) A company is an associate of another company—

(a) if the same person has control of both, or a person has control of one and persons who are his associates, or he and persons who are his associates, have control of the other; or

(b) if a group of two or more persons has control of each company, and the groups either consist of the same persons or could be regarded as consisting of the same persons by treating (in one or more cases) a member of either group as replaced by a person of whom he is an associate.

(5B) A company is an associate of another person if that person has control of it or if that person and persons who are his associates together have control of it.

(5C) For the purposes of this section a person shall be taken to have control of a company if—

(a) the directors of the company or of another company which has control of it (or any of them) are accustomed to act in accordance with his directions or instructions; or

(b) he is entitled to exercise, or control the exercise of, one third or more of the voting power at any general meeting of the company or of another company which has control of it,

and where two or more persons together satisfy either of the above conditions, they shall be taken to have control of the company.]

(6) [In subsections (5), (5A), (5B) and (5C) above,] "company" includes any body corporate (whether incorporated in Great Britain or elsewhere).

(7) The Secretary of State may by regulations—

(a) amend the foregoing provisions of this section so as to provide further categories of persons who, for the purposes of this Act, are to be associates of other persons; and

(b) provide that any or all of subsections (2) to (6) above (or any subsection added by virtue of paragraph (a) above) shall cease to apply, whether in whole or in part, or shall apply subject to such modifications as he may specify in the regulations;

and he may in the regulations make such incidental or transitional provision as he considers appropriate.

NOTES

Repealed as noted at the beginning of this Act.

Sub-s (2): words in square brackets substituted by the Civil Partnership Act 2004, s 261(2), Sch 28, para 40.

Sub-s (3): words in square brackets substituted by the Bankruptcy (Scotland) Regulations 2008, SSI 2008/82, reg 8(1), (2).

Sub-s (4): para (b) and word "and" immediately preceding it repealed by the Bankruptcy and Debt Advice (Scotland) Act 2014, s 56(2), Sch 4, subject to transitional provisions and savings in SSI 2014/261, arts 4, 12 at **[2.91]**, **[2.99]**; words in square brackets substituted by the Civil Partnership Act 2004, s 261(2), Sch 28, para 40.

Sub-ss (5A)–(5C): inserted by SSI 2008/82, reg 8(1), (3).

Sub-s (6): words in square brackets substituted by SSI 2008/82, reg 8(1), (4).

Modification: this section is modified in its application for the purposes of the Pensions Act 1995, s 40, by the Occupational Pension Schemes (Investment) Regulations 2005, SI 2005/3378, reg 10(2), and for the purposes of the Pensions Act 1995, s 23(3)(b) at **[17.117]**, and ss 27, 28, by s 123(2), (3) of the 1995 Act.

Regulations: the Bankruptcy (Scotland) Regulations 2008, SSI 2008/82 at **[16.262]**.

[5.175]

75 Amendments, repeals and transitional provisions

(1) Subject to subsection (3) below—

(a) the enactments mentioned in Part I of Schedule 7 to this Act shall have effect subject to the amendments respectively specified in that Schedule, being amendments consequential on the provisions of this Act;

(b) Part II of that Schedule, which re-enacts certain provisions of the Bankruptcy (Scotland) Act 1913 repealed by this Act, shall have effect.

(2) The enactments set out in columns 1 and 2 of Schedule 8 to this Act are, subject to subsection (3) below, hereby repealed to the extent specified in the third column of that Schedule.

(3) Subject to subsections (4) and (5) below, nothing in this Act shall affect any of the enactments repealed or amended by this Act in their operation in relation to a sequestration as regards which the award was made before the coming into force of this section.

(4) Where a debtor's estate has been sequestrated before the coming into force of this section but he has not been discharged, the debtor shall be discharged on the expiry of—

(a) 2 years after such coming into force; or

(b) 3 years after the date of sequestration,

whichever expires later:

Provided that, not later than 3 months before the date on which the debtor is due to be discharged under this subsection, the trustee in the sequestration or any creditor may apply to the sheriff for a deferment of that discharge; and subsections (4) to (8) of section 54 of this Act shall apply in relation to that application by the trustee as they apply in relation to an application under subsection (3) of that section . . .

(5) Section 63 of this Act shall apply in a case where before the coming into force of this section sequestration of a debtor's estate has been awarded under the Bankruptcy (Scotland) Act 1913 but the debtor has not yet been discharged, subject to the following modifications—

(a) in subsections (1)(a) and (2)(c) for the words "this Act" there shall be substituted the words "the Bankruptcy (Scotland) Act 1913";

(b) . . . and

(c) in subsection (2)(b) for the words "24 of this Act" there shall be substituted the words "64 of the Bankruptcy (Scotland) Act 1913".

(6) The apparent insolvency of a debtor may be constituted for the purposes of this Act notwithstanding that the circumstance founded upon to constitute the apparent insolvency occurred on a date before the coming into force of section 7 of this Act; and, for those purposes, the apparent insolvency shall be deemed to have been constituted on that date:

Provided that apparent insolvency shall be constituted by virtue of this subsection only on grounds which would have constituted notour bankruptcy under the Bankruptcy (Scotland) Act 1913.

(7) Where a debtor whose estate is sequestrated after the commencement of this subsection is liable, by virtue of a transaction entered into before that date, to pay royalties or a share of the profits to any person in respect of any copyright or interest in copyright comprised in the sequestrated estate, section 102 of the Bankruptcy (Scotland) Act 1913 (trustee's powers in relation to copyright) shall apply in relation to the . . . trustee as it applied before its repeal in relation to a trustee in bankruptcy under the said Act of 1913.

(8) Where sequestration of a debtor's estate is awarded under this Act a person shall not be guilty of an offence under any provision of this Act in respect of anything done before the date of commencement of that provision but, notwithstanding the repeal by this Act of the Bankruptcy (Scotland) Act 1913, he shall be guilty of an offence under that Act in respect of anything done before that date which would have been an offence under that Act if the award of sequestration had been made under that Act.

(9) Unless the context otherwise requires, any reference in any enactment or document to notour bankruptcy, or to a person being notour bankrupt, shall be construed as a reference to apparent insolvency, or to a person being apparently insolvent, within the meaning of section 7 of this Act.

(10) Unless the context otherwise requires, any reference in any enactment or document to a person's estate being sequestrated under the Bankruptcy (Scotland) Act 1913 shall be construed as, or as including, a reference to its being sequestrated under this Act; and analogous references shall be construed accordingly.
(11) Unless the context otherwise requires, any reference in any enactment or document to a trustee in sequestration or to a trustee in bankruptcy shall be construed as a reference to a . . . trustee, within the meaning of this Act; and analogous expressions shall be construed accordingly.
(12) Unless the context otherwise requires, any reference in any enactment or document—
(a) to a "gratuitous alienation" shall be construed as including a reference to an alienation challengeable under section 34(1) of this Act or under section 615A(1) of the Companies Act 1985;
(b) to a "fraudulent preference" or to an "unfair preference" shall be construed as including a reference to—
(i) an unfair preference within the meaning of this Act;
(ii) a preference created as is mentioned in subsection (1) of section 36 of this Act (as applied by section 615B of the said Act of 1985), by a transaction to which subsection (4) of the said section 36 (as so applied) applies.

NOTES

Repealed as noted at the beginning of this Act.

Sub-s (4): words "by the permanent trustee" (omitted) repealed by the Bankruptcy and Diligence etc (Scotland) Act 2007, s 226(2), Sch 6, Pt 1, subject to transitional provisions and savings in SSI 2008/115, arts 5–7, 10, 15 at **[2.51]–[2.53]**, **[2.56]**, **[2.57]**.

Sub-s (5): para (b) repealed by the Bankruptcy and Diligence etc (Scotland) Act 2007, s 226(2), Sch 6, Pt 1, subject to transitional provisions and savings in SSI 2008/115, arts 5–7, 10, 15 at **[2.51]–[2.53]**, **[2.56]**, **[2.57]**, and previously read as follows:

"(b) in subsections (2)(b) and (4) the word "permanent" shall be omitted;"

Sub-s (7): word "permanent" (omitted) repealed by the Bankruptcy and Diligence etc (Scotland) Act 2007, s 226(2), Sch 6, Pt 1, subject to transitional provisions and savings in SSI 2008/115, arts 5–7, 10, 15 at **[2.51]–[2.53]**, **[2.56]**, **[2.57]**.

Sub-s (11): words "permanent trustee, or in a case where no permanent trustee has been elected or appointed an interim" (omitted) repealed by the Bankruptcy and Diligence etc (Scotland) Act 2007, s 226(2), Sch 6, Pt 1, subject to transitional provisions and savings in SSI 2008/115, arts 5–7, 10, 15 at **[2.51]–[2.53]**, **[2.56]**, **[2.57]**.

[5.176]
76 Receipts and expenses
(1) Any—
(a) payments received by the Secretary of State under section 58(3) of this Act; or
(b) amounts handed over to him in accordance with section 53 of this Act by virtue of the insertion provided for in paragraph 9 of Schedule 2 to this Act,
shall be paid by him into the Consolidated Fund.
(2) There shall be paid out of moneys provided by Parliament—
(a) any amount of outlays and remuneration payable in accordance with section 53 of this Act by virtue of the insertion mentioned in subsection (1)(b) above;
(b) any administrative expenses incurred by the Secretary of State under this Act; and
(c) any increase attributable to this Act in the sums so payable under any other Act.

NOTES

Repealed as noted at the beginning of this Act.

[5.177]
77 Crown application
The application of this Act to the Crown is to the Crown as creditor only.

NOTES

Repealed as noted at the beginning of this Act.

[5.178]
78 Short title, commencement and extent
(1) This Act may be cited as the Bankruptcy (Scotland) Act 1985.
(2) This Act, except this section, shall come into force on such day as the Secretary of State may by order made by statutory instrument appoint; and different days may be so appointed for different purposes and for different provisions.
(3) An order under subsection (2) above may contain such transitional provisions and savings as appear to the Secretary of State necessary or expedient in connection with the provisions brought into force (whether wholly or partly) by the order.
(4) Without prejudice to section 75(3) to (5) of this Act, this Act applies to sequestrations as regards which the petition—
(a) is presented on or after the date of coming into force of section 5 of this Act; or
(b) was presented before, but in respect of which no award of sequestration has been made by, that date.
(5) This Act, except the provisions mentioned in subsection (6) below, extends to Scotland only.

(6) The provisions referred to in subsection (5) above are sections 8(5), 22(8) (including that subsection as applied by section 48(7)), 46, 55 and 73(5), paragraph 16(b) of Schedule 4 and paragraph 3 of Schedule 5.

NOTES

Repealed as noted at the beginning of this Act.

Orders: the Bankruptcy (Scotland) Act 1985 (Commencement) Order 1985, SI 1985/1924; the Bankruptcy (Scotland) Act 1985 (Commencement) Order 1986, SI 1986/78; the Bankruptcy (Scotland) Act 1985 (Commencement No 2) Order 1986, SI 1986/1913.

SCHEDULES

[SCHEDULE A1
DEBTOR TO WHOM SECTION 5(2ZA) APPLIES: APPLICATION OF ACT

(introduced by section 5(2ZE))

Modification of certain provisions of Act

[5.179]

1 (1) Where section 5(2ZA) applies in relation to a debtor, this Act applies subject to the modifications mentioned in sub-paragraphs (2) to (6).

(2) Section 3(1) applies as if paragraphs (e) and (f) were omitted.

(3) Section 20 applies as if for subsection (1) there were substituted—

"(1) This section applies where the Accountant in Bankruptcy receives by virtue of section 5(6A) the statement of assets and liabilities in relation to a debtor to whom section 5(2ZA) applies.

(1A) As soon as practicable, the Accountant in Bankruptcy must prepare a statement of the debtor's affairs so far as within the knowledge of the Accountant in Bankruptcy stating that, because section 5(2ZA) applies to the debtor, no claims may be submitted by creditors under section 22 or 48.

(1B) The Accountant in Bankruptcy must send a copy of the statement prepared under subsection (1A) to every known creditor of the debtor.".

(4) Section 43A applies as if for subsection (2) there were substituted—

"(2) The Accountant in Bankruptcy may at any time before the discharge of the debtor require the debtor to give an account in writing, in such form as may be prescribed, of the debtor's current state of affairs.".

(5) Section 58A applies as if—

(a) subsections (3) to (4C) and (7)(a) were omitted, and

(b) for subsection (5) there were substituted—

"(5) The debtor or any creditor may, before the expiry of the period of 14 days beginning with the day on which the debtor is discharged under section 54C(1), appeal to the sheriff against the discharge of the Accountant in Bankruptcy in respect of the Accountant in Bankruptcy's actings as trustee.".

(6) Sections 21A, 22, 23, 24, 25, 26 to 27, 48, 52 and 62(2A) do not apply.

Accountant in Bankruptcy's duty to consider whether paragraph 1 should cease to apply

2 (1) This paragraph applies where paragraph 1 applies in relation to a debtor.

(2) If the Accountant in Bankruptcy considers that the circumstances mentioned in any of sub-paragraphs (3) to (6) apply in relation to the debtor, the Accountant in Bankruptcy must consider whether paragraph 1 should cease to apply in relation to the debtor.

(3) The circumstances are—

(a) the Accountant in Bankruptcy becomes aware that the debtor application submitted under section 5 contains an error, and

(b) the nature of the error is such that the debtor was not at that time a debtor to whom section 5(2ZA) applies.

(4) The circumstances are—

(a) the Accountant in Bankruptcy becomes aware that the debtor application submitted under section 5 deliberately misrepresents or fails to state a fact that was the case at the time of the application, and

(b) the nature of the misrepresentation or the omission of the fact is such that the debtor was not at that time a debtor to whom section 5(2ZA) applies.

(5) The circumstances are that, at any time after the date on which the debtor application is made—

(a) the total value of the debtor's assets (leaving out of account any liabilities and any assets that would not vest in a trustee under section 33(1)) exceeds £5000 (or such other amount as may be prescribed), or

(b) the Accountant in Bankruptcy assesses the debtor under the common financial tool as being able to make a contribution.

(6) The circumstances are that, at any time after the date of sequestration—

(a) the Accountant in Bankruptcy is not satisfied that the debtor has co-operated with the trustee, and
(b) the Accountant in Bankruptcy considers that it would be of financial benefit to the estate of the debtor and in the interests of the creditors if paragraph 1 were to cease to have effect.

(7) The Scottish Ministers may by regulations modify this paragraph—
(a) by modifying the circumstances in which paragraph 1 ceases to have effect,
(b) in consequence of any modification made under paragraph (a).

Procedure where Accountant in Bankruptcy considers paragraph 1 should cease to apply

3 (1) If the Accountant in Bankruptcy considers under paragraph 2(2) that paragraph 1 should cease to apply in relation to a debtor, the Accountant in Bankruptcy must notify the debtor of that fact and the matters mentioned in sub-paragraph (2).

(2) The matters are—
(a) the circumstances mentioned in paragraph 2 which the Accountant in Bankruptcy considers apply in relation to the debtor, and
(b) that the debtor may make representations to the Accountant in Bankruptcy within the period of 14 days beginning with the giving of notification under sub-paragraph (1).

(3) On the expiry of the period mentioned in sub-paragraph (2)(b) and after having taken into account any representations made by the debtor under that sub-paragraph, the Accountant in Bankruptcy must decide whether paragraph 1 should cease to apply in relation to the debtor.

(4) If the Accountant in Bankruptcy decides that paragraph 1 should cease to apply in relation to the debtor, the Accountant in Bankruptcy must, as soon as practicable after reaching that decision, give notice in writing to the debtor of the decision and the effect of it.

Debtor's right of appeal against decision under paragraph 3

4 (1) This paragraph applies where the Accountant in Bankruptcy gives notice to a debtor under paragraph 3(4).

(2) The debtor may appeal to the sheriff against the decision.

(3) An appeal must be lodged not later than 14 days after the day on which notice is given.

(4) If the sheriff grants the appeal, paragraph 1 continues to apply in relation to the debtor.

(5) If the sheriff refuses the appeal or if it is abandoned or withdrawn, paragraph 1 ceases to apply in relation to the debtor.

Decision that paragraph 1 ceases to have effect: modification of certain provisions of Act

5 (1) Where paragraph 1 ceases to have effect in relation to a debtor, this Act applies subject to sub-paragraphs (2) to (4).

(2) The debtor must send to the trustee a statement of assets and liabilities—
(a) where no appeal is taken under paragraph 4, before the expiry of the period of 7 days beginning with the expiry of the period during which an appeal may be made under that paragraph,
(b) where an appeal is refused or, as the case may be, abandoned or withdrawn, before the expiry of the period of 7 days beginning with the day on which notice is given of the outcome of the appeal or, as the case may be, its abandonment or withdrawal.

(3) Section 21A applies as if in subsection (2), for "sequestration is awarded" there were substituted "paragraph 1 of Schedule A1 ceases to have effect in relation to the debtor".

(4) Section 43A applies as if for subsection (2) there were substituted—

"(2) The trustee must require the debtor to give an account in writing, in such form as may be prescribed, of the debtor's current state of affairs—
(a) before the expiry of the period of 60 days beginning with the day on which paragraph 1 of Schedule A1 ceases to have effect in relation to the debtor,
(b) on the expiry of the period of 6 months beginning with the day on which the account is given under paragraph (a), and
(c) on the expiry of each subsequent period of 6 months.".]

NOTES

Commencement: 30 June 2014 (for the purpose of making regulations); 1 April 2015 (otherwise).

Schedule inserted by the Bankruptcy and Debt Advice (Scotland) Act 2014, s 5(2), Sch 1, subject to transitional provisions and savings in SSI 2014/261, arts 4, 12 at **[2.91]**, **[2.99]**.

Repealed as noted at the beginning of this Act.

SCHEDULE 1
DETERMINATION OF AMOUNT OF CREDITOR'S CLAIM

Sections 5(5) and 22(9)

Amount which may be claimed generally

[5.180]

1. (1) Subject to the provisions of this Schedule, the amount in respect of which a creditor shall be entitled to claim shall be the accumulated sum of principal and any interest which is due on the debt as at the date of sequestration.

(2) If a debt does not depend on a contingency but would not be payable but for the sequestration until after the date of sequestration, the amount of the claim shall be calculated as if the debt were payable on the date of sequestration but subject to the deduction of interest at the rate specified in section 51(7) of this Act from the said date until the date for payment of the debt.

(3) In calculating the amount of his claim, a creditor shall deduct any discount (other than any discount for payment in cash) which is allowable by contract or course of dealing between the creditor and the debtor or by the usage of trade.

Claims for aliment and periodical allowance on divorce

2. (1) A person entitled to aliment, however arising, from a living debtor as at the date of sequestration, or from a deceased debtor immediately before his death, shall not be entitled to include in the amount of his claim—

(a) any unpaid aliment for any period before the date of sequestration unless the amount of the aliment has been quantified by court decree or by any legally binding obligation which is supported by evidence in writing, and,

[(i)] in the case of spouses (or, where the aliment is payable to a divorced person in respect of a child, former spouses)[, or

(ii) in the case of civil partners (or, where the aliment is payable to a former civil partner in respect of a child after dissolution of a civil partnership, former civil partners),]

they were living apart during that period;

(b) any aliment for any period after the date of sequestration.

(2) Sub-paragraph (1) above shall apply to a periodical allowance payable on divorce [or on dissolution of a civil partnership]—

(a) by virtue of a court order; or

(b) under any legally binding obligation which is supported by evidence in writing, as it applies to aliment and as if for the words from "in the case"[, where they first occur] to "they" there were substituted the words "the payer and payee".

Debts depending on contingency

3. (1) Subject to sub-paragraph (2) below, the amount which a creditor shall be entitled to claim shall not include a debt in so far as its existence or amount depends upon a contingency.

(2) On an application by the creditor—

(a) to the . . . trustee; or

(b) if there is no . . . trustee, to the [Accountant in Bankruptcy],

the . . . trustee or [Accountant in Bankruptcy] shall put a value on the debt in so far as it is contingent, and the amount in respect of which the creditor shall then be entitled to claim shall be that value but no more; and, where the contingent debt is an annuity, a cautioner may not then be sued for more than that value.

[(3) An interested person may apply to the Accountant in Bankruptcy for a review of a valuation under sub-paragraph (2) by the trustee.

(4) An application under sub-paragraph (3) must be made before the expiry of the period of 14 days beginning with the day of the valuation.

(5) If an application under subsection (3) is made, the Accountant in Bankruptcy must—

(a) take into account any representations made by an interested person before the expiry of the period of 21 days beginning with the day on which the application is made, and

(b) confirm or vary the valuation before the expiry of the period of 28 days beginning with the day on which the application is made.

(6) An interested person may appeal to the sheriff against a decision by the Accountant in Bankruptcy under subsection (5)(b) before the expiry of the period of 14 days beginning with the day of the decision.

(7) The Accountant in Bankruptcy may refer a case to the sheriff for a direction before making a decision under sub-paragraph (5)(b).

(8) An appeal to the sheriff under sub-paragraph (6) may not be made in relation to a matter on which the Accountant in Bankruptcy has applied to the sheriff for a direction under sub-paragraph (7).]

Debts due under composition contracts

4. Where in the course of a sequestration the debtor is discharged following approval by the sheriff of a composition offered by the debtor but the sequestration is subsequently revived, the amount in respect of which a creditor shall be entitled to claim shall be the same amount as if the composition had not been so approved less any payment already made to him under the composition contract.

Secured debts

5. (1) In calculating the amount of his claim, a secured creditor shall deduct the value of any security as estimated by him—

Provided that if he surrenders, or undertakes in writing to surrender, a security for the benefit of the debtor's estate, he shall not be required to make a deduction of the value of that security.

(2) The . . . trustee may, at any time after the expiry of 12 weeks from the date of sequestration, require a secured creditor at the expense of the debtor's estate to discharge the security or convey or assign it to the . . . trustee on payment to the creditor of the value specified by the creditor; and the amount in respect of which the creditor shall then be entitled to claim shall be any balance of his debt remaining after receipt of such payment.

(3) In calculating the amount of his claim, a creditor whose security has been realised shall deduct the amount (less the expenses of realisation) which he has received, or is entitled to receive, from the realisation.

Valuation of claims against partners for debts of the partnership

6. Where a creditor claims in respect of a debt of a partnership, against the estate of one of its partners, the creditor shall estimate the value of—

(a) the debt to the creditor from the firm's estate where that estate has not been sequestrated; or

(b) the creditor's claim against that estate where it has been sequestrated, and deduct that value from his claim against the partner's estate; and the amount in respect of which he shall be entitled to claim on the partner's estate shall be the balance remaining after that deduction has been made.

NOTES

Repealed as noted at the beginning of this Act.

Para 2: sub-para (1)(a)(i) numbered as such, and words in square brackets in sub-para (1) and words in first pair of square brackets in sub-para (2) inserted, by the Civil Partnership Act 2004, s 261(2), Sch 28, para 41; words in second pair of square brackets in sub-para (2) inserted by the Bankruptcy and Debt Advice (Scotland) Act 2014, s 56(1), Sch 3, paras 2, 36, subject to transitional provisions and savings in SSI 2014/261, arts 4, 12 at **[2.91]**, **[2.99]**.

Para 3: word "permanent" omitted from sub-para (2) in both places repealed by the Bankruptcy and Diligence etc (Scotland) Act 2007, s 226(2), Sch 6, Pt 1, subject to transitional provisions and savings in SSI 2008/115, arts 5–7, 10, 15 at **[2.51]–[2.53]**, **[2.56]**, **[2.57]**; words in square brackets in sub-para (2) substituted for original word "sheriff" and sub-paras (3)–(8) substituted for original sub-para (3), by the Bankruptcy and Debt Advice (Scotland) Act 2014, s 37, subject to transitional provisions and savings in SSI 2014/261, arts 4, 12 at **[2.91]**, **[2.99]**. Sub-para (3) previously read as follows (with word omitted repealed by the Bankruptcy and Diligence etc (Scotland) Act 2007, s 226(2), Sch 6, Pt 1, subject to transitional provisions and savings in SSI 2008/115, arts 5–7, 10, 15)—

> "(3) Any interested person may appeal to the sheriff against a valuation under sub paragraph (2) above by the . . . trustee, and the sheriff may affirm or vary that valuation.".

Para 4: repealed by the Bankruptcy and Debt Advice (Scotland) Act 2014, s 56(2), Sch 4, subject to transitional provisions and savings in SSI 2014/261, arts 4, 12 at **[2.91]**, **[2.99]**; words "by the sheriff" repealed by the Bankruptcy and Diligence etc (Scotland) Act 2007, s 21(13), as from a day to be appointed.

Para 5: word "permanent" omitted repealed by the Bankruptcy and Diligence etc (Scotland) Act 2007, s 226(2), Sch 6, Pt 1, subject to transitional provisions and savings in SSI 2008/115, arts 5–7, 10, 15 at **[2.51]–[2.53]**, **[2.56]**, **[2.57]**.

SCHEDULE 2
ADAPTATION OF PROCEDURE ETC UNDER THIS ACT WHERE PERMANENT TRUSTEE NOT ELECTED

Sections 23(4), 24(5) and 28(5)

[5.181]

1. *[Except where the permanent trustee is the Accountant in Bankruptcy,] section 24(2) shall, in so far as it relates to qualifications for continuing to act as permanent trustee, apply to a permanent trustee appointed, as it applies to one elected, under this Act.*

[2. (1) In place of section 25, sub-paragraph (2) below shall have effect.

(2) The sheriff clerk shall issue to the permanent trustee an act and warrant in such form as shall be prescribed by the Court of Session by act of sederunt.

2A. *Sections 26 and 26A shall apply as if for any reference to the confirmation of the permanent trustee in office there was substituted a reference to the permanent trustee receiving the act and warrant issued in pursuance of paragraph 2(2) above.]*

[3. (1) In place of subsections (1A) to (5) of section 28, sub-paragraph (2) below shall have effect.

(2) Where the permanent trustee resigns under subsection (1) of section 28 of this Act or dies—

(a) the Accountant in Bankruptcy; or

(b) such person as may be nominated by the Accountant in Bankruptcy (being a person who is not ineligible for election as permanent trustee under section 24(2) of this Act) if that person consents to the nomination, may apply to the sheriff for appointment as permanent trustee; and, on such an application being made, the sheriff shall appoint the Accountant in Bankruptcy or, as the case may be, the person nominated by him to be the permanent trustee.]

[4. (1) Section 29 shall have effect as follows.

(2) Where the permanent trustee is the Accountant in Bankruptcy, subsections (1) to (6) shall not have effect.

(3) In any other case—

(a) subsection (5) shall not have effect but sub-paragraph (2) of paragraph 3 above shall apply where the permanent trustee has been removed from office under subsection (1)(b) of section 29 of this Act or following an appeal under subsection (4) of that section as that sub-paragraph applies where he resigns or dies; and

(b) subsection (6) shall have effect as if for the words from "(b)" to the end there were substituted the words—

"(b) appoint as permanent trustee—

(i) the Accountant in Bankruptcy; or

(ii) such person as may be nominated by the Accountant in Bankruptcy (being a person who is not ineligible for election as permanent trustee under section 24(2) of this Act) if that person consents to the nomination."

(4) In every case—

(a) subsection (7) shall not have effect; and

(b) subsection (8) shall have effect as if for the word "(5)" there were substituted the word "(6)".]

5. Where an appointment is made under paragraph 3(3), or by virtue of paragraph [4(3)(a) or (b)], above the provisions of this Act shall continue to have effect as regards the sequestration subject to such modifications and with such further provisions as are set out in this Schedule.

6. Section 30 shall not have effect, and, in any sequestration to which this Schedule applies by virtue of section 28(5) of this Act, any commissioners already holding office shall cease to do so.

7. In section 39[, subsection (1) shall not have effect where the permanent trustee is the Accountant in Bankruptcy and]—

(a) in subsection (1), the reference to the permanent trustee's confirmation in office shall be construed as a reference to his receiving the act and warrant issued under paragraph 2(2) of this Schedule;

[(b) in subsection (2) the words "but if there are commissioners only with the consent of the commissioners, the creditors or the court" shall not have effect, and—

(i) if the permanent trustee is the Accountant in Bankruptcy, no consent shall be required for the actings mentioned in that subsection; and

(ii) in any other case, the consent of the Accountant in Bankruptcy shall be required for such actings.]

[7A. In section 43 (money received by permanent trustee) for subsection (1) there shall be substituted the following subsection—

"(1) Subject to subsection (2) below, all money received by—

(a) the Accountant in Bankruptcy in respect of his actings as permanent trustee shall be deposited by him in the name of the debtor's estate or in the name of the Secretary of State in an appropriate bank or institution;

(b) the permanent trustee (where he is not the Accountant in Bankruptcy) in the exercise of his functions shall be deposited by him in the name of the debtor's estate in an appropriate bank or institution.".]

8. [Except where the permanent trustee is the Accountant in Bankruptcy,] any power under section 44 or 45 to apply to the sheriff for an order requiring attendance shall be exerciseable only with the consent of the Accountant in Bankruptcy (unless, in the case of section 45(1), the Accountant in Bankruptcy has requested the application).

[9. (1) Where the permanent trustee is the Accountant in Bankruptcy, section 53 shall have effect as follows.

(2) For subsections (1) to (7) there shall be substituted the following subsections—

"(1) At the end of each accounting period, the Accountant in Bankruptcy shall prepare accounts of his intromissions with the debtor's estate, and he shall make a determination of his fees and outlays calculated in accordance with regulations made under section 69A of this Act.

(2) Such accounts and determination shall be available for inspection by the debtor and the creditors not later than 6 weeks after the end of the accounting period to which they relate.

(3) In making a determination as mentioned in subsection (1) above, the Accountant in Bankruptcy may take into account any adjustment which he may wish to make in the amount of his remuneration fixed in respect of any earlier accounting period.

(4) Not later than 8 weeks after the end of an accounting period, the debtor or any creditor may appeal to the sheriff against the determination of the Accountant in Bankruptcy; and the decision of the sheriff on such an appeal shall be final.

(5) On the expiry of the period within which an appeal may be made under subsection (4) above, the Accountant in Bankruptcy shall pay to the creditors their dividends in accordance with the scheme of division."

(3) In subsection (10) for the words "the audited" there shall be substituted the word "his".]

NOTES

Repealed as noted at the beginning of this Act.

Schedule repealed by the Bankruptcy and Diligence etc (Scotland) Act 2007, s 11(6), subject to transitional provisions and savings in SSI 2008/115, arts 5–7, 10, 15 at **[2.51]–[2.53]**, **[2.56]**, **[2.57]**.

Para 1: words in square brackets inserted by the Bankruptcy (Scotland) Act 1993, s 11(3), Sch 1, para 30(1), (2), subject to s 12(6) thereof, at **[5.194]** and to the Bankruptcy (Scotland) Act 1993 Commencement and Savings Order 1993, SI 1993/438, arts 4, 5, at **[16.58]**, **[16.59]**.

Paras 2, 2A: substituted for original para 2 by the Bankruptcy (Scotland) Act 1993, s 11(3), Sch 1, para 30(1), (3), subject to s 12(6) thereof, at **[5.194]** and to SI 1993/438, arts 4, 5, at **[16.58]**, **[16.59]**.

Paras 3, 4: substituted by the Bankruptcy (Scotland) Act 1993, s 11(3), Sch 1, para 30(1), (4), (5), subject to s 12(6) thereof, at **[5.194]** and to SI 1993/438, arts 4, 5, at **[16.58]**, **[16.59]**.

Para 5: words in square brackets substituted by the Bankruptcy (Scotland) Act 1993, s 11(3), Sch 1, para 30(1), (6), subject to s 12(6) thereof, at **[5.194]** and to SI 1993/438, arts 4, 5, at **[16.58]**, **[16.59]**.

Para 7: words in first pair of square brackets inserted and sub-para (b) substituted by the Bankruptcy (Scotland) Act 1993, s 11(3), Sch 1, para 30(1), (7), subject to s 12(6) thereof, at **[5.194]** and to SI 1993/438, arts 4, 5, at **[16.58]**, **[16.59]**.

Para 7A: inserted by the Bankruptcy (Scotland) Act 1993, s 11(3), Sch 1, para 30(1), (8), subject to s 12(6) thereof, at **[5.194]** and to SI 1993/438, arts 4, 5, at **[16.58]**, **[16.59]**.

Para 8: words in square brackets inserted by the Bankruptcy (Scotland) Act 1993, s 11(3), Sch 1, para 30(1), (9), subject to s 12(6) thereof, at **[5.194]** and to SI 1993/438, arts 4, 5, at **[16.58]**, **[16.59]**.

Para 9: substituted by the Bankruptcy (Scotland) Act 1993, s 11(3), Sch 1, para 30(1), (10), subject to s 12(6) thereof, at **[5.194]** and to SI 1993/438, arts 4, 5, at **[16.58]**, **[16.59]**.

Acts of Sederunt: Act of Sederunt (Bankruptcy Rules) 1993, SI 1993/921.

[SCHEDULE 2A
MODIFICATION OF DUTIES OF PERMANENT TRUSTEE IN SUMMARY ADMINISTRATION

[5.182]

1. The permanent trustee shall comply with the requirements of sections 3 and 39 of this Act only in so far as, in his view, it would be of financial benefit to the estate of the debtor and in the interests of creditors to do so.

2. The permanent trustee shall, until the debtor is discharged under this Act, at the end of—
- *(a) the period of 6 months beginning with the date of sequestration; and*
- *(b) each subsequent period of 6 months, require the debtor to give an account in writing of his current state of affairs.*

3. (1) Where the Accountant in Bankruptcy is not the permanent trustee, the permanent trustee shall comply with any general or specific directions given to him by the Accountant in Bankruptcy.

(2) Directions given under this paragraph may be given in respect of any particular case, all cases or any class or description of case.

4. (1) The permanent trustee shall, as soon as a certificate for the summary administration of the sequestration of the debtor's estate has been granted, publish in the Edinburgh Gazette a notice stating that such a certificate has been granted and that he has been appointed permanent trustee and, where no notice under section 15(6) of this Act has been published in respect of the sequestration—
- *(a) stating that sequestration of the debtor's estate has been awarded; and*
- *(b) inviting the submission of claims to him.*

(2) A notice under sub-paragraph (1) above shall also contain such additional information as may be prescribed.

5. Except in the case of an application for the grant of a certificate for the summary administration of the sequestration of the debtor's estate under section 25(2A) of this Act, Schedule 2 to this Act shall have effect in respect of a sequestration to which this Schedule applies.]

NOTES

Schedule inserted by the Bankruptcy (Scotland) Act 1993, s 6(2), subject to s 12(6) thereof, at **[5.194]** and to the Bankruptcy (Scotland) Act 1993 Commencement and Savings Order 1993, SI 1993/438, arts 4, 5, at **[16.58]**, **[16.59]**.

Repealed as noted at the beginning of this Act.

Repealed by the Bankruptcy and Diligence etc (Scotland) Act 2007, s 28(1), (3), subject to transitional provisions and savings in SSI 2008/115, arts 5–7, 10, 15 at **[2.51]**–**[2.53]**, **[2.56]**, **[2.57]**.

SCHEDULE 3
PREFERRED DEBTS

Section 51

PART I
LIST OF PREFERRED DEBTS

[5.183]

1–3. . . .

Contributions to occupational pension schemes, etc

4. Any sum which is owed by the debtor and is a sum to which [Schedule 4 to the Pension Schemes Act 1993] (contributions to occupational pension scheme and state scheme premiums) applies.

Remuneration of employees, etc

5. (1) So much of any amount which—
- (a) is owed by the debtor to a person who is or has been an employee of the debtor, and
- (b) is payable by way of remuneration in respect of the whole or any part of the period of four months next before the relevant date,

as does not exceed the prescribed amount.

(2) An amount owed by way of accrued holiday remuneration, in respect of any period of employment before the relevant date, to a person whose employment by the debtor has been terminated, whether before, on or after that date.

(3) So much of any sum owed in respect of money advanced for the purpose as has been applied for the payment of a debt which, if it had not been paid, would have been a debt falling within sub-paragraph (1) or (2) above.

6. So much of any amount which—

(a) is ordered, whether before or after the relevant date, to be paid by the debtor under the Reserve Forces (Safeguard of Employment) Act 1985; and

(b) is so ordered in respect of a default made by the debtor before that date in the discharge of his obligations under that Act,

as does not exceed such amount as may be prescribed.

[Levies on coal and steel production

6A. Any sums due at the relevant date from the debtor in respect of—

(a) the levies on the production of coal and steel referred to in Articles 49 and 50 of the ECSC Treaty, or

(b) any surcharge for delay provided for in Article 50(3) of that Treaty and Article 6 of Decision 3/52 of the High Authority of the Coal and Steel Community.]

[Debts owed to the Financial Services Compensation Scheme

6AA. Any debt owed by the debtor to the scheme manager of the Financial Services Compensation Scheme under section 215(2A) of the Financial Services and Markets Act 2000.]

[Deposits covered by Financial Services Compensation Scheme

6B. So much of any amount owed at the relevant date by the debtor in respect of an eligible deposit as does not exceed the compensation that would be payable in respect of the deposit under the Financial Services Compensation Scheme to the person or persons to whom the amount is owed.]

[Other deposits

6C. So much of any amount owed at the relevant date by the debtor to one or more eligible persons in respect of an eligible deposit as exceeds any compensation that would be payable in respect of the deposit under the Financial Services Compensation Scheme to that person or those persons.

6D. An amount owed at the relevant date by the debtor to one or more eligible persons in respect of a deposit that—

(a) was made through a non-EEA branch of a credit institution authorised by the competent authority of an EEA state, and

(b) would have been an eligible deposit if it had been made through an EEA branch of that credit institution.]

NOTES

Repealed as noted at the beginning of this Act.

Para 1: repealed by the Enterprise Act 2002, ss 251(2)(a), 278(2), Sch 26, subject to transitional provisions in relation to the abolition of preferential status for Crown debts in cases which were started before 15 September 2003 (see the Enterprise Act 2002 (Commencement No 4 and Transitional Provisions and Savings) Order 2003, SI 2003/2093, art 4 at **[2.27]**). Para 1, as amended by the Income Tax (Earnings and Pensions) Act 2003, s 722, Sch 6, Pt 2, para 153, previously read as follows:

"**1.** (1) Sums due at the relevant date from the debtor on account of deductions of income tax from emoluments paid during the period of twelve months next before that date, being deductions which the debtor was liable to make under [PAYE regulations], less the amount of the repayments of income tax which the debtor was liable to make during that period.

(2) Sums due at the relevant date from the debtor in respect of such deductions as are required to be made by the debtor for that period under section [559 of the Income and Corporation Taxes Act 1988] (subcontractors in the construction industry).".

Para 2: repealed by the Enterprise Act 2002, ss 251(2)(b), 278(2), Sch 26, subject to transitional provisions as noted to para 1 above. Para 2, as amended by the Finance Act 1991, s 7, Sch 2, para 21, the Finance Act 1993, s 36(3), the Finance Act 1994, ss 40, 64, Sch 6, para 13, Sch 7, para 7(3), (4), the Finance Act 1996, s 60, Sch 5, Pt III, para 12(2), (3), the Finance Act 1997, ss 13(2), 113, Sch 2, Pt II, para 6, Sch 18, Pt II, the Finance Act 2000, s 30, Sch 7, para 2(1) and the Finance Act 2001, s 27, Sch 5, para 18(1), previously read as follows:

"**2.** (1) Any value added tax which is referable to the period of six months next before the relevant date.

[(1A) Any insurance premium tax which is referable to the period of six months next before the relevant date.]

[(1B) Any landfill tax which is referable to the period of six months next before the relevant date.]

[(1C) Any climate change levy which is referable to the period of six months next before the relevant date.]

[(1D) Any aggregates levy which is referable to the period of six months next before the relevant date.]

(2) The amount of any car tax which is due at the relevant date from the debtor and which became due within a period of twelve months next before that date.

(3) Any amount which is due—

(a) by way of general betting duty[, bingo duty or gaming duty], or

(b) under section 12(1) of the Betting and Gaming Duties Act 1981 (general betting duty and pool betting duty recoverable from agent collecting stakes), . . .

(c) . . .

from the debtor at the relevant date and which became due within the period of twelve months next before that date.

[(4) The amount of any excise duty on beer which is due at the relevant date from the debtor and which became due within a period of 6 months next before that date.]

[(5) Any amount which is due by way of lottery duty from the debtor at the relevant date and which became due within the period of 12 months next before that date.]

[(6) Any amount which is due by way of air passenger duty from the debtor at the relevant date and which became due within the period of six months next before that date.]".

Para 3: repealed by the Enterprise Act 2002, ss 251(2)(c), 278(2), Sch 26, subject to transitional provisions as noted to para 1 above, and originally read as follows:

"3. (1) All sums which on the relevant date are due from the debtor on account of Class 1 or Class 2 contributions under the Social Security Act 1975 or the Social Security (Northern Ireland) Act 1975 and which became due from the debtor in the twelve months next before the relevant date.

(2) All sums which on the relevant date have been assessed on and are due from the debtor on account of Class 4 contributions under either of the said Acts of 1975, being sums which—

(a) are due to the Commissioners of Inland Revenue (rather than to the Secretary of State or a Northern Ireland department); and

(b) are assessed on the debtor up to 5th April next before the relevant date,

but not exceeding, in the whole, any one year's assessment.".

Para 4: words in square brackets substituted by the Pension Schemes Act 1993, s 190, Sch 8, para 17.

Para 6A: inserted, together with preceding cross-heading, by the Insolvency (ECSC Levy Debts) Regulations 1987, SI 1987/2093, reg 3.

Para 6AA: inserted, together with preceding cross-heading, by the Deposit Guarantee Scheme Regulations 2015, SI 2015/486, reg 16(a).

Para 6B: inserted by the Financial Services (Banking Reform) Act 2013, s 13(3).

Paras 6C, 6D: inserted by the Banks and Building Societies (Depositor Preference and Priorities) Order 2014, SI 2014/3486, art 28(1), (3)(a), except in relation to any insolvency proceedings commenced before 1 January 2015 (as to the meaning of this, see further the note "SI 2014/3486, art 3" to the Insolvency Act 1986, s 4 at **[1.5]**).

Regulations: the Bankruptcy (Scotland) Regulations 2014, SSI 2014/225 at **[16.267]**.

PART II
INTERPRETATION OF PART I

Meaning of "the relevant date"

[5.184]

7. In Part I of this Schedule "the relevant date" means—

(a) in relation to a debtor (other than a deceased debtor), the date of sequestration; and

(b) in relation to a deceased debtor, the date of his death.

8–8C. . . .

[Periods to which aggregates levy referable

8D. (1) For the purpose of paragraph 2(1D) of Part I of this Schedule—

(a) where the whole of the accounting period to which any aggregates levy is attributable falls within the period of six months next before the relevant date ('the relevant period'), the whole amount of that levy shall be referable to the relevant period; and

(b) in any other case the amount of any aggregates levy which shall be referable to the relevant period shall be the proportion of the levy which is equal to such proportion (if any) of the accounting period in question as falls within the relevant period.

(2) In sub-paragraph (1) above "accounting period" shall be construed in accordance with Part II of the Finance Act 2001.]

Amounts payable by way of remuneration

9. (1) For the purposes of paragraph 5 of Part I of this Schedule a sum is payable by the debtor to a person by way of remuneration in respect of any period if—

(a) it is paid as wages or salary (whether payable for time or for piece work or earned wholly or partly by way of commission) in respect of services rendered to the debtor in that period; or

(b) it is an amount falling within sub-paragraph (2) below and is payable by the debtor in respect of that period.

(2) An amount falls within this sub-paragraph if it is—

(a) a guarantee payment under section 12(1) of the Employment Protection (Consolidation) Act 1978 (employee without work to do for a day or part of a day),

(b) remuneration on suspension on medical grounds under section 19 of that Act,

(c) any payment for the time off under section 27(3) (trade-union duties), 31(3) (looking for work, etc) or 31A(4) (ante-natal care) of that Act,

(d) . . .

(e) remuneration under a protective award made by an industrial tribunal under section 101 of the Employment Protection Act 1975 (redundancy dismissal with compensation).

(3) For the purposes of paragraph 5(2) of Part I of this Schedule, holiday remuneration shall be deemed, in the case of a person whose employment has been terminated by or in consequence of the award of sequestration of his employer's estate, to have accrued to that person in respect of any period of

employment if, by virtue of that person's contract of employment or of any enactment (including an order made or direction given under any enactment), that remuneration would have accrued in respect of that period if that person's employment had continued until he became entitled to be allowed the holiday.

(4) Without prejudice to the preceding provisions of this paragraph—

(a) any remuneration payable by the debtor to a person in respect of a period of holiday or of absence from work through sickness or other good cause is deemed to be wages or, as the case may be, salary in respect of services rendered to the debtor in that period; and

(b) references in this paragraph to remuneration in respect of a period of holiday include references to any sums which, if they had been paid, would have been treated for the purposes of the enactments relating to social services as earnings in respect of that period.

[Meaning of scheme manager

9ZA. In paragraph 6AA "the scheme manager" has the meaning given in section 212(1) of the Financial Services and Markets Act 2000.]

[Meaning of eligible deposit

9A. (1) In [paragraphs 6B to 6D] "eligible deposit" means a deposit in respect of which the person, or any of the persons, to whom it is owed would be eligible for compensation under the Financial Services Compensation Scheme.

(2) For [the purposes of those paragraphs and this paragraph] a "deposit" means rights of the kind described in paragraph 22 of Schedule 2 to the Financial Services and Markets Act 2000 (deposits).

[(3) In paragraphs 6C and 6D, "eligible person" means—

(a) an individual, or

(b) a micro-enterprise, a small enterprise or a medium-sized enterprise, each of those terms having the meaning given in Article 2.1(107) of the Directive 2014/59/EU of 15th May 2014 establishing a framework for the recovery and resolution of credit institutions and investment firms.

(4) In paragraph 6D—

(a) "credit institution" has the meaning given in Article 4.1(1) of the capital requirements regulation;

(b) "EEA branch" means a branch, as defined in Article 4.1(17) of the capital requirements regulation, which is established in an EEA state;

(c) "non-EEA branch" means a branch, as so defined, which is established in a country which is not an EEA state;

and for this purpose "the capital requirements regulation" means Regulation (EU) No 575/2013 of the European Parliament and of the Council of 26th June 2013 on prudential requirements for credit institutions and investment firms and amending Regulation (EU) No 648/2012.]]

Transitional Provisions

10. Regulations under paragraph 5 or 6 of Part I of this Schedule may contain such transitional provisions as may appear to the Secretary of State necessary or expedient.

NOTES

Repealed as noted at the beginning of this Act.

Para 8: repealed by the Enterprise Act 2002, s 278(2), Sch 26, subject to transitional provisions in relation to the abolition of preferential status for Crown debts in cases which were started before 15 September 2003 (see the Enterprise Act 2002 (Commencement No 4 and Transitional Provisions and Savings) Order 2003, SI 2003/2093, art 4 at **[2.27]**). Para 8, as amended by the Value Added Tax Act 1994, s 100(1), Sch 14, para 9, previously read as follows:

> **"8.** (1) For the purpose of paragraph 2(1) of Part I of this Schedule—
>
> (a) where the whole of the prescribed accounting period to which any value added tax is attributable falls within the period of six months next before the relevant date ("the relevant period"), the whole amount of that tax shall be referable to the relevant period; and
>
> (b) in any other case the amount of any value added tax which shall be referable to the relevant period shall be the proportion of the tax which is equal to such proportion (if any) of the accounting reference period in question as falls within the relevant period.
>
> (2) In sub-paragraph (1) above "prescribed accounting period" has the same meaning as in the [Value Added Tax Act 1994].".

Para 8A: inserted by the Finance Act 1994, s 64, Sch 7, para 7(3), (5); repealed by the Enterprise Act 2002, s 278(2), Sch 26, subject to transitional provisions as noted to para 8 above. Para 8A previously read as follows:

> **"8A.** (1) For the purpose of paragraph 2(1A) of Part I of this Schedule—
>
> (a) where the whole of the accounting period to which any insurance premium tax is attributable falls within the period of six months next before the relevant date ("the relevant period"), the whole amount of that tax shall be referable to the relevant period; and
>
> (b) in any other case the amount of any insurance premium tax which shall be referable to the relevant period shall be the proportion of the tax which is equal to such proportion (if any) of the accounting period in question as falls within the relevant period.
>
> (2) In sub-paragraph (1) above "accounting period" shall be construed in accordance with Part III of the Finance Act 1994.".

Para 8B: inserted by the Finance Act 1996, s 60, Sch 5, Pt III, para 12(2), (4); repealed by the Enterprise Act 2002, s 278(2), Sch 26, subject to transitional provisions as noted to para 8 above. Para 8B previously read as follows:

"**8B.** (1) For the purpose of paragraph 2(1B) of Part I of this Schedule—
(a) where the whole of the accounting period to which any landfill tax is attributable falls within the period of six months next before the relevant date ("the relevant period"), the whole amount of that tax shall be referable to the relevant period; and
(b) in any other case the amount of any landfill tax which shall be referable to the relevant period shall be the proportion of the tax which is equal to such proportion (if any) of the accounting period in question as falls within the relevant period.

(2) In sub-paragraph (1) above "accounting period" shall be construed in accordance with Part III of the Finance Act 1996.".

Para 8C: inserted by the Finance Act 2000, s 30, Sch 7, para 2(2); repealed by the Enterprise Act 2002, s 278(2), Sch 26, subject to transitional provisions as noted to para 8 above. Para 8C previously read as follows:

"**8C.** (1) For the purpose of paragraph 2(1C) of Part I of this Schedule—
(a) where the whole of the accounting period to which any climate change levy is attributable falls within the period of six months next before the relevant date ("the relevant period"), the whole amount of that levy shall be referable to the relevant period; and
(b) in any other case the amount of any climate change levy which shall be referable to the relevant period shall be the proportion of the levy which is equal to such proportion (if any) of the accounting period in question as falls within the relevant period.

(2) In sub-paragraph (1) "accounting period" shall be construed in accordance with Schedule 6 to the Finance Act 2000.".

Para 8D: inserted by the Finance Act 2001, s 27, Sch 5, para 18(2).

Para 9: sub-para (2)(d) repealed by the Social Security Act 1986, s 86, Sch 10, Pt IV, para 80, Sch 11.

Para 9ZA: inserted, together with preceding cross-heading, by the Deposit Guarantee Scheme Regulations 2015, SI 2015/486, reg 16(b).

Para 9A: inserted by the Financial Services (Banking Reform) Act 2013, s 13(4); words in square brackets in sub-paras (1), (2) substituted (for original words "paragraph 6B" and "this purpose" respectively) and sub-paras (3), (4) added, by the Banks and Building Societies (Depositor Preference and Priorities) Order 2014, SI 2014/3486, art 28(1), (3)(b), except in relation to any insolvency proceedings commenced before 1 January 2015 (as to the meaning of this, see further the note "SI 2014/3486, art 3" to the Insolvency Act 1986, s 4 at **[1.5]**).

Employment Protection (Consolidation) Act 1978: the whole Act is now repealed. Sections 12(1), 19, 31(3), 31A(4) were repealed by the Employment Rights Act 1996, s 45, Sch 3, Pt I; s 27 was repealed by the Trade Union and Labour Relations (Consolidation) Act 1992, s 300(1), Sch 1.

Employment Protection Act 1975, s 101: repealed by the Trade Union and Labour Relations (Consolidation) Act 1992, s 300(1), Sch 1.

[SCHEDULE 3A
INFORMATION TO BE INCLUDED IN THE SEDERUNT BOOK

(introduced by section 62(2A))

[5.185]

1 A copy of a debtor application made under section 5(2)(a).

2 A copy of a petition presented under section 5(2)(b).

3 Where the trustee is the Accountant in Bankruptcy, a copy of a statement of assets and liabilities sent to the Accountant in Bankruptcy in accordance with section 5(6A).

4 A copy of an award of sequestration granted under section 12(1) or (3).

5 A copy of a warrant to cite the debtor granted under section 12(2).

6 Where the trustee is not the Accountant in Bankruptcy—
(a) the audited accounts sent to the trustee by the Accountant in Bankruptcy in accordance with section 13A(5)(d), and
(b) the determination fixing the amount of the outlays and remuneration payable to the interim trustee sent to the trustee by the Accountant in Bankruptcy in accordance with section 13A(5)(d).

7 Where the trustee is the Accountant in Bankruptcy—
(a) the accounts audited by the Accountant in Bankruptcy in accordance with section 13A(5)(a), and
(b) the determination fixing the amount of the outlays and remuneration payable to the interim trustee issued in accordance with section 13A(5)(b).

8 Where the Accountant in Bankruptcy is appointed as interim trustee and the sheriff awards sequestration in accordance with section 13B(1)(a)—
(a) the accounts of the Accountant in Bankruptcy's intromissions (if any) with the debtor's estate;, and
(b) the determination of the Accountant in Bankruptcy's fees and outlays calculated in accordance with regulations made under section 69A.

9 A copy of any—
(a) order recalling or refusing to recall an award of sequestration by the sheriff under section 17 and sent to the trustee under section 17(8)(b)(ii),
(b) grant or refusal to grant a recall of an award of sequestration under section 17D(1), 17E(6) or 17G.

10 A copy of any order under section 41(1)(b)(ii) or 41A(1)(b)(ii) sent to the trustee under section 17(8)(b).

11 Where the trustee is a replacement trustee appointed under section 25 and the Accountant in Bankruptcy was not the original trustee—
- (a) a copy of any determination fixing the amount of the outlays and remuneration payable to the original trustee and of the original trustee's audited accounts which is sent to the trustee under section 26(3)(b)(ii),
- (b) upon appointment, such information as is appropriate to provide a record of the sequestration process before the trustee's appointment as replacement trustee (except that no entry is to be made in relation to any written comments made by the original trustee under section 20(2)), and
- (c) an entry recording any certificate of discharge issued to the original trustee under section 27.

12 Where the trustee is not the Accountant in Bankruptcy, a copy of a statement of assets and liabilities sent to the trustee under section 19(1) or (2).

13 A copy of a notice given under section 21A(2).

14 Where the trustee is not the Accountant in Bankruptcy, a copy of a report made under section 21B(1)(a).

15 Where the trustee is a replacement trustee appointed under section 25 and the Accountant in Bankruptcy was the original trustee, upon appointment, such information as is appropriate to provide a record of the sequestration process before the trustee's appointment as replacement trustee.

16 A copy of any initial proposal for the debtor's contribution provided by the trustee under section 32A(1)(b).

17 A copy of a debtor contribution order applying to the debtor.

18 A copy of any decree issued under section 34 affecting the sequestrated estate.

19 A copy of any decree of recall issued following an application under section 35(2).

20 A copy of any decree issued under section 36 affecting the sequestrated estate.

21 The inventory and valuation of the estate made up and maintained in accordance with section 38(1)(b).

22 A copy of an account given by the debtor under section 43A(2).

23 The debtor's deposition at an examination subscribed under section 47(5).

24 A copy of the record of an examination sent to the Accountant in Bankruptcy under section 47(6).

25 An appropriate entry in relation to the production of any document to the trustee in accordance with section 48(7), stating the date when it was produced to the trustee.

26 Where the trustee accepts or rejects a claim under section 49, the decision on the claim, specifying—
- (a) the amount of the claim accepted by the trustee,
- (b) the category of debt, and the value of any security, as decided by the trustee, and
- (c) if the claim is rejected, the reasons.

27 A copy of a decision of the Accountant in Bankruptcy under section 49(6C)(b) and of the sheriff under section 49(6D).

28 An agreement or determination in respect of the accounting period under section 52(2)(b)(i) or (ii).

29 Where the trustee is not the Accountant in Bankruptcy, the audited accounts, the scheme of division and the final determination in relation to the trustee's outlays and remuneration, as mentioned in section 53.

30 A copy the certificate of discharge given to the debtor under section 54(2) or 54A(2) or 54F.

31 A copy the certificate deferring discharge where the debtor cannot be traced issued under section 54D(4)(b) or (6)(b).

32 Where the Accountant in Bankruptcy has acted as trustee, after making the final division of the debtor's estate—
- (a) the Accountant in Bankruptcy's final accounts of the Accountant in Bankruptcy's intromissions (if any) with the debtor's estate,
- (b) the scheme of division (if any), and
- (c) a determination of the Accountant in Bankruptcy's fees and outlays calculated in accordance with regulations made under section 69A.

33 Where the Accountant in Bankruptcy has acted as trustee and is discharged from all liability as mentioned in section 58A(7), an appropriate entry in relation to such discharge.

34 A decision of the court under section 63 and of the Accountant in Bankruptcy under section 63A.

35 A copy of a decree arbitral or, as the case may be, an appropriate entry recording the compromise referred to in section 65.

36 The minutes of the meeting mentioned in paragraph 7 of Schedule 6.

37 A copy of the minutes of any meeting sent to the Accountant in Bankruptcy in accordance with paragraph 16 of Schedule 6.

38 Where a meeting of commissioners is called in accordance with paragraph 17 of Schedule 6—
(a) a record of the deliberations of the commissioners at the meeting,
(b) where the trustee is not clerk in accordance with paragraph 21 of Schedule 6, a record of the deliberations of the commissioners transmitted by the commissioner acting as clerk, such commissioner to authenticate the insertion when made, and
(c) in relation to any matter agreed without a meeting, the minute recording that agreement signed in accordance with paragraph 23 of Schedule 6.".

39 A copy of any decision (including any determination, direction, award, acceptance, rejection, adjudication, requirement, declaration, order or valuation) relating to the sequestration which is—
(a) issued by the Accountant in Bankruptcy, and
(b) not otherwise mentioned in this Schedule.

40 A copy of any decree, interlocutory decree, direction or order relating to the sequestration which is—
(a) granted by the court, and
(b) not otherwise mentioned in this Schedule.]

NOTES

Commencement: 1 April 2015.

Schedule inserted by the Bankruptcy and Debt Advice (Scotland) Act 2014, s 23(4), Sch 2, subject to transitional provisions and savings in SSI 2014/261, arts 4, 12 at **[2.91]**, **[2.99]**.

Repealed as noted at the beginning of this Act.

SCHEDULE 4
DISCHARGE ON COMPOSITION

Section 56

[5.186]

1. (1) At any time after the sheriff clerk issues the act and warrant to the permanent trustee, an offer of composition may be made by or on behalf of the debtor, in respect of his debts, to the . . . trustee.

(2) Any offer of composition shall specify caution or other security to be provided for its implementation.

2. The . . . trustee[, where he is not the Accountant in Bankruptcy,] shall submit the offer of composition along with a report thereon to the commissioners or, if there are no commissioners, to the Accountant in Bankruptcy.

3. The commissioners or, if there are no commissioners, the Accountant in Bankruptcy—
(a) if they consider (or he considers) that the offer of composition will be timeously implemented and that, if the rules set out in section 51 of, and Schedule 1 to, this Act were applicable, its implementation would secure payment of a dividend of at least 25p in the £ in respect of the ordinary debts; and
(b) if satisfied with the caution or other security specified in the offer; shall recommend that the offer should be placed before the creditors.

4. Where a recommendation is made that the offer of composition should be placed before the creditors, the . . . trustee shall—
(a) intimate the recommendation to the debtor and record it in the sederunt book;
(b) publish in the Edinburgh Gazette a notice stating that an offer of composition has been made and where its terms may be inspected;
(c) invite every creditor known to him to accept or reject the offer by completing a prescribed form sent by the permanent trustee with the invitation and returning the completed form to him; and
(d) send along with the prescribed form a report—
(i) summarising the offer and the present state of the debtor's affairs and the progress in realising his estate; and
(ii) estimating, if the offer is accepted, the expenses to be met in concluding the sequestration proceedings and the dividend which would be payable in respect of the ordinary debts if the rules set out in section 51 of, and Schedule 1 to, this Act were applied.

5. (1) The permanent trustee shall determine from the completed prescribed forms duly received by him that the offer of composition has been accepted by the creditors, if a majority in number and not less than two-thirds in value of the creditors known to him have accepted it, and otherwise shall determine that they have rejected it.

(2) For the purposes of this paragraph, a prescribed form shall be deemed to be duly received by the permanent trustee if it is received by him not later than 14 days after the date on which it was sent to the creditor.

(3) The permanent trustee shall intimate in writing his determination under this paragraph to the debtor and any other person by whom the offer of composition was made and shall insert his determination in the sederunt book.

6. Where the permanent trustee determines that the creditors have accepted the offer of composition, he shall submit to the sheriff—

(a) a statement that he has so determined;

(b) a copy of the report mentioned in paragraph 4(d) of this Schedule; and

(c) a declaration by the debtor as to the matters mentioned in sub-paragraphs (i) and (iii) of section 54(4)(b) of this Act.

7. (1) The sheriff shall, on the receipt by him of the documents mentioned in paragraph 6 of this Schedule, fix a date and time for a hearing to consider whether or not to approve the offer of composition.

(2) The permanent trustee shall then send to every creditor known to him a notice in writing stating—

(a) that he has determined that the creditors have accepted the offer of composition;

(b) that a hearing has been fixed by the sheriff to consider whether or not to approve the offer;

(c) the place, date and time of the hearing; and

(d) that the recipient of the notice may make representations at the hearing as to whether or not the offer of composition should be approved.

8. (1) At the hearing the sheriff shall examine the documents and hear any representations and thereafter shall make an order—

(a) if he is satisfied that a majority in number and not less than two-thirds in value of the creditors known to the permanent trustee have accepted the offer of composition and that the terms of the offer are reasonable, approving the offer; and

(b) if he is not so satisfied, refusing to approve the offer of composition.

(2) The sheriff may make an order approving the offer of composition, notwithstanding that there has been a failure to comply with any provision of this Schedule.

(3) The debtor or any creditor may within 14 days of the order being made appeal against an order approving or refusing to approve the offer of composition.

9. (1) Where the offer of composition is approved, the . . . trustee[, where he is not the Accountant in Bankruptcy,] shall—

(a) submit to the commissioners or, if there are no commissioners, to the Accountant in Bankruptcy, his accounts of his intromissions with the debtor's estate for audit and a claim for the outlays reasonably incurred by him and for his remuneration; and where the said documents are submitted to the commissioners, he shall send a copy of them to the Accountant in Bankruptcy;

(b) take all reasonable steps to ensure that the interim trustee (where he is a different person) has submitted, or submits, to the Accountant in Bankruptcy his accounts and his claim for his outlays and remuneration.

[(1A) Where the offer of composition is approved and the . . . trustee is the Accountant in Bankruptcy, the . . . trustee shall prepare accounts of his intromissions with the debtor's estate and he shall make a determination of his fees and outlays calculated in accordance with regulations made under section 69A of this Act.]

(2) Subsections (3), (4), (6) and (10) of section 53 of this Act shall apply, subject to any necessary modifications, in respect of the accounts and claim submitted under sub-paragraph (1)(a) above as they apply in respect of the accounts and claim submitted under section 53(1) of this Act.

[(3) Subsections (2), (3), (4), (5) and (10) of section 53 of this Act as adapted by *paragraph 9(2) and (3) of Schedule 2 to* this Act shall apply, subject to any necessary modifications, in respect of the accounts and determination prepared under sub-paragraph (1A) above as they apply in respect of the accounts and determination prepared under the said section 53 as so adapted.]

10. As soon as the procedure under paragraph 9 of this Schedule has been completed, there shall be *lodged with the sheriff clerk*—

(a) by the *permanent trustee*, a declaration that all necessary charges in connection with the sequestration have been paid or that satisfactory provision has been made in respect of the payment of such charges;

(b) by or on behalf of the debtor, the bond of caution or other security for payment of the composition.

11. Once the documents have been lodged under paragraph 10 of this Schedule, the sheriff shall make an order discharging the debtor and the permanent trustee; and subsection (7) of section 54 of this Act shall apply in relation to an order under this paragraph as it applies in relation to an order under subsection (6) of that section.

12. *An order under paragraph 11* of this Schedule discharging the . . . trustee shall have the effect of discharging him from all liability (other than any liability arising from fraud) to the creditors or to the debtor in respect of any act or omission of the . . . trustee in exercising the functions conferred on him by this Act.

13. Notwithstanding that an offer of composition has been made, the sequestration shall proceed as if no such offer of composition has been made until the discharge of the debtor becomes effective; and the sequestration shall thereupon cease.

14. A creditor who has not submitted a claim under section 48 of this Act before *the sheriff makes an order approving* an offer of composition [is approved] shall not be entitled to make any demand against a person offering the composition on behalf of the debtor or against a cautioner in the offer; but this paragraph is without prejudice to any right of such a creditor to a dividend out of the debtor's estate equal to the dividend which creditors of the same class are entitled to receive under the composition.

15. A debtor may make two, but no more than two, offers of composition in the course of a sequestration.

16. [(1)] On *an order under paragraph 11 of this Schedule discharging the debtor becoming effective*—

(a) the debtor shall be re-invested in his estate as existing at the date of the order;
(b) the debtor shall, subject to paragraph 14 of this Schedule, be discharged of all debts for which he was liable at the date of sequestration (other than any debts mentioned in section 55(2) of this Act); and
(c) the claims of creditors in the sequestration shall be converted into claims for their respective shares in the composition.

[(2) The discharge of the debtor by virtue of *an order under paragraph 11 above* shall not affect any right of a secured creditor—

(a) for a debt in respect of which the debtor has been discharged to enforce his security for payment of the debt and any interest due and payable on the debt until the debt is paid in full; or
(b) for an obligation in respect of which the debtor has been discharged to enforce his security in respect of the obligation.]

17. (1) *Without prejudice to any rule of law relating to the reduction of court decrees,* the Court of Session, on the application of any creditor, may recall the *order of the sheriff approving the offer of composition and* discharging the debtor and the . . . trustee where it is satisfied—

(a) that there has been, or is likely to be, default in payment of the composition or of any instalment thereof; or
(b) that for any reason the composition cannot be proceeded with or cannot be proceeded with without undue delay or without injustice to the creditors.

(2) The effect of a decree of recall under this paragraph where the debtor has already been discharged shall be to revive the sequestration:

Provided that the revival of the sequestration shall not affect the validity of any transaction which has been entered into by the debtor since his discharge with a person who has given value and has acted in good faith.

(3) Where the . . . trustee has been discharged, the Court may, on pronouncing a decree of recall under this paragraph, appoint a judicial factor to administer the debtor's estate, and give the judicial factor such order as it thinks fit as to that administration.

(4) The clerk of the court shall send a copy of a decree of recall under this paragraph to the . . . trustee or judicial factor for insertion in the sederunt book.

18. (1) *Without prejudice to any rule of law relating to the reduction of court decrees*, the Court of Session, on the application of any creditor, may reduce an *order under paragraph 11* of this Schedule discharging a debtor where it is satisfied that a payment was made or a preference granted or that a payment or preference was promised for the purpose of facilitating the obtaining of the debtor's discharge.

(2) The Court may, whether or not it pronounces a decree of reduction under this paragraph, order a creditor who has received a payment or preference in connection with the debtor's discharge to surrender the payment or the value of the preference to the debtor's estate.

(3) Where the . . . trustee has been discharged, the Court may, on pronouncing a decree of reduction under this paragraph, appoint a judicial factor to administer the debtor's estate, and give the judicial factor such order as it thinks fit as to that administration.

(4) The clerk of court shall send a copy of a decree of reduction under this paragraph to the . . . trustee or judicial factor for insertion in the sederunt book.

NOTES

Repealed as noted at the beginning of this Act.

Repealed by the Bankruptcy and Debt Advice (Scotland) Act 2014, s 18(3), subject to transitional provisions and savings in SSI 2014/261, arts 4, 12 at **[2.91]**, **[2.99]**.

Para 1: for the words "clerk issues the act and warrant to the permanent" there are substituted the words "or, as the case may be, the Accountant in Bankruptcy appoints the", as from a day to be appointed, and word "permanent" (omitted) repealed by the Bankruptcy and Diligence etc (Scotland) Act 2007, ss 21(1), (2), 226(2), Sch 6, Pt 1, subject to transitional provisions and savings in SSI 2008/115, arts 5–7, 10, 15 at **[2.51]–[2.53]**, **[2.56]**, **[2.57]**.

Para 2: word "permanent" (omitted) repealed by the Bankruptcy and Diligence etc (Scotland) Act 2007, s 226(2), Sch 6, Pt 1, subject to transitional provisions and savings in SSI 2008/115, arts 5–7, 10, 15 at **[2.51]–[2.53]**, **[2.56]**, **[2.57]**; words in square brackets inserted by the Bankruptcy (Scotland) Act 1993, s 11(3), Sch 1, para 31(1), (2), subject to s 12(6) thereof, at **[5.194]** and to the Bankruptcy (Scotland) Act 1993 Commencement and Savings Order 1993, SI 1993/438, arts 4, 5, at **[16.58]**, **[16.59]**.

Para 4: word "permanent" (omitted) repealed by the Bankruptcy and Diligence etc (Scotland) Act 2007, s 226(2), Sch 6, Pt 1, subject to transitional provisions and savings in SSI 2008/115, arts 5–7, 10, 15 at **[2.51]–[2.53]**, **[2.56]**, **[2.57]**; sub-paras (c), (d) substituted by new sub-para (c), by the Bankruptcy and Diligence etc (Scotland) Act 2007, s 21(1), (3), as from 1 April 2008 for the purpose of making regulations or orders, subject to transitional provisions as noted above, and as from a day to be appointed for remaining purposes, as follows:

"(c) not later than 1 week after the date of publication of such notice, send to every creditor known to him—
(i) a copy of the terms of offer; and
(ii) such other information as may be prescribed.".

Paras 5–8: substituted by new paras 5–8, 8A, 8B, by the Bankruptcy and Diligence etc (Scotland) Act 2007, s 21(1), (4), as from 1 April 2008 for the purpose of making regulations or orders, subject to transitional provisions and savings in SSI 2008/115, arts 5–7, 10, 15 at **[2.51]–[2.53]**, **[2.56]**, **[2.57]**, and as from a day to be appointed for remaining purposes, as follows:

"**5.** The notice mentioned in paragraph 4(b) of this Schedule shall be in the prescribed form and shall contain such information as may be prescribed.

6. Where, within the period of 5 weeks beginning with the date of publication of the notice under paragraph 4(b) of this Schedule, the trustee has not received notification in writing from a majority in number or not less than one third in value of the creditors that they reject the offer of composition, the offer of composition shall be approved by the trustee.

7. Where the trustee has received notification within the period and to the extent mentioned in paragraph 6 of this Schedule, the offer of composition shall be rejected by the trustee.

8. Any creditor who has been sent a copy of the terms of the offer as referred to in paragraph 4(c)(i) of this Schedule and who has not notified the trustee as mentioned in paragraph 6 of this Schedule that he objects to the offer shall be treated for all purposes as if he had accepted the offer.

8A. (1) The Scottish Ministers may by regulations amend paragraphs 4 to 8 of this Schedule by replacing them, varying them or adding to or deleting anything from them.

(2) Regulations made under sub-paragraph (1) above may contain such amendments of this Act as appear to the Scottish Ministers to be necessary in consequence of any amendment made by the regulations to the said paragraphs 4 to 8.

8B. (1) Where an offer of composition is approved, a creditor who has not been sent a copy of the terms of the offer as mentioned in paragraph 4(c)(i) of this Schedule or who has notified the trustee of his rejection of the offer as mentioned in paragraph 6 of this Schedule may, not more than 28 days after the expiry of the period mentioned in said paragraph 6, appeal to the Accountant in Bankruptcy against such approval.

(2) In determining an appeal under sub-paragraph (1) above, the Accountant in Bankruptcy may—
(a) approve or reject the offer of composition; and
(b) make such other determination in consequence of that approval or rejection as he thinks fit.".

Para 9: words in square brackets in sub-para (1), and the whole of sub-paras (1A), (3), inserted, by the Bankruptcy (Scotland) Act 1993, s 11(3), Sch 1, para 31(1), (3), subject to s 12(6) thereof, at **[5.194]** and to SI 1993/438, arts 4, 5, at **[16.58]**, **[16.59]**; for the words "paragraph 9(2) and (3) of Schedule 2 to" in sub-para (3) there are substituted the words "section 53A of", as from a day to be appointed, and word "permanent" omitted in each place repealed, by the Bankruptcy and Diligence etc (Scotland) Act 2007, ss 21(1), (5), 226(2), Sch 6, Pt 1, subject to transitional provisions and savings in SSI 2008/115, arts 5–7, 10, 15 at **[2.51]–[2.53]**, **[2.56]**, **[2.57]**.

Para 10: for the words "lodged with the sheriff clerk" there are substituted the words "sent to the Accountant in Bankruptcy" and for the words "permanent trustee" in sub-para (a) there are substituted the words "trustee (where he is not the Accountant in Bankruptcy)" by the Bankruptcy and Diligence etc (Scotland) Act 2007, s 21(1), (6), as from a day to be appointed.

Para 11: substituted by the Bankruptcy and Diligence etc (Scotland) Act 2007, s 21(1), (7), as from 1 April 2008 for the purpose of making regulations or orders, subject to transitional provisions and savings in SSI 2008/115, arts 5–7, 10, 15 at **[2.51]–[2.53]**, **[2.56]**, **[2.57]**, and as from a day to be appointed for remaining purposes, as follows:

"**11.** (1) Where the documents have been sent to the Accountant in Bankruptcy under paragraph 10 of this Schedule and either—
(a) the period mentioned in paragraph 8B(1) of this Schedule has expired; or
(b) the Accountant in Bankruptcy, in determining an appeal under said paragraph 8B(1), has approved the offer of composition,

the Accountant in Bankruptcy shall grant the certificates of discharge referred to in sub-paragraph (2) below.

(2) Those certificates are—
(a) a certificate discharging the debtor; and
(b) a certificate discharging the trustee.

(3) A certificate granted under sub-paragraph (1) above shall be in the prescribed form.

(4) The Accountant in Bankruptcy shall—
(a) send a certified copy of the certificate discharging the debtor to the keeper of the register of inhibitions for recording in that register; and
(b) send a copy of that certificate to the trustee who shall insert it in the sederunt book or, where the Accountant in Bankruptcy is the trustee, insert a copy of that certificate in the sederunt book.".

Para 12: for the words "An order under paragraph 11" there are substituted the words "A certificate granted under paragraph 11(1)", as from a day to be appointed, and word "permanent" omitted in both places repealed by the Bankruptcy and Diligence etc (Scotland) Act 2007, ss 21(1), (8), 226(2), Sch 6, Pt 1, subject to transitional provisions and savings in SSI 2008/115, arts 5–7, 10, 15 at **[2.51]–[2.53]**, **[2.56]**, **[2.57]**.

Para 14: words "the sheriff makes an order approving" repealed and words in square brackets inserted by the Bankruptcy and Diligence etc (Scotland) Act 2007, s 21(1), (9), as from a day to be appointed.

Para 16: original para renumbered as sub-para (1) and the whole of sub-para (2) inserted, by the Bankruptcy (Scotland) Act 1993, s 11(3), Sch 1, para 31(1), (4). Note that by s 11(3) of, and Sch 1, para 31(5) to, that Act, the amendment made to para 16 is deemed always to have had effect; for the words from "an order under" to "debtor becoming effective" in sub-para (1) there are substituted the words "the granting of a certificate under paragraph 11(1) of this Schedule discharging the debtor" and for the words "an order under paragraph 11 above" in sub-para (2) there are substituted the words "the granting of a certificate under paragraph 11(1) of this Schedule" by the Bankruptcy and Diligence etc (Scotland) Act 2007, s 21(1), (10), as from a day to be appointed.

Para 17: words from "Without prejudice to" to "of court decrees," repealed and for the words "order of the sheriff approving the offer of composition and" there are substituted the words "approval of the offer of composition and the granting of certificates" by the Bankruptcy and Diligence etc (Scotland) Act 2007, s 21(1), (11), as from a day to be appointed; word "permanent" omitted in each place repealed by the Bankruptcy and Diligence etc (Scotland) Act 2007, s 226(2), Sch 6, Pt 1, subject to transitional provisions and savings in SSI 2008/115, arts 5–7, 10, 15 at **[2.51]–[2.53]**, **[2.56]**, **[2.57]**.

Para 18: in sub-para (1), words from "Without prejudice to" to "of court decrees," repealed and for the words "an order under paragraph 11" there are substituted the words "a certificate granted under paragraph 11(1)" by the Bankruptcy and Diligence etc (Scotland) Act 2007, s 21(1), (12), as from a day to be appointed; word "permanent" omitted from sub-paras (3), (4) repealed by the Bankruptcy and Diligence etc (Scotland) Act 2007, s 226(2), Sch 6, Pt 1, subject to transitional provisions and savings in SSI 2008/115, arts 5–7, 10, 15 at **[2.51]–[2.53]**, **[2.56]**, **[2.57]**.

SCHEDULE 5
VOLUNTARY TRUST DEEDS FOR CREDITORS

Section 59

Remuneration of trustee

[5.187]

1. Whether or not provision is made in the trust deed for auditing the trustee's accounts and for determining the method of fixing the trustee's remuneration or whether or not the trustee and the creditors have agreed on such auditing and the method of fixing the remuneration, the debtor, the trustee or any creditor may, at any time before the final distribution of the debtor's estate among the creditors, have the trustee's accounts audited by and his remuneration fixed by the Accountant in Bankruptcy.

[Accountant in Bankruptcy's power to carry out audit

1A. The Accountant in Bankruptcy may, at any time, audit the trustee's accounts and fix his remuneration.]

Registration of notice of inhibition

2. (1) The trustee, from time to time after the trust deed has been delivered to him, may cause a notice in such form as shall be prescribed by the Court of Session by act of sederunt to be recorded in the register of inhibitions *and adjudications*; and such recording shall have the same effect as the recording in that register of letters of inhibition against the debtor.

(2) The trustee, after the debtor's estate has been finally distributed among his creditors or the trust deed has otherwise ceased to be operative, shall cause to be so recorded a notice in such form as shall be prescribed as aforesaid recalling the notice recorded under sub-paragraph (1) above.

Lodging of claim to bar effect of limitation of actions

3. The submission of a claim by a creditor to the trustee acting under a trust deed shall bar the effect of any enactment or rule of law relating to limitation of actions in any part of the United Kingdom.

Valuation of claims

4. Unless the trust deed otherwise provides, Schedule 1 to this Act shall apply in relation to a trust deed as it applies in relation to a sequestration but subject to the following modifications—

(a) in paragraphs 1, 2 and 5 for the word "sequestration" wherever it occurs there shall be substituted the words "granting of the trust deed";

(b) in paragraph 3—

(i) in sub-paragraph (2), for the words from the beginning of paragraph (a) to "or sheriff" there shall be substituted the words "the trustee"; and

(ii) . . .

(c) paragraph 4 shall be omitted; and

(d) . . .

Protected trust deeds

[5. (1) The Scottish Ministers may by regulations make provision as to—

(a) the conditions which require to be fulfilled in order for a trust deed to be granted the status of a protected trust deed;

(b) the consequences of a trust deed being granted that status;

(c) the rights of any creditor who does not accede to a trust deed which is granted protected status;

(d) the extent to which a debtor may be discharged, by virtue of a protected trust deed, from his liabilities or from such liabilities or class of liabilities as may be prescribed in the regulations;

(e) the circumstances in which a debtor may bring to an end the operation of a trust deed in respect of which the conditions provided for under sub-paragraph (a) above are not fulfilled;

(f) the administration of the trust under a protected trust deed (including provision about the remuneration payable to the trustee).

(2) Regulations under this paragraph may—

(a) make provision enabling applications to be made to the court;

[(aa) . . .]

(b) contain such amendments of this Act as appear to the Scottish Ministers to be necessary in consequence of any other provision of the regulations.]

NOTES

Repealed as noted at the beginning of this Act.

Para 1A: inserted, together with preceding cross-heading, by the Bankruptcy and Diligence etc (Scotland) Act 2007, s 23(1), subject to transitional provisions and savings in SSI 2008/115, arts 5–7, 10, 15 at **[2.51]–[2.53]**, **[2.56]**, **[2.57]**.

Para 2: words "and adjudications" repealed by the Bankruptcy and Diligence etc (Scotland) Act 2007, s 226(2), Sch 6, Pt 1, as from a day to be appointed.

Para 4: sub-paras (b)(ii), (d) repealed by the Bankruptcy and Diligence etc (Scotland) Act 2007, s 226(2), Sch 6, Pt 1, subject to transitional provisions and savings in SSI 2008/115, arts 5–7, 10, 15 at **[2.51]**–**[2.53]**, **[2.56]**, **[2.57]**, and previously read as follows:

"(ii) in sub-paragraph (3), for the reference to the permanent trustee there shall be substituted a reference to the trustee;".

"(d) in paragraph 5(2) for the references to the permanent trustee there shall be substituted references to the trustee.";

sub-para (c) repealed by the Bankruptcy and Debt Advice (Scotland) Act 2014, s 56(2), Sch 4, subject to transitional provisions and savings in SSI 2014/261, arts 4, 12 at **[2.91]**, **[2.99]**.

Para 5: substituted for paras 5–13, by the Bankruptcy and Diligence etc (Scotland) Act 2007, s 20(1), except in relation to protected trust deeds granted before 1 April 2008; para (2)(aa) inserted by the Home Owner and Debtor Protection (Scotland) Act 2010, s 13(2) and repealed by the Bankruptcy and Debt Advice (Scotland) Act 2014, s 56(2), Sch 4.

Prior to the substitution by the 2007 Act, paras 5–13 (as amended) and the notes thereto, read as follows:

"[**5.** (1) Paragraphs 6 and 7 of this Schedule shall apply in respect of a trust deed if—

(a) the trustee is a person who would not be disqualified under section 24(2) of this Act from acting as the permanent trustee if the debtor's estate were being sequestrated;

(b) after the trust deed has been delivered to him, the trustee publishes in the Edinburgh Gazette the notice specified in sub-paragraph (3) below;

(c) not later than one week after the date of publication of such notice, the trustee sends to every creditor known to him—

(i) a copy of the trust deed;

(ii) a copy of the notice; and

(iii) such other information as may be prescribed;

(d) within the period of 5 weeks beginning with the date of publication of such notice, the trustee has not received notification in writing from a majority in number or not less than one third in value of the creditors that they object to the trust deed and do not wish to accede to it; and

(e) immediately after the expiry of the said period of 5 weeks, the trustee sends to the Accountant in Bankruptcy for registration in the register of insolvencies a copy of the trust deed with a certificate endorsed thereon that it is a true copy and that he has not received notification as mentioned in sub-sub-paragraph (d) above.

(2) Any creditor who has been sent a copy of the notice referred to in sub-paragraph (1)(b) above and who has not notified the trustee as mentioned in sub-paragraph (1)(d) above that he objects to the trust deed shall be treated for all purposes as if he had acceded to the trust deed; and any reference in this Act to a creditor who has acceded to a trust deed shall include a reference to a creditor who is treated for all purposes as if he had so acceded.

(3) The notice mentioned in sub-paragraph (1)(b) above shall be in the prescribed form and shall contain such information as may be prescribed.

(4) The Secretary of State may by regulations amend sub-paragraphs (1) to (3) above by replacing them, varying them or adding to or deleting anything from them.

(5) Regulations made under sub-paragraph (4) above may contain such amendments of this Act as appear to the Secretary of State to be necessary in consequence of any amendment made by the regulations to the said sub-paragraphs (1) to (3).]

6. Where the provisions of paragraph 5 of this Schedule have been fulfilled, then—

[(a) subject to paragraph 7 of this Schedule, a creditor who has—

(i) not been sent a copy of the notice as mentioned in paragraph 5(1)(c) above; or

(ii) notified the trustee of his objection to the trust deed as mentioned in paragraph 5(1)(d) above,

shall have no higher right to recover his debt than a creditor who has acceded to the trust deed;]

(b) the debtor may not petition for the sequestration of his estate while the trust deed subsists.

7. (1) A qualified creditor [who has not been sent a copy of the notice as mentioned in paragraph 5(1)(c) above or who has notified the trustee of his objection to the trust deed as mentioned in paragraph 5(1)(d) above] may present a petition for sequestration of the debtor's estate—

(a) not later than 6 weeks after the date of publication of the notice under [paragraph 5(1)(b)] of this Schedule; but

(b) subject to section 8(1)(b) of this Act, at any time if he avers that the provision for distribution of the estate is or is likely to be unduly prejudicial to a creditor or class of creditors.

(2) The court may award sequestration in pursuance of sub-paragraph (1)(a) above if it considers that to do so would be in the best interests of the creditors.

(3) The court shall award sequestration in pursuance of sub-paragraph (1)(b) above if, but only if, it is satisfied that the creditor's said averment is correct.

8. In this Act a trust deed in respect of which paragraphs 6 and 7 of this Schedule apply is referred to as a "protected trust deed".

9. Where the trustee under a protected trust deed has made the final distribution of the estate among the creditors, he shall, not more than 28 days after the final distribution, send to the Accountant in Bankruptcy for registration in the register of insolvencies—

(a) a statement in the prescribed form indicating how the estate was realised and distributed; and

(b) a certificate to the effect that the distribution was in accordance with the trust deed.

10. Where the trustee under a protected trust deed has obtained a discharge from the creditors who have acceded to the trust deed he shall forthwith give notice of the discharge—

(a) by sending the notice by recorded delivery to every creditor known to him [who has not been sent a copy of the notice as mentioned in paragraph 5(1)(c) above or who has notified the trustee of his objection to the trust deed as mentioned in paragraph 5(1)(d) above]; and

(b) by sending the notice to the Accountant in Bankruptcy who shall register the fact of the discharge in the register of insolvencies,

and, except where the court makes an order under paragraph 12 below, the sending of such notice to a creditor [who has not been sent a copy of the notice as mentioned in paragraph 5(1)(c) above or who has notified the trustee of his objection to the trust deed as mentioned in paragraph 5(1)(d) above] shall be effective to make the discharge binding upon that creditor.

Creditors not acceding to protected trust deed

11. A creditor [who has not been sent a copy of the notice as mentioned in paragraph 5(1)(c) above or who has notified the trustee of his objection to the trust deed as mentioned in paragraph 5(1)(d) above] may, not more than 28 days after notice has been sent under paragraph 10 above, apply to the court for an order under paragraph 12 below.

12. Where, on an application by a creditor under paragraph 11 above, the court is satisfied (on grounds other than those on which a petition under paragraph 7(1)(b) above was or could have been presented by that creditor) that the intromissions of the trustee under the protected trust deed with the estate of the debtor have been so unduly prejudicial to that creditor's claim that he should not be bound by the discharge it may order that he shall not be so bound.

13. Where the court makes an order under paragraph 12 above, the clerk of the court shall send a copy of the order to—

(a) the trustee; and

(b) the Accountant in Bankruptcy who shall register the copy of the order in the register of insolvencies.

NOTES

Repealed as noted at the beginning of this Act.

Para 5: substituted by the Bankruptcy (Scotland) Act 1993, s 11(3), Sch 1, para 32(1), (2), subject to s 12(6) thereof, at **[5.194]** and to the Bankruptcy (Scotland) Act 1993 Commencement and Savings Order 1993, SI 1993/438, arts 4, 5, at **[16.58]**, **[16.59]**.

Para 6: sub-para (a) substituted by the Bankruptcy (Scotland) Act 1993, s 11(3), Sch 1, para 32(1), (3), subject to s 12(6) thereof, at **[5.194]** and to SI 1993/438, arts 4, 5, at **[16.58]**, **[16.59]**.

Paras 7, 10, 11: words in square brackets substituted by the Bankruptcy (Scotland) Act 1993, s 11(3), Sch 1, para 32(1), (4)–(6), subject to s 12(6) thereof, at **[5.194]** and to SI 1993/438, arts 4, 5, at **[16.58]**, **[16.59]**.".

Regulations: the Protected Trust Deeds (Scotland) Regulations 2013, SSI 2013/318 at **[16.266]**; the Common Financial Tool etc (Scotland) Regulations 2014, SSI 2014/290.

Acts of Sederunt: Act of Sederunt (Rules of Court Amendment No 1) (Bankruptcy Rules) 1993, SI 1993/514; Act of Sederunt (Bankruptcy Rules) 1993, SI 1993/921; Act of Sederunt (Rules of the Court of Session 1994), SI 1994/1443 at **[16.60]**; the Act of Sederunt (Sheriff Court Bankruptcy Rules) 2008, SSI 2008/119 at **[16.263]**.

Modification: in relation to the application of this Schedule, with modifications, in respect of the Lloyd's of London insurance market, see the Insurers (Reorganisation and Winding Up) Regulations 2004, SI 2004/353, reg 33 (as modified by Insurers (Reorganisation and Winding Up) (Lloyd's) Regulations 2005, SI 2005/1998, regs 32, 40(1)–(4), (11)).

SCHEDULE 6
MEETINGS OF CREDITORS AND COMMISSIONERS

Section 66

PART I
MEETINGS OF CREDITORS OTHER THAN THE STATUTORY MEETING

Calling of meeting

[5.188]

1. The . . . trustee shall call a meeting of creditors if required to do so by—

(a) order of the [sheriff];

(b) one-tenth in number or one-third in value of the creditors;

(c) a commissioner; or

(d) the Accountant in Bankruptcy.

2. A meeting called under paragraph 1 above shall be held not later than 28 days after the issuing of the order of the [sheriff] under sub-paragraph (a) of that paragraph or the receipt by the . . . trustee of the requirement under sub-paragraph (b), (c) or (d) thereof.

3. The . . . trustee or a commissioner who has given written notice to him may at any time call a meeting of creditors.

4. The . . . trustee or a commissioner calling a meeting under paragraph 1 or 3 above shall, not less than 7 days before the date fixed for the meeting, notify—

(a) every creditor known to him; and

(b) the Accountant in Bankruptcy,

of the date, time and place fixed for the holding of the meeting and its purpose.

5. (1) Where a requirement has been made under paragraph 1 above but no meeting has been called by the . . . trustee, the Accountant in Bankruptcy may, of his own accord or on the application of any creditor, call a meeting of creditors.

(2) The Accountant in Bankruptcy calling a meeting under this paragraph shall, not less than 7 days before the date fixed for the meeting, take reasonable steps to notify the creditors of the date, time and place fixed for the holding of the meeting and its purpose.

6. It shall not be necessary to notify under paragraph 4 or 5 of this Schedule any creditor whose accepted claim is less than £50 for such sum as may be prescribed, unless the creditor has requested in writing such notification.

Role of . . . trustee at meeting

7. (1) At the commencement of a meeting, the chairman shall be the . . . trustee who as chairman shall, after carrying out his duty under section 49(1) of this Act, invite the creditors to elect one of their number as chairman in his place and shall preside over the election.

(2) If a chairman is not elected in pursuance of this paragraph, the . . . trustee shall remain the chairman throughout the meeting.

(3) The . . . trustee shall arrange for a record to be made of the proceedings at the meeting . . .

Appeals

8. The . . . trustee, a creditor or any other person having an interest may, within 14 days after the date of a meeting called under paragraph 1 or 3 above, appeal to the sheriff against a resolution of the creditors at the meeting.

NOTES

Repealed as noted at the beginning of this Act.

Word "permanent" (omitted in each place) repealed and word in square brackets in paras (1), (2) substituted for original word "court" by the Bankruptcy and Diligence etc (Scotland) Act 2007, ss 36, 226(2), Sch 1, paras 1, 61(a), Sch 6, Pt 1, subject to transitional provisions and savings in SSI 2008/115, arts 5–7, 10, 15 at **[2.51]–[2.53]**, **[2.56]**, **[2.57]**.

Para 7: words "and he shall insert the minutes of the meeting in the sederunt book" omitted in the second place in sub-para (3) repealed by the Bankruptcy and Debt Advice (Scotland) Act 2014, s 56(2), Sch 4, subject to transitional provisions and savings in SSI 2014/261, arts 4, 12 at **[2.91]**, **[2.99]**

PART II
ALL MEETINGS OF CREDITORS

Validity of proceedings

[5.189]

9. No proceedings at a meeting shall be invalidated by reason only that any notice or other document relating to the calling of the meeting which is required to be sent or given under any provision of this Act has not been received by, or come to the attention of, any creditor before the meeting.

Locus of meeting

10. Every meeting shall be held in such place (whether or not in the sheriffdom) as is, in the opinion of the person calling the meeting, the most convenient for the majority of the creditors.

Mandatories

11. (1) A creditor may authorise in writing any person to represent him at a meeting.

(2) A creditor shall lodge any authorisation given under sub-paragraph (1) above with . . . the . . . trustee before the commencement of the meeting.

(3) Any reference in paragraph 7(1) of this Schedule and the following provisions of this Part of this Schedule to a creditor shall include a reference to a person authorised by him under this paragraph.

Quorum

12. The quorum at any meeting shall be one creditor.

Voting at meeting

13. Any question at a meeting shall be determined by a majority in value of the creditors who vote on that question.

Objections by creditors

14. (1) The chairman at any meeting may allow or disallow any objection by a creditor, other than (if the chairman is not the . . . trustee) an objection relating to a creditor's claim.

(2) Any person aggrieved by the determination of the chairman in respect of an objection may appeal therefrom to the sheriff.

(3) If the chairman is in doubt whether to allow or disallow an objection, the meeting shall proceed as if no objection had been made, except that for the purposes of appeal the objection shall be deemed to have been disallowed.

Adjournment of meeting

15. (1) If no creditor has appeared at a meeting at the expiry of a period of half an hour after the time appointed for the commencement of the meeting, the chairman [may] adjourn the meeting to such other day as the chairman [may] appoint, being not less than 7 nor more than 21 days after the day on which the meeting was adjourned.

(2) The chairman may, with the consent of a majority in value of the creditors who vote on the matter, adjourn a meeting.

(3) Any adjourned meeting shall be held at the same time and place as the original meeting, unless in the resolution for the adjournment of the meeting another time or place is specified.

Minutes of meeting

16. The minutes of every meeting shall be signed by the chairman and within 14 days of the meeting a copy of the minutes shall be sent to the Accountant in Bankruptcy.

NOTES

Repealed as noted at the beginning of this Act.

Para 11: words "the interim trustee or, as the case may be," and "permanent" omitted from sub-para (2) respectively, repealed by the Bankruptcy and Diligence etc (Scotland) Act 2007, s 226(2), Sch 6, Pt 1, subject to transitional provisions and savings in SSI 2008/115, arts 5–7, 10, 15 at **[2.51]–[2.53]**, **[2.56]**, **[2.57]**.

Para 14: word "permanent" omitted from sub-para (1) repealed by the Bankruptcy and Diligence etc (Scotland) Act 2007, s 226(2), Sch 6, Pt 1, subject to transitional provisions and savings in SSI 2008/115, arts 5–7, 10, 15 at **[2.51]–[2.53]**, **[2.56]**, **[2.57]**.

Para 15: in sub-para (1), word in both pairs of square brackets substituted for original word "shall" by the Bankruptcy and Diligence etc (Scotland) Act 2007, s 36, Sch 1, paras 1, 61(b), subject to transitional provisions and savings in SSI 2008/115, arts 5–7, 10, 15 at **[2.51]–[2.53]**, **[2.56]**, **[2.57]**.

PART III
MEETING OF COMMISSIONERS

[5.190]

17. The . . . trustee may call a meeting of commissioners at any time, and shall call a meeting of commissioners—

(a) on being required to do so by order of the [sheriff]; or

(b) on being requested to do so by the Accountant in Bankruptcy or any commissioner.

18. If the . . . trustee fails to call a meeting of commissioners within 14 days of being required or requested to do so under paragraph 17 of this Schedule, a commissioner may call a meeting of commissioners.

19. The . . . trustee shall give the commissioners at least 7 days notice of a meeting called by him, unless the commissioners decide that they do not require such notice.

20. The . . . trustee shall act as clerk at meetings . . .

21. If the commissioners are considering the performance of the functions of the . . . trustee under any provision of this Act, he shall withdraw from the meeting if requested to do so by the commissioners; and in such a case a commissioner shall act as clerk, shall transmit a record of the deliberations of the commissioners to the . . . trustee . . .

22. The quorum at a meeting of commissioners shall be one commissioner and the commissioners may act by a majority of the commissioners present at the meeting.

23. Any matter may be agreed by the commissioners without a meeting if such agreement is unanimous and is subsequently recorded in a minute signed by the commissioners . . .

NOTES

Repealed as noted at the beginning of this Act.

Word "permanent" omitted repealed and word in square brackets in para 17 substituted for original word "court" by the Bankruptcy and Diligence etc (Scotland) Act 2007, ss 36, 226(2), Sch 1, paras 1, 61(a), Sch 6, Pt 1, subject to transitional provisions and savings in SSI 2008/115, arts 5–7, 10, 15 at **[2.51]–[2.53]**, **[2.56]**, **[2.57]**.

Words omitted from paras 20, 21, 23 repealed by the Bankruptcy and Debt Advice (Scotland) Act 2014, s 56(2), Sch 4, subject to transitional provisions and savings in SSI 2014/261, arts 4, 12 at **[2.91]**, **[2.99]**.

SCHEDULE 7

Section 75(1)

(Pt I contains consequential amendments which, in so far as unrepealed and relevant to this work, have been incorporated at the appropriate place.)

PART II
RE-ENACTMENT OF CERTAIN PROVISIONS OF BANKRUPTCY (SCOTLAND) ACT 1913 (C 20)

Arrestments and Poindings

[5.191]

24. (1) Subject to sub-paragraph (2) below, all arrestments and [attachments] which have been executed within 60 days prior to the constitution of the apparent insolvency of the debtor, or within four months thereafter, shall be ranked *pari passu* as if they had all been executed on the same date.

(2) Any such arrestment which is executed on the dependence of an action shall be followed up without undue delay.

(3) Any creditor judicially producing in a process relative to the subject of such arrestment or [attachment] liquid grounds of debt or decree of payment within 60 days or four months referred to in sub-paragraph (1) above shall be entitled to rank as if he had executed an arrestment or [an attachment]; and if [in the meantime the first or any subsequent arrester obtains] a decree of furthcoming, and recovers payment, or [an attaching] creditor carries through [an auction] [or receives payment in respect of a [attached] article upon its redemption], he shall be accountable for the sum recovered to those who, by virtue of this Act, may be eventually found to have a right to a ranking *pari passu* thereon, and shall be liable in an action at their instance for payment to them proportionately, after allowing out of the fund the expense of such recovery.

(4) Arrestments executed for attaching the same effects of the debtor after the period of four months subsequent to the constitution of his apparent insolvency shall not compete with those within the said periods prior or subsequent thereto, but may rank with each other on any reversion of the fund attached in accordance with any enactment or rule of law relating thereto.

(5) Any reference in the foregoing provisions of this paragraph to a debtor shall be construed as including a reference to an entity whose apparent insolvency may, by virtue of subsection [(4)] of section 7 of this Act, be constituted under subsection (1) of that section.

(6) This paragraph shall apply in respect of arrestments and poindings which have been executed either before or after the coming into force of this paragraph.

(7) The repeal of the Bankruptcy (Scotland) Act 1913 shall not affect the equalisation of arrestments and poindings (whether executed before or after the coming into force of this paragraph) in consequence of the constitution of notour bankruptcy under that Act.

[(8) Nothing in this paragraph shall apply to an earnings arrestment, a current maintenance arrestment or a conjoined arrestment order.]

Exemptions from stamp or other duties for conveyances, deeds etc relating to sequestrated estates

25. Any—

(a) conveyance, assignation, instrument, discharge, writing, or deed relating solely to the estate of a debtor which has been or may be sequestrated, either under this or any former Act, being estate which after the execution of such conveyance, assignation, instrument, discharge, writing, or deed, shall be and remain the property of such debtor, for the benefit of his creditors, or the . . . trustee appointed or chosen under or by virtue of such sequestration,

(b) discharge to such debtor,

(c) deed, assignation, instrument, or writing for reinvesting the debtor in the estate,

(d) article of roup or sale, or submission,

(e) other instrument or writing whatsoever relating solely to the estate of any such debtor; and

(f) other deed or writing forming part of the proceedings ordered under sequestration, shall be exempt from all stamp duties or other Government duty.

NOTES

Repealed as noted at the beginning of this Act.

Para 24: word in square brackets in sub-para (1) and words in first, second, fourth, fifth and seventh (inner) pairs of square brackets in sub-para (3) substituted by the Debt Arrangement and Attachment (Scotland) Act 2002, s 61, Sch 3, Pt 1, para 15(1), (5), subject to a saving in s 59 of that Act in relation to a poinding in respect of which a warrant sale has been completed before 30 December 2002; words in third pair of square brackets in para (3) substituted (for original words "the first or any subsequent arrester obtains in the meantime" by the Bankruptcy and Debt Advice (Scotland) Act 2014, s 56(1), Sch 3, paras 2, 37, subject to transitional provisions and savings in SSI 2014/261, arts 4, 12 at **[2.91]**, **[2.99]**; words in sixth (outer) pair of square brackets in sub-para (3) inserted and whole of sub-para (8) added by the Debtors (Scotland) Act 1987, s 108(1), Sch 6, para 28; in sub-para (5), figure in square brackets substituted for original figure "(5)" by the Bankruptcy and Diligence etc (Scotland) Act 2007, s 36, Sch 1, paras 1, 62, subject to transitional provisions and savings in SSI 2008/115, arts 5–7, 10, 15 at **[2.51]–[2.53]**, **[2.56]**, **[2.57]**.

Para 25: words "interim or permanent" omitted from sub-para (a) repealed by the Bankruptcy and Diligence etc (Scotland) Act 2007, s 226(2), Sch 6, Pt 1, subject to transitional provisions and savings in SSI 2008/115, arts 5–7, 10, 15 at **[2.51]–[2.53]**, **[2.56]**, **[2.57]**.

SCHEDULE 8

(*Sch 8 contains repeals only.*)

BANKRUPTCY (SCOTLAND) ACT 1993

(1993 c 6)

An Act to amend the Bankruptcy (Scotland) Act 1985; and for connected purposes

[18 February 1993]

NOTES

This Act is repealed by the Bankruptcy (Scotland) Act 2016, s 234(2), Sch 9, Pt 1, as from 30 November 2016, subject to transitional provisions and savings in s 234(3)–(8) thereof at **[5.432]**.

1–8 (*Outside the scope of this work.*)

[5.192]

9 Remuneration of permanent trustee

(1) This section applies in the case of any sequestration in respect of which the petition is presented during the period beginning with the day on which this Act is passed and ending with the commencement of section 2 of this Act, being a sequestration to which Schedule 2 to the 1985 Act applies and in respect of which the permanent trustee is entitled to payment of his outlays and remuneration by virtue of paragraph 9 of that Schedule.

(2) In the case of any sequestration to which this section applies, section 53 of the 1985 Act shall apply for the purposes of the determination of the remuneration and outlays of the permanent trustee subject to the provisions of regulations made under this section.

(3) Regulations under this section may prescribe—

(a) the work in respect of which remuneration and outlays may be claimed, including work undertaken while the permanent trustee was acting as interim trustee;
(b) an amount which shall be paid in respect of remuneration and outlays in respect of any sequestration to which this section applies; and
(c) a scale of fees relating to the nature and extent of work undertaken to apply for the purposes of determining the remuneration and outlays in respect of any such sequestration.

(4) Such regulations may enable the Accountant in Bankruptcy, having taken into account the matters mentioned in paragraphs (a) and (b) of section 53(4) of the 1985 Act, to determine whether, in relation to any sequestration to which this section applies, the remuneration and outlays shall be—
(a) the amount mentioned in subsection (3)(b) above; or
(b) determined by reference to the scale mentioned in subsection (3)(c) above.

(5) Section 72 of the 1985 Act shall apply to regulations made under this section as it applies to regulations made under that Act.

(6) A determination by the Accountant in Bankruptcy in pursuance of regulations made under this section may be appealed to the sheriff in accordance with subsection (6) of the said section 53.

NOTES

Repealed as noted at the beginning of this Act.

[5.193]
10 Finance

(1) There shall be paid into the Consolidated Fund any fees received by the Accountant in Bankruptcy in pursuance of regulations made under section 69A of the 1985 Act.

(2) There shall be paid out of money provided by Parliament—
(a) any fees paid in pursuance of section 1B(4) of the 1985 Act as inserted by section 1(1) of this Act;
(b) any administrative expenses incurred by the Secretary of State under this Act; and
(c) any increase attributable to this Act in the sums so payable under any other Act.

NOTES

Repealed as noted at the beginning of this Act.

11 (*Outside the scope of this work.*)

[5.194]
12 Short title, interpretation, commencement and extent

(1) This Act may be cited as the Bankruptcy (Scotland) Act 1993.

(2) Expressions used in this Act and in the 1985 Act shall have the same meaning in this Act as they do in that Act.

(3) The following provisions shall come into force on the day on which this Act is passed, namely—
section 8;
section 9;
this section; and
paragraphs 22(5), 23 and 31(4) and (5) of Schedule 1 and, so far as relating to those paragraphs, section 11.

(4) Subject to subsection (3) above, this Act shall come into force on such day as the Secretary of State may by order made by statutory instrument appoint; and different days may be so appointed for different purposes and for different provisions.

(5) An order under subsection (4) above may contain such transitional provisions and savings as appear to the Secretary of State necessary or expedient in connection with the provisions brought into force (whether wholly or partly) by the order.

(6) Notwithstanding anything in an order made under subsection (4) above, nothing in any provision commenced by such an order shall have effect as regards any sequestration in respect of which the petition is presented before such commencement.

(7) Subject to subsection (8) below, this Act extends to Scotland only.

(8) The amendment by this Act of an enactment which extends to England and Wales or Northern Ireland extends also to England and Wales or, as the case may be, Northern Ireland.

NOTES

Repealed as noted at the beginning of this Act.
Orders: the Bankruptcy (Scotland) Act 1993 Commencement and Savings Order 1993, SI 1993/438.

SCHEDULES 1 AND 2

(*Schs 1, 2 outside the scope of this work.*)

BANKRUPTCY (SCOTLAND) ACT 2016

(2016 asp 21)

ARRANGEMENT OF SECTIONS

PART 1
APPLICATION OR PETITION FOR SEQUESTRATION

Applications and petitions

1 Sequestration . . . [5.195]
2 Sequestration of estate of living debtor . . . [5.196]
3 Debt advice and information package . . . [5.197]
4 Money advice . . . [5.198]
5 Sequestration of estate of deceased debtor . . . [5.199]
6 Sequestration of other estates . . . [5.200]
7 Qualified creditor and qualified creditors . . . [5.201]
8 Debtor applications: general . . . [5.202]
9 Certificate for sequestration . . . [5.203]
10 Death or withdrawal . . . [5.204]
11 Debtor application: provision of information . . . [5.205]
12 Petition for sequestration of estate: provision of information . . . [5.206]
13 Further provisions relating to presentation of petitions . . . [5.207]
14 Further provisions relating to debtor applications . . . [5.208]
14A Main proceedings in Scotland: undertaking by trustee in respect of assets in another EU member State . . . [5.209]
14B Main proceedings in another member State: approval of undertaking offered by member State insolvency practitioner to local creditors in the UK . . . [5.210]

Jurisdiction

15 Jurisdiction . . . [5.211]

Meaning of "apparent insolvency"

16 Meaning of "apparent insolvency" . . . [5.212]

Concurrent proceedings

17 Concurrent proceedings for sequestration or analogous remedy . . . [5.213]
18 Powers in relation to concurrent proceedings . . . [5.214]

Creditor's oath

19 Creditor's oath . . . [5.215]

PART 2
SEQUESTRATION: AWARD AND RECALL

Incomplete or inappropriate debtor applications

20 Debtor application: incomplete application . . . [5.216]
21 Refusal of debtor application: inappropriate application . . . [5.217]

Award of sequestration

22 When sequestration is awarded . . . [5.218]
23 Circumstances in which sequestration is not to be awarded in pursuance of section 22(5) . . . [5.219]
23A Effect of sequestration on land attachment . . . [5.220]
24 Effect of sequestration on diligence generally . . . [5.221]
25 Effect of sequestration on diligence: estate of deceased debtor . . . [5.222]
26 Registration of warrant or determination of debtor application . . . [5.223]
27 Further matters in relation to award of sequestration . . . [5.224]
28 Benefit from another estate . . . [5.225]

Recall of sequestration

29 Petitions for recall of sequestration . . . [5.226]
30 Recall of sequestration by sheriff . . . [5.227]
31 Application to Accountant in Bankruptcy for recall of sequestration . . . [5.228]
32 Application under section 31: further procedure . . . [5.229]
33 Determination where amount of outlays and remuneration not agreed . . . [5.230]
34 Recall of sequestration by Accountant in Bankruptcy . . . [5.231]
35 Recall where Accountant in Bankruptcy trustee . . . [5.232]
36 Application for recall: remit to sheriff . . . [5.233]
37 Recall of sequestration by Accountant in Bankruptcy: review and appeal . . . [5.234]

38 Effect of recall of sequestration . . . . . [5.235]

PART 3
INITIAL STAGES OF SEQUESTRATION, STATUTORY MEETING AND TRUSTEE VOTE

Initial stages

39 Interim preservation of estate . . . . . [5.236]
40 Offences in relation to interim preservation of estate . . . . . [5.237]
41 Statement of assets and liabilities etc . . . . . [5.238]
42 Duties on receipt of list of assets and liabilities . . . . . [5.239]

Statutory meeting

43 Statutory meeting . . . . . [5.240]
44 Calling of statutory meeting . . . . . [5.241]
45 Procedure where no statutory meeting called . . . . . [5.242]
46 Submission of claims for voting purposes . . . . . [5.243]
47 Offences in relation to submission of claims for voting purposes . . . . . [5.244]
48 Proceedings before trustee vote . . . . . [5.245]

Trustee vote

49 Trustee vote . . . . . [5.246]

PART 4
TRUSTEES AND COMMISSIONERS

Trustees

50 Functions of trustee . . . . . [5.247]
51 Appointment of trustee . . . . . [5.248]
52 Application to Accountant in Bankruptcy by trustee for a direction . . . . . [5.249]

Interim trustees

53 Functions of interim trustee . . . . . [5.250]
54 Appointment of interim trustee . . . . . [5.251]
55 Removal, resignation etc of interim trustee . . . . . [5.252]
56 Termination of interim trustee's functions where not appointed trustee . . . . . [5.253]
57 Appeal or review by virtue of section 56 . . . . . [5.254]
58 Termination of Accountant in Bankruptcy's functions as interim trustee where not appointed trustee . . . . . [5.255]
59 Review or appeal by virtue of section 58 . . . . . [5.256]

Replacement trustees

60 Appointment of replacement trustee . . . . . [5.257]
61 Procedure in application to Accountant in Bankruptcy under section 60 . . . . . [5.258]
62 Procedure in application under section 60, or appeal under section 61, to sheriff . . . . . [5.259]
63 Termination of original trustee's functions . . . . . [5.260]
64 Accountant in Bankruptcy's intromissions in capacity of original trustee . . . . . [5.261]
65 Discharge of original trustee . . . . . [5.262]
66 Replacement of trustee acting in more than one sequestration . . . . . [5.263]
67 Further provision as regards replacement under section 66 . . . . . [5.264]
68 Review of determination or appointment under section 66 . . . . . [5.265]

Resignation or death of trustee

69 Resignation or death of trustee . . . . . [5.266]

Removal of trustee and appointment of new trustee

70 Removal of trustee other than where trustee is unable to act or should no longer continue to act: general . . . . . [5.267]
71 Removal of trustee other than where trustee is unable to act or should no longer continue to act: review, appeal and election of new trustee . . . . . [5.268]
72 Removal of trustee where trustee is unable to act or should no longer continue to act: general . [5.269]
73 Removal of trustee where trustee is unable to act or should no longer continue to act: review, appeal and election of new trustee . . . . . [5.270]
74 Election or appointment of new trustee by virtue of section 71(6) or 73(1) . . . . . [5.271]
75 Further provision as regards election or appointment of new trustee . . . . . [5.272]

Commissioners

76 Commissioners . . . . . [5.273]
77 Election, resignation and removal of commissioners . . . . . [5.274]

PART 5
VESTING ETC

Vesting

78 Vesting of estate at date of sequestration .....[5.275]
79 Provision supplementary to section 78 and interpretation of Part 5 .....[5.276]
80 Property subject to restraint order .....[5.277]
81 Property released from detention .....[5.278]
82 Property in respect of which receivership or administration order is made .....[5.279]
83 Property in respect of which realisation order is made .....[5.280]
84 Property subject to certain orders where confiscation order discharged or quashed .....[5.281]
85 Vesting of income received by debtor after sequestration .....[5.282]
86 Further provision as regards vesting of estate .....[5.283]
87 Dealings and circumstances of debtor after sequestration .....[5.284]

Limitation on vesting

88 Limitation on vesting .....[5.285]

PART 6
DEBTOR'S CONTRIBUTION

Common financial tool

89 Assessment of debtor's contribution .....[5.286]

Payments by debtor following sequestration

90 Debtor contribution order: general .....[5.287]
91 Debtor contribution order: payment period and intervals .....[5.288]
92 Debtor contribution order: review and appeal .....[5.289]
93 Effect of debtor contribution order .....[5.290]
94 Deductions from debtor's earnings and other income .....[5.291]
95 Variation and removal of debtor contribution order by trustee .....[5.292]
96 Payment break .....[5.293]
97 Sections 95 and 96: review and appeal .....[5.294]

PART 7
SAFEGUARDING INTERESTS OF CREDITORS

Gratuitous alienations and unfair preferences

98 Gratuitous alienations .....[5.295]
99 Unfair preferences .....[5.296]

Recall of certain orders

100 Recall of order for payment of capital sum on divorce or on dissolution of civil partnership .....[5.297]

Excessive contributions

101 Recovery of excessive pension contributions .....[5.298]
102 Orders under section 101 .....[5.299]
103 Orders under section 101: supplementary .....[5.300]
104 Excessive contributions in pension-sharing cases: general .....[5.301]
105 Excessive contributions in pension-sharing cases: recovery orders .....[5.302]
106 Recovery orders: supplementary .....[5.303]
107 References in Part 7 to "the 1889 Act" and to "the 1999 Act" .....[5.304]

PART 8
ADMINISTRATION OF ESTATE BY TRUSTEE

General

108 Taking possession of estate by trustee .....[5.305]
109 Management and realisation of estate .....[5.306]

Contractual Powers and Money Received

110 Contractual powers of trustee .....[5.307]
111 Money received by trustee .....[5.308]

Debtor's home

112 Debtor's family home .....[5.309]
113 Power of trustee in relation to debtor's family home .....[5.310]

Rights of spouse or civil partner

114 Protection of rights of spouse against arrangements intended to defeat them .....[5.311]
115 Protection of rights of civil partner against arrangements intended to defeat them .....[5.312]

Account of state of affairs

116 Debtor's account of state of affairs . . . [5.313]

Financial education for debtor

117 Financial education for debtor . . . [5.314]

PART 9
EXAMINATION OF DEBTOR

Private and public examination

118 Private examination . . . [5.315]
119 Public examination . . . [5.316]
120 Provisions ancillary to sections 118 and 119 . . . [5.317]

Conduct of examination

121 Conduct of examination . . . [5.318]

PART 10
CLAIMS, DIVIDENDS AND DISTRIBUTION ETC

Submission and adjudication of claims

122 Submission of claims to trustee . . . [5.319]
123 Evidence as to validity or amount of claim . . . [5.320]
124 False claims etc . . . [5.321]
125 Further provision as to claims . . . [5.322]
126 Adjudication of claims: general . . . [5.323]
127 Adjudication of claims: review and appeal . . . [5.324]

Entitlement to vote and draw a dividend

128 Voting and drawing a dividend . . . [5.325]

Distribution

129 Priority in distribution . . . [5.326]
130 Accounting periods . . . [5.327]
131 Distribution in accordance with accounting periods . . . [5.328]

Procedure after end of accounting period

132 Submission of accounts and scheme of division . . . [5.329]
133 Audit of accounts and determination as to outlays and remuneration payable to trustee . . . [5.330]
134 Appeal against determination as to outlays and remuneration payable to trustee . . . [5.331]
135 Further provision as to procedure after end of accounting period . . . [5.332]
136 Procedure after end of accounting period where Accountant in Bankruptcy is trustee . . . [5.333]

PART 11
DISCHARGE

Discharge of debtor

137 Discharge of debtor where Accountant in Bankruptcy not trustee . . . [5.334]
138 Discharge of debtor where Accountant in Bankruptcy trustee . . . [5.335]
139 Discharge of debtor: review and appeal . . . [5.336]
140 Discharge of debtor to whom section 2(2) applies . . . [5.337]
141 Deferral of discharge where debtor cannot be traced . . . [5.338]
142 Debtor not traced: new trustee . . . [5.339]
143 Debtor not traced: subsequent debtor contact . . . [5.340]
144 Subsequent debtor contact: review and appeal . . . [5.341]
145 Effect of discharge under section 137, 138 or 140 . . . [5.342]
146 Discharge under section 140: conditions . . . [5.343]
147 Section 146: sanctions . . . [5.344]

Discharge of trustee

148 Discharge of trustee . . . [5.345]
149 Further provision as regards discharge of trustee . . . [5.346]
150 Unclaimed dividends . . . [5.347]
151 Discharge of Accountant in Bankruptcy . . . [5.348]

PART 12
ASSETS DISCOVERED AFTER DISCHARGE OF TRUSTEE

152 Assets discovered after discharge of trustee: appointment of trustee . . . [5.349]
153 Assets discovered after discharge of trustee: notice . . . [5.350]
154 Assets discovered after discharge of trustee: appeal . . . [5.351]

PART 13
BANKRUPTCY RESTRICTIONS ORDERS AND INTERIM BANKRUPTCY RESTRICTIONS ORDERS

Bankruptcy restrictions orders

155 Bankruptcy restrictions order . . . [5.352]
156 Grounds for making bankruptcy restrictions order . . . [5.353]
157 Bankruptcy restrictions order: application of section 218(13) . . . [5.354]
158 Timing for making a bankruptcy restrictions order . . . [5.355]
159 Duration of bankruptcy restrictions order and application for revocation or variation . . . [5.356]

Interim bankruptcy restrictions orders

160 Interim bankruptcy restrictions orders . . . [5.357]

Effect of recall of sequestration

161 Bankruptcy restrictions orders and interim bankruptcy restrictions orders: effect of recall of sequestration . . . [5.358]

PART 14
VOLUNTARY TRUST DEEDS FOR CREDITORS

General

162 Voluntary trust deeds for creditors . . . [5.359]

Protected trust deeds: protected status

163 Protected status: general . . . [5.360]

Conditions for protected status

164 Protected status: the debtor . . . [5.361]
165 Protected status: the trustee . . . [5.362]
166 Exclusion of a secured creditor from trust deed . . . [5.363]
167 Statements in and advice regarding trust deed . . . [5.364]
168 Payment of debtor's contribution . . . [5.365]
169 Notice in register of insolvencies . . . [5.366]
170 Documents to be sent to creditors . . . [5.367]

Registration for protected status

171 Registration for protected status . . . [5.368]

Effect of Protected Status etc

172 Effect of protected status: general . . . [5.369]
173 Effect of protected status on diligence against earnings . . . [5.370]
173A Effect of protected status on essential supplies . . . [5.371]
174 Deductions by virtue of protected trust deed from debtor's earnings . . . [5.372]
175 Agreement in respect of debtor's heritable property . . . [5.373]
176 Dividend payments . . . [5.374]
177 Sequestration petition by qualified creditor . . . [5.375]
178 Creditor's application as respects intromissions of trustee . . . [5.376]

Administration, accounting and discharge

179 Directions to trustee under protected trust deed . . . [5.377]
180 Information and notification obligations of trustee under protected trust deed . . . [5.378]
181 Administration of trust under protected trust deed . . . [5.379]
182 Retention of documents by trustee under protected trust deed . . . [5.380]
183 Remuneration payable to trustee under protected trust deed . . . [5.381]
184 Protected trust deed: discharge of debtor . . . [5.382]
185 Student loans . . . [5.383]
186 Protected trust deed: discharge of trustee . . . [5.384]
187 Electronic delivery of notices etc under this Part . . . [5.385]

Appeals and directions

188 Protected trust deed: appeal . . . [5.386]
189 Protected trust deed: sheriff's direction . . . [5.387]

Application for conversion to sequestration

190 Application for conversion to sequestration . . . [5.388]
191 Contents of affidavit required under section 190(2) . . . [5.389]
192 Powers of Accountant in Bankruptcy on application for conversion to sequestration . . . [5.390]

Part 14: General

193 Interpretation of Part 14 . . . [5.391]
194 Regulations modifying Part 14 . . . [5.392]

PART 15
MORATORIUM ON DILIGENCE

195 Moratorium on diligence: notice of intention to make debtor application under section 2(1)(a) .[5.393]
196 Moratorium on diligence: notice of intention to make debtor application under section 6 .[5.394]
197 Moratorium on diligence following notice under section 195(1) or 196(1) .[5.395]
198 Period of moratorium .[5.396]

PART 16
ACCOUNTANT IN BANKRUPTCY

Appointment

199 Accountant in Bankruptcy .[5.397]

Functions

200 Supervisory functions of Accountant in Bankruptcy .[5.398]
201 Performance of certain functions of Accountant in Bankruptcy .[5.399]
202 Further duty of Accountant in Bankruptcy .[5.400]

Directions to accountant in bankruptcy

203 Directions to Accountant in Bankruptcy .[5.401]

Conduct of proceedings in the sheriff court

204 Conduct of proceedings in the sheriff court .[5.402]

Fees for accountant in bankruptcy

205 Fees for Accountant in Bankruptcy .[5.403]

PART 17
MISCELLANEOUS

206 Liabilities and rights of co-obligants .[5.404]
207 Member State insolvency practitioner deemed creditor .[5.405]
208 Trustee's duty to provide certain notices and copies of documents to member State insolvency practitioner .[5.406]
209 Extortionate credit transactions .[5.407]
210 Sederunt book and other documents .[5.408]
211 Power of court to cure defects in procedure .[5.409]
212 Power of Accountant in Bankruptcy to cure defects in procedure .[5.410]
213 Decision under section 212(1): review .[5.411]
214 Review of decision by Accountant in Bankruptcy: grounds of appeal .[5.412]
215 Debtor to co-operate with trustee .[5.413]
216 Arbitration and compromise .[5.414]
217 Meetings of creditors and commissioners .[5.415]
218 General offences by debtor etc .[5.416]
219 General offences: supplementary and penalties .[5.417]
220 Summary proceedings .[5.418]
221 Outlays of insolvency practitioner in actings as interim trustee or trustee .[5.419]
222 Supplies by utilities .[5.420]
223 Disqualification provisions: power to make regulations .[5.421]
224 Regulations: applications to Accountant in Bankruptcy etc .[5.422]

PART 18
GENERAL

225 Regulations: general .[5.423]
226 Modification of regulation making powers .[5.424]
227 Variation of references to time, money etc .[5.425]
228 Interpretation .[5.426]
229 Meaning of "associate" .[5.427]
230 "Associates": regulations for the purposes of section 229 .[5.428]
231 Proceedings under EU insolvency proceedings regulation: modified definition of "estate" .[5.429]
232 Crown application .[5.430]
233 Re-enactment .[5.431]
234 Modifications, repeals, savings, revocations and transitional provisions .[5.432]
235 Continuity of the law .[5.433]
236 Sequestrations to which this Act applies .[5.434]
237 Commencement .[5.435]
238 Short title .[5.436]

SCHEDULES

Schedule 1—Debtor to Whom Section 2(2) Applies: Application of Act. . . . .[5.437]
Schedule 2—Determination of Amount of Creditor's Claim. . . . .[5.438]
Schedule 3—Preferred Debts
Part 1—List of Preferred Debts . . . .[5.439]
Part 2—Interpretation of Part 1 . . . .[5.440]
Schedule 4—Voluntary Trust Deeds for Creditors. . . . .[5.441]
Schedule 5—Information to be Included in the Sederunt Book . . . .[5.442]
Schedule 6—Meetings of Creditors and Commissioners
Part 1—Meetings of Creditors other than the Statutory Meeting . . . .[5.443]
Part 2—All Meetings of Creditors . . . .[5.444]
Part 3—Meetings of Commissioners . . . .[5.445]
Schedule 7—Re-Enactment of Sections 10 and 189 of the Bankruptcy (Scotland) Act 1913 . . . .[5.446]

An Act of the Scottish Parliament to consolidate the Bankruptcy (Scotland) Act 1985, the Bankruptcy (Scotland) Act 1993, Part 1 of the Bankruptcy and Diligence etc (Scotland) Act 2007, Part 2 of the Home Owner and Debtor Protection (Scotland) Act 2010, the Bankruptcy and Debt Advice (Scotland) Act 2014, the Protected Trust Deeds (Scotland) Regulations 2013 and related enactments.

28 April 2016

PART 1
APPLICATION OR PETITION FOR SEQUESTRATION

Applications and petitions

[5.195]

1 Sequestration

The estate of a debtor may be sequestrated in accordance with the provisions of this Act.

NOTES

Commencement: 30 November 2016.

[5.196]

2 Sequestration of estate of living debtor

(1) The sequestration of the estate of a living debtor is—
- (a) by debtor application made by the debtor, if subsection (2) or (8) applies to the debtor, or
- (b) on the petition of—
  - (i) a qualified creditor, or qualified creditors, if the debtor is apparently insolvent,
  - (ii) a temporary administrator,
  - (iii) a member State [insolvency practitioner] appointed in main proceedings, or
  - (iv) a trustee acting under a trust deed if a condition mentioned in subsection (7) is satisfied.

(2) This subsection applies to the debtor where—
- (a) the debtor—
  - (i) has been assessed by the common financial tool as requiring to make no debtor's contribution, or
  - (ii) has been in receipt of payments, of a kind prescribed, for a period of at least 6 months ending with the day on which the debtor application is made,
- (b) the total amount of the debtor's debts (including interest) at the date the debtor application is made is—
  - (i) not less than £1,500 or such other amount as may be prescribed, and
  - (ii) not more than £17,000 or such other amount as may be prescribed,
- (c) the total value of the debtor's assets (leaving out of account any liabilities) on the date the debtor application is made does not exceed £2,000 or such other amount as may be prescribed,
- (d) no single asset of the debtor has a value which exceeds £1,000 or such other amount as may be prescribed,
- (e) the debtor does not own land,
- (f) the debtor has been granted, within the prescribed period and in accordance with section 9, a certificate for sequestration of the debtor's estate,
- (g) in the 10 years ending on the day before the day on which the debtor application is made or such other period as may be prescribed, no award of sequestration has been made against the debtor in pursuance of an application made by the debtor by virtue of this subsection, and
- (h) in the 5 years ending on the day before the day on which the debtor application is made, no award of sequestration has been made against the debtor in pursuance of—
  - (i) an application made by the debtor other than by virtue of this subsection, or
  - (ii) a petition.

(3) For the purposes of subsection (2)(c) and (d)—
- (a) any property of the debtor is not to be regarded as an asset if, under any provision of this or any other enactment, it would be excluded from vesting in AiB as trustee,
- (b) if the debtor reasonably requires the use of a vehicle, any vehicle owned by the debtor the value of which does not exceed £3,000 or such other amount as may be prescribed is not to be regarded as an asset, and
- (c) any other property of the debtor that is of a prescribed type is not to be regarded as an asset.

(4) For the purposes of subsection (2)(c) and (d), the Scottish Ministers may by regulations make provision about how the value of the debtor's assets is to be determined.
(5) The Scottish Ministers may by regulations modify subsection (2).
(6) Schedule 1 makes further provision about the application of certain provisions of this Act in relation to a debtor to whom subsection (2) applies.
(7) The conditions mentioned in subsection (1)(b)(iv) are—
(a) that the debtor has failed to comply—
(i) with an obligation imposed on the debtor under the trust deed, being an obligation with which the debtor reasonably could have complied, or
(ii) with an instruction reasonably given to, or requirement reasonably made of, the debtor by the trustee for the purposes of the trust deed, or
(b) that the trustee avers in the trustee's petition that it would be in the best interests of the creditors that an award of sequestration be made.
(8) This subsection applies to the debtor where—
(a) the total amount of the debtor's debts (including interest) at the date the debtor application is made is not less than £3,000 or such sum as may be prescribed,
(b) an award of sequestration has not been made against the debtor in the 5 years ending on the day before the date the debtor application is made,
(c) the debtor has obtained the advice of a money adviser in accordance with section 4(1),
(d) the debtor has given a statement of undertakings (including an undertaking to pay to the trustee, after the award of sequestration of the debtor's estate, an amount determined using the common financial tool), and
(e) the debtor—
(i) is apparently insolvent,
(ii) has been granted, within the prescribed period and in accordance with section 9, a certificate for sequestration of the debtor's estate, or
(iii) has granted a trust deed which, by reason of creditors objecting, or not agreeing, to it is not a protected trust deed.
(9) For the purposes of subsection (8)(e)(i), the debtor is not apparently insolvent by reason only of granting a trust deed or of giving notice to creditors as mentioned in section 16(1)(c).
(10) In subsection (8)(e)(ii), "the prescribed period" means such period, ending immediately before the date the debtor application is made, as may be prescribed under section 9(4)(b).

NOTES

Commencement: 30 November 2016.

Sub-s (1): words in square brackets substituted for original word "liquidator" by the Insolvency (Regulation (EU) 2015/848) (Miscellaneous Amendments) (Scotland) Regulations 2017, SSI 2017/210, regs 4(1), (2), 9, as from 26 June 2017, except in relation to proceedings opened before that date.

Regulations: the Bankruptcy (Scotland) Regulations 2016, SSI 2016/397 at **[16.401]**.

[5.197]
3 Debt advice and information package
(1) No petition may be presented under section 2(1)(b)(i) unless the qualified creditor has, or qualified creditors have, provided the debtor, by such time prior to the presentation of the petition as may be prescribed, with a debt advice and information package.
(2) In this Act, "debt advice and information package" means the debt advice and information package referred to in section 10(5) of the 2002 Act.

NOTES

Commencement: 30 November 2016.

Regulations: the Bankruptcy (Scotland) Regulations 2016, SSI 2016/397 at **[16.401]**.

[5.198]
4 Money advice
(1) An application for the sequestration of a living debtor's estate may not be made unless the debtor has obtained from a money adviser advice on—
(a) the debtor's financial circumstances,
(b) the effect of the proposed sequestration,
(c) the preparation of the application, and
(d) such other matters as may be prescribed.
(2) In this Act, "money adviser" means a person who—
(a) is not an associate of the debtor, and
(b) is of a prescribed description or falls within a prescribed class.

NOTES

Commencement: 30 November 2016.

Regulations: the Bankruptcy (Scotland) Regulations 2016, SSI 2016/397 at **[16.401]**.

[5.199]
5 Sequestration of estate of deceased debtor
The sequestration of the estate of a deceased debtor is—
(a) by debtor application made by the executor, or a person entitled to be appointed as executor, on the estate,

(b) on the petition of a qualified creditor, or qualified creditors, of the deceased debtor,
(c) on the petition of a temporary administrator,
(d) on the petition of a member State [insolvency practitioner] appointed in main proceedings, or
(e) on the petition of a trustee acting under a trust deed.

NOTES

Commencement: 30 November 2016.

Para (d): words in square brackets substituted for original word "liquidator" by the Insolvency (Regulation (EU) 2015/848) (Miscellaneous Amendments) (Scotland) Regulations 2017, SSI 2017/210, regs 4(1), (3), 9, as from 26 June 2017, except in relation to proceedings opened before that date.

[5.200]

6 Sequestration of other estates

(1) The estate belonging to any of the following (or held for or jointly by, as the case may be, the trustees, partners or members of any of the following) may be sequestrated—
(a) a trust in respect of debts incurred by it,
(b) a partnership (including a dissolved partnership),
(c) a body corporate,
(d) an unincorporated body,
(e) a limited partnership (including a dissolved limited partnership) within the meaning of the Limited Partnerships Act 1907.

(2) But it is not competent to sequestrate the estate of any of the following—
(a) a company registered under the Companies Act 2006,
(b) a limited liability partnership, or
(c) any other entity if it is an entity in respect of which an enactment provides, expressly or by implication, that sequestration is incompetent.

(3) The sequestration of a trust estate in respect of debts incurred by the trust is—
(a) by debtor application made by a majority of trustees, with the concurrence of a qualified creditor or qualified creditors, or
(b) on the petition of—
(i) a temporary administrator,
(ii) a member State [insolvency practitioner] appointed in main proceedings, or
(iii) a qualified creditor or qualified creditors, if the trustees as such are apparently insolvent.

(4) The sequestration of the estate of a partnership is—
(a) by debtor application made by the partnership where the partnership is apparently insolvent,
(b) by debtor application made by the partnership with the concurrence of a qualified creditor or qualified creditors, or
(c) on the petition of—
(i) a temporary administrator,
(ii) a member State [insolvency practitioner] appointed in main proceedings,
(iii) a trustee acting under a trust deed, or
(iv) a qualified creditor or qualified creditors, if the partnership is apparently insolvent.

(5) For the purposes of an application under subsection (4)(a), section 16(4) is to be read as if—
(a) the word "either", and
(b) the words "or if any of the partners is apparently insolvent for a debt of the partnership",

were omitted.

(6) A petition under subsection (4)(c) may be combined with a petition for the sequestration of the estate of any of the partners as an individual where that individual is apparently insolvent.

(7) The sequestration of the estate of a body corporate or of an unincorporated body is—
(a) by debtor application made by a person authorised to act on behalf of the body, with the concurrence of a qualified creditor or qualified creditors, or
(b) on the petition of—
(i) a temporary administrator,
(ii) a member State [insolvency practitioner] appointed in main proceedings, or
(iii) a qualified creditor or qualified creditors, if the body is apparently insolvent.

(8) The application of this Act to the sequestration of the estate of a limited partnership is subject to such modifications as may be prescribed.

(9) Subsections (3)(a) of section 8 and (3) to (6) of section 10 apply for the purposes of this section as they apply for the purposes of their respective sections.

NOTES

Commencement: 30 November 2016.

Sub-ss (3), (4), (7): words in square brackets substituted for original word "liquidator" by the Insolvency (Regulation (EU) 2015/848) (Miscellaneous Amendments) (Scotland) Regulations 2017, SSI 2017/210, regs 4(1), (4), 9, as from 26 June 2017, except in relation to proceedings opened before that date.

Regulations: the Bankruptcy (Scotland) Regulations 2016, SSI 2016/397 at **[16.401]**.

[5.201]

7 Qualified creditor and qualified creditors

(1) In this Act—

"qualified creditor" means a creditor who, at the date of the presentation of the petition, or as the case may be at the date the debtor application is made, is a creditor of the debtor in respect of relevant debts which amount (or of one such debt which amounts) to not less than £3,000 or such sum as may be prescribed, and

"qualified creditors" means creditors who, at the date in question, are creditors of the debtor in respect of relevant debts which amount in aggregate to not less than £3,000 or such sum as may be prescribed.

(2) In the definitions of "qualified creditor" and "qualified creditors" in subsection (1) "relevant debts" means liquid or illiquid debts (other than contingent or future debts or amounts payable under a confiscation order) whether secured or unsecured.

(3) In subsection (2), "confiscation order" means a confiscation order under Part 2, 3 or 4 of the Proceeds of Crime Act 2002.

(4) Paragraphs 1(1) and (3), 2(1)(a) and (2) and 5 of schedule 2 apply in order to ascertain the amount of the debt or debts for the purposes of subsection (1) as those paragraphs apply in order to ascertain the amount which a creditor is entitled to claim but as if for any reference to the date of sequestration there were substituted a reference to the date of the presentation of the petition or, as the case may be, the date the debtor application is made.

NOTES

Commencement: 30 November 2016.

[5.202]

8 Debtor applications: general

(1) Any debtor application must be made to AiB.

(2) A debtor application must—

(a) include a declaration by the money adviser who provided the advice referred to in section 4(1) that such advice has been given, and

(b) specify the name and address of the money adviser.

(3) The debtor must send to AiB along with the application—

(a) a statement of assets and liabilities, and

(b) a statement of undertakings.

(4) If the debtor—

(a) fails, in a statement of assets and liabilities sent to AiB in accordance with subsection (3)(a), to disclose a material fact, or

(b) makes in such a statement a material misstatement,

then the debtor commits an offence.

(5) A person who commits an offence under subsection (4) is liable on summary conviction to a fine not exceeding level 5 on the standard scale or to imprisonment for a term not exceeding 3 months or both to such fine and to such imprisonment.

(6) In any proceedings for an offence under subsection (4), it is a defence to show that the accused had a reasonable excuse for the failure in question or, as the case may be, for making the statement in question.

NOTES

Commencement: 30 November 2016.

Regulations: the Bankruptcy (Scotland) Regulations 2016, SSI 2016/397 at **[16.401]**.

[5.203]

9 Certificate for sequestration

(1) A certificate for sequestration of the estate of a debtor is a certificate granted by a money adviser certifying that the debtor is unable to pay debts as they become due.

(2) A certificate may be granted only on the debtor applying for it.

(3) A money adviser must grant a certificate if, and only if, the debtor can demonstrate that the debtor is unable to pay debts as they become due.

(4) The Scottish Ministers may—

(a) by regulations make provision about certification by a money adviser, including—

(i) the form and manner in which a certification must be made,

(ii) the fee, if any, which a money adviser is entitled to charge for or in connection with granting a certificate,

(b) prescribe a period for the purpose of section 2(2)(f) or (8)(e)(ii).

NOTES

Commencement: 30 November 2016.

Regulations: the Bankruptcy (Scotland) Regulations 2016, SSI 2016/397 at **[16.401]**.

[5.204]

10 Death or withdrawal

(1) Where, after a petition for sequestration is presented but before the sequestration is awarded, the debtor dies then, if the petitioner is a creditor, the proceedings are to continue in accordance with this Act so far as circumstances will permit.

(2) Where, after a debtor application is made but before the sequestration is awarded, the debtor dies then the application falls.

(3) Where, after a petition for sequestration is presented but before the sequestration is awarded, a creditor who is the petitioner withdraws or dies, there may be sisted in the place of that creditor any creditor who both was a qualified creditor at the date when the petition was presented and is a qualified creditor at the date of the sist.
(4) Where, after a petition for sequestration is presented but before the sequestration is awarded, a creditor who has lodged answers to the petition withdraws or dies, there may be sisted in the place of that creditor any other creditor.
(5) Where, after a debtor application is made but before the sequestration is awarded, a creditor who concurs in the application withdraws or dies, any other creditor may, if the conditions mentioned in subsection (6) are met, notify AiB that the other creditor concurs in the application in place of the creditor who has withdrawn or died.
(6) The conditions are that the other creditor—
(a) was a qualified creditor at the date when the debtor application was made, and
(b) is a qualified creditor at the date of the notification.

NOTES
Commencement: 30 November 2016.

[5.205]
11 Debtor application: provision of information
(1) Where a debtor application is made other than under section 5(a), the debtor must state in the application—
(a) whether or not the debtor's centre of main interests is situated in the United Kingdom or in another member State, and
(b) whether or not the debtor possesses an establishment in the United Kingdom or in another member State.
(2) Where a debtor application is made by an executor under section 5(a) the executor must state in the application—
(a) whether or not the debtor's centre of main interests was situated in the United Kingdom or in another member State, and
(b) whether or not the debtor possessed an establishment in the United Kingdom or in another member State.
(3) If, to the debtor's knowledge, there is a member State [insolvency practitioner] appointed in main proceedings in relation to the debtor, the debtor is, as soon as reasonably practicable, to send a copy of the debtor application to that member State [insolvency practitioner].

NOTES
Commencement: 30 November 2016.
Sub-s (3): words in square brackets substituted for original word "liquidator" by the Insolvency (Regulation (EU) 2015/848) (Miscellaneous Amendments) (Scotland) Regulations 2017, SSI 2017/210, regs 4(1), (5), 9, as from 26 June 2017, except in relation to proceedings opened before that date.

[5.206]
12 Petition for sequestration of estate: provision of information
(1) A petitioner for sequestration of the estate of a debtor is, in so far as it is within the petitioner's knowledge, to state in the petition—
(a) whether or not the debtor's centre of main interests is situated in the United Kingdom or in another member State, and
(b) whether or not the debtor possesses an establishment in the United Kingdom or in another member State.
(2) If, to the petitioner's knowledge, there is a member State [insolvency practitioner] appointed in main proceedings in relation to the debtor, the petitioner is, as soon as reasonably practicable, to send a copy of the petition to that member State [insolvency practitioner].

NOTES
Commencement: 30 November 2016.
Sub-s (2): words in square brackets substituted for original word "liquidator" by the Insolvency (Regulation (EU) 2015/848) (Miscellaneous Amendments) (Scotland) Regulations 2017, SSI 2017/210, regs 4(1), (6), 9, as from 26 June 2017, except in relation to proceedings opened before that date.

[5.207]
13 Further provisions relating to presentation of petitions
(1) The petitioner is, on the day the petition for sequestration is presented under section 2, 5 or 6, to send a copy of the petition to AiB.
(2) A petition for the sequestration of the estate of a debtor (other than a limited partnership or a deceased debtor) may be presented—
(a) by a qualified creditor or qualified creditors only if the apparent insolvency founded on in the petition was constituted within 4 months before the date of presentation of the petition, or
(b) at any time by—
(i) a trustee acting under a trust deed,
(ii) a temporary administrator, or
(iii) a member State [insolvency practitioner] appointed in main proceedings.
(3) A petition for the sequestration of the estate of a limited partnership may be presented—

(a) by a qualified creditor or qualified creditors only if the apparent insolvency founded on in the petition was constituted within 4 months (or such other period as may be prescribed) before the date of presentation of the petition, or
(b) at any time by—
(i) a trustee acting under a trust deed,
(ii) a temporary administrator, or
(iii) a member State [insolvency practitioner] appointed in main proceedings.

(4) A petition for the sequestration of the estate of a deceased debtor may be presented—
(a) by a qualified creditor or qualified creditors—
(i) in a case where the apparent insolvency of the debtor founded on in the petition was constituted within 4 months before the date of death, at any time, and
(ii) in any other case (whether or not apparent insolvency has been constituted), not earlier than 6 months after the date of death, or
(b) at any time by—
(i) a person entitled to be appointed as executor of the estate,
(ii) a trustee acting under a trust deed,
(iii) a temporary administrator, or
(iv) a member State [insolvency practitioner] appointed in main proceedings.

(5) The presentation of a petition for sequestration bars the effect of any enactment or rule of law relating to the limitation of actions.

(6) Where, before sequestration is awarded, it becomes apparent that a petitioning creditor was ineligible to petition, that person must withdraw, or as the case may be withdraw from, the petition; but another creditor may be sisted in that person's place.

NOTES

Commencement: 30 November 2016.

Sub-ss (2), (3), (4): words in square brackets substituted for original word "liquidator" by the Insolvency (Regulation (EU) 2015/848) (Miscellaneous Amendments) (Scotland) Regulations 2017, SSI 2017/210, regs 4(1), (7), 9, as from 26 June 2017, except in relation to proceedings opened before that date.

[5.208]

14 Further provisions relating to debtor applications

(1) A debtor application may be made at any time; but this subsection is subject to subsections (2) and (3).

(2) A debtor application made in relation to the estate of a limited partnership may be made—
(a) at any time unless a time is prescribed, and
(b) if a time is prescribed, within that time.

(3) Any intromission by an executor with the deceased debtor's estate after the 12 months mentioned in subsection (4) is deemed an intromission without title unless, within that period, the executor—
(a) makes a debtor application under section 5(a), or
(b) petitions for the appointment of a judicial factor to administer the estate.

(4) The 12 months referred to in subsection (3) is the 12 months following the day on which the executor knew, or ought to have known, that the estate was absolutely insolvent and likely to remain so.

(5) The making of, or concurrence in, a debtor application bars the effect of any enactment or rule of law relating to the limitation of actions.

(6) Where, before sequestration is awarded, it becomes apparent that a creditor concurring in a debtor application was ineligible to concur, AiB must withdraw the ineligible creditor from the application.

(7) But another creditor may concur in place of the ineligible creditor; and if the other creditor does concur in place of the ineligible creditor, the other creditor must notify AiB of that fact.

NOTES

Commencement: 30 November 2016.

[5.209]

[14A Main proceedings in Scotland: undertaking by trustee in respect of assets in another EU member State

(1) This section applies where a trustee in sequestration or acting under a protected trust deed in main proceedings proposes to give an undertaking under Article 36 of the EU insolvency proceedings regulation in respect of assets located in another member State.

(2) In addition to the requirements as to form and content set out in Article 36 the proposed undertaking must contain—
(a) the heading "Proposed Undertaking under Article 36 of the EU Insolvency Regulation (2015/848)",
(b) identification details for the main proceedings,
(c) identification and contact details for the trustee, and
(d) a description of the effect of the undertaking if approved.

(3) The proposed undertaking must be delivered to all local creditors in the member State concerned of whose address the trustee is aware.

(4) Where the undertaking is rejected the trustee must inform every creditor known to the trustee of the rejection of the undertaking as soon as reasonably practicable.

(5) Where the undertaking is approved the trustee must as soon as reasonably practicable send a copy of the undertaking to every creditor known to the trustee with a notice—
(a) informing them of the approval of the undertaking, and

(b) describing its effect (so far as they have not already been given this information under subsection (2)(d)).

(6) The trustee may advertise details of the undertaking in the other member State in such manner as the trustee thinks fit.]

NOTES

Commencement: 26 June 2017, except in relation to proceedings opened before that date.

Inserted, together with s 14B, by the Insolvency (Regulation (EU) 2015/848) (Miscellaneous Amendments) (Scotland) Regulations 2017, SSI 2017/210, regs 4(1), (8), 9, as from 26 June 2017, except in relation to proceedings opened before that date.

[5.210]

[14B Main proceedings in another member State: approval of undertaking offered by member State insolvency practitioner to local creditors in the UK

(1) This section applies where a member State insolvency practitioner proposes an undertaking under Article 36 of the EU insolvency proceedings regulation and the secondary proceedings which the undertaking is intended to avoid would be sequestration or a protected trust deed.

(2) A decision on approval of the undertaking by local creditors shall be taken as if it were a decision taken by a company's creditors to approve a proposed company voluntary arrangement under section 4A of the Insolvency Act 1986.

(3) Without prejudice to the generality of subsection (2), Rules 1.12 to 1.16E(c) of the Insolvency (Scotland) Rules 1986 apply to that decision.

(4) The member State insolvency practitioner must publish a notice in the Edinburgh Gazette of the undertaking containing—

(a) the fact that the undertaking was approved,

(b) the date the undertaking was approved, and

(c) a description of the effect of the undertaking.]

NOTES

Commencement: 26 June 2017, except in relation to proceedings opened before that date.

Inserted as noted to s 14A at **[5.209]**.

Jurisdiction

[5.211]

15 Jurisdiction

(1) Where a petition is presented for the sequestration of the estate of a debtor (whether living or deceased), the sheriff has jurisdiction if, at the relevant time, the debtor—

(a) had an established place of business in the sheriffdom, or

(b) was habitually resident in the sheriffdom.

(2) AiB may determine a debtor application for the sequestration of the estate of a living or deceased debtor if, at the relevant time, the debtor—

(a) had an established place of business in Scotland, or

(b) was habitually resident in Scotland.

(3) Where a petition is presented for the sequestration of the estate of an entity which may be sequestrated by virtue of section 6, the sheriff has jurisdiction if the entity—

(a) had at the relevant time an established place of business in the sheriffdom, or

(b) was constituted or formed under Scots law and at any time carried on business in the sheriffdom.

(4) AiB may determine a debtor application for the sequestration of the estate of such an entity if the entity—

(a) had at the relevant time an established place of business in Scotland, or

(b) was constituted or formed under Scots law and at any time carried on business in Scotland.

(5) Even where a person (whether living or deceased) does not fall within subsection (1), the sheriff has jurisdiction in respect of the sequestration of that person's estate if—

(a) a petition has been presented for the sequestration of the estate of a partnership of which the person is, or was at the relevant time before dying, a partner, and

(b) the process of that sequestration is still current.

(6) Subsection (7) applies as regards any proceedings under this Act which—

(a) may be brought before a sheriff, and

(b) relate either to a debtor application or to the sequestration of a debtor's estate following any such application.

(7) The proceedings are to be brought before the sheriff who, under subsection (1) or (3), would have jurisdiction in respect of a petition for sequestration of the debtor's estate.

(8) References in this section to "the relevant time" are to any time in the year immediately preceding (as the case may be)—

(a) the date of presentation of the petition,

(b) the date the debtor application is made, or

(c) the debtor's date of death.

(9) This section is subject to Article 3 of the [EU] insolvency proceedings regulation.

NOTES

Commencement: 30 November 2016.

Sub-s (9): word in square brackets substituted for original word "EC" by the Insolvency (Regulation (EU) 2015/848) (Miscellaneous Amendments) (Scotland) Regulations 2017, SSI 2017/210, regs 4(1), (9), 9, as from 26 June 2017, except in relation to proceedings opened before that date.

Meaning of "apparent insolvency"

[5.212]

16 Meaning of "apparent insolvency"

(1) The apparent insolvency of a debtor is constituted, or where the debtor is already apparently insolvent again constituted, whenever—

(a) the debtor's estate is sequestrated,

(b) the debtor is adjudged bankrupt in England and Wales or in Northern Ireland,

(c) the debtor gives written notice to the debtor's creditors that the debtor has ceased to pay the debtor's debts in the ordinary course of business (but the debtor must not, at the time notice is so given, be a person whose property—

(i) is affected by a restraint order,

(ii) is detained under or by virtue of a relevant detention power, or

(iii) is subject to a confiscation or charging order),

(d) the debtor becomes subject to main proceedings in a member State other than the United Kingdom,

(e) the debtor grants a trust deed,

(f) following the service on the debtor of a duly executed charge for payment of a debt, the days of charge expire without payment (unless the circumstances are shown to be such as are mentioned in subsection (2)),

(g) a decree of adjudication of any part of the debtor's estate is granted, either for payment or in security (unless the circumstances are shown to be such as are mentioned in subsection (2)),

(h) a debt constituted by a decree or document of debt, as defined in section 10 of the 2002 Act, is being paid by the debtor under a debt payment programme under Part 1 of that Act and the programme is revoked (unless the circumstances are shown to be such as are mentioned in subsection (2)), or

(i) a creditor of the debtor, in respect of a liquid debt which amounts to (or liquid debts which in aggregate amount to) not less than £1,500 or such sum as may be prescribed, serves on the debtor, by personal service by an officer of court, a demand in the prescribed form requiring the debtor either to pay the debt (or debts) or to find security for its (or their) payment and the condition set out in subsection (3) is met.

(2) The circumstances are—

(a) that at the time of the occurrence, the debtor was able and willing to pay the debtor's debts as they became due, or

(b) that, but for the debtor's property being affected by a restraint order or being subject to a confiscation order or charging order, the debtor would at that time have been able to pay those debts as they became due.

(3) The condition is that the debtor does not, within 3 weeks after the date of service—

(a) comply with the demand, or

(b) intimate to the creditor, by recorded delivery, that the debtor—

(i) denies that there is a debt, or

(ii) denies that the sum claimed by the creditor as the debt is immediately payable.

(4) The apparent insolvency of a partnership is constituted (or as the case may be again constituted) either—

(a) in accordance with subsection (1), or

(b) if any of the partners is apparently insolvent for a debt of the partnership.

(5) The apparent insolvency of an unincorporated body is constituted (or as the case may be again constituted) either—

(a) if a person representing the body is apparently insolvent for a debt of the body, or

(b) if a person holding property for the body in a fiduciary capacity is apparently insolvent for such a debt.

(6) Notwithstanding subsection (2) of section 6, the apparent insolvency of an entity such as is mentioned in that subsection may be constituted (or as the case may be again constituted) under subsection (1); and any reference to the debtor in subsections (1) to (3) and (7) is, except where the context otherwise requires, to be construed as including a reference to such an entity.

(7) The debtor's apparent insolvency continues—

(a) if constituted under paragraph (a) or (b) of subsection (1), until the debtor's discharge,

(b) if constituted under paragraph (c), (e), (f), (g), (h) or (i) of that subsection, until the debtor becomes able to pay the debtor's debts and pays them as they become due, or

(c) if constituted under paragraph (d) of that subsection, until the main proceedings end.

(8) In this section—

"charging order" means an order made under section 78 of the Criminal Justice Act 1988 or under section 27 of the Drug Trafficking Act 1994,

"confiscation order" means a confiscation order made under Part 2, 3 or 4 of the Proceeds of Crime Act 2002,

"liquid debt" does not include a sum payable under a confiscation order,

"relevant detention power" means section 44A, 47J, 47K, 47M, 47P, 122A, 127J, 127K, 127M, 127P, 193A, 195J, 195K, 195M or 195P of the Proceeds of Crime Act 2002, and

"restraint order" means a restraint order made under Part 2, 3 or 4 of that Act of 2002.

NOTES

Commencement: 30 November 2016.

Concurrent proceedings

[5.213]

17 Concurrent proceedings for sequestration or analogous remedy

(1) If, in the course of sequestration proceedings (referred to in this section and in section 18 as the "instant proceedings"), a person who is a petitioner for sequestration, the debtor, or a creditor concurring in a debtor application is or becomes aware of any of the circumstances mentioned in subsection (2), that person must as soon as may be take the action mentioned in subsection (3).

(2) The circumstances are that, notwithstanding the instant proceedings—

(a) a petition for sequestration of the debtor's estate is before a sheriff,
(b) such sequestration has been awarded,
(c) a debtor application has been made in relation to the debtor's estate,
(d) sequestration has been awarded by virtue of any such application,
(e) a petition for the appointment of a judicial factor on the debtor's estate is before a court,
(f) such a judicial factor has been appointed,
(g) a petition is before a court for the winding up of the debtor under Part 4 or 5 of the Insolvency Act 1986 or section 372 of the Financial Services and Markets Act 2000,
(h) an application for an analogous remedy in respect of the debtor's estate is proceeding, or
(i) such an analogous remedy is in force.

(3) The action is—

(a) where the instant proceedings are by petition for sequestration, to notify the sheriff to whom that petition was presented of the circumstances in question,
(b) where the instant proceedings are by debtor application, to notify AiB of those circumstances.

(4) A petitioner who fails to comply with subsection (1) may be made liable for the expenses of presenting the petition for sequestration.

(5) A debtor who fails so to comply commits an offence.

(6) A debtor who commits an offence under subsection (5) is liable on summary conviction to a fine not exceeding level 5 on the standard scale.

(7) A creditor concurring in a debtor application who fails so to comply may be made liable for the expenses of making the debtor application.

(8) In this section and in section 18, "analogous remedy" means—

(a) in relation to England and Wales—
 (i) an individual voluntary arrangement or bankruptcy order under the Insolvency Act 1986,
 (ii) an administration order under section 112 of the County Courts Act 1984, or
 (iii) a remedy having the like effect to any of those mentioned in sub-paragraphs (i) and (ii) or to sequestration, and
(b) in relation to Northern Ireland or to any other country, a remedy having the like effect as a remedy mentioned in paragraph (a).

NOTES

Commencement: 30 November 2016.

[5.214]

18 Powers in relation to concurrent proceedings

(1) Where, in the course of instant proceedings (see section 17(1)) which are by petition, any of the circumstances mentioned in paragraphs (a) to (g) of section 17(2) exists, the sheriff to whom the petition in the instant proceedings was presented may, on the sheriff's own motion or at the instance of the debtor, of a creditor or of any other person having an interest—

(a) allow the petition to proceed,
(b) sist it, or
(c) dismiss it.

(2) Without prejudice to subsection (1), where, in the course of such instant proceedings, any of the circumstances mentioned in paragraph (a), (b), (e), (f) or (g) of section 17(2) exists, the Court of Session may, on the Court's own motion or at the instance of the debtor, of a creditor or of any other person having an interest—

(a) direct the sheriff before whom the petition in the instant proceedings is pending or the sheriff before whom the other petition is pending, to sist or dismiss the petition in the instant proceedings or, as the case may be, the other petition, or
(b) order the petitions to be heard together.

(3) Without prejudice to subsection (1), where, in the course of such instant proceedings, any of the circumstances mentioned in paragraph (c) or (d) of section 17(2) exists, the sheriff to whom the petition in the instant proceedings was presented may, on the sheriff's own motion or at the instance of the debtor, of a creditor or of any other person having an interest, direct AiB to dismiss the debtor application.

(4) AiB must recall an award of sequestration if—

(a) the award was by virtue of a debtor application, and
(b) the sheriff directs AiB to dismiss the debtor application.

(5) The effect of the recall of an award of sequestration is, so far as practicable, to restore the debtor and any other person affected by the sequestration to the position the debtor or, as the case may be, the other person would have been in if the sequestration had not been awarded.

(6) A recall of an award of sequestration does not—
(a) affect the interruption of prescription caused by—
(i) the presentation of the petition for sequestration,
(ii) the making of the debtor application, or
(iii) the submission of a claim under section 46 or 122,
(b) invalidate any transaction entered into before such recall by the interim trustee, or by the trustee, with a person acting in good faith, or
(c) affect a bankruptcy restrictions order which has not been revoked under section 161(1)(a).
(7) Without delay after granting recall of an award of sequestration under subsection (4), AiB must send a certified copy of the decision to the Keeper of the Register of Inhibitions for recording in that register.
(8) Where, in the course of instant proceedings which are by debtor application, any of the circumstances mentioned in paragraphs (a) to (g) of section 17(2) exists, AiB may dismiss the debtor application in the instant proceedings.
(9) Subsection (10) applies where, in respect of the same estate—
(a) a petition for sequestration is pending before a sheriff, and
(b) an application for an analogous remedy (see section 17(8)) is proceeding or an analogous remedy is in force.
(10) The sheriff, on the sheriff's own motion or at the instance of the debtor, of a creditor or of any other person having an interest, may—
(a) allow the petition for sequestration to proceed,
(b) sist it, or
(c) dismiss it.
(11) Subsection (12) applies where, in respect of the same estate—
(a) a debtor application has been made and is not yet determined, and
(b) an application for an analogous remedy is proceeding or an analogous remedy is in force.
(12) AiB may proceed to determine the application or may dismiss it.

NOTES

Commencement: 30 November 2016.

Creditor's oath

[5.215]

19 Creditor's oath

(1) Every creditor who is—
(a) a petitioner for sequestration,
(b) a creditor who concurs in a debtor application, or
(c) a qualified creditor who becomes sisted under subsection (3) of section 10 (or under that subsection as applied by section 6(9)),

must produce an oath, in the prescribed form, made by or on behalf of the creditor.
(2) The oath may be made—
(a) in the United Kingdom, before any person entitled to administer an oath there,
(b) outwith the United Kingdom, before—
(i) a British diplomatic or consular officer, or
(ii) any person authorised to administer an oath or affirmation under the law of the place where the oath is made.
(3) The identity of the creditor and the identity of the person before whom the oath is made, and their authority to make and to administer the oath respectively, are presumed to be correctly stated unless the contrary is established.
(4) Any seal or signature on the oath is presumed to be authentic unless the contrary is established.
(5) If the oath contains an error or has omitted a fact—
(a) the sheriff to whom the petition was presented, or
(b) in the case of a creditor concurring in a debtor application, AiB,

may at any time before sequestration is awarded allow another oath to be produced rectifying the original oath.
(6) This section applies to the making of that other oath as it applies to the making of the original oath.
(7) The creditor must produce, along with the oath—
(a) an account or voucher (according to the nature of the debt) which constitutes prima facie evidence of the debt, and
(b) if a petitioning creditor, such evidence as is available to the creditor to show the apparent insolvency of the debtor.

NOTES

Commencement: 30 November 2016.
Regulations: the Bankruptcy (Scotland) Regulations 2016, SSI 2016/397 at **[16.401]**.

PART 2
SEQUESTRATION: AWARD AND RECALL

Incomplete or inappropriate debtor applications

[5.216]

20 Debtor application: incomplete application

(1) This section applies where a debtor application is made and AiB considers that—
(a) the application is incomplete,

(b) further information is required in relation to the application,
(c) further evidence is required to substantiate any fact relevant to the application, or
(d) any fee or charge applicable to the application is outstanding.

(2) AiB must specify by notice in writing to the debtor—
(a) any further information which must be provided,
(b) any further evidence which must be provided, and
(c) any fee or charge to be paid.

(3) Any information, evidence, fee or charge to be provided or paid under subsection (2) must be provided or paid within 21 days (or such greater number of days as may be specified by AiB) beginning with the day on which notice is sent under that subsection.

(4) AiB may refuse to award sequestration if, after the expiry of the days referred to in subsection (3), AiB considers that—
(a) the application remains incomplete,
(b) the debtor has provided insufficient information or evidence under subsection (2)(a) or (b), or
(c) any fee or charge applicable to the application remains outstanding.

NOTES

Commencement: 30 November 2016.

[5.217]

21 Refusal of debtor application: inappropriate application

(1) This section applies where a debtor application is made and AiB considers that an award of sequestration may not be appropriate in the circumstances of the case.

(2) AiB must specify by notice in writing to the debtor—
(a) the reason why AiB considers the application may not be appropriate, and
(b) any further information which must be provided within 21 days (or such greater number of days as may be specified by AiB) beginning with the day on which notice is sent under this subsection.

(3) AiB may refuse to award sequestration if, after the expiry of the days referred to in subsection (2)(b), AiB remains of the view that an award of sequestration would be inappropriate in the circumstances of the case.

NOTES

Commencement: 30 November 2016.

Award of sequestration

[5.218]

22 When sequestration is awarded

(1) Where a debtor application (other than an application under section 5(a)) is made and neither section 20 nor section 21 applies, AiB must award sequestration forthwith if satisfied—
(a) that the application is made in accordance with—
(i) this Act, and
(ii) any provisions made under this Act,
(b) that section 2(8) applies to the debtor, and
(c) that the provisions of section 8(3)(a) have been complied with.

(2) Where a debtor application is made under section 5(a), AiB must award sequestration forthwith if satisfied—
(a) that the application has been made in accordance with this Act and with any provisions made under this Act, and
(b) that the provisions of section 8(3)(a) have been complied with.

(3) Where a petition for sequestration of the estate of a debtor is presented by—
(a) a creditor, or
(b) a trustee acting under a trust deed,

the sheriff must grant warrant to cite the debtor to appear before the sheriff on such date as is specified in the warrant to show cause why sequestration should not be awarded.

(4) Any date specified under subsection (3) must be—
(a) no fewer than 6, and
(b) no more than 14,

days after the date of citation.

(5) The sheriff must forthwith award sequestration on that petition on being satisfied—
(a) if the debtor has not appeared, that proper citation has been made of the debtor,
(b) that the petition has been presented in accordance with this Act,
(c) that the provisions of section 13(1) have been complied with,
(d) that in the case of a petition by a trustee—
(i) at least one of the conditions in section 2(7)(a) applies, or
(ii) the petition includes an averment in accordance with section 2(7)(b), and
(e) that, in the case of a petition by a creditor, the requirements of this Act relating to apparent insolvency have been fulfilled.

(6) But subsection (5) is subject to section 23.

(7) In this Act, "the date of sequestration" means—
(a) where a debtor application is made, the date on which sequestration is awarded,

(b) where the petition for sequestration is presented by a creditor, or by a trustee acting under a trust deed, and sequestration is awarded, the date on which the sheriff granted warrant under subsection (3) (or, where more than one warrant is so granted, the date on which the first warrant is so granted).

NOTES

Commencement: 30 November 2016.

[5.219]

23 Circumstances in which sequestration is not to be awarded in pursuance of section 22(5)

(1) Sequestration must not be awarded in pursuance of section 22(5) if—

(a) cause is shown why sequestration cannot competently be awarded,

(b) the debtor forthwith pays or satisfies, or produces written evidence of the payment or satisfaction of—

(i) the debt in respect of which the debtor became apparently insolvent, and

(ii) any other debt due by the debtor to the petitioner and to any creditor concurring in the petition.

(2) Where the sheriff is satisfied that the debtor will, within 42 days beginning with the day the debtor appears before the sheriff, pay or satisfy the debts mentioned in sub-paragraphs (i) and (ii) of subsection (1)(b), the sheriff may continue the petition for no more than 42 days.

(3) The sheriff may continue the petition for such period as the sheriff thinks fit if satisfied—

(a) that a debt payment programme, under Part 1 of the 2002 Act, relating to the debts mentioned in sub-paragraphs (i) and (ii) of subsection (1)(b) has been applied for and has not yet been approved or rejected, or

(b) that such a debt payment programme will be applied for.

NOTES

Commencement: 30 November 2016.

[5.220]

[23A Effect of sequestration on land attachment

(1) No land attachment of the heritable property of a debtor, created within the 6 months before the date of sequestration (whether or not subsisting at that date), is effectual to create a preference for the creditor.

(2) A creditor who creates a land attachment within the 6 months mentioned in subsection (1) is entitled to payment, out of the attached land or out of the proceeds of sale of it, of the expenses incurred—

(a) in obtaining the extract of the decree, or other document, containing the warrant for land attachment, and

(b) in serving the charge for payment, registering the notice of land attachment, serving a copy of that notice, and registering certificate of service of that copy.

(3) A notice of land attachment—

(a) registered on or after the date of sequestration against land forming part of the debtor's heritable estate (including any estate vesting under section 86(5) in the trustee in the sequestration) is of no effect,

(b) registered before that date and in relation to which, by that date, no land attachment is created is of no effect.

(4) It is not competent for a creditor to insist in a land attachment—

(a) created over the debtor's heritable estate before the beginning of the 6 months mentioned in subsection (1), and

(b) which subsists on the date of sequestration.

(5) But subsection (4) is subject to subsections (6) to (9).

(6) Where, in execution of a warrant for sale, a contract to sell the land has been concluded—

(a) the trustee must concur in and ratify the deed implementing that contract, and

(b) the appointed person must account for and pay to the trustee in the sequestration any balance of the proceeds of sale (being the balance which would, but for the sequestration, be due to the debtor) after disbursing those proceeds in accordance with section 116 of the Bankruptcy and Diligence etc (Scotland) Act 2007 (disbursement of proceeds of sale of attached land).

(7) Subsection (6) does not apply where the deed implementing the contract is not registered within 28 days beginning with the day on which—

(a) the certified copy of the order of the sheriff granting warrant is recorded, under subsection (1)(a) of section 26, in the Register of Inhibitions, or

(b) the certified copy of the determination of AiB awarding sequestration is recorded, under subsection (2) of that section, in that register.

(8) Where a decree of foreclosure has been granted but an extract of it has not been registered, the creditor may proceed to complete title to the land by registering that extract provided that the creditor does so before the expiry of the days mentioned in subsection (7).

(9) The Scottish Ministers may, as they think fit, prescribe a period in substitution for the days mentioned in subsection (7); and a different period may be prescribed for the purposes of subsection (8) than is prescribed for the purposes of subsection (7).

(10) Expressions used in this section which also occur in Chapter 2 of Part 4 of the Bankruptcy and Diligence etc (Scotland) Act 2007 have the same meanings in this section as they have in that Chapter.]

NOTES

Commencement: 30 November 2016.

Inserted by the Bankruptcy and Diligence etc (Scotland) Act 2007, s 127A(1), (2) (as inserted by the Bankruptcy (Scotland) Act 2016, s 234(1), Sch 8, para 24(1), (2)).

[5.221]

24 Effect of sequestration on diligence generally

(1) The order of the sheriff, or as the case may be the determination of the debtor application by AiB, awarding sequestration has, as from the date of sequestration, in relation to diligence done (whether before or after that date) in respect of any part of the estate of the debtor, the effect mentioned in subsection (2).

(2) The effect is of—

(a) a decree of adjudication of the heritable estate of the debtor for payment of debts duly recorded in the Register of Inhibitions on the date of sequestration,

(b) an arrestment in execution and decree of furthcoming,

(c) an arrestment in execution and warrant for sale, and

(d) an attachment,

in favour of the creditors according to their respective entitlements.

(3) Where an inhibition on the estate of the debtor takes effect within the 60 days before the date of sequestration, any relevant right of challenge vests, at the date of sequestration, in the trustee in the sequestration as does any right of the inhibitor to receive payment for the discharge of the inhibition.

(4) But subsection (3) neither entitles the trustee to receive any payment made to the inhibitor before the date of sequestration nor affects the validity of anything done before that date in consideration of such payment.

(5) In subsection (3), "any relevant right of challenge" means any right to challenge a deed voluntarily granted by the debtor if it is a right which vested in the inhibitor by virtue of the inhibition.

(6) No arrestment, money attachment, interim attachment or attachment of the debtor's estate (including any estate vesting in the trustee under section 86(5)) executed—

(a) within the 60 days before the date of sequestration and whether or not subsisting at that date, or

(b) on or after that date,

is effectual to create a preference for the arrester or attacher.

(7) The estate so arrested or attached is, or any funds released under section 73J(2) of the Debtors (Scotland) Act 1987 (automatic release of funds) or the proceeds of sale of such estate are, to be handed over to the trustee.

(8) An arrester or attacher whose arrestment, money attachment, interim attachment or attachment is executed within the period mentioned in subsection (6)(a) is entitled to payment, out of the arrested or attached estate or out of the proceeds of the sale of such estate, of the expenses incurred—

(a) in obtaining—

(i) warrant for interim attachment, or

(ii) the extract of the decree or other document on which the arrestment, money attachment or attachment proceeded,

(b) in executing the arrestment, money attachment, interim attachment or attachment, and

(c) in taking any further action in respect of the diligence.

(9) Nothing in subsections (6) to (8) applies to an earnings arrestment, a current maintenance arrangement, a conjoined arrestment order or a deduction from earnings order under the Child Support Act 1991.

NOTES

Commencement: 30 November 2016.

[5.222]

25 Effect of sequestration on diligence: estate of deceased debtor

(1) [Sections 23A(1) and (2) and 24 apply] to the estate of a deceased debtor which—

(a) has been sequestrated within 12 months after the date of death, or

(b) was absolutely insolvent at that date and in respect of which a judicial factor has been appointed under section 11A of the Judicial Factors (Scotland) Act 1889 within 12 months after that date,

but with the modifications mentioned in subsection (2).

(2) The modifications are that—

(a) any reference to the date of sequestration is to be construed as a reference to the date of death, and

(b) any reference to the debtor is to be construed as a reference to the deceased debtor.

(3) It is not competent, on or after the date of sequestration, for any creditor . . . to be confirmed as executor-creditor on the estate.

(4) Subsections (5) and (6) apply where, within 12 months after the debtor's death—

(a) the debtor's estate is sequestrated, or

(b) a judicial factor is appointed under section 11A of the Judicial Factors (Scotland) Act 1889 to administer the debtor's estate and that estate is absolutely insolvent.

(5) No confirmation as executor-creditor on that estate at any time after the debtor's death is effectual in a question with the trustee or the judicial factor.

(6) But the executor-creditor is entitled—

(a) out of the estate, or

(b) out of the proceeds of sale of the estate,

to the expenses incurred by the executor-creditor in obtaining the confirmation.

NOTES

Commencement: 30 November 2016.

Sub-s (1): words in square brackets substituted by the Bankruptcy and Diligence etc (Scotland) Act 2007, s 127A(1), (3)(a) (as inserted by the Bankruptcy (Scotland) Act 2016, s 234(1), Sch 8, para 24(1), (2)).

Sub-s (3): words omitted repealed by the Bankruptcy and Diligence etc (Scotland) Act 2007, s 127A(1), (3)(b) (as inserted by the Bankruptcy (Scotland) Act 2016, s 234(1), Sch 8, para 24(1), (2)).

[5.223]

26 Registration of warrant or determination of debtor application

(1) On the sheriff granting warrant under section 22(3) the sheriff clerk must forthwith send—

(a) a certified copy of the order granting the warrant to the Keeper of the Register of Inhibitions for recording in that register,

(b) a copy of that order to AiB, and

(c) where the debtor is taking part in a debt payment programme under Part 1 of the 2002 Act, a copy of that order to the DAS administrator ("DAS administrator" having the meaning given by regulation 2(1) of the Debt Arrangement Scheme (Scotland) Regulations 2011 (SSI 2011/141)).

(2) On awarding sequestration on a debtor application AiB must forthwith send a certified copy of AiB's determination of the application to the Keeper of the Register of Inhibitions for recording in that register.

(3) Recording under subsection (1)(a) or (2) has the effect, as from the date of sequestration, of an inhibition and of a citation in an adjudication of the debtor's heritable estate at the instance of the creditors who subsequently have claims in the sequestration accepted under section 126.

(4) The effect mentioned in subsection (3) expires—

(a) on the recording by virtue of section 27(11)(a) of a certified copy of an order refusing to award sequestration or by virtue of section 30(9)(a) of a certified copy of an order recalling an award of sequestration,

(b) on the recording by virtue of section 18(7), 34(4) or 35(7) of a certified copy of a decision, or

(c) if the effect has not earlier expired by virtue of paragraph (a) or (b), at the end of 3 years beginning with the date of sequestration.

(5) But subsection (4)(c) is subject to subsections (6) and (7).

(6) The trustee may if not discharged send a memorandum, in a form prescribed by act of sederunt, to the Keeper of the Register of Inhibitions for recording in that register before the expiry of—

(a) the 3 years mentioned in subsection (4)(c), or

(b) a period for which the effect mentioned in subsection (3) has been renewed by virtue of subsection (7).

(7) The recording of a memorandum sent in accordance with subsection (6) renews the effect mentioned in subsection (3) for 3 years beginning with the expiry of—

(a) the 3 years mentioned in subsection (4)(c), or

(b) as the case may be, the period mentioned in subsection (6)(b).

(8) The trustee may, if appointed or reappointed under section 152, send a memorandum in a form prescribed by act of sederunt to the Keeper of the Register of Inhibitions for recording in that register before the expiry of that appointment.

(9) The recording of a memorandum sent in accordance with subsection (8) imposes the effect mentioned in subsection (3) for 3 years beginning with the day of notification in accordance with section 153(1).

NOTES

Commencement: 30 November 2016.

Rules: the Act of Sederunt (Sheriff Court Bankruptcy Rules) 2016, SSI 2016/313 at **[16.322]**.

[5.224]

27 Further matters in relation to award of sequestration

(1) On application the sheriff may, at any time after sequestration has been awarded, transfer the sequestration to any other sheriff.

(2) But subsection (1) is subject to subsection (3).

(3) The debtor may, with the leave of the sheriff, appeal to the Sheriff Appeal Court against such a transfer.

(4) Where the sheriff makes an order refusing to award sequestration, the petitioner may appeal against the order within 14 days after the date on which the order is made.

(5) If, following a debtor application, AiB refuses to award sequestration, the debtor or a creditor concurring in the application may apply to AiB for a review of the refusal.

(6) Any application under subsection (5) must be made within 14 days beginning with the day on which AiB refuses to award sequestration.

(7) If an application under subsection (5) is made, AiB must—

(a) take into account any representations made by an interested person within 21 days beginning with the day on which the application is made, and

(b) confirm the refusal, or award sequestration, within 28 days beginning with that day.

(8) If AiB confirms the refusal to award sequestration under subsection (7)(b), the debtor or a creditor concurring in the application may, within 14 days beginning with the day of that confirmation, appeal to the sheriff.

(9) An award of sequestration is not subject to review otherwise than by recall under—

(a) section 18(4),

(b) sections 29 and 30,
(c) section 34, or
(d) section 35.

(10) Subsection (9) is without prejudice to any right to bring an action of reduction of an award of sequestration.

(11) Where a petition for sequestration is presented by a creditor, or by a trustee acting under a trust deed, the sheriff clerk is—

(a) on the final determination or the abandonment of any appeal under subsection (4) in relation to the petition, or (if there is no such appeal) within the 14 days mentioned in that subsection, to send a certified copy of the order refusing to award sequestration to the Keeper of the Register of Inhibitions for recording in that register,
(b) to send forthwith a copy of that order to—
  (i) AiB, and
  (ii) where the debtor is taking part in a debt payment programme under Part 1 of the 2002 Act, the DAS administrator ("DAS administrator" having the meaning given by regulation 2(1) of the Debt Arrangement Scheme (Scotland) Regulations 2011 (SSI 2011/141)).

(12) Where sequestration has been awarded the process of sequestration is not to fall asleep.

NOTES

Commencement: 30 November 2016.

[5.225]
28 Benefit from another estate

(1) Where a debtor learns, whether before or after the date of sequestration, that the debtor may derive benefit from another estate, the debtor must as soon as practicable after that date inform—

(a) the trustee in the sequestration, of that fact, and
(b) the person who is administering that other estate, of the sequestration.

(2) A debtor who fails to comply with subsection (1) commits an offence.

(3) A debtor who commits an offence under subsection (2) is liable, on summary conviction, to a fine not exceeding level 5 on the standard scale.

NOTES

Commencement: 30 November 2016.

Recall of sequestration

[5.226]
29 Petitions for recall of sequestration

(1) A petition for recall of an award of sequestration may be presented to the sheriff by—

(a) the debtor,
(b) any creditor,
(c) any other person having an interest (whether or not a person who was a petitioner for, or concurred in a debtor application for, the sequestration),
(d) the trustee in the sequestration, or
(e) AiB.

(2) Such a petition may not be presented to the sheriff if the only ground is that the debtor has paid, or is able to pay, the debtor's debts in full.

(3) Subsection (2) does not apply where—

(a) sequestration was awarded following a petition of a qualified creditor or qualified creditors, and
(b) a petition for recall of the award of sequestration includes the ground that the debtor was not apparently insolvent.

(4) A copy of the petition, along with a notice stating that the recipient of the notice may lodge answers to the petition within 14 days after service of the notice, must be served by the petitioner on—

(a) the debtor,
(b) any person who was a petitioner for, or concurred in a debtor application for, the sequestration,
(c) the trustee, and
(d) AiB.

(5) On service, under subsection (4), of a copy of the petition AiB must enter particulars of the petition in the register of insolvencies.

(6) A petition under this section may be presented at any time.

(7) But subsection (6) is subject to sections 114(3) and 115(3).

(8) Notwithstanding that a petition has been presented under this section, the proceedings in the sequestration are to continue as if the petition had not been presented until the recall is granted.

(9) But subsection (8) is subject to section 30(7).

(10) Subsection (11) applies where a petitioner under this section, or a person who has lodged answers to the petition, withdraws or dies.

(11) Any person—

(a) entitled to present, or
(b) entitled to lodge answers to,

a petition under this section may be sisted in place of the person who has withdrawn or died.

NOTES
Commencement: 30 November 2016.

[5.227]
30 Recall of sequestration by sheriff
(1) The sheriff may recall the award of sequestration if satisfied that in all the circumstances of the case (including those arising after the date of the award) it is appropriate to do so.
(2) In particular, the sheriff may recall the award if satisfied—
(a) that the debtor has paid the debtor's debts in full,
(b) that a majority in value of the creditors reside in a country other than Scotland and that it is more appropriate for the debtor's estate to be administered in that other country, or
(c) that another award of sequestration of the estate, or of an analogous remedy, as defined in section 17(8), has (or other such awards have) been granted.
(3) Where another award of sequestration of the debtor's estate has been granted, the sheriff may, after such intimation as the sheriff considers necessary, recall an award (whether or not the award in respect of which the petition for recall was presented).
(4) Where the sheriff intends to recall an award of sequestration on the ground that the debtor has paid the debtor's debts in full, the order recalling the award may not—
(a) be made before the payment in full of the outlays and remuneration of the trustee and of the interim trustee, or
(b) be subject to any conditions which are to be fulfilled before the order takes effect.
(5) On or before recalling an award of sequestration, the sheriff—
(a) must make provision for the payment of the outlays and remuneration of the trustee in the sequestration (see section 50(1)) and of any interim trustee (see section 53(1))—
(i) by directing that such payment must be made out of the debtor's estate, or
(ii) by requiring that a person who was a party to the petition for sequestration, or as the case may be to the debtor application, must pay the whole or any part of those outlays and remuneration,
(b) may direct that payment of the expenses of a creditor who was a petitioner for sequestration, or concurred in the debtor's application for sequestration, must be made out of the debtor's estate, and
(c) may make any further order the sheriff considers necessary or reasonable in all the circumstances of the case.
(6) Subsection (5)(b) is without prejudice to subsection (8).
(7) Where the sheriff considers that it is inappropriate to recall, or to refuse to recall, an award of sequestration forthwith, the sheriff may order that the proceedings in the sequestration are to continue but are to be subject to such conditions as the sheriff may think fit.
(8) The sheriff may make such order in relation to the expenses in a petition for recall as the sheriff thinks fit.
(9) The sheriff clerk must send—
(a) a certified copy of any order recalling an award of sequestration to the Keeper of the Register of Inhibitions for recording in that register, and
(b) a copy of any interim or final order recalling, or refusing to recall, an award of sequestration or a copy of any order under section 114(3)(b) or 115(3)(b)—
(i) to AiB, and
(ii) if AiB is not the trustee in the sequestration, to the trustee in the sequestration.

NOTES
Commencement: 30 November 2016.

[5.228]
31 Application to Accountant in Bankruptcy for recall of sequestration
(1) An application for recall of an award of sequestration may be made to AiB on the ground that the debtor has paid or is able to pay the debtor's debts in full.
(2) An application may be made by—
(a) the debtor,
(b) any creditor (whether or not a person who was a petitioner for, or concurred in a debtor application for, the sequestration),
(c) the trustee (where AiB is not the trustee), or
(d) any other person having an interest (whether or not a person who was a petitioner for the sequestration).
(3) The person making an application must, at the same time as applying to AiB, give to the persons mentioned in subsection (4)—
(a) a copy of the application, and
(b) a notice informing the recipient that the person has a right to make representations to AiB in relation to the application within 21 days beginning with the day on which the notice is given.
(4) The persons are—
(a) the debtor (where the debtor is not the applicant),
(b) any person who was a petitioner for, or concurred in a debtor application for, the sequestration, and
(c) the trustee.

(5) Despite an application being made, the proceedings in the sequestration are to continue as if the application had not been made until a recall of an award of sequestration is granted under section 34(1) (subject to any conditions imposed under section 34(3)).

(6) Where the applicant withdraws the application or dies, AiB may continue the application by substituting any person mentioned in subsection (2) for the applicant.

NOTES

Commencement: 30 November 2016.

[5.229]

32 Application under section 31: further procedure

(1) This section applies where an application is made under section 31.

(2) The trustee must prepare a statement on the debtor's affairs so far as within the knowledge of the trustee.

(3) The trustee must submit the statement to AiB—

(a) at the same time as the trustee makes the application under section 31, or

(b) where that application is made by another person, within 21 days beginning with the day on which notice is given under section 31(3)(b).

(4) The statement must—

(a) indicate whether the debtor has agreed to—

(i) the interim trustee's claim for outlays reasonably incurred and for remuneration for work reasonably undertaken by the interim trustee (including any outlays and remuneration which are yet to be incurred), and

(ii) the trustee's claim for outlays reasonably incurred and for remuneration for work reasonably undertaken by the trustee (including any outlays and remuneration which are yet to be incurred),

(b) state whether or not the debtor's debts have been paid in full (including the payment of the outlays and remuneration of the interim trustee and of the trustee),

(c) where the debtor's debts have not been so paid—

(i) provide details of any debt which has not been paid, and

(ii) indicate whether, in the opinion of the trustee, the debtor's assets are likely to be sufficient to pay the debts in full (including the payment of the outlays and remuneration of the interim trustee and of the trustee) within 8 weeks beginning with the day on which the statement is submitted, and

(d) provide details of any distribution of the debtor's estate.

(5) The trustee must notify every creditor known to the trustee that the application has been made—

(a) where it is made by the trustee, within 7 days beginning with the day on which it is made, and

(b) where it is made by a person other than the trustee, within 7 days beginning with the day on which notice is given under section 31(3)(b).

(6) If a creditor has not previously submitted a claim under section 46 or 122, the creditor must, in order to be included in the statement made by the trustee, submit a claim.

(7) That claim must be submitted—

(a) in accordance with section 46(2) to (4), and

(b) within 14 days beginning with the day on which notice is given under subsection (5).

(8) If any creditor submits a claim in accordance with subsection (7), the trustee must update and re-submit the statement within 7 days after the days mentioned in paragraph (b) of that subsection have expired.

(9) The trustee must update and re-submit the statement if—

(a) the statement previously submitted did not state in accordance with subsection (4)(b) that the debtor's debts have been paid in full, and

(b) before the day on which the application is determined by AiB, the trustee is able to make that statement.

NOTES

Commencement: 30 November 2016.

[5.230]

33 Determination where amount of outlays and remuneration not agreed

(1) This section applies where—

(a) AiB receives an application under section 31, and

(b) the statement submitted by the trustee under section 32 indicates that the amount of the outlays and remuneration of the trustee is not agreed.

(2) The trustee must—

(a) at the same time as submitting the statement under section 32, provide AiB with—

(i) the trustee's accounts of the trustee's intromissions with the debtor's estate for audit, and

(ii) details of the trustee's claim for outlays reasonably incurred and for remuneration for work reasonably undertaken by the trustee (including any outlays and remuneration which are yet to be incurred), and

(b) provide AiB with such other information in relation to that claim as may reasonably be requested by AiB.

(3) AiB must, within 28 days after the days mentioned in section 32(7)(b) have expired, issue a determination fixing the amount of the outlays and of the remuneration payable to the trustee.

(4) AiB may, within the 28 days mentioned in subsection (3), determine the expenses reasonably incurred by a creditor who was a petitioner for, or as the case may be concurred in a debtor application for, sequestration.

(5) Subsections (2) to (4) of section 133 apply to AiB for the purpose of issuing a determination in accordance with subsection (3) as they apply to the commissioners or to AiB for the purpose of fixing an amount under that section.

NOTES

Commencement: 30 November 2016.

[5.231]

34 Recall of sequestration by Accountant in Bankruptcy

(1) AiB may recall an award of sequestration if—

(a) the trustee has notified AiB, in the statement submitted under section 32, that the debtor's debts have been paid in full (including the outlays and remuneration of the interim trustee and the trustee), and

(b) AiB is satisfied that in all the circumstances it is appropriate to do so.

(2) AiB may not recall an award of sequestration after—

(a) where no appeal in made under section 37(5)(a), the day which is 8 weeks after the day on which the statement was first submitted under section 32(3), or

(b) where such an appeal is made, such later day which is 14 days after the day on which the appeal is finally determined or abandoned.

(3) If AiB does not under subsection (1) recall an award of sequestration, the sequestration must continue but is to be subject to such conditions as AiB thinks fit.

(4) Without delay after granting recall under subsection (1), AiB must send a certified copy of the decision to the Keeper of the Register of Inhibitions for recording in that register.

NOTES

Commencement: 30 November 2016.

[5.232]

35 Recall where Accountant in Bankruptcy trustee

(1) This section applies where AiB—

(a) is the trustee, and

(b) considers recall of an award of sequestration should be granted on the ground that the debtor has paid, or is able to pay, the debtor's debts in full (including the outlays and remuneration of the interim trustee and the trustee).

(2) AiB must notify the debtor and every creditor known to AiB that AiB considers subsection (1) applies.

(3) If a creditor has not previously submitted a claim under section 46 or 122, the creditor must, in order for the creditor's claim to a dividend out of the debtor's estate to be considered, submit a claim.

(4) The claim must be submitted—

(a) in accordance with section 46(2) to (4), and

(b) within 14 days beginning with the day on which notice is given under subsection (2).

(5) Before recalling an award of sequestration AiB must—

(a) take into account any representations made by an interested person within 21 days beginning with the day on which notice is given under subsection (2), and

(b) make a determination of AiB's fees and outlays calculated in accordance with regulations under section 205.

(6) AiB may recall an award of sequestration if satisfied that—

(a) the debtor has paid the debtor's debts in full (including the outlays and remuneration of the interim trustee and the trustee),

(b) those debts were paid in full within 8 weeks after the days mentioned in subsection (5)(a) have expired, and

(c) in all the circumstances it is appropriate to recall it.

(7) Without delay after recalling an award of sequestration under subsection (6), AiB must send a certified copy of the decision to the Keeper of the Register of Inhibitions for recording in that register.

NOTES

Commencement: 30 November 2016.

[5.233]

36 Application for recall: remit to sheriff

(1) AiB may, at any time before deciding under section 34(1) whether to recall an award of sequestration, remit to the sheriff an application made under section 31.

(2) AiB may, at any time before deciding under section 35(6) whether to recall an award of sequestration, remit the case to the sheriff.

(3) If an application is remitted under subsection (1) or (2), the sheriff may dispose of the application or the case in accordance with section 30 as if it were a petition presented by AiB under section 29.

NOTES

Commencement: 30 November 2016.

[5.234]

37 Recall of sequestration by Accountant in Bankruptcy: review and appeal

(1) A person mentioned in subsection (2) may apply to AiB for a review of—
  (a) a decision of AiB under section 34(1) or 35(6) to recall, or refuse to recall, an award of sequestration, or
  (b) a determination of AiB under section 33(4).

(2) The persons are—
  (a) the debtor,
  (b) any creditor,
  (c) the trustee, and
  (d) any other person having an interest.

(3) Any application under subsection (1) must be made within 14 days beginning with the day on which the decision or, as the case may be, the determination or requirement is made.

(4) If an application under subsection (1) is made, AiB must—
  (a) take into account any representations made by an interested person within 21 days beginning with the day on which the application is made, and
  (b) confirm, amend or revoke the decision, determination or requirement within 28 days beginning with that date.

(5) A person mentioned in subsection (2) may, within 14 days beginning with the day on which the decision, determination or requirement is made, appeal to the sheriff against—
  (a) a determination of AiB under section 33(3) or 35(5)(b), or
  (b) a decision of AiB under subsection (4)(b).

(6) Any decision of the sheriff on an appeal relating to a determination of AiB under section 33(3) or 35(5)(b) is final.

NOTES

Commencement: 30 November 2016.

[5.235]

38 Effect of recall of sequestration

(1) The effect of the recall of an award of sequestration is, so far as practicable, to restore the debtor and any other person affected by the sequestration to the position the debtor, or, as the case may be, the other person, would have been in if the sequestration had not been awarded.

(2) But subsection (1) is subject to subsection (3).

(3) A recall of an award of sequestration is not to—
  (a) affect the interruption of prescription caused by—
    (i) the presentation of the petition for sequestration,
    (ii) the making of the debtor application, or
    (iii) the submission of a claim under section 46 or 122,
  (b) invalidate any transaction entered into before such recall by the interim trustee, or by the trustee in the sequestration, with a person acting in good faith, or
  (c) affect a bankruptcy restrictions order which has not been revoked under section 161(1)(a).

NOTES

Commencement: 30 November 2016.

PART 3
INITIAL STAGES OF SEQUESTRATION, STATUTORY MEETING AND TRUSTEE VOTE

Initial stages

[5.236]

39 Interim preservation of estate

(1) An interim trustee may, in pursuance of the function conferred by section 53(1), give general or particular directions to the debtor relating to the management of the debtor's estate.

(2) In exercising the function so conferred, an interim trustee may—
  (a) require the debtor to deliver up to the interim trustee—
    (i) any money or valuables, or
    (ii) any document relating to the debtor's business or financial affairs,
  belonging to, or in the possession of, the debtor or under the debtor's control,
  (b) place in safe custody anything mentioned in paragraph (a),
  (c) require the debtor to deliver up to the interim trustee any perishable goods belonging to the debtor or under the debtor's control,
  (d) arrange for the sale or disposal of such goods,
  (e) make, or cause to be made, an inventory or valuation of any property belonging to the debtor,
  (f) require the debtor to implement any transaction entered into by the debtor,
  (g) effect or maintain insurance policies in respect of the business or property of the debtor, or
  (h) carry on any business of the debtor or borrow money in so far as it is necessary for the interim trustee to do so to safeguard the debtor's estate.

(3) Section 111 applies to an interim trustee as it applies to a trustee.

(4) The sheriff, on the application of an interim trustee, may—

(a) on cause shown, grant a warrant authorising the interim trustee to enter the house where the debtor resides or the debtor's business premises and to search for and take possession of anything mentioned in subsection (2)(a) or (c) (if need be, by opening shut and lock-fast places), or

(b) make such other order to safeguard the debtor's estate as the sheriff thinks appropriate.

(5) Where AiB is the interim trustee, the debtor may apply to AiB for a review of a direction under subsection (1) on the ground that the direction is unreasonable.

(6) If an application under subsection (5) is made, AiB must—

(a) take into account any representations made by an interested person within 21 days beginning with the day on which the application is made, and

(b) confirm, amend or revoke the direction (whether or not substituting a new direction) within 28 days beginning with that day.

(7) The sheriff may, on an application made by the debtor made within 14 days beginning with the day on which AiB makes a decision under subsection (6)(b)—

(a) set aside a direction under subsection (1) or (6)(b) if the sheriff considers the direction to be unreasonable, and

(b) in any event, give such directions to the debtor regarding the management of the debtor's estate as the sheriff considers appropriate.

(8) The debtor must comply with a direction—

(a) under subsection (1) pending a decision by AiB under subsection (6)(b), and

(b) under subsection (6)(b) pending the final determination of any appeal (subject to any interim order of the sheriff).

(9) Where AiB is not the interim trustee, the sheriff, on an application by the debtor on the grounds that a direction under subsection (1) is unreasonable, may—

(a) set aside the direction if the sheriff considers it to be unreasonable, and

(b) in any event, give such directions to the debtor regarding the management of the debtor's estate as the sheriff considers appropriate.

(10) But, subject to any interim order of the sheriff, the debtor must comply with the direction appealed against pending the final determination of the appeal.

NOTES

Commencement: 30 November 2016.

[5.237]

40 Offences in relation to interim preservation of estate

(1) If a debtor—

(a) fails without reasonable excuse to comply with a direction under subsection (1), (6)(b), (7)(b) or (9)(b), or a requirement under subsection (2)(a), (c) or (f), of section 39, or

(b) obstructs the interim trustee where the interim trustee is acting in pursuance of subsection (4)(a) of that section,

then the debtor commits an offence.

(2) A person who commits an offence under subsection (1) is liable—

(a) on summary conviction, to a fine not exceeding the statutory maximum, or—

(i) in a case where the person has previously been convicted of an offence inferring dishonest appropriation of property or an attempt at dishonest appropriation of property, to imprisonment for a term not exceeding 6 months, or

(ii) in any other case, to imprisonment for a term not exceeding 3 months,

or both to a fine not exceeding the statutory maximum and to such imprisonment as is mentioned, in relation to the case in question, in sub-paragraph (i) or (ii), or

(b) on conviction on indictment—

(i) to a fine, or

(ii) to imprisonment for a term not exceeding 2 years,

or both to a fine and to such imprisonment.

NOTES

Commencement: 30 November 2016.

[5.238]

41 Statement of assets and liabilities etc

(1) Where a debtor has made a debtor application then, within 7 days after the appointment of the trustee in the sequestration under section 51 (where the trustee is not AiB), the debtor must send to the trustee such statement of assets and liabilities as was sent to AiB in pursuance of section 8(3)(a).

(2) Where a petitioner for sequestration is a creditor, or a trustee acting under a trust deed, then, within 7 days after having been notified by the trustee as mentioned in section 51(13) the debtor must send to the trustee a statement of assets and liabilities.

(3) If the debtor—

(a) fails to disclose any material fact in a statement of assets and liabilities sent to the trustee in accordance with subsection (1) or (2), or

(b) makes a material misstatement in any such statement,

then the debtor commits of an offence.

(4) A person who commits an offence under subsection (3) is liable on summary conviction to a fine not exceeding level 5 on the standard scale or to imprisonment for a term not exceeding 3 months (or both to such fine and to such imprisonment).
(5) In any proceedings for an offence under subsection (3), it is a defence for the accused to show that the accused had a reasonable excuse for the failure to disclose or for the making of the misstatement.

NOTES
Commencement: 30 November 2016.

[5.239]
42 Duties on receipt of list of assets and liabilities
(1) As soon as practicable after a trustee has received a statement of assets and liabilities—
(a) the trustee must prepare a statement of the debtor's affairs so far as within the knowledge of the trustee, and
(b) if, in the trustee's opinion, the debtor's assets are unlikely to be sufficient to pay any dividend whatsoever in respect of the debts mentioned in section 129(1)(e) to (i) the trustee is so to indicate in the statement prepared under paragraph (a).
(2) Not later—
(a) than 4 days before the date fixed for the statutory meeting, or
(b) where the trustee does not intend to hold such a meeting, than 60 days after the date on which the sequestration is awarded,
the trustee must send to AiB the statement, copy statement and comments mentioned in subsection (3).
(3) The statement, copy statement and comments are—
(a) the statement of assets and liabilities (unless that statement has already been received by AiB by virtue of section 8(3)(a)),
(b) subject to subsection (4), a copy of the statement prepared under subsection (1)(a), and
(c) written comments by the trustee indicating what in the trustee's opinion are the causes of the insolvency and to what extent the conduct of the debtor may have contributed to the insolvency.
(4) The trustee need not send the copy mentioned in subsection (3)(b) if the trustee has, in accordance with section 108(1)(c), sent a copy of the inventory and valuation to AiB.
(5) The written comments made under subsection (3)(c) are absolutely privileged.
(6) Subsections (2) and (5) do not apply in any case where AiB is the trustee.

NOTES
Commencement: 30 November 2016.

Statutory meeting

[5.240]
43 Statutory meeting
A meeting of creditors called under section 44 is referred to in this Act as "the statutory meeting".

NOTES
Commencement: 30 November 2016.

[5.241]
44 Calling of statutory meeting
(1) The statutory meeting may be held at such time and place as the trustee in the sequestration may determine.
(2) But subsection (1) is subject to subsections (6) and (7).
(3) Not later than—
(a) 60 days after the date on which sequestration is awarded, or
(b) such greater number of days after that date as the sheriff may, on cause shown, allow,
the trustee must give notice to every creditor known to the trustee of whether or not the trustee intends to call the statutory meeting.
(4) A notice under subsection (3)—
(a) must be accompanied by a copy of the trustee's statement of the debtor's affairs, and
(b) where the trustee is notifying an intention not to hold the statutory meeting, must inform creditors of the effect of subsections (5) and (6).
(5) Within 7 days after the giving of notice under subsection (3), any creditor may request the trustee to call the statutory meeting.
(6) Where a request under subsection (5) is made (or requests under that subsection are made) by not less than ¼ in value of the debtor's creditors, the trustee must call the statutory meeting not later than—
(a) 28 days after the date on which notice is given under subsection (3), or
(b) such greater number of days after that date as the sheriff may, on cause shown, allow.
(7) Where the trustee gives notice under subsection (3) that the trustee intends to call the statutory meeting, that meeting must be called within 28 days after the date on which the notice is given.
(8) No fewer than 7 days before the date fixed for the statutory meeting, the trustee—
(a) must notify every creditor known to the trustee of the date, time and place of the meeting, and
(b) must in the notification—
(i) invite the submission of such claims as have not already been submitted, and
(ii) inform the creditors of the trustee's duties under section 48(4).
(9) The creditors may continue the statutory meeting to a date not later than—
(a) 7 days after the days mentioned in subsection (7) have expired, or

(b) such greater number of days after that expiry as the sheriff may, on cause shown, allow.

NOTES

Commencement: 30 November 2016.

[5.242]

45 Procedure where no statutory meeting called

(1) Where the trustee in the sequestration does not call the statutory meeting and the 7 days mentioned in section 44(5) expire, the trustee must forthwith make a report to AiB on the circumstance of the sequestration.

(2) But subsection (1) does not apply if AiB is the trustee.

NOTES

Commencement: 30 November 2016.

[5.243]

46 Submission of claims for voting purposes

(1) For the purposes of voting at the statutory meeting a creditor (in this section and in section 47 referred to as "C") must, in accordance with this section, submit a claim to the trustee in the sequestration at or before the meeting.

(2) C submits a claim under this section by producing to the trustee—

(a) a statement of claim in the prescribed form, and

(b) an account or voucher (according to the nature of the debt) which constitutes prima facie evidence of the debt.

(3) But the trustee may dispense with any requirement under subsection (2) in respect of any debt or of any class of debt.

(4) Where C neither resides, nor has a place of business, in the United Kingdom, the trustee—

(a) must, if the trustee knows where C does reside or have a place of business and if no notification has been given to C under section 44(3), write to C informing C that C may submit a claim under this section, and

(b) may allow C to submit an informal claim in writing.

(5) If C has produced a statement of claim in accordance with subsection (2), C may at any time before the statutory meeting produce, in place of that statement of claim, another statement of claim specifying a different amount for C's claim.

(6) C may, in such circumstances as may be prescribed, state the amount of C's claim in foreign currency.

(7) The trustee must, on production of any document to the trustee under this section—

(a) initial the document,

(b) keep a record of it, stating the date on which it was produced to the trustee, and

(c) if requested by the person producing it, return it (if it is not a statement of claim) to that person.

(8) The submission of a claim under this section bars the effect of any enactment or rule of law relating to the limitation of actions.

(9) Schedule 2 has effect for determining the amount in respect of which C is entitled to claim.

NOTES

Commencement: 30 November 2016.

Regulations: the Bankruptcy (Scotland) Regulations 2016, SSI 2016/397 at **[16.401]**.

[5.244]

47 Offences in relation to submission of claims for voting purposes

(1) Subsections (2) and (3) apply where C produces under section 46—

(a) a statement of claim,

(b) account,

(c) voucher, or

(d) other evidence,

which is false.

(2) C commits an offence unless C shows that C neither knew nor had reason to believe that the statement of claim, account, voucher or other evidence was false.

(3) The debtor commits an offence if the debtor—

(a) knew, or became aware, that the statement of claim, account, voucher or other evidence was false, and

(b) failed, as soon as practicable after acquiring such knowledge, to report to the trustee that the statement of claim, account, voucher or other evidence was false.

(4) A person who commits an offence under subsection (2) or (3) is liable—

(a) on summary conviction, to a fine not exceeding the statutory maximum, or—

(i) in a case where the person has previously been convicted of an offence inferring dishonest appropriation of property or an attempt at dishonest appropriation of property, to imprisonment for a term not exceeding 6 months, or

(ii) in any other case, to imprisonment for a term not exceeding 3 months,

or both to a fine not exceeding the statutory maximum and to such imprisonment as is mentioned, in relation to the case in question, in sub-paragraph (i) or (ii), or

(b) on conviction on indictment, to a fine, to imprisonment for a term not exceeding 2 years or both to a fine and to such imprisonment.

NOTES
Commencement: 30 November 2016.

[5.245]
48 Proceedings before trustee vote
(1) At the commencement of the statutory meeting the trustee in the sequestration must chair the meeting and, as the person chairing it, is—
(a) for the purposes of subsection (3), to accept or reject in whole or in part the claim of each creditor (and if the amount of the claim is stated in foreign currency, to convert that amount into sterling, in such manner as may be prescribed, at the rate of exchange prevailing at the close of business on the date of sequestration),
(b) on that being done, to invite the creditors to elect one of their number to chair the meeting in place of the trustee,
(c) to preside over the election, and
(d) to arrange for a record to be made of the proceedings at the meeting.
(2) But, if no person is elected in pursuance of subsection (1)(b), the trustee must chair the statutory meeting throughout.
(3) The acceptance of a claim in whole or in part under paragraph (a) of that subsection is, subject to section 49(6), to determine the entitlement of a creditor to vote at the statutory meeting.
(4) On the conclusion of the proceedings under subsection (1)—
(a) the trustee must make available for inspection—
(i) the statement of assets and liabilities, and
(ii) the statement prepared under section 42(1),
(b) the trustee must answer to the best of the trustee's ability any questions,
(c) the trustee must consider any representations put to the trustee by the creditors which relate to the debtor's—
(i) assets and business or financial affairs, or
(ii) conduct in relation to such assets and affairs,
(d) after the trustee considers any such representations as are mentioned in paragraph (c) if, in the trustee's opinion, the debtor's assets are unlikely to be sufficient to pay any dividend whatsoever in respect of the debts mentioned in paragraphs (e) to (i) of section 129(1), the trustee is so to indicate,
(e) the trustee must determine whether it is necessary to revise the trustee's statement of the debtor's affairs, and
(f) if the trustee does so determine, the trustee must revise the statement either at, or as soon as may be after, the statutory meeting.
(5) Where the trustee does carry out such a revision, the trustee is as soon as possible after the statutory meeting to send a copy of the revised statement to every creditor known to the trustee.

NOTES
Commencement: 30 November 2016.
Regulations: the Bankruptcy (Scotland) Regulations 2016, SSI 2016/397 at **[16.401]**.

Trustee vote

[5.246]
49 Trustee vote
(1) At the statutory meeting the creditors are, at the conclusion of the proceedings under section 48(4), to proceed to a vote at which they are—
(a) to confirm the appointment of the trustee appointed under section 51 (referred to in this section and in Part 4 as the "original trustee"), or
(b) to elect another person as the trustee in the sequestration (referred to in this section and in that Part as the "replacement trustee").
(2) The vote is referred to in this Act as a "trustee vote".
(3) None of the persons listed in subsection (5) is eligible for election as replacement trustee.
(4) No one who becomes a person so listed after being elected as replacement trustee is qualified to continue to act as trustee.
(5) The persons are—
(a) the debtor,
(b) a person not qualified to act as an insolvency practitioner,
(c) a person who, though qualified to act as an insolvency practitioner, is not qualified to act as such in relation to the debtor,
(d) a person who holds an interest opposed to the general interests of the creditors,
(e) a person who has not given an undertaking, in writing, to act as trustee, and
(f) AiB.
(6) None of the persons listed in subsection (7) is entitled to vote in the trustee vote.
(7) The persons are—
(a) anyone who, other than by succession, acquires after the date of sequestration a debt due by the debtor, and
(b) any creditor to the extent that the creditor's debt is a postponed debt.
(8) Where AiB is the original trustee, if no creditor entitled to vote in the trustee vote attends the statutory meeting or no replacement trustee is elected, AiB must—

(a) forthwith report the proceedings at the statutory meeting to the sheriff, and
(b) continue to act as the trustee.

(9) Where AiB is not the original trustee, if no creditor entitled to vote in the trustee vote attends the statutory meeting or no replacement trustee is elected, the original trustee must—
(a) forthwith—
(i) notify AiB accordingly, and
(ii) report the proceedings at the statutory meeting to the sheriff, and
(b) continue to act as the trustee in the sequestration.

NOTES

Commencement: 30 November 2016.

PART 4
TRUSTEES AND COMMISSIONERS

Trustees

[5.247]

50 Functions of trustee

(1) In every sequestration there is to be a trustee, whose general functions are—
(a) to recover, manage and realise the estate of the debtor, whether situated in Scotland or elsewhere,
(b) to distribute the estate among the debtor's creditors according to their respective entitlements,
(c) to ascertain the reasons for the debtor's insolvency and the circumstances surrounding it,
(d) to ascertain the state of the debtor's liabilities and assets,
(e) to maintain, for the purpose of providing an accurate record of the sequestration process, a sederunt book during the trustee's term of office,
(f) to keep regular accounts of the trustee's intromissions with the debtor's estate, such accounts being available for inspection at all reasonable times by the commissioners, if there are any, the creditors and the debtor, and
(g) whether or not the trustee is still acting in the sequestration, to supply AiB with such information as AiB considers necessary to enable AiB to discharge AiB's functions under this Act.

(2) The trustee, in performing the trustee's functions under this Act, must have regard to advice offered to the trustee by the commissioners, if there are any.

(3) Where the trustee has reasonable grounds—
(a) to suspect that an offence has been committed in relation to a sequestration—
(i) by the debtor in respect of the debtor's assets, the debtor's dealings with them or the debtor's conduct in relation to the debtor's business or financial affairs, or
(ii) by a person other than the debtor in that person's dealings with the debtor, the interim trustee or the trustee in respect of the debtor's assets, business or financial affairs, or
(b) to believe that any behaviour on the part of the debtor is of a kind that would result in a sheriff granting, under section 156(1), an application for a bankruptcy restrictions order,

the trustee must report the matter to AiB.

(4) A report under subsection (3) is absolutely privileged.

(5) Subsections (1)(g) and (3) do not apply in any case where AiB is the trustee.

(6) Where AiB is the trustee, AiB may apply to the sheriff for directions in relation to any particular matter arising in the sequestration.

(7) The debtor, a creditor or any other person having an interest may, if dissatisfied with any act, omission or decision of the trustee, apply to the sheriff in that regard.

(8) On an application under subsection (7), the sheriff may confirm, revoke, or modify the decision in question, confirm or annul the act in question, give the trustee directions or make such order as the sheriff thinks fit.

(9) The trustee must comply with the requirements of subsections (1)(a) to (d) and (2) only in so far as, in the trustee's view, to do so would be—
(a) of financial benefit to the debtor's estate, and
(b) in the interests of the creditors.

NOTES

Commencement: 30 November 2016.

[5.248]

51 Appointment of trustee

(1) Subsection (2) applies where the sheriff awards sequestration of the debtor's estate and the petition for the sequestration—
(a) nominates a person to be the trustee in the sequestration,
(b) states that the person—
(i) is qualified to act as an insolvency practitioner, and
(ii) has given an undertaking to act as the trustee in the sequestration, and
(c) has, annexed to it, a copy of the undertaking.

(2) The sheriff may, if—
(a) it appears to the sheriff that the person is so qualified and has given the undertaking, and
(b) no interim trustee is appointed under section 54(1),

appoint the person to be the trustee in the sequestration.

(3) Where the sheriff—

(a) awards sequestration of the debtor's estate,
(b) does not, under subsection (2), appoint a person to be the trustee in the sequestration, and
(c) no interim trustee is appointed under section 54(1),

the sheriff must appoint AiB to be the trustee in the sequestration.

(4) Subsections (5) and (7) apply where the sheriff—
(a) awards sequestration of the debtor's estate, and
(b) an interim trustee is appointed under section 54(1).

(5) The sheriff may appoint—
(a) the interim trustee, or
(b) subject to subsection (6), such other person as may be nominated by the petitioner,

to be the trustee in the sequestration.

(6) A person nominated under subsection (5)(b) may be appointed to be the trustee in the sequestration only if—
(a) it appears to the sheriff that the person is qualified to act as an insolvency practitioner and has given an undertaking to act as the trustee in the sequestration, and
(b) a copy of the undertaking has been lodged with the sheriff.

(7) Where the sheriff does not, under subsection (5), appoint a person to be the trustee in the sequestration, the sheriff must appoint AiB to be the trustee in the sequestration.

(8) Subsection (9) applies where AiB awards sequestration of the debtor's estate and the debtor application—
(a) nominates a person to be the trustee in the sequestration,
(b) states that the person—
(i) is qualified to act as an insolvency practitioner, and
(ii) has given an undertaking to act as the trustee in the sequestration, and
(c) has, annexed to it, a copy of the undertaking.

(9) AiB may, if it appears to AiB that the person is so qualified and has given that undertaking, appoint the person to be the trustee in the sequestration.

(10) But subsection (9) is subject to subsection (11).

(11) AiB is not to make an appointment under subsection (9) where—
(a) the debtor application is made by a debtor to whom section 2(2) applies, and
(b) AiB awards sequestration of the debtor's estate.

(12) Where AiB—
(a) awards sequestration of the debtor's estate, and
(b) does not, under subsection (9), appoint a person to be the trustee in the sequestration,

AiB is deemed to be appointed the trustee in the sequestration.

(13) Where a trustee is appointed in a sequestration for which the petition is presented by a creditor, or by a trustee acting under a trust deed, the appointee must, as soon as practicable, notify the debtor of the appointment.

(14) The trustee must, at the same time as notifying the debtor under subsection (13), send to the debtor for signature by the debtor a statement of undertakings in the form prescribed.

NOTES

Commencement: 30 November 2016.

Regulations: the Bankruptcy (Scotland) Regulations 2016, SSI 2016/397 at **[16.401]**.

[5.249]

52 Application to Accountant in Bankruptcy by trustee for a direction

(1) This section applies where AiB is not the trustee in the sequestration.

(2) The trustee may apply to AiB for a direction in relation to any particular matter arising in the sequestration.

(3) Before giving any such direction, AiB may refer the matter to the sheriff by making an application for a direction in relation to the matter.

(4) The trustee may apply to AiB for a review of a direction given by AiB under this section.

(5) An application for a review under subsection (4) may not be made—
(a) by an interim trustee,
(b) after the expiry of 14 days beginning with the day on which notice of the direction by AiB is given to the trustee, or
(c) in relation to a matter on which AiB has applied to the sheriff for a direction under subsection (3).

(6) If an application for a review under subsection (4) is made, AiB must—
(a) take into account any representations made by the trustee, the debtor, any creditor or any other person having an interest, within 21 days beginning with the day on which the application is made, and
(b) confirm, amend or revoke the direction within 28 days beginning with that day.

(7) The trustee may, within 14 days beginning with the day of a decision of AiB under subsection (6)(b), appeal to the sheriff against that decision.

NOTES

Commencement: 30 November 2016.

Interim trustees

[5.250]

53 Functions of interim trustee

(1) An interim trustee's general function is to safeguard the debtor's estate pending the determination of the petition for sequestration.

(2) An interim trustee, whether or not still acting in the sequestration, must supply AiB with such information as AiB considers necessary to enable AiB to discharge AiB's functions under this Act.

NOTES

Commencement: 30 November 2016.

[5.251]

54 Appointment of interim trustee

(1) Where a petition for sequestration is presented by a creditor, or by a trustee acting under a trust deed, the sheriff may appoint an interim trustee before sequestration is awarded if—

(a) the debtor consents, or

(b) the trustee acting under the trust deed or any creditor shows cause.

(2) For the purposes of the appointment of an interim trustee under subsection (1)—

(a) where a person is nominated as mentioned in subsection (1)(a) of section 51 and the provisions of that subsection apply, the sheriff may appoint that person, and

(b) where such a person is not appointed, the sheriff must appoint AiB.

(3) Where an interim trustee is appointed under subsection (1), the appointee is, as soon as practicable, to notify the debtor of the appointment.

(4) The interim trustee must, at the same time as notifying the debtor under subsection (3), send to the debtor for signature by the debtor a statement of undertakings in the form prescribed.

NOTES

Commencement: 30 November 2016.

Regulations: the Bankruptcy (Scotland) Regulations 2016, SSI 2016/397 at **[16.401]**.

[5.252]

55 Removal, resignation etc of interim trustee

(1) This section applies where—

(a) an interim trustee is appointed under section 54(1), and

(b) the petition for sequestration has not been determined.

(2) Where, under section 200(4) the sheriff removes an interim trustee from office the sheriff must, on the application of AiB, appoint a new interim trustee.

(3) Without prejudice to that section or to subsection (2), where the sheriff is satisfied—

(a) that the interim trustee is unable to act—

(i) for a reason mentioned in subsection (4), or

(ii) by, under or by virtue of any other provision of this Act, or

(b) that the interim trustee's conduct has been such that the interim trustee should no longer continue to act in the sequestration,

then, on the application of the debtor, a creditor or AiB, the sheriff must remove the interim trustee from office and appoint a new interim trustee.

(4) The reasons are—

(a) that the interim trustee is incapable (within the meaning of section 1(6) of the Adults with Incapacity (Scotland) Act 2000), or

(b) that the interim trustee has some incapacity by virtue of which the interim trustee is unable to act as interim trustee.

(5) An interim trustee (not being AiB) may apply to the sheriff for authority to resign office; and if the sheriff is, in respect of the applicant, satisfied as is mentioned in subsection (3), the sheriff must grant the application.

(6) Where, following an application under subsection (5) the interim trustee resigns office, the sheriff must appoint a new interim trustee.

(7) Where the interim trustee dies, the sheriff must, on the application of the debtor, a creditor or AiB, appoint a new interim trustee.

(8) A person (other than AiB) may not be appointed to act as interim trustee in a sequestration if the person is ineligible, by virtue of section 49(3), for election as a replacement trustee.

(9) An interim trustee who, by virtue of subsection (8), is prohibited from acting as such must forthwith make an application under subsection (5).

(10) Subsections (1) to (3) of section 51 apply as regards the appointment of an interim trustee under this section as if, for any reference—

(a) to the sheriff awarding sequestration of the debtor's estate, there were substituted a reference to the sheriff appointing a new interim trustee, and

(b) to the petition for sequestration, there were substituted a reference to the application under this section for the appointment of a new interim trustee.

NOTES

Commencement: 30 November 2016.

[5.253]
56 Termination of interim trustee's functions where not appointed trustee

(1) This section applies where an interim trustee (not being AiB) is appointed under section 54(1) and the sheriff—

(a) awards sequestration and appoints another person as trustee under subsection (5) or (7) of section 51, or

(b) refuses to award sequestration.

(2) Where the sheriff awards sequestration and appoints another person as trustee in the sequestration, the interim trustee—

(a) must hand over to the other person everything in the interim trustee's possession which relates to the sequestration, and

(b) on that being done, must cease to act in the sequestration.

(3) The sheriff may make such order in relation to liability for the outlays and remuneration of the interim trustee as may be appropriate.

(4) Within 3 months after the sheriff awards, or refuses to award, sequestration the interim trustee must—

(a) submit to AiB—
  (i) the interim trustee's accounts for intromissions (if any) with the debtor's estate,
  (ii) a claim for outlays reasonably incurred by the interim trustee, and
  (iii) a claim for remuneration for work reasonably undertaken by the interim trustee, and

(b) send a copy of the interim trustee's accounts and claims to—
  (i) the debtor,
  (ii) the petitioner, and
  (iii) in a case where sequestration is awarded, the trustee and all creditors known to the interim trustee.

(5) On a submission being made under subsection (4)(a), AiB must—

(a) audit the accounts,

(b) issue a determination fixing the amount of the outlays and remuneration payable to the interim trustee,

(c) send a copy of the determination to—
  (i) the interim trustee, and
  (ii) the persons mentioned in subsection (4)(b), and

(d) where a trustee (not being AiB) is appointed in the sequestration, send a copy of the audited accounts and of the determination to the trustee.

(6) On receiving a copy of the determination sent under subsection (5)(c)(i), the interim trustee may apply to AiB for a certificate of discharge.

(7) The grant of a certificate of discharge under this section by AiB has the effect of discharging the interim trustee from all liability (other than any liability arising from fraud)—

(a) to the debtor,

(b) to the petitioner, or

(c) to the creditors,

in respect of any act or omission of the interim trustee in exercising the functions conferred on the interim trustee by this Act.

NOTES

Commencement: 30 November 2016.

[5.254]
57 Appeal or review by virtue of section 56

(1) The interim trustee, or any person mentioned in subsection (4)(b) of section 56 may, within 14 days after the issuing of the determination under subsection (5)(b) of that section, appeal to the sheriff against the determination.

(2) The decision of the sheriff on an appeal under subsection (1) is final.

(3) The interim trustee must send to the persons mentioned in subsection (4)(b) of section 56 notice of any application under subsection (6) of that section and must inform them—

(a) that they may make written representations relating to it to AiB within 14 days after such notification, and

(b) of the effect mentioned in subsection (7) of that section.

(4) On the expiry of the 14 days mentioned in subsection (3)(a) AiB must, after considering any representations made to AiB—

(a) grant or refuse to grant the certificate of discharge, and

(b) notify accordingly the persons mentioned in section 56(4)(b).

(5) The interim trustee or any person mentioned in section 56(4)(b) may apply to AiB for a review of a determination under subsection (4).

(6) Any application under subsection (5) must be made within 14 days after the determination is issued.

(7) If an application under subsection (5) is made, AiB must—

(a) take into account any representations made by an interested person within 21 days beginning with the day on which the application is made, and

(b) confirm, amend or revoke the determination within 28 days beginning with that day.

(8) The interim trustee, or any person mentioned in subsection (4)(b) of section 56, may, within 14 days after a decision under subsection (7)(b), appeal to the sheriff against the decision.

(9) If, following an appeal under subsection (8), the sheriff determines that a certificate of discharge—

(a) which has been refused should be granted under section 56, the sheriff must order AiB to grant it,

(b) which has been granted should have been refused, the sheriff must revoke the certificate.

(10) Following any appeal under subsection (8), the sheriff clerk must send a copy of the decree of the sheriff to AiB.

(11) The decision of the sheriff on an appeal under subsection (8) is final.

NOTES

Commencement: 30 November 2016.

[5.255]

58 Termination of Accountant in Bankruptcy's functions as interim trustee where not appointed trustee

(1) This section applies where AiB is appointed as interim trustee under section 54(1) and the sheriff—

(a) awards sequestration and appoints another person as trustee under section 51(5), or

(b) refuses to award sequestration.

(2) Where the sheriff awards sequestration and appoints another person as trustee in the sequestration, AiB—

(a) must hand over to the other person everything in AiB's possession which relates to the sequestration, and

(b) on that being done, must cease to act in the sequestration.

(3) The sheriff may make such order in relation to liability for the outlays and remuneration of AiB as may be appropriate.

(4) Within 3 months after the sheriff awards, or refuses to award, sequestration AiB must—

(a) send to the debtor and the petitioner—

(i) AiB's accounts for intromissions (if any) with the debtor's estate,

(ii) a determination of AiB's fees and outlays, calculated in accordance with regulations made under section 205, and

(iii) the notice mentioned in subsection (5), and

(b) in a case where sequestration is awarded, send a copy of those accounts, that determination and that notice to all creditors known to AiB.

(5) The notice is a notice in writing stating—

(a) that AiB has commenced procedure under this Act leading to discharge in respect of AiB's actings as interim trustee,

(b) that an application for a review may be made under section 59(1),

(c) that an appeal may be made to the sheriff under section 59(4), and

(d) that, in the circumstances mentioned in subsection (6), AiB is discharged from any liability incurred while acting as interim trustee.

(6) Subsection (7) applies where—

(a) the requirements of this section have been complied with, and

(b) either no appeal is made under section 59(4) or any such appeal is refused as regards the discharge of AiB.

(7) AiB is discharged from all liability (other than any liability arising from fraud)—

(a) to the debtor,

(b) to the petitioner, or

(c) to the creditors,

in respect of any act or omission of AiB in exercising the functions of interim trustee conferred on AiB by this Act.

NOTES

Commencement: 30 November 2016.

[5.256]

59 Review or appeal by virtue of section 58

(1) The debtor, the petitioner or any creditor may apply to AiB for a review of the discharge of AiB in respect of AiB's actings as interim trustee.

(2) Any application under subsection (1) must be made within 14 days beginning with the day on which notice is sent under section 58(4)(a)(iii) or (b).

(3) If an application for a review under subsection (1) is made, AiB must—

(a) take into account any representations made, within 21 days beginning with the day on which the application is made, by an interested person, and

(b) confirm or revoke the discharge within 28 days beginning with that day.

(4) The debtor, the petitioner or any creditor may appeal to the sheriff within 14 days beginning with—

(a) the day on which notice is sent under section 58(4)(a)(iii) or (b), against the determination mentioned in section 58(4)(a)(ii), or

(b) the day of a decision by AiB under subsection (3)(b), against that decision.

(5) The sheriff clerk must, following an appeal under subsection (4), send a copy of the decree to AiB.

(6) The decision of the sheriff on an appeal under subsection (4) is final.

NOTES

Commencement: 30 November 2016.

Replacement trustees

[5.257]

60 Appointment of replacement trustee

(1) This section applies where a replacement trustee is elected by virtue of a trustee vote.

(2) On the election of the replacement trustee the original trustee must immediately make a report of the proceedings at the statutory meeting—

(a) where the original trustee was not AiB, to AiB, or

(b) where the original trustee was AiB, to the sheriff.

(3) The debtor, a creditor, the original trustee, the replacement trustee or AiB may object to any matter connected with the election—

(a) in the case of an objection by a person other than AiB, by applying to AiB,

(b) in the case of an objection by AiB, by application to the sheriff.

(4) Any objection under subsection (3) must—

(a) specify the grounds on which the objection is taken, and

(b) be made within 4 days beginning with the day of the statutory meeting.

(5) If there is no timeous objection under subsection (3), AiB must without delay declare the elected person to be the trustee in the sequestration.

(6) No expense in objecting under this section is to fall on the debtor's estate.

NOTES

Commencement: 30 November 2016.

[5.258]

61 Procedure in application to Accountant in Bankruptcy under section 60

(1) This section applies where an application is made to AiB under section 60(3)(a).

(2) AiB must—

(a) without delay give the original trustee, the replacement trustee, the objector and any other interested person an opportunity to make written submissions on the application, and

(b) make a decision.

(3) If AiB decides—

(a) to reject the objection in the application, AiB must without delay declare the elected person to be the trustee in the sequestration,

(b) to sustain the objection in the application, AiB must order the original trustee to arrange a new meeting at which a new trustee vote must be held.

(4) Sections 48, 49, 60 and 62, and this section, apply in relation to a meeting arranged by virtue of subsection (3)(b).

(5) The original trustee, the replacement trustee, the objector and any other interested party may apply to AiB for a review of a decision under subsection (2)(b).

(6) Any application under subsection (5) must be made within 14 days beginning with the day on which notice of the decision is given.

(7) If an application for a review under subsection (5) is made, AiB must—

(a) take into account any representations made by an interested party within 21 days beginning with the day on which the application is made, and

(b) confirm, amend or revoke the decision within 28 days beginning with that day.

(8) The trustee, the objector or any other interested party may, within 14 days beginning with the day of a decision of AiB under subsection (7)(b), appeal to the sheriff against that decision.

(9) No expense in objecting under this section is to fall on the debtor's estate.

NOTES

Commencement: 30 November 2016.

[5.259]

62 Procedure in application under section 60, or appeal under section 61, to sheriff

(1) This section applies where there is—

(a) an application by AiB under section 60(3)(b), or

(b) an appeal under section 61(8).

(2) The sheriff must—

(a) without delay give the parties an opportunity to be heard on the application, and

(b) make a decision.

(3) If the sheriff decides—

(a) to reject an objection to the appointment of an elected person, the sheriff must without delay declare the elected person to be the trustee in the sequestration and make an order appointing the elected person to be the trustee in the sequestration, or

(b) to sustain such an objection, the sheriff must order the original trustee to arrange a new meeting at which a new trustee vote must be held.

(4) Sections 48, 49, 60, 61 and this section, apply in relation to a meeting arranged by virtue of subsection (3)(b).

(5) Any declaration, appointment or decision of the sheriff under this section is final.

NOTES

Commencement: 30 November 2016.

[5.260]

63 Termination of original trustee's functions

(1) This section applies where—

(a) a replacement trustee is appointed under section 60, and

(b) the original trustee is not AiB.

(2) On the appointment of the replacement trustee, the original trustee—

(a) must hand over to the replacement trustee everything in the original trustee's possession which relates to the sequestration, including—

(i) the statement of assets and liabilities,

(ii) a copy of the statement of the debtor's affairs prepared under section 42(1)(a) (as revised under section 48(4)(f) if so revised), and

(iii) a copy of the written comments sent under section 42(2)), and

(b) on that being done, must cease to act in the sequestration.

(3) Within 3 months after the appointment of the replacement trustee, the original trustee must—

(a) submit to AiB—

(i) the original trustee's accounts for intromissions (if any) with the debtor's estate,

(ii) a claim for outlays reasonably incurred, and for remuneration for work reasonably undertaken, by the original trustee, and

(b) send to the replacement trustee a copy of what is submitted under paragraph (a).

(4) Where the original trustee was appointed under section 54(1) as the interim trustee in the sequestration, the original trustee's accounts and the claim referred to in subsection (3)(a)(ii) must include accounts and a claim for the period of the original trustee's appointment as interim trustee.

(5) On a submission being made under subsection (3)(a), AiB must—

(a) audit the accounts,

(b) issue a determination fixing the amount of the outlays and remuneration payable to the original trustee, and

(c) send a copy of—

(i) the determination to the original trustee, and

(ii) the audited accounts and the determination to the replacement trustee.

(6) The original trustee, the replacement trustee, the debtor or any creditor may appeal to the sheriff against the determination within 14 days after it is issued.

(7) The decision of the sheriff on an appeal under subsection (6) is final.

NOTES

Commencement: 30 November 2016.

[5.261]

64 Accountant in Bankruptcy's intromissions in capacity of original trustee

(1) This section applies where AiB was the original trustee and some other person is appointed as replacement trustee under section 60.

(2) On the appointment of the replacement trustee AiB—

(a) must hand over to that person everything in AiB's possession—

(i) which relates to the sequestration, and

(ii) which AiB obtained in the capacity of original trustee (including the statement of assets and liabilities), and

(b) on that being done, must cease to act as trustee.

(3) AiB must, within 3 months after the appointment of the replacement trustee, supply to that person—

(a) AiB's accounts of AiB's intromissions (if any) as original trustee with the debtor's estate,

(b) a determination of AiB's fees and outlays calculated in accordance with regulations under section 205, and

(c) a copy of the notice mentioned in subsection (4)(b).

(4) AiB must send to the debtor and to all creditors known to AiB—

(a) a copy of the determination mentioned in subsection (3)(b), and

(b) a notice in writing stating—

(i) that AiB has commenced procedure under this Act leading to discharge in respect of AiB's actings as trustee,

(ii) that the accounts of AiB's intromissions (if any) with the debtor's estate are available for inspection at such address as AiB may determine,

(iii) that an application for a review may be made under subsection (5),

(iv) that an appeal may be made to the sheriff under subsection (8), and

(v) the effect of subsections (10) and (11).

(5) The replacement trustee, the debtor or any creditor may apply to AiB for a review of the discharge of AiB in respect of AiB's actings as trustee.

(6) Any application under subsection (5) must be made within 14 days beginning with the day on which notice is sent under subsection (4)(b).

(7) If an application under subsection (5) is made, AiB must—

(a) take into account any representations made by an interested person within 21 days beginning with the day on which the application is made, and

(b) confirm or revoke the discharge within 28 days beginning with that day.

(8) The replacement trustee, the debtor or any creditor may appeal to the sheriff within 14 days beginning with—

(a) the day on which notice is sent under subsection (4)(b), against the determination mentioned in subsection (3)(b), or

(b) the day of a decision of AiB under subsection (7)(b), against that decision.

(9) The decision of the sheriff on an appeal under subsection (8) is final.

(10) Subsection (11) applies where—

(a) the requirements of this section have been complied with, and

(b) either no appeal is made under subsection (8) or any such appeal is refused as regards the discharge of AiB.

(11) AiB is discharged from all liability (other than liability arising from fraud) to the creditors or to the debtor in respect of any act or omission of AiB in exercising the functions of trustee in the sequestration.

NOTES

Commencement: 30 November 2016.

[5.262]

65 Discharge of original trustee

(1) On receiving a copy of the determination of AiB sent under section 63(5)(c)(i) the original trustee may apply to AiB for a certificate of discharge.

(2) The original trustee must send notice of the application to the debtor, to all creditors known to the original trustee and to the replacement trustee and must inform the debtor—

(a) that the debtor, the replacement trustee or any creditor may, in relation to the application, make written representations to AiB within 14 days after such notification,

(b) that the audited accounts of the original trustee's intromissions (if any) with the debtor's estate are available for inspection at the original trustee's office and that a copy of those accounts has been sent to the replacement trustee, and

(c) of the effect mentioned in subsection (11).

(3) On the expiry of the 14 days mentioned in subsection (2)(a) AiB must, after considering any representations duly made to AiB—

(a) grant or refuse to grant the certificate of discharge, and

(b) notify accordingly (in addition to the original trustee) the debtor, the replacement trustee and all creditors who have made such representations.

(4) The original trustee, the replacement trustee, the debtor or any creditor who has made representations by virtue of subsection (2)(a) may apply to AiB for a review of a determination under subsection (3).

(5) Any application under subsection (4) must be made within 14 days beginning with the day on which that determination is issued.

(6) If an application under subsection (4) is made, AiB must—

(a) take into account any representations made by an interested person within 21 days beginning with the day on which the application is made, and

(b) confirm, amend or revoke the determination (whether or not granting a certificate of discharge) within 28 days beginning with that day.

(7) The original trustee, the replacement trustee, the debtor or any creditor who has made representations by virtue of subsection (2)(a) may, within 14 days after a decision under subsection (6)(b), appeal to the sheriff against that decision.

(8) If, on such appeal, the sheriff determines that a certificate of discharge which has been refused should be granted the sheriff must order AiB to grant it.

(9) The sheriff clerk must send a copy of the sheriff's decree to AiB.

(10) The decision of the sheriff on an appeal under subsection (7) is final.

(11) The grant of a certificate of discharge under this section by AiB has the effect of discharging the original trustee from all liability (other than liability arising from fraud) to the creditors, or to the debtor, in respect of any act or omission of the original trustee in exercising the functions conferred on the original trustee by this Act.

(12) This section does not apply where AiB is the original trustee.

NOTES

Commencement: 30 November 2016.

[5.263]

66 Replacement of trustee acting in more than one sequestration

(1) This section applies where a trustee acting as such in two or more sequestrations—

(a) dies,

(b) ceases, by virtue of section 49(4), to be qualified to continue to act as trustee, or

(c) becomes subject to the circumstances mentioned in subsection (2).

(2) The circumstances are that there is—

(a) a conflict of interest affecting the trustee, or

(b) a change in the personal circumstances of the trustee,

which prevents the trustee from carrying out the trustee's functions, or makes it impracticable for the trustee to carry out those functions.

(3) AiB may, in a case where subsection (1)(b) or (c) applies, determine that the trustee is removed from office in each sequestration in which the trustee has ceased to be qualified.

(4) AiB may appoint as the trustee in each sequestration in which the former trustee was acting a person—

(a) determined by AiB, and

(b) who consents to the appointment.

(5) A person may not be appointed under subsection (4) if the person is ineligible, by virtue of section 49(3), for election as a replacement trustee.

(6) If, in relation to any sequestration, AiB determines that no person is to be appointed under subsection (4), AiB is deemed to be the trustee in that sequestration.

(7) A determination or appointment under this section may be made—

(a) on the application of any person having an interest, or

(b) without an application, where AiB proposes to make a determination or appointment of AiB's own accord.

(8) The applicant must notify all interested persons where an application is made under subsection (7)(a).

(9) AiB must notify all interested persons where AiB proposes to make a determination or appointment by virtue of subsection (7)(b).

(10) A notice under subsection (8) or (9) must inform the recipient that the recipient has a right to make representations to AiB, in relation to the application or to the proposed determination or appointment, within 14 days beginning with the day on which the notice is given.

NOTES

Commencement: 30 November 2016.

[5.264]

67 Further provision as regards replacement under section 66

(1) Before making a determination or appointment under section 66, AIB must take into account any representations made by an interested person.

(2) AiB must notify any determination or appointment under section 66 to—

(a) the former trustee (or, where the former trustee has died, the former trustee's representatives),

(b) the debtor,

(c) the trustee appointed under section 66 (where the trustee appointed is not AiB), and

(d) each sheriff who awarded sequestration or to whom sequestration was transferred under section 27(1).

(3) The trustee appointed under section 66—

(a) must notify the determination or appointment under that section to every creditor known to the trustee,

(b) may require—

(i) delivery of all documents (other than the former trustee's accounts) relating to each sequestration in which the former trustee was acting and in the possession of the former trustee or of the former trustee's representatives,

(ii) delivery of a copy of the former trustee's accounts, and

(iii) the former trustee, or the former trustee's representatives, to submit the trustee's accounts for audit to the commissioners or, if there are no commissioners, to AiB.

(4) Where the trustee appointed under section 66 requires submission in accordance with subsection (3)(b)(iii), the commissioners or, as the case may be, AiB must issue a determination fixing the amount of the outlays and remuneration payable to the former trustee, or the former trustee's representatives, in accordance with section 132.

NOTES

Commencement: 30 November 2016.

[5.265]

68 Review of determination or appointment under section 66

(1) A person mentioned in section 67(2)(a) or (b) or (3)(a) may apply to AiB for a review of any determination or appointment under that section.

(2) Any application under subsection (1) must be made within 14 days beginning with the day on which notice of the determination or appointment is given.

(3) If an application under subsection (1) is made, AiB must—

(a) take into account any representations made by an interested person within 21 days beginning with the day on which the application is made, and

(b) confirm, amend or revoke the determination or appointment within 28 days beginning with that day.

(4) A person mentioned in section 67(2)(a) or (b) or (3)(a) may, within 14 days beginning with the day of a decision of AiB under subsection (3)(b), appeal to the sheriff against that decision.

(5) AiB may refer a case to the court for a direction before—

(a) making any determination or appointment under section 66,

(b) issuing any determination under section 67(4), or

(c) undertaking any review under this section.

(6) Any appeal under subsection (4) or referral under subsection (5) must be made—

(a) by a single petition to the Court of Session where the appeal relates to two or more sequestrations and the sequestrations are, by virtue of section 15, in different sheriffdoms, and

(b) in any other case, to the sheriff.

NOTES

Commencement: 30 November 2016.

Resignation or death of trustee

[5.266]

69 Resignation or death of trustee

(1) The trustee in the sequestration (in this section referred to as "T") may apply to AiB for authority to resign office and AiB must grant the application where satisfied that—

(a) T is unable to act (whether by, under or by virtue of a provision of this Act or from any other cause), or

(b) T's conduct has been such that T should no longer continue to act in the sequestration.

(2) AiB may make the granting of an application under subsection (1) subject—

(a) to the election of a new trustee, and

(b) to such other conditions as AiB thinks appropriate in all the circumstances of the case.

(3) Where AiB grants an application under subsection (1), then—

(a) except where paragraph (b) applies, the commissioners, or if there are no commissioners AiB, must call a meeting of the creditors, to be held within 28 days after T resigns, for the election by the creditors of a new trustee, and

(b) if the application is granted subject to the election of a new trustee, T must call a meeting of the creditors, to be held within 28 days after the granting of the application, for such an election.

(4) Where the commissioners become, or if there are no commissioners AiB becomes, aware that T has died, they or as the case may be AiB are, as soon as practicable after becoming so aware, to call a meeting of creditors for the election by the creditors of a new trustee.

(5) The preceding provisions of this Part in relation to the election of a replacement trustee and the appointment of that trustee also apply, subject to any necessary modifications, in relation to the election and appointment of a new trustee in pursuance of subsections (1) to (3) or subsection (4).

(6) Where no new trustee is elected in pursuance of subsection (3) or (4), AiB may appoint as the new trustee in the sequestration—

(a) a person who applies to AiB within 14 days beginning with the day of the meeting arranged under subsection (3) or (4), or

(b) any other person as may be determined by AiB and who consents to the appointment.

(7) A person may not be appointed under subsection (6) if the person is ineligible, by virtue of section 49(3), for election as a replacement trustee.

(8) If, after the expiry of the days mentioned in subsection (6)(a), AiB determines that no person is to be appointed under subsection (6), AiB is deemed to be the new trustee in the sequestration.

(9) The new trustee (in this subsection and in subsection (11) referred to as "NT") may require—

(a) delivery to NT of all documents relating to the sequestration and in the possession of T or T's representatives (except that, in the case of T's accounts, NT is entitled to delivery only of a copy),

(b) T or T's representatives to submit T's accounts for audit to the commissioners or, if there are no commissioners, to AiB.

(10) The commissioners are, or if there are no commissioners AiB is, to issue a determination fixing the amount of the outlays and remuneration payable to T or T's representatives in accordance with section 133.

(11) T or T's representatives, NT, the debtor or any creditor may within 14 days after a determination under subsection (10) is issued—

(a) by the commissioners, appeal against it to AiB,

(b) by AiB, appeal against it to the sheriff.

(12) A decision of AiB under subsection (11)(a) is appealable to the sheriff.

(13) The decision of the sheriff on an appeal under subsection (11)(b) or (12) is final.

NOTES

Commencement: 30 November 2016.

Removal of trustee and appointment of new trustee

[5.267]

70 Removal of trustee other than where trustee is unable to act or should no longer continue to act: general

(1) The trustee in the sequestration (in this section and in sections 71 to 73 referred to as "T") may be removed from office—

(a) by the creditors at a meeting called for the purpose if they also forthwith elect a new trustee, or

(b) by order made by AiB if AiB is satisfied that, on the basis of circumstances other than those mentioned in section 72(2), there are reasons to remove T from office.

(2) An order removing T in accordance with subsection (1)(b) may be made—

(a) on the application of—

(i) the commissioners, or

(ii) a person representing not less than ¼ in value of the creditors, or

(b) in any other case where AiB is satisfied as mentioned in that subsection.

(3) "Creditors", in subsection (1)(a), does not include—

(a) anyone who, other than by succession, acquires after the date of sequestration a debt due by the debtor, or

(b) any creditor to the extent that the creditor's debt is a postponed debt.

(4) AiB must—

(a) order any application by a person mentioned in subsection (2)(a) to be served on T,

(b) enter particulars of the application in the register of insolvencies, and

(c) before deciding whether or not to make an order under subsection (1)(b), give T the opportunity to make representations.

(5) AiB may—

(a) in ordering, or

(b) instead of ordering,

the removal of T from office under subsection (1)(b), make such further or other order as AiB thinks fit.

(6) This section and sections 71 to 75 do not apply where AiB is the trustee in the sequestration.

(7) This section is without prejudice to section 200(4).

NOTES

Commencement: 30 November 2016.

[5.268]

71 Removal of trustee other than where trustee is unable to act or should no longer continue to act: review, appeal and election of new trustee

(1) T, the commissioners or any creditor may apply to AiB for a review of any decision of AiB under section 70(1)(b) or (5).

(2) Any application under subsection (1) must be made within 14 days beginning with the day on which the decision is given.

(3) If an application under subsection (1) for a review is made, AiB must—

(a) take into account any representations made by an interested person within 21 days beginning with the day on which the application is made, and

(b) confirm, amend or revoke the decision within 28 days beginning with that day.

(4) T, the commissioners or any creditor may, within 14 days beginning with the day on which a decision of AiB under subsection (3)(b) is given, appeal to the sheriff against that decision.

(5) Subsection (6) applies where T has been removed from office—

(a) under section 70(1)(b),

(b) under section 200(4),

(c) following a review under subsection (1), or

(d) following an appeal under subsection (4).

(6) The commissioners (or if there are no commissioners AiB) must call a meeting of creditors, to be held within 28 days after the removal, for the election by the creditors of a new trustee.

(7) AiB may refer a case to the sheriff for a direction before—

(a) making an order under section 70(1)(b) or (5), or

(b) undertaking any review under this section.

(8) An application for a review under subsection (1) may not be made in relation to a matter on which AiB has applied to the sheriff for a direction under subsection (7).

NOTES

Commencement: 30 November 2016.

[5.269]

72 Removal of trustee where trustee is unable to act or should no longer continue to act: general

(1) If AiB is satisfied that any of the circumstances mentioned in subsection (2) apply, AiB may—

(a) declare the office of trustee to have become, or to be, vacant, and

(b) make any necessary order—

(i) to enable the sequestration of the estate to proceed, or

(ii) to safeguard the estate pending the election of a new trustee.

(2) The circumstances are that—

(a) T is unable to act (whether by, under or by virtue of a provision of this Act or from any other cause whatsoever other than death), or

(b) T's conduct has been such that T should no longer continue to act in the sequestration.

(3) The declaration under subsection (1)(a), and any order under subsection (1)(b), may be made—

(a) on the application of the commissioners, of the debtor or of a creditor, or

(b) in any other case where AiB is satisfied as mentioned in subsection (1).

(4) AiB must order such intimation of an application by a person mentioned in subsection (3)(a) as AiB considers necessary.

(5) This section is without prejudice to section 200(4).

NOTES

Commencement: 30 November 2016.

[5.270]

73 Removal of trustee where trustee is unable to act or should no longer continue to act: review, appeal and election of new trustee

(1) If AiB makes a declaration under section 72(1)(a), the commissioners (or if there are no commissioners AiB) must call a meeting of creditors, to be held within 28 days beginning with the day of the declaration, for the election of a new trustee by the creditors.

(2) T, the commissioners, the debtor or any creditor may apply to AiB for a review of any declaration made under section 72(1)(a) or of any order made under section 72(1)(b).

(3) Any application under subsection (2) must be made within 14 days beginning with the day of the declaration.

(4) If an application under subsection (2) is made, AiB must—

(a) take into account any representations made by an interested person within 21 days beginning with the day on which the application is made, and
(b) confirm, amend or revoke the declaration or order within 28 days beginning with that day.
(5) T, the commissioners, the debtor or any creditor may, within 14 days beginning with the day of any decision of AiB under subsection (4)(b), appeal to the sheriff against that decision.
(6) AiB may refer a case to the sheriff for a direction before—
(a) making any declaration or any order under section 72(1), or
(b) undertaking any review under this section.
(7) An application for a review under subsection (2) may not be made in relation to a matter on which AiB has applied to the sheriff for a direction under subsection (6).

NOTES
Commencement: 30 November 2016.

[5.271]
74 Election or appointment of new trustee by virtue of section 71(6) or 73(1)
The preceding provisions of this Part in relation to the election of a replacement trustee and the appointment of that trustee also apply, subject to any necessary modifications, in relation to the election and appointment of a new trustee by virtue of section 71(6) or 73(1).

NOTES
Commencement: 30 November 2016.

[5.272]
75 Further provision as regards election or appointment of new trustee
Subsections (6) to (13) of section 69 apply for the purposes of sections 70 to 74 as those subsections apply for the purposes of section 69.

NOTES
Commencement: 30 November 2016.

Commissioners

[5.273]
76 Commissioners
In any sequestration there may be elected, in accordance with section 77, commissioners, whose general functions are—
(a) to supervise the intromissions of the trustee in the sequestration with the sequestrated estate, and
(b) to advise the trustee.

NOTES
Commencement: 30 November 2016.

[5.274]
77 Election, resignation and removal of commissioners
(1) At the statutory meeting or at any subsequent meeting of creditors, the creditors (other than any such person as is listed in section 49(7)) may, from among the creditors or their mandatories, elect a commissioner or commissioners (or a new or additional commissioner or new or additional commissioners).
(2) No more than 5 commissioners are to hold office in any one sequestration at any one time.
(3) None of the persons listed in subsection (5) is eligible for election as a commissioner.
(4) Nor is anyone who becomes a person so listed after being elected as a commissioner entitled to continue to act as a commissioner.
(5) The persons are—
(a) any person listed in paragraph (a) or (d) of section 49(5), and
(b) a person who is an associate of the debtor or of the trustee in the sequestration.
(6) A commissioner may resign office at any time.
(7) A commissioner may be removed from office—
(a) if the commissioner is a mandatory of a creditor (see paragraphs 14 to 16 of schedule 6), by the creditor recalling the mandate and intimating in writing to the trustee that it is recalled,
(b) by the creditors (other than any such person as is listed in section 49(7)) at a meeting called for the purpose, or
(c) by order of the sheriff if the sheriff is satisfied that the commissioner is no longer acting in the interests of the efficient conduct of the sequestration.
(8) An order under subsection (7)(c) may be made on the application of—
(a) AiB,
(b) a person representing not less than ¼ in value of the creditors, or
(c) the trustee.
(9) The sheriff must—
(a) order an application by a person mentioned in subsection (8) to be served on the commissioner,
(b) order that the application be intimated to every creditor who has given a mandate to the commissioner, and
(c) before deciding whether or not to make an order under subsection (7)(c), give the commissioner the opportunity to make representations.

(10) On an application under subsection (7)(c), the sheriff may—
(a) in ordering the removal of the commissioner from office, make such further order as the sheriff thinks fit, or
(b) instead of removing the commissioner from office, make such other order as the sheriff thinks fit.
(11) The trustee, AiB, any commissioner or any creditor may, within 14 days after a decision of the sheriff on an application under subsection (7)(c), appeal against that decision.
(12) Subsection (7) is without prejudice to section 200(4).

NOTES
Commencement: 30 November 2016.

PART 5
VESTING ETC

Vesting

[5.275]
78 Vesting of estate at date of sequestration
(1) The whole estate of the debtor vests for the benefit of the creditors in the trustee in the sequestration, by virtue of the trustee's appointment, as at the date of sequestration.
(2) But subsection (1) is subject to section 88.
(3) It is not competent for—
(a) the trustee, or
(b) any person deriving title from the trustee,
to complete title, before the expiry of the period mentioned in subsection (4), to any heritable property in Scotland vested in the trustee by virtue of the trustee's appointment.
(4) The period is 28 days (or such other period as may be prescribed) beginning with the day on which the certified copy of—
(a) the order of the sheriff granting warrant is recorded under subsection (1)(a) of section 26 in the Register of Inhibitions, or
(b) the determination of AiB awarding sequestration is recorded under subsection (2) of that section in that register.
(5) The exercise by the trustee of any power conferred on the trustee by this Act, in respect of any heritable estate vested in the trustee by virtue of that person's appointment, is not challengeable on the ground of a prior inhibition.
(6) Where the debtor has an uncompleted title to any heritable estate in Scotland, the trustee may complete title to that estate either in the trustee's own name or in the name of the debtor.
(7) But completion of title in the name of the debtor does not validate by accretion any unperfected right in favour of a person other than the trustee.
(8) Moveable property in respect of which, but for this subsection—
(a) delivery or possession, or
(b) intimation of assignation,
would be required in order to complete title vests in the trustee, by virtue of the trustee's appointment, as if at the date of sequestration (as the case may be) the trustee had taken delivery or possession of the property or had made intimation of its assignation to the trustee.
(9) Any non-vested contingent interest which the debtor has vests in the trustee as if an assignation of that interest had been executed by the debtor (and intimation of assignation made) at the date of sequestration.
(10) Any non-vested contingent interest vested in the trustee by virtue of subsection (9) is, where it remains so vested as at the date which is 4 years after the date of sequestration, re-invested in the debtor as if an assignation of that interest had been executed by the trustee (and intimation of assignation made) at that date.
(11) A person claiming a right to any estate claimed by the trustee may apply to the sheriff for the estate to be excluded from such vesting, a copy of the application being served on the trustee.
(12) The sheriff must grant the application if satisfied that the estate should not be so vested.
(13) Where any successor of a deceased debtor whose estate has been sequestrated has made up title to, or is in possession of, any part of that estate, the sheriff may on the application of the trustee order the successor to convey such estate to the trustee.

NOTES
Commencement: 30 November 2016.

[5.276]
79 Provision supplementary to section 78 and interpretation of Part 5
(1) In subsection (1) of section 78, the "whole estate of the debtor" means the debtor's whole estate at the date of sequestration (wherever situated) including—
(a) any income or estate vesting in the debtor on the date of sequestration,
(b) any property of the debtor title to which has not been completed by another person deriving right from the debtor, and
(c) the capacity to exercise and to take proceedings for exercising all such powers in, over or in respect of any property as—
(i) might have been exercised by the debtor for the debtor's own benefit as at, or on, the date of sequestration, or

(ii) might be exercised on a relevant date.

(2) But subsection (1) is subject to subsection (3) and to section 231.

(3) The "whole estate of the debtor" does not include any interest of the debtor as tenant under—

(a) a tenancy which is an assured tenancy within the meaning of Part 2 of the Housing (Scotland) Act 1988,

(b) a protected tenancy within the meaning of the Rent (Scotland) Act 1984 in respect of which, by virtue of Part 8 of that Act, no premium can lawfully be required as a condition of assignation, . . .

(c) a Scottish secure tenancy within the meaning of the Housing (Scotland) Act 2001[; or

(d) a private residential tenancy within the meaning of the Private Housing (Tenancies) (Scotland) Act 2016].

(4) On the date on which the trustee serves notice to that effect on the debtor, the interest of the debtor as tenant under any of the tenancies referred to in subsection (3) forms part of the debtor's estate and vests in the trustee as if it had vested in the trustee under section 86(5).

(5) In this Part "relevant date" means a date after the date of sequestration and before the date which is 4 years after the date of sequestration.

NOTES

Commencement: 30 November 2016.

Sub-s (3): word omitted from para (b) repealed and para (d) inserted together with word immediately preceding it, by the Private Housing (Tenancies) (Scotland) Act 2016 (Consequential Provisions) Regulations 2017, SSI 2017/405, reg 4.

[5.277]

80 Property subject to restraint order

(1) Subsection (2) applies where—

(a) property is excluded from the debtor's estate by virtue of section 420(2)(a) of the Proceeds of Crime Act 2002 (property subject to a restraint order),

(b) an order under section 50, 67A, 128, 131A, 198 or 215A of that Act has not been made in respect of the property,

(c) the restraint order is discharged, and

(d) immediately after the discharge of the restraint order the property is not detained under or by virtue of section 44A, 47J, 122A, 127J, 193A or 195J of that Act.

(2) The property vests in the trustee in the sequestration as part of the debtor's estate.

(3) But subsection (2) does not apply to the proceeds of property realised by a management receiver under section 49(2)(d) or 197(2)(d) of that Act (realisation of property to meet receiver's outlays and remuneration).

NOTES

Commencement: 30 November 2016.

[5.278]

81 Property released from detention

(1) Subsection (2) applies where—

(a) property is excluded from the debtor's estate by virtue of section 420(2)(b) of the Proceeds of Crime Act 2002 (property detained under certain provisions),

(b) no order is in force in respect of the property under section 41, 50, 120, 128, 190 or 198 of that Act, and

(c) the property is released.

(2) The property vests in the trustee in the sequestration as part of the debtor's estate.

NOTES

Commencement: 30 November 2016.

[5.279]

82 Property in respect of which receivership or administration order is made

(1) Subsection (2) applies where—

(a) property is excluded from the debtor's estate by virtue of section 420(2)(c) of the Proceeds of Crime Act 2002 (property in respect of which an order for the appointment of a receiver or administrator under certain provisions of that Act is in force),

(b) a confiscation order is made under section 6, 92 or 156 of that Act,

(c) the amount payable under the confiscation order is fully paid, and

(d) any of the property remains in the hands of the receiver or administrator (as the case may be).

(2) The property vests in the trustee in the sequestration as part of the debtor's estate.

NOTES

Commencement: 30 November 2016.

[5.280]

83 Property in respect of which realisation order is made

(1) Subsection (2) applies where—

(a) property is excluded from the debtor's estate by virtue of section 420(2)(d) of the Proceeds of Crime Act 2002 (property in respect of which an order has been made authorising realisation of the property by an appropriate officer),

(b) a confiscation order is made under section 6, 92 or 156 of that Act,
(c) the amount payable under the confiscation order is fully paid, and
(d) any of the property remains in the hands of the appropriate officer.

(2) The property vests in the trustee in the sequestration as part of the debtor's estate.

NOTES

Commencement: 30 November 2016.

[5.281]

84 Property subject to certain orders where confiscation order discharged or quashed

(1) Subsection (2) applies where—
(a) property is excluded from the debtor's estate by virtue of section 420(2)(a), (b), (c) or (d) of the Proceeds of Crime Act 2002 (property excluded from debtor's estate),
(b) a confiscation order is made under section 6, 92 or 156 of that Act, and
(c) the confiscation order is discharged under section 30, 114 or 180 of that Act (as the case may be) or quashed under that Act or in pursuance of any enactment relating to appeals against conviction or sentence.

(2) Any such property vests in the trustee in the sequestration as part of the debtor's estate if it is in the hands of—
(a) a receiver appointed under Part 2 or 4 of that Act,
(b) an administrator appointed under Part 3 of that Act, or
(c) an appropriate officer (within the meaning of section 41A, 120A or 190A of that Act).

(3) But subsection (2) does not apply to the proceeds of property realised by a management receiver under section 49(2)(d) or 197(2)(d) of that Act (realisation of property to meet receiver's outlays and remuneration).

NOTES

Commencement: 30 November 2016.

[5.282]

85 Vesting of income received by debtor after sequestration

(1) Any income, of whatever nature, received by the debtor on a relevant date, other than income arising from the estate which is vested in the trustee in the sequestration, is to vest in the debtor.

(2) But subsection (1) is subject to sections 90 to 97.

NOTES

Commencement: 30 November 2016.

[5.283]

86 Further provision as regards vesting of estate

(1) Diligence in respect of a debt or obligation mentioned in subsection (2) is not competent against income vesting in the debtor under section 85.

(2) The debt or obligation is one in respect of which the debtor, if discharged under section 137, 138 or 140, would be discharged under section 145.

(3) For the purposes of subsection (1), diligence includes the making of a deduction from earnings order under the Child Support Act 1991.

(4) Subsection (5) applies where any estate, wherever situated—
(a) is acquired by the debtor on a relevant date, and
(b) would have vested in the trustee in the sequestration if it had been part of the debtor's estate on the date of sequestration.

(5) The estate vests in the trustee for the benefit of the creditors as at the date of acquisition.

(6) A person who holds estate vesting in the trustee under subsection (5) is, on production to the person of a copy of the order certified by the sheriff clerk, or as the case may be by AiB, appointing the trustee, to convey or deliver the estate to the trustee.

(7) But such a person incurs no liability to the trustee except to account for any proceeds of the conveyance which are in the person's hands if the person has, in good faith and without knowledge of the sequestration, conveyed the estate—
(a) to the debtor, or
(b) to anyone on the instructions of the debtor.

(8) The trustee is not entitled, by virtue of subsections (4) to (7), to any remedy against an appropriate bank or institution (in this section and in section 87(7) referred to as a "bank") in respect of a banking transaction entered into before the receipt by the bank of a notice under subsection (9) (whether or not the bank is aware of the sequestration).

(9) Where the trustee knows, or becomes aware, of any estate vested in the trustee under section 78 or this section which comprises funds held by a bank, the trustee must serve a notice on the bank—
(a) informing the bank of the sequestration, and
(b) specifying reasonable detail in order to allow the bank to identify the debtor and the funds held.

(10) A notice under subsection (9)—
(a) must be in writing and may be sent—
(i) by first class post or by using a registered or recorded delivery postal service to the bank, or
(ii) in some other manner (including by electronic means) which the trustee reasonably considers likely to cause it to be delivered to the bank on the same or next day, and

(b) is deemed to have been received the day after it is sent.

(11) Subsections (4) to (8) are without prejudice to—

(a) section 85, and

(b) any right acquired in the estate in good faith and for value.

NOTES

Commencement: 30 November 2016.

[5.284]

87 Dealings and circumstances of debtor after sequestration

(1) The debtor must immediately notify the trustee in the sequestration—

(a) of any assets acquired by the debtor on a relevant date, or

(b) of any other substantial change in the debtor's financial circumstances.

(2) A debtor who fails to comply with subsection (1) commits an offence.

(3) A debtor who commits an offence under subsection (2) is liable on summary conviction—

(a) to a fine not exceeding level 5 on the standard scale,

(b) to imprisonment for a term not exceeding 3 months, or

(c) both to such fine and to such imprisonment.

(4) Any dealing of, or with, the debtor and relating to the debtor's estate vested in the trustee under section 78 or 86 is of no effect in a question with the trustee.

(5) But subsection (4) does not apply where the person seeking to uphold the dealing establishes that the trustee—

(a) has abandoned to the debtor the property to which the dealing relates,

(b) has expressly or impliedly authorised the dealing, or

(c) is otherwise personally barred from challenging the dealing.

(6) Nor does subsection (4) apply where the person seeking to uphold the dealing establishes both—

(a) that the dealing is—

(i) the performance of an obligation undertaken before the date of sequestration by a person obliged to the debtor in the obligation,

(ii) the purchase from the debtor of goods for which the purchaser has given value to the debtor or is willing to give value to the trustee, or

(iii) one which satisfies the conditions mentioned in subsection (10), and

(b) that the person dealing with the debtor was, at the time when the dealing occurred, unaware of the sequestration and had at that time no reason to believe that the debtor's estate had been sequestrated or was the subject of sequestration proceedings.

(7) Nor does subsection (4) apply where the dealing is a banking transaction entered into before the receipt by the bank of a notice under section 86(9) (whether or not the bank is aware of the sequestration).

(8) Where the trustee has abandoned heritable property to the debtor, notice (in such form as may be prescribed) given to the debtor by the trustee is sufficient evidence that the property is vested in the debtor.

(9) Where notice is given under subsection (8), the trustee is as soon as reasonably practicable after giving it to record a certified copy of it in the Register of Inhibitions.

(10) The conditions are that—

(a) the dealing constitutes—

(i) the transfer of incorporeal moveable property, or

(ii) the creation, transfer, variation or extinguishing of a real right in heritable property,

for which the person dealing with the debtor has given adequate consideration to the debtor or is willing to give adequate consideration to the trustee,

(b) the dealing requires the delivery of a deed, and

(c) the delivery occurs during the period beginning with the date of sequestration and ending 7 days after the day on which—

(i) the certified copy of the order of the sheriff granting warrant is recorded in the Register of Inhibitions under section 26(1)(a), or

(ii) the certified copy of the determination of AiB awarding sequestration is recorded in that register under section 26(2).

NOTES

Commencement: 30 November 2016.

Regulations: the Bankruptcy (Scotland) Regulations 2016, SSI 2016/397 at **[16.401]**.

Limitation on vesting

[5.285]

88 Limitation on vesting

(1) The following property of the debtor does not vest in the trustee in the sequestration—

(a) any property—

(i) kept outside a dwellinghouse, and

(ii) in respect of which attachment is, by virtue of section 11(1) of the 2002 Act, incompetent,

(b) any property—

(i) kept inside a dwellinghouse, and

(ii) not a non-essential asset for the purposes of Part 3 of that Act, and

(c) property held on trust by the debtor for any other person.

(2) The vesting of the debtor's estate in the trustee in the sequestration does not affect the right of hypothec of a landlord.
(3) Sections 78, 85 and 86 are without prejudice to the right of any secured creditor which is preferable to the rights of the trustee.

NOTES
Commencement: 30 November 2016.

PART 6
DEBTOR'S CONTRIBUTION

Common financial tool

[5.286]
89 Assessment of debtor's contribution

(1) The Scottish Ministers may by regulations specify a method (the "common financial tool") to be used to assess an appropriate amount of a living debtor's income (the "debtor's contribution") to be paid to a trustee after the sequestration of the debtor's estate.
(2) Regulations under subsection (1) may in particular prescribe—
  (a) a method for assessing a debtor's financial circumstances (including the debtor's assets, income, liabilities and expenditure),
  (b) a method for determining a reasonable amount of expenditure for a debtor after the sequestration of the debtor's estate,
  (c) the proportion of a debtor's income that is to constitute the debtor's contribution,
  (d) that a method determined by another person must be used (with or without modification in accordance with regulations made under subsection (1)) as the common financial tool.
(3) The common financial tool must ensure that the amount of reasonable expenditure for a debtor is not less than the total amount of any income received by the debtor by way of guaranteed minimum pension (within the meaning of the Pension Schemes Act 1993).
(4) The common financial tool must ensure that an amount is allowed for—
  (a) aliment for the debtor, and
  (b) the debtor's relevant obligations.
(5) The "debtor's relevant obligations" are any obligation of—
  (a) aliment owed by the debtor ("obligation of aliment" having the meaning given by section 1(2) of the Family Law (Scotland) Act 1985),
  (b) the debtor to make a periodical allowance to a former spouse or former civil partner, and
  (c) the debtor to pay child support maintenance under the Child Support Act 1991.
(6) The amount allowed for the debtor's relevant obligations referred to in paragraphs (a) and (b) of subsection (5) need not be sufficient for compliance with a subsisting order or agreement as regards the aliment or periodical allowance.

NOTES
Commencement: 30 November 2016.
Regulations: the Bankruptcy (Scotland) Regulations 2016, SSI 2016/397 at **[16.401]**.

Payments by debtor following sequestration

[5.287]
90 Debtor contribution order: general

(1) AiB must make an order fixing the debtor's contribution (a "debtor contribution order")—
  (a) in the case of a debtor application, at the same time as awarding sequestration of the debtor's estate,
  (b) in the case of an award of sequestration following a petition under section 2(1)(b), after considering initial proposals for the debtor's contribution provided by the trustee.
(2) In a case referred to in subsection (1)(b), the trustee must send initial proposals for the debtor's contribution within 6 weeks beginning with the date of the award of sequestration.
(3) In making a debtor contribution order, AiB must use the common financial tool to assess the debtor's contribution.
(4) A debtor contribution order may fix the amount of the debtor's contribution as zero.
(5) A debtor contribution order may be made irrespective of sections 11 and 12 of the Welfare Reform and Pensions Act 1999.
(6) A debtor contribution order may provide that a third person must pay to the trustee a specified proportion of money due to the debtor by way of income.
(7) Where a third person pays a sum of money to the trustee in accordance with subsection (6), the third person is discharged from any liability to the debtor to the extent of the sum so paid.
(8) AiB must, immediately following the making of a debtor contribution order, give written notice of the order to—
  (a) the debtor,
  (b) the trustee, and
  (c) any third person mentioned in the order.
(9) A debtor contribution order must not take effect on a date before the expiry of 14 days beginning with the day of notification of the order.

NOTES

Commencement: 30 November 2016.

[5.288]

91 Debtor contribution order: payment period and intervals

(1) A debtor contribution order must contain provision requiring the debtor to pay the debtor's contribution (if not zero)—

(a) during the payment period, and

(b) at regular intervals determined by the person making or varying the order.

(2) In subsection (1)(a), "payment period" means—

(a) the 48 months beginning with the date of the first payment,

(b) such shorter period as is determined by the person making or varying the order, or

(c) such longer period as is—

(i) determined by the trustee where there is a period during which the debtor did not pay an amount required under the debtor contribution order, or

(ii) agreed by the debtor and the trustee.

(3) The person making or varying the order may determine a shorter period under subsection (2)(b) only if, in the opinion of that person, the value of—

(a) the debtor's contribution during the shorter period, and

(b) any other estate of the debtor taken possession of by the trustee,

would be sufficient to allow a distribution of the debtor's estate to meet in full all of the debts mentioned in section 129.

(4) AiB must, when making a debtor contribution order—

(a) determine the date of the first payment, or

(b) in a case where the debtor's contribution is fixed as zero, determine the date which is to be deemed the date of the first payment under the order.

NOTES

Commencement: 30 November 2016.

[5.289]

92 Debtor contribution order: review and appeal

(1) The debtor, the trustee or any other interested person may apply to AiB for a review of a debtor contribution order.

(2) An application under subsection (1) must be made within 14 days beginning with the day on which the order is made.

(3) If an application under subsection (1) is made, the order is suspended until the determination of that review by AiB.

(4) If an application under subsection (1) is made, AiB must—

(a) take into account any representations made by an interested person within 21 days beginning with the day on which the application is made, and

(b) confirm, amend or revoke the order within 28 days beginning with that day.

(5) The trustee or the debtor may, within 14 days beginning with the date of any decision of AiB under subsection (4)(b), appeal to the sheriff against that decision.

NOTES

Commencement: 30 November 2016.

[5.290]

93 Effect of debtor contribution order

(1) The debtor must pay to the trustee any debtor's contribution (if not zero)—

(a) as fixed by AiB in making the debtor contribution order, or

(b) as varied in accordance with section 95.

(2) The requirement to pay the debtor's contribution applies irrespective of the debtor's discharge.

(3) If the value of the debtor's estate and income when taken possession of by the trustee is sufficient to allow a distribution of the debtor's estate to meet in full all of the debts mentioned in section 129, any debtor contribution order ceases to have effect.

NOTES

Commencement: 30 November 2016.

[5.291]

94 Deductions from debtor's earnings and other income

(1) Subsections (2) to (6) apply where, under a debtor contribution order—

(a) the debtor is required to pay to the trustee an amount from the debtor's earnings or other income, or

(b) in accordance with section 90(6), a third person is required to pay to the trustee money otherwise due to the debtor by way of income.

(2) The debtor must give the person mentioned in subsection (3) an instruction to make—

(a) deductions of specified amounts from the debtor's earnings or other income, and

(b) payments to the trustee of the amounts so deducted.

(3) The person—

(a) in the case of an amount to be paid from the debtor's earnings from employment, is the person by whom the debtor is employed,
(b) in the case of an amount to be paid from other earnings or income of the debtor, is a third person who is required to pay the earnings or income to the debtor, and
(c) in the case mentioned in subsection (1)(b), is the third person who is required to pay the income to the trustee.

(4) The trustee may give the person mentioned in subsection (3) an instruction of the type mentioned in subsection (2) if the debtor fails—
(a) to comply with the requirements imposed by that subsection, and
(b) to pay the debtor's contribution in respect of 2 payment intervals applying by virtue of the debtor contribution order.

(5) A person mentioned in subsection (3) must comply with an instruction provided in accordance with subsection (2) or (4).

(6) Where the person by whom the debtor is employed or another third person pays a sum of money to the trustee in accordance with this section, that person is discharged from any liability to the debtor to the extent of the sum so paid.

(7) The Scottish Ministers may by regulations make provision about instructions to be provided under this section, including in particular—
(a) the form in which an instruction must be made,
(b) the manner in which an instruction provided in accordance with subsection (2) or (4) affects the recipient of that instruction, and
(c) the consequence of any failure of a recipient of an instruction provided in accordance with subsection (2) or (4) to comply with the duty imposed by subsection (5).

NOTES

Commencement: 30 November 2016.
Regulations: the Bankruptcy (Scotland) Regulations 2016, SSI 2016/397 at **[16.401]**.

[5.292]

95 Variation and removal of debtor contribution order by trustee

(1) The trustee may vary or quash a debtor contribution order—
(a) on the application of the debtor, following any change in the debtor's circumstances,
(b) if the trustee considers it to be appropriate, following any such change, or
(c) if the trustee considers it to be appropriate when—
(i) sending a report to AiB under section 137(4), or
(ii) granting a discharge under section 138(2).

(2) In deciding whether to vary or quash a debtor contribution order, the trustee must use the common financial tool to assess the debtor's contribution.

(3) A decision by the trustee under subsection (1)(b) must not take effect before the expiry of 14 days beginning with the day on which the decision is made.

(4) The trustee must notify in writing the persons mentioned in subsection (5) immediately following—
(a) any variation or quashing of a debtor contribution order, or
(b) any refusal of an application as respects such an order.

(5) The persons are—
(a) the debtor,
(b) AiB (if the trustee is not AiB),
(c) any third person required to make a payment under the debtor contribution order or under section 94(5), and
(d) any other interested person.

NOTES

Commencement: 30 November 2016.

[5.293]

96 Payment break

(1) The trustee may, on the application of the debtor, extend the payment period of a debtor contribution order by granting a payment break.

(2) A "payment break" is a period not exceeding 6 months during which payments under the debtor contribution order are deferred.

(3) A debtor may apply for a payment break if—
(a) there has been a reduction of at least 50% in the debtor's disposable income (as determined using the common financial tool) as a result of any of the circumstances mentioned in subsection (4) arising in relation to the debtor, and
(b) the debtor has not previously applied for a payment break in relation to a debtor contribution order applying after the sequestration of the debtor's estate.

(4) The circumstances are—
(a) a period of unemployment or a change in employment,
(b) a period of leave from employment because of—
(i) the birth or adoption of a child, or
(ii) the need to care for a dependant,
(c) a period of illness of the debtor,
(d) a divorce,
(e) a dissolution of civil partnership,

(f) a separation from a person to whom the debtor is married or with whom the debtor is in civil partnership, and

(g) the death of a person who, along with the debtor, cared for a dependant of the debtor.

(5) An application for a payment break must specify the period during which the debtor wishes payments to be deferred.

(6) If, in the opinion of the trustee, a payment break is fair and reasonable, the trustee may grant it on such conditions and for such period as the trustee thinks fit.

(7) The trustee must notify in writing the grant of a payment break to—

(a) the debtor,

(b) AiB (if the trustee is not AiB), and

(c) any third person required to make a payment under the debtor contribution order.

(8) If the trustee decides not to grant a payment break, the trustee must notify the debtor of that decision and of the reasons for that decision.

(9) The payment period in a debtor contribution order is deemed to be varied by the addition to the period of any payment break granted under this section.

NOTES

Commencement: 30 November 2016.

[5.294]

97 Sections 95 and 96: review and appeal

(1) The debtor or any other interested person may apply to AiB for a review of a decision by the trustee under section 95 or 96.

(2) Any application under subsection (1) must be made within 14 days beginning with the day on which the decision is made.

(3) If an application under subsection (1) relates to a decision by the trustee under section 95(1)(b), the decision is suspended until the determination of that review by AiB.

(4) If an application under subsection (1) is made, AiB must—

(a) take into account any representations made by an interested person within 21 days beginning with the day on which the application is made, and

(b) confirm, amend or revoke the decision within 28 days beginning with that day.

(5) The trustee or the debtor may, within 14 days beginning with the date of any decision of AiB under subsection (4)(b), appeal to the sheriff against that decision.

NOTES

Commencement: 30 November 2016.

PART 7
SAFEGUARDING INTERESTS OF CREDITORS

Gratuitous alienations and unfair preferences

[5.295]

98 Gratuitous alienations

(1) Subsection (2) applies where—

(a) by an alienation (whether before or after the coming into force of this Act) by a debtor—

(i) any of the debtor's property has been transferred, or

(ii) any claim or right of the debtor has been discharged or renounced,

(b) any of the following has occurred—

(i) the debtor's estate has been sequestrated (other than, in the case of an individual, after the debtor has died),

(ii) the debtor has granted a trust deed which has become a protected trust deed,

(iii) the debtor has died and within 12 months after the date of death the debtor's estate has been sequestrated, or

(iv) the debtor has died, the debtor's estate was absolutely insolvent at the date of death and within those 12 months a judicial factor has been appointed under section 11A of the 1889 Act (see section 107) to administer that estate, and

(c) the alienation took place on a relevant day.

(2) The alienation is challengeable by—

(a) any creditor who is a creditor by virtue of a debt incurred on or before (as the case may be) the date of sequestration, the granting of the trust deed or the debtor's death, or

(b) (as the case may be) the trustee in the sequestration, the trustee acting under the trust deed or the judicial factor.

(3) For the purposes of paragraph (c) of subsection (1), the day on which an alienation takes place is the day on which the alienation becomes completely effectual.

(4) In that paragraph, "relevant day" means, if the alienation has the effect of favouring—

(a) a person who is an associate of the debtor, a day not earlier than 5 years before, or

(b) any other person, a day not earlier than 2 years before,

(as the case may be) the date of sequestration, the granting of the trust deed or the date of death.

(5) On a challenge being brought under subsection (2), the court must grant decree—

(a) of reduction, or

(b) for such restoration of property to the debtor's estate, or such other redress, as may be appropriate.

(6) Except that the court is not to grant such decree if the person seeking to uphold the alienation establishes—

(a) that immediately, or at any other time, after the alienation the debtor's assets were greater than the debtor's liabilities,

(b) that the alienation was made for adequate consideration, or

(c) that the alienation was—

(i) a birthday, Christmas or other conventional gift, or

(ii) a gift made, for a charitable purpose, to a person who is not an associate of the debtor, being a gift which, having regard to all the circumstances, it was reasonable for the debtor to make.

(7) Subsection (6) is without prejudice to any right acquired, in good faith and for value, from or through the transferee in the alienation.

(8) In subsection (6)(c)(ii), "charitable purpose" means any charitable, benevolent or philanthropic purpose whether or not it is charitable within the meaning of any rule of law.

(9) For the purposes of subsections (1) to (8), an alienation in implementation of a prior obligation is deemed to be one for which there was no consideration, or no adequate consideration, to the extent that the prior obligation was undertaken for no consideration, or no adequate consideration.

(10) This section is without prejudice to the operation of section 2 of the Married Women's Policies of Assurance (Scotland) Act 1880 (which provides that a policy of assurance may be effected in trust for spouse, future spouse and children) including the operation of that section as applied by section 132 of the Civil Partnership Act 2004.

(11) A trustee in a sequestration, a trustee acting under a protected trust deed or a judicial factor appointed under section 11A of the 1889 Act has the same right as a creditor has under any rule of law to challenge an alienation of a debtor made for no consideration or for no adequate consideration.

NOTES

Commencement: 30 November 2016.

[5.296]

99 Unfair preferences

(1) Subsection (5) applies to a transaction entered into (whether before or after the coming into force of this Act) by a debtor which has the effect of creating a preference in favour of a creditor to the prejudice of the general body of creditors, being a preference created not earlier than 6 months before—

(a) the date of sequestration of the debtor's estate (if, in the case of an individual, a date within the debtor's lifetime),

(b) the granting by the debtor of a trust deed which has become a protected trust deed,

(c) the debtor's death where, within 12 months after the date of death—

(i) the debtor's estate is sequestrated,

(ii) a judicial factor is appointed under section 11A of the 1889 Act to administer the debtor's estate and that estate was absolutely insolvent at the date of death.

(2) But subsection (5) does not apply to—

(a) a transaction in the ordinary course of trade or business,

(b) a payment in cash for a debt which when it was paid had become payable,

(c) a transaction by which the parties undertake reciprocal obligations (whether the performance by the parties of their respective obligations is to occur at the same time or at different times),

(d) the granting of a mandate by a debtor authorising an arrestee to pay over the arrested funds, or part of the arrested funds, to the arrester where—

(i) there has been a decree for payment or a warrant for summary diligence, and

(ii) the decree or warrant has been preceded by an arrestment on the dependence of the action or followed by an arrestment in execution.

(3) Paragraphs (b) and (c) of subsection (2) are to be disregarded if the transaction in question was collusive with the purpose of prejudicing the general body of creditors.

(4) For the purposes of subsection (1), the day on which a preference is created is the day on which it becomes completely effectual.

(5) The transaction is challengeable by—

(a) any creditor who is a creditor by virtue of a debt incurred on or before (as the case may be) the date of sequestration, the granting of the protected trust deed or the debtor's death, or

(b) (as the case may be) the trustee in the sequestration, the trustee acting under the protected trust deed or the judicial factor.

(6) On a challenge being brought under subsection (5) the court, if satisfied that the transaction challenged is a transaction to which that subsection applies, must grant decree—

(a) of reduction, or

(b) for such restoration of property to the debtor's estate, or such other redress, as may be appropriate.

(7) Subsection (6) is without prejudice to any right acquired, in good faith and for value, from or through the creditor in whose favour the preference was created.

(8) A trustee in a sequestration, a trustee acting under a protected trust deed or a judicial factor appointed under section 11A of the 1889 Act has the same right as a creditor has under any rule of law to challenge a preference created by a debtor.

NOTES

Commencement: 30 November 2016.

Recall of certain orders

[5.297]

100 Recall of order for payment of capital sum on divorce or on dissolution of civil partnership

(1) This section applies where—

(a) a court has, under section 8(2) of the Family Law (Scotland) Act 1985 and whether before or after the coming into force of this Act, made—

(i) an order for the payment by a debtor of a capital sum,

(ii) an order for the transfer of property by the debtor, or

(iii) a pension sharing order,

(b) on the date of the making of the order the debtor was absolutely insolvent or was rendered so by implementation of the order, and

(c) within 5 years after the making of the order—

(i) the debtor's estate has been sequestrated other than on the death of the debtor,

(ii) the debtor has granted a trust deed which has (whether or not within the 5 years) become a protected trust deed,

(iii) the debtor has died and, within 12 months after the date of death, the debtor's estate has been sequestrated, or

(iv) the debtor has died and, within those 12 months, a judicial factor has been appointed under section 11A of the 1889 Act to administer the debtor's estate.

(2) The court, on the application of (as the case may be) the trustee in the sequestration, the trustee acting under the trust deed or the judicial factor, may make an order for recall of the order in question and—

(a) for the repayment to the applicant of the whole or part of any sum already paid under the order,

(b) for the return to the applicant of all or part of any property already transferred under the order, or

(c) (where such property has been sold) for payment to the applicant of all or part of the proceeds of sale.

(3) But before making an order under subsection (2), the court must have regard to all the circumstances including, in particular, the financial and other circumstances (in so far as made known to the court) of the person against whom the order would be made.

NOTES

Commencement: 30 November 2016.

Excessive contributions

[5.298]

101 Recovery of excessive pension contributions

(1) Where a debtor's estate has been sequestrated and the debtor—

(a) has rights under an approved pension arrangement, or

(b) has excluded rights under an unapproved pension arrangement,

the trustee in the sequestration may apply to the court for an order under this section.

(2) Subsection (3) applies where the court is satisfied—

(a) that the rights under the arrangement are to any extent, and whether directly or indirectly, the fruits of relevant contributions, and

(b) that the making of any of the relevant contributions ("the excessive contributions") has unfairly prejudiced the debtor's creditors.

(3) The court may make such order as it thinks fit for restoring the position to what it would have been had the excessive contributions not been made.

(4) Subsection (5) applies where the court is satisfied that the value of the rights under the arrangement is, as a result of rights of the debtor under—

(a) the arrangement, or

(b) any other pension arrangement,

having at any time become subject to a debit under section 29(1)(a) of the 1999 Act (see section 107), less than it would otherwise have been.

(5) Where this subsection applies—

(a) any relevant contributions which were represented by the rights which became subject to the debit are, for the purposes of subsection (2), to be taken to be contributions of which the rights under the arrangement are the fruits, and

(b) where the relevant contributions represented by the rights under the arrangement (including those so represented by virtue of paragraph (a)) are not all excessive contributions, relevant contributions which are represented by the rights under the arrangement otherwise than by virtue of paragraph (a) are to be treated as excessive contributions before any which are so represented by virtue of that paragraph.

(6) In subsections (2) to (5), "relevant contributions" means contributions to the arrangement or to any other pension arrangement—

(a) which the debtor has at any time made on the debtor's own behalf, or

(b) which have at any time been made on the debtor's behalf.

(7) The court must, in determining whether it is satisfied under subsection (2)(b), consider in particular—

(a) whether any of the contributions were made for the purpose of putting assets beyond the reach of, or of any of, the debtor's creditors, and

(b) whether the total amount of any contributions—

(i) made by or on behalf of the debtor to pension arrangements, and
(ii) represented (whether directly or indirectly) by rights under approved pension arrangements or excluded rights under unapproved pensions arrangements,

is an amount which is excessive in view of the debtor's circumstances when those contributions were made.

(8) For the purposes of this section and of sections 102 and 103, rights of a debtor under an unapproved pension arrangement are excluded rights if they are rights which are excluded from the debtor's estate by virtue of regulations under section 12 of the 1999 Act.

(9) In the recovery provisions (see section 103(7))—

"approved pension arrangement" has the same meaning as in section 11 of the 1999 Act, and
"unapproved pension arrangement" has the same meaning as in section 12 of that Act.

NOTES

Commencement: 30 November 2016.

[5.299]

102 Orders under section 101

(1) Without prejudice to the generality of section 101(3), an order under that section may include provision—

(a) requiring the person responsible for the arrangement to pay an amount to the trustee,
(b) adjusting the liabilities of the arrangement in respect of the debtor,
(c) adjusting any liabilities of the arrangement in respect of any other person that derive, directly or indirectly, from rights of the debtor under the arrangement,
(d) for the recovery by the person responsible for the arrangement (whether by deduction from any amount which that person is ordered to pay or otherwise) of costs incurred by that person in complying in the debtor's case with any requirement under section 103(1) or in giving effect to the order.

(2) In subsection (1), references to adjusting the liabilities of the arrangement in respect of a person include, in particular, reducing the amount of any benefit or future benefit to which that person is entitled under the arrangement.

(3) In subsection (1)(c), the reference to liabilities of the arrangement does not include liabilities in respect of a person which result from giving effect to an order or provision falling within section 28(1) of the 1999 Act (pension sharing orders).

(4) The maximum amount which the person responsible for an arrangement may be required to pay by an order under section 101 is the lesser of—

(a) the amount of the excessive contributions, and
(b) the value of the debtor's rights under the arrangement (if the arrangement is an approved pension arrangement) or of the debtor's excluded rights under the arrangement (if the arrangement is an unapproved pension arrangement).

(5) An order under section 101 which requires the person responsible for an arrangement to pay an amount ("the restoration amount") to the trustee must provide for the liabilities of the arrangement to be correspondingly reduced.

(6) For the purposes of subsection (5), liabilities are correspondingly reduced if the difference between—

(a) the amount of the liabilities immediately before the reduction, and
(b) their amount immediately after the reduction,

is equal to the restoration amount.

(7) An order under section 101 in respect of an arrangement—

(a) is binding on the person responsible for the arrangement, and
(b) overrides provisions of the arrangement to the extent that they conflict with the provisions of the order.

NOTES

Commencement: 30 November 2016.

[5.300]

103 Orders under section 101: supplementary

(1) The person responsible for—

(a) an approved pension arrangement under which a debtor has rights,
(b) an unapproved pension arrangement under which a debtor has excluded rights, or
(c) a pension arrangement under which a debtor has at any time had rights,

must, on the trustee in the sequestration making a written request, provide the trustee with such information about the arrangement and rights as the trustee may reasonably require for, or in connection with, the making of applications under section 101.

(2) Nothing in—

(a) any provision of section 159 of the Pension Schemes Act 1993 or section 91 of the Pensions Act 1995 (which prevent assignation and the making of orders that restrain a person from receiving anything which the person is prevented from assigning),
(b) any provision of any enactment (whether passed or made before or after the passing of the 1999 Act) corresponding to any of the provisions mentioned in paragraph (a), or
(c) any provision of the arrangement in question corresponding to any of those provisions,

applies to a court exercising its powers under section 101.

(3) Where any sum is required by an order under section 101 to be paid to the trustee, that sum is to be comprised in the debtor's estate.
(4) Regulations made by the Secretary of State may, for the purposes of the recovery provisions, make provision about the calculation and verification of—
(a) any such value as is mentioned in section 102(4)(b),
(b) any such amounts as are mentioned in section 102(6)(a) and (b).
(5) The power conferred by subsection (4) includes power to provide for calculation or verification—
(a) in such manner as may, in the particular case, be approved by a prescribed person, or
(b) in accordance with guidance from time to time prepared by a prescribed person.
(6) References in the recovery provisions to the person responsible for a pension arrangement are to—
(a) the trustees, managers or provider of the arrangement, or
(b) the person having, in relation to the arrangement, functions corresponding to those of a trustee, manager or provider.
(7) In this section and in section 101, "the recovery provisions" means this section and sections 101 and 102.
(8) Regulations under subsection (4) may contain such incidental, supplemental and transitional provisions as appear to the Secretary of State necessary or expedient.
(9) In subsection (5), "prescribed" means prescribed by the regulations.

NOTES
Commencement: 30 November 2016.

[5.301]
104 Excessive contributions in pension-sharing cases: general
(1) For the purposes of section 98, a pension-sharing transaction is taken—
(a) to be a transaction, entered into by the transferor (in this section referred to as "TR") with the transferee (in this section referred to as "TE"), by which the appropriate amount is transferred by TR to TE, and
(b) to be capable of being an alienation challengeable under that section only so far as it is a transfer of so much of the appropriate amount as is recoverable.
(2) For the purposes of section 99, a pension-sharing transaction is taken—
(a) to be something (namely a transfer of the appropriate amount to TE) done by TR, and
(b) to be capable of being an unfair preference given to TE only so far as it is a transfer of so much of the appropriate amount as is recoverable.
(3) For the purposes of section 100, a pension-sharing transaction is taken—
(a) to be a pension sharing order made by the court under section 8(2) of the Family Law (Scotland) Act 1985, and
(b) to be an order capable of being recalled under that section only so far as it is a payment or transfer of so much of the appropriate amount as is recoverable.
(4) Subsection (5) applies where—
(a) an alienation is challenged under section 98,
(b) a transaction is challenged under section 99, or
(c) an application is made under section 100 for the recall of an order made in divorce proceedings.
(5) If any question arises as to whether, or the extent to which, the appropriate amount in the case of a pension-sharing transaction is recoverable, the question must be determined in accordance with subsections (6) to (10).
(6) The court is first to determine the extent, if any, to which TR's rights under the shared arrangement at the time of the transaction appear to have been, whether directly or indirectly, the fruits of contributions ("personal contributions") to the shared arrangement or any other pension arrangement—
(a) which TR has at any time made on TR's own behalf, or
(b) which have at any time been made on TR's behalf.
(7) Where it appears that those rights were to any extent the fruits of personal contributions, the court is then to determine the extent, if any, to which those rights appear to have been the fruits of personal contributions whose making has unfairly prejudiced TR's creditors ("the unfair contributions").
(8) If it appears to the court that the extent to which those rights were the fruits of the unfair contributions is such that the transfer of the appropriate amount could have been made out of rights under the shared arrangement which were not the fruits of the unfair contributions, then the appropriate amount is not recoverable.
(9) If it appears to the court that the transfer could not have been wholly so made, then the appropriate amount is recoverable to the extent to which it appears to the court that the transfer could not have been so made.
(10) In making the determination mentioned in subsection (7) the court must consider in particular—
(a) whether any of the personal contributions were made for the purpose of putting assets beyond the reach of TR's creditors or any of them, and
(b) whether the total amount of any personal contributions represented, at the time the pension sharing arrangement was made, by rights under pension arrangements is an amount which is excessive in view of TR's circumstances when those contributions were made.
(11) In this section and sections 105 and 106—
"appropriate amount", in relation to a pension-sharing transaction, means the appropriate amount in relation to that transaction for the purposes of section 29(1) of the 1999 Act (creation of pension credits and debits),
"pension-sharing transaction" means an order or provision falling within section 28(1) of that Act (orders and agreements which activate pension-sharing),

"shared arrangement", in relation to a pension-sharing transaction, means the pension arrangement to which the transaction relates,

"transferee" (or "TE"), in relation to a pension-sharing transaction, means the person for whose benefit the transaction is made, and

"transferor" (or "TR"), in relation to a pension-sharing transaction, means the person to whose rights the transaction relates.

NOTES

Commencement: 30 November 2016.

[5.302]

105 Excessive contributions in pension-sharing cases: recovery orders

(1) In this section and section 106, "recovery order" means, in any proceedings to which section 104 applies—

(a) a decree granted under section 98(5),

(b) a decree granted under section 99(6), or

(c) an order made under section 100(2).

(2) A recovery order may include provision—

(a) requiring the person responsible for a pension arrangement in which TE (see section 104(11)) has acquired rights derived directly or indirectly from the pension-sharing transaction (again see that section) to pay an amount to the trustee,

(b) adjusting the liabilities of the pension arrangement in respect of TE,

(c) adjusting any liabilities of the pension arrangement in respect of any other person that derive, directly or indirectly, from rights of TE under the arrangement,

(d) for the recovery by the person responsible for the pension arrangement (whether by deduction from any amount which that person is ordered to pay or otherwise) of costs incurred by that person in complying in the debtor's case with any requirement under section 106(1) or in giving effect to the order.

(3) Subsection (2) is without prejudice to the generality of section 98(5), 99(6) or 100(2).

(4) In subsection (2), references to adjusting the liabilities of a pension arrangement in respect of a person include, in particular, reducing the amount of any benefit or future benefit to which that person is entitled under the arrangement.

(5) The maximum amount which the person responsible for an arrangement may be required to pay by a recovery order is the smallest of—

(a) so much of the appropriate amount (see section 104(11)) as is recoverable in accordance with section 104,

(b) so much, if any, of the amount of the unfair contributions (within the meaning given by section 104(7)) as is not recoverable by way of an order under section 101 containing provision such as is mentioned in section 102(1)(a), and

(c) the value of the debtor's rights under the arrangement acquired by TE as a consequence of the transfer of the appropriate amount.

(6) A recovery order which requires the person responsible for an arrangement to pay an amount ("the restoration amount") to the trustee must provide for the liabilities of the arrangement to be correspondingly reduced.

(7) For the purposes of subsection (6), liabilities are correspondingly reduced if the difference between—

(a) the amount of the liabilities immediately before the reduction, and

(b) their amount immediately after the reduction,

is equal to the restoration amount.

(8) A recovery order in respect of an arrangement—

(a) is binding on the person responsible for the arrangement, and

(b) overrides provisions of the arrangement to the extent that they conflict with the provisions of the order.

NOTES

Commencement: 30 November 2016.

[5.303]

106 Recovery orders: supplementary

(1) The person responsible for a pension arrangement under which TE has, at any time, acquired rights by virtue of the transfer of the appropriate amount (see section 104(11)) is, on the trustee making a written request, to provide the trustee with such information about the arrangement and the rights under it of TR and TE as the trustee may reasonably require for, or in connection with, the making of an application for a recovery order.

(2) Nothing in the provisions mentioned in subsection (3) applies to a court exercising its power to make a recovery order (see section 105(1)).

(3) The provisions are—

(a) any provision of section 159 of the Pension Schemes Act 1993 or section 91 of the Pensions Act 1995 (which prevent assignation and the making of orders which restrain a person from receiving anything the person is prevented from assigning),

(b) any provision of any enactment (whether passed or made before or after the passing of the 1999 Act) corresponding to any of the provisions mentioned in paragraph (a), or

(c) any provision of the arrangement in question corresponding to any of those provisions.

(4) Regulations may, for the purposes of the recovery provisions, make provision about the calculation and verification of—
(a) any such value as is mentioned in section 105(5)(c),
(b) any such amounts as are mentioned in section 105(7)(a) and (b).
(5) The power conferred by subsection (4) includes power to provide for calculation or verification—
(a) in such manner as may, in the particular case, be approved by a prescribed person, or
(b) in accordance with guidance from time to time prepared by a prescribed person.
(6) References in the recovery provisions to the person responsible for a pension arrangement are to—
(a) the trustees, managers or providers of the arrangement, or
(b) the person having, in relation to the arrangement, functions corresponding to those of a trustee, manager or provider.
(7) In this section—
"prescribed" means prescribed by regulations,
"the recovery provisions" means this section and sections 98, 99, 100 and 105, and
"regulations" means regulations made by the Secretary of State.
(8) Regulations under the recovery provisions may contain such incidental, supplemental and transitional provisions as appear to the Secretary of State necessary or expedient.

NOTES

Commencement: 30 November 2016.

[5.304]

107 References in Part 7 to "the 1889 Act" and to "the 1999 Act"

In this Part, references—
to "the 1889 Act" are to the Judicial Factors (Scotland) Act 1889, and
to "the 1999 Act" are to the Welfare Reform and Pensions Act 1999.

NOTES

Commencement: 30 November 2016.

PART 8
ADMINISTRATION OF ESTATE BY TRUSTEE

General

[5.305]

108 Taking possession of estate by trustee

(1) The trustee in the sequestration must—
(a) for the purpose of recovering the estate of the debtor under section 50(1)(a), take possession as soon as may be after the trustee's appointment—
(i) of the debtor's whole estate so far as vesting in the trustee under sections 78 and 86, and
(ii) of any document in the debtor's possession or control relating to the debtor's assets or the debtor's business or financial affairs,
(b) make up and maintain an inventory and valuation of the estate, and
(c) forthwith thereafter send a copy of the inventory and valuation to AiB.
(2) Paragraph (a) of subsection (1) is subject to section 113.
(3) The trustee is entitled to have access to, and to make a copy of, any document relating to the assets or the business or financial affairs of the debtor—
(a) sent by or on behalf of the debtor to a third party, and
(b) in the third party's hands.
(4) If a person obstructs the trustee in the trustee's exercise, or attempted exercise, of a power conferred by subsection (3), the sheriff may, on the trustee's application, order the person to cease obstructing the trustee.
(5) The trustee may require delivery to the trustee of any title deed or other document of the debtor, even if a right of lien is claimed over it.
(6) Subsection (5) is without prejudice to any preference of the holder of the lien.

NOTES

Commencement: 30 November 2016.

[5.306]

109 Management and realisation of estate

(1) The trustee in the sequestration, as soon as may be after the trustee's appointment, must consult with AiB concerning the exercise of the trustee's functions under section 50(1)(a).
(2) The trustee must comply with any general or specific directions given to the trustee (as the case may be)—
(a) by the creditors,
(b) on the application under this subsection of the commissioners, by the sheriff, or
(c) by AiB,
as to the exercise by the trustee of such functions.
(3) But subsection (2) is subject to subsections (4), (9) and (12).
(4) Subsections (1) and (2) do not apply where the trustee is AiB.
(5) The trustee may—
(a) carry on or close down any business of the debtor,

(b) bring, defend or continue any legal proceedings relating to the estate of the debtor,
(c) create a security over any part of the estate,
(d) where any right, option or other power forms part of the debtor's estate, make payments or incur liabilities with a view to obtaining, for the benefit of the creditors, any property which is the subject of the right, option or power,
(e) borrow money in so far as it is necessary for the trustee to do so to safeguard the debtor's estate, and
(f) effect or maintain insurance policies in respect of the business or property of the debtor.

(6) Any sale of the debtor's estate by the trustee may either be by public sale or by private bargain.

(7) The following rules apply to the sale of any part of the debtor's heritable estate over which a heritable security is held by a creditor or creditors if the rights of the secured creditor or creditors are preferable to those of the trustee—
(a) the trustee may sell that part only with the concurrence of every such creditor unless the trustee obtains a sufficiently high price to discharge every such security,
(b) the following acts are precluded—
(i) the taking of steps by a creditor to enforce the creditor's security over the part after the trustee has intimated to the creditor that the trustee intends to sell the part,
(ii) the commencement by the trustee of the procedure for the sale of the part after the creditor has intimated to the trustee that the creditor intends to commence the procedure for its sale,
(c) except that where the trustee or a creditor has given intimation under paragraph (b) but has unduly delayed in proceeding with the sale then, if authorised by the sheriff in the case of—
(i) sub-paragraph (i) of that paragraph, any creditor to whom intimation has been given may enforce the creditor's security, or
(ii) sub-paragraph (ii) of that paragraph, the trustee may sell the part.

(8) The function of the trustee under section 50(1)(a) to realise the debtor's estate includes the function of selling, with or without recourse against the estate, debts owing to the estate.

(9) The trustee may sell any perishable goods without complying with any directions given to the trustee under subsection (2)(a) or (c) if the trustee considers that compliance with such directions would adversely affect the sale.

(10) The validity of the title of any purchaser is not challengeable on the ground that there has been a failure to comply with a requirement of this section.

(11) It is not competent for the trustee or an associate of the trustee, or for any commissioner, to purchase any of the debtor's estate in pursuance of this section.

(12) The trustee—
(a) must comply with the requirements of subsection (7) of this section, and
(b) may do anything permitted by this section,

only in so far as, in the trustee's view, it would be of financial benefit to the estate of the debtor, and in the interests of the creditors, to do so.

NOTES

Commencement: 30 November 2016.

Contractual Powers and Money Received

[5.307]

110 Contractual powers of trustee

(1) The trustee in the sequestration may, as respects any contract entered into by the debtor before the date of sequestration—
(a) adopt it (except where adoption is precluded by its express or implied terms) if the trustee considers that its adoption would be beneficial to the administration of the debtor's estate, or
(b) refuse to adopt it.

(2) But subsection (1) is subject to subsections (3) and (10).

(3) The trustee must, within 28 days after the receipt by the trustee of a request in writing from any party to a contract entered into by the debtor, adopt or refuse to adopt the contract.

(4) The 28 days mentioned in subsection (3) may be extended—
(a) in a case where AiB is the trustee, by the sheriff on the application of AiB, and
(b) in any other case, by AiB on the application of the trustee.

(5) The trustee may, within 14 days beginning with the day of the decision, apply to AiB for a review of a decision of AiB under subsection (4)(b).

(6) If an application for a review under subsection (5) is made, AiB must—
(a) take into account any representations made by an interested party within 21 days beginning with the day on which the application is made, and
(b) confirm, amend or revoke the decision within 28 days beginning with that day.

(7) The trustee may, within 14 days beginning with the day of the decision, appeal to the sheriff against a decision by AiB under subsection (6)(b).

(8) AiB may refer a case to the sheriff for a direction before—
(a) making a decision under subsection (4)(b), or
(b) undertaking any review under this section.

(9) An application for a review under subsection (5) may not be made in relation to a matter on which AiB has applied to the sheriff for a direction under subsection (8).

(10) If, within the 28 days mentioned in subsection (3) or as the case may be within the longer period allowed by virtue of subsection (4), the trustee does not reply in writing to a request under subsection (3), the trustee is deemed to have refused to adopt the contract.

(11) The trustee may enter into any contract where the trustee considers that to do so would be beneficial for the administration of the debtor's estate.

NOTES

Commencement: 30 November 2016.

[5.308]

111 Money received by trustee

(1) All money received by the trustee in the sequestration in the exercise of the trustee's functions must be deposited by the trustee in the name of the debtor's estate in an interest-bearing account in an appropriate bank or institution.

(2) But subsection (1) is subject to subsections (3) and (5).

(3) In any case where the trustee is AiB, all money received by AiB in the exercise of AiB's functions as trustee must be deposited by AiB in an interest-bearing account in an appropriate bank or institution—

(a) in the name of the debtor's estate, or

(b) in the name of the Scottish Ministers.

(4) But subsection (3) is subject to subsection (5).

(5) The trustee may at any time retain in the trustee's hands a sum not exceeding £200 or such other sum as may be prescribed.

NOTES

Commencement: 30 November 2016.

Debtor's home

[5.309]

112 Debtor's family home

(1) This section applies where a debtor's sequestrated estate includes any right or interest in the debtor's family home.

(2) At the end of 3 years beginning with the date of sequestration, the right or interest—

(a) ceases to form part of the debtor's sequestrated estate, and

(b) is reinvested in the debtor (without disposition, conveyance, assignation or other transfer).

(3) Subsection (2) does not apply if—

(a) during the 3 years mentioned in subsection (2), the trustee in the sequestration—

(i) disposes of or otherwise realises the right or interest,

(ii) concludes missives for sale of the right or interest,

(iii) sends a memorandum to the Keeper of the Register of Inhibitions under section 26(6),

(iv) completes title in the Land Register of Scotland, or as the case may be in the Register of Sasines, in relation to the right or interest,

(v) commences proceedings to obtain the authority of the sheriff under section 113(1)(b) to sell or dispose of the right or interest,

(vi) commences proceedings in an action for division and sale of the family home,

(vii) commences proceedings in an action for the purpose of obtaining vacant possession of the family home,

(viii) enters with the debtor into an agreement such as is mentioned in subsection (4), or

(ix) commences an action under section 98 in respect of the right or interest, or

(b) the trustee in the sequestration—

(i) does not, at any time during the 3 years mentioned in subsection (2), know about the facts giving rise to a right of action under section 98, but

(ii) commences an action under that section reasonably soon after becoming aware of those facts.

(4) The agreement referred to in subsection (3)(a)(viii) is an agreement that the debtor is to incur a specified liability to the debtor's estate (with or without interest from the date of the agreement) in consideration of which the right or interest is to—

(a) cease to form part of the debtor's sequestrated estate, and

(b) be reinvested in the debtor (without disposition, conveyance, assignation or other transfer).

(5) If the debtor does not inform the trustee or AiB of the right or interest within 3 months beginning with the date of sequestration then the 3 years mentioned in subsection (2) is to be taken—

(a) not to begin with the date of sequestration, but

(b) to begin instead with the date on which the trustee becomes aware of the right or interest.

(6) The sheriff may, on the trustee's application, substitute for the 3 years mentioned in subsection (2) a longer period—

(a) in prescribed circumstances, and

(b) in such other circumstances as the sheriff thinks appropriate.

(7) The Scottish Ministers may, by regulations—

(a) make provision for this section to have effect with the substitution, in such circumstances as may be specified in the regulations, of a shorter period for the 3 years mentioned in subsection (2),

(b) prescribe circumstances in which this section does not apply,

(c) prescribe circumstances in which a sheriff may disapply this section,

(d) make provision requiring the trustee to give notice that this section applies or does not apply,

(e) make provision about compensation,

(f) make such provision as they consider necessary or expedient in consequence of regulations made under paragraphs (a) to (e), or

(g) modify sub-paragraphs (i) to (viii) of subsection (3)(a) so as to—

(i) add or remove a matter, or
(ii) vary a matter,
referred to in that subsection.

(8) In this section, "family home" has the same meaning as in section 113.

NOTES

Commencement: 30 November 2016.

[5.310]

113 Power of trustee in relation to debtor's family home

(1) Before the trustee in the sequestration (in this section referred to as "T"), or the trustee acting under the trust deed (in this section referred to as "TU"), sells or disposes of any right or interest in the debtor's family home, T or TU must—

(a) obtain the relevant consent, or
(b) where unable to obtain that consent, obtain the authority of the sheriff in accordance with subsection (2) or as the case may be (3).

(2) Where T or TU requires to obtain the authority of the sheriff in terms of subsection (1)(b), the sheriff, after having regard to all the circumstances of the case including—

(a) the needs and financial resources of the debtor's spouse or former spouse,
(b) the needs and financial resources of the debtor's civil partner or former civil partner,
(c) the needs and financial resources of any child of the family,
(d) the interests of the creditors, and
(e) the length of the period during which (whether before or after the relevant date) the family home was used as a residence by any of the persons referred to in paragraphs (a) to (c),

may refuse to grant the application or may postpone the granting of the application for such period (not exceeding 3 years) as the sheriff may consider reasonable in the circumstances or may grant the application subject to such conditions as the sheriff may prescribe.

(3) Subsection (2) applies to an action brought by T or TU—

(a) for division and sale of, or
(b) for the purpose of obtaining vacant possession of,

the debtor's family home as that subsection applies to an application under subsection (1)(b).

(4) Before commencing proceedings to obtain the authority of the sheriff under subsection (2) or (3), T or TU must give notice of the proceedings to the local authority in whose area the home is situated.

(5) Notice under subsection (4) must be given in such form and manner as may be prescribed.

(6) For the purposes of subsection (3), any reference in subsection (2) to the granting of the application is to be construed as a reference to the granting of decree in the action.

(7) In this section—

"family home" means any property in which, at the relevant date, the debtor had a right or interest (whether alone or in common with another person), being property which was occupied at that date as a residence—

(a) by—
(i) the debtor and the debtor's spouse or civil partner,
(ii) the debtor's spouse or civil partner,
(iii) the debtor's former spouse or former civil partner,
in any of those cases, whether with or without a child of the family, or
(b) by the debtor with a child of the family,

"child of the family" includes—

(a) any child or grandchild of either—
(i) the debtor, or
(ii) the debtor's spouse or civil partner (or former spouse or civil partner), and
(b) any person who has been brought up or accepted by either—
(whatever age the child, grandchild or person may be),
(i) the debtor, or
(ii) the debtor's spouse or civil partner (or former spouse or civil partner),
as if a child of the debtor, spouse, civil partner or former spouse or civil partner,

"relevant consent" means, in relation to the sale or disposal of any right or interest in a family home—

(a) in a case where the family home is occupied by the debtor's spouse or civil partner (or former spouse or civil partner), the consent of the spouse or civil partner (or as the case may be former spouse or civil partner) whether or not the family home is also occupied by the debtor,
(b) where paragraph (a) does not apply, in a case where the family home is occupied by the debtor with a child of the family, the consent of the debtor, and

"relevant date" means the day immediately preceding the date of sequestration or, as the case may be, the day immediately preceding the date the trust deed was granted.

NOTES

Commencement: 30 November 2016.
Regulations: the Bankruptcy (Scotland) Regulations 2016, SSI 2016/397 at **[16.401]**.

Rights of spouse or civil partner

[5.311]

114 Protection of rights of spouse against arrangements intended to defeat them

(1) Subsections (2) and (3) apply where a debtor's sequestrated estate includes a matrimonial home in respect of which—

(a) the debtor, immediately before the date the order was made appointing the trustee, was an entitled spouse, and

(b) the other spouse is a non-entitled spouse.

(2) Where the trustee in the sequestration knows—

(a) that the debtor is married to the non-entitled spouse, and

(b) where the non-entitled spouse is residing,

the trustee must inform the non-entitled spouse, within 14 days beginning with the date mentioned in subsection (1)(a), of the fact that sequestration of the debtor's estate has been awarded, of the right of petition which exists under section 29 and of the effect of subsection (3).

(3) On the petition under section 29 of the non-entitled spouse presented either within 40 days beginning with the date mentioned in subsection (1)(a) or within 10 weeks beginning with the date of the award of sequestration the sheriff, if satisfied that the purpose of the petition for sequestration, or as the case may be the debtor application, was wholly or mainly to defeat the occupancy rights of the non-entitled spouse, may—

(a) under section 30, recall the sequestration, or

(b) make such order as the sheriff thinks appropriate to protect the occupancy rights of the non-entitled spouse.

(4) The reference in subsection (1)(a) to the date the order is made appointing the trustee is, in a case where more than one trustee is appointed in the sequestration, to be construed as a reference to the date the first order is made appointing a trustee.

(5) In this section—

"entitled spouse" and "non-entitled spouse" are to be construed in accordance with section 6 of the Matrimonial Homes (Family Protection) (Scotland) Act 1981,

"matrimonial home" has the meaning given by section 22 of that Act, and

"occupancy rights" has the meaning given by section 1(4) of that Act.

NOTES

Commencement: 30 November 2016.

[5.312]

115 Protection of rights of civil partner against arrangements intended to defeat them

(1) Subsections (2) and (3) apply where a debtor's sequestrated estate includes a family home in respect of which—

(a) the debtor, immediately before the date the order was made appointing the trustee, was an entitled partner, and

(b) the other partner in the civil partnership is a non-entitled partner.

(2) Where the trustee in the sequestration knows—

(a) that the debtor is in civil partnership with the non-entitled partner, and

(b) where the non-entitled partner is residing,

the trustee must inform the non-entitled partner, within 14 days beginning with the date mentioned in subsection (1)(a), of the fact that sequestration of the debtor's estate has been awarded, of the right of petition which exists under section 29 and of the effect of subsection (3).

(3) On the petition under section 29 of the non-entitled partner presented either within 40 days beginning with the date mentioned in subsection (1)(a) or within 10 weeks beginning with the date of the award of sequestration the sheriff, if satisfied that the purpose of the petition for sequestration, or as the case may be the debtor application, was wholly or mainly to defeat the occupancy rights of the non-entitled partner, may—

(a) under section 30, recall the sequestration, or

(b) make such order as the sheriff thinks appropriate to protect the occupancy rights of the non-entitled partner.

(4) The reference in subsection (1)(a) to the date the order is made appointing the trustee is, in a case where more than one trustee is appointed in the sequestration, to be construed as a reference to the date the first order is made appointing a trustee.

(5) In this section—

"entitled partner" and "non-entitled partner" are to be construed in accordance with section 101 of the Civil Partnership Act 2004,

"family home" has the meaning given by section 135 of that Act, and

"occupancy rights" means the rights conferred by section 101(1) of that Act.

NOTES

Commencement: 30 November 2016.

Account of state of affairs

[5.313]

116 Debtor's account of state of affairs

(1) This section applies to a debtor who—

(a) has not been discharged under this Act, or

(b) is subject to a debtor contribution order.

(2) The trustee in the sequestration must, at the end of—

(a) 6 months beginning with the date of sequestration, and

(b) each subsequent 6 months,

require the debtor to give an account in writing, in such form as may be prescribed, of the debtor's current state of affairs.

NOTES

Commencement: 30 November 2016.

Regulations: the Bankruptcy (Scotland) Regulations 2016, SSI 2016/397 at **[16.401]**.

Financial education for debtor

[5.314]

117 Financial education for debtor

(1) The trustee must notify a living debtor that the debtor is required to undertake a prescribed course of financial education (a "financial education course") specified by the trustee if, in the opinion of the trustee—

(a) any of the circumstances mentioned in subsection (2) applies, and

(b) undertaking the course would be appropriate for the debtor.

(2) The circumstances are—

(a) that in the 5 years ending on the date on which the sequestration was awarded—

(i) the debtor's estate was sequestrated,

(ii) the debtor granted a protected trust deed,

(iii) an analogous remedy (as defined in section 17(8)) was in force in respect of the debtor, or

(iv) the debtor participated in a debt management programme under which the debtor made regular payments,

(b) that the debtor is subject to, or under investigation with a view to an application being made for, a bankruptcy restrictions order,

(c) that the trustee considers that the pattern of the debtor's behaviour, whether before or after the award of sequestration, is such that the debtor would benefit from a financial education course, and

(d) that the debtor agrees to undertake a financial education course.

(3) The trustee must decide whether to issue a notification under subsection (1)—

(a) within 6 months beginning with the date of the award of sequestration, and

(b) in a case where section 143 applies, as soon as reasonably practicable after—

(i) the trustee ascertains the whereabouts of the debtor, or

(ii) the debtor makes contact with the trustee.

(4) A debtor must not be required to undertake or, as the case may be, complete the financial course specified by the trustee if, in the opinion of the trustee, the debtor—

(a) is unable to participate in the course as a result of the debtor's health (including by reason of disability or of physical or mental illness), or

(b) has completed a financial education course in the 5 years ending on the date on which the sequestration of the debtor's estate was awarded.

(5) Regulations under subsection (1) may in particular—

(a) prescribe the content, format and method of delivery of a course,

(b) prescribe different courses for different circumstances, or

(c) make provision for particular courses to be specified by a trustee where particular circumstances in subsection (2) apply.

(6) In subsection (2)(a)(iv), "debt management programme" includes in particular a programme approved in accordance with section 2 of the 2002 Act.

NOTES

Commencement: 30 November 2016.

Regulations: the Bankruptcy (Scotland) Regulations 2016, SSI 2016/397 at **[16.401]**.

PART 9
EXAMINATION OF DEBTOR

Private and public examination

[5.315]

118 Private examination

(1) The trustee in the sequestration may request—

(a) the debtor to appear before the trustee and to give information relating to the debtor's assets, the debtor's dealings with them or the debtor's conduct in relation to the debtor's business or financial affairs, or

(b) the debtor's spouse or civil partner, or any other person who the trustee believes can give such information to give that information.

(2) In this Act any such spouse, civil partner or other person is referred to as a "relevant person".

(3) The trustee may, if the trustee considers it necessary, apply to the sheriff for an order to be made under subsection (4).

(4) On an application under subsection (3), the sheriff may make an order requiring the debtor or a relevant person to attend for private examination before the sheriff on a date and at a time specified in the order.

(5) But subsection (4) is subject to section 120(3).
(6) A date specified in an order under subsection (4) must be not earlier than 8 days nor later than 16 days after the date of the order.
(7) A person who fails without reasonable excuse to comply with an order under subsection (4) commits an offence.
(8) A person who commits an offence under subsection (7) is liable, on summary conviction—
 (a) to a fine not exceeding level 5 on the standard scale, or
 (b) to imprisonment for a term not exceeding 3 months,
or both to such fine and to such imprisonment.
(9) Where the debtor is an entity whose estate may be sequestrated by virtue of section 6(1), the references, in this section and in sections 119 to 121, to the debtor are to be construed, unless the context otherwise requires, as references to a person representing the entity.

NOTES

Commencement: 30 November 2016.

[5.316]
119 Public examination
(1) At least 8 weeks before the end of the first accounting period the trustee in the sequestration—
 (a) may, or
 (b) if requested to do so by AiB or by the commissioners (if any) or by ¼ in value of the creditors, must,
apply to the sheriff for an order for the public examination before the sheriff of the debtor, or of a relevant person, relating to the debtor's assets, the debtor's dealings with those assets or the debtor's conduct in relation to the debtor's business or financial affairs.
(2) Except that on cause shown such application may be made by the trustee at any time.
(3) On an application under subsection (1), the sheriff must make an order requiring the debtor or the relevant person to attend for examination before the sheriff in open court on a date and at a time specified in the order.
(4) But subsection (3) is subject to section 120(3).
(5) A date specified in an order under subsection (3) must be not earlier than 8 days nor later than 16 days after the date of the order.
(6) On the sheriff making an order under subsection (3), the trustee must—
 (a) send to AiB a notice in such form, and containing such particulars, as may be prescribed,
 (b) send a copy of the notice—
  (i) to every creditor known to the trustee, and
  (ii) where the order is in respect of a relevant person, to the debtor, and
 (c) inform each person sent a copy under paragraph (b) that the person may participate in the examination.
(7) AiB must enter particulars of the notice sent under subsection (6)(a) in the register of insolvencies.
(8) A person who fails without reasonable excuse to comply with an order under subsection (3) commits an offence.
(9) A person who commits an offence under subsection (8) is liable, on summary conviction—
 (a) to a fine not exceeding level 5 on the standard scale, or
 (b) to imprisonment for a term not exceeding 3 months,
or both to such fine and to such imprisonment.

NOTES

Commencement: 30 November 2016.
Regulations: the Bankruptcy (Scotland) Regulations 2016, SSI 2016/397 at **[16.401]**.

[5.317]
120 Provisions ancillary to sections 118 and 119
(1) If a debtor or relevant person is residing in Scotland, the sheriff may on the application of the trustee grant a warrant (which may be executed by a messenger-at-arms or sheriff officer anywhere in Scotland) to apprehend the debtor or relevant person and to have the apprehended person taken to the place of the examination.
(2) But a warrant under subsection (1) must not be granted unless the sheriff is satisfied that it is necessary to grant it to secure the attendance of the debtor or relevant person at the examination.
(3) If the debtor or relevant person is for any good reason prevented from attending for examination, the sheriff may grant a commission to take the examination of the debtor or relevant person (the commissioner being, in this section and in section 121, referred to as an "examining commissioner").
(4) Subsection (3) is without prejudice to subsection (5).
(5) The sheriff or the examining commissioner may at any time adjourn the examination to such day as the sheriff or examining commissioner may fix.
(6) The sheriff or examining commissioner may order the debtor or a relevant person to produce for inspection any document—
 (a) in the custody or control of the person so ordered, and
 (b) relating to the debtor's assets, the debtor's dealings with those assets or the debtor's conduct in relation to the debtor's business or financial affairs,
and to deliver the document or a copy of the document to the trustee in the sequestration for further examination by the trustee.

NOTES

Commencement: 30 November 2016.

Conduct of examination

[5.318]

121 Conduct of examination

(1) The examination, whether before the sheriff or an examining commissioner, must be taken on oath.

(2) At the examination—

(a) the trustee in the sequestration (or a solicitor or counsel acting on behalf of the trustee) and, in the case of public examination, any creditor may question the debtor or a relevant person, and

(b) the debtor may question a relevant person,

as to any matter relating to the debtor's assets, the debtor's dealings with those assets or the debtor's conduct in relation to the debtor's business or financial affairs.

(3) The debtor or a relevant person—

(a) is required to answer any question relating to the debtor's assets, the debtor's dealings with those assets or the debtor's conduct in relation to the debtor's business or financial affairs, and

(b) is not excused from answering any such question on the ground—

(i) that the answer may incriminate, or tend to incriminate, the person questioned, or

(ii) of confidentiality.

(4) Except that—

(a) a statement made by the debtor or a relevant person in answer to any such question is not admissible in evidence in any subsequent criminal proceedings against the person making it (except where the proceedings are in respect of a charge of perjury relating to the statement), and

(b) a person subject to examination is not required to disclose any information received from a person not called for examination if the information is confidential between the two persons.

(5) The rules relating to the recording of evidence in ordinary causes specified in the first schedule of the Sheriff Courts (Scotland) Act 1907 apply in relation to the recording of evidence at the examination before the sheriff or examining commissioner.

(6) The debtor's deposition at the examination must be subscribed by the debtor and by the sheriff (or, as the case may be, the examining commissioner).

(7) The trustee must send a copy of the record of the examination to AiB.

(8) A relevant person is entitled, as if the person were a witness in an ordinary civil cause in the sheriff court, to fees or allowances in respect of the person's attendance at the examination.

(9) Except that the sheriff may disallow or restrict the entitlement to such fees or allowances if the sheriff thinks it appropriate to do so in all the circumstances.

NOTES

Commencement: 30 November 2016.

PART 10
CLAIMS, DIVIDENDS AND DISTRIBUTION ETC

Submission and adjudication of claims

[5.319]

122 Submission of claims to trustee

(1) A creditor must submit a claim in accordance with this section to the trustee in the sequestration in order to obtain an adjudication as to that person's entitlement—

(a) to vote at a meeting of creditors other than the statutory meeting, or

(b) (so far as funds are available) to a dividend out of the debtor's estate in respect of any accounting period.

(2) Where the claim is by virtue of—

(a) paragraph (a) of subsection (1), it must be submitted at or before the meeting,

(b) paragraph (b) of that subsection, it must be submitted in accordance with subsection (4).

(3) But subsection (1) is subject to subsections (4), (7) and (8) and to section 131(6) to (9).

(4) A creditor must, in order to obtain an adjudication as to the creditor's entitlement (so far as funds are available) to a dividend out of the debtor's estate, submit a claim to the trustee not later than the relevant day.

(5) The "relevant day", in relation to a creditor, means—

(a) where notice is given to the creditor under section 44(3), the day which is 120 days after the day on which that notice is given,

(b) where no such notice is given, the day which is 120 days after the day on which the trustee gives notice to the creditor inviting the submission of claims.

(6) If a creditor submits a claim to the trustee after the relevant day, the trustee may, in respect of any accounting period, provide an adjudication as to the creditor's entitlement (so far as funds are available) to a dividend out of the debtor's estate if—

(a) the claim is submitted not later than 8 weeks before the end of the accounting period, and

(b) there were exceptional circumstances which prevented the claim from being submitted before the relevant day.

(7) Subsection (8) applies as regards a claim submitted by a creditor—

(a) under section 46 and accepted in whole or in part by the trustee for the purpose of voting at the statutory meeting, or
(b) under this section and not rejected in whole.

(8) The claim is deemed to have been re-submitted for the purpose of obtaining an adjudication as to the creditor's entitlement both to vote at any subsequent meeting and (so far as funds are available) to a dividend in respect of an accounting period or as the case may be of any subsequent accounting period.

(9) A creditor submits a claim under this section by producing to the trustee—
(a) a statement of claim in the prescribed form, and
(b) an account or voucher (according to the nature of the debt) which constitutes prima facie evidence of the debt.

(10) But the trustee, with the consent of the commissioners if any, may dispense with any requirement under subsection (9) in respect of any debt or of any class of debt.

(11) Where a creditor (in this subsection referred to as "C") neither resides, nor has a place of business, in the United Kingdom, the trustee—
(a) must, if the trustee knows where C does reside or have a place of business and if no notification has been given to C under section 44(3), write to C informing C that C may submit a claim under this section, and
(b) may allow C to submit an informal claim in writing.

(12) Where a creditor has submitted a claim under this section (or under section 46 a statement of claim which has been deemed re-submitted as mentioned in subsection (8)), the creditor may at any time submit a further claim under this section specifying a different amount for the creditor's claim.

(13) But a secured creditor is not entitled to produce a further claim specifying a different value for the security at any time after the trustee requires the secured creditor to discharge, or convey or assign, the security under paragraph 4(3) of schedule 2.

NOTES

Commencement: 30 November 2016.

[5.320]

123 Evidence as to validity or amount of claim

(1) The trustee in the sequestration, for the purpose of being satisfied as to the validity or amount of a claim submitted by a creditor under section 122, may require—
(a) the creditor to produce further evidence, or
(b) any other person who the trustee believes can produce relevant evidence to produce such evidence.

(2) If the creditor (or as the case may be the other person) refuses or delays to do so, the trustee may apply to the sheriff for an order requiring the creditor (or the other person) to attend for private examination before the sheriff.

(3) At any private examination under subsection (2)—
(a) a solicitor or counsel may act on behalf of the trustee, or
(b) the trustee may appear on the trustee's own behalf.

(4) Sections 118(4) to (7) and 121(1) apply, subject to any necessary modifications, to the examination of the creditor (or the other person) as they apply to the examination of a relevant person.

(5) References in subsections (1) and (4) to the creditor in a case where the creditor is an entity mentioned in section 6(1) are to be construed, unless the context otherwise requires, as references to a person representing the entity.

NOTES

Commencement: 30 November 2016.

[5.321]

124 False claims etc

(1) Subsections (2) and (3) apply where a creditor produces under section 122 or 123—
(a) a statement of claim,
(b) account,
(c) voucher, or
(d) other evidence,

which is false.

(2) The creditor commits an offence unless it is shown that the creditor neither knew nor had reason to believe that the statement of claim, account, voucher or other evidence was false.

(3) The debtor commits an offence if the debtor—
(a) knew, or became aware, that the statement of claim, account, voucher or other evidence was false, and
(b) failed, as soon as practicable after acquiring such knowledge, to report to the trustee that the statement of claim, account, voucher or other evidence was false.

(4) A person convicted of an offence under subsection (2) or (3) is liable—
(a) on summary conviction, to a fine not exceeding the statutory maximum, or—
(i) in a case where the person has previously been convicted of an offence inferring dishonest appropriation of property or an attempt at dishonest appropriation of property, to imprisonment for a term not exceeding 6 months, or
(ii) in any other case, to imprisonment for a term not exceeding 3 months,

or both to a fine not exceeding the statutory maximum and to such imprisonment as is mentioned, in relation to the case in question, in sub-paragraph (i) or (ii), or

(b) on conviction on indictment—
(i) to a fine, or
(ii) to imprisonment for a term not exceeding 2 years,
or both to a fine and to such imprisonment.

NOTES

Commencement: 30 November 2016.

[5.322]

125 Further provision as to claims

(1) A creditor may, in such circumstances as may be prescribed, state the amount of the creditor's claim under section 122 in foreign currency.

(2) The trustee in the sequestration must, on production of any document to the trustee for the purposes of any of sections 122 to 124—

(a) initial the document, and

(b) if requested by the person producing it, return it (if it is not a statement of claim) to that person.

(3) The submission of a claim under section 122 bars the effect of any enactment or rule of law relating to the limitation of actions.

(4) Schedule 2 has effect for determining the amount in respect of which the creditor is entitled to claim.

NOTES

Commencement: 30 November 2016.

[5.323]

126 Adjudication of claims: general

(1) At the commencement of every meeting of creditors (other than the statutory meeting) the trustee in the sequestration must, for the purposes of section 128 so far as it relates to voting at the meeting, accept or reject the claim of each creditor.

(2) Subsection (3) applies where funds are available for payment of a dividend out of the debtor's estate in respect of an accounting period.

(3) For the purpose of determining who is entitled to such a dividend, the trustee—

(a) must, not later than 4 weeks before the end of the period, accept or reject every claim submitted (or deemed to have been re-submitted) to the trustee under this Act, and

(b) must, at the same time, make a decision on any matter required to be specified under paragraph (a) or (b) of subsection (7).

(4) The trustee must then, as soon as reasonably practicable, send a list of every claim so accepted or rejected (including its amount and whether it has been accepted or rejected) to the debtor and to every creditor known to the trustee.

(5) If the amount of a claim is stated in foreign currency, the trustee in adjudicating under subsection (1) or (3) on the claim must convert the amount into sterling, in such manner as may be prescribed, at the rate of exchange prevailing at the close of business on the date of sequestration.

(6) Where the trustee rejects a claim, the trustee must forthwith notify the claimant, giving reasons for the rejection.

(7) Where the trustee accepts or rejects a claim, the trustee must record the trustee's decision on the claim, specifying—

(a) the amount of the claim accepted by the trustee,

(b) the category of debt, and the value of any security, as decided by the trustee, and

(c) if the trustee is rejecting the claim, the trustee's reasons for doing so.

(8) Any reference in this section or in section 127 to the acceptance or rejection of a claim is to be construed as a reference to the acceptance or rejection of the claim in whole or in part.

NOTES

Commencement: 30 November 2016.
Regulations: the Bankruptcy (Scotland) Regulations 2016, SSI 2016/397 at **[16.401]**.

[5.324]

127 Adjudication of claims: review and appeal

(1) The debtor or any creditor may apply to AiB for a review of—

(a) the acceptance or rejection of any claim, or

(b) a decision in respect of any matter requiring to be specified under section 126(7)(a) or (b).

(2) The debtor may make an application under subsection (1) only if the debtor satisfies AiB that the debtor has, or is likely to have, a pecuniary interest in the outcome of the review.

(3) Any application under subsection (1) must be made, in the case of a review relating to an acceptance or rejection—

(a) under subsection (1) of section 126, within 14 days beginning with the day of the decision to accept or reject the claim, and

(b) under subsection (3) of that section, within 28 days beginning with that day.

(4) If an application under subsection (1) is made, AiB must—

(a) take into account any representations made by an interested party within 21 days beginning with the day on which the application is made, and

(b) confirm, amend or revoke the decision within 28 days beginning with that day.

(5) The debtor or any creditor may, within 14 days beginning with the day of a decision by AiB under subsection (4)(b), appeal to the sheriff against that decision.
(6) The debtor may appeal under subsection (5) only if the debtor satisfies the sheriff that the debtor has, or is likely to have, a pecuniary interest in the outcome of the appeal.

NOTES

Commencement: 30 November 2016.

Entitlement to vote and draw a dividend

[5.325]

128 Voting and drawing a dividend

(1) A creditor whose claim has been accepted in whole or in part by the trustee in the sequestration or on review or appeal under section 127 is entitled, in a case where the acceptance is under (or on review or appeal arising from)—
- (a) section 126(1), to vote on any matter at the meeting of creditors for the purpose of voting at which the claim is accepted, or
- (b) section 126(3), to payment out of the debtor's estate of a dividend in respect of the accounting period for the purposes of which the claim is accepted.

(2) But—
- (a) paragraph (a) of subsection (1) is subject to sections 70(1)(a) and 77(1) and (7)(b), and
- (b) the entitlement mentioned in paragraph (b) of that subsection arises only in so far as the estate has funds available, having regard to section 129, to make the payment in question.

(3) No vote may be cast, by virtue of a debt, more than once on any resolution put to a meeting of creditors.
(4) Where a creditor—
- (a) is entitled to vote under this section,
- (b) has lodged the creditor's claim in one or more sets of other proceedings, and
- (c) votes (either in person or by proxy) on a resolution put to the meeting,

only the creditor's vote is to be counted.
(5) Subsection (6) applies where—
- (a) a creditor has lodged the creditor's claim in more than one set of other proceedings, and
- (b) more than one member State [insolvency practitioner] seeks to vote by virtue of the claim.

(6) The entitlement to vote by virtue of the claim is exercisable by the member State [insolvency practitioner] in main proceedings whether or not the creditor has lodged the claim in those proceedings.
(7) For the purposes of subsections (4) to (6), "other proceedings" means main proceedings, secondary proceedings or territorial proceedings in a member State other than the United Kingdom.

NOTES

Commencement: 30 November 2016.

Sub-ss (5), (6): words in square brackets substituted for original word "liquidator" by the Insolvency (Regulation (EU) 2015/848) (Miscellaneous Amendments) (Scotland) Regulations 2017, SSI 2017/210, regs 4(1), (10), 9, as from 26 June 2017, except in relation to proceedings opened before that date.

Distribution

[5.326]

129 Priority in distribution

(1) The funds of the debtor's estate must be distributed by the trustee in the sequestration to meet the following debts in the order in which they are mentioned—
- (a) the outlays and remuneration of an interim trustee in the administration of the debtor's estate,
- (b) the outlays and remuneration of the trustee in the sequestration in the administration of the debtor's estate,
- (c) where the debtor has died—
  - (i) deathbed and funeral expenses reasonably incurred, and
  - (ii) expenses reasonably incurred in administering the deceased's estate,
- (d) the expenses reasonably incurred by a creditor who is a petitioner for, or concurs in a debtor application for, sequestration,
- (e) ordinary preferred debts (excluding any interest which has accrued on those debts to the date of sequestration),
- (f) secondary preferred debts (excluding any interest which has accrued on those debts to the date of sequestration),
- (g) ordinary debts (that is to say, debts which are neither secured debts nor debts mentioned in any other paragraph of this subsection),
- (h) interest, between the date of sequestration and the date of payment of the debt, at the rate specified in subsection (10) on—
  - (i) the ordinary preferred debts,
  - (ii) the secondary preferred debts, and
  - (iii) the ordinary debts,
- (i) any postponed debt.

(2) In this Act—

"preferred debt" means a debt listed in Part 1 of schedule 3 of this Act,
"ordinary preferred debt" means a debt within any of paragraphs 1 to 6 of that Part, and
"secondary preferred debt" means a debt within paragraph 7 or 8 of that Part.

(3) Part 2 of that schedule has effect for the interpretation of Part 1 of that schedule.

(4) In this Act, "postponed debt" means—
(a) a loan made to the debtor, in consideration of a share of the profits in the debtor's business, which is postponed under section 3 of the Partnership Act 1890 to the claims of other creditors,
(b) a loan made to the debtor by the debtor's spouse or civil partner, or
(c) a creditor's right to—
(i) anything vesting in the trustee by virtue of a successful challenge under section 98, or
(ii) the proceeds of sale of anything so vesting.
(5) A debt falling within any of paragraphs (c) to (i) of subsection (1) has the same priority as any other debt falling within the same paragraph and, where the funds of the estate are inadequate to enable the debts mentioned in the paragraph in question to be paid in full, those debts are to abate in equal proportions.
(6) Any surplus remaining after all the debts mentioned in this section have been paid in full must be made over to the debtor or the debtor's successors or assignees.
(7) In subsection (6), "surplus"—
(a) includes any kind of estate, but
(b) does not include any unclaimed dividend.
(8) Subsection (6) is subject to [Article 49 of the EU] insolvency proceedings regulation (which provides that any surplus in secondary proceedings is to be transferred to main proceedings).
(9) Nothing in this section affects—
(a) any right of a secured creditor which is preferable to the rights of the trustee,
(b) any preference of the holder of a lien over a title deed, or other document, which has been delivered to the trustee in accordance with a requirement under section 108(5).
(10) The rate of interest referred to in paragraph (h) of subsection (1) is whichever is the greater of—
(a) the prescribed rate at the date of sequestration, and
(b) the rate applicable to that debt apart from the sequestration.

NOTES

Commencement: 30 November 2016.

Sub-s (8): words in square brackets substituted for original words "Article 35 of the EC" by the Insolvency (Regulation (EU) 2015/848) (Miscellaneous Amendments) (Scotland) Regulations 2017, SSI 2017/210, regs 4(1), (11), 9, as from 26 June 2017, except in relation to proceedings opened before that date.

Regulations: the Bankruptcy (Scotland) Regulations 2016, SSI 2016/397 at **[16.401]**.

[5.327]
130 Accounting periods

(1) The trustee in the sequestration must make up accounts of the trustee's intromissions with the debtor's estate in respect of each accounting period.
(2) In this Act, "accounting period" is to be construed as follows—
(a) the first accounting period is the period of 12 months, or such shorter period as may be determined or agreed in accordance with subsection (5), either period beginning with the date on which sequestration is awarded, and
(b) any subsequent accounting period is the period of 12 months beginning when its immediately preceding accounting period ends.
(3) But—
(a) paragraph (a) of subsection (2) is subject to subsection (4), and
(b) paragraph (b) of subsection (2) is subject to the exception that—
(i) in a case where AiB is not the trustee, the trustee and the commissioners (or, if there are no commissioners, the trustee and AiB) agree, or
(ii) in a case where AiB is the trustee, the trustee determines,
an accounting period is to be some other period beginning when its immediately preceding accounting period ends, it is that other period.
(4) Where the trustee was appointed under section 54(1) as interim trustee in the sequestration, the first accounting period is—
(a) the period—
(i) beginning with the date of the appointment as interim trustee, and
(ii) ending on the date 12 months after that on which sequestration is awarded, or
(b) such shorter period as may be determined or agreed in accordance with subsection (5).
(5) This subsection applies where the trustee considers that the funds of the debtor's estate are sufficient to pay a dividend in accordance with section 131(1) in respect of—
(a) in a case where the trustee is AiB, a shorter period of not less than 6 months determined by AiB, and
(b) in any other case, a shorter period of not less than 6 months agreed—
(i) between the trustee and the commissioners, or
(ii) if there are no commissioners, between the trustee and AiB.
(6) An agreement under sub-paragraph (i), or determination under sub-paragraph (ii), of subsection (3)(b)—
(a) may be made in respect of one accounting period or more,
(b) may be made before the beginning of the accounting period in relation to which it has effect and, in any event, is not to have effect unless made before the day on which that accounting period would, but for the agreement or determination, have ended, and
(c) may provide for different accounting periods to be of different duration.

NOTES

Commencement: 30 November 2016.

[5.328]

131 Distribution in accordance with accounting periods

(1) The trustee in the sequestration must pay, under section 135(1), a dividend out of the estate in respect of each accounting period—

(a) if the funds of the debtor's estate are sufficient, and

(b) after making allowance for future contingencies.

(2) But subsection (1) is subject to the following subsections.

(3) The trustee may pay—

(a) the debts mentioned in paragraphs (a) to (d) of section 129(1), other than the trustee's own remuneration, at any time,

(b) the preferred debts at any time but only with the consent of the commissioners or, if there are no commissioners, of AiB.

(4) If, in respect of an accounting period, the trustee—

(a) is not ready to pay a dividend, or

(b) considers it would be inappropriate to pay a dividend because the expense of doing so would be disproportionate to the amount of the dividend,

the trustee may, with the consent of the commissioners or, if there are no commissioners, of AiB, postpone the payment to a date not later than the time for payment of a dividend in respect of the next accounting period.

(5) Where a review or appeal is made under section 127 as respects the acceptance or rejection of a creditor's claim, the trustee must, at the time of payment of dividends and until the review or appeal is determined, set aside an amount which would be sufficient, if the determination in the review or appeal were to provide for the creditor's claim being accepted in full, to pay a dividend in respect of that claim.

(6) Subsection (7) applies where a creditor—

(a) has failed to produce evidence in support of the creditor's claim earlier than 8 weeks before the end of an accounting period on being required to do so under section 123(1), and

(b) has given a reason for such failure which is acceptable to the trustee.

(7) The trustee must set aside, for such time as is reasonable to enable the creditor to produce that evidence or any other evidence that will enable the trustee to be satisfied under that section, an amount which would be sufficient, were the claim accepted in full, to pay a dividend in respect of that claim.

(8) Where a creditor submits a claim to the trustee later than 8 weeks before the end of an accounting period but more than 8 weeks before the end of a subsequent accounting period in respect of which, after making allowance for future contingencies, funds are available for the payment of a dividend, the trustee must, if the trustee accepts the claim in whole or in part, pay to the creditor—

(a) the same dividend as has, or dividends as have, already been paid to creditors of the same class in respect of any accounting period or periods, and

(b) whatever dividend may be payable to the creditor in respect of the subsequent accounting period mentioned above.

(9) Paragraph (a) of subsection (8) is without prejudice to any dividend which has already been paid.

(10) In the declaration of, and payment of, a dividend, a payment must not be made more than once by virtue of the same debt.

(11) Any dividend paid in respect of a claim must be paid to the creditor.

NOTES

Commencement: 30 November 2016.

Procedure after end of accounting period

[5.329]

132 Submission of accounts and scheme of division

(1) Within 2 weeks after the end of an accounting period the trustee in the sequestration must, in respect of that period, submit to the commissioners (or, if there are no commissioners, to AiB))—

(a) the trustee's accounts of the trustee's intromissions with the estate of the debtor for audit and, where funds are available after making allowance for future contingencies, a scheme of division of the divisible funds, and

(b) a claim for the outlays reasonably incurred by the trustee and for the trustee's remuneration.

(2) Where documents mentioned in subsection (1) are submitted to the commissioners, the trustee must send a copy of them to AiB.

(3) All accounts in respect of legal services incurred by the trustee are, before they are paid by the trustee, to be submitted for taxation to the auditor of the court before which the sequestration is pending.

(4) But subsection (3) is subject to subsection (5).

(5) The trustee may pay the account without submitting it for taxation where—

(a) any such account has been agreed between the trustee and the person entitled to payment in respect of that account,

(b) the trustee is not an associate of that person, and

(c) the commissioners have (or, if there are no commissioners, AiB has) determined that the account need not be submitted for taxation.

(6) This section and sections 133 to 135 do not apply where AiB is the trustee in the sequestration.

NOTES

Commencement: 30 November 2016.

[5.330]

133 Audit of accounts and determination as to outlays and remuneration payable to trustee

(1) Within 6 weeks after the end of an accounting period—

(a) the commissioners (or, as the case may be, AiB)—

(i) may audit the accounts, and

(ii) must issue a determination fixing the amount of the outlays and the remuneration payable to the trustee in the sequestration, and

(b) the trustee must make the audited accounts, scheme of division and that determination available for inspection by the debtor and the creditors.

(2) The basis for fixing the amount of the remuneration payable to the trustee may be a commission calculated by reference to the value of the debtor's estate which has been realised by the trustee.

(3) But there is in any event to be taken into account—

(a) the work which, having regard to that value, was reasonably undertaken by the trustee, and

(b) the extent of the trustee's responsibilities in administering the debtor's estate.

(4) In fixing the amount of such remuneration in respect of any accounting period, the commissioners (or, as the case may be, AiB) may take into account any adjustment which the commissioners or AiB may wish to make in the amount of remuneration fixed in respect of any earlier accounting period.

NOTES

Commencement: 30 November 2016.

[5.331]

134 Appeal against determination as to outlays and remuneration payable to trustee

(1) Not later than 8 weeks after the end of an accounting period the trustee in the sequestration, the debtor or any creditor may appeal against a determination issued under section 133(1)(a)(ii)—

(a) to AiB where it is a determination of the commissioners, and

(b) to the sheriff where it is a determination of AiB.

(2) But subsection (1) is subject to subsection (4).

(3) The determination of AiB in an appeal under paragraph (a) of subsection (1) is appealable to the sheriff (whose decision on an appeal under this subsection or under paragraph (b) of subsection (1) is final).

(4) The debtor may appeal under subsection (1) if, and only if, the debtor satisfies AiB, or as the case may be the sheriff, that the debtor has, or is likely to have, a pecuniary interest in the outcome of the appeal.

(5) Before the debtor or a creditor appeals under subsection (1) or (3), the debtor or, as the case may be, the creditor must give notice to the trustee of the intention to appeal.

NOTES

Commencement: 30 November 2016.

[5.332]

135 Further provision as to procedure after end of accounting period

(1) The trustee in the sequestration must pay to the creditors their dividends in accordance with the scheme of division on—

(a) the expiry of the 8 weeks mentioned in section 134(1), or

(b) if there is an appeal under that subsection, on the final determination of the last such appeal.

(2) There must be deposited by the trustee, in an appropriate bank or institution, any dividend—

(a) allocated to a creditor but not cashed or uplifted, or

(b) dependent on a claim in respect of which an amount has been set aside under subsection (5) or (7) of section 131.

(3) If a creditor's claim is revalued, the trustee may—

(a) in paying any dividend to that creditor, make such adjustment to it as the trustee considers necessary to take account of that revaluation, or

(b) require the creditor to repay to the trustee the whole or part of a dividend already paid to the creditor.

NOTES

Commencement: 30 November 2016.

[5.333]

136 Procedure after end of accounting period where Accountant in Bankruptcy is trustee

(1) In any case where AiB is the trustee in the sequestration, AiB must at the end of each accounting period—

(a) prepare accounts of AiB's intromissions with the estate of the debtor, and

(b) make a determination of AiB's fees and outlays calculated in accordance with regulations under section 205.

(2) Such accounts and determination must be available for inspection by the debtor and the creditors by not later than 6 weeks after the end of the accounting period to which they relate.

(3) In making a determination as mentioned in subsection (1), AiB may take into account any adjustment which AiB may wish to make in the amount of AiB's remuneration fixed in respect of any earlier accounting period.
(4) Not later than 8 weeks after the end of an accounting period the debtor or any creditor may appeal to the sheriff against AiB's determination.
(5) But subsection (4) is subject to subsection (7).
(6) The decision of the sheriff on an appeal under subsection (4) is final.
(7) The debtor may appeal under subsection (4) if, and only if, the debtor satisfies the sheriff that the debtor has, or is likely to have, a pecuniary interest in the outcome of the appeal.
(8) Before the debtor or a creditor appeals under subsection (4), the debtor or as the case may be the creditor must give notice to AiB of the intention to appeal.
(9) On the expiry of the 8 weeks mentioned in subsection (4), AiB must pay to the creditors their dividends in accordance with the scheme of division.
(10) There must be deposited by AiB, in an appropriate bank or institution, any dividend—
(a) allocated to a creditor but not cashed or uplifted, or
(b) dependent on a claim in respect of which an amount has been set aside under subsection (5) or (7) of section 131.
(11) If a creditor's claim is revalued, AiB may—
(a) in paying any dividend to that creditor, make such adjustment to it as AiB considers necessary to take account of that revaluation, or
(b) require the creditor to repay to AiB the whole or part of a dividend already paid to the creditor.

NOTES
Commencement: 30 November 2016.

PART 11
DISCHARGE

Discharge of debtor

[5.334]
137 Discharge of debtor where Accountant in Bankruptcy not trustee
(1) This section applies where AiB is not the trustee.
(2) AiB may, by granting a certificate of discharge in the prescribed form, discharge the debtor at any time after the date which is 12 months after the date on which sequestration is awarded.
(3) Before deciding whether to discharge the debtor under subsection (2), AiB must—
(a) consider the report provided by the trustee under subsection (4), and
(b) take into account any representations received during the 28 days mentioned in subsection (6)(b).
(4) The trustee must prepare and send a report to AiB—
(a) without delay after the date which is 10 months after the date on which sequestration is awarded, and
(b) if the debtor is not otherwise discharged, before sending to AiB the documentation referred to in section 148(1)(b)(i).
(5) The report must include—
(a) information about—
(i) the debtor's assets, liabilities, financial affairs and business affairs,
(ii) the debtor's conduct in relation to those assets, liabilities and affairs,
(iii) the sequestration, and
(iv) the debtor's conduct in the course of the sequestration,
(b) a statement of whether, in the opinion of the trustee, the debtor has as at the date of the report—
(i) complied with any debtor contribution order,
(ii) co-operated with the trustee in accordance with section 215,
(iii) complied with the statement of undertakings,
(iv) made a full and fair surrender of the debtor's estate,
(v) made a full disclosure of all claims which the debtor is entitled to make against any other persons, and
(vi) delivered to the trustee every document under the debtor's control relating to the debtor's estate, financial affairs or business affairs, and
(c) a statement of whether the trustee has, as at the date that the report is sent to AiB, carried out all of the trustee's functions in accordance with section 50.
(6) The trustee must, at the same time as sending a report to AiB under this section, give to the debtor and to every creditor known to the trustee—
(a) a copy of the report, and
(b) a notice informing the recipient that the recipient has a right to make representations to AiB in relation to the report within 28 days beginning with the day on which the notice is given.
(7) A discharge under this section is not to take effect before the expiry of 14 days beginning with the day of notification of the decision.

NOTES
Commencement: 30 November 2016.
Regulations: the Bankruptcy (Scotland) Regulations 2016, SSI 2016/397 at **[16.401]**.

[5.335]
138 Discharge of debtor where Accountant in Bankruptcy trustee
(1) This section applies where AiB is the trustee.
(2) AiB may, by granting a certificate of discharge in the prescribed form, discharge the debtor at any time after the date which is 12 months after the date on which sequestration is awarded.
(3) AiB must, as soon as practicable after the date which is 12 months after the date on which sequestration is awarded—
(a) decide whether to discharge the debtor under subsection (2),
(b) notify the debtor and every creditor known to AiB of that decision, and
(c) send a report to those persons.
(4) The report must give an account of—
(a) the debtor's assets, liabilities, financial affairs and business affairs,
(b) the debtor's conduct in relation to those assets, liabilities and affairs,
(c) the sequestration, and
(d) the debtor's conduct in the course of the sequestration, including compliance with the statement of undertakings.
(5) Subsection (6) applies where—
(a) AiB refuses to discharge the debtor under subsection (2), and
(b) the debtor is not otherwise discharged.
(6) AiB must, as soon as practicable after the date which is 12 months after the date of the refusal—
(a) decide whether to discharge or refuse to discharge the debtor under subsection (2),
(b) notify the debtor and every creditor known to AiB of that decision, and
(c) send a report giving an account of the matters mentioned in subsection (4) to those persons.
(7) Discharge under this section is not to take effect before the expiry of 14 days beginning with the day of notification of the decision to discharge.

NOTES
Commencement: 30 November 2016.
Regulations: the Bankruptcy (Scotland) Regulations 2016, SSI 2016/397 at **[16.401]**.

[5.336]
139 Discharge of debtor: review and appeal
(1) The trustee or the debtor may apply to AiB for a review of a decision to refuse to discharge the debtor under section 137(2) or 138(2).
(2) Any creditor may apply to AiB for a review of a decision to discharge the debtor under section 137(2) or 138(2).
(3) Any application under subsection (1) or (2) must be made within 14 days beginning with the day of the notification of the decision in question.
(4) If an application is made under subsection (2), the discharge is suspended until the determination of the review by AiB.
(5) If an application is made under subsection (1) or (2), AiB must—
(a) take into account any representations made by an interested person within 21 days beginning with the day on which the application is made, and
(b) confirm or revoke the decision within 28 days beginning with that day.
(6) The debtor, the trustee or any creditor may appeal to the sheriff, against any decision of AiB under subsection (5)(b), within 14 days beginning with the day of the decision.

NOTES
Commencement: 30 November 2016.

[5.337]
140 Discharge of debtor to whom section 2(2) applies
(1) Where section 2(2) applies to a debtor, the debtor is discharged on the date which is 6 months after the date on which sequestration is awarded.
(2) A debtor may, following discharge, apply to AiB for a certificate of discharge in the prescribed form.

NOTES
Commencement: 30 November 2016.
Regulations: the Bankruptcy (Scotland) Regulations 2016, SSI 2016/397 at **[16.401]**.

[5.338]
141 Deferral of discharge where debtor cannot be traced
(1) Subsection (2) applies where the trustee—
(a) having made reasonable inquiries, is unable to ascertain the whereabouts of the debtor, and
(b) as a result is unable to carry out the trustee's functions in accordance with section 50.
(2) The trustee must—
(a) notify the debtor by sending to the last known address of the debtor a deferral notice in the prescribed form,
(b) give a deferral notice to every creditor known to the trustee, and
(c) where the trustee is not AiB, apply in the prescribed form to AiB for a deferral.
(3) Any deferral application under subsection (2)(c) must be made by the trustee—
(a) no earlier than the date which is 8 months after the date on which sequestration is awarded, and

(b) no later than the date which is 10 months after the date on which sequestration is awarded.

(4) After receiving a deferral application, AiB must—

(a) take into account any representations made by an interested person within 14 days beginning with the day on which the application is made, and

(b) if satisfied of the matters mentioned in subsection (5), issue a certificate deferring discharge indefinitely.

(5) The matters are—

(a) that the trustee is unable to ascertain the whereabouts of the debtor, and

(b) it would not be reasonably practicable for the trustee to continue to search for the debtor.

(6) Where AiB is the trustee and has given a deferral notice in accordance with subsection (2)(b), AiB must—

(a) take into account any representations made by an interested person within 14 days beginning with the day on which the deferral notice is given, and

(b) if satisfied that it would not be reasonably practicable to continue to search for the debtor, issue a certificate deferring discharge indefinitely.

(7) Where a certificate is issued under subsection (4)(b) or (6)(b), AiB must make an appropriate entry in the register of insolvencies.

NOTES

Commencement: 30 November 2016.

Regulations: the Bankruptcy (Scotland) Regulations 2016, SSI 2016/397 at **[16.401]**.

[5.339]

142 Debtor not traced: new trustee

(1) This section applies where a certificate is issued under section 141(4)(b).

(2) The trustee may apply to AiB, in the prescribed form, for authority to resign office.

(3) An application under subsection (2) must include details of every creditor known to the trustee.

(4) An application under subsection (2) may not be made—

(a) if, after the certificate is issued, the trustee ascertains the whereabouts of the debtor or the debtor makes contact with the trustee, or

(b) after the date which is 6 months after that on which the certificate is issued.

(5) Where an application is made under subsection (2), AiB must issue to the trustee who made the application a notice in the prescribed form granting the application.

(6) Where a notice is issued under subsection (5)—

(a) AiB is deemed to be the trustee,

(b) AiB must notify every creditor known to AiB that AiB is deemed to be the trustee,

(c) the former trustee is not entitled to recover, other than by a claim in the final distribution of the debtor's estate, outlays and remuneration payable under sections 132 and 133, and

(d) subsections (9) to (13) of section 69 apply in relation to the appointment of AiB as the new trustee as they apply in relation to the appointment of a new trustee under that section.

NOTES

Commencement: 30 November 2016.

Regulations: the Bankruptcy (Scotland) Regulations 2016, SSI 2016/397 at **[16.401]**.

[5.340]

143 Debtor not traced: subsequent debtor contact

(1) This section applies where—

(a) a certificate is issued under section 141(4)(b) or (6)(b), and

(b) the trustee ascertains the whereabouts of the debtor or the debtor makes contact with the trustee.

(2) Where AiB is the trustee, AiB may discharge the debtor at any time after the date which is 12 months after that on which—

(a) the whereabouts of the debtor were ascertained, or

(b) the debtor made contact with the trustee.

(3) Where AiB is not the trustee, the trustee must prepare and send a report to AiB without delay after the date which is 10 months after the earlier of—

(a) the date on which the whereabouts of the debtor were ascertained by the trustee, and

(b) the date on which the debtor made contact with the trustee.

(4) If the trustee sends a report to AiB under subsection (3)—

(a) the report must include the matters which, in a report sent to AiB, are included in accordance with subsection (5) of section 137, and

(b) subsection (6) of that section applies to a report sent under this section as it applies to a report sent in accordance with subsection (4) of that section.

(5) After receiving a report under subsection (3), AiB may discharge the debtor by granting a certificate of discharge in the prescribed form.

(6) Before deciding whether to discharge the debtor under subsection (5), AiB must—

(a) consider the report prepared under subsection (3), and

(b) take into account any representations received during the 28 days mentioned in subsection (6)(b) of section 137 (as applied in accordance with subsection (4)).

(7) Discharge under subsection (2) or (5) is not to take effect before the expiry of 14 days beginning with the day of notification of the decision to discharge.

(8) Discharge under subsection (2) or (5) is deemed for the purposes of section 145 to have been given under section 137(2).

NOTES

Commencement: 30 November 2016.

[5.341]

144 Subsequent debtor contact: review and appeal

(1) The debtor may apply to AiB for a review of a decision under section 143(2) or (5) to refuse to discharge the debtor.

(2) Any creditor may apply to AiB for a review of a decision under section 143(2) or (5) to discharge the debtor.

(3) Any application under subsection (1) or (2) must be made within 14 days beginning with the day of notification of the decision in question.

(4) If an application for a review under subsection (2) is made, the discharge is suspended until the determination of that review by AiB.

(5) If an application for a review under subsection (1) or (2) is made, AiB must—

(a) take into account any representations made by an interested person within 21 days beginning with the day on which the application is made, and

(b) confirm or revoke the decision within 28 days beginning with the day on which the application is made.

(6) The debtor, the trustee or any creditor may appeal to the sheriff against any decision of AiB under subsection (5)(b) within 14 days beginning with the day of the decision.

NOTES

Commencement: 30 November 2016.

[5.342]

145 Effect of discharge under section 137, 138 or 140

(1) On the discharge of the debtor under section 137, 138 or 140 the debtor is discharged of all debts and obligations contracted by the debtor, or for which the debtor was liable, at the date of sequestration.

(2) Subsection (1) is subject to subsections (3) and (5).

(3) The debtor is not discharged by virtue of subsection (1) from—

(a) any liability to pay a fine or other penalty due to the Crown,

(b) any liability to pay a fine imposed in a justice of the peace court (or a district court),

(c) any liability under a compensation order (within the meaning of section 249 of the Criminal Procedure (Scotland) Act 1995,

(d) any liability to forfeiture of a sum of money deposited in court under section 24(6) of the Criminal Procedure (Scotland) Act 1995,

(e) any liability incurred by reason of fraud or breach of trust,

(f) any obligation to pay—

(i) aliment, or any sum of an alimentary nature, under any enactment or rule of law, or

(ii) any periodical allowance payable on divorce by virtue of a court order or under an obligation, or

(g) the obligation imposed on the debtor by section 215.

(4) The obligations mentioned in paragraph (f) of subsection (3) do not include—

(a) aliment, or a periodical allowance, which could be included in the amount of a creditor's claim under paragraph 2 of schedule 2, or

(b) child support maintenance within the meaning of the Child Support Act 1991 which was unpaid in respect of any period before the date of sequestration of—

(i) any person by whom it was due to be paid, or

(ii) any employer by whom it was, or was due to be, deducted under section 31(5) of that Act.

(5) The discharge of the debtor under section 137, 138 or 140 does not affect any right of a secured creditor for an obligation in respect of which the debtor has been discharged, to enforce the security in respect of that obligation.

(6) In subsection (3)(a), the reference to a fine or other penalty due to the Crown includes a reference to a confiscation order made under Part 2, 3 or 4 of the Proceeds of Crime Act 2002.

(7) Nothing in this section affects regulations in relation to which section 73B of the Education (Scotland) Act 1980 (regulations relating to student loans) applies.

NOTES

Commencement: 30 November 2016.

[5.343]

146 Discharge under section 140: conditions

(1) This section applies where a debtor is discharged under section 140.

(2) During the relevant period the debtor must comply with the condition in subsection (3) before the debtor, either alone or jointly with another person, obtains credit—

(a) to the extent of £2,000 (or such other sum as may be prescribed) or more, or

(b) of any amount where, at the time of obtaining credit, the debtor has debts amounting to £1,000 (or such other sum as may be prescribed) or more.

(3) The condition is that the debtor must inform the person who is providing credit to the debtor (or, as the case may be, jointly to the debtor and another person) that the debtor is required to comply with the conditions in this section.

(4) During the relevant period, the debtor must not engage (whether directly or indirectly) in a business under a name other than that to which the discharge relates unless the debtor complies with the condition in subsection (5).

(5) The condition is that the debtor must inform any person with whom the debtor enters into any business transaction of the name of the business to which the discharge relates.

(6) In this section, "relevant period" means the 6 months beginning with the date of discharge.

NOTES

Commencement: 30 November 2016.

[5.344]

147 Section 146: sanctions

(1) If a debtor fails to comply with the requirement imposed by subsection (2) or (4) of section 146, that section applies in relation to the debtor as if the relevant period were the 12 months beginning with the date of discharge.

(2) If a debtor fails to comply with the requirement imposed by subsection (2) or (4) of section 146 during the period when the section applies in relation to the debtor by virtue of subsection (1), the debtor commits an offence.

(3) A debtor who commits an offence under subsection (2) is liable on summary conviction—

- (a) to a fine not exceeding the statutory maximum,
- (b) to imprisonment for—
  - (i) a term not exceeding 3 months, or
  - (ii) if the person has previously been convicted of an offence inferring dishonest appropriation of property (or an attempt at such appropriation), a term not exceeding 6 months, or
- (c) both to such fine and to such imprisonment.

(4) A debtor who commits an offence under subsection (2) is liable on conviction on indictment—

- (a) to a fine,
- (b) to imprisonment for a term not exceeding 2 years, or
- (c) both to such fine and to such imprisonment.

NOTES

Commencement: 30 November 2016.

Discharge of trustee

[5.345]

148 Discharge of trustee

(1) After the trustee in the sequestration has made a final division of the debtor's estate and has inserted the trustee's final audited accounts in the sederunt book, the trustee—

- (a) must pay to AiB any unclaimed dividends and unapplied balances,
- (b) on that being done—
  - (i) must send to AiB the sederunt book (in the format specified by subsection (2)) and a copy of the audited accounts, and
  - (ii) may at the same time apply to AiB for a certificate of discharge.

(2) The trustee must send an electronic version of the sederunt book in such format as AiB may from time to time direct.

(3) AiB must deposit any unclaimed dividends and any unapplied balances paid to AiB under subsection (1)(a) in an appropriate bank or institution.

(4) The trustee must send, to the debtor and to all the creditors known to the trustee, notice of any application under subsection (1)(b)(ii) and must inform the debtor and such creditors—

- (a) that written representations relating to the application may be made by them to AiB within 14 days after the notification,
- (b) that the sederunt book is available for inspection following a request made to AiB and contains the audited accounts of, and scheme of division in, the sequestration, and
- (c) of the effect mentioned in subsection (7).

(5) On the expiry of the 14 days mentioned in subsection (4)(a), AiB, after examining the documents sent to AiB and considering any representations duly made to AiB, must—

- (a) grant or refuse to grant the certificate of discharge, and
- (b) notify accordingly—
  - (i) the trustee,
  - (ii) the debtor, and
  - (iii) all creditors who made such representations.

(6) Any certificate of discharge granted under subsection (5)—

- (a) must take effect after the expiry of the 14 days mentioned in section 149(2), and
- (b) has no effect if an application for review is made under section 149(1).

(7) The grant of a certificate of discharge under this section has the effect of discharging the trustee from all liability (other than any liability arising from fraud)—

- (a) to the debtor, or
- (b) to the creditors,

in respect of any act or omission of the trustee in exercising the functions conferred on the trustee by this Act (including, where the trustee was also the interim trustee, the functions of interim trustee).

(8) This section and section 149 do not apply in any case where AiB is trustee.

NOTES

Commencement: 30 November 2016.

[5.346]

149 Further provision as regards discharge of trustee

(1) The trustee, the debtor or any creditor who has made representations under subsection (4)(a) of section 148 may apply to AiB for a review of a determination under subsection (5) of that section.

(2) Any application under subsection (1) must be made within 14 days beginning with the day of the determination.

(3) If an application for a review under subsection (1) is made, AiB must—

(a) take into account any representations made, within 21 days beginning with the day on which the application is made, by an interested person, and

(b) confirm, amend or revoke the determination (whether or not issuing a new certificate of discharge) within 28 days beginning with that day.

(4) Within 14 days after a decision under subsection (3)(b)—

(a) the trustee,

(b) the debtor, or

(c) any creditor who made representations under section 148(4)(a),

may appeal against the decision to the sheriff.

(5) If, on an appeal under subsection (4), the sheriff determines that a certificate of discharge which has been refused should be granted the sheriff must order AiB to grant it.

(6) The sheriff clerk must send AiB a copy of the sheriff's decree.

(7) The decision of the sheriff on an appeal under subsection (4) is final.

(8) Where a certificate of discharge is granted under section 148 or by virtue of this section, AiB must make an appropriate entry in—

(a) the register of insolvencies, and

(b) in the sederunt book.

(9) The provisions of this section apply (subject to any necessary modifications)—

(a) where a trustee has died, to the trustee's executor, or

(b) where a trustee has resigned office or been removed from office, to that trustee,

as they apply to a trustee who has made a final division of the debtor's estate in accordance with the preceding provisions of this Act.

NOTES

Commencement: 30 November 2016.

[5.347]

150 Unclaimed dividends

(1) Any person producing evidence of that person's right may apply to AiB to receive a dividend deposited under section 148(3) or 151(2), if the application is made not later than 7 years after the date of deposit.

(2) If AiB is satisfied of that person's right to the dividend, AiB must authorise the bank or institution in which the deposit was made to pay to the person the amount of the dividend and of any interest which has accrued on the dividend.

(3) AiB is, at the expiry of 7 years from the date of deposit of any unclaimed dividend or unapplied balance under section 148(3) or 151(2), to hand over the deposit receipt or other voucher relating to the dividend or balance to the Scottish Ministers who on that being done are entitled to payment of the amount due (principal and interest) from the bank or institution in which the deposit was made.

NOTES

Commencement: 30 November 2016.

[5.348]

151 Discharge of Accountant in Bankruptcy

(1) This section applies where AiB has acted as the trustee in the sequestration.

(2) AiB must deposit any unclaimed dividends and any unapplied balances in an appropriate bank or institution.

(3) AiB must send to the debtor and to all creditors known to AiB—

(a) a determination of AiB's fees and outlays calculated in accordance with regulations under section 205,

(b) a notice in writing stating—

(i) that AiB has commenced the procedure under this Act leading to discharge in respect of AiB's actings as trustee,

(ii) that the sederunt book relating to the sequestration is available for inspection following a request made to AiB,

(iii) that an application for review may be made under subsection (4),

(iv) that an appeal may be made to the sheriff under subsection (7), and

(v) the effect of subsections (9) and (10).

(4) The debtor or any creditor may apply to AiB for review of the discharge of AiB in respect of AiB's actings as trustee.

(5) Any application under subsection (4) must be made within 14 days beginning with the day on which notice is sent under subsection (3)(b).

(6) If an application under subsection (4) is made, AiB must—
(a) take into account any representations made by an interested person within 21 days beginning with the day on which the application is made, and
(b) confirm or revoke the discharge within 28 days beginning with that day.
(7) The debtor or any creditor may, within 14 days beginning with the day on which a decision is made by AiB under subsection (6)(b), appeal to the sheriff against that decision.
(8) The decision of the sheriff on an appeal under subsection (7) is final.
(9) Subsection (10) applies where—
(a) the requirements of this section have been complied with, and
(b) no appeal is made under subsection (7) or such an appeal is made but is refused as regards the discharge of AiB.
(10) AiB is discharged from all liability (other than any liability arising from fraud)—
(a) to the debtor, or
(b) to the creditors,
in respect of any act or omission of AiB in exercising the functions of trustee in the sequestration (including, where the trustee was also the interim trustee, the functions of interim trustee).

NOTES
Commencement: 30 November 2016.

PART 12
ASSETS DISCOVERED AFTER DISCHARGE OF TRUSTEE

[5.349]
152 Assets discovered after discharge of trustee: appointment of trustee
(1) This section applies where—
(a) the trustee is discharged—
(i) under section 148,
(ii) by virtue of section 149, or
(iii) under section 151, and
(b) after that discharge but within 5 years beginning with the date on which sequestration is awarded, the trustee or AiB becomes aware of any newly identified estate with a value of not less than £1,000 (or such other sum as may be prescribed).
(2) In this section, "newly identified estate" means any part of the debtor's estate which—
(a) vested in the trustee in accordance with section 78 or 86, and
(b) was not, before the trustee was discharged, known to the trustee.
(3) AiB may—
(a) in a case where the trustee was discharged under section 148—
(i) on the application of the trustee who was discharged, reappoint that person as trustee on the debtor's estate, or
(ii) appoint AiB as trustee on that estate, or
(b) in a case where AiB was discharged under section 151, reappoint AiB as trustee on that estate.
(4) AiB may make an appointment or reappointment under subsection (3) only if, in the opinion of AiB, the value of the newly identified estate is likely to exceed the costs of—
(a) the appointment or reappointment, and
(b) the recovery, management, realisation and distribution of the newly identified estate.
(5) Where the trustee was discharged under section 148 and applies for reappointment under subsection (3)(a)(i), the discharged trustee must provide to AiB the information mentioned in subsection (8)(a) to (c).
(6) Where the trustee was discharged under section 148 and does not apply for reappointment under subsection (3)(a)(i), the discharged trustee must—
(a) provide AiB with details of any newly identified estate that the discharged trustee becomes aware of, where that estate has a value not less than the value mentioned in subsection (1), and
(b) if requested by AiB, provide AiB with the information mentioned in subsection (8)(b) and (c).
(7) Where AiB was discharged under section 151, AiB must record and consider the information mentioned in subsection (8).
(8) The information is—
(a) the estimated value of the newly identified estate,
(b) the reason why the newly identified estate forms part of the debtor's estate,
(c) the reason why the newly identified estate was not recovered,
(d) the estimated outlays and remuneration of the trustee following an appointment or reappointment under subsection (3), and
(e) the likely distribution under section 129 following such an appointment or reappointment.
(9) This section is without prejudice to any other right to take action following the discharge of the trustee.

NOTES
Commencement: 30 November 2016.

[5.350]
153 Assets discovered after discharge of trustee: notice
(1) AiB must notify the debtor and any other person AiB considers to have an interest where—
(a) an application is made under section 152(3)(a)(i), or
(b) AiB proposes to make an appointment or reappointment under section 152(3)(a)(ii) or (b).

(2) A notice under subsection (1) must inform the recipient that the recipient has a right to make representations to AiB, within 14 days beginning with the day on which the notice is given, in relation to the application or the proposed appointment or reappointment.

(3) Before making an appointment or reappointment under section 152, AiB must take into account any representations made by an interested person.

(4) If AiB makes an appointment or reappointment under section 152, AiB must as soon as is practicable notify the debtor of the appointment or reappointment.

(5) Any notice under subsection (4) must include information in relation to the debtor's duty, under section 215, to co-operate with the trustee.

NOTES

Commencement: 30 November 2016.

[5.351]

154 Assets discovered after discharge of trustee: appeal

Where AiB makes or refuses to make an appointment or reappointment under section 152, an interested person may, within 14 days after AiB's decision, appeal to the sheriff against that decision.

NOTES

Commencement: 30 November 2016.

PART 13
BANKRUPTCY RESTRICTIONS ORDERS AND INTERIM BANKRUPTCY RESTRICTIONS ORDERS

Bankruptcy restrictions orders

[5.352]

155 Bankruptcy restrictions order

(1) Where sequestration of a living debtor's estate is awarded, an order (to be known as a "bankruptcy restrictions order") in respect of the debtor may be made—

(a) by AiB, or

(b) on the application of AiB, by the sheriff.

(2) If AiB proposes to make a bankruptcy restrictions order, AiB must so notify the debtor.

(3) A notice under subsection (2) must inform the debtor that the debtor has a right to make representations to AiB in relation to the proposed bankruptcy restrictions order.

(4) Before making a bankruptcy restrictions order, AiB must take into account any representations made by the debtor.

NOTES

Commencement: 30 November 2016.

[5.353]

156 Grounds for making bankruptcy restrictions order

(1) A bankruptcy restrictions order must be made if AiB, or as the case may be the sheriff, thinks it appropriate having regard to the conduct, whether before or after the date of sequestration, of the debtor.

(2) AiB, or as the case may be the sheriff, is in particular to take into account any of the following kinds of behaviour on the part of the debtor—

(a) failing to keep records which account for a loss of property—

(i) by the debtor, or

(ii) by a business carried on by the debtor,

where the loss occurred in the period beginning 2 years before the date of presentation of the petition for sequestration, or as the case may be the date the debtor application was made, and ending with the date of the application for a bankruptcy restrictions order,

(b) failing to produce records of that kind on demand by—

(i) AiB,

(ii) the interim trustee, or

(iii) the trustee in the sequestration,

(c) failing to supply accurate information to an authorised person for the purpose of the granting under section 9 of a certificate for sequestration of the debtor's estate,

(d) making a gratuitous alienation, or any other alienation, for no consideration or for no adequate consideration, which a creditor has, under any rule of law, right to challenge,

(e) creating an unfair preference, or any other preference, which a creditor has, under any rule of law, right to challenge,

(f) making an excessive pension contribution,

(g) failing to supply goods or services which were wholly or partly paid for, where the failure has given rise to a claim submitted by a creditor under section 46 or 122,

(h) trading at a time before the date of sequestration when the debtor knew, or ought to have known, that the debtor was unable to meet the debtor's debts,

(i) incurring, before the date of sequestration, a debt which the debtor had no reasonable expectation of being able to pay,

(j) failing to account satisfactorily to the sheriff, AiB, the interim trustee or the trustee, for—

(i) a loss of property, or

(ii) an insufficiency of property to meet the debtor's debts,
(k) carrying on any gambling, speculation or extravagance—
(i) which may have contributed materially to, or increased the extent of, the debtor's debts, or
(ii) which took place between the date of presentation of the petition for sequestration, or as the case may be the date the debtor application was made, and the date on which sequestration is awarded,
(l) neglect of business affairs, being neglect of a kind which may have contributed materially to, or increased the extent of, the debtor's debts,
(m) fraud or breach of trust,
(n) failing to co-operate with—
(i) AiB,
(ii) the interim trustee, or
(iii) the trustee in the sequestration.

(3) AiB, or as the case may be the sheriff, must in particular also consider whether the debtor—
(a) has previously been sequestrated, and
(b) remained undischarged from that sequestration at any time during the 5 years ending with the date of the sequestration to which the application relates.

(4) For the purposes of subsection (2)—
"excessive pension contribution" is to be construed in accordance with section 101, and
"gratuitous alienation" means an alienation challengeable under section 98.

NOTES
Commencement: 30 November 2016.

[5.354]
157 Bankruptcy restrictions order: application of section 218(13)

(1) Where—
(a) AiB thinks it appropriate, AiB may, or
(b) as the case may be, the sheriff thinks it appropriate, the sheriff may,
specify in a bankruptcy restrictions order that section 218(13) is to apply to the debtor, during the period the debtor is subject to the order, as if the debtor were a debtor within the meaning of section 219(2)(a).

(2) But for the purposes of subsection (1), section 219(2) has effect as if, for paragraph (c) of that section, there were substituted—

"(c) the "relevant information" about the status of the debtor is the information that (as the case may be)—
(i) the debtor is subject to a bankruptcy restrictions order, or
(ii) where the debtor's estate has been sequestrated and the debtor has not been discharged, that fact.".

NOTES
Commencement: 30 November 2016.

[5.355]
158 Timing for making a bankruptcy restrictions order

(1) AiB must make, or apply to the sheriff for, any bankruptcy restrictions order within the period which begins with the date of sequestration and ends with the date on which the debtor's discharge becomes effective.

(2) But subsection (1) is subject to subsection (3).

(3) After the end of the period referred to in subsection (1), AiB may—
(a) make a bankruptcy restrictions order, or
(b) make an application for a bankruptcy restrictions order,
with the permission of the sheriff.

NOTES
Commencement: 30 November 2016.

[5.356]
159 Duration of bankruptcy restrictions order and application for revocation or variation

(1) A bankruptcy restrictions order—
(a) comes into force when made, and
(b) ceases to have effect at the end of a day specified, for the purposes of this paragraph, in the order.

(2) The day specified under subsection (1)(b)—
(a) in the case of an order made by AiB—
(i) must not be before the expiry of 2 years beginning with the day on which the order is made, but
(ii) must be within 5 years beginning with that day, and
(b) in the case of an order made by the sheriff—
(i) must not be before the expiry of the 5 years beginning with the day on which the order is made, but
(ii) must be within 15 years beginning with that day.

(3) On an application by the debtor, the person mentioned in subsection (4) may—
(a) revoke a bankruptcy restrictions order, or
(b) vary it.
(4) The person is, in the case of a bankruptcy restrictions order —
(a) made by AiB, AiB, and
(b) made by the sheriff, the sheriff.
(5) If an application under subsection (3) is made to AiB, AiB must—
(a) take into account any representations made, within 21 days beginning with the day on which the application is made, by an interested person, and
(b) confirm, revoke or vary the order within 28 days beginning with that day.
(6) The debtor may appeal to the sheriff against any decision of AiB under subsection (5)(b) within 14 days beginning with the date of the decision.
(7) The sheriff may—
(a) in determining such an appeal, or
(b) otherwise on an application by AiB,
make an order providing that the debtor may not make another application under subsection (3) for such period as may be specified in the order.
(8) Variation under subsection (3)(b) may include providing for such an order to cease to have effect at the end of a day earlier than that specified under subsection (1)(b).

NOTES

Commencement: 30 November 2016.

Interim bankruptcy restrictions orders

[5.357]

160 Interim bankruptcy restrictions orders

(1) Subsection (2) applies at any time—
(a) after AiB notifies the debtor under section 155(2) that AiB proposes to make a bankruptcy restrictions order, and
(b) before AiB decides whether to make the order.
(2) AiB may make an interim bankruptcy restrictions order if AiB thinks—
(a) that there are *prima facie* grounds to suggest that a bankruptcy restrictions order will be made, and
(b) that it is in the public interest to make such an order.
(3) Subsection (4) applies at any time between—
(a) the making of an application to the sheriff for a bankruptcy restrictions order, and
(b) the determination of that application.
(4) The sheriff may, on the application of AiB, make an interim bankruptcy restrictions order if the sheriff thinks—
(a) that there are *prima facie* grounds to suggest that the application for the bankruptcy restrictions order will be successful, and
(b) that it is in the public interest to make an interim bankruptcy restrictions order.
(5) An interim bankruptcy restrictions order—
(a) has the same effect as a bankruptcy restrictions order, and
(b) comes into force on being made.
(6) An interim bankruptcy restrictions order ceases to have effect—
(a) where it was made by AiB, on AiB deciding whether or not to make a bankruptcy restrictions order,
(b) where it was made by the sheriff, on the determination of the application for the bankruptcy restrictions order, or
(c) if the sheriff discharges it on the application of AiB or of the debtor.
(7) Where a bankruptcy restrictions order is made in respect of a debtor who is subject to an interim bankruptcy restrictions order, subsection (2) of section 159 has effect in relation to the bankruptcy restrictions order as if the reference in that subsection to the day the order is made were a reference to the day the interim bankruptcy restrictions order is made.

NOTES

Commencement: 30 November 2016.

Effect of recall of sequestration

[5.358]

161 Bankruptcy restrictions orders and interim bankruptcy restrictions orders: effect of recall of sequestration

(1) Where an award of sequestration of a debtor's estate is recalled under section 30(1)—
(a) the sheriff may revoke any bankruptcy restrictions order or interim bankruptcy restrictions order in force in respect of the debtor, and
(b) no new bankruptcy restrictions order or interim bankruptcy restrictions order may be made in respect of the debtor.
(2) Where the sheriff refuses to revoke, under subsection (1)(a), a bankruptcy restrictions order or interim bankruptcy restrictions order the debtor may, within 28 days after the date on which the award of sequestration is recalled, appeal to the Sheriff Appeal Court against the refusal.
(3) The decision of the Sheriff Appeal Court on an appeal under subsection (2) is final.
(4) Where an award of sequestration of a debtor's estate is recalled under section 34(1) or 35(6)—

(a) AiB may revoke any bankruptcy restrictions order or interim bankruptcy restrictions order in force in respect of the debtor, and
(b) no new bankruptcy restrictions order or interim bankruptcy restrictions order may be made in respect of the debtor.

(5) Where AiB refuses to revoke under subsection (4) a bankruptcy restrictions order or interim bankruptcy restrictions order, the debtor may apply to AiB for a review of the refusal.

(6) Any application under subsection (5) must be made within 14 days beginning with the day on which the award of sequestration is recalled.

(7) If an application under subsection (5) is made, AiB must—
(a) take into account any representations made by an interested person within 21 days beginning with the day on which the application is made, and
(b) confirm the refusal or revoke the order within 28 days beginning with that day.

(8) The debtor may appeal to the sheriff against any decision of AiB under subsection (7)(b) within 14 days beginning with the day of the decision.

(9) The decision of the sheriff on an appeal under subsection (8) is final.

NOTES

Commencement: 30 November 2016.

PART 14
VOLUNTARY TRUST DEEDS FOR CREDITORS

General

[5.359]
162 Voluntary trust deeds for creditors

Sections 163 to 193 and schedule 4 have effect in relation to voluntary trust deeds executed on or after the date on which this Part comes into force.

NOTES

Commencement: 30 November 2016.

Protected trust deeds: protected status

[5.360]
163 Protected status: general

(1) A trust deed has protected status (and is to be known as a "protected trust deed") where—
(a) the conditions set out in sections 164, 165, 166(2) (where it applies) and 167 to 170 are met, and
(b) the deed is registered under section 171(2) in the register of insolvencies.

(2) And it has that status from the date on which it is so registered (that date being, in this Part, referred to as the "date of protection").

NOTES

Commencement: 30 November 2016.

Conditions for protected status

[5.361]
164 Protected status: the debtor

(1) The debtor must be—
(a) a living individual who,
(b) a partnership which,
(c) a limited partnership (within the meaning of the Limited Partnerships Act 1907) which,
(d) a trust which,
(e) a corporate body which, or
(f) an unincorporated body which,

grants a trust deed for a single estate.

(2) The debtor must not be—
(a) a debtor whose estate has been sequestrated if the trustee in the sequestration has not been discharged under section 148 or 151, or
(b) an entity referred to in section 6(2).

(3) The total amount of the debtor's debts (including interest) as at the date on which the debtor grants the trust deed must be not less than £5,000.

NOTES

Commencement: 30 November 2016.

[5.362]
165 Protected status: the trustee

The trustee under the trust deed must be a person who would not be disqualified under section 49(3) to (5) from acting as the replacement trustee were the debtor's estate being sequestrated.

NOTES

Commencement: 30 November 2016.

[5.363]

166 Exclusion of a secured creditor from trust deed

(1) The conditions set out in subsection (2) apply where a secured creditor is, by virtue of an agreement such as is mentioned in paragraph (b)(ii) of the definition of "trust deed" in section 228(1) (in this Part referred to as "the trust deed definition"), excluded from a trust deed.

(2) Before the debtor grants the trust deed—

(a) the trustee must provide the debtor and the secured creditor with a valuation, made by a chartered surveyor or other suitably qualified person, of the dwellinghouse (or part) which is to be excluded from the estate conveyed as mentioned in paragraph (b)(i) of the trust deed definition,

(b) the debtor must, in such form as may be prescribed for the purposes of this paragraph, request obtaining the secured creditor's agreement not to claim under the trust deed for any of the debt in respect of which the security is held, and

(c) any agreement so obtained must be set out in such form as may be prescribed for the purposes of this paragraph.

NOTES

Commencement: 30 November 2016.

Regulations: the Protected Trust Deeds (Forms) (Scotland) Regulations 2016, SSI 2016/398 at **[16.438]**.

[5.364]

167 Statements in and advice regarding trust deed

(1) The trust deed must state—

(a) that, subject to any exclusion mentioned in paragraph (b)(i) of the trust deed definition, all of the debtor's estate (other than property listed in section 88(1) or which would be excluded under any other provision of this Act or of any other enactment from vesting in the trustee of a sequestrated estate) is conveyed to the trustee, and

(b) that the debtor agrees to convey to the trustee, for the benefit of creditors generally, any estate (wherever situated) which—

(i) is acquired by the debtor during the 4 years beginning with the date on which the trust deed is granted, and

(ii) would have been conveyed to the trustee by virtue of paragraph (a) had it been part of the debtor's estate on the date on which the trust deed was granted.

(2) Where the debtor's dwellinghouse, or part of the debtor's dwellinghouse, is excluded as mentioned in paragraph (b)(i) of the trust deed definition from the estate conveyed to the trustee, the trust deed must also include details—

(a) of any secured creditor who has agreed not to claim under the trust deed for any of the debt in respect of which the security is held, and

(b) of that debt.

(3) Before the debtor grants the trust deed—

(a) the trustee must advise the debtor that granting the deed may result—

(i) in the debtor's estate being sequestrated,

(ii) in the debtor's being refused credit, whether before or after the debtor's discharge under section 184,

(iii) subject to any exclusion mentioned in paragraph (b)(i) of the trust deed definition, in the debtor's not being able to remain in the debtor's current place of residence,

(iv) subject to any such exclusion, in the debtor's being required to relinquish property which the debtor owns,

(v) in the debtor's being required to make contributions from income for the benefit of creditors,

(vi) in damage to the debtor's business interests and employment prospects, and

(vii) in the fact of the debtor's having granted a trust deed becoming public information,

(b) the trustee must provide the debtor with a copy of a debt advice and information package, and

(c) the trustee and the debtor must both sign a statement to the effect that the trustee has fulfilled the duties referred to in this subsection.

NOTES

Commencement: 30 November 2016.

[5.365]

168 Payment of debtor's contribution

(1) The trust deed must state that the debtor is, during the payment period mentioned in subsection (2), to pay any contributions from income for the benefit of creditors (including, where the debtor is an individual, any contribution required by the common financial tool) at regular intervals.

(2) The payment period is—

(a) a period of 48 months beginning with the date on which the trust deed is granted,

(b) such period shorter than 48 months as is determined by the trustee, or

(c) such period longer than 48 months as is—

(i) determined by the trustee where there has been a period during which the debtor has not paid those contributions, or

(ii) agreed between the debtor and the trustee.

(3) The trustee may, under subsection (2)(b), determine a shorter payment period only if, in the trustee's opinion, payment of those contributions (from income or otherwise) during that period would allow distribution of the debtor's estate to meet in full the total amount, as at the date on which the debtor grants the trust deed, of the debtor's debts (including interest).

(4) Where the debtor is an individual, those contributions must be such as to result, over the payment period, in the payment of a sum less than the total amount, as at the date on which the debtor grants the trust deed, of the debtor's debts (including interest).

(5) In calculating those contributions for the purposes of subsections (1) and (4), the whole of the debtor's surplus income over the amount allowed for expenditure in the statement of the debtor's income and expenditure supplied under section 170(1)(d)(ii) must be applied.

NOTES

Commencement: 30 November 2016.

[5.366]

169 Notice in register of insolvencies

After the trust deed has been delivered to the trustee, the trustee must without delay send a notice in such form as may be prescribed for the purposes of this section to AiB for publication by registration in the register of insolvencies.

NOTES

Commencement: 30 November 2016.

Regulations: the Protected Trust Deeds (Forms) (Scotland) Regulations 2016, SSI 2016/398 at **[16.438]**.

[5.367]

170 Documents to be sent to creditors

(1) Not later than 7 days after the date of registration under section 169, the trustee must send to every creditor known to the trustee (other than any secured creditor who has, as mentioned in paragraph (b)(ii) of the trust deed definition, agreed not to claim under the trust deed for any of the debt in respect of which the security is held)—

(a) a copy of the trust deed,

(b) a copy of such form as may be prescribed for the purposes of a creditor making a statement of claim,

(c) a copy of the notice mentioned in section 169,

(d) a statement of the debtor's affairs, prepared by the trustee, containing—

(i) a list of the debtor's assets and liabilities,

(ii) a statement of the debtor's income and expenditure as at the date on which the trust deed was granted (being, where the debtor is a living individual, a statement in the [form prescribed for that purpose by the Protected Trust Deeds (Forms) (Scotland) Regulations 2016]),

(iii) a statement as to the extent to which those assets and that income will not vest in the trustee,

(iv) a statement as to whether, and if so on what basis, the [EU] insolvency proceedings regulation applies to the trust deed,

(v) if the [EU] insolvency proceedings regulation does apply to the trust deed, a statement as to whether the proceedings are main proceedings or territorial proceedings,

(vi) a statement as to whether the creditors are likely to be paid a dividend and the amount of the dividend that is expected to be paid,

(vii) if the case is one in which there is an exclusion such as is mentioned in paragraph (b)(i) of the trust deed definition, a statement by the trustee, on the basis of the information for the time being available to the trustee, as to what the effect of that exclusion is likely to be on any such dividend,

(viii) a statement that the trustee on request must provide a copy of any valuation held by the trustee which has been made by a third party and which relates to an asset of the debtor, any statement showing the amount due by the debtor under a security and any document showing the income for the time being of the debtor,

(ix) a copy of any agreement referred to in section 175(1),

(x) a statement explaining the conditions which require to be fulfilled before the trust deed will become a protected trust deed and the consequences of its so becoming,

(xi) details of any protected trust deed in respect of which, in the 6 months preceding publication of the notice provided for in section 169, the debtor has been discharged in terms of section 184(1) (or regulation 24(1) of the Protected Trust Deeds (Scotland) Regulations 2013 (SSI 2013/318)) or been refused a letter of discharge under section 184(8) (or regulation 24(8) of those regulations), and

(xii) where a secured creditor's agreement has been obtained by virtue of paragraph (b) of section 166(2), a statement containing the valuation made by virtue of paragraph (a) of that section and a statement of the amount owed, in respect of the security held, to that creditor, and

(e) a statement, in such form as may be prescribed for the purposes of this paragraph, of the trustee's anticipated realisations from the trust deed.

(2) The trust deed must be acceded to by the creditors to whom the trustee is required by subsection (1) to send documents (those creditors being in this Part referred to as "the notified creditors") but is deemed to have been acceded to by them unless, within the relevant period, the trustee receives notification in writing from a majority in number, or no fewer than ? in value, of them that they object to the trust deed being granted protected status.

NOTES

Commencement: 30 November 2016.

Sub-s (1): words in square brackets in para (d)(ii) substituted by the Protected Trust Deeds (Forms) (Scotland) Regulations 2016, SSI 2016/398, reg 2(2); word in square brackets in para (d)(iv), (v) substituted for original word "EC" by the Insolvency (Regulation (EU) 2015/848) (Miscellaneous Amendments) (Scotland) Regulations 2017, SSI 2017/210, regs 4(1), (12), 9, as from 26 June 2017, except in relation to proceedings opened before that date.

Regulations: the Protected Trust Deeds (Forms) (Scotland) Regulations 2016, SSI 2016/398 at **[16.438]**.

Registration for protected status

[5.368]

171 Registration for protected status

(1) As soon as reasonably practicable after the expiry of the relevant period (and in any event within 4 weeks after that expiry), the trustee must send to AiB for registration in the register of insolvencies—

(a) a copy of the trust deed,

(b) either—

(i) a copy of every form of agreement obtained by virtue of section 166(2)(c), or

(ii) a statement by the trustee that no such form of agreement has been obtained,

(c) a statement by the trustee that those creditors, if any, who have objected in writing to the trust deed during the relevant period do not constitute a majority in number, or ? or more in value, of the creditors,

(d) a copy of the statement referred to in section 167(3)(c),

(e) a copy of the statement referred to in section 170(1)(d),

(f) a copy of any agreement referred to in section 175(1),

(g) a statement, in the form prescribed for the purposes of section 170(1)(e), of the trustee's anticipated realisations from the trust deed,

(h) where the debtor, being a living individual, makes a contribution from income—

(i) a statement that the amount of the contribution is in accordance with the common financial tool as assessed by the trustee, and

(ii) any evidence or explanation required in applying the common financial tool,

[(i) a statement by the trustee, in the form prescribed for that purpose in the Protected Trust Deeds (Forms) (Scotland) Regulations 2016, that—

(i) the documents and statements required under paragraphs (a) to (h) of this subsection accompany the statement, and

(ii) the conditions set out in sections 164 to 170 have been met].

(2) AiB must register the trust deed in the register of insolvencies if—

(a) AiB has received all the documents required to be sent under subsection (1),

(b) the conditions set out in sections 164 to 170 have been met, and

(c) AiB is satisfied, in accordance with the common financial tool, with the amount of the contribution determined.

(3) Subsection (4) applies where AiB notifies the trustee either—

(a) that the trust deed is registered in the register of insolvencies, or

(b) that such registration is refused.

(4) The trustee must, within 7 days after being so notified, notify the debtor and every creditor known to the trustee that the trust deed is so registered or refused.

NOTES

Commencement: 30 November 2016.

Sub-s (1): para (i) added by the Protected Trust Deeds (Forms) (Scotland) Regulations 2016, SSI 2016/398, reg 2(4).

Effect of Protected Status etc

[5.369]

172 Effect of protected status: general

(1) Where a trust deed has protected status then—

(a) subject to section 177, a creditor who (either or both)—

(i) is not a notified creditor, or

(ii) notified the trustee, during the relevant period, of objection to the trust deed,

has no higher right to recover the debt than a creditor who has acceded to, or been deemed by virtue of section 170(2) to have acceded to, the trust deed, and

(b) an application for sequestration of the debtor's estate may not be made by the debtor while the trust deed subsists.

(2) A creditor ceases to be deemed (by virtue of section 170(2)) to have acceded to a trust deed if the trustee refuses a request by the debtor to apply to AiB for discharge in terms of section 184(8).

(3) Where a secured creditor's agreement has been obtained by virtue of section 166(2)(b) and the trust deed becomes a protected trust deed, that creditor is not entitled—

(a) to make a claim under the protected trust deed for any of the debt in respect of which the security is held,

(b) to do diligence against the assets conveyed to the trustee under the protected trust deed, or

(c) to petition for the sequestration of the debtor during the subsistence of the protected trust deed.

NOTES

Commencement: 30 November 2016.

[5.370]

173 Effect of protected status on diligence against earnings

(1) This section applies where a trust deed has protected status.

(2) On the date of protection, any current earnings arrestment, maintenance arrestment, or, subject to subsection (3), conjoined arrestment order ceases to have effect.

(3) Any sum paid, before the date of protection, by the employer to the sheriff clerk under a conjoined arrestment order must be disbursed by the sheriff clerk under section 64 of the Debtors (Scotland) Act 1987 even if the date of disbursement is after the date of protection.

(4) A deduction from earnings order under that Act of 1987 is not competent after the date of protection to secure the payment of any amount due by the debtor under a maintenance calculation (within the meaning of that Act) in respect of which a claim could be made under the trust deed.

(5) The execution of an earnings arrestment or the making of a conjoined arrestment order is not competent, after the date of protection, to enforce a debt in respect of which the creditor is entitled to make a claim under the trust deed.

NOTES

Commencement: 30 November 2016.

[5.371]

[173A Effect of protected status on essential supplies

(1) An insolvency-related term of a contract for the supply of essential goods or services to a debtor ceases to have effect if—

(a) a trust deed granted by the debtor is granted protected status, and

(b) the supply is for the purpose of a business which is or has been carried on by or on behalf of the debtor.

(2) An insolvency-related term of a contract does not cease to have effect by virtue of subsection (1) to the extent that—

(a) it provides for the contract or the supply to terminate, or any other thing to take place, because the individual becomes subject to an insolvency procedure other than a trust deed,

(b) it entitles a supplier to terminate the contract or the supply, or do any other thing, because the individual becomes subject to an insolvency procedure other than a trust deed, or

(c) it entitles a supplier to terminate the contract or the supply because of an event that occurs, or may occur, after a trust deed granted by the debtor is granted protected status.

(3) Where an insolvency-related term of a contract ceases to have effect under this section the supplier may—

(a) terminate the contract, if the condition in subsection (4) is met,

(b) terminate the supply, if the condition in subsection (7) is met.

(4) The condition in this subsection is that—

(a) the trustee under the trust deed consents to the termination of the contract,

(b) on application by the supplier the court grants permission for the termination of the contract, or

(c) any charges in respect of the supply that are incurred after the date of protection of the trust deed are not paid within the period of 28 days beginning with the day on which payment is due.

(5) An application by the supplier under subsection (4)(b) is to be made to the sheriff who, had a petition for sequestration of the estate been presented at the date the trust deed was granted, would have had jurisdiction to hear that petition in terms of section 15(1) or (3).

(6) The court may grant permission under subsection (4)(b) only if satisfied that the continuation of the contract would cause the supplier hardship.

(7) The condition in this subsection is that—

(a) the supplier gives written notice to the trustee under the trust deed that the supply will be terminated unless the trustee personally guarantees the payment of any charges in respect of the continuation of the supply after the date of protection of the trust deed, and

(b) the trustee does not give that guarantee within the period of 14 days beginning with the day the notice is received.

(8) For the purposes of securing that the interests of suppliers are protected, where—

(a) an insolvency-related term of a contract (the "original term") ceases to have effect by virtue of subsection (1), and

(b) a subsequent trust deed granted by the debtor is granted protected status,

the contract is treated for the purposes of subsections (1) to (7) as if, immediately before the subsequent trust deed granted by the debtor is granted protected status, it included an insolvency-related term identical to the original term.

(9) A contract for the supply of essential goods or services is a contract for a supply mentioned in section 222(4).

(10) An insolvency-related term of a contract for the supply of essential goods or services to a debtor is a provision of the contract under which—

(a) the contract or the supply would terminate, or any other thing would take place, because a trust deed granted by the debtor is granted protected status,

(b) the supplier would be entitled to terminate the contract or the supply, or to do any other thing, because a trust deed granted by the debtor is granted protected status, or

(c) the supplier would be entitled to terminate the contract or the supply because of an event that occurred before a trust deed granted by the debtor is granted protected status.

(11) Subsection (1) does not have effect in relation to a contract entered into before 1st August 2017.]

NOTES

Commencement: 1 August 2017.

Inserted by the Public Services Reform (Corporate Insolvency and Bankruptcy) (Scotland) Order 2017, SSI 2017/209, art 6.

[5.372]

174 Deductions by virtue of protected trust deed from debtor's earnings

(1) This section applies where—

(a) a debtor is required to pay to the trustee, by virtue of a protected trust deed, a contribution from income for the benefit of creditors,

(b) in respect of that contribution, an amount is required to be paid from the debtor's earnings from employment, and

(c) the debtor has failed on two consecutive occasions to pay that amount to the trustee.

(2) Following a request by the trustee, the debtor must give the debtor's employer an instruction, in such form as may be prescribed for the purposes of this section, to make—

(a) deductions of specified amounts from the debtor's earnings, and

(b) payments to the trustee of the amounts so deducted.

(3) The trustee may give the debtor's employer an instruction, in such form as may be prescribed for the purposes of this section (being a form to the same effect as is mentioned in subsection (2)), if the debtor fails to comply with the requirement imposed by that subsection.

(4) If agreed between the debtor and the trustee, the debtor may give the debtor's employer a variation to an instruction mentioned in subsection (2).

(5) The employer must comply with any instruction given in accordance with subsection (2) or (3) (or, if an instruction under subsection (2) is varied in accordance with subsection (4), with that instruction as so varied).

(6) The instruction having been delivered, the employer must, while it is in effect—

(a) deduct the sum specified in it on every pay day, and

(b) pay the sum deducted to the trustee as soon as it is reasonable to do so.

(7) Where an employer fails without good cause to make a payment due under an instruction, the employer is—

(a) liable to pay on demand by a trustee the amount that should have been paid, and

(b) not entitled to recover from a debtor the amount paid to the debtor in breach of the instruction.

(8) An employer may, on making a payment due under an instruction—

(a) charge a fee equivalent to the fee chargeable for the time being under section 71 (employer's fee for operating diligence against earnings) of the Debtors (Scotland) Act 1987, and

(b) deduct that fee from the balance due to the debtor.

(9) The trustee must, without delay after the discharge of a debtor under section 184, notify in writing any person who has received an instruction under subsection (2) or (3) (or an instruction under subsection (2) varied in accordance with subsection (4)) that the instruction is recalled.

NOTES

Commencement: 30 November 2016.

Regulations: the Protected Trust Deeds (Forms) (Scotland) Regulations 2016, SSI 2016/398 at **[16.438]**.

[5.373]

175 Agreement in respect of debtor's heritable property

(1) Subject to the conditions in subsection (2), the trustee may, in such form as may be prescribed for the purposes of this section as at the date on which the trust deed is granted, agree—

(a) not to realise any specified heritable estate of the debtor which has been conveyed to the trustee,

(b) to relinquish the trustee's interest in respect of such heritable estate, and

(c) to recall any notice of inhibition in respect of such heritable estate in accordance with paragraph 3(3) of schedule 4.

(2) The conditions are that the debtor must—

(a) pay any amount determined by the trustee by a date so determined,

(b) pay a monthly amount so determined for a period so determined (being, in a case where there is a contribution from income, a period following the payment period applicable by virtue of section 168(2)), and

(c) co-operate with the administration of the trust.

(3) The amount of the debtor's payments under paragraphs (a) and (b) of subsection (2) must be determined in accordance with a valuation made by a chartered surveyor, or other qualified third party, of the debtor's heritable estate as at the date of grant of the trust deed.

(4) If the debtor fails to fulfil a condition mentioned in subsection (2), the trustee may withdraw from the agreement.

(5) The trustee must, as soon as is practicable, send a copy of the agreement (in the form mentioned in subsection (1)) to AiB and to every creditor known to the trustee other than any secured creditor who has, as mentioned in paragraph (b)(ii) of the trust deed definition, agreed not to claim under the trust deed for any of the debt in respect of which the security is held.

(6) This section does not apply to the debtor's dwellinghouse (or any part of that dwellinghouse) if the dwellinghouse or part is, by virtue of an exclusion such as is mentioned in paragraph (b)(i) of the trust deed definition, excluded from the estate conveyed to the trustee.

NOTES

Commencement: 30 November 2016.

Regulations: the Protected Trust Deeds (Forms) (Scotland) Regulations 2016, SSI 2016/398 at **[16.438]**.

[5.374]

176 Dividend payments

(1) If the funds of the debtor's estate are sufficient, the trustee must pay a dividend out of it to the creditors no later than 6 weeks after the end of—

(a) a first dividend period of 24 months beginning with the date on which the trust deed is granted, and

(b) any subsequent dividend period of 6 months beginning with the end of the previous dividend period.

(2) The funds of the debtor's estate are "sufficient" if, after—

(a) deduction of the trustee's fees and of any outlays payable under this Part, and

(b) making allowance for future contingencies,

a dividend may be paid to the creditors amounting to at least 5 pence for each pound sterling of the debtor's debt, as at the date of protection, under the trust deed.

NOTES

Commencement: 30 November 2016.

[5.375]

177 Sequestration petition by qualified creditor

(1) A qualified creditor who is not a notified creditor or who has notified the trustee of objection to the trust deed within the relevant period may—

(a) not later than 5 weeks after the date of registration under section 169 of the notice mentioned in that section, or

(b) at any time if the creditor avers that the provision for distribution of the estate is, or is likely to be, unduly prejudicial to a creditor or class of creditors,

present a petition to the sheriff for sequestration of the debtor's estate.

(2) Subsection (1)(b) is subject to section 13(2)(a).

(3) The sheriff may award sequestration in pursuance of—

(a) subsection (1)(a), only if satisfied that to do so would be in the best interests of the creditors, and

(b) subsection (1)(b), only if satisfied that the creditor's averment is correct.

NOTES

Commencement: 30 November 2016.

[5.376]

178 Creditor's application as respects intromissions of trustee

(1) A creditor who is not sent a copy of the notice mentioned in section 169 or who has notified the trustee of objection to the trust deed within the relevant period may apply to the sheriff under this section.

(2) Where on such an application the sheriff is satisfied, on grounds other than those on which a petition under section 177(1)(b) has been or could have been presented by the creditor, that the intromissions of the trustee with the estate of the debtor have been so unduly prejudicial to the creditor's claim that the creditor should not be bound by the trustee's discharge, the sheriff may order that the creditor is not to be so bound.

(3) On the sheriff making an order under subsection (2), the sheriff clerk must—

(a) send a copy of the order to the trustee, and

(b) send a copy of the order to AiB for registration in the register of insolvencies.

(4) Any application under subsection (1) must be made within 28 days after the registration in the register of insolvencies of the trustee's statement of realisation and distribution of estate under the protected trust deed, as mentioned in section 186(8)(b).

(5) The sheriff to whom the application may be made is the sheriff to whom a petition for sequestration would be brought in respect of the debtor by virtue of section 15(1) or (3).

NOTES

Commencement: 30 November 2016.

Administration, accounting and discharge

[5.377]

179 Directions to trustee under protected trust deed

(1) AiB may give directions to the trustee under a protected trust deed as to how the trustee should conduct the administration of the trust.

(2) On a direction being issued by virtue of subsection (1) its terms must be intimated to the debtor and to all known creditors.

(3) The direction may be issued on the initiative of AiB or (at AiB's discretion) on the request of the trustee, the debtor or any creditor.

(4) The trustee must, unless subsection (5) applies, comply with the direction within 30 days beginning with the day on which the direction is given.

(5) Where the trustee has appealed under section 188(1)(c) and the appeal has been dismissed by the sheriff or withdrawn by the trustee, the trustee must comply with the direction within 30 days beginning with the day of dismissal or withdrawal.
(6) If it appears to AiB that the trustee has failed, without reasonable excuse, to comply with the direction, AiB may report the matter to the sheriff who, after hearing the trustee on the matter, may—
(a) censure the trustee, or
(b) make such other order as the circumstances of the case require.

NOTES
Commencement: 30 November 2016.

[5.378]
180 Information and notification obligations of trustee under protected trust deed
(1) Where the trustee under a protected trust deed makes a determination to shorten or lengthen the payment period by virtue of section 168, the trustee must without delay notify the debtor accordingly.
(2) Whether or not still acting in the administration of the trust under a protected trust deed, the trustee must supply AiB with such information relating to the trust deed as AiB considers necessary to enable AiB to discharge AiB's functions under this Act.
(3) If it appears to AiB that the trustee has failed, without reasonable excuse, to supply information to AiB which is requested in accordance with subsection (2), AiB may report the matter to the sheriff who, after hearing the trustee on the matter, may—
(a) censure the trustee, or
(b) make such other order as the circumstances of the case require.
(4) On the trustee under a protected trust deed being replaced with a new trustee, the new trustee must without delay notify AiB accordingly.

NOTES
Commencement: 30 November 2016.

[5.379]
181 Administration of trust under protected trust deed
(1) At intervals of not more than 12 months (the first such interval beginning with the date on which the trust deed was granted) and within 6 weeks after the end of each interval, the trustee under a protected trust deed must send the trustee's accounts of the trustee's intromissions with the debtor's estate in administering the trust during the period in question—
(a) to the debtor,
(b) to each creditor, and
(c) (unless they are sent under section 186) to AiB.
(2) At such intervals the trustee must send to AiB, the debtor and each creditor a report, in such form as may be prescribed for the purposes of this subsection, on the management of the trust during the period in question.
(3) Subsection (4) applies where—
(a) within 21 days after the date on which the report is sent, the trustee receives notification in writing from—
(i) a majority in number, or
(ii) no fewer than ? in value,
of the creditors that they object to a course of action recommended in the report, and
(b) the expected final dividend to ordinary creditors set out in the report is at least 20% lower than the expected dividend to ordinary creditors set out in the form prescribed for the purposes of section 170(1)(e).
(4) The trustee must request under section 179(3) a direction as to the administration of the trust.
(5) The debtor or any creditor may, within 14 days after receiving a statement by virtue of subsection (1), require AiB to exercise the function mentioned in section 200(1)(a) (in so far as relating to trustees under protected trust deeds) by carrying out an examination of the administration of the trust by the trustee.
(6) In determining the amount of any contribution from income to be made by the debtor—
(a) the trustee may take account of any social security benefit paid to the debtor, but
(b) any contribution must not include an amount derived from social security benefit.

NOTES
Commencement: 30 November 2016.
Regulations: the Protected Trust Deeds (Forms) (Scotland) Regulations 2016, SSI 2016/398 at **[16.438]**.

[5.380]
182 Retention of documents by trustee under protected trust deed
The trustee under a protected trust deed must retain the following documents (or copies of those documents) for at least 12 months after the date of the trustee's discharge by the creditors under section 186—
(a) the trust deed,
(b) the statement mentioned in section 167(3)(c),
(c) the notice mentioned in section 169,
(d) the statement mentioned in section 170(1)(d),
(e) all statements of objection or accession received from creditors,

(f) the statement of anticipated realisations provided for in section 170(1)(e),
(g) any written agreement relating to the debtor's heritable estate and mentioned in section 175(1),
(h) all reports sent under section 181(2),
(i) any adjudication on a creditor's claim,
(j) any scheme of division among creditors,
(k) any circular sent to creditors with accounts,
(l) the debtor's discharge from the trust deed,
(m) the application to creditors for the trustee's discharge,
(n) the statement of realisation and distribution provided for in section 186(8)(b),
(o) any decree, interlocutory decree, direction or order granted by the court and relating to the administration of the trust, and
(p) any other document relating to the administration of the trust if it is a document which AiB, by notice to the trustee prior to the trustee's discharge, identifies as a document the trustee should retain.

NOTES

Commencement: 30 November 2016.

[5.381]

183 Remuneration payable to trustee under protected trust deed

(1) For work done by the trustee in administering the trust, the trustee under a protected trust deed is entitled to remuneration consisting only of—

(a) a fixed fee which must be set out in a form prescribed for the purposes of this paragraph,
(b) an additional fee based on a percentage of the total assets and contributions realised by the trustee, being a fee set out in a form so prescribed, and
(c) outlays incurred—
  (i) after the date on which the trust deed is granted, or
  (ii) before that date on a single valuation of any item of the debtor's heritable estate specified or valued in such a valuation.

(2) In the event of unforeseen circumstances the fixed fee may by increased by—

(a) approval by a majority in value of the notified creditors, or
(b) approval by AiB (all notified creditors having first been asked to approve the increase).

(3) AiB must approve an increase in the fixed fee if satisfied—

(a) that a majority in value of the notified creditors have not refused to approve the increase, and
(b) that the increase is required for work to be completed by the trustee for the benefit of the creditors generally, being work which was not foreseen in submitting a form by virtue of section 170(1)(e).

(4) In deciding whether or not to grant the approval mentioned in subsection (2)(b), AiB may determine the amount of any increase in the fixed fee.

(5) The trustee is entitled to include work done in seeking to comply with section 166(2) (whether or not a secured creditor has agreed not to claim under the trust deed) in the fixed fee and any outlays incurred.

(6) Any debt due to a third party for work done before the granting of the trust deed does not rank higher than any other creditor's claim.

(7) The trustee is entitled to recover from the debtor's estate any audit fee charged by AiB under paragraph 1 or 2 of schedule 4 in accordance with such rate as may be prescribed under section 205.

(8) AiB may, at any time, audit the trustee's accounts and fix the outlays of the trustee in the administration of the trust.

NOTES

Commencement: 30 November 2016.

Regulations: the Protected Trust Deeds (Forms) (Scotland) Regulations 2016, SSI 2016/398 at **[16.438]**.

[5.382]

184 Protected trust deed: discharge of debtor

(1) If the conditions set out in subsection (2) are met then, subject to subsections (6) and (9) and to section 185(1)—

(a) the debtor falls to be discharged from all debts and obligations —
  (i) in terms of the protected trust deed, or
  (ii) for which the debtor was liable as at the date that deed was granted, and
(b) the trustee under the protected trust deed must send—
  (i) to AiB, an application for discharge of the debtor from the trust deed (being an application in such form as may be prescribed for the purposes of this paragraph), and
  (ii) to the debtor, a copy of that application.

(2) The conditions are—

(a) that the trustee makes a statement (being a statement in such form as may be prescribed for the purposes of this paragraph) that, to the best of the trustee's knowledge, the debtor has—
  (i) met the debtor's obligations in terms of the trust deed, and
  (ii) co-operated with the administration of the trust, and
(b) any notice of inhibition under paragraph 3 of schedule 4 has been recalled or has expired.

(3) Subject to subsection (9), on receipt of the application referred to in subsection (1)(b)(i), AiB must register it in the register of insolvencies and the date of discharge is the date on which it is so registered.

(4) AiB must without delay notify the trustee of—

(a) the fact of registration, and
(b) the date of the debtor's discharge.

(5) The trustee must, within 7 days after receipt of the notification mentioned in subsection (4), notify the debtor and every creditor known to the trustee of the information set out in that notification.

(6) The letter of discharge does not—

(a) discharge the debtor from—
(i) any liability arising after the date on which the protected trust deed was granted,
(ii) any liability or obligation mentioned in section 145(3),
(iii) any liability for a debt in respect of which a security is held if the secured creditor has, as mentioned in paragraph (b)(ii) of the trust deed definition, agreed not to claim under the trust deed for any of the debt in respect of which the security is held, or
(b) affect the rights of a secured creditor.

(7) For the purposes of subsection (2)(a)(i), it is not a failure to meet the debtor's obligations for the debtor to refuse to —

(a) consent to the sale of the debtor's dwellinghouse (or of a part of that dwellinghouse) if the dwellinghouse or part is excluded, as mentioned in paragraph (b)(i) of the trust deed definition, from the estate conveyed to the trustee,
(b) give a relevant consent in terms of section 113(1)(a).

(8) If, on request by the debtor or as soon as reasonably practicable after the end of the period for which payments are required under the trust deed, the trustee refuses to apply to AiB for discharge of the debtor, the trustee must—

(a) inform the debtor by notice in writing—
(i) of the fact and the reason for the refusal,
(ii) that the debtor is not discharged from the debtor's debts and obligations in terms of the trust deed, and
(iii) of the debtor's right to apply to the sheriff for a direction under section 189(1), and
(b) send a copy of the notice to AiB within 21 days after the date of issue of the notice.

(9) AiB may refuse to register under subsection (3) an application sent under subsection (1)(b)(i) if not satisfied that the debtor has—

(a) met the debtor's obligations in terms of the trust deed, or
(b) co-operated with the administration of the trust.

(10) If AiB does so refuse, AiB must provide written notification of the refusal and of the reason for it to the trustee and the debtor.

(11) Within 7 days after the date on which the trustee receives any such notification as is mentioned in subsection (10), the trustee must send a copy of it to every creditor known to the trustee.

NOTES

Commencement: 30 November 2016.
Regulations: the Protected Trust Deeds (Forms) (Scotland) Regulations 2016, SSI 2016/398 at **[16.438]**.

[5.383]
185 Student loans

(1) Section 184 does not affect the right to recover any debt arising from a student loan.

(2) In subsection (1), "student loan" means a loan made by virtue of—

(a) section 73(f) of the Education (Scotland) Act 1980,
(b) section 1 of the Education (Student Loans) Act 1990,
(c) section 22 of the Teaching and Higher Education Act 1998, or
(d) Article 3 of the Education (Student Support) (Northern Ireland) Order 1998 (SI 1998/1760).

NOTES

Commencement: 30 November 2016.

[5.384]
186 Protected trust deed: discharge of trustee

(1) This section applies where a trustee under a protected trust deed has made the final distribution of the trust estate among the creditors.

(2) Within 28 days after the date of final distribution, the trustee must apply for discharge to such of those creditors as have acceded (or are deemed to have acceded) to the trust deed.

(3) Any application under subsection (2) must be in such form as may be prescribed for the purposes of that subsection.

(4) The trustee must send AiB by the date of application—

(a) a copy of the application, and
(b) the accounts of the trustee's intromissions for the last period for which accounts must be sent under section 181(1).

(5) For the purposes of subsection (2), the "date of final distribution" is the date on which all of the estate distributed has been placed beyond the control of the trustee.

(6) A creditor who does not respond to the application within 14 days after it is made is deemed to have agreed to the trustee's discharge.

(7) If a majority of the creditors in value consent to the application the trustee is discharged.

(8) On being discharged, the trustee must within 28 days of the discharge—

(a) inform AiB of the discharge,
(b) send AiB, for registration in the register of insolvencies, a statement of realisation and distribution of estate under the protected trust deed, and

(c) send AiB, where accounts submitted under subsection (4)(b) require to be revised, a copy of the revised accounts.

(9) A statement under subsection (8)(b) must be in such form as may be prescribed for the purposes of that subsection.

(10) Where the trustee's discharge is granted under this section, the discharge also applies as regards any previous trustee under the trust deed unless, under section 189, a person with an interest obtains an order to the contrary from the sheriff.

NOTES

Commencement: 30 November 2016.

Regulations: the Protected Trust Deeds (Forms) (Scotland) Regulations 2016, SSI 2016/398 at **[16.438]**.

[5.385]

187 Electronic delivery of notices etc under this Part

(1) Any notice or document authorised or required under this Part may be given, delivered or sent by electronic means, provided the intended recipient—

(a) has consented (whether in the specific case or generally) to electronic delivery and has not withdrawn that consent, and

(b) has supplied an electronic address for delivery.

(2) In the absence of evidence to the contrary, a notice or other document is presumed to have been delivered under this Part where—

(a) the sender can produce a copy of the electronic message—

(i) which contained the notice or other document or to which the notice or other document was attached, and

(ii) which shows the time and date the message was sent, and

(b) that electronic message was sent to the address supplied under subsection (1)(b).

(3) This section does not apply where some other form of delivery is required by rules of court or by order of the court.

NOTES

Commencement: 30 November 2016.

Appeals and directions

[5.386]

188 Protected trust deed: appeal

(1) The persons mentioned in subsection (2) may appeal to the sheriff against—

(a) any refusal by AiB to register a trust deed if it is a refusal on the grounds that AiB is not satisfied as mentioned in section 171(2)(c),

(b) any determination by AiB fixing the remuneration payable to the trustee under a protected trust deed,

(c) any direction under section 179(1) to the trustee, or

(d) any refusal by AiB under section 184(9).

(2) The persons are—

(a) the trustee,

(b) the debtor, if able to satisfy the sheriff that the debtor has, or is likely to have, a pecuniary interest in the outcome of the appeal, and

(c) any creditor, if able to satisfy the sheriff that the creditor has, or is likely to have any such interest in that outcome.

(3) The trustee may appeal to the sheriff against a refusal by the creditors to grant the trustee's discharge under section 186(2).

(4) The debtor may appeal to the sheriff against a refusal by the trustee to apply under section 184(1)(b)(i) for the debtor's discharge.

(5) Any appeal under subsection (1) must be made within 21 days after the refusal, determination or direction appealed against.

(6) The sheriff to whom any appeal under this section is to be made is the sheriff who, had a petition for the sequestration of the estate been presented at the date the trust deed was granted, would have had jurisdiction to hear that petition in terms of section 15(1) or (3).

(7) The decision of the sheriff on an appeal under this section is final.

NOTES

Commencement: 30 November 2016.

[5.387]

189 Protected trust deed: sheriff's direction

(1) Any person with an interest may at any time apply to the sheriff for a direction as regards the administration of a trust under a protected trust deed.

(2) A direction by virtue of subsection (1) may include—

(a) any order the sheriff thinks fit to make in the interests of justice, or

(b) an order to cure any defect in procedure.

(3) The sheriff to whom any application under this section is to be made is the sheriff who, had a petition for the sequestration of the estate been presented at the date the trust deed was granted, would have had jurisdiction to hear that petition in terms of section 15(1) or (3).

NOTES

Commencement: 30 November 2016.

Application for conversion to sequestration

[5.388]

190 Application for conversion to sequestration

(1) This section applies where a member State [insolvency practitioner] proposes to apply to AiB for the conversion under [Article 51 of the EU] insolvency proceedings regulation (conversion of [secondary insolvency] proceedings) of a protected trust deed into sequestration.

(2) An affidavit complying with section 191 must be—

(a) prepared and sworn, and

(b) submitted to AiB in support of the application.

(3) The application and affidavit required under subsection (2) are to be served on—

(a) the debtor,

(b) the trustee, and

(c) such other person as may be prescribed.

NOTES

Commencement: 30 November 2016.

Sub-s (1): words in first, second and third pairs of square brackets substituted for original words "liquidator", "Article 37 of the EC" and "earlier" respectively, by the Insolvency (Regulation (EU) 2015/848) (Miscellaneous Amendments) (Scotland) Regulations 2017, SSI 2017/210, regs 4(1), (13), 9, as from 26 June 2017, except in relation to proceedings opened before that date.

[5.389]

191 Contents of affidavit required under section 190(2)

(1) An affidavit required under section 190(2) must—

(a) state that main proceedings have been opened in relation to the debtor in a member State other than the United Kingdom,

[(b) state that the member State insolvency practitioner believes that the conversion of the protected trust deed into sequestration would be most appropriate as regards the interests of the local creditors(a) and coherence between the main and secondary proceedings,]

(c) contain such other information as the member State [insolvency practitioner] considers will be of assistance to AiB—

(i) in deciding whether to make an order under section 192, and

(ii) if AiB were to do so, in considering the need for any consequential provision that would be necessary or desirable, and

(d) contain such other matters as may be prescribed.

(2) Any affidavit under this section must be sworn by, or on behalf of, the member State [insolvency practitioner].

NOTES

Commencement: 30 November 2016.

Sub-s (1): para (b) substituted and words in square brackets in para (c) substituted for original word "liquidator", by the Insolvency (Regulation (EU) 2015/848) (Miscellaneous Amendments) (Scotland) Regulations 2017, SSI 2017/210, regs 4(1), (14), 9, as from 26 June 2017, except in relation to proceedings opened before that date. Para (b) originally read as follows:

"(b) state that the member State liquidator believes that the conversion of the protected trust deed into a sequestration would prove to be in the interests of the creditors in the main proceedings,".

Sub-s (2): words in square brackets substituted for original word "liquidator" by SSI 2017/210, regs 4(1), (14)(b), 9, as from 26 June 2017, except in relation to proceedings opened before that date.

[5.390]

192 Powers of Accountant in Bankruptcy on application for conversion to sequestration

(1) After considering an application for conversion of a protected trust deed into a sequestration, AiB may make such order as AiB thinks fit.

(2) If AiB makes an order for conversion into sequestration, the order may contain all such consequential provisions as AiB thinks necessary or desirable.

(3) The provisions of this Act apply to an order made by AiB under subsection (1) as if the order were a determination by AiB of a debtor application—

(a) under section 22(1), and

(b) in relation to which the member State [insolvency practitioner] is a concurring creditor.

(4) On AiB making an order for conversion into sequestration under subsection (1), any expenses properly incurred as expenses of the administration of the trust deed in question become a first charge on the debtor's estate.

NOTES

Commencement: 30 November 2016.

Sub-s (3): words in square brackets substituted for original word "liquidator" by the Insolvency (Regulation (EU) 2015/848) (Miscellaneous Amendments) (Scotland) Regulations 2017, SSI 2017/210, regs 4(1), (15), 9, as from 26 June 2017, except in relation to proceedings opened before that date.

Part 14: General

[5.391]
193 Interpretation of Part 14
In this Part—

. . .

"the date of protection" has the meaning given by section 163(2),

"the date of protection" has the meaning given by section 163(2),

"the notified creditors" has the meaning given by section 170(2),

"the relevant period" means the period of 5 weeks beginning with the date of registration of the notice referred to in section 169,

"remuneration" means reasonable fees and outlays, and

"the trust deed definition" has the meaning given by section 166(1).

NOTES

Commencement: 30 November 2016.

Definition "the Common Financial Statement" (omitted) repealed by the Protected Trust Deeds (Forms) (Scotland) Regulations 2016, SSI 2016/398, reg 2(3).

[5.392]
194 Regulations modifying Part 14

(1) The Scottish Ministers may by regulations modify (or add to) the provisions of this Part but, subject to subsections (2) and (3), only in so far as corresponding modifications or additions might, before the coming into force of this Part, have been made by virtue of paragraph 5(1) of schedule 5 of the Bankruptcy (Scotland) Act 1985 to the Protected Trust Deeds (Scotland) Regulations 2013 (SSI 2013/318).

(2) Regulations under subsection (1) may make provision enabling applications to be made to the court.

(3) Regulations under subsection (1) may contain such modifications of the provisions of this Act as appear to the Scottish Ministers to be necessary in consequence of those regulations.

NOTES

Commencement: 30 November 2016.

Regulations: the Protected Trust Deeds (Forms) (Scotland) Regulations 2016, SSI 2016/398 at **[16.438]**.

PART 15
MORATORIUM ON DILIGENCE

[5.393]
195 Moratorium on diligence: notice of intention to make debtor application under section 2(1)(a)

(1) A person may give written notice to AiB of the person's intention—

(a) to make a debtor application under section 2(1)(a),

(b) to seek to fulfil the conditions required in order for a trust deed granted by or on behalf of that person to be granted the status of protected trust deed, or

(c) to apply for the approval of a debt payment programme in accordance with section 2 of the 2002 Act.

(2) A person may not give notice under subsection (1) if that person has given such notice in the immediately preceding 12 months.

(3) AiB must, without delay after receipt of a notice under subsection (1), enter in the registers mentioned in subsection (4)—

(a) the name of the person who gave the notice, and

(b) such other information as AiB considers appropriate in relation to that person.

(4) The registers are—

(a) the register of insolvencies, and

(b) the register of debt payment programmes (in this Part referred to as the "DAS register") established and maintained in accordance with section 7 of the 2002 Act.

NOTES

Commencement: 30 November 2016.

[5.394]
196 Moratorium on diligence: notice of intention to make debtor application under section 6

(1) A person may give written notice to AiB of the person's intention to make a debtor application under section 6.

(2) A person may not give notice under subsection (1) in respect of an estate if any person has given such notice in respect of the same estate in the immediately preceding 12 months.

(3) AiB must, without delay after receipt of a notice under subsection (1), enter in the register of insolvencies—

(a) the name of the person who is the subject of the notice, and

(b) such other information as AiB considers appropriate in relation to that person.

NOTES

Commencement: 30 November 2016.

[5.395]

197 Moratorium on diligence following notice under section 195(1) or 196(1)

(1) This section applies where a person gives notice under section 195(1) or 196(1).

(2) A moratorium on diligence applies in relation to the person who is the subject of the notice for the moratorium period determined in accordance with section 198.

(3) While a moratorium on diligence applies in relation to the person it is not competent—

(a) to serve a charge for payment in respect of any debt owed by the person, or

(b) to commence or execute any diligence to enforce payment of any debt owed by the person,

(c) to found on any debt owed by the person in presenting, or concurring in the presentation of, a petition for sequestration of the person's estate, or

(d) where an arrestment mentioned in subsection (1) of section 73J of the Debtors (Scotland) Act 1987 has been granted in respect of funds due to the person, to release funds to the creditor under subsection (2) of that section.

(4) The moratorium period applying in relation to the person must be disregarded for the purpose of determining the period mentioned in subsection (3) of that section 73J.

(5) Despite subsection (3)(b), it is competent to—

(a) auction an article which has been attached in accordance with the 2002 Act where—

(i) notice has been given to the debtor under section 27(4) of that Act, or

(ii) the article has been removed, or notice of removal has been given, under section 53 of that Act,

(b) implement a decree of furthcoming,

(c) implement a decree or order for sale of a ship (or of a share of a ship) or cargo, or

(d) execute—

(i) an earnings arrestment,

(ii) a current maintenance arrestment, or

(iii) a conjoined arrestment order,

which came into effect before the day on which the moratorium period in relation to the person began.

NOTES

Commencement: 30 November 2016.

[5.396]

198 Period of moratorium

(1) The moratorium period applying in relation to a person is the period which—

(a) begins on the day on which an entry is made under section 195(3) or 196(3) in the register of insolvencies, and

(b) ends on—

(i) the day which is 6 weeks after that day,

(ii) such earlier day as is mentioned in subsection (2), or

(iii) if subsection (3), (5) or (7) applies, such later day as is determined in accordance with subsection (4), (6) or (8).

(2) The earlier day is the day on which, in relation to the person who is the subject of the moratorium—

(a) an entry is made in the register of insolvencies recording the award of sequestration of the estate,

(b) an entry is made in the register of insolvencies recording that a trust deed granted by the person has been granted or refused protected status,

(c) an entry is made in the DAS register recording the approval of a debt payment programme in accordance with section 2 of the 2002 Act, or

(d) written notice is given to AiB—

(i) by the person withdrawing the notice given under section 195(1), or

(ii) by or on behalf of the person withdrawing the notice given under section 196(1).

(3) This subsection applies if, on the day which is 6 weeks after the day on which the moratorium began under subsection (1)(a)—

(a) a debtor application has been made for sequestration of the estate of the person who is the subject of the moratorium,

(b) the moratorium has not ended by virtue of subsection (2)(a), and

(c) no decision has been made by AiB under section 27(7)(b).

(4) Where subsection (3) applies, the moratorium period ends on—

(a) the day on which an entry is made in the register of insolvencies recording the award of sequestration of the estate,

(b) in the case of refusal to award sequestration—

(i) the day of the expiry of the period applying by virtue of section 27(6) where no application for review is made under section 27(5), or

(ii) the day on which a decision is made by AiB under section 27(7)(b) where an application for review is made, or

(c) the day on which written notice is given to AiB—

(i) by the person withdrawing the notice given under section 195(1), or

(ii) by or on behalf of the person withdrawing the notice given under section 196(1).

(5) This subsection applies if, on the day which is 6 weeks after the day on which the moratorium began under subsection (1)(a)—

(a) an entry has been made in the register of insolvencies recording an application for a trust deed granted by or on behalf of the person who is the subject of the moratorium to be granted the status of protected trust deed, and
(b) the moratorium has not ended by virtue of subsection (2)(b).

(6) Where subsection (5) applies, the moratorium period ends on—
(a) the day on which an entry is made in the register of insolvencies recording that the trust deed granted by or on behalf of the person has been granted the status of protected trust deed,
(b) where such an entry is not made, the day which is 13 weeks after the day on which the moratorium began under subsection (1)(a), or
(c) the day on which written notice is given to AiB by the person withdrawing the notice given under section 195(1).

(7) This subsection applies if, on the day which is 6 weeks after the day on which the moratorium began under subsection (1)(a)—
(a) the person who is the subject of the moratorium has applied for approval of a debt payment programme under section 2 of the 2002 Act,
(b) the moratorium has not ended by virtue of subsection (2)(c), and
(c) the application has not been determined.

(8) Where subsection (7) applies, the moratorium period ends on—
(a) the day on which an entry is made in the DAS register recording the approval of the debt payment programme in accordance with section 2 of the 2002 Act,
(b) in the case of a rejection of a debt payment programme, the day on which an entry is made in the DAS register recording the rejection, or
(c) the day on which written notice is given to AiB by the person withdrawing the notice given under section 195(1).

NOTES

Commencement: 30 November 2016.

PART 16
ACCOUNTANT IN BANKRUPTCY

Appointment

[5.397]

199 Accountant in Bankruptcy

(1) The Accountant in Bankruptcy (in this Act referred to as "AiB") is appointed by the Scottish Ministers and is an officer of the court.

(2) The Scottish Ministers may appoint a member of the staff of AiB—
(a) to be Depute Accountant in Bankruptcy, and
(b) as Depute Accountant in Bankruptcy, to exercise all the functions of AiB at any time when AiB is unable to do so.

NOTES

Commencement: 30 November 2016.

Functions

[5.398]

200 Supervisory functions of Accountant in Bankruptcy

(1) AiB has, in the administration of sequestration and personal insolvency, the following general functions—
(a) as regards interim trustees (not being AiB), trustees in sequestrations (not being AiB), trustees under protected trust deeds and commissioners—
(i) supervision of the performance by them of the functions conferred on them by this Act, or by any other enactment or by any rule of law, and
(ii) the investigation of any complaints made against them,
(b) the determination of debtor applications,
(c) the maintenance of a register (in this Act referred to as the "register of insolvencies"), in such form as may be prescribed,
(d) the preparation of an annual report, and
(e) such other functions as may from time to time be conferred on AiB by the Scottish Ministers.

(2) The register of insolvencies is to contain particulars of—
(a) persons who are the subject of notices under sections 195(1) and 196(1),
(b) estates which have been sequestrated,
(c) trust deeds sent to AiB for registration,
(d) bankruptcy restrictions orders and interim bankruptcy restrictions orders,
(e) the winding up and receivership of business associations which the Court of Session has jurisdiction to wind up, and
(f) any other document specified in regulations made under subsection (1) or any other enactment.

(3) The annual report must be presented to the Scottish Ministers and the Court of Session and must contain—
(a) statistical information relating to—
(i) the state of all sequestrations of which particulars have been registered in the register of insolvencies during the year to which the report relates,

(ii) the winding up and receivership of business associations of which particulars have been registered in the register of insolvencies during the year to which the report relates,

(b) particulars of trust deeds registered as protected trust deeds in that year, and

(c) particulars of the performance of AiB's functions under this Act.

(4) If it appears to AiB that a person mentioned in subsection (1)(a) has failed, without reasonable excuse, to perform a duty imposed on that person by any provision of this Act, or by any other enactment or by any rule of law, AiB must report the matter to the sheriff who, after hearing the person on the matter, may—

(a) remove the person from office,

(b) censure the person, or

(c) make such other order as the circumstances of the case may require.

(5) Subsection (6) applies where AiB has reasonable grounds to suspect that an offence has been committed—

(a) by a person mentioned in subsection (1)(a) in the performance of the person's functions under this Act or any other enactment or any rule of law,

(b) in relation to a sequestration, by the debtor in respect of the debtor's assets, the debtor's dealings with them or the debtor's conduct in relation to the debtor's business or financial affairs, or

(c) in relation to a sequestration, by a person other than the debtor in that person's dealings with the debtor, the interim trustee or the trustee in the sequestration in respect of the debtor's assets or the debtor's business or financial affairs.

(6) AiB must report the matter to the Lord Advocate.

(7) AiB must—

(a) make the register of insolvencies available for inspection at all reasonable times, and

(b) provide any person, on request, with a certified copy of an entry in the register.

(8) Regulations under subsection (1)(c) may in particular prescribe circumstances where information need not be in included in the register of insolvencies if, in the opinion of AiB, inclusion of the information would be likely to jeopardise the safety or welfare of any person.

(9) In subsections (2) and (3), "business association" has the meaning given in section C2 of Part 2 of schedule 5 of the Scotland Act 1998.

NOTES

Commencement: 30 November 2016.

Regulations: the Bankruptcy (Scotland) Regulations 2016, SSI 2016/397 at **[16.401]**.

[5.399]

201 Performance of certain functions of Accountant in Bankruptcy

(1) The functions of AiB, other than functions conferred by section 200, may be carried out on AiB's behalf by any member of AiB's staff authorised by AiB to do so.

(2) Without prejudice to subsection (1), AiB may appoint, on such terms and conditions as AiB considers appropriate, such persons as AiB considers fit to perform on AiB's behalf any of AiB's functions in respect of the sequestration of the estate of any debtor.

(3) A person appointed under subsection (2) must comply with such general or specific directions as AiB may from time to time give to such person as to the performance of those functions.

(4) AiB may pay a person so appointed such fee as AiB may consider appropriate.

NOTES

Commencement: 30 November 2016.

[5.400]

202 Further duty of Accountant in Bankruptcy

AiB is, on receiving any notice under section 109(1) of the Insolvency Act 1986 in relation to a community interest company, to forward a copy of that notice to the Regulator of Community Interest Companies.

NOTES

Commencement: 30 November 2016.

Directions to accountant in bankruptcy

[5.401]

203 Directions to Accountant in Bankruptcy

(1) The Scottish Ministers may, after consultation with the Lord President of the Court of Session, give AiB general directions as to the performance of AiB's functions under this Act.

(2) Directions under this section may be given in respect of—

(a) all cases, or

(b) any class or description of cases,

but are not to be given in respect of a particular case.

(3) AiB must comply with any directions given under this section.

NOTES

Commencement: 30 November 2016.

Conduct of proceedings in the sheriff court

[5.402]
204 Conduct of proceedings in the sheriff court
(1) A person authorised by AiB may conduct civil proceedings in the sheriff court in relation to a function of AiB (including the functions listed in section 200).
(2) In subsection (1), "civil proceedings" are proceedings which are not in respect of an offence.

NOTES
Commencement: 30 November 2016.

Fees for accountant in bankruptcy

[5.403]
205 Fees for Accountant in Bankruptcy
(1) The Scottish Ministers may prescribe—
(a) the fees and outlays to be payable to AiB in respect of the exercise of any of AiB's functions under this Act,
(b) the time at or by which, and the manner in which, such fees and outlays are to be paid, and
(c) the circumstances, if any, in which AiB may allow—
(i) exemption from payment, or
(ii) the remission or modification of payment,
of any such fees or outlays.
(2) The Secretary of State may prescribe by regulations—
(a) the fees and outlays to be payable to AiB in respect of the exercise of any of AiB's functions under the Insolvency Act 1986,
(b) the time at or by which, and the manner in which, such fees and outlays are to be paid, and
(c) the circumstances, if any, in which AiB may allow—
(i) exemption from payment, or
(ii) the remission or modification of payment,
of any such fees or outlays.

NOTES
Commencement: 30 November 2016.
Regulations: the Bankruptcy Fees (Scotland) Revocation Regulations 2017, SSI 2017/97.

PART 17
MISCELLANEOUS

[5.404]
206 Liabilities and rights of co-obligants
(1) Where a creditor has an obligant bound to the creditor along with the debtor for the whole or part of the debt, the obligant is not freed or discharged from the obligant's liability for the debt by reason of the discharge of the debtor or by virtue of the creditor's voting or drawing a dividend or assenting to, or not opposing, the discharge of the debtor.
(2) Subsection (3) applies where—
(a) the creditor has had a claim accepted in whole or in part, and
(b) the obligant holds a security over any part of the debtor's estate
(3) The obligant must account to the trustee in the sequestration so as to put the estate in the same position as if the obligant had paid the debt to the creditor and thereafter had had the obligant's claim accepted in whole or in part in the sequestration after deduction of the value of the security.
(4) The obligant may require and obtain at the obligant's own expense from the creditor an assignation of the debt on payment of the amount of the debt and on that being done may in respect of the debt submit a claim, and vote and draw a dividend, if otherwise legally entitled to do so.
(5) Subsection (4) is without prejudice to any right, under any rule of law, of a co-obligant who has paid the debt.
(6) In this section, "obligant" includes cautioner.

NOTES
Commencement: 30 November 2016.

[5.405]
207 Member State [insolvency practitioner] deemed creditor
For the purposes of this Act, and without prejudice to the generality of the right to participate referred to in [paragraph 3 of Article 45 of the EU] insolvency proceedings regulation (exercise of creditors' rights), a member State [insolvency practitioner] appointed in relation to a debtor is deemed to be a creditor in the sum due to creditors in proceedings in relation to which the member State [insolvency practitioner] holds office.

NOTES
Commencement: 30 November 2016.
Words "insolvency practitioner" in square brackets in each place they appear substituted for original word "liquidator" and other words in square brackets substituted for original words "paragraph 3 of Article 32 of the EC", by the Insolvency

(Regulation (EU) 2015/848) (Miscellaneous Amendments) (Scotland) Regulations 2017, SSI 2017/210, regs 4(1), (16), (17), 9, as from 26 June 2017, except in relation to proceedings opened before that date.

[5.406]
208 Trustee's duty to provide certain notices and copies of documents to member State [insolvency practitioner]

(1) This section applies where a member State [insolvency practitioner] has been appointed in relation to a debtor.

(2) Where an interim trustee or a trustee in the sequestration must—

(a) give notice to the sheriff or AiB, or

(b) provide a copy of a document to the sheriff or AiB,

the interim trustee or trustee in the sequestration must also give such notice, or provide such a copy, to the member State [insolvency practitioner].

(3) Subsection (2) is without prejudice to the generality of the obligations imposed by [Article 41 of the EU] insolvency proceedings regulation (duty to co-operate and communicate information).

(4) In subsection (2)(b), "document" includes an order of court.

NOTES

Commencement: 30 November 2016.

Section heading, sub-ss (1), (2): words in square brackets substituted for original word "liquidator" by the Insolvency (Regulation (EU) 2015/848) (Miscellaneous Amendments) (Scotland) Regulations 2017, SSI 2017/210, regs 4(1), (18)(a), (19), 9, as from 26 June 2017, except in relation to proceedings opened before that date.

Sub-s (3): words in square brackets substituted for original words "Article 31 of the EC" by SSI 2017/210, regs 4(1), (18)(b), 9, as from 26 June 2017, except in relation to proceedings opened before that date.

[5.407]
209 Extortionate credit transactions

(1) This section applies where—

(a) a debtor is, or has been, party to a transaction for, or involving, the provision of credit to the debtor, and

(b) the debtor's estate is sequestrated.

(2) The sheriff may, on the application of the trustee in the sequestration, make an order with respect to the transaction if the transaction—

(a) is, or was, extortionate, and

(b) was not entered into more than 3 years before the date of sequestration.

(3) For the purposes of this section a transaction is extortionate if, having regard to the risk accepted by the person providing the credit—

(a) the terms of the transaction are, or were, such as to require grossly exorbitant payments to be made (whether unconditionally or in certain contingencies) in respect of the provision of the credit, or

(b) the transaction otherwise grossly contravened ordinary principles of fair dealing.

(4) It is to be presumed, unless the contrary is proved, that a transaction with respect to which an application is made under this section is, or as the case may be was, extortionate.

(5) An order under this section with respect to a transaction may contain such one or more of the following as the sheriff thinks fit—

(a) provision setting aside the whole or part of any obligation created by the transaction,

(b) provision otherwise varying the terms of the transaction or varying the terms on which any security for the purposes of the transaction is held,

(c) provision requiring any person who is a party to the transaction to pay to the trustee any sums paid to that person, by virtue of the transaction, by the debtor,

(d) provision requiring any person to surrender to the trustee any property held by the person as security for the purposes of the transaction,

(e) provision directing accounts to be taken between any persons.

(6) Any sums required to be paid, or property required to be surrendered, to the trustee in accordance with an order under this section vest in the trustee.

(7) The powers conferred by this section are exercisable, in relation to a transaction, concurrently with any powers exercisable under this Act in relation to that transaction as a gratuitous alienation or unfair preference.

(8) In this section, "credit" has the same meaning as in the Consumer Credit Act 1974.

NOTES

Commencement: 30 November 2016.

[5.408]
210 Sederunt book and other documents

(1) Whoever by virtue of this Act for the time being holds the sederunt book must make it available for inspection at all reasonable hours by any interested party; but this subsection is subject to subsection (2).

(2) As regards any case in which the person on whom a duty is imposed by subsection (1) is AiB, the Scottish Ministers may by regulations—

(a) limit the period for which the duty is so imposed, and

(b) prescribe conditions in accordance with which the duty is to be carried out.

(3) The trustee must insert in the sederunt book the information listed in schedule 5.

(4) The Scottish Ministers may by regulations modify schedule 5.

(5) An entry in the sederunt book is sufficient evidence of the facts stated in that entry, (except where the entry is founded on by the trustee in the sequestration in the trustee's own interest).
(6) Notwithstanding any provision of this Act, the trustee is not bound to insert in the sederunt book a document of a confidential nature.
(7) The trustee is not bound to exhibit to a person other than a commissioner or AiB any document in the trustee's possession which is of a confidential nature.
(8) An extract from the register of insolvencies bearing to be signed by AiB is sufficient evidence of the facts stated in the extract.

NOTES

Commencement: 30 November 2016.

[5.409]

211 Power of court to cure defects in procedure

(1) On the application of a person having an interest, the sheriff may—
- (a) if there has been a failure to comply with a requirement of this Act (or of regulations under this Act), make an order—
  - (i) waiving the failure, and
  - (ii) so far as practicable, restoring any person prejudiced by the failure to the position that person would have been in but for the failure, or
- (b) if for any reason anything required or authorised to be done in, or in connection with, the sequestration process cannot be done, make such order as may be necessary to enable the thing to be done.

(2) An order under subsection (1) may waive a failure to comply with a requirement mentioned in section 212(1)(a) or (b) only if the failure relates to—
- (a) a document to be lodged with the sheriff,
- (b) a document issued by the sheriff, or
- (c) a time limit specified in relation to proceedings before the sheriff or a document relating to those proceedings.

(3) In an order under subsection (1), the sheriff may impose such conditions, including conditions as to expenses, as the sheriff thinks fit and may—
- (a) authorise, or dispense with, the performance of any act in the sequestration process,
- (b) appoint as trustee on the debtor's estate AiB or a person who would be eligible to be elected under section 49 (whether or not in place of an existing trustee),
- (c) extend or waive a time limit specified in or under this Act.

(4) Subsection (5) applies where the sheriff, or as the case may be the Court of Session, considers that a remit from the sheriff to the Court of Session is desirable because of the importance or complexity of the matters raised by an application under subsection (1).
(5) The application—
- (a) may at any time be so remitted—
  - (i) of the sheriff's own accord, or
  - (ii) on an application by a person having an interest, and
- (b) must be so remitted, if the Court of Session so directs on an application by any such person.

NOTES

Commencement: 30 November 2016.

[5.410]

212 Power of Accountant in Bankruptcy to cure defects in procedure

(1) AiB may make an order—
- (a) correcting a clerical or incidental error in a document required by or under this Act, or
- (b) waiving a failure—
  - (i) to comply with a time limit specified by or under this Act, and
  - (ii) for which no provision is made by or under this Act.

(2) An order under subsection (1) may be made—
- (a) on the application of any person having an interest, or
- (b) without an application if AiB proposes to correct or waive a matter mentioned in that subsection.

(3) The applicant must notify all interested persons where an application is made under subsection (2)(a).
(4) AiB must notify all interested persons where AiB proposes to make an order by virtue of subsection (2)(b).
(5) A notice under subsection (3) or (4) must inform the recipient that the recipient has a right to make representations to AiB in relation to the application or the proposed order within 14 days beginning with the day on which the notice is given.
(6) Before making an order under subsection (1), AiB must take into account any representations made by an interested person.
(7) An order under subsection (1) may—
- (a) so far as practicable, restore any person prejudiced by the error or failure to the position that person would have been in but for the error or failure, and
- (b) impose such conditions, including conditions as to expenses, as AiB thinks fit.

(8) After making an order under subsection (1) which affects a matter recorded in the Register of Inhibitions, AiB must without delay send a certified copy of the order to the keeper of that register for recording in that register.

NOTES

Commencement: 30 November 2016.

[5.411]

213 Decision under section 212(1): review

(1) An interested person may apply to AiB for a review of a decision of AiB to make, or refuse to make, an order under section 212(1).

(2) Any application under subsection (1) must be made within 14 days beginning with the day of that decision.

(3) If an application under subsection (1) is made, AiB must—

- (a) take into account any representations made by an interested person within 21 days beginning with the day on which the application is made, and
- (b) confirm, amend or revoke the decision within 28 days beginning with the day on which the application is made.

(4) An interested person may appeal to the sheriff against a decision by AiB under subsection (3)(b) within 14 days beginning with the day of that decision.

(5) The decision of the sheriff on an appeal under subsection (4) is final.

NOTES

Commencement: 30 November 2016.

[5.412]

214 Review of decision by Accountant in Bankruptcy: grounds of appeal

(1) For the avoidance of doubt, an appeal under a provision mentioned in subsection (2) may be made on—

- (a) a matter of fact,
- (b) a point of law, or
- (c) the merits.

(2) The provisions are—

- (a) section 27(8),
- (b) section 37(5),
- (c) section 52(7),
- (d) section 57(8),
- (e) section 59(4),
- (f) section 61(8),
- (g) section 64(8),
- (h) section 65(7),
- (i) section 68(4),
- (j) section 71(4),
- (k) section 73(5),
- (l) section 92(5),
- (m) section 97(5),
- (n) section 110(7),
- (o) section 127(5),
- (p) section 139(6),
- (q) section 144(6),
- (r) section 149(4),
- (s) section 151(7),
- (t) section 161(8),
- (u) section 213(4), and
- (v) paragraph 3(9) of schedule 2.

NOTES

Commencement: 30 November 2016.

[5.413]

215 Debtor to co-operate with trustee

(1) The debtor must take every practicable step (and in particular must execute any document) which may be necessary to enable the trustee in the sequestration to perform the functions conferred on the trustee by this Act.

(2) If the sheriff, on the trustee's application, is satisfied—

- (a) that the debtor has failed to execute a document in compliance with subsection (1), the sheriff may authorise the sheriff clerk to do so, or
- (b) that the debtor has failed to comply in any other respect with that subsection, the sheriff may order the debtor to do so.

(3) The execution, by virtue of paragraph (a) of subsection (2), of a document by the sheriff clerk has the like force and effect in all respects as if it had been executed by the debtor.

(4) If the debtor fails to comply with an order under subsection (2)(b) then the debtor commits an offence.

(5) If the debtor is convicted of an offence under subsection (4) then the debtor is liable—

- (a) on summary conviction, to a fine not exceeding the statutory maximum, or—

(i) in a case where the debtor has previously been convicted of an offence inferring dishonest appropriation of property or an attempt at dishonest appropriation of property, to imprisonment for a term not exceeding 6 months, or
(ii) in any other case, to imprisonment for a term not exceeding 3 months,

or both to a fine not exceeding the statutory maximum and to such imprisonment as is mentioned, in relation to the case in question, in sub-paragraph (i) or (ii),

(b) on conviction on indictment—
(i) to a fine or to imprisonment for a term not exceeding 2 years, or
(ii) both to a fine and to such imprisonment.

(6) In this section, "debtor" includes a debtor discharged under this Act.

NOTES

Commencement: 30 November 2016.

[5.414]

216 Arbitration and compromise

(1) The trustee in the sequestration may (but if there are commissioners then only with their consent or with the consent of the creditors or of the sheriff)—
(a) refer to arbitration any claim or question, of whatever nature, arising in the course of the sequestration, or
(b) make a compromise with regard to any claim, of whatever nature, made against or on behalf of the sequestrated estate.

(2) Where a claim or question is referred to arbitration under this section, AiB may vary any time limit for carrying out a procedure under this Act.

(3) A decree arbitral on a reference under paragraph (a) of subsection (1), or a compromise under paragraph (b) of that subsection, is binding on the creditors and on the debtor.

NOTES

Commencement: 30 November 2016.

[5.415]

217 Meetings of creditors and commissioners

Part 1 of schedule 6 has effect in relation to meetings of creditors other than the statutory meeting, Part 2 in relation to all meetings of creditors and Part 3 in relation to meetings of commissioners.

NOTES

Commencement: 30 November 2016.

[5.416]

218 General offences by debtor etc

(1) Subsection (2) applies where, during the relevant period, a debtor makes a false statement in relation to the debtor's assets or financial or business affairs —
(a) to a creditor, or
(b) to a person concerned in the administration of the debtor's estate.

(2) Unless the debtor shows that the debtor neither knew nor had reason to believe that the statement was false, the debtor commits an offence.

(3) Subsection (4) applies where, during the relevant period, a debtor or some other person acting in the debtor's interest (whether or not with the debtor's authority)—
(a) destroys,
(b) damages,
(c) conceals,
(d) disposes of, or
(e) removes from Scotland,

any part of the debtor's estate or any document relating to the debtor's assets or business or financial affairs.

(4) Unless the perpetrator shows that it was not done with intent to prejudice the creditors, the perpetrator commits an offence.

(5) If, after the date of sequestration of the estate of a debtor, the debtor (being a person who is absent from Scotland) fails when required by the court to come to Scotland for any purpose connected with the administration of that estate, then the debtor commits an offence.

(6) Subsection (7) applies where, during the relevant period, a debtor or some other person acting in the debtor's interest (whether or not with the debtor's authority) falsifies any document relating to the debtor's assets or business or financial affairs.

(7) Unless the perpetrator shows that the perpetrator had no intention to mislead the trustee, a commissioner or any creditor, the perpetrator commits an offence.

(8) If a debtor whose estate is sequestrated—
(a) knows that a person has falsified a document relating to the debtor's assets or business or financial affairs, and
(b) fails, within one month of acquiring that knowledge, to report it to the trustee in the sequestration,

then the debtor commits an offence.

(9) Subsection (10) applies where, during the relevant period, a person (in this subsection and in subsection (10) referred to as "P") who is absolutely insolvent—

(a) transfers anything to another person for an inadequate consideration, or
(b) grants an unfair preference to any of P's creditors.

(10) Unless P shows that it was not done with intent to prejudice P's creditors, P commits an offence.

(11) Subsection (12) applies where, at any time in the period of one year ending with the sequestration of the estate of a debtor who is engaged in trade or business, the debtor otherwise than in the ordinary course of the trade or business pledges or disposes of property which the debtor has obtained on credit and has not paid for.

(12) Unless the debtor shows that it was not done with intent to prejudice the debtor's creditors, the debtor commits an offence.

(13) If a debtor, either alone or jointly with another person, obtains credit—
(a) to the extent of £2,000 or such other sum as may be prescribed or more, or
(b) of any amount where, at the time the credit is obtained, the debtor has debts amounting to £1,000 or such other sum as may be prescribed or more,

without giving the person from whom the credit is obtained the relevant information about the debtor's status, then the debtor commits an offence.

NOTES

Commencement: 30 November 2016.

[5.417]

219 General offences: supplementary and penalties

(1) For the purpose of calculating an amount of credit mentioned in subsection (13) of section 218 or of debts mentioned in paragraph (b) of that subsection, no account is to be taken of any credit obtained or, as the case may be, of any liability for charges in respect of—
(a) any of the supplies mentioned in section 222(4), and
(b) any council tax (within the meaning of section 99(1) of the Local Government Finance Act 1992.

(2) For the purposes of section 218(13)—
(a) "debtor" means—
(i) a person whose estate has been sequestrated,
(ii) a person who has been adjudged bankrupt in England and Wales or in Northern Ireland, or
(iii) a person subject to a bankruptcy restrictions order, or a bankruptcy restrictions undertaking, made in England and Wales,

being, in the case of a person mentioned in sub-paragraph (i) or (ii), a person who has not been discharged,
(b) the reference to the debtor obtaining credit includes a reference to a case where goods—
(i) are hired to the debtor under a hire-purchase agreement, or
(ii) are agreed to be sold to the debtor under a conditional sale agreement, and
(c) the "relevant information" about the status of the debtor is the information that (as the case may be)—
(i) the debtor's estate has been sequestrated and that the debtor has not been discharged,
(ii) the debtor is an undischarged bankrupt in England and Wales or in Northern Ireland, or
(iii) the debtor is subject to a bankruptcy restrictions order, or a bankruptcy restrictions undertaking, made in England and Wales.

(3) In section 218—

"the relevant period" means the period commencing one year immediately before the date of sequestration of the debtor's estate and ending with the debtor's discharge, and

references to intent to prejudice creditors include references to intent to prejudice an individual creditor.

(4) If a person does, or fails to do, in England and Wales or in Northern Ireland anything which if done, or as the case may be not done, in Scotland is an offence under section 218(2), (4), (7), (8), (10) or (12), then that person commits an offence under the subsection in question.

(5) A person convicted of an offence under section 218 is liable—
(a) on summary conviction, to a fine not exceeding the statutory maximum, or—
(i) in a case where the person has previously been convicted of an offence inferring dishonest appropriation of property or an attempt at dishonest appropriation of property, to imprisonment for a term not exceeding 6 months, or
(ii) in any other case, to imprisonment for a term not exceeding 3 months,

or both to a fine not exceeding the statutory maximum and to such imprisonment as is mentioned, in relation to the case in question, in sub-paragraph (i) or (ii), or
(b) on conviction on indictment, to a fine, or—
(i) in the case of an offence under section 218(2), (4), (7) or (12), to imprisonment for a term not exceeding 5 years, or
(ii) in any other case, to imprisonment for a term not exceeding 2 years,

or both to a fine and to such imprisonment as is mentioned, in relation to the case in question, in sub-paragraph (i) or (ii).

NOTES

Commencement: 30 November 2016.

[5.418]
220 Summary proceedings
(1) Summary proceedings for an offence under this Act may be commenced at any time within 12 months after the date on which evidence sufficient in the opinion of the Lord Advocate to justify the proceedings comes to the Lord Advocate's knowledge.
(2) But such proceedings must not be commenced by virtue of this section more than 3 years after the commission of the offence.
(3) Section 136(3) of the Criminal Procedure (Scotland) Act 1995 (date of commencement of summary proceedings) has effect for the purposes of this section as it has for the purposes of that section.
(4) For the purposes of subsection (1), a certificate of the Lord Advocate as to the date on which the evidence in question came to the Lord Advocate's knowledge is conclusive evidence of the date on which it did so.

NOTES
Commencement: 30 November 2016.

[5.419]
221 Outlays of insolvency practitioner in actings as interim trustee or trustee
The Scottish Ministers may, by regulations, provide for the premium (or a proportionate part of the premium) of any bond of caution or other security required, for the time being, to be given by an insolvency practitioner to be taken into account as part of the outlays of the practitioner in the practitioner's actings as an interim trustee or as trustee in the sequestration.

NOTES
Commencement: 30 November 2016.
Regulations: the Bankruptcy (Scotland) Regulations 2016, SSI 2016/397 at **[16.401]**.

[5.420]
222 Supplies by utilities
(1) This section applies where on any day ("the relevant day")—
 (a) sequestration is awarded in a case where a debtor application was made,
 (b) a warrant is granted under section 22(3) in a case where the petition was presented by a creditor or by a trustee acting under a trust deed, or
 (c) the debtor grants a trust deed.
(2) If a request falling within subsection (3) is made for the giving, after the relevant day, of any of the supplies mentioned in subsection (4), the supplier—
 (a) may make it a condition of the giving of the supply that the office holder personally guarantee the payment of any charges in respect of the supply, and
 (b) is not to make it a condition (or to do anything which has the effect of making it a condition) of the giving of the supply that any outstanding charges in respect of a supply given to the debtor before the relevant day are paid.
(3) A request falls within this subsection if it is made—
 (a) by or with the concurrence of the office holder, and
 (b) for the purposes of any business which is, or has been, carried on by or on behalf of the debtor.
(4) The supplies are—
 (a) a supply of gas by a gas supplier, within the meaning of Part 1 of the Gas Act 1986,
 [(aa) a supply of gas by a person within paragraph 1 of schedule 2A of the Gas Act 1986 (supply by landlords etc),]
 (b) a supply of electricity by an electricity supplier, within the meaning of Part 1 of the Electricity Act 1989,
 [(ba) a supply of electricity by a class of person within Class A (small suppliers) or Class B (resale) of schedule 4 of the Electricity (Class Exemptions from the Requirement for a Licence) Order 2001 (SI 2001/3270),]
 (c) a supply of water by Scottish Water, . . .
 [(ca) a supply of water by a water services provider within the meaning of the Water Services etc (Scotland) Act 2005,
 (cb) a supply of water by a person who has an interest in the premises to which the supply is given,]
 (d) a supply of communications services by a provider of a public electronic communications service,
 [(e) a supply of communications services by a person who carries on a business which includes giving such supplies, and
 (f) a supply of goods or services mentioned in subsection (5A) by a person who carries on a business which includes giving such supplies, where the supply is for the purpose of enabling or facilitating anything to be done by electronic means.]
(5) In subsection (4)(d) "communications services" do not include electronic communications services to the extent that they are used to broadcast, or otherwise transmit, programme services (within the meaning of the Communications Act 2003).
[(5A) The goods and services referred to in subsection (4)(f) are—
 (a) point of sale terminals,
 (b) computer hardware and software,
 (c) information, advice and technical assistance in connection with the use of information technology,
 (d) data storage and processing,

(e) website hosting.]

(6) In this section, "the office holder" means, as the case may be—

(a) the interim trustee,

(b) the trustee in the sequestration, or

(c) the trustee acting under a trust deed.

NOTES

Commencement: 30 November 2016.

Sub-s (4): paras (aa), (ba), (ca), (cb), (e), (f) inserted and word omitted from para (c) repealed by the Public Services Reform (Corporate Insolvency and Bankruptcy) (Scotland) Order 2017, SSI 2017/209, art 7(1), (2).

Sub-s (5A): inserted by SSI 2017/209, art 7(1), (3).

[5.421]

223 Disqualification provisions: power to make regulations

(1) The Scottish Ministers may make regulations under this section in relation to a disqualification provision.

(2) A "disqualification provision" is a provision, made by or under any enactment, which disqualifies (whether permanently or temporarily and whether absolutely or conditionally) a relevant debtor or a category of relevant debtors from—

(a) being elected or appointed to an office or position,

(b) holding an office or position, or

(c) becoming or remaining a member of a body or group.

(3) In subsection (2), the reference to a provision which disqualifies a person conditionally includes a reference to a provision which enables the person to be dismissed.

(4) Regulations under subsection (1) may repeal or revoke the disqualification provision.

(5) Regulations under subsection (1) may amend, or modify the effect of, the disqualification provision—

(a) so as to reduce the category of relevant debtors to whom the disqualification provision applies,

(b) so as to extend the disqualification provision to some or all natural persons who are subject to a bankruptcy restrictions order,

(c) so that the disqualification provision applies only to some or all natural persons who are subject to a bankruptcy restrictions order,

(d) so as to make the application of the disqualification provision wholly or partly subject to the discretion of a specified person, body or group.

(6) Regulations made by virtue of subsection (5)(d) may provide for a discretion to be subject to—

(a) the approval of a specified person or body,

(b) appeal to a specified person, body, court or tribunal.

(7) The Scottish Ministers may be specified for the purposes of subsection (5)(d) or (6)(a) or (b).

(8) In this section, "bankruptcy restrictions order" includes—

(a) a bankruptcy restrictions order made under paragraph 1 of schedule 4A of the Insolvency Act 1986, and

(b) a bankruptcy restrictions undertaking entered into under paragraph 7 of that schedule.

(9) In this section, "relevant debtor" means a debtor—

(a) whose estate has been sequestrated,

(b) who has granted (or on whose behalf has been granted) a trust deed,

(c) who has been adjudged bankrupt by a court in England and Wales or in Northern Ireland, or

(d) who, in England and Wales or in Northern Ireland, has made an agreement with the debtor's creditors—

(i) for a composition in satisfaction of the debtor's debts,

(ii) for a scheme of arrangement of the debtor's affairs, or

(iii) for some other kind of settlement or arrangement.

(10) Regulations under this section may make—

(a) provision generally or for a specified purpose only,

(b) different provision for different purposes, and

(c) transitional, consequential or incidental provision.

NOTES

Commencement: 30 November 2016.

[5.422]

224 Regulations: applications to Accountant in Bankruptcy etc

(1) The Scottish Minsters may, by regulations, make provision in relation to the procedure to be followed in relation to—

(a) an application to AiB under this Act,

(b) an application to AiB for a review under this Act,

(c) any other decision made by AiB under this Act.

(2) In this section, "decision" includes any appointment, determination, direction, award, acceptance, rejection, adjudication, requirement, declaration, order or valuation made by AiB.

(3) Regulations under subsection (1) may in particular make provision for, or in connection with—

(a) the procedure to be followed by the person making an application,

(b) the form of any report or other document that may be required for the purposes of an application or a decision,

(c) the form of a statement of undertakings that must be given by the debtor when making a debtor application,
(d) time limits applying in relation to the procedure,
(e) the procedure to be followed in connection with the production and recovery of documents relating to an application or a decision,
(f) the procedure to be followed (including provision about those entitled to participate) in determining an application or making a decision, and
(g) the procedure to be followed after an application is determined or a decision is made.

(4) Regulations under subsection (1) may—
(a) include such supplementary, incidental or consequential provision as the Scottish Minsters consider appropriate, or
(b) modify any enactment (including this Act).

(5) This section is without prejudice to section 194.

NOTES

Commencement: 30 November 2016.

Regulations: the Bankruptcy (Applications and Decisions) (Scotland) Regulations 2016, SSI 2016/295 at **[16.295]**; the Bankruptcy (Scotland) Regulations 2016, SSI 2016/397 at **[16.401]**.

PART 18
GENERAL

[5.423]

225 Regulations: general

(1) This section relates to regulations made under this Act by the Scottish Ministers.

(2) Such regulations may make different provision for different cases or classes of case.

(3) Subject to subsections (4) and (5), the regulations are subject to the negative procedure.

(4) Regulations under—
(a) section 2(4), (5) or (8)(a), 4(2)(b), 7(1), 9(4), 89(1), 94(7), 112(7)(g), 166(2)(b) or (c), 169, 170(1)(b) or (e), 174(2) or (3), 175(1), 181(2), 183(1)(a) or (b), 184(1)(b) or (2)(a), 186(3) or (9), 194(1) or 223,
(b) section 224(1) and containing provisions which add to, replace or omit any part of the text of an Act or of an Act of the Scottish Parliament, or
(c) paragraph 2(7) of schedule 1,

are subject to the affirmative procedure.

(5) Regulations made under section 237(2) are not subject to the negative procedure or to the affirmative procedure.

NOTES

Commencement: 29 April 2016.

Regulations: the Bankruptcy (Applications and Decisions) (Scotland) Regulations 2016, SSI 2016/295 at **[16.295]**; the Bankruptcy (Scotland) Regulations 2016, SSI 2016/397 at **[16.401]**; the Protected Trust Deeds (Forms) (Scotland) Regulations 2016, SSI 2016/398 at **[16.438]**; the Bankruptcy Fees (Scotland) Revocation Regulations 2017, SSI 2017/97.

[5.424]

226 Modification of regulation making powers

Any power in a provision of this Act to make regulations may, in so far as the provision relates to a matter to which the [EU] insolvency proceedings regulation applies, be exercised for the purpose of making provision in consequence of the [EU} insolvency proceedings regulation.

NOTES

Commencement: 29 April 2016.

Word in square brackets in both places substituted for original word "EC" by the Insolvency (Regulation (EU) 2015/848) (Miscellaneous Amendments) (Scotland) Regulations 2017, SSI 2017/210, regs 4(1), (20), 9, as from 26 June 2017, except in relation to proceedings opened before that date.

[5.425]

227 Variation of references to time, money etc

For any reference in this Act to—
(a) a period of time,
(b) an amount of money, or
(c) a fraction,

there may be prescribed, in substitution, some other period or as the case may be some other amount or fraction.

NOTES

Commencement: 30 November 2016.

Regulations: the Bankruptcy (Applications and Decisions) (Scotland) Regulations 2016, SSI 2016/295 at **[16.295]**.

[5.426]

228 Interpretation

(1) In this Act, unless the context otherwise requires—

"the 2002 Act" means the Debt Arrangement and Attachment (Scotland) Act 2002,

"Accountant in Bankruptcy" (or "AiB") is to be construed in accordance with section 199,
"accounting period" is to be construed in accordance with section 130(2),
"apparent insolvency" and "apparently insolvent" are to be construed in accordance with section 16,
"appropriate bank or institution" means—

(a) the Bank of England,

(b) a person who has permission under Part 4 of the Financial Services and Markets Act 2000 to accept deposits,

(c) an EEA firm of the kind mentioned in paragraph 5(b) of schedule 3 of that Act which has permission under paragraph 15 of that schedule (as a result of qualifying for authorisation under paragraph 12 of that schedule) to accept deposits, or

(d) a person who is exempt from the general prohibition in respect of accepting deposits as a result of an exemption order made under section 38(1) of that Act,

"associate" is to be construed in accordance with section 229,
"bankruptcy restrictions order" has the meaning given by section 155(1),
"business" means the carrying on of any activity, whether for profit or not,
"centre of main interests" has the same meaning as in the [EU] insolvency proceedings regulation,
"commissioner", except in the expression "examining commissioner", is to be construed in accordance with section 76,
"common financial tool" has the meaning given by section 89(1),
"court" means Court of Session or sheriff,
"creditor" includes a member State [insolvency practitioner] deemed to be a creditor under section 207,
"DAS register" has the meaning given by section 195(4)(b),
"date of sequestration" has the meaning given by section 22(7),
"debt advice and information package" has the meaning given by section 3(2),
"debtor" includes, without prejudice to the expression's generality, an entity whose estate may be sequestrated by virtue of section 6, a deceased debtor, a deceased debtor's executor or a person entitled to be appointed a deceased debtor's executor,
"debtor application" means an application for sequestration made to AiB under section 2(1)(a), 5(a) or 6(3)(a), (4)(b) or (7)(a),
"debtor contribution order" has the meaning given by section 90(1),
"debtor's contribution" has the meaning given by section 89(1),
"the EC insolvency proceedings regulation" means Council Regulation (EC) No 1346/2000 of 29 May 2000 on insolvency proceedings,
"establishment" has the meaning given by [Article 2(10) of the EU] insolvency proceedings regulation,
["the EU insolvency proceedings regulation" means Regulation (EU) 2015/848 of the European Parliament and of the Council on insolvency proceedings,]
"examination" means a private examination under section 118 or a public examination under section 119,
"examining commissioner" is to be construed in accordance with section 120(3),
"interim bankruptcy restrictions order" is to be construed in accordance with section 160,
"interim trustee" is to be construed in accordance with sections 53 and 54,
"main proceedings" means proceedings opened in accordance with Article 3(1) of the [EU] insolvency proceedings regulation and falling within the definition of insolvency proceedings in [Article 2(4)] of that regulation and—

(a) in relation to *England and Wales and* Scotland, set out in Annex A to that regulation under the heading "United Kingdom", and

(b) in relation to another member State, set out in Annex A to that regulation under the heading relating to that member State,

["member State insolvency practitioner" means a person falling within the definition of insolvency practitioner in Article 2(5) of the EU insolvency proceedings regulation appointed in proceedings to which it applies in a member State other than the United Kingdom,]
"money adviser" has the meaning given by section 4(2),
"ordinary debt" is to be construed in accordance with section 129(1)(g),
"original trustee" is to be construed in accordance with section 49(1)(a),
"postponed debt" has the meaning given by section 129(4),
"preferred debt" has the meaning given by section 129(2),
"prescribed" means prescribed by regulations made by the Scottish Ministers,
"protected trust deed" is to be construed in accordance with section 163,
"qualified creditor" and "qualified creditors" are to be construed in accordance with section 7(1),
"qualified to act as an insolvency practitioner" is to be construed in accordance with section 390 of the Insolvency Act 1986 (persons not qualified to act as insolvency practitioners),
"register of insolvencies" has the meaning given by section 200(1)(c),
"relevant person" has the meaning given by section 118(2),
"replacement trustee" is to be construed in accordance with section 49(1)(b),
["secondary proceedings" means proceedings opened in accordance with Articles 3(2) and (3) of the EU insolvency proceedings regulation which are set out in Annex A to that regulation—

(a) n relation to Scotland, under the heading "United Kingdom", and

(b) in relation to another member State, under the heading relating to that member State,]

"secured creditor" means a creditor who holds a security for a debt over any part of the debtor's estate,

"security" means any security, heritable or moveable, or any right of lien, retention or preference,
"sederunt book" means the sederunt book maintained under section 50(1)(e),
"sequestration proceedings" includes a debtor application (and analogous expressions are to be construed accordingly),
"statement of assets and liabilities" means a document (including a copy of a document) in such form as may be prescribed containing—
(a) a list of the debtor's assets and liabilities,
(b) a list of the debtor's income and expenditure, and
(c) such other information as may be prescribed,
"statement of undertakings" means the statement of debtor undertakings sent to the debtor under section 51(14) or 54(4) or, in the case of a debtor application, given by the debtor in making the application,
"statutory meeting" has the meaning given by section 43,
"temporary administrator" means a temporary administrator referred to by [Article 52 of the EU] insolvency proceedings regulation,
"territorial proceedings" means any proceedings opened in accordance with Articles 3(2) and 3(4) of the EC insolvency proceedings regulation, falling within the definition of insolvency proceedings in [Article 2(4)] of that regulation and—
(a) in relation to *England and Wales and* Scotland, set out in Annex A to that regulation under the heading "United Kingdom", and
(b) in relation to another member State, set out in Annex A to that regulation under the heading relating to that member State,
"trust deed" means—
(a) a voluntary trust deed granted by or on behalf of a debtor whereby the debtor's estate (other than such of that estate as would not, under any provision of this or any other enactment, vest in the trustee were that estate sequestrated) is conveyed to the trustee for the benefit of the debtor's creditors generally, and
(b) any other trust deed which would fall within paragraph (a) but for—
(i) the exclusion from the estate conveyed to the trustee of the whole or part of the debtor's dwellinghouse, where a secured creditor holds a security over it, and
(ii) the fact that the debtor's estate is not conveyed to the trustee for the benefit of creditors generally because the secured creditor has, at the debtor's request, agreed before the trust deed is granted not to claim under the trust deed for any of the debt in respect of which the security is held,
"trustee vote" is to be construed in accordance with section 49(1) and (2), and
"unfair preference" means a preference created as is mentioned in subsection (1) of section 99 by a transaction to which subsection (5) of that section applies.

(2) The expressions in the definition of "appropriate bank or institution" in subsection (1) must be read with—
(a) section 22 of the Financial Services and Markets Act 2000,
(b) any relevant order under that section, and
(c) schedule 2 of that Act.

(3) In paragraph (b)(i) of the definition of "trust deed" in subsection (1), "the debtor's dwellinghouse" means a dwellinghouse (including any yard, garden, outbuilding or other pertinents) which, on the day immediately preceding the date the trust deed was granted—
(a) the debtor (whether alone or in common with any other person)—
(i) owned, or
(ii) leased under a long lease ("long lease" having the same meaning as in section 9(2) of the Land Registration etc (Scotland) Act 2012), and
(b) was the debtor's sole or main residence.

(4) For the purposes of subsection (3)(b), a dwellinghouse may be the debtor's sole or main residence irrespective of whether it is used, to any extent, by the debtor for the purposes of any profession, trade or business.

(5) Any reference in this Act to a debtor being absolutely insolvent is to be construed as a reference to the debtor's liabilities being greater than the debtor's assets; and any reference to a debtor's estate being absolutely insolvent is to be construed accordingly.

(6) Any reference in this Act to value of the creditors is, in relation to any matter, a reference to the value of their claims as accepted for the purposes of that matter.

(7) Any reference in this Act to "the creditors" in the context of their giving consent or doing any other thing is, unless the context otherwise requires, to be construed as a reference to the majority in value of such creditors as vote in that context at a meeting of creditors.

(8) Any reference in this Act to any of the actings mentioned in subsection (9) barring the effect of any enactment or rule of law relating to the limitation of actions is to be construed as a reference to that act having the same effect, for the purposes of that enactment or rule of law, as an effective acknowledgement of the creditor's claim.

(9) The actings are—
(a) the presentation of a petition for sequestration,
(b) the concurrence in a debtor application, and
(c) the submission of a claim.

(10) Any reference in this Act to any such enactment as is mentioned in subsection (8) does not include a reference to an enactment which implements or gives effect to any international agreement or obligation.

(11) Any reference in this Act, however expressed, to the time when a petition for sequestration is presented is to be construed as a reference to the time when the petition is received by the sheriff clerk.
(12) Any reference in this Act, however expressed, to the time when a debtor application is made is to be construed as a reference to the time when the application is received by AiB.

NOTES

Commencement: 29 April 2016.

Regulations: the Bankruptcy (Scotland) Regulations 2016, SSI 2016/397 at **[16.401]**.

Sub-s (1) is amended by the Insolvency (Regulation (EU) 2015/848) (Miscellaneous Amendments) (Scotland) Regulations 2017, SSI 2017/210, regs 4(1), (21), 9, as from 26 June 2017, except in relation to proceedings opened before that date, as follows:

—in definition "centre of main interests", word in square brackets substituted for original word "EC";
—in definition "creditor", words in square brackets substituted for original word "liquidator";
—definition "the EC insolvency proceedings regulation" in italics repealed;
—in definition "establishment" words in square brackets substituted for original words "Article 2(h) of the EC";
—definition "the EU insolvency proceedings regulation" inserted;
—in definition "main proceedings" words in first and second pairs of square brackets substituted for original words "EC" and "Article 2(a)" respectively and words in italics repealed;
—definitions "member State insolvency practitioner" and "secondary proceedings" substituted and those definitions originally read as follows:

"member State liquidator" means a person falling within the definition of liquidator in Article 2(b) of the EC insolvency proceedings regulation appointed in proceedings to which it applies in a member State other than the United Kingdom,
"secondary proceedings" means proceedings opened in accordance with Articles 3(2) and 3(3) of the EC insolvency proceedings regulation, falling within the definition of winding-up proceedings in Article 2(c) of that regulation and—
(a) in relation to England and Wales and Scotland, set out in Annex B to that regulation under the heading "United Kingdom", and
(b) in relation to another member State, set out in Annex B to that regulation under the heading relating to that member State,";

—in definition "temporary administrator" words in square brackets substituted for original words "Article 38 of the EC"; and
—in definition "territorial proceedings" words in square brackets substituted for original words "Article 2(a)" and words in italics repealed.

[5.427]

229 Meaning of "associate"

(1) For the purposes of this Act, any question whether a person is an associate of another person must be determined in accordance with the following provisions of this section.
(2) Subsection (1) is subject to section 230(1).
(3) And any reference, whether in the following provisions of this section or in regulations under section 230(1), to a person being an associate of another person is to be taken to be a reference to their being associates of each other.
(4) A person (in this subsection referred to as "A") is an associate of a natural person (in this subsection referred to as "B") if A is—
(a) B's spouse or civil partner,
(b) a relative of B or of B's spouse or civil partner, or
(c) the spouse or civil partner of such a relative.
(5) A person (in this subsection referred to as "C") is an associate of any person (in this subsection referred to as "D") with whom C is in partnership and of any person who is an associate of D.
(6) A firm is an associate of any person who is a member of the firm.
(7) For the purposes of this section, a person (in this subsection referred to as "E") is a relative of a natural person (in this subsection referred to as "F") if E is F's brother, sister, uncle, aunt, nephew, niece, lineal ancestor or lineal descendant treating any relationship of the half-blood as a relationship of the whole-blood and the stepchild or adopted child of someone (in this subsection referred to as "S") as S's child.
(8) References in this section to a spouse or civil partner include references to a former spouse or civil partner and a reputed spouse or civil partner.
(9) A person (in this subsection referred to as "G") is an associate of any person whom G employs or by whom G is employed.
(10) For the purposes of subsection (9), any director or other officer of a company is to be treated as employed by the company.
(11) A company is an associate of another company if—
(a) the same person has control of both, or if a person (in this subsection referred to as "H") has control of one and persons who are H's associates have control of the other, or
(b) a group of two or more persons has control of each company and the groups either—
(i) consist of the same persons, or
(ii) could be regarded as consisting of the same persons by treating (in one case or more) a member of either group as replaced by a person of whom that member is an associate.
(12) A company is an associate of another person (in this subsection referred to as "J") if—
(a) J has control of it, or
(b) J and persons who are J's associates together have control of it.
(13) For the purposes of this section, a person (in this subsection referred to as "K") is taken to have control of a company—
(a) if the directors of the company, or of another company which has control of it, (or any of them) are accustomed to act in accordance with K's directions or instructions, or

(b) if K is entitled to exercise, or control the exercise of, ? or more of the voting power at any general meeting of the company or of another company which has control of the company.

(14) Where two or more persons together satisfy either of the conditions mentioned in subsection (13), they are taken to have control of the company.

(15) In subsections (10) to (14), "company" includes any body corporate (whether incorporated in Great Britain or elsewhere).

NOTES

Commencement: 29 April 2016.

[5.428]

230 "Associates": regulations for the purposes of section 229

(1) The Scottish Ministers may by regulations—

(a) amend section 229 so as to provide further categories of persons who, for the purposes of this Act, are to be associates of other persons, and

(b) provide that any or all of subsections (4) to (15) of that section (or any subsection added to that section by virtue of paragraph (a))—

(i) is to cease to apply, whether in whole or in part, or

(ii) is to apply subject to such modifications as they may specify in the regulations.

(2) The Scottish Ministers may in the regulations make such incidental or transitional provision as they consider appropriate.

NOTES

Commencement: 29 April 2016.

[5.429]

231 Proceedings under [EU] insolvency proceedings regulation: modified definition of "estate"

In the application of this Act to insolvency proceedings under the [EU] insolvency proceedings regulation, a reference to "estate" is a reference to estate which may be dealt with in those proceedings.

NOTES

Commencement: 30 November 2016.

Word in square brackets in section heading and text substituted for original word "EC" by the Insolvency (Regulation (EU) 2015/848) (Miscellaneous Amendments) (Scotland) Regulations 2017, SSI 2017/210, regs 4(1), (22), (23), 9, as from 26 June 2017, except in relation to proceedings opened before that date.

[5.430]

232 Crown application

This Act binds the Crown as creditor only.

NOTES

Commencement: 30 November 2016.

[5.431]

233 Re-enactment

Schedule 7, derived from Part 2 of schedule 7 of the Bankruptcy (Scotland) Act 1985 (and re-enacting sections 10 and 189 of the Bankruptcy (Scotland) Act 1913), has effect.

NOTES

Commencement: 30 November 2016.

[5.432]

234 Modifications, repeals, savings, revocations and transitional provisions

(1) Schedule 8 makes provision for the modification of enactments.

(2) The enactments mentioned in schedule 9 are repealed, or as the case may be revoked, to the extent mentioned in the second column of that schedule.

(3) Nothing in this Act affects—

(a) any of the enactments repealed, revoked or amended by this Act in the enactment's operation in relation to—

(i) a sequestration as regards which the petition was presented, or the debtor application was made before, or

(ii) a trust deed executed before,

the coming into force of this Act, or

(b) any power to repeal, revoke or amend any such enactment, in so far as the power relates to such operation of the enactment.

(4) The apparent insolvency of a debtor may be constituted for the purposes of this Act even though the circumstance founded on for such constitution occurred on a date before the coming into force of this Act; and for those purposes the apparent insolvency is taken to have been constituted on the date in question.

(5) If a debtor whose estate is sequestrated after the coming into force of this Act is liable, by virtue of a transaction entered into before the date on which section 102 of the Bankruptcy (Scotland) Act 1913 was repealed, to pay royalties or a share of the profits to any person in respect of copyright, or interest in copyright, comprised in the sequestrated estate, then that section applies in relation to the trustee in the sequestration as it applied, before its repeal, in relation to any trustee in bankruptcy (within the meaning of that Act).

(6) Where sequestration of a debtor's estate is awarded under this Act a person—

(a) does not commit an offence under any provision of this Act in respect of anything done before the date of commencement of that provision, but

(b) instead commits an offence under the Bankruptcy (Scotland) Act 1985 (or as the case may be under the Bankruptcy (Scotland) Act 1913) in respect of anything so done which would have been an offence under that Act if the award of sequestration had been made under that Act.

(7) Unless the context otherwise requires, any reference in any enactment or document—

(a) to notour bankruptcy, or to a person being notour bankrupt, is to be construed as a reference to apparent insolvency, or to a person being apparently insolvent, within the meaning of section 16 of this Act,

(b) to a person's estate being sequestrated under the Bankruptcy (Scotland) Act 1913 or the Bankruptcy (Scotland) Act 1985 is to be construed as, or as including, a reference to its being sequestrated under this Act, and

(c) to a trustee in sequestration or to a trustee in bankruptcy, is to be construed as a reference to a trustee in a sequestration within the meaning of this Act,

(analogous references being construed accordingly).

(8) Unless the context otherwise requires, any reference in any enactment or document—

(a) to a "gratuitous alienation" is to be construed as including a reference to an alienation challengeable under section 98(2), or

(b) to a "fraudulent preference" or to an "unfair preference" is to be construed as including a reference to an unfair preference within the meaning of this Act.

NOTES

Commencement: 30 November 2016.

Regulations: the Bankruptcy (Scotland) Regulations 2016, SSI 2016/397 at **[16.401]**.

[5.433]

235 Continuity of the law

(1) The repeal and re-enactment of a provision by this Act does not affect the continuity of the law.

(2) Anything done, or having effect as if done, under (or for the purposes of or in reliance on) a provision repealed by this Act, being a provision in force or effective immediately before the coming into force of this Act, has effect after that coming into force as if done under (or for the purposes of or in reliance on) the corresponding provision of this Act.

(3) Any reference (express or implied) in this Act or in any other enactment or document to a provision of this Act is to be construed, so far as the context permits, as including, as respects times, circumstances or purposes in relation to which the corresponding repealed provision had effect, a reference to that corresponding provision.

(4) Any reference (express or implied) in any enactment or document to a provision repealed by this Act is to be construed, so far as the context permits, as including, as respects times, circumstances or purposes in relation to which the corresponding provision of this Act has effect, a reference to that corresponding provision.

(5) Subsections (1) to (4) have effect in place of section 19(3) to (5) of the Interpretation and Legislative Reform (Scotland) Act 2010 (effect of repeal and re-enactment); but nothing in this section affects any other provision of that Act.

(6) This section is without prejudice to section 234(3) and to any specific transitional provision or saving contained in this Act.

(7) References in this section to this Act include subordinate legislation made under or by virtue of this Act.

NOTES

Commencement: 30 November 2016.

[5.434]

236 Sequestrations to which this Act applies

This Act applies to sequestrations as regards which the petition is presented, or the debtor application is made on or after the day on which this section comes into force.

NOTES

Commencement: 30 November 2016.

[5.435]

237 Commencement

(1) This section and sections 225, 226, 228 to 230 and 238 come into force on the day after Royal Assent.

(2) The remaining provisions of this Act come into force on such day as the Scottish Ministers may by regulations appoint.

(3) Different days may, under subsection (2), be appointed for different purposes and for different provisions.

NOTES

Commencement: 29 April 2016.

[5.436]

238 Short title

The short title of this Act is the Bankruptcy (Scotland) Act 2016.

NOTES

Commencement: 29 April 2016.

SCHEDULES

SCHEDULE 1
DEBTOR TO WHOM SECTION 2(2) APPLIES: APPLICATION OF ACT

(introduced by section 2(6))

Modification of certain provisions of Act

[5.437]

1 (1) Where section 2(2) applies in relation to a debtor, this Act applies subject to the modifications mentioned in sub-paragraphs (2) to (6).

(2) Section 42 applies as if for subsection (1) there were substituted—

"(1) This section applies where AiB receives by virtue of section 8(3)(a) the statement of assets and liabilities in relation to a debtor to whom section 2(2) applies.

(1A) As soon as practicable, AiB must prepare a statement of the debtor's affairs, so far as within the knowledge of AiB, stating that, because 2(2) applies in relation to the debtor, no claims may be submitted by creditors under section 46 or 122.

(1B) AiB must send a copy of the statement prepared under subsection (1A) to every known creditor of the debtor.".

(3) Section 50(1) applies as if paragraphs (e) and (f) were omitted.

(4) Section 116 applies as if for subsection (2) there were substituted—

"(2) AiB may at any time before the discharge of the debtor require the debtor to give an account in writing, in such form as may be prescribed, of the debtor's current state of affairs.".

(5) Section 151 applies as if—

(a) subsections (2) to (6) and (9)(a) were omitted, and

(b) for subsection (7) there were substituted—

"(7) The debtor or any creditor may, within 14 days beginning with the day on which the debtor is discharged under section 140(1), appeal to the sheriff against the discharge of AiB in respect of AiB's actings as trustee.".

(6) Sections 44, 46, 48, 49, 60, 63 to 65, 122, 131 and 210(3) do not apply.

Accountant in Bankruptcy's duty to consider whether paragraph 1 should cease to have effect

2 (1) This paragraph applies where paragraph 1 applies in relation to a debtor.

(2) If AiB considers that the circumstances mentioned in any of sub-paragraphs (3) to (6) apply in relation to the debtor, AiB must consider whether paragraph 1 should cease to have effect in relation to the debtor.

(3) The circumstances are that—

(a) AiB becomes aware the debtor application submitted under section 2 contains an error, and

(b) the nature of the error is such that the debtor was not at the time of application a debtor to whom section 2(2) applies.

(4) The circumstances are that—

(a) AiB becomes aware that the debtor application submitted under section 2 deliberately misrepresents, or fails to state, a fact that was the case at the time of application, and

(b) the nature of the misrepresentation or the omission of the fact is such that the debtor was not at that time a debtor to whom section 2(2) applies.

(5) The circumstances are that, at any time after the date on which the debtor application is made—

(a) the total value of the debtor's assets (leaving out of account any liabilities and any assets that, under section 88(1), would not vest in a trustee) exceeds £5,000 or such other sum as may be prescribed, or

(b) AiB assesses the debtor, under the common financial tool, as being able to make a contribution.

(6) The circumstances are that, at any time after the date of sequestration—

(a) AiB is not satisfied that the debtor has co-operated with the trustee, and

(b) AiB considers that if paragraph 1 were to cease to have effect it would be—

(i) of financial benefit to the estate of the debtor, and

(ii) in the interests of the creditors.

(7) The Scottish Ministers may by regulations modify this paragraph—
(a) by modifying the circumstances in which paragraph 1 ceases to have effect,
(b) in consequence of any modification made under sub-paragraph (7)(a).

Procedure where Accountant in Bankruptcy considers paragraph 1 should cease to have effect

3 (1) If AiB considers under paragraph 2(2) that paragraph 1 should cease to have effect in relation to a debtor, AiB must notify the debtor of that fact and of the matters mentioned in sub-paragraph (2).

(2) The matters are—
(a) the circumstances mentioned in paragraph 2 which AiB considers apply in relation to the debtor, and
(b) that the debtor may make representations to AiB within 14 days beginning with the giving of notification under sub-paragraph (1).

(3) On the expiry of the 14 days mentioned in sub-paragraph (2)(b) and after having taken into account any representations made by the debtor under that sub-paragraph, AIB must decide whether paragraph 1 should cease to have effect in relation to the debtor.

(4) If AiB decides that paragraph 1 should cease to have effect in relation to the debtor, AiB must, as soon as practicable after reaching that decision, give notice in writing to the debtor—
(a) of the decision, and
(b) of the effect of the decision.

Debtor's right of appeal against decision under paragraph 3

4 (1) This paragraph applies where AiB gives notice to a debtor under paragraph 3(4).

(2) The debtor may appeal to the sheriff against the decision.

(3) Any such appeal must be lodged within 14 days after the day on which the notice is given.

(4) If the sheriff grants the appeal, paragraph 1 continues to have effect in relation to the debtor.

(5) If the sheriff refuses the appeal, or if it is abandoned or withdrawn, paragraph 1 ceases to have effect in relation to the debtor.

Decision that paragraph 1 ceases to have effect: modification of certain provisions of Act

5 (1) Where paragraph 1 ceases to have effect in relation to a debtor, this Act applies subject to sub-paragraphs (2) to (4).

(2) The debtor must send to the trustee a statement of assets and liabilities—
(a) where no appeal is taken under paragraph 4, within 7 days beginning with the expiry of the period during which an appeal may be made under that paragraph, or
(b) where an appeal is refused or, as the case may be, abandoned or withdrawn, within 7 days beginning with—
(i) the day on which notice is given of the outcome of the appeal, or
(ii) as the case may be, its abandonment or withdrawal.

(3) Section 44 applies as if, in subsection (3)(a), for the words "sequestration is awarded" there were substituted "paragraph 1 of schedule 1 ceases to have effect in relation to the debtor".

(4) Section 116 applies as if for subsection (2) there were substituted—

"(2) The trustee in the sequestration must require the debtor to give an account in writing, in such form as may be prescribed, of the debtor's current state of affairs—
(a) within 60 days beginning with the day on which paragraph 1 of schedule 1 ceases to have effect in relation to the debtor,
(b) on the expiry of 6 months beginning with the day on which the account is given under paragraph (a), and
(c) on the expiry of each subsequent 6 months.".

NOTES

Commencement: 30 November 2016.
Regulations: the Bankruptcy (Scotland) Regulations 2016, SSI 2016/397 at **[16.401]**.

SCHEDULE 2
DETERMINATION OF AMOUNT OF CREDITOR'S CLAIM

(introduced by sections 7(4), 46(9) and 125(4))

Amount which may be claimed generally

[5.438]

1 (1) Subject to the provisions of this schedule, the amount in respect of which a creditor is entitled to claim is the accumulated sum of principal and any interest which is due on the debt as at the date of sequestration.

(2) If a debt does not depend on a contingency but would not be payable but for the sequestration until after the date of the sequestration, the amount of the claim must be calculated as if the debt were payable on that date but subject to the deduction of interest at the rate specified in section 129(10) from that date until the date for payment of the debt.

(3) In calculating the amount of a creditor's claim, the creditor must deduct any discount (other than any discount for payment in cash) which is allowable by contract or course of dealing between the creditor and the debtor or by the usage of trade.

Claims for aliment and for periodical allowance on divorce or on dissolution of civil partnership

2 (1) A person entitled to aliment, however arising, from a living debtor as at the date of sequestration, or from a deceased debtor immediately before the debtor's death, is not entitled to include in the amount of the person's claim—

(a) any unpaid aliment for any period before the date of sequestration unless the amount of the aliment has been quantified by court decree or by any legally binding obligation which is supported by evidence in writing, and—

(i) in the case of spouses (or, where the aliment is payable to a divorced person in respect of a child, former spouses), or

(ii) in the case of civil partners (or, where the aliment is payable to a former civil partner in respect of a child after dissolution of a civil partnership, former civil partners),

they were living apart during that period, or

(b) any aliment for a period after the date of sequestration.

(2) Sub-paragraph (1) applies to a periodical allowance payable on divorce or on dissolution of a civil partnership—

(a) by virtue of a court order, or

(b) under any legally binding obligation which is supported by evidence in writing,

as it applies to aliment and as if, for sub-paragraphs (i) and (ii) of sub-paragraph (1)(a) and the word "they" which immediately follows sub-paragraph (ii), there were substituted "the payer and payee".

Debts depending on contingency

3 (1) The amount which a creditor is entitled to claim does not include a debt in so far as its existence or amount depend on a contingency.

(2) But sub-paragraph (1) is subject to sub-paragraph (3).

(3) On an application by the creditor—

(a) to the trustee in the sequestration, or

(b) if there is no trustee, to AiB,

the trustee, or AiB, must put a value on the debt in so far as it is contingent.

(4) The amount in respect of which the creditor is then entitled to claim is that value but no more.

(5) And where the contingent debt is an annuity, a cautioner may not then be sued for more than that value.

(6) An interested person may apply to AiB for a review of a valuation under sub-paragraph (3) by the trustee.

(7) Any application under sub-paragraph (6) must be made within 14 days beginning with the day of the valuation.

(8) If an application under sub-paragraph (6) is made, AiB must—

(a) take into account any representations made by an interested person within 21 days beginning with the day on which the application is made, and

(b) confirm or vary the valuation within 28 days beginning with that day.

(9) An interested person may appeal to the sheriff against a decision by AiB under sub-paragraph (8)(b) within 14 days beginning with the day of the decision.

(10) AiB may refer a case to the sheriff for a direction before making a decision under sub-paragraph (8)(b).

(11) An appeal to the sheriff under sub-paragraph (9) may not be made in relation to a matter on which AiB has applied for a direction under sub-paragraph (10).

Secured debts

4 (1) A secured creditor, in calculating the amount of the secured creditor's claim, must deduct the value of any security as estimated by the secured creditor.

(2) But if the secured creditor surrenders, or undertakes in writing to surrender, a security for the benefit of the debtor's estate, the secured creditor is not required to make a deduction of the value of that security.

(3) The trustee in the sequestration may, at any time after the expiry of 12 weeks after the date of sequestration, require the secured creditor, at the expense of the debtor's estate, to discharge the security or convey or assign it to the trustee on payment to the creditor of the value specified by the creditor.

(4) The amount in respect of which the creditor is then entitled to claim is any balance of the creditor's debt remaining after receipt of the payment.

(5) A creditor whose security has been realised, in calculating the amount of the creditor's claim, must deduct the amount (less the expenses of realisation) which the creditor has received, or is entitled to receive, from the realisation.

Valuation of claims against partners for debts of the partnership

5 (1) Where a creditor claims, in respect of a debt of a partnership, against the estate of one of its partners, the creditor must estimate the value of—

(a) the debt to the creditor from the firm's estate where that estate has not been sequestrated, or

(b) the creditor's claim against that estate where it has been sequestrated,

and deduct that value from the creditor's claim against the partner's estate.

(2) The amount in respect of which the creditor is entitled to claim on the partner's estate is the balance remaining after that deduction is made.

NOTES

Commencement: 30 November 2016.

SCHEDULE 3
PREFERRED DEBTS

(introduced by section 129(2) and (3))

PART 1
LIST OF PREFERRED DEBTS

Contributions to occupational pension schemes etc

[5.439]

1 Any sum which is owed by the debtor and is a sum to which schedule 4 of the Pension Schemes Act 1993 (contributions to occupational pension scheme and state scheme premiums) applies.

Remuneration of employees etc

2 (1) So much of any amount which—

(a) is owed by the debtor to a person who is or has been an employee of the debtor, and

(b) is payable by way of remuneration in respect of the whole or any part of the 4 months which immediately precedes the relevant date,

as does not exceed the prescribed amount.

(2) An amount owed by way of accrued holiday remuneration, in respect of any period of employment before the relevant date, to a person whose employment by the debtor has been terminated (whether before, on or after that date).

(3) So much of any amount owed in respect of money advanced for the purpose as has been applied for the payment of a debt which, if it had not been paid, would have been a debt falling within sub-paragraph (1) or (2).

3 So much of any amount which—

(a) is ordered, whether before or after the relevant date, to be paid by the debtor under the Reserve Forces (Safeguard of Employment) Act 1985, and

(b) is so ordered in respect of a default made by the debtor before that date in the discharge of the debtor's obligations under that Act,

as does not exceed such amount as may be prescribed.

Levies on coal and steel production

4 Any sums due at the relevant date from the debtor in respect of—

(a) the levies on the production of coal and steel referred to in Articles 49 and 50 of the Treaty establishing the European Coal and Steel Community, or

(b) any surcharge for delay provided for in Article 50(3) of that Treaty and Article 6 of Decision 3/52 of the High Authority of that Community.

Debts owed to the Financial Services Compensation Scheme

5 Any debt owed by the debtor to the scheme manager of the Financial Services Compensation Scheme under section 215(2A) of the Financial Services and Markets Act 2000.

Deposits covered by Financial Services Compensation Scheme

6 So much of any amount owed at the relevant date by the debtor in respect of an eligible deposit as does not exceed the compensation that would be payable in respect of the deposit under the Financial Services Compensation Scheme to the person or persons to whom the amount is owed.

Other deposits

7 So much of any amount owed at the relevant date by the debtor to one or more eligible persons in respect of an eligible deposit as exceeds any compensation that would be payable in respect of the deposit under the Financial Services Compensation Scheme to that person or those persons.

8 An amount owed at the relevant date by the debtor to one or more eligible persons in respect of a deposit which—

(a) was made through a non-EEA branch of a credit institution authorised by the competent authority of an EEA state, and

(b) would have been an eligible deposit if it had been made through an EEA branch of that credit institution.

NOTES

Commencement: 30 November 2016.

PART 2
INTERPRETATION OF PART 1

Meaning of "the relevant date"

[5.440]

9 In Part 1, "the relevant date" means—

(a) in relation to a debtor other than a deceased debtor, the date of sequestration, and

(b) in relation to a deceased debtor, the date of death.

Amounts payable by way of remuneration

10 (1) For the purposes of paragraph 2, a sum is payable by the debtor to a person by way of remuneration in respect of any period if—

(a) it is paid as wages or salary (whether payable for time or for piece work or earned wholly or partly by way of commission) in respect of services rendered to the debtor in that period, or

(b) it is an amount falling within sub-paragraph (2) and is payable by the debtor in respect of that period.

(2) An amount falls within this sub-paragraph if it is—

(a) a guarantee payment under section 28(1) to (3) of the Employment Rights Act 1996 (entitlement to payment for workless day),

(b) a payment for time off under section 53(1) (looking for new employment or making arrangements for training for future employment) or 56(1) (antenatal care) of that Act,

(c) remuneration on suspension on medical grounds under section 64 of that Act,

(d) a payment for time off under section 169(1) of the Trade Union and Labour Relations (Consolidation) Act 1992 (trade union duties), or

(e) remuneration under a protective award made by an employment tribunal under section 189 of that Act (redundancy dismissal with compensation).

(3) For the purposes of paragraph 2(2), holiday remuneration is deemed, in the case of a person ("P") whose employment has been terminated by or in consequence of the award of sequestration of P's employer's estate, to have accrued to P in respect of a period of employment if, by virtue of P's contract of employment or of any enactment, that remuneration would have accrued in respect of that period if P's employment had continued until P became entitled to be allowed the holiday.

(4) In sub-paragraph (3), "enactment" includes an order made or direction given under an enactment.

(5) Without prejudice to the preceding provisions of this paragraph—

(a) any remuneration payable by the debtor to a person in respect of a period—

(i) of holiday, or

(ii) of absence from work through sickness or other good cause,

is deemed to be wages, or as the case may be salary, in respect of services rendered to the debtor in that period, and

(b) references in this paragraph to remuneration in respect of a period of holiday include references to any sums which, if they had been paid, would have been treated for the purposes of the enactments relating to social services as earnings in respect of that period.

Meaning of "prescribed"

11 In paragraphs 2 and 3, "prescribed" means prescribed by regulations made by the Secretary of State.

Meaning of "scheme manager"

12 In paragraph 5, "the scheme manager" has the meaning given in section 212(1) of the Financial Services and Markets Act 2000.

Meaning of "eligible deposit"

13 (1) In paragraphs 6 to 8, "eligible deposit" means a deposit in respect of which the person, or any of the persons, to whom it is owed would be eligible for compensation under the Financial Services Compensation Scheme.

(2) For the purposes of those paragraphs and of this paragraph, a "deposit" means rights of the kind described in paragraph 22 of schedule 2 of the Financial Services and Markets Act 2000 (deposits).

(3) In paragraphs 7 and 8, "eligible person" means—

(a) an individual, or

(b) a micro-enterprise, a small enterprise or a medium-sized enterprise, each of those terms having the meaning given in Article 2.1(107) of the Directive 2014/59/EU of 15th May 2014 establishing a framework for the recovery and resolution of credit institutions and investment firms.

(4) In paragraph 8—

(a) "credit institution" has the meaning given in Article 4.1(1) of the capital requirements regulation,

(b) "EEA branch" means a branch, as defined in Article 4.1(17) of the capital requirements regulation, which is established in an EEA state, and

(c) "non-EEA branch" means a branch, as so defined, which is established in a country which is not an EEA state.

(5) In sub-paragraph (4)(a) and (b), "the capital requirements regulation" means Regulation (EU) No 575/2013 of the European Parliament and of the Council of 26 June 2013 on prudential requirements for credit institutions and investment firms and amending regulation (EU) NO 648/2012.

Transitional provisions

14 Regulations under paragraph 2 or 3 may contain such transitional provisions as may appear to the Secretary of State necessary or expedient.

NOTES

Commencement: 30 November 2016.

SCHEDULE 4
VOLUNTARY TRUST DEEDS FOR CREDITORS

(introduced by section 162)

Remuneration of trustee

[5.441]

1 Whether or not—

(a) provision is made in the trust deed for auditing the accounts of the trustee in the sequestration and for determining the method of fixing the trustee's remuneration, or

(b) the trustee and the creditors have agreed on such auditing and the method of fixing that remuneration,

the debtor, the trustee or any creditor may, at any time before the final distribution of the debtor's estate among the creditors, have the trustee's accounts audited by, and the trustee's remuneration fixed by, AiB.

Accountant in Bankruptcy's power to carry out audit

2 AiB may, at any time, audit the trustee's accounts and fix the trustee's remuneration.

Registration of notice of inhibition

3 (1) The trustee, from time to time after the trust deed is delivered to the trustee, may cause a notice in such form as is prescribed by act of sederunt to be recorded in the Register of Inhibitions.

(2) Such recording has the same effect as the recording in that register of letters of inhibition against the debtor.

(3) The trustee, after—

(a) the debtor's estate has been distributed finally among the debtor's creditors, or

(b) the trust deed has otherwise ceased to be operative,

must cause a notice in such form as is so prescribed to be recorded in that register recalling the notice recorded under sub-paragraph (1).

Lodging of claim to bar effect of limitation of actions

4 The submission to the trustee, acting under a trust deed, of a claim by a creditor bars the effect of any enactment or rule of law relating to limitation of actions.

Valuation of claims

5 (1) Unless the trust deed otherwise provides, schedule 2 applies in relation to a trust deed as it applies to a sequestration but subject to the following modifications.

(2) In paragraphs 1, 2 and 4, for the word "sequestration", wherever it occurs, there is substituted "granting of the trust deed".

(3) In paragraph 3(3), for paragraphs (a) and (b) and the words "the trustee or sheriff" which immediately follow paragraph (b) there is substituted "the trustee".

NOTES

Commencement: 30 November 2016.

Rules: the Act of Sederunt (Sheriff Court Bankruptcy Rules) 2016, SSI 2016/313 at **[16.322]**.

SCHEDULE 5
INFORMATION TO BE INCLUDED IN THE SEDERUNT BOOK

(introduced by section 210(3))

[5.442]

1 A copy of the debtor application made under section 2(1)(a).

2 A copy of the petition presented under section 2(1)(b).

3 Where the trustee is AiB, a copy of the statement of assets and liabilities sent to AiB in accordance with section 8(3)(a).

[3A Any undertaking given by the trustee approved under Article 36 of the EU insolvency proceedings regulation.]

4 A copy of the award of sequestration under section 22(1) or (5).

5 A copy of the warrant to cite the debtor granted under section 22(3).

6 Where the trustee is not AiB—

(a) the audited accounts sent to the trustee by AiB in accordance with section 56(5)(d), and

(b) the determination fixing the amount of the outlays and remuneration payable to the interim trustee sent to the trustee by AiB in accordance with that section.

7 Where the trustee is AiB—

(a) the accounts audited by AiB in accordance with section 56(5)(a), and

(b) the determination, issued in accordance with section 56(5)(b), fixing the amount of the outlays and remuneration payable to the interim trustee.

8 Where AiB is appointed interim trustee and the sheriff awards sequestration in accordance with section 58(1)(a)—
(a) the accounts of AiB's intromissions (if any) with the debtor's estate, and
(b) the determination of AiB's fees and outlays calculated in accordance with regulations under section 205.

9 A copy of—
(a) an order—
(i) recalling or refusing to recall an award of sequestration by the sheriff under section 30, and
(ii) sent to the trustee under subsection (9)(b)(ii) of that section, or
(b) a grant of (or a refusal to grant), under section 34(1), 35(6) or 37, recall of an award of sequestration.

10 A copy of an order under section 114(3)(b) or 115(3)(b) sent to the trustee under section 30(9)(b).

11 Where the trustee is a replacement trustee appointed under section 60—
(a) a copy of the audited accounts, and determination, sent under section 63(5)(c)(ii),
(b) on that appointment, such information as is appropriate to provide a record of the sequestration process before that appointment (except that no entry is to be made in relation to any written comments made by the original trustee under section 42(3)(c)), and
(c) an entry recording a certificate of discharge issued to the original trustee under section 65.

12 Where the trustee is not AiB, a copy of a statement of assets and liabilities sent to the trustee under section 41(1) or (2).

13 A copy of a notice given under section 44(3).

14 Where the trustee is not AiB, a copy of a report made under section 45(1).

15 Where the trustee is a replacement trustee appointed under section 60 and AiB was the original trustee, on that appointment, such information as is appropriate to provide a record of the sequestration process before that appointment.

16 A copy of an initial proposal for the debtor's contribution provided by the trustee under section 90(1)(b).

17 A copy of a debtor contribution order applying to the debtor.

18 A copy of a decree issued under section 98 affecting the sequestrated estate.

19 A copy of a decree of recall issued following an application under section 100(2).

20 A copy of a decree under section 99 affecting the sequestrated estate.

21 The inventory and valuation of the estate, made up and maintained in accordance with section 108(1)(b).

22 A copy of an account given by the debtor under section 116(2).

23 The debtor's deposition at an examination subscribed under section 121(6).

24 A copy of the record of an examination sent to AiB under section 121(7).

25 An appropriate entry in relation to the production of any document to the trustee in accordance with section 125(2), stating the date when it was produced to the trustee.

26 Where the trustee accepts or rejects a claim under section 126, the decision on the claim, specifying—
(a) the amount of the claim accepted by the trustee,
(b) the category of debt, and the value of any security, as decided by the trustee, and
(c) if the claim is rejected, the reason.

27 A copy of a decision of AiB under subsection (4)(b) of section 127 and of the sheriff under subsection (5) of that section.

28 An agreement or determination in respect of the accounting period under section 130(3)(b)(i) or (ii).

29 Where the trustee is not AiB, the audited accounts, the scheme of division and the final determination in relation to the trustee's outlays and remuneration as mentioned in section 136.

30 A copy of the certificate of discharge given to the debtor under section 137(2), 138(2) or 143(5).

31 A copy of the certificate deferring discharge where the debtor cannot be traced issued under section 141(4)(b) or (6)(b).

32 Where AiB has acted as trustee, after making the final division of the debtor's estate—
(a) AiB's final accounts of AiB's intromissions (if any) with the debtor's estate,

(b) the scheme of division (if any), and
(c) a determination of AiB's fees and outlays calculated in accordance with regulations under section 205.

33 Where AiB has acted as trustee and is discharged from all liability as mentioned in section 151(10), an appropriate entry in relation to such discharge.

34 A decision of the court under section 211 and of AiB under section 212.

35 A copy of a decree arbitral or, as the case may be, an appropriate entry recording the compromise referred to in section 216(1)(b).

36 The minutes of the meeting referred to in paragraphs 8 to 10 of schedule 6.

37 A copy of the minutes of a meeting sent to AiB in accordance with paragraph 25 of that schedule.

38 Where a meeting of commissioners is called in accordance with paragraph 26 of that schedule—
(a) a record of the deliberations of the commissioners at the meeting,
(b) where the trustee is not clerk in accordance with paragraph 30 of that schedule, a record of the deliberations of the commissioners transmitted by the commissioner acting as clerk (such commissioner to authenticate the insertion when made), and
(c) in relation to any matter agreed without a meeting, the minute recording that agreement signed in accordance with paragraph 32(b) of that schedule.

39 A copy of any decision (including any determination, direction, award, acceptance, rejection, adjudication, requirement, declaration, order or valuation) relating to the sequestration which is—
(a) issued by AiB, and
(b) not otherwise mentioned in this schedule.

40 A copy of any decree, interlocutory decree, direction or order relating to the sequestration which is—
(a) granted by the court, and
(b) not otherwise mentioned in this schedule.

NOTES

Commencement: 30 November 2016.

Para 3A: inserted by the Insolvency (Regulation (EU) 2015/848) (Miscellaneous Amendments) (Scotland) Regulations 2017, SSI 2017/210, regs 4(1), (24), 9, as from 26 June 2017, except in relation to proceedings opened before that date.

SCHEDULE 6
MEETINGS OF CREDITORS AND COMMISSIONERS

(introduced by section 217)

PART 1
MEETINGS OF CREDITORS OTHER THAN THE STATUTORY MEETING

Calling of meeting

[5.443]

1 The trustee in the sequestration must call a meeting of creditors if required to do so—
(a) by order of the sheriff,
(b) by ? in number or ? in value of the creditors,
(c) by a commissioner, or
(d) by AiB.

2 Any such meeting must be held not later than 28 days after—
(a) the issuing of the order under paragraph 1(a), or
(b) the receipt by the trustee of the requirement under paragraph 1(b), (c) or (d).

3 The trustee, or a commissioner who has given notice to the trustee, may at any time call a meeting of creditors.

4 The trustee, calling a meeting under paragraph 1 or 3, or a commissioner, calling a meeting under paragraph 3, is no fewer than 7 days before the date fixed for the meeting to notify—
(a) every creditor known to the trustee or, as the case may be, to the commissioner, and
(b) AiB,

of the date, time and place fixed for the holding of the meeting and of the meeting's purpose.

5 Where—
(a) a requirement has been made under paragraph 1, but
(b) no meeting has been called by the trustee,

AiB may, of AiB's own accord or on the application of any creditor, call a meeting of creditors.

6 AiB, calling a meeting under paragraph 5, is no fewer than 7 days before the date fixed for the meeting to take reasonable steps to notify the creditors of the date, time and place fixed for the holding of the meeting and of the meeting's purpose.

7 It is not necessary to notify under paragraph 4 or 6 any creditor whose accepted claim is less than £50 or such sum as may be prescribed, unless the creditor has in writing requested such notification.

Role of trustee at meeting

8 At the commencement of a meeting the trustee is to be the person chairing the meeting and as such is, after carrying out the trustee's duties under section 126(1)—

(a) to invite the creditors to elect one of their number to chair the meeting in the trustee's place, and
(b) to preside over the election.

9 If no person is elected in pursuance of paragraph 8, the trustee must chair the meeting throughout.

10 The trustee is to arrange for a record to be made of the proceedings at the meeting.

Appeals

11 The trustee, a creditor or any other person having an interest may, within 14 days after the date of a meeting called under paragraph 4 or 6, appeal to the sheriff against a resolution of the creditors at the meeting.

NOTES

Commencement: 30 November 2016.

PART 2
ALL MEETINGS OF CREDITORS

Validity of proceedings

[5.444]

12 No proceedings at a meeting are invalidated by reason only that a notice or other document relating to the calling of the meeting, being a notice required to be sent or given under a provision of this Act, has not been received by, or come to the attention of, any creditor before the meeting.

Locus of meeting

13 Every meeting must be held in such place (whether or not in the sheriffdom) as is, in the opinion of the person calling the meeting, the most convenient for the majority of the creditors.

Mandatories

14 A creditor may authorise in writing a person to represent the creditor at a meeting.

15 A creditor must lodge with the trustee, before the commencement of the meeting, any authorisation given under paragraph 14.

16 Any reference in paragraph 8, or in the following provisions of this Part, to a creditor includes a reference to a person authorised under paragraph 14 by a creditor.

Quorum

17 The quorum at any meeting is one creditor.

Voting at meeting

18 Any question at a meeting is to be determined by a majority in value of the creditors who vote on that question.

Objections by creditors

19 At any meeting the person chairing it may allow or disallow any objection by a creditor, other than (if the person chairing the meeting is not the trustee) an objection relating to a creditor's claim.

20 A person aggrieved by the determination of the person chairing the meeting in respect of an objection may appeal to the sheriff against the determination.

21 If the person chairing the meeting is in doubt as to whether to allow or disallow an objection, the meeting must proceed as if no objection had been made, except that for the purposes of appeal the objection is to be deemed to have been disallowed.

Adjournment of meeting

22 If no creditor has appeared at a meeting by half an hour after the time appointed for its commencement, the person chairing the meeting may adjourn it to such other day as that person may appoint, being a day no fewer than 7, nor more than 21, days after that on which the meeting is adjourned.

23 The person chairing the meeting may, with the consent of a majority in value of the creditors who vote on a resolution to adjourn a meeting, adjourn the meeting.

24 Any adjourned meeting must be held at the same time and place as the original meeting, unless in the resolution another time or place is specified.

Minutes of meeting

25 The minutes of every meeting must be signed by the person who chaired the meeting and within 14 days after the meeting must be sent to AiB.

NOTES

Commencement: 30 November 2016.

PART 3
MEETINGS OF COMMISSIONERS

[5.445]

26 The trustee—

(a) may call a meeting of commissioners at any time, and

(b) must call such a meeting—

(i) on being required to do so by order of the sheriff, or

(ii) on being requested to do so by AiB or by any commissioner.

27 If the trustee fails to call a meeting of commissioners within 14 days after being required or requested to do so under paragraph 26, a commissioner may call a meeting of commissioners.

28 The trustee must give the commissioners at least 7 days' notice of a meeting called by the trustee unless the commissioners decide that they do not require such notice.

29 The trustee is to act as clerk at a meeting of commissioners.

30 If the commissioners are considering the performance of the functions of the trustee under any provision of this Act, the trustee must withdraw from the meeting if requested to do so by the commissioners and in such a case a commissioner must—

(a) act as clerk, and

(b) transmit a record of the deliberations of the commissioners to the trustee.

31 The quorum at a meeting of commissioners is one commissioner and the commissioners may act by a majority of the commissioners present at the meeting.

32 Any matter may be agreed by the commissioners without a meeting if such agreement—

(a) is unanimous, and

(b) is subsequently recorded in a minute signed by the commissioners.

NOTES

Commencement: 30 November 2016.

SCHEDULE 7
RE-ENACTMENT OF SECTIONS 10 AND 189 OF THE BANKRUPTCY (SCOTLAND) ACT 1913

(introduced by section 233)

Arrestments and attachments

[5.446]

1 (1) Subject to sub-paragraph (2), all arrestments and attachments which have been executed within 60 days prior to the constitution of the apparent insolvency of the debtor, or within 4 months after its constitution, rank *pari passu* as if they had all been executed on the same date.

(2) Any such arrestment which is executed on the dependence of an action must be followed up without undue delay.

(3) A creditor judicially producing, in a process relative to the subject of such arrestment or attachment, liquid grounds of debt or decree of payment within the 60 days or 4 months referred to in sub-paragraph (1) is entitled to rank as if the creditor had executed an arrestment or an attachment.

(4) If, in the meantime—

(a) the first or any subsequent arrester obtains a decree of furthcoming and recovers payment, that arrester, or

(b) an attaching creditor carries through an auction or receives payment in respect of an attached article upon its redemption, that attaching creditor,

is accountable for the sum recovered to those who, by virtue of this Act, may eventually be found to have a ranking *pari passu* on the sum; and is liable in an action at their instance for payment to them proportionately, after allowing out of the fund the expense of such recovery.

(5) Arrestments executed for attaching the same effects of the debtor after the 4 months subsequent to the constitution of the debtor's apparent insolvency do not compete with those within the 60 days or 4 months referred to in sub-paragraph (1) but may rank with each other on any reversion of the fund attached in accordance with any enactment or rule of law relating to such ranking.

(6) Any reference in sub-paragraphs (1) to (5) to a debtor is to be construed as including a reference to an entity whose apparent insolvency may, by virtue of subsection (6) of section 16 of this Act, be constituted under subsection (1) of that section.

(7) This paragraph applies in respect of arrestments and attachments executed whether before or after the coming into force of this Act.

(8) Nothing in this paragraph applies to an earnings arrestment, a current maintenance arrestment or a conjoined arrestment order.

Exemptions from stamp or other duties for conveyances, deeds etc relating to sequestrated estates

2 Any—
- (a) conveyance, assignation, instrument, discharge, writing or deed relating solely to the estate of a debtor which has been or may be sequestrated, under either this or any former Act, being estate which after the execution of the document in question is and remains the property of the debtor, for the benefit of the debtor's creditors, or of the trustee in the sequestration,
- (b) discharge to the debtor,
- (c) deed, assignation, instrument, or writing for reinvesting the debtor in the estate,
- (d) article of roup or sale, or submission,
- (e) other instrument or writing whatsoever relating solely to the estate of the debtor, and
- (f) other deed or writing forming part of the proceedings ordered under such sequestration,

is exempt from all stamp duties or other Government duty.

NOTES

Commencement: 30 November 2016.

SCHEDULES 8 AND 9

(Schs 8, 9 contain amendments, repeals and revocations which, in so far as relevant to this work, have been incorporated at the appropriate place.)

PART 6
INSOLVENCY RULES

INSOLVENCY RULES 1986 (NOTE)

(SI 1986/1925)

[6.1]

NOTES

These Rules are revoked and replaced by the Insolvency (England and Wales) Rules 2016, SI 2016/1024, r 2, Sch 1, as from 6 April 2017, subject to transitional provisions in Sch 2 thereto at **[6.935]**. The Insolvency (England and Wales) Rules 2016, SI 2016/1024 are set out in full at **[6.2]**.

Continued application of the Insolvency Rules 1986:

As to the continued application of these 1986 Rules in relation to special insolvency regimes, see the Insolvency (England and Wales) Rules 2016 (Consequential Amendments and Savings) Rules 2017, SI 2017/369, r 3 at **[6.947]**.

See also the Small Business, Enterprise and Employment Act 2015 (Consequential Amendments, Savings and Transitional Provisions) Regulations 2018, SI 2018/208, regs 24, 25, which provide as follows:

24 Savings in relation to special insolvency rules

(1) Despite the revocation of the Insolvency Rules 1986, those Rules apply as they applied before they were revoked for the purposes of the application of—

(a) the Bank Insolvency (England and Wales) Rules 2009 (SI 2009/356 at **[7.93]**);

(b) the Bank Administration (England and Wales) Rules 2009 (SI 2009/357 at **[7.386]**);

(c) the Building Society Special Administration (England and Wales) Rules 2010 (SI 2010/2580 at **[7.483]**); and

(d) the Building Society Insolvency (England and Wales) Rules 2010 (SI 2010/2581 at **[7.546]**).

(2) Despite the revocation of the Insolvency Rules, Rule 12A.30 of, and Schedule 4 to, the Insolvency Rules 1986 (forms for use in insolvency proceedings) apply as they applied before they were revoked for the purpose of prescribing forms for the statement of affairs required to be delivered and for any statement of concurrence required to be submitted under rule 54 of the Investment Bank Special Administration (England and Wales) Rules 2011, SI 2011/1301 (at **[7.1711]**).

25 Savings in relation to insolvency proceedings

(1) Despite the revocation of the Insolvency Rules, those Rules apply as they applied before they were revoked for the purposes of—

(a) a proposal to a society and its creditors for a voluntary arrangement within the meaning given in section 1 of the Insolvency Act 1986 as applied in relation to a relevant society by article 2(1) of the 2014 Order;

(b) the administration of a society under Part 2 of the Insolvency Act 1986 as applied by article 2(2) of the 2014 Order; and

(c) proceedings instituted in England and Wales for the winding up of a relevant scheme (within the meaning given in regulation 17(1)(a) of the Collective Investment in Transferable Securities (Contractual Scheme) Regulations 2013).

(2) In this regulation—

"the 2014 Order" means the Co-operative and Community Benefit Societies and Credit Unions (Arrangements, Reconstructions and Administration) Order 2014 (SI 2014/229 at **[7.1425]**); and

"society" means a relevant society within the meaning given in article 1(2) of the 2014 Order which the courts in England and Wales have jurisdiction to wind up.

The Insolvency Rules 1986 as they stood at 1 August 2016 are to be found in the 18th edition of this Handbook; they have been omitted from the current edition due to reasons of space. Provisions of the 1986 Rules that have been amended since publication of the 18th edition are set out below, together with notes relating to those provisions.

THE THIRD GROUP OF PARTS

PART 7
COURT PROCEDURE AND PRACTICE

CHAPTER 8
APPEALS IN INSOLVENCY PROCEEDINGS

7.47 Appeals and reviews of court orders [in corporate insolvency]

(1) Every court having jurisdiction [for the purposes of Parts 1 to 4 of the Act and Parts 1 to 4 of the Rules,] may review, rescind or vary any order made by it in the exercise of that jurisdiction.

[(2) Appeals in civil matters in proceedings under Parts 1 to 4 of the Act and Parts 1 to 4 of the Rules lie as follows—

[(a) where the decision appealed against is made by a district judge sitting in the county court hearing centre specified in the first column of the table in Schedule 2D—

(i) to a High Court Judge sitting in a district registry; or

(ii) to a Registrar in Bankruptcy of the High Court,

as specified in the corresponding entry in the second column of the table;

(b) to a High Court Judge where the decision appealed against is made by—

(i) a Circuit Judge sitting in the county court;

(ii) a Master;

(iii) a Registrar in Bankruptcy of the High Court, if that decision is made at first instance; or

(iv) a district judge sitting in a district registry;

(c) to the Civil Division of the Court of Appeal where the decision appealed against is made by a Registrar in Bankruptcy of the High Court, if that decision is an appeal from a decision made by a District Judge; and

(d) to the Civil Division of the Court of Appeal where the decision appealed against is made by a High Court Judge.]]

(3) [The county court] is not, in the exercise of its jurisdiction [for the purposes of Parts 1 to 4 of the Act and Parts 1 to 4 of the Rules], subject to be restrained by the order of any other court, and no appeal lies from its decision in the exercise of that jurisdiction except as provided by this Rule.

(4) Any application for the rescission of a winding-up order shall be made within [5 business] days after the date on which the order was made.

[(5) In this rule—

"Circuit Judge sitting in the county court" means a judge sitting pursuant to section 5(1)(a) of the County Courts Act 1984;

"Civil Division of the Court of Appeal" means the division of the Court of Appeal established by section 3(1) of the Senior Courts Act 1981;

"Chancery Division of the High Court" means the division of the High Court established by section 5(1)(a) of the Senior Courts Act 1981;

"county court" means the court established by section A1 of the County Courts Act 1984;

"district judge" means a person appointed a district judge under section 6(1) of the County Courts Act 1984;

"district judge sitting in a district registry" means a district judge sitting in an assigned district registry as a district judge of the High Court under section 100 of the Senior Courts Act 1981;

"district registry" means a district registry of the High Court under section 99 of the Senior Courts Act 1981;

"High Court Judge" means a judge listed in section 4(1) of the Senior Courts Act 1981;

"Master" means a person appointed to the office of Master, Chancery Division under section 89(1) of the Senior Courts Act 1981;

"Registrar in Bankruptcy of the High Court" means a person appointed to the office of Registrar in Bankruptcy of the High Court under section 89(1) of the Senior Courts Act 1981;

and for the purposes of each definition a person appointed to act as a deputy for any person holding that office is included.]

NOTES

Rule heading: words in square brackets substituted for original words "(winding up)" by the Insolvency (Amendment) Rules 2010, SI 2010/686, r 2, Sch 1, para 466(1), (2), subject to transitional provisions in r 6(1) of, and Sch 4, para 1 to, the 2010 Rules (see 18th edition of this Handbook).

Para (1): words in square brackets substituted for original words "under the Act to wind up companies" by SI 2010/686, r 2, Sch 1, para 466(1), (3), subject to transitional provisions in r 6(1) of, and Sch 4, para 1 to, the 2010 Rules (see 18th edition of this Handbook).

Para (2): substituted by SI 2010/686, r 2, Sch 1, para 466(1), (4), subject to transitional provisions in r 6(1) of, and Sch 4, para 1 to, the 2010 Rules (see 18th edition of this Handbook), and previously read as follows:

"(2) An appeal from a decision made in the exercise of that jurisdiction by a county court or by a registrar of the High Court lies to a single judge of the High Court; and an appeal from a decision of that judge on such an appeal lies, with the leave of that judge or the Court of Appeal, to the Court of Appeal.";

sub-paras (a)–(d) substituted for original sub-paras (a), (b), by the Insolvency (Amendment) (No 2) Rules 2016, SI 2016/903, rr 2, 3, 6, as from 3 October 2016, except where a person has filed a notice of appeal or applied for permission to appeal before that date. Sub-paras (a), (b) previously read as follows—

"(a) to a single judge of the High Court where the decision appealed against is made by the county court or the registrar;

(b) to the Civil Division of the Court of Appeal from a decision of a single judge of the High Court.".

Para (3): words in first pair of square brackets substituted by the Insolvency (Commencement of Proceedings) and Insolvency Rules 1986 (Amendment) Rules 2014, SI 2014/817, r 4, Sch 2, para 16; words in second pair of square brackets substituted for original words "to wind up companies" by SI 2010/686, r 2, Sch 1, para 466(1), (5), subject to transitional provisions in r 6(1) of, and Sch 4, para 1 to, the 2010 Rules (see 18th edition of this Handbook).

Para (4): words in square brackets substituted for original number "7" by SI 2010/686, r 2, Sch 1, para 466(1), (6), subject to transitional provisions in r 6(1) of, and Sch 4, para 1 to, the 2010 Rules (see 18th edition of this Handbook).

Para (5): added by SI 2016/903, rr 2, 4, 6, as from 3 October 2016, except where a person has filed a notice of appeal or applied for permission to appeal before that date.

PART 13
INTERPRETATION AND APPLICATION

13.13 Expressions used generally

(1) . . .

(2) "The Department" means [the Department for Business, Energy and Industrial Strategy].

[(2A)]–(19) . . .

NOTES

Paras (1), (2A)–(19): see 18th edition of this Handbook.

Para (2): words in square brackets substituted by the Secretaries of State for Business, Energy and Industrial Strategy, for International Trade and for Exiting the European Union and the Transfer of Functions (Education and Skills) Order 2016, SI 2016/992, art 14, Schedule, para 15, as from 9 November 2016.

SCHEDULES

[SCHEDULE 2D
DESTINATION OF APPEALS FROM DECISIONS OF DISTRICT JUDGES IN INSOLVENCY MATTERS

County Court Hearing Centre	*Destination of Appeal*
Aberystwyth	Cardiff District Registry
Aylesbury	Registrar in Bankruptcy
Banbury	Birmingham District Registry
Barnsley	Leeds District Registry
Barnstaple	Bristol District Registry
Barrow-in-Furness	Liverpool District Registry or Manchester District Registry
Bath	Bristol District Registry

Bedford	Birmingham District Registry
Birkenhead	Liverpool District Registry or Manchester District Registry
Birmingham	Birmingham District Registry
Blackburn	Liverpool District Registry or Manchester District Registry
Blackpool	Liverpool District Registry or Manchester District Registry
Blackwood	Cardiff District Registry
Bolton	Liverpool District Registry or Manchester District Registry
Boston	Birmingham District Registry
Bournemouth and Poole	Registrar in Bankruptcy
Bradford	Leeds District Registry
Bridgend	Cardiff District Registry
Brighton	Registrar in Bankruptcy
Bristol	Bristol District Registry
Burnley	Liverpool District Registry or Manchester District Registry
Bury	Liverpool District Registry or Manchester District Registry
Bury St Edmunds	Registrar in Bankruptcy
Caernarfon	Cardiff District Registry
Cambridge	Registrar in Bankruptcy
Canterbury	Registrar in Bankruptcy
Cardiff	Cardiff District Registry
Carlisle	Liverpool District Registry or Manchester District Registry
Caernarfon	Cardiff District Registry
County Court at Central London	Registrar in Bankruptcy
Chelmsford	Registrar in Bankruptcy
Chester	Liverpool District Registry or Manchester District Registry
Chesterfield	Leeds District Registry
Colchester	Registrar in Bankruptcy
Coventry	Birmingham District Registry
Crewe	Liverpool District Registry or Manchester District Registry
Croydon	Registrar in Bankruptcy
Darlington	Newcastle District Registry
Derby	Birmingham District Registry
Doncaster	Leeds District Registry
Dudley	Birmingham District Registry
Durham	Leeds District Registry or Newcastle District Registry
Eastbourne	Registrar in Bankruptcy
Exeter	Bristol District Registry
Gloucester and Cheltenham	Bristol District Registry
Great Grimsby	Leeds District Registry
Guildford	Registrar in Bankruptcy
Halifax	Leeds District Registry
Harrogate	Leeds District Registry
Hastings	Registrar in Bankruptcy
Haverfordwest	Cardiff District Registry
Hereford	Bristol District Registry
Hertford	Registrar in Bankruptcy
Huddersfield	Leeds District Registry
Ipswich	Registrar in Bankruptcy
Kendal	Liverpool District Registry or Manchester District Registry
Kings Lynn	Registrar in Bankruptcy
Kingston-upon-Hull	Leeds District Registry
Kingston-upon-Thames	Registrar in Bankruptcy
Lancaster	Liverpool District Registry or Manchester District Registry
Leeds	Leeds District Registry
Leicester	Birmingham District Registry
Lincoln	Leeds District Registry or Birmingham District Registry

Liverpool	Liverpool District Registry or Manchester District Registry
Llangefni	Cardiff District Registry
Luton	Registrar in Bankruptcy
Maidstone	Registrar in Bankruptcy
Manchester	Manchester District Registry
Merthyr Tydfil	Cardiff District Registry
Middlesbrough	Newcastle District Registry
Milton Keynes	Birmingham District Registry
Newcastle upon Tyne	Newcastle District Registry
Newport (Gwent)	Cardiff District Registry
Newport (Isle of Wight)	Registrar in Bankruptcy
Northampton	Birmingham District Registry
Norwich	Registrar in Bankruptcy
Nottingham	Birmingham District Registry
Oldham	Liverpool District Registry or Manchester District Registry
Oxford	Registrar in Bankruptcy
Peterborough	Registrar in Bankruptcy
Plymouth	Bristol District Registry
Pontypridd	Cardiff District Registry
Portsmouth	Registrar in Bankruptcy
Port Talbot Justice Centre	Cardiff District Registry
Preston	Liverpool District Registry or Manchester District Registry
Reading	Registrar in Bankruptcy
Rhyl	Cardiff District Registry
Romford	Registrar in Bankruptcy
Salisbury	Registrar in Bankruptcy
Scarborough	Leeds District Registry
Scunthorpe	Leeds District Registry
Sheffield	Leeds District Registry
Slough	Registrar in Bankruptcy
Southampton	Registrar in Bankruptcy
Southend-on-Sea	Registrar in Bankruptcy
Stafford	Birmingham District Registry
St Albans	Registrar in Bankruptcy
Stockport	Liverpool District Registry or Manchester District Registry
Stoke-on-Trent	Manchester District Registry
Sunderland	Newcastle District Registry
Swansea	Cardiff District Registry
Swindon	Bristol District Registry
Tameside	Liverpool District Registry or Manchester District Registry
Taunton	Bristol District Registry
Telford	Birmingham District Registry
Torquay & Newton Abbot	Bristol District Registry
Truro	Bristol District Registry
Tunbridge Wells	Registrar in Bankruptcy
Wakefield	Leeds District Registry
Walsall	Birmingham District Registry
Warrington	Liverpool District Registry or Manchester District Registry
Warwick	Birmingham District Registry
Welshpool & Newton	Cardiff District Registry
West Cumbria	Liverpool District Registry or Manchester District Registry
Wigan	Liverpool District Registry or Manchester District Registry
Winchester	Registrar in Bankruptcy
Wolverhampton	Birmingham District Registry
Worcester	Birmingham District Registry
Wrexham	Cardiff District Registry

Yeovil	Bristol District Registry
York	Leeds District Registry]

NOTES

Commencement: 3 October 2016.

Inserted by the Insolvency (Amendment) (No 2) Rules 2016, SI 2016/903, rr 2, 5, 6, Schedule, except where a person has filed a notice of appeal or applied for permission to appeal before 3 October 2016.

INSOLVENCY (ENGLAND AND WALES) RULES 2016

(SI 2016/1024)

ARRANGEMENT OF RULES

INTRODUCTORY RULES

1 Citation and commencement .[6.2]
2 Revocations .[6.3]
3 Extent and application .[6.4]
4 Transitional and savings provisions .[6.5]
5 Power of Secretary of State to regulate certain matters .[6.6]
6 Punishment of offences .[6.7]
7 Review .[6.8]

PART 1
SCOPE, INTERPRETATION, TIME AND RULES ABOUT DOCUMENTS

CHAPTER 1
SCOPE OF THESE RULES

1.1 Scope .[6.9]

CHAPTER 2
INTERPRETATION

1.2 Defined terms .[6.10]
1.3 Calculation of time periods .[6.11]

CHAPTER 3
FORM AND CONTENT OF DOCUMENTS

1.4 Requirement for writing and form of documents .[6.12]
1.5 Authentication .[6.13]
1.6 Information required to identify persons and proceedings etc .[6.14]
1.7 Reasons for stating that proceedings are or will be main, secondary etc under the EU Regulation .[6.15]
1.8 Prescribed format of documents .[6.16]
1.9 Variations from prescribed contents .[6.17]

CHAPTER 4
STANDARD CONTENTS OF GAZETTE NOTICES AND THE GAZETTE AS EVIDENCE ETC

1.10 Contents of notices to be gazetted under the Act or Rules .[6.18]
1.11 Standard contents of all notices .[6.19]
1.12 Gazette notices relating to a company .[6.20]
1.13 Gazette notices relating to a bankruptcy .[6.21]
1.14 The Gazette: evidence, variations and errors .[6.22]

CHAPTER 5
STANDARD CONTENTS OF NOTICES ADVERTISED OTHERWISE THAN IN THE GAZETTE

1.15 Standard contents of notices advertised otherwise than in the Gazette .[6.23]
1.16 Non-Gazette notices relating to a company .[6.24]
1.17 Non-Gazette notices relating to a bankruptcy .[6.25]
1.18 Non-Gazette notices: other provisions .[6.26]

CHAPTER 6
STANDARD CONTENTS OF DOCUMENTS TO BE DELIVERED TO THE REGISTRAR OF COMPANIES

1.19 Standard contents of documents delivered to the registrar of companies .[6.27]
1.20 Registrar of companies: covering notices .[6.28]
1.21 Standard contents of all documents .[6.29]
1.22 Standard contents of documents relating to the office of office-holders .[6.30]
1.23 Standard contents of documents relating to other documents .[6.31]

1.24 Standard contents of documents relating to court orders . . . [6.32]
1.25 Standard contents of returns or reports of decisions . . . [6.33]
1.26 Standard contents of returns or reports of matters considered by company members by correspondence . . . [6.34]
1.27 Standard contents of documents relating to other events . . . [6.35]

CHAPTER 7
STANDARD CONTENTS OF NOTICES FOR DELIVERY TO OTHER PERSONS ETC
1.28 Standard contents of notices to be delivered to persons other than the registrar of companies . . [6.36]
1.29 Standard contents of all notices . . . [6.37]
1.30 Standard contents of notices relating to the office of office-holders . . . [6.38]
1.31 Standard contents of notices relating to documents . . . [6.39]
1.32 Standard contents of notices relating to court proceedings or orders . . . [6.40]
1.33 Standard contents of notices of the results of decisions . . . [6.41]
1.34 Standard contents of returns or reports of matters considered by company members by correspondence . . . [6.42]

CHAPTER 8
APPLICATIONS TO THE COURT
1.35 Standard contents and authentication of applications to the court under Parts 1 to 11 of the Act . . . [6.43]

CHAPTER 9
DELIVERY OF DOCUMENTS AND OPTING OUT (SECTIONS 246C, 248A, 379C AND 383A)
1.36 Application of Chapter . . . [6.44]
1.37 Delivery to the creditors and opting out . . . [6.45]
1.38 Creditor's election to opt out . . . [6.46]
1.39 Office-holder to provide information to creditors on opting-out . . . [6.47]
1.40 Delivery of documents to authorised recipients . . . [6.48]
1.41 Delivery of documents to joint office-holders . . . [6.49]
1.42 Postal delivery of documents. . . . [6.50]
1.43 Delivery by document exchange. . . . [6.51]
1.44 Personal delivery of documents . . . [6.52]
1.45 Electronic delivery of documents . . . [6.53]
1.46 Electronic delivery of documents to the court . . . [6.54]
1.47 Electronic delivery of notices to enforcement officers . . . [6.55]
1.48 Electronic delivery by office-holders . . . [6.56]
1.49 Use of website by office-holder to deliver a particular document (sections 246B and 379B) . . [6.57]
1.50 General use of website to deliver documents . . . [6.58]
1.51 Retention period for documents made available on websites . . . [6.59]
1.52 Proof of delivery of documents . . . [6.60]
1.53 Delivery of proofs and details of claims . . . [6.61]

CHAPTER 10
INSPECTION OF DOCUMENTS, COPIES AND PROVISION OF INFORMATION
1.54 Right to copies of documents . . . [6.62]
1.55 Charges for copies of documents provided by the office-holder . . . [6.63]
1.56 Offence in relation to inspection of documents . . . [6.64]
1.57 Right to list of creditors . . . [6.65]
1.58 Confidentiality of documents: grounds for refusing inspection . . . [6.66]

PART 2
COMPANY VOLUNTARY ARRANGEMENTS (CVA)

CHAPTER 1
PRELIMINARY
2.1 Interpretation . . . [6.67]

CHAPTER 2
THE PROPOSAL FOR A CVA (SECTION 1)
2.2 Proposal for a CVA: general principles and amendment . . . [6.68]
2.3 Proposal: contents. . . . [6.69]

CHAPTER 3
PROCEDURE FOR A CVA WITHOUT A MORATORIUM
2.4 Procedure for proposal where the nominee is not the liquidator or the administrator (section 2). . . . [6.70]
2.5 Information for the official receiver . . . [6.71]
2.6 Statement of affairs (section 2(3)) . . . [6.72]

2.7 Application to omit information from statement of affairs delivered to creditors . . . .[6.73]
2.8 Additional disclosure for assistance of nominee where the nominee is not the liquidator or administrator . . . .[6.74]
2.9 Nominee's report on proposal where the nominee is not the liquidator or administrator (section 2(2)) . . . .[6.75]
2.10 Replacement of nominee (section 2(4)) . . . .[6.76]

CHAPTER 4
PROCEDURE FOR A CVA WITH A MORATORIUM

2.11 Statement of affairs (paragraph 6(1)(b) of Schedule A1) . . . .[6.77]
2.12 Application to omit information from a statement of affairs . . . .[6.78]
2.13 The nominee's statement (paragraph 6(2) of Schedule A1) . . . .[6.79]
2.14 Documents filed with court to obtain a moratorium (paragraph 7(1) of Schedule A1) . . . .[6.80]
2.15 Notice and advertisement of beginning of a moratorium . . . .[6.81]
2.16 Notice of continuation of a moratorium where physical meeting of creditors is summoned (paragraph 8(3B) of Schedule A1) . . . .[6.82]
2.17 Notice of decision extending or further extending a moratorium (paragraph 36 of Schedule A1) . . . .[6.83]
2.18 Notice of court order extending or further extending or continuing or renewing a moratorium (paragraph 34(2) of Schedule A1) . . . .[6.84]
2.19 Advertisement of end of a moratorium (paragraph 11(1) of Schedule A1) . . . .[6.85]
2.20 Disposal of charged property etc during a moratorium . . . .[6.86]
2.21 Withdrawal of nominee's consent to act (paragraph 25(5) of Schedule A1) . . . .[6.87]
2.22 Application to the court to replace the nominee (paragraph 28 of Schedule A1) . . . .[6.88]
2.23 Notice of appointment of replacement nominee . . . .[6.89]
2.24 Applications to court to challenge nominee's actions etc (paragraphs 26 and 27 of Schedule A1) . . . .[6.90]

CHAPTER 5
CONSIDERATION OF THE PROPOSAL BY THE COMPANY MEMBERS AND CREDITORS

2.25 Consideration of proposal: common requirements (section 3) . . . .[6.91]
2.26 Members' consideration at a meeting . . . .[6.92]
2.27 Creditors' consideration by a decision procedure . . . .[6.93]
2.28 Timing of decisions on proposal . . . .[6.94]
2.29 Creditors' approval of modified proposal . . . .[6.95]
2.30 Notice of members' meeting and attendance of officers . . . .[6.96]
2.31 Requisition of physical meeting by creditors . . . .[6.97]
2.32 Non-receipt of notice by members . . . .[6.98]
2.33 Proposal for alternative supervisor . . . .[6.99]
2.34 Chair at meetings . . . .[6.100]
2.35 Members' voting rights . . . .[6.101]
2.36 Requisite majorities of members . . . .[6.102]
2.37 Notice of order made under section 4A(6) or paragraph 36(5) of Schedule A1 . . . .[6.103]
2.38 Report of consideration of proposal under section 4(6) and (6A) or paragraph 30(3) and (4) of Schedule A1 . . . .[6.104]

CHAPTER 6
ADDITIONAL MATTERS CONCERNING AND FOLLOWING APPROVAL OF CVA

2.39 Hand-over of property etc to supervisor . . . .[6.105]
2.40 Revocation or suspension of CVA . . . .[6.106]
2.41 Supervisor's accounts and reports . . . .[6.107]
2.42 Production of accounts and records to the Secretary of State . . . .[6.108]
2.43 Fees and expenses . . . .[6.109]
2.44 Termination or full implementation of CVA . . . .[6.110]

CHAPTER 7
TIME RECORDING INFORMATION

2.45 Provision of information . . . .[6.111]

PART 3
ADMINISTRATION

CHAPTER 1
INTERPRETATION FOR THIS PART

3.1 Interpretation for Part 3 . . . .[6.112]
3.2 Proposed administrator's statement and consent to act . . . .[6.113]

CHAPTER 2
APPOINTMENT OF ADMINISTRATOR BY COURT

3.3 Administration application (paragraph 12 of Schedule B1) . . . .[6.114]

Part 6 Insolvency Rules

3.4 Administration application made by the directors . . . [6.115]
3.5 Administration application by the supervisor of a CVA . . . [6.116]
3.6 Witness statement in support of administration application . . . [6.117]
3.7 Filing of application . . . [6.118]
3.8 Service of application . . . [6.119]
3.9 Notice to enforcement agents charged with distress or other legal process, etc . . . [6.120]
3.10 Notice of other insolvency proceedings . . . [6.121]
3.11 Intervention by holder of qualifying floating charge (paragraph 36(1)(b) of Schedule B1) . . . [6.122]
3.12 The hearing . . . [6.123]
3.13 The order . . . [6.124]
3.14 Order on an application under paragraph 37 or 38 of Schedule B1 . . . [6.125]
3.15 Notice of administration order . . . [6.126]

CHAPTER 3
APPOINTMENT OF ADMINISTRATOR BY HOLDER OF FLOATING CHARGE

3.16 Notice of intention to appoint . . . [6.127]
3.17 Notice of appointment . . . [6.128]
3.18 Filing of notice with the court . . . [6.129]
3.19 Appointment by floating charge holder after administration application made . . . [6.130]
3.20 Appointment taking place out of court business hours: procedure . . . [6.131]
3.21 Appointment taking place out of court business hours: content of notice . . . [6.132]
3.22 Appointment taking place out of court business hours: legal effect . . . [6.133]

CHAPTER 4
APPOINTMENT OF ADMINISTRATOR BY COMPANY OR DIRECTORS

3.23 Notice of intention to appoint . . . [6.134]
3.24 Notice of appointment after notice of intention to appoint . . . [6.135]
3.25 Notice of appointment without prior notice of intention to appoint . . . [6.136]
3.26 Notice of appointment: filing with the court . . . [6.137]

CHAPTER 5
NOTICE OF ADMINISTRATOR'S APPOINTMENT

3.27 Publication of administrator's appointment . . . [6.138]

CHAPTER 6
STATEMENT OF AFFAIRS

3.28 Interpretation . . . [6.139]
3.29 Statement of affairs: notice requiring and delivery to the administrator (paragraph 47(1) of Schedule B1) . . . [6.140]
3.30 Statement of affairs: content (paragraph 47 of Schedule B1) . . . [6.141]
3.31 Statement of affairs: statement of concurrence . . . [6.142]
3.32 Statement of affairs: filing . . . [6.143]
3.33 Statement of affairs: release from requirement and extension of time . . . [6.144]
3.34 Statement of affairs: expenses . . . [6.145]

CHAPTER 7
ADMINISTRATOR'S PROPOSALS

3.35 Administrator's proposals: additional content . . . [6.146]
3.36 Administrator's proposals: statement of pre-administration costs . . . [6.147]
3.37 Advertising administrator's proposals and notices of extension of time for delivery of proposals (paragraph 49 of Schedule B1) . . . [6.148]
3.38 Seeking approval of the administrator's proposals . . . [6.149]
3.39 Invitation to creditors to form a creditors' committee . . . [6.150]
3.40 Notice of extension of time to seek approval . . . [6.151]
3.41 Notice of the creditors' decision on the administrator's proposals (paragraph 53(2)) . . . [6.152]
3.42 Administrator's proposals: revision . . . [6.153]
3.43 Notice of result of creditors' decision on revised proposals (paragraph 54(6)) . . . [6.154]

CHAPTER 8
LIMITED DISCLOSURE OF STATEMENTS OF AFFAIRS AND PROPOSALS

3.44 Application of Chapter . . . [6.155]
3.45 Orders limiting disclosure of statement of affairs etc . . . [6.156]
3.46 Order for disclosure by administrator . . . [6.157]
3.47 Rescission or amendment of order for limited disclosure . . . [6.158]
3.48 Publication etc of statement of affairs or statement of proposals . . . [6.159]

CHAPTER 9
DISPOSAL OF CHARGED PROPERTY

3.49 Disposal of charged property . . . [6.160]

CHAPTER 10
EXPENSES OF THE ADMINISTRATION

3.50 Expenses . . . [6.161]
3.51 Order of priority . . . [6.162]
3.52 Pre-administration costs . . . [6.163]

CHAPTER 11
EXTENSION AND ENDING OF ADMINISTRATION

3.53 Interpretation . . . [6.164]
3.54 Application to extend an administration and extension by consent (paragraph 76(2) of Schedule B1) . . . [6.165]
3.55 Notice of automatic end of administration (paragraph 76 of Schedule B1) . . . [6.166]
3.56 Notice of end of administration when purposes achieved (paragraph 80(2) of Schedule B1) . . . [6.167]
3.57 Administrator's application for order ending administration (paragraph 79 of Schedule B1) . . . [6.168]
3.58 Creditor's application for order ending administration (paragraph 81 of Schedule B1) . . . [6.169]
3.59 Notice by administrator of court order . . . [6.170]
3.60 Moving from administration to creditors' voluntary winding up (paragraph 83 of Schedule B1) . . . [6.171]
3.61 Moving from administration to dissolution (paragraph 84 of Schedule B1) . . . [6.172]

CHAPTER 12
REPLACING THE ADMINISTRATOR

3.62 Grounds for resignation . . . [6.173]
3.63 Notice of intention to resign . . . [6.174]
3.64 Notice of resignation (paragraph 87 of Schedule B1) . . . [6.175]
3.65 Application to court to remove administrator from office . . . [6.176]
3.66 Notice of vacation of office when administrator ceases to be qualified to act . . . [6.177]
3.67 Deceased administrator . . . [6.178]
3.68 Application to replace . . . [6.179]
3.69 Appointment of replacement or additional administrator . . . [6.180]
3.70 Administrator's duties on vacating office . . . [6.181]

PART 4
RECEIVERSHIP

CHAPTER 1
APPOINTMENT OF JOINT RECEIVERS OR MANAGERS TO WHOM PART 3 OF THE ACT APPLIES (OTHER THAN THOSE APPOINTED UNDER SECTION 51 (SCOTTISH RECEIVERSHIPS))

4.1 Receivers or managers appointed under an instrument: acceptance of appointment (section 33) . . . [6.182]

CHAPTER 2
ADMINISTRATIVE RECEIVERS (OTHER THAN IN SCOTTISH RECEIVERSHIPS)

4.2 Application of Chapter 2 . . . [6.183]
4.3 Interpretation . . . [6.184]
4.4 Administrative receiver's security . . . [6.185]
4.5 Publication of appointment of administrative receiver (section 46(1)) . . . [6.186]
4.6 Requirement to provide a statement of affairs (section 47(1)) . . . [6.187]
4.7 Statement of affairs: contents and delivery of copy (section 47(2)) . . . [6.188]
4.8 Statement of affairs: statement of concurrence . . . [6.189]
4.9 Statement of affairs: retention by administrative receiver . . . [6.190]
4.10 Statement of affairs: release from requirement and extension of time (section 47(5)) . . . [6.191]
4.11 Statement of affairs: expenses . . . [6.192]
4.12 Limited disclosure . . . [6.193]
4.13 Administrative receiver's report to the registrar of companies and secured creditors (section 48(1)) . . . [6.194]
4.14 Copy of report for unsecured creditors (section 48(2)) . . . [6.195]
4.15 Invitation to creditors to form a creditors' committee . . . [6.196]
4.16 Disposal of charged property (section 43(1)) . . . [6.197]
4.17 Summary of receipts and payments . . . [6.198]
4.18 Resignation . . . [6.199]
4.19 Deceased administrative receiver . . . [6.200]
4.20 Other vacation of office . . . [6.201]
4.21 Notice to registrar of companies (section 45(4)) . . . [6.202]

CHAPTER 3
NON-ADMINISTRATIVE RECEIVERS AND THE PRESCRIBED PART

4.22 Application of Chapter 3 . . . [6.203]

4.23 Report to creditors . . . [6.204]
4.24 Receiver to deal with prescribed part . . . [6.205]

PART 5
MEMBERS' VOLUNTARY WINDING UP

CHAPTER 1
STATUTORY DECLARATION OF SOLVENCY (SECTION 89)

5.1 Statutory declaration of solvency: requirements additional to those in section 89. . . . [6.206]

CHAPTER 2
THE LIQUIDATOR

5.2 Appointment by the company . . . [6.207]
5.3 Meetings in members' voluntary winding up of authorised deposit-takers . . . [6.208]
5.4 Appointment by the court (section 108) . . . [6.209]
5.5 Cost of liquidator's security (section 390(3)) . . . [6.210]
5.6 Liquidator's resignation. . . . [6.211]
5.7 Removal of liquidator by the court . . . [6.212]
5.8 Removal of liquidator by company meeting . . . [6.213]
5.9 Delivery of proposed final account to members (section 94) . . . [6.214]
5.10 Final account prior to dissolution (section 94) . . . [6.215]
5.11 Deceased liquidator . . . [6.216]
5.12 Loss of qualification as insolvency practitioner . . . [6.217]
5.13 Liquidator's duties on vacating office . . . [6.218]
5.14 Application by former liquidator to the Secretary of State for release (section 173(2)(b)) . . . [6.219]
5.15 Power of court to set aside certain transactions entered into by liquidator . . . [6.220]
5.16 Rule against improper solicitation by or on behalf of the liquidator. . . . [6.221]

CHAPTER 3
SPECIAL MANAGER

5.17 Application for and appointment of special manager (section 177) . . . [6.222]
5.18 Security . . . [6.223]
5.19 Failure to give or keep up security . . . [6.224]
5.20 Accounting . . . [6.225]
5.21 Termination of appointment. . . . [6.226]

CHAPTER 4
CONVERSION TO CREDITORS' VOLUNTARY WINDING UP

5.22 Statement of affairs (section 95(3)) . . . [6.227]

PART 6
CREDITORS' VOLUNTARY WINDING UP

CHAPTER 1
APPLICATION OF PART 6

6.1 Application of Part 6 . . . [6.228]

CHAPTER 2
STATEMENT OF AFFAIRS AND OTHER INFORMATION

6.2 Statement of affairs made out by the liquidator under section 95(1A) . . . [6.229]
6.3 Statement of affairs made out by the directors under section 99(1). . . . [6.230]
6.4 Additional requirements as to statements of affairs . . . [6.231]
6.5 Statement of affairs: statement of concurrence. . . . [6.232]
6.6 Order limiting disclosure of statement of affairs etc . . . [6.233]
6.7 Expenses of statement of affairs and decisions sought from creditors . . . [6.234]
6.8 Delivery of accounts to liquidator (section 235). . . . [6.235]
6.9 Expenses of assistance in preparing accounts . . . [6.236]

CHAPTER 3
NOMINATION AND APPOINTMENT OF LIQUIDATORS AND INFORMATION TO CREDITORS

6.10 Application of the rules in this Chapter. . . . [6.237]
6.11 Nomination of liquidator and information to creditors on conversion from members' voluntary winding up (section 96) . . . [6.238]
6.12 Creditors' decision on appointment other than at a meeting (conversion from members' voluntary winding up) . . . [6.239]
6.13 Information to creditors and contributories (conversion of members' voluntary winding up into creditors' voluntary winding up) . . . [6.240]
6.14 Information to creditors and appointment of liquidator . . . [6.241]
6.15 Information to creditors and contributories . . . [6.242]

6.16 Further information where administrator becomes liquidator (paragraph 83(3) of Schedule B1) .[6.243]
6.17 Report by director etc .[6.244]
6.18 Decisions on nomination .[6.245]
6.19 Invitation to creditors to form a liquidation committee .[6.246]

CHAPTER 4
THE LIQUIDATOR

6.20 Appointment by creditors or by the company .[6.247]
6.21 Power to fill vacancy in office of liquidator .[6.248]
6.22 Appointment by the court (section 100(3) or 108) .[6.249]
6.23 Advertisement of appointment .[6.250]
6.24 Cost of liquidator's security (section 390(3)) .[6.251]
6.25 Liquidator's resignation and replacement .[6.252]
6.26 Removal of liquidator by creditors .[6.253]
6.27 Removal of liquidator by the court .[6.254]
6.28 Final account prior to dissolution (section 106) .[6.255]
6.29 Deceased liquidator .[6.256]
6.30 Loss of qualification as insolvency practitioner .[6.257]
6.31 Vacation of office on making of winding-up order .[6.258]
6.32 Liquidator's duties on vacating office .[6.259]
6.33 Application by former liquidator for release (section 173(2)(b)) .[6.260]
6.34 Power of court to set aside certain transactions .[6.261]
6.35 Rule against improper solicitation .[6.262]
6.36 Permission for exercise of powers by liquidator .[6.263]

CHAPTER 5
SPECIAL MANAGER

6.37 Application for and appointment of special manager (section 177) .[6.264]
6.38 Security .[6.265]
6.39 Failure to give or keep up security .[6.266]
6.40 Accounting .[6.267]
6.41 Termination of appointment .[6.268]

CHAPTER 6
PRIORITY OF PAYMENT OF COSTS AND EXPENSES, ETC

6.42 General rule as to priority .[6.269]
6.43 Saving for powers of the court .[6.270]

CHAPTER 7
LITIGATION EXPENSES AND PROPERTY SUBJECT TO A FLOATING CHARGE

6.44 Interpretation .[6.271]
6.45 Requirement for approval or authorisation .[6.272]
6.46 Request for approval or authorisation .[6.273]
6.47 Grant of approval or authorisation .[6.274]
6.48 Application to the court by the liquidator .[6.275]

PART 7
WINDING UP BY THE COURT

CHAPTER 1
APPLICATION OF PART

7.1 Application of Part 7 .[6.276]

CHAPTER 2
THE STATUTORY DEMAND (SECTIONS 123(1)(A) AND 222(1)(A))

7.2 Interpretation .[6.277]
7.3 The statutory demand .[6.278]

CHAPTER 3
PETITION FOR WINDING-UP ORDER

7.4 Application of this Chapter .[6.279]
7.5 Contents of petition .[6.280]
7.6 Verification of petition .[6.281]
7.7 Petition: presentation and filing .[6.282]
7.8 Court to which petition is to be presented where the company is subject to a CVA or is in administration .[6.283]
7.9 Copies of petition to be served on company or delivered to other persons .[6.284]
7.10 Notice of petition .[6.285]

7.11 Persons entitled to request a copy of petition . . . [6.286]
7.12 Certificate of compliance . . . [6.287]
7.13 Permission for the petitioner to withdraw . . . [6.288]
7.14 Notice by persons intending to appear . . . [6.289]
7.15 List of appearances . . . [6.290]
7.16 Witness statement in opposition . . . [6.291]
7.17 Substitution of creditor or contributory for petitioner . . . [6.292]
7.18 Order for substitution of petitioner . . . [6.293]
7.19 Notice of adjournment . . . [6.294]
7.20 Order for winding up by the court . . . [6.295]
7.21 Notice to official receiver of winding-up order . . . [6.296]
7.22 Delivery and notice of the order . . . [6.297]
7.23 Petition dismissed . . . [6.298]
7.24 Injunction to restrain presentation or notice of petition . . . [6.299]

CHAPTER 4
PETITION BY A CONTRIBUTORY OR A RELEVANT OFFICE-HOLDER

7.25 Interpretation and application of rules in Chapter 3 . . . [6.300]
7.26 Contents of petition for winding-up order by a contributory . . . [6.301]
7.27 Petition presented by a relevant office-holder . . . [6.302]
7.28 Verification of petition . . . [6.303]
7.29 Presentation and service of petition . . . [6.304]
7.30 Request to appoint former administrator or supervisor as liquidator (section 140) . . . [6.305]
7.31 Hearing of petition . . . [6.306]
7.32 Order for winding up by the court of a company in administration or where there is a supervisor of a CVA in relation to the company . . . [6.307]

CHAPTER 5
PROVISIONAL LIQUIDATOR

7.33 Application for appointment of provisional liquidator (section 135) . . . [6.308]
7.34 Deposit by applicant . . . [6.309]
7.35 Order of appointment of provisional liquidator . . . [6.310]
7.36 Notice of appointment of provisional liquidator . . . [6.311]
7.37 Security . . . [6.312]
7.38 Remuneration . . . [6.313]
7.39 Termination of appointment . . . [6.314]

CHAPTER 6
STATEMENT OF AFFAIRS AND OTHER INFORMATION

7.40 Notice requiring statement of affairs (section 131) . . . [6.315]
7.41 Statement of affairs . . . [6.316]
7.42 Statement of affairs: statement of concurrence . . . [6.317]
7.43 Order limiting disclosure of statement of affairs etc . . . [6.318]
7.44 Release from duty to submit statement of affairs: extension of time (section 131) . . . [6.319]
7.45 Statement of affairs: expenses . . . [6.320]
7.46 Delivery of accounts to official receiver . . . [6.321]
7.47 Further disclosure . . . [6.322]

CHAPTER 7
REPORTS AND INFORMATION TO CREDITORS AND CONTRIBUTORIES

7.48 Reports by official receiver . . . [6.323]
7.49 Reports by official receiver: estimate of prescribed part . . . [6.324]
7.50 Further information where winding up follows administration . . . [6.325]
7.51 Notice of stay of winding up . . . [6.326]

CHAPTER 8
THE LIQUIDATOR

7.52 Choosing a person to be liquidator . . . [6.327]
7.53 Appointment of liquidator by creditors or contributories . . . [6.328]
7.54 Decision on nomination . . . [6.329]
7.55 Invitation to creditors and contributories to form a liquidation committee . . . [6.330]
7.56 Appointment by the court . . . [6.331]
7.57 Appointment by the Secretary of State . . . [6.332]
7.58 Cost of liquidator's security (section 390(3)) . . . [6.333]
7.59 Appointment to be gazetted and notice given to registrar of companies . . . [6.334]
7.60 Hand-over of assets by official receiver to liquidator . . . [6.335]
7.61 Liquidator's resignation . . . [6.336]

7.62 Notice to official receiver of intention to vacate office . . . . . [6.337]
7.63 Decision of creditors to remove liquidator . . . . . [6.338]
7.64 Procedure on removal by creditors. . . . . [6.339]
7.65 Removal of liquidator by the court (section 172(2)). . . . . [6.340]
7.66 Removal of liquidator by the Secretary of State (section 172(4)) . . . . . [6.341]
7.67 Deceased liquidator . . . . . [6.342]
7.68 Loss of qualification as insolvency practitioner . . . . . [6.343]
7.69 Application by liquidator for release (section 174(4)(b) or (d)) . . . . . [6.344]
7.70 Release of official receiver . . . . . [6.345]
7.71 Final account prior to dissolution (section 146) . . . . . [6.346]
7.72 Relief from, or variation of, duty to report . . . . . [6.347]
7.73 Liquidator's duties on vacating office . . . . . [6.348]
7.74 Power of court to set aside certain transactions . . . . . [6.349]
7.75 Rule against improper solicitation . . . . . [6.350]

CHAPTER 9
DUTIES AND POWERS OF LIQUIDATOR

7.76 General duties of liquidator. . . . . [6.351]
7.77 Permission for exercise of powers by liquidator . . . . . [6.352]
7.78 Enforced delivery up of company's property (section 234). . . . . [6.353]

CHAPTER 10
SETTLEMENT OF LIST OF CONTRIBUTORIES

7.79 Delegation to liquidator of power to settle list of contributories. . . . . [6.354]
7.80 Duty of liquidator to settle list (section 148). . . . . [6.355]
7.81 Contents of list . . . . . [6.356]
7.82 Procedure for settling list . . . . . [6.357]
7.83 Application to court for variation of the list . . . . . [6.358]
7.84 Variation of, or addition to, the list . . . . . [6.359]
7.85 Costs of applications to vary etc the list of contributories . . . . . [6.360]

CHAPTER 11
CALLS ON CONTRIBUTORIES

7.86 Making of calls by the liquidator (sections 150 and 160). . . . . [6.361]
7.87 Sanction of the liquidation committee for making a call . . . . . [6.362]
7.88 Application to court for permission to make a call (sections 150 and 160). . . . . [6.363]
7.89 Order giving permission to make a call. . . . . [6.364]
7.90 Making and enforcement of the call. . . . . [6.365]
7.91 Court order to enforce payment of call by a contributory. . . . . [6.366]

CHAPTER 12
SPECIAL MANAGER

7.92 Application of this Chapter and interpretation . . . . . [6.367]
7.93 Appointment and remuneration of special manager (section 177) . . . . . [6.368]
7.94 Security . . . . . [6.369]
7.95 Failure to give or keep up security . . . . . [6.370]
7.96 Accounting . . . . . [6.371]
7.97 Termination of appointment. . . . . [6.372]

CHAPTER 13
PUBLIC EXAMINATION OF COMPANY OFFICERS AND OTHERS (SECTION 133)

7.98 Applications relating to promoters, past managers etc (section 133(1)(c)) . . . . . [6.373]
7.99 Request by a creditor for a public examination (section 133(2)). . . . . [6.374]
7.100 Request by a contributory for a public examination . . . . . [6.375]
7.101 Further provisions about requests by a creditor or contributory for a public examination. . . . [6.376]
7.102 Order for public examination . . . . . [6.377]
7.103 Notice of the public examination. . . . . [6.378]
7.104 Examinee unfit for examination. . . . . [6.379]
7.105 Procedure at public examination . . . . . [6.380]
7.106 Adjournment . . . . . [6.381]
7.107 Expenses of examination . . . . . [6.382]

CHAPTER 14
PRIORITY OF PAYMENT OF COSTS AND EXPENSES, ETC

7.108 General rule as to priority. . . . . [6.383]
7.109 Winding up commencing as voluntary . . . . . [6.384]
7.110 Saving for powers of the court (section 156) . . . . . [6.385]

Part 6 Insolvency Rules

CHAPTER 15
LITIGATION EXPENSES AND PROPERTY SUBJECT TO A FLOATING CHARGE

7.111 Interpretation .... [6.386]
7.112 Priority of litigation expenses .... [6.387]
7.113 Requirement for approval or authorisation of litigation expenses .... [6.388]
7.114 Requests for approval or authorisation .... [6.389]
7.115 Grant of approval or authorisation .... [6.390]
7.116 Application to the court by the liquidator .... [6.391]

CHAPTER 16
MISCELLANEOUS RULES

Sub-division A: Return of capital

7.117 Application to court for order authorising return of capital .... [6.392]
7.118 Procedure for return .... [6.393]

Sub-division B: Dissolution after winding up

7.119 Secretary of State's directions under sections 203 and 205 and appeal .... [6.394]

PART 8
INDIVIDUAL VOLUNTARY ARRANGEMENTS (IVA)

CHAPTER 1
PRELIMINARY

8.1 Interpretation .... [6.395]

CHAPTER 2
PREPARATION OF THE DEBTOR'S PROPOSAL FOR AN IVA

8.2 Proposal for an IVA: general principles and amendment .... [6.396]
8.3 Proposal: contents .... [6.397]
8.4 Notice of nominee's consent .... [6.398]
8.5 Statement of affairs (section 256 and 256A) .... [6.399]
8.6 Application to omit information from statement of affairs delivered to creditors .... [6.400]
8.7 Additional disclosure for assistance of nominee .... [6.401]

CHAPTER 3
CASES IN WHICH AN APPLICATION FOR AN INTERIM ORDER IS MADE

8.8 Application for interim order .... [6.402]
8.9 Court in which application is to be made .... [6.403]
8.10 Order granting a stay .... [6.404]
8.11 Hearing of the application .... [6.405]
8.12 The interim order .... [6.406]
8.13 Action to follow making of an interim order .... [6.407]
8.14 Order extending period of an interim order (section 256(4)) .... [6.408]
8.15 Nominee's report on the proposal .... [6.409]
8.16 Order extending period of interim order to enable the creditors to consider the proposal (section 256(5)) .... [6.410]
8.17 Replacement of the nominee (section 256(3)) .... [6.411]
8.18 Consideration of the nominee's report .... [6.412]

CHAPTER 4
CASES WHERE NO INTERIM ORDER IS TO BE OBTAINED

8.19 Nominee's report (section 256A) .... [6.413]
8.20 Court or hearing centre to which applications must be made where no interim order .... [6.414]
8.21 Replacement of the nominee (section 256A(4)) .... [6.415]

CHAPTER 5
CONSIDERATION OF THE PROPOSAL BY THE CREDITORS

8.22 Consideration of the proposal .... [6.416]
8.23 Proposals for an alternative supervisor .... [6.417]
8.24 Report of the creditors' consideration of a proposal .... [6.418]

CHAPTER 6
ACTION FOLLOWING APPROVAL OF AN IVA

8.25 Hand-over of property, etc to supervisor .... [6.419]
8.26 Report to the Secretary of State of the approval of an IVA .... [6.420]
8.27 Revocation or suspension of an IVA (section 262) .... [6.421]
8.28 Supervisor's accounts and reports .... [6.422]
8.29 Production of accounts and records to the Secretary of State .... [6.423]
8.30 Fees and expenses .... [6.424]

8.31 Termination or full implementation of the IVA. . . . . [6.425]

CHAPTER 7
APPLICATIONS TO ANNUL BANKRUPTCY ORDERS UNDER SECTION 261(2)(A) AND (B)

8.32 Application by the bankrupt to annul the bankruptcy order (section 261(2)(a)) . . . . . [6.426]
8.33 Application by the official receiver to annul the bankruptcy order (section 261(2)(b)) . . . . . [6.427]
8.34 Order annulling bankruptcy. . . . . [6.428]
8.35 Notice of order . . . . . [6.429]
8.36 Advertisement of order . . . . . [6.430]
8.37 Trustee's final account. . . . . [6.431]

CHAPTER 8
TIME RECORDING INFORMATION

8.38 Provision of information . . . . . [6.432]

PART 9
DEBT RELIEF ORDERS

CHAPTER 1
INTERPRETATION

9.1 Debtor's family . . . . . [6.433]
9.2 Excluded debts. . . . . [6.434]

CHAPTER 2
APPLICATION FOR A DEBT RELIEF ORDER

9.3 Application for a debt relief order: information required in the application . . . . . [6.435]
9.4 Delivery of application . . . . . [6.436]
9.5 Role of approved intermediary. . . . . [6.437]

CHAPTER 3
VERIFYING THE APPLICATION AND DETERMINING THE DEBTOR'S INCOME AND PROPERTY

9.6 Prescribed verification checks: conditions in paragraphs 1 to 8 of Schedule 4ZA of the Act . . . [6.438]
9.7 Determination of debtor's monthly surplus income . . . . . [6.439]
9.8 Determination of value of the debtor's property (paragraph 8 of Schedule 4ZA). . . . . [6.440]
9.9 Property to be excluded in determining the value of a debtor's property. . . . . [6.441]

CHAPTER 4
MAKING OR REFUSAL OF A DEBT RELIEF ORDER

9.10 Contents of debt relief order . . . . . [6.442]
9.11 Other steps to be taken by official receiver or debtor upon making of the order. . . . . [6.443]
9.12 Prescribed information for creditors on making of debt relief order. . . . . [6.444]
9.13 Refusal of application for debt relief order . . . . . [6.445]

CHAPTER 5
OBJECTION AND REVOCATION

9.14 Meaning of "creditor" . . . . . [6.446]
9.15 Creditor's objection to a debt relief order (section 251K) . . . . . [6.447]
9.16 Official receiver's response to objection under section 251K. . . . . [6.448]
9.17 Creditor's request that a debt relief order be revoked (section 251L(4)) . . . . . [6.449]
9.18 Procedure in revoking or amending a debt relief order (section 251L) . . . . . [6.450]
9.19 Debtor's notification of official receiver of matters in section 251J(3) or (5) . . . . . [6.451]
9.20 Death of debtor during a moratorium period under a debt relief order . . . . . [6.452]

CHAPTER 6
APPLICATIONS TO THE COURT

9.21 Notice of application to court under section 251M . . . . . [6.453]
9.22 Court in which applications under sections 251M or 251N are to be made . . . . . [6.454]
9.23 Creditor's bankruptcy petition: creditor consents to making application for a debt relief order. . . . . [6.455]
9.24 Extension of moratorium period . . . . . [6.456]

CHAPTER 7
PERMISSION TO ACT AS A DIRECTOR, ETC

9.25 Application for permission under the Company Directors Disqualification Act 1986 . . . . . . [6.457]
9.26 Report of official receiver. . . . . [6.458]
9.27 Court's order on application . . . . . [6.459]

PART 10
BANKRUPTCY

CHAPTER 1
THE STATUTORY DEMAND

10.1 The statutory demand (section 268) . . . . . [6.460]

Part 6 Insolvency Rules

10.2 Service of statutory demand .....[6.461]
10.3 Proof of service of statutory demand .....[6.462]
10.4 Application to set aside statutory demand .....[6.463]
10.5 Hearing of application to set aside .....[6.464]

CHAPTER 2
CREDITORS' BANKRUPTCY PETITIONS

Preliminary

10.6 Application and interpretation .....[6.465]
10.7 Contents of petition .....[6.466]
10.8 Identification of debtor .....[6.467]
10.9 Identification of debt .....[6.468]
10.10 Verification of petition .....[6.469]
10.11 Court in which petition is to be presented .....[6.470]
10.12 Procedure for presentation and filing of petition .....[6.471]
10.13 Application to Chief Land Registrar to register petition .....[6.472]
10.14 Service of petition and delivery of copies .....[6.473]
10.15 Death of debtor before service .....[6.474]
10.16 Amendment of petition .....[6.475]
10.17 Security for costs .....[6.476]
10.18 Debtor's notice of opposition to petition .....[6.477]
10.19 Notice by persons intending to appear .....[6.478]
10.20 List of appearances .....[6.479]
10.21 Hearing of petition .....[6.480]
10.22 Postponement of hearing .....[6.481]
10.23 Adjournment of the hearing .....[6.482]
10.24 Decision on the hearing .....[6.483]
10.25 Vacating registration on withdrawal of petition .....[6.484]
10.26 Non-appearance of petitioning creditor .....[6.485]
10.27 Substitution of petitioner .....[6.486]
10.28 Order for substitution of petitioner .....[6.487]
10.29 Change of carriage of petition .....[6.488]
10.31 Contents of bankruptcy order .....[6.489]
10.32 Delivery and notice of the order .....[6.490]
10.33 Application to Chief Land Registrar to register bankruptcy order .....[6.491]

CHAPTER 3
DEBTORS' BANKRUPTCY APPLICATIONS

10.34 Preliminary .....[6.492]
10.35 Bankruptcy application for a bankruptcy order .....[6.493]
10.36 Procedure for making a bankruptcy application and communication with the adjudicator .....[6.494]
10.37 Application to the Chief Land Registrar to register a bankruptcy application .....[6.495]
10.38 Verification checks .....[6.496]
10.39 Determination of the bankruptcy application .....[6.497]
10.40 The determination period .....[6.498]
10.41 Settlement and contents of bankruptcy order .....[6.499]
10.42 Refusal to make a bankruptcy order and contents of notice of refusal .....[6.500]
10.43 Review of refusal to make a bankruptcy order .....[6.501]
10.44 Appeal to the court following a review of refusal to make a bankruptcy order .....[6.502]
10.45 Action to follow making of order .....[6.503]
10.46 Application to the Chief Land Registrar .....[6.504]
10.47 The bankruptcy file .....[6.505]
10.48 Court to which applications are to be made .....[6.506]

CHAPTER 4
THE INTERIM RECEIVER

10.49 Application for appointment of interim receiver (section 286) .....[6.507]
10.50 Deposit .....[6.508]
10.51 Order of appointment .....[6.509]
10.52 Security .....[6.510]
10.53 Remuneration .....[6.511]
10.54 Termination of appointment .....[6.512]

CHAPTER 5
DISCLOSURE OF THE BANKRUPT'S AFFAIRS

Sub-division A: creditor's petition

10.55 Notice requiring statement of affairs (section 288) . . . [6.513]
10.56 Statement of affairs . . . [6.514]
10.57 Limited disclosure . . . [6.515]
10.58 Requirement to submit statement of affairs and extension of time (section 288(3)) . . . [6.516]
10.59 Expenses of assisting bankrupt to prepare statement of affairs . . . [6.517]
10.60 Delivery of accounts to official receiver . . . [6.518]
10.61 Further disclosure . . . [6.519]

Sub-division B: Bankruptcy application

10.62 Preliminary . . . [6.520]
10.63 Delivery of accounts to official receiver . . . [6.521]
10.64 Expenses of preparing accounts . . . [6.522]
10.65 Further disclosure . . . [6.523]

Sub-division C: Reports by the official receiver

10.66 Reports by the official receiver . . . [6.524]

CHAPTER 6
THE TRUSTEE IN BANKRUPTCY

Sub-division A: appointment and associated formalities

10.67 Appointment by creditors of new trustee . . . [6.525]
10.68 Certification of appointment . . . [6.526]
10.69 Cost of the trustee's security (section 390(3)) . . . [6.527]
10.70 Creditors' decision to appoint a trustee . . . [6.528]
10.71 Appointment by the court (section 291A(2)) . . . [6.529]
10.72 Appointment by the Secretary of State . . . [6.530]
10.73 Authentication of trustee's appointment . . . [6.531]
10.74 Appointment to be gazetted . . . [6.532]
10.75 Hand-over of bankrupt's estate by official receiver to trustee . . . [6.533]
10.76 Invitation to creditors to form a creditors' committee . . . [6.534]

Sub-division B: resignation and removal

10.77 Trustee's resignation and appointment of replacement (section 298(7)) . . . [6.535]
10.78 Decision of creditors to remove trustee (section 298(1)) . . . [6.536]
10.79 Procedure on removal by creditors . . . [6.537]
10.80 Removal of trustee by the court (section 298(1)) . . . [6.538]
10.81 Removal of trustee by the Secretary of State (section 298(5)) . . . [6.539]
10.82 Notice of resignation or removal . . . [6.540]
10.83 Release of removed trustee (section 299) . . . [6.541]
10.84 Deceased trustee . . . [6.542]
10.85 Loss of qualification as insolvency practitioner (section 298(6)) . . . [6.543]

Sub-division C: release on completion of administration of bankrupt's estate

10.86 Release of official receiver on completion of administration (section 299) . . . [6.544]
10.87 Vacation of office on completion of bankruptcy (sections 298(8) and 331) . . . [6.545]
10.88 Rule as to reporting . . . [6.546]
10.89 Notice to official receiver of intention to vacate office . . . [6.547]
10.90 Trustee's duties on vacating office . . . [6.548]
10.91 Power of the court to set aside certain transactions . . . [6.549]
10.92 Rule against improper solicitation . . . [6.550]
10.93 Enforcement of trustee's obligations to official receiver (section 305(3)) . . . [6.551]

CHAPTER 7
SPECIAL MANAGER

10.94 Application for and order of appointment of special manager (section 370) . . . [6.552]
10.95 Security . . . [6.553]
10.96 Failure to give or keep up security . . . [6.554]
10.97 Accounting . . . [6.555]
10.98 Termination of appointment . . . [6.556]

CHAPTER 8
PUBLIC EXAMINATION OF BANKRUPT

10.99 Order for public examination of bankrupt . . . [6.557]

Part 6 Insolvency Rules

10.100 Notice of public examination . . . [6.558]
10.101 Order for public examination requested by creditors . . . [6.559]
10.102 Bankrupt unfit for examination . . . [6.560]
10.103 Procedure at public examination . . . [6.561]
10.104 Adjournment . . . [6.562]
10.105 Expenses of examination . . . [6.563]

CHAPTER 9
REPLACEMENT OF EXEMPT PROPERTY
10.106 Purchase of replacement property . . . [6.564]
10.107 Money provided in lieu of sale . . . [6.565]

CHAPTER 10
INCOME PAYMENTS ORDERS
10.108 Interpretation . . . [6.566]
10.109 Application for income payments order (section 310) . . . [6.567]
10.110 Order for income payments order . . . [6.568]
10.111 Action to follow making of order . . . [6.569]
10.112 Variation of order . . . [6.570]
10.113 Order to payer of income: administration . . . [6.571]
10.114 Review of order . . . [6.572]

CHAPTER 11
INCOME PAYMENTS AGREEMENTS
10.114A Interpretation . . . [6.573]
10.115 Approval of income payments agreements . . . [6.574]
10.116 Acceptance of income payments agreements . . . [6.575]
10.117 Variation of income payments agreements . . . [6.576]

CHAPTER 12
APPLICATIONS FOR PRODUCTION OF DOCUMENTS BY HER MAJESTY'S REVENUE AND CUSTOMS (SECTION 369)
10.118 Application for order . . . [6.577]
10.119 Making and service of the order . . . [6.578]
10.120 Custody of documents . . . [6.579]

CHAPTER 13
MORTGAGED PROPERTY
10.121 Interpretation . . . [6.580]
10.122 Claim by mortgagee of land . . . [6.581]
10.123 Power of court to order sale . . . [6.582]
10.124 Proceeds of sale . . . [6.583]

CHAPTER 14
AFTER-ACQUIRED PROPERTY
10.125 Duties of bankrupt in relation to after-acquired property . . . [6.584]
10.126 Trustee's recourse to person to whom property disposed . . . [6.585]

CHAPTER 15
PERMISSION TO ACT AS DIRECTOR, ETC
10.127 Interpretation . . . [6.586]
10.128 Application for permission . . . [6.587]
10.129 Report of official receiver . . . [6.588]
10.130 Court's order on application . . . [6.589]
10.131 Costs under this Chapter . . . [6.590]

CHAPTER 16
ANNULMENT OF BANKRUPTCY ORDER
10.132 Application for annulment . . . [6.591]
10.133 Report by trustee . . . [6.592]
10.134 Applicant's claim that remuneration or expenses are excessive . . . [6.593]
10.135 Power of court to stay proceedings . . . [6.594]
10.136 Notice to creditors who have not proved . . . [6.595]
10.137 The hearing . . . [6.596]
10.138 Matters to be proved under section 282(1)(b) . . . [6.597]
10.139 Notice to creditors . . . [6.598]
10.140 Other matters arising on annulment . . . [6.599]
10.141 Trustee's final account . . . [6.600]

CHAPTER 17
DISCHARGE

10.142 Application for suspension of discharge . . . [6.601]
10.143 Lifting of suspension of discharge . . . [6.602]
10.144 Certificate of discharge from bankruptcy order made otherwise than on a bankruptcy application . . . [6.603]
10.145 Certificate of discharge from bankruptcy order made on a bankruptcy application . . . [6.604]
10.146 Bankrupt's debts surviving discharge . . . [6.605]
10.147 Costs under this Chapter . . . [6.606]

CHAPTER 18
PRIORITY OF PAYMENT OF COSTS ETC OUT OF THE BANKRUPT'S ESTATE

10.148 Expenses . . . [6.607]
10.149 General rule as to priority . . . [6.608]

CHAPTER 19
SECOND BANKRUPTCY

10.150 Scope of this Chapter . . . [6.609]
10.151 General duty of existing trustee . . . [6.610]
10.152 Delivery up to later trustee . . . [6.611]
10.153 Existing trustee's expenses . . . [6.612]

CHAPTER 20
CRIMINAL BANKRUPTCY

10.153A Application . . . [6.613]
10.154 Contents of petition . . . [6.614]
10.155 Status and functions of Official Petitioner . . . [6.615]
10.156 Interim receivership . . . [6.616]
10.157 Proof of bankruptcy debts and notice of order . . . [6.617]
10.158 Rules not applying in criminal bankruptcy . . . [6.618]
10.159 Annulment of criminal bankruptcy order . . . [6.619]
10.160 Application by bankrupt for discharge . . . [6.620]
10.161 Report of official receiver . . . [6.621]
10.162 Order of discharge . . . [6.622]
10.163 Deferment of issue of order pending appeal . . . [6.623]
10.164 Costs under this Chapter . . . [6.624]

CHAPTER 21
MISCELLANEOUS RULES IN BANKRUPTCY

10.165 Amendment of title of proceedings . . . [6.625]
10.166 Application for redirection order . . . [6.626]
10.167 Bankrupt's home: property falling within section 283A . . . [6.627]
10.168 Application in relation to the vesting of an interest in a dwelling-house (registered land) . . . [6.628]
10.169 Vesting of bankrupt's interest (unregistered land) . . . [6.629]
10.170 Vesting of bankrupt's estate: substituted period . . . [6.630]
10.171 Charging order . . . [6.631]

PART 11
BANKRUPTCY AND DEBT RELIEF RESTRICTIONS ORDERS AND UNDERTAKINGS AND THE INSOLVENCY REGISTERS

CHAPTER 1
INTERPRETATION

11.1 References to the Secretary of State . . . [6.632]

CHAPTER 2
BANKRUPTCY AND DEBT RELIEF RESTRICTIONS ORDERS (SCHEDULES 4ZB AND 4A)

11.2 Application for a bankruptcy or debt relief restrictions order . . . [6.633]
11.3 Service of the application on the bankrupt or debtor . . . [6.634]
11.4 The bankrupt's or debtor's evidence opposing an application . . . [6.635]
11.5 Making a bankruptcy or debt relief restrictions order . . . [6.636]

CHAPTER 3
INTERIM BANKRUPTCY AND DEBT RELIEF RESTRICTIONS ORDERS

11.6 Application for an interim bankruptcy or debt relief restrictions order . . . [6.637]
11.7 Making an interim bankruptcy or debt relief restrictions order . . . [6.638]
11.8 Application to set aside an interim order . . . [6.639]
11.9 Order setting aside an interim order . . . [6.640]

CHAPTER 4
BANKRUPTCY RESTRICTIONS AND DEBT RELIEF RESTRICTIONS UNDERTAKINGS

11.10 Acceptance of a bankruptcy restrictions or a debt relief restrictions undertaking . . . [6.641]
11.11 Notification . . . [6.642]
11.12 Application to annul a bankruptcy restrictions or a debt relief restrictions undertaking . . . [6.643]

CHAPTER 5
INSOLVENCY REGISTERS: GENERAL

11.13 Maintenance of the registers and inspection . . . [6.644]

CHAPTER 6
INDIVIDUAL INSOLVENCY REGISTER

11.14 Entry of information on the individual insolvency register: IVAs . . . [6.645]
11.15 Deletion of information from the individual insolvency register: IVAs . . . [6.646]
11.16 Entry of information on to the individual insolvency register: bankruptcy orders . . . [6.647]
11.17 Deletion of information from the individual insolvency register: bankruptcy orders . . . [6.648]
11.18 Entry of information on to the individual insolvency register: debt relief orders . . . [6.649]
11.19 Deletion of information from the individual insolvency register: debt relief orders . . . [6.650]

CHAPTER 7
BANKRUPTCY AND DEBT RELIEF RESTRICTIONS REGISTER

11.20 Bankruptcy restrictions and debt relief restrictions orders and undertakings: entry of information on the registers . . . [6.651]
11.21 Deletion of information from the registers . . . [6.652]

CHAPTER 8
RECTIFICATION OF REGISTERS AND DEATH OF PERSONS ON REGISTER

11.22 Rectification of the registers . . . [6.653]
11.23 Death of a person about whom information is held on a register . . . [6.654]

PART 12
COURT PROCEDURE AND PRACTICE

CHAPTER 1
GENERAL

Application of the Civil Procedure Rules 1998

12.1 Court rules and practice to apply . . . [6.655]
12.2 Performance of functions by the Court . . . [6.656]

CHAPTER 2
COMMENCEMENT OF INSOLVENCY PROCEEDINGS IN THE COUNTY COURT

12.3 Commencement of insolvency proceedings under Parts 1 to 7 of the Act (corporate insolvency proceedings) . . . [6.657]
12.4 Commencement of insolvency proceedings under Parts 7A to 11 of the Act (personal insolvency proceedings; bankruptcy) . . . [6.658]
12.5 Allocation of proceedings to the London Insolvency District . . . [6.659]

CHAPTER 3
MAKING APPLICATIONS TO COURT: GENERAL

12.6 Preliminary . . . [6.660]
12.7 Filing of application . . . [6.661]
12.8 Fixing the venue . . . [6.662]
12.9 Service or delivery of application . . . [6.663]
12.10 Hearing in urgent case . . . [6.664]
12.11 Directions . . . [6.665]
12.12 Hearing and determination without notice . . . [6.666]
12.13 Adjournment of the hearing of an application . . . [6.667]

CHAPTER 4
MAKING APPLICATIONS TO COURT: SPECIFIC APPLICATIONS

Sub-division A: Applications in connection with section 176A (prescribed part)

12.14 Applications under section 176A(5) to disapply section 176A . . . [6.668]
12.15 Notice of application under section 176A(5) . . . [6.669]
12.16 Notice of an order under section 176A(5) . . . [6.670]

Sub-division B: Applications for private examination (sections 236, 251N and 366)

12.17 Application of this sub-division and interpretation . . . [6.671]
12.18 Contents of application . . . [6.672]
12.19 Order for examination etc . . . [6.673]

12.20 Procedure for examination . . . [6.674]
12.21 Record of examination . . . [6.675]
12.22 Costs of proceedings under sections 236, 251N and 366 . . . [6.676]

Sub-division C—persons unable to manage own property or affairs

12.23 Application and interpretation . . . [6.677]
12.24 Appointment of another person to act . . . [6.678]
12.25 Witness statement in support of application . . . [6.679]
12.26 Service of notices following appointment . . . [6.680]

CHAPTER 5
OBTAINING INFORMATION AND EVIDENCE

12.27 Further information and disclosure . . . [6.681]
12.28 Witness statements and reports . . . [6.682]
12.29 Evidence provided by the official receiver, an insolvency practitioner or a special manager . . . [6.683]

CHAPTER 6
TRANSFER OF PROCEEDINGS

Sub-division A: General

12.30 General power of transfer . . . [6.684]
12.31 Proceedings commenced in the wrong court . . . [6.685]
12.32 Applications for transfer . . . [6.686]
12.33 Procedure following order for transfer . . . [6.687]
12.34 Consequential transfer of other proceedings . . . [6.688]

Sub-division B: Block transfer of cases where insolvency practitioner has died etc

12.35 Interpretation . . . [6.689]
12.36 Power to make a block transfer order . . . [6.690]
12.37 Application for a block transfer order . . . [6.691]
12.38 Action following application for a block transfer order . . . [6.692]

CHAPTER 7
THE COURT FILE

12.39 The court file . . . [6.693]
12.40 Office copies of documents . . . [6.694]

CHAPTER 8
COSTS

12.41 Application of Chapter and interpretation . . . [6.695]
12.42 Requirement to assess costs by the detailed procedure . . . [6.696]
12.43 Procedure where detailed assessment is required . . . [6.697]
12.44 Costs of officers charged with execution of writs or other process . . . [6.698]
12.45 Petitions presented by insolvent companies . . . [6.699]
12.46 Costs paid otherwise than out of the insolvent estate . . . [6.700]
12.47 Awards of costs against an office-holder, the adjudicator or the official receiver . . . [6.701]
12.48 Applications for costs . . . [6.702]
12.49 Costs and expenses of petitioners and other specified persons . . . [6.703]
12.50 Final costs certificate . . . [6.704]

CHAPTER 9
ENFORCEMENT PROCEDURES

12.51 Enforcement of court orders . . . [6.705]
12.52 Orders enforcing compliance . . . [6.706]
12.53 Warrants (general provisions) . . . [6.707]
12.54 Warrants under sections 134 and 364 . . . [6.708]
12.55 Warrants under sections 236, 251N and 366 . . . [6.709]
12.56 Warrants under section 365 . . . [6.710]
12.57 Execution overtaken by judgment debtor's insolvency . . . [6.711]

CHAPTER 10
APPEALS

12.58 Application of Chapter . . . [6.712]
12.59 Appeals and reviews of court orders in corporate insolvency . . . [6.713]
12.60 Appeals in bankruptcy by the Secretary of State . . . [6.714]
12.61 Procedure on appeal . . . [6.715]
12.62 Appeals against decisions of the Secretary of State or official receiver . . . [6.716]

CHAPTER 11
COURT ORDERS, FORMAL DEFECTS AND SHORTHAND WRITERS

12.63 Court orders . . . [6.717]
12.64 Formal defects . . . [6.718]
12.65 Shorthand writers: nomination etc . . . [6.719]

PART 13
OFFICIAL RECEIVERS

13.1 Official receivers in court . . . [6.720]
13.2 Persons entitled to act on official receiver's behalf . . . [6.721]
13.3 Application for directions . . . [6.722]
13.4 Official receiver's expenses . . . [6.723]
13.5 Official receiver not to be appointed liquidator or trustee . . . [6.724]

PART 14
CLAIMS BY AND DISTRIBUTIONS TO CREDITORS IN ADMINISTRATION, WINDING UP AND BANKRUPTCY

CHAPTER 1
APPLICATION AND INTERPRETATION

14.1 Application of Part 14 and interpretation . . . [6.725]

CHAPTER 2
CREDITORS' CLAIMS IN ADMINISTRATION, WINDING UP AND BANKRUPTCY

14.2 Provable debts . . . [6.726]
14.3 Proving a debt . . . [6.727]
14.4 Requirements for proof . . . [6.728]
14.5 Costs of proving . . . [6.729]
14.6 Allowing inspection of proofs . . . [6.730]
14.7 Admission and rejection of proofs for dividend . . . [6.731]
14.8 Appeal against decision on proof . . . [6.732]
14.9 Office-holder not liable for costs under rule 14.8 . . . [6.733]
14.10 Withdrawal or variation of proof . . . [6.734]
14.11 Exclusion of proof by the court . . . [6.735]
14.12 Administration and winding up by the court: debts of insolvent company to rank equally . . . [6.736]
14.13 Administration and winding up: division of unsold assets . . . [6.737]
14.14 Administration and winding up: estimate of value of debt . . . [6.738]
14.15 Secured creditor: value of security . . . [6.739]
14.16 Secured creditor: surrender for non-disclosure . . . [6.740]
14.17 Secured creditor: redemption by office-holder . . . [6.741]
14.18 Secured creditor: test of security's value . . . [6.742]
14.19 Realisation or surrender of security by creditor . . . [6.743]
14.20 Discounts . . . [6.744]
14.21 Debts in foreign currency . . . [6.745]
14.22 Payments of a periodical nature . . . [6.746]
14.23 Interest . . . [6.747]
14.24 Administration: mutual dealings and set-off . . . [6.748]
14.25 Winding up: mutual dealings and set-off . . . [6.749]

CHAPTER 3
DISTRIBUTION TO CREDITORS IN ADMINISTRATION, WINDING UP AND BANKRUPTCY

14.26 Application of Chapter to a particular class of creditors and to distributions . . . [6.750]
14.27 Declaration and distribution of dividends in a winding up . . . [6.751]
14.28 Gazette notice of intended first dividend or distribution . . . [6.752]
14.29 Individual notices to creditors etc of intended dividend or distribution . . . [6.753]
14.30 Contents of notice of intention to declare a dividend or make a distribution . . . [6.754]
14.31 Further contents of notice to creditors owed small debts etc . . . [6.755]
14.32 Admission or rejection of proofs following last date for proving . . . [6.756]
14.33 Postponement or cancellation of dividend . . . [6.757]
14.34 Declaration of dividend . . . [6.758]
14.35 Notice of declaration of a dividend . . . [6.759]
14.36 Last notice about dividend in a winding up . . . [6.760]
14.37 Contents of last notice about dividend (administration, winding up and bankruptcy) . . . [6.761]
14.38 Sole or final dividend . . . [6.762]
14.39 Administration and winding up: provisions as to dividends . . . [6.763]
14.40 Supplementary provisions as to dividends and distributions . . . [6.764]
14.41 Secured creditors . . . [6.765]

14.42 Disqualification from dividend .[6.766]
14.43 Assignment of right to dividend .[6.767]
14.44 Debt payable at future time .[6.768]
14.45 Administration and winding up: non-payment of dividend .[6.769]

PART 15
DECISION MAKING

CHAPTER 1
APPLICATION OF PART

15.1 Application of Part .[6.770]

CHAPTER 2
DECISION PROCEDURES

15.2 Interpretation .[6.771]
15.3 The prescribed decision procedures .[6.772]
15.4 Electronic voting .[6.773]
15.5 Virtual meetings .[6.774]
15.6 Physical meetings .[6.775]
15.7 Deemed consent (sections 246ZF and 379ZB) .[6.776]

CHAPTER 3
NOTICES, VOTING AND VENUES FOR DECISIONS

15.8 Notices to creditors of decision procedure .[6.777]
15.9 Voting in a decision procedure .[6.778]
15.10 Venue for decision procedure .[6.779]
15.11 Notice of decision procedures or of seeking deemed consent: when and to whom delivered .[6.780]
15.12 Notice of decision procedure by advertisement only .[6.781]
15.13 Gazetting and advertisement of meeting .[6.782]
15.14 Notice to company officers, bankrupts etc in respect of meetings .[6.783]
15.15 Non-receipt of notice of decision .[6.784]
15.16 Decisions on remuneration and conduct .[6.785]

CHAPTER 4
DECISION MAKING IN PARTICULAR PROCEEDINGS

15.17 Decisions in winding up of authorised deposit-takers .[6.786]

CHAPTER 5
REQUISITIONED DECISIONS

15.18 Requisitions of decision .[6.787]
15.19 Expenses and timing of requisitioned decision .[6.788]

CHAPTER 6
CONSTITUTION OF MEETINGS

15.20 Quorum at meetings .[6.789]
15.21 Chair at meetings .[6.790]
15.22 The chair—attendance, interventions and questions .[6.791]

CHAPTER 7
ADJOURNMENT AND SUSPENSION OF MEETINGS

15.23 Adjournment by chair .[6.792]
15.24 Adjournment of meetings to remove a liquidator or trustee .[6.793]
15.25 Adjournment in absence of chair .[6.794]
15.26 Proofs in adjournment .[6.795]
15.27 Suspension .[6.796]

CHAPTER 8
CREDITORS' VOTING RIGHTS AND MAJORITIES

15.28 Creditors' voting rights .[6.797]
15.29 Scheme manager's voting rights .[6.798]
15.30 Claim made in proceedings in other member States .[6.799]
15.31 Calculation of voting rights .[6.800]
15.32 Calculation of voting rights: special cases .[6.801]
15.33 Procedure for admitting creditors' claims for voting .[6.802]
15.34 Requisite majorities .[6.803]
15.35 Appeals against decisions under this Chapter .[6.804]

CHAPTER 9
EXCLUSIONS FROM MEETINGS

15.36 Action where person excluded .[6.805]

15.37 Indication to excluded person . . . . [6.806]
15.38 Complaint . . . . [6.807]

CHAPTER 10
CONTRIBUTORIES' VOTING RIGHTS AND MAJORITIES

15.39 Contributories' voting rights and requisite majorities . . . . [6.808]

CHAPTER 11
RECORDS

15.40 Record of a decision . . . . [6.809]

CHAPTER 12
COMPANY MEETINGS

15.41 Company meetings . . . . [6.810]
15.42 Remote attendance: notification requirements . . . . [6.811]
15.43 Location of company meetings . . . . [6.812]
15.44 Action where person excluded . . . . [6.813]
15.45 Indication to excluded person . . . . [6.814]
15.46 Complaint . . . . [6.815]

PART 16
PROXIES AND CORPORATE REPRESENTATION

16.1 Application and interpretation . . . . [6.816]
16.2 Specific and continuing proxies . . . . [6.817]
16.3 Blank proxy . . . . [6.818]
16.4 Use of proxies . . . . [6.819]
16.5 Use of proxies by the chair . . . . [6.820]
16.6 Right of inspection and retention of proxies . . . . [6.821]
16.7 Proxy-holder with financial interest . . . . [6.822]
16.9 Instrument conferring authorisation to represent corporation . . . . [6.823]

PART 17
CREDITORS' AND LIQUIDATION COMMITTEES

CHAPTER 1
INTRODUCTORY

17.1 Scope and interpretation . . . . [6.824]

CHAPTER 2
FUNCTIONS OF A COMMITTEE

17.2 Functions of a committee . . . . [6.825]

CHAPTER 3
MEMBERSHIP AND FORMALITIES OF FORMATION OF A COMMITTEE

17.3 Number of members of a committee . . . . [6.826]
17.4 Eligibility for membership of creditors' or liquidation committee . . . . [6.827]
17.5 Establishment of committees . . . . [6.828]
17.6 Liquidation committee established by contributories . . . . [6.829]
17.7 Notice of change of membership of a committee . . . . [6.830]
17.8 Vacancies: creditor members of creditors' or liquidation committee . . . . [6.831]
17.9 Vacancies: contributory members of liquidation committee . . . . [6.832]
17.10 Resignation . . . . [6.833]
17.11 Termination of membership . . . . [6.834]
17.12 Removal . . . . [6.835]
17.13 Cessation of liquidation committee in a winding up when creditors are paid in full . . . . [6.836]

CHAPTER 4
MEETINGS OF COMMITTEE

17.14 Meetings of committee . . . . [6.837]
17.15 The chair at meetings . . . . [6.838]
17.16 Quorum . . . . [6.839]
17.17 Committee-members' representatives . . . . [6.840]
17.18 Voting rights and resolutions . . . . [6.841]
17.19 Resolutions by correspondence . . . . [6.842]
17.20 Remote attendance at meetings of committee . . . . [6.843]
17.21 Procedure for requests that a place for a meeting should be specified . . . . [6.844]

CHAPTER 5
SUPPLY OF INFORMATION BY THE OFFICE-HOLDER TO THE COMMITTEE

17.22 Notice requiring office-holder to attend the creditors' committee (administration and administrative receivership) (paragraph 57(3)(a) of Schedule B1 and

section 49(2)) . . . . . [6.845]
17.23 Office-holder's obligation to supply information to the committee (winding up and bankruptcy) . . . . . [6.846]

CHAPTER 6
MISCELLANEOUS

17.24 Expenses of members etc . . . . . [6.847]
17.25 Dealings by committee members and others . . . . . [6.848]
17.26 Dealings by committee members and others: administration and administrative receivership . . . . . [6.849]
17.27 Formal defects . . . . . [6.850]
17.28 Special rule for winding up by the court and bankruptcy: functions vested in the Secretary of State . . . . . [6.851]

CHAPTER 7
WINDING UP BY THE COURT FOLLOWING AN ADMINISTRATION

17.29 Continuation of creditors' committee. . . . . . [6.852]

PART 18
REPORTING AND REMUNERATION OF OFFICE-HOLDERS
CHAPTER 1
INTRODUCTORY

18.1 Scope of Part 18 and interpretation . . . . . [6.853]

CHAPTER 2
PROGRESS REPORTS

18.2 Reporting by the office-holder . . . . . [6.854]
18.3 Contents of progress reports in administration, winding up and bankruptcy . . . . . [6.855]
18.4 Information about remuneration . . . . . [6.856]
18.5 Information about pre-administration costs . . . . . [6.857]
18.6 Progress reports in administration: timing . . . . . [6.858]
18.7 Progress reports in voluntary winding up: timing . . . . . [6.859]
18.8 Progress reports in winding up by the court and bankruptcy: timing . . . . . [6.860]
18.9 Creditors' and members' requests for further information in administration, winding up and bankruptcy . . . . . [6.861]
18.10 Administration, creditors' voluntary liquidation and compulsory winding up: reporting distribution of property to creditors under rule 14.13 . . . . . [6.862]
18.11 Voluntary winding up: reporting arrangement under section 110 . . . . . [6.863]
18.12 Members' voluntary winding up: reporting distribution to members other than under section 110 . . . . . [6.864]
18.13 Bankruptcy proceedings: reporting distribution of property to creditors under section 326 . . [6.865]

CHAPTER 3
FINAL ACCOUNTS IN WINDING UP AND FINAL REPORTS IN BANKRUPTCY

18.14 Contents of final account (winding up) and final report (bankruptcy) . . . . . [6.866]

CHAPTER 4
REMUNERATION AND EXPENSES IN ADMINISTRATION, WINDING UP AND BANKRUPTCY

18.15 Application of Chapter . . . . . [6.867]
18.16 Remuneration: principles . . . . . [6.868]
18.17 Remuneration of joint office-holders . . . . . [6.869]
18.18 Remuneration: procedure for initial determination in an administration . . . . . [6.870]
18.19 Remuneration: procedure for initial determination in a members' voluntary winding up . . . [6.871]
18.20 Remuneration: procedure for initial determination in a creditors' voluntary winding up or a winding up by the court . . . . . [6.872]
18.21 Remuneration: procedure for initial determination in a bankruptcy . . . . . [6.873]
18.22 Application of scale fees where creditors fail to fix the basis of the office-holder's remuneration . . . . . [6.874]
18.23 Remuneration: application to the court to fix the basis . . . . . [6.875]
18.24 Remuneration: administrator, liquidator or trustee seeking increase etc . . . . . [6.876]
18.25 Application for an increase etc in remuneration: the general rule . . . . . [6.877]
18.26 First exception: administrator has made a statement under paragraph 52(1)(b) of Schedule B1 . . . . . [6.878]
18.27 Second exception: administrator who had applied for increase etc under rule 18.24 becomes liquidator . . . . . [6.879]
18.28 Remuneration: recourse by administrator, liquidator or trustee to the court . . . . . [6.880]
18.29 Remuneration: review at request of administrator, liquidator or trustee . . . . . [6.881]
18.30 Remuneration: exceeding the fee estimate . . . . . [6.882]
18.31 Remuneration: new administrator, liquidator or trustee . . . . . [6.883]

18.32 Remuneration: apportionment of set fees . . . . [6.884]
18.33 Remuneration: variation of the application of rules 18.29, 18.30 and 18.32 . . . . [6.885]
18.34 Remuneration and expenses: application to court by a creditor or member on grounds that remuneration or expenses are excessive . . . . [6.886]
18.35 Remuneration and expenses: application to court by a bankrupt on grounds that remuneration or expenses are excessive . . . . [6.887]
18.36 Applications under rules 18.34 and 18.35 where the court has given permission for the application . . . . [6.888]
18.37 Applications under rule 18.34 where the court's permission is not required for the application . . . . [6.889]
18.38 Remuneration of a liquidator or trustee who realises assets on behalf of a secured creditor . . [6.890]

PART 19
DISCLAIMER IN WINDING UP AND BANKRUPTCY

19.1 Application of this Part . . . . [6.891]
19.2 Notice of disclaimer (sections 178 and 315) . . . . [6.892]
19.3 Notice of disclaimer to interested persons (sections 178 and 315) . . . . [6.893]
19.4 Notice of disclaimer of leasehold property (sections 179 and 317) . . . . [6.894]
19.5 Notice of disclaimer in respect of a dwelling house (bankruptcy) (section 318) . . . . [6.895]
19.6 Additional notices of disclaimer . . . . [6.896]
19.7 Records . . . . [6.897]
19.8 Application for permission to disclaim in bankruptcy (section 315(4)) . . . . [6.898]
19.9 Application by interested party for decision on disclaimer (sections 178(5) and 316) . . . . [6.899]
19.10 Disclaimer presumed valid and effective . . . . [6.900]
19.11 Application for exercise of court's powers under section 181 (winding up) or section 320 (bankruptcy) . . . . [6.901]

PART 20
DEBTORS AND THEIR FAMILIES AT RISK OF VIOLENCE: ORDERS NOT TO DISCLOSE CURRENT ADDRESS

20.1 Application of this Part and interpretation . . . . [6.902]
20.2 Proposed IVA (order for non-disclosure of current address) . . . . [6.903]
20.3 IVA (order for non-disclosure of current address) . . . . [6.904]
20.4 Debt relief application (order for non-disclosure of current address) . . . . [6.905]
20.5 Bankruptcy application (order for non-disclosure of current address) . . . . [6.906]
20.6 Bankruptcy and debt relief proceedings (order for non-disclosure of current address) . . . . [6.907]
20.7 Additional provisions in respect of orders under rule 20.6(4) . . . . [6.908]

PART 21
THE EU REGULATION

21.1 Interpretation for this Part . . . . [6.909]
21.1A Standard contents of applications to court under the EU Regulation . . . . [6.910]
21.2 Conversion into winding up proceedings or bankruptcy: application . . . . [6.911]
21.3 Conversion into winding up proceedings or bankruptcy: court order . . . . [6.912]
21.4 Confirmation of creditors' voluntary winding up: application . . . . [6.913]
21.5 Confirmation of creditors' voluntary winding up: court order . . . . [6.914]
21.6 Confirmation of creditors' voluntary winding up: notice to member State liquidator . . . . [6.915]
21.7 Proceedings in another member State: duty to give notice . . . . [6.916]
21.8 Member State liquidator: rules on creditors' participation in proceedings . . . . [6.917]
21.9 Main proceedings in England and Wales: undertaking by office-holder in respect of assets in another member State (Article 36 of the EU Regulation) . . . . [6.918]
21.10 Main proceedings in another member State: approval of undertaking offered by the member State liquidator to local creditors in the UK . . . . [6.919]
21.11 Powers of an office-holder or member State liquidator in proceedings concerning members of a group of companies (Article 60 of the EU Regulation) . . . . [6.920]
21.12 Group coordination proceedings (Section 2 of Chapter 5 of the EU Regulation) . . . . [6.921]
21.13 Group coordination order (Article 68 EU Regulation) [. . . . [6.922]
21.14 Delivery of group coordination order to registrar of companies . . . . [6.923]
21.15 Office-holder's report . . . . [6.924]
21.16 Publication of opening of proceedings by a member State liquidator . . . . [6.925]
21.17 Notice by office-holder that insolvency proceedings in another member State are closed etc . . . . [6.926]

PART 22
PERMISSION TO ACT AS DIRECTOR ETC OF COMPANY WITH A PROHIBITED NAME (SECTION 216)

22.1 Preliminary . . . . [6.927]
22.2 Application for permission under section 216(3) . . . . [6.928]

22.3 Power of court to call for liquidator's report . . . . . . [6.929]
22.4 First excepted case . . . . . . [6.930]
22.5 Statement as to the effect of the notice under rule 22.4(2) . . . . . . [6.931]
22.6 Second excepted case . . . . . . [6.932]
22.7 Third excepted case . . . . . . [6.933]

SCHEDULES

Schedule 1—Revocations . . . . . . [6.934]
Schedule 2—Transitional and savings provisions . . . . . . [6.935]
Schedule 3—Punishment of offences under these Rules. . . . . . . [6.936]
Schedule 4—Service of documents . . . . . . [6.937]
Schedule 5—Calculation of time periods . . . . . . [6.938]
Schedule 6—Insolvency jurisdiction of county court hearing centres . . . . . . [6.939]
Schedule 7—Information to be provided in the bankruptcy application
Part I. . . . . . . [6.940]
Part II . . . . . . [6.941]
Schedule 8—Additional information to be provided in the bankruptcy application . . . . . . [6.942]
Schedule 9—Information to be given to creditors . . . . . . [6.943]
Schedule 10—Destination of appeals from decisions of District Judges in corporate insolvency matters . . . . . . [6.944]
Schedule 11—Determination of insolvency office-holder's remuneration . . . . . . [6.945]

NOTES

Made: 18 October 2016.
Authority: Insolvency Act 1986, ss 411, 412.
Commencement: 6 April 2017.

INTRODUCTORY RULES

[6.2]

1 Citation and commencement

These Rules may be cited as the Insolvency (England and Wales) Rules 2016 and come into force on 6th April 2017.

NOTES

Commencement: 6 April 2017.
This rule derived from the Insolvency Rules 1986, SI 1986/1925, r 0.1.

[6.3]

2 Revocations

The Rules listed in Schedule 1 are revoked.

NOTES

Commencement: 6 April 2017.

[6.4]

3 Extent and application

(1) These Rules extend to England and Wales only.

(2) These Rules as they relate to company voluntary arrangements under Part 1 of the Act, administration under Part 2 of the Act and winding up under Parts 4 and 5 of the Act apply in relation to companies which the courts in England and Wales have jurisdiction to wind up.

(3) These Rules do not apply to receivers appointed under section 51 (Scottish receivership).

NOTES

Commencement: 6 April 2017.
This rule derived from the Insolvency Rules 1986, SI 1986/1925, r 0.3.

[6.5]

4 Transitional and savings provisions

The transitional and savings provisions set out in Schedule 2 have effect.

NOTES

Commencement: 6 April 2017.
This rule derived from the Insolvency Rules 1986, SI 1986/1925, r 13.14.

[6.6]

5 Power of the Secretary of State to regulate certain matters

(1) Under paragraph 27 of Schedule 8 and paragraph 30 of Schedule 9 to the Act, the Secretary of State may, subject to the Act and the Rules made under it, make regulations with respect to any matter provided for in the Rules relating to the carrying out of the functions of—

(a) a liquidator, provisional liquidator, administrator or administrative receiver of a company;
(b) an interim receiver appointed under section 286; and
(c) a trustee of a bankrupt's estate.

(2) The regulations that may be made may include, without prejudice to the generality of paragraph (1), provision with respect to the following matters arising in companies winding up and individual bankruptcy—

(a) the preparation and keeping by liquidators, trustees, provisional liquidators, interim receivers and the official receiver, of books, accounts and other records, and their production to such persons as may be authorised or required to inspect them;
(b) the auditing of liquidators' and trustees' accounts;
(c) the manner in which liquidators and trustees are to act in relation to the insolvent company's or bankrupt's books, papers and other records, and the manner of their disposal by the responsible office-holder or others;
(d) the supply of copies of documents relating to the insolvency and the affairs of the insolvent company or individual (on payment, in such cases as may be specified by the regulations, of the specified fee)—
 (i) by the liquidator in company insolvency to creditors and members of the company, contributories in its winding up and the liquidation committee; and
 (ii) by the trustee in bankruptcy to creditors and the creditors' committee;
(e) the manner in which insolvent estates are to be distributed by liquidators and trustees, including provision with respect to unclaimed funds and dividends;
(f) the manner in which moneys coming into the hands of a liquidator or trustee in the course of the administration of the proceedings are to be handled and invested, and the payment of interest on sums which have been paid into the Insolvency Services Account under regulations made by virtue of this sub-paragraph;
(g) the amount (or the manner of determining the amount) to be paid to the official receiver as remuneration when acting as provisional liquidator, liquidator, interim receiver or trustee.

(3) Regulations made under this rule may—

(a) confer a discretion on the court;
(b) make non-compliance with any of the regulations a criminal offence;
(c) make different provision for different cases, including different provision for different areas; and
(d) contain such incidental, supplemental and transitional provisions as may appear to the Secretary of State necessary or expedient.

NOTES

Commencement: 6 April 2017.
This rule derived from the Insolvency Rules 1986, SI 1986/1925, r 12.1.

[6.7]

6 Punishment of offences

Schedule 3 sets out the punishments for certain contraventions of these Rules.

NOTES

Commencement: 6 April 2017.
This rule derived from the Insolvency Rules 1986, SI 1986/1925, r 12.21, Sch 5.

[6.8]

7 Review

(1) The Secretary of State must from time to time—

(a) carry out a review of these Rules;
(b) set out the conclusions of the review in a report; and
(c) publish the report.

(2) The report must in particular—

(a) set out the objectives intended to be achieved by the regulatory system established by these Rules;
(b) assess the extent to which those objectives are achieved; and
(c) assess whether those objectives remain appropriate and, if so, the extent to which they could be achieved with a system that imposes less regulation.

(3) The first report under this rule must be published before the end of the period of five years beginning with the day on which these Rules come into force.

(4) Reports under this rule are afterwards to be published at intervals not exceeding five years.

NOTES

Commencement: 6 April 2017.

PART 1
SCOPE, INTERPRETATION, TIME AND RULES ABOUT DOCUMENTS

CHAPTER 1 SCOPE OF THESE RULES

[6.9]
1.1 Scope

(1) These Rules are made to give effect to Parts 1 to 11 of the Insolvency Act 1986 and to the [EU Regulation].

(2) Consequently references to insolvency proceedings and requirements relating to such proceedings are, unless the context requires otherwise, limited to proceedings in respect of Parts 1 to 11 of the Act and the [EU Regulation] (whether or not court proceedings).

NOTES

Commencement: 6 April 2017.

This rule derived from the Insolvency Rules 1986, SI 1986/1925, r 13.7.

Paras (1), (2): words in square brackets substituted by the Insolvency (England and Wales) and Insolvency (Scotland) (Miscellaneous and Consequential Amendments) Rules 2017, SI 2017/1115, rr 22, 23(1).

CHAPTER 2 INTERPRETATION

[Note: the terms which are defined in rule 1.2 include some terms defined by the Act for limited purposes which are applied generally by these Rules. Such terms have the meaning given by the Act for those limited purposes.]

[6.10]
1.2 Defined terms

(1) In these Rules, unless otherwise stated, a reference to a Part or a Schedule is to a Part of, or Schedule to, these Rules.

(2) In these Rules—

"the Act" means the Insolvency Act 1986, and—

(a) a reference to a numbered section without mention of another Act is to that section of the Act; and

(b) a reference to Schedule A1, B1, 4ZA, 4ZB or 4A is to that Schedule to the Act;

"appointed person" means a person as described in paragraph (3) who is appointed by an office-holder (other than the official receiver);

"Article 1.2 undertaking" means one of the following within the meaning of Article 1.2 of [Regulation (EU) 2015/848 of the European Parliament and of the Council ("the EU Regulations")]—

(a) an insurance undertaking;

(b) a credit institution;

(c) an investment undertaking which provides services involving the holding of funds or securities for third parties;

(d) a collective investment undertaking;

[Note: "associate" is defined by section 435];

["attendance" and "attend" a person attends, or is in attendance at, a meeting who is present or attends remotely in accordance with section 246A or rule 15.6, or who participates in a virtual meeting, whether that person attends the meeting or virtual meeting in person, by proxy, or by corporate representative (in accordance with section 434B or section 323 of the Companies Act, as applicable);]

"authenticate" means to authenticate in accordance with rule 1.5;

"authorised deposit-taker" means a person with permission under Part 4A of the Financial Services and Markets Act 2000 to accept deposits; this definition must be read with—

(a) section 22 of that Act and any relevant order under that section; and

(b) Schedule 2 to that Act;

[Note: "bankrupt's estate" is defined in section 283];

"bankruptcy application" means the bankruptcy application submitted by the debtor to the adjudicator requesting the making of a bankruptcy order against the debtor;

"bankruptcy file" means the file opened by the adjudicator in accordance with rule 10.47;

"bankruptcy restrictions register" means the register referred to in rule 11.13(2) of matters relating to bankruptcy restrictions orders, interim bankruptcy restrictions orders and bankruptcy restrictions undertakings;

"business day" means, for the purposes of these Rules as they relate to Parts 7A to 10 of the Act (insolvency of individuals; bankruptcy), any day other than a Saturday, a Sunday, Christmas Day, Good Friday or a day which is a bank holiday in England and Wales [Note: for the purposes of these Rules as they relate to Parts 1 to 7 of the Act (company insolvency; company winding up) section 251 defines "business day" as including additionally a day which is a bank holiday in Scotland];

"centre of main interests" has the same meaning as in the [EU Regulation];

"certificate of service" means a certificate of service which complies with the requirements in Schedule 4;

"Companies Act" means the Companies Act 2006;

[Note: the term "connected" used of a person in relation to a company is defined in section 249 of the Act];

"consumer" means an individual acting for purposes that are wholly or mainly outside that individual's trade, business, craft or profession;

[Note: "contributory" is defined by section 79];

"convener" means an office-holder or other person who seeks a decision in accordance with Part 15 of these Rules;

[Note: "the court" is defined by section 251 for the purposes of these Rules as they relate to Parts 1 to 7 of the Act (company insolvency; company winding up) and by section 385(1) for the purposes of these Rules as they relate to Parts 7A to 10 of the Act (insolvency of individuals; bankruptcy);

"CPR" means the Civil Procedure Rules 1998;

"credit reference agency" means a person authorised or permitted by the Financial Conduct Authority to carry on the regulated activity of providing credit references;

"CVA" means a voluntary arrangement in relation to a company under Part 1 of the Act;

"debt" is defined in rule 14.1(3) for the purposes of administration and winding up and "small debt" is also defined in rule 14.1(3) for administration, winding up and bankruptcy [Note: debt is defined in section 385(1) for the purposes of these Rules as they relate to Parts 7A to 10 of the Act (insolvency of individuals; bankruptcy)];

"debt relief restrictions register" means the register referred to in rule 11.13(2) of matters relating to debt relief restrictions orders and debt relief restrictions undertakings;

"decision date" and "decision procedure" are to be interpreted in accordance with rule 15.2 and Part 15;

"decision procedure" means a decision procedure prescribed by rule 15.3;

[Note: "deemed consent procedure" is defined in section 246ZF for corporate insolvency and 379ZB for individual insolvency; rule 15.7 makes further provision about deemed consent];

"deliver" and "delivery" are to be interpreted in accordance with Chapter 9 of Part 1;

"deliver to the creditors" and similar expressions in these Rules and the Act are to be interpreted in accordance with rule 1.37;

[Note: "distress" is defined in section 436 as including the procedure in Schedule 12 to the Tribunals, Courts and Enforcement Act 2007 (c 15), and references to levying distress, seizing goods and related expressions are to be construed accordingly];

"document" includes a written notice or statement or anything else in writing capable of being delivered to a recipient;

[[Note: EU Regulation is defined for the purposes of these Rules by section 436 of the Act as Regulation (EU) No 2015/848 of the European Parliament and of the Council]].

"enforcement agent" means a person authorised by section 63(2) of the Tribunals, Courts and Enforcement Act 2007 to act as an enforcement agent;

"enforcement officer" means an individual who is authorised to act as an enforcement officer under the Courts Act 2003;

"fees estimate" means a written estimate that specifies—

- (a) details of the work the insolvency practitioner ("the IP") and the IP's staff propose to undertake;
- (b) the hourly rate or rates the IP and the IP's staff propose to charge for each part of that work;
- (c) the time the IP anticipates each part of that work will take;
- (d) whether the IP anticipates it will be necessary to seek approval or further approval under Chapter 4 of Part 18; and
- (e) the reasons it will be necessary to seek such approval under these Rules;

"file with the court" and similar expressions in these Rules means deliver to the court for filing and such references are to be read as including "submit" and "submission" to the court in the Act (except in sections 236 and 366);

"the Gazette", which has the meaning given in section 251 for the purposes of these Rules as they relate to Parts 1 to 7 of the Act (company insolvency; company winding up), has that meaning for the purposes of these Rules as they relate to Parts 7A to 10 of the Act;

"Gazette notice" means a notice which is, has been or is to be gazetted;

"to gazette" means to advertise once in the Gazette;

"general regulations" means regulations made by the Secretary of State under introductory rule 5;

"hearing centre" means a hearing centre of the County Court;

[Note: "hire-purchase agreement" is defined by section 436(1) as having the same meaning as in the Consumer Credit Act 1974 for the purposes of the Act and by paragraph 1 of Schedule A1 (company voluntary arrangement) for the purposes of that Schedule and by paragraph 111(1) of Schedule B1 (administration) for the purposes of that Schedule];

"identification details" and similar references to information identifying persons, proceedings, etc are to be interpreted in accordance with rule 1.6;

"individual insolvency register" means the register referred to in rule 11.13(1) of matters relating to bankruptcies, debt relief orders and IVAs;

"individual register" has the meaning given by rule 217(1) of the Land Registration Rules 2003;

"insolvent estate" means—

- (a) in relation to a company insolvency, the company's assets;
- (b) in relation to a bankruptcy, a petition or an application for bankruptcy, the bankrupt's estate (as defined in section 283);
- (c) or otherwise the debtor's property;

"IP number" means the number assigned to an office-holder as an insolvency practitioner by the Secretary of State;

"IVA" means a voluntary arrangement in relation to an individual under Part 8 of the Act;

"judge" includes [an Insolvency and Companies Court Judge] unless the context otherwise requires;

"London Insolvency District" has the meaning given by section 374 of the Act and the London Insolvency District (County Court at Central London) Order 2014;

["main proceedings" means proceedings opened in accordance with Article 3(1) of the EU Regulation and falling within the definition of insolvency proceedings in Article 2(4) of that Regulation and which—

(a) in relation to England and Wales, are set out in Annex A to that Regulation under the heading "United Kingdom"; and

(b) in relation to another member State, are set out under the heading relating to that member State;]

"meeting" in relation to a person's creditors or contributories means either a "physical meeting" or a "virtual meeting" as defined in rule 15.2, unless the contrary intention is given;

"member State liquidator" means [a person falling within the definition of "insolvency practitioner" in Article 2(5)] of the [EU Regulation] appointed in proceedings to which the] EU Regulation] applies in a member State other than the United Kingdom;

"nominated person" means a person who has been required under section 47 or 131 to make out and submit a statement as to the affairs of a company in administrative receivership or being wound up by the court;

[Note: "nominee" is defined in section 1(2) in relation to company voluntary arrangements and section 253(2) in relation to individual voluntary arrangements];

["non-EU proceedings"] means insolvency proceedings which are not main, secondary or territorial proceedings;

"office-holder" means a person who under the Act or these Rules holds an office in relation to insolvency proceedings and includes a nominee;

"permission" of the court is to be read as including "leave of the court" in the Act and in the Company Directors' Disqualification Act 1986;

"petitioner" or "petitioning creditor" includes a person who has been substituted as such or has been given carriage of the petition;

"physical meeting" means a meeting as described in section 246ZE(9) or 379ZA(9);

"Practice Direction" means a direction as to the practice and procedure of a court within the scope of the CPR;

"prescribed order of priority" means the order of priority of payments of expenses set out in—

(a) Chapter 10 of Part 3 for administration proceedings;

(b) Chapter 6 of Part 6 for creditors' voluntary winding up proceedings;

(c) Chapter 14 of Part 7 for winding up by the court proceedings; and

(d) Chapter 18 of Part 10 for bankruptcy proceedings;

"prescribed part" has the same meaning as in section 176A(2)(a) and the Insolvency Act 1986 (Prescribed Part) Order 2003;

"progress report" means a report which complies with Chapter 2 of Part 18;

[Note: "property" is defined by section 436(1) of the Act];

"prove" and "proof" have the following meaning—

(a) a creditor who claims for a debt in writing is referred to as proving that debt;

(b) the document by which the creditor makes the claim is referred to as that creditor's proof; and

(c) for the purpose of voting, or objecting to a deemed consent, in an administration, an administrative receivership, a creditors' voluntary winding up, a CVA or an IVA, the requirements for a proof are satisfied by the convener or chair having been notified by the creditor in writing of a debt;

"proxy" and "blank proxy" are to be interpreted in accordance with Part 16;

"qualified to act as an insolvency practitioner" in relation to a company, debtor or bankrupt has the meaning given by section 390 of the Act;

[Note: "records" are defined in section 436(1) of the Act]

"registered land" has the meaning given by section 132(1) of the Land Registration Act 2002;

"registrar" means [an Insolvency and Companies Court Judge] and unless the context requires otherwise includes a District Judge—

(a) in a District Registry of the High Court; and

(b) in a hearing centre with relevant insolvency jurisdiction;

"residential address" means the current residential address of an individual or, if that is not known, the last known residential address;

["secondary proceedings" means proceedings opened in accordance with Article 3(2) and (3) of the EU Regulation and falling within the definition of insolvency proceedings in Article 2(4) of that Regulation and which—

(a) in relation to England and Wales, are set out are set out in Annex A to that Regulation under the heading "United Kingdom";

(b) and in relation to another member State are set out under the heading relating to that member State;]

"serve" and "service" are to be interpreted in respect of a particular document by reference to Schedule 4;

"solicitor" means a solicitor of the Senior Courts and, in relation to England and Wales, includes any other person who, for the purpose of the Legal Services Act 2007 is an authorised person in relation to an activity which constitutes the conduct of litigation (within the meaning of that Act);

"standard contents" means—

(a) for a Gazette notice, the standard contents set out in Chapter 4 of this Part;

(b) for a notice to be advertised other than in the Gazette, the standard contents set out in Chapter 5 of Part 1;

(c) for a document to be delivered to the registrar of companies, the standard contents set out in Chapter 6 of Part 1;

(d) for notices to be delivered to other persons, the standard contents set out in Chapter 7 of Part 1;

(e) for applications to the court the standard contents set out in Chapter 8 of Part 1;

"standard fee for copies" means 15 pence per A4 or A5 page or 30 pence per A3 page;

"statement of proposals" means a statement made by an administrator under paragraph 49 of Schedule B1 setting out proposals for achieving the purpose of an administration;

"statement of truth" means a statement of truth made in accordance with Part 22 of the CPR;

"temporary administrator" means a temporary administrator referred to in [Article 52 of the EU Regulation];

["territorial proceedings" means proceedings opened in accordance with Article 3(2) and (4) of the EU Regulation and falling within the definition of insolvency proceedings in Article 2(4) of that Regulation and which—

(a) in relation to England and Wales, are set out in Annex A to the EU Regulation under the heading "United Kingdom"; and

(b) in relation to another member State, are set out under the heading relating to that member State;]

"trustee" has the same meaning throughout these Rules as they relate to the insolvency of individuals as it has for bankruptcy in section 385(1);

"venue" in relation to any proceedings, attendance before the court, decision procedure or meeting means the time, date and place or platform for the proceedings, attendance, decision procedure or meeting;

"virtual meeting" has the meaning given by rule 15.2(2);

"winding up by the court" means a winding up under section 122(1), 124A or 221;

"witness statement" means a witness statement verified by a statement of truth made in accordance with Part 32 of the CPR;

[Note: "writing": section 436B(1) of the Act provides that a reference to a thing in writing includes that thing in electronic form; subsection (2) excludes certain documents from the application of subsection (1); and

"written resolution" in respect of a private company refers to a written resolution passed in accordance with Chapter 2 of Part 13 of the Companies Act].

(3) An appointed person in relation to a company, debtor or bankrupt must be—

(a) qualified to act as an insolvency practitioner in relation to that company, debtor or bankrupt; or

(b) a person experienced in insolvency matters who is—

(i) a member or employee of the office-holder's firm, or

(ii) an employee of the office-holder.

(4) A fee or remuneration is charged when the work to which it relates is done.

NOTES

Commencement: 6 April 2017.

This rule derived from the Insolvency Rules 1986, SI 1986/1925, r 0.2, Pt 13.

Para (2): definition ""attendance" and "attend"" substituted by the Insolvency (England and Wales) (Amendment) Rules 2017, SI 2017/366, rr 3, 4; words in square brackets in definitions "centre of main interests" and "temporary administrator" substituted by the Insolvency (England and Wales) and Insolvency (Scotland) (Miscellaneous and Consequential Amendments) Rules 2017, SI 2017/1115, rr 22, 23(2), 24.

Words in square brackets in definitions "judge" and "registrar" substituted by the Alteration of Judicial Titles (Registrar in Bankruptcy of the High Court) Order 2018, SI 2018/130, art 3, Schedule, para 14(a)(i).

Para (2) is also amended by the Insolvency Amendment (EU 2015/848) Regulations 2017, SI 2017/702, regs 2, 3, Schedule, Pt 2, paras 32, 33, as from 26 June 2017, except in relation to proceedings opened before that date, as follows:

In the definition of "Article 1.2 undertaking" the words in square brackets were substituted for the original words "Council Regulation (EC) No 1346/2000 ("the EC Regulations")".

The note following the definition of "document" was substituted for original note "[Note: EC Regulation is defined for the purposes of these Rules by section 436 of the Act as Council Regulation (EC) No1346/2000]".

Definitions "main proceedings", "secondary proceedings" and "territorial proceedings" substituted and originally read as follows:

""main proceedings" means proceedings opened in accordance with Article 3(1) of the EC Regulation and falling within the definition of insolvency proceedings in Article 2(a) of the EC Regulation and which—

(a) in relation to England and Wales, are set out in Annex A to the EC Regulation under the heading "United Kingdom"; and

(b) in relation to another member State, are set out in Annex A to the EC Regulation under the heading relating to that member State;

"secondary proceedings" means proceedings opened in accordance with Articles 3(2) and 3(3) of the EC Regulation and falling within the definition of winding-up proceedings in Article 2(c) of the EC Regulation and which—

(a) in relation to England and Wales, are set out in Annex B to the EC Regulation under the heading "United Kingdom"; and

(b) in relation to another member State, are set out in Annex B to the EC Regulation under the heading relating to that member State;

"territorial proceedings" means proceedings opened in accordance with Articles 3(2) and 3(4) of the EC Regulation which fall within the definition of insolvency proceedings in Article 2(a) of that Regulation and—

(a) in relation to England and Wales, are set out in Annex A to the EC Regulation under the heading "United Kingdom"; and

(b) in relation to another member State, are set out in Annex A to the EC Regulation under the heading relating to that member State;".

In the definition "member State liquidator" the words in first pair of square brackets were substituted for the original words "a person falling within the definition of liquidator in Article 2(b)", and the words in second and third pairs of square brackets were substituted for the original words "EC Regulation".

In the definition "non-EU proceedings" words in square brackets substituted for the original words "non-EC proceedings".

[6.11]

1.3 Calculation of time periods

The rules set out in Schedule 5 apply to the calculation of the beginning and end of time periods under these Rules.

NOTES

Commencement: 6 April 2017.

This rule derived from the Insolvency Rules 1986, SI 1986/1925, r 12A.55.

CHAPTER 3 FORM AND CONTENT OF DOCUMENTS

[6.12]

1.4 Requirement for writing and form of documents

(1) A notice or statement must be in writing unless the Act or these Rules provide otherwise.

(2) A document in electronic form must be capable of being—

(a) read by the recipient in electronic form; and

(b) reproduced by the recipient in hard-copy form.

NOTES

Commencement: 6 April 2017.

This rule derived from the Insolvency Rules 1986, SI 1986/1925, r 12A.7.

[6.13]

1.5 Authentication

(1) A document in electronic form is sufficiently authenticated—

(a) if the identity of the sender is confirmed in a manner specified by the recipient; or

(b) where the recipient has not so specified, if the communication contains or is accompanied by a statement of the identity of the sender and the recipient has no reason to doubt the truth of that statement.

(2) A document in hard-copy form is sufficiently authenticated if it is signed.

(3) If a document is authenticated by the signature of an individual on behalf of—

(a) a body of persons, the document must also state the position of that individual in relation to the body;

(b) a body corporate of which the individual is the sole member, the document must also state that fact.

NOTES

Commencement: 6 April 2017.

This rule derived from the Insolvency Rules 1986, SI 1986/1925, r 12A.9.

[6.14]

1.6 Information required to identify persons and proceedings etc

(1) Where the Act or these Rules require a document to identify, or to contain identification details in respect of, a person or proceedings, or to provide contact details for an office-holder, the information set out in the table must be given.

(2) Where a requirement relates to a proposed office-holder, the information set out in the table in respect of an office-holder must be given with any necessary adaptations.

Bankrupt	(a) full name; and (b) residential address (subject to any order for limited disclosure made under Part 20).

Company where it is the subject of the proceedings	In the case of a registered company— (c) the registered name; (d) for a company incorporated in England and Wales under the Companies Act or a previous Companies Act, its registered number; (e) for a company incorporated outside the United Kingdom— (i) the country or territory in which it is incorporated, (ii) the number, if any, under which it is registered, and (iii) the number, if any, under which it is registered as an overseas company under Part 34 of the Companies Act. In the case of an unregistered company— (f) its name; and (g) the postal address of any principal place of business.
Company other than one which is the subject of the proceedings	In the case of a registered company— (h) the registered name; (i) for a company incorporated in any part of the United Kingdom under the Companies Act or a previous Companies Act, its registered number; (j) for a company incorporated outside the United Kingdom— (i) the country or territory in which it is incorporated, (ii) the number, if any, under which it is registered; and (k) the number, if any, under which it is registered as an overseas company under Part 34 of the Companies Act; (l) In the case of an unregistered company— (i) its name, and (ii) the postal address of any principal place of business.
Debtor	(m) full name; and (n) residential address (subject to any order for limited disclosure made under Part 20).
Office-holder	(o) the name of the office-holder; and (p) the nature of the appointment held by the office-holder.
Contact details for an office-holder	(q) a postal address for the office-holder; and (r) either an email address, or a telephone number, through which the office-holder may be contacted.
Proceedings	(s) for proceedings relating to a company, the information identifying the company; (t) for proceedings relating to an individual, the full name of the bankrupt or debtor; (u) the full name of the court or hearing centre in which the proceedings are, or are to be, conducted or where documents relating to the proceedings have been or will be filed; and, if applicable, (v) any number assigned to those proceedings by the court, the hearing centre or the adjudicator.

NOTES

Commencement: 6 April 2017.

[6.15]
1.7 Reasons for stating that proceedings are or will be main, secondary etc under the [EU Regulation]

Where these Rules require reasons to be given for a statement that proceedings are or will be main, secondary or territorial or [non-EU proceedings], the reasons must include—

(a) for a company—

(i) the centre of main interests,

(ii) the place of the registered office within the meaning of Article 3(1) of the [EU Regulation] and where appropriate an explanation why this is not the same as the centre of main interests, or

(iii) that there is no registered office if that be the case in [non-EU proceedings];

(b) for a debtor, the centre of main interests.

NOTES

Commencement: 6 April 2017.

Words in square brackets substituted by the Insolvency (England and Wales) and Insolvency (Scotland) (Miscellaneous and Consequential Amendments) Rules 2017, SI 2017/1115, rr 22, 23(3), (4), 30(1), (2).

[6.16]
1.8 Prescribed format of documents

(1) Where a rule sets out requirements as to the contents of a document any title required by the rule must appear at the beginning of the document.

(2) Any other contents required by the rule (or rules where more than one apply to a particular document) must be provided in the order listed in the rule (or rules) or in another order which the maker of the document considers would be convenient for the intended recipient.

NOTES

Commencement: 6 April 2017.

[6.17]
1.9 Variations from prescribed contents

(1) Where a rule sets out the required contents of a document, the document may depart from the required contents if—

(a) the circumstances require such a departure (including where the requirement is not applicable in the particular case); or

(b) the departure (whether or not intentional) is immaterial.

(2) However this rule does not apply to the required content of a statutory demand on a company set out in rule 7.3 and on an individual set out in rule 10.1.

NOTES

Commencement: 6 April 2017.

CHAPTER 4 STANDARD CONTENTS OF GAZETTE NOTICES AND THE GAZETTE AS EVIDENCE ETC

[Note: (1) the requirements in Chapter 4 must be read with rule 1.6 which sets out the information required to identify an office-holder, a company etc;

(2) this Chapter does not apply to the notice of a liquidator's appointment prescribed under section 109 by SI 1987/752.]

[6.18]
1.10 Contents of notices to be gazetted under the Act or Rules

(1) Where the Act or these Rules require or permit a notice to be gazetted, the notice must also contain the standard contents set out in this Chapter in addition to any content specifically required by the Act or any other provision of these Rules.

(2) Information which this Chapter requires to be included in a Gazette notice may be omitted if it is not reasonably practicable to obtain it.

NOTES

Commencement: 6 April 2017.

This rule derived from the Insolvency Rules 1986, SI 1986/1925, rr 12A.33, 12A.36.

[6.19]
1.11 Standard contents of all notices

(1) A notice must identify the proceedings, if it is relevant to the particular notice, identify the office-holder and state—

(a) the office-holder's contact details;

(b) the office-holder's IP number (except for the official receiver);

(c) the name of any person other than the office-holder who may be contacted about the proceedings; and

(d) the date of the office-holder's appointment.

(2) This rule does not apply to a notice under rule 22.4(3) (Permission to act as a director: first excepted case).

NOTES

Commencement: 6 April 2017.

This rule derived from the Insolvency Rules 1986, SI 1986/1925, rr 12A.33, 12A.36.

[6.20]

1.12 Gazette notices relating to a company

(1) A notice relating to a registered company must also state—

- (a) its registered office;
- (b) any principal trading address if this is different from its registered office;
- (c) any name under which it was registered in the period of 12 months before the date of the commencement of the proceedings which are the subject of the Gazette notice; and
- (d) any other name or style (not being a registered name)—
  - (i) under which the company carried on business, and
  - (ii) in which any debt owed to a creditor was incurred.

(2) A notice relating to an unregistered company must also identify the company and specify any name or style—

- (a) under which the company carried on business; and
- (b) in which any debt owed to a creditor was incurred.

NOTES

Commencement: 6 April 2017.

This rule derived from the Insolvency Rules 1986, SI 1986/1925, rr 12A.33, 12A.36.

[6.21]

1.13 Gazette notices relating to a bankruptcy

A notice relating to a bankruptcy must also identify the bankrupt and state—

- (a) any other address at which the bankrupt has resided in the period of 12 months before the making of the bankruptcy order;
- (b) any principal trading address if different from the bankrupt's residential address;
- (c) the bankrupt's date of birth;
- (d) the bankrupt's occupation;
- (e) any other name by which the bankrupt has been known; and
- (f) any name or style (other than the bankrupt's own name) under which—
  - (i) the bankrupt carried on business, and
  - (ii) any debt owed to a creditor was incurred.

NOTES

Commencement: 6 April 2017.

This rule derived from the Insolvency Rules 1986, SI 1986/1925, rr 12A.35, 12A.36.

[6.22]

1.14 The Gazette: evidence, variations and errors

(1) A copy of the Gazette containing a notice required or permitted by the Act or these Rules to be gazetted is evidence of any facts stated in the notice.

(2) Where the Act or these Rules require an order of the court or of the adjudicator to be gazetted, a copy of the Gazette containing the notice may be produced in any proceedings as conclusive evidence that the order was made on the date specified in the notice.

(3) Where an order of the court or of the adjudicator which is gazetted has been varied, or any matter has been erroneously or inaccurately gazetted, the person whose responsibility it was to gazette the order or other matter must as soon as is reasonably practicable cause the variation to be gazetted or a further entry to be made in the Gazette for the purpose of correcting the error or inaccuracy.

NOTES

Commencement: 6 April 2017.

This rule derived from the Insolvency Rules 1986, SI 1986/1925, r 12A.37.

CHAPTER 5 STANDARD CONTENTS OF NOTICES ADVERTISED OTHERWISE THAN IN THE GAZETTE

[Note: the requirements in Chapter 5 must be read with rule 1.6 which sets out the information required to identify an office-holder, a company etc]

[6.23]

1.15 Standard contents of notices advertised otherwise than in the Gazette

(1) Where the Act or these Rules provide that a notice may be advertised otherwise than in the Gazette the notice must contain the standard contents set out in this Chapter (in addition to any content specifically required by the Act or any other provision of these Rules).

(2) A notice must, if it is relevant to the particular notice, identify the office-holder and specify the office-holder's contact details.

(3) Information which this Chapter requires to be included in a notice may be omitted if it is not reasonably practicable to obtain it.

NOTES

Commencement: 6 April 2017.

This rule derived from the Insolvency Rules 1986, SI 1986/1925, rr 12A.38, 12A.41.

[6.24]

1.16 Non-Gazette notices relating to a company

A notice relating to a company must also identify the proceedings and state—

(a) the company's principal trading address;

(b) any name under which the company was registered in the 12 months before the date of the commencement of the proceedings which are the subject of the notice; and

(c) any name or style (not being a registered name) under which—

(i) the company carried on business, and

(ii) any debt owed to a creditor was incurred.

NOTES

Commencement: 6 April 2017.

This rule derived from the Insolvency Rules 1986, SI 1986/1925, rr 12A.39, 12A.41.

[6.25]

1.17 Non-Gazette notices relating to a bankruptcy

A notice relating to a bankruptcy must also identify the proceedings, identify the bankrupt and state—

(a) any other address at which the bankrupt has resided in the period of 12 months before the making of the bankruptcy order;

(b) any principal trading address if different from the bankrupt's residential address;

(c) the bankrupt's date of birth;

(d) the bankrupt's occupation;

(e) any other name by which the bankrupt has been known; and

(f) any name or style (other than the bankrupt's own name) under which—

(i) the bankrupt carried on business, and

(ii) any debt owed to a creditor was incurred.

NOTES

Commencement: 6 April 2017.

This rule derived from the Insolvency Rules 1986, SI 1986/1925, rr 12A.40, 12A.41.

[6.26]

1.18 Non-Gazette notices: other provisions

Information which this Chapter requires to be stated in a notice must be included in an advertisement of that notice in a way that is clear and comprehensible.

NOTES

Commencement: 6 April 2017.

This rule derived from the Insolvency Rules 1986, SI 1986/1925, r 12A.41.

CHAPTER 6 STANDARD CONTENTS OF DOCUMENTS TO BE DELIVERED TO THE REGISTRAR OF COMPANIES

[Note: the requirements in Chapter 6 must be read with rule 1.6 which sets out the information required to identify an office-holder, a company etc]

[6.27]

1.19 Standard contents of documents delivered to the registrar of companies

(1) Where the Act or these Rules require a document to be delivered to the registrar of companies the document must contain the standard contents set out in this Chapter (in addition to any content specifically required by the Act or any other provision of these Rules).

(2) A document of more than one type must satisfy the requirements which apply to each.

(3) However requirements as to the contents of a document which is to be delivered to another person at the same time as the registrar of companies may be satisfied by delivering to that other person a copy of the document delivered to the registrar.

NOTES

Commencement: 6 April 2017.

This rule derived from the Insolvency Rules 1986, SI 1986/1925, rr 12A.42, 12A.43.

[6.28]

1.20 Registrar of companies: covering notices

(1) This rule applies where the Act or these Rules require an office-holder to deliver any of the following documents to the registrar of companies—

(a) an account (including a final report) or a summary of receipts and payments;

(b) an administrative receiver's report under section 48(1);
(c) a court order;
(d) a declaration of solvency;
(e) a direction of the Secretary of State under section 203 or 205;
(f) a notice of disclaimer;
(g) a statement of administrator's proposals (including a statement of revised proposals);
(h) a statement of affairs;
(i) a statement of concurrence;
(j) a notice of an administrator's resignation under paragraph 87(2) of Schedule B1;
(k) a notice of a liquidator's death which the official receiver is required to deliver under rule [7.67(3)(b)];
(l) a notice that a liquidator has vacated office on loss of qualification to act which the official receiver is required to deliver under rule [7.68(4)(b)];
(m) any report including—
  (i) a final report,
  (ii) a progress report (including a final progress report),
  (iii) a report of a creditors' decision under paragraph 53(2) or 54(6) of Schedule B1, and
  (iv) a report of a decision approving a CVA under section 4(6) and [(6A)] or paragraph 30(3) and (4) of Schedule A1 to the Act;
(n) a copy of the notice that a CVA has been fully implemented or terminated that the supervisor is required to deliver under rule 2.44(3);
[(o) an undertaking given under Article 36 of the EU Regulation.]

(2) The office-holder must deliver to the registrar of companies with a document mentioned in paragraph (1) a notice containing the standard contents required by this Part.

(3) Such a notice may relate to more than one document where those documents relate to the same proceedings and are delivered together to the registrar of companies.

NOTES

Commencement: 6 April 2017.

Para (1): figures in square brackets in sub-paras (k), (l), (m) substituted by the Insolvency (England and Wales) (Amendment) Rules 2017, SI 2017/366, rr 3, 6; sub-para (o) added by the Insolvency Amendment (EU 2015/848) Regulations 2017, SI 2017/702, regs 2, 3, Schedule, Pt 2, paras 32, 34, as from 26 June 2017, except in relation to proceedings opened before that date.

[6.29]

1.21 Standard contents of all documents

(1) A document to be delivered to the registrar of companies must—
(a) identify the company;
(b) state—
  (i) the nature of the document,
  (ii) the section of the Act, the paragraph of Schedule A1 or B1 or the rule under which the document is delivered,
  (iii) the date of the document,
  (iv) the name and address of the person delivering the document, and
  (v) the capacity in which that person is acting in relation to the company; and
(c) be authenticated by the person delivering the document.

(2) Where the person delivering the document is the office-holder, the address may be omitted if it has previously been notified to the registrar of companies in the proceedings and is unchanged.

NOTES

Commencement: 6 April 2017.

This rule derived from the Insolvency Rules 1986, SI 1986/1925, r 12A.43.

[6.30]

1.22 Standard contents of documents relating to the office of office-holders

(1) A document relating to the office of the office-holder must also identify the office-holder and state—
(a) the date of the event of which notice is delivered or of the notice (as applicable);
(b) where the document relates to an appointment, the person, body or court making the appointment;
(c) where the document relates to the termination of an appointment, the reason for that termination; and
(d) the contact details for the office-holder.

(2) Where the person delivering the document is the office-holder, the address may be omitted if it has previously been notified to the registrar of companies in the proceedings and is unchanged.

NOTES

Commencement: 6 April 2017.

This rule derived from the Insolvency Rules 1986, SI 1986/1925, r 12A.44.

[6.31]

1.23 Standard contents of documents relating to other documents

A document relating to another document must also state—

(a) the nature of the other document;
(b) the date of the other document; and
(c) where the other document relates to a period of time, the period of time to which it relates.

NOTES

Commencement: 6 April 2017.
This rule derived from the Insolvency Rules 1986, SI 1986/1925, r 12A.45.

[6.32]
1.24 Standard contents of documents relating to court orders

A document relating to a court order must also specify—
(a) the nature of the order; and
(b) the date of the order.

NOTES

Commencement: 6 April 2017.
This rule derived from the Insolvency Rules 1986, SI 1986/1925, r 12A.46.

[6.33]
1.25 Standard contents of returns or reports of decisions

A return or report of a decision procedure, deemed consent procedure or meeting must also state—
(a) the purpose of the procedure or meeting;
(b) a description of the procedure or meeting used;
(c) in the case of a decision procedure or meeting, the venue;
(d) whether, in the case of a meeting, the required quorum was in place;
(e) the outcome (including any decisions made or resolutions passed); and
(f) the date of any decision made or resolution passed.

NOTES

Commencement: 6 April 2017.
This rule derived from the Insolvency Rules 1986, SI 1986/1925, r 12A.47.

[6.34]
1.26 Standard contents of returns or reports of matters considered by company members by correspondence

A return or report of a matter, consideration of which has been sought from the members of a company by correspondence, must also state—
(a) the purpose of the consideration; and
(b) the outcome of the consideration (including any resolutions passed or deemed to be passed).

NOTES

Commencement: 6 April 2017.
This rule derived from the Insolvency Rules 1986, SI 1986/1925, r 12A.47.

[6.35]
1.27 Standard contents of documents relating to other events

A document relating to any other event must also state—
(a) the nature of the event, including the section of the Act, the paragraph of Schedule A1 or B1 or the rule under which it took place; and
(b) the date on which the event occurred.

NOTES

Commencement: 6 April 2017.
This rule derived from the Insolvency Rules 1986, SI 1986/1925, r 12A.48.

CHAPTER 7 STANDARD CONTENTS OF NOTICES FOR DELIVERY TO OTHER PERSONS ETC

[Note: the requirements in Chapter 7 must be read with rule 1.6 which sets out the information required to identify an office-holder, a company etc]

[6.36]
1.28 Standard contents of notices to be delivered to persons other than the registrar of companies

(1) Where the Act or these Rules require a notice to be delivered to a person other than the registrar of companies in respect of proceedings under Parts 1 to 11 of the Act or the [EU Regulation], the notice must contain the standard contents set out in this Chapter (in addition to any content specifically required by the Act or another provision of these Rules).

(2) A notice of more than one type must satisfy the requirements which apply to each.

(3) However, the requirements in respect of a document which is to be delivered to another person at the same time as the registrar of companies may be satisfied by delivering to that other person a copy of the document delivered to the registrar.

NOTES

Commencement: 6 April 2017.

Para (1): words in square brackets substituted by the Insolvency (England and Wales) and Insolvency (Scotland) (Miscellaneous and Consequential Amendments) Rules 2017, SI 2017/1115, rr 22, 23(5).

[6.37]

1.29 Standard contents of all notices

A notice must—

(a) state the nature of the notice;
(b) identify the proceedings;
(c) in the case of proceedings relating to an individual, identify the bankrupt or debtor;
(d) state the section of the Act, the paragraph of Schedule A1 or B1 or the rule under which the notice is given; and
(e) in the case of a notice delivered by the office-holder, state the contact details for the office-holder.

NOTES

Commencement: 6 April 2017.

[6.38]

1.30 Standard contents of notices relating to the office of office-holders

A notice relating to the office of the office-holder must also identify the office-holder and state—

(a) the date of the event of which notice is delivered;
(b) where the notice relates to an appointment, the person, body or court making the appointment; and
(c) where the notice relates to the termination of an appointment, the reason for that termination.

NOTES

Commencement: 6 April 2017.

[6.39]

1.31 Standard contents of notices relating to documents

A notice relating to a document must also state—

(a) the nature of the document;
(b) the date of the document; and
(c) where the document relates to a period of time the period of time to which the document relates.

NOTES

Commencement: 6 April 2017.

[6.40]

1.32 Standard contents of notices relating to court proceedings or orders

A notice relating to court proceedings must also identify those proceedings and if the notice relates to a court order state—

(a) the nature of the order; and
(b) the date of the order.

NOTES

Commencement: 6 April 2017.

[6.41]

1.33 Standard contents of notices of the results of decisions

A notice of the result of a decision procedure, deemed consent procedure or meeting must also state—

(a) the purpose of the procedure or meeting;
(b) a description of the procedure or meeting used;
(c) in the case of a decision procedure or meeting, the venue;
(d) whether, in the case of a meeting, the required quorum was in place; and
(e) the outcome (including any decisions made or resolutions passed).

NOTES

Commencement: 6 April 2017.

[6.42]

1.34 Standard contents of returns or reports of matters considered by company members by correspondence

A return or report of a matter, consideration of which has been sought from the members of a company by correspondence, must also specify—

(a) the purpose of the consideration; and
(b) the outcome of the consideration (including any resolutions passed or deemed to be passed).

NOTES

Commencement: 6 April 2017.

CHAPTER 8 APPLICATIONS TO THE COURT

[Note: the requirements in Chapter 8 must be read with rule 1.6 which sets out the information required to identify an office-holder, a company etc]

[6.43]

1.35 Standard contents and authentication of applications to the court under Parts 1 to 11 of the Act

(1) This rule applies to applications to court under Parts 1 to 11 of the Act (other than an application for an administration order, a winding up petition or a bankruptcy petition).

(2) The application must state—

- (a) that the application is made under the Act or these Rules (as applicable);
- (b) the section of the Act or paragraph of a Schedule to the Act or the number of the rule under which it is made;
- (c) the names of the parties;
- (d) the name of the bankrupt, debtor or company which is the subject of the insolvency proceedings to which the application relates;
- (e) the court (and where applicable, the division or district registry of that court) or hearing centre in which the application is made;
- (f) where the court has previously allocated a number to the insolvency proceedings within which the application is made, that number;
- (g) the nature of the remedy or order applied for or the directions sought from the court;
- (h) the names and addresses of the persons on whom it is intended to serve the application or that no person is intended to be served;
- (i) where the Act or Rules require that notice of the application is to be delivered to specified persons, the names and addresses of all those persons (so far as known to the applicant); and
- (j) the applicant's address for service.

(3) The application must be authenticated by or on behalf of the applicant or the applicant's solicitor.

NOTES

Commencement: 6 April 2017.
This rule derived from the Insolvency Rules 1986, SI 1986/1925, r 7.3.

CHAPTER 9 DELIVERY OF DOCUMENTS AND OPTING OUT (SECTIONS 246C, 248A, 379C AND 383A)

[6.44]

1.36 Application of Chapter

[Note: the registrar's rules include provision for the electronic delivery of documents.]

(1) This Chapter applies where a document is required under the Act or these Rules to be delivered, filed, forwarded, furnished, given, sent, or submitted in respect of proceedings under Parts 1 to 11 of the Act or the [EU Regulation] unless the Act, a rule or an order of the court makes different provision including one requiring service of the document.

(2) However in respect of delivery of a document to the registrar of companies—

- (a) subject to sub-paragraph (b) only the following rules in this Chapter apply: rules 1.42 (postal delivery of documents), 1.43 (delivery by document exchange), 1.44 (personal delivery) and 1.52 (proof of delivery of documents);
- (b) the registrar's rules made under sections 1068 and 1117 of the Companies Act apply to determine the date when any document is received by the registrar of companies.

NOTES

Commencement: 6 April 2017.
Para (1): words in square brackets substituted by the Insolvency (England and Wales) and Insolvency (Scotland) (Miscellaneous and Consequential Amendments) Rules 2017, SI 2017/1115, rr 22, 23(6).

[6.45]

1.37 Delivery to the creditors and opting out

(1) Where the Act or a rule requires an office-holder to deliver a document to the creditors, or the creditors in a class, the requirement is satisfied by the delivery of the document to all such creditors of whose address the office-holder is aware other than opted-out creditors [unless the opt out does not apply].

(2) Where a creditor has opted out from receiving documents, the opt out does not apply to—

- (a) a notice which the Act requires to be delivered to all creditors without expressly excluding opted-out creditors;
- (b) a notice of a change in the office-holder or the contact details for the office-holder;
- (c) a notice as provided for by sections 246C(2) or 379C(2) (notices of distributions, intended distributions and notices required to be given by court order); or

Part 6 Insolvency Rules

(d) a document which these Rules requires to accompany a notice within sub-paragraphs (a) to (c).

(3) The office-holder must begin to treat a creditor as an opted-out creditor as soon as reasonably practicable after delivery of the creditor's election to opt out.

(4) An office-holder in any consecutive insolvency proceedings of a different kind under Parts 1 to 11 of the Act in respect of the same company or individual who is aware that a creditor was an opted-out creditor in the earlier proceedings must treat the creditor as an opted out creditor in the consecutive proceedings.

NOTES

Commencement: 6 April 2017.

This rule derived from the Insolvency Rules 1986, SI 1986/1925, rr 4.44, 6.74.

Para (1): words in square brackets substituted by the Insolvency (England and Wales) (Amendment) Rules 2017, SI 2017/366, rr 3, 5.

[6.46]

1.38 Creditor's election to opt out

(1) A creditor may at any time elect to be an opted-out creditor.

(2) The creditor's election to opt out must be by a notice in writing authenticated and dated by the creditor.

(3) The creditor must deliver the notice to the office-holder.

(4) A creditor becomes an opted-out creditor when the notice is delivered to the office-holder.

(5) An opted-out creditor—

(a) will remain an opted-out creditor for the duration of the proceedings unless the opt out is revoked; and

(b) is deemed to be an opted-out creditor in respect of any consecutive insolvency proceedings under Parts 1 to 11 of the Act of a different kind relating to the same company or individual.

(6) The creditor may at any time revoke the election to opt out by a further notice in writing, authenticated and dated by the creditor and delivered to the office-holder.

(7) The creditor ceases to be an opted-out creditor from the date the notice is received by the office-holder.

NOTES

Commencement: 6 April 2017.

[6.47]

1.39 Office-holder to provide information to creditors on opting-out

(1) The office-holder must, in the first communication with a creditor, inform the creditor in writing that the creditor may elect to opt out of receiving further documents relating to the proceedings.

(2) The communication must contain—

(a) identification and contact details for the office-holder;

(b) a statement that the creditor has the right to elect to opt out of receiving further documents about the proceedings unless—

(i) the Act requires a document to be delivered to all creditors without expressly excluding opted-out creditors,

(ii) it is a notice relating to a change in the office-holder or the office-holder's contact details, or

(iii) it is a notice of a dividend or proposed dividend or a notice which the court orders to be sent to all creditors or all creditors of a particular category to which the creditor belongs;

(c) a statement that opting-out will not affect the creditor's entitlement to receive dividends should any be paid to creditors;

(d) a statement that unless these Rules provide to the contrary opting-out will not affect any right the creditor may have to vote in a decision procedure or a participate in a deemed consent procedure in the proceedings although the creditor will not receive notice of it;

(e) a statement that a creditor who opts out will be treated as having opted out in respect of any consecutive insolvency proceedings of a different kind in respect of the same company or individual; and

(f) information about how the creditor may elect to be or cease to be an opted-out creditor.

NOTES

Commencement: 6 April 2017.

[6.48]

1.40 Delivery of documents to authorised recipients

Where under the Act or these Rules a document is to be delivered to a person (other than by being served on that person), it may be delivered instead to any other person authorised in writing to accept delivery on behalf of the first-mentioned person.

NOTES

Commencement: 6 April 2017.

This rule derived from the Insolvency Rules 1986, SI 1986/1925, r 12A.5.

[6.49]

1.41 Delivery of documents to joint office-holders

Where there are joint office-holders in insolvency proceedings, delivery of a document to one of them is to be treated as delivery to all of them.

NOTES

Commencement: 6 April 2017.

This rule derived from the Insolvency Rules 1986, SI 1986/1925, r 12A.15.

[6.50]

1.42 Postal delivery of documents

(1) A document is delivered if it is sent by post in accordance with the provisions of this rule.

(2) First class or second class post may be used to deliver a document except where these Rules require first class post to be used.

(3) Unless the contrary is shown—

(a) a document sent by first class post is treated as delivered on the second business day after the day on which it is posted;

(b) a document sent by second class post is treated as delivered on the fourth business day after the day on which it is posted;

(c) where a post-mark appears on the envelope in which a document was posted, the date of that post-mark is to be treated as the date on which the document was posted.

(4) In this rule "post-mark" means a mark applied by a postal operator which records the date on which a letter entered the postal system of the postal operator.

NOTES

Commencement: 6 April 2017.

This rule derived from the Insolvency Rules 1986, SI 1986/1925, r 12A.3.

[6.51]

1.43 Delivery by document exchange

(1) A document is delivered to a member of a document exchange if it is delivered to that document exchange.

(2) Unless the contrary is shown, a document is treated as delivered—

(a) one business day after the day it is delivered to the document exchange where the sender and the intended recipient are members of the same document exchange; or

(b) two business days after the day it is delivered to the departure facility of the sender's document exchange where the sender and the intended recipient are members of different document exchanges.

NOTES

Commencement: 6 April 2017.

[6.52]

1.44 Personal delivery of documents

A document is delivered if it is personally delivered in accordance with the rules for personal service in CPR Part 6.

NOTES

Commencement: 6 April 2017.

This rule derived from the Insolvency Rules 1986, SI 1986/1925, r 12A.2.

[6.53]

1.45 Electronic delivery of documents

(1) A document is delivered if it is sent by electronic means and the following conditions apply.

(2) The conditions are that the intended recipient of the document has—

(a) given actual or deemed consent for the electronic delivery of the document;

(b) not revoked that consent before the document is sent; and

(c) provided an electronic address for the delivery of the document.

(3) Consent may relate to a specific case or generally.

(4) For the purposes of paragraph (2)(a) an intended recipient is deemed to have consented to the electronic delivery of a document by the office-holder where the intended recipient and the person who is the subject of the insolvency proceedings had customarily communicated with each other by electronic means before the proceedings commenced.

(5) Unless the contrary is shown, a document is to be treated as delivered by electronic means to an electronic address where the sender can produce a copy of the electronic communication which—

(a) contains the document; and

(b) shows the time and date the communication was sent and the electronic address to which it was sent.

(6) Unless the contrary is shown, a document sent electronically is treated as delivered to the electronic address to which it is sent at 9.00 am on the next business day after it was sent.

NOTES

Commencement: 6 April 2017.

This rule derived from the Insolvency Rules 1986, SI 1986/1925, r 12A.10.

[6.54]

1.46 Electronic delivery of documents to the court

(1) A document may not be delivered to a court by electronic means unless this is expressly permitted by the CPR, a Practice Direction, or these Rules.

(2) A document delivered by electronic means is to be treated as delivered to the court at the time it is recorded by the court as having been received or otherwise as the CPR, a Practice Direction or these Rules provide.

NOTES

Commencement: 6 April 2017.

This rule derived from the Insolvency Rules 1986, SI 1986/1925, r 12A.14.

[6.55]

1.47 Electronic delivery of notices to enforcement officers

Where anything in the Act or these Rules provides for the delivery of a notice to an enforcement officer or enforcement agent, it may be delivered by electronic means to a person who has been authorised to receive such a notice on behalf of a specified enforcement officer or enforcement agent or on behalf of enforcement officers or enforcement agents generally.

NOTES

Commencement: 6 April 2017.

This rule derived from the Insolvency Rules 1986, SI 1986/1925, r 12A.29.

[6.56]

1.48 Electronic delivery by office-holders

(1) Where an office-holder delivers a document by electronic means, the document must contain, or be accompanied by, a statement that the recipient may request a hard copy of the document and a telephone number, email address and postal address that may be used to make that request.

(2) An office-holder who receives such a request must deliver a hard copy of the document to the recipient free of charge within five business days of receipt of the request.

NOTES

Commencement: 6 April 2017.

This rule derived from the Insolvency Rules 1986, SI 1986/1925, r 12A.11.

[6.57]

1.49 Use of website by office-holder to deliver a particular document (sections 246B and 379B)

[Note: rule 3.54(3) allows notice of an extension to an administration to be given on a website, and rules 2.25(6) and 8.22(5) do likewise in respect of notice of the result of the consideration of a proposal for a CVA and an IVA respectively.]

(1) This rule applies for the purposes of sections 246B and 379B (use of websites).

(2) An office-holder who is required to deliver a document to any person may (except where personal delivery is required) satisfy that requirement by delivering a notice to that person which contains—

(a) a statement that the document is available for viewing and downloading on a website;

(b) the website's address and any password necessary to view and download the document; and

(c) a statement that the person to whom the notice is delivered may request a hard copy of the document with a telephone number, email address and postal address which may be used to make that request.

(3) An office-holder who receives such a request must deliver a hard copy of the document to the recipient free of charge within five business days of receipt of the request.

(4) A document to which a notice under paragraph (2) relates must—

(a) remain available on the website for the period required by rule 1.51; and

(b) be in a format that enables it to be downloaded within a reasonable time of an electronic request being made for it to be downloaded.

(5) A document which is delivered to a person by means of a website in accordance with this rule, is deemed to have been delivered—

(a) when the document is first made available on the website; or

(b) when the notice under paragraph (2) is delivered to that person, if that is later.

NOTES

Commencement: 6 April 2017.

This rule derived from the Insolvency Rules 1986, SI 1986/1925, r 12A.12.

[6.58]

1.50 General use of website to deliver documents

(1) The office-holder may deliver a notice to each person to whom a document will be required to be delivered in the insolvency proceedings which contains—

(a) a statement that future documents in the proceedings other than those mentioned in paragraph (2) will be made available for viewing and downloading on a website without notice to the recipient and that the office-holder will not be obliged to deliver any such documents to the recipient of the notice unless it is requested by that person;

(b) a telephone number, email address and postal address which may be used to make a request for a hard copy of a document;

(c) a statement that the recipient of the notice may at any time request a hard copy of any or all of the following—

(i) all documents currently available for viewing on the website,

(ii) all future documents which may be made available there, and

(d) the address of the website, any password required to view and download a relevant document from that site.

(2) A statement under paragraph (1)(a) does not apply to the following documents—

(a) a document for which personal delivery is required;

(b) a notice under rule 14.29 of intention to declare a dividend; and

(c) a document which is not delivered generally.

(3) A document is delivered generally if it is delivered to some or all of the following classes of persons—

(a) members,

(b) contributories,

(c) creditors;

(d) any class of members, contributories or creditors.

(4) An office-holder who has delivered a notice under paragraph (1) is under no obligation—

(a) to notify a person to whom the notice has been delivered when a document to which the notice applies has been made available on the website; or

(b) to deliver a hard copy of such a document unless a request is received under paragraph (1)(c).

(5) An office-holder who receives such a request—

(a) in respect of a document which is already available on the website must deliver a hard copy of the document to the recipient free of charge within five business days of receipt of the request; and

(b) in respect of all future documents must deliver each such document in accordance with the requirements for delivery of such a document in the Act and these Rules.

(6) A document to which a statement under paragraph (1)(a) applies must—

(a) remain available on the website for the period required by rule 1.51; and

(b) must be in such a format as to enable it to be downloaded within a reasonable time of an electronic request being made for it to be downloaded.

(7) A document which is delivered to a person by means of a website in accordance with this rule, is deemed to have been delivered—

(a) when the relevant document was first made available on the website; or

(b) if later, when the notice under paragraph (1) was delivered to that person.

(8) Paragraph (7) does not apply in respect of a person who has made a request under paragraph (1)(c)(ii) for hard copies of all future documents.

NOTES

Commencement: 6 April 2017.

This rule derived from the Insolvency Rules 1986, SI 1986/1925, r 12A.13.

[6.59]

1.51 Retention period for documents made available on websites

(1) This rule applies to a document which is made available on a website under rules 1.49, 1.50, 2.25(6) (notice of the result of the consideration of a proposal for a CVA), 3.54(3) (notice of an extension to an administration) and 8.22(4) (notice of the result of the consideration of a proposal for an IVA).

(2) Such a document must continue to be made available on the website until two months after the end of the particular insolvency proceedings or the release of the last person to hold office as the office-holder in those proceedings.

NOTES

Commencement: 6 April 2017.

This rule derived from the Insolvency Rules 1986, SI 1986/1925, rr 12A.12, 12A.13.

[6.60]

1.52 Proof of delivery of documents

(1) A certificate complying with this rule is proof that a document has been duly delivered to the recipient in accordance with this Chapter unless the contrary is shown.

(2) A certificate must state the method of delivery and the date of the sending, posting or delivery (as the case may be).

(3) In the case of the official receiver or the adjudicator the certificate must be given by—
(a) the official receiver or the adjudicator; or
(b) a member of the official receiver's or adjudicator's staff.

(4) In the case of an office-holder other than the official receiver or the adjudicator the certificate must be given by—
(a) the office-holder;
(b) the office-holder's solicitor; or
(c) a partner or an employee of either of them.

(5) In the case of a person other than an office-holder the certificate must be given by that person and must state—
(a) that the document was delivered by that person; or
(b) that another person (named in the certificate) was instructed to deliver it.

(6) A certificate under this rule may be endorsed on a copy of the document to which it relates.

NOTES

Commencement: 6 April 2017.
This rule derived from the Insolvency Rules 1986, SI 1986/1925, r 12A.8.

[6.61]
1.53 Delivery of proofs and details of claims

(1) Once a proof has, or details of a claim have, been delivered to an office-holder in accordance with these Rules that proof or those details need not be delivered again; and accordingly, where a provision of these Rules requires delivery of a proof or details of a claim by a certain time, that requirement is satisfied if the proof has or the details have already been delivered.

(2) Paragraph (1) also applies to those cases set out in rule 14.3(2)(a) and (b) where a creditor who has proved in insolvency proceedings is deemed to have proved in an insolvency proceedings which immediately follows that proceeding.

NOTES

Commencement: 6 April 2017.
This rule derived from the Insolvency Rules 1986, SI 1986/1925, rr 4.54, 6.81.

CHAPTER 10 INSPECTION OF DOCUMENTS, COPIES AND PROVISION OF INFORMATION

[6.62]
1.54 Right to copies of documents

Where the Act, in relation to proceedings under Parts 1 to 11 of the Act, or these Rules give a person the right to inspect documents, that person has a right to be supplied on request with copies of those documents on payment of the standard fee for copies.

NOTES

Commencement: 6 April 2017.
This rule derived from the Insolvency Rules 1986, SI 1986/1925, r 12A.52.

[6.63]
1.55 Charges for copies of documents provided by the office-holder

Except where prohibited by these Rules, an office-holder is entitled to require the payment of the standard fee for copies of documents requested by a creditor, member, contributory or member of a liquidation or creditors' committee.

NOTES

Commencement: 6 April 2017.
This rule derived from the Insolvency Rules 1986, SI 1986/1925, r 12A.53.

[6.64]
1.56 Offence in relation to inspection of documents

(1) It is an offence for a person who does not have a right under these Rules to inspect a relevant document falsely to claim to be a creditor, a member of a company or a contributory of a company with the intention of gaining sight of the document.

(2) A relevant document is one which is on the court file, the bankruptcy file or held by the office-holder or any other person and which a creditor, a member of a company or a contributory of a company has the right to inspect under these Rules.

(3) A person guilty of an offence under this rule is liable to imprisonment or a fine, or both.

NOTES

Commencement: 6 April 2017.
This rule derived from the Insolvency Rules 1986, SI 1986/1925, r 12.18.

[6.65]
1.57 Right to list of creditors

(1) This rule applies to—

(a) administration;
(b) creditors' voluntary winding up;
(c) winding up by the court; and
(d) bankruptcy.

(2) A creditor has the right to require the office-holder to provide a list of the names and addresses of the creditors and the amounts of their respective debts unless—
(a) a statement of affairs has been filed with the court or delivered to the registrar of companies; or
(b) the information is available for inspection on the bankruptcy file.

(3) The office-holder on being required to provide such a list—
(a) must deliver it to the person requiring the list as soon as reasonably practicable; and
(b) may charge the standard fee for copies for a hard copy.

(4) The office-holder may omit the name and address of a creditor if the office-holder thinks its disclosure would be prejudicial to the conduct of the proceedings or might reasonably be expected to lead to violence against any person.

(5) In such a case the list must include—
(a) the amount of that creditor's debt; and
(b) a statement that the name and address of the creditor has been omitted for that debt.

NOTES

Commencement: 6 April 2017.
This rule derived from the Insolvency Rules 1986, SI 1986/1925, r 12A.54.

[6.66]
1.58 Confidentiality of documents: grounds for refusing inspection

(1) Where an office-holder considers that a document forming part of the records of the insolvency proceedings—
(a) should be treated as confidential; or
(b) is of such a nature that its disclosure would be prejudicial to the conduct of the proceedings or might reasonably be expected to lead to violence against any person;

the office-holder may decline to allow it to be inspected by a person who would otherwise be entitled to inspect it.

(2) The persons to whom the office-holder may refuse inspection include members of a liquidation committee or a creditors' committee.

(3) Where the office-holder refuses inspection of a document, the person wishing to inspect it may apply to the court which may reconsider the office-holder's decision.

(4) The court's decision may be subject to such conditions (if any) as it thinks just.

NOTES

Commencement: 6 April 2017.
This rule derived from the Insolvency Rules 1986, SI 1986/1925, r 12A.51.

PART 2
COMPANY VOLUNTARY ARRANGEMENTS (CVA)

CHAPTER 1 PRELIMINARY

[6.67]
2.1 Interpretation

In this Part—

"nominee" and "supervisor" include the proposed nominee or supervisor in relation to a proposal for a CVA; and
"proposal" means a proposal for a CVA.

NOTES

Commencement: 6 April 2017.

CHAPTER 2 THE PROPOSAL FOR A CVA (SECTION 1)

[Note: (1) section 1 of the Act sets out who may propose a CVA;

(2) a document required by the Act or these Rules must also contain the standard contents set out in Part 1.]

[6.68]
2.2 Proposal for a CVA: general principles and amendment

(1) A proposal must—
(a) contain identification details for the company;
(b) explain why the proposer thinks a CVA is desirable;
(c) explain why the creditors are expected to agree to a CVA; and
(d) be authenticated and dated by the proposer.

(2) The proposal may be amended with the nominee's agreement in writing in the following cases.

(3) The first case is where—
  (a) no steps have been taken to obtain a moratorium;
  (b) the nominee is not the liquidator or administrator of the company; and
  (c) the nominee's report has not been filed with the court under section 2(2).

(4) The second case is where—
  (a) the proposal is made with a view to obtaining a moratorium; and
  (b) the nominee's statement under paragraph 6(2) of Schedule A1 (nominee's opinion on prospects of CVA being approved etc) has not yet been submitted to the directors.

NOTES

Commencement: 6 April 2017.

This rule derived from the Insolvency Rules 1986, SI 1986/1925, r 1.3.

[6.69]

2.3 Proposal: contents

(1) The proposal must set out the following so far as known to the proposer—

Assets	(a) the company's assets, with an estimate of their respective values; (b) which assets are charged and the extent of the charge; (c) which assets are to be excluded from the CVA; and (d) particulars of any property to be included in the CVA which is not owned by the company, including details of who owns such property, and the terms on which it will be available for inclusion;
Liabilities	(e) the nature and amount of the company's liabilities; (f) how the company's liabilities will be met, modified, postponed or otherwise dealt with by means of the CVA and in particular— (i) how preferential creditors and creditors who are, or claim to be, secured will be dealt with, (ii) how creditors who are connected with the company will be dealt with, (iii) if the company is not in administration or liquidation whether, if the company did go into administration or liquidation, there are circumstances which might give rise to claims under section 238 (transactions at an undervalue), section 239 (preferences), section 244 (extortionate credit transactions), or section 245 (floating charges invalid), and (iv) where there are circumstances that might give rise to such claims, whether, and if so what, provision will be made to indemnify the company in respect of them;
Nominee's fees and expenses	(g) the amount proposed to be paid to the nominee by way of fees and expenses;
Supervisor	(h) identification and contact details for the supervisor; (i) confirmation that the supervisor is qualified to act as an insolvency practitioner in relation to the company and the name of the relevant recognised professional body which is the source of the supervisor's authorisation; (j) how the fees and expenses of the supervisor will be determined and paid; (k) the functions to be performed by the supervisor; (l) where it is proposed that two or more supervisors be appointed a statement whether acts done in connection with the CVA may be done by any one or more of them or must be done by all of them;

Guarantees and proposed guarantees	(m) whether any, and if so what, guarantees have been given in respect of the company's debts, specifying which of the guarantors are persons connected with the company; (n) whether any, and if so what, guarantees are proposed to be offered for the purposes of the CVA and, if so, by whom and whether security is to be given or sought;
Timing	(o) the proposed duration of the CVA; (p) the proposed dates of distributions to creditors, with estimates of their amounts;
Type of proceedings	(q) whether the proceedings will be main, territorial or [non-EU proceedings] with reasons;
Conduct of the business	(r) how the business of the company will be conducted during the CVA;
Further credit facilities	(s) details of any further proposed credit facilities for the company, and how the debts so arising are to be paid;
Handling of funds arising	(t) the manner in which funds held for the purposes of the CVA are to be banked, invested or otherwise dealt with pending distribution to creditors; (u) how funds held for the purpose of payment to creditors, and not so paid on the termination of the CVA, will be dealt with; (v) how the claim of any person bound by the CVA by virtue of section 5(2)(b)(ii) or paragraph 37(2)(b)(ii) of Schedule A1 will be dealt with;
Address (where moratorium proposed)	(w) where the proposal is made in relation to a company that is eligible for a moratorium (in accordance with paragraphs 2 and 3 of Schedule A1) with a view to obtaining a moratorium under Schedule A1, the address to which the documents referred to in paragraph 6(1) of that Schedule must be delivered; and
Other matters	(x) any other matters that the proposer considers appropriate to enable members and creditors to reach an informed decision on the proposal.

(2) Where the proposal is made by the directors, an estimate so far as known to them of—

(a) the value of the prescribed part if the proposal for the CVA is not accepted and the company goes into liquidation (whether or not the liquidator might be required under section 176A to make the prescribed part available for the satisfaction of unsecured debts); and

(b) the value of the company's net property (as defined by section 176A(6)) on the date that the estimate is made.

(3) Where the proposal is made by the administrator or liquidator the following so far as known to the office-holder—

(a) an estimate of—

(i) the value of the prescribed part (whether or not the administrator or liquidator might be required under section 176A to make the prescribed part available for the satisfaction of unsecured debts), and

(ii) the value of the company's net property (as defined by section 176A(6)); and

(b) a statement as to whether the administrator or liquidator proposes to make an application to the court under section 176A(5) and if so the reasons for the application; and

(c) details of the nature and amount of the company's preferential creditors.

(4) Information may be excluded from an estimate under paragraph (2) or (3)(a) if the inclusion of the information could seriously prejudice the commercial interests of the company.

(5) If the exclusion of such information affects the calculation of the estimate, the proposal must include a statement to that effect.

NOTES

Commencement: 6 April 2017.

This rule derived from the Insolvency Rules 1986, SI 1986/1925, r 1.3.

Para (1): words in square brackets in the Table substituted by the Insolvency (England and Wales) and Insolvency (Scotland) (Miscellaneous and Consequential Amendments) Rules 2017, SI 2017/1115, rr 22, 30(3).

CHAPTER 3 PROCEDURE FOR A CVA WITHOUT A MORATORIUM

[Note: a document required by the Act or these Rules must also contain the standard contents set out in Part 1.]

[6.70]
2.4 Procedure for proposal where the nominee is not the liquidator or the administrator (section 2)

(1) This rule applies where the nominee is not the same person as the liquidator or the administrator.

(2) A nominee who consents to act must deliver a notice of that consent to the proposer as soon as reasonably practicable after the proposal has been submitted to the nominee under section 2(3).

(3) The notice must state the date the nominee received the proposal.

(4) The period of 28 days in which the nominee must submit a report to the court under section 2(2) begins on the date the nominee received the proposal as stated in the notice.

NOTES

Commencement: 6 April 2017.
This rule derived from the Insolvency Rules 1986, SI 1986/1925, r 1.4.

[6.71]
2.5 Information for the official receiver

Where the company is being wound up by the court, the liquidator must deliver to the official receiver—
(a) a copy of the proposal; and
(b) the name and address of the nominee (if the nominee is not the liquidator).

NOTES

Commencement: 6 April 2017.
This rule derived from the Insolvency Rules 1986, SI 1986/1925, r 1.10.

[6.72]
2.6 Statement of affairs (section 2(3))

(1) The statement of the company's affairs required by section 2(3) must contain the following—
(a) a list of the company's assets, divided into such categories as are appropriate for easy identification, and with each category given an estimated value;
(b) in the case of any property on which a claim against the company is wholly or partly secured, particulars of the claim, and of how and when the security was created;
(c) the names and addresses of the preferential creditors, with the amounts of their respective claims;
(d) the names and addresses of the unsecured creditors with the amounts of their respective claims;
(e) particulars of any debts owed by the company to persons connected with it;
(f) particulars of any debts owed to the company by persons connected with it;
(g) the names and addresses of the company's members, with details of their respective shareholdings; and
(h) any other particulars that the nominee in writing requires to be provided for the purposes of making the nominee's report on the proposal to the court.

(2) The statement must be made up to a date not earlier than two weeks before the date of the proposal.

(3) However the nominee may allow the statement to be made up to an earlier date (but not more than two months before the date of the proposal) where that is more practicable.

(4) Where the statement is made up to an earlier date, the nominee's report to the court on the proposal must explain why.

(5) The statement of affairs must be verified by a statement of truth made by the proposer.

(6) Where the proposal is made by the directors, only one director need make the statement of truth.

NOTES

Commencement: 6 April 2017.
This rule derived from the Insolvency Rules 1986, SI 1986/1925, r 1.5.

[6.73]
2.7 Application to omit information from statement of affairs delivered to creditors

The nominee, the directors or any person appearing to the court to have an interest, may apply to the court for a direction that specified information be omitted from the statement of affairs as delivered to the creditors where disclosure of that information would be likely to prejudice the conduct of the CVA or might reasonably be expected to lead to violence against any person.

NOTES

Commencement: 6 April 2017.
This rule derived from the Insolvency Rules 1986, SI 1986/1925, r 1.56.

[6.74]

2.8 Additional disclosure for assistance of nominee where the nominee is not the liquidator or administrator

(1) This rule applies where the nominee is not the administrator or the liquidator of the company.

(2) If it appears to the nominee that the nominee's report to the court cannot properly be prepared on the basis of information in the proposal and statement of affairs, the nominee may require the proposer to provide—

- (a) more information about the circumstances in which, and the reasons why, a CVA is being proposed;
- (b) particulars of any previous proposals which have been made in relation to the company under Part 1 of the Act; and
- (c) any further information relating to the company's affairs which the nominee thinks necessary for the purposes of the report.

(3) The nominee may require the proposer to inform the nominee whether, and if so in what circumstances, any person who is, or has been at any time in the two years before the date the nominee received the proposal, a director or officer of the company has—

- (a) been concerned in the affairs of any other company (whether or not incorporated in England and Wales) or limited liability partnership which has been the subject of insolvency proceedings;
- (b) been made bankrupt;
- (c) been the subject of a debt relief order; or
- (d) entered into an arrangement with creditors.

(4) The proposer must give the nominee such access to the company's accounts and records as the nominee may require to enable the nominee to consider the proposal and prepare the nominee's report.

NOTES

Commencement: 6 April 2017.

This rule derived from the Insolvency Rules 1986, SI 1986/1925, r 1.6.

[6.75]

2.9 Nominee's report on proposal where the nominee is not the liquidator or administrator (section 2(2))

(1) The nominee's report must be filed with the court under section 2(2) accompanied by—

- (a) a copy of the report;
- (b) a copy of the proposal (as amended under rule 2.2(2), if that is the case); and
- (c) a copy of the statement of the company's affairs or a summary of it.

(2) The report must state—

- (a) why the nominee considers the proposal does or does not have a reasonable prospect of being approved and implemented; and
- (b) why the members and the creditors should or should not be invited to consider the proposal.

(3) The court must endorse the nominee's report and the copy of it with the date of filing and deliver the copy to the nominee.

(4) The nominee must deliver a copy of the report to the company.

NOTES

Commencement: 6 April 2017.

This rule derived from the Insolvency Rules 1986, SI 1986/1925, r 1.7.

[6.76]

2.10 Replacement of nominee (section 2(4))

(1) A person (other than the nominee) who intends to apply to the court under section 2(4) for the nominee to be replaced must deliver a notice that such an application is intended to be made to the nominee at least five business days before filing the application with the court.

(2) A nominee who intends to apply under that section to be replaced must deliver a notice that such an application is intended to be made to the person intending to make the proposal, or the proposer, at least five business days before filing the application with the court.

(3) The court must not appoint a replacement nominee unless a statement by the replacement nominee has been filed with the court confirming that person—

- (a) consents to act; and
- (b) is qualified to act as an insolvency practitioner, in relation to the company.

NOTES

Commencement: 6 April 2017.

This rule derived from the Insolvency Rules 1986, SI 1986/1925, r 1.8.

CHAPTER 4 PROCEDURE FOR A CVA WITH A MORATORIUM

[Note: a document required by the Act or these Rules must also contain the standard contents set out in Part 1.]

[6.77]
2.11 Statement of affairs (paragraph 6(1)(b) of Schedule A1)

(1) The statement of affairs required by paragraph 6(1)(b) of Schedule A1 must contain the same information as is required by rule 2.6.

(2) The statement must be made up to a date not earlier than two weeks before the date of the proposal.

(3) However the nominee may allow the statement to be made up to an earlier date (but not more than two months before the proposal) where that is more practicable.

(4) Where the statement is made up to an earlier date, the nominee's statement to the directors on the proposal must explain why.

(5) The statement of affairs must be verified by a statement of truth made by at least one director.

NOTES

Commencement: 6 April 2017.
This rule derived from the Insolvency Rules 1986, SI 1986/1925, r 1.37.

[6.78]
2.12 Application to omit information from a statement of affairs

The nominee, the directors or any person appearing to the court to have an interest, may apply to the court for a direction that specified information be omitted from the statement of affairs as delivered to the creditors where disclosure of that information would be likely to prejudice the conduct of the CVA or might reasonably be expected to lead to violence against any person.

NOTES

Commencement: 6 April 2017.
This rule derived from the Insolvency Rules 1986, SI 1986/1925, r 1.56.

[6.79]
2.13 The nominee's statement (paragraph 6(2) of Schedule A1)

(1) The nominee must submit to the directors the statement required by paragraph 6(2) of Schedule A1 within 28 days of the submission to the nominee of the proposal.

(2) The statement must—
  (a) include the name and address of the nominee; and
  (b) be authenticated and dated by the nominee.

(3) A statement which contains an opinion on all the matters referred to in paragraph 6(2) must—
  (a) explain why the nominee has formed that opinion; and
  (b) if the nominee is willing to act, be accompanied by a statement of the nominee's consent to act in relation to the proposed CVA.

(4) The statement of the nominee's consent must—
  (a) include the name and address of the nominee;
  (b) state that the nominee is qualified to act as an insolvency practitioner in relation to the company; and
  (c) be authenticated and dated by the nominee.

NOTES

Commencement: 6 April 2017.
This rule derived from the Insolvency Rules 1986, SI 1986/1925, r 1.38.

[6.80]
2.14 Documents filed with court to obtain a moratorium (paragraph 7(1) of Schedule A1)

(1) The statement of the company's affairs which the directors file with the court under paragraph 7(1)(b) of Schedule A1 must be the same as the statement they submit to the nominee under paragraph 6(1)(b) of that Schedule.

(2) The statement required by paragraph 7(1)(c) of that Schedule that the company is eligible for a moratorium must—
  (a) be made by the directors;
  (b) state that the company meets the requirements of paragraph 3 of Schedule A1 and is not a company which falls within paragraph 2(2) of that Schedule;
  (c) confirm that the company is not ineligible for a moratorium under paragraph 4 of that Schedule; and
  (d) be authenticated and dated by the directors.

[(2A) A statement from the nominee whether the proceedings will be main, secondary, territorial or [non-EU proceedings] with the reasons for so stating must also be filed with the court.]

(3) The statement required by paragraph 7(1)(d) of that Schedule that the nominee has consented to act must be in the same terms as the statement referred to in rule 2.13(3)(b) and (4).

(4) The statement of the nominee's opinion required by paragraph 7(1)(e) of that Schedule—
  (a) must be the same as the statement of opinion required by paragraph 6(2) of that Schedule; and
  (b) must be filed with the court not later than ten business days after it was submitted to the directors.

(5) The documents filed with the court under paragraph 7(1) of that Schedule must be accompanied by four copies of a schedule, authenticated and dated by the directors, identifying the company and listing all the documents filed.

(6) The court must endorse the copies of the schedule with the date on which the documents were filed and deliver three copies of the endorsed schedule to the directors.

NOTES

Commencement: 6 April 2017.

This rule derived from the Insolvency Rules 1986, SI 1986/1925, r 1.39.

Para (2A): inserted by the Insolvency Amendment (EU 2015/848) Regulations 2017, SI 2017/702, regs 2, 3, Schedule, Pt 2, paras 32, 35, as from 26 June 2017, except in relation to proceedings opened before that date; words in square brackets substituted by the Insolvency (England and Wales) and Insolvency (Scotland) (Miscellaneous and Consequential Amendments) Rules 2017, SI 2017/1115, rr 22, 30(4).

[6.81]

2.15 Notice and advertisement of beginning of a moratorium

(1) The directors must as soon as reasonably practicable after delivery to them of the endorsed copies of the schedule deliver two copies of the schedule to the nominee and one to the company.

(2) After delivery of the copies of the schedule, the nominee—

(a) must as soon as reasonably practicable gazette a notice of the coming into force of the moratorium; and

(b) may advertise the notice in such other manner as the nominee thinks fit.

(3) The notice must specify—

(a) the nature of the business of the company;

(b) that a moratorium under section 1A has come into force; and

(c) the date on which it came into force.

(4) The nominee must as soon as reasonably practicable deliver a notice of the coming into force of the moratorium to—

(a) the registrar of companies;

(b) the company; and

(c) any petitioning creditor of whose address the nominee is aware.

(5) The notice must specify—

(a) the date on which the moratorium came into force; and

(b) the court with which the documents to obtain the moratorium were filed.

(6) The nominee must deliver a notice of the coming into force of the moratorium and the date on which it came into force to—

(a) any enforcement agent or other officer who to the knowledge of the nominee is charged with distress or other legal process, against the company or its property; and

(b) any person who to the nominee's knowledge has distrained against the company or its property.

NOTES

Commencement: 6 April 2017.

This rule derived from the Insolvency Rules 1986, SI 1986/1925, r 1.40.

[6.82]

2.16 Notice of continuation of a moratorium where physical meeting of creditors is summoned (paragraph 8(3B) of Schedule A1)

(1) This rule applies where under paragraph 8(3B)(b) and (3C) of Schedule A1 the moratorium continues after the initial period of 28 days referred to in paragraph 8(3) of that Schedule because a physical meeting of the company's creditors is first summoned to take place after the end of that period.

(2) The nominee must file with the court and deliver to the registrar of companies a notice of the continuation as soon as reasonably practicable after summoning such a meeting of the company's creditors.

(3) The notice must—

(a) identify the company;

(b) give the name and address of the nominee;

(c) state the date on which the notice of the meeting was sent to the creditors under rule 15.6;

(d) state the date for which the meeting is summoned;

(e) state that under paragraph 8(3B)(b) and (3C) of Schedule A1 the moratorium will be continued to that date; and

(f) be authenticated and dated by the nominee.

NOTES

Commencement: 6 April 2017.

[6.83]

2.17 Notice of decision extending or further extending a moratorium (paragraph 36 of Schedule A1)

(1) This rule applies where the moratorium is extended, or further extended by a decision which takes effect under paragraph 36 of Schedule A1.

(2) The nominee must, as soon as reasonably practicable, file with the court and deliver to the registrar of companies a notice of the decision.

(3) The notice must—

(a) identify the company;
(b) give the name and address of the nominee;
(c) state the date on which the moratorium was extended or further extended;
(d) state the new expiry date of the moratorium; and
(e) be authenticated and dated by the nominee.

NOTES

Commencement: 6 April 2017.
This rule derived from the Insolvency Rules 1986, SI 1986/1925, r 1.41.

[6.84]

2.18 Notice of court order extending or further extending or continuing or renewing a moratorium (paragraph 34(2) of Schedule A1)

Where the court makes an order extending, further extending, renewing or continuing a moratorium, the nominee must, as soon as reasonably practicable, deliver to the registrar of companies a notice stating the new expiry date of the moratorium.

NOTES

Commencement: 6 April 2017.
This rule derived from the Insolvency Rules 1986, SI 1986/1925, r 1.41.

[6.85]

2.19 Advertisement of end of a moratorium (paragraph 11(1) of Schedule A1)

(1) After the moratorium ends, the nominee—

(a) must, as soon as reasonably practicable, gazette a notice of its coming to an end; and
(b) may advertise the notice in such other manner as the nominee thinks fit.

(2) The notice must state—

(a) the nature of the company's business;
(b) that a moratorium under section 1A has ended; and
(c) the date on which it came to an end.

(3) The nominee must, as soon as reasonably practicable—

(a) file with the court a notice specifying the date on which the moratorium ended; and
(b) deliver such a notice to—
(i) the registrar of companies,
(ii) the company, and
(iii) the creditors.

(4) The notice to the court must—

(a) identify the company;
(b) give the name and address of the nominee; and
(c) be authenticated and dated by the nominee.

NOTES

Commencement: 6 April 2017.
This rule derived from the Insolvency Rules 1986, SI 1986/1925, r 1.42.

[6.86]

2.20 Disposal of charged property etc during a moratorium

(1) This rule applies where the company applies to the court under paragraph 20 of Schedule A1 for permission to dispose of—

(a) property subject to a security; or
(b) goods under a hire-purchase agreement.

(2) The court must fix a venue for hearing the application.

(3) The company must as soon as reasonably practicable deliver a notice of the venue to the holder of the security or the owner of the goods under the agreement.

(4) If an order is made, the court must deliver two sealed copies of the order to the company and the company must deliver one of them to the holder or owner as soon as reasonably practicable.

NOTES

Commencement: 6 April 2017.
This rule derived from the Insolvency Rules 1986, SI 1986/1925, r 1.43.

[6.87]

2.21 Withdrawal of nominee's consent to act (paragraph 25(5) of Schedule A1)

(1) A nominee who withdraws consent to act, must file with the court and otherwise deliver a notice under paragraph 25(5) of Schedule A1 as soon as reasonably practicable.

(2) The notice filed with the court must—

(a) identify the company;

(b) give the name and address of the nominee;
(c) specify the date on which the nominee withdrew consent;
(d) state, with reference to the reasons at paragraph 25(2) of that Schedule, why the nominee withdrew consent; and
(e) be authenticated and dated by the nominee.

NOTES

Commencement: 6 April 2017.
This rule derived from the Insolvency Rules 1986, SI 1986/1925, r 1.44.

[6.88]
2.22 Application to the court to replace the nominee (paragraph 28 of Schedule A1)

(1) Directors who intend to make an application under paragraph 28 of Schedule A1 for the nominee to be replaced must deliver a notice of the intention to make the application to the nominee at least five business days before filing the application with the court.

(2) A nominee who intends to make an application under that paragraph to be replaced must deliver notice of the intention to make the application to the directors at least five business days before filing the application with the court.

(3) The court must not appoint a replacement nominee unless a statement by the replacement nominee has been filed with the court confirming that person—
(a) consents to act; and
(b) is qualified to act as an insolvency practitioner in relation to the company.

NOTES

Commencement: 6 April 2017.
This rule derived from the Insolvency Rules 1986, SI 1986/1925, r 1.45.

[6.89]
2.23 Notice of appointment of replacement nominee

(1) A person appointed as a replacement nominee must as soon as reasonably practicable deliver a notice of the appointment to the registrar of companies and the former nominee and, where the appointment is not by the court, file a notice of the appointment with the court.

(2) The notice filed with the court must—
(a) identify the company;
(b) give the name and address of the replacement nominee;
(c) specify the date on which the replacement nominee was appointed to act; and
(d) be authenticated and dated by the replacement nominee.

NOTES

Commencement: 6 April 2017.
This rule derived from the Insolvency Rules 1986, SI 1986/1925, r 1.46.

[6.90]
2.24 Applications to court to challenge nominee's actions etc (paragraphs 26 and 27 of Schedule A1)

A person intending to make an application to the court under paragraph 26 or 27 of Schedule A1 must deliver a notice of the intention to make the application to the nominee at least five business days before filing the application with the court.

NOTES

Commencement: 6 April 2017.
This rule derived from the Insolvency Rules 1986, SI 1986/1925, r 1.47.

CHAPTER 5 CONSIDERATION OF THE PROPOSAL BY THE COMPANY MEMBERS AND CREDITORS

[Note: a document required by the Act or these Rules must also contain the standard contents set out in Part 1.]

[6.91]
2.25 Consideration of proposal: common requirements (section 3)

(1) The nominee must invite the members of the company to consider a proposal by summoning a meeting of the company as required by section 3.

(2) The nominee must invite the creditors to consider the proposal by way of a decision procedure.

[(2A) The nominee must examine whether there is jurisdiction to open the proceedings and must specify in the nominee's comments on the proposal required by paragraphs (3)(d)(iii) and (5)(a)(iii) whether the proceedings will be main, secondary, territorial or non-EU proceedings with the reasons for so stating.]

(3) In the case of the members, the nominee must deliver to every person whom the nominee believes to be a member a notice which must—
(a) identify the proceedings;

(b) state the venue for the meeting;
(c) state the effect of the following—
   (i) rule 2.35 about members' voting rights,
   (ii) rule 2.36 about the requisite majority of members for passing resolutions, and
   (iii) rule 15.35 about rights of appeal; and
(d) be accompanied by—
   (i) a copy of the proposal,
   (ii) a copy of the statement of affairs, or if the nominee thinks fit a summary including a list of creditors with the amounts of their debts,
   (iii) the nominee's comments on the proposal, unless the nominee is the administrator or liquidator [in which case the comments required are limited to stating whether the proceedings will be main, secondary, territorial or non-EU proceedings with the reasons for so stating], and
   (iv) details of each resolution to be voted on.

(4) In the case of the creditors, the nominee must deliver to each creditor a notice in respect of the decision procedure which complies with rule 15.8 so far as is relevant.

(5) The notice must also—
(a) be accompanied by—
   (i) a copy of the proposal,
   (ii) a copy of the statement of affairs, or if the nominee thinks fit a summary including a list of creditors with the amounts of their debts, and
   (iii) the nominee's comments on the proposal, unless the nominee is the administrator or liquidator; and
(b) state how a creditor may propose a modification to the proposal, and how the nominee will deal with such a proposal for a modification.

(6) The notice may also state that the results of the consideration of the proposal will be made available for viewing and downloading on a website and that no other notice will be delivered to the creditors or members (as the case may be).

(7) Where the results of the consideration of the proposal are to be made available for viewing and downloading on a website the nominee must comply with the requirements for use of a website to deliver a document set out in rule 1.49(2)(a) to (c), (3) and (4) with any necessary adaptations and rule 1.49(5)(a) applies to determine the time of delivery of the document.

NOTES

Commencement: 6 April 2017.

This rule derived from the Insolvency Rules 1986, SI 1986/1925, rr 1.9, 1.11, 1.48.

Para (2A): inserted by the Insolvency Amendment (EU 2015/848) Regulations 2017, SI 2017/702, regs 2, 3, Schedule, Pt 2, paras 32, 36(1), (2), as from 26 June 2017, except in relation to proceedings opened before that date.

Para (3): words in square brackets in sub-para (d)(iii) inserted by SI 2017/702, regs 2, 3, Schedule, Pt 2, paras 32, 36(1), (3), as from 26 June 2017, except in relation to proceedings opened before that date.

[6.92]

2.26 Members' consideration at a meeting

(1) Where the nominee invites the members to consider the proposal at a meeting the notice to members under rule 2.25(3) must also—
(a) specify the purpose of and venue for the meeting; and
(b) be accompanied by a blank proxy.

(2) The nominee must have regard to the convenience of those invited to attend when fixing the venue for a meeting (including the resumption of an adjourned meeting).

(3) The date of the meeting (except where the nominee is the administrator or liquidator of the company) must not be more than 28 days from the date on which—
(a) the nominee's report is filed with the court under rule 2.9; or
(b) the moratorium came into force.

NOTES

Commencement: 6 April 2017.

This rule derived from the Insolvency Rules 1986, SI 1986/1925, rr 1.9, 1.11, 1.48.

[6.93]

2.27 Creditors' consideration by a decision procedure

Where the nominee is inviting the creditors to consider the proposal by a decision procedure, the decision date must be not less than 14 days from the date of delivery of the notice and not more than 28 days from the date—
(a) the nominee's report is filed with the court under rule 2.9; or
(b) the moratorium came into force.

NOTES

Commencement: 6 April 2017.

This rule derived from the Insolvency Rules 1986, SI 1986/1925, rr 1.9, 1.11, 1.48.

[6.94]
2.28 Timing of decisions on proposal

(1) The decision date for the creditors' decision procedure may be on the same day as, or on a different day to, the meeting of the company.

(2) But the creditors' decision on the proposal must be made before the members' decision.

(3) The members' decision must be made not later than five business days after the creditors' decision.

(4) For the purpose of this rule, the timing of the members' decision is either the date and time of the meeting of the company or, where the nominee invites members to consider the proposal by correspondence, the deadline for receipt of members' votes.

NOTES

Commencement: 6 April 2017.
This rule derived from the Insolvency Rules 1986, SI 1986/1925, r 1.13.

[6.95]
2.29 Creditors' approval of modified proposal

(1) This rule applies where a decision is sought from the creditors following notice to the nominee of proposed modifications to the proposal from the company's directors under paragraph 31(7) of Schedule A1.

(2) The decision must be sought by a decision procedure with a decision date within 14 days of the date on which the directors gave notice to the nominee of the modifications.

(3) The creditors must be given at least seven days' notice of the decision date.

NOTES

Commencement: 6 April 2017.

[6.96]
2.30 Notice of members' meeting and attendance of officers

(1) A notice under rule [2.25(3)] summoning a meeting of the company must be delivered at least 14 days before the day fixed for the meeting to all the members and to—

(a) every officer or former officer of the company whose presence the nominee thinks is required; and
(b) all other directors of the company.

(2) Every officer or former officer who receives such a notice stating that the nominee thinks that person's attendance is required is required to attend the meeting.

NOTES

Commencement: 6 April 2017.
This rule derived from the Insolvency Rules 1986, SI 1986/1925, rr 1.9, 1.11, 1.48.
Para (1): figure in square brackets substituted by the Insolvency (England and Wales) and Insolvency (Scotland) (Miscellaneous and Consequential Amendments) Rules 2017, SI 2017/1115, rr 2, 3.

[6.97]
2.31 Requisition of physical meeting by creditors

(1) This rule applies where the creditors requisition a physical meeting to consider a proposal (with or without modifications) in accordance with section 246ZE and rule 15.6.

(2) The meeting must take place within 14 days of the date on which the prescribed proportion of creditors have required the meeting to take place.

[(3) A notice summoning a meeting of the creditors must be delivered to the creditors at least seven days before the day fixed for the meeting.]

NOTES

Commencement: 6 April 2017.
Para (3): substituted by the Insolvency (England and Wales) (Amendment) Rules 2017, SI 2017/366, rr 3, 7.

[6.98]
2.32 Non-receipt of notice by members

Where in accordance with the Act or these Rules the members are invited to consider a proposal, the consideration is presumed to have duly taken place even if not everyone to whom the notice is to be delivered receives it.

NOTES

Commencement: 6 April 2017.
This rule derived from the Insolvency Rules 1986, SI 1986/1925, r 12A.4.

[6.99]
2.33 Proposal for alternative supervisor

(1) If in response to a notice inviting—

(a) members to consider the proposal by correspondence; or
(b) creditors to consider the proposal other than at a meeting,

a member or creditor proposes that a person other than the nominee be appointed as supervisor, that person's consent to act and confirmation of being qualified to act as an insolvency practitioner in relation to the company must be delivered to the nominee by the deadline in the notice of the decision by correspondence or by the decision date (as the case may be).

(2) If, at either a meeting of the company or the creditors to consider the proposal, a resolution is moved for the appointment of a person other than the nominee to be supervisor, the person moving the resolution must produce to the chair at or before the meeting—

(a) confirmation that the person proposed as supervisor is qualified to act as an insolvency practitioner in relation to the company; and

(b) that person's written consent to act (unless that person is present at the meeting and there signifies consent to act).

NOTES

Commencement: 6 April 2017.

This rule derived from the Insolvency Rules 1986, SI 1986/1925, r 1.22.

[6.100]

2.34 Chair at meetings

The chair of a meeting under this Part must be the nominee or an appointed person.

NOTES

Commencement: 6 April 2017.

This rule derived from the Insolvency Rules 1986, SI 1986/1925, r 1.14.

[6.101]

2.35 Members' voting rights

(1) A member is entitled to vote according to the rights attaching to the member's shares in accordance with the articles of the company.

(2) A member's shares include any other interest that person may have as a member of the company.

(3) The value of a member for the purposes of voting is determined by reference to the number of votes conferred on that member by the company's articles.

NOTES

Commencement: 6 April 2017.

This rule derived from the Insolvency Rules 1986, SI 1986/1925, rr 1.18, 1.51.

[6.102]

2.36 Requisite majorities of members

(1) A resolution is passed by members by correspondence or at a meeting of the company when a majority (in value) of those voting have voted in favour of it.

(2) This is subject to any express provision to the contrary in the articles.

(3) A resolution is not passed by correspondence unless at least one member has voted in favour of it.

NOTES

Commencement: 6 April 2017.

This rule derived from the Insolvency Rules 1986, SI 1986/1925, rr 1.20, 1.53.

[6.103]

2.37 Notice of order made under section 4A(6) or paragraph 36(5) of Schedule A1

(1) This rule applies where the court makes an order under section 4A(6) or paragraph 36(5) of Schedule A1.

(2) The member who applied for the order must deliver a sealed copy of it to—

(a) the proposer; and

(b) the supervisor (if there is one different to the proposer).

(3) If the directors are the proposer a single copy may be delivered to the company at its registered office.

(4) The supervisor, or the proposer where there is no supervisor, must as soon as reasonably practicable deliver a notice that the order has been made to every person who had received a notice to vote on the matter or who is affected by the order.

(5) The member who applied for the order must, within five business days of the order, deliver a copy to the registrar of companies.

NOTES

Commencement: 6 April 2017.

This rule derived from the Insolvency Rules 1986, SI 1986/1925, r 1.22A.

[6.104]

2.38 Report of consideration of proposal under section 4(6) and (6A) or paragraph 30(3) and (4) of Schedule A1

(1) A report [or reports as the case may be] must be prepared of the consideration of a proposal under section 4(6) and (6A) or paragraph 30(3) and (4) of Schedule A1 by the convener or, in the case of a meeting, the chair.

(2) The report must—

(a) state whether the proposal was approved or rejected and whether by the creditors alone or by both the creditors and members and, in either case, whether any approval was with any modifications;

(b) list the creditors and members who voted or attended or who were represented at the meeting or decision procedure (as applicable) used to consider the proposal, setting out (with their respective values) how they voted on each resolution [or whether they abstained];

(c) identify which of those creditors were considered to be connected with the company;

(d) if the proposal was approved, state with reasons whether the proceedings are main, territorial or [non-EU proceedings]; and

(e) include such further information as the nominee or the chair thinks it appropriate to make known to the court.

(3) A copy of the report must be filed with the court, within four business days of . . . the date of the company meeting.

(4) The court must endorse the copy of the report with the date of filing.

(5) The chair (in the case of a company meeting) or otherwise the convener must give notice of the result of the consideration of the proposal to everyone who was invited to consider the proposal or to whom notice of a decision procedure or meeting was delivered as soon as reasonably practicable after a copy of the report is filed with the court.

(6) Where the decision approving the CVA has effect under section 4A or paragraph 36 of Schedule A1 with or without modifications, the supervisor must as soon as reasonably practicable deliver a copy of the convener's report or, in the case of a meeting, the chair's report to the registrar of companies.

NOTES

Commencement: 6 April 2017.

This rule derived from the Insolvency Rules 1986, SI 1986/1925, r 1.24.

Para (1): words in square brackets inserted by the Insolvency (England and Wales) (Amendment) Rules 2017, SI 2017/366, rr 3, 8(1).

Para (2): words in square brackets in sub-para (b) inserted by SI 2017/366, rr 3, 8(2); words in square brackets in sub-para (d) substituted by the Insolvency (England and Wales) and Insolvency (Scotland) (Miscellaneous and Consequential Amendments) Rules 2017, SI 2017/1115, rr 22, 30(5).

Para (3): words omitted revoked by SI 2017/366, rr 3, 8(3).

CHAPTER 6 ADDITIONAL MATTERS CONCERNING AND FOLLOWING APPROVAL OF CVA

[Note: a document required by the Act or these Rules must also contain the standard contents set out in Part 1.]

[6.105]

2.39 Hand-over of property etc to supervisor

(1) Where the decision approving a CVA has effect under section 4A or paragraph 36 of Schedule A1, and the supervisor is not the same person as the proposer, the proposer must, as soon as reasonably practicable, do all that is required to put the supervisor in possession of the assets included in the CVA.

(2) Where the company is in administration or liquidation and the supervisor is not the same person as the administrator or liquidator, the supervisor must—

(a) before taking possession of the assets included in the CVA, deliver to the administrator or liquidator an undertaking to discharge the balance referred to in paragraph (3) out of the first realisation of assets; or

(b) upon taking possession of the assets included in the CVA, discharge such balance.

(3) The balance is any balance due to the administrator or liquidator, or to the official receiver not acting as liquidator—

(a) by way of fees or expenses properly incurred and payable under the Act or these Rules; and

(b) on account of any advances made in respect of the company together with interest on such advances at the rate specified in section 17 of the Judgments Act 1838 at the date on which the company entered administration or went into liquidation.

(4) The administrator or liquidator, or the official receiver not acting as liquidator, has a charge on the assets included in the CVA in respect of any sums comprising such balance, subject only to the deduction from realisations by the supervisor of the proper costs and expenses of such realisations.

(5) The supervisor must from time to time out of the realisation of assets—

(a) discharge all guarantees properly given by the administrator or liquidator for the benefit of the company; and

(b) pay all the expenses of the administrator or liquidator or of the official receiver not acting as liquidator.

(6) Sums due to the official receiver take priority over those due to any other person under this rule.

NOTES

Commencement: 6 April 2017.

This rule derived from the Insolvency Rules 1986, SI 1986/1925, rr 1.23, 1.54.

[6.106]

2.40 Revocation or suspension of CVA

(1) This rule applies where the court makes an order of revocation or suspension under section 6 or paragraph 38 of Schedule A1.

(2) The applicant for the order must deliver a sealed copy of it to—

(a) the proposer; and

(b) the supervisor (if different).

(3) If the directors are the proposer a single copy of the order may be delivered to the company at its registered office.

(4) If the order includes a direction by the court under section 6(4)(b) or (c) or under paragraph 38(4)(b) or (c) of Schedule A1 for [action to be taken], the applicant for the order must deliver a notice that the order has been made to the person who is directed to take such action.

(5) The proposer must—

(a) as soon as reasonably practicable deliver a notice that the order has been made to all of those persons to whom a notice to consider the matter was delivered or who appear to be affected by the order;

(b) within five business days of delivery of a copy of the order (or within such longer period as the court may allow), deliver (if applicable) a notice to the court advising that it is intended to make a revised proposal to the company and its creditors, or to invite re-consideration of the original proposal.

(6) The applicant for the order must deliver a copy of the order to the registrar of companies within five business days of the making of the order with a notice which must contain the date on which the voluntary arrangement took effect.

NOTES

Commencement: 6 April 2017.

This rule derived from the Insolvency Rules 1986, SI 1986/1925, r 1.25.

Para (4): words in square brackets substituted by the Insolvency (England and Wales) (Amendment) Rules 2017, SI 2017/366, rr 3, 9.

[6.107]

2.41 Supervisor's accounts and reports

(1) The supervisor must keep accounts and records where the CVA authorises or requires the supervisor—

(a) to carry on the business of the company;

(b) to realise assets of the company; or

(c) otherwise to administer or dispose of any of its funds.

(2) The accounts and records which must be kept are of the supervisor's acts and dealings in, and in connection with, the CVA, including in particular records of all receipts and payments of money.

(3) The supervisor must preserve any such accounts and records which were kept by any other person who has acted as supervisor of the CVA and are in the supervisor's possession.

(4) The supervisor must deliver reports on the progress and prospects for the full implementation of the CVA to—

(a) the registrar of companies;

(b) the company;

(c) the creditors bound by the CVA;

(d) subject to paragraph (10) below, the members; and

(e) if the company is not in liquidation, the company's auditors (if any) for the time being.

(5) The notice which accompanies the report when delivered to the registrar of companies must contain the date on which the voluntary arrangement took effect.

(6) The first report must cover the period of 12 months commencing on the date on which the CVA was approved and a further report must be made for each subsequent period of 12 months.

(7) Each report must be delivered within the period of two months after the end of the 12 month period.

(8) Such a report is not required if the obligation to deliver a final report under rule 2.44 . . . arises in the two month period.

(9) Where the supervisor is authorised or required to do any of the things mentioned in paragraph (1), the report must—

(a) include or be accompanied by a summary of receipts and payments required to be recorded by virtue of paragraph (2); or

(b) state that there have been no such receipts and payments.

(10) The court may, on application by the supervisor, dispense with the delivery of such reports or summaries to members, either altogether or on the basis that the availability of the report to members is to be advertised by the supervisor in a specified manner.

NOTES

Commencement: 6 April 2017.

This rule derived from the Insolvency Rules 1986, SI 1986/1925, r 1.26A.

Para (8): figure omitted revoked by the Insolvency (England and Wales) (Amendment) Rules 2017, SI 2017/366, rr 3, 10.

[6.108]

2.42 Production of accounts and records to the Secretary of State

(1) The Secretary of State may during the CVA, or after its full implementation or termination, require the supervisor to produce for inspection (either at the premises of the supervisor or elsewhere)—

(a) the supervisor's accounts and records in relation to the CVA; and

(b) copies of reports and summaries prepared in compliance with rule 2.41.

(2) The Secretary of State may require the supervisor's accounts and records to be audited and, if so, the supervisor must provide such further information and assistance as the Secretary of State requires for the purposes of audit.

NOTES

Commencement: 6 April 2017.

This rule derived from the Insolvency Rules 1986, SI 1986/1925, r 1.27.

[6.109]

2.43 Fees and expenses

The fees and expenses that may be incurred for the purposes of the CVA are—

(a) fees for the nominee's services agreed with the company (or, as the case may be, the administrator or liquidator) and disbursements made by the nominee before the decision approving the CVA takes effect under section 4A or paragraph 36 of Schedule A1;

(b) fees or expenses which—

(i) are sanctioned by the terms of the CVA, or

(ii) where they are not sanctioned by the terms of the CVA would be payable, or correspond to those which would be payable, in an administration or winding up.

NOTES

Commencement: 6 April 2017.

This rule derived from the Insolvency Rules 1986, SI 1986/1925, r 1.28.

[6.110]

2.44 Termination or full implementation of CVA

(1) Not more than 28 days after the full implementation or termination of the CVA the supervisor must deliver a notice that the CVA has been fully implemented or terminated to all the members and those creditors who are bound by the arrangement.

(2) The notice must state the date the CVA took effect and must be accompanied by a copy of a report by the supervisor which—

(a) summarises all receipts and payments in relation to the CVA;

(b) explains any departure from the terms of the CVA as it originally had effect;

(c) if the CVA has terminated, sets out the reasons why; and

(d) includes (if applicable) a statement as to the amount paid to any unsecured creditors by virtue of section 176A.

(3) The supervisor must within the 28 days mentioned above send to the registrar of companies and file with the court a copy of the notice to creditors and of the supervisor's report.

(4) The supervisor must not vacate office until after the copies of the notice and report have been delivered to the registrar of companies and filed with the court.

NOTES

Commencement: 6 April 2017.

This rule derived from the Insolvency Rules 1986, SI 1986/1925, r 1.29.

CHAPTER 7 TIME RECORDING INFORMATION

[Note: a document required by the Act or these Rules must also contain the standard contents set out in Part 1.]

[6.111]

2.45 Provision of information

(1) This rule applies where the remuneration of the nominee or the supervisor has been fixed on the basis of the time spent.

(2) A person who is acting, or has acted within the previous two years, as—

(a) a nominee in relation to a proposal; or

(b) the supervisor in relation to a CVA;

must, within 28 days of receipt of a request from a person mentioned in paragraph (3), deliver free of charge to that person a statement complying with paragraphs (4) and (5).

(3) The persons are—

Part 6 Insolvency Rules

(a) any director of the company; and
(b) where the proposal has been approved, any creditor or member.

(4) The statement must cover the period which—
(a) in the case of a person who has ceased to act as nominee or supervisor in relation to a company, begins with the date of appointment as nominee or supervisor and ends with the date of ceasing to act; and
(b) in any other case, consists of one or more complete periods of six months beginning with the date of appointment and ending most nearly before the date of receiving the request.

(5) The statement must set out—
(a) the total number of hours spent on the matter during that period by the nominee or supervisor, and any staff;
(b) for each grade of staff engaged on the matter, the average hourly rate at which work carried out by staff in that grade is charged; and
(c) the number of hours spent on the matter by each grade of staff during that period.

NOTES

Commencement: 6 April 2017.
This rule derived from the Insolvency Rules 1986, SI 1986/1925, r 1.55.

PART 3
ADMINISTRATION

CHAPTER 1 INTERPRETATION FOR THIS PART

[Note: a document required by the Act or these Rules must also contain the standard contents set out in Part 1.]

[6.112]
3.1 Interpretation for Part 3

In this Part—

"pre-administration costs" means fees charged, and expenses incurred by the administrator, or another person qualified to act as an insolvency practitioner in relation to the company, before the company entered administration but with a view to it doing so; and

"unpaid pre-administration costs" means pre-administration costs which had not been paid when the company entered administration.

NOTES

Commencement: 6 April 2017.
This rule derived from the Insolvency Rules 1986, SI 1986/1925, r 2.33(2A).

[6.113]
3.2 Proposed administrator's statement and consent to act

(1) References in this Part to a consent to act are to a statement by a proposed administrator headed "Proposed administrator's statement and consent to act" which contains the following—
(a) identification details for the company immediately below the heading;
(b) a certificate that the proposed administrator is qualified to act as an insolvency practitioner in relation to the company;
(c) the proposed administrator's IP number;
(d) the name of the relevant recognised professional body which is the source of the proposed administrator's authorisation to act in relation to the company;
(e) a statement that the proposed administrator consents to act as administrator of the company;
(f) a statement whether or not the proposed administrator has had any prior professional relationship with the company and if so a short summary of the relationship;
(g) the name of the person by whom the appointment is to be made or the applicant in the case of an application to the court for an appointment; and
(h) a statement that the proposed administrator is of the opinion that the purpose of administration is reasonably likely to be achieved in the particular case.

(2) The statement and consent to act must be authenticated and dated by the proposed administrator.

(3) Where a number of persons are proposed to be appointed to act jointly or concurrently as the administrator of a company, each must make a separate statement and consent to act.

NOTES

Commencement: 6 April 2017.
This rule derived from the Insolvency Rules 1986, SI 1986/1925, Sch 4, Fm 2.2.

CHAPTER 2 APPOINTMENT OF ADMINISTRATOR BY COURT

[Note: a document required by the Act or these Rules must also contain the standard contents set out in Part 1.]

[6.114]

3.3 Administration application (paragraph 12 of Schedule B1)

(1) An administration application in relation to a company must be headed "Administration application" and must identify the company immediately below the heading.

(2) The application must contain—

(a) the name of the applicant;

(b) a statement whether the application is being made by—

(i) the company under paragraph 12(1)(a) of Schedule B1,

(ii) the directors of the company under paragraph 12(1)(b) of Schedule B1,

(iii) a single creditor under paragraph 12(1)(c) of Schedule B1,

(iv) a creditor under paragraph 12(1)(c) of Schedule B1 on behalf of that creditor and others,

(v) the holder of a qualifying floating charge under paragraph 35 or 37 of Schedule B1 (specifying which),

(vi) the liquidator of the company under paragraph 38 of Schedule B1,

(vii) the supervisor of a CVA under section 7(4)(b), or

(viii) a designated officer of a magistrates' court under section 87A of the Magistrates' Courts Act 1980;

(c) if the application is made by a creditor on behalf of that creditor and others, the names of the others;

(d) if the application is made by the holder of a qualifying floating charge, details of the charge including the date of the charge, the date on which it was registered and the maximum amount if any secured by the charge;

(e) if the company is registered under the Companies Act—

(i) any issued and called-up capital, the number of shares into which the capital is divided, the nominal value of each share and the amount of capital paid up or treated as paid up; or

(ii) that it is a company limited by guarantee;

(f) particulars of the principal business carried on by the company;

(g) a statement whether the company is an Article 1.2 undertaking;

(h) a statement whether the proceedings flowing from the appointment will be main, secondary, territorial or [non-EU proceedings] and that the reasons for the statement are set out in the witness statement in support of the application made under rule 3.6;

(i) except where the applicant is the holder of a qualifying floating charge and is making the application under paragraph 35 of Schedule B1, a statement that the applicant believes, for the reasons set out in the witness statement in support of the application that the company is, or is likely to become, unable to pay its debts;

(j) the name and address of the proposed administrator;

(k) the address for service of the applicant;

(l) the statement that the applicant requests the court—

(i) to make an administration order in relation to the company,

(ii) to appoint the proposed person to be administrator, and

(iii) to make such ancillary order as the applicant may request, and such other order as the court thinks appropriate.

(3) The application must be authenticated by the applicant or the applicant's solicitor and dated.

NOTES

Commencement: 6 April 2017.

This rule derived from the Insolvency Rules 1986, SI 1986/1925, Sch 4, Fm 2.1.

Para (2): words in square brackets in sub-para (h) substituted by the Insolvency (England and Wales) and Insolvency (Scotland) (Miscellaneous and Consequential Amendments) Rules 2017, SI 2017/1115, rr 22, 30(6).

[6.115]

3.4 Administration application made by the directors

After an application by the directors for an administration order is filed it is to be treated for all purposes as an application by the company.

NOTES

Commencement: 6 April 2017.

This rule derived from the Insolvency Rules 1986, SI 1986/1925, r 2.3(2).

[6.116]

3.5 Administration application by the supervisor of a CVA

After an application by the supervisor of a CVA for an administration order in respect of the company has been served on the company as required by rule 3.8(3)(d) it is to be treated for all purposes as an application by the company.

NOTES

Commencement: 6 April 2017.

This rule derived from the Insolvency Rules 1986, SI 1986/1925, r 2.2(4).

[6.117]

3.6 Witness statement in support of administration application

(1) If an administration application is to be made by—

(a) the company, a witness statement must be made by one of the following stating that the person making the statement does so on behalf of the company—
 (i) one of the directors,
 (ii) the secretary of the company, or
 (iii) the supervisor of a CVA;

(b) the company's directors, a witness statement must be made by one of the following stating that the person making it does so on behalf of the directors—
 (i) one of the directors, or
 (ii) the secretary of the company;

(c) a single creditor, a witness statement must be made by—
 (i) that creditor, or
 (ii) a person acting under that creditor's authority;

(d) two or more creditors, a witness statement must be made by a person acting under the authority of them all, whether or not one of their number.

(2) In a case falling within paragraph (1)(c)(ii) or (d), the witness statement must state the nature of the authority of the person making it and the means of that person's knowledge of the matters to which the witness statement relates.

(3) The witness statement must contain—

(a) a statement of the company's financial position, specifying (to the best of the applicant's knowledge and belief) the company's assets and liabilities, including contingent and prospective liabilities;

(b) details of any security known or believed to be held by creditors of the company, and whether in any case the security is such as to confer power on the holder to appoint an administrative receiver or to appoint an administrator under paragraph 14 of Schedule B1;

(c) a statement that an administrative receiver has been appointed if that is the case;

(d) details of any insolvency proceedings in relation to the company, including any petition that has been presented for the winding up of the company so far as known to the applicant;

(e) where it is intended to appoint a number of persons as administrators, a statement of the matters relating to the exercise of their functions set out in paragraph 100(2) of Schedule B1;

(f) the reasons for the statement that the proceedings will be main, secondary, territorial or [non-EU proceedings]; and

(g) any other matters which, in the applicant's opinion, will assist the court in deciding whether to make such an order.

(4) Where the application is made by the holder of a qualifying floating charge under paragraph 35 or 37 of Schedule B1, the witness statement must give sufficient details to satisfy the court that the applicant is entitled to appoint an administrator under paragraph 14 of Schedule B1.

(5) Where the application is made under paragraph 37 or 38 of Schedule B1 in relation to a company in liquidation, the witness statement must also contain—

(a) details of the existing insolvency proceedings, the name and address of the liquidator, the date the liquidator was appointed and by whom;

(b) the reasons why it has subsequently been considered appropriate that an administration application should be made; and

(c) any other matters that would, in the applicant's opinion, assist the court in deciding whether to make provision in relation to matters arising in connection with the liquidation.

NOTES

Commencement: 6 April 2017.

This rule derived from the Insolvency Rules 1986, SI 1986/1925, rr 2.2–2.4, 2.11.

Para (3): words in square brackets in sub-para (f) substituted by the Insolvency (England and Wales) and Insolvency (Scotland) (Miscellaneous and Consequential Amendments) Rules 2017, SI 2017/1115, rr 22, 30(7).

[6.118]

3.7 Filing of application

(1) The application must be filed with the court together with the witness statement in support and the proposed administrator's consent to act.

(2) The court must fix a venue for the hearing of the application.

(3) There must also be filed, at the same time as the application or at any time after that, a sufficient number of copies of the application and the statement for service in accordance with rule 3.8.

(4) Each of the copies filed must—

(a) have applied to it the seal of the court;

(b) be endorsed with—
 (i) the date and time of filing, and
 (ii) the venue fixed by the court; and

(c) be delivered by the court to the applicant.

NOTES

Commencement: 6 April 2017.

This rule derived from the Insolvency Rules 1986, SI 1986/1925, r 2.5.

[6.119]

3.8 Service of application

(1) In this rule, references to the application are to a copy of the application and witness statement delivered by the court under rule 3.7(4)(c).

(2) Notification for the purposes of paragraph 12(2) of Schedule B1 must be by service of the application.

(3) The applicant must serve the application on the following (in addition to serving it on the persons referred to in paragraph 12(2)(a) to (c) of Schedule B1)—
- (a) any administrative receiver of the company;
- (b) if there is a petition pending for the winding up of the company on—
  - (i) the petitioner, and
  - (ii) any provisional liquidator;
- (c) any member State liquidator appointed in main proceedings in relation to the company;
- (d) the company, if the application is made by anyone other than the company or its directors;
- (e) any supervisor of a CVA in relation to the company; and
- (f) the proposed administrator.

(4) The certificate of service must be filed with the court as soon as reasonably practicable after service and in any event not later than the business day before the hearing of the application.

NOTES

Commencement: 6 April 2017.

This rule derived from the Insolvency Rules 1986, SI 1986/1925, r 2.6.

[6.120]

3.9 Notice to enforcement agents charged with distress or other legal process, etc

The applicant must as soon as reasonably practicable after filing the application deliver a notice of its being made to—
- (a) any enforcement agent or other officer who to the knowledge of the applicant is charged with distress or other legal process against the company or its property; and
- (b) any person who to the knowledge of the applicant has distrained against the company or its property.

NOTES

Commencement: 6 April 2017.

This rule derived from the Insolvency Rules 1986, SI 1986/1925, r 2.7.

[6.121]

3.10 Notice of other insolvency proceedings

After the application has been filed and until an order is made, it is the duty of the applicant to file with the court notice of the existence of any insolvency proceedings in relation to the company, as soon as the applicant becomes aware of them—
- (a) anywhere in the world, in the case of a company registered under the Companies Act in England and Wales;
- (b) in any EEA State (including the United Kingdom), in the case of a company incorporated in an EEA State other than the United Kingdom; or
- (c) in any member State other than Denmark, in the case of a company not incorporated in an EEA State.

NOTES

Commencement: 6 April 2017.

This rule derived from the Insolvency Rules 1986, SI 1986/1925, r 2.5.

[6.122]

3.11 Intervention by holder of qualifying floating charge (paragraph 36(1)(b) of Schedule B1)

(1) Where the holder of a qualifying floating charge applies to the court under paragraph 36(1)(b) of Schedule B1 to have a specified person appointed as administrator, the holder must produce to the court—
- (a) the written consent of the holder of any prior qualifying floating charge;
- (b) the proposed administrator's consent to act; and
- (c) sufficient evidence to satisfy the court that the holder is entitled to appoint an administrator under paragraph 14 of Schedule B1.

(2) If an administration order is made appointing the specified person, the costs of the person who made the administration application and of the applicant under paragraph 36(1)(b) of Schedule B1 are, unless the court orders otherwise, to be paid as an expense of the administration.

NOTES

Commencement: 6 April 2017.

This rule derived from the Insolvency Rules 1986, SI 1986/1925, r 2.10.

[6.123]
3.12 The hearing

(1) At the hearing of the administration application, any of the following may appear or be represented—

(a) the applicant;
(b) the company;
(c) one or more of the directors;
(d) any administrative receiver;
(e) any person who has presented a petition for the winding up of the company;
(f) the proposed administrator;
(g) any member State liquidator appointed in main proceedings in relation to the company;
(h) the holder of any qualifying floating charge;
(i) any supervisor of a CVA;
(j) with the permission of the court, any other person who appears to have an interest which justifies appearance.

(2) If the court makes an administration order, the costs of the applicant, and of any other person whose costs are allowed by the court, are payable as an expense of the administration.

NOTES

Commencement: 6 April 2017.
This rule derived from the Insolvency Rules 1986, SI 1986/1925, r 2.12.

[6.124]
3.13 The order

(1) Where the court makes an administration order the court's order must be headed "Administration order" and must contain the following—

(a) identification details for the proceedings;
(b) the name and title of the judge making the order;
(c) the address for service of the applicant;
(d) details of any other parties (including the company) appearing and by whom represented;
(e) an order that during the period the order is in force the affairs, business and property of the company is to be managed by the administrator;
(f) the name of the person appointed as administrator;
(g) an order that that person is appointed as administrator of the company;
(h) a statement that the court is satisfied either that the [EU Regulation] does not apply or that it does;
(i) where the [EU Regulation] does apply, a statement whether the proceedings are main, secondary or territorial proceedings;
(j) the date of the order (and if the court so orders the time); and
(k) such other provisions if any as the court thinks just.

(2) Where two or more administrators are appointed the order must also specify (as required by paragraph 100(2) of Schedule B1)—

(a) which functions (if any) are to be exercised by those persons acting jointly; and
(b) which functions (if any) are to be exercised by any or all of those persons.

NOTES

Commencement: 6 April 2017.
This rule derived from the Insolvency Rules 1986, SI 1986/1925, r 2.13, Sch 4, Fm 2.4B.
Para (1): words in square brackets in sub-paras (h), (i) substituted by the Insolvency (England and Wales) and Insolvency (Scotland) (Miscellaneous and Consequential Amendments) Rules 2017, SI 2017/1115, rr 22, 23(7).

[6.125]
3.14 Order on an application under paragraph 37 or 38 of Schedule B1

Where the court makes an administration order in relation to a company on an application under paragraph 37 or 38 of Schedule B1, the court must also include in the order—

(a) in the case of a liquidator appointed in a voluntary winding up, the removal of that liquidator from office;
(b) provision for payment of the expenses of the winding up;
(c) such provision as the court thinks just relating to—
  (i) any indemnity given to the liquidator,
  (ii) the release of the liquidator,
  (iii) the handling or realisation of any of the company's assets in the hands of or under the control of the liquidator, and
  (iv) other matters arising in connection with the winding up; and
(d) such other provisions if any as the court thinks just.

NOTES

Commencement: 6 April 2017.
This rule derived from the Insolvency Rules 1986, SI 1986/1925, r 2.13.

[6.126]

3.15 Notice of administration order

(1) If the court makes an administration order, it must as soon as reasonably practicable deliver two sealed copies of the order to the applicant.

(2) The applicant must as soon as reasonably practicable deliver a sealed copy of the order to the person appointed as administrator.

(3) If the court makes an order under sub-paragraph (d) or (f) of paragraph 13(1) of Schedule B1, it must give directions as to the persons to whom, and how, notice of that order is to be delivered.

NOTES

Commencement: 6 April 2017.

This rule derived from the Insolvency Rules 1986, SI 1986/1925, r 2.14.

CHAPTER 3 APPOINTMENT OF ADMINISTRATOR BY HOLDER OF FLOATING CHARGE

[Note: a document required by the Act or these Rules must also contain the standard contents set out in Part 1.]

[6.127]

3.16 Notice of intention to appoint

(1) This rule applies where the holder of a qualifying floating charge ("the appointer") gives a notice under paragraph 15(1)(a) of Schedule B1 of intention to appoint an administrator under paragraph 14 and files a copy of the notice with the court under paragraph 44(2).

(2) The notice filed with the court must be headed "Notice of intention to appoint an administrator by holder of qualifying floating charge" and must contain the following—

(a) identification details for the proceedings;
(b) the name and address of the appointer;
(c) a statement that the appointer intends to appoint an administrator of the company;
(d) the name and address of the proposed administrator;
(e) a statement that the appointer is the holder of the qualifying floating charge in question and that it is now enforceable;
(f) details of the charge, the date upon which it was registered and the maximum amount if any secured by the charge;
(g) a statement that the notice is being given in accordance with paragraph 15(1)(a) of Schedule B1 to the holder of every prior floating charge which satisfies paragraph 14(2) of that Schedule;
(h) the names and addresses of the holders of such prior floating charges and details of the charges;
(i) a statement whether the company is or is not subject to insolvency proceedings at the date of the notice, and details of the proceedings if it is;
(j) a statement whether the company is an Article 1.2 undertaking; and
(k) a statement whether the proceedings flowing from the appointment will be main, secondary, territorial or [non-EU proceedings] with reasons for the statement.

(3) The notice must be authenticated by the appointer or the appointer's solicitor and dated.

(4) The filing of the copy with the court under paragraph 44(2) of Schedule B1 must be done at the same time as notice is given in accordance with paragraph 15(1)(a).

(5) The giving of notice under paragraph 15(1)(a) must be by service of the notice.

NOTES

Commencement: 6 April 2017.

This rule derived from the Insolvency Rules 1986, SI 1986/1925, r 2.15, Sch 4, Fm 2.5B.

Para (2): words in square brackets in sub-para (k) substituted by the Insolvency (England and Wales) and Insolvency (Scotland) (Miscellaneous and Consequential Amendments) Rules 2017, SI 2017/1115, rr 22, 30(8).

[6.128]

3.17 Notice of appointment

(1) Notice of an appointment under paragraph 14 of Schedule B1 must be headed "Notice of appointment of an administrator by holder of a qualifying floating charge" and must contain—

(a) identification details for the proceedings;
(b) the name and address of the appointer;
(c) a statement that the appointer has appointed the person named as administrator of the company;
(d) the name and address of the person appointed as administrator;
(e) a statement that a copy of the administrator's consent to act accompanies the notice;
(f) a statement that the appointer is the holder of the qualifying floating charge in question and that it is now enforceable;
(g) details of the charge including the date of the charge, the date on which it was registered and the maximum amount if any secured by the charge;
(h) one of the following statements—
   (i) that notice has been given in accordance with paragraph 15(1)(a) of Schedule B1 to the holder of every prior floating charge which satisfies paragraph 14(2) of that Schedule, that two business days have elapsed from the date the last such notice was given (if more than one) and—

(aa) that a copy of every such notice was filed with the court under paragraph 44(2) of Schedule B1, and the date of that filing (or the latest date of filing if more than one), or

(bb) that a copy of every such notice accompanies the notice of appointment but was not filed with the court under paragraph 44(2) of Schedule B1,

(ii) that the holder of every such floating charge to whom notice was given has consented in writing to the making of the appointment and that a copy of every consent accompanies the notice of appointment,

(iii) that the holder of every such floating charge has consented in writing to the making of the appointment without notice having been given to all and that a copy of every consent accompanies the notice of appointment, or

(iv) that there is no such floating charge;

(i) a statement whether the company is or is not subject to insolvency proceedings at the date of the notice, and details of the proceedings if it is;

(j) a statement whether the company is an Article 1.2 undertaking;

(k) a statement whether the proceedings flowing from the appointment will be main, secondary, territorial or [non-EU proceedings] and the reasons for so stating; and

(l) a statement that the appointment is in accordance with Schedule B1.

(2) Where two or more administrators are appointed the notice must also specify (as required by paragraph 100(2) of Schedule B1)—

(a) which functions (if any) are to be exercised by those persons acting jointly; and

(b) which functions (if any) are to be exercised by any or all of those persons.

(3) The statutory declaration included in the notice in accordance with paragraph 18(2) of Schedule B1 must be made not more than five business days before the notice is filed with the court.

NOTES

Commencement: 6 April 2017.

This rule derived from the Insolvency Rules 1986, SI 1986/1925, r 2.16, Sch 4, Fm 2.6B.

Para (1): words in square brackets in sub-para (k) substituted by the Insolvency (England and Wales) and Insolvency (Scotland) (Miscellaneous and Consequential Amendments) Rules 2017, SI 2017/1115, rr 22, 30(9).

[6.129]

3.18 Filing of notice with the court

(1) Three copies of the notice of appointment must be filed with the court, accompanied by—

(a) the administrator's consent to act; and

(b) either—

(i) evidence that the appointer has given notice as required by paragraph 15(1)(a) of Schedule B1; or

(ii) copies of the written consent of all those required to give consent in accordance with paragraph 15(1)(b) of Schedule B1.

(2) The court must apply the seal of the court to the copies of the notice, endorse them with the date and time of filing and deliver two of the sealed copies to the appointer.

(3) The appointer must as soon as reasonably practicable deliver one of the sealed copies to the administrator.

(4) This rule is subject to rules 3.20 and 3.21 (appointment made out of court business hours).

NOTES

Commencement: 6 April 2017.

This rule derived from the Insolvency Rules 1986, SI 1986/1925, r 2.17.

[6.130]

3.19 Appointment by floating charge holder after administration application made

(1) This rule applies where the holder of a qualifying floating charge, after receiving notice that an administration application has been made, appoints an administrator under paragraph 14 of Schedule B1.

(2) The holder must as soon as reasonably practicable deliver a copy of the notice of appointment to—

(a) the person making the administration application; and

(b) the court in which the application has been made.

NOTES

Commencement: 6 April 2017.

This rule derived from the Insolvency Rules 1986, SI 1986/1925, r 2.18.

[6.131]

3.20 Appointment taking place out of court business hours: procedure

(1) When (but only when) the court is closed, the holder of a qualifying floating charge may file a notice of appointment with the court by—

(a) faxing it to a designated telephone number; or

(b) emailing it, or attaching it to an email, to a designated email address.

(2) The notice must specify the name of the court (and hearing centre if applicable) that has jurisdiction.

(3) The Lord Chancellor must designate the telephone number and email address.

(4) The Secretary of State must publish the designated telephone number and email address on the Insolvency Service webpages and deliver notice of them to any person requesting them from the Insolvency Service.

(5) The appointer must ensure that—

(a) a fax transmission report giving the time and date of the fax transmission and the telephone number to which the notice was faxed and containing a copy of the first page (in part or in full) of the document faxed is created by the fax machine that is used to fax the notice; or

(b) a hard copy of the email is created giving the time and date of the email and the address to which it was sent.

(6) The appointer must retain the fax transmission report or hard copy of the email.

(7) The appointer must deliver a notice to the administrator of the filing of the notice of appointment as soon as reasonably practicable.

(8) The copy of the faxed or emailed notice of appointment as received by the Courts Service must be delivered by the Lord Chancellor as soon as reasonably practicable to the court specified in the notice as the court having jurisdiction in the case, to be placed on the relevant court file.

(9) The appointer must take to the court on the next occasion that the court is open for business—

(a) three copies of the faxed or emailed notice of appointment;

(b) the fax transmission report or hard copy required by paragraph (5);

(c) all supporting documents referred to in the notice in accordance with rule 3.21(1) which are in the appointer's possession; and

(d) a statement providing reasons for the out-of-hours filing of the notice of appointment, including why it would have been damaging to the company or its creditors not to have so acted.

(10) The copies of the notice must be sealed by the court and endorsed with—

(a) the date and time when, according to the appointer's fax transmission report or hard copy of the email, the notice was faxed or sent; and

(b) the date when the notice and accompanying documents were delivered to the court.

(11) The court must deliver two of the sealed copies of the notice of appointment to the appointer.

(12) The appointer must, as soon as reasonably practicable, deliver one of the copies to the administrator.

(13) The reference—

(a) to the Insolvency Service in paragraph (4) means the Secretary of State acting by means of the Insolvency Service; and

(b) to the Courts Service in paragraph (8) means the Lord Chancellor acting by means of Her Majesty's Courts and Tribunals Service.

NOTES

Commencement: 6 April 2017.

This rule derived from the Insolvency Rules 1986, SI 1986/1925, r 2.19.

[6.132]

3.21 Appointment taking place out of court business hours: content of notice

(1) Notice of an appointment filed in accordance with rule 3.20 must be headed "Notice of appointment of an administrator by holder of a qualifying floating charge", identify the company immediately below the heading and must contain—

(a) the name and address of the appointer;

(b) a statement that the appointer has appointed the person named as administrator of the company;

(c) the name and address of the person appointed as administrator;

(d) a statement that the appointer is the holder of the qualifying floating charge in question and that it is now enforceable;

(e) details of the charge, the date upon which it was registered and the maximum amount secured by the charge;

(f) one of the following statements—

(i) that notice has been given in accordance with paragraph 15(1)(a) of Schedule B1 to the holder of every prior floating charge which satisfies paragraph 14(2) of that Schedule, that a copy of every such notice was filed with the court under paragraph 44(2) of that Schedule, the date of that filing (or the latest date of filing if more than one) and that two business days have elapsed [since notice was given under paragraph 15(1)(a) of Schedule B1],

(ii) that notice has been given in accordance with paragraph 15(1)(a) of Schedule B1 to the holder of every prior floating charge which satisfies paragraph 14(2) of that Schedule and that a copy of every such notice is in the appointer's possession but was not filed with the court under paragraph 44(2) of that Schedule,

(iii) that the holder of every such floating charge to whom notice was given has consented to the making of the appointment and that a copy of every consent [in writing] is in the appointer's possession,

(iv) that the holder of every such floating charge has consented to the making of the appointment without notice having been given to all and that a copy of every consent [in writing] is in the appointer's possession, or

(v) that there is no such floating charge;

(g) a statement whether the company is or is not subject to insolvency proceedings at the date of the notice, and details of the proceedings if it is;
(h) a statement whether the company is an Article 1.2 undertaking . . . ;
(i) a statement whether the proceedings flowing from the appointment will be main, secondary, territorial or [non-EU proceedings] [and that a statement of the reasons for stating this is in the appointer's possession];
(j) an undertaking that the following will be delivered to the court on the next occasion on which the court is open—
 (i) any document referred to in the notice in accordance with rule 3.20 as being in the appointer's possession,
 (ii) the fax transmission report or hard copy of the email, and
 (iii) the statement of reasons for out-of-hours filing;
(k) a statement that the proposed administrator consents to act; and
(l) a statement that the appointment is in accordance with Schedule B1.

(2) Where two or more administrators are appointed the notice must also specify (as required by paragraph 100(2) of Schedule B1)—
(a) which functions (if any) are to be exercised by those persons acting jointly; and
(b) which functions (if any) are to be exercised by any or all of those persons.

(3) The statutory declaration included in the notice in accordance with paragraph 18(2) of Schedule B1 must be made not more than five business days before the notice is filed with the court.

NOTES

Commencement: 6 April 2017.

This rule derived from the Insolvency Rules 1986, SI 1986/1925, r 2.19(1), Sch 4, Fm 2.7B.

Para (1): words in square brackets in sub-para (f)(i) substituted, words in square brackets in sub-para (f)(iii), (iv) inserted, words omitted from sub-para (h) revoked, and words in second pair of square brackets in sub-para (i) inserted, by the Insolvency (England and Wales) (Amendment) Rules 2017, SI 2017/366, rr 3, 12; words in first pair of square brackets in sub-para (i) substituted by the Insolvency (England and Wales) and Insolvency (Scotland) (Miscellaneous and Consequential Amendments) Rules 2017, SI 2017/1115, rr 22, 30(10).

[6.133]

3.22 Appointment taking place out of court business hours: legal effect

(1) The filing of a notice in accordance with rule 3.20 has the same effect for all purposes as the filing of a notice of appointment in accordance with rule 3.18.

(2) The appointment—
(a) takes effect from the date and time of the fax transmission or sending of the email; but
(b) ceases to have effect if the requirements of rule 3.20(9) are not completed on the next occasion the court is open for business.

(3) Where any question arises in relation to the date and time that the notice of appointment was filed with the court, it is a presumption capable of rebuttal that the date and time shown on the appointer's fax transmission report or hard copy of the email is the date and time at which the notice was filed.

NOTES

Commencement: 6 April 2017.

This rule derived from the Insolvency Rules 1986, SI 1986/1925, r 2.19(2).

CHAPTER 4 APPOINTMENT OF ADMINISTRATOR BY COMPANY OR DIRECTORS

[Note: a document required by the Act or these Rules must also contain the standard contents set out in Part 1.]

[6.134]

3.23 Notice of intention to appoint

(1) If paragraph 26 of Schedule B1 requires a notice of intention to appoint an administrator under paragraph 22 of that Schedule then the notice must be headed "Notice of intention to appoint an administrator by company or directors" and must contain the following—
(a) identification details for the proceedings;
(b) a statement that the company or the directors, as the case may be, intend to appoint an administrator of the company;
(c) the name and address of the proposed administrator;
(d) the names and addresses of the persons to whom notice is being given in accordance with paragraph 26(1) of Schedule B1;
(e) a statement that each of those persons is or may be entitled to appoint—
 (i) an administrative receiver of the company, or
 (ii) an administrator of the company under paragraph 14 of Schedule B1;
(f) a statement that the company has not within the preceding 12 months been—
 (i) in administration;
 (ii) the subject of a moratorium under Schedule A1 which ended on a date when no CVA was in force; or
 (iii) the subject of a CVA which was made during a moratorium under Schedule A1 and which ended prematurely within the meaning of section 7B;
(g) a statement that in relation to the company there is no—

(i) petition for winding up which has been presented but not yet disposed of,
(ii) administration application which has not yet been disposed of, or
(iii) administrative receiver in office;

(h) a statement whether the company is an Article 1.2 undertaking;

(i) a statement whether the proceedings flowing from the appointment will be main, secondary, territorial or [non-EU proceedings] and the reasons for so stating;

(j) a statement that the notice is accompanied (as appropriate) by either—
(i) a copy of the resolution of the company to appoint an administrator, or
(ii) a record of the decision of the directors to appoint an administrator; and

(k) a statement that if a recipient of the notice who is named in paragraph (e) wishes to consent in writing to the appointment that person may do so but that after five business days have expired from delivery of the notice the appointer may make the appointment although such a recipient has not replied.

(2) The notice must be accompanied by—
(a) a copy of the resolution of the company to appoint an administrator, where the company intends to make the appointment, or
(b) a record of the decision of the directors, where the directors intend to make the appointment.

(3) The giving of notice under paragraph 26(1) of Schedule B1 must be by service of the notice.

(4) If notice of intention to appoint is given under paragraph 26(1) of Schedule B1, a copy of the notice under paragraph 26(2) must be [sent] at the same time to—
(a) any enforcement agent or other officer who, to the knowledge of the person giving the notice, is charged with distress or other legal process against the company;
(b) any person who, to the knowledge of the person giving the notice, has distrained against the company or its property;
(c) any supervisor of a CVA; and
(d) the company, if the company is not intending to make the appointment.

(5) The giving of notice under paragraph 26(2) of Schedule B1 must be by service of the notice.

(6) The statutory declaration accompanying the notice in accordance with paragraph 27(2) of Schedule B1 must—
(a) if it is not made by the person making the appointment, indicate the capacity in which the person making the declaration does so; and
(b) be made not more than five business days before the notice is filed with the court.

NOTES

Commencement: 6 April 2017.

This rule derived from the Insolvency Rules 1986, SI 1986/1925, r 2.20, Sch 4, Fm 2.8B.

Para (1): words in square brackets substituted by the Insolvency (England and Wales) and Insolvency (Scotland) (Miscellaneous and Consequential Amendments) Rules 2017, SI 2017/1115, rr 22, 30(11).

Para (4): word in square brackets substituted by the Insolvency (England and Wales) (Amendment) Rules 2017, SI 2017/366, rr 3, 13.

[6.135]

3.24 Notice of appointment after notice of intention to appoint

(1) Notice of an appointment under paragraph 22 of Schedule B1 (when notice of intention to appoint has been given under paragraph 26) must be headed "Notice of appointment of an administrator by a company (where a notice of intention to appoint has been given)" or "Notice of appointment of an administrator by the directors of a company (where a notice of intention to appoint has been given)" and must contain—
(a) identification details for the company immediately below the heading;
(b) a statement that the company has, or the directors have, as the case may be, appointed the person named as administrator of the company;
(c) the name and address of the person appointed as administrator;
(d) a statement that a copy of the administrator's consent to act accompanies the notice;
(e) a statement that the company is, or the directors are, as the case may be, entitled to make an appointment under paragraph 22 of Schedule B1;
(f) a statement that the appointment is in accordance with Schedule B1;
(g) a statement whether the company is an Article 1.2 undertaking;
(h) a statement whether the proceedings flowing from the appointment will be main, secondary, territorial or [non-EU proceedings] and the reasons for so stating;
(i) a statement that the company has, or the directors have, as the case may be, given notice of their intention to appoint in accordance with paragraph 26(1) of Schedule B1, that a copy of the notice was filed with the court, the date of that filing and either—
(i) that five business days have elapsed [since notice was given under paragraph 26 of Schedule B1], or
(ii) that each person to whom the notice was given has consented to the appointment; and
(j) the date and time of the appointment.

(2) Where two or more administrators are appointed the notice must also specify (as required by paragraph 100(2) of Schedule B1)—
(a) which functions (if any) are to be exercised by those persons acting jointly; and
(b) which functions (if any) are to be exercised by any or all of those persons.

(3) The statutory declaration included in the notice in accordance with paragraph 29(2) of Schedule B1 must be made not more than five business days before the notice is filed with the court.

(4) If the statutory declaration is not made by the person making the appointment it must indicate the capacity in which the person making the declaration does so.

NOTES

Commencement: 6 April 2017.

This rule derived from the Insolvency Rules 1986, SI 1986/1925, r 2.23, 2.24, Sch 4, Fm 2.9B.

Para (1): words in square brackets in sub-para (h) substituted by the Insolvency (England and Wales) and Insolvency (Scotland) (Miscellaneous and Consequential Amendments) Rules 2017, SI 2017/1115, rr 22, 30(12); words in square brackets in sub-para (i) substituted by the Insolvency (England and Wales) (Amendment) Rules 2017, SI 2017/366, rr 3, 14.

[6.136]

3.25 Notice of appointment without prior notice of intention to appoint

(1) Notice of an appointment under paragraph 22 of Schedule B1 (when notice of intention to appoint has not been given under paragraph 26) must be headed "Notice of appointment of an administrator by a company (where a notice of intention to appoint has not been given)" or "Notice of appointment of an administrator by the directors of a company (where a notice of intention to appoint has not been given)" and must identify the company immediately below the heading.

(2) The notice must state the following—

- (a) that the company has, or the directors have, as the case may be, appointed the person specified under sub-paragraph (b) as administrator of the company;
- (b) the name and address of the person appointed as administrator;
- (c) that a copy of the administrator's consent to act accompanies the notice;
- (d) that the company is or the directors are, as the case may be, entitled to make an appointment under paragraph 22 of Schedule B1;
- (e) that the appointment is in accordance with Schedule B1;
- (f) that the company has not within the preceding 12 months been—
  - (i) in administration,
  - (ii) the subject of a moratorium under Schedule A1 which ended on a date when no CVA was in force, or
  - (iii) the subject of a CVA which was made during a moratorium under Schedule A1 and which ended prematurely within the meaning of section 7B;
- (g) that in relation to the company there is no—
  - (i) petition for winding up which has been presented but not yet disposed of,
  - (ii) administration application which has not yet been disposed of, or
  - (iii) administrative receiver in office;
- (h) whether the company is an Article 1.2 undertaking;
- (i) whether the proceedings flowing from the appointment will be main, secondary, territorial or [non-EU proceedings] and the reasons for so stating;
- (j) that the notice is accompanied by—
  - (i) a copy of the resolution of the company to appoint an administrator, or
  - (ii) a record of the decision of the directors to appoint an administrator; and
- (k) the date and time of the appointment.

(3) Where two or more administrators are appointed the notice must also specify (as required by paragraph 100(2) of Schedule B1)—

- (a) which functions (if any) are to be exercised by those persons acting jointly; and
- (b) which functions (if any) are to be exercised by any or all of those persons.

(4) The statutory declaration included in the notice in accordance with paragraphs 29(2) and 30 of Schedule B1 must—

- (a) if the declaration is made on behalf of the person making the appointment, indicate the capacity in which the person making the declaration does so; and
- (b) be made not more than five business days before the notice is filed with the court.

NOTES

Commencement: 6 April 2017.

This rule derived from the Insolvency Rules 1986, SI 1986/1925, r 2.25, Sch 4, Fm 2.8B.

Para (2): words in square brackets in sub-para (i) substituted by the Insolvency (England and Wales) and Insolvency (Scotland) (Miscellaneous and Consequential Amendments) Rules 2017, SI 2017/1115, rr 22, 30(13).

[6.137]

3.26 Notice of appointment: filing with the court

(1) Three copies of the notice of appointment must be filed with the court, accompanied by—

- (a) the administrator's consent to act; and
- (b) the written consent of all those persons to whom notice was given in accordance with paragraph 26(1) of Schedule B1 unless the period of notice set out in paragraph 26(1) has expired.

(2) Where a notice of intention to appoint an administrator has not been given, the copies of the notice of appointment must also be accompanied by—

- (a) a copy of the resolution of the company to appoint an administrator, where the company is making the appointment; or

(b) a record of the decision of the directors, where the directors are making the appointment.

(3) The court must apply to the copies the seal of the court, endorse them with the date and time of filing and deliver two of the sealed copies to the appointer.

(4) The appointer must as soon as reasonably practicable deliver one of the sealed copies to the administrator.

NOTES

Commencement: 6 April 2017.

This rule derived from the Insolvency Rules 1986, SI 1986/1925, r 2.26.

CHAPTER 5 NOTICE OF ADMINISTRATOR'S APPOINTMENT

[Note: a document required by the Act or these Rules must also contain the standard contents set out in Part 1.]

[6.138]

3.27 Publication of administrator's appointment

(1) The notice of appointment, to be published by the administrator as soon as reasonably practicable after appointment under paragraph 46(2)(b) of Schedule B1, must be gazetted and may be advertised in such other manner as the administrator thinks fit.

(2) The notice of appointment must state the following—

(a) that an administrator has been appointed;

(b) the date of the appointment; and

(c) the nature of the business of the company.

(3) The administrator must, as soon as reasonably practicable after the date specified in paragraph 46(6) of Schedule B1, deliver a notice of the appointment—

(a) if a receiver or an administrative receiver has been appointed, to that person;

(b) if there is pending a petition for the winding up of the company, to the petitioner (and also to the provisional liquidator, if any);

(c) to any enforcement officer, enforcement agent or other officer who, to the administrator's knowledge, is charged with distress or other legal process against the company or its property;

(d) to any person who, to the administrator's knowledge, has distrained against the company or its property; and

(e) any supervisor of a CVA.

(4) Where, under Schedule B1 or these Rules, the administrator is required to deliver a notice of the appointment to the registrar of companies or any other person, it must be headed "Notice of administrator's appointment" and must contain—

(a) the administrator's name and address and IP number;

(b) identification details for the proceedings; and

(c) a statement that the administrator has been appointed as administrator of the company;

(5) The notice must be authenticated and dated by the administrator.

NOTES

Commencement: 6 April 2017.

This rule derived from the Insolvency Rules 1986, SI 1986/1925, r 2.27.

CHAPTER 6 STATEMENT OF AFFAIRS

[Note: a document required by the Act or these Rules must also contain the standard contents set out in Part 1.]

[6.139]

3.28 Interpretation

In this Chapter—

"nominated person" means a relevant person who has been required by the administrator to make out and deliver to the administrator a statement of affairs; and

"relevant person" means a person mentioned in paragraph 47(3) of Schedule B1.

NOTES

Commencement: 6 April 2017.

This rule derived from the Insolvency Rules 1986, SI 1986/1925, r 2.28(1).

[6.140]

3.29 Statement of affairs: notice requiring and delivery to the administrator (paragraph 47(1) of Schedule B1)

[Note: see section 234(1) and 235(1) for the application of section 235 to administrators.]

(1) A requirement under paragraph 47(1) of Schedule B1 for one or more relevant persons to provide the administrator with a statement of the affairs of the company must be made by a notice delivered to each such person.

(2) The notice must be headed "Notice requiring statement of affairs" and must—

(a) require each nominated person to whom the notice is delivered to prepare and submit to the administrator a statement of the affairs of the company;
(b) inform each nominated person of—
 (i) the names and addresses of all others (if any) to whom the same notice has been delivered,
 [(ii) the requirement to deliver the statement of affairs to the administrator no later than eleven days after receipt of the notice requiring the statement of affairs;] and
 (iii) the effect of paragraph 48(4) of Schedule B1 (penalty for non-compliance) and section 235 (duty to co-operate with the office-holder).

(3) The administrator must inform each nominated person to whom notice is delivered that a document for the preparation of the statement of affairs capable of completion in compliance with rule 3.30 will be supplied if requested.

(4) The nominated person (or one of them, if more than one) must deliver the statement of affairs to the administrator with the statement of truth required by paragraph 47(2)(a) of Schedule B1 and a copy of each statement.

NOTES

Commencement: 6 April 2017.
This rule derived from the Insolvency Rules 1986, SI 1986/1925, r 2.28, Sch 4, Fm 2.14B.
Para (2): sub-para (b)(ii) substituted by the Insolvency (England and Wales) (Amendment) Rules 2017, SI 2017/366, rr 3, 15.

[6.141]
3.30 Statement of affairs: content (paragraph 47 of Schedule B1)

[Note: paragraph 47(2)(a) of Schedule B1 requires the statement of affairs to be verified by a statement of truth.]

(1) The statement of the company's affairs must be headed "Statement of affairs" and must—
(a) identify the company immediately below the heading; and
(b) state that it is a statement of the affairs of the company on a specified date, being the date on which it entered administration.

(2) The statement of affairs must contain (in addition to the matters required by paragraph 47(2) of Schedule B1)—
(a) a summary of the assets of the company, setting out the book value and the estimated realisable value of—
 (i) any assets subject to a fixed charge,
 (ii) any assets subject to a floating charge,
 (iii) any uncharged assets, and
 (iv) the total value of all the assets available for preferential creditors;
(b) a summary of the liabilities of the company, setting out—
 (i) the amount of preferential debts,
 (ii) an estimate of the deficiency with respect to preferential debts or the surplus available after paying the preferential debts,
 (iii) an estimate of the prescribed part, if applicable,
 (iv) an estimate of the total assets available to pay debts secured by floating charges,
 (v) the amount of debts secured by floating charges,
 (vi) an estimate of the deficiency with respect to debts secured by floating charges or the surplus available after paying the debts secured by fixed or floating charges,
 (vii) the amount of unsecured debts (excluding preferential debts),
 (viii) an estimate of the deficiency with respect to unsecured debts or the surplus available after paying unsecured debts,
 (ix) any issued and called-up capital, and
 (x) an estimate of the deficiency with respect to, or surplus available to, members of the company;
(c) a list of the company's creditors with the further particulars required by paragraph (3) indicating—
 (i) any creditors under hire-purchase, chattel leasing or conditional sales agreements, and
 (ii) any creditors claiming retention of title over property in the company's possession; and
(d) the name and address of each member of the company and the number, nominal value and other details of the shares held by each member.

(3) The list of creditors required by paragraph 47(2) of Schedule B1 and paragraph (2)(c) of this rule must contain the details required by paragraph (4) except where paragraphs (5) and (6) apply.

(4) The particulars required by paragraph (3) are as follows—
(a) the name and postal address of the creditor;
(b) the amount of the debt owed to the creditor;
(c) details of any security held by the creditor;
(d) the date on which the security was given; and
(e) the value of any such security.

(5) Paragraph (6) applies where the particulars required by paragraph (4) relate to creditors who are either—
(a) employees or former employees of the company; or
(b) consumers claiming amounts paid in advance for the supply of goods or services.

(6) Where this paragraph applies—

(a) the statement of affairs itself must state separately for each of paragraph (5)(a) and (b) the number of such creditors and the total of the debts owed to them; and
(b) the particulars required by paragraph (4) must be set out in separate schedules to the statement of affairs for each of paragraphs (5)(a) and (b).

NOTES

Commencement: 6 April 2017.
This rule derived from the Insolvency Rules 1986, SI 1986/1925, r 2.29, Sch 4, Fm 2.14B.

[6.142]
3.31 Statement of affairs: statement of concurrence

(1) The administrator may require a relevant person to deliver to the administrator a statement of concurrence.

(2) A statement of concurrence is a statement, verified by a statement of truth, that that person concurs in the statement of affairs submitted by a nominated person.

(3) The administrator must inform the nominated person who has been required to submit a statement of affairs that the relevant person has been required to deliver a statement of concurrence.

(4) The nominated person must deliver a copy of the statement of affairs to every relevant person who has been required to submit a statement of concurrence.

(5) A statement of concurrence—
(a) must identify the company; and
(b) may be qualified in relation to matters dealt with in the statement of affairs where the relevant person—
(i) is not in agreement with the statement of affairs,
(ii) considers the statement of affairs to be erroneous or misleading, or
(iii) is without the direct knowledge necessary for concurring with it.

(6) The relevant person must deliver the required statement of concurrence together with a copy to the administrator before the end of the period of five business days (or such other period as the administrator may agree) beginning with the day on which the relevant person receives the statement of affairs.

NOTES

Commencement: 6 April 2017.
This rule derived from the Insolvency Rules 1986, SI 1986/1925, r 2.29(2).

[6.143]
3.32 Statement of affairs: filing

(1) The administrator must as soon as reasonably practicable deliver to the registrar of companies a copy of—
(a) the statement of affairs; and
(b) any statement of concurrence.

(2) However, the administrator must not deliver to the registrar of companies with the statement of affairs any schedule required by rule 3.30(6)(b).

(3) The requirement to deliver the statement of affairs is subject to any order of the court made under rule 3.45 that the statement of affairs or a specified part must not be delivered to the registrar of companies.

NOTES

Commencement: 6 April 2017.
This rule derived from the Insolvency Rules 1986, SI 1986/1925, r 2.29(7).

[6.144]
3.33 Statement of affairs: release from requirement and extension of time

(1) The power of the administrator under paragraph 48(2) of Schedule B1 to revoke a requirement to provide a statement of affairs or to extend the period within which it must be submitted may be exercised upon the administrator's own initiative or at the request of a nominated person who has been required to provide it.

(2) The nominated person may apply to the court if the administrator refuses that person's request for a revocation or extension.

(3) On receipt of an application, the court may, if it is satisfied that no sufficient cause is shown for it, dismiss it without giving notice to any party other than the applicant.

(4) Unless the application is dismissed, the court must fix a venue for it to be heard.

(5) The applicant must, at least 14 days before any hearing, deliver to the administrator a notice stating the venue with a copy of the application and of any evidence on which the applicant intends to rely.

(6) The administrator may do either or both of the following—
(a) file a report of any matters which the administrator thinks ought to be drawn to the court's attention; or
(b) appear and be heard on the application.

(7) If a report is filed, the administrator must deliver a copy of it to the applicant not later than five business days before the hearing.

(8) Sealed copies of any order made on the application must be delivered by the court to the applicant and the administrator.

(9) On an application under this rule, the applicant's costs must be paid by the applicant in any event, but the court may order that an allowance of all or part of them be payable as an expense of the administration.

NOTES

Commencement: 6 April 2017.
This rule derived from the Insolvency Rules 1986, SI 1986/1925, r 2.31.

[6.145]
3.34 Statement of affairs: expenses

(1) The expenses of a nominated person which the administrator considers to have been reasonably incurred in making a statement of affairs or of a relevant person in making a statement of concurrence must be paid by the administrator as an expense of the administration.

(2) A decision by the administrator that expenses were not reasonably incurred (and are therefore not payable as an expense of the administration) may be appealed to the court.

NOTES

Commencement: 6 April 2017.
This rule derived from the Insolvency Rules 1986, SI 1986/1925, r 2.32.

CHAPTER 7 ADMINISTRATOR'S PROPOSALS

[Note: a document required by the Act or these Rules must also contain the standard contents set out in Part 1.]

[6.146]
3.35 Administrator's proposals: additional content

(1) The administrator's statement of proposals made under paragraph 49 of Schedule B1 (which is required by paragraph 49(4) to be delivered to the registrar of companies, creditors and members) must identify the proceedings and, in addition to the matters set out in paragraph 49, contain—

- (a) any other trading names of the company;
- (b) details of the administrator's appointment, including—
  - (i) the date of appointment,
  - (ii) the person making the application or appointment, and
  - (iii) where a number of persons have been appointed as administrators, details of the matters set out in paragraph 100(2) of Schedule B1 relating to the exercise of their functions;
- (c) the names of the directors and secretary of the company and details of any shareholdings in the company which they may have;
- (d) an account of the circumstances giving rise to the appointment of the administrator;
- (e) the date the proposals are delivered to the creditors;
- (f) if a statement of the company's affairs has been submitted—
  - (i) a copy or summary of it, except so far as an order under rule 3.45 or 3.46 limits disclosure of it, and excluding any schedule referred to in rule 3.30(6)(b), or the particulars relating to individual creditors contained in any such schedule,
  - (ii) details of who provided the statement of affairs, and
  - (iii) any comments which the administrator may have upon the statement of affairs;
- (g) if an order under rule 3.45 or 3.46 has been made—
  - (i) a statement of that fact, and
  - (ii) the date of the order;
- (h) if no statement of affairs has been submitted—
  - (i) details of the financial position of the company at the latest practicable date (which must, unless the court orders otherwise, be a date not earlier than that on which the company entered administration), and
  - (ii) an explanation as to why there is no statement of affairs;
- (i) a full list of the company's creditors in accordance with paragraph (2) if either—
  - (i) no statement of affairs has been submitted, or
  - (ii) a statement of affairs has been submitted but it does not include such a list, or the administrator believes the list included is less than full;
- (j) a statement of—
  - (i) how it is envisaged the purpose of the administration will be achieved, and
  - (ii) how it is proposed that the administration will end, including, where it is proposed that the administration will end by the company moving to a creditors' voluntary winding up—
    - (aa) details of the proposed liquidator,
    - (bb) where applicable, the declaration required by section 231, and
    - (cc) a statement that the creditors may, before the proposals are approved, nominate a different person as liquidator in accordance with paragraph 83(7)(a) of Schedule B1 and rule 3.60(6)(b);
- (k) a statement of either—
  - (i) the method by which the administrator has decided to seek a decision from creditors as to whether they approve the proposals, or

(ii) the administrator's reasons for not seeking a decision from creditors;

(l) the manner in which the affairs and business of the company—

(i) have, since the date of the administrator's appointment, been managed and financed, including, where any assets have been disposed of, the reasons for the disposals and the terms upon which the disposals were made, and

(ii) will, if the administrator's proposals are approved, continue to be managed and financed;

(m) a statement whether the proceedings are main, secondary, territorial or [non-EU proceedings]; and

(n) any other information that the administrator thinks necessary to enable creditors to decide whether or not to approve the proposals.

(2) The list of creditors required by paragraph (1)(i) must contain the details required by sub-paragraph (3) except where paragraphs (4) and (5) apply;

(3) The particulars required by paragraph (2) are as follows and must be given in this order—

(a) the name and postal address of the creditor;

(b) the amount of the debt owed to the creditor;

(c) details of any security held by the creditor;

(d) the date on which any such security was given; and

(e) the value of any such security;

(4) This paragraph applies where the particulars required by paragraph (3) relate to creditors who are either—

(a) employees or former employees of the company; or

(b) consumers claiming amounts paid in advance for the supply of goods and services.

(5) Where paragraph (4) applies—

(a) the list of creditors required by paragraph (1)(i) must state separately for each of paragraphs (4)(a) and (b) the number of the creditors and the total of the debts owed to them; and

(b) the particulars required by paragraph (3) in respect of such creditors must be set out in separate schedules to the list of creditors for each of sub-paragraphs (4)(a) and (b); and

(c) the administrator must not deliver any such schedule to the registrar of companies with the statement of proposals.

(6) Except where the administrator proposes a CVA in relation to the company, the statement made by the administrator under paragraph 49 of Schedule B1 must also include—

(a) to the best of the administrator's knowledge and belief, an estimate of the value of—

(i) the prescribed part (whether or not the administrator might be required under section 176A to make the prescribed part available for the satisfaction of unsecured debts), and

(ii) the company's net property (as defined by section 176A(6)); and

(b) a statement whether the administrator proposes to make an application to the court under section 176A(5) and if so the reason for the application.

(7) The administrator may exclude from an estimate under paragraph (6)(a) information the disclosure of which could seriously prejudice the commercial interests of the company.

(8) If the exclusion of such information affects the calculation of an estimate, the report must say so.

(9) The document containing the statement of proposals must include a statement of the basis on which it is proposed that the administrator's remuneration should be fixed by a decision in accordance with Chapter 4 of Part 18 of these Rules.

(10) Where applicable the document containing the statement of proposals must include—

(a) a statement of any pre-administration costs charged or incurred by the administrator or, to the administrator's knowledge, by any other person qualified to act as an insolvency practitioner in relation to the company;

(b) a statement that the payment of any unpaid pre-administration costs as an expense of the administration is—

(i) subject to approval under rule 3.52, and

(ii) not part of the proposals subject to approval under paragraph 53 of Schedule B1.

NOTES

Commencement: 6 April 2017.

This rule derived from the Insolvency Rules 1986, SI 1986/1925, r 2.33.

Para (1): words in square brackets in sub-para (m) substituted by the Insolvency (England and Wales) and Insolvency (Scotland) (Miscellaneous and Consequential Amendments) Rules 2017, SI 2017/1115, rr 22, 30(14).

[6.147]

3.36 Administrator's proposals: statement of pre-administration costs

A statement of pre-administration costs under rule 3.35(10)(a) must include—

(a) details of any agreement under which the fees were charged and expenses incurred, including the parties to the agreement and the date on which the agreement was made;

(b) details of the work done for which the fees were charged and expenses incurred;

(c) an explanation of why the work was done before the company entered administration and how it had been intended to further the achievement of an objective in paragraph 3(1) of Schedule B1 in accordance with sub-paragraphs (2) to (4) of that paragraph;

(d) a statement of the amount of the pre-administration costs, setting out separately—

(i) the fees charged by the administrator,
(ii) the expenses incurred by the administrator,
(iii) the fees charged (to the administrator's knowledge) by any other person qualified to act as an insolvency practitioner in relation to the company (and, if more than one, by each separately), and
(iv) the expenses incurred (to the administrator's knowledge) by any other person qualified to act as an insolvency practitioner in relation to the company (and, if more than one, by each separately);

(e) a statement of the amounts of pre-administration costs which have already been paid (set out separately as under sub-paragraph (d));
(f) the identity of the person who made the payment or, if more than one person made the payment, the identity of each such person and of the amounts paid by each such person set out separately as under sub-paragraph (d); and
(g) a statement of the amounts of unpaid pre-administration costs (set out separately as under sub-paragraph (d)).

NOTES

Commencement: 6 April 2017.

This rule derived from the Insolvency Rules 1986, SI 1986/1925, r 2.33(2A), (2B).

[6.148]

3.37 Advertising administrator's proposals and notices of extension of time for delivery of proposals (paragraph 49 of Schedule B1)

(1) A notice published by the administrator under paragraph 49(6) of Schedule B1 must—
(a) identify the proceedings and contain the registered office of the company;
(b) be advertised in such manner as the administrator thinks fit; and
(c) be published as soon as reasonably practicable after the administrator has delivered the statement of proposals to the company's creditors but no later than eight weeks (or such other period as may be agreed by the creditors or as the court may order) from the date on which the company entered administration.

(2) Where the court orders, on an application by the administrator under paragraph 107 of Schedule B1, an extension of the period in paragraph 49(5) of Schedule B1 for delivering copies of the statement of proposals, the administrator must as soon as reasonably practicable after the making of the order deliver a notice of the extension to—
(a) the creditors of the company;
(b) the members of the company of whose address the administrator is aware; and
(c) the registrar of companies.

(3) The notice must—
(a) identify the proceedings;
(b) state the date to which the court has ordered an extension; and
(c) contain the registered office of the company.

(4) The administrator is taken to comply with paragraph [(2)(b)] if the administrator publishes a notice complying with paragraph (5).

(5) The notice must—
(a) contain the information required by paragraph (3);
(b) be advertised in such manner as the administrator thinks fit;
(c) state that members may request in writing a copy of the notice of the extension, and state the address to which to write; and
(d) be published as soon as reasonably practicable after the administrator has delivered the notice of the extension to the company's creditors.

NOTES

Commencement: 6 April 2017.

This rule derived from the Insolvency Rules 1986, SI 1986/1925, r 2.33.

Para (4): figure in square brackets substituted by the Insolvency (England and Wales) and Insolvency (Scotland) (Miscellaneous and Consequential Amendments) Rules 2017, SI 2017/1115, rr 2, 4.

[6.149]

3.38 Seeking approval of the administrator's proposals

(1) This rule applies where the administrator is required by paragraph 51 of Schedule B1 to seek approval from the company's creditors of the statement of proposals made under paragraph 49 of that Schedule.

(2) The statement of proposals delivered under paragraph 49(4) of Schedule B1 must be accompanied by a notice to the creditors of the decision procedure in accordance with rule 15.8.

(3) The administrator may seek a decision using deemed consent in which case the requirements in rule 15.7 also apply to the notice.

(4) Where the administrator has made a statement under paragraph 52(1) of Schedule B1 and has not sought a decision on approval from creditors, the proposal will be deemed to have been approved unless a decision has been requested under paragraph 52(2) of Schedule B1.

(5) Where under paragraph (4) the proposal is deemed to have been approved the administrator must, as soon as reasonably practicable after the expiry of the period for requisitioning a decision set out in rule 15.18(2), deliver a notice of the date of deemed approval to the registrar of companies, the court and any creditor to whom the administrator has not previously delivered the proposal.

(6) The notice must contain—
- (a) identification details for the proceedings;
- (b) the name of the administrator;
- (c) the date the administrator was appointed; and
- (d) the date on which the statement of proposals was delivered to the creditors.

(7) A copy of the statement of proposals, with the statements required by rule 3.35(5), must accompany the notice given to the court and to any creditors to whom a copy of the statement of proposals has not previously been delivered.

NOTES

Commencement: 6 April 2017.
This rule derived from the Insolvency Rules 1986, SI 1986/1925, r 2.34.

[6.150]
3.39 Invitation to creditors to form a creditors' committee

(1) Where the administrator is required to seek a decision from the company's creditors under rule 3.38, the administrator must at the same time deliver to the creditors a notice inviting them to decide whether a creditors' committee should be established if sufficient creditors are willing to be members of the committee.

(2) The notice must also invite nominations for membership of the committee, such nominations to be received by the administrator by a date to be specified in the notice.

(3) The notice must state that any nominations—
- (a) must be delivered to the administrator by the specified date; and
- (b) can only be accepted if the administrator is satisfied as to the creditor's eligibility under rule 17.4.

(4) A notice under this rule must also be delivered to the creditors at any other time when the administrator seeks a decision from creditors and a creditors' committee has not already been established at that time.

NOTES

Commencement: 6 April 2017.

[6.151]
3.40 Notice of extension of time to seek approval

(1) Where the court orders an extension to the period set out in paragraph 51(2) of Schedule B1, the administrator must deliver a notice of the extension as soon as reasonably practicable to each person mentioned in paragraph 49(4) of Schedule B1.

(2) The notice must contain identification details for the proceedings and the date to which the court has ordered an extension.

(3) The administrator is taken to have complied with paragraph (1) as regards members of the company if the administrator publishes a notice complying with paragraph (4).

(4) The notice must—
- (a) be advertised in such manner as the administrator thinks fit;
- (b) state that members may request in writing a copy of the notice of the extension, and state the address to which to write; and
- (c) be published as soon as reasonably practicable after the administrator has delivered the notice of the extension to the company's creditors.

NOTES

Commencement: 6 April 2017.
This rule derived from the Insolvency Rules 1986, SI 1986/1925, r 2.34.

[6.152]
3.41 Notice of the creditors' decision on the administrator's proposals (paragraph 53(2))

(1) In addition to delivering a report to the court and the registrar of companies (in accordance with paragraph 53(2) of Schedule B1) the administrator must deliver a report to—
- (a) the company's creditors (accompanied by a copy of the statement of proposals, with the statement required by rule 3.35(10)(a) and (b), if it has not previously been delivered to the creditor); and
- (b) every other person to whom a copy of the statement of proposals was delivered.

(2) A report mentioned in paragraph (1) must contain—
- (a) identification details for the proceedings;
- (b) details of decisions taken by the creditors including details of any modifications to the proposals which were approved by the creditors; and
- (c) the date such decisions were made.

(3) A copy of the statement of proposals, with any statements required by rule 3.35(9) and (10), must accompany the report to the court.

NOTES

Commencement: 6 April 2017.

This rule derived from the Insolvency Rules 1986, SI 1986/1925, r 2.46.

[6.153]

3.42 Administrator's proposals: revision

(1) Where paragraph 54(1) of Schedule B1 applies, the statement of the proposed revision which is required to be delivered to the creditors must be delivered with a notice of the decision procedure in accordance with rule 15.8.

(2) The statement must identify the proceedings and include—
- (a) any other trading names of the company;
- (b) details of the administrator's appointment, including—
  - (i) the date of appointment, and
  - (ii) the person making the application or appointment;
- (c) the names of the directors and secretary of the company and details of any shareholdings in the company which they may have;
- (d) a summary of the original proposals and the reason or reasons for proposing a revision;
- (e) details of the proposed revision, including details of the administrator's assessment of the likely impact of the proposed revision upon creditors generally or upon each class of creditors;
- (f) where the proposed revision relates to the ending of the administration by a creditors' voluntary winding up and the nomination of a person to be the proposed liquidator of the company—
  - (i) details of the proposed liquidator,
  - (ii) where applicable, the declaration required by section 231, and
  - (iii) a statement that the creditors may, before the proposals are approved, nominate a different person as liquidator in accordance with paragraph 83(7)(a) of Schedule B1 and rule 3.60(6)(b); and
- (g) any other information that the administrator thinks necessary to enable creditors to decide whether or not to vote for the proposed revisions.

(3) The administrator may seek a decision using deemed consent in which case the requirements in rule 15.7 also apply to the notice.

(4) The period within which, subject to paragraph 54(3) of Schedule B1, the administrator must send a copy of the statement to every member of the company of whose address the administrator is aware is five business days after sending the statement of the proposed revision to the creditors.

(5) Notice under paragraph 54(3) and (4) of Schedule B1 must—
- (a) be advertised in such manner as the administrator thinks fit as soon as reasonably practicable after the administrator has sent the statement to the creditors; and
- (b) state that members may request in writing a copy of the proposed revision, and state the address to which to write.

[(6) A copy of the statement of revised proposals under rule 3.43(3) must be delivered to the registrar of companies not later than five days after the report under rule 3.43(1) is delivered.]

NOTES

Commencement: 6 April 2017.

This rule derived from the Insolvency Rules 1986, SI 1986/1925, r 2.45.

Para (6): added by the Insolvency (England and Wales) (Amendment) Rules 2017, SI 2017/366, rr 3, 16.

[6.154]

3.43 Notice of result of creditors' decision on revised proposals (paragraph 54(6))

(1) In addition to delivering a report to the court and the registrar of companies (in accordance with paragraph 54(6) of Schedule B1) the administrator must deliver a report to—
- (a) the company's creditors (accompanied by a copy of the original statement of proposals and the revised statement of proposals if the administrator had not delivered notice of the decision procedure or deemed consent procedure to the creditor); and
- (b) every other person to whom a copy of the original statement of proposals was delivered.

(2) A report mentioned in paragraph (1) must contain—
- (a) identification details for the proceedings;
- (b) the date of the revised proposals;
- (c) details of decisions taken by the creditors including details of any modifications to the revised proposals which were approved by the creditors; and
- (d) the date such decisions were made.

(3) A copy of the statement of revised proposals must accompany the notice to the court.

NOTES

Commencement: 6 April 2017.

This rule derived from the Insolvency Rules 1986, SI 1986/1925, r 2.46.

CHAPTER 8 LIMITED DISCLOSURE OF STATEMENTS OF AFFAIRS AND PROPOSALS

[Note: a document required by the Act or these Rules must also contain the standard contents set out in Part 1.]

[6.155]
3.44 Application of Chapter

This Chapter applies to the disclosure of information which would be likely to prejudice the conduct of the administration or might reasonably be expected to lead to violence against any person.

NOTES

Commencement: 6 April 2017.
This rule derived from the Insolvency Rules 1986, SI 1986/1925, r 2.30.

[6.156]
3.45 Orders limiting disclosure of statement of affairs etc

(1) If the administrator thinks that the circumstances in rule 3.44 apply in relation to the disclosure of—
- (a) the whole or part of the statement of the company's affairs;
- (b) any of the matters specified in rule 3.35(1)(h) and (i) (administrator's proposals); or
- (c) a statement of concurrence,

the administrator may apply to the court for an order in relation to the particular document or a specified part of it.

(2) The court may order that the whole of or a specified part of a document referred to in paragraph (1)(a) to (c) must not be delivered to the registrar of companies or, in the case of the statement of proposals, to creditors or members of the company.

(3) The administrator must as soon as reasonably practicable deliver to the registrar of companies—
- (a) a copy of the order;
- (b) the statement of affairs, statement of proposals and any statement of concurrence to the extent provided by the order; and
- (c) if the order relates to the statement of proposals, an indication of the nature of the matter in relation to which the order was made.

(4) If the order relates to the statement of proposals, the administrator must as soon as reasonably practicable also deliver to the creditors and members of the company—
- (a) the statement of proposals to the extent provided by the order; and
- (b) an indication of the nature of the matter in relation to which the order was made.

NOTES

Commencement: 6 April 2017.
This rule derived from the Insolvency Rules 1986, SI 1986/1925, rr 2.30, 2.33A.

[6.157]
3.46 Order for disclosure by administrator

(1) A creditor may apply to the court for an order that the administrator disclose any of the following in relation to which an order has been made under rule 3.45(2)—
- (a) a statement of affairs;
- (b) a specified part of it;
- (c) a part of a statement of proposals; or
- (d) statement of concurrence.

(2) The application must be supported by a witness statement.

(3) The applicant must deliver to the administrator notice of the application at least three business days before the hearing.

(4) In an order for disclosure, the court may include conditions as to confidentiality, duration, the scope of the order in the event of any change of circumstances or such other matters as it thinks just.

NOTES

Commencement: 6 April 2017.
This rule derived from the Insolvency Rules 1986, SI 1986/1925, r 2.30(4).

[6.158]
3.47 Rescission or amendment of order for limited disclosure

(1) If there is a material change in circumstances rendering an order for limited disclosure under rule 3.45(2) wholly or partially unnecessary, the administrator must, as soon as reasonably practicable after the change, apply to the court for the order to be rescinded or amended.

(2) If the court makes such an order, the administrator must as soon as reasonably practicable deliver to the registrar of companies—
- (a) a copy of the order; and
- (b) the statement of affairs, the statement of proposals and any statement of concurrence to the extent provided by the order.

(3) If the order relates to the statement of proposals, the administrator must as soon as reasonably practicable also deliver to the creditors and members the statement of proposals to the extent allowed by the order.

NOTES

Commencement: 6 April 2017.

This rule derived from the Insolvency Rules 1986, SI 1986/1925, r 2.30(7).

[6.159]

3.48 Publication etc of statement of affairs or statement of proposals

(1) CPR Part 31 does not apply to an application under rule 3.45, 3.46 or 3.47.

(2) If, after the administrator has sent a statement of proposals under paragraph 49(4) of Schedule B1, a statement of affairs is delivered to the registrar of companies in accordance with rule 3.47(2) as the result of the rescission or amendment of an order, the administrator must deliver to the creditors a copy or summary of the statement of affairs as delivered to the registrar of companies.

(3) The administrator is taken to comply with the requirements for delivery to members of the company in rule 3.45(4) or 3.47(3) if the administrator publishes the required notice.

(4) The required notice must—

- (a) be advertised in such manner as the administrator thinks fit;
- (b) state that members can request in writing—
  - (i) a copy of the statement of proposals to the extent provided by the order, and
  - (ii) an indication of the nature of the matter in relation to which the order was made;
- (c) state the address to which such a written request is to be made; and
- (d) be published as soon as reasonably practicable after the administrator has delivered the statement of proposals to the extent provided by the order to the company's creditors.

NOTES

Commencement: 6 April 2017.

This rule derived from the Insolvency Rules 1986, SI 1986/1925, r 2.30(8)–(10).

CHAPTER 9 DISPOSAL OF CHARGED PROPERTY

[Note: a document required by the Act or these Rules must also contain the standard contents set out in Part 1.]

[6.160]

3.49 Disposal of charged property

(1) This rule applies where the administrator applies to the court under paragraph 71 or 72 of Schedule B1 for authority to dispose of—

- (a) property which is subject to a security other than a floating charge; or
- (b) goods in the possession of the company under a hire-purchase agreement.

(2) The court must fix a venue for the hearing of the application.

(3) As soon as reasonably practicable after the court has done so, the administrator must deliver notice of the venue to the holder of the security or the owner of the goods.

(4) If an order is made under paragraph 71 or 72 of Schedule B1, the court must deliver two sealed copies to the administrator.

(5) The administrator must deliver—

- (a) one of the sealed copies to the holder of the security or the owner of the goods; and
- (b) a copy of the sealed order to the registrar of companies.

NOTES

Commencement: 6 April 2017.

This rule derived from the Insolvency Rules 1986, SI 1986/1925, r 2.66.

CHAPTER 10 EXPENSES OF THE ADMINISTRATION

[Note: a document required by the Act or these Rules must also contain the standard contents set out in Part 1.]

[6.161]

3.50 Expenses

(1) All fees, costs, charges and other expenses incurred in the course of the administration are to be treated as expenses of the administration.

(2) The expenses associated with the prescribed part must be paid out of the prescribed part.

(3) The cost of the security required by section 390(3) for the proper performance of the administrator's functions is an expense of the administration.

(4) For the purposes of paragraph 99 of Schedule B1, a former administrator's remuneration and expenses comprise all the items in rule 3.51(2).

NOTES

Commencement: 6 April 2017.

This rule derived from the Insolvency Rules 1986, SI 1986/1925, rr 2.67, 12.2.

[6.162]
3.51 Order of priority

(1) Where there is a former administrator, the items in paragraph 99 of Schedule B1 are payable in priority to the expenses in this rule.

(2) Subject to paragraph (1) and to any court order under paragraph (3) the expenses of the administration are payable in the following order of priority—

(a) expenses properly incurred by the administrator in performing the administrator's functions;
(b) the cost of any security provided by the administrator in accordance with the Act or these Rules;
(c) where an administration order was made, the costs of the applicant and any person appearing on the hearing of the application whose costs were allowed by the court;
(d) where the administrator was appointed otherwise than by order of the court—
    (i) the costs and expenses of the appointer in connection with the making of the appointment, and
    (ii) the costs and expenses incurred by any other person in giving notice of intention to appoint an administrator;
(e) any amount payable to a person in respect of assistance in the preparation of a statement of affairs or statement of concurrence;
(f) any allowance made by order of the court in respect of the costs on an application for release from the obligation to submit a statement of affairs or deliver a statement of concurrence;
(g) any necessary disbursements by the administrator in the course of the administration (including any [costs referred to in Articles 30 or 59 of the EU Regulation and] expenses incurred by members of the creditors' committee or their representatives and allowed for by the administrator under rule 17.24, but not including any payment of corporation tax in circumstances referred to in sub-paragraph (j) below);
(h) the remuneration or emoluments of any person who has been employed by the administrator to perform any services for the company, as required or authorised under the Act or these Rules;
(i) the administrator's remuneration the basis of which has been fixed under Part 18 and unpaid pre-administration costs approved under rule 3.52; and
(j) the amount of any corporation tax on chargeable gains accruing on the realisation of any asset of the company (irrespective of the person by whom the realisation is effected).

(3) If the assets are insufficient to satisfy the liabilities, the court may make an order as to the payment out of the assets of the expenses incurred in the administration in such order of priority as the court thinks just.

NOTES

Commencement: 6 April 2017.

This rule derived from the Insolvency Rules 1986, SI 1986/1925, r 2.67.

Para (2): words in square brackets in sub-para (g) inserted by the Insolvency Amendment (EU 2015/848) Regulations 2017, SI 2017/702, regs 2, 3, Schedule, Pt 2, paras 32, 37, as from 26 June 2017, except in relation to proceedings opened before that date.

[6.163]
3.52 Pre-administration costs

(1) Where the administrator has made a statement of pre-administration costs under rule 3.35(10)(a), the creditors' committee may determine whether and to what extent the unpaid pre-administration costs set out in the statement are approved for payment.

(2) Paragraph (3) applies where—

(a) there is no creditors' committee;
(b) there is a creditors' committee but it does not make the necessary determination; or
(c) the creditors' committee does make the necessary determination but the administrator or other insolvency practitioner who has charged fees or incurred expenses as pre-administration costs considers the amount determined to be insufficient.

(3) When this paragraph applies, determination of whether and to what extent the unpaid pre-administration costs are approved for payment must be—

(a) by a decision of the creditors through a decision procedure; or
(b) in a case where the administrator has made a statement under paragraph 52(1)(b) of Schedule B1, by—
    (i) the consent of each of the secured creditors, or
    (ii) if the administrator has made, or intends to make, a distribution to preferential creditors, by—
        (aa) the consent of each of the secured creditors, and
        (bb) a decision of the preferential creditors in a decision procedure.

(4) The administrator must call a meeting of the creditors' committee or seek a decision of creditors by a decision procedure if so requested for the purposes of paragraphs (1) to (3) by another insolvency practitioner who has charged fees or incurred expenses as pre-administration costs; and the administrator must deliver notice of the meeting or decision procedure within 28 days of receipt of the request.

(5) The administrator (where the fees were charged or expenses incurred by the administrator) or other insolvency practitioner (where the fees were charged or expenses incurred by that practitioner) may apply to the court for a determination of whether and to what extent the unpaid pre-administration costs are approved for payment if either—

(a) there is no determination under paragraph (1) or (3); or

(b) there is such a determination but the administrator or other insolvency practitioner who has charged fees or incurred expenses as pre-administration costs considers the amount determined to be insufficient.

(6) Where there is a creditors' committee the administrator or other insolvency practitioner must deliver at least 14 days' notice of the hearing to the members of the committee; and the committee may nominate one or more of its members to appear, or be represented, and to be heard on the application.

(7) If there is no creditors' committee, notice of the application must be delivered to such one or more of the company's creditors as the court may direct, and those creditors may nominate one or more of their number to appear or be represented, and to be heard on the application.

(8) The court may, if it appears to be a proper case, order the costs of the application, including the costs of any member of the creditors' committee appearing or being represented on it, or of any creditor so appearing or being represented, to be paid as an expense of the administration.

(9) Where the administrator fails to call a meeting of the creditors' committee or seek a decision from creditors in accordance with paragraph (4), the other insolvency practitioner may apply to the court for an order requiring the administrator to do so.

NOTES

Commencement: 6 April 2017.
This rule derived from the Insolvency Rules 1986, SI 1986/1925, r 2.67A.

CHAPTER 11 EXTENSION AND ENDING OF ADMINISTRATION

[Note: a document required by the Act or these Rules must also contain the standard contents set out in Part 1.]

[6.164]
3.53 Interpretation

"Final progress report" means in this Chapter, and in Part 18 in so far as it relates to final progress reports in an administration, a progress report which includes a summary of—

(a) the administrator's proposals;
(b) any major amendments to, or deviations from, those proposals;
(c) the steps taken during the administration; and
(d) the outcome.

NOTES

Commencement: 6 April 2017.
This rule derived from the Insolvency Rules 1986, SI 1986/1925, r 2.110.

[6.165]
3.54 Application to extend an administration and extension by consent (paragraph 76(2) of Schedule B1)

(1) This rule applies where an administrator makes an application to the court for an order, or delivers a notice to the creditors requesting their consent, to extend the administrator's term of office under paragraph 76(2) of Schedule B1.

(2) The application or the notice must state the reasons why the administrator is seeking an extension.

(3) A request to the creditors may contain or be accompanied by a notice that if the extension is granted a notice of the extension will be made available for viewing and downloading on a website and that no other notice will be delivered to the creditors.

(4) Where the result of a request to the creditors is to be made available for viewing and downloading on a website, the notice must comply with the requirements for use of a website to deliver documents set out in rule 1.49(2)(a) to (c), (3) and (4) with any necessary modifications and rule 1.49(5)(a) applies to determine the time of delivery of the document.

(5) Where the court makes an order extending the administrator's term of office, the administrator must as soon as reasonably practicable deliver to the creditors a notice of the order together with the reasons for seeking the extension given in the application to the court.

(6) Where the administrator's term of office has been extended with the consent of creditors, the administrator must as soon as reasonably practicable deliver a notice of the extension to the creditors except where paragraph (3) applies.

(7) The notices which paragraph 78(5)(b) of Schedule B1 require to be delivered to the registrar of companies must also identify the proceedings.

NOTES

Commencement: 6 April 2017.
This rule derived from the Insolvency Rules 1986, SI 1986/1925, r 2.112.

[6.166]
3.55 Notice of automatic end of administration (paragraph 76 of Schedule B1)

(1) This rule applies where—

(a) the appointment of an administrator has ceased to have effect; and
(b) the administrator is not required by any other rule to give notice of that fact.

(2) The former administrator must, as soon as reasonably practicable, and in any event within five business days of the date on which the appointment has ceased, deliver to the registrar of companies and file with the court a notice accompanied by a final progress report.

(3) The notice must be headed "Notice of automatic end of administration" and identify the company immediately below the heading.

(4) The notice must contain—

- (a) identification details for the proceedings;
- (b) the former administrator's name and address;
- (c) a statement that that person had been appointed administrator of the company;
- (d) the date of the appointment;
- (e) the name of the person who made the appointment or the administration application, as the case may be;
- (f) a statement that the appointment has ceased to have effect;
- (g) the date on which the appointment ceased to have effect; and
- (h) a statement that a copy of the final progress report accompanies the notice.

(5) The notice must be authenticated by the administrator and dated.

(6) A copy of the notice and accompanying final progress report must be delivered as soon as reasonably practicable to—

- (a) the directors of the company; and
- (b) all other persons to whom notice of the administrator's appointment was delivered.

(7) A former administrator who makes default in complying with this rule is guilty of an offence and liable to a fine and, for continued contravention, to a daily default fine.

NOTES

Commencement: 6 April 2017.

This rule derived from the Insolvency Rules 1986, SI 1986/1925, r 2.111.

[6.167]

3.56 Notice of end of administration when purposes achieved (paragraph 80(2) of Schedule B1)

(1) Where an administrator who was appointed under paragraph 14 or 22 of Schedule B1 thinks that the purpose of administration has been sufficiently achieved, the notice ("notice of end of administration") which the administrator may file with the court and deliver to the registrar of companies under paragraph 80(2) of Schedule B1 must be headed "Notice of end of administration" and identify the company immediately below the heading.

(2) The notice must contain—

- (a) identification details for the proceedings;
- (b) the administrator's name and address;
- (c) a statement that that person has been appointed administrator of the company;
- (d) the date of the appointment;
- (e) the name of the person who made the appointment or the administration application, as the case may be;
- (f) a statement that the administrator thinks that the purpose of the administration has been sufficiently achieved;
- (g) a statement that a copy of the final progress report accompanies the notice; and
- (h) a statement that the administrator is filing the notice with the court and delivering a copy to the registrar of companies.

(3) The notice must be authenticated by the administrator and dated.

(4) The notice must be accompanied by a final progress report.

(5) The notice filed with the court must also be accompanied by a copy of the notice.

(6) The court must endorse the notice and the copy with the date and time of filing, seal the copy and deliver it to the administrator.

(7) The prescribed period within which the administrator, under paragraph 80(4) of Schedule B1, must send a copy of the notice to the creditors is five business days from the filing of the notice.

(8) The copy notice sent to creditors must be accompanied by the final progress report.

(9) The administrator must within the same period deliver a copy of the notice and the final progress report to all other persons (other than the creditors and the registrar of companies) to whom notice of the administrator's appointment was delivered.

(10) The administrator is taken to have complied with the requirement in paragraph 80(4) of Schedule B1 to give notice to the creditors if, within five business days of filing the notice with the court, the administrator gazettes a notice which—

- (a) states that the administration has ended, and the date on which it ended;
- (b) undertakes that the administrator will provide a copy of the notice of end of administration to any creditor of the company who applies in writing; and
- (c) specifies the address to which to write.

(11) The Gazette notice may be advertised in such other manner as the administrator thinks fit.

NOTES

Commencement: 6 April 2017.

This rule derived from the Insolvency Rules 1986, SI 1986/1925, r 2.113.

[6.168]
3.57 Administrator's application for order ending administration (paragraph 79 of Schedule B1)

(1) An application to court by the administrator under paragraph 79 of Schedule B1 for an order ending an administration must be accompanied by—

(a) a progress report for the period since—
  (i) the last progress report (if any), or
  (ii) if there has been no previous progress report, the date on which the company entered administration;

(b) a statement indicating what the administrator thinks should be the next steps for the company (if applicable); and

(c) where the administrator makes the application because of a requirement decided by the creditors, a statement indicating with reasons whether or not the administrator agrees with the requirement.

(2) Where the application is made other than because of a requirement by a decision of the creditors—

(a) the administrator must, at least five business days before the application is made, deliver notice of the administrator's intention to apply to court to—
  (i) the person who made the administration application or appointment, and
  (ii) the creditors; and

(b) the application must be accompanied by—
  (i) a statement that notice has been delivered to the creditors, and
  (ii) copies of any response from creditors to that notice.

(3) Where the application is in conjunction with a petition under section 124 for an order to wind up the company, the administrator must, at least five business days before the application is filed, deliver notice to the creditors as to whether the administrator intends to seek appointment as liquidator.

NOTES

Commencement: 6 April 2017.

This rule derived from the Insolvency Rules 1986, SI 1986/1925, r 2.114.

[6.169]
3.58 Creditor's application for order ending administration (paragraph 81 of Schedule B1)

(1) Where a creditor applies to the court under paragraph 81 of Schedule B1 for an order ending an administration, a copy of the application must be delivered, not less than five business days before the date fixed for the hearing, to—

(a) the administrator;

(b) the person who made the administration application or appointment; and

(c) where the appointment was made under paragraph 14 of Schedule B1, the holder of the floating charge by virtue of which the appointment was made (if different to (b)).

(2) Any of those persons may appear at the hearing of the application.

(3) Where the court makes an order under paragraph 81 ending the administration, the court must deliver a copy of the order to the administrator.

NOTES

Commencement: 6 April 2017.

This rule derived from the Insolvency Rules 1986, SI 1986/1925, r 2.115.

[6.170]
3.59 Notice by administrator of court order

Where the court makes an order ending the administration, the administrator must as soon as reasonably practicable deliver a copy of the order and of the final progress report to—

(a) the registrar of companies;

(b) the directors of the company; and

(c) all other persons to whom notice of the administrator's appointment was delivered.

NOTES

Commencement: 6 April 2017.

This rule derived from the Insolvency Rules 1986, SI 1986/1925, r 2.116.

[6.171]
3.60 Moving from administration to creditors' voluntary winding up (paragraph 83 of Schedule B1)

[Note: the information referred to in paragraph (5) is required to be included in the first progress report of the liquidator. See rule 18.3(5).]

(1) This rule applies where the administrator delivers to the registrar of companies a notice under paragraph 83(3) of Schedule B1 of moving from administration to creditors' voluntary winding up.

(2) The notice must contain—

(a) identification details for the proceedings;

(b) the name of the person who made the appointment or the administration application, as the case may be; and

(c) the name and IP number of the proposed liquidator.

(3) The notice to the registrar of companies must be accompanied by a copy of the administrator's final progress report.

(4) A copy of the notice and the final progress report must be sent as soon as reasonably practicable after delivery of the notice to all those persons to whom notice of the administrator's appointment was delivered in addition to the creditors (as required by paragraph 83(5)(b)).

(5) The person who ceases to be administrator on the registration of the notice must inform the person who becomes liquidator of anything which happens after the date of the final progress report and before the registration of the notice which the administrator would have included in the final report had it happened before the date of the report.

(6) For the purposes of paragraph 83(7)(a) of Schedule B1, a person is nominated by the creditors as liquidator by—

- (a) their approval of the statement of the proposed liquidator in the administrator's proposals or revised proposals; or
- (b) their nomination of a different person, through a decision procedure, before their approval of the proposals or revised proposals.

(7) Where the creditors nominate a different person, the nomination must, where applicable, include the declaration required by section 231.

NOTES

Commencement: 6 April 2017.

This rule derived from the Insolvency Rules 1986, SI 1986/1925, r 2.117A.

[6.172]

3.61 Moving from administration to dissolution (paragraph 84 of Schedule B1)

(1) This rule applies where the administrator delivers to the registrar of companies a notice under paragraph 84(1) of Schedule B1 of moving from administration to dissolution.

(2) The notice must identify the proceedings.

(3) As soon as reasonably practicable after sending the notice, the administrator must deliver a copy of the notice to all persons to whom notice of the administrator's appointment was delivered (in addition to the creditors mentioned in paragraph 84(5)(b) [but excluding opted-out creditors]).

(4) A final progress report must accompany the notice to the registrar of companies and every copy filed or otherwise delivered.

(5) Where a court makes an order under paragraph 84(7) of Schedule B1 it must, where the applicant is not the administrator, deliver a copy of the order to the administrator.

(6) The administrator must deliver a copy of the order to the registrar of companies with the notice required by paragraph 84(8).

NOTES

Commencement: 6 April 2017.

This rule derived from the Insolvency Rules 1986, SI 1986/1925, r 2.118.

Para (3): words in square brackets inserted by the Insolvency (England and Wales) and Insolvency (Scotland) (Miscellaneous and Consequential Amendments) Rules 2017, SI 2017/1115, rr 2, 5.

CHAPTER 12 REPLACING THE ADMINISTRATOR

[Note: a document required by the Act or these Rules must also contain the standard contents set out in Part 1.]

[6.173]

3.62 Grounds for resignation

(1) The administrator may resign—

- (a) on grounds of ill health;
- (b) because of the intention to cease to practise as an insolvency practitioner; or
- (c) because the further discharge of the duties of administrator is prevented or made impractical by—
  - (i) a conflict of interest, or
  - (ii) a change of personal circumstances.

(2) The administrator may, with the permission of the court, resign on other grounds.

NOTES

Commencement: 6 April 2017.

This rule derived from the Insolvency Rules 1986, SI 1986/1925, r 2.119.

[6.174]

3.63 Notice of intention to resign

(1) The administrator must give at least five business days' notice of intention—

- (a) to resign in a case falling within rule 3.62(1); or
- (b) to apply for the court's permission to resign in a case falling within rule 3.62(2).

(2) The notice must contain—

- (a) identification details for the proceedings;

Part 6 Insolvency Rules

(b) the date of the appointment of the administrator;
(c) the name of the person who made the appointment or the administration application, as the case may be.

(3) The notice must also contain—
(a) the date with effect from which the administrator intends to resign; or
(b) where the administrator was appointed by an administration order, the date on which the administrator intends to file with the court an application for permission to resign.

(4) The notice must be delivered—
(a) to any continuing administrator of the company;
(b) to the creditors' committee (if any);
(c) if there is neither a continuing administrator nor a creditors' committee, to—
  (i) the company, and
  (ii) the company's creditors;
(d) to the member State liquidator appointed in relation to the company (if there is one);
(e) where the administrator was appointed by the holder of a qualifying floating charge under paragraph 14 of Schedule B1, to—
  (i) the person who appointed the administrator, and
  (ii) all holders of prior qualifying floating charges;
(f) where the administrator was appointed by the company or the directors of the company under paragraph 22 of Schedule B1, to—
  (i) the appointer, and
  (ii) all holders of qualifying floating charges.

(5) The notice must be accompanied by a summary of the administrator's receipts and payments.

NOTES

Commencement: 6 April 2017.
This rule derived from the Insolvency Rules 1986, SI 1986/1925, r 2.120.

[6.175]
3.64 Notice of resignation (paragraph 87 of Schedule B1)

(1) A resigning administrator must, within five business days of delivering the notice under paragraph 87(2) of Schedule B1, deliver a copy of the notice to—
(a) the registrar of companies;
(b) all persons, other than the person who made the appointment, to whom notice of intention to resign was delivered under rule 3.63; and
(c) except where the appointment was by administration order, file a copy of the notice with the court.

(2) The notice must contain—
(a) identification details for the proceedings;
(b) the date of the appointment of the administrator; and
(c) the name of the person who made the appointment or the administration application, as the case may be.

(3) The notice must state—
(a) the date from which the resignation is to have effect; and
(b) where the resignation is with the permission of the court, the date on which permission was given.

(4) Where an administrator was appointed by an administration order, notice of resignation under paragraph 87(2)(a) of Schedule B1 must be given by filing the notice with the court.

NOTES

Commencement: 6 April 2017.
This rule derived from the Insolvency Rules 1986, SI 1986/1925, r 2.121.

[6.176]
3.65 Application to court to remove administrator from office

(1) An application for an order under paragraph 88 of Schedule B1 that the administrator be removed from office must state the grounds on which the order is requested.

(2) A copy of the application must be delivered, not less than five business days before the date fixed for the hearing—
(a) to the administrator;
(b) to the person who—
  (i) made the application for the administration order, or
  (ii) appointed the administrator;
(c) to the creditors' committee (if any);
(d) to any continuing administrator appointed to act jointly or concurrently; and
(e) where there is neither a creditors' committee nor a continuing administrator appointed, to the company and the creditors, including any floating charge holders.

(3) The court must deliver to the applicant a copy of any order removing the administrator.

(4) The applicant must deliver a copy—

(a) as soon as reasonably practicable, and in any event within five business days of the copy order being delivered, to the administrator; and
(b) within five business days of the copy order being delivered, to—
(i) all other persons to whom notice of the application was delivered, and
(ii) the registrar of companies.

NOTES
Commencement: 6 April 2017.
This rule derived from the Insolvency Rules 1986, SI 1986/1925, r 2.122.

[6.177]
3.66 Notice of vacation of office when administrator ceases to be qualified to act
An administrator who has ceased to be qualified to act as an insolvency practitioner in relation to the company and gives notice in accordance with paragraph 89 of Schedule B1 must also deliver notice to the registrar of companies.

NOTES
Commencement: 6 April 2017.
This rule derived from the Insolvency Rules 1986, SI 1986/1925, r 2.123.

[6.178]
3.67 Deceased administrator
(1) If the administrator dies a notice of the fact and date of death must be filed with the court.
(2) The notice must be filed as soon as reasonably practicable by one of the following—
(a) a surviving administrator;
(b) a member of the deceased administrator's firm (if the deceased was a member or employee of a firm);
(c) an officer of the deceased administrator's company (if the deceased was an officer or employee of a company); or
(d) a personal representative of the deceased administrator.
(3) If such a notice has not been filed within the 21 days following the administrator's death then any other person may file the notice.
(4) The person who files the notice must also deliver a notice to the registrar of companies which contains—
(a) identification details for the proceedings;
(b) the name of the person who made the appointment or the administration application, as the case may be;
(c) the date of the appointment of the administrator; and
(d) the fact and date of death.

NOTES
Commencement: 6 April 2017.
This rule derived from the Insolvency Rules 1986, SI 1986/1925, r 2.124.

[6.179]
3.68 Application to replace
(1) Where an application to court is made under paragraph 91(1) or 95 of Schedule B1 to appoint a replacement administrator, the application must be accompanied by the proposed replacement administrator's consent to act.
(2) Where the application is made under paragraph 91(1), a copy of the application must be delivered—
(a) to the person who made the application for the administration order;
(b) to any person who has appointed an administrative receiver of the company;
(c) to any person who is or may be entitled to appoint an administrative receiver of the company;
(d) to any person who is or may be entitled to appoint an administrator of the company under paragraph 14 of Schedule B1;
(e) to any administrative receiver of the company;
(f) if there is pending a petition for the winding up of the company, to—
(i) the petitioner, and
(ii) any provisional liquidator;
(g) to any member State liquidator appointed in main proceedings in relation to the company;
(h) to the company, if the application is made by anyone other than the company;
(i) to any supervisor of any CVA in relation to the company; and
(j) to the proposed administrator.
(3) Where the application is made under paragraph 95, the application must be accompanied by a witness statement setting out the applicant's belief as to the matters set out in that paragraph.
(4) Rules 3.12, 3.13, and 3.15(1) and (2) apply to applications made under paragraph 91(1) and 95 of Schedule B1, with any necessary modifications.

NOTES
Commencement: 6 April 2017.
This rule derived from the Insolvency Rules 1986, SI 1986/1925, r 2.125.

[6.180]

3.69 Appointment of replacement or additional administrator

Where a replacement administrator is appointed or an additional administrator is appointed to act—

(a) the following apply—

(i) rule 3.17 (notice of appointment) the requirement as to the heading in paragraph (1) and paragraphs (1)(a) to (f), and (2),

(ii) rule 3.18 (filing of notice with court) paragraphs (1)(a) and (b)(ii), (2) and (3),

(iii) rule 3.24 (notice of appointment after notice of intention to appoint) paragraphs (1)(a) to (d) and (2),

(iv) rule 3.25 (notice of appointment without prior notice of intention to appoint) paragraphs (1), (2)(a) to (c) and (3),

(v) rule 3.26 (notice of appointment: filing with the court) paragraphs (1)(a), (3) and (4), and

(vi) rule 3.27 (publication of administrator's appointment) paragraphs (1), (2)(a) and (b), (3) and (4);

(b) the replacement or additional administrator must deliver notice of the appointment to the registrar of companies; and

(c) all documents must clearly identify the appointment as of a replacement administrator or an additional administrator.

NOTES

Commencement: 6 April 2017.

This rule derived from the Insolvency Rules 1986, SI 1986/1925, rr 2.126–2.128.

[6.181]

3.70 Administrator's duties on vacating office

(1) An administrator who ceases to be in office as a result of removal, resignation or ceasing to be qualified to act as an insolvency practitioner in relation to the company must as soon as reasonably practicable deliver to the person succeeding as administrator—

(a) the assets (after deduction of any expenses properly incurred and distributions made by the departing administrator);

(b) the records of the administration, including correspondence, proofs and other documents relating to the administration while it was within the responsibility of the departing administrator; and

(c) the company's records.

(2) An administrator who makes default in complying with this rule is guilty of an offence and liable to a fine and, for continued contravention, to a daily default fine.

NOTES

Commencement: 6 April 2017.

This rule derived from the Insolvency Rules 1986, SI 1986/1925, r 2.129.

PART 4
RECEIVERSHIP

[Note: for the application of this Part see introductory rule 3.]

CHAPTER 1 APPOINTMENT OF JOINT RECEIVERS OR MANAGERS TO WHOM PART 3 OF THE ACT APPLIES (OTHER THAN THOSE APPOINTED UNDER SECTION 51 (SCOTTISH RECEIVERSHIPS))

[Note: a document required by the Act or these Rules must also contain the standard contents set out in Part 1.]

[6.182]

4.1 Receivers or managers appointed under an instrument: acceptance of appointment (section 33)

(1) This Chapter applies to all receivers to whom Part 3 of the Act applies [(other than those appointed under section 51 (Scottish Receiverships))].

(2) Where two or more persons are appointed as joint receivers or managers of a company's property under powers contained in an instrument—

(a) each of them must accept the appointment in accordance with section 33 as if each were a sole appointee;

(b) the joint appointment takes effect only when all of them have accepted; and

(c) the joint appointment is deemed to have been made at the time at which the instrument of appointment was received by or on behalf of all of them.

(3) A person who is appointed as the sole or joint receiver or manager of a company's property under powers contained in an instrument and accepts the appointment in accordance with section 33(1)(a), but not in writing, must confirm the acceptance in writing to the person making the appointment within five business days.

(4) The written acceptance or confirmation of acceptance must contain—

(a) the name and address of the appointer;

(b) the name and address of the appointee;

(c) the name of the company concerned;

(d) the time and date of receipt of the instrument of appointment; and
(e) the time and date of acceptance.

(5) Acceptance or confirmation of acceptance of appointment as a receiver or manager of a company's property, whether under the Act or these Rules, may be given by any person (including, in the case of a joint appointment, any joint appointee) duly authorised for that purpose on behalf of the receiver or manager.

NOTES

Commencement: 6 April 2017.

This rule derived from the Insolvency Rules 1986, SI 1986/1925, r 3.1.

Para (1): words in square brackets inserted by the Insolvency (England and Wales) (Amendment) Rules 2017, SI 2017/366, rr 3, 17.

CHAPTER 2 ADMINISTRATIVE RECEIVERS (OTHER THAN IN SCOTTISH RECEIVERSHIPS)

[Note: a document required by the Act or these Rules must also contain the standard contents set out in Part 1.]

[6.183]
4.2 Application of Chapter 2

This Chapter applies to administrative receivers (other than those appointed under section 51 (Scottish receiverships)).

NOTES

Commencement: 6 April 2017.

[6.184]
4.3 Interpretation

In this Chapter—

"nominated person" means a relevant person who has been required by the administrative receiver to make out and deliver to the administrative receiver a statement of affairs; and

"relevant person" means a person mentioned in section 47(3).

NOTES

Commencement: 6 April 2017.

[6.185]
4.4 Administrative receiver's security

The cost of the administrative receiver's security required by section 390(3) for the proper performance of the administrative receiver's functions is an expense of the administrative receivership.

NOTES

Commencement: 6 April 2017.

This rule derived from the Insolvency Rules 1986, SI 1986/1925, r 12A.56.

[6.186]
4.5 Publication of appointment of administrative receiver (section 46(1))

(1) The notice which an administrative receiver is required by section 46(1) to send to the company and the creditors on being appointed must contain—

(a) identification details for the company;
(b) any other registered name of the company in the 12 months before the date of the appointment;
(c) any name under which the company has traded at any time in those 12 months, if substantially different from its then registered name;
(d) the name and address of the person appointed;
(e) the date of the appointment;
(f) the name of the person who made the appointment;
(g) the date of the instrument conferring the power under which the appointment was made;
(h) a brief description of the instrument; and
(i) a brief description of any assets of the company in relation to which the appointment is not made.

(2) The notice which an administrative receiver is required by section 46(1) to publish—

(a) must be gazetted;
(b) may be advertised in such other manner as the administrative receiver thinks fit; and
(c) must state—
  (i) that an administrative receiver has been appointed,
  (ii) the date of the appointment,
  (iii) the name of the person who made the appointment, and
  (iv) the nature of the business of the company.

NOTES

Commencement: 6 April 2017.

This rule derived from the Insolvency Rules 1986, SI 1986/1925, r 3.2.

Part 6 Insolvency Rules

[6.187]
4.6 Requirement to provide a statement of affairs (section 47(1))

[Note: see sections 234(1) and 235(1) for the application of section 235 to administrative receivers.]

(1) A requirement under section 47(1) for a nominated person to make out and submit to the administrative receiver a statement of the affairs of the company must be made by a notice delivered to such a person.

(2) The notice must be headed "Notice requiring statement of affairs" and must—
- (a) identify the company immediately below the heading;
- (b) require the recipient to prepare and submit to the administrative receiver a statement of the affairs of the company; and
- (c) inform each recipient of—
  - (i) the name and address of any other nominated person to whom a notice has been delivered,
  - (ii) the date by which the statement must be delivered to the administrative receiver, and
  - (iii) the effect of sections 47(6) (penalty for non-compliance) and 235 (duty to co-operate with the office-holder).

(3) The administrative receiver must inform each nominated person that a document for the preparation of the statement of affairs capable of completion in compliance with rule 4.7 can be supplied if requested.

NOTES
Commencement: 6 April 2017.
This rule derived from the Insolvency Rules 1986, SI 1986/1925, r 3.3.

[6.188]
4.7 Statement of affairs: contents and delivery of copy (section 47(2))

[Note: section 47(2) requires the statement of affairs to be verified by a statement of truth.]

(1) The statement of affairs must be headed "Statement of affairs" and must state that it is a statement of the affairs of the company on a specified date, being the date on which the administrative receiver was appointed.

(2) The statement of affairs must contain, in addition to the matters required by section 47(2)—
- (a) a summary of the assets of the company, setting out the book value and the estimated realisable value of—
  - (i) any assets subject to a fixed charge,
  - (ii) any assets subject to a floating charge,
  - (iii) any uncharged assets, and
  - (iv) the total assets available for preferential creditors;
- (b) a summary of the liabilities of the company, setting out—
  - (i) the amount of preferential debts,
  - (ii) an estimate of the deficiency with respect to preferential debts or the surplus available after paying the preferential debts,
  - (iii) an estimate of the prescribed part, if applicable,
  - (iv) an estimate of the total assets available to pay debts secured by floating charges,
  - (v) the amount of debts secured by floating charges,
  - (vi) an estimate of the deficiency with respect to debts secured by floating charges or the surplus available after paying the debts secured by floating charges,
  - (vii) the amount of unsecured debts (excluding preferential debts and any deficiency with respect to debts secured by floating charges),
  - (viii) an estimate of the deficiency with respect to unsecured debts or the surplus available after paying unsecured debts (excluding preferential debts and any deficiency with respect to debts secured by fixed and floating charges),
  - (ix) any issued and called-up capital, and
  - (x) an estimate of the deficiency with respect to, or surplus available to, members of the company;
- (c) a list of the company's creditors with the further particulars required by paragraph (3) indicating—
  - (i) any creditors under hire-purchase, chattel leasing or conditional sale agreements,
  - (ii) any creditors who are consumers claiming amounts paid in advance for the supply of goods or services, and
  - (iii) any creditors claiming retention of title over property in the company's possession.

(3) The particulars required by section 47(2) and paragraph (2)(c) of this rule to be included in the statement of affairs relating to each creditor are as follows—
- (a) the name and postal address;
- (b) the amount of the debt owed to the creditor;
- (c) details of any security held by the creditor;
- (d) the date the security was given; and
- (e) the value of any such security.

(4) Paragraph (5) applies where the particulars required by paragraph (3) relate to creditors who are either—
- (a) employees or former employees of the company; or
- (b) consumers claiming amounts paid in advance for the supply of goods or services.

(5) Where this paragraph applies—

(a) the statement of affairs must state separately for each of paragraphs (4)(a) and (b) the number of such creditors and the total of the debts owed to them; and
(b) the particulars required by paragraph (3) must be set out in separate schedules to the statement of affairs for each of paragraphs (4)(a) and (b).

(6) The nominated person who makes the statement of truth required by section 47(2) (or if more than one, by one of them) must deliver the statement of affairs together with a copy to the administrative receiver.

NOTES

Commencement: 6 April 2017.
This rule derived from the Insolvency Rules 1986, SI 1986/1925, r 3.4(1), Sch 4, Fm 3.2.

[6.189]
4.8 Statement of affairs: statement of concurrence

(1) The administrative receiver may require a relevant person to deliver to the administrative receiver a statement of concurrence.

(2) A statement of concurrence is a statement, verified by a statement of truth, that that person concurs in the statement of affairs submitted by a nominated person.

(3) The administrative receiver must inform the nominated person who has been required to submit a statement of affairs that the relevant person has been required to deliver a statement of concurrence.

(4) The nominated person must deliver a copy of the statement of affairs to every relevant person who has been required to deliver a statement of concurrence.

(5) A statement of concurrence—
(a) must identify the company; and
(b) may be qualified in relation to matters dealt with in the statement of affairs where the relevant person—
(i) is not in agreement with the statement of affairs,
(ii) considers the statement to be erroneous or misleading, or
(iii) is without the direct knowledge necessary for concurring in it.

(6) The relevant person must deliver the required statement of concurrence together with a copy to the administrative receiver before the end of the period of five business days (or such other period as the administrative receiver may agree) beginning with the day on which the relevant person receives the statement of affairs.

NOTES

Commencement: 6 April 2017.
This rule derived from the Insolvency Rules 1986, SI 1986/1925, r 3.4(2)–(5).

[6.190]
4.9 Statement of affairs: retention by administrative receiver

The administrative receiver must retain the verified statement of affairs and each statement of concurrence as part of the records of the receivership.

NOTES

Commencement: 6 April 2017.
This rule derived from the Insolvency Rules 1986, SI 1986/1925, r 3.4(6).

[6.191]
4.10 Statement of affairs: release from requirement and extension of time (section 47(5))

(1) The administrative receiver may exercise the power in section 47(5) to release a person from an obligation to submit a statement of affairs imposed under section 47(1) or (2), or to grant an extension of time, either on the administrative receiver's own discretion or at the request of a nominated person.

(2) A nominated person may apply to the court if the administrative receiver refuses that person's request.

(3) On receipt of an application, the court may, if it is satisfied that no sufficient cause is shown for it, dismiss it without giving notice to any party other than the applicant.

(4) The applicant must, at least 14 days before any hearing, deliver to the administrative receiver a notice stating the venue with a copy of the application and of any evidence on which the applicant intends to rely.

(5) The administrative receiver may do either or both of the following—
(a) file a report of any matters which the administrative receiver thinks ought to be drawn to the court's attention; or
(b) appear and be heard on the application.

(6) If a report is filed, the administrative receiver must deliver a copy of it to the applicant not later than five business days before the hearing.

(7) Sealed copies of any order made on the application must be delivered by the court to the applicant and the administrative receiver.

(8) On any application under this rule, the applicant's costs must be paid by the applicant in any event; but the court may order that an allowance of all or part of them be payable out of the assets under the administrative receiver's control.

NOTES

Commencement: 6 April 2017.
This rule derived from the Insolvency Rules 1986, SI 1986/1925, r 3.6.

[6.192]
4.11 Statement of affairs: expenses

(1) The administrative receiver must pay, out of the assets under the administrative receiver's control, the expenses which the administrative receiver considers to have been reasonably incurred by—
- (a) a nominated person in making a statement of affairs and statement of truth; or
- (b) a relevant person in making a statement of concurrence.

(2) Any decision by the administrative receiver under this rule is subject to appeal to the court.

NOTES

Commencement: 6 April 2017.
This rule derived from the Insolvency Rules 1986, SI 1986/1925, r 3.7.

[6.193]
4.12 Limited disclosure

(1) This rule applies where the administrative receiver thinks that disclosure of the whole or part of a statement of the company's affairs or a statement of concurrence would be likely to prejudice the conduct of the receivership or might reasonably be expected to lead to violence against any person.

(2) The administrative receiver may apply to the court for an order in respect of—
- (a) the statement of affairs; or
- (b) a statement of concurrence;

and the court may order that the whole or any specified part of the statement of affairs or a statement of concurrence must not be open to inspection except with permission of the court.

(3) The court's order may include directions regarding the delivery of documents to the registrar of companies and the disclosure of relevant information to other persons.

NOTES

Commencement: 6 April 2017.
This rule derived from the Insolvency Rules 1986, SI 1986/1925, r 3.5.

[6.194]
4.13 Administrative receiver's report to the registrar of companies and secured creditors (section 48(1))

(1) The report which under section 48(1) an administrative receiver is to send to the registrar of companies must be accompanied by a copy of any statement of affairs under section 47 and any statement of concurrence under rule 4.8.

(2) However the administrative receiver must not deliver to the registrar of companies with the statement of affairs any schedule required by rule 4.7(5)(b).

(3) The duty to send a copy of the report to the registrar of companies is subject to any order for limited disclosure made under rule 4.12.

(4) If a statement of affairs or statement of concurrence is submitted to the administrative receiver after the report is sent to the registrar of companies, the administrative receiver must deliver a copy of it to the registrar of companies as soon as reasonably practicable after its receipt by the administrative receiver.

(5) The report must contain (in addition to the matters required by section 48(1)) estimates to the best of the administrative receiver's knowledge and belief of—
- (a) the value of the prescribed part (whether or not the administrative receiver might be required under section 176A to make the prescribed part available for the satisfaction of unsecured debts); and
- (b) the value of the company's net property (as defined by section 176A(6)).

(6) The administrative receiver may exclude from an estimate under paragraph (5) information the disclosure of which could seriously prejudice the commercial interests of the company.

(7) If the exclusion of such information affects the calculation of an estimate, the report must say so.

(8) If the administrative receiver proposes to make an application to court under section 176A(5) the report must say so and give the reason for the application.

NOTES

Commencement: 6 April 2017.
This rule derived from the Insolvency Rules 1986, SI 1986/1925, r 3.8.

[6.195]
4.14 Copy of report for unsecured creditors (section 48(2))

A notice under section 48(2)(b) stating an address to which unsecured creditors should write for copies of an administrative receiver's report under that section—

(a) must be gazetted;
(b) may be advertised in such other manner as the administrative receiver thinks fit; and
(c) must be accompanied by a notice under rule 4.15.

NOTES
Commencement: 6 April 2017.
This rule derived from the Insolvency Rules 1986, SI 1986/1925, r 3.8.

[6.196]
4.15 Invitation to creditors to form a creditors' committee

(1) An administrative receiver must deliver to the creditors with the report under section 48(1) a notice inviting the creditors to decide whether a creditors' committee should be established if sufficient creditors are willing to be members of the committee.

(2) The notice must also invite nominations for membership of the committee, such nominations to be received by the administrative receiver by a date to be specified in the notice.

(3) The notice must state that any nominations—
(a) must be delivered to the administrative receiver by the specified date; and
(b) can only be accepted if the administrative receiver is satisfied as to the creditor's eligibility under rule 17.4.

NOTES
Commencement: 6 April 2017.

[6.197]
4.16 Disposal of charged property (section 43(1))

(1) This rule applies where an administrative receiver applies to the court under section 43(1) for authority to dispose of property of the company which is subject to a security.

(2) The court must fix a venue for the hearing of the application.

(3) As soon as reasonably practicable after the court has fixed the venue, the administrative receiver must deliver notice of the venue to the person who is the holder of the security.

(4) If an order is made under section 43(1), the court must deliver two sealed copies to the administrative receiver and the administrative receiver must deliver one of them to the holder of the security.

NOTES
Commencement: 6 April 2017.
This rule derived from the Insolvency Rules 1986, SI 1986/1925, r 3.31.

[6.198]
4.17 Summary of receipts and payments

(1) The administrative receiver must deliver a summary of receipts and payments as receiver to the registrar of companies, the company and to the person who made the appointment, and to each member of the creditors' committee.

(2) The notice delivered to the registrar of companies under rule 1.20 must contain the date of the appointment of the administrative receiver.

(3) The summary must be delivered to those persons within two months after—
(a) the end of the period of 12 months from the date of being appointed;
(b) the end of every subsequent period of 12 months; and
(c) ceasing to act as administrative receiver (unless there is a joint administrative receiver who continues in office).

(4) The summary must show receipts and payments—
(a) during the relevant period of 12 months; or
(b) where the administrative receiver has ceased to act, during the period—
(i) from the end of the last 12-month period to the time when the administrative receiver so ceased, or
(ii) if there has been no previous summary, since being appointed.

(5) This rule is without prejudice to the administrative receiver's duty to produce proper accounts otherwise than as above.

(6) An administrative receiver who makes default in complying with this rule is guilty of an offence and liable to a fine and, for continued contravention, to a daily default fine.

NOTES
Commencement: 6 April 2017.
This rule derived from the Insolvency Rules 1986, SI 1986/1925, r 3.32.

[6.199]
4.18 Resignation

(1) An administrative receiver must deliver notice of intention to resign at least five business days before the date the resignation is intended to take effect to—
(a) the person by whom the appointment was made;

(b) the company or, if it is then in liquidation, the liquidator; and
(c) the members of the creditors' committee.

(2) The notice must specify the date on which the administrative receiver intends the resignation to take effect.

NOTES
Commencement: 6 April 2017.
This rule derived from the Insolvency Rules 1986, SI 1986/1925, r 3.33.

[6.200]
4.19 Deceased administrative receiver

(1) If the administrative receiver dies a notice of the fact and date of death must be delivered as soon as reasonably practicable to—
(a) the person by whom the appointment was made;
(b) the registrar of companies;
(c) the company or, if it is in liquidation, the liquidator; and
(d) the members of the creditors' committee.

(2) The notice must be delivered by one of the following—
(a) a surviving joint administrative receiver;
(b) a member of the deceased administrative receiver's firm (if the deceased was a member or employee of a firm);
(c) an officer of the deceased administrative receiver's company (if the deceased was an officer or employee of a company); or
(d) a personal representative of the deceased administrative receiver.

(3) If such a notice has not been delivered within 21 days following the administrative receiver's death then any other person may deliver the notice.

NOTES
Commencement: 6 April 2017.
This rule derived from the Insolvency Rules 1986, SI 1986/1925, r 3.34.

[6.201]
4.20 Other vacation of office

An administrative receiver, on vacating office on completion of the administrative receivership, or in consequence of ceasing to be qualified to act as an insolvency practitioner in relation to the company, must as soon as reasonably practicable deliver a notice of doing so to—
(a) the person by whom the appointment was made;
(b) the company or, if it is then in liquidation, the liquidator; and
(c) the members of the creditors' committee.

NOTES
Commencement: 6 April 2017.
This rule derived from the Insolvency Rules 1986, SI 1986/1925, r 3.35.

[6.202]
4.21 Notice to registrar of companies (section 45(4))

Where an administrative receiver's office is vacated other than by death, the notice to the registrar of companies required by section 45(4) may be given by delivering to the registrar of companies the notice required by section 859K(3) of the Companies Act.

NOTES
Commencement: 6 April 2017.
This rule derived from the Insolvency Rules 1986, SI 1986/1925, r 3.35(2).

CHAPTER 3 NON-ADMINISTRATIVE RECEIVERS AND THE PRESCRIBED PART

[Note: a document required by the Act or these Rules must also contain the standard contents set out in Part 1.]

[6.203]
4.22 Application of Chapter 3

This Chapter applies where a receiver (other than an administrative receiver) is appointed by the court or otherwise under a charge which was created as a floating charge; and section 176A applies.

NOTES
Commencement: 6 April 2017.
This rule derived from the Insolvency Rules 1986, SI 1986/1925, r 3.39.

[6.204]
4.23 Report to creditors

(1) Within three months (or such longer period as the court may allow) of the date of the appointment, the receiver must deliver to the creditors—

(a) a notice of the appointment; and
(b) a report.

(2) The report must contain estimates to the best of the receiver's knowledge and belief of—
(a) the value of the prescribed part (whether or not the receiver might be required under section 176A to make the prescribed part available for the satisfaction of unsecured debts); and
(b) the value of company's net property (as defined by section 176A(6)).

(3) The receiver may exclude from an estimate under paragraph (2) information the disclosure of which could seriously prejudice the commercial interests of the company.

(4) If the exclusion of such information affects the calculation of an estimate, the report must say so.

(5) If the receiver proposes to make an application to court under section 176A(5) the report must say so and give the reason for the application.

(6) The report must also state whether, and if so why, the receiver proposes to present a petition for the winding up of the company.

(7) The receiver may, instead of delivering the report under paragraph (1), cause a notice to be gazetted and may advertise that notice in such other manner as the receiver thinks fit where—
(a) full details of the unsecured creditors of the company are not available to the receiver; or
(b) the receiver thinks it is otherwise impracticable to deliver such a report.

(8) A notice under paragraph (7) must contain the matters required to be included in the receiver's report.

NOTES

Commencement: 6 April 2017.
This rule derived from the Insolvency Rules 1986, SI 1986/1925, r 3.39.

[6.205]
4.24 Receiver to deal with prescribed part

(1) The receiver—
(a) may present a petition for the winding up of the company if the ground of the petition is that in section 122(1)(f); and
(b) must deliver to any administrator or liquidator the sums representing the prescribed part.

(2) If there is no administrator or liquidator the receiver must—
(a) apply to the court for directions as to the manner in which to discharge the duty under section 176A(2)(a); and
(b) act in accordance with any directions given.

NOTES

Commencement: 6 April 2017.
This rule derived from the Insolvency Rules 1986, SI 1986/1925, r 3.40.

PART 5
MEMBERS' VOLUNTARY WINDING UP

CHAPTER 1 STATUTORY DECLARATION OF SOLVENCY (SECTION 89)

[Note: a document required by the Act or these Rules must also contain the standard contents set out in Part 1.]

[6.206]
5.1 Statutory declaration of solvency: requirements additional to those in section 89

[Note: the "official rate" referred to in paragraph (1)(b) is defined in section 251 as being the rate referred to in section 189(4).]

(1) The statutory declaration of solvency required by section 89 must identify the company and state—
(a) the name and a postal address for each director making the declaration (which may be the director's service address provided for by section 163 of the Companies Act);
(b) either—
(i) that all of the directors, or
(ii) that a majority of the directors,
have made a full inquiry into the company's affairs and that, having done so, they have formed the opinion that the company will be able to pay its debts in full together with interest at the official rate within a specified period (which must not exceed 12 months) from the commencement of the winding up; and
(c) that the declaration is accompanied by a statement of the company's assets and liabilities as at a date which is stated (being the latest practicable date before the making of the declaration as required by section 89(2)(b)).

(2) The statement of the company's assets and liabilities must contain—
(a) the date of the statement;
(b) a statement that the statement shows the assets of the company at estimated realisable values and liabilities of the company expected to rank as at the date referred to in sub-paragraph (1)(c);
(c) a summary of the assets of the company, setting out the estimated realisable value of—
(i) any assets subject to a fixed charge,

Part 6 Insolvency Rules

(ii) any assets subject to a floating charge,
(iii) any uncharged assets; and
(iv) the total value of all the assets available to preferential creditors;

(d) the value of each of the following secured liabilities of the company expected to rank for payment—
(i) liabilities secured on specific assets, and
(ii) liabilities secured by floating charges;

(e) a summary of the unsecured liabilities of the company expected to rank for payment;
(f) the estimated costs of the winding up and other expenses;
(g) the estimated amount of interest accruing until payment of debts in full; and
(h) the estimated value of any surplus after paying debts in full together with interest at the official rate.

NOTES

Commencement: 6 April 2017.
This rule derived from the Insolvency Rules 1986, SI 1986/1925, Sch 4, Fm 4.70.

CHAPTER 2 THE LIQUIDATOR

[Note: a document required by the Act or these Rules must also contain the standard contents set out in Part 1.]

[6.207]
5.2 Appointment by the company

(1) This rule applies where the liquidator is appointed by the company.

(2) The chair of the meeting, or a director or the secretary of the company in the case of a written resolution of a private company, must certify the appointment when the appointee has provided to the person certifying the appointment a statement to the effect that the appointee is an insolvency practitioner qualified under the Act to be the liquidator and consents to act.

(3) The certificate must be authenticated and dated by the person who certifies the appointment and must contain—

(a) identification details for the company;
(b) identification and contact details for the person appointed as liquidator;
(c) the date the liquidator was appointed; and
(d) a statement that the appointee—
(i) provided a statement of being qualified to act as an insolvency practitioner in relation to the company,
(ii) has consented to act, and
(iii) was appointed liquidator of the company.

(4) Where two or more liquidators are appointed the certificate must also specify (as required by section 231) whether any act required or authorised under any enactment to be done by the liquidator is to be done by all or any one or more of them.

(5) The person who certifies the appointment must deliver the certificate as soon as reasonably practicable to the liquidator, who must keep it as part of the records of the winding up.

(6) Not later than 28 days from the liquidator's appointment, the liquidator must deliver notice of the appointment to the creditors of the company.

NOTES

Commencement: 6 April 2017.
This rule derived from the Insolvency Rules 1986, SI 1986/1925, r 4.139.

[6.208]
5.3 Meetings in members' voluntary winding up of authorised deposit-takers

(1) This rule applies to a meeting of the members of an authorised deposit-taker at which it is intended to propose a resolution for its winding up.

(2) Notice of such a meeting of the company must be delivered by the directors to the Financial Conduct Authority and to the scheme manager established under section 212(1) of the Financial Services and Markets Act 2000.

(3) The notice to the Financial Conduct Authority and the scheme manager must be the same as delivered to members of the company.

(4) The scheme manager is entitled to be represented at any meeting of which it is required by this rule to be given notice.

NOTES

Commencement: 6 April 2017.
This rule derived from the Insolvency Rules 1986, SI 1986/1925, r 4.72.

[6.209]
5.4 Appointment by the court (section 108)

(1) This rule applies where the liquidator is appointed by the court under section 108.

(2) The order of the court must contain—

(a) the name of the court (and hearing centre if applicable) in which the order is made;
(b) the name and title of the judge making the order;
(c) identification details for the company;
(d) the name and address of the applicant;
(e) the capacity in which the applicant made the application;
(f) identification details for the proposed liquidator;
(g) a statement that the appointee has filed with the court a statement to the effect that the appointee is an insolvency practitioner qualified to act as the liquidator and consents to act;
(h) an order that the proposed liquidator, having filed a statement of being qualified to act as an insolvency practitioner in relation to the company and having consented to act, is appointed liquidator of the company from the date of the order, or such other date as the court orders; and
(i) the date of the order.

(3) Where two or more liquidators are appointed the order must also specify (as required by section 231) whether any act required or authorised under any enactment to be done by the liquidator is to be done by all or any one or more of them.

(4) The court must deliver a sealed copy of the order to the liquidator, whose appointment takes effect from the date of the order or from such other date as the court orders.

(5) Not later than 28 days from the liquidator's appointment, the liquidator must deliver notice of the appointment to the creditors of the company.

NOTES

Commencement: 6 April 2017.
This rule derived from the Insolvency Rules 1986, SI 1986/1925, r 4.140.

[6.210]
5.5 Cost of liquidator's security (section 390(3))

The cost of the liquidator's security required by section 390(3) for the proper performance of the liquidator's functions is an expense of the winding up.

NOTES

Commencement: 6 April 2017.
This rule derived from the Insolvency Rules 1986, SI 1986/1925, r 12A.56.

[6.211]
5.6 Liquidator's resignation

(1) A liquidator may resign only—
(a) on grounds of ill health;
(b) because of the intention to cease to practise as an insolvency practitioner;
(c) because the further discharge of the duties of liquidator is prevented or made impractical by—
(i) a conflict of interest, or
(ii) a change of personal circumstances;
(d) where two or more persons are acting as liquidator jointly and it is the opinion of both or all of them that it is no longer expedient that there should continue to be that number of joint liquidators.

(2) Before resigning, the liquidator must deliver a notice to the members of the company—
(a) stating the liquidator's intention to resign; and
(b) calling a meeting for the members to consider whether a replacement should be appointed;
except where the resignation is under sub-paragraph (1)(d).

(3) The notice must be accompanied by a summary of the liquidator's receipts and payments.

(4) The notice may suggest the name of a replacement liquidator.

(5) The date of the meeting must be not more than five business days before the date on which the liquidator intends to give notice of resignation to the registrar of companies under section 171(5).

(6) The resigning liquidator's release is effective 21 days after the date of delivery of the notice of resignation to the registrar of companies under section 171(5), unless the court orders otherwise.

NOTES

Commencement: 6 April 2017.
This rule derived from the Insolvency Rules 1986, SI 1986/1925, r 4.142(3).

[6.212]
5.7 Removal of liquidator by the court

(1) This rule applies where an application is made to the court for the removal of the liquidator, or for an order directing the liquidator to summon a company meeting for the purpose of removing the liquidator.

(2) On receipt of an application, the court may, if it is satisfied that no sufficient cause is shown for it, dismiss it without giving notice to any party other than the applicant.

(3) Unless the application is dismissed, the court must fix a venue for it to be heard.

(4) The applicant must, at least 14 days before any hearing, deliver to the liquidator a notice stating the venue with a copy of the application and of any evidence on which the applicant intends to rely.

(5) A respondent may apply for security for the costs of the application and the court may make such an order if it is satisfied, having regard to all the circumstances of the case, that it is just to make such an order.

(6) The liquidator may do either or both of the following at such a hearing—
 (a) file a report of any matters which the liquidator thinks ought to be drawn to the court's attention; or
 (b) appear and be heard on the application.

(7) On a successful application the court's order must contain the following—
 (a) the name of the court (and hearing centre if applicable) in which the order is made;
 (b) the name and title of the judge making the order;
 (c) identification details for the company;
 (d) the name and address of the applicant;
 (e) the capacity in which the applicant made the application;
 (f) identification and contact details for the liquidator (or former liquidator);
 (g) an order either—
  (i) that the liquidator is removed from office, or
  (ii) that the liquidator must summon a [company meeting] on or before a date which is stated in the order for the purpose of considering the liquidator's removal from office; and
 (h) the date of the order.

(8) The order of the court may include such provision as the court thinks just relating to matters arising in connection with the removal.

(9) The costs of the application are not payable as an expense of the winding up unless the court orders otherwise.

(10) Where the court removes the liquidator—
 (a) it must deliver the sealed order of removal to the former liquidator; and
 (b) the former liquidator must deliver a copy of the order to the registrar of companies as soon as reasonably practicable.

(11) If the court appoints a new liquidator, rule 5.4 applies.

NOTES

Commencement: 6 April 2017.

This rule derived from the Insolvency Rules 1986, SI 1986/1925, r 4.143.

Para (7): words in square brackets in sub-para (g)(ii) substituted by the Insolvency (England and Wales) (Amendment) Rules 2017, SI 2017/366, rr 3, 18.

[6.213]

5.8 Removal of liquidator by company meeting

A liquidator removed by a meeting of the company must as soon as reasonably practicable deliver notice of the removal to the registrar of companies.

NOTES

Commencement: 6 April 2017.

This rule derived from the Insolvency Rules 1986, SI 1986/1925, r 4.142.

[6.214]

5.9 Delivery of proposed final account to members (section 94)

(1) The liquidator must deliver a notice to the members accompanied by the proposed final account required by section 94(1) and rule 18.14 giving them a minimum of eight weeks' notice of a specified date on which the liquidator intends to deliver the final account as required by section 94(2).

(2) The notice must inform the members that when the company's affairs are fully wound up—
 (a) the liquidator will make up the final account and deliver it to the members; and
 (b) when the final account is delivered to the registrar of companies the liquidator will be released under section 171(6).

(3) The affairs of the company are not fully wound up until the latest of—
 (a) the period referred to in paragraph (1) having expired without the liquidator receiving any request for information under rule 18.9 or the filing of any application to court under that rule or under rule 18.34 (application to court on the grounds that the liquidator's remuneration or expenses are excessive);
 (b) any request for information under rule 18.9 having been finally determined (including any applications to court under that rule); or
 (c) any application to the court under rule 18.34 having been finally determined.

(4) However the liquidator may conclude that the company's affairs are fully wound up before the period referred to in paragraph (1) has expired if every member confirms in writing to the liquidator that they do not intend to make any such request or application.

NOTES

Commencement: 6 April 2017.

This rule derived from the Insolvency Rules 1986, SI 1986/1925, r 4.126A.

[6.215]
5.10 Final account prior to dissolution (section 94)

(1) The contents of the final account which the liquidator is required to make up under section 94 must comply with the requirements of rule 18.14.

(2) When the account is delivered to the members under section 94(2) it must be accompanied by a notice which states that—
- (a) the company's affairs are fully wound up;
- (b) the liquidator having delivered copies of the account to the members must, within 14 days of the date on which the account is made up, deliver a copy of the account to the registrar of companies; and
- (c) the liquidator will vacate office and be released under section 171 on delivering the final account to the registrar of companies.

(3) The copy of the account which the liquidator must deliver to the registrar of companies under section 94(3) must be accompanied by a notice stating that the liquidator has delivered the final account of the winding up to the members in accordance with section 94(2).

NOTES

Commencement: 6 April 2017.
This rule derived from the Insolvency Rules 1986, SI 1986/1925, r 4.126A.

[6.216]
5.11 Deceased liquidator

(1) If the liquidator dies a notice of the fact and date of death must be delivered as soon as reasonably practicable to—
- (a) one of the company's directors; and
- (b) the registrar of companies.

(2) One of the following must deliver the notice—
- (a) a surviving joint liquidator;
- (b) a member of the deceased liquidator's firm (if the deceased was a member or employee of a firm);
- (c) an officer of the deceased liquidator's company (if the deceased was an officer or employee of a company); or
- (d) a personal representative of the deceased liquidator.

(3) If such notice has not been delivered within the 21 days following the liquidator's death then any other person may deliver the notice.

NOTES

Commencement: 6 April 2017.
This rule derived from the Insolvency Rules 1986, SI 1986/1925, r 4.145.

[6.217]
5.12 Loss of qualification as insolvency practitioner

(1) This rule applies where the liquidator vacates office on ceasing to be qualified to act as an insolvency practitioner in relation to the company.

(2) A notice of the fact must be delivered as soon as reasonably practicable to the registrar of companies and the Secretary of State by one of the following—
- (a) the liquidator who has vacated office;
- (b) a continuing joint liquidator; or
- (c) the recognised professional body which was the source of the vacating liquidator's authorisation to act in relation to the company.

(3) Each notice must be authenticated and dated by the person delivering the notice.

NOTES

Commencement: 6 April 2017.
This rule derived from the Insolvency Rules 1986, SI 1986/1925, r 4.146.

[6.218]
5.13 Liquidator's duties on vacating office

A liquidator who ceases to be in office as a result of removal, resignation or ceasing to be qualified to act as an insolvency practitioner in relation to the company, must as soon as reasonably practicable deliver to the succeeding liquidator—
- (a) the assets (after deduction of any expenses properly incurred, and distributions made, by the former liquidator);
- (b) the records of the winding up, including correspondence, proofs and other documents relating to the winding up; and
- (c) the company's documents and other records.

NOTES

Commencement: 6 April 2017.
This rule derived from the Insolvency Rules 1986, SI 1986/1925, r 4.148.

[6.219]
5.14 Application by former liquidator to the Secretary of State for release (section 173(2)(b))

(1) This rule applies to a liquidator who—
(a) is removed by the court;
(b) vacates office on ceasing to be qualified to act as an insolvency practitioner in relation to the company; or
(c) vacates office in consequence of the court making a winding-up order against the company.

(2) Where the former liquidator applies to the Secretary of State for release the application must contain—
(a) identification details for the former liquidator;
(b) identification details for the company;
(c) the circumstances under which the former liquidator ceased to act as liquidator; and
(d) a statement that the former liquidator is applying to the Secretary of State for release.

(3) The application must be authenticated and dated by the former liquidator.

(4) When the Secretary of State gives a release, the Secretary of State must deliver—
(a) a certificate of the release to the former liquidator; and
(b) a notice of the release to the registrar of companies.

(5) Release is effective from the date of the certificate or such other date as the certificate specifies.

NOTES

Commencement: 6 April 2017.
This rule derived from the Insolvency Rules 1986, SI 1986/1925, rr 4.144(2), 4.147.

[6.220]
5.15 Power of court to set aside certain transactions entered into by liquidator

(1) If in dealing with the estate the liquidator enters into any transaction with a person who is an associate of the liquidator, the court may, on the application of any interested person , set the transaction aside and order the liquidator to compensate the company for any loss suffered in consequence of it.

(2) This does not apply if either—
(a) the transaction was entered into with the prior consent of the court; or
(b) it is shown to the court's satisfaction that the transaction was for value, and that it was entered into by the liquidator without knowing, or having any reason to suppose, that the person concerned was an associate.

(3) Nothing in this rule is to be taken as prejudicing the operation of any rule of law or equity relating to a liquidator's dealings with trust property, or the fiduciary obligations of any person.

NOTES

Commencement: 6 April 2017.
This rule derived from the Insolvency Rules 1986, SI 1986/1925, r 4.149.

[6.221]
5.16 Rule against improper solicitation by or on behalf of the liquidator

(1) Where the court is satisfied that any improper solicitation has been used by or on behalf of the liquidator in obtaining proxies or procuring the liquidator's appointment, it may order that no remuneration be allowed as an expense of the winding up to any person by whom, or on whose behalf, the solicitation was exercised.

(2) An order of the court under this Rule overrides any resolution of the members, or any other provision of these Rules relating to the liquidator's remuneration.

NOTES

Commencement: 6 April 2017.
This rule derived from the Insolvency Rules 1986, SI 1986/1925, r 4.150.

CHAPTER 3 SPECIAL MANAGER

[Note: a document required by the Act or these Rules must also contain the standard contents set out in Part 1.]

[6.222]
5.17 Application for and appointment of special manager (section 177)

(1) An application by the liquidator under section 177 for the appointment of a special manager must be supported by a report setting out the reasons for the application.

(2) The report must include the applicant's estimate of the value of the business or property in relation to which the special manager is to be appointed.

(3) The court's order appointing a special manager must have the title "Order of Appointment of Special Manager" and must contain—
(a) the name of the court (and hearing centre if applicable) in which the order is made;
(b) the name and title of the judge making the order;
(c) identification details for the proceedings;
(d) the name and address of the applicant;

(e) the name and address of the proposed special manager;
(f) an order that the proposed special manager is appointed as special manager of the company;
(g) details of the special manager's responsibility over the company's business or property;
(h) the powers to be entrusted to the special manager under section [177(3)];
(i) the time allowed for the special manager to give the required security for the appointment;
(j) the duration of the special manager's appointment, being one of the following—
 (i) for a fixed period stated in the order;
 (ii) until the occurrence of a specified event; or
 (iii) until the court makes a further order;
(k) the order that the special manager's remuneration will be fixed from time to time by the court; and
(l) the date of the order and the date on which it takes effect if different.

(4) The appointment of the special manager may be renewed by order of the court.

(5) The acts of the special manager are valid notwithstanding any defect in the special manager's appointment or qualifications.

NOTES

Commencement: 6 April 2017.

This rule derived from the Insolvency Rules 1986, SI 1986/1925, r 4.206.

Para (3): figure in square brackets in sub-para (h) substituted by the Insolvency (England and Wales) (Amendment) Rules 2017, SI 2017/366, rr 3, 19.

[6.223]

5.18 Security

(1) The appointment of the special manager does not take effect until the person appointed has given (or, if the court allows, undertaken to give) security to the liquidator for the appointment.

(2) A person appointed as special manager may give security either specifically for a particular winding up, or generally for any winding up in relation to which that person may be appointed as special manager.

(3) The amount of the security must be not less than the value of the business or property in relation to which the special manager is appointed, as estimated in the liquidator's report which accompanied the application for appointment.

(4) When the special manager has given security to the liquidator, the liquidator must file with the court a certificate as to the adequacy of the security.

(5) The cost of providing the security must be paid in the first instance by the special manager, but the special manager is entitled to be reimbursed as an expense of the winding up.

NOTES

Commencement: 6 April 2017.

This rule derived from the Insolvency Rules 1986, SI 1986/1925, r 4.207.

[6.224]

5.19 Failure to give or keep up security

(1) If the special manager fails to give the required security within the time stated in the order of appointment, or any extension of that time that may be allowed, the liquidator must report the failure to the court, which may discharge the order appointing the special manager.

(2) If the special manager fails to keep up the security, the liquidator must report the failure to the court, which may remove the special manager, and make such order as it thinks just as to costs.

(3) If the court discharges the order appointing the special manager, or makes an order removing the special manager, the court must give directions as to whether any, and if so what, steps should be taken for the appointment of another special manager.

NOTES

Commencement: 6 April 2017.

This rule derived from the Insolvency Rules 1986, SI 1986/1925, r 4.208.

[6.225]

5.20 Accounting

(1) The special manager must produce accounts, containing details of the special manager's receipts and payments, for the approval of the liquidator.

(2) The accounts must be for—
(a) each three month period for the duration of the special manager's appointment; and
(b) any shorter period ending with the termination of the special manager's appointment.

(3) When the accounts have been approved, the special manager's receipts and payments must be added to those of the liquidator.

NOTES

Commencement: 6 April 2017.

This rule derived from the Insolvency Rules 1986, SI 1986/1925, r 4.209.

Part 6 Insolvency Rules

[6.226]
5.21 Termination of appointment

(1) If the liquidator thinks that the appointment of the special manager is no longer necessary or beneficial for the company, the liquidator must apply to the court for directions, and the court may order the special manager's appointment to be terminated.

(2) The liquidator must also make such an application if the members pass a resolution requesting that the appointment be terminated.

NOTES

Commencement: 6 April 2017.
This rule derived from the Insolvency Rules 1986, SI 1986/1925, r 4.210.

CHAPTER 4 CONVERSION TO CREDITORS' VOLUNTARY WINDING UP

[6.227]
5.22 Statement of affairs (section 95(3))

The rules in Chapter 2 of Part 6 apply to the statement of affairs made out by the liquidator under section 95(1A) where the liquidator is of the opinion that the company will be unable to pay its debts in full (together with interest at the official rate) within the period stated in the directors' declaration under section 89.

NOTES

Commencement: 6 April 2017.
This rule derived from the Insolvency Rules 1986, SI 1986/1925, r 4.34.

PART 6
CREDITORS' VOLUNTARY WINDING UP

CHAPTER 1 APPLICATION OF PART 6

[6.228]
6.1 Application of Part 6

(1) This Part applies to a creditors' voluntary winding up.

(2) However where a company moves from administration to creditors' voluntary winding up by the registration of a notice under paragraph 83(3) of Schedule B1 the following rules do not apply—

6.2 to 6.7 (statement of affairs etc);
6.11 to 6.15 (information to creditors and contributories and appointment of liquidator);
6.17 (report by directors etc);
6.18 (decisions on nomination);
6.20 (appointment by creditors or by the company);
6.22 (appointment by the court (section 100(3) or 108), other than in respect of appointments under section 108); and
6.23 (advertisement of appointment).

NOTES

Commencement: 6 April 2017.
This rule derived from the Insolvency Rules 1986, SI 1986/1925, r 4.1(6).

CHAPTER 2 STATEMENT OF AFFAIRS AND OTHER INFORMATION

[Note: a document required by the Act or these Rules must also contain the standard contents set out in Part 1.]

[6.229]
6.2 Statement of affairs made out by the liquidator under section 95(1A)

[Note: (1) section 95(4A) requires the statement of affairs to be verified by a statement of truth;

(2) the "official rate" referred to in paragraph (2)(c) is defined in section 251 as being the rate referred to in section 189(4)).]

(1) This rule applies to the statement of affairs made out by the liquidator under section 95(1A) (effect of company's insolvency in members' voluntary winding up).

(2) The statement of affairs must be headed "Statement of affairs" and must contain—

(a) identification details for the company;
(b) a statement that it is a statement of the affairs of the company on a date which is specified, being the date of the opinion formed by the liquidator under section 95(1);
(c) a statement that as at that date, the liquidator formed the opinion that the company would be unable to pay its debts in full (together with interest at the official rate) within the period stated in the directors' declaration of solvency made under section 89; and
(d) the date it is made.

(3) The statement of affairs must be delivered by the liquidator to the registrar of companies within five business days after the completion of the decision procedure or deemed consent procedure referred to in rule 6.11 in respect of the appointment of the liquidator.

(4) However the liquidator must not deliver to the registrar of companies with the statement of affairs any schedule required by rule 6.4(4)(b).

NOTES

Commencement: 6 April 2017.

This rule derived from the Insolvency Rules 1986, SI 1986/1925, r 4.34, Sch 4, Fm 4.18.

[6.230]

6.3 Statement of affairs made out by the directors under section 99(1)

[Note: section 99(2A) requires the statement of affairs to be verified by a statement of truth.]

(1) This rule applies to the statement of affairs made out by the directors under section 99(1).

(2) The statement of affairs must be headed "Statement of affairs" and must contain—

- (a) identification details for the company;
- (b) a statement that it is a statement of the affairs of the company on a date which is specified, being a date not more than 14 days before the date of the resolution for winding up; and
- (c) the date it is made.

(3) If a creditor requests a copy of the statement of affairs at a time when no liquidator is appointed the directors must deliver a copy to the creditor.

(4) The directors must deliver the statement of affairs to the liquidator as soon as reasonably practicable after the liquidator is appointed.

(5) The liquidator must deliver the statement of affairs to the registrar of companies within five business days after the completion of the decision procedure or deemed consent procedure referred to in rule 6.14 in respect of the appointment of the liquidator.

(6) However the liquidator must not deliver to the registrar of companies with the statement of affairs any schedule required by rule 6.4(4)(b).

NOTES

Commencement: 6 April 2017.

This rule derived from the Insolvency Rules 1986, SI 1986/1925, r 4.34, Sch 4, Fm 4.19.

[6.231]

6.4 Additional requirements as to statements of affairs

(1) A statement of affairs under section 95(1A) or 99(1) must also contain—

- (a) a list of the company's shareholders, with the following details about each shareholder—
  - (i) name and postal address,
  - (ii) the type of shares held,
  - (iii) the nominal amount of the shares held,
  - (iv) the number of shares held,
  - (v) the amount per share called up, and
  - (vi) the total amount called up;
- (b) the total amount of shares called up held by all shareholders;
- (c) a summary of the assets of the company, setting out the book value and estimated realisable value of—
  - (i) any assets subject to a fixed charge,
  - (ii) any assets subject to a floating charge,
  - (iii) any uncharged assets, and
  - (iv) the total value of all the assets available for preferential creditors;
- (d) a summary of the liabilities of the company, setting out—
  - (i) the amount of preferential debts,
  - (ii) an estimate of the deficiency with respect to preferential debts or the surplus available after paying the preferential debts,
  - (iii) an estimate of the prescribed part, if applicable,
  - (iv) an estimate of the total assets available to pay debts secured by floating charges,
  - (v) the amount of debts secured by floating charges,
  - (vi) an estimate of the deficiency with respect to debts secured by floating charges or the surplus available after paying the debts secured by fixed or floating charges,
  - (vii) the amount of unsecured debts (excluding preferential debts),
  - (viii) an estimate of the deficiency with respect to unsecured debts or the surplus available after paying unsecured debts,
  - (ix) any issued and called-up capital, and
  - (x) an estimate of the deficiency with respect to, or surplus available to, members of the company;
- (e) a list of the company's creditors with the further particulars required by paragraph (2) indicating—
  - (i) any creditors under hire-purchase, chattel leasing or conditional sale agreements,
  - (ii) any creditors who are consumers claiming amounts paid in advance of the supply of goods or services, and
  - (iii) any creditors claiming retention of title over property in the company's possession.

(2) The further particulars required by this paragraph relating to each creditor are as follows—

- (i) the name and postal address,
- (ii) amount of the debt owed to the creditor, (as required by section 95(4) or 99(2)),

Part 6 Insolvency Rules

(iii) details of any security held by the creditor,
(iv) the date the security was given, and
(v) the value of any such security.

(3) Paragraph (4) applies where the particulars required by paragraph (2) relate to creditors who are either—

(a) employees or former employees of the company; or
(b) consumers claiming amounts paid in advance for the supply of goods or services.

(4) Where this paragraph applies—

(a) the statement of affairs must state separately for each of paragraphs (3)(a) and (b) the number of such creditors and the total of the debts owed to them; and
(b) the particulars required by paragraph (2) must be set out in separate schedules to the statement of affairs for each of paragraphs (3)(a) and (b).

NOTES

Commencement: 6 April 2017.

This rule derived from the Insolvency Rules 1986, SI 1986/1925, Sch 4, Fms 4.18, 4.19.

[6.232]

6.5 Statement of affairs: statement of concurrence

(1) The liquidator may require a director ("the relevant person") to deliver to the liquidator a statement of concurrence.

(2) A statement of concurrence is a statement that the relevant person concurs in the statement of affairs submitted by another director.

(3) The liquidator must inform the director who has been required to submit a statement of affairs that the relevant person has been required to deliver a statement of concurrence.

(4) The director who has been required to submit the statement of affairs must deliver a copy to every relevant person who has been required to submit a statement of concurrence.

(5) A statement of concurrence—

(a) must identify the company; and
(b) may be qualified in relation to matters dealt with in the statement of affairs, where the maker of the statement of concurrence—
(i) is not in agreement with the statement of affairs,
(ii) considers the statement of affairs to be erroneous or misleading, or
(iii) is without the direct knowledge necessary for concurring with it.

(6) The relevant person must deliver the required statement of concurrence, verified by a statement of truth, to the liquidator together with a copy before the end of the period of five business days (or such other period as the liquidator may agree) beginning with the day on which the relevant person receives the statement of affairs.

(7) The liquidator must deliver the verified statement of concurrence to the registrar of companies.

NOTES

Commencement: 6 April 2017.

This rule derived from the Insolvency Rules 1986, SI 1986/1925, r 4.34(5).

[6.233]

6.6 Order limiting disclosure of statement of affairs etc

(1) Where the liquidator thinks that disclosure of the whole or part of the statement of affairs or of any statement of concurrence would be likely to prejudice the conduct of the winding up or might reasonably be expected to lead to violence against any person, the liquidator may apply to the court for an order that the statement of affairs, statement of concurrence or any specified part of them must not be delivered to the registrar of companies.

(2) The court may order that the whole or a specified part of the statement of affairs or a statement of concurrence must not be delivered to the registrar of companies.

(3) The liquidator must as soon as reasonably practicable deliver to the registrar of companies a copy of the order, the statement of affairs and any statement of concurrence to the extent allowed by the order.

NOTES

Commencement: 6 April 2017.

This rule derived from the Insolvency Rules 1986, SI 1986/1925, r 4.35.

[6.234]

6.7 Expenses of statement of affairs and decisions sought from creditors

(1) Any reasonable and necessary expenses of preparing the statement of affairs under section 99 may be paid out of the company's assets, either before or after the commencement of the winding up, as an expense of the winding up.

(2) Any reasonable and necessary expenses of the decision procedure or deemed consent procedure to seek a decision from the creditors on the nomination of a liquidator under rule 6.14 may be paid out of the company's assets, either before or after the commencement of the winding up, as an expense of the winding up.

(3) Where payment under paragraph (1) or (2) is made before the commencement of the winding up, the directors must deliver to the creditors with the statement of affairs a statement of the amount of the payment and the identity of the person to whom it was made.

(4) The liquidator appointed under section 100 may make such a payment, but if there is a liquidation committee, the liquidator must deliver to the committee at least five business days' notice of the intention to make it.

(5) However such a payment may not be made to the liquidator, or to any associate of the liquidator, otherwise than with the approval of the liquidation committee, the creditors, or the court.

(6) This is without prejudice to the court's powers under rule 7.109 (voluntary winding up superseded by winding up by the court).

NOTES

Commencement: 6 April 2017.

This rule derived from the Insolvency Rules 1986, SI 1986/1925, r 4.38.

[6.235]

6.8 Delivery of accounts to liquidator (section 235)

(1) A person who is specified in section 235(3) must deliver to the liquidator accounts of the company of such nature, as at such date, and for such period, as the liquidator requires.

(2) The period for which the liquidator may require accounts may begin from a date up to three years before the date of the resolution for winding up, or from an earlier date to which audited accounts of the company were last prepared.

(3) The accounts must, if the liquidator so requires, be verified by a statement of truth.

(4) The accounts (verified by a statement of truth if so required) must be delivered to the liquidator within 21 days from the liquidator's request, or such longer period as the liquidator may allow.

NOTES

Commencement: 6 April 2017.

This rule derived from the Insolvency Rules 1986, SI 1986/1925, r 4.40.

[6.236]

6.9 Expenses of assistance in preparing accounts

(1) Where the liquidator requires a person to deliver accounts under rule 6.8 the liquidator may, with the approval of the liquidation committee (if there is one) and as an expense of the winding up, employ a person or firm to assist that person in the preparation of the accounts.

(2) The person who is required to deliver accounts may request an allowance of all or part of the expenses to be incurred in employing a person or firm to assist in preparing the accounts.

(3) A request for an allowance must be accompanied by an estimate of the expenses involved.

(4) The liquidator must only authorise the employment of a named person or a named firm approved by the liquidator.

(5) The liquidator may, with the approval of the liquidation committee (if there is one), authorise such an allowance, payable as an expense of the winding up.

NOTES

Commencement: 6 April 2017.

This rule derived from the Insolvency Rules 1986, SI 1986/1925, r 4.41.

CHAPTER 3 NOMINATION AND APPOINTMENT OF LIQUIDATORS AND INFORMATION TO CREDITORS

[Note: a document required by the Act or these Rules must also contain the standard contents set out in Part 1.]

[6.237]

6.10 Application of the rules in this Chapter

(1) The rules in this Chapter apply as follows.

(2) Rules 6.11 to 6.13 only apply to a conversion from a members' voluntary winding up to a creditors' voluntary winding up.

(3) Rule 6.16 only applies where the administrator becomes the liquidator in a voluntary winding up which follows an administration.

(4) Rules 6.14, 6.15 and 6.17 only apply to a creditors' voluntary winding up which has not been commenced by a conversion from a members' voluntary winding up or an administration.

(5) Rules 6.18 and 6.19 apply to all creditors' voluntary windings up.

NOTES

Commencement: 6 April 2017.

[6.238]

6.11 Nomination of liquidator and information to creditors on conversion from members' voluntary winding up (section 96)

(1) This rule applies in respect of the conversion of a members' voluntary winding up to a creditors' voluntary winding up under section 96.

(2) The liquidator must seek a nomination from the creditors for a liquidator in the creditors' voluntary winding up by—

(a) a decision procedure; or

(b) the deemed consent procedure.

(3) The liquidator must deliver to the creditors a copy of the statement of affairs required by section 95(1A) and Chapter 2 of this Part together with a notice which complies with rules 15.7 or 15.8 so far as are relevant.

(4) The notice must also contain—

(a) identification and contact details for the existing liquidator; and

(b) a statement that if no person is nominated by the creditors then the existing liquidator will be the liquidator in the creditors' voluntary winding up.

(5) The decision date in the notice must be not later than 28 days from the date under section 95(1) that the liquidator formed the opinion that the company will be unable to pay its debts in full.

(6) Subject to paragraph (9), the creditors must be given at least 14 days' notice of the decision date.

(7) Paragraph (8) applies where—

(a) the liquidator has sought a decision from creditors on the nomination of a liquidator by the deemed consent procedure; but

(b) the level of objections to the proposed nomination have meant, under section 246ZF, that no nomination is deemed to have been made.

(8) Where this paragraph applies, the liquidator must seek a nomination from creditors by way of a decision procedure in accordance with this rule, the decision date to be as soon as reasonably practicable, but no more than 28 days from the date that the level of objections had the effect that no nomination was deemed to have been made.

(9) Where paragraph (8) applies, the creditors must be given at least seven days' notice of the decision date.

(10) Where the liquidator is required by rule 15.6 to summon a physical meeting as a result of requests from creditors received in response to a notice delivered under this rule, the physical meeting must be summoned to take place—

(a) within 28 days of the date on which the threshold for requiring a physical meeting was met; and

(b) with at least 14 days' notice.

NOTES

Commencement: 6 April 2017.

[6.239]

6.12 Creditors' decision on appointment other than at a meeting (conversion from members' voluntary winding up)

(1) This rule applies where the creditors' decision on the nomination of a liquidator in a conversion of a members' into a creditors' voluntary winding up is intended to be sought otherwise than through a meeting or through the deemed consent procedure, including where the conditions in rule 6.11(7) are met and the liquidator, under rule 6.11(8), goes on to seek a nomination from creditors by way of a decision procedure other than a meeting.

(2) Instead of delivering a notice of the decision procedure or deemed consent procedure under rule 6.11, the liquidator must deliver a notice to creditors inviting them to make proposals for the nomination of a liquidator.

(3) Such a notice must—

(a) identify any liquidator for whom a proposal which is in compliance with paragraph 4 has already been received;

(b) explain that the liquidator is not obliged to seek the creditors' views on any proposal that does not meet the requirements of paragraphs (4) and (5); and

(c) be accompanied by the statement of affairs unless that has previously been delivered to the creditor.

(4) Any proposal must state the name and contact details of the proposed liquidator, and contain a statement that the proposed liquidator is qualified to act as an insolvency practitioner in relation to the company and has consented to act as liquidator of the company.

(5) Any proposal must be received by the liquidator within five business days of the date of the notice under paragraph (2).

(6) Within two business days of the end of the period referred to in paragraph (5), the liquidator must [send] a notice to creditors of a decision procedure under rule 6.11.

NOTES

Commencement: 6 April 2017.

Para (6): word in square brackets substituted by the Insolvency (England and Wales) (Amendment) Rules 2017, SI 2017/366, rr 3, 23.

[6.240]

6.13 Information to creditors and contributories (conversion of members' voluntary winding up into creditors' voluntary winding up)

(1) The liquidator must deliver to the creditors and contributories within 28 days of the conversion of a members' voluntary winding up into a creditors' voluntary winding up under section 96 a notice which must contain—

(a) the date the winding up became a creditors' voluntary winding up;

(b) a report of the decision procedure or deemed consent procedure which took place under rule [6.11]; and

(c) the information required by paragraph (3).

(2) The notice must be accompanied by a copy of the statement of affairs or a summary except where the notice is being delivered to a creditor to whom a copy of the statement of affairs has previously been delivered under section 95(1A).

(3) The required information is an estimate to the best of the liquidator's knowledge and belief of—

(a) the value of the prescribed part (whether or not the liquidator might be required under section 176A to make the prescribed part available for the satisfaction of unsecured debts); and

(b) the value of the company's net property (as defined by section 176A(6)).

(4) The liquidator may exclude from an estimate under paragraph (3) information the disclosure of which could seriously prejudice the commercial interests of the company.

(5) If the exclusion of such information affects the calculation of an estimate, the report must say so.

(6) If the liquidator proposes to make an application to court under section 176A(5) the report must say so and give the reason for the application.

NOTES

Commencement: 6 April 2017.

This rule derived from the Insolvency Rules 1986, SI 1986/1925, r 4.49.

Para (1): figure in square brackets in sub-para (b) substituted by the Insolvency (England and Wales) (Amendment) Rules 2017, SI 2017/366, rr 3, 22.

[6.241]

6.14 Information to creditors and appointment of liquidator

(1) This rule applies in respect of the appointment of a liquidator under section 100.

(2) The directors of the company must deliver to the creditors a notice seeking their decision on the nomination of a liquidator by—

(a) the deemed consent procedure; or

(b) a virtual meeting.

(3) The decision date for the decision of the creditors on the nomination of a liquidator must be not earlier than three business days after the notice under paragraph (2) is delivered but not later than 14 days after the resolution is passed to wind up the company.

(4) Where the directors have sought a decision from the creditors through the deemed consent procedure under paragraph (2)(a) but, pursuant to section 246ZF(5)(a) (deemed consent procedure), more than the specified number of creditors object so that the decision cannot be treated as having been made, the directors must then seek a decision from the creditors on the nomination of a liquidator by holding a physical meeting under rule 15.6 (physical meetings) as if a physical meeting had been required under section 246ZE(4) (decisions by creditors and contributories: general).

(5) Where paragraph (4) applies, the meeting must not be held earlier than three business days after the notice under rule 15.6(3) is delivered or later than 14 days after the level of objections reach that described in paragraph (4).

(6) A request for a physical meeting under section 246ZE must be made in accordance with rule 15.6 except that—

(a) such a request may be made at any time between the delivery of the notice under paragraph (2) and the decision date under paragraph (3); and

(b) the decision date where this paragraph applies must be not earlier than three business days after the notice under rule 15.6(3) is delivered and not later than 14 days after the level of requests reach that described in section 246ZE.

(7) The directors must deliver to the creditors a copy of the statement of affairs required under section 99 of the Act not later than on the business day before the decision date.

(8) A notice delivered under paragraph (2), in addition to the information required by rules 15.7 (deemed consent) and 15.8 (notices to creditors of decision procedure), must contain—

(a) the date the resolution to wind up is to be considered or was passed;

(b) identification and contact details of any liquidator nominated by the company;

(c) a statement of either—

(i) the name and address of a person qualified to act as an insolvency practitioner in relation to the company who during the period before the decision date, will furnish creditors free of charge with such information concerning the company's affairs as they may reasonably require, or

(ii) a place in the relevant locality where, on the two business days falling next before the decision date, a list of the names and addresses of the company's creditors will be available for inspection free of charge; and

Part 6 Insolvency Rules

(d) where the notice is sent to creditors in advance of the copy of the statement of affairs, a statement that the directors, before the decision date and before the end of the period of seven days beginning with the day after the day on which the company passed a resolution for winding up, are required by section 99 of the Insolvency Act 1986—
   (i) to make out a statement in the prescribed form as to the affairs of the company, and
   (ii) send the statement to the company's creditors.

(9) Where the company's principal place of business in England or Wales was situated in different localities at different times during the relevant period, the duty imposed by sub-paragraph (8)(c)(ii) above applies separately in relation to each of those localities.

(10) Where the company had no place of business in England or Wales during the relevant period, the reference in paragraph (9) to the company's principal place of business in England or Wales are replaced by references to its registered office.

(11) In paragraph (9), "the relevant period" means the period of six months immediately preceding the day on which the notices referred to in paragraph (2) were delivered.

(12) Where a virtual or physical meeting is held under this rule and a liquidator has already been nominated by the company, the liquidator or an appointed person must attend any meeting held under this rule and report on any exercise of the liquidator's powers under section 112, 165 or 166 of the Act.

(13) A director who is in default in seeking a decision on the nomination of a liquidator in accordance with this rule is guilty of an offence and is liable to a fine.

NOTES

Commencement: 6 April 2017.

This rule derived from the Insolvency Rules 1986, SI 1986/1925, r 4.49.

[6.242]

6.15 Information to creditors and contributories

(1) The liquidator must deliver to the creditors and contributories within 28 days of the appointment of the liquidator under section 100 a notice which must—
   (a) be accompanied by a statement of affairs or a summary where the notice is delivered to any contributory or creditor to whom the notice under rule 6.14 was not delivered;
   (b) [be accompanied by] a report on the decision procedure or deemed consent procedure under rule 6.14; and
   (c) be accompanied by the information required by paragraph (2).

(2) The required information is an estimate to the best of the liquidator's knowledge and belief of—
   (a) the value of the prescribed part (whether or not the liquidator might be required under section 176A to make the prescribed part available for the satisfaction of unsecured debts); and
   (b) the value of the company's net property (as defined by section 176A(6)).

(3) The liquidator may exclude from an estimate under paragraph (2) information the disclosure of which could seriously prejudice the commercial interests of the company.

(4) If the exclusion of such information affects the calculation of an estimate, the report must say so.

(5) If the liquidator proposes to make an application to court under section 176A(5) the report must say so and give the reason for the application.

NOTES

Commencement: 6 April 2017.

This rule derived from the Insolvency Rules 1986, SI 1986/1925, r 4.49.

Para (1): words in square brackets inserted by the Insolvency (England and Wales) and Insolvency (Scotland) (Miscellaneous and Consequential Amendments) Rules 2017, SI 2017/1115, rr 2, 6.

[6.243]

6.16 Further information where administrator becomes liquidator (paragraph 83(3) of Schedule B1)

(1) This rule applies where an administrator becomes liquidator on the registration of a notice under paragraph 83(3) of Schedule B1, and becomes aware of creditors not formerly known to that person as administrator.

(2) The liquidator must deliver to those creditors a copy of any statement delivered by the administrator to creditors in accordance with paragraph 49(4) of Schedule B1 and rule 3.35.

NOTES

Commencement: 6 April 2017.

This rule derived from the Insolvency Rules 1986, SI 1986/1925, r 4.49A.

[6.244]

6.17 Report by director etc

(1) Where the statement of affairs sent to creditors under section 99(1) does not, or will not, state the company's affairs at the decision date for the creditors' nomination of a liquidator, the directors of the company must cause a report (written or oral) to be made to the creditors in accordance with this rule on any material transactions relating to the company occurring between the date of the making of the statement and the decision date.

(2) In the case of a decision being taken through a meeting, the report must be made at the meeting by the director chairing the meeting or by another person with knowledge of the relevant matters.

(3) Where the deemed consent procedure is used, the report must be delivered to creditors as soon as reasonably practicable after the material transaction takes place in the same manner as the deemed consent procedure.

(4) Where the decision date is within the period of three business days from the delivery of a report under paragraph (3), this rule extends the decision date until the end of that period notwithstanding the requirement in rule 6.14(3) relating to the timing of the decision date.

(5) On delivery of a report under paragraph (3), the directors must notify the creditors of the effects of paragraph (4).

(6) A report under this rule must be recorded in the record of the decision under rule 15.40.

NOTES

Commencement: 6 April 2017.

This rule derived from the Insolvency Rules 1986, SI 1986/1925, r 4.53B.

[6.245]

6.18 Decisions on nomination

(1) In the case of a decision on the nomination of a liquidator—

(a) if on any vote there are two nominees, the person who obtains the most support is appointed;

(b) if there are three or more nominees, and one of them has a clear majority over both or all the others together, that one is appointed; and

(c) in any other case, the convener or chair must continue to take votes (disregarding at each vote any nominee who has withdrawn and, if no nominee has withdrawn, the nominee who obtained the least support last time) until a clear majority is obtained for any one nominee.

(2) In the case of a decision being made at a meeting, the chair may at any time put to the meeting a resolution for the joint nomination of any two or more nominees.

NOTES

Commencement: 6 April 2017.

This rule derived from the Insolvency Rules 1986, SI 1986/1925, r 4.63.

[6.246]

6.19 Invitation to creditors to form a liquidation committee

(1) Where any decision is sought from the company's creditors—

(a) in a creditors' voluntary winding up; or

(b) where a members' voluntary winding up is converting in a creditors' voluntary winding up;

the convener of the decision must at the same time deliver to the creditors a notice inviting them to decide whether a liquidation committee should be established if sufficient creditors are willing to be members of the committee.

(2) The notice must also invite nominations for membership of the committee, such nominations to be received by a date specified in the notice.

(3) The notice must state that nominations—

(a) must be delivered to the convener by the specified date; and

(b) can only be accepted if the convener is satisfied as to the creditor's eligibility under rule 17.4.

NOTES

Commencement: 6 April 2017.

CHAPTER 4 THE LIQUIDATOR

[Note: a document required by the Act or these Rules must also contain the standard contents set out in Part 1.]

[6.247]

6.20 Appointment by creditors or by the company

(1) This rule applies where a person is appointed as liquidator by creditors or the company.

[(2) The liquidator's appointment takes effect from the date of the passing of the resolution of the company or, where the creditors decide to appoint a person who is not the person appointed by the company, from the relevant decision date.]

(3) Their appointment must be certified by—

(a) the convener or chair of the decision procedure or deemed consent procedure; or

(b) in respect of an appointment by the company the chair of the company meeting or a director or the secretary of the company (in the case of a written resolution).

(4) The person who certifies the appointment must not do so unless and until the proposed liquidator ("the appointee") has provided that person with a statement of being an insolvency practitioner qualified under the Act to be the liquidator and of consenting to act.

(5) The certificate must be authenticated and dated by the person who certifies the appointment and must contain—

(a) identification details for the company;

(b) identification and contact details for the person appointed as liquidator;
(c) the date of the meeting of the company or conclusion of the decision procedure or deemed consent procedure when the liquidator was appointed;
(d) a statement that the appointee—
    (i) has provided a statement of being qualified to act as an insolvency practitioner in relation to the company,
    (ii) has consented to act, and
    (iii) was appointed liquidator of the company.

(6) Where two or more liquidators are appointed the certificate must also specify (as required by section 231) whether any act required or authorised under any enactment to be done by the liquidator is to be done by all or any one or more of them.

(7) The person who certifies the appointment must deliver the certificate as soon as reasonably practicable to the liquidator, who must keep it as part of the records of the winding up.

NOTES

Commencement: 6 April 2017.

This rule derived from the Insolvency Rules 1986, SI 1986/1925, r 4.101.

Para (2): substituted by the Insolvency (England and Wales) (Amendment) Rules 2017, SI 2017/366, rr 3, 24.

[6.248]

6.21 Power to fill vacancy in office of liquidator

Where a vacancy in the office of liquidator occurs in the manner mentioned in section 104 a decision procedure to fill the vacancy may be initiated by any creditor or, if there was more than one liquidator, by the continuing liquidator or liquidators.

NOTES

Commencement: 6 April 2017.

This rule derived from the Insolvency Rules 1986, SI 1986/1925, r 4.101A.

[6.249]

6.22 Appointment by the court (section 100(3) or 108)

(1) This rule applies where the liquidator is appointed by the court under section 100(3) or 108.

(2) The court's order must not be made unless and until the proposed liquidator has filed with the court a statement of being qualified under the Act to act as an insolvency practitioner in relation to the company and of consenting to act.

(3) The order of the court must contain—
(a) the name of the court (and hearing centre if applicable) in which the order is made;
(b) the name and title of the judge making the order;
(c) the date on which it is made;
(d) identification details for the company;
(e) the name and postal address of the applicant;
(f) the capacity in which the applicant made the application;
(g) identification details for the proposed liquidator; and
(h) an order that the proposed liquidator, having filed a statement of being qualified to act as an insolvency practitioner in relation to the company and having consented to act, is appointed liquidator of the company from the date of the order, or such other date as the court orders.

(4) Where two or more liquidators are appointed the order must also specify (as required by section 231) whether any act required or authorised under any enactment to be done by the liquidator is to be done by all or any one or more of them.

(5) The court must deliver a sealed copy of the order to the liquidator.

(6) Within 28 days from appointment, the liquidator must—
(a) deliver a notice of the appointment to creditors of the company; or
(b) advertise the appointment in accordance with any directions given by the court.

NOTES

Commencement: 6 April 2017.

This rule derived from the Insolvency Rules 1986, SI 1986/1925, r 4.103.

[6.250]

6.23 Advertisement of appointment

(1) A liquidator appointed in a voluntary winding up in addition to delivering a notice of the appointment in accordance with section 109(1) may advertise the notice in such other manner as the liquidator thinks fit.

(2) The notice must state—
(a) that a liquidator has been appointed; and
(b) the date of the appointment.

(3) The liquidator must initially bear the expense of giving notice under this rule but is entitled to be reimbursed for the expenditure as an expense of the winding up.

NOTES

Commencement: 6 April 2017.

This rule derived from the Insolvency Rules 1986, SI 1986/1925, r 4.106A.

[6.251]

6.24 Cost of liquidator's security (section 390(3))

The cost of the liquidator's security required by section 390(3) for the proper performance of the liquidator's functions is an expense of the winding up.

NOTES

Commencement: 6 April 2017.

This rule derived from the Insolvency Rules 1986, SI 1986/1925, r 12A.56.

[6.252]

6.25 Liquidator's resignation and replacement

(1) A liquidator may resign only—

(a) on grounds of ill health;

(b) because of the intention to cease to practise as an insolvency practitioner;

(c) because the further discharge of the duties of liquidator is prevented or made impractical by—

(i) a conflict of interest, or

(ii) or a change of personal circumstances; or

(d) where two or more persons are acting as liquidator jointly and it is the opinion of both or all of them that it is no longer expedient that there should continue to be that number of joint liquidators.

(2) Before resigning the liquidator must invite the creditors by a decision procedure, or by deemed consent, to consider whether a replacement should be appointed except where the resignation is under paragraph (1)(d).

(3) The notice of the decision procedure or of deemed consent must—

(a) state the liquidator's intention to resign;

(b) state that under rule 6.25(7) of these Rules the liquidator will be released 21 days after the date of delivery of the notice of resignation to the registrar of companies under section 171(5), unless the court orders otherwise; and

(c) comply with rules 15.7 and 15.8 so far as are relevant.

(4) The notice may suggest the name of a replacement liquidator.

(5) The notice must be accompanied by a summary of the liquidator's receipts and payments.

(6) The decision date must be not more than five business days before the date on which the liquidator intends to give notice of resignation to the registrar of companies under section 171(5).

(7) The resigning liquidator's release is effective 21 days after the date of delivery of the notice of resignation to the registrar of companies under section 171(5), unless the court orders otherwise.

NOTES

Commencement: 6 April 2017.

This rule derived from the Insolvency Rules 1986, SI 1986/1925, r 4.108.

[6.253]

6.26 Removal of liquidator by creditors

(1) Where the creditors decide that the liquidator be removed, the convener of the decision procedure or the chair of the meeting (as the case may be) must as soon as reasonably practicable deliver the certificate of the liquidator's removal to the removed liquidator.

(2) The removed liquidator must deliver a notice of the removal to the registrar of companies as soon as reasonably practicable.

NOTES

Commencement: 6 April 2017.

This rule derived from the Insolvency Rules 1986, SI 1986/1925, r 4.117.

[6.254]

6.27 Removal of liquidator by the court

(1) This rule applies where an application is made to the court for the removal of the liquidator, or for an order directing the liquidator to initiate a decision procedure of creditors for the purpose of removing the liquidator.

(2) On receipt of an application, the court may, if it is satisfied that no sufficient cause is shown for it, dismiss it without giving notice to any party other than the applicant.

(3) Unless the application is dismissed, the court must fix a venue for it to be heard.

(4) The applicant must, at least 14 days before any hearing, deliver to the liquidator a notice stating the venue with a copy of the application and of any evidence on which the applicant intends to rely.

(5) A respondent may apply for security for the costs of the application and the court may make such an order if it is satisfied, having regard to all the circumstances of the case, that it is just to make such an order.

(6) The liquidator may do either or both of the following—

(a) file a report of any matters which the liquidator thinks ought to be drawn to the court's attention; or
(b) appear and be heard on the application.

(7) The costs of the application are not payable as an expense of the winding up unless the court orders otherwise.

(8) On a successful application the court's order must contain the following—
(a) the name of the court (and hearing centre if applicable) in which the order is made;
(b) the name and title of the judge making the order;
(c) identification details for the company;
(d) the name and postal address of the applicant;
(e) the capacity in which the applicant made the application;
(f) identification and contact details for the liquidator;
(g) an order either—
(i) that the liquidator is removed from office from the date of the order (unless the order specifies otherwise), or
(ii) that the liquidator must initiate a decision procedure of the company's creditors (specifying which procedure is to be used) on or before a date stated in the order for the purpose of considering the liquidator's removal from office; and
(h) the date of the order.

(9) Where the court removes the liquidator—
(a) it must deliver the sealed order of removal to the former liquidator; and
(b) the former liquidator must deliver a copy of the order to the registrar of companies as soon as reasonably practicable.

(10) If the court appoints a new liquidator rule 6.22 applies.

NOTES

Commencement: 6 April 2017.
This rule derived from the Insolvency Rules 1986, SI 1986/1925, r 4.120.

[6.255]
6.28 Final account prior to dissolution (section 106)

(1) The final account which the liquidator is required to make up under section 106(1) and deliver to members and creditors must comply with the requirements of rule 18.14.

(2) When the account is delivered to the creditors it must be accompanied by a notice which states—
(a) that the company's affairs are fully wound up;
(b) that the creditors have the right to request information from the liquidator under rule 18.9;
(c) that the creditors have the right to challenge the liquidator's remuneration and expenses under rule 18.34;
(d) that a creditor may object to the release of the liquidator by giving notice in writing to the liquidator before the end of the prescribed period;
(e) that the prescribed period is the period ending at the later of—
(i) eight weeks after delivery of the notice, or
(ii) if any request for information under rule 18.9 or any application to court under that rule or rule 18.34 is made, when that request or application is finally determined;
(f) that the liquidator will vacate office under section 171 on delivering to the registrar of companies the final account and notice saying whether any creditor has objected to release; and
(g) that the liquidator will be released under section 173 at the same time as vacating office unless any of the company's creditors objected to the liquidator's release.

(3) The copy of the account which the liquidator delivers to the registrar of companies under section 106(3) must be accompanied by a notice containing the statement required by section 106(3)(a) of whether any creditors have objected to the liquidator's release.

(4) Where a creditor has objected to the liquidator's release rule 6.33 applies to an application by the liquidator to the Secretary of State for release.

(5) The liquidator is not obliged to prepare or deliver any progress report which may become due under these Rules in the period between the date to which the final account is made up and the date when the account is delivered to the registrar of companies under section 106(3)(a).

NOTES

Commencement: 6 April 2017.
This rule derived from the Insolvency Rules 1986, SI 1986/1925, r 4.126.

[6.256]
6.29 Deceased liquidator

(1) If the liquidator dies a notice of the fact and date of death must be delivered as soon as reasonably practicable—
(a) where there is a liquidation committee, to the members of that committee; and
(b) to the registrar of companies.

(2) The notice must be delivered by one of the following—
(a) a surviving joint liquidator;

(b) a member of the deceased liquidator's firm (if the deceased was a member or employee of a firm);
(c) an officer of the deceased liquidator's company (if the deceased was an officer or employee of a company); or
(d) a personal representative of the deceased liquidator.

(3) If such a notice has not been delivered within the 21 days following the liquidator's death then any other person may deliver the notice.

NOTES

Commencement: 6 April 2017.
This rule derived from the Insolvency Rules 1986, SI 1986/1925, r 4.133.

[6.257]
6.30 Loss of qualification as insolvency practitioner

(1) This rule applies where the liquidator vacates office on ceasing to be qualified to act as an insolvency practitioner in relation to the company.

(2) A notice of the fact must be delivered as soon as reasonably practicable to the registrar of companies and the Secretary of State by one of the following—
(a) the liquidator who has vacated office;
(b) a continuing joint liquidator;
(c) the recognised professional body which was the source of the vacating liquidator's authorisation to act in relation to the company.

(3) Each notice must be authenticated and dated by the person delivering the notice.

NOTES

Commencement: 6 April 2017.
This rule derived from the Insolvency Rules 1986, SI 1986/1925, r 4.135.

[6.258]
6.31 Vacation of office on making of winding-up order

Where the liquidator vacates office in consequence of the court making a winding-up order against the company, rule 6.33 applies in relation to the application to the Secretary of State for release of the liquidator.

NOTES

Commencement: 6 April 2017.
This rule derived from the Insolvency Rules 1986, SI 1986/1925, r 4.136.

[6.259]
6.32 Liquidator's duties on vacating office

A liquidator who ceases to be in office in consequence of removal, resignation or ceasing to be qualified as an insolvency practitioner in relation to the company, must as soon as reasonably practicable deliver to the succeeding liquidator—
(a) the assets (after deduction of any expenses properly incurred, and distributions made, by the former liquidator);
(b) the records of the winding up, including correspondence, proofs and other documents; and
(c) the company's records.

NOTES

Commencement: 6 April 2017.
This rule derived from the Insolvency Rules 1986, SI 1986/1925, r 4.138.

[6.260]
6.33 Application by former liquidator for release (section 173(2)(b))

(1) An application to the Secretary of State by a former liquidator for release under section 173(2)(b) must contain—
(a) identification and contact details for the former liquidator;
(b) identification details for the company;
(c) details of the circumstances under which the liquidator has ceased to act as liquidator;
(d) a statement that the former liquidator of the company is applying to the Secretary of State for a certificate of release as liquidator as a result of the circumstances specified in the application.

(2) The application must be authenticated and dated by the former liquidator.

(3) When the Secretary of State releases the former liquidator, the Secretary of State must certify the release and deliver the certificate to the former liquidator whose release is effective from the date of the certificate or such other date as the certificate specifies.

(4) The Secretary of State must deliver a notice of the release to the registrar of companies.

NOTES

Commencement: 6 April 2017.
This rule derived from the Insolvency Rules 1986, SI 1986/1925, r 4.122(3), Sch 4, Fm 4.41.

[6.261]

6.34 Power of court to set aside certain transactions

(1) If in dealing with the insolvent estate the liquidator enters into any transaction with a person who is an associate of the liquidator, the court may, on the application of any interested person, set the transaction aside and order the liquidator to compensate the company for any loss suffered in consequence of it.

(2) This does not apply if either—

(a) the transaction was entered into with the prior consent of the court; or

(b) it is shown to the court's satisfaction that the transaction was for value, and that it was entered into by the liquidator without knowing, or having any reason to suppose, that the person concerned was an associate.

(3) Nothing in this rule is to be taken as prejudicing the operation of any rule of law or equity relating to a liquidator's dealings with trust property or the fiduciary obligations of any person.

NOTES

Commencement: 6 April 2017.

This rule derived from the Insolvency Rules 1986, SI 1986/1925, r 4.149.

[6.262]

6.35 Rule against improper solicitation

(1) Where the court is satisfied that any improper solicitation has been used by or on behalf of the liquidator in obtaining proxies or procuring the liquidator's appointment, it may order that no remuneration be allowed as an expense of the winding up to any person by whom, or on whose behalf, the solicitation was exercised.

(2) An order of the court under this rule overrides any resolution of the liquidation committee or the creditors, or any other provision of these Rules relating to the liquidator's remuneration.

NOTES

Commencement: 6 April 2017.

This rule derived from the Insolvency Rules 1986, SI 1986/1925, r 4.150.

[6.263]

6.36 Permission for exercise of powers by liquidator

(1) Where these Rules require permission for the liquidator to exercise a power any permission given must not be a general permission but must relate to a particular proposed exercise of the liquidator's power.

(2) A person dealing with the liquidator in good faith and for value is not concerned to enquire whether any such permission has been given.

(3) Where the liquidator has done anything without such permission, the court or the liquidation committee may, for the purpose of enabling the liquidator to meet the liquidator's expenses out of the assets, ratify what the liquidator has done; but neither may do so unless satisfied that the liquidator has acted in a case of urgency and has sought ratification without undue delay.

(4) In this rule "permission" includes "sanction".

NOTES

Commencement: 6 April 2017.

This rule derived from the Insolvency Rules 1986, SI 1986/1925, r 4.184.

CHAPTER 5 SPECIAL MANAGER

[Note: a document required by the Act or these Rules must also contain the standard contents set out in Part 1.]

[6.264]

6.37 Application for and appointment of special manager (section 177)

(1) An application by the liquidator under section 177 for the appointment of a special manager must be supported by a report setting out the reasons for the application.

(2) The report must include the applicant's estimate of the value of the business or property in relation to which the special manager is to be appointed.

(3) The court's order appointing a special manager must have the title "Order of Appointment of Special Manager" and must contain—

(a) the name of the court (and hearing centre if applicable) in which the order is made;

(b) the name and title of the judge making the order;

(c) identification details for the proceedings;

(d) the name and address of the applicant;

(e) the name and address of the proposed special manager;

(f) the order that that the proposed special manager is appointed as special manager of the company from the date of the order (or otherwise as the order provides);

(g) details of the special manager's responsibility over the company's business or property;

(h) the powers entrusted to the special manager under section [177(3)];

(i) the time allowed for the special manager to give the required security for the appointment;

(j) the duration of the special manager's appointment, being one of the following—
 (i) for a fixed period stated in the order,
 (ii) until the occurrence of a specified event, or
 (iii) until the court makes a further order;
(k) the order that the special manager's remuneration will be fixed from time to time by the court; and
(l) the date of the order.

(4) The appointment of the special manager may be renewed by order of the court.

(5) The acts of the special manager are valid notwithstanding any defect in the special manager's appointment or qualifications.

NOTES

Commencement: 6 April 2017.

This rule derived from the Insolvency Rules 1986, SI 1986/1925, r 4.206.

Para (3): figure in square brackets in sub-para (h) substituted by the Insolvency (England and Wales) (Amendment) Rules 2017, SI 2017/366, rr 3, 20.

[6.265]
6.38 Security

(1) The appointment of the special manager does not take effect until the person appointed has given (or, if the court allows, undertaken to give) security to the applicant for the appointment.

(2) A person appointed as special manager may give security either specifically for a particular winding up, or generally for any winding up in relation to which that person may be appointed as special manager.

(3) The amount of the security must be not less than the value of the business or property in relation to which the special manager is appointed, as estimated in the applicant's report which accompanied the application for appointment.

(4) When the special manager has given security to the applicant, the applicant must file with the court a certificate as to the adequacy of the security.

(5) The cost of providing the security must be paid in the first instance by the special manager; but the special manager is entitled to be reimbursed as an expense of the winding up, in the prescribed order of priority.

NOTES

Commencement: 6 April 2017.

This rule derived from the Insolvency Rules 1986, SI 1986/1925, r 4.207.

[6.266]
6.39 Failure to give or keep up security

(1) If the special manager fails to give the required security within the time stated in the order of appointment, or any extension of that time that may be allowed, the liquidator must report the failure to the court which may discharge the order appointing the special manager.

(2) If the special manager fails to keep up the security, the liquidator must report the failure to the court, which may remove the special manager, and make such order as it thinks just as to costs.

(3) If the court discharges the order appointing the special manager or makes an order removing the special manager, the court must give directions as to whether any, and if so what, steps should be taken for the appointment of another special manager.

NOTES

Commencement: 6 April 2017.

This rule derived from the Insolvency Rules 1986, SI 1986/1925, r 4.208.

[6.267]
6.40 Accounting

(1) The special manager must produce accounts, containing details of the special manager's receipts and payments, for the approval of the liquidator.

(2) The account must be for—
(a) each three month period for the duration of the special manager's appointment;
(b) any shorter period ending with the termination of the special manager's appointment.

(3) When the accounts have been approved, the special manager's receipts and payments must be added to those of the liquidator.

NOTES

Commencement: 6 April 2017.

This rule derived from the Insolvency Rules 1986, SI 1986/1925, r 4.209.

[6.268]
6.41 Termination of appointment

(1) If the liquidator thinks that the employment of the special manager is no longer necessary or beneficial for the company, the liquidator must apply to the court for directions, and the court may order the special manager's appointment to be terminated.

(2) The liquidator must also make such an application if the creditors decide that the appointment should be terminated.

NOTES

Commencement: 6 April 2017.

This rule derived from the Insolvency Rules 1986, SI 1986/1925, r 4.210.

CHAPTER 6 PRIORITY OF PAYMENT OF COSTS AND EXPENSES, ETC

[6.269]

6.42 General rule as to priority

(1) All fees, costs, charges and other expenses incurred in the course of the winding up are to be treated as expenses of the winding up.

(2) The expenses of the winding up are payable out of—

(a) assets of the company available for the payment of general creditors, including—

(i) proceeds of any legal action which the liquidator has power to bring in the liquidator's own name or in the name of the company,

(ii) proceeds arising from any award made under any arbitration or other dispute resolution procedure which the liquidator has power to bring in the liquidator's own name or in the name of the company,

(iii) any payments made under any compromise or other agreement intended to avoid legal action or recourse to arbitration or to any other dispute resolution procedure, and

(iv) payments made as a result of an assignment or a settlement of any such action, arbitration or other dispute resolution procedure in lieu of or before any judgment being given or award being made; and

(b) subject as provided in rules 6.44 to 6.48, property comprised in or subject to a floating charge created by the company.

(3) The expenses associated with the prescribed part must be paid out of the prescribed part.

(4) Subject as provided in rules 6.44 to 6.48, the expenses are payable in the following order of priority—

(a) expenses which are properly chargeable or incurred by the liquidator in preserving, realising or getting in any of the assets of the company or otherwise in the preparation, conduct or assignment of any legal proceedings, arbitration or other dispute resolution procedures, which the liquidator has power to bring in the liquidator's own name or bring or defend in the name of the company or in the preparation or conduct of any negotiations intended to lead or leading to a settlement or compromise of any legal action or dispute to which the proceedings or procedures relate;

(b) the cost of any security provided by the liquidator or special manager under the Act or these Rules;

(c) the remuneration of the special manager (if any);

(d) any amount payable to a person employed or authorised, under Chapter 2 of this Part, to assist in the preparation of a statement of affairs or of accounts;

(e) the costs of employing a shorthand writer on the application of the liquidator;

(f) any necessary disbursements by the liquidator in the course of the administration of the winding up (including any [costs referred to in Articles 30 or 59 of the EU Regulation and] expenses incurred by members of the liquidation committee or their representatives and allowed by the liquidator under rule 17.24, but not including any payment of corporation tax in circumstances referred to in sub-paragraph (i));

(g) the remuneration or emoluments of any person who has been employed by the liquidator to perform any services for the company, as required or authorised by or under the Act or these Rules;

(h) the remuneration of the liquidator, up to an amount not exceeding that which is payable under Schedule 11 (determination of insolvency office-holder's remuneration);

(i) the amount of any corporation tax on chargeable gains accruing on the realisation of any asset of the company (irrespective of the person by whom the realisation is effected);

(j) the balance, after payment of any sums due under sub-paragraph (h) above, of any remuneration due to the liquidator; and

(k) any other expenses properly chargeable by the liquidator in carrying out the liquidator's functions in the winding up.

NOTES

Commencement: 6 April 2017.

This rule derived from the Insolvency Rules 1986, SI 1986/1925, rr 4.218, 12.2.

Para (4): words in square brackets in sub-para (f) inserted by the Insolvency Amendment (EU 2015/848) Regulations 2017, SI 2017/702, regs 2, 3, Schedule, Pt 2, paras 32, 38, as from 26 June 2017, except in relation to proceedings opened before that date.

[6.270]

6.43 Saving for powers of the court

Nothing in these Rules—

(a) applies to or affects the powers of any court, in proceedings by or against the company, to order costs to be paid by the company, or the liquidator; or

(b) affects the rights of any person to whom such costs are ordered to be paid.

NOTES

Commencement: 6 April 2017.

This rule derived from the Insolvency Rules 1986, SI 1986/1925, r 4.220.

CHAPTER 7 LITIGATION EXPENSES AND PROPERTY SUBJECT TO A FLOATING CHARGE

[Note: a document required by the Act or these Rules must also contain the standard contents set out in Part 1.]

[6.271]

6.44 Interpretation

(1) In this Chapter—

"approval" and "authorisation" respectively mean—

(a) where yet to be incurred, the approval; and

(b) where already incurred, the authorisation;

of expenses specified in section [176ZA(1)];

"the creditor" means—

(a) a preferential creditor of the company; or

(b) a holder of a debenture secured by, or a holder of, a floating charge created by the company;

"legal proceedings" means—

(a) proceedings under sections 212, 213, 214, 238, 239, 244 and 423 and any arbitration or other dispute resolution proceedings invoked for purposes corresponding to those to which the sections relate and any other proceedings, including arbitration or other dispute resolution procedures, which a liquidator has power to bring in the liquidator's own name for the purpose of preserving, realising, or getting in any of the assets of the company;

(b) legal actions and proceedings, arbitration or any other dispute resolution procedures which a liquidator has power to bring or defend in the name of the company; and

(c) negotiations intended to lead or leading to a settlement or compromise of any action, proceeding or procedure to which sub-paragraphs (a) or (b) relate;

"litigation expenses" means expenses of a winding up which—

(a) are properly chargeable or incurred in the preparation or conduct of any legal proceedings; and

(b) as expenses in the winding up, exceed, or in the opinion of the liquidator are likely to exceed (and only in so far as they exceed or are likely to exceed), in the aggregate £5,000; and

"specified creditor" means a creditor identified under rule 6.45(2).

(2) Litigation expenses will not have the priority provided by section 176ZA over any claims to property comprised in or subject to a floating charge created by the company and must not be paid out of any such property unless and until approved or authorised in accordance with rules 6.45 to 6.48.

NOTES

Commencement: 6 April 2017.

This rule derived from the Insolvency Rules 1986, SI 1986/1925, r 4.218A.

Para (1): figure in square brackets in the definition of "approval" and "authorisation" substituted by the Insolvency (England and Wales) (Amendment) Rules 2017, SI 2017/366, rr 3, 25.

[6.272]

6.45 Requirement for approval or authorisation

(1) Subject to rules 6.46 to 6.48, either paragraphs (3) and (4) apply or paragraph (5) applies where, in the course of winding up a company, the liquidator—

(a) ascertains that property is comprised in or subject to a floating charge;

(b) has personally instituted or proposes to institute or continue legal proceedings or is in the process of defending or proposes to defend any legal proceeding brought or likely to be brought against the company; and

(c) before or at any stage in those proceedings, is of the opinion that—

(i) the assets of the company available for payment of general creditors are or will be insufficient to pay litigation expenses; and

(ii) in order to pay litigation expenses the liquidator will have to have recourse to property comprised in or subject to a floating charge created by the company.

(2) As soon as reasonably practicable after the date on which the liquidator forms the opinion referred to in paragraph (1), the liquidator must identify the creditor who, in the liquidator's opinion at that time—

(a) has a claim to property comprised in or subject to a floating charge created by the company; and

(b) taking into account the value of that claim and any subsisting property then comprised in or secured by such a charge, appears to the liquidator to be the creditor most immediately likely of any persons having such claims to receive some payment in respect of a claim but whose claim would not be paid in full.

(3) The liquidator must request from the specified creditor the approval or authorisation of such amount for litigation expenses as the liquidator thinks fit.

(4) Where the liquidator identifies two or more specified creditors, the liquidator must seek from each of them approval or authorisation of such amount of litigation expenses as the liquidator thinks fit, apportioned between them ("the apportioned amount") according to the value of the property to the extent covered by their charges.

(5) For so long as the conditions specified in paragraph (1) subsist, the liquidator may, in the course of a winding up, make such further requests to the specified creditor or creditors for approval or authorisation of such further amount for litigation expenses as the liquidator thinks fit to be paid out of property comprised in or subject to a floating charge created by the company, taking into account any amount for litigation expenses previously approved or authorised and the value of the property comprised in or subject to the floating charge.

NOTES

Commencement: 6 April 2017.
This rule derived from the Insolvency Rules 1986, SI 1986/1925, r 4.218B.

[6.273]
6.46 Request for approval or authorisation

(1) All requests made by the liquidator for approval or authorisation must include the following—
- (a) a statement describing the nature of the legal proceedings, including, where relevant, the statutory provision under which proceedings are or are to be brought and the grounds upon which the liquidator relies;
- (b) a statement specifying the amount or apportioned amount of litigation expenses for which approval or authorisation is sought ("the specified amount");
- (c) notice that approval or authorisation or other reply to the request must be made in writing within 28 days from the date of its being received ("the specified time limit"); and
- (d) a statement explaining the consequences of a failure to reply within the specified time limit.

(2) Where anything in paragraph (1) requires the inclusion of any information, the disclosure of which could be seriously prejudicial to the winding up of the company, the liquidator may—
- (a) exclude such information from any of the above statements or notices if accompanied by a statement to that effect; or
- (b) include it on terms—
  - (i) that bind the creditor to keep the information confidential; and
  - (ii) that include an undertaking on the part of the liquidator to apply to the court for an order that so much of the information as may be kept in the files of the court is not to be open to public inspection.

(3) The creditor may within the specified time limit apply to the liquidator in writing for such further particulars as is reasonable and in such a case, the time limit specified in paragraph (1)(c) will apply from the date of the creditor's receipt of the liquidator's response to any such request.

(4) Where the liquidator requires the approval or authorisation of two or more creditors, the liquidator must deliver a request to each creditor, containing the matters listed in paragraph (1) and also giving—
- (a) the number of creditors concerned;
- (b) the total value of their claims, or if not known, as it is estimated to be by the liquidator immediately before delivering any such request; and
- (c) to each preferential creditor, notice that approval or authorisation of the specified amount will be taken to be given where a majority in value of those preferential creditors who respond within the specified time limit are in favour of it; or
- (d) where rule 6.45 applies, notice to the specified creditors that the amount of litigation expenses will be apportioned between them in accordance with that rule and notice of the value of the portion allocated to, and the identity of, the specified creditors affected by that apportionment.

NOTES

Commencement: 6 April 2017.
This rule derived from the Insolvency Rules 1986, SI 1986/1925, r 4.218C.

[6.274]
6.47 Grant of approval or authorisation

(1) Where the liquidator fails to include in the liquidator's request any one of the matters, statements or notices required to be specified by paragraph (1) or paragraphs (1) and (4), of rule 6.46, the request for approval or authorisation will be treated as not having been made.

(2) Subject to paragraphs (3), (4) and (5), approval or authorisation will be taken to have been given where the specified amount has been requested by the liquidator, and—
- (a) that amount is approved or authorised within the specified time limit; or
- (b) a different amount is approved or authorised within the specified time limit and the liquidator considers it sufficient.

(3) Where the liquidator requires the approval or authorisation of two or more preferential creditors, approval or authorisation will be taken to be given where a majority in value of those who respond within the specified time limit approve or authorise—
- (a) the specified amount; or
- (b) a different amount which the liquidator considers sufficient.

(4) Where a majority in value of two or more preferential creditors propose an amount other than that specified by the liquidator, they will be taken to have approved or authorised an amount equal to the lowest of the amounts so proposed.

(5) In any case in which there is no response in writing within the specified time limit to the liquidator's request—

(a) at all, or

(b) at any time following the liquidator's provision of further particulars under rule 6.46(3),

the liquidator's request will be taken to have been approved or authorised from the date of the expiry of that time limit.

NOTES

Commencement: 6 April 2017.

This rule derived from the Insolvency Rules 1986, SI 1986/1925, r 4.218D.

[6.275]

6.48 Application to the court by the liquidator

(1) In the circumstances specified below the court may, on the application of the liquidator, approve or authorise such amount of litigation expenses as it thinks just.

(2) Except where paragraph (3) applies, the liquidator may apply to the court for an order approving or authorising an amount for litigation expenses only where the specified creditor (or, if more than one, any one of them)—

(a) is or is intended to be a defendant in the legal proceedings in relation to which the litigation expenses have been or are to be incurred; or

(b) has been requested to approve or authorise the amount specified under rule 6.46(1)(b) and has—

(i) declined to approve or authorise, as the case may be, the specified amount;

(ii) approved or authorised an amount which is less than the specified amount and which lesser amount the liquidator considers insufficient; or

(iii) made such application for further particulars or other response to the liquidator's request as is, in the liquidator's opinion, unreasonable.

(3) Where the liquidator thinks that circumstances are such that the liquidator requires urgent approval or authorisation of litigation expenses, the liquidator may apply to the court for approval or authorisation either—

(a) without seeking approval or authorisation from the specified creditor; or

(b) if sought, before the expiry of the specified time limit.

(4) The court may grant such application for approval or authorisation—

(a) if the liquidator satisfies the court of the urgency of the case; and

(b) subject to such terms and conditions as the court thinks just.

(5) The liquidator must, at the same time as making any application to the court under this rule, deliver copies of it to the specified creditor, unless the court orders otherwise.

(6) The specified creditor (or, if more than one, any one of them) is entitled to be heard on any such application unless the court orders otherwise.

(7) The court may grant approval or authorisation subject to such terms and conditions as it may think just, including terms and conditions relating to the amount or nature of the litigation expenses and as to any obligation to make further applications to the court under this rule.

(8) The costs of the liquidator's application under this rule, including the costs of any specified creditor appearing or represented on it, are an expense of the winding up unless the court orders otherwise.

NOTES

Commencement: 6 April 2017.

This rule derived from the Insolvency Rules 1986, SI 1986/1925, r 4.218E.

PART 7
WINDING UP BY THE COURT

CHAPTER 1 APPLICATION OF PART

[6.276]

7.1 Application of Part 7

This Part applies to winding up by the court.

NOTES

Commencement: 6 April 2017.

CHAPTER 2 THE STATUTORY DEMAND (SECTIONS 123(1)(A) AND 222(1)(A))

[6.277]

7.2 Interpretation

A demand served by a creditor on a company under section 123(1)(a) (registered companies) or 222(1)(a) (unregistered companies) is referred to in this Part as "a statutory demand".

NOTES

Commencement: 6 April 2017.

This rule derived from the Insolvency Rules 1986, SI 1986/1925, r 4.4.

[6.278]

7.3 The statutory demand

(1) A statutory demand must be headed either "Statutory Demand under section 123(1)(a) of the Insolvency Act 1986" or "Statutory Demand under section 222(1)(a) of the Insolvency Act 1986" (as applicable) and must contain—

(a) identification details for the company;
(b) the registered office of the company (if any);
(c) the name and address of the creditor;
(d) either a statement that the demand is made under section 123(1)(a) or a statement that it is made under section 222(1)(a);
(e) the amount of the debt and the consideration for it (or, if there is no consideration, the way in which it arises);
(f) if the demand is founded on a judgment or order of a court, details of the judgment or order;
(g) if the creditor is entitled to the debt by way of assignment, details of the original creditor and any intermediary assignees;
(h) a statement that the company must pay the debt claimed in the demand within 21 days of service of the demand on the company after which the creditor may present a winding-up petition unless the company offers security for the debt and the creditor agrees to accept security or the company compounds the debt with the creditor's agreement;
(i) the name of an individual with whom an officer or representative of the company may communicate with a view to securing or compounding the debt to the creditor's satisfaction;
(j) the named individual's address, electronic address and telephone number (if any);
(k) a statement that the company has the right to apply to the court for an injunction restraining the creditor from presenting or advertising a petition for the winding up of the company; and
(l) the name of the court (and hearing centre if applicable) to which, according to the present information, the company must make the application ($21 the High Court, the County Court at Central London or a named hearing centre of the County Court, as the case may be).

(2) The following must be separately identified in the demand (if claimed) with the amount or rate of the charge and the grounds on which payment is claimed—

(a) any charge by way of interest of which notice had not previously been delivered to the company as included in its liability; and
(b) any other charge accruing from time to time.

(3) The amount claimed for such charges must be limited to that which has accrued due at the date of the demand.

(4) The demand must be dated, and authenticated either by the creditor, or a person authorised to make the demand on the creditor's behalf.

(5) A demand which is authenticated by a person other than the creditor must state that the person is authorised to make the demand on the creditor's behalf and state the person's relationship to the creditor.

NOTES

Commencement: 6 April 2017.

This rule derived from the Insolvency Rules 1986, SI 1986/1925, rr 4.5, 4.6, Sch 4, Fm 4.1.

CHAPTER 3 PETITION FOR WINDING-UP ORDER

[Notes: (1) for petitions by a contributory or relevant office-holder (an administrator, administrative receiver or supervisor of a CVA) see Chapter 4; (2) a document required by the Act or these Rules must also contain the standard contents set out in Part 1.]

[6.279]

7.4 Application of this Chapter

(1) This Chapter applies subject to rule 7.25 to—

(a) a petition for winding up presented by a contributory; or
(b) a petition for winding up presented by a relevant office-holder of the company.

(2) "Relevant office-holder" in this Part means an administrator, administrative receiver and supervisor of a CVA.

NOTES

Commencement: 6 April 2017.

[6.280]

7.5 Contents of petition

(1) The petition must contain—

(a) the name of the court (and hearing centre if applicable);
(b) the name and address of the petitioner;
(c) identification details for the company subject to the petition;

(d) the company's registered office (if any);
(e) the date the company was incorporated and the enactment under which it was incorporated;
(f) the total number of issued shares of the company and the manner in which they are divided up;
(g) the aggregate nominal value of those shares;
(h) the amount of capital paid up or credited as paid up;
(i) a statement of the nature of the company's business if known;
(j) the grounds on which the winding-up order is sought;
(k) where the ground for the winding-up order is section 122(1)(a), a statement that the company has by special resolution resolved that the company be wound up by the court and the date of such resolution;
(l) where the ground for the winding-up order is section 122(1)(f) or 221(5)(b) and a statutory demand has been served on the company, a statement that such a demand has been served and the date of service and that the company is insolvent and unable to pay its debts;
(m) a statement whether the company is an Article 1.2 undertaking;
(n) a statement whether the proceedings will be main, secondary, territorial or [non-EU proceedings] and that the reasons for so stating are given in a witness statement;
(o) a statement that in the circumstances it is just and equitable that the company should be wound up;
(p) a statement that the petitioner therefore applies for an order that the company may be wound up by the court under the Act, or that such other order may be made as the court thinks just;
(q) the name and address of any person on whom the petitioner intends to serve the petition; and
(r) the contact details of the petitioner's solicitor (if any).

(2) The petition must also contain a blank box for the court to complete with the details of the venue for hearing the petition.

NOTES

Commencement: 6 April 2017.

This rule derived from the Insolvency Rules 1986, SI 1986/1925, Sch 4, Fm 4.2.

Para (1): words in square brackets in sub-para (n) substituted by the Insolvency (England and Wales) and Insolvency (Scotland) (Miscellaneous and Consequential Amendments) Rules 2017, SI 2017/1115, rr 22, 30(15).

[6.281]
7.6 Verification of petition

(1) The petition must be verified by a statement of truth.

(2) Where the petition is in respect of debts due to different creditors then the debt to each creditor must be verified separately.

(3) A statement of truth which is not contained in or endorsed upon the petition must identify the petition and must contain—
(a) identification details for the company;
(b) the name of the petitioner; and
(c) the name of the court (and hearing centre if applicable) in which the petition is to be presented.

(4) The statement of truth must be authenticated and dated by or on behalf of the petitioner.

(5) Where the person authenticating the statement of truth is not the petitioner, or one of the petitioners, the statement of truth must state—
(a) the name and postal address of the person making the statement;
(b) the capacity in which, and the authority by which, the person authenticates the statement; and
(c) the means of that person's knowledge of the matters verified in the statement of truth.

(6) If the petition is based on a statutory demand, and more than four months have elapsed between the service of the demand and the presentation of the petition, a witness statement must explain the reasons for the delay.

(7) A statement of truth verifying more than one petition must include in its title the names of the companies to which it relates and must set out, in relation to each company, the statements relied on by the petitioner; and a clear and legible photocopy of the statement of truth must be filed with each petition which it verifies.

(8) The witness statement must give the reasons for the statement that the proceedings will be main, secondary, territorial or [non-EU proceedings].

NOTES

Commencement: 6 April 2017.

This rule derived from the Insolvency Rules 1986, SI 1986/1925, r 4.12.

Para (8): words in square brackets substituted by the Insolvency (England and Wales) and Insolvency (Scotland) (Miscellaneous and Consequential Amendments) Rules 2017, SI 2017/1115, rr 22, 30(16).

[6.282]
7.7 Petition: presentation and filing

(1) The petition must be filed with the court.

(2) A petition may not be filed unless—
(a) a receipt for the deposit payable to the official receiver is produced on presentation of the petition; or
(b) the Secretary of State has given notice to the court that the petitioner has made suitable alternative arrangements for the payment of the deposit and that notice has not been revoked.

(3) A notice of alternative arrangements for the deposit may be revoked by a further notice filed with the court.

(4) The court must fix a venue for hearing the petition, and this must be endorsed on the petition and the copies.

(5) Each copy of the petition must have the seal of the court applied to it, and must be delivered to the petitioner.

NOTES

Commencement: 6 April 2017.
This rule derived from the Insolvency Rules 1986, SI 1986/1925, r 4.7.

[6.283]

7.8 Court to which petition is to be presented where the company is subject to a CVA or is in administration

(1) A petition which is filed in relation to a company for which there is in force a CVA must be presented to the court or hearing centre to which the nominee's report under section 2 was submitted or where the documents for a moratorium under section 1A were filed.

(2) A petition which is filed in relation to a company which is in administration must be presented to the court or hearing centre of the court having jurisdiction for the administration.

NOTES

Commencement: 6 April 2017.
This rule derived from the Insolvency Rules 1986, SI 1986/1925, r 4.7.

[6.284]

7.9 Copies of petition to be served on company or delivered to other persons

(1) Where this rule requires the petitioner to serve a copy of the petition on the company or deliver a copy to another person the petitioner must, when filing the petition with the court, file an additional copy with the court for each such person.

(2) Where the petitioner is not the company the petitioner must serve a sealed copy of the petition on the company in accordance with Schedule 4.

(3) If, to the petitioner's knowledge—

(a) the company is in the course of being wound up voluntarily, the petitioner must deliver a copy of the petition to the liquidator;
(b) an administrative receiver has been appointed in relation to the company, or the company is in administration, the petitioner must deliver a copy of the petition to the receiver or the administrator;
(c) there is in force for the company a CVA, the petitioner must deliver a copy of the petition to the supervisor of the CVA; or
(d) there is a member State liquidator appointed in main proceedings in relation to the company, the petitioner must deliver a copy to that person.

(4) If either the Financial Conduct Authority or Prudential Regulation Authority is entitled to be heard at the hearing of the petition in accordance with section 371 of the Financial Services and Markets Act 2000, the petitioner must deliver a copy of the petition to the Financial Conduct Authority or Prudential Regulation Authority (as appropriate).

(5) Where this rule requires the petitioner to deliver a copy of the petition to any other person that copy must be delivered within three business days after the day on which the petition is served on the company or where the petitioner is the company within three business days of the company receiving the sealed petition.

NOTES

Commencement: 6 April 2017.
This rule derived from the Insolvency Rules 1986, SI 1986/1925, r 4.10.

[6.285]

7.10 Notice of petition

(1) Unless the court otherwise directs, the petitioner must give notice of the petition.

(2) The notice must state—

(a) that a petition has been presented for the winding up of the company;
(b) in the case of an overseas company, the address at which service of the petition was effected;
(c) the name and address of the petitioner;
(d) the date on which the petition was presented;
(e) the venue fixed for the hearing of the petition;
(f) the name and address of the petitioner's solicitor (if any); and
(g) that any person intending to appear at the hearing (whether to support or oppose the petition) must give notice of that intention in accordance with rule 7.14.

(3) The notice must be gazetted.

(4) The notice must be made to appear—

(a) if the petitioner is the company itself, not less than seven business days before the day appointed for the hearing; and

(b) otherwise, not less than seven business days after service of the petition on the company, nor less than seven business days before the day appointed for the hearing.

(5) The court may dismiss the petition if notice of it is not given in accordance with this rule.

NOTES

Commencement: 6 April 2017.

This rule derived from the Insolvency Rules 1986, SI 1986/1925, r 4.11.

[6.286]

7.11 Persons entitled to request a copy of petition

If a director, contributory or creditor requests a hard copy of the petition from the solicitor for the petitioner, or the petitioner, if acting in person, and pays the standard fee for copies the solicitor or petitioner must deliver the copy within two business days.

NOTES

Commencement: 6 April 2017.

This rule derived from the Insolvency Rules 1986, SI 1986/1925, r 4.13.

[6.287]

7.12 Certificate of compliance

(1) The petitioner or the petitioner's solicitor must, at least five business days before the hearing of the petition, file with the court a certificate of compliance with rules 7.9 and 7.10 relating to service and notice of the petition.

(2) The certificate must be authenticated and dated by the petitioner or the petitioner's solicitor and must state—

(a) the date of presentation of the petition;
(b) the date fixed for the hearing; and
(c) the date or dates on which the petition was served and notice of it was given in compliance with rules 7.9 and 7.10.

(3) A copy of or, where that is not reasonably practicable, a statement of the content of, any notice given must be filed with the court with the certificate.

(4) The court may, if it thinks just, dismiss the petition if this rule is not complied with.

NOTES

Commencement: 6 April 2017.

This rule derived from the Insolvency Rules 1986, SI 1986/1925, r 4.14.

[6.288]

7.13 Permission for the petitioner to withdraw

(1) The court may order that the petitioner has permission to withdraw the petition on such terms as to costs as the parties may agree if at least five business days before the first hearing the petitioner, on an application without notice to any other party, satisfies the court that—

(a) notice of the petition has not been given under rule 7.10;
(b) no notices in support or in opposition to the petition have been received by the petitioner; and
(c) the company consents to an order being made under this rule.

(2) The order must contain—

(a) identification details for the company;
(b) the date the winding-up petition was presented;
(c) the name and postal address of the applicant;
(d) a statement that upon the application made without notice to any other party by the applicant named in the order the court is satisfied that notice of the petition has not been given, that no notices in support of or in opposition to the petition have been received by the petitioner and that the company consents to this order; and
(e) an order that, with the permission of the court, the petition is withdrawn.

NOTES

Commencement: 6 April 2017.

This rule derived from the Insolvency Rules 1986, SI 1986/1925, r 4.15.

[6.289]

7.14 Notice by persons intending to appear

(1) A creditor or contributory who intends to appear on the hearing of the petition must deliver a notice of intention to appear to the petitioner.

(2) The notice must contain—

(a) the name and address of the creditor or contributory, and any telephone number and reference which may be required for communication with that person or with any other person (also to be specified in the notice) authorised to speak or act on the creditor's or contributory's behalf;
(b) the date of the presentation of the petition and a statement that the notice relates to the matter of that petition;
(c) the date of the hearing of the petition;
(d) for a creditor, the amount and nature of the debt due from the company to the creditor;

(e) for a contributory, the number of shares held in the company;
(f) a statement whether the creditor or contributory intends to support or oppose the petition;
(g) where the creditor or contributory is represented by a solicitor or other agent, the name, postal address, telephone number and any reference number of that person and details of that person's position with or relationship to the creditor or contributory; and
(h) the name and postal address of the petitioner.

(3) The notice must be authenticated and dated by or on behalf of the creditor or contributory delivering it.

(4) Where the person authenticating the notice is not the creditor or contributory the notice must state the name and postal address of the person making the statement and the capacity in which, and the authority by which, the person authenticates the notice.

(5) The notice must be delivered to the petitioner or the petitioner's solicitor at the address shown in the court records, or in the notice of the petition required by rule 7.10.

(6) The notice must be delivered so as to reach the petitioner (or the petitioner's solicitor) not later than 4pm on the business day before that which is appointed for the hearing (or, where the hearing has been adjourned, for the adjourned hearing).

(7) A person who fails to comply with this rule may appear on the hearing of the petition only with the permission of the court.

NOTES

Commencement: 6 April 2017.
This rule derived from the Insolvency Rules 1986, SI 1986/1925, r 4.16.

[6.290]
7.15 List of appearances

(1) The petitioner must prepare for the court a list of the creditors and contributories who have given notice under rule 7.14.

(2) The list must contain—
(a) the date of the presentation of the petition;
(b) the date of the hearing of the petition;
(c) a statement that the creditors and contributories listed have delivered notice that they intend to appear at the hearing of the petition;
(d) their names and addresses;
(e) the amount each creditor claims to be owed;
(f) the number of shares claimed to be held by each contributory;
(g) the name and postal address of any solicitor for a person listed; and
(h) whether each person listed intends to support the petition, or to oppose it.

(3) On the day appointed for the hearing of the petition, a copy of the list must be handed to the court before the hearing commences.

(4) If the court gives a person permission to appear under rule 7.14(7), then the petitioner must add that person to the list with the same particulars.

NOTES

Commencement: 6 April 2017.
This rule derived from the Insolvency Rules 1986, SI 1986/1925, r 4.17.

[6.291]
7.16 Witness statement in opposition

(1) If the company intends to oppose the petition, it must not later than five business days before the date fixed for the hearing—
(a) file with the court a witness statement in opposition; and
(b) deliver a copy of the witness statement to the petitioner or the petitioner's solicitor.

(2) The witness statement must contain—
(a) identification details for the proceedings;
(b) a statement that the company intends to oppose the making of a winding-up order; and
(c) a statement of the grounds on which the company opposes the making of the order.

NOTES

Commencement: 6 April 2017.
This rule derived from the Insolvency Rules 1986, SI 1986/1925, r 4.18.

[6.292]
7.17 Substitution of creditor or contributory for petitioner

(1) This rule applies where the petitioner—
(a) is subsequently found not to have been entitled to present the petition;
(b) fails to give notice of the petition in accordance with rule 7.10;
(c) consents to withdraw the petition, or to allow it to be dismissed, consents to an adjournment, or fails to appear in support of the petition when it is called on in court on the day originally fixed for the hearing, or on a day to which it is adjourned; or
(d) appears, but does not apply for an order in the terms requested in the petition.

(2) The court may, on such terms as it thinks just, substitute as petitioner—
- (a) a creditor or contributory who in its opinion would have a right to present a petition and who wishes to prosecute it; or
- (b) a member State liquidator who has been appointed in main proceedings in relation to the company, and who wishes to prosecute the petition.

NOTES

Commencement: 6 April 2017.
This rule derived from the Insolvency Rules 1986, SI 1986/1925, r 4.19.

[6.293]
7.18 Order for substitution of petitioner

An order for substitution of a petitioner must contain—
- (a) identification details for the proceedings;
- (b) the name of the original petitioner;
- (c) the name of the creditor, contributory or member State liquidator ("the named person") who is substituted as petitioner;
- (d) a statement that the named person has requested to be substituted as petitioner under rule 7.17;
- (e) the following orders—
  - (i) either—
    - (aa) that the named person must pay the statutory deposit to the court and that, upon such payment being made, the statutory deposit paid by the original petitioner is to be repaid to the original petitioner by the official receiver, or
    - (bb) where the named person is the subject of a notice to the court by the Secretary of State under rule 7.7(2)(b) (notice of alternative arrangements for the payment of deposit) that the statutory deposit paid by the original petitioner is to be repaid to the original petitioner by the official receiver;
  - (ii) that the named person be substituted as petitioner in place of the original petitioner and that the named person may amend the petition accordingly,
  - (iii) that the named person must within a period specified in the order file a statement of truth of the statements in the amended petition,
  - (iv) that not later than before the adjourned hearing of the petition, by a date specified in the order, the named person must serve a sealed copy of the amended petition on the company and deliver a copy to any other person to whom the original petition was delivered,
  - (v) that the hearing of the amended petition be adjourned to the venue specified in the order, and
  - (vi) that the question of the costs of the original petitioner and of the statutory deposit (if appropriate) be reserved until the final determination of the amended petition;
- (f) the venue of the adjourned hearing; and
- (g) the date of the order.

NOTES

Commencement: 6 April 2017.

[6.294]
7.19 Notice of adjournment

(1) If the court adjourns the hearing of the petition the petitioner must as soon as reasonably practicable deliver a notice of the making of the order of adjournment and of the venue for the adjourned hearing to—
- (a) the company; and
- (b) any creditor or contributory who has given notice under rule 7.14 but was not present at the hearing.

(2) The notice must identify the proceedings.

NOTES

Commencement: 6 April 2017.
This rule derived from the Insolvency Rules 1986, SI 1986/1925, r 4.18A.

[6.295]
7.20 Order for winding up by the court

(1) An order for winding-up by the court must contain—
- (a) identification details for the proceedings;
- (b) the name and title of the judge making the order;
- (c) the name and postal address of the petitioner;
- (d) the nature of the petitioner which entitles that person to present the petition (eg the company, a creditor, or a regulator);
- (e) the date of presentation of the petition;
- (f) an order that the company be wound up by the court under the Act;
- (g) a statement whether the proceedings are main, secondary, territorial or [non-EU proceedings];
- (h) an order that the petitioner's costs of the petition be paid out of the assets of the company (unless the court determines otherwise);

Part 6 Insolvency Rules

(i) if applicable, an order that the costs of other persons as specified in the order be paid out of the assets of the company;
(j) the date of the order; and
(k) a statement that an official receiver attached to the court is by virtue of the order liquidator of the company, or

(2) The order may contain such additional terms concerning costs as the court thinks just.

NOTES

Commencement: 6 April 2017.

Para (1): words in square brackets in sub-para (g) substituted by the Insolvency (England and Wales) and Insolvency (Scotland) (Miscellaneous and Consequential Amendments) Rules 2017, SI 2017/1115, rr 22, 30(17).

[6.296]
7.21 Notice to official receiver of winding-up order

(1) When a winding-up order has been made, the court must deliver notice of the fact to the official receiver as soon as reasonably practicable.

(2) The notice must have the title "Notice to Official Receiver of Winding-up Order" and must contain—
(a) identification details for the proceedings;
(b) the company's registered office;
(c) the date of presentation of the petition;
(d) the date of the winding-up order; and
(e) the name and postal address of the petitioner or the petitioner's solicitor.

NOTES

Commencement: 6 April 2017.

This rule derived from the Insolvency Rules 1986, SI 1986/1925, r 4.20, Sch 4, Fm 4.13.

[6.297]
7.22 Delivery and notice of the order

(1) As soon as reasonably practicable after making a winding-up order, the court must deliver to the official receiver two copies of the order sealed with the seal of the court.

(2) The official receiver must deliver—
(a) a sealed copy of the order to the company; and
(b) a copy of the order to the registrar of companies (in compliance with section 130(1)).

(3) As an alternative to delivering a sealed copy of the order to the company, the court may direct that the sealed copy be delivered to such other person or persons, as the court directs.

(4) The official receiver—
(a) must cause a notice of the order to be gazetted as soon as reasonably practicable; and
(b) may advertise a notice of the order in such other manner as the official receiver thinks fit.

(5) The notice must state—
(a) that a winding-up order has been made in relation to the company; and
(b) the date of the order.

NOTES

Commencement: 6 April 2017.

This rule derived from the Insolvency Rules 1986, SI 1986/1925, r 4.21.

[6.298]
7.23 Petition dismissed

(1) Unless the court otherwise directs, when a petition is dismissed the petitioner must give a notice of the dismissal as soon as reasonably practicable.

(2) The notice must be—
(a) gazetted; or
(b) advertised in accordance with any directions of the court.

(3) The notice must contain—
(a) a statement that a petition for the winding up of the company has been dismissed;
(b) in the case of an overseas company, the address at which service of the petition was effected;
(c) the name and address of the petitioner;
(d) the date on which the petition was presented;
(e) the date on which the petition was gazetted or otherwise advertised; and
(f) the date of the hearing at which the petition was dismissed.

(4) The company may itself gazette notice of the dismissal where—
(a) the petitioner is not the company; and
(b) the petitioner has not given notice in accordance with paragraphs (1) to (3) within 21 days of the date of the hearing at which the petition was dismissed.

NOTES

Commencement: 6 April 2017.

This rule derived from the Insolvency Rules 1986, SI 1986/1925, r 4.21B.

[6.299]

7.24 Injunction to restrain presentation or notice of petition

(1) An application by a company for an injunction restraining a creditor from presenting a petition for the winding up of the company must be made to a court having jurisdiction to wind up the company.

(2) An application by a company for an injunction restraining a creditor from giving notice of a petition for the winding up of a company must be made to the court or hearing centre in which the petition is pending.

NOTES

Commencement: 6 April 2017.

This rule derived from the Insolvency Rules 1986, SI 1986/1925, r 4.6A.

CHAPTER 4 PETITION BY A CONTRIBUTORY OR A RELEVANT OFFICE-HOLDER

[Note: (1) "relevant office-holder" is defined in rule 7.4(2); (2) a document required by the Act or these Rules must also contain the standard contents set out in Part 1.]

[6.300]

7.25 Interpretation and application of rules in Chapter 3

(1) The following rules in Chapter 3 apply subject to paragraph (2), with the necessary modifications, to a petition under this Chapter by a contributory or a relevant office-holder—

rule 7.8 (court to which petition is to be presented where the company is subject to a CVA or is in administration);
rule 7.9(1), (4) and (5) (copies of petition to be served on other persons);
rule 7.11 (persons entitled to request a copy of petition);
rule 7.14 (notice by persons intending to appear);
rule 7.15 (list of appearances);
rule 7.19 (notice of adjournment);
rule 7.20 (order for winding up by the court) except where rule 7.32 applies (petition by administrator or where there is a supervisor);
rule 7.21 (notice to official receiver of winding-up order); and
rule 7.22 (delivery and notice of the order).

(2) The following rules apply to petitions under this Chapter presented by a relevant office-holder—

rule 7.23 (petition dismissed); and
rule 7.24 (injunction to restrain presentation or notice of petition).

NOTES

Commencement: 6 April 2017.

This rule derived from the Insolvency Rules 1986, SI 1986/1925, r 4.24.

[6.301]

7.26 Contents of petition for winding-up order by a contributory

(1) A petition presented by a contributory must contain—

(a) the name of the court (and hearing centre if applicable);
(b) the name and postal address of the petitioner;
(c) identification details for the company subject to the petition;
(d) the company's registered office (if any);
(e) the date the company was incorporated and the enactment under which it was incorporated;
(f) the total number of issued shares of the company and the manner in which they are divided up;
(g) the aggregate nominal value of those shares;
(h) the amount of capital paid up or credited as paid up;
(i) a statement of the nature of the company's business if known;
(j) the number and total value of the shares held by the petitioner;
(k) a statement whether the shares held by the petitioner—
  (i) were allotted to the petitioner on the incorporation of the company,
  (ii) have been registered in the name of the petitioner for more than six months in the last 18 months, or
  (iii) devolved upon the petitioner through the death of the former holder of the shares;
(l) the grounds on which the winding-up order is sought;
(m) a statement whether the company is an Article 1.2 undertaking;
(n) a statement whether the proceedings will be main, secondary, territorial or [non-EU proceedings] and that the reasons for so stating are given in the form of a witness statement;
(o) a statement that in the circumstances it is just and equitable that the company should be wound up;
(p) a statement that the petitioner therefore applies for an order that the company may be wound up by the court under the Act, or that such other order may be made as the court thinks just;
(q) the name and postal address of any person on whom the petitioner intends to serve the petition; and
(r) the contact details of the petitioner's solicitor (if any).

(2) The petition must also contain a blank box for the court to complete with the details of the venue for hearing the petition.

Part 6 Insolvency Rules

NOTES

Commencement: 6 April 2017.

This rule derived from the Insolvency Rules 1986, SI 1986/1925, Sch 4, Fm 4.14.

Para (1): words in square brackets in sub-para (n) substituted by the Insolvency (England and Wales) and Insolvency (Scotland) (Miscellaneous and Consequential Amendments) Rules 2017, SI 2017/1115, rr 22, 30(18).

[6.302]
7.27 Petition presented by a relevant office-holder

(1) A petition by a relevant office-holder must be expressed to be the petition of the company by the office-holder.

(2) The petition must contain the particulars required by rule 7.26 (other than paragraph (1)(j) and (k) and the following (as applicable)—

- (a) identification details for the office-holder;
- (b) the full name of the court or hearing centre in which the proceedings are being conducted or where documents relating to the proceedings are filed;
- (c) the court case number;
- (d) the date the insolvency proceedings in respect of which the office-holder holds office commenced; and
- (e) where the office-holder is an administrator, an application under paragraph 79 of Schedule B1, requesting that the appointment of the administrator should cease to have effect.

NOTES

Commencement: 6 April 2017.

This rule derived from the Insolvency Rules 1986, SI 1986/1925, r 4.7.

[6.303]
7.28 Verification of petition

(1) The petition must be verified by a statement of truth.

(2) A statement of truth which is not contained in or endorsed upon the petition must identify the petition and must contain—

- (a) identification details for the company;
- (b) the name of the petitioner; and
- (c) the name of the court (and hearing centre if applicable) in which the petition is to be presented.

(3) The statement of truth must be authenticated and dated by or on behalf of the petitioner.

(4) Where the person authenticating the statement of truth is not the petitioner, or one of the petitioners, the statement of truth must state—

- (a) the name and postal address of the person making the statement;
- (b) the capacity in which, and the authority by which, the person authenticates the statement; and
- (c) the means of the person's knowledge of the matters verified in the statement of truth.

(5) A statement of truth verifying more than one petition must include in its title the names of the companies to which it relates and must set out, in relation to each company, the statements relied on by the petitioner; and a clear and legible photocopy of the statement of truth must be filed with each petition which it verifies.

(6) The reasons for the statement that the proceedings will be main, secondary, territorial or [non-EU proceedings] must be given in a witness statement.

NOTES

Commencement: 6 April 2017.

This rule derived from the Insolvency Rules 1986, SI 1986/1925, Sch 4, Fm 4.14.

Para (6): words in square brackets substituted by the Insolvency (England and Wales) and Insolvency (Scotland) (Miscellaneous and Consequential Amendments) Rules 2017, SI 2017/1115, rr 22, 30(19).

[6.304]
7.29 Presentation and service of petition

(1) The petition with one copy must be filed with the court.

(2) The petition may not be filed unless a receipt for the deposit payable to the official receiver is produced on presentation of the petition.

(3) The court must fix a hearing for a return day on which, unless the court otherwise directs, the petitioner and the company must attend before the court for—

- (a) directions to be given in relation to the procedure on the petition; or
- (b) the hearing of the petition where—
  - (i) it is presented by a relevant office-holder, and
  - (ii) the court considers it just in all the circumstances.

(4) On fixing the return day, the court must deliver to the petitioner a sealed copy of the petition endorsed with the return day and time of hearing.

(5) The petitioner must serve a sealed copy of the petition on the company at least 14 days before the return day.

(6) Where a member State liquidator has been appointed in main proceedings in relation to the company, the petitioner must deliver a copy of the petition to the member State liquidator.

NOTES

Commencement: 6 April 2017.

This rule derived from the Insolvency Rules 1986, SI 1986/1925, r 4.22.

[6.305]

7.30 Request to appoint former administrator or supervisor as liquidator (section 140)

(1) This rule applies where a petition requests under section 140 the appointment of a former administrator or supervisor as liquidator.

(2) The person whose appointment is sought ("the appointee") must, not less than two business days before the return day fixed under rule 7.29(3), file with the court a report including particulars of—

(a) the date on which the appointee delivered notice to creditors of the company, of the appointee's intention to seek appointment as liquidator, such date to be at least seven business days before the day on which the report is filed; and

(b) details of any response from creditors to that notice, including any objections to the proposed appointment.

NOTES

Commencement: 6 April 2017.

This rule derived from the Insolvency Rules 1986, SI 1986/1925, r 4.7.

[6.306]

7.31 Hearing of petition

(1) On the return day, or at any time after it, the court—

(a) must, where the petition is presented by a person who is not a relevant office-holder, give directions;

(b) may, in any other case, give directions; or

(c) may, in either case, make any such order as it sees fit.

(2) In particular, the court may give directions relating to the following matters—

(a) service or delivery of the petition, whether in connection with the venue for a further hearing, or for any other purpose;

(b) whether particulars of claim and defence are to be delivered, and generally as to the procedure on the petition;

(c) whether and if so by what means, notice of the petition is to be given;

(d) the manner in which any evidence is to be provided at any hearing before the judge and in particular (but without prejudice to the generality of the above) as to—

(i) the taking of evidence wholly or in part by witness statement or orally,

(ii) the cross-examination of any person who has made a witness statement, and

(iii) the matters to be dealt with in evidence; and

(e) any other matter affecting the procedure on the petition or in connection with the hearing and disposal of the petition.

(3) In giving directions the court must consider whether a copy of the petition should be served on or delivered to any of the persons specified in rule 7.9.

NOTES

Commencement: 6 April 2017.

This rule derived from the Insolvency Rules 1986, SI 1986/1925, r 4.23.

[6.307]

7.32 Order for winding up by the court of a company in administration or where there is a supervisor of a CVA in relation to the company

(1) An order for winding-up by the court of a company in administration or where there is a supervisor of a CVA in relation to the company must contain—

(a) identification details for the proceedings;

(b) the name and title of the judge making the order;

(c) the name and postal address of the administrator or supervisor of the company;

(d) the date of the administrator's or supervisor's appointment;

(e) the date of presentation of the petition;

(f) where there is an administrator, an order that the administrator's appointment ceases to have effect;

(g) an order that the company be wound up by the court under the Act;

(h) a statement whether the proceedings are main, secondary, territorial or [non-EU proceedings]; and

(i) the name and address of the person appointed as liquidator of the company (if applicable);

(j) an order that—

(i) an official receiver attached to the court is by virtue of the order liquidator of the company, or

(ii) that the administrator or the supervisor (as the case may be) specified in the order is appointed liquidator of the company; and

(k) the date of the order.

(2) The order may contain such additional terms as to the costs as the court thinks just.

(3) Where the court appoints the former administrator or the supervisor as liquidator paragraphs (3)(c), (4), (7), (8) and (9) of rule 7.56 apply.

NOTES

Commencement: 6 April 2017.

This rule derived from the Insolvency Rules 1986, SI 1986/1925, r 4.20, Sch 4, Fm 4.12.

Para (1): words in square brackets in sub-para (h) substituted by the Insolvency (England and Wales) and Insolvency (Scotland) (Miscellaneous and Consequential Amendments) Rules 2017, SI 2017/1115, rr 22, 30(20).

CHAPTER 5 PROVISIONAL LIQUIDATOR

[Note: a document required by the Act or these Rules must also contain the standard contents set out in Part 1.]

[6.308]
7.33 Application for appointment of provisional liquidator (section 135)

(1) An application to the court for the appointment of a provisional liquidator under section 135 may be made by—
- (a) the petitioner;
- (b) a creditor of the company;
- (c) a contributory;
- (d) the company;
- (e) the Secretary of State;
- (f) a temporary administrator;
- (g) a member State liquidator appointed in main proceedings (including in accordance with [Article 37 of the EU Regulation]); or
- (h) any person who under any enactment would be entitled to present a petition for the winding up of the company.

(2) The application must be supported by a witness statement stating—
- (a) the grounds on which it is proposed that a provisional liquidator should be appointed;
- (b) if some person other than the official receiver is proposed to be appointed, that that person has consented to act and, to the best of the applicant's belief, is qualified to act as an insolvency practitioner in relation to the company;
- (c) whether or not the official receiver has been informed of the application and, if so, whether a copy of it has been delivered to the official receiver;
- (d) whether to the applicant's knowledge—
  - (i) there has been proposed or is in force for the company a CVA;
  - (ii) an administrator or administrative receiver is acting in relation to the company; or
  - (iii) a liquidator has been appointed for its voluntary winding up; and
- (e) the applicant's estimate of the value of the assets in relation to which the provisional liquidator is to be appointed
- [(f) a statement whether the proceedings will be main, secondary, territorial or non-EU proceedings with the reasons for so stating.]

(3) The applicant must deliver copies of the application and the witness statement in support to the official receiver, who may attend the hearing and make any representations which the official receiver thinks appropriate.

(4) If for any reason it is not practicable to deliver copies of the application and statement to the official receiver before the hearing, the applicant must inform the official receiver of the application in sufficient time for the official receiver to be able to attend.

(5) If satisfied that sufficient grounds are shown for the appointment the court may appoint a provisional liquidator on such terms as it thinks just.

NOTES

Commencement: 6 April 2017.

This rule derived from the Insolvency Rules 1986, SI 1986/1925, r 4.25.

Para (1): words in square brackets in sub-para (g) substituted by the Insolvency (England and Wales) and Insolvency (Scotland) (Miscellaneous and Consequential Amendments) Rules 2017, SI 2017/1115, rr 22, 26.

Para (2): sub-para (f) inserted by the Insolvency Amendment (EU 2015/848) Regulations 2017, SI 2017/702, regs 2, 3, Schedule, Pt 2, paras 32, 39, as from 26 June 2017, except in relation to proceedings opened before that date.

[6.309]
7.34 Deposit by applicant

(1) An applicant for an order appointing the official receiver as provisional liquidator must, before the order is made, deposit with the official receiver, or otherwise secure to the official receiver's satisfaction, such sum as the court directs to cover the official receiver's remuneration and expenses.

(2) If the sum deposited or secured proves to be insufficient, the court may, on the application of the official receiver, order the applicant for the appointment to deposit or secure an additional sum.

(3) If such additional sum is not deposited or secured within two business days after service of the order on the applicant then the court may discharge the order appointing the official receiver as provisional liquidator.

(4) If a winding-up order is made after a provisional liquidator has been appointed, any money deposited under this rule must (unless it is required because the assets are insufficient to pay the remuneration and expenses of the provisional liquidator) be repaid to the person depositing it (or as that person may direct) as an expense of the winding up, in the prescribed order of priority.

NOTES

Commencement: 6 April 2017.

This rule derived from the Insolvency Rules 1986, SI 1986/1925, r 4.27.

[6.310]
7.35 Order of appointment of provisional liquidator

(1) The order appointing the provisional liquidator must have the title "Order of appointment of Provisional Liquidator" and contain—
- (a) the name of the court (and hearing centre if applicable) in which the order is made;
- (b) the name and title of the judge making the order;
- (c) the name and postal address of the applicant;
- (d) identification details for the company;
- (e) the statement that the court is satisfied—
  - (i) that the company is unable to pay its debts (if applicable), and
  - (ii) that the proceedings are main, secondary, territorial or [non-EU proceedings], as the case may be;
- (f) an order either that—
  - (i) upon the sum, which is specified in the order, being deposited by the applicant with the official receiver, the official receiver is appointed provisional liquidator of the company, or
  - (ii) the person specified in the order is appointed provisional liquidator of the company;
- (g) identification and contact details for the provisional liquidator, where the provisional liquidator is not the official receiver;
- (h) details of the functions to be carried out by the provisional liquidator in relation to the company's affairs;
- (i) a notice to the officers of the company that they are required by section 235 to give the provisional liquidator all the information the provisional liquidator may reasonably require relating to the company's property and affairs and to attend upon the provisional liquidator at such times as the provisional liquidator may reasonably require; and
- (j) the date of the order.

(2) Where two or more provisional liquidators are appointed the order must also specify (as required by section 231) whether any act required or authorised under any enactment to be done by the provisional liquidator is to be done by all or any one or more of them.

(3) The court must, as soon as reasonably practicable after the order is made, deliver copies of the order as follows—
- (a) if the official receiver is the provisional liquidator, two sealed copies to the official receiver;
- (b) if another person is appointed as provisional liquidator—
  - (i) two sealed copies to that person, and
  - (ii) one copy to the official receiver;
- (c) if there is an administrative receiver acting in relation to the company, one sealed copy to the administrative receiver.

(4) The official receiver or other person appointed as provisional liquidator must as soon as reasonably practicable deliver a sealed copy of the order to either—
- (a) the company, or
- (b) the liquidator, if a liquidator was appointed for the company's voluntary winding-up.

(5) The official receiver or other person appointed as provisional liquidator must as soon as reasonably practicable deliver a copy of the order to the registrar of companies.

NOTES

Commencement: 6 April 2017.

This rule derived from the Insolvency Rules 1986, SI 1986/1925, r 4.26, Sch 4, Fm 4.15.

Para (1): words in square brackets in sub-para (e) substituted by the Insolvency (England and Wales) and Insolvency (Scotland) (Miscellaneous and Consequential Amendments) Rules 2017, SI 2017/1115, rr 22, 30(21).

[6.311]
7.36 Notice of appointment of provisional liquidator

(1) The provisional liquidator must as soon as reasonably practicable after receipt of the copy of the order of appointment give notice of appointment unless the court directs otherwise.

(2) The notice—
- (a) must be gazetted; and
- (b) may be advertised in such other manner as the provisional liquidator thinks fit.

(3) The notice must state—
- (a) that a provisional liquidator has been appointed; and
- (b) the date of the appointment.

NOTES

Commencement: 6 April 2017.

This rule derived from the Insolvency Rules 1986, SI 1986/1925, r 4.25A.

[6.312]
7.37 Security

(1) This rule applies where an insolvency practitioner is appointed as provisional liquidator.

(2) The cost of providing the security required under the Act must be paid in the first instance by the provisional liquidator, however—

(a) if a winding-up order is not made, the person appointed is entitled to be reimbursed out of the property of the company, and the court may make an order on the company accordingly; and

(b) if a winding-up order is made, the person appointed is entitled to be reimbursed as an expense of the winding up in the prescribed order of priority.

(3) If the provisional liquidator fails to give or keep up the required security, the court may remove the provisional liquidator, and make such order as it thinks just as to costs.

(4) If an order is made under this rule removing the provisional liquidator, or discharging the order appointing the provisional liquidator, the court must give directions as to whether any, and if so what, steps should be taken for the appointment of another person in the place of the removed or discharged provisional liquidator.

NOTES

Commencement: 6 April 2017.

This rule derived from the Insolvency Rules 1986, SI 1986/1925, rr 4.28, 4.29.

[6.313]
7.38 Remuneration

(1) The remuneration of the provisional liquidator (other than the official receiver) is to be fixed by the court from time to time on the application of the provisional liquidator.

(2) In fixing the remuneration of the provisional liquidator, the court must take into account—

(a) the time properly given by the provisional liquidator and the staff of the provisional liquidator in attending to the company's affairs;

(b) the complexity of the case;

(c) any respects in which, in connection with the company's affairs, there falls on the provisional liquidator any responsibility of an exceptional kind or degree;

(d) the effectiveness with which the provisional liquidator appears to be carrying out, or to have carried out, the duties of the provisional liquidator; and

(e) the value and nature of the property with which the provisional liquidator has to deal.

(3) Without prejudice to any order the court may make as to costs, the remuneration of the provisional liquidator (whether the official receiver or another) must be paid to the provisional liquidator, and the amount of any expenses incurred by the provisional liquidator (including the remuneration and expenses of any special manager appointed under section 177) reimbursed—

(a) if a winding-up order is not made, out of the property of the company;

(b) if a winding-up order is made, as an expense of the winding up, in the prescribed order of priority; and

(c) in either case (if the relevant funds are insufficient), out of the deposit under rule 7.34.

(4) Unless the court otherwise directs, where a winding up order is not made, the provisional liquidator may retain out of the company's property such sums or property as are or may be required for meeting the remuneration and expenses of the provisional liquidator.

(5) Where a person other than the official receiver has been appointed provisional liquidator, and the official receiver has taken any steps for the purpose of obtaining a statement of affairs or has performed any other duty under these Rules, the provisional liquidator must pay the official receiver such sum (if any) as the court may direct.

NOTES

Commencement: 6 April 2017.

This rule derived from the Insolvency Rules 1986, SI 1986/1925, r 4.30.

[6.314]
7.39 Termination of appointment

(1) The appointment of the provisional liquidator may be terminated by the court on the application of the provisional liquidator, or a person specified in rule 7.33(1).

(2) If the provisional liquidator's appointment terminates, in consequence of the dismissal of the winding-up petition or otherwise, the court may give such directions as it thinks just relating to the accounts of the provisional liquidator's administration or any other matters which it thinks appropriate.

(3) The provisional liquidator must give notice of termination of the appointment as provisional liquidator, unless the termination is on the making of a winding-up order or the court directs otherwise.

(4) The notice referred to in paragraph (3)—

(a) must be delivered to the registrar of companies as soon as reasonably practicable;

(b) must be gazetted as soon as reasonably practicable; and

(c) may be advertised in such other manner as the provisional liquidator thinks fit.

(5) The notice under paragraph (3) must state—

(a) that the appointment as provisional liquidator has been terminated;
(b) the date of that termination; and
(c) that the appointment terminated otherwise than on the making of a winding-up order.

NOTES

Commencement: 6 April 2017.
This rule derived from the Insolvency Rules 1986, SI 1986/1925, r 4.31.

CHAPTER 6 STATEMENT OF AFFAIRS AND OTHER INFORMATION

[Note: a document required by the Act or these Rules must also contain the standard contents set out in Part 1.]

[6.315]

7.40 Notice requiring statement of affairs (section 131)

(1) Where, under section 131, the official receiver requires a nominated person to provide the official receiver with a statement of the affairs of the company, the official receiver must deliver a notice to that person.

(2) The notice must be headed "Notice requiring statement of affairs" and must—
(a) identify the company immediately below the heading;
(b) require a nominated person to prepare and submit to the official receiver a statement of affairs of the company;
(c) inform the nominated person—
(i) of the names and addresses of any other nominated person to whom such a notice has been delivered, and
(ii) of the date by which the statement must be delivered; and
(d) state the effect of section 131(7) (penalty for non-compliance) and section 235 (duty to co-operate) as it applies to the official receiver.

(3) The official receiver must inform the nominated person that a document for the preparation of the statement of affairs capable of completion in compliance with rule 7.41 can be supplied by the official receiver if requested.

NOTES

Commencement: 6 April 2017.
This rule derived from the Insolvency Rules 1986, SI 1986/1925, r 4.32.

[6.316]

7.41 Statement of affairs

(1) The statement of affairs must be headed "Statement of affairs" and must contain—
(a) identification details for the company;
(b) a statement that it is a statement of the affairs of the company on a date which is specified, being—
(i) the date of the winding-up order, or
(ii) the date directed by the official receiver;
(c) a list of the company's shareholders with the following information about each one—
(i) name and postal address,
(ii) the type of shares held,
(iii) the nominal amount of the shares held,
(iv) the number of shares held,
(v) the amount per share called up, and
(vi) the total amount of shares called up;
(d) the total amount of shares called up held by all shareholders;
(e) a summary of the assets of the company, setting out the book value and estimated realisable value of—
(i) any assets subject to a fixed charge,
(ii) any assets subject to a floating charge,
(iii) any uncharged assets, and
(iv) the total value of all the assets available for preferential creditors;
(f) a summary of the liabilities of the company, setting out—
(i) the amount of preferential debts,
(ii) an estimate of the deficiency with respect to preferential debts or the surplus available after paying the preferential debts,
(iii) an estimate of the prescribed part, if applicable,
(iv) an estimate of the total assets available to pay debts secured by floating charges,
(v) the amount of debts secured by floating charges,
(vi) an estimate of the deficiency with respect to debts secured by floating charges or the surplus available after paying the debts secured by fixed or floating charges,
(vii) the amount of unsecured debts (excluding preferential debts),
(viii) an estimate of the deficiency with respect to unsecured debts or the surplus available after paying unsecured debts,
(ix) any issued and called-up capital, and

(x) an estimate of the deficiency with respect to, or surplus available to, members of the company;

(g) a list of the company's creditors (as required by section 131(2)) with the following particulars required by paragraph (2) indicating—

(i) any creditors under hire-purchase, chattel leasing or conditional sale agreements,

(ii) any creditors who are consumers claiming amounts paid in advance of the supply of goods or services, and

(iii) any creditors claiming retention of title over property in the company's possession.

(2) The particulars required by this paragraph are as follows—

(i) the name and postal address,

(ii) the amount of the debt owed to the creditor,

(iii) details of any security held by the creditor,

(iv) the date the security was given, and

(v) the value of any such security.

(3) Paragraph (4) applies where the particulars required by paragraph (2) relate to creditors who are either—

(a) employees or former employees of the company; or

(b) consumers claiming amounts paid in advance for the supply of goods or services.

(4) Where this paragraph applies—

(a) the statement of affairs itself must state separately for each of paragraph (3)(a) and (b) the number of such creditors and the total of the debts owed to them; and

(b) the particulars required by paragraph (2) in respect of those creditors must be set out in separate schedules to the statement of affairs for each of paragraph (3)(a) and (b).

(5) The statement of affairs must be verified by a statement of truth by the nominated person, or all of them if more than one, making the statement of affairs.

(6) The nominated person (or one of them, if more than one) must deliver the statement of affairs verified as required by paragraph (5) to the official receiver together with a copy.

(7) The official receiver must deliver the verified copy of the statement of affairs and any statements of concurrence delivered under rule 7.42 to the registrar of companies.

(8) However the official receiver must not deliver to the registrar of companies with the statement of affairs any schedule required by paragraph (4)(b).

NOTES

Commencement: 6 April 2017.

This rule derived from the Insolvency Rules 1986, SI 1986/1925, Sch 4, Fm 4.17.

[6.317]

7.42 Statement of affairs: statement of concurrence

(1) The official receiver may require a person mentioned in section 131(3) ("a relevant person") to deliver to the official receiver a statement of concurrence.

(2) A statement of concurrence is a statement, verified by a statement of truth, that that person concurs in the statement of affairs submitted by a nominated person.

(3) The official receiver must inform the nominated person who has been required to submit a statement of affairs that the relevant person has been required to deliver a statement of concurrence.

(4) The nominated person must deliver a copy of the statement of affairs to every relevant person who has been required to submit a statement of concurrence.

(5) A statement of concurrence—

(a) must identify the company; and

(b) may be qualified in relation to matters dealt with in the statement of affairs, where the relevant person—

(i) is not in agreement with the statement of affairs,

(ii) considers the statement of affairs to be erroneous or misleading, or

(iii) is without the direct knowledge necessary for concurring in it.

(6) The relevant person must deliver the required statement of concurrence (with a copy) to the official receiver before the end of the period of five business days (or such other period as the official receiver may agree) beginning with the day on which the relevant person receives the statement of affairs.

NOTES

Commencement: 6 April 2017.

This rule derived from the Insolvency Rules 1986, SI 1986/1925, r 4.33.

[6.318]

7.43 Order limiting disclosure of statement of affairs etc

(1) Where the official receiver thinks that disclosure of the whole or part of the statement of affairs or of any statement of concurrence would be likely to prejudice the conduct of the winding up or might reasonably be expected to lead to violence against any person, the official receiver may apply to the court for an order that the statement of affairs, statement of concurrence or any specified part of them must not be filed with the registrar of companies.

(2) The court may order that the whole or a specified part of the statement of affairs or of a statement of concurrence must not be delivered to the registrar of companies.

(3) The official receiver must as soon as reasonably practicable deliver to the registrar of companies a copy of the order, and the statement of affairs and any statement of concurrence to the extent allowed by the order.

NOTES

Commencement: 6 April 2017.

This rule derived from the Insolvency Rules 1986, SI 1986/1925, r 4.35.

[6.319]

7.44 Release from duty to submit statement of affairs: extension of time (section 131)

(1) The official receiver may exercise the power in section 131(5) to release a person from an obligation to submit a statement of affairs imposed under section 131(1) or (2), or to grant an extension of time, either at the official receiver's own discretion, or at the request of a nominated person.

(2) A nominated person may apply to the court for a release or an extension of time if the official receiver refuses that person's request.

(3) On receipt of an application, the court may, if it is satisfied that no sufficient cause is shown for it, dismiss it without giving notice to any party other than the applicant.

(4) Unless the application is dismissed, the court must fix a venue for it to be heard.

(5) The applicant must, at least 14 days before any hearing, deliver to the official receiver a notice stating the venue with a copy of the application and of any evidence on which the applicant intends to rely.

(6) The official receiver may do either or both of the following—

- (a) file a report of any matters which the official receiver thinks ought to be drawn to the court's attention; or
- (b) appear and be heard on the application.

(7) If a report is filed, the official receiver must deliver a copy of it to the applicant not later than five business days before the hearing.

(8) The court must deliver sealed copies of any order made on the application to the nominated person and the official receiver.

(9) The applicant must pay the applicant's own costs in any event and, unless and to the extent that the court orders otherwise those costs will not be an expense of the winding up.

NOTES

Commencement: 6 April 2017.

This rule derived from the Insolvency Rules 1986, SI 1986/1925, r 4.36.

[6.320]

7.45 Statement of affairs: expenses

(1) If a nominated person cannot personally prepare a proper statement of affairs, the official receiver may, as an expense of the winding up, employ a person or firm to assist in the preparation of the statement.

(2) At the request of a nominated person, made on the grounds that the nominated person cannot personally prepare a proper statement, the official receiver may authorise an allowance, payable as an expense of the winding up, of all or part of the expenses to be incurred by the nominated person in employing a person or firm to assist the nominated person in preparing it.

(3) Any such request by the nominated person must be accompanied by an estimate of the expenses involved; and the official receiver must only authorise the employment of a named person or a named firm, approved by the official receiver.

(4) An authorisation given by the official receiver under this rule must be subject to such conditions (if any) as the official receiver thinks fit to impose relating to the manner in which any person may obtain access to relevant documents and other records.

(5) Nothing in this rule relieves a nominated person from any obligation relating to the preparation, verification and submission of the statement of affairs, or to the provision of information to the official receiver or the liquidator.

(6) Any payment made as an expense of the winding up under this rule must be made in the prescribed order of priority.

(7) Paragraphs (2) to (6) of this rule may be applied, on application to the official receiver by any nominated person, in relation to the making of a statement of concurrence.

NOTES

Commencement: 6 April 2017.

This rule derived from the Insolvency Rules 1986, SI 1986/1925, r 4.37.

Part 6 Insolvency Rules

[6.321]
7.46 Delivery of accounts to official receiver

(1) Any of the persons specified in section 235(3) must, at the request of the official receiver, deliver to the official receiver accounts of the company of such nature, as at such date, and for such period, as the official receiver may specify.

(2) The period specified may begin from a date up to three years before the date of the presentation of the winding-up petition, or from an earlier date to which audited accounts of the company were last prepared.

(3) The court may, on the official receiver's application, require accounts for any earlier period.

(4) Rule 7.45 applies (with the necessary modifications) in relation to accounts to be delivered under this rule as it applies in relation to the statement of affairs.

(5) The accounts must, if the official receiver so requires, be verified by a statement of truth and (whether or not so verified) be delivered to the official receiver within 21 days of the request under paragraph (1), or such longer period as the official receiver may allow.

NOTES

Commencement: 6 April 2017.

This rule derived from the Insolvency Rules 1986, SI 1986/1925, r 4.39.

[6.322]
7.47 Further disclosure

(1) The official receiver may at any time require a nominated person to deliver (in writing) further information amplifying, modifying or explaining any matter contained in the statement of affairs, or in accounts delivered under the Act or these Rules.

(2) The information must, if the official receiver so directs, be verified by a statement of truth, and (whether or not so verified) be delivered to the official receiver within 21 days of the requirement under paragraph (1), or such longer period as the official receiver may allow.

NOTES

Commencement: 6 April 2017.

This rule derived from the Insolvency Rules 1986, SI 1986/1925, r 4.42.

CHAPTER 7 REPORTS AND INFORMATION TO CREDITORS AND CONTRIBUTORIES

[Note: a document required by the Act or these Rules must also contain the standard contents set out in Part 1.]

[6.323]
7.48 Reports by official receiver

(1) The official receiver must deliver a report on the winding up and the state of the company's affairs to the creditors and contributories at least once after the making of the winding-up order.

(2) The report must contain—

(a) identification details for the proceedings;
(b) contact details for the official receiver;
(c) a summary of the assets and liabilities of the company as known to the official receiver at the date of the report;
(d) such comments on the summary and the company's affairs as the official receiver thinks fit; and
(e) any other information of relevance to the creditors or contributories.

(3) The official receiver may apply to the court to be relieved of any duty imposed by this rule or to be authorised to carry out the duty in another way.

(4) On such an application the court must have regard to the cost of carrying out the duty, to the amount of the assets available, and to the extent of the interest of creditors or contributories, or any particular class of them.

(5) If proceedings in a winding-up are stayed by order of the court any duty of the official receiver to deliver a report under this rule ceases.

NOTES

Commencement: 6 April 2017.

This rule derived from the Insolvency Rules 1986, SI 1986/1925, rr 4.43, 4.45, 4.46.

[6.324]
7.49 Reports by official receiver: estimate of prescribed part

(1) The official receiver must include in a report under rule 7.48(1) estimates to the best of the official receiver's knowledge and belief of the value of—

(a) the prescribed part (whether or not the official receiver might be required under section 176A to make the prescribed part available for the satisfaction of unsecured debts); and
(b) the company's net property (as defined by section 176A(6)).

(2) If the official receiver (as liquidator) proposes to make an application to court under section 176A(5) the report must say so and give the reason for the application.

(3) The official receiver may exclude from an estimate under paragraph (1) information the disclosure of which could seriously prejudice the commercial interests of the company.

(4) If the exclusion of such information affects the calculation of the estimate, the report must say so.

NOTES

Commencement: 6 April 2017.

This rule derived from the Insolvency Rules 1986, SI 1986/1925, r 4.43.

[6.325]

7.50 Further information where winding up follows administration

(1) This rule applies where an administrator is appointed by the court under section 140 as the company's liquidator and becomes aware of creditors not formerly known to that person as administrator.

(2) The liquidator must deliver to those creditors a copy of any statement previously sent by the administrator to creditors in accordance with paragraph 49(4) of Schedule B1 and rule 3.35.

NOTES

Commencement: 6 April 2017.

This rule derived from the Insolvency Rules 1986, SI 1986/1925, r 4.49A.

[6.326]

7.51 Notice of stay of winding up

Where the court grants a stay in a winding up it may include in its order such requirements on the company as it thinks just with a view to bringing the stay to the notice of creditors and contributories.

NOTES

Commencement: 6 April 2017.

This rule derived from the Insolvency Rules 1986, SI 1986/1925, r 4.48(2).

CHAPTER 8 THE LIQUIDATOR

[Note: a document required by the Act or these Rules must also contain the standard contents set out in Part 1.]

[6.327]

7.52 Choosing a person to be liquidator

(1) This rule applies where nominations are sought by the official receiver from the company's creditors and contributories under section 136 for the purpose of choosing a person to be liquidator of the company in place of the official receiver.

(2) The official receiver must deliver to the creditors and contributories a notice inviting proposals for a liquidator.

(3) The notice must explain that the official receiver is not obliged to seek the creditors' views on any proposals that do not meet the requirements of paragraphs (4) and (5).

(4) A proposal must state the name and contact details of the proposed liquidator, and contain a statement that the proposed liquidator is qualified to act as an insolvency practitioner in relation to the company and has consented to act as liquidator of the company.

(5) A proposal must be received by the official receiver within five business days of the date of the notice under paragraph (2).

(6) Following the end of the period for inviting proposals under paragraph (2), where any proposals are received the official receiver must seek a decision on the nomination of a liquidator from the creditors (on any proposals received from creditors) and from the contributories (on any proposals received from contributories) by—

(a) a decision procedure; or

(b) the deemed consent procedure.

(7) Where a decision is sought under paragraph (6) following the official receiver's decision under section 136(5)(a) to seek a nomination, the decision date must be not more than four months from the date of the winding-up order.

(8) Where the official receiver is required under section 136(5)(c) to seek such a decision, the official receiver must send a notice to the creditors and contributories which complies with rule 15.7 or 15.8 so far as relevant.

(9) The notice must also—

(a) identify any liquidator proposed to be nominated by a creditor (in the case of a notice to creditors) or by a contributory (in the case of a notice to contributories) in accordance with this rule; and

(b) contain a statement explaining the effect of section 137(2) (duty of official receiver to consider referral of need for appointment of liquidator to the Secretary of State where no person is chosen to be liquidator).

(10) The decision date in the notice must be no later than 21 days after the date for receiving proposals has passed.

(11) The creditors and contributories must be given at least 14 days' notice of the decision date.

(12) Where no proposal is received by the official receiver under paragraph (2), the official receiver has no obligation to seek a decision from creditors or contributories on a liquidator.

(13) Nothing in this rule affects the official receiver's ability under section 137(1), at any time when liquidator of the company, to apply to the Secretary of State to appoint a liquidator in place of the official receiver.

NOTES

Commencement: 6 April 2017.

This rule derived from the Insolvency Rules 1986, SI 1986/1925, r 4.50.

[6.328]
7.53 Appointment of liquidator by creditors or contributories

(1) This rule applies where a person is appointed as liquidator by the creditors or contributories.

(2) The convener of the decision procedure or deemed consent procedure, or the chair in the case of a meeting must certify the appointment, but not unless and until the appointee has provided to the convener or the chair a statement to the effect that the appointee is an insolvency practitioner qualified under the Act to be the liquidator and consents to act.

(3) The certificate must be authenticated and dated by the convener or chair and must—

- (a) identify the company;
- (b) identify and provide contact details for the person appointed as liquidator;
- (c) state the date on which the liquidator was appointed;
- (d) state that the appointee—
  - (i) has provided a statement of being qualified to act as an insolvency practitioner in relation to the company,
  - (ii) has consented to act, and
  - (iii) was appointed as liquidator of the company.

(4) Where two or more liquidators are appointed the certificate must also specify (as required by section 231) whether any act required or authorised under any enactment to be done by the liquidator is to be done by all or any one or more of them.

(5) The liquidator's appointment is effective from the date on which the appointment is certified, that date to be endorsed on the certificate.

(6) The convener or chair (if that person is not the official receiver) must deliver the certificate to the official receiver.

(7) The official receiver must in any case deliver the certificate to the liquidator.

NOTES

Commencement: 6 April 2017.

This rule derived from the Insolvency Rules 1986, SI 1986/1925, r 4.100.

[6.329]
7.54 Decision on nomination

(1) In the case of a decision on the nomination of a liquidator—

- (a) if on any vote there are two nominees, the person who obtains the most support is appointed;
- (b) if there are three or more nominees, and one of them has a clear majority over both or all the others together, that one is appointed; and
- (c) in any other case, the convener or chair must continue to take votes (disregarding at each vote any nominee who has withdrawn and, if no nominee has withdrawn, the nominee who obtained the least support last time) until a clear majority is obtained for any one nominee.

(2) In the case of a decision being made at a meeting, the chair may at any time put to the meeting a resolution for the joint nomination of any two or more nominees.

NOTES

Commencement: 6 April 2017.

This rule derived from the Insolvency Rules 1986, SI 1986/1925, r 4.63.

[6.330]
7.55 Invitation to creditors and contributories to form a liquidation committee

(1) Where a decision is sought from the company's creditors and contributories on the appointment of a liquidator, the convener of the decision must at the same time deliver to the creditors and contributories a notice inviting them to decide whether a liquidation committee should be established if sufficient creditors are willing to be members of the committee.

(2) The notice must also invite nominations for membership of the committee, such nominations to be received by a date specified in the notice.

(3) The notice must—

- (a) state that nominations must be delivered to the convener by the specified date;
- (b) state, in the case of creditors, that nominations can only be accepted if the convener is satisfied as to the creditors' eligibility under rule 17.4; and
- (c) explain the effect of section 141(2) and (3) on whether a committee is to be established under Part 17.

NOTES

Commencement: 6 April 2017.

[6.331]

7.56 Appointment by the court

(1) This rule applies where the liquidator is appointed by the court under section 139(4) (different persons nominated by creditors and contributories) or section 140 (winding up following administration or CVA).

(2) The court must not make the order unless and until the person being appointed has filed with the court a statement to the effect that that person is an insolvency practitioner, duly qualified under the Act to be the liquidator, and consents to act.

(3) The order of the court must contain—

(a) identification details for the proceedings;

(b) the name and title of the judge making the order;

(c) the name and postal address of the applicant;

(d) the capacity in which the applicant made the application;

(e) identification and contact details for the proposed liquidator;

(f) a statement that the proposed liquidator has filed—

(i) a statement of qualification to act as an insolvency practitioner in relation to the company, and

(ii) a consent to act;

(g) the order that the proposed liquidator is appointed liquidator of the company; and

(h) the date on which the order is made.

(4) Where two or more liquidators are appointed the order must also specify (as required by section 231) whether any act required or authorised under any enactment to be done by the liquidator is to be done by all or any one or more of them.

(5) The court must deliver two copies of the order to the official receiver one of which must be sealed.

(6) The official receiver must deliver the sealed copy of the order to the person appointed as liquidator.

(7) The liquidator's appointment takes effect from the date of the order or such other date as the court orders.

(8) Within 28 days from appointment, the liquidator must—

(a) deliver notice of the appointment to the creditors and to the contributories of the company of whom the liquidator is aware; or

(b) advertise the appointment in accordance with any directions given by the court.

(9) In the notice under this rule the liquidator must—

(a) state whether the liquidator proposes to seek decisions from creditors and contributories for the purpose of establishing a liquidation committee, or proposes only to seek a decision from creditors for that purpose; and

(b) if the liquidator does not propose to seek any such decision, set out the powers of the creditors under the Act to require the liquidator to seek one.

NOTES

Commencement: 6 April 2017.

This rule derived from the Insolvency Rules 1986, SI 1986/1925, r 4.102.

[6.332]

7.57 Appointment by the Secretary of State

(1) This rule applies where the official receiver applies to the Secretary of State to appoint a liquidator in place of the official receiver, or refers to the Secretary of State the need for an appointment.

(2) If the Secretary of State makes an appointment, the Secretary of State must deliver a copy of the certificate of appointment to the official receiver, who must deliver it to the person appointed.

(3) The certificate must specify the date from which the liquidator's appointment is to be effective.

NOTES

Commencement: 6 April 2017.

This rule derived from the Insolvency Rules 1986, SI 1986/1925, r 4.104.

[6.333]

7.58 Cost of liquidator's security (section 390(3))

The cost of the liquidator's security required by section 390(3) for the proper performance of the liquidator's functions is an expense of the winding up.

NOTES

Commencement: 6 April 2017.

This rule derived from the Insolvency Rules 1986, SI 1986/1925, r 12A.56.

[6.334]

7.59 Appointment to be gazetted and notice given to registrar of companies

(1) The liquidator—

(a) must gazette a notice of the appointment as soon as reasonably practicable after appointment; and
(b) may advertise the notice in such other manner as the liquidator thinks fit.

(2) The notice must state—
(a) that a liquidator has been appointed; and
(b) the date of the appointment.

(3) As soon as reasonably practicable the liquidator must deliver notice of the appointment to the registrar of companies.

NOTES
Commencement: 6 April 2017.
This rule derived from the Insolvency Rules 1986, SI 1986/1925, r 4.106A.

[6.335]
7.60 Hand-over of assets by official receiver to liquidator

(1) This rule only applies where the liquidator is appointed in succession to the official receiver acting as liquidator.

(2) When the liquidator's appointment takes effect, the official receiver must as soon as reasonably practicable do all that is required for putting the liquidator into possession of the assets.

(3) On taking possession of the assets, the liquidator must discharge any balance due to the official receiver on account of—
(a) expenses properly incurred by the official receiver and payable under the Act or these Rules; and
(b) any advances made by the official receiver in respect of the assets, together with interest on such advances at the rate specified in section 17 of the Judgments Act 1838 at the date of the winding-up order.

(4) Alternatively, the liquidator may (before taking office) give to the official receiver a written undertaking to discharge any such balance out of the first realisation of assets.

(5) The official receiver has a charge on the assets in respect of any sums due to the official receiver under paragraph (3) until they have been discharged, subject only to the deduction from realisations by the liquidator of the proper costs and expenses of such realisations.

(6) The liquidator must from time to time out of the realisation of assets discharge all guarantees properly given by the official receiver for the benefit of the insolvent estate, and must pay all the official receiver's expenses.

(7) The official receiver must give to the liquidator all such information relating to the affairs of the company and the course of the winding up as the official receiver considers to be reasonably required for the effective discharge by the liquidator of the liquidator's duties.

(8) The official receiver must also deliver to the liquidator a copy of any report made by the official receiver under Chapter 7 of Part 7.

NOTES
Commencement: 6 April 2017.
This rule derived from the Insolvency Rules 1986, SI 1986/1925, r 4.107.

[6.336]
7.61 Liquidator's resignation

(1) A liquidator may resign only—
(a) on grounds of ill health;
(b) because of the intention to cease to practise as an insolvency practitioner;
(c) because the further discharge of the duties of liquidator is prevented or made impracticable by—
(i) a conflict of interest, or
(ii) a change of personal circumstances;
(d) where two or more persons are acting as liquidator jointly, and it is the opinion of both or all of them that it is no longer expedient that there should continue to be that number of joint liquidators.

(2) Before resigning, the liquidator must deliver a notice to creditors, and invite the creditors by a decision procedure, or by deemed consent procedure, to consider whether a replacement should be appointed, except where the resignation is under sub-paragraph (1)(d).

(3) The notice must—
(a) state the liquidator's intention to resign;
(b) state that under rule 7.61(7) of these Rules the liquidator will be released 21 days after the date of delivery of the notice of resignation to the court under section 172(6), unless the court orders otherwise; and
(c) comply with rule 15.7 or 15.8 so far as applicable.

(4) The notice may suggest the name of a replacement liquidator.

(5) The notice must be accompanied by a summary of the liquidator's receipts and payments.

(6) The decision date must be not more than five business days before the date on which the liquidator intends to give notice under section 172(6).

(7) The resigning liquidator's release is effective 21 days after the date on which the notice of resignation under section 172(6) is filed with the court.

NOTES

Commencement: 6 April 2017.

This rule derived from the Insolvency Rules 1986, SI 1986/1925, r 4.108(4).

[6.337]

7.62 Notice to official receiver of intention to vacate office

(1) This rule applies where the liquidator intends to vacate office, whether by resignation or otherwise, and as a result there will be a vacancy in the office of liquidator (so that by virtue of section 136(3) the official receiver is liquidator until the vacancy is filled).

(2) The liquidator must deliver notice of that intention to the official receiver at least 21 days before the liquidator intends to vacate office.

(3) The liquidator must include in the notice to the official receiver the following details of any property of the company which has not been realised, applied, distributed or otherwise fully dealt with in the winding up—

- (a) the nature of the property;
- (b) its value (or the fact that it has no value);
- (c) its location;
- (d) any action taken by the liquidator to deal with the property or any reason for the liquidator not dealing with it; and
- (e) the current position in relation to it.

NOTES

Commencement: 6 April 2017.

This rule derived from the Insolvency Rules 1986, SI 1986/1925, r 4.137.

[6.338]

7.63 Decision of creditors to remove liquidator

(1) This rule applies where the convener of the decision procedure or chair of the meeting (as the case may be) is other than the official receiver, and a decision is made, using a decision procedure, to remove the liquidator

(2) The convener or chair must within three business days of the decision to remove the liquidator deliver a certificate to that effect to the official receiver.

(3) If the creditors decided to appoint a new liquidator, the certificate of the new liquidator's appointment must also be delivered to the official receiver within that time; and the certificate must comply with the requirements in rule 7.53.

(4) The certificate of the liquidator's removal must—

- (a) identify the company;
- (b) identify and provide contact details for the removed liquidator;
- (c) state that the creditors of the company decided on the date specified in the certificate that the liquidator specified in the certificate be removed from office as liquidator of the company;
- (d) state the decision procedure used, and the decision date;
- (e) state that the creditors either—
  - (i) did not decide against the liquidator being released, or
  - (ii) decided that the liquidator should not be released; and
- (f) be authenticated and dated by the convener or chair.

(5) The liquidator's removal is effective from the date of the certificate of removal.

NOTES

Commencement: 6 April 2017.

This rule derived from the Insolvency Rules 1986, SI 1986/1925, r 7.113.

[6.339]

7.64 Procedure on removal by creditors

(1) Where the creditors have decided that the liquidator be removed, the official receiver must file the certificate of removal with the court.

(2) The official receiver must deliver a copy of the certificate as soon as reasonably practicable to the removed liquidator and deliver a notice of the removal to the registrar of companies.

NOTES

Commencement: 6 April 2017.

This rule derived from the Insolvency Rules 1986, SI 1986/1925, r 4.116.

[6.340]

7.65 Removal of liquidator by the court (section 172(2))

(1) This rule applies where an application is made to the court under section 172(2) for the removal of the liquidator, or for an order directing the liquidator to initiate a decision procedure of creditors for the purpose of removing the liquidator.

(2) On receipt of an application, the court may, if it is satisfied that no sufficient cause is shown for it, dismiss it without giving notice to any party other than the applicant.

Part 6 Insolvency Rules

(3) Unless the application is dismissed, the court must fix a venue for it to be heard.

(4) The applicant must, at least 14 days before any hearing, deliver to the liquidator and the official receiver a notice stating the venue with a copy of the application and of any evidence on which the applicant intends to rely.

(5) A respondent may apply for security for costs of the application and the court may make such an order if it is satisfied, having regard to all the circumstances of the case, that it is just to make such an order.

(6) The liquidator and the official receiver may do either or both of the following—

(a) file a report of any matters which the liquidator or the official receiver thinks ought to be drawn to the court's attention; or

(b) appear and be heard on the application.

(7) On a successful application the court's order must contain—

(a) the name of the court (and hearing centre if applicable) in which the order is made;

(b) the name and title of the judge making the order;

(c) the name and postal address of the applicant;

(d) the capacity in which the applicant made the application;

(e) identification and contact details for the liquidator;

(f) identification details for the company;

(g) an order either—

(i) that the liquidator is removed from office; or

(ii) that the liquidator must initiate a decision procedure of the company's creditors (specifying which procedure is to be used) on or before the date specified in the order for the purpose of considering the liquidator's removal from office; and

(h) the date the order is made.

(8) The costs of the application are not payable as an expense of the winding up unless the court orders otherwise.

(9) Where the court removes the liquidator—

(a) it must deliver the sealed order of removal to the former liquidator and a copy of the order to the official receiver; and

(b) the former liquidator must deliver a copy of the order to the registrar of companies as soon as reasonably practicable.

(10) If the court appoints a new liquidator, rule 7.56 applies.

NOTES

Commencement: 6 April 2017.

This rule derived from the Insolvency Rules 1986, SI 1986/1925, r 4.119.

[6.341]

7.66 Removal of liquidator by the Secretary of State (section 172(4))

(1) This rule applies where the Secretary of State decides to direct under section 172(4) the removal of a liquidator appointed by the Secretary of State.

(2) Before doing so the Secretary of State must deliver to the liquidator and the official receiver a notice of the Secretary of State's decision and the grounds for the decision.

(3) The notice must specify a period within which the liquidator may make representations against implementation of the decision.

(4) If the Secretary of State directs the removal of the liquidator, the Secretary of State must as soon as reasonably practicable—

(a) deliver notice of the Secretary of State's decision to the registrar of companies, the liquidator and the official receiver; and

(b) file notice of the decision with the court.

(5) Where the Secretary of State directs the liquidator be removed the court may make any order that it could have made if the liquidator had been removed by the court.

NOTES

Commencement: 6 April 2017.

This rule derived from the Insolvency Rules 1986, SI 1986/1925, r 4.123.

[6.342]

7.67 Deceased liquidator

(1) If the liquidator (not being the official receiver) dies a notice of the fact and date of death must be delivered to the official receiver by one of the following—

(a) a surviving joint liquidator;

(b) a member of the deceased liquidator's firm (if the deceased was a member or employee of a firm);

(c) an officer of the deceased liquidator's company (if the deceased was an officer or employee of a company);

(d) a personal representative of the deceased liquidator.

(2) If no such notice has been delivered within the 21 days following the liquidator's death then any other person may deliver the notice.

(3) The official receiver must—

(a) file notice of the death with the court, for the purpose of fixing the date of the deceased liquidator's release under section 174(4)(a); and

(b) deliver a copy of the notice to the registrar of companies.

NOTES

Commencement: 6 April 2017.

This rule derived from the Insolvency Rules 1986, SI 1986/1925, r 4.132.

[6.343]

7.68 Loss of qualification as insolvency practitioner

(1) This rule applies where the liquidator vacates office on ceasing to be qualified to act as an insolvency practitioner in relation to the company.

(2) A notice of the fact must be delivered as soon as reasonably practicable to the official receiver by one of the following—

(a) the liquidator who has vacated office;

(b) a continuing joint liquidator;

(c) the recognised professional body which was the source of the vacating liquidator's authorisation to act in relation to the company.

(3) The notice must be authenticated and dated by the person delivering the notice.

(4) The official receiver must—

(a) deliver a notice of receiving such a notice to the Secretary of State; and

(b) deliver a copy to the registrar of companies.

NOTES

Commencement: 6 April 2017.

This rule derived from the Insolvency Rules 1986, SI 1986/1925, r 4.134.

[6.344]

7.69 Application by liquidator for release (section 174(4)(b) or (d))

(1) An application by a liquidator to the Secretary of State for release under section 174(4)(b) or (d) must contain—

(a) identification details for the proceedings;

(b) identification and contact details for the liquidator;

(c) a statement that the liquidator of the company is applying to the Secretary of State to grant the liquidator with a certificate of the liquidator's release as liquidator as a result of the circumstances specified in the application;

(d) details of the circumstances referred to in sub-paragraph (c) under which the liquidator has ceased to act as liquidator.

(2) The application must be authenticated and dated by the liquidator.

(3) When the Secretary of State releases the former liquidator, the Secretary of State must certify the release and deliver the certificate to the former liquidator whose release is effective from the date of the certificate or such other date as the certificate specifies.

(4) The Secretary of State must deliver notice of the release to the registrar of companies.

NOTES

Commencement: 6 April 2017.

This rule derived from the Insolvency Rules 1986, SI 1986/1925, r 4.121.

[6.345]

7.70 Release of official receiver

(1) The official receiver must, before giving notice to the Secretary of State under section 174(3) (that the winding up is for practical purposes complete), deliver notice of intention to do so to the creditors.

(2) The notice must be accompanied by a summary of the official receiver's receipts and payments as liquidator.

(3) The summary of receipts and payments must also include a statement as to the amount paid to unsecured creditors under section 176A (prescribed part).

(4) When the Secretary of State has determined the date from which the official receiver's release is to be effective, the Secretary of State must—

(a) notify the official receiver of the release; and

(b) deliver a notice of the release to the registrar of companies accompanied by the summary of the official receiver's receipts and payments.

NOTES

Commencement: 6 April 2017.

This rule derived from the Insolvency Rules 1986, SI 1986/1925, r 4.124.

[6.346]
7.71 Final account prior to dissolution (section 146)

(1) The final account which the liquidator is required to make up under section 146(2) and deliver to creditors must comply with the requirements of rule 18.14.

(2) When the account is delivered to the creditors it must be accompanied by a notice which states—
- (a) that the company's affairs are fully wound up;
- (b) that the creditor has the right to request information from the liquidator under rule 18.9;
- (c) that a creditor has the right to challenge the liquidator's remuneration and expenses under rule 18.34;
- (d) that a creditor may object to the release of the liquidator by giving notice in writing to the liquidator before the end of the prescribed period;
- (e) that the prescribed period is the period ending at the later of—
  - (i) eight weeks after delivery of the notice, or
  - (ii) if any request for information under rule 18.9 or any application to court under that rule or rule 18.34 is made when that request or application is finally determined;
- (f) that the liquidator will vacate office under section 172(8) as soon as the liquidator has complied with section 146(4) by filing with the court and delivering to the registrar of companies the final account and notice containing the statement required by section 146(4)(b) of whether any creditors have objected to the liquidator's release; and
- (g) that the liquidator will be released under section 174(4)(d)(ii) at the same time as vacating office unless any of the creditors objected to the release.

(3) The liquidator must deliver a copy of the notice under section 146(4) to the Secretary of State.

(4) Rule 7.69 applies to an application by the liquidator to the Secretary of State for release.

NOTES

Commencement: 6 April 2017.

This rule derived from the Insolvency Rules 1986, SI 1986/1925, r 4.125.

[6.347]
7.72 Relief from, or variation of, duty to report

(1) The court may, on the application of the liquidator or the official receiver, relieve the liquidator or official receiver of any duty imposed on the liquidator or official receiver by rule 7.70 or rule 7.71, or authorise the liquidator or official receiver to carry out the duty in a way other than required by either of those rules.

(2) In considering whether to act under this rule, the court must have regard to the cost of carrying out the duty, to the amount of the assets available, and to the extent of the interest of creditors or contributories, or any particular class of them.

NOTES

Commencement: 6 April 2017.

This rule derived from the Insolvency Rules 1986, SI 1986/1925, r 4.125A.

[6.348]
7.73 Liquidator's duties on vacating office

(1) A liquidator who ceases to be in office in consequence of removal, resignation or ceasing to be qualified to act as an insolvency practitioner in relation to the company, must as soon as reasonably practicable deliver to the successor as liquidator—
- (a) the assets (after deduction of any expenses properly incurred, and distributions made, by the previous liquidator);
- (b) the records of the winding up, including correspondence, proofs and other documents relating to the winding up while it was within the former liquidator's responsibility; and
- (c) the company's documents and other records.

(2) Where the liquidator vacates office under section 172(8) (final report to creditors), the liquidator must deliver to the official receiver the company's documents and other records which have not already been disposed of in accordance with general regulations in the course of the winding up.

NOTES

Commencement: 6 April 2017.

This rule derived from the Insolvency Rules 1986, SI 1986/1925, r 4.138.

[6.349]
7.74 Power of court to set aside certain transactions

(1) If in dealing with the insolvent estate the liquidator enters into any transaction with a person who is an associate of the liquidator, the court may, on the application of any interested person, set the transaction aside and order the liquidator to compensate the company for any loss suffered in consequence of it.

(2) This does not apply if either—
- (a) the transaction was entered into with the prior consent of the court; or
- (b) it is shown to the court's satisfaction that the transaction was for value, and that it was entered into by the liquidator without knowing, or having any reason to suppose, that the person concerned was an associate.

(3) Nothing in this rule is to be taken as prejudicing the operation of any rule of law or equity relating to a liquidator's dealings with trust property, or the fiduciary obligations of any person.

NOTES

Commencement: 6 April 2017.

This rule derived from the Insolvency Rules 1986, SI 1986/1925, r 4.149.

[6.350]

7.75 Rule against improper solicitation

(1) Where the court is satisfied that any improper solicitation has been used by or on behalf of the liquidator in obtaining proxies or procuring the liquidator's appointment, it may order that no remuneration be allowed as an expense of the winding up to any person by whom, or on whose behalf, the solicitation was exercised.

(2) An order of the court under this rule overrides any resolution of the liquidation committee or the creditors, or any other provision of these Rules relating to the liquidator's remuneration.

NOTES

Commencement: 6 April 2017.

This rule derived from the Insolvency Rules 1986, SI 1986/1925, r 4.150.

CHAPTER 9 DUTIES AND POWERS OF LIQUIDATOR

[Note: a document required by the Act or these Rules must also contain the standard contents set out in Part 1.]

[6.351]

7.76 General duties of liquidator

(1) The duties which the Act imposes on the court relating to the collection of the company's assets and their application in discharge of the company's liabilities are discharged by the liquidator as an officer of the court subject to its control.

(2) In the discharge of the liquidator's duties, the liquidator, for the purposes of acquiring and retaining possession of the company's property, has the same powers as a receiver appointed by the High Court, and the court may on the application of the liquidator enforce such acquisition or retention accordingly.

NOTES

Commencement: 6 April 2017.

This rule derived from the Insolvency Rules 1986, SI 1986/1925, r 4.179.

[6.352]

7.77 Permission for exercise of powers by liquidator

(1) Where the Act or these Rules require permission for the liquidator to exercise a power any permission given must not be a general permission but must relate to a particular proposed exercise of the liquidator's power.

(2) A person dealing with the liquidator in good faith and for value is not concerned to enquire whether any such permission has been given.

(3) Where the liquidator has done anything without such permission, the court or the liquidation committee may, for the purpose of enabling the liquidator to meet the liquidator's expenses out of the assets, ratify what the liquidator has done; but neither must do so unless satisfied that the liquidator has acted in a case of urgency and has sought ratification without undue delay.

(4) In this rule "permission" includes "sanction".

NOTES

Commencement: 6 April 2017.

This rule derived from the Insolvency Rules 1986, SI 1986/1925, r 4.184.

[6.353]

7.78 Enforced delivery up of company's property (section 234)

(1) The powers conferred on the court by section 234 (enforced delivery of company property) are exercisable by the liquidator or, where a provisional liquidator has been appointed, by the provisional liquidator.

(2) Any person on whom a requirement under section 234(2) is imposed by the liquidator or provisional liquidator must, without avoidable delay, comply with it.

NOTES

Commencement: 6 April 2017.

This rule derived from the Insolvency Rules 1986, SI 1986/1925, r 4.185.

CHAPTER 10 SETTLEMENT OF LIST OF CONTRIBUTORIES

[Note: a document required by the Act or these Rules must also contain the standard contents set out in Part 1.]

[6.354]
7.79 Delegation to liquidator of power to settle list of contributories

(1) The duties of the court under section 148 in relation to settling the list of contributories are, by virtue of these Rules and in accordance with section 160, delegated to the liquidator.

(2) The liquidator's duties in settling the list of contributories are performed as an officer of the court subject to the court's control.

NOTES

Commencement: 6 April 2017.

This rule derived from the Insolvency Rules 1986, SI 1986/1925, r 4.195.

[6.355]
7.80 Duty of liquidator to settle list (section 148)

The liquidator must, as soon as reasonably possible after the liquidator's appointment, exercise the court's power to settle a list of the company's contributories for the purposes of section 148 and, with the court's approval, rectify the register of members.

NOTES

Commencement: 6 April 2017.

This rule derived from the Insolvency Rules 1986, SI 1986/1925, r 4.196.

[6.356]
7.81 Contents of list

(1) The list must identify—

(a) the several classes of the company's shares (if more than one); and

(b) the several classes of contributories, distinguishing between those who are contributories in their own right and those who are so as representatives of, or liable for the debts of, others.

(2) In the case of each contributory the list must state—

(a) the address of the contributory;

(b) the number and class of shares, or the extent of any other interest to be attributed to the contributory; and

(c) if the shares are not fully paid up, the amounts which have been called up and paid in respect of them (and the equivalent, if any, where the interest of the contributory is other than shares).

NOTES

Commencement: 6 April 2017.

This rule derived from the Insolvency Rules 1986, SI 1986/1925, r 4.197.

[6.357]
7.82 Procedure for settling list

(1) Having settled the list, the liquidator must as soon as reasonably practicable deliver a notice, to each person included in the list, that this has been done.

(2) The notice given to each person must state—

(a) in what character, and for what number of shares or what interest, that person is included in the list;

(b) what amounts have been called up and paid up in respect of the shares or interest; and

(c) that in relation to any shares or interest not fully paid up, that person's inclusion in the list may result in the unpaid capital being called.

(3) The notice must inform a person to whom it is given that, if that person objects to any entry in, or omission from, the list, that person should so inform the liquidator in writing within 21 days from the date of the notice.

(4) On receipt of an objection, the liquidator must within 14 days deliver a notice to the objector either—

(a) that the liquidator has amended the list (specifying the amendment); or

(b) that the liquidator considers the objection to be not well-founded and declines to amend the list.

(5) The notice must in either case inform the objector of the effect of rule 7.83.

NOTES

Commencement: 6 April 2017.

This rule derived from the Insolvency Rules 1986, SI 1986/1925, r 4.198.

[6.358]
7.83 Application to court for variation of the list

(1) If a person ("the objector") objects to any entry in, or exclusion from, the list of contributories as settled by the liquidator and, notwithstanding notice by the liquidator declining to amend the list, the objector maintains the objection, the objector may apply to the court for an order removing the entry objected to or (as the case may be) otherwise amending the list.

(2) The application must be made within 21 days of the delivery to the applicant of the liquidator's notice under rule 7.82(4).

NOTES

Commencement: 6 April 2017.

This rule derived from the Insolvency Rules 1986, SI 1986/1925, r 4.199.

[6.359]

7.84 Variation of, or addition to, the list

The liquidator may from time to time vary or add to the list of contributories as previously settled by the liquidator, but subject in all respects to the preceding rules in this Chapter.

NOTES

Commencement: 6 April 2017.

This rule derived from the Insolvency Rules 1986, SI 1986/1925, r 4.200.

[6.360]

7.85 Costs of applications to vary etc the list of contributories

Where a person applies to set aside or vary any act or decision of the liquidator in settling the list of contributories then—

- (a) the liquidator (if other than the official receiver) is not liable for any costs incurred by that person in relation to the application unless the court makes an order to that effect; and
- (b) the official receiver is not personally liable for such costs.

NOTES

Commencement: 6 April 2017.

This rule derived from the Insolvency Rules 1986, SI 1986/1925, r 4.201.

CHAPTER 11 CALLS ON CONTRIBUTORIES

[Note: a document required by the Act or these Rules must also contain the standard contents set out in Part 1.]

[6.361]

7.86 Making of calls by the liquidator (sections 150 and 160)

(1) Subject as follows the powers relating to the making of calls on contributories are exercisable by the liquidator as an officer of the court.

(2) However as provided by section 160(2) the making of a call requires either the sanction of the liquidation committee or the court's special permission.

NOTES

Commencement: 6 April 2017.

This rule derived from the Insolvency Rules 1986, SI 1986/1925, r 4.202.

[6.362]

7.87 Sanction of the liquidation committee for making a call

(1) Where the liquidator proposes to make a call, and there is a liquidation committee, the liquidator may summon a meeting of the committee for the purpose of obtaining its sanction.

(2) The liquidator must deliver a notice of the meeting to each member of the committee giving at least five business days' notice of the meeting.

(3) The notice must state the purpose of making the call and the proposed amount of the call.

NOTES

Commencement: 6 April 2017.

This rule derived from the Insolvency Rules 1986, SI 1986/1925, r 4.203.

[6.363]

7.88 Application to court for permission to make a call (sections 150 and 160)

(1) Where the liquidator proposes to make a call the liquidator may apply to the court without notice to any other party for permission to make a call on any contributories of the company.

(2) The application must state the amount of the proposed call, and the contributories on whom it is to be made.

(3) The application must be supported by a witness statement accompanied by a schedule.

(4) The witness statement must have the title "Witness statement of liquidator in support of application for call" and must contain—

- (a) identification and contact details for the liquidator;
- (b) identification details for the company;
- (c) the number of persons on the list of contributories settled by the liquidator;
- (d) the total number of shares to which the proposed call relates;
- (e) the statement that in addition to the amount of the assets of the company mentioned in the schedule the liquidator believes a further sum will be required to satisfy the debts and liabilities of the company, and pay the expenses of and incidental to the winding up;
- (f) the additional sum required;

(g) a statement that in order to provide the additional sum it is necessary to make a call upon the persons on the settled list of contributories, and that as it is probable that some of those contributories will partly or wholly fail to pay the amount of the call, the liquidator believes that it is necessary that a call of a specified amount per share be made in order to realise the amount required;
(h) the specified amount per share.

(5) The accompanying schedule must show—
(a) the amount due in respect of debts already proved;
(b) the estimated amount of—
(i) further liabilities of the company, and
(ii) the expenses of the winding up;
(c) the total of the amounts referred to in sub-paragraphs (a) and (b); and
(d) a list of the assets in hand belonging to the company with their total value.

(6) The schedule must be verified by a statement of truth made by the liquidator.

NOTES

Commencement: 6 April 2017.
This rule derived from the Insolvency Rules 1986, SI 1986/1925, r 4.204, Sch 4, Fm 4.56.

[6.364]
7.89 Order giving permission to make a call

(1) The court's order giving permission to make a call must have the title "Order giving permission to make a call" and must contain—
(a) the name of the court (and hearing centre if applicable) in which the order is made;
(b) the name and title of the judge making the order;
(c) identification and contact details for the liquidator;
(d) identification details for the company;
(e) an order that the liquidator may make a call of the amount per share specified in the order on the contributories who are specified in the order;
(f) the amount per share of the call;
(g) the names of the contributories of the company on whom the liquidator is to make the call;
(h) an order that each such contributory must on or before the date specified in the order pay to the liquidator of the company the amount due from that contributory in respect of the call; and
(i) the date of the order.

(2) The court may direct that notice of the order be delivered to the contributories concerned, or to other contributories, or may direct that the notice be publicly advertised.

NOTES

Commencement: 6 April 2017.
This rule derived from the Insolvency Rules 1986, SI 1986/1925, Sch 4, Fm 4.57.

[6.365]
7.90 Making and enforcement of the call

(1) The liquidator must deliver a notice of the call to each of the contributories concerned.
(2) The notice must contain—
(a) identification details for the company;
(b) identification and contact details for the liquidator;
(c) a statement that a call on the contributories specified in the notice of the amount per share stated in the notice was sanctioned by—
(i) a resolution of the liquidation committee of the company passed on the date which is stated in the notice, or
(ii) an order of the court named in the notice on the date which is stated in the notice;
(d) the amount per share of the call;
(e) the amount or balance due from the contributory to whom the notice is addressed in respect of the call;
(f) the date by which the sum must be paid;
(g) a warning to the contributory that, if the required sum is not paid by the date specified in the notice, interest at the rate specified in the notice will be charged on the unpaid amount from that date until payment; and
(h) the specified annual interest rate.

(3) The notice must be accompanied by a copy of the resolution of the liquidation committee sanctioning the call or of the court's order giving permission as the case may be.

NOTES

Commencement: 6 April 2017.
This rule derived from the Insolvency Rules 1986, SI 1986/1925, r 4.205, Sch 4, Fm 4.58.

[6.366]
7.91 Court order to enforce payment of call by a contributory

(1) The court may make an order to enforce payment of the amount due from a contributory.
(2) The order must have the title "Order for payment of call due from contributory" and must contain—

(a) the name of the court (and hearing centre if applicable) in which the order is made;
(b) identification and contact details for the liquidator who made the application;
(c) the name and title of the judge making the order;
(d) identification details for the company;
(e) the name and postal address of the contributory who is the subject of the order;
(f) the amount per share of the call;
(g) an order that the contributory pay the liquidator the sum stated in the order in respect of the call on or before the date stated in the order or within four business days after service of the order whichever is the later;
(h) an order that the contributory pay the liquidator interest at the rate stated in the order for the period commencing from the date specified in the order to the date of payment;
(i) an order that the contributory pay the liquidator a stated sum in respect of the liquidator's costs of the application within the same period as the amount of the call must be paid;
(j) a warning to the contributory that if the required sums are not paid within the time specified in the order further steps will be taken to compel the contributory to comply with the order; and
(k) the date of the order.

NOTES

Commencement: 6 April 2017.
This rule derived from the Insolvency Rules 1986, SI 1986/1925, r 4.205, Sch 4, Fm 4.59.

CHAPTER 12 SPECIAL MANAGER

[Note: a document required by the Act or these Rules must also contain the standard contents set out in Part 1.]

[6.367]
7.92 Application of this Chapter and interpretation

This Chapter applies to applications for the appointment of a special manager by a liquidator and by a provisional liquidator (where one has been appointed), and so references to the liquidator are to be read as including a provisional liquidator.

NOTES

Commencement: 6 April 2017.

[6.368]
7.93 Appointment and remuneration of special manager (section 177)

(1) An application made by the liquidator under section 177 for the appointment of a special manager must be supported by a report setting out the reasons for the application.

(2) The report must include the applicant's estimate of the value of the business or property in relation to which the special manager is to be appointed.

(3) The court's order appointing the special manager must have the title "Order of appointment of special manager" and must contain—
(a) identification details for the proceedings;
(b) the name and address of the person who made the application;
(c) the name and title of the judge making the order;
(d) the name and address of the proposed special manager;
(e) the order that the proposed special manager is appointed as special manager of the company;
(f) details of the special manager's responsibility over the company's business or property;
(g) the powers to be entrusted to the special manager under section [177(3)];
(h) the time allowed for the special manager to give the required security for the appointment;
(i) the duration of the special manager's appointment being one of the following—
(i) for a fixed period stated in the order,
(ii) until the occurrence of a specified event, or
(iii) until the court makes a further order;
(j) an order that the special manager's remuneration will be fixed from time to time by the court; and
(k) the date of the order.

(4) The appointment of a special manager may be renewed by order of the court.

(5) The special manager's remuneration will be fixed from time to time by the court.

(6) The acts of the special manager are valid notwithstanding any defect in the special manager's appointment or qualifications.

NOTES

Commencement: 6 April 2017.
This rule derived from the Insolvency Rules 1986, SI 1986/1925, r 4.206.
Para (3): figure in square brackets in sub-para (g) substituted by the Insolvency (England and Wales) (Amendment) Rules 2017, SI 2017/366, rr 3, 21.

Part 6 Insolvency Rules

[6.369]
7.94 Security

(1) The appointment of the special manager does not take effect until the person appointed has given (or, if the court allows, undertaken to give) security to the applicant for the appointment.

(2) A person appointed as a special manager may give security either specifically for a particular winding up, or generally for any winding up in relation to which that person may be employed as special manager.

(3) The amount of the security must be not less than the value of the business or property in relation to which the special manager is appointed, as estimated in the applicant's report which accompanied the application for appointment.

(4) When the special manager has given security to the applicant that person must file with the court a certificate as to the adequacy of the security.

(5) The cost of providing the security must be paid in the first instance by the special manager; but—
- (a) where a winding-up order is not made, the special manager is entitled to be reimbursed out of the property of the company, and the court may order accordingly; and
- (b) where a winding-up order is made, the special manager is entitled to be reimbursed as an expense of the winding up in the prescribed order of priority.

NOTES

Commencement: 6 April 2017.
This rule derived from the Insolvency Rules 1986, SI 1986/1925, r 4.207.

[6.370]
7.95 Failure to give or keep up security

(1) If the special manager fails to give the required security within the time allowed for that purpose by the order of appointment, or any extension of that time that may be allowed, the liquidator must report the failure to the court, which may discharge the order appointing the special manager.

(2) If the special manager fails to keep up the security, the liquidator must report the failure to the court, which may remove the special manager, and make such order as it thinks just as to costs.

(3) If the court discharges the order appointing the special manager or makes an order removing the special manager, the court must give directions as to whether any, and if so what, steps should be taken for the appointment of another special manager.

NOTES

Commencement: 6 April 2017.
This rule derived from the Insolvency Rules 1986, SI 1986/1925, r 4.208.

[6.371]
7.96 Accounting

(1) The special manager must produce accounts, containing details of the special manager's receipts and payments, for the approval of the liquidator.

(2) The accounts must be for—
- (a) each three month period for the duration of the special manager's appointment; or
- (b) any shorter period ending with the termination of the special manager's appointment.

(3) When the accounts have been approved, the special manager's receipts and payments must be added to those of the liquidator.

NOTES

Commencement: 6 April 2017.
This rule derived from the Insolvency Rules 1986, SI 1986/1925, r 4.209.

[6.372]
7.97 Termination of appointment

(1) The special manager's appointment terminates—
- (a) if the winding-up petition is dismissed; or
- (b) in a case where a provisional liquidator was appointed under section 135, if the appointment is discharged without a winding-up order having been made.

(2) If the liquidator is of the opinion that the employment of the special manager is no longer necessary or beneficial for the company, the liquidator must apply to the court for directions, and the court may order the special manager's appointment to be terminated.

(3) The liquidator must make the same application if the creditors decide that the appointment should be terminated.

NOTES

Commencement: 6 April 2017.
This rule derived from the Insolvency Rules 1986, SI 1986/1925, r 4.210.

CHAPTER 13 PUBLIC EXAMINATION OF COMPANY OFFICERS AND OTHERS (SECTION 133)

[Note: a document required by the Act or these Rules must also contain the standard contents set out in Part 1.]

[6.373]

7.98 Applications relating to promoters, past managers etc (section 133(1)(c))

(1) An application under section 133(1) for the public examination of a person falling within paragraph (c) of subsection (1) (promoters, past managers, etc) must be accompanied by a report by the official receiver indicating—

(a) the grounds on which the official receiver thinks the person is within that paragraph; and

(b) whether the official receiver thinks it is likely that the order can be served on the person at a known address and, if so, by what means.

(2) If the official receiver thinks that there is no reasonable certainty that service at a known address will be effective, the court may direct that the order be served by some means other than, or in addition to, service in such manner.

NOTES

Commencement: 6 April 2017.

This rule derived from the Insolvency Rules 1986, SI 1986/1925, r 4.211.

[6.374]

7.99 Request by a creditor for a public examination (section 133(2))

(1) A request made under section 133(2) by a creditor to the official receiver for the public examination of a person must contain—

(a) identification details for the company;

(b) the name and postal address of the creditor;

(c) the name and postal address of the proposed examinee;

(d) a description of the relationship which the proposed examinee has, or has had, with the company;

(e) a request by the creditor to the official receiver to apply to the court for a public examination of the proposed examinee under section 133(2);

(f) the amount of the creditor's claim in the winding up;

(g) a statement that the total amount of the creditor's and any concurring creditors' claims is believed to represent not less than one-half in value of the debts of the company;

(h) a statement that the creditor understands the requirement to deposit with the official receiver such sum as the official receiver may determine to be appropriate by way of security for the expenses of holding a public examination; and

(i) a statement that the creditor believes that a public examination is required for the reason stated in the request.

(2) The request must be authenticated and dated by the creditor.

(3) The request must be accompanied by—

(a) a list of the creditors concurring with the request and the amounts of their respective claims in the winding up, with their respective values; and

(b) from each concurring creditor, confirmation of the creditor's concurrence.

NOTES

Commencement: 6 April 2017.

This rule derived from the Insolvency Rules 1986, SI 1986/1925, r 4.213.

[6.375]

7.100 Request by a contributory for a public examination

(1) A request made under section 133(2) by a contributory to the official receiver for the public examination of a person must contain—

(a) identification details for the company;

(b) the name and postal address of the contributory;

(c) the name and postal address of the proposed examinee;

(d) a description of the relationship which the proposed examinee has, or has had, with the company;

(e) a request by the contributory to the official receiver to apply to the court for a public examination of the proposed examinee under section 133(2);

(f) the number of shares held in the company by the contributory;

(g) the number of votes to which the contributory is entitled;

(h) a statement that the total amount of the contributory's and any concurring contributories' shares and votes is believed to represent not less than three-quarters in value of the company's contributories;

(i) a statement that the contributory understands the requirement to deposit with the official receiver such sum as the official receiver may determine to be appropriate by way of security for the expenses of holding a public examination; and

(j) a statement that the contributory believes that a public examination is required for the reason specified in the request.

(2) The request must be authenticated and dated by the contributory.

(3) The request must be accompanied by—

(a) a list of the contributories concurring with the request and the number of shares and votes each holds in the company; and

(b) from each concurring contributory, confirmation of the concurrence and of the number of shares and votes held in the company.

NOTES

Commencement: 6 April 2017.

This rule derived from the Insolvency Rules 1986, SI 1986/1925, r 4.213.

[6.376]

7.101 Further provisions about requests by a creditor or contributory for a public examination

(1) A request by a creditor or contributory for a public examination does not require the support of concurring creditors or contributories if the requisitioning creditor's debt or, as the case may be, requisitioning contributory's shares, is sufficient alone under section 133(2).

(2) Before the official receiver makes the requested application, the creditor or contributory requesting the examination must deposit with the official receiver such sum (if any) as the official receiver determines is appropriate as security for the expenses of the public examination (if ordered).

(3) The official receiver must make the application for the examination—

(a) within 28 days of receiving the creditor's or contributory's request (if no security is required under paragraph (2); or

(b) within 28 days of the creditor or contributory (as the case may be) depositing the required security.

(4) However if the official receiver thinks the request is unreasonable, the official receiver may apply to the court for an order to be relieved from making the application.

(5) If the application for an order under paragraph (4) is made without notice to any other party and the court makes such an order then the official receiver must deliver a notice of the order as soon as reasonably practicable to the creditors or contributories who requested the examination.

(6) If the court dismisses the official receiver's application under paragraph (4), the official receiver must make the application under section 133(2) as soon as reasonably practicable.

NOTES

Commencement: 6 April 2017.

This rule derived from the Insolvency Rules 1986, SI 1986/1925, rr 4.213(3), (4), 4.214(5).

[6.377]

7.102 Order for public examination

(1) An order for a public examination must have the title "Order for Public Examination" and must contain the following—

(a) identification details for the proceedings;

(b) the name and title of the judge making the order;

(c) the name and postal address of the person to be examined;

(d) the venue for the public examination;

(e) the order that the person named in the order must attend the specified venue for the purpose of being publicly examined;

(f) the date of the order; and

(g) a warning to the person to be examined that failure without reasonable excuse to attend the public examination at the time and place specified in the order will make the person liable to be arrested without further notice under section 134(2); and that the person will also be guilty of contempt of court under section 134(1) and be liable to be committed to prison or fined.

(2) The official receiver must serve a copy of the order on the person to be examined as soon as reasonably practicable after the order is made.

(3) The court must rescind an order for the public examination of a person who was said to fall within section 133(1)(c) if that person satisfies the court that it is not so.

[Note: rule 81.9 (as amended) of the CPR requires a warning as mentioned in paragraph (1)(g) to be displayed prominently on the front of the order.]

NOTES

Commencement: 6 April 2017.

This rule derived from the Insolvency Rules 1986, SI 1986/1925, Sch 4, Fm 4.61.

[6.378]

7.103 Notice of the public examination

(1) The official receiver must give at least 14 days' notice of the public examination to—

(a) the liquidator (if a liquidator has been nominated or appointed);

(b) the special manager (if a special manager has been appointed); and

(c) the creditors and all the contributories of the company who are known to the official receiver (subject to any contrary direction of the court).

(2) Where the official receiver thinks fit additional notice of the order may be given by gazetting the notice.

(3) The official receiver may in addition to gazetting the notice advertise it in such other manner as the official receiver thinks fit;

(4) The notice must state—

(a) the purpose of the public examination; and

(b) the venue.

(5) Unless the court directs otherwise, the official receiver must not give notice under paragraph (2) of an order relating to a person falling within section 133(1)(c) until at least five business days have elapsed since the examinee was served with the order.

NOTES

Commencement: 6 April 2017.

This rule derived from the Insolvency Rules 1986, SI 1986/1925, r 4.212.

[6.379]

7.104 Examinee unfit for examination

(1) Where the examinee is a person who lacks capacity within the meaning of the Mental Capacity Act 2005 or is unfit to undergo or attend for public examination, the court may—

(a) stay the order for the examinee's public examination; or

(b) order that it is to be conducted in such manner and at such place as it thinks just.

(2) The applicant for an order under paragraph (1) must be—

(a) a person who has been appointed by a court in the United Kingdom or elsewhere to manage the affairs of, or to represent, the examinee;

(b) a person who appears to the court to be a suitable person to make the application; or

(c) the official receiver.

(3) Where the application is made by a person other than the official receiver, then—

(a) the application must, unless the examinee is a person who lacks capacity within the meaning of the Mental Capacity Act 2005, be supported by the witness statement of a registered medical practitioner as to the examinee's mental and physical condition;

(b) at least five business days' notice of the application must be given to the official receiver and the liquidator (if other than the official receiver); and

(c) before any order is made on the application, the applicant must deposit with the official receiver such sum as the latter certifies to be necessary for the additional expenses of an examination.

(4) An order must contain—

(a) identification details for the proceedings;

(b) the name and postal address of the applicant;

(c) the name and title of the judge making the order;

(d) the capacity in which the applicant (other than the official receiver) made the application;

(e) the name and postal address of the examinee;

(f) the date of the order for the examinee's public examination ("the original order");

(g) a statement that the court is satisfied that the examinee specified in the order lacks capacity within the meaning of the Mental Capacity Act 2005 to manage and administer the examinee's property and affairs or is unfit to undergo a public examination;

(h) an order that—

(i) the original order is to be stayed on the grounds that the examinee is unfit to undergo a public examination, or

(ii) the original order is varied (as specified in this order) on the grounds that the examinee is unfit to attend the public examination fixed by the original order; and

(i) the date of the order.

(5) Where a person other than the official receiver makes the application, the court may order that some or all of the expenses of the examination are to be payable out of the deposit under paragraph (3)(c), instead of as an expense of the winding up.

(6) Where the application is made by the official receiver it may be made without notice to any other party, and may be supported by evidence set out in a report by the official receiver to the court.

NOTES

Commencement: 6 April 2017.

This rule derived from the Insolvency Rules 1986, SI 1986/1925, r 4.214.

[6.380]

7.105 Procedure at public examination

(1) At the public examination the examinee must—

(a) be examined on oath; and

(b) answer all the questions which the court puts, or allows to be put.

(2) A person allowed by section 133(4) to question the examinee may—

(a) with the approval of the court appear by an appropriately qualified legal representative; or

(b) in writing authorise another person to question the examinee on that person's behalf.

Part 6 Insolvency Rules

(3) The examinee may at the examinee's own expense employ an appropriately qualified legal representative, who may put to the examinee such questions as the court may allow for the purpose of enabling the examinee to explain or qualify any answers given by the examinee, and may make representations on behalf of the examinee.

(4) The court must have such record made of the examination as the court thinks proper.

(5) The record may, in any proceedings (whether under the Act or otherwise) be used as evidence of any statement made by the examinee in the course of the public examination.

(6) If criminal proceedings have been instituted against the examinee, and the court is of the opinion that continuing the hearing might prejudice a fair trial of those proceedings, the hearing may be adjourned.

NOTES

Commencement: 6 April 2017.

This rule derived from the Insolvency Rules 1986, SI 1986/1925, r 4.215.

[6.381]

7.106 Adjournment

[Note: rule 81.9 (as amended) of the CPR requires a warning as mentioned in paragraph (3) to be displayed prominently on the front of the order.]

(1) The court may adjourn the public examination from time to time, either to a fixed date or generally.

(2) Where the examination has been adjourned generally, the court may at any time on the application of the official receiver or of the examinee—

(a) fix a venue for the resumption of the examination; and

(b) give directions as to the manner in which, and the time within which, notice of the resumed public examination is to be given to persons entitled to take part in it.

(3) An order adjourning the public examination to a fixed date must contain a warning to the examinee that failure without reasonable excuse to attend the public examination at the time and place specified in the order will make the examinee liable to be arrested without further notice under section 134(2); and that the examinee will also be guilty of contempt of court under section 134(1) and be liable to be committed to prison or fined.

(4) Where an application to resume an examination is made by the examinee, the court may grant it on terms that the examinee must pay the expenses of giving the notices required by paragraph (2) and that, before a venue for the resumed public examination is fixed, the examinee must deposit with the official receiver such sum as the official receiver considers necessary to cover those expenses.

NOTES

Commencement: 6 April 2017.

This rule derived from the Insolvency Rules 1986, SI 1986/1925, r 4.216.

[6.382]

7.107 Expenses of examination

(1) Where a public examination of the examinee has been ordered by the court on a request by a creditor under rule 7.99 or by a contributory under rule 7.100, the court may order that some or all of the expenses of the examination are to be paid out of the deposit required under those rules, instead of as an expense of the winding up.

(2) The costs and expenses of a public examination do not fall on the official receiver personally.

NOTES

Commencement: 6 April 2017.

This rule derived from the Insolvency Rules 1986, SI 1986/1925, r 4.217.

CHAPTER 14 PRIORITY OF PAYMENT OF COSTS AND EXPENSES, ETC

[6.383]

7.108 General rule as to priority

(1) All fees, costs, charges and other expenses incurred in the course of the winding up are to be treated as expenses of the winding up.

[(2) The expenses of the winding up are payable out of—

(a) assets of the company available for the payment of general creditors, including—

(i) proceeds of any legal action which the liquidator has power to bring in the liquidator's own name or in the name of the company;

(ii) proceeds arising from any award made under any arbitration or other dispute resolution procedure which the liquidator has power to bring in the liquidator's own name or in the name of the company;

(iii) any payments made under any compromise or other agreement intended to avoid legal action or recourse to arbitration or to any other dispute resolution procedure;

(iv) payments made as a result of an assignment or a settlement of any such action, arrangement or procedure in lieu of or before any judgment being given or award being made; and

(b) subject as provided in rules 7.111 to 7.116, property comprised in or subject to a floating charge created by the company.]

(3) The expenses associated with the prescribed part must be paid out of the prescribed part.

(4) Subject as provided in rules 7.112 to 7.116, the expenses are payable in the following order of priority—

(a) the following expenses, which rank equally in order of priority—

(i) expenses that are properly chargeable or incurred by the provisional liquidator in carrying out the functions conferred on the provisional liquidator by the court,

(ii) expenses that are properly chargeable or incurred by the official receiver or the liquidator in preserving, realising or getting in any of the assets of the company or otherwise in the preparation, conduct or assignment of any legal proceedings, arbitration or other dispute resolution procedures, which the official receiver or liquidator has power to bring in the official receiver's or liquidator's own name or bring or defend in the name of the company or in the preparation or conduct of any negotiations intended to lead or leading to a settlement or compromise of any legal action or dispute to which the proceedings or procedures relate,

(iii) expenses that relate to the employment of a shorthand writer, if appointed by an order of the court made at the instance of the official receiver in connection with an examination, and

(iv) expenses that are incurred in holding a hearing under rule 7.104 (examinee unfit) where the application for it was made by the official receiver;

(b) any other expenses incurred or disbursements made by the official receiver or under the official receiver's authority, including those incurred or made in carrying on the business of the company;

(c) the fees payable under any order made under section 414 or section 415A, including those payable to the official receiver (other than the fee referred to in sub-paragraph (d)), and any remuneration payable to the official receiver under general regulations;

(d) the fee payable under any order made under section 414 for the performance by the official receiver of the general duties of the official receiver and any repayable sum deposited under any such order as security for the fee;

(e) the cost of any security provided by a provisional liquidator, liquidator or special manager in accordance with the Act or these Rules;

(f) the remuneration of the provisional liquidator (if any);

(g) any sum deposited on an application for the appointment of a provisional liquidator;

(h) the costs of the petitioner, and of any person appearing on the petition whose costs are allowed by the court;

(i) the remuneration of the special manager (if any);

(j) any amount payable to a person employed or authorised, under Chapter 6 of this Part, to assist in the preparation of a statement of affairs or of accounts;

(k) any allowance made, by order of the court, in respect of costs on an application for release from the obligation to submit a statement of affairs, or for an extension of time for submitting such a statement;

(l) the costs of employing a shorthand writer in any case other than one appointed by an order of the court at the instance of the official receiver in connection with an examination;

(m) any necessary disbursements by the liquidator in the course of the administration of the winding up (including any [costs referred to in Articles 30 or 59 of the EU Regulation and] expenses incurred by members of the liquidation committee or their representatives and allowed by the liquidator under rule 17.24, but not including any payment of corporation tax in circumstances referred to in sub-paragraph (p));

(n) the remuneration or emoluments of any person who has been employed by the liquidator to perform any services for the company, as required or authorised by or under the Act or these Rules;

(o) the remuneration of the liquidator, up to an amount not exceeding that which is payable under Schedule 11 (determination of insolvency office-holder's remuneration);

(p) the amount of any corporation tax on chargeable gains accruing on the realisation of any asset of the company (irrespective of the person by whom the realisation is effected);

(q) the balance, after payment of any sums due under sub-paragraph (o) above, of any remuneration due to the liquidator; and

(r) any other expenses properly chargeable by the liquidator in carrying out the liquidator's functions in the winding up.

NOTES

Commencement: 6 April 2017.

This rule derived from the Insolvency Rules 1986, SI 1986/1925, rr 4.218, 12.2.

Para (2): substituted by the Insolvency (England and Wales) (Amendment) Rules 2017, SI 2017/366, rr 3, 26.

Para (4): words in square brackets in sub-para (m) inserted by the Insolvency Amendment (EU 2015/848) Regulations 2017, SI 2017/702, regs 2, 3, Schedule, Pt 2, paras 32, 40, as from 26 June 2017, except in relation to proceedings opened before that date.

[6.384]
7.109 Winding up commencing as voluntary

Where the winding up by the court immediately follows a voluntary winding up (whether members' voluntary or creditors' voluntary), such remuneration of the voluntary liquidator and costs and expenses of the voluntary winding up as the court may allow are to rank in priority with the expenses specified in rule 7.108(4)(a).

NOTES

Commencement: 6 April 2017.
This rule derived from the Insolvency Rules 1986, SI 1986/1925, r 4.219.

[6.385]
7.110 Saving for powers of the court (section 156)

(1) The priorities laid down by rules 7.108 and 7.109 are subject to the power of the court to make orders under section 156, where the assets are insufficient to satisfy the liabilities.

(2) Nothing in those rules—
- (a) applies to or affects the power of any court, in proceedings by or against the company, to order costs to be paid by the company, or the liquidator; or
- (b) affects the rights of any person to whom such costs are ordered to be paid.

NOTES

Commencement: 6 April 2017.
This rule derived from the Insolvency Rules 1986, SI 1986/1925, r 4.220.

CHAPTER 15 LITIGATION EXPENSES AND PROPERTY SUBJECT TO A FLOATING CHARGE

[Note: a document required by the Act or these Rules must also contain the standard contents set out in Part 1.]

[6.386]
7.111 Interpretation

In this Chapter—

"approval" and "authorisation" respectively mean—
- (a) where yet to be incurred, the approval, and
- (b) where already incurred, the authorisation,

of expenses specified in section 176ZA(3);

"the creditor" means—
- (a) a preferential creditor of the company; or
- (b) a holder of a debenture secured by, or a holder of, a floating charge created by the company;

"legal proceedings" means—
- (a) proceedings under sections 212, 213, 214, 238, 239, 244 and 423 and any arbitration or other dispute resolution proceedings invoked for purposes corresponding to those to which the sections relate and any other proceedings, including arbitration or other dispute resolution procedures, which a liquidator has power to bring in the liquidator's own name for the purpose of preserving, realising, or getting in any of the assets of the company;
- (b) legal actions and proceedings, arbitration or any other dispute resolution procedures which a liquidator has power to bring or defend in the name of the company; and
- (c) negotiations intended to lead or leading to a settlement or compromise of any action, proceeding or procedure to which sub-paragraphs (a) or (b) relate;

"litigation expenses" means expenses of a winding up which—
- (a) are properly chargeable or incurred in the preparation or conduct of any legal proceedings; and
- (b) as expenses in the winding up, exceed, or in the opinion of the liquidator are likely to exceed (and only in so far as they exceed or are likely to exceed), in the aggregate £5,000; and

"specified creditor" means a creditor identified under rule 7.113(2).

NOTES

Commencement: 6 April 2017.
This rule derived from the Insolvency Rules 1986, SI 1986/1925, r 4.218A.

[6.387]
7.112 Priority of litigation expenses

Litigation expenses will not have the priority provided by section 176ZA over any claims to property comprised in or subject to a floating charge created by the company and must not be paid out of any such property unless and until approved or authorised in accordance with rules 7.113 to 7.116.

NOTES

Commencement: 6 April 2017.
This rule derived from the Insolvency Rules 1986, SI 1986/1925, r 4.218A(2).

[6.388]
7.113 Requirement for approval or authorisation of litigation expenses

(1) Subject to rules 7.114 to 7.116 either paragraphs (3) and (4) apply or paragraph (5) applies where, in the course of winding up a company, the liquidator—

(a) ascertains that property is comprised in or subject to a floating charge;
(b) has personally instituted or proposes to institute or continue legal proceedings or is in the process of defending or proposes to defend any legal proceeding brought or likely to be brought against the company; and
(c) before or at any stage in those proceedings, is of the opinion that—
 (i) the assets of the company available for payment of general creditors are or will be insufficient to pay litigation expenses, and
 (ii) in order to pay litigation expenses the liquidator will have to have recourse to property comprised in or subject to a floating charge created by the company.

(2) As soon as reasonably practicable after the date on which the liquidator forms the opinion referred to in paragraph (1), the liquidator must identify the creditor who, in the liquidator's opinion at that time—

(a) has a claim to property comprised in or subject to a floating charge created by the company; and
(b) taking into account the value of that claim and any subsisting property then comprised in or secured by such a charge, appears to the liquidator to be the creditor most immediately likely of any persons having such claims to receive some payment in respect of a claim but whose claim would not be paid in full.

(3) The liquidator must request from the specified creditor the approval or authorisation of such amount for litigation expenses as the liquidator thinks fit.

(4) Where the liquidator identifies two or more specified creditors, the liquidator must seek from each of them approval or authorisation of such amount of litigation expenses as the liquidator thinks fit, apportioned between them ("the apportioned amount") according to the value of the property to the extent covered by their charges.

(5) For so long as the conditions specified in paragraph (1) subsist, the liquidator may, in the course of a winding up, make such further requests to the specified creditor or creditors for approval or authorisation of such further amount for litigation expenses as the liquidator thinks fit to be paid out of property comprised in or subject to a floating charge created by the company, taking into account any amount for litigation expenses previously approved or authorised and the value of the property comprised in or subject to the floating charge.

NOTES

Commencement: 6 April 2017.
This rule derived from the Insolvency Rules 1986, SI 1986/1925, r 4.218B.

[6.389]
7.114 Requests for approval or authorisation

(1) All requests made by the liquidator for approval or authorisation must include the following—

(a) a statement describing the nature of the legal proceedings, including, where relevant, the statutory provision under which proceedings are or are to be brought and the grounds upon which the liquidator relies;
(b) a statement specifying the amount or apportioned amount of litigation expenses for which approval or authorisation is sought ("the specified amount");
(c) notice that approval or authorisation or other reply to the request must be made in writing within 28 days from the date of its being received ("the specified time limit"); and
(d) a statement explaining the consequences of a failure to reply within the specified time limit.

(2) Where anything in paragraph (1) requires the inclusion of any information, the disclosure of which could be seriously prejudicial to the winding up of the company, the liquidator may—

(a) exclude such information from any of the above statements or notices if accompanied by a statement to that effect; or
(b) include it on terms—
 (i) that bind the creditor to keep the information confidential, and
 (ii) that include an undertaking on the part of the liquidator to apply to the court for an order that so much of the information as may be kept in the files of the court, is not be open to public inspection.

(3) The creditor may within the specified time limit apply to the liquidator in writing for such further particulars as is reasonable and in such a case, the time limit specified in paragraph (1)(c) will apply from the date of the creditor's receipt of the liquidator's response to any such request.

(4) Where the liquidator requires the approval or authorisation of two or more creditors, the liquidator must deliver a request to each creditor, containing the matters listed in paragraph (1) and also giving—

(a) the number of creditors concerned;
(b) the total value of their claims, or if not known, as it is estimated to be by the liquidator immediately before delivering any such request; and
(c) to each preferential creditor, notice that approval or authorisation of the specified amount will be taken to be given where a majority in value of those preferential creditors who respond within the specified time limit are in favour of it; or
(d) where rule 7.113 applies, notice to the specified creditors that the amount of litigation expenses will be apportioned between them in accordance with that rule and notice of the value of the portion allocated to, and the identity of, the specified creditors affected by that apportionment.

NOTES

Commencement: 6 April 2017.

This rule derived from the Insolvency Rules 1986, SI 1986/1925, r 4.218C.

[6.390]

7.115 Grant of approval or authorisation

(1) Where the liquidator fails to include in the liquidator's request any one of the matters, statements or notices required by paragraph (1) or paragraphs (1) and (4), of rule 7.114, the request for approval or authorisation will be treated as not having been made.

(2) Subject to paragraphs (3), (4) and (5), approval or authorisation will be taken to have been given where the specified amount has been requested by the liquidator, and—

(a) that amount is approved or authorised within the specified time limit; or

(b) a different amount is approved or authorised within the specified time limit and the liquidator considers it sufficient.

(3) Where the liquidator requires the approval or authorisation of two or more preferential creditors, approval or authorisation will be taken to be given where a majority in value of those who respond within the specified time limit approve or authorise—

(a) the specified amount; or

(b) a different amount which the liquidator considers sufficient.

(4) Where a majority in value of two or more preferential creditors propose an amount other than that specified by the liquidator, they will be taken to have approved or authorised an amount equal to the lowest of the amounts so proposed.

(5) In any case in which there is no response in writing within the specified time limit to the liquidator's request—

(a) at all; or

(b) at any time following the liquidator's provision of further particulars under rule 7.114(3);

the liquidator's request will be taken to have been approved or authorised from the date of the expiry of that time limit.

NOTES

Commencement: 6 April 2017.

This rule derived from the Insolvency Rules 1986, SI 1986/1925, r 4.218D.

[6.391]

7.116 Application to the court by the liquidator

(1) In the circumstances specified below the court may, upon the application of the liquidator, approve or authorise such amount of litigation expenses as it thinks just.

(2) Except where paragraph (3) applies, the liquidator may apply to the court for an order approving or authorising an amount for litigation expenses only where the specified creditor (or, if more than one, any of them)—

(a) is or is intended to be a defendant in the legal proceedings in relation to which the litigation expenses have been or are to be incurred; or

(b) has been requested to approve or authorise the amount specified under rule 7.114(1)(b) and has—

(i) declined to approve or authorise, as the case may be, the specified amount,

(ii) approved or authorised an amount which is less than the specified amount and which lesser amount the liquidator considers insufficient, or

(iii) made such application for further particulars or other response to the liquidator's request as is, in the liquidator's opinion, unreasonable.

(3) Where the liquidator thinks that circumstances are such that the liquidator requires urgent approval or authorisation of litigation expenses, the liquidator may apply to the court for approval or authorisation either—

(a) without seeking approval or authorisation from the specified creditor; or

(b) if sought, before the expiry of the specified time limit.

(4) The court may grant such application for approval or authorisation—

(a) if the liquidator satisfies the court of the urgency of the case; and

(b) subject to such terms and conditions as the court thinks just.

(5) The liquidator must, at the same time as making any application to the court under this rule, deliver copies of it to the specified creditor, unless the court orders otherwise.

(6) The specified creditor (or, if more than one, any of them) is entitled to be heard on any such application unless the court orders otherwise.

(7) The court may grant approval or authorisation subject to such terms and conditions as it may think just, including terms and conditions relating to the amount or nature of the litigation expenses and as to any obligation to make further applications to the court under this rule.

(8) The costs of the liquidator's application under this rule, including the costs of any specified creditor appearing or represented on it, will be an expense of the winding up unless the court orders otherwise.

NOTES

Commencement: 6 April 2017.

This rule derived from the Insolvency Rules 1986, SI 1986/1925, r 4.218E.

CHAPTER 16 MISCELLANEOUS RULES

[Note: a document required by the Act or these Rules must also contain the standard contents set out in Part 1.]

Sub-division A: Return of capital

[6.392]

7.117 Application to court for order authorising return of capital

(1) This rule applies where the liquidator intends to apply to the court for an order authorising a return of capital.

(2) The application must be accompanied by a list of the persons to whom the return is to be made.

(3) The list must include the same details of those persons as appears in the settled list of contributories, with any necessary alterations to take account of matters after settlement of the list, and the amount to be paid to each person.

(4) Where the court makes an order authorising the return, it must deliver a sealed copy of the order to the liquidator.

NOTES

Commencement: 6 April 2017.

This rule derived from the Insolvency Rules 1986, SI 1986/1925, r 4.221.

[6.393]

7.118 Procedure for return

(1) The liquidator must inform each person to whom a return is made of the rate of return per share, and whether it is expected that any further return will be made.

(2) Any payments made by the liquidator by way of the return may be delivered by post, unless for any reason another method of making the payment has been agreed with the payee.

NOTES

Commencement: 6 April 2017.

This rule derived from the Insolvency Rules 1986, SI 1986/1925, r 4.222.

Sub-division B: Dissolution after winding up

[6.394]

7.119 Secretary of State's directions under sections 203 and 205 and appeal

(1) This rule applies where the Secretary of State gives a direction under—

(a) section 203 (where official receiver applies to the registrar of companies for a company's early dissolution); or

(b) section 205 (application by interested person for postponement of dissolution).

(2) The Secretary of State must deliver the direction to the applicant for it.

(3) The applicant must deliver a copy of the direction to the registrar of companies, to comply with section 203(5) or, as the case may be, section 205(6).

(4) Following an appeal under section 203(4) or 205(4) (against a decision of the Secretary of State under the applicable section) the court must deliver a sealed copy of its order to the person in whose favour the appeal was determined.

(5) That person must deliver a copy to the registrar of companies to comply with section 203(5) or, as the case may be, section 205(6).

NOTES

Commencement: 6 April 2017.

This rule derived from the Insolvency Rules 1986, SI 1986/1925, rr 4.224, 4.225.

PART 8
INDIVIDUAL VOLUNTARY ARRANGEMENTS (IVA)

CHAPTER 1 PRELIMINARY

[6.395]

8.1 Interpretation

In this Part—

"authorised person" means the official receiver where the official receiver is authorised to act as nominee or supervisor under section 389B(1) of the Act;

"nominee" and "supervisor" include the proposed nominee or supervisor in relation to a proposal for an IVA; and

"proposal" means a proposal for an IVA.

NOTES

Commencement: 6 April 2017.

CHAPTER 2 PREPARATION OF THE DEBTOR'S PROPOSAL FOR AN IVA

[Note: a document required by the Act or these Rules must also contain the standard contents set out in Part 1.]

[6.396]
8.2 Proposal for an IVA: general principles and amendment

(1) A proposal must—
- (a) identify the debtor;
- (b) explain why the debtor thinks an IVA is desirable;
- (c) explain why the creditors are expected to agree to an IVA; and
- (d) be authenticated and dated by the debtor.

(2) The proposal may be amended with the nominee's agreement in writing at any time up to the filing of the nominee's report with the court under section 256, or the submission of the nominee's report to the creditors under section 256A.

NOTES

Commencement: 6 April 2017.

This rule derived from the Insolvency Rules 1986, SI 1986/1925, r 5.3.

[6.397]
8.3 Proposal: contents

The proposal must set out the following so far as known to the debtor—

Assets	(a) the debtor's assets, with an estimate of their respective values; (b) which assets are charged and the extent of the charge; (c) which assets are to be excluded from the IVA; and (d) particulars of any property to be included in the IVA which is not owned by the debtor including details of who owns such property and the terms on which it will be available for inclusion;
Liabilities	(e) the nature and amount of the debtor's liabilities; (f) how the debtor's liabilities will be met, modified, postponed or otherwise dealt with by means of the IVA and, in particular— (i) how preferential creditors and creditors who are, or claim to be, secured will be dealt with, (ii) how creditors who are associates of the debtor will be dealt with, (iii) if the debtor is an undischarged bankrupt, whether any claim has been made under section 339 (transactions at an undervalue), section 340 (preferences), or section 343 (extortionate credit transactions) and, if it has, whether, and if so what, provision is being made to indemnify the bankrupt's estate in respect of such a claim; and (iv) if the debtor is not an undischarged bankrupt whether there are circumstances which might give rise to a claim as referred to in sub-paragraph (iii) if the debtor were made bankrupt and, where there are such circumstances, whether and, if so what, provision will be made to indemnify the bankrupt's estate in respect of such a claim;
Nominee's fees and expenses	(g) the amount proposed to be paid to the nominee by way of fees and expenses;
Supervisor	(h) identification and contact details for the supervisor; (i) confirmation that the supervisor is qualified to act as an insolvency practitioner (or is an authorised person) in relation to the debtor and the name of the relevant recognised professional body which is the source of the supervisor's authorisation; (j) how the fees and expenses of the supervisor will be determined and paid; (k) the functions to be undertaken by the supervisor; (l) where it is proposed that two or more supervisors be appointed, a statement whether acts done in connection with the IVA may be done by any one or more of them or must be done by all of them;

Guarantees and proposed guarantees	(m) whether any, and if so what, guarantees have been given in respect of the debtor's debts, specifying which of the guarantors are associates of the debtor; (n) whether any guarantees are proposed to be offered for the purposes of the IVA, and if so what, by whom and whether security is to be given or sought;
Timing	(o) the proposed duration of the IVA; (p) the proposed dates of distributions to creditors, with estimates of their amounts;
Type of proceedings	(q) whether the proceedings will be main, territorial or [non-EU proceedings] with reasons;
Conduct of business	(r) if the debtor has any business, how that business will be conducted during the IVA;
Further credit facilities	(s) details of any further proposed credit facilities for the debtor and how the debts so arising are to be paid;
Handling of funds arising	(t) the manner in which funds held for the purposes of the IVA are to be banked, invested or otherwise dealt with pending distribution to creditors; (u) how funds held for the purpose of payment to creditors, and not so paid on the termination of the IVA, will be dealt with; (v) how the claim of any person bound by the IVA by virtue of section 260(2)(b)(ii) will be dealt with;
Other proposals	(w) whether another proposal in relation to the debtor has been submitted within the 24 months before the date of the submission of the proposal to the nominee— (i) for approval by the creditors and, if so, (aa) whether that proposal was approved or rejected, (bb) whether, if approved, the IVA was completed or was terminated, and (cc) in what respects such a proposal, where rejected, differs from the current proposal; (ii) to the court in connection with an application for an interim order under section 253 and, if so, whether the interim order was made;
Other matters	(x) any other matters which the debtor considers appropriate to enable creditors to reach an informed decision on the proposal.

NOTES

Commencement: 6 April 2017.

This rule derived from the Insolvency Rules 1986, SI 1986/1925, r 5.3.

Words in square brackets in the Table entry "Type of proceedings" substituted by the Insolvency (England and Wales) and Insolvency (Scotland) (Miscellaneous and Consequential Amendments) Rules 2017, SI 2017/1115, rr 22, 30(22).

[6.398]

8.4 Notice of nominee's consent

(1) A nominee who consents to act must deliver a notice of that consent to the debtor as soon as reasonably practicable after the proposal has been submitted to the nominee under section 256(2) or 256A(2).

(2) The notice must state the date the nominee received the proposal.

NOTES

Commencement: 6 April 2017.

This rule derived from the Insolvency Rules 1986, SI 1986/1925, r 5.4.

[6.399]

8.5 Statement of affairs (section 256 and 256A)

(1) The statement of affairs which the debtor is required to submit to the nominee under either section 256(2) or 256A(2) must contain—

(a) a list of the debtor's assets, divided into such categories as are appropriate for easy identification, and with each category given an estimated value;

(b) in the case of any property on which a claim against the debtor is wholly or partly secured, particulars of the claim and of how and when the security was created;

(c) the names and addresses of the preferential creditors with the amounts of their respective claims;

(d) the names and addresses of the unsecured creditors, with the amounts of their respective claims;

(e) particulars of any debts owed by the debtor to persons who are associates of the debtor;

(f) particulars of any debts owed to the debtor by persons who are associates of the debtor; and

(g) any other particulars that the nominee in writing requires to be provided for the purposes of making the nominee's report on the proposal to the court or to the creditors (as the case may be).

(2) The statement must be made up to a date not earlier than two weeks before the date of the proposal.

(3) However the nominee may allow the statement to be made up to a date that is earlier than two weeks (but no earlier than two months) before the date of the proposal where that is more practicable.

(4) If the statement is made up to an earlier date the nominee's report must explain why an earlier date was allowed.

(5) The statement must be verified by a statement of truth made by the debtor.

(6) Where the debtor is an undischarged bankrupt and has already delivered a statement of affairs under section 288 the debtor need not submit a statement of affairs to the nominee under section 256(2) or 256A(2) unless the nominee requires a further statement of affairs to supplement or amplify the earlier one.

NOTES

Commencement: 6 April 2017.

This rule derived from the Insolvency Rules 1986, SI 1986/1925, r 5.5.

[6.400]

8.6 Application to omit information from statement of affairs delivered to creditors

The nominee, the debtor or any person appearing to the court to have an interest may, if any information in the statement of affairs would be likely to prejudice the conduct of the IVA or might reasonably be expected to lead to violence against any person, apply to the court for an order that specified information be omitted from any statement of affairs required to be delivered to the creditors.

NOTES

Commencement: 6 April 2017.

This rule derived from the Insolvency Rules 1986, SI 1986/1925, r 5.68.

[6.401]

8.7 Additional disclosure for assistance of nominee

(1) If it appears to the nominee that the report to the court under section 256(1) or to the creditors under section 256A(3) cannot properly be prepared on the basis of information in the proposal and statement of affairs, the nominee may require the debtor to provide—

(a) more information about the circumstances in which, and the reasons why, an IVA is being proposed;

(b) more information about any proposals of the kind referred to in rule 8.3(w);

(c) information about any proposals which have at any time been made by the debtor under Part 8 of the Act; and

(d) any further information relating to the debtor's affairs which the nominee thinks necessary for the purposes of the report.

(2) The nominee may require the debtor to inform the nominee whether and in what circumstances the debtor has at any time—

(a) been concerned in the affairs of a company wherever incorporated or limited liability partnership which has become the subject of insolvency proceedings;

(b) been made bankrupt;

(c) been the subject of a debt relief order; or

(d) entered into an arrangement with creditors.

(3) The debtor must give the nominee such access to the debtor's accounts and records as the nominee requires to enable the nominee to consider the debtor's proposal and prepare the report on it.

NOTES

Commencement: 6 April 2017.

This rule derived from the Insolvency Rules 1986, SI 1986/1925, r 5.6.

CHAPTER 3 CASES IN WHICH AN APPLICATION FOR AN INTERIM ORDER IS MADE

[Note: a document required by the Act or these Rules must also contain the standard contents set out in Part 1.]

[6.402]

8.8 Application for interim order

(1) An application to the court for an interim order under Part 8 of the Act must be accompanied by a witness statement containing—

(a) the reasons for making the application;

(b) information about any action, execution, other legal process or the levying of any distress which, to the debtor's knowledge, has been commenced against the debtor or the debtor's property;

(c) a statement that the debtor is an undischarged bankrupt or is able to make a bankruptcy application;

(d) a statement that no previous application for an interim order has been made by or in relation to the debtor in the period of 12 months ending with the date of the witness statement; and

(e) a statement that a person named in the witness statement is willing to act as nominee in relation to the proposal and is qualified to act as an insolvency practitioner (or is an authorised person) in relation to the debtor.

(2) The witness statement must be accompanied by a copy of—

(a) the proposal; and

(b) the notice of the nominee's consent to act.

(3) When the application and the witness statement have been filed, the court must fix a venue for the hearing of the application.

(4) The applicant must deliver a notice of the hearing and the venue at least two business days before the hearing to—

(a) the nominee;

(b) the debtor, the official receiver or the trustee (whichever is not the applicant) where the debtor is an undischarged bankrupt; and

(c) any creditor who (to the debtor's knowledge) has presented a bankruptcy petition against the debtor where the debtor is not an undischarged bankrupt.

(5) A notice under section 253(4) must contain the name and address of the nominee.

NOTES

Commencement: 6 April 2017.

This rule derived from the Insolvency Rules 1986, SI 1986/1925, r 5.7.

[6.403]

8.9 Court in which application is to be made

(1) An application must be made—

(a) to the court (and hearing centre if applicable), if any, which has the conduct of the bankruptcy, where the debtor is an undischarged bankrupt; or

(b) to the court (and hearing centre if applicable) determined in accordance with rule 10.48.

(2) The application must contain sufficient information to establish that it is made to the appropriate court or hearing centre.

NOTES

Commencement: 6 April 2017.

This rule derived from the Insolvency Rules 1986, SI 1986/1925, r 5.8.

[6.404]

8.10 Order granting a stay

A court order under section 254(1)(b) granting a stay pending hearing of an application must identify the proceedings and contain—

(a) the section number of the Act under which it is made;

(b) details of the action, execution or other legal process which is stayed;

(c) the date on which the application for an interim order will be heard; and

(d) the date that the order granting the stay is made.

NOTES

Commencement: 6 April 2017.

This rule derived from the Insolvency Rules 1986, SI 1986/1925, Sch 4, Fm 5.1.

[6.405]

8.11 Hearing of the application

(1) A person to whom a notice of the hearing of the application for an interim order was (or should have been) delivered under rule 8.8(4) may appear or be represented at the hearing.

(2) The court must take into account any representations made by or on behalf of such a person (in particular, as to whether an order should contain such provision as is referred to in section 255(3) (provisions as to the conduct of the bankruptcy etc) and (4) (provisions staying proceedings in bankruptcy etc).

(3) If the court makes an interim order, it must fix a venue for consideration of the nominee's report for a date no later than the date on which the order ceases to have effect.

NOTES

Commencement: 6 April 2017.

This rule derived from the Insolvency Rules 1986, SI 1986/1925, r 5.9.

[6.406]

8.12 The interim order

An interim order must contain—

(a) identification details for the proceedings;

(b) the section number of the Act under which it is made;

(c) a statement that the order has effect from its making until the end of the period of 14 days beginning on the day after the date on which it is made;

(d) particulars of the effect of the order (as set out in section 252(2));

(e) an order that the report of the nominee be delivered to the court no later than two business days before the date fixed for the court's consideration of the report;
(f) particulars of any orders made under section 255(3) and (4);
(g) where the debtor is an undischarged bankrupt and the applicant is not the official receiver, an order that the applicant delivers, as soon as reasonably practicable, a copy of the interim order to the official receiver;
(h) the venue for the court's consideration of the nominee's report; and
(i) the date of the order.

NOTES

Commencement: 6 April 2017.
This rule derived from the Insolvency Rules 1986, SI 1986/1925, Sch 4, Fm 5.2.

[6.407]
8.13 Action to follow making of an interim order

(1) The court must deliver at least two sealed copies of the interim order to the applicant.

(2) As soon as reasonably practicable, the applicant must deliver—
(a) one copy to the nominee and, where the debtor is an undischarged bankrupt, another copy to the official receiver (unless the official receiver was the applicant); and
(b) a notice that the order has been made to any other person to whom a notice of the hearing of the application for an interim order was (or should have been) delivered under rule 8.8(4) and who was not in attendance or represented at the hearing.

NOTES

Commencement: 6 April 2017.
This rule derived from the Insolvency Rules 1986, SI 1986/1925, r 5.10.

[6.408]
8.14 Order extending period of an interim order (section 256(4))

An order under section 256(4) extending the period for which an interim order has effect must contain—
(a) identification details for the proceedings;
(b) a statement that the application is that of the nominee for an extension of the period under section 256(4) for which an interim order is to have effect;
(c) an order that the period for which the interim order has effect is extended to a specified date;
(d) particulars of the effect (as set out in section 252(2)) of the interim order;
(e) an order that the report of the nominee be delivered to the court no later two business days before the date fixed for the court's consideration of the nominee's report;
(f) particulars of any orders made under section 255(3) or (4);
(g) where the debtor is an undischarged bankrupt and the applicant is not the official receiver, an order that the applicant deliver, as soon as reasonably practicable, a copy of the order to the official receiver;
(h) the venue for the court's consideration of the report; and
(i) the date of the order.

NOTES

Commencement: 6 April 2017.
This rule derived from the Insolvency Rules 1986, SI 1986/1925, Sch 4, Fm 5.3.

[6.409]
8.15 Nominee's report on the proposal

(1) The nominee's report under section 256 must be filed with the court not less than two business days before the interim order ceases to have effect, accompanied by—
(a) a copy of the report;
(b) a copy of the proposal (as amended, if applicable, under rule 8.2(2); and
(c) a copy of any statement of affairs or a summary of such a statement.

(2) The nominee must also deliver a copy of the report to the debtor.

(3) The nominee's report must explain whether or not the nominee considers that the proposal has a reasonable prospect of being approved and implemented and whether or not creditors should be invited to consider the proposal.

(4) The court must endorse the nominee's report and the copy of it with the date on which they were filed and return the copy to the nominee.

(5) Where the debtor is an undischarged bankrupt, the nominee must deliver to the official receiver and any trustee, a copy of—
(a) the proposal;
(b) the nominee's report; and
(c) any statement of affairs or summary of such a statement.

(6) Where the debtor is not an undischarged bankrupt, the nominee must deliver a copy of each of those documents to any person who has presented a bankruptcy petition against the debtor.

NOTES

Commencement: 6 April 2017.

This rule derived from the Insolvency Rules 1986, SI 1986/1925, r 5.11.

[6.410]

8.16 Order extending period of interim order to enable the creditors to consider the proposal (section 256(5))

An order under section 256(5) extending the period for which an interim order has effect to enable creditors to consider the proposal must contain—

(a) identification details for the proceedings;

(b) the section number of the Act under which it is made;

(c) the date that the nominee's report was filed;

(d) a statement that for the purpose of enabling the creditors to consider the proposal, the period for which the interim order has effect is extended to a specified date;

(e) a statement that the nominee will be inviting the creditors to consider the proposal and details of the decision procedure the nominee intends to use;

(f) where the debtor is an undischarged bankrupt and the nominee is not the official receiver, an order that the nominee deliver, as soon as reasonably practicable, a copy of the order to the official receiver; and

(g) the date of the order.

NOTES

Commencement: 6 April 2017.

This rule derived from the Insolvency Rules 1986, SI 1986/1925, Sch 4, Fm 5.3.

[6.411]

8.17 Replacement of the nominee (section 256(3))

(1) A debtor who intends to apply under section 256(3)(a) or (b) for the nominee to be replaced must deliver a notice to the nominee that such an application is intended to be made at least five business days before filing the application with the court.

(2) A nominee who intends to apply under section 256(3)(b) to be replaced must deliver a notice to the debtor that such an application is intended to be made at least five business days before filing the application with the court.

(3) The court must not appoint a replacement nominee unless the replacement nominee has filed with the court a statement confirming—

(a) that person is qualified to act as an insolvency practitioner (or is an authorised person) in relation to the debtor; and

(b) that person's consent to act.

NOTES

Commencement: 6 April 2017.

This rule derived from the Insolvency Rules 1986, SI 1986/1925, r 5.12.

[6.412]

8.18 Consideration of the nominee's report

(1) A person to whom a notice was (or should have been) delivered under rule 8.8(4) may appear or be represented at the court's hearing to consider the nominee's report.

(2) Rule 8.13 applies to any order made by the court at the hearing.

NOTES

Commencement: 6 April 2017.

This rule derived from the Insolvency Rules 1986, SI 1986/1925, r 5.13.

CHAPTER 4 CASES WHERE NO INTERIM ORDER IS TO BE OBTAINED

[Note: a document required by the Act or these Rules must also contain the standard contents set out in Part 1.]

[6.413]

8.19 Nominee's report (section 256A)

(1) The nominee's report under section 256A(3) must explain whether or not the nominee considers that the proposal has a reasonable prospect of being approved and implemented and whether or not creditors should be invited to consider the proposal.

[(1A) The nominee must examine whether there is jurisdiction to open the proceedings and must specify in the nominee's report whether the proceedings will be main, secondary, territorial on non-EU proceedings with the reasons for so stating.]

(2) The report must contain sufficient information to enable a person to identify (in accordance with rule 8.20) the appropriate court or hearing centre in which to file an application relating to the proposal or the IVA.

(3) The nominee must also deliver a copy of the report to the debtor.

(4) Where the nominee gives an opinion in the affirmative on the matters referred to in section 256A(3)(a) and (b), the copy of the report delivered by the nominee to each of the creditors must be accompanied by—

(a) a statement that an application for an interim order under section 253 is not being made;
(b) a copy of the proposal (as amended, if applicable, under rule 8.2(2));
(c) a copy of any statement of affairs or a summary of such a statement; and
(d) a copy of the notice of the nominee's consent to act.

(5) In such a case the nominee must also deliver those documents within 14 days (or such longer period as the court may allow) of receipt of the document and statement referred to in section 256A(2) to—
(a) the official receiver and any trustee, where the debtor is an undischarged bankrupt; and
(b) any person who has presented a bankruptcy petition against the debtor.

(6) Where the nominee gives an opinion in the negative on the matters referred to in section 256A(3)(a) and (b) the nominee must within 14 days (or such longer period as the court may allow) of receipt of the document and statement referred to in section 256A(2)—
(a) deliver a copy of the report to the creditors; and
(b) give the reasons for that opinion to the debtor.

NOTES

Commencement: 6 April 2017.

This rule derived from the Insolvency Rules 1986, SI 1986/1925, r 5.14A.

Para (1A): inserted by the Insolvency Amendment (EU 2015/848) Regulations 2017, SI 2017/702, regs 2, 3, Schedule, Pt 2, paras 32, 41, as from 26 June 2017, except in relation to proceedings opened before that date.

[6.414]

8.20 Court or hearing centre to which applications must be made where no interim order

(1) This rule applies where the nominee has made a report under section 256A(3).

(2) Any application relating to a proposal or an IVA must be made—
(a) to the court or hearing centre, if any, which has the conduct of the bankruptcy, where the debtor is an undischarged bankrupt; or
(b) to the court or hearing centre determined in accordance with rule 10.48.

(3) The application must contain sufficient information to establish that it is made to the appropriate court or hearing centre.

(4) The applicant must file with the court (in addition to the documents in support of the application) such other documents required by this Part as the applicant considers may assist the court in determining the application.

NOTES

Commencement: 6 April 2017.

This rule derived from the Insolvency Rules 1986, SI 1986/1925, r 5.14B.

[6.415]

8.21 Replacement of the nominee (section 256A(4))

(1) A debtor who intends to apply under section 256A(4)(a) or (b) for the nominee to be replaced must deliver a notice of the intention to make the application to the nominee at least five business days before filing the application with the court.

(2) A nominee who intends to apply under section 256A(4)(b) to be replaced must deliver a notice of the intention to make such an application to the debtor at least five business days before filing the application with the court.

(3) The court must not appoint a replacement nominee unless the replacement nominee has filed with the court a statement confirming—
(a) that person is qualified to act as an insolvency practitioner (or is an authorised person) in relation to the debtor; and
(b) that person's consent to act.

NOTES

Commencement: 6 April 2017.

This rule derived from the Insolvency Rules 1986, SI 1986/1925, r 5.14B.

CHAPTER 5 CONSIDERATION OF THE PROPOSAL BY THE CREDITORS

[Note: a document required by the Act or these Rules must also contain the standard contents set out in Part 1.]

[6.416]

8.22 Consideration of the proposal

(1) This rule applies where the nominee is required to seek a decision from the debtor's creditors as to whether they approve the debtor's proposal.

(2) The nominee must deliver to each creditor a notice which complies with rule 15.8 so far as is relevant.

(3) The notice must also contain—
(a) identification details for the proceedings;
(b) where an interim order has not been obtained, details of the court or hearing centre to which an application relating to the proposal or the IVA must be made under rule 8.20(2);

(c) where an interim order is in force, details of the court or hearing centre in which the nominee's report on the debtor's proposal has been filed under section 256;
(d) a statement as to how a person entitled to vote for the proposal may propose a modification to it, and how the nominee will deal with such a proposal for a modification.

(4) The notice may contain or be accompanied by a notice that the results of the consideration of the proposal will be made available for viewing and downloading on a website and that no other notice will be delivered to the creditors to whom the notice under this rule was sent.

(5) Where the results of the consideration of the proposal are to be made available for viewing and downloading on a website the nominee must comply with the requirements for use of a website to deliver a document set out in rule 1.49(2)(a) to (c), (3) and (4) with any necessary adaptations and rule 1.49(5)(a) applies to determine the time of delivery of the document.

(6) The notice must be accompanied by the following (unless they have been delivered already under rule 8.19)—
(a) a copy of the proposal;
(b) a copy of the statement of affairs, or a summary including a list of creditors with the amounts of their debts; and
(c) a copy of the nominee's report on the proposal.

(7) The decision date must be not less than 14 days from the date of delivery of the notice and not more than 28 days from the date on which—
(a) the nominee received the document and statement of affairs referred to in section 256A(2) in a case where an interim order has not been obtained; or
(b) the nominee's report was considered by the court in a case where an interim order is in force.

NOTES

Commencement: 6 April 2017.
This rule derived from the Insolvency Rules 1986, SI 1986/1925, r 5.17.

[6.417]
8.23 Proposals for an alternative supervisor

(1) If in response to a notice of a decision procedure to consider the proposal other than at a meeting, a creditor proposes that a person other than the nominee be appointed as supervisor, that person's consent to act and confirmation of being qualified to act as an insolvency practitioner (or being an authorised person) in relation to the debtor must be delivered to the nominee by the creditor.

(2) If at a creditors' meeting to consider the proposal a resolution is moved for the appointment of a person other than the nominee to be supervisor, that person must produce to the chair at or before the meeting—
(a) confirmation of being qualified to act as an insolvency practitioner (or being an authorised person) in relation to the debtor; and
(b) written consent to act (unless the person is present at the meeting and signifies consent).

NOTES

Commencement: 6 April 2017.
This rule derived from the Insolvency Rules 1986, SI 1986/1925, r 5.25.

[6.418]
8.24 Report of the creditors' consideration of a proposal

(1) A report of the creditors' consideration of a proposal must be prepared by the convener or, if the proposal is considered at a meeting, by the chair.

(2) The report must—
(a) state whether the proposal was approved or rejected and, if approved, with what (if any) modifications;
[(b) list the creditors who voted or attended or who were represented at the meeting or decision procedure (as applicable) used to consider the proposal, setting out (with their respective values) how they voted on each resolution or whether they abstained;]
(c) if the proposal was approved, state whether the proceedings are main, territorial or [non-EU proceedings] and the reasons for so stating; and
(d) include such further information as the nominee or the chair thinks appropriate.

(3) Where an interim order was obtained a copy of the report must be filed with the court, within four business days of the decision date.

(4) The court must endorse the copy of the report with the date of filing.

(5) The nominee must give notice of the result of the consideration to—
(a) everyone who was invited to consider the proposal and to whom notice of the decision procedure was delivered;
(b) any other creditor; and
(c) where the debtor is an undischarged bankrupt, the official receiver and any trustee.

(6) The notice must be given—
(a) where an interim order was obtained, as soon as reasonably practicable after a copy of the report is filed with the court; or
(b) where an interim order was not obtained, within four business days of the decision date.

NOTES

Commencement: 6 April 2017.

This rule derived from the Insolvency Rules 1986, SI 1986/1925, r 5.27.

Para (2): sub-para (b) substituted by the Insolvency (England and Wales) (Amendment) Rules 2017, SI 2017/366, rr 3, 27; words in square brackets in sub-para (c) substituted by the Insolvency (England and Wales) and Insolvency (Scotland) (Miscellaneous and Consequential Amendments) Rules 2017, SI 2017/1115, rr 22, 30(23).

CHAPTER 6 ACTION FOLLOWING APPROVAL OF AN IVA

[Note: a document required by the Act or these Rules must also contain the standard contents set out in Part 1.]

[6.419]

8.25 Hand-over of property, etc to supervisor

(1) As soon as reasonably practicable after the IVA is approved, the debtor or, where the debtor is an undischarged bankrupt, the official receiver or any trustee must do all that is required to put the supervisor in possession of the assets included in the IVA.

(2) Where the debtor is an undischarged bankrupt, the supervisor must—

- (a) before taking possession of the assets included in the IVA, deliver to the official receiver or any trustee an undertaking to discharge the balance due to the official receiver or trustee out of the first realisation of the assets; or
- (b) upon taking possession of the assets included in the IVA, discharge such balance.

(3) The balance is any balance due to the official receiver or any trustee—

- (a) by way of fees or expenses properly incurred and payable under the Act or these Rules; and
- (b) on account of any advances made in respect of the bankrupt's estate, together with interest on such advances at the rate specified in section 17 of the Judgments Act 1838 at the date of the bankruptcy order.

(4) Where the debtor is an undischarged bankrupt, the official receiver and any trustee have a charge on the assets included in the IVA in respect of any sums comprising such balance, subject only to the deduction by the supervisor from realisations of the proper costs and expenses of realisation.

(5) Any sums due to the official receiver take priority over those due to any trustee.

(6) The supervisor must from time to time out of the realisation of assets—

- (a) discharge all guarantees properly given by the official receiver or any trustee for the benefit of the bankrupt's estate; and
- (b) pay the expenses of the official receiver and any trustee.

NOTES

Commencement: 6 April 2017.

This rule derived from the Insolvency Rules 1986, SI 1986/1925, r 5.26.

[6.420]

8.26 Report to the Secretary of State of the approval of an IVA

(1) After the creditors approve an IVA the nominee, appointed person or the chair must deliver a report containing the required information to the Secretary of State.

(2) The report must be delivered as soon as reasonably practicable, and in any event within 14 days after the report that the creditors have approved the IVA has been filed with the court under rule 8.24(3) or the notice that the creditors have approved the IVA has been sent to the creditors under rule 8.24(5) as the case may be.

(3) The required information is—

- (a) identification details for the debtor;
- (b) the debtor's gender;
- (c) the debtor's date of birth;
- (d) any name by which the debtor was or is known, not being the name in which the debtor has entered into the IVA;
- (e) the date on which the IVA was approved by the creditors; and
- (f) the name and address of the supervisor.

(4) A person who is appointed to act as a supervisor as a replacement of another person, or who vacates that office must deliver a notice of that fact to the Secretary of State as soon as reasonably practicable.

NOTES

Commencement: 6 April 2017.

This rule derived from the Insolvency Rules 1986, SI 1986/1925, r 5.29.

[6.421]

8.27 Revocation or suspension of an IVA (section 262)

(1) This rule applies where the court makes an order of revocation or suspension under section 262.

(2) The applicant for the order must deliver a sealed copy of it to—

- (a) the debtor (if different from the applicant);
- (b) the supervisor; and

(c) where the debtor is an undischarged bankrupt, the official receiver and any trustee (in either case, if different from the applicant).

(3) If the order includes a direction by the court under section 262(4)(b) for a matter to be considered further by a decision procedure, the applicant for the order must deliver a notice that the order has been made to the person who is directed to take such action.

(4) The debtor, or the trustee (if the debtor is an undischarged bankrupt) must—

(a) as soon as reasonably practicable deliver a notice that the order has been made to everyone to whom a notice to consider the matter by a decision procedure was delivered or who appears to be affected by the order; and

(b) within five business days of delivery of a copy of the order (or within such longer period as the court may allow), deliver, if applicable, a notice to the court advising that it is intended to make a revised proposal to the creditors, or to invite re-consideration of the original proposal.

(5) The applicant for the order must, within five business days of the making of the order deliver a notice of the order to the Secretary of State.

(6) The applicant for the order must, within five business days of the expiry of any order of suspension, deliver a notice of the expiry to the Secretary of State.

NOTES

Commencement: 6 April 2017.

This rule derived from the Insolvency Rules 1986, SI 1986/1925, r 5.30.

[6.422]

8.28 Supervisor's accounts and reports

(1) The supervisor must keep accounts and records where the IVA authorises or requires the supervisor—

(a) to carry on the business of the debtor or trade on behalf of or in the name of the debtor;

(b) to realise assets of the debtor or, where the debtor is an undischarged bankrupt, belonging to the bankrupt's estate; or

(c) otherwise to administer or dispose of any funds of the debtor or the bankrupt's estate.

(2) The accounts and records which must be kept are of the supervisor's acts and dealings in, and in connection with, the IVA, including in particular records of all receipts and payments of money.

(3) The supervisor must preserve any such accounts and records which were kept by any other person who has acted as supervisor of the IVA and are in the supervisor's possession.

(4) The supervisor must deliver reports on the progress and prospects for the full implementation of the IVA to—

(a) the debtor; and

(b) the creditors bound by the IVA.

(5) The first report must cover the period of 12 months commencing on the date on which the IVA was approved and a further report must be made for each subsequent period of 12 months.

(6) Each report must be delivered within the period of two months after the end of the 12 month period.

(7) Such a report is not required if an obligation to deliver a report under rule 8.31 . . . arises in the two months after the end of the period.

(8) Where the supervisor is authorised or required to do any of the things mentioned in paragraph (1), the report—

(a) must include or be accompanied by a summary of receipts and payments which paragraph (2) requires to be recorded; or

(b) where there have been no such receipts and payments, must say so.

NOTES

Commencement: 6 April 2017.

This rule derived from the Insolvency Rules 1986, SI 1986/1925, r 5.31A.

Para (7): figure omitted revoked by the Insolvency (England and Wales) (Amendment) Rules 2017, SI 2017/366, rr 3, 11.

[6.423]

8.29 Production of accounts and records to the Secretary of State

(1) The Secretary of State may during the IVA or after its full implementation or termination require the supervisor to produce for inspection (either at the supervisor's premises or elsewhere)—

(a) the supervisor's accounts and records in relation to the IVA; and

(b) copies of reports and summaries prepared in compliance with rule 8.28.

(2) The Secretary of State may require any accounts and records produced under this rule to be audited and, if so, the supervisor must provide such further information and assistance as the Secretary of State requires for the purposes of the audit.

NOTES

Commencement: 6 April 2017.

This rule derived from the Insolvency Rules 1986, SI 1986/1925, r 5.32.

[6.424]

8.30 Fees and expenses

The fees and expenses that may be incurred for the purposes of the IVA are—

(a) fees for the nominee's services agreed with the debtor, the official receiver or any trustee;
(b) disbursements made by the nominee before the approval of the IVA; and
(c) fees or expenses which—
  (i) are sanctioned by the terms of the IVA, or
  (ii) where they are not sanctioned by the terms of the IVA, would be payable, or correspond to those which would be payable, in the debtor's bankruptcy.

NOTES

Commencement: 6 April 2017.
This rule derived from the Insolvency Rules 1986, SI 1986/1925, r 5.33.

[6.425]
8.31 Termination or full implementation of the IVA

(1) Not more than 28 days after the full implementation or termination of the IVA the supervisor must deliver a notice that the IVA has been fully implemented or terminated to the debtor and the creditors bound by the IVA.

(2) The notice must state the date the IVA took effect.

(3) The notice must be accompanied by a copy of a report by the supervisor which—
(a) summarises all receipts and payments in relation to the IVA;
(b) explains any departure from the terms of the IVA as approved by the creditors; and
(c) if the IVA has terminated, sets out the reasons why.

(4) The supervisor must within the 28 days mentioned above—
(a) deliver a copy of the notice and report to the Secretary of State; and
(b) if the creditors were invited to consider the proposal following a report under section 256(1)(aa), file a copy of the notice and report with the court.

(5) The supervisor must not vacate office until the notice and report have been delivered to the Secretary of State.

NOTES

Commencement: 6 April 2017.
This rule derived from the Insolvency Rules 1986, SI 1986/1925, r 5.34.

CHAPTER 7 APPLICATIONS TO ANNUL BANKRUPTCY ORDERS UNDER SECTION 261(2)(A) AND (B)

[Note: a document required by the Act or these Rules must also contain the standard contents set out in Part 1.]

[6.426]
8.32 Application by the bankrupt to annul the bankruptcy order (section 261(2)(a))

(1) An application by bankrupt to the court under section 261(2)(a) must be supported by a witness statement stating—
(a) that the IVA has been approved by the creditors;
(b) the date of the approval; and
(c) that the 28 day period in section 262(3)(a) for applications to be made under section 262(1) has expired and no applications or appeals remain to be disposed of.

(2) The application and witness statement must be filed with the court and the court must deliver a notice of the venue for the hearing to the bankrupt.

(3) Not less than five business days before the date of the hearing, the bankrupt must deliver a notice of the venue, with a copy of the application and witness statement, to—
(a) the official receiver;
(b) any trustee (if different to the official receiver); and
(c) the supervisor.

(4) The official receiver, any such trustee and the supervisor may attend the hearing or be represented and bring to the court's attention any matters which seem to them to be relevant.

NOTES

Commencement: 6 April 2017.
This rule derived from the Insolvency Rules 1986, SI 1986/1925, rr 5.51, 5.52.

[6.427]
8.33 Application by the official receiver to annul the bankruptcy order (section 261(2)(b))

(1) An application by the official receiver to the court under section 261(2)(b) to annul a bankruptcy order must be supported by a report stating—
(a) the grounds on which it is made;
(b) that the time period in paragraph (2) has expired; and
(c) that the official receiver is not aware that any application under section 262 or appeal remains to be disposed of.

(2) The official receiver must not make such an application before the expiry of the period of 42 days beginning with the day on which—

(a) the nominee filed the report of the creditors' consideration with the court, where the creditors considered the proposal under section 257 following a report to a court under section 256(1)(aa); or

(b) the nominee delivered a notice to the creditors of the result of their consideration, where the creditors considered the proposal under section 257 following a report to the creditors under section 256A(3).

(3) The application and the report must be filed with the court and the court must deliver a notice of the venue for the hearing to the official receiver.

(4) Not less than five business days before the date of the hearing, the official receiver must deliver a notice of the venue, with a copy of the application and the report, to the bankrupt.

NOTES

Commencement: 6 April 2017.

This rule derived from the Insolvency Rules 1986, SI 1986/1925, rr 5.54, 5.55.

[6.428]

8.34 Order annulling bankruptcy

(1) An order under section 261(2) annulling a bankruptcy order must contain—

(a) identification details the proceedings;

(b) the section number of the Act under which the order is made;

(c) the name and address of the applicant;

(d) a statement that it appears that an IVA under section 258 has been approved and implemented and the date of approval;

(e) a statement that there has been no application under section 262 for the revocation or suspension of the IVA and that the time period for making such an application has expired;

(f) where the applicant is the official receiver under section 261(2)(b) that the time period in rule 8.33(2) has expired;

(g) the order that the relevant bankruptcy order, identified by its date and the name of the bankrupt as set out in the bankruptcy order, be annulled;

(h) if appropriate, an order that the relevant bankruptcy petition (identified by the date of its presentation) or the relevant bankruptcy application (identified by the date it was made) (as the case may be) be dismissed;

(i) where there is a trustee, an order in respect of the trustee's release, having regard to rule 8.37;

(j) an order that the registration of the bankruptcy petition or bankruptcy application as a pending action at the Land Charges Department of HM Land Registry be vacated (identified by the date of registration and reference number);

(k) an order that the registration of the bankruptcy order on the register of writs and orders affecting land at the Land Charges Department of HM Land Registry be vacated (identified by date of registration and reference number);

(l) the date the order is made;

(m) a notice to the effect that if the former bankrupt requires notice of the order to be gazetted and advertised in the same manner as the bankruptcy order was advertised, the bankrupt must deliver a notice to the official receiver within 28 days; and

(n) a notice to the effect that it is the responsibility of the former bankrupt and in the former bankrupt's interest to ensure that any registration of the petition or bankruptcy application and of the bankruptcy order at the Land Charges Department of HM Land Registry and any entries relating to the petition or bankruptcy application and bankruptcy order in any registered titles at HM Land Registry are cancelled (such a notice giving relevant HM Land Registry contact details and referring to relevant Registry guidance).

(2) The court must deliver a sealed copy of the order to—

(a) the former bankrupt;

(b) the official receiver;

(c) any trustee (if different to the official receiver); and

(d) the supervisor.

NOTES

Commencement: 6 April 2017.

This rule derived from the Insolvency Rules 1986, SI 1986/1925, Sch 4, Fm 5.7.

[6.429]

8.35 Notice of order

(1) An official receiver, who has delivered a notice of the debtor's bankruptcy to the creditors, must, as soon as reasonably practicable, deliver a notice of an annulment under section 261(2) to them.

(2) Expenses incurred by the official receiver in delivering a notice under this rule are a charge in the official receiver's favour on the property of the former bankrupt, whether or not actually in the hands of the former bankrupt.

(3) Where any such property is in the hands of any person other than the former bankrupt, the official receiver's charge is valid subject only to any costs that may be incurred by that person in effecting realisation of the property for the purpose of satisfying the charge.

NOTES

Commencement: 6 April 2017.

This rule derived from the Insolvency Rules 1986, SI 1986/1925, rr 5.53, 5.56.

[6.430]
8.36 Advertisement of order

(1) The former bankrupt may in writing within 28 days of the date of an order for annulment under section 261(2) require the official receiver—

(a) to cause a notice of the order to be gazetted; and
(b) to advertise the order in the same manner as the bankruptcy order was advertised.

(2) The official receiver must comply with any such requirement as soon as reasonably practicable.

(3) The notice must state—

(a) the name of the former bankrupt;
(b) the date on which the bankruptcy order was made;
(c) that the bankruptcy order has been annulled;
(d) the date of the annulment order; and
(e) the grounds of the annulment.

(4) Where the former bankrupt has died, or is a person lacking capacity to manage the person's own affairs (within the meaning of the Mental Capacity Act 2005), the references to the former bankrupt in paragraph (1) are to be read as references to the personal representative of the same or, as the case may be, a person appointed by the court to represent or act for the former bankrupt.

NOTES

Commencement: 6 April 2017.
This rule derived from the Insolvency Rules 1986, SI 1986/1925, r 5.60.

[6.431]
8.37 Trustee's final account

(1) The making of an order under section 261(2) does not of itself release the trustee from any duty or obligation imposed by or under the Act or these Rules to account for all of the trustee's transactions in connection with the former bankrupt's estate.

(2) As soon as reasonably practicable after the making of an order, the trustee must—

(a) deliver a copy of the final account of the trustee to the Secretary of State; and
(b) file a copy of that account with the court.

(3) The final account must include a summary of the trustee's receipts and payments.

(4) The trustee is released from such time as the court may determine, having regard to whether paragraph (2) of this rule has been complied with.

NOTES

Commencement: 6 April 2017.
This rule derived from the Insolvency Rules 1986, SI 1986/1925, r 5.61.

CHAPTER 8 TIME RECORDING INFORMATION

[Note: a document required by the Act or these Rules must also contain the standard contents set out in Part 1.]

[6.432]
8.38 Provision of information

(1) This rule applies where the remuneration of the nominee or the supervisor has been fixed on the basis of time spent.

(2) A person who is acting, or has acted within the previous two years as—

(a) a nominee in relation to a proposal; or
(b) the supervisor in relation to an IVA;

must, within 28 days of receipt of a request from a person mentioned in paragraph (3), deliver free of charge to that person a statement complying with paragraph (4) and (5).

(3) The persons are—

(a) the debtor; and
(b) where the proposal has been approved, a creditor bound by the IVA.

(4) The statement must cover the period which—

(a) in the case of a person who has ceased to act as nominee or supervisor in relation to an IVA, begins with the date of that person's appointment as nominee or supervisor and ends with the date of ceasing to act; and
(b) in any other case, consists of one or more complete periods of six months beginning with the date of appointment and ending most nearly before the date of receiving the request.

(5) The statement must set out—

(i) the total number of hours spent on the matter during that period by the nominee or supervisor, and by any staff,
(ii) for each grade of staff engaged on the matter, the average hourly rate at which work carried out by staff in that grade is charged, and
(iii) the number of hours spent on the matter by each grade of staff during that period.

NOTES

Commencement: 6 April 2017.

This rule derived from the Insolvency Rules 1986, SI 1986/1925, r 5.66.

PART 9
DEBT RELIEF ORDERS

CHAPTER 1 INTERPRETATION

[Notes: (1) a debt relief order under Part 7A of the Act may be made in respect of "qualifying debts" (as defined in section 251A(2)); these do not include "excluded debts" which are prescribed by rule 9.2 for the purposes of section 251A(4).

(2) "approved intermediaries" and "competent authority" are defined in section 251U of the Act for purposes of Part 7A of the Act.]

[6.433]
9.1 Debtor's family

In this Part the expression "debtor's family" has the same meaning in relation to a debtor as it has in section 385(1) in relation to a bankrupt.

NOTES

Commencement: 6 April 2017.

[6.434]
9.2 Excluded debts

(1) For the purposes of Part 7A of the Act debts of the following descriptions are prescribed under section 251A(4) as "excluded debts"—

(a) any fine imposed for an offence and any obligation (including an obligation to pay a lump sum or to pay costs) arising under an order made in family proceedings or any obligation arising under a maintenance assessment or maintenance calculation made under the Child Support Act 1991;

(b) any debt or liability to which a debtor is or may become subject in respect of any sum paid or payable to the debtor as a student by way of a loan and which the debtor receives whether before or after the debt relief order is made;

(c) any obligation arising under a confiscation order made under section 1 of the Drug Trafficking Offences Act 1986, section 1 of the Criminal Justice (Scotland) Act 1987, section 71 of the Criminal Justice Act 1988, or Parts 2, 3 or 4 of the Proceeds of Crime Act 2002;

(d) any debt which consists of a liability to pay damages for negligence, nuisance or breach of a statutory, contractual or other duty, or to pay damages by virtue of Part 1 of the Consumer Protection Act 1987, being in either case damages in respect of the death of or personal injury (including any disease or other impairment of physical or mental condition) to any person; and

(e) any obligation arising from a payment out of the social fund under section 138(1)(b) of the Social Security Contributions and Benefits Act 1992 by way of crisis loan or budgeting loan.

(2) In paragraph (1)(a) "family proceedings" and "fine" have the meanings given by section 281(8) (which applies the Magistrates' Courts Act 1980 and the Matrimonial and Family Proceedings Act 1984).

(3) In paragraph (1)(b) "loan" means a loan made under—

(a) regulations made under section 22(1) of the Teaching and Higher Education Act 1998; or

(b) the Education (Student Loans) Act 1990, or that Act as it continues in force by virtue of any savings made, in connection with its repeal by the Teaching and Higher Education Act 1998, by an order made under section 46(4) of that Act; . . .

[and includes any interest on the loan and any penalties or charges incurred in connection with it.]

NOTES

Commencement: 6 April 2017.

This rule derived from the Insolvency Rules 1986, SI 1986/1925, r 5A.2.

Para (3): word omitted from sub-para (b) revoked and words in square brackets substituted for original sub-para (c) by the Insolvency (England and Wales) (Amendment) Rules 2017, SI 2017/366, rr 3, 28.

CHAPTER 2 APPLICATION FOR A DEBT RELIEF ORDER

[Note: a document required by the Act or these Rules must also contain the standard contents set out in Part 1.]

[6.435]
9.3 Application for a debt relief order: information required in the application

(1) An application for a debt relief order under section 251A must state the matters set out in paragraphs (2) to (9) (which are prescribed for the purposes of section 251B(2)(c)) as they are at the date of the application as well as the matters referred to in section 251B(2)(a) (list of the debtor's debts at the date of the application) and 251B(2)(b) (details of any security held in respect of those debts).

(2) The application must identify the debtor and state—

Part 6 Insolvency Rules

(a) the debtor's occupation (if any);
(b) the debtor's gender;
(c) the debtor's date of birth;
(d) the debtor's places of residence during the three years before the date of the application;
(e) any other name used by the debtor for any purpose;
(f) the name, address and nature of any business carried on by the debtor, including any business carried on by—
 (i) a firm or partnership of which the debtor is a member;
 (ii) an agent or manager for the debtor or for such firm or partnership;
(g) any other liabilities (including those imposed by an order of the court) to which the debtor is subject;
(h) the address of the creditor to whom each debt is owed;
(i) the total amount of the debtor's monthly income from all sources (see rule 9.7(1));
(j) the sources of that income and the amount from each source;
(k) particulars of the expenditure which the debtor claims is necessary to meet the monthly reasonable domestic needs of the debtor and the debtor's family, including the purpose and the amount of that expenditure;
(l) the total amount available from any source to meet the claimed monthly reasonable domestic needs of the debtor and the debtor's family (see rule 9.7(2)); and
(m) particulars of the debtor's property and its total estimated value (see rules 9.8 and 9.9).

(3) The debtor must also state in the application—
(a) whether or not at the date of the application the debtor—
 (i) has given a preference to any person during the period of two years ending with the application date,
 (ii) has entered into a transaction with any person at an undervalue during the period of two years ending with the application date,
 (iii) is domiciled in England and Wales,
 (iv) at any time during the period of three years ending with the application date—
  (aa) was resident,
  (bb) had a place of residence, or
  (cc) carried on business,
 in England and Wales,
 (v) is an undischarged bankrupt,
 (vi) is subject to a debt relief order,
 (vii) has been subject to a debt relief order in the six years ending with the application date,
 (viii) is subject to an interim order or an IVA under Part 8 of the Act, or
 (ix) is subject to a bankruptcy restrictions order or undertaking or debt relief restrictions order or undertaking; and
(b) whether at the date of the application—
 (i) a bankruptcy petition has been presented against the debtor,
 (ii) a bankruptcy application has been made by the debtor,
 (iii) any debt management arrangements (see section 251F) are in force in relation to the debtor, and
 (iv) any other legal action has been taken against the debtor in relation to any of the debtor's existing debts.

(4) In the application, the debtor must deduct from each debt all trade and other discounts which are available to the debtor, except any discount for immediate or early settlement.

(5) Where any debts were incurred or are payable in a foreign currency, the amount of those debts must be converted into sterling at a single exchange rate for that currency prevailing on the relevant date.

(6) A creditor who considers that the rate is unreasonable may apply to the court.

(7) If the court finds that the rate is unreasonable it may itself determine the rate.

(8) Where a debt consists of unpaid payments of a periodical nature, the amount of the debt will consist of any amounts due and unpaid up to the application date.

(9) Where at the application date any payment was accruing due, the amount of the debt will be so much as would have fallen due at that date, if accruing from day to day.

(10) A debtor may include a debt of which payment is not yet due at the date of the application if it is for a liquidated sum payable at some certain future time.

(11) In the application, the debtor must also—
(a) consent to the official receiver making checks for the purpose of verifying that the debtor complies with the conditions to which the making of a debt relief order is subject;
(b) state that the debtor is unable to pay the debts;
(c) request a debt relief order; and
(d) indicate the date on which the application is completed.

(12) The debtor must deliver to the approved intermediary such information and such documents as will enable the intermediary to substantiate the information in the application, including information about each debt, the amount of the debt and the name and address of the creditor.

NOTES

Commencement: 6 April 2017.

This rule derived from the Insolvency Rules 1986, SI 1986/1925, r 5A.3.

[6.436]
9.4 Delivery of application

(1) An application for a debt relief order must be completed and delivered to the official receiver in electronic form and by electronic means.

(2) The preconditions for delivering a document electronically set out in rule 1.45(2) do not apply to applications for debt relief orders.

(3) In the event of any malfunction or error in the operation of the electronic form or means of delivery, the official receiver must inform the competent authorities and approved intermediaries—

(a) that approved intermediaries may complete and deliver applications in hard copy for a specified period; and

(b) of the postal address to which such applications are to be delivered and of any terms or conditions to which the use of the address is subject.

(4) Such an application completed in hard copy may not be delivered by fax.

NOTES

Commencement: 6 April 2017.

This rule derived from the Insolvency Rules 1986, SI 1986/1925, r 5A.4.

[6.437]
9.5 Role of approved intermediary

(1) The approved intermediary, through whom the application for a debt relief order is to be made, must create an application for a debt relief order in the name of the debtor as soon as reasonably practicable after being asked by the debtor to do so.

(2) The approved intermediary may assist the debtor—

(a) to identify what information is required to complete the application;

(b) based upon the documentation and information supplied by the debtor, to ascertain whether—

(i) the debtor appears to have debts not exceeding the prescribed amount,

(ii) the debtor's surplus income does not exceed the prescribed amount, and

(iii) the value of the debtor's property does not exceed the prescribed amount; and

(c) to ensure that the application (if made) is completed in full.

(3) The approved intermediary must draw the debtor's attention to—

(a) all the conditions to which an application for, and the making of, a debt relief order is subject;

(b) the possible consequences of the debtor making any false representation or omission in the application; and

(c) the fact that verification checks will be made for the purpose of verifying that the debtor complies with the conditions to which the making of a debt relief order is subject and the requirement for the debtor to consent to such checks being made.

(4) The approved intermediary must deliver the application to the official receiver as soon as reasonably practicable after being instructed by the debtor to do so.

NOTES

Commencement: 6 April 2017.

This rule derived from the Insolvency Rules 1986, SI 1986/1925, r 5A.5.

CHAPTER 3 VERIFYING THE APPLICATION AND DETERMINING THE DEBTOR'S INCOME AND PROPERTY

[6.438]
9.6 Prescribed verification checks: conditions in paragraphs 1 to 8 of Schedule 4ZA of the Act

(1) For the purposes of section 251D(4) and (5) and the conditions in paragraphs 1 to 8 of Schedule 4ZA of the Act, the prescribed verification checks are those searches or enquiries specified in this rule.

(2) For the purpose of verifying a debtor's connection with England and Wales on the application date, verification checks made in, or with, one or more of the following—

(a) the electoral registers for the areas in England and Wales in which the debtor claims to reside or to carry on business or to have resided or carried on business at the date of the application;

(b) the individual insolvency register;

(c) the bankruptcy restrictions register;

(d) the debt relief restrictions register;

(e) a credit reference agency.

(3) Verification checks made in one or more of the registers specified in paragraph (4), for the purpose of verifying that a debtor—

(a) is not, on the determination date—

(i) an undischarged bankrupt,

(ii) subject to a bankruptcy restrictions order or undertaking,

(iii) subject to a debt relief restrictions order or undertaking,

(iv) subject to an IVA; or

(b) has not been the subject of a debt relief order in the period of six years ending with the determination date.

(4) The registers referred to in paragraph (3) are—

(a) the individual insolvency register;

Part 6 Insolvency Rules

(b) the bankruptcy restrictions register; and
(c) the debt relief restrictions register.

(5) Verification checks made in, or with, one or more of the sources specified in paragraph (6) for the purpose of verifying—
(a) that the debtor is not subject to an interim order on the determination date;
(b) whether a creditor's bankruptcy petition has been presented against the debtor before the determination date;
(c) whether the debtor has made a bankruptcy application before the determination date;
(d) whether proceedings in relation to any such bankruptcy application have finally been disposed of before the determination date;
(e) where a creditor's bankruptcy petition has been presented against the debtor before the determination date, the status of the proceedings in relation to the petition and whether the person who presented the petition has consented to the making of the application for a debt relief order.

(6) The sources are—
(a) the individual insolvency register;
(b) county or other court records;
(c) a credit reference agency.

(7) Verification checks made with a credit reference agency, for the purpose of verifying that each of the following does not exceed the prescribed amount—
(a) the amount of the debtor's overall indebtedness;
(b) the amount of the debtor's monthly surplus income; or
(c) the total value of the debtor's property.

NOTES

Commencement: 6 April 2017.
This rule derived from the Insolvency Rules 1986, SI 1986/1925, r 5A.7.

[6.439]
9.7 Determination of debtor's monthly surplus income

(1) For the purposes of this Part, the income of a debtor comprises every payment in the nature of income which is from time to time made to the debtor or to which the debtor from time to time becomes entitled, including any payment in respect of the carrying on of a business or in respect of an office or employment and any payment under a pension scheme.

(2) In determining the monthly surplus income of a debtor, the official receiver must take into account any contribution made by a member of the debtor's family to the amount necessary for the reasonable domestic needs of the debtor and the debtor's family.

NOTES

Commencement: 6 April 2017.
This rule derived from the Insolvency Rules 1986, SI 1986/1925, r 5A.8.

[6.440]
9.8 Determination of value of the debtor's property (paragraph 8 of Schedule 4ZA)

(1) The official receiver in determining the total value of the debtor's property for the purposes of determining whether the condition in paragraph 8 of Schedule 4ZA is met must treat as a debtor's property for the purposes of this Part—
(a) all property belonging to or vested in the debtor on the determination date; and
(b) any property which by virtue of any of the following provisions of this Part is comprised in or is treated as falling within the preceding sub-paragraph.

(2) For the purposes of this Part—
(a) property, in relation to a debtor, includes references to any power exercisable by the debtor over or in relation to property except in so far as the power is exercisable over or in relation to property which is not or is deemed not for the time being to be the property of the debtor and cannot be exercised for the benefit of the debtor;
(b) a power exercisable over or in relation to property is deemed for the purposes of this Part to vest in the person entitled to exercise it at the time of the transaction or event by virtue of which it is exercisable by that person (whether or not it becomes so exercisable at that time);
(c) property belonging to or vested in the debtor so belongs or vests in the debtor subject to the rights of any person other than the debtor (whether as a secured creditor of the debtor or otherwise).

(3) In determining the value of the debtor's property the descriptions of property set out in rule 9.9 must be excluded.

NOTES

Commencement: 6 April 2017.
This rule derived from the Insolvency Rules 1986, SI 1986/1925, r 5A.9.

[6.441]

9.9 Property to be excluded in determining the value of a debtor's property

(1) For the purposes of determining the value of a person's property under rule 9.8, the official receiver must disregard—

(a) a single domestic motor vehicle belonging to or vested in the debtor if—

(i) it has been especially adapted for use by the debtor because of a physical impairment that has a substantial and long-term adverse effect on the debtor's ability to carry out normal day-to-day activities, subject to paragraph (2), or

(ii) the maximum potential realisable value of the vehicle is less than £1,000 (the prescribed amount);

(b) subject to paragraph (3), such tools, books and other items of equipment as are necessary to the debtor for use personally in the debtor's employment, business or vocation;

(c) subject to paragraph (3), such clothing, bedding, furniture, household equipment and provisions as are necessary for satisfying the basic domestic needs of the debtor and the debtor's family;

(d) property held by the debtor on trust for any other person;

(e) the right of nomination to a vacant ecclesiastical benefice;

(f) a tenancy which is an assured tenancy or an assured agricultural occupancy, within the meaning of Part 1 of the Housing Act 1988, and the terms of which inhibit an assignment as mentioned in section 127(5) of the Rent Act 1977;

(g) a protected tenancy, within the meaning of the Rent Act 1977, in relation to which, by virtue of any provision of Part 9 of that Act, no premium can lawfully be required as a condition of assignment;

(h) a tenancy of a dwelling-house by virtue of which the debtor is, within the meaning of the Rent (Agriculture) Act 1976, a protected occupier of the dwelling-house, and the terms of which inhibit an assignment as mentioned in section 127(5) of the Rent Act 1977;

(i) a secure tenancy, within the meaning of Part 4 of the Housing Act 1985, which is not capable of being assigned, except in the cases mentioned in section 91(3) of that Act; and

(j) any right of the debtor under an approved pension arrangement (as defined by section 11 of the Welfare Reform and Pensions Act 1999).

(2) The amount the official receiver must disregard under paragraph (1)(a)(i) is limited to the value of a reasonable replacement where it appears to the official receiver that the realisable value of the vehicle to be disregarded exceeds the cost of a reasonable replacement for it.

(3) The amount the official receiver must disregard under paragraph (1)(b) or (c) is limited to the value of a reasonable replacement where it appears to the official receiver that the realisable value of the whole or a part of the property to be disregarded exceeds the cost of a reasonable replacement for that property or that part.

(4) A vehicle or other property is a reasonable replacement if it is reasonably adequate for meeting the needs met by the other vehicle or other property.

NOTES

Commencement: 6 April 2017.

This rule derived from the Insolvency Rules 1986, SI 1986/1925, r 5A.10.

CHAPTER 4 MAKING OR REFUSAL OF A DEBT RELIEF ORDER

[Note: a document required by the Act or these Rules must also contain the standard contents set out in Part 1.]

[6.442]

9.10 Contents of debt relief order

A debt relief order must contain—

(a) the debtor's identification details;

(b) the date of, and the reference number allocated to, the debtor's application;

(c) a list of the debtor's qualifying debts as at the application date, specifying the amount owed and the creditor's name, address and reference (if any); and

(d) the date on which the order was made.

NOTES

Commencement: 6 April 2017.

This rule derived from the Insolvency Rules 1986, SI 1986/1925, r 5A.11.

[6.443]

9.11 Other steps to be taken by official receiver or debtor upon making of the order

(1) In addition to delivering a copy of the order to the debtor under section 251E, the official receiver must—

(a) deliver a notice of the making and date of the order to the approved intermediary through whom the debtor's application was made; and

(b) cause an entry to be made in the individual insolvency register in accordance with rule 11.18.

(2) If there are other debt management arrangements or an attachment of earnings order in force in relation to the debtor, the official receiver must deliver a notice of the making of the debt relief order to the court, or the body, as the case may be, responsible for making the debt management arrangements or order.

NOTES

Commencement: 6 April 2017.
This rule derived from the Insolvency Rules 1986, SI 1986/1925, r 5A.12.

[6.444]
9.12 Prescribed information for creditors on making of debt relief order

The official receiver must deliver a notice to each creditor to whom a qualifying debt specified in the order is owed, of—

(a) the making, the date and the reference number of the order;
(b) the effect of the order;
(c) the matters to which a creditor may object under section 251K; and
(d) the name, address and telephone number of the official receiver delivering the notice and the address to which any objection under that section may or must be delivered.

NOTES

Commencement: 6 April 2017.
This rule derived from the Insolvency Rules 1986, SI 1986/1925, r 5A.13.

[6.445]
9.13 Refusal of application for debt relief order

If the official receiver refuses an application for a debt relief order, the official receiver must deliver a notice to the debtor stating that the official receiver refused the application, and the reason why it has been refused.

NOTES

Commencement: 6 April 2017.
This rule derived from the Insolvency Rules 1986, SI 1986/1925, r 5A.6.

CHAPTER 5 OBJECTION AND REVOCATION

[Note: a document required by the Act or these Rules must also contain the standard contents set out in Part 1.]

[6.446]
9.14 Meaning of "creditor"

In this Chapter, "creditor" means a person specified in a debt relief order as a creditor to whom a qualifying debt is owed.

NOTES

Commencement: 6 April 2017.
This rule derived from the Insolvency Rules 1986, SI 1986/1925, r 5A.14.

[6.447]
9.15 Creditor's objection to a debt relief order (section 251K)

(1) The prescribed period under section 251K(2)(a) for a creditor to object to a debt relief order during the moratorium period is within 30 days of the date on which a notice of the making of the order was delivered to the creditor.

(2) The objection must be made in writing to the official receiver and must contain—

(a) the name and address of the creditor;
(b) the name of the debtor and the reference number of the order;
(c) the matters under section 251K to which the creditor objects;
(d) a statement of which of the prescribed grounds for objection the creditor relies upon;
(e) a statement of the facts on which the creditor relies; and
(f) information and documents in support of the grounds and the facts on which the creditor relies.

(3) The prescribed grounds for objection are that—

(a) there is an error in, or an omission from, something specified in the debt relief order;
(b) a bankruptcy order has been made in relation to the debtor;
(c) the debtor has made a proposal under Part 8 of the Act;
(d) the official receiver should not have been satisfied that—
 (i) the debts specified in the order were qualifying debts of the debtor as at the application date,
 (ii) the conditions specified in Part 1 of Schedule 4ZA were met, or
 (iii) the conditions specified in Part 2 of that Schedule were met; or
(e) the official receiver should have been satisfied that the official receiver was permitted to make an order in spite of any failure to meet the conditions referred to in sub-paragraphs (d)(ii) and (iii).

NOTES

Commencement: 6 April 2017.
This rule derived from the Insolvency Rules 1986, SI 1986/1925, r 5A.14.

[6.448]

9.16 Official receiver's response to objection under section 251K

(1) After considering a creditor's objection to a debt relief order in accordance with section 251K, the official receiver, if minded to revoke or amend the debt relief order, must deliver to the debtor—

(a) particulars of the objection;
(b) the grounds and facts upon which the creditor relies;
(c) an invitation to the debtor to deliver any comments on them to the official receiver within 21 days of delivery of the particulars; and
(d) the address to which the debtor's comments must be delivered.

(2) Before deciding whether to revoke or amend the debt relief order, the official receiver must consider any comments made by the debtor provided they are received within the 21 day period.

(3) After coming to a decision on the objection the official receiver must deliver a notice of the decision to the creditor within 14 days.

(4) If the official receiver has decided to make an application under section 251M(2) then the official receiver must treat the creditor as a person interested in the application under rule 9.21(3)(b) (if the creditor would not otherwise be such).

NOTES

Commencement: 6 April 2017.
This rule derived from the Insolvency Rules 1986, SI 1986/1925, r 5A.15.

[6.449]

9.17 Creditor's request that a debt relief order be revoked (section 251L(4))

(1) A creditor may request that the official receiver revoke a debt relief order under section 251L(4) because either or both of the conditions in paragraphs 7 and 8 of Schedule 4ZA are not met at any time after the debt relief order was made.

(2) The request must contain—

(a) the name and address of the creditor;
(b) the name of the debtor and the reference number of the order;
(c) which of the conditions under paragraph 7 and 8 of Schedule 4ZA are not met;
(d) a statement of the facts on which the creditor relies; and
(e) information and documents supporting the facts which are relied upon.

(3) After coming to a decision on the request the official receiver must deliver a notice of the decision to the creditor within 14 days.

(4) If the official receiver has decided to make an application under section 251M(2) then the official receiver must treat the creditor as a person interested in the application under rule 9.21(3)(b) (if the creditor would not otherwise be such).

NOTES

Commencement: 6 April 2017.
This rule derived from the Insolvency Rules 1986, SI 1986/1925, r 5A.16.

[6.450]

9.18 Procedure in revoking or amending a debt relief order (section 251L)

(1) The official receiver must as soon as reasonably practicable after deciding to revoke a debt relief order under section 251L deliver notice of the decision to the debtor and the creditors.

(2) The notice must contain—

(a) identification details for the debtor;
(b) the date and reference number of the debt relief order;
(c) the reasons for revocation; and
(d) the date (under subsection (5) or (7) of section 251L) on or from which the revocation has effect.

(3) Where the official receiver—

(a) has delivered notices under paragraph (1) of the revocation of a debt relief order from a specified date; and
(b) thinks it appropriate under section 251L(7) to revoke the debt relief order with immediate effect before the specified date;

the official receiver must deliver a notice of the new date to anyone who previously received a notice under paragraph (1).

(4) The official receiver must cause the entry in the individual insolvency register relating to the order to be amended so far as information concerning the order has not already been deleted under rule 11.19.

(5) Where the debtor has died during the moratorium period rule 9.20 applies.

(6) The official receiver must as soon as reasonably practicable after amending a debt relief order deliver a notice of the amendment to the debtor and the creditors.

(7) The notice must contain—

(a) identification details for the debtor and the date and reference number of the debt relief order;
(b) the amendment;
(c) the date on which the amendment was made; and
(d) the reasons for it.

Part 6 Insolvency Rules

(8) The official receiver must as soon as reasonably practicable cause the entry in the individual insolvency register relating to the amended debt relief order to be amended accordingly.

NOTES

Commencement: 6 April 2017.
This rule derived from the Insolvency Rules 1986, SI 1986/1925, r 5A.16.

[6.451]

9.19 Debtor's notification of official receiver of matters in section 251J(3) or (5)

(1) The debtor must deliver a notice to the official receiver as soon as reasonably practicable after the debtor becomes aware of an error in, or omission from, the information supplied to the official receiver in, or in support of, the application.

(2) The notice must state the nature of the error or omission and the reason for it.

(3) The debtor must deliver a notice to the official receiver as soon as reasonably practicable after the debtor becomes aware of a change in the debtor's circumstances between the application date and the determination date that would affect (or would have affected) the determination of the application.

(4) The notice must state the nature of the change and the date of the change.

(5) Where a debt relief order is made and—

- (a) the debtor's income increases during the moratorium period applicable to the order, the debtor must as soon as reasonably practicable after the date of the increase deliver a notice to the official receiver stating—
  - (i) the amount of the increase,
  - (ii) the reason for it,
  - (iii) the date of the increase, and
  - (iv) its expected duration;
- (b) the debtor acquires property or property is devolved upon the debtor during that period, the debtor must as soon as reasonably practicable after the date of the acquisition or devolution deliver a notice to the official receiver stating—
  - (i) the nature of the acquisition or devolution,
  - (ii) the date of the acquisition or devolution,
  - (iii) the reason for it, and
  - (iv) its value;
- (c) the debtor becomes aware of any error in or omission from any information supplied by the debtor to the official receiver after the determination date, the debtor must as soon as reasonably practicable after the date on which the debtor becomes aware of it deliver a notice to the official receiver, stating—
  - (i) the nature of the error or omission,
  - (ii) the reason for it, and
  - (iii) the date on which the debtor became aware of it.

NOTES

Commencement: 6 April 2017.
This rule derived from the Insolvency Rules 1986, SI 1986/1925, r 5A.17.

[6.452]

9.20 Death of debtor during a moratorium period under a debt relief order

(1) This rule applies where a debtor dies during a moratorium period under a debt relief order.

(2) The official receiver must, as soon as reasonably practicable after being informed of the death of the debtor—

- (a) cause a note of the fact and the date of the death to be entered on the individual insolvency register under rule 11.23;
- (b) revoke the debt relief order; and
- (c) deliver a notice of the revocation to—
  - (i) the creditors, and
  - (ii) the personal representatives of the debtor.

(3) The notice of revocation must—

- (a) state the reason for the revocation; and
- (b) specify the date on which the revocation took effect.

NOTES

Commencement: 6 April 2017.
This rule derived from the Insolvency Rules 1986, SI 1986/1925, r 5A.27.

CHAPTER 6 APPLICATIONS TO THE COURT

[Note: a document required by the Act or these Rules must also contain the standard contents set out in Part 1.]

[6.453]

9.21 Notice of application to court under section 251M

(1) This rule applies to applications to the court under section 251M.

(2) Where the application is made by a person who is dissatisfied by an act, omission or decision of the official receiver in connection with a debt relief order or an application for a debt relief order the applicant must deliver a notice—

(a) if the applicant is the debtor, to the official receiver and any creditor specified in the debt relief order or in the application for the debt relief order; or

(b) if the applicant is a person other than the debtor, to the official receiver and the debtor.

(3) Where the application is made by the official receiver for directions or an order in relation to a matter arising in connection with a debt relief order or an application for such an order, the official receiver must deliver notice to—

(a) the debtor; and

(b) any person appearing to the official receiver to have an interest in the application.

NOTES

Commencement: 6 April 2017.

This rule derived from the Insolvency Rules 1986, SI 1986/1925, r 5A.19.

[6.454]

9.22 Court in which applications under sections 251M or 251N are to be made

(1) An application to the court under section 251M or 251N must be made to—

(a) the County Court at Central London, where the proceedings are allocated to the London Insolvency District under rule 12.5(a)(i) to (iv);

(b) the High Court, where the proceedings are allocated to the London Insolvency District under rule 12.5(a)(v);

(c) the debtor's own hearing centre as determined under paragraph (3) (subject to paragraph (4)), in any other case where the debtor is resident in England and Wales.

(2) The application may be filed either with the debtor's own hearing centre or with the High Court if—

(a) the debtor is not resident in England and Wales but was resident or carried on business in England and Wales within the six months immediately before the application is filed with the court; and

(b) the proceedings are not allocated to the London Insolvency District.

(3) In this rule the debtor's own hearing centre is—

(a) where the debtor has carried on business in England and Wales within the six months immediately before the application is filed with the court, the hearing centre which serves the insolvency district where for the longest period during those six months—

(i) the debtor carried on business, or

(ii) the principal place of business was located, if business was carried on in more than one insolvency district; or

(b) where the debtor has not carried on business in England and Wales within the six months immediately before the application is filed with the court, the hearing centre which serves the insolvency district where the debtor resided for the longest period during those six months.

(4) Where, for whatever reason, it is not possible for the application to be filed with the debtor's own hearing centre, the applicant may, with a view to expediting the application, file the application—

(a) where paragraph (3)(a) applies, with—

(i) the hearing centre for the insolvency district in which the debtor resides, or

(ii) the hearing centre specified in Schedule 6 as the nearest full-time hearing centre to the hearing centre specified in paragraph (3)(a), or paragraph (i) as the case may be; or

(b) where paragraph (3)(b) applies, with the hearing centre specified in Schedule 6 as being the nearest full-time hearing centre to that specified in paragraph (3)(b).

(5) The application must contain sufficient information to establish that it is brought in the appropriate court, and where the application is made to the County Court, the appropriate hearing centre.

NOTES

Commencement: 6 April 2017.

This rule derived from the Insolvency Rules 1986, SI 1986/1925, r 5A.21.

[6.455]

9.23 Creditor's bankruptcy petition: creditor consents to making application for a debt relief order

(1) This rule applies where before the determination of an application for a debt relief order, a creditor's petition for bankruptcy has been presented against a debtor and the proceedings in relation to the petition remain before the court.

(2) In this rule "the debt" means the debt to which the creditor's bankruptcy petition relates.

(3) If, on the hearing of the petition, the petitioner consents to the debtor making an application for a debt relief order in relation to the debt the court must—

(a) refer the debtor to an approved intermediary for the purpose of making an application for a debt relief order in relation to the debtor and the debt noting the consent of the creditor on the order for referral; and

(b) stay the proceedings on the petition in relation to the debt on such terms and conditions as it thinks just.

(4) The debtor must deliver to the approved intermediary as soon as reasonably practicable after the making of the order of referral—

(a) a sealed copy of the order; and
(b) copies of the petition and the creditor's statutory demand (if there was one).

(5) The approved intermediary must, on receipt of the order and the copies, as soon as reasonably practicable after the application for a debt relief order has been made, deliver them to the official receiver endorsed with the name of the debtor and the number of the application to which they relate.

(6) If, following the reference by the court, a debt relief order is made in relation to the debt, the petition must be dismissed in relation to it unless the court otherwise directs.

NOTES

Commencement: 6 April 2017.
This rule derived from the Insolvency Rules 1986, SI 1986/1925, r 5A.23.

[6.456]
9.24 Extension of moratorium period

Where the moratorium period applicable to a debt relief order is extended—
(a) notice of the extension, and the period of extension must be delivered—
  (i) where extended by the court, to the official receiver, who must deliver a copy to the debtor and to the creditors specified in the debt relief order,
  (ii) where extended by the official receiver, to the debtor and to the creditors specified in the debt relief order; and
(b) the official receiver must cause to be entered in the individual insolvency register—
  (i) that such an extension has been made in relation to the debtor,
  (ii) the date on which the extension was made,
  (iii) its duration, and
  (iv) the date of the anticipated end of the moratorium period.

NOTES

Commencement: 6 April 2017.
This rule derived from the Insolvency Rules 1986, SI 1986/1925, r 5A.20.

CHAPTER 7 PERMISSION TO ACT AS A DIRECTOR, ETC

[Note: a document required by the Act or these Rules must also contain the standard contents set out in Part 1.]

[6.457]
9.25 Application for permission under the Company Directors Disqualification Act 1986

(1) This rule relates to an application for permission under section 11 of the Company Directors Disqualification Act 1986, to act as director of, or to take part or be concerned in the promotion, formation or management of a company by a person—
(a) in relation to whom a moratorium period under a debt relief order applies; or
(b) in relation to whom a debt relief restrictions order or undertaking is in force.

(2) The application must be supported by a witness statement which must contain identification details for the company and specify—
(a) the nature of its business or intended business, and the place or places where that business is, or is to be, carried on;
(b) in the case of a company which has not yet been incorporated, whether it is, or is to be, a private or a public company;
(c) the persons who are, or are to be, principally responsible for the conduct of its affairs (whether as directors, shadow directors, managers or otherwise);
(d) the manner and capacity in which the applicant for permission proposes to take part or be concerned in the promotion or formation of the company or, as the case may be, its management; and
(e) the emoluments and other benefits to be obtained by virtue of the matters referred to in paragraph (d).

(3) The court must fix a venue for the hearing of the application, and must deliver a notice to the applicant for permission accordingly.

NOTES

Commencement: 6 April 2017.
This rule derived from the Insolvency Rules 1986, SI 1986/1925, r 5A.24.

[6.458]
9.26 Report of official receiver

(1) The applicant for permission must, not less than 28 days before the date fixed for the hearing, deliver to the official receiver, notice of the venue, accompanied by copies of the application and the witness statement under rule 9.25.

(2) The official receiver may, not less than 14 days before the date fixed for the hearing, file with the court a report of any matters which the official receiver considers ought to be drawn to the court's attention.

(3) A copy of the report must be delivered by the official receiver, as soon as reasonably practicable after it is filed, to the applicant for permission.

(4) The applicant for permission may, not later than five business days before the date of the hearing, file with the court a notice specifying any statements in the official receiver's report which are to be denied or disputed.

(5) If a notice is filed under paragraph (4), the applicant for permission must deliver copies of it, not less than three business days before the date of the hearing, to the official receiver.

(6) The official receiver may appear on the hearing of the application, and may make representations and put to the applicant for permission such questions as the court may allow.

NOTES

Commencement: 6 April 2017.

This rule derived from the Insolvency Rules 1986, SI 1986/1925, r 5A.25.

[6.459]

9.27 Court's order on application

(1) If the court grants the application for permission under section 11 of the Company Directors Disqualification Act 1986, its order must specify that which by virtue of the order the applicant has permission to do.

(2) The court may at the same time, having regard to any representations made by the official receiver on the hearing of the application, exercise in relation to the moratorium period or the debt relief order to which the applicant for permission is subject, any power which it has under section 251M.

(3) Whether or not the application is granted, copies of the order must be delivered by the court to the applicant and the official receiver.

NOTES

Commencement: 6 April 2017.

This rule derived from the Insolvency Rules 1986, SI 1986/1925, r 5A.26.

PART 10
BANKRUPTCY

CHAPTER 1 THE STATUTORY DEMAND

[Note: a document required by the Act or these Rules must also contain the standard contents set out in Part 1.]

[6.460]

10.1 The statutory demand (section 268)

(1) A statutory demand under section 268 must contain—

(a) the heading either "Statutory demand under section 268(1) (debt payable immediately) of the Insolvency Act 1986" or "Statutory demand under section 268(2) (debt not immediately payable)";

(b) identification details for the debtor;

(c) the name and address of the creditor;

(d) a statement of the amount of the debt, and the consideration for it (or, if there is no consideration, the way in which it arises);

(e) if the demand is made under section 268(1) and founded on a judgment or order of a court, the date of the judgment or order and the court in which it was obtained;

(f) if the demand is made under section 268(2), a statement of the grounds on which it is alleged that the debtor appears to have no reasonable prospect of paying the debt;

(g) if the creditor is entitled to the debt by way of assignment, details of the original creditor and any intermediary assignees;

(h) a statement that if the debtor does not comply with the demand bankruptcy proceedings may be commenced;

(i) the date by which the debtor must comply with the demand, if bankruptcy proceedings are to be avoided;

(j) a statement of the methods of compliance which are open to the debtor;

(k) a statement that the debtor has the right to apply to the court to have the demand set aside;

(l) a statement that rule 10.4(4) of the Insolvency (England and Wales) Rules 2016 states to which court such an application must be made; and name the court or hearing centre of the County Court to which, according to the present information, the debtor must make the application ($21 the High Court, the County Court at Central London or a named hearing centre of the County Court as the case may be);

(m) a statement that any application to set aside the demand must be made within 18 days of service on the debtor; and

(n) a statement that if the debtor does not apply to set aside the demand within 18 days or otherwise deal with this demand within 21 days after its service the debtor could be made bankrupt and the debtor's property and goods taken away.

(2) Where the statutory demand is served by a Minister of the Crown or a Government Department the statutory demand must explain that the debtor may alternatively apply to set aside the demand to the High Court or the County Court at Central London (as the case may be) if the Minister or Department intends to present a bankruptcy petition to one of them.

(3) A demand must name one or more individuals with whom the debtor may communicate with a view to—

(a) securing or compounding the debt to the satisfaction of the creditor; or

(b) establishing to the creditor's satisfaction that there is a reasonable prospect that the debt will be paid when it falls due.

(4) The postal address, electronic address and telephone number (if any) of the named individual must be given.

(5) A demand must be dated and authenticated either by the creditor or by a person who is authorised to make the demand on the creditor's behalf

(6) A demand which is authenticated by a person other than the creditor must state that the person is authorised to make the demand on the creditor's behalf and state the person's relationship to the creditor.

(7) If the amount claimed in the demand includes—

(a) any charge by way of interest of which notice had not previously been delivered to the debtor as a liability of the debtor's; or

(b) any other charge accruing from time to time,

the amount or rate of the charge must be separately identified, and the grounds on which payment of it is claimed must be stated.

(8) The amount claimed for such charges must be limited to that which has accrued at the date of the demand.

(9) If the creditor holds any security in respect of the debt, the full amount of the debt must be specified, but—

(a) the demand must specify the nature of the security, and the value which the creditor puts upon it at the date of the demand; and

(b) the demand must claim payment of the full amount of the debt, less the specified value of the security.

[(10) When the statutory demand is to be served out of the jurisdiction, the time limits of 18 days and 21 days referred to in sub-paragraphs 10.1(1)(m) and (n) above must be amended as follows—

(a) for any reference to 18 days there must be substituted the number of days which is the appropriate number of days set out in the table accompanying the Practice Direction supplementing Section IV of CPR Part 6 plus 4 days; and

(b) for any reference to 21 days there must be substituted the number of days which is the appropriate number of days set out in the table accompanying the Practice Direction supplementing Section IV of CPR Part 6 plus 7 days.]

NOTES

Commencement: 6 April 2017.

This rule derived from the Insolvency Rules 1986, SI 1986/1925, rr 6.1, 6.2.

Para (10): added by the Insolvency (England and Wales) and Insolvency (Scotland) (Miscellaneous and Consequential Amendments) Rules 2017, SI 2017/1115, rr 2, 7.

[6.461]

10.2 Service of statutory demand

A creditor must do all that is reasonable to bring the statutory demand to the debtor's attention and, if practicable in the particular circumstances, serve the demand personally.

NOTES

Commencement: 6 April 2017.

This rule derived from the Insolvency Rules 1986, SI 1986/1925, r 6.3.

[6.462]

10.3 Proof of service of statutory demand

(1) Where section 268 requires a statutory demand to be served before the petition, a certificate of service of the demand must be filed with the court with the petition.

(2) The certificate must be verified by a statement of truth and be accompanied by a copy of the demand served.

(3) If the demand has been served personally on the debtor, the statement of truth must be made by the person who served the demand unless service has been acknowledged in writing by the debtor or a person authorised to accept service.

(4) If service has been acknowledged in writing either by—

(a) the debtor; or

(b) a person who is authorised to accept service on the debtor's behalf and who has stated that this is the case in the acknowledgement of service;

then the certificate of service must be authenticated either by the creditor or by a person acting on the creditor's behalf, and the acknowledgement of service must accompany the certificate.

(5) If the demand has been served other than personally and there is no acknowledgement of service, the certificate must be authenticated by a person or persons having direct personal knowledge of the means adopted for serving the statutory demand, and must contain the following information—

(a) the steps taken to serve the demand; and
(b) a date by which, to the best of the knowledge, information and belief of the person authenticating the certificate, the demand will have come to the debtor's attention.

(6) Where paragraph (5) applies the statutory demand is deemed to have been served on the debtor on the date referred to in paragraph (5)(b) unless the court determines otherwise.

NOTES

Commencement: 6 April 2017.

This rule derived from the Insolvency Rules 1986, SI 1986/1925, r 6.11.

[6.463]

10.4 Application to set aside statutory demand

(1) The debtor may apply to the court for an order setting aside the statutory demand.

(2) The application must be made within 18 days from the date of the service of the statutory demand.

(3) The application must—

(a) identify the debtor;
(b) state that the application is for an order that the statutory demand be set aside;
(c) state the date of the statutory demand; and
(d) be dated and authenticated by the debtor, or by a person authorised to act on the debtor's behalf.

(4) The application must be made to the court or hearing centre—

(a) determined in accordance with rule 10.48; or
(b) to which rule 10.11(1) requires a petition to be presented if—
   (i) the creditor serving the statutory demand is a Minister of the Crown or a government Department,
   (ii) the debt in respect of which the statutory demand is made, or part of it equal to or exceeding the bankruptcy level (within the meaning of section 267), is the subject of a judgment or order of a court, and
   (iii) the statutory demand—
      (aa) specifies the date of the judgment or order and the court in which it was obtained, and
      (bb) indicates the creditor's intention to present a bankruptcy petition against the debtor in the High Court or the County Court at Central London as the case may be.

(5) The time within which the debtor must comply with the statutory demand ceases to run on the date the application is filed with the court, subject to any order of the court under rule 10.5.

(6) The debtor's application must be accompanied by a copy of the statutory demand, where it is in the debtor's possession, and supported by a witness statement containing the following—

(a) the date on which the debtor became aware of the statutory demand;
(b) the grounds on which the debtor claims that it should be set aside; and
(c) any evidence in support of the application.

NOTES

Commencement: 6 April 2017.

This rule derived from the Insolvency Rules 1986, SI 1986/1925, r 6.4.

[6.464]

10.5 Hearing of application to set aside

(1) On receipt of an application to set aside a statutory demand, the court may, if satisfied that no sufficient cause is shown for it, dismiss it without giving notice of the application to the creditor.

(2) The time for complying with the statutory demand runs again from the date the application is dismissed under paragraph (1).

(3) Unless the application is dismissed under paragraph (1), the court must fix a venue for it to be heard, and must give at least five business days' notice to—

(a) the debtor or, if the debtor's application was made by a solicitor acting for the debtor, to the solicitor;
(b) the creditor; and
(c) whoever is named in the statutory demand as the person with whom the debtor may communicate about the demand (or the first such if more than one).

(4) On the hearing of the application, the court must consider the evidence then available to it, and may either determine the application or adjourn it, giving such directions as it thinks appropriate.

(5) The court may grant the application if—

(a) the debtor appears to have a counterclaim, set-off or cross demand which equals or exceeds the amount of the debt specified in the statutory demand;
(b) the debt is disputed on grounds which appear to the court to be substantial;
(c) it appears that the creditor holds some security in relation to the debt claimed by the demand, and either rule 10.1(9) is not complied with in relation to it, or the court is satisfied that the value of the security equals or exceeds the full amount of the debt; or
(d) the court is satisfied, on other grounds, that the demand ought to be set aside.

(6) An order setting aside a statutory demand must contain—
- (a) identification details for the debtor;
- (b) the date of the hearing of the application;
- (c) the date of the statutory demand;
- (d) an order that the statutory demand be set aside;
- (e) details of any further order in the matter; and
- (f) the date of the order.

(7) Where the creditor holds some security in relation to the debt and has complied with rule 10.1(9) but the court is satisfied that the statutory demand undervalues the security, the court may order the creditor to amend the demand (but without prejudice to the creditor's right to present a bankruptcy petition by reference to the original demand as so amended).

(8) If the court dismisses the application, it must make an order authorising the creditor to present a bankruptcy petition either as soon as reasonably practicable, or on or after a date specified in the order.

(9) The court must deliver a copy of any order under paragraphs (6) to (8) to the creditor as soon as reasonably practicable.

NOTES

Commencement: 6 April 2017.
This rule derived from the Insolvency Rules 1986, SI 1986/1925, r 6.5.

CHAPTER 2 CREDITORS' BANKRUPTCY PETITIONS

Preliminary

[Note: a document required by the Act or these Rules must also contain the standard contents set out in Part 1.]

[6.465]
10.6 Application and interpretation

(1) This Chapter relates to a creditor's petition and making a bankruptcy order on such a petition.

(2) In this Chapter "the debt" means the debt in relation to which the petition is presented.

(3) This Chapter also applies to a petition under section 264(1)(c) by a supervisor of, or person bound by, an IVA , with any necessary modifications.

NOTES

Commencement: 6 April 2017.
This rule derived from the Insolvency Rules 1986, SI 1986/1925, r 6.6.

[6.466]
10.7 Contents of petition

(1) The petition must state—
- (a) the name and postal address of the petitioner;
- (b) where the petitioner is represented by a solicitor, the name, postal address and telephone number of the solicitor;
- (c) that the petitioner requests that the court make a bankruptcy order against the debtor;
- (d) whether—
  - (i) the debtor's centre of main interests is within a member State,
  - (ii) the debtor's centre of main interests is not within a member State, or
  - (iii) the debtor carries on business as an Article 1.2 undertaking;
- (e) whether the debtor—
  - (i) is resident in England and Wales, or
  - (ii) is not resident in England and Wales;
- (f) whether the petition is presented to—
  - (i) the High Court,
  - (ii) the County Court at Central London, or
  - (iii) a specified hearing centre; and
- (g) the reasons why the court or hearing centre to which the petition is presented is the correct court or hearing centre under rule 10.11.

(2) If the petition is based on a statutory demand, and more than four months have elapsed between the service of the demand and the presentation of the petition, the petition must explain the reasons for the delay.

(3) The petition must also contain a blank box for the court to complete with the details of the venue for hearing the petition.

NOTES

Commencement: 6 April 2017.
This rule derived from the Insolvency Rules 1986, SI 1986/1925, Sch 4, Fms 6.7–6.10.

[6.467]
10.8 Identification of debtor

(1) The petition must state the following matters about the debtor, so far as they are within the petitioner's knowledge—

(a) the debtor's identification details;
(b) the occupation (if any) of the debtor;
(c) the name or names in which the debtor carries on business, if other than the name of the debtor, and whether, in the case of any business of a specified nature, the debtor carries it on alone or with others;
(d) the nature of the debtor's business, and the address or addresses at which it is carried on;
(e) any name or names, other than the name of the debtor, in which the debtor has carried on business at or after the time when the debt was incurred, and whether the debtor has done so alone or with others;
(f) any address or addresses at which the debtor has resided or carried on business at or after that time, and the nature of that business; and
(g) whether the centre of main interests or an establishment of the debtor (as defined in [Article 2(10) of the EU Regulation]) is in another member State.

(2) The particulars of the debtor given under this rule determine the title of the proceedings.

(3) If to the petitioner's knowledge the debtor has used any name other than the one specified under paragraph (1)(a), that fact must be stated in the petition.

NOTES

Commencement: 6 April 2017.

This rule derived from the Insolvency Rules 1986, SI 1986/1925, r 6.7.

Para (1): words in square brackets in sub-para (g) substituted by the Insolvency (England and Wales) and Insolvency (Scotland) (Miscellaneous and Consequential Amendments) Rules 2017, SI 2017/1115, rr 22, 27.

[6.468]

10.9 Identification of debt

(1) The petition must state for each debt in relation to which it is presented—
(a) the amount of the debt, the consideration for it (or, if there is no consideration, the way in which it arises) and the fact that it is owed to the petitioner;
(b) when the debt was incurred or became due;
(c) if the amount of the debt includes any charge by way of interest not previously notified to the debtor as a liability of the debtor's, the amount or rate of the charge (separately identified);
(d) if the amount of the debt includes any other charge accruing from time to time, the amount or rate of the charge (separately identified);
(e) the grounds on which any such a charge is claimed to form part of the debt, provided that the amount or rate must, in the case of a petition based on a statutory demand, be limited to that claimed in the demand;
(f) that the debt is unsecured (subject to section 269); and
(g) either—
  (i) that the debt is for a liquidated sum payable immediately, and the debtor appears to be unable to pay it, or
  (ii) that the debt is for a liquidated sum payable at some certain, future time (that time to be specified), and the debtor appears to have no reasonable prospect of being able to pay it.

(2) Where the debt is one for which, under section 268, a statutory demand must have been served on the debtor, the petition must—
(a) specify the date and manner of service of the statutory demand; and
(b) state that, to the best of the creditor's knowledge and belief—
  (i) the demand has been neither complied with nor set aside in accordance with these Rules, and
  (ii) that no application to set it aside is outstanding.

(3) If the case is within section 268(1)(b) (unsatisfied execution or process in respect of judgment debt, etc) the petition must state which court issued the execution or other process and give particulars of the return.

[(4) The court may decline to file the petition if not satisfied that the creditor has discharged the obligation imposed by rule 10.2.]

NOTES

Commencement: 6 April 2017.

This rule derived from the Insolvency Rules 1986, SI 1986/1925, r 6.8.

Para (4): added by the Insolvency (England and Wales) and Insolvency (Scotland) (Miscellaneous and Consequential Amendments) Rules 2017, SI 2017/1115, rr 2, 8.

[6.469]

10.10 Verification of petition

(1) The petition must be verified by a statement of truth.

(2) If the petition relates to debts to different creditors, the debt to each creditor must be separately verified.

(3) A statement of truth which is not contained in or endorsed upon the petition which it verifies must be sufficient to identify the petition and must contain—
(a) the name of the debtor;
(b) the name of the petitioner; and
(c) the court or hearing centre in which the petition is to be presented.

(4) The statement of truth must be authenticated and dated by or on behalf of the petitioner.

(5) Where the person authenticating the statement of truth is not the petitioner, or one of the petitioners, the statement of truth must state—

(a) the name and postal address of the authenticating person;

(b) the capacity in which, and the authority by which, that person authenticates the statement of truth; and

(c) the means of the authenticating person's knowledge of the matters verified.

NOTES

Commencement: 6 April 2017.

This rule derived from the Insolvency Rules 1986, SI 1986/1925, r 6.12.

[6.470]

10.11 Court in which petition is to be presented

(1) Where the proceedings are allocated to the London Insolvency District under rule 12.5(a)(i) to (iv) or (b), the creditor must present the petition to—

(a) the High Court where the debt is £50,000 or more; or

(b) the County Court at Central London where the debt is less than £50,000.

(2) Where the proceedings are allocated to the London Insolvency District under rule 12.5(a)(v), (c) or (d), the creditor must present the petition to the High Court.

(3) Where the debtor is resident in England and Wales and the proceedings are not allocated to the London Insolvency District, the creditor must present the petition to the debtor's own hearing centre.

(4) The debtor's own hearing centre is—

(a) where the debtor has carried on business in England and Wales within the six months immediately preceding the presentation of the petition, the hearing centre for the insolvency district where for the longest period during those six months—

(i) the debtor carried on business, or

(ii) the principal place of business was located, if business was carried on in more than one insolvency district; or

(b) where the debtor has not carried on business in England and Wales within the six months immediately preceding the presentation of the petition, the hearing centre for the insolvency district where the debtor resided for the longest period during those six months.

(5) If the debtor is not resident in England and Wales but was resident or carried on business in England and Wales within the six months immediately preceding the presentation of the petition and the proceedings are not allocated to the London Insolvency District, the petition may be presented either to the debtor's own hearing centre or to the High Court.

(6) Unless paragraph (2) applies, where to the petitioner's knowledge there is in force for the debtor an IVA under Part 8 of the Act, the petition must be presented to the court or hearing centre—

(a) to which the nominee's report under section 256 was submitted;

(b) to which an application has been made, where a nominee has made a report under section 256A(3); or

(c) as determined under paragraphs (1) to (5) in any other case.

(7) The petition must contain sufficient information to establish that it is presented in the appropriate court and, where the court is the County Court, the appropriate hearing centre.

NOTES

Commencement: 6 April 2017.

This rule derived from the Insolvency Rules 1986, SI 1986/1925, r 6.9A.

[6.471]

10.12 Procedure for presentation and filing of petition

(1) The petition must be filed with the court.

(2) A petition may not be filed unless—

(a) a receipt for the deposit payable to the official receiver is produced on presentation of the petition; or

(b) the Secretary of State has given notice to the court that the petitioner has made suitable alternative arrangements in accordance with an order made under section 415(3) for the payment of the deposit and that notice has not been revoked.

(3) A notice of alternative arrangements for the deposit may be revoked by a further notice filed with the court.

(4) The following copies of the petition must also be filed with the court with the petition—

(a) one for service on the debtor;

(b) one copy for the supervisor, if to the petitioner's knowledge there is in force for the debtor an IVA under Part 8 of the Act, and the petitioner is not the supervisor of the IVA; and

(c) one copy for the liquidator, if to the petitioner's knowledge there is a member State liquidator appointed in main proceedings in relation to the debtor.

(5) The date and time of filing the petition must be endorsed on the petition and on the copies.

(6) The court must fix a venue for hearing the petition, and this must also be endorsed on the petition and the copies.

(7) Each copy of the petition must have the seal of the court applied to it and must be delivered to the petitioner.

NOTES

Commencement: 6 April 2017.

This rule derived from the Insolvency Rules 1986, SI 1986/1925, r 6.10.

[6.472]

10.13 Application to Chief Land Registrar to register petition

(1) When the petition is filed, the court must as soon as reasonably practicable deliver to the Chief Land Registrar an application for registration of the petition in the register of pending actions.

(2) The application must contain—

(a) a statement that the court is applying for registration of a petition in bankruptcy proceedings as a pending action with the Chief Land Registrar under section 5 of the Land Charges Act 1972;

(b) the debtor's name;

(c) the debtor's gender, if known;

(d) details of the debtor's trade, profession or occupation, including any trading name and, in the case of a partnership, the name and gender, if known, of each of the other partners;

(e) the postal address for each known place of residence of the debtor, including the debtor's business address where the court considers it to be appropriate for the purpose of the notice;

(f) the relevant key number allocated by the Land Charges Department;

(g) the name of the court (and hearing centre if applicable);

(h) the number and date of the petition; and

(i) the name and postal address of the petitioner.

(3) The application must be sealed and dated by the court.

(4) A separate application must be completed for each debtor and for any alternative name by which the debtor has been or is known (other than any trading name).

NOTES

Commencement: 6 April 2017.

This rule derived from the Insolvency Rules 1986, SI 1986/1925, r 6.13.

[6.473]

10.14 Service of petition and delivery of copies

(1) The petitioner must serve the petition on the debtor in accordance with Schedule 4 (Service of documents).

(2) If to the petitioner's knowledge there is in force for the debtor an IVA , and the petitioner is not the supervisor of the IVA, a copy of the petition must be delivered by the petitioner to the supervisor.

(3) If to the petitioner's knowledge, there is a member State liquidator appointed in main proceedings in relation to the debtor, a copy of the petition must be delivered by the petitioner to the member State liquidator.

NOTES

Commencement: 6 April 2017.

This rule derived from the Insolvency Rules 1986, SI 1986/1925, r 6.14.

[6.474]

10.15 Death of debtor before service

If the debtor dies before service of the petition, the court may order service to be effected on the debtor's personal representative, or on such other person as it thinks just.

NOTES

Commencement: 6 April 2017.

This rule derived from the Insolvency Rules 1986, SI 1986/1925, r 6.16.

[6.475]

10.16 Amendment of petition

The petition may be amended at any time after presentation with the court's permission.

NOTES

Commencement: 6 April 2017.

This rule derived from the Insolvency Rules 1986, SI 1986/1925, r 6.22.

[6.476]

10.17 Security for costs

(1) This rule applies where the debt is a liquidated sum payable at some future time, it being claimed in the petition that the debtor appears to have no reasonable prospect of being able to pay it.

(2) The debtor may apply for an order that the petitioning creditor give security for the debtor's costs.

(3) The nature and amount of the security to be ordered is in the court's discretion.

(4) If an order for security is made then the petition may not be heard until the whole amount of the security has been given.

NOTES

Commencement: 6 April 2017.

This rule derived from the Insolvency Rules 1986, SI 1986/1925, r 6.17.

[6.477]

10.18 Debtor's notice of opposition to petition

(1) A debtor who intends to oppose the making of a bankruptcy order must not less than five business days before the day fixed for the hearing—

(a) file a notice with the court; and

(b) deliver a copy of the notice to the petitioning creditor or the petitioner's solicitor.

(2) The notice must—

(a) identify the proceedings;

(b) state that the debtor intends to oppose the making of a bankruptcy order; and

(c) state the grounds on which the debtor opposes the making of the order.

NOTES

Commencement: 6 April 2017.

This rule derived from the Insolvency Rules 1986, SI 1986/1925, r 6.21.

[6.478]

10.19 Notice by persons intending to appear

(1) A creditor or a member State liquidator appointed in main proceedings in relation to the debtor who intends to appear on the hearing of the petition must deliver a notice of intention to appear to the petitioner.

(2) The notice must contain the following—

(a) the name and address of the person, and any telephone number and reference which may be required for communication with that creditor or with any other person (also to be specified in the notice) authorised to speak or act on the person's behalf;

(b) the date of the presentation of the bankruptcy petition and a statement that the notice relates to the matter of that petition;

(c) the date of the hearing of the petition;

(d) in the case of a creditor, the amount and nature of the debt due from the debtor to the creditor;

(e) whether the person intends to support or oppose the petition;

(f) where the person is represented by a solicitor or other agent, the name, postal address, telephone number and reference number (if any) of that person and details of that person's position with or relationship to the creditor or member State liquidator; and

(g) the name and postal address of the petitioner.

(3) The notice must be authenticated and dated by the person delivering it.

(4) The notice must be delivered to the petitioner or the petitioner's solicitor at the address shown in the court records.

(5) The notice must be delivered so as to reach the petitioner (or the petitioner's solicitor) not later than 4pm on the business day before that which is appointed for the hearing (or, where the hearing has been adjourned, for the adjourned hearing).

(6) A person who fails to comply with this rule may appear and be heard on the hearing of the petition only with the permission of the court.

NOTES

Commencement: 6 April 2017.

This rule derived from the Insolvency Rules 1986, SI 1986/1925, r 6.23.

[6.479]

10.20 List of appearances

(1) The petitioner must prepare for the court a list of the persons who have delivered a notice under rule 10.19 of their intention to appear.

(2) The list must contain—

(a) the date of the presentation of the bankruptcy petition;

(b) the date of the hearing of the petition;

(c) a statement that the persons listed have delivered notice that they intend to appear at the hearing of the petition;

(d) the name and address of each person who has delivered notice of intention to appear;

(e) in the case of creditors, the amount owed to each such creditor;

(f) the name and postal address of any solicitor for a person listed; and

(g) whether each person listed intends to support the petition, or to oppose it.

(3) On the day appointed for hearing the petition, a copy of the list must be handed to the court before the hearing commences.

(4) If the court gives a person permission to appear under rule 10.19(6) then the petitioner must add that person to the list with the same particulars.

NOTES

Commencement: 6 April 2017.

This rule derived from the Insolvency Rules 1986, SI 1986/1925, r 6.24.

[6.480]

10.21 Hearing of petition

(1) The petition may not be heard until at least 14 days have elapsed since it was served on the debtor.

(2) However the court may, on such terms as it thinks just, hear the petition at an earlier date, if—

- (a) it appears that the debtor has absconded;
- (b) the court is satisfied that it is a proper case for an expedited hearing; or
- (c) the debtor consents to a hearing within the 14 days.

(3) The following persons may appear and be heard—

- (a) the petitioning creditor;
- (b) the debtor;
- (c) the supervisor of any IVA in force for the debtor; and
- (d) any person who has delivered a notice under rule 10.19.

NOTES

Commencement: 6 April 2017.

This rule derived from the Insolvency Rules 1986, SI 1986/1925, r 6.18.

[6.481]

10.22 Postponement of hearing

(1) The petitioner may, if the petition has not been served, apply to the court to appoint another day for the hearing.

(2) The application must state the reasons why the petition has not been served.

(3) Costs of the application may not be allowed in the proceedings except by order of the court.

(4) If the court appoints another day for the hearing, the petitioner must as soon as reasonably practicable deliver notice of that day to any person who delivered notice of intention to appear under rule 10.19 and to any person who must be served with a copy of the petition under rule 10.14.

NOTES

Commencement: 6 April 2017.

This rule derived from the Insolvency Rules 1986, SI 1986/1925, r 6.28.

[6.482]

10.23 Adjournment of the hearing

(1) This rule applies if the court adjourns the hearing of a bankruptcy petition.

(2) The order of adjournment must identify the proceedings and contain—

- (a) the date of the presentation of the petition;
- (b) the order that the further hearing of the petition be adjourned to the venue specified in the order;
- (c) the venue of the adjourned hearing; and
- (d) the date of the order.

(3) Unless the court otherwise directs, the petitioner must as soon as reasonably practicable deliver a notice of the order of adjournment to—

- (a) the debtor; and
- (b) any person who has delivered a notice of intention to appear under rule 10.19 but was not present at the hearing.

(4) The notice of the order of adjournment must identify the proceedings and—

- (a) contain—
  - (i) the date of the presentation of the petition,
  - (ii) the date the order of adjournment was made, and
  - (iii) the venue for the adjourned hearing; and
- (b) be authenticated and dated by the petitioner or the petitioner's solicitor.

NOTES

Commencement: 6 April 2017.

This rule derived from the Insolvency Rules 1986, SI 1986/1925, r 6.29.

[6.483]

10.24 Decision on the hearing

(1) On the hearing of the petition, the court may make a bankruptcy order if satisfied that the statements in the petition are true, and that the debt on which it is founded has not been paid, or secured or compounded.

(2) If the petition is brought in relation to a judgment debt, or a sum ordered by any court to be paid, the court may stay or dismiss the petition on the ground that an appeal is pending from the judgment or order, or that execution of the judgment has been stayed.

(3) An order dismissing or giving permission to withdraw a bankruptcy petition must contain—

- (a) identification details for the proceedings;

Part 6 Insolvency Rules

(b) the date of the presentation of the bankruptcy petition;
(c) the name, postal address and description of the applicant;
(d) a statement that the petition has been heard;
(e) the order that the petition be dismissed or that, with the permission of the court, the petition is withdrawn;
(f) details of any further terms of the order;
(g) the date and reference number of the registration of the petition as a pending action with the Chief Land Registrar;
(h) an order that the entry relating to the petition in the register of pending actions be vacated on the debtor's application; and
(i) the date of the order.

(4) The order must notify the debtor that it is the debtor's responsibility and in the debtor's interest to ensure that the registration of the petition as an entry, both with the Chief Land Registrar and in the title register of any property owned by the debtor, is cancelled.

(5) In the case of a petition preceded by a statutory demand, the petition will not be dismissed on the ground only that the amount of the debt was over-stated in the demand, unless the debtor, within the time allowed for complying with the demand, delivered a notice to the creditor disputing the validity of the demand on that ground; but, in the absence of such notice, the debtor is deemed to have complied with the demand if the correct amount is paid within the time allowed.

NOTES

Commencement: 6 April 2017.
This rule derived from the Insolvency Rules 1986, SI 1986/1925, r 6.25.

[6.484]
10.25 Vacating registration on withdrawal of petition

If the petition is withdrawn by permission of the court, the court must deliver to the debtor two sealed copies of the order (one for the Chief Land Registrar).

NOTES

Commencement: 6 April 2017.
This rule derived from the Insolvency Rules 1986, SI 1986/1925, r 6.27.

[6.485]
10.26 Non-appearance of petitioning creditor

A petitioning creditor who fails to appear on the hearing of the petition may not present a petition either alone or jointly with any other person against the same debtor in respect of the same debt without the permission of the court to which the previous petition was presented.

NOTES

Commencement: 6 April 2017.
This rule derived from the Insolvency Rules 1986, SI 1986/1925, r 6.26.

[6.486]
10.27 Substitution of petitioner

(1) This rule applies where the petitioner—
(a) is subsequently found not to have been entitled to present the petition;
(b) consents to withdraw the petition or to allow it to be dismissed;
(c) consents to an adjournment;
(d) fails to appear in support of the petition when it is called on in court on the day originally fixed for the hearing, or on a day to which it is adjourned; or
(e) appears, but does not apply for an order in the terms of the petition.

(2) The court may, on such terms as it thinks just, substitute as petitioner a person who—
(a) has delivered a notice under rule 10.19 of intention to appear at the hearing;
(b) is willing to prosecute the petition; and
(c) was, in the case of a creditor, at the date on which the petition was presented, in such a position in relation to the debtor as would have enabled the creditor on that date to present a bankruptcy petition in relation to a debt or debts owed to that creditor by the debtor, paragraphs (a) to (d) of section 267(2) being satisfied in relation to that debt or those debts.

NOTES

Commencement: 6 April 2017.
This rule derived from the Insolvency Rules 1986, SI 1986/1925, r 6.30.

[6.487]
10.28 Order for substitution of petitioner

The order for substitution of a petitioner must contain—
(a) identification details for the proceedings;
(b) the date of the hearing of the petition;
(c) the name of the original petitioner;
(d) the name of the person who is willing to prosecute the petition ("the named person");
(e) a statement that the named person meets the requirements of rule 10.27(2);

(f) details of the statutory demand or return of the enforcement officer or enforcement agent;
(g) the following orders—
  (i) that upon payment by the named person of the statutory deposit to the court the statutory deposit paid by the original petitioner to the court be repaid to the original petitioner by the official receiver,
  (ii) that the named person be substituted as petitioner in place of the original petitioner and that the relevant person may amend the petition accordingly,
  (iii) that the named person must within five business days from the date of the order file a copy of the amended petition together with a statement of truth verifying the amended petition,
  (iv) that at least 14 days before the date of the adjourned hearing of the petition the named person must serve upon the debtor a sealed copy of the amended petition,
  (v) that the hearing of the amended petition be adjourned to the venue specified in the order, and
  (vi) that the question of the costs of the original petitioner and of the statutory deposit (if appropriate) be reserved until the final determination of the amended petition;
(h) the venue of the adjourned hearing; and
(i) the date of the order.

NOTES

Commencement: 6 April 2017.
This rule derived from the Insolvency Rules 1986, SI 1986/1925, Sch 4, Fm 6.24A.

[6.488]

10.29 Change of carriage of petition

(1) On the hearing of the petition, a person who has delivered notice under rule 10.19 of intention to appear at the hearing, may apply to the court for an order giving that person carriage of the petition in place of the petitioner, but without requiring any amendment of the petition.

(2) The court may, on such terms as it thinks just, make a change of carriage order if satisfied that—
(a) the applicant is an unpaid and unsecured creditor of the debtor or a member State liquidator appointed in main proceedings in relation to the debtor; and
(b) the petitioner either—
  (i) intends by any means to secure the postponement, adjournment, dismissal or withdrawal of the petition, or
  (ii) does not intend to prosecute the petition, either diligently or at all.

(3) The court must not make such an order if satisfied that the petitioner's debt has been paid, secured or compounded by means of—
(a) a disposition of property made by some person other than the debtor; or
(b) a disposition of the debtor's own property made with the approval of, or ratified by, the court.

(4) A change of carriage order may be made whether or not the petitioner appears at the hearing.

(5) If the order is made, the person given the carriage of the petition is entitled to rely on all evidence previously provided in the proceedings.

(6) The change of carriage order will contain—
(a) identification details for the proceedings;
(b) the date of the hearing of the petition;
(c) the name of the person who is willing to be given carriage of the petition ("the relevant person");
(d) a statement that the relevant person is a creditor of the debtor or a member State liquidator appointed in main proceedings in relation to the debtor;
(e) the name of the original petitioner;
(f) a statement that the relevant person has applied for an order under this rule to have carriage of the petition in place of the original petitioner;
(g) the order that the relevant person must within a period which is specified in the order serve upon the debtor and the original petitioner a sealed copy of the order;
(h) the order that the further hearing of the petition be adjourned to the venue specified in the order;
(i) the venue of the adjourned hearing;
(j) the order that the question of the costs of the original petitioner be reserved until the final determination of the petition; and
(k) the date of the order.

NOTES

Commencement: 6 April 2017.
This rule derived from the Insolvency Rules 1986, SI 1986/1925, r 6.31.

[6.489]

10.31 Contents of bankruptcy order

(1) The bankruptcy order must identify the proceedings and contain—
(a) the name and address of the petitioner;
(b) the date of the presentation of the petition;
(c) the details of the debtor as provided under rule 10.8(1)(a) to (g);
(d) the order that the person named is made bankrupt;
(e) the order either—

(i) that the court being satisfied that the [EU Regulation] applies declares that the proceedings are main, secondary or territorial proceedings (as the case may be) as defined in Article 3 of the [EU Regulation], or
(ii) that the court is satisfied that the [EU Regulation] does not apply in relation to the proceedings;
(f) a statement that the official receiver (or one of them) attached to the court is by virtue of the order trustee of the bankrupt's estate;
(g) a notice of the bankrupt's duties in relation to the official receiver under section 291, and in particular to the bankrupt's duty to give the official receiver such inventory of the bankrupt's estate and such other information, and to attend on the official receiver at such times, as the official receiver may reasonably require; and
(h) the date and time of the order.

(2) If the petitioner is represented by a solicitor the order is to be endorsed with the name, address, telephone number and reference of the solicitor.

(3) Subject to section 346 (effect of bankruptcy on enforcement procedures), the order may include provision staying any action or proceeding against the bankrupt.

NOTES

Commencement: 6 April 2017.

This rule derived from the Insolvency Rules 1986, SI 1986/1925, r 6.33.

Para (1): words in square brackets substituted by the Insolvency (England and Wales) and Insolvency (Scotland) (Miscellaneous and Consequential Amendments) Rules 2017, SI 2017/1115, rr 22, 23(8).

[6.490]

10.32 Delivery and notice of the order

(1) As soon as reasonably practicable after making a bankruptcy order the court must deliver two sealed copies of the order to the official receiver.

(2) The official receiver must as soon as reasonably practicable deliver a sealed copy of the order to the bankrupt.

(3) On receipt of the sealed copies of the bankruptcy order the official receiver—
(a) must as soon as reasonably practicable—
(i) deliver an application for registration of the order containing the particulars specified in rule 10.33 to the Chief Land Registrar, for registration in the register of writs and orders affecting land, and
(ii) cause notice of the order to be gazetted;
(b) must cause an entry to be made in the individual insolvency register in accordance with rule 11.16; and
(c) may cause notice of the order to be advertised in such other manner as the official receiver thinks fit.

(4) The notice to be gazetted and any notice to be advertised must state—
(a) that a bankruptcy order has been made against the bankrupt;
(b) the date and time of the making of the bankruptcy order;
(c) the name and address of the petitioning creditor; and
(d) the date of presentation of the petition.

(5) The court may, on the application of the bankrupt or a creditor, order the official receiver to suspend action under paragraph (3) and rule 11.16, pending a further order of the court.

(6) An application for such action to be suspended must be supported by a witness statement stating the grounds on which it is made.

(7) Where an order to suspend such action is made, the applicant must deliver a copy of the order to the official receiver as soon as reasonably practicable.

NOTES

Commencement: 6 April 2017.

This rule derived from the Insolvency Rules 1986, SI 1986/1925, r 6.34.

[6.491]

10.33 Application to Chief Land Registrar to register bankruptcy order

(1) The application for registration of the bankruptcy order delivered to the Chief Land Registrar under rule 10.32 must contain—
(a) identification details for the proceedings;
(b) a statement that the official receiver is applying for registration of a bankruptcy order in the register of writs and orders under section 6 of the Land Charges Act 1972;
(c) the name of the bankrupt;
(d) the bankrupt's gender, if known;
(e) details of the bankrupt's trade, profession or occupation, including any trading name and, in the case of a partnership, the name and gender, if known, of each of the other partners;
(f) the postal address for each known place of residence of the bankrupt, including the bankrupt's business address where the official receiver considers it to be appropriate for the purpose of the notice;
(g) the relevant key number allocated by the Chief Land Registrar;
(h) the date of the bankruptcy order; and

(i) the name and postal address of the petitioner.

(2) The application must be authenticated and dated by the official receiver.

(3) A separate application must be completed for each address and for any alternative name by which the bankrupt has been or is known (other than any trading name).

NOTES

Commencement: 6 April 2017.

This rule derived from the Insolvency Rules 1986, SI 1986/1925, Sch 4, Fm 6.26.

CHAPTER 3 DEBTORS' BANKRUPTCY APPLICATIONS

[Note: a document required by the Act or these Rules must also contain the standard contents set out in Part 1.]

[6.492]

10.34 Preliminary

This Chapter relates to a debtor's bankruptcy application and the making of a bankruptcy order on the application of a debtor.

NOTES

Commencement: 6 April 2017.

This rule derived from the Insolvency Rules 1986, SI 1986/1925, r 6.37.

[6.493]

10.35 Bankruptcy application for a bankruptcy order

(1) In the bankruptcy application the debtor must—

(a) state that the debtor is unable to pay the debtor's debts;

(b) request that the adjudicator make a bankruptcy order against the debtor;

(c) state that the debtor is not aware of any pending bankruptcy petition;

(d) state whether a bankruptcy order has been made in respect of any of the debts which are the subject of the bankruptcy application;

(e) state whether the debtor has taken debt advice before completing the bankruptcy application;

(f) consent to verification checks being made by the adjudicator;

(g) provide the information set out in Schedule 7;

(h) provide the additional information set out in Schedule 8;

(i) state that the information provided in accordance with this rule is accurate and up-to-date at the date of the bankruptcy application; and

(j) state that the prescribed fee and deposit have been paid in full.

(2) The bankruptcy application must be authenticated by the debtor.

NOTES

Commencement: 6 April 2017.

This rule derived from the Insolvency Rules 1986, SI 1986/1925, r 6.38, Schs 2A, 2B.

[6.494]

10.36 Procedure for making a bankruptcy application and communication with the adjudicator

(1) The bankruptcy application must be completed in accordance with these Rules in electronic form and delivered to the adjudicator by electronic means unless otherwise agreed with the adjudicator in accordance with paragraph (4).

(2) For the purposes of rule 10.35(1)(i) the date of the bankruptcy application is the date that the debtor submits the bankruptcy application to the adjudicator under these Rules.

(3) A bankruptcy application is made when its receipt has been acknowledged by the adjudicator by electronic or other means.

(4) In the event of any malfunction or error in the operation of the electronic form or means of delivery, the adjudicator must—

(a) agree that debtors may, for a specified period, complete and deliver bankruptcy applications in another format; and

(b) provide an alternative means of delivery for the bankruptcy application and details of any terms or conditions to which their use is subject.

(5) If a bankruptcy application is completed in hard copy, it may not be delivered by fax.

(6) Where the debtor has given an electronic address in the bankruptcy application, the adjudicator must so far as reasonably practicable communicate with the debtor by electronic means.

(7) Unless the contrary is shown, a document (other than a bankruptcy application) is to be treated as delivered by electronic means to an electronic address where the sender can produce a copy of the electronic communication which—

(a) contains the document; and

(b) shows the time and date the communication was sent and the electronic address to which it was sent.

(8) Unless the contrary is shown, a document (other than a bankruptcy application) is to be treated as delivered to the electronic address to which it is sent at 9.00am on the next business day after it was sent.

Part 6 Insolvency Rules

(9) Rule 1.45 does not apply to electronic delivery of documents between a debtor and the adjudicator.

NOTES

Commencement: 6 April 2017.

This rule derived from the Insolvency Rules 1986, SI 1986/1925, r 6.39.

[6.495]

10.37 Application to the Chief Land Registrar to register a bankruptcy application

(1) When a bankruptcy application is made, the adjudicator must as soon as reasonably practicable deliver to the Chief Land Registrar an application for registration of the bankruptcy application, in the register of pending actions.

(2) The application must contain—

- (a) a statement that the adjudicator is applying for registration of a bankruptcy application as a pending action under section 5 of the Land Charges Act 1972;
- (b) the debtor's name and any alternative name by which the debtor has been or is known;
- (c) the debtor's date of birth;
- (d) the debtor's gender, if known;
- (e) the debtor's occupation, including any trading name;
- (f) the postal address for each known place of residence of the debtor;
- (g) the debtor's business address where the adjudicator considers it appropriate for the purpose of the application;
- (h) the relevant key number allocated by the Chief Land Registrar;
- (i) the reference allocated to the bankruptcy application; and
- (j) the date of the bankruptcy application.

(3) The application must be authenticated and dated by the adjudicator.

NOTES

Commencement: 6 April 2017.

This rule derived from the Insolvency Rules 1986, SI 1986/1925, r 6.40.

[6.496]

10.38 Verification checks

For the purpose of determining whether the adjudicator can make a bankruptcy order, verification checks may be made in, or with, one or more of the following—

- (a) the electoral registers for such districts in England and Wales as the adjudicator considers appropriate to determine the identity and residence of the debtor;
- (b) the individual insolvency register;
- (c) the official receiver; or
- (d) a credit reference agency.

NOTES

Commencement: 6 April 2017.

This rule derived from the Insolvency Rules 1986, SI 1986/1925, r 6.41.

[6.497]

10.39 Determination of the bankruptcy application

(1) The adjudicator must determine whether to make a bankruptcy order within the determination period referred to in rule 10.40.

(2) In reaching a determination, the adjudicator must have regard to whether the requirements of section 263K of the Act are met.

(3) During the determination period the adjudicator may request such further information from the debtor as the adjudicator considers is necessary in order to make the determination, such information to be provided in writing or at the request of the adjudicator, to be provided orally.

(4) Subject to paragraph (5), the adjudicator must make a determination from the information provided under rule 10.35(1)(g), any further information provided under paragraph (3) and from the verification checks.

(5) Before determining that the requirements of section 263K are not met, the adjudicator must have regard to the additional information provided under rule 10.35(1)(h).

NOTES

Commencement: 6 April 2017.

This rule derived from the Insolvency Rules 1986, SI 1986/1925, r 6.42.

[6.498]

10.40 The determination period

(1) The determination period is 28 days from the date the bankruptcy application is made.

(2) Where the adjudicator requests further information from the debtor more than 14 days after the date the bankruptcy application is made, the determination period is extended by 14 days.

(3) A failure to make a determination within the determination period is a refusal.

NOTES

Commencement: 6 April 2017.

This rule derived from the Insolvency Rules 1986, SI 1986/1925, r 6.43.

[6.499]

10.41 Settlement and contents of bankruptcy order

(1) The bankruptcy order must be settled by the adjudicator.

(2) The bankruptcy order must contain—

(a) the information set out in Part 1 of Schedule 7;

(b) the date of delivery of the bankruptcy application on which the order is made;

(c) the order that upon reading the application it is ordered that person named be made bankrupt;

(d) the order either—

(i) that the adjudicator being satisfied that the [EU Regulation] applies declares that the proceedings are main, secondary or territorial proceedings (as the case may be) as defined in Article 3 of the [EU Regulation], or

(ii) that the adjudicator is satisfied that the [EU Regulation] does not apply in relation to the proceedings;

(e) a statement that the official receiver (or one of them) attached to the court is, by virtue of the order, trustee of the bankrupt's estate; and

(f) a notice of the bankrupt's duties in relation to the official receiver under section 291(4) (duties of bankrupt in relation to the official receiver), and in particular to the bankrupt's duty to give the official receiver such inventory of the bankrupt's estate and such other information, and to attend on the official receiver at such times, as the official receiver may reasonably require.

NOTES

Commencement: 6 April 2017.

This rule derived from the Insolvency Rules 1986, SI 1986/1925, r 6.44.

Para (2): words in square brackets substituted by the Insolvency (England and Wales) and Insolvency (Scotland) (Miscellaneous and Consequential Amendments) Rules 2017, SI 2017/1115, rr 22, 23(9).

[6.500]

10.42 Refusal to make a bankruptcy order and contents of notice of refusal

(1) Where the adjudicator determines that the requirements of section 263K are not met, the adjudicator must refuse to make a bankruptcy order.

(2) The adjudicator must deliver notice of the refusal to make a bankruptcy order to the debtor as soon as reasonably practicable after the refusal to make the bankruptcy order under paragraph (1) or under rule 10.40(3).

(3) The notice of refusal must state—

(a) the reason or reasons for the refusal to make a bankruptcy order;

(b) that the debtor may request that the adjudicator review the decision to refuse to make a bankruptcy order within 14 days from the date of delivery of the notice of refusal;

(c) that where a review is requested it will be a review of the information that was available to the adjudicator at the date when the adjudicator refused to make a bankruptcy order;

(d) that following a review, the adjudicator must either—

(i) confirm the refusal to make a bankruptcy order; or

(ii) make a bankruptcy order against the debtor; and

(e) where the adjudicator confirms the refusal following a review, that the debtor may appeal to the court against the decision within 28 days from the date of delivery of the notice of confirmation of the refusal.

NOTES

Commencement: 6 April 2017.

This rule derived from the Insolvency Rules 1986, SI 1986/1925, r 6.45.

[6.501]

10.43 Review of refusal to make a bankruptcy order

(1) The debtor may request the adjudicator to review the decision to refuse to make a bankruptcy order within 14 days from the date of delivery of the notice of refusal.

(2) The debtor must give reasons for requesting a review but the request may not include additional information that was not available to the adjudicator when the determination was made.

(3) Where the adjudicator makes a bankruptcy order following a review, the bankruptcy order must be settled by the adjudicator in accordance with rule 10.41.

(4) Where the adjudicator confirms the refusal to make a bankruptcy order, the adjudicator must deliver notice to the debtor as soon as reasonably practicable.

(5) The notice will state—

(a) the reason or reasons for confirming the refusal to make the bankruptcy order; and

(b) that the debtor may appeal to the court against the decision within 28 days from the date of delivery of the confirmation of the notice of refusal.

NOTES

Commencement: 6 April 2017.

This rule derived from the Insolvency Rules 1986, SI 1986/1925, r 6.46.

[6.502]

10.44 Appeal to the court following a review of refusal to make a bankruptcy order

(1) Following a decision by the adjudicator to confirm the refusal to make a bankruptcy order, a debtor may appeal the decision to the court.

(2) An appeal under this rule must be made within 28 days from the date of delivery of the confirmation of the notice of refusal.

(3) The appeal must set out the grounds for the appeal.

(4) The court must either—
 (a) dismiss the application; or
 (b) make a bankruptcy order against the debtor.

(5) The bankruptcy order must contain—
 (a) the information set out in Part 1 of Schedule 7;
 (b) the date of delivery of the bankruptcy application on which the order is made;
 (c) the date and time of the making of the order; and
 (d) a statement that the order has been made following an appeal to the court under this rule.

(6) The adjudicator is not personally liable for costs incurred by any person in respect of an application under this rule.

(7) As soon as reasonably practicable after the making of the bankruptcy order the court must deliver sealed copies of the order to the debtor and the official receiver.

NOTES

Commencement: 6 April 2017.

This rule derived from the Insolvency Rules 1986, SI 1986/1925, r 6.47.

[6.503]

10.45 Action to follow making of order

(1) As soon as reasonably practicable following the making of the bankruptcy order the adjudicator must deliver copies of the bankruptcy order to the debtor and the official receiver.

(2) On the application of the bankrupt to the official receiver, the official receiver must deliver to the bankrupt a hard copy of the bankruptcy order.

(3) Subject to paragraph (5), on receipt of the bankruptcy order, the official receiver—
 (a) must as soon as reasonably practicable—
  (i) deliver an application to the Chief Land Registrar for registration of the bankruptcy order in the register of writs and orders affecting land, and
  (ii) must cause notice of the bankruptcy order to be gazetted;
 (b) may cause notice of the bankruptcy order to be advertised in such other manner as the official receiver thinks fit; and
 (c) must cause an entry to be made in the individual insolvency register in accordance with rule 11.16.

(4) The notice to be gazetted under paragraph (3)(a)(ii) and any notice to be advertised under paragraph (3)(b) must state—
 (a) that a bankruptcy order has been made against the bankrupt;
 (b) the date of the bankruptcy order;
 (c) that the bankruptcy order was made on the debtor's own bankruptcy application; and
 (d) the date of delivery of the bankruptcy application.

(5) The court may, on the application of the bankrupt or a creditor, order the official receiver to suspend action under paragraph (3), pending a further order of the court.

(6) An application for such action to be suspended must be supported by a witness statement stating the grounds on which it is made.

(7) Where an order is made to suspend such action, the applicant must deliver a copy of it to the official receiver as soon as reasonably practicable.

NOTES

Commencement: 6 April 2017.

This rule derived from the Insolvency Rules 1986, SI 1986/1925, r 6.48.

[6.504]

10.46 Application to the Chief Land Registrar

(1) The application to the Chief Land Registrar for registration of the bankruptcy order under rule 10.45 must contain—
 (a) a statement that the official receiver is applying for registration of a bankruptcy order made by the adjudicator in the register of writs and orders under section 6 of the Land Charges Act 1972;
 (b) the bankrupt's name and any alternative names by which the bankrupt has been or is known;
 (c) the bankrupt's date of birth;

(d) the bankrupt's gender, if known;
(e) the bankrupt's occupation including any trading name;
(f) the postal address for each known place of residence of the bankrupt;
(g) the bankrupt's business address where the official receiver considers it appropriate for the purpose of the application;
(h) the relevant key number allocated by the Chief Land Registrar;
(i) the reference allocated to the bankruptcy order; and
(j) the date of the bankruptcy order.

(2) The application must be authenticated and dated by the official receiver.

NOTES

Commencement: 6 April 2017.
This rule derived from the Insolvency Rules 1986, SI 1986/1925, r 6.49.

[6.505]
10.47 The bankruptcy file

(1) On receipt of a bankruptcy application, the adjudicator must open a file on which the adjudicator must place the bankruptcy application and any documents which are filed with the adjudicator under this Chapter.

(2) As soon as reasonably practicable following the making of the bankruptcy order the adjudicator must deliver the bankruptcy file to the official receiver.

(3) The official receiver must place on the bankruptcy file—
(a) any documents delivered to the official receiver by the court; and
(b) any notices delivered to the official receiver under these Rules.

(4) The following persons may inspect the bankruptcy file—
(a) the court;
(b) the trustee;
(c) the Secretary of State; and
(d) the bankrupt.

(5) Following the making of a bankruptcy order, a creditor may inspect the following information and documents filed on the bankruptcy file—
(a) the information provided to the adjudicator and set out in Schedule 9;
(b) the bankruptcy order; and
(c) directions and orders of the court, if any.

(6) The right to inspect the bankruptcy file may be exercised on that person's behalf by a person authorised to do so by that person.

(7) Any person who is not otherwise entitled to inspect the bankruptcy file (or any part of it) may do so if the court gives permission.

(8) The court may direct that the bankruptcy file, a document (or part of it) must not be made available under this rule without the permission of the court.

(9) An application for a direction to withhold the bankruptcy file, a document (or part of it) may be made by—
(a) the official receiver;
(b) the trustee; or
(c) any person appearing to the court to have an interest.

(10) An application under this rule for—
(a) permission to inspect the bankruptcy file; or
(b) a direction to withhold the bankruptcy file, a document (or part of it),
may be made without notice to any other party, but the court may direct that notice must be delivered to any person who would be affected by its decision.

NOTES

Commencement: 6 April 2017.
This rule derived from the Insolvency Rules 1986, SI 1986/1925, r 6.50.

[6.506]
10.48 Court to which applications are to be made

(1) An application to the court under this Chapter must be made to the debtor's own hearing centre where the debtor is resident in England and Wales.

(2) If the debtor is not resident in England and Wales but was resident or carried on business in England and Wales within the six months immediately preceding the making of the bankruptcy application, an application may be made to the debtor's own hearing centre or to the High Court.

(3) In this rule the debtor's own hearing centre is—
(a) where the debtor has carried on business in England and Wales within the six months immediately preceding the filing with the court of the application, the hearing centre for the insolvency district where for the longest period during those six months—
(i) the debtor carried on business, or
(ii) the principal place of business was located, if business was carried on in more than one insolvency district; or

Part 6 Insolvency Rules

(b) where the debtor has not carried on business in England and Wales within the six months immediately before making the application to the court, the hearing centre for the insolvency district where the debtor resided for the longest period during those six months.

(4) Where, for whatever reason, it is not possible for the application to be made to the debtor's own hearing centre, the applicant may, with a view to expediting the application, make the application—

(a) where paragraph (3)(a) applies, to—

(i) the hearing centre for the insolvency district in which the debtor resides, or

(ii) whichever court or hearing centre is specified in Schedule 6 as being the nearest full-time court or hearing centre in relation to—

(aa) the hearing centre in paragraph (3)(a), or

(bb) the hearing centre in paragraph (4)(a)(i); or

(b) where paragraph (3)(b) applies, whichever court or hearing centre is specified in Schedule 6 as being the nearest full-time court or hearing centre in relation to the court in that paragraph.

(5) The application must contain sufficient information to establish that it is brought in the appropriate court or hearing centre.

NOTES

Commencement: 6 April 2017.

This rule derived from the Insolvency Rules 1986, SI 1986/1925, r 6.50A.

CHAPTER 4 THE INTERIM RECEIVER

[Note: a document required by the Act or these Rules must also contain the standard contents set out in Part 1.]

[6.507]
10.49 Application for appointment of interim receiver (section 286)

(1) An application to the court under section 286 for the appointment of the official receiver or an insolvency practitioner as interim receiver may be made by—

(a) a creditor;

(b) the debtor;

(c) a temporary administrator; or

(d) a member State liquidator appointed in main proceedings (including in accordance with [Article 37 of the EU Regulation]).

(2) The application must be supported by a witness statement stating—

(a) the grounds on which it is proposed that the interim receiver should be appointed;

(b) whether or not the official receiver has been informed of the application and, if so, whether a copy of it has been delivered to that person;

(c) if the proposed interim receiver is an insolvency practitioner, that the insolvency practitioner has consented to act;

(d) whether to the applicant's knowledge there has been proposed or is in force an IVA; and

(e) the applicant's estimate of the value of the property or business in relation to which the interim receiver is to be appointed

[(f) a statement whether the proceedings will be main, secondary, territorial or non-EU proceedings with the reasons for so stating.]

(3) The applicant must deliver copies of the application and the witness statement to the proposed interim receiver and to the official receiver.

(4) If for any reason it is not practicable to deliver a copy of the application to the proposed interim receiver that person must be informed of the application in sufficient time to be able to be present at the hearing.

(5) The official receiver may attend the hearing of the application and make representations.

(6) If satisfied that sufficient grounds are shown for the appointment, the court may appoint an interim receiver on such terms as it thinks just.

NOTES

Commencement: 6 April 2017.

This rule derived from the Insolvency Rules 1986, SI 1986/1925, r 6.51.

Para (1): words in square brackets in sub-para (d) substituted for original words "Article 29 of the EC Regulation" by the Insolvency Amendment (EU 2015/848) Regulations 2017, SI 2017/702, regs 2, 3, Schedule, Pt 2, paras 32, 42(a), as from 26 June 2017, except in relation to proceedings opened before that date.

Para (2): sub-para (f) inserted by SI 2017/702, regs 2, 3, Schedule, Pt 2, paras 32, 42(b), as from 26 June 2017, except in relation to proceedings opened before that date.

[6.508]
10.50 Deposit

(1) An applicant for an order appointing the official receiver as interim receiver must, before the order is made, deposit with the official receiver, or otherwise secure to the official receiver's satisfaction, such sum as the court directs to cover the official receiver's remuneration and expenses.

(2) If the sum proves to be insufficient, the court may, on the application of the official receiver, order the applicant to deposit or secure an additional sum.

(3) If such additional sum is not deposited or secured within two business days after service of the order on the applicant the court may discharge the order appointing the official receiver as interim receiver.

(4) If a bankruptcy order is made after an interim receiver has been appointed, any money deposited under this rule must (unless it is required because the assets are insufficient to pay the remuneration and expenses of the interim receiver, or the deposit was made by the debtor out of the debtor's own property) be repaid to the person depositing it (or as that person may direct) out of the bankrupt's estate, in the prescribed order of priority.

NOTES

Commencement: 6 April 2017.

This rule derived from the Insolvency Rules 1986, SI 1986/1925, r 6.53.

[6.509]

10.51 Order of appointment

(1) The order appointing the interim receiver must contain—

(a) identification details for the proceedings;

(b) the name and title of the judge making the order;

(c) the name and postal address of the applicant;

(d) identification details for the debtor;

(e) the statement that the court is satisfied—

(i) that the debtor is unable to pay the debtor's debts, and

(ii) that the proceedings are main, secondary, territorial or [non-EU proceedings] (as the case may be);

(f) the order either that—

(i) upon the applicant depositing the sum specified in the order with the official receiver, the official receiver is appointed interim receiver of the property of the debtor, or

(ii) the person specified in the order is appointed interim receiver of the property of the debtor;

(g) identification and contact details for the interim receiver, where the interim receiver is not the official receiver;

(h) details of the nature, together with a short description, of the property of which the interim receiver is to take possession;

(i) details of the duties to be carried out by the interim receiver in relation to the debtor's affairs;

(j) a notice to the debtor stating that the debtor must give the interim receiver all the information about the debtor's property that the interim receiver may require in order to carry out the functions imposed on the interim receiver by the order; and

(k) the date of the order.

(2) The court must, as soon as reasonably practicable after the order is made, deliver two sealed copies of the order to the person appointed interim receiver.

(3) The interim receiver must as soon as reasonably practicable deliver a sealed copy of the order to the debtor.

NOTES

Commencement: 6 April 2017.

This rule derived from the Insolvency Rules 1986, SI 1986/1925, r 6.52, Sch 4, Fm 6.32.

Para (1): words in square brackets in sub-para (e) substituted by the Insolvency (England and Wales) and Insolvency (Scotland) (Miscellaneous and Consequential Amendments) Rules 2017, SI 2017/1115, rr 22, 30(24).

[6.510]

10.52 Security

(1) This rule applies where an insolvency practitioner is appointed as interim receiver under section 286.

(2) The cost of providing the security required under the Act must be paid in the first instance by the interim receiver.

(3) If a bankruptcy order is not made, the person so appointed is entitled to be reimbursed out of the property of the debtor, and the court may make an order on the debtor accordingly.

(4) If a bankruptcy order is made, the person so appointed is entitled to be reimbursed out of the bankrupt's estate in the prescribed order of priority.

(5) If the interim receiver fails to give or keep up the required security, the court may remove the interim receiver, and make such order as it thinks just as to costs.

(6) If an order is made under this rule removing the interim receiver, or discharging the order appointing the interim receiver, the court must give directions as to whether any, and if so what, steps should be taken for the appointment of another person as interim receiver.

NOTES

Commencement: 6 April 2017.

This rule derived from the Insolvency Rules 1986, SI 1986/1925, r 6.54.

[6.511]
10.53 Remuneration

(1) The remuneration of an interim receiver (other than the official receiver) must be fixed by the court from time to time on application of the interim receiver.

(2) In fixing the remuneration of the interim receiver, the court must take into account—

(a) the time properly given by the interim receiver and staff of the interim receiver in attending to the debtor's affairs;
(b) the complexity of the case;
(c) any respects in which, in connection with the debtor's affairs, there falls on the interim receiver any responsibility of an exceptional kind or degree;
(d) the effectiveness with which the interim receiver appears to be carrying out, or to have carried out, the duties of the interim receiver; and
(e) the value and nature of the property with which the interim receiver has to deal.

(3) Without prejudice to any order the court may make as to costs, the interim receiver's remuneration (whether the official receiver or another) must be paid to the interim receiver, and the amount of any expenses incurred by the interim receiver (including the remuneration and expenses of any special manager appointed under section 370) reimbursed—

(a) if a bankruptcy order is not made, out of the property of the debtor; and
(b) if a bankruptcy order is made, out of the bankrupt's estate in the prescribed order of priority; or
(c) in either case (the relevant funds being insufficient), out of any deposit under rule 10.50.

(4) Unless the court otherwise directs, if a bankruptcy order is not made, the interim receiver may retain out of the debtor's property such sums or property as are or may be required for meeting the remuneration and expenses of the interim receiver.

(5) Where a person other than the official receiver has been appointed interim receiver, and the official receiver has taken any steps for the purpose of obtaining a statement of affairs or has performed any other duty under these Rules, the interim receiver must pay the official receiver such sum (if any) as the court may direct.

NOTES

Commencement: 6 April 2017.
This rule derived from the Insolvency Rules 1986, SI 1986/1925, r 6.56.

[6.512]
10.54 Termination of appointment

(1) The appointment of the interim receiver may be terminated by the court on the application of the interim receiver, or a person specified in rule 10.49(1).

(2) If the interim receiver's appointment terminates, in consequence of the dismissal of the bankruptcy petition or otherwise, the court may give such directions as it thinks just relating to the accounts of the interim receiver's administration and any other matters which it thinks appropriate.

NOTES

Commencement: 6 April 2017.
This rule derived from the Insolvency Rules 1986, SI 1986/1925, r 6.57.

CHAPTER 5 DISCLOSURE OF THE BANKRUPT'S AFFAIRS

[Note: a document required by the Act or these Rules must also contain the standard contents set out in Part 1.]

Sub-division A: creditor's petition

[6.513]
10.55 Notice requiring statement of affairs (section 288)

(1) Where, under section 288, the official receiver requires a bankrupt to provide the official receiver with a statement of affairs, the official receiver must deliver a notice to the bankrupt.

(2) The notice must be headed "Notice requiring statement of affairs" and must—

(a) require the bankrupt to prepare and submit to the official receiver a statement of affairs;
(b) inform the bankrupt of the date by which the statement must be delivered; and
(c) state the effect of section 288(4) (penalty for non-compliance) and section 291 (duty to co-operate).

(3) The official receiver must deliver instructions for the preparation of the statement of affairs with the notice.

NOTES

Commencement: 6 April 2017.
This rule derived from the Insolvency Rules 1986, SI 1986/1925, r 6.58.

[6.514]
10.56 Statement of affairs

(1) The statement of affairs must contain—

(a) identification details for the proceedings;
(b) identification details for the bankrupt;

(c) the date of the bankruptcy order;
(d) a list of the bankrupt's secured creditors giving in relation to each—
 (i) the name and postal address,
 (ii) the amount owed to the creditor, and
 (iii) particulars of the property of the bankrupt which is claimed by the creditor to clear or reduce the creditor's debt and the value of that property;
(e) a list of unsecured creditors giving in relation to each—
 (i) the name and postal address of the creditor,
 (ii) the amount the creditor claims the bankrupt owes to that creditor, and
 (iii) the amount the bankrupt thinks is owed by the bankrupt to that creditor;
(f) a list of the bankrupt's total assets (which must include anything not previously mentioned in the statement of affairs which may be of value) divided into the following categories and giving the value of each asset listed—
 (i) cash at the bank or building society,
 (ii) household furniture and belongings,
 (iii) life policies,
 (iv) money owed to the bankrupt,
 (v) stock in trade,
 (vi) motor vehicles, and
 (vii) other property; and
(g) the total value of the assets listed under paragraph (f).

(2) The bankrupt must authenticate and date each page of the statement of affairs.

(3) The statement of affairs must be verified by a statement of truth and delivered to the official receiver, together with one copy.

(4) The official receiver must file the verified statement with the court.

NOTES

Commencement: 6 April 2017.
This rule derived from the Insolvency Rules 1986, SI 1986/1925, rr 6.59, 6.60, Sch 4, Fm 6.33A.

[6.515]
10.57 Limited disclosure

Where the official receiver thinks that disclosure of the whole or part of the statement of affairs would be likely to prejudice the conduct of the bankruptcy or might reasonably be expected to lead to violence against any person, the official receiver may apply to the court for an order that the statement of affairs or any specified part of it either—
(a) must not be filed with the court; or
(b) must be filed separately and not open to inspection otherwise than with permission of the court.

NOTES

Commencement: 6 April 2017.
This rule derived from the Insolvency Rules 1986, SI 1986/1925, r 6.61.

[6.516]
10.58 Requirement to submit statement of affairs and extension of time (section 288(3))

(1) The official receiver may exercise the power in section 288(3) to require the bankrupt to submit a statement of affairs under section 288(3) and to grant an extension of time, either on the official receiver's own initiative, or at the bankrupt's request.

(2) A bankrupt required to submit a statement of affairs under paragraph (1) may apply to the court for a release or extension of time, if the official receiver has refused to release the bankrupt from that requirement or grant an extension.

(3) On receipt of an application, the court may, if it is satisfied that no sufficient cause is shown for it, dismiss it without giving notice to any party other than the applicant.

(4) Unless the application is dismissed, the court must fix a venue for it to be heard.

(5) The applicant must, at least 14 days before any hearing, deliver to the official receiver a notice stating the venue with a copy of the application and any evidence on which the applicant intends to rely.

(6) The official receiver may do either or both of the following—
(a) file a report of any matters which the official receiver thinks ought to be drawn to the court's attention; or
(b) appear and be heard on the application.

(7) If such a report is filed, the official receiver must deliver a copy of it to the bankrupt not later than five business days before the hearing.

(8) The court must deliver sealed copies of any order made on the application to the bankrupt and the official receiver.

(9) The bankrupt must pay the bankrupt's costs of the application in any event and, unless and to the extent the court orders otherwise, no allowance in respect of them will be made out of the bankrupt's estate.

NOTES

Commencement: 6 April 2017.

This rule derived from the Insolvency Rules 1986, SI 1986/1925, r 6.62.

[6.517]
10.59 Expenses of assisting bankrupt to prepare statement of affairs

(1) If the bankrupt cannot personally prepare a proper statement of affairs, the official receiver may, at the expense of the bankrupt's estate, employ a person or firm to assist in the preparation of the statement.

(2) At the request of the bankrupt, made on the grounds that the bankrupt cannot personally prepare a proper statement, the official receiver may authorise an allowance payable out of the bankrupt's estate (in accordance with the prescribed order of priority) of all or part of the expenses to be incurred by the bankrupt in employing a person or firm to assist the bankrupt in preparing it.

(3) The bankrupt's request must be accompanied by an estimate of the expenses involved, and the official receiver must only authorise the employment of a named person or named firm approved by the official receiver.

(4) The official receiver may make the authorisation subject to such conditions (if any) as the official receiver thinks fit relating to the manner in which any person may obtain access to relevant documents and other records.

(5) Nothing in this rule relieves the bankrupt from any obligation relating to the preparation, verification and submission of a statement of affairs, or to the provision of information to the official receiver or the trustee.

NOTES

Commencement: 6 April 2017.
This rule derived from the Insolvency Rules 1986, SI 1986/1925, r 6.63.

[6.518]
10.60 Delivery of accounts to official receiver

(1) The bankrupt must, at the request of the official receiver, deliver to the official receiver accounts relating to the bankrupt's affairs of such nature, as at such date and for such period as the official receiver may specify.

(2) The period specified may begin from a date up to three years before the date of the presentation of the bankruptcy petition.

(3) The court may, on the official receiver's application, require accounts for any earlier period.

(4) Rule 10.59 (expenses of assisting bankrupt to prepare statement of affairs) applies to accounts to be delivered under this rule as it applies to the statement of affairs.

(5) The accounts must, if the official receiver so requires, be verified by a statement of truth, and (whether or not so verified) delivered to the official receiver within 21 days of the request, or such longer period as the official receiver may allow.

NOTES

Commencement: 6 April 2017.
This rule derived from the Insolvency Rules 1986, SI 1986/1925, rr 6.64, 6.65.

[6.519]
10.61 Further disclosure

(1) The official receiver may at any time require the bankrupt to deliver in writing further information amplifying, modifying or explaining any matter contained in the bankrupt's statement of affairs, or in accounts delivered under the Act or these Rules.

(2) The information must, if the official receiver directs, be verified by a statement of truth, and (whether or not verified) delivered to the official receiver within 21 days from the date of the requirement, or such longer period as the official receiver may allow.

NOTES

Commencement: 6 April 2017.
This rule derived from the Insolvency Rules 1986, SI 1986/1925, r 6.66.

Sub-division B: Bankruptcy application

[6.520]
10.62 Preliminary

The rules in this sub-division apply in relation to further disclosure which is required of a bankrupt where the bankruptcy order was made on a bankruptcy application.

NOTES

Commencement: 6 April 2017.
This rule derived from the Insolvency Rules 1986, SI 1986/1925, r 6.67.

[6.521]
10.63 Delivery of accounts to official receiver

(1) The bankrupt must, at the request of the official receiver, deliver to the official receiver accounts relating to the bankrupt's affairs of such nature, as at such date and for such period as the official receiver may specify.

(2) The specified period may begin from a date up to three years preceding the date of the bankruptcy application.

(3) The accounts must, if the official receiver so requires, be verified by a statement of truth, and (whether or not so verified) be delivered to the official receiver within 21 days of the request or such longer period as the official receiver may allow.

(4) The court may, on the official receiver's application, require accounts in respect of any earlier period.

NOTES

Commencement: 6 April 2017.

This rule derived from the Insolvency Rules 1986, SI 1986/1925, rr 6.69, 670.

[6.522]

10.64 Expenses of preparing accounts

(1) If the bankrupt cannot personally prepare adequate accounts under rule 10.63, the official receiver may, at the expense of the bankrupt's estate, employ a person or firm to assist in their preparation.

(2) At the request of the bankrupt, made on the grounds that the bankrupt cannot personally prepare the accounts, the official receiver may authorise an allowance payable out of the bankrupt's estate (in accordance with the prescribed order of priority) of all or part of the expenses to be incurred by the bankrupt in employing a person or firm to assist the bankrupt in their preparation.

(3) The bankrupt's request must be accompanied by an estimate of the expenses involved; and the official receiver must only authorise the employment of a named person or a named firm, being in either case approved by the official receiver.

(4) The official receiver may make the authorisation subject to such conditions (if any) as the official receiver thinks fit relating to the manner in which any person may obtain access to relevant documents and other records.

(5) Nothing in this rule relieves the bankrupt from any obligation relating to the preparation and delivery of accounts, or to the provision of information to the official receiver or the trustee.

NOTES

Commencement: 6 April 2017.

This rule derived from the Insolvency Rules 1986, SI 1986/1925, r 6.71.

[6.523]

10.65 Further disclosure

(1) The official receiver may at any time require the bankrupt to deliver in writing further information amplifying, modifying or explaining any matter contained in the bankruptcy application, or in accounts delivered under the Act or these Rules.

(2) The information must, if the official receiver so directs, be verified by a statement of truth, and (whether or not so verified) delivered to the official receiver within 21 days from the date of the requirement, or such longer period as the official receiver may allow.

NOTES

Commencement: 6 April 2017.

This rule derived from the Insolvency Rules 1986, SI 1986/1925, r 6.72.

Sub-division C: Reports by the official receiver

[6.524]

10.66 Reports by the official receiver

(1) The official receiver must deliver a report on the bankruptcy and the bankrupt's affairs to the creditors at least once after the making of the bankruptcy order.

(2) The report must contain—

(a) identification details for the proceedings;

(b) contact details for the official receiver;

(c) a summary of the assets and liabilities of the bankrupt as known to the official receiver at the date of the report;

(d) such comments on the summary and the bankrupt's affairs as the official receiver thinks fit; and

(e) any other information of relevance to the creditors.

(3) The official receiver may apply to the court to be relieved of any duty imposed by this rule or to be authorised to carry out the duty in another way.

(4) On such an application the court must have regard to the cost of carrying out the duty, to the amount of the assets available, and to the extent of the interest of creditors or any particular class of them.

(5) If a bankruptcy order is annulled, any duty of the official receiver to deliver a report under this rule ceases.

NOTES

Commencement: 6 April 2017.

This rule derived from the Insolvency Rules 1986, SI 1986/1925, rr 6.73, 6.75–678.

CHAPTER 6 THE TRUSTEE IN BANKRUPTCY

[Note: a document required by the Act or these Rules must also contain the standard contents set out in Part 1.]

Sub-division A: appointment and associated formalities

[6.525]
10.67 Appointment by creditors of new trustee

(1) This rule applies where the bankrupt's creditors decide to remove a trustee in bankruptcy under section 298 but do not, as part of the decision procedure to remove the trustee, appoint a new trustee.

(2) The existing trustee must send the creditors a notice inviting proposals for a new trustee.

(3) The notice must contain a statement explaining the effect of section 298(4B) (decision of creditors to remove a trustee does not take effect until creditors appoint another trustee).

(4) The notice must also explain that the existing trustee is not obliged to seek the creditors' views on any proposals that do not meet the requirements of paragraphs (5) and (6).

(5) Any proposal must state the name and contact details of the proposed trustee, and contain a statement that the proposed trustee is qualified to act as an insolvency practitioner in relation to the bankrupt and has consented to act as trustee.

(6) Any proposal must be received by the existing trustee within five business days of the date of the notice.

(7) Following the end of the period for inviting proposals under paragraph (2) of this rule, where any proposals are received the existing trustee must seek a decision from the creditors on the appointment of a replacement trustee by—

(a) a decision procedure; or
(b) the deemed consent procedure.

(8) Where paragraph (7) applies, the existing trustee must send the creditors a notice which complies with rules 15.7 and 15.8 so far as are relevant.

(9) The notice must also identify any person proposed to be nominated as trustee in accordance with this rule.

(10) The decision date in the notice must be no later than 14 days after the date for receiving proposals has passed.

(11) The creditors must be given at least seven days' notice of the decision date.

(12) A notice inviting proposals for a new trustee under paragraph (2) may be sent before or after the date of the decision to remove the trustee.

(13) Nothing in this rule affects the official receiver's ability under section 296(1), at any time when trustee, to apply to the Secretary of State to appoint a trustee instead of the official receiver.

NOTES

Commencement: 6 April 2017.

This rule derived from the Insolvency Rules 1986, SI 1986/1925, r 6.120.

[6.526]
10.68 Certification of appointment

(1) This rule applies where a person has been appointed as trustee by a decision of the creditors.

(2) The convener or the chair (as the case may be) must certify the appointment, but not unless and until the appointee has delivered to the convener or chair a statement that the appointee is an insolvency practitioner qualified to act as trustee in relation to the bankrupt and consents to act.

(3) The trustee's appointment takes effect from the date on which the appointment is certified, that date to be endorsed on the certificate.

(4) The certificate must contain—

(a) identification details for the proceedings;
(b) identification details for the bankrupt;
(c) identification and contact details for the person appointed as trustee;
(d) the date on which the creditors made the appointment; and
(e) the statement that the appointee—
 (i) has provided a statement of being qualified to act as an insolvency practitioner in relation to the bankrupt,
 (ii) has consented to act, and
 (iii) was appointed trustee of the bankrupt's estate.

(5) The certificate must be authenticated and dated by the person who certifies the appointment.

(6) Where two or more trustees are appointed the certificate must also specify (as required by section 292(3)) the circumstances in which the trustees must act together and the circumstances in which one or more of them may act for the others.

(7) The convener or chair (if that person is not the official receiver) must deliver the certificate to the official receiver.

(8) The official receiver must in any case deliver the certificate to the trustee.

NOTES

Commencement: 6 April 2017.

This rule derived from the Insolvency Rules 1986, SI 1986/1925, r 6.120, Sch 4, Fms 6.40, 6.41 .

[6.527]
10.69 Cost of the trustee's security (section 390(3))

The cost of the trustee's security required by section 390(3) for the proper performance of the trustee's functions is an expense of the bankruptcy.

NOTES

Commencement: 6 April 2017.
This rule derived from the Insolvency Rules 1986, SI 1986/1925, r 12A.56.

[6.528]
10.70 Creditors' decision to appoint a trustee

(1) In the case of a decision on the appointment of a trustee—

(a) if on any vote there are two nominees for appointment, the person who obtains the most support is appointed;

(b) if there are three or more nominees, and one of them has a clear majority over both or all the others together, that one is appointed; and

(c) in any other case the convener or chair must continue to take votes (disregarding at each vote any nominee who has withdrawn and, if no nominee has withdrawn, the nominee who obtained the least support last time) until a clear majority is obtained for any one nominee.

(2) In the case of a decision being made at a meeting, the chair may at any time put to the meeting a resolution for the joint appointment of any two or more nominees.

NOTES

Commencement: 6 April 2017.
This rule derived from the Insolvency Rules 1986, SI 1986/1925, r 6.88.

[6.529]
10.71 Appointment by the court (section 291A(2))

(1) This rule applies where the court appoints the trustee under section 291A(2).

(2) The court's order must not be made unless and until the proposed appointee has filed with the court a statement that the proposed appointee is an insolvency practitioner, qualified to act as the trustee in relation to the bankrupt and consents to act.

(3) The order of the court must contain—

(a) identification details the proceedings;

(b) the name and title of the judge making the order;

(c) the name and postal address of the applicant;

(d) the capacity in which the applicant made the application;

(e) identification and contact details for the person appointed as trustee;

(f) a statement that that the appointee has filed a statement of qualification to act as an insolvency practitioner in relation to the bankrupt and of consent to act;

(g) the order that the appointee is appointed trustee of the bankrupt's estate; and

(h) the date of the order.

(4) Where two or more trustees are appointed the order must also specify (as required by section 292(3)) the circumstances in which the trustees must act together and the circumstances in which one or more of them may act for the others.

(5) The court must deliver two copies of the order, one of which must be sealed, to the official receiver.

(6) The official receiver must deliver the sealed copy of the order to the person appointed as trustee.

(7) The trustee's appointment takes effect from the date of the order.

NOTES

Commencement: 6 April 2017.
This rule derived from the Insolvency Rules 1986, SI 1986/1925, r 6.121, Sch 4, Fms 6.42, 6.43.

[6.530]
10.72 Appointment by the Secretary of State

(1) This rule applies where the official receiver—

(a) refers the need for an appointment of a trustee to the Secretary of State under section 300(4); or

(b) applies to the Secretary of State under section 296 to make the appointment.

(2) If the Secretary of State makes an appointment the Secretary of State must deliver a copy of the certificate of appointment to the official receiver, who must deliver it to the person appointed.

(3) The certificate must specify the date from which the trustee's appointment is to be effective.

NOTES

Commencement: 6 April 2017.
This rule derived from the Insolvency Rules 1986, SI 1986/1925, r 6.122.

[6.531]
10.73 Authentication of trustee's appointment

Where a trustee is appointed under any of rules 10.70, 10.71 or 10.72, a sealed copy of the order of appointment or (as the case may be) a copy of the certificate of the trustee's appointment may in any proceedings be adduced as proof that the trustee is duly authorised to exercise the powers and perform the duties of trustee of the bankrupt's estate.

NOTES

Commencement: 6 April 2017.
This rule derived from the Insolvency Rules 1986, SI 1986/1925, r 6.123.

[6.532]
10.74 Appointment to be gazetted

(1) As soon as reasonably practicable after appointment a trustee appointed by a decision of the bankrupt's creditors—
(a) must gazette a notice of the appointment; and
(b) may advertise the notice in other such manner as the trustee thinks fit.

(2) The notice must state—
(a) that a trustee has been appointed by a decision of creditors; and
(b) the date of the appointment.

NOTES

Commencement: 6 April 2017.
This rule derived from the Insolvency Rules 1986, SI 1986/1925, r 6.124.

[6.533]
10.75 Hand-over of bankrupt's estate by official receiver to trustee

(1) This rule applies where a trustee is appointed in succession to the official receiver acting as trustee.

(2) When the trustee's appointment takes effect, the official receiver must as soon as reasonably practicable do all that is required for putting the trustee into possession of the bankrupt's estate.

(3) On taking possession of the bankrupt's estate, the trustee must discharge any balance due to the official receiver on account of—
(a) expenses properly incurred by the official receiver and payable under the Act or these Rules; and
(b) any advances made by the official receiver in respect of the bankrupt's estate, together with interest on such advances at the rate specified in section 17 of the Judgments Act 1838 on the date of the bankruptcy order.

(4) Alternatively, the trustee may (before taking office) deliver to the official receiver a written undertaking to discharge any such balance out of the first realisation of assets.

(5) The official receiver has a charge on the bankrupt's estate in respect of any sums due under paragraph (3) until they have been discharged, subject only to the deduction from realisations by the trustee of the costs and expenses of such realisations.

(6) The trustee must from time to time out of the realisation of assets discharge all guarantees properly given by the official receiver for the benefit of the bankrupt's estate, and must pay all the official receiver's expenses.

(7) The official receiver must give to the trustee all the information relating to the affairs of the bankrupt and the course of the bankruptcy which the official receiver considers to be reasonably required for the effective discharge by the trustee of the trustee's duties in relation to the bankrupt's estate.

(8) The official receiver must also deliver to the trustee any report of the official receiver under rule 10.66.

NOTES

Commencement: 6 April 2017.
This rule derived from the Insolvency Rules 1986, SI 1986/1925, r 6.125.

[6.534]
10.76 Invitation to creditors to form a creditors' committee

(1) Where the trustee seeks any decision from the bankrupt's creditors, the trustee must at the same time deliver to the creditors a notice inviting them to decide whether a creditors' committee should be established if sufficient creditors are willing to be members of the committee.

(2) The notice must also invite nominations for membership of the committee, such nominations to be received by a date specified in the notice.

(3) The notice must state that nominations—
(a) must be delivered to the trustee by the specified date; and
(b) can only be accepted if the convener is satisfied as to the creditors' eligibility under rule 17.4.

NOTES

Commencement: 6 April 2017.

Sub-division B: resignation and removal

[6.535]

10.77 Trustee's resignation and appointment of replacement (section 298(7))

(1) A trustee may resign under section 298(7) only—

(a) on grounds of ill health;

(b) because of the intention to cease to practise as an insolvency practitioner;

(c) because the further discharge of the duties of trustee is prevented or made impracticable by—

(i) a conflict of interest, or

(ii) a change of personal circumstances; or

(d) where two or more persons are acting as trustee jointly, and it is the opinion of both or all of them that it is no longer expedient that there should continue to be that number of joint trustees.

(2) Before resigning, the trustee must invite the creditors to consider, either by a decision procedure or by the deemed consent procedure, whether a replacement should be appointed except where the resignation is under sub-paragraph (1)(d).

(3) The notice to the creditors must—

(a) state the trustee's intention to resign;

(b) state that under rule 10.77(8) of the Insolvency (England and Wales) Rules 2016, the trustee will be released 21 days after the date of delivery of the notice of resignation to the prescribed person under section 298(7), unless the court orders otherwise; and

(c) comply with rule 15.7 or 15.8 so far as applicable.

(4) The notice may suggest the name of a replacement trustee.

(5) The notice must be accompanied by a summary of the trustee's receipts and payments.

(6) The decision date must be not more than five business days before the date on which the trustee intends to give notice under section 298(7).

(7) The trustee must deliver a copy of the notice to the official receiver and the bankrupt.

(8) The resigning trustee's release is effective 21 days after the date on which the notice of resignation under section 298(7) is filed with the court in a bankruptcy based on a petition or, delivered to the official receiver in a bankruptcy based on a debtor's application.

NOTES

Commencement: 6 April 2017.

This rule derived from the Insolvency Rules 1986, SI 1986/1925, r 6.126.

[6.536]

10.78 Decision of creditors to remove trustee (section 298(1))

(1) Where the convener of the decision procedure or chair of a meeting of creditors is other than the official receiver, and a decision is taken to remove the trustee, the convener or chair must, within three business days, deliver a certificate to that effect to the official receiver.

(2) If the creditors have decided to appoint a new trustee, the certificate of the new trustee's appointment must also be delivered to the official receiver within three business days from the date of that decision and rule 10.68 must be complied with in relation to it.

(3) The certificate of the trustee's removal must be authenticated and dated by the convener or chair and—

(a) identify the bankrupt;

(b) identify and provide contact details for the removed trustee;

(c) state that the creditors decided that the trustee specified in the certificate be removed from office as trustee of the bankrupt's estate;

(d) state the decision date and the decision procedure used; and

(e) state that the creditors either—

(i) did not decide against the trustee being released, or

(ii) decided that the trustee should not be released.

(4) The trustee's removal is effective from the date of the certificate of removal.

NOTES

Commencement: 6 April 2017.

This rule derived from the Insolvency Rules 1986, SI 1986/1925, rr 6.127, 6.129.

[6.537]

10.79 Procedure on removal by creditors

(1) Where the creditors have decided that the trustee be removed, the official receiver must in a bankruptcy based on a petition file the certificate of removal with the court.

(2) The official receiver must deliver a copy of the certificate to the removed trustee.

NOTES

Commencement: 6 April 2017.

This rule derived from the Insolvency Rules 1986, SI 1986/1925, r 6.131.

[6.538]
10.80 Removal of trustee by the court (section 298(1))

(1) This rule applies where an application is made to the court under section 298(1) for the removal of the trustee, or for an order directing the trustee to initiate a creditors' decision procedure for the purpose of removing the trustee.

(2) On receipt of an application, the court may, if it is satisfied that no sufficient cause is shown for it, dismiss it without giving notice to any party other than the applicant.

(3) Unless the application is dismissed, the court must fix a venue for it to be heard.

(4) The applicant must, at least 14 days before any hearing, deliver to the trustee and the official receiver a notice stating the venue with a copy of the application and of any evidence on which the applicant intends to rely.

(5) A respondent may apply for security for the costs of the application and the court may make such an order if it is satisfied, having regard to all the circumstances of the case, that it is just to make such an order.

(6) The trustee and the official receiver may do either or both of the following—
- (a) file a report of any matters which the trustee or the official receiver thinks ought to be drawn to the court's attention; or
- (b) appear and be heard on the application.

(7) The costs of the application are not payable as an expense of the bankruptcy unless the court orders otherwise.

(8) On a successful application the court's order must contain—
- (a) identification details for the proceedings;
- (b) the name and title of the judge making the order;
- (c) the name and postal address of the applicant;
- (d) a statement as to the capacity in which the applicant made the application;
- (e) identification and contact details for the trustee;
- (f) an order that either—
  - (i) the trustee is removed from office, or
  - (ii) the trustee must instigate a creditors' decision procedure on or before the date specified in the order for the purpose of considering the trustee's removal from office;
- (g) details of any further order in the matter; and
- (h) the date of the order.

(9) Where the court removes the trustee it must deliver a sealed copy of the order of removal to the trustee and a copy to the official receiver.

(10) If the court appoints a new trustee, rule 10.71 applies.

NOTES

Commencement: 6 April 2017.
This rule derived from the Insolvency Rules 1986, SI 1986/1925, r 6.132.

[6.539]
10.81 Removal of trustee by the Secretary of State (section 298(5))

(1) This rule applies where the Secretary of State decides to remove a trustee appointed by the Secretary of State.

(2) Before doing so the Secretary of State must deliver to the trustee and the official receiver a notice of the Secretary of State's decision and the grounds for the decision.

(3) The notice must specify a period within which the trustee may make representations against implementation of the decision.

(4) If the Secretary of State directs the removal of the trustee, the Secretary of State must as soon as reasonably practicable—
- (a) deliver the notice to the trustee and the official receiver; and
- (b) where the bankruptcy was based upon a petition, file a notice of the decision with the court.

(5) Where the Secretary of State directs the trustee be removed, the court may make any order that it could have made if the trustee had been removed by the court.

NOTES

Commencement: 6 April 2017.
This rule derived from the Insolvency Rules 1986, SI 1986/1925, r 6.133.

[6.540]
10.82 Notice of resignation or removal

Where a new trustee is appointed in place of one who has resigned or been removed, the new trustee must, in the notice of appointment, state that the predecessor trustee has resigned or, as the case may be, been removed and (if it be the case) has been given release.

NOTES

Commencement: 6 April 2017.
This rule derived from the Insolvency Rules 1986, SI 1986/1925, r 6.134.

[6.541]

10.83 Release of removed trustee (section 299)

(1) Where the trustee is removed by a creditors' decision procedure the certificate of removal must state whether or not the creditors decided against the trustee's release.

(2) Where the creditors decided against release, the trustee's application to the Secretary of State for release under subsection 299(3)(b) must—

- (a) identify the proceedings;
- (b) identify the bankrupt;
- (c) identify and provide contact details for the trustee;
- (d) provide details of the circumstances under which the trustee has ceased to act as trustee;
- (e) state that the trustee is applying to the Secretary of State for a certificate of the trustee's release as a trustee as a result of the circumstances specified in the application; and
- (f) be authenticated and dated by the trustee.

(3) When the Secretary of State gives the release, the Secretary of State must certify it accordingly and file the certificate with the court in a bankruptcy based on a creditor's petition.

(4) The Secretary of State must deliver a copy of the certificate to the official receiver and former trustee whose release is effective from the date of the certificate or such other date as the certificate specifies.

NOTES

Commencement: 6 April 2017.

This rule derived from the Insolvency Rules 1986, SI 1986/1925, r 6.135.

[6.542]

10.84 Deceased trustee

(1) If the trustee (not being the official receiver) dies, notice of the fact and date of death must be delivered to the official receiver by one of the following—

- (a) a surviving joint trustee;
- (b) a member or partner in the deceased trustee's firm (if the deceased was a member, partner or employee of a firm);
- (c) an officer of the deceased trustee's company (if the deceased was an officer or employee of a company); or
- (d) a personal representative of the deceased trustee.

(2) If no such notice has been delivered within 21 days following the trustee's death then any other person may deliver the notice.

(3) In a bankruptcy based on a creditor's petition the official receiver must file notice of the death with the court.

(4) The date of the deceased trustee's release under section 299(3)(a) is—

- (a) the date of the filing of the notice with the court where the bankruptcy is based on a creditor's petition; or
- (b) the date of delivery of the notice under paragraph (1) to the official receiver where the bankruptcy is based on a debtor's application.

NOTES

Commencement: 6 April 2017.

This rule derived from the Insolvency Rules 1986, SI 1986/1925, r 6.143.

[6.543]

10.85 Loss of qualification as insolvency practitioner (section 298(6))

(1) This rule applies where the trustee vacates office under section 298(6), on ceasing to be qualified to act as an insolvency practitioner in relation to the bankrupt.

(2) A notice of the fact must be delivered as soon as reasonably practicable to the official receiver by one of the following—

- (a) the trustee who has vacated office;
- (b) a continuing joint trustee;
- (c) the recognised professional body which was the source of the vacating trustee's authorisation to act in relation to the bankrupt.

(3) The notice must be authenticated and dated by the person delivering the notice.

(4) On receiving such a notice the official receiver must—

- (a) deliver a copy of the notice to the Secretary of State; and
- (b) file a copy of the notice with the court where the bankruptcy was based on a creditor's petition.

(5) Rule 10.83(2) to (4) applies in relation to the trustee's application for release under section 299(3)(b).

NOTES

Commencement: 6 April 2017.

This rule derived from the Insolvency Rules 1986, SI 1986/1925, r 6.144.

Part 6 Insolvency Rules

Sub-division C: release on completion of administration of bankrupt's estate

[6.544]

10.86 Release of official receiver on completion of administration (section 299)

(1) Before giving a notice that the administration of the bankrupt's estate is for practical purposes complete to the Secretary of State under section 299(2), the official receiver must deliver a notice of intention to do so to the creditors and to the bankrupt.

(2) The notice must be accompanied by a summary of the official receiver's receipts and payments as trustee.

(3) When the Secretary of State has determined the date from which the official receiver's release is effective, the Secretary of State must—

(a) where the bankruptcy was based on a bankruptcy application, deliver a notice of release to the official receiver; or

(b) in all other cases, file a notice of the release with the court.

(4) The Secretary of State's notice to the court must be accompanied by the summary of the official receiver's receipts and payments.

NOTES

Commencement: 6 April 2017.

This rule derived from the Insolvency Rules 1986, SI 1986/1925, r 6.136.

[6.545]

10.87 Vacation of office on completion of bankruptcy (sections 298(8) and 331)

(1) The report which the trustee is required to make under section 331(2A)(a) must comply with the requirements of rule 18.14.

(2) A copy of the notice and report that is sent to creditors under section 331(2) and (2A) must be sent to the bankrupt as soon as is reasonably practicable after notice is given to creditors under that provision.

(3) The notice under section 331(2) must also state—

(a) that the creditors have the right to request information from the trustee under rule 18.9;

(b) that the creditors have the right to challenge the trustee's remuneration and expenses under rule 18.34;

(c) that the bankrupt has a right to challenge the trustee's remuneration and expenses under rule 18.35;

(d) that the creditors may object to the trustee's release by giving notice in writing to the trustee before the end of the prescribed period;

(e) that the prescribed period is the period ending at the later of—

(i) eight weeks after delivery of the notice; or

(ii) if any request for information under rule 18.9 or any application to the court under that rule, rule 18.34 or rule 18.35 is made when that request or application is finally determined;

(f) that the trustee will vacate office under section 298(8) when, after the end of the prescribed period, the trustee files with the court a notice that the trustee has given notice to the creditors under section 331; and

(g) that the trustee will be released under section 299(3)(d) at the same time as vacating office unless any of the creditors objected to the trustee's release.

(4) The notice under section 298(8) must be authenticated and dated by the trustee.

(5) The notice must be accompanied by a copy of the final report.

(6) The trustee must deliver a copy of the notice under section 298(8) to—

(a) the Secretary of State; and

(b) the official receiver.

(7) Rule 10.83(2) to (4) applies to an application by the trustee to the Secretary of State for release.

NOTES

Commencement: 6 April 2017.

This rule derived from the Insolvency Rules 1986, SI 1986/1925, r 6.137.

[6.546]

10.88 Rule as to reporting

(1) The court may, on the application of the trustee or official receiver, relieve the applicant of any duty imposed on the applicant by rule 10.86 and 10.87 and rule 18.14 (contents of final report), or authorise the applicant to carry out the duty in any other way.

(2) In considering whether to relieve the applicant, the court must have regard to the cost of carrying out the duty, to the amount of the funds available in the bankrupt's estate, and to the extent of the interest of creditors or any particular class of them.

NOTES

Commencement: 6 April 2017.

This rule derived from the Insolvency Rules 1986, SI 1986/1925, r 6.137A.

[6.547]
10.89 Notice to official receiver of intention to vacate office

(1) This rule applies where the trustee intends to vacate office, whether by resignation or otherwise, and as a result there will be a vacancy in the office of trustee (so that by virtue of section 300 the official receiver is trustee until the vacancy is filled).

(2) The trustee must deliver notice of that intention to the official receiver at least 21 days before the trustee intends to vacate office.

(3) The notice must include the following details of any property which has not been realised, applied, distributed or otherwise fully dealt with in the bankruptcy—
- (a) the nature of the property;
- (b) its value (or that it has no value);
- (c) its location;
- (d) any action taken by the trustee to deal with the property or any reason for the trustee not dealing with it; and
- (e) the current position in relation to it.

NOTES

Commencement: 6 April 2017.
This rule derived from the Insolvency Rules 1986, SI 1986/1925, r 6.145.

[6.548]
10.90 Trustee's duties on vacating office

A trustee who ceases to be in office in consequence of removal, resignation or ceasing to be qualified to act as an insolvency practitioner in relation to the bankrupt, must as soon as reasonably practicable deliver to the successor as trustee—
- (a) the assets of the bankrupt's estate (after deduction of any expenses properly incurred, and distributions made, by the trustee);
- (b) the records of the bankruptcy, including correspondence, proofs and other documents relating to the bankruptcy while it was within the trustee's responsibility, and
- (c) the bankrupt's documents and other records.

NOTES

Commencement: 6 April 2017.
This rule derived from the Insolvency Rules 1986, SI 1986/1925, r 6.146.

[6.549]
10.91 Power of the court to set aside certain transactions

(1) If in dealing with the bankrupt's estate the trustee enters into any transaction with a person who is an associate of the trustee, the court may, on the application of any interested person, set the transaction aside and order the trustee to compensate the bankrupt's estate for any loss suffered in consequence of it.

(2) This does not apply if either—
- (a) the transaction was entered into with the prior consent of the court; or
- (b) it is shown to the court's satisfaction that the transaction was for value, and that it was entered into by the trustee without knowing, or having any reason to suppose, that the person concerned was an associate.

(3) Nothing in this rule is to be taken as prejudicing the operation of any rule of law or equity relating to a trustee's dealings with trust property, or the fiduciary obligations of any person.

NOTES

Commencement: 6 April 2017.
This rule derived from the Insolvency Rules 1986, SI 1986/1925, r 6.147.

[6.550]
10.92 Rule against improper solicitation

(1) Where the court is satisfied that any improper solicitation has been used by or on behalf of the trustee in obtaining proxies or procuring the trustee's appointment, it may order that no remuneration be allowed out of the bankrupt's estate to any person by whom, or on whose behalf, the solicitation was exercised.

(2) An order of the court under this rule overrides any decision of the creditors' committee or the creditors, or any other provision of these Rules relating to the trustee's remuneration.

NOTES

Commencement: 6 April 2017.
This rule derived from the Insolvency Rules 1986, SI 1986/1925, r 6.148.

[6.551]
10.93 Enforcement of trustee's obligations to official receiver (section 305(3))

(1) On the application of the official receiver, the court may make such orders as it thinks necessary to enforce the duties of the trustee under section 305(3).

(2) An order of the court under this rule may provide that all costs of and incidental to the official receiver's application must be borne by the trustee.

Part 6 Insolvency Rules

NOTES

Commencement: 6 April 2017.

This rule derived from the Insolvency Rules 1986, SI 1986/1925, r 6.149.

CHAPTER 7 SPECIAL MANAGER

[Note: a document required by the Act or these Rules must also contain the standard contents set out in Part 1.]

[6.552]
10.94 Application for and order of appointment of special manager (section 370)

[Note: section 377 provides that the acts of the special manager are valid notwithstanding any defect in the special manager's appointment or qualifications.]

(1) An application by the interim receiver or trustee under section 370 for the appointment of a special manager must be supported by a report setting out the reasons for the application. The report must include the applicant's estimate of the value of the bankrupt's estate, property or business in relation to which the special manager is to be appointed.

(2) The court's order appointing the special manager must contain—
- (a) identification details for the proceedings;
- (b) the name and title of the judge making the order;
- (c) the name and postal address of the applicant;
- (d) the name and postal address of the proposed special manager;
- (e) an order that the proposed special manager is appointed as special manager;
- (f) details of the special manager's responsibility over the debtor's property or the bankrupt's estate;
- (g) the powers entrusted to the special manager under section 370(4);
- (h) the time allowed for the special manager to give the required security for the appointment;
- (i) the duration of the special manager's appointment, being one of the following—
  - (i) for a fixed period stated in the order,
  - (ii) until the occurrence of a specified event, or
  - (iii) until the court makes a further order;
- (j) an order that the special manager's remuneration will be fixed from time to time by the court; and
- (k) the date of the order.

(3) The appointment of a special manager may be renewed by order of the court.

NOTES

Commencement: 6 April 2017.

This rule derived from the Insolvency Rules 1986, SI 1986/1925, r 6.167, Sch 4, Fm 6.54.

[6.553]
10.95 Security

(1) The appointment of the special manager does not take effect until the person appointed has given (or, if the court allows, undertaken to give) security to the applicant for the appointment.

(2) A person appointed as special manager may give security either specifically for a particular bankruptcy, or generally for any bankruptcy in relation to which that person may be appointed as special manager.

(3) The amount of the security must be not less than the value of the bankrupt's estate, property or business in relation to which the special manager is appointed, as estimated in the applicant's report which accompanied the application for appointment.

(4) When the special manager has given security to the applicant, the applicant must file with the court a certificate as to the adequacy of the security.

(5) The cost of providing the security must be paid in the first instance by the special manager; but—
- (a) where a bankruptcy order is not made, the special manager is entitled to be reimbursed out of the property of the debtor, and the court may order accordingly; and
- (b) where a bankruptcy order is made, the special manager is entitled to be reimbursed out of the bankrupt's estate in the prescribed order of priority.

NOTES

Commencement: 6 April 2017.

This rule derived from the Insolvency Rules 1986, SI 1986/1925, r 6.168.

[6.554]
10.96 Failure to give or keep up security

(1) If the special manager fails to give the required security within the time stated for that purpose by the order of appointment, or any extension of that time that may be allowed, the interim receiver or trustee (as the case may be) must report the failure to the court, which may discharge the order appointing the special manager.

(2) If the special manager fails to keep up the security, the interim receiver or trustee must report the failure to the court, which may remove the special manager, and make such order as it thinks just as to costs.

(3) If the court discharges the order appointing the special manager or makes an order removing the special manager, the court must give directions as to whether any, and if so what, steps should be taken for the appointment of another special manager.

NOTES

Commencement: 6 April 2017.
This rule derived from the Insolvency Rules 1986, SI 1986/1925, r 6.169.

[6.555]
10.97 Accounting

(1) The special manager must produce accounts, containing details of the special manager's receipts and payments, for the approval of the trustee.

(2) The accounts must be for—
 (a) each three month period for the duration of the special manager's appointment; or
 (b) any shorter period ending with the termination of the special manager's appointment.

(3) When the accounts have been approved, the special manager's receipts and payments must be added to those of the trustee.

NOTES

Commencement: 6 April 2017.
This rule derived from the Insolvency Rules 1986, SI 1986/1925, r 6.170.

[6.556]
10.98 Termination of appointment

(1) The special manager's appointment terminates if—
 (a) the bankruptcy petition is dismissed; or
 (b) in a case where an interim receiver was appointed under section 286, the appointment is discharged without a bankruptcy order having been made.

(2) If the interim receiver or the trustee thinks that the appointment of the special manager is no longer necessary or beneficial to the bankrupt's estate, the interim receiver or the trustee must apply to the court for directions, and the court may order the special manager's appointment to be terminated.

(3) The interim receiver or the trustee must make such an application if the creditors decide that the appointment should be terminated.

NOTES

Commencement: 6 April 2017.
This rule derived from the Insolvency Rules 1986, SI 1986/1925, r 6.171.

CHAPTER 8 PUBLIC EXAMINATION OF BANKRUPT

[Note: a document required by the Act or these Rules must also contain the standard contents set out in Part 1.]

[6.557]
10.99 Order for public examination of bankrupt

[Note: rule 81.9 (as amended) of the CPR requires a warning as mentioned in paragraph (2)(f) to be displayed prominently on the front of the order.]

(1) This rule applies to a court order for the public examination of a bankrupt made on an application by the official receiver under section 290.

(2) The order must have the title "Order for public examination" and contain—
 (a) identification details for the proceedings;
 (b) the name and the title of the judge making the order;
 (c) an order that the bankrupt must attend the venue specified in the order for the purpose of being publicly examined;
 (d) the venue for the public examination;
 (e) the date of the order; and
 (f) a warning that if the bankrupt fails without reasonable excuse to attend the public examination at the time and place specified in the order the bankrupt will be liable to be arrested without further notice under section 364(1) and may be held to be in contempt of court under section 290(5) and imprisoned or fined.

(3) The official receiver must serve a copy of the court's order on the bankrupt as soon as reasonably practicable after the order is made.

NOTES

Commencement: 6 April 2017.
This rule derived from the Insolvency Rules 1986, SI 1986/1925, r 6.172, Sch 4, Fm 6.55.

[6.558]
10.100 Notice of public examination

(1) The official receiver must deliver at least 14 days' notice of the public examination to—
 (a) any trustee or special manager; and
 (b) subject to any contrary direction of the court, every creditor of the bankrupt who is known to the official receiver.

(2) Where the official receiver thinks fit, a notice of the order must be gazetted not less than 14 days before the day fixed for the hearing.

(3) The official receiver may advertise the notice in such other manner as the official receiver thinks fit.

(4) The notice must state the purpose of the examination hearing and the venue.

NOTES

Commencement: 6 April 2017.
This rule derived from the Insolvency Rules 1986, SI 1986/1925, r 6.172.

[6.559]
10.101 Order for public examination requested by creditors

(1) A notice by a creditor to the official receiver, under section 290(2), requesting the bankrupt to be publicly examined must be accompanied by—
 (a) a list of the creditors concurring with the request with the name and postal address of each and the amount of their respective claims; and
 (b) confirmation by each creditor of that creditor's concurrence; and
 (c) a statement of the reasons why the public examination is requested.

(2) The request must be authenticated and dated by the creditor giving the notice.

(3) A list of concurring creditors is not required if the requisitioning creditor's debt alone is at least one half in value of the bankrupt's creditors.

(4) Before the official receiver makes the requested application, the creditor requesting the examination must deposit with the official receiver such sum (if any) as the official receiver determines is appropriate as security for the expenses of the public examination, if ordered.

(5) The official receiver must make the application for the examination—
 (a) within 28 days of receiving the creditor's request (if no security is required under paragraph (4)); or
 (b) within 28 days of the creditor depositing such security if security is requested.

(6) However, if the official receiver thinks the request is unreasonable, the official receiver may apply to the court for an order to be relieved from making the application.

(7) If the court so orders, and the application for the order was made without notice to any other party, the official receiver must deliver a copy of the order as soon as reasonably practicable to the requisitionist.

(8) If such an application is dismissed, the official receiver's application under section 290(2) must be made as soon as reasonably practicable on conclusion of the hearing of the application first mentioned.

NOTES

Commencement: 6 April 2017.
This rule derived from the Insolvency Rules 1986, SI 1986/1925, r 6.173.

[6.560]
10.102 Bankrupt unfit for examination

[Note: rule 81.9 (as amended) of the CPR requires a warning as mentioned in paragraph (6) to be displayed prominently on the front of the order.]

(1) Where the bankrupt is a person who lacks capacity within the meaning of the Mental Capacity Act 2005 or is unfit to undergo or attend for public examination, the court may—
 (a) stay the order for the bankrupt's public examination; or
 (b) direct that it will be conducted in a manner and place the court thinks just.

(2) An application for an order under paragraph (1) must be made—
 (a) by a person who has been appointed by a court in the United Kingdom or elsewhere to manage the affairs of, or to represent, the bankrupt;
 (b) by a person who appears to the court to be a suitable person to make the application; or
 (c) by the official receiver.

(3) Where an application is made by a person other than the official receiver, then—
 (a) the application must, unless the bankrupt is a person who lacks capacity within the meaning of the Mental Capacity Act 2005, be supported by a witness statement by a registered medical practitioner as to the bankrupt's mental and physical condition;
 (b) at least five business days' notice of the application must be delivered to the official receiver and the trustee (if one is appointed); and
 (c) before any order is made on the application, the applicant must deposit with the official receiver such sum as the official receiver determines is necessary for the additional expenses of an examination.

(4) The court may order that some or all of the expenses of the examination are to be payable out of the deposit under paragraph (3)(c), instead of out of the bankrupt's estate.

(5) The order must contain—
- (a) identification details for the proceedings;
- (b) the name and title of the judge making the order;
- (c) the date of the original order for the public examination of the bankrupt;
- (d) the name and postal address of the applicant;
- (e) a statement as to the capacity in which the applicant (other than the official receiver) made the application;
- (f) a statement that the court is satisfied that the bankrupt is a person who lacks capacity within the meaning of the Mental Capacity Act 2005 to manage and administer the bankrupt's property and affairs or is unfit to undergo a public examination;
- (g) an order either that—
  - (i) the original order is stayed on the grounds that the bankrupt is unfit to undergo a public examination, or
  - (ii) the original order is varied (as specified in this order) on the grounds that the bankrupt is unfit to attend the public examination fixed by the original order; and
- (h) the date of the order.

(6) If the original order is varied, the order must also contain a warning to the bankrupt, which must be displayed prominently on the front page of the order, stating that if the bankrupt fails without reasonable excuse to attend the public examination at the time and place set out in the order the bankrupt—
- (a) may be arrested without further notice under section 364(1); and
- (b) may be held to be in contempt of court under section 290(5) and imprisoned or fined.

(7) Where the application is made by the official receiver, it may be made without notice to any other party, and may be supported by evidence set out in a report by the official receiver to the court.

NOTES

Commencement: 6 April 2017.
This rule derived from the Insolvency Rules 1986, SI 1986/1925, r 6.174.

[6.561]
10.103 Procedure at public examination

(1) At the public examination the bankrupt must—
- (a) be examined on oath; and
- (b) answer all the questions the court puts, or allows to be put.

(2) A person allowed by section 290(4) to question the bankrupt may—
- (a) with the approval of the court be represented by an appropriately qualified legal representative;
- (b) in writing authorise another person to question the bankrupt on that person's behalf.

(3) The bankrupt may at the bankrupt's own expense instruct an appropriately qualified legal representative, who may put such questions as the court may allow to the bankrupt for the purpose of enabling the bankrupt to explain or qualify any answers given by the bankrupt, and may make representations on the bankrupt's behalf.

(4) The court must have such record made of the examination as the court thinks proper.

(5) The record may, in any proceedings (whether under the Act or otherwise) be used as evidence of any statement made by the bankrupt in the course of the bankrupt's public examination.

(6) If criminal proceedings have been instituted against the bankrupt, and the court is of the opinion that the continuance of the hearing might prejudice a fair trial of those proceedings, the hearing may be adjourned.

NOTES

Commencement: 6 April 2017.
This rule derived from the Insolvency Rules 1986, SI 1986/1925, r 6.175.

[6.562]
10.104 Adjournment

[Note: rule 81.9 (as amended) of the CPR requires a warning as mentioned in paragraph (2) to be displayed prominently on the front of the order.]

(1) The court may adjourn the public examination from time to time, either to a fixed date or generally.

(2) The order of adjournment of the public examination to a fixed date must contain a warning to the bankrupt, which must be displayed prominently on the front page of the order, stating that if the bankrupt fails without reasonable excuse to attend the public examination at the time and place set out in the order the bankrupt—
- (a) may be arrested without further notice under section 364(1); and
- (b) may be held to be in contempt of court under section 290(5) and imprisoned or fined.

(3) Where the examination has been adjourned generally, the court may at any time on the application of the official receiver or of the bankrupt—
- (a) fix a venue for the resumption of the examination; and
- (b) give directions as to the manner in which, and the time within which, notice of the resumed public examination is to be given to persons entitled to take part in it.

(4) Where such an application is made by the bankrupt, the court may grant it on terms that the expenses of giving the notices required by that paragraph must be paid by the bankrupt and that, before a venue for the resumed public examination is fixed, the bankrupt must deposit with the official receiver such sum as the official receiver considers necessary to cover those expenses.

(5) Where the examination is adjourned, the official receiver may, there and then, make an application under section 279(3) (suspension of automatic discharge).

(6) If the court makes such an order suspending the bankrupt's discharge, then the court must deliver copies of the order to the official receiver, the trustee and the bankrupt.

NOTES

Commencement: 6 April 2017.

This rule derived from the Insolvency Rules 1986, SI 1986/1925, r 6.176.

[6.563]

10.105 Expenses of examination

(1) Where a public examination of the bankrupt has been ordered by the court on a creditor's request under rule 10.101, the court may order that some or all of the expenses of the examination are to be paid out of the deposit under rule 10.101, instead of out of the bankrupt's estate.

(2) The costs and expenses of a public examination do not fall on the official receiver personally.

NOTES

Commencement: 6 April 2017.

This rule derived from the Insolvency Rules 1986, SI 1986/1925, r 6.177.

CHAPTER 9 REPLACEMENT OF EXEMPT PROPERTY

[6.564]

10.106 Purchase of replacement property

(1) A purchase of replacement property under section 308(3) may be made either before or after the realisation by the trustee of the value of the property vesting in the trustee under the section.

(2) The trustee is under no obligation to apply funds to the purchase of a replacement for property vested in the trustee, unless and until the trustee has sufficient funds in the bankrupt's estate for that purpose.

NOTES

Commencement: 6 April 2017.

This rule derived from the Insolvency Rules 1986, SI 1986/1925, r 6.187.

[6.565]

10.107 Money provided in lieu of sale

(1) The following applies where a third party proposes to the trustee that the third party should provide the bankrupt's estate with a sum of money enabling the bankrupt to be left in possession of property which would otherwise be made to vest in the trustee under section 308.

(2) The trustee may accept that proposal, if satisfied that it is a reasonable one, and that the bankrupt's estate will benefit to the extent of the value of the property in question less the cost of a reasonable replacement.

NOTES

Commencement: 6 April 2017.

This rule derived from the Insolvency Rules 1986, SI 1986/1925, r 6.188.

CHAPTER 10 INCOME PAYMENTS ORDERS

[Note: a document required by the Act or these Rules must also contain the standard contents set out in Part 1.]

[6.566]

10.108 Interpretation

In this Chapter the "permitted fee" means the amount which is prescribed for the purposes of section 7(4)(a) of the Attachment of Earnings Act 1971.

NOTES

Commencement: 6 April 2017.

[6.567]

10.109 Application for income payments order (section 310)

(1) Where the trustee applies for an income payments order under section 310, the court must fix a venue for the hearing of the application.

(2) Notice of the application and the venue must be delivered by the trustee to the bankrupt at least 28 days before the day fixed for the hearing, together with a copy of the trustee's application and a short statement of the grounds on which it is made.

(3) The notice must inform the bankrupt that—

(a) the bankrupt is required to attend the hearing unless at least five business days before the date fixed for the hearing the bankrupt files with the court and delivers to the trustee, consent to an order being made in the terms of the application; and

(b) if the bankrupt attends, the bankrupt will be given an opportunity to show cause why the order should not be made, or why a different order should be made to that applied for by the trustee.

(4) The notice must be authenticated and dated by the trustee.

NOTES

Commencement: 6 April 2017.

This rule derived from the Insolvency Rules 1986, SI 1986/1925, r 6.189.

[6.568]

10.110 Order for income payments order

An order under section 310 must have the title "Income Payments Order" and must contain—

(a) identification details for the proceedings;

(b) identification and contact details for the trustee;

(c) a statement that the bankrupt has or has not consented to the order (as the case may be);

(d) the order that it appears to the court that the sum which is specified in the order should be paid to the trustee in accordance with the payments schedule detailed in the order until the date specified in the order;

(e) the order that the bankrupt must pay to the trustee the sum referred to in paragraph (e) in accordance with the payments schedule out of the bankrupt's income, the first of such instalments to be made on or before the date specified in the order; and

(f) the date of the order.

NOTES

Commencement: 6 April 2017.

This rule derived from the Insolvency Rules 1986, SI 1986/1925, Sch 4, Fms 6.65, 6.66.

[6.569]

10.111 Action to follow making of order

(1) Where the court makes an income payments order, the trustee must deliver a sealed copy of the order to the bankrupt as soon as reasonably practicable after it is made.

(2) If the order is made under section 310(3)(b), a sealed copy of the order must also be delivered by the trustee to the person to whom the order is directed.

NOTES

Commencement: 6 April 2017.

This rule derived from the Insolvency Rules 1986, SI 1986/1925, r 6.190.

[6.570]

10.112 Variation of order

(1) If an income payments order is made under section 310(3)(a), and the bankrupt does not comply with it, the trustee may apply to the court for the order to be varied, so as to take effect under section 310(3)(b) as an order to the payer of the relevant income.

(2) The trustee's application under this rule may be made without notice to any other party.

(3) The order must contain—

(a) identification details for the proceedings;

(b) identification and contact details for the trustee who made the application;

(c) the name and address of the payer;

(d) a statement that the applicant is the trustee of the bankrupt;

(e) the date of the income payments order;

(f) a statement that it appears to the court that the bankrupt has failed to comply with the income payments order;

(g) the order that the income payments order be varied to the effect that the payer specified in this order do take payment in accordance with the payments schedule detailed in this order out of the bankrupt's income and that the first instalment must be paid on the date specified in the order; and that the payer must deliver the sums deducted to the trustee; and

(h) the date of the order.

(4) The court must deliver sealed copies of any order made on the application to the trustee and the bankrupt as soon as reasonably practicable after the order is made.

(5) In the case of an order varying or discharging an income payments order made under section 310(3)(b), the court must deliver an additional sealed copy of the order to the trustee, for delivery as soon as reasonably practicable to the payer of the relevant income.

NOTES

Commencement: 6 April 2017.

This rule derived from the Insolvency Rules 1986, SI 1986/1925, r 6.191, Sch 4, Fm 6.67.

[6.571]
10.113 Order to payer of income: administration

(1) Where a person receives notice of an income payments order under section 310(3)(b), with reference to income otherwise payable by that person to the bankrupt, that person ("the payer") must make the necessary arrangements for compliance with the order as soon as reasonably practicable.

(2) When making any payment to the trustee, the payer may deduct the permitted fee towards the clerical and administrative costs of compliance with the income payments order.

(3) The payer must give to the bankrupt a statement of any amount deducted by the payer under paragraph (2).

(4) Where a payer receives notice of an income payments order imposing on the payer a requirement under section 310(3)(b), and either—

(a) the payer is then no longer liable to make to the bankrupt any payment of income; or
(b) having made payments in compliance with the order, the payer ceases to be so liable;

the payer must as soon as reasonably practicable deliver notice of that fact to the trustee.

NOTES

Commencement: 6 April 2017.
This rule derived from the Insolvency Rules 1986, SI 1986/1925, r 6.192.

[6.572]
10.114 Review of order

(1) Where an income payments order is in force, either the trustee or the bankrupt may apply to the court for the order to be varied or discharged.

(2) If the application is made by the trustee, rule 10.109 applies (with any necessary modification) as in the case of an application for an income payments order.

(3) If the application is made by the bankrupt, it must be accompanied by a short statement of the grounds on which it is made.

(4) On receipt of an application, the court may, if it is satisfied that no sufficient cause is shown for it, dismiss it without giving notice to any party other than the applicant.

(5) Unless the application is dismissed, the court must fix a venue for it to be heard.

(6) The applicant must, at least 28 days before any hearing, deliver to the trustee or the bankrupt (whichever of them is not the applicant) a notice stating the venue with—

(a) a copy of the application; and
(b) where the applicant is the bankrupt, a copy of the statement of the grounds for the application referred to in paragraph (3).

(7) The trustee may do either or both of the following—

(a) file a report of any matters which the trustee thinks ought to be drawn to the court's attention; or
(b) appear and be heard on the application.

(8) The trustee must file a copy of a report under paragraph (7)(a) with the court not less than five business days before the date fixed for the hearing and must deliver a copy of it to the bankrupt.

(9) The court order must contain—

(a) identification details for the proceedings;
(b) the name and title of the judge making the order;
(c) the name and postal address of the applicant;
(d) an order that the income payments order specified is varied as specified;
(e) the date of the income payments order referred to in paragraph (d);
(f) details of how the income payments order is varied by this order; and
(g) the date of the order.

(10) Sealed copies of any order made on the application must be delivered by the court to the trustee, the bankrupt and the payer (if other than the bankrupt) as soon as reasonably practicable after the order is made.

NOTES

Commencement: 6 April 2017.
This rule derived from the Insolvency Rules 1986, SI 1986/1925, r 6.193, Fm 6.68.

CHAPTER 11 INCOME PAYMENTS AGREEMENTS

[Note: a document required by the Act or these Rules must also contain the standard contents set out in Part 1.]

[6.573]
[10.114A Interpretation

In this Chapter, the "permitted fee" means the amount which is prescribed for the purposes of section 7(4)(a) of the Attachment of Earnings Act 1971.]

NOTES

Commencement: 6 April 2017.
Inserted by the Insolvency (England and Wales) (Amendment) Rules 2017, SI 2017/366, rr 3, 29.

[6.574]
10.115 Approval of income payments agreements

(1) An income payments agreement can only be entered into before the bankrupt's discharge.

(2) The official receiver or trustee must provide a draft of the agreement to the bankrupt for the bankrupt's approval.

(3) Within 14 days or such longer period as may be specified by the official receiver or trustee from the date on which the income payments agreement was delivered, the bankrupt must—

(a) if the bankrupt decides to approve the agreement, authenticate the agreement and return it to the official receiver or trustee; or

(b) if the bankrupt decides not to approve the agreement, deliver a notice of that decision specifying the bankrupt's reasons for not approving the agreement to the official receiver or trustee.

NOTES

Commencement: 6 April 2017.

This rule derived from the Insolvency Rules 1986, SI 1986/1925, r 6.193A.

[6.575]
10.116 Acceptance of income payments agreements

(1) On receipt by the official receiver or trustee of the authenticated income payments agreement, the official receiver or trustee must authenticate and date it at which time it will come into force and a copy must be delivered to the bankrupt.

(2) Where the agreement provides for payments by a third person in accordance with section 310A(1)(b), a notice of the agreement must be delivered by the official receiver or trustee to that person.

(3) The notice must—

(a) identify the bankrupt;

(b) state that an income payments agreement has been made, the date of it, and that it provides for the payment by the third person of sums owed to the bankrupt (or a part of those sums) to be paid to the official receiver or trustee;

(c) state the name and address of the third person;

(d) state the amount of money to be paid to the official receiver or trustee from the bankrupt's income, the period over which the payments are to be made, and the intervals at which the sums are to be paid; and

(e) identify and provide contact details for the official receiver or trustee and details of how and where the sums are to be paid.

(4) When making any payment to the official receiver or the trustee a person who has received notice of an income payments agreement with reference to income otherwise payable by that person to the bankrupt may deduct the permitted fee towards the clerical and administrative costs of compliance with the income payments agreement.

(5) The payer must give to the bankrupt a statement of any amount deducted by the payer under paragraph (4).

NOTES

Commencement: 6 April 2017.

This rule derived from the Insolvency Rules 1986, SI 1986/1925, r 6.193B.

[6.576]
10.117 Variation of income payments agreements

(1) Where an application is made to court for variation of an income payments agreement, the application must be accompanied by a copy of the agreement.

(2) Where the bankrupt applies to the court for variation of an income payments agreement under section 310A(6)(b), the bankrupt must deliver a copy of the application and notice of the venue to the official receiver or trustee (whichever is appropriate) at least 28 days before the date fixed for the hearing.

(3) When the official receiver or trustee applies to the court for variation of an income payments agreement under section 310A(6)(b), the official receiver or trustee must deliver a copy of the application and notice of the venue to the bankrupt at least 28 days before the date fixed for the hearing.

(4) The court may order the variation of an income payments agreement under section 310A.

(5) The court order must contain—

(a) identification details for the proceedings;

(b) the name and title of the judge making the order;

(c) the name and postal address of the applicant

(d) the order that the income payments agreement be varied as specified;

(e) the date of the income payments agreement referred to in paragraph (d);

(f) details of how the income payments agreement is varied by the order; and

(g) the date of the order.

(6) Where the court orders an income payments agreement under section 310A(1)(a) to be varied, so as to be an agreement under section 310A(1)(b) providing that a third person is to make payments to the trustee or the official receiver, the official receiver or trustee must deliver a notice of the agreement to that person in accordance with rule 10.116(2).

Part 6 Insolvency Rules

(7) A person who has received notice of an income payments agreement relating to income otherwise payable by that person to the bankrupt may deduct the permitted fee towards the clerical and administrative costs of compliance with the agreement when making any payment to the official receiver or the trustee.

(8) The payer must give the bankrupt a statement of any amount deducted under paragraph (7).

NOTES

Commencement: 6 April 2017.

This rule derived from the Insolvency Rules 1986, SI 1986/1925, Sch 4, Fm 6.81.

CHAPTER 12 APPLICATIONS FOR PRODUCTION OF DOCUMENTS BY HER MAJESTY'S REVENUE AND CUSTOMS (SECTION 369)

[Note: a document required by the Act or these Rules must also contain the standard contents set out in Part 1.]

[6.577]
10.118 Application for order

(1) An application by the official receiver or the trustee for an order under section 369 (order for production of documents) must specify (with such details as will enable the order, if made, to be most easily complied with) the documents the production of which is sought, naming the official to whom the order is to be addressed.

(2) The court must fix a venue for the hearing of the application.

(3) The applicant must deliver notice of the venue, accompanied by a copy of the application to the Commissioners for Her Majesty's Revenue and Customs ("the Commissioners") at least 28 days before the hearing.

(4) The notice must require the Commissioners, not later than five business days before the date fixed for the hearing of the application, to inform the court whether they consent or object to the making of an order.

(5) If the Commissioners consent to the making of an order, the statement must include the name of the official to whom the order should be addressed, if other than the one named in the application.

(6) If the Commissioners object to the making of an order, they must file with the court a statement of their grounds of objection not less than five business days before the hearing of the application and must ensure that an official of theirs attends the hearing.

(7) The Commissioners must deliver a copy of the statement of objections to the applicant as soon as reasonably practicable.

NOTES

Commencement: 6 April 2017.

This rule derived from the Insolvency Rules 1986, SI 1986/1925, r 6.194.

[6.578]
10.119 Making and service of the order

(1) The court may make the order applied for, with any modifications which appear appropriate, having regard to any representations made on behalf of the Commissioners.

(2) The order—

(a) may be addressed to an official of Her Majesty's Revenue and Customs other than the one named in the application;

(b) must specify a time, not less than 28 days after service on the official to whom the order is addressed, within which compliance is required; and

(c) may include requirements as to the manner in which documents to which the order relates are to be produced.

(3) A sealed copy of the order must be served by the applicant on the official to whom it is addressed.

(4) If the official is unable to comply with the order because the relevant documents are not in the possession of the official, and the official has been unable to obtain possession of them, the official must file with the court a statement as to the reasons for the official's non-compliance.

(5) The official must deliver a copy of the statement referred to in paragraph (4) to the applicant as soon as reasonably practicable.

NOTES

Commencement: 6 April 2017.

This rule derived from the Insolvency Rules 1986, SI 1986/1925, r 6.195.

[6.579]
10.120 Custody of documents

When, in compliance with an order under section 369, original documents are produced, any person who, by order of the court under section 369(2), has possession or custody of those documents is responsible to the court for their safe keeping as, and return when, directed.

NOTES

Commencement: 6 April 2017.

This rule derived from the Insolvency Rules 1986, SI 1986/1925, r 6.196.

CHAPTER 13 MORTGAGED PROPERTY

[Note: a document required by the Act or these Rules must also contain the standard contents set out in Part 1.]

[6.580]

10.121 Interpretation

For the purposes of this Chapter "land" includes any interest in, or right over, land.

NOTES

Commencement: 6 April 2017.

This rule derived from the Insolvency Rules 1986, SI 1986/1925, r 6.197.

[6.581]

10.122 Claim by mortgagee of land

(1) Any person claiming to be the legal or equitable mortgagee of land belonging to the bankrupt may apply to the court for an order directing that the land be sold.

(2) The court, if satisfied as to the applicant's title, may direct accounts to be taken and enquiries made to ascertain—

(a) the principal, interest and costs due under the mortgage; and

(b) where the mortgagee has been in possession of the land or any part of it, the rents and profits, dividends, interest, or other proceeds received by the mortgagee or on the mortgagee's behalf.

(3) The court may also give directions in relation to any mortgage (whether prior or subsequent) on the same property, other than that of the applicant.

(4) For the purpose of those accounts and enquiries, and of making title to the purchaser, any of the parties may be examined by the court, and must produce on oath before the court all such documents in their custody or under their control relating to the bankrupt's estate as the court may direct.

(5) The court may under paragraph (4) order any of the parties to clarify any matter which is in dispute in the proceedings or give additional information in relation to any such matter and CPR Part 18 (further information) applies to any such order.

(6) In any proceedings between a mortgagor and mortgagee, or the trustee of either of them, the court may order accounts to be taken and enquiries made in like manner as in the Chancery Division of the High Court.

NOTES

Commencement: 6 April 2017.

This rule derived from the Insolvency Rules 1986, SI 1986/1925, r 6.197.

[6.582]

10.123 Power of court to order sale

(1) The court may order that the land, or any specified part of it, be sold and any party bound by the order and in possession of the land or part, or in receipt of the rents and profits from it, may be ordered to deliver possession or receipt to the purchaser or to such other person as the court may direct.

(2) The court may—

(a) permit the person having the conduct of the sale to sell the land in such manner as that person thinks fit; or

(b) direct that the land be sold as directed by the order.

(3) The court's order may contain directions—

(a) appointing the person to have the conduct of the sale;

(b) fixing the manner of sale (whether by contract conditional on the court's approval, private treaty, public auction, or otherwise);

(c) settling the particulars and conditions of sale;

(d) for obtaining evidence of the value of the property and for fixing a reserve or minimum price;

(e) requiring particular persons to join in the sale and conveyance;

(f) requiring the payment of the purchase money into court, or to trustees or others; or

(g) if the sale is to be by public auction, fixing the security (if any) to be given by the auctioneer, and the auctioneer's remuneration.

(4) The court may direct that, if the sale is to be by public auction, the mortgagee may bid on the mortgagee's own behalf.

(5) Nothing in this rule or rule 10.124 affects the rights in rem of creditors or third parties protected under [Article 8 of the EU Regulation].

NOTES

Commencement: 6 April 2017.

This rule derived from the Insolvency Rules 1986, SI 1986/1925, r 6.198

Para (5): words in square brackets substituted by the Insolvency (England and Wales) and Insolvency (Scotland) (Miscellaneous and Consequential Amendments) Rules 2017, SI 2017/1115, rr 22, 25(1).

[6.583]
10.124 Proceeds of sale

(1) The proceeds of sale must be applied as follows—
- (a) first in payment of—
  - (i) the trustee's expenses in relation to the application to the court,
  - (ii) the trustee's expenses of the sale and attendance at it, and
  - (iii) any costs of the trustee arising from the taking of accounts, and making of enquiries, as directed by the court under rule 10.122;
- (b) secondly, in payment of the amount found due to any mortgagee, for principal, interest and costs; and
- (c) the balance must be retained by or paid to the trustee.

(2) Where the proceeds of the sale are insufficient to pay in full the amount found due to any mortgagee, the mortgagee is entitled to prove as a creditor for any deficiency, and to receive dividends rateably with other creditors, but not so as to disturb any dividend already declared.

NOTES
Commencement: 6 April 2017.
This rule derived from the Insolvency Rules 1986, SI 1986/1925, r 6.199.

CHAPTER 14 AFTER-ACQUIRED PROPERTY

[6.584]
10.125 Duties of bankrupt in relation to after-acquired property

(1) The notice to be given by the bankrupt to the trustee, under section 333(2), of property acquired by, or devolving upon, the bankrupt, or of any increase of the bankrupt's income, must be given within 21 days of the bankrupt becoming aware of the relevant facts.

(2) The bankrupt must not, without the trustee's consent in writing, dispose of such property or income within the period of 42 days beginning with the date of giving the notice.

(3) If the bankrupt disposes of property before giving the notice required by this rule or contrary to paragraph (2), it is the bankrupt's duty as soon as reasonably practicable to disclose to the trustee the name and address of the person to whom the property was disposed, and to provide any other information which may be necessary to enable the trustee to trace the property and recover it for the bankrupt's estate.

(4) Paragraphs (1) to (3) do not apply to property acquired by the bankrupt in the ordinary course of a business carried on by the bankrupt.

(5) A bankrupt who carries on a business must, when required by the trustee, deliver to the trustee—
- (a) information about the business, showing the total of goods bought and sold and services supplied and the profit or loss arising from the business; and
- (b) fuller details including accounts of the business.

NOTES
Commencement: 6 April 2017.
This rule derived from the Insolvency Rules 1986, SI 1986/1925, r 6.200.

[6.585]
10.126 Trustee's recourse to person to whom property disposed

(1) Where property has been disposed of by the bankrupt, before giving the notice required by section 333(2) or otherwise in contravention of rule 10.125, the trustee may serve notice on the person to whom the property was disposed, claiming the property as part of the bankrupt's estate by virtue of section 307.

(2) The trustee's notice must be served within 28 days of the trustee becoming aware of the identity of the person to whom the property was disposed and an address at which that person can be served.

NOTES
Commencement: 6 April 2017.
This rule derived from the Insolvency Rules 1986, SI 1986/1925, r 6.201.

CHAPTER 15 PERMISSION TO ACT AS DIRECTOR, ETC

[Note: a document required by the Act or these Rules must also contain the standard contents set out in Part 1.]

[6.586]
10.127 Interpretation

In this Chapter a bankrupt includes a person in relation to whom a bankruptcy restrictions order is in force.

NOTES
Commencement: 6 April 2017.

This rule derived from the Insolvency Rules 1986, SI 1986/1925, r 6.202A.

[6.587]
10.128 Application for permission

(1) An application under section 11 of the Company Directors Disqualification Act 1986 by the bankrupt for permission to act as director of, or to take part or be concerned in the promotion, formation or management of a company, must be supported by a witness statement.

(2) The witness statement must identify the company and specify—

(a) the nature of its business or intended business, and the place or places where that business is, or is to be, carried on;

(b) whether it is, or in the case of a company which has not yet been incorporated is to be, a private or a public company;

(c) the persons who are, or are to be, principally responsible for the conduct of its affairs (whether as directors, shadow directors, managers or otherwise);

(d) the manner and capacity in which the applicant proposes to take part or be concerned in the promotion or formation of the company or, as the case may be, its management; and

(e) the emoluments and other benefits to be obtained from the directorship.

(3) The court must fix a venue for hearing the bankrupt's application and deliver notice of the hearing to the bankrupt.

NOTES

Commencement: 6 April 2017.

This rule derived from the Insolvency Rules 1986, SI 1986/1925, r 6.203.

[6.588]
10.129 Report of official receiver

(1) The bankrupt must, not less than 28 days before the date fixed for the hearing, deliver to the official receiver and the trustee (if different) notice of the venue, accompanied by copies of the application and the witness statement under rule 10.128.

(2) The official receiver may, not less than 14 days before the date fixed for the hearing, file with the court a report of any matters which the official receiver considers ought to be drawn to the court's attention.

(3) The official receiver must deliver a copy of the report to the bankrupt and to the trustee (if not the official receiver) as soon as reasonably practicable after it is filed.

(4) Where a copy of the report is delivered by post under paragraph (3) it must be delivered by first class post.

(5) The bankrupt may, not later than five business days before the date of the hearing, file with the court a notice specifying any statements in the official receiver's report which the bankrupt intends to deny or dispute.

(6) If the bankrupt files such a notice, the bankrupt must deliver copies of it, not less than three business days before the date of the hearing, to the official receiver and the trustee.

(7) The official receiver and the trustee may appear on the hearing of the application, and may make representations and put to the bankrupt such questions as the court may allow.

NOTES

Commencement: 6 April 2017.

This rule derived from the Insolvency Rules 1986, SI 1986/1925, r 6.204.

[6.589]
10.130 Court's order on application

(1) A court order granting the bankrupt permission under section 11 of the Company Directors Disqualification Act 1986 must specify what the bankrupt has permission to do.

(2) The court, having regard to any representations made by the trustee on the hearing of the application, may—

(a) include in the order provision varying an income payments order or an income payments agreement already in force in relation to the bankrupt; or

(b) if no income payments order is in force, make one.

(3) Whether or not the application is granted, copies of the order must be delivered by the court to the bankrupt, the official receiver and the trustee (if different).

NOTES

Commencement: 6 April 2017.

This rule derived from the Insolvency Rules 1986, SI 1986/1925, r 6.205.

[6.590]
10.131 Costs under this Chapter

In no case do any costs or expenses arising under this Chapter fall on the official receiver personally.

NOTES

Commencement: 6 April 2017.

This rule derived from the Insolvency Rules 1986, SI 1986/1925, r 6.222.

CHAPTER 16 ANNULMENT OF BANKRUPTCY ORDER

[Note: a document required by the Act or these Rules must also contain the standard contents set out in Part 1.]

[6.591]
10.132 Application for annulment

(1) An application to the court under section 282(1) for the annulment of a bankruptcy order must specify whether it is made—

(a) under subsection (1)(a) (claim that the order ought not to have been made); or
(b) under subsection (1)(b) (debts and expenses of the bankruptcy all paid or secured).

(2) The application must be supported by a witness statement stating the grounds on which it is made.

(3) Where the application is made under section 282(1)(b), the witness statement must contain all the facts by reference to which, under the Act and these Rules, the court may be satisfied that the condition in section 282(1)(b) applies before annulling the bankruptcy order.

(4) A copy of the application and the witness statement in support must be filed with the court.

(5) The court must deliver notice of the venue fixed for the hearing to the applicant.

(6) Where the application is made under section 282(1)(a) the applicant must deliver notice of the venue, accompanied by copies of the application and the supporting witness statement, to the official receiver, the trustee (if different), and the person on whose petition the bankruptcy order was made in sufficient time to enable them to be present at the hearing.

(7) Where the application is made under section 282(1)(b) the applicant must deliver notice of the venue, accompanied by copies of the application and the supporting witness statement, to the official receiver and the trustee (if different) not less than 28 days before the hearing.

(8) Where the applicant is not the bankrupt, all notices, documents and evidence required by this Chapter to be delivered to another party by the applicant must also be delivered to the bankrupt.

NOTES

Commencement: 6 April 2017.
This rule derived from the Insolvency Rules 1986, SI 1986/1925, r 6.206.

[6.592]
10.133 Report by trustee

(1) The following applies where the application is made under section 282(1)(b) (debts and expenses of the bankruptcy all paid or secured).

(2) Not less than 21 days before the date fixed for the hearing, the trustee must file with the court a report relating to the following matters—

(a) the circumstances leading to the bankruptcy;
(b) a summary of the bankrupt's assets and liabilities at the date of the bankruptcy order and at the date of the application;
(c) details of any creditors who are known to the trustee to have claims, but have not proved; and
(d) such other matters as the person making the report considers to be, in the circumstances, necessary for the information of the court.

(3) Where the trustee is other than the official receiver, the report must also include a statement of—

(a) the trustee's remuneration;
(b) the basis fixed for the trustee's remuneration under rule 18.16; and
(c) the expenses incurred by the trustee.

(4) The report must include particulars of the extent to which, and the manner in which, the debts and expenses of the bankruptcy have been paid or secured.

(5) In so far as debts and expenses are unpaid but secured, the person making the report must state in it whether and to what extent that person considers the security to be satisfactory.

(6) A copy of the report must be delivered to the applicant as soon as reasonably practicable after it is filed with the court and the applicant may file a further witness statement in answer to statements made in the report.

(7) Copies of any such witness statement must be delivered by the applicant to the official receiver and the trustee (if different).

(8) If the trustee is other than the official receiver, a copy of the trustee's report must be delivered to the official receiver at least 21 days before the hearing.

(9) The official receiver may then file an additional report, a copy of which must be delivered to the applicant and the trustee (if not the official receiver) at least five business days before the hearing.

NOTES

Commencement: 6 April 2017.
This rule derived from the Insolvency Rules 1986, SI 1986/1925, r 6.207.

[6.593]

10.134 Applicant's claim that remuneration or expenses are excessive

(1) Where the trustee is other than the official receiver and application for annulment is made under section 282(1)(b), the applicant may also apply to the court for one or more of the orders in paragraph (4) on the ground that the remuneration charged, or expenses incurred, by the trustee are in all the circumstances excessive.

(2) Application for such an order must be made no later than five business days before the date fixed for the hearing of the application for annulment and be accompanied by a copy of any evidence which the applicant intends to provide in support.

(3) The applicant must deliver a copy of the application and of any evidence accompanying it to the trustee as soon as reasonably practicable after the application is made.

(4) If the court annuls the bankruptcy order under section 282(1)(b) and considers the application to be well-founded, it must also make one or more of the following orders—

- (a) an order reducing the amount of remuneration which the trustee was entitled to charge;
- (b) an order that some or all of the remuneration or expenses in question be treated as not being bankruptcy expenses;
- (c) an order that the trustee or the trustee's personal representative pay to the applicant the amount of the excess of remuneration or expenses or such part of the excess as the court may specify; and
- (d) any other order that the court thinks just.

NOTES

Commencement: 6 April 2017.

This rule derived from the Insolvency Rules 1986, SI 1986/1925, r 6.207A.

[6.594]

10.135 Power of court to stay proceedings

(1) The court may, in advance of the hearing, make an order staying any proceedings which it thinks ought, in the circumstances of the application, to be stayed.

(2) Except in relation to an application for an order staying all or any part of the proceedings in the bankruptcy, application for an order under this rule may be made without notice to any other party.

(3) Where an application is made under this rule for an order staying all or any part of the proceedings in the bankruptcy, the applicant must deliver copies of the application to the official receiver and the trustee, if other than the official receiver, in sufficient time to enable them to be present at the hearing and make representations.

(4) Where the court makes an order under this rule staying all or any part of the proceedings in the bankruptcy, the rules in this Chapter nevertheless continue to apply to any application for, or other matters in connection with, the annulment of the bankruptcy order.

(5) If the court makes an order under this rule, it must deliver copies of the order to the applicant, the official receiver and the trustee (if different).

NOTES

Commencement: 6 April 2017.

This rule derived from the Insolvency Rules 1986, SI 1986/1925, r 6.208.

[6.595]

10.136 Notice to creditors who have not proved

Where the application for annulment is made under section 282(1)(b) and it has been reported to the court under rule 10.133(2)(c) that there are known creditors of the bankrupt who have not proved, the court may—

- (a) direct the trustee or, if no trustee has been appointed, the official receiver to deliver notice of the application to such of those creditors as the court thinks ought to be informed of it, with a view to their proving for their debts within 21 days;
- (b) direct the trustee or, if no trustee has been appointed, the official receiver to advertise the fact that the application has been made, so that creditors who have not proved may do so within a specified time; and
- (c) adjourn the application meanwhile, for any period not less than 35 days.

NOTES

Commencement: 6 April 2017.

This rule derived from the Insolvency Rules 1986, SI 1986/1925, r 6.209.

[6.596]

10.137 The hearing

(1) The trustee must attend the hearing of the application under section 282 unless the court directs otherwise.

(2) The official receiver, if not the trustee, may attend, but is not required to do so unless the official receiver has filed a report under rule 10.133.

(3) If the court makes an order on the application or on an application under rule 10.134, it must deliver copies of the order to the applicant, the official receiver and (if other) the trustee.

(4) An order of annulment under section 282 must contain—

(a) identification details for the proceedings;

(b) the name and address of the applicant;

(c) the date of the bankruptcy order;

(d) the date of the filing of the bankruptcy petition or the making of the bankruptcy application;

(e) the date and reference number of the registration of the bankruptcy petition or bankruptcy application as a pending action with the Chief Land Registrar;

(f) the date and reference number of the registration of the bankruptcy order on the register of writs and orders affecting land with the Chief Land Registrar;

(g) a statement that it appears to the court that—

(i) the bankruptcy order ought not to have been made, or

(ii) the bankruptcy debts and expenses of the bankruptcy have all been paid or secured to the satisfaction of the court;

and that under section 282(2) the bankruptcy order ought to be annulled;

(h) an order—

(i) that the bankruptcy order specified in the order is annulled,

(ii) that the bankruptcy petition or bankruptcy application specified in the order be dismissed, and

(iii) that the registration of the petition or the bankruptcy application as a pending action with the Chief Land Registrar and of the bankruptcy order with the Chief Land Registrar specified in the order be vacated upon application made by the bankrupt; and

(i) the date of the order.

(5) The order must contain a notice to the bankrupt stating—

(a) should the bankrupt require notice of the order to be gazetted and to be advertised in the same manner as the bankruptcy order was advertised, the bankrupt must within 28 days deliver notice of that requirement to the official receiver; and

(b) it is the bankrupt's responsibility and in the bankrupt's interest to ensure that the registration of the petition or bankruptcy application and of the bankruptcy order with the Chief Land Registrar are cancelled.

[(6) The adjudicator is not in any event to be liable for costs arising on an application under section 282.]

NOTES

Commencement: 6 April 2017.

This rule derived from the Insolvency Rules 1986, SI 1986/1925, r 6.210.

Para (6): added by the Insolvency (England and Wales) (Amendment) Rules 2017, SI 2017/366, rr 3, 30.

[6.597]
10.138 Matters to be proved under section 282(1)(b)

(1) This rule applies in relation to the matters which—

(a) must, in an application under section 282(1)(b), be proved to the satisfaction of the court; and

(b) may be taken into account by the court on hearing such an application.

(2) Subject to the following paragraph, all bankruptcy debts which have been proved must have been—

(a) paid in full; or

(b) secured in full to the satisfaction of the court.

(3) If a debt is disputed, or a creditor who has proved can no longer be traced, the bankrupt must have given such security (in the form of money paid into court, or a bond entered into with approved sureties) as the court considers adequate to satisfy any sum that may subsequently be proved to be due to the creditor concerned and (if the court thinks just) costs.

(4) Where such security has been given in the case of an untraced creditor, the court may direct that particulars of the alleged debt, and the security, be advertised in such manner as it thinks just.

(5) If the court directs such advertisement and no claim on the security is made within 12 months from the date of the advertisement (or the first advertisement, if more than one), the court must, on application, order the security to be released.

(6) In determining whether to annul a bankruptcy order under section 282(1)(b), the court may, if it thinks just and without prejudice to the generality of its discretion under section 282(1), take into account whether any sums have been paid or payment of any sums has been secured in respect of post-commencement interest on the bankruptcy debts which have been proved.

(7) For the purposes of paragraphs (2) and (6), security includes an undertaking given by a solicitor and accepted by the court.

(8) For the purposes of paragraph (6), "post-commencement interest" means interest on the bankruptcy debts at the rate specified in section 328(5) in relation to periods during which those debts have been outstanding since the commencement of the bankruptcy.

NOTES

Commencement: 6 April 2017.

This rule derived from the Insolvency Rules 1986, SI 1986/1925, r 6.211.

[6.598]
10.139 Notice to creditors

(1) Where the official receiver has delivered notice of the debtor's bankruptcy to the creditors and the bankruptcy order is annulled, the official receiver must as soon as reasonably practicable deliver notice of the annulment to them.

(2) Expenses incurred by the official receiver in delivering such notice are a charge in the official receiver's favour on the property of the former bankrupt, whether or not the property is actually in the official receiver's hands.

(3) Where any property is in the hands of a trustee or any person other than the former bankrupt, the official receiver's charge is subject to any costs that may be incurred by the trustee or that other person in effecting realisation of the property for the purpose of satisfying the charge.

NOTES

Commencement: 6 April 2017.
This rule derived from the Insolvency Rules 1986, SI 1986/1925, r 6.212.

[6.599]
10.140 Other matters arising on annulment

(1) Within 28 days of the making of an order under section 282, the former bankrupt may require the official receiver to publish a notice of the making of the order in accordance with paragraphs (2) and (4).

(2) As soon as reasonably practicable the notice must be—
(a) gazetted; and
(b) advertised in the same manner as the bankruptcy order to which it relates was advertised.

(3) The notice must state—
(a) the name of the former bankrupt;
(b) the date on which the bankruptcy order was made;
(c) that the bankruptcy order against the former bankrupt has been annulled under section 282(1); and
(d) the date of the annulment.

(4) Where the former bankrupt—
(a) has died; or
(b) is a person lacking capacity to manage the person's own affairs (within the meaning of the Mental Capacity Act 2005);

the reference to the former bankrupt in paragraph (1) is to be read as referring to the former bankrupt's personal representative or, as the case may be, a person appointed by the court to represent or act for the former bankrupt.

NOTES

Commencement: 6 April 2017.
This rule derived from the Insolvency Rules 1986, SI 1986/1925, r 6.213.

[6.600]
10.141 Trustee's final account

(1) Where a bankruptcy order is annulled under section 282, this does not of itself release the trustee from any duty or obligation, imposed on the trustee by or under the Act or these Rules, to account for all of the trustee's transactions in connection with the former bankrupt's estate.

(2) The trustee must deliver a copy of the trustee's final account to the Secretary of State as soon as practicable after the court's order annulling the bankruptcy order.

(3) The trustee must file a copy of the final account with the court.

(4) The final account must include a summary of the trustee's receipts and payments in the administration, and contain a statement to the effect that the trustee has reconciled the account with that which is held by the Secretary of State in respect of the bankruptcy.

(5) The trustee is released from such time as the court may determine, having regard to whether—
(a) the trustee has delivered the final accounts under paragraph (2); and
(b) any security given under rule 10.138 has been, or will be, released.

NOTES

Commencement: 6 April 2017.
This rule derived from the Insolvency Rules 1986, SI 1986/1925, r 6.214.

CHAPTER 17 DISCHARGE

[Note: a document required by the Act or these Rules must also contain the standard contents set out in Part 1.]

[6.601]
10.142 Application for suspension of discharge

(1) The following applies where the official receiver or trustee (if different) applies to the court for an order under section 279(3) (suspension of automatic discharge), but not where the official receiver makes that application under rule 10.104 on the adjournment of the bankrupt's public examination.

(2) The official receiver or trustee must file, with the application, evidence in support setting out the reasons why it appears that such an order should be made.

(3) The court must fix a venue for the hearing of the application, and deliver notice of it to the official receiver, the trustee, and the bankrupt.

(4) Copies of the official receiver's report under this rule must be delivered by the official receiver to the bankrupt and any trustee who is not the official receiver, so as to reach them at least 21 days before the date fixed for the hearing.

(5) Copies of the trustee's evidence in support of the application must be delivered by the trustee to the official receiver and the bankrupt at least 21 days before the date fixed for the hearing.

(6) If the bankrupt intends to deny or dispute any statements in the official receiver's or trustee's evidence in support then the bankrupt must not later than five business days before the date of the hearing, file with the court a notice specifying the statements which the bankrupt intends to deny or dispute.

(7) If the bankrupt files such a notice under paragraph (6), the bankrupt must deliver copies of it, not less than three business days before the date of the hearing, to the official receiver and any trustee.

(8) If the court makes an order suspending the bankrupt's discharge, copies of the order must be delivered by the court to the official receiver, any trustee and the bankrupt.

(9) An order of suspension of discharge under section 279(3) must be headed "Suspension of Discharge" and must contain—

- (a) identification details for the proceedings;
- (b) the name and title of the judge making the order;
- (c) identification and contact details for the applicant who will be the official receiver or the trustee;
- (d) the date of the bankruptcy order;
- (e) a statement that it appears to the court that the bankrupt has failed or is failing to comply with the bankrupt's obligations under the Act for the reasons specified in the order;
- (f) a statement in what respect the bankrupt has failed to comply with the bankrupt's obligations under the Act;
- (g) an order that the relevant period for the purpose of section 279 will cease to run for either—
  - (i) a specified period, or
  - (ii) until specified conditions have been fulfilled;
- (h) the period or conditions referred to in paragraph (g); and
- (i) the date of the order.

NOTES

Commencement: 6 April 2017.

This rule derived from the Insolvency Rules 1986, SI 1986/1925, r 6.215.

[6.602]

10.143 Lifting of suspension of discharge

(1) Where the court has made an order under section 279(3) that the period specified in section 279(1) will cease to run, the bankrupt may apply to it for the order to be discharged.

(2) The court must fix a venue for the hearing of the application and deliver notice of it to the bankrupt.

(3) The bankrupt must, not less than 28 days before the date fixed for the hearing, deliver notice of the venue with a copy of the application to the official receiver and any trustee.

(4) The official receiver and the trustee may appear and be heard on the bankrupt's application.

(5) Whether or not they appear, the official receiver and trustee may file with the court a report containing evidence in support of any matters which either of them considers ought to be drawn to the court's attention.

(6) If the court made an order under section 279(3)(b), the court may request a report from the official receiver or the trustee as to whether or not the condition specified in the order has been fulfilled.

(7) Copies of a report filed under paragraph (5) or requested by the court under paragraph (6) must be delivered by the official receiver or trustee to the bankrupt and to either the official receiver or trustee (depending on which has filed the report), not later than 14 days before the hearing.

(8) The bankrupt may, not later than five business days before the date of the hearing, file with the court a notice specifying any statements in the official receiver's or trustee's report which the bankrupt intends to deny or dispute.

(9) If the bankrupt files such a notice, the bankrupt must deliver copies of it to the official receiver and the trustee not less than three business days before the date of the hearing.

(10) If on the bankrupt's application the court discharges the order under section 279(3) (being satisfied that the period specified in section 279(1) should begin to run again), it must deliver to the bankrupt a certificate that it has done so, and must deliver copies of the certificate to the official receiver and the trustee (if different).

(11) The court's order lifting the suspension of discharge must contain—

- (a) identification details for the proceedings;
- (b) the name and title of the judge making the order;
- (c) the date and terms of the order made under section 279;
- (d) a statement that the bankrupt specified in the order has made the application;
- (e) a statement whether or not the court has taken into consideration the report of the official receiver or of the trustee or both in this matter;

(f) an order discharging the order suspending discharge; and
(g) state the date of the order.

(12) The certificate that the order suspending discharge has been lifted must contain—
(a) identification details for the proceedings;
(b) the date of the bankruptcy order;
(c) the date of the order suspending discharge;
(d) a statement that the court has made—
(i) the bankruptcy order specified in this order against the bankrupt specified in this order, and
(ii) the order suspending the bankrupt's discharge specified in this order;
(e) a statement that it is certified that the order of suspension of discharge was lifted on the date specified in this order; and
(f) the date of the certificate.

NOTES

Commencement: 6 April 2017.
This rule derived from the Insolvency Rules 1986, SI 1986/1925, r 6.216.

[6.603]
10.144 Certificate of discharge from bankruptcy order made otherwise than on a bankruptcy application

(1) A bankrupt may apply to the court for a certificate of discharge where the bankruptcy order was made otherwise than on a bankruptcy application.

(2) Where it appears to the court that the bankrupt is discharged, whether by expiration of time or otherwise, the court must deliver a certificate of discharge to the former bankrupt.

(3) The certificate of discharge must be headed "Certificate of Discharge" and must contain—
(a) identification details for the proceedings;
(b) the date of the bankruptcy order;
(c) the statement that the former bankrupt was discharged from bankruptcy;
(d) the date of discharge from bankruptcy; and
(e) the date of the certificate.

(4) The certificate must also state—
(a) that the former bankrupt may request in writing notice of the discharge to be gazetted and advertised in the same manner as the bankruptcy order; and
(b) that such a request must be delivered to the official receiver within 28 days of the making of the certificate of discharge.

(5) As soon as reasonably practicable after delivery of such a request to the official receiver the notice of discharge must be gazetted, and advertised in the same manner as the bankruptcy order.

(6) The notice must contain—
(a) the name of the former bankrupt;
(b) the date of the bankruptcy order;
(c) the statement that a certificate of discharge has been delivered to the former bankrupt;
(d) the date of the certificate; and
(e) the date from which the discharge is effective.

(7) An application for a notice of discharge and a request in writing that the notice be gazetted and advertised may be made by the former bankrupt's personal representative or, as the case may be, a person appointed by the court to represent or act for the former bankrupt where the former bankrupt—
(a) has died; or
(b) is a person lacking capacity to manage the person's own affairs (within the meaning of the Mental Capacity Act 2005).

NOTES

Commencement: 6 April 2017.
This rule derived from the Insolvency Rules 1986, SI 1986/1925, rr 6.219(3), 6.220.

[6.604]
10.145 Certificate of discharge from bankruptcy order made on a bankruptcy application

(1) A bankrupt may apply to the official receiver for a certificate of discharge where the bankruptcy order was made on a bankruptcy application.

(2) The bankrupt must send the application to the official receiver with the prescribed fee.

(3) Where it appears to the official receiver that the bankrupt is discharged, the official receiver must deliver a certificate of discharge to the former bankrupt by electronic means.

(4) The certificate of discharge must be headed "Certificate of Discharge" and must contain—
(a) identification details for the former bankrupt;
(b) the date of the bankruptcy order;
(c) a statement that the former bankrupt was discharged from bankruptcy;
(d) the date of discharge from the bankruptcy; and
(e) the date of the certificate.

(5) The certificate must also state—

(a) that the former bankrupt may request in writing notice of the discharge to be gazetted and advertised in the same manner as the bankruptcy order; and
(b) that such a request must be delivered to the official receiver within 28 days of the making of the certificate of discharge.

(6) As soon as reasonably practicable after delivery of such a request to the official receiver the notice of discharge must be gazetted, and advertised in the same manner as the bankruptcy order.

(7) The notice must contain—
(a) the name of the former bankrupt;
(b) the date of the bankruptcy order;
(c) the statement that a certificate of discharge has been delivered to the former bankrupt;
(d) the date of the certificate; and
(e) the date from which the discharge is effective.

(8) An application for a notice of discharge and a request in writing that the notice be gazetted and advertised may be made by the former bankrupt's personal representative or, as the case may be, a person appointed by the court to represent or act for the former bankrupt where the former bankrupt—
(a) has died; or
(b) is a person lacking capacity to manage the person's own affairs (within the meaning of the Mental Capacity Act 2005).

NOTES

Commencement: 6 April 2017.
This rule derived from the Insolvency Rules 1986, SI 1986/1925, rr 6.219(3), 6.220.

[6.605]
10.146 Bankrupt's debts surviving discharge

[Note: see also section 281 (effect of discharge).]

Discharge does not release the bankrupt from any obligation arising—
(a) under a confiscation order made under section 1 of the Drug Trafficking Offences Act 1986;
(b) under a confiscation order made under section 1 of the Criminal Justice (Scotland) Act 1987;
(c) under a confiscation order made under section 71 of the Criminal Justice Act 1988;
(d) under a confiscation order made under Parts 2, 3 or 4 of the Proceeds of Crime Act 2002; or
(e) from a payment out of the social fund under section 138(1)(b) of the Social Security Contributions and Benefits Act 1992 by way of crisis loan or budgeting loan.

NOTES

Commencement: 6 April 2017.
This rule derived from the Insolvency Rules 1986, SI 1986/1925, r 6.223.

[6.606]
10.147 Costs under this Chapter

In no case do any costs or expenses arising under this Chapter fall on the official receiver personally.

NOTES

Commencement: 6 April 2017.
This rule derived from the Insolvency Rules 1986, SI 1986/1925, r 6.222.

CHAPTER 18 PRIORITY OF PAYMENT OF COSTS ETC OUT OF THE BANKRUPT'S ESTATE

[Note: a document required by the Act or these Rules must also contain the standard contents set out in Part 1.]

[6.607]
10.148 Expenses

All fees, costs, charges and other expenses incurred in the course of the bankruptcy are to be treated as expenses of the bankruptcy.

NOTES

Commencement: 6 April 2017.
This rule derived from the Insolvency Rules 1986, SI 1986/1925, r 12.2.

[6.608]
10.149 General rule as to priority

The expenses of the bankruptcy are payable out of the bankrupt's estate in the following order of priority—
(a) expenses or costs which—
(i) are properly chargeable or incurred by the official receiver or the trustee in preserving, realising or getting in any of the assets of the bankrupt or otherwise relating to the conduct of any legal proceedings which [the official receiver or the trustee] has power to bring (whether the claim on which the proceedings are based forms part of the bankrupt's estate or otherwise) or defend,
(ii) relate to the employment of a shorthand writer, if appointed by an order of the court made at the instance of the official receiver in connection with an examination, or

(iii) are incurred in holding an examination under rule 10.102 (examinee unfit) where the application was made by the official receiver;

(b) any other expenses incurred or disbursements made by the official receiver or under the official receiver's authority, including those incurred or made in carrying on the business of a debtor or bankrupt;

(c) the fees payable under any order made under section 415 or 415A, including those payable to the official receiver (other than the fee referred to in sub-paragraph (d)), and any remuneration payable to the official receiver under general regulations;

[(d) the fee payable under any order made under section 415 for the performance by the official receiver of the general duties of the official receiver and any repayable sum deposited under any such order as security for the fee;]

(e) . . .

(f) the cost of any security provided by an interim receiver, trustee or special manager in accordance with the Act or these Rules;

(g) the remuneration of the interim receiver (if any);

(h) any sum deposited on an application for the appointment of an interim receiver;

(i) the costs of the petitioner, and of any person appearing on the petition whose costs are allowed by the court;

(j) the remuneration of the special manager (if any);

(k) any amount payable to a person or firm employed or authorised, under rules 10.59, 10.60 or 10.64, to assist in the preparation of a statement of affairs or of accounts;

(l) any allowance made, by order of the court, in respect of costs on an application for release from the obligation to submit a statement of affairs, or for an extension of time for submitting such a statement;

(m) the costs of employing a shorthand writer in any case other than one appointed by an order of the court at the instance of the official receiver in connection with an examination;

(n) any necessary disbursements by the trustee in the course of the trustee's administration (including any expenses incurred by members of the creditors' committee or their representatives and allowed by the trustee under rule 17.24, but not including any [costs referred to in Article 30 of the EU Regulation and] payment of capital gains tax in circumstances referred to in sub-paragraph (q));

(o) the remuneration or emoluments of any person (including the bankrupt) who has been employed by the trustee to perform any services for the bankrupt's estate, as required or authorised by or under the Act or these Rules;

(p) the remuneration of the trustee, up to any amount not exceeding that which is payable under Schedule 11;

(q) the amount of any capital gains tax on chargeable gains accruing on the realisation of any asset of the bankrupt (irrespective of the person by whom the realisation is effected);

(r) the balance, after payment of any sums due under sub-paragraph (p), of any remuneration due to the trustee; and

(s) any other expenses properly chargeable by the trustee in carrying out the trustee's functions in the bankruptcy.

NOTES

Commencement: 6 April 2017.

This rule derived from the Insolvency Rules 1986, SI 1986/1925, r 6.224.

Words in square brackets in para (a)(i) substituted by the Insolvency (England and Wales) (Amendment) Rules 2017, SI 2017/366, rr 3, 31; para (d) substituted and para (e) revoked by the Insolvency (England and Wales) and Insolvency (Scotland) (Miscellaneous and Consequential Amendments) Rules 2017, SI 2017/1115, rr 2, 9.

words in square brackets in para (n) inserted by the Insolvency Amendment (EU 2015/848) Regulations 2017, SI 2017/702, regs 2, 3, Schedule, Pt 2, paras 32, 43, as from 26 June 2017, except in relation to proceedings opened before that date.

CHAPTER 19 SECOND BANKRUPTCY

[Note: a document required by the Act or these Rules must also contain the standard contents set out in Part 1.]

[6.609]
10.150 Scope of this Chapter

[Note: "the earlier bankruptcy", "the existing trustee" and "the later bankruptcy" are defined in section 334(1).]

The rules in this Chapter relate to the manner in which, in the case of a second bankruptcy, the existing trustee is to deal with property and money to which section 334(3) applies until there is a trustee of the bankrupt's estate in the later bankruptcy.

NOTES

Commencement: 6 April 2017.

This rule derived from the Insolvency Rules 1986, SI 1986/1925, r 6.225.

[6.610]
10.151 General duty of existing trustee

(1) The existing trustee must take into custody or under control the property and money to which section 334(3) applies so far as this has not already been done in the earlier bankruptcy.

(2) Where any of that property consists of perishable goods, or goods the value of which is likely to diminish if they are not disposed of, the existing trustee has power to sell or otherwise dispose of those goods.

(3) The proceeds of such a sale or disposal must be held, under the existing trustee's control, with the other property and money comprised in the bankrupt's estate.

NOTES

Commencement: 6 April 2017.

This rule derived from the Insolvency Rules 1986, SI 1986/1925, r 6.226.

[6.611]

10.152 Delivery up to later trustee

The existing trustee must, if requested by the later trustee for the purposes of the later bankruptcy, deliver to the later trustee as soon as reasonably practicable all the property and money in the existing trustee's custody or under the existing trustee's control under rule 10.151.

NOTES

Commencement: 6 April 2017.

This rule derived from the Insolvency Rules 1986, SI 1986/1925, r 6.227.

[6.612]

10.153 Existing trustee's expenses

Any expenses incurred by the existing trustee in compliance with section 335(1) and this Chapter must be paid out of, and are a charge on, all of the property and money referred to in section 334(3), whether in the hands of the existing trustee or of the later trustee for the purposes of the later bankruptcy.

NOTES

Commencement: 6 April 2017.

This rule derived from the Insolvency Rules 1986, SI 1986/1925, r 6.228.

CHAPTER 20 CRIMINAL BANKRUPTCY

[Note: a document required by the Act or these Rules must also contain the standard contents set out in Part 1.]

[6.613]

[10.153A Application

The rules in this chapter apply to proceedings arising out of criminal bankruptcy orders.]

NOTES

Commencement: 6 April 2017.

Inserted by the Insolvency (England and Wales) (Amendment) Rules 2017, SI 2017/366, rr 3, 32.

[6.614]

10.154 Contents of petition

The petition must contain—

(a) identification details for the debtor;
(b) the name and postal address of the petitioner if other than the Official Petitioner;
(c) the occupation (if any) of the debtor;
(d) any other address at which the debtor has resided at or after the time the petition debt was incurred;
(e) any other name by which the debtor is or has been known;
(f) the trading name, business address and nature of the business of any business carried on by the debtor;
(g) details of any other businesses which have been carried on by the debtor at or after the time the petition debt was incurred;
(h) a statement that the petitioner requests that court make a bankruptcy order against the debtor;
(i) a statement that a criminal bankruptcy order was made against the debtor at the court specified in this petition and that an office copy of the order accompanies the petition;
(j) the name of the court that made the criminal bankruptcy order;
(k) a statement that the criminal bankruptcy order—
  (i) remains in force, or
  (ii) was amended by the Court of Appeal on the date specified in this petition, that an office copy of the order of the Court of Appeal accompanies the petition and that the order as amended by the Court of Appeal remains in force;
(l) a statement that according to the criminal bankruptcy order the debtor is indebted to the persons specified in this petition as having suffered loss or damage in the aggregate sum of the amount of loss or damage suffered specified in this petition;
(m) the names and addresses of the persons referred to in paragraph (k); and
(n) the amount of loss or damage suffered referred to in paragraph (k).

NOTES

Commencement: 6 April 2017.

This rule derived from the Insolvency Rules 1986, SI 1986/1925, Sch 4, Fm 6.79.

[6.615]
10.155 Status and functions of Official Petitioner

(1) The Official Petitioner is to be treated for all purposes of the Act and these Rules as a creditor of the bankrupt.

(2) The Official Petitioner may attend or be represented at any meeting of creditors, and is to be given any notice under the Act or these Rules which is required or authorised to be delivered to creditors; and the requirements of these Rules as to the delivery and use of proxies do not apply to the Official Petitioner.

NOTES

Commencement: 6 April 2017.
This rule derived from the Insolvency Rules 1986, SI 1986/1925, r 6.230.

[6.616]
10.156 Interim receivership

The rules in Chapter 4 of this Part about the appointment of an interim receiver apply in criminal bankruptcy only in so far as they provide for the appointment of the official receiver as interim receiver.

NOTES

Commencement: 6 April 2017.
This rule derived from the Insolvency Rules 1986, SI 1986/1925, r 6.231.

[6.617]
10.157 Proof of bankruptcy debts and notice of order

(1) The making of a bankruptcy order on a criminal bankruptcy petition does not affect the right of creditors to prove for their debts arising otherwise than in consequence of the criminal proceedings.

(2) A person specified in a criminal bankruptcy order as having suffered loss or damage must be treated as a creditor of the bankrupt; and a copy of the order is sufficient evidence of that person's claim, subject to its being shown by any party to the bankruptcy proceedings that the loss or damage actually suffered was more or (as the case may be) less than the amount specified in the order.

(3) The requirements of these Rules about proofs do not apply to the Official Petitioner.

(4) In criminal bankruptcy, notice of the making of the bankruptcy order and blank proofs must be delivered by the official receiver to every creditor who is known to the official receiver within 12 weeks from the making of the bankruptcy order.

NOTES

Commencement: 6 April 2017.
This rule derived from the Insolvency Rules 1986, SI 1986/1925, r 6.232.

[6.618]
10.158 Rules not applying in criminal bankruptcy

The following rules do not apply in criminal bankruptcy—

(a) . . .
(b) Chapter 6 of this Part, except rules 10.86 (release of official receiver) and 10.91 (power of court to set aside transactions);
(c) rule 15.21(a) and (b) (chair at meetings); and
(d) Part 17 (creditors' and liquidation committees).

NOTES

Commencement: 6 April 2017.
This rule derived from the Insolvency Rules 1986, SI 1986/1925, r 6.234.
Para (a): revoked by the Insolvency (England and Wales) (Amendment) Rules 2017, SI 2017/366, rr 3, 33.

[6.619]
10.159 Annulment of criminal bankruptcy order

Chapter 16 of this Part (annulment of bankruptcy order) applies to an application to the court under section 282(2) as it applies to an application under section 282(1), with any necessary modifications.

NOTES

Commencement: 6 April 2017.
This rule derived from the Insolvency Rules 1986, SI 1986/1925, r 6.234(3).

[6.620]
10.160 Application by bankrupt for discharge

(1) A bankrupt who applies under section 280 for an order of discharge must deliver notice of the application to the official receiver, and deposit with the official receiver such sum as the official receiver may require for the purpose of covering the costs of the application.

(2) The court, if satisfied that the bankrupt has complied with paragraph (1), must fix a venue for the hearing of the application, and give at least 42 days' notice of it to the official receiver and the bankrupt.

(3) The official receiver must deliver notice of the application and venue to—

(a) the trustee; and

(b) every creditor who, to the official receiver's knowledge, has a claim outstanding against the bankrupt's estate which has not been satisfied.

(4) These notices must be delivered not later than 14 days before the date fixed for the hearing of the bankrupt's application.

NOTES

Commencement: 6 April 2017.

This rule derived from the Insolvency Rules 1986, SI 1986/1925, r 6.217.

[6.621]

10.161 Report of official receiver

(1) Where the bankrupt makes an application under section 280, the official receiver must, at least 21 days before the date fixed for the hearing of the application, file with the court a report containing—

(a) particulars of any failure by the bankrupt to comply with the bankrupt's obligations under Parts 8 to 11 of the Act;

(b) the circumstances surrounding the present bankruptcy, and those surrounding any previous bankruptcy of the bankrupt;

(c) the extent to which, in the present and in any previous bankruptcy, the bankrupt's liabilities have exceeded the bankrupt's assets; and

(d) particulars of any distribution which has been, or is expected to be, made to creditors in the present bankruptcy or, if such is the case, that there has been and is to be no distribution; and

(e) any other matters which in the official receiver's opinion ought to be brought to the court's attention.

(2) The official receiver must deliver a copy of the report to the bankrupt and the trustee, so as to reach them at least 14 days before the date of the hearing of the application under section 280.

(3) The bankrupt may, not later than five business days before the date of the hearing, file with the court a notice specifying any statements in the official receiver's report which the bankrupt intends to deny or dispute.

(4) Such a notice must be authenticated and dated by the bankrupt and must contain the bankrupt's name and postal address.

(5) The bankrupt must deliver copies of such a notice to the official receiver and the trustee not less than three business days before the date of the hearing.

(6) The official receiver, the trustee and any creditor may appear on the hearing of the bankrupt's application, and may make representations and put to the bankrupt such questions as the court allows.

NOTES

Commencement: 6 April 2017.

This rule derived from the Insolvency Rules 1986, SI 1986/1925, r 6.218.

[6.622]

10.162 Order of discharge

(1) An order of the court under section 280(2)(b) (discharge absolutely) or (c) (discharge subject to conditions relating to income or property) must contain—

(a) the name of the court;

(b) identification details for the bankrupt;

(c) the date of the bankruptcy order;

(d) the date of the report of the official receiver in the matter;

(e) the statement that the court has taken into consideration the report of the official receiver specified in the order as to the bankrupt's conduct and affairs, including the bankrupt's conduct during the bankruptcy;

(f) an order—

(i) that the bankrupt be discharged absolutely, or

(ii) that the bankrupt be discharged but that the bankrupt's discharge be suspended until the conditions specified in the order are fulfilled;

(g) the date on which the order is made;

(h) the date on which the order takes effect; and

(i) any conditions required to be fulfilled for discharge.

(2) Copies of any order made on an application by the bankrupt for discharge under section 280 must be delivered by the court to the bankrupt, the trustee and the official receiver.

(3) The order must contain a notice to the bankrupt stating that should the bankrupt require notice of the order to be gazetted and to be advertised in the same manner as the bankruptcy order was advertised, then the bankrupt must within 28 days deliver a notice of that requirement to the official receiver

NOTES

Commencement: 6 April 2017.

This rule derived from the Insolvency Rules 1986, SI 1986/1925, r 6.219.

[6.623]
10.163 Deferment of issue of order pending appeal

An order made by the court on an application by the bankrupt for discharge under section 280 must not be drawn up or gazetted until the time allowed for appealing has expired or, if an appeal is entered, until the appeal has been determined.

NOTES

Commencement: 6 April 2017.
This rule derived from the Insolvency Rules 1986, SI 1986/1925, r 6.221.

[6.624]
10.164 Costs under this Chapter

In no case do any costs or expenses arising under this Chapter fall on the official receiver personally.

NOTES

Commencement: 6 April 2017.

CHAPTER 21 MISCELLANEOUS RULES IN BANKRUPTCY

[Note: a document required by the Act or these Rules must also contain the standard contents set out in Part 1.]

[6.625]
10.165 Amendment of title of proceedings

(1) At any time after the making of a bankruptcy order, the official receiver may amend the title of the proceedings.

(2) An official receiver who amends the title of proceedings must as soon as reasonably practicable—
- (a) where the bankruptcy is on the petition of a creditor, file a notice of the amendment with the court;
- (b) where the bankruptcy is on the application of a debtor, file a notice of the amendment on the bankruptcy file; and
- (c) make an application to the Chief Land Registrar to amend the register of writs and orders.

(3) If the official receiver thinks fit to gazette the amendment then it must be gazetted as soon as reasonably practicable, and may be advertised in such other manner as the official receiver thinks fit.

(4) The notice must—
- (a) state that the title of the proceedings has been amended; and
- (b) specify the amendment.

NOTES

Commencement: 6 April 2017.
This rule derived from the Insolvency Rules 1986, SI 1986/1925, r 6.35.

[6.626]
10.166 Application for redirection order

(1) This rule applies where the official receiver or trustee other than the official receiver makes an application to the court under section 371(1) (re-direction of bankrupt's letters etc).

(2) The application must be made without notice to the bankrupt or any other person, unless the court directs otherwise.

(3) Where the applicant is the official receiver the applicant must file with the court with the application a report setting out the reasons why the order is sought.

(4) Where the applicant is the trustee the applicant must file with the court a witness statement setting out the reasons why the order is sought.

(5) The court must fix a venue for the hearing of the application if the court thinks just and deliver notice to the applicant.

(6) The court may make an order on such conditions as it thinks just.

(7) The order must identify the person on whom it is to be served, and need not be served on the bankrupt unless the court so directs.

NOTES

Commencement: 6 April 2017.
This rule derived from the Insolvency Rules 1986, SI 1986/1925, r 6.235A.

[6.627]
10.167 Bankrupt's home: property falling within section 283A

(1) Where it appears to a trustee that section 283A(1) applies, the trustee must deliver notice as soon as reasonably practicable to—
- (a) the bankrupt;
- (b) the bankrupt's spouse or civil partner (in a case falling within section 283A(1)(b)); and
- (c) the former spouse or former civil partner of the bankrupt (in a case falling within section 283A(1)(c)).

Part 6 Insolvency Rules

(2) Such a notice must contain—
(a) the name of the bankrupt;
(b) the address of the dwelling-house;
(c) if the dwelling-house is registered land, the title number; and
(d) the date by which the trustee must have delivered the notice.

(3) A trustee must not deliver such a notice any later than 14 days before the third anniversary of the bankruptcy order or, 14 days before the third anniversary of when the official receiver or trustee became aware of the property.

NOTES

Commencement: 6 April 2017.
This rule derived from the Insolvency Rules 1986, SI 1986/1925, r 6.237.

[6.628]
10.168 Application in relation to the vesting of an interest in a dwelling-house (registered land)

(1) This rule applies where—
(a) the bankrupt's estate includes an interest in a dwelling-house which at the date of bankruptcy was the sole or principal residence of—
(i) the bankrupt,
(ii) the bankrupt's spouse or civil partner, or
(iii) a former spouse or former civil partner of the bankrupt; and
(b) the dwelling-house is registered land; and
(c) an entry has been made relating to the bankruptcy in the individual register of the dwelling-house or the register has been altered to reflect the vesting of the bankrupt's interest in a trustee in bankruptcy.

(2) Where such an interest ceases to be comprised in the bankrupt's estate and vests in the bankrupt under either section 283A(2) or 283A(4) of the Act, or under section 261(8) of the Enterprise Act 2002, the trustee must, within five business days of the vesting, make such application to the Chief Land Registrar as is necessary to show in the individual register of the dwelling-house that the interest has vested in the bankrupt.

(3) The trustee's application must be made in accordance with the Land Registration Act 2002 and must be accompanied by—
(a) evidence of the trustee's appointment (where not previously provided to the Chief Land Registrar); and
(b) a certificate from the trustee stating that the interest has vested in the bankrupt under section 283A(2) or 283A(4) of the Act or section 261(8) of the Enterprise Act 2002 (whichever is appropriate).

(4) As soon as reasonably practicable after making such an application, the trustee must deliver notice of the application—
(a) to the bankrupt; and
(b) to the bankrupt's spouse, former spouse, civil partner or former civil partner if the dwelling-house was the sole or principal residence of that person.

(5) The trustee must deliver notice of the application to every person who (to the trustee's knowledge) claims an interest in, or is under any liability in relation to, the dwelling-house.

NOTES

Commencement: 6 April 2017.
This rule derived from the Insolvency Rules 1986, SI 1986/1925, r 6.237A.

[6.629]
10.169 Vesting of bankrupt's interest (unregistered land)

(1) Where an interest in a dwelling-house which at the date of the bankruptcy was the sole or principal residence of—
(a) the bankrupt;
(b) the bankrupt's spouse or civil partner; or
(c) a former spouse or former civil partner of the bankrupt;

ceases to be comprised in the bankrupt's estate and vests in the bankrupt under either section 283A(2) or 283A(4) of the Act or section 261(8) of the Enterprise Act 2002 and the dwelling-house is unregistered land, the trustee must as soon as reasonably practicable deliver to the bankrupt a certificate as to the vesting.

(2) Such a certificate is conclusive proof that the interest mentioned in paragraph (1) has vested in the bankrupt.

(3) As soon as reasonably practicable after delivering the certificate, the trustee must deliver a copy of the certificate to the bankrupt's spouse, former spouse, civil partner or former civil partner if the dwelling-house was the sole or principal residence of that person.

(4) The trustee must deliver a copy of the certificate to every person who (to the trustee's knowledge) claims an interest in, or is under any liability relating to, the dwelling-house.

NOTES

Commencement: 6 April 2017.
This rule derived from the Insolvency Rules 1986, SI 1986/1925, r 6.237B.

[6.630]

10.170 Vesting of bankrupt's estate: substituted period

[Note: section 283A(6)(b) gives the court the power to impose a longer period than the three years mentioned in section 283A(2) in such circumstances as the court thinks appropriate.]

(1) For the purposes of section 283A(2) the period of one month is substituted for the period of three years set out in that section where the trustee has delivered notice to the bankrupt that the trustee considers—

(a) the continued vesting of the property in the bankrupt's estate to be of no benefit to creditors; or
(b) the re-vesting to the bankrupt will make dealing with the bankrupt's estate more efficient.

(2) The one month period starts from the date of the notice.

NOTES

Commencement: 6 April 2017.
This rule derived from the Insolvency Rules 1986, SI 1986/1925, rr 6.237C, 6.237CA.

[6.631]

10.171 Charging order

(1) This rule applies where the trustee applies to the court under section 313 for an order imposing a charge on property consisting of an interest in a dwelling-house.

(2) The respondents to the application must be—

(a) any spouse or former spouse or civil partner or former civil partner of the bankrupt having or claiming to have an interest in the property;
(b) any other person appearing to have an interest in the property; and
(c) such other persons as the court may direct.

(3) The trustee must make a report to the court, containing the following particulars—

(a) the extent of the bankrupt's interest in the property;
(b) the amount which, at the date of the application, remains owing to unsecured creditors of the bankrupt; and
(c) an estimate of the cost of realising the interest.

(4) The terms of the charge to be imposed must be agreed between the trustee and the bankrupt or in the absence of an agreement must be settled by the court.

(5) The rate of interest applicable under section 313(2) is the rate specified in section 17 of the Judgments Act 1838 on the day on which the charge is imposed, and the rate must be stated in the court's order imposing the charge.

(6) The court's order must also—

(a) describe the property to be charged;
(b) state whether the title to the property is registered and, if it is, specify the title number;
(c) set out the extent of the bankrupt's interest in the property which has vested in the trustee;
(d) indicate by reference to any, or the total, amount which is payable otherwise than to the bankrupt out of the bankrupt's estate and of interest on that amount, how the amount of the charge to be imposed is to be ascertained;
(e) set out the conditions (if any) imposed by the court under section 3(1) of the Charging Orders Act 1979; and
(f) identify the date any property charged under section 313 will cease to be comprised in the bankrupt's estate and will, subject to the charge (and any prior charge), vest in the bankrupt.

(7) The date referred to in paragraph (6)(f) must be that of the registration of the charge in accordance with section 3(2) of the Charging Orders Act 1979 unless the court is of the opinion that a different date is appropriate.

(8) Where the court order is capable of giving rise to an application under the Land Charges Act 1972 or the Land Registration Act 2002 the trustee must, as soon as reasonably practicable after the making of the court order or at the appropriate time, make the appropriate application to the Chief Land Registrar.

(9) The appropriate application is—

(a) an application under section 6(1)(a) of the Land Charges Act 1972 (application for registration in the register of writs and orders affecting land); or
(b) an application under the Land Registration Act 2002 for an entry in the register in relation to the charge imposed by the order; and such application under that Act as is necessary to show in the individual register or registers of the dwelling-house that the interest has vested in the bankrupt.

(10) In determining the value of the bankrupt's interest for the purposes of paragraph (6)(c), the court must disregard that part of the value of the property in which the bankrupt's interest subsists which is equal to the value of—

(a) any loans secured by mortgage or other charge against the property;
(b) any other third party interest; and
(c) the reasonable costs of sale.

NOTES

Commencement: 6 April 2017.
This rule derived from the Insolvency Rules 1986, SI 1986/1925, r 6.237D, Sch 4, Fm 6.79A.

PART 11
BANKRUPTCY AND DEBT RELIEF RESTRICTIONS ORDERS AND UNDERTAKINGS AND THE INSOLVENCY REGISTERS

CHAPTER 1 INTERPRETATION

[6.632]
11.1 References to the Secretary of State

References to the Secretary of State in Chapters 2 and 3 include the official receiver acting on the direction of the Secretary of State in making an application for—

(a) a bankruptcy restrictions order or an interim bankruptcy restrictions order in accordance with paragraph 1(2)(b) or 5(3)(b) respectively of Schedule 4A; or

(b) a debt relief restrictions order or an interim debt relief restrictions order in accordance with paragraph 1(2)(b) or 5(3)(b) respectively of Schedule 4ZB.

NOTES

Commencement: 6 April 2017.

This rule derived from the Insolvency Rules 1986, SI 1986/1925, rr 6.240, 6.252.

CHAPTER 2 BANKRUPTCY AND DEBT RELIEF RESTRICTIONS ORDERS (SCHEDULES 4ZB AND 4A)

[Note: a document required by the Act or these Rules must also contain the standard contents set out in Part 1.]

[6.633]
11.2 Application for a bankruptcy or debt relief restrictions order

(1) An application by the Secretary of State to the court for a bankruptcy restrictions order under paragraph 1 of Schedule 4A, or for a debt relief restrictions order under paragraph 1 of Schedule 4ZB, must be supported by a report by the Secretary of State.

(2) The report must—

(a) set out the conduct which the Secretary of State thinks justifies making a bankruptcy restrictions order or a debt relief restrictions order; and

(b) contain the evidence on which the Secretary of State relies in support of the application.

(3) Any evidence in support of the application provided by a person other than the Secretary of State must be given in a witness statement.

(4) The date for the hearing must be at least eight weeks after the date when the court fixes the venue for the hearing.

NOTES

Commencement: 6 April 2017.

This rule derived from the Insolvency Rules 1986, SI 1986/1925, rr 6.241, 6.253.

[6.634]
11.3 Service of the application on the bankrupt or debtor

(1) The Secretary of State must serve a notice of the application and the venue on the bankrupt or debtor not more than 14 days after the application is filed with the court.

(2) The notice must be accompanied by—

(a) a copy of the application;

(b) a copy of the Secretary of State's report;

(c) a copy of any other evidence filed in support of the application; and

(d) a document for completion as an acknowledgement of service.

(3) The bankrupt or debtor must file the acknowledgement of service, indicating whether or not the application is contested, not more than 14 days after service of the application.

(4) A bankrupt or debtor who fails to file an acknowledgement of service within that time may attend the hearing of the application but may not take part in the hearing unless the court gives permission.

NOTES

Commencement: 6 April 2017.

This rule derived from the Insolvency Rules 1986, SI 1986/1925, rr 6.242, 6.254.

[6.635]
11.4 The bankrupt's or debtor's evidence opposing an application

(1) A bankrupt or debtor who wishes to oppose the application must—

(a) file with the court any evidence for the court to take into consideration within 28 days of service of the application; and

(b) serve a copy of it on the Secretary of State within three business days of filing the evidence with the court.

(2) The Secretary of State must file with the court any evidence in reply within 14 days from receiving the copy of the bankrupt's or debtor's evidence, and must serve a copy of that evidence on the bankrupt or debtor as soon as reasonably practicable.

NOTES

Commencement: 6 April 2017.
This rule derived from the Insolvency Rules 1986, SI 1986/1925, rr 6.243, 6.255.

[6.636]

11.5 Making a bankruptcy or debt relief restrictions order

(1) The court may make a bankruptcy restrictions order or a debt relief restrictions order whether or not the bankrupt or debtor appears or has filed evidence.

(2) Where the court makes such an order, it must deliver two sealed copies to the Secretary of State as soon as reasonably practicable.

(3) As soon as reasonably practicable after receiving the sealed copies, the Secretary of State must deliver one of them to the bankrupt or debtor.

NOTES

Commencement: 6 April 2017.
This rule derived from the Insolvency Rules 1986, SI 1986/1925, rr 6.244, 6.256.

CHAPTER 3 INTERIM BANKRUPTCY AND DEBT RELIEF RESTRICTIONS ORDERS

[Note: a document required by the Act or these Rules must also contain the standard contents set out in Part 1.]

[6.637]

11.6 Application for an interim bankruptcy or debt relief restrictions order

(1) An application by the Secretary of State to the court for an interim bankruptcy restrictions order under paragraph 5 of Schedule 4A or an interim debt relief restrictions order under paragraph 5 of Schedule 4ZB, must be supported by a report by the Secretary of State.

(2) The report must—

(a) set out the conduct which the Secretary of State thinks justifies making an interim bankruptcy restrictions order or an interim debt relief restrictions order; and

(b) contain the evidence on which the Secretary of State relies in support of the application including evidence of why it would be in the public interest to make such an order.

(3) Any evidence in support of the application provided by a person other than the Secretary of State must be given in a witness statement.

(4) The Secretary of State must deliver a notice of the application to the bankrupt or debtor at least two business days before the date set for the hearing unless the court directs otherwise.

(5) The notice must be accompanied by—

(a) a copy of the application;

(b) a copy of the Secretary of State's report;

(c) a copy of any other evidence filed in support of the application; and

(d) a document for completion as an acknowledgement of service.

(6) The bankrupt or debtor may file with the court evidence for the court to take into consideration and may appear at the hearing.

NOTES

Commencement: 6 April 2017.
This rule derived from the Insolvency Rules 1986, SI 1986/1925, rr 6.245, 6.246, 6.257, 6.258.

[6.638]

11.7 Making an interim bankruptcy or debt relief restrictions order

(1) The court may make an interim bankruptcy restrictions order or interim debt relief restrictions order whether or not the bankrupt or debtor appears or has filed evidence.

(2) Where the court makes such an order, it must deliver two sealed copies of the order to the Secretary of State as soon as reasonably practicable.

(3) As soon as reasonably practicable after receiving the sealed copies, the Secretary of State must deliver one of them to the bankrupt or debtor.

NOTES

Commencement: 6 April 2017.
This rule derived from the Insolvency Rules 1986, SI 1986/1925, rr 6.247, 6.259.

[6.639]

11.8 Application to set aside an interim order

(1) A bankrupt subject to an interim bankruptcy restrictions order or a debtor subject to an interim debt relief restrictions order may apply to the court to set the order aside.

(2) The application must be supported by a witness statement stating the grounds on which it is made.

(3) The bankrupt or debtor must deliver to the Secretary of State, not less than five business days before the hearing—

(a) a notice of the venue;

(b) a copy of the application; and
(c) a copy of the supporting witness statement.

(4) The Secretary of State may attend the hearing and call the attention of the court to any matter which seems to be relevant, and may give evidence or call witnesses.

NOTES

Commencement: 6 April 2017.
This rule derived from the Insolvency Rules 1986, SI 1986/1925, rr 6.248, 6.260.

[6.640]
11.9 Order setting aside an interim order

(1) Where the court sets aside an interim bankruptcy restrictions order or an interim debt relief restrictions order, it must deliver two sealed copies of the order to the Secretary of State as soon as reasonably practicable.

(2) As soon as reasonably practicable after receiving the sealed copies, the Secretary of State must deliver one of them to the bankrupt or debtor.

NOTES

Commencement: 6 April 2017.
This rule derived from the Insolvency Rules 1986, SI 1986/1925, rr 6.248(5), (6), 260(5), (6).

CHAPTER 4 BANKRUPTCY RESTRICTIONS AND DEBT RELIEF RESTRICTIONS UNDERTAKINGS

[Note: a document required by the Act or these Rules must also contain the standard contents set out in Part 1.]

[6.641]
11.10 Acceptance of a bankruptcy restrictions or a debt relief restrictions undertaking

(1) A bankruptcy restrictions undertaking authenticated by the bankrupt is accepted by the Secretary of State for the purposes of paragraph 9 of Schedule 4A when the Secretary of State authenticates the undertaking.

(2) A debt relief restrictions undertaking authenticated by a person in relation to whom a debt relief order has been made is accepted by the Secretary of State for the purposes of paragraph 9 of Schedule 4ZB when the Secretary of State authenticates the undertaking.

NOTES

Commencement: 6 April 2017.
This rule derived from the Insolvency Rules 1986, SI 1986/1925, rr 6.249, 6.261.

[6.642]
11.11 Notification

(1) The Secretary of State must, as soon as reasonably practicable after accepting a bankruptcy restrictions undertaking or a debt relief restrictions undertaking, deliver copies to the person who offered the undertaking and to the official receiver.

(2) In the case of a bankruptcy restrictions undertaking the Secretary of State must also file a copy with the court in the case of a creditor's bankruptcy petition or on the bankruptcy file in the case of a debtor's bankruptcy application.

NOTES

Commencement: 6 April 2017.
This rule derived from the Insolvency Rules 1986, SI 1986/1925, rr 6.250, 6.262.

[6.643]
11.12 Application to annul a bankruptcy restrictions or a debt relief restrictions undertaking

(1) An application by a bankrupt or debtor to annul or vary an undertaking under paragraph 9(3)(a) or (b) of Schedule 4A or paragraph 9(3)(a) or (b) of Schedule 4ZB must be supported by a witness statement stating the grounds on which the application is made.

(2) The bankrupt or debtor must, at least 28 days before the date fixed for the hearing, deliver to the Secretary of State—
(a) a notice of the venue;
(b) a copy of the application; and
(c) a copy of the supporting witness statement.

(3) The Secretary of State may attend the hearing and call the attention of the court to any matter which seems to be relevant, and may give evidence or call witnesses.

(4) Where the court annuls or varies a bankruptcy restrictions undertaking or debt relief restrictions undertaking, it must deliver two sealed copies of the order to the Secretary of State as soon as reasonably practicable.

(5) As soon as reasonably practicable after receiving the sealed copies, the Secretary of State must deliver one of them to the bankrupt or debtor.

NOTES

Commencement: 6 April 2017.

This rule derived from the Insolvency Rules 1986, SI 1986/1925, rr 6.251, 6.263.

CHAPTER 5 INSOLVENCY REGISTERS: GENERAL

[6.644]

11.13 Maintenance of the registers and inspection

(1) The Secretary of State must maintain the individual insolvency register of matters relating to bankruptcies, debt relief orders and IVAs in accordance with Chapter 6.

(2) The Secretary of State must maintain the bankruptcy restrictions register and the debt relief restrictions register in accordance with Chapter 7.

(3) The registers must be available to be searched electronically by members of the public at any time unless there is malfunction or error in the electronic operation of the registers.

(4) Any person may request the official receiver to make a search of the registers on any business day between 9am and 5pm.

(5) An obligation under this Part to enter information on, or delete information from, a register, must be performed as soon as is reasonably practicable after it arises.

NOTES

Commencement: 6 April 2017.

This rule derived from the Insolvency Rules 1986, SI 1986/1925, r 6A.1.

CHAPTER 6 INDIVIDUAL INSOLVENCY REGISTER

[6.645]

11.14 Entry of information on the individual insolvency register: IVAs

(1) This rule applies where—
- (a) an IVA has been accepted by the debtor's creditors; and
- (b) the Secretary of State receives any of the following—
  - (i) a report under rule 8.26 (report on approval of IVA), or
  - (ii) a notice under rules 8.27(5) (notice of revocation or suspension of IVA), 8.27(6) (notice of expiry of suspension) or 8.31 (notice that the IVA has been terminated or fully implemented).

(2) The Secretary of State must enter the following on the individual insolvency register—
- (a) the debtor's identification details;
- (b) the debtor's date of birth;
- (c) the date on which the IVA was approved by the creditors;
- (d) the debtor's gender;
- (e) any name other than the name in which the debtor entered into IVA by which the debtor was or is known;
- (f) a statement as to whether the IVA has been—
  - (i) completed in accordance with its terms,
  - (ii) terminated, or
  - (iii) revoked; and
- (g) the name and address of the supervisor.

(3) This rule is subject to any court order for the non-disclosure of the debtor's current address made under rule 20.2 (debtors at risk of violence: proposed IVA) or 20.3 (debtors at risk of violence: IVA).

NOTES

Commencement: 6 April 2017.

This rule derived from the Insolvency Rules 1986, SI 1986/1925, r 6A.2A.

[6.646]

11.15 Deletion of information from the individual insolvency register: IVAs

The Secretary of State must delete from the individual insolvency register all information concerning an IVA three months after receiving one of the following—
- (a) a notice under rule 8.27(5) of the making of a revocation order in relation to the IVA; or
- (b) a notice under rule 8.31(3) of the termination or full implementation of the IVA.

NOTES

Commencement: 6 April 2017.

This rule derived from the Insolvency Rules 1986, SI 1986/1925, r 6A.3.

[6.647]

11.16 Entry of information on to the individual insolvency register: bankruptcy orders

(1) Where the official receiver receives a copy of a bankruptcy order from the court under rule 10.32, or from the adjudicator under rule 10.45, the official receiver must cause the following to be entered on the individual insolvency register—

(a) the matters listed in rules 10.8 or the information set out in Part 1 of Schedule 7, relating to the debtor as they are stated in the bankruptcy petition or bankruptcy application;
(b) the date of the bankruptcy order; and
(c) identification details for the proceedings.

(2) The official receiver must cause to be entered on to the individual insolvency register the following information—
(a) the bankrupt's identification details and date of birth;
(b) the bankrupt's gender and occupation (if any);
(c) the date of a previous bankruptcy order or debt relief order (if any) made against the bankrupt in the period of six years before the latest bankruptcy order (if there is more than one such previous order only the latest and excluding any bankruptcy order that was annulled or any debt relief order that was revoked);
(d) any name by which the bankrupt was known, not being the name in which the individual was made bankrupt;
(e) the address of any business carried on by the bankrupt and the name in which that business was carried on if carried on in a name other than the name in which the individual was made bankrupt;
(f) the name and address of any insolvency practitioner appointed to act as trustee in bankruptcy;
(g) the address at which the official receiver may be contacted;
(h) the automatic discharge date under section 279; and
(i) where a bankruptcy order is annulled or rescinded by the court, the fact that such an order has been made, the date on which it is made and (if different) the date on which it has effect.

(3) Where the official receiver receives a copy of an order under rule 10.104(6) or 10.142(8) suspending the bankrupt's discharge the official receiver must cause to be entered on to the individual insolvency register—
(a) the fact that such an order has been made; and
(b) the period for which the discharge has been suspended or that the relevant period has ceased to run until the fulfilment of conditions specified in the order.

(4) Where the official receiver receives under rule 10.143(10) a copy of a certificate of the discharge of an order under section 279(3) the official receiver must cause the following to be entered on the individual insolvency register—
(a) that the court has discharged the order made under section 279(3); and
(b) the new date of discharge of the bankrupt.

(5) Where the order discharging the order under section 279(3) is subsequently rescinded by the court, the official receiver must cause the register to be amended accordingly.

(6) Where a bankrupt is discharged from bankruptcy under section 279(1), the official receiver must cause the fact and date of such discharge to be entered in the individual insolvency register.

(7) This rule is subject to any court order for the non-disclosure of the debtor's current address made under rule 20.5 (persons at risk of violence: bankruptcy application) or 20.6 (debtors at risk of violence: bankruptcy and debt relief proceedings).

NOTES

Commencement: 6 April 2017.

This rule derived from the Insolvency Rules 1986, SI 1986/1925, r 6A.4.

[6.648]

11.17 Deletion of information from the individual insolvency register: bankruptcy orders

The Secretary of State must delete from the individual insolvency register all information concerning a bankruptcy where—
(a) the bankruptcy order has been annulled under section 261(2)(a), 261(2)(b) or section 282(1)(b) and a period of three months has elapsed since a notice of the annulment was delivered to the official receiver;
(b) the bankrupt has been discharged from the bankruptcy and a period of three months has elapsed from the date of discharge;
(c) the bankruptcy order is annulled under section 282(1)(a) and 28 days have elapsed since a notice of the annulment was delivered to the official receiver under rule 10.137(3); or
(d) an order has been made by the court under section 375 rescinding the bankruptcy order and 28 days have elapsed since receipt by the official receiver.

NOTES

Commencement: 6 April 2017.

This rule derived from the Insolvency Rules 1986, SI 1986/1925, r 6A.5.

[6.649]

11.18 Entry of information on to the individual insolvency register: debt relief orders

(1) The official receiver must cause to be entered on to the individual insolvency register after the making of a debt relief order the following information relating to the order or the debtor—
(a) as they are stated in the debtor's application—
(i) the debtor's identification details and date of birth,
(ii) the debtor's gender and occupation (if any),

(iii) the name or names in which the debtor has carried on business, if other than the debtor's true name, and
(iv) the nature of the debtor's business and the address or addresses at which the debtor carries or has carried it on and whether alone or with others;
(b) the date of the debt relief order;
(c) the reference number of the order;
(d) the date of the end of the moratorium period; and
(e) the date of a previous bankruptcy order or a debt relief order (if any) made against the debtor in the period of six years before the latest debt relief order (if there is more than one such order only the latest and excluding any bankruptcy order that was annulled or debt relief order that was revoked).

(2) Except where information concerning a debt relief order has been deleted under rule 11.19, the official receiver must also cause to be entered on the register in relation to the order—
(a) where the moratorium period is terminated early, the fact that such has happened, the date of early termination and whether the early termination is on revocation of the debt relief order or by virtue of any other enactment;
(b) where the moratorium period is extended, the fact that such has happened, the date on which the extension was made, its duration and the date of the new anticipated end of the moratorium period; or
(c) where the debtor is discharged from all qualifying debts, the date of such discharge.

(3) This rule is subject to any court order for the non-disclosure of the debtor's current address made under rule 20.4 (debtors at risk of violence: debt relief application) or 20.6 (debtors at risk of violence: bankruptcy and debt relief proceedings).

NOTES

Commencement: 6 April 2017.
This rule derived from the Insolvency Rules 1986, SI 1986/1925, r 6A.5A.

[6.650]
11.19 Deletion of information from the individual insolvency register: debt relief orders

The Secretary of State must delete from the individual insolvency register all information concerning a debt relief order where three months have elapsed from the date on which—
(a) the debt relief order has been revoked; or
(b) the debtor has been discharged from the qualifying debts.

NOTES

Commencement: 6 April 2017.
This rule derived from the Insolvency Rules 1986, SI 1986/1925, r 6A.5B.

CHAPTER 7 BANKRUPTCY AND DEBT RELIEF RESTRICTIONS REGISTER

[6.651]
11.20 Bankruptcy restrictions and debt relief restrictions orders and undertakings: entry of information on the registers

(1) Where any of the following orders are made against a bankrupt or a debtor the Secretary of State must enter on the bankruptcy restrictions register or debt relief restrictions register as appropriate the specified information—
(a) an interim bankruptcy restrictions order;
(b) a bankruptcy restrictions order;
(c) an interim debt relief restrictions order; or
(d) a debt relief restrictions order.

(2) The specified information is—
(a) the bankrupt's or debtor's identification details;
(b) the bankrupt's or debtor's gender;
(c) the bankrupt's or debtor's occupation (if any);
(d) a statement that an interim bankruptcy restrictions order, a bankruptcy restrictions order, an interim debt relief restrictions order or a debt relief restrictions order has been made against the bankrupt or debtor;
(e) the date of the order;
(f) the court in which the order was made and the court or order reference number; and
(g) the duration of the order.

(3) Where a bankruptcy restrictions undertaking is given by a bankrupt or a debt relief restrictions undertaking is given by a debtor, the Secretary of State must enter on to the bankruptcy restrictions or debt relief restrictions register—
(a) the bankrupt's or debtor's identification details;
(b) the bankrupt's or debtor's gender;
(c) the bankrupt's or debtor's occupation (if any);
(d) a statement that a bankruptcy restrictions undertaking or debt relief restrictions undertaking has been given;
(e) the date of the acceptance of the bankruptcy restrictions undertaking or debt relief restrictions undertaking by the Secretary of State; and

(f) the duration of the bankruptcy restrictions undertaking or debt relief restrictions undertaking.

(4) This rule is subject to any court order for the non-disclosure of the debtor's current address made under rules 20.6 (debtors at risk of violence: bankruptcy and debt relief proceedings) or 20.7 (additional provisions in respect of order under rule 20.6(4)).

NOTES

Commencement: 6 April 2017.
This rule derived from the Insolvency Rules 1986, SI 1986/1925, rr 6A.6, 6A.7A.

[6.652]
11.21 Deletion of information from the registers

The Secretary of State must delete from the bankruptcy restrictions register or debt relief restrictions register all information relating to an interim bankruptcy restrictions order, bankruptcy restrictions order, interim debt relief restrictions order, debt relief restrictions order, bankruptcy restrictions undertaking or debt relief restrictions undertaking after—

(a) receipt of notice that the order or undertaking has ceased to have effect; or
(b) the expiry of the order or undertaking.

NOTES

Commencement: 6 April 2017.
This rule derived from the Insolvency Rules 1986, SI 1986/1925, rr 6A.7, 6A.7B.

CHAPTER 8 RECTIFICATION OF REGISTERS AND DEATH OF PERSONS ON REGISTER

[6.653]
11.22 Rectification of the registers

Where the Secretary of State becomes aware of an inaccuracy in information on the individual insolvency register, the bankruptcy restrictions register or the debt relief restrictions register, the Secretary of State must rectify the inaccuracy as soon as reasonably practicable.

NOTES

Commencement: 6 April 2017.
This rule derived from the Insolvency Rules 1986, SI 1986/1925, r 6A.8.

[6.654]
11.23 Death of a person about whom information is held on a register

Where the Secretary of State receives notice of the date of the death of a person in relation to whom information is held on any of the registers, the Secretary of State must cause the fact and date of the person's death to be entered on to the register.

NOTES

Commencement: 6 April 2017.
This rule derived from the Insolvency Rules 1986, SI 1986/1925, r 6A.8(2).

PART 12
COURT PROCEDURE AND PRACTICE

CHAPTER 1 GENERAL

Application of the Civil Procedure Rules 1998

[6.655]
12.1 Court rules and practice to apply

(1) The provisions of the CPR (including any related Practice Directions) apply for the purposes of proceedings under Parts 1 to 11 of the Act with any necessary modifications, except so far as disapplied by or inconsistent with these Rules.

(2) All insolvency proceedings must be allocated to the multi-track for which CPR Part 29 makes provision, and accordingly those provisions of the CPR which provide for directions questionnaires and track allocation do not apply.

(3) CPR Part 32 applies to a false statement in a document verified by a statement of truth made under these Rules as it applies to a false statement in a document verified by a statement of truth made under CPR Part 22.

NOTES

Commencement: 6 April 2017.
This rule derived from the Insolvency Rules 1986, SI 1986/1925, r 7.51A.

[6.656]
12.2 Performance of functions by the Court

(1) Anything to be done under or by virtue of the Act or these Rules by, to or before the court may be done by, to or before a judge, District Judge or a registrar.

(2) The registrar or District Judge may authorise any act of a formal or administrative character which is not by statute that person's responsibility to be carried out by the chief clerk or any other officer of the court acting on that person's behalf, in accordance with directions given by the Lord Chancellor.

(3) The hearing of an application must be in open court unless the court directs otherwise.

NOTES

Commencement: 6 April 2017.

This rule derived from the Insolvency Rules 1986, SI 1986/1925, r 7.6A.

CHAPTER 2 COMMENCEMENT OF INSOLVENCY PROCEEDINGS IN THE COUNTY COURT

[A document required by the Act or these Rules must also contain the standard contents set out in Part 1.]

[6.657]

12.3 Commencement of insolvency proceedings under Parts 1 to 7 of the Act (corporate insolvency proceedings)

(1) Where section 117 of the Act, as extended in its application by section 251, gives jurisdiction to the County Court in respect of proceedings under Parts 1 to 7 of the Act any such proceedings when they are commenced in the County Court may only be commenced in the hearing centre which serves the area in which the company's registered office is situated.

(2) However if the registered office is situated in an area served by a hearing centre for which Schedule 6 lists an alternative court or hearing centre then any such proceedings in the County Court may only be commenced in that alternative court or hearing centre.

NOTES

Commencement: 6 April 2017.

This rule derived from the Insolvency (Commencement of Proceedings) and Insolvency Rules 1986 (Amendment) Rules 2014, SI 2014/817, r 2.

[6.658]

12.4 Commencement of insolvency proceedings under Parts 7A to 11 of the Act (personal insolvency proceedings; bankruptcy)

(1) Proceedings under Parts 7A to 11 of the Act that are allocated in accordance with rule 12.5 to the London Insolvency District when they are commenced in the County Court may only be commenced in the County Court at Central London.

(2) Elsewhere such proceedings when they are commenced in the County Court may only be commenced in the hearing centre determined in accordance with these Rules.

(3) However if the hearing centre so determined is one for which Schedule 6 lists an alternative hearing centre then such proceedings when they are commenced in the County Court may only be commenced in that alternative hearing centre.

NOTES

Commencement: 6 April 2017.

This rule derived from the Insolvency (Commencement of Proceedings) and Insolvency Rules 1986 (Amendment) Rules 2014, SI 2014/817, r 3.

[6.659]

12.5 Allocation of proceedings to the London Insolvency District

The following proceedings are allocated to the London Insolvency District—

(a) bankruptcy petitions or applications in relation to a debt relief order under section 251M (powers of court in relation to debt relief orders) or 251N (inquiry into debtor's dealings and property) where—

(i) the debtor is resident in England and Wales and within the six months immediately preceding the presentation of the petition or the making of the application the debtor carried on business within the area of the London Insolvency District—

(aa) for the greater part of those six months, or

(bb) for a longer period in those six months than in any other insolvency district,

(ii) the debtor is resident in England and Wales and within the six months immediately preceding the presentation of the petition or the making of the application the debtor did not carry on business in England and Wales but resided within the area of the London Insolvency District for—

(aa) the greater part of those six months, or

(bb) a longer period in those six months than in any other insolvency district,

(iii) the debtor is not resident in England and Wales but within the six months immediately preceding the presentation of the petition or the making of the application carried on business within the area of the London Insolvency District,

(iv) the debtor is not resident in England and Wales and within the 6 months immediately preceding the presentation of the petition or the making of the application did not carry on business in England and Wales but resided within the area of the London Insolvency District, or

(v) the debtor is not resident in England and Wales and within the 6 months immediately preceding the presentation of the petition or the making of the application the debtor neither carried on business nor resided in England and Wales;

(b) creditors' bankruptcy petitions presented by a Minister of the Crown or a Government Department, where either—

(i) in any statutory demand on which the petition is based the creditor has indicated the intention to present a bankruptcy petition to a court exercising jurisdiction in relation to the London Insolvency District, or

(ii) the petition is presented under section 267(2)(c) on the grounds specified in section 268(1)(b);

(c) bankruptcy petitions—

(i) where the petitioner is unable to ascertain the place where the debtor resides or, if the debtor carries on business in England and Wales, both where the debtor resides and where the debtor carries on business, or

(ii) where the debtor is a member of a partnership and—

(aa) the partnership is being wound up by the High Court sitting in London; or

(bb) a petition for the winding up of the partnership has been presented to the High Court sitting in London and at the time of the presentation of the bankruptcy petition, the petition for the winding up of the partnership has not been fully disposed of; and

(d) bankruptcy petitions based on criminal bankruptcy orders under section 264(1)(d).

NOTES

Commencement: 6 April 2017.

This rule derived from the Insolvency Rules 1986, SI 1986/1925, r 7.10ZA.

CHAPTER 3 MAKING APPLICATIONS TO COURT: GENERAL

[Note: (1) a document required by the Act or these Rules must also contain the standard contents set out in Part 1 and an application to court must also contain the standard contents set out in rule 1.35;

(2) Paragraphs 3 and 4 of Schedule 5 make provision in relation to the court's power to extend the time for doing anything required by these Rules;

(3) the rules about the applications referred to in rule 12.6 are found in Chapter 2 of Part 3 (administration applications); Chapter 3 of Part 7 (petition for winding up order by creditor) and Chapter 4 of Part 7 (petition for winding up by contributory or office-holder) and Chapter 2 of Part 10 (creditor's bankruptcy petitions).]

[6.660]
12.6 Preliminary

This Chapter applies to an application made to the court except—

(a) an administration application under Part 2 of the Act;

(b) a petition for a winding-up order under Part 4 of the Act; and

(c) a creditor's petition for a bankruptcy order under Part 9 of the Act.

NOTES

Commencement: 6 April 2017.

This rule derived from the Insolvency Rules 1986, SI 1986/1925, r 7.1.

[6.661]
12.7 Filing of application

[Note: see rule 1.46 for electronic delivery of documents to the court.]

An application filed with the court in hard-copy form must be accompanied by one copy and a number of additional copies equal to the number of persons who are to be served with the application.

NOTES

Commencement: 6 April 2017.

This rule derived from the Insolvency Rules 1986, SI 1986/1925, r 7.4(1).

[6.662]
12.8 Fixing the venue

When an application is filed the court must fix a venue for it to be heard unless—

(a) it considers it is not appropriate to do so;

(b) the rule under which the application is brought provides otherwise; or

(c) the case is one to which rule 12.12 applies.

NOTES

Commencement: 6 April 2017.

This rule derived from the Insolvency Rules 1986, SI 1986/1925, r 7.4(2).

[6.663]
12.9 Service or delivery of application

(1) The applicant must serve a sealed copy of the application, endorsed with the venue for the hearing, on the respondent named in the application unless the court directs or these Rules provide otherwise.

(2) The court may also give one or more of the following directions—
- (a) that the application be served upon persons other than those specified by the relevant provision of the Act or these Rules;
- (b) that service upon, or the delivery of a notice to any person may be dispensed with;
- (c) that such persons be notified of the application and venue in such other a way as the court specifies; or
- (d) such other directions as the court sees fit.

(3) A sealed copy of the application must be served, or notice of the application and venue must be delivered, at least 14 days before the date fixed for its hearing unless—
- (a) the provision of the Act or these Rules under which the application is made makes different provision;
- (b) the case is urgent and the court acts under rule 12.10; or
- (c) the court extends or abridges the time limit.

NOTES

Commencement: 6 April 2017.

This rule derived from the Insolvency Rules 1986, SI 1986/1925, r 7.4(3)–(5).

[6.664]
12.10 Hearing in urgent case

(1) Where the case is urgent, the court may (without prejudice to its general power to extend or abridge time limits) hear the application immediately with or without notification to, or the attendance of, other parties.

(2) The application may be heard on terms providing for the filing or service of documents, notification, or the carrying out of other formalities as the court thinks just.

NOTES

Commencement: 6 April 2017.

This rule derived from the Insolvency Rules 1986, SI 1986/1925, r 7.4(6).

[6.665]
12.11 Directions

The court may at any time give such directions as it thinks just as to—
- (a) service or notice of the application on or to any person;
- (b) whether particulars of claim and defence are to be delivered and generally as to the procedure on the application including whether a hearing is necessary;
- (c) the matters to be dealt with in evidence; and
- (d) the manner in which any evidence is to be provided and in particular as to—
  - (i) the taking of evidence wholly or partly by witness statement or orally,
  - (ii) any report to be made by an office-holder, and
  - (iii) the cross-examination of the maker of a witness statement or of a report.

NOTES

Commencement: 6 April 2017.

This rule derived from the Insolvency Rules 1986, SI 1986/1925, r 7.10(3).

[6.666]
12.12 Hearing and determination without notice

(1) Where the Act and these Rules do not require service of a sealed copy of the application on, or notice of it to be delivered to, any person, the court may—
- (a) hear the application as soon as reasonably practicable;
- (b) fix a venue for the application to be heard, in which case rule 12.9 applies to the extent that it is relevant; or
- (c) determine the application without a hearing.

(2) However nothing in the Act or these Rules is to be taken as prohibiting the applicant from giving notice.

NOTES

Commencement: 6 April 2017.

This rule derived from the Insolvency Rules 1986, SI 1986/1925, r 7.5A.

[6.667]
12.13 Adjournment of the hearing of an application

(1) The court may adjourn the hearing of an application on such terms as it thinks just.

(2) The court may give directions as to the manner in which any evidence is to be provided at a resumed hearing and in particular as to—
- (a) the taking of evidence wholly or partly by witness statement or orally;

(b) the cross-examination of the maker of a witness statement; or
(c) any report to be made by an office-holder.

NOTES
Commencement: 6 April 2017.
This rule derived from the Insolvency Rules 1986, SI 1986/1925, r 7.10(1), (2).

CHAPTER 4 MAKING APPLICATIONS TO COURT: SPECIFIC APPLICATIONS

[Note: a document required by the Act or these Rules must also contain the standard contents set out in Part 1.]

Sub-division A: Applications in connection with section 176A (prescribed part)

[6.668]
12.14 Applications under section 176A(5) to disapply section 176A

(1) An application under section 176A(5) must be accompanied by a witness statement of the liquidator, administrator or receiver.
(2) The witness statement must state—
(a) the type of insolvency proceedings in which the application arises;
(b) a summary of the financial position of the company;
(c) the information substantiating the applicant's view that the cost of making a distribution to unsecured creditors would be disproportionate to the benefits; and
(d) whether any other office-holder is acting in relation to the company and, if so, that office-holder's address.

NOTES
Commencement: 6 April 2017.
This rule derived from the Insolvency Rules 1986, SI 1986/1925, r 7.3A.

[6.669]
12.15 Notice of application under section 176A(5)

(1) An application under section 176A(5) may be made without the application being served upon, or notification to any other party.
(2) However the office-holder making the application must notify any other office-holder who is acting in relation to the company including any member State liquidator.

NOTES
Commencement: 6 April 2017.
This rule derived from the Insolvency Rules 1986, SI 1986/1925, r 7.4A.

[6.670]
12.16 Notice of an order under section 176A(5)

(1) Where the court makes an order under section 176A(5), the court must, as soon as reasonably practicable, deliver the sealed order to the applicant and a sealed copy to any other office-holder.
(2) The liquidator, administrator or receiver must, as soon as reasonably practicable, deliver notice of the order to each creditor unless the court directs otherwise.
(3) The court may direct that the requirement in paragraph (2) is complied with if a notice is published by the liquidator, administrator or receiver which states that the court has made an order disapplying the requirement to set aside the prescribed part.
(4) As soon as reasonably practicable the notice—
(a) must be gazetted; and
(b) may be advertised in such other manner as the liquidator, administrator, or receiver thinks fit.
(5) The liquidator, administrator or receiver must deliver a copy of the order to the registrar of companies as soon as reasonably practicable after the making of the order.

NOTES
Commencement: 6 April 2017.
This rule derived from the Insolvency Rules 1986, SI 1986/1925, r 12A. 57.

Sub-division B: Applications for private examination (sections 236, 251N and 366)

[Note: for rules about public examinations see Chapter 13 of Part 7 and Chapter 8 of Part 10.]

[6.671]
12.17 Application of this sub-division and interpretation

(1) The rules in this sub-division apply to applications to the court for an order under—
(a) section 236 (inquiry into company's dealings);
(b) section 251N (debt relief orders—inquiry into dealings and property of debtor); and
(c) section 366 (inquiry into bankrupt's dealings and property) including section 366 as it applies by virtue of section 368.
(2) In this sub-division—
"applicable section" means section 236, 251N or 366; and

"the insolvent" means the company, the debtor or the bankrupt as the case may be.

NOTES

Commencement: 6 April 2017.

This rule derived from the Insolvency Rules 1986, SI 1986/1925, r 9.1.

[6.672]

12.18 Contents of application

(1) An application to the court under section 236, 251N or 366 must state—

(a) the grounds on which it is made; and

(b) which one or more of the following orders is sought—

(i) for the respondent to appear before the court,

(ii) for the respondent to clarify any matter which is in dispute in the proceedings or to give additional information in relation to any such matter (if so Part 18 CPR (further information) applies to any such order),

(iii) for the respondent to submit witness statements (if so, particulars must be given of the matters to be included), or

(iv) for the respondent to produce books, papers or other records (if so, the items in question to be specified).

(2) An application under an applicable section may be made without notice to any other party.

(3) The court may, whatever the order sought in the application, make any order which it has power to make under the applicable section.

NOTES

Commencement: 6 April 2017.

This rule derived from the Insolvency Rules 1986, SI 1986/1925, r 9.2.

[6.673]

12.19 Order for examination etc

(1) Where the court orders the respondent to appear before it, it must specify the venue for the appearance.

(2) The date must not be less than 14 days from the date of the order.

(3) If the respondent is ordered to file with the court a witness statement or a written account, the order must specify—

(a) the matters which are to be dealt with in it; and

(b) the time within which it is to be delivered.

(4) If the order is to produce documents or other records, the time and manner of compliance must be specified.

(5) The applicant must serve a copy of the order on the respondent as soon as reasonably practicable.

NOTES

Commencement: 6 April 2017.

This rule derived from the Insolvency Rules 1986, SI 1986/1925, r 9.3.

[6.674]

12.20 Procedure for examination

(1) The applicant may attend an examination of the respondent, in person, or be represented by an appropriately qualified legal representative, and may put such questions to the respondent as the court may allow.

(2) Unless the applicant objects, the following persons may attend the examination with the permission of the court and may put questions to the respondent (but only through the applicant)—

(a) any person who could have applied for an order under the applicable section; and

(b) any creditor who has provided information on which the application was made under section 236 or 366.

(3) If the respondent is ordered to clarify any matter or to give additional information, the court must direct the respondent as to the questions which the respondent is required to answer, and as to whether the respondent's answers (if any) are to be made in a witness statement.

(4) The respondent may employ an appropriately qualified legal representative at the respondent's own expense, who may—

(a) put to the respondent such questions as the court may allow for the purpose of enabling the respondent to explain or qualify any answers given by the respondent; and

(b) make representations on the respondent's behalf.

(5) Such written record of the examination must be made as the court thinks proper and such record must be read either to or by the respondent and authenticated by the respondent at a venue fixed by the court.

(6) The record may, in any proceedings (whether under the Act or otherwise), be used as evidence against the respondent of any statement made by the respondent in the course of the respondent's examination.

NOTES

Commencement: 6 April 2017.

This rule derived from the Insolvency Rules 1986, SI 1986/1925, r 9.4.

[6.675]

12.21 Record of examination

(1) Unless the court otherwise directs, the record of questions put to the respondent, the respondent's answers and any witness statement or written account delivered to the court by the respondent in compliance with an order of the court under the applicable section are not to be filed with the court.

(2) The documents listed in paragraph (3) may not be inspected without the permission of the court, except by—

(a) the applicant for an order under the applicable section; or

(b) any person who could have applied for such an order in relation to the affairs of the same insolvent.

(3) The documents are—

(a) the record of the respondent's examination;

(b) copies of questions put to the respondent or proposed to be put to the respondent and answers to questions given by the respondent;

(c) any witness statement by the respondent; and

(d) any document on the court file that shows the grounds for the application for the order.

(4) The court may from time to time give directions as to the custody and inspection of any documents to which this rule applies, and as to the provision of copies of, or extracts from, such documents.

NOTES

Commencement: 6 April 2017.

This rule derived from the Insolvency Rules 1986, SI 1986/1925, r 9.5.

[6.676]

12.22 Costs of proceedings under sections 236, 251N and 366

(1) Where the court has ordered an examination of a person under an applicable section, and it appears to it that the examination was made necessary because information had been unjustifiably refused by the respondent, it may order that the respondent pay the costs of the examination.

(2) Where the court makes an order against a person under—

(a) section 237(1) or 367(1) (to deliver up property in any person's possession which belongs to the insolvent estate); or

(b) section 237(2) or 367(2) (to pay any amount in discharge of a debt due to the insolvent);

the costs of the application for the order may be ordered by the court to be paid by the respondent.

(3) Subject to paragraphs (1) and (2), the applicant's costs must, unless the court orders otherwise, be paid—

(a) in relation to a company insolvency, as an expense of the insolvency proceedings; and

(b) in relation to an individual insolvency, but not in proceedings relating to debt relief orders or applications for debt relief orders, out of the bankrupt's estate or (as the case may be) the debtor's property.

(4) A person summoned to attend for examination must be tendered a reasonable sum for travelling expenses incurred in connection with that person's attendance but any other costs falling on that person are at the court's discretion.

(5) Where the examination is on the application of the official receiver otherwise than in the capacity of liquidator or trustee, no order may be made for the payment of costs by the official receiver.

NOTES

Commencement: 6 April 2017.

This rule derived from the Insolvency Rules 1986, SI 1986/1925, r 9.6.

Sub-division C—persons unable to manage own property or affairs

[6.677]

12.23 Application and interpretation

(1) This sub-division applies where it appears to the court in insolvency proceedings that a person affected by the proceedings is unable to manage and administer that person's own property and affairs by reason of—

(a) lacking capacity within the meaning of the Mental Capacity Act 2005;

(b) suffering from a physical affliction; or

(c) disability.

(2) Such a person is referred to in this sub-division as "the incapacitated person".

NOTES

Commencement: 6 April 2017.

This rule derived from the Insolvency Rules 1986, SI 1986/1925, r 7.43.

[6.678]
12.24 Appointment of another person to act

(1) The court may appoint such person as it thinks just to appear for, represent or act for the incapacitated person.

(2) The appointment may be made either generally or for the purpose of a particular application or proceeding, or for the exercise of particular rights or powers which the incapacitated person might have exercised but for that person's incapacity.

(3) The court may make the appointment either of its own motion or on application by—
- (a) a person who has been appointed by a court in the United Kingdom or elsewhere to manage the affairs of, or to represent, the incapacitated person;
- (b) any person who appears to the court to be a suitable person to make the application;
- (c) the official receiver; or
- (d) the office-holder.

(4) An application may be made without notice to any other party.

(5) However the court may require such notice of the application as it thinks necessary to be delivered to the incapacitated person, or any other person, and may adjourn the hearing of the application to enable the notice to be delivered.

NOTES

Commencement: 6 April 2017.
This rule derived from the Insolvency Rules 1986, SI 1986/1925, r 7.43.

[6.679]
12.25 Witness statement in support of application

An application under rule 12.24(3) must be supported by a witness statement made by a registered medical practitioner as to the mental or physical condition of the incapacitated person.

NOTES

Commencement: 6 April 2017.
This rule derived from the Insolvency Rules 1986, SI 1986/1925, r 7.45A.

[6.680]
12.26 Service of notices following appointment

Any notice served on, or sent to, a person appointed under rule 12.24 has the same effect as if it had been served on, or delivered to, the incapacitated person.

NOTES

Commencement: 6 April 2017.
This rule derived from the Insolvency Rules 1986, SI 1986/1925, r 7.46.

CHAPTER 5 OBTAINING INFORMATION AND EVIDENCE

[Note: a document required by the Act or these Rules must also contain the standard contents set out in Part 1.]

[6.681]
12.27 Further information and disclosure

(1) A party to insolvency proceedings in court may apply to court for an order—
- (a) that in accordance with CPR Part 18 (further information) another party—
  - (i) clarify a matter that is in dispute in the proceedings, or
  - (ii) give additional information in relation to such a matter; or
- (b) for disclosure from any person in accordance with CPR Part 31 (disclosure and inspection of documents).

(2) An application under this rule may be made without notice to any other party.

NOTES

Commencement: 6 April 2017.
This rule derived from the Insolvency Rules 1986, SI 1986/1925, r 7.60.

[6.682]
12.28 Witness statements and reports

(1) Where the Act or these Rules require evidence as to a matter, such evidence may be given by witness statement unless—
- (a) in a specific case a rule or the Act makes different provision; or
- (b) the court otherwise directs.

(2) Unless either the provision of the Act or rule under which the application is made provides otherwise, or the court directs otherwise—
- (a) if the applicant intends to rely at the first hearing on evidence in a witness statement or report, the applicant must file the witness statement or report with the court and serve a copy of it on the respondent not less than 14 days before the date fixed for the hearing; and

Part 6 Insolvency Rules

(b) where the respondent intends to oppose the application and rely for that purpose on evidence contained in a witness statement or report, the respondent must file the witness statement or report with the court and serve a copy on the applicant not less than five business days before the date fixed for the hearing.

(3) The court may order a person who has made a witness statement or report to attend for cross-examination.

(4) Where a person who has been ordered to attend fails to do so the witness statement or report must not be used in evidence without the court's permission.

NOTES

Commencement: 6 April 2017.

This rule derived from the Insolvency Rules 1986, SI 1986/1925, rr 7.7A, 7.8.

[6.683]

12.29 Evidence provided by the official receiver, an insolvency practitioner or a special manager

(1) Where in insolvency proceedings a witness statement is made by an office-holder, the office-holder must state—

(a) the capacity in which the office-holder is acting; and

(b) the office-holder's address.

(2) The following may file a report with the court instead of a witness statement in all insolvency proceedings—

(a) the official receiver; and

(b) the adjudicator.

(3) The following may file a report with the court instead of a witness statement unless the application involves other parties or the court otherwise directs—

(a) an administrator;

(b) a provisional liquidator;

(c) a liquidator;

(d) an interim receiver;

(e) a trustee; and

(f) a special manager.

(4) Where a report is filed instead of a witness statement, the report must be treated for the purpose of rule 12.28 and any hearing before the court as if it were a witness statement.

NOTES

Commencement: 6 April 2017.

This rule derived from the Insolvency Rules 1986, SI 1986/1925, r 7.9.

CHAPTER 6 TRANSFER OF PROCEEDINGS

[Note: a document required by the Act or these Rules must also contain the standard contents set out in Part 1.]

Sub-division A: General

[6.684]

12.30 General power of transfer

(1) The High Court may order insolvency proceedings which are pending in that court to be transferred to a specified hearing centre.

(2) The County Court may order insolvency proceedings which are pending in a hearing centre to be transferred either to the High Court or another hearing centre.

(3) A judge of the High Court may order insolvency proceedings which are pending in the County Court to be transferred to the High Court.

(4) The court may order a transfer of proceedings—

(a) of its own motion;

(b) on the application of the official receiver; or

(c) on the application of a person appearing to the court to have an interest in the proceedings.

(5) Winding-up proceedings may only be transferred to a hearing centre in which proceedings to wind up companies may be commenced under the Act or to the County Court at Central London.

(6) Bankruptcy proceedings or proceedings relating to a debt relief order may only be transferred to a hearing centre in which bankruptcy proceedings may be commenced under the Act.

(7) A case in a schedule under rule 12.37(8) may be transferred solely for the purposes of rule 12.38 (action following application for a block transfer order) by—

(a) the registrar to or from the High Court; and

(b) the District Judge of the hearing centre to which the application is made, to or from that hearing centre.

NOTES

Commencement: 6 April 2017.

This rule derived from the Insolvency Rules 1986, SI 1986/1925, r 7.11.

[6.685]
12.31 Proceedings commenced in the wrong court

Where insolvency proceedings are commenced in the wrong court or hearing centre, that court may order—

(a) the proceedings be transferred to the court or hearing centre in which they ought to have been commenced;

(b) the proceedings be continued in the court in which they have been commenced; or

(c) the proceedings be struck out.

NOTES

Commencement: 6 April 2017.

This rule derived from the Insolvency Rules 1986, SI 1986/1925, r 7.12.

[6.686]
12.32 Applications for transfer

(1) An application by the official receiver for proceedings to be transferred must be accompanied by a report by the official receiver.

(2) The report must set out the reasons for the transfer, and include a statement either that—

(a) the petitioner, or the debtor in proceedings relating to a debt relief order, consents to the transfer; or

(b) the petitioner or such a debtor has been given at least 14 days' notice of the official receiver's application.

(3) If the court is satisfied from the report that the proceedings can be conducted more conveniently in another court or hearing centre, it must order that the proceedings be transferred to that court or hearing centre.

(4) A person other than the official receiver who applies for the transfer of winding up or bankruptcy proceedings or proceedings relating to a debt relief order must deliver a notice that such an application is intended to be made at least 14 days' before filing the application with the court to—

(a) the official receiver attached to the court or hearing centre in which the proceedings are pending; and

(b) the official receiver attached to the court or hearing centre to which it is proposed that they should be transferred.

NOTES

Commencement: 6 April 2017.

This rule derived from the Insolvency Rules 1986, SI 1986/1925, r 7.13.

[6.687]
12.33 Procedure following order for transfer

(1) Where a court makes an order for the transfer of proceedings under rule 12.30 (other than paragraph (7) of that rule), it must as soon as reasonably practicable deliver to the transferee court or hearing centre a sealed copy of the order, and the file of the proceedings.

(2) A transferee court (or hearing centre) which receives such an order and the file in winding up or bankruptcy proceedings or proceedings relating to a debt relief order must, as soon as reasonably practicable, deliver notice of the transfer to the official receiver attached to that court or hearing centre and the transferor court respectively.

(3) Where the High Court makes a transfer order under rule 12.30(7)—

(a) it must deliver sealed copies of the order—

(i) to the hearing centre from which the proceedings are transferred, and

(ii) in winding up or bankruptcy proceedings or proceedings relating to a debt relief order, to the official receiver attached to that hearing centre and the High Court respectively; and

(b) the hearing centre must deliver the file of the proceedings to the High Court.

NOTES

Commencement: 6 April 2017.

This rule derived from the Insolvency Rules 1986, SI 1986/1925, r 7.14.

[6.688]
12.34 Consequential transfer of other proceedings

(1) This rule applies where—

(a) the High Court has—

(i) made a winding-up order,

(ii) appointed a provisional liquidator,

(iii) made a bankruptcy order, or

(iv) appointed an interim receiver; or

(b) winding-up or bankruptcy proceedings have been transferred to the High Court from the County Court.

(2) A judge of any division of the High Court may, of that judge's own motion, order the transfer to that division of any such proceedings as are mentioned below and are pending against the company or individual concerned ("the insolvent") either in another division of the High Court or in a court in England and Wales other than the High Court.

(3) Paragraph (2) is subject to rule 30.5(4) CPR (transfer between divisions and to and from a specialist list).

(4) The proceedings which may be transferred are those brought by or against the insolvent for the purpose of enforcing a claim against the insolvent estate, or brought by a person other than the insolvent for the purpose of enforcing any such claim (including in either case proceedings of any description by a debenture-holder or mortgagee).

(5) Where any such proceedings are transferred, they must be listed before a registrar for directions or final disposal as the registrar sees fit.

NOTES

Commencement: 6 April 2017.
This rule derived from the Insolvency Rules 1986, SI 1986/1925, r 7.15.

Sub-division B: Block transfer of cases where insolvency practitioner has died etc

[6.689]
12.35 Interpretation

In this Sub-division—

"outgoing office-holder" has the meaning given in rule 12.36(1);
"replacement office-holder" has the meaning given in rule 12.36(1);
"block transfer order" has the meaning given in rule 12.36(2);
"substantive application" is that part of the application in rule 12.37(1)(c) and (d).

NOTES

Commencement: 6 April 2017.
This rule derived from the Insolvency Rules 1986, SI 1986/1925, r 7.10A.

[6.690]
12.36 Power to make a block transfer order

(1) This rule applies where an office-holder ('the outgoing office-holder')—
- (a) dies;
- (b) retires from practice; or
- (c) is otherwise unable or unwilling to continue in office;

and it is expedient to transfer some or all of the cases in which the outgoing office-holder holds office to one or more office-holders ('the replacement office-holder') in a single transaction.

(2) In a case to which this rule applies the court has the power to make an order ('a block transfer order') appointing a replacement office-holder in the place of the outgoing office-holder to be—
- (a) liquidator in any winding up (including a case where the official receiver is the liquidator by virtue of section 136);
- (b) administrator in any administration;
- (c) trustee in a bankruptcy (including a case where the official receiver is the trustee by virtue of section 300); or
- (d) supervisor of a CVA or an IVA.

(3) The replacement office-holder must be—
- (a) qualified to act as an insolvency practitioner in relation to the company or bankrupt; or
- (b) where the replacement office-holder is to be appointed supervisor of an IVA—
  - (i) qualified to act as an insolvency practitioner in relation to the debtor, or
  - (ii) a person authorised so to act.

NOTES

Commencement: 6 April 2017.
This rule derived from the Insolvency Rules 1986, SI 1986/1925, r 7.10B.

[6.691]
12.37 Application for a block transfer order

(1) An application for a block transfer order may be made to the registrar or District Judge for—
- (a) the transfer to the High Court of the cases specified in the schedule to the application under paragraph (8);
- (b) the transfer of the cases back to the court or hearing centre from which they were transferred when a replacement office-holder has been appointed;
- (c) the removal of the outgoing office-holder by the exercise of any of the powers in paragraph (2);
- (d) the appointment of a replacement office-holder by the exercise of any of the powers in paragraph (3); or
- (e) such other order or direction as may be necessary or expedient in connection with any of the matters referred to above.

(2) The powers referred to in paragraph (1)(c) are those in—
- (a) section 7(5) and paragraph 39(6) of Schedule A1 (CVA);
- (b) section 19, paragraph 88 of Schedule B1 and rule 12.36(2) (administration);
- (c) section 108 (voluntary winding up);
- (d) section 172(2) and rule 12.36(2) (winding up by the court);
- (e) section 263(5) (IVA); and
- (f) section 298 and rule 12.36(2) (bankruptcy).

(3) The powers referred to in paragraph (1)(d) are those in—
(a) section 7(5) and paragraph 39(6) of Schedule A1 (CVA);
(b) section 13, paragraphs 63, 91 and 95 of Schedule B1 and rule 12.36(2) (administration);
(c) section 108 (voluntary winding up);
(d) section 168(3) and (5) and rule 12.36(2) (winding up by the court);
(e) section 263(5) (IVA); and
(f) sections 298 and 303(2) and rule 12.36(2) (bankruptcy).

(4) Subject to paragraph (5), the application may be made by any of the following—
(a) the outgoing office-holder (if able and willing to do so);
(b) any person who holds office jointly with the outgoing office-holder;
(c) any person who is proposed to be appointed as the replacement office-holder;
(d) any creditor in a case subject to the application;
(e) the recognised professional body which was the source of the outgoing office-holder's authorisation; or
(f) the Secretary of State.

(5) Where one or more outgoing office-holder in the schedule under paragraph (8) is an administrator, an application may not be made unless the applicant is a person permitted to apply to replace that office-holder under section 13 or paragraph 63, 91 or 95 of Schedule B1 or such a person is joined as applicant in relation to the replacement of that office-holder.

(6) An applicant (other than the Secretary of State) must deliver a notice of the intended application to the Secretary of State on or before the date the application is made.

(7) The following must be made a respondent to the application and served with it—
(a) the outgoing office-holder (if not the applicant or deceased);
(b) any person who holds office jointly with the outgoing office-holder; and
(c) such other person as the registrar or District Judge directs.

(8) The application must contain a schedule setting out—
(a) identification details for the proceedings; and
(b) the capacity in which the outgoing office-holder was appointed.

(9) The application must be supported by evidence—
(a) setting out the circumstances as a result of which it is expedient to appoint a replacement office-holder; and
(b) exhibiting the consent to act of each person who is proposed to be appointed as replacement office-holder.

(10) Where all the cases in the schedule under paragraph (8) are in the County Court—
(a) the application may be made to a District Judge of a convenient hearing centre in which insolvency proceedings of such type may be commenced; and
(b) this rule applies with appropriate modifications.

NOTES

Commencement: 6 April 2017.

This rule derived from the Insolvency Rules 1986, SI 1986/1925, r 7.10C.

[6.692]

12.38 Action following application for a block transfer order

(1) The registrar or District Judge may in the first instance consider the application without a hearing and make such order as the registrar or District Judge thinks just.

(2) In the first instance, the registrar or District Judge may do any of the following—
(a) make an order directing the transfer to the High Court of those cases not already within its jurisdiction for the purpose only of the substantive application;
(b) if the documents are considered to be in order and the matter is considered straightforward, make an order on the substantive application;
(c) give any directions which are considered to be necessary including (if appropriate) directions for the joinder of any additional respondents or requiring the service of the application on any person or requiring additional evidence to be provided; or
(d) if an order is not made on the substantive application, give directions for the further consideration of the substantive application by the registrar or District Judge or a judge of the Chancery Division.

(3) The applicant must ensure that a sealed copy of every order transferring any case to the High Court and of every order which is made on a substantive application is filed with the court having jurisdiction over each case affected by such order.

(4) In any case other than an application relating to the appointment of an administrator, in deciding to what extent (if any) the costs of making an application under this rule should be paid as an expense of the insolvency proceedings to which the application relates, the factors to which the court must have regard include—
(a) the reasons for the making of the application;
(b) the number of cases to which the application relates;
(c) the value of assets comprised in those cases; and
(d) the nature and extent of the costs involved.

(5) Where an application relates to the appointment of an administrator and is made by a person under section 13 or paragraph 63, 91 or 95 of Schedule B1, the costs of making that application are to be paid as an expense of the administration to which the application relates unless the court directs otherwise.

(6) Notice of any appointment made under this rule must be delivered—

(a) to the Secretary of State as soon as reasonably practicable; and

(b) to—

(i) the creditors, and

(ii) such other persons as the court may direct, in such manner as the court may direct.

(7) Where the application was made to the District Judge under rule 12.37(10) this rule applies with appropriate modifications.

NOTES

Commencement: 6 April 2017.

This rule derived from the Insolvency Rules 1986, SI 1986/1925, r 7.10D.

CHAPTER 7 THE COURT FILE

[Note: a document required by the Act or these Rules must also contain the standard contents set out in Part 1.]

[6.693]

12.39 The court file

(1) Where documents are filed with the court under the Act or these Rules, the court must open and maintain a court file and place those documents on the file.

(2) However where a bankruptcy file has been opened under rule 10.47, documents filed with the court under the Act or these Rules must be placed on the bankruptcy file.

(3) The following may inspect the court file, or obtain from the court a copy of the court file, or of any document in the court file—

(a) the office-holder in the proceedings;

(b) the Secretary of State; and

(c) a creditor who provides the court with a statement confirming that that person is a creditor of the company or the individual to whom the proceedings relate.

(4) The same right to inspect and obtain copies is exercisable—

(a) in proceedings under Parts 1 to 7 of the Act, by—

(i) an officer or former officer of the company to which the proceedings relate, or

(ii) a member of the company or a contributory in its winding up;

(b) in proceedings relating to an IVA, by the debtor;

(c) in bankruptcy proceedings, by—

(i) the bankrupt,

(ii) a person against whom a bankruptcy petition has been presented, or

(iii) a person who has been served with a statutory demand under section 268;

(d) in proceedings relating to a debt relief order, by the debtor.

(5) The right to inspect and obtain copies may be exercised on a person's behalf by someone authorised to do so by that person.

(6) Other persons may inspect the file or obtain copies if the court gives permission.

(7) The right to a copy of a document is subject to payment of the fee chargeable under an order made under section 92 of the Courts Act 2003.

(8) Inspection of the file, with permission if required, may be at any reasonable time.

(9) The court may direct that the file, a document (or part of it) or a copy of a document (or part of it) must not be made available under paragraph (3), (4) or (5) without the permission of the court.

(10) An application for a direction under paragraph (9) may be made by—

(a) the official receiver;

(b) the office-holder in the proceedings; or

(c) any person appearing to the court to have an interest.

(11) The following applications may be made without notice to any other party, but the court may direct that notice must be delivered to any person who would be affected by its decision—

(a) an application for permission to inspect the file or obtain a copy of a document under paragraph (6); and

(b) an application for a direction under paragraph (9).

(12) If, for the purposes of powers conferred by the Act or these Rules, the Secretary of State or the official receiver makes a request to inspect or requests the transmission of the file of insolvency proceedings, the court must comply with the request (unless the file is for the time being in use for the court's own purposes).

NOTES

Commencement: 6 April 2017.

This rule derived from the Insolvency Rules 1986, SI 1986/1925, r 7.31A.

[6.694]
12.40 Office copies of documents

(1) The court must provide an office copy of a document from the court file to a person who has under these Rules the right to inspect the court file where that person has requested such a copy and paid the appropriate fee under rule 12.39(7).

(2) A person's right under this rule may be exercised on that person's behalf by someone authorised to do so by that person.

(3) An office copy must be in such form as the registrar or District Judge thinks appropriate, and must bear the court's seal.

NOTES

Commencement: 6 April 2017.
This rule derived from the Insolvency Rules 1986, SI 1986/1925, r 7.61.

CHAPTER 8 COSTS

[Note: a document required by the Act or these Rules must also contain the standard contents set out in Part 1.]

[6.695]
12.41 Application of Chapter and interpretation

(1) This Chapter applies to costs of and in connection with insolvency proceedings.

(2) In this Chapter "costs" includes charges and expenses.

(3) CPR Parts 44 and 47 (which relate to costs) apply to such costs.

NOTES

Commencement: 6 April 2017.
This rule derived from the Insolvency Rules 1986, SI 1986/1925, r 7.33A.

[6.696]
12.42 Requirement to assess costs by the detailed procedure

(1) Where the costs of any person are payable as an expense out of the insolvent estate, the amount payable must be decided by detailed assessment unless agreed between the office-holder and the person entitled to payment.

(2) In the absence of agreement, the office-holder—
- (a) may serve notice requiring the person entitled to payment to commence detailed assessment proceedings in accordance with CPR Part 47; and
- (b) must serve such notice (except in an administrative receivership) where a liquidation or creditors' committee formed in relation to the insolvency proceedings resolves that the amount of the costs must be decided by detailed assessment.

(3) Detailed assessment proceedings must be commenced in the court to which the insolvency proceedings are allocated or, where in relation to a company there is no such court, any court having jurisdiction to wind up the company.

(4) Where the costs of any person employed by an office-holder in insolvency proceedings are required to be decided by detailed assessment or fixed by order of the court, the office-holder may make payments on account to such person in respect of those costs if that person undertakes in writing—
- (a) to repay as soon as reasonably practicable any money which may, when detailed assessment is made, prove to have been overpaid; and
- (b) to pay interest on any such sum as is mentioned in sub-paragraph (a) at the rate specified in section 17 of the Judgments Act 1838 on the date payment was made and for the period beginning with the date of payment and ending with the date of repayment.

(5) In any proceedings before the court (including proceedings on a petition), the court may order costs to be decided by detailed assessment.

(6) Unless otherwise directed or authorised, the costs of a trustee in bankruptcy or a liquidator are to be allowed on the standard basis for which provision is made in—
- (a) CPR rule 44.3 (basis of assessment); and
- (b) CPR rule 44.4 (factors to be taken into account when deciding the amount of costs).

NOTES

Commencement: 6 April 2017.
This rule derived from the Insolvency Rules 1986, SI 1986/1925, r 7.34A.

[6.697]
12.43 Procedure where detailed assessment is required

(1) The costs officer must require a certificate of employment before making a detailed assessment of the costs of a person employed in insolvency proceedings by the office-holder.

(2) The certificate must be endorsed on the bill and signed by the office-holder and must include—
- (a) the name and address of the person employed;
- (b) details of the functions to be carried out under the employment; and
- (c) a note of any special terms of remuneration which have been agreed.

Part 6 Insolvency Rules

(3) A person whose costs in insolvency proceedings are required to be decided by detailed assessment must, on being required in writing to do so by the office-holder, commence detailed assessment proceedings in accordance with CPR Part 47 (procedure for detailed assessment of costs and default provisions).

(4) If that person does not commence such proceedings within 3 months of being required to do so under paragraph (3), or within such further time as the court, on application, may permit, the office-holder may deal with the insolvent estate without regard to any claim for costs by that person, whose claim is forfeited by such failure to commence proceedings.

(5) Where in any such case such a claim for costs lies additionally against an office-holder in the office-holder's personal capacity, that claim is also forfeited by such failure to commence proceedings.

(6) Where costs have been incurred in insolvency proceedings in the High Court and those proceedings are subsequently transferred to the County Court, all costs of those proceedings directed by the court or otherwise required to be assessed may nevertheless, on the application of the person who incurred the costs, be ordered to be decided by detailed assessment in the High Court.

NOTES

Commencement: 6 April 2017.
This rule derived from the Insolvency Rules 1986, SI 1986/1925, r 7.35.

[6.698]
12.44 Costs of officers charged with execution of writs or other process

(1) This rule applies where an enforcement officer, or other officer charged with execution of the writ or other process—

- (a) is required under section 184(2) or 346(2) to deliver up goods or money; or
- (b) has under section 184(3) or 346(3) deducted costs from the proceeds of an execution or money paid to that officer.

(2) The office-holder may require in writing that the amount of the enforcement officer's or other officer's bill of costs be decided by detailed assessment and where such a requirement is made rule 12.43 (procedure where detailed assessment is required) applies.

(3) Where, in the case of a deduction of the kind mentioned in paragraph (1)(b), any amount deducted is disallowed at the conclusion of the detailed assessment proceedings, the enforcement officer must as soon as reasonably practicable pay a sum equal to that disallowed to the office-holder for the benefit of the insolvent estate.

NOTES

Commencement: 6 April 2017.
This rule derived from the Insolvency Rules 1986, SI 1986/1925, r 7.36.

[6.699]
12.45 Petitions presented by insolvent companies

(1) This rule applies where a winding-up petition is presented by a company against itself.

(2) A solicitor acting for the company must in the solicitor's bill of costs give credit for any sum or security received by the solicitor as a deposit from the company on account of the costs and expenses to be incurred in respect of the filing and prosecution of the petition and the deposit must be noted by the costs officer on the final costs certificate.

(3) Where an order is made on a petition presented by the company and before the presentation of that petition a petition had been presented by a creditor, no costs are to be allowed to the company or that company's solicitor out of the insolvent estate unless the court considers that—

- (a) the insolvent estate has benefited by the company's conduct; or
- (b) there are otherwise special circumstances justifying the allowance of costs.

NOTES

Commencement: 6 April 2017.
This rule derived from the Insolvency Rules 1986, SI 1986/1925, r 7.37A.

[6.700]
12.46 Costs paid otherwise than out of the insolvent estate

Where the amount of costs is decided by detailed assessment under an order of the court directing that those costs are to be paid otherwise than out of the insolvent estate, the costs officer must note on the final costs certificate by whom, or the manner in which, the costs are to be paid.

NOTES

Commencement: 6 April 2017.
This rule derived from the Insolvency Rules 1986, SI 1986/1925, r 7.38.

[6.701]
12.47 Awards of costs against an office-holder, the adjudicator or the official receiver

Without prejudice to any provision of the Act or Rules by virtue of which the official receiver or the adjudicator is not in any event to be liable for costs and expenses, where an office-holder, the adjudicator or the official receiver (where the official receiver is not acting as an office-holder) is made a party to any proceedings on the application of another party to the proceedings, the office-holder, the adjudicator or official receiver is not to be personally liable for the costs unless the court otherwise directs.

NOTES

Commencement: 6 April 2017.

This rule derived from the Insolvency Rules 1986, SI 1986/1925, r 7.39.

[6.702]

12.48 Applications for costs

(1) This rule applies where a party to, or person affected by, any proceedings in an insolvency applies to the court for an order allowing their costs, or part of them, of or incidental to the proceedings, and that application is not made at the time of the proceedings.

(2) The applicant must serve a sealed copy of the application—

- (a) in proceedings other than proceedings relating to a debt relief order—
  - (i) on the office-holder, and
  - (ii) in a winding up by the court or a bankruptcy, on the official receiver; or
- (b) in proceedings relating to a debt relief order, on the official receiver.

(3) The office-holder and, where appropriate, the official receiver may appear on an application to which paragraph (2)(a) applies.

(4) The official receiver may appear on an application to which paragraph (2)(b) applies.

(5) No costs of or incidental to the application are to be allowed to the applicant unless the court is satisfied that the application could not have been made at the time of the proceedings.

NOTES

Commencement: 6 April 2017.

This rule derived from the Insolvency Rules 1986, SI 1986/1925, r 7.40.

[6.703]

12.49 Costs and expenses of petitioners and other specified persons

(1) The petitioner is not to receive an allowance as a witness for attending the hearing of the petition.

(2) However the costs officer may allow that person's expenses of travelling and subsistence in attending the hearing.

(3) The bankrupt, the debtor or an officer of the insolvent company to which the proceedings relate is not to receive an allowance as a witness in an examination or other proceedings before the court except as directed by the court.

NOTES

Commencement: 6 April 2017.

This rule derived from the Insolvency Rules 1986, SI 1986/1925, r 7.41.

[6.704]

12.50 Final costs certificate

(1) A final costs certificate of the costs officer is final and conclusive as to all matters which have not been objected to in the manner provided for under the rules of the court.

(2) Where it is proved to the satisfaction of a costs officer that a final costs certificate has been lost or destroyed, the costs officer may issue a duplicate.

NOTES

Commencement: 6 April 2017.

This rule derived from the Insolvency Rules 1986, SI 1986/1925, r 7.42.

CHAPTER 9 ENFORCEMENT PROCEDURES

[Note: a document required by the Act or these Rules must also contain the standard contents set out in Part 1.]

[6.705]

12.51 Enforcement of court orders

(1) In any insolvency proceedings, orders of the court may be enforced in the same manner as a judgment to the same effect.

(2) Where an order in insolvency proceedings is made, or any process is issued, by the County Court, the order or process may be enforced, executed and dealt with by any hearing centre, as if it had been made or issued for the enforcement of a judgment or order to the same effect made by that hearing centre.

(3) Paragraph (2) applies whether or not the other hearing centre is one in which such insolvency proceedings may be commenced.

(4) Where a warrant for the arrest of a person is issued by the High Court, the warrant may be discharged by the County Court where the person who is the subject of the warrant—

- (a) has been brought before a hearing centre in which insolvency proceedings may be commenced; and
- (b) has given to the County Court a satisfactory undertaking to comply with the obligations that apply to that person under the Act or these Rules.

Part 6 Insolvency Rules

NOTES

Commencement: 6 April 2017.

This rule derived from the Insolvency Rules 1986, SI 1986/1925, r 7.19.

[6.706]

12.52 Orders enforcing compliance

(1) The court may, on application by the competent person, make such orders as it thinks necessary for the enforcement of obligations falling on any person in accordance with—

(a) paragraph 47 of Schedule B1 (duty to submit statement of affairs in administration);

(b) section 47(duty to submit statement of affairs in administrative receivership);

(c) section 131 (duty to submit statement of affairs in a winding up);

(d) section 143(2) (liquidator to furnish information, books, papers, etc); or

(e) section 235 (duty of various persons to co-operate with office-holder).

(2) The competent person for this purpose is—

(a) under paragraph 47 of Schedule B1, the administrator;

(b) under section 47, the administrative receiver;

(c) under section 131 or 143(2), the official receiver; and

(d) under section 235, the official receiver, the administrator, the administrative receiver, the liquidator or the provisional liquidator, as the case may be.

(3) An order of the court under this rule may provide that all costs of and incidental to the application for it are to be borne by the person against whom the order is made.

NOTES

Commencement: 6 April 2017.

This rule derived from the Insolvency Rules 1986, SI 1986/1925, r 7.20.

[6.707]

12.53 Warrants (general provisions)

(1) A warrant issued by the court under any provision of the Act must be addressed to such officer of the High Court or of the County Court as the warrant specifies, or to any constable.

(2) The persons referred to in sections 134(2), 236(5), 251N(5), 364(1), 365(3) and 366(3) (court's powers of enforcement) as the prescribed officer of the court are—

(a) in the case of the High Court, the tipstaff and the tipstaff's assistants of the court; and

(b) in the case of the County Court, a bailiff.

(3) In this Chapter references to property include books, papers and other documents and records.

NOTES

Commencement: 6 April 2017.

This rule derived from the Insolvency Rules 1986, SI 1986/1925, r 7.21.

[6.708]

12.54 Warrants under sections 134 and 364

When a person ("the arrested person") is arrested under a warrant issued by the court under section 134 (officer of company failing to attend for public examination), or section 364 (arrest of debtor or bankrupt)—

(a) the arresting officer must give the arrested person into the custody of—

(i) the court in a case where the court is ready and able to deal with the arrested person, or

(ii) where the court is not ready and able, the governor of the prison named in the warrant (or where that prison is not able to accommodate the arrested person, the governor of such other prison with appropriate facilities which is able to accommodate the arrested person), who must keep the arrested person in custody until such time as the court orders otherwise and must produce that person before the court at its next sitting; and

(b) any property in the arrested person's possession which may be seized must, as directed by the warrant, be—

(i) delivered to whoever is specified in the warrant as authorised to receive it, or otherwise dealt with in accordance with the directions in the warrant, or

(ii) kept by the officer seizing it pending the receipt of written orders from the court as to its disposal.

NOTES

Commencement: 6 April 2017.

This rule derived from the Insolvency Rules 1986, SI 1986/1925, r 7.22.

[6.709]

12.55 Warrants under sections 236, 251N and 366

(1) When a person is arrested under a warrant issued under section 236 (inquiry into insolvent company's dealings), 251N (the equivalent in relation to debt relief orders) or 366 (the equivalent in bankruptcy), the arresting officer must as soon as reasonably practicable bring the arrested person before the court issuing the warrant in order that the arrested person may be examined.

(2) If the arrested person cannot immediately be brought up for examination, the officer must deliver that person into the custody of the governor of the prison named in the warrant (or where that prison is not able to accommodate the arrested person, the governor of such other prison with appropriate facilities which is able to accommodate the arrested person), who must keep the arrested person in custody and produce that person before the court as it may from time to time direct.

(3) After arresting the person named in the warrant, the officer must as soon as reasonably practicable report to the court the arrest or delivery into custody (as the case may be) and apply to the court to fix a venue for the arrested person's examination.

(4) The court must appoint the earliest practicable time for the examination, and must—

(a) direct the governor of the prison to produce the arrested person for examination at the time and place appointed; and

(b) as soon as reasonably practicable deliver notice of the venue to the applicant for the warrant.

(5) Where any property in the arrested person's possession is seized, the property must, as directed by the warrant, be—

(a) delivered to whoever is specified in the warrant as authorised to receive it, or otherwise dealt with in accordance with the directions in the warrant; or

(b) kept by the officer seizing it pending the receipt of written orders from the court as to its disposal.

NOTES

Commencement: 6 April 2017.

This rule derived from the Insolvency Rules 1986, SI 1986/1925, r 7.23.

[6.710]

12.56 Warrants under section 365

(1) A warrant issued under section 365(3) (search of premises not belonging to the bankrupt) must authorise any person executing it to seize any property of the bankrupt found as a result of the execution of the warrant.

(2) Any property seized under a warrant issued under section 365(2) or (3) must, as directed by the warrant, be—

(a) delivered to whoever is specified in the warrant as authorised to receive it, or otherwise dealt with in accordance with the directions in the warrant; or

(b) kept by the officer seizing it pending the receipt of written orders from the court as to its disposal.

NOTES

Commencement: 6 April 2017.

This rule derived from the Insolvency Rules 1986, SI 1986/1925, r 7.25.

[6.711]

12.57 Execution overtaken by judgment debtor's insolvency

(1) This rule applies where execution has been taken out against property of a judgment debtor, and notice is delivered to the enforcement officer or other officer charged with the execution—

(a) under section 184(1) (that a winding-up order has been made against the debtor, or that a provisional liquidator has been appointed, or that a resolution for voluntary winding up has been passed);

(b) under section 184(4) (that a winding-up petition has been presented, or a winding-up order made, or that a meeting has been called at which there is to be proposed a resolution for voluntary winding up, or that such a resolution has been passed);

(c) under section 346(2) (that a judgment debtor has been made bankrupt); or

(d) under section 346(3)(b) (that a bankruptcy petition has been presented or a bankruptcy application has been made in relation to the debtor).

(2) Subject to paragraph (3) and rule 1.47, the notice must be delivered to the office of the enforcement officer or of the officer charged with the execution—

(a) by hand; or

(b) by any other means of delivery which enables proof of receipt of the document at the relevant address.

(3) Where the execution is in the County Court then if—

(a) there is filed with the hearing centre in charge of such execution in relation to the judgment debtor a winding-up or bankruptcy petition; or

(b) there is made by the hearing centre in charge of such execution in relation to the judgment debtor a winding-up order or an order appointing a provisional liquidator, or a bankruptcy order or an order appointing an interim receiver;

section 184 or 346 is deemed satisfied in relation to the requirement of a notice to be served on, or delivered to, the officer in charge of the execution.

NOTES

Commencement: 6 April 2017.

This rule derived from the Insolvency Rules 1986, SI 1986/1925, r 12A.28.

CHAPTER 10 APPEALS

[Note: a document required by the Act or these Rules must also contain the standard contents set out in Part 1.]

[6.712]

12.58 Application of Chapter

CPR Part 52 (appeals) applies to appeals under this Chapter as varied by any applicable Practice Direction.

NOTES

Commencement: 6 April 2017.

This rule derived from the Insolvency Rules 1986, SI 1986/1925, r 7.49A.

[6.713]

12.59 Appeals and reviews of court orders in corporate insolvency

(1) Every court having jurisdiction for the purposes of Parts 1 to 7 of the Act and the corresponding Parts of these Rules, may review, rescind or vary any order made by it in the exercise of that jurisdiction.

(2) Appeals in civil matters in proceedings under Parts 1 to 7 of the Act and the corresponding Parts of these Rules lie as follows—

(a) where the decision appealed against is made by a District Judge sitting in a hearing centre specified in the first column of the table in Schedule 10—
   (i) to a High Court Judge sitting in a district registry, or
   (ii) to [an Insolvency and Companies Court Judge];
   as specified in the second column of the table;

(b) to a High Court Judge where the decision appealed against is made by—
   (i) a Circuit Judge sitting in the County Court,
   (ii) a Master,
   (iii) [an Insolvency and Companies Court Judge], if that decision is made at first instance, or
   (iv) a District Judge sitting in a district registry;

(c) to the Civil Division of the Court of Appeal where the decision appealed against is made by [an Insolvency and Companies Court Judge], if that decision is an appeal from a decision made by a District Judge; and

(d) to the Civil Division of the Court of Appeal where the decision is made by a High Court Judge.

(3) Any application for the rescission of a winding-up order must be made within five business days after the date on which the order was made.

(4) In this rule—

"Circuit Judge sitting in the county court" means a judge sitting pursuant to section 5(1)(a) of the County Courts Act 1984;

"Civil Division of the Court of Appeal" means the division of the Court of Appeal established by section 3(1) of the Senior Courts Act 1981;

"county court" means the court established by section A1 of the County Courts Act 1984;

"District Judge" means a person appointed a District Judge under section 6(1) of the County Courts Act 1984;

"District Judge sitting in a district registry" means a District Judge sitting in an assigned district registry as a District Judge of the High Court under section 100 of the Senior Courts Act 1981;

"district registry" means a district registry of the High Court under section 99 of the Senior Courts Act 1981;

"High Court Judge" means a judge listed in section 4(1) of the Senior Courts Act 1981;

["Insolvency and Companies Court Judge" means a person appointed to the office of Insolvency and Companies Court Judge under section 89(1) of the Senior Courts Act 1981;]

"Master" means a person appointed to the office of Master, Chancery Division under section 89(1) of the Senior Courts Act 1981;

"Registrar in Bankruptcy of the High Court" means a person appointed to the office of Registrar in Bankruptcy of the High Court under section 89(1) of the Senior Courts Act 1981;

and for the purposes of each definition a person appointed to act as a deputy for any person holding that office is included.

NOTES

Commencement: 6 April 2017.

This rule derived from the Insolvency Rules 1986, SI 1986/1925, r 7.47.

Para (2): words in square brackets substituted by the Alteration of Judicial Titles (Registrar in Bankruptcy of the High Court) Order 2018, SI 2018/130, art 3, Schedule, para 14(a)(ii).

Para (4): definition "Insolvency and Companies Court Judge" inserted and definition "Registrar in Bankruptcy of the High Court" (omitted) revoked, by SI 2018/130, art 3, Schedule, para 14(b).

[6.714]

12.60 Appeals in bankruptcy by the Secretary of State

In bankruptcy proceedings, an appeal lies at the instance of the Secretary of State from any order of the court made on an application for the rescission or annulment of a bankruptcy order, or for the bankrupt's discharge.

NOTES

Commencement: 6 April 2017.
This rule derived from the Insolvency Rules 1986, SI 1986/1925, r 7.48.

[6.715]
12.61 Procedure on appeal

(1) An appeal against a decision at first instance may be brought only with the permission of the court which made the decision or of the court that has jurisdiction to hear the appeal.

(2) An appellant must file an appellant's notice within 21 days after the date of the decision of the court that the appellant wishes to appeal.

NOTES

Commencement: 6 April 2017.
This rule derived from the Insolvency Rules 1986, SI 1986/1925, r 7.49A.

[6.716]
12.62 Appeals against decisions of the Secretary of State or official receiver

An appeal under the Act or these Rules against a decision of the Secretary of State or the official receiver must be brought within 28 days of delivery of notice of the decision.

NOTES

Commencement: 6 April 2017.
This rule derived from the Insolvency Rules 1986, SI 1986/1925, r 7.50.

CHAPTER 11 COURT ORDERS, FORMAL DEFECTS AND SHORTHAND WRITERS

[Note: a document required by the Act or these Rules must also contain the standard contents set out in Part 1.]

[6.717]
12.63 Court orders

Notwithstanding any requirement in these Rules as to the contents of a court order the court may make such other order or in such form as the court thinks just.

NOTES

Commencement: 6 April 2017.

[6.718]
12.64 Formal defects

No insolvency proceedings will be invalidated by any formal defect or any irregularity unless the court before which objection is made considers that substantial injustice has been caused by the defect or irregularity and that the injustice cannot be remedied by any order of the court.

NOTES

Commencement: 6 April 2017.
This rule derived from the Insolvency Rules 1986, SI 1986/1925, r 7.55.

[6.719]
12.65 Shorthand writers: nomination etc

(1) The court may in writing nominate a person to be official shorthand writer to the court.

(2) The court may, at any time in the course of insolvency proceedings, appoint a shorthand writer to take down evidence of a person examined under section 133, 236, 251N, 290 or 366.

(3) Where the official receiver applies to the court for an order appointing a shorthand writer, the official receiver must name the person the official receiver proposes for the appointment.

(4) The remuneration of a shorthand writer appointed in insolvency proceedings must be paid by the party at whose instance the appointment was made, or out of the insolvent estate, or otherwise, as the court may direct.

(5) Any question arising as to the rates of remuneration payable under this rule must be determined by the court.

NOTES

Commencement: 6 April 2017.
This rule derived from the Insolvency Rules 1986, SI 1986/1925, rr 7.16, 7.17.

PART 13
OFFICIAL RECEIVERS

[6.720]
13.1 Official receivers in court

(1) Judicial notice must be taken of the appointment under sections 399 to 401 of official receivers and deputy official receivers.

(2) Official receivers and deputy official receivers have a right of audience in insolvency proceedings, whether in the High Court or the County Court.

NOTES

Commencement: 6 April 2017.
This rule derived from the Insolvency Rules 1986, SI 1986/1925, r 10.1.

[6.721]
13.2 Persons entitled to act on official receiver's behalf

(1) In the absence of the official receiver authorised to act in a particular case, an officer authorised in writing for the purpose by the Secretary of State, or by the official receiver, may with the permission of the court, act on the official receiver's behalf and in the official receiver's place—

(a) in any examination under section 133, 236, 251N, 290 or 366; and
(b) in relation to any application to the court.

(2) In case of emergency, where there is no official receiver capable of acting, anything to be done by, to or before the official receiver may be done by, to or before the registrar or District Judge.

NOTES

Commencement: 6 April 2017.
This rule derived from the Insolvency Rules 1986, SI 1986/1925, r 10.2.

[6.722]
13.3 Application for directions

The official receiver may apply to the court for directions in relation to any matter arising in insolvency proceedings.

NOTES

Commencement: 6 April 2017.
This rule derived from the Insolvency Rules 1986, SI 1986/1925, r 10.3.

[6.723]
13.4 Official receiver's expenses

(1) Any expenses (including damages) incurred by the official receiver (in whatever capacity the official receiver may be acting) in connection with proceedings taken against the official receiver in insolvency proceedings are to be treated as expenses of the insolvency proceedings.

(2) The official receiver has a charge on the insolvent estate in respect of any sums due to the official receiver under paragraph (1) in connection with insolvency proceedings other than proceedings relating to debt relief orders or applications for debt relief orders.

NOTES

Commencement: 6 April 2017.
This rule derived from the Insolvency Rules 1986, SI 1986/1925, r 10.4.

[6.724]
13.5 Official receiver not to be appointed liquidator or trustee

The official receiver may not be appointed as liquidator or trustee by any decision of creditors or (in a winding up) contributories or the company.

NOTES

Commencement: 6 April 2017.
This rule derived from the Insolvency Rules 1986, SI 1986/1925, r 4.101B.

PART 14
CLAIMS BY AND DISTRIBUTIONS TO CREDITORS IN ADMINISTRATION, WINDING UP AND BANKRUPTCY

CHAPTER 1 APPLICATION AND INTERPRETATION

[6.725]
14.1 Application of Part 14 and interpretation

[Note: "bankruptcy debt" and related expressions are defined in relation to bankruptcy in section 382.]

(1) This Part applies to administration, winding up and bankruptcy proceedings.

(2) The definitions in this rule apply to administration, winding up and bankruptcy proceedings except as otherwise stated.

(3) "Debt", in relation to winding up and administration, means (subject to the next paragraph) any of the following—

- (a) any debt or liability to which the company is subject at the relevant date;
- (b) any debt or liability to which the company may become subject after the relevant date by reason of any obligation incurred before that date;
- (c) any interest provable as mentioned in rule 14.23;

"small debt" means a debt (being the total amount owed to a creditor) which does not exceed £1,000 (which amount is prescribed for the purposes of paragraph 13A of Schedule 8 to the Act and paragraph 18A of Schedule 9 to the Act);

"dividend", in relation to a members' voluntary winding up, includes a distribution;

"provable debt" has the meaning given in rule 14.2; and

"relevant date" means—

- (a) in the case of an administration which was not immediately preceded by a winding up, the date on which the company entered administration,
- (b) in the case of an administration which was immediately preceded by a winding up, the date on which the company went into liquidation,
- (c) in the case of a winding up which was not immediately preceded by an administration, the date on which the company went into liquidation,
- (d) in the case of a winding up which was immediately preceded by an administration, the date on which the company entered administration, and
- (e) in the case of a bankruptcy, the date of the bankruptcy order.

(4) For the purposes of any provision of the Act or these Rules about winding up or administration, any liability in tort is a debt provable in the winding up or administration, if either—

- (a) the cause of action has accrued at the relevant date; or
- (b) all the elements necessary to establish the cause of action exist at that date except for actionable damage.

(5) For the purposes of references in any provision of the Act or these Rules about winding up or administration to a debt or liability, it is immaterial whether the debt or liability is present or future, whether it is certain or contingent, or whether its amount is fixed or liquidated, or is capable of being ascertained by fixed rules or as a matter of opinion; and references in any such provision to owing a debt are to be read accordingly.

(6) In any provision of the Act or these Rules about winding up or administration, except in so far as the context otherwise requires, "liability" means (subject to paragraph (4)) a liability to pay money or money's worth, including any liability under an enactment, a liability for breach of trust, any liability in contract, tort or bailment, and any liability arising out of an obligation to make restitution.

NOTES

Commencement: 6 April 2017.

This rule derived from the Insolvency Rules 1986, SI 1986/1925, r 13.12.

CHAPTER 2 CREDITORS' CLAIMS IN ADMINISTRATION, WINDING UP AND BANKRUPTCY

[Note: a document required by the Act or these Rules must also contain the standard contents set out in Part 1.]

[6.726]

14.2 Provable debts

(1) All claims by creditors except as provided in this rule, are provable as debts against the company or bankrupt, whether they are present or future, certain or contingent, ascertained or sounding only in damages.

(2) The following are not provable—

- (a) an obligation arising under a confiscation order made under—
  - (i) section 1 of the Drug Trafficking Offences Act 1986,
  - (ii) section 1 of the Criminal Justice (Scotland) Act 1987,
  - (iii) section 71 of the Criminal Justice Act 1988, or
  - (iv) Parts 2, 3 or 4 of the Proceeds of Crime Act 2002;
- (b) an obligation arising from a payment out of the social fund under section 138(1)(b) of the Social Security Contributions and Benefits Act 1992 by way of crisis loan or budgeting loan.
- (c) in bankruptcy—
  - (i) a fine imposed for an offence,
  - (ii) an obligation (other than an obligation to pay a lump sum or to pay costs) arising under an order made in family proceedings, or
  - (iii) an obligation arising under a maintenance assessment made under the Child Support Act 1991.

(3) In paragraph (2)(c), "fine" and "family proceedings" have the meanings given by section 281(8) (which applies the Magistrates Courts Act 1980 and the Matrimonial and Family Proceedings Act 1984).

(4) The following claims are not provable until after all other claims of creditors have been paid in full with interest under sections 189(2) (winding up), section 328(4) (bankruptcy) and rule 14.23 (payment of interest)—

(a) a claim arising by virtue of section 382(1)(a) of the Financial Services and Markets Act 2000 (restitution orders), unless it is also a claim arising by virtue of sub-paragraph (b) of that section (a person who has suffered loss etc); or
(b) in administration and winding up, a claim which by virtue of the Act or any other enactment is a claim the payment of which in a bankruptcy, an administration or a winding up is to be postponed.

(5) Nothing in this rule prejudices any enactment or rule of law under which a particular kind of debt is not provable, whether on grounds of public policy or otherwise.

NOTES

Commencement: 6 April 2017.

This rule derived from the Insolvency Rules 1986, SI 1986/1925, r 12.3.

[6.727]

14.3 Proving a debt

(1) A creditor wishing to recover a debt must submit a proof to the office-holder unless—
(a) this rule or an order of the court provides otherwise; or
(b) it is a members' voluntary winding up in which case the creditor is not required to submit a proof unless the liquidator requires one to be submitted.

(2) A creditor is deemed to have proved—
(a) in a winding up immediately preceded by an administration, where the creditor has already proved in the administration; or
(b) in an administration immediately preceded by a winding up, where the creditor has already proved in the winding up.

(3) A creditor is deemed to have proved for the purposes of determination and payment of a dividend but not otherwise where—
(a) the debt is a small debt;
(b) a notice has been delivered to the creditor of intention to declare a dividend or make a distribution under rule 14.29 which complies with rule 14.31 (further contents of notice to creditors owed small debts); and
(c) the creditor has not advised the office-holder that the debt is incorrect or not owed in response to the notice.

NOTES

Commencement: 6 April 2017.

This rule derived from the Insolvency Rules 1986, SI 1986/1925, rr 2.72, 4.73, 6.96.

[6.728]

14.4 Requirements for proof

(1) A proof must—
(a) be made out by, or under the direction of, the creditor and authenticated by the creditor or a person authorised on the creditor's behalf;
(b) state the creditor's name and address;
(c) if the creditor is a company, identify the company;
(d) state the total amount of the creditor's claim (including any value added tax) as at the relevant date, less any payments made after that date in relation to the claim, any deduction under rule 14.20 and any adjustment by way of set-off in accordance with rules 14.24 and 14.25;
(e) state whether or not the claim includes any outstanding uncapitalised interest;
(f) contain particulars of how and when the debt was incurred by the company or the bankrupt;
(g) contain particulars of any security held, the date on which it was given and the value which the creditor puts on it;
(h) provide details of any reservation of title in relation to goods to which the debt relates;
(i) provide details of any document by reference to which the debt can be substantiated;
(j) be dated and authenticated; and
(k) state the name, postal address and authority of the person authenticating the proof (if someone other than the creditor).

(2) Where sub-paragraph (i) applies the document need not be delivered with the proof unless the office-holder has requested it.

(3) The office-holder may call for the creditor to produce any document or other evidence which the office-holder considers is necessary to substantiate the whole or any part of a claim.

NOTES

Commencement: 6 April 2017.

This rule derived from the Insolvency Rules 1986, SI 1986/1925, rr 2.72(3), 4.73, 4.75, 6.98.

[6.729]

14.5 Costs of proving

Unless the court orders otherwise—
(a) each creditor bears the cost of proving for that creditor's own debt, including costs incurred in providing documents or evidence under rule 14.4 (3);

(b) in an administration or winding up, costs incurred by the office-holder in estimating the value of a debt under rule 14.14 are payable out of the assets as an expense of the administration or winding up; and
(c) in a bankruptcy, costs incurred by the office-holder in estimating the value of a debt under section 322(3) fall on the bankrupt's estate as an expense of the bankruptcy.

NOTES
Commencement: 6 April 2017.
This rule derived from the Insolvency Rules 1986, SI 1986/1925, rr 2.74, 4.78, 6.100.

[6.730]
14.6 Allowing inspection of proofs

The office-holder must, so long as proofs delivered to the office-holder are in the possession of the office-holder, allow them to be inspected, at all reasonable times on any business day, by the following—
(a) a creditor who has delivered a proof (unless the proof has been wholly rejected for purposes of dividend or otherwise, or withdrawn);
(b) a member or contributory of the company or, in the case of a bankruptcy, the bankrupt; and
(c) a person acting on behalf of any of the above.

NOTES
Commencement: 6 April 2017.
This rule derived from the Insolvency Rules 1986, SI 1986/1925, rr 2.75. 4.79, 6.101.

[6.731]
14.7 Admission and rejection of proofs for dividend

(1) The office-holder may admit or reject a proof for dividend (in whole or in part).

(2) If the office-holder rejects a proof in whole or in part, the office-holder must deliver to the creditor a statement of the office-holder's reasons for doing so, as soon as reasonably practicable.

NOTES
Commencement: 6 April 2017.
This rule derived from the Insolvency Rules 1986, SI 1986/1925, rr 2.77, 4.82, 6.105.

[6.732]
14.8 Appeal against decision on proof

(1) If a creditor is dissatisfied with the office-holder's decision under rule 14.7 in relation to the creditor's own proof (including a decision whether the debt is preferential), the creditor may apply to the court for the decision to be reversed or varied.

(2) The application must be made within 21 days of the creditor receiving the statement delivered under rule 14.7(2).

(3) A member, a contributory, any other creditor or, in a bankruptcy, the bankrupt, if dissatisfied with the office-holder's decision admitting, or rejecting the whole or any part of, a proof or agreeing to revalue a creditor's security under rule 14.15, may make such an application within 21 days of becoming aware of the office-holder's decision.

(4) The court must fix a venue for the application to be heard.

(5) The applicant must deliver notice of the venue to the creditor who delivered the proof in question (unless it is the applicant's own proof) and the office-holder.

(6) The office-holder must, on receipt of the notice, file the relevant proof with the court, together (if appropriate) with a copy of the statement sent under rule 14.7(2).

(7) After the application has been heard and determined, a proof which was submitted by the creditor in hard copy form must be returned by the court to the office-holder.

NOTES
Commencement: 6 April 2017.
This rule derived from the Insolvency Rules 1986, SI 1986/1925, rr 2.78, 4.83, 6.105.

[6.733]
14.9 Office-holder not liable for costs under rule 14.8

(1) The official receiver is not personally liable for costs incurred by any person in respect of an application under rule 14.8.

(2) An office-holder other than the official receiver is not personally liable for costs incurred by any person in respect of an application under rule 14.8 unless the court orders otherwise.

NOTES
Commencement: 6 April 2017.
This rule derived from the Insolvency Rules 1986, SI 1986/1925, rr 2.78(6), 4.83(6), 6.105(6).

[6.734]
14.10 Withdrawal or variation of proof

(1) A creditor may withdraw a proof at any time by delivering a written notice to the office-holder.

(2) The amount claimed by a creditor's proof may be varied at any time by agreement between the creditor and the office-holder.

NOTES

Commencement: 6 April 2017.

This rule derived from the Insolvency Rules 1986, SI 1986/1925, rr 2.79, 4.84, 6.106.

[6.735]

14.11 Exclusion of proof by the court

(1) The court may exclude a proof or reduce the amount claimed—

(a) on the office-holder's application, where the office-holder thinks that the proof has been improperly admitted, or ought to be reduced; or

(b) on the application of a creditor, a member, a contributory or a bankrupt, if the office-holder declines to interfere in the matter.

(2) Where application is made under paragraph (1), the court must fix a venue for the application to be heard.

(3) The applicant must deliver notice of the venue—

(a) in the case of an application by the office-holder, to the creditor who submitted the proof; and

(b) in the case of an application by a creditor, a member, a contributory or a bankrupt, to the office-holder and to the creditor who made the proof (if not the applicant).

NOTES

Commencement: 6 April 2017.

This rule derived from the Insolvency Rules 1986, SI 1986/1925, rr 2.80, 4.85, 6.107.

[6.736]

14.12 Administration and winding up by the court: debts of insolvent company to rank equally

[Note: for the equivalent rule for voluntary liquidation see section 107 of the Act and for bankruptcy section 328 of the Act.]

(1) This rule applies in an administration and a winding up by the court.

(2) Debts other than preferential debts rank equally between themselves and, after the preferential debts, must be paid in full unless the assets are insufficient for meeting them, in which case they abate in equal proportions between themselves.

NOTES

Commencement: 6 April 2017.

This rule derived from the Insolvency Rules 1986, SI 1986/1925, rr 2.69, 4.181 .

[6.737]

14.13 Administration and winding up: division of unsold assets

[Note: in respect of bankruptcy see section 326 (distribution of property in specie).]

(1) This rule applies in an administration or in a winding up of a company (other than a members' voluntary winding up) to any property which from its peculiar nature or other special circumstances cannot be readily or advantageously sold.

(2) The office-holder may with the required permission divide the property in its existing form among the company's creditors according to its estimated value.

(3) The required permission is—

(a) the permission of the creditors' committee in an administration or, if there is no creditors' committee, the creditors; and

(b) the permission of the liquidation committee in a winding up, or, if there is no liquidation committee, the creditors (without prejudice to provisions of the Act about disclaimer).

NOTES

Commencement: 6 April 2017.

This rule derived from the Insolvency Rules 1986, SI 1986/1925, rr 2.71, 4.183.

[6.738]

14.14 Administration and winding up: estimate of value of debt

(1) In an administration or in a winding up, the office-holder must estimate the value of a debt that does not have a certain value because it is subject to a contingency or for any other reason.

(2) The office-holder may revise such an estimate by reference to a change of circumstances or to information becoming available to the office-holder.

(3) The office-holder must inform the creditor of the office-holder's estimate and any revision.

(4) Where the value of a debt is estimated under this rule or by the court under section 168(3) or (5), the amount provable in the case of that debt is that of the estimate for the time being.

NOTES

Commencement: 6 April 2017.

This rule derived from the Insolvency Rules 1986, SI 1986/1925, rr 2.81, 4.86.

[6.739]
14.15 Secured creditor: value of security

(1) A secured creditor may, with the agreement of the office-holder or the permission of the court, at any time alter the value which that creditor has put upon a security in a proof.

(2) Paragraph (3) applies where a secured creditor—

(a) being the applicant for the administration order or the appointer of the administrator, has in the application or the notice of appointment put a value on the security;

(b) being the petitioner in winding-up or bankruptcy proceedings, has put a value on the security in the petition; or

(c) has voted in respect of the unsecured balance of the debt.

(3) Where this paragraph applies—

(a) the secured creditor may re-value the security only with the agreement of the office-holder or the permission of the court; and

(b) where the revaluation was by agreement, the office-holder must deliver a notice of the revaluation to the creditors within five business days after the office-holder's agreement.

NOTES

Commencement: 6 April 2017.

This rule derived from the Insolvency Rules 1986, SI 1986/1925, rr 2.90, 4.95, 6.115.

[6.740]
14.16 Secured creditor: surrender for non-disclosure

(1) If a secured creditor fails to disclose a security in a proof, the secured creditor must surrender that security for the general benefit of creditors, unless the court, on application by the secured creditor, relieves the secured creditor from the effect of this rule on the grounds that the omission was inadvertent or the result of honest mistake.

(2) If the court grants that relief, it may require or allow the creditor's proof to be amended, on such terms as may be just.

(3) Nothing in this rule or in rules 14.17 or 14.18 affects the rights in rem of creditors or third parties protected under [Article 8 of the EU Regulation].

NOTES

Commencement: 6 April 2017.

This rule derived from the Insolvency Rules 1986, SI 1986/1925, rr 2.91, 4.96, 6.116.

Para (3): words in square brackets substituted by the Insolvency (England and Wales) and Insolvency (Scotland) (Miscellaneous and Consequential Amendments) Rules 2017, SI 2017/1115, rr 22, 25(2).

[6.741]
14.17 Secured creditor: redemption by office-holder

(1) The office-holder may at any time deliver a notice to a creditor whose debt is secured that the office-holder proposes, at the expiration of 28 days from the date of the notice, to redeem the security at the value put upon it in the creditor's proof.

(2) The creditor then has 21 days (or such longer period as the office-holder may allow) in which to alter the value of the security in accordance with rule 14.15.

(3) If the creditor alters the value of the security with the permission of the office-holder or the court then the office-holder may only redeem at the new value.

(4) If the office-holder redeems the security the cost of transferring it is payable as an expense out of the insolvent estate.

(5) A creditor whose debt is secured may at any time deliver a notice to the office-holder requiring the office-holder to elect whether or not to redeem the security at the value then placed on it.

(6) The office-holder then has three months in which to redeem the security or elect not to redeem the security.

NOTES

Commencement: 6 April 2017.

This rule derived from the Insolvency Rules 1986, SI 1986/1925, rr 2.92, 4.97, 6.117.

[6.742]
14.18 Secured creditor: test of security's value

(1) If the office-holder is dissatisfied with the value which a secured creditor puts on a security in the creditor's proof the office-holder may require any property comprised in the security to be offered for sale.

(2) The terms of sale will be as agreed between the office-holder and the secured creditor, or as the court may direct.

(3) If the sale is by auction, the office-holder on behalf of the company or the insolvent estate and the creditor may bid.

(4) This rule does not apply if the value of the security has been altered with the court's permission.

NOTES

Commencement: 6 April 2017.

This rule derived from the Insolvency Rules 1986, SI 1986/1925, rr 2.93, 4.98, 6.118.

[6.743]
14.19 Realisation or surrender of security by creditor

(1) If a creditor who has valued a security subsequently realises the security (whether or not at the instance of the office-holder)—

(a) the net amount realised must be treated in all respects (including in relation to any valuation in a proof) as an amended valuation made by the creditor; and
(b) the creditor may prove for the balance of the creditor's debt.

(2) A creditor who voluntarily surrenders a security may prove for the whole of the creditor's debt as if it were unsecured.

NOTES

Commencement: 6 April 2017.
This rule derived from the Insolvency Rules 1986, SI 1986/1925, rr 2.83, 2.94, 4.88, 4.99, 6.119.

[6.744]
14.20 Discounts

All trade and other discounts (except a discount for immediate or early settlement) which would have been available to the company or the debtor but for the insolvency proceedings must be deducted from the claim.

NOTES

Commencement: 6 April 2017.
This rule derived from the Insolvency Rules 1986, SI 1986/1925, rr 2.84, 4.89, 6.110.

[6.745]
14.21 Debts in foreign currency

(1) A proof for a debt incurred or payable in a foreign currency must state the amount of the debt in that currency.

(2) The office-holder must convert all such debts into sterling at a single rate for each currency determined by the office-holder by reference to the exchange rates prevailing on the relevant date.

(3) On the next occasion when the office-holder communicates with the creditors the office-holder must advise them of any rate so determined.

(4) A creditor who considers that the rate determined by the office-holder is unreasonable may apply to the court.

(5) If on hearing the application the court finds that the rate is unreasonable it may itself determine the rate.

(6) This rule does not apply to the conversion of foreign currency debts in an application for a debt relief order.

NOTES

Commencement: 6 April 2017.
This rule derived from the Insolvency Rules 1986, SI 1986/1925, rr 2.86, 4.91, 6.111.

[6.746]
14.22 Payments of a periodical nature

(1) In the case of rent and other payments of a periodical nature, the creditor may prove for any amounts due and unpaid up to the relevant date.

(2) Where at that date any payment was accruing due, the creditor may prove for so much as would have been due at that date, if accruing from day to day.

NOTES

Commencement: 6 April 2017.
This rule derived from the Insolvency Rules 1986, SI 1986/1925, rr 2.87, 4.92, 6.112.

[6.747]
14.23 Interest

[Note: provision for the payment of interest out of a surplus remaining after payment of the debts is made by section 189(2) in respect of winding up and section 328(4) in respect of bankruptcy.]

(1) Where a debt proved in insolvency proceedings bears interest, that interest is provable as part of the debt except in so far as it is payable in respect of any period after the relevant date.

(2) In the circumstances set out below the creditor's claim may include interest on the debt for periods before the relevant date although not previously reserved or agreed.

(3) If the debt is due by virtue of a written instrument and payable at a certain time, interest may be claimed for the period from that time to the relevant date.

(4) If the debt is due otherwise, interest may only be claimed if demand for payment of the debt was made in writing by or on behalf of the creditor, and notice was delivered that interest would be payable from the date of the demand to the date of the payment, before—

(a) the relevant date, in respect of administration or winding up; or
(b) the presentation of the bankruptcy petition or the bankruptcy application.

(5) Interest under paragraph (4) may only be claimed for the period from the date of the demand to the relevant date and, for the purposes of the Act and these Rules, must be charged at a rate not exceeding that mentioned in paragraph (6).

(6) The rate of interest to be claimed under paragraphs (3) and (4) is the rate specified in section 17 of the Judgments Act 1838 on the relevant date.

(7) In an administration—
(a) any surplus remaining after payment of the debts proved must, before being applied for any other purpose, be applied in paying interest on those debts in respect of the periods during which they have been outstanding since the relevant date;
(b) all interest payable under sub-paragraph (a) ranks equally whether or not the debts on which it is payable rank equally; and
(c) the rate of interest payable under sub-paragraph (a) is whichever is the greater of the rate specified under paragraph (6) and the rate applicable to the debt apart from the administration.

NOTES

Commencement: 6 April 2017.
This rule derived from the Insolvency Rules 1986, SI 1986/1925, rr 2.88, 4.93, 6.113.

[6.748]
14.24 Administration: mutual dealings and set-off

(1) This rule applies in an administration where the administrator intends to make a distribution and has delivered a notice under rule 14.29.

(2) An account must be taken as at the date of the notice of what is due from the company and a creditor to each other in respect of their mutual dealings and the sums due from the one must be set off against the sums due from the other.

(3) If there is a balance owed to the creditor then only that balance is provable in the administration.

(4) If there is a balance owed to the company that must be paid to the administrator as part of the assets.

(5) However if all or part of the balance owed to the company results from a contingent or prospective debt owed by the creditor then the balance (or that part of it which results from the contingent or prospective debt) must be paid in full (without being discounted under rule 14.44) if and when that debt becomes due and payable.

(6) In this rule—
"obligation" means an obligation however arising, whether by virtue of an agreement, rule of law or otherwise; and
"mutual dealings" means mutual credits, mutual debts or other mutual dealings between the company and a creditor proving or claiming to prove for a debt in the administration but does not include any of the following—
(a) a debt arising out of an obligation incurred after the company entered administration;
(b) a debt arising out of an obligation incurred at a time when the creditor had notice that—
(i) an application for an administration order was pending, or
(ii) any person had delivered notice of intention to appoint an administrator;
(c) a debt arising out of an obligation where—
(i) the administration was immediately preceded by a winding up, and
(ii) at the time when the obligation was incurred the creditor had notice that a decision had been sought from creditors under section 100 on the nomination of a liquidator or that a winding-up petition was pending;
(d) a debt arising out of an obligation incurred during a winding up which immediately preceded the administration; or
(e) a debt which has been acquired by a creditor by assignment or otherwise, under an agreement between the creditor and another party where that agreement was entered into—
(i) after the company entered administration,
(ii) at a time when the creditor had notice that an application for an administration order was pending,
(iii) at a time when the creditor had notice that any person had given notice of intention to appoint an administrator,
(iv) where the administration was immediately preceded by a winding up, at a time when the creditor had notice that a decision had been sought from creditors under section 100 on the nomination of a liquidator or that a winding-up petition was pending, or
(v) during a winding up which immediately preceded the administration.

(7) A sum must be treated as being due to or from the company for the purposes of paragraph (2) whether—
(a) it is payable at present or in the future;
(b) the obligation by virtue of which it is payable is certain or contingent; or
(c) its amount is fixed or liquidated, or is capable of being ascertained by fixed rules or as a matter of opinion.

(8) For the purposes of this rule—

(a) rule 14.14 applies to an obligation which, by reason of its being subject to a contingency or for any other reason, does not bear a certain value;

(b) rules 14.21 to 14.23 apply to sums due to the company which—

(i) are payable in a currency other than sterling,

(ii) are of a periodical nature, or

(iii) bear interest; and

(c) rule 14.44 applies to a sum due to or from the company which is payable in the future.

NOTES

Commencement: 6 April 2017.

This rule derived from the Insolvency Rules 1986, SI 1986/1925, r 2.85.

[6.749]

14.25 Winding up: mutual dealings and set-off

(1) This rule applies in a winding up where, before the company goes into liquidation, there have been mutual dealings between the company and a creditor of the company proving or claiming to prove for a debt in the liquidation.

(2) An account must be taken of what is due from the company and the creditor to each other in respect of their mutual dealings and the sums due from the one must be set off against the sums due from the other.

(3) If there is a balance owed to the creditor then only that balance is provable in the winding up.

(4) If there is a balance owed to the company then that must be paid to the liquidator as part of the assets.

(5) However if all or part of the balance owed to the company results from a contingent or prospective debt owed by the creditor then the balance (or that part of it which results from the contingent or prospective debt) must be paid in full (without being discounted under rule 14.44) if and when that debt becomes due and payable.

(6) In this rule—

"obligation" means an obligation however arising, whether by virtue of an agreement, rule of law or otherwise; and

"mutual dealings" means mutual credits, mutual debts or other mutual dealings between the company and a creditor proving or claiming to prove for a debt in the winding up but does not include any of the following—

(a) a debt arising out of an obligation incurred at a time when the creditor had notice that—

(i) a decision had been sought from creditors on the nomination of a liquidator under section 100, or

(ii) a petition for the winding up of the company was pending;

(b) a debt arising out of an obligation where—

(i) the liquidation was immediately preceded by an administration, and

(ii) at the time the obligation was incurred the creditor had notice that an application for an administration order was pending or a person had delivered notice of intention to appoint an administrator; and

(c) a debt arising out of an obligation incurred during an administration which immediately preceded the liquidation;

(d) a debt which has been acquired by a creditor by assignment or otherwise, under an agreement between the creditor and another party where that agreement was entered into—

(i) after the company went into liquidation,

(ii) at a time when the creditor had notice that a decision had been sought from creditors under section 100 on the nomination of a liquidator,

(iii) at a time when the creditor had notice that a winding-up petition was pending,

(iv) where the winding up was immediately preceded by an administration at a time when the creditor had notice that an application for an administration order was pending or a person had delivered notice of intention to appoint an administrator, or

(v) during an administration which immediately preceded the winding up.

(7) A sum must be treated as being due to or from the company for the purposes of paragraph (2) whether—

(a) it is payable at present or in the future;

(b) the obligation by virtue of which it is payable is certain or contingent; or

(c) its amount is fixed or liquidated, or is capable of being ascertained by fixed rules or as a matter of opinion.

(8) For the purposes of this rule—

(a) rule 14.14 applies to an obligation which, by reason of its being subject to a contingency or for any other reason, does not bear a certain value;

(b) rules 14.21 to 14.23 apply to sums due to the company which—

(i) are payable in a currency other than sterling,

(ii) are of a periodical nature, or

(iii) bear interest; and

(c) rule 14.44 applies to a sum due to or from the company which is payable in the future.

NOTES

Commencement: 6 April 2017.
This rule derived from the Insolvency Rules 1986, SI 1986/1925, r 4.90.

CHAPTER 3 DISTRIBUTION TO CREDITORS IN ADMINISTRATION, WINDING UP AND BANKRUPTCY

[Note: a document required by the Act or these Rules must also contain the standard contents set out in Part 1.]

[6.750]

14.26 Application of Chapter to a particular class of creditors and to distributions

(1) This Chapter applies where the office-holder makes, or proposes to make, a distribution to any class of creditors other than secured creditors.

(2) Where the distribution is to a particular class of creditors in an administration, a reference in this Chapter to creditors is a reference to that class of creditors only.

NOTES

Commencement: 6 April 2017.
This rule derived from the Insolvency Rules 1986, SI 1986/1925, r 2.95(5).

[6.751]

14.27 Declaration and distribution of dividends in a winding up

[Note: section 324 makes provision in respect of such a declaration and distribution in a bankruptcy.]

Whenever a liquidator in a creditors' voluntary winding up or a winding up by the court has sufficient funds in hand for the purpose the liquidator must, while retaining such sums as may be necessary for the expenses of the winding up, declare and distribute dividends among the creditors in respect of the debts which they have proved.

NOTES

Commencement: 6 April 2017.
This rule derived from the Insolvency Rules 1986, SI 1986/1925, r 4.180.

[6.752]

14.28 Gazette notice of intended first dividend or distribution

(1) Subject to paragraphs (2) and (4) where the office-holder intends to declare a first dividend or distribution the office-holder must gazette a notice containing—

- (a) a statement that the office-holder intends to declare a first dividend or distribution;
- (b) the date by which and place to which proofs must be delivered; and
- (c) in the case of a members' voluntary winding up, where the dividend or distribution is to be a sole or final distribution, a statement that the distribution may be made without regard to the claim of any person in respect of a debt not proved.

(2) Where the intended dividend is only to preferential creditors the office-holder need only gazette a notice if the office-holder thinks fit.

(3) The office-holder may in addition advertise such a notice in such other manner (if any) as the office-holder thinks fit.

(4) Paragraph (1) does not apply where the office-holder has previously, by a notice which has been gazetted, invited creditors to prove their debts.

NOTES

Commencement: 6 April 2017.
This rule derived from the Insolvency Rules 1986, SI 1986/1925, rr 11.2, 2.95, 4.182A.

[6.753]

14.29 Individual notices to creditors etc of intended dividend or distribution

(1) The office-holder must deliver a notice of the intention to make a distribution to creditors or declare a dividend—

- (a) to the creditors in an administration; and
- (b) to all creditors in a winding up or a bankruptcy who have not proved (including any creditors who are owed small debts and are not deemed under rule 14.3(3) to have proved as a result of a previous notice under rule 14.29).

(2) Where the intended dividend is only for preferential creditors, the office-holder is only required to deliver such a notice to the preferential creditors.

(3) Where the office-holder intends to declare a dividend to unsecured creditors in an administration or winding-up the notice must also state the value of the prescribed part unless there is no prescribed part or the court has made an order under section 176A(5).

NOTES

Commencement: 6 April 2017.

This rule derived from the Insolvency Rules 1986, SI 1986/1925, rr 2.95, 11.2.

[6.754]
14.30 Contents of notice of intention to declare a dividend or make a distribution

A notice under rule 14.29 must contain the following—

(a) a statement that the office-holder intends to make a distribution to creditors or declare a dividend (as the case may be) within the period of two months from the last date for proving;
(b) a statement whether the proposed distribution or dividend is interim or final;
(c) the last date by which proofs may be delivered which must be—
  (i) the same date for all creditors who prove, and
  (ii) not less than 21 days from the date of notice;
(d) a statement of the place to which proofs must be delivered;
(e) the additional information required by rule 14.31 where the office-holder intends to treat a small debt as proved for the purposes of paying a dividend; and
(f) in the case of a members' voluntary winding up, where the distribution is to be a sole or final distribution, a statement that the distribution may be made without regard to the claim of any person in respect of a debt not proved.

NOTES

Commencement: 6 April 2017.
This rule derived from the Insolvency Rules 1986, SI 1986/1925, rr 2.95(4), 11.2.

[6.755]
14.31 Further contents of notice to creditors owed small debts etc

(1) The office-holder may treat a debt, which is a small debt according to the accounting records or the statement of affairs of the company or bankrupt, as if it were proved for the purpose of paying a dividend.

(2) Where the office-holder intends to treat such a debt as if it were proved the notice delivered under rule 14.29 must—

(a) state the amount of the debt which the office-holder believes to be owed to the creditor according to the accounting records or statement of affairs of the company or the bankrupt (as the case may be);
(b) state that the office-holder will treat the debt which is stated in notice, being for £1,000 or less, as proved for the purposes of paying a dividend unless the creditor advises the office-holder that the amount of the debt is incorrect or that no debt is owed;
(c) require the creditor to notify the office-holder by the last date for proving if the amount of the debt is incorrect or if no debt is owed; and
(d) inform the creditor that where the creditor advises the office-holder that the amount of the debt is incorrect the creditor must also submit a proof in order to receive a dividend.

(3) The information required by paragraph (2)(a) may take the form of a list of small debts which the office-holder intends to treat as proved which includes that owed to the particular creditor to whom the notice is being delivered.

NOTES

Commencement: 6 April 2017.

[6.756]
14.32 Admission or rejection of proofs following last date for proving

(1) Unless the office-holder has already dealt with them, the office-holder must within 14 days of the last date for proving set out in the notice under rule 14.29—

(a) admit or reject (in whole or in part) proofs delivered to the office-holder; or
(b) make such provision in relation to them as the office-holder thinks fit.

(2) The office-holder is not obliged to deal with a proof delivered after the last date for proving, but the office-holder may do so if the office-holder thinks fit.

(3) In the declaration of a dividend a payment must not be made more than once in respect of the same debt.

(4) Subject to rule 14.43 (assignment of right to dividend), payment must only be made to the creditor in a case where both the creditor and a member State liquidator have proved in relation to the same debt.

NOTES

Commencement: 6 April 2017.
This rule derived from the Insolvency Rules 1986, SI 1986/1925, rr 2.96, 11.3.

[6.757]
14.33 Postponement or cancellation of dividend

(1) The office-holder may postpone or cancel the dividend in the period of two months from the last date for proving if an application is made to the court for the office-holder's decision on a proof to be reversed or varied, or for a proof to be excluded, or for a reduction of the amount claimed.

(2) The office-holder may postpone a dividend if the office-holder considers that due to the nature of the affairs of the person to whom the proceedings relate there is real complexity in admitting or rejecting proofs of claims submitted.

(3) Where the dividend is postponed or cancelled a new notice under rule 14.29 will be required if the dividend is paid subsequently.

NOTES

Commencement: 6 April 2017.
This rule derived from the Insolvency Rules 1986, SI 1986/1925, rr 2.96A, 11.4.

[6.758]
14.34 Declaration of dividend

(1) The office-holder must declare the dividend in the two month period referred to in rule 14.30(a) in accordance with the notice of intention to declare a dividend unless the office-holder has had cause to postpone or cancel the dividend.

(2) The office-holder must not declare a dividend so long as there is pending an application to the court to reverse or vary a decision of the office-holder on a proof, or to exclude a proof or to reduce the amount claimed unless the court gives permission.

(3) If the court gives such permission, the office-holder must make such provision in relation to the proof as the court directs.

NOTES

Commencement: 6 April 2017.
This rule derived from the Insolvency Rules 1986, SI 1986/1925, rr 2.97, 115.

[6.759]
14.35 Notice of declaration of a dividend

(1) Where the office-holder declares a dividend the office-holder must deliver notice of that fact to all creditors who have proved for their debts (subject to paragraph (5)).

(2) The notice declaring a dividend may be delivered at the same time as the dividend is distributed.

(3) The notice must include the following in relation to the insolvency proceedings—

- (a) the amounts raised from the sale of assets, indicating (so far as practicable) amounts raised by the sale of particular assets;
- (b) the payments made by the office-holder in carrying out the office-holder's functions;
- (c) the provision (if any) made for unsettled claims, and funds (if any) retained for particular purposes;
- (d) the total amount to be distributed and the rate of dividend; and
- (e) whether, and if so when, any further dividend is expected to be declared.

(4) In an administration, a creditors' voluntary winding-up or a winding up by the court, where the administrator or liquidator intends to make a distribution to unsecured creditors, the notice must also state the value of the prescribed part unless there is no prescribed part or the court has made an order under section 176A(5).

(5) Where the office-holder declares a dividend for preferential creditors only, the notice under paragraph (1) need only be delivered to those preferential creditors who have proved for their debts.

NOTES

Commencement: 6 April 2017.
This rule derived from the Insolvency Rules 1986, SI 1986/1925, rr 2.98, 2.99, 11.6.

[6.760]
14.36 Last notice about dividend in a winding up

[Note: section 330 contains the requirement to deliver such a notice in a bankruptcy.]

(1) When the liquidator in a winding up has realised all the company's assets or so much of them as can, in the liquidator's opinion, be realised without needlessly prolonging the winding up, the liquidator must deliver a notice as provided for in this Chapter, either—

- (a) of intention to declare a final dividend; or
- (b) that no dividend, or further dividend, will be declared.

(2) The notice must contain the particulars required by rule 14.30, 14.31, 14.37 or 14.38 as the case may be and must require claims against the assets to be established by a date set out in the notice.

NOTES

Commencement: 6 April 2017.
This rule derived from the Insolvency Rules 1986, SI 1986/1925, r 4.186.

[6.761]
14.37 Contents of last notice about dividend (administration, winding up and bankruptcy)

(1) This rule applies in an administration, winding up or bankruptcy.

(2) If the office-holder delivers notice to creditors that the office-holder is unable to declare any dividend or (as the case may be) any further dividend, the notice must contain a statement to the effect either—

- (a) that no funds have been realised; or
- (b) that the funds realised have already been distributed or used or allocated for paying the expenses of the insolvency proceedings.

(3) The information required by paragraph (2) may be included in a progress report.

NOTES

Commencement: 6 April 2017.

This rule derived from the Insolvency Rules 1986, SI 1986/1925, rr 2.100, 11.7.

[6.762]

14.38 Sole or final dividend

[Note: see section 330 in respect of a dividend in a bankruptcy.]

(1) Where, in an administration or winding up, it is intended that the distribution is to be a sole or final dividend, after the date specified as the last date for proving in the notice under rule 14.29, the office-holder—

- (a) in a winding up, must pay any outstanding expenses of the winding up out of the assets;
- (b) in an administration, must—
  - (i) pay any outstanding expenses of a winding up (including any of the items mentioned in rule 6.42 or 7.108 (as appropriate)) or provisional winding up that immediately preceded the administration,
  - (ii) pay any items payable in accordance with the provisions of paragraph 99 of Schedule B1,
  - (iii) pay any amount outstanding (including debts or liabilities and the administrator's own remuneration and expenses) which would, if the administrator were to cease to be the administrator of the company, be payable out of the property of which he had custody or control in accordance with the provisions of paragraph 99, and
  - (iv) declare and distribute that dividend without regard to the claim of any person in respect of a debt not already proved; or
- (c) in a members' voluntary winding up may, and in every other case must, declare and distribute that dividend without regard to the claim of any person in respect of a debt not already proved.

(2) The reference in paragraph (1)(b)(iv) and (c) to debts that have not been proved does not include small debts treated as proved by the office-holder.

(3) The court may, on the application of any person, postpone the date specified in the notice.

NOTES

Commencement: 6 April 2017.

This rule derived from the Insolvency Rules 1986, SI 1986/1925, rr 2.68, 4.186.

[6.763]

14.39 Administration and winding up: provisions as to dividends

[Note: see section 324(4) in respect of such provisions in bankruptcy.]

In an administration or winding up, in the calculation and distribution of a dividend the office-holder must make provision for—

- (a) any debts which are the subject of claims which have not yet been determined; and
- (b) disputed proofs and claims.

NOTES

Commencement: 6 April 2017.

This rule derived from the Insolvency Rules 1986, SI 1986/1925, r 4.182(1).

[6.764]

14.40 Supplementary provisions as to dividends and distributions

(1) A creditor is not entitled to disturb the payment of any dividend or making of any distribution because—

- (a) the amount claimed in the creditor's proof is increased after payment of the dividend;
- (b) in an administration, a creditors' voluntary winding up or a winding up by the court the creditor did not prove for a debt before the declaration of the dividend; or
- (c) in a members' voluntary winding up, the creditor did not prove for a debt before the last date for proving or increases the claim in proof after that date.

(2) However the creditor is entitled to be paid a dividend or receive a distribution which the creditor has failed to receive out of any money for the time being available for the payment of a further dividend or making a further distribution.

(3) Such a dividend must be paid or distribution made before that money is applied to the payment of any further dividend or making of any further distribution.

(4) If, after a creditor's proof has been admitted, the proof is withdrawn or excluded, or the amount of it is reduced, the creditor is liable to repay to the office-holder, for the credit of the insolvency proceedings, any amount overpaid by way of dividend.

NOTES

Commencement: 6 April 2017.

This rule derived from the Insolvency Rules 1986, SI 1986/1925, rr 2.101, 4.182(2), 11.8.

[6.765]

14.41 Secured creditors

(1) The following applies where a creditor alters the value of a security after a dividend has been declared.

(2) If the alteration reduces the creditor's unsecured claim ranking for dividend, the creditor must as soon as reasonably practicable repay to the office-holder, for the credit of the administration or of the insolvent estate, any amount received by the creditor as dividend in excess of that to which the creditor would be entitled, having regard to the alteration of the value of the security.

(3) If the alteration increases the creditor's unsecured claim, the creditor is entitled to receive from the office-holder, out of any money for the time being available for the payment of a further dividend, before any such further dividend is paid, any dividend or dividends which the creditor has failed to receive, having regard to the alteration of the value of the security.

(4) The creditor is not entitled to disturb any dividend declared (whether or not distributed) before the date of the alteration.

NOTES

Commencement: 6 April 2017.

This rule derived from the Insolvency Rules 1986, SI 1986/1925, rr 2.102, 6.109, 11.9.

[6.766]

14.42 Disqualification from dividend

If a creditor contravenes any provision of the Act or these Rules relating to the valuation of securities, the court may, on the application of the office-holder, order that the creditor be wholly or partly disqualified from participation in any dividend.

NOTES

Commencement: 6 April 2017.

This rule derived from the Insolvency Rules 1986, SI 1986/1925, rr 2.103, 11.10.

[6.767]

14.43 Assignment of right to dividend

(1) If a person entitled to a dividend ("the entitled person") delivers notice to the office-holder that the entitled person wishes the dividend to be paid to another person, or that the entitled person has assigned the entitlement to another person, the office-holder must pay the dividend to that other person accordingly.

(2) A notice delivered under this rule must specify the name and address of the person to whom payment is to be made.

NOTES

Commencement: 6 April 2017.

[6.768]

14.44 Debt payable at future time

(1) Where a creditor has proved for a debt of which payment is not due at the date of the declaration of a dividend, the creditor is entitled to the dividend equally with other creditors, but subject as follows.

(2) For the purpose of dividend (and no other purpose) the amount of the creditor's admitted proof must be discounted by applying the following formula—

$$X / 1.05^n$$

where—

(a) "X" is the value of the admitted proof; and

(b) "n" is the period beginning with the relevant date and ending with the date on which the payment of the creditor's debt would otherwise be due, expressed in years (part of a year being expressed as a decimal fraction of a year).

NOTES

Commencement: 6 April 2017.

This rule derived from the Insolvency Rules 1986, SI 1986/1925, rr 2.89, 2.105, 4.94, 6.114, 11.13.

[6.769]

14.45 Administration and winding up: non-payment of dividend

[Note: see section 325(2) for equivalent provisions in respect of bankruptcy.]

(1) No action lies against the office-holder in an administration or winding up for payment of a dividend.

(2) However, if the office-holder refuses to pay a dividend the court may, if it thinks just, order the office-holder to pay it and also to pay, out of the office-holder's own money—

(a) interest on the dividend, at the rate for the time being specified in section 17 of the Judgments Act 1838, from the time when it was withheld; and

(b) the costs of the proceedings in which the order to pay is made.

NOTES

Commencement: 6 April 2017.

This rule derived from the Insolvency Rules 1986, SI 1986/1925, rr 2.70(3), 4.182(3).

PART 15
DECISION MAKING

CHAPTER 1 APPLICATION OF PART

[6.770]

15.1 Application of Part

In this Part—

(a) Chapters 2 to 11 apply where the Act or these Rules require a decision to be made by a qualifying decision procedure, or by a creditors' decision procedure or permit a decision to be made by the deemed consent procedure; and

(b) Chapter 12 applies to company meetings.

NOTES

Commencement: 6 April 2017.

CHAPTER 2 DECISION PROCEDURES

[Note: a document required by the Act or these Rules must also contain the standard contents set out in Part 1.]

[6.771]

15.2 Interpretation

(1) In these Rules—

"decision date" means—

(a) in the case of a decision to be made at a meeting, the date of the meeting;

(b) in the case of a decision to be made either by a decision procedure other than a meeting or by the deemed consent procedure, the date the decision is to be made or deemed to have been made;

and a decision falling within paragraph (b) is to be treated as made at 23:59 on the decision date;

"decision procedure" means a qualifying decision procedure or a creditors' decision procedure as prescribed by rule 15.3;

"electronic voting" includes any electronic system which enables a person to vote without the need to attend at a particular location to do so;

"physical meeting" means a meeting as described in section 246ZE(9) or 379ZA(9);

"virtual meeting" means a meeting where persons who are not invited to be physically present together may participate in the meeting including communicating directly with all the other participants in the meeting and voting (either directly or via a proxy-holder);

(2) The decision date is to be set at the discretion of the convener, but must be not less than 14 days from the date of delivery of the notice, except where the table in rule 15.11 requires a different period or the court directs otherwise.

(3) The rules in Chapters 2 to 11 about decision procedures of creditors apply with any necessary modifications to decision making by contributories.

(4) In particular, in place of the requirement for percentages or majorities in decision making by creditors to be determined by value, where the procedure seeks a decision from contributories value must be determined on the percentage of voting rights in accordance with rule 15.39.

NOTES

Commencement: 6 April 2017.

[6.772]

15.3 The prescribed decision procedures

[Note: under sections 246ZE and 379ZA a decision may not be made by a creditors' meeting (a physical meeting) unless the prescribed proportion of the creditors request in writing that the decision be made by such a meeting.]

The following decision procedures are prescribed as decision procedures under sections 246ZE and 379ZA by which a convener may seek a decision under the Act or these Rules from creditors—

(a) correspondence;

(b) electronic voting;

(c) virtual meeting;

(d) physical meeting; . . .

(e) any other decision making procedure which enables all creditors who are entitled to participate in the making of the decision to participate equally.

NOTES

Commencement: 6 April 2017.

Word omitted from para (d) revoked by the Insolvency (England and Wales) (Amendment) Rules 2017, SI 2017/366, rr 3, 35.

[6.773]
15.4 Electronic voting

Where the decision procedure uses electronic voting—

(a) the notice delivered to creditors must give them any necessary information as to how to access the voting system including any password required;

(b) except where electronic voting is being used at a meeting, the voting system must be a system capable of enabling a creditor to vote at any time between the notice being delivered and the decision date; and

(c) in the course of a vote the voting system must not provide any creditor with information concerning the vote cast by any other creditor.

NOTES

Commencement: 6 April 2017.

[6.774]
15.5 Virtual meetings

Where the decision procedure uses a virtual meeting the notice delivered to creditors must contain—

(a) any necessary information as to how to access the virtual meeting including any telephone number, access code or password required; and

(b) a statement that the meeting may be suspended or adjourned by the chair of the meeting (and must be adjourned if it is so resolved at the meeting).

NOTES

Commencement: 6 April 2017.

[6.775]
15.6 Physical meetings

(1) A request for a physical meeting may be made before or after the notice of the decision procedure or deemed consent procedure has been delivered, but must be made not later than five business days after the date on which the convener delivered the notice of the decision procedure or deemed consent procedure unless these Rules provide to the contrary.

(2) It is the convener's responsibility to check whether any requests for a physical meeting are submitted before the deadline and if so whether in aggregate they meet or surpass one of the thresholds requiring a physical meeting under sections 246ZE(7) or 379ZA(7).

(3) Where the prescribed proportion of creditors require a physical meeting the convener must summon the meeting by giving notice which complies with rule 15.8 so far as applicable and which must also contain a statement that the meeting may be suspended or adjourned by the chair of the meeting (and must be adjourned if it is so resolved at the meeting).

(4) In addition, the notice under paragraph (3) must inform the creditors that as a result of the requirement to hold a physical meeting the original decision procedure or the deemed consent procedure is superseded.

(5) The convener must send the notice under paragraph (3) not later than three business days after one of the thresholds requiring a physical meeting has been met or surpassed.

(6) The convener—

(a) may permit a creditor to attend a physical meeting remotely if the convener receives a request to do so in advance of the meeting; and

(b) must include in the notice of the meeting a statement explaining the convener's discretion to permit remote attendance.

(7) In this rule, attending a physical meeting "remotely" means attending and being able to participate in the meeting without being in the place where the meeting is being held.

[(8) For the purpose of determining whether the thresholds under section 246ZE(7) or 379ZA(7) are met, the convener must calculate the value of the creditor's debt by reference to rule 15.31.]

NOTES

Commencement: 6 April 2017.

Para (8): added by the Insolvency (England and Wales) (Amendment) Rules 2017, SI 2017/366, rr 3, 36.

[6.776]
15.7 Deemed consent (sections 246ZF and 379ZB)

[Note: the deemed consent procedure cannot be used to make a decision on remuneration of any person, or where the Act, these Rules or any other legislation requires a decision to be made by a decision procedure.]

(1) This rule makes further provision about the deemed consent procedure to that set out in sections 246ZF and 379ZB.

(2) A notice seeking deemed consent must, in addition to the requirements of section 246ZF or 379ZB (as applicable) comply with the requirements of rule 15.8 so far as applicable and must also contain—

(a) a statement that in order to object to the proposed decision a creditor must have delivered a notice, stating that the creditor so objects, to the convener not later than the decision date together with a proof in respect of the creditor's claim in accordance with these Rules failing which the objection will be disregarded;

(b) a statement that it is the convener's responsibility to aggregate any objections to see if the threshold is met for the decision to be taken as not having been made; and

(c) a statement that if the threshold is met the deemed consent procedure will terminate without a decision being made and if a decision is sought again on the same matter it will be sought by a decision procedure.

(3) In this rule, the threshold is met where the appropriate number of relevant creditors (as defined in sections 246ZF and 379ZB) have objected to the proposed decision.

(4) For the purpose of aggregating objections, the convener may presume the value of relevant creditors' claims to be the value of claims by those creditors who, in the convener's view, would have been entitled to vote had the decision been sought by a decision procedure in accordance with this Part, even where those creditors had not already met the criteria for such entitlement to vote.

(5) The provisions of rules 15.31(2) (calculation of voting rights), 15.32 (calculation of voting rights: special cases) and 15.33 (procedure for admitting creditors' claims for voting) apply to the admission or rejection of a claim for the purpose of the convener deciding whether or not an objection should count towards the total aggregated objections.

(6) A decision of the convener on the aggregation of objections under this rule is subject to appeal under rule 15.35 as if it were a decision under Chapter 8 of this Part.

NOTES

Commencement: 6 April 2017.

CHAPTER 3 NOTICES, VOTING AND VENUES FOR DECISIONS

[Note: a document required by the Act or these Rules must also contain the standard contents set out in Part 1.]

[6.777]

15.8 Notices to creditors of decision procedure

(1) This rule sets out the requirements for notices to creditors where a decision is sought by a decision procedure.

(2) The convener must deliver a notice to every creditor who is entitled to notice of the procedure.

(3) The notice must contain the following—

(a) identification details for the proceedings;

(b) details of the decision to be made or of any resolution on which a decision is sought;

(c) a description of the decision procedure which the convener is using, and arrangements, including the venue, for the decision procedure;

(d) a statement of the decision date;

(e) . . . a statement of by when the creditor must have delivered a proof in respect of the creditor's claim in accordance with these Rules failing which a vote by the creditor will be disregarded;

(f) a statement that a creditor whose debt is treated as a small debt in accordance with rule 14.31(1) must still deliver a proof if that creditor wishes to vote;

(g) a statement that a creditor who has opted out from receiving notices may nevertheless vote if the creditor provides a proof in accordance with paragraph (e);

(h) in the case of a decision to remove a liquidator in a creditors' voluntary winding-up or a winding up by the court, a statement drawing the attention of creditors to section 173(2)[, 174(2)] or 174(4) (which relate to the release of the liquidator), as appropriate;

(i) in the case of a decision to remove a trustee in a bankruptcy, a statement drawing the attention of creditors to section [299(1) or] 299(3) (which relates to the release of the trustee);

(j) in the case of a decision in relation to a proposed CVA or IVA, a statement of the effects of the relevant provisions of the following—

(i) rule 15.28 about creditors' voting rights,

(ii) rule 15.31 about the calculation of creditors' voting rights, and

(iii) rule 15.34 about the requisite majority of creditors for making decisions;

(k) except in the case of a physical meeting, a statement that creditors who meet the thresholds in sections 246ZE(7) or 379ZA(7) may, within five business days from the date of delivery of the notice, require a physical meeting to be held to consider the matter;

(l) in the case of a meeting, a statement that any proxy must be delivered to the convener or chair before it may be used at the meeting;

(m) in the case of a meeting, a statement that, where applicable, a complaint may be made in accordance with rule 15.38 and the period within which such a complaint may be made; and

(n) a statement that a creditor may appeal a decision in accordance with rule 15.35, and the relevant period under rule 15.35 within which such an appeal may be made.

(4) The notice must be authenticated and dated by the convener.

(5) Where the decision procedure is a meeting the notice must be accompanied by a blank proxy complying with rule 16.3.

(6) This rule does not apply if the court orders under rule 15.12 that notice of a decision procedure be given by advertisement only.

NOTES

Commencement: 6 April 2017.

This rule derived from the Insolvency Rules 1986, SI 1986/1925, rr 1.9, 1.48, 2.34, 4.50, 4.51, 4.54, 5.17, 6.79, 6.81.

Para (3): words omitted from sub-para (e) revoked and figure and words in square brackets in sub-paras (h), (i) substituted by the Insolvency (England and Wales) (Amendment) Rules 2017, SI 2017/366, rr 3, 37.

[6.778]

15.9 Voting in a decision procedure

(1) In order to be counted in a decision procedure other than where votes are cast at a meeting, votes must—

(a) be received by the convener on or before the decision date; and

(b) in the case of a vote cast by a creditor, be accompanied by a proof in respect of the creditor's claim unless it has already been given to the convener.

(2) In an administration, an administrative receivership, a creditors' voluntary winding up, a winding up by the court or a bankruptcy a vote must be disregarded if—

(a) a proof in respect of the claim is not received by the convener on or before the decision date or, in the case of a meeting, 4pm on the business day before the decision date unless under rule 15.26 or 15.28(1)(b)(ii) (as applicable) the chair is content to accept the proof later; or

(b) the convener decides, in the application of Chapter 8 of this Part, that the creditor is not entitled to cast the vote.

(3) For the decision to be made, the convener must receive at least one valid vote on or before the decision date.

NOTES

Commencement: 6 April 2017.

This rule derived from the Insolvency Rules 1986, SI 1986/1925, rr 2.38, 3.11, 4.50, 4.51, 4.54, 6.79, 6.81.

[6.779]

15.10 Venue for decision procedure

The convener must have regard to the convenience of those invited to participate when fixing the venue for a decision procedure (including the resumption of an adjourned meeting).

NOTES

Commencement: 6 April 2017.

This rule derived from the Insolvency Rules 1986, SI 1986/1925, rr 1.13, 2.35, 3.9, 4.60, 5.18, 6.86.

[6.780]

15.11 Notice of decision procedures or of seeking deemed consent: when and to whom delivered

[Note: when an office-holder is obliged to give notice to "the creditors", this is subject to rule 1.37, which limits the obligation to giving notice to those creditors of whose address the office-holder is aware.]

(1) Notices of decision procedures, and notices seeking deemed consent, must be delivered in accordance with the following table.

Proceedings	*Decisions*	*Persons to whom notice must be delivered*	*Minimum notice required*
administration	decisions of creditors	the creditors who had claims against the company at the date when the company entered administration (except for those who have subsequently been paid in full)	14 days
administrative receivership	decisions of creditors	the creditors	14 days
creditors' voluntary winding up	decisions of creditors for appointment of liquidator (including any decision made at the same time on the liquidator's remuneration or the establishment of a liquidation committee)	the creditors	14 days on conversion from members' voluntary liquidation, 7 days on conversion from member's voluntary liquidation where deemed consent has been objected to and in other cases, 3 business days

Proceedings	*Decisions*	*Persons to whom notice must be delivered*	*Minimum notice required*
creditors' voluntary winding up or a winding up by the court	decisions of creditors to consider whether a replacement should be appointed after a liquidator's resignation	the creditors	28 days
winding up by the court	decisions of creditors to consider whether to remove or replace the liquidator (other than after a liquidator's resignation)	the creditors and the official receiver	14 days
creditors' voluntary winding up or a winding up by the court	other decisions of creditors	the creditors	14 days
winding up by the court	decisions of contributories	every person appearing (by the company's records or otherwise) to be a contributory	14 days
proposed CVA	decisions of creditors	the creditors	7 days for a decision on proposed modifications to the proposal from the company's directors under paragraph 31(7) of Schedule A1; 7 days for consideration of proposal where physical meeting requisitioned; in other cases, 14 days
proposed IVA	decisions of creditors	the creditors	14 days
bankruptcy	decisions of creditors to consider whether a replacement should be appointed after the resignation of a trustee	the creditors and the official receiver	28 days
bankruptcy	decisions of creditors to consider removing the trustee	the creditors and the official receiver	14 days
bankruptcy	decisions of creditors on appointment of new trustee following removal of previous trustee (including any decision made at the same time on the establishment of a creditors' committee)	the creditors	7 days
bankruptcy	other decisions of creditors	the creditors	14 days
[Main proceedings in another member State	Approval under Article 36(5) of the EU Regulation of proposed undertaking offered by a member State liquidator	all the local creditors in the United Kingdom	14 days]

(2) This rule does not apply where the court orders under rule 15.12 that notice of a decision procedure be given by advertisement only.

NOTES

Commencement: 6 April 2017.

This rule derived from the Insolvency Rules 1986, SI 1986/1925, rr 1.9, 1.48, 2.35, 3.9, 4.50, 4.54, 5.17, 6.79, 6.81.

Para (1): table entry in square brackets added by the Insolvency Amendment (EU 2015/848) Regulations 2017, SI 2017/702, regs 2, 3, Schedule, Pt 2, paras 32, 44, as from 26 June 2017, except in relation to proceedings opened before that date.

[6.781]
15.12 Notice of decision procedure by advertisement only

(1) The court may order that notice of a decision procedure is to be given by advertisement only and not by individual notice to the persons concerned.

(2) In considering whether to make such an order, the court must have regard to the relative cost of advertisement as against the giving of individual notices, the amount of assets available and the extent of the interest of creditors, members and contributories or any particular class of them.

(3) The advertisement must meet the requirements for a notice under rule 15.8(3), and must also state—

(a) that the court ordered that notice of the decision procedure be given by advertisement only; and
(b) the date of the court's order.

NOTES

Commencement: 6 April 2017.
This rule derived from the Insolvency Rules 1986, SI 1986/1925, rr 2.37A, 4.59, 6.85.

[6.782]
15.13 Gazetting and advertisement of meeting

(1) In an administration, a creditors' voluntary winding up, a winding up by the court, or a bankruptcy, where a decision is being sought by a meeting the convener must gazette a notice of the procedure stating—

(a) that a meeting of creditors or contributories is to take place;
(b) the venue for the meeting;
(c) the purpose of the meeting; and
(d) the time and date by which, and place at which, those attending must deliver proxies and proofs (if not already delivered) in order to be entitled to vote.

(2) The notice must also state—

(a) who is the convener in respect of the decision procedure; and
(b) if the procedure results from a request of one or more creditors, the fact that it was so summoned and the section of the Act under which it was summoned.

(3) The notice must be gazetted before or as soon as reasonably practicable after notice of the meeting is delivered in accordance with these Rules.

(4) Information to be gazetted under this rule may also be advertised in such other manner as the convener thinks fit.

(5) The convener may gazette other decision procedures or the deemed consent procedure in which case the equivalent information to that required by this rule must be stated in the notice.

NOTES

Commencement: 6 April 2017.
This rule derived from the Insolvency Rules 1986, SI 1986/1925, rr 2.34, 4.50, 4.53C, 4.53D, 6.79.

[6.783]
15.14 Notice to company officers, bankrupts etc in respect of meetings

(1) In a proposal for a CVA, an administration, a creditors' voluntary winding up or a winding up by the court notice to participate in a creditors' meeting must be delivered to every present or former officer of the company whose presence the convener thinks is required and that person is required to attend the meeting.

(2) In a bankruptcy, notice of a meeting must be delivered to the bankrupt who is required to attend the meeting unless paragraph (3) applies.

(3) In a bankruptcy, where the bankrupt is not required to attend the meeting, the notice must state—

(a) that the bankrupt is not required to attend the meeting;
(b) that if the bankrupt wishes to attend, the bankrupt should tell the convener as soon as reasonably practicable;
(c) that whether the bankrupt will be allowed to participate in the meeting is at the discretion of the chair; and
(d) that the decision of the chair as to what intervention, if any, the bankrupt may make is final.

(4) Notices under this rule must be delivered in compliance with the minimum notice requirements set out in rule 15.2(2) or in compliance with an order of the court under rule 15.12.

NOTES

Commencement: 6 April 2017.
This rule derived from the Insolvency Rules 1986, SI 1986/1925, rr 1.16, 2.34(2), 4.58, 6.84.

[6.784]
15.15 Non-receipt of notice of decision

Where a decision is sought by a notice in accordance with the Act or these Rules, the decision procedure or deemed consent procedure is presumed to have been duly initiated and conducted, even if not everyone to whom the notice is to be delivered has received it.

NOTES

Commencement: 6 April 2017.

This rule derived from the Insolvency Rules 1986, SI 1986/1925, r 12A.4.

[6.785]
15.16 Decisions on remuneration and conduct

(1) This rule applies in relation to a decision or resolution which is proposed in an administration, a creditors' voluntary winding up, a winding up by the court or a bankruptcy and which affects a person in relation to that person's remuneration or conduct as administrator, liquidator or trustee (actual, proposed or former).

(2) The following may not vote on such a decision or resolution whether as a creditor, contributory, proxy-holder or corporate representative, except so far as permitted by rule 16.7 (proxy-holder with financial interest)—
- (a) that person;
- (b) the partners and employees of that person; and
- (c) the officers and employees of the company of which that person is a director, officer or employee.

NOTES

Commencement: 6 April 2017.
This rule derived from the Insolvency Rules 1986, SI 1986/1925, rr 4.63, 6.88.

CHAPTER 4 DECISION MAKING IN PARTICULAR PROCEEDINGS

[Note: a document required by the Act or these Rules must also contain the standard contents set out in Part 1.]

[6.786]
15.17 Decisions in winding up of authorised deposit-takers

(1) This rule applies in a creditors' voluntary winding up or a winding up by the court of an authorised deposit-taker.

(2) The directors of a company must deliver a notice of a meeting of the company at which it is intended to propose a resolution for its winding up to the Financial Conduct Authority and to the scheme manager established under section 212(1) of the Financial Services and Markets Act 2000.

(3) These notices must be the same as those delivered to members of the company.

(4) Where any decision is sought for the purpose of considering whether a replacement should be appointed after the liquidator's resignation, removing the liquidator or appointing a new liquidator, the convener must also deliver a copy of the notice by which such a decision is sought to the Financial Conduct Authority and the scheme manager.

(5) A scheme manager who is required by this rule to be given notice of a meeting is entitled to be represented at the meeting.

NOTES

Commencement: 6 April 2017.
This rule derived from the Insolvency Rules 1986, SI 1986/1925, r 4.72.

CHAPTER 5 REQUISITIONED DECISIONS

[Note: a document required by the Act or these Rules must also contain the standard contents set out in Part 1.]

[6.787]
15.18 Requisitions of decision

[Note: this rule is concerned with requests by creditors or contributories for a decision, rather than requests for decisions to be made by way of a physical meeting under sections 246ZE(3) or 379ZA(3).]

(1) In this Chapter, "requisitioned decision" means a decision on nominations requested to be sought under section 136(5)(c) or a decision requested to be sought under section 168(2), 171(2)(b), 171(3A), 172(3), 298(4)(c) or 314(7) or paragraph 52(2) or 56(1) of Schedule B1.

(2) A request for a decision to be sought under paragraph 52(2) of Schedule B1 must be delivered within 8 business days of the date on which the administrator's statement of proposals is delivered.

(3) The request for a requisitioned decision must include a statement of the purpose of the proposed decision and either—
- (a) a statement of the requesting creditor's claim or contributory's value, together with—
  - (i) a list of the creditors or contributories concurring with the request and of the amounts of their respective claims or values, and
  - (ii) confirmation of concurrence from each creditor or contributory concurring; or
- (b) a statement of the requesting creditor's debt or contributory's value and that that alone is sufficient without the concurrence of other creditors or contributories.

(4) A decision procedure must be instigated under section 171(2)(b) for the removal of the liquidator, other than a liquidator appointed by the court under section 108, if 25% in value of the company's creditors, excluding those who are connected with the company, request it.

(5) Where a decision procedure under section 171(2)(b), 171(3), 171(3A) or 298(4)(c) is to be instigated, or is proposed to be instigated, the court may, on the application of any creditor, give directions as to the decision procedure to be used and any other matter which appears to the court to require regulation or control.

(6) Where the official receiver receives a request under section 136(5)(c) and it appears that it is properly made, the official receiver must withdraw any notices previously given under section 136(5)(b) and act in accordance with Chapter 2 as if the official receiver had decided under section 136 to seek nominations.

NOTES

Commencement: 6 April 2017.
This rule derived from the Insolvency Rules 1986, SI 1986/1925, rr 2.37, 4.57, 6.83.

[6.788]
15.19 Expenses and timing of requisitioned decision

(1) The convener must, not later than 14 days from receipt of a request for a requisitioned decision, provide the requesting creditor with itemised details of the sum to be deposited as security for payment of the expenses of such procedure.

(2) The convener is not obliged to initiate the decision procedure or deemed consent procedure (where applicable) until either—
- (a) the convener has received the required sum; or
- (b) the period of 14 days has expired without the convener having informed the requesting creditor or contributory of the sum required to be deposited as security.

(3) A requisitioned decision must be made—
- (a) where requested under section 136(5)(c), within three months; or
- (b) in any other case, within 28 days;

of the date on which the earlier of the events specified in paragraph (2) of this rule occurs.

(4) The expenses of a requisitioned decision must be paid out of the deposit (if any) unless—
- (a) the creditors decide that they are to be payable as an expense of the administration, winding up or bankruptcy, as the case may be; and
- (b) in the case of a decision of contributories, the creditors are first paid in full, with interest.

(5) The notice of a requisitioned decision of creditors must contain a statement that the creditors may make a decision as in paragraph (4)(a) of this rule.

(6) Where the creditors do not so decide, the expenses must be paid by the requesting creditor or contributory to the extent that the deposit (if any) is not sufficient.

(7) To the extent that the deposit (if any) is not required for payment of the expenses, it must be repaid to the requesting creditor or contributory.

NOTES

Commencement: 6 April 2017.
This rule derived from the Insolvency Rules 1986, SI 1986/1925, rr 2.37, 4.57(2), 4.61(3), (5), 6.83(2), 6.87.

CHAPTER 6 CONSTITUTION OF MEETINGS

[6.789]
15.20 Quorum at meetings

(1) A meeting is not competent to act unless a quorum is in attendance.

(2) A quorum is—
- (a) in the case of a meeting of creditors, at least one creditor entitled to vote; and
- (b) in the case of a meeting of contributories, at least two contributories entitled to vote, or all the contributories, if their number does not exceed two.

(3) Where the provisions of this rule as to quorum are satisfied by the attendance of the chair alone or the chair and one additional person, but the chair is aware, either by virtue of proofs and proxies received or otherwise, that one or more additional persons would, if attending, be entitled to vote, the chair must delay the start of the meeting by at least 15 minutes after the appointed time.

NOTES

Commencement: 6 April 2017.
This rule derived from the Insolvency Rules 1986, SI 1986/1925, r 12A.21.

[6.790]
15.21 Chair at meetings

[(1)] The chair of a meeting must be—
- (a) the convener;
- (b) an appointed person; or
- (c) in cases where the convener is the official receiver, a person appointed by the official receiver.

[(2) However, where a decision on the appointment of a liquidator under rule 6.14(2)(b), 6.14(4) or 6.14(6) is made by a meeting or a virtual meeting, the chair of the meeting must be the convener.]

Part 6 Insolvency Rules

NOTES

Commencement: 6 April 2017.

This rule derived from the Insolvency Rules 1986, SI 1986/1925, rr 2.36, 3.10, 4.55, 4.56, 5.19, 6.82.

Para (2) is added by the Insolvency (England and Wales) (Amendment) Rules 2017, SI 2017/366, rr 3, 38 and the original text of r 15.21 is renumbered as para (1) accordingly.

[6.791]

15.22 The chair—attendance, interventions and questions

The chair of a meeting may—

(a) allow any person who has given reasonable notice of wishing to attend to participate in a virtual meeting or to be admitted to a physical meeting;

(b) decide what intervention, if any, may be made at—

(i) a meeting of creditors by any person attending who is not a creditor, or

(ii) a meeting of contributories by any person attending who is not a contributory; and

(c) decide what questions may be put to—

(i) any present or former officer of the company, or

(ii) the bankrupt or debtor.

NOTES

Commencement: 6 April 2017.

This rule derived from the Insolvency Rules 1986, SI 1986/1925, rr 4.58, 6.84.

CHAPTER 7 ADJOURNMENT AND SUSPENSION OF MEETINGS

[6.792]

15.23 Adjournment by chair

(1) The chair may (and must if it is so resolved) adjourn a meeting for not more than 14 days, but subject to any direction of the court and to rule 15.24.

(2) Further adjournment under this rule must not be to a day later than 14 days after the date on which the meeting was originally held (subject to any direction by the court).

(3) But in a case relating to a proposed CVA, the chair may, and must if the meeting so resolves, adjourn a meeting held under paragraph 29(1) of Schedule A1 to a day which is not more than 14 days after the date on which the moratorium (including any extension) ends.

NOTES

Commencement: 6 April 2017.

This rule derived from the Insolvency Rules 1986, SI 1986/1925, rr 1.21, 1.53, 2.35, 3.14, 4.65(3), 5.24, 6.91.

[6.793]

15.24 Adjournment of meetings to remove a liquidator or trustee

If the chair of a meeting to remove the liquidator or trustee in a creditors' voluntary winding up, a winding up by the court or a bankruptcy is the liquidator or trustee or the liquidator's or trustee's nominee and a resolution has been proposed for the liquidator's or trustee's removal, the chair must not adjourn the meeting without the consent of at least one-half (in value) of the creditors attending and entitled to vote.

NOTES

Commencement: 6 April 2017.

This rule derived from the Insolvency Rules 1986, SI 1986/1925, rr 4.113, 4.114, 6.129.

[6.794]

15.25 Adjournment in absence of chair

(1) In an administration, administrative receivership, a creditors' voluntary winding up, a winding up by the court or a bankruptcy, if no one attends to act as chair within 30 minutes of the time fixed for a meeting to start, then the meeting is adjourned to the same time and place the following week or, if that is not a business day, to the business day immediately following.

(2) If no one attends to act as chair within 30 minutes of the time fixed for the meeting after a second adjournment under this rule, then the meeting comes to an end.

NOTES

Commencement: 6 April 2017.

This rule derived from the Insolvency Rules 1986, SI 1986/1925, rr 2.35(5), 4.65(6A), 6.91(4A).

[6.795]

15.26 Proofs in adjournment

Where a meeting in an administration, an administrative receivership, a creditors' voluntary winding-up, a winding up by the court or a bankruptcy is adjourned, proofs may be used if delivered not later than 4pm on the business day immediately before resumption of the adjourned meeting, or later than that time where the chair is content to accept the proof.

NOTES

Commencement: 6 April 2017.

This rule derived from the Insolvency Rules 1986, SI 1986/1925, rr 2.35, 4.65(7), 6.91(5).

[6.796]

15.27 Suspension

The chair of a meeting may, without an adjournment, declare the meeting suspended for one or more periods not exceeding one hour in total (or, in exceptional circumstances, such longer total period during the same day at the chair's discretion).

NOTES

Commencement: 6 April 2017.

This rule derived from the Insolvency Rules 1986, SI 1986/1925, rr 1.21, 1.53, 2.35, 3.14, 4.65, 5.24, 6.90.

CHAPTER 8 CREDITORS' VOTING RIGHTS AND MAJORITIES

[Note: a document required by the Act or these Rules must also contain the standard contents set out in Part 1.]

[6.797]

15.28 Creditors' voting rights

(1) In an administration, an administrative receivership, a creditors' voluntary winding up, a winding up by the court and a bankruptcy, a creditor is entitled to vote in a decision procedure or to object to a decision proposed using the deemed consent procedure only if—

- (a) the creditor has, subject to rule 15.29, delivered to the convener a proof of the debt claimed in accordance with paragraph (3), including any calculation for the purposes of rule 15.31 or 15.32, and
- (b) the proof was received by the convener—
  - (i) not later than the decision date, or in the case of a meeting, 4pm on the business day before the meeting, or
  - (ii) in the case of a meeting, later than the time given in sub-paragraph (i) where the chair is content to accept the proof; and
- (c) the proof has been admitted for the purposes of entitlement to vote.

(2) In the case of a meeting, a proxy-holder is not entitled to vote on behalf of a creditor unless the convener or chair has received the proxy intended to be used on behalf of that creditor.

(3) A debt is claimed in accordance with this paragraph if it is—

- (a) claimed as due from the company or bankrupt to the person seeking to be entitled to vote; or
- (b) in relation to a member State liquidator, claimed to be due to creditors in proceedings in relation to which that liquidator holds office.

(4) The convener or chair may call for any document or other evidence to be produced if the convener or chair thinks it necessary for the purpose of substantiating the whole or any part of a claim.

(5) In a decision relating to a proposed CVA or IVA every creditor, secured or unsecured, who has notice of the decision procedure is entitled to vote in respect of that creditor's debt.

(6) Where a decision is sought in an administration under rule 3.52(3)(b) (pre-administration costs), rule 18.18(4) (remuneration: procedure for initial determination in an administration) or rule 18.26(2) (first exception: administrator has made statement under paragraph 52(1)(b) of Schedule B1), creditors are entitled to participate to the extent stated in those paragraphs.

NOTES

Commencement: 6 April 2017.

This rule derived from the Insolvency Rules 1986, SI 1986/1925, rr 1.17, 1.49, 2.38, 3.11, 4.67, 4.68, 5.21, 6.93, 6.93A.

[6.798]

15.29 Scheme manager's voting rights

(1) For the purpose of voting in a creditors' voluntary winding up or a winding up by the court of an authorised deposit-taker at which the scheme manager established under section 212(1) of the Financial Services and Markets Act 2000 is entitled to be represented under rule 15.17 (but not for any other purpose), the manager may deliver, instead of a proof, a statement containing—

- (a) the names of the creditors of the company in relation to whom an obligation of the scheme manager has arisen or may reasonably be expected to arise;
- (b) the amount of each such obligation; and
- (c) the total amount of all such obligations.

(2) The manager may from time to time deliver a further statement; and each such statement supersedes any previous statement.

NOTES

Commencement: 6 April 2017.

This rule derived from the Insolvency Rules 1986, SI 1986/1925, Sch 1, paras 2–4, 6.

[6.799]

15.30 Claim made in proceedings in other member States

(1) Where a creditor in an administration, a creditors' voluntary winding up, a winding up by the court or a bankruptcy—

(a) is entitled to vote under rule 15.28(1) (as determined, where that be the case, in accordance with rule 15.35);

(b) has made the claim in other proceedings; and

(c) votes on a resolution in a decision procedure;

and a member State liquidator casts a vote in respect of the same claim, only the creditor's vote is to be counted.

(2) Where in an administration, a creditors' voluntary winding up, a winding up by the court or a bankruptcy—

(a) a creditor has made a claim in more than one set of other proceedings; and

(b) more than one member State liquidator seeks to vote in respect of that claim;

the entitlement to vote in respect of that claim is exercisable by the member State liquidator in the main proceedings, whether or not the creditor has made the claim in the main proceedings.

(3) In this rule, "other proceedings" mean main, secondary or territorial proceedings in another member State.

NOTES

Commencement: 6 April 2017.

This rule derived from the Insolvency Rules 1986, SI 1986/1925, rr 2.38, 4.67, 6.93.

[6.800]

15.31 Calculation of voting rights

(1) Votes are calculated according to the amount of each creditor's claim—

(a) in an administration, as at the date on which the company entered administration, less—

(i) any payments that have been made to the creditor after that date in respect of the claim, and

(ii) any adjustment by way of set-off which has been made in accordance with rule 14.24 or would have been made if that rule were applied on the date on which the votes are counted;

(b) in an administrative receivership, as at the date of the appointment of the receiver, less any payments that have been made to the creditor after that date in respect of the claim;

(c) in a creditors' voluntary winding up, a winding up by the court or a bankruptcy, as set out in the creditor's proof to the extent that it has been admitted;

(d) in a proposed CVA—

(i) at the date the company went into liquidation where the company is being wound up,

(ii) at the date the company entered into administration (less any payments made to the creditor after that date in respect of the claim) where it is in administration,

(iii) at the beginning of the moratorium where a moratorium has been obtained (less any payments made to the creditor after that date in respect of the claim), or

(iv) where (i) to (iii) do not apply, at the decision date;

(e) in a proposed IVA—

(i) where the debtor is not an undischarged bankrupt—

(aa) at the date of the interim order, where there is an interim order in force,

(bb) otherwise, at the decision date,

(ii) where the debtor is an undischarged bankrupt, at the date of the bankruptcy order.

(2) A creditor may vote in respect of a debt of an unliquidated or unascertained amount if the convener or chair decides to put upon it an estimated minimum value for the purpose of entitlement to vote and admits the claim for that purpose.

(3) But in relation to a proposed CVA or IVA, a debt of an unliquidated or unascertained amount is to be valued at £1 for the purposes of voting unless the convener or chair or an appointed person decides to put a higher value on it.

(4) Where a debt is wholly secured its value for voting purposes is nil.

(5) Where a debt is partly secured its value for voting purposes is the value of the unsecured part.

(6) However, the value of the debt for voting purposes is its full value without deduction of the value of the security in the following cases—

(a) where the administrator has made a statement under paragraph 52(1)(b) of Schedule B1 and the administrator has been requested to seek a decision under paragraph 52(2); and

(b) where, in a proposed CVA, there is a decision on whether to extend or further extend a moratorium or to bring a moratorium to an end before the end of the period of any extension.

(7) No vote may be cast in respect of a claim more than once on any resolution put to the meeting; and for this purpose (where relevant), the claim of a creditor and of any member State liquidator in relation to the same debt are a single claim.

(8) A vote cast in a decision procedure which is not a meeting may not be changed.

(9) Paragraph (7) does not prevent a creditor or member State liquidator from—

(a) voting in respect of less than the full value of an entitlement to vote; or

(b) casting a vote one way in respect of part of the value of an entitlement and another way in respect of some or all of the balance of that value.

NOTES

Commencement: 6 April 2017.

This rule derived from the Insolvency Rules 1986, SI 1986/1925, rr 1.17(2), (3), 1.49(3), 1.52(3), 2.38(4), 2.40(2), 3.11(4), 5.21(2), (3), 5.41(2), 6.93.

[6.801]

15.32 Calculation of voting rights: special cases

(1) In an administration, a creditor under a hire-purchase agreement is entitled to vote in respect of the amount of the debt due and payable by the company on the date on which the company entered administration.

(2) In calculating the amount of any debt for the purpose of paragraph (1), no account is to be taken of any amount attributable to the exercise of any right under the relevant agreement so far as the right has become exercisable solely by virtue of—

- (a) the making of an administration application;
- (b) a notice of intention to appoint an administrator or any matter arising as a consequence of the notice; or
- (c) the company entering administration.

(3) Any voting rights which a creditor might otherwise exercise in respect of a claim in a creditors' voluntary winding up or a winding up by the court of an authorised deposit-taker are reduced by a sum equal to the amount of that claim in relation to which the scheme manager, by virtue of its having delivered a statement under rule 15.29, is entitled to exercise voting rights.

NOTES

Commencement: 6 April 2017.

This rule derived from the Insolvency Rules 1986, SI 1986/1925, r 2.42, Sch 1.

[6.802]

15.33 Procedure for admitting creditors' claims for voting

(1) The convener or chair in respect of a decision procedure must ascertain entitlement to vote and admit or reject claims accordingly.

(2) The convener or chair may admit or reject a claim in whole or in part.

(3) If the convener or chair is in any doubt whether a claim should be admitted or rejected, the convener or chair must mark it as objected to and allow votes to be cast in respect of it, subject to such votes being subsequently declared invalid if the objection to the claim is sustained.

NOTES

Commencement: 6 April 2017.

This rule derived from the Insolvency Rules 1986, SI 1986/1925, rr 1.17A, 1.50, 2.39, 4.70, 5.21(1)–(4), 5.22, 6.94(1), (3).

[6.803]

15.34 Requisite majorities

(1) A decision is made by creditors when a majority (in value) of those voting have voted in favour of the proposed decision, except where this rule provides otherwise.

[(2) In the case of an administration, a decision is not made if those voting against it include more than half in value of the creditors to whom notice of the decision procedure was delivered who are not, to the best of the convener's or chair's belief, persons connected with the company.]

(3) Each of the following decisions in a proposed CVA is made when three-quarters or more (in value) of those responding vote in favour of it—

- (a) a decision approving a proposal or a modification;
- (b) a decision extending or further extending a moratorium; or
- (c) a decision bringing a moratorium to an end before the end of the period of any extension.

(4) In a proposed CVA a decision is not made if more than half of the total value of the unconnected creditors vote against it.

(5) For the purposes of paragraph (4)—

- (a) a creditor is unconnected unless the convener or chair decides that the creditor is connected with the company;
- (b) in deciding whether a creditor is connected reliance may be placed on the information provided by the company's statement of affairs or otherwise in accordance with these Rules; and
- (c) the total value of the unconnected creditors is the total value of those unconnected creditors whose claims have been admitted for voting.

(6) In a case relating to a proposed IVA—

- (a) a decision approving a proposal or a modification is made when three-quarters or more (in value) of those responding vote in favour of it;
- (b) a decision is not made if more than half of the total value of creditors who are not associates of the debtor vote against it.

(7) For the purposes of paragraph (6)—

- (a) a creditor is not an associate of the debtor unless the convener or chair decides that the creditor is an associate of the debtor;

Part 6 Insolvency Rules

(b) in deciding whether a creditor is an associate of the debtor, reliance may be placed on the information provided by the debtor's statement of affairs or otherwise in accordance with these Rules; and

(c) the total value of the creditors who are not associates of the debtor is the total value of the creditors who are not associates of the debtor whose claims have been admitted for voting.

NOTES

Commencement: 6 April 2017.

This rule derived from the Insolvency Rules 1986, SI 1986/1925, rr 1.19, 1.52, 2.43, 3.15, 4.63, 5.23, 6.88.

Para (2): substituted by the Insolvency (England and Wales) (Amendment) Rules 2017, SI 2017/366, rr 3, 39.

[6.804]

15.35 Appeals against decisions under this Chapter

(1) A decision of the convener or chair under this Chapter is subject to appeal to the court by a creditor, by a contributory, or by the bankrupt or debtor (as applicable).

(2) In a proposed CVA, an appeal against a decision under this Chapter may also be made by a member of the company.

(3) If the decision is reversed or varied, or votes are declared invalid, the court may order another decision procedure to be initiated or make such order as it thinks just but, in a CVA or IVA, the court may only make an order if it considers that the circumstances which led to the appeal give rise to unfair prejudice or material irregularity.

(4) An appeal under this rule may not be made later than 21 days after the decision date.

(5) However, the previous paragraph does not apply in a proposed CVA or IVA, where an appeal may not be made after the end of the period of 28 days beginning with the day—

(a) in a proposed CVA, on which the first of the reports required by section 4(6) or paragraph 30(3) of Schedule A1 was filed with the court; or

(b) in a proposed IVA—

(i) where an interim order has not been obtained, on which the notice of the result of the consideration of the proposal required by section 259(1)(a) has been given, or

(ii) otherwise, on which the report required by section 259(1)(b) is made to the court.

(6) The person who made the decision is not personally liable for costs incurred by any person in relation to an appeal under this rule unless the court makes an order to that effect.

(7) The court may not make an order under paragraph (6) if the person who made the decision in a winding up by the court or a bankruptcy is the official receiver or a person nominated by the official receiver.

NOTES

Commencement: 6 April 2017.

This rule derived from the Insolvency Rules 1986, SI 1986/1925, rr 1.17A, 1.50, 1.52, 2.39, 3.12, 4.70, 5.22, 5.23, 5.42, 6.94.

CHAPTER 9 EXCLUSIONS FROM MEETINGS

[Note: a document required by the Act or these Rules must also contain the standard contents set out in Part 1.]

[6.805]

15.36 Action where person excluded

(1) In this rule and rules 15.37 and 15.38, an "excluded person" means a person who has taken all steps necessary to attend a virtual meeting or has been permitted by the convener to attend a physical meeting remotely under the arrangements which—

(a) have been put in place by the convener of the meeting; but

(b) do not enable that person to attend the whole or part of that meeting.

(2) Where the chair becomes aware during the course of the meeting that there is an excluded person, the chair may—

(a) continue the meeting;

(b) declare the meeting void and convene the meeting again; or

(c) declare the meeting valid up to the point where the person was excluded and adjourn the meeting.

(3) Where the chair continues the meeting, the meeting is valid unless—

(a) the chair decides in consequence of a complaint under rule 15.38 to declare the meeting void and hold the meeting again; or

(b) the court directs otherwise.

(4) Without prejudice to paragraph (2), where the chair becomes aware during the course of the meeting that there is an excluded person, the chair may, at the chair's discretion and without an adjournment, declare the meeting suspended for any period up to 1 hour.

NOTES

Commencement: 6 April 2017.

This rule derived from the Insolvency Rules 1986, SI 1986/1925, r 12A.23.

[6.806]
15.37 Indication to excluded person

(1) A creditor who claims to be an excluded person may request an indication of what occurred during the period of that person's claimed exclusion.

(2) A request under paragraph (1) must be made in accordance with paragraph (3) as soon as reasonably practicable, and in any event, not later than 4pm on the business day following the day on which the exclusion is claimed to have occurred.

(3) A request under paragraph (1) must be made to—
(a) the chair where it is made during the course of the business of the meeting; or
(b) the convener where it is made after the conclusion of the business of the meeting.

(4) Where satisfied that the person making the request is an excluded person, the person to whom the request is made under paragraph (3) must deliver the requested indication to the excluded person as soon as reasonably practicable, and in any event, not later than 4pm on the business day following the day on which the request was made under paragraph (1).

NOTES
Commencement: 6 April 2017.
This rule derived from the Insolvency Rules 1986, SI 1986/1925, r 12A.24.

[6.807]
15.38 Complaint

(1) A person may make a complaint who—
(a) is, or claims to be, an excluded person; or
(b) attends the meeting and claims to have been adversely affected by the actual, apparent or claimed exclusion of another person.

(2) The complaint must be made to the appropriate person who is—
(a) the chair, where the complaint is made during the course of the meeting; or
(b) the convener, where it is made after the meeting.

(3) The complaint must be made as soon as reasonably practicable and, in any event, no later than 4pm on the business day following—
(a) the day on which the person was, appeared or claimed to be excluded; or
(b) where an indication is sought under rule 15.37, the day on which the complainant received the indication.

(4) The appropriate person must, as soon as reasonably practicable following receipt of the complaint,—
(a) consider whether there is an excluded person;
(b) where satisfied that there is an excluded person, consider the complaint; and
(c) where satisfied that there has been prejudice, take such action as the appropriate person considers fit to remedy the prejudice.

(5) Paragraph (6) applies where the appropriate person is satisfied that the complainant is an excluded person and—
(a) a resolution was voted on at the meeting during the period of the person's exclusion; and
(b) the excluded person asserts how the excluded person intended to vote on the resolution.

(6) Where the appropriate person is satisfied that if the excluded person had voted as that person intended it would have changed the result of the resolution, then the appropriate person must, as soon as reasonably practicable,—
(a) count the intended vote as having been cast in that way;
(b) amend the record of the result of the resolution;
(c) where notice of the result of the resolution has been delivered to those entitled to attend the meeting, deliver notice to them of the change and the reason for it; and
(d) where notice of the result of the resolution has yet to be delivered to those entitled to attend the meeting, the notice must include details of the change and the reason for it.

(7) Where satisfied that more than one complainant is an excluded person, the appropriate person must have regard to the combined effect of the intended votes.

(8) The appropriate person must deliver notice to the complainant of any decision as soon as reasonably practicable.

(9) A complainant who is not satisfied by the action of the appropriate person may apply to the court for directions and any application must be made no more than two business days from the date of receiving the decision of the appropriate person.

NOTES
Commencement: 6 April 2017.
This rule derived from the Insolvency Rules 1986, SI 1986/1925, r 12A. 25.

CHAPTER 10 CONTRIBUTORIES' VOTING RIGHTS AND MAJORITIES

[6.808]
15.39 Contributories' voting rights and requisite majorities

In a decision procedure for contributories—

(a) voting rights are as at a general meeting of the company, subject to any provision of the articles affecting entitlement to vote, either generally or at a time when the company is in liquidation; and

(b) a decision is made if more than one half of the votes cast by contributories are in favour.

NOTES

Commencement: 6 April 2017.

This rule derived from the Insolvency Rules 1986, SI 1986/1925, rr 4.63, 4.69.

CHAPTER 11 RECORDS

[6.809]

15.40 Record of a decision

(1) The convener or chair must cause a record of the decision procedure to be kept.

(2) In the case of a meeting, the record must be in the form of a minute of the meeting.

(3) The record must be authenticated by the convener or chair and be retained by the office-holder as part of the records of the insolvency proceedings in question.

(4) The record must identify the proceedings, and must include—

(a) in the case of a decision procedure of creditors, a list of the names of the creditors who participated and their claims;

(b) in the case of a decision procedure of contributories, a list of the names of the contributories who participated;

(c) where a decision is taken on the election of members of a creditors' committee or liquidation committee, the names and addresses of those elected;

(d) a record of any change to the result of the resolution made under rule 15.38(6) and the reason for any such change; and

(e) in any case, a record of every decision made and how creditors voted.

(5) Where a decision is sought using the deemed consent procedure, a record must be made of the procedure, authenticated by the convener, and must be retained by the office-holder as part of the records of the insolvency proceedings in question.

(6) The record under paragraph (5) must—

(a) identify the proceedings;

(b) state whether or not the decision was taken; and

(c) contain a list of the creditors or contributories who objected to the decision, and in the case of creditors, their claims.

(7) A record under this rule must also identify any decision procedure (or the deemed consent procedure) by which the decision had previously been sought.

NOTES

Commencement: 6 April 2017.

This rule derived from the Insolvency Rules 1986, SI 1986/1925, rr 2.44A, 3.15, 4.71, 6.95.

CHAPTER 12 COMPANY MEETINGS

[6.810]

15.41 Company meetings

(1) Unless the Act or these Rules provide otherwise, a company meeting must be called and conducted, and records of the meeting must be kept—

(a) in accordance with the law of England and Wales, including any applicable provision in or made under the Companies Act, in the case of a company incorporated—

(i) in England and Wales, or

(ii) outside the United Kingdom other than in an EEA state;

(b) in accordance with the law of that state applicable to meetings of the company in the case of a company incorporated in an EEA state other than the United Kingdom.

(2) For the purpose of this rule, reference to a company meeting called and conducted to resolve, decide or determine a particular matter includes a reference to that matter being resolved, decided or determined by written resolution of a private company passed in accordance with section 288 of the Companies Act.

(3) In an administration—

(a) in summoning any company meeting the administrator must have regard to the convenience of the members when fixing the venue; and

(b) the chair of the meeting must be either the administrator or an appointed person.

NOTES

Commencement: 6 April 2017.

This rule derived from the Insolvency Rules 1986, SI 1986/1925, r 2.49(5A).

[6.811]

15.42 Remote attendance: notification requirements

When a meeting is to be summoned and held in accordance with section 246A(3), the convener must notify all those to whom notice of the meeting is being given of—

(a) the ability of a person claiming to be an excluded person to request an indication in accordance with rule 15.45;
(b) the ability of a person within rule 15.46(1) to make a complaint in accordance with that rule; and
(c) in either case, the period within which a request or complaint must be made.

NOTES
Commencement: 6 April 2017.

[6.812]
15.43 Location of company meetings

(1) This rule applies to a request to the convener of a meeting under section 246A(9) to specify a place for the meeting.

(2) The request must be accompanied by
(a) a list of the members making or concurring with the request and their voting rights, and
(b) from each person concurring, confirmation of that person's concurrence.

(3) The request must be delivered to the convener within seven business days of the date on which the convener delivered the notice of the meeting in question.

(4) Where the convener considers that the request has been properly made in accordance with the Act and this rule, the convener must—
(a) deliver notice to all those previously given notice of the meeting—
(i) that it is to be held at a specified place, and
(ii) as to whether the date and time are to remain the same or not;
(b) set a venue (including specification of a place) for the meeting, the date of which must be not later than 28 days after the original date for the meeting; and
(c) deliver at least 14 days' notice of that venue to all those previously given notice of the meeting;

and the notices required by sub-paragraphs (a) and (c) may be delivered at the same or different times.

(5) Where the convener has specified a place for the meeting in response to a request to which this rule applies, the chair of the meeting must attend the meeting by being present in person at that place.

NOTES
Commencement: 6 April 2017.
This rule derived from the Insolvency Rules 1986, SI 1986/1925, r 12A.22.

[6.813]
15.44 Action where person excluded

(1) In this rule and rules 15.45 and 15.46, an "excluded person" means a person who has taken all steps necessary to attend a company meeting under the arrangements which—
(a) have been put in place by the convener of the meeting under section 246A(6); but
(b) do not enable that person to attend the whole or part of that meeting.

(2) Where the chair becomes aware during the course of the meeting that there is an excluded person, the chair may—
(a) continue the meeting;
(b) declare the meeting void and convene the meeting again; or
(c) declare the meeting valid up to the point where the person was excluded and adjourn the meeting.

(3) Where the chair continues the meeting, the meeting is valid unless—
(a) the chair decides in consequence of a complaint under rule 15.46 to declare the meeting void and hold the meeting again; or
(b) the court directs otherwise.

(4) Without prejudice to paragraph (2), where the chair becomes aware during the course of the meeting that there is an excluded person, the chair may, in the chair's discretion and without an adjournment, declare the meeting suspended for any period up to 1 hour.

NOTES
Commencement: 6 April 2017.
This rule derived from the Insolvency Rules 1986, SI 1986/1925, r 12A.23.

[6.814]
15.45 Indication to excluded person

(1) A person who claims to be an excluded person may request an indication of what occurred during the period of that person's claimed exclusion.

(2) A request under paragraph (1) must be made in accordance with paragraph (3) as soon as reasonably practicable, and in any event, not later than 4pm on the business day following the day on which the exclusion is claimed to have occurred.

(3) A request under paragraph (1) must be made to—
(a) the chair where it is made during the course of the business of the meeting; or
(b) the convener where it is made after the conclusion of the business of the meeting.

(4) Where satisfied that the person making the request is an excluded person, the person to whom the request is made under paragraph (3) must deliver the requested indication to the excluded person as soon as reasonably practicable, and in any event, not later than 4pm on the business day following the day on which the request was made under paragraph (1).

NOTES

Commencement: 6 April 2017.
This rule derived from the Insolvency Rules 1986, SI 1986/1925, r 12A.24.

[6.815]
15.46 Complaint

(1) A person may make a complaint who—
- (a) is, or claims to be, an excluded person; or
- (b) attends the meeting and claims to have been adversely affected by the actual, apparent or claimed exclusion of another person.

(2) The complaint must be made to the appropriate person who is—
- (a) the chair, where the complaint is made during the course of the meeting; or
- (b) the convener, where it is made after the meeting.

(3) The complaint must be made as soon as reasonably practicable and, in any event, no later than 4pm on the business day following—
- (a) the day on which the person was, appeared or claimed to be excluded; or
- (b) where an indication is sought under rule 15.45, the day on which the complainant received the indication.

(4) The appropriate person must, as soon as reasonably practicable following receipt of the complaint,—
- (a) consider whether there is an excluded person;
- (b) where satisfied that there is an excluded person, consider the complaint; and
- (c) where satisfied that there has been prejudice, take such action as the appropriate person considers fit to remedy the prejudice.

(5) Paragraph (6) applies where the appropriate person is satisfied that the complainant is an excluded person and—
- (a) a resolution was voted on at the meeting during the period of the person's exclusion; and
- (b) the excluded person asserts how the excluded person intended to vote on the resolution.

(6) Where the appropriate person is satisfied that if the excluded person had voted as that person intended it would have changed the result of the resolution, then the appropriate person must, as soon as reasonably practicable,—
- (a) count the intended vote as having been cast in that way;
- (b) amend the record of the result of the resolution;
- (c) where notice of the result of the resolution has been delivered to those entitled to attend the meeting, deliver notice to them of the change and the reason for it; and
- (d) where notice of the result of the resolution has yet to be delivered to those entitled to attend the meeting, the notice must include details of the change and the reason for it.

(7) Where satisfied that more than one complainant is an excluded person, the appropriate person must have regard to the combined effect of the intended votes.

(8) The appropriate person must deliver notice to the complainant of any decision as soon as reasonably practicable.

(9) A complainant who is not satisfied by the action of the appropriate person may apply to the court for directions and any application must be made no more than two business days from the date of receiving the decision of the appropriate person.

NOTES

Commencement: 6 April 2017.
This rule derived from the Insolvency Rules 1986, SI 1986/1925, r 12A.25.

PART 16
PROXIES AND CORPORATE REPRESENTATION

[Note: a document required by the Act or these Rules must also contain the standard contents set out in Part 1.]

[6.816]
16.1 Application and interpretation

(1) This Part applies in any case where a proxy is given in relation to a meeting or proceedings under the Act or these Rules, or where a corporation authorises a person to represent it.

(2) References in this Part to "the chair" are to the chair of the meeting for which a specific proxy is given or at which a continuing proxy is exercised.

NOTES

Commencement: 6 April 2017.

[6.817]
16.2 Specific and continuing proxies

(1) A "proxy" is a document made by a creditor, member or contributory which directs or authorises another person ("the proxy-holder") to act as the representative of the creditor, member or contributory at a meeting or meetings by speaking, voting, abstaining, or proposing resolutions.

(2) A proxy may be either—
- (a) a specific proxy which relates to a specific meeting; or
- (b) a continuing proxy for the insolvency proceedings.

(3) A specific proxy must—
- (a) direct the proxy-holder how to act at the meeting by giving specific instructions;
- (b) authorise the proxy-holder to act at the meeting without specific instructions; or
- (c) contain both direction and authorisation.

(4) A proxy is to be treated as a specific proxy for the meeting which is identified in the proxy unless it states that it is a continuing proxy for the insolvency proceedings.

(5) A continuing proxy must authorise the proxy-holder to attend, speak, vote or abstain, or to propose resolutions without giving the proxy-holder any specific instructions how to do so.

(6) A continuing proxy may be superseded by a proxy for a specific meeting or withdrawn by a written notice to the office-holder.

(7) A creditor, member or contributory may appoint more than one person to be proxy-holder but if so—
- (a) their appointment is as alternates; and
- (b) only one of them may act as proxy-holder at a meeting.

(8) The proxy-holder must be an individual.

NOTES

Commencement: 6 April 2017.

This rule derived from the Insolvency Rules 1986, SI 1986/1925, r 8.1.

[6.818]
16.3 Blank proxy

(1) A "blank proxy" is a document which—
- (a) complies with the requirements in this rule; and
- (b) when completed with the details specified in paragraph (3) will be a proxy as described in rule 16.2.

[(2) A blank proxy must state that the creditor, member or contributory named in the document (when completed) appoints a person who is named or identified as the proxy-holder of the creditor, member or contributory.]

(3) The specified details are—
- (a) the name and address of the creditor, member or contributory;
- (b) either the name of the proxy-holder or the identification of the proxy-holder (eg the chair of the meeting or the official receiver); . . .
- [(c) a statement that the proxy is either—
  - (i) for a specific meeting, which is identified in the proxy, or
  - (ii) a continuing proxy for the proceedings; and
- (d) if the proxy is for a specific meeting, instructions as to the extent to which the proxy holder is directed to vote in a particular way, to abstain or to propose any resolution.]

[(4) When it is delivered, a blank proxy must not have inserted into it the name or description of any person as proxy-holder or as a nominee for the office-holder, or instructions as to how a person appointed as proxy-holder is to act.]

(5) A blank proxy must have a note to the effect that the proxy may be completed with the name of the person or the chair of the meeting who is to be proxy-holder.

NOTES

Commencement: 6 April 2017.

This rule derived from the Insolvency Rules 1986, SI 1986/1925, r 8.2.

Para (2): substituted by the Insolvency (England and Wales) (Amendment) Rules 2017, SI 2017/366, rr 3, 40(a).

Para (3): word omitted from sub-para (b) revoked and sub-paras (c), (d) substituted for original sub-para (c), by SI 2017/366, rr 3, 40(b), (c).

Para (4): substituted by the Insolvency (England and Wales) and Insolvency (Scotland) (Miscellaneous and Consequential Amendments) Rules 2017, SI 2017/1115, rr 2, 10.

[6.819]
16.4 Use of proxies

(1) A proxy for a specific meeting must be delivered to the chair before the meeting.

(2) A continuing proxy must be delivered to the office-holder and may be exercised at any meeting which begins after the proxy is delivered.

(3) A proxy may be used at the resumption of the meeting after an adjournment, but if a different proxy is given for use at a resumed meeting, that proxy must be delivered to the chair before the start of the resumed meeting.

(4) Where a specific proxy directs a proxy-holder to vote for or against a resolution for the nomination or appointment of a person as office-holder, the proxy-holder may, unless the proxy states otherwise, vote for or against (as the proxy-holder thinks fit) a resolution for the nomination or appointment of that person jointly with another or others.

(5) A proxy-holder may propose a resolution which is one on which the proxy-holder could vote if someone else proposed it.

(6) Where a proxy gives specific directions as to voting, this does not, unless the proxy states otherwise, prohibit the proxy-holder from exercising discretion how to vote on a resolution which is not dealt with by the proxy.

(7) The chair may require a proxy used at a meeting to be the same as or substantially similar to the blank proxy delivered for that meeting or to a blank proxy previously delivered which has been completed as a continuing proxy.

NOTES

Commencement: 6 April 2017.

This rule derived from the Insolvency Rules 1986, SI 1986/1925, rr 8.2, 8.3.

[6.820]
16.5 Use of proxies by the chair

(1) Where a proxy appoints the chair (however described in the proxy) as proxy-holder the chair may not refuse to be the proxy-holder.

(2) Where the office-holder is appointed as proxy-holder but another person acts as chair of the meeting, that other person may use the proxies as if that person were the proxy-holder.

(3) Where, in a meeting of creditors in an administration, creditors' voluntary winding up, winding up by the court or a bankruptcy, the chair holds a proxy which requires the proxy-holder to vote for a particular resolution and no other person proposes that resolution the chair must propose it unless the chair considers that there is good reason for not doing so.

(4) If the chair does not propose such a resolution, the chair must as soon as reasonably practicable after the meeting deliver a notice of the reason why that was not done to the creditor, member or contributory.

NOTES

Commencement: 6 April 2017.

This rule derived from the Insolvency Rules 1986, SI 1986/1925, rr 1.15, 2.36, 4.64, 5.20, 6.89, 8.3(3).

[6.821]
16.6 Right of inspection and retention of proxies

(1) A person attending a meeting is entitled, immediately before or in the course of the meeting, to inspect proxies and associated documents delivered to the chair or to any other person in accordance with the notice convening the meeting.

(2) The chair must—
- (a) retain the proxies used for voting at a meeting where the chair is the office-holder, or
- (b) deliver them as soon as reasonably practicable after the meeting to the office-holder.

(3) The office-holder must allow proxies, so long as they remain in the office-holder's hands, to be inspected at all reasonable times on any business day by—
- (a) a creditor, in the case of proxies used at a meeting of creditors;
- (b) a member of the company or a contributory, in the case of proxies used at a meeting of the company, or a meeting of contributories;
- (c) a director of the company in the case of corporate insolvency proceedings; or
- (d) the debtor or the bankrupt in the case of personal insolvency proceedings.

(4) A creditor in paragraph (3)(a) is a person who has delivered a proof in the proceedings, but does not include a person whose claim has been wholly rejected.

(5) However the right of inspection is subject to rule 1.58 (confidentiality of documents—grounds for refusing inspection).

NOTES

Commencement: 6 April 2017.

This rule derived from the Insolvency Rules 1986, SI 1986/1925, rr 8.4, 8.5.

[6.822]
16.7 Proxy-holder with financial interest

(1) A proxy-holder must not vote for a resolution which would—
- (a) directly or indirectly place the proxy-holder or any associate of the proxy-holder in a position to receive any remuneration, fees or expenses from the insolvent estate; or
- (b) fix or change the amount of or the basis of any remuneration, fees or expenses receivable by the proxy-holder or any associate of the proxy-holder out of the insolvent estate.

(2) However a proxy-holder may vote for such a resolution if the proxy specifically directs the proxy-holder to vote in that way.

(3) Where an office-holder is appointed as proxy-holder and that proxy is used under rule 16.5(2) by another person acting as chair, the office-holder is deemed to be an associate of the person acting as chair.

NOTES

Commencement: 6 April 2017.

This rule derived from the Insolvency Rules 1986, SI 1986/1925, r 8.6.

[6.823]

16.9 Instrument conferring authorisation to represent corporation

(1) A person authorised to represent a corporation (other than as a proxy-holder) at a meeting of creditors or contributories must produce to the chair—

(a) the instrument conferring the authority; or

(b) a copy of it certified as a true copy by—

(i) two directors,

(ii) a director and the secretary, or

(iii) a director in the presence of a witness who attests the director's signature.

(2) The instrument conferring the authority must have been executed in accordance with section 44(1) to (3) of the Companies Act unless the instrument is the constitution of the corporation.

NOTES

Commencement: 6 April 2017.

This rule derived from the Insolvency Rules 1986, SI 1986/1925, r 8.7.

PART 17
CREDITORS' AND LIQUIDATION COMMITTEES

CHAPTER 1 INTRODUCTORY

[6.824]

17.1 Scope and interpretation

(1) This Part applies to the establishment and operation of—

(a) a creditors' committee in an administration;

(b) a creditors' committee in an administrative receivership;

(c) a liquidation committee in a creditors' voluntary winding up;

(d) a liquidation committee in a winding up by the court; and

(e) a creditors' committee in a bankruptcy.

(2) In this Part—

"contributory member" means a member of a liquidation committee appointed by the contributories; and

"creditor member" means a member of a liquidation committee appointed by the creditors.

NOTES

Commencement: 6 April 2017.

CHAPTER 2 FUNCTIONS OF A COMMITTEE

[6.825]

17.2 Functions of a committee

In addition to any functions conferred on a committee by any provision of the Act, the committee is to—

(a) assist the office-holder in discharging the office-holder's functions; and

(b) act in relation to the office-holder in such manner as may from time to time be agreed.

NOTES

Commencement: 6 April 2017.

This rule derived from the Insolvency Rules 1986, SI 1986/1925, rr 2.52, 3.18.

CHAPTER 3 MEMBERSHIP AND FORMALITIES OF FORMATION OF A COMMITTEE

[Note: (1) a document required by the Act or these Rules must also contain the standard contents set out in Part 1;

(2) see sections 215, 362, 363, 365, 371 and 374 of the Financial Services and Markets Act 2000 (c 8) for the rights of persons appointed by a scheme manager, the Financial Conduct Authority and the Prudential Regulation Authority to attend committees and make representations.]

[6.826]

17.3 Number of members of a committee

[Note: section 101(1) provides that a liquidation committee in a creditors' voluntary winding up may not have more than five members.]

(1) A committee in an administration, administrative receivership or a bankruptcy must have at least three members but not more than five members.

(2) A liquidation committee in a creditors' voluntary winding up appointed pursuant to section 101 must have at least three members.

(3) A liquidation committee in a winding up by the court established under section 141 must have—
(a) at least three and not more than five members elected by the creditors; and
(b) where the grounds on which the company was wound up do not include inability to pay its debts, and where the contributories so decide, up to three contributory members elected by the contributories.

NOTES

Commencement: 6 April 2017.
This rule derived from the Insolvency Rules 1986, SI 1986/1925, rr 2.50, 3.16.

[6.827]
17.4 Eligibility for membership of creditors' or liquidation committee

(1) This rule applies to a creditors' committee in an administration, an administrative receivership, and a bankruptcy and to a liquidation committee in a creditors' voluntary winding up and a winding up by the court.

(2) A creditor is eligible to be a member of such a committee if—
(a) the person has proved for a debt;
(b) the debt is not fully secured; and
(c) neither of the following apply—
(i) the proof has been wholly disallowed for voting purposes, or
(ii) the proof has been wholly rejected for the purpose of distribution or dividend.

(3) No person can be a member as both a creditor and a contributory.

(4) A body corporate may be a member of a creditors' committee, but it cannot act otherwise than by a representative appointed under rule 17.17.

NOTES

Commencement: 6 April 2017.
This rule derived from the Insolvency Rules 1986, SI 1986/1925, rr 2.50, 3.16, 4.152, 6.150.

[6.828]
17.5 Establishment of committees

(1) Where the creditors, or where applicable, contributories, decide that a creditors' or liquidation committee should be established, the convener or chair of the decision procedure [or convener of the deemed consent process] (if not the office-holder) must—
(a) as soon as reasonably practicable deliver a notice of the decision to the office-holder (or to the person appointed as office-holder); and
(b) where a decision has also been made as to membership of the committee, inform the office-holder of the names and addresses of the persons elected to be members of the committee.

(2) Before a person may act as a member of the committee that person must agree to do so.

(3) A person's proxy-holder attending a meeting establishing the committee or, in the case of a corporation, its duly appointed representative, may give such agreement (unless the proxy or instrument conferring authority contains a statement to the contrary).

(4) Where a decision has been made to establish a committee but not as to its membership, the office-holder must seek a decision from the creditors (about creditor members of the committee) and, where appropriate in a winding up by the court, a decision from contributories (about contributory members of the committee).

[(5) The committee is not established (and accordingly cannot act) until the office-holder has sent a notice of its membership in order to comply with paragraph (9) or (10).]

(6) The notice must contain the following—
(a) a statement that the committee has been duly constituted;
(b) identification details for any company that is a member of the committee;
(c) the full name and address of each member that is not a company.

(7) The notice must be authenticated and dated by the office-holder.

(8) The notice must be delivered as soon as reasonably practicable after the minimum number of persons required by rule 17.3 have agreed to act as members and been elected.

(9) Where the notice relates to a liquidation committee or a creditors' committee other than in a bankruptcy the office-holder must, as soon as reasonably practicable, deliver the notice to the registrar of companies.

(10) Where the notice relates to a creditors' committee in a bankruptcy the office-holder must, as soon as reasonably practicable—
(a) in bankruptcy proceedings based on a petition file the notice with the court; and
(b) in bankruptcy proceedings based on a bankruptcy application deliver the notice to the official receiver.

NOTES

Commencement: 6 April 2017.
This rule derived from the Insolvency Rules 1986, SI 1986/1925, rr 2.51, 3.17, 4.153, 6.151.
Para (1): words in square brackets inserted by the Insolvency (England and Wales) and Insolvency (Scotland) (Miscellaneous and Consequential Amendments) Rules 2017, SI 2017/1115, rr 2, 11(1), (2).
Para (5): substituted by SI 2017/1115, rr 2, 11(1), (3).

[6.829]

17.6 Liquidation committee established by contributories

(1) This rule applies where, under section 141, the creditors do not decide that a liquidation committee should be established, or decide that a committee should not be established.

(2) The contributories may decide to appoint one of their number to make application to the court for an order requiring the liquidator to seek a further decision from the creditors on whether to establish a liquidation committee; and—

- (a) the court may, if it thinks that there are special circumstances to justify it, make such an order; and
- (b) the creditors' decision sought by the liquidator in compliance with the order is deemed to have been a decision under section 141.

(3) If the creditors decide under paragraph (2)(b) not to establish a liquidation committee, the contributories may establish a committee.

(4) The committee must then consist of at least three, and not more than five, contributories elected by the contributories; and rule 17.5 applies, substituting for the reference to rule 17.3 in rule 17.5(8) a reference to this paragraph.

NOTES

Commencement: 6 April 2017.

This rule derived from the Insolvency Rules 1986, SI 1986/1925, r 4.154.

[6.830]

17.7 Notice of change of membership of a committee

(1) The office-holder must deliver or file a notice if there is a change in membership of the committee.

(2) The notice must contain the following—

- (a) the date of the original notice in respect of the constitution of the committee and the date of the last notice of membership given under this rule (if any);
- (b) a statement that this notice of membership replaces the previous notice;
- (c) identification details for any company that is a member of the committee;
- (d) the full name and address of any member that is not a company;
- (e) a statement whether any member has become a member since the issue of the previous notice;
- (f) the identification details for a company or otherwise the full name of any member named in the previous notice who is no longer a member and the date the membership ended.

(3) The notice must be authenticated and dated by the office-holder.

(4) Where the notice relates to a liquidation committee or a creditors' committee other than in a bankruptcy the office-holder must, as soon as reasonably practicable, deliver the notice to the registrar of companies.

(5) Where the notice relates to a creditors' committee in a bankruptcy the office-holder must, as soon as reasonably practicable—

- (a) in bankruptcy proceedings based on a petition file the notice with the court; and
- (b) in bankruptcy proceedings based on a bankruptcy application deliver the notice to the official receiver.

NOTES

Commencement: 6 April 2017.

This rule derived from the Insolvency Rules 1986, SI 1986/1925, rr 2.51, 3.17, 4.153, 6.151.

[6.831]

17.8 Vacancies: creditor members of creditors' or liquidation committee

(1) This rule applies if there is a vacancy among the creditor members of a creditors' or liquidation committee or where the number of creditor members of the committee is fewer than the maximum allowed.

(2) A vacancy need not be filled if—

- (a) the office-holder and a majority of the remaining creditor members agree; and
- (b) the total number of creditor members does not fall below three.

(3) The office-holder may appoint a creditor, who is qualified under rule 17.4 to be a member of the committee, to fill a vacancy or as an additional member of the committee, if—

- (a) a majority of the remaining creditor members of the committee (provided there are at least two) agree to the appointment; and
- (b) the creditor agrees to act.

(4) Alternatively, the office-holder may seek a decision from creditors to appoint a creditor (with that creditor's consent) to fill the vacancy.

(5) Where the vacancy is filled by an appointment made by a decision of creditors which is not convened or chaired by the office-holder, the convener or chair must report the appointment to the office-holder.

NOTES

Commencement: 6 April 2017.

This rule derived from the Insolvency Rules 1986, SI 1986/1925, rr 2.59, 3.25, 4.163, 6.160.

[6.832]
17.9 Vacancies: contributory members of liquidation committee

(1) This rule applies if there is a vacancy among the contributory members of a liquidation committee or where the number of contributory members of the committee is fewer than the maximum allowed under rule 17.3(3)(b) or 17.6(4) as the case may be.

(2) A vacancy need not be filled if—
- (a) the liquidator and a majority of the remaining contributory members agree; and
- (b) in the case of a committee of contributories only, the number of members does not fall below three.

(3) The liquidator may appoint a contributory to be a member of the committee, to fill a vacancy or as an additional member of the committee, if—
- (a) a majority of the remaining contributory members of the committee (provided there are at least two) agree to the appointment; and
- (b) the contributory agrees to act.

(4) Alternatively, the office-holder may seek a decision from contributories to appoint a contributory (with that contributory's consent) to fill the vacancy.

(5) Where the vacancy is filled by an appointment made by a decision of contributories which is not convened or chaired by the office-holder, the convener or chair must report the appointment to the office-holder.

NOTES

Commencement: 6 April 2017.
This rule derived from the Insolvency Rules 1986, SI 1986/1925, r 4.164.

[6.833]
17.10 Resignation

A member of a committee may resign by informing the office-holder in writing.

NOTES

Commencement: 6 April 2017.
This rule derived from the Insolvency Rules 1986, SI 1986/1925, rr 2.56, 3.22, 4.160, 6.157.

[6.834]
17.11 Termination of membership

A person's membership of a committee is automatically terminated if that person—
- (a) becomes bankrupt, in which case the person's trustee in bankruptcy replaces the bankrupt as a member of the committee;
- (b) is a person to whom a moratorium period under a debt relief order applies;
- (c) neither attends nor is represented at three consecutive meetings (unless it is resolved at the third of those meetings that this rule is not to apply in that person's case);
- (d) has ceased to be eligible to be a member of the committee under rule 17.4;
- (e) ceases to be a creditor or is found never to have been a creditor;
- (f) ceases to be a contributory or is found never to have been a contributory.

NOTES

Commencement: 6 April 2017.
This rule derived from the Insolvency Rules 1986, SI 1986/1925, rr 2.57, 3.23, 4.161, 6.158.

[6.835]
17.12 Removal

(1) A creditor member of a committee may be removed by a decision of the creditors through a decision procedure and in the case of a liquidation committee a contributory member of the committee may be removed by a decision of contributories through a decision procedure.

(2) At least 14 days' notice must be given of a decision procedure under this rule.

NOTES

Commencement: 6 April 2017.
This rule derived from the Insolvency Rules 1986, SI 1986/1925, rr 2.58, 3.24, 4.162, 6.159.

[6.836]
17.13 Cessation of liquidation committee in a winding up when creditors are paid in full

(1) Where the creditors have been paid in full together with interest in accordance with section 189, the liquidator must deliver to the registrar of companies a notice to that effect.

(2) On the delivery of the notice the liquidation committee ceases to exist.

(3) The notice must—
- (a) identify the liquidator;
- (b) contain a statement by the liquidator certifying that the creditors of the company have been paid in full with interest in accordance with section 189; and
- (c) be authenticated and dated by the liquidator.

NOTES

Commencement: 6 April 2017.

This rule derived from the Insolvency Rules 1986, SI 1986/1925, r 4.171A.

CHAPTER 4 MEETINGS OF COMMITTEE

[Note: a document required by the Act or these Rules must also contain the standard contents set out in Part 1.]

[6.837]

17.14 Meetings of committee

(1) Meetings of the committee must be held when and where determined by the office-holder.

(2) The office-holder must call a first meeting of the committee to take place within six weeks of the committee's establishment.

(3) After the calling of the first meeting, the office-holder must call a meeting—

(a) if so requested by a member of the committee or a member's representative (the meeting then to be held within 21 days of the request being received by the office-holder); and

(b) for a specified date, if the committee has previously resolved that a meeting be held on that date.

(4) The office-holder must give five business days' notice of the venue of a meeting to each member of the committee (or a member's representative, if designated for that purpose), except where the requirement for notice has been waived by or on behalf of a member.

(5) Waiver may be signified either at or before the meeting.

NOTES

Commencement: 6 April 2017.

This rule derived from the Insolvency Rules 1986, SI 1986/1925, rr 2.52, 3.18, 4.156, 6.153.

[6.838]

17.15 The chair at meetings

The chair at a meeting of a committee must be the office-holder or an appointed person.

NOTES

Commencement: 6 April 2017.

This rule derived from the Insolvency Rules 1986, SI 1986/1925, rr 2.53, 3.19, 4.157, 6.154.

[6.839]

17.16 Quorum

A meeting of a committee is duly constituted if due notice of it has been delivered to all the members, and at least two of the members are in attendance or represented.

NOTES

Commencement: 6 April 2017.

This rule derived from the Insolvency Rules 1986, SI 1986/1925, rr 2.54, 3.20, 4.158, 6.155.

[6.840]

17.17 Committee-members' representatives

(1) A member of the committee may, in relation to the business of the committee, be represented by another person duly authorised by the member for that purpose.

(2) A person acting as a committee-member's representative must hold a letter of authority entitling that person to act (either generally or specifically) and authenticated by or on behalf of the committee-member.

(3) A proxy or an instrument conferring authority (in respect of a person authorised to represent a corporation) is to be treated as a letter of authority to act generally (unless the proxy or instrument conferring authority contains a statement to the contrary).

(4) The chair at a meeting of the committee may call on a person claiming to act as a committee-member's representative to produce a letter of authority, and may exclude that person if no letter of authority is produced at or by the time of the meeting or if it appears to the chair that the authority is deficient.

(5) A committee member may not be represented by—

(a) another member of the committee;

(b) a person who is at the same time representing another committee-member;

(c) a body corporate;

(d) an undischarged bankrupt;

(e) a person whose estate has been sequestrated and who has not been discharged;

(f) a person to whom a moratorium period under a debt relief order applies;

(g) a person who is subject to a company directors disqualification order or a company directors disqualification undertaking; or

(h) a person who is subject to a bankruptcy restrictions order (including an interim order), a bankruptcy restrictions undertaking, a debt relief restrictions order (including an interim order) or a debt relief restrictions undertaking.

(6) Where a representative authenticates any document on behalf of a committee-member the fact that the representative authenticates as a representative must be stated below the authentication.

NOTES

Commencement: 6 April 2017.

This rule derived from the Insolvency Rules 1986, SI 1986/1925, rr 2.55, 3.21, 4.159, 6.156.

[6.841]

17.18 Voting rights and resolutions

(1) At a meeting of the committee, each member (whether the member is in attendance or is represented by a representative) has one vote.

(2) A resolution is passed when a majority of the members attending or represented have voted in favour of it.

(3) Every resolution passed must be recorded in writing and authenticated by the chair, either separately or as part of the minutes of the meeting, and the record must be kept with the records of the proceedings.

NOTES

Commencement: 6 April 2017.

This rule derived from the Insolvency Rules 1986, SI 1986/1925, rr 2.60, 3.26, 4.165, 4.166, 6.161.

[6.842]

17.19 Resolutions by correspondence

(1) The office-holder may seek to obtain the agreement of the committee to a resolution by delivering to every member (or the member's representative designated for the purpose) details of the proposed resolution.

(2) The details must be set out in such a way that the recipient may indicate agreement or dissent and where there is more than one resolution may indicate agreement to or dissent from each one separately.

(3) A member of the committee may, within five business days from the delivery of details of the proposed resolution, require the office-holder to summon a meeting of the committee to consider the matters raised by the proposed resolution.

(4) In the absence of such a request, the resolution is passed by the committee if a majority of the members (excluding any who are not permitted to vote by reason of rule 17.25(4)) deliver notice to the office-holder that they agree with the resolution.

(5) A copy of every resolution passed under this rule, and a note that the agreement of the committee was obtained, must be kept with the records of the proceedings.

NOTES

Commencement: 6 April 2017.

This rule derived from the Insolvency Rules 1986, SI 1986/1925, rr 2.61, 3.27, 4.167, 6.162.

[6.843]

17.20 Remote attendance at meetings of committee

(1) Where the office-holder considers it appropriate, a meeting may be conducted and held in such a way that persons who are not present together at the same place may attend it.

(2) A person attends such a meeting who is able to exercise that person's right to speak and vote at the meeting.

(3) A person is able to exercise the right to speak at a meeting when that person is in a position to communicate during the meeting to all those attending the meeting any information or opinions which that person has on the business of the meeting.

(4) A person is able to exercise the right to vote at a meeting when—

(i) that person is able to vote, during the meeting, on resolutions or determinations put to the vote at the meeting, and

(ii) that person's vote can be taken into account in determining whether or not such resolutions or determinations are passed at the same time as the votes of all the other persons attending the meeting.

(5) Where such a meeting is to be held the office-holder must make whatever arrangements the office-holder considers appropriate to—

(a) enable those attending the meeting to exercise their rights to speak or vote; and

(b) verify the identity of those attending the meeting and to ensure the security of any electronic means used to enable attendance.

(6) A requirement in these Rules to specify a place for the meeting may be satisfied by specifying the arrangements the office-holder proposes to enable persons to exercise their rights to speak or vote where in the reasonable opinion of the office-holder—

(a) a meeting will be attended by persons who will not be present together at the same place; and

(b) it is unnecessary or inexpedient to specify a place for the meeting.

(7) In making the arrangements referred to in paragraph (6) and in forming the opinion referred to in paragraph (6)(b), the office-holder must have regard to the legitimate interests of the committee members or their representatives attending the meeting in the efficient despatch of the business of the meeting.

(8) Where the notice of a meeting does not specify a place for the meeting the office-holder must specify a place for the meeting if at least one member of the committee requests the office-holder to do so in accordance with rule 17.21.

NOTES

Commencement: 6 April 2017.
This rule derived from the Insolvency Rules 1986, SI 1986/1925, r 12A.26.

[6.844]
17.21 Procedure for requests that a place for a meeting should be specified

(1) This rule applies to a request to the office-holder under rule 17.20(8) to specify a place for the meeting.

(2) The request must be made within three business days of the date on which the office-holder delivered the notice of the meeting in question.

(3) Where the office-holder considers that the request has been properly made in accordance with this rule, the office-holder must—

(a) deliver notice to all those previously given notice of the meeting—
  (i) that it is to be held at a specified place, and
  (ii) as to whether the date and time are to remain the same or not;
(b) fix a venue for the meeting, the date of which must be not later than seven business days after the original date for the meeting; and
(c) give three business days' notice of the venue to all those previously given notice of the meeting.

(4) The notices required by sub-paragraphs (a) and (c) may be delivered at the same or different times.

(5) Where the office-holder has specified a place for the meeting in response to a request under rule 17.20(8), the chair of the meeting must attend the meeting by being present in person at that place.

NOTES

Commencement: 6 April 2017.
This rule derived from the Insolvency Rules 1986, SI 1986/1925, r 12A.27.

CHAPTER 5 SUPPLY OF INFORMATION BY THE OFFICE-HOLDER TO THE COMMITTEE

[Note: a document required by the Act or these Rules must also contain the standard contents set out in Part 1.]

[6.845]
17.22 Notice requiring office-holder to attend the creditors' committee (administration and administrative receivership) (paragraph 57(3)(a) of Schedule B1 and section 49(2))

[Note: in an administration paragraph 57(3) of Schedule B1 enables the creditors' committee to require the administrator to provide the committee with information: section 49(2) makes similar provision in an administrative receivership.]

(1) This rule applies where—

(a) a committee in an administration resolves under paragraph 57(3)(a) of Schedule B1 to require the attendance of an administrator; or
(b) a committee in an administrative receivership resolves under section 49(2) to require the attendance of the administrative receiver.

(2) The notice delivered to the office-holder requiring the office-holder's attendance must be—

(a) accompanied by a copy of the resolution; and
(b) authenticated by a member of the committee.

(3) A member's representative may authenticate the notice for the member.

(4) The meeting at which the office-holder's attendance is required must be fixed by the committee for a business day, and must be held at such time and place as the office-holder determines.

(5) Where the office-holder so attends, the committee may elect one of their number to be chair of the meeting in place of the office-holder or an appointed person.

NOTES

Commencement: 6 April 2017.
This rule derived from the Insolvency Rules 1986, SI 1986/1925, rr 2.62, 3.28.

[6.846]
17.23 Office-holder's obligation to supply information to the committee (winding up and bankruptcy)

[Note: see section 49(2) and paragraph 57(2) of Schedule B1 for the office-holder's duty in an administrative receivership and an administration to supply information to the creditors' committee.]

(1) This rule applies in relation to a creditors' voluntary winding up, a winding up by the court and a bankruptcy.

(2) The office-holder must deliver a report to every member of the liquidation committee or the creditors' committee (as appropriate) containing the information required by paragraph (3)—

(a) not less than once in every period of six months (unless the committee agrees otherwise); and

(b) when directed to do so by the committee.

(3) The required information is a report setting out—

(a) the position generally in relation to the progress of the proceedings; and

(b) any matters arising in connection with them to which the office-holder considers the committee's attention should be drawn.

(4) The office-holder must, as soon as reasonably practicable after being directed by the committee—

(a) deliver any report directed under paragraph (2)(b);

(b) comply with a request by the committee for information.

(5) However the office-holder need not comply with such a direction where it appears to the office-holder that—

(a) the direction is frivolous or unreasonable;

(b) the cost of complying would be excessive, having regard to the relative importance of the information; or

(c) there are insufficient assets to enable the office-holder to comply.

(6) Where the committee has come into being more than 28 days after the appointment of the office-holder, the office-holder must make a summary report to the members of the committee of what actions the office-holder has taken since the office-holder's appointment, and must answer such questions as they may put to the office-holder relating to the office-holder's conduct of the proceedings so far.

(7) A person who becomes a member of the committee at any time after its first establishment is not entitled to require a report under this rule by the office-holder of any matters previously arising, other than a summary report.

(8) Nothing in this rule disentitles the committee, or any member of it, from having access to the office-holder's record of the proceedings, or from seeking an explanation of any matter within the committee's responsibility.

NOTES

Commencement: 6 April 2017.

This rule derived from the Insolvency Rules 1986, SI 1986/1925, rr 4.155, 4.168, 6.152, 6.163.

CHAPTER 6 MISCELLANEOUS

[Note: a document required by the Act or these Rules must also contain the standard contents set out in Part 1.]

[6.847]

17.24 Expenses of members etc

(1) The office-holder must pay, as an expense of the insolvency proceedings, the reasonable travelling expenses directly incurred by members of the committee or their representatives in attending the committee's meetings or otherwise on the committee's business.

(2) The requirement for the office-holder to pay the expenses does not apply to a meeting of the committee held within six weeks of a previous meeting, unless the meeting is summoned by the office-holder.

NOTES

Commencement: 6 April 2017.

This rule derived from the Insolvency Rules 1986, SI 1986/1925, rr 2.63, 3.29, 4.169, 6.164.

[6.848]

17.25 Dealings by committee members and others

(1) This rule applies in a creditors' voluntary winding up, a winding up by the court and a bankruptcy to a person who is, or has been in the preceding 12 months—

(a) a member of the committee;

(b) a member's representative; or

(c) an associate of a member, or of a member's representative.

(2) Such a person must not enter into a transaction as a result of which that person would—

(a) receive as an expense of the insolvency proceedings a payment for services given or goods supplied in connection with the administration of the insolvent estate;

(b) obtain a profit from the administration of the insolvent estate; or

(c) acquire an asset forming part of the insolvent estate.

(3) However such a transaction may be entered into—

(a) with the prior sanction of the committee, where it is satisfied (after full disclosure of the circumstances) that the person will be giving full value in the transaction;

(b) with the prior permission of the court; or

(c) if that person does so as a matter of urgency, or by way of performance of a contract in force before the start of the insolvency proceedings, and that person obtains the court's permission for the transaction, having applied for it without undue delay.

(4) Neither a member nor a representative of a member who is to participate directly or indirectly in a transaction may vote on a resolution to sanction that transaction.

(5) The court may, on the application of an interested person—

(a) set aside a transaction on the ground that it has been entered into in contravention of this rule; and

(b) make such other order about the transaction as it thinks just, including an order requiring a person to whom this rule applies to account for any profit obtained from the transaction and compensate the insolvent estate for any resultant loss.

(6) The court will not make an order under the previous paragraph in respect of an associate of a member of the committee or an associate of a member's representative, if satisfied that the associate or representative entered into the relevant transaction without having any reason to suppose that in doing so the associate or representative would contravene this rule.

(7) The costs of the application are not payable as an expense of the insolvency proceedings unless the court orders otherwise.

NOTES

Commencement: 6 April 2017.
This rule derived from the Insolvency Rules 1986, SI 1986/1925, rr 4.170, 6.165.

[6.849]
17.26 Dealings by committee members and others: administration and administrative receivership

(1) This rule applies in an administration and administrative receivership.

(2) Membership of the committee does not prevent a person from dealing with the company provided that a transaction is in good faith and for value.

(3) The court may, on the application of an interested person—

(a) set aside a transaction which appears to it to be contrary to this rule; and

(b) make such other order about the transaction as it thinks just including an order requiring a person to whom this rule applies to account for any profit obtained from the transaction and compensate the company for any resultant loss.

NOTES

Commencement: 6 April 2017.
This rule derived from the Insolvency Rules 1986, SI 1986/1925, rr 2.64, 3.30.

[6.850]
17.27 Formal defects

[Note: section 377 makes similar provision to paragraph (1) for the validity of acts of the creditors' committee in a bankruptcy.]

(1) The acts of a creditors' committee or a liquidation committee are valid notwithstanding any defect in the appointment, election or qualifications of a member of the committee or a committee-member's representative or in the formalities of its establishment.

(2) This rule does not apply to the creditors' committee in a bankruptcy.

NOTES

Commencement: 6 April 2017.
This rule derived from the Insolvency Rules 1986, SI 1986/1925, rr 2.65, 3.30A, 4.172A.

[6.851]
17.28 Special rule for winding up by the court and bankruptcy: functions vested in the Secretary of State

(1) At any time when the functions of a committee in a winding up by the court or a bankruptcy are vested in the Secretary of State under section 141(4) or (5) or section 302(1) or (2), requirements of the Act or these Rules about notices to be delivered, or reports to be made, to the committee by the office-holder do not apply, otherwise than as enabling the committee to require a report as to any matter.

(2) Where the committee's functions are so vested under section 141(5) or 302(2), they may be exercised by the official receiver.

NOTES

Commencement: 6 April 2017.
This rule derived from the Insolvency Rules 1986, SI 1986/1925, rr 4.172, 6.166.

CHAPTER 7 WINDING UP BY THE COURT FOLLOWING AN ADMINISTRATION

[Note: a document required by the Act or these Rules must also contain the standard contents set out in Part 1.]

[6.852]
17.29 Continuation of creditors' committee

[Note: paragraph 83(8)(f) of Schedule B1 makes similar provision to this rule for the liquidation committee to continue where the administration is followed by a creditors' voluntary winding up.]

(1) This rule applies where—
   (a) a winding-up order has been made by the court on the application of the administrator under paragraph 79 of Schedule B1;
   (b) the court makes an order under section 140(1) appointing the administrator as the liquidator; and
   (c) a creditors' committee was in existence immediately before the winding-up order was made.

(2) The creditors' committee shall continue in existence after the date of the order as if appointed as a liquidation committee under section 141.

(3) However, subject to rule 17.8(3)(a), the committee cannot act until—
   (a) the minimum number of persons required by rule 17.3 have agreed to act as members of the liquidation committee (including members of the former creditors' committee and any other who may be appointed under rule 17.8); and
   (b) the liquidator has delivered a notice of continuance of the committee to the registrar of companies.

(4) The notice must be delivered as soon as reasonably practicable after the minimum number of persons required have agreed to act as members or, if applicable, been appointed.

(5) The notice must contain—
   (a) a statement that the former creditors' committee is continuing in existence;
   (b) identification details for any company that is a member of the committee;
   (c) the full name and address of each member that is not a company.

(6) The notice must be authenticated and dated by the office-holder.

NOTES

Commencement: 6 April 2017.
This rule derived from the Insolvency Rules 1986, SI 1986/1925, rr 4.173, 4.174A, 4.176, 4.178.

PART 18
REPORTING AND REMUNERATION OF OFFICE-HOLDERS

[Note: this Part does not apply to the official receiver acting as an office-holder.]

CHAPTER 1 INTRODUCTORY

[6.853]
18.1 Scope of Part 18 and interpretation

(1) This Part applies to administration, winding up and bankruptcy.

(2) However this Part does not apply to the official receiver as office-holder or in respect of any period for which the official receiver is the office-holder.

(3) In particular an office-holder other than the official receiver is not required to make any report in respect of a period during which the official receiver was office-holder.

(4) In this Part "committee" means either or both of a creditors' committee and a liquidation committee as the context requires.

NOTES

Commencement: 6 April 2017.

CHAPTER 2 PROGRESS REPORTS

[Note: a document required by the Act or these Rules must also contain the standard contents set out in Part 1.]

[6.854]
18.2 Reporting by the office-holder

The office-holder in an administration, winding up or bankruptcy must prepare and deliver reports in accordance with this Chapter.

NOTES

Commencement: 6 April 2017.

[6.855]
18.3 Contents of progress reports in administration, winding up and bankruptcy

[Note: see rule 3.53 for provisions about the contents of a final progress report in an administration.]

(1) The office-holder's progress report in an administration, winding up and bankruptcy must contain the following—
   (a) identification details for the proceedings;
   (b) identification details for the bankrupt;
   (c) identification and contact details for the office-holder;
   (d) the date of appointment of the office-holder and any changes in the office-holder in accordance with paragraphs (3) and (4);
   (e) details of progress during the period of the report, including a summary account of receipts and payments during the period of the report;
   (f) the information relating to remuneration and expenses required by rule 18.4;

(g) the information relating to distributions required by rules 18.10 to 18.13 as applicable;
(h) details of what remains to be done; and
(i) any other information of relevance to the creditors.

(2) The receipts and payments account in a final progress report must state the amount paid to unsecured creditors by virtue of the application of section 176A.

(3) A change in the office-holder is only required to be shown in the next report after the change.

(4) However if the current office-holder is seeking the repayment of pre-administration expenses from a former office-holder the change in office-holder must continue to be shown until the next report after the claim is settled.

(5) Where the period of an administrator's appointment is extended the next progress report after the date the extension is granted must contain details of the extension.

(6) Where an administration has converted to a voluntary winding up the first progress report by the liquidator must include a note of any information received by the liquidator from the former administrator under rule 3.60(5) (matters occurring after the date of the administrator's final progress report).

NOTES

Commencement: 6 April 2017.

This rule derived from the Insolvency Rules 1986, SI 1986/1925, rr 2.47, 4.49B, 4.49C, 6.78A.

[6.856]

18.4 Information about remuneration

(1) The information relating to remuneration and expenses referred to in rule 18.3(1)(f) is as follows—
(a) the basis fixed for the remuneration of the office-holder under rules 18.16 and 18.18 to 18.21 as applicable, (or, if not fixed at the date of the report, the steps taken during the period of the report to fix it);
(b) if the basis of remuneration has been fixed, a statement of—
(i) the remuneration charged by the office-holder during the period of the report, and
(ii) where the report is the first to be made after the basis has been fixed, the remuneration charged by the office-holder during the periods covered by the previous reports, together with a description of the things done by the office-holder during those periods in respect of which the remuneration was charged;
(c) where the basis of the remuneration is fixed as a set amount under rule 18.16(2)(c), it may be shown as that amount without any apportionment to the period of the report;
(d) a statement of the expenses incurred by the office-holder during the period of the report;
(e) a statement setting out whether at the date of the report—
[(i) in a case other than a members' voluntary winding up, the remuneration expected to be charged by the office-holder is likely to exceed the fees estimate under rule 18.16(4) or any approval given,]
(ii) the expenses incurred or expected to be incurred are likely to exceed, or have exceeded, the details given to the creditors prior to the determination of the basis of remuneration, and
(iii) the reasons for that excess; and
(f) a statement of the rights of creditors [or], in a members' voluntary winding up, of members—
(i) to request information about remuneration or expenses under rule 18.9, and
(ii) to challenge the office-holder's remuneration and expenses under rule 18.34.

(2) The information about remuneration and expenses is required irrespective of whether payment was made in respect of them during the period of the report.

NOTES

Commencement: 6 April 2017.

This rule derived from the Insolvency Rules 1986, SI 1986/1925, rr 2.47, 4.49B, 4.49C, 6.78A.

Para (1): sub-para (e)(i) and word in square brackets in sub-para (f) substituted by the Insolvency (England and Wales) (Amendment) Rules 2017, SI 2017/366, rr 3, 41.

[6.857]

18.5 Information about pre-administration costs

(1) Where the administrator has made a statement of pre-administration costs under rule 3.35(10)(a)—
(a) if they are approved under rule 3.52, the first progress report after the approval must include a statement setting out the date of the approval and the amounts approved;
(b) while any of the costs remain unapproved each successive report must include a statement of any steps taken to get approval.

(2) However if either the administrator has decided not to seek approval, or another insolvency practitioner entitled to seek approval has told the administrator of that practitioner's decision not to seek approval then—
(a) the next report after that must include a statement of whichever is the case; and
(b) no statement under paragraph (1)(b) is required in subsequent reports.

NOTES

Commencement: 6 April 2017.

This rule derived from the Insolvency Rules 1986, SI 1986/1925, r 2.67A.

[6.858]
18.6 Progress reports in administration: timing

(1) The administrator's progress report in an administration must cover the periods of—
 (a) six months starting on the date the company entered administration; and
 (b) each subsequent period of six months.

(2) The periods for which progress reports are required under paragraph (1) are unaffected by any change in the administrator.

(3) However where an administrator ceases to act the succeeding administrator must, as soon as reasonably practicable after being appointed, deliver a notice to the creditors of any matters about which the succeeding administrator thinks the creditors should be informed.

(4) The administrator must deliver a copy of a report to the registrar of companies and the creditors within one month of the end of the period covered by the report unless the report is a final progress report under rule 3.55.

(5) An administrator who makes default in delivering a progress report within the time limit in paragraph (4) is guilty of on offence and liable to a fine and, for continued contravention, to a daily default fine.

NOTES

Commencement: 6 April 2017.

This rule derived from the Insolvency Rules 1986, SI 1986/1925, r 2.47(3), (6).

[6.859]
18.7 Progress reports in voluntary winding up: timing

(1) This rule applies for the purposes of sections 92A and 104A and prescribes the periods for which reports must be made.

(2) The liquidator's progress reports in a voluntary winding up must cover the periods of—
 (a) 12 months starting on the date the liquidator is appointed; and
 (b) each subsequent period of 12 months.

(3) The periods for which progress reports are required under paragraph (2) are unaffected by any change in the liquidator.

(4) However where a liquidator ceases to act the succeeding liquidator must, as soon as reasonably practicable after being appointed, deliver a notice to the members (in a members' voluntary winding up) or to members and creditors (in a creditors' voluntary winding up) of any matters about which the succeeding liquidator thinks the members or creditors should be informed.

(5) A progress report is not required for any period which ends after [a notice is delivered under rule 5.9(1) (members' voluntary winding up) or after] the date to which a final account is made up under section . . . 106 and is delivered by the liquidator . . . to members and creditors (creditors' voluntary winding up).

(6) The liquidator must [deliver] a copy of each progress report within two months after the end of the period covered by the report to—
 (a) the registrar of companies (who is a prescribed person for the purposes of sections 92A and 104A);
 (b) the members; and
 (c) in a creditors' voluntary liquidation, the creditors.

NOTES

Commencement: 6 April 2017.

This rule derived from the Insolvency Rules 1986, SI 1986/1925, r 4.49C.

Para (5): words in square brackets inserted and words omitted in both places revoked by the Insolvency (England and Wales) (Amendment) Rules 2017, SI 2017/366, rr 3, 42(1).

Para (6): word in square brackets substituted by SI 2017/366, rr 3, 42(2).

[6.860]
18.8 Progress reports in winding up by the court and bankruptcy: timing

(1) The liquidator or trustee's progress report in a winding up by the court or bankruptcy must cover the periods of—
 (a) 12 months starting on the date a person other than the official receiver is appointed liquidator or trustee; and
 (b) each subsequent period of 12 months.

(2) The periods for which progress reports are required under paragraph (1) are unaffected by any change in the liquidator or trustee unless at any time the official receiver becomes liquidator or trustee in succession to another person in which case—
 (a) the current reporting period under paragraph (1) ends; and
 (b) if a person other than the official receiver is subsequently appointed as liquidator or trustee a new period begins under paragraph (1)(a).

(3) Where a liquidator or trustee ceases to act the succeeding liquidator or trustee must as soon as reasonably practicable after being appointed, deliver a notice to the creditors of any matters about which the succeeding liquidator or trustee thinks the creditors should be informed.

(4) A progress report is not required for any period which ends after the date to which a final account or report is made up under section 146 (winding up by the court) or section 331 (bankruptcy) and is delivered by the liquidator or the trustee to the creditors.

(5) In a winding up by the court, the liquidator must deliver a copy of the progress report to the registrar of companies, the members of the company and the creditors within two months of the end of the period covered by the report.

(6) In a bankruptcy, the trustee must deliver a copy of the progress report to the creditors within two months of the end of the period covered by the report.

NOTES

Commencement: 6 April 2017.

This rule derived from the Insolvency Rules 1986, SI 1986/1925, rr 4.49B, 6.78A(3).

[6.861]

18.9 Creditors' and members' requests for further information in administration, winding up and bankruptcy

(1) The following may make a written request to the office-holder for further information about remuneration or expenses (other than pre-administration costs in an administration) set out in a progress report under rule 18.4(1)(b), (c) or (d) or a final report [or account] under rule 18.14—

(a) a secured creditor;

(b) an unsecured creditor with the concurrence of at least 5% in value of the unsecured creditors (including the creditor in question);

(c) members of the company in a members' voluntary winding up with at least 5% of the total voting rights of all the members having the right to vote at general meetings of the company;

(d) any unsecured creditor with the permission of the court; or

(e) any member of the company in a members' voluntary winding up with the permission of the court.

(2) A request, or an application to the court for permission, by such a person or persons must be made or filed with the court (as applicable) within 21 days of receipt of the report [or account] by the person, or by the last of them in the case of an application by more than one member or creditor.

(3) The office-holder must, within 14 days of receipt of such a request respond to the person or persons who requested the information by—

(a) providing all of the information requested;

(b) providing some of the information requested; or

(c) declining to provide the information requested.

(4) The office-holder may respond by providing only some of the information requested or decline to provide the information if—

(a) the time or cost of preparation of the information would be excessive; or

(b) disclosure of the information would be prejudicial to the conduct of the proceedings;

(c) disclosure of the information might reasonably be expected to lead to violence against any person; or

(d) the office-holder is subject to an obligation of confidentiality in relation to the information.

(5) An office-holder who does not provide all the information or declines to provide the information must inform the person or persons who requested the information of the reasons for so doing.

(6) A creditor, and a member of the company in a members' voluntary winding up, who need not be the same as the creditor or members who requested the information, may apply to the court within 21 days of—

(a) the office-holder giving reasons for not providing all of the information requested; or

(b) the expiry of the 14 days within which an office-holder must respond to a request.

(7) The court may make such order as it thinks just on an application under paragraph (6).

NOTES

Commencement: 6 April 2017.

This rule derived from the Insolvency Rules 1986, SI 1986/1925, rr 2.48A, 4.49E, 6.78C.

Paras (1), (2): words in square brackets inserted by the Insolvency (England and Wales) (Amendment) Rules 2017, SI 2017/366, rr 3, 43.

[6.862]

18.10 Administration, creditors' voluntary liquidation and compulsory winding up: reporting distribution of property to creditors under rule 14.13

(1) This rule applies where in an administration, creditors' voluntary liquidation or compulsory winding up there has been a distribution of property to creditors under rule 14.13.

(2) In any account or summary of receipts and payments which is required to be included in an account or report prepared under a rule listed in paragraph (3) the office-holder must—

(a) state the estimated value of the property divided among the creditors of the company during the period to which the account or summary relates; and

(b) provide details of the basis of the valuation as a note to the account or summary of receipts and payments.

(3) Paragraph (2) applies to the following—

(a) rule 3.63 (administrator's intention to resign);

(b) rule 6.25 (liquidator's resignation and replacement);
(c) rule 7.61 (liquidator's resignation);
(d) rule 18.3 (contents of progress report); and
(e) rule 18.14 (contents of final account (winding up) and final report (bankruptcy)).

NOTES

Commencement: 6 April 2017.
This rule derived from the Insolvency Rules 1986, SI 1986/1925, r 4.49F.

[6.863]

18.11 Voluntary winding up: reporting arrangement under section 110

(1) This rule applies where in a voluntary winding up there has been an arrangement under section 110 and a distribution to members has taken place under section 110(2) or (4).

(2) In any account or summary of receipts and payments which is required to be included in an account or report prepared under a section or rule listed in paragraph (3) the liquidator must—
(a) state the estimated value during the period to which the account or report relates of—
(i) the property transferred to the transferee,
(ii) the property received from the transferee, and
(iii) the property distributed to members under section 110(2) or (4); and
(b) provide details of the basis of the valuation as a note to the account or summary of receipts and payments.

(3) Paragraph (2) applies to the following—
(a) section 92A and rule 18.7 (members' voluntary winding up: progress report to company at year's end);
(b) section 94 and rule 18.14 (members' voluntary winding up: final account prior to dissolution);
(c) section 104A (creditors' voluntary winding up: progress report to company and creditors at year's end);
(d) section 106 and rules 6.28 and 18.14 (creditors' voluntary winding up: final account prior to dissolution).

NOTES

Commencement: 6 April 2017.
This rule derived from the Insolvency Rules 1986, SI 1986/1925, r 4.49F.

[6.864]

18.12 Members' voluntary winding up: reporting distribution to members other than under section 110

(1) This rule applies where in a members' voluntary winding up there has been a distribution of property to members in its existing form other than under an arrangement under section 110.

(2) In any account or summary of receipts and payments which is required to be included in an account or report prepared under a section or rule listed in paragraph (3) the liquidator must—
(a) state the estimated value of the property distributed to the members of the company during the period to which the account or report relates; and
(b) provide details of the basis of the valuation as a note to the account or summary of receipts and payments.

(3) Paragraph (2) applies to the following—
(a) section 92A (progress report);
(b) section 94 (final account prior to dissolution);
(c) rule 5.6 (liquidator's resignation).

NOTES

Commencement: 6 April 2017.
This rule derived from the Insolvency Rules 1986, SI 1986/1925, r 4.49G.

[6.865]

18.13 Bankruptcy proceedings: reporting distribution of property to creditors under section 326

(1) This rule applies in bankruptcy where there has been a distribution of property to creditors under section 326.

(2) In an account or report which the trustee is required to prepare under a section or rule listed in paragraph (3) the trustee must—
(a) state the estimated value of the property distributed among the creditors during the period to which the account or report relates; and
(b) provide details of the basis of the valuation in a note to the account or report.

(3) Paragraph (2) applies to the following—
(a) section 331 (final report to creditors in bankruptcy);
(b) rule 10.77 (consideration of appointment of replacement trustee); and
(c) Chapters 2 and 3 of this Part.

NOTES

Commencement: 6 April 2017.
This rule derived from the Insolvency Rules 1986, SI 1986/1925, r 6.78D.

CHAPTER 3 FINAL ACCOUNTS IN WINDING UP AND FINAL REPORTS IN BANKRUPTCY

[Note: a document required by the Act or these Rules must also contain the standard contents set out in Part 1.]

[6.866]
18.14 Contents of final account (winding up) and final report (bankruptcy)

(1) The liquidator's final account under section 94, 106 or 146 or the trustee's final report under section 331 must contain an account of the liquidator's administration of the winding up or of the trustee's administration of the bankruptcy including——
(a) a summary of the office-holder's receipts and payments, including details of the office-holder's remuneration and expenses; and
(b) details of the basis fixed for the office-holder's remuneration.

(2) The liquidator's final account under section 106 or 146(1)(a) must also include a statement as to the amount paid to unsecured creditors by virtue of section 176A.

(3) The final account or report to creditors or members must also contain—
(a) details of the remuneration charged and expenses incurred by the office-holder during the period since the last progress report (if any);
(b) a description of the things done by the office-holder in that period in respect of which the remuneration was charged and the expenses incurred; and
(c) a summary of the receipts and payments during that period.

(4) If the basis of the office-holder's remuneration had not been fixed by the date to which the last progress report was made up, the final account or report must also include details of the remuneration charged in the period of any preceding progress report in which details of remuneration were not included.

(5) Where the basis of remuneration has been fixed as a set amount, it is sufficient for the office-holder to state that amount and to give details of the expenses charged within the period in question.

NOTES

Commencement: 6 April 2017.
This rule derived from the Insolvency Rules 1986, SI 1986/1925, rr 4.125, 4.126, 4.126A, 4.49D, 6.78B.

CHAPTER 4 REMUNERATION AND EXPENSES IN ADMINISTRATION, WINDING UP AND BANKRUPTCY

[Note: a document required by the Act or these Rules must also contain the standard contents set out in Part 1.]

[6.867]
18.15 Application of Chapter

(1) This Chapter applies to the remuneration of—
(a) an administrator;
(a) a liquidator; and
(b) a trustee in bankruptcy.

(2) This Chapter does not apply to the remuneration of a provisional liquidator or an interim receiver.

NOTES

Commencement: 6 April 2017.

[6.868]
18.16 Remuneration: principles

(1) An administrator, liquidator or trustee in bankruptcy is entitled to receive remuneration for services as office-holder.

(2) The basis of remuneration must be fixed—
(a) as a percentage of the value of—
(i) the property with which the administrator has to deal, or
(ii) the assets which are realised, distributed or both realised and distributed by the liquidator or trustee;
(b) by reference to the time properly given by the office-holder and the office-holder's staff in attending to matters arising in the administration, winding up or bankruptcy; or
(c) as a set amount.

(3) The basis of remuneration may be one or a combination of the bases set out in paragraph (2) and different bases or percentages may be fixed in respect of different things done by the office-holder.

(4) Where an office-holder, other than in a members' voluntary winding up, proposes to take all or any part of the remuneration on the basis set out in paragraph (2)(b), the office-holder must, prior to the determination of which of the bases set out in paragraph (2) are to be fixed, deliver to the creditors—
(a) a fees estimate; and
(b) details of the expenses the office-holder considers will be, or are likely to be, incurred.

(5) The fees estimate and details of expenses given under paragraph (4) may include remuneration expected to be charged and expenses expected to be incurred if the administrator becomes the liquidator where the administration moves into winding up.

(6) An office-holder, other than in a members' voluntary winding up, must deliver to the creditors the information required under paragraph (7) before the determination of which of the bases set out in paragraph (2) is or are to be fixed, unless the information has already been delivered under paragraph (4).

(7) The information the office-holder is required to give under this paragraph is—

(a) the work the office-holder proposes to undertake; and

(b) details of the expenses the office-holder considers will be, or are likely to be, incurred.

(8) The matters to be determined in fixing the basis of remuneration are—

(a) which of the bases set out in paragraph (2) is or are to be fixed and (where appropriate) in what combination;

(b) the percentage or percentages (if any) to be fixed under paragraphs (2)(a) and (3);

(c) the amount (if any) to be set under paragraph (2)(c).

(9) In arriving at that determination, regard must be had to the following—

(a) the complexity (or otherwise) of the case;

(b) any respects in which, in connection with the company's or bankrupt's affairs, there falls on the office-holder, any responsibility of an exceptional kind or degree;

(c) the effectiveness with which the office-holder appears to be carrying out, or to have carried out, the office-holder's duties; and

(d) the value and nature of the property with which the office-holder has to deal.

(10) A proposed liquidator in respect of a creditors' voluntary winding up may deliver to the creditors the information required by paragraphs (4) or (6) before becoming liquidator in which case that person is not required to deliver that information again if that person is appointed as liquidator.

NOTES

Commencement: 6 April 2017.

This rule derived from the Insolvency Rules 1986, SI 1986/1925, rr 2.106, 4.127, 4.418A, 6.138.

[6.869]

18.17 Remuneration of joint office-holders

Where there are joint office-holders it is for them to agree between themselves how the remuneration payable should be apportioned; and any dispute arising between them may be referred—

(a) to the committee, to the creditors (by a decision procedure) or (in a members' voluntary winding up) the company in general meeting, for settlement by resolution; or

(b) to the court, for settlement by order.

NOTES

Commencement: 6 April 2017.

This rule derived from the Insolvency Rules 1986, SI 1986/1925, rr 2.106(7), 4.128(2), 6.139(2).

[6.870]

18.18 Remuneration: procedure for initial determination in an administration

(1) This rule applies to the determination of the officer-holder's remuneration in an administration.

(2) It is for the committee to determine the basis of remuneration.

(3) If the committee fails to determine the basis of the remuneration or there is no committee then the basis of remuneration must be fixed by a decision of the creditors by a decision procedure [except in a case under paragraph (4)].

(4) Where the administrator has made a statement under paragraph 52(1)(b) of Schedule B1 that there are insufficient funds for distribution to unsecured creditors other than out of the prescribed part and either there is no committee, or the committee fails to determine the basis of remuneration, the basis of the administrator's remuneration may be fixed by—

(a) the consent of each of the secured creditors; or

(b) if the administrator has made or intends to make a distribution to preferential creditors—

(i) the consent of each of the secured creditors, and

(ii) a decision of the preferential creditors in a decision procedure.

NOTES

Commencement: 6 April 2017.

This rule derived from the Insolvency Rules 1986, SI 1986/1925, rr 2.106, 2.106(5A).

Para (3): words in square brackets added by the Insolvency (England and Wales) (Amendment) Rules 2017, SI 2017/366, rr 3, 44.

[6.871]

18.19 Remuneration: procedure for initial determination in a members' voluntary winding up

In a members' voluntary winding up, it is for the company in general meeting to determine the basis of remuneration.

NOTES

Commencement: 6 April 2017.

[6.872]

18.20 Remuneration: procedure for initial determination in a creditors' voluntary winding up or a winding up by the court

(1) This rule applies to the determination of the office-holder's remuneration in a creditors' voluntary winding up or a winding up by the court.

(2) It is for the committee to determine the basis of remuneration.

(3) If the committee fails to determine the basis of remuneration or there is no committee then the basis of remuneration may be fixed by a decision of the creditors by a decision procedure.

(4) However where an administrator becomes liquidator in either of the following two cases the basis of remuneration fixed under rule 18.18 for the administrator is treated as having been fixed for the liquidator, and paragraphs (2) and (3) do not apply.

(5) The two cases are where—

(a) a company which is in administration moves into winding up under paragraph 83 of Schedule B1 and the administrator becomes the liquidator; and

(b) a winding-up order is made immediately upon the appointment of an administrator ceasing to have effect and the court under section 140(1) appoints as liquidator the person whose appointment as administrator has ceased to have effect.

NOTES

Commencement: 6 April 2017.

This rule derived from the Insolvency Rules 1986, SI 1986/1925, r 4.127.

[6.873]

18.21 Remuneration: procedure for initial determination in a bankruptcy

(1) This rule applies to the determination of the office-holder's remuneration in a bankruptcy.

(2) It is for the committee to determine the basis of remuneration.

(3) If the committee fails to determine the basis of the remuneration or there is no committee then the basis of the remuneration may be fixed by a decision of the creditors by a decision procedure.

NOTES

Commencement: 6 April 2017.

This rule derived from the Insolvency Rules 1986, SI 1986/1925, r 6.138.

[6.874]

18.22 Application of scale fees where creditors fail to fix the basis of the office-holder's remuneration

(1) This rule applies where in a winding up by the court or bankruptcy, the liquidator or trustee—

(a) has requested the creditors to fix the basis of remuneration under rule 18.20(3) or 18.21(3) as applicable and the creditors have not done so; or

(b) in any event if the basis of remuneration is not fixed by the creditors within 18 months after the date of the liquidator's or trustee's appointment.

(2) The liquidator or trustee is entitled to such sum as is arrived at (subject to paragraph (3)) by—

(a) applying the realisation scale set out in Schedule 11 to the moneys received by the liquidator or trustee from the realisation of the assets of the company or bankrupt (including any Value Added Tax on the realisation but after deducting any sums paid to secured creditors in respect of their securities and any sums spent out of money received in carrying on the business of the company or bankrupt); and

(b) adding to the sum arrived at under sub-paragraph (a) such sum as is arrived at by applying the distribution scale set out in Schedule 11 to the value of assets distributed to creditors of the company or bankrupt (including payments made in respect of preferential debts) and to contributories.

(3) In a bankruptcy that part of the trustee's remuneration calculated under paragraph (2) by reference to the realisation scale must not exceed such sum as is arrived at by applying the realisation scale to such part of the bankrupt's assets as are required to pay—

(a) the bankruptcy debts (including any interest payable by virtue of section 328(4)) to the extent required to be paid by these Rules (ignoring those debts paid otherwise than out of the proceeds of the realisation of the bankrupt's assets or which have been secured to the satisfaction of the court);

(b) the expenses of the bankruptcy other than—

(i) fees or the remuneration of the official receiver, and

(ii) any sums spent out of money received in carrying on the business of the bankrupt;

(c) fees payable by virtue of any order made under section 415; and

(d) the remuneration of the official receiver.

NOTES

Commencement: 6 April 2017.

This rule derived from the Insolvency Rules 1986, SI 1986/1925, rr 4.127A, 6.138A.

[6.875]

18.23 Remuneration: application to the court to fix the basis

(1) If the basis of the administrator's remuneration or the liquidator's remuneration in a voluntary winding up is not fixed under rules 18.18 to 18.20 (as applicable) then the administrator or liquidator must apply to the court for it to be fixed.

(2) Before making such an application the liquidator or administrator must attempt to fix the basis in accordance with rules 18.18 to 18.20.

(3) An application under this rule may not be made more than 18 months after the date of the administrator's or liquidator's appointment.

(4) In a members' voluntary winding up—

- (a) the liquidator must deliver at least 14 days' notice of such an application to the company's contributories, or such one or more of them as the court may direct; and
- (b) the contributories may nominate one or more of their number to appear, or be represented, and to be heard on the application.

NOTES

Commencement: 6 April 2017.

This rule derived from the Insolvency Rules 1986, SI 1986/1925, rr 2.106(6), 4.127(7), 4.148A(6).

[6.876]

18.24 Remuneration: administrator, liquidator or trustee seeking increase etc

An office-holder who considers the rate or amount of remuneration fixed to be insufficient or the basis fixed to be inappropriate may—

- (a) request the creditors to increase the rate or amount or change the basis in accordance with rules 18.25 to 18.27;
- (b) apply to the court for an order increasing the rate or amount or changing the basis in accordance with rule 18.28.

NOTES

Commencement: 6 April 2017.

This rule derived from the Insolvency Rules 1986, SI 1986/1925, rr 2.17, 4.129A, 6.140A.

[6.877]

18.25 Application for an increase etc in remuneration: the general rule

(1) This rule applies to a request by an office-holder in accordance with rule 18.24 for an increase in the rate or amount of remuneration or a change in the basis.

(2) Subject to the exceptions set out in rules 18.26 and 18.27, where the basis of the office-holder's remuneration has been fixed by the committee an administrator, liquidator or trustee may make such a request to the creditors for approval by a decision procedure.

NOTES

Commencement: 6 April 2017.

This rule derived from the Insolvency Rules 1986, SI 1986/1925, rr 2.107(1), 4.129A, 6.140A.

[6.878]

18.26 First exception: administrator has made a statement under paragraph 52(1)(b) of Schedule B1

(1) This exception applies in an administration where—

- (a) the basis of the administrator's remuneration has been fixed by the committee; and
- (b) the administrator has made a statement under paragraph 52(1)(b) of Schedule B1.

(2) A request by the administrator for an increase in the rate or amount of remuneration or a change in the basis must be approved by—

- (a) the consent of each of the secured creditors; or
- (b) if the administrator has made or intends to make a distribution to preferential creditors—
  - (i) the consent of each of the secured creditors, and
  - (ii) a decision of the preferential creditors in a decision procedure.

NOTES

Commencement: 6 April 2017.

This rule derived from the Insolvency Rules 1986, SI 1986/1925, r 2.107(2).

[6.879]

18.27 Second exception: administrator who had applied for increase etc under rule 18.24 becomes liquidator

(1) This exception applies in a liquidation where—

- (a) an administrator has become the liquidator;
- (b) the remuneration had been determined by the committee in the preceding administration;
- (c) the basis of the liquidator's remuneration is treated under rule 18.20(4) and (5) as being that which was fixed in the administration; and
- (d) the administrator had subsequently requested an increase under rule 18.24.

(2) A request by the liquidator for an increase in the rate or amount of remuneration or a change in the basis may only be made by application to the court.

(3) Rule 18.28(6) to (8) apply to such an application.

NOTES

Commencement: 6 April 2017.

This rule derived from the Insolvency Rules 1986, SI 1986/1925, r 4.127(5A).

[6.880]

18.28 Remuneration: recourse by administrator, liquidator or trustee to the court

(1) This rule applies to an application by an office-holder to the court in accordance with rule 18.24 for an increase in the rate or amount of remuneration or change in the basis.

(2) An administrator may make such an application where the basis of the administrator's remuneration has been fixed—

- (a) by the committee and the administrator has requested that the rate or amount be increased or the basis changed by decision of the creditors (by a decision procedure), but the creditors have not changed it;
- (b) by decision of the creditors (by decision procedure); or
- (c) by the approval of either the secured creditors or the preferential creditors or both in a case where the administrator has made a statement under paragraph 52(1)(b) of Schedule B1.

(3) A liquidator may make such an application where the basis of the liquidator's remuneration has been fixed—

- (a) by the committee, and the liquidator has requested that the rate or amount be increased or the basis changed by decision of the creditors (by a decision procedure), but the creditors have not changed it;
- (b) by decision of the creditors (by a decision procedure);
- (c) under rule 18.20(4) and (5) or 18.22; or
- (d) in a members' voluntary winding up, by the company in general meeting.

(4) A trustee may make such an application where the trustee's remuneration has been fixed—

- (a) by the committee and the trustee has requested that the amount be increased or the basis changed by decision of the creditors (by a decision procedure), but the creditors have not changed it;
- (b) by decision of the creditors (by a decision procedure); or
- (c) under rule 18.22.

(5) Where an application is made under paragraph (2)(c), the administrator must deliver notice to each of the creditors whose approval was sought under rule 18.18(4).

(6) The office-holder must deliver a notice of the application at least 14 days before the hearing as follows—

- (a) in an administration, a creditors' voluntary winding up, a winding up by the court or a bankruptcy—
  - (i) to the members of the committee, or
  - (ii) if there is no committee to such one or more of the creditors as the court may direct;
- (b) in a members' voluntary winding up, to the company's contributories, or such one or more of them as the court may direct.

(7) The committee, the creditors or the contributories (as the case may be) may nominate one or more of their number to appear or be represented and to be heard on the application.

(8) The court may, if it appears to be a proper case (including in a members' voluntary winding up), order the costs of the office-holder's application, including the costs of any member of the committee appearing or being represented on it, or of any creditor or contributory so appearing or being represented on it, to be paid as an expense of the estate.

NOTES

Commencement: 6 April 2017.

This rule derived from the Insolvency Rules 1986, SI 1986/1925, rr 2.108, 4.130, 6.141.

[6.881]

18.29 Remuneration: review at request of administrator, liquidator or trustee

(1) Where, after the basis of the office-holder's remuneration has been fixed, there is a material and substantial change in the circumstances which were taken into account in fixing it, the office-holder may request that the basis be changed.

(2) The request must be made—

- (a) to the company, where in a members' voluntary liquidation the company fixed the basis in general meeting;
- (b) to the committee, where the committee fixed the basis;
- (c) to the creditors or a particular class of creditors where the creditors or that class of creditors fixed the basis;
- (d) by application to the court, where the court fixed the basis;
- (e) to the committee if there is one and otherwise to the creditors where, in a winding up or bankruptcy, the remuneration was determined under rule 18.22.

(3) The preceding provisions of this Chapter which apply to the fixing of the office-holder's remuneration apply to a request for a change as appropriate.

(4) However the exception in rule 18.27 which would require such an application to be made to the court in the circumstances there set out does not apply.

(5) Any change in the basis of remuneration applies from the date of the request under paragraph (2) and not for any earlier period.

NOTES

Commencement: 6 April 2017.

This rule derived from the Insolvency Rules 1986, SI 1986/1925, rr 2.109A, 4.131A, 6.142A.

[6.882]

18.30 Remuneration: exceeding the fee estimate

(1) The office-holder must not draw remuneration in excess of the total amount set out in the fees estimate without approval.

(2) The request for approval must be made—

(a) where the committee fixed the basis, to that committee;

(b) where the creditors or a class of creditors fixed the basis, to the creditors or that class of creditors;

(c) where the court fixed the basis, to the court;

and rules 18.16 to 18.23 apply as appropriate.

(3) The request for approval must specify—

(a) the reasons why the office-holder has exceeded, or is likely to exceed, the fees estimate;

(b) the additional work the office-holder has undertaken or proposes to undertake;

(c) the hourly rate or rates the office-holder proposes to charge for each part of that additional work;

(d) the time that additional work has taken or the office-holder expects that work will take;

(e) whether the office-holder anticipates that it will be necessary to seek further approval; and

(f) the reasons it will be necessary to seek further approval.

NOTES

Commencement: 6 April 2017.

This rule derived from the Insolvency Rules 1986, SI 1986/1925, rr 2.109AB, 4.131AB, 6.142AB.

[6.883]

18.31 Remuneration: new administrator, liquidator or trustee

(1) This rule applies where a new administrator, liquidator or trustee is appointed in place of another.

(2) Any decision, determination, resolution or court order in effect under the preceding provisions of this Chapter immediately before the former office-holder ceased to hold office (including any application of scale fees under rule 18.22) continues to apply in relation to the remuneration of the new office-holder until a further decision, determination, resolution or court order is made in accordance with those provisions.

NOTES

Commencement: 6 April 2017.

This rule derived from the Insolvency Rules 1986, SI 1986/1925, rr 2.109B, 4.131B, 4.148D, 6.142B.

[6.884]

18.32 Remuneration: apportionment of set fees

(1) This rule applies where the basis of the office-holder's remuneration is a set amount under rule 18.16(2)(c) and the office-holder ceases (for whatever reason) to hold office before the time has elapsed or the work has been completed in respect of which the amount was set.

(2) A request or application may be made to determine what portion of the amount should be paid to the former office-holder or the former office-holder's personal representative in respect of the time which has actually elapsed or the work which has actually been done.

(3) The request or application may be made by—

(a) the former office-holder or the former office-holder's personal representative within the period of 28 days beginning with the date upon which the former office-holder ceased to hold office; or

(b) the office-holder for the time being in office, if the former office-holder or the former office-holder's personal representative has not applied by the end of that period.

(4) The request or application to determine the portion must be made to the relevant person being—

(a) the company, where the company is in members' voluntary liquidation and it fixed the basis in general meeting;

(b) the committee, where the committee fixed the basis;

(c) the creditors or a class of creditors where the creditors or that class fixed the basis;

(d) the court where the court fixed the basis.

(5) In an administration where the circumstances set out in rule 18.18(4) apply the relevant person is to be determined under that paragraph.

(6) The person making the request or application must deliver a copy of it to the office-holder for the time being or to the former office-holder or the former office-holder's personal representative, as the case may be ("the recipient").

(7) The recipient may, within 21 days of receipt of the copy of the request or application, deliver notice of intent to make representations to the relevant person or to appear or be represented before the court on an application to the court.

(8) No determination may be made upon the request or application until either—
- (a) the expiry of the 21 days, or
- (b) if the recipient delivers a notice of intent, the recipient has been given the opportunity to make representations or to appear or be represented.

(9) Where the former office-holder or the former office-holder's personal representative (whether or not the original person making the request or application) considers that the portion so determined is insufficient that person may apply—
- (a) to the creditors for a decision increasing the portion, in the case of a determination by the committee;
- (b) to the court, in the case of a decision or resolution (as the case may be) of—
  - (i) the creditors (whether under paragraph (4)(c) or under sub-paragraph (a)), or
  - (ii) the company in general meeting.

(10) Paragraphs (6) to (8) apply to an application under paragraph (9) as appropriate.

NOTES

Commencement: 6 April 2017.

This rule derived from the Insolvency Rules 1986, SI 1986/1925, rr 2.109C, 4.131C, 4148E, 6.142C.

[6.885]
18.33 Remuneration: variation of the application of rules 18.29, 18.30 and 18.32

(1) This rule applies where the basis of remuneration has been fixed in accordance with rule 18.18(4) and all of the following apply—
- (a) there is now, or is likely to be, sufficient property to enable a distribution to be made to unsecured creditors other than by virtue of section 176A(2)(a); and
- (b) the administrator or liquidator in a winding up which immediately follows an administration makes a request under rule 18.29, 18.30 or 18.32.

(2) A request under 18.29, 18.30 or 18.32, must be made—
- (a) where there is a committee, to the committee; or
- (b) where there is no committee, to the creditors for a decision by decision procedure.

NOTES

Commencement: 6 April 2017.

This rule derived from the Insolvency Rules 1986, SI 1986/1925, rr 2.109D, 4.131D.

[6.886]
18.34 Remuneration and expenses: application to court by a creditor or member on grounds that remuneration or expenses are excessive

(1) This rule applies to an application in an administration, a winding-up or a bankruptcy made by a person mentioned in paragraph (2) on the grounds that—
- (a) the remuneration charged by the office-holder is in all the circumstances excessive;
- (b) the basis fixed for the office-holder's remuneration under rules 18.16, 18.18, 18.19, 18.20 and 18.21 (as applicable) is inappropriate; or
- (c) the expenses incurred by the office-holder are in all the circumstances excessive.

(2) The following may make such an application for one or more of the orders set out in rule 18.36 or 18.37 as applicable—
- (a) a secured creditor,
- (b) an unsecured creditor with either—
  - (i) the concurrence of at least 10% in value of the unsecured creditors (including that creditor), or
  - (ii) the permission of the court, or
- (c) in a members' voluntary winding up—
  - (i) members of the company with at least 10% of the total voting rights of all the members having the right to vote at general meetings of the company, or
  - (ii) a member of the company with the permission of the court.

(3) The application by a creditor or member must be made no later than eight weeks after receipt by the applicant of the progress report under rule 18.3, or final report or account under rule 18.14 which first reports the charging of the remuneration or the incurring of the expenses in question ("the relevant report").

NOTES

Commencement: 6 April 2017.

This rule derived from the Insolvency Rules 1986, SI 1986/1925, rr 2.109, 4.131, 4.148C, 6.142.

[6.887]
18.35 Remuneration and expenses: application to court by a bankrupt on grounds that remuneration or expenses are excessive

[Note: where a bankrupt is applying for an annulment under section 282(1)(b) the bankrupt may also make an application in respect of the trustee's remuneration or expenses. See rule 10.134.]

(1) A bankrupt may, with the permission of the court, make an application on the grounds that—
  (a) the remuneration charged by the office-holder is in all the circumstances excessive;
  (b) the expenses incurred by the office-holder are in all the circumstances excessive.

(2) The bankrupt may make such an application for one or more of the orders set out in rule 18.36(4).

(3) The application must be made no later than eight weeks after receipt by the bankrupt of the report under rule 10.87.

(4) The court must not give the bankrupt permission to make an application unless the bankrupt shows that—
  (a) there is (or would be but for the remuneration or expenses in question); or
  (b) it is likely that there will be (or would be but for the remuneration or expenses in question),

a surplus of assets to which the bankrupt would be entitled.

(5) Paragraph (4) is without prejudice to the generality of the matters which the court may take into account in determining whether to give the bankrupt permission.

NOTES

Commencement: 6 April 2017.

This rule derived from the Insolvency Rules 1986, SI 1986/1925, r 6.142.

[6.888]

18.36 Applications under rules 18.34 and 18.35 where the court has given permission for the application

(1) This rule applies to applications made with permission under rules 18.34 and 18.35.

(2) Where the court has given permission, it must fix a venue for the application to be heard.

(3) The applicant must, at least 14 days before the hearing, deliver to the office-holder a notice stating the venue and accompanied by a copy of the application and of any evidence on which the applicant intends to rely.

(4) If the court considers the application to be well-founded, it must make one or more of the following orders—
  (a) an order reducing the amount of remuneration which the office-holder is entitled to charge;
  (b) an order reducing any fixed rate or amount;
  (c) an order changing the basis of remuneration;
  (d) an order that some or all of the remuneration or expenses in question is not to be treated as expenses of the administration, winding up or bankruptcy;
  (e) an order for the payment of the amount of the excess of remuneration or expenses or such part of the excess as the court may specify by—
    (i) the administrator or liquidator or the administrator's or liquidator's personal representative to the company, or
    (ii) the trustee or the trustee's personal representative to such person as the court may specify as property comprised in the bankrupt's estate;
  (f) any other order that it thinks just.

(5) An order under paragraph (4)(b) or (c) may only be made in respect of periods after the period covered by the relevant report.

(6) Unless the court orders otherwise the costs of the application must be paid by the applicant, and are not payable as an expense of the administration, winding up or bankruptcy.

NOTES

Commencement: 6 April 2017.

This rule derived from the Insolvency Rules 1986, SI 1986/1925, rr 2.109, 4.131, 4.148C, 6.142.

[6.889]

18.37 Applications under rule 18.34 where the court's permission is not required for the application

(1) On receipt of an application under rule 18.34 for which the court's permission is not required, the court may, if it is satisfied that no sufficient cause is shown for the application, dismiss it without giving notice to any party other than the applicant.

(2) Unless the application is dismissed, the court must fix a venue for it to be heard.

(3) The applicant must, at least 14 days before any hearing, deliver to the office-holder a notice stating the venue with a copy of the application and of any evidence on which the applicant intends to rely.

(4) If the court considers the application to be well-founded, it must make one or more of the following orders—
  (a) an order reducing the amount of remuneration which the office-holder is entitled to charge;
  (b) an order reducing any fixed rate or amount;
  (c) an order changing the basis of remuneration;
  (d) an order that some or all of the remuneration or expenses in question be treated as not being expenses of the administration or winding up or bankruptcy;
  (e) an order for the payment of the amount of the excess of remuneration or expenses or such part of the excess as the court may specify by—
    (i) the administrator or liquidator or the administrator's or liquidator's personal representative to the company, or

(ii) the trustee or the trustee's personal representative to such person as the court may specify as property comprised in the bankrupt's estate;

(f) any other order that it thinks just.

(5) An order under paragraph (4)(b) or (c) may only be made in respect of periods after the period covered by the relevant report.

(6) Unless the court orders otherwise the costs of the application must be paid by the applicant, and are not payable as an expense of the administration or as winding up or bankruptcy.

NOTES

Commencement: 6 April 2017.

This rule derived from the Insolvency Rules 1986, SI 1986/1925, rr 2.109, 4.131, 4.148C, 6.142.

[6.890]

18.38 Remuneration of a liquidator or trustee who realises assets on behalf of a secured creditor

(1) A liquidator or trustee who realises assets on behalf of a secured creditor is entitled to such sum by way of remuneration as is arrived at as follows, unless the liquidator or trustee has agreed otherwise with the secured creditor—

(a) in a winding up—

(i) where the assets are subject to a charge which when created was a mortgage or a fixed charge, such sum as is arrived at by applying the realisation scale in Schedule 11 to the monies received in respect of the assets realised (including any sums received in respect of Value Added Tax on them but after deducting any sums spent out of money received in carrying on the business of the company),

(ii) where the assets are subject to a charge which when created was a floating charge such sum as is arrived at by—

(aa) first applying the realisation scale in Schedule 11 to monies received by the liquidator from the realisation of the assets (including any Value Added Tax on the realisation but ignoring any sums received which are spent in carrying on the business of the company),

(bb) then by adding to the sum arrived at under sub-paragraph (a)(ii)(aa) such sum as is arrived at by applying the distribution scale in Schedule 11 to the value of the assets distributed to the holder of the charge and payments made in respect of preferential debts; or

(b) in a bankruptcy such sum as is arrived at by applying the realisation scale in Schedule 11 to the monies received in respect of the assets realised (including any Value Added Tax on them).

(2) The sum to which the liquidator or trustee is entitled must be taken out of the proceeds of the realisation.

NOTES

Commencement: 6 April 2017.

This rule derived from the Insolvency Rules 1986, SI 1986/1925, rr 4.127B, 6.139.

PART 19
DISCLAIMER IN WINDING UP AND BANKRUPTCY

[Note: a document required by the Act or these Rules must also contain the standard contents set out in Part 1.]

[6.891]

19.1 Application of this Part

This Part applies to disclaimer by a liquidator under section 178 (winding up) and by a trustee under section 315 (bankruptcy).

NOTES

Commencement: 6 April 2017.

This rule derived from the Insolvency Rules 1986, SI 1986/1925, rr 4.187, 6.178.

[6.892]

19.2 Notice of disclaimer (sections 178 and 315)

(1) An office-holder's notice of disclaimer of property under section 178 (winding up) or section 315 (bankruptcy) must (as appropriate)—

(a) have the title—

(i) "Notice of disclaimer under section 178 of the Insolvency Act 1986" (in the case of a winding up), or

(ii) "Notice of disclaimer under section 315 of the Insolvency Act 1986" (in the case of a bankruptcy);

(b) identify the company or the bankrupt;

(c) identify and provide contact details for the office-holder;

(d) contain such particulars of the property disclaimed as will enable it to be easily identified;

(e) state—

(i) that the liquidator of the company disclaims all the company's interest in the property, or

Part 6 Insolvency Rules

(ii) that the trustee of the bankrupt's estate disclaims all the bankrupt's interest in the property.

(2) The notice must be authenticated and dated by the office-holder.

(3) If the property consists of registered land—

(a) the notice must state the registered title number; and

(b) the office-holder must deliver a copy of the notice to the Chief Land Registrar as soon as reasonably practicable after authenticating the notice.

(4) The liquidator must, as soon as reasonably practicable after authenticating the notice, deliver a copy of the notice to the registrar of companies.

(5) The trustee must, as soon as reasonably practicable after authenticating the notice, file a copy of the notice—

(a) with the court; or

(b) where the bankruptcy is based on a bankruptcy application, on the bankruptcy file.

(6) If the property consists of land or buildings the nature of the interest must be stated in the notice.

(7) The date of disclaimer for the purposes of section 178(4)(a) (winding up) or section 315(3)(a) (bankruptcy) is the date on which the liquidator or trustee authenticated the notice.

NOTES

Commencement: 6 April 2017.

This rule derived from the Insolvency Rules 1986, SI 1986/1925, rr 4.187, 6.178.

[6.893]

19.3 Notice of disclaimer to interested persons (sections 178 and 315)

(1) The office-holder must deliver a copy of the notice of disclaimer within seven business days after the date of the notice to every person who (to the office-holder's knowledge)—

(a) claims an interest in the disclaimed property;

(b) is under any liability in relation to the property, not being a liability discharged by the disclaimer; and

(c) if the disclaimer is of an unprofitable contract, is a party to the contract or has an interest under it.

(2) If it subsequently comes to the office-holder's knowledge that a person has an interest in the disclaimed property which would have entitled that person to receive a copy of the notice under paragraph (1) then the office-holder must deliver a copy to that person as soon as reasonably practicable.

(3) If it subsequently comes to the office-holder's knowledge that a person has an interest in the disclaimed property which would have entitled that person to receive a copy of the notice under rule 19.4 or 19.5 then the office-holder must serve a copy on that person as soon as reasonably practicable.

(4) The office-holder is not required to deliver or serve a copy of a notice under paragraph (2) or (3) if—

(a) the office-holder is satisfied that the person has already been made aware of the disclaimer and its date, or

(b) the court, on the office-holder's application, orders that delivery or service of a copy is not required in the particular case.

NOTES

Commencement: 6 April 2017.

This rule derived from the Insolvency Rules 1986, SI 1986/1925, rr 4.188, 6.179.

[6.894]

19.4 Notice of disclaimer of leasehold property (sections 179 and 317)

Where a notice of disclaimer relates to leasehold property the office-holder must serve any copies of the notice of disclaimer which are required by either section 179 (winding up) or section 317 (bankruptcy) within seven business days after the date of the notice of disclaimer.

NOTES

Commencement: 6 April 2017.

This rule derived from the Insolvency Rules 1986, SI 1986/1925, rr 4.188(2), 6.179(2).

[6.895]

19.5 Notice of disclaimer in respect of a dwelling house (bankruptcy) (section 318)

(1) This rule applies in a bankruptcy where the disclaimer is of property in a dwelling house.

(2) The trustee must serve any copies of the notice of disclaimer which are required by section 318 within seven business days after the date of the notice of disclaimer.

(3) A notice, or copy notice in relation to the disclaimer by a trustee of property in a dwelling house which is to be served on a person under the age of 18 may be served on the person's parent or guardian.

NOTES

Commencement: 6 April 2017.

This rule derived from the Insolvency Rules 1986, SI 1986/1925, r 6.179(3), (4).

[6.896]
19.6 Additional notices of disclaimer

An office-holder who is disclaiming property may at any time deliver a copy of the notice of the disclaimer to any other person whom the office-holder thinks ought, in the public interest or otherwise, to be informed of the disclaimer.

NOTES

Commencement: 6 April 2017.
This rule derived from the Insolvency Rules 1986, SI 1986/1925, rr 4.189, 6.180.

[6.897]
19.7 Records

The office-holder must include in the records of the insolvency a record of—

(a) the name and address of each person to whom a copy of the notice of disclaimer has been delivered or served under rules 19.3 to 19.6, with the nature of the person's interest;
(b) the date on which the copy of the notice was delivered to or served on that person;
(c) the date on which the liquidator delivered a copy of the notice to the registrar of companies;
(d) the date on which the trustee filed a copy of the notice with the court or on the bankruptcy file; and
(e) if applicable, the date on which a copy of the notice was delivered to the Chief Land Registrar.

NOTES

Commencement: 6 April 2017.
This rule derived from the Insolvency Rules 1986, SI 1986/1925, rr 4.190A, 6.181A.

[6.898]
19.8 Application for permission to disclaim in bankruptcy (section 315(4))

(1) This rule applies where section 315(4) requires the trustee to obtain the court's permission to disclaim property claimed for the bankrupt's estate under section 307 or 308.

(2) The trustee may apply for permission without notice to any other party.

(3) The application must be accompanied by a report—

(a) containing such particulars of the property as will enable it to be easily identified;
(b) setting out the reasons why, the property having been claimed for the bankrupt's estate, the trustee is now applying for the court's permission to disclaim it; and
(c) stating the persons (if any) who have been informed of the trustee's intention to make the application.

(4) If the report says that any person has consented to the disclaimer, a copy of that consent must accompany the report.

(5) The court may grant the permission, and may, before doing so—

(a) order that notice of the application be delivered to all such persons who, if the property is disclaimed, will be entitled to apply for a vesting or other order under section 320; and
(b) fix a venue for the hearing of the application.

NOTES

Commencement: 6 April 2017.
This rule derived from the Insolvency Rules 1986, SI 1986/1925, r 6.182.

[6.899]
19.9 Application by interested party for decision on disclaimer (sections 178(5) and 316)

(1) This rule applies where an interested party makes an application under section 178(5) (winding up) or section 316 (bankruptcy) to the office-holder in respect of any property.

(2) The applicant must deliver the application to the office-holder and must provide proof of delivery in accordance with rule 1.52 if requested.

(3) If in a bankruptcy the trustee cannot disclaim the property concerned without the court's permission and the trustee applies for permission within the period of 28 days mentioned in section 316(1)(b), then the court must extend the time allowed for giving notice of disclaimer to a date not earlier than the date fixed for hearing the application.

NOTES

Commencement: 6 April 2017.
This rule derived from the Insolvency Rules 1986, SI 1986/1925, rr 4.191A, 6.183.

[6.900]
19.10 Disclaimer presumed valid and effective

Any disclaimer of property by the office-holder is presumed valid and effective, unless it is proved that the office-holder has been in breach of the office-holder's duties relating to the giving of notice of disclaimer or otherwise under sections 178 to 180 (winding up) or sections 315 to 319 (bankruptcy), or under this Part.

NOTES

Commencement: 6 April 2017.

This rule derived from the Insolvency Rules 1986, SI 1986/1925, rr 4.193, 6.185.

[6.901]

19.11 Application for exercise of court's powers under section 181 (winding up) or section 320 (bankruptcy)

(1) This rule applies to an application under section 181 (winding up) or section 320 (bankruptcy) for a court order to vest or deliver disclaimed property.

(2) The application must be made within three months of the applicant becoming aware of the disclaimer, or of the applicant receiving a copy of the office-holder's notice of disclaimer delivered under rule 19.3 to 19.6, whichever is the earlier.

(3) The applicant must file with the application a witness statement stating—

(a) whether the application is made under—

(i) section 181(2)(a) (claim of interest in the property),

(ii) section 181(2)(b) (liability not discharged),

(iii) section 320(2)(a) (claim of interest in the property),

(iv) section 320(2)(b) (liability not discharged), or

(v) section 320(2)(c) (occupation of a dwelling-house);

(b) the date on which the applicant received a copy of the office-holder's notice of disclaimer, or otherwise became aware of the disclaimer; and

(c) the grounds of the application and the order sought.

(4) The court must fix a venue for hearing the application.

(5) The applicant must, not later than five business days before the date fixed, deliver to the office-holder notice of the venue, accompanied by copies of the application and the filed witness statement.

(6) On hearing the application, the court may give directions as to any other persons to whom notice of the application and the grounds on which it is made should be delivered.

(7) The court must deliver sealed copies of any order made on the application to the applicant and the office-holder.

(8) If the property disclaimed is of a leasehold nature, or in a bankruptcy is property in a dwelling house, and section 179 (winding up), 317 or 318 (bankruptcy) applies to suspend the effect of the disclaimer, the court's order must include a direction giving effect to the disclaimer.

(9) However, paragraph (8) does not apply if, before the order is drawn up, other applications under section 181 (winding up) or section 320 (bankruptcy) are pending in relation to the same property.

NOTES

Commencement: 6 April 2017.

This rule derived from the Insolvency Rules 1986, SI 1986/1925, rr 4.194, 6.186.

PART 20
DEBTORS AND THEIR FAMILIES AT RISK OF VIOLENCE: ORDERS NOT TO DISCLOSE CURRENT ADDRESS

[Note: a document required by the Act or these Rules must also contain the standard contents set out in Part 1.]

[6.902]

20.1 Application of this Part and interpretation

(1) The rules in this Part apply where disclosure or continuing disclosure of the current address or whereabouts of a debtor to other persons (whether to the public generally or to specific persons) might reasonably be expected to lead to violence against the debtor or against a person who normally resides with the debtor as a member of the debtor's family.

(2) In this Part—

"current address" means the debtor's residential address and any address at which the debtor currently carries on business; and

"family" in the expression "debtor's family" has the same meaning in relation to a debtor other than a bankrupt as is provided by section 385(1) in respect of a bankrupt.

NOTES

Commencement: 6 April 2017.

This rule derived from the Insolvency Rules 1986, SI 1986/1925, rr 5.67(2), 5A.18(1), 6.235B(2).

[6.903]

20.2 Proposed IVA (order for non-disclosure of current address)

(1) This rule applies where a debtor intends to make a proposal for an IVA and has received notice of consent to act from the nominee.

(2) The debtor may make an application for an order as set out in paragraph (4) for the non-disclosure of the debtor's current address.

(3) The application must be accompanied by a witness statement referring to this rule and containing sufficient evidence to satisfy the court that rule 20.1(1) applies.

(4) If the court is satisfied that the circumstances set out in rule 20.1(1) apply, the court may order that if the IVA is approved—

(a) the debtor's current address must be omitted from—

(i) any part of the court file of the proceedings in relation to the debtor's IVA which is open to inspection,

(ii) the debtor's identification details required to be entered on the individual insolvency register under rule 11.14,

(iii) any notice or advertisement under rule 8.36 of an order under section 261 to annul the bankruptcy order where an IVA is approved; and

(b) where there is a requirement in these Rules to identify the debtor, the debtor's identification details must not include details of the debtor's current address.

(5) Where the court makes such an order, it may further order that the details to be entered on the individual insolvency register must include instead such other details of the debtor's addresses or whereabouts as the court thinks just, including details of any address at which the debtor has previously resided or carried on business.

NOTES

Commencement: 6 April 2017.

This rule derived from the Insolvency Rules 1986, SI 1986/1925, r 5.67.

[6.904]

20.3 IVA (order for non-disclosure of current address)

(1) This rule applies where a debtor has entered into an IVA.

(2) The following may make an application for an order as set out in paragraph (4) for the non-disclosure of the debtor's current address—

(a) the debtor;

(b) the supervisor;

(c) the official receiver (whether acting as a supervisor or otherwise); and

(d) the Secretary of State.

(3) The application must be accompanied by a witness statement referring to this rule and containing sufficient evidence to satisfy the court that rule 20.1(1) applies.

(4) If the court is satisfied that the circumstances set out in rule 20.1(1) apply, the court may order that—

(a) the debtor's current address must be omitted from—

(i) any part of the court file of the proceedings in relation to the debtor which is open to inspection,

(ii) the debtor's identification details entered or required to be entered on the individual insolvency register under rule 11.14, and

(iii) any notice or advertisement under rule 8.35 of an order under section 261 to annul the bankruptcy order where an IVA is approved; and

(b) where there is a requirement in these Rules to identify the debtor, the debtor's identification details must not include the debtor's current address.

(5) Where the court makes such an order, it may further order that the details to be entered on the individual insolvency register must include instead such other details of the debtor's addresses or whereabouts as the court thinks just, including details of any address at which the debtor has previously resided or carried on business.

NOTES

Commencement: 6 April 2017.

This rule derived from the Insolvency Rules 1986, SI 1986/1925, r 5.67.

[6.905]

20.4 Debt relief application (order for non-disclosure of current address)

(1) This rule applies where a debtor intends to make a debt relief application and has been issued with a unique identifier for the application.

(2) The debtor may make an application for an order as set out in paragraph (4) for the non-disclosure of the debtor's current address.

(3) The application must be accompanied by a witness statement referring to this rule and containing sufficient evidence to satisfy the court that rule 20.1(1) applies.

(4) If the court is satisfied that the circumstances set out in rule 20.1(1) apply, the court may order that if a debt relief order is made—

(a) the debtor's current address must be omitted from—

(i) any part of the court file of the proceedings in relation to the debtor which is open to inspection, and

(ii) the debtor's identification details required to be entered on the individual insolvency register under rule 11.18; and

(b) where there is a requirement in these Rules to identify the debtor, the debtor's identification must not include the debtor's current address.

(5) Where the court makes such an order, it may further order that the details to be entered on the individual insolvency register must include instead such other details of the debtor's addresses or whereabouts as the court thinks just, including details of any address at which the debtor has previously resided or carried on business.

NOTES

Commencement: 6 April 2017.

This rule derived from the Insolvency Rules 1986, SI 1986/1925, r 5A.18.

[6.906]

20.5 Bankruptcy application (order for non-disclosure of current address)

(1) This rule applies where a debtor intends to make a bankruptcy application and has been issued with a unique identifier for the application.

(2) The debtor may make an application for an order as set out in paragraph (4) for the non-disclosure of the debtor's current address.

(3) The application must be accompanied by a witness statement referring to this rule and containing sufficient evidence to satisfy the court that rule 20.1(1) applies.

(4) If the court is satisfied that the circumstances set out in rule 20.1(1) apply, the court may order that if a bankruptcy order is made—

(a) the debtor's current address must be omitted from—

(i) any part of the bankruptcy file which is open to inspection,

(ii) the details in respect of the debtor to be entered on the individual insolvency register under rule 11.16,

(iii) the details in respect of the debtor to be entered in the bankruptcy order; and

(b) where there is a requirement in these Rules to identify the debtor, the debtor's identification details must not include the debtor's current address.

(5) Where the court makes an order under paragraph (4), it may further order that such other details of the debtor's addresses or whereabouts as the court thinks just, including details of any address at which the debtor has previously resided or carried on business, are to be included in—

(a) the details in respect of the debtor kept on or to be entered on the individual insolvency register under rule 11.16;

(b) the details in respect of the debtor included on the bankruptcy file; or

(c) the description of the debtor to be inserted in the bankruptcy order.

NOTES

Commencement: 6 April 2017.

This rule derived from the Insolvency Rules 1986, SI 1986/1925, r 6.50B.

[6.907]

20.6 Bankruptcy and debt relief proceedings (order for non-disclosure of current address)

(1) For the purposes of this rule, "debtor" means a person subject to a bankruptcy order, a debt relief order, a bankruptcy restrictions order, a debt relief restrictions order, a bankruptcy restrictions undertaking or a debt relief restrictions undertaking.

(2) The following may make an application for an order as set out in paragraph (4) for the non-disclosure of the debtor's current address—

(a) the debtor;

(b) the official receiver; or

(c) in respect of a bankruptcy order, a bankruptcy restrictions order or a bankruptcy restrictions undertaking, the trustee or the Secretary of State.

(3) The application must be accompanied by a witness statement referring to this rule and containing sufficient evidence to satisfy the court that rule 20.1(1) applies.

(4) If the court is satisfied that the circumstances set out in rule 20.1(1) apply, the court may order that—

(a) the debtor's current address must be omitted from—

(i) any part of the court file or bankruptcy file of the proceedings in relation to the debtor which is open to inspection,

(ii) the debtor's identification details entered or required to be entered on the individual insolvency register under rule 11.16 (bankruptcy orders), rule 11.18 (debt relief orders), or the bankruptcy restrictions register or the debt relief restrictions register under 11.20 (as the case may be), and

(iii) the details in respect of the debtor to be entered in the bankruptcy order or debt relief order;

(b) the full title of the proceedings must be amended by the omission of the debtor's current address; and

(c) where there is a requirement in these Rules to identify the debtor, the debtor's identification details must not include the debtor's current address.

(5) Where the court makes an order under paragraph (4), it may further order that such other details of the debtor's addresses or whereabouts as the court thinks just, including details of any address at which the debtor has previously resided or carried on business, are to be included in—

(a) the full title of any proceedings;

(b) the details in respect of the debtor kept on or to be entered on the relevant register; or

(c) the description of the debtor to be inserted in the bankruptcy order or the debt relief order.

NOTES

Commencement: 6 April 2017.

This rule derived from the Insolvency Rules 1986, SI 1986/1925, rr 5A.18, 6.235B.

[6.908]

20.7 Additional provisions in respect of orders under rule 20.6(4)

(1) This rule applies where the court is making an order under rule 20.6(4) in respect of a debtor who is subject to a bankruptcy order, a bankruptcy restrictions order or a bankruptcy restrictions undertaking.

(2) The court may make either or both of the following further orders—

(a) that the details of the debtor required to be included in any notice to be gazetted or otherwise advertised must not include the debtor's current address; and.

(b) that the details of the debtor required to be included in any such notice to be gazetted or otherwise advertised must instead of the debtor's current address include such other details of the debtor's addresses or whereabouts as the court thinks just, including details of any address at which the debtor has previously resided or carried on business.

(3) Where the court makes an order under rule 20.6(4) amending the full title of the proceedings by the omission of the debtor's current address from the description of the debtor, the official receiver—

(a) must as soon as reasonably practicable deliver notice of it to the Chief Land Registrar, for corresponding amendment of the register; and

(b) may cause notice of the order to be—

(i) gazetted, or

(ii) both gazetted and delivered in such other manner as the official receiver thinks fit.

(4) A notice of the amendment of the title of the proceedings which is published in accordance with paragraph (3)—

(a) must omit the current address of the debtor;

(b) must contain the amended title of the proceedings, and the date of the bankruptcy order; and

(c) must not include the description under which the proceedings were previously published.

NOTES

Commencement: 6 April 2017.

PART 21
[THE EU REGULATION]

[Note: a document required by the Act or these Rules must also contain the standard contents set out in Part 1.]

NOTES

Part heading: substituted for the original words "The EC Regulation" by the Insolvency Amendment (EU 2015/848) Regulations 2017, SI 2017/702, regs 2, 3, Schedule, Pt 2, paras 32, 45, as from 26 June 2017, except in relation to proceedings opened before that date.

[6.909]

21.1 Interpretation for this Part

In this Part—

["winding-up proceedings" means insolvency proceedings listed in the United Kingdom entry in Annex A to the EU Regulation other than voluntary arrangements where they relate to individuals, bankruptcy or sequestration;] and

"conversion into winding-up proceedings" refers to an order under [Article 51 of the EU Regulation (conversion of secondary insolvency proceedings)] [that winding-up proceedings of one kind are converted into winding-up proceedings of another kind.]

NOTES

Commencement: 6 April 2017.

Definition "winding-up proceedings" substituted by the Insolvency Amendment (EU 2015/848) Regulations 2017, SI 2017/702, regs 2, 3, Schedule, Pt 2, paras 32, 46(a), as from 26 June 2017, except in relation to proceedings opened before that date, and originally read as follows—

""winding-up proceedings" are the winding-up proceedings within the meaning of Article 2(c) of the EC Regulation listed under the United Kingdom entry in Annex B to that Regulation, other than bankruptcy and sequestration proceedings;".

In the definition "conversion into winding-up proceedings" words in square brackets substituted by SI 2017/702, regs 2, 3, Schedule, Pt 2, paras 32, 46(b), as from 26 June 2017, except in relation to proceedings opened before that date, and the definition originally read as follows—

""conversion into winding-up proceedings" refers to an order under Article 37 of the EC Regulation (conversion of earlier proceedings) that—

(a) a CVA be converted into administration proceedings the purposes of which are limited to the winding up of the company through administration and exclude the purpose contained in paragraph 3(1)(a) of Schedule B1;

(b) the purposes of an administration be limited to the winding up of the company through administration and exclude the purpose contained in paragraph 3(1)(a) of Schedule B1; or

(c) a CVA or an administration be converted into—

(i) a creditors' voluntary winding up, or
(ii) a winding up by the court.".

[6.910]
[21.1A Standard contents of applications to court under the EU Regulation

Where an application is made to the court under the EU Regulation the standard contents set out in rule 1.35 apply to the application with any necessary adaptations except in so far as these Rules make specific provision for such an application.]

NOTES

Commencement: 26 June 2017.

Inserted by the Insolvency Amendment (EU 2015/848) Regulations 2017, SI 2017/702, regs 2, 3, Schedule, Pt 2, paras 32, 47, except in relation to proceedings opened before 26 June 2017.

[6.911]
21.2 Conversion into winding up proceedings or bankruptcy: application

[[Note: "Local creditor" is defined in Article 2(11) of the EU Regulation.]]

(1) This rule applies where a member State liquidator in main proceedings applies to the court under [Article 51 of the EU Regulation] for—

[(a) conversion of winding-up proceedings of one kind into winding-up proceedings of another kind; or
(b) conversion of an IVA into bankruptcy or of bankruptcy into an IVA;]

(2) A witness statement made by or on behalf of the member State liquidator must be filed with the court in support of the application.

(3) The witness statement must state—

(a) that main proceedings have been opened in relation to the company or, as the case may be, the debtor in a member State other than the United Kingdom;
(b) the belief of the person making the statement that the conversion of the CVA or administration into winding-up proceedings or the IVA into a bankruptcy [would be most appropriate as regards the interests of the local creditors and coherence between the main and secondary insolvency proceedings];
(c) where the application is for conversion into winding-up proceedings of a CVA or an administration, in the opinion of the person making the statement, into which proceedings the CVA or administration should be converted; and
(d) all other matters that, in the opinion of the member State liquidator, would assist the court in—
 (i) deciding whether to make such an order, and
 (ii) considering whether and, if so, what consequential provision to include.

(4) The application and the witness statement must be served upon—

(a) the company or the debtor, as the case may be; and
(b) the supervisor or the administrator, as the case may be.

NOTES

Commencement: 6 April 2017.

This rule derived from the Insolvency Rules 1986, SI 1986/1925, rr 1.31, 1.32, 2.130, 2.131, 5.62, 5.63.

Note following the rule heading inserted by the Insolvency Amendment (EU 2015/848) Regulations 2017, SI 2017/702, regs 2, 3, Schedule, Pt 2, paras 32, 48, as from 26 June 2017, except in relation to proceedings opened before that date.

Para (1): words in first pair of square brackets substituted for the original words "Article 37 of the EC Regulation", and paras (a), (b) substituted, by SI 2017/702, regs 2, 3, Schedule, Pt 2, paras 32, 48(a), (b), as from 26 June 2017, except in relation to proceedings opened before that date. Paras (a), (b) originally read as follows—

"(a) conversion into winding-up proceedings of a CVA or an administration, or
(b) conversion of an IVA into a bankruptcy.".

Para (3): words in square brackets substituted for the original words "would prove to be in the interests of the creditors in the main proceedings", by SI 2017/702, regs 2, 3, Schedule, Pt 2, paras 32, 48(c), as from 26 June 2017, except in relation to proceedings opened before that date.

[6.912]
21.3 Conversion into winding up proceedings or bankruptcy: court order

(1) On hearing an application for conversion into winding-up proceedings, or conversion of an IVA into a bankruptcy the court may, subject to [Article 51 of the EU Regulation], make such order as it thinks just.

(2) An order for conversion into winding-up proceedings may—

(a) provide that the company be wound up as if a resolution for voluntary winding up under section 84 were passed on the day on which the order is made; and
(b) contain such consequential provisions as the court thinks just.

(3) An order for the conversion of an IVA into a bankruptcy may contain such consequential provisions as the court thinks just.

NOTES

Commencement: 6 April 2017.

This rule derived from the Insolvency Rules 1986, SI 1986/1925, rr 1.33, 2.132, 5.64.

Para (1): words in square brackets substituted by the Insolvency (England and Wales) and Insolvency (Scotland) (Miscellaneous and Consequential Amendments) Rules 2017, SI 2017/1115, rr 22, 28.

[6.913]

21.4 Confirmation of creditors' voluntary winding up: application

(1) This rule applies where—

(a) a company has passed a resolution for voluntary winding up, and either—

(i) no declaration of solvency has been made in accordance with section 89, or

(ii) a declaration made under section 89—

(aa) has no effect by virtue of section 89(2), or

(bb) is treated as not having been made by virtue of section 96; or

(b) a company has moved from administration to creditors' voluntary winding up in accordance with paragraph 83 of Schedule B1.

(2) The liquidator may apply to court for an order confirming the winding up as a creditors' voluntary winding up for the purposes of the [EU Regulation].

(3) The application must be supported by a witness statement made by the liquidator which must contain—

(a) identification details for the liquidator and the company;

(b) the date on which the resolution for voluntary winding up was passed;

(c) a statement that the application is accompanied by the documents required by paragraph (4);

(d) a statement that the documents required by paragraph (4)(c) and (d) are true copies of the originals; and

(e) a statement whether the proceedings will be main proceedings, secondary proceedings or territorial proceedings [and the reasons for so stating].

(4) The liquidator must file with the court—

(a) two copies of the application;

(b) evidence of having been appointed liquidator of the company;

(c) a copy of—

(i) the resolution for voluntary winding up, or

(ii) the notice of moving from administration to creditors' voluntary winding up sent by the administrator to the registrar of companies under paragraph 83(3) of Schedule B1; and

(d) a copy of—

(i) the statement of affairs required by section 99 or under paragraph 47 of Schedule B1, or

(ii) the information included in the administrator's statement of proposals under rule 3.35(1)(h).

NOTES

Commencement: 6 April 2017.

This rule derived from the Insolvency Rules 1986, SI 1986/1925, r 7.62(1)–(3).

Para (2): words in square brackets substituted by the Insolvency (England and Wales) and Insolvency (Scotland) (Miscellaneous and Consequential Amendments) Rules 2017, SI 2017/1115, rr 22, 23(10).

Para (3): words in square brackets in sub-para (e) added by the Insolvency Amendment (EU 2015/848) Regulations 2017, SI 2017/702, regs 2, 3, Schedule, Pt 2, paras 32, 49, as from 26 June 2017, except in relation to proceedings opened before that date.

[6.914]

21.5 Confirmation of creditors' voluntary winding up: court order

(1) On an application under the preceding rule, the court may make an order confirming the creditors' voluntary winding up.

(2) It may do so without a hearing.

(3) If the court makes an order confirming the creditors' voluntary winding up, it must affix its seal to the application.

(4) A member of the court staff may deal with an application under this rule.

NOTES

Commencement: 6 April 2017.

This rule derived from the Insolvency Rules 1986, SI 1986/1925, r 7.62(5)–(8).

[6.915]

21.6 Confirmation of creditors' voluntary winding up: notice to member State liquidator

(1) Where the court has confirmed the creditors' voluntary winding up, the liquidator must as soon as reasonably practicable give notice to any member State liquidator appointed in relation to the company.

(2) Paragraph (1) is without prejudice to the liquidator's obligation in [Article 54 of the EU Regulation] (duty to inform creditors in other member States) in relation to the creditors' voluntary winding up.

NOTES

Commencement: 6 April 2017.

This rule derived from the Insolvency Rules 1986, SI 1986/1925, r 7.63.

Para (2): words in square brackets substituted by the Insolvency (England and Wales) and Insolvency (Scotland) (Miscellaneous and Consequential Amendments) Rules 2017, SI 2017/1115, rr 22, 29.

[6.916]

21.7 [Proceedings in another member State: duty to give notice]

(1) This rule applies where—

(a) the supervisor of a CVA or an IVA, an administrator, a liquidator[, provisional liquidator, interim receiver] or a trustee in bankruptcy is required to give notice, or provide a copy of a document (including an order of court), to the court, the registrar of companies or the official receiver . . .

(b) . . .

(2) Where not already required to do so by [Article 41 of the EU Regulation], the supervisor, administrator, liquidator[, provisional liquidator, interim receiver] or trustee must also give notice or provide a copy to[—

(a) any member State liquidator; or

(b) where the supervisor, administrator, liquidator, provisional liquidator, interim receiver or trustee knows that an application has been made to commence insolvency proceedings in another member State but a member State liquidator has not yet been appointed to the court to which that application has been made.]

NOTES

Commencement: 6 April 2017.

This rule derived from the Insolvency Rules 1986, SI 1986/1925, rr 1.34, 2.133, 4.231, 5.65, 6238, 6.239.

Rule heading: substituted for the original words "Member State liquidator: duty to give notice" by the Insolvency Amendment (EU 2015/848) Regulations 2017, SI 2017/702, regs 2, 3, Schedule, Pt 2, paras 32, 50(a), as from 26 June 2017, except in relation to proceedings opened before that date.

Paras (1), (2): words in square brackets inserted or substituted and words omitted revoked by SI 2017/702, regs 2, 3, Schedule, Pt 2, paras 32, 50(b). (c), as from 26 June 2017, except in relation to proceedings opened before that date. Paras (1), (2) originally read as follows—

"(1) This rule applies where—

(a) the supervisor of a CVA or an IVA, an administrator, a liquidator or a trustee in bankruptcy is required to give notice, or provide a copy of a document (including an order of court), to the court, the registrar of companies or the official receiver; and

(b) a member State liquidator has been appointed in relation to a company.

(2) Where not already required to do so by Article 31 of the EC Regulation, the supervisor, administrator, liquidator or trustee must also give notice or provide a copy to the member State liquidator.".

[6.917]

21.8 Member State liquidator: rules on creditors' participation in proceedings

(1) The provisions in these Rules apply to a member State liquidator's participation in proceedings in accordance with [Article 45 of the EU Regulation] (exercise of creditors' rights) in the same manner as they do to creditors' participation in those proceedings.

(2) In this rule, "creditors' participation"—

(a) includes the following matters—

(i) requesting and being provided with information, including inspecting or obtaining copies of documents or files,

(ii) being provided with notices or other documents,

(iii) participating and voting in decision procedures,

(iv) the establishment and operation of creditor committees,

(v) proving in respect of debts and receipt of dividends, and

(vi) applying to the court and appearing at hearings; and

(b) is limited to creditors' participation from the time of the opening of proceedings in accordance with [Article 2(8) of the EU Regulation].

NOTES

Commencement: 6 April 2017.

This rule derived from the Insolvency Rules 1986, SI 1986/1925, rr 2.133, 4.231, 6.238, 6.239, 7.64, 8.8.

Para (1): words in square brackets substituted for the original words "Article 32(3) of the EC Regulation" by the Insolvency Amendment (EU 2015/848) Regulations 2017, SI 2017/702, regs 2, 3, Schedule, Pt 2, paras 32, 51(a), as from 26 June 2017, except in relation to proceedings opened before that date.

Para (2): words in square brackets in sub-para (b) substituted for the original words "Article 2(f) of the EC Regulation" by SI 2017/702, regs 2, 3, Schedule, Pt 2, paras 32, 51(b), as from 26 June 2017, except in relation to proceedings opened before that date.

[6.918]

[21.9 Main proceedings in England and Wales: undertaking by office-holder in respect of assets in another member State (Article 36 of the EU Regulation)

[Note: "local creditor" is defined in Article 2(11) of the EU Regulation.]

(1) This rule applies where an office-holder in main proceedings proposes to give an undertaking under Article 36 of the EU Regulation in respect of assets located in another member State.

(2) The following requirements apply in respect of the proposed undertaking.

(3) In addition to the requirements as to form and content set out in Article 36 the undertaking must contain—

(a) the heading "Proposed Undertaking under Article 36 of the EU Insolvency Regulation (2015/848)";

(b) identification details for the main proceedings;
(c) identification and contact details for the office-holder; and
(d) a description of the effect of the undertaking if approved.

(4) The proposed undertaking must be delivered to all the local creditors in the member State concerned of whose address the office-holder is aware.

(5) Where the undertaking is rejected the office-holder must inform all the creditors of the company of the rejection of the undertaking as soon as reasonably practicable.

(6) Where the undertaking is approved the office-holder must as soon as reasonably practicable—

(a) send a copy of the undertaking to all the creditors with a notice informing them of the approval of the undertaking and of its effect (so far as they have not already been given this information under paragraph (3)(d));
(b) in the case of a bankruptcy file the undertaking on the court file or the bankruptcy file as the case may be;
(c) where the insolvency proceedings relate to a registered company deliver a copy of the undertaking to the registrar of companies.

(7) The office-holder may advertise details of the undertaking in the other member State in such manner as the office-holder thinks fit.]

NOTES

Commencement: 26 June 2017.

Rules 21.9–21.17 inserted by the Insolvency Amendment (EU 2015/848) Regulations 2017, SI 2017/702, regs 2, 3, Schedule, Pt 2, paras 32, 52, except in relation to proceedings opened before 26 June 2017.

[6.919]

[21.10 Main proceedings in another member State: approval of undertaking offered by the member State liquidator to local creditors in the UK

(1) This rule applies where a member State liquidator proposes an undertaking under Article 36 and the secondary proceedings which the undertaking is intended to avoid would be insolvency proceedings to which these Rules apply.

(2) The decision by the local creditors whether to approve the undertaking must be made by a decision procedure subject to the rules which apply to the approval of a CVA (with any necessary modifications) and subject as follows.

(3) In Part 15 the rules in Chapters 1 to 9 and 11 apply to the decision procedure (with any necessary modifications) except for the following—

15.7, 15.12, 15.14, 15.16–15.19, 15.24, 15.29 to 15.30.

(4) Where the main proceedings relate to a registered company the member State liquidator must deliver a copy of the approved undertaking to the registrar of companies.

(5) Where the main proceedings relate to an individual the member State liquidator must gazette a notice of the undertaking containing—

(a) the fact that the undertaking was approved;
(b) the date the undertaking was approved; and
(c) a description of the effect of the undertaking.]

NOTES

Inserted as noted to r 21.9 at **[6.918]**.

[6.920]

[21.11 Powers of an office-holder or member State liquidator in proceedings concerning members of a group of companies (Article 60 of the EU Regulation)

Where an office-holder or a member State liquidator makes an application in accordance with paragraph (1)(b) of Article 60 of the EU Regulation the application must state with reasons why the applicant thinks the matters set out in points (i) to (iv) of that paragraph apply.]

NOTES

Inserted as noted to r 21.9 at **[6.918]**.

[6.921]

[21.12 Group coordination proceedings (Section 2 of Chapter 5 of the EU Regulation)

(1) An application to open group coordination proceedings must be headed "Application under Article 61 of Regulation (EU) 2015/848 to open group coordination proceedings" and must, in addition to the requirements in Article 61 contain—

(a) identification and contact details for the office-holder making the application;
(b) identification details for the insolvency proceedings by virtue of which the office-holder is making the application;
(c) identification details for the insolvency proceedings in respect of each company which is a member of the group;
(d) contact details for the office-holders and member state liquidators appointed in those proceedings;
(e) identification details for any insolvency proceedings in respect of a member of the group which are not to be subject to the coordination because of an objection to being included; and

(f) if relevant, a copy of any such agreement as is mentioned in Article 66 of the EU Regulation.

(2) "office-holder" in this rule includes [as the context requires] a person holding office in insolvency proceedings in relation to the company in Scotland or Northern Ireland, and a member State liquidator.]

NOTES

Inserted as noted to r 21.9 at **[6.918]**.

Para (2): words in square brackets inserted by the Insolvency (England and Wales) and Insolvency (Scotland) (Miscellaneous and Consequential Amendments) Rules 2017, SI 2017/1115, rr 2, 12.

[6.922]

[21.13 Group coordination order (Article 68 EU Regulation)

[Note: an order opening group coordination proceedings must also contain the matters set out in Article 68(1)(a) to (c).]

(1) An order opening group coordination proceedings must also contain—

(a) identification details for the insolvency proceedings by virtue of which the office-holder is making the application;

(b) identification and contact details for the office-holder making the application;

(c) identification details for the insolvency proceedings which are subject to the coordination;

(d) identification details for any insolvency proceedings for a member of the group which are not subject to the coordination because of an objection to being included.

(2) The office-holder who made the application must deliver a copy of the order to the coordinator and to any person who is, in respect of proceedings subject to the coordination—

(a) an office-holder,

(b) a person holding office in insolvency proceedings in relation to the company in Scotland or Northern Ireland, and

(c) a member State liquidator.]

NOTES

Inserted as noted to r 21.9 at **[6.918]**.

[6.923]

[21.14 Delivery of group coordination order to registrar of companies

An office-holder in respect of insolvency proceedings subject to coordination must deliver a copy of the group coordination order to the registrar of companies.]

NOTES

Inserted as noted to r 21.9 at **[6.918]**.

[6.924]

[21.15 Office-holder's report

(1) This rule applies where, under the second paragraph of Article 70(2) of the EU Regulation, an office-holder is required to give reasons for not following the coordinator's recommendations or the group coordination plan.

(2) Those reasons must be given as soon as reasonably practicable by a notice to all the creditors.

(3) Those reasons may be given in the next progress report where doing so satisfies the requirement to give the reasons as soon as reasonably practicable.]

NOTES

Inserted as noted to r 21.9 at **[6.918]**.

[6.925]

[21.16 Publication of opening of proceedings by a member State liquidator

(1) This rule applies where—

(a) a company subject to insolvency proceedings has an establishment in England and Wales; and

(b) a member State liquidator is required or authorised under Article 28 of the EU Regulation to publish a notice.

(2) The notice must be published in the Gazette.]

NOTES

Inserted as noted to r 21.9 at **[6.918]**.

[6.926]

[21.17 Statement by member State liquidator that insolvency proceedings in another member State are closed etc

A statement by a member State liquidator under any of sections 201, 202, 205 or paragraph 84 of Schedule B1 informing the registrar of companies that the insolvency proceedings in another member State are closed or that the member State liquidator consents to the dissolution must contain—

(a) identification details for the company; and

(b) identification details for the member State liquidator.]

NOTES

Inserted as noted to r 21.9 at **[6.918]**.

PART 22
PERMISSION TO ACT AS DIRECTOR ETC OF COMPANY WITH A PROHIBITED NAME (SECTION 216)

[Note: a document required by the Act or these Rules must also contain the standard contents set out in Part 1.]

[6.927]
22.1 Preliminary

(1) The rules in this Part—
- (a) relate to permission required under section 216 (restriction on re-use of name of company in insolvent liquidation) for a person to act as mentioned in section 216(3) in relation to a company with a prohibited name;
- (b) prescribe the cases excepted from that provision, that is to say, in which a person to whom the section applies may so act without that permission; and
- (c) apply to all windings up to which section 216 applies.

NOTES

Commencement: 6 April 2017.
This rule derived from the Insolvency Rules 1986, SI 1986/1925, r 4.226.

[6.928]
22.2 Application for permission under section 216(3)

(1) At least 14 days' notice of any application for permission to act in any of the circumstances which would otherwise be prohibited by section 216(3) must be given by the applicant to the Secretary of State, who may—
- (a) appear at the hearing of the application; and
- (b) whether or not appearing at the hearing, make representations.

NOTES

Commencement: 6 April 2017.
This rule derived from the Insolvency Rules 1986, SI 1986/1925, r 4.227A.

[6.929]
22.3 Power of court to call for liquidator's report

When considering an application for permission under section 216, the court may call on the liquidator, or any former liquidator, of the liquidating company for a report of the circumstances in which the company became insolvent and the extent (if any) of the applicant's apparent responsibility for its doing so.

NOTES

Commencement: 6 April 2017.
This rule derived from the Insolvency Rules 1986, SI 1986/1925, r 4.227A(2).

[6.930]
22.4 First excepted case

(1) This rule applies where—
- (a) a person ("the person") was within the period mentioned in section 216(1) a director, or shadow director, of an insolvent company that has gone into insolvent liquidation; and
- (b) the person acts in all or any of the ways specified in section 216(3) in connection with, or for the purposes of, the carrying on (or proposed carrying on) of the whole or substantially the whole of the business of the insolvent company where that business (or substantially the whole of it) is (or is to be) acquired from the insolvent company under arrangements—
  - (i) made by its liquidator, or
  - (ii) made before the insolvent company entered into insolvent liquidation by an office-holder acting in relation to it as administrator, administrative receiver or supervisor of a CVA.

(2) The person will not be taken to have contravened section 216 if prior to that person acting in the circumstances set out in paragraph (1) a notice is, in accordance with the requirements of paragraph (3),—
- (a) given by the person, to every creditor of the insolvent company whose name and address—
  - (i) is known by that person, or
  - (ii) is ascertainable by that person on the making of such enquiries as are reasonable in the circumstances; and
- (b) published in the Gazette.

(3) The notice referred to in paragraph (2)—
- (a) may be given and published before the completion of the arrangements referred to in paragraph (1)(b) but must be given and published no later than 28 days after their completion;
- (b) must contain—

(i) identification details for the company,
(ii) the name and address of the person,
(iii) a statement that it is the person's intention to act (or, where the insolvent company has not entered insolvent liquidation, to act or continue to act) in all or any of the ways specified in section 216(3) in connection with, or for the purposes of, the carrying on of the whole or substantially the whole of the business of the insolvent company,
(iv) the prohibited name or, where the company has not entered into insolvent liquidation, the name under which the business is being, or is to be, carried on which would be a prohibited name in respect of the person in the event of the insolvent company entering insolvent liquidation,
(v) a statement that the person would not otherwise be permitted to undertake those activities without the leave of the court or the application of an exception created by Rules made under the Insolvency Act 1986,
(vi) a statement that breach of the prohibition created by section 216 is a criminal offence, and
(vii) a statement as set out in rule 22.5 of the effect of issuing the notice under rule 22.4(2);

(c) where the company is in administration, has an administrative receiver appointed or is subject to a CVA, must contain,—
(i) the date that the company entered administration, had an administrative receiver appointed or a CVA approved (whichever is the earliest), and
(ii) a statement that the person was a director of the company on that date; and

(d) where the company is in insolvent liquidation, must contain—
(i) the date that the company entered insolvent liquidation, and
(ii) a statement that the person was a director of the company during the 12 months ending with that date.

(4) Notice may in particular be given under this rule—
(a) prior to the insolvent company entering insolvent liquidation where the business (or substantially the whole of the business) is, or is to be, acquired by another company under arrangements made by an office-holder acting in relation to the insolvent company as administrator, administrative receiver or supervisor of a CVA (whether or not at the time of the giving of the notice the person is a director of that other company); or
(b) at a time when the person is a director of another company where—
(i) the other company has acquired, or is to acquire, the whole, or substantially the whole, of the business of the insolvent company under arrangements made by its liquidator, and
(ii) it is proposed that after the giving of the notice a prohibited name should be adopted by the other company.

(5) Notice may not be given under this rule by a person who has already acted in breach of section 216.

NOTES
Commencement: 6 April 2017.
This rule derived from the Insolvency Rules 1986, SI 1986/1925, r 4.228.

[6.931]
22.5 Statement as to the effect of the notice under rule 22.4(2)

The statement as to the effect of the notice under rule 22.4(2) must be as set out below—

"Section 216(3) of the Insolvency Act 1986 lists the activities that a director of a company that has gone into insolvent liquidation may not undertake unless the court gives permission or there is an exception in the Insolvency Rules made under the Insolvency Act 1986. (This includes the exceptions in Part 22 of the Insolvency (England and Wales) Rules 2016.) These activities are—
(a) acting as a director of another company that is known by a name which is either the same as a name used by the company in insolvent liquidation in the 12 months before it entered liquidation or is so similar as to suggest an association with that company;
(b) directly or indirectly being concerned or taking part in the promotion, formation or management of any such company; or
(c) directly or indirectly being concerned in the carrying on of a business otherwise than through a company under a name of the kind mentioned in (a) above.

This notice is given under rule 22.4 of the Insolvency (England and Wales) Rules 2016 where the business of a company which is in, or may go into, insolvent liquidation is, or is to be, carried on otherwise than by the company in liquidation with the involvement of a director of that company and under the same or a similar name to that of that company.

The purpose of giving this notice is to permit the director to act in these circumstances where the company enters (or has entered) insolvent liquidation without the director committing a criminal offence and in the case of the carrying on of the business through another company, being personally liable for that company's debts.

Notice may be given where the person giving the notice is already the director of a company which proposes to adopt a prohibited name."

NOTES
Commencement: 6 April 2017.
This rule derived from the Insolvency Rules 1986, SI 1986/1925, r 4.228.

[6.932]
22.6 Second excepted case

(1) Where a person to whom section 216 applies as having been a director or shadow director of the liquidating company applies for permission of the court under that section not later than seven business days from the date on which the company went into liquidation, the person may, during the period specified in paragraph (2) below, act in any of the ways mentioned in section 216(3), notwithstanding that the person does not have the permission of the court under that section.

(2) The period referred to in paragraph (1) begins with the day on which the company goes into liquidation and ends either on the day falling six weeks after that date or on the day on which the court disposes of the application for permission under section 216, whichever of those days occurs first.

NOTES

Commencement: 6 April 2017.
This rule derived from the Insolvency Rules 1986, SI 1986/1925, r 4.229.

[6.933]
22.7 Third excepted case

The court's permission under section 216(3) is not required where the company there referred to though known by a prohibited name within the meaning of the section—

(a) has been known by that name for the whole of the period of 12 months ending with the day before the liquidating company went into liquidation; and
(b) has not at any time in those 12 months been dormant within the meaning of section 1169(1), (2) and (3)(a) of the Companies Act.

NOTES

Commencement: 6 April 2017.
This rule derived from the Insolvency Rules 1986, SI 1986/1925, r 4.230.

SCHEDULE 1
REVOCATIONS

Introductory rule 2

[6.934]

The Insolvency Rules 1986	1986/1925
The Insolvency (Amendment) Rules 1987	1987/1919
The Insolvency (Amendment) Rules 1989	1989/397
The Insolvency (Amendment) Rules 1991	1991/495
The Insolvency (Amendment) Rules 1993	1993/602
The Insolvency (Amendment) Rules 1995	1995/586
The Insolvency (Amendment) Rules 1999	1999/359
The Insolvency (Amendment) (No 2) Rules 1999	1999/1022
The Insolvency (Amendment) Rules 2001	2001/763
The Insolvency (Amendment) Rules 2002	2002/1307
The Insolvency (Amendment) (No 2) Rules 2002	2002/2712
The Insolvency (Amendment) Rules 2003	2003/1730
The Insolvency (Amendment) Rules 2004	2004/584
The Insolvency (Amendment) (No 2) Rules 2004	2004/1070
The Insolvency (Amendment) Rules 2005	2005/527
The Insolvency (Amendment) Rules 2006	2006/1272
The Insolvency (Amendment) Rules 2007	2007/1974
The Insolvency (Amendment) Rules 2008	2008/737
The Insolvency (Amendment) Rules 2009	2009/642
The Insolvency (Amendment No 2) Rules 2009	2009/2472
The Insolvency (Amendment) Rules 2010	2010/686
The Insolvency (Amendment) (No 2) Rules 2010	2010/734
The Insolvency (Amendment) Rules 2011	2011/785
The Insolvency (Amendment) Rules 2012	2012/469
The Insolvency (Amendment) Rules 2013	2013/2135
The Insolvency (Commencement of Proceedings) and Insolvency Rules 1986 (Amendment) Rules 2014	2014/817
The Insolvency (Amendment) Rules 2015	2015/443
The Insolvency (Amendment) Rules 2016	2016/187

The Insolvency (Amendment) (No 2) Rules 2016	2016/903

NOTES

Commencement: 6 April 2017.

SCHEDULE 2
TRANSITIONAL AND SAVINGS PROVISIONS

Introductory rule 4

General

[6.935]

1 In this Schedule—

"the 1986 Rules" means the Insolvency Rules 1986 as they had effect immediately before the commencement date and a reference to "1986 rule" followed by a rule number is a reference to a rule in the 1986 Rules; and

"the commencement date" means the date these Rules come into force.

Requirement for office-holder to provide information to creditors on opting out

2 (1) Rule 1.39, which requires an office-holder to provide information to a creditor on the right to opt out under rule 1.38 in the first communication to the creditor, does not apply to an office-holder who has delivered the first communication before the commencement date.

(2) However, such an office-holder may choose to deliver information on the right to opt out in which case the communication to the creditor must contain the information required by rule 1.39(2).

Electronic communication

3 (1) Rule 1.45(4) does not apply where the relevant proceedings commenced before the commencement date.

(2) In this paragraph "commenced" means—

(a) the delivery of a proposal for a voluntary arrangement to the intended nominee;
(b) the appointment of an administrator under paragraph 14 or 22 of Schedule B1;
(c) the making of an administration order;
(d) the appointment of an administrative receiver;
(e) the passing or deemed passing of a resolution to wind up a company;
(f) the making of a winding-up order; or
(g) the making of a bankruptcy order.

Statements of affairs

4 (1) The provisions of these Rules relating to statements of affairs in administration, administrative receivership, company winding up and bankruptcy do not apply and the following rules in the 1986 Rules continue to apply where relevant proceedings commenced before the commencement date and a person is required to provide a statement of affairs—

(a) 1986 rules 2.28 to 2.32 (administration);
(b) 1986 rules 3.3 to 3.8 (administrative receivership);
(c) 1986 rules 4.32 to 4.42 (company winding up); and
(d) 1986 rules 6.58 to 6.72 (bankruptcy).

(2) In this paragraph "commenced" means—

(a) the appointment of an administrator under paragraph 14 or 22 of Schedule B1;
(b) the making of an administration order;
(c) the appointment of an administrative receiver
(d) the passing or deemed passing of a resolution to wind up a company;
(e) the making of a winding-up order; or
(f) the making of a bankruptcy order.

Savings in respect of meetings taking place on or after the commencement date and resolutions by correspondence

5 (1) This paragraph applies where on or after the commencement date—

(a) a creditors' or contributories' meeting is to be held as a result of a notice issued before that date in relation to a meeting for which provision is made by the 1986 Rules or the 1986 Act;
(b) a meeting is to be held as a result of a requisition by a creditor or contributory made before that date;
(c) a meeting is to be held as a result of a statement made under paragraph 52(1)(b) of Schedule B1 and a request is made before that date which obliges the administrator to summon an initial creditors' meeting;
(d) a . . . meeting is required by [sections 93 or 105] of the 1986 Act in the winding up of a company where the resolution to wind up was passed before 6th April 2010.

(2) Where a meeting is to be held under sub-paragraph (1)(a) to (1)(d), Part 15 of these Rules does not apply and the 1986 Rules relating to the following continue to apply—

(a) the requirement to hold the meeting;
(b) notice and advertisement of the meeting;
(c) governance of the meeting;

(d) recording and taking minutes of the meeting;
(e) the report or return of the meeting;
(f) membership and formalities of establishment of liquidation and creditors' committees where the resolution to form the committee is passed at the meeting;
(g) the office-holder's resignation or removal at the meeting;
(h) the office-holder's release;
(i) fixing the office-holder's remuneration;
(j) . . .
(k) hand-over of assets to a supervisor of a voluntary arrangement where the proposal is approved at the meeting;
(l) the notice of the appointment of a supervisor of a voluntary arrangement where the appointment is made at the meeting;
(m) the advertisement of appointment of a trustee in bankruptcy where the appointment is made at the meeting;
(n) claims that remuneration is or that other expenses are excessive; and
(o) complaints about exclusion at the meeting.

(3) Where, before the commencement date, the office-holder sought to obtain a resolution by correspondence under 1986 rule 2.48, 4.63A or 6.88A, the 1986 Rules relating to resolutions by correspondence continue to apply and sub-paragraph (2) applies to any meeting that those rules require the office-holder to summon.

(4) However, any application to the court in respect of such a meeting or vote is to be made in accordance with Part 12 of these Rules.

Savings in respect of final meetings taking place on or after the commencement date

6 (1) This paragraph applies where—
(a) before the commencement date—
(i) a final report to creditors has been sent under 1986 rule 4.49D (final report to creditors in liquidation),
(ii) a final report to creditors and bankrupt has been sent under 1986 rule 6.78B (final report to creditors and bankrupt), or
(iii) a meeting has been called under [sections 94, 106, 146 or 331] of the 1986 Act (final meeting . . .); and
(b) a meeting under section 94, 106, 146 or 331 of the 1986 Act is held on or after the commencement date.

(2) Where a meeting is held to which this paragraph applies, Part 15 of these Rules does not apply and the 1986 Rules relating to the following continue to apply—
(a) the requirement to hold the meeting;
(b) notice and advertisement of the meeting;
(c) governance of the meeting;
(d) recording and taking minutes of the meeting;
(e) the form and content of the final report;
(f) the office-holder's resignation or removal;
(g) the office-holder's release;
(h) fixing the office-holder's remuneration;
(i) requests for further information from creditors;
(j) claims that remuneration is or other expenses are excessive; and
(k) complaints about exclusion at the meeting.

(3) However, any application to the court in respect of such a meeting is to be made in accordance with Part 12 of these Rules.

Progress reports and statements to the registrar of companies

7 (1) Where an obligation to prepare a progress report arises before the commencement date but has not yet been fulfilled the following provisions of the 1986 Rules continue to apply—
(a) 1986 rule 2.47 (reports to creditors in administration;
(b) 1986 rules 4.49B and 4.49C (progress reports—winding up); and
(c) 1986 rule 6.78A (reports to creditors in bankruptcy).

(2) Where before the commencement date, a conversion notice under paragraph 83 of Schedule B1 was sent to the registrar of companies . . . , 1986 rule 2.117A(1) continues to apply . . . .

(3) The provisions of these Rules relating to progress reporting do not apply—
(a) in the case of a bankruptcy, where the bankruptcy order was made on a petition presented before 6th April 2010; or
(b) in the case of a winding up, where the winding-up order was made on a petition presented before 6th April 2010.

(4) Where a voluntary winding up commenced before 6th April 2010, 1986 rule 4.223-CVL as it had effect immediately before that date, continues to apply.

[(5) Where rules 18.6, 18.7 or 18.8 prescribe the periods for which progress reports must be made but before the commencement date an office-holder has ceased to act[, or an administrator has sent a progress report to creditors in support of a request for their consent to an extension of the administration,] resulting in a change in reporting period under 1986 rule 2.47(3A), 2.47(3B) 4.49B(5), 4.49C(3), or 6.78A(4), the period for which reports must be made is the period for which reports were required to be made under the 1986 Rules immediately before the commencement date.]

Foreign currency

8 (1) Where, before the commencement date an amount stated in a foreign currency on an application, claim or proof of debt is converted into sterling by the office-holder under 1986 rule 2.86, 1986 rule 4.91, 1986 rule 5A.3 or 1986 rule 6.111, the office-holder and any successor to the office-holder must continue to use that exchange rate for subsequent conversions of that currency into sterling for the purpose of distributing any assets of the insolvent estate.

(2) However when an office-holder, convener, appointed person or chair uses an exchange rate to convert an application, claim or proof in a foreign currency into sterling solely for voting purposes before the commencement date, it does not prevent the office-holder from using an alternative rate for subsequent conversions.

CVA moratoria

9 Where, before the commencement date, the directors of a company submit to the nominee the documents required under paragraph 6(1) of Schedule A1, the 1986 Rules relating to moratoria continue to apply to that proposed voluntary arrangement.

Priority of expenses of voluntary arrangements

10 1986 rule 4.21A (expenses of CVA in a liquidation) and 1986 rule 6.46A (expenses of IVA in a bankruptcy) continue to apply where a winding up or bankruptcy petition is presented or a bankruptcy application is made (as the case may be) before the commencement date.

General powers of liquidator

11 1986 rule 4.184 (General powers of liquidator) continues to apply as regards a person dealing in good faith and for value with a liquidator and in respect of the power of the court or the liquidation committee to ratify anything done by the liquidator without permission before the amendments made to sections 165 and 167 of the Act by section 120(2) and (3) of the Small Business, Enterprise and Employment Act 2015 (which removed the requirements for the liquidator to obtain such permission) came into force.

Fast-track voluntary arrangements

12 Where a fast-track voluntary arrangement is in effect on the commencement date the following 1986 Rules continue to apply to it after the commencement date—
- (a) 1986 rules 5.35 to 5.50 (fast-track voluntary arrangement);
- (b) 1986 rules 5.57 to 5.59 (application by official receiver to annul a bankruptcy order under section 263D(3)); and
- (c) 1986 rules 5.60 to 5.61 (other matters arising on annulments under sections 261(2)(a), 261(2)(b) or 263D(3)).

First trustee in bankruptcy

13 On the commencement date the official receiver becomes trustee of the bankrupt's estate where—
- (a) a bankruptcy order was made before the commencement date; and
- (b) no trustee has yet been appointed.

Applications before the court

14 (1) [Subject to paragraph (1A), where] an application to court is filed or a petition is presented under the Act or under the 1986 Rules before the commencement date and the court remains seised of that application or petition on the commencement date, the 1986 rules continue to apply to that application or petition.

[(1A) Where the 1986 Rules apply by virtue of paragraph (1) they are to apply as though—
- (a) in rules 7.47(2)(a)(ii), (b)(iii) and (c) and 13.2(3A)(a) for "a Registrar in Bankruptcy of the High Court" there were substituted "an Insolvency and Companies Court Judge", and
- (b) in rule 7.47(5), for the words "Registrar in Bankruptcy of the High Court" both times they appear there were substituted "Insolvency and Companies Court Judge.]

(2) For the purpose of paragraph (1), the court is no longer seised of an application when—
- (a) it makes an order having the effect of determining of the application; or
- (b) in relation to a petition for bankruptcy or winding up when—
  - (i) the court makes a bankruptcy order or a winding up order,
  - (ii) the court dismisses the petition, or
  - (iii) the petition is withdrawn.

(3) Any application to the court to review, rescind[, vary] or appeal an order made under paragraph [14(2)] is to be made in accordance with Part 12 of these Rules.

Forms

15 A form contained in Schedule 4 to the 1986 Rules may be used on or after the commencement date if—
- (a) the form is used to provide a statement of affairs pursuant to paragraph 4 of this Schedule;
- (b) the form relates to a meeting held under the 1986 Rules as described in paragraph 5(1) of this Schedule;
- (c) the form is required for the administration of a fast-track voluntary arrangement pursuant to paragraph 12 of this Schedule;
- (d) the form is required because before the commencement date, the office-holder sought to obtain the passing of a resolution by correspondence; or

(e) the form relates to any application to the court or petition presented before the commencement date.

Registers

16 (1) The Secretary of State must maintain on the individual insolvency register, the bankruptcy restrictions register and the debt relief restrictions register information which is on the registers immediately before the commencement date.

(2) The Secretary of State must also enter on the appropriate register referred to in paragraph (1) information received (but not yet entered on the register) before the commencement date.

(3) The Court's power under Part 20 to order that information must not be entered in those registers where there is a risk of violence applies equally to information received by the Secretary of State before the commencement date but not yet entered on a register.

(4) Any obligation in Part 11 to delete information from a register or to rectify a register applies equally to information entered on the register before these rules come into force.

Administrations commenced before 15th September 2003

17 The 1986 Rules continue to apply to administrations where the petition for an administration order was presented before 15th September 2003.

Set-off in insolvency proceedings commenced before 1st April 2005

18 Where before 1st April 2005 a company has entered administration or gone into liquidation, the office-holder, when calculating any set-off must apply the 1986 Rules as they had effect immediately before 1st April 2005.

Calculating the value of future debts in insolvency proceedings commenced before 1st April 2005

19 Where before 1st April 2005 a company has entered administration or gone into liquidation or a bankruptcy order has been made, the office-holder, when calculating the value of a future debt for the purpose of dividend (and no other purpose) must apply the 1986 Rules as they had effect immediately before 1st April 2005.

Obligations arising under family proceedings where bankruptcy order is made on or before 31 March 2005

20 Rule 12.3 of the 1986 Rules applies, without the amendments made by rule 44 of the Insolvency (Amendment) Rules 2005 to an obligation arising under an order made in family proceedings in any case where a bankruptcy order was made on or before 31 March 2005.

Insolvency practitioner [fees and expenses] estimates

21 (1) [Rules 18.4(1)(e), 18.16(4) to (10), and 18.30 do not apply in a case where before 1st October 2015—]

(a) the appointment of an administrator took effect;
(b) a liquidator was nominated under section 100(2), or 139(3) of the Act;
(c) a liquidator was appointed under section 139(4) or 140 of the Act;
(d) a person was directed by the court or appointed to be a liquidator under section 100(3) of the Act;
(e) a liquidator was nominated or the administrator became the liquidator under paragraph 83(7) of Schedule B1 to the Act; or
(f) a trustee of a bankrupt's estate was appointed.

(2) Paragraphs (4) and (5) of rule 18.20 do not apply where an administrator was appointed before 1st October 2015 and—

(a) the company is wound up under paragraph 83 of Schedule B1 on or after the commencement date and the administrator becomes the liquidator; or
(b) a winding-up order is made upon the appointment of an administrator ceasing to have effect on or after the commencement date and the court under section 140(1) appoints as liquidator the person whose appointment as administrator has ceased to have effect.

[Transitional provision for companies entering administration before 6th April 2010 and moving to voluntary liquidation between 6th April 2010 and 8th December 2017 inclusive of those dates

22 Where—

(a) a company goes into administration before 6th April 2010; and
(b) the company goes into voluntary liquidation under paragraph 83 of Schedule B1 between 6th April 2010 and 8th December 2017 inclusive of those dates;

the 1986 Rules as amended by the Insolvency (Amendment) Rules 2010( ) apply to the extent necessary to give effect to section 104A of the Act notwithstanding that by virtue of paragraph 1(6)(a) or (b) of Schedule 4 to the Insolvency (Amendment) Rules 2010 those amendments to the Insolvency Rules 1986 would otherwise not apply.]

NOTES

Commencement: 6 April 2017.

Para 5: in sub-para (1)(d) word omitted revoked and words in square brackets substituted, and sub-para (2)(j) revoked, by the Insolvency (England and Wales) (Amendment) Rules 2017, SI 2017/366, rr 3, 45, 46.

Para 6: in sub-para (1)(a)(iii), words in square brackets substituted and words omitted revoked by SI 2017/366, rr 3, 47.

Para 7: words omitted from sub-para (2) in both places revoked and sub-para (5) added, by SI 2017/366, rr 3, 48, 49; words in square brackets in sub-para (5) inserted by the Insolvency (England and Wales) and Insolvency (Scotland) (Miscellaneous and Consequential Amendments) Rules 2017, SI 2017/1115, rr 2, 13(1), (2).

Para 14: words in square brackets in sub-para (1) substituted and sub-para (1A) inserted by the Alteration of Judicial Titles (Registrar in Bankruptcy of the High Court) Order 2018, SI 2018/130, art 3, Schedule, para 14(c); in sub-para (3), word in square brackets inserted and figure in square brackets substituted by SI 2017/1115, rr 2, 13(1), (3).

Para 21: words in square brackets in the heading and sub-para (1) substituted by SI 2017/1115, rr 2, 13(1), (4), (5).

Para 22: substituted together with preceding heading by SI 2017/1115, rr 2, 13(1), (6), (7).

SCHEDULE 3
PUNISHMENT OF OFFENCES UNDER THESE RULES

Introductory rule 6

[6.936]

Rule creating offence	General nature of the offence	Mode of prosecution	Punishment	Daily default fine (if applicable)
1.56(3)	Falsely claiming to be a person entitled to inspect a document with the intention of gaining sight of it.	1 On indictment. 2 Summary.	2 years, or a fine, or both. 6 months, or a fine, or both.	Not applicable.
3.55(7)	Former administrator failing to file a notice of automatic end of administration and progress report.	Summary.	Level 3 on the standard scale.	One tenth of level 3 on the standard scale.
3.70(2)	Failing to comply with administrator's duties on vacating office.	Summary.	Level 3 on the standard scale.	One tenth of level 3 on the standard scale.
4.17(6)	Administrative receiver failing to deliver required accounts of receipts and payments.	Summary.	Level 3 on the standard scale.	One tenth of level 3 on the standard scale.
6.14(13)	Directors failing to seek a decision on the nomination of a liquidator.	1 On indictment. 2 Summary.	1 A fine. 2 A fine.	Not applicable.
18.6(5)	Administrator failing to deliver required progress reports in accordance with rule 18.6.	Summary.	Level 3 on the standard scale.	One tenth of level 3 on the standard scale.

NOTES

Commencement: 6 April 2017.

This Schedule derived from the Insolvency Rules 1986, SI 1986/1925, Sch 5.

SCHEDULE 4
SERVICE OF DOCUMENTS

Rule 1.2(2)

[6.937]
1 (1) This Schedule sets out the requirements for service where a document is required to be served.

(2) Service is to be carried out in accordance with Part 6 of the CPR as that Part applies to either a "claim form" or a "document other than the claim form" except where this Schedule provides otherwise or the court otherwise approves or directs.

(3) However, where a document is required or permitted to be served at a company's registered office service may be effected at a previous registered office in accordance with section 87(2) of the Companies Act.

(4) In the case of an overseas company service may be effected in any manner provided for by section 1139(2) of the Companies Act.

(5) If for any reason it is impracticable to effect service as provided for in paragraphs (2) to (4) then service may be effected in such other manner as the court may approve or direct.

(6) The third column of the table below sets out which documents are treated as "claim forms" for the purposes of applying Part 6 of the CPR and which are "documents other than the claim form" (called in this Schedule "other documents").

(7) The fourth column of the table sets out modifications to Part 6 of the CPR which apply to the service of documents listed in the first and second columns.

(8) Part 6 of the CPR applies to the service of documents outside the jurisdiction with such modifications as the court may approve or direct.

Service of winding-up petitions

2 (1) A winding-up petition must be served at a company's registered office by handing it to a person at that address who—
- (a) at the time of service acknowledges being a director, other officer or employee of the company;
- (b) is, to the best of the knowledge and belief of the person serving the petition, a director, other officer or employee of the company; or
- (c) acknowledges being authorised to accept service of documents on the company's behalf.

(2) However if there is no one of the kind mentioned in sub-paragraph (1) at the registered office, the petition may be served by depositing it at or about the registered office in such a way that it is likely to come to the notice of a person attending the office.

(3) Sub-paragraph (4) applies if—
- (a) for any reason it is not practicable to serve a petition at a company's registered office;
- (b) the company has no registered office; or
- (c) the company is an unregistered company.

(4) Where this paragraph applies the petition may be served—
- (a) by leaving it at the company's last known principal place of business in England and Wales in such a way that it is likely to come to the attention of a person attending there; or
- (b) on the secretary or a director, manager or principal officer of the company, wherever that person may be found.

Service of administration application (paragraph 12 of Schedule B1)

3 (1) An application to the court for an administration order must be served by delivering the documents as follows—
- (a) on the company at its registered office or if service at its registered office is not practicable at its last known principal place of business in England and Wales;
- (b) on any other person at that person's proper address.

(2) A person's proper address is any which he has previously notified as the address for service, but if the person has not notified such an address then the documents may be served at that person's usual or last known address.

(3) Paragraph (4) sets out the proper address for service for an authorised deposit-taker who—
- (a) has appointed, or is or may be entitled to appoint, an administrative receiver of the company; or
- (b) is, or may be, entitled to appoint an administrative receiver of the company under paragraph 14 of Schedule B1; and
- (c) has not notified an address for service.

(4) The proper address for service is—
- (a) that of an office of the authorised-deposit taker where the applicant knows the company maintains a bank account; or
- (b) where the applicant doesn't know of any such office, the registered office; or
- (c) if there is no such registered office the usual or last known address.

Service on joint office-holders

4 Service of a document on one of joint office-holders is to be treated as service on all of them.

Service of orders staying proceedings

5 (1) This paragraph applies where the court makes an order staying an action, execution or other legal process against—

(a) the property of a company; or
(b) the property or person of an individual debtor or bankrupt.

(2) The order may be served within the jurisdiction by serving a sealed copy at the address for service of—

(a) the claimant; or
(b) another party having the carriage of the proceedings to be stayed.

Certificate of service

6 (1) The service of an application or petition must be verified by a certificate of service.

(2) The certificate of service must—

(a) identify the application or petition;
(b) identify the company, where the application or petition relates to a company;
(c) identify the debtor, where the application relates to an individual;
(d) identify the applicant or petitioner;
(e) specify—
  (i) the court or hearing centre in which the application was made or at which the petition was filed, and the court reference number,
  (ii) the date of the application or petition,
  (iii) whether the copy served was a sealed copy,
  (iv) the person(s) served, and
  (v) the manner of service and the date of service; and
(f) be verified by a statement of truth.

[(3) Where the court has directed that service be effected in a particular manner, the certificate must be accompanied by a sealed copy of the order directing such manner of service.]

Table of requirements for service

Rule (or section)	***Document***	***Whether treated as claim form or other document***	***Modifications to Part 6 of the CPR which apply unless the court directs otherwise***
3.8	Administration application	Claim form	Service in accordance with paragraph 3 of this Schedule. The applicant must serve the application.
3.16 (& Para 15 of Sch B1)	Notice of intention to appoint administrator by a floating charge holder	[Other document]	The appointer must serve the notice.
3.23 (& para 26 of Sch B1)	Notice of intention to appoint administrator by company or directors	[Other document]	Service on the company at its registered office or if that is not practicable, at its last known principal place of business in England and Wales.
7.3	Statutory demand on a company under section 123(1) or 222(1)(a) (unregistered companies)		[Note: the requirements for service of a statutory demand are set out in sections 123(1) and 222(1)(a) respectively.]
7.9 and 7.29	Winding-up petition	Claim form	Service in accordance with paragraph 2 of this Schedule. The petitioner must serve the petition.
7.34	Court order for additional deposit to be paid—provisional liquidator	Other document	
7.99	Court order to enforce payment of a call	Other document	
7.102	Court order for public examination served on examinee	Other document	
10.2	Statutory demand (bankruptcy)	Other document	Service in accordance with rule 10.2.
10.14	Bankruptcy petition (creditor's)	Claim form	Personal service. The petitioner must serve the petition.

Rule (or section)	*Document*	*Whether treated as claim form or other document*	*Modifications to Part 6 of the CPR which apply unless the court directs otherwise*
10.29	Court order—change of carriage of petition	Other document	
10.50	Court order for additional deposit to be paid—interim receiver	Other document	
10.99	Court order for public examination served on bankrupt	Other document	
10.119	Court order for disclosure by HMRC	Other document	
10.126	Notice to recipient of after acquired property	Other document	
10.166	Court order for post redirection	Other document	
11.3	Application for debt relief restrictions order (DRRO) or bankruptcy restrictions order (BRO)	Claim form	The applicant must serve the application.
11.4	Service of evidence for DRRO or BRO	Other document	
12.9	Applications to court generally (where service required)	Claim form	The applicant must serve the application.
12.19	Court order for private examination	Other document	Personal service. The applicant must serve the order.
12.28(2)	Witness statement of evidence	Other document	
12.37(7)	Application for block transfer order	Claim form	The applicant must serve the application.
12.42	Notice requiring person to assess costs by detailed assessment	Other document	
12.48	Application for costs	Claim form	The applicant must serve the application.
19.4 (& sections 179 and 317)	Notice of disclaimer (leasehold property)	Other document	
19.5 (& section 318)	Notice of disclaimer (dwelling house)	Other document	
21.2	Application for conversion into winding up /bankruptcy under [EU Regulation]	Claim form	The applicant must serve the application.
Paragraph 5(1) of this Schedule	Order staying proceedings	Other document	The applicant must serve the order.

NOTES

Commencement: 6 April 2017.

Para 1 derived from the Insolvency Rules 1986, SI 1986/1925, rr 12A.17, 12A.20; para 2 derived from the Insolvency Rules 1986, SI 1986/1925, rr 4.8, 4.22; para 3 derived from the Insolvency Rules 1986, SI 1986/1925, r 12A.19; para 4 derived from the Insolvency Rules 1986, SI 1986/1925, rr 7.56, 12A.18; para 5 derived from the Insolvency Rules 1986, SI 1986/1925, rr 2.8, 2.9, 4.9A, 6.15A.

Para 6: sub-para (3) substituted and words in square brackets in entry relating to r 21.2 in the Table substituted, by the Insolvency (England and Wales) and Insolvency (Scotland) (Miscellaneous and Consequential Amendments) Rules 2017, SI 2017/1115, rr 2, 14, 22, 23(11); words "Other document" in square brackets in the third column of the Table substituted by the Insolvency (England and Wales) (Amendment) Rules 2017, SI 2017/366, rr 3, 50.

SCHEDULE 5
CALCULATION OF TIME PERIODS

Rule 1.3

[Note: section 376 of the Act contains a power for the court to extend the time for doing anything required by the Act or these Rules under the Second Group of Parts (Insolvency of Individuals; bankruptcy).]

[6.938]
1 The rules in CPR 2.8 with the exception of paragraph (4) apply for the calculation of periods expressed in days in the Act and these Rules.

2 (1) This paragraph applies for the calculation of periods expressed in months.

(2) The beginning and the end of a period expressed in months is to be determined as follows—

- (a) if the beginning of the period is specified—
  - (i) the month in which the period ends is the specified number of months after the month in which it begins, and
  - (ii) the date in the month on which the period ends is—
    - [(aa) the day before the date corresponding to the date in the month on which it begins, or]
    - (bb) if there is no such date in the month in which it ends, the last day of that month;
- (b) if the end of the period is specified—
  - (i) the month in which the period begins is the specified number of months before the month in which it ends, and
  - (ii) the date in the month on which the period begins is—
    - [(aa) the day after the date corresponding to the date in the month on which it ends, or]
    - (bb) if there is no such date in the month in which it begins, the last day of that month.

3 The provisions of CPR rule 3.1(2)(a) (the court's general powers of management) apply so as to enable the court to extend or shorten the time for compliance with anything required or authorised to be done by these Rules.

4 Paragraph 3 is subject to any time limits expressly stated in the Act and to any specific powers in the Act or these Rules to extend or shorten the time for compliance.

NOTES

Commencement: 6 April 2017.

This Schedule derived from the Insolvency Rules 1986, SI 1986/1925, r 12.55.

Para 2: sub-paras (2)(a)(ii)(aa), (2)(b)(ii)(aa) substituted by the Insolvency (England and Wales) (Amendment) Rules 2017, SI 2017/366, rr 3, 51.

SCHEDULE 6
INSOLVENCY JURISDICTION OF COUNTY COURT HEARING CENTRES

Rule 9.22

[Note: where the entry "London Insolvency District" appears in this table, jurisdiction under Parts 1 to 7 of the Act is conferred on the High Court as a result of article 6B of the High Court and County Courts Jurisdiction Order 1991 (SI 1991/724) which was inserted by the High Court and County Courts Jurisdiction (Amendment) Order 2014 (SI 2014/821).]

[6.939]

Country court hearing centre	*Destination of Appeal*
Aberystwyth	Cardiff or Caernarfon District Registry
Banbury	Birmingham District Registry
Barnsley	Leeds District Registry
Barnstaple	Bristol District Registry
Barrow-in-Furness	Liverpool District Registry or Manchester District Registry
Bath	Bristol District Registry
Bedford	Birmingham District Registry
Birkenhead	Liverpool District Registry or Manchester District Registry
Birmingham	Birmingham District Registry
Blackburn	Liverpool District Registry or Manchester District Registry
Blackpool	Liverpool District Registry or Manchester District Registry
Blackwood	Cardiff District Registry
Bolton	Liverpool District Registry or Manchester District Registry
Boston	Birmingham District Registry
Bournemouth and Poole	Registrar in Bankruptcy
Bradford	Leeds District Registry

Part 6 Insolvency Rules

Country court hearing centre	*Destination of Appeal*
Brighton	Registrar in Bankruptcy
Bristol	Bristol District Registry
Burnley	Liverpool District Registry or Manchester District Registry
Bury	Liverpool District Registry or Manchester District Registry
Bury St Edmunds	Registrar in Bankruptcy
Caernarfon	Cardiff District Registry
Cambridge	Registrar in Bankruptcy
Canterbury	Registrar in Bankruptcy
Cardiff	Cardiff District Registry
Carlisle	Liverpool District Registry or Manchester District Registry
Caernarfon	Cardiff District Registry or Caernarfon District Registry
County Court at Central London	Registrar in Bankruptcy
Chelmsford	Registrar in Bankruptcy
Chester	Liverpool District Registry or Manchester District Registry
Chesterfield	Leeds District Registry
Colchester	Registrar in Bankruptcy
Coventry	Birmingham District Registry
Crewe	Liverpool District Registry or Manchester District Registry
Croydon	Registrar in Bankruptcy
Darlington	Newcastle District Registry
Derby	Birmingham District Registry
Doncaster	Leeds District Registry
Dudley	Birmingham District Registry
Durham	Leeds District Registry or Newcastle District Registry
Eastbourne	Registrar in Bankruptcy
Exeter	Bristol District Registry
Gloucester and Cheltenham	Bristol District Registry
Great Grimsby	Leeds District Registry
Guildford	Registrar in Bankruptcy
Halifax	Leeds District Registry
Harrogate	Leeds District Registry
Hastings	Registrar in Bankruptcy
Haverfordwest	Cardiff District Registry
Hereford	Bristol District Registry
Hertford	Registrar in Bankruptcy
Huddersfield	Leeds District Registry
Ipswich	Registrar in Bankruptcy
Kendal	Liverpool District Registry or Manchester District Registry
Kingston-upon-Hull	Leeds District Registry
Kingston-upon-Thames	Registrar in Bankruptcy
Lancaster	Liverpool District Registry or Manchester District Registry
Leeds	Leeds District Registry
Leicester	Birmingham District Registry
Lincoln	Leeds District Registry or Birmingham District Registry
Liverpool	Liverpool District Registry or Manchester District Registry
Llangefni	Cardiff District Registry or Caernarfon District Registry
Luton	Registrar in Bankruptcy
Maidstone	Registrar in Bankruptcy
Manchester	Manchester District Registry
Merthyr Tydfil	Cardiff District Registry
Middlesbrough	Newcastle District Registry

Country court hearing centre	*Destination of Appeal*
Milton Keynes	Birmingham District Registry
Newcastle upon Tyne	Newcastle District Registry
Newport (Gwent)	Cardiff District Registry
Newport (Isle of Wight)	Registrar in Bankruptcy
Northampton	Birmingham District Registry
Norwich	Registrar in Bankruptcy
Nottingham	Birmingham District Registry
Oldham	Liverpool District Registry or Manchester District Registry
Oxford	Registrar in Bankruptcy
Peterborough	Registrar in Bankruptcy
Plymouth	Bristol District Registry
Pontypridd	Cardiff District Registry
Portsmouth	Registrar in Bankruptcy
Port Talbot	Cardiff District Registry
Prestatyn	Cardiff District Registry or Caernarfon District Registry
Preston	Liverpool District Registry or Manchester District Registry
Reading	Registrar in Bankruptcy
Rhyl	Cardiff District Registry or Caernarfon District Registry
Romford	Registrar in Bankruptcy
Salisbury	Registrar in Bankruptcy
Scarborough	Leeds District Registry
Scunthorpe	Leeds District Registry
Sheffield	Leeds District Registry
Slough	Registrar in Bankruptcy
Southampton	Registrar in Bankruptcy
Southend-on-Sea	Registrar in Bankruptcy
Stafford	Birmingham District Registry
St Albans	Registrar in Bankruptcy
Stockport	Liverpool District Registry or Manchester District Registry
Stoke-on-Trent	Manchester District Registry
Sunderland	Newcastle District Registry
Swansea	Cardiff District Registry
Swindon	Bristol District Registry
Taunton	Bristol District Registry
Telford	Birmingham District Registry
Torquay & Newton Abbot	Bristol District Registry
Truro	Bristol District Registry
Tunbridge Wells	Registrar in Bankruptcy
Wakefield	Leeds District Registry
Walsall	Birmingham District Registry
Warwick	Birmingham District Registry
Welshpool & Newton	Cardiff District Registry
West Cumbria	Liverpool District Registry or Manchester District Registry
Wigan	Liverpool District Registry or Manchester District Registry
Winchester	Registrar in Bankruptcy
Wolverhampton	Birmingham District Registry
Worcester	Birmingham District Registry
Wrexham	Cardiff District Registry or Caernarfon District Registry
Yeovil	Bristol District Registry
York	Leeds District Registry

NOTES

Commencement: 6 April 2017.

This Schedule derived from the Insolvency Rules 1986, SI 1986/1925, Sch 2 and the Insolvency (Commencement of Proceedings) and Insolvency Rules 1986 (Amendment) Rules 2014, SI 2014/817.

SCHEDULE 7
INFORMATION TO BE PROVIDED IN THE BANKRUPTCY APPLICATION

Rule 10.35

PART 1

Debtor's personal information

[6.940]

1 Debtor's title.

2 Debtor's identification details.

3 Any previous name or other names by which the debtor is known or has been known during the last five years immediately before the date of the bankruptcy application.

NOTES

Commencement: 6 April 2017.

This Part of this Schedule derived from the Insolvency Rules 1986, SI 1986/1925, r 6.38, Schs 2A, 2B.

PART 2

Additional personal information

[6.941]

4 Debtor's contact telephone number.

5 Debtor's email address (if any).

6 Debtor's date of birth.

7 Debtor's National Insurance number.

8 Debtor's gender.

9 Any previous address at which the debtor has resided during the three years immediately before the date of the bankruptcy application.

10 Whether the debtor is—
- (a) single;
- (b) married;
- (c) divorced;
- (d) co-habiting;
- (e) separated;
- (f) widowed;
- (g) a civil partner;
- (h) a former civil partner; or
- (i) a surviving civil partner.

11 All occupants of the debtor's household and in relation to each person—
- (a) name;
- (b) age;
- (c) relationship to the debtor; and
- (d) whether or not that person is dependent on the debtor.

12 Any other person dependent on the debtor and in relation to each person—
- (a) name;
- (b) age;
- (c) postal address; and
- (d) reason for that person's dependency on the debtor.

Occupation and employment details

13 Debtor's occupation (if any).

14 Debtor's employment status.

15 Where the debtor is employed—
- (a) date when the debtor commenced the employment; and
- (b) name and address of the employer.

16 Where the debtor is unemployed—
- (a) date when the debtor was last employed;
- (b) date when the debtor commenced the employment; and

(c) name and address of the last employer.

17 Where the debtor has worked for any previous employers during the 12 months immediately before the date of the bankruptcy application—

(a) dates of that employment; and
(b) name and address of those employers.

18 Where the debtor is, or has been, self-employed other than as a partner in a partnership, during the three years preceding the date of the bankruptcy application, in respect of each business—

(a) date when the business commenced trading;
(b) name and trading address of the business;
(c) name or names, other than the debtor's name, in which the debtor carried on business;
(d) nature of the business;
(e) trading address or addresses of the business and any address or addresses at which the debtor has carried on business during the period in which any of the debtor's bankruptcy debts were incurred; and
(f) the date the business ceased trading, if applicable.

19 Where the debtor traded in a partnership at any time in the three years immediately preceding the date of the bankruptcy application, in respect of each partnership—

(a) date the partnership commenced;
(b) name and trading address of the partnership;
(c) trading address or addresses of the partnership and any address or addresses at which the partnership has carried on business during or after the time when any of the debtor's bankruptcy debts were incurred; and
(d) date the partnership ceased, if applicable.

20 Where the debtor is, or has been, a director or involved in the management of a company during the 12 months immediately preceding the date of the bankruptcy application—

(a) name and contact details for each company; and
(b) in the case of any company mentioned in accordance with sub paragraph (a) that is subject to any insolvency proceedings, the office-holder and contact details for that office-holder.

Creditors

21 In respect of each creditor—

(a) name and address;
(b) account number or reference (if known);
(c) date the debt was incurred;
(d) the amount the creditor claims the debtor owes the creditor; and
(e) where the debt is secured, the property of the debtor which is claimed by the creditor to clear or reduce the creditor's debt.

22 Where the debtor has an interest in a property, in relation to each property, its address.

Legal proceedings

23 Where the debtor is, or has been in the five years immediately preceding the date of the bankruptcy application, involved in proceedings for divorce, separation or the dissolution of a civil partnership—

(a) identity of the proceedings;
(b) nature of the proceedings; and
(c) date and details of any resolution of those proceedings and any agreed settlement, whether formal or informal, and any gifts or transfers of property that occurred in, or as a result, of those proceedings.

24 Where the debtor is involved in proceedings, other than proceedings for divorce, separation or the dissolution of a civil partnership—

(a) identity of the proceedings;
(b) nature of the proceedings; and
(c) date and details of any interim settlement, whether formal or informal, and any interim orders.

Assets and liabilities

25 Total value of assets.

26 Total value of liabilities.

27 Debtor's net monthly income from all sources.

28 Debtor's monthly surplus income calculated by reference to paragraphs 23 to 30 of Schedule 8 (additional information to be provided in the bankruptcy application).

NOTES

Commencement: 6 April 2017.
This Part of this Schedule derived from the Insolvency Rules 1986, SI 1986/1925, r 6.38, Schs 2A, 2B.

SCHEDULE 8
ADDITIONAL INFORMATION TO BE PROVIDED IN THE BANKRUPTCY APPLICATION

Rule 10.35

Disposal of assets

[6.942]

1 Where in the five years preceding the date on which the bankruptcy application is made the debtor has entered into a transaction at an undervalue within the meaning of section 339(1), given a preference within the meaning of section 340(2), has rights or excluded rights under section 342A(3) of the Act or placed an asset into a trust for the benefit of any person, including the surrender of life, endowment and pension policies, in respect of each asset—
- (a) description of the asset;
- (b) date the debtor gave away, transferred or sold the asset;
- (c) consideration given, if any;
- (d) name and address of the person to whom the debtor sold, transferred or gave away the asset;
- (e) relationship of that person to the debtor;
- (f) if relevant, name of the trustees and beneficiaries or class of beneficiaries;
- (g) estimated market value of the asset at the date of the bankruptcy application;
- (h) net proceeds (if any) (less any charges and legal fees).

2 Where in the five years preceding the date on which the bankruptcy application is made the debtor has disposed of or sold any property at market value or disposed of, sold at market value or realised any life, endowment and pension policies in respect of each asset—
- (a) description of the asset;
- (b) date the debtor disposed of, sold at market value or realised the asset; and
- (c) net proceeds (if any) (less any charges and legal fees).

Financial arrangements with creditors

3 Where the debtor has been made bankrupt in the two years immediately preceding the date of the bankruptcy application—
- (a) date of the bankruptcy order; and
- (b) reference allocated by the official receiver.

4 Where the debtor has entered into a debt relief order in the two years immediately preceding the date of the bankruptcy application—
- (a) date of the debt relief order; and
- (b) reference allocated by the official receiver.

5 Where the debtor has, or has had, an IVA in the two years immediately preceding the date of the bankruptcy application, the date of the arrangement.

6 Where the debtor has, or has had, an arrangement in force with creditors, other than an IVA in the two years immediately preceding the date of the bankruptcy application, the date and nature of the arrangement.

Legal and financial advisers

7 Where a solicitor has acted for or on behalf of the debtor in the five years immediately preceding the date of the bankruptcy application, in relation to each solicitor—
- (a) name, address and reference of the solicitor; and
- (b) nature and date of the transaction or transactions on which the solicitor advised or acted.

8 Where an accountant, book keeper or other financial adviser has acted for or on behalf of the debtor in the five years immediately preceding the date of the bankruptcy application, in relation to each accountant, book keeper and financial adviser—
- (a) name, address and reference; and
- (b) dates of acting for the debtor.

Business affairs of a self-employed debtor

9 Where the debtor traded in a partnership at any time in the three years immediately preceding the date of the bankruptcy application, in respect of each partnership—
- (a) names and addresses of each of the partners;
- (b) name or names, other than the partners' names, in which the partnership carried on business; and
- (c) the nature of the partnership business.

10 Where the debtor is or has been self-employed (other than as a partner in a partnership) at any time in the three years immediately preceding the date of the bankruptcy application—
- (a) Value Added Tax number, where the business was registered for Value Added Tax;
- (b) address where the debtor's books of account and other accounting records are kept; and
- (c) where the debtor holds records on a computer, details of which records are held, what software is used (including any passwords) and where the computer is located.

11 Where the debtor is or has been self-employed (including a partner in a partnership) at any time in the three years immediately preceding the date of the bankruptcy application—

(a) name and address of any person employed by the debtor immediately preceding the bankruptcy application; and
(b) whether—
(i) the debtor owes any employee or former employee any money, and
(ii) any employee or former employee has or may claim that the debtor owes that person some money.

Financial affairs—assets

12 The nature and value of each asset belonging to the debtor.

13 Where any asset is owned jointly with another person—
(a) name and address of that joint owner; and
(b) relationship of that person to the debtor.

14 Where any asset is subject to the rights of any person (other than a joint owner), whether as a secured creditor of the debtor or otherwise, in respect of each asset—
(a) nature of third party rights;
(b) account number or reference of that creditor or creditors; and
(c) amount each creditor claims is owed to them.

15 Where the debtor holds or has held in the last two years any bank, building society, credit union or national savings account including any joint, business or dormant accounts, in respect of each account—
(a) name, address and sort code of the bank or supplier;
(b) account number; and
(c) whether or not the debtor's regular income is paid into the account.

16 Where the debtor owns a motor vehicle or has disposed of any vehicle during the 12 months immediately preceding the date of the bankruptcy application, in respect of each motor vehicle—
(a) make and model;
(b) registration number;
(c) what the motor vehicle is [or was] used for by the debtor
(d) save where the motor vehicle has been disposed of, the location of the motor vehicle; and
(e) where the motor vehicle has been disposed of, the date of disposal and any proceeds from that disposal.

17 Where the debtor regularly uses a motor vehicle that the debtor does not own, in respect of each motor vehicle—
(a) make and model;
(b) registration number;
(c) name and address of the owner; and
(d) debtor's relationship to the vehicle's owner.

18 Where the debtor owns any property consisting of land or buildings, in respect of each property—
(a) type of and description of the property;
(b) who lives at the property and their relationship to the debtor;
(c) any income received by the debtor from the property; and
(d) nature of the insurance policy currently in force in relation to the property and the expiry date of that insurance policy.

19 Where the debtor rents or leases a property, in respect of each property—
(a) who lives at the property and their relationship to the debtor;
(b) monthly rent;
(c) name and address of the landlord and any managing agent.

20 Where the debtor has an interest in any other property, in respect of each property—
(a) nature of the interest;
(b) type of and description of the property;
(c) who lives at the property and their relationship to the debtor;
(d) name and address of the person who permits the debtor to use the property;
(e) amount paid by the debtor to the person who permits the debtor to use the property;
(f) any income received by the debtor from the property; and
(g) whether or not there is a written agreement.

21 Where the debtor resides at a property in which the debtor has no interest, the basis on which the debtor resides at that property.

22 Where the debtor has or has held within the five years immediately before the date of the bankruptcy application any occupational pension, personal pension, endowment or other life policy in relation to each policy—
(a) type of policy;
(b) name and address of the pension, endowment or life assurance company or broker;
(c) policy number;
(d) approximate date when the policy was taken out;
(e) estimated value of policy;
(f) amount (if any) being received now by the debtor and the frequency of those payments; and

(g) name of the beneficiary or beneficiaries of the policy.

Financial affairs—income and expenditure

23 Debtor's total annual income from all sources, the sources of that income and the amount from each source.

24 Total annual household income from all sources, the sources of that income and the amount from each source.

25 Current (or last) income tax reference number.

26 Monthly national insurance.

27 Mean monthly tax.

28 Where the debtor has any current attachment of earnings orders in force, in respect of each attachment of earnings order—
(a) name of creditor;
(b) name of the court that made the attachment of earnings order.

29 Particulars of the debtor's mean monthly expenditure which the debtor claims is necessary to meet the monthly reasonable domestic needs of the debtor's family, including the objective and the amount of that expenditure.

30 Particulars of the debtor's monthly expenditure not otherwise provided under this Schedule.

Enforcement officers and enforcement agents

31 Where an enforcement officer or enforcement agent has visited the debtor in the last six months—
(a) name of the creditor by whom the relevant debt is claimed;
(b) date of initial visit;
(c) description and estimated value of property seized.

Cause of insolvency

32 Why the debt was incurred.

33 Date when the debtor first experienced difficulty in paying some or all of the debtor's debts.

34 Reasons for the debtor not having enough money to pay some or all of the debtor's debts.

35 Where the debtor has gambled any money through betting or gambling during the last two years, how much the debtor has gambled.

NOTES

Commencement: 6 April 2017.

This Schedule derived from the Insolvency Rules 1986, SI 1986/1925, r 6.38, Schs 2A, 2B.

Para 16: words in square brackets in sub-para (c) inserted by the Insolvency (England and Wales) (Amendment) Rules 2017, SI 2017/366, rr 3, 52.

SCHEDULE 9
INFORMATION TO BE GIVEN TO CREDITORS

Rule 10.47

[6.943]

1 Title of the debtor.

2 Debtor's identification details.

3 Any previous name or other names by which the debtor is known or has been known during the last five years immediately before the date of the bankruptcy application.

4 Any previous address at which the debtor has resided at during the three years immediately before the date of the bankruptcy application.

5 Name and address for each creditor.

6 Amount each creditor claims is due.

7 Debtor's occupation (if any).

8 Debtor's employment status.

9 Where the debtor is, or has been, self-employed other than as a partner in a partnership, during the three years preceding the date of the bankruptcy application, in respect of each business—
(a) name and trading address of the business;
(b) name or names, other than the debtor's name, in which the debtor carried on business;
(c) nature of the business;

(d) trading address or addresses of the business and any address or addresses at which the debtor has carried on business during the period in which any of the debtor's bankruptcy debts were incurred; and

(e) where the business has ceased trading, the date when the business ceased trading.

10 Total value of assets.

11 Total value of liabilities.

12 Where in the five years preceding the date of the bankruptcy application the debtor has given away, placed into a trust for the benefit of any person, given a preference within the meaning of section 340 of the Act, has rights or excluded rights under section 342A of the Act or has transferred or sold for less than its true value any assets that the debtor owned, either alone or jointly, including the surrender of life, endowment and pension policies in relation to each asset—

(a) description of the asset;

(b) date the debtor gave away, transferred or sold the asset;

(c) relationship of that person to the debtor;

(d) estimated market value or true value of the asset at the date of the bankruptcy application;

(e) value at which the asset was given away, transferred or sold; and

(f) net proceeds (if any) (less any charges and legal fees).

13 Where any asset is owned jointly with another person, the nature of the asset.

14 Where any asset is subject to the rights of any person (other than a joint owner), whether as a secured creditor of the debtor or otherwise, in respect of each asset, the nature of third party rights.

15 Where the debtor owns a motor vehicle or has disposed of any vehicle during the 12 months immediately preceding the date of the bankruptcy application, in respect of each motor vehicle—

(a) make, model and year of manufacture;

(b) what the motor vehicle is [or was] used for by the debtor;

(c) save where the motor vehicle has been disposed of, the location of the motor vehicle;

(d) where the motor vehicle has been disposed of, the date of disposal and any proceeds from that disposal.

16 Where the debtor regularly uses a motor vehicle that the debtor does not own, [in relation to] each motor vehicle—

(a) make and model; and

(b) debtor's relationship to the vehicle's owner.

17 Where the debtor owns or has an interest in any property, [in respect of] each property—

(a) address;

(b) type of and description of the property;

(c) nature of the interest

(d) value of that interest; and

(e) any income received by the debtor from the property.

18 Where the debtor holds or has held within the five years immediately before the date of the bankruptcy application any occupational pension, personal pension, endowment or other life policy [in respect of] each policy—

(a) type of policy;

(b) approximate date when the policy was taken out; and

(c) estimated value of policy.

19 Debtor's net monthly income from all sources.

20 Debtor's monthly surplus income after taking into account any contribution made by a member of the debtor's family to the amount necessary for the reasonable domestic needs of the debtor and the debtor's family.

21 Current (or last) income tax reference number.

22 [In respect of] each creditor—

(a) name and address;

(b) date the debt was incurred;

(c) the amount the creditor claims the debtor owes the creditor;

(d) where the debt is secured, the property of the debtor which is claimed by the creditor to clear of reduce the creditor's debt.

NOTES

Commencement: 6 April 2017.

This Schedule derived from the Insolvency Rules 1986, SI 1986/1925, Sch 2C.

Para 15: words in square brackets inserted by the Insolvency (England and Wales) (Amendment) Rules 2017, SI 2017/366, rr 3, 53.

Paras 16, 17, 18, 22: words in square brackets substituted by SI 2017/366, rr 3, 54, 55.

SCHEDULE 10
DESTINATION OF APPEALS FROM DECISIONS OF DISTRICT JUDGES IN CORPORATE INSOLVENCY MATTERS

Rule 12.59

[6.944]

Country court hearing centre	*Destination of Appeal*
Aberystwyth	Cardiff or Caernarfon District Registry
Banbury	Birmingham District Registry
Barnsley	Leeds District Registry
Barnstaple	Bristol District Registry
Barrow-in-Furness	Liverpool District Registry or Manchester District Registry
Bath	Bristol District Registry
Bedford	Birmingham District Registry
Birkenhead	Liverpool District Registry or Manchester District Registry
Birmingham	Birmingham District Registry
Blackburn	Liverpool District Registry or Manchester District Registry
Blackpool	Liverpool District Registry or Manchester District Registry
Blackwood	Cardiff District Registry
Bolton	Liverpool District Registry or Manchester District Registry
Boston	Birmingham District Registry
Bournemouth and Poole	Registrar in Bankruptcy
Bradford	Leeds District Registry
Brighton	Registrar in Bankruptcy
Bristol	Bristol District Registry
Burnley	Liverpool District Registry or Manchester District Registry
Bury	Liverpool District Registry or Manchester District Registry
Bury St Edmunds	Registrar in Bankruptcy
Caernarfon	Cardiff District Registry
Cambridge	Registrar in Bankruptcy
Canterbury	Registrar in Bankruptcy
Cardiff	Cardiff District Registry
Carlisle	Liverpool District Registry or Manchester District Registry
Caernarfon	Cardiff District Registry or Caernarfon District Registry
County Court at Central London	Registrar in Bankruptcy
Chelmsford	Registrar in Bankruptcy
Chester	Liverpool District Registry or Manchester District Registry
Chesterfield	Leeds District Registry
Colchester	Registrar in Bankruptcy
Coventry	Birmingham District Registry
Crewe	Liverpool District Registry or Manchester District Registry
Croydon	Registrar in Bankruptcy
Darlington	Newcastle District Registry
Derby	Birmingham District Registry
Doncaster	Leeds District Registry
Dudley	Birmingham District Registry
Durham	Leeds District Registry or Newcastle District Registry
Eastbourne	Registrar in Bankruptcy
Exeter	Bristol District Registry
Gloucester and Cheltenham	Bristol District Registry
Great Grimsby	Leeds District Registry
Guildford	Registrar in Bankruptcy
Halifax	Leeds District Registry
Harrogate	Leeds District Registry

Hastings	Registrar in Bankruptcy
Haverfordwest	Cardiff District Registry
Hereford	Bristol District Registry
Hertford	Registrar in Bankruptcy
Huddersfield	Leeds District Registry
Ipswich	Registrar in Bankruptcy
Kendal	Liverpool District Registry or Manchester District Registry
Kingston-upon-Hull	Leeds District Registry
Kingston-upon-Thames	Registrar in Bankruptcy
Lancaster	Liverpool District Registry or Manchester District Registry
Leeds	Leeds District Registry
Leicester	Birmingham District Registry
Lincoln	Leeds District Registry or Birmingham District Registry
Liverpool	Liverpool District Registry or Manchester District Registry
Llangefni	Cardiff District Registry or Caernarfon District Registry
Luton	Registrar in Bankruptcy
Maidstone	Registrar in Bankruptcy
Manchester	Manchester District Registry
Merthyr Tydfil	Cardiff District Registry
Middlesbrough	Newcastle District Registry
Milton Keynes	Birmingham District Registry
Newcastle upon Tyne	Newcastle District Registry
Newport (Gwent)	Cardiff District Registry
Newport (Isle of Wight)	Registrar in Bankruptcy
Northampton	Birmingham District Registry
Norwich	Registrar in Bankruptcy
Nottingham	Birmingham District Registry
Oldham	Liverpool District Registry or Manchester District Registry
Oxford	Registrar in Bankruptcy
Peterborough	Registrar in Bankruptcy
Plymouth	Bristol District Registry
Pontypridd	Cardiff District Registry
Portsmouth	Registrar in Bankruptcy
Port Talbot	Cardiff District Registry
Prestatyn	Cardiff District Registry or Caernarfon District Registry
Preston	Liverpool District Registry or Manchester District Registry
Reading	Registrar in Bankruptcy
Rhyl	Cardiff District Registry or Caernarfon District Registry
Romford	Registrar in Bankruptcy
Salisbury	Registrar in Bankruptcy
Scarborough	Leeds District Registry
Scunthorpe	Leeds District Registry
Sheffield	Leeds District Registry
Slough	Registrar in Bankruptcy
Southampton	Registrar in Bankruptcy
Southend-on-Sea	Registrar in Bankruptcy
Stafford	Birmingham District Registry
St Albans	Registrar in Bankruptcy
Stockport	Liverpool District Registry or Manchester District Registry
Stoke-on-Trent	Manchester District Registry
Sunderland	Newcastle District Registry
Swansea	Cardiff District Registry

Swindon	Bristol District Registry
Taunton	Bristol District Registry
Telford	Birmingham District Registry
Torquay & Newton Abbot	Bristol District Registry
Truro	Bristol District Registry
Tunbridge Wells	Registrar in Bankruptcy
Wakefield	Leeds District Registry
Walsall	Birmingham District Registry
Warwick	Birmingham District Registry
Welshpool & Newton	Cardiff District Registry
West Cumbria	Liverpool District Registry or Manchester District Registry
Wigan	Liverpool District Registry or Manchester District Registry
Winchester	Registrar in Bankruptcy
Wolverhampton	Birmingham District Registry
Worcester	Birmingham District Registry
Wrexham	Cardiff District Registry or Caernarfon District Registry
Yeovil	Bristol District Registry
York	Leeds District Registry

NOTES

Commencement: 6 April 2017.

SCHEDULE 11
DETERMINATION OF INSOLVENCY OFFICE-HOLDER'S REMUNERATION

Rule 18.22

[6.945]

This table sets out the realisation and distribution scales for determining the remuneration of trustees and liquidators.

The realisation scale	
on the first £5,000	20%
on the next £5,000	15%
on the next £90,000	10%
on all further sums realised	5%

The distribution scale	
on the first £5,000	10%
on the next £5,000	7.5%
on the next £90,000	5%
on all further sums distributed	2.5%.

NOTES

Commencement: 6 April 2017.

This Schedule derived from the Insolvency Rules 1986, SI 1986/1925, Sch 6.

INSOLVENCY (ENGLAND AND WALES) RULES 2016 (CONSEQUENTIAL AMENDMENTS AND SAVINGS) RULES 2017

(SI 2017/369)

NOTES

Made: 9 March 2017.

Authority: Insolvency Act 1986, ss 411, 412.

Commencement: 6 April 2017.

[6.946]

1 Citation and commencement

These Rules may be cited as the Insolvency (England and Wales) Rules 2016 (Consequential Amendments and Savings) Rules 2017 and come into force on 6th April 2017.

NOTES

Commencement: 6 April 2017.

2 (*Rule 2 introduces Schs 1 and 2 (amendments to primary and subordinate legislation).*)

[6.947]

3 Savings in relation to special insolvency rules

The Insolvency Rules 1986, as they had effect immediately before 6th April 2017, insofar as they apply to proceedings under the following instruments, continue to have effect for the purposes of the application of—

(a) the Railway Administration Order 2001;
(b) the Limited Liability Partnerships Regulations 2001;
(c) the Energy Act 2004;
(d) the Energy Administration Rules 2005;
(e) the PPP Administration Order Rules 2007;
(f) the Water Industry (Special Administration) Rules 2009;
(g) the Energy Act 2011;
(h) the Charitable Incorporated Organisations (Insolvency and Dissolution) Regulations 2012;
(i) the Energy Supply Company Administration Rules 2013; and
(j) the Postal Administration Rules 2013.

NOTES

Commencement: 6 April 2017.

SCHEDULES 1, 2

(*Schs 1 and 2 contain amendments to primary and subordinate legislation; in so far as they are relevant to this work they have been incorporated at the appropriate place.*)

PART 7
SPECIAL INSOLVENCY REGIMES—ENGLAND AND WALES

A
AIR TRAFFIC

TRANSPORT ACT 2000

(2000 c 38)

ARRANGEMENT OF SECTIONS

PART I
AIR TRAFFIC

CHAPTER I
AIR TRAFFIC SERVICES

Administration orders etc

26 Protection of licence companies etc . . . . [7.1]
27 Duty to make order . . . . [7.2]
28 Power to make order . . . . [7.3]
29 Air traffic administration orders . . . . [7.4]
30 Petitions and orders: supplementary . . . . [7.5]
31 Government financial help . . . . [7.6]
32 Guarantees under section 31 . . . . [7.7]
33 Northern Ireland . . . . [7.8]

PART V
MISCELLANEOUS AND SUPPLEMENTARY

Supplementary

275 Commencement . . . . [7.9]
279 Extent . . . . [7.10]
280 Short title . . . . [7.11]

SCHEDULES

Schedule 1—Air traffic administration orders: General
Part I—Modifications of 1986 Act . . . . [7.12]
Part II—Other provisions . . . . [7.13]
Schedule 2—Air traffic administration orders: Schemes . . . . [7.14]
Schedule 3—Air traffic administration orders: Northern Ireland . . . . [7.15]

An Act to make provision about transport

[30 November 2000]

NOTES

Note that the Insolvency Act 1986, Pt II (ss 8–27), which dealt with administration orders (the subject-matter of most of the provisions of this Act reproduced here), is substituted by the Enterprise Act 2002, s 248(1), subject to savings and transitional provisions (i) in a case where a petition for an administration order has been presented before 15 September 2003 (see the Enterprise Act 2002 (Commencement No 4 and Transitional Provisions and Savings) Order 2003, SI 2003/2093, art 3 at **[2.26]**), and (ii) in relation to special administration regimes (see s 249 of the 2002 Act at **[2.10]**). The administration of companies is now dealt with in Sch B1 to the 1986 Act at **[1.575]**.

PART I
AIR TRAFFIC

CHAPTER I AIR TRAFFIC SERVICES

1–25 (*Outside the scope of this work.*)

Administration orders etc

[7.1]

26 Protection of licence companies etc

(1) No licence company may be wound up voluntarily.

(2) No application may be made to a court for an administration order under Part II of the 1986 Act in relation to a licence company, and—

(a) anything purporting to be such an application is of no effect;

(b) no administration order may be made under that Part in relation to a licence company.

(3) No step may be taken by a person to enforce any security over the property of a licence company unless the person has given to the Secretary of State and the CAA at least 14 days' notice of his intention to take the step.

(4) No application for the winding up of a licence company may be made by a person other than the Secretary of State unless the person has given to the Secretary of State and the CAA at least 14 days' notice of his intention to make the application.
(5) In subsection (3) "security" and "property" have the same meanings as in Parts I to VII of the 1986 Act.
(6) In this section and sections 27 to 30—
(a) references to a licence company are to a company which holds a licence;
(b) references to the 1986 Act are to the Insolvency Act 1986.

[7.2]
27 Duty to make order
(1) This section applies if an application is made to any court for the winding up of a licence company.
(2) The Secretary of State and the CAA are entitled to be heard by the court.
(3) The court must not make a winding up order or appoint a provisional liquidator.
(4) But if the court is satisfied that it would be appropriate to make a winding up order if the company were not a licence company, it must instead make an air traffic administration order.
(5) The Secretary of State and the CAA may propose a person to manage the company's affairs, business and property while an air traffic administration order is in force; and if they do the court must appoint that person.
(6) A reference to the court is to the court which (but for this section) would have jurisdiction to wind up the company.

[7.3]
28 Power to make order
(1) The court may make an air traffic administration order in relation to a licence company if—
(a) an application by petition is made by the Secretary of State or by the CAA with his consent, and
(b) the court is satisfied that one or more of the following four conditions is satisfied.
(2) The first condition is that the company is or is likely to be unable to pay its debts.
(3) The second condition is that—
(a) the Secretary of State certifies that but for section 27 it would be appropriate for him to petition for the company's winding up under section 124A of the 1986 Act (petition following inspectors' report etc), and
(b) but for section 27 it would be just and equitable (as mentioned in section 124A) for the company to be wound up.
(4) The third condition is that—
(a) there has been or is or is likely to be a contravention by the company of a section 8 duty,
(b) no notice has been served under section 22(10) or (11) in relation to the contravention or apprehended contravention, and
(c) the contravention or apprehended contravention is serious enough to make it inappropriate for the company to continue to hold the licence concerned.
(5) The fourth condition is that—
(a) a final or provisional order has been made or confirmed in relation to a section 8 duty or a licence condition,
(b) the order is not the subject of proceedings under section 23, and
(c) there has been or is or is likely to be such a contravention of the order by the company as to make it inappropriate for it to continue to hold the licence concerned.
(6) For the purposes of subsection (2) a company is unable to pay its debts if it is deemed to be unable to do so under section 123 of the 1986 Act.
(7) A reference in subsection (4) or (5) to a section 8 duty or to a licence condition or to a final or provisional order is to be construed in accordance with section 20.
(8) A reference to the court is to the court which (but for section 27) would have jurisdiction to wind up the company.

[7.4]
29 Air traffic administration orders
(1) An air traffic administration order made under section 27 or 28 is an order directing that in the period while the order is in force the company's affairs, business and property are to be managed by a person appointed by the court—
(a) for the achievement of the following two purposes, and
(b) in a manner which protects the interests of the company's members and creditors.
(2) The first purpose is—
(a) the transfer to another company, as a going concern, of so much of the licence company's undertaking as it is necessary to transfer to ensure that its licensed activities may be properly carried out, or
(b) the transfer to different companies of different parts of the licence company's undertaking, as going concerns, where the parts together constitute so much of its undertaking as is described in paragraph (a).
(3) The second purpose is the carrying on, pending the transfer, of the licence company's licensed activities.
(4) A reference to a licence company's licensed activities is to the activities which the licence concerned authorises the company to carry out.
(5) In subsection (1) "business" and "property" have the same meanings as in the 1986 Act.
(6) The reference in subsection (1) to the court is to the court making the order.

[7.5]
30 Petitions and orders: supplementary
(1) A petition under section 28 above cannot be withdrawn except with the court's leave.
(2) Section 9(4) and (5) of the 1986 Act (court's powers) apply on the hearing of a petition under section 28 above as they apply on the hearing of a petition for an administration order.
(3) Section 10(1), (2), (4) and (5) of the 1986 Act (effect of petition) apply in the case of a petition under section 28 above as if—
(a) the reference in subsection (1) to an administration order were to an air traffic administration order;
(b) the reference in subsection (1)(c) to proceedings included a reference to proceedings under or for the purposes of section 20 above;
(c) in subsection (1)(c) after "its property" there were inserted ", and no right of re-entry or forfeiture may be enforced against the company in respect of any land,";
(d) subsection (2)(b) and (c) were omitted.
(4) Schedules 1 and 2 contain provisions relating to air traffic administration orders.
(5) The power given by section 411 of the 1986 Act to make rules applies for the purpose of giving effect to the air traffic administration order provisions as it applies for the purpose of giving effect to Parts I to VII of that Act, but taking references to those Parts as references to those provisions.
(6) The air traffic administration order provisions are sections 27 to 29, this section and Schedules 1 and 2.
(7) The reference in subsection (1) to the court is to the court to which the application by petition is made.

[7.6]
31 Government financial help
(1) If an air traffic administration order is in force in relation to a company the Secretary of State may—
(a) make grants or loans to the company of such sums as he thinks appropriate to facilitate the achievement of the order's purposes;
(b) agree to indemnify the air traffic administrator in respect of liabilities incurred and loss or damage sustained by him in connection with carrying out his functions under the order.
(2) The Secretary of State may guarantee, in such manner and on such terms as he thinks fit, the repayment of the principal of, the payment of interest on and the discharge of any other financial obligation in connection with any sum borrowed from any person by a company in relation to which an air traffic administration order is in force when the guarantee is given.
(3) The terms on which a grant is made under this section may require all or part of it to be repaid to the Secretary of State if there is a contravention of the other terms on which it is made.
(4) A loan made under this section must be repaid to the Secretary of State at such times and by such methods, and interest must be paid to him at such rates and times, as may be specified in directions given by him from time to time.
(5) Subsections (3) and (4) do not prejudice any provision applied in relation to the company by Schedule 1.
(6) A grant, loan, agreement to indemnify, guarantee or direction under this section requires the Treasury's consent.
(7) The air traffic administrator is the person appointed by the court to achieve the purposes of the air traffic administration order.

[7.7]
32 Guarantees under section 31
(1) This section applies to a guarantee given under section 31.
(2) Immediately after a guarantee is given the Secretary of State must lay a statement of it before each House of Parliament.
(3) If a sum is paid out for fulfilling a guarantee, as soon as possible after the end of each relevant financial year the Secretary of State must lay a statement relating to the sum before each House of Parliament.
(4) If any sums are paid out for fulfilling a guarantee the borrowing company must make to the Secretary of State at such times and in such manner as may be specified in directions given by him from time to time—
(a) payments of such amounts as he may specify in such directions in or towards repayment of the sums paid out, and
(b) payments of interest at such rate as he may specify in such directions on what is outstanding in respect of sums paid out.
(5) Subsection (4) does not prejudice any provision applied in relation to the borrowing company by Schedule 1.
(6) A direction under this section requires the Treasury's consent.
(7) Relevant financial years are financial years starting with that in which the sum is paid out and ending with that in which all liability in respect of the principal of the sum and interest on it is finally discharged.
(8) The borrowing company is the company which borrowed the sums in respect of which the guarantee was given.

[7.8]
33 Northern Ireland

Schedule 3 contains provisions relating to Northern Ireland.

34–254 (*Ss 34–40, ss 41–107 (Chs II–VI), ss 108–254 (Pts II–IV) outside the scope of this work.*)

PART V
MISCELLANEOUS AND SUPPLEMENTARY

255–272 (*Outside the scope of this work.*)

Supplementary

273, 274 (*Outside the scope of this work.*)

[7.9]
275 Commencement

(1) Subject as follows, the preceding provisions of this Act come into force in accordance with provision made by the Secretary of State by order made by statutory instrument; and different provision may be made for different purposes.

(2)–(5) (*Outside the scope of this work.*)

NOTES

Orders: various commencement orders have been made under this section. The order relevant to the provisions of this Act reproduced here is the Transport Act 2000 (Commencement No 3) Order 2001, SI 2001/57.

276–278 (*Outside the scope of this work.*)

[7.10]
279 Extent

(1) Parts II and III, and the repeals relating to those Parts, and sections 255 and 256, 265, 267 and 268 and 270 and 271, and the repeals in Part V(2) of Schedule 31, extend only to England and Wales.

(2) Subject as follows, Part IV, sections 257 to 260 (and Schedule 29), sections 261 to 263 (and Schedule 30) and sections 264, 266 and 269, and Part V(1) of Schedule 31, extend only to England and Wales and Scotland.

(3) The amendments made by Parts I and IV, and the repeals and revocations relating to those Parts, have the same extent as the enactments to which they relate (except where it is otherwise provided).

(4) Sections 247 and 250, paragraph 14 of Schedule 14 and Schedule 26 extend to England and Wales, Scotland and Northern Ireland.

[7.11]
280 Short title

This Act may be cited as the Transport Act 2000.

SCHEDULES

SCHEDULE 1
AIR TRAFFIC ADMINISTRATION ORDERS: GENERAL

Section 30

PART I
MODIFICATIONS OF 1986 ACT

Introduction

[7.12]
1. This Part of this Schedule applies if an air traffic administration order is made.

General application of provisions of 1986 Act

2. Sections 11 to 23 and 27 of the 1986 Act (which relate to administration orders under Part II of that Act) apply with the modifications specified in this Part of this Schedule.

General modifications

3. In those sections as applied by this Part of this Schedule—

(a) references to an administration order are to an air traffic administration order, and

(b) references to an administrator are to an air traffic administrator.

Effect of order

4. In section 11 of the 1986 Act (effect of order) as applied by this Part of this Schedule—

(a) the requirement in subsection (1)(a) that any petition for the winding up of the company shall be dismissed does not prejudice the air traffic administration order if it is made by virtue of section 27 above,

(b) the reference in subsection (3)(d) to proceedings includes a reference to any proceedings under or for the purposes of section 20 above, and

(c) subsection (3)(d) has effect as if after "its property" there were inserted ", and no right of re-entry or forfeiture may be enforced against the company in respect of any land,".

Appointment of air traffic administrator

5. In section 13 of the 1986 Act (appointment of administrator) as applied by this Part of this Schedule for subsection (3) substitute—

"(3) An application for an order under subsection (2) may be made—
(a) by the Secretary of State,
(b) by the CAA with the Secretary of State's consent,
(c) by any continuing air traffic administrator of the company, or
(d) where there is no such air traffic administrator, by the company, the directors or any creditor or creditors of the company."

General powers of air traffic administrator

6. (1) Section 14 of the 1986 Act (general powers of administrator) as applied by this Part of this Schedule has effect as follows.

(2) In subsection (1)(b) the reference to the powers specified in Schedule 1 to the 1986 Act includes a reference to a power to act on behalf of the company—
(a) for the purposes of this Part, or
(b) for the purposes of the exercise or performance of any power or duty which is conferred or imposed on the company by virtue of its holding a licence.

(3) In subsection (4) the reference to a power conferred by the company's [articles of association] includes a reference to a power conferred by virtue of the company's holding a licence.

Power to deal with charged property

7. (1) Section 15 of the 1986 Act (power to deal with charged property) as applied by this Part of this Schedule has effect as follows.

(2) In subsection (2) for "the purpose or one or more of the purposes specified in the administration order" substitute "one or both of the purposes of the administration order".

(3) In subsection (5)(b) for "in the open market by a willing vendor" substitute "for the best price which is reasonably available on a sale which is consistent with the purposes of the air traffic administration order".

Duties of air traffic administrator

8. (1) Section 17 of the 1986 Act (duties of administrator) as applied by this Part of this Schedule has effect as follows.

(2) For subsection (2) substitute—

"(2) Subject to any directions of the court, it shall be the duty of the air traffic administrator to manage the affairs, business and property of the company in accordance with proposals under section 23 as they are revised from time to time."

(3) In subsection (3) omit paragraph (a).

Discharge of order

9. (1) Section 18 of the 1986 Act (discharge and variation of administration order) as applied by this Part of this Schedule has effect as follows.

(2) For subsections (1) and (2) substitute—

"(1) An application for an air traffic administration order to be discharged may be made—
(a) by the air traffic administrator, on the ground that the purposes of the order have been achieved; or
(b) by the Secretary of State or (with his consent) by the CAA, on the ground that it is no longer necessary that those purposes are achieved."

(3) In subsection (3) omit the words "or vary".

(4) In subsection (4)—
(a) omit the words "or varied" and "or variation", and
(b) after "to the registrar of companies" insert ", to the CAA and to the Secretary of State".

Notice of making of order

10. In section 21(2) of the 1986 Act (notice of order to be given by administrator) as applied by this Part of this Schedule after "to the registrar of companies" insert ", to the CAA, to the Secretary of State".

Statement of proposals

11. In section 23 of the 1986 Act (statement of proposals) as applied by this Part of this Schedule for subsections (1) and (2) substitute—

"(1) Where an air traffic administration order has been made, the air traffic administrator shall, within 3 months (or such longer period as the court may allow) after the making of the order, send a statement of his proposals for achieving the purposes of the order—

(a) to the Secretary of State,
(b) to the CAA,
(c) to all creditors of the company (so far as he is aware of their addresses), and
(d) to the registrar of companies.

(2) The air traffic administrator may from time to time revise those proposals.

(2A) If the air traffic administrator proposes to make revisions which appear to him to be substantial, he shall before making them send a statement of the proposed revisions—
(a) to the Secretary of State,
(b) to the CAA,
(c) to all creditors of the company (so far as he is aware of their addresses), and
(d) to the registrar of companies.

(2B) The air traffic administrator shall give a copy of any statement under subsection (1) or (2A) to all members of the company before the end of the period described in subsection (1) or, as the case may be, before making the revisions.

(2C) The requirement in subsection (2B) is satisfied if the administrator—
(a) sends a copy of the statement to all members of the company (so far as he is aware of their addresses), or
(b) publishes in the prescribed manner a notice stating an address to which members should write for copies of the statement to be sent to them free of charge."

Applications to court

12. (1) Section 27 of the 1986 Act (protection of interests of creditors and members) as applied by this Part of this Schedule has effect as follows.

(2) After subsection (1) insert—

"(1A) If a creditor or member of the company makes an application under subsection (1), the court shall give notice of the application to the Secretary of State, who shall be entitled to be heard by the court in connection with the application.

(1B) At any time when an air traffic administration order is in force the Secretary of State or (with his consent) the CAA may apply to the court by petition for an order under this section on one or both of the following grounds.

(1C) The first ground is that the air traffic administrator has exercised or is exercising or proposing to exercise his powers in relation to the company in a manner which will not best ensure the achievement of the purposes of the order.

(1D) The second ground is that he has exercised or is exercising or proposing to exercise his powers in relation to the company in a manner which involves a contravention of—
(a) a condition of the licence granted under Chapter I of Part I of the Transport Act 2000, or
(b) a duty imposed by section 8(1) of that Act, or
(c) any other requirement imposed on the company by virtue of its holding the licence."

(3) Omit subsection (3).

(4) In subsection (4) omit the words "Subject as above".

(5) After that subsection insert—

"(4A) Provision may be made by virtue of subsection (4)(d) that the air traffic administration order is to be discharged from such date as may be specified in the order unless, before that date, such measures are taken as the court thinks fit for the purpose of protecting the interests of creditors."

(6) For subsection (6) substitute—

"(6) Where an air traffic administration order is discharged, the air traffic administrator shall within 14 days after the date on which the discharge takes effect send [a copy] of the order under this section—
(a) to the Secretary of State,
(b) to the CAA, and
(c) to the registrar of companies;

and if, without reasonable excuse, the air traffic administrator fails to comply with this subsection, he is liable to a fine and, for continued contravention, to a daily default fine."

NOTES

Paras 6, 12: words in square brackets substituted by the Companies Act 2006 (Consequential Amendments, Transitional Provisions and Savings) Order 2009, SI 2009/1941, art 2(1), Sch 1, para 184(1), (7).

PART II
OTHER PROVISIONS

General adaptations

[7.13]
13. (1) References in the 1986 Act (except in sections 8 to 10 and 24 to 26), or in any other enactment passed before the day on which this Act is passed, to an administration order under Part II of that Act, to an application for such an order and to an administrator include references (respectively) to an air traffic administration order, to an application for an air traffic administration order and to an air traffic administrator.

(2) References in the 1986 Act, or in any other enactment passed before the day on which this Act is passed, to an enactment contained in Part II of that Act include references to that enactment as applied by section 30 above or Part I of this Schedule.

(3) But—
- (a) sub-paragraph (1) applies in relation to a reference in an enactment contained in Part II of the 1986 Act only so far as necessary for the purposes of the operation of the provisions of that Part as so applied;
- (b) sub-paragraphs (1) and (2) apply subject to Part I of this Schedule.

Saving

14. The provisions of this Schedule are without prejudice to the power conferred by section 411 of the 1986 Act (company insolvency rules) as modified by paragraph 13(1) and (2).

Interpretation

15. (1) In this Schedule "the 1986 Act" means the Insolvency Act 1986.

(2) For the purposes of this Schedule and any modification of the 1986 Act made by this Schedule—
- (a) an air traffic administration order is an order made under section 27 or 28 above;
- (b) an air traffic administrator is a person appointed by the court to achieve the purposes of an air traffic administration order;
- (c) the CAA is the Civil Aviation Authority.

SCHEDULE 2
AIR TRAFFIC ADMINISTRATION ORDERS: SCHEMES

Section 30

Application of Schedule

[7.14]
1. This Schedule applies if—
- (a) the court has made an air traffic administration order in relation to a licence company (the existing licence company), and
- (b) it is proposed that on and after the appointed day another company (the new licence company) should carry out licensed activities in respect of all or part of a licensed area.

Interpretation

2. For the purposes of this Schedule—
- (a) an air traffic administration order is an order made under section 27 or 28;
- (b) an air traffic administrator is a person appointed by the court to achieve the purposes of an air traffic administration order;
- (c) the court is the court which (but for section 27) would have jurisdiction to wind up the existing licence company;
- (d) references to the existing licence company and the new licence company must be construed in accordance with paragraph 1;
- (e) references to a licence company are to be construed in accordance with section 26;
- (f) other licence companies are licence companies, other than the existing licence company and the new licence company;
- (g) licensed activities are activities which the licence concerned authorises the existing licence company to carry out;
- (h) a licensed area is an area in respect of which the licence concerned authorises the existing licence company to provide air traffic services;
- (i) the appointed day is a day which falls before the discharge of the air traffic administration order takes effect and which is appointed by the court for the purposes of this Schedule.

Making and modification of schemes

3. (1) The existing licence company, acting with the consent of the new licence company and, in relation to the matters affecting them, of any other licence companies, may make a scheme designed to secure that the new licence company carries out licensed activities in respect of all or part of the licensed area.

(2) No scheme takes effect unless it is approved by the Secretary of State after consulting the CAA.

(3) If a scheme is submitted to the Secretary of State for approval he may modify the scheme before approving it.

(4) But no modification may be made unless the following consent—

(a) the new licence company,
(b) the existing licence company, and
(c) in relation to the matters affecting them, any other licence companies.

(5) A scheme comes into force on the appointed day.

(6) At any time after a scheme has come into force, if he thinks it appropriate the Secretary of State may by order provide that the scheme is to be taken for all purposes to have come into force with the modifications specified in the order.

(7) But the Secretary of State may not make an order under sub-paragraph (6) unless the following consent—
(a) the existing licence company,
(b) the new licence company, and
(c) in relation to the provisions of the order which affect them, any other licence companies.

(8) An order under sub-paragraph (6)—
(a) may make, with effect from the coming into force of the scheme to which it relates, any such provision as could have been made by the scheme, and
(b) in connection with giving effect to that provision from that time, may make such supplementary, consequential and transitional provision as the Secretary of State thinks appropriate.

Effect on licence

4. (1) A scheme may provide for a licence held by the existing licence company to have effect, with such modifications as the scheme may specify, as if the licence had been granted to the new licence company.

(2) If different schemes are made in relation to different parts of the licensed area—
(a) each scheme has effect as if there were a separate licence in respect of each part, and
(b) each licence has effect as if it had been granted to the company which is the new licence company under the scheme concerned.

Property, rights and liabilities

5. A scheme may provide for the transfer of property, rights and liabilities from the existing licence company to the new licence company.

6. (1) In determining whether and in what manner to exercise the powers under paragraph 3 to approve and modify a scheme, the Secretary of State must have regard to the need to ensure that a scheme allocates property, rights and liabilities to the new licence company in such manner as appears to the Secretary of State to be appropriate.

(2) In deciding what is appropriate the Secretary of State must take into account the licensed activities which will be carried out on or after the appointed day by any of—
(a) the new licence company,
(b) the existing licence company, and
(c) any other licence companies.

7. (1) When a scheme comes into force, it has effect without more so as to transfer to the new licence company the property, rights and liabilities to which the scheme relates.

(2) A scheme may divide the property, rights or liabilities of the existing licence company and in connection with that division may—
(a) create for the existing licence company, the new licence company or any other licence companies an interest in or right over any property to which the scheme relates;
(b) create new rights and liabilities as between any two or more of those companies with respect to the subject-matter of the scheme;
(c) in connection with any provision made by virtue of paragraph (a) or (b), make incidental provision as to the interests, rights and liabilities of other persons with respect to the subject-matter of the scheme.

(3) A scheme may impose duties on the existing licence company, the new licence company and any other licence company to take all such steps as may be necessary to secure that—
(a) any interest, right or liability created by virtue of paragraph (a) or (b) of sub-paragraph (2), and
(b) any incidental provision made by virtue of paragraph (c) of that sub-paragraph, has effect.

(4) A scheme may require the new licence company and any other licence companies to provide consideration in respect of the transfer or creation of property, rights and liabilities by means of the scheme.

(5) A requirement imposed under sub-paragraph (4) is enforceable in the same way as if the property, rights and liabilities had been created or transferred, and (if the case so requires) had been capable of being created or transferred, by agreement between the parties.

(6) The property, rights and liabilities of the existing licence company which may be transferred in accordance with a scheme include—
(a) property, rights and liabilities which the existing licence company would not otherwise be capable of transferring or assigning;
(b) property, rights and liabilities to which the existing licence company may become entitled or subject after the making of the scheme and before the appointed day;
(c) property situated anywhere in the United Kingdom or elsewhere;
(d) rights and liabilities under enactments;

(e) rights and liabilities under the law of any part of the United Kingdom or of any country or territory outside the United Kingdom.

(7) If a scheme makes a person entitled to possession of a document, the provision that may be made by virtue of sub-paragraph (2)(b) includes—

(a) provision for treating that person as having given another person an acknowledgement in writing of the right of that other person to the production of the document and to delivery of copies of it,

(b) provision applying section 64 of the Law of Property Act 1925 (production and safe custody of documents) to that acknowledgement,

(c) provision that, where a scheme transfers any interest in land or other property situated in Scotland, subsections (1) and (2) of section 16 of the Land Registration (Scotland) Act 1979 (omission of certain clauses in deeds) are to have effect in relation to the transfer as if the transfer had been effected by deed and as if from each of those subsections the words "unless specially qualified" had been omitted, and

(d) provision applying section 9 of the Conveyancing Act 1881 (which is the equivalent in Northern Ireland to section 64 of the Law of Property Act 1925) to that acknowledgement.

(8) Sub-paragraph (9) applies if a transfer authorised by sub-paragraph (6)(a) would (were it not so authorised)—

(a) give rise to a contravention or liability by reason of a provision relating to the terms on which the existing licence company is entitled or subject to the property, right or liability transferred, or

(b) give rise to an interference with any interest or right by reason of such a provision.

(9) In such a case the transfer does not give rise to such a contravention, liability or interference.

(10) The provision referred to in sub-paragraph (8) may arise under an enactment or agreement or otherwise.

8. (1) A scheme may impose duties on the existing licence company and on the new licence company to take all such steps as may be necessary to secure that the vesting in the new licence company, by virtue of the scheme, of any foreign property, right or liability is effective under the relevant foreign law.

(2) A scheme may require the existing licence company to comply with any directions given by the new licence company in performing any duty imposed on the existing licence company by virtue of a provision included in the scheme under sub-paragraph (1).

(3) A scheme may provide that, until the vesting of any foreign property, right or liability of the existing licence company in the new licence company is effective under the relevant foreign law, it is the duty of the existing licence company—

(a) to hold that property or right for the benefit of the new licence company, or

(b) to discharge that liability on behalf of the new licence company.

(4) A scheme may provide that in specified cases foreign property, rights or liabilities acquired or incurred by an existing licence company after the scheme comes into force are immediately to become property, rights or liabilities of the new licence company; and in relation to such property, rights or liabilities the scheme may make provision equivalent to that in sub-paragraphs (1) to (3).

(5) Nothing in any provision included in a scheme by virtue of this paragraph affects the law of any part of the United Kingdom as it applies to the vesting of any foreign property, right or liability in the new licence company by virtue of the scheme.

(6) References in this paragraph to any foreign property, right or liability are references to any property, right or liability as respects which any issue arising in any proceedings would have to be determined (in accordance with the rules of private international law) by reference to the law of a country or territory outside the United Kingdom.

(7) Any expenses incurred by an existing licence company in consequence of any provision included in a scheme by virtue of this paragraph must be met by the new licence company.

(8) Duties imposed on an existing licence company or a new licence company by virtue of this paragraph are enforceable in the same way as if they were imposed by a contract between the existing licence company and the new licence company.

Supplementary provisions of schemes

9. (1) A scheme may contain supplementary, consequential and transitional provision for the purposes of, or in connection with, any provision of the scheme.

(2) In particular a scheme may provide—

(a) that for purposes connected with any transfers made in accordance with the scheme (including the transfer of rights and liabilities under an enactment) the new licence company is to be treated as the same person in law as the existing licence company;

(b) that (so far as may be necessary for the purposes of or in connection with any such transfers) agreements made, transactions effected and other things done by or in relation to the existing licence company are to be treated as made, effected or done by or in relation to the new licence company;

(c) that (so far as may be necessary for the purposes of or in connection with any such transfers) references in any agreement (whether or not in writing) or in any document to, or to any officer of, the existing licence company are to have effect with such modifications as the scheme may specify;

(d) that proceedings commenced by or against the existing licence company are to be continued by or against the new licence company;
(e) that contracts of employment with the existing licence company are not to terminate and that periods of employment with the existing licence company are to count for all purposes as periods of employment with the new licence company;
(f) that disputes about the effect of the scheme between the existing licence company and the new licence company, between either of them and any other licence company or between different companies which are other licence companies are to be referred to such arbitration as may be specified in or determined under the scheme;
(g) that determinations on such arbitrations are conclusive for all purposes;
(h) that certificates given jointly by two or more of the licence companies mentioned in paragraph (f) as to the effect of the scheme as between the licence companies giving the certificates are conclusive for all purposes.

Assistance

10. (1) The new licence company, the existing licence company and any other licence companies which are likely to be affected by a scheme must provide the Secretary of State with all such information and other assistance as the Secretary of State may reasonably require for the purposes of, or in connection with, the exercise of any power conferred by paragraph 3.

(2) If a company without reasonable excuse fails to do anything required of it by sub-paragraph (1) it is guilty of an offence and liable on summary conviction to a fine not exceeding level 5 on the standard scale.

Effect of air traffic administration order

11. While an air traffic administration order is in force in relation to an existing licence company anything which the company is permitted or required to do—
(a) by paragraph 3 or 10, or
(b) in consequence of any provision of a scheme,
is effective only if it is done on the company's behalf by its air traffic administrator.

SCHEDULE 3
AIR TRAFFIC ADMINISTRATION ORDERS: NORTHERN IRELAND

Section 33

[7.15]

1. In their application to a licence company formed and registered [under the Companies Act 2006 in Northern Ireland], sections 26 to 32 and Schedules 1 and 2 have effect with the modifications made by this Schedule.

2. (1) Section 26 is modified as follows.

(2) In subsection (2) for "Part II of the 1986 Act" substitute "Part III of the 1989 Order".

(3) In subsection (5) for "Parts I to VII of the 1986 Act" substitute "Parts II to VII of the 1989 Order".

(4) In subsection (6)—
(a) for "the 1986 Act" substitute "the 1989 Order", and
(b) for "the Insolvency Act 1986" substitute "the Insolvency (Northern Ireland) Order 1989".

3. (1) Section 28 is modified as follows.

(2) In subsection (3) for paragraph (a) substitute—

"(a) the Secretary of State certifies that but for section 27 it would in his opinion be appropriate for the Department of Enterprise, Trade and Investment to petition for the company's winding up under Article 104A of the 1989 Order (petition following inspectors' report etc), and".

(3) In subsection (3)(b) for "section 124A" substitute "Article 104A".

(4) In subsection (6) for "section 123 of the 1986 Act" substitute "Article 103 of the 1989 Order".

4. In section 29(5) for "the 1986 Act" substitute "the 1989 Order".

5. (1) Section 30 is modified as follows.

(2) In subsection (2) for "Section 9(4) and (5) of the 1986 Act" substitute "Article 22(4) and (5) of the 1989 Order".

(3) In subsection (3)—
(a) for "Section 10(1), (2), (4) and (5) of the 1986 Act" substitute "Article 23(1), (2) and (4) of the 1989 Order";
(b) in paragraphs (a), (b), (c) and (d) for "subsection" substitute "paragraph".

(4) In subsection (5)—
(a) for "section 411 of the 1986 Act" substitute "Article 359 of the 1989 Order", and
(b) for "Parts I to VII of that Act" substitute "Parts II to VII of that Order".

6. For Schedule 1 substitute—

"SCHEDULE 1

AIR TRAFFIC ADMINISTRATION ORDERS: GENERAL

PART I

MODIFICATIONS OF 1989 ORDER

Introduction

1. This Part of this Schedule applies if an air traffic administration order is made in Northern Ireland.

General application of provisions of 1989 Order

2. Articles 24 to 35 and 39 of the 1989 Order (which relate to administration orders under Part III of that Order) apply with the modifications specified in this Part of this Schedule.

General modifications

3. In those Articles as applied by this Part of this Schedule—

(a) references to an administration order are to an air traffic administration order, and

(b) references to an administrator are to an air traffic administrator.

Effect of order

4. In Article 24 of the 1989 Order (effect of order) as applied by this Part of this Schedule—

(a) the requirement in paragraph (1)(a) that any petition for the winding up of the company shall be dismissed does not prejudice the air traffic administration order if it is made by virtue of section 27 above,

(b) the reference in paragraph (3)(d) to proceedings includes a reference to any proceedings under or for the purposes of section 20 above, and

(c) paragraph (3)(d) has effect as if after "its property" there were inserted ", and no right of re-entry or forfeiture may be enforced against the company in respect of any land,".

Appointment of air traffic administrator

5. In Article 26 of the 1989 Order (appointment of administrator) as applied by this Part of this Schedule for paragraph (3) substitute—

"(3) An application for an order under paragraph (2) may be made—

(a) by the Secretary of State,

(b) by the CAA with the Secretary of State's consent,

(c) by any continuing air traffic administrator of the company, or

(d) where there is no such air traffic administrator, by the company, the directors or any creditor or creditors of the company."

General powers of air traffic administrator

6. (1) Article 27 of the 1989 Order (general powers of administrator) as applied by this Part of this Schedule has effect as follows.

(2) In paragraph (1)(b) the reference to the powers specified in Schedule 1 to the 1989 Order includes a reference to a power to act on behalf of the company—

(a) for the purposes of this Part, or

(b) for the purposes of the exercise or performance of any power or duty which is conferred or imposed on the company by virtue of its holding a licence.

(3) In paragraph (4) the reference to a power conferred by the company's [articles of association] includes a reference to a power conferred by virtue of the company's holding a licence.

Power to deal with charged property

7. (1) Article 28 of the 1989 Order (power to deal with charged property) as applied by this Part of this Schedule has effect as follows.

(2) In paragraph (2) for "the purpose or one or more of the purposes specified in the administration order" substitute "one or both of the purposes of the administration order".

(3) In paragraph (5)(b) for "in the open market by a willing vendor" substitute "for the best price which is reasonably available on a sale which is consistent with the purposes of the air traffic administration order".

Duties of air traffic administrator

8. (1) Article 29 of the 1989 Order (duties of administrator) as applied by this Part of this Schedule has effect as follows.

(2) For paragraph (2) substitute—

"(2) Subject to any directions of the High Court, it shall be the duty of the air traffic administrator to manage the affairs, business and property of the company in accordance with proposals under Article 35 as they are revised from time to time."

(3) In paragraph (3) omit sub-paragraph (a).

Part 7A Special Insolvency Regimes

Discharge of order

9. (1) Article 30 of the 1989 Order (discharge and variation of administration order) as applied by this Part of this Schedule has effect as follows.

(2) For paragraphs (1) and (2) substitute—

"(1) An application for an air traffic administration order to be discharged may be made—

(a) by the air traffic administrator, on the ground that the purposes of the order have been achieved; or

(b) by the Secretary of State or (with his consent) by the CAA, on the ground that it is no longer necessary that those purposes are achieved."

(3) In paragraph (3) omit the words "or vary".

(4) In paragraph (4)—

(a) omit the words "or varied" and "or variation", and

(b) after "to the registrar" insert ", to the CAA and to the Secretary of State".

Notice of making of order

10. In Article 33(2) of the 1989 Order (notice of order to be given by administrator) as applied by this Part of this Schedule after "to the registrar" insert ", to the CAA, to the Secretary of State".

Statement of proposals

11. In Article 35 of the 1989 Order (statement of proposals) as applied by this Part of this Schedule for paragraphs (1) and (2) substitute—

"(1) Where an air traffic administration order has been made, the air traffic administrator shall, within 3 months (or such longer period as the High Court may allow) after the making of the order, send a statement of his proposals for achieving the purposes of the order—

(a) to the Secretary of State,

(b) to the CAA,

(c) to all creditors of the company (so far as he is aware of their addresses), and

(d) to the registrar.

(2) The air traffic administrator may from time to time revise those proposals.

(2A) If the air traffic administrator proposes to make revisions which appear to him to be substantial, he shall before making them send a statement of the proposed revisions—

(a) to the Secretary of State,

(b) to the CAA,

(c) to all creditors of the company (so far as he is aware of their addresses), and

(d) to the registrar.

(2B) The air traffic administrator shall give a copy of any statement under paragraph (1) or (2A) to all members of the company before the end of the period described in paragraph (1) or, as the case may be, before making the revisions.

(2C) The requirement in paragraph (2B) is satisfied if the administrator—

(a) sends a copy of the statement to all members of the company (so far as he is aware of their addresses), or

(b) publishes in the prescribed manner a notice stating an address to which members should write for copies of the statement to be sent to them free of charge."

Applications to court

12. (1) Article 39 of the 1989 Order (protection of interests of creditors and members) as applied by this Part of this Schedule has effect as follows.

(2) After paragraph (1) insert—

"(1A) If a creditor or member of the company makes an application under paragraph (1), the court shall give notice of the application to the Secretary of State, who shall be entitled to be heard by the court in connection with the application.

(1B) At any time when an air traffic administration order is in force the Secretary of State or (with his consent) the CAA may apply to the court by petition for an order under this Article on one or both of the following grounds.

(1C) The first ground is that the air traffic administrator has exercised or is exercising or proposing to exercise his powers in relation to the company in a manner which will not best ensure the achievement of the purposes of the order.

(1D) The second ground is that he has exercised or is exercising or proposing to exercise his powers in relation to the company in a manner which involves a contravention of—

(a) a condition of the licence granted under Chapter I of Part I of the Transport Act 2000, or

(b) a duty imposed by section 8(1) of that Act, or

(c) any other requirement imposed on the company by virtue of its holding the licence."

(3) Omit paragraph (3).

(4) In paragraph (4) omit the words "Subject to paragraph (3),".

(5) After that paragraph insert—

"(4A) Provision may be made by virtue of paragraph (4)(d) that the air traffic administration order is to be discharged from such date as may be specified in the order unless, before that date, such measures are taken as the court thinks fit for the purpose of protecting the interests of creditors."

(6) For paragraph (6) substitute—

"(6) Where an air traffic administration order is discharged, the air traffic administrator shall within 14 days after the date on which the discharge takes effect send [a copy] of the order under this Article—

(a) to the Secretary of State,

(b) to the CAA, and

(c) to the registrar;

and if, without reasonable excuse, the air traffic administrator contravenes this paragraph, he shall be guilty of an offence and, for continued contravention, he shall be guilty of a continuing offence."

PART II
OTHER PROVISIONS

General adaptations

13. (1) References in the 1989 Order (except in Articles 21 to 23 and 36 to 38), or in any other enactment passed before the day on which this Act is passed, to an administration order under Part III of that Order, to an application for such an order and to an administrator include references (respectively) to an air traffic administration order, to an application for an air traffic administration order and to an air traffic administrator.

(2) References in the 1989 Order, or in any other enactment passed before the day on which this Act is passed, to an enactment contained in Part III of that Order include references to that enactment as applied by section 30 above or Part I of this Schedule.

(3) But—

(a) sub-paragraph (1) applies in relation to a reference in an enactment contained in Part III of the 1989 Order only so far as necessary for the purposes of the operation of the provisions of that Part as so applied;

(b) sub-paragraphs (1) and (2) apply subject to Part I of this Schedule.

Saving

14. The provisions of this Schedule are without prejudice to the power conferred by Article 359 of the 1989 Order (insolvency rules) as modified by paragraph 13(1) and (2).

Interpretation

15. (1) In this Schedule "the 1989 Order" means the Insolvency (Northern Ireland) Order 1989.

(2) For the purposes of this Schedule and any modification of the 1989 Order made by this Schedule—

(a) an air traffic administration order is an order made under section 27 or 28 above;

(b) an air traffic administrator is a person appointed by the court to achieve the purposes of an air traffic administration order;

(c) the CAA is the Civil Aviation Authority."

NOTES

Paras 1, 6 (in substituted Sch 1, paras 6, 12): words in square brackets substituted by the Companies Act 2006 (Consequential Amendments, Transitional Provisions and Savings) Order 2009, SI 2009/1941, art 2(1), Sch 1, para 184(1), (8).

SCHEDULES 4–31

(*Schs 4–31 outside the scope of this work.*)

B
BANKS

BANKS (ADMINISTRATION PROCEEDINGS) ORDER 1989

(SI 1989/1276)

NOTES

Made: 24 July 1989.

Authority: Insolvency Act 1986, s 422.

Commencement: 23 August 1989.

This Order was revoked by the Banks (Former Authorised Institutions) (Insolvency) Order 2006, SI 2006/3107, art 2(1), subject to transitional provisions in art 2(2) thereof at **[7.22]**, in relation to proceedings begun before 15 December 2006.

[7.16]

1 Citation and commencement

This Order may be cited as the Banks (Administration Proceedings) Order 1989 and shall come into force on 23rd August 1989.

NOTES

Revoked as noted at the beginning of this Order.

[7.17]

[1A Interpretation

In this Order, "former authorised institution" means a company which—

(a) continues to have a liability in respect of a deposit which was held by it in accordance the Banking Act 1979 or the Banking Act 1987, and

(b) is not an authorised person within the meaning of the Financial Services and Markets Act 2000.]

NOTES

Inserted by the Financial Services and Markets Act 2000 (Consequential Amendments and Repeals) Order 2001, SI 2001/3649, art 398(1), (2).

Revoked as noted at the beginning of this Order.

[7.18]

2 Application of provisions in the Insolvency Act 1986 with modifications in relation to companies which are . . . former authorised institutions . . .

The provisions in Part II of the Insolvency Act 1986 shall apply in relation to those . . . former authorised institutions . . . which are companies within the meaning of section 735 of the Companies Act 1985 with the modifications specified in the Schedule to this Order (any reference to a numbered section in the Schedule being, unless otherwise provided, to a section of the Insolvency Act 1986) and accordingly the provisions of the first Group of Parts of the Insolvency Act 1986 apply in relation to such institutions with such modifications.

NOTES

Revoked as noted at the beginning of this Order.

Article heading: words omitted revoked by the Financial Services and Markets Act 2000 (Consequential Amendments and Repeals) Order 2001, SI 2001/3649, art 398(1), (3).

Words omitted revoked by the Financial Services and Markets Act 2000 (Consequential Amendments) Order 2002, SI 2002/1555, art 34(1), (2).

[7.19]

3 Application

This Order shall not apply in relation to petitions for administration orders presented before it comes into force or in relation to administration orders made upon such petitions.

NOTES

Revoked as noted at the beginning of this Order.

SCHEDULE
MODIFICATIONS OF PART II OF THE INSOLVENCY ACT 1986 IN RELATION TO COMPANIES WHICH ARE . . . FORMER AUTHORISED INSTITUTIONS . . .

Article 2

[7.20]

[1. Subsection (1A) of section 8, and the definition of "relevant deposit" in subsection (1B), apply in relation to a former authorised institution as they apply in relation to an authorised deposit taker.]

2. In [section 8(5)] paragraph (b) shall be omitted.

Part 7B Special Insolvency Regimes

3. In section 9(1), after the words "the directors", there shall be inserted the words "or by the [Financial Services Authority],".

4. In section 9(2)(a), after the word "company", there shall be inserted the words "to the [Financial Services Authority] (unless it is a petitioner),".

5. At the end of section 13(3)(c) there shall be added the words "or (d) by the [Financial Services Authority].".

6. In section 23(1)(a), after the words "registrar of companies" there shall be inserted the words ", the [Financial Services Authority]".

7. In section 25(2)(a), after the words "their addresses") there shall be inserted the words "and the [Financial Services Authority]".

8. In section 27(1), after the words "in force," there shall be inserted the words "the [Financial Services Authority], [the scheme manager, within the meaning of the Financial Services and Markets Act 2000], or".

9. In section 27(1)(a), for the words "(including at least himself") there shall be substituted the words "(including, where the applicant is a creditor or member, at least himself)".

NOTES

Revoked as noted at the beginning of this Order.

Schedule heading: words omitted revoked by the Financial Services and Markets Act 2000 (Consequential Amendments and Repeals) Order 2001, SI 2001/3649, art 398(1), (4).

Para 1: substituted by SI 2001/3649, art 398(1), (5).

Para 2: words in square brackets substituted by the Financial Services and Markets Act 2000 (Consequential Amendments) Order 2002, SI 2002/1555, art 34(1), (3).

Paras 3–7: words in square brackets substituted by the Bank of England Act 1998 (Consequential Amendments of Subordinate Legislation) Order 1998, SI 1998/1129, art 2, Sch 1, para 9.

Para 8: words in first pair of square brackets substituted by SI 1998/1129, art 2, Sch 1, para 9; words in second pair of square brackets substituted by SI 2001/3649, art 398(1), (6).

BANKS (FORMER AUTHORISED INSTITUTIONS) (INSOLVENCY) ORDER 2006

(SI 2006/3107)

NOTES

Made: 20 November 2006.

Authority: Insolvency Act 1986, s 422.

Commencement: 15 December 2006.

[7.21]

1 Citation and commencement

(1) This Order may be cited as the Banks (Former Authorised Institutions) (Insolvency) Order 2006 and shall come into force on 15th December 2006 ("the commencement date").

(2) In this Order, "the 1986 Act" means the Insolvency Act 1986.

[7.22]

2 Revocation of the Banks (Administration Proceedings) Order 1989

(1) Subject to paragraph (2), the Banks (Administration Proceedings) Order 1989 ("the 1989 Order") is revoked.

(2) The 1989 Order shall continue in effect for the purposes of any proceedings begun before the commencement date under the first Group of Parts of the 1986 Act in relation to a former authorised institution within the meaning of Article 1A of that Order.

[7.23]

3 Modification of first Group of Parts of the Insolvency Act 1986 in their application to companies that are former authorised institutions

(1) This article applies to a person of the kind mentioned in section 422(1) of the 1986 Act that is a company within the meaning of section 735(1) of the Companies Act 1985.

(2) The first Group of Parts of the 1986 Act shall apply in relation to a person to which this article applies with the modifications set out in the Schedule to this Order.

SCHEDULE
MODIFICATIONS OF PART 2 OF THE INSOLVENCY ACT IN ITS APPLICATION TO COMPANIES THAT ARE FORMER AUTHORISED INSTITUTIONS

Article 3

[7.24]
1. References to a numbered paragraph in this Schedule are references to the paragraph so numbered in Schedule B1 to the Insolvency Act 1986.

2. In their application to a person falling within article 3(1), section 8 of, and Schedule B1 to, the 1986 Act shall apply subject to the modifications set out below.

3. Paragraph 9 shall apply with the omission of sub-paragraph (1).

4. For paragraph 12(1) there is substituted—

"**12.** (1) An application to the court for an administration order in respect of a company ("an administration application") may be made only by—
(a) the company,
(b) the directors of the company,
(c) one or more creditors of the company,
[(d) the Financial Conduct Authority,
(da) the Prudential Regulation Authority,];
(e) the designated officer for a magistrates' court in exercise of the power conferred by section 87A of the Magistrates' Courts Act 1980 (c 43) (fine imposed on company), or
(f) a combination of persons listed in paragraphs (a) to (e).

[(1A) Where an administration application is made to which the Financial Conduct Authority is not a party, the applicant shall, as soon as is reasonably practicable after the making of the application, give notice of the making of the application to the Financial Conduct Authority.

(1B) Where an administration application is made to which the Prudential Regulation Authority is not a party, the applicant shall, as soon as is reasonably practicable after the making of the application, give notice of the making of the application to the Prudential Regulation Authority.]".

5. For paragraph 22 there is substituted—

"**22.** (1) Subject as set out in this paragraph—
(a) a company may appoint an administrator; and
(b) the directors of a company may appoint an administrator.

(2) An administrator may not be appointed under this paragraph without the consent in writing of the [Financial Conduct Authority and the Prudential Regulation Authority].

(3) The written consent under paragraph (2) must be filed in court—
(a) at the same time that any notice of intention to appoint under paragraph 26 is filed in court pursuant to paragraph 27; or
(b) where no such notice of intention to appoint is required to be given, at the same time that notice of appointment is filed under paragraph 29.".

6. After paragraph 91 there is inserted—

"**91A.** Where the administrator was appointed by administration order, the court may replace the administrator on an application under this paragraph made by the [Financial Conduct Authority or the Prudential Regulation Authority].

91B. Where the administrator was appointed otherwise than by administration order any replacement administrator may only be appointed with the consent of the [Financial Conduct Authority or the Prudential Regulation Authority].".

7. After paragraph 116 there is inserted—

"*Miscellaneous–Powers of the [Financial Conduct Authority and Prudential Regulation Authority]*

117.
(1) . . .

(2) The [Financial Conduct Authority and the Prudential Regulation Authority] is entitled to be heard at the hearing of an administration application or at any other court hearing in relation to the company pursuant to any provision of Schedule B1.

(3) Any notice or other document required to be sent to a creditor of the company must also be sent to the [Financial Conduct Authority and the Prudential Regulation Authority].

(4) The [Financial Conduct Authority or the Prudential Regulation Authority] may apply to the court under paragraph 74 and in such a case paragraphs 74(1)(a) and 74(1)(b) shall have effect as if for the words "harm the interests of the applicant (whether alone or in common with some or all other members or creditors)" there were substituted the words "harm the interests of some or all members or creditors".

[(4A) The Financial Conduct Authority and the Prudential Regulation Authority are entitled to participate (but not vote) in a qualifying decision procedure by which a decision about any matter is sought from the creditors of the company.]

(5) A person appointed for the purpose by the [Financial Conduct Authority or the Prudential Regulation Authority] is entitled—

(a) to attend any meeting of creditors of the company summoned under this Act;
(b) to attend any meeting of a committee established under paragraph 57; and
(c) to make representations as to any matter for decision at such a meeting.".

[8.

Where this Schedule applies in relation to the administration in Scotland of a person referred to in article 3(1), paragraph 117 of Schedule B1 (treated as inserted by paragraph 7) has effect as if sub-paragraph (4A) were omitted.]

NOTES

Paras 4–6: words in square brackets substituted, and words omitted revoked, by the Financial Services Act 2012 (Consequential Amendments and Transitional Provisions) Order 2013, SI 2013/472, art 3, Sch 2, para 117.

Para 7: in the text which is treated as inserted in Schedule B1 to the 1986 Act, sub-para (4A) is inserted by the Small Business, Enterprise and Employment Act 2015 (Consequential Amendments, Savings and Transitional Provisions) Regulations 2018, SI 2018/208, reg 11(a); other words in square brackets substituted, and words omitted revoked, by SI 2013/472, art 3, Sch 2, para 117.

Para 8: added by SI 2018/208, reg 11(b).

BANKING ACT 2009

(2009 c 1)

ARRANGEMENT OF SECTIONS

PART 1
SPECIAL RESOLUTION REGIME

CHAPTER 3
SPECIAL RESOLUTION ACTION

Exercise of powers: general

7 General conditions . . . [7.25]

CHAPTER 7
GENERAL PROVISIONS

89K Insolvency Proceedings . . . [7.26]

PART 2
BANK INSOLVENCY

Introduction

90 Overview . . . [7.27]
91 Interpretation: "bank" . . . [7.28]
92 Interpretation: "the court" . . . [7.29]
93 Interpretation: other expressions . . . [7.30]

Bank insolvency order

94 The order . . . [7.31]
95 Application . . . [7.32]
96 Grounds for applying . . . [7.33]
97 Grounds for making . . . [7.34]
98 Commencement . . . [7.35]

Process of bank liquidation

99 Objectives . . . [7.36]
100 Liquidation committee . . . [7.37]
101 Liquidation committee: supplemental . . . [7.38]
102 Objective 1: (a) or (b)? . . . [7.39]
103 General powers, duties and effect . . . [7.40]
104 Additional general powers . . . [7.41]
105 Status of bank liquidator . . . [7.42]

Tenure of bank liquidator

106 Term of appointment . . . [7.43]
107 Resignation . . . [7.44]
108 Removal by court . . . [7.45]
109 Removal by creditors . . . [7.46]
110 Disqualification . . . [7.47]
111 Release . . . [7.48]
112 Replacement . . . [7.49]

Termination of process, &c

113 Company voluntary arrangement . . . [7.50]
114 Administration . . . [7.51]
115 Dissolution . . . [7.52]
116 Dissolution: supplemental . . . [7.53]

Other processes

117 Bank insolvency as alternative order . . . [7.54]
118 Voluntary winding-up . . . [7.55]
119 Exclusion of other procedures . . . [7.56]
120 Notice to PRA of preliminary steps . . . [7.57]
120A Notice to the regulators and the Bank of England of preliminary steps . . . [7.58]
121 Disqualification of directors . . . [7.59]
122 Application of insolvency law . . . [7.60]

Miscellaneous

127 Insolvency Services Account . . . [7.61]
129 Co-operation between courts . . . [7.62]
129A Banks not regulated by PRA . . . [7.63]
135 Consequential provision . . . [7.64]

PART 3
BANK ADMINISTRATION

Introduction

136 Overview . . . [7.65]
137 Objectives . . . [7.66]
138 Objective 1: supporting private sector purchaser or resolution company . . . [7.67]
139 Objective 1: duration . . . [7.68]
140 Objective 2: "normal" administration . . . [7.69]

Process

141 Bank administration order . . . [7.70]
142 Application . . . [7.71]
143 Grounds for applying . . . [7.72]
144 Grounds for making . . . [7.73]
145 General powers, duties and effect . . . [7.74]
168 Consequential provision . . . [7.75]

PART 7
MISCELLANEOUS
Investment banks

232 Definition . . . [7.76]
233 Insolvency regulations . . . [7.77]
234 Regulations: details . . . [7.78]
235 Regulations: procedure . . . [7.79]
236 Review . . . [7.80]

PART 8
GENERAL

263 Commencement . . . [7.81]
264 Extent . . . [7.82]
265 Short title . . . [7.83]

An Act to make provision about banking

[12 February 2009]

PART 1
SPECIAL RESOLUTION REGIME

1–3, 3A, 3B *((Chs 1, 2) outside the scope of this work.)*

[CHAPTER 3 SPECIAL RESOLUTION ACTION]

NOTES

Chapter heading: inserted by the Bank Recovery and Resolution Order 2014, SI 2014/3329, arts 2, 7.

4–6E *(Outside the scope of this work.)*

Part 7B Special Insolvency Regimes

Exercise of powers: general

[7.25]

7 General conditions

[(1) A stabilisation power may be exercised in respect of a bank only if—
(a) the PRA is satisfied that Condition 1 is met, and
(b) the Bank of England is satisfied that Conditions 2, 3 and 4 are met.

(2) Condition 1 is that the bank is failing or likely to fail.

(3) Condition 2 is that, having regard to timing and other relevant circumstances, it is not reasonably likely that (ignoring the stabilisation powers) action will be taken by or in respect of the bank that will result in Condition 1 ceasing to be met.

(4) Condition 3 is that the exercise of the power is necessary having regard to the public interest in the advancement of one or more of the special resolution objectives.

(5) Condition 4 is that one or more of the special resolution objectives would not be met to the same extent by the winding up of the bank (whether under Part 2 or otherwise).

(5A) The PRA must treat Condition 1 as met if satisfied that it would be met but for financial assistance provided by—
(a) the Treasury, or
(b) the Bank of England,
disregarding ordinary market assistance offered by the Bank on its usual terms.

(5B) The Bank of England must treat Condition 2 as met if satisfied that it would be met but for financial assistance of the kind mentioned in subsection (5A).

(5C) For the purposes of Condition 1, a bank is failing or likely to fail if—
(a) it is failing, or is likely to fail, to satisfy the threshold conditions in circumstances where that failure would justify the variation or cancellation by the PRA under section 55J of the Financial Services and Markets Act 2000 of the bank's permission under Part 4A of that Act to carry on one or more regulated activities,
(b) the value of the assets of the bank [is less than the amount of its liabilities,]
(c) the bank is unable to pay its debts or other liabilities as they fall due,
(d) [paragraph (b) or (c) (or both)] will, in the near future, apply to the bank, or
(e) extraordinary public financial support is required in respect of the bank and subsection (5E) does not apply to that support.

(5D) "The threshold conditions" means the threshold conditions, as defined by subsection (1) of section 55B of the Financial Services and Markets Act 2000, for which the PRA is treated as responsible under subsection (2) of that section.

(5E) This subsection applies where, in order to remedy a serious disturbance in the economy of the United Kingdom and preserve financial stability, the extraordinary public financial support takes any of the following forms—
(a) a State guarantee to back liquidity facilities provided by central banks,
(b) a State guarantee of newly issued liabilities,
(c) an injection of own funds, or purchase of capital instruments, at prices and on terms that do not confer an advantage upon the bank, where none of the circumstances referred to in subsection (5C)(a), (b), (c) or (d) are present at the time the public support is granted and none of Cases 1 to 4 in section 6A apply.

(5F) Before determining that Condition 1 is met, the PRA must consult the Bank of England.

(5G) Before determining whether or not Condition 2 is met, the Bank of England must consult—
(a) the PRA,
(b) the FCA, and
(c) the Treasury.

(5H) Before determining that Conditions 3 and 4 are met, the Bank must consult—
(a) the PRA,
(b) the FCA, and
(c) the Treasury.]

(6) The special resolution objectives are not relevant to Conditions 1 and 2.

(7) The conditions for applying for and making a bank insolvency order are set out in sections 96 and 97.

(8) The conditions for applying for and making a bank administration order are set out in sections 143 and 144.

NOTES

Sub-ss (1)–(5H): substituted, for sub-ss (1)–(5), by the Bank Recovery and Resolution Order 2014, SI 2014/3329, arts 2, 12; in sub-s (5C) words in square brackets substituted by the Bank Recovery and Resolution Order 2016, SI 2016/1239, arts 2, 7.

7A–89JA *(Ss 7A–83, ss 83ZA–89JA (Chs 4–6) outside the scope of this work.)*

[CHAPTER 7 GENERAL PROVISIONS

[7.26]

89K Insolvency Proceedings

(1) If—
(a) a stabilisation power has been exercised in respect of a relevant firm, or
(b) the conditions in section 7 are met in relation to a relevant firm,
insolvency proceedings may not be commenced in relation to that firm except by, or with the consent of, the Bank of England.

(2) For the purposes of subsection (1), the commencement of insolvency proceedings means—
(a) making an application for an administration order;
(b) presenting a petition for winding up;
(c) proposing a resolution for voluntary winding up;
(d) appointing an administrator.
(3) In this section—
(a) "relevant firm" means—
(i) a bank, building society, investment firm, financial holding company, mixed financial holding company or a mixed activity holding company, or
(ii) a financial institution which is a subsidiary undertaking of an entity within sub-paragraph (i);
(b) "building society" has the meaning given in the Building Societies Act 1986;
(c) "financial holding company" has the meaning given in Article 4.1(2) of the capital requirements regulation;
(d) "financial institution" has the meaning given in Article 4.1(26) of the capital requirements regulation;
(e) "mixed activity holding company" has the meaning given in Article 4.1(22) of the capital requirements regulation;
(f) "mixed financial holding company" has the meaning given in Article 2.15 of Directive 2002/87/EC of the European Parliament and of the Council of 16th December 2002 on the supplementary supervision of credit institutions, insurance undertakings and investment firms in a financial conglomerate.]

NOTES

Commencement: 1 January 2015.

Chapter 7 (ss 89K–89M) inserted by the Bank Recovery and Resolution Order 2014, SI 2014/3329, arts 2, 103.

89L, 89M *(Ss 89L, 89M outside the scope of this work.)*

PART 2
BANK INSOLVENCY

NOTES

Modifications: this Part is applied with modifications in respect of building societies, by the Building Societies (Insolvency and Special Administration) Order 2009, SI 2009/805, art 3, Sch 1, Pts 1, 2 at **[7.475]**, **[7.479]**, **[7.480]**, and applied with modifications in relation to special administration (bank insolvency), by the Investment Bank Special Administration Regulations 2011, SI 2011/245, reg 9, Sch 1, para 6 at **[7.1669]**, **[7.1704]**.

Introduction

[7.27]

90 Overview

(1) This Part provides for a procedure to be known as bank insolvency.
(2) The main features of bank insolvency are that—
(a) a bank enters the process by court order,
(b) the order appoints a bank liquidator,
(c) the bank liquidator aims to arrange for the bank's eligible depositors to have their accounts transferred or to receive their compensation from the FSCS,
(d) the bank liquidator then winds up the bank, and
(e) for those purposes, the bank liquidator has powers and duties of liquidators, as applied and modified by the provisions of this Part.
(3) The Table describes the provisions of this Part.

Sections	*Topic*
Sections 90 to 93	Introduction
Sections 94 to 98	Bank insolvency order
Sections 99 to 105	Process of bank liquidation
Sections 106 to 112	Tenure of bank liquidator
Sections 113 to 116	Termination of process, &c
Sections 117 to 122	Other processes
Sections 123 to 135	Miscellaneous

[7.28]

91 Interpretation: "bank"

(1) In this Part "bank" means a UK institution which has permission under [Part 4A] of the Financial Services and Markets Act 2000 to carry on the regulated activity of accepting deposits (within the meaning of section 22 of that Act, taken with Schedule 2 and any order under section 22).
(2) But "bank" does not include—
(a) a building society within the meaning of section 119 of the Building Societies Act 1986,
(b) a credit union within the meaning of section 31 of the Credit Unions Act 1979, or
(c) any other class of institution excluded by an order made by the Treasury.

Part 7B Special Insolvency Regimes

(3) In subsection (1) "UK institution" means an institution which is incorporated in, or formed under the law of any part of, the United Kingdom.
(4) An order under subsection (2)(c)—
(a) shall be made by statutory instrument, and
(b) may not be made unless a draft has been laid before and approved by resolution of each House of Parliament.
(5) Section 130 makes provision for the application of this Part to building societies.
(6) Section 131 makes provision for the application of this Part to credit unions.

NOTES

Sub-s (1): words in square brackets substituted by the Financial Services Act 2012, s 106, Sch 17, Pt 2, paras 29, 30.
Orders: the Banking Act 2009 (Exclusion of Insurers) Order 2010, SI 2010/35.

[7.29]
92 Interpretation: "the court"
In this Part "the court" means—
(a) in England and Wales, the High Court,
(b) in Scotland, the Court of Session, and
(c) in Northern Ireland, the High Court.

[7.30]
93 Interpretation: other expressions
[(1) In this Part—
(a) "the PRA" means the Prudential Regulation Authority, and
(b) "the FCA" means the Financial Conduct Authority.]
(2) In this Part a reference to "the FSCS" is a reference to—
(a) the Financial Services Compensation Scheme (established under Part 15 of the Financial Services and Markets Act 2000), or
(b) where appropriate, the scheme manager of that Scheme.
(3) In this Part "eligible depositors" means depositors who are eligible for compensation under the FSCS.
(4) For the purposes of a reference in this Part to inability to pay debts—
(a) a bank that is in default on an obligation to pay a sum due and payable under an agreement, is to be treated as unable to pay its debts, and
(b) section 123 of the Insolvency Act 1986 (inability to pay debts) also applies; and
for the purposes of paragraph (a) "agreement" means an agreement the making or performance of which constitutes or is part of a regulated activity carried on by the bank.
(5) Expressions used in this Part and in the Insolvency Act 1986 have the same meaning as in that Act.
(6) Expressions used in this Part and in the Companies Act 2006 have the same meaning as in that Act.
(7) A reference in this Part to action includes a reference to inaction.
(8) The expression "fair" is used in this Part as a shorter modern equivalent of the expression "just and equitable" (and is not therefore intended to exclude the application of any judicial or other practice relating to the construction and application of that expression).

NOTES

Sub-s (1): substituted by the Financial Services Act 2012, s 106, Sch 17, Pt 2, paras 29, 31.

Bank insolvency order

[7.31]
94 The order
(1) A bank insolvency order is an order appointing a person as the bank liquidator of a bank.
(2) A person is eligible for appointment as a bank liquidator if qualified to act as an insolvency practitioner [in relation to the bank].
(3) An appointment may be made only if the person has consented to act.
(4) A bank insolvency order takes effect in accordance with section 98; and—
(a) the process of a bank insolvency order having effect may be described as "bank insolvency" in relation to the bank, and
(b) while the order has effect the bank may be described as being "in bank insolvency".

NOTES

Sub-s (2): words in square brackets inserted by the Deregulation Act 2015, the Small Business, Enterprise and Employment Act 2015 and the Insolvency (Amendment) Act (Northern Ireland) 2016 (Consequential Amendments and Transitional Provisions) Regulations 2017, SI 2017/400, reg 5(1), (2).

[7.32]
95 Application
(1) An application for a bank insolvency order may be made to the court by—
(a) the Bank of England,
(b) the [PRA], or
(c) the Secretary of State.
(2) An application must nominate a person to be appointed as the bank liquidator.
(3) The bank must be given notice of an application, in accordance with rules under section 411 of the Insolvency Act 1986 (as applied by section 125 below).

NOTES

Sub-s (1): word in square brackets in para (b) substituted by the Financial Services Act 2012, s 106, Sch 17, Pt 2, paras 29, 32.

[7.33]

96 Grounds for applying

(1) In this section—

(a) Ground A is that a bank is unable, or likely to become unable, to pay its debts,

(b) Ground B is that the winding up of a bank would be in the public interest, and

(c) Ground C is that the winding up of a bank would be fair.

(2) The Bank of England may apply for a bank insolvency order only if—

(a) . . . the [PRA] is satisfied that [Condition 1 in section 7 is met], and

(b) the Bank of England is satisfied—

[(ia) that Condition 2 in section 7 is met,]

(i) that the bank has eligible depositors, and

(ii) that Ground A or C applies.

(3) The [PRA] may apply for a bank insolvency order only if—

[(a) the Bank of England [is satisfied that Condition 2 in section 7 is met, and]]

(b) the [PRA] is satisfied—

(i) that [Condition 1 in section 7 is met],

(ii) that the bank has eligible depositors, and

(iii) that Ground A or C applies.

(4) The Secretary of State may apply for a bank insolvency order only if satisfied—

(a) that the bank has eligible depositors, and

(b) that Ground B applies.

(5) The sources of information on the basis of which the Secretary of State may be satisfied of the matters specified in subsection (4) include those listed in section 124A(1) of the Insolvency Act 1986 (petition for winding up on grounds of public interest).

NOTES

Sub-s (2): words omitted from para (a) repealed by the Bank of England and Financial Services Act 2016, s 16, Sch 2, Pt 2, paras 52, 56(1), (2); word in first pair of square brackets in para (a) substituted by the Financial Services Act 2012, s 106, Sch 17, Pt 2, paras 29, 33; words in second pair of square brackets in para (a) substituted, and para (b)(ia) inserted, by the Bank Recovery and Resolution Order 2014, SI 2014/3329, arts 2, 104(1), (2).

Sub-s (3): word "PRA" in square brackets in both places substituted by the Financial Services Act 2012, s 106, Sch 17, Pt 2, paras 29, 33; para (a) and words in square brackets in para (b)(i) substituted by SI 2014/3329, arts 2, 104(1), (3); words in square brackets in para (a) substituted by the Bank of England and Financial Services Act 2016, s 16, Sch 2, Pt 2, paras 52, 56(1), (3).

[7.34]

97 Grounds for making

(1) The court may make a bank insolvency order on the application of the Bank of England or the [PRA] if satisfied—

(a) that the bank has eligible depositors, and

(b) that Ground A or C of section 96 applies.

(2) The court may make a bank insolvency order on the application of the Secretary of State if satisfied—

(a) that the bank has eligible depositors, and

(b) that Grounds B and C of section 96 apply.

(3) On an application for a bank insolvency order the court may—

(a) grant the application in accordance with subsection (1) or (2),

(b) adjourn the application (generally or to a specified date), or

(c) dismiss the application.

NOTES

Sub-s (1): word in square brackets substituted by the Financial Services Act 2012, s 106, Sch 17, Pt 2, paras 29, 34.

[7.35]

98 Commencement

(1) A bank insolvency order shall be treated as having taken effect in accordance with this section.

(2) In the case where—

(a) notice has been given to the [PRA] under section 120 of an application for an administration order or a petition for a winding up order, and

(b) the [PRA] or the Bank of England applies for a bank insolvency order in the period of 2 weeks specified in Condition 3 in that section,

the bank insolvency order is treated as having taken effect when the application or petition was made or presented.

(3) In any other case, the bank insolvency order is treated as having taken effect when the application for the order was made.

(4) Unless the court directs otherwise on proof of fraud or mistake, proceedings taken in the bank insolvency, during the period for which it is treated as having had effect, are treated as having been taken validly.

NOTES

Sub-s (2): words in square brackets substituted by the Financial Services Act 2012, s 106, Sch 17, Pt 2, paras 29, 35.

Process of bank liquidation

[7.36]

99 Objectives

(1) A bank liquidator has two objectives.

(2) Objective 1 is to work with the FSCS so as to ensure that as soon as is reasonably practicable each eligible depositor—

(a) has the relevant account transferred to another financial institution, or

(b) receives payment from (or on behalf of) the FSCS.

(3) Objective 2 is to wind up the affairs of the bank so as to achieve the best result for the bank's creditors as a whole.

(4) Objective 1 takes precedence over Objective 2 (but the bank liquidator is obliged to begin working towards both objectives immediately upon appointment).

[7.37]

100 Liquidation committee

(1) Following a bank insolvency order a liquidation committee must be established, for the purpose of ensuring that the bank liquidator properly exercises the functions under this Part.

[(2) The liquidation committee is to consist initially of—

(a) two individuals nominated by the Bank of England,

(b) one individual nominated by the PRA,

(c) one individual nominated by the FCA, and

(d) one individual nominated by the FSCS.]

(3) The bank liquidator must report to the liquidation committee about any matter—

(a) on request, or

(b) which the bank liquidator thinks is likely to be of interest to the liquidation committee.

(4) In particular, the bank liquidator—

(a) must keep the liquidation committee informed of progress towards Objective 1 in section 99, and

(b) must notify the liquidation committee when in the bank liquidator's opinion Objective 1 in section 99 has been achieved entirely or so far as is reasonably practicable.

(5) As soon as is reasonably practicable after receiving notice under subsection (4)(b) the liquidation committee must either—

(a) resolve that Objective 1 in section 99 has been achieved entirely or so far as is reasonably practicable (a "full payment resolution"), or

(b) apply to the court under section 168(5) of the Insolvency Act 1986 (as applied by section 103 below).

(6) Where a liquidation committee passes a full payment resolution—

(a) the bank liquidator must summon a meeting of creditors,

(b) the meeting may elect 2 or 4 individuals as new members of the liquidation committee,

(c) those individuals replace the members nominated by the Bank of England[, the PRA and the FCA],

(d) the FSCS may resign from the liquidation committee (in which case 3 or 5 new members may be elected under paragraph (b)), and

(e) if no individuals are elected under paragraph (b), or the resulting committee would have fewer than 3 members or an even number of members, the liquidation committee ceases to exist at the end of the meeting.

(7) Subject to provisions of this section, rules under section 411 of the Insolvency Act 1986 (as amended by section 125 below) may make provision about—

(a) the establishment of liquidation committees,

(b) the membership of liquidation committees,

(c) the functions of liquidation committees, and

(d) the proceedings of liquidation committees.

NOTES

Sub-s (2): substituted by the Financial Services Act 2012, s 106, Sch 17, Pt 2, paras 29, 36(1), (2).

Sub-s (6): words in square brackets substituted by the Financial Services Act 2012, s 106, Sch 17, Pt 2, paras 29, 36(1), (3).

[7.38]

101 Liquidation committee: supplemental

(1) A meeting of the liquidation committee may be summoned—

(a) by any of the members, or

(b) by the bank liquidator.

(2) While the liquidation committee consists of the initial members (or their nominated replacements) a meeting is quorate only if all the members are present.

(3) A person aggrieved by any action of the liquidation committee before it has passed a full payment resolution may apply to the court, which may make any order (including an order for the repayment of money).

(4) The court may (whether on an application under subsection (3), on the application of a bank liquidator or otherwise) make an order that the liquidation committee is to be treated as having passed a full payment resolution.

(5) If a liquidation committee fails to comply with section 100(5) the bank liquidator must apply to the court—

(a) for an order under subsection (4) above, or

(b) for directions under or by virtue of section 168(3) or 169(2) of the Insolvency Act 1986 as applied by section 103 below.

(6) A nominating body under section 100(2) may replace its nominee at any time.

(7) After the removal of the nominated members under section 100(6)(c) the [PRA, the FCA] and the Bank of England—

(a) may attend meetings of the liquidation committee,

(b) are entitled to copies of documents relating to the liquidation committee's business,

(c) may make representations to the liquidation committee, and

(d) may participate in legal proceedings relating to the bank insolvency.

(8) Where a liquidation committee ceases to exist by virtue of section 100(6)(e)—

(a) it may be re-formed by a creditors' meeting summoned by the bank liquidator for the purpose, and

(b) the bank liquidator must summon a meeting for the purpose if requested to do so by one-tenth in value of the bank's creditors.

(9) Where a liquidation committee ceases to exist by virtue of section 100(6)(e) and has not been re-formed under subsection (8) above or under section 141(2) or 142(2) of the Insolvency Act 1986 (as applied by section 103 below)—

(a) ignore a reference in this Part to the liquidation committee,

(b) for section 113(2) to (4) substitute requirements for the bank liquidator, before making a proposal—

(i) to produce a final report,

(ii) to send copies in accordance with section 113(2)(b),

(iii) to make it available in accordance with section 113(2)(c), and

(iv) to be satisfied as specified in section 113(4)(b),

(c) ignore Condition 2 in section 114, and

(d) for section 115(1) to (5) substitute a power for the bank liquidator to apply to the Secretary of State or Accountant of Court for release and requirements that before making an application the bank liquidator must—

(i) produce a final report,

(ii) send copies in accordance with section 115(2)(b),

(iii) make it available in accordance with section 115(2)(c), and

(iv) notify the court and the registrar of companies of the intention to vacate office and to apply for release.

NOTES

Sub-s (7): word in square brackets substituted by the Financial Services Act 2012, s 106, Sch 17, Pt 2, paras 29, 37.

[7.39]

102 Objective 1: (a) or (b)?

(1) As soon as is reasonably practicable, a liquidation committee must recommend the bank liquidator to pursue—

(a) Objective 1(a) in section 99,

(b) Objective 1(b) in section 99, or

(c) Objective 1(a) for one specified class of case and Objective 1(b) for another.

(2) In making a recommendation the liquidation committee must consider—

(a) the desirability of achieving Objective 1 as quickly as possible, and

(b) Objective 2 in section 99.

(3) If the liquidation committee thinks that the bank liquidator is failing to comply with their recommendation, they must apply to the court for directions under section 168(5) of the Insolvency Act 1986 (as applied by section 103 below).

(4) Where the liquidation committee has not made a recommendation the bank liquidator may apply to the court under section 101(3); and the court may, in particular, make a direction in lieu of a recommendation if the liquidation committee fail to make one within a period set by the court.

[7.40]

103 General powers, duties and effect

(1) A bank liquidator may do anything necessary or expedient for the pursuit of the Objectives in section 99.

(2) The following provisions of this section provide for—

(a) general powers and duties of bank liquidators (by application of provisions about liquidators), and

(b) the general process and effects of bank insolvency (by application of provisions about winding up).

(3) The provisions set out in the Table apply in relation to bank insolvency as in relation to winding up, with—

(a) the modifications set out in subsection (4),

(b) any other modification specified in the Table, and

(c) any other necessary modification.

(4) The modifications are that—

(a) a reference to the liquidator is a reference to the bank liquidator,

(b) a reference to winding up is a reference to bank insolvency,

(c) a reference to winding up by the court is a reference to the imposition of bank insolvency by order of the court,

(d) a reference to being wound up under Part IV or V of the Insolvency Act 1986 is a reference to being made the subject of a bank insolvency order,

(e) a reference to the commencement of winding up is a reference to the commencement of bank insolvency,

(f) a reference to going into liquidation is a reference to entering bank insolvency,

(g) a reference to a winding-up order is a reference to a bank insolvency order, and

(h) [except where otherwise specified in the Table,] a reference to a company is a reference to the bank.

(5) Powers conferred by this Act, by the Insolvency Act 1986 (as applied) and the Companies Acts are in addition to, and not in restriction of, any existing powers of instituting proceedings against a contributory or debtor of a bank, or the estate of any contributory or debtor, for the recovery of any call or other sum.

(6) A reference in an enactment or other document to anything done under a provision applied by this Part includes a reference to the provision as applied.

[(7) In the Table "Schedule 9 to the 2015 Act" means Schedule 9 to the Small Business, Enterprise and Employment Act 2015 (further amendments relating to the abolition of requirements to hold meetings: company insolvency).]

TABLE OF APPLIED PROVISIONS

Provision of Insolvency Act 1986	***Subject***	***Modification or comment***
Section 127	Avoidance of property dispositions	Ignore section 127(2).
Section 128	Avoidance of attachment, &c	
Section 130	Consequences of winding-up order	Ignore section 130(4).
Section 131	Company's statement of affairs	(a) Treat references to the official receiver as references to the bank liquidator. (b) A creditor or contributory of the bank is entitled to receive a copy of a statement under section 131 on request to the bank liquidator.
Section 135	Provisional appointment	(a) Treat the reference to the presentation of a winding-up petition as a reference to the making of an application for a bank insolvency order. (b) Subsection (2) applies in relation to England and Wales and Scotland (and subsection (3) does not apply). (c) Ignore the reference to the official receiver. (d) Only a person who is qualified to act as an insolvency practitioner [in relation to the bank] and who consents to act may be appointed. (e) A provisional bank liquidator may not pay dividends to creditors. (f) The appointment of a provisional bank liquidator lapses on the appointment of a bank liquidator.
Section 141	Liquidation Committee (England and Wales)	[Ignore the amendment made by paragraph 36 of Schedule 9 to the 2015 Act.] The application of section 141 is subject to— (a) sections 100, 101 and 109 of this Act,

TABLE OF APPLIED PROVISIONS

Provision of Insolvency Act 1986	***Subject***	***Modification or comment***
		(b) rules under section 411 (as applied by section 125 of this Act) which may, in particular, adapt section 141 to reflect (i) the fact that the bank liquidator is appointed by the court and (ii) the possibility of calling creditors' meetings under other provisions, and (c) the omission of references to the official receiver.
Section 142	Liquidation Committee (Scotland)	[Ignore the amendments made by paragraph 37 of Schedule 9 to the 2015 Act.] The application of section 142 is subject to— (a) sections 100, 101 and 109 of this Act, (b) rules under section 411 (as applied by section 125 of this Act) which may, in particular, adapt section 142 to reflect (i) the fact that the bank liquidator is appointed by the court and (ii) the possibility of calling creditors' meetings under other provisions, and (c) the omission of references to the official receiver.
Section 143	General functions of liquidator	(a) Section 143(1) is subject to Objective 1 in section 99 above. (b) Ignore section 143(2).
Section 144	Custody of property	
Section 145	Vesting of property	
Section 146	*Duty to summon final meeting*	*Section 146 is not applied—but section 115 below makes similar provision.*
Section 147	Power to stay or sist proceedings	An application may be made only by— (a) the bank liquidator, (b) the [PRA], (c) the Bank of England, (d) the FSCS, or (e) a creditor or contributory (but only if the liquidation committee has passed a full payment resolution).
Section 148	List of contributories and application of assets	*By virtue of the Insolvency Rules the functions under this section are largely delegated to the liquidator—rules by virtue of section 125 may achieve a similar delegation to the bank liquidator.*
Section 149	Debts due from contributories	
Section 150	Power to make calls	
Section 152	Order on contributory: evidence	
Section 153	Exclusion of creditors	
Section 154	Adjustment of rights of contributories	
Section 155	Inspection of books by creditors	In making or considering whether to make an order under section 155 the court shall have regard to Objective 1 in section 99 above.
Section 156	Payment of expenses of winding up	

Part 7B Special Insolvency Regimes

TABLE OF APPLIED PROVISIONS		
Provision of Insolvency Act 1986	***Subject***	***Modification or comment***
Section 157	Attendance at company meetings (Scotland)	
Section 158	Power to arrest absconding contributory	
Section 159	*Powers to be cumulative*	*Section 159 is not applied—but subsection (5) above makes similar provision.*
Section 160	Delegation of powers to liquidator (England and Wales)	[Ignore the amendment made by paragraph 39 of Schedule 9 to the 2015 Act.]
Section 161	Orders for calls on contributories (Scotland)	
Section 162	Appeals from orders (Scotland)	An appeal may be brought only if the liquidation committee has passed a full payment resolution.
Section 167 and Schedule 4	General powers of liquidator	(a) An application to the court may not be made under section 167(3) unless the liquidation committee has passed a full payment resolution (although a creditor or contributory may apply to the court with respect to any action (or inaction) of the liquidation committee, under section 101(3) above). (b) In exercising or considering whether to exercise a power under Schedule 4 the bank liquidator shall have regard to Objective 1 in section 99. (c) A reference to the liquidation committee is to the liquidation committee established by section 100. (d) The power in paragraph 4 of Schedule 4 includes the power to submit matters to arbitration. *Some additional general powers are conferred by section 104 below.*
Section 168	Supplementary powers of liquidator	[(za) Ignore the amendment made by paragraph 41 of Schedule 9 to the 2015 Act.] (a) A direction or request under section 168(2) has no effect unless the liquidation committee has passed a full payment resolution. (b) Section 168(5) also applies in the case of the imposition of bank insolvency by order of the Court of Session. (c) An application to the court may not be made under section 168(5) unless the liquidation committee has passed a full payment resolution (except as provided in section 100 or 102 above).
Section 169	Supplementary powers (Scotland)	(a) . . . (b) Powers of the bank liquidator by virtue of section 169(2) are subject to Objective 1 in section 99 above.
Section 170	Liquidator's duty to make returns	The liquidation committee is added to the list of persons able to apply under section 170(2).
Section 172	Removal of liquidator	*Section 172 is not applied to a bank liquidator—but section 108 makes similar provision.*

TABLE OF APPLIED PROVISIONS

Provision of Insolvency Act 1986	***Subject***	***Modification or comment***
		Section 172(1), (2) and (5) are applied to a provisional bank liquidator.
Section 174	*Release of liquidator*	*Section 174 is not applied—but section 115 makes similar provision.*
Section 175	Preferential debts	
Section 176	Preferential charge on goods restrained	
Section 176ZA	Expenses of winding up	
[Section 176ZB	Application of proceeds of office-holder claims]	
Section 176A	Share of assets for unsecured creditors	
Section 177	Appointment of special manager	
Section 178	Power to disclaim onerous property	
Section 179	Disclaimer of leaseholds	
Section 180	Land subject to rentcharge	
Section 181	Disclaimer: powers of court	
Section 182	Leaseholds	
Section 183	Effect of execution or attachment (England and Wales)	
Section 184	Execution of writs (England and Wales)	
Section 185	Effect of diligence (Scotland)	In the application of [section 24(1) and (2) of the Bankruptcy (Scotland) Act 2016] the reference to an order of the court awarding winding up is a reference to the making of the bank insolvency order.
Section 186	Rescission of contracts by court	
Section 187	Transfer of assets to employees	
Section 188	Publicity	
Section 189	Interest on debts	
Section 190	Exemption from stamp duty	
Section 191	Company's books as evidence	
Section 192	Information about pending liquidations	
Section 193	Unclaimed dividends (Scotland)	
Section 194	Resolutions passed at adjourned meetings	[Section 194 applies as it applied before its repeal by paragraph 46 of Schedule 9 to the 2015 Act.]
Section 195	Meetings to ascertain wishes of creditors or contributories	[(a) Ignore the amendments made by paragraph 47 of Schedule 9 to the 2015 Act.]
		[(b)] The power to have regard to the wishes of creditors and contributories is subject to Objective 1 in section 99.
Section 196	Judicial notice of court documents	

Part 7B Special Insolvency Regimes

TABLE OF APPLIED PROVISIONS		
Provision of Insolvency Act 1986	***Subject***	***Modification or comment***
Section 197	Commission for receiving evidence	
Section 198	Court order for examination of persons (Scotland)	
Section 199	Costs of application for leave to proceed (Scotland)	
Section 200	Affidavits	
Section 206	Fraud in anticipation of winding up	
Section 207	Transactions in fraud of creditors	
Section 208	Misconduct in course of winding up	[Ignore the amendment made by paragraph 52 of Schedule 9 to the 2015 Act.]
Section 209	Falsification of company's books	
Section 210	Material omissions	
Section 211	False representations to creditors	
Section 212	Summary remedy against directors, &c	
Section 213	Fraudulent trading	
[Section 214	Wrongful trading	(a) Treat the reference in subsection (2)(b) to entering insolvent administration as a reference to entering bank administration under Part 3 of this Act at a time when the bank's assets are insufficient for the payment of its debts and other liabilities and the expenses of the administration. (b) Ignore subsection (6A).]
Section 215	Sections 213 & 214: procedure	
Section 216	Restriction on re-use of company names	
Section 217	Personal liability for debts	
Section 218	Prosecution of officers and members of company	(a) Ignore subsections (4) and (6). (b) In subsection (3), treat the second reference to the official receiver as a reference to the Secretary of State. (c) In subsection (5) treat the reference to subsection (4) as a reference to subsection (3).
Section 219	Obligations under section 218	
Section 231	Appointment of 2 or more persons	
Section 232	Validity of acts	
Section 233	Utilities	
Section 234	Getting in company's property	
Section 235	Co-operation with liquidator	Ignore references to the official receiver
Section 236	Inquiry into company's dealings	Ignore references to the official receiver

TABLE OF APPLIED PROVISIONS		
Provision of Insolvency Act 1986	***Subject***	***Modification or comment***
Section 237	Section 236: enforcement by court	
Section 238	Transactions at undervalue (England and Wales)	Anything done by the bank in connection with the exercise of a stabilisation power under Part 1 of this Act is not a transaction at an undervalue for the purposes of section 238.
Section 239	Preferences (England and Wales)	Action taken by the bank in connection with the exercise of a stabilisation power under Part 1 of this Act does not amount to giving a preference for the purpose of section 239.
Section 240	Sections 238 & 239: relevant time	
Section 241	Orders under sections 238 & 239	Having notice of the relevant proceedings means having notice of— (a) an application by the Bank of England, the [PRA] or the Secretary of State for a bank insolvency order, or (b) notice under section 120 below.
Section 242	Gratuitous alienations (Scotland)	Anything done by the bank in connection with the exercise of a stabilisation power under Part 1 of this Act is not a gratuitous alienation for the purpose of section 242 or any other rule of law.
Section 243	Unfair preferences (Scotland)	Action taken by the bank in connection with the exercise of a stabilisation power under Part 1 of this Act does not amount to an unfair preference for the purpose of section 243 or any other rule of law.
Section 244	Extortionate credit transactions	
Section 245	Avoidance of floating charges	
Section 246	Unenforceability of liens	
[Section 246ZD	Power to assign certain causes of action]	
Sections 386 & 387, and Schedule 6 (and Schedule 4 to the Pension Schemes Act 1993)	Preferential debts	
Section 389	Offence of acting without being qualified	Treat references to acting as an insolvency practitioner as references to acting as a bank liquidator.

TABLE OF APPLIED PROVISIONS

Provision of Insolvency Act 1986	*Subject*	*Modification or comment*
[Sections 390 to 391T	Authorisation and regulation of insolvency practitioners	(a) In section 390 treat references to acting as an insolvency practitioner as references to acting as a bank liquidator. (b) Read subsection (2) of that section (as so modified) as if after "authorised" there were inserted "to act as an insolvency practitioner". (c) An order under section 391 has effect in relation to any provision applied for the purposes of bank insolvency. (d) In sections 390A, 390B(1) and (3), 391O(1)(b) and 391R(3)(b), in a reference to authorisation or permission to act as an insolvency practitioner in relation to (or only in relation to) companies the reference to companies has effect without the modification in subsection (4)(h) of this section. (e) In sections 391Q(2)(b) and 391S(3)(e) the reference to a company has effect without the modification in subsection (4)(h) of this section.]
Sections 423–425	Transactions defrauding creditors	Anything done by the bank in connection with the exercise of a stabilisation power under Part 1 of this Act is not a transaction at an undervalue for the purposes of section 423.
Sections 430 to 432 and Schedule 10	Offences	
Section 433	Statements: admissibility	For section 433(1)(a) and (b) substitute a reference to a statement prepared for the purposes of a provision of this Part.

NOTES

Note: the table following sub-s (7) is reproduced as it appears in the original Queen's printer's copy. The entries in italics appear in italics in the original and do not represent amendments to the text.

Sub-s (4): words in square brackets in para (h) inserted by the Deregulation Act 2015, the Small Business, Enterprise and Employment Act 2015 and the Insolvency (Amendment) Act (Northern Ireland) 2016 (Consequential Amendments and Transitional Provisions) Regulations 2017, SI 2017/400, reg 5(1), (3).

Sub-s (7): inserted by the Small Business, Enterprise and Employment Act 2015 (Consequential Amendments, Savings and Transitional Provisions) Regulations 2018, SI 2018/208, reg 5(1), (2).

The table following sub-s (7) has been amended as follows:

Words in square brackets in the entry relating to s 134 inserted, words omitted from the entry relating to s 169 repealed, entries relating to ss 176ZB and 246ZD inserted, and entry relating to s 214 substituted, by SI 2017/400, reg 5(1), (4)(a)–(e).

Words in square brackets in the entries relating to ss 141, 142, 160, 168, 194, 195, and 208 inserted by SI 2018/208, reg 5(1), (3).

In entries relating to ss 147 and 241, words in square brackets substituted by the Financial Services Act 2012, s 106, Sch 17, Pt 2, paras 29, 38.

In entry relating to s 185, words in square brackets substituted (for the original words "section 37(1) of the Bankruptcy (Scotland) Act 1985") by the Bankruptcy (Scotland) Act 2016 (Consequential Provisions and Modifications) Order 2016, SI 2016/1034, art 7(1), (3), Sch 1, para 32, as from 30 November 2016 (except in relation to (i) a sequestration as regards which the petition is presented, or the debtor application is made before that date; or (ii) a trust deed executed before that date).

Entries relating to ss 390–391T substituted (for the original entries relating to ss 390 and 391) by SI 2017/400, reg 5(1), (4)(f), subject to transitional provisions as noted below.

Transitional provisions: Regulation 17 of the 2017 Regulations provides—

> "(1) Regulations 5(4)(f) and (10)(e) and 10(5)(e) and (8)(b), so far as they relate to sections 391O to 391R (court sanction of insolvency practitioners in public interest cases), have effect in relation to a person who acts as an insolvency practitioner in any relevant proceedings on or after the commencement date, but disregarding any conduct of that person before that date.
>
> (2) Paragraph (1) applies notwithstanding that the date of the person's authorisation to act as an insolvency practitioner or appointment to act in the relevant proceedings precedes the commencement date.
>
> (3) "Relevant proceedings" means any proceedings of a kind specified in regulation 14(2)(a), (b), (c) and (e).".

Note for the purposes of reg 17 as set out above that the commencement date is 7 April 2017. Note also that the proceedings specified in reg 14(2)(a), (b), (c) and (e) are: (a) bank insolvency under Part 2 of the 2009 Act or bank administration under Part 3 of that Act; (b) building society insolvency under Part 2 of the 2009 Act (as applied by section 90C of the Building

Societies Act 1986); (c) building society special administration under Part 3 of the 2009 Act (as applied by section 90C of the Building Societies Act 1986); and (e) special administration, special administration (bank insolvency) or special administration (bank administration) under the Investment Bank Special Administration Regulations 2011.

[7.41]
104 Additional general powers
(1) A bank liquidator has the following powers.
(2) Power to effect and maintain insurances in respect of the business and property of the bank.
(3) Power to do all such things (including the carrying out of works) as may be necessary for the realisation of the property of the bank.
(4) Power to make any payment which is necessary or incidental to the performance of the bank liquidator's functions.

NOTES

Applied with modifications, for the purposes of an authorised bank, by the Scottish and Northern Ireland Banknote Regulations 2009, SI 2009/3056, reg 29, Sch 1, Pt 1, para 4.

[7.42]
105 Status of bank liquidator
A bank liquidator is an officer of the court.

Tenure of bank liquidator

[7.43]
106 Term of appointment
A bank liquidator appointed by bank insolvency order remains in office until vacating office—
(a) by resigning under section 107,
(b) on removal under section 108 or 109,
(c) on disqualification under section 110,
(d) on the appointment of a replacement in accordance with section 112,
(e) in accordance with sections 113 to 115, or
(f) on death.

[7.44]
107 Resignation
(1) A bank liquidator may resign by notice to the court.
(2) Rules under section 411 of the Insolvency Act 1986 (as applied by section 125 below) may restrict a bank liquidator's power to resign.
(3) Resignation shall take effect in accordance with those rules (which shall include provision about release).

[7.45]
108 Removal by court
(1) A bank liquidator may be removed by order of the court on the application of—
(a) the liquidation committee,
(b) the [PRA], or
(c) the Bank of England.
(2) Before making an application the [PRA] must consult . . . [the FCA].
(3) Before making an application the Bank of England must consult . . . [the FCA].
(4) A bank liquidator removed by order has release with effect from a time determined by—
(a) the Secretary of State, or
(b) in the case of a bank liquidator in Scotland, the Accountant of Court.

NOTES

Sub-s (1): words in square brackets substituted by the Financial Services Act 2012, s 106, Sch 17, Pt 2, paras 29, 39(1), (2).
Sub-s (2): word in first pair of square brackets substituted, and words in second pair of square brackets inserted, by the Financial Services Act 2012, s 106, Sch 17, Pt 2, paras 29, 39(1), (23); words omitted repealed by the Bank of England and Financial Services Act 2016, s 16, Sch 2, Pt 2, paras 52, 57(1), (2).
Sub-s (3): words omitted repealed by the Bank of England and Financial Services Act 2016, s 16, Sch 2, Pt 2, paras 52, 57(1), (3); words in square brackets substituted by the Financial Services Act 2012, s 106, Sch 17, Pt 2, paras 29, 39(1), (4).

[7.46]
109 Removal by creditors
(1) A bank liquidator may be removed by resolution of a meeting of creditors held pursuant to section 195 of the Insolvency Act 1986 (as applied by section 103 above) provided that the following conditions are met.
(2) Condition 1 is that the liquidation committee has passed a full payment resolution.
(3) Condition 2 is that the notice given to creditors of the meeting includes notice of intention to move a resolution removing the bank liquidator.
(4) Condition 3 is that the Bank of England[, the PRA and the FCA]—
(a) receive notice of the meeting, and
(b) are given an opportunity to make representations to it.
(5) A bank liquidator who is removed under this section has release with effect—
(a) from the time when the court is informed of the removal, or

(b) if the meeting removing the bank liquidator resolves to disapply paragraph (a), from a time determined by—
(i) the Secretary of State, or
(ii) in the case of a bank liquidator in Scotland, the Accountant of Court.

NOTES

Sub-s (4): words in square brackets substituted by the Financial Services Act 2012, s 106, Sch 17, Pt 2, paras 29, 40.

[7.47]
110 Disqualification

(1) If a bank liquidator ceases to be qualified to act as an insolvency practitioner [in relation to the bank], the appointment lapses.

(2) A bank liquidator whose appointment lapses under subsection (1) has release with effect from a time determined by—
(a) the Secretary of State, or
(b) in the case of a bank liquidator in Scotland, the Accountant of Court.

NOTES

Sub-s (1): words in square brackets inserted by the Deregulation Act 2015, the Small Business, Enterprise and Employment Act 2015 and the Insolvency (Amendment) Act (Northern Ireland) 2016 (Consequential Amendments and Transitional Provisions) Regulations 2017, SI 2017/400, reg 5(1), (5).

[7.48]
111 Release

A bank liquidator who is released is discharged from all liability in respect of acts or omissions in the bank insolvency and otherwise in relation to conduct as bank liquidator (but without prejudice to the effect of section 212 of the Insolvency Act 1986 as applied by section 103 above).

[7.49]
112 Replacement

(1) Where a bank liquidator vacates office the Bank of England must as soon as is reasonably practicable appoint a replacement bank liquidator.

(2) But where a bank liquidator is removed by resolution of a meeting of creditors under section 109—
(a) a replacement may be appointed by resolution of the meeting, and
(b) failing that, subsection (1) above applies.

Termination of process, &c

[7.50]
113 Company voluntary arrangement

(1) A bank liquidator may make a proposal in accordance with section 1 of the Insolvency Act 1986 (company voluntary arrangement).

(2) Before making a proposal the bank liquidator—
(a) shall present a final report on the bank liquidation to the liquidation committee,
(b) shall send a copy of the report to—
[(i) the PRA,
(ia) the FCA,]
(ii) the FSCS,
(iii) the Bank of England,
(iv) the Treasury, and
(v) the registrar of companies, and
(c) shall make the report available to members, creditors and contributories on request.

(3) A proposal may be made only with the consent of the liquidation committee.

(4) The liquidation committee may consent only if—
(a) it has passed a full payment resolution, and
(b) the bank liquidator is satisfied, as a result of arrangements made with the FSCS, that any depositor still eligible for compensation under the scheme will be dealt with in accordance with section 99(2)(a) or (b).

(5) The bank liquidator must be the nominee (see section 1(2) of the 1986 Act).

(6) Part 1 of the 1986 Act shall apply to a proposal made by a bank liquidator, with the following modifications.

(7) In section 3 (summoning of meetings) subsection (2) (and not (1)) applies.

(8) The action that may be taken by the court under section 5(3) (effect of approval) includes suspension of the bank insolvency order.

(9) On the termination of a company voluntary arrangement the bank liquidator may apply to the court to lift the suspension of the bank insolvency order.

NOTES

Sub-s (2): paras (b)(i), (ia) substituted, for original para (b)(i), by the Financial Services Act 2012, s 106, Sch 17, Pt 2, paras 29, 41.

[7.51]
114 Administration

(1) A bank liquidator who thinks that administration would achieve a better result for the bank's creditors as a whole than bank insolvency may apply to the court for an administration order (under paragraph 38 of Schedule B1 to the Insolvency Act 1986).
(2) An application may be made only if the following conditions are satisfied.
(3) Condition 1 is that the liquidation committee has passed a full payment resolution.
(4) Condition 2 is that the liquidation committee has resolved that moving to administration might enable the rescue of the bank as a going concern.
(5) Condition 3 is that the bank liquidator is satisfied, as a result of arrangements made with the FSCS, that any depositors still eligible for compensation under the scheme will receive their payments or have their accounts transferred during administration.

[7.52]
115 Dissolution

(1) A bank liquidator who thinks that the winding up of the bank is for practical purposes complete shall summon a final meeting of the liquidation committee.
(2) The bank liquidator—
  (a) shall present a final report on the bank insolvency to the meeting,
  (b) shall send a copy of the report to—
    [(i) the PRA,
    (ia) the FCA,]
    (ii) the FSCS,
    (iii) the Bank of England,
    (iv) the Treasury, and
    (v) the registrar of companies, and
  (c) shall make the report available to members, creditors and contributories on request.
(3) At the meeting the liquidation committee shall—
  (a) consider the report, and
  (b) decide whether to release the bank liquidator.
(4) If the liquidation committee decides to release the bank liquidator, the bank liquidator—
  (a) shall notify the court and the registrar of companies, and
  (b) vacates office, and has release, when the court is notified.
(5) If the liquidation committee decides not to release the bank liquidator, the bank liquidator may apply to the Secretary of State for release; if the application is granted, the bank liquidator—
  (a) vacates office when the application is granted, and
  (b) has release from a time determined by the Secretary of State.
(6) In the case of a bank liquidator in Scotland, a reference in subsection (5) to the Secretary of State is a reference to the Accountant of Court.
(7) On receipt of a notice under subsection (4)(a) the registrar of companies shall register it.
(8) At the end of the period of 3 months beginning with the day of the registration of the notice, the bank is dissolved (subject to deferral under section 116).

NOTES

Sub-s (2): paras (b)(i), (ia) substituted, for original para (b)(i), by the Financial Services Act 2012, s 106, Sch 17, Pt 2, paras 29, 42.

[7.53]
116 Dissolution: supplemental

(1) The Secretary of State may by direction defer the date of dissolution under section 115, on the application of a person who appears to the Secretary of State to be interested.
(2) An appeal to the court lies from any decision of the Secretary of State on an application for a direction under subsection (1).
(3) Subsection (1) does not apply where the bank insolvency order was made by the court in Scotland; but the court may by direction defer the date of dissolution on an application by a person appearing to the court to have an interest.
(4) A person who obtains deferral under subsection (1) or (3) shall, within 7 days after the giving of the deferral direction, deliver a copy of the direction to the registrar of companies for registration.
(5) A person who without reasonable excuse fails to comply with subsection (4) is liable to a fine and, for continued contravention, to a daily default fine, in each case of the same amount as for a contravention of section 205(6) of the Insolvency Act 1986 (dissolution).
(6) The bank liquidator may give the notice summoning the final meeting under section 115 above at the same time as giving notice of any final distribution of the bank's property; but, if summoned for an earlier date the meeting shall be adjourned (and, if necessary, further adjourned) until a date on which the bank liquidator is able to report to the meeting that the winding up of the bank is for practical purposes complete.
(7) A bank liquidator must retain sufficient sums to cover the expenses of the final meeting under section 115 above.

Other processes

[7.54]
117 Bank insolvency as alternative order

(1) On a petition for a winding up order or an application for an administration order in respect of a bank the court may, instead, make a bank insolvency order.

(2) A bank insolvency order may be made under subsection (1) only—

(a) on the application of the [PRA] made with the consent of . . . [the FCA], or

(b) on the application of the Bank of England.

NOTES

Sub-s (2): in para (a) word in first pair of square brackets substituted and words in second pair of square brackets inserted by the Financial Services Act 2012, s 106, Sch 17, Pt 2, paras 29, 43; words omitted repealed by the Bank of England and Financial Services Act 2016, s 16, Sch 2, Pt 2, paras 52, 58.

[7.55]
118 Voluntary winding-up

A resolution for voluntary winding up of a bank under section 84 of the Insolvency Act 1986 shall have no effect without the prior approval of the court.

[7.56]
119 Exclusion of other procedures

(1) The following paragraphs of Schedule B1 to the Insolvency Act 1986 (administration) apply to a bank insolvency order as to an administration order.

(2) Those paragraphs are—

(a) paragraph 40 (dismissal of pending winding-up petition), and

(b) paragraph 42 (moratorium on insolvency proceedings).

(3) For that purpose—

(a) a reference to an administration order is a reference to a bank insolvency order,

(b) a reference to a company being in administration is a reference to a bank being in bank insolvency, and

(c) a reference to an administrator is a reference to a bank liquidator.

[7.57]
120 Notice to [PRA] of preliminary steps

(1) An application for an administration order in respect of a bank may not be determined unless the conditions below are satisfied.

(2) A petition for a winding up order in respect of a bank may not be determined unless the conditions below are satisfied.

(3) A resolution for voluntary winding up of a bank may not be made unless the conditions below are satisfied.

(4) An administrator of a bank may not be appointed unless the conditions below are satisfied.

(5) Condition 1 is that [the PRA and the Bank of England have] been notified—

(a) by the applicant for an administration order, that the application has been made,

(b) by the petitioner for a winding up order, that the petition has been presented,

(c) by the bank, that a resolution for voluntary winding up may be made, or

(d) by the person proposing to appoint an administrator, of the proposed appointment.

(6) Condition 2 is that a copy of the notice complying with Condition 1 has been filed [(in Scotland, lodged)] with the court (and made available for public inspection by the court).

(7) Condition 3 is that—

(a) the period of [7 days], beginning with the day on which the notice is received, has ended, or

[(b) both—

(i) the Bank of England has informed the person who gave the notice that it does not intend to exercise a stabilisation power under Part 1 in relation to the firm (and Condition 5 has been met, if applicable), and

(ii) each of the PRA and the Bank of England has informed the person who gave the notice that it does not intend to apply for a bank insolvency order.]

(8) Condition 4 is that no application for a bank insolvency order is pending.

[(8A) Condition 5—

(a) applies only if a resolution instrument has been made under section 12A with respect to the bank in the 3 months ending with the date on which the PRA receives the notification under Condition 1, and

(b) is that the Bank of England has informed the person who gave the notice that it consents to the insolvency procedure to which the notice relates going ahead.]

(9) Arranging for the giving of notice in order to satisfy Condition 1 can be a step with a view to minimising the potential loss to a bank's creditors for the purpose of section 214 of the Insolvency Act 1986 (wrongful trading).

(10) [Where notice has been given under Condition 1]—

(a) . . .

(b) the [PRA] shall inform the person who gave the notice, within the period in Condition 3(a), whether it intends to apply for a bank insolvency order, . . .

(c) if the Bank of England decides to apply for a bank insolvency order or to exercise a stabilisation power under Part 1, the Bank shall inform the person who gave the notice, within the period in Condition 3(a)[, and

(d) if Condition 5 applies, the Bank of England must, within the period in Condition 3(a), inform the person who gave the notice whether or not it consents to the insolvency procedure to which the notice relates going ahead.]

[(11) References in this section to the insolvency procedure to which the notice relates are to the procedure for the determination, resolution or appointment in question (see subsections (1) to (4)).]

NOTES

Section heading: word in square brackets substituted by the Financial Services Act 2012, s 106, Sch 17, Pt 2, paras 29, 44(1), (2).

Sub-s (5): words in square brackets substituted by the Bank Recovery and Resolution Order 2014, SI 2014/3329, arts 2, 105(1), (2). Note that the Queen's Printer's copy of SI 2014/3329 substitutes the words in square brackets for the original word "PRA", which would result in a duplicate "the" appearing in the text. It is assumed this is a drafting error and has been corrected accordingly.

Sub-s (6): words in square brackets inserted by the Financial Services Act 2012, s 106, Sch 17, Pt 2, paras 29, 44(1), (3).

Sub-s (7): words in square brackets substituted by SI 2014/3329, arts 2, 105(1), (3).

Sub-s (8A): inserted by the Financial Services (Banking Reform) Act 2013, s 17(1), Sch 2, Pt 1, paras 1, 10(b).

Sub-s (10): words in first pair of square brackets substituted, and para (a) repealed, by SI 2014/3329, arts 2, 105(1), (4); word in square brackets in para (b) substituted by the Financial Services Act 2012, s 106, Sch 17, Pt 2, paras 29, 44(1), (2); word omitted from para (b) repealed, and para (d) and word immediately preceding it added, by the Financial Services (Banking Reform) Act 2013, s 17, Sch 2, Pt 1, paras 1, 10(a).

Sub-s (11): added by the Financial Services (Banking Reform) Act 2013, s 17(1), Sch 2, Pt 1, paras 1, 10(d).

[7.58]

[120A Notice to the regulators and the Bank of England of preliminary steps

(1) Section 120 shall apply to relevant firms as it applies to banks, except that for this purpose—

(a) subsections (5) and (10) of that section have effect as if any reference to the PRA were a reference to the appropriate regulator, and

(b) subsection (7) has effect as if for paragraph (b) there were substituted—

"(b) the Bank of England has informed the person who gave the notice that it does not intend to exercise a stabilisation power under Part 1 in relation to the firm (and Condition 5 has been met, if applicable)."

(2) In this section—

(a) "relevant firm" means—

(i) a financial holding company, investment firm, mixed financial holding company or a mixed activity holding company, or

(ii) a financial institution which is a subsidiary undertaking of a bank or an entity within paragraph (a)(i);

(b) "financial holding company" has the meaning given in Article 4.1(2) of the capital requirements regulation (within the meaning of section 3);

(c) "financial institution" has the meaning given in Article 4.1(26) of the capital requirements regulation (within the meaning of section 3);

(d) "mixed activity holding company" has the meaning given in Article 4.1(22) of the capital requirements regulation (within the meaning of section 3);

(e) "mixed financial holding company" has the meaning given in Article 2.15 of Directive 2002/87/EC of the European Parliament and of the Council of 16th December 2002 on the supplementary supervision of credit institutions, insurance undertakings and investment firms in a financial conglomerate.

(3) In this section, references to "the appropriate regulator" are—

(a) to the PRA, in relation to a PRA-authorised person; and

(b) to the FCA in relation to any other authorised person.]

NOTES

Commencement: 1 January 2015.

Inserted by the Bank Recovery and Resolution Order 2014, SI 2014/3329, arts 2, 106.

[7.59]

121 Disqualification of directors

(1) In this section "the Disqualification Act" means the Company Directors Disqualification Act 1986.

(2) In the Disqualification Act—

(a) a reference to liquidation includes a reference to bank insolvency,

(b) a reference to winding up includes a reference to making or being subject to a bank insolvency order,

(c) a reference to becoming insolvent includes a reference to becoming subject to a bank insolvency order, and

(d) a reference to a liquidator includes a reference to a bank liquidator.

[(3) For the purposes of the application of section 7A of the Disqualification Act (office-holder's report on conduct of directors) to a bank which is subject to a bank insolvency order—

(a) the "office-holder" is the bank liquidator,

(b) the "insolvency date" means the date on which the bank insolvency order is made, and

(c) subsections (9) to (11) are omitted.]

(4) *(Inserts the Company Directors Disqualification Act 1986, s 21A at* **[4.40]***.)*

NOTES

Sub-s (3): substituted by the Deregulation Act 2015, the Small Business, Enterprise and Employment Act 2015 and the Insolvency (Amendment) Act (Northern Ireland) 2016 (Consequential Amendments and Transitional Provisions) Regulations 2017, SI 2017/400, reg 5(1), (6).

[7.60]
122 Application of insolvency law

(1) The Secretary of State and the Treasury may by order made jointly—

(a) provide for an enactment about insolvency to apply to bank insolvency (with or without specified modifications);

(b) amend, or modify the application of, an enactment about insolvency in consequence of this Part.

(2) An order under subsection (1)—

(a) shall be made by statutory instrument, and

(b) may not be made unless a draft has been laid before and approved by resolution of each House of Parliament.

Miscellaneous

123–126 (*Ss 123, 124 outside the scope of this work; s 125 amends the Insolvency Act 1986, ss 411, 413, Sch 8 at* **[1.522]**, **[1.524]**, **[1.593]**; *s 126 amends s 414 of the 1986 Act at* **[1.525]**.)

[7.61]
127 Insolvency Services Account

A bank liquidator who obtains money by realising assets in the course of the bank insolvency must pay it into the Insolvency Services Account (kept by the Secretary of State).

128 (*Amends the Insolvency Act 1986, s 433 at* **[1.550]**.)

[7.62]
129 Co-operation between courts

(1) Provisions of or by virtue of this Part are "insolvency law" for the purposes of section 426 of the Insolvency Act 1986 (co-operation between courts).

(2) (Amends the Insolvency Act 1986, s 426 at **[1.540]**.)

[7.63]
[129A Banks not regulated by PRA

(1) In the application of this Part to an FCA-regulated bank the modifications specified in the Table apply.

(2) In this section—

"FCA-regulated bank" means a bank which does not carry on any activity which is a PRA-regulated activity for the purposes of the Financial Services and Markets Act 2000;

"immediate group" has the meaning given by section 421ZA of the Financial Services and Markets Act 2000;

"PRA-authorised person" has the meaning given by section 2B(5) of that Act.

Provision	***Modification***	
Section 95	Treat the reference to the PRA in subsection (1) as a reference to the FCA.	
Section 96	[(a)	Read subsection (2)(a) as "the FCA has informed the Bank of England that the FCA is satisfied that Condition 1 in section 7 is met,
	(b)	Treat the references to the PRA in subsection (3) as references to the FCA.
	(ba)	Read subsection (3)(a) as "the Bank of England—(i) has informed the FCA that it is satisfied that Condition 2 in section 7 is met, and (ii) has consented to the application,".]
	(c)	The FCA must consult the PRA before applying for a bank insolvency order.
Section 97	Treat the reference to the PRA in subsection (1) as a reference to the FCA.	
Section 98	Treat the references to the PRA in subsection (2) as references to the FCA.	
Section 100	(a)	Treat the reference to two individuals in subsection (2)(a) as a reference to one individual.
	(b)	Ignore subsection (2)(b).
	(c)	Ignore the reference to the PRA in subsection (6)(c).
Section 101	Ignore the reference to the PRA in subsection (7).	

Provision	*Modification*	
Section 103	In the Table, in the entries relating to sections 147 and 241 of the Insolvency Act 1986, treat the reference to the PRA as a reference to the FCA.	
Section 108	(a)	Treat the reference to the PRA in subsections (1) and (2) as a reference to the FCA.
	[(b)	Treat the reference in subsection (2) to the FCA as a reference to the Bank of England.]
	(c)	. . .
Section 109	Ignore the reference to the PRA in subsection (4).	
Section 113	Ignore subsection (2)(b)(i).	
Section 115	Ignore subsection (2)(b)(i).	
Section 117	(a)	Treat the reference to the PRA in subsection (2) as a reference to the FCA.
	[(b)	Treat the reference in subsection (2) to the FCA as a reference to the Bank of England.]
Section 120	(a)	Treat the references to the PRA in subsections (5), (7) and (10) as references to the FCA.
	(b)	Ignore the duty to inform the FCA in subsection (10)(a).]

NOTES

Inserted by the Financial Services Act 2012, s 106, Sch 17, Pt 2, paras 29, 45.

Table: in the entry for s 96, in column 2, paras (a), (b), (ba) substituted for original paras (a), (b), in the entry for s 108, in column 2, para (b) substituted and para (c) repealed, and in the entry for s 117, in column 2, para (b) substituted, by the Bank of England and Financial Services Act 2016, s 16, Sch 2, Pt 2, paras 52, 59.

130–134 (*For s 130 see* **[7.471]**; *ss 131–134 outside the scope of this work.*)

[7.64]

135 Consequential provision

(1) The Treasury may by order make provision in consequence of this Part.

(2) An order may, in particular, amend or modify the effect of an enactment (including a fiscal enactment) passed before the commencement of this Part.

(3) An order—

(a) shall be made by statutory instrument, and

(b) may not be made unless a draft has been laid before and approved by resolution of each House of Parliament.

NOTES

Orders: the Banking Act 2009 (Parts 2 and 3 Consequential Amendments) Order 2009, SI 2009/317.

PART 3
BANK ADMINISTRATION

NOTES

Application to Multiple Transfers: as to the application of this Part to multiple transfers, see the Banking Act 2009 (Bank Administration) (Modification for Application to Multiple Transfers) Regulations 2009, SI 2009/313.

Banks in Temporary Public Ownership: as to the application of this Part to banks in temporary public ownership, see the Banking Act 2009 (Bank Administration) (Modification for Application to Banks in Temporary Public Ownership) Regulations 2009, SI 2009/312.

Building Societies: this Part is applied with modifications in respect of building societies, by the Building Societies (Insolvency and Special Administration) Order 2009, SI 2009/805, art 3, Sch 1, Pts 1, 3 at **[7.475]**, **[7.479]**, **[7.481]**.

Bank administration: this Part is applied with modifications in relation to a special administration (bank administration), by the Investment Bank Special Administration Regulations 2011, SI 2011/245, reg 9, Sch 2, para 6 at **[7.1669]**, **[7.1705]**.

Introduction

[7.65]

136 Overview

(1) This Part provides for a procedure to be known as bank administration.

(2) The main features of bank administration are that—

(a) it is used where part of the business of a bank is sold to a commercial purchaser in accordance with section 11 or transferred to a [resolution company] in accordance with section 12 [or 12ZA] (and it can also be used in certain cases of multiple transfers under Part 1),

(b) the court appoints a bank administrator on the application of the Bank of England,

Part 7B Special Insolvency Regimes

(c) the bank administrator is able and required to ensure that the non-sold or non-transferred part of the bank ("the residual bank") provides services or facilities required to enable the commercial purchaser ("the private sector purchaser") or the transferee ("the [resolution company]") to operate effectively, and

(d) in other respects the process is the same as for normal administration under the Insolvency Act 1986, subject to specified modifications.

(3) The Table describes the provisions of this Part.

Sections	***Topic***
Sections 136 to 140	Introduction
Sections 141 to 148	Process
Sections 149 to [152A]	Multiple transfers
Sections 153 and 154	Termination
Sections 155 to 168	Miscellaneous

NOTES

Sub-s (2): words in first and third pairs of square brackets substituted and words in second pair of square brackets inserted, by the Bank Recovery and Resolution Order 2016, SI 2016/1239, arts 2, 26(1), (2).

Sub-s (3): figure in square brackets substituted by the Financial Services (Banking Reform) Act 2013, s 17(1), Sch 2, Pt 1, paras 1, 28.

[7.66]

137 Objectives

(1) A bank administrator has two objectives—

(a) Objective 1: support for commercial purchaser or [resolution company] (see section 138), and

(b) Objective 2: "normal" administration (see section 140).

(2) Objective 1 takes priority over Objective 2 (but a bank administrator is obliged to begin working towards both objectives immediately upon appointment).

NOTES

Sub-s (1): words in square brackets substituted by the Bank Recovery and Resolution Order 2016, SI 2016/1239, arts 2, 26(1), (3).

[7.67]

138 Objective 1: supporting private sector purchaser or [resolution company]

(1) Objective 1 is to ensure the supply to the private sector purchaser or [resolution company] of such services and facilities as are required to enable it, in the opinion of the Bank of England, to operate effectively.

(2) For the purposes of Objective 1—

(a) the reference to services and facilities includes a reference to acting as transferor or transferee under a supplemental or reverse property transfer instrument [(including a bridge bank supplemental property transfer instrument or bridge bank supplemental reverse property transfer instrument)], and

(b) the reference to "supply" includes a reference to supply by persons other than the residual bank.

(3) In the case of bank administration following a private sector purchase the bank administrator must co-operate with any request of the Bank of England to enter into an agreement for the residual bank to provide services or facilities to the private sector purchaser; and—

(a) in pursuing Objective 1 the bank administrator must have regard to the terms of that or any other agreement entered into between the residual bank and the private sector purchaser,

(b) in particular, the bank administrator must avoid action that is likely to prejudice performance by the residual bank of its obligations in accordance with those terms,

(c) if in doubt about the effect of those terms the bank administrator may apply to the court for directions under paragraph 63 of Schedule B1 to the Insolvency Act 1986 (applied by section 145 below), and

(d) the private sector purchaser may refer to the court a dispute about any agreement with the residual bank, by applying for directions under paragraph 63 of Schedule B1.

(4) In the case of bank administration following transfer to a [resolution company], the bank administrator must co-operate with any request of the Bank of England to enter into an agreement for the residual bank to provide services or facilities to the [resolution company]; and—

(a) the bank administrator must avoid action that is likely to prejudice performance by the residual bank of its obligations in accordance with an agreement,

(b) the bank administrator must ensure that so far as is reasonably practicable an agreement entered into includes provision for consideration at market rate,

(c) paragraph (b) does not prevent the bank administrator from entering into an agreement on any terms that the bank administrator thinks necessary in pursuit of Objective 1, and

(d) this subsection does not apply after Objective 1 ceases.

(5) Where a bank administrator requires the Bank of England's consent or approval to any action in accordance with this Part, the Bank may withhold consent or approval only on the grounds that the action might prejudice the achievement of Objective 1.

NOTES

Words in square brackets in sub-s (2)(a) inserted and all other words in square brackets substituted by the Bank Recovery and Resolution Order 2016, SI 2016/1239, arts 2, 26(1), (4).

[7.68]

139 Objective 1: duration

(1) Objective 1 ceases if the Bank of England notifies the bank administrator that the residual bank is no longer required in connection with the private sector purchaser or [resolution company].

(2) A bank administrator who thinks that Objective 1 is no longer required may apply to the court for directions under paragraph 63 of Schedule B1 to the Insolvency Act 1986 (applied by section 145 below); and the court may direct the Bank of England to consider whether to give notice under subsection (1) above.

(3) If immediately upon the making of a bank administration order the Bank of England thinks that the residual bank is not required in connection with the private sector purchaser or [resolution company], the Bank of England may give a notice under subsection (1).

(4) A notice under subsection (1) is referred to in this Part as an "Objective 1 Achievement Notice".

NOTES

Sub-ss (1), (3): words in square brackets substituted by the Bank Recovery and Resolution Order 2016, SI 2016/1239, arts 2, 26(1), (5).

[7.69]

140 Objective 2: "normal" administration

(1) Objective 2 is to—

(a) rescue the residual bank as a going concern ("Objective 2(a)"), or

(b) achieve a better result for the residual bank's creditors as a whole than would be likely if the residual bank were wound up without first being in bank administration ("Objective 2(b)").

(2) In pursuing Objective 2 a bank administrator must aim to achieve Objective 2(a) unless of the opinion either—

(a) that it is not reasonably practicable to achieve it, or

(b) that Objective 2(b) would achieve a better result for the residual bank's creditors as a whole.

(3) In pursuing Objective 2(b) in bank administration following transfer to a [resolution company], the bank administrator may not realise any asset unless—

(a) the asset is on a list of realisable assets agreed between the bank administrator and the Bank of England, or

(b) the Bank of England has given an Objective 1 Achievement Notice.

NOTES

Sub-s (3): words in square brackets substituted by the Bank Recovery and Resolution Order 2016, SI 2016/1239, arts 2, 26(1), (6).

Process

[7.70]

141 Bank administration order

(1) A bank administration order is an order appointing a person as the bank administrator of a bank.

(2) A person is eligible for appointment as a bank administrator if qualified to act as an insolvency practitioner [in relation to the bank].

(3) An appointment may be made only if the person has consented to act.

(4) A bank administration order takes effect in accordance with its terms; and—

(a) the process of a bank administration order having effect may be described as "bank administration" in relation to the bank, and

(b) while the order has effect the bank may be described as being "in bank administration".

NOTES

Sub-s (2): words in square brackets inserted by the Deregulation Act 2015, the Small Business, Enterprise and Employment Act 2015 and the Insolvency (Amendment) Act (Northern Ireland) 2016 (Consequential Amendments and Transitional Provisions) Regulations 2017, SI 2017/400, reg 5(1), (7).

[7.71]

142 Application

(1) An application for a bank administration order may be made to the court by the Bank of England.

(2) An application must nominate a person to be appointed as the bank administrator.

(3) The bank must be given notice of an application, in accordance with rules under section 411 of the Insolvency Act 1986 (as applied by section 160 below).

[7.72]

143 Grounds for applying

(1) The Bank of England may apply for a bank administration order in respect of a bank if the following conditions are met.

(2) Condition 1 is that the Bank of England has made or intends to make a property transfer instrument in respect of the bank in accordance with section 11(2)[, 12(2) or 12ZA(3)].

(3) Condition 2 is that the Bank of England is satisfied that the residual bank—

(a) is unable to pay its debts, or
(b) is likely to become unable to pay its debts as a result of the property transfer instrument which the Bank intends to make.

NOTES

Sub-s (2): words in square brackets substituted by the Bank Recovery and Resolution Order 2016, SI 2016/1239, arts 2, 26(1), (7).

[7.73]

144 Grounds for making

(1) The court may make a bank administration order if satisfied that the conditions in section 143 were met.

(2) On an application for a bank administration order the court may—

(a) grant the application,
(b) adjourn the application (generally or to a specified date), or
(c) dismiss the application.

[7.74]

145 General powers, duties and effect

(1) A bank administrator may do anything necessary or expedient for the pursuit of the Objectives in section 137.

(2) The following provisions of this section provide for—

(a) general powers and duties of bank administrators (by application of provisions about administrators), and
(b) the general process and effects of bank administration (by application of provisions about administration).

(3) The provisions set out in the Tables apply in relation to bank administration as in relation to administration, with—

(a) the modifications set out in subsection (4),
(b) any other modification specified in the Tables, and
(c) any other necessary modification.

(4) The modifications are that—

(a) a reference to the administrator is a reference to the bank administrator,
(b) a reference to administration is a reference to bank administration,
(c) a reference to an administration order is a reference to a bank administration order,
(d) [except where otherwise specified in Table 2,] a reference to a company is a reference to the bank,
(e) a reference to the purpose of administration is a reference to the Objectives in section 137, and
(f) in relation to provisions of the Insolvency Act 1986 other than Schedule B1 [and section 246ZB], the modifications in section 103 above apply (but converting references into references to bank administration or administrators rather than to bank insolvency or liquidators).

(5) Powers conferred by this Act, by the Insolvency Act 1986 (as applied) and the Companies Acts are in addition to, and not in restriction of, any existing powers of instituting proceedings against a contributory or debtor of a bank, or the estate of any contributory or debtor, for the recovery of any call or other sum.

(6) A reference in an enactment or other document to anything done under a provision applied by this Part includes a reference to the provision as applied.

[(7) In the Tables "Schedule 9 to the 2015 Act" means Schedule 9 to the Small Business, Enterprise and Employment Act 2015 (further amendments relating to the abolition of requirements to hold meetings: company insolvency).]

TABLE 1: APPLIED PROVISIONS: INSOLVENCY ACT 1986, SCHEDULE B1

Provision of Sch B1	*Subject*	*Modification or comment*
Para 40(1)(a)	Dismissal of pending winding-up petition	
Para 41	Dismissal of administrative or other receiver	
Para 42	Moratorium on insolvency proceedings	Ignore sub-paras (4) and (5).
Para 43	Moratorium on other legal process	(a) In the case of bank administration following transfer to a [resolution company], unless the Bank of England has given an Objective 1 Achievement Notice consent of the bank administrator may not be given for the purposes of Para 43 without the approval of the Bank of England.

TABLE 1: APPLIED PROVISIONS: INSOLVENCY ACT 1986, SCHEDULE B1		
Provision of Sch B1	*Subject*	*Modification or comment*
		(b) In the case of bank administration following transfer to a [resolution company], unless the Bank of England has given an Objective 1 Achievement Notice, in considering whether to give permission under sub-Para (6) to a winding-up the court must have regard to the Objectives in section 137.
		(c) In considering whether to give permission for the purposes of Para 43 the court must have regard to the Objectives in section 137.
Para 44(1)(a) and (5)	Interim moratorium	
Para 46	Announcement of appointment	Ignore sub-Para (6)(b) and (c).
Paras 47 & 48	Statement of affairs	
Para 49	Administrator's proposals	(a) Para 49 does not apply unless the Bank of England has given an Objective 1 Achievement Notice; *for bank administrator's proposals before the Bank of England has given an Objective 1 Achievement Notice, see section 147.*
		(b) Treat the reference in sub-Para (1) to the purpose of administration as a reference to Objective 2.
		(c) Before making proposals under sub-Para (1) in the case of bank administration following transfer to a [resolution company], the bank administrator must consult the Bank of England about the chances of a payment to the residual bank from a scheme established by resolution fund order under section 49(3).
		(d) Treat the reference in sub-Para (2)(b) to the Objective mentioned in Para 3(1)(a) or (b) as a reference to Objective 2(a).
		(e) Ignore sub-Para(3)(b).
		[(ea) Ignore the amendment made by paragraph 10(2) of Schedule 9 to the 2015 Act.]
		(f) Treat references in sub-Para (5) to the company's entering administration as references to satisfaction of the condition in Para (a) above.
Paras 50–58	Creditors' meeting	[(za) Ignore the repeal of Paras 50 and 58 by paragraph 10(3) and (22) of Schedule 9 to the 2015 Act.
		(zb) Ignore the amendments of Paras 51 to 57 made by paragraph 10(4) to (21) of Schedule 9 to the 2015 Act.]
		(a) Treat references in Para 51(2) to the company's entering administration as references to the giving of an Objective 1 Achievement Notice.
		(b) The bank administrator may comply with a request under Para 56(1)(a) only if satisfied that it will not prejudice pursuit of Objective 1 in section 137.
		(c) A creditors' meeting may not establish a creditors' committee in reliance on Para 57 until the Bank of England has given an Objective 1 Achievement Notice.

TABLE 1: APPLIED PROVISIONS: INSOLVENCY ACT 1986, SCHEDULE B1

Provision of Sch B1	*Subject*	*Modification or comment*
		(d) Until that time the Bank of England shall have the functions of the creditors' committee.
Para 59	General powers	A bank administrator may not rely on Para 59 (or subsection (1) above) for the purpose of recovering property transferred by property transfer instrument.
Para 60 and Schedule 1	General powers	(a) The exercise of powers under Schedule 1 is subject to section 137(2).
		(b) In the case of bank administration following transfer to a [resolution company], until the Bank of England has given an Objective 1 Achievement Notice powers under the following paragraphs of Schedule 1 may be exercised only with the Bank of England's consent: 2, 3, 11, 14, 15, 16, 17, 18 and 21.
Para 61	Directors	
Para 62	Power to call meetings of creditors	[Ignore the amendment made by paragraph 10(23) of Schedule 9 to the 2015 Act.]
Para 63	Application to court for directions	(a) Before the Bank of England has given an Objective 1 Achievement Notice, the bank administrator may apply for directions if unsure whether a proposed action would prejudice the pursuit of Objective 1; and before making an application in reliance on this paragraph the bank administrator must give notice to the Bank of England, which shall be entitled to participate in the proceedings.
		(b) In making directions the court must have regard to the Objectives in section 137.
Para 64	Management powers.	
Para 65	Distribution to creditors	(a) In the case of bank administration following transfer to a [resolution company], until the Bank of England has given an Objective 1 Achievement Notice a bank administrator may make a distribution only with the Bank of England's consent. [(b) Where paragraph (a) applies, ignore sub-para (3).]
Para 66	Payments	
Para 67	Taking custody of property	
Para 68	Management	Before the approval of proposals under Para 53 a bank administrator shall manage the bank's affairs, business and property in accordance with principles agreed between the bank administrator and the Bank of England.
Para 69	Agency	
Para 70	Floating charges	The bank administrator may take action only if satisfied that it will not prejudice pursuit of Objective 1 in section 137.
Para 71	Fixed charges	The court may make an order only if satisfied that it will not prejudice pursuit of Objective 1 in section 137.

TABLE 1: APPLIED PROVISIONS: INSOLVENCY ACT 1986, SCHEDULE B1		
Provision of Sch B1	*Subject*	*Modification or comment*
Para 72	Hire-purchase property	In the case of administration following transfer to a [resolution company], until the Bank of England has given an Objective 1 Achievement Notice an application may be made only with the Bank of England's consent.
Para 73	Protection for secured and preferential creditors	(a) Treat a reference to proposals as including a reference to the principles specified in the modification of Para 68 set out above.
		(b) Para 73(1)(a) does not apply until the Bank of England has given an Objective 1 Achievement Notice.
Para 74	Challenge to administrator's conduct	[(za) Ignore the amendment made by paragraph 10(24) of Schedule 9 to the 2015 Act.]
		(a) The Bank of England may make an application to the court, on any grounds, including grounds of insufficient pursuit of Objective 1 in section 137 (in addition to applications that may anyway be made under Para 74).
		(b) Until the Bank of England has given an Objective 1 Achievement Notice, an order may be made on the application of a creditor only if the court is satisfied that it would not prejudice pursuit of Objective 1 in section 137.
Para 75	Misfeasance	In addition to applications that may anyway be made under Para 75, an application may be made by the bank administrator or the Bank of England.
[Para 79	Termination: successful rescue	(a) Ignore sub-para (2).
		(b) *See section 153.*]
Para 84	Termination: no more assets for distribution	*See section 154.*
Para 85	Discharge of administration order	
Para 86	Notice to Companies Registrar of end of administration	*See section 153.*
Para 87	Resignation	A bank administrator may resign only by notice in writing—
		(a) to the court, copied to the Bank of England, or
		(b) in the case of a bank administrator appointed by the creditors' committee under Para 90, to the creditors' committee.
Para 88	Removal	Until the Bank of England has given an Objective 1 Achievement Notice, an application for an order may be made only with the Bank of England's consent.
Para 89	Disqualification	The notice under sub-Para (2) must be given to the Bank of England.
Paras 90 & 91	Replacement	(a) Until an Objective 1 Notice has been given, the Bank of England, and nobody else, may make an application under Para 91(1).
		(b) After that, either the Bank of England or a creditors' committee may apply.
		(c) Ignore Para 91(1)(b) to (e) and (2).

TABLE 1: APPLIED PROVISIONS: INSOLVENCY ACT 1986, SCHEDULE B1		
Provision of Sch B1	***Subject***	***Modification or comment***
Para 96	Substitution of floating charge-holder	Para 96 applies to a bank administrator, but—
		(a) only after an Objective 1 Achievement Notice has been given, and
		(b) ignoring references to priority of charges.
Para 98	Discharge	[Ignore the amendments made by paragraph 10(36) to (38) of Schedule 9 to the 2015 Act.] Discharge takes effect—
		(a) where the person ceases to be bank administrator before an Objective 1 Achievement Notice has been given, at a time determined by the Bank of England, and
		(b) otherwise, at a time determined by resolution of the creditors' committee (for which purpose ignore sub-Para (3)).
Para 99	Vacation of office: charges and liabilities	In the application of sub-Para (3), payments may be made only—
		(a) in accordance with directions of the Bank of England, and
		(b) if the Bank is satisfied that they will not prejudice Objective 1 in section 137.
Paras 100–103	Joint administrators	Until an Objective 1 Achievement Notice has been given, an application under Para 103 may be made only by the Bank of England.
Para 104	Validity	
Para 106 (and section 430 and Schedule 10)	Fines	[Ignore the amendments made by paragraph 11 of Schedule 9 to the 2015 Act.]
Paras 107–109	Extension of time limits	(a) Until an Objective 1 Achievement Notice has been given, an application under Para 107 may be made only with the Bank of England's consent.
		(b) In considering an application under Para 107 the court must have regard to Objective 1 in section 137.
		[(ba) Ignore the amendments of Para 108 made by paragraph 10(39) to (43) of Schedule 9 to the 2015 Act.]
		(c) In Para 108(1) "consent" means consent of the Bank of England.
Para 110	*Amendment of provisions about time*	*An order under Para 110 may amend a provision of the Schedule as it applies by virtue of this section (whether or not in the same way as it amends the provision as it applies otherwise).*
Para 111	Interpretation	[Ignore the amendment made by paragraph 10(44) of Schedule 9 to the 2015 Act.]
[Paras 112–114	Scotland miscellaneous	

TABLE 1: APPLIED PROVISIONS: INSOLVENCY ACT 1986, SCHEDULE B1

Provision of Sch B1	*Subject*	*Modification or comment*
Para 115	Scotland: floating charges	(a) In Scotland, on the giving by the Bank of England of consent as provided for in Para 65 (as applied by this section), any floating charge granted by the bank attaches to the property which is subject to the charge, unless it has already so attached, but only if the distribution concerned is to be made to creditors of the residual bank who are neither secured creditors nor preferential creditors and otherwise than by virtue of section 176A(2)(a) (as applied by this section).
		(b) Where paragraph (a) applies, ignore sub-paras (1A) and (1B).
Para 116	Scotland: payment to holder of floating charge subject to rights]	

TABLE 2: APPLIED PROVISIONS: OTHER PROVISIONS OF THE INSOLVENCY ACT 1986

Section	*Subject*	*Modification or comment*
Section 135	Provisional appointment	(a) Treat the reference to the presentation of a winding-up petition as a reference to the making of an application for a bank administration order.
		(b) Subsection (2) applies in relation to England and Wales and Scotland (and subsection (3) does not apply).
		(c) Ignore the reference to the official receiver.
		(d) Only a person who is qualified to act as an insolvency practitioner [in relation to the bank] and who consents to act may be appointed.
		(e) The court may only confer on a provisional bank administrator functions in connection with the pursuance of Objective 1; and section 138(2)(a) does not apply before a bank administration order is made.
		(f) A provisional bank administrator may not pursue Objective 2.
		(g) The appointment of a provisional bank administrator lapses on the appointment of a bank administrator.
		(h) Section 172(1), (2) and (5) apply to a provisional bank administrator.
Section 168(4) (and Para 13 of Schedule 4)	Discretion in managing and distributing assets	In the case of bank administration following transfer to a [resolution company], until the Bank of England has given an Objective 1 Achievement Notice distribution may be made only—
		(a) with the Bank of England's consent, or
		(b) out of assets which have been designated as realisable by agreement between the bank administrator and the Bank of England.
[Section 176ZB	Application of proceeds of office-holder claims]	

Part 7B Special Insolvency Regimes

TABLE 2: APPLIED PROVISIONS: OTHER PROVISIONS OF THE INSOLVENCY ACT 1986

Section	*Subject*	*Modification or comment*
Section 176A	Unsecured creditors	In the case of bank administration following transfer to a [resolution company], until the Bank of England has given an Objective 1 Achievement Notice distribution may be made in reliance on s. 176A only—
		(a) with the Bank of England's consent, or
		(b) out of assets which have been designated as realisable by agreement between the bank administrator and the Bank of England.
Section 178	Disclaimer of onerous property	In the case of bank administration following transfer to a [resolution company], until the Bank of England has given an Objective 1 Achievement Notice notice of disclaimer may be given only with the Bank of England's consent.
Section 179	Disclaimer of leaseholds	
Section 180	Land subject to rent-charge	
Section 181	Disclaimer: powers of court	
Section 182	Leaseholds	
Section 188	Publicity	
Section 213	*Fraudulent trading*	
Section 214	*Wrongful trading*	*Ignore subsection (6).*
Section 233	Utilities	
[Section 233A	Further protection of utilities]	
Section 234	Getting in company's property	
Section 235	Co-operation with liquidator	
Section 236	Inquiry into company's dealings	
Section 237	Section 236: enforcement by court	
Section 238	Transactions at undervalue (England and Wales)	
Section 239	Preferences (England and Wales)	
Section 240	Ss. 238 & 239: relevant time	
Section 241	Orders under ss. 238 & 239	(a) In considering making an order in reliance on section 241 the court must have regard to Objective 1 of section 137.
		(b) Ignore subsections (2A)(a) and (3) to (3C).
Section 242	Gratuitous alienations (Scotland)	
Section 243	Unfair preferences (Scotland)	In considering the grant of a decree under subsection (5) the court must have regard to Objective 1 of section 137.
Section 244	Extortionate credit transactions	
Section 245	Avoidance of floating charges	

TABLE 2: APPLIED PROVISIONS: OTHER PROVISIONS OF THE INSOLVENCY ACT 1986		
Section	***Subject***	***Modification or comment***
Section 246	Unenforceability of liens	
[Section 246ZA	Fraudulent trading: administration	
Section 246ZB	Wrongful trading: administration	(a) Treat the reference in subsection (2)(b) to going into insolvent liquidation as a reference to entering bank insolvency under Part 2 of this Act at a time when the bank's assets are insufficient for the payment of its debts and other liabilities and the expenses of the bank insolvency.
		(b) Ignore subsection (6)(b).
Section 246ZC	Proceedings under section 246ZA or 246ZB	
Section 246ZD	Power to assign certain causes of action]	
Sections 386 & 387, and Schedule 6 (and Schedule 4 to the Pension Schemes Act 1993)	Preferential debts	
Section 389	Offence of acting without being qualified	Treat references to acting as an insolvency practitioner as references to acting as a bank administrator.
[Sections 390 to 391T	Authorisation and regulation of insolvency practitioners	(a) In section 390 treat references to acting as an insolvency practitioner as references to acting as a bank administrator.
		(b) Read subsection (2) of that section (as so modified) as if after "authorised" there were inserted "to act as an insolvency practitioner".
		(c) An order under section 391 has effect in relation to any provision applied for the purposes of bank administration.
		(d) In sections 390A, 390B(1) and (3), 391O(1)(b) and 391R(3)(b), in a reference to authorisation or permission to act as an insolvency practitioner in relation to (or only in relation to) companies the reference to companies has effect without the modification in subsection (4)(d) of this section.
		(e) In sections 391Q(2)(b) and 391S(3)(e) the reference to a company has effect without the modification in subsection (4)(d) of this section.]
Sections 423–425	Transactions defrauding creditors	(a) In considering granting leave under section 424(1) the court must have regard to Objective 1 of section 137.
		(b) In considering making an order in reliance on section 425 the court must have regard to Objective 1 of section 137.
Sections 430–432 & Schedule 10	Offences	
Section 433	Statements: admissibility	For section 433(1)(a) and (b) substitute a reference to a statement prepared for the purposes of a provision of this Part.

NOTES

Sub-s (7): inserted by the Small Business, Enterprise and Employment Act 2015 (Consequential Amendments, Savings and Transitional Provisions) Regulations 2018, SI 2018/208, reg 5(1), (4).

The tables following sub-s (7) have been amended as follows:

Note: the tables above are reproduced as they appear in the original Queen's printer's copy. Ie, certain entries appear in italics in the original version of this Act (except entries relating to ss 213 and 214 which are italicised due to their repeal (as noted below)).

The words "resolution company" in square brackets in each place that they occur in Tables 1 and 2 were substituted by the Bank Recovery and Resolution Order 2016, SI 2016/1239, arts 2, 26(1), (8).

Table 1:

In the entry relating to para 49, para (ea) was inserted by SI 2018/208, reg 5(1), (5)(a).

In the entry relating to paras 50–58, paras (za) and (zb) were inserted by SI 2018/208, reg 5(1), (5)(b).

The words in square brackets in the entries relating to paras 62, 98, 106 and 111 were inserted by SI 2018/208, reg 5(1), (5)(c), (e), (f), (h).

Words in square brackets in the entry relating to para 65 substituted, and entries relating to paras 112–116 substituted, by the Deregulation Act 2015, the Small Business, Enterprise and Employment Act 2015 and the Insolvency (Amendment) Act (Northern Ireland) 2016 (Consequential Amendments and Transitional Provisions) Regulations 2017, SI 2017/400, reg 5(1), (9).

In the entry relating to para 74, para (za) was inserted by SI 2018/208, reg 5(1), (5)(d).

Entry relating to para 79 substituted (for the original entry relating to para 80) by the Financial Services Act 2010, s 21(1), (6).

In the entry relating to paras 107–109, para (ba) was inserted by SI 2018/208, reg 5(1), (5)(g).

Table 2:

Words in square brackets in para (d) of the entry relating to s 135 inserted, and entries relating to ss 176ZB and ss 246ZA–246ZD inserted, by SI 2017/400, reg 5(1), (10)(a), (b), (d).

Entries relating to ss 213 and 214 repealed by SI 2017/400, reg 5(1), (10)(c), subject to transitional provisions as follows: Regulation 15 of the 2017 Regulations provides (note that the "commencement date" is 7 April 2017)—

"(1) Sections 246ZA to 246ZC (administration: penalisation of directors etc) do not apply in relation to—

(a) any relevant proceedings commenced before the commencement date; or

(b) the administration of a building society under Part 2 of the 1986 Act (as applied by section 90A of the Building Societies Act 1986) commenced before the commencement date.

(2) Regulation 5(10)(c) (the omission of the entries for section 213 and 214 of the 1986 Act in Table 2 in section 145 of the 2009 Act) does not apply in relation to any relevant proceedings commenced before the commencement date.

(3) "Relevant proceedings" means—

(a) bank administration under Part 3 of the 2009 Act; or

(b) building society special administration under Part 3 of the 2009 Act (as applied by section 90C of the Building Societies Act 1986).".

Entries relating to s 390–391T substituted (for the original entries relating to ss 390 and 391 by SI 2017/400, reg 5(1), (10)(e), subject to transitional provisions as noted to s 103 at **[7.40]**.

146–167 *(Ss 146–157, 159, 163, 164, 165(1), 166, 167 outside the scope of this work; for s 158 see* **[7.472]***; s 160 amends the Insolvency Act 1986, ss 411, 413 at* **[1.522]**, **[1.524]***; s 161 amends s 414 of the 1986 Act at* **[1.525]***; s 162 amends s 433 of the 1986 Act at* **[1.550]**, *s 165(2) amends s 426 of the 1986 Act at* **[1.540]**.)

[7.75]

168 Consequential provision

(1) The Treasury may by order make provision in consequence of this Part.

(2) An order may, in particular, amend or modify the effect of an enactment (including a fiscal enactment) passed before the commencement of this Part.

(3) An order—

(a) shall be made by statutory instrument, and

(b) may not be made unless a draft has been laid before and approved by resolution of each House of Parliament.

NOTES

Orders: the Banking Act 2009 (Parts 2 and 3 Consequential Amendments) Order 2009, SI 2009/317.

169–227 *((Pts 4–6) outside the scope of this work.)*

PART 7
MISCELLANEOUS

228–231 (*Outside the scope of this work.*)

Investment banks

[7.76]

232 Definition

(1) In this group of sections "investment bank" means an institution which satisfies the following conditions.

(2) Condition 1 is that the institution has permission under [Part 4A] of the Financial Services and Markets Act 2000 to carry on the regulated activity of—

(a) safeguarding and administering investments,

(b) dealing in investments as principal, or

(c) dealing in investments as agent.

(3) Condition 2 is that the institution holds client assets.

(4) In this group of sections "client assets" means assets which an institution has undertaken to hold for a client (whether or not on trust and whether or not the undertaking has been complied with).

(5) Condition 3 is that the institution is incorporated in, or formed under the law of any part of, the United Kingdom.

[(5A) In subsection (4), "assets"—

(a) includes money, but

(b) does not include anything which an institution holds for the purposes of carrying on an insurance mediation activity unless—

(i) the activity arises in the course of carrying on an investment activity, or

(ii) the institution has elected, in relation to the thing, to comply with rules that would apply in relation to it if the activity were not an insurance mediation activity.

(5B) In this section—

"rules" means general rules (within the meaning of the Financial Services and Markets Act 2000) made by virtue of [section 137B(1)] of that Act;

"insurance mediation activity" has the meaning given by paragraph 2(5) of Schedule 6 to that Act (read as mentioned in paragraph 2(6) of that Schedule); and

"investment activity" means—

(a) anything that falls within the definition of "investment services and activities" in section 417(1) of that Act; or

(b) anything that is "designated investment business" within the meaning of the [Financial Conduct Authority Handbook or the Prudential Regulation Authority Handbook].]

(6) The Treasury may by order—

(a) provide that a specified class of institution, which has a permission under Part 4 of the Financial Services and Markets Act 2000 to carry on a regulated activity, is to be treated as an investment bank for the purpose of this group of sections;

(b) provide that a specified class of institution is not to be treated as an investment bank for the purpose of this group of sections;

(c) provide that assets of a specified kind, or held in specified circumstances, are to be or not to be treated as client assets for the purpose of this group of sections;

(d) amend a provision of this section in consequence of provision under paragraph (a), (b) or (c).

[(7) The Treasury may by order amend the definition of "investment activity" in subsection (5B), including by defining that term by reference to rules or guidance made by the PRA or the FCA under the Financial Services and Markets Act 2000.]

NOTES

Sub-s (2): words in square brackets substituted by the Financial Services Act 2012, s 106, Sch 17, Pt 4, paras 52, 55(1), (2).

Sub-s (5A): inserted, together with sub-s (5B), by the Investment Bank (Amendment of Definition) Order 2011, SI 2011/239, art 3.

Sub-s (5B): inserted, together with sub-s (5A), by SI 2011/239, art 3; in definition "rules" words in square brackets substituted by the Financial Services Act 2012, s 106, Sch 17, Pt 4, paras 52, 55(1), (3); in definition "investment activity" words in square brackets substituted by the Financial Services Act 2012 (Consequential Amendments) Order 2013, SI 2013/636, art 2, Schedule, para 10.

Sub-s (7): added by the Financial Services Act 2012, s 106, Sch 17, Pt 4, paras 52, 55(1), (4).

Orders: the Investment Bank (Amendment of Definition) Order 2011, SI 2011/239 at **[7.1659]**.

[7.77]

233 Insolvency regulations

(1) The Treasury may by regulations ("investment bank insolvency regulations")—

(a) modify the law of insolvency in its application to investment banks;

(b) establish a new procedure for investment banks where—

(i) they are unable, or are likely to become unable, to pay their debts (within the meaning of section 93(4)), or

(ii) their winding up would be fair (within the meaning of section 93(8)).

(2) Investment bank insolvency regulations may, in particular—

(a) apply or replicate (with or without modifications) or make provision similar to provision made by or under the Insolvency Act 1986 or Part 2 or 3 of this Act;

(b) establish a new procedure either (i) to operate for investment banks in place of liquidation or administration (under the Insolvency Act 1986), or (ii) to operate alongside liquidation or administration in respect of a particular part of the business or affairs of investment banks.

(3) In making investment bank insolvency regulations the Treasury shall have regard to the desirability of—

(a) identifying, protecting, and facilitating the return of, client assets,

(b) protecting creditors' rights,

(c) ensuring certainty for investment banks, creditors, clients, liquidators and administrators,

(d) minimising the disruption of business and markets, and

(e) maximising the efficiency and effectiveness of the financial services industry in the United Kingdom.

(4) A reference to returning client assets includes a reference to—

(a) transferring assets to another institution, and

(b) returning or transferring assets equivalent to those which an institution undertook to hold for clients.

NOTES

Regulations: the Investment Bank Special Administration Regulations 2011, SI 2011/245 at **[7.1661]**.

[7.78]

234 Regulations: details

(1) Investment bank insolvency regulations may provide for a procedure to be instituted—

(a) by a court, or

(b) by the action of one or more specified classes of person.

(2) Investment bank insolvency regulations may—

(a) confer functions on persons appointed in accordance with the regulations (which may, in particular, (i) be similar to the functions of a liquidator or administrator under the Insolvency Act 1986, or (ii) involve acting as a trustee of client assets), and

(b) specify objectives to be pursued by a person appointed in accordance with the regulations.

(3) Investment bank insolvency regulations may make the application of a provision depend—

(a) on whether an investment bank is, or is likely to become, unable to pay its debts,

(b) on whether the winding up of an investment bank would be fair, or

(c) partly on those and partly on other considerations.

(4) Investment bank insolvency regulations may make provision about the relationship between a procedure established by the regulations and—

(a) liquidation or administration under the Insolvency Act 1986,

(b) bank insolvency or bank administration under Part 2 or 3 of this Act, and

(c) provision made by or under any other enactment in connection with insolvency.

(5) Regulations by virtue of subsection (4) may, in particular—

(a) include provision for temporary or permanent moratoria;

(b) amend an enactment.

(6) Investment bank insolvency regulations may include provision—

(a) establishing a mechanism for determining which assets are client assets (subject to section 232);

(b) establishing a mechanism for determining that assets are to be, or not to be, treated as client assets (subject to section 232);

(c) about the treatment of client assets;

(d) about the treatment of unsettled transactions (and related collateral);

(e) for the transfer to another financial institution of assets or transactions;

(f) for the creation or enforcement of rights (including rights that take preference over creditors' rights) in respect of client assets or other assets;

(g) indemnifying a person who is exercising or purporting to exercise functions under or by virtue of the regulations;

(h) for recovery of assets transferred in error.

(7) Provision may be included under subsection (6)(f) only to the extent that the Treasury think it necessary having regard to the desirability of protecting both—

(a) client assets, and

(b) creditors' rights.

(8) Investment bank insolvency regulations may confer functions on—

(a) a court or tribunal,

[(b) the Prudential Regulation Authority,

(ba) the Financial Conduct Authority,]

(c) the Financial Services Compensation Scheme (established under Part 15 of the Financial Services and Markets Act 2000),

(d) the scheme manager of that Scheme, and

(e) any other specified person.

(9) Investment bank insolvency regulations may include provision about institutions that are or were group undertakings (within the meaning of section 1161(5) of the Companies Act 2006) of an investment bank.

(10) Investment bank insolvency regulations may replicate or apply, with or without modifications, a power to make procedural rules.

(11) Investment bank insolvency regulations may include provision for assigning or apportioning responsibility for the cost of the application of a procedure established or modified by the regulations.

NOTES

Sub-s (8): paras (b), (ba) substituted, for original para (b), by the Financial Services Act 2012, s 106, Sch 17, Pt 4, paras 52, 56.

[7.79]

235 Regulations: procedure

(1) Investment bank insolvency regulations shall be made by statutory instrument.

(2) Investment bank insolvency regulations may not be made unless a draft has been laid before and approved by resolution of each House of Parliament.

(3) The Treasury must consult before laying draft investment bank insolvency regulations before Parliament.

(4) If the power to make investment bank insolvency regulations has not been exercised before the end of the period of 2 years beginning with the date on which this Act is passed, it lapses.

(5) An order under section 232(6)—

(a) shall be made by statutory instrument, and

(b) may not be made unless a draft has been laid before and approved by resolution of each House of Parliament.

[(6) An order under section 232(7)—

(a) is to be made by statutory instrument, and

(b) is subject to annulment in pursuance of a resolution of either House of Parliament.]

NOTES

Sub-s (6): added by the Financial Services Act 2012, s 106, Sch 17, Pt 4, paras 52, 57.

[7.80]

236 Review

(1) The Treasury shall arrange for a review of the effect of any investment bank insolvency regulations.
(2) The review must be completed during the period of 2 years beginning with the date on which the regulations come into force.
(3) The Treasury shall appoint one or more persons to conduct the review; and a person appointed must have expertise in connection with the law of insolvency or financial services.
(4) The review must consider, in particular—
(a) how far the regulations are achieving the objectives specified in section 233(3), and
(b) whether the regulations should continue to have effect.
(5) The review must result in a report to the Treasury.
(6) The Treasury shall lay a copy of the report before Parliament.
(7) If a review recommends further reviews—
(a) the Treasury may arrange for the further reviews, and
(b) subsections (3) to (6) (and this subsection) shall apply to them.

237–256 (*Outside the scope of this work.*)

PART 8
GENERAL

257–262 (*Ss 257, 258, 260–262 outside the scope of this work; for s 259 see* **[7.473]**.)

[7.81]

263 Commencement

(1) The preceding provisions of this Act shall come into force in accordance with provision made by the Treasury by order.
(2) Subsection (1) does not apply to section 254, which comes into force at the end of the period of 2 months beginning with the date of Royal Assent.
(3) An order under subsection (1)—
(a) may make provision generally or only in relation to specific provisions or purposes,
(b) may make different provision for different provisions or purposes,
(c) may include incidental or transitional provision (including savings), and
(d) shall be made by statutory instrument.
(4) Where the Treasury or another authority are required to consult or take other action before exercising a power or fulfilling a duty to make legislation or to do any other thing under, by virtue of or in connection with this Act, the Treasury or other authority may rely on consultation or other action carried out before the commencement of the relevant provision of this Act.

NOTES

Orders: the Banking Act 2009 (Commencement No 1) Order 2009, SI 2009/296; the Banking Act 2009 (Commencement No 2) Order 2009, SI 2009/1296; the Banking Act 2009 (Commencement No 3) Order 2009, SI 2009/2038; the Banking Act 2009 (Commencement No 4) Order 2009, SI 2009/3000; the Banking Act 2009 (Commencement No 5) Order 2016, SI 2016/598.

[7.82]

264 Extent

(1) This Act extends to—
(a) England and Wales,
(b) Scotland, and
(c) Northern Ireland.
(2) But—
(a) sections 253 and 254 extend to Scotland only, and
(b) an amendment of an enactment has the same extent as the enactment (or the relevant part).

[7.83]

265 Short title

This Act may be cited as the Banking Act 2009.

BANKING ACT 2009 (PARTS 2 AND 3 CONSEQUENTIAL AMENDMENTS) ORDER 2009

(SI 2009/317)

NOTES

Made: 19 February 2009.
Authority: Banking Act 2009, ss 135, 168.
Commencement: 21 February 2009.

Modification: this Order is applied, with modifications in respect of building societies, by the Building Societies (Insolvency and Special Administration) Order 2009, SI 2009/805, art 18, Sch 2, paras 1(a), 2, 3 at **[7.478]**, **[7.482]**.

ARRANGEMENT OF ARTICLES

PART 1
INTRODUCTION

1 Citation and commencement . . . . . [7.84]
2 Interpretation . . . . . [7.85]

PART 2
GENERAL MODIFICATIONS TO LEGISLATION

3 . . . . . [7.86]

PART 3
SPECIFIC MODIFICATIONS AND AMENDMENTS TO LEGISLATION

4 Finance (No 2) Act 1992 . . . . . [7.87]
5 Financial Services and Markets Act 2000 . . . . . [7.88]
6 Companies Act 2006 . . . . . [7.89]
7 Dormant Bank and Building Society Accounts Act 2008 . . . . . [7.90]
8 Pension Protection Fund (Entry Rules) Regulations 2005 . . . . . [7.91]

SCHEDULES

Schedule—Legislation Subject to the General Modifications in Part 2 . . . . . [7.92]

PART 1
INTRODUCTION

[7.84]
1 Citation and commencement

This Order may be cited as the Banking Act 2009 (Parts 2 and 3 Consequential Amendments) Order 2009 and comes into force on 21st February 2009.

[7.85]
2 Interpretation

In this Order—

"the 2009 Act" means the Banking Act 2009.

PART 2
GENERAL MODIFICATIONS TO LEGISLATION

[7.86]
3

(1) So far as the enactments set out in the Schedule ("the listed enactments") apply in relation to liquidation and administration, they apply with the modifications set out in paragraphs (2) to (4).

(2) The modifications relating to bank insolvency under Part 2 of the 2009 Act are that references to—
- (a) "liquidator" include a reference to a bank liquidator under Part 2 of the 2009 Act;
- (b) "provisional liquidator" include a reference to a provisional bank liquidator under Part 2 of the 2009 Act;
- (c) "liquidation" or "insolvent liquidation" include a reference to bank insolvency under Part 2 of the 2009 Act;
- (d) "winding up" or "winding up by the court" include a reference to bank insolvency under Part 2 of the 2009 Act (and a reference to the "commencement of winding up" in this context is to the commencement of bank insolvency);
- (e) "winding up order" include a reference to a bank insolvency order under Part 2 of the 2009 Act;
- (f) "wound up" include a reference to a bank having been put into bank insolvency under Part 2 of the 2009 Act; and
- (g) "winding up petition" or "petition to wind up" include an application for bank insolvency under Part 2 of the 2009 Act.

(3) The modifications relating to bank administration under Part 3 of the 2009 Act are that references to—
- (a) "administrator" include a reference to a bank administrator under Part 3 of the 2009 Act;
- (b) "administration" or "insolvent administration" include a reference to a bank administration under Part 3 of the 2009 Act;
- (c) "administration order" include a reference to a bank administration order under Part 3 of the 2009 Act; and
- (d) "provisional liquidator" include a reference to a provisional bank administrator under Part 3 of the 2009 Act.

(4) The modifications relating to bank insolvency or bank administration under Parts 2 and 3 of the 2009 Act are that references to—

(a) "insolvency legislation" or "the law of insolvency" include Parts 2 and 3 of the 2009 Act and the provisions of the Insolvency Act 1986 and the Insolvency (Northern Ireland) Order 1989 as applied by those Parts;

(b) a person acting as an "insolvency practitioner" (as defined in section 388 of the Insolvency Act 1986) include a person acting as a bank liquidator or bank administrator under Parts 2 and 3 of the 2009 Act;

(c) the provisions of the Insolvency Act 1986 and the Insolvency (Northern Ireland) Order 1989, in the context of bank insolvency or bank administration, shall be read to include those provisions as applied and modified by sections 103 and 145 of the 2009 Act; and

(d) the provisions of the Insolvency Rules 1986, the Insolvency Rules (Northern Ireland) 1991 and the Insolvency (Scotland) Rules 1986, in the context of bank insolvency or bank administration, shall be read to include those provisions as applied and modified by rules made under section 411(1A) of the Insolvency Act 1986 in relation to bank insolvency, and under section 411(1B) of the Insolvency Act 1986 in relation to bank administration.

NOTES

Note that the Insolvency Rules 1986, SI 1986/1925 are revoked and replaced (as from 6 April 2017 and subject to transitional provisions) by the Insolvency (England and Wales) Rules 2016, SI 2016/1024 at **[6.2]**.

PART 3
SPECIFIC MODIFICATIONS AND AMENDMENTS TO LEGISLATION

[7.87]

4 Finance (No 2) Act 1992

(1) The following provision of the Finance (No 2) Act 1992 applies with the modification set out in this article.

(2) Paragraph 2 of Schedule 12 (Banks etc in Compulsory Liquidation) is to be read as if it included the following—

> "(3A) Where the company is a bank (as defined in section 91 of the Banking Act 2009), bank insolvency proceedings shall be taken to have commenced against the bank when the application for a bank insolvency order is made to the court under section 95 of the Banking Act 2009.".

[7.88]

5 Financial Services and Markets Act 2000

(1) The following provisions of the Financial Services and Markets Act 2000 apply with the modifications set out in this article.

(2) In section 215 (Rights of the scheme in relevant person's insolvency)—

(a) in subsection (3), the reference to making an administration application is to be read as including making an application for a bank administration order under section 142 of the 2009 Act, and

(b) subsection (4) is to be read as if it read the following—

> "(4) In the case of a bank insolvency (as defined in Part 2 of the Banking Act 2009), if the scheme manager decides, pursuant to section 100(6)(d) of that Act, not to remain on the liquidation committee, the scheme manager shall retain the rights it usually enjoys in respect of the winding up of a relevant person under section 371(3) and (4).".

(3) In section 355 (Interpretation of Part 24), the definition of "court" is to be read as if ", unless otherwise provided," were inserted after the word "means".

(4) In section 361 (Administrator's duty to report to Authority), references to—

(a) "administration" are to be read as including a reference to bank administration under Part 3 of the 2009 Act; and

(b) "the administrator" are to be read as including the bank administrator under Part 3 of the 2009 Act.

(5) In section 362 (Authority's powers to participate in proceedings)—

(a) references to "court"—

(i) in the context of a bank administration under Part 3 of the 2009 Act in England, Wales or Northern Ireland, are to be read as meaning the High Court, and

(ii) in the context of a bank administration under Part 3 of the 2009 Act in Scotland, are to be read as meaning the Court of Session,

(b) in subsection (1), the reference to making an administration application is to be read as including making an application for a bank administration order under section 142 of the 2009 Act, and

(c) in subsections (4) and (4A), references to paragraph 74 of Schedule B1 to the Insolvency Act 1986 and paragraph 75 of Schedule B1 to the Insolvency (Northern Ireland) Order 1989 are to be read as including references to those provisions as applied and modified by section 145 of the 2009 Act.

(6) In section 370 (Liquidator's duty to report to Authority), references to "liquidator" are to be read as including a reference to a bank liquidator under Part 2 of the 2009 Act.

(7) In section 375 (Authority's right to apply for an order), references to the provisions of the Insolvency Act 1986 and the Insolvency (Northern Ireland) Order 1989 are to be read as including references to those provisions as applied and modified by section 103 and section 134 of the 2009 Act.

[7.89]

6 Companies Act 2006

(1) The following provisions of the Companies Act 2006 apply with the modifications set out in this article.

(2) In section 461 (permitted disclosure of information obtained under compulsory powers)—

(a) subsection (4)(c) is to be read so as to include the 2009 Act in the list of enactments in that subsection;

(b) in subsection (4)(g) is to be read so as to include the 2009 Act in the list of enactments in that subsection.

(3) Any references in Part 35 (the registrar of companies) to the Insolvency Act 1986 and the Insolvency (Northern Ireland) Order 1989 are to be read as including a reference to Parts 2 and 3 of the 2009 Act.

(4) Where an application is made to the court for—

(a) a bank insolvency order under Part 2 of the 2009 Act,

(b) the appointment of a provisional bank liquidator under section 135 of the Insolvency Act 1986 or article 115 of the Insolvency (Northern Ireland) Order 1989, as applied by section 103 of the 2009 Act,

(c) a bank administration order under Part 3 of the 2009 Act, or

(d) the appointment of a provisional bank administrator under section 135 of the Insolvency Act 1986 or article 115 of the Insolvency (Northern Ireland) Order 1989, as applied by section 145 of the 2009 Act,

sections 1139 and 1140 (service of documents on company, directors, secretaries and others) have effect subject to the provisions for service set out in Parts 2 or 3 of the 2009 Act and in rules made under section 411 of the Insolvency Act 1986 in respect of those Parts.

(5) In Part 2 of Schedule 2 (Specified Descriptions of Disclosures)—

(a) paragraph 25 is to be read so as to include the 2009 Act in the list of enactments in that paragraph, and

(b) paragraph 46 is to be read so as to include the 2009 Act in the list of enactments in that paragraph.

(6) In Part 2 of Schedule 11A (Specified Descriptions of Disclosures)—

(a) paragraph 30 is to be read so as to include the 2009 Act in the list of enactments in that paragraph, and

(b) paragraph 52 is to be read so as to include the 2009 Act in the list of enactments in that paragraph.

[7.90]

7 Dormant Bank and Building Society Accounts Act 2008

(1) This article applies to a reclaim fund established under the Dormant Bank and Building Society Accounts Act 2008 if, under sections 1 or 2 of that Act, the balance of a customer's dormant account is transferred into that reclaim fund from a bank which is a bank within the meaning of section 91 of the 2009 Act.

(2) Where that reclaim fund is unable, or likely to be unable, to satisfy a claim against it, the fact that it ceases to be authorised does not prevent the operation of the Financial Services Compensation Scheme under section 213 of the Financial Services and Markets Act 2000 in respect of it; and for that purpose, the reclaim fund is a relevant person within the meaning of section 213(9), despite the lapse of authorisation.

[7.91]

8 Pension Protection Fund (Entry Rules) Regulations 2005

(1) The Pension Protection Fund (Entry Rules) Regulations 2005 are amended as follows.

(2) In regulation 6 (Circumstances in which insolvency proceedings in relation to the employer are stayed or come to an end), after paragraph (1)(a)(v) insert—

"(vi) where the company is a bank (as defined in section 91 of the Banking Act 2009), the bank insolvency procedure is stayed under section 130 of the Insolvency Act 1986 (as applied by section 103 of the Banking Act 2009), or the bank insolvency order is rescinded or discharged, except in circumstances where the court has made an administration order in accordance with section 114 of the Banking Act 2009.".

9 (*Amends the Pension Protection Fund (Entry Rules) Regulations (Northern Ireland) 2005 (outside the scope of this work).*)

SCHEDULE
LEGISLATION SUBJECT TO THE GENERAL MODIFICATIONS IN PART 2

Article 3(1)

Primary Legislation

[7.92]
Taxes Management Act 1970

Prescription and Limitation (Scotland) Act 1973

Companies Act 1985

Companies (Northern Ireland) Order 1986

Debtors (Scotland) Act 1987

Income and Corporation Taxes Act 1988

Companies Act 1989

Companies (No 2) (Northern Ireland) Order 1990

Taxation of Chargeable Gains Act 1992

Finance (No 2) Act 1992

Pension Schemes Act 1993

Pension Schemes (Northern Ireland) Act 1993

Pensions Act 1995

Pensions (Northern Ireland) Order 1995

Proceeds of Crime (Scotland) Act 1995

Finance Act 1996

Employment Rights Act 1996

Employment Rights (Northern Ireland) Order 1996

Terrorism Act 2000

Finance Act 2000

International Criminal Court Act 2001

International Criminal Court (Scotland) Act 2001

Finance Act 2002

Proceeds of Crime Act 2002

Debt Arrangement and Attachment (Scotland) Act 2002

Finance Act 2003

Pensions Act 2004

Pensions (Northern Ireland) Order 2005

Companies Act 2006

Bankruptcy and Diligence (Scotland) Act 2007

Finance Act 2008

Dormant Bank and Building Society Accounts Act 2008

Secondary Legislation

Insolvent Companies (Disqualification of Unfit Directors) Proceedings Rules 1987

Financial Markets and Insolvency Regulations 1991

Financial Markets and Insolvency Regulations (Northern Ireland) 1991

Insolvency Regulations 1994

Non-Domestic Rating (Unoccupied Property) (Scotland) Regulations 1994

Insolvent Companies (Reports on Conduct of Directors) Rules 1996

Financial Markets and Insolvency Regulations 1996

Financial Markets and Insolvency Regulations (Northern Ireland) 1996

Individual Savings Account Regulations 1998

Corporation Tax (Simplified Arrangements for Group Relief) Regulations 1999

Financial Markets and Insolvency (Settlement Finality) Regulations 1999

Financial Collateral Arrangements (No 2) Regulations 2003

Insolvency Practitioners and Insolvency Services Account (Fees) Order 2003

Insolvent Companies (Reports on Conduct of Directors) Rules (Northern Ireland) 2003

Insolvent Companies (Disqualification of Unfit Directors) Proceedings Rules (Northern Ireland) 2003

Land Registration Rules 2003

Credit Institutions (Reorganisation and Winding Up) Regulations 2004

Insolvency Practitioners Regulations 2005

Pension Protection Fund (Entry Rules) Regulations 2005

Pension Protection Fund (Entry Rules) Regulations (Northern Ireland) 2005

Gender Recognition (Disclosure of Information) (England, Wales and Northern Ireland) Order 2005

Gender Recognition (Disclosure of Information) (Scotland) Order 2005

Financial Assistance Scheme Regulations 2005

Insolvency Practitioners Regulations (Northern Ireland) 2006

Insolvency Practitioners and Insolvency Account (Fees) Order (Northern Ireland) 2006

Land Registration (Scotland) Rules 2006

Companies (Cross-Border Mergers) Regulations 2007

Regulated Covered Bonds Regulations 2008

BANK INSOLVENCY (ENGLAND AND WALES) RULES 2009

(SI 2009/356)

NOTES

Made: 23 February 2009.

Authority: Insolvency Act 1986, s 411(1A)(a), (2), (2C), (3).

Commencement: 25 February 2009.

Note: these Rules apply certain provisions of the Insolvency Rules 1986, SI 1986/1925, subject to a number of general and specific modifications. The Insolvency Rules 1986, SI 1986/1925 are revoked and replaced (as from 6 April 2017 and subject to transitional provisions) by the Insolvency (England and Wales) Rules 2016, SI 2016/1024 at **[6.2]**.

ARRANGEMENT OF RULES

PART 1
INTRODUCTORY PROVISIONS

1 Citation and commencement . . . [7.93]
2 Extent . . . [7.94]
3 Application of rules, construction and interpretation . . . [7.95]
4 Overview . . . [7.96]
5 Forms . . . [7.97]
6 Time limits . . . [7.98]

PART 2
APPLICATION FOR ORDER

7 Filing of application . . . [7.99]
8 Service of application . . . [7.100]
9 Proof of service . . . [7.101]
10 Other persons to receive copy of application . . . [7.102]
11 Verification of application . . . [7.103]
12 Persons entitled to copy of application . . . [7.104]
13 Certificate of compliance . . . [7.105]
14 Leave for the applicant to withdraw . . . [7.106]
15 Witness statement in opposition . . . [7.107]

16 Making, transmission and advertisement of order [7.108]
17 Authentication of bank liquidator's appointment [7.109]
18 Initial duties of bank liquidation committee [7.110]
19 Expenses of voluntary arrangement [7.111]

PART 3
PROVISIONAL BANK LIQUIDATOR
20 Appointment of provisional bank liquidator [7.112]
21 Notice of appointment [7.113]
22 Order of appointment [7.114]
23 Security [7.115]
24 Failure to give or keep up security [7.116]
25 Remuneration [7.117]
26 Termination of appointment [7.118]

PART 4
STATEMENT OF AFFAIRS AND OTHER INFORMATION
27 Notice requiring statement of affairs [7.119]
28 Verification and filing [7.120]
29 Limited disclosure [7.121]
30 Release from duty to submit statement of affairs; extension of time [7.122]
31 Expenses of statement of affairs [7.123]
32 Submission of accounts [7.124]
33 Further disclosure [7.125]

PART 5
INFORMATION TO CREDITORS AND CONTRIBUTORIES
34 Report by bank liquidator [7.126]
35 Meaning of "creditors" [7.127]
36 Report where statement of affairs lodged [7.128]
37 Statement of affairs dispensed with [7.129]
38 General rule as to reporting [7.130]
39 Bank insolvency stayed [7.131]

PART 6
MEETINGS OF CREDITORS AND CONTRIBUTORIES
RULES OF GENERAL APPLICATION
40 First meeting [7.132]
41 Business at first meetings of creditors and contributories [7.133]
42 General power to call meetings [7.134]
43 The chair at meetings [7.135]
44 Requisitioned meetings: general [7.136]
45 Requisitioned meetings: reforming the liquidation committee [7.137]
46 Attendance at meetings of bank's personnel [7.138]
47 Notice of meetings by advertisement only [7.139]
48 Venue [7.140]
49 Expenses of summoning meetings [7.141]
50 Resolutions [7.142]
51 Chair of meeting as proxy-holder [7.143]
52 Suspension and adjournment [7.144]
53 Entitlement to vote (creditors) [7.145]
54 Entitlement to vote (contributories) [7.146]
55 Admission and rejection of proof (creditors' meetings) [7.147]
56 Record of proceedings [7.148]

PART 7
PROOF OF DEBTS
57 Meaning of "prove" [7.149]
58 Supply of forms [7.150]
59 Contents of proof [7.151]
60 Claim established by witness statement [7.152]
61 Cost of proving [7.153]
62 Bank liquidator to allow inspection of proofs [7.154]
63 New bank liquidator appointed [7.155]
64 Admission and rejection of proofs for dividend [7.156]
65 Appeal against decision on proof [7.157]
66 Withdrawal or variation of proof [7.158]

67 Expunging of proof by the court ....[7.159]
68 Estimate of quantum ....[7.160]
69 Negotiable instruments, etc ....[7.161]
70 Secured creditors ....[7.162]
71 Discounts ....[7.163]
72 Mutual credits and set-off ....[7.164]
73 Disapplication of set off for eligible depositors ....[7.165]
74 Debt in foreign currency ....[7.166]
75 Payments of a periodical nature ....[7.167]
76 Interest ....[7.168]
77 Debt payable at future time ....[7.169]

PART 8
SECURED CREDITORS

78 Value of security ....[7.170]
79 Surrender for non-disclosure ....[7.171]
80 Redemption by liquidator ....[7.172]
81 Test of security's value ....[7.173]
82 Realisation of security by creditor ....[7.174]

PART 9
THE BANK LIQUIDATOR

CHAPTER 1
GENERAL

83 Remuneration of bank liquidator ....[7.175]
84 Replacement of bank liquidator by creditors ....[7.176]
85 Authentication of bank liquidator's appointment ....[7.177]
86 Appointment to be advertised and registered ....[7.178]

CHAPTER 2
RESIGNATION AND REMOVAL

87 Creditors' meeting to be notified of the bank liquidator's resignation ....[7.179]
88 Action following acceptance of resignation ....[7.180]
89 Advertisement of resignation ....[7.181]
90 Meeting of creditors to remove bank liquidator ....[7.182]
91 Court's power to regulate meetings under rule 90 ....[7.183]
92 Procedure on removal ....[7.184]
93 Advertisement of removal ....[7.185]
94 Removal of bank liquidator by the court ....[7.186]
95 Release of resigning or removed bank liquidator ....[7.187]

CHAPTER 3
RELEASE ON COMPLETION OF WINDING UP

96 Final meeting ....[7.188]
97 Rule as to reporting ....[7.189]

CHAPTER 4
REMUNERATION

98 Fixing of remuneration ....[7.190]
99 Bank liquidator's entitlement to remuneration where it is not fixed under rule 98 ....[7.191]
100 Bank liquidator's remuneration where he realises assets on behalf of chargeholder ....[7.192]
101 Other matters affecting remuneration ....[7.193]
102 Recourse of bank liquidator to meeting of creditors ....[7.194]
103 Recourse to the court ....[7.195]
104 Creditors' claim that remuneration is excessive ....[7.196]
105 Primacy of Objective 1 ....[7.197]

CHAPTER 5
SUPPLEMENTARY PROVISIONS

106 Replacement Bank liquidator ....[7.198]
107 Bank liquidator deceased ....[7.199]
108 Loss of qualification as insolvency practitioner ....[7.200]
109 Resignation of the bank liquidator ....[7.201]
110 Notice to Bank of England of intention to vacate office ....[7.202]

111 Bank liquidator's duties on vacating office .[7.203]
112 Power of court to set aside certain transactions .[7.204]
113 Rule against solicitation .[7.205]

PART 10
THE LIQUIDATION COMMITTEE

114 Application of rules in this Part .[7.206]
115 Membership of committee .[7.207]
116 Formalities of establishment .[7.208]
117 Committee established by contributories .[7.209]
118 Obligations of liquidator to committee .[7.210]
119 Meetings of the committee .[7.211]
120 The chair at meetings .[7.212]
121 Quorum .[7.213]
122 Committee-members' representatives .[7.214]
123 Resignation .[7.215]
124 Termination of membership .[7.216]
125 Removal .[7.217]
126 Vacancy (creditor members) .[7.218]
127 Vacancy (contributory members) .[7.219]
128 Voting rights and resolutions .[7.220]
129 Resolutions by post .[7.221]
130 Liquidator's reports .[7.222]
131 Expenses of members, etc .[7.223]
132 Dealings by committee-members and others .[7.224]
133 Composition of committee when creditors paid in full .[7.225]
134 Committee's functions vested in the Secretary of State .[7.226]
135 Formal defects .[7.227]

PART 11
COLLECTION AND DISTRIBUTION OF BANK'S ASSETS BY BANK LIQUIDATOR

136 General duties of bank liquidator .[7.228]
137 General qualification on powers .[7.229]
138 Manner of distributing assets .[7.230]
139 Debts of insolvent company to rank equally .[7.231]
140 Supplementary provisions as to dividend .[7.232]
141 Division of unsold assets .[7.233]
142 General powers of the liquidator .[7.234]
143 Enforced delivery up of company's property .[7.235]
144 Final distribution .[7.236]

PART 12
DISCLAIMER

145 Liquidator's notice of disclaimer .[7.237]
146 Communication of disclaimer to persons interested .[7.238]
147 Additional notices .[7.239]
148 Duty to keep court informed .[7.240]
149 Application by interested party under s 178(5) .[7.241]
150 Interest in property to be declared on request .[7.242]
151 Disclaimer presumed valid and effective .[7.243]
152 Application for exercise of court's powers under s 181 .[7.244]

PART 13
SETTLEMENT OF LIST OF CONTRIBUTORIES

153 Preliminary .[7.245]
154 Primacy of Objective 1 .[7.246]
155 Duty of liquidator to settle list .[7.247]
156 Form of list .[7.248]
157 Procedure for settling list .[7.249]
158 Application to court for variation of the list .[7.250]
159 Variation of, or addition to, the list .[7.251]
160 Costs not to fall on bank liquidator .[7.252]

PART 14
CALLS

161 Calls by bank liquidator .[7.253]
162 Control by bank liquidation committee .[7.254]

163 Application to court for leave to make a call .....[7.255]
164 Making and enforcement of the call .....[7.256]

PART 15
SPECIAL MANAGER

165 Appointment and remuneration .....[7.257]
166 Security .....[7.258]
167 Failure to give or keep up security .....[7.259]
168 Accounting .....[7.260]
169 Termination of appointment .....[7.261]

PART 16
ORDER OF PAYMENT AS TO COSTS, ETC OUT OF ASSETS

170 General rule as to priority .....[7.262]
171 Litigation expenses and property subject to a floating charge—general application .....[7.263]
172 Litigation expenses and property subject to a floating charge—requirement for approval or authorisation .....[7.264]
173 Litigation expenses and property subject to a floating charge—request for approval or authorisation .....[7.265]
174 Litigation expenses and property subject to a floating charge—grant of approval or authorisation .....[7.266]
175 Litigation expenses and property subject to a floating charge—application to court by the bank liquidator .....[7.267]
176 Saving for powers of the court .....[7.268]

PART 17
MISCELLANEOUS RULES

CHAPTER 1
RETURN OF CAPITAL

177 Application to court for order authorising return of capital .....[7.269]
178 Procedure for return of capital .....[7.270]

CHAPTER 2
CONCLUSION OF BANK INSOLVENCY

179 Secretary of State's directions under section 116 of the 2009 Act .....[7.271]
180 Procedure following appeal under section 116 of the 2009 Act .....[7.272]

CHAPTER 3
LEAVE TO ACT AS DIRECTOR, ETC OF BANK WITH PROHIBITED NAME

181 Preliminary .....[7.273]
182 Application for leave under s 216(3) before passing of full payment resolution .....[7.274]
183 Consideration of application for leave under s 216(3) .....[7.275]
184 First excepted case .....[7.276]
185 Second excepted case .....[7.277]
186 Third excepted case .....[7.278]
187 Further exception .....[7.279]

PART 18
COURT PROCEDURE AND PRACTICE

CHAPTER 1
APPLICATIONS (GENERAL)

188 Preliminary .....[7.280]
189 Interpretation .....[7.281]
190 Form and contents of application .....[7.282]
191 Application under section 176A(5) to disapply section 176A .....[7.283]
192 Filing and service of application .....[7.284]
193 Notice of application under section 176A(5) .....[7.285]
194 Other hearings without notice .....[7.286]
195 Hearing of application .....[7.287]
196 Use of evidence .....[7.288]
197 Filing and service of witness statements .....[7.289]
198 Use of reports .....[7.290]
199 Adjournment of hearings: directions .....[7.291]

CHAPTER 3
SHORTHAND WRITERS

200 Nomination and appointment of shorthand writers .....[7.292]

201 Remuneration . . . . . [7.293]

CHAPTER 4
ENFORCEMENT PROCEDURES

202 Enforcement of court orders . . . . . [7.294]
203 Orders enforcing compliance with the rules . . . . . [7.295]
204 Warrants (general provisions) . . . . . [7.296]
205 Warrants under section 236 . . . . . [7.297]

CHAPTER 5
COURT RECORDS AND RETURNS

206 Title of proceedings . . . . . [7.298]
207 Court records . . . . . [7.299]
208 Inspection of records . . . . . [7.300]
209 File of court proceedings and inspection . . . . . [7.301]

CHAPTER 6
COSTS AND DETAILED ASSESSMENT

211 Application of the CPR . . . . . [7.302]
212 Requirement to assess costs by the detailed procedure . . . . . [7.303]
213 Procedure where detailed assessment required . . . . . [7.304]
214 Costs of officers charged with executions of writs or other process . . . . . [7.305]
215 Costs paid otherwise than out of the insolvent estate . . . . . [7.306]
216 Award of costs against responsible insolvency practitioner . . . . . [7.307]
217 Application for costs . . . . . [7.308]
218 Costs and expenses of witnesses . . . . . [7.309]
219 Final costs certificate . . . . . [7.310]

CHAPTER 7
PERSONS INCAPABLE OF MANAGING THEIR AFFAIRS

220 Introductory . . . . . [7.311]
221 Appointment of another person to act . . . . . [7.312]
222 Witness statement in support of application . . . . . [7.313]
223 Service of notices following appointment . . . . . [7.314]

CHAPTER 8
APPEALS IN BANK INSOLVENCY PROCEEDINGS

224 Appeals and review of court orders . . . . . [7.315]
225 Procedure on appeal . . . . . [7.316]
226 Appeal against a decision of the Secretary of State . . . . . [7.317]

CHAPTER 9
GENERAL

227 Principal court rules and practice to apply . . . . . [7.318]
228 Right of attendance . . . . . [7.319]
229 Restriction on concurrent proceedings and remedies . . . . . [7.320]
230 Security in court . . . . . [7.321]
231 Payment into court . . . . . [7.322]
232 Further information and disclosure . . . . . [7.323]
233 Office copies of documents . . . . . [7.324]

PART 19
PROXIES AND COMPANY REPRESENTATION

234 Definition of "proxy" . . . . . [7.325]
235 Issue and use of forms . . . . . [7.326]
236 Use of proxies at meetings . . . . . [7.327]
237 Retention of proxies . . . . . [7.328]
238 Right of inspection . . . . . [7.329]
239 Proxy-holder with financial interest . . . . . [7.330]
240 Company representation . . . . . [7.331]

PART 20
EXAMINATION OF PERSONS CONCERNED IN BANK INSOLVENCY

241 Preliminary . . . . . [7.332]
242 Form and contents of application . . . . . [7.333]
243 Order for examination, etc . . . . . [7.334]
244 Procedure for examination . . . . . [7.335]
245 Record of examination . . . . . [7.336]
246 Costs of proceedings . . . . . [7.337]

PART 21
DECLARATION AND PAYMENT OF DIVIDEND

247 Preliminary . . . [7.338]
248 Notice of intended dividend . . . [7.339]
249 Final admission/rejection of proofs . . . [7.340]
250 Postponement or cancellation of dividend . . . [7.341]
251 Decision to declare dividend . . . [7.342]
252 Notice of declaration . . . [7.343]
253 Notice of no, or no further, dividend . . . [7.344]
254 Proof altered after payment of dividend . . . [7.345]
255 Secured creditors . . . [7.346]
256 Disqualification from dividend . . . [7.347]
257 Assignment of right to dividend . . . [7.348]
258 Preferential creditors . . . [7.349]
259 Debt payable at future time . . . [7.350]

PART 22
MISCELLANEOUS AND GENERAL

260 Power of Secretary of State or Treasury to regulate certain matters . . . [7.351]
261 Costs, expenses, etc . . . [7.352]
262 Provable debts . . . [7.353]
263 Notices . . . [7.354]
264 Quorum at meeting of creditors or contributories . . . [7.355]
265 Evidence of proceedings at meetings . . . [7.356]
266 Documents issuing from Secretary of State . . . [7.357]
267 Insolvency practitioner's security . . . [7.358]
268 Time limits . . . [7.359]
269 Service by post . . . [7.360]
270 General provisions as to service . . . [7.361]
271 Service outside the jurisdiction . . . [7.362]
272 Confidentiality of documents . . . [7.363]
273 Notices sent simultaneously to the same person . . . [7.364]
274 Right to copy documents . . . [7.365]
275 Charge for copy documents . . . [7.366]
276 Non-receipt of notice of meeting . . . [7.367]
277 Right to have list of creditors . . . [7.368]
278 False claim of status as creditor, etc . . . [7.369]
279 Execution overtaken by judgement debtor's insolvency . . . [7.370]
280 The Gazette . . . [7.371]
281 Punishment of offences . . . [7.372]
282 Notice of order under section 176A(5) . . . [7.373]

PART 23
INTERPRETATION

283 Introductory . . . [7.374]
284 "The court"; "the registrar" . . . [7.375]
285 "Give notice", etc . . . [7.376]
286 Notice, etc to solicitors . . . [7.377]
287 Notice to joint bank liquidators . . . [7.378]
288 "Insolvent estate" . . . [7.379]
289 "Responsible insolvency practitioner", etc . . . [7.380]
290 "The appropriate fee" . . . [7.381]
291 "Debt", "liability" . . . [7.382]
292 Expressions used generally . . . [7.383]
293 The Schedule . . . [7.384]

SCHEDULES

Schedule . . . [7.385]

PART 1
INTRODUCTORY PROVISIONS

[7.93]

1 Citation and commencement

These Rules may be cited as the Bank Insolvency (England and Wales) Rules 2009 and come into force on 25th February 2009.

[7.94]

2 Extent

These Rules extend to England and Wales only.

[7.95]

3 Application of rules, construction and interpretation

(1) These Rules apply in relation to a bank undergoing the procedure in Part 2 of the Banking Act 2009 known as bank insolvency.

(2) In these Rules—

"the 1985 Act" means the Companies Act 1985;

"the 1986 Act" means the Insolvency Act 1986 (and includes those provisions as applied by section 103 of the 2009 Act);

"the 1986 Rules" means the Insolvency Rules 1986 [including all the amendments to them up to and including those made by the Insolvency (Amendment) (No 2) Rules 2009];

"the 2006 Act" means the Companies Act 2006;

"the 2009 Act" means the Banking Act 2009;

["the appropriate regulator" in relation to a bank means—

(a) if the bank is a PRA-authorised person (within the meaning of the Financial Services and Markets Act 2000), the Prudential Regulation Authority and the Financial Conduct Authority;

(b) in any other case, the Financial Conduct Authority;]

"bank" means the bank (as defined by section 91(1) of the 2009 Act) which is or is to be the subject of the bank insolvency order;

"CPR" means the Civil Procedure Rules 1998;

. . .

"the FSCS" means the Financial Services Compensation Scheme (established under Part 15 of the Financial Services and Markets Act 2000) or, where appropriate, the scheme manager of that scheme;

"the insolvent" means the bank that has been put into bank insolvency;

"liquidation committee" means the committee established pursuant to section 100 of the 2009 Act;

"personal service" has the meaning given in Part 6 of the CPR;

"registered address" has the meaning given by section 1140 of the 2006 Act;

"sealed" means sealed with the seal of the court under which the application was made[;] and

"statement of truth" has the meaning set out in Part 22 of the CPR.

(3) These Rules consist of—

(a) the rules set out in full;

(b) in the case of a rule applying a rule in Part 4, 7, 8, 9, 11, 12 or 13 of the 1986 Rules, the rule so applied with—

(i) the modifications set out in paragraph (4),

(ii) the modifications contained in the rule applying it, and

(iii) any other necessary modification;

(c) the Schedule, which applies the relevant schedules of the 1986 Rules.

(4) The modifications are that where applicable, a reference to—

(a) the 1986 Act (or to "the Act") is a reference to that Act as applied, with modifications, by the 2009 Act, (and includes, where appropriate, a reference to Part 2 of the 2009 Act.)

(b) the 1986 Rules (or to "the Rules") is a reference to these Rules,

(c) an affidavit is a reference to a witness statement,

(d) the commencement of winding up is a reference to the commencement of bank insolvency,

(e) the chairman is a reference to the chair,

(f) a reference to a company is a reference to a bank,

(g) going into liquidation is a reference to entering bank insolvency,

(h) insolvency proceedings is a reference to bank insolvency proceedings,

(i) the official receiver should be ignored unless otherwise stated,

(j) a petition for winding up is a reference to an application for bank insolvency under section 95 of the 2009 Act,

(k) a petitioner is a reference to an applicant,

(l) the provisional liquidator is a reference to the provisional bank liquidator,

(m) winding up is a reference to bank insolvency,

(n) winding up by the court is a reference to a bank being placed into bank insolvency by the court, and

(o) a winding-up order is a reference to a bank insolvency order.

(5) Expressions used—

(a) both in a rule set out in full and in Part 2 of the 2009 Act, or

(b) both in a modification to a rule from the 1986 Rules applied by these Rules and in Part 2 of the 2009 Act,

have the same meaning as in Part 2 of the 2009 Act.

(6) Where a rule applies a rule of the 1986 Rules and modifies that rule by inserting or substituting text—

(a) any reference in the modified rule to the 2009 Rules is a reference to these rules;
(b) expressions inserted or substituted have the same meaning as in these rules.

(7) Where a rule in the 1986 Rules (Rule A) contains a reference to another such rule (Rule B) and—

(a) both Rule A and Rule B are applied by these Rules, or
(b) Rule A is applied by and the provision in Rule B to which Rule A refers is substantially repeated in these Rules,

the reference in Rule A shall be treated, for the purpose of these Rules, as being, respectively, to the rule in these Rules that applies Rule B or the provision in these Rules that substantially repeats the provision in Rule B.

(8) Where a rule (Rule A) refers to another rule (Rule B), and Rule B applies a rule of the 1986 Rules (Rule C) with or without modifications, the reference in Rule A includes [a reference to Rule C as applied by Rule B].

(9) Any notice or document required to [be] sent electronically [pursuant to these Rules] shall be treated as having been sent to the person if—

(a) it is sent by email to the person's last known email address, and
(b) the email contains a prompt asking the person for an electronic receipt saying that the email has been read.

(10) Where [these Rules] provide for a witness statement (either expressly, or through the application of the 1986 Rules as modified above)—

(a) that statement is a reference to a witness statement verified by a statement of truth in accordance with Part 22 of the CPR, and
(b) if the statement is made by the bank liquidator or provisional bank liquidator, the statement should state as such and should include the address at which that person works.

NOTES

Para (2): in definition "the 1986 Rules" words in square brackets inserted and in definition "sealed" semi-colon in square brackets substituted by the Bank Insolvency (England and Wales) (Amendment) Rules 2010, SI 2010/2579, rr 3, 4(a); definition "the appropriate regulator" inserted and definition "the FSA" (omitted) revoked by the Financial Services Act 2012 (Consequential Amendments and Transitional Provisions) Order 2013, SI 2013/472, art 3, Sch 2, para 163(a).

Para (8): words in square brackets substituted by SI 2010/2579, rr 3, 4(b).

Para (9): word in first pair of square brackets inserted and words in second pair of square brackets substituted by SI 2010/2579, rr 3, 4(c).

Para (10): words in square brackets substituted by SI 2010/2579, rr 3, 4(d).

Note that the Insolvency Rules 1986, SI 1986/1925 are revoked and replaced (as from 6 April 2017 and subject to transitional provisions) by the Insolvency (England and Wales) Rules 2016, SI 2016/1024 at **[6.2]**.

[7.96]
4 Overview

The purpose of these Rules is to provide a procedure for the appointment of a bank liquidator and the operation of bank insolvency under Part 2 of the 2009 Act in England and Wales.

[7.97]
5 Forms

(1) This [rule] applies where a provision of these Rules—

(a) applies a provision of [the 1986 Rules] which requires the use of a prescribed form, or
(b) makes provision similar to that made by a provision of those Rules which requires the use of a prescribed form.

(2) The form prescribed for the purposes of those Rules is to be used with any modification that the person using the form thinks desirable to reflect the nature of bank insolvency (whether or not the modification is set out in a Practice Form issued by the Treasury for that purpose).

NOTES

Para (1): words in square brackets substituted by the Bank Insolvency (England and Wales) (Amendment) Rules 2010, SI 2010/2579, rr 3, 5.

[7.98]
6 Time [limits]

(1) Where by any provision of the 1986 Act, the 2009 Act or these Rules, the time for doing anything is limited, the court may extend the time, either before or after it has expired, on such terms, if any, as it thinks fit.

(2) If the court's consideration of whether to extend the time for doing anything takes place before a full payment resolution has been passed, the court shall only extend the time if it considers that the resulting delay will not significantly prejudice the achievement of Objective 1.

NOTES

Provision heading: word in square brackets substituted by the Bank Insolvency (England and Wales) (Amendment) Rules 2010, SI 2010/2579, rr 3, 6.

PART 2
APPLICATION FOR ORDER

[7.99]

7 Filing of application

(1) The application for a bank insolvency order, verified by witness statement in accordance with rule 11, shall be filed in court.

(2) There shall be filed with the application—

(a) 1 copy for service on the bank,
(b) 1 copy to be attached to the proof of service, and
(c) further copies to be sent to [the] persons under rule 10.

(3) The court shall fix the venue, date and time for the hearing of the application and in doing so shall have regard to—

(a) the desirability of the application being heard as soon as is reasonably practicable, and
(b) the need to give the bank a reasonable opportunity to attend.

(4) Each of the copies issued to the applicant shall be sealed and be endorsed with the venue, date and time for the hearing.

(5) Any application filed in relation to a bank in respect of which there is in force a voluntary arrangement under Part 1 of the 1986 Act shall be filed in accordance with this rule, but a copy of that application shall also be sent to the court to which the nominee's report under section 2 of the 1986 Act was submitted, if that is not the same court.

NOTES

Para (2): word in square brackets substituted by the Bank Insolvency (England and Wales) (Amendment) Rules 2010, SI 2010/2579, rr 3, 7.

[7.100]

8 Service of application

(1) The applicant shall serve the bank with a sealed copy of the application.

(2) The application shall be served on the bank by personal service at its registered office.

(3) In paragraph (2) "registered office" means—

(a) the place which is specified, in the bank's statement delivered under section 9 of the 2006 Act or, before that section comes into force, section 10 of the 1985 Act as the intended situation of its registered office on incorporation, or
(b) if notice has been given by the bank to the registrar of companies under section 87 of the 2006 Act or, before that section comes into force, section 287 of the 1985 Act, the place specified in that notice or, as the case may be, in the last such notice.

(4) Service of the application at the registered office may be effected in any of the following ways—

(a) it may be handed to a person who there and then acknowledges that they are, or to the best of the server's knowledge, information and belief are, a director or other officer, or employee, of the bank, or
(b) it may be handed to a person who there and then acknowledges that they are authorised to accept service documents on the company's behalf, or
(c) in the absence of such person as is mentioned in sub-paragraphs (a) and (b), it may be deposited at or about the registered office in such a way that it is likely to come to the notice of a person attending the office.

(5) If for any reason it is impracticable to effect service as provided by paragraph (2) or (4), the application may be served in such other manner as the court may approve or direct.

(6) Application for permission of the court under paragraph (5) may be made without notice to the bank, stating in a witness statement what steps have been taken to comply with paragraph (2) or (4), and the reasons why it is impracticable to effect service as there provided.

(7) If the bank or its legal representatives fail to attend the hearing, the court may make the bank insolvency order in its absence if satisfied that the application has been served in accordance with this rule.

[7.101]

9 Proof of service

Apply rule 4.9 of the 1986 Rules.

[7.102]

10 Other persons to receive copy of application

(1) The applicant shall [send 2 copies] of the application to—

(a) the proposed bank liquidator,
(b) the Bank of England, (if it is not the applicant,)
[(c) the Financial Conduct Authority, (if it is not the applicant);

(ca) if the bank is a PRA-authorised person (within the meaning of the Financial Services and Markets Act 2000) and the applicant is not the Prudential Regulation Authority, that Authority;]
(d) the FSCS,
(e) . . . any person who has given notice to the [Financial Conduct Authority or the Prudential Regulation Authority] in respect of the bank under section 120 of the Banking Act 2009,
(f) if there is in force for the bank a voluntary arrangement under Part 1 of the 1986 Act, the supervisor of that arrangement, and
(g) if an administrative receiver has been appointed in relation to the bank, that receiver,

in accordance with paragraph (2).

(2) [One] copy shall be sent electronically as soon as practicable and the other [(a sealed copy)] shall be sent by first class post on the business day on which the application is served on the bank.

(3) Any of the persons in sub-paragraph (1) will have the right to attend and be heard at the hearing of the application.

NOTES

Para (1): words in first pair of square brackets substituted and word omitted revoked by the Bank Insolvency (England and Wales) (Amendment) Rules 2010, SI 2010/2579, rr 3, 8(a); sub-paras (c), (ca) substituted and words in square brackets in sub-para (e) substituted by the Financial Services Act 2012 (Consequential Amendments and Transitional Provisions) Order 2013, SI 2013/472, art 3, Sch 2, para 163(b).

Para (2): word in first pair of square brackets substituted and words in second pair of square brackets inserted by SI 2010/2579, rr 3, 8(b).

[7.103]
11 Verification of application

(1) This applies where an application has been filed at the court under rule 7 above.

(2) A witness statement shall be attached to the application to state that the statements in the application are true, or are true to the best of the applicant's knowledge, information and belief.

(3) The witness statement [shall] identify the person making the statement and [shall] include the capacity in which that person makes the statement and the basis for that person's knowledge of the matters set out in the application.

(4) The witness statement is, unless proved otherwise, evidence of the statements in the application.

NOTES

Para (3): word in square brackets in both places it occurs substituted by the Bank Insolvency (England and Wales) (Amendment) Rules 2010, SI 2010/2579, rr 3, 9.

[7.104]
12 Persons entitled to copy of application

(1) Every contributory or creditor of the bank is entitled to a copy of the application on request from the applicant.

(2) The applicant shall respond to any request for a copy of the application as soon as reasonably practicable after the application has been made on payment of the appropriate fee.

[7.105]
13 Certificate of compliance

(1) Apply rule 4.14 of the 1986 Rules.

(2) In paragraph (1) the period for filing shall be as soon as reasonably practicable before the hearing of the application.

(3) In paragraph (2), leave out the words "[a copy or]" to the end, and insert—

"A witness statement made by the proposed bank liquidator to the effect that—
(c) the person is qualified to act as an insolvency practitioner in accordance with section 390 of the 1986 Act, and
(d) the person consents to act as the bank liquidator,

shall be filed in court with the certificate."

NOTES

Para (3): words in square brackets substituted by the Bank Insolvency (England and Wales) (Amendment) Rules 2010, SI 2010/2579, rr 3, 10.

[7.106]
14 Leave for the applicant to withdraw

Apply rule 4.15 of the 1986 Rules. Leave out "at least 5 days" and ignore sub-paragraph (a).

[7.107]
15 Witness statement in opposition

(1) If the bank intends to oppose an application, the bank . . . may (but need not) file a witness statement in opposition in court.

(2) A statement under paragraph (1) must be filed before the hearing of the application and a copy must be served on the applicant, before the hearing.

(3) The statement may be served on the applicant by personal service or by electronic means.

(4) The statement should also be sent to the persons in rule 10(1) before the hearing by personal service or by electronic means.

[(5) The fact that the bank has not filed a statement under this rule shall not prevent it being heard at the hearing.]

NOTES

Para (1): words omitted revoked by the Bank Insolvency (England and Wales) (Amendment) Rules 2010, SI 2010/2579, rr 3, 11(a).

Para (5): substituted by SI 2010/2579, rr 3, 11(b).

[7.108]

16 Making, transmission and advertisement of order

(1) The court shall not make a bank insolvency order unless the person nominated to be appointed as the bank liquidator in the application for the order has filed in court a witness statement under rule 13.

(2) When the bank insolvency order has been made the court shall immediately send 5 sealed copies (or such larger number as the bank liquidator may have requested) to the bank liquidator.

(3) The court shall also, if practicable, immediately send a [copy] of the order to the bank liquidator electronically.

(4) The bank liquidator shall serve a sealed copy of the order on the bank at its registered office and, where the bank liquidator knows the bank's email address, will send an electronic copy to the bank.

(5) The bank liquidator shall send [2 copies] of the order—

- (a) to the Bank of England, the [appropriate regulator] and the FSCS . . .
- (b) to the registrar of companies in accordance with section 130(1) of the 1986 Act (as applied by the 2009 Act);
- [(c) if there is in force for the bank a voluntary arrangement under Part 1 of the 1986 Act, the supervisor of that arrangement; and
- (d) if an administrative receiver has been appointed in relation to the bank, that receiver,

in accordance with paragraph (5A)].

[(5A) One copy shall be sent electronically as soon as practicable and the other (a sealed copy) shall be sent by first class post on the business day on which the order is served on the bank.]

[(6) The bank liquidator—

- (a) shall cause notice of the order to be gazetted as soon as reasonably practicable; and
- (b) may advertise notice of the order in such other manner as the bank liquidator thinks fit.]

NOTES

Para (3): word in square brackets substituted by the Bank Insolvency (England and Wales) (Amendment) Rules 2010, SI 2010/2579, rr 3, 12(a).

Para (5): words in first pair of square brackets substituted, words omitted revoked, and words in third pair of square brackets inserted, by SI 2010/2579, rr 3, 12(b); words in second pair of square brackets substituted by the Financial Services Act 2012 (Consequential Amendments and Transitional Provisions) Order 2013, SI 2013/472, art 3, Sch 2, para 163(f).

Para (5A): inserted by SI 2010/2579, rr 3, 12(c).

Para (6): substituted by SI 2010/2579, rr 3, 12(d).

[7.109]

17 Authentication of bank liquidator's appointment

A sealed copy of the court's order may in any proceedings be adduced as proof that the person appointed is duly authorised to exercise the powers and perform the duties of the bank liquidator in the bank insolvency.

[7.110]

18 Initial duties of bank liquidation committee

(1) As soon as reasonably practicable after the making of a bank insolvency order, the liquidation committee [shall] meet the bank liquidator for the purpose of discussing which of the objectives, or combination of objectives, mentioned in section 102(1) of the 2009 Act, the committee should recommend the bank liquidator to pursue.

(2) If the bank liquidator and every individual on the liquidation committee agree, the meeting may be held by audio or video conference.

(3) The liquidation committee [shall] make its recommendation to the bank liquidator at the meeting.

(4) The Bank of England [shall] confirm the liquidation committee's recommendation in writing as soon as practicable after the meeting.

(5) As soon as practicable after the making of a bank insolvency order, the liquidation committee shall also pass a resolution as to the terms on which, in accordance with rule 98, the bank liquidator is to be remunerated.

(6) Until a full payment resolution has been passed, the bank liquidation committee—

- (a) shall take decisions and pass resolutions by a simple majority, and
- (b) for the purpose of taking decisions and passing resolutions, may communicate by any means that its members consider convenient.

NOTES

Paras (1), (3), (4): words in square brackets substituted by the Bank Insolvency (England and Wales) (Amendment) Rules 2010, SI 2010/2579, rr 3, 13.

[7.111]

19 Expenses of voluntary arrangement

Apply rule 4.21A of the 1986 Rules.

PART 3
PROVISIONAL BANK LIQUIDATOR

[7.112]

20 Appointment of provisional bank liquidator

(1) . . .

(2) An application to the court for the appointment of a provisional bank liquidator under section 135 of the Act may be made—

(a) by the Bank of England,

[(b) by the Financial Conduct Authority, with the consent of the Bank of England;

(ba) if the bank is a PRA-authorised person (within the meaning of the Financial Services and Markets Act 2000), by the Prudential Regulation Authority with the consent of the Bank of England;]

(c) by the Secretary of State.

(3) The application must be supported by a witness statement stating—

(a) the grounds upon which it is proposed that the provisional bank liquidator should be appointed;

(b) that the person to be appointed has consented to act,

(c) that the person to be appointed is qualified to act as an insolvency practitioner,

(d) whether to the applicant's knowledge—

(i) there has been proposed or is in force for the bank a company voluntary arrangement under Part 1 of the 1986 Act, or

(ii) an administrative receiver is acting in relation to the bank.

(e) the applicant's estimate of the value of the assets in respect of which the provisional bank liquidator is to be appointed, and

(f) the functions the applicant wishes to be carried out by the provisional bank liquidator in relation to the bank's affairs.

(4) The court may on the application, if satisfied that sufficient grounds are shown for the appointment, make it on such terms as it thinks fit.

NOTES

Para (1): revoked by the Bank Insolvency (England and Wales) (Amendment) Rules 2010, SI 2010/2579, rr 3, 14.

Para (2): sub-paras (b), (ba) substituted by the Financial Services Act 2012 (Consequential Amendments and Transitional Provisions) Order 2013, SI 2013/472, art 3, Sch 2, para 163(c).

[7.113]

21 Notice of appointment

[(1)] Where a provisional bank liquidator has been appointed, the court shall notify the applicant and the person appointed.

[(2) Unless the court otherwise directs, on receipt of the notification under paragraph (1) the provisional bank liquidator shall give notice of that appointment as soon as reasonably practicable. Such notice—

(a) shall be gazetted; and

(b) may be advertised in such other manner as the provisional bank liquidator thinks fit.]

NOTES

Para (1): numbered as such by the Bank Insolvency (England and Wales) (Amendment) Rules 2010, SI 2010/2579, rr 3, 15.

Para (2): added by SI 2010/2579, rr 3, 15.

[7.114]

22 Order of appointment

(1) The order of appointment shall specify the functions to be carried out by the provisional bank liquidator in relation to the bank's affairs.

(2) The court shall, immediately after the order is made, send 4 sealed copies of the order (or such larger number as the provisional bank liquidator may have requested), to the provisional bank liquidator.

(3) The court shall also, if practicable, immediately send a [copy] of the order to the provisional bank liquidator electronically.

(4) The provisional bank liquidator shall serve a sealed copy of the order on the bank at its registered office and, where the provisional bank liquidator knows the bank's email address, will send an electronic copy to the bank.

(5) The bank liquidator shall send [2 copies] of the order—

(a) to the Bank of England, the [appropriate regulator], and the FSCS . . .

(b) to the registrar of companies, . . .

(c) (if applicable) to any administrative receiver of the bank[; and]

[(d) if there is in force for the bank a voluntary arrangement under Part 1 of the 1986 Act, the supervisor of that arrangement,

in accordance with paragraph (6)].

[(6) One copy shall be sent electronically as soon as practicable and the other (a sealed copy) shall be sent by first class post on the business day on which the order is served on the bank.]

NOTES

Para (3): word in square brackets substituted by the Bank Insolvency (England and Wales) (Amendment) Rules 2010, SI 2010/2579, rr 3, 16(a).

Para (5): words in first pair of square brackets substituted, words omitted revoked and words in third and fourth pairs of square brackets inserted by SI 2010/2579, rr 3, 16(b); words in third pair of square brackets substituted by the Financial Services Act 2012 (Consequential Amendments and Transitional Provisions) Order 2013, SI 2013/472, art 3, Sch 2, para 163(f).

Para (6): inserted by SI 2010/2579, rr 3, 16(c).

[7.115]
23 Security

Apply rule 4.28 of the 1986 Rules.

[7.116]
24 Failure to give or keep up security

Apply rule 4.29 of the 1986 Rules.

[7.117]
25 Remuneration

Apply rule 4.30 of the 1986 Rules. Ignore paragraph (4).

[7.118]
26 Termination of appointment

(1) Apply rule 4.31 of the 1986 Rules.

(2) At the end insert—

"(3) On the making of a bank insolvency order the appointment of the provisional bank liquidator shall terminate.".

PART 4
STATEMENT OF AFFAIRS AND OTHER INFORMATION

[7.119]
27 Notice requiring statement of affairs

(1) Apply rule 4.32 of the 1986 Rules. For "official receiver", substitute "[bank liquidator]".

(2) . . .

NOTES

Para (1): words in square brackets substituted by the Bank Insolvency (England and Wales) (Amendment) Rules 2010, SI 2010/2579, rr 3, 17(a).

Para (2): revoked by SI 2010/2579, rr 3, 17(b).

[7.120]
28 Verification and filing

(1) Apply rule 4.33 of the 1986 Rules. [For "official receiver" substitute "bank liquidator"]

(2) For paragraph (6), substitute—

"(6) The bank liquidator shall file the statement of affairs in court and shall send a copy of it to the registrar of companies."

(3) Ignore paragraph (7).

NOTES

Para (1): words in square brackets inserted by the Bank Insolvency (England and Wales) (Amendment) Rules 2010, SI 2010/2579, rr 3, 18.

[7.121]
29 Limited disclosure

(1) Apply rule 4.35 of the 1986 Rules. In paragraph (1), for "official receiver", substitute "[bank liquidator]".

(2) After paragraph (1), insert—

"(1A) The [bank liquidator] may also apply to the court for an order of limited disclosure in respect of those depositors of the bank who, at the time of the making of the statement of affairs, still have a claim against the bank in respect of their deposits."

NOTES

Para (1): words in square brackets substituted by the Bank Insolvency (England and Wales) (Amendment) Rules 2010, SI 2010/2579, rr 3, 19.

Para (2): in the Insolvency Rules 1986, r 4.35(1A) (as set out) words in square brackets substituted by SI 2010/2579, rr 3, 19.

[7.122]
30 Release from duty to submit statement of affairs; extension of time

Apply rule 4.36 of the 1986 Rules. For "official receiver" substitute "bank liquidator."

[7.123]
31 Expenses of statement of affairs

Apply rule 4.37 of the 1986 Rules. For "official receiver", substitute "[bank liquidator]".

NOTES

Words in square brackets substituted by the Bank Insolvency (England and Wales) (Amendment) Rules 2010, SI 2010/2579, rr 3, 20.

[7.124]
32 Submission of accounts

Apply rule 4.39 of the 1986 Rules. For "official receiver", substitute "[bank liquidator]".

NOTES

Words in square brackets substituted by the Bank Insolvency (England and Wales) (Amendment) Rules 2010, SI 2010/2579, rr 3, 21.

[7.125]
33 Further disclosure

Apply rule 4.42 of the 1986 Rules. For "official receiver", substitute "[bank liquidator]".

NOTES

Words in square brackets substituted by the Bank Insolvency (England and Wales) (Amendment) Rules 2010, SI 2010/2579, rr 3, 22.

PART 5
INFORMATION TO CREDITORS AND CONTRIBUTORIES

[7.126]
34 Report by bank liquidator

(1) The bank liquidator shall, at least once after the making of the bank insolvency order, make a report with respect to the proceedings in the bank insolvency and the state of the bank's affairs.

(2) Regardless of whether the liquidation committee has passed a full payment resolution, the first report under paragraph (1) shall be, within 8 weeks of the commencement of the bank insolvency, made publicly available on the bank's website [and the bank liquidator shall send a copy of it to any creditor or contributory on request].

(3) The bank liquidator shall include in the report under paragraph (1)—

- (a) a statement that the proceedings are being held in the High Court and the relevant court reference number;
- (b) the full name, registered office address, registered companies house number and any other trading names of the bank;
- (c) details relating to the bank liquidator's appointment, including the date of appointment, and where there are joint liquidators, details of—
  - (i) which functions (if any) are to be exercised by the persons appointed acting jointly, and
  - (ii) which functions (if any) are to be exercised by any of all of the persons appointed.
- (d) the names of the directors and secretary of the bank and details of any shareholdings in the bank that they have;
- (e) an account of the circumstances giving rise to the bank insolvency;
- (f) if a statement of affairs has been submitted, a copy of that statement;
- (g) if a statement of affairs has yet to be submitted—
  - (i) subject to sub paragraph (ii), the names, addresses and details of any [debts owed to the creditors], including details of any security held (or, in the case of depositors who still are creditors of the bank at the time the report is made, a single statement of their aggregate debt),
  - (ii) details of the financial position of the bank at the latest practicable date (which must, unless the court orders otherwise, be a date not earlier than the commencement of bank insolvency);
- (h) the basis upon it has been proposed under rule 41, or, if the full payment resolution has yet to be passed, rule 18, that the bank liquidator's remuneration has been fixed;
- (i) to the best of the bank liquidator's knowledge and belief—
  - (i) an estimate of the value of the prescribed part (within the meaning of section 176A of the 1986 Act) regardless of whether—

(aa) the bank liquidator proposes to make an application to the court under section 176A(5) of that Act, or

(bb) section 176A(3) of that Act applies, and

(ii) an estimate of the value of the company's net property;

(j) whether, and if so, why, the bank liquidator proposes to make an application to court under section 176A(5) of the 1986 Act;

(k) a summary of—

(i) how Objective 1 is being or has been achieved and an estimate of the costs to the bank liquidator of achieving it,

(ii) the manner in which the affairs and business of the bank not involved in the achievement of Objective 1 have, since the commencement of the bank insolvency; been managed and financed, including, where any assets have been disposed of, the reasons for such disposals and the terms upon which such disposals were made, and

(iii) how the affairs and business of the bank will continue to be managed and financed; and

(l) an explanation of how it is envisaged the [objectives of the bank liquidator] will be achieved, including whether a dividend will be paid and an estimate as to the amount of this dividend and how it is proposed that the bank liquidation shall end.

(4) Nothing in this rule is to be taken as requiring either estimate mentioned in paragraph (3) to include any information the disclosure of which could seriously prejudice the commercial interests of the company. If such information is excluded from the calculation the estimate shall be accompanied by a statement to that effect.

(5) The bank liquidator shall file with the court a copy of any report sent under this rule.

NOTES

Para (2): words in square brackets inserted by the Bank Insolvency (England and Wales) (Amendment) Rules 2010, SI 2010/2579, rr 3, 23(a).

Para (3): words in square brackets substituted by SI 2010/2579, rr 3, 23(b).

[7.127]

35 Meaning of "creditors"

Apply rule 4.44 of the 1986 Rules.

[7.128]

36 Report where statement of affairs lodged

Apply rule 4.45 of the 1986 Rules. For "official receiver", substitute "[bank liquidator]".

NOTES

Words in square brackets substituted by the Bank Insolvency (England and Wales) (Amendment) Rules 2010, SI 2010/2579, rr 3, 24.

[7.129]

37 Statement of affairs dispensed with

Apply rule 4.46 of the 1986 Rules. [In paragraphs (2) and (3), for "official receiver" substitute "bank liquidator".]

NOTES

Words in square brackets inserted by the Bank Insolvency (England and Wales) (Amendment) Rules 2010, SI 2010/2579, rr 3, 25.

[7.130]

38 General rule as to reporting

(1) Apply rule 4.47 of the 1986 Rules. [For "official receiver" substitute "bank liquidator".]

(2), (3) . . .

NOTES

Para (1): words in square brackets inserted by the Bank Insolvency (England and Wales) (Amendment) Rules 2010, SI 2010/2579, rr 3, 26(a).

Paras (2), (3): revoked by SI 2010/2579, rr 3, 26(b).

[7.131]

39 Bank insolvency stayed

(1) Apply rule 4.48 of the 1986 Rules. [For "official receiver" substitute "bank liquidator".]

(2), (3) . . .

NOTES

Para (1): words in square brackets substituted by the Bank Insolvency (England and Wales) (Amendment) Rules 2010, SI 2010/2579, rr 3, 27(a).

Paras (2), (3): revoked by SI 2010/2579, rr 3, 27(b).

PART 6
MEETINGS OF CREDITORS AND CONTRIBUTORIES
RULES OF GENERAL APPLICATION

[7.132]
40 First meeting

(1) Once the liquidation committee passes a full payment resolution the bank liquidator shall—
(a) immediately summon a meeting of the bank's creditors and a meeting of the bank's contributories, and
(b) fix a venue, date and time for the meetings,
and the date must be within 3 months of the date on which the full payment resolution was passed.

(2) When the venue, date and time of the meetings have been fixed the bank liquidator shall give notice of the meetings to—
(a) the court,
(b) every creditor who is known to the bank liquidator or is identified in the bank's statement of affairs,
(c) every person appearing (by the bank's books or otherwise) to be a contributory of the bank, and
(d) each member of the liquidation committee,
. . .

[(2A) The bank liquidator—
(a) shall gazette the notice of the meetings as soon as reasonably practicable; and
(b) may advertise it in such other manner as the bank liquidator thinks fit.]

(3) In giving the notice mentioned in paragraph (2) the bank liquidator shall, if practicable, indicate whether the present intention of the FSCS is to resign from the liquidation committee at the meeting.

(4) Notice to the court and the members of the liquidation committee shall be given immediately; notice to creditors and contributories shall be given, and the advertisements placed to appear, at least 21 days before the date fixed for the meeting.

(5) The notice to creditors shall specify a time and date, not more than 4 days before the date fixed for the meeting, by which they must lodge proofs and (if applicable) proxies, in order to be entitled to vote at the meeting.

(6) The FSCS is entitled to be represented at the meeting and Schedule 1 to the 1986 Rules, as applied by rule 293, has effect with respect to its voting rights at such a meeting.

(7) Meetings summoned under this rule are known respectively as "the first meeting of creditors" and "the first meeting of contributories", and jointly as "the first meetings in the bank liquidation."

NOTES

Para (2): words omitted revoked by the Bank Insolvency (England and Wales) (Amendment) Rules 2010, SI 2010/2579, rr 3, 28(a).

Para (2A): inserted by SI 2010/2579, rr 3, 28(b).

[7.133]
41 Business at first meetings of creditors and contributories

(1) At the first meeting of creditors the FSCS shall state whether or not it is resigning from the liquidation committee.

(2) At that meeting those creditors present (or represented by proxy) may—
(a) where the FSCS has not resigned, elect 2 or 4 individuals as new members of the liquidation committee,
(b) where the FSCS has resigned, elect 3 or 5 individuals as new members of the liquidation committee,
in place of the members nominated by the Bank of England and the [appropriate regulator]. In accordance with section 100(6)(d) of the 2009 Act, the liquidation committee ceases to exist at the end of the meeting if no individuals are elected as mentioned or if the resulting committee would have fewer than 3 members or an even number of members. The maximum number of committee members will be 5.

(3) At the first meeting of creditors no resolutions shall be taken other than the following—
(a) if an application has been made to the court by the creditors under rule 94 for the court to direct the bank liquidator to summon a meeting of creditors for the purpose of removing him, and the court has directed that a resolution may be passed to that effect at the first meeting of creditors,—
 (i) a resolution to remove the bank liquidator (or a resolution to remove 1 or more of the bank liquidators if joint liquidators were originally appointed), and
 (ii) a resolution to appoint a named insolvency practitioner to be bank liquidator or 2 or more insolvency practitioners as joint liquidators;
(b) if no individuals have been elected to form a liquidation committee under paragraph (2), a resolution specifying the terms on which the liquidator is to be remunerated, or to defer consideration of that matter;
(c) where 2 or more persons are appointed jointly to act as bank liquidator, a resolution specifying which acts are to be done by both of them, all of them or by only 1;
(d) a resolution to adjourn the meeting for not more than 3 weeks; and
(e) any other resolutions which the chair thinks it right to allow for special reasons.

(4) At the first meeting of contributories, no resolutions shall be taken other than the following—

(a) if no individuals have been elected to form a liquidation committee under paragraph (2), a resolution to form a liquidation committee (and rule 117 shall then apply);
(b) a resolution to adjourn the meeting for not more than 3 weeks;
(c) any other resolutions which the chair thinks it right to allow for special reasons.

NOTES

Para (2): words in square brackets substituted by the Financial Services Act 2012 (Consequential Amendments and Transitional Provisions) Order 2013, SI 2013/472, art 3, Sch 2, para 163(f).

[7.134]
42 General power to call meetings

(1) Apply rule 4.54 of the 1986 Rules.

(2) Where the bank liquidator has been directed to summon a meeting of creditors under section 195 of the Act (as applied by section 109 of the 2009 Act) for the purpose of removing the bank liquidator, the bank liquidator shall give notice of the meeting to the Bank of England and the [appropriate regulator].

NOTES

Para (2): words in square brackets substituted by the Financial Services Act 2012 (Consequential Amendments and Transitional Provisions) Order 2013, SI 2013/472, art 3, Sch 2, para 163(f).

[7.135]
43 The chair at meetings

(1) Meetings shall be chaired by the bank liquidator or a person nominated in writing by the bank liquidator.

(2) A person nominated under paragraph (1) must be—
(a) qualified to act as an insolvency practitioner in accordance with section 390 of the 1986 Act, or
(b) an employee of the bank liquidator or of the bank liquidator's firm who is experienced in insolvency matters.

[7.136]
44 Requisitioned meetings: general

(1) Apply rule 4.57 of the 1986 Rules.

[7.137]
45 Requisitioned meetings: reforming the liquidation committee

(1) Rule 4.57 of the 1986 Rules also applies where—
(a) the liquidation committee has ceased to exist at the end of the first meeting of creditors under rule 41 and no further steps have been taken to [re-establish] that committee; and
(b) the bank liquidator has been requested, by no less than one-tenth in value of the bank's creditors, to summon a meeting for the purpose of re-establishing the liquidation committee.

(2) Where a meeting is requisitioned to re-establish the liquidation committee, the time periods set out in rule 4.57 of the 1986 Rules may be expedited by the bank liquidator [at the request] of the bank's creditors.

(3) The bank liquidator shall give notice of the meeting to the [appropriate regulator] and Bank of England.

(4) Rule 41(1) and (2) shall apply at this meeting as if it were the first meeting of creditors.

NOTES

Paras (1), (2): words in square brackets substituted by the Bank Insolvency (England and Wales) (Amendment) Rules 2010, SI 2010/2579, rr 3, 29.

Para (3): words in square brackets substituted by the Financial Services Act 2012 (Consequential Amendments and Transitional Provisions) Order 2013, SI 2013/472, art 3, Sch 2, para 163(f).

[7.138]
46 Attendance at meetings of bank's personnel

Apply rule 4.58 of the 1986 Rules.

[7.139]
47 Notice of meetings by advertisement only

Apply rule 4.59 of the 1986 Rules.

[7.140]
48 Venue

Apply rule 4.60 of the 1986 Rules.

[7.141]
49 Expenses of summoning meetings

Apply rule 4.61 of the 1986 Rules.

[7.142]
50 Resolutions

Apply rule 4.63 of the 1986 Rules.

[7.143]
51 Chair of meeting as proxy-holder

Apply rule 4.64 of the 1986 Rules.

[7.144]
52 Suspension and adjournment

(1) Apply rule 4.65 of the 1986 Rules.

(2) In paragraph (3), leave out "or, as the case may be, 4.114—CVL(3)".

[7.145]
53 Entitlement to vote (creditors)

(1) Apply rule 4.67 of the 1986 Rules.

(2) Ignore paragraph (ii) of paragraph (1)(a) and paragraph (8).

(3) In paragraph (9), ignore the reference to paragraph (8).

[7.146]
54 Entitlement to vote (contributories)

Apply rule 4.69 of the 1986 Rules.

[7.147]
55 Admission and rejection of proof (creditors' meetings)

Apply rule 4.70 of the 1986 Rules. For paragraph (5) substitute—

> "(5) The chair is not personally liable for costs incurred by any person in respect of an application under this rule unless the court makes an application to that effect.".

[7.148]
56 Record of proceedings

Apply rule 4.71 of the 1986 Rules.

PART 7
PROOF OF DEBTS

[7.149]
57 Meaning of "prove"

(1) Apply rule 4.73 of the 1986 Rules.

(2) In paragraph (5), for "or a Government Department" substitute ", a Government Department or the FSCS".

(3) Ignore paragraphs (2), and (8).

[7.150]
58 Supply of forms

Apply rule 4.74 of the 1986 Rules.

[7.151]
59 Contents of proof

Apply rule 4.75 of the 1986 Rules.

[7.152]
60 Claim established by [witness statement]

Apply rule 4.77 of the 1986 Rules. Ignore paragraph (3).

NOTES

Provision heading: words in square brackets substituted by the Bank Insolvency (England and Wales) (Amendment) Rules 2010, SI 2010/2579, rr 3, 30.

[7.153]
61 Cost of proving

(1) Apply rule 4.78 of the 1986 Rules.

(2) In paragraph (1), leave out "or 4.76—CVL".

[7.154]
62 Bank liquidator to allow inspection of proofs

Apply rule 4.79 of the 1986 Rules.

[7.155]
63 New bank liquidator appointed

Apply rule 4.81 of the 1986 Rules.

[7.156]
64 Admission and rejection of proofs for dividend

Apply rule 4.82 of the 1986 Rules.

[7.157]
65 Appeal against decision on proof

(1) Apply rule 4.83 of the 1986 Rules.

(2) For paragraph (6) substitute—

"(6) The bank liquidator is not personally liable for costs incurred by any person in respect of an application under this rule unless the court makes an order to that effect.".

[7.158]
66 Withdrawal or variation of proof

Apply rule 4.84 of the 1986 Rules.

[7.159]
67 Expunging of proof by the court

Apply rule 4.85 of the 1986 Rules.

[7.160]
68 Estimate of quantum

Apply rule 4.86 of the 1986 Rules.

[7.161]
69 Negotiable instruments, etc

Apply rule 4.87 of the 1986 Rules.

[7.162]
70 Secured creditors

Apply rule 4.88 of the 1986 Rules.

[7.163]
71 Discounts

Apply rule 4.89 of the 1986 Rules.

[7.164]
72 Mutual credits and set-off

[(1)] This rule applies where, before the bank goes into bank insolvency, there have been mutual credits, mutual debts or other mutual dealings between the company and any creditor of the bank proving or claiming to prove for a debt in the bank insolvency.

[(2)] The reference in paragraph (1) to mutual credits, mutual debts or other mutual dealings does not include—

(a) any debt arising out of an obligation incurred at a time when the creditor had notice that—
  (i) a meeting of creditors had been summoned under section 98 of the 1986 Act,
  (ii) a petition for the winding up of the bank was pending, or
  (iii) an application for a bank insolvency order in respect of the bank was pending;

(b) any debt which has been acquired by a creditor on assignment or otherwise, pursuant to an agreement between the creditor and any other party where that agreement was entered into—
  (i) after the commencement of bank insolvency,
  (ii) at a time when the creditor had notice that a meeting of creditors had been summoned under section 98,
  (iii) at a time when the creditor had notice that a winding up petition was pending, or
  (iv) at a time when the creditor had notice that an application for a bank insolvency order in respect of the bank was pending.

[(3)] An account shall be taken of what is due from each party to the other in respect of the mutual dealings, and the sums due from [one] party shall be set off against the sums due from the other.

[(4)] A sum shall be regarded as being due to or from the bank for the purposes of [paragraph 3] whether—

(a) it is payable at present or in the future;
(b) the obligation by virtue of which it is payable is certain or contingent; or
(c) its amount is fixed or liquidated, or is capable of being ascertained by fixed rules or as a matter of opinion.

[(5)] Rule 4.86 of the 1986 Rules shall apply for the purposes [of this rule] to any obligation to or from the bank which, by reason of its being subject to any contingency or for any other reason, does not bear a certain value.

[(6)] Rules 74 to 76 shall apply for the purposes of this [rule] in relation to any sums due to the bank which—
(a) are payable in a currency other than sterling,
(b) are of a periodical nature, or
(c) bear interest.

[(7)] Rule 259 shall apply for the purposes of this rule to any sum due to or from the bank which is payable in the future.

[(8)] Subject to rule 73, only the balance (if any) of the account owed to the creditor is provable in the liquidation. Alternatively the balance (if any) owed to the company shall be paid to the bank liquidator as part of the assets except where all or part of the balance result from a contingent or prospective debt owed by the creditor and in such a case the balance (or that part of it which results from the contingent or prospective debt) shall be paid if and when that debt becomes due and payable.

[(9)] In this rule, "obligation" means an obligation however arising, whether by virtue of an agreement, rule of law or otherwise.

NOTES

Para (1): numbered as such by the Bank Insolvency (England and Wales) (Amendment) Rules 2010, SI 2010/2579, rr 3, 31(a).

Paras (2), (7)–(9): renumbered as such by SI 2010/2579, rr 3, 31(a).

Paras (3)–(6): renumbered as such and words in square brackets substituted by SI 2010/2579, rr 3, 31.

[7.165]
73 Disapplication of set off for eligible depositors

(1) This rule applies if the [appropriate regulator] Rules allow the FSCS to make gross payments of compensation.

[(2) Rule 72 shall apply but, for the purpose of determining the sums due from the bank to the eligible depositor in respect of protected deposits under rule 72(3)—
(a) where the total of sums held by the bank for the depositor in respect of protected deposits is no more than the amount prescribed as the maximum compensation payable in respect of protected deposits under Part 15 of the Financial Services and Markets Act 2000 ("the limit"), then paragraph (3) applies; and
(b) where the sums exceed the limit, then paragraph (4) applies.]

(3) [Where this paragraph applies] there shall be deemed to have been no mutual dealings, regardless of whether there are any sums due from the depositor to the bank, and the sum due to the . . . depositor from the bank will be the total of the sums held by the bank for that depositor in respect of the protected deposits.

(4) [Where this paragraph applies] then—
(a) any mutual dealings shall be treated as being mutual dealings only in relation to the amount by which [the total of sums due to the depositor] exceeds that limit, and
(b) the sums due from the bank to [the depositor in respect of the protected deposits] will be—
[(i) the amount by which that total exceeds the limit, set off against the amounts due to the bank from the depositor in accordance with rule 72(3), and
(ii) the sums held by the bank for the depositor in respect of protected deposits up to the limit].

(5) Any arrangements with regard to [set-off] between the bank and the eligible depositor in existence before the commencement of bank insolvency shall be subject to this rule [in so far as they relate to protected deposits].

[(6) In this rule—
"eligible depositor" has the meaning given by section 93(3) of the 2009 Act;
["appropriate regulator rules" means the rules, as amended from time to time, made under section 213 of the Financial Services and Markets Act 2000 by the Financial Conduct Authority or the Prudential Regulation Authority;]
"protected deposit" means a protected deposit within the meaning given by [appropriate regulator] Rules].

NOTES

Para (1): words in square brackets substituted by the Financial Services Act 2012 (Consequential Amendments and Transitional Provisions) Order 2013, SI 2013/472, art 3, Sch 2, para 163(g).

Para (2): substituted by the Bank Insolvency (England and Wales) (Amendment) Rules 2010, SI 2010/2579, rr 3, 32(a).

Para (3): words in square brackets substituted and words omitted revoked by SI 2010/2579, rr 3, 32(b).

Para (4): words in square brackets substituted by SI 2010/2579, rr 3, 32(c).

Para (5): word in first pair of square brackets substituted and words in second pair of square brackets inserted by SI 2010/2579, rr 3, 32(d).

Para (6): substituted by SI 2010/2579, rr 3, 32(e); words in square brackets substituted by SI 2013/472, art 3, Sch 2, para 163(d), (g).

[7.166]
74 Debt in foreign currency

Apply rule 4.91 of the 1986 Rules. In paragraph (1), leave out from "or, if" to the end.

[7.167]
75 Payments of a periodical nature

Apply rule 4.92 of the 1986 Rules. In paragraph (1), leave out from "or, if" to the end.

[7.168]
76 Interest

Apply rule 4.93 of the 1986 Rules. In paragraph (1), leave out from "or, if" to the end.

[7.169]
77 Debt payable at future time

(1) Apply rule 4.94 of the 1986 Rules.

(2) Leave out from "or, if" to "entered administration".

PART 8
SECURED CREDITORS

[7.170]
78 Value of security

Apply rule 4.95 of the 1986 Rules.

[7.171]
79 Surrender for non-disclosure

Apply rule 4.96 of the 1986 Rules. Ignore paragraph (3).

[7.172]
80 Redemption by liquidator

Apply rule 4.97 of the 1986 Rules.

[7.173]
81 Test of security's value

Apply rule 4.98 of the 1986 Rules.

[7.174]
82 Realisation of security by creditor

Apply rule 4.99 of the 1986 Rules.

PART 9
THE BANK LIQUIDATOR

CHAPTER 1 GENERAL

[7.175]
83 Remuneration of bank liquidator

(1) This rule applies where—
- (a) the liquidation committee has ceased to exist as mentioned in rule 41(1),
- (b) the committee has not been reformed at a meeting of creditors held under either rule [41, 44 or 45], and
- (c) the committee has not been reformed at a meeting of contributories held under rule 117.

(2) Where this rule applies the creditors may, at the first or any subsequent meeting of creditors, pass a resolution as to the terms on which, in accordance with rule 98, the bank liquidator is to be remunerated.

(3) Where such a resolution is passed—
- (a) it supersedes any resolution as to the remuneration of the bank liquidator passed by the liquidation committee before the first meeting of creditors, and
- (b) the bank liquidator shall be paid under the resolution passed by the bank liquidation committee under rule 18(5) in respect of the performance of his functions before the day on which the creditors' resolution is passed and under the creditors' resolution in respect of the performance of his functions on and after that day.

NOTES

Para (1): words in square brackets substituted by the Bank Insolvency (England and Wales) (Amendment) Rules 2010, SI 2010/2579, rr 3, 33.

[7.176]
84 Replacement of bank liquidator by creditors

(1) Apply rule 4.100 of the 1986 Rules.

(2) For paragraph (1) substitute—

"(1) This rule applies where a person is appointed as bank liquidator by a meeting of creditors."

(3) For paragraph (4) substitute—

"(4) The chairman of the meeting shall—
- (a) send the certificate to the new bank liquidator,

(b) send a copy of the certificate to the Bank of England and the [appropriate regulator], and
(c) file a copy of the certificate in court."

NOTES

Para (3): words in square brackets substituted by the Financial Services Act 2012 (Consequential Amendments and Transitional Provisions) Order 2013, SI 2013/472, art 3, Sch 2, para 163(f).

[7.177]
85 Authentication of bank liquidator's appointment

Apply rule 4.105 of the 1986 Rules). Leave out from "or (as" to "the Act".

[7.178]
86 Appointment to be advertised and registered

(1) This rule applies where the bank liquidator is appointed by a meeting of the creditors or by the Bank of England under rule 106.

[(2) The bank liquidator shall, after receiving the certificate of appointment, give notice of that appointment as soon as reasonably practicable. Such notice—
(a) shall be gazetted; and
(b) may be advertised in such other manner as the bank liquidator thinks fit.]

(3) The expense of giving notice under this rule shall be borne in the first instance by the bank liquidator; but he is entitled to be reimbursed as an expense of the bank insolvency.

(4) The bank liquidator shall immediately notify his appointment to the registrar of companies.

NOTES

Para (2): substituted by the Bank Insolvency (England and Wales) (Amendment) Rules 2010, SI 2010/2579, rr 3, 34.

CHAPTER 2 RESIGNATION AND REMOVAL

[7.179]
87 Creditors' meeting to be notified of the bank liquidator's resignation

(1) Apply rule 4.108 of the 1986 Rules.

(2) For paragraph (1), substitute—

"(1) Before resigning office, the bank liquidator must obtain the consent of the Bank of England and must call a meeting of creditors to notify them of this.
(1A) The notice summoning the meeting shall indicate that this is the purpose, or one of the purposes, of the meeting and shall draw the attention of the creditors to rule 95 with respect to the bank liquidator's release.
(1B) The notice in [paragraph] (1A) shall enclose a copy of the Bank of England's consent."

(3) For paragraph (2) substitute—

"(2) Copies of the notice and of the account mentioned in paragraph (3) shall be sent to the court, the Bank of England and the [appropriate regulator].".

NOTES

Para (2): in the Insolvency Rules 1986, r 4.108(1B) (as set out) word in square brackets inserted by the Bank Insolvency (England and Wales) (Amendment) Rules 2010, SI 2010/2579, rr 3, 35.

Para (3): words in square brackets substituted by the Financial Services Act 2012 (Consequential Amendments and Transitional Provisions) Order 2013, SI 2013/472, art 3, Sch 2, para 163(f).

[7.180]
88 Action following acceptance of resignation

(1) This rule applies where a meeting is summoned to notify the creditors of the bank liquidator's resignation

(2) The meeting [shall] resolve whether to give the bank liquidator their release.

[(3) If the meeting resolves not to release the bank liquidator, the bank liquidator shall be given a copy of that resolution and rule 95 applies.]

(4) After the meeting the bank liquidator shall file the notice of his resignation in court and [shall] send copies of the notice to the Bank of England, the [appropriate regulator] and the registrar of companies.

(5) The bank liquidator's resignation is effective as from the date on which the court receives the notice of [that] resignation, and the court [shall] endorse that date on the notice.

NOTES

Paras (2), (5): words in square brackets substituted by the Bank Insolvency (England and Wales) (Amendment) Rules 2010, SI 2010/2579, rr 3, 36(a), (c).

Para (3): substituted by SI 2010/2579, rr 3, 36(b).

Para (4): word in first pair of square brackets substituted by SI 2010/2579, rr 3, 36(a), (c); words in second pair of square brackets substituted by the Financial Services Act 2012 (Consequential Amendments and Transitional Provisions) Order 2013, SI 2013/472, art 3, Sch 2, para 163(f).

[7.181]
89 Advertisement of resignation

Apply rule 4.112 of the 1986 Rules.

[7.182]
90 Meeting of creditors to remove bank liquidator

(1) Apply rule 4.113 of the 1986 Rules.

(2) In paragraph (1), for "section 174(4)" substitute "section 109 of the Banking Act 2009".

(3) In paragraph (2), for "official receiver" substitute "Bank of England and the [appropriate regulator]".

(4) [For paragraph (4)] substitute—

"(4) Where the meeting passes a resolution that—
(a) the bank liquidator be removed;
(b) a new bank liquidator be appointed, or
(c) the bank liquidator not to be given their release
the bank liquidator [shall] be given a copy of that resolution and if it has been resolved to remove the bank liquidator, the bank liquidator [shall] be given a certificate to that effect."

(5) For paragraph (5) substitute—

"(5) If the creditors have resolved to appoint a new bank liquidator, the certificate of [that] appointment shall also be sent to the registrar of companies within that time and rule 4.100 shall apply."

NOTES

Para (3): words in square brackets substituted by the Financial Services Act 2012 (Consequential Amendments and Transitional Provisions) Order 2013, SI 2013/472, art 3, Sch 2, para 163(f).

Paras (4), (5): words in square brackets substituted by the Bank Insolvency (England and Wales) (Amendment) Rules 2010, SI 2010/2579, rr 3, 37.

[7.183]
91 Court's power to regulate meetings under rule 90

Apply rule 4.115 of the 1986 Rules. Leave out "or 4.114—CVL".

[7.184]
92 Procedure on removal

(1) Apply rule 4.116 of the 1986 Rules.

(2) For "official receiver", wherever it appears, substitute "out-going bank liquidator".

(3) For paragraph (3) substitute—

"(3) A copy of the certificate so endorsed shall be sent by the court to the outgoing bank liquidator and [to any new bank liquidator appointed]."

(4) Ignore paragraph (4).

NOTES

Para (3): in the Insolvency Rules 1986, r 4.116(3) (as set out) words in square brackets substituted by the Bank Insolvency (England and Wales) (Amendment) Rules 2010, SI 2010/2579, rr 3, 38.

[7.185]
93 Advertisement of removal

Apply rule 4.118 of the 1986 Rules.

[7.186]
94 Removal of bank liquidator by the court

(1) Apply rule 4.119 of the 1986 Rules.

(2) After paragraph (1) insert—

"[(1A)] If the liquidation committee has not yet passed a full payment resolution, the court shall dismiss any application under paragraph (1) where the application is made by someone other than the Bank of England, the [Financial Conduct Authority, the Prudential Regulation Authority] or the liquidation committee."

(3) In paragraph (2), for "at least 7 days' notice" substitute—

"(a) if the application is made before the passing of a full payment resolution, such notice as is reasonable in all the circumstances, and
(b) if the application is made after the passing of a full payment resolution, at least 7 days' notice.".

(4) In paragraph (4), leave out ", at least 14 days before the hearing,".

(5) After paragraph (4) insert—

"(4A) The notice and copies mentioned in paragraph (4) shall be sent—

(a) if the application is made before the passing of a full payment resolution, within such time so as to give the bank liquidator notice of the hearing as is reasonable in all the circumstances, and

(b) if the application is made after the passing of a full payment resolution, at least 14 days before the hearing.".

(6) In paragraph (6)—

(a) in sub-paragraph (a), for "official receiver" substitute "Bank of England and the [appropriate regulator]" and at the end insert "and", and

(b) leave out "and" at the end of sub-paragraph (b), and sub-paragraph (c).

NOTES

Para (2): in the Insolvency Rules 1986, r 4.119 (as set out) para (1A) renumbered as such by the Bank Insolvency (England and Wales) (Amendment) Rules 2010, SI 2010/2579, rr 3, 39; words in second pair of square brackets substituted by the Financial Services Act 2012 (Consequential Amendments and Transitional Provisions) Order 2013, SI 2013/472, art 3, Sch 2, para 163(e).

Para (6): words in square brackets substituted by the Financial Services Act 2012 (Consequential Amendments and Transitional Provisions) Order 2013, SI 2013/472, art 3, Sch 2, para 163(f).

[7.187]

95 Release of resigning or removed bank liquidator

(1) Apply rule 4.121 of the 1986 Rules.

(2) In paragraph (1), for "accepted by" substitute "notified to".

(3) For rule 4.109 substitute "rule 88 of the [2009 Rules]".

(4) In paragraph (3)—

(a) in sub paragraph (a) for "receive his resignation" substitute "be notified of his resignation"; and

(b) leave out "or" at the end of sub-paragraph (a) and at the end of sub-paragraph (b) insert—

", or

(c) the bank liquidator resigns, and the Bank of England has refused his release,".

(5) For paragraph (4) substitute—

"(4) When the Secretary of State gives the release, he shall certify it accordingly, file the certificate in court and send a copy to the registrar of companies."

NOTES

Para (3): words in square brackets substituted by the Bank Insolvency (England and Wales) (Amendment) Rules 2010, SI 2010/2579, rr 3, 40.

CHAPTER 3 RELEASE ON COMPLETION OF WINDING UP

[7.188]

96 Final meeting

(1) The bank liquidator shall give at least 14 days' notice of the final meeting of the liquidation committee to be held under section 115 of the 2009 Act to the following—

(a) the [appropriate regulator],

(b) the FSCS,

(c) the Bank of England,

(d) the Treasury,

(e) the registrar of companies, and

(f) the members of the liquidation committee.

(2) The bank liquidator's final report to be laid before the meeting under that section shall contain an account of the liquidator's administration of the winding up, including—

(a) details as to how Objective 1 was achieved having regard, in particular, to the expenses of the bank liquidator in connection with that Objective,

(b) a summary of the bank liquidator's receipts and payments,

(c) a statement that the bank liquidator has reconciled his account with that which is held by the Secretary of State in respect of the winding up, and

(d) a statement as to the amount paid to unsecured creditors by virtue of the application of section 176A (prescribed part) of the 1986 Act.

(3) At the same time that notice of the final meeting is sent out, the bank liquidator shall file the final report in court and send it to the registrar of companies.

[(4) The bank liquidator shall give notice to all creditors and contributories that the final report is available, either on request to the bank liquidator or at Companies House, and shall cause that notice to be gazetted (and may advertise the notice by such other method as the bank liquidator sees fit) at least 14 days before the final meeting is held.]

(5) At the final meeting, the liquidation committee may question the bank liquidator with respect to any matter contained in the final report, and may resolve against the bank liquidator being released.

(6) The bank liquidator shall give notice to the court that the final meeting has been held and the notice shall state whether or not he has been given his release.

(7) Where the liquidation committee does not resolve against the bank liquidator's release, the bank liquidator vacates office at the end of the meeting and has his release when the notice in paragraph (6) is filed in court.

(8) If there is no quorum present at the final meeting, the bank liquidator shall report to the court that a final meeting was summoned in accordance with section 115 of the 2009 Act, but there was no quorum present; and the final meeting is then deemed to have been held, and the liquidation committee not to have resolved against the bank liquidator being released.

(9) If the liquidation committee resolves against the bank liquidator having his release then rule 95 applies.

NOTES

Para (1): words in square brackets substituted by the Financial Services Act 2012 (Consequential Amendments and Transitional Provisions) Order 2013, SI 2013/472, art 3, Sch 2, para 163(f).

Para (4): substituted by the Bank Insolvency (England and Wales) (Amendment) Rules 2010, SI 2010/2579, rr 3, 41.

[7.189]
97 Rule as to reporting

Apply rule 4.125A of the 1986 Rules. [For "Rule 4.124 or 4.125" substitute "Rule 96 of the 2009 Rules"].

NOTES

Words in square brackets substituted by the Bank Insolvency (England and Wales) (Amendment) Rules 2010, SI 2010/2579, rr 3, 42.

CHAPTER 4 REMUNERATION

[7.190]
98 Fixing of remuneration

(1) Apply rule 4.127 of the 1986 Rules.

(2) In paragraph (3), leave out from the beginning to "receiver".

(3) For paragraph (5) substitute—

"(5) If, under rule 41(2), the liquidation committee ceases to exist at the end of the first meeting of creditors, [the terms on which the bank liquidator is to be remunerated determined] by the initial liquidation committee under rule 18 can be redetermined by a resolution of a meeting of creditors, and paragraph (4) applies to the determination of the creditors as it does to the determination of the liquidation committee."

(4) In paragraph (6), for the words from the beginning to "his" substitute "Where the bank liquidator's".

NOTES

Para (3): in the Insolvency Rules 1986, r 4.127(5) (as set out) words in square brackets substituted by the Bank Insolvency (England and Wales) (Amendment) Rules 2010, SI 2010/2579, rr 3, 43.

[7.191]
99 Bank liquidator's entitlement to remuneration where it is not fixed under rule 98

(1) Apply rule 4.127A of the 1986 Rules.

(2) In paragraph (1), for the words from "liquidator" to "his" substitute "bank liquidator's".

(3) In paragraph (2), after "Schedule 6" add "to the 1986 Rules as applied by [the Schedule to the 2009 Rules]".

NOTES

Para (3): words in square brackets substituted by the Bank Insolvency (England and Wales) (Amendment) Rules 2010, SI 2010/2579, rr 3, 44.

[7.192]
100 Bank liquidator's remuneration where he realises assets on behalf of chargeholder

(1) Apply rule 4.127B of the 1986 Rules.

(2) In paragraph (1), for the words from "liquidator" to "and" substitute "bank liquidator".

(3) In paragraphs (2) and (3), after "Schedule 6" add "to the 1986 Rules as applied by [the Schedule to the 2009 Rules]".

NOTES

Para (3): words in square brackets substituted by the Bank Insolvency (England and Wales) (Amendment) Rules 2010, SI 2010/2579, rr 3, 45.

[7.193]
101 Other matters affecting remuneration

Apply rule 4.128 of the 1986 Rules.

[7.194]
102 Recourse of bank liquidator to meeting of creditors

Apply rule 4.129 of the 1986 Rules.

[7.195]
103 Recourse to the court

Apply rule 4.130 of the 1986 Rules.

[7.196]
104 Creditors' claim that remuneration is excessive

Apply rule 4.131 of the 1986 Rules.

[7.197]
105 Primacy of Objective 1

Nothing done under a rule in this chapter may prejudice the achievement of Objective 1.

CHAPTER 5 SUPPLEMENTARY PROVISIONS

[7.198]
106 Replacement Bank liquidator

(1) Where the bank liquidator vacates his office for any reason (including death) other than by removal by a meeting of creditors in accordance with rule 90, the Bank of England shall appoint a new bank liquidator as soon as practicable.

[(2) Where a bank liquidator has been removed by a meeting of creditors, and no resolution has been passed by that meeting to appoint a new bank liquidator, the Bank of England shall appoint a new bank liquidator as soon as practicable.]

(3) The Bank of England shall file in court the document appointing the new bank liquidator ("[the certificate of appointment]") together with statements to the effect that the new bank liquidator—

(a) is qualified to act as an insolvency practitioner in accordance with section 390 of the 1986 Act, and

(b) consents to act as the bank liquidator.

(4) The bank liquidator shall send a copy of the [certificate of appointment] to the [appropriate regulator] and registrar of companies.

(5) . . .

NOTES

Para (2): substituted by the Bank Insolvency (England and Wales) (Amendment) Rules 2010, SI 2010/2579, rr 3, 46(a).

Para (3): words in square brackets substituted by SI 2010/2579, rr 3, 46(b), (c).

Para (4): words in first pair of square brackets substituted by SI 2010/2579, rr 3, 46(b), (c); words in second pair of square brackets substituted by the Financial Services Act 2012 (Consequential Amendments and Transitional Provisions) Order 2013, SI 2013/472, art 3, Sch 2, para 163(f).

Para (5): revoked by SI 2010/2579, rr 3, 46(d).

[7.199]
107 Bank liquidator deceased

(1) Unless notice of the death of the bank liquidator has been given under paragraph (2) or (3), it is the duty of the bank liquidator's personal representatives, where the bank liquidator has died, to give notice of that fact to the Bank of England and the liquidation committee, specifying the date of the death.

(2) If the deceased bank liquidator was a partner in a firm, notice may be given to the Bank of England, the [appropriate regulator] and liquidation committee by a partner in the firm who is qualified to act as an insolvency practitioner, or is a member of any body recognised by the Secretary of State for the authorisation of insolvency practitioners.

(3) Notice of the death may also be given by any person producing the relevant death certificate or a copy of it to the Bank of England, the [appropriate regulator] and the liquidation committee.

(4) The Bank of England shall give notice to the court, for the purpose of fixing the date of the deceased bank liquidator's release.

NOTES

Paras (2), (3): words in square brackets substituted by the Financial Services Act 2012 (Consequential Amendments and Transitional Provisions) Order 2013, SI 2013/472, art 3, Sch 2, para 163(f).

[7.200]
108 Loss of qualification as insolvency practitioner

(1) Apply rule 4.134 of the 1986 Rules. For paragraph (2) substitute—

"(2) The bank liquidator shall immediately give notice of his doing to the Bank of England.
(3) The Bank of England shall file a copy of this notice in court."

[7.201]
109 Resignation of the bank liquidator

(1) This rule applies where the bank liquidator was appointed by the bank insolvency order or by the Bank of England.

(2) The bank liquidator can only resign—
  (a) after the liquidation committee have passed a full payment resolution, and
  (b) with the consent of the Bank of England.

(3) Before calling a meeting of creditors under rule 87 to receive notice of the bank liquidator's resignation, the bank liquidator must write to the Bank of England notifying it of the intention to resign.

(4) The Bank of England shall notify the bank liquidator in writing within 21 days as to whether it consents to the resignation; if the Bank of England does not consent to the resignation, it shall set out its reasons in writing.

(5) The bank liquidator, if not content with the Bank of England's response, may apply to the Court for directions under section 168(3) of the 1986 Act.

[7.202]
110 Notice to Bank of England of intention to vacate office

(1) This rule applies where the bank liquidator was appointed by a meeting of creditors.

(2) Apply rule 4.137 of the 1986 Rules.

(3) For "official receiver", wherever it appears, substitute "Bank of England" and for "receive his resignation" substitute "be notified of his resignation".

[7.203]
111 Bank liquidator's duties on vacating office

Apply rule 4.138 of the 1986 Rules. Ignore paragraph (3).

[7.204]
112 Power of court to set aside certain transactions

(1) Apply rule 4.149 of the 1986 Rules.

(2) In paragraph (2)—
  (a) leave out "either", and
  (b) leave out "or" at the end of sub-paragraph (a), and after sub-paragraph (b) insert—

  ", or
  (c) it is shown to the court's satisfaction that the transaction was entered into by the liquidator for the purpose of achieving Objective 1.".

[7.205]
113 Rule against solicitation

(1) Apply rule 4.150 of the 1986 Rules.

PART 10
THE LIQUIDATION COMMITTEE

[7.206]
114 Application of rules in this Part

The rules in this Part apply only in relation to the liquidation committee established . . . after a full payment resolution has been passed.

NOTES

Words omitted revoked by the Bank Insolvency (England and Wales) (Amendment) Rules 2010, SI 2010/2579, rr 3, 47.

[7.207]
115 Membership of committee

(1) Apply rule 4.152 of the 1986 Rules.

(2) For paragraph (1) substitute—

["(1) Subject to rule 41(1) of the 2009 Rules and rule 4.154 as applied by rule 117 of the 2009 Rules, the liquidation committee shall consist of either 3 or 5 creditors of the bank, elected by the meeting of creditors held under rule 41 of the 2009 Rules."]

(3) Ignore paragraphs (2), (4) and (7) and ignore any reference to contributory members in paragraph (6).

NOTES

Para (2): the Insolvency Rules 1986, r 4.152(1) (as set out) substituted by the Bank Insolvency (England and Wales) (Amendment) Rules 2010, SI 2010/2579, rr 3, 48.

[7.208]
116 Formalities of establishment

Apply rule 4.153 of the 1986 Rules . . .

NOTES

Words omitted revoked by the Bank Insolvency (England and Wales) (Amendment) Rules 2010, SI 2010/2579, rr 3, 49.

[7.209]
117 Committee established by contributories

(1) Apply rule 4.154 of the 1986 Rules.

(2) For paragraph (1) substitute—

"(1) This rule applies where the outcome of the creditors' meeting summoned by the bank liquidator under rule 41 of the . . . 2009 Rules is, (by virtue of rule 41 (2)), that the liquidation committee ceases to exist at the end of the meeting.".

(3) In paragraph (2), for "that section" substitute "section 141 of the Act".

(4) In paragraph (4) for "at least 3 and not more than 5", substitute "3 or 5".

NOTES

Para (2): in the Insolvency Rules 1986, r 4.154(1) (as set out) words omitted revoked by the Bank Insolvency (England and Wales) (Amendment) Rules 2010, SI 2010/2579, rr 3, 50.

[7.210]
118 Obligations of liquidator to committee

Apply rule 4.155 of the 1986 Rules.

[7.211]
119 Meetings of the committee

Apply rule 4.156 of the 1986 Rules.

[7.212]
120 The chair at meetings

Apply rule 4.157 of the 1986 Rules.

[7.213]
121 Quorum

A meeting of the committee is duly constituted if due notice of it has been given to all the members, and at least 2 members are present or represented.

[7.214]
122 Committee-members' representatives

Apply rule 4.159 of the 1986 Rules . . .

NOTES

Words omitted revoked by the Bank Insolvency (England and Wales) (Amendment) Rules 2010, SI 2010/2579, rr 3, 51.

[7.215]
123 Resignation

Apply rule 4.160 of the 1986 Rules.

[7.216]
124 Termination of membership

Apply rule 4.161 of the 1986 Rules.

[7.217]
125 Removal

Apply rule 4.162 of the 1986 Rules.

[7.218]
126 Vacancy (creditor members)

Apply rule 4.163 of the 1986 Rules.

[7.219]
127 Vacancy (contributory members)

Apply rule 4.164 of the 1986 Rules.

[7.220]
128 Voting rights and resolutions

Apply rule 4.165 of the 1986 Rules.

[7.221]
129 Resolutions by post

Apply rule 4.167 of the 1986 Rules.

[7.222]
130 Liquidator's reports

Apply rule 4.168 of the 1986 Rules.

[7.223]
131 Expenses of members, etc

Apply rule 4.169 of the 1986 Rules.

[7.224]
132 Dealings by committee-members and others

Apply rule 4.170 of the 1986 Rules.

[7.225]
133 Composition of committee when creditors paid in full

(1) Apply rule 4.171 of the 1986 Rules.

(2) For paragraph (4) substitute—

"(4) The members of the liquidation committee will cease to be members at the end of the final meeting held under rule 96 of the [2009 Rules]."

NOTES

Para (2): in the Insolvency Rules 1986, r 4.171(4) (as set out) words in square brackets substituted by the Bank Insolvency (England and Wales) (Amendment) Rules 2010, SI 2010/2579, rr 3, 52.

[7.226]
134 Committee's functions vested in the Secretary of State

Apply rule 4.172 of the 1986 Rules. Ignore paragraph (2).

[7.227]
135 Formal defects

Apply rule 4.172A of the 1986 Rules.

PART 11
COLLECTION AND DISTRIBUTION OF BANK'S ASSETS BY BANK LIQUIDATOR

[7.228]
136 General duties of bank liquidator

Apply rule 4.179 of the 1986 Rules.

[7.229]
137 General qualification on powers

In exercising any power conferred on the bank liquidator by this Part before a full payment resolution has been passed, the bank liquidator shall exercise it consistently with Objective 1.

[7.230]
138 Manner of distributing assets

Apply rule 4.180 of the 1986 Rules.

[7.231]
139 Debts of insolvent company to rank equally

Apply rule 4.181 of the 1986 Rules.

[7.232]
140 Supplementary provisions as to dividend

Apply rule 4.182 of the 1986 Rules.

[7.233]
141 Division of unsold assets

Apply rule 4.183 of the 1986 Rules.

[7.234]
142 General powers of the liquidator

Apply rule 4.184 of the 1986 Rules. In paragraph (1) leave out "section 165(2) or".

[7.235]
143 Enforced delivery up of company's property

Apply rule 4.185 of the 1986 Rules.

[7.236]
144 Final distribution

Apply rule 4.186 of the 1986 Rules. For "Part 11 of the Rules", substitute "Part 21 of the 2009 Rules".

PART 12
DISCLAIMER

[7.237]
145 Liquidator's notice of disclaimer

Apply rule 4.187 of the 1986 Rules.

[7.238]
146 Communication of disclaimer to persons interested

Apply rule 4.188 of the 1986 Rules.

[7.239]
147 Additional notices

Apply rule 4.189 of the 1986 Rules.

[7.240]
148 Duty to keep court informed

Apply rule 4.190 of the 1986 Rules.

[7.241]
149 Application by interested party under s 178(5)

Apply rule 4.191 of the 1986 Rules.

[7.242]
150 Interest in property to be declared on request

Apply rule 4.192 of the 1986 Rules.

[7.243]
151 Disclaimer presumed valid and effective

Apply rule 4.193 of the 1986 Rules. For "Chapter" substitute "Part".

[7.244]
152 Application for exercise of court's powers under s 181

Apply rule 4.194 of the 1986 Rules.

PART 13
SETTLEMENT OF LIST OF CONTRIBUTORIES

[7.245]
153 Preliminary

Apply rule 4.195 of the 1986 Rules.

[7.246]
154 Primacy of Objective 1

Where the bank liquidator considers that the carrying out of a duty imposed by a rule in this Part would prejudice the achievement of Objective 1, the bank liquidator shall postpone the carrying out of that duty until [the bank liquidator] considers that the carrying out of the duty would no longer be likely to prejudice the achievement of that Objective.

NOTES

Words in square brackets substituted by the Bank Insolvency (England and Wales) (Amendment) Rules 2010, SI 2010/2579, rr 3, 53.

[7.247]
155 Duty of liquidator to settle list

Apply rule 4.196 of the 1986 Rules.

[7.248]
156 Form of list

Apply rule 4.197 of the 1986 Rules.

[7.249]
157 Procedure for settling list

Apply rule 4.198 of the 1986 Rules.

[7.250]
158 Application to court for variation of the list

Apply rule 4.199 of the 1986 Rules.

[7.251]
159 Variation of, or addition to, the list

Apply rule 4.200 of the 1986 Rules . . .

NOTES

Words omitted revoked by the Bank Insolvency (England and Wales) (Amendment) Rules 2010, SI 2010/2579, rr 3, 54.

[7.252]
160 Costs not to fall on bank liquidator

The bank liquidator is not personally liable for any costs incurred by a person in respect of an application to set aside or vary the bank liquidator's act or decision in settling the list of contributories, or varying or adding to the list, unless the court makes an order to that effect.

PART 14
CALLS

[7.253]
161 Calls by [bank] liquidator

Apply rule 4.202 of the 1986 Rules.

NOTES

Provision heading: word in square brackets substituted by the Bank Insolvency (England and Wales) (Amendment) Rules 2010, SI 2010/2579, rr 3, 55.

[7.254]
162 Control by bank liquidation committee

Apply rule 4.203 of the 1986 Rules.

[7.255]
163 Application to court for leave to make a call

Apply rule 4.204 of the 1986 Rules.

[7.256]
164 Making and enforcement of the call

Apply rule 4.205 of the 1986 Rules.

PART 15
SPECIAL MANAGER

[7.257]
165 Appointment and remuneration

Apply rule 4.206 of the 1986 Rules.

[7.258]
166 Security

Apply rule 4.207 of the 1986 Rules.

[7.259]
167 Failure to give or keep up security

Apply rule 4.208 of the 1986 Rules.

[7.260]
168 Accounting

Apply rule 4.209 of the 1986 Rules.

[7.261]
169 Termination of appointment

Apply rule 4.210 of the 1986 Rules.

PART 16
ORDER OF PAYMENT AS TO COSTS, ETC OUT OF ASSETS

[7.262]
170 General rule as to priority

(1) Apply rule 4.218 of the 1986 Rules.

(2) In paragraph (3)—

(a) ignore sub-paragraphs (a)(iii) and (iv), (b), and (d),

(b) in sub-paragraph (c) leave out the words from "or section 415A" to the end, and

(c) in sub-paragraph (la), leave out the words from "in any case" to the end.

[7.263]
171 Litigation expenses and property subject to a floating charge—general application

Apply rule 4.218A of the 1986 Rules.

[7.264]
172 Litigation expenses and property subject to a floating charge—requirement for approval or authorisation

Apply rule 4.218B of the 1986 Rules.

[7.265]
173 Litigation expenses and property subject to a floating charge—request for approval or authorisation

Apply rule 4.218C of the 1986 Rules.

[7.266]
174 Litigation expenses and property subject to a floating charge—grant of approval or authorisation

Apply rule 4.218D of the 1986 Rules.

[7.267]
175 Litigation expenses and property subject to a floating charge—application to court by the bank liquidator

Apply rule 4.218E of the 1986 Rules.

[7.268]
176 Saving for powers of the court

Apply rule 4.220 of the 1986 Rules.

PART 17
MISCELLANEOUS RULES

CHAPTER 1 RETURN OF CAPITAL

[7.269]
177 Application to court for order authorising return of capital

Apply rule 4.221 of the 1986 Rules.

[7.270]
178 Procedure for return of capital

Apply rule 4.222 of the 1986 Rules.

CHAPTER 2 CONCLUSION OF BANK INSOLVENCY

[7.271]
179 Secretary of State's directions under [section] 116 of the 2009 Act

(1) Where the Secretary of State gives a direction under section 116 of the 2009 Act (application by an interested person for postponement of dissolution) the Secretary of State shall send 2 copies of the direction to that applicant.

(2) Of those copies, 1 shall be sent by the applicant to the registrar of companies to comply with section 116(4) of the 2009 Act.

NOTES

Provision heading: word in square brackets substituted by the Bank Insolvency (England and Wales) (Amendment) Rules 2010, SI 2010/2579, rr 3, 56.

[7.272]
180 Procedure following appeal under [section] 116 of the 2009 Act

Following an appeal under section 116(2) of the 2009 Act (against a decision of the Secretary of State under that section) the court shall send 2 sealed copies of its order to the person in whose favour the appeal was determined, and that party shall send 1 of the copies to the registrar of companies.

NOTES

Provision heading: word in square brackets substituted by the Bank Insolvency (England and Wales) (Amendment) Rules 2010, SI 2010/2579, rr 3, 57.

CHAPTER 3 LEAVE TO ACT AS DIRECTOR, ETC OF BANK WITH PROHIBITED NAME

[7.273]
181 Preliminary

Apply rule 4.226 of the 1986 Rules. In paragraph (c), leave out the words from "whether" to the end.

[7.274]
182 Application for leave under s 216(3) before passing of full payment resolution

Where an application for leave under section 216 of the 1986 Act is made before a full payment resolution has been passed, it may only be made with the consent of the bank liquidator.

[7.275]

183 Consideration of application for leave under s 216(3)

Apply rule 4.227 of the 1986 Rules.

[7.276]

184 First excepted case

Apply rule 4.228 of the 1986 Rules. In paragraph (1)(b)(ii) ignore the reference to administrator.

[7.277]

185 Second excepted case

Apply rule 4.229 of the 1986 Rules . . .

NOTES

Words omitted revoked by the Bank Insolvency (England and Wales) (Amendment) Rules 2010, SI 2010/2579, rr 3, 58.

[7.278]

186 Third excepted case

Apply rule 4.230 of the 1986 Rules. In paragraph (a), for "liquidating company went into liquidation" substitute "bank went into bank insolvency".

[7.279]

187 Further exception

The court's leave under section 216(3) of the Act is not required in respect of anything done by a person in connection with the exercise of a stabilisation power under Part 1 of the 2009 Act.

PART 18
COURT PROCEDURE AND PRACTICE

CHAPTER 1 APPLICATIONS (GENERAL)

[7.280]

188 Preliminary

This Part applies to any application made to the court under [Part 2 of] the 2009 Act or these Rules except an application under section 95 of the 2009 Act for a bank insolvency order.

NOTES

Words in square brackets inserted by the Bank Insolvency (England and Wales) (Amendment) Rules 2010, SI 2010/2579, rr 3, 59.

[7.281]

189 Interpretation

Apply rule 7.2 of the 1986 Rules. [In paragraph (1), leave out from the second "and" to the end of the paragraph.]

NOTES

Words in square brackets added by the Bank Insolvency (England and Wales) (Amendment) Rules 2010, SI 2010/2579, rr 3, 60.

[7.282]

190 Form and contents of application

Apply rule 7.3 of the 1986 Rules.

[7.283]

191 Application under section 176A(5) to disapply section 176A

(1) Apply rule 7.3A of the 1986 Rules.

(2) In paragraph (1), ignore "administrator or receiver."

(3) Ignore paragraph (2)(a).

[7.284]

192 Filing and service of application

Apply rule 7.4 of the 1986 Rules.

[7.285]

193 Notice of application under section 176A(5)

Apply rule 7.4A of the 1986 Rules. Leave out the words from "save that notice" to the end.

[7.286]

194 Other hearings without notice

Apply rule 7.5 of the 1986 Rules.

[7.287]
195 Hearing of application

Apply rule 7.6 of the 1986 Rules.

[7.288]
196 Use of evidence

Apply rule 7.7 of the 1986 Rules.

[7.289]
197 Filing and service of witness statements

Apply rule 7.8 of the 1986 Rules. Ignore paragraph (2).

[7.290]
198 Use of reports

(1) Unless the application involves other parties, or the court orders otherwise, a report may be filed in court instead of a witness statement by—
  (a) the bank liquidator,
  (b) the provisional bank liquidator, or
  (c) the special manager.

(2) In any case where a report is filed instead of a witness statement, the report shall be treated for the purposes of rule 197, and any hearing before the court, as if it were a witness statement.

[7.291]
199 Adjournment of hearings: directions

Apply rule 7.10 of the 1986 Rules. [In paragraph (2)(c)(iii), for "Rule 7.9(1)(b)" substitute "Rule 198(1) of the 2009 Rules".]

NOTES

Words in square brackets inserted by the Bank Insolvency (England and Wales) (Amendment) Rules 2010, SI 2010/2579, rr 3, 61.

CHAPTER 3 SHORTHAND WRITERS

[7.292]
200 Nomination and appointment of shorthand writers

(1) Apply rule 7.16 of the 1986 Rules.

(2) In paragraph (1) leave out "and, in a county court, the registrar".

(3) In paragraph (2) leave out "133" and "[251N,] 290 or 366".

(4) Ignore paragraph (3).

NOTES

Para (3): reference in square brackets inserted by the Bank Insolvency (England and Wales) (Amendment) Rules 2010, SI 2010/2579, rr 3, 62.

[7.293]
201 Remuneration

Apply rule 7.17 of the 1986 Rules.

CHAPTER 4 ENFORCEMENT PROCEDURES

[7.294]
202 Enforcement of court orders

(1) Apply rule 7.19 of the 1986 Rules.

(2) Ignore paragraph (2).

[7.295]
203 Orders enforcing compliance with the rules

(1) The court may, on the application of the bank liquidator (or the provisional bank liquidator as the case may be,) make such orders as it thinks necessary for the enforcement of obligations falling on any person in accordance with—
  (a) section 143(2) (liquidator to furnish information, books, papers etc) of the 1986 Act or
  (b) section 235 (duty to cooperate with liquidator) of that Act.

(2) An order of the court under this rule may provide that all the costs of and incidental to the application for it shall be borne by the person against whom the order is made.

[7.296]
204 Warrants (general provisions)

(1) A warrant issued by the court under any provision of the 1986 Act shall be addressed to such officer of the High Court as the warrant specifies, or to any constable.

(2) The person described in section 236(5) of the 1986 Act as the prescribed officer of the court is the tipstaff and his assistants of the court.

(3) In this Chapter, references to property include books, papers and records.

[7.297]
205 Warrants under section 236

Apply rule 7.23 of the 1986 Rules. In paragraph (1), leave out "[251N] or 366 (the equivalent in bankruptcy)".

NOTES

Reference in square brackets inserted by the Bank Insolvency (England and Wales) (Amendment) Rules 2010, SI 2010/2579, rr 3, 63.

CHAPTER 5 COURT RECORDS AND RETURNS

[7.298]
206 Title of proceedings

Every proceeding under Part 2 of the 2009 Act shall, with any necessary additions, be titled "IN THE MATTER OF . . . . (naming the bank to which the proceedings relate) AND IN THE MATTER OF THE BANKING ACT 2009".

[7.299]
207 Court records

Apply rule 7.27 of the 1986 Rules.

[7.300]
208 Inspection of records

Apply rule 7.28 of the 1986 Rules.

[7.301]
209 File of court proceedings and inspection

(1) The Court shall open and maintain a file for each bank insolvency and (subject to the direction of the registrar) all documents relating to that bank insolvency shall be placed on that file.

(2) Where a file has been opened under paragraph (1), the following have the right, at all reasonable times, to inspect that file—

- (a) the bank liquidator,
- (b) any person stating in writing that they are a creditor of the bank to which the bank insolvency relates,
- (c) a member of the bank,
- (d) any person who is, or at any time has been, a director or officer of the bank to which the bank insolvency relates,
- (e) any person who is a contributory of the bank to which the bank insolvency relates, and
- (f) the Bank of England, the [appropriate regulator] and the FSCS.

(3) The right of inspection conferred on any person by paragraph (2) may be exercised on their behalf by a person properly authorised by them.

(4) Any person may, with permission of the court, inspect the file.

(5) The right of inspection conferred by this rule is not exercisable in respect of documents, or parts of documents, which the court has directed (either generally or specially) are not to be open to inspection without the court's permission.

(6) An application for a direction of the court under paragraph (5) may be made by the bank liquidator or by any party appearing to the court to have an interest in the bank insolvency.

(7) If, for the purposes of powers conferred by the 1986 Act, the 2009 Act or these rules, the Secretary of State wishes to inspect the file on a bank insolvency and requests the court to transmit the file, the court shall comply with the request or, if the file is for the time being in use for the court's own purposes, as soon as the file is no longer in such use.

[(8) Rule 208 applies in respect of the file in any bank insolvency as it applies in respect of court records.]

NOTES

Para (2): words in square brackets substituted by the Financial Services Act 2012 (Consequential Amendments and Transitional Provisions) Order 2013, SI 2013/472, art 3, Sch 2, para 163(f).

Para (8): substituted by the Bank Insolvency (England and Wales) (Amendment) Rules 2010, SI 2010/2579, rr 3, 64.

210 (*Revoked by the Bank Insolvency (England and Wales) (Amendment) Rules 2010, SI 2010/2579, rr 3, 65.*)

CHAPTER 6 COSTS AND DETAILED ASSESSMENT

[7.302]
211 Application of the CPR

Apply rule 7.33 of the 1986 Rules.

[7.303]
212 Requirement to assess costs by the detailed procedure

(1) Apply rule 7.34 of the 1986 Rules.

(2) In paragraph (1)—
(a) for "company insolvency" and "liquidation" substitute "bank insolvency",
(b) ignore sub-paragraph (b), and
(c) for the words from "court to which" to the end substitute "High Court".

(3) In paragraph (2), leave out "or creditors".

(4) In paragraph (5), for "trustee in bankruptcy or a liquidator" substitute "bank liquidator."

(5) Ignore paragraph (6).

[7.304]
213 Procedure where detailed assessment required

Apply rule 7.35 of the 1986 Rules. Ignore paragraph (6).

[7.305]
214 Costs of officers charged with executions of writs or other process

(1) Apply rule 7.36 of the 1986 Rules.

(2) In paragraph (1)(a), leave out "or 346(2)".

(3) In paragraph (1)(b), leave out "or 346(3)".

[7.306]
215 Costs paid otherwise than out of the insolvent estate

Apply rule 7.38 of the 1986 Rules.

[7.307]
216 Award of costs against responsible insolvency practitioner

(1) Apply rule 7.39 of the 1986 Rules.

(2) Leave out from the beginning to "expenses" and "the official receiver or".

[7.308]
217 Application for costs

(1) Apply rule 7.40 of the 1986 Rules.

(2) In paragraph (1) for "insolvency" substitute "bank insolvency".

(3) In paragraph (2), leave out the words from ", and, in winding up" to the end.

(4) In paragraph (3), leave out "and, where appropriate, the official receiver".

[(5) Ignore paragraph (3A).]

NOTES

Para (5): added by the Bank Insolvency (England and Wales) (Amendment) Rules 2010, SI 2010/2579, rr 3, 66.

[7.309]
218 Costs and expenses of witnesses

(1) Apply rule 7.41 of the 1986 Rules.

(2) In paragraph (1), leave out "the bankrupt or [the debtor or]".

(3) Ignore paragraph (2).

NOTES

Para (2): words in square brackets inserted by the Bank Insolvency (England and Wales) (Amendment) Rules 2010, SI 2010/2579, rr 3, 67.

[7.310]
219 Final costs certificate

Apply rule 7.42 of the 1986 Rules.

CHAPTER 7 PERSONS INCAPABLE OF MANAGING THEIR AFFAIRS

[7.311]
220 Introductory

Apply rule 7.43 of the 1986 Rules. In paragraph (1), for (a), substitute "by reason of being a protected person within the meaning of Part 21 of the CPR or".

[7.312]
221 Appointment of another person to act

Apply rule 7.44 of the 1986 Rules. Ignore paragraph (3)(c).

[7.313]
222 Witness statement in support of application

(1) Apply rule 7.45 of the 1986 Rules.

(2) In paragraph (1) leave out from the beginning to "receiver".

(3) Ignore paragraph (2).

[7.314]
223 Service of notices following appointment

Apply rule 7.46 of the 1986 Rules.

CHAPTER 8 APPEALS IN BANK INSOLVENCY PROCEEDINGS

[7.315]
224 Appeals and review of court orders

(1) The High Court may review, rescind or vary any order made by it in the exercise of its jurisdiction under Part 2 of the Banking Act 2009.

(2) An appeal from a decision of a registrar of the High Court lies, with the permission of the registrar or a judge of the High Court, to a single judge of the High Court, and a second appeal lies, with the permission of the Court of Appeal to the Court of Appeal.

(3) An appeal of a decision of first instance of a judge of the High Court lies, with the permission of the judge or the Court of Appeal, to the Court of Appeal.

(4) . . .

NOTES

Para (4): revoked by the Bank Insolvency (England and Wales) (Amendment) Rules 2010, SI 2010/2579, rr 3, 68.

[7.316]
225 Procedure on appeal

Part 52 of the CPR applies with regard to the procedure for appeals.

[7.317]
226 Appeal against a decision of the Secretary of State

Apply rule 7.50 of the 1986 Rules. Ignore . . . paragraph (2).

NOTES

Words omitted revoked by the Bank Insolvency (England and Wales) (Amendment) Rules 2010, SI 2010/2579, rr 3, 69.

CHAPTER 9 GENERAL

[7.318]
227 Principal court rules and practice to apply

(1) The CPR and the practice and procedure of the High Court (including any practice direction) apply to bank insolvency proceedings in the High Court, with any necessary modifications, except so far as inconsistent with these Rules.

(2) All bank insolvency proceedings shall be allocated to the multi-track for which CPR Part 29 makes provision . . . , accordingly those provisions of the CPR which provide for allocation questionnaires and track allocation do not apply.

NOTES

Para (2): word omitted revoked by the Bank Insolvency (England and Wales) (Amendment) Rules 2010, SI 2010/2579, rr 3, 70.

[7.319]
228 Right of attendance

Apply rule 7.53 of the 1986 Rules. In paragraph (1) for "company insolvency proceedings" substitute "bank insolvency proceedings".

[7.320]
229 Restriction on concurrent proceedings and remedies

Where in a bank insolvency, the court makes an order staying any action, execution or legal process against the property of the bank, service of the order may be effected by delivering a sealed copy [to the address for service of the claimant or other person having carriage of the proceedings to be stayed].

NOTES

Words in square brackets substituted by the Bank Insolvency (England and Wales) (Amendment) Rules 2010, SI 2010/2579, rr 3, 71.

[7.321]
230 Security in court

Apply rule 7.58 of the 1986 Rules.

Part 7B Special Insolvency Regimes

[7.322]
231 Payment into court

Apply rule 7.59 of the 1986 Rules.

[7.323]
232 Further information and disclosure

(1) Apply rule 7.60 of the 1986 Rules.

(2) After paragraph (2) insert—

> "(3) Before the passing of a full payment resolution the court shall only grant an order on an application under paragraph (1)(b) if satisfied that granting the order is unlikely to prejudice the achievement of Objective 1."

[7.324]
233 Office copies of documents

Apply rule 7.61 of the 1986 Rules.

PART 19
PROXIES AND COMPANY REPRESENTATION

[7.325]
234 Definition of "proxy"

(1) Apply rule 8.1 of the 1986 Rules.

(2) In paragraph (2) leave out "company".

[(3) In paragraph (4), for "chairman of the meeting" to "official receiver" substitute "chair of the meeting or the bank liquidator.".]

NOTES

Para (3): substituted by the Bank Insolvency (England and Wales) (Amendment) Rules 2010, SI 2010/2579, rr 3, 72.

[7.326]
235 Issue and use of forms

Apply rule 8.2 of the 1986 Rules.

[7.327]
236 Use of proxies at meetings

Apply rule 8.3 of the 1986 Rules. Ignore paragraph (2).

[7.328]
237 Retention of proxies

Apply rule 8.4 of the 1986 Rules.

[7.329]
238 Right of inspection

(1) Apply rule 8.5 of the 1986 Rules.

(2) . . .

(3) For paragraph (2) substitute—

> "(2) The reference in paragraph (1) to creditors is to those creditors who have proved their debts, but this does not include a person whose proof has been wholly rejected for purposes of voting, dividend or otherwise.".

(4) Ignore paragraph (3)(b).

NOTES

Para (2): revoked by the Bank Insolvency (England and Wales) (Amendment) Rules 2010, SI 2010/2579, rr 3, 73.

[7.330]
239 Proxy-holder with financial interest

Apply rule 8.6 of the 1986 Rules.

[7.331]
[240 Company representation

Apply rule 8.7 of the 1986 Rules. In paragraph (1) omit "of creditors or".]

NOTES

Substituted by the Bank Insolvency (England and Wales) (Amendment) Rules 2010, SI 2010/2579, rr 3, 74.

PART 20
EXAMINATION OF PERSONS CONCERNED IN BANK INSOLVENCY

[7.332]
241 Preliminary

(1) The rules in this Part relate to applications to the court for an order under section 236 of the 1986 Act (inquiry into company's dealings when it is, or is alleged to be, insolvent).

(2) The following definitions apply—
- (a) the person in respect of whom an order is applied for is "the respondent",
- (b) "the applicable section" is section 236 of the 1986 Act, and
- (c) the bank is "the insolvent".

[7.333]
242 Form and contents of application

Apply rule 9.2 of the 1986 Rules.

[7.334]
243 Order for examination, etc

Apply rule 9.3 of the 1986 Rules.

[7.335]
244 Procedure for examination

Apply rule 9.4 of the 1986 Rules. [In paragraph (4), omit "or 366".]

NOTES

Words in square brackets inserted by the Bank Insolvency (England and Wales) (Amendment) Rules 2010, SI 2010/2579, rr 3, 75.

[7.336]
245 Record of examination

Apply rule 9.5 of the 1986 Rules.

[7.337]
246 Costs of proceedings

(1) Apply rule 9.6 of the 1986 Rules.

(2) In paragraph (2)(a) leave out "or 367(1)" and in paragraph (2)(b) leave out "or 367(2)".

(3) In paragraph (3)(a), for "company insolvency" substitute "bank insolvency".

(4) Ignore paragraph (3)(b).

(5) Ignore paragraph (5).

PART 21
DECLARATION AND PAYMENT OF DIVIDEND

[7.338]
247 Preliminary

(1) The rules in this Part relate to the declaration and payment of dividends in a bank insolvency.

(2) In this Part—

"creditors" means those creditors of the bank of whom the bank liquidator is aware, or who are identified in the bank's statement of affairs and

"the insolvent" means the bank.

[7.339]
248 Notice of intended dividend

Apply rule 11.2 of the 1986 Rules. Ignore paragraph (1)(b).

[7.340]
249 Final admission/rejection of proofs

Apply rule 11.3 of the 1986 Rules. Ignore paragraph (4).

[7.341]
250 Postponement or cancellation of dividend

Apply rule 11.4 of the 1986 Rules.

[7.342]
251 Decision to declare dividend

Apply rule 11.5 of the 1986 Rules.

[7.343]
252 Notice of declaration

(1) Apply rule 11.6 of the 1986 Rules.

(2) Ignore paragraph (1)(b).

(3) In paragraph (2), after (b), add—

"(ba) expenses incurred by the bank liquidator in the achievement of objective 1 under section 99 of the Banking Act 2009."

[7.344]
253 Notice of no, or no further, dividend

Apply rule 11.7 of the 1986 Rules.

[7.345]
254 Proof altered after payment of dividend

Apply rule 11.8 of the 1986 Rules.

[7.346]
255 Secured creditors

Apply rule 11.9 of the 1986 Rules.

[7.347]
256 Disqualification from dividend

Apply rule 11.10 of the 1986 Rules.

[7.348]
257 Assignment of right to dividend

Apply rule 11.11 of the 1986 Rules.

[7.349]
258 Preferential creditors

Apply rule 11.12 of the 1986 Rules.

[7.350]
259 Debt payable at future time

Apply rule 11.13 of the 1986 Rules. For paragraph (3) substitute "In paragraph (2), "relevant date" means the date of the commencement of bank insolvency."

PART 22
MISCELLANEOUS AND GENERAL

[7.351]
260 Power of Secretary of State or Treasury to regulate certain matters

(1) As provided for in paragraph 27 of Schedule 8 to the 1986 Act, either the Secretary of State or the Treasury may, subject to the Act and to these Rules, make regulations with respect to any matter provided for in these Rules relating to the carrying out of the functions of a bank liquidator or provisional bank liquidator, including, without prejudice to the generality of the above, provision with respect to the following matters arising in bank insolvency—

- (a) the preparation and keeping by bank liquidators and provisional bank liquidators of books, accounts and other records, and their production to such persons as may be authorised or required to inspect them;
- (b) the auditing of bank liquidators' accounts;
- (c) the manner in which bank liquidators are to act in relation to the bank's books, papers and other records, and the manner of their disposal by the bank liquidator or others;
- (d) the supply by the bank liquidator to creditors and contributories and to the liquidation committee of copies of documents relating to the bank insolvency and the affairs of the bank (on payment, in such cases as may be specified in the regulations, of a fee.);
- (e) the manner in which insolvent estates are to be distributed by the bank liquidator, including provision with respect to unclaimed funds and dividends;
- (f) the manner in which monies coming into the hands of the bank liquidator are to be handled and invested and the payment of interest on sums which, in pursuance of regulations made under this sub-paragraph, have been paid into the Insolvency Services Account[.]

(2) Regulations made under paragraph (1) may—

- (a) confer a discretion on the court,
- (b) make non-compliance with any of the regulations a criminal offence,
- (c) make different provision for different cases, including different provision for different areas, and
- (d) contain such incidental, supplemental and transitional provisions as may appear to the Secretary of State or the Treasury as necessary or expedient.

NOTES

Para (1): in sub-para (f) full stop in square brackets substituted by the Bank Insolvency (England and Wales) (Amendment) Rules 2010, SI 2010/2579, rr 3, 76.

[7.352]
261 Costs, expenses, etc

(1) All fees, costs, charges and other expenses incurred in the course of bank insolvency, except for any money paid by the FSCS to eligible depositors in pursuance of [Objective 1], and any expense incurred by the FSCS in this process, are to be regarded as expenses of the bank insolvency.

(2) The costs associated with the [prescribed part] shall be paid out of that [prescribed part].

NOTES

Para (1): words in square brackets substituted by the Bank Insolvency (England and Wales) (Amendment) Rules 2010, SI 2010/2579, rr 3, 77(a).

Para (2): words in square brackets substituted by SI 2010/2579, rr 3, 77(b).

[7.353]
262 Provable debts

(1) Subject to paragraphs (2) and (3) in a bank insolvency all claims by creditors are provable as debts against the bank, whether they are present or future, certain or contingent, ascertained or sounding only in damages.

(2) Any obligation arising under a confiscation order made under Parts 2, 3 or 4 of the Proceeds of Crime Act 2002 is not provable.

(3) The following are not provable except at a time when all other claims of creditors in the insolvency proceedings (other than any of a kind mentioned in this paragraph) have been paid in full with interest under section 189(2) of the 1986 Act—

(a) any claim arising by virtue of section 382(1)(a) of the Financial Services and Markets Act 2000, not being a claim arising by virtue of section 382(1)(b) of that Act; or

(b) any claim which by virtue of the 1986 Act or any enactment is a claim the payment of which in the bank insolvency is to be postponed.

(4) Nothing in this rule prejudices any enactment or rule of law under which a particular kind of debt is not provable, whether on grounds of public policy or otherwise.

[7.354]
263 Notices

(1) Apply rule 12.4 of the 1986 Rules.

(2) Ignore references to the official receiver.

[7.355]
264 Quorum at meeting of creditors or contributories

(1) Apply rule 12.4A of the 1986 Rules.

(2) For paragraph (3) substitute—

["(3) For the purposes of this rule the reference to creditors or contributories necessary to constitute a quorum is to those persons present or represented by proxy by any person (including the chair) including, in the case of contributories, persons duly represented under section 323 of the 2006 Act."]

NOTES

Para (2): the Insolvency Rules 1986, r 12.4A(3) (as set out) substituted by the Bank Insolvency (England and Wales) (Amendment) Rules 2010, SI 2010/2579, rr 3, 78.

[7.356]
265 Evidence of proceedings at meetings

Apply rule 12.5 of the 1986 Rules.

[7.357]
266 Documents issuing from Secretary of State

Apply rule 12.6 of the 1986 Rules . . .

NOTES

Words omitted revoked by the Bank Insolvency (England and Wales) (Amendment) Rules 2010, SI 2010/2579, rr 3, 79.

[7.358]
267 Insolvency practitioner's security

(1) Apply rule 12.8 of the 1986 Rules.

(2) For paragraph (2) substitute—

"(2) It is the duty of the liquidation committee in a bank insolvency to review from time to time the adequacy of the bank liquidator's security.".

[7.359]
268 Time limits

Apply rule 12.9(1) of the 1986 Rules as regards time limits for anything required or authorised to be done by these Rules.

[7.360]
269 Service by post

Apply rule 12.10 of the 1986 Rules.

[7.361]
270 General provisions as to service

CPR Part 6 (service of documents) applies as regards any matter relating to the service of documents and the giving of notice in bank insolvency proceedings except in cases where a rule makes provision as to the service of a document or the giving of a notice.

[7.362]
271 Service outside the jurisdiction

(1) CPR Part 6 applies as regards any matter relating to the service of documents in Scotland and Northern Ireland except in cases where a rule makes provision as to the service of a document or the giving of a notice.

(2) Where for the purposes of bank insolvency proceedings any process or order of the court, or other document, is required to be served on a person who is not in the United Kingdom—

- (a) with regard to the service of documents to which a rule makes provision, the court may order service to be effected within such time, on such person, at such place and in such manner as it thinks fit, and may also require such proof of service as it thinks fit,
- (b) with regard to the service of documents otherwise, [CPR Rules 6.40(3) to 6.46] apply.

(3) An application under paragraph (2)(a) shall be supported by a witness statement stating—

- (a) the grounds on which the application is made, and
- (b) in what place or country the person to be served is, or probably may be found.

NOTES

Para (2): words in square brackets in sub-para (b) substituted by the Bank Insolvency (England and Wales) (Amendment) Rules 2010, SI 2010/2579, rr 3, 80.

[7.363]
272 Confidentiality of documents

(1) Apply rule 12.13 of the 1986 Rules.

(2) In paragraph (2) ignore the reference to a creditors' committee.

[7.364]
273 Notices sent simultaneously to the same person

Apply rule 12.14 of the 1986 Rules.

[7.365]
274 Right to copy documents

Apply rule 12.15 of the 1986 Rules.

[7.366]
275 Charge for copy documents

Apply rule 12.15A of the 1986 Rules.

[7.367]
276 Non-receipt of notice of meeting

Apply rule 12.16 of the 1986 Rules.

[7.368]
277 Right to have list of creditors

(1) Where a creditor has the right under these Rules to inspect documents on the court file, the creditor may require the bank liquidator to send them a list of the bank's creditors and the amounts of their respective debts.

(2) Paragraph (1) does not apply if a statement of the bank's affairs has been filed in court or filed with the registrar of companies.

(3) The bank liquidator must respond to a request in paragraph (1) but may charge the appropriate fee for doing so.

[7.369]
278 False claim of status as creditor, etc

Apply rule 12.18 of the 1986 Rules.

[7.370]
279 Execution overtaken by judgement debtor's insolvency

(1) This rule applies where execution has been taken out against property of a judgment debtor, and notice is given to the enforcement officer or other officer charged with the execution under section 184(1) of the 1986 Act (that a bank insolvency order has been made against the debtor, or that a provisional bank liquidator has been appointed).

(2) The notice shall be in writing and be delivered by personal service at, or sent by recorded delivery to, the office of the enforcement officer or (as the case may be) of the officer charged with the execution.

[7.371]
280 The Gazette

Apply rule 12.20 of the 1986 Rules.

[7.372]
281 Punishment of offences

Apply rule 12.21 of the 1986 Rules . . .

NOTES

Words omitted revoked by the Bank Insolvency (England and Wales) (Amendment) Rules 2010, SI 2010/2579, rr 3, 81.

[7.373]
282 Notice of order under section 176A(5)

(1) Apply rule 12.22 of the 1986 Rules. For references to "the liquidator, administrator or receiver" read "bank liquidator".

PART 23
INTERPRETATION

[7.374]
283 Introductory

This Part of the Rules has effect for their interpretation and application; and any definition given in this Part (and in any provision of the 1986 Rules applied by this Part) applies except, and in so far as, the context requires otherwise.

[7.375]
284 "The court"; "the registrar"

(1) Apply rule 13.2 of the 1986 Rules.

(2) Ignore paragraphs (3) and (5).

(3) In paragraph (4), for "company insolvency proceedings" substitute "bank insolvency proceedings."

[7.376]
285 "Give notice", etc

Apply rule 13.3 of the 1986 Rules. [In paragraph (3), leave out from "except" to the end of the paragraph.]

NOTES

Words in square brackets inserted by the Bank Insolvency (England and Wales) (Amendment) Rules 2010, SI 2010/2579, rr 3, 82.

[7.377]
286 Notice, etc to solicitors

Apply rule 13.4 of the 1986 Rules.

[7.378]
287 Notice to joint bank liquidators

Where 2 or more persons are acting jointly as the bank liquidator, delivery of a document to 1 of them is to be treated as delivery to them all.

[7.379]
288 "Insolvent estate"

References to "the insolvent estate" are to the assets of the bank.

[7.380]
289 "Responsible insolvency practitioner", etc

In relation to a bank insolvency, "the responsible insolvency practitioner" means the person acting in the bank insolvency as the bank liquidator or provisional bank liquidator.

[7.381]
290 "The appropriate fee"

"The appropriate fee" means 15 pence per A4 or A5 page, and 30 pence per A3 page.

[7.382]
291 "Debt", "liability"

(1) Apply rule 13.12 of the 1986 Rules.

(2) Ignore paragraph (5).

[7.383]
292 Expressions used generally

(1) Apply rule 13.13 of the 1986 Rules.

(2) In paragraph (1) for "Rules 1.7" to "6.23" substitute "rule 10 of the Bank Insolvency Rules 2009".

(3) In paragraph (5), after "Secretary of State" insert "or the Treasury".

(4) In paragraph (7), for "Chapter 20 of Part 4 of these Rules, or Chapter 23 of Part 6" substitute "Part 16 of the [2009 Rules]".

(5) Ignore paragraphs (8) to (14).

(6) In paragraph (15), after "section 176A(2)(a)" insert "as applied by section 103 of the Banking Act 2009".

NOTES

Para (4): words in square brackets substituted by the Bank Insolvency (England and Wales) (Amendment) Rules 2010, SI 2010/2579, rr 3, 83.

[7.384]
293 The Schedule

The Schedule, which applies relevant schedules to the 1986 Rules to these rules with modifications, has effect.

SCHEDULE

[7.385]
1. The following [Schedules] to the 1986 Rules are applied to these Rules—

(a) Schedule 1. Ignore all references to rule 4.72 and for paragraph (1) substitute—

"**1.** This Schedule applies where a bank insolvency order (as defined under Part 2 of the Banking Act 2009) has been made in respect of a bank".

(b) Schedule 5; and

(c) Schedule 6.

NOTES

Para 1: word in square brackets substituted by the Bank Insolvency (England and Wales) (Amendment) Rules 2010, SI 2010/2579, rr 3, 84.

BANK ADMINISTRATION (ENGLAND AND WALES) RULES 2009

(SI 2009/357)

NOTES

Made: 23 February 2009.

Authority: Insolvency Act 1986, s 411(1B)(a), (2), (2D).

Commencement: 25 February 2009.

Note: these Rules apply certain provisions of the Insolvency Rules 1986, SI 1986/1925, subject to a number of general and specific modifications. The Insolvency Rules 1986, SI 1986/1925 are revoked and replaced (as from 6 April 2017 and subject to transitional provisions) by the Insolvency (England and Wales) Rules 2016, SI 2016/1024 at **[6.2]**.

ARRANGEMENT OF RULES

PART 1
INTRODUCTION

1 Citation . . . [7.386]
2 Commencement . . . [7.387]
3 Extent . . . [7.388]
4, 5 Interpretation . . . [7.389], [7.390]
6 Overview . . . [7.391]
7 Forms . . . [7.392]

PART 2
APPLICATION FOR BANK ADMINISTRATION ORDER

8 Introduction . . . [7.393]
9, 10 Content of application . . . [7.394], [7.395]
11 Statement of proposed bank administrator . . . [7.396]
12 Bank of England witness statement . . . [7.397]
13, 14 Filing . . . [7.398], [7.399]
15–19 Service. . . . [7.400]–[7.404]
20 Other notification. . . . [7.405]
21 Venue . . . [7.406]

22 Hearing . . . . . . [7.407]
23 The order . . . . . . [7.408]
24, 25 Notice of order . . . . . . [7.409], [7.410]
26 Costs . . . . . . [7.411]

PART 3
PROCESS OF BANK ADMINISTRATION

27 Introduction . . . . . . [7.412]
28 Bank administrator's proposals: Objective 1 Stage . . . . . . [7.413]
29–34 Bank administrator's proposals: Objective 2 Stage . . . . . . [7.414]–[7.420]
35–38 Reports to creditors . . . . . . [7.421]–[7.424]
39 Removal of bank administrator in Objective 1 Stage . . . . . . [7.425]
40–46 Appointment of provisional bank administrator . . . . . . [7.426]–[7.432]
47 Additional joint bank administrator . . . . . . [7.433]
47A Disapplication of set-off for protected deposits . . . . . . [7.434]
48 End of administration: successful rescue . . . . . . [7.435]
49 End of administration: dissolution . . . . . . [7.436]

PART 4
COURT PROCEDURE AND PRACTICE

50 Introduction . . . . . . [7.437]
51 Title of proceedings . . . . . . [7.438]
52–57 Right to inspect file . . . . . . [7.439]–[7.444]

PART 5
APPLICATION OF INSOLVENCY RULES 1986

58, 59 General application . . . . . . [7.445], [7.446]
60 General modifications . . . . . . [7.447]
61 Table of applications and specific modifications . . . . . . [7.448]

PART 1
INTRODUCTION

[7.386]
1 Citation

These Rules may be cited as the Bank Administration (England and Wales) Rules 2009.

[7.387]
2 Commencement

These Rules come into force on 25th February 2009.

[7.388]
3 Extent

These Rules extend to England and Wales only.

[7.389]
4 Interpretation

(1) The following expressions used in these Rules take their meaning from the Banking Act 2009 . . .—

(a) "bank" (s 2),
(b) "bank administration" (s 141(4)(a)),
(c) "bank administration order" (s 141(1)),
(d) "bank administrator" (s 141(1)),
[(da) "Bank of England" (s 256B(1)),]
(e) "bridge bank" (s 136(2)),
(f) "the court" (the High Court—s 166(1)),
(g) . . .
(h) "Objective 1" (support for commercial purchaser or bridge bank—ss 137 & 138),
(i) "Objective 1 Achievement Notice" (s 139(4)),
(j) "Objective 2" (normal administration—ss 137 & 140),
(k) "private sector purchaser" (s 136(2)),
(l) "property transfer instrument" (s 33),
(m) "residual bank" (s 136(2)), and
(n) "resolution fund order" (s 49(3)).

(2) Expressions used in the Companies Act 2006 have the same meaning [in these Rules].

NOTES

Para (1): first words omitted revoked by the Bank Administration (England and Wales) (Amendment) Rules 2010, SI 2010/2583, rr 3, 4(a); sub-para (da) inserted by the Bank of England and Financial Services (Consequential Amendments)

Part 7B Special Insolvency Regimes

Regulations 2017, SI 2017/80, reg 2, Schedule, para 30; sub-para (g) revoked by the Financial Services Act 2012 (Consequential Amendments and Transitional Provisions) Order 2013, SI 2013/472, art 3, Sch 2, para 164(a).

Para (2): words in square brackets substituted by SI 2010/2583, rr 3, 4(b).

[7.390]
5

In these Rules—

(a) "the FSCS" means the scheme manager of the Financial Services Compensation Scheme (established under Part 15 of the Financial Services and Markets Act 2000),

[(aa) "the appropriate regulator" in relation to a bank means—

(a) if the bank is a PRA-authorised person (within the meaning of the Financial Services and Markets Act 2000), the Prudential Regulation Authority and the Financial Conduct Authority;

(bb) in any other case, the Financial Conduct Authority;]

(b) "the Objective 1 Stage" means the period during which a bank administration order is in force before the Bank of England gives an Objective 1 Achievement Notice,

(c) "the Objective 2 Stage" means the period during which a bank administration order is in force after the Bank of England gives an Objective 1 Achievement Notice,

[(ca) a reference to "the Insolvency Rules 1986" is a reference to those Rules including all amendments to them up to and including those made by the Insolvency (Amendment) (No 2) Rules 2009,]

(d) a reference to personal service is a reference to personal service in accordance with Part 6 of the Civil Procedure Rules 1998,

(e) a reference to the CPR is to the Civil Procedure Rules 1998, and

(f) a reference to a witness statement (including a reference implied by the application of an enactment) is a reference to a witness statement—

(i) verified by a statement of truth in accordance with Part 22 of the CPR, and

(ii) if made by a bank administrator, stating that the statement is made in that capacity and giving the address at which the bank administrator works,

[(g) the purpose of bank administration" is a reference to the objectives of bank administration in section 137 of the Banking Act 2009].

NOTES

Para (aa): inserted by the Financial Services Act 2012 (Consequential Amendments and Transitional Provisions) Order 2013, SI 2013/472, art 3, Sch 2, para 164(b).

Paras (ca), (g) inserted by the Bank Administration (England and Wales) (Amendment) Rules 2010, SI 2010/2583, rr 3, 5.

Note that the Insolvency Rules 1986, SI 1986/1925 are revoked and replaced (as from 6 April 2017 and subject to transitional provisions) by the Insolvency (England and Wales) Rules 2016, SI 2016/1024 at **[6.2]**.

[7.391]
6 Overview

The purpose of these Rules is to prescribe a procedure for the appointment of a bank administrator, and the operation of bank administration, under Part 3 of the Banking Act 2009 in England and Wales.

[7.392]
7 Forms

(1) This Rule applies where a provision of these Rules—

(a) applies a provision of the Insolvency Rules 1986 which requires the use of a prescribed form, or

(b) makes provision similar to that made by a provision of those Rules which requires the use of a prescribed form.

(2) The form prescribed for the purposes of those Rules is to be used, with any modification that the person using the form thinks desirable to reflect the nature of bank administration (whether or not the modification is set out in a Practice Form issued by the Treasury for that purpose).

PART 2
APPLICATION FOR BANK ADMINISTRATION ORDER

[7.393]
8 Introduction

This Part makes specific provision for a number of aspects of applications for bank administration orders; Part 5 applies a number of provisions of the Insolvency Rules 1986 to applications for bank administration orders (with specified modifications).

[7.394]
9 Content of application

An application by the Bank of England for a bank administration order in respect of a bank must specify—

(a) the full name of the bank,

(b) any other trading names,

(c) the address of the bank's registered office,

(d) an email address for the bank,

(e) the address of the Bank of England, and

(f) the identity of the person (or persons) nominated for appointment as bank administrator.

[7.395]
10

If the bank has notified the Bank of England of an address for service which is, because of special circumstances, to be used in place of the registered office, that address shall be specified under Rule 9(c).

[7.396]
11 Statement of proposed bank administrator

An application must be accompanied by a statement by the proposed bank administrator—

(a) specifying the name and address of the person (or of each person) proposed to be appointed,
(b) giving that person's (or each person's) consent to act,
(c) giving details of the person's (or each person's) qualification to act as an insolvency practitioner, and
(d) giving details of any prior professional relationship that the person (or any of them) has had with the bank.

[7.397]
12 Bank of England witness statement

(1) An application for a bank administration order in respect of a bank must be accompanied by a witness statement made on behalf of the Bank of England—

(a) certifying that the conditions for applying for a bank administration order, set out in section 143 of the Banking Act 2009, are met in respect of the bank,
(b) stating the bank's current financial position to the best of the Bank of England's knowledge and belief (including actual, contingent and prospective assets and liabilities),
(c) specifying any security which the Bank of England knows or believes to be held by a creditor of the bank,
(d) specifying whether any security confers power to appoint an administrator under paragraph 14 of Schedule B1 to the Insolvency Act 1986 (holder of qualifying floating charge) or an administrative receiver (and whether an administrative receiver has been appointed),
(e) specifying any insolvency proceedings which have been instituted in respect of the bank (including any process notified to the [Financial Conduct Authority or the Prudential Regulation Authority] under section 120 of the Banking Act 2009),
(f) giving details of the property transfer instrument which the Bank of England has made or intends to make in respect of the bank,
(g) where the property transfer instrument has not yet been made, explaining what effect it is likely to have on the bank's financial position,
(h) specifying how functions are to be apportioned where more than one person is to be appointed as bank administrator (stating, in particular, whether functions are to be exercisable jointly or concurrently), and
(i) including any other material which the Bank of England thinks may help the court to decide whether to make the bank administration order.

(2) The statement [must] identify the person [making] the statement and [must] include the capacity in which that person makes the statement and the basis for that person's knowledge of the matters set out in the statement.

NOTES

Para (1): words in square brackets substituted by the Financial Services Act 2012 (Consequential Amendments and Transitional Provisions) Order 2013, SI 2013/472, art 3, Sch 2, para 164(c).

Para (2): words in square brackets substituted by the Bank Administration (England and Wales) (Amendment) Rules 2010, SI 2010/2583, rr 3, 6.

[7.398]
13 Filing

The application, and its accompanying documents, must be filed with the court, together with enough copies of the application and accompanying documents for service under Rule 15.

[7.399]
14

Each filed copy—

(a) shall have the seal of the court applied to it,
(b) shall be endorsed with the date and time of filing,
(c) shall be endorsed with the venue for the hearing of the application (fixed by the court under Rule 21), and
(d) shall be issued to the Bank of England.

[7.400]
15 Service

The Bank of England shall serve the application—

(a) on the bank,
(b) on the person (or each of the persons) nominated for appointment as bank administrator,

(c) on any person whom the Bank of England knows to be entitled to appoint an administrator under paragraph 14 of Schedule B1 to the Insolvency Act 1986 or an administrative receiver,
(d) on any person who has given notice to the [appropriate regulator] in respect of the bank under section 120 of the Banking Act 2009 (bank insolvency: notice of preliminary steps of other insolvency procedures), and
(e) if the property transfer instrument was made or is to be made under section 11(2)(b) of the Banking Act 2009 (transfer to commercial purchaser), on each transferee.

NOTES

Para (d): words in square brackets substituted by the Financial Services Act 2012 (Consequential Amendments and Transitional Provisions) Order 2013, SI 2013/472, art 3, Sch 2, para 164(g).

[7.401]
16

Service under [Rule 15] must be service of a sealed and endorsed copy of the application and its accompanying documents issued under Rule 14.

NOTES

Words in square brackets substituted by the Bank Administration (England and Wales) (Amendment) Rules 2010, SI 2010/2583, rr 3, 7.

[7.402]
17

Service must be effected as soon as is reasonably practicable, having regard in particular to the need to give the bank's representatives a reasonable opportunity to attend the hearing.

[7.403]
18

(1) Service must be effected—
(a) by personal service to an address that the person has notified to the Bank of England as an address for service,
(b) by personal service to the person's registered office (where no address for service has been notified),
(c) by personal service to the person's usual or last known principal place of business in England and Wales (where there is no registered office and no address for service has been notified), or
(d) in such other manner and at such a place as the court may direct.

(2) If the Bank of England knows of an email address that is habitually used for business purposes by a person on whom service is required, the Bank must (in addition to personal service) as soon as is reasonably practicable send by email an electronic copy of a sealed and endorsed copy of the application and its accompanying documents.

[7.404]
19

(1) Service of the application shall be verified by a witness statement specifying the date on which, and the manner in which, service was effected.

(2) The witness statement, with a sealed copy of the application exhibited to it, shall be filed with the court—
(a) as soon as is reasonably practicable, and
(b) in any event, before the hearing of the application.

[7.405]
20 Other notification

As soon as is reasonably practicable after filing the application the Bank of England must notify—
(a) any enforcement officer or other officer whom the Bank of England knows to be charged with effecting an execution or other legal process against the bank or its property,
(b) any person whom the Bank of England knows to have distrained against the bank or its property, and
(c) the [appropriate regulator].

NOTES

Para (c): words in square brackets substituted by the Financial Services Act 2012 (Consequential Amendments and Transitional Provisions) Order 2013, SI 2013/472, art 3, Sch 2, para 164(g).

[7.406]
21 Venue

(1) The court shall fix the venue for the hearing when the application is filed.

(2) In fixing the venue the court shall have regard to—
(a) the desirability of the application being heard as soon as is reasonably practicable, and
(b) the need for the bank's representatives to be able to reach the venue in time for the hearing.

[7.407]
22 Hearing

At the hearing of the application, any of the following may appear or be represented—

(a) the Bank of England,
(b) the [appropriate regulator],
(c) the bank,
(d) a director of the bank,
(e) the person (or a person) nominated for appointment as bank administrator,
(f) any person who has given notice to the [appropriate regulator] in respect of the bank under section 120 of the Banking Act 2009 (bank insolvency: notice of preliminary steps of other insolvency procedures), and
(g) with the permission of the court, any other person who appears to have an interest.

NOTES

Paras (b), (f): words in square brackets substituted by the Financial Services Act 2012 (Consequential Amendments and Transitional Provisions) Order 2013, SI 2013/472, art 3, Sch 2, para 164(g).

[7.408]
23 The order

A bank administration order must be in the form specified in Rule 2.12(2) of the Insolvency Rules 1986, with such variations, if any, as the circumstances may require.

[7.409]
24 Notice of order

If the court makes a bank administration order, it shall send 4 [or, if the bank is a PRA-authorised person (within the meaning of the Financial Services and Markets Act 2000), 5] sealed copies to the Bank of England.

NOTES

Words in square brackets substituted by the Financial Services Act 2012 (Consequential Amendments and Transitional Provisions) Order 2013, SI 2013/472, art 3, Sch 2, para 164(d).

[7.410]
25

The Bank of England shall as soon as is reasonably practicable send—

(a) one sealed copy to the bank administrator,
[(b) one sealed copy to the Financial Conduct Authority,
(ba) if the bank is a PRA-authorised person (within the meaning of the Financial Services and Markets Act 2000), one sealed copy to the Prudential Regulation Authority, and]
(c) one sealed copy to the FSCS.

NOTES

Paras (b), (ba): substituted for original para (b) by the Financial Services Act 2012 (Consequential Amendments and Transitional Provisions) Order 2013, SI 2013/472, art 3, Sch 2, para 164(e).

[7.411]
26 Costs

If the court makes a bank administration order, the following are payable as an expense of the bank administration—

(a) the Bank of England's costs of making the application, and
(b) any other costs allowed by the court.

PART 3
PROCESS OF BANK ADMINISTRATION

[7.412]
27 Introduction

This Part makes specific provision for a number of aspects of bank administration; Part 5 applies a number of provisions of the Insolvency Rules 1986 to bank administration (with specified modifications).

[7.413]
28 Bank administrator's proposals: Objective 1 Stage

(1) This Rule makes provision about the statement of proposals which the bank administrator is required to make in the Objective 1 Stage under section 147 of the Banking Act 2009.

(2) In addition to the information required by section 147 the statement must include—

(a) details of the court where the proceedings are and the court reference number,
(b) the full name, any other trading names, the registered address and registered number of the bank,
(c) details of the bank administrator's appointment (including the date),
(d) in the case of joint bank administrators, details of the apportionment of functions,
(e) the names of the directors and secretary of the bank and details of any shareholdings in the bank they have,

Part 7B Special Insolvency Regimes

(f) an account of the circumstances giving rise to the application for the appointment of the bank administrator,
(g) if a statement of the bank's affairs has been submitted, a copy or summary of it with the bank administrator's comments, if any,
(h) if an order limiting the disclosure of the statement of affairs has been made under Rule 2.30 of the Insolvency Rules 1986 (as applied by Rule 58 below), a statement of that fact, as well as—
  (i) details of who provided the statement of affairs,
  (ii) the date of the order for limited disclosure, and
  (iii) the details or a summary of the details that are not subject to that order,
(i) if a full statement of affairs is not provided, the names, addresses and debts of the creditors including details of any security held (or, in the case of depositors, a single statement of their aggregate debt),
(j) if no statement of affairs has been submitted, details of the financial position of the bank at the latest practicable date (which must, unless the court otherwise orders, be a date not earlier than that on which the bank entered bank administration), a list of the bank's creditors including their names, addresses and details of their debts, including any security held, (or, in the case of depositors, a single statement of their aggregate debt), and an explanation as to why there is no statement of affairs,
(k) the basis upon which it is proposed that the bank administrator's remuneration should be fixed under Rule 2.106 of the Insolvency Rules 1986 (as applied by Rule 58),
(l) how the bank administrator proposes to pursue Objective 1,
(m) whether the bank administrator proposes to pursue Objective 2(a) or Objective 2(b),
(n) if the bank administrator proposes to pursue Objective 2(a), how it is envisaged the purpose of the bank administration will be achieved in the Objective 2 Stage,
(o) if the bank administrator proposes to pursue Objective 2(b)—
  (i) how it is envisaged the purpose of the bank administration will be achieved in the Objective 2 Stage, and
  (ii) how it is proposed that the bank administration shall end (winding-up or voluntary arrangement, in accordance with section 154 of the Banking Act 2009),
(p) the manner in which the affairs and business of the bank have been managed and financed since the date of the bank administrator's appointment (including the reasons for and terms of any disposal of assets), and
(q) the manner in which the affairs and business of the bank will be managed and financed if the bank administrator's proposals are approved.

(3) The statement—
(a) may exclude information, the disclosure of which could seriously prejudice the commercial interests of the bank or of the bridge bank or private sector purchaser, and
(b) must include a statement of any exclusion.

[7.414]
29 Bank administrator's proposals: Objective 2 Stage

(1) This Rule makes provision about the statement of proposals which the bank administrator is required to make under paragraph 49 of Schedule B1 to the Insolvency Act 1986 as it applies during the Objective 2 Stage (in accordance with Table 1 in section 145(6) of the Banking Act 2009).

(2) The statement must include—
(a) details of the court where the proceedings are and the court reference number,
(b) the full name, any other trading names, the registered address and registered number of the bank,
(c) details of the bank administrator's appointment (including the date),
(d) in the case of joint bank administrators, details of the apportionment of functions,
(e) the names of the directors and secretary of the bank and details of any shareholdings in the bank they have,
(f) an account of the circumstances giving rise to the application for the appointment of the bank administrator,
(g) if a statement of the bank's affairs has been submitted, a copy or summary of it with the bank administrator's comments, if any,
(h) if an order limiting the disclosure of the statement of affairs has been made under Rule 2.30 of the Insolvency Rules 1986 (as applied by Rule 58 below), a statement of that fact, as well as—
  (i) details of who provided the statement of affairs,
  (ii) the date of the order for limited disclosure, and
  (iii) the details or a summary of the details that are not subject to that order,
(i) if a full statement of affairs is not provided, the names, addresses and debts of the creditors including details of any security held (or, in the case of depositors, a single statement of their aggregate debt),
(j) if no statement of affairs has been submitted, details of the financial position of the bank at the latest practicable date (which must, unless the court otherwise orders, be a date not earlier than that on which the bank entered bank administration), a list of the bank's creditors including their names, addresses and details of their debts including any security held, (or, in the case of depositors, a single statement of their aggregate debt), and an explanation as to why there is no statement of affairs,
(k) the basis upon which it is proposed that the bank administrator's remuneration should be fixed under Rule 2.106 of the Insolvency Rules 1986 (as applied by Rule 58 below),

(l) details of whether (and why) the bank administrator proposes to apply to the court under section 176A(5) of the Insolvency Act 1986 (omission of distribution to unsecured creditors: as applied by Table 2 in section 145(6) of the Banking Act 2009) (unless the bank administrator intends to propose a company voluntary arrangement),
(m) an estimate of the value of the prescribed part for the purposes of section 176A (unless the bank administrator intends to propose a company voluntary arrangement) certified as being made to the best of the bank administrator's knowledge and belief,
(n) an estimate of the value of the bank's net property (unless the bank administrator intends to propose a company voluntary arrangement) certified as being made to the best of the bank administrator's knowledge and belief,
(o) whether the bank administrator proposes to pursue Objective 2(a) or Objective 2(b),
(p) if the bank administrator proposes to pursue Objective 2(a), how it is envisaged the purpose of the bank administration will be achieved,
(q) if the bank administrator proposes to pursue Objective 2(b)—
 (i) how it is envisaged the purpose of the bank administration will be achieved, and
 (ii) how it is proposed that the bank administration shall end (winding-up or voluntary arrangement, in accordance with section 154 of the Banking Act 2009),
(r) if the bank administrator has decided not to call a meeting of creditors, the reasons,
(s) the manner in which the affairs and business of the bank have been managed and financed since the date of the bank administrator's appointment (including the reasons for and terms of any disposal of assets),
(t) the manner in which the affairs and business of the bank will be managed and financed if the bank administrator's proposals are approved, and
(u) any other information which the bank administrator thinks necessary to enable creditors to decide whether or not to vote for the approval of the proposals.

(3) In the case of bank administration following transfer to a bridge bank under section 12(2) of the Banking Act 2009—
(a) the statement under paragraph 49 of Schedule B1 must state whether any payment is to be made to the bank from a scheme under a resolution fund order, or
(b) if that information is unavailable when the statement under paragraph 49 is made, the bank administrator must issue a supplemental statement when the information is available.

(4) The statement—
(a) may exclude information, the disclosure of which could seriously prejudice the commercial interests of the bank, and
(b) must include a statement of any exclusion.

[7.415]
30
If the bank administrator thinks that the statement made under section 147 of the Banking Act 2009 in accordance with Rule 28 contains information required by Rule 29(2), the statement under paragraph 49 of Schedule B1 to the Insolvency Act 1986 (as applied by Table 1 in section 145(6) of the Banking Act 2009) may consist of the statement under section 147, with such additions, modifications and supplemental information as the bank administrator thinks necessary—
(a) to comply with Rule 29(2), and
(b) to bring the statement under section 147 up to date.

[7.416]
[30A
Where the statement of proposals is sent to creditors in accordance with paragraph 49(4)(b) of Schedule B1 (as applied by Table 1 in section 145(6) of the Banking Act 2009), it must be sent to the [appropriate regulator] and the FSCS at the same time.]

NOTES

Inserted by the Bank Administration (England and Wales) (Amendment) Rules 2010, SI 2010/2583, rr 3, 8.

Words in square brackets substituted by the Financial Services Act 2012 (Consequential Amendments and Transitional Provisions) Order 2013, SI 2013/472, art 3, Sch 2, para 164(g).

[7.417]
31
Where the court orders an extension of the period of time under paragraph 49(5) of Schedule B1 on an application by the bank administrator under paragraph 107 (as applied by Table 1 in section 145(6) of the Banking Act 2009), the bank administrator must notify the persons set out in paragraph 49(4) as soon as is reasonably practicable after the making of the order.

[7.418]
32
Where the bank administrator has made a statement under paragraph 52(1) of Schedule B1 (as applied by Table 1 in section 145(6) of the Banking Act 2009) and has not called an initial meeting of creditors, the proposals issued in accordance with Rule 29 above will be deemed to have been approved by the creditors (if no meeting has been requisitioned under paragraph 52(2) within the period set out in Rule 2.37(1) of the Insolvency Rules 1986—as applied by Rule 58 below).

[7.419]
33

Where the bank administrator intends to apply to the court . . . for the bank administration to cease before the statement of proposals is sent to creditors in accordance with paragraph 49 of Schedule B1, the bank administrator must, at least 10 days before making the application . . . , send to all known creditors of the bank a report containing the information required by Rule 29(2).

NOTES

Words omitted revoked by the Bank Administration (England and Wales) (Amendment) Rules 2010, SI 2010/2583, rr 3, 9.

[7.420]
34

[(1) Where the bank administrator wishes to publish a notice under paragraph 49(6) of Schedule B1 (as applied by Table 1 in section 145(6) of the Banking Act 2009), the notice shall be advertised in such manner as the bank administrator thinks fit.]

(2) The notice must—

(a) state the full name of the bank,

(b) state the full name and address of the bank administrator,

(c) give details of the bank administrator's appointment, and

(d) specify an address to which members can write for a copy of the statement of proposals.

(3) The notice must be published as soon as is reasonably practicable after the bank administrator sends the statement of proposals to the bank's creditors but no later than 8 weeks (or such other period as may be agreed by the creditors or as the court may order) from the date that the bank entered bank administration.

NOTES

Para (1): substituted by the Bank Administration (England and Wales) (Amendment) Rules 2010, SI 2010/2583, rr 3, 10.

[7.421]
35 Reports to creditors

(1) "Progress report" means a report which includes—

(a) details of the court where the proceedings are and the relevant court reference number,

(b) full details of the bank's name, address of registered office and companies house registered number, and other trading names of the bank,

(c) full details of the bank administrator's name and address and date of appointment, including any changes in office-holder,

(d) in the case of joint bank administrators, details of the apportionment of functions,

(e) details of any extensions of the initial period of appointment,

(f) details of progress during the period of the report, including a receipts and payments account (as detailed in paragraph (2) below),

(g) details of any assets that remain to be realised,

(h) details of any amounts received from a scheme under a resolution fund order, and

(i) any other information likely to be relevant to the creditors.

(2) A receipts and payments account must state what assets of the bank have been realised, for what value, and what payments have been made to creditors or others.

(3) The account must be in the form of an abstract showing receipts and payments during the period of the report; and where the bank administrator has ceased to act, the receipts and payments account shall include a statement as to the amount paid to unsecured creditors by virtue of the application of section 176A of the Insolvency Act 1986 (prescribed part).

(4) During the Objective 1 Stage, a progress report must include details of—

(a) the extent of the business of the bank that has been transferred,

(b) any property, rights or liabilities that have been transferred, or which the bank administrator expects to be transferred, under a power in Part 1 of the Banking Act 2009 (special resolution regime),

(c) any requirements imposed on the residual bank, for the purpose of the pursuit of Objective 1, under a power in [Part 1], and

(d) the arrangements for managing and financing the bank during the Objective 1 Stage.

(5) In complying with paragraph (4)(c) and (d) a report—

(a) may exclude information, the disclosure of which could seriously prejudice the commercial interests of the bank or of the bridge bank or private sector purchaser, and

(b) must include a statement of any exclusion.

NOTES

Para (4): words in square brackets in sub-para (c) substituted by the Bank Administration (England and Wales) (Amendment) Rules 2010, SI 2010/2583, rr 3, 11.

[7.422]
36

A progress report must be produced for—

(a) the first period of 6 months of the bank administration,

(b) every subsequent period of 6 months, and

(c) when the bank administrator ceases to act, the period from the date of the previous report (or, if there was none, from the beginning of the bank administration) until the administrator ceases to act.

[7.423]
37

(1) The bank administrator must send a copy of each progress report within 28 days of the end of the period covered by the report, to—

(a) the creditors,
(b) the court,
(c) the Bank of England,
(d) the [appropriate regulator],
(e) the FSCS, and
(f) the registrar of companies.

(2) Instead of complying with paragraph (1)(a) the bank administrator may publish the progress report on its internet website (and take appropriate steps to draw attention to it [and send a copy of it to any creditor on request]).

(3) The court may, on the bank administrator's application—

(a) extend the period specified in paragraph (1),
(b) make any other order about the content of a progress report.

NOTES

Para (1): words in square brackets substituted by the Financial Services Act 2012 (Consequential Amendments and Transitional Provisions) Order 2013, SI 2013/472, art 3, Sch 2, para 164(g).

Para (2): words in square brackets added by the Bank Administration (England and Wales) (Amendment) Rules 2010, SI 2010/2583, rr 3, 12.

[7.424]
38

(1) A bank administrator who fails to comply with Rules 36 and 37 is liable to a fine and, for continued contravention, to a daily default fine.

(2) For that purpose, failure to comply with Rules 36 and 37 shall be treated in the same way as failure to comply with Rule 2.47 of the Insolvency Rules 1986.

[7.425]
39 Removal of bank administrator in Objective 1 Stage

(1) This Rule is about an application for removal of a bank administrator made by the Bank of England during the Objective 1 Stage (in accordance with the modifications for the application of paragraph 91 of Schedule B1 to the Insolvency Act 1986 in Table 1 in section 145(6) of the Banking Act 2009).

(2) The rules for service of notice of the application, other notification of the application and for the hearing shall be as for the application to appoint a bank administrator under Part 2 of these Rules.

(3) But both the person proposed to be appointed as a replacement and the existing bank administrator are entitled to be served and heard.

[7.426]
40 Appointment of provisional bank administrator

An application to the court for the appointment of a provisional bank administrator under section 135 of the Insolvency Act 1986 (as applied by Table 2 in section 145(6) of the Banking Act 2009) may be made by the Bank of England.

[7.427]
41

The application must be supported by a witness statement stating—

(a) why the Bank of England thinks that a provisional bank administrator should be appointed,
(b) that the person to be appointed has consented to act,
(c) that the person to be appointed is qualified to act as an insolvency practitioner,
(d) whether, to the Bank of England's knowledge, a company voluntary arrangement under Part 1 of the Insolvency Act 1986 has been proposed or is in force in respect of the bank,
(e) whether, to the Bank of England's knowledge, an administrative receiver is acting in respect of the bank, and
(f) the Bank of England's estimate of the value of the assets in respect of which the provisional bank administrator is to be appointed.

[7.428]
42

If satisfied that sufficient grounds are shown for the appointment, the court may make it on such terms as it thinks fit.

[7.429]
43

An order appointing a provisional bank administrator must specify the functions to be carried out in relation to the bank's affairs.

[7.430]
[44

If the court makes an order appointing a provisional bank administrator, as soon as reasonably practicable the court shall send 4 sealed copies of the order to the person appointed (and 1 additional copy by email if possible).]

NOTES

Substituted by the Bank Administration (England and Wales) (Amendment) Rules 2010, SI 2010/2583, rr 3, 13.

[7.431]
45

(1) As soon as is reasonably practicable after appointment a provisional bank administrator must send a copy of the order of appointment to—
- (a) the bank,
- [(aa) any administrative receiver of the bank,]
- (b) the [appropriate regulator], . . .
- [(ba) the FSCS, and]
- (c) the registrar of companies (together with the form specified in Rule 4.26(3)(ii) of the Insolvency Rules 1986, with such variations, if any, as the circumstances may require).

(2) Notice to the bank must be given by service in accordance with Rule 18 above.

[(3) Unless the court otherwise directs, on receipt of the order of appointment, as soon as reasonably practicable, the provisional bank administrator shall give notice of that appointment. Such notice—
- (a) shall be gazetted; and
- (b) may be advertised in such other manner as the provisional bank administrator thinks fit.]

NOTES

Para (1): sub-paras (aa), (ba) inserted and word omitted from sub-para (b) revoked, by the Bank Administration (England and Wales) (Amendment) Rules 2010, SI 2010/2583, rr 3, 14(a); words in square brackets in sub-para (b) substituted by the Financial Services Act 2012 (Consequential Amendments and Transitional Provisions) Order 2013, SI 2013/472, art 3, Sch 2, para 164(g).

Para (3): added by SI 2010/2583, rr 3, 14(b).

[7.432]
46

The Bank of England may disclose the fact and terms of an order appointing a provisional bank administrator to any person whom the Bank thinks has a sufficient business interest.

[7.433]
47 Additional joint bank administrator

(1) The process for the appointment of an additional joint bank administrator is the same as for the initial appointment of a bank administrator.

(2) The existing bank administrator (or each of them) is entitled to a copy of the application and may—
- (a) file written representations, and
- (b) be heard at the hearing.

(3) An application for the appointment of an additional joint bank administrator may be made during the Objective 1 Stage only by the Bank of England.

(4) Rule 58 below applies Rules 2.127 and 2.128 of the Insolvency Rules 1986 (notification and advertisement of the appointment of an additional joint administrator).

[7.434]
[47A Disapplication of set-off for protected deposits

(1) This rule applies if—
- (a) [appropriate regulator] Rules allow the FSCS to make gross payments of compensation in respect of protected deposits; and
- (b) all or part of a creditor's claim against the bank is in respect of protected deposits.

(2) Rule 2.85 of the Insolvency Rules 1986 shall apply, but for the purpose of determining the sums due from the bank to an eligible depositor in respect of protected deposits under rule 2.85(3)—
- (a) where the total of the sums held by the bank for the depositor in respect of protected deposits is no more than the amount prescribed as the maximum compensation payable in respect of protected deposits under Part 15 of the Financial Services and Markets Act 2000 ("the limit"), then paragraph (3) applies; and
- (b) where the sums held exceed the limit, then paragraph (4) applies.

(3) Where this paragraph applies, there shall be deemed to have been no mutual dealings, regardless of whether there are any sums due from the depositor to the bank, and the sum due to the depositor from the bank will be the total of the sums held by the bank for that depositor in respect of the protected deposits.

(4) Where this paragraph applies then—
(a) any mutual dealings shall be treated as being mutual dealings only in relation to the amount by which the total of the sums due to the depositor exceeds the limit, and
(b) the sums due from the bank to the depositor in respect of the protected deposits will be—
(i) the amount by which that total exceeds the limit, set off against the amounts due to the bank from the depositor in accordance with rule 2.85(3); and
(ii) the sums held by the bank for the depositor in respect of protected deposits up to the limit.

(5) Any arrangements with regard to set-off between the bank and the eligible depositor in existence before the date of the notice referred to in rule 2.85(1) shall be subject to this rule in so far as they relate to protected deposits.

(6) In this rule—
"eligible depositor" has the meaning given to it by section 93(3) of the Banking Act 2009;
["appropriate regulator rules" means the rules, as amended from time to time, made by the Financial Conduct Authority or the Prudential Regulation Authority under section 213 of the Financial Services and Markets Act 2000;]
"protected deposit" means a protected deposit within the meaning given by the [appropriate regulator] Rules held by the bank at the date of the notice referred to in rule 2.85(1).]

NOTES

Inserted by the Bank Administration (England and Wales) (Amendment) Rules 2010, SI 2010/2583, rr 3, 15.

Paras (1), (6): words in square brackets substituted by the Financial Services Act 2012 (Consequential Amendments and Transitional Provisions) Order 2013, SI 2013/472, art 3, Sch 2, para 164(f), (g).

[7.435]

48 End of administration: successful rescue

(1) This Rule supplements section 153 of the Banking Act 2009 (end of bank administration where bank administrator satisfied that Objective 2(a) has been achieved).

[(2) The bank administrator's application under paragraph 79 of Schedule B1 to the Insolvency Act 1986 (as applied by section 153 of the Banking Act 2009) ("the application") shall have attached to it a progress report for the period from the date of the previous report (or, if there was none, from the beginning of the bank administration) and a statement indicating what the bank administrator thinks should be the next steps for the bank.]

(3) . . .

[(4) Before making the application, the bank administrator must send a copy of the application and the progress report to—
(a) the Bank of England,
(b) the [appropriate regulator],
(c) the FSCS, and
(d) the registrar of companies.]

(5) [Copies under paragraphs (4)(b) and (c) must be sent] at least 7 days' before the hearing of the application . . .

[(6) Within 5 business days of filing the application with the court, the bank administrator must gazette a notice undertaking to provide a copy of the application to any creditor of the bank. This notice may also be published in such other manner as the bank administrator thinks fit.]

[(7) The application must certify compliance with the preceding paragraphs of this rule.]

(8) If the court is satisfied that the conditions in section 153(1) of the Banking Act 2009 have been met it shall—
(a) discharge the bank administration order, and
(b) notify the bank administrator, who shall notify the registrar of companies.

NOTES

Para (2): substituted by the Bank Administration (England and Wales) (Amendment) Rules 2010, SI 2010/2583, rr 3, 16(a).

Para (3): revoked by SI 2010/2583, rr 3, 16(b).

Para (4): substituted by SI 2010/2583, rr 3, 16(c); words in square brackets substituted by the Financial Services Act 2012 (Consequential Amendments and Transitional Provisions) Order 2013, SI 2013/472, art 3, Sch 2, para 164(g).

Para (5): words in square brackets substituted and words omitted revoked by SI 2010/2583, rr 3, 16(d).

Paras (6), (7): substituted by SI 2010/2583, rr 3, 16(e), (f).

[7.436]

49 End of administration: dissolution

(1) This Rule supplements section 154(2)(a) of the Banking Act 2009 (bank administrator giving notice under paragraph 84 of Schedule B1 to the Insolvency Act 1986 that there are no more assets for distribution, and moving to dissolution).

(2) The bank administrator's notice under paragraph 84—
(a) must be filed with the court in Form 2.35B (the form specified in rule 2.118 of the Insolvency Rules 1986 subject to Rule 7(2) above), and
(b) must be accompanied by a final progress report.

(3) The notice shall not take effect until the court discharges the bank administration order on the application of the bank administrator.

(4) Before applying for discharge the bank administrator must send a copy of the notice under paragraph 84 and the progress report to—

(a) the registrar of companies, and

(b) each person who received notice of the bank administrator's appointment.

(5) After the expiry of the period mentioned in paragraph 84(6) (and subject to extension under paragraph 84(7)) if the court discharges the bank administration order—

(a) the notice takes effect as specified in paragraph 84(6),

(b) the court shall notify the bank administrator, who shall notify the registrar of companies.

(6) If the court makes an order under paragraph 84(7) it shall notify the bank administrator in Form 2.36B (the form specified in rule 2.118 of the Insolvency Rules 1986 subject to Rule 7(2) above), who shall notify the registrar of companies.

PART 4
COURT PROCEDURE AND PRACTICE

[7.437]
50 Introduction

This Part makes specific provision for a number of aspects of proceedings under Part 3 of the Banking Act 2009 (bank administration); Part 5 of these Rules applies a number of provisions of the Insolvency Rules 1986 to proceedings under the 2009 Act (with specified modifications).

[7.438]
51 Title of proceedings

Proceedings under Part 3 of the Banking Act 2009 shall be entitled "IN THE MATTER OF . . . (naming the bank to which the proceedings relate) AND IN THE MATTER OF PART 3 OF THE BANKING ACT 2009".

[7.439]
52 Right to inspect file

(1) The court must open and maintain a file for each set of bank administration proceedings.

(2) All documents relating to the bank administration are to be placed on the file, subject to any direction of the registrar.

[(2A) No bank administration proceedings shall be filed in the Central Office of the High Court.]

(3) The following have the right, at all reasonable times, to inspect the court's file in respect of bank administration proceedings—

(a) the bank administrator or provisional bank administrator,

(b) a person who is or was a director or officer of the bank,

(c) a member of the bank,

(d) any person stating himself in writing to be a creditor of the bank,

(e) any person stating himself in writing to be a contributory in respect of the bank,

(f) the Bank of England,

(g) the [appropriate regulator], and

(h) the FSCS.

NOTES

Para (2A): inserted by the Bank Administration (England and Wales) (Amendment) Rules 2010, SI 2010/2583, rr 3, 17.

Para (3): words in square brackets substituted by the Financial Services Act 2012 (Consequential Amendments and Transitional Provisions) Order 2013, SI 2013/472, art 3, Sch 2, para 164(g).

[7.440]
53

A right of inspection may be exercised on a person's behalf by anyone authorised by him in writing.

[7.441]
54

Any person may, with permission of the court, inspect the court's file in respect of bank administration proceedings.

[7.442]
55

A right of inspection is not exercisable in the case of documents, or parts of documents, as to which the court directs that they are not to be made open to inspection without the court's permission; and an application for a direction may be made by—

(a) the bank administrator or provisional bank administrator, or

(b) any person appearing to the court to have an interest.

[7.443]
56

Rule 7.28(2) and (3) of the Insolvency Rules 1986 (as applied by Rule 58 below) apply in respect of the court's file of bank administration proceedings as they apply in respect of court records.

[7.444]
57

Proceedings under sections 213 and 214 of the Insolvency Act 1986 (fraudulent and wrongful trading) shall be conducted in accordance with section 215 of that Act subject to the modifications specified in section 145 of the Banking Act 2009.

PART 5
APPLICATION OF INSOLVENCY RULES 1986

[7.445]
58 General application

The provisions of the Insolvency Rules 1986 listed in the Table in Rule 61 apply for the purposes of bank administration and applications for bank administration.

[7.446]
59

For that purpose the rules apply with—
(a) the general modifications set out in Rule 60,
(b) any specific modification set out in the Table in Rule 61, and
(c) any other necessary modification.

[7.447]
60 General modifications

The general modifications are that—
(a) a reference to an administrator or liquidator is to be treated as a reference to the bank administrator,
(b) a reference to administration or liquidation is to be treated as a reference to bank administration,
(c) a reference to a provisional liquidator is to be treated as a reference to a provisional bank administrator,
(d) a reference to a winding-up order is to be treated as a reference to a bank administration order,
(e) a reference to a petition for a winding-up order is to be treated as a reference to an application for a bank administration order,
(f) a reference to insolvency proceedings is to be treated as a reference to bank administration (or proceedings for bank administration),
(g) a reference to the responsible insolvency practitioner is to be treated as a reference to the bank administrator or provisional bank administrator,
(h) all references to the Official Receiver are to be ignored,
(i) all references to the county courts are to be ignored,
(j) all references to the EC regulation or to the appointment of a member State liquidator are to be ignored,
(k) a reference to the company is to be treated as a reference to the bank,
(l) a reference to an affadavit is to be treated as to a witness statement verified by a statement of truth in accordance with Part 22 of the CPR,
(m) a reference in the rules to a paragraph of Schedule B1 to the Insolvency Act 1986 is to be treated as a reference to that paragraph as applied and modified by section 145 of the Banking Act 2009, and
(n) a reference to the Insolvency Act 1986 includes a reference to Part 3 of the Banking Act 2009.

[7.448]
61 Table of applications and specific modifications

This Rule contains the Table of applied provisions of the Insolvency Rules 1986.

Rule	*Subject*	*Specific modifications*
Preparatory steps		
2.27	Notification and advertisement of administrator's appointment	. . .
2.28	Notice requiring statement of affairs	
2.29	Verification and filing	
2.30	Limited disclosure	On an application for disclosure under paragraph (4) any of the following may appear and be heard, or make written representations— (a) the bank administrator, (b) the Bank of England, and (c) the [appropriate regulator].

Rule	*Subject*	*Specific modifications*
2.31	Release from duty to submit statement of affairs; extension of time	On an application under paragraph (2) for release or extension of time any of the following may appear and be heard, or make written representations— (a) the bank administrator, (b) the Bank of England, and (c) the [appropriate regulator].
2.32	Expenses of statement of affairs	
Bank administrator's proposals and creditors' meetings		
2.33	*Administrator's proposals*	*Rule 2.33 is not applied—but equivalent provision is made by Part 3 of these Rules.*
2.34	Meetings to consider administrator's proposals	(1) Rule 2.34 applies in the Objective 2 Stage. (2) The [appropriate regulator] and the FSCS are added to the list in paragraph (2) of persons entitled to notice.
2.35	Creditors' meetings generally	The [appropriate regulator] and the FSCS are added to the list in paragraph (3) of persons to whose convenience the bank administrator is to have regard.
2.36	Chairman at meetings	
2.37	Meeting requisitioned by creditors	Treat the reference to the administrator's statement of proposals as a reference to the bank administrator's statement of proposals in accordance with Rule 29 above.
2.38	Entitlement to vote	
2.39	Admission and rejection of claims	
2.40	Secured creditors	
2.41	Holders of negotiable instruments	
2.42	Hire-purchase, conditional sale and chattel leasing agreements	
2.43	Resolutions	
2.44	Minutes	
2.45	Revision of the administrator's proposals	In paragraph (2)(c) ignore the reference to the person making the appointment.
2.46	Notice to creditors	
2.47	*Reports to creditors*	*Rule 2.47 is not applied—but equivalent provision is made by Part 3 of these Rules.*
2.48	Correspondence instead of creditors' meetings	
2.49	Venue and conduct of company meeting	
Creditors' committee		
2.50	Constitution of committee	*(A creditors' committee cannot be established until the Objective 2 Stage—see the modifications for the application of paragraphs 50 to 58 of Schedule B1 to the Insolvency Act 1986 in Table 1 in section 145 of the Banking Act 2009.)*
2.51	Formalities of establishment	

Rule	***Subject***	***Specific modifications***
2.52	Functions and meetings of the committee	
2.53	The chairman at meetings	
2.54	Quorum	
2.55	Committee-members' representatives	
2.56	Resignation	
2.57	Termination of membership	
2.58	Removal	
2.59	Vacancies	
2.60	Procedure at meetings	
2.61	Resolutions of creditors' committee by post	
2.62	Information from administrator	
2.63	Expenses of members	
2.64	Members dealing with the company	In respect of any application to set aside a transaction under paragraph (2)— (a) notice of the application must be given to the [appropriate regulator], and (b) the [appropriate regulator] may appear and be heard.
2.65	Formal defects	
Process of administration		
2.66	Application to court to dispose of charged property	If an application is made during the Objective 1 Stage, then in addition to the requirements of Rule 2.66— (a) the bank administrator must notify the Bank of England of the time and place of the hearing, (b) the Bank of England may appear, and (c) if an order is made the bank administrator must send a copy to the Bank of England as soon as is reasonably practicable.
2.67	Priority of expenses of administration	In addition to the matters listed in Rule 2.67(1), expenses in connection with provisional bank administration are payable in the following order of priority— (a) the cost of any security provided by the provisional bank administrator takes priority equally with security provided by the bank administrator, and (b) the remuneration of the provisional bank administrator ranks next, and (c) any deposit lodged on an application for the appointment of a provisional bank administrator ranks next.

Rule	*Subject*	*Specific modifications*
2.68	Distributions to creditors: introduction	*(Distributions in the case of bank administration following transfer to a bridge bank under section 12(2) of the Banking Act 2009 and during the Objective 1 Stage require the Bank of England's consent—see the modification for the application of paragraph 65 of Schedule B1 to the Insolvency Act 1986 in Table 1 in section 145 of the Banking Act 2009.)*
2.69	Debts of insolvent company to rank equally	
2.70	Dividends: supplementary	
2.71	Division of unsold assets	
2.72	Proving a debt	
2.73	Claim established by witness statement	
2.74	Costs of proving	
2.75	Administrator to allow inspection of proofs	
2.76	New administrator: transfer of proofs	
2.77	Admission and rejection of proofs for dividend	
2.78	Appeal against decision on proof	In respect of any application under Rule 2.78(1) or (2)— (a) notice of the application must be given to the [appropriate regulator] and (b) the [appropriate regulator]
2.79	Withdrawal or variation of proof	
2.80	Expunging of proof by the court	In respect of any application under Rule 2.80(1)(b)— (a) notice of the application must be given to the [appropriate regulator] and (b) the [appropriate regulator]
2.81	Estimate of quantum of claims	
2.82	Negotiable instruments etc	
2.83	Secured creditors	
2.84	Discounts	
2.85	Mutual credit and set-off	[Where all or part of a creditor's claim against the bank is in respect of protected deposits (see rule 47A(6)), rule 47A applies instead.]
2.86	Debt in foreign currency	
2.87	Periodical payments	
2.88	Interest	
2.89	Debt payable in future	
2.90	Value of security	
2.91	Surrender for non-disclosure	
2.92	Redemption by administrator	
2.93	Test of security's value	
2.94	Realisation of security by creditor	

Rule	*Subject*	*Specific modifications*
2.95	Notice of proposed distribution	The following are added to the list of those entitled to receive notice under Rule 2.95(2)— (a) the [appropriate regulator] (b) the FSCS (c) during the Objective 1 Stage of a bank administration following transfer to a bridge bank under section 12(2) of the Banking Act 2009
2.96	Admission or rejection of proofs	
2.97	Declaration of dividend	
2.98	Notice of declaration of dividend	(1) The following are added to the list of those entitled to receive notice under Rule 2.98(1)— (a) the [appropriate regulator] (b) the FSCS (c) during the Objective 1 Stage of a bank administration following transfer to a bridge bank under section 12(2) of the Banking Act 2009 (2) In the case of bank administration following transfer to a bridge bank under section 12(2) of the Banking Act 2009 and during the Objective 1 Stage
2.99	Payment of dividends etc	
2.100	Notice of no dividend or no further dividend	The bank administrator must copy any notice under Rule 2.100 to— (a) the [appropriate regulator] (b) the FSCS (c) the Bank of England
2.101	Proof altered after payment of dividend	
2.102	Secured creditors	
2.103	Disqualification from dividend	In respect of any application for disqualification under Rule 2.103— (a) notice of the application must be given to the [appropriate regulator], and (b) the [appropriate regulator] may appear and be heard.
2.104	Assignment of right to dividend	
2.105	Debt payable in future	The "relevant date" is the date of the bank administration order.
The bank administrator		
2.106	Fixing of remuneration	(1) In the Objective 1 Stage the Bank of England shall fix the bank administrator's remuneration in accordance with Rule 2.106(2)(a) or (b). (2) In the Objective 2 Stage, Rule 2.106 applies (but pending action under paragraphs (3) or (5) arrangements established by the Bank of England in the Objective 1 Stage shall continue to apply).

Rule	*Subject*	*Specific modifications*
2.107	Recourse to meeting of creditors	
2.108	Recourse to the court	(1) In respect of remuneration fixed by the Bank of England— (a) Rule 2.108 applies as if references to the creditors' committee were references to the Bank of England, and (b) the court shall have regard to Objective 1. (2) In respect of any application under Rule 2.108— (a) notice of the application must be given to the [appropriate regulator], and (b) the [appropriate regulator] may appear and be heard.
2.109	Creditors' claim that remuneration is excessive	Rule 2.109 applies only during the Objective 2 Stage.
4.127B and Schedule 6	Remuneration where assets realised on behalf of chargeholder	
Ending administration		
2.110	Final progress report	(1) The reference to Rule 2.47 is to be treated as a reference to Rule 35 above. (2) In the case of bank administration following transfer to a bridge bank under section 12(2) of the Banking Act 2009 the final progress report— (a) must not be made until the bank administrator is satisfied that any payment likely to be made to the bank from a scheme under a resolution fund order has been made, and (b) must state whether any payment has been received and, if so, its amount.
. . .		. . .
2.114	Application to court by administrator	[Rule 2.114 is not applied—but equivalent provision is made by Part 3 of these Rules.]
2.118	Moving from administration to dissolution	*Rule 2.118 is not applied—but equivalent provision is made by Part 3 of these Rules.*
Replacing bank administrator		
2.119	Grounds for resignation	During the Objective 1 Stage the Bank of England's consent, as well as the court's permission, is required for resignation under paragraph (2).
2.120	Notice of intention to resign	The Bank of England and the [appropriate regulator] are added to the list of those entitled to notice under paragraph (1).
2.121	Notice of resignation	

Rule	Subject	Specific modifications
2.122	Application to court to remove administrator	*(An application may be made during the Objective 1 Stage only with the Bank of England's consent—see the modifications for the application of paragraph 88 of Schedule B1 to the Insolvency Act 1986 in Table 1 in section 145 of the Banking Act 2009.)* (1) An application must state either— (a) that the Bank of England has consented to its being made, or (b) that the Objective 1 Stage has ended. (2) The [appropriate regulator] is added to the list of those entitled to notice under paragraph (2).
2.123	Notice of vacation of office on ceasing to be qualified	
2.124	Death of administrator	
2.125	Application to replace	Rule 2.125 is applied during the Objective 2 Stage only (and ignoring references to paragraph 95 of Schedule B1). *(For equivalent provision about application for removal by the Bank of England during the Objective 1 Stage (in accordance with the modifications for the application of paragraph 91 of Schedule B1 to the Insolvency Act 1986 in Table 1 in section 145 of the Banking Act 2009) see Part 3 of these Rules.*
2.126	Notification and advertisement of replacement	
2.127	Notification and advertisement of appointment of joint administrator	
2.128	Notice to registrar of companies of replacement or addition	
2.129	Duties on vacating office	
Provisional bank administrator (see application of section 135 of the Insolvency Act 1986 in Table 2 in section 145 of the Banking Act 2009)		
4.25	*Appointment*	*Rule 4.25 is not applied—but equivalent provision is made by Part 3 of these Rules.*
4.25A	*Notice of appointment*	*Rule 4.25A is not applied—but equivalent provision is made by Part 3 of these Rules.*
4.26	*Order of appointment*	*Rule 4.26 is not applied—but equivalent provision is made by Part 3 of these Rules.*
4.28	Security	
4.29	Failure to give or keep up security	
4.30	Remuneration	Ignore paragraph (4).
4.31	Termination of appointment	(1) An application for termination may be made by— (a) the provisional bank administrator, or (b) the Bank of England. (2) A provisional bank administrator's appointment terminates on the making of a bank administration order.

Rule	*Subject*	*Specific modifications*
Disclaimer		
4.187	Notice of disclaimer	*(In the case of bank administration following transfer to a bridge bank under section 12(2) of the Banking Act 2009 notice may be given during the Objective 1 Stage only with the Bank of England's consent—see the modifications for the application of section 178 of the Insolvency Act 1986 in Table 2 in section 145 of the Banking Act 2009.)*
4.188	Communication to interested persons	
4.189	Additional notices	
4.190	Duty to keep court informed	
4.191	Application by interested party	
4.192	Interest in property to be declared on request	
4.193	Disclaimer presumed valid and effective	
4.194	Application for exercise of court's powers under section 181 of the Insolvency Act 1986	*(Section 181 is applied by Table 2 in section 145 of the Banking Act 2009.)*
Court procedure and practice		
7.1	Application of Chapter 1 of Part 7	Chapter 1 does not apply to an application for a bank administration order (which is addressed in Part 2 of these Rules).
7.2	Interpretation	
7.3	Form and contents of application	
7.3A	Application to disapply section 176A of the Insolvency Act 1986	
7.4	Filing and service of application	
7.4A	Notice of application under section 176A of the Insolvency Act 1986	
7.5	Other hearings *ex parte*	
7.6	Hearing of application	
7.7	Use of witness statement evidence	
7.8	Filing and service of witness statements	
7.9	Use of reports	
7.10	Adjournment of hearings; directions	
7.16	Nomination and appointment of shorthand writers	
7.17	Remuneration of shorthand writers	
7.19	Enforcement of court orders	
7.20	Orders enforcing compliance with Rules	
7.21	Warrants	
7.23	Warrants under section 236	
7.27	Court records	

Rule	*Subject*	*Specific modifications*
7.28	Inspection of records	
. . .	. . .	
7.31	*Right to inspect court file*	*Rule 7.31 is not applied—but equivalent provision is made in Part 4 of these Rules.*
. . .	. . .	
7.33	Costs: application of the Civil Proceedings Rules	
7.34	Requirement to assess costs by the detailed procedure	
7.35	Procedure where detailed assessment required	
7.36	Costs of execution or other process	
7.38	Costs paid otherwise than out of the insolvent estate	
7.39	Award of costs against responsible insolvency practitioner	
7.40	Application for costs	
7.41	Costs and expenses of witnesses	
7.42	Final costs certificate	
7.43	Persons who lack capacity to manage their affairs: introductory	
7.44	Appointment of another person to act	
7.45	Witness statement in support of application	
7.46	Services of notices following appointment	
7.47	Appeals and reviews of court orders	. . .
7.49	Procedure on appeal	
7.51	Principal court rules and practice to apply	*(The reference to the CPR, the practice and procedure of the High Court and of the county court is to be treated as a reference to the CPR (Part 52).)*
7.53	Right of attendance	
7.54	Insolvency practitioner's solicitor	
7.55	Formal defects	
7.56	Restriction on concurrent proceedings and remedies	
7.58	Security in court	
7.59	Payment into court	
7.60	Further information and disclosure	
7.61	Office copies of documents	
Proxies		
8.1	Definition of proxy	
8.2	Issue and use of forms	
8.3	Use of proxies at meetings	
8.4	Retention of proxies	
8.5	Right of inspection of proxies	

Rule	*Subject*	*Specific modifications*
8.6	Proxy-holder with financial interest	
8.7	Company representation	[In paragraph (1) omit "of creditors or"]
Examination of persons		
9.1	Preliminary	(1) *Part 9 applies to applications under section 236 of the Insolvency Act 1986 (inquiry into company's dealings) as applied by Table 2 in section 145 of the Banking Act 2009.* (2) Treat a reference to "the insolvent" as a reference to the bank.
9.2	Form and contents of application	
9.3	Order for examination	
9.4	Procedure for examination	
9.5	Record of examination	
9.6	Costs of proceedings	
. . .	. . .	. . .
Miscellaneous and general		
12.1	Regulation of specified administrative matters	A reference to the Secretary of State includes a reference to the Treasury.
12.2	Costs and expenses	
12.3	Provable debts	
12.4	Notices	
12.4A	Quorum at meetings	. . .
12.5	Evidence of proceedings at meeting	
12.6	Documents issued by Secretary of State	
12.8	Insolvency practitioner's security	
12.9	Time-limits	
12.10	Service by post	*(Rule 12.10 applies subject to express provision about service made in these Rules.)*
12.11	Service and notice: general	Part 6 of the CPR applies subject to any provision of these rules.
12.12	Service outside jurisdiction	Part 6 of the CPR applies with regard to service in Scotland or Northern Ireland, subject to any provision of these rules. Where service is to take place outside the United Kingdom, where these rules provide for service, the court may direct how that service is to be effect. With regard to service otherwise, Part 6 of the CPR applies.
12.13	Confidentiality of documents	
12.14	Notices sent simultaneously to same person	
12.15	Right to copy documents	
12.15A	Charge for copy documents	
12.16	Non-receipt of notice of meeting	
12.17	Right to have list of creditors	
12.18	False claim of status as creditor	
12.20	Gazette	

Rule	Subject	Specific modifications
12.21 and Schedule 5	Punishment of offences	
12.22	Notice of order under section 176A of the Insolvency Act 1986	
13.1 to 13.13	Interpretation and application	

NOTES

Words "appropriate regulator" in square brackets substituted in each place by the Financial Services Act 2012 (Consequential Amendments and Transitional Provisions) Order 2013, SI 2013/472, art 3, Sch 2, para 164(g).

In entries relating to rules 2.27, 7.47, 12.4A, words omitted from column 3 revoked by the Bank Administration (England and Wales) (Amendment) Rules 2010, SI 2010/2583, rr 3, 18(a), (f), (i).

In entry relating to rule 2.85, in column 3 words in square brackets inserted by SI 2010/2583, rr 3, 18(b).

Entries relating to rules 2.113, 7.30, 7.32, 11.1–11.13 (all omitted) revoked by SI 2010/2583, rr 3, 18(c), (e), (h).

In entries relating to rules 2.114, 8.7, in column 3 words in square brackets substituted by SI 2010/2583, rr 3, 18(d), (g).

Note: the italicised text in the table above is as set out in the original and does not represent amendments to the text.

C
BUILDING SOCIETIES

BUILDING SOCIETIES ACT 1986

(1986 c 53)

ARRANGEMENT OF SECTIONS

PART X
DISSOLUTION, WINDING UP, MERGERS, TRANSFER OF BUSINESS

Dissolution and winding up

86 Modes of dissolution and winding up . . . . [7.449]
87 Dissolution by consent. . . . . [7.450]
88 Voluntary winding up . . . . [7.451]
89 Winding up by court: grounds and petitioners . . . . [7.452]
89A Building society insolvency as alternative order . . . . [7.453]
90 Application of winding up legislation to building societies. . . . . [7.454]
90A Application of other companies insolvency legislation to building societies . . . . [7.455]
90B Power to alter priorities on dissolution and winding up. . . . . [7.456]
90C Application of bank insolvency and administration legislation to building societies. . . . . [7.457]
90D Notice to the FCA and the PRA of preliminary steps . . . . [7.458]
90E Disqualification of directors. . . . . [7.459]
91 Power of court to declare dissolution of building society void . . . . [7.460]
92 Supplementary . . . . [7.461]

PART XI
MISCELLANEOUS AND SUPPLEMENTARY AND CONVEYANCING SERVICES

General

125 Short title . . . . [7.462]
126 Commencement. . . . . [7.463]

SCHEDULES

Schedule 15—Application of companies winding up legislation to building societies
Part I—General mode of application . . . . [7.464]
Part II—Modified Application of Insolvency Act 1986 Parts IV, 6, 7, 12 and 13 and Schedule 10 . [7.465]
Part III—Modified application of Insolvency (Northern Ireland) Order 1989 Parts V, 11 and 12. . . [7.466]
Part IV—Dissolution of building society wound up (England and Wales, Scotland and Northern Ireland) . . . . [7.467]
Schedule 15A—Application of other companies insolvency legislation to building societies
Part I—General mode of application . . . . [7.468]
Part II—Modified Application of Parts I to III, 6, 7, 12 and 13 of Insolvency Act 1986 . . . . [7.469]
Part III—Modified application of Parts II, III, 4 and 12 of Insolvency (Northern Ireland) Order 1989 . . . . [7.470]

An Act to make fresh provision with respect to building societies and further provision with respect to conveyancing service

[25 July 1986]

1–85 *((Pts I–IX) outside the scope of this work.)*

PART X
DISSOLUTION, WINDING UP, MERGERS, TRANSFER OF BUSINESS

Dissolution and winding up

[7.449]
86 Modes of dissolution and winding up

(1) A building society—
(a) may be dissolved by consent of the members, or
(b) may be wound up voluntarily or by the court,

in accordance with this Part; and a building society may not, except where it is dissolved by virtue of section 93(5), 94(10) or 97(9), [or following building society insolvency or building society special administration,] be dissolved or wound up in any other manner.

(2) A building society which is in the course of dissolution by consent, or is being wound up voluntarily, may be wound up by the court.

NOTES

Sub-s (1): words in square brackets inserted by the Building Societies (Insolvency and Special Administration) Order 2009, SI 2009/805, art 7.

[7.450]

87 Dissolution by consent

(1) A building society may be dissolved by an instrument of dissolution, with the consent (testified by their signature of that instrument) of three-quarters of the members of the society, holding not less than two-thirds of the number of shares in the society.

(2) An instrument of dissolution under this section shall set out—

(a) the liabilities and assets of the society in detail;
(b) the number of members, and the amount standing to their credit in the accounting records of the society;
(c) the claims of depositors and other creditors, and the provision to be made for their payment;
(d) the intended appropriation or division of the funds and property of the society;
(e) the names of one or more persons to be appointed as trustees for the purposes of the dissolution, and their remuneration.

(3) An instrument of dissolution made with consent given and testified as mentioned in subsection (1) above may be altered with the like consent, testified in the like manner.

(4) The provisions of this Act shall continue to apply in relation to a building society as if the trustees appointed under the instrument of dissolution were the board of directors of the society.

(5) The trustees, within 15 days of the necessary consent being given and testified (in accordance with subsection (1) above) to—

(a) an instrument of dissolution, or
(b) any alteration to such an instrument,

shall give notice to the [FCA and, if the society is a PRA-authorised person, the PRA] of the fact and, except in the case of an alteration to an instrument, of the date of commencement of the dissolution, enclosing a copy of the instrument or altered instrument, as the case may be; and if the trustees fail to comply with this subsection they shall each be liable on summary conviction to a fine not exceeding level 3 on the standard scale.

(6) An instrument of dissolution under this section, or an alteration to such an instrument, shall be binding on all members of the society as from the date on which the copy of the instrument or altered instrument, as the case may be, is placed in the public file of the society under subsection (10) below.

(7) The trustees shall, within 28 days from the termination of the dissolution, give notice to the [FCA and, if the society is a PRA-authorised person, the PRA] of the fact and the date of the termination, enclosing an account and balance sheet signed and certified by them as correct, and showing the assets and liabilities of the society at the commencement of the dissolution, and the way in which those assets and liabilities have been applied and discharged; and, if they fail to do so they shall each be liable on summary conviction—

(a) to a fine not exceeding level 2 on the standard scale, and
(b) in the case of a continuing offence, to an additional fine not exceeding £10 for every day during which the offence continues.

(8) Except with the consent of the [appropriate authority], no instrument of dissolution, or alteration of such an instrument, shall be of any effect if the purpose of the proposed dissolution or alteration is to effect or facilitate the transfer of the society's engagements to any other society [or the transfer of its business to a company].

(9) Any provision in a resolution or document that members of a building society proposed to be dissolved shall accept investments in a company or another society (whether in shares, deposits or any other form) in or towards satisfaction of their rights in the dissolution shall be conclusive evidence of such a purpose as is mentioned in subsection (8) above.

(10) The [FCA] shall keep in the public file of the society any notice or other document received by it under subsection (5) or (7) above and shall record in that file the date on which the notice or document is placed in it.

NOTES

Sub-ss (5), (7), (10): words in square brackets substituted by the Financial Services Act 2012 (Mutual Societies) Order 2013, SI 2013/496, art 2(b), Sch 8, paras 1, 31(1)–(3), (5).

Sub-s (8): words in first pair of square brackets substituted by SI 2013/496, art 2(b), Sch 8, paras 1, 31(1), (4); words in second pair of square brackets substituted by the Building Societies Act 1997, s 43, Sch 7, para 38.

[7.451]

88 Voluntary winding up

(1) A building society may be wound up voluntarily under the applicable winding up legislation if it resolves by special resolution that it be wound up voluntarily[, but a resolution may not be passed if—

(a) the conditions in section 90D are not satisfied, or
(b) the society is in building society insolvency or building society special administration].

[(1A) A resolution under subsection (1) shall have no effect without the prior approval of the court.]

(2) A copy of any special resolution passed for the voluntary winding up of a building society shall be sent by the society [to the FCA and, if the society is a PRA-authorised person, the PRA] within 15 days after it is passed; and the [FCA must keep a copy] in the public file of the society.

(3) A copy of any such resolution shall be annexed to every copy of the memorandum or of the rules issued after the passing of the resolution.

(4) If a building society fails to comply with subsection (2) or (3) above the society shall be liable on summary conviction to a fine not exceeding level 3 on the standard scale and so shall any officer who is also guilty of the offence.
(5) For the purposes of this section, a liquidator of the society shall be treated as an officer of it.

NOTES

Sub-s (1): words in square brackets inserted by the Building Societies (Insolvency and Special Administration) Order 2009, SI 2009/805, art 4.

Sub-s (1A): inserted by SI 2009/805, art 4.

Sub-s (2): words in square brackets substituted by the Financial Services Act 2012 (Mutual Societies) Order 2013, SI 2013/496, art 2(b), Sch 8, paras 1, 32.

[7.452]

89 Winding up by court: grounds and petitioners

(1) A building society may be wound up under the applicable winding up legislation by the court on any of the following grounds in addition to the grounds referred to or specified in section 37(1), that is to say, if—
- (a) the society has by special resolution resolved that it be wound up by the court;
- (b) the number of members is reduced below ten;
- (c) the number of directors is reduced below two;
- (d) being a society registered as a building society under this Act or the repealed enactments, the society has not been [given permission under [Part 4A] of the Financial Services and Markets Act 2000 to accept deposits] and more than three years has expired since it was so registered;
- [(e) the society's permission under [Part 4A] of the Financial Services and Markets Act 2000 to accept deposits has been cancelled (and no such permission has subsequently been given to it);]
- (f) the society exists for an illegal purpose;
- (g) the society is unable to pay its debts; or
- (h) the court is of the opinion that it is just and equitable that the society should be wound up.

(2) Except as provided by subsection (3) below, section 37 or the applicable winding up legislation, a petition for the winding up of a building society may be presented by—
- [(a) the FCA, after consulting the PRA if the society is a PRA-authorised person,
- (aa) if the society is a PRA-authorised person, the PRA, after consulting the FCA,]
- (b) the building society or its directors,
- (c) any creditor or creditors (including any contingent or any prospective creditor), or
- (d) any contributory or contributories,

or by all or any of those parties, together or separately.

(3) A contributory may not present a petition unless either—
- (a) the number of members is reduced below ten, or
- (b) the share in respect of which he is a contributory has been held by him, or has devolved to him on the death of a former holder and between them been held, for at least six months before the commencement of the winding up.

(4) For the purposes of this section, in relation to a building society,—
- (a) . . .
- [(b) the reference to its existing for an illegal purpose includes a reference to its existing after it has ceased to comply with the requirement imposed by section 5(1)(a) (purpose or principal purpose).]

(5) In this section, "contributory" has the same meaning as in paragraph 9(2) or, as the case may be, paragraph 37(2) of Schedule 15 to this Act.

NOTES

Sub-s (1): words in first (outer) pair of square brackets in para (d) and the whole of para (e) substituted by the Financial Services and Markets Act 2000 (Mutual Societies) Order 2001, SI 2001/2617, art 13(1), Sch 3, Pt II, paras 131, 175(a)(i), (ii); for transitional provisions see art 13(3), Sch 5, paras 17, 23 thereto; words in second (inner) pair of square brackets in para (d) and words in square brackets in para (e) substituted by the Financial Services Act 2012 (Mutual Societies) Order 2013, SI 2013/496, art 2(b), Sch 8, paras 1, 33(1), (2).

Sub-s (2): paras (a), (aa) substituted for the original para (a) by SI 2013/496, art 2(b), Sch 8, paras 1, 33(1), (3).

Sub-s (4): para (a) repealed by SI 2001/2617, art 13(1), (2), Sch 3, Pt II, paras 131, 175(b), Sch 4; para (b) substituted by the Building Societies Act 1997, s 43, Sch 7, para 39 (as to the coming into force of this amendment, see s 92 of this Act and the note "Commencement" at **[7.461]**).

[7.453]

[89A Building society insolvency as alternative order

(1) On a petition for a winding up order or an application for an administration order in respect of a building society the court may, instead, make a building society insolvency order (under section 94 of the Banking Act 2009 as applied by section 90C above).

(2) A building society insolvency order may be made under subsection (1) only—
- (a) on the application of the [appropriate authority] made with the consent of the Bank of England, or
- (b) on the application of the Bank of England.]

NOTES

Inserted by the Building Societies (Insolvency and Special Administration) Order 2009, SI 2009/805, art 5.

Sub-s (2): words in square brackets in para (a) substituted by the Financial Services Act 2012 (Mutual Societies) Order 2013, SI 2013/496, art 2(b), Sch 8, paras 1, 34.

[7.454]

90 Application of winding up legislation to building societies

(1) In this section "the companies winding up legislation" means the enactments applicable in relation to England and Wales, Scotland or Northern Ireland which are specified in paragraph 1 of Schedule 15 to this Act (including any enactment which creates an offence by any person arising out of acts or omissions occurring before the commencement of the winding up).

(2) In its application to the winding up of a building society, by virtue of section 88(1) or 89(1), the companies winding up legislation shall have effect with the modifications effected by Parts I to III of Schedule 15 to this Act; and the supplementary provisions of Part IV of that Schedule shall also have effect in relation to such a winding up.

(3) In sections 37, 88, 89 and 103, "the applicable winding up legislation" means the companies winding up legislation as so modified.

[7.455]

[90A Application of other companies insolvency legislation to building societies

For the purpose of—

(a) enabling voluntary arrangements to be approved in relation to building societies,
(b) enabling administration orders to be made in relation to building societies, and
(c) making provision with respect to persons appointed in England and Wales[, Scotland] or Northern Ireland as receivers and managers[, or receivers,] of building societies' property,

the enactments specified in paragraph 1(2) of Schedule 15A to this Act shall apply in relation to building societies with the modifications specified in that Schedule.]

NOTES

Inserted by the Building Societies Act 1997, s 39(1).

Words in square brackets in para (c) inserted by the Building Societies (Floating Charges and Other Provisions) Order 2016, SI 2016/679, art 3, in relation to a floating charge created by a building society on or after 28 June 2016.

Application: this section is applied, with modifications, for the purposes of a relevant building society, by the Building Societies (Financial Assistance) Order 2010, SI 2010/1188, art 10 at **[18.216]**.

The substitution of the Insolvency Act 1986, Pt II (administration orders) by the Enterprise Act 2002, s 248(1), (2), Sch 16, does not affect building societies for which special arrangements for the administration procedure have been made by this section and Sch 15A at **[7.468]**, with modifications; see s 249 of the 2002 Act at **[2.10]**.

[7.456]

[90B Power to alter priorities on dissolution and winding up

(1) The Treasury may by order make provision for the purpose of ensuring that, on the winding up, or dissolution by consent, of a building society, any assets available for satisfying the society's liabilities to creditors or to shareholders are applied in satisfying those liabilities pari passu.

(2) Liabilities to creditors do not include—

(a) liabilities in respect of subordinated deposits;
(b) liabilities in respect of preferential debts;
(c) any other category of liability which the Treasury specifies in the order for the purposes of this paragraph.

(3) Liabilities to shareholders do not include liabilities in respect of deferred shares.

(4) A preferential debt is a debt which constitutes a preferential debt for the purposes of any of the enactments specified in paragraph 1 of Schedule 15 to this Act (or which would constitute such a debt if the society were being wound up).

(5) An order under this section may—

(a) make amendments of this Act;
(b) make different provision for different purposes;
(c) make such consequential, supplementary, transitional and saving provision as appears to the Treasury to be necessary or expedient.

(6) The power to make an order under this section is exercisable by statutory instrument but no such order may be made unless a draft of it has been laid before and approved by a resolution of each House of Parliament.]

NOTES

Commencement: 20 November 2014.

Inserted by the Building Societies (Funding) and Mutual Societies (Transfers) Act 2007, s 2.

Orders: the Banks and Building Societies (Depositor Preference and Priorities) Order 2014, SI 2014/3486.

[7.457]

[90C Application of bank insolvency and administration legislation to building societies

(1) Parts 2 (Bank Insolvency) and 3 (Bank Administration) of the Banking Act 2009 shall apply in relation to building societies with any modifications specified in an order made under section 130 or 158 of that Act and with the modifications specified in subsection (2) below.

(2) In the application of Parts 2 and 3 of that Act to building societies—

(a) references to "bank" (except in the term "bridge bank" and the terms specified in paragraphs (b) and (c)) have effect as references to "building society";

(b) references to "bank insolvency", "bank insolvency order", "bank liquidation" and "bank liquidator" have effect as references to "building society insolvency", "building society insolvency order", "building society liquidation" and "building society liquidator";

(c) references to "bank administration", "bank administration order" and "bank administrator" have effect as references to "building society special administration", "building society special administration order" and "building society special administrator".]

NOTES

Inserted by the Building Societies (Insolvency and Special Administration) Order 2009, SI 2009/805, art 2.

[7.458]

[90D Notice to the [FCA and the PRA] of preliminary steps

(1) An application for an administration order in respect of a building society may not be determined unless the conditions below are satisfied.

(2) A petition for a winding up order in respect of a building society may not be determined unless the conditions below are satisfied.

(3) A resolution for voluntary winding up of a building society may not be passed unless the conditions below are satisfied.

(4) An administrator of a building society may not be appointed unless the conditions below are satisfied.

(5) Condition 1 is that the [FCA[, the Bank of England] and, if the society is a PRA-authorised person, the PRA have] been notified—

(a) by the applicant for an administration order, that the application has been made,

(b) by the petitioner for a winding up order, that the petition has been presented,

(c) by the building society, that a resolution for voluntary winding up may be passed, or

(d) by the person proposing to appoint an administrator, of the proposed appointment.

(6) Condition 2 is that a copy of the notice complying with Condition 1 has been filed with the court (and made available for public inspection by the court).

(7) Condition 3 is that—

(a) the period of [7 days], beginning with the day on which the notice is received, has ended, or

[(b) both—

(i) the Bank of England has informed the person who gave the notice that it does not intend to exercise a stabilisation power under Part 1 of the Banking Act 2009 in relation to the building society (and condition 5 has been met, if applicable), and

(ii) each of the PRA and the Bank of England has informed the person who gave the notice that it does not intend to apply for a building society insolvency order (under section 95 of the Banking Act 2009 as applied by section 90C).]

(8) Condition 4 is that no application for a building society insolvency order is pending.

[(8A) Condition 5—

(a) applies only if a resolution instrument has been made under section 12A of the Banking Act 2009 with respect to the building society in the three months ending with the date on which the Bank of England receives the notification under Condition 1, and

(b) is that the Bank of England has informed the person who gave the notice that it consents to the insolvency procedure to which the notice relates going ahead.]

(9) Arranging for the giving of notice in order to satisfy Condition 1 can be a step with a view to minimising the potential loss to a building society's creditors for the purpose of section 214 of the Insolvency Act 1986 (wrongful trading) or Article 178 (wrongful trading) of the Insolvency (Northern Ireland) Order 1989 as applied in relation to building societies by section 90 of, and Schedule 15 to, this Act.

(10) Where [the society is a PRA-authorised person and] [notice has been given under Condition 1]—

(a) . . .

(b) the [PRA] shall inform the person who gave the notice, within the period in Condition 3(a), whether it intends to apply for a building society insolvency order, . . .

(c) if the Bank of England decides to apply for a building society insolvency order or to exercise a stabilisation power under Part 1 of the Banking Act 2009, the Bank shall inform the person who gave the notice, within the period in Condition 3(a)[; and

[(d) if Condition 5 applies, the Bank of England must, within the period in Condition 3(a), inform the person who gave the notice whether or not it consents to the insolvency procedure to which the notice relates going ahead.]

[(11) Where the society is not a PRA-authorised person and [notice has been received under Condition 1]—

(a) . . .

(b) if the Bank of England decides to apply for a building society insolvency order or to exercise a stabilisation power under Part 1 of the Banking Act 2009, the Bank shall inform the person who gave the notice, within the period in Condition 3(a)[; and

(c) if Condition 5 applies, the Bank of England must, within the period in Condition 3(a), inform the person who gave the notice whether or not it consents to the insolvency procedure to which the notice relates going ahead].]

[(12) References in this section to the insolvency procedure to which the notice relates are to the procedure for the determination, resolution or appointment in question (see subsections (1) to (4)).]]

NOTES

Inserted, together with s 90E, by the Building Societies (Insolvency and Special Administration) Order 2009, SI 2009/805, art 6.

Section heading: words in square brackets substituted by the Financial Services Act 2012 (Mutual Societies) Order 2013, SI 2013/496, art 2(b), Sch 8, paras 1, 35(1), (6).

Sub-s (5): words in first (outer) pair of square brackets substituted by SI 2013/496, art 2(b), Sch 8, paras 1, 35(1), (2); words in second (inner) pair of square brackets inserted by the Building Societies (Bail-in) Order 2014, SI 2014/3344, art 4(1), (2).

Sub-s (7): words in square brackets in para (a), and para (b) substituted by SI 2014/3344, art 4(1), (3).

Sub-ss (8A), (12): inserted and added respectively by SI 2014/3344, art 4(1), (4), (7).

Sub-s (10): words in first pair of square brackets inserted, and word in third pair of square brackets substituted, by SI 2013/496, art 2(b), Sch 8, paras 1, 35(1), (4); words in second pair of square brackets substituted, para (a) and word omitted from para (b) repealed, and para (d) and word immediately preceding it added, by SI 2014/3344, art 4(1), (5).

Sub-s (11): added by SI 2013/496, art 2(b), Sch 8, paras 1, 35(1), (5); words in first pair of square brackets substituted, para (a) repealed, and para (c) and word immediately preceding it added by SI 2014/3344, art 4(1), (6).

[7.459]

[90E Disqualification of directors

(1) In this section "the Disqualification Act" means the Company Directors Disqualification Act 1986.

(2) In the Disqualification Act—

(a) a reference to liquidation includes a reference to building society insolvency and a reference to building society special administration,

(b) a reference to winding up includes a reference to making or being subject to a building society insolvency order and a reference to making or being subject to a building society special administration order,

(c) a reference to becoming insolvent includes a reference to becoming subject to a building society insolvency order and a reference to becoming subject to a building society special administration order, and

(d) a reference to a liquidator includes a reference to a building society liquidator and a reference to a building society special administrator.

[(3) For the purposes of the application of section 7A of the Disqualification Act (office-holder's report on conduct of directors) to a building society which is subject to a building society insolvency order—

(a) the "office-holder" is the building society liquidator,

(b) the "insolvency date" means the date on which the building society insolvency order is made, and

(c) subsections (9) to (11) are omitted.

(4) For the purposes of the application of that section to a building society which is subject to a building society special administration order—

(a) the "office-holder" is the building society special administrator,

(b) the "insolvency date" means the date on which the building society special administration order is made, and

(c) subsections (9) to (11) are omitted.]

(5) In the application of this section to Northern Ireland, references to the Disqualification Act are to the Company Directors Disqualification (Northern Ireland) Order 2002 and [in subsections (3) and (4)—

(a) the reference to section 7A of the Disqualification Act is a reference to Article 10A of that Order (office-holder's report on conduct of directors), and

(b) the reference to subsections (9) to (11) of that section is a reference to paragraphs (9) to (11) of that Article.]]

NOTES

Inserted as noted to s 90D at **[7.458]**.

Sub-ss (3), (4): substituted by the Small Business, Enterprise and Employment Act 2015 and the Insolvency (Amendment) Act (Northern Ireland) 2016 (Consequential Amendments and Transitional Provisions) Regulations 2017, SI 2017/400, reg 2(1), (2)(a).

Sub-s (5): words in square brackets substituted by SI 2017/400, reg 2(1), (2)(b).

[7.460]

91 Power of court to declare dissolution of building society void

(1) Where a building society has been dissolved under section 87 or following a winding up, [building society insolvency or building society special administration,] the High Court or, in relation to a society whose principal office was in Scotland, the Court of Session, may, at any time within 12 years after the date on which the society was dissolved, make an order under this section declaring the dissolution to have been void.

(2) An order under this section may be made, on such terms as the court thinks fit, on an application by the trustees under section 87 or the liquidator, [building society liquidator or building society special administrator,] as the case may be, or by any other person appearing to the Court to be interested.

(3) When an order under this section is made, such proceedings may be taken as might have been taken if the society had not been dissolved.

(4) The person on whose application the order is made shall, within seven days of its being so made, or such further time as the Court may allow, [furnish the FCA and, if the society is a PRA-authorised person, the PRA] with a copy of the order; and the [FCA must keep a copy] in the public file of the society.

(5) If a person fails to comply with subsection (4) above, he shall be liable on summary conviction—

(a) to a fine not exceeding level 3 on the standard scale, and

(b) in the case of a continuing offence, to an additional fine not exceeding £40 for every day during which the offence continues.

NOTES

Sub-ss (1) (2): words in square brackets inserted by the Building Societies (Insolvency and Special Administration) Order 2009, SI 2009/805, art 8.

Sub-s (4): words in square brackets substituted by the Financial Services Act 2012 (Mutual Societies) Order 2013, SI 2013/496, art 2(b), Sch 8, paras 1, 36.

[7.461]
[92 Supplementary

Where at any time a building society is being wound up or dissolved by consent, [or is in building society insolvency or building society special administration,] a borrowing member shall not be liable to pay any amount other than one which, at that time, is payable under the mortgage or other security by which his indebtedness to the society in respect of the loan is secured.]

NOTES

Substituted by the Building Societies Act 1997, s 43, Sch 7, para 40.

Words in square brackets inserted by the Building Societies (Insolvency and Special Administration) Order 2009, SI 2009/805, art 9.

Commencement: the effect of the Building Societies Act 1997 (Commencement No 3) Order 1997, SI 1997/2668, art 2(2), (3), (5), Schedule, Pt II (made under s 47(3) of the 1997 Act) is that the substitution of this section by the Building Societies Act 1997 (and the amendment to s 89 at **[7.452]**) comes into force as follows: (i) on 1 December 1997, for all purposes, in the case of any existing building society (as defined by Sch 8, para 1(7) to the 1997 Act) which sent the central office a record of alterations to its purpose or principal purpose, its powers and its rules, in accordance with Sch 8, para 1(1) to that Act, where the alterations were specified as taking effect on or before 1 December 1997 and the record of the alterations was registered by the central office under Sch 8, para 1(3) to that Act, on or before that date; (ii) in the case of any other existing building society for all purposes, except the limited purpose mentioned in SI 1997/2668, art 2(4), on the date on which the record of alterations to its purpose or principal purpose, its powers and its rules takes effect under Sch 8, para 1(5) or 2(6), to the 1997 Act, or is registered under Sch 8, para 3(3)(a) to that Act; (iii) on 1 December 1997, for all purposes, in the case of any building society registered after 30 November 1997.

92A–103 (*Outside the scope of this work.*)

PART XI
MISCELLANEOUS AND SUPPLEMENTARY AND CONVEYANCING SERVICES

104–124 (*Outside the scope of this work.*)

General

[7.462]
125 Short title

This Act may be cited as the Building Societies Act 1986.

[7.463]
126 Commencement

(1) This Act shall come into operation as follows.

(2) (*Outside the scope of this work.*)

(3) The remaining provisions of this Act, except sections 121, . . . 125, this section, in Schedule 20, paragraph 7 (and section 120(4) so far as it relates to that paragraph) and . . . , shall come into operation on such day as the Treasury may appoint by order made by statutory instrument and different days may be appointed for different provisions or different purposes.

(4), (5) (*Outside the scope of this work.*)

NOTES

Sub-s (3): words omitted repealed by the Statute Law (Repeals) Act 2004.

Orders: the Building Societies Act 1986 (Commencement No 1) Order 1986, SI 1986/1560; the Building Societies Act 1986 (Commencement No 2) Order 1989, SI 1989/1083.

SCHEDULES 1–14

(*Schs 1–14 outside the scope of this work.*)

SCHEDULE 15
APPLICATION OF COMPANIES WINDING UP LEGISLATION TO BUILDING SOCIETIES

Section 90

PART I
GENERAL MODE OF APPLICATION

[7.464]

1. The enactments which comprise the companies winding up legislation (referred to in this Schedule as "the enactments") are the provisions of—

(a) Parts IV, VI, VII[, XII and XIII] of the Insolvency Act 1986, or

Part 7C Special Insolvency Regimes

[(b) Articles 5 to 8 of Part I and Parts V, VII and XI of the Insolvency (Northern Ireland) Order 1989; or]

in so far as they relate to offences under any such enactment, sections 430 and 432 of, and Schedule 10 to, the Insolvency Act 1986 or [Articles 2(6) and 373 of, and Schedule 7 to, the Insolvency (Northern Ireland) Order 1989].

[**1A.** In this Schedule—

"deposit" means rights of the kind described in—

(a) paragraph 22 of Schedule 2 to the Financial Services and Markets Act 2000 (deposits); or

(b) section 1(2)(b) of the Dormant Bank and Building Society Accounts Act 2008 (balances transferred under that Act to authorised reclaim fund); and

"relevant deposit" means—

(a) an "eligible deposit" within the meaning given by paragraph 15C(1) of Schedule 6 to the Insolvency Act 1986 (categories of preferential debts) or a deposit of the kind mentioned in paragraph 15BB of that Schedule; or

(b) an "eligible deposit" within the meaning given by paragraph 21(1) of Schedule 4 to the Insolvency (Northern Ireland) Order 1989 (categories of preferential debts) or a deposit of the kind mentioned in paragraph 20 of that Schedule.]

2. Subject to the following provisions of this Schedule, the enactments apply to the winding up of building societies as they apply to the winding up of companies limited by shares and [registered under the Companies Act 2006 in England and Wales or Scotland or (as the case may be) in Northern Ireland.]

3. (1) The enactments shall, in their application to building societies, have effect with the substitution—

(a) for "company" of "building society" [(except as otherwise specified in paragraphs 33B and 55G below)];

(b) for "the registrar of companies" or "the registrar" of "the [Financial Conduct Authority]";

(c) for "the articles" of "the rules"; and

(d) for "registered office" of "principal office".

(2) In the application of the enactments to building societies—

[(aa) every reference to a company registered in Scotland shall have effect as a reference to a building society whose principal office is situated in Scotland;]

[(ab) a reference to the debts of a company includes a reference to sums due to shareholding members of a building society in respect of deposits;]

(a) every reference to the officers, or to a particular officer, of a company shall have effect as a reference to the officers, or to the corresponding officer, of the building society and as including a person holding himself out as such an officer; and

[(b) every reference to an administrative receiver shall be omitted.]

4. (1) Where any of the enactments as applied to building societies requires a notice or other document to be sent to the [FCA], it shall have effect as if it required the [FCA] to keep the notice or document in the public file of the society concerned and to record in that file the date on which the notice or document is placed in it.

(2) Where any of the enactments, as so applied, refers to the registration, or to the date of registration, of such a notice or document, that enactment shall have effect as if it referred to the placing of the notice or document in the public file or (as the case may be) to the date on which it was placed there.

5. Any enactment which specifies a money sum altered by order under section 416 of the Insolvency Act 1986, or, as the case may be, [Article 362 of the Insolvency (Northern Ireland) Order 1989], (powers to alter monetary limits) applies with the effect of the alteration.

NOTES

Para 1: words in first pair of square brackets substituted by the Companies Act 1989, ss 211(2), 212, Sch 24; words in second and third pairs of square brackets substituted by the Insolvency (Northern Ireland) Order 1989, SI 1989/2405, art 381(2), Sch 9, Pt II, para 45(a).

Para 1A: inserted by the Banks and Building Societies (Depositor Preference and Priorities) Order 2014, SI 2014/3486, art 32(1), (2).

Para 2: words in square brackets substituted by the Companies Act 2006 (Consequential Amendments, Transitional Provisions and Savings) Order 2009, SI 2009/1941, art 2(1), Sch 1, para 87(1), (11)(a).

Para 3: words in square brackets in sub-para (1)(a) inserted by the Small Business, Enterprise and Employment Act 2015 and the Insolvency (Amendment) Act (Northern Ireland) 2016 (Consequential Amendments and Transitional Provisions) Regulations 2017, SI 2017/400, reg 2(1), (3)(a); words in square brackets in sub-para (1)(b) substituted by the Financial Services Act 2012 (Mutual Societies) Order 2013, SI 2013/496, art 2(b), Sch 8, paras 1, 57(1), (2); sub-para (2)(aa) inserted by the Financial Services and Markets Act 2000 (Consequential Amendments and Repeals) Order 2001, SI 2001/3649, art 200(1); sub-para (2)(b) substituted by the Building Societies Act 1997, s 43, Sch 7, para 65; sub-para (2)(ab) inserted by SI 2014/3486, art 32(1), (3).

Para 4: words in square brackets substituted by SI 2013/496, art 2(b), Sch 8, paras 1, 57(1), (3).

Para 5: words in square brackets substituted by SI 1989/2405, art 381(2), Sch 9, Pt II, para 45(b).

Application: para 3 is applied, with modifications, for the purposes of a relevant building society, by the Building Societies (Financial Assistance) Order 2010, SI 2010/1188, art 9(1), (2) at **[18.215]**.

PART II
MODIFIED APPLICATION OF INSOLVENCY ACT 1986 PARTS IV[, [6, 7,] 12 AND 13] [AND SCHEDULE 10]

Preliminary

[7.465]

6. In this Part of this Schedule, Part IV of the Insolvency Act 1986 is referred to as "Part IV"; and that Act is referred to as "the Act".

[6ZA. Parts 4, 6, 7 and 12 of, and Schedule 10 to, the Act, in their application to building societies, have effect without the amendments of those Parts and that Schedule made by—

(a) section 122 of the Small Business, Enterprise and Employment Act 2015 (abolition of requirements to hold meetings: company insolvency);

(b) section 124 of that Act (ability for creditors to opt not to receive certain notices: company insolvency); and

(c) Part 1 of Schedule 9 to that Act (sections 122 to 125: further amendments).]

[6A. In the following provisions of the Act a reference to the creditors, general creditors or unsecured creditors of a company includes a reference to every shareholding member of the building society to whom a sum due from the society in relation to the member's shareholding is due in respect of a deposit—

(a) subsection (1) of section 143 (general functions of liquidator in winding up by the court);

(b) subsection (3) of section 149 (debts due from contributory to company);

(c) subsection (4) of section 168 (supplementary powers (England and Wales));

(d) subsection (2)(b) of section 175 (preferential debts (general provision));

(e) subsection (1) of section 176ZA (payment of expenses of winding up (England and Wales));

. . .

(f) subsections (3)(b) and (5)(a) of section 176A (share of assets for unsecured creditors);

[(g) subsection (1)(e) of section 391O (direct sanctions orders);

(h) subsection (5) of section 391Q (direct sanctions order: conditions); and

(i) subsection (3)(e) of section 391R (direct sanctions direction instead of order).]]

Members of a building society as contributories in winding up

7. (1) Section 74 (liability of members) of the Act is modified as follows.

(2) In subsection (1), the reference to any past member shall be omitted.

(3) Paragraphs (a) to (d) of subsection (2) shall be omitted; and so shall subsection (3).

[(3A) In paragraph (f) of subsection (2) the reference to a sum due to a member of the company by way of dividends, profits or otherwise does not include a sum due to a shareholding member of a building society in respect of a deposit.]

(4) The extent of the liability of a member of a building society in a winding up shall not exceed the extent of his liability under paragraph 6 of Schedule 2 to this Act.

8. Sections 75 to 78 and 83 in Chapter I of Part IV (miscellaneous provisions not relevant to building societies) do not apply.

9. (1) Section 79 (meaning of "contributory") of the Act does not apply.

(2) In the enactments as applied to a building society, "contributory"—

(a) means every person liable to contribute to the assets of the society in the event of its being wound up, and

(b) for the purposes of all proceedings for determining, and all proceedings prior to the determination of, the persons who are to be deemed contributories, includes any person alleged to be a contributory, and

(c) includes persons who are liable to pay or contribute to the payment of—

(i) any debt or liability of the building society being wound up, or

(ii) any sum for the adjustment of rights of members among themselves, or

(iii) the expenses of the winding up;

but does not include persons liable to contribute by virtue of a declaration by the court under section 213 (imputed responsibility for fraudulent trading) or section 214 (wrongful trading) of the Act.

Voluntary winding up

10. (1) Section 84 of the Act does not apply.

(2) In the enactments as applied to a building society, the expression "resolution for voluntary winding up" means a resolution passed under section 88(1) of this Act.

11. In subsection (1) of section 101 (appointment of liquidation committee) of the Act, the reference to functions conferred on a liquidation committee by or under that Act shall have effect as a reference to its functions by or under that Act as applied to building societies.

12. (1) Section 107 (distribution of property) of the Act does not apply; and the following applies in its place.

Part 7C Special Insolvency Regimes

(2) Subject to the provisions of Part IV relating to preferential payments, a building society's property in a voluntary winding up shall be applied in satisfaction of the society's liabilities to creditors . . . pari passu and, subject to that application, in accordance with the rules of the society.

[(3) In sub-paragraph (2) the reference to the society's liabilities to creditors includes a reference to the society's liabilities to shareholding members of the society in respect of deposits which are not relevant deposits.]

13. Sections 110 and 111 (liquidator accepting shares, etc as consideration for sale of company property) of the Act do not apply.

14. Section 116 (saving for certain rights) of the Act shall also apply in relation to the dissolution by consent of a building society as it applies in relation to its voluntary winding up.

Winding up by the court

15. In sections 117 (High Court and county court jurisdiction) and 120 (Court of Session and sheriff court jurisdiction) of the Act, each reference to a company's share capital paid up or credited as paid up shall have effect as a reference to the amount standing to the credit of shares in a building society as shown by the latest balance sheet.

[**16.** (1) Section 122 (circumstances in which company may be wound up by the court) of the Act does not apply in relation to a building society whose principal office is situated in England and Wales.

(2) Section 122 has effect in relation to a building society whose principal office is situated in Scotland as if subsection (1) were omitted.]

17. Section 124 (application for winding up) of the Act does not apply.

18. (1) In section 125 (powers of court on hearing of petition) of the Act, subsection (1) applies with the omission of the words from "but the court" to the end of the subsection.

(2) The conditions which the court may impose under section 125 of the Act include conditions for securing—

(a) that the building society be dissolved by consent of its members under section 87, or

(b) that the society amalgamates with, or transfers its engagements to, another building society under section 93 or 94, or

(c) that the society transfers its business to a company under section 97,

and may also include conditions for securing that any default which occasioned the petition be made good and that the costs, or in Scotland the expenses, of the proceedings on that petition be defrayed by the person or persons responsible for the default.

19. Section 126 (power of court, between petition and winding-up order, to stay or restrain proceedings against company) of the Act has effect with the omission of subsection (2).

20. If, before the presentation of a petition for the winding up by the court of a building society, an instrument of dissolution under section 87 is placed in the society's public file, section 129(1) (commencement of winding up by the court) of the Act shall also apply in relation to the date on which the instrument is so placed and to any proceedings in the course of the dissolution as it applies to the commencement date for, and proceedings in, a voluntary winding up.

21. (1) Section 130 of the Act (consequences of winding-up order) shall have effect with the following modifications.

(2) Subsections (1) and (3) shall be omitted.

(3) A building society shall, within 15 days of a winding-up order being made in respect of it, give notice of the order [to the FCA and, if the society is a PRA-authorised person, the PRA]; and the [FCA must] keep the notice in the public file of the society.

(4) If a building society fails to comply with sub-paragraph (3) above, it shall be liable on summary conviction to a fine not exceeding level 3 on the standard scale; and so shall any officer who is also guilty of the offence.

22. Section 140 (appointment of liquidator by court in certain circumstances) of the Act does not apply.

23. In the application of sections 141(1) and 142(1) (liquidation committees), of the Act to building societies, the references to functions conferred on a liquidation committee by or under that Act shall have effect as references to its functions by or under that Act as so applied.

[**23A.** Section 143 (general functions of liquidator in winding up by the court) of the Act has effect as if after subsection (1) there were inserted—

> "(1A) Subject to the provisions of Part 4 relating to preferential payments, a building society's property in the winding up shall be applied in satisfaction of the society's liabilities to creditors pari passu and, subject to that application, in accordance with the rules of the society.
>
> (1B) In subsection (1A) the reference to the society's liabilities to creditors includes a reference to the society's liabilities to shareholding members of the society in respect of deposits which are not relevant deposits.".]

24. The conditions which the court may impose under section 147 (power to stay or sist winding up) of the Act shall include those specified in paragraph 18(2) above.

25. Section 154 (adjustment of rights of contributories) of the Act shall have effect with the modification that any surplus is to be distributed in accordance with the rules of the society.

26. *In section 165(2) (liquidator's powers) of the Act, the reference to an extraordinary resolution shall have effect as a reference to a special resolution.*

Winding up: general

27. Section 187 (power to make over assets to employees) of the Act does not apply.

28. (1) In section 201 (dissolution: voluntary winding up) of the Act, subsection (2) applies without the words from "and on the expiration" to the end of the subsection and, in subsection (3), the word "However" shall be omitted.

(2) Sections 202 to 204 (early dissolution) of the Act do not apply.

29. In section 205 (dissolution: winding up by the court) of the Act, subsection (2) applies with the omission of the words from "and, subject" to the end of the subsection; and in subsections (3) and (4) references to the Secretary of State shall have effect as references to the [appropriate authority].

Penal provisions

30. Sections 216 and 217 of the Act (restriction on re-use of name) do not apply.

31. (1) Sections 218 and 219 (prosecution of delinquent officers) of the Act do not apply in relation to offences committed by members of a building society acting in that capacity.

(2) Sections 218(5) of the Act and subsections (1) and (2) of section 219 of the Act do not apply.

(3) The references in subsections (3) and (4) of section 219 of the Act to the Secretary of State shall have effect as references to the [FCA]; and the reference in subsection (3) to section 218 of the Act shall have effect as a reference to that section as supplemented by paragraph 32 below.

32. (1) Where a report is made to the prosecuting authority (within the meaning of section 218) under section 218(4) of the Act, in relation to an officer of a building society, he may, if he thinks fit, refer the matter to the [FCA] for further enquiry.

(2) On such a reference to it the [FCA] shall exercise its power under section 55(1) of this Act to appoint one or more investigators to investigate and report on the matter.

(3) An answer given by a person to a question put to him in exercise of the powers conferred by section 55 on a person so appointed may be used in evidence against the person giving it.

Preferential debts

33. Section 387 (meaning in Schedule 6 of "the relevant date") of the Act applies with the omission of subsections (2) and (4) to (6).

[Insolvency practitioners: their qualification and regulation

33A Section 390 of the Act (persons not qualified to act as insolvency practitioners) has effect as if for subsection (2) there were substituted—

> "(2) A person is not qualified to act as an insolvency practitioner in relation to a building society at any time unless at that time the person is fully authorised to act as an insolvency practitioner or partially authorised to act as an insolvency practitioner only in relation to companies.".

33B (1) In the following provisions of the Act, in a reference to authorisation or permission to act as an insolvency practitioner in relation to (or only in relation to) companies, the reference to companies has effect without the modification in paragraph 3(1)(a) above—

(a) sections 390A and 390B(1) and (3) (authorisation of insolvency practitioners); and

(b) sections 391O(1)(b) and 391R(3)(b) (court sanction of insolvency practitioners in public interest cases).

(2) In sections 391Q(2)(b) (direct sanctions order: conditions) and 391S(3)(e) (power for Secretary of State to obtain information) of the Act the reference to a company has effect without the modification in paragraph 3(1)(a) above.]

NOTES

Part heading: words in first (outer) pair of square brackets substituted by the Small Business, Enterprise and Employment Act 2015 and the Insolvency (Amendment) Act (Northern Ireland) 2016 (Consequential Amendments and Transitional Provisions) Regulations 2017, SI 2017/400, reg 2(1), (3)(b); words in second (inner) and third pairs of square brackets inserted by the Small Business, Enterprise and Employment Act 2015 (Consequential Amendments, Savings and Transitional Provisions) Regulations 2018, SI 2018/208, reg 2(1), (2)(a).

Para 6ZA: inserted by SI 2018/208, reg 2(1), (2)(b).

Para 6A: inserted by the Banks and Building Societies (Depositor Preference and Priorities) Order 2014, SI 2014/3486, art 33(1), (2); word omitted from sub-para (e) repealed and sub-paras (g)–(i) inserted by SI 2017/400, reg 2(1), (3)(c).

Para 7: sub-para (3A) inserted by SI 2014/3486, art 33(1), (3).

Para 12: words omitted from sub-para (2) repealed by the Financial Services and Markets Act 2000 (Mutual Societies) Order 2001, SI 2001/2617, art 13(1), (2), Sch 3, Pt II, paras 131, 209(d), Sch 4; sub-para (3) added by SI 2014/3486, art 33(1), (4).

Para 16: substituted by the Building Societies (Floating Charges and Other Provisions) Order 2016, SI 2016/679, art 2, in relation to a floating charge created by a building society on or after 28 June 2016. Para 16 originally read as follows:

"16. Section 122 (circumstances in which company may be wound up by the court) of the Act does not apply.".

Paras 21, 29, 31, 32: words in square brackets substituted by the Financial Services Act 2012 (Mutual Societies) Order 2013, SI 2013/496, art 2(b), Sch 8, paras 1, 57(1), (4)–(7).

Para 23A: inserted by SI 2014/3486, art 33(1), (5).

Para 26: repealed by the Companies Act 2006 (Commencement No 3, Consequential Amendments, Transitional Provisions and Savings) Order 2007, SI 2007/2194, art 10, Sch 4, Pt 3, para 49(1), Sch 5, in relation to written resolutions for which the circulation date is on or after 1 October 2007 and to resolutions passed at a meeting of which notice is given on or after that date; see SI 2007/2194, arts 1(3)(a), 10(1), (2), 12, Sch 4, Pt 3, para 49(2).

Paras 33A, 33B: inserted, together with preceding heading, by SI 2017/400, reg 2(1), (3)(d).

Application: para 33 is applied, with modifications, for the purposes of a relevant building society, by the Building Societies (Financial Assistance) Order 2010, SI 2010/1188, art 9(1), (3) at **[18.215]**.

[PART III
MODIFIED APPLICATION OF INSOLVENCY (NORTHERN IRELAND) ORDER 1989 PARTS V[, 11 AND 12]

Preliminary

[7.466]

34. In this Part of this Schedule, Part V of the Insolvency (Northern Ireland) Order 1989 is referred to as "Part V", that Order is referred to as "the Order" and references to "Articles" are references to Articles of that Order.

[34A. In the following provisions a reference to the creditors, general creditors or unsecured creditors of a company includes a reference to every shareholding member of the building society to whom a sum due from the society in relation to the member's shareholding is due in respect of a deposit—

(a) paragraph (1) of Article 121 (general functions of liquidator in winding up by the High Court);
(b) paragraph (3) of Article 127 (debts due from contributory to company);
(c) paragraph (4) of Article 143 (supplementary powers);
(d) paragraph (2)(b) of Article 149 (preferential debts (general provision));
(e) paragraph (1) of Article 150ZA (payment of expenses of winding up);
(f) paragraphs (3)(b) and (5)(a) of Article 150A (share of assets for unsecured creditors);
[(g) paragraph (1)(e) of Article 350O (direct sanctions orders);
(h) paragraph (5) of Article 350Q (direct sanctions order: conditions); and
(i) paragraph (3)(e) of Article 350R (direct sanctions direction instead of order).]]

Members of a building society as contributories in winding up

35. (1) Article 61 (liability of members) is modified as follows.

(2) In paragraph (1), the reference to any past member shall be omitted.

(3) Sub-paragraphs (a) to (d) of paragraph (2) shall be omitted; and so shall paragraph (3).

[(3A) In sub-paragraph (f) of paragraph (2) the reference to a sum due to a member of the company by way of dividends, profits or otherwise does not include a sum due to a shareholding member of a building society in respect of a deposit.]

(4) The extent of the liability of a member of a building society in a winding up shall not exceed the extent of his liability under paragraph 6 of Schedule 2 to this Act.

36. Articles 62 to 65 and 69 in Chapter I of Part V (miscellaneous provisions not relevant to building societies) do not apply.

37. In the enactments as applied to a building society, "contributory"—

(a) means every person liable to contribute to the assets of the society in the event of its being wound up, and
(b) for the purposes of all proceedings for determining, and all proceedings prior to the determination of, the persons who are to be deemed contributories, includes any person alleged to be a contributory, and
(c) includes persons who are liable to pay or contribute to the payment of—
    (i) any debt or liability of the building society being wound up, or
    (ii) any sum for the adjustment of rights of members among themselves, or
    (iii) the expenses of the winding up;

but does not include persons liable to contribute by virtue of a declaration by the Court under Article 177 (imputed responsibility for fraudulent trading) or Article 178 (wrongful trading).

Voluntary winding up

38. (1) Article 70 does not apply.

(2) In the enactments as applied to a building society, the expression "resolution for voluntary winding up" means a resolution passed under section 88(1) of this Act.

39. In paragraph (1) of Article 87 (appointment of liquidation committee), the reference to functions conferred on a liquidation committee by or under the Order shall have effect as a reference to its functions by or under the Order as applied to building societies.

40. (1) Article 93 (distribution of property) does not apply; and the following applies in its place.

(2) Subject to the provisions of Part V relating to preferential payments, a building society's property in a voluntary winding up shall be applied in satisfaction of the society's liabilities to creditors . . . pari passu and, subject to that application, in accordance with the rules of the society.

[(3) In sub-paragraph (2) the reference to the society's liabilities to creditors includes a reference to the society's liabilities to shareholding members of the society in respect of deposits which are not relevant deposits.]

41. Articles 96 and 97 (liquidator accepting shares, etc, as consideration for sale of company property) do not apply.

42. Article 101 (saving for certain rights) shall also apply in relation to the dissolution by consent of a building society as it applies in relation to its voluntary winding up.

Winding up by the High Court

43. Article 102 (circumstances in which company may be wound up by the High Court) does not apply.

44. Article 104 (application for winding up) does not apply.

45. (1) In Article 105 (powers of High Court on hearing of petition), paragraph (1) applies with the omission of the words from "but the Court" to the end of the paragraph.

(2) The conditions which the High Court may impose under Article 105 include conditions for securing—

(a) that the building society be dissolved by consent of its members under section 87, or

(b) that the society amalgamates with, or transfers its engagements to, another building society under section 93 or 94, or

(c) that the society transfers its business to a company under section 97,

and may also include conditions for securing that any default which occasioned the petition be made good and that the costs of the proceedings on that petition be defrayed by the person or persons responsible for the default.

46. Article 106 (power of High Court, between petition and winding-up order, to stay or restrain proceedings against company) has effect with the omission of paragraph (2).

47. If, before the presentation of a petition for the winding up by the High Court of a building society, an instrument of dissolution under section 87 is placed in the society's public file, Article 109(1) (commencement of winding up by the High Court) shall also apply in relation to the date on which the instrument is so placed and to any proceedings in the course of the dissolution as it applies to the commencement date for, and proceedings in, a voluntary winding up.

48. (1) Article 110 (consequences of winding-up order) shall have effect with the following modifications.

(2) Paragraphs (1) and (3) shall be omitted.

(3) A building society shall, within 15 days of a winding-up order being made in respect of it, give notice of the order [to the FCA and, if the society is a PRA-authorised person, the PRA]; and [the FCA must] keep the notice in the public file of the society.

(4) If a building society fails to comply with sub-paragraph (3) above, it shall be liable on summary conviction to a fine not exceeding level 3 on the standard scale; and so shall any officer who is also guilty of the offence.

49. Article 119 (appointment of liquidator by High Court in certain circumstances) does not apply.

50. In the application of Article 120(1) (liquidation committee) to building societies, the references to functions conferred on a liquidation committee by or under the Order shall have effect as references to its functions by or under the Order as so applied.

[**50A.** Article 121 (general functions of liquidator in winding up by the High Court) of the Order has effect as if after paragraph (1) there were inserted—

> "(1A) Subject to the provisions of Part V relating to preferential payments, a building society's property in the winding up shall be applied in satisfaction of the society's liabilities to creditors pari passu and, subject to that application, in accordance with the rules of the society.
>
> (1B) In paragraph (1A) the reference to the society's liabilities to creditors includes a reference to the society's liabilities to shareholding members of the society in respect of deposits which are not relevant deposits.".]

51. The conditions which the High Court may impose under Article 125 (power to stay winding up) shall include those specified in paragraph 45(2) above.

52. Article 132 (adjustment of rights of contributories) shall have effect with the modification that any surplus is to be distributed in accordance with the rules of the society.

53. *In Article 140(2) (liquidator's powers), the reference to an extraordinary resolution shall have effect as a reference to a special resolution.*

Winding up: general

54. Article 158 (power to make over assets to employees) does not apply.

55. (1) In Article 166 (dissolution: voluntary winding up), paragraph (2) applies without the words from "and on the expiration" to the end of the paragraph and, in paragraph (3), the word "However" shall be omitted.

(2) Articles 167 and 168 (early dissolution) do not apply.

55A. In Article 169 (dissolution: winding up by the High Court) paragraph (1) applies with the omission of the words from "and, subject" to the end of the paragraph; and in paragraphs (2) and (3) references to the Department shall have effect as references to the [appropriate authority].

Penal provisions

55B. Articles 180 and 181 (restriction on re-use of name) do not apply.

55C. (1) Articles 182 and 183 (prosecution of delinquent officers) do not apply in relation to offences committed by members of a building society acting in that capacity.

(2) Article 182(4) and paragraphs (1) and (2) of Article 183 do not apply.

(3) The references in paragraphs (3) and (5) of Article 183 to the Department shall have effect as references to the [FCA]; and the reference in paragraph (3) to Article 182 shall have effect as a reference to that Article as supplemented by paragraph 55D below.

55D. (1) Where a report is made to the prosecuting authority (within the meaning of Article 182) under Article 182(3), in relation to an officer of a building society, he may, if he thinks fit, refer the matter to the [FCA] for further enquiry.

(2) On such a reference to it the [FCA] shall exercise its power under section 55(1) of this Act to appoint one or more investigators to investigate and report on the matter.

(3) An answer given by a person to a question put to him in exercise of the powers conferred by section 55 on a person so appointed may be used in evidence against the person giving it.

Preferential debts

55E. Article 347 (meaning in Schedule 4 of "the relevant date") applies with the omission of paragraphs (2) and (4) to (6).

[Insolvency practitioners: their qualification and regulation

55F. Article 349 (persons not qualified to act as insolvency practitioners) has effect as if for paragraph (2) there were substituted—

> "(2) A person is not qualified to act as an insolvency practitioner in relation to a building society at any time unless at that time the person is fully authorised to act as an insolvency practitioner or partially authorised to act as an insolvency practitioner only in relation to companies.".

55G. (1) In the following provisions of the Order, in a reference to authorisation or permission to act as an insolvency practitioner in relation to (or only in relation to) companies, the reference to companies has effect without the modification in paragraph 3(1)(a) above—

(a) Articles 349A and 349B(1) and (3) (authorisation of insolvency practitioners); and

(b) Articles 350O(1)(b) and 350R(3)(b) (court sanction of insolvency practitioners in public interest cases).

(2) In Articles 350Q(2)(b) (direct sanctions order: conditions) and 350S(3)(e) (power for Department to obtain information) the reference to a company has effect without the modification in paragraph 3(1)(a) above.]]

NOTES

Substituted by the Insolvency (Northern Ireland) Order 1989, SI 1989/2405, art 381(2), Sch 9, Pt II, para 45(c).

Part heading: words in square brackets substituted by the Small Business, Enterprise and Employment Act 2015 and the Insolvency (Amendment) Act (Northern Ireland) 2016 (Consequential Amendments and Transitional Provisions) Regulations 2017, SI 2017/400, reg 2(1), (3)(e).

Para 34A: inserted by the Banks and Building Societies (Depositor Preference and Priorities) Order 2014, SI 2014/3486, art 34(1), (2); word omitted from sub-para (e) repealed and sub-paras (g)–(i) inserted by SI 2017/400, reg 2(1), (3)(f).

Para 35: sub-para (3A) inserted by SI 2014/3486, art 34(1), (3).

Para 40: words omitted from sub-para (2) repealed by the Financial Services and Markets Act 2000 (Mutual Societies) Order 2001, SI 2001/2617, art 13(1), (2), Sch 3, Pt II, paras 131, 209(d), Sch 4; sub-para (3) added by SI 2014/3486, art 34(1), (4).

Paras 48, 55A, 55C, 55D: words in square brackets substituted by the Financial Services Act 2012 (Mutual Societies) Order 2013, SI 2013/496, art 2(b), Sch 8, paras 1, 57(1), (8)–(11).

Para 50A: inserted by SI 2014/3486, art 34(1), (5).

Para 53: repealed by the Companies Act 2006 (Commencement No 3, Consequential Amendments, Transitional Provisions and Savings) Order 2007, SI 2007/2194, art 10, Sch 4, Pt 3, para 49(1), Sch 5, in relation to written resolutions for which the circulation date is on or after 1 October 2007 and to resolutions passed at a meeting of which notice is given on or after that date; see SI 2007/2194, arts 1(3)(a), 10(1), (2), 12, Sch 4, Pt 3, para 49(2).

Paras 55F, 55G: inserted, together with preceding heading, by SI 2017/400, reg 2(1), (3)(g).

Application: para 55E is applied, with modifications, for the purposes of a relevant building society, by the Building Societies (Financial Assistance) Order 2010, SI 2010/1188, art 9(1), (4) at **[18.215]**.

PART IV
DISSOLUTION OF BUILDING SOCIETY WOUND UP (ENGLAND AND WALES, SCOTLAND AND NORTHERN IRELAND)

[7.467]
56. (1) Where a building society has been wound up voluntarily, it is dissolved as from 3 months from the date of the placing in the public file of the society of the return of the final meetings of the society and its creditors made by the liquidator under—

(a) section 94 or (as the case may be) 106 of the Insolvency Act 1986 (as applied to building societies), or on such other date as is determined in accordance with section 201 of that Act, or

(b) Article [80 or (as the case may be) 92 of the Insolvency (Northern Ireland) Order 1989] (as so applied), or on such other date as is determined in accordance with that Article,

as the case may be.

(2) Where a building society has been wound up by the court, it is dissolved as from 3 months from the date of the placing in the public file of the society of—

(a) the liquidator's notice under section 172(8) of the Insolvency Act 1986 (as applied to building societies) [or, as the case may be, Article 146(7) of the Insolvency (Northern Ireland) Order 1989 (as applied to building societies)], or

(b) the notice of the completion of the winding up from the official receiver or the [official receiver for Northern Ireland],

or on such other date as is determined in accordance with section 205 of that Act [or Article 169 of that Order], as the case may be.

57. [(1) Sections 1012 to 1023 and 1034 of the Companies Act 2006 (property of dissolved company) apply in relation to the property of a dissolved building society (whether dissolved under section 87 or following its winding up) as they apply in relation to the property of a dissolved company.]

(2) Paragraph 3(1) above shall apply to those sections for the purpose of their application to building societies.

[(3) Any reference in those sections to restoration to the register shall be read as a reference to the effect of an order under section 91 of this Act.]

Insolvency rules and fees: England and Wales and Scotland

58. (1) Rules may be made under section 411 of the Insolvency Act for the purpose of giving effect, in relation to building societies, to the provisions of the applicable winding up legislation.

(2) An order made by the competent authority under section 414 of the Insolvency Act 1986 may make provision for fees to be payable under that section in respect of proceedings under the applicable winding up legislation and the performance by the official receiver or the Secretary of State of functions under it.

Insolvency rules and fees: Northern Ireland

59. (1) Rules may be made under [Article 359 of the Insolvency (Northern Ireland) Order 1989] for the purpose of giving effect in relation to building societies, to the provisions of the applicable winding up legislation.

[(2) An Order made by the Department of Economic Development under Article 361 of the Insolvency (Northern Ireland) Order 1989 may make provision for fees to be payable under that Article in respect of proceedings under the applicable winding-up legislation and the performance by the official receiver for Northern Ireland or that Department of functions under it.]

NOTES

Para 56: words in first and third pairs of square brackets substituted and words in second and fourth pairs of square brackets inserted by the Insolvency (Northern Ireland) Order 1989, SI 1989/2405, art 381(2), Sch 9, Pt II, para 45(d).

Para 57: sub-para (1) substituted and sub-para (3) substituted, for the original sub-paras (3), (4), by the Companies Act 2006 (Consequential Amendments, Transitional Provisions and Savings) Order 2009, SI 2009/1941, art 2(1), Sch 1, para 87(1), (11)(b), (c).

Para 59: words in square brackets substituted by SI 1989/2405, art 381(2), Sch 9, Pt II, para 45(e).

[SCHEDULE 15A
APPLICATION OF OTHER COMPANIES INSOLVENCY LEGISLATION TO BUILDING SOCIETIES

Section 90A

PART I
GENERAL MODE OF APPLICATION

[7.468]
1. (1) Subject to the provisions of this Schedule, the enactments specified in sub-paragraph (2) below (referred to in this Schedule as "the enactments") apply in relation to building societies as they apply in relation to companies limited by shares and [registered under the Companies Act 2006 in England and Wales or Scotland or (as the case may be) in Northern Ireland].

(2) The enactments referred to in sub-paragraph (1) above are—

(a) Parts I [(except section 1A)][, II [and 3, section 176ZB (in Part 4), and]] VI, VII, XII and XIII, section 434 and Part XVIII of the Insolvency Act 1986, or

(b) [Part I, Part II (except Article 14A), Parts III,] IV, VII, XI and XII and Article 378 of the Insolvency (Northern Ireland) Order 1989,

and, in so far as they relate to offences under any such enactment, sections 430 and 432 of; and Schedule 10 to, the Insolvency Act 1986 or Article 2(6) and 373 of, and Schedule 7 to, the Insolvency (Northern Ireland) Order 1989.

2. (1) The enactments shall, in their application to building societies, have effect with the substitution—

(a) for "company" of "building society" [(except as otherwise specified in paragraphs 27H and 54 below)];
(b) for "the registrar of companies" or "the registrar" of "the [Financial Conduct Authority]";
(c) for "the articles" of "the rules"; and
(d) for "registered office" of "principal office".

(2) In the application of the enactments to building societies—

[(aa) every reference to a company registered in Scotland shall have effect as a reference to a building society whose principal office is situated in Scotland;]
(a) every reference to the officers, or to a particular officer, of a company shall have effect as a reference to the officers, or to the corresponding officer, of the building society and as including a person holding himself out as such an officer; and
(b) every reference to an administrative receiver[, other than a reference in section 29(2), 72A or 251 of the Insolvency Act 1986 or in Article 5(1) or 59A of the Insolvency (Northern Ireland) Order 1989] shall be omitted.

3. (1) Where any of the enactments as applied to building societies requires a notice or other document to be sent to the [FCA], it shall have effect as if it required the [FCA] to keep the notice or document in the public file of the society concerned and to record in that file the date on which the notice or document is placed in it.

(2) Where any of the enactments, as so applied, refers to the registration, or to the date of registration, of such a notice or document, that enactment shall have effect as if it referred to the placing of the notice or document in the public file or (as the case may be) to the date on which it was placed there.

[(3) Any reference in any of the enactments, as so applied, to the register shall have effect as a reference to the public file.]

4. (1) Rules may be made under section 411 of the Insolvency Act 1986 or, as the case may be, Article 359 of the Insolvency (Northern Ireland) Order 1989 for the purpose of giving effect, in relation to building societies, to the provisions of the enactments.

(2) An order made by the competent authority under section 414 of the Insolvency Act 1986 may make provision for fees to be payable under that section in respect of proceedings under the enactments and the performance by the official receiver or the Secretary of State of functions under them.

(3) An order made by the Department of Economic Development under Article 361 of the Insolvency (Northern Ireland) Order 1989 may make provision for fees to be payable under that Article in respect of proceedings under the enactments and the performance by the official receiver or that Department of functions under them.

5. Any enactment which specifies a money sum altered by order under section 416 of the Insolvency Act 1986, or, as the case may be, Article 362 of the Insolvency (Northern Ireland) Order 1989, (powers to alter monetary limits) applies with the effect of the alteration.

[5A. In this Schedule—

"deposit" and "relevant deposit" have the meaning given by paragraph 1A of Schedule 15; and
"scheme manager" has the same meaning as in the Financial Services and Markets Act 2000.]]

NOTES

Inserted by the Building Societies Act 1997, s 39(2), Sch 6.

Para 1: words in square brackets in sub-para (1) substituted by the Companies Act 2006 (Consequential Amendments, Transitional Provisions and Savings) Order 2009, SI 2009/1941, art 2(1), Sch 1, para 87(1), (12)(a); words in first pair of square brackets in sub-para (2)(a) inserted by the Insolvency Act 2000, s 2(b), Sch 2, Pt II, para 14(1), (2); figures in second (outer) pair of square brackets in sub-para (2)(a) substituted for original words "and II, Chapter I of Part III, Parts", by the Building Societies (Floating Charges and Other Provisions) Order 2016, SI 2016/679, art 4(1), (2)(a), in relation to a floating charge created by a building society on or after 28 June 2016; words in third (inner) pair of square brackets in sub-para (2)(a) substituted by the Small Business, Enterprise and Employment Act 2015 and the Insolvency (Amendment) Act (Northern Ireland) 2016 (Consequential Amendments and Transitional Provisions) Regulations 2017, SI 2017/400, reg 2(1), (4)(a); words in square brackets in sub-para (2)(b) substituted by the Insolvency (Northern Ireland) Order 2002, SI 2002/3152 (NI 6), art 4(b), Sch 2, Pt II, para 14(1), (2).

Para 2: words in square brackets in sub-para (1)(a) inserted by SI 2017/400, reg 2(1), (4)(b); words in square brackets in sub-para (1)(b) substituted by the Financial Services Act 2012 (Mutual Societies) Order 2013, SI 2013/496, art 2(b), Sch 8, para 58(1), (2); sub-para (2)(aa) inserted by the Financial Services and Markets Act 2000 (Consequential Amendments and Repeals) Order 2001, SI 2001/3649, art 200(2); words in square brackets in sub-para (2)(b) inserted by SI 2016/679, art 4(1), (2)(b), in relation to a floating charge created by a building society on or after 28 June 2016.

Para 3: words in square brackets in sub-para (1) substituted by SI 2013/496, art 2(b), Sch 8, para 58(1), (3); sub-para (3) added by SI 2016/679, art 4(1), (2)(c), in relation to a floating charge created by a building society on or after 28 June 2016.

Para 5A: added by the Financial Services and Markets Act 2000 (Mutual Societies) Order 2001, SI 2001/2617, art 13(1), Sch 3, Pt II, paras 131, 210(d); substituted by SI 2016/679, art 4(1), (2)(d), in relation to a floating charge created by a building society on or after 28 June 2016. Para 5A previously read as follows:

"[5A. In this Schedule, "scheme manager" has the same meaning as in the Financial Services and Markets Act 2000.]".

Application: paras 1, 2 are applied, with modifications, for the purposes of a relevant building society, by the Building Societies (Financial Assistance) Order 2010, SI 2010/1188, art 11(1)–(3) at **[18.217]**.

[PART II
MODIFIED APPLICATION OF [PARTS I TO III[, 6, 7, 12 AND 13]] OF INSOLVENCY ACT 1986

NOTES

Part heading: words in first (outer) pair of square brackets substituted for original words "Parts I and II and Chapter I of Part III", by the Building Societies (Floating Charges and Other Provisions) Order 2016, SI 2016/679, art 4(1), (3)(a), in relation to a floating charge created by a building society on or after 28 June 2016; words in second (inner) pair of square brackets substituted by the Small Business, Enterprise and Employment Act 2015 (Consequential Amendments, Savings and Transitional Provisions) Regulations 2018, SI 2018/208, reg 2(1), (3)(a).

Preliminary

[7.469]

6. In this Part of this Schedule, the Insolvency Act 1986 is referred to as "the Act".

[6A. Parts 1, 3, 6, 7 and 12 of the Act, in their application to building societies, have effect without the amendments of those Parts made by—
- (a) section 122 of the Small Business, Enterprise and Employment Act 2015 (abolition of requirements to hold meetings: company insolvency);
- (b) section 124 of that Act (ability for creditors to opt not to receive certain notices: company insolvency); and
- (c) Part 1 of Schedule 9 to that Act (sections 122 to 125: further amendments).]

Voluntary arrangements

7. Section 1 of the Act (proposals for voluntary arrangements) has effect as if—
- (a) it required any proposal under Part I of the Act to be so framed as to enable a building society to comply with the requirements of this Act; and
- (b) any reference to debts included a reference to liabilities owed to the holders of shares in a building society.

8. In section 2 (procedure where nominee is not liquidator or administrator) and section 3 (summoning of meetings) of the Act as applied to a building society, any reference to a meeting of the society is a reference to—
- (a) a meeting of both shareholding and borrowing members of the society; and
- (b) a meeting of shareholding members alone.

[and subsection (1) of section 2 shall have effect with the omission of the words from "and the directors" to the end].

[8A. In subsection (2) of section 4A of the Act (approval of arrangement) as applied to a building society, paragraph (b) and the word "or" immediately preceding that paragraph are omitted.]

9. In section 6 of the Act (challenge of decisions) as applied to a building society, "contributory"—
- (a) means every person liable to contribute to the assets of the society in the event of its being wound up, and
- (b) for the purposes of all proceedings for determining, and all proceedings prior to the determination of; the persons who are to be deemed contributories, includes any person alleged to be a contributory, and
- (c) includes persons who are liable to pay or contribute to the payment of—
  - (i) any debt or liability of the building society being wound up, or
  - (ii) any sum for the adjustment of rights of members among themselves, or
  - (iii) the expenses of the winding up;

but does not include persons liable to contribute by virtue of a declaration by the court under section 213 (imputed responsibility for fraudulent trading) or section 214 (wrongful trading) of the Act.

[9A. In section 7A of the Act (prosecution of delinquent officers) as applied to a building society—
- (a) in subsection (2), for paragraphs (i) and (ii) there is substituted "the [FCA]",
- (b) subsections (3) to (7) are omitted,
- (c) in subsection (8), for "Secretary of State" there is substituted "[FCA]".]

Administration orders

10. (1) Section 8 of the Act (power of court to make administration order) has effect as if it included provision that, where—
- (a) an application for an administration order to be made in relation to a building society is made by the [FCA or the PRA] (with or without other parties); and
- (b) the society has defaulted in an obligation to pay any sum due and payable in respect of any deposit or share,

the society shall be deemed for the purposes of subsection (1) to be unable to pay its debts.

(2) In subsection (3) of that section, paragraph (c) and, in subsection (4) of that section, the words from "nor where" to the end are omitted.

Part 7C Special Insolvency Regimes

11. (1) Subsection (1) of section 9 of the Act (application for administration order) as applied to a building society has effect as if—

(a) it enabled an application to the court for an administration order to be by petition presented, with or without other parties, by the [FCA or the PRA] or by a shareholding member entitled under section 89(3) of this Act to petition for the winding up of the society; and

(b) the words from "or by the clerk" to "on companies)" were omitted.

(2) In subsection (2)(a) of that section as so applied, the reference to any person who has appointed, or is or may be entitled to appoint, an administrative receiver of the society is a reference to the [FCA or the PRA] (unless it is a petitioner).

(3) Subsection (3) of that section, and in subsection (4) of that section, the words "Subject to subsection (3)," are omitted.

12. In section 10 of the Act (effect of application for administration order), the following are omitted, namely—

(a) in subsection (2), paragraphs (b) and (c); and

(b) subsection (3).

13. In section 11 of the Act (effect of administration order), the following are omitted, namely—

(a) in subsection (1), paragraph (b) and the word "and" immediately preceding that paragraph;

(b) in subsection (3), paragraph (b);

(c) in subsection (4), the words "an administrative receiver of the company has vacated office under subsection (1)(b), or"; and

(d) subsection (5).

14. In subsection (1) of section 12 of the Act (notification of administration order), the reference to every invoice, order for goods or business letter is a reference to every statement of account, order for goods or services, business letter or advertisement.

15. Subsection (3) of section 13 of the Act (appointment of administrator) has effect as if it enabled an application for an order under subsection (2) of that section to be made by the [FCA or the PRA].

16. (1) Subject to sub-paragraph (2) below, section 14 of the Act (general powers of administrator) has effect as if it required the administrator of a building society, in exercising his powers under that section—

(a) to ensure compliance with the provisions of this Act; and

(b) not to appoint to be a director any person who is not a fit and proper person to hold that position.

(2) Sub-paragraph (1)(a) above does not apply in relation to section 5, 6 or 7 of this Act . . .

(3) In subsection (4) of that section as applied to a building society, the reference to any power conferred by the Act or [the Companies Acts] or by [the company's articles] is a reference to any power conferred by this Act or by the society's memorandum or rules.

(4) . . .

17. (1) Subject to sub-paragraph (3) below, paragraph 16 of Schedule 1 to the Act (powers of administrators) as applied to a building society has effect as if it conferred power to transfer liabilities in respect of deposits with or shares in the society.

(2) No transfer under that paragraph shall be a transfer of engagements for the purposes of Part X of this Act.

(3) No transfer under that paragraph which, apart from sub-paragraph (2) above, would be a transfer of engagements for the purposes of that Part shall be made unless it is approved by the court, or by meetings summoned under section 23(1) or 25(2) of the Act (as modified by paragraph 21 or 23 below).

18. . . .

19. (1) Section 17 of the Act (general duties of administrator) has effect as if, instead of the requirement imposed by subsection (3), it required the administrator of a building society to summon a meeting of the society's creditors if—

(a) he is requested, in accordance with the rules, to do so by 500 of the society's creditors, or by one-tenth, in number or value, of those creditors, or

(b) he is directed to do so by the court.

(2) That section also has effect as if it required the administrator of a building society to summon a meeting of the society's shareholding members if—

(a) he is requested, in accordance with the rules, to do so by 500 of the society's shareholding members, or by one-tenth, in number, of those members, or

(b) he is directed to do so by the court.

20. . . .

21. (1) Subsection (1) of section 23 of the Act (statement of proposals) as applied to a building society has effect as if—

(a) the reference to the [Financial Conduct Authority] included a reference to the [scheme manager];

(b) the reference to all creditors included a reference to all holders of shares in the society; and

(c) the reference to a meeting of the society's creditors included a reference to a meeting of holders of shares in the society.

(2) In subsection (2) of that section as so applied, references to members of the society do not include references to holders of shares in the society.

22. Section 24 of the Act (consideration of proposals by creditors' meeting) as applied to a building society has effect as if any reference to a meeting of creditors included a reference to a meeting of holders of shares in the society.

23. (1) Section 25 of the Act (approval of substantial revisions) as applied to a building society has effect as if—

(a) subsection (2) required the administrator to send a statement in the prescribed form of his proposed revisions to the [FCA, to the PRA]; and

(b) the reference in that subsection to a meeting of creditors included a reference to a meeting of holders of shares in the society.

(2) In subsection (3) of that section as so applied, references to members of the society do not include references to holders of shares in the society.

24. Subsection (1) of section 27 of the Act (protection of interests of creditors and members) has effect—

(a) as if it enabled the [[FCA, the PRA] or the scheme manager] to apply to the court by petition for an order under that section; and

(b) in relation to an application by the [[FCA, the PRA] or the scheme manager], as if the words "(including at least himself)" were omitted.

Receivers and managers

25. In section 38 of the Act (receivership accounts), "prescribed" means prescribed by regulations made by statutory instrument by the [Treasury].

26. In subsection (1) of section 39 of the Act (notification that receiver or manager appointed), the reference to every invoice, order for goods or business letter is a reference to every statement of account, order for goods or services, business letter or advertisement.

[27. Subsection (3) of section 40 of the Act (payment of debts out of assets subject to floating charge), as applied to a building society, has effect as if the reference to general creditors included a reference to shareholding members of the society in respect of deposits which are not relevant deposits.

27A. Sections 42 to 49 of the Act (administrative receivers) are omitted.

27B. Subsection (1) of section 51 of the Act (power to appoint receiver), as applied to a building society, has effect as if for the words "an incorporated company (whether a company registered under the Companies Act 2006 or not)" there were substituted "a building society".

27C. Subsection (3) of section 59 of the Act (priority of debts), as applied to a building society, has effect as if the reference to ordinary creditors included a reference to shareholding members of the society in respect of deposits which are not relevant deposits.

27D. Subsection (1) of section 67 of the Act (report by receiver), as applied to a building society, has effect as if—

(a) the reference to the Financial Conduct Authority included a reference to the scheme manager; and

(b) in paragraph (d) the reference to other creditors included a reference to shareholding members of the society in respect of deposits which are not relevant deposits.

27E. Subsection (1) of section 70 of the Act (interpretation for Chapter 2), as applied to a building society, has effect as if—

(a) in the definition of "company" for the words "an incorporated company (whether or not a company registered under the Companies Act 2006)" there were substituted "a building society"; and

(b) the definition of "the register" were omitted.

27F. Chapter 4 of Part 3 of the Act (prohibition of appointment of administrative receiver), as applied to a building society, has effect as if—

(a) in section 72A (floating charge holder not to appoint administrative receiver)—

  (i) in subsections (1) and (2) the word "qualifying" and in subsection (3) the definition of "holder of a qualifying floating charge in respect of a company's property" were omitted; and

  (ii) subsections (4)(a), (5) and (6) were omitted; and

(b) sections 72B to 72H(a) (exceptions to prohibition) were omitted.]]

[Insolvency practitioners: their qualification and regulation

27G. Section 390 of the Act (persons not qualified to act as insolvency practitioners) has effect as if for subsection (2) there were substituted—

"(2) A person is not qualified to act as an insolvency practitioner in relation to a building society at any time unless at that time the person is fully authorised to act as an insolvency practitioner or partially authorised to act as an insolvency practitioner only in relation to companies.".

27H. (1) In the following provisions of the Act, in a reference to authorisation or permission to act as an insolvency practitioner in relation to (or only in relation to) companies the reference to companies has effect without the modification in paragraph 2(1)(a) above—

(a) sections 390A and 390B(1) and (3) (authorisation of insolvency practitioners); and

(b) sections 391O(1)(b) and 391R(3)(b) (court sanction of insolvency practitioners in public interest cases).

(2) In sections 391Q(2)(b) (direct sanctions order: conditions) and 391S(3)(e) (power for Secretary of State to obtain information) of the Act the reference to a company has effect without the modification in paragraph 2(1)(a) above.

27I. In sections 391O, 391Q and 391R of the Act a reference to the creditors of a company includes a reference to every shareholding member of the building society to whom a sum due from the society in relation to the member's shareholding is due in respect of a deposit.]

NOTES

Inserted as noted to Pt I at **[7.468]**.

Para 6A: inserted by the Small Business, Enterprise and Employment Act 2015 (Consequential Amendments, Savings and Transitional Provisions) Regulations 2018, SI 2018/208, reg 2(1), (3)(b).

Para 8: words in square brackets added by the Insolvency Act 2000, s 2(b), Sch 2, Pt II, para 14(1), (3).

Para 8A: inserted by the Insolvency Act 2000, s 2(b), Sch 2, Pt II, para 14(1), (3).

Para 9A: inserted by the Insolvency Act 2000, s 2(b), Sch 2, Pt II, para 14(1), (4); words in square brackets substituted by the Financial Services Act 2012 (Mutual Societies) Order 2013, SI 2013/496, art 2(b), Sch 8, para 58(1), (4).

Paras 10, 11, 15: words in square brackets substituted by SI 2013/496, art 2(b), Sch 8, para 58(1), (5).

Para 16: words omitted from sub-para (2) and the whole of sub-para (4) repealed by SI 2001/2617, art 13(1), (2), Sch 3, Pt II, paras 131, 210(f), (g), Sch 4; words in square brackets in sub-para (3) substituted by the Companies Act 2006 (Consequential Amendments, Transitional Provisions and Savings) Order 2009, SI 2009/1941, art 2(1), Sch 1, para 87(1), (12)(b).

Paras 18, 20: repealed by the Financial Services (Banking Reform) Act 2013, s 138, Sch 9, paras 1, 4(2)(a), (b).

Para 21: words in first pair of square brackets substituted by SI 2013/496, art 2(b), Sch 8, para 58(1), (7); words in second pair of square brackets substituted by the Financial Services and Markets Act 2000 (Mutual Societies) Order 2001, SI 2001/2617, art 13(1), Sch 3, Pt II, paras 131, 210(h)(ii).

Para 23: words in square brackets substituted by SI 2013/496, art 2(b), Sch 8, para 58(1), (6).

Para 24: words in first (outer) pair of square brackets in sub-paras (a) and (b) substituted by SI 2001/2617, art 13(1), Sch 3, Pt II, paras 131, 210(i), (k); words in second (inner) pair of square brackets substituted by SI 2013/496, art 2(b), Sch 8, para 58(1), (8).

Para 25: word in square brackets substituted by SI 2001/2617, arts 4(1)(c), 13(1), Sch 1, Pt III, Sch 3, Pt II, paras 131, 210(l); for transitional provisions in relation to transferred functions, see art 5 thereof.

Paras 27, 27A–27F: substituted (for original para 27) by the Building Societies (Floating Charges and Other Provisions) Order 2016, SI 2016/679, art 4(1), (3)(b), in relation to a floating charge created by a building society on or after 28 June 2016. Para 27 previously read as follows:

"**27.** Section 40 (payment of debts out of assets subject to floating charge) and sections 42 to 49 (administrative receivers) of the Act are omitted.".

Paras 27G, 27H, 27I: inserted by the Small Business, Enterprise and Employment Act 2015 and the Insolvency (Amendment) Act (Northern Ireland) 2016 (Consequential Amendments and Transitional Provisions) Regulations 2017, SI 2017/400, reg 2(1), (4)(d).

Application: paras 11–13, 18, 20, 27 are applied, with modifications, for the purposes of a relevant building society, by the Building Societies (Financial Assistance) Order 2010, SI 2010/1188, art 11(1), (4)–(6) at **[18.217]**.

[PART III
MODIFIED APPLICATION OF PARTS II, III[, 4 AND 12] OF INSOLVENCY (NORTHERN IRELAND) ORDER 1989

NOTES

Part heading: words in square brackets inserted by the Small Business, Enterprise and Employment Act 2015 and the Insolvency (Amendment) Act (Northern Ireland) 2016 (Consequential Amendments and Transitional Provisions) Regulations 2017, SI 2017/400, reg 2(1), (4)(e).

Preliminary

[7.470]

28. In this Part of this Schedule, the Insolvency (Northern Ireland) Order 1989 is referred to as "the Order".

Voluntary arrangements

29. Article 14 of the Order (proposals for voluntary arrangements) has effect as if—

(a) it required any proposal under Part II of the Order to be so framed as to enable a building society to comply with the requirements of this Act; and

(b) any reference to debts included a reference to liabilities owed to the holders of shares in a building society.

30. In Article 15 (procedure where nominee is not liquidator or administrator) and Article 16 (summoning of meetings) of the Order as applied to a building society, any reference to meetings of the society is a reference to—

(a) a meeting of both shareholding and borrowing members of the society; and

(b) a meeting of shareholding members alone

[and paragraph (1) of Article 15 shall have effect with the omission of the words from "and the directors" to the end.]

[30A. In paragraph (2) of Article 17A of the Order (approval of arrangement) as applied to a building society, sub-paragraph (b) and the word "or" immediately preceding that sub-paragraph are omitted.]

31. In Article 19 of the Order (challenge of decisions) as applied to a building society, "contributory"—

(a) means every person liable to contribute to the assets of the society in the event of its being wound up, and

(b) for the purposes of all proceedings for determining, and all proceedings prior to the determination of, the persons who are to be deemed contributories, includes any person alleged to be a contributory, and

(c) includes persons who are liable to pay or contribute to the payment of—

(i) any debt or liability of the building society being wound up, or

(ii) any sum for the adjustment of rights of members among themselves, or

(iii) the expenses of the winding up;

but does not include persons liable to contribute by virtue of a declaration by the High Court under Article 177 (imputed responsibility for fraudulent trading) or Article 178 (wrongful trading) of the Order.

[31A. (1) In Article 20A of the Order (prosecution of delinquent officers) as applied to a building society—

(a) in paragraph (2) for the words "the Department", in each place where they occur, there are substituted the words "[each of the Financial Conduct Authority and the Prudential Regulation Authority]",

(b) paragraphs (3)–(7) are omitted,

(c) in paragraph (8)—

(i) after the words "Northern Ireland" there are inserted the words "or the [Financial Conduct Authority or the Prudential Regulation Authority]", and

(ii) after the words "Northern Ireland" and the words "the Director", in the second place where they occur, there are inserted the words "or the [Financial Conduct Authority or the Prudential Regulation Authority]",

(d) in paragraph (9) after the words "for Northern Ireland" there are inserted he words "or the [Financial Conduct Authority or the Prudential Regulation Authority]".]

Administration orders

32. (1) Article 21 of the Order (power of High Court to make administration order) has effect as if it included provision that, where—

(a) an application for an administration order to be made in relation to a building society is made by the [FCA or the PRA] (with or without other parties); and

(b) the society has defaulted in an obligation to pay any sum due and payable in respect of any deposit or share,

the society shall be deemed for the purposes of paragraph (1) to be unable to pay its debts.

(2) In paragraph (3) of that Article, sub-paragraph (c) and, in paragraph (4) of that Article, the words from "nor where" to the end are omitted.

33. (1) Paragraph (1) of Article 22 of the Order (application for administration order) as applied to a building society has effect as if—

(a) it enabled an application to the High Court for an administration order to be by petition presented, with or without other parties, by the [FCA, by the PRA] or by a shareholding member entitled under section 89(3) of this Act to petition for the winding up of the society; and

(b) the words from "or by the chief clerk" to "on companies)", in the second place where they occur, were omitted.

(2) In paragraph (2)(a) of that Article as so applied, the reference to any person who has appointed, or is or may be entitled to appoint, an administrative receiver of the society is a reference to the [FCA or, as the case may be, the PRA] (unless it is a petitioner).

(3) Paragraph (3) of that Article, and in paragraph (4) of that Article, the words "Subject to paragraph (3)," are omitted.

34. In Article 23 of the Order (effect of application for administration order), the following are omitted, namely—

(a) in paragraph (2), sub-paragraphs (b) and (c); and

(b) paragraph (3).

35. In Article 24 of the Order (effect of administration order), the following are omitted, namely—

(a) in paragraph (1), sub-paragraph (b) and the word "and" immediately preceding that sub-paragraph;

(b) in paragraph (3), sub-paragraph (b);

(c) in paragraph (4), the words "an administrative receiver of the company has vacated office under paragraph (1)(b), or"; and

(d) paragraph (5).

36. In paragraph (1) of Article 25 of the Order (notification of administration order), the reference to every invoice, order for goods or business letter is a reference to every statement of account, order for goods or services, business letter or advertisement.

37. Paragraph (3) of Article 26 of the Order (appointment of administrator) has effect as if it enabled an application for an order under paragraph (2) of that Article to be made by [the FCA and the PRA].

38. (1) Subject to sub-paragraph (2) below, Article 27 of the Order (general powers of administrator) has effect as if it required the administrator of a building society, in exercising his powers under that Article—

(a) to ensure compliance with the provisions of this Act; and

(b) not to appoint to be a director any person who is not a fit and proper person to hold that position.

(2) Sub-paragraph (1)(a) above does not apply in relation to section 5, 6 or 7 of this Act . . .

(3) In paragraph (4) of that Article as applied to a building society, the reference to any power conferred by the Order or [the Companies Acts] or by [the company's articles] is a reference to any power conferred by this Act or by the society's memorandum or rules.

(4) . . .

39. (1) Subject to sub-paragraph (3) below, paragraph 17 of Schedule 1 to the Order (powers of administrators) as applied to a building society has effect as if it conferred power to transfer liabilities in respect of deposits with or shares in the society.

(2) No transfer under that paragraph shall be a transfer of engagements for the purposes of Part X of this Act.

(3) No transfer under that paragraph which, apart from sub-paragraph (2) above, would be a transfer of engagements for the purposes of that Part shall be made unless it is approved by the High Court, or by meetings summoned under Article 35(1) or 37(2) of the Order (as modified by paragraph 43 or 45 below).

40. . . .

41. (1) Article 29 of the Order (general duties of administrator) has effect as if, instead of the requirement imposed by paragraph (3), it required the administrator of a building society to summon a meeting of the society's creditors if—

(a) he is requested, in accordance with the rules, to do so by 500 of the society's creditors, or by one-tenth, in number or value, of those creditors, or

(b) he is directed to do so by the High Court.

(2) That Article also has effect as if it required the administrator of a building society to summon a meeting of the society's shareholding members if—

(a) he is requested, in accordance with the rules, to do so by 500 of the society's shareholding members, or by one-tenth, in number, of those members, or

(b) he is directed to do so by the High Court.

42. . . .

43. (1) Paragraph (1) of Article 35 of the Order (statement of proposals) as applied to a building society has effect as if—

(a) the reference to the [Financial Conduct Authority] included a reference to the [scheme manager];

(b) the reference to all creditors included a reference to all holders of shares in the society; and

(c) the reference to a meeting of the society's creditors included a reference to a meeting of holders of shares in the society.

(2) In paragraph (2) of that Article as so applied, references to members of the society do not include references to holders of shares in the society.

44. Article 36 of the Order (consideration of proposals by creditors' meeting) as applied to a building society has effect as if any reference to a meeting of creditors included a reference to a meeting of holders of shares in the society.

45. (1) Article 37 of the Order (approval of substantial revisions) as applied to a building society has effect as if—

(a) paragraph (2) required the administrator to send a statement in the prescribed form of his proposed revisions to the [[FCA, to the PRA] and to the scheme manager]; and

(b) the reference in that paragraph to a meeting of creditors included a reference to a meeting of holders of shares in the society.

(2) In paragraph (3) of that Article as so applied, references to members of the society do not include references to holders of shares in the society.

46. Paragraph (1) of Article 39 of the Order (protection of interests of creditors and members) has effect—

(a) as if it enabled the [[FCA, the PRA] or the scheme manager] to apply to the High Court by petition for an order under that section; and

(b) in relation to an application by the [[FCA, the PRA] or the scheme manager], as if the words "(including at least himself)" were omitted.

Receivers and managers

47. In Article 48 of the Order (receivership accounts), "prescribed" means prescribed by regulations made by statutory instrument by the [Treasury].

48. In paragraph (1) of Article 49 of the Order (notification that receiver or manager appointed), the reference to every invoice, order for goods or business letter is a reference to every statement of account, order for goods or services, business letter or advertisement.

[**49.** Paragraph (3) of Article 50 of the Order (payment of debts out of assets subject to floating charge), as applied to a building society, has effect as if the reference to general creditors included a reference to shareholding members of the society in respect of deposits which are not relevant deposits.

50. Articles 52 to 59 of the Order (administrative receivers) are omitted.

51. Article 59A of the Order (floating charge holder not to appoint administrative receiver), as applied to a building society, has effect as if—

(a) in paragraph (1) the word "qualifying" were omitted; and
(b) paragraphs (2), (3)(a), (4) and (5) were omitted.

52. Articles 59B to 59J of the Order (exceptions to prohibition) are omitted.]]

[Insolvency practitioners: their qualification and regulation

53. Article 349 of the Order (persons not qualified to act as insolvency practitioners) has effect as if for paragraph (2) there were substituted—

"(2) A person is not qualified to act as an insolvency practitioner in relation to a building society at any time unless at that time the person is fully authorised to act as an insolvency practitioner or partially authorised to act as an insolvency practitioner only in relation to companies.".

54. (1) In the following provisions of the Order, in a reference to authorisation or permission to act as an insolvency practitioner in relation to (or only in relation to) companies the reference to companies has effect without the modification in paragraph 2(1)(a) above—

(a) Articles 349A and 349B(1) and (3) (authorisation of insolvency practitioners); and
(b) Articles 350O(1)(b) and 350R(3)(b) (court sanction of insolvency practitioners in public interest cases).

(2) In Articles 350Q(2)(b) (direct sanctions order: conditions) and 350S(3)(e) (power for Department to obtain information) of the Order the reference to a company has effect without the modification in paragraph 2(1)(a) above.

55. In Articles 350O, 350Q and 350R of the Order a reference to the creditors of a company includes a reference to every shareholding member of the building society to whom a sum due from the society in relation to the member's shareholding is due in respect of a deposit.]

NOTES

Inserted as noted to Pt I at **[7.468]**.

Para 30: words in square brackets added by the Insolvency (Northern Ireland) Order 2002, SI 2002/3152 (NI 6), art 4(b), Sch 2, Pt II, para 14(1), (3).

Para 30A: inserted by SI 2002/3152 (NI 6), art 4(b), Sch 2, Pt II, para 14(1), (3).

Para 31A: inserted by SI 2002/3152 (NI 6), art 4(b), Sch 2, Pt II, para 14(1), (4); words in square brackets substituted by the Financial Services Act 2012 (Mutual Societies) Order 2013, SI 2013/496, art 2(b), Sch 8, para 58(1), (9).

Paras 32, 33, 37: words in square brackets substituted by SI 2013/496, art 2(b), Sch 8, para 58(1), (10)–(12).

Para 38: words omitted from sub-para (2), and the whole of sub-para (4), repealed by SI 2001/2617, art 13(1), (2), Sch 3, Pt II, paras 131, 210(n), (o), Sch 4; words in first pair of square brackets in sub-para (3) substituted by the Companies Act 2006 (Commencement No 3, Consequential Amendments, Transitional Provisions and Savings) Order 2007, SI 2007/2194, art 10, Sch 4, Pt 3, para 50, subject to savings in art 12 thereof; words in second pair of square brackets in sub-para (3) substituted by the Companies Act 2006 (Consequential Amendments, Transitional Provisions and Savings) Order 2009, SI 2009/1941, art 2(1), Sch 1, para 87(1), (12)(c).

Paras 40, 42: repealed by the Financial Services (Banking Reform) Act 2013, s 138, Sch 9, paras 1, 4(2)(c), (d).

Para 43: words in first pair of square brackets substituted by SI 2013/496, art 2(b), Sch 8, para 58(1), (13); words in second pair of square brackets substituted by the Financial Services and Markets Act 2000 (Mutual Societies) Order 2001, SI 2001/2617, art 13(1), Sch 3, Pt II, paras 131, 210(p).

Para 45: words in first (outer) pair of square brackets substituted by SI 2001/2617, art 13(1), Sch 3, Pt II, paras 131, 210(q); words in second (inner) pair of square brackets substituted by SI 2013/496, art 2(b), Sch 8, para 58(1), (14).

Para 46: words in first (outer) pair of square brackets in sub-paras (a), (b) substituted by SI 2001/2617, art 13(1), Sch 3, Pt II, paras 131, 210(r), (s); words in second (inner) pair of square brackets in sub-paras (a), (b) substituted by SI 2013/496, art 2(b), Sch 8, para 58(1), (15).

Para 47: word in square brackets substituted by SI 2001/2617, arts 4(1)(c), 13(1), Sch 1, Pt III, Sch 3, Pt II, paras 131, 210(t); for transitional provisions in relation to transferred functions, see art 5 thereof.

Paras 49–52: substituted (for original para 49) by the Building Societies (Floating Charges and Other Provisions) Order 2016, SI 2016/679, art 4(1), (4), in relation to a floating charge created by a building society on or after 28 June 2016. Para 49 previously read as follows:

"**49.** Article 50 (payment of debts out of assets subject to floating charge) and Articles 52 to 59 (administrative receivers) of the Order are omitted.".

Paras 53–55: inserted by the Small Business, Enterprise and Employment Act 2015 and the Insolvency (Amendment) Act (Northern Ireland) 2016 (Consequential Amendments and Transitional Provisions) Regulations 2017, SI 2017/400, reg 2(1), (4)(f).

Application: paras 33–35, 40, 42, 49 are applied, with modifications, for the purposes of a relevant building society, by the Building Societies (Financial Assistance) Order 2010, SI 2010/1188, art 11(1), (7)–(9) at **[18.217]**.

SCHEDULES 16–21

(*Schs 16–21 outside the scope of this work.*)

BANKING ACT 2009

(2009 c 1)

An Act to make provision about banking

[12 February 2009]

1–89 ((*Pt 1*) *outside the scope of this work.*)

PART 2
BANK INSOLVENCY

90–122 (*For ss 90–122 see* **[7.27]–[7.60]**.)

Miscellaneous

123–129 (*Ss 123–126 outside the scope of this work; for ss 127–129A see* **[7.61]–[7.63]**.)

[7.471]

130 Building societies

(1) The Treasury may by order provide for this Part to apply to building societies (within the meaning of section 119 of the Building Societies Act 1986) as it applies to banks, subject to modifications set out in the order.

(2) An order may—

(a) amend the Building Societies Act 1986 or any other enactment which relates, or in so far as it relates, to building societies;

(b) amend an enactment amended by this Part;

(c) replicate, with or without modifications, any provision of this Part;

(d) apply a provision made under or by virtue of this Part, with or without modifications, to this Part as it applies to building societies.

(3) An order—

(a) shall be made by statutory instrument, and

(b) may not be made unless a draft has been laid before and approved by resolution of each House of Parliament.

(4) Provision made under or by virtue of this Part may make special provision in relation to the application of this Part to building societies.

NOTES

See further, in relation to the application of this section, with modifications, in respect of building societies: the Building Societies (Insolvency and Special Administration) Order 2009, SI 2009/805, art 3, Sch 1, Pt 1, Pt 2, paras 6, 23 at **[7.475]**, **[7.479]**, **[7.480]**.

Orders: the Building Societies (Insolvency and Special Administration) Order 2009, SI 2009/805 at **[7.474]**; the Building Societies (Insolvency and Special Administration) (Amendment) Order 2010, SI 2010/1189.

131–135 (*Ss 131–134 outside the scope of this work; for s 135 see* **[7.64]**.)

PART 3
BANK ADMINISTRATION

136–154 (*For ss 136–145 see* **[7.65]–[7.74]**; *ss 146–154 outside the scope of this work.*)

Miscellaneous

155–157 (*Outside the scope of this work.*)

[7.472]

158 Building societies

(1) The Treasury may by order provide for this Part to apply to building societies (within the meaning of section 119 of the Building Societies Act 1986) as it applies to banks, subject to modifications set out in the order.

(2) An order may—

(a) amend the Building Societies Act 1986 or any other enactment which relates, or in so far as it relates, to building societies;

(b) amend an enactment amended by this Part;

(c) replicate, with or without modifications, any provision of this Part;

(d) apply a provision made under or by virtue of this Part, with or without modifications, to this Part as it applies to building societies.

(3) An order—

(a) shall be made by statutory instrument, and

(b) may not be made unless a draft has been laid before and approved by resolution of each House of Parliament.

(4) Provision made under or by virtue of this Part may make special provision in relation to the application of this Part to building societies.

NOTES

See further, in relation to the application of this section, with modifications, in respect of building societies: the Building Societies (Insolvency and Special Administration) Order 2009, SI 2009/805, art 3, Sch 1, Pt 1, Pt 3, paras 24, 36 at **[7.475]**, **[7.479]**, **[7.481]**.

Orders: the Building Societies (Insolvency and Special Administration) Order 2009, SI 2009/805 at **[7.474]**; the Building Societies (Insolvency and Special Administration) (Amendment) Order 2010, SI 2010/1189.

159–256A (*Ss 159–168, ss 169–256A (Pts 4–7) outside the scope of this work.*)

PART 8
GENERAL

257–258A (*Outside the scope of this work.*)

[7.473]
259 Statutory instruments

(1) A statutory instrument under this Act—
- (a) may make provision that applies generally or only for specified purposes, cases or circumstances,
- (b) may make different provision for different purposes, cases or circumstances, and
- (c) may include incidental, consequential or transitional provision.

(2)–(6) (*Outside the scope of this work.*)

260–265 (*Ss 260–262 outside the scope of this work; for ss 263–265 see* **[7.81]–[7.83]**.)

BUILDING SOCIETIES (INSOLVENCY AND SPECIAL ADMINISTRATION) ORDER 2009

(SI 2009/805)

NOTES

Made: 29 March 2009 (3.06 pm).
Authority: Banking Act 2009, ss 130, 158, 259(1).
Commencement: 29 March 2009.

ARRANGEMENT OF ARTICLES

1 Citation and interpretation . . . [7.474]
3 . . . [7.475]
16 Rules . . . [7.476]
17 Northern Ireland . . . [7.477]
18 Application of subordinate legislation under Parts 2 and 3 of the 2009 Act . . . [7.478]

SCHEDULES

Schedule 1—Modified Application of Parts 2 and 3 of the Banking Act 2009 to Building Societies
Part 1—General Mode of Application . . . [7.479]
Part 2—Modified Application of Part 2 of the 2009 Act . . . [7.480]
Part 3—Modified Application of Part 3 of the 2009 Act . . . [7.481]
Schedule 2—Modified Application of Subordinate Legislation . . . [7.482]

[7.474]
1 Citation and interpretation

(1) This Order may be cited as the Building Societies (Insolvency and Special Administration) Order 2009.

(2) In this Order—
"the 1986 Act" means the Building Societies Act 1986;
"the 2009 Act" means the Banking Act 2009.

2 (*Inserts the Building Societies Act 1986, s 90C at* **[7.457]**.)

[7.475]
3

Schedule 1 to this Order specifies modifications to Parts 2 and 3 of the 2009 Act as they apply in relation to building societies.

4–15 (*Arts 4–9 amend the Building Societies Act 1986 as follows: art 4 amends s 88 at* **[7.451]**, *art 5 inserts s 89A at* **[7.453]**, *art 6 inserts ss 90D, 90E at* **[7.458]**, **[7.459]**, *art 7 amends s 86(1) at* **[7.449]**, *art 8 amends s 91 at* **[7.460]***, and art 9 amends s 92 at* **[7.461]***; arts 10, 11, 15 make amendments outside the scope of this work; art 12 inserts the Company Directors Disqualification Act 1986, s 21C at* **[4.42]***; art 13 inserts the Insolvency Act 1986, s 411(3A) at* **[1.522]***; art 14 inserts the Insolvency Act 1986, s 414(8C) at* **[1.525]**.)

[7.476]
16 Rules

Section 413(2) of the Insolvency Act 1986 (rules: duty to consult Insolvency Rules Committee) shall not apply to the first set of rules made in relation to building society insolvency or to the first set of rules made in relation to building society special administration.

[7.477]
17 Northern Ireland

In the application of this Order to Northern Ireland—

(a) a reference to an enactment is to be treated as a reference to the equivalent enactment having effect in relation to Northern Ireland,

(b) where this Order amends an enactment an equivalent amendment (incorporating any necessary modification) is made to the equivalent enactment having effect in relation to Northern Ireland, and

(c) a reference to the Secretary of State is to be treated as a reference to the Department of Enterprise, Trade and Investment.

[7.478]
18 Application of subordinate legislation under Parts 2 and 3 of the 2009 Act

Schedule 2 applies subordinate legislation made under Parts 2 and 3 of the 2009 Act in relation to building societies, with the modifications set out in that Schedule.

SCHEDULES

SCHEDULE 1
MODIFIED APPLICATION OF PARTS 2 AND 3 OF THE BANKING ACT 2009 TO BUILDING SOCIETIES

Article 3

PART 1
GENERAL MODE OF APPLICATION

General mode of application and interpretation

[7.479]

1. This Schedule specifies modifications to Part 2 (Bank Insolvency) and Part 3 (Bank Administration) of the 2009 Act as they apply in relation to building societies by virtue of section 90C of the 1986 Act.

2. (1) Parts 2 and 3 of the 2009 Act apply to building societies with the following general modifications (in addition to the general modifications set out in section 90C(2) of the 1986 Act)—

(a) for "company" in each place where it appears (except in section 151) substitute "building society";

(b) a reference to depositors includes a reference to holders of shares in the society;

(c) a reference to a provision in Part 1 (Special Resolution Regime) of the 2009 Act is a reference to that provision as applied to building societies with any modifications by section 84 of the 2009 Act (application of Part 1: general);

(d) a reference to a provision in Part 2 or 3 of the 2009 Act is a reference to that provision as applied in relation to building societies by section 90C of the 1986 Act with any modifications specified in that section or this Schedule.

3. Where a provision of Part 2 or 3 of the 2009 Act applies a provision of the Insolvency Act 1986 or the Companies Act 2006, the provision so applied has effect in relation to building societies with the following modifications—

(a) for "articles" substitute "rules";

(b) [except where otherwise specified in this Schedule,] for "company" substitute "building society";

(c) for "registered office" substitute "principal office";

(d) for "registrar of companies" or "registrar" substitute "[FCA]";

(e) for "resolution for voluntary winding up" substitute "resolution passed under section 88(1) of the Building Societies Act 1986";

(f) every reference to a company registered in Scotland has effect as a reference to a building society whose principal office is situated in Scotland;

(g) every reference to the officers, or to a particular officer, of a company has effect as a reference to the officers, or to the corresponding officer, of the building society and as including a person holding himself out as such an officer;

(h) every reference to a voluntary arrangement under Part 1 of the Insolvency Act 1986 has effect as a reference to a voluntary arrangement under that Part as applied in relation to building societies by section 90A of, and Schedule 15A to, the Building Societies Act 1986;

(i) any requirement to send a notice or other document, or make a report, to the registrar of companies, has effect as a requirement to send that notice or document, or make that report, to the [FCA] and for the [FCA] to place it on the public file of the society concerned.

4. In Parts 2 and 3 of the 2009 Act, and in any provision of the Insolvency Act 1986 applied by those Parts, "contributory", in relation to a building society—

(a) means every person liable to contribute to the assets of the society in the event of its being wound up, and

(b) for the purposes of all proceedings for determining, and all proceedings prior to the determination of, the persons who are deemed to be contributories, includes any person alleged to be a contributory, and

(c) includes persons who are liable to pay or contribute to the payment of—

(i) any debt or liability of the building society being wound up, or

(ii) any sum for the adjustment of rights of members among themselves, or

(iii) the expenses of the winding up,

but does not include persons liable to contribute by virtue of a declaration by the court under section 213 (imputed responsibility for fraudulent trading) or 214 (wrongful trading) of the Insolvency Act 1986.

5. Expressions used in this Schedule (including in text inserted or substituted by this Schedule) have the same meaning as in the Building Societies Act 1986.

NOTES

Para 3: words in square brackets in sub-para (b) inserted by the Small Business, Enterprise and Employment Act 2015 and the Insolvency (Amendment) Act (Northern Ireland) 2016 (Consequential Amendments and Transitional Provisions) Regulations 2017, SI 2017/400, reg 8(1), (2); words in square brackets in sub-paras (d), (i) substituted by the Financial Services Act 2012 (Mutual Societies) Order 2013, SI 2013/496, art 2(c), Sch 11, para 16(1), (2).

PART 2
MODIFIED APPLICATION OF PART 2 OF THE 2009 ACT

[7.480]

6. This Part sets out modifications to Part 2 of the 2009 Act (Bank Insolvency) as it applies in relation to building societies by virtue of section 90C of the 1986 Act.

Introduction

7. Ignore section 91 of the 2009 Act (interpretation: "bank").

8. Subsections (5) and (6) of section 93 of the 2009 Act (interpretation: other expressions) do not apply in relation to any expression defined in this Schedule.

Building society insolvency order

9. In section 95 of the 2009 Act (application), in subsection (1), ignore paragraph (c).

10. In section 96 of the 2009 Act (grounds for applying)—

(a) in subsection (1), ignore paragraph (b);

(b) ignore subsections (4) and (5).

11. In section 97 of the 2009 Act (grounds for making)—

(a) ignore subsection (2);

(b) in subsection (3), ignore "or (2)".

12. In section 98 of the 2009 Act (commencement), in subsection (2)(a), for "section 120" substitute "section 90D of the Building Societies Act 1986".

Process of building society liquidation

13. (1) In section 103 of the 2009 Act (general powers, duties and effect), in subsection (4) ignore paragraph (h).

(2) In that section, the table (Insolvency Act 1986) applies with the modifications set out in this paragraph.

(3) For the entry for section 154 substitute—

"Section 154	Adjustment of rights of contributories	Any surplus is to be distributed in accordance with the rules of the society.".

(4) Ignore the entry for section 187 (transfer of assets to employees).

Part 7C Special Insolvency Regimes

[(4A) For the entry for section 195 substitute—

"Section 195	Meetings to ascertain wishes of creditors or contributories	(a)	The power to have regard to the wishes of creditors and contributories is subject to Objective 1 in section 99.
		(b)	In subsection (3), for "the number of votes conferred on each contributory by the Companies Act or the articles", substitute "the value of the shares each contributory holds in the building society".".]

(5) Ignore the entries for sections 216 (restriction on re-use of names) and 217 (personal liability for debts).

(6) For the entries for sections 218 and 219 substitute—

"Section 218	Prosecution of officers and members of company	(a)	the section does not apply in relation to offences committed by members of a building society acting in that capacity.
		(b)	In subsection (3), treat the second reference to the official receiver as a reference to the Secretary of State.
		(c)	Ignore subsections (4), (5) and (6).
		(d)	Where a report is made to the Secretary of State under subsection (3), the Secretary of State may refer the matter to the [FCA or the PRA] for further enquiry.
		(e)	On such a reference to it the [FCA or, as the case may be, the PRA] shall exercise its power under section 55(1) of the Building Societies Act 1986 to appoint one or more competent persons to investigate and report on the matter.
Section 219	Obligations under section 218	(a)	The section does not apply in relation to offences committed by members of a building society acting in that capacity.
		(b)	Subsection (1) of section 219 does not apply.
		(c)	Subsections (2), (2A) and (2B) of section 219 apply in relation to the powers referred to in the entry above for section 218.
		(d)	In subsections (3) and (4) of section 219 the references to the Secretary of State shall have effect as references to the [FCA or, as the case may be, the PRA].".

[(6A) For the entry for sections 390 to 391T substitute—

"Sections 390 to 391T Authorisation and regulation of insolvency practitioners	(a) In section 390 treat references to acting as an insolvency practitioner as references to acting as a building society liquidator. (b) For subsection (2) of that section substitute— "(2) A person is not qualified to act as a building society liquidator at any time unless at that time the person is fully authorised to act as an insolvency practitioner or partially authorised to act as an insolvency practitioner only in relation to companies.". (c) An order under section 391 has effect in relation to any provision applied for the purposes of building society insolvency. (d) In sections 390A, 390B(1) and (3), 391O(1)(b) and 391R(3)(b), in a reference to authorisation or permission to act as an insolvency practitioner in relation to (or only in relation to) companies the reference to companies has effect without the modification in paragraph 3(b) of this Schedule. (e) In sections 391Q(2)(b) and 391S(3)(e) the reference to a company has effect without the modification in paragraph 3(b) of this Schedule. (f) In sections 391O, 391Q and 391R a reference to the creditors of a company includes a reference to every shareholding member of the building society to whom a sum due from the society in relation to the member's shareholding is due in respect of a deposit.]

(7) For the entry for sections 423–425 substitute—

"Sections 423–425	Transactions defrauding creditors	(a)	Sections 423–425 apply only where a building society insolvency order is made.
		(b)	Anything done by the building society in connection with the exercise of a stabilisation power under Part 1 of this Act as applied to building societies by section 84 of this Act is not a transaction at an undervalue for the purposes of section 423.".

Termination of process, &c

14. In section 113 of the 2009 Act (voluntary arrangement)—
- (a) in subsection (1), at the end insert "as applied in relation to building societies by section 90A of, and Schedule 15A to, the Building Societies Act 1986";
- (b) in subsection (2), ignore paragraph (b)(v);
- (c) in subsection (6) at the end insert "and with the modifications made by Schedule 15A to the Building Societies Act 1986".

15. In section 114 of the 2009 Act (administration)—
- (a) in subsection (1), for "(under paragraph 38 of Schedule B1 to the Insolvency Act 1986)" substitute "(under section 9 of the Insolvency Act 1986 as applied in relation to building societies by section 90A of, and Schedule 15A to, the Building Societies Act 1986)";
- (b) in subsection (4), for "the rescue of the bank as a going concern" substitute "the survival of the building society, and the whole or any part of its undertaking, as a going concern".

16. In section 115 of the 2009 Act (dissolution)—
- (a) in subsection (2), ignore paragraph (b)(v);
- (b) in subsection (4), for "registrar of companies" substitute "[FCA]";
- (c) in subsection (7), for "the registrar of companies shall register it" substitute "the [FCA] shall place it on the public file of the society concerned";
- (d) In subsection (8), for "the day of the registration of the notice" substitute "the day on which the notice is placed on the public file of the society".
- [(e) after subsection (8) insert—

"(9) Sections 1012 to 1023 and 1034 of the Companies Act 2006 (provisions as to property of dissolved company) apply in relation to the property of a building society dissolved under this section as they apply to the property of a dissolved company.".]

[**17.** In section 116 of the 2009 Act (dissolution: supplemental)—
- (a) in subsections (1) and (2) the references to the Secretary of State have effect as references to the [FCA];

(b) for subsection (4) substitute—

"(4) On giving a direction under subsection (1) the [FCA] shall place it on the public file of the society concerned.";

(c) ignore subsection (5).]

18. . . .

Other processes

19. Ignore sections 117 (insolvency as alternative order) and 118 (voluntary winding-up) of the 2009 Act.

20. (1) Ignore section 119 of the 2009 Act (exclusion of other procedures); this paragraph, and section 88(1)(b) of the 1986 Act, make equivalent provision.

(2) A petition for the winding-up of a building society shall be dismissed on the making of a building society insolvency order in respect of the building society.

(3) Where a building society is in building society insolvency, no order may be made for the winding-up of the building society.

21. Ignore sections 120 (notice to [PRA] of preliminary steps) and 121 (disqualification of directors) of the 2009 Act.

Miscellaneous

22. In section 124 of the 2009 Act (transfer of accounts), after subsection (2) insert—

"(2A) The arrangements may—

(a) cancel shares in the building society;

(b) confer rights and impose liabilities in place of cancelled shares (whether by way of actual or deemed shares in a transferee building society or by way of other rights and liabilities in relation to a transferee bank).".

23. Ignore sections 130 (building societies), 131 (credit unions), 132 (partnerships) and 133 (Scottish partnerships) of the 2009 Act.

NOTES

Para 13: sub-para (4A) inserted by the Building Societies (Insolvency and Special Administration) (Amendment) Order 2010, SI 2010/1189, art 2(1), (2)(a); in sub-para (6) words in square brackets substituted by the Financial Services Act 2012 (Mutual Societies) Order 2013, SI 2013/496, art 2(c), Sch 11, para 16(1), (3); sub-para (6A) inserted by the Small Business, Enterprise and Employment Act 2015 and the Insolvency (Amendment) Act (Northern Ireland) 2016 (Consequential Amendments and Transitional Provisions) Regulations 2017, SI 2017/400, reg 8(1), (3).

Para 16: words in square brackets in sub-paras (b), (c) substituted by SI 2013/496, art 2(c), Sch 11, para 16(1), (4); sub-para (e) inserted by SI 2010/1189, art 2(1), (2)(b).

Para 17: substituted by SI 2010/1189, art 2(1), (2)(c); words in square brackets substituted by SI 2013/496, art 2(c), Sch 11, para 16(1), (5).

Para 18: revoked by SI 2010/1189, art 2(1), (2)(d).

Para 21: words in square brackets substituted by SI 2013/496, art 2(c), Sch 11, para 16(1), (6).

PART 3
MODIFIED APPLICATION OF PART 3 OF THE 2009 ACT

[7.481]

24. This Part sets out modifications to Part 3 of the 2009 Act (Bank Administration) as it applies in relation to building societies by virtue of section 90C of the 1986 Act.

Introduction

25. In section 140 of the 2009 Act (objective 2: "normal" administration) the references in subsections (1) and (2) to the residual building society's creditors as a whole include references to all holders of shares in the society.

Process

26. In section 145 of the 2009 Act (general powers, duties and effect), in subsection (4) omit paragraph (d).

27. (1) In section 145, table 1 (Schedule B1 to the Insolvency Act 1986) applies with the modifications set out in this paragraph.

(2) For the entries for paras 59 to 64, see paragraph 29 below.

(3) For the entry for para 65, substitute—

"Para 65	Distribution	(a) In sub para (1) the reference to a creditors includes a reference to a shareholding member.

		(b)	In the case of building society special administration following transfer to a bridge bank, until the Bank of England has given an Objective 1 Achievement Notice a bank administrator may make a distribution only with the Bank of England's consent.
		[(c)	Where paragraph (b) applies, ignore sub para. (3).]".

(4) For the entry for para 75, substitute—

"Para 75	Misfeasance	(a)	In addition to applications that may anyway be made under para 75, an application may be made by the building society special administrator or the Bank of England.
		(b)	An application may not be made by a borrowing member.".

[(5) For the entry for para 80 (termination: successful rescue) substitute—

"Para 79	Termination: successful rescue	(a)	Ignore sub-para (2).
		(b)	*See section 153.*".]

(6) Ignore the entry for para 84 (termination: no more assets for distribution): paragraph 30 below makes equivalent provision.

(7) For the entry for para 111 (interpretation) substitute—

"Para 111	Interpretation	Ignore sub-paragraphs (1A) and (1B)".

28. (1) In section 145, table 2 (other provisions of the Insolvency Act 1986) applies with the modifications set out in this paragraph.

(2) For the entry for section 168(4) (and para 13 of Schedule 4) substitute—

"Section 168(4) (and para 13 of Schedule 4)	Discretion in managing and distributing assets	(a)	In the case of building society special administration following transfer to a bridge bank, until the Bank of England has given an Objective 1 Achievement Notice distribution may be made only (i) with the Bank of England's consent or (ii) out of assets which have been designated as realisable by agreement between the bank administrator and the Bank of England.
		(b)	In subsection (4) the references to creditors includes a reference to shareholding members.".

[(2A) For the entry for sections 390 to 391T substitute—

Part 7C Special Insolvency Regimes

"Sections 390 to 391T Authorisation and regulation of insolvency practitioners	(a) In section 390 treat references to acting as an insolvency practitioner as references to acting as a building society special administrator. (b) For subsection (2) of that section substitute— "(2) A person is not qualified to act as a building society special administrator at any time unless at that time the person is fully authorised to act as an insolvency practitioner or partially authorised to act as an insolvency practitioner only in relation to companies.". (c) An order under section 391 has effect in relation to any provision applied for the purposes of building society special administration. (d) In sections 390A, 390B(1) and (3), 391O(1)(b) and 391R(3)(b), in a reference to authorisation or permission to act as an insolvency practitioner in relation to (or only in relation to) companies the reference to companies has effect without the modification in paragraph 3(b) of this Schedule. (e) In sections 391Q(2)(b) and 391S(3)(e) the reference to a company has effect without the modification in paragraph 3(b) of this Schedule. (f) In sections 391O, 391Q and 391R a reference to the creditors of a company includes a reference to every shareholding member of the building society to whom a sum due from the society in relation to the member's shareholding is due in respect of a deposit."]

(3) For the entry for sections 423–425 substitute—

"Section 423–425	Transactions defrauding creditors	(a)	Sections 423–425 apply only where a building society special administration order is made.
		(b)	In considering granting leave under section 424(1) the court must have regard to Objective 1 of section 134.
		(c)	In considering making an order in reliance on section 425 the court must have regard to Objective 1 of section 137.".

General powers of administrator

29. (1) This paragraph modifies the application of paragraphs 59 to 64 of Schedule B1 to the Insolvency Act 1986 (general powers of administrator); the modifications have effect in addition to those set out for those paragraphs in table 1 in section 145 of the 2009 Act.

(2) Subject to sub-paragraph (3), paragraphs 59 to 64 of Schedule B1 have effect as if they required the building society special administrator, in exercising powers under those paragraphs—

(a) to ensure compliance with the provisions of the Building Societies Act 1986, and

(b) not to appoint to be a director any person who is not a fit and proper person to hold that position.

(3) Sub-paragraph (2)(a) does not apply in relation to section 5, 6 or 7 of the Building Societies Act 1986.

No more assets for distribution

30. (1) This paragraph makes provision equivalent to paragraph 84 of Schedule B1 to the Insolvency Act 1986 (termination: no more assets for distribution).

(2) A building society special administrator who thinks that the building society has no property which might permit a distribution to its creditors and shareholding members must send a notice to that effect to the [FCA and the PRA].

(3) The court may on the application of the building society special administrator disapply sub-paragraph (2) in respect of the building society.

(4) On receipt of a notice under sub-paragraph (2) the [FCA] must place it on the public file of the building society and record in that file the date on which it was placed there.

(5) The appointment of the building society special administrator ceases to have effect on the date on which the notice under sub-paragraph (2) is placed in the public file of the society.

(6) A building society special administrator who sends a notice under sub-paragraph (2) must as soon as is reasonably practicable—

(a) file a copy of the notice with the court, and

(b) send a copy of the notice to each creditor and shareholding member whose address is known.

(7) The building society is dissolved at the end of the period of three months beginning with the date on which the notice under sub-paragraph (2) was placed in its public file.

(8) On an application in respect of a building society by the building society special administrator or another interested person the court may—

(a) extend the period specified in sub-paragraph (7),

(b) suspend that period, or

(c) disapply sub-paragraph (7).

(9) Where an order is made under sub-paragraph (8) in respect of a building society the building society special administrator shall as soon as is reasonably practicable notify the [FCA and, where relevant, the PRA].

(10) A building society special administrator who fails without reasonable excuse to comply with sub-paragraph (6) commits an offence.

(11) An offence under sub-paragraph (10) shall be treated for all purposes as an offence under paragraph 84(9) of Schedule B1 to the Insolvency Act 1986.

[(12) Sections 1012 to 1023 and 1034 of the Companies Act 2006 (provisions as to property of dissolved company) apply in relation to the property of a building society dissolved under this paragraph as they apply in relation to the property of a dissolved company.]

. . .

31. . . .

Multiple transfers

32. (1) In section 152 of the 2009 Act (property transfer from temporary public ownership), in subsection (1)—

(a) for paragraph (a) substitute—

"(a) make an order under section 85 (temporary public ownership) in respect of a building society, and";

(b) in paragraph (b) for "(or from another bank which is or was in the same group as the bank)" substitute "(or from a bank which is or was in the same group as the building society").

(2) Where the Treasury make an order under section 85 in respect of a building society, and later make a property transfer order from a bank which was in the same group as the building society, Part 3 of the 2009 Act, and any subordinate legislation made under that Part, applies to the transferor bank without the modifications made by section 90C of the Building Societies Act 1986 and this Order.

[Property transfer from transferred institution

32ZA. Where a resolution instrument makes provision under section 84A of the 2009 Act in respect of a building society, in section 152A of the 2009 Act (property transfer from transferred institution)—

(a) the first reference in paragraphs (a) and (b) of subsection (1) to a bank (which would otherwise apply as mentioned in section 90C(2)(a) of the 1986 Act) is to be read as a reference—

(i) to the successor company (defined in section 84D(8) of the 2009 Act), or

(ii) in a case within section 84D(1)(b) of the 2009 Act, to the successor company or its specified parent undertaking (defined in section 84D(8) of the 2009 Act);

(b) in paragraph (a) of subsection (1) ignore the reference to a bank's parent undertaking;

(c) in paragraph (b) of subsection (1) ignore "or from another a bank which is or was in the same group as the bank"; and

(d) the reference in subsection (1) to sections 12A(2) and 41A(2) of the 2009 Act and the reference in subsection (2) to section 41A(2) is to those section as applied and modified by section 84D(2) of the 2009 Act.]

Termination

[32A. In section 153 of the 2009 Act (successful rescue), for subsections (2) and (3) substitute—

"(2) The building society special administrator shall make an application under paragraph 79 of Schedule B1 to the Insolvency Act 1986 (court ending administration on achievement of objectives).

(3) A building society special administrator who makes an application in accordance with subsection (2) must send a copy to the [FCA and the PRA].".]

33. In section 154 of the 2009 Act (winding-up or voluntary arrangement)—

(a) in subsection (2), in paragraph (a), the reference to paragraph 84 of Schedule B1 to the Insolvency Act 1986 has effect as a reference to paragraph 30 of this Schedule;

(b) in that subsection, in paragraph (b), at the end insert "as applied in relation to building societies by section 90A of, and Schedule 15A to, the Building Societies Act 1986";

(c) in subsection (3), at the end insert "and with the modifications made by Schedule 15A to the Building Societies Act 1986".

Miscellaneous

34. Ignore section 155 of the 2009 Act (disqualification of directors).

35. (1) Ignore section 157 of the 2009 Act (other processes); this paragraph makes equivalent provision.

(2) Before exercising an insolvency power in respect of a residual building society [the FCA or the PRA] must give notice to the Bank of England, which may participate in any proceedings arising out of the exercise of the power.

(3) In sub-paragraph (2)—
(a) "residual building society" means a building society all or part of whose business has been transferred to a commercial purchaser or to a bridge bank in accordance with section 11 or section 12 of the 2009 Act respectively (as applied with modifications by section 84 of the 2009 Act), and
(b) "insolvency power" means—
(i) [the power of the FCA or PRA] to apply to the court for an administration order (see paragraph 11(1) of Schedule 15A to the Building Societies Act 1986), and
(ii) [the power of the FCA or PRA] to present a petition for the winding-up of a building society (see sections 37(1) and 89(2) of the Building Societies Act 1986).

36. Ignore sections 158 (building societies), 159 (credit unions), 163 (partnerships) and 164 (Scottish partnerships) of the 2009 Act.

37. Subsections (4) and (5) of section 166 of the 2009 Act (interpretation: general) do not apply to expressions defined in this Schedule.

NOTES

Para 27: in sub-para (3), in the substituted entry for para 65, words in square brackets in the third column substituted by the Small Business, Enterprise and Employment Act 2015 and the Insolvency (Amendment) Act (Northern Ireland) 2016 (Consequential Amendments and Transitional Provisions) Regulations 2017, SI 2017/400, reg 8(1), (4)(a); sub-para (5) substituted by the Building Societies (Insolvency and Special Administration) (Amendment) Order 2010, SI 2010/1189, art 2(1), (2)(e).

Para 28: sub-para (2A) inserted by SI 2017/400, reg 8(1), (4)(b).

Para 30: words in square brackets in sub-paras (2), (4) substituted by the Financial Services Act 2012 (Mutual Societies) Order 2013, SI 2013/496, art 2(c), Sch 11, para 16(1), (7); words in square brackets in sub-para (9) substituted by the Financial Services Act 2012 (Consequential Amendments and Transitional Provisions) Order 2013, SI 2013/472, art 3, Sch 2, para 169; sub-para (12) inserted by SI 2010/1189, art 2(1), (2)(f).

Para 31: revoked by SI 2010/1189, art 2(1), (2)(g).

Para 32ZA: inserted by the Building Societies (Bail-in) Order 2014, SI 2014/3344, art 5.

Para 32A: inserted by SI 2010/1189, art 2(1), (2)(h); words in square brackets substituted by SI 2013/496, art 2(c), Sch 11, para 16(1), (8).

Para 35: words in square brackets substituted by the Financial Services Act 2012 (Consequential Amendments and Transitional Provisions) Order 2013, SI 2013/472, art 3, Sch 2, para 169.

SCHEDULE 2
MODIFIED APPLICATION OF SUBORDINATE LEGISLATION

Article 18

[7.482]

1. The following instruments apply in relation to building societies as they apply in relation to banks, with the modifications set out in this Schedule—
(a) the Banking Act 2009 (Parts 2 and 3 Consequential Amendments) Order 2009;
(b) the Bank Administration (Sharing Information) Regulations 2009;
(c) the Banking Act 2009 (Bank Administration) (Modification for Application to Multiple Transfers) Regulations 2009;
(d) the Banking Act 2009 (Bank Administration) (Modification for Application to Banks in Temporary Public Ownership) Regulations 2009.

2. The following general modifications apply to all of the instruments referred to in paragraph 1—
(a) references to "bank" (except in the term "bridge bank") have effect as references to "building society";
(b) references to "bank administration", "bank administration order" and "bank administrator" have effect as references to "building society special administration", "building society special administration order" and "building society special administrator";
(c) references to Part 1 of the 2009 Act, or to any provision in that Part, have effect as references to that Part, or that provision, as applied to building societies with any modifications by section 84 of the 2009 Act (application of Part 1: general);
(d) references to Part 2 or 3 of the 2009 Act, or to any provision in Part 2 or Part 3, have effect as references to that Part, or that provision, as applied in relation to building societies by section 90C of the 1986 Act with any modifications specified in that section or in Schedule 1 to this Order.

3. The modifications to the Banking Act 2009 (Parts 2 and 3 Consequential Amendments) Order 2009 (in addition to the modifications set out in paragraph 2) are—
(a) references to "bank insolvency", "bank insolvency order" and "bank liquidator" are references to "building society insolvency", "building society insolvency order" and "building society liquidator";
(b) ignore article 4 (Finance (No 2) Act 1992);
(c) ignore article 5 (Financial Services and Markets Act 2000);
(d) ignore article 6 (Companies Act 2006);
(e) in article 7 (Dormant Bank and Building Society Accounts Act 2008), for "bank which is a bank within the meaning of section 91 of the 2009 Act" substitute "building society within the meaning of section 119 of the Building Societies Act 1986";
[(ea) after article 8 insert—

"8A (1) The Pension Protection Fund (Entry Rules) Regulations 2005 apply with the following modifications.
(2) In regulation 9(1) and (2) (confirmation of scheme status by insolvency practitioner), the references to "company" are to be read as references to "building society".
(3) In regulation 10(3) (confirmation of scheme status by Board), the reference to "company" is to be read as a reference to "building society".";

(eb) after article 9 insert—

"9A (1) The Pension Protection Fund (Entry Rules) Regulations (Northern Ireland) 2005 apply with the following modifications.
(2) In regulation 9(1) and (2) (confirmation of scheme status by insolvency practitioner), the references to "company" are to be read as references to "building society".
(3) In regulation 10(3) (confirmation of scheme status by Board), the reference to "company" is to be read as a reference to "building society".";]

(f) in the Schedule, ignore any enactment which does not apply in relation to building societies.

4. The modifications to the Banking Act 2009 (Bank Administration) (Modification for Application to Multiple Transfers) Regulations 2009 (in addition to the modifications set out in paragraph 2) are—
(a) in regulation 1(2), ignore the definition of "a bank in temporary public ownership";
(b) in regulation 3(1)(a), for "a share transfer order, in respect of the securities issued by a bank (or a bank's holding company)" substitute "an order under section 85 of the Act (temporary public ownership) in respect of a building society".

5. The modifications to the Banking Act 2009 (Bank Administration) (Modification for Application to Banks in Temporary Public Ownership) Regulations 2009 (in addition to the modifications set out in paragraph 2) are—
(a) in regulation 2(1), for "a share transfer order to transfer the securities of a bank or a bank's holding company into temporary public ownership", substitute "an order under section 85 (temporary public ownership) of the Act in respect of a building society";
(b) ignore references to a bank holding company.

NOTES

Para 3: sub-paras (ea), (eb) inserted by the Building Societies (Insolvency and Special Administration) (Amendment) Order 2010, SI 2010/1189, art 2(1), (3).

BUILDING SOCIETY SPECIAL ADMINISTRATION (ENGLAND AND WALES) RULES 2010

(SI 2010/2580)

NOTES

Made: 20 October 2010.
Authority: Insolvency Act 1986, s 411(1B)(a), (2), (2D), (3).
Commencement: 15 November 2010.
Note: these Rules apply certain provisions of the Insolvency Rules 1986, SI 1986/1925, subject to a number of general and specific modifications. The Insolvency Rules 1986, SI 1986/1925 are revoked and replaced (as from 6 April 2017 and subject to transitional provisions) by the Insolvency (England and Wales) Rules 2016, SI 2016/1024 at **[6.2]**.

ARRANGEMENT OF RULES

PART 1
INTRODUCTION

1 Citation .....[7.483]
2 Commencement .....[7.484]
3 Extent .....[7.485]
4, 5 Interpretation .....[7.486], [7.487]
6 Overview .....[7.488]
7 Forms .....[7.489]

PART 2
APPLICATION FOR BUILDING SOCIETY SPECIAL ADMINISTRATION ORDER

8 Introduction .....[7.490]
9, 10 Content of application .....[7.491], [7.492]
11 Statement of proposed building society special administrator .....[7.493]
12 Bank of England witness statement .....[7.494]
13, 14 Filing .....[7.495], [7.496]
15–19 Service .....[7.497]–[7.501]
20 Other notification .....[7.502]
21 Venue .....[7.503]

22 Hearing . . . [7.504]
23 The order . . . [7.505]
24, 25 Notice of order. . . . [7.506], [7.507]
26 Costs. . . . [7.508]

PART 3
PROCESS OF BUILDING SOCIETY SPECIAL ADMINISTRATION
27 Introduction . . . [7.509]
28 Building society special administrator's proposals: Objective 1 Stage. . . . [7.510]
29–35 Building society special administrator's proposals: Objective 2 Stage. . . . [7.511]–[7.517]
36–39 Reports to creditors . . . [7.521]
40 Removal of special administrator in Objective 1 Stage . . . [7.522]
41–47 Appointment of provisional special administrator . . . [7.523]–[7.529]
48 Additional joint special administrator . . . [7.530]
49 Disapplication of set-off for protected deposits. . . . [7.531]
50 End of special administration: successful rescue . . . [7.532]
51 End of special administration: dissolution. . . . [7.533]

PART 4
COURT PROCEDURE AND PRACTICE
52 Introduction . . . [7.534]
53 Title of proceedings . . . [7.535]
54–59 Right to inspect file . . . [7.536]–[7.541]

PART 5
APPLICATION OF INSOLVENCY RULES 1986
60, 61 General application . . . [7.542], [7.543]
62 General modifications . . . [7.544]
63 Table of applications and specific modifications . . . [7.545]

PART 1
INTRODUCTION

[7.483]
1 Citation

These Rules may be cited as the Building Society Special Administration (England and Wales) Rules 2010.

[7.484]
2 Commencement

These Rules come into force on 15th November 2010.

[7.485]
3 Extent

These Rules extend to England and Wales only.

[7.486]
4 Interpretation

(1) In these Rules—
- (a) "the 2009 Order" means the Building Societies (Insolvency and Special Administration) Order 2009;
- (b) "building society" means a building society incorporated (or deemed to be incorporated) under the Building Societies Act 1986;
- (c) "building society special administration", "building society special administration order" and "building society special administrator" have the same meaning as in the Building Societies Act 1986 (see sections 90C(2) and 119(1) of that Act);
- (d) "contributory", in relation to a building society—
  - (i) means every person liable to contribute to the assets of the society in the event of its being wound up, and
  - (ii) for the purposes of all proceedings for determining, and all proceedings prior to the determination of, the persons who are deemed to be contributories, includes any person alleged to be a contributory, and
  - (iii) includes persons who are liable to pay or contribute to the payment of any debt or liability of the building society, or any sum for the adjustment of rights of members among themselves, or the expenses of the winding up,

  but does not include persons liable to contribute by virtue of a declaration by the court under section 213 (fraudulent trading) or 214 (wrongful trading) of the Insolvency Act 1986;
- (e) "principal office" means—

(i) the place which is specified in a building society's memorandum sent to the [FCA] under paragraph 1(1)(c) of Schedule 2 to the Building Societies Act 1986 as the address of its principal office, or
(ii) if notice has been given by a building society to the [FCA] under paragraph 11(2) of that Schedule (change of principal office), the place specified in that notice or, as the case may be, in the last such notice;

(f) "registered name", in relation to a building society, means the name of the society which is for the time being registered with the [FCA];
(g) "society", "special administration", "special administration order" and "special administrator" mean respectively building society, building society special administration, building society special administration order and building society special administrator;
(h) the following expressions have the same meaning as in Part 1 or Part 3 of the Banking Act 2009—
[(ai) "the Bank of England" (s 256B(1)),]
(i) "bridge bank" (s 136(2)),
(ii) "the court" (the High Court—s 166(1)),
[(iii) "the FCA" (the Financial Conduct Authority—s 166(2)),]
(iv) "Objective 1" (support for commercial purchaser or bridge bank—ss 137 & 138),
(v) "Objective 1 Achievement Notice" (s 139(4)),
(vi) "Objective 2" (normal administration—ss 137 & 140),
[(via) "the PRA" (the Prudential Regulation Authority—s 166(2)),]
(vii) "private sector purchaser" (s 136(2)),
(viii) "property transfer instrument" (s 33),
(ix) "residual building society" (s 136(2)), and
(x) "resolution fund order" (s 49(3));
(i) any reference to Part 1 of the Banking Act 2009 (Special Resolution Regime), or to any provision in that Part, is a reference to that Part or to that provision as applied, with modifications, by section 84 of that Act;
(j) any reference to Part 3 of the Banking Act 2009 (Bank Administration), or to any provision in that Part, is a reference to that Part or to that provision as applied and modified by section 90C of the Building Societies Act 1986 and by any order made under section 158 of the Banking Act 2009;
(k) any reference to the Insolvency Rules 1986 is a reference to those Rules including all amendments to them up to and including those made by the Insolvency (Amendment) (No 2) Rules 2009.

(2) Other expressions used in these Rules, where used in relation to building societies, have the same meaning as in the Building Societies Act 1986.

NOTES

Para (1): words in square brackets in sub-paras (e), (f), and sub-para (h)(iii) substituted, and sub-para (h)(via) inserted, by the Financial Services Act 2012 (Mutual Societies) Order 2013, SI 2013/496, art 2(c), Sch 11, para 19(1), (2); sub-para (h)(ai) inserted by the Bank of England and Financial Services (Consequential Amendments) Regulations 2017, SI 2017/80, reg 2, Schedule, para 36.

Note that the Insolvency Rules 1986, SI 1986/1925 are revoked and replaced (as from 6 April 2017 and subject to transitional provisions) by the Insolvency (England and Wales) Rules 2016, SI 2016/1024 at **[6.2]**.

[7.487]
5

In these Rules—
(a) "the FSCS" means the scheme manager of the Financial Services Compensation Scheme (established under Part 15 of the Financial Services and Markets Act 2000),
(b) "the Objective 1 Stage" means the period during which a building society special administration order is in force before the Bank of England gives an Objective 1 Achievement Notice,
(c) "the Objective 2 Stage" means the period during which a building society special administration order is in force after the Bank of England gives an Objective 1 Achievement Notice,
(d) a reference to personal service is a reference to personal service in accordance with Part 6 of the Civil Procedure Rules 1998,
(e) a reference to the CPR is to the Civil Procedure Rules 1998, and
(f) a reference to a witness statement (including a reference implied by the application of an enactment) is a reference to a witness statement—
(i) verified by a statement of truth in accordance with Part 22 of the CPR, and
(ii) if made by a building society special administrator, stating that the statement is made in that capacity and giving the address at which the special administrator works, and
(g) "the purpose of the special administration" is a reference to the objectives of building society administration in section 137 of the Banking Act 2009.

[7.488]
6 Overview

The purpose of these Rules is to prescribe a procedure for the appointment of a building society special administrator, and the operation of building society special administration, under Part 3 of the Banking Act 2009 in England and Wales.

[7.489]
7 Forms

(1) This Rule applies where a provision of these Rules—

(a) applies a provision of the Insolvency Rules 1986 which requires the use of a prescribed form, or
(b) makes provision similar to that made by a provision of those Rules which requires the use of a prescribed form.

(2) The form prescribed for the purposes of those Rules is to be used, with any modification that the person using the form thinks desirable to reflect the nature of building society special administration (whether or not the modification is set out in a Practice Form issued by the Treasury for that purpose).

PART 2
APPLICATION FOR BUILDING SOCIETY SPECIAL ADMINISTRATION ORDER

[7.490]
8 Introduction

This Part makes specific provision for a number of aspects of applications for building society special administration orders; Part 5 applies a number of provisions of the Insolvency Rules 1986 to applications for building society special administration orders (with specified modifications).

[7.491]
9 Content of application

An application by the Bank of England for a building society special administration order in respect of a building society must specify—

(a) the registered name of the building society,
(b) any other trading names,
(c) the address of the society's principal office,
(d) an email address for the society,
(e) the address of the Bank of England, and
(f) the identity of the person (or persons) nominated for appointment as building society special administrator.

[7.492]
10

If the building society has notified the Bank of England of an address for service which is, because of special circumstances, to be used in place of the principal office, that address shall be specified under Rule 9(c).

[7.493]
11 Statement of proposed building society special administrator

An application must be accompanied by a statement by the proposed building society special administrator—

(a) specifying the name and address of the person (or of each person) proposed to be appointed,
(b) giving that person's (or each person's) consent to act,
(c) giving details of the person's (or each person's) qualification to act as an insolvency practitioner, and
(d) giving details of any prior professional relationship that the person (or any of them) has had with the building society.

[7.494]
12 Bank of England witness statement

(1) An application for a building society special administration order in respect of a building society must be accompanied by a witness statement made on behalf of the Bank of England—

(a) certifying that the conditions for applying for a building society special administration order, set out in section 143 of the Banking Act 2009, are met in respect of the society,
(b) stating the society's current financial position to the best of the Bank of England's knowledge and belief (including actual, contingent and prospective assets and liabilities),
(c) specifying any security which the Bank of England knows or believes to be held by a creditor of the building society,
(d) specifying whether any security confers power to appoint an administrative receiver (and whether an administrative receiver has been appointed),
(e) specifying any insolvency proceedings which have been instituted in respect of the society (including any process notified to the [FCA and where relevant the PRA] under section 90D of the Building Societies Act 1986),
(f) giving details of the property transfer instrument which the Bank of England has made or intends to make in respect of the society,
(g) where the property transfer instrument has not yet been made, explaining what effect it is likely to have on the society's financial position,
(h) specifying how functions are to be apportioned where more than one person is to be appointed as building society special administrator (stating, in particular, whether functions are to be exercisable jointly or concurrently), and
(i) including any other material which the Bank of England thinks may help the court to decide whether to make the special administration order.

(2) The statement must identify the person making the statement and must include the capacity in which that person makes the statement and the basis for that person's knowledge of the matters set out in the statement.

NOTES

Para (1): words in square brackets substituted by the Financial Services Act 2012 (Consequential Amendments and Transitional Provisions) Order 2013, SI 2013/472, art 3, Sch 2, para 190(1), (2).

[7.495]

13 Filing

The application, and its accompanying documents, must be filed with the court, together with enough copies of the application and accompanying documents for service under Rule 15.

[7.496]

14

Each filed copy—

(a) shall have the seal of the court applied to it,
(b) shall be endorsed with the date and time of filing,
(c) shall be endorsed with the venue for the hearing of the application (fixed by the court under Rule 21), and
(d) shall be issued to the Bank of England.

[7.497]

15 Service

The Bank of England shall serve the application—

(a) on the building society,
(b) on the person (or each of the persons) nominated for appointment as building society special administrator,
(c) on any person whom the Bank of England knows to be entitled to appoint an administrative receiver,
(d) on any person who has given notice to the [FCA and, where relevant, the PRA] in respect of the building society under section 90D of the Building Societies Act 1986 (notice to the [FCA and PRA] of preliminary steps), and
(e) if the property transfer instrument was made or is to be made under section 11(2)(b) of the Banking Act 2009 (transfer to commercial purchaser), on each transferee.

NOTES

Para (d): words in square brackets substituted by the Financial Services Act 2012 (Mutual Societies) Order 2013, SI 2013/496, art 2(c), Sch 11, para 19(1), (3).

[7.498]

16

Service under Rule 15 must be service of a sealed and endorsed copy of the application and its accompanying documents issued under Rule 14.

[7.499]

17

Service must be effected as soon as is reasonably practicable, having regard in particular to the need to give the building society's representatives a reasonable opportunity to attend the hearing.

[7.500]

18

(1) Service must be effected—

(a) by personal service to an address that the person has notified to the Bank of England as an address for service,
(b) by personal service to the person's registered office or principal office (where no address for service has been notified),
(c) by personal service to the person's usual or last known principal place of business in England and Wales (where there is no registered office or principal office and no address for service has been notified), or
(d) in such other manner and at such a place as the court may direct.

(2) If the Bank of England knows of an email address that is habitually used for business purposes by a person on whom service is required, the Bank must (in addition to personal service) as soon as is reasonably practicable send by email an electronic copy of a sealed and endorsed copy of the application and its accompanying documents.

[7.501]

19

(1) Service of the application shall be verified by a witness statement specifying the date on which, and the manner in which, service was effected.

(2) The witness statement, with a sealed copy of the application exhibited to it, shall be filed with the court—

(a) as soon as is reasonably practicable, and
(b) in any event, before the hearing of the application.

[7.502]
20 Other notification

As soon as is reasonably practicable after filing the application the Bank of England must notify—
(a) any enforcement officer or other officer whom the Bank of England knows to be charged with effecting an execution or other legal process against the building society or its property,
(b) any person whom the Bank of England knows to have distrained against the building society or its property, and
(c) the [FCA and where relevant the PRA].

NOTES

Para (c): words in square brackets substituted by the Financial Services Act 2012 (Consequential Amendments and Transitional Provisions) Order 2013, SI 2013/472, art 3, Sch 2, para 190(1), (3).

[7.503]
21 Venue

(1) The court shall fix the venue for the hearing when the application is filed.
(2) In fixing the venue the court shall have regard to—
(a) the desirability of the application being heard as soon as is reasonably practicable, and
(b) the need to give the building society a reasonable opportunity to attend.

[7.504]
22 Hearing

At the hearing of the application, any of the following may appear or be represented—
(a) the Bank of England,
(b) the FSA,
(c) the building society,
(d) a director of the building society,
(e) the person (or a person) nominated for appointment as building society special administrator,
(f) any person who has given notice to the [FCA and, where relevant, the PRA] in respect of the building society under section 90D of the Building Societies Act 1986 (notice to the [FCA and PRA] of preliminary steps), and
(g) with the permission of the court, any other person who appears to have an interest.

NOTES

Para (f): words in square brackets substituted by the Financial Services Act 2012 (Mutual Societies) Order 2013, SI 2013/496, art 2(c), Sch 11, para 19(1), (4).

Note: at the date of going to press the reference to the FSA in para (b) has not been amended to reflect the transfer of that body's functions to the FCA and the PRA.

[7.505]
23 The order

A building society special administration order must be in the form specified in Rule 2.12(2) of the Insolvency Rules 1986, with such variations, if any, as the circumstances may require.

[7.506]
24 Notice of order

If the court makes a building society special administration order, it shall send [four or, if the building society is a PRA-authorised person (within the meaning of the Financial Services and Markets Act 2000), five] sealed copies to the Bank of England.

NOTES

Words in square brackets substituted by the Financial Services Act 2012 (Consequential Amendments and Transitional Provisions) Order 2013, SI 2013/472, art 3, Sch 2, para 190(1), (4).

[7.507]
25

The Bank of England shall as soon as is reasonably practicable send—
(a) one sealed copy to the building society special administrator,
(b) one sealed copy to the [FCA and where relevant the PRA], and
(c) one sealed copy to the FSCS.

NOTES

Para (b): words in square brackets substituted by the Financial Services Act 2012 (Consequential Amendments and Transitional Provisions) Order 2013, SI 2013/472, art 3, Sch 2, para 190(1), (5).

[7.508]
26 Costs

If the court makes a building society special administration order, the following are payable as an expense of the building society special administration—

(a) the Bank of England's costs of making the application, and
(b) any other costs allowed by the court.

PART 3
PROCESS OF BUILDING SOCIETY SPECIAL ADMINISTRATION

[7.509]
27 Introduction

This Part makes specific provision for a number of aspects of building society special administration; Part 5 applies a number of provisions of the Insolvency Rules 1986 to building society special administration (with specified modifications).

[7.510]
28 Building society special administrator's proposals: Objective 1 Stage

(1) This Rule makes provision about the statement of proposals which the building society special administrator is required to make in the Objective 1 Stage under section 147 of the Banking Act 2009.

(2) In addition to the information required by section 147 the statement must include—
  (a) details of the court where the proceedings are and the court reference number,
  (b) the registered name, any other trading names and the address of the principal office of the building society,
  (c) details of the special administrator's appointment (including the date),
  (d) in the case of joint special administrators, details of the apportionment of functions,
  (e) the names of the directors, secretary and chief executive of the society and details of any shares they hold in the society,
  (f) an account of the circumstances giving rise to the application for the appointment of the special administrator,
  (g) if a statement of the society's affairs has been submitted, a copy or summary of it with the special administrator's comments, if any,
  (h) if an order limiting the disclosure of the statement of affairs has been made under Rule 2.30 of the Insolvency Rules 1986 (as applied by Rule 60 below), a statement of that fact, as well as—
    (i) details of who provided the statement of affairs,
    (ii) the date of the order for limited disclosure, and
    (iii) the details or a summary of the details that are not subject to that order,
  (i) if a full statement of affairs is not provided—
    (i) the names, addresses and debts of the creditors including details of any security held (or, in the case of depositors, a single statement of their aggregate debt), and
    (ii) details of the shares issued by the society (including the types of shares issued and the number of each type in issue),
  (j) if no statement of affairs has been submitted—
    (i) details of the financial position of the society at the latest practicable date (which must, unless the court otherwise orders, be a date not earlier than that on which the society entered special administration),
    (ii) a list of the society's creditors including their names, addresses and details of their debts, including any security held, (or, in the case of depositors, a single statement of their aggregate debt),
    (iii) details of the shares issued by the society (including the types of shares issued and the number of each type in issue), and
    (iv) an explanation as to why there is no statement of affairs,
  (k) the basis upon which it is proposed that the special administrator's remuneration should be fixed under Rule 2.106 of the Insolvency Rules 1986 (as applied by Rule 60),
  (l) how the special administrator proposes to pursue Objective 1,
  (m) whether the special administrator proposes to pursue Objective 2(a) or Objective 2(b),
  (n) if the special administrator proposes to pursue Objective 2(a), how it is envisaged the purpose of the special administration will be achieved in the Objective 2 Stage,
  (o) if the special administrator proposes to pursue Objective 2(b)—
    (i) how it is envisaged the purpose of the special administration will be achieved in the Objective 2 Stage, and
    (ii) how it is proposed that the special administration shall end (winding-up or voluntary arrangement, in accordance with section 154 of the Banking Act 2009),
  (p) the manner in which the affairs and business of the society have been managed and financed since the date of the special administrator's appointment (including the reasons for and terms of any disposal of assets), and
  (q) the manner in which the affairs and business of the society will be managed and financed if the special administrator's proposals are approved.

(3) The statement—
  (a) may exclude information, the disclosure of which could seriously prejudice the commercial interests of the society or of the bridge bank or private sector purchaser, and
  (b) must include a statement of any exclusion.

[7.511]
29 Building society special administrator's proposals: Objective 2 Stage

(1) This Rule makes provision about the statement of proposals which the special administrator is required to make under paragraph 49 of Schedule B1 to the Insolvency Act 1986 as it applies during the Objective 2 Stage (in accordance with Table 1 in section 145(6) of the Banking Act 2009).

(2) The statement must include—

(a) details of the court where the proceedings are and the court reference number,

(b) the registered name, any other trading names, and the principal office of the society,

(c) details of the special administrator's appointment (including the date),

(d) in the case of joint special administrators, details of the apportionment of functions,

(e) the names of the directors, secretary and chief executive of the society and details of any shares they hold in the society,

(f) an account of the circumstances giving rise to the application for the appointment of the special administrator,

(g) if a statement of the society's affairs has been submitted, a copy or summary of it with the special administrator's comments, if any,

(h) if an order limiting the disclosure of the statement of affairs has been made under Rule 2.30 of the Insolvency Rules 1986 (as applied by Rule 60 below), a statement of that fact, as well as—

(i) details of who provided the statement of affairs,

(ii) the date of the order for limited disclosure, and

(iii) the details or a summary of the details that are not subject to that order,

(i) if a full statement of affairs is not provided—

(i) the names, addresses and debts of the creditors including details of any security held (or, in the case of depositors, a single statement of their aggregate debt),

(ii) details of the shares issued by the society (including the types of shares issued and the number of each type in issue),

(j) if no statement of affairs has been submitted—

(i) details of the financial position of the society at the latest practicable date (which must, unless the court otherwise orders, be a date not earlier than that on which the society entered special administration),

(ii) a list of the society's creditors including their names, addresses and details of their debts including any security held, (or, in the case of depositors, a single statement of their aggregate debt),

(iii) details of the shares issued by the society (including the types of shares issued and the number of each type in issue), and

(iv) an explanation as to why there is no statement of affairs,

(k) the basis upon which it is proposed that the special administrator's remuneration should be fixed under Rule 2.106 of the Insolvency Rules 1986 (as applied by Rule 60 below),

(l) details of whether (and why) the special administrator proposes to apply to the court under section 176A(5) of the Insolvency Act 1986 (omission of distribution to unsecured creditors: as applied by Table 2 in section 145(6) of the Banking Act 2009) (unless the special administrator intends to propose a voluntary arrangement),

(m) an estimate of the value of the prescribed part for the purposes of section 176A (unless the special administrator intends to propose a voluntary arrangement) certified as being made to the best of the special administrator's knowledge and belief,

(n) an estimate of the value of the society's net property (unless the special administrator intends to propose a voluntary arrangement) certified as being made to the best of the special administrator's knowledge and belief,

(o) whether the special administrator proposes to pursue Objective 2(a) or Objective 2(b),

(p) if the special administrator proposes to pursue Objective 2(a), how it is envisaged the purpose of the special administration will be achieved,

(q) if the special administrator proposes to pursue Objective 2(b)—

(i) how it is envisaged the purpose of the special administration will be achieved, and

(ii) how it is proposed that the special administration shall end (winding-up or voluntary arrangement, in accordance with section 154 of the Banking Act 2009),

(r) if the special administrator has decided not to call a meeting of creditors, the reasons,

(s) the manner in which the affairs and business of the society have been managed and financed since the date of the special administrator's appointment (including the reasons for and terms of any disposal of assets),

(t) the manner in which the affairs and business of the society will be managed and financed if the special administrator's proposals are approved, and

(u) any other information which the special administrator thinks necessary to enable creditors to decide whether or not to vote for the approval of the proposals.

(3) In the case of special administration following transfer to a bridge bank under section 12(2) of the Banking Act 2009—

(a) the statement under paragraph 49 of Schedule B1 must state whether any payment is to be made to the society from a scheme under a resolution fund order, or

(b) if that information is unavailable when the statement under paragraph 49 is made, the special administrator must issue a supplemental statement when the information is available.

(4) The statement—

(a) may exclude information, the disclosure of which could seriously prejudice the commercial interests of the society, and

(b) must include a statement of any exclusion.

[7.512]
30

If the special administrator thinks that the statement made under section 147 of the Banking Act 2009 in accordance with Rule 28 contains information required by Rule 29(2), the statement under paragraph 49 of Schedule B1 to the Insolvency Act 1986 (as applied by Table 1 in section 145(6) of the Banking Act 2009) may consist of the statement under section 147, with such additions, modifications and supplemental information as the special administrator thinks necessary—

(a) to comply with Rule 29(2), and
(b) to bring the statement under section 147 up to date.

[7.513]
31

Where the statement of proposals is sent to creditors, in accordance with paragraph 49(4)(b) of Schedule B1 (as applied by Table 1 in section 145(6) of the Banking Act 2009), it must be sent to the [FCA and where relevant the PRA] and the FSCS at the same time.

NOTES

Words in square brackets substituted by the Financial Services Act 2012 (Consequential Amendments and Transitional Provisions) Order 2013, SI 2013/472, art 3, Sch 2, para 190(1), (6).

[7.514]
32

Where the court orders an extension of the period of time under paragraph 49(5) of Schedule B1 on an application by the special administrator under paragraph 107 (as applied by Table 1 in section 145(6) of the Banking Act 2009), the special administrator must notify the persons set out in paragraph 49(4) as soon as is reasonably practicable after the making of the order.

[7.515]
33

Where the special administrator has made a statement under paragraph 52(1) of Schedule B1 (as applied by Table 1 in section 145(6) of the Banking Act 2009) and has not called an initial meeting of creditors, the proposals issued in accordance with Rule 29 above will be deemed to have been approved by the creditors (if no meeting has been requisitioned under paragraph 52(2) within the period set out in Rule 2.37(1) of the Insolvency Rules 1986—as applied by Rule 60 below).

[7.516]
34

Where the special administrator intends to apply to the court under paragraph 79 of Schedule B1 (as applied by the 2009 Order) for the special administration to cease before the statement of proposals is sent to creditors in accordance with paragraph 49 of Schedule B1, the special administrator must, at least 10 days before making the application, send to all known creditors of the society a report containing the information required by Rule 29(2).

[7.517]
35

(1) Where the special administrator wishes to publish a notice under paragraph 49(6) of Schedule B1 (as applied by Table 1 in section 145(6) of the Banking Act 2009), the notice shall be advertised in such manner as the special administrator thinks fit.

(2) The notice must—

(a) state the full name of the society,
(b) state the full name and address of the special administrator,
(c) give details of the special administrator's appointment, and
(d) specify an address to which members can write for a copy of the statement of proposals.

(3) The notice must be published as soon as is reasonably practicable after the special administrator sends the statement of proposals to the society's creditors but no later than 8 weeks (or such other period as may be agreed by the creditors or as the court may order) from the date that the society entered special administration.

[7.518]
36 Reports to creditors

(1) "Progress report" means a report which includes—

(a) details of the court where the proceedings are and the relevant court reference number,
(b) full details of the society's registered name, principal office and other trading names,
(c) full details of the special administrator's name and address and date of appointment, including any changes in office-holder,
(d) in the case of joint special administrators, details of the apportionment of functions,
(e) details of any extensions of the initial period of appointment,
(f) details of progress during the period of the report, including a receipts and payments account (as detailed in paragraph (2) below),
(g) details of any assets that remain to be realised,

(h) details of any amounts received from a scheme under a resolution fund order, and
(i) any other information likely to be relevant to the creditors.

(2) A receipts and payments account must state what assets of the society have been realised, for what value, and what payments have been made to creditors or others.

(3) The account must be in the form of an abstract showing receipts and payments during the period of the report; and where the special administrator has ceased to act, the receipts and payments account shall include a statement as to the amount paid to unsecured creditors by virtue of the application of section 176A of the Insolvency Act 1986 (share of assets for unsecured creditors).

(4) During the Objective 1 Stage, a progress report must include details of—
(a) the extent of the business of the society that has been transferred,
(b) any property, rights or liabilities that have been transferred, or which the special administrator expects to be transferred, under a power in Part 1 of the Banking Act 2009 (Special Resolution Regime),
(c) any requirements imposed on the residual building society, for the purpose of the pursuit of Objective 1, under a power in Part 1, and
(d) the arrangements for managing and financing the society during the Objective 1 Stage.

(5) In complying with paragraph (4)(c) and (d) a report—
(a) may exclude information, the disclosure of which could seriously prejudice the commercial interests of the society or of the bridge bank or private sector purchaser, and
(b) must include a statement of any exclusion.

[7.519]
37

A progress report must be produced for—
(a) the first period of 6 months of the special administration,
(b) every subsequent period of 6 months, and
(c) when the special administrator ceases to act, the period from the date of the previous report (or, if there was none, from the beginning of the special administration) until the administrator ceases to act.

[7.520]
38

(1) The special administrator must send a copy of each progress report within 28 days of the end of the period covered by the report, to
(a) the creditors and shareholding members,
(b) the court,
(c) the Bank of England,
(d) the [FCA and where relevant the PRA], and
(e) the FSCS.

(2) Instead of complying with paragraph (1)(a) the special administrator may publish the progress report on its internet website (and take appropriate steps to draw attention to it) and send a copy of it to any creditors and shareholding members on request.

(3) The court may, on the special administrator's application—
(a) extend the period specified in paragraph (1),
(b) make any other order about the content of a progress report.

NOTES

Para (1): words in square brackets substituted by the Financial Services Act 2012 (Consequential Amendments and Transitional Provisions) Order 2013, SI 2013/472, art 3, Sch 2, para 190(1), (7).

[7.521]
39

(1) A special administrator who fails to comply with Rules 37 and 38 is liable to a fine and, for continued contravention, to a daily default fine.

(2) For that purpose, failure to comply with Rules 37 and 38 shall be treated in the same way as failure to comply with Rule 2.47 of the Insolvency Rules 1986.

[7.522]
40 Removal of special administrator in Objective 1 Stage

(1) This Rule is about an application for removal of a special administrator made by the Bank of England during the Objective 1 Stage (in accordance with the modifications for the application of paragraph 91 of Schedule B1 to the Insolvency Act 1986 in Table 1 in section 145(6) of the Banking Act 2009).

(2) The rules for service of notice of the application, other notification of the application and for the hearing shall be as for the application to appoint a special administrator under Part 2 of these Rules.

(3) But both the person proposed to be appointed as a replacement and the existing special administrator are entitled to be served and heard.

[7.523]
41 Appointment of provisional special administrator

An application to the court for the appointment of a provisional special administrator under section 135 of the Insolvency Act 1986 (as applied by Table 2 in section 145(6) of the Banking Act 2009) may be made by the Bank of England.

[7.524]
42

The application must be supported by a witness statement stating—
- (a) why the Bank of England thinks that a provisional special administrator should be appointed,
- (b) that the person to be appointed has consented to act,
- (c) that the person to be appointed is qualified to act as an insolvency practitioner,
- (d) whether, to the Bank of England's knowledge, a voluntary arrangement under Part 1 of the Insolvency Act 1986 (as applied in relation to building societies by section 90A of, and Schedule 15A to, the Building Societies Act 1986) has been proposed or is in force in respect of the society,
- (e) whether, to the Bank of England's knowledge, an administrative receiver is acting in respect of the society, and
- (f) the Bank of England's estimate of the value of the assets in respect of which the provisional special administrator is to be appointed.

[7.525]
43

If satisfied that sufficient grounds are shown for the appointment, the court may make it on such terms as it thinks fit.

[7.526]
44

An order appointing a provisional special administrator must specify the functions to be carried out in relation to the society's affairs.

[7.527]
45

If the court makes an order appointing a provisional special administrator, as soon as reasonably practicable the court shall send four [or, if the building society is a PRA-authorised person (within the meaning of the Financial Services and Markets Act 2000), five] sealed copies of the order to the person appointed (and one additional copy by email if possible).

NOTES

Words in square brackets inserted by the Financial Services Act 2012 (Consequential Amendments and Transitional Provisions) Order 2013, SI 2013/472, art 3, Sch 2, para 190(1), (8).

[7.528]
46

(1) As soon as is reasonably practicable after appointment a provisional special administrator must send a copy of the order of appointment to—
- (a) the society,
- (b) any administrative receiver of the society,
- (c) the [FCA and where relevant the PRA] (together with the form specified in Rule 4.26(3)(ii) of the Insolvency Rules 1986, with such variations, if any, as the circumstances may require), and
- (d) the FSCS.

(2) Notice to the society must be given by service in accordance with Rule 18 above.

(3) Unless the court otherwise directs, on receipt of the order of appointment, as soon as reasonably practicable, the provisional special administrator shall give notice of that appointment. Such notice—
- (a) shall be gazetted; and
- (b) may be advertised in such other manner as the provisional special administrator thinks fit.

NOTES

Para (1): words in square brackets substituted by the Financial Services Act 2012 (Consequential Amendments and Transitional Provisions) Order 2013, SI 2013/472, art 3, Sch 2, para 190(1), (9).

[7.529]
47

The Bank of England may disclose the fact and terms of an order appointing a provisional special administrator to any person whom the Bank thinks has a sufficient business interest.

[7.530]
48 Additional joint special administrator

(1) The process for the appointment of an additional joint special administrator is the same as for the initial appointment of a special administrator.

(2) The existing special administrator (or each of them) is entitled to a copy of the application and may—

(a) file written representations, and

(b) be heard at the hearing.

(3) An application for the appointment of an additional joint special administrator may be made during the Objective 1 Stage only by the Bank of England.

(4) Rule 60 below applies Rules 2.127 and 2.128 of the Insolvency Rules 1986 (notification and advertisement of appointment of joint administrator).

[7.531]

49 Disapplication of set-off for protected deposits

(1) This rule applies if—

(a) [the appropriate regulator's rules] allow the FSCS to make gross payments of compensation in respect of protected deposits; and

(b) all or part of a creditor's claim against the building society is in respect of protected deposits.

(2) In respect of protected deposits Rule 2.85 of the Insolvency Rules 1986 (as applied by Rule 60 below) shall apply and, for the purpose of determining the sums due from the building society to an eligible depositor under rule 2.85(3)—

(a) where the total of the sums held by the building society for the eligible depositor in respect of protected deposits is no more than the prescribed limit then paragraph (3) applies; and

(b) where the sums held exceed the prescribed limit, then paragraph (4) applies.

(3) Where this paragraph applies, there shall be deemed to have been no mutual dealings, regardless of whether there are any sums due from the depositor to the building society, and the sum due to the eligible depositor from the building society in respect of the protected deposits will be the total of the sums held by the building society for that depositor in respect of those deposits.

(4) Where this paragraph applies then—

(a) any mutual dealings shall be treated as being mutual dealings only in relation to the amount by which the total of the sums due to the eligible depositor exceeds the prescribed limit, and

(b) the sums due from the building society to the eligible depositor in respect of protected deposits will be—

(i) the amount by which that total exceeds the prescribed limit, set off in accordance with rule 2.85(3); and

(ii) the sums held by the bank for the eligible depositor in respect of protected deposits up to the prescribed limit.

(5) Any arrangements with regard to set-off between the building society and the eligible depositor in existence before the date of the notice referred to in rule 2.85(1) shall be subject to this rule in so far as they relate to protected deposits.

(6) In this rule—

"eligible depositor" has the meaning given to it by section 93(3) of the Banking Act 2009;

["appropriate regulator's rules" means the rules, as amended from time to time, made under section 213 of the Financial Services and Markets Act 2000 by—

(a) if the building society is a PRA-authorised person (within the meaning of that Act), the PRA or the FCA;

(b) in any other case, the FCA;]

"prescribed limit" means the amount prescribed as the maximum compensation payable in respect of protected deposits under Part 15 of the Financial Services and Markets Act 2000; and

"protected deposit" means a protected deposit within the meaning given by the [appropriate regulator's rules] held by the building society at the date of the notice referred to in rule 2.85(1) but does not include a share in the society held by an eligible depositor.

NOTES

Paras (1), (6): words in square brackets substituted by the Financial Services Act 2012 (Consequential Amendments and Transitional Provisions) Order 2013, SI 2013/472, art 3, Sch 2, para 190(1), (10).

[7.532]

50 End of special administration: successful rescue

(1) This Rule supplements section 153 of the Banking Act 2009 (successful rescue).

(2) The special administrator's application under paragraph 79 of Schedule B1 to the Insolvency Act (as applied by section 153 of the Banking Act 2009) (the "application") must have attached to it a progress report for the period from the date of the previous report (or, if there was none, from the beginning of the special administration) and a statement indicating what the administrator thinks should be the next step for the society.

(3) Before making the application the special administrator must send a copy of the application and the progress report referred to in paragraph 2 to—

(a) the Bank of England,

(b) the [FCA and where relevant the PRA], and

(c) the FSCS.

(4) Notice under paragraph (3)(b) and (c) must be sent at least 7 days before the hearing of the application.

(5) Within 5 business days of filing the application with the court, the special administrator must gazette a notice undertaking to provide a copy of the application to any creditor or shareholding member of the society.

(6) The notice in paragraph (5) may also be published in such other manner as the special administrator thinks fit.

(7) The application must certify compliance with the preceding paragraphs of this Rule.

(8) If the court is satisfied that the conditions in section 153(1) of the Banking Act 2009 have been met it shall—

- (a) discharge the special administration order, and
- (b) notify the special administrator, who shall notify the [FCA and where relevant the PRA].

NOTES

Paras (3), (8): words in square brackets substituted by the Financial Services Act 2012 (Consequential Amendments and Transitional Provisions) Order 2013, SI 2013/472, art 3, Sch 2, para 190(1), (11).

[7.533]

51 End of special administration: dissolution

(1) This Rule supplements section 154(2)(a) of the Banking Act 2009.

(2) The special administrator's notice under paragraph 30 of Schedule 1 to the 2009 Order—

- (a) must be filed with the court in Form 2.35B (the form specified in rule 2.118 of the Insolvency Rules 1986 subject to Rule 7(2) above), and
- (b) must be accompanied by a final progress report.

(3) The notice shall not take effect until the court discharges the special administration order on the application of the special administrator.

(4) Before applying for discharge the special administrator must send a copy of the notice referred to in paragraph (2) and the final progress report to—

- (a) the [FCA and where relevant the PRA], and
- (b) each person who received notice of the special administrator's appointment.

(5) After the expiry of the period mentioned in paragraph 30(7) of Schedule 1 to the 2009 Order (and subject to extension under paragraph 30(8) of that Schedule) if the court discharges the special administration order—

- (a) the notice takes effect as specified in paragraph 30(7) of that Schedule,
- (b) the court shall notify the special administrator, who shall notify the [FCA and where relevant the PRA].

(6) If the court makes an order under paragraph 30(8) of Schedule 1 to the 2009 Order it shall notify the special administrator in Form 2.36B (the form specified in rule 2.118 of the 1986 Rules subject to Rule 7(2) above), who shall notify the [FCA and where relevant the PRA].

NOTES

Paras (4)–(6): words in square brackets substituted by the Financial Services Act 2012 (Consequential Amendments and Transitional Provisions) Order 2013, SI 2013/472, art 3, Sch 2, para 190(1), (12).

PART 4
COURT PROCEDURE AND PRACTICE

[7.534]

52 Introduction

This Part makes specific provision for a number of aspects of proceedings for building society special administration under Part 3 of the Banking Act 2009; Part 5 of these Rules applies a number of provisions of the Insolvency Rules 1986 to proceedings for building society special administration under the Banking Act 2009 (with specified modifications).

[7.535]

53 Title of proceedings

Proceedings for building society special administration under Part 3 of the Banking Act 2009 shall be entitled "IN THE MATTER OF . . . . (naming the society to which the proceedings relate) AND IN THE MATTER OF PART 3 OF THE BANKING ACT 2009".

[7.536]

54 Right to inspect file

(1) The court must open and maintain a file for each set of building society special administration proceedings.

(2) All documents relating to the special administration are to be placed on the file, subject to any direction of the registrar.

(3) No special administration proceedings shall be filed in the Central Office of the High Court.

(4) The following have the right, at all reasonable times, to inspect the court's file in respect of special administration proceedings—

- (a) the special administrator or provisional special administrator,
- (b) a person who is or was a director or officer of the society,
- (c) a member of the society,

(d) any person stating himself in writing to be a creditor of the society,
(e) any person stating himself in writing to be a contributory in respect of the society,
(f) the Bank of England,
(g) the [FCA and where relevant the PRA], and
(h) the FSCS.

NOTES

Para (4): words in square brackets substituted by the Financial Services Act 2012 (Consequential Amendments and Transitional Provisions) Order 2013, SI 2013/472, art 3, Sch 2, para 190(1), (13).

[7.537]
55

A right of inspection may be exercised on a person's behalf by anyone authorised by that person in writing.

[7.538]
56

Any person may, with permission of the court, inspect the court's file in respect of special administration proceedings.

[7.539]
57

A right of inspection is not exercisable in the case of documents, or parts of documents, as to which the court directs that they are not to be made open to inspection without the court's permission; and an application for a direction may be made by—
(a) the special administrator or provisional special administrator, or
(b) any person appearing to the court to have an interest.

[7.540]
58

Rule 7.28(2) and (3) of the Insolvency Rules 1986 (as applied by Rule 60 below) applies in respect of the court's file of special administration proceedings as it applies in respect of court records.

[7.541]
59

Proceedings under sections 213 and 214 of the Insolvency Act 1986 (fraudulent and wrongful trading) shall be conducted in accordance with section 215 of that Act subject to the modifications specified in section 145 of the Banking Act 2009.

PART 5
APPLICATION OF INSOLVENCY RULES 1986

[7.542]
60 General application

The provisions of the Insolvency Rules 1986 listed in the Table in Rule 63 apply for the purposes of building society special administration and applications for special administration.

[7.543]
61

For that purpose the rules apply with—
(a) the general modifications set out in Rule 62,
(b) any specific modification set out in the Table in Rule 63, and
(c) any other necessary modification.

[7.544]
62 General modifications

The general modifications are that—
(a) a reference to an administrator or liquidator is to be treated as a reference to the building society special administrator,
(b) a reference to administration or liquidation is to be treated as a reference to building society special administration,
(c) a reference to a provisional liquidator is to be treated as a reference to a provisional building society special administrator,
(d) a reference to a winding-up order is to be treated as a reference to a building society special administration order,
(e) a reference to a petition for a winding-up order is to be treated as a reference to an application for a building society special administration order,
(f) a reference to insolvency proceedings is to be treated as a reference to building society special administration (or proceedings for special administration),
(g) a reference to the responsible insolvency practitioner is to be treated as a reference to the building society special administrator or provisional special administrator,
(h) all references to the Official Receiver are to be ignored,

(i) all references to the county courts are to be ignored,
(j) all references to the EC regulation or to the appointment of a member State liquidator are to be ignored,
(k) a reference to the company is to be treated as a reference to the building society,
(l) a reference to an affidavit is to be treated as to a witness statement verified by a statement of truth in accordance with Part 22 of the CPR,
(m) a reference to the officers, or to a particular officer, of a company is to be treated as a reference to the officers, or to the corresponding officer, of a building society and as including a person holding himself out as such an officer,
(n) a reference to a contributory is to be treated as a reference to a contributory within the meaning of these Rules (see rule 4(1)(d)),
(o) a reference to the registered office of the company is to be treated as a reference to the principal office of the building society,
(p) a reference to sending or giving a document or notice to, or filing it with, the registrar of companies is to be treated as a reference to sending the document or notice to the [FCA] for placing on the public file of the society,
(q) a reference to a voluntary arrangement under Part 1 of the Insolvency Act 1986 is to be treated as a reference to a voluntary arrangement under that Part as applied in relation to building societies by section 90A of, and Schedule 15A to, the Building Societies Act 1986,
(r) a reference in the rules to a paragraph of Schedule B1 to the Insolvency Act 1986 is to be treated as a reference to that paragraph as applied and modified by section 145 of the Banking Act 2009, by section 90C of the Building Societies Act 1986 and by any order made under section 158 of the Banking Act 2009, and
(s) a reference to the Insolvency Act 1986 includes a reference to Part 3 of the Banking Act 2009.

NOTES

Para (p): words in square brackets substituted by the Financial Services Act 2012 (Consequential Amendments and Transitional Provisions) Order 2013, SI 2013/472, art 3, Sch 2, para 190(1), (14).

[7.545]

63 Table of applications and specific modifications

This Rule contains the Table of applied provisions of the Insolvency Rules 1986.

Rule	*Subject*	*Specific modifications*
Preparatory steps		
2.27	Notification and advertisement of administrator's appointment	
2.28	Notice requiring statement of affairs	
2.29	Verification and filing	
2.30	Limited disclosure	On an application for disclosure under paragraph (4) any of the following may appear and be heard, or make written representations— (a) the special administrator, (b) the Bank of England, and (c) the [FCA and where relevant the PRA].
2.31	Release from duty to submit statement of affairs; extension of time	On an application under paragraph (2) for release or extension of time any of the following may appear and be heard, or make written representations— (a) the special administrator, (b) the Bank of England, and (c) the [FCA and where relevant the PRA].
2.32	Expenses of statement of affairs	
Special administrator's proposals and creditors' meetings		
2.33	Administrator's proposals	Rule 2.33 is not applied—but equivalent provision is made by Part 3 of these Rules.
2.34	Meetings to consider administrator's proposals	(1) Rule 2.34 applies in the Objective 2 Stage.

Part 7C Special Insolvency Regimes

Rule	Subject	Specific modifications
		(2) The [FCA and where relevant the PRA] and the FSCS are added to the list in paragraph (2) of persons entitled to notice.
2.35	Creditors' meetings generally	The [FCA and where relevant the PRA] and the FSCS are added to the list in paragraph (3) of persons to whose convenience the special administrator is to have regard.
2.36	Chairman at meetings	
2.37	Meeting requisitioned by creditors	Treat the reference to the administrator's statement of proposals as a reference to the special administrator's statement of proposals in accordance with Rule 29 above.
2.38	Entitlement to vote	
2.39	Admission and rejection of claims	
2.40	Secured creditors	
2.41	Holders of negotiable instruments	
2.42	Hire-purchase, conditional sale and chattel leasing agreements	
2.43	Resolutions	
2.44	Minutes	
2.45	Revision of the administrator's proposals	In paragraph (2)(c) ignore the reference to the person making the appointment.
2.46	Notice to creditors	
2.47	Reports to creditors	Rule 2.47 is not applied—but equivalent provision is made by Part 3 of these Rules.
2.48	Correspondence instead of creditors' meetings	
2.49	Venue and conduct of company meeting	In paragraph (5) the reference to a general meeting of the company summoned under the company's articles of association, and in accordance with the applicable provisions of the Companies Act, has effect as a reference to a general meeting of the society summoned under the society's rules, and in accordance with the applicable provisions of the Building Societies Act 1986.
Creditors' committee		
2.50	Constitution of committee	*(A creditors' committee cannot be established until the Objective 2 Stage—see the modifications for the application of paragraphs 50 to 58 of Schedule B1 to the Insolvency Act 1986 in Table 1 in section 145 of the Banking Act 2009.)*
2.51	Formalities of establishment	
2.52	Functions and meetings of the committee	
2.53	The chairman at meetings	
2.54	Quorum	
2.55	Committee-members' representatives	
2.56	Resignation	
2.57	Termination of membership	

Rule	*Subject*	*Specific modifications*
2.58	Removal	
2.59	Vacancies	
2.60	Procedure at meetings	
2.61	Resolutions of creditors' committee by post	
2.62	Information from administrator	
2.63	Expenses of members	
2.64	Members' dealing with the society	In respect of any application to set aside a transaction under paragraph (2)— (a) notice of the application must be given to the [FCA and where relevant the PRA], and (b) the [FCA and where relevant the PRA] may appear and be heard.
2.65	Formal defects	
Process of administration		
2.66	Disposal of charged property	If an application is made during the Objective 1 Stage, then in addition to the requirements of Rule 2.66— (a) the special administrator must notify the Bank of England of the time and place of the hearing, (b) the Bank of England may appear, and (c) if an order is made the special administrator must send a copy to the Bank of England as soon as is reasonably practicable.
2.67	Expenses of the administration	In addition to the matters listed in Rule 2.67(1), expenses in connection with provisional special administration are payable in the following order of priority— (a) the cost of any security provided by the provisional special administrator takes priority equally with security provided by the special administrator, and (b) the remuneration of the provisional special administrator ranks next, and (c) any deposit lodged on an application for the appointment of a provisional special administrator ranks next.
2.68	Distributions to creditors: introduction	In paragraphs (1) and (2), references to creditors include references to shareholding members. *(Distributions in the case of special administration following transfer to a bridge bank under section 12(2) of the Banking Act 2009 and during the Objective 1 Stage require the Bank of England's consent—see the modification of the application of paragraph 65 of Schedule B1 to the Insolvency Act 1986 in Table 1 in section 145 of the Banking Act 2009.)*

Part 7C Special Insolvency Regimes

Rule	*Subject*	*Specific modifications*
2.69	Debts of the insolvent company to rank equally	"Debts" do not include any amounts owing from the society to a member in respect of shares.
2.70	Dividends: supplementary	
2.71	Division of unsold assets	
2.72	Proving a debt	
2.73	Claim established by witness statement	
2.74	Costs of proving	
2.75	Administrator to allow inspection of proofs	
2.76	New administrator appointed	
2.77	Admission and rejection of proofs for dividend	
2.78	Appeal against decision on proof	In respect of any application under Rule 2.78(1) or (2)— (a) notice of the application must be given to the [FCA and where relevant the PRA] and, during the Objective 1 Stage, the Bank of England, and (b) the [FCA and where relevant the PRA], and the Bank of England during the Objective 1 Stage, may appear and be heard.
2.79	Withdrawal or variation of proof	
2.80	Expunging of proof by the court	In respect of any application under Rule 2.80(1)(b)— (a) notice of the application must be given to the [FCA and where relevant the PRA] and, during the Objective 1 Stage, the Bank of England, and (b) the [FCA and where relevant the PRA], and the Bank of England during the Objective 1 Stage, may appear and be heard.
2.81	Estimate of quantum	
2.82	Negotiable instruments, etc	
2.83	Secured creditors	
2.84	Discounts	
2.85	Mutual credit and set-off	In addition to the matters listed in Rule 2.85(2)(a) to (e), "mutual dealings" does not include any mutual dealings between the society and a creditor who is also a shareholding member of the society in respect of shares held by that person in the society. Where the conditions in paragraph (1) of Rule 49 of these Rules are met, Rule 2.85 applies with the modifications set out in Rule 49 in addition to the modifications set out above.
2.86	Debt in foreign currency	
2.87	Payments of a periodical nature	
2.88	Interest	
2.89	Debt payable in future	
2.90	Value of security	

Rule	*Subject*	*Specific modifications*
2.91	Surrender for non-disclosure	
2.92	Redemption by administrator	
2.93	Test of security's value	
2.94	Realisation of security by creditor	
2.95	Notice of proposed distribution	(1) The notice in Rule 2.95(1) must also be given where the special administrator is proposing to make a distribution to shareholding members. (2) The following are added to the list of those entitled to receive notice under Rule 2.95(2)— (a) the [FCA and where relevant the PRA], (b) the FSCS, (c) shareholding members of the society, and (d) during the Objective 1 Stage of a special administration following transfer to a bridge bank under section 12(2) of the Banking Act 2009, the Bank of England. (3) The notice in Rule 2.95(1) shall state, where applicable, that the distribution is to shareholding members of the society. (4) In Rule 2.95(4)(a) the reference to a distribution to creditors includes, where appropriate, a distribution to shareholding members.
2.96	Admission or rejection of proofs	
2.97	Declaration of dividend	In Rule 2.97(1) the reference to one or more classes of creditor includes a reference to one or more classes of shareholding member.
2.98	Notice of declaration of dividend	(1) The following are added to the list of those entitled to receive notice under Rule 2.98(1)— (a) the [FCA and where relevant the PRA], (b) the FSCS, (c) Shareholding members of the society, and (d) During the Objective 1 Stage of a special administration following transfer to a bridge bank under section 12(2) of the Banking Act 2009, the Bank of England.

Rule	*Subject*	*Specific modifications*
		(2) In the case of special administration following transfer to a bridge bank under section 12(2) of the Banking Act 2009 and during the Objective 1 Stage, the particulars required by Rule 2.98(2) include details of any payment made from a scheme under a resolution fund order. (3) The particulars required by Rule 2.98(2) include, where appropriate, details of any distribution to shareholding members.
2.99	Payment of dividends and related matters	In Rule 2.99(2) the reference to any creditor includes a reference to any shareholding member.
2.100	Notice of no dividend, or no further dividend	(1) The special administrator must copy any notice under Rule 2.100 to— (a) the [FCA and where relevant the PRA], (b) The FSCS, and (c) the Bank of England, in a case where it consented to a distribution under Rule 2.68 (as applied above). (2) In Rule 2.100 the reference to creditors includes a reference to shareholding members.
2.101	Proof altered after payment of dividend	
2.102	Secured creditors	
2.103	Disqualification from dividend	In respect of any application for disqualification under Rule 2.103— (a) notice of the application must be given to the [FCA and where relevant the PRA], and (b) the [FCA and where relevant the PRA] may appear and be heard.
2.104	Assignment of right to dividend	
2.105	Debt payable at future time	The "relevant date" is the date of the special administration order.
The special administrator		
2.106	Fixing of remuneration	(1) In the Objective 1 Stage the Bank of England shall fix the special administrator's remuneration in accordance with Rule 2.106(2). (2) In the Objective 2 Stage, Rule 2.106 applies (but pending action under paragraphs (3) or (5) arrangements established by the Bank of England in the Objective 1 Stage shall continue to apply).
2.107	Recourse to meeting of creditors	
2.108	Recourse to the court	(1) In respect of remuneration fixed by the Bank of England—

Rule	*Subject*	*Specific modifications*
		(a) Rule 2.108 applies as if references to the creditors' committee were references to the Bank of England, and (b) the court shall have regard to the achievement of Objective 1. (2) In respect of any application under Rule 2.108— (a) notice of the application must be given to the [FCA and where relevant the PRA], and (b) the [FCA and where relevant the PRA] may appear and be heard.
2.109	Creditors' claim that remuneration is excessive	Rule 2.109 applies only during the Objective 2 Stage.
4.127B and Schedule 6	Remuneration where assets realised on behalf of chargeholder	
Ending administration		
2.110	Final progress reports	(1) The reference to Rule 2.47 is to be treated as a reference to Rule 36 above. (2) In the case of special administration following transfer to a bridge bank under section 12(2) of the Banking Act 2009 the final progress report— (a) must not be made until the special administrator is satisfied that any payment likely to be made to the society from a scheme under a resolution fund order has been made, and (b) must state whether any payment has been received and, if so, its amount.
2.114	Application to court by administrator	Rule 2.114 is not applied—but equivalent provision is made by Part 3 of these Rules.
2.118	Moving from administration to dissolution	Rule 2.118 is not applied—but equivalent provision is made by Part 3 of these Rules.
Replacing special administrator		
2.119	Grounds for resignation	During the Objective 1 Stage the Bank of England's consent, as well as the court's permission, is required for resignation under paragraph (2).
2.120	Notice of intention to resign	The Bank of England and the [FCA and where relevant the PRA] are added to the list of those entitled to notice under paragraph (1).
2.121	Notice of resignation	

Rule	Subject	Specific modifications
2.122	Application to court to remove administrator from office	*(An application may be made during the Objective 1 Stage only with the Bank of England's consent—see the modifications for the application of paragraph 88 of Schedule B1 to the Insolvency Act 1986 in Table 1 in section 145 of the Banking Act 2009.)* (1) An application must state either— (a) that the Bank of England has consented to its being made, or (b) that the Objective 1 Stage has ended. (2) The [FCA and where relevant the PRA] is added to the list of those entitled to notice under paragraph (2).
2.123	Notice of vacation of office on ceasing to be qualified	
2.124	Death of administrator	
2.125	Application to replace	Rule 2.125 is applied during the Objective 2 Stage only (and ignoring references to paragraph 95 of Schedule B1). *(For equivalent provision about application for removal by the Bank of England during the Objective 1 Stage (in accordance with the modifications for the application of paragraph 91 of Schedule B1 to the Insolvency Act 1986 in Table 1 in section 145 of the Banking Act 2009) see Part 3 of these Rules.)*
2.126	Notification and advertisement of replacement	
2.127	Notification and advertisement of appointment of joint administrator	
2.128	Notice to [FCA] of replacement or addition	
2.129	Duties on vacating office	
Provisional special administrator (see application of section 135 of the Insolvency Act 1986 in Table 2 in section 145 of the Banking Act 2009)		
4.25	Appointment	Rule 4.25 is not applied—but equivalent provision is made by Part 3 of these Rules.
4.25A	Notice of appointment	Rule 4.25A is not applied—but equivalent provision is made by Part 3 of these Rules.
4.26	Order of appointment	Rule 4.26 is not applied—but equivalent provision is made by Part 3 of these Rules.
4.28	Security	
4.29	Failure to give or keep up security	
4.30	Remuneration	Ignore paragraph (4).
4.31	Termination of appointment	(1) An application for termination may be made by— (a) the provisional special administrator, or (b) the Bank of England.

Rule	***Subject***	***Specific modifications***
		(2) A provisional special administrator's appointment terminates on the making of a special administration order.
Disclaimer		
4.187	Notice of disclaimer	*(In the case of special administration following transfer to a bridge bank under section 12(2) of the Banking Act 2009 notice may be given during the Objective 1 Stage only with the Bank of England's consent—see the modifications for the application of section 178 of the Insolvency Act 1986 in Table 2 in section 145 of the Banking Act 2009.)*
4.188	Communication to interested persons	
4.189	Additional notices	
4.190	Duty to keep court informed	
4.191	Application by interested party	
4.192	Interest in property to be declared on request	
4.193	Disclaimer presumed valid and effective	
4.194	Application for exercise of court's powers under section 181 of the Insolvency Act 1986	*(Section 181 is applied by Table 2 in section 145 of the Banking Act 2009.)*
Court procedure and practice		
7.1	Application of Chapter 1 of Part 7	Chapter 1 does not apply to an application for a special administration order (which is addressed in Part 2 of these Rules).
7.2	Interpretation	
7.3	Form and contents of application	
7.3A	Application to disapply section 176A of the Insolvency Act 1986	
7.4	Filing and service of application	
7.4A	Notice of application under section 176A of the Insolvency Act 1986	
7.5	Other hearings ex parte	
7.6	Hearing of application	
7.7	Use of witness statement evidence	
7.8	Filing and service of witness statements	
7.9	Use of reports	
7.10	Adjournment of hearings; directions	
7.16	Nomination and appointment of shorthand writers	
7.17	Remuneration of shorthand writers	
7.19	Enforcement of court orders	
7.20	Orders enforcing compliance with Rules	
7.21	Warrants	
7.23	Warrants under section 236	
7.27	Court records	
7.28	Inspection of records	
7.31	Right to inspect court file	Rule 7.31 is not applied—but equivalent provision is made in Part 4 of these Rules.

Rule	*Subject*	*Specific modifications*
7.33	Costs: application of the Civil Procedure Rules	
7.34	Requirement to assess costs by the detailed procedure	
7.35	Procedure where detailed assessment required	
7.36	Costs of execution or other process	
7.38	Costs paid otherwise than out of the insolvent estate	
7.39	Award of costs against responsible insolvency practitioner	
7.40	Application for costs	
7.41	Costs and expenses of witnesses	
7.42	Final costs certificate	
7.43	Persons who lack capacity to manage their affairs: introductory	
7.44	Appointment of another person to act	
7.45	Witness statement in support of application	
7.46	Services of notices following appointment	
7.47	Appeals and reviews of court orders	
7.49	Procedure on appeal	
7.51	Principal court rules and practice to apply	*(The reference to the CPR, the practice and procedure of the High Court and of the county court is to be treated as a reference to the CPR (Part 52).)*
7.53	Right of attendance	
7.54	Insolvency practitioner's solicitor	
7.55	Formal defects	
7.56	Restriction on concurrent proceedings and remedies	
7.58	Security in court	
7.59	Payment into court	
7.60	Further information and disclosure	
7.61	Office copies of documents	
Proxies		
8.1	Definition of proxy	
8.2	Issue and use of forms	
8.3	Use of proxies at meetings	
8.4	Retention of proxies	
8.5	Right of inspection of proxies	
8.6	Proxy-holder with financial interest	
Examination of persons		
9.1	Preliminary	1 Part 9 applies to applications under section 236 of the Insolvency Act 1986 (inquiry into society's dealings) as applied by Table 2 in section 145 of the Banking Act 2009. 2 Treat a reference to "the insolvent" as a reference to the society.
9.2	Form and contents of application	
9.3	Order for examination, etc	

Rule	*Subject*	*Specific modifications*
9.4	Procedure for examination	
9.5	Record of examination	
9.6	Costs of proceedings	
Miscellaneous and general		
12.1	Regulation of specified administrative matters	A reference to the Secretary of State includes a reference to the Treasury.
12.2	Costs, expenses, etc	
12.3	Provable debts	
12.4	Notices	
12.4A	Quorum at meetings	
12.5	Evidence of proceedings at meeting	
12.6	Documents issuing from Secretary of State	
12.8	Insolvency practitioner's security	
12.9	Time-limits	
12.10	Service by post	*(Rule 12.10 applies subject to express provision about service made in these Rules.)*
12.11	Service and notice: general	Part 6 of the CPR applies subject to any provision of these rules.
12.12	Service outside jurisdiction	Part 6 of the CPR applies with regard to service in Scotland or Northern Ireland, subject to any provision of these rules. Where service is to take place outside the United Kingdom, where these rules provide for service, the court may direct how that service is to be effected. With regard to service otherwise, Part 6 of the CPR applies.
12.13	Confidentiality of documents	
12.14	Notices sent simultaneously to same person	
12.15	Right to copy documents	
12.15A	Charge for copy documents	
12.16	Non-receipt of notice of meeting	
12.17	Right to have list of creditors	
12.18	False claim of status as creditor, etc	
12.20	Gazette	
12.21 and Schedule 5	Punishment of offences	
12.22	Notice of order under section 176A of the Insolvency Act 1986	
13.1 to 13.13	Interpretation and application	

NOTES

Words in square brackets substituted by the Financial Services Act 2012 (Consequential Amendments and Transitional Provisions) Order 2013, SI 2013/472, art 3, Sch 2, para 190(1), (15).

Note: the italicised text in the table above is as set out in the original and does not represent amendments to the text.

BUILDING SOCIETY INSOLVENCY (ENGLAND AND WALES) RULES 2010

(SI 2010/2581)

NOTES

Made: 20 October 2010.

Authority: Insolvency Act 1986, s 411(1A)(a), (2), (2C), (3), (3A).

Part 7C Special Insolvency Regimes

Commencement: 15 November 2010.
Note: these Rules apply certain provisions of the Insolvency Rules 1986, SI 1986/1925, subject to a number of general and specific modifications. The Insolvency Rules 1986, SI 1986/1925 are revoked and replaced (as from 6 April 2017 and subject to transitional provisions) by the Insolvency (England and Wales) Rules 2016, SI 2016/1024 at **[6.2]**.

ARRANGEMENT OF RULES

PART 1
INTRODUCTORY PROVISIONS

1 Citation and commencement . . . . [7.546]
2 Extent . . . . [7.547]
3 Application of Rules, construction and interpretation . . . . [7.548]
4 Overview . . . . [7.549]
5 Forms . . . . [7.550]
6 Time limits . . . . [7.551]

PART 2
APPLICATION FOR ORDER

7 Filing of application . . . . [7.552]
8 Service of application . . . . [7.553]
9 Proof of service . . . . [7.554]
10 Other persons to receive copy of application . . . . [7.555]
11 Verification of application . . . . [7.556]
12 Persons entitled to copy of application . . . . [7.557]
13 Certificate of compliance . . . . [7.558]
14 Leave for the applicant to withdraw . . . . [7.559]
15 Witness statement in opposition . . . . [7.560]
16 Making, transmission and advertisement of order . . . . [7.561]
17 Authentication of building society liquidator's appointment . . . . [7.562]
18 Initial duties of building society liquidation committee . . . . [7.563]
19 Expenses of voluntary arrangement . . . . [7.564]

PART 3
PROVISIONAL BUILDING SOCIETY LIQUIDATOR

20 Appointment of provisional building society liquidator . . . . [7.565]
21 Notice of appointment . . . . [7.566]
22 Order of appointment . . . . [7.567]
23 Security . . . . [7.568]
24 Failure to give or keep up security . . . . [7.569]
25 Remuneration . . . . [7.570]
26 Termination of appointment . . . . [7.571]

PART 4
STATEMENT OF AFFAIRS AND OTHER INFORMATION

27 Notice requiring statement of affairs . . . . [7.572]
28 Verification and filing . . . . [7.573]
29 Limited disclosure . . . . [7.574]
30 Release from duty to submit statement of affairs; extension of time . . . . [7.575]
31 Expenses of statement of affairs . . . . [7.576]
32 Submission of accounts . . . . [7.577]
33 Further disclosure . . . . [7.578]

PART 5
INFORMATION TO CREDITORS AND CONTRIBUTORIES

34 Report by building society liquidator . . . . [7.579]
35 Meaning of "creditors" . . . . [7.580]
36 Report where statement of affairs lodged . . . . [7.581]
37 Statement of affairs dispensed with . . . . [7.582]
38 General rule as to reporting . . . . [7.583]
39 Building society insolvency stayed . . . . [7.584]

PART 6
MEETINGS OF CREDITORS AND CONTRIBUTORIES

40 Meaning of "contributories" . . . . [7.585]
41 First meeting . . . . [7.586]
42 Business at first meetings of creditors and contributories . . . . [7.587]
43 General power to call meetings . . . . [7.588]
44 The chair at meetings . . . . [7.589]

45 Requisitioned meetings: general . . . [7.590]
46 Requisitioned meetings: reforming the liquidation committee . . . [7.591]
47 Attendance at meetings of building society's personnel . . . [7.592]
48 Notice of meetings by advertisement only . . . [7.593]
49 Venue . . . [7.594]
50 Expenses of summoning meetings . . . [7.595]
51 Resolutions . . . [7.596]
52 Chair of meeting as proxy-holder . . . [7.597]
53 Suspension and adjournment . . . [7.598]
54 Entitlement to vote (creditors) . . . [7.599]
55 Entitlement to vote (contributories) . . . [7.600]
56 Admission and rejection of proof (creditors' meetings) . . . [7.601]
57 Record of proceedings . . . [7.602]

PART 7
PROOF OF DEBTS

58 Meaning of "prove" . . . [7.603]
59 Supply of forms . . . [7.604]
60 Contents of proof . . . [7.605]
61 Claim established by witness statement . . . [7.606]
62 Cost of proving . . . [7.607]
63 Building society liquidator to allow inspection of proofs . . . [7.608]
64 New building society liquidator appointed . . . [7.609]
65 Admission and rejection of proofs for dividend . . . [7.610]
66 Appeal against decision on proof . . . [7.611]
67 Withdrawal or variation of proof . . . [7.612]
68 Expunging of proof by the court . . . [7.613]
69 Estimate of quantum . . . [7.614]
70 Negotiable instruments, etc . . . [7.615]
71 Secured creditors . . . [7.616]
72 Discounts . . . [7.617]
73 Mutual credits and set-off . . . [7.618]
74 Disapplication of set-off for eligible depositors . . . [7.619]
75 Debt in foreign currency . . . [7.620]
76 Payments of a periodical nature . . . [7.621]
77 Interest . . . [7.622]
78 Debt payable at future time . . . [7.623]

PART 8
SECURED CREDITORS

79 Value of security . . . [7.624]
80 Surrender for non-disclosure . . . [7.625]
81 Redemption by liquidator . . . [7.626]
82 Test of security's value . . . [7.627]
83 Realisation of security by creditor . . . [7.628]

PART 9
THE BUILDING SOCIETY LIQUIDATOR

CHAPTER 1
GENERAL

84 Remuneration of building society liquidator . . . [7.629]
85 Replacement of building society liquidator by creditors . . . [7.630]
86 Authentication of building society liquidator's appointment . . . [7.631]
87 Appointment to be advertised and registered . . . [7.632]

CHAPTER 2
RESIGNATION AND REMOVAL

88 Creditors' meeting to be notified of the building society liquidator's resignation . . . [7.633]
89 Action following acceptance of resignation . . . [7.634]
90 Advertisement of resignation . . . [7.635]
91 Meeting of creditors to remove building society liquidator . . . [7.636]
92 Court's power to regulate meetings under rule 89 . . . [7.637]
93 Procedure on removal . . . [7.638]
94 Advertisement of removal . . . [7.639]
95 Removal of building society liquidator by the court . . . [7.640]

96 Release of resigning or removed building society liquidator . . . . [7.641]

CHAPTER 3
RELEASE ON COMPLETION OF WINDING UP

97 Final meeting . . . . [7.642]
98 Rule as to reporting . . . . [7.643]

CHAPTER 4
REMUNERATION

99 Fixing of remuneration . . . . [7.644]
100 Building society liquidator's entitlement to remuneration where it is not fixed under rule 99 . . . . [7.645]
101 Building society liquidator's remuneration where he realises assets on behalf of chargeholder . . . . [7.646]
102 Other matters affecting remuneration. . . . . [7.647]
103 Recourse of building society liquidator to meeting of creditors. . . . . [7.648]
104 Recourse to the court. . . . . [7.649]
105 Creditors' claim that remuneration is excessive. . . . . [7.650]
106 Primacy of Objective 1 . . . . [7.651]

CHAPTER 5
SUPPLEMENTARY PROVISIONS

107 Replacement building society liquidator . . . . [7.652]
108 Building society liquidator deceased . . . . [7.653]
109 Loss of qualification as insolvency practitioner . . . . [7.654]
110 Resignation of the building society liquidator. . . . . [7.655]
111 Notice to Bank of England of intention to vacate office . . . . [7.656]
112 Building society liquidator's duties on vacating office . . . . [7.657]
113 Power of court to set aside certain transactions . . . . [7.658]
114 Rule against solicitation . . . . [7.659]

PART 10
THE LIQUIDATION COMMITTEE

115 Application of rules in this Part. . . . . [7.660]
116 Membership of committee . . . . [7.661]
117 Formalities of establishment. . . . . [7.662]
118 Committee established by contributories. . . . . [7.663]
119 Obligations of liquidator to committee. . . . . [7.664]
120 Meetings of the committee . . . . [7.665]
121 The chair at meetings . . . . [7.666]
122 Quorum . . . . [7.667]
123 Committee-members' representatives. . . . . [7.668]
124 Resignation . . . . [7.669]
125 Termination of membership . . . . [7.670]
126 Removal . . . . [7.671]
127 Vacancy (creditor members). . . . . [7.672]
128 Vacancy (contributory members) . . . . [7.673]
129 Voting rights and resolutions . . . . [7.674]
130 Resolutions by post. . . . . [7.675]
131 Liquidator's reports. . . . . [7.676]
132 Expenses of members, etc . . . . [7.677]
133 Dealings by committee-members and others . . . . [7.678]
134 Composition of committee when creditors paid in full. . . . . [7.679]
135 Committee's functions vested in the Secretary of State . . . . [7.680]
136 Formal defects . . . . [7.681]

PART 11
COLLECTION AND DISTRIBUTION OF BUILDING SOCIETY'S ASSETS BY BUILDING SOCIETY LIQUIDATOR

137 General duties of building society liquidator . . . . [7.682]
138 General qualification on powers . . . . [7.683]
139 Manner of distributing assets . . . . [7.684]
140 Debts of insolvent building society to rank equally . . . . [7.685]
141 Supplementary provisions as to dividend . . . . [7.686]
142 Division of unsold assets . . . . [7.687]
143 General powers of the liquidator . . . . [7.688]
144 Enforced delivery up of building society's property . . . . [7.689]

145 Final distribution . . . . [7.690]

PART 12
DISCLAIMER

146 Liquidator's notice of disclaimer . . . . [7.691]
147 Communication of disclaimer to persons interested . . . . [7.692]
148 Additional notices . . . . [7.693]
149 Duty to keep court informed . . . . [7.694]
150 Application by interested party under section 178(5). . . . . [7.695]
151 Interest in property to be declared on request. . . . . [7.696]
152 Disclaimer presumed valid and effective. . . . . [7.697]
153 Application for exercise of court's powers under s 181 . . . . [7.698]

PART 13
SETTLEMENT OF LIST OF CONTRIBUTORIES

154 Preliminary . . . . [7.699]
155 Primacy of Objective 1 . . . . [7.700]
156 Duty of liquidator to settle list . . . . [7.701]
157 Form of list . . . . [7.702]
158 Procedure for settling list . . . . [7.703]
159 Application to court for variation of the list. . . . . [7.704]
160 Variation of, or addition to, the list. . . . . [7.705]
161 Costs not to fall on building society liquidator . . . . [7.706]

PART 14
CALLS

162 Calls by building society liquidator . . . . [7.707]
163 Control by building society liquidation committee . . . . [7.708]
164 Application to court for leave to make a call . . . . [7.709]
165 Making and enforcement of the call . . . . [7.710]

PART 15
SPECIAL MANAGER

166 Appointment and remuneration . . . . [7.711]
167 Security . . . . [7.712]
168 Failure to give or keep up security . . . . [7.713]
169 Accounting . . . . [7.714]
170 Termination of appointment . . . . [7.715]

PART 16
ORDER OF PAYMENT AS TO COSTS, ETC OUT OF ASSETS

171 General rule as to priority . . . . [7.716]
172 Litigation expenses and property subject to a floating charge—general application . . . . [7.717]
173 Litigation expenses and property subject to a floating charge—requirement for approval or authorisation . . . . [7.718]
174 Litigation expenses and property subject to a floating charge—request for approval or authorisation . . . . [7.719]
175 Litigation expenses and property subject to a floating charge—grant of approval or authorisation . . . . [7.720]
176 Litigation expenses and property subject to a floating charge—application to court by the building society liquidator. . . . . [7.721]
177 Saving for powers of the court . . . . [7.722]

PART 17
MISCELLANEOUS RULES

CHAPTER 1
RETURN OF CAPITAL

178 Application to court for order authorising return of capital . . . . [7.723]
179 Procedure for return of capital . . . . [7.724]

CHAPTER 2
CONCLUSION OF BUILDING SOCIETY INSOLVENCY

180 Appropriate regulator's directions under section 116 of the Banking Act . . . . [7.725]
181 Procedure following appeal under section 116 of the Banking Act. . . . . [7.726]

PART 18
COURT PROCEDURE AND PRACTICE

CHAPTER 1
APPLICATIONS (GENERAL)

182 Preliminary . . . . [7.727]

Part 7C Special Insolvency Regimes

183 Interpretation . . . [7.728]
184 Form and contents of application . . . [7.729]
185 Application under section 176A(5) to disapply section 176A . . . [7.730]
186 Filing and service of application . . . [7.731]
187 Notice of application under section 176A(5) . . . [7.732]
188 Other hearings without notice . . . [7.733]
189 Hearing of application . . . [7.734]
190 Use of evidence . . . [7.735]
191 Filing and service of witness statements . . . [7.736]
192 Use of reports . . . [7.737]
193 Adjournment of hearings: directions . . . [7.738]

CHAPTER 2
SHORTHAND WRITERS

194 Nomination and appointment of shorthand writers . . . [7.739]
195 Remuneration . . . [7.740]

CHAPTER 3
ENFORCEMENT PROCEDURES

196 Enforcement of court orders . . . [7.741]
197 Orders enforcing compliance with the Rules . . . [7.742]
198 Warrants (general provisions) . . . [7.743]
199 Warrants under section 236 . . . [7.744]

CHAPTER 4
COURT RECORDS AND RETURNS

200 Title of proceedings . . . [7.745]
201 Court records . . . [7.746]
202 Inspection of records . . . [7.747]
203 File of court proceedings and inspection . . . [7.748]

CHAPTER 5
COSTS AND DETAILED ASSESSMENT

204 Application of the CPR . . . [7.749]
205 Requirement to assess costs by the detailed procedure . . . [7.750]
206 Procedure where detailed assessment required . . . [7.751]
207 Costs of officers charged with executions of writs or other process . . . [7.752]
208 Costs paid otherwise than out of the insolvent estate . . . [7.753]
209 Award of costs against responsible insolvency practitioner . . . [7.754]
210 Application for costs . . . [7.755]
211 Costs and expenses of witnesses . . . [7.756]
212 Final costs certificate . . . [7.757]

CHAPTER 6
PERSONS INCAPABLE OF MANAGING THEIR AFFAIRS

213 Introductory . . . [7.758]
214 Appointment of another person to act . . . [7.759]
215 Witness statement in support of application . . . [7.760]
216 Service of notices following appointment . . . [7.761]

CHAPTER 7
APPEALS IN BUILDING SOCIETY INSOLVENCY PROCEEDINGS

217 Appeals and review of court orders . . . [7.762]
218 Procedure on appeal . . . [7.763]
219 Appeal against a decision of the Secretary of State . . . [7.764]

CHAPTER 8
GENERAL

220 Principal court rules and practice to apply . . . [7.765]
221 Right of attendance . . . [7.766]
222 Restriction on concurrent proceedings and remedies . . . [7.767]
223 Security in court . . . [7.768]
224 Payment into court . . . [7.769]
225 Further information and disclosure . . . [7.770]
226 Office copies of documents . . . [7.771]

PART 19
PROXIES

227 Definition of "proxy" . . . [7.772]

228 Issue and use of forms . . . [7.773]
229 Use of proxies at meetings . . . [7.774]
230 Retention of proxies . . . [7.775]
231 Right of inspection . . . [7.776]
232 Proxy-holder with financial interest . . . [7.777]

PART 20
EXAMINATION OF PERSONS CONCERNED IN BUILDING SOCIETY INSOLVENCY

233 Preliminary . . . [7.778]
234 Form and contents of application . . . [7.779]
235 Order for examination, etc . . . [7.780]
236 Procedure for examination . . . [7.781]
237 Record of examination . . . [7.782]
238 Costs of proceedings . . . [7.783]

PART 21
DECLARATION AND PAYMENT OF DIVIDEND

239 Preliminary . . . [7.784]
240 Notice of intended dividend . . . [7.785]
241 Final admission/rejection of proofs . . . [7.786]
242 Postponement or cancellation of dividend . . . [7.787]
243 Decision to declare dividend . . . [7.788]
244 Notice of declaration . . . [7.789]
245 Notice of no, or no further, dividend . . . [7.790]
246 Proof altered after payment of dividend . . . [7.791]
247 Secured creditors . . . [7.792]
248 Disqualification from dividend . . . [7.793]
249 Assignment of right to dividend . . . [7.794]
250 Preferential creditors . . . [7.795]
251 Debt payable at future time . . . [7.796]

PART 22
MISCELLANEOUS AND GENERAL

252 Power of Secretary of State or Treasury to regulate certain matters . . . [7.797]
253 Costs, expenses, etc . . . [7.798]
254 Provable debts . . . [7.799]
255 Notices . . . [7.800]
256 Quorum at meeting of creditors or contributories . . . [7.801]
257 Evidence of proceedings at meetings . . . [7.802]
258 Documents issuing from Secretary of State . . . [7.803]
259 Insolvency practitioner's security . . . [7.804]
260 Time limits . . . [7.805]
261 Service by post . . . [7.806]
262 General provisions as to service . . . [7.807]
263 Service outside the jurisdiction . . . [7.808]
264 Confidentiality of documents . . . [7.809]
265 Notices sent simultaneously to the same person . . . [7.810]
266 Right to copy documents . . . [7.811]
267 Charge for copy documents . . . [7.812]
268 Non-receipt of notice of meeting . . . [7.813]
269 Right to have list of creditors . . . [7.814]
270 False claim of status as creditor, etc . . . [7.815]
271 Execution overtaken by judgement debtor's insolvency . . . [7.816]
272 The Gazette . . . [7.817]
273 Punishment of offences . . . [7.818]
274 Notice of order under section 176A(5) . . . [7.819]

PART 23
INTERPRETATION

275 Introductory . . . [7.820]
276 "The court"; "the registrar" . . . [7.821]
277 "Give notice", etc . . . [7.822]
278 Notice, etc to solicitors . . . [7.823]
279 Notice to joint building society liquidators . . . [7.824]
280 "Insolvent estate" . . . [7.825]
281 "Responsible insolvency practitioner", etc . . . [7.826]
282 "The appropriate fee" . . . [7.827]

283 "Debt", "liability" . . . . [7.828]
284 Expressions used generally . . . . [7.829]
285 The Schedule . . . . [7.830]

SCHEDULES

Schedule . . . . [7.831]

PART 1
INTRODUCTORY PROVISIONS

[7.546]
1 Citation and commencement

These Rules may be cited as the Building Society Insolvency (England and Wales) Rules 2010 and come into force on 15th November 2010.

[7.547]
2 Extent

These Rules extend to England and Wales only.

[7.548]
3 Application of Rules, construction and interpretation

(1) These Rules apply in relation to a building society undergoing the procedure in Part 2 of the Banking Act 2009, as applied and modified by section 90C of the Building Societies Act 1986 and by any order made under section 130 of the Banking Act, known as building society insolvency.

(2) In these Rules—

"the 1986 Rules" means the Insolvency Rules 1986 including all amendments to them up to and including those made by the Insolvency (Amendment) (No 2) Rules 2009;

"the 2009 Order" means the Building Societies (Insolvency and Special Administration) Order 2009;

"the 2010 Rules" mean these Rules;

["the appropriate regulator", in relation to a building society, means—

(a) if the building society is a PRA-authorised person (within the meaning of the Financial Services and Markets Act 2000), the Prudential Regulation Authority and the Financial Conduct Authority (except in rules 20, 74, 95(2) and 180 when it means the Prudential Regulation Authority or the Financial Conduct Authority);

(b) in any other case, the Financial Conduct Authority;]

"the Banking Act" means the Banking Act 2009;

"the Building Societies Act" means the Building Societies Act 1986;

"building society" means a building society incorporated under the Building Societies Act;

"building society insolvency", "building society insolvency order" and "building society liquidator" have the same meaning as in the Building Societies Act (see section 90C(2));

"contributory", in relation to a building society and subject as provided in rule 40—

(i) means every person liable to contribute to the assets of the society in the event of its being wound up, and

(ii) for the purposes of all proceedings for determining, and all proceedings prior to the determination of, the persons who are deemed to be contributories, includes any person alleged to be a contributory, and

(iii) includes persons who are liable to pay or contribute to the payment of any debt or liability of the building society, or any sum for the adjustment of rights of members among themselves, or the expenses of the winding up,

but does not include persons liable to contribute by virtue of a declaration by the court under section 213 (fraudulent trading) or 214 (wrongful trading) of the Insolvency Act;

"CPR" means the Civil Procedure Rules 1998;

"eligible depositor" means a depositor who is eligible for compensation under the FSCS;

. . .

"the FSCS" means the Financial Services Compensation Scheme (established under Part 15 of the Financial Services and Markets Act 2000) or, where appropriate, the scheme manager of that scheme;

"the Insolvency Act" means the Insolvency Act 1986;

"liquidation committee" means the committee established pursuant to section 100 of the Banking Act;

"Objective 1" has the same meaning as in Part 2 of the Banking Act (see section 99(2));

"personal service" has the meaning given in Part 6 of the CPR;

"principal office" means—

(b) the place which is specified in the building society's memorandum sent to the [Financial Conduct Authority] under paragraph 1(1)(c) of Schedule 2 to the Building Societies Act as the address of its principal office; or

(c) if notice has been given by the building society to the [Financial Conduct Authority] under paragraph 11(2) of that Schedule (change of principal office), the place specified in that notice or, as the case may be, in the last such notice;

"registered name" in relation to a building society means the name of the society which is for the time being registered with the [Financial Conduct Authority]; and "sealed" means sealed with the seal of the court under which the application was made.

(3) Other expressions used in these Rules, where used in relation to building societies, have the same meaning as in the Building Societies Act.

(4) In these Rules—

(a) any reference to Part 2 of the Banking Act (Bank Insolvency), or to any provision in that Part, is a reference to that Part or provision as applied and modified by section 90C of the Building Societies Act and by any order made under section 130 of the Banking Act;

(b) any reference to any provision of the Insolvency Act that is not applied by Part 2 of the Banking Act, is a reference to that provision as applied and modified by section 90A of, and Schedule 15A to, the Building Societies Act;

(c) any reference to any provision of the Insolvency Act which is applied by Part 2 of the Banking Act is a reference to that provision as applied and modified by section 90C of the Building Societies Act and by any order made under section 130 of the Banking Act.

(5) These Rules consist of—

(a) the rules set out in full;

(b) in the case of a rule applying a rule in Part 4, 7, 8, 9, 11, 12 or 13 of the 1986 Rules, the rule so applied with—

(i) the modifications set out in paragraph (6),

(ii) the modifications contained in the rule applying it, and

(iii) any other necessary modification;

(c) the Schedule, which applies the relevant schedules of the 1986 Rules.

(6) The modifications are that where applicable, a reference to—

(a) any provision of the Insolvency Act that is applied by Part 2 of the Banking Act is a reference to that provision as applied and modified by section 90C of the Building Societies Act and by any order made under section 130 of the Banking Act;

(b) any provision of the Insolvency Act that is not applied by Part 2 of the Banking Act is a reference to that provision as applied and modified by section 90A of, and Schedule 15A to, the Building Societies Act;

(c) the 1986 Rules (or "the Rules") is a reference to these Rules;

(d) an affidavit is a reference to a witness statement;

(e) ex parte is a reference to without notice;

(f) the commencement of winding up is a reference to the commencement of building society insolvency;

(g) the chairman is a reference to the chair;

(h) a company is a reference to a building society;

(i) going into liquidation is a reference to entering building society insolvency;

(j) insolvency proceedings is a reference to building society insolvency proceedings;

(k) the official receiver should be ignored unless otherwise stated;

(l) a petition for winding up is a reference to an application for building society insolvency under section 95 of the Banking Act;

(m) a petitioner is a reference to an applicant;

(n) the provisional liquidator is a reference to the provisional building society liquidator;

(o) winding up is a reference to building society insolvency;

(p) winding up by the court is a reference to a building society being placed into building society insolvency by the court;

(q) a winding-up order is a reference to a building society insolvency order;

(r) the registered office is a reference to the principal office within the meaning of these Rules;

(s) the articles is a reference to the rules of the building society;

(t) the officers, or a particular officer of a company, is a reference to the officers, or the corresponding officer, of the building society and includes a person holding themself out as such an officer;

(u) the registrar of companies or the registrar is a reference to the [Financial Conduct Authority];

(v) contributory is a reference to a contributory in relation to a building society within the meaning of these Rules.

(7) Expressions used—

(a) both in a rule set out in full and in Part 2 of the Banking Act, or

(b) both in a modification to a rule from the 1986 Rules applied by these Rules and in Part 2 of the Banking Act,

have the same meaning as in Part 2 of the Banking Act.

(8) Expressions used—

(a) both in a rule set out in full and in the Building Societies Act, or

(b) both in a modification to a rule from the 1986 Rules applied by these Rules and in the Building Societies Act,

have the same meaning as in the Building Societies Act.

(9) Where a rule applies a rule of the 1986 Rules and modifies that rule by inserting or substituting text—

(a) any reference in the modified rule to the 2010 Rules is a reference to these Rules;

(b) expressions inserted or substituted have the same meaning as in these Rules.

(10) Where a rule in the 1986 Rules (Rule A) contains a reference to another such rule (Rule B) and—

(a) both Rule A and Rule B are applied by these Rules, or

(b) Rule A is applied by and the provision in Rule B to which Rule A refers is substantially repeated in these Rules,

the reference in Rule A shall be treated, for the purpose of these Rules, as being, respectively, to the rule in these Rules that applies Rule B or the provision in these Rules that substantially repeats the provision in Rule B.

(11) Where a rule (Rule A) refers to another rule (Rule B), and Rule B applies a rule of the 1986 Rules (Rule C) with or without modifications, the reference in Rule A includes a reference to Rule C as applied by Rule B.

(12) Any notice or document required to be sent electronically pursuant to these Rules shall be treated as having been sent to the person if—

(a) it is sent by email to the person's last known email address, and

(b) the email contains a prompt asking the person for an electronic receipt saying that the email has been read.

(13) Where these Rules provide for a witness statement (either expressly, or through the application of the 1986 Rules as modified above)—

(a) that statement is a reference to a witness statement verified by a statement of truth in accordance with Part 22 of the CPR, and

(b) if the statement is made by the building society liquidator or provisional building society liquidator, the statement should state as such and should include the address at which that person works.

NOTES

Para (2): definition "the appropriate regulator" inserted, definition "the FSA" (omitted) revoked and words in square brackets in definitions "principal office" and "registered name" substituted by the Financial Services Act 2012 (Consequential Amendments and Transitional Provisions) Order 2013, SI 2013/472, art 3, Sch 2, para 191(1), (2).

Para (6): words in square brackets substituted by SI 2013/472, art 3, Sch 2, para 191(1), (2).

Note that in the Queen's Printer copy of these rules, there is no sub-para (a) in the definition "principal office" in para (2).

[7.549]

4 Overview

The purpose of these Rules is to provide a procedure for the appointment of a building society liquidator and the operation of building society insolvency under Part 2 of the Banking Act in England and Wales.

[7.550]

5 Forms

(1) This rule applies where a provision of these rules—

(a) applies a provision of the 1986 Rules which requires the use of a prescribed form, or

(b) makes provision similar to that made by a provision of those Rules which requires the use of a prescribed form.

(2) The form prescribed for the purposes of those Rules is to be used with any modification that the person using the form thinks desirable to reflect the nature of building society insolvency (whether or not the modification is set out in a Practice Form issued by the Treasury for that purpose).

[7.551]

6 Time limits

(1) Where by any provision of the Insolvency Act, the Banking Act or these Rules, the time for doing anything is limited, the court may extend the time, either before or after it has expired, on such terms, if any, as it thinks fit.

(2) If the court's consideration of whether to extend the time for doing anything takes place before a full payment resolution has been passed, the court shall only extend the time if it considers that the resulting delay will not significantly prejudice the achievement of Objective 1.

PART 2
APPLICATION FOR ORDER

[7.552]

7 Filing of application

(1) The application for a building society insolvency order, verified by witness statement in accordance with rule 11, shall be filed in court.

(2) There shall be filed with the application—

(a) one copy for service on the building society,

(b) one copy to be attached to the proof of service, and

(c) further copies to be sent to the persons under rule 10.

(3) The court shall fix the venue, date and time for the hearing of the application and in doing so shall have regard to—

(a) the desirability of the application being heard as soon as is reasonably practicable, and

(b) the need to give the building society a reasonable opportunity to attend.

(4) Each of the copies issued to the applicant shall be sealed and be endorsed with the venue, date and time for the hearing.

(5) Any application filed in relation to a building society in respect of which there is in force a voluntary arrangement under Part 1 of the Insolvency Act shall be filed in accordance with this rule, but a copy of that application shall also be sent to the court to which the nominee's report under section 2 of the Insolvency Act was submitted, if that is not the same court.

[7.553]

8 Service of application

(1) The applicant shall serve the building society with a sealed copy of the application.

(2) The application shall be served on the building society at its principal office.

(3) Service of the application at the principal office may be effected in any of the following ways—

(a) it may be handed to a person who there and then acknowledges that they are, or, to the best of the server's knowledge, information and belief, are, a director or other officer, or employee, of the building society, or

(b) it may be handed to a person who there and then acknowledges that they are authorised to accept service of documents on the building society's behalf, or

(c) in the absence of such person as is mentioned in sub-paragraphs (a) and (b), it may be deposited at or about the principal office in such a way that it is likely to come to the notice of a person attending the office.

(4) If for any reason it is impracticable to effect service as provided by paragraph (2) or (3), the application may be served in such other manner as the court may approve or direct.

(5) Application for permission of the court under paragraph (4) may be made without notice to the building society, stating in a witness statement what steps have been taken to comply with paragraph (2) or (3), and the reasons why it is impracticable to effect service as there provided.

(6) If the building society or its legal representatives fail to attend the hearing, the court may make the building society insolvency order in its absence if satisfied that the application has been served in accordance with this rule.

[7.554]

9 Proof of service

Apply rule 4.9 of the 1986 Rules.

[7.555]

10 Other persons to receive copy of application

(1) The applicant shall send two copies of the application to—

(a) the proposed building society liquidator,

(b) the Bank of England (if it is not the applicant),

(c) the [appropriate regulator] (if it is not the applicant),

(d) the FSCS,

(e) any person who has given notice to the [appropriate regulator] in respect of the building society under section 90D of the Building Societies Act,

(f) if there is in force for the building society a voluntary arrangement under Part 1 of the Insolvency Act, the supervisor of that arrangement, and

(g) if an administrative receiver has been appointed in relation to the building society, that receiver,

in accordance with paragraph (2).

(2) One copy shall be sent electronically as soon as practicable and the other (a sealed copy) shall be sent by first class post on the business day on which the application is served on the building society.

(3) Any of the persons in sub-paragraph (1) will have the right to attend and be heard at the hearing of the application.

NOTES

Para (1): words in square brackets substituted by the Financial Services Act 2012 (Consequential Amendments and Transitional Provisions) Order 2013, SI 2013/472, art 3, Sch 2, para 191(1), (5).

[7.556]

11 Verification of application

(1) This applies where an application has been filed in court under rule 7.

(2) A witness statement shall be attached to the application to state that the statements in the application are true, or are true to the best of the applicant's knowledge, information and belief.

(3) The witness statement shall identify the person making the statement and shall include the capacity in which that person makes the statement and the basis for that person's knowledge of the matters set out in the application.

(4) The witness statement is, unless proved otherwise, evidence of the statements in the application.

[7.557]

12 Persons entitled to copy of application

(1) Every contributory or creditor of the building society is entitled to a copy of the application on request from the applicant.

(2) The applicant shall respond to any request for a copy of the application as soon as reasonably practicable after the application has been made on payment of the appropriate fee.

[7.558]
13 Certificate of compliance

(1) Apply rule 4.14 of the 1986 Rules.

(2) In paragraph (1) the period for filing shall be as soon as reasonably practicable before the hearing of the application.

(3) In paragraph (2), leave out the words "a copy or" to the end.

(4) After paragraph (2) insert—

"(2A) A witness statement made by the proposed building society liquidator to the effect that—
(a) the person is qualified to act as an insolvency practitioner in accordance with section 390 of the Insolvency Act, and
(b) the person consents to act as the building society liquidator,
shall be filed in court with the certificate.".

[7.559]
14 Leave for the applicant to withdraw

Apply rule 4.15 of the 1986 Rules. Leave out "at least 5 days" and ignore sub-paragraph (a).

[7.560]
15 Witness statement in opposition

(1) If the building society intends to oppose an application, the building society may (but need not) file a witness statement in opposition in court.

(2) A statement under paragraph (1) must be filed before the hearing of the application and a copy must be served on the applicant, before the hearing.

(3) The statement may be served on the applicant by personal service or by electronic means.

(4) The statement should also be sent to the persons in rule 10(1) before the hearing.

(5) The fact that the building society has not filed a statement under this rule shall not prevent the building society from being heard at the hearing.

[7.561]
16 Making, transmission and advertisement of order

(1) The court shall not make a building society insolvency order unless the person nominated to be appointed as the building society liquidator in the application for the order has filed in court a witness statement under rule 13.

(2) When the building society insolvency order has been made the court shall immediately send five sealed copies (or such larger number as the building society liquidator may have requested) to the building society liquidator.

(3) The court shall also, if practicable, immediately send a copy of the order to the building society liquidator electronically.

(4) The building society liquidator shall serve a sealed copy of the order on the building society at its principal office and, where the building society liquidator knows the building society's email address, shall send an electronic copy to the building society.

(5) The building society liquidator shall send two copies of the order to—
(a) the Bank of England,
(b) the [appropriate regulator],
(c) the FSCS,
(d) if there is in force for the building society a voluntary arrangement under Part 1 of the Insolvency Act, the supervisor of that arrangement, and
(e) if an administrative receiver has been appointed in relation to the building society, that administrative receiver,
in accordance with paragraph (6).

(6) One copy shall be sent electronically as soon as practicable and the other (a sealed copy) shall be sent by first class post on the business day on which the order is served on the building society.

(7) The building society liquidator—
(a) shall cause notice of the order to be gazetted as soon as reasonably practicable, and
(b) may advertise notice of the order in such other manner as the building society liquidator thinks fit.

NOTES

Para (5): words in square brackets substituted by the Financial Services Act 2012 (Consequential Amendments and Transitional Provisions) Order 2013, SI 2013/472, art 3, Sch 2, para 191(1), (5).

[7.562]
17 Authentication of building society liquidator's appointment

A sealed copy of the court's order may in any proceedings be adduced as proof that the person appointed is duly authorised to exercise the powers and perform the duties of the building society liquidator in the building society insolvency.

[7.563]

18 Initial duties of building society liquidation committee

(1) As soon as reasonably practicable after the making of a building society insolvency order, the liquidation committee shall meet the building society liquidator for the purpose of discussing which of the objectives, or combination of objectives, mentioned in section 102(1) of the Banking Act, the committee should recommend the building society liquidator to pursue.

(2) If the building society liquidator and every individual on the liquidation committee agree, the meeting may be held by audio or video conference.

(3) The liquidation committee shall make its recommendation to the building society liquidator at the meeting.

(4) The Bank of England shall confirm the liquidation committee's recommendation in writing as soon as practicable after the meeting.

(5) As soon as practicable after the making of a building society insolvency order, the liquidation committee shall also pass a resolution as to the terms on which, in accordance with rule 99, the building society liquidator is to be remunerated.

(6) Until a full payment resolution has been passed, the building society liquidation committee—

- (a) shall take decisions and pass resolutions by a simple majority, and
- (b) for the purpose of taking decisions and passing resolutions, may communicate by any means that its members consider convenient.

[7.564]

19 Expenses of voluntary arrangement

Apply rule 4.21A of the 1986 Rules.

PART 3
PROVISIONAL BUILDING SOCIETY LIQUIDATOR

[7.565]

20 Appointment of provisional building society liquidator

(1) An application to the court for the appointment of a provisional building society liquidator under section 135 of the Insolvency Act may be made—

- (a) by the Bank of England,
- (b) by the [appropriate regulator] (with the consent of the Bank of England).

(2) The application must be supported by a witness statement stating—

- (a) the grounds upon which it is proposed that the provisional building society liquidator should be appointed,
- (b) that the person to be appointed has consented to act,
- (c) that the person to be appointed is qualified to act as an insolvency practitioner,
- (d) whether to the applicant's knowledge—
  - (i) there has been proposed or is in force for the building society a voluntary arrangement under Part 1 of the Insolvency Act, or
  - (ii) an administrative receiver is acting in relation to the building society,
- (e) the applicant's estimate of the value of the assets in respect of which the provisional building society liquidator is to be appointed, and
- (f) the functions the applicant wishes to be carried out by the provisional building society liquidator in relation to the building society's affairs.

(3) The court may on the application, if satisfied that sufficient grounds are shown for the appointment, make it on such terms as it thinks fit.

NOTES

Para (1): words in square brackets substituted by the Financial Services Act 2012 (Consequential Amendments and Transitional Provisions) Order 2013, SI 2013/472, art 3, Sch 2, para 191(1), (5).

[7.566]

21 Notice of appointment

(1) Where a provisional building society liquidator has been appointed, the court shall notify the applicant and the person appointed.

(2) Unless the court otherwise directs, on receipt of the notification under paragraph (1), the provisional liquidator shall give notice of that appointment as soon as reasonably practicable. Such notice—

- (a) shall be gazetted, and
- (b) may be advertised in such other manner as the provisional liquidator thinks fit.

[7.567]

22 Order of appointment

(1) The order of appointment shall specify the functions to be carried out by the provisional building society liquidator in relation to the building society's affairs.

(2) The court shall, immediately after the order is made, send four sealed copies of the order (or such larger number as the provisional building society liquidator may have requested), to the provisional building society liquidator.

(3) The court shall also, if practicable, immediately send a copy of the order to the provisional building society liquidator electronically.

(4) The provisional building society liquidator shall serve a sealed copy of the order on the building society at its principal office and, where the provisional building society liquidator knows the building society's email address, shall send an electronic copy to the building society.

(5) The provisional building society liquidator shall send two copies of the order to—

(a) the Bank of England,

(b) the [appropriate regulator],

(c) the FSCS,

(d) if there is in force for the building society a voluntary arrangement under Part 1 of the Insolvency Act, the supervisor of that arrangement, and

(e) if an administrative receiver has been appointed in relation to the building society, that administrative receiver,

in accordance with paragraph (6).

(6) One copy shall be sent electronically as soon as practicable and the other (a sealed copy) shall be sent by first class post on the business day on which the order is served on the building society.

NOTES

Para (5): words in square brackets substituted by the Financial Services Act 2012 (Consequential Amendments and Transitional Provisions) Order 2013, SI 2013/472, art 3, Sch 2, para 191(1), (5).

[7.568]
23 Security

Apply rule 4.28 of the 1986 Rules.

[7.569]
24 Failure to give or keep up security

Apply rule 4.29 of the 1986 Rules.

[7.570]
25 Remuneration

Apply rule 4.30 of the 1986 Rules. Ignore paragraph (4).

[7.571]
26 Termination of appointment

(1) Apply rule 4.31 of the 1986 Rules.

(2) After paragraph (2) insert—

"(2A) On the making of a building society insolvency order the appointment of the provisional building society liquidator shall terminate.".

PART 4
STATEMENT OF AFFAIRS AND OTHER INFORMATION

[7.572]
27 Notice requiring statement of affairs

(1) Apply rule 4.32 of the 1986 Rules. For "official receiver", substitute "building society liquidator".

[7.573]
28 Verification and filing

(1) Apply rule 4.33 of the 1986 Rules. For "official receiver" substitute "building society liquidator".

(2) For paragraph (6), substitute—

"(6) The building society liquidator shall file the statement of affairs in court and shall send a copy of it to the [appropriate regulator].".

(3) Ignore paragraph (7).

NOTES

Para (2): words in square brackets substituted by the Financial Services Act 2012 (Consequential Amendments and Transitional Provisions) Order 2013, SI 2013/472, art 3, Sch 2, para 191(1), (5).

[7.574]
29 Limited disclosure

(1) Apply rule 4.35 of the 1986 Rules. In paragraph (1), for "official receiver", substitute "building society liquidator".

(2) After paragraph (1), insert—

"(1A) The building society liquidator may also apply to the court for an order of limited disclosure in respect of those depositors of the building society who, at the time of the making of the statement of affairs, still have a claim against the building society in respect of their deposits.".

[7.575]
30 Release from duty to submit statement of affairs; extension of time

Apply rule 4.36 of the 1986 Rules. For "official receiver" substitute "building society liquidator."

[7.576]
31 Expenses of statement of affairs

Apply rule 4.37 of the 1986 Rules. For "official receiver", substitute "building society liquidator".

[7.577]
32 Submission of accounts

Apply rule 4.39 of the 1986 Rules. For "official receiver", substitute "building society liquidator".

[7.578]
33 Further disclosure

Apply rule 4.42 of the 1986 Rules. For "official receiver", substitute "building society liquidator".

PART 5
INFORMATION TO CREDITORS AND CONTRIBUTORIES

[7.579]
34 Report by building society liquidator

(1) The building society liquidator shall, at least once after the making of the building society insolvency order, make a report with respect to the proceedings in the building society insolvency and the state of the building society's affairs.

(2) Regardless of whether the liquidation committee has passed a full payment resolution, the first report under paragraph (1) shall be, within eight weeks of the commencement of the building society insolvency, made publicly available on the building society's website and the building society liquidator shall send a copy of it to any creditor or contributory on request.

(3) The building society liquidator shall include in the report under paragraph (1)—

(a) a statement that the proceedings are being held in the High Court and the relevant court reference number;

(b) the full registered name of the building society, any other trading names of the building society, and the address of its principal office;

(c) details relating to the building society liquidator's appointment, including the date of appointment, and, where there are joint liquidators, details of—

(i) which functions (if any) are to be exercised by the persons appointed acting jointly, and

(ii) which functions (if any) are to be exercised by any or all of the persons appointed;

(d) the names of the directors, chief executive and secretary of the building society and details of any shares in the building society that they have;

(e) an account of the circumstances giving rise to the building society insolvency;

(f) if a statement of affairs has been submitted, a copy of that statement;

(g) if a statement of affairs has yet to be submitted—

(i) the names, addresses and details of any debts owed to the creditors, including details of any security held (or, in the case of depositors who are still creditors of the building society at the time the report is made, a single statement of their aggregate debt),

(ii) details of the shares issued by the society (including the types of shares issued and the number of each type in issue), and

(iii) details of the financial position of the building society at the latest practicable date (which must, unless the court orders otherwise, be a date not earlier than the commencement of building society insolvency);

(h) the basis upon which it has been proposed under rule 42, or, if the full payment resolution has yet to be passed, rule 18, that the building society liquidator's remuneration be fixed;

(i) to the best of the building society liquidator's knowledge and belief—

(i) an estimate of the value of the prescribed part (within the meaning of section 176A of the Insolvency Act) regardless of whether—

(aa) the building society liquidator proposes to make an application to the court under section 176A(5) of that Act, or

(bb) section 176A(3) of that Act applies, and

(ii) an estimate of the value of the building society's net property;

(j) whether, and if so, why, the building society liquidator proposes to make an application to court under section 176A(5) of the Insolvency Act;

(k) a summary of—

(i) how Objective 1 is being or has been achieved and an estimate of the costs to the building society liquidator of achieving it,

(ii) the manner in which the affairs and business of the building society not involved in the achievement of Objective 1 have, since the commencement of the building society insolvency, been managed and financed, including, where any assets have been disposed of, the reasons for such disposals and the terms upon which such disposals were made, and

(iii) how the affairs and business of the building society will continue to be managed and financed; and

(l) an explanation of how it is envisaged the objectives of the building society liquidator will be achieved, including whether a dividend will be paid, an estimate as to the amount of this dividend, and how it is proposed that the building society liquidation shall end.

(4) Nothing in this rule is to be taken as requiring either estimate mentioned in paragraph (3)(i) to include any information the disclosure of which could seriously prejudice the commercial interests of the building society. If such information is excluded from the calculation the estimate shall be accompanied by a statement to that effect.

(5) The building society liquidator shall file with the court a copy of any report sent under this rule.

[7.580]
35 Meaning of "creditors"

Apply rule 4.44 of the 1986 Rules.

[7.581]
36 Report where statement of affairs lodged

Apply rule 4.45 of the 1986 Rules. For "official receiver", substitute "building society liquidator".

[7.582]
37 Statement of affairs dispensed with

Apply rule 4.46 of the 1986 Rules. For "official receiver", substitute "building society liquidator".

[7.583]
38 General rule as to reporting

Apply rule 4.47 of the 1986 Rules. For "official receiver", substitute "building society liquidator".

[7.584]
39 Building society insolvency stayed

Apply rule 4.48 of the 1986 Rules. For "official receiver", substitute "building society liquidator".

PART 6
MEETINGS OF CREDITORS AND CONTRIBUTORIES

[7.585]
40 Meaning of "contributories"

For the purposes of this Part, "contributories" does not include the borrowing members of the society (see paragraph 5(2) of Schedule 2 to the Building Societies Act).

[7.586]
41 First meeting

(1) Once the liquidation committee passes a full payment resolution the building society liquidator shall—

(a) immediately summon a meeting of the building society's creditors and a meeting of the building society's contributories, and

(b) fix a venue, date and time for the meetings,

and the date must be within three months of the date on which the full payment resolution was passed.

(2) When the venue, date and time of the meetings have been fixed the building society liquidator shall give notice of the meetings to—

(a) the court,

(b) every creditor who is known to the building society liquidator or is identified in the building society's statement of affairs,

(c) every person appearing (by the building society's books or otherwise) to be a contributory of the building society, and

(d) each member of the liquidation committee.

(3) The building society liquidator—

(a) shall gazette the notice of the meeting as soon as reasonably practicable, and

(b) may advertise it in such other manner as the building society liquidator thinks fit.

(4) In giving the notice mentioned in paragraph (2) the building society liquidator shall, if practicable, indicate whether the present intention of the FSCS is to resign from the liquidation committee at the meeting.

(5) Notice to the court and the members of the liquidation committee shall be given immediately; notice to creditors and contributories shall be given, and the advertisements placed to appear, at least 21 days before the date fixed for the meeting.

(6) The notice to creditors shall specify a time and date, not more than four days before the date fixed for the meeting, by which they must lodge proofs and (if applicable) proxies, in order to be entitled to vote at the meeting.

(7) The FSCS is entitled to be represented at the meeting and Schedule 1 to the 1986 Rules, as applied by rule 285, has effect with respect to its voting rights at such a meeting.

(8) Meetings summoned under this rule are known respectively as "the first meeting of creditors" and "the first meeting of contributories", and jointly as "the first meetings in the building society liquidation".

[7.587]

42 Business at first meetings of creditors and contributories

(1) At the first meeting of creditors the FSCS shall state whether or not it is resigning from the liquidation committee.

(2) At that meeting those creditors present (or represented by proxy) may—

(a) where the FSCS has not resigned, elect two or four individuals as new members of the liquidation committee,

(b) where the FSCS has resigned, elect three or five individuals as new members of the liquidation committee,

in place of the members nominated by the Bank of England and the [appropriate regulator]. In accordance with section 100(6)(e) of the Banking Act, the liquidation committee ceases to exist at the end of the meeting if no individuals are elected as mentioned or if the resulting committee would have fewer than three members or an even number of members. The maximum number of committee members will be five.

(3) At the first meeting of creditors no resolutions shall be taken other than the following—

(a) if an application has been made to the court by the creditors under rule 95 for the court to direct the building society liquidator to summon a meeting of creditors for the purpose of removing the building society liquidator, and the court has directed that a resolution may be passed to that effect at the first meeting of creditors,—

(i) a resolution to remove the building society liquidator (or a resolution to remove one or more of the building society liquidators if joint liquidators were originally appointed), and

(ii) a resolution to appoint a named insolvency practitioner to be building society liquidator or two or more insolvency practitioners as joint liquidators;

(b) if no individuals have been elected to form a liquidation committee under paragraph (2), a resolution specifying the terms on which the liquidator is to be remunerated, or to defer consideration of that matter;

(c) where two or more persons are appointed jointly to act as building society liquidator, a resolution specifying which acts are to be done by both of them, all of them or by only one;

(d) a resolution to adjourn the meeting for not more than three weeks; and

(e) any other resolutions which the chair thinks it right to allow for special reasons.

(4) At the first meeting of contributories, no resolutions shall be taken other than the following—

(a) if no individuals have been elected to form a liquidation committee under paragraph (2), a resolution to form a liquidation committee (and rule 118 shall then apply);

(b) a resolution to adjourn the meeting for no more than three weeks;

(c) any other resolutions which the chair thinks it right to allow for special reasons.

(5) The FSCS shall be entitled to be a member of any liquidation committee formed where the liquidation committee has ceased to exist at the end of the first meeting of the creditors.

NOTES

Para (2): words in square brackets substituted by the Financial Services Act 2012 (Consequential Amendments and Transitional Provisions) Order 2013, SI 2013/472, art 3, Sch 2, para 191(1), (5).

[7.588]

43 General power to call meetings

(1) Apply rule 4.54 of the 1986 Rules.

(2) Where the building society liquidator has been directed to summon a meeting of creditors under section 195 of the Insolvency Act (as applied by section 109 of the Banking Act) for the purpose of removing the building society liquidator, the building society liquidator shall give notice of the meeting to the Bank of England and the [appropriate regulator].

NOTES

Para (2): words in square brackets substituted by the Financial Services Act 2012 (Consequential Amendments and Transitional Provisions) Order 2013, SI 2013/472, art 3, Sch 2, para 191(1), (5).

[7.589]

44 The chair at meetings

(1) Meetings shall be chaired by the building society liquidator or a person nominated in writing by the building society liquidator.

(2) A person nominated under paragraph (1) must be—

(a) qualified to act as an insolvency practitioner in accordance with section 390 of the Insolvency Act, or

(b) an employee of the building society liquidator or of the building society liquidator's firm who is experienced in insolvency matters.

[7.590]

45 Requisitioned meetings: general

Apply rule 4.57 of the 1986 Rules. In rule 4.57(4)(a) for "the amount for which they may vote at any meeting" substitute "the value of the shares held by them in the society".

[7.591]
46 Requisitioned meetings: reforming the liquidation committee

(1) Rule 4.57 of the 1986 Rules also applies where—

(a) the liquidation committee has ceased to exist at the end of the first meeting of creditors under rule 42 and no further steps have been taken to re-establish that committee; and

(b) the building society liquidator has been requested, by no less than one-tenth in value of the building society's creditors, to summon a meeting for the purpose of re-establishing the liquidation committee.

(2) Where a meeting is requisitioned to re-establish the liquidation committee, the time periods set out in rule 4.57 of the 1986 Rules may be expedited by the building society liquidator at the request of the building society's creditors.

(3) The building society liquidator shall give notice of the meeting to the [appropriate regulator] and Bank of England.

(4) Rule 42(1) and (2) shall apply at this meeting as if it were the first meeting of creditors.

NOTES

Para (3): words in square brackets substituted by the Financial Services Act 2012 (Consequential Amendments and Transitional Provisions) Order 2013, SI 2013/472, art 3, Sch 2, para 191(1), (5).

[7.592]
47 Attendance at meetings of building society's personnel

Apply rule 4.58 of the 1986 Rules.

[7.593]
48 Notice of meetings by advertisement only

Apply rule 4.59 of the 1986 Rules.

[7.594]
49 Venue

Apply rule 4.60 of the 1986 Rules.

[7.595]
50 Expenses of summoning meetings

Apply rule 4.61 of the 1986 Rules.

[7.596]
51 Resolutions

Apply rule 4.63 of the 1986 Rules. In rule 4.63(1) for "the number of votes conferred on each contributory by the company's articles" substitute "the value of the shares each contributory holds in the building society".

[7.597]
52 Chair of meeting as proxy-holder

Apply rule 4.64 of the 1986 Rules.

[7.598]
53 Suspension and adjournment

(1) Apply rule 4.65 of the 1986 Rules.

(2) In paragraph (3), leave out "or, as the case may be, 4.114—CVL(3)".

[7.599]
54 Entitlement to vote (creditors)

(1) Apply rule 4.67 of the 1986 Rules.

(2) Ignore paragraph (ii) of paragraph (1)(a) and paragraph (8).

(3) In paragraph (9), ignore the reference to paragraph (8).

[7.600]
55 Entitlement to vote (contributories)

Apply rule 4.69 of the 1986 Rules.

[7.601]
56 Admission and rejection of proof (creditors' meetings)

Apply rule 4.70 of the 1986 Rules. For paragraph (5) substitute—

"(5) The chair is not personally liable for costs incurred by any person in respect of an application under this rule unless the court makes an order to that effect.".

[7.602]
57 Record of proceedings

Apply rule 4.71 of the 1986 Rules.

PART 7
PROOF OF DEBTS

[7.603]
58 Meaning of "prove"

(1) Apply rule 4.73 of the 1986 Rules.

(2) In paragraph (5), for "or a Government Department" substitute ", a Government Department or the FSCS".

(3) Ignore paragraphs (2) and (8).

[7.604]
59 Supply of forms

Apply rule 4.74 of the 1986 Rules.

[7.605]
60 Contents of proof

Apply rule 4.75 of the 1986 Rules.

[7.606]
61 Claim established by witness statement

Apply rule 4.77 of the 1986 Rules. Ignore paragraph (3).

[7.607]
62 Cost of proving

(1) Apply rule 4.78 of the 1986 Rules.

(2) In paragraph (1) leave out "or 4.76—CVL".

[7.608]
63 Building society liquidator to allow inspection of proofs

Apply rule 4.79 of the 1986 Rules.

[7.609]
64 New building society liquidator appointed

Apply rule 4.81 of the 1986 Rules.

[7.610]
65 Admission and rejection of proofs for dividend

Apply rule 4.82 of the 1986 Rules.

[7.611]
66 Appeal against decision on proof

(1) Apply rule 4.83 of the 1986 Rules.

(2) For paragraph (6) substitute—

> "(6) The building society liquidator is not personally liable for costs incurred by any person in respect of an application under this rule unless the court makes an order to that effect.".

[7.612]
67 Withdrawal or variation of proof

Apply rule 4.84 of the 1986 Rules.

[7.613]
68 Expunging of proof by the court

Apply rule 4.85 of the 1986 Rules.

[7.614]
69 Estimate of quantum

Apply rule 4.86 of the 1986 Rules.

[7.615]
70 Negotiable instruments, etc

Apply rule 4.87 of the 1986 Rules.

[7.616]
71 Secured creditors

Apply rule 4.88 of the 1986 Rules.

[7.617]
72 Discounts

Apply rule 4.89 of the 1986 Rules.

[7.618]
73 Mutual credits and set-off

(1) This rule applies where, before the building society goes into building society insolvency, there have been mutual credits, mutual debts or other mutual dealings between the society and any creditor of the society proving or claiming to prove for a debt in the building society insolvency.

(2) The reference in paragraph (1) to mutual credits, mutual debts or other mutual dealings does not include—

- (a) any debt arising out of an obligation incurred at a time when the creditor had notice that—
  - (i) a meeting of creditors had been summoned under section 98 of the Insolvency Act,
  - (ii) a petition for the winding up of the building society was pending, or
  - (iii) an application for a building society insolvency order in respect of the building society was pending;
- (b) any debt which has been acquired by a creditor on assignment or otherwise, pursuant to an agreement between the creditor and any other party where that agreement was entered into—
  - (i) after the commencement of building society insolvency,
  - (ii) at a time when the creditor had notice that a meeting of creditors had been summoned under section 98,
  - (iii) at a time when the creditor had notice that a winding up petition was pending, or
  - (iv) at a time when the creditor had notice that an application for a building society insolvency order in respect of the building society was pending;
- (c) any mutual dealings between the building society and a creditor who is also a shareholding member of the building society in respect of shares held by that person in the building society.

(3) An account shall be taken of what is due from each party to the other in respect of the mutual dealings, and the sums due from one party shall be set off against the sums due from the other.

(4) A sum shall be regarded as being due to or from the building society for the purposes of paragraph (3) whether—

- (a) it is payable at present or in the future;
- (b) the obligation by virtue of which it is payable is certain or contingent; or
- (c) its amount is fixed or liquidated, or is capable of being ascertained by fixed rules or as a matter of opinion.

(5) Rule 4.86 of the 1986 Rules shall apply for the purposes of this rule to any obligation to or from the building society which, by reason of its being subject to any contingency or for any other reason, does not bear a certain value.

(6) Rules 75 to 77 shall apply for the purposes of this rule in relation to any sums due to the building society which—

- (a) are payable in a currency other than sterling,
- (b) are of a periodical nature, or
- (c) bear interest.

(7) Rule 251 shall apply for the purposes of this rule to any sum due to or from the building society which is payable in the future.

(8) Subject to rule 74, only the balance (if any) of the account owed to the creditor is provable in the liquidation. Alternatively the balance (if any) owed to the building society shall be paid to the building society liquidator as part of the assets except where all or part of the balance results from a contingent or prospective debt owed by the creditor and in such a case the balance (or that part of it which results from the contingent or prospective debt) shall be paid if and when that debt becomes due and payable.

(9) In this rule, "obligation" means an obligation however arising, whether by virtue of an agreement, rule of law or otherwise.

[7.619]
74 Disapplication of set-off for eligible depositors

(1) This rule applies if the [the appropriate regulator's rules] allow the FSCS to make gross payments of compensation.

(2) In respect of protected deposits Rule 73 shall apply and, for the purpose of determining the sums due from the building society to an eligible depositor under rule 73(3)—

- (a) where the total of the sums held by the building society for the eligible depositor in respect of protected deposits is no more than the prescribed limit, then paragraph (3) applies; and
- (b) where the sums held exceed the prescribed limit, then paragraph (4) applies.

(3) Where this paragraph applies, there shall be deemed to have been no mutual dealings, regardless of whether there are any sums due from the depositor to the building society, and the sum due to the eligible depositor from the building society in respect of the protected deposits will be the total of the sums held by the building society for that depositor in respect of those deposits.

(4) Where this paragraph applies then—

- (a) any mutual dealings shall be treated as being mutual dealings only in relation to the amount by which that total exceeds the prescribed limit, and
- (b) the sums due from the building society to the eligible depositor in respect of the protected deposits will be—
  - (i) the amount by which that total exceeds the prescribed limit, set off in accordance with rule 73(3); and
  - (ii) the sums held by the building society for the eligible depositor in respect of protected deposits up to the prescribed limit.

(5) Any arrangements with regard to set-off between the building society and the eligible depositor in existence before the commencement of building society insolvency shall be subject to this rule, insofar as they relate to protected deposits.

(6) In this rule—

["appropriate regulator's rules" means the rules, as amended from time to time, made under section 213 of the Financial Services and Markets Act 2000 by—

(a) if the building society is a PRA-authorised person (within the meaning of that Act), the Prudential Regulation Authority or the Financial Conduct Authority; or

(b) in any other case, the Financial Conduct Authority;]

"prescribed limit" means the amount prescribed as the maximum compensation payable in respect of protected deposits under Part 15 of the Financial Services and Markets Act 2000; and

"protected deposit" means a protected deposit within the meaning given by the [the appropriate regulator's rules] but does not include a share in the society held by an eligible depositor.

NOTES

Para (1): words in square brackets substituted by the Financial Services Act 2012 (Consequential Amendments and Transitional Provisions) Order 2013, SI 2013/472, art 3, Sch 2, para 191(1), (3)(a).

Para (6): definition "the appropriate regulator's rules" substituted for definition "FSA Rules" and words in square brackets in definition "protected deposit" substituted by SI 2013/472, art 3, Sch 2, para 191(1), (3)(b).

[7.620]
75 Debt in foreign currency

Apply rule 4.91 of the 1986 Rules. In paragraph (1), leave out from "or, if" to the end.

[7.621]
76 Payments of a periodical nature

Apply rule 4.92 of the 1986 Rules. In paragraph (1), leave out from "or, if" to the end.

[7.622]
77 Interest

Apply rule 4.93 of the 1986 Rules. In paragraph (1), leave out from "or, if" to the end.

[7.623]
78 Debt payable at future time

(1) Apply rule 4.94 of the 1986 Rules.

(2) Leave out from "or, if" to "entered administration".

PART 8
SECURED CREDITORS

[7.624]
79 Value of security

Apply rule 4.95 of the 1986 Rules.

[7.625]
80 Surrender for non-disclosure

Apply rule 4.96 of the 1986 Rules. Ignore paragraph (3).

[7.626]
81 Redemption by liquidator

Apply rule 4.97 of the 1986 Rules.

[7.627]
82 Test of security's value

Apply rule 4.98 of the 1986 Rules.

[7.628]
83 Realisation of security by creditor

Apply rule 4.99 of the 1986 Rules.

PART 9
THE BUILDING SOCIETY LIQUIDATOR

CHAPTER 1 GENERAL

[7.629]
84 Remuneration of building society liquidator

(1) This rule applies where—

(a) the liquidation committee has ceased to exist as mentioned in rule 42(2),

(b) the committee has not been reformed at a meeting of creditors held under rule 42, 45 or 46, and

(c) the committee has not been reformed at a meeting of contributories held under rule 118.

(2) Where this rule applies the creditors may, at the first or any subsequent meeting of creditors, pass a resolution as to the terms on which, in accordance with rule 99, the building society liquidator is to be remunerated.

(3) Where such a resolution is passed—

(a) it supersedes any resolution as to the remuneration of the building society liquidator passed by the liquidation committee before the first meeting of creditors, and

(b) the building society liquidator shall be paid under the resolution passed by the liquidation committee under rule 18(5) in respect of the performance of the building society liquidator's functions before the day on which the creditors' resolution is passed and under the creditors' resolution in respect of the performance of the building society liquidator's functions on and after that day.

[7.630]

85 Replacement of building society liquidator by creditors

(1) Apply rule 4.100 of the 1986 Rules.

(2) For paragraph (1) substitute—

"(1) This rule applies where a person is appointed as building society liquidator by a meeting of creditors.".

(3) For paragraph (4) substitute—

"(4) The chair of the meeting shall—

(a) send the certificate to the new building society liquidator,

(b) send a copy of the certificate to the Bank of England and the [appropriate regulator], and

(c) file a copy of the certificate in court.".

NOTES

Para (3): words in square brackets substituted by the Financial Services Act 2012 (Consequential Amendments and Transitional Provisions) Order 2013, SI 2013/472, art 3, Sch 2, para 191(1), (5).

[7.631]

86 Authentication of building society liquidator's appointment

Apply rule 4.105 of the 1986 Rules. Leave out from "or (as" to "the Act".

[7.632]

87 Appointment to be advertised and registered

(1) This rule applies where the building society liquidator is appointed by a meeting of the creditors or by the Bank of England under rule 107.

(2) The building society liquidator shall, after receiving the certificate of appointment, as soon as reasonably practicable give notice of that appointment. Such notice—

(a) shall be gazetted; and

(b) may be advertised in such other manner as the building society liquidator thinks fit.

(3) The expense of giving notice under this rule shall be borne in the first instance by the building society liquidator; but the building society liquidator is entitled to be reimbursed as an expense of the building society insolvency.

(4) The building society liquidator shall immediately notify the appointment to the [appropriate regulator].

NOTES

Para (4): words in square brackets substituted by the Financial Services Act 2012 (Consequential Amendments and Transitional Provisions) Order 2013, SI 2013/472, art 3, Sch 2, para 191(1), (5).

CHAPTER 2 RESIGNATION AND REMOVAL

[7.633]

88 Creditors' meeting to be notified of the building society liquidator's resignation

(1) Apply rule 4.108 of the 1986 Rules.

(2) For paragraph (1), substitute—

"(1) Before resigning office, the building society liquidator must obtain the consent of the Bank of England and must call a meeting of creditors to notify them of this.

(1A) The notice summoning the meeting shall indicate that this is the purpose, or one of the purposes, of the meeting and shall draw the attention of the creditors to rule 96 with respect to the building society liquidator's release.

(1B) The notice in paragraph (1A) shall enclose a copy of the Bank of England's consent.".

(3) For paragraph (2) substitute—

"(2) Copies of the notice and of the account mentioned in paragraph (3) shall be sent to the court, the Bank of England and the [appropriate regulator].".

NOTES

Para (3): words in square brackets substituted by the Financial Services Act 2012 (Consequential Amendments and Transitional Provisions) Order 2013, SI 2013/472, art 3, Sch 2, para 191(1), (5).

[7.634]

89 Action following acceptance of resignation

(1) This rule applies where a meeting is summoned to notify the creditors of the building society liquidator's resignation.

(2) The meeting shall resolve whether to give the building society liquidator their release.

(3) If the meeting resolves not to release the building society liquidator, the building society liquidator shall be given a copy of that resolution and rule 96 applies.

(4) After the meeting the building society liquidator shall file the notice of resignation in court and shall send copies of the notice to the Bank of England and the [appropriate regulator].

(5) The building society liquidator's resignation is effective as from the date on which the court receives the notice of that resignation, and the court shall endorse that date on the notice.

NOTES

Para (4): words in square brackets substituted by the Financial Services Act 2012 (Consequential Amendments and Transitional Provisions) Order 2013, SI 2013/472, art 3, Sch 2, para 191(1), (5).

[7.635]

90 Advertisement of resignation

Apply rule 4.112 of the 1986 Rules.

[7.636]

91 Meeting of creditors to remove building society liquidator

(1) Apply rule 4.113 of the 1986 Rules.

(2) In paragraph (1), for "section 174(4)" substitute "section 109 of the Banking Act 2009".

(3) In paragraph (2), for "official receiver" substitute "Bank of England and the [appropriate regulator]".

(4) For paragraph (4) substitute—

"(4) Where the meeting passes a resolution that—
(a) the building society liquidator be removed,
(b) a new building society liquidator be appointed, or
(c) the building society liquidator not be given their release,
the building society liquidator shall be given a copy of that resolution and if it has been resolved to remove the building society liquidator, the building society liquidator shall be given a certificate to that effect.".

(5) For paragraph (5) substitute—

"(5) If the creditors have resolved to appoint a new building society liquidator, the certificate of that appointment shall also be sent to the [appropriate regulator] and rule 4.100 shall apply.".

NOTES

Paras (3), (5): words in square brackets substituted by the Financial Services Act 2012 (Consequential Amendments and Transitional Provisions) Order 2013, SI 2013/472, art 3, Sch 2, para 191(1), (5).

[7.637]

92 Court's power to regulate meetings under rule 89

Apply rule 4.115 of the 1986 Rules. Leave out "or 4.114—CVL".

[7.638]

93 Procedure on removal

(1) Apply rule 4.116 of the 1986 Rules.

(2) For "official receiver", wherever it appears, substitute "out-going building society liquidator".

(3) For paragraph (3) substitute—

"(3) A copy of the certificate so endorsed shall be sent by the court to the outgoing building society liquidator and to any new building society liquidator appointed.".

(4) Ignore paragraph (4).

[7.639]

94 Advertisement of removal

Apply rule 4.118 of the 1986 Rules.

[7.640]
95 Removal of building society liquidator by the court

(1) Apply rule 4.119 of the 1986 Rules.

(2) After paragraph (1) insert—

"(1A) If the liquidation committee has not yet passed a full payment resolution, the court shall dismiss any application under paragraph (1) where the application is made by someone other than the Bank of England, the [appropriate regulator] or the liquidation committee.".

(3) In paragraph (2), for "at least 7 days' notice" substitute—

"(a) if the application is made before the passing of a full payment resolution, such notice as is reasonable in all the circumstances, and
(b) if the application is made after the passing of a full payment resolution, at least 7 days' notice.".

(4) In paragraph (4), leave out ", at least 14 days before the hearing,".

(5) After paragraph (4) insert—

"(4A) The notice and copies mentioned in paragraph (4) shall be sent—
(a) if the application is made before the passing of a full payment resolution, within such time so as to give the building society liquidator notice of the hearing as is reasonable in all the circumstances, and
(b) if the application is made after the passing of a full payment resolution, at least 14 days before the hearing.".

(6) In paragraph (6)—
(a) in sub-paragraph (a), for "official receiver" substitute "Bank of England and the [appropriate regulator]" and at the end insert "and", and
(b) leave out "and" at the end of sub-paragraph (b), and sub-paragraph (c).

NOTES

Paras (2), (6): words in square brackets substituted by the Financial Services Act 2012 (Consequential Amendments and Transitional Provisions) Order 2013, SI 2013/472, art 3, Sch 2, para 191(1), (5).

[7.641]
96 Release of resigning or removed building society liquidator

(1) Apply rule 4.121 of the 1986 Rules.

(2) In paragraph (1), for "accepted by" substitute "notified to".

(3) For rule 4.109 substitute "rule 89 of the 2010 Rules".

(4) In paragraph (3)—
(a) in sub paragraph (a) for "receive his resignation" substitute "be notified of his resignation"; and
(b) leave out "or" at the end of sub-paragraph (a) and at the end of sub-paragraph (b) insert "or" and—

"(c) the building society liquidator resigns, and the Bank of England has refused his release,".

(5) For paragraph (4) substitute—

"(4) When the Secretary of State gives the release, he shall certify it accordingly, file the certificate in court and send a copy to the [appropriate regulator].".

NOTES

Para (5): words in square brackets substituted by the Financial Services Act 2012 (Consequential Amendments and Transitional Provisions) Order 2013, SI 2013/472, art 3, Sch 2, para 191(1), (5).

CHAPTER 3 RELEASE ON COMPLETION OF WINDING UP

[7.642]
97 Final meeting

(1) The building society liquidator shall give at least 14 days' notice of the final meeting of the liquidation committee to be held under section 115 of the Banking Act to the following—
(a) the [appropriate regulator],
(b) the FSCS,
(c) the Bank of England,
(d) the Treasury, and
(e) the members of the liquidation committee.

(2) The building society liquidator's final report to be laid before the meeting under that section shall contain an account of the liquidator's administration of the winding up, including—
(a) details as to how Objective 1 was achieved having regard, in particular, to the expenses of the building society liquidator in connection with that Objective,
(b) a summary of the building society liquidator's receipts and payments,
(c) a statement that the building society liquidator has reconciled his account with that which is held by the Secretary of State in respect of the winding up, and

(d) a statement as to the amount paid to unsecured creditors by virtue of the application of section 176A (prescribed part) of the 1986 Act.

(3) At the same time that notice of the final meeting is sent out, the building society liquidator shall file the final report in court and send it to the [appropriate regulator].

(4) The building society liquidator shall give notice to all creditors and contributories that the final report is available, either on request to the building society liquidator or from the [appropriate regulator], and shall cause that notice to be gazetted and to be advertised by such other method as the liquidator sees fit at least 14 days before the final meeting is held.

(5) At the final meeting, the liquidation committee may question the building society liquidator with respect to any matter contained in the final report, and may resolve against the building society liquidator being released.

(6) The building society liquidator shall give notice to the court that the final meeting has been held and the notice shall state whether or not he has been given his release.

(7) Where the liquidation committee does not resolve against the building society liquidator's release, the building society liquidator vacates office at the end of the meeting and has his release when the notice in paragraph (6) is filed in court.

(8) If there is no quorum present at the final meeting, the building society liquidator shall report to the court that a final meeting was summoned in accordance with section 115 of the Banking Act, but there was no quorum present; and the final meeting is then deemed to have been held, and the liquidation committee not to have resolved against the building society liquidator being released.

(9) If the liquidation committee resolves against the building society liquidator having his release then rule 96 applies.

NOTES

Paras (1), (3), (4): words in square brackets substituted by the Financial Services Act 2012 (Consequential Amendments and Transitional Provisions) Order 2013, SI 2013/472, art 3, Sch 2, para 191(1), (5).

[7.643]
98 Rule as to reporting

Apply rule 4.125A of the 1986 Rules. For "Rule 4.124 or 4.125" substitute "Rule 97 of the 2010 Rules".

CHAPTER 4 REMUNERATION

[7.644]
99 Fixing of remuneration

(1) Apply rule 4.127 of the 1986 Rules.

(2) In paragraph (3), leave out from the beginning to "receiver".

(3) For paragraph (5) substitute—

"(5) If, under rule 42(2) of the 2010 Rules, the liquidation committee ceases to exist at the end of the first meeting of creditors, the terms on which the building society liquidator is to be remunerated determined by the initial liquidation committee under rule 18 of the 2010 Rules can be re-determined by a resolution of a meeting of creditors, and paragraph (4) applies to the determination of the creditors as it does to the determination of the liquidation committee.".

(4) In paragraph (6), for the words from the beginning to "his" substitute "Where the building society liquidator's".

[7.645]
100 Building society liquidator's entitlement to remuneration where it is not fixed under rule 99

(1) Apply rule 4.127A of the 1986 Rules.

(2) In paragraph (1), for the words from "liquidator" to "his" substitute "building society liquidator's".

(3) In paragraph (2), after "Schedule 6" add "to the 1986 Rules as applied by the Schedule to the 2010 Rules".

[7.646]
101 Building society liquidator's remuneration where he realises assets on behalf of chargeholder

(1) Apply rule 4.127B of the 1986 Rules.

(2) In paragraph (1), for the words from "liquidator" to "and" substitute "building society liquidator".

(3) In paragraphs (2) and (3), after "Schedule 6" add "to the 1986 Rules as applied by the Schedule to the 2010 Rules".

[7.647]
102 Other matters affecting remuneration

Apply rule 4.128 of the 1986 Rules.

[7.648]
103 Recourse of building society liquidator to meeting of creditors

Apply rule 4.129 of the 1986 Rules.

[7.649]
104 Recourse to the court

Apply rule 4.130 of the 1986 Rules.

[7.650]
105 Creditors' claim that remuneration is excessive

(1) Apply rule 4.131 of the 1986 Rules.

(2) In paragraph (1) at the end insert "The FSCS may also apply to the Court for such an order on those grounds".

[7.651]
106 Primacy of Objective 1

Nothing done under a rule in this Chapter may prejudice the achievement of Objective 1.

CHAPTER 5 SUPPLEMENTARY PROVISIONS

[7.652]
107 Replacement building society liquidator

(1) Where the building society liquidator vacates office for any reason (including death) other than by removal by a meeting of creditors in accordance with rule 91, the Bank of England shall appoint a new building society liquidator as soon as practicable.

(2) Where a building society liquidator has been removed by a meeting of creditors and no resolution has been passed by that meeting to appoint a new building society liquidator, the Bank of England shall appoint a new building society liquidator as soon as practicable.

(3) The Bank of England shall file in court the document appointing the new building society liquidator ("the certificate of appointment") together with statements to the effect that the new building society liquidator—

- (a) is qualified to act as an insolvency practitioner in accordance with section 390 of the Insolvency Act, and
- (b) consents to act as the building society liquidator.

(4) The building society liquidator shall send a copy of the certificate of appointment to the [appropriate regulator].

NOTES

Para (4): words in square brackets substituted by the Financial Services Act 2012 (Consequential Amendments and Transitional Provisions) Order 2013, SI 2013/472, art 3, Sch 2, para 191(1), (5).

[7.653]
108 Building society liquidator deceased

(1) Unless notice of the death of the building society liquidator has been given under paragraph (2) or (3), it is the duty of the building society liquidator's personal representatives, where the building society liquidator has died, to give notice of that fact to the Bank of England and the liquidation committee, specifying the date of the death.

(2) If the deceased building society liquidator was a partner in a firm, notice may be given to the Bank of England, the [appropriate regulator] and the liquidation committee by a partner in the firm who is qualified to act as an insolvency practitioner, or is a member of any body recognised by the Secretary of State for the authorisation of insolvency practitioners.

(3) Notice of the death may also be given by any person producing the relevant death certificate or a copy of it to the Bank of England, the [appropriate regulator] and the liquidation committee.

(4) The Bank of England shall give notice to the court, for the purpose of fixing the date of the deceased building society liquidator's release.

NOTES

Paras (2), (3): words in square brackets substituted by the Financial Services Act 2012 (Consequential Amendments and Transitional Provisions) Order 2013, SI 2013/472, art 3, Sch 2, para 191(1), (5).

[7.654]
109 Loss of qualification as insolvency practitioner

(1) Apply rule 4.134 of the 1986 Rules. For paragraph (2) substitute—

"(2) The building society liquidator shall immediately give notice of his doing so to the Bank of England.

(3) The Bank of England shall file a copy of this notice in court.".

[7.655]
110 Resignation of the building society liquidator

(1) This rule applies where the building society liquidator was appointed by the court (in the building society insolvency order) or by the Bank of England.

(2) The building society liquidator can only resign—

- (a) after the liquidation committee have passed a full payment resolution, and
- (b) with the consent of the Bank of England.

(3) Before calling a meeting of creditors under rule 88 to receive notice of the building society liquidator's resignation, the building society liquidator must write to the Bank of England notifying it of the intention to resign.

(4) The Bank of England shall notify the building society liquidator in writing within 21 days as to whether it consents to the resignation; if the Bank of England does not consent to the resignation, it shall set out its reasons in writing.

(5) The building society liquidator, if not content with the Bank of England's response, may apply to the court for directions under section 168(3) of the Insolvency Act.

[7.656]
111 Notice to Bank of England of intention to vacate office

(1) This rule applies where the building society liquidator was appointed by a meeting of creditors.

(2) Apply rule 4.137 of the 1986 Rules.

(3) For "official receiver", wherever it appears, substitute "Bank of England" and for "receive his resignation" substitute "be notified of his resignation".

[7.657]
112 Building society liquidator's duties on vacating office

Apply rule 4.138 of the 1986 Rules. Ignore paragraph (3).

[7.658]
113 Power of court to set aside certain transactions

(1) Apply rule 4.149 of the 1986 Rules.

(2) In paragraph (2)—
- (a) leave out "either", and
- (b) leave out "or" at the end of sub-paragraph (a), and after sub-paragraph (b) insert ", or" and—

  "(c) it is shown to the court's satisfaction that the transaction was entered into by the building society liquidator for the purpose of achieving Objective 1.".

[7.659]
114 Rule against solicitation

(1) Apply rule 4.150 of the 1986 Rules.

PART 10
THE LIQUIDATION COMMITTEE

[7.660]
115 Application of rules in this Part

The rules in this Part apply only in relation to the liquidation committee established after a full payment resolution has been passed.

[7.661]
116 Membership of committee

(1) Apply rule 4.152 of the 1986 Rules.

(2) For paragraph (1) substitute—

"(1) Subject to rule 42(2) and (5) of the 2010 Rules, rule 4.154 as applied by rule 118 of the 2010 Rules and rule 4.171 as applied by rule 134 of the 2010 Rules, the liquidation committee shall consist of either three or five creditors of the company, elected by the meeting of creditors held under rule 42 of those Rules.".

(3) Ignore paragraphs (2), (4) and (7).

[7.662]
117 Formalities of establishment

Apply rule 4.153 of the 1986 Rules.

[7.663]
118 Committee established by contributories

(1) Apply rule 4.154 of the 1986 Rules.

(2) For paragraph (1) substitute—

"(1) This rule applies where the outcome of the creditors' meeting summoned by the building society liquidator under rule 42 of the 2010 Rules is, (by virtue of rule 42(2)), that the liquidation committee ceases to exist at the end of the meeting.".

(3) In paragraph (2), for "that section" substitute "section 141 of the Act".

(4) In paragraph (4) for "at least 3 and not more than 5", substitute "three or five".

[7.664]
119 Obligations of liquidator to committee

Apply rule 4.155 of the 1986 Rules.

[7.665]
120 Meetings of the committee

(1) Apply rule 4.156 of the 1986 Rules.

(2) In paragraph (2)(a), after "representative" insert "or the FSCS".

[7.666]
121 The chair at meetings

Apply rule 4.157 of the 1986 Rules.

[7.667]
122 Quorum

Subject to rule 4.171(6A) of the 1986 Rules as inserted by rule 134(3) of these rules, a meeting of the committee is duly constituted if due notice of it has been given to all the members, and at least two members are present or represented.

[7.668]
123 Committee-members' representatives

Apply rule 4.159 of the 1986 Rules.

[7.669]
124 Resignation

Apply rule 4.160 of the 1986 Rules.

[7.670]
125 Termination of membership

Apply rule 4.161 of the 1986 Rules.

[7.671]
126 Removal

Apply rule 4.162 of the 1986 Rules.

[7.672]
127 Vacancy (creditor members)

Apply rule 4.163 of the 1986 Rules.

[7.673]
128 Vacancy (contributory members)

Apply rule 4.164 of the 1986 Rules.

[7.674]
129 Voting rights and resolutions

Apply rule 4.165 of the 1986 Rules. In paragraph (1), leave out "creditor".

[7.675]
130 Resolutions by post

(1) Apply rule 4.167 of the 1986 Rules.

(2) In paragraph (3), after "committee" insert "or the FSCS".

[7.676]
131 Liquidator's reports

Apply rule 4.168 of the 1986 Rules.

[7.677]
132 Expenses of members, etc

Apply rule 4.169 of the 1986 Rules.

[7.678]
133 Dealings by committee-members and others

Apply rule 4.170 of the 1986 Rules.

[7.679]
134 Composition of committee when creditors paid in full

(1) Apply rule 4.171 of the 1986 Rules.

(2) In paragraph (6)—

(a) at the beginning, insert "Subject to paragraph (6A) below";
(b) after "under paragraph (1)" insert "or since the FSCS has ceased to be on the committee";
(c) at the end, insert "subject to paragraph (6A) below".

(3) After paragraph (6) insert—

"(6A) The liquidation committee continues to exist and can act so long as it consists of at least the FSCS."

[7.680]
135 Committee's functions vested in the Secretary of State
Apply rule 4.172 of the 1986 Rules. Ignore paragraph (2).

[7.681]
136 Formal defects
Apply rule 4.172A of the 1986 Rules.

PART 11
COLLECTION AND DISTRIBUTION OF BUILDING SOCIETY'S ASSETS BY BUILDING SOCIETY LIQUIDATOR

[7.682]
137 General duties of building society liquidator
Apply rule 4.179 of the 1986 Rules.

[7.683]
138 General qualification on powers
In exercising any power conferred on the building society liquidator by this Part before a full payment resolution has been passed, the building society liquidator shall exercise it consistently with Objective 1.

[7.684]
139 Manner of distributing assets
Apply rule 4.180 of the 1986 Rules.

[7.685]
140 Debts of insolvent building society to rank equally
Apply rule 4.181 of the 1986 Rules.

[7.686]
141 Supplementary provisions as to dividend
Apply rule 4.182 of the 1986 Rules.

[7.687]
142 Division of unsold assets
Apply rule 4.183 of the 1986 Rules.

[7.688]
143 General powers of the liquidator
Apply rule 4.184 of the 1986 Rules. In paragraph (1) leave out "section 165(2) or".

[7.689]
144 Enforced delivery up of building society's property
Apply rule 4.185 of the 1986 Rules.

[7.690]
145 Final distribution
Apply rule 4.186 of the 1986 Rules. For "Part 11 of the Rules", substitute "Part 21 of the 2010 Rules".

PART 12
DISCLAIMER

[7.691]
146 Liquidator's notice of disclaimer
Apply rule 4.187 of the 1986 Rules.

[7.692]
147 Communication of disclaimer to persons interested
Apply rule 4.188 of the 1986 Rules.

[7.693]
148 Additional notices
Apply rule 4.189 of the 1986 Rules.

[7.694]
149 Duty to keep court informed
Apply rule 4.190 of the 1986 Rules.

[7.695]
150 Application by interested party under section 178(5)
Apply rule 4.191 of the 1986 Rules.

[7.696]
151 Interest in property to be declared on request

Apply rule 4.192 of the 1986 Rules.

[7.697]
152 Disclaimer presumed valid and effective

Apply rule 4.193 of the 1986 Rules. For "Chapter" substitute "Part".

[7.698]
153 Application for exercise of court's powers under s 181

Apply rule 4.194 of the 1986 Rules.

PART 13
SETTLEMENT OF LIST OF CONTRIBUTORIES

[7.699]
154 Preliminary

Apply rule 4.195 of the 1986 Rules.

[7.700]
155 Primacy of Objective 1

Where the building society liquidator considers that the carrying out of a duty imposed by a rule in this Part would prejudice the achievement of Objective 1, the building society liquidator shall postpone the carrying out of that duty until the building society liquidator considers that the carrying out of the duty would no longer be likely to prejudice the achievement of that Objective.

[7.701]
156 Duty of liquidator to settle list

Apply rule 4.196 of the 1986 Rules.

[7.702]
157 Form of list

Apply rule 4.197 of the 1986 Rules.

[7.703]
158 Procedure for settling list

Apply rule 4.198 of the 1986 Rules.

[7.704]
159 Application to court for variation of the list

Apply rule 4.199 of the 1986 Rules.

[7.705]
160 Variation of, or addition to, the list

Apply rule 4.200 of the 1986 Rules.

[7.706]
161 Costs not to fall on building society liquidator

The building society liquidator is not personally liable for any costs incurred by a person in respect of an application to set aside or vary the building society liquidator's act or decision in settling the list of contributories, or varying or adding to the list, unless the court makes an order to that effect.

PART 14
CALLS

[7.707]
162 Calls by building society liquidator

Apply rule 4.202 of the 1986 Rules.

[7.708]
163 Control by building society liquidation committee

Apply rule 4.203 of the 1986 Rules.

[7.709]
164 Application to court for leave to make a call

Apply rule 4.204 of the 1986 Rules.

[7.710]
165 Making and enforcement of the call

Apply rule 4.205 of the 1986 Rules.

PART 15
SPECIAL MANAGER

[7.711]
166 Appointment and remuneration
Apply rule 4.206 of the 1986 Rules.

[7.712]
167 Security
Apply rule 4.207 of the 1986 Rules.

[7.713]
168 Failure to give or keep up security
Apply rule 4.208 of the 1986 Rules.

[7.714]
169 Accounting
Apply rule 4.209 of the 1986 Rules.

[7.715]
170 Termination of appointment
Apply rule 4.210 of the 1986 Rules.

PART 16
ORDER OF PAYMENT AS TO COSTS, ETC OUT OF ASSETS

[7.716]
171 General rule as to priority

(1) Apply rule 4.218 of the 1986 Rules.

(2) In paragraph (3)—
- (a) ignore sub-paragraphs (a)(iii) and (iv), (b), and (d),
- (b) in sub-paragraph (c) leave out the words from "or section 415A" to the end,
- (c) in sub-paragraph (la), leave out the words from "in any case" to the end.

[7.717]
172 Litigation expenses and property subject to a floating charge—general application
Apply rule 4.218A of the 1986 Rules.

[7.718]
173 Litigation expenses and property subject to a floating charge—requirement for approval or authorisation
Apply rule 4.218B of the 1986 Rules.

[7.719]
174 Litigation expenses and property subject to a floating charge—request for approval or authorisation
Apply rule 4.218C of the 1986 Rules.

[7.720]
175 Litigation expenses and property subject to a floating charge—grant of approval or authorisation
Apply rule 4.218D of the 1986 Rules.

[7.721]
176 Litigation expenses and property subject to a floating charge—application to court by the building society liquidator
Apply rule 4.218E of the 1986 Rules.

[7.722]
177 Saving for powers of the court
Apply rule 4.220 of the 1986 Rules.

PART 17
MISCELLANEOUS RULES

CHAPTER 1 RETURN OF CAPITAL

[7.723]
178 Application to court for order authorising return of capital
Apply rule 4.221 of the 1986 Rules.

[7.724]
179 Procedure for return of capital

Apply rule 4.222 of the 1986 Rules.

CHAPTER 2 CONCLUSION OF BUILDING SOCIETY INSOLVENCY

[7.725]
180 [Appropriate regulator]'s directions under section 116 of the Banking Act

Where the [appropriate regulator] gives a direction under section 116 of the Banking Act (application by an interested person for postponement of dissolution) the [appropriate regulator] shall send a copy of the direction to that applicant.

NOTES

Words in square brackets substituted by the Financial Services Act 2012 (Consequential Amendments and Transitional Provisions) Order 2013, SI 2013/472, art 3, Sch 2, para 191(1), (5).

[7.726]
181 Procedure following appeal under section 116 of the Banking Act

Following an appeal under section 116(2) of the Banking Act (against a decision of [the Financial Conduct Authority or the Prudential Regulation Authority] under that section) the court shall send two sealed copies of its order to the person in whose favour the appeal was determined, and that person shall send one of the copies to [the regulator in question].

NOTES

Words in square brackets substituted by the Financial Services Act 2012 (Consequential Amendments and Transitional Provisions) Order 2013, SI 2013/472, art 3, Sch 2, para 191(1), (4).

PART 18
COURT PROCEDURE AND PRACTICE

CHAPTER 1 APPLICATIONS (GENERAL)

[7.727]
182 Preliminary

This Part applies to any application made to the court under Part 2 of the Banking Act or these Rules except an application under section 95 of the Banking Act for a building society insolvency order.

[7.728]
183 Interpretation

Apply rule 7.2 of the 1986 Rules. In paragraph (1) ignore from the second "and" to the end of the paragraph.

[7.729]
184 Form and contents of application

Apply rule 7.3 of the 1986 Rules.

[7.730]
185 Application under section 176A(5) to disapply section 176A

(1) Apply rule 7.3A of the 1986 Rules.

(2) In paragraph (1), ignore "administrator or receiver."

(3) Ignore paragraph (2)(a).

[7.731]
186 Filing and service of application

Apply rule 7.4 of the 1986 Rules.

[7.732]
187 Notice of application under section 176A(5)

Apply rule 7.4A of the 1986 Rules. Leave out the words from "save that notice" to the end.

[7.733]
188 Other hearings without notice

Apply rule 7.5 of the 1986 Rules.

[7.734]
189 Hearing of application

Apply rule 7.6 of the 1986 Rules.

[7.735]
190 Use of evidence

Apply rule 7.7 of the 1986 Rules.

[7.736]
191 Filing and service of witness statements

Apply rule 7.8 of the 1986 Rules. Ignore paragraph (2).

[7.737]
192 Use of reports

(1) Unless the application involves other parties, or the court orders otherwise, a report may be filed in court instead of a witness statement by—

(a) the building society liquidator,
(b) the provisional building society liquidator, or
(c) the special manager.

(2) In any case where a report is filed instead of a witness statement, the report shall be treated for the purposes of rule 191, and any hearing before the court, as if it were a witness statement.

[7.738]
193 Adjournment of hearings: directions

Apply rule 7.10 of the 1986 Rules. In paragraph (2)(c)(iii), for "Rule 7.9(1)(b)" substitute "Rule 192(1) of the 2010 Rules".

CHAPTER 2 SHORTHAND WRITERS

[7.739]
194 Nomination and appointment of shorthand writers

(1) Apply rule 7.16 of the 1986 Rules.

(2) In paragraph (1) leave out "and, in a county court, the registrar".

(3) In paragraph (2) leave out "133" and "251N, 290 or 366".

(4) Ignore paragraph (3).

[7.740]
195 Remuneration

Apply rule 7.17 of the 1986 Rules.

CHAPTER 3 ENFORCEMENT PROCEDURES

[7.741]
196 Enforcement of court orders

(1) Apply rule 7.19 of the 1986 Rules.

(2) Ignore paragraph (2).

[7.742]
197 Orders enforcing compliance with the Rules

(1) The court may, on the application of the building society liquidator or the provisional building society liquidator as the case may be, make such orders as it thinks necessary for the enforcement of obligations falling on any person in accordance with—

(a) section 143(2) (liquidator to furnish information, books, papers etc) of the Insolvency Act or
(b) section 235 (duty to cooperate with liquidator) of that Act.

(2) An order of the court under this rule may provide that all the costs of and incidental to the application for it shall be borne by the person against whom the order is made.

[7.743]
198 Warrants (general provisions)

(1) A warrant issued by the court under any provision of the 1986 Act shall be addressed to such officer of the High Court as the warrant specifies, or to any constable.

(2) The person described in section 236(5) of the Insolvency Act as the prescribed officer of the court is the tipstaff and his assistants of the court.

(3) In this Chapter, references to property include books, papers and records.

[7.744]
199 Warrants under section 236

Apply rule 7.23 of the 1986 Rules. In paragraph (1), leave out "251N or 366 (the equivalent in bankruptcy)".

CHAPTER 4 COURT RECORDS AND RETURNS

[7.745]
200 Title of proceedings

Every proceeding under Part 2 of the Banking Act shall, with any necessary additions, be titled "IN THE MATTER OF . . . . (naming the building society to which the proceedings relate) AND IN THE MATTER OF THE BANKING ACT 2009".

[7.746]
201 Court records

Apply rule 7.27 of the 1986 Rules.

[7.747]
202 Inspection of records

Apply rule 7.28 of the 1986 Rules.

[7.748]
203 File of court proceedings and inspection

(1) The Court shall open and maintain a file for each building society insolvency and (subject to the direction of the registrar) all documents relating to that building society insolvency shall be placed on that file.

(2) Where a file has been opened under paragraph (1), the following have the right, at all reasonable times, to inspect that file—
- (a) the building society liquidator,
- (b) any person stating in writing that they are a creditor of the building society to which the building society insolvency relates,
- (c) a member of the building society,
- (d) any person who is, or at any time has been, a director or officer of the building society to which the building society insolvency relates,
- (e) any person who is a contributory of the building society to which the building society insolvency relates, and
- (f) the Bank of England, the [appropriate regulator] and the FSCS.

(3) The right of inspection conferred on any person by paragraph (2) may be exercised on their behalf by a person properly authorised by them.

(4) Any person may, with permission of the court, inspect the file.

(5) The right of inspection conferred by this rule is not exercisable in respect of documents, or parts of documents, which the court has directed (either generally or specially) are not to be open to inspection without the court's permission.

(6) An application for a direction of the court under paragraph (5) may be made by the building society liquidator or by any party appearing to the court to have an interest in the building society insolvency.

(7) If, for the purposes of powers conferred by the Insolvency Act, the Banking Act or these Rules, the Secretary of State wishes to inspect the file on a building society insolvency and requests the court to transmit the file, the court shall comply with the request or, if the file is for the time being in use for the court's own purposes, as soon as the file is no longer in such use.

(8) Rule 202 applies in respect of the court's file on any building society insolvency as it applies in respect of court records of general insolvency proceedings.

NOTES

Para (2): words in square brackets substituted by the Financial Services Act 2012 (Consequential Amendments and Transitional Provisions) Order 2013, SI 2013/472, art 3, Sch 2, para 191(1), (5).

CHAPTER 5 COSTS AND DETAILED ASSESSMENT

[7.749]
204 Application of the CPR

Apply rule 7.33 of the 1986 Rules.

[7.750]
205 Requirement to assess costs by the detailed procedure

(1) Apply rule 7.34 of the 1986 Rules.

(2) In paragraph (1)—
- (a) for "company insolvency" and "liquidation" substitute "building society insolvency",
- (b) ignore sub-paragraph (b), and
- (c) for the words from "court to which" to the end substitute "High Court".

(3) In paragraph (2), leave out "or creditors".

(4) In paragraph (5), for "trustee in bankruptcy or a liquidator" substitute "building society liquidator."

(5) Ignore paragraph (6).

[7.751]
206 Procedure where detailed assessment required

Apply rule 7.35 of the 1986 Rules. Ignore paragraph (6).

[7.752]
207 Costs of officers charged with executions of writs or other process

(1) Apply rule 7.36 of the 1986 Rules.

(2) In paragraph (1)(a), leave out "or 346(2)".

(3) In paragraph (1)(b), leave out "or 346(3)".

[7.753]
208 Costs paid otherwise than out of the insolvent estate

Apply rule 7.38 of the 1986 Rules.

[7.754]
209 Award of costs against responsible insolvency practitioner

(1) Apply rule 7.39 of the 1986 Rules.

(2) Leave out from the beginning to "expenses" and "the official receiver or".

[7.755]
210 Application for costs

(1) Apply rule 7.40 of the 1986 Rules.

(2) In paragraph (1) for "insolvency" substitute "building society insolvency".

(3) In paragraph (2), leave out the words from ", and, in winding up" to the end.

(4) In paragraph (3), leave out "and, where appropriate, the official receiver".

(5) Ignore paragraph (3A).

[7.756]
211 Costs and expenses of witnesses

(1) Apply rule 7.41 of the 1986 Rules.

(2) In paragraph (1), leave out "the bankrupt or the debtor or".

(3) Ignore paragraph (2).

[7.757]
212 Final costs certificate

Apply rule 7.42 of the 1986 Rules.

CHAPTER 6 PERSONS INCAPABLE OF MANAGING THEIR AFFAIRS

[7.758]
213 Introductory

Apply rule 7.43 of the 1986 Rules. In paragraph (1), for (a), substitute "by reason of being a protected person within the meaning of Part 21 of the CPR or".

[7.759]
214 Appointment of another person to act

Apply rule 7.44 of the 1986 Rules. Ignore paragraph (3)(c).

[7.760]
215 Witness statement in support of application

(1) Apply rule 7.45 of the 1986 Rules.

(2) In paragraph (1) leave out from the beginning to "receiver".

(3) Ignore paragraph (2).

[7.761]
216 Service of notices following appointment

Apply rule 7.46 of the 1986 Rules.

CHAPTER 7 APPEALS IN BUILDING SOCIETY INSOLVENCY PROCEEDINGS

[7.762]
217 Appeals and review of court orders

(1) The High Court may review, rescind or vary any order made by it in the exercise of its jurisdiction under Part 2 of the Banking Act.

(2) An appeal from a decision of a registrar of the High Court lies, with the permission of the registrar or a judge of the High Court, to a single judge of the High Court, and a second appeal lies, with the permission of the Court of Appeal, to the Court of Appeal.

(3) An appeal of a decision of first instance of a judge of the High Court lies, with the permission of the judge or the Court of Appeal, to the Court of Appeal.

[7.763]
218 Procedure on appeal

Part 52 of the CPR applies with regard to the procedure for appeals.

[7.764]
219 Appeal against a decision of the Secretary of State

Apply rule 7.50 of the 1986 Rules. Ignore paragraph (2).

CHAPTER 8 GENERAL

[7.765]
220 Principal court rules and practice to apply

(1) The CPR and the practice and procedure of the High Court (including any practice direction) apply to building society insolvency proceedings in the High Court, with any necessary modifications, except so far as inconsistent with these Rules.

(2) All building society insolvency proceedings shall be allocated to the multi-track for which CPR Part 29 makes provision, accordingly those provisions of the CPR which provide for allocation questionnaires and track allocation do not apply.

[7.766]
221 Right of attendance

Apply rule 7.53 of the 1986 Rules. In paragraph (1) for "company insolvency proceedings" substitute "building society insolvency proceedings".

[7.767]
222 Restriction on concurrent proceedings and remedies

Where in a building society insolvency, the court makes an order staying any action, execution or legal process against the property of the building society, service of the order may be effected by delivering a sealed copy to the address for service of the claimant or other person having the carriage of the proceedings to be stayed.

[7.768]
223 Security in court

Apply rule 7.58 of the 1986 Rules.

[7.769]
224 Payment into court

Apply rule 7.59 of the 1986 Rules.

[7.770]
225 Further information and disclosure

(1) Apply rule 7.60 of the 1986 Rules.

(2) After paragraph (2) insert—

"(3) Before the passing of a full payment resolution the court shall only grant an order on an application under paragraph (1)(b) if satisfied that granting the order is unlikely to prejudice the achievement of Objective 1.".

[7.771]
226 Office copies of documents

Apply rule 7.61 of the 1986 Rules.

PART 19
PROXIES

[7.772]
227 Definition of "proxy"

(1) Apply rule 8.1 of the 1986 Rules.

(2) In paragraph (2) leave out "company".

(3) In paragraph (4), for "chairman of the meeting" to "official receiver" substitute "chair of the meeting or the building society liquidator".

[7.773]
228 Issue and use of forms

Apply rule 8.2 of the 1986 Rules.

[7.774]
229 Use of proxies at meetings

Apply rule 8.3 of the 1986 Rules. Ignore paragraph (2).

[7.775]
230 Retention of proxies

Apply rule 8.4 of the 1986 Rules.

[7.776]
231 Right of inspection

(1) Apply rule 8.5 of the 1986 Rules.

(2) In paragraph (1)(b), for "a company's members or" substitute "the building society's" and for "company or of its" substitute "building society's".

(3) For paragraph (2) substitute—

"(2) The reference in paragraph (1) to creditors is to those creditors who have proved their debts, but this does not include a person whose proof has been wholly rejected for purposes of voting, dividend or otherwise.".

(4) Ignore paragraph (3)(b).

[7.777]
232 Proxy-holder with financial interest

Apply rule 8.6 of the 1986 Rules.

PART 20
EXAMINATION OF PERSONS CONCERNED IN BUILDING SOCIETY INSOLVENCY

[7.778]
233 Preliminary

(1) The rules in this Part relate to applications to the court for an order under section 236 of the Insolvency Act (inquiry into company's dealings when it is, or is alleged to be, insolvent).

(2) The following definitions apply—
  (a) the person in respect of whom an order is applied for is "the respondent",
  (b) "the applicable section" is section 236 of the Insolvency Act, and
  (c) the building society is "the insolvent".

[7.779]
234 Form and contents of application

Apply rule 9.2 of the 1986 Rules.

[7.780]
235 Order for examination, etc

Apply rule 9.3 of the 1986 Rules.

[7.781]
236 Procedure for examination

Apply rule 9.4 of the 1986 Rules. In paragraph (4) leave out "or 366".

[7.782]
237 Record of examination

Apply rule 9.5 of the 1986 Rules.

[7.783]
238 Costs of proceedings

(1) Apply rule 9.6 of the 1986 Rules.

(2) In paragraph (2)(a) leave out "or 367(1)" and in paragraph (2)(b) leave out "or 367(2)".

(3) Ignore paragraph (3)(b).

(4) Ignore paragraph (5).

PART 21
DECLARATION AND PAYMENT OF DIVIDEND

[7.784]
239 Preliminary

(1) The rules in this Part relate to the declaration and payment of dividends in a building society insolvency.

(2) In this Part—

"creditors" means those creditors of the building society of whom the building society liquidator is aware, or who are identified in the building society's statement of affairs, and

"the insolvent" means the building society.

[7.785]
240 Notice of intended dividend

Apply rule 11.2 of the 1986 Rules. Ignore paragraph (1)(b).

[7.786]
241 Final admission/rejection of proofs

Apply rule 11.3 of the 1986 Rules. Ignore paragraph (4).

[7.787]
242 Postponement or cancellation of dividend

Apply rule 11.4 of the 1986 Rules.

[7.788]
243 Decision to declare dividend

Apply rule 11.5 of the 1986 Rules.

[7.789]
244 Notice of declaration

(1) Apply rule 11.6 of the 1986 Rules.

(2) Ignore paragraph (1)(b).

(3) In paragraph (2), after (b), add—

"(ba) expenses incurred by the building society liquidator in the achievement of Objective 1 under section 99 of the Banking Act.".

[7.790]
245 Notice of no, or no further, dividend

Apply rule 11.7 of the 1986 Rules.

[7.791]
246 Proof altered after payment of dividend

Apply rule 11.8 of the 1986 Rules.

[7.792]
247 Secured creditors

Apply rule 11.9 of the 1986 Rules.

[7.793]
248 Disqualification from dividend

Apply rule 11.10 of the 1986 Rules.

[7.794]
249 Assignment of right to dividend

Apply rule 11.11 of the 1986 Rules.

[7.795]
250 Preferential creditors

Apply rule 11.12 of the 1986 Rules.

[7.796]
251 Debt payable at future time

Apply rule 11.13 of the 1986 Rules. For paragraph (3) substitute—

"(3) In paragraph (2), "relevant date" means the date of the commencement of building society insolvency.".

PART 22
MISCELLANEOUS AND GENERAL

[7.797]
252 Power of Secretary of State or Treasury to regulate certain matters

(1) As provided for in paragraph 27 of Schedule 8 to the Insolvency Act, either the Secretary of State or the Treasury may, subject to the Act and to these Rules, make regulations with respect to any matter provided for in these Rules relating to the carrying out of the functions of a building society liquidator or provisional building society liquidator, including, without prejudice to the generality of the above, provision with respect to the following matters arising in building society insolvency—

(a) the preparation and keeping by building society liquidators and provisional building society liquidators of books, accounts and other records, and their production to such persons as may be authorised or required to inspect them;
(b) the auditing of building society liquidators' accounts;
(c) the manner in which building society liquidators are to act in relation to the building society's books, papers and other records, and the manner of their disposal by the building society liquidator or others;
(d) the supply by the building society liquidator to creditors and contributories and to the liquidation committee of copies of documents relating to the building society insolvency and the affairs of the building society (on payment, in such cases as may be specified in the regulations, of a fee);
(e) the manner in which insolvent estates are to be distributed by the building society liquidator, including provision with respect to unclaimed funds and dividends;
(f) the manner in which monies coming into the hands of the building society liquidator are to be handled and invested and the payment of interest on sums which, in pursuance of regulations made under this sub-paragraph, have been paid into the Insolvency Services Account.

(2) Regulations made under paragraph (1) may—

(a) confer a discretion on the court;
(b) make non-compliance with any of the regulations a criminal offence;
(c) make different provision for different cases, including different provision for different areas; and
(d) contain such incidental, supplemental and transitional provisions as may appear to the Secretary of State or the Treasury as necessary or expedient.

[7.798]
253 Costs, expenses, etc

(1) All fees, costs, charges and other expenses incurred in the course of building society insolvency, except for any money paid by the FSCS to eligible depositors in pursuance of Objective 1, and any expense incurred by the FSCS in this process, are to be regarded as expenses of the building society insolvency.

(2) The costs associated with the prescribed part (within the meaning of section 176A of the Insolvency Act) shall be paid out of that prescribed part.

[7.799]
254 Provable debts

(1) Subject to paragraphs (2) and (3) in a building society insolvency all claims by creditors are provable as debts against the building society, whether they are present or future, certain or contingent, ascertained or sounding only in damages.

(2) Any obligation arising under a confiscation order made under Parts 2, 3 or 4 of the Proceeds of Crime Act 2002 is not provable.

(3) The following are not provable except at a time when all other claims of creditors in the insolvency proceedings (other than any of a kind mentioned in this paragraph) have been paid in full with interest under section 189(2) of the Insolvency Act—

(a) any claim arising by virtue of section 382(1)(a) of the Financial Services and Markets Act 2000, not being a claim arising by virtue of section 382(1)(b) of that Act; or

(b) any claim which by virtue of the Insolvency Act or any enactment is a claim the payment of which in the building society insolvency is to be postponed.

(4) Nothing in this rule prejudices any enactment or rule of law under which a particular kind of debt is not provable, whether on grounds of public policy or otherwise.

[7.800]
255 Notices

(1) Apply rule 12.4 of the 1986 Rules.

(2) Ignore references to the official receiver.

[7.801]
256 Quorum at meeting of creditors or contributories

(1) Apply rule 12.4A of the 1986 Rules.

(2) For paragraph (3) substitute—

"(3) For the purposes of this rule, the reference to the creditor or contributories necessary to constitute a quorum is to those persons present or represented by proxy by any person (including the chair)."

[7.802]
257 Evidence of proceedings at meetings

Apply rule 12.5 of the 1986 Rules.

[7.803]
258 Documents issuing from Secretary of State

Apply rule 12.6 of the 1986 Rules.

[7.804]
259 Insolvency practitioner's security

(1) Apply rule 12.8 of the 1986 Rules.

(2) For paragraph (2) substitute—

"(2) It is the duty of the liquidation committee in a building society insolvency to review from time to time the adequacy of the building society liquidator's security.".

[7.805]
260 Time limits

Apply rule 12.9(1) of the 1986 Rules as regards time limits for anything required or authorised to be done by these Rules.

[7.806]
261 Service by post

Apply rule 12.10 of the 1986 Rules.

[7.807]
262 General provisions as to service

CPR Part 6 (service of documents) applies as regards any matter relating to the service of documents and the giving of notice in building society insolvency proceedings except in cases where a rule makes provision as to the service of a document or the giving of a notice.

[7.808]
263 Service outside the jurisdiction

(1) CPR Part 6 applies as regards any matter relating to the service of documents in Scotland and Northern Ireland except in cases where a rule makes provision as to the service of a document or the giving of a notice.

(2) Where for the purposes of building society insolvency proceedings any process or order of the court, or other document, is required to be served on a person who is not in the United Kingdom—

(a) with regard to the service of documents in relation to which a rule makes provision, the court may order service to be effected within such time, on such person, at such place and in such manner as it thinks fit, and may also require such proof of service as it thinks fit,

(b) with regard to the service of documents otherwise, CPR Rules 6.40(3) to 6.46 apply.

(3) An application under paragraph (2)(a) shall be supported by a witness statement stating—

(a) the grounds on which the application is made, and

(b) in what place or country the person to be served is, or probably may be found.

[7.809]
264 Confidentiality of documents

(1) Apply rule 12.13 of the 1986 Rules.

(2) In paragraph (2) ignore the reference to a creditors' committee.

[7.810]
265 Notices sent simultaneously to the same person

Apply rule 12.14 of the 1986 Rules.

[7.811]
266 Right to copy documents

Apply rule 12.15 of the 1986 Rules.

[7.812]
267 Charge for copy documents

Apply rule 12.15A of the 1986 Rules.

[7.813]
268 Non-receipt of notice of meeting

Apply rule 12.16 of the 1986 Rules.

[7.814]
269 Right to have list of creditors

(1) Where a creditor has the right under these Rules to inspect documents on the court file, the creditor may require the building society liquidator to send them a list of the building society's creditors and the amounts of their respective debts.

(2) Paragraph (1) does not apply if a statement of the building society's affairs has been filed in court or filed with the [appropriate regulator].

(3) The building society liquidator must respond to a request in paragraph (1) but may charge the appropriate fee for doing so.

NOTES

Para (2): words in square brackets substituted by the Financial Services Act 2012 (Consequential Amendments and Transitional Provisions) Order 2013, SI 2013/472, art 3, Sch 2, para 191(1), (5).

[7.815]
270 False claim of status as creditor, etc

Apply rule 12.18 of the 1986 Rules.

[7.816]
271 Execution overtaken by judgement debtor's insolvency

(1) This rule applies where execution has been taken out against property of a judgment debtor, and notice is given to the enforcement officer or other officer charged with the execution under section 184(1) of the Insolvency Act (that a building society insolvency order has been made against the debtor, or that a provisional building society liquidator has been appointed).

(2) The notice shall be in writing and be delivered by personal service at, or sent by recorded delivery to, the office of the enforcement officer or (as the case may be) of the officer charged with the execution.

[7.817]
272 The Gazette

Apply rule 12.20 of the 1986 Rules.

[7.818]
273 Punishment of offences

Apply rule 12.21 of the 1986 Rules.

[7.819]

274 Notice of order under section 176A(5)

Apply rule 12.22 of the 1986 Rules. For references to "the liquidator, administrator or receiver" substitute "building society liquidator".

PART 23
INTERPRETATION

[7.820]

275 Introductory

This Part of the Rules has effect for their interpretation and application; and any definition given in this Part (and in any provision of the 1986 Rules applied by this Part) applies except, and in so far as, the context requires otherwise.

[7.821]

276 "The court"; "the registrar"

(1) Apply rule 13.2 of the 1986 Rules.

(2) Ignore paragraphs (3) and (5).

[7.822]

277 "Give notice", etc

Apply rule 13.3 of the 1986 Rules. In paragraph (3) leave out from "except" to the end of the paragraph.

[7.823]

278 Notice, etc to solicitors

Apply rule 13.4 of the 1986 Rules.

[7.824]

279 Notice to joint building society liquidators

Where two or more persons are acting jointly as the building society liquidator, delivery of a document to one of them is to be treated as delivery to them all.

[7.825]

280 "Insolvent estate"

References to "the insolvent estate" are to the assets of the building society.

[7.826]

281 "Responsible insolvency practitioner", etc

In relation to a building society insolvency, "the responsible insolvency practitioner" means the person acting in the building society insolvency as the building society liquidator or provisional building society liquidator.

[7.827]

282 "The appropriate fee"

"The appropriate fee" means 15 pence per A4 or A5 page, and 30 pence per A3 page.

[7.828]

283 "Debt", "liability"

(1) Apply rule 13.12 of the 1986 Rules.

(2) Ignore paragraph (5).

[7.829]

284 Expressions used generally

(1) Apply rule 13.13 of the 1986 Rules.

(2) In paragraph (1) for "Rules 1.7" to "6.23" substitute "rule 10 of the 2009 Rules".

(3) In paragraph (5), after "Secretary of State" insert "or the Treasury".

(4) In paragraph (7), for "Chapter 20 of Part 4 of these Rules, or Chapter 23 of Part 6" substitute "Part 16 of the 2010 Rules".

(5) Ignore paragraphs (8) to (14).

(6) In paragraph (15), after "section 176A(2)(a)" insert "as applied by section 103 of the Banking Act 2009".

[7.830]

285 The Schedule

The Schedule, which applies relevant schedules to the 1986 Rules to these Rules with modifications, has effect.

SCHEDULE

[7.831]

286 The following Schedules to the 1986 Rules are applied to these Rules—

(a) Schedule 1. Ignore all references to "rule 4.72" and for paragraph (1) substitute—

> **"1.** This Schedule applies where a building society insolvency order (see section 90C of the Building Societies Act 1986) has been made in respect of a building society".

(b) Schedule 5; and

(c) Schedule 6.

NOTES

Note: the Queen's Printer copy of this Schedule contains only one provision, numbered "286".

D
CONTRACTUAL SCHEMES

FINANCIAL SERVICES AND MARKETS ACT 2000

(2000 c 8)

An Act to make provision about the regulation of financial services and markets; to provide for the transfer of certain statutory functions relating to building societies, friendly societies, industrial and provident societies and certain other mutual societies; and for connected purposes

[14 June 2000]

NOTES

Only the section relevant to contractual schemes is reproduced here.

PART XVII
COLLECTIVE INVESTMENT SCHEMES

CHAPTER I INTERPRETATION

[7.832]

[235A Contractual schemes

(1) In this Part "contractual scheme" means—

(a) a co-ownership scheme; or

(b) a partnership scheme.

(2) In this Part "co-ownership scheme" means a collective investment scheme which satisfies the conditions in subsection (3).

(3) The conditions are—

(a) that the arrangements constituting the scheme are contractual;

(b) that they are set out in a deed that is entered into between the operator and a depositary and meets the requirements of subsection (4);

(c) that the scheme does not constitute a body corporate, a partnership or a limited partnership;

(d) that the property subject to the scheme is held by, or to the order of, a depositary; and

(e) that either—

(i) the property is beneficially owned by the participants as tenants in common (or, in Scotland, is the common property of the participants); or

(ii) where the arrangements constituting the scheme provide for such pooling as is mentioned in section 235(3)(a) in relation to separate parts of the property, each part is beneficially owned by the participants in that part as tenants in common (or, in Scotland, is the common property of the participants in that part).

(4) The deed—

(a) must contain a statement that the arrangements are intended to constitute a co-ownership scheme as defined in section 235A of the Financial Services and Markets Act 2000;

(b) must make provision for the issue and redemption of units;

(c) must—

(i) prohibit the transfer of units,

(ii) allow units to be transferred only if specified conditions are met, or

(iii) where the arrangements constituting the scheme provide for such pooling as is mentioned in section 235(3)(a) in relation to separate parts of the property, in relation to each separate part make provision falling within sub-paragraph (i) or (ii);

(d) must authorise the operator—

(i) to acquire, manage and dispose of property subject to the scheme; and

(ii) to enter into contracts which are binding on participants for the purposes of, or in connection with, the acquisition, management or disposal of property subject to the scheme; and

(e) must make provision requiring the operator and depositary to wind up the scheme in specified circumstances.

(5) In this Part "partnership scheme" means a collective investment scheme which satisfies the conditions in subsection (6).

(6) The conditions are—

(a) that the scheme is a limited partnership;

[(aa) that the limited partnership is not designated under section 8(2) of the Limited Partnerships Act 1907 as a private fund limited partnership;]

(b) that the limited partnership—

(i) at any time has only one general partner; and

(ii) on formation has only one limited partner, who is a person nominated by the general partner ("the nominated partner");

(c) that the arrangements constituting the partnership are set out in a deed that is entered into between the general partner and the nominated partner;

(d) that the deed prohibits such pooling as is mentioned in section 235(3)(a) in relation to separate parts of the property; and
(e) that the deed provides that if an authorisation order is made in respect of the limited partnership under section 261D(1)—
(i) the property subject to the scheme is to be held by, or to the order of, a person appointed to be a depositary;
(ii) the limited partners, other than the nominated partner, are to be the participants in the scheme; and
(iii) the partnership is not dissolved on any person ceasing to be a limited partner provided that there remains at least one limited partner.

(7) In this section "general partner", "limited partner" and "limited partnership" have the same meaning as in the Limited Partnerships Act 1907.

(8) In this Part "contractual scheme deed" means—
(a) in relation to a co-ownership scheme, the deed referred to in subsection (3)(b); and
(b) in relation to a partnership scheme, the deed referred to in subsection (6)(c).]

NOTES

Inserted by the Collective Investment in Transferable Securities (Contractual Scheme) Regulations 2013, SI 2013/1388, reg 3(1), (5).

Sub-s (6): para (aa) inserted by the Legislative Reform (Private Fund Limited Partnerships) Order 2017, SI 2017/514, art 3.

COLLECTIVE INVESTMENT IN TRANSFERABLE SECURITIES (CONTRACTUAL SCHEME) REGULATIONS 2013

(SI 2013/1388)

NOTES

Made: 5 June 2013.
Authority: European Communities Act 1972, s 2(2).
Commencement: 6 June 2013.

ARRANGEMENT OF REGULATIONS

PART 1
CITATION, COMMENCEMENT AND INTERPRETATION

1 Citation and commencement .....[7.833]
2 Interpretation .....[7.834]

PART 5
WINDING UP INSOLVENT CONTRACTUAL SCHEMES

17 Co-ownership schemes: winding up by the court .....[7.835]
19 Partnership schemes: liability of the general partner (Scotland) .....[7.836]

SCHEDULES

Schedule 2—Co-ownership Schemes: Application of the Insolvency Act 1986 and the Insolvency (Northern Ireland) Order 1989
Part 1—Interpretation .....[7.837]
Part 2—Application of the 1986 Act and the 1989 Order with Modifications .....[7.838]
Part 3—Table of Applied Provisions of the 1986 Act .....[7.839]
Part 4—Table of Applied Provisions of the 1989 Order .....[7.840]
Schedule 3—Co-ownership Schemes: Application of the Insolvency Rules 1986
Part 1—Application of Rules with Modifications .....[7.841]
Part 2—Table of Specific Modifications of the Insolvency Rules 1986 .....[7.842]
Schedule 4—Co-ownership Schemes: Application of the Insolvency (Scotland) Rules 1986
Part 1—Application of Rules with Modifications .....[7.843]
Part 2—Table of Specific Modifications of the Insolvency (Scotland) Rules 1986 .....[7.844]
Schedule 5—Co-ownership Schemes: Application of the Insolvency Rules (Northern Ireland) 1991
Part 1—Application of Rules with Modifications .....[7.845]
Part 2—Table of Specific Modifications of the Insolvency Rules (Northern Ireland) 1991 .....[7.846]

PART 1
CITATION, COMMENCEMENT AND INTERPRETATION

[7.833]
1 Citation and commencement

These Regulations may be cited as the Collective Investment in Transferable Securities (Contractual Scheme) Regulations 2013, and come into force on the day after the day on which they are made.

[7.834]

2 Interpretation

In these Regulations—

"the 1986 Act" means the Insolvency Act 1986;

"the 1989 Order" means the Insolvency (Northern Ireland) Order 1989;

"authorised contract" has the meaning given in section 261M(1) of FSMA;

"authorised contractual scheme" has the meaning given in section 237(3) of FSMA;

"depositary" has the meaning given in section 237(2) of FSMA;

"the FCA" means the Financial Conduct Authority;

"FSMA" means the Financial Services and Markets Act 2000;

"operator" has the meaning given in section 237(2) of FSMA;

"participant" has the meaning given in section 235(2) of FSMA;

"partnership scheme" has the meaning given in section 235A(5) of FSMA;

"stand-alone co-ownership scheme" has the meaning given in section 237(8) of FSMA;

"sub-scheme" has the meaning given in section 237(7) of FSMA;

"umbrella co-ownership scheme" has the meaning given in section 237(5) of FSMA; and

"units" has the meaning given in section 237(2) of FSMA.

3–16 *((Pts 2–4) Reg 3 inserts the Financial Services and Markets Acts 2000, s 235A at* **[7.832]** *and amends provisions of the 2000 Act which are outside the scope of this work; regs 4–16 outside the scope of this work.)*

PART 5
WINDING UP INSOLVENT CONTRACTUAL SCHEMES

[7.835]

17 Co-ownership schemes: winding up by the court

(1) In this regulation and in Schedules 2 to 5—

(a) each of the following is a "relevant scheme"—

(i) a stand-alone co-ownership scheme;

(ii) a sub-scheme of an umbrella co-ownership scheme;

(b) in relation to a relevant scheme—

(i) a reference to a creditor is a reference to a person to whom a sum is or may become payable in respect of a debt of the relevant scheme;

(ii) a reference to a debt is a reference to any debt or obligation incurred for the purposes of, or in connection with, the acquisition, management or disposal of property subject to the relevant scheme;

(iii) a reference to a liability is a reference to any liability (including any contingent or prospective liability) of the participants in the relevant scheme for a debt of the relevant scheme; and

(c) in relation to a sub-scheme of an umbrella co-ownership scheme, a reference to the operator or the depositary is a reference to the operator or the depositary of the umbrella co-ownership scheme in relation to which that sub-scheme forms a separate pool of the contributions of the participants and the profits and income out of which payments are made to them.

(2) Subject to the provisions of this regulation, a relevant scheme may be wound up under the 1986 Act or the 1989 Order as if it were an unregistered company (within the meaning of the 1986 Act or the 1989 Order as the case may be).

(3) The High Court has jurisdiction to wind up a relevant scheme if the depositary of the relevant scheme has a place of business situated in England and Wales or Northern Ireland.

(4) The Court of Session has jurisdiction to wind up a relevant scheme if the depositary of the relevant scheme has a place of business situated in Scotland.

(5) If the depositary of a relevant scheme has a place of business situated in Northern Ireland, the relevant scheme may not be wound up under Part 5 of the 1986 Act (winding up of unregistered companies) unless the depositary has a place of business situated in England and Wales or Scotland, or in both England and Wales and Scotland.

(6) If the depositary of a relevant scheme has a place of business situated in England and Wales or Scotland, the relevant scheme may not be wound up under Part 6 of the 1989 Order (winding up of unregistered companies) unless the depositary has a place of business situated in Northern Ireland.

(7) If the depositary of a relevant scheme has a place of business situated in both England and Wales and Scotland—

(a) the High Court has jurisdiction to wind up the relevant scheme if the winding up proceedings are instituted in England and Wales; and

(b) the Court of Session has jurisdiction to wind up the relevant scheme if the winding up proceedings are instituted in Scotland.

(8) Schedules 2 to 5 (which make provision about the application in relation to the winding up of relevant schemes of provisions in the 1986 Act, the 1989 Order, the Insolvency Rules 1986, the Insolvency (Scotland) Rules 1986 and the Insolvency Rules (Northern Ireland) 1991) have effect.

(9) An application to the High Court or the Court of Session for the winding up of a relevant scheme is to be made by petition presented—

(a) by the operator or any creditor of the relevant scheme;

(b) by the FCA;

(c) in a case falling within section 124A of the 1986 Act (petition for winding up on grounds of public interest), as modified by Schedule 2, by the Secretary of State; or

(d) in a case falling within Article 104A of the 1989 Order (petition for winding up on grounds of public interest), as modified by Schedule 2, by the Department of Enterprise, Trade and Investment.

(10) The operator of a relevant scheme, upon presenting a petition for the winding up of the relevant scheme or being served with such a petition, must immediately—

(a) cease entering into contracts which are binding on the participants;

(b) cease making payments under authorised contracts; and

(c) except where the operator has already done so pursuant to a direction given by the FCA, cease the issue and redemption of units under the relevant scheme.

(11) Where the court makes an order dismissing a petition presented for the winding up of a relevant scheme, the prohibitions imposed by paragraph (10) cease to apply in relation to the scheme upon the making of the order.

(12) Where, upon hearing a petition presented for the winding up of a relevant scheme, the court makes a winding-up order, the operator ceases to have the authority which was given in relation to the relevant scheme in accordance with section 235A(4)(d) of FSMA.

(13) A relevant scheme is not an unincorporated body for the purposes of section 6(1) of the Bankruptcy (Scotland) Act 1985 (sequestration of other estates).

(14) Section 370 of FSMA (liquidator's duty to report to FCA and PRA) has effect with the following modifications in relation to a relevant scheme which is being wound up on a petition presented by any person—

(a) in paragraph (a) of subsection (1) and paragraph (a) of subsection (2) the reference to a body is to be read as a reference to the relevant scheme; and

(b) in paragraph (b) of subsection (1) and paragraph (b) of subsection (2) the reference to the body is to be read as a reference to the operator or the depositary of the relevant scheme.

NOTES

Note that the Insolvency Rules 1986, SI 1986/1925 are revoked and replaced (as from 6 April 2017 and subject to transitional provisions) by the Insolvency (England and Wales) Rules 2016, SI 2016/1024 at **[6.2]**. See further, the Small Business, Enterprise and Employment Act 2015 (Consequential Amendments, Savings and Transitional Provisions) Regulations 2018, SI 2018/208. Regulation 25(1)(c) of the 2018 Regulations provides that, despite the revocation of the Insolvency Rules 1986, those Rules apply as they applied before they were revoked for the purposes of proceedings instituted in England and Wales for the winding up of a relevant scheme (within the meaning given in sub-para (1)(a) above).

18 (*Outside the scope of this work.*)

[7.836]

19 Partnership schemes: liability of the general partner (Scotland)

(1) In this regulation—

"the Act" means the Bankruptcy (Scotland) Act 1985;

"authorisation order" means an order made under section 261D(1) of FSMA;

"authorised partnership" means a partnership scheme in respect of which an authorisation order has been made (even if revoked); and

"relevant debts and obligations", in relation to an authorised partnership, means debts and obligations of the partnership which are incurred while the authorisation order made in respect of the partnership is in force.

(2) The Act has effect with the following modifications in its application to an authorised partnership—

(a) in section 6 (sequestration of other estates), in subsection (4), paragraph (b) is to be read as if after sub-paragraph (i) there were inserted—

"(ia) the Financial Conduct Authority;";

(b) the following provisions are to be read as if after the words "presented by a creditor" there were inserted ", the Financial Conduct Authority"—

(i) in section 2 (appointment and functions of the trustee in the sequestration), subsections (5) and (7)(a);

(ii) in section 12 (when sequestration is awarded), subsections (2), (3) and (4)(b);

(iii) in section 15 (further provisions relating to award of sequestration), subsection (5);

(iv) in section 70 (supplies by utilities), subsection (1)(b); and

(c) in section 12, in subsection (3)(d), after "a creditor" insert "or the Financial Conduct Authority".

(3) Where sequestration of the estate of an authorised partnership is awarded under section 12(1) or (3) of the Act, the general partner of the partnership has no personal liability for relevant debts and obligations.

(4) Paragraph (3) is without prejudice to the power of the court to make an order compelling the general partner to repay, restore or account for any money or property, or to contribute to the assets of the partnership, if the general partner has misapplied or retained, or become accountable for, any money or other property of the partnership, or been guilty of any misfeasance or breach of any fiduciary or other duty in relation to the partnership.

20–25 ((*Pts 6–8) outside the scope of this work.*)

SCHEDULE 1

(Sch 1 sets out an amendment, mentioned in reg 13, to the Limited Partnerships (Forms) Rules 2009, SI 2009/2160 (outside the scope of this work).)

SCHEDULE 2
CO-OWNERSHIP SCHEMES: APPLICATION OF THE INSOLVENCY ACT 1986 AND THE INSOLVENCY (NORTHERN IRELAND) ORDER 1989

Regulation 17(8)

PART 1
INTERPRETATION

[7.837]

1 In this Schedule and in Schedules 3, 4 and 5—

(a) unless otherwise specified, a reference to a section is a reference to a section of the 1986 Act;
(b) a reference to an Article is a reference to an Article of the 1989 Order; and
(c) a reference to a participant, in relation to a relevant scheme, is a reference to the participant as a holder of units in that scheme (and not in any other capacity).

2 Unless the context otherwise requires, in this Schedule and in Schedules 3, 4 and 5—

(a) a reference to an authorised contract is a reference to an authorised contract entered into by the operator;
(b) a reference to the depositary is a reference to the depositary of a relevant scheme—
  (i) in relation to which a petition has been presented under regulation 17(9); or
  (ii) which is being wound up by the court following the presentation of such a petition;
(c) a reference to the operator is a reference to the operator of such a scheme; and
(d) a reference to the participants is a reference to the participants in such a scheme.

PART 2
APPLICATION OF THE 1986 ACT AND THE 1989 ORDER WITH MODIFICATIONS

[7.838]

3 In relation to the winding up of a relevant scheme under the 1986 Act, the provisions set out in the Table in Part 3 of this Schedule apply with—

(a) the general modifications set out in paragraph 5;
[(aa) the modifications specified in paragraph 6 in relation to provision about creditors' meetings and creditors' notices;]
(b) any other modification specified in the Table; and
(c) any other necessary modification.

4 In relation to the winding up of a relevant scheme under the 1989 Order, the provisions set out in the Table in Part 4 of this Schedule apply with—

(a) the general modifications set out in paragraph 5;
(b) any other modification specified in the Table; and
(c) any other necessary modification.

5 Unless the context otherwise requires and subject to any modification specified in the Table in Part 3 or 4 of this Schedule which has a contrary effect, the general modifications are that—

(a) a reference to a company includes a reference to a relevant scheme;
(b) a reference to a voluntary winding up or a resolution for voluntary winding up of a company is to be ignored;
(c) a reference to a creditor of a company is to be read as a reference to a creditor of a relevant scheme;
(d) a reference to a contributory or to a meeting of contributories is to be ignored;
(e) a reference to the making or recovery of a call is to be ignored;
(f) a reference to a member of a company or to a register or meeting of members is to be ignored;
(g) a reference to the property, assets, estate or effects of a company is to be read as a reference to the property subject to a relevant scheme;
(h) a reference to any books, papers or records belonging to the company is to be read as a reference to books, papers or records affecting or relating to the affairs of, or the property subject to, the relevant scheme;
(i) a reference to an action or proceeding against a company is to be read as a reference to an action or a proceeding brought against the operator for the resolution of any matter relating to a relevant scheme;
(j) a reference to a debt, obligation or liability of a company is to be read as a reference to a debt or liability of a relevant scheme;
(k) a reference to the registrar of companies or to the Accountant in Bankruptcy or to the registrar of companies and the Accountant in Bankruptcy is to be read as a reference to the FCA;
(l) a reference to an officer (other than a past officer) of the company is to be read as a reference to—
  (i) a director of the operator or of the depositary; or
  (ii) a person employed by the operator or by the depositary; and

(m) a reference to a past officer of the company is to be read as a reference to—
 (i) a previous director of the operator or of the depositary;
 (ii) someone who is, or was previously, a director of a person who has been replaced as the operator or the depositary, and was a director when that person was the operator or the depositary;
 (iii) a person who was previously employed by the operator or by the depositary; or
 (iv) someone who is, or was previously, employed by a person who has been replaced as the operator or the depositary, and was so employed when that person was the operator or the depositary.

[6 The modifications relating to provision about creditors' meetings and creditors' notices are that—
 (a) sections 136 to 139, 141, 142, 146, 160, 168, 172, 174, 195, 208 and 246A of the 1986 Act have effect without the amendments of those sections made by Part 1 of Schedule 9 to the Small Business, Enterprise and Employment Act 2015 (further amendments relating to the abolition of requirements to hold meetings; opted-out creditors: company insolvency); and
 (b) section 194 applies as it applied before its repeal by paragraph 46 of that Schedule.]

NOTES

In para 3, sub-para (aa) inserted, and para 6 added, by the Small Business, Enterprise and Employment Act 2015 (Consequential Amendments, Savings and Transitional Provisions) Regulations 2018, SI 2018/208, reg 14.

PART 3
TABLE OF APPLIED PROVISIONS OF THE 1986 ACT

[7.839]

Provision of the 1986 Act	*Modification*
Part 4 (winding up of companies registered under the Companies Acts)	
Chapter 6 (winding up by the court)	
Section 121 (power to remit winding up to Lord Ordinary)	
Section 124A (petition for winding-up on grounds of public interest)	
Section 125 (powers of court on hearing of petition)	This section is to be read as if subsection (2) were omitted.
Section 126 (power to stay or restrain proceedings against company)	Subsection (1) is to be read as if for the words "the company, or any creditor" there were substituted "the Financial Conduct Authority, the operator or any creditor of the relevant scheme".
Section 127 (avoidance of property dispositions, etc)	In subsection (1), the reference to any transfer of shares or alteration in the status of the company's members is to be read as a reference to any issue, transfer or redemption of units in the relevant scheme.
Section 128 (avoidance of attachments, etc)	This section is to be read as if for subsections (1) and (2) there were substituted— "Where a relevant scheme is being wound up by the court, any attachment, sequestration, distress or execution put in force against the property subject to the relevant scheme after the commencement of the winding up is void.".
Section 129 (commencement of winding up by the court)	
Section 130 (consequences of winding-up order)	In subsection (1) the first reference to the company is to be read as a reference to the operator. This section is to be read as if subsection (4) were omitted.
Section 131 (company's statement of affairs)	In subsection (3)(a) the reference to officers of the company is to be read as a reference to the operator and the depositary. Subsection (3) is to be read as if paragraphs (c) and (d) were omitted.
Section 132 (investigation by official receiver)	
Section 133 (public examination of officers)	Subsection (1) is to be read as if for paragraph (b) there were substituted— "(b) has acted as liquidator of the relevant scheme;". In subsection (1) the reference to the dissolution of the company is to be read as a reference to the completion of winding up of the relevant scheme.
Section 134 (enforcement of section 133)	

Section 135 (appointment and powers of provisional liquidator)	
Section 136 (functions of official receiver in relation to office of liquidator)	Subsection (1) is to be read as if the words ", subject to section 140 below," were omitted.
Section 137 (appointment by Secretary of State)	
Section 138 (appointment of liquidator in Scotland)	This section is to be read as if subsection (4) were omitted.
Section 139 (choice of liquidator at meetings of creditors and contributories)	This section is to be read as if for subsections (3) and (4) there were substituted— "(3) The liquidator shall be the person (if any) nominated by the creditors.".
Section 141 (liquidation committee (England and Wales))	This section is to be read as if subsection (3) were omitted.
Section 142 (liquidation committee (Scotland))	This section is to be read as if— (a) in subsection (1) for the words from "separate meetings" to "(as the case may be)" there were substituted "a meeting of creditors has been summoned for the purpose of choosing a person to be liquidator,"; (b) in subsection (3) the words ", if appointed by the court otherwise than under section 139(4)(a)," were omitted; and (c) subsection (4) were omitted.
Section 143 (general functions in winding up by the court)	
Section 144 (custody of company's property)	In subsection (1) the reference to all the property and things in action to which the company is or appears to be entitled is to be read as a reference to all property which is or appears to be subject to the relevant scheme and all things in action relating to that property.
Section 145 (vesting of company property in liquidator)	Subsection (1) is to be read as if the words "or held by trustees on its behalf" were omitted.
Section 146 (duty to summon final meeting)	
Section 147 (power to stay or sist winding up)	Subsection (2) is to be read as if after the words "the official receiver" there were inserted "or the liquidator". In subsection (3) the first reference to the company is to be read as a reference to the operator.
Section 153 (power to exclude creditors not proving in time)	
Section 155 (inspection of books by creditors, etc)	In subsection (1) the reference to books and papers in the company's possession is to be read as a reference to such books and papers affecting or relating to the affairs of, or the property subject to, the relevant scheme as are in the possession of the operator or the depositary.
Section 156 (payment of expenses of winding up)	
Section 157 (attendance at company meetings (Scotland))	In this section the reference to the winding up by the court of a company registered in Scotland is to be read as a reference to the winding up of a relevant scheme by the Court of Session.
Section 159 (powers of court to be cumulative)	In this section the references to a debtor of the company are to be read as references to a person by whom a debt is, or may become, payable to the operator in respect of any liability (including any contingent or prospective liability) incurred under an authorised contract.
Section 160 (delegation of powers to liquidator (England and Wales))	
Section 162 (appeals from orders in Scotland)	
Chapter 7 (liquidators)	

Section 163 (style and title of liquidators)	
Section 164 (corrupt inducement affecting appointment)	
Section 167 (winding up by the court)	Subsection (2)(a) is to be read as if for the words "a person who is connected with the company (within the meaning of section 249 in Part VII)" there were substituted "the operator or the depositary of the relevant scheme or a person who is an associate of the operator or depositary".
Section 168 (supplementary powers (England and Wales))	
Section 169 (supplementary powers (Scotland))	. . .
Section 170 (enforcement of liquidator's duty to make returns, etc)	
Section 172 (removal, etc (winding up by the court))	
Section 174 (release (winding up by the court))	
Chapter 8 (provisions of general application in winding up)	
Section 178 (power to disclaim onerous property)	In subsection (4) each reference to the company is to be read as a reference to the participants and the depositary.
Section 179 (disclaimer of leaseholds)	In subsection (1) the reference to a person claiming under the company as underlessee or mortgagee is to be read as a reference to a person claiming as underlessee or mortgagee under the leasehold title which is held by the depositary (or a person nominated by the depositary to hold the leasehold title).
Section 180 (land subject to rentcharge)	
Section 181 (powers of court (general))	
Section 182 (powers of court (leaseholds))	In this section— (a) a reference to a person claiming under the company as underlessee or mortgagee is to be read as a reference to a person claiming as underlessee or mortgagee under the leasehold title which is held by the depositary (or a person nominated by the depositary to hold the leasehold title); and (b) a reference to the company, in relation to any reference to liabilities, obligations, estates, incumbrances or interests, is to be read as a reference to the lessee.
Section 186 (rescission of contracts by the court)	In subsection (1) the references to a contract made with the company are to be read as references to an authorised contract.
Section 188 (notification that company is in liquidation)	This section is to be read as if for subsections (1) and (2) there were substituted— "(1) When a relevant scheme is being wound up by the court— (a) every business letter (whether in hard copy, electronic or any other form) issued by the operator, the depositary or a liquidator of the relevant scheme, and (b) any website which relates to the relevant scheme and for which the operator or the depositary is responsible, must contain a statement that the relevant scheme is being wound up. (2) If default is made in complying with this section, any of the following persons who knowingly and wilfully authorises or permits the default, namely, the operator, the depositary and any liquidator of the relevant scheme, is liable to a fine.".
Section 189 (interest on debts)	
Section 190 (documents exempt from stamp duty)	In subsection (2) the reference to a company registered in England and Wales is to be read as a reference to a relevant scheme being wound up by the High Court. In subsection (3) the reference to a company registered in Scotland is to be read as a reference to a relevant scheme being wound up by the Court of Session.
Section 192 (information as to pending liquidations)	

Section 194 (resolutions passed at adjourned meetings)	
Section 195 (meetings to ascertain wishes of creditors or contributories)	
Section 196 (judicial notice of court documents)	
Section 197 (commission for receiving evidence)	
Section 198 (court order for examination of persons in Scotland)	
Section 199 (costs of application for leave to proceed (Scottish companies))	This section is to be read as if— (a) for the words from "a company" to "Scotland" there were substituted "the operator of a relevant scheme which is being wound up in Scotland (for the resolution of any matter relating to that scheme)"; and (b) for the words "the company" there were substituted "the operator".
Section 200 (affidavits etc in United Kingdom and overseas)	
Chapter 10 (malpractice before and during liquidation; penalisation of companies and company officers; investigations and prosecutions)	
Section 206 (fraud, etc in anticipation of winding up)	In subsection (1)(a) the reference to a debt due to the company is to be read as a reference to a debt which is, or may become, payable to the operator in respect of any liability (including any contingent or prospective liability) incurred under an authorised contract. This section is to be read as if subsection (3) were omitted.
Section 207 (transactions in fraud of creditors)	In subsection (1)(b) the reference to any unsatisfied judgment or order for the payment of money obtained against the company is to be read as a reference to any unsatisfied judgment or order for the payment of money to a creditor of the relevant scheme.
Section 208 (misconduct in course of winding up)	In subsection (1)(a) the reference to the disposal by the company of any part of the company's property is to be read as a reference to the disposal by the operator of part of the property subject to the relevant scheme. This section is to be read as if subsection (3) were omitted.
Section 209 (falsification of company's books)	In subsection (1) the reference to any register, book of account or document belonging to the company is to be read as a reference to any register, book of account or document affecting or relating to the affairs of, or the property subject to, the relevant scheme.
Section 210 (material omissions from statement relating to company's affairs)	This section is to be read as if subsection (3) were omitted.
Section 211 (false representations to creditors)	This section is to be read as if subsection (2) were omitted.
Section 212 (summary remedy against delinquent directors, liquidators, etc)	Subsection (1)(a) is to be read as if the reference to an officer of the company included a reference to the operator and the depositary.
Section 213 (fraudulent trading)	
Section 214 (wrongful trading)	In subsections (1) and (2) a reference to a director of a company is to be read as a reference to the operator or depositary of a relevant scheme. This section is to be read as if— (a) after subsection (2) there were inserted— "(2A) The condition specified in subsection (2)(b) is taken to be satisfied in relation to the operator or depositary of a relevant scheme if, at some time before the commencement of the winding up, a director or employee of the operator or depositary knew or ought to have concluded that there was no reasonable prospect that the relevant scheme would avoid going into insolvent liquidation."; and (b) subsection (7) were omitted.
	In subsections (4) and (5) a reference to a director of a company is to be read as a reference to the operator or depositary of a relevant scheme or a director or employee of the operator or depositary.

Part 7D Special Insolvency Regimes

Section 215 (proceedings under sections 213, 214)	
Section 218 (prosecution of delinquent officers and members of company)	
Section 219 (obligations arising under section 218)	In subsection (3) the reference to every agent of the company is to be read as a reference to the operator and the depositary and every person who, at the request of the operator or the depositary, has provided the services of banker, solicitor or auditor or professional services of any other description in relation to the relevant scheme.
Part 5 (winding up of unregistered companies)	
Section 220 (meaning of "unregistered company")	
Section 221 (winding up of unregistered companies)	This section is to be read as if— (a) subsections (2), (3) and (7) were omitted; (b) in subsection (4) the words ", except in accordance with the EC Regulation" were omitted; and (c) in subsection (5)— (i) paragraph (a) were omitted; and (ii) for paragraph (b) there were substituted— "(b) if the operator of a relevant scheme is unable to pay the debts of that scheme out of the property subject to it.".
Section 222 (inability to pay debts: unpaid creditor for £750 or more)	In subsection (1)(a) and (b) each reference to the company is to be read as a reference to the operator.
Section 224 (inability to pay debts: other cases)	In subsection (1)(a) the reference to execution or other process issued in favour of a creditor against the company or any person authorised to be sued as nominal defendant on its behalf is to be read as a reference to execution or other process issued in favour of a creditor of the relevant scheme against the property subject to that scheme.
Section 229 (provisions of this Part to be cumulative)	
Part 6 (miscellaneous provisions applying to companies which are insolvent or in liquidation)	
Section 230 (holders of office to be qualified insolvency practitioners)	
Section 231 (appointment to office of two or more persons)	
Section 232 (validity of office-holder's acts)	
Section 234 (getting in the company's property)	In subsection (2) the reference to any property, books, papers or records to which the company appears to be entitled is to be read as a reference to any property that appears to be property subject to the relevant scheme, and to any books, papers or records that appear to affect or relate to that property or to the affairs of the relevant scheme.
Section 235 (duty to co-operate with office-holder)	Subsection (3) is to be read as if— (a) in paragraph (a) the reference to officers of the company included a reference to the operator and the depositary; and (b) paragraphs (c) and (d) were omitted.
Section 236 (inquiry into company's dealings, etc)	In subsection (2)(b) the reference to any person supposed to be indebted to the company is to be read as a reference to a person by whom, it is supposed, a debt is, or may become, payable to the operator in respect of any liability (including any contingent or prospective liability) incurred under an authorised contract. In subsection (3) the reference to dealings with the company is to be read as a reference to dealings with any matter affecting or relating to the affairs of, or the property subject to, the relevant scheme.
Section 237 (court's enforcement powers under s 236)	In subsection (2) the reference to any person who is indebted to the company is to be read as a reference to a person by whom a debt is, or may become, payable to the operator in respect of any liability (including any contingent or prospective liability) incurred under an authorised contract.

Section 238 (transactions at an undervalue (England and Wales))	In subsections (2) and (3) the reference to the company is to be read as a reference to the operator or the depositary. In subsection (4)— (a) in paragraphs (a) and (b) the second reference to the company is to be read as a reference to the participants in a relevant scheme; and (b) each other reference to a company is to be read as a reference to the operator or depositary of the relevant scheme. Subsection (5) is to be read as if for paragraph (a) there were substituted— "(a) that the operator or the depositary, in entering into the transaction, did so in good faith and for the purposes of carrying on the business of the relevant scheme, and".
Section 239 (preferences (England and Wales))	In subsections (2) and (3) the reference to the company is to be read as a reference to the operator or the depositary. Subsection (4) is to be read as if for the words from "a company" to the end there were substituted— "the operator or depositary of a relevant scheme gives a preference to a person if— (a) that person is one of the creditors of the relevant scheme or a surety or guarantor for any of the debts or liabilities of the relevant scheme, and (b) the operator or depositary does anything or suffers anything to be done which (in either case) has the effect of putting that person into a position which, in the event of the relevant scheme going into insolvent liquidation, will be better than the position that person would have been in if that thing had not been done.". In subsection (5) the reference to the company which gave the preference is to be read as a reference to the operator or the depositary in giving the preference. In subsection (6)— (a) the first reference to a company is to be read as a reference to the operator or depositary of a relevant scheme; and (b) the reference to a person connected with the company is to be read as a reference to a person who is an associate (within the meaning of section 435) of the operator or depositary of the relevant scheme.
Section 240 ("relevant time" under sections 238, 239)	In subsections (1) and (2)— (a) a reference to a company, except the second reference in subsection (2), is to be read as a reference to the operator or depositary of a relevant scheme; and (b) the reference to a person who is connected with the company is to be read as a reference to a person who is an associate (within the meaning of section 435) of the operator or depositary of the relevant scheme. In subsection (2) the reference to the inability of the company to pay its debts within the meaning of section 123 is to be read as a reference to the inability of the operator of a relevant scheme to pay the debts of that scheme within the meaning of section 222 or 224 (as modified by this Schedule).
Section 241 (orders under sections 238, 239)	In this section a reference to a company is to be read as a reference to the operator or the depositary, except— (a) in subsection (1)(a), where the reference to the company is to be read as a reference to the liquidator of the relevant scheme; (b) in subsection (1)(c), where the reference to security given by the company is to be read as a reference to security over any property subject to the relevant scheme; (c) in subsection (1)(g), where the first reference to the company is to be read as a reference to the liquidator of the relevant scheme; (d) in subsection (2), with respect to the reference to a creditor of the company; and (e) in subsection (3C).
Section 242 (gratuitous alienations (Scotland))	In subsection (1)(a) the reference to an alienation by the company is to be read as a reference to an alienation by the operator or the depositary. In subsection (2)(a) the reference to any claim or right of the company is to be read as a reference to any claim that may be made or any right that may be exercised by the operator for the benefit of the participants. In subsections (3)(a) and (4)(c) the reference to an associate of the company is to be read as a reference to an associate (within the meaning of section 435) of the operator or the depositary. In subsection (7) the reference to an alienation of a company is to be read as a reference to an alienation by the operator or the depositary.
Section 243 (unfair preferences (Scotland))	In subsection (1) a reference to a transaction entered into by a company is to be read as a reference to a transaction entered into by the operator or the depositary. In subsection (2)(d) the reference to a company is to be read as a reference to the operator or the depositary.
Section 246 (unenforceability of liens on books, etc)	
[Section 246ZD (power to assign certain causes of action)]	

Section 246A (remote attendance at meetings)	
Section 246B (use of websites)	
Part 7 (interpretation for first group of Parts)	
Section 247 ("insolvency" and "go into liquidation")	This section is to be read as if— (a) in subsection (2), for the words from "it passes a resolution" to the end there were substituted "an order for its winding up is made by the court"; and (b) subsection (3) were omitted.
Section 248 ("secured creditor" etc)	
Section 249 ("connected" with a company)	This section is to be read as if the words from ", a person" to "and" were omitted.
Section 251 (expressions used generally)	This section is to be read as if the existing provision were subsection (1) and after that provision there were inserted— "(2) In Parts 4, 5 and 6— (a) a reference to the depositary of a relevant scheme is a reference to the depositary (within the meaning given in section 237(2) of the Financial Services and Markets Act 2000 ("FSMA")) of that scheme; (b) a reference to the operator of a relevant scheme is a reference to the operator (within the meaning given in section 237(2) of FSMA) of that scheme; (c) a reference to the participants in a relevant scheme is a reference to the participants (within the meaning given in section 235(2) of FSMA) in that scheme; (d) a reference to— (i) a relevant scheme, (ii) a creditor or a debt of a relevant scheme, or (iii) the operator or the depositary in relation to a relevant scheme which is a sub-scheme of an umbrella co-ownership scheme, is to be construed in accordance with regulation 17(1) of the Collective Investment in Transferable Securities (Contractual Scheme) Regulations 2013.".
Part 13 (insolvency practitioners and their qualification)	
Section 388 (meaning of "act as insolvency practitioner")	In subsection (4), the definition of "company" is to be read as if the reference to a company that may be wound up under Part 5 of the 1986 Act included a reference to a relevant scheme.
Section 389 (acting without qualification an offence)	
[Section 390 (persons not qualified to act as insolvency practitioners)	This section is to be read as if for subsection (2) there were substituted— "(2) A person is not qualified to act at any time as an insolvency practitioner in relation to a relevant scheme [unless at that time the person is fully authorised to act as an insolvency practitioner or partially authorised to act as an insolvency practitioner only in relation to companies]."]
[Section 390A (authorisation of insolvency practitioners) Sections 391 to 391T (regulation of insolvency practitioners)	In these sections a reference to a company, except in a reference to creditors of a company, is to be read without modification by this Schedule.]
Part 17 (miscellaneous and general)	
Sections 430 (provision introducing Schedule of punishments) Section 431 (summary proceedings) Section 432 (offences by bodies corporate)	These sections are to be read as if a reference to an offence under the 1986 Act or a provision of that Act, in so far as it is a reference to an offence under a provision of that Act that is applied by these Regulations, is to be read as a reference to the offence under that provision as so applied.
Part 17A (supplementary provisions)	
Section 434C (legal professional privilege)	
Schedule 4 (powers of liquidator in a winding up)	

Schedule 4 (powers of liquidator in a winding up)	Schedule 4 is to be read as if— (a) paragraphs 8 and 11 were omitted; (b) the power in paragraph 4 included a power to bring or defend any action or other legal proceeding which would otherwise be brought or defended by the operator on behalf of the participants; (c) the power in paragraph 7 included a power to do all acts and execute all deeds, receipts and other documents which would otherwise be done or executed by the operator on behalf of the participants; and (d) the power in paragraph 9 included a power to draw, accept, make and indorse any bill of exchange or promissory note with the same effect as if the bill or note had been drawn, accepted, made or indorsed by the operator in the course of the business of the relevant scheme. (e) Paragraph 5 is to be read as subject to the requirements in regulation 17(10) to cease making payments under authorised contracts and to cease the issue and redemption of units.
Schedule 10 (punishment of offences under the 1986 Act)	
Schedule 10 (punishment of offences under the 1986 Act)	Schedule 10 is to be read as if a reference to a provision which is applied by these Regulations were a reference to that provision as so applied.

NOTES

Words omitted from the entry relating to s 169 revoked, and entry relating to s 246ZD inserted, by the Deregulation Act 2015, the Small Business, Enterprise and Employment Act 2015 and the Insolvency (Amendment) Act (Northern Ireland) 2016 (Consequential Amendments and Transitional Provisions) Regulations 2017, SI 2017/400, reg 11(1), (2)(a), (b).

Entry relating to s 390 inserted by the Deregulation Act 2015 (Insolvency) (Consequential Amendments and Transitional and Savings Provisions) Order 2015, SI 2015/1641, art 5, Sch 2, para 2; words in square brackets substituted by SI 2017/400, reg 11(1), (2)(c).

Entry relating to ss 390A–391T inserted by the Small Business, Enterprise and Employment Act 2015 (Consequential Amendments) (Insolvency and Company Directors Disqualification) Regulations 2015, SI 2015/1651, reg 6; subsequently substituted by SI 2017/400, reg 11(1), (2)(d).

PART 4
TABLE OF APPLIED PROVISIONS OF THE 1989 ORDER

[7.840]

Provision of the 1989 Order	*Modification*
Part 1 (Introductory)	
Article 2 (general interpretation)	
Article 3 ("act as insolvency practitioner")	In paragraph (4), the definition of "company" is to be read as if the reference to a company that may be wound up under Part 6 of the 1989 Order included a reference to a relevant scheme.
Article 4 ("associate")	

Article 5 (interpretation of Parts 2 to 7 of the 1989 Order)	This Article is to be read as if— (a) the definition of "the registrar" were omitted; and (b) after paragraph (1) there were inserted— "(2) In Parts 5, 6 and 7— (a) a reference to the depositary of a relevant scheme is a reference to the depositary (within the meaning given in section 237(2) of the Financial Services and Markets Act 2000 ("FSMA")) of that scheme; (b) a reference to the operator of a relevant scheme is a reference to the operator (within the meaning given in section 237(2) of FSMA) of that scheme; (c) a reference to the participants in a relevant scheme is a reference to the participants (within the meaning given in section 235(2) of FSMA) in that scheme; (d) a reference to the registrar is to be read as a reference to the Financial Conduct Authority; and (e) a reference to— (i) a relevant scheme, (ii) a creditor or a debt of a relevant scheme, or (iii) the operator or the depositary in relation to a relevant scheme which is a sub-scheme of an umbrella co-ownership scheme, is to be construed in accordance with regulation 17(1) of the Collective Investment in Transferable Securities (Contractual Scheme) Regulations 2013.".
Article 6 ("insolvency" and "go into liquidation")	This Article is to be read as if— (a) in paragraph (2), for the words from "it passes a resolution" to the end there were substituted "an order for its winding up is made by the High Court"; and (b) paragraph (3) were omitted.
Part 5 (winding up of companies registered under the Companies Act 2006)	
Chapter 6 (winding up by the High Court)	
Article 104A (petition for winding up on grounds of public interest)	
Article 105 (powers of High Court on hearing of petition)	This Article is to be read as if paragraph (2) were omitted.
Article 106 (power to stay or restrain proceedings against company)	Paragraph (1) is to be read as if for the words "the company, or any creditor" there were substituted "the Financial Conduct Authority, the operator or any creditor of the relevant scheme".
Article 107 (avoidance of property dispositions, etc)	In paragraph (1), the reference to any transfer of shares or alteration in the status of the company's members is to be read as a reference to any issue, transfer or redemption of units in the relevant scheme.
Article 108 (avoidance of sequestration or distress)	
Article 109 (commencement of winding up by the High Court)	
Article 110 (consequences of winding-up order)	In paragraph (1) the reference to the company is to be read as a reference to the operator. This Article is to be read as if paragraph (4) were omitted.

Article 111 (company's statement of affairs)	In paragraph (3)(a) the reference to officers of the company is to be read as a reference to the operator and the depositary. Paragraph (3) is to be read as if sub-paragraphs (c) and (d) were omitted.
Article 112 (investigation by official receiver)	
Article 113 (public examination of officers)	Paragraph (1) is to be read as if for sub-paragraph (b) there were substituted— "(b) has acted as liquidator of the relevant scheme;". In paragraph (1) the reference to the dissolution of the company is to be read as a reference to the completion of winding up of the relevant scheme.
Article 114 (enforcement of Article 113)	
Article 115 (appointment and powers of provisional liquidator)	
Article 116 (functions of official receiver in relation to office of liquidator)	Paragraph (1) is to be read as if the words ", subject to Article 119," were omitted.
Article 117 (appointment by Department)	
Article 118 (choice of liquidator at meetings of creditors and contributories)	This Article is to be read as if for paragraphs (3) and (4) there were substituted— "(3) The liquidator shall be the person (if any) nominated by the creditors.".
Article 120 (liquidation committee)	This Article is to be read as if paragraph (3) were omitted.
Article 121 (general functions in winding up by the High Court)	
Article 122 (custody of company's property)	In this Article the reference to all the property to which the company is or appears to be entitled is to be read as a reference to all property which is or appears to be subject to the relevant scheme.
Article 123 (vesting of company property in liquidator)	Paragraph (1) is to be read as if the words "or held by trustees on its behalf" were omitted.
Article 124 (duty to summon final meeting)	
Article 125 (power to stay winding up)	Paragraph (2) is to be read as if after the words "the official receiver" there were inserted "or the liquidator". In paragraph (3) the reference to the company is to be read as a reference to the operator.
Article 131 (power to exclude creditors not proving in time)	
Article 133 (inspection of books by creditors, etc)	In paragraph (1) the reference to books and papers in the company's possession is to be read as a reference to such books and papers affecting or relating to the affairs of, or the property subject to, the relevant scheme as are in the possession of the operator or the depositary.
Article 134 (payment of expenses of winding up)	
Article 136 (powers of High Court to be cumulative)	In this Article the references to any debtor of the company are to be read as references to a person by whom a debt is, or may become, payable to the operator in respect of any liability (including any contingent or prospective liability) incurred under an authorised contract.
Article 137 (delegation of powers to liquidator)	
Chapter 7 (liquidators)	

Article 138 (style and title of liquidators)	
Article 139 (corrupt inducement affecting appointment)	
Article 142 (winding up by the High Court)	Paragraph (2)(a) is to be read as if for the words "a person who is connected with the company (within the meaning given by Article 7)" there were substituted "the operator or the depositary of the relevant scheme or a person who is an associate of the operator or depositary".
Article 143 (supplementary powers)	
Article 144 (enforcement of liquidator's duty to make returns, etc)	
Article 146 (removal, etc (winding up by the High Court))	
Article 148 (release (winding up by the High Court))	
Chapter 8 (provisions of general application in winding up)	
Article 152 (power to disclaim onerous property)	In paragraph (3) each reference to the company is to be read as a reference to the participants and the depositary.
Article 153 (disclaimer of leaseholds)	In paragraph (1) the reference to a person claiming under the company as underlessee or mortgagee is to be read as a reference to a person claiming as underlessee or mortgagee under the leasehold title which is held by the depositary (or a person nominated by the depositary to hold the leasehold title).
Article 154 (land subject to rentcharge)	
Article 155 (powers of High Court (general)	
Article 156 (powers of High Court (leaseholds))	In this Article— (a) a reference to a person claiming under the company as underlessee or mortgagee is to be read as a reference to a person claiming as underlessee or mortgagee under the leasehold title which is held by the depositary (or a person nominated by the depositary to hold the leasehold title); and (b) a reference to the company, in relation to any reference to liabilities, obligations, estates, incumbrances or interests, is to be read as a reference to the lessee.
Article 157 (rescission of contracts by the High Court)	In paragraph (1) the references to a contract made with the company are to be read as references to an authorised contract.
Article 159 (notification that company is in liquidation)	This Article is to be read as if for paragraphs (1) and (2) there were substituted— "(1) When a relevant scheme is being wound up by the High Court— (a) every business letter (whether in hard copy, electronic or any other form) issued by the operator, the depositary or a liquidator of the relevant scheme, and (b) any website which relates to the relevant scheme and for which the operator or the depositary is responsible, must contain a statement that the relevant scheme is being wound up. (2) If default is made in complying with this Article, any of the following persons who knowingly and wilfully authorises or permits the default, namely, the operator, the depositary and any liquidator of the relevant scheme, shall be guilty of an offence.".

Article 160 (interest on debts)	
Article 162 (information as to pending liquidations)	
Article 163 (resolutions passed at adjourned meetings)	
Article 164 (meeting to ascertain wishes of creditors or contributories)	
Article 165 (affidavits, etc, in United Kingdom and elsewhere)	
Chapter 10 (malpractice before and during liquidation; penalisation of companies and company officers; investigations and prosecutions)	
Article 170 (fraud, etc in anticipation of winding up)	In paragraph (1)(a) the reference to a debt due to the company is to be read as a reference to a debt which is, or may become, payable to the operator in respect of any liability (including any contingent or prospective liability) incurred under an authorised contract. This Article is to be read as if paragraph (3) were omitted.
Article 171 (transactions in fraud of creditors)	In paragraph (1)(b) the reference to any unsatisfied judgment or order for the payment of money obtained against the company is to be read as a reference to any unsatisfied judgment or order for the payment of money to a creditor of the relevant scheme.
Article 172 (misconduct in course of winding up)	In paragraph (1)(a) the reference to the disposal by the company of any part of the company's property is to be read as a reference to the disposal by the operator of part of the property subject to the relevant scheme. This Article is to be read as if paragraph (3) were omitted.
Article 173 (falsification of company's books)	In this Article the reference to any register, accounting records or document belonging to the company is to be read as a reference to any register, accounting records or document affecting or relating to the affairs of, or the property subject to, the relevant scheme.
Article 174 (material omissions from statement relating to company's affairs)	This Article is to be read as if paragraph (3) were omitted.
Article 175 (false representations to creditors)	This Article is to be read as if paragraph (2) were omitted.
Article 176 (summary remedy against delinquent directors, liquidators, etc)	Paragraph (1)(a) is to be read as if the reference to an officer of the company included a reference to the operator and the depositary.
Article 177 (fraudulent trading)	
Article 178 (wrongful trading)	In paragraphs (1) and (2) a reference to a director of a company is to be read as a reference to the operator or depositary of a relevant scheme. This Article is to be read as if— (c) after paragraph (2) there were inserted— "(2A) The condition specified in paragraph (2)(b) is taken to be satisfied in relation to the operator or depositary of a relevant scheme if, at some time before the commencement of the winding up, a director or employee of the operator or depositary knew or ought to have concluded that there was no reasonable prospect that the relevant scheme would avoid going into insolvent liquidation"; and (d) paragraph (7) were omitted.

	In paragraphs (4) and (5) a reference to a director of a company is to be read as a reference to the operator or depositary of a relevant scheme or a director or employee of the operator or depositary.
Article 179 (proceedings under Articles 177 and 178)	
Article 182 (prosecution of delinquent officers and members of company)	
Article 183 (obligations arising under Article 182)	In paragraph (3) the reference to every agent of the company is to be read as a reference to the operator and the depositary and every person who, at the request of the operator or the depositary, has provided the services of banker, solicitor or auditor or professional services of any other description in relation to the relevant scheme.
Part 6 (winding up of unregistered companies)	
Article 184 (meaning of "unregistered company")	
Article 185 (winding up of unregistered companies)	This Article is to be read as if— (a) paragraph (2) were omitted; (b) in paragraph (3) the words ", except in accordance with the EC Regulation" were omitted; and (c) in paragraph (4)— (i) sub-paragraph (a) were omitted; and (ii) for sub-paragraph (b) there were substituted— "(b) if the operator of a relevant scheme is unable to pay the debts of that scheme out of the property subject to it.".
Article 186 (inability to pay debts: unpaid creditor for £750 or more)	In paragraph (1)(a) and (b) each reference to the company is to be read as a reference to the operator. Paragraph (1)(a) is to be read as if the words "in Northern Ireland" were omitted.
Article 188 (inability to pay debts: other cases)	In paragraph (1)(b) the reference to execution or other process issued in favour of a creditor against the company or any person authorised to be sued as nominal defendant on its behalf is to be read as a reference to execution or other process issued in favour of a creditor of the relevant scheme against the property subject to that scheme.
Article 193 (provisions of this Part to be cumulative)	
Part 7 (miscellaneous provisions applying to companies which are insolvent or in liquidation)	
Article 194 (holders of office to be qualified insolvency practitioners)	
Article 195 (appointment to office of two or more persons)	
Article 196 (validity of office-holder's acts)	
Article 198 (getting in the company's property)	In paragraph (2) the reference to any property, books, papers or records to which the company appears to be entitled is to be read as a reference to any property that appears to be property subject to the relevant scheme, and to any books, papers or records that appear to affect or relate to that property or to the affairs of the relevant scheme.

Article 199 (duty to co-operate with office-holder)	Paragraph (3) is to be read as if— (a) in sub-paragraph (a) the reference to officers of the company included a reference to the operator and the depositary; and (b) sub-paragraphs (c) and (d) were omitted.
Article 200 (inquiry into company's dealings, etc)	In paragraph (2)(b) the reference to any person supposed to be indebted to the company is to be read as a reference to a person by whom, it is supposed, a debt is, or may become, payable to the operator in respect of any liability (including any contingent or prospective liability) incurred under an authorised contract. In paragraph (3) the reference to dealings with the company is to be read as a reference to dealings with any matter affecting or relating to the affairs of, or the property subject to, the relevant scheme.
Article 201 (High Court's enforcement powers under Article 200)	In paragraph (2) the reference to any person who is indebted to the company is to be read as a reference to a person by whom a debt is, or may become, payable to the operator in respect of any liability (including any contingent or prospective liability) incurred under an authorised contract.
Article 202 (transactions at an undervalue)	In paragraphs (2) and (3) the reference to the company is to be read as a reference to the operator or the depositary. In paragraph (4)— (a) in sub-paragraphs (a) and (b) the second reference to the company is to be read as a reference to the participants in a relevant scheme; and (b) each other reference to a company is to be read as a reference to the operator or depositary of the relevant scheme. Paragraph (5) is to be read as if for sub-paragraph (a) there were substituted— "(a) that the operator or the depositary, in entering into the transaction, did so in good faith and for the purposes of carrying on the business of the relevant scheme, and".
Article 203 (preferences)	In paragraphs (2) and (3) the reference to the company is to be read as a reference to the operator or the depositary. Paragraph (4) is to be read as if for the words from "a company" to the end there were substituted— "the operator or depositary of a relevant scheme gives a preference to a person if— (a) that person is one of the creditors of the relevant scheme or a surety or guarantor for any of the debts or liabilities of the relevant scheme, and (b) the operator or depositary does anything or suffers anything to be done which (in either case) has the effect of putting that person into a position which, in the event of the relevant scheme going into insolvent liquidation, will be better than the position that person would have been in if that thing had not been done.".

	In paragraph (5) the reference to the company which gave the preference is to be read as a reference to the operator or the depositary in giving the preference. In paragraph (6)— (a) the first reference to a company is to be read as a reference to the operator or depositary of a relevant scheme; and (b) the reference to a person connected with the company is to be read as a reference to a person who is an associate (within the meaning of Article 4) of the operator or depositary of the relevant scheme.
Article 204 ("relevant time" under Articles 202, 203)	In paragraphs (1) and (2)— (a) a reference to a company, except the second reference in paragraph (2), is to be read as a reference to the operator or depositary of a relevant scheme; and (b) the reference to a person who is connected with the company is to be read as a reference to a person who is an associate (within the meaning of Article 4) of the operator or depositary of the relevant scheme. In paragraph (2) the reference to the inability of the company to pay its debts within the meaning of Article 103 is to be read as a reference to the inability of the operator of a relevant scheme to pay the debts of that scheme within the meaning of Article 186 or 188 (as modified by this Schedule).
Article 205 (orders under Articles 202, 203)	In this Article a reference to a company is to be read as a reference to the operator or the depositary, except— (a) in paragraph (1)(a), where the reference to the company is to be read as a reference to the liquidator of the relevant scheme; (b) in paragraph (1)(c), where the reference to security given by the company is to be read as a reference to security over any property subject to the relevant scheme; (c) in paragraph (1)(g), where the first reference to the company is to be read as a reference to the liquidator of the relevant scheme; (d) in paragraph (2), with respect to the reference to a creditor of the company; and (e) in paragraph (3C).
Article 208 (unenforceability of liens on books, etc)	
Part 12 (insolvency practitioners and their qualification)	
Article 348 (acting as insolvency practitioner without qualification)	
[Article 349 (persons not qualified to act as insolvency practitioner) Article 349A (authorisation of insolvency practitioners) Articles 350 to 350T (regulation of insolvency practitioners)	This Article is to be read as if for paragraph (2) there were substituted— "(2) A person is not qualified to act at any time as an insolvency practitioner in relation to a relevant scheme unless at that time the person is fully authorised to act as an insolvency practitioner or partially authorised to act as an insolvency practitioner only in relation to companies.". In these Articles a reference to a company, except in a reference to creditors of a company, is to be read without modification by this Schedule.]
Part 14 (miscellaneous)	

Article 373 (prosecution and punishment of offences) Article 374 (summary proceedings)	These Articles are to be read as if a reference to an offence under the 1989 Order or a provision of that Order, in so far as it is a reference to an offence under a provision of that Order that is applied by these Regulations, is to be read as a reference to the offence under that provision as so applied.
Part 15 (supplementary provisions)	
Article 385 (legal professional privilege)	
Schedule 2 (powers of liquidator in a winding up)	
Schedule 2 (powers of liquidator in a winding up)	Schedule 2 is to be read as if— (a) paragraphs 9 and 12 were omitted; (b) the power in paragraph 4 included a power to bring or defend any action or other legal proceeding which would otherwise be brought or defended by the operator on behalf of the participants; (c) the power in paragraph 8 included a power to do all acts and execute all deeds, receipts and other documents which would otherwise be done or executed by the operator on behalf of the participants; and (d) the power in paragraph 10 included a power to draw, accept, make and indorse any bill of exchange or promissory note with the same effect as if the bill or note had been drawn, accepted, made or indorsed by the operator in the course of the business of the relevant scheme. Paragraph 5 is to be read as subject to the requirements in regulation 17(10) to cease making payments under authorised contracts and to cease the issue and redemption of units.
Schedule 7 (punishment of offences under the 1989 Order)	
Schedule 7 (punishment of offences under the 1989 Order)	Schedule 7 is to be read as if a reference to a provision which is applied by these Regulations were a reference to that provision as so applied.

NOTES

Entries relating to Articles 349, 349A, 350–350T inserted by the Deregulation Act 2015, the Small Business, Enterprise and Employment Act 2015 and the Insolvency (Amendment) Act (Northern Ireland) 2016 (Consequential Amendments and Transitional Provisions) Regulations 2017, SI 2017/400, reg 11(1), (3).

SCHEDULE 3
CO-OWNERSHIP SCHEMES: APPLICATION OF THE INSOLVENCY RULES 1986

Regulation 17(8)

PART 1
APPLICATION OF RULES WITH MODIFICATIONS

[7.841]

1 In relation to the winding up of a relevant scheme by the High Court under the 1986 Act, Parts 4 and 7 to 13 of the Insolvency Rules 1986, in so far as they apply to the winding up of an unregistered company, apply with—

(a) the general modifications set out in paragraph 2;
(b) any other modification specified in the Table in Part 2 of this Schedule; and
(c) any other necessary modification.

2 Unless the context otherwise requires and subject to any modification specified in the Table in Part 2 of this Schedule which has a contrary effect, the general modifications are that—

(a) a reference to a company includes a reference to a relevant scheme;
(b) a reference to a voluntary winding up or a resolution for voluntary winding up of a company is to be ignored;
(c) in any provision relating to—
    (i) the service on a company of a petition, demand or order, or the giving or sending by a company of any notice or other document,

Part 7D Special Insolvency Regimes

(ii) the provision to a company of any explanation or other information, or
(iii) an application to the court by a company or by any person in relation to a company,

a reference to the company is to be read as a reference to the operator or, in the case of a provision that has effect in relation to a company before the presentation of a winding-up petition, the operator of a relevant scheme in relation to which a written demand has been served under section 222(1)(a) (as applied by Schedule 2);

(d) a reference to a creditor of a company is to be read as a reference to a creditor of the relevant scheme;
(e) a reference to a contributory or to a meeting of contributories is to be ignored;
(f) a reference to a member of a company or to a register of members is to be ignored;
(g) a reference to the estate or to the property or assets of a company is to be read as a reference to the property subject to the relevant scheme;
(h) a reference to a debt or liability of a company is to be read as a reference to a debt or liability of the relevant scheme; and
(i) a reference to the registrar of companies is to be read as a reference to the FCA.

NOTES

Note that the Insolvency Rules 1986, SI 1986/1925 are revoked and replaced (as from 6 April 2017 and subject to transitional provisions) by the Insolvency (England and Wales) Rules 2016, SI 2016/1024 at **[6.2]**.

PART 2
TABLE OF SPECIFIC MODIFICATIONS OF THE INSOLVENCY RULES 1986

[7.842]

Rule	***Subject***	***Modification***
Part 4 (companies winding up)		
Chapter 1 (the scheme of this Part of the Rules)		
4.2	Winding up by the court: the various forms of petition	Paragraph (2) is to be read as if— (a) the reference to the company included a reference to the operator of a relevant scheme; and (b) the words "the directors," and "the official receiver," were omitted.
Chapter 2 (the statutory demand)		
4.4	Preliminary	In paragraph (2) the reference to a company is to be read as a reference to the operator of a relevant scheme.
4.5	Form and content of statutory demand	In paragraph (2)(a) the reference to the company's liability is to be read as a reference to the liability of the relevant scheme in relation to which the statutory demand has been served.
4.6	Information to be given in statutory demand	In paragraph (1)(c) the reference to the company is to be read as a reference to the operator of the relevant scheme in relation to which the statutory demand has been served.
Chapter 3 (petition to winding-up order)		
4.6A	Injunction to restrain presentation or advertisement of petition	The first reference to a company is to be read as a reference to the operator of a relevant scheme.
4.7	Presentation and filing of petition	Paragraph (3) is to be read as if the words "who is a person other than the company" were omitted.
4.8	Service of petition	This Rule is to be read as if paragraph (2) required the petition is to be served at the registered office or principal place of business of the operator and of the depositary. Paragraphs (3) to (5) apply in relation to the operator and in relation to the depositary as they apply in relation to a company on which a petition is served.

Rule	*Subject*	*Modification*
4.9A	Proof of service	The certificate of service must specify (instead of the particulars in paragraph (2)(a) and (b)) the name of the relevant scheme and the name and registered office (or principal place of business) of the operator and of the depositary.
4.10	Other persons to receive copies of petition	This Rule is to be read as if there were substituted for paragraphs (1) to (4)— "(1) The petitioner must send a copy of the petition to the FCA.".
4.12	Verification of petition	A statement of truth which is not contained in or endorsed upon the petition which it verifies must specify (instead of the particulars in paragraph (3A)(a)) the name of the relevant scheme and of the operator and the depositary.
4.13	Persons entitled to copy of petition	This Rule is to be read as if the word "director," were omitted.
4.15	Permission for petitioner to withdraw	In paragraph (c) the reference to the company is to be read as a reference to the operator and the depositary.
4.18	Witness statement in opposition	In this Rule— (a) each reference to the company is to be read as a reference to the operator; and (b) paragraph (1) is to be read as if it required the operator to file a witness statement only with the depositary's consent.
Chapter 4 (petition by contributories)		
4.22 to 4.24	Petition by contributories	These Rules do not apply.
Chapter 5 (provisional liquidator)		
4.25	Appointment of provisional liquidator	Paragraph (1) is to be read as if it provided that an application for the appointment of a provisional liquidator may be made by the operator, the depositary, the FCA or a creditor.
4.28	Security	In paragraph (2)(a) the reference to the making of an order on the company is to be read as a reference to the making of an order on the operator and the depositary.
Chapter 6 (statement of affairs and other information)		
4.39	Submission of accounts	A reference to the accounts of the company is to be read as a reference to the accounts relating to the affairs of the relevant scheme.
Chapter 7 (information to creditors and contributories)		
4.43	Reports by official receiver	This Rule is to be read as if paragraphs (1A) and (1B) were omitted.
4.48	Winding up stayed	In paragraph (2) the reference to the company is to be read as a reference to the operator.

Rule	*Subject*	*Modification*
4.49B	Reports to creditors and members – winding up by the court	The progress report must include full details (instead of the details in paragraph (1)(b)) of the name of the relevant scheme and the name and registered office (or principal place of business) of the operator and of the depositary. Paragraph (2) is to be read as if the words from "and, where the liquidator" to the end were omitted. In paragraph (7) the reference to the members of the company is to be read as a reference to the operator and the depositary.
Chapter 8 (meetings of creditors and contributories)		
4.58	Attendance at meetings of company's personnel	A reference to the company's personnel is to be read as a reference to— (a) the operator and the depositary; and (b) the directors and employees of the operator and the depositary.
Chapter 9 (proof of debts in a liquidation)		
4.79	Liquidator to allow inspection of proofs	The reference to any contributory of the company is to be read as a reference to the operator or the depositary.
4.83	Appeal against decision on proof	In paragraphs (2) and (4A) a reference to a contributory is to be read as a reference to the operator or the depositary. In paragraph (4A) the reference to the company is to be read as a reference to the operator for the benefit of the participants.
4.90	Mutual credits and set-off	A reference to mutual credits, mutual debts or other mutual dealings between the company and any creditor is to be read as a reference to mutual credits etc between the operator on behalf of the participants and a creditor, and a reference to any obligation to or from the company, or any sum due or owed to, or due from, the company is to be read accordingly.
Chapter 10 (secured creditors)		
4.98	Test of security's value	In paragraph (2) the reference to the liquidator on behalf of the company is to be read as a reference to the liquidator acting in the best interests of the relevant scheme.
Chapter 11 (the liquidator)		
4.124	Release of official receiver	This Rule is to be read as if paragraph (2A) were omitted.
4.125	Final meeting	This Rule is to be read as if paragraph (2A) were omitted.
4.128	Other matters affecting remuneration	Paragraph (3) is to be read as if for the words "act on behalf of the company" there were substituted "act in the liquidation".
4.131	Creditors' claim that remuneration is or other expenses are excessive	Paragraph (4)(e) is to be read as if it required the amount to which it refers to be paid to the operator for the benefit the relevant scheme.

Rule	*Subject*	*Modification*
4.138	Liquidator's duties on vacating office	A reference to the company's books, papers and other records is to be read as a reference to all books, papers and other records affecting or relating to the affairs of, or the property subject to, the relevant scheme.
4.149	Power of court to set aside certain transactions	Paragraph (1) is to be read as if the court's power to order the liquidator to compensate the company for loss suffered in consequence of a transaction which is set aside included power to order the liquidator, by way of compensation for loss suffered in consequence of such a transaction, to contribute any sum to the property subject to the relevant scheme.
Chapter 12 (the liquidation committee)		
4.152	Membership of committee	Paragraph (1) is to be read as if the words "Subject to Rule 4.154 below," were omitted.
4.154	Committee established by contributories	This Rule does not apply.
4.171A	Composition of committee when creditors paid in full	This Rule is to be read as if— (a) at the end of paragraph (2) there were inserted "and the committee is abolished"; and (b) paragraphs (3) and (4) were omitted.
Chapter 14 (collection and distribution of company's assets by liquidator		
4.181	Debts of insolvent company to rank equally	This Rule is to be read as if the references to preferential debts were omitted.
Chapter 15 (disclaimer)		
4.188	Communication of disclaimer to persons interested	In paragraph (2) the reference to a person who claims under the company as underlessee or mortgagee is to be read as a reference to a person claiming as underlessee or mortgagee under the leasehold title which is held by the depositary (or a person nominated by the depositary to hold the leasehold title).
Chapters 16, 17 and 18		
4.195 to 4.201	Settlement of list of contributories	These Rules do not apply.
4.202 to 4.205	Calls	These Rules do not apply.
4.206 to 4.210	Special manager	These Rules do not apply.
Chapter 19 (public examination of company officers and others)		
4.213	Order on request by creditors or contributories	In paragraph (2) the reference to the relationship which the proposed examinee has, or has had, to the company is to be read as a reference to that person's interest in the relevant scheme or dealings with the operator.
Chapter 20 (order of payment of costs, etc, out of assets)		

Rule	*Subject*	*Modification*
4.218	General rule as to priority	Paragraph (2) is to be read as if sub-paragraph (b) were omitted. Paragraph (3) is to be read as if the words "Subject as provided in Rules 4.218A to 4.218E," were omitted. In paragraphs (2) and (3) a reference to any legal action or proceedings or any arbitration or other dispute resolution procedure which the liquidator has power to bring or defend in the name of the company is to be read as a reference to such action, proceedings or procedure which the liquidator has power to bring or defend on behalf of the participants.
4.218A to 4.218E	Litigation expenses and property subject to a floating charge	These Rules do not apply.
4.220	Saving for powers of the court	In paragraph (2)— (a) the reference to proceedings by or against the company is to be read as a reference to proceedings brought by or against the operator for the resolution of any matter relating to the relevant scheme; and (b) the reference to the power of any court to order costs to be paid by the company is to be read as a reference to the power of any court to order costs to be paid out of the property subject to the relevant scheme.
Chapters 21, 22 and 23		
4.221 to 4.225	Miscellaneous rules	These Rules do not apply.
4.226 to 4.230	Permission to act as director, etc, of company with prohibited name	These Rules do not apply.
4.231	EC Regulation—member state liquidator	This Rule does not apply.
Part 7 (court procedure and practice)		
7.1	Preliminary	The reference to a petition for a winding-up order under Part IV is to be read as a reference to a petition presented under regulation 17(9).
7.31A	Court file	In paragraph (4)(a)— (a) the reference to an officer or former officer of the company is to be read as a reference to the operator and the depositary; and (b) the reference to a member of the company is to be read as a reference to a participant.
7.41	Costs and expenses of witnesses	In paragraph (1) the reference to an officer of the insolvent company is to be read as a reference to— (a) the operator or any person who is employed by the operator; or (b) the depositary or any person who is employed by the depositary.
7.56	Service of orders staying proceedings	The reference to the property of a company is to be read as a reference to the property subject to a relevant scheme.
Part 8 (proxies and company representation)		

Rule	*Subject*	*Modification*
8.5	Right of inspection	In paragraph (3) the right of inspection exercisable in the case of an insolvent company by its directors is exercisable in the case of the relevant scheme by the operator or the depositary.
Part 11 (declaration and payment of dividend (winding up and bankruptcy))		
11.6	Notice of declaration	This Rule is to be read as if paragraph (2A) were omitted.
Part 12 (miscellaneous and general)		
12.18	False claim of status as creditor, etc	In paragraph (1)— (a) each reference to the Rules is to be read as a reference to the Rules as modified by this Schedule; and (b) the reference to the members of a company is to be read, in relation to the winding up of a relevant scheme, as a reference to— (i) the operator or depositary of the relevant scheme; or (ii) the participants in it.
Part 12A (provisions of general effect)		
12A.18	Service of orders staying proceedings	In paragraph (1)(a) the reference to the property of a company is to be read as a reference to the property subject to a relevant scheme.
12A.30	Forms for use in insolvency proceedings	Any form prescribed for use by paragraph (1) which is used in proceedings for winding up a relevant scheme is to be read with the modifications set out in this Schedule (so far as applicable for the form concerned). The requirement in paragraph (2) to use a form with such variations as the circumstances may require includes a requirement to use it with such variations as are necessary to take account of applicable modifications.
12A.34 and 12A.39	Notices relating to companies	Instead of the particulars given in each of these Rules a notice must specify the name of the relevant scheme and the name and registered office (or principal place of business) of the operator and of the depositary.
12A.43	Information to be contained in all notifications to the registrar	A notification must specify (instead of the particulars in paragraphs (a) and (b)) the name of the relevant scheme and the name of the operator and of the depositary.
12A.53	Charge for copy documents	The first reference to a member is to be read as a reference to a participant.

NOTES

Note that the Insolvency Rules 1986, SI 1986/1925 are revoked and replaced (as from 6 April 2017 and subject to transitional provisions) by the Insolvency (England and Wales) Rules 2016, SI 2016/1024 at **[6.2]**.

SCHEDULE 4
CO-OWNERSHIP SCHEMES: APPLICATION OF THE INSOLVENCY (SCOTLAND) RULES 1986

Regulation 17(8)

PART 1
APPLICATION OF RULES WITH MODIFICATIONS

[7.843]

1 In relation to the winding up of a relevant scheme by the Court of Session under the 1986 Act, Rule 0.2 (interpretation) and Parts 4 and 7 of the Insolvency (Scotland) Rules 1986, in so far as they apply to the winding up of an unregistered company, apply with—

(a) the general modifications set out in paragraph 2;
(b) any other modification specified in the Table in Part 2 of this Schedule; and
(c) any other necessary modification.

2 Unless the context otherwise requires and subject to any modification specified in the Table in Part 2 of this Schedule which has a contrary effect, the general modifications are that—

(a) a reference to a company includes a reference to a relevant scheme;
(b) a reference to a voluntary winding up or a resolution for voluntary winding up of a company is to be ignored;
(c) in any provision relating to—
  (i) the possession or control of any books, papers, records or other property,
  (ii) sending any documents or records to a third party, or
  (iii) the giving or sending of any notice,

  a reference to the company is to be read as a reference to the operator of the relevant scheme;
(d) a reference to a creditor of a company is to be read as a reference to a creditor of the relevant scheme;
(e) a reference to a contributory or to a meeting of contributories is to be ignored;
(f) a reference to a member of a company is to be ignored;
(g) a reference to the property or assets of a company is to be read as a reference to the property subject to the relevant scheme;
(h) a reference to a debt or liability of a company is to be read as a reference to a debt or liability of the relevant scheme;
(i) a reference to the registrar of companies or to the Accountant in Bankruptcy or to the registrar of companies and the Accountant in Bankruptcy is to be read as a reference to the FCA; and
(j) where a Rule of the Insolvency (Scotland) Rules 1986 applies a provision of the Bankruptcy (Scotland) Act 1985 which contains a reference to the debtor (except in the expression "the debtor's estate"), the Rule is to be read as if it modified the provision concerned by requiring that reference to be read as a reference to the operator.

PART 2
TABLE OF SPECIFIC MODIFICATIONS OF THE INSOLVENCY (SCOTLAND) RULES 1986

[7.844]

Rule	*Subject*	*Modification*
Part 4 (winding up by the court)		
Chapter 1 (provisional liquidator)		
4.1	Appointment of provisional liquidator	Paragraph (1) is to be read as if the words "or by the company itself," were omitted.
4.3	Caution	Paragraph (a) is to be read as if the words "against the company" were omitted.
Chapter 3 (information)		
4.10	Information to creditors and contributories	This Rule is to be read as if paragraph (1A) were omitted.
Chapter 4 (meeting of creditors and contributories)		

Rule	***Subject***	***Modification***
4.12	First meetings in the liquidation	This Rule is to be read as if— (a) in paragraph (1) for the words from "under section 138(3)" to "as the case may be," there were substituted "the interim liquidator summons"; (b) for paragraphs (2) and (2A) there were substituted— "(2) That meeting is to be known as "the first meeting of creditors" and must be summoned for a date not later than 42 days after the date of the winding-up order or such longer period as the court may allow."; and (c) paragraph (4) were omitted.
4.14	Attendance at meetings of company's personnel	This Rule is to be read as if paragraph (3) were omitted. A reference to the company's personnel is to be read as a reference to— (a) the operator and the depositary; and (b) the directors and employees of the operator and the depositary.
Chapter 5 (claims in liquidation)		
4.16	Application of the Bankruptcy (Scotland) Act 1985	This Rule is to be read, in relation to section 49 of the Bankruptcy (Scotland) Act 1985, as if it included a modification of subsection (6A) having the effect that the operator may appeal if, and only if, it satisfies the sheriff that the participants have, or are likely to have, a pecuniary interest in the outcome of the appeal. In paragraph (2) the expression in column 2 of the table which is substituted for a reference to the expression "Debtor" in column 1 of the table is to be read, in relation to sections 22(5) and 44(2) of the Bankruptcy (Scotland) Act 1985, as a reference to— (c) the operator; or (d) a director or employee of the operator.
4.17	Claims in foreign currency	In paragraph (1) each reference to the company is to be read as a reference to the operator.
Chapter 6 (the liquidator)		
4.18	Appointment of liquidator by the court	Paragraph (1) is to be read as if the words from ", 139(4)" to the end were omitted.
4.19	Appointment by creditors or contributories	Paragraph (2) is to be read as if the words "Subject to section 139(4)" were omitted.

Rule	*Subject*	*Modification*
4.22	Taking possession and realisation of the company's assets	In paragraph (1)(a) the reference to any property, books, papers or records to which the company appears to be entitled is to be read as a reference to any property that appears to be property subject to the relevant scheme, and to any books, papers or records that appear to affect or relate to that property or to the affairs of the relevant scheme. In paragraph (4) the reference to any title deed or other document or record of the company is to be read as a reference to any title deed or other document or record that affects or relates to the property subject to the relevant scheme or to the affairs of the relevant scheme.
4.28	Resignation of liquidator	Paragraph (2) is to be read as if the words from "and a statement" to the end were omitted.
4.31	Final meeting	Paragraph (2) is to be read as if the words from "and a statement" to the end were omitted.
4.38	Power of court to set aside certain transactions	Paragraph (1) is to be read as if the court's power to order the liquidator to compensate the company for loss suffered in consequence of a transaction which is set aside included power to order the liquidator, by way of compensation for loss suffered in consequence of such a transaction, to contribute any sum to the property subject to the relevant scheme.
Chapter 7 (the liquidation committee)		
4.41	Membership of committee	Paragraph (1) is to be read as if the words "Subject to Rule 4.43 below," were omitted.
4.43	Committee established by contributories	This Rule does not apply.
4.59	Composition of committee when creditors paid in full	This Rule is to be read as if— (a) at the end of paragraph (3) there were inserted "and the committee is abolished"; and (b) paragraphs (4) to (7) were omitted.
Chapter 9 (distribution of company's assets by liquidator)		
4.66	Order of priority in distribution	Paragraph (4) is to be read as if the words "Subject to the provisions of section 175," were omitted. In paragraph (5) the reference to the members is to be read as a reference to the participants.
4.67	Order of priority of expenses of liquidation	In paragraph (3)— (a) the reference to proceedings by or against the company is to be read as a reference to proceedings brought by or against the operator for the resolution of any matter relating to the relevant scheme; and (b) the reference to the power of any court to order expenses to be paid by the company is to be read as a reference to the power of any court to order expenses to be paid out of the property subject to the relevant scheme.

Rule	*Subject*	*Modification*
4.68	Application of the Bankruptcy (Scotland) Act 1985 (procedure after end of accounting period)	This Rule is to be read, in relation to section 53 of the Bankruptcy (Scotland) Act 1985, as if it included a modification of subsection (6A) having the effect that the operator may appeal if, and only if, it satisfies the Accountant in Bankruptcy or, as the case may be, the sheriff that the participants have, or are likely to have, a pecuniary interest in the outcome of the appeal.
Chapter 10 (special manager)		
4.69 to 4.73	Special manager	These Rules do not apply.
Chapter 11 (public examination of company officers and others)		
4.75	Order on request by creditors or contributories	In paragraph (2) the reference to the proposed examinee's relationship to the company is to be read as a reference to that person's interest in the relevant scheme or dealings with the operator.
Chapters 13, 14 and 15		
4.78 to 4.82	Company with prohibited name	These Rules do not apply.
4.83 and 4.84	EC Regulation	These Rules do not apply.
Part 7 (provisions of general application)		
Chapter 2 (proxies and company representation)		
7.18	Right of inspection	In paragraph (3) the right of inspection exercisable in the case of an insolvent company by its directors is exercisable in the case of the relevant scheme by the operator or the depositary.
Chapter 3 (miscellaneous)		
7.21A and 7.21B	Contents of notices	Instead of the particulars in paragraph (3) of each of these Rules all notices published must specify the name of the relevant scheme and the name and registered office (or principal place of business) of the operator and of the depositary.
7.26	Right to list of creditors and copy documents	In paragraph (2A) the first reference to a member is to be read as a reference to a participant.
7.27	Confidentiality of documents	In paragraph (1)(b) the reference, in relation to the winding up of a company, to the company's members is to be read, in relation to the winding up of a relevant scheme, as a reference to— (a) the operator or depositary of the relevant scheme; or (b) the participants in it.
7.30	Forms for use in insolvency proceedings	Any form prescribed for use by this Rule which is used in proceedings for winding up a relevant scheme is to be read with the modifications set out in this Schedule (so far as applicable for the form concerned). The reference to the use of a form with such variations as circumstances require includes a reference to its use with such variations as are necessary to take account of applicable modifications.

Part 7D Special Insolvency Regimes

Rule	Subject	Modification
7.32	Power of court to cure defects in procedure	The table in paragraph (2) is to be read as if the entry for the expression "Debtor" were omitted. In the entry for the expression "Permanent trustee" the reference to "Responsible insolvency practitioner" is to be read as a reference to the responsible insolvency practitioner in proceedings for winding up the relevant scheme.
7.33	Sederunt book	Paragraph (7) is to be read as if for sub-paragraph (d) there were substituted— "(d) in the case of a winding up, the date on which the liquidator vacates office under section 172(8) or the date of a certificate of release issued by the Accountant of Court".
7.34	Disposal of company's books, papers and other records	In paragraphs (1), (2) and (3) a reference to the company's books, papers and records is to be read as a reference to all books, papers and other records affecting or relating to the affairs of, or the property subject to, the relevant scheme. In paragraph (3) the reference to the date which is 12 months after the dissolution of the company shall be read as a reference to the date which is 12 months after the date of a notice given by the liquidator in compliance with Rule 4.31(4) which states that the liquidator has been released.
7.36	Information about time spent on a case	In paragraph (2)(b) the reference, in relation to a company, to any director is to be read, in relation to a relevant scheme, as a reference to the operator or depositary of the relevant scheme.

SCHEDULE 5
CO-OWNERSHIP SCHEMES: APPLICATION OF THE INSOLVENCY RULES (NORTHERN IRELAND) 1991

Regulation 17(8)

PART 1
APPLICATION OF RULES WITH MODIFICATIONS

[7.845]

1 In relation to the winding up of a relevant scheme under the 1989 Order, Rules 0.1 to 0.7 (introductory provisions), Parts 4 and 7 to 12 of the Insolvency Rules (Northern Ireland) 1991, in so far as they apply to the winding up of an unregistered company, apply with—

(a) the general modifications set out in paragraphs 2 and 3;
(b) any other modification specified in the Table in Part 2 of this Schedule; and
(c) any other necessary modification.

2 Unless the context otherwise requires and subject to any modification specified in the Table in Part 2 of this Schedule which has a contrary effect, the general modifications are the modifications made in sub-paragraphs (a) to (h) of paragraph 2 of Schedule 3 (read as if set out in this paragraph), except that sub-paragraph (c) is to be read as if for "section 222(1)(a)" there were substituted "Article 186(1)".

3 A reference to the registrar is to be read as a reference to the FCA.

PART 2
TABLE OF SPECIFIC MODIFICATIONS OF THE INSOLVENCY RULES (NORTHERN IRELAND) 1991

[7.846]

Rule	Subject	Modification
Part 4 (companies winding up)		

Rule	*Subject*	*Modification*
Chapter 1 (the scheme of Part 4)		
4.002	Winding up by the court: the various forms of petition	Paragraph (2) is to be read as if— (a) the reference to the company included a reference to the operator of a relevant scheme; and (b) the words "the directors," and "the official receiver," were omitted.
Chapter 2 (the statutory demand)		
4.004	Preliminary	In paragraph (2) the reference to a company is to be read as a reference to the operator of a relevant scheme.
4.005	Form and content of statutory demand	In paragraph (2)(a) the reference to the company's liability is to be read as a reference to the liability of the relevant scheme in relation to which the statutory demand has been served.
4.006	Information to be given in statutory demand	In paragraph (1)(c) the reference to the company is to be read as a reference to the operator of the relevant scheme in relation to which the statutory demand has been served.
Chapter 3 (petition to winding-up order)		
4.007	Presentation and filing of petition	Paragraph (3) is to be read as if the words "If the petitioner is other than the company itself," were omitted.
4.008	Service of petition	This Rule is to be read as if paragraph (2) required the petition is to be served at the registered office or principal place of business of the operator and of the depositary. Paragraphs (3) to (5) apply in relation to the operator and in relation to the depositary as they apply in relation to a company on which a petition is served.
4.010	Other persons to receive copies of petition	This Rule is to be read as if there were substituted for paragraphs (1) to (5)— "(1) The petitioner must send a copy of the petition to the FCA.".
4.011	Notice and advertisement of petition	The advertisement must state (instead of the particulars in paragraph (5)(a)) the name of the relevant scheme, the name and registered office (or principal place of business) of the operator and of the depositary and, if service of the petition was effected overseas, the address at which it was effected.
4.013	Persons entitled to copy of petition	This Rule is to be read as if the word "director," were omitted.
4.015	Dismissal or withdrawal of petition	In paragraph (1)(c) the reference to the company is to be read as a reference to the operator and the depositary.
4.018	Affidavit by company in opposition	In this Rule— (a) each reference to the company is to be read as a reference to the operator; and (b) paragraph (1) is to be read as if it required the operator to file an affidavit only with the depositary's consent.
Chapter 4 (petition by contributories)		
4.024 to 4.026	Petition by contributories	These Rules do not apply.
Chapter 5 (provisional liquidator)		

Part 7D Special Insolvency Regimes

Rule	Subject	Modification
4.027	Appointment of provisional liquidator	Paragraph (1) is to be read as if it provided that an application for the appointment of a provisional liquidator may be made by the operator, the depositary, the FCA or a creditor.
4.031	Security	In paragraph (2)(a) the reference to the making of an order on the company is to be read as a reference to the making of an order on the operator and the depositary.
Chapter 6 (Statement of affairs and other information)		
4.043	Submission of accounts	A reference to the accounts of the company is to be read as a reference to the accounts relating to the affairs of the relevant scheme.
Chapter 7 (information to creditors and contributories)		
4.047	Reports by official receiver	This Rule is to be read as if paragraphs (1A) and (1B) were omitted.
4.052	Winding up stayed	In paragraph (2) the reference to the company is to be read as a reference to the operator.
Chapter 8 (meetings of creditors and contributories)		
4.065	Attendance at meetings of company's personnel	A reference to the company's personnel is to be read as a reference to— (a) the operator and the depositary; and (b) the directors and employees of the operator and the depositary.
Chapter 9 (proof of debts in a liquidation)		
4.085	Liquidator to allow inspection of proofs	The reference to any contributory of the company is to be read as a reference to the operator or the depositary.
4.089	Appeal against decision on proof	In paragraph (3) the reference to a contributory is to be read as a reference to the operator or the depositary.
4.096	Mutual credits and set-off	A reference to mutual credits, mutual debts or other mutual dealings between the company and any creditor is to be read as a reference to mutual credits etc between the operator on behalf of the participants and a creditor, and a reference to any obligation to or from the company, or any sum due or owed to, or due from, the company is to be read accordingly.
Chapter 10 (secured creditors)		
4.104	Test of security's value	In paragraph (2) the reference to the liquidator on behalf of the company is to be read as a reference to the liquidator acting in the best interests of the relevant scheme.
Chapter 11 (the liquidator)		
4.131	Release of official receiver	This Rule is to be read as if paragraph (2A) were omitted.
4.132	Final meeting	This Rule is to be read as if paragraph (2A) were omitted.
4.135	Other matters affecting remuneration	Paragraph (3) is to be read as if for the words "act on behalf of the company" there were substituted "act in the liquidation".

Rule	***Subject***	***Modification***
4.145	Liquidator's duties on vacating office	A reference to the company's books, papers and other records is to be read as a reference to all books, papers and other records affecting or relating to the affairs of, or the property subject to, the relevant scheme.
4.157	Power of court to set aside certain transactions	Paragraph (1) is to be read as if the court's power to order the liquidator to compensate the company for loss suffered in consequence of a transaction which is set aside included power to order the liquidator, by way of compensation for loss suffered in consequence of such a transaction, to contribute any sum to the property subject to the relevant scheme.
Chapter 12 (the liquidation committee)		
4.160	Membership of committee	Paragraph (1) is to be read as if the words "Subject to Rule 4.162," were omitted.
4.162	Committee established by contributories	This Rule does not apply.
4.179	Composition of committee when creditors paid in full	This Rule is to be read as if— (a) at the end of paragraph (4) there were inserted "and the committee is abolished"; and (b) paragraphs (5) to (9) were omitted.
Chapter 14 (collection and distribution of company's assets by liquidator		
4.190	Debts of insolvent company to rank equally	This Rule is to be read as if the references to preferential debts were omitted.
Chapter 15 (disclaimer)		
4.198	Communication of disclaimer to persons interested	In paragraph (2) the reference to a person who claims under the company as underlessee or mortgagee is to be read as a reference to a person claiming as underlessee or mortgagee under the leasehold title which is held by the depositary (or a person nominated by the depositary to hold the leasehold title).
Chapters 16, 17 and 18		
4.205 to 4.211	Settlement of list of contributories	These Rules do not apply.
4.212 to 4.215	Calls	These Rules do not apply.
4.216 to 4.220	Special manager	These Rules do not apply.
Chapter 19 (public examination of company officers and others)		
4.223	Order on request by creditors or contributories	In paragraph (3) the reference to the relationship which the proposed examinee has, or has had, to the company is to be read as a reference to that person's interest in the relevant scheme or dealings with the operator.
Chapter 20 (order of payment of costs out of assets)		

Rule	Subject	Modification
4.228	General rule as to priority	Paragraph (2) is to be read as if sub-paragraph (b) were omitted. Paragraph (3) is to be read as if the words "Subject as provided in Rules 4.228A to 4.228E," were omitted. In paragraphs (2) and (3) a reference to any legal action or proceedings or any arbitration or other dispute resolution procedure which the liquidator has power to bring or defend in the name of the company is to be read as a reference to such action, proceedings or procedure which the liquidator has power to bring or defend on behalf of the participants.
4.228A to 4.228E	Litigation expenses and property subject to a floating charge	These Rules do not apply.
4.230	Saving for powers of the court	In paragraph (2)— (a) the reference to proceedings by or against the company is to be read as a reference to proceedings brought by or against the operator for the resolution of any matter relating to the relevant scheme; and (b) the reference to the power of any court to order costs to be paid by the company is to be read as a reference to the power of any court to order costs to be paid out of the property subject to the relevant scheme.
Chapter 21 (miscellaneous rules)		
4.231 and 4.232	Order authorising a return of capital	These Rules do not apply.
4.233	Statement to registrar under Article 162	This Rule is to be read as if paragraph (2) were omitted.
4.234 and 4.235	Dissolution after winding up	These Rules do not apply.
Chapters 22 and 23		
4.236 to 4.240	Leave to act as director, etc, of company with prohibited name	These Rules do not apply.
4.241	EC Regulation—member state liquidator	This Rule does not apply.
Part 7 (court procedure and practice)		
7.05	Preliminary	The reference to a petition for a winding-up order under Part V is to be read as a reference to a petition presented under regulation 17(9).
7.27	Right to inspect the file	In paragraph (2)(a)— (a) the reference to a director or officer of the company is to be read as a reference to the operator and the depositary; and (b) the reference to a member of the company is to be read as a reference to a participant.
7.37	Costs and expenses of witnesses	In paragraph (1) the reference to an officer of the insolvent company is to be read as a reference to— (a) the operator or any person who is employed by the operator; or (b) the depositary or any person who is employed by the depositary.
7.51	Restriction on concurrent proceedings and remedies	The reference to the property of a company is to be read as a reference to the property subject to a relevant scheme.

Rule	*Subject*	*Modification*
Part 8 (proxies and company representation)		
8.5	Right of inspection	In paragraph (3) the right of inspection exercisable in the case of an insolvent company by its directors is exercisable in the case of the relevant scheme by the operator or the depositary.
Part 12 (miscellaneous and general)		
12.08	Forms for use in insolvency proceedings	Any form prescribed for use by this Rule which is used in proceedings for winding up a relevant scheme is to be read with the modifications set out in this Schedule (so far as applicable for the form concerned). This Rule is to be read, in relation to such a form, as subject to a requirement to vary the form as necessary to take account of applicable modifications.
12.17	Charge for copy documents	The first reference to a member is to be read as a reference to a participant.
12.20	False claim of status as creditor, etc	In paragraph (1)— (a) each reference to the Rules is to be read as a reference to the Rules as modified by this Schedule; and (b) the reference to the members of a company is to be read, in relation to the winding up of a relevant scheme, as a reference to— (i) the operator or depositary of the relevant scheme; or (ii) the participants in it.

E
ENERGY COMPANIES

ENERGY ACT 2004

(2004 c 20)

ARRANGEMENT OF SECTIONS

PART 2
SUSTAINABILITY AND RENEWABLE ENERGY SOURCES

CHAPTER 3
DECOMMISSIONING OF OFFSHORE INSTALLATIONS

Implementation of decommissioning programmes

110A Protection of funds held for purposes of decommissioning . . . . [7.847]
110B Section 110A: supplemental . . . . [7.848]

PART 3
ENERGY REGULATION

CHAPTER 3
SPECIAL ADMINISTRATION REGIME FOR ENERGY LICENSEES

Energy administration orders

154 Energy administration orders . . . . [7.849]
155 Objective of an energy administration . . . . [7.850]
156 Applications for energy administration orders. . . . . [7.851]
157 Powers of court . . . . [7.852]
158 Energy administrators . . . . [7.853]
159 Conduct of administration, transfer schemes etc . . . . [7.854]

Restrictions on other insolvency procedures

160 Restrictions on winding-up orders . . . . [7.855]
161 Restrictions on voluntary winding up . . . . [7.856]
162 Restrictions on making of ordinary administration orders . . . . [7.857]
163 Restrictions on administrator appointments by creditors etc. . . . . [7.858]
164 Restrictions on enforcement of security . . . . [7.859]

Financial support for companies in administration

165 Grants and loans . . . . [7.860]
166 Indemnities . . . . [7.861]
167 Guarantees where energy administration order is made . . . . [7.862]

Licence modifications relating to energy administration

168 Modifications of particular or standard conditions . . . . [7.863]
169 Licence conditions to secure funding of energy administration . . . . [7.864]

Supplemental provision of Chapter 3 of Part 3

170 Modification of Chapter 3 of Part 3 under Enterprise Act 2002 . . . . [7.865]
171 Interpretation of Chapter 3 of Part 3 . . . . [7.866]

PART 4
MISCELLANEOUS AND SUPPLEMENTAL
Supplemental

196 General interpretation . . . . [7.867]
198 Short title, commencement and extent . . . . [7.868]

SCHEDULES

Schedule 20—Conduct of Energy Administration
Part 1—Application of Schedule B1 to the 1986 Act . . . . [7.869]
Part 2—Modifications of Schedule B1 . . . . [7.870]
Part 3—Further Schedule B1 Modifications for Non-GB companies . . . . [7.871]
Part 4—Other Modifications. . . . . [7.872]
Schedule 21—Energy Transfer Schemes . . . . [7.873]

An Act to make provision for the decommissioning and cleaning up of installations and sites used for, or contaminated by, nuclear activities; to make provision relating to the civil nuclear industry; to make provision about radioactive waste; to make provision for the development, regulation and encouragement of the use of renewable energy sources; to make further provision in connection with the regulation of the gas and electricity industries; to make provision for the imposition of charges in connection with the carrying out of the Secretary of State's functions relating to energy matters; to make provision for giving effect to international agreements relating to pipelines and offshore installations; and for connected purposes

[22 July 2004]

NOTES

Note: the Insolvency Rules 1986, SI 1986/1925 are revoked and replaced (as from 6 April 2017 and subject to transitional provisions) by the Insolvency (England and Wales) Rules 2016, SI 2016/1024 at **[6.2]**, however, the Insolvency (England and Wales) Rules 2016 (Consequential Amendments and Savings) Rules 2017, SI 2017/369, r 3(c) at **[6.947]** provides that the Insolvency Rules 1986 as they had effect immediately before 6 April 2017 and insofar as they apply to proceedings under this Act, continue to have effect for the purposes of the application of this Act.

See also the Deregulation Act 2015 and Small Business, Enterprise and Employment Act 2015 (Consequential Amendments) (Savings) Regulations 2017, SI 2017/540, reg 4(1), (2)(c) and the Insolvency Amendment (EU 2015/848) Regulations 2017, SI 2017/702, reg 4 at **[2.103]**, for savings in relation to the Insolvency Act 1986 in so far as it applies to proceedings under this Act.

1–80 *((Pt 1) outside the scope of this work.)*

PART 2
SUSTAINABILITY AND RENEWABLE ENERGY SOURCES

81–104 *((Chs 1, 2) outside the scope of this work.)*

CHAPTER 3 DECOMMISSIONING OF OFFSHORE INSTALLATIONS

105–108 *(Outside the scope of this work.)*

Implementation of decommissioning programmes

109, 110 *(Outside the scope of this work.)*

[7.847]

[110A Protection of funds held for purposes of decommissioning

(1) This section applies where any security in relation to the carrying out of an approved decommissioning programme, or for compliance with the conditions of its approval, has been provided by a person ("the security provider") by way of a trust or other arrangements.

(2) In this section a reference to "the protected assets" is a reference to the security and any property or rights in which it consists.

(3) The manner in which, and purposes for which, the protected assets are to be applied and enforceable (whether in the event of the security provider's insolvency or otherwise) is to be determined in accordance with the trust or other arrangements.

(4) For the purposes of subsection (3), no regard is to be had to so much of the Insolvency Act 1986, the Insolvency (Northern Ireland) Order 1989 or any other enactment or rule of law as, in its operation in relation to the security provider or any conduct of the security provider, would—

(a) prevent or restrict the protected assets from being applied in accordance with the trust or other arrangement, or

(b) prevent or restrict their enforcement for the purposes of being so applied.

(5) In subsection (4) "enactment" includes an instrument made under an enactment.]

NOTES

Inserted, together with s 110B, by the Energy Act 2008, s 70(1).

[7.848]

[110B Section 110A: supplemental

(1) The [appropriate Minister] may direct a security provider to publish specified information about the protected assets.

(2) A direction under this section may specify—

(a) the time when the information must be published, and

(b) the manner of publication.

(3) If a security provider fails to comply with a direction, the [appropriate Minister] or a creditor of the security provider may make an application to the court under this section.

(4) If, on an application under this section, the court decides that the security provider has failed to comply with the direction, it may order the security provider to take such steps as the court directs for securing that the direction is complied with.

(5) In this section—

"the protected assets" has the same meaning as in section 110A;

"security provider" means a person who has provided security in relation to which that section applies.

(6) In subsections (3) and (4) references to "the court" are references—

(a) to the High Court, in relation to an application in England and Wales or Northern Ireland, or

(b) to the Court of Session, in relation to an application in Scotland.]

NOTES

Inserted as noted to s 110A at **[7.847]**.

Sub-ss (1), (3): words in square brackets substituted by the Scotland Act 2016, s 62(1), (10), subject to transitional provisions and savings in SI 2017/300, regs 3(2), 4.

111–132 *(Ss 111–114, ss 115–132 (Chs 4, 5) outside the scope of this work.)*

PART 3
ENERGY REGULATION

133–153 *((Chs 1, 2) outside the scope of this work.)*

CHAPTER 3 SPECIAL ADMINISTRATION REGIME FOR ENERGY LICENSEES

NOTES

Modification: this Chapter (including Schs 20, 21) is applied with modifications in relation to esc administration orders, by the Energy Act 2011, s 96 at **[7.1065]**.

Energy administration orders

[7.849]

154 Energy administration orders

(1) In this Chapter "energy administration order" means an order which—

(a) is made by the court in relation to a protected energy company; and

(b) directs that, while the order is in force, the affairs, business and property of the company are to be managed by a person appointed by the court.

(2) The person appointed in relation to a company for the purposes of an energy administration order is referred to in this Chapter as the energy administrator of the company.

(3) The energy administrator of a company must manage its affairs, business and property, and exercise and perform all his powers and duties as such, so as to achieve the objective set out in[—

(a) section 155(1), and

(b) section 155(9) (if and to the extent that section 155(9) applies in relation to the company).]

(4) In relation to an energy administration order applying to a non-GB company, references in this section to the affairs, business and property of the company are references only to its affairs and business so far as carried on in Great Britain and to its property in Great Britain.

(5) In this Chapter—

"protected energy company" means a company which is the holder of a relevant licence; and

"relevant licence" means—

(a) a licence granted under section 6(1)(b) or (c) of the 1989 Act (transmission and distribution licences for electricity); or

(b) a licence granted under section 7 of the Gas Act 1986 (licensing of gas transporters).

NOTES

Sub-s (3): sub-paras (a), (b) substituted by the Energy Act 2013, s 48(1), (2).

[7.850]

155 Objective of an energy administration

(1) The objective of an energy administration is to secure—

(a) that the company's system is and continues to be maintained and developed as an efficient and economical system; and

(b) that it becomes unnecessary, by one or both of the following means, for the energy administration order to remain in force for that purpose.

(2) Those means are—

(a) the rescue as a going concern of the company subject to the energy administration order; and

(b) transfers falling within subsection (3).

(3) A transfer falls within this subsection if it is a transfer as a going concern—

(a) to another company, or

(b) as respects different parts of the undertaking of the company subject to the energy administration order, to two or more different companies,

of so much of that undertaking as it is appropriate to transfer for the purpose of achieving the objective of the energy administration.

(4) The means by which transfers falling within subsection (3) may be effected include, in particular—

(a) a transfer of the undertaking of the company subject to the energy administration order, or of a part of its undertaking, to a wholly-owned subsidiary of that company; and

(b) a transfer to a company of securities of a wholly-owned subsidiary to which there has been a transfer falling within paragraph (a).

(5) The objective of an energy administration may be achieved by transfers falling within subsection (3) to the extent only that—

(a) the rescue as a going concern of the company subject to the energy administration order is not reasonably practicable or is not reasonably practicable without such transfers;

(b) the rescue of that company as a going concern will not achieve that objective or will not do so without such transfers;

(c) such transfers would produce a result for the company's creditors as a whole that is better than the result that would be produced without them; or
(d) such transfers would, without prejudicing the interests of those creditors as a whole, produce a result for the company's members as a whole that is better than the result that would be produced without them.

(6) In this section "the company's system", in relation to an energy administration, means—
(a) the system of electricity distribution or of electricity transmission, or
(b) the pipe-line system for the conveyance of gas,

which the company subject to the energy administration order has been maintaining as the holder of a relevant licence.

(7) In this section "efficient and economical", in relation to a system for electricity distribution or electricity transmission, includes co-ordinated.

[(8) Subsection (9) applies if the company in relation to which an energy administration order is made has functions conferred by or by virtue of—
(a) Chapter 2, 3 or 4 of Part 2 of the Energy Act 2013, or
(b) an order made under section 46 of that Act (power of Secretary of State to transfer certain functions).

(9) The objective of an energy administration (in addition to the objective mentioned in subsection (1)) is to secure—
(a) that those functions are and continue to be carried out in an efficient and effective manner; and
(b) that it becomes unnecessary, by one or both of the means mentioned in subsection (2), for the energy administration order to remain in force for that purpose.

(10) The duty under section 154(3), so far as it relates to the objective mentioned in subsection (9)—
(a) applies only to the extent that securing that objective is not inconsistent with securing the objective mentioned in subsection (1);
(b) ceases to apply in respect of any function of a company if an order is made under section 46 of the Energy Act 2013 as a result of which the function is transferred from that company to another person.]

NOTES

Sub-ss (8)–(10): added by the Energy Act 2013, s 48(1), (3).

[7.851]

156 Applications for energy administration orders

(1) An application for an energy administration order in relation to a company may be made only—
(a) by the Secretary of State; or
(b) with the consent of the Secretary of State, by GEMA.

(2) The applicant for an energy administration order in relation to a company must give notice of the application to—
(a) every person who has appointed an administrative receiver of the company;
(b) every person who is or may be entitled to appoint an administrative receiver of the company;
(c) every person who is or may be entitled to make an appointment in relation to the company under paragraph 14 of Schedule B1 to the 1986 Act (appointment of administrators by holders of floating charges); and
(d) such other persons as may be prescribed by energy administration rules.

(3) The notice must be given as soon as reasonably practicable after the making of the application.

(4) In this section "administrative receiver" means—
(a) an administrative receiver within the meaning given by section 251 of the 1986 Act for the purposes of Parts 1 to 7 of that Act; or
(b) a person whose functions in relation to a non-GB company—
(i) are equivalent to those of an administrative receiver; and
(ii) relate only to the affairs and business of the company so far as carried on in Great Britain and to its property in Great Britain.

[7.852]

157 Powers of court

(1) On hearing an application for an energy administration order, the court has the following powers—
(a) it may make the order;
(b) it may dismiss the application;
(c) it may adjourn the hearing conditionally or unconditionally;
(d) it may make an interim order;
(e) it may treat the application as a winding-up petition and make any order the court could make under section 125 of the 1986 Act (power of court on hearing winding-up petition);
(f) it may make any other order which the court thinks appropriate.

(2) The court may make an energy administration order in relation to a company only if it is satisfied—
(a) that the company is unable to pay its debts;
(b) that it is likely to be unable to pay its debts; or
(c) that, on a petition by the Secretary of State under section 124A of the 1986 Act (petition for winding up on grounds of public interest), it would be just and equitable (disregarding the objective of the energy administration) to wind up the company in the public interest.

(3) The court must not make an energy administration order in relation to a company on the ground set out in subsection (2)(c) unless the Secretary of State has certified to the court that the case is one in which he considers (disregarding the objective of the energy administration) that it would be appropriate for him to petition under section 124A of the 1986 Act.

(4) The court has no power to make an energy administration order in relation to a company which—
- (a) is in administration under Schedule B1 to the 1986 Act; or
- (b) has gone into liquidation (within the meaning of section 247(2) of that Act).

(5) An energy administration order comes into force—
- (a) at the time appointed by the court; or
- (b) if no time is so appointed, when the order is made.

(6) An interim order under subsection (1)(d) may, in particular—
- (a) restrict the exercise of a power of the company or of its directors; or
- (b) make provision conferring a discretion on a person qualified to act as an insolvency practitioner in relation to the company.

(7) Where the company in relation to which an application is made is a non-GB company, the reference in subsection (6)(a) to restricting the exercise of a power of the company or of its directors is a reference only to restricting the exercise of such a power—
- (a) within Great Britain; or
- (b) in relation to the company's affairs or business so far as carried on in Great Britain, or to its property in Great Britain.

(8) For the purposes of this section a company is unable to pay its debts if—
- (a) it is a company which is deemed to be so unable under section 123 of the 1986 Act (definition of inability to pay debts); or
- (b) it is an unregistered company which is deemed, by virtue of any of sections 222 to 224 of that Act, to be so unable for the purposes of section 221 of that Act (winding-up of unregistered companies), or which would be so deemed if it were an unregistered company for the purposes of those sections.

[7.853]

158 Energy administrators

(1) The energy administrator of a company—
- (a) is an officer of the court; and
- (b) in exercising and performing his powers and duties in relation to the company, is the company's agent.

(2) The management by the energy administrator of a company of any affairs, business or property of the company must be carried out for the purpose of achieving the objective of the energy administration as quickly and as efficiently as is reasonably practicable.

(3) The energy administrator of a company must exercise and perform his powers and duties in the manner which, so far as it is consistent with the objective of the energy administration to do so, best protects—
- (a) the interests of the creditors of the company as a whole; and
- (b) subject to those interests, the interests of the members of the company as a whole.

(4) A person is not to be the energy administrator of a company unless he is a person qualified to act as an insolvency practitioner in relation to the company.

(5) Where the court makes an appointment in a case in which two or more persons will be the energy administrator of a company after the appointment, the appointment must set out—
- (a) which (if any) of the powers and duties of an energy administrator are to be exercisable or performed only by those persons acting jointly;
- (b) the circumstances (if any) in which powers and duties of an energy administrator are to be exercisable, or may be performed, by one of the persons appointed to be the energy administrator, or by particular appointees, acting alone; and
- (c) the circumstances (if any) in which things done in relation to one of the persons appointed to be the energy administrator, or in relation to particular appointees, are to be treated as done in relation to all of them.

[7.854]

159 Conduct of administration, transfer schemes etc

(1) Schedule 20 (which applies the provisions of Schedule B1 to the 1986 Act about ordinary administration orders and certain other enactments to energy administration orders) has effect.

(2) Schedule 21 (which makes provision for transfer schemes to achieve the objective of an energy administration) has effect.

(3) The power to make rules conferred by section 411 of the 1986 Act (company insolvency rules) shall apply for the purpose of giving effect to this Chapter as it applies for the purpose of giving effect to Parts 1 to 7 of that Act and, accordingly, as if references in that section to those Parts included references to this Chapter [(including this Chapter as applied by section 96 of the Energy Act 2011)].

NOTES

Sub-s (3): words in square brackets inserted by the Energy Act 2011, s 97.

Rules: the Energy Administration Rules 2005, SI 2005/2483 at **[7.874]**; the Energy Administration (Scotland) Rules 2006, SI 2006/772 at **[16.178]**; the Energy Supply Company Administration Rules 2013, SI 2013/1046 at **[7.1074]**; the Energy Supply Company Administration (Scotland) Rules 2013, SI 2013/1047.

Restrictions on other insolvency procedures

[7.855]
160 Restrictions on winding-up orders

(1) This section applies where a petition for the winding-up of a protected energy company is presented by a person other than the Secretary of State.

(2) The court is not to exercise its powers on a winding-up petition unless—

(a) notice of the petition has been served both on the Secretary of State and on GEMA; and
(b) a period of at least fourteen days has elapsed since the service of the last of those notices to be served.

(3) If an application for an energy administration order in relation to the company is made to the court in accordance with section 156(1) before a winding-up order is made on the petition, the court may exercise its powers under section 157, instead of exercising its powers on a winding-up petition.

(4) References in this section to the court's powers on a winding-up petition are references to—

(a) its powers under section 125 of the 1986 Act (other than its power of adjournment); and
(b) its powers under section 135 of that Act.

[7.856]
161 Restrictions on voluntary winding up

(1) A protected energy company has no power to pass a resolution for voluntary winding up without the permission of the court.

(2) Such permission may be granted only on an application made by the company.

(3) The court is not to grant permission on such an application unless—

(a) notice of the application has been served both on the Secretary of State and on GEMA; and
(b) a period of at least fourteen days has elapsed since the service of the last of those notices to be served.

(4) If an application for an energy administration order in relation to the company is made to the court in accordance with section 156(1) after an application for permission under this section has been made and before it is granted, the court may exercise its powers under section 157, instead of granting permission.

(5) In this section "a resolution for voluntary winding up" has the same meaning as in the 1986 Act.

[7.857]
162 Restrictions on making of ordinary administration orders

(1) This section applies where an ordinary administration application is made in relation to a protected energy company by a person other than the Secretary of State.

(2) The court must dismiss the application if—

(a) an energy administration order is in force in relation to the company; or
(b) an energy administration order has been made in relation to the company but is not yet in force.

(3) Where subsection (2) does not apply, the court, on hearing the application, must not exercise its powers under paragraph 13 of Schedule B1 to the 1986 Act (other than its power of adjournment) unless—

(a) notice of the application has been served both on the Secretary of State and on GEMA;
(b) a period of at least fourteen days has elapsed since the service of the last of those notices to be served; and
(c) there is no application for an energy administration order that is outstanding.

(4) Paragraph 44 of Schedule B1 to the 1986 Act (interim moratorium) does not prevent, or require the permission of the court for, the making of an application for an energy administration order.

(5) Upon the making of an energy administration order in relation to a protected energy company, the court must dismiss any ordinary administration application made in relation to that company which is outstanding.

(6) In this section "ordinary administration application" means an application in accordance with paragraph 12 of Schedule B1 to the 1986 Act.

[7.858]
163 Restrictions on administrator appointments by creditors etc

(1) No step is to be taken by any person to make an appointment in relation to a company under paragraph 14 or 22 of Schedule B1 to the 1986 Act (powers of holder of floating charge and of the company itself and of its directors to appoint administrators) if—

(a) an energy administration order is in force in relation to the company;
(b) an energy administration order has been made in relation to the company but is not yet in force; or
(c) an application for such an order is outstanding.

(2) In the case of a protected energy company to which subsection (1) does not apply, an appointment in relation to that company under paragraph 14 or 22 of Schedule B1 to the 1986 Act takes effect only if each of the conditions mentioned in subsection (3) is met.

(3) Those conditions are—

(a) that a copy of every document in relation to the appointment that is filed or lodged with the court in accordance with paragraph 18 or 29 of Schedule B1 to the 1986 Act (documents to be filed or lodged for appointment of administrator) has been served both on the Secretary of State and on GEMA;
(b) that a period of fourteen days has elapsed since the service of the last of those copies to be served;

(c) that there is no outstanding application to the court for an energy administration order in relation to the company in question; and
(d) that the making of an application for such an order has not resulted in the making of an energy administration order which is in force or is still to come into force.

(4) Paragraph 44 of Schedule B1 to the 1986 Act (interim moratorium) does not prevent, or require the permission of the court for, the making of an application for an energy administration order at any time before the appointment takes effect.

[7.859]
164 Restrictions on enforcement of security

(1) No step to enforce a security over property of a protected energy company is to be taken by any person, unless—
(a) notice of his intention to do so has been served both on the Secretary of State and on GEMA; and
(b) a period of at least fourteen days has elapsed since the service of the last of those notices to be served.

(2) In the case of a protected energy company which is a non-GB company, the reference in subsection (1) to the property of the company is a reference only to its property in Great Britain.

Financial support for companies in administration

[7.860]
165 Grants and loans

(1) This section applies where an energy administration order has been made in relation to a company.
(2) The Secretary of State may make grants or loans to the company of such amounts as it appears to him appropriate to pay or lend for achieving the objective of the energy administration.
(3) A grant or loan under this section may be made in whatever manner, and on whatever terms, the Secretary of State considers appropriate.
(4) The terms on which a grant may be made under this section include, in particular, terms requiring the whole or a part of the grant to be repaid to the Secretary of State if there is a contravention of the other terms on which the grant is made.
(5) The terms on which a loan may be made under this section include, in particular, terms requiring—
(a) the loan to be repaid at such times and by such methods, and
(b) interest to be paid on the loan at such rates and at such times,
as the Secretary of State may from time to time direct.
(6) The consent of the Treasury is required—
(a) for the making of a grant or loan under this section; and
(b) for the giving by the Secretary of State of a direction under subsection (5).
(7) The Secretary of State must pay sums received by him by virtue of this section into the Consolidated Fund.

[7.861]
166 Indemnities

(1) This section applies where an energy administration order has been made in relation to a company.
(2) The Secretary of State may agree to indemnify persons in respect of one or both of the following—
(a) liabilities incurred in connection with the exercise and performance by the energy administrator of his powers and duties; and
(b) loss or damage sustained in that connection.
(3) The agreement may be made in whatever manner, and on whatever terms, the Secretary of State considers appropriate.
[(3AA) As soon as practicable after agreeing to indemnify persons under this section, the Secretary of State must lay a statement of the agreement before Parliament.]
(4) If sums are paid by the Secretary of State in consequence of an indemnity agreed to under this section, the company must pay him—
(a) such amounts in or towards the repayment to him of those sums as he may direct; and
(b) interest, at such rates as he may direct, on amounts outstanding under this subsection.
(5) Payments to the Secretary of State under subsection (4) must be made at such times and in such manner as he may determine.
(6) Subsection (4) does not apply in the case of a sum paid by the Secretary of State for indemnifying a person in respect of a liability to the company in relation to which the energy administration order was made.
[(6A) Where a sum has been paid out by the Secretary of State in consequence of an indemnity agreed to under this section, the Secretary of State must lay a statement relating to that sum before Parliament—
(a) as soon as practicable after the end of the financial year in which that sum is paid out; and
(b) (except where subsection (4) does not apply in the case of the sum) as soon as practicable after the end of each subsequent relevant financial year.
(6B) In relation to a sum paid out in consequence of an indemnity, a financial year is a relevant financial year for the purposes of subsection (6A) unless—
(a) before the beginning of that year, the whole of that sum has been repaid to the Secretary of State under subsection (4); and
(b) the company in question is not at any time during that year subject to liability to pay interest on amounts that became due under that subsection in respect of that sum.]
(7) The consent of the Treasury is required—
(a) for the doing of anything by the Secretary of State under subsection (2);

(b) for the giving by him of any direction under subsection (4); and
(c) for the making of a determination under subsection (5).

(8) The power of the Secretary of State to agree to indemnify persons—
(a) is confined to a power to agree to indemnify persons in respect of liabilities, loss and damage incurred or sustained by them as relevant persons; but
(b) includes power to agree to indemnify persons (whether or not they are identified or identifiable at the time of the agreement) who subsequently become relevant persons.

(9) A person is a relevant person for the purposes of this section if he is—
(a) the energy administrator;
(b) an employee of the energy administrator;
(c) a member or employee of a firm of which the energy administrator is a member;
(d) a member or employee of a firm of which the energy administrator is an employee;
(e) a member of a firm of which the energy administrator was an employee or member at a time when the order was in force;
(f) a body corporate which is the employer of the energy administrator;
(g) an officer, employee or member of such a body corporate.

(10) For the purposes of subsection (9)—
(a) the references to the energy administrator are to be construed, where two or more persons are appointed to act as the energy administrator, as references to any one or more of them; and
(b) the references to a firm of which a person was a member or employee at a particular time include references to a firm which holds itself out to be the successor of a firm of which he was a member or employee at that time.

(11) The Secretary of State must pay sums received by him by virtue of subsection (4) into the Consolidated Fund.

NOTES

Sub-s (3AA): inserted by the Energy Act 2011, s 93(1), (2).
Sub-ss (6A), (6B): inserted by the Energy Act 2011, s 93(1), (3).

[7.862]
167 Guarantees where energy administration order is made

(1) This section applies where an energy administration order has been made in relation to a company.

(2) The Secretary of State may guarantee—
(a) the repayment of any sum borrowed by the company while the energy administration order is in force;
(b) the payment of interest on such a sum; and
(c) the discharge of any other financial obligation of the company in connection with the borrowing of such a sum.

(3) The Secretary of State may give a guarantee under this section in such manner, and on such terms, as he thinks fit.

(4) As soon as practicable after giving a guarantee under this section, the Secretary of State must lay a statement of the guarantee before Parliament.

(5) If sums are paid out by the Secretary of State under a guarantee given under this section, the company must pay him—
(a) such amounts in or towards the repayment to him of those sums as he may direct; and
(b) interest, at such rates as he may direct, on amounts outstanding under this subsection.

(6) Payments to the Secretary of State under subsection (5) must be made at such times, and in such manner, as he may from time to time direct.

(7) Where a sum has been paid out by the Secretary of State under a guarantee given under this section, he must lay a statement relating to that sum before Parliament—
(a) as soon as practicable after the end of the financial year in which that sum is paid out; and
(b) as soon as practicable after the end of each subsequent relevant financial year.

(8) In relation to a sum paid out under a guarantee, a financial year is a relevant financial year for the purposes of subsection (7) unless—
(a) before the beginning of that year, the whole of that sum has been repaid to the Secretary of State under subsection (5); and
(b) the company in question is not at any time during that year subject to liability to pay interest on amounts that became due under that subsection in respect of that sum.

(9) The consent of the Treasury is required—
(a) for the giving of a guarantee under this section; and
(b) for the giving by the Secretary of State of a direction under subsection (5) or (6).

(10) The Secretary of State must pay sums received by him by virtue of subsection (5) into the Consolidated Fund.

Licence modifications relating to energy administration

[7.863]
168 Modifications of particular or standard conditions

(1) Where the Secretary of State considers it appropriate to do so in connection with the provision made by this Chapter, he may make—
(a) modifications of the conditions of a gas or electricity licence held by a particular person;
(b) modifications of the standard conditions of such licences of any type.

(2) The power to make modifications under this section includes power to make incidental, consequential or transitional modifications.

(3) Before making a modification under this section, the Secretary of State must consult—
(a) the holder of any licence being modified; and
(b) such other persons as he considers appropriate.

(4) Subsection (3) may be satisfied by consultation that took place wholly or partly before the commencement of this section.

(5) The Secretary of State must publish every modification made by him under this section.

(6) The publication must be in such manner as the Secretary of State considers appropriate.

(7) A modification under subsection (1)(a) of part of a standard condition of a licence does not prevent any other part of the condition from continuing to be regarded as a standard condition for the purposes of Part 1 of the 1989 Act or Part 1 of the Gas Act 1986 (c 44).

(8) Where the Secretary of State makes modifications under subsection (1)(b) of the standard conditions of licences of any type, GEMA must—
(a) make (as nearly as may be) the same modifications of those standard conditions for the purposes of their incorporation in licences of that type granted after that time; and
(b) publish the modifications in such manner as it considers appropriate.

(9) The Secretary of State's powers under this section are exercisable only during the eighteen months beginning with the commencement of this section.

(10) In section 81(2) of the Utilities Act 2000 (c 27) (standard conditions of licences under Part 1 of the Gas Act), for "such modifications of the conditions made under Part I of the 1986 Act" substitute "any modifications made under Part 1 of the 1986 Act or under the Energy Act 2004".

(11) In this section "gas or electricity licence" means a licence for the purposes of section 5 of the Gas Act 1986 (c 44) or section 4 of the 1989 Act (prohibition on unlicensed activities).

[7.864]
169 Licence conditions to secure funding of energy administration

(1) The modifications that may be made under section 168 include, in particular, modifications imposing conditions requiring the holder of the licence—
(a) so to modify the charges imposed by him for anything done by him in the carrying on of the licensed activities as to raise such amounts as may be determined by or under the conditions; and
(b) to pay the amounts so raised to such persons as may be so determined for the purpose of—
(i) their applying those amounts in making good any shortfall in the property available for meeting the expenses of an energy administration; or
(ii) enabling those persons to secure that those amounts are so applied.

(2) Those modifications may include modifications imposing on the licence holder an obligation to apply amounts paid to him in pursuance of conditions falling within subsection (1)(a) or (b) in making good any such shortfall.

(3) For the purposes of this section—
(a) there is a shortfall in the property available for meeting the costs of an energy administration if, in a case where a company is or has been subject to an energy administration order, the property available (apart from conditions falling within subsection (1) or (2)) for meeting relevant debts is insufficient for meeting them; and
(b) amounts are applied in making good that shortfall if they are paid in or towards discharging so much of a relevant debt as cannot be met out of the property otherwise available for meeting relevant debts.

(4) In this section "relevant debt", in relation to a case in which a company is or has been subject to an energy administration order, means an obligation—
(a) to make payments in respect of the expenses or remuneration of any person as the energy administrator of that company;
(b) to make a payment in discharge of a debt or liability of that company arising out of a contract entered into at a time when the order was in force by the person who at that time was the energy administrator of that company;
(c) to repay the whole or a part of a grant made to that company under section 165;
(d) to repay a loan made to the company under that section, or to pay interest on such a loan;
(e) to make a payment under section 166(4); or
(f) to make a payment under section 167(5).

Supplemental provision of Chapter 3 of Part 3

[7.865]
170 Modification of Chapter 3 of Part 3 under Enterprise Act 2002

(1) The power to modify or apply enactments conferred on the Secretary of State by each of the sections of the Enterprise Act 2002 (c 40) mentioned in subsection (2) includes power to make such consequential modifications of this Chapter [(including this Chapter as applied by section 96 of the Energy Act 2011)] as he considers appropriate in connection with any other provision made under that section.

(2) Those sections are—
(a) sections 248 and 277 (amendments consequential on that Act); and
(b) section 254 (power to apply insolvency law to foreign companies).

NOTES

Sub-s (1): words in square brackets inserted by the Energy Act 2011, s 100(3).

[7.866]

171 Interpretation of Chapter 3 of Part 3

(1) In this Chapter—

"the 1986 Act" means the Insolvency Act 1986 (c 45);

"business", "member", "property" and "security" have the same meanings as in the 1986 Act;

["company" means—

(a) a company registered under the Companies Act 2006, or

(b) an unregistered company;]

["court", in relation to a company, means the court—

(a) having jurisdiction to wind up the company, or

(b) that would have such jurisdiction apart from section 221(2) or 441(2) of the Insolvency Act 1986 (exclusion of winding up jurisdiction in case of companies having principal place of business in, or incorporated in, Northern Ireland);]

"energy administration order" has the meaning given by section 154(1);

"energy administration rules" means rules made under section 411 of the 1986 Act by virtue of section 159(3) of this Act;

"energy administrator" has the meaning given by section 154(2) and is to be construed in accordance with subsection (2) of this section;

["non-GB company" means a company incorporated outside Great Britain;]

"objective of the energy administration" is to be construed in accordance with section 155;

"protected energy company" has the meaning given by section 154(5);

"relevant licence" has the meaning given by section 154(5);

["unregistered company" means a company that is not registered under the Companies Act 2006.]

(2) In this Chapter references to the energy administrator of a company—

(a) include references to a person appointed under paragraph 91 or 103 of Schedule B1 to the 1986 Act, as applied by Part 1 of Schedule 20 to this Act, to be the energy administrator of that company; and

(b) where two or more persons are appointed to be the energy administrator of that company, are to be construed in accordance with the provision made under section 158(5).

(3) References in this Chapter to a person qualified to act as an insolvency practitioner in relation to a company are to be construed in accordance with Part 13 of the 1986 Act (insolvency practitioners and their qualifications); but as if references in that Part to a company included references to a [Northern Ireland company].

(4) For the purposes of this Chapter an application made to the court is outstanding if it—

(a) has not yet been granted or dismissed; and

(b) has not been withdrawn.

(5) For the purposes of subsection (4) an application is not to be taken as having been dismissed if an appeal against the dismissal of the application, or a subsequent appeal, is pending.

(6) An appeal shall be treated as pending for the purposes of subsection (5) if—

(a) such an appeal has been brought and has been neither determined nor withdrawn;

(b) an application for permission to appeal has been made but has not been determined or withdrawn; or

(c) no such appeal has been brought and the period for bringing an appeal is still running.

(7) References in this Chapter to Schedule B1 to the 1986 Act, or to a provision of that Schedule (except the references in subsection (2) of this section), are references to that Schedule or that provision without the modifications made by Part 1 of Schedule 20 to this Act.

[(8) In this section "Northern Ireland company" means a company registered under the Companies Act 2006 in Northern Ireland.]

NOTES

Sub-s (1): definitions "company", "court", "non-GB company" and "unregistered company" substituted by the Companies Act 2006 (Consequential Amendments, Transitional Provisions and Savings) Order 2009, SI 2009/1941, art 2(1), Sch 1, para 220(1), (4).

Sub-s (3): words in square brackets substituted by SI 2009/1941, art 2(1), Sch 1, para 220(1), (5).

Sub-s (8): substituted by SI 2009/1941, art 2(1), Sch 1, para 220(1), (6).

172–187 (*(Ch 4) outside the scope of this work.*)

PART 4
MISCELLANEOUS AND SUPPLEMENTAL

188–191 (*Outside the scope of this work.*)

Supplemental

192–195 (*Outside the scope of this work.*)

[7.867]

196 General interpretation

(1) In this Act—

"the 1965 Act" means the Nuclear Installations Act 1965 (c 57);

"the 1989 Act" means the Electricity Act 1989 (c 29);

"the 1993 Act" means the Radioactive Substances Act 1993 (c 12);

"affirmative resolution procedure" is to be construed in accordance with section 192(3);

"BNFL" means the Nuclear Fuels Company (within the meaning of the Atomic Energy Authority Act 1971 (c 11));
"contravention" includes a failure to comply, and cognate expressions are to be construed accordingly;
"documents" includes accounts, drawings, written representations and records of any description;
"electronic communications network" has the same meaning as in the Communication Act 2003 (c 21);
"enactment" [(except in Chapter 5 of Part 2)] includes Acts of the Scottish Parliament and Northern Ireland legislation;
"financial year" means a period of twelve months ending with 31st March;
"GEMA" means the Gas and Electricity Markets Authority;
"modification" includes omission, addition or alteration, and cognate expressions are to be construed accordingly;
"the NDA" means the Nuclear Decommissioning Authority established by section 1;
"negative resolution procedure" is to be construed in accordance with section 192(2);
"nuclear site licence" has the same meaning as in the 1965 Act;
"nuclear transfer scheme" means a scheme under section 38;
"pensions, allowances or gratuities" is to be construed in accordance with subsection (2);
"securities", in relation to a body corporate, includes shares, debentures, debenture stock, bonds and other securities of the body corporate, whether or not constituting a charge on the assets of the body corporate;
"shares" includes stock;
"subordinate legislation" has the same meaning as in the Interpretation Act 1978 (c 30);
"subsidiary" and "wholly-owned subsidiary" have the meanings given by [section 1159 of the Companies Act 2006];
"the UKAEA" means the United Kingdom Atomic Energy Authority.

(2) In this Act—
(a) references to pensions, allowances or gratuities include references to any similar benefits provided on death or retirement; and
(b) references to the payment of pensions, allowances or gratuities to or in respect of a person include references to the making of payments towards the provision of the payment of pensions, allowances or gratuities to or in respect of that person.

NOTES

Sub-s (1): definition "the 1993 Act" repealed, in relation to England and Wales, by the Environmental Permitting (England and Wales) Regulations 2010, SI 2010/675, regs 107, 109(1), Sch 26, Pt 1, para 17(1), (4), Sch 28; words in square brackets in definition "enactment" inserted by the Climate Change Act 2008, s 78, Sch 7, paras 1, 7(1), (4); words in square brackets in definition "subsidiary" substituted by the Companies Act 2006 (Consequential Amendments, Transitional Provisions and Savings) Order 2009, SI 2009/1941, art 2(1), Sch 1, para 220(1), (7).

Modification: this section is applied with modifications in relation to esc administration orders, by the Energy Act 2011, s 96(1), (5) at **[7.1065]**.

197 (*Outside the scope of this work.*)

[7.868]
198 Short title, commencement and extent
(1) This Act may be cited as the Energy Act 2004.
(2) This Act (apart from this section) shall come into force on such day as the Secretary of State may by order appoint; and different days may be appointed for different purposes.
(3) Subject to subsection (4) of this section, this Act extends to Northern Ireland.
(4) The following provisions of this Act do not extend to Northern Ireland—
(a)–(c) (*outside the scope of this work*);
(d) Part 3 (with the exception of section 151(5)).

NOTES

Orders: at present, 11 commencement orders have been made under this section. The orders relevant to the provisions of this Act printed in this work are the Energy Act 2004 (Commencement No 2) Order 2004, SI 2004/2184 and the Energy Act 2004 (Commencement No 3) Order 2004, SI 2004/2575.

SCHEDULES 1–19

(*Schs 1–19 outside the scope of this work.*)

SCHEDULE 20
CONDUCT OF ENERGY ADMINISTRATION

Section 159

PART 1
APPLICATION OF SCHEDULE B1 TO THE 1986 ACT

Application of Schedule B1 provisions

[7.869]
1. (1) The provisions of Schedule B1 to the 1986 Act specified in paragraph 2 of this Schedule are to have effect in relation to energy administration orders—

(a) as they have effect in relation to administration orders under that Schedule; but
(b) with the modifications set out in Part 2 of this Schedule.

(2) Those provisions as modified by Part 2 of this Schedule are to have effect in the case of [a non-GB company] with the further modifications for which provision is made by or under Part 3 of this Schedule.

2. Those provisions of Schedule B1 to the 1986 Act are paragraphs 1, 40 to 50, 54, 59 to 68, 70 to 75, 79, 83 to 91, 98 to 107 and 109 to 116.

NOTES

Para 1: words in square brackets substituted by the Companies Act 2006 (Consequential Amendments, Transitional Provisions and Savings) Order 2009, SI 2009/1941, art 2(1), Sch 1, para 220(1), (11)(a).

PART 2
MODIFICATIONS OF SCHEDULE B1

Introductory

[7.870]

3. The modifications set out in this Part of this Schedule to the provisions of Schedule B1 to the 1986 Act specified in paragraph 2 apply where those provisions have effect by virtue of Part 1 of this Schedule.

General modifications of the applicable provisions

4. In those provisions—
(a) for "administration application" in each place where it occurs substitute "energy administration application";
(b) for "administration order" in each place where it occurs substitute "energy administration order";
(c) for "administrator" in each place where it occurs substitute "energy administrator";
(d) for "enters administration" in each place where it occurs substitute "enters energy administration";
(e) for "in administration" in each place where it occurs substitute "in energy administration";
(f) for "purpose of administration" in each place where it occurs (other than in paragraph 111(1)) substitute "objective of the energy administration".

Specific modifications

5. (1) In paragraph 1, for sub-paragraph (1) (which defines "administrator") substitute—

"(1) In this Schedule "energy administrator", in relation to a company, means a person appointed by the court for the purposes of an energy administration order to manage the company's affairs, business and property."

(2) In sub-paragraph (2) of that paragraph, for "Act" substitute "Schedule".

6. In paragraph 40 (dismissal of pending winding-up petition), omit sub-paragraphs (1)(b), (2) and (3).

7. In paragraph 42 (moratorium on insolvency proceedings), omit sub-paragraphs (4) and (5).

8. In paragraph 44 (interim moratorium), omit sub-paragraphs (2) to (4), (6) and (7)(a) to (c).

9. In paragraph 46(6) (date for notifying administrator's appointment), for paragraphs (a) to (c) substitute "the date on which the energy administration order comes into force".

10. (1) In sub-paragraph (2)(b) of paragraph 49 (administrator's proposals) for "objective mentioned in paragraph 3(1)(a) or (b) cannot be achieved" substitute "objective of the energy administration should be achieved by means other than just a rescue of the company as a going concern".
(2) After sub-paragraph (4)(a) of that paragraph insert—

"(aa) to the Secretary of State and to GEMA,".

11. For paragraph 54 (revision of administrator's proposals) substitute—

"**54.** (1) The energy administrator of a company may on one or more occasions revise the proposals included in the statement made under paragraph 49 in relation to the company.
(2) Where the energy administrator thinks that a revision by him is substantial, he must send a copy of the revised proposals—
(a) to the registrar of companies,
(b) to the Secretary of State and to GEMA,
(c) to every creditor of the company of whose claim and address he is aware, and
(d) to every member of the company of whose address he is aware.
(3) A copy sent in accordance with sub-paragraph (2) must be sent within the prescribed period.
(4) The energy administrator is to be taken to have complied with sub-paragraph (2)(d) if he publishes, in the prescribed manner, a notice undertaking to provide a copy of the revised proposals free of charge to any member of the company who applies in writing to a specified address.
(5) The energy administrator commits an offence if he fails without reasonable excuse to comply with this paragraph."

12. In paragraph 60 (powers of an administrator), the existing text is to be sub-paragraph (1) and after that sub-paragraph insert—

"(2) The energy administrator of a company has the power to act on behalf of the company for the purposes of any enactment or subordinate legislation which confers a power on the company, or imposes a duty on it.

(3) In sub-paragraph (2) "enactment" has the same meaning as in the Energy Act 2004."

13. (1) In paragraph 68 (management duties of an administrator), for sub-paragraph (1)(a) to (c) substitute

"the proposals as—

(a) set out in the statement made under paragraph 49 in relation to the company, and

(b) from time to time revised under paragraph 54,

for achieving the objective of the energy administration."

(2) For sub-paragraph (3)(a) to (d) of that paragraph substitute "the directions are consistent with the achievement of the objective of the energy administration".

14. In paragraphs 71(3)(b) and 72(3)(b) (handling of secured property), for "market" substitute "the appropriate".

15. In paragraph 73(3) (which contains a reference to the administrator's proposals), for "or modified" substitute "under paragraph 54".

16. (1) In paragraph 74 (challenge to administrator's conduct), for sub-paragraph (2) substitute—

"(2) Where a company is in energy administration, a person mentioned in sub-paragraph (2A) may apply to the court claiming that the energy administrator is conducting himself in a manner preventing the achievement of the objective of the energy administration as quickly and efficiently as is reasonably practicable.

(2A) The persons who may apply to the court under sub-paragraph (2) are—

(a) the Secretary of State;

(b) with the consent of the Secretary of State, GEMA;

(c) a creditor or member of the company."

(2) In sub-paragraph (6) of that paragraph, for paragraphs (a) to (c) substitute—

"(a) a voluntary arrangement approved under Part 1, or

(b) a compromise or arrangement sanctioned under [section 899 of the Companies Act 2006] (compromise with creditors and members)."

(3) After that sub-paragraph insert—

"(7) In the case of a claim made otherwise than by the Secretary of State or GEMA, the court may grant a remedy or relief or make an order under this paragraph only if it has given the Secretary of State or GEMA a reasonable opportunity of making representations about the claim and the proposed remedy, relief or order.

(8) The court may grant a remedy or relief or make an order on an application under this paragraph only if it is satisfied, in relation to the matters that are the subject of the application, that the energy administrator—

(a) is acting,

(b) has acted, or

(c) is proposing to act,

in a way that is inconsistent with the achievement of the objective of the energy administration as quickly and as efficiently as is reasonably practicable.

(9) Before the making of an order of the kind mentioned in sub-paragraph (4)(d)—

(a) the court must notify the energy administrator of the proposed order and of a period during which he is to have the opportunity of taking steps falling within sub-paragraphs (10) to (12); and

(b) the period notified must have expired without the taking of such of those steps as the court thinks should have been taken;

and that period must be a reasonable period.

(10) In the case of a claim under sub-paragraph (1)(a), the steps referred to in sub-paragraph (9) are—

(a) ceasing to act in a manner that unfairly harms the interests to which the claim relates;

(b) remedying any harm unfairly caused to those interests; and

(c) steps for ensuring that there is no repetition of conduct unfairly causing harm to those interests.

(11) In the case of a claim under sub-paragraph (1)(b), the steps referred to in sub-paragraph (9) are steps for ensuring that the interests to which the claim relates are not unfairly harmed.

(12) In the case of a claim under sub-paragraph (2), the steps referred to in sub-paragraph (9) are—

(a) ceasing to act in a manner preventing the achievement of the objective of the energy administration as quickly and as efficiently as is reasonably practicable;

(b) remedying the consequences of the energy administrator having acted in such a manner; and

(c) steps for ensuring that there is no repetition of conduct preventing the achievement of the objective of the energy administration as quickly and as efficiently as is reasonably practicable."

17. In paragraph 75(2) (misfeasance), after paragraph (b) insert—

"(ba) a person appointed as an administrator of the company under the provisions of this Act, as they have effect in relation to administrators other than energy administrators,".

18. (1) In paragraph 79 (end of administration), for sub-paragraphs (1) and (2) substitute—

"(1) On an application made by a person mentioned in sub-paragraph (2), the court may provide for the appointment of an energy administrator of a company to cease to have effect from a specified time.

(2) An application may be made to the court under this paragraph—

(a) by the Secretary of State,

(b) with the consent of the Secretary of State, by GEMA, or

(c) with the consent of the Secretary of State, by the energy administrator."

(2) Omit sub-paragraph (3) of that paragraph.

19. In paragraph 83(3) (notice to registrar when moving to voluntary liquidation), after "may" insert ", with the consent of the Secretary of State or of GEMA,".

20. (1) In paragraph 84 (notice to registrar when moving to dissolution), in sub-paragraph (1), for "to the registrar of companies" substitute—

"(a) to the Secretary of State and to GEMA; and

(b) if directed to do so by either the Secretary of State or GEMA, to the registrar of companies."

(2) Omit sub-paragraph (2) of that paragraph.

(3) In sub-paragraphs (3) to (6) of that paragraph, for "(1)", wherever occurring, substitute "(1)(b)".

21. In paragraph 87 (resignation of administrator), for sub-paragraph (2)(a) to (d) substitute "by notice in writing to the court".

22. In paragraph 89 (administrator ceasing to be qualified), for sub-paragraph (2)(a) to (d) substitute "to the court".

23. In paragraph 90 (filling vacancy in office of administrator), for "Paragraphs 91 to 95 apply" substitute "Paragraph 91 applies".

24. (1) In paragraph 91 (vacancies in court appointments), for sub-paragraph (1) substitute—

"(1) The court may replace the energy administrator on an application made—

(a) by the Secretary of State;

(b) with the consent of the Secretary of State, by GEMA; or

(c) where more than one person was appointed to act jointly as the energy administrator, by any of those persons who remains in office."

(2) Omit sub-paragraph (2) of that paragraph.

25. In paragraph 98 (discharge from liability on vacation of office), omit sub-paragraphs (2)(b) and (3).

26. (1) In paragraph 99 (charges and liabilities upon vacation of office by administrator), in sub-paragraph (4), for the words from the beginning to "cessation", where first occurring, substitute "A sum falling within sub-paragraph (4A)".

(2) After that sub-paragraph insert—

"(4A) A sum falls within this sub-paragraph if it is—

(a) a sum payable in respect of a debt or liability arising out of a contract that was entered into before cessation by the former energy administrator or a predecessor;

(b) a sum that must be repaid by the company in respect of a grant that was made before cessation under section 165 of the Energy Act 2004 as is mentioned in subsection (4) of that section;

(c) a sum that must be repaid by the company in respect of a loan made before cessation under that section or that must be paid by the company in respect of interest payable on such a loan;

(d) a sum payable by the company under subsection (4) of section 166 of that Act in respect of an agreement to indemnify made before cessation; or

(e) a sum payable by the company under subsection (5) of section 167 of that Act in respect of a guarantee given before cessation."

(3) In sub-paragraph (5) of that paragraph, for "(4)" substitute "(4A)(a)".

27. In paragraph 100 (joint and concurrent administrators), omit sub-paragraph (2).

28. In paragraph 101(3) (joint administrators), after "87 to" insert "91, 98 and".

29. (1) In paragraph 103 (appointment of additional administrators), in sub-paragraph (2)—
(a) omit the words from the beginning to "order";
(b) for paragraph (a) substitute—

"(a) the Secretary of State,
(aa) GEMA, or".

(2) After that sub-paragraph insert—

"(2A) The consent of the Secretary of State is required for an application by GEMA for the purposes of sub-paragraph (2)."

(3) Omit sub-paragraphs (3) to (5) of that paragraph.

30. In paragraph 106 (penalties), omit sub-paragraph (2)(a), (b), (f), (g), (i) and (l) to (n).

31. In paragraph 109 (references to extended periods), omit "or 108".

32. (1) In sub-paragraph (1) of paragraph 111 (interpretation)—
(a) omit the definitions of "correspondence", "holder of a qualifying floating charge", "market value", "the purpose of administration" and "unable to pay its debts";
(b) after the definition of "administrator" (as amended by virtue of paragraph 4 of this Schedule) insert—

""appropriate value" means the best price which would be reasonably available on a sale which is consistent with the achievement of the objective of the energy administration;"

(c) for the definition of "company" substitute—

""company", "court" and "energy administration order" have the same meanings as in Chapter 3 of Part 3 of the Energy Act 2004;"

(d) after the definition of "creditors' meeting" insert—

""energy administration application" means an application to the court for an energy administration order under Chapter 3 of Part 3 of the Energy Act 2004;
"GEMA" means the Gas and Electricity Markets Authority;"

(e) after the definition of "hire purchase agreement" insert—

""objective", in relation to an energy administration, is to be construed in accordance with section 155 of the Energy Act 2004;
"prescribed" means prescribed by energy administration rules within the meaning of Chapter 3 of Part 3 of the Energy Act 2004;".

(2) After sub-paragraph (3) of that paragraph insert—

"(4) For the purposes of this Schedule a reference to an energy administration order includes a reference to an appointment under paragraph 91 or 103."

NOTES

Para 16: words in square brackets substituted for original words "section 425 of the Companies Act" by the Companies Act 2006 (Consequential Amendments etc) Order 2008, SI 2008/948, art 3(1)(b), Sch 1, Pt 2, para 230, subject to transitional provisions and savings in arts 6, 11, 12 thereof.

PART 3
FURTHER SCHEDULE B1 MODIFICATIONS FOR [NON-GB COMPANIES]

Introductory

[7.871]

33. (1) Where the provisions of Schedule B1 to the 1986 Act specified in paragraph 2 of this Schedule (as modified by Part 2 of this Schedule) have effect in relation to [a non-GB company], they shall do so subject to the further modifications that are set out—
(a) in this Part of this Schedule; or
(b) in an order made by the Secretary of State for the purposes of this paragraph.

(2) An order under this paragraph may include modifications of paragraphs 35 to 40.
(3) An order under this paragraph is subject to the negative resolution procedure.

34. In paragraphs 35 to 40—
(a) the provisions of Schedule B1 to the 1986 Act that are specified in paragraph 2 are referred to as the applicable provisions; and
(b) references to those provisions, or to provisions comprised in them, are references to those provisions as modified by Part 2 of this Schedule.

Modifications

35. In the case of [a non-GB company]—
(a) paragraphs 42(2), 83 and 84 of Schedule B1 to the 1986 Act do not apply;

(b) paragraphs 46(4), 49(4)(a), 54(2)(a), 71(5) and (6), 72(4) and (5) and 86 of that Schedule apply only if the company is subject to a requirement imposed [by regulations under section 1043 or 1046 of the Companies Act 2006 (unregistered UK companies or overseas companies)]; and
(c) paragraph 61 of that Schedule does not apply . . .

36. (1) The applicable provisions and Schedule 1 to the 1986 Act (as applied by paragraph 60(1) of Schedule B1 to that Act) are to be construed . . . by reference to the limitation imposed upon the scope of the energy administration order in question by virtue of section 154(4) of this Act.

(2) Sub-paragraph (1) has effect, in particular, so that—
(a) a power conferred, or duty imposed, upon the energy administrator by or under the applicable provisions or Schedule 1 to the 1986 Act is to be construed as being conferred or imposed only in relation to the affairs and business of the company so far as carried on in Great Britain and to its property in Great Britain;
(b) references to the affairs, business or property of the company are to be construed as references to its affairs or business so far as carried on in Great Britain or to its property in Great Britain;
(c) references to goods in the company's possession are to be construed as references to goods in the possession of the company in Great Britain;
(d) references to premises let to the company are to be construed as references to premises let to the company in Great Britain;
(e) references to legal process instituted or continued against the company or property of the company are to be construed as references to such legal process relating to the affairs or business of the company so far as carried on in Great Britain or to its property in Great Britain.

37. (1) Paragraph 41 of Schedule B1 to the 1986 Act (dismissal of receivers) has effect . . . as if—
(a) for sub-paragraph (1) there were substituted the sub-paragraphs set out in sub-paragraph (2) of this paragraph; and
(b) sub-paragraphs (2) to (4) of that paragraph were omitted.

(2) The sub-paragraphs treated as substituted for paragraph 41(1) are—

"(1) Where an energy administration order takes effect in respect of a company—
(a) a person appointed to perform functions equivalent to those of an administrative receiver, and
(b) if the energy administrator so requires, a person appointed to perform functions equivalent to those of a receiver,

shall refrain, during the period specified in sub-paragraph (1A), from performing those functions in Great Britain or in relation to any of the company's property in Great Britain.

(1A) That period is—
(a) in the case of a person mentioned in sub-paragraph (1)(a), the period while the company is in energy administration; and
(b) in the case of a person mentioned in sub-paragraph (1)(b), during so much of that period as is after the date on which he is required by the energy administrator to refrain from performing his functions."

38. Paragraph 43(6A) of Schedule B1 to the 1986 Act (moratorium on appointment to receiverships) has effect . . . as if for "An administrative receiver" there were substituted "A person with functions equivalent to those of an administrative receiver".

39. Paragraph 44(7) of Schedule B1 to the 1986 Act (proceedings to which interim moratorium does not apply) has effect . . . as if for paragraph (d) there were substituted—

"(d) the carrying out of his functions by a person who (whenever his appointment) has functions equivalent to those of an administrative receiver of the company."

40. Paragraph 64 of Schedule B1 to the 1986 Act (general powers of administrator) has effect . . . as if—
(a) in sub-paragraph (1), after "power" there were inserted "in relation to the affairs or business of the company so far as carried on in Great Britain or to its property in Great Britain"; and
(b) in sub-paragraph (2)(b), after "instrument" there were inserted "or by the law of the place where the company is incorporated".

NOTES

Part heading: words in square brackets substituted by the Companies Act 2006 (Consequential Amendments, Transitional Provisions and Savings) Order 2009, SI 2009/1941, art 2(1), Sch 1, para 220(1), (11)(b).

Para 33: words in square brackets substituted by SI 2009/1941, art 2(1), Sch 1, para 220(1), (11)(c).

Para 35: words in square brackets substituted and words omitted repealed by SI 2009/1941, art 2(1), Sch 1, para 220(1), (11)(d).

Paras 36–40: words omitted repealed by SI 2009/1941, art 2(1), Sch 1, para 220(1), (11)(e).

PART 4
OTHER MODIFICATIONS

General modifications

[7.872]

41. (1) Subject to paragraph 42, every reference falling within sub-paragraph (2) which is contained—
(a) in a provision of the 1986 Act (other than Schedule B1), or

(b) in any other enactment passed before this Act,

shall have effect as including a reference to whatever corresponds to it for the purposes of this paragraph.

(2) Those references are those (however expressed) which are or include references to—

(a) an administrator appointed by an administration order;
(b) an administration order;
(c) an application for an administration order;
(d) a company in administration;
(e) entering into administration;
(f) Schedule B1 or a provision of that Schedule.

(3) For the purposes of this paragraph—

(a) an energy administrator corresponds to an administrator appointed by an administration order;
(b) an energy administration order corresponds to an administration order;
(c) an application for an energy administration order corresponds to an application for an administration order;
(d) a company in energy administration corresponds to a company in administration;
(e) entering into energy administration corresponds to entering into administration;
(f) what corresponds to Schedule B1 or a provision of that Schedule is that Schedule or that provision as applied by Part 1 of this Schedule.

42. (1) Paragraph 41, in its application to section 1(3) of the 1986 Act, does not entitle the energy administrator of an unregistered company to make a proposal under Part 1 of that Act (company voluntary arrangements).

(2) Paragraph 41 does not confer any right under section 7(4) of the 1986 Act (implementation of voluntary arrangements) for a supervisor of voluntary arrangements to apply for an energy administration order in relation to a protected energy company.

(3) Paragraph 41 does not apply to section 359 of the Financial Services and Markets Act 2000 (c 8) ([administration order]).

Modifications of 1986 Act

43. In section 5 of the 1986 Act (effect of approval of voluntary arrangements) after subsection (4) insert—

"(5) Where the company is in energy administration, the court shall not make an order or give a direction under subsection (3) unless—

(a) the court has given the Secretary of State or the Gas and Electricity Markets Authority a reasonable opportunity of making representations to it about the proposed order or direction; and
(b) the order or direction is consistent with the objective of the energy administration.

(6) In subsection (5) "in energy administration" and "objective of the energy administration" are to be construed in accordance with Schedule B1 to this Act, as applied by Part 1 of Schedule 20 to the Energy Act 2004."

44. (1) Section 6 of that Act (challenge of decisions in relation to voluntary arrangements) is amended as follows.

(2) In subsection (2) for "this section" substitute "subsection (1)".

(3) After that subsection insert—

"(2A) Subject to this section, where a voluntary arrangement in relation to a company in energy administration is approved at the meetings summoned under section 3, an application to the court may be made—

(a) by the Secretary of State, or
(b) with the consent of the Secretary of State, by the Gas and Electricity Markets Authority,

on the ground that the voluntary arrangement is not consistent with the achievement of the objective of the energy administration."

(4) In subsection (4) after "subsection (1)" insert "or, in the case of an application under subsection (2A), as to the ground mentioned in that subsection".

(5) After subsection (7) insert—

"(8) In this section "in energy administration" and "objective of the energy administration" are to be construed in accordance with Schedule B1 to this Act, as applied by Part 1 of Schedule 20 to the Energy Act 2004."

45. In section 129(1A) of that Act (commencement of winding up), the reference to paragraph 13(1)(e) of Schedule B1 includes a reference to section 157(1)(e) of this Act.

Power to make further modifications

46. (1) The Secretary of State may by order make such modifications of—

(a) the 1986 Act, or
(b) any other enactment passed before this Act that relates to insolvency or makes provision by reference to anything that is or may be done under the 1986 Act,

as he considers appropriate in relation to any provision made by or under this Chapter [(including this Chapter as applied by section 96 of the Energy Act 2011)].

(2) An order under this paragraph may also make modifications of this Part of this Schedule.

(3) The power to make an order containing provision authorised by this paragraph is subject to the affirmative resolution procedure.

Interpretation of Part 4 of Schedule

47. In this Part of this Schedule—

"administration order", "administrator", "enters administration" and "in administration" are to be construed in accordance with Schedule B1 (disregarding Part 1 of this Schedule);

"enters energy administration" and "in energy administration" are to be construed in accordance with Schedule B1 (as applied by Part 1 of this Schedule);

"Schedule B1" means Schedule B1 to the 1986 Act.

NOTES

Para 42: words in square brackets substituted by the Financial Services Act 2012, s 114(1), Sch 18, Pt 2, para 101.

Para 46: words in square brackets in sub-para (1) inserted by the Energy Act 2011, s 101(2).

SCHEDULE 21
ENERGY TRANSFER SCHEMES

Section 159

Application of Schedule

[7.873]

1. This Schedule applies where—

(a) the court has made an energy administration order in relation to a company (the "old energy company"); and

(b) it is proposed that a transfer falling within section 155(3) be made to another company (the "new energy company").

2. It is for the energy administrator, while the energy administration order is in force, to act on behalf of the old energy company in the doing of anything that it is authorised or required to do by or under this Schedule.

Making of energy transfer schemes

3. (1) The old energy company may—

(a) with the consent of the new energy company, and

(b) for the purpose of giving effect to the proposed transfer,

make a scheme under this Schedule for the transfer of property, rights and liabilities from the old energy company to the new energy company (an "energy transfer scheme").

(2) Such a scheme may be made only at a time when the energy administration order is in force in relation to the old energy company.

(3) An energy transfer scheme may set out the property, rights and liabilities to be transferred in one or more of the following ways—

(a) by specifying or describing them in particular;

(b) by identifying them generally by reference to, or to a specified part of, the undertaking of the old energy company; or

(c) by specifying the manner in which they are to be determined.

(4) An energy transfer scheme shall take effect in accordance with paragraph 8 at the time appointed by the court.

(5) But the court must not appoint a time for a scheme to take effect unless that scheme has been approved by the Secretary of State.

(6) The Secretary of State may modify an energy transfer scheme before approving it, but only modifications to which both the old energy company and the new energy company have consented may be made.

(7) In deciding whether to approve an energy transfer scheme, the Secretary of State must have regard, in particular, to—

(a) the public interest; and

(b) the effect the scheme is likely to have (if any) upon the interests of third parties.

(8) Before approving an energy transfer scheme, the Secretary of State must consult GEMA.

(9) The old energy company and the new energy company each have a duty to provide the Secretary of State with all information and other assistance that he may reasonably require for the purposes of, or in connection with, the exercise of the powers conferred on him by this paragraph.

Provision that may be made by a scheme

4. (1) An energy transfer scheme may contain provision—

(a) for the creation, in favour of the old energy company or the new energy company, of an interest or right in or in relation to property transferred in accordance with the scheme;

(b) for giving effect to a transfer to the new energy company by the creation, in favour of that company, of an interest or right in or in relation to property retained by the old energy company;

(c) for the creation of new rights and liabilities (including rights of indemnity and duties to indemnify) as between the old energy company and the new energy company;
(d) in connection with any provision made under this sub-paragraph, provision making incidental provision as to the interests, rights and liabilities of other persons with respect to the property, rights and liabilities to which the scheme relates.

(2) The property, rights and liabilities of the old energy company that may be transferred in accordance with an energy transfer scheme include—
(a) property, rights and liabilities that would not otherwise be capable of being transferred or assigned by the old energy company;
(b) property acquired, and rights and liabilities arising, in the period after the making of the scheme but before it takes effect;
(c) rights and liabilities arising after it takes effect in respect of matters occurring before it takes effect;
(d) property situated anywhere in Great Britain or elsewhere;
(e) rights and liabilities under the law of a part of Great Britain or of a place outside Great Britain;
(f) rights and liabilities under an enactment, [EU] instrument or subordinate legislation.

(3) The transfers to which effect may be given by an energy transfer scheme include transfers of interests and rights that are to take effect in accordance with the scheme as if there were—
(a) no such requirement to obtain a person's consent or concurrence,
(b) no such liability in respect of a contravention of any other requirement, and
(c) no such interference with any interest or right,
as there would be, in the case of a transaction apart from this Act, by reason of a provision falling within sub-paragraph (4).

(4) A provision falls within this sub-paragraph to the extent that it has effect (whether under an enactment or agreement or otherwise) in relation to the terms on which the old energy company is entitled, or subject, to anything to which the transfer relates.

(5) Sub-paragraph (6) applies where (apart from that sub-paragraph) a person would be entitled, in consequence of anything done or likely to be done by or under this Act in connection with an energy transfer scheme—
(a) to terminate, modify, acquire or claim an interest or right; or
(b) to treat an interest or right as modified or terminated.

(6) That entitlement—
(a) shall not be enforceable in relation to that interest or right until after the transfer of the interest or right by the scheme; and
(b) shall then be enforceable in relation to the interest or right only in so far as the scheme contains provision for the interest or right to be transferred subject to whatever confers that entitlement.

(7) Sub-paragraphs (3) to (6) have effect where shares in a subsidiary of the old energy company are transferred—
(a) as if the reference in sub-paragraph (4) to the terms on which the old energy company is entitled or subject to anything to which the transfer relates included a reference to the terms on which the subsidiary is entitled or subject to anything immediately before the transfer takes effect; and
(b) in relation to an interest or right of the subsidiary, as if the references in sub-paragraph (6) to the transfer of the interest or right included a reference to the transfer of the shares.

(8) Sub-paragraphs (3) and (4) apply to the creation of an interest or right by an energy transfer scheme as they apply to the transfer of an interest or right.

Transfer of licences

5. (1) The provision that may be made by an energy transfer scheme includes the transfer of a relevant licence from the old energy company to the new energy company.

(2) Such a transfer may relate to the whole or any part of the licence.

(3) Where such a transfer relates to a part of the licence, the provision made under sub-paragraph (1) may include—
(a) provision apportioning responsibility between the old energy company and the new energy company in relation to—
 (i) the making of payments required by conditions included in the licence;
 (ii) ensuring compliance with any other requirements of the conditions included in the licence; and
(b) provision making incidental modifications to the terms and conditions of the licence.

(4) References in this paragraph to a part of a licence are references to one or both of—
(a) a part of the activities authorised by the licence;
(b) a part of the area in relation to which the holder of the licence is authorised to carry on those activities.

Powers and duties under statutory provisions

6. (1) The provision that may be made by an energy transfer scheme includes provision for some or all of the powers and duties to which this paragraph applies—
(a) to be transferred to the new energy company; or
(b) to become powers and duties that are exercisable, or must be performed, concurrently by the old energy company and the new energy company.

(2) Provision falling within sub-paragraph (1) may apply to powers and duties only in so far as they are exercisable or required to be performed in the area specified or described in the provision.

(3) The powers and duties to which this paragraph applies are the powers and duties conferred or imposed upon the old energy company by or under an enactment, so far as those powers and duties are connected with—

(a) the undertaking of the old energy company to the extent the energy transfer scheme relates to that undertaking; or

(b) any property, rights or liabilities to be transferred in accordance with the scheme.

(4) The powers and duties mentioned in sub-paragraph (3) include, in particular, powers and duties relating to the carrying out of works or the acquisition of land.

Supplemental provisions relating to transfers

7. (1) An energy transfer scheme may make incidental, supplemental, consequential and transitional provision in connection with the other provisions of the scheme.

(2) Such provision may include different provision for different cases or different purposes.

(3) In particular, an energy transfer scheme may make provision, in relation to a provision of the scheme—

(a) for the new energy company to be treated as the same person in law as the old energy company;

(b) for agreements made, transactions effected or other things done by or in relation to the old energy company to be treated, so far as may be necessary for the purposes of or in connection with a transfer in accordance with the scheme, as made, effected or done by or in relation to the new energy company;

(c) for references in an agreement, instrument or other document to the old energy company or to an employee or office holder with the old energy company to have effect, so far as may be necessary for the purposes of or in connection with a transfer in accordance with the scheme, with such modifications as are specified in the scheme;

(d) that the effect of any transfer in accordance with the scheme in relation to contracts of employment with the old energy company is not to terminate any of those contracts but is to be that periods of employment with that company are to count for all purposes as periods of employment with the new energy company;

(e) for proceedings commenced by or against the old energy company to be continued by or against the new energy company.

(4) Sub-paragraph (3)(c) does not apply to references in an enactment or in subordinate legislation.

(5) An energy transfer scheme may make provision for disputes as to the effect of the scheme between the old energy company and the new energy company to be referred to such arbitration as may be specified in or determined under the scheme.

(6) Where a person is entitled, in consequence of an energy transfer scheme, to possession of a document relating in part to the title to land or other property in England and Wales, or to the management of such land or other property—

(a) the scheme may provide for that person to be treated as having given another person an acknowledgement in writing of the right of that other person to production of the document and to delivery of copies of it; and

(b) section 64 of the Law of Property Act 1925 (c 20) (production and safe custody of documents) shall have effect accordingly, and on the basis that the acknowledgement did not contain an expression of contrary intention.

(7) Where a person is entitled, in consequence of an energy transfer scheme, to possession of a document relating in part to the title to land or other property in Scotland or to the management of such land or other property, subsections (1) and (2) of section 16 of the Land Registration (Scotland) Act 1979 (c 33) (omission of certain clauses in deeds) shall have effect in relation to the transfer—

(a) as if the transfer had been effected by deed; and

(b) as if the words "unless specially qualified" were omitted from each of those subsections.

(8) In this paragraph references to a transfer in accordance with an energy transfer scheme include references to the creation in accordance with such a scheme of an interest, right or liability.

Effect of scheme

8. (1) In relation to each provision of an energy transfer scheme for the transfer of property, rights or liabilities, or for the creation of interests, rights or liabilities—

(a) this Act shall have effect so as, without further assurance, to vest the property or interests, or those rights or liabilities, in the transferee at the time appointed by the court for the purposes of paragraph 3(4); and

(b) the provisions of that scheme in relation to that property or those interests, or those rights or liabilities, shall have effect from that time.

(2) In this paragraph "the transferee"—

(a) in relation to property, rights or liabilities transferred by an energy transfer scheme, means the new energy company; and

(b) in relation to interests, rights or liabilities created by such a scheme, means the person in whose favour, or in relation to whom, they are created.

(3) In its application to Scotland, sub-paragraph (1) has effect with the omission of the words "without further assurance".

Subsequent modification of scheme

9. (1) The Secretary of State may by notice to the old energy company and the new energy company modify an energy transfer scheme after it has taken effect, but only modifications to which both the old energy company and the new energy company have consented may be made.

(2) The notice must specify the time at which it is to take effect (the "modification time").

(3) Where a notice is issued under this paragraph in relation to an energy transfer scheme, as from the modification time, the scheme shall for all purposes be treated as having taken effect, at the time appointed for the purposes of paragraph 3(4), with the modifications made by the notice.

(4) Those modifications may make—

(a) any provision that could have been included in the scheme when it took effect at the time appointed for the purposes of paragraph 3(4); and

(b) transitional provision in connection with provision falling within paragraph (a).

(5) In deciding whether to modify an energy transfer scheme, the Secretary of State must have regard, in particular, to—

(a) the public interest; and

(b) the effect the modification is likely to have (if any) upon the interests of third parties.

(6) Before modifying an energy transfer scheme that has taken effect, the Secretary of State must consult GEMA.

(7) The old energy company and the new energy company each have a duty to provide the Secretary of State with all information and other assistance that he may reasonably require for the purposes of, or in connection with, the exercise of the powers conferred on him by this paragraph.

Transfers in the case of non-GB companies

10. Where the old energy company is a non-GB company, the property, rights and liabilities of that company which may be transferred by an energy transfer scheme, or in relation to which interests, rights or liabilities may be created by such a scheme, are confined to—

(a) property of the old energy company in Great Britain;

(b) rights and liabilities arising in relation to any such property; and

(c) rights and liabilities arising in connection with the affairs and business of the company so far as carried on in Great Britain.

Provision relating to foreign property etc

11. (1) Where there is a transfer in accordance with an energy transfer scheme of—

(a) any foreign property, or

(b) a foreign right or liability,

the old energy company and the new energy company must each take all requisite steps to secure that the vesting of the foreign property, right or liability in the new energy company is effective under the relevant foreign law.

(2) Until the vesting of the foreign property, right or liability in the new energy company in accordance with the energy transfer scheme is effective under the relevant foreign law, the old energy company must—

(a) hold the property or right for the benefit of the new energy company; or

(b) discharge the liability on behalf of the new energy company.

(3) The old energy company must comply with any directions given to it by the new energy company in relation to the performance of the obligations under sub-paragraphs (1) and (2) of the old energy company.

(4) Nothing in sub-paragraphs (1) to (3) prejudices the effect under the law of a part of Great Britain of the vesting of a foreign property, right or liability in the new energy company in accordance with an energy transfer scheme.

(5) Where—

(a) any foreign property, right or liability is acquired or incurred in respect of any other property, right or liability by a company, and

(b) by virtue of this paragraph, the company holds the other property or right for the benefit of the new energy company or is required to discharge the liability on behalf of the new energy company,

the property, right or liability acquired or incurred shall immediately become the property, right or liability of the new energy company.

(6) The provisions of sub-paragraphs (1) to (5) shall have effect in relation to foreign property, rights or liabilities transferred to the new energy company under sub-paragraph (5) as they have effect in the case of property, rights and liabilities transferred in accordance with an energy transfer scheme.

(7) References in this paragraph to foreign property, or to a foreign right or liability, are references to any property, right or liability as respects which an issue arising in any proceedings would be determined (in accordance with the rules of private international law) by reference to the law of a country or territory outside Great Britain.

(8) Expenses incurred under this paragraph by a company as the company from which anything is transferred shall be met by the new energy company.

(9) An obligation imposed under this paragraph in relation to property, rights or liabilities shall be enforceable as if contained in a contract between the old energy company and the new energy company.

Application of Schedule to transfers to subsidiaries

12. Where the proposed transfer falling within subsection (3) of section 155 is a transfer of the kind mentioned in subsection (4)(a) of that section, this Schedule shall have effect in relation to that transfer as if—

(a) paragraph 3(1)(a) were omitted; and

(b) paragraph 3(6) had effect with "the old energy company has consented may be made" substituted for the words from "both" onwards.

Interpretation

13. In this Schedule—

"energy transfer scheme" has the meaning given by paragraph 3(1);

"new energy company" has the meaning given by paragraph 1;

"third party", in relation to an energy transfer scheme or any modification of such a scheme, means a person who is neither—

(a) the old energy company; nor

(b) the new energy company.

NOTES

Para 4: reference in square brackets in sub-para (2)(f) substituted by the Treaty of Lisbon (Changes in Terminology) Order 2011, SI 2011/1043, art 6(1)(d).

SCHEDULES 22, 23

(*Schs 22, 23 outside the scope of this work.*)

ENERGY ADMINISTRATION RULES 2005

(SI 2005/2483)

NOTES

Made: 2 September 2005.

Authority: Insolvency Act 1986, s 411; Energy Act 2004, s 159(3).

Commencement: 1 October 2005.

Note: the Insolvency Rules 1986, SI 1986/1925 are revoked and replaced (as from 6 April 2017 and subject to transitional provisions) by the Insolvency (England and Wales) Rules 2016, SI 2016/1024 at **[6.2]**, however, the Insolvency (England and Wales) Rules 2016 (Consequential Amendments and Savings) Rules 2017, SI 2017/369, r 3(d) at **[6.947]** provides that the Insolvency Rules 1986 as they had effect immediately before 6 April 2017 and insofar as they apply to proceedings under the Energy Administration Rules 2005, continue to have effect for the purposes of the application of the 2005 Rules.

See also the Deregulation Act 2015 and Small Business, Enterprise and Employment Act 2015 (Consequential Amendments) (Savings) Regulations 2017, SI 2017/540, reg 4(1), (2)(d) and the Insolvency Amendment (EU 2015/848) Regulations 2017, SI 2017/702, reg 4 at **[2.103]**, for savings in relation to the Insolvency Act 1986 in so far as it applies to proceedings under these Rules.

ARRANGEMENT OF RULES

PART 1
INTRODUCTORY PROVISIONS

1 Citation and commencement . . . [7.874]
2 Construction and interpretation . . . [7.875]
3 Extent . . . [7.876]

PART 2
APPOINTMENT OF ENERGY ADMINISTRATOR BY COURT

4 Affidavit in support of energy administration application . . . [7.877]
5 Form of application . . . [7.878]
6 Contents of application and affidavit in support . . . [7.879]
7 Filing of application . . . [7.880]
8 Service of application . . . [7.881]
9 Notice to officers charged with execution of writs or other process, etc . . . [7.882]
10 Manner in which service to be effected . . . [7.883]
11 Proof of service . . . [7.884]
12 The hearing . . . [7.885]
13 Notice of energy administration order . . . [7.886]

PART 3
PROCESS OF ENERGY ADMINISTRATION

14 Notification and advertisement of energy administrator's appointment . . . [7.887]
15 Notice requiring statement of affairs . . . [7.888]
16 Verification and filing . . . [7.889]

17 Limited disclosure . . . . . [7.890]
18 Release from duty to submit statement of affairs; extension of time . . . . . [7.891]
19 Expenses of statement of affairs . . . . . [7.892]
20 Energy administrator's proposals . . . . . [7.893]

PART 4
MEETINGS AND REPORTS

CHAPTER 1
CREDITORS' MEETINGS

21 Creditors' meetings generally . . . . . [7.894]
22 The chairman at meetings . . . . . [7.895]
23 Creditors' meeting for nomination of alternative liquidator . . . . . [7.896]
24 Entitlement to vote . . . . . [7.897]
25 Admission and rejection of claims . . . . . [7.898]
26 Secured creditors . . . . . [7.899]
27 Holders of negotiable instruments . . . . . [7.900]
28 Hire-purchase, conditional sale and chattel leasing agreements . . . . . [7.901]
29 Resolutions . . . . . [7.902]
30 Minutes . . . . . [7.903]
31 Revision of the energy administrator's proposals . . . . . [7.904]
32 Reports to creditors . . . . . [7.905]

CHAPTER 2
COMPANY MEETINGS

33 Venue and conduct of company meeting . . . . . [7.906]

PART 5
DISPOSAL OF CHARGED PROPERTY

34 Authority to dispose of property . . . . . [7.907]

PART 6
EXPENSES OF THE ENERGY ADMINISTRATION

35 Priority of expenses of energy administration . . . . . [7.908]

PART 7
DISTRIBUTION OF CREDITORS

CHAPTER 1
APPLICATION OF PART AND GENERAL

36 Distribution to creditors generally . . . . . [7.909]
37 Debts of insolvent company to rank equally . . . . . [7.910]
38 Supplementary provisions as to dividend . . . . . [7.911]
39 Division of unsold assets . . . . . [7.912]

CHAPTER 2
MACHINERY OF PROVING A DEBT

40 Proving a debt . . . . . [7.913]
41 Claim established by affidavit . . . . . [7.914]
42 Costs of proving . . . . . [7.915]
43 Energy administrator to allow inspection of proofs . . . . . [7.916]
44 New energy administrator appointed . . . . . [7.917]
45 Admission and rejection of proofs for dividend . . . . . [7.918]
46 Appeal against decision on proof . . . . . [7.919]
47 Withdrawal or variation of proof . . . . . [7.920]
48 Expunging of proof by the court . . . . . [7.921]

CHAPTER 3
QUANTIFICATION OF CLAIMS

49 Estimate of quantum . . . . . [7.922]
50 Negotiable instruments, etc . . . . . [7.923]
51 Secured creditors . . . . . [7.924]
52 Discounts . . . . . [7.925]
53 Mutual credits and set-off . . . . . [7.926]
54 Debt in foreign currency . . . . . [7.927]
55 Payments of a periodical nature . . . . . [7.928]
56 Interest . . . . . [7.929]
57 Debt payable at future time . . . . . [7.930]
58 Value of security . . . . . [7.931]

59 Surrender for non-disclosure . . . [7.932]
60 Redemption by energy administrator . . . [7.933]
61 Test of security's value . . . [7.934]
62 Realisation of security by creditor . . . [7.935]
63 Notice of proposed distribution . . . [7.936]
64 Admission or rejection of proofs . . . [7.937]
65 Declaration of dividend . . . [7.938]
66 Notice of declaration of a dividend . . . [7.939]
67 Payments of dividends and related matters . . . [7.940]
68 Notice of no dividend, or no further dividend . . . [7.941]
69 Proof altered after payment of dividend . . . [7.942]
70 Secured creditors . . . [7.943]
71 Disqualification from dividend . . . [7.944]
72 Assignment of right to dividend . . . [7.945]
73 Debt payable at future time . . . [7.946]

PART 8
THE ENERGY ADMINISTRATOR

74 Fixing of remuneration . . . [7.947]

PART 9
ENDING ENERGY ADMINISTRATION

75 Final progress reports . . . [7.948]
76 Application to court . . . [7.949]
77 Notification by energy administrator of court order . . . [7.950]
78 Moving from energy administration to creditors' voluntary liquidation . . . [7.951]
79 Moving from energy administration to dissolution . . . [7.952]
80 Provision of information to the Secretary of State . . . [7.953]

PART 10
REPLACING ENERGY ADMINISTRATOR

81 Grounds for resignation . . . [7.954]
82 Notice of intention to resign . . . [7.955]
83 Notice of resignation . . . [7.956]
84 Application to court to remove energy administrator from office . . . [7.957]
85 Notice of vacation of office when energy administrator ceases to be qualified to act . . . [7.958]
86 Energy administrator deceased . . . [7.959]
87 Application to replace . . . [7.960]
88 Notification and advertisement of appointment of replacement energy administrator . . . [7.961]
89 Notification and advertisement of appointment of joint energy administrator . . . [7.962]
90 Notification to registrar of companies . . . [7.963]
91 Energy administrator's duties on vacating office . . . [7.964]

PART 11
COURT PROCEDURE AND PRACTICE

CHAPTER 1
APPLICATIONS

92 Preliminary . . . [7.965]
93 Interpretation . . . [7.966]
94 Form and contents of application . . . [7.967]
95 Application under section 176A(5) of the 1986 Act to disapply section 176A of the 1986 Act . . . [7.968]
96 Filing and service of application . . . [7.969]
97 Notice of application under section 176A(5) of the 1986 Act . . . [7.970]
98 Other hearings *ex parte* . . . [7.971]
99 Hearing of application . . . [7.972]
100 Use of affidavit evidence . . . [7.973]
101 Filing and service of affidavits . . . [7.974]
102 Use of reports . . . [7.975]
103 Adjournment of hearings; directions . . . [7.976]

CHAPTER 2
SHORTHAND WRITERS

104 Nomination and appointment of shorthand writers . . . [7.977]
105 Remuneration . . . [7.978]

CHAPTER 3
ENFORCEMENT PROCEDURES

106 Enforcement of court orders . . . [7.979]
107 Orders enforcing compliance with the Rules . . . [7.980]
108 Warrant under section 236 of the 1986 Act . . . [7.981]

CHAPTER 4
COURT RECORDS AND RETURNS

109 Title of proceedings . . . [7.982]
110 Court records . . . [7.983]
111 Inspection of records . . . [7.984]
112 File of court proceedings . . . [7.985]
113 Right to inspect file . . . [7.986]
114 Filing of Gazette notices and advertisements . . . [7.987]

CHAPTER 5
COSTS AND DETAILED ASSESSMENT

115 Application of CPR . . . [7.988]
116 Requirement to assess costs by the detailed procedure . . . [7.989]
117 Procedure where detailed assessment required . . . [7.990]
118 Costs paid otherwise than out of the assets of the protected energy company . . . [7.991]
119 Award of costs against energy administrator . . . [7.992]
120 Application for costs . . . [7.993]
121 Costs and expenses of witnesses . . . [7.994]
122 Final costs certificate . . . [7.995]

CHAPTER 6
PERSONS INCAPABLE OF MANAGING THEIR AFFAIRS

123 Introductory . . . [7.996]
124 Appointment of another person to act . . . [7.997]
125 Affidavit in support of application . . . [7.998]
126 Services of notices following appointment . . . [7.999]

CHAPTER 7
APPEALS IN ENERGY ADMINISTRATION PROCEEDINGS

127 Appeals and reviews of energy administration orders . . . [7.1000]
128 Procedure on appeal . . . [7.1001]

CHAPTER 8
GENERAL

129 Principal court rules and practice to apply . . . [7.1002]
130 Right of audience . . . [7.1003]
131 Right of attendance . . . [7.1004]
132 Energy administrator's solicitor . . . [7.1005]
133 Formal defects . . . [7.1006]
134 Restriction on concurrent proceedings and remedies . . . [7.1007]
135 Affidavits . . . [7.1008]
136 Security in court . . . [7.1009]
137 Payment into court . . . [7.1010]
138 Further information and disclosure . . . [7.1011]
139 Office copies of documents . . . [7.1012]

PART 12
PROXIES AND COMPANY REPRESENTATION

140 Definition of proxy . . . [7.1013]
141 Issue and use of forms . . . [7.1014]
142 Use of proxies at meetings . . . [7.1015]
143 Retention of proxies . . . [7.1016]
144 Right of inspection . . . [7.1017]
145 Proxy-holder with financial interest . . . [7.1018]
146 Company representation . . . [7.1019]

PART 13
EXAMINATION OF PERSONS IN ENERGY ADMINISTRATION PROCEEDINGS

147 Preliminary . . . [7.1020]
148 Form and contents of application . . . [7.1021]
149 Order for examination, etc . . . [7.1022]
150 Procedure for examination . . . [7.1023]

151 Record of examination . . . [7.1024]
152 Costs of proceedings under section 236 . . . [7.1025]

PART 14
MISCELLANEOUS AND GENERAL

153 Power of Secretary of State to regulate certain matters . . . [7.1026]
154 Costs, expenses, etc . . . [7.1027]
155 Provable debts . . . [7.1028]
156 Notices . . . [7.1029]
157 Quorum at meeting of creditors . . . [7.1030]
158 Evidence of proceedings at meetings . . . [7.1031]
159 Documents issuing from Secretary of State . . . [7.1032]
160 Forms for use in energy administration proceedings . . . [7.1033]
161 Energy administrator's security . . . [7.1034]
162 Time-limits . . . [7.1035]
163 Service by post . . . [7.1036]
164 General provisions as to service and notice . . . [7.1037]
165 Service outside the jurisdiction . . . [7.1038]
166 Confidentiality of documents . . . [7.1039]
167 Notices sent simultaneously to the same person . . . [7.1040]
168 Right to copy documents . . . [7.1041]
169 Charge for copy documents . . . [7.1042]
170 Non-receipt of notice of meeting . . . [7.1043]
171 Right to have list of creditors . . . [7.1044]
172 False claim of status as creditor . . . [7.1045]
173 The Gazette . . . [7.1046]
174 Punishment of offences . . . [7.1047]
175 Notice of order under section 176A(5) of the 1986 Act . . . [7.1048]

PART 15
INTERPRETATION AND APPLICATION

176 Introductory . . . [7.1049]
177 "The court"; "the registrar" . . . [7.1050]
178 "Give notice" etc . . . [7.1051]
179 Notice, etc to solicitors . . . [7.1052]
180 Notice to joint energy administrators . . . [7.1053]
181 "Venue" . . . [7.1054]
182 "Energy administration proceedings" . . . [7.1055]
183 "The appropriate fee" . . . [7.1056]
184 "Debt", "liability" . . . [7.1057]
185 "Authorised deposit-taker and former authorised deposit-taker" . . . [7.1058]
186 Expressions used generally . . . [7.1059]
187 Application . . . [7.1060]

SCHEDULES

Schedule 1—Forms . . . [7.1061]
Schedule 2—Punishment of Offences under the Rules . . . [7.1062]

PART 1
INTRODUCTORY PROVISIONS

[7.874]
1 Citation and commencement

These Rules may be cited as the Energy Administration Rules 2005 and shall come into force on 1st October 2005.

[7.875]
2 Construction and interpretation

(1) In these Rules—

"the 1986 Act" means the Insolvency Act 1986;

"the 2004 Act" means the Energy Act 2004;

"administrative receiver" has the same meaning as in section 156(4) of the 2004 Act;

"the Companies Act" means the Companies Act 1985;

"CPR" means the Civil Procedure Rules 1998 and "CPR" followed by a Part or rule number means the Part or rule with that number in those Rules;

"enforcement officer" means an individual who is authorised to act as an enforcement officer under the Courts Act 2003;

"GEMA" means the Gas and Electricity Markets Authority;
"insolvency proceedings" has the same meaning as in Rule 13.7 of the Insolvency Rules;
"the Insolvency Rules" means the Insolvency Rules 1986;
"qualifying floating charge" has the same meaning as in paragraph 14(2) of Schedule B1 to the 1986 Act, without the modifications made by Schedule 20 to the 2004 Act;
"the Rules" means the Energy Administration Rules 2005.

(2) References in the Rules to *ex parte* hearings shall be construed as references to hearings without notice being served on any other party; references to applications made *ex parte* as references to applications made without notice being served on any other party and other references which include the expression "*ex parte*" shall be similarly construed.

(3) References to provisions of Schedule B1 to the 1986 Act are references to those provisions as modified and applied by Schedule 20 to the 2004 Act unless otherwise stated.

(4) References to other provisions of the 1986 Act are, where those provisions have been modified by Schedule 20 to the 2004 Act, references to those provisions as so modified.

(5) Where the protected energy company is a non-GB company within the meaning of section 171 of the 2004 Act, references in the Rules to the affairs, business and property of the company are references only to its affairs and business so far as carried on in Great Britain and to its property in Great Britain unless otherwise stated.

(6) Where the protected energy company is an unregistered company, any requirement to send information to the registrar of companies applies only if the company is subject to a requirement imposed by virtue of section 691(1) or 718 of the Companies Act.

(7) Subject to paragraphs (1), (2), (3), (4), (5) and (6), Part 15 of the Rules has effect for their interpretation and application.

NOTES

Note: the Insolvency Rules 1986, SI 1986/1925 are revoked and replaced (as from 6 April 2017 and subject to transitional provisions) by the Insolvency (England and Wales) Rules 2016, SI 2016/1024 at **[6.2]**, however, the Insolvency (England and Wales) Rules 2016 (Consequential Amendments and Savings) Rules 2017, SI 2017/369, r 3(d) provides that the Insolvency Rules 1986 as they had effect immediately before 6 April 2017 and insofar as they apply to proceedings under the Energy Administration Rules 2005, continue to have effect for the purposes of the application of the 2005 Rules.

[7.876]
3 Extent

The Rules apply in relation to protected energy companies which the courts in England and Wales have jurisdiction to wind up.

PART 2
APPOINTMENT OF ENERGY ADMINISTRATOR BY COURT

[7.877]
4 Affidavit in support of energy administration application

Where it is proposed to apply to the court for an energy administration order to be made in relation to a protected energy company, the energy administration application shall be in Form EA1 and an affidavit complying with Rule 6 must be prepared and sworn, with a view to its being filed with the court in support of the application.

[7.878]
5 Form of application

(1) The application shall state by whom it is made and the applicant's address for service.

(2) Where it is made by GEMA, the application shall contain a statement that it is made with the consent of the Secretary of State.

(3) There shall be attached to the application a written statement which shall be in Form EA2 by each of the persons proposed to be energy administrator stating—
- (a) that he consents to accept the appointment; and
- (b) details of any prior professional relationship(s) that he has had with the protected energy company to which he is to be appointed as energy administrator.

[7.879]
6 Contents of application and affidavit in support

(1) The energy administration application shall state that the company is a protected energy company.

(2) The application shall state one or both of the following—
- (a) the applicant's belief that the protected energy company is, or is likely to be, unable to pay its debts;
- (b) the Secretary of State has certified that it would be appropriate for him to petition for the winding up of the protected energy company under section 124A of the 1986 Act (petition for winding up on grounds of public interest).

(3) There shall be attached to the application an affidavit in support which shall contain—
- (a) a statement of the protected energy company's financial position, specifying (to the best of the applicant's knowledge and belief) the company's assets and liabilities, including contingent and prospective liabilities;

(b) details of any security known or believed to be held by the creditors of the protected energy company and whether in any case the security is such as to confer power on the holder to appoint an administrative receiver or to appoint an administrator under paragraph 14 of Schedule B1 to the 1986 Act, without the modifications made by Schedule 20 to the 2004 Act. If an administrative receiver has been appointed, that fact shall be stated;

(c) details of any insolvency proceedings in relation to the protected energy company including any petition that has been presented for the winding up of the protected energy company so far as within the immediate knowledge of the applicant;

(d) details of any notice served in accordance with section 164 of the 2004 Act by any person intending to enforce any security over the protected energy company's assets, so far as within the immediate knowledge of the applicant;

(e) details of any step taken to enforce any such security, so far as within the immediate knowledge of the applicant;

(f) details of any application for leave of the court to pass a resolution for the voluntary winding up of the protected energy company, so far as within the immediate knowledge of the applicant;

(g) where it is intended to appoint a number of persons as energy administrators, details of the matters set out in section 158(5) of the 2004 Act regarding the exercise of the powers and duties of the energy administrator;

(h) any other matters which, in the opinion of those intending to make the application for an energy administration order, will assist the court in deciding whether to make such an order, so far as lying within the knowledge or belief of the applicant.

[7.880]

7 Filing of application

(1) The application (and all supporting documents) shall be filed with the court, with a sufficient number of copies for service and use as provided by Rule 8.

(2) Each of the copies filed shall have applied to it the seal of the court and be issued to the applicant; and on each copy there shall be endorsed the date and time of filing.

(3) The court shall fix a venue for the hearing of the application and this also shall be endorsed on each copy of the application issued under paragraph (2).

(4) After the application is filed, it is the duty of the applicant to notify the court in writing of the existence of any insolvency proceedings, in relation to the protected energy company, as soon as the applicant becomes aware of them.

[7.881]

8 Service of application

(1) In the following paragraphs of this Rule, references to the application are to a copy of the application issued by the court under Rule 7(2) together with the affidavit in support of it and the documents attached to the application.

(2) Notification for the purposes of section 156(2) of the 2004 Act shall be by way of service in accordance with Rule 10, verified in accordance with Rule 11.

(3) The application shall be served in addition to those persons referred to in section 156(2) of the 2004 Act—

(a) if an administrative receiver has been appointed, on him;

(b) if there is pending an administration application under Schedule B1 to the 1986 Act, without the modifications made by Schedule 20 to the 2004 Act, on the applicant;

(c) if there is pending a petition for the winding-up of the protected energy company, on the petitioner (and also on the provisional liquidator, if any);

(d) on any creditor who has served notice in accordance with section 164 of the 2004 Act of his intention to enforce his security over property of the protected energy company;

(e) on the person proposed as energy administrator;

(f) on the protected energy company;

(g) if the applicant is the Secretary of State, on GEMA;

(h) if the applicant is GEMA, on the Secretary of State;

(i) if a supervisor of a voluntary arrangement under Part I of the 1986 Act has been appointed, on him.

[7.882]

9 Notice to officers charged with execution of writs or other process, etc

The applicant shall as soon as reasonably practicable after filing the application give notice of its being made to—

(a) any enforcement officer or other officer who to the applicant's knowledge is charged with an execution or other legal process against the protected energy company or its property; and

(b) any person who to the applicant's knowledge has distrained against the protected energy company or its property.

[7.883]

10 Manner in which service to be effected

(1) Service of the application in accordance with Rule 8 shall be effected by the applicant, or the applicant's solicitor, or by a person instructed by the applicant or the applicant's solicitor, not less than 2 days before the date fixed for the hearing.

(2) Service shall be effected as follows—

(a) on the protected energy company (subject to paragraph (3) below), by delivering the documents to its registered office;

(b) on any other person (subject to paragraph (4) below), by delivering the documents to his proper address;

(c) in either case, in such other manner as the court may direct.

(3) If delivery to a protected energy company's registered office is not practicable or if the protected energy company is an unregistered company, service may be effected by delivery to its last known principal place of business in England and Wales.

(4) Subject to paragraph (5), for the purposes of paragraph (2)(b) above, a person's proper address is any which he has previously notified as his address for service; but if he has not notified any such address, service may be effected by delivery to his usual or last known address.

(5) In the case of a person who—

(a) is an authorised deposit-taker or a former authorised deposit-taker;

(b)

(i) has appointed, or is or may be entitled to appoint, an administrative receiver of the protected energy company, or

(ii) is, or may be entitled to appoint an administrator of the protected energy company under paragraph 14 of Schedule B1 to the 1986 Act, without the modifications made by Schedule 20 to the 2004 Act; and

(c) has not notified an address for service,

the proper address is the address of an office of that person where, to the knowledge of the applicant, the protected energy company maintains a bank account or, where no such office is known to the applicant, the registered office of that person, or, if there is no such office, his usual or last known address.

(6) Delivery of the documents to any place or address may be made by leaving them there, or sending them by first class post.

[7.884]

11 Proof of service

(1) Service of the application shall be verified by an affidavit of service in Form EA3, specifying the date on which, and the manner in which, service was effected.

(2) The affidavit of service, with a sealed copy of the application exhibited to it, shall be filed with the court as soon as reasonably practicable after service, and in any event not less than 1 day before the hearing of the application.

[7.885]

12 The hearing

(1) At the hearing of the energy administration application, any of the following may appear or be represented—

(a) the Secretary of State;

(b) GEMA;

(c) the protected energy company;

(d) one or more of the directors;

(e) if an administrative receiver has been appointed, that person;

(f) any person who has presented a petition for the winding-up of the protected energy company;

(g) the person proposed for appointment as energy administrator;

(h) any person that is the holder of a qualifying floating charge;

(i) any person who has applied to the court for an administration order under Schedule B1 to the 1986 Act, without the modifications made by Schedule 20 to the 2004 Act;

(j) any creditor who has served notice in accordance with section 164 of the 2004 Act of his intention to enforce his security over the protected energy company's property;

(k) any supervisor of a voluntary arrangement under Part I of the 1986 Act;

(l) with the permission of the court, any other person who appears to have an interest justifying his appearance.

(2) If the court makes an energy administration order, it shall be in Form EA4.

(3) If the court makes an energy administration order, the costs of the applicant, and of any person whose costs are allowed by the court, are payable as an expense of the energy administration.

[7.886]

13 Notice of energy administration order

(1) If the court makes an energy administration order, it shall as soon as reasonably practicable send two sealed copies of the order to the person who made the application.

(2) The applicant shall send a sealed copy of the order as soon as reasonably practicable to the person appointed as energy administrator.

(3) If the court makes an order under section 157(1)(d) of the 2004 Act or any other order under section 157(1)(f) of the 2004 Act, it shall give directions as to the persons to whom, and how, notice of that order is to be given.

PART 3
PROCESS OF ENERGY ADMINISTRATION

[7.887]
14 Notification and advertisement of energy administrator's appointment

(1) The energy administrator shall advertise his appointment once in the Gazette, and once in such newspaper as he thinks most appropriate for ensuring that the appointment comes to the notice of the protected energy company's creditors. The advertisement shall be in Form EA5.

(2) The energy administrator shall, as soon as reasonably practicable after the date specified in paragraph 46(6) of Schedule B1 to the 1986 Act, give notice of his appointment—

(a) if the application for the energy administration order was made by the Secretary of State, to GEMA;
(b) if the application for the energy administration order was made by GEMA, to the Secretary of State;
(c) if a receiver or an administrative receiver has been appointed, to him;
(d) if there is pending a petition for the winding up of the protected energy company, to the petitioner (and to the provisional liquidator, if any);
(e) to any person who has applied to the court for an administration order under Schedule B1 to the 1986 Act, without the modifications made by Schedule 20 to the 2004 Act, in relation to the protected energy company;
(f) to any enforcement officer who, to the energy administrator's knowledge, is charged with execution or other legal process against the protected energy company;
(g) to any person who, to the energy administrator's knowledge, has distrained against the protected energy company or its property;
(h) to any supervisor of a voluntary arrangement under Part I of the 1986 Act;
(i) to any holder of a qualifying floating charge who, to the energy administrator's knowledge, has served notice in accordance with section 163 of the 2004 Act that he is seeking to appoint an administrator; and
(j) to any creditor who, to the energy administrator's knowledge, has served notice in accordance with section 164 of the 2004 Act of his intention to enforce his security over property of the protected energy company.

(3) Where, under a provision of Schedule B1 to the 1986 Act or these Rules, the energy administrator is required to send a notice of his appointment to any person, he shall do so in Form EA6.

[7.888]
15 Notice requiring statement of affairs

(1) In this Part "relevant person" shall have the meaning given to it in paragraph 47(3) of Schedule B1 to the 1986 Act.

(2) The energy administrator shall send notice in Form EA7 to each relevant person whom he determines appropriate requiring him to prepare and submit a statement of the protected energy company's affairs.

(3) The notice shall inform each of the relevant persons—

(a) of the names and addresses of all others (if any) to whom the same notice has been sent;
(b) of the time within which the statement must be delivered;
(c) of the effect of paragraph 48(4) of Schedule B1 to the 1986 Act (penalty for non-compliance); and
(d) of the application to him, and to each other relevant person, of section 235 of the 1986 Act (duty to provide information, and to attend on the energy administrator, if required).

(4) The energy administrator shall furnish each relevant person to whom he has sent notice in Form EA7 with the forms required for the preparation of the statement of affairs.

[7.889]
16 Verification and filing

(1) The statement of the protected energy company's affairs shall be in Form EA8, contain all the particulars required by that form and shall be verified by a statement of truth by the relevant person.

(2) The energy administrator may require any relevant person to submit a statement of concurrence in Form EA9 stating that he concurs in the statement of affairs. Where the energy administrator does so, he shall inform the person making the statement of affairs of that fact.

(3) The statement of affairs shall be delivered by the relevant person making the statement of truth, together with a copy, to the energy administrator. The relevant person shall also deliver a copy of the statement of affairs to all those persons whom the energy administrator has required to make a statement of concurrence.

(4) A person required to submit a statement of concurrence shall do so before the end of the period of 5 business days (or such other period as the energy administrator may agree) beginning with the day on which the statement of affairs being concurred with is received by him.

(5) A statement of concurrence may be qualified in respect of matters dealt with in the statement of affairs, where the maker of the statement of concurrence is not in agreement with the relevant person, or he considers the statement of affairs to be erroneous or misleading, or he is without the direct knowledge necessary for concurring with it.

(6) Every statement of concurrence shall be verified by a statement of truth and be delivered to the energy administrator by the person who makes it, together with a copy of it.

(7) Subject to Rule 17 below, the energy administrator shall as soon as reasonably practicable send to the registrar of companies and file with the court a Form EA10 together with a copy of the statement of affairs and any statement of concurrence.

[7.890]
17 Limited disclosure

(1) Where the energy administrator thinks that it would prejudice the conduct of the energy administration for the whole or part of the statement of the protected energy company's affairs to be disclosed, he may apply to the court for an order of limited disclosure in respect of the statement, or any specified part of it.

(2) The court may, on such application, order that the statement or, as the case may be, the specified part of it, shall not be filed with the registrar of companies.

(3) The energy administrator shall as soon as reasonably practicable send to the registrar of companies a Form EA10 together with a copy of the order and the statement of affairs (to the extent provided by the order) and any statement of concurrence.

(4) If a creditor seeks disclosure of a statement of affairs or a specified part of it in relation to which an order has been made under this Rule, he may apply to the court for an order that the energy administrator disclose it or a specified part of it. The application shall be supported by written evidence in the form of an affidavit.

(5) The applicant shall give the energy administrator notice of his application at least 3 days before the hearing.

(6) The court may make any order for disclosure subject to any conditions as to confidentiality, duration, the scope of the order in the event of any change of circumstances, or other matters as it sees fit.

(7) If there is a material change in circumstances rendering the limit on disclosure or any part of it unnecessary, the energy administrator shall, as soon as reasonably practicable after the change, apply to the court for the order or any part of it to be rescinded.

(8) The energy administrator shall, as soon as reasonably practicable after the making of an order under paragraph (7) above, file with the registrar of companies Form EA10 together with a copy of the statement of affairs to the extent provided by the order.

(9) When the statement of affairs is filed in accordance with paragraph (8), the energy administrator shall, where he has sent a statement of proposals under paragraph 49 of Schedule B1 to the 1986 Act, provide the creditors with a copy of the statement of affairs as filed, or a summary thereof.

(10) The provisions of Part 31 of the CPR shall not apply to an application under this Rule.

[7.891]
18 Release from duty to submit statement of affairs; extension of time

(1) The power of the energy administrator under paragraph 48(2) of Schedule B1 to the 1986 Act to give a release from the obligation imposed by paragraph 47(1) of Schedule B1 to the 1986 Act, or to grant an extension of time, may be exercised at the energy administrator's own discretion, or at the request of any relevant person.

(2) A relevant person may, if he requests a release or extension of time and it is refused by the energy administrator, apply to the court for it.

(3) The court may, if it thinks that no sufficient cause is shown for the application, dismiss it without a hearing but it shall not do so without giving the relevant person at least 7 days' notice, upon receipt of which the relevant person may request the court to list the application for a without notice hearing. If the application is not dismissed, the court shall fix a venue for it to be heard, and give notice to the relevant person accordingly.

(4) The relevant person shall, at least 14 days before the hearing, send to the energy administrator a notice stating the venue and accompanied by a copy of the application and of any evidence which he (the relevant person) intends to adduce in support of it.

(5) The energy administrator may appear and be heard on the application and, whether or not he appears, he may file a written report of any matters which he considers ought to be drawn to the court's attention.

If such a report is filed, a copy of it shall be sent by the energy administrator to the relevant person, not later than 5 days before the hearing.

(6) Sealed copies of any order made on the application shall be sent by the court to the relevant person and the energy administrator.

(7) On any application under this Rule the relevant person's costs shall be paid in any event by him and, unless the court otherwise orders, no allowance towards them shall be made out of the assets.

[7.892]
19 Expenses of statement of affairs

(1) A relevant person making the statement of the protected energy company's affairs or statement of concurrence shall be allowed, and paid by the energy administrator out of his receipts, any expenses incurred by the relevant person in so doing which the energy administrator considers reasonable.

(2) Any decision by the energy administrator under this Rule is subject to appeal to the court.

(3) Nothing in this Rule relieves a relevant person of any obligation with respect to the preparation, verification and submission of the statement of affairs, or to the provision of information to the energy administrator.

[7.893]
20 Energy administrator's proposals

(1) The energy administrator shall, under paragraph 49 of Schedule B1 to the 1986 Act, make a statement which he shall send to the registrar of companies attached to Form EA11.

(2) The statement shall include, in addition to those matters set out in paragraph 49 of Schedule B1 to the 1986 Act—

(a) details of the court where the proceedings are and the relevant court reference number;
(b) the full name, registered address, registered number and any other trading names of the protected energy company;
(c) details relating to his appointment as energy administrator, including the date of appointment and whether the application was made by the Secretary of State or GEMA and, where there are joint energy administrators, details of the matters set out in section 158(5) of the 2004 Act;
(d) the names of the directors and secretary of the protected energy company and details of any shareholdings in the protected energy company they may have;
(e) an account of the circumstances giving rise to the appointment of the energy administrator;
(f) if a statement of the protected energy company's affairs has been submitted, a copy or summary of it, with the energy administrator's comments, if any;
(g) if an order limiting the disclosure of the statement of affairs (under Rule 17) has been made, a statement of that fact, as well as—
  (i) details of who provided the statement of affairs;
  (ii) the date of the order of limited disclosure; and
  (iii) the details or a summary of the details that are not subject to that order;
(h) if a full statement of affairs is not provided, the names, addresses and debts of the creditors including details of any security held;
(i) if no statement of affairs has been submitted, details of the financial position of the protected energy company at the latest practicable date (which must, unless the court otherwise orders, be a date not earlier than that on which the protected energy company entered energy administration), a list of the protected energy company's creditors including their names, addresses and details of their debts, including any security held, and an explanation as to why there is no statement of affairs;
(j) (except where the energy administrator proposes a voluntary arrangement in relation to the protected energy company and subject to paragraph (3))—
  (i) to the best of the energy administrator's knowledge and belief—
    (aa) an estimate of the value of the prescribed part (whether or not he proposes to make an application to court under section 176A(5) of the 1986 Act or section 176A(3) of the 1986 Act applies); and
    (bb) an estimate of the value of the protected energy company's net property; and
  (ii) whether, and, if so, why, the energy administrator proposes to make an application to court under section 176A(5) of the 1986 Act;
(k) how it is envisaged the objective of the energy administration will be achieved and how it is proposed that the energy administration shall end. If a creditors' voluntary liquidation is proposed, details of the proposed liquidator must be provided, and a statement that, in accordance with paragraph 83(7) of Schedule B1 to the 1986 Act and Rule 78(3), creditors may nominate a different person as the proposed liquidator, provided that the nomination is made at a meeting of creditors called for that purpose;
(l) the manner in which the affairs and business of the protected energy company—
  (i) have, since the date of the energy administrator's appointment, been managed and financed, including, where any assets have been disposed of, the reasons for such disposals and the terms upon which such disposals were made; and
  (ii) will continue to be managed and financed; and
(m) such other information (if any) as the energy administrator thinks necessary.

(3) Nothing in paragraph (2)(j) is to be taken as requiring any such estimate to include any information, the disclosure of which could seriously prejudice the commercial interests of the protected energy company. If such information is excluded from the calculation the estimate shall be accompanied by a statement to that effect.

(4) Where the court orders, upon an application by the energy administrator under paragraph 107 of Schedule B1 to the 1986 Act, an extension of the period of time in paragraph 49(5) of Schedule B1 to the 1986 Act, the energy administrator shall notify in Form EA12 all the persons set out in paragraph 49(4) of Schedule B1 to the 1986 Act as soon as reasonably practicable after the making of the order.

(5) Where the energy administrator wishes to publish a notice under paragraph 49(6) of Schedule B1 to the 1986 Act he shall publish the notice once in such newspaper as he thinks most appropriate for ensuring that the notice comes to the attention of the protected energy company's members. The notice shall—

(a) state the full name of the protected energy company;
(b) state the full name and address of the energy administrator;
(c) give details of the energy administrator's appointment; and
(d) specify an address to which members can write for a copy of the statement of proposals.

(6) This notice must be published as soon as reasonably practicable after the energy administrator sends his statement of proposals to the protected energy company's creditors but no later than 8 weeks (or such other period as the court may order) from the date that the protected energy company entered energy administration.

PART 4
MEETINGS AND REPORTS
CHAPTER 1 CREDITORS' MEETINGS

[7.894]
21 Creditors' meetings generally

(1) This Rule applies to creditors' meetings summoned by the energy administrator under paragraph 62 of Schedule B1 to the 1986 Act.

(2) Notice of a creditors' meeting shall be in Form EA13.

(3) In fixing the venue for the meeting, the energy administrator shall have regard to the convenience of creditors and the meeting shall be summoned for commencement between 10.00 and 16.00 hours on a business day, unless the court otherwise directs.

(4) Subject to paragraphs (6) and (7) below and Rule 23, at least 14 days' notice of the meeting shall be given to all creditors who are known to the energy administrator and had claims against the protected energy company at the date when the protected energy company entered energy administration unless that creditor has subsequently been paid in full; and the notice shall—

- (a) specify the purpose of the meeting;
- (b) contain a statement of the effect of Rule 24 (entitlement to vote); and
- (c) contain the forms of proxy.

(5) If within 30 minutes from the time fixed for the commencement of the meeting there is no person present to act as chairman, the meeting stands adjourned to the same time and place in the following week or, if that day is not a business day, to the business day immediately following.

(6) The meeting may be adjourned once, if the chairman thinks fit, but not for more than 14 days from the date on which it was fixed to commence, subject to the direction of the court.

(7) If a meeting is adjourned the energy administrator shall as soon as reasonably practicable notify the creditors of the venue of the adjourned meeting.

[7.895]
22 The chairman at meetings

(1) At any meeting of creditors summoned by the energy administrator, either he shall be chairman, or a person nominated by him in writing to act in his place.

(2) A person so nominated must be either—

- (a) one who is qualified to act as an insolvency practitioner in relation to the protected energy company, or
- (b) an employee of the energy administrator or his firm who is experienced in insolvency matters.

[7.896]
23 Creditors' meeting for nomination of alternative liquidator

(1) Where under Rule 20(2)(k) or 31(2)(g), the energy administrator has proposed that the protected energy company enter creditors' voluntary liquidation once the energy administration has ended, the energy administrator shall, in the circumstances detailed in paragraph (2), call a meeting of creditors for the purpose of nominating a person other than the person named as proposed liquidator in the energy administrator's proposals or revised proposals.

(2) The energy administrator shall call a meeting of creditors where such a meeting is requested by creditors of the protected energy company whose debts amount to at least 25 per cent of the total debts of the protected energy company.

(3) The request for a creditors' meeting for the purpose set out in paragraph (1) shall be in Form EA14. A request for such a meeting shall be made within 21 days of the date on which the energy administrator's statement of proposals is sent out, or where revised proposals have been sent out and a proposed revision relates to the ending of the energy administration by a creditors' voluntary liquidation, within 21 days from the date on which the revised statement of proposals is sent out.

(4) A request under this Rule shall include—

- (a) a list of creditors concurring with the request, showing the amounts of their respective debts in the energy administration; and
- (b) from each creditor concurring, written confirmation of his concurrence,

but sub-paragraph (a) does not apply if the requesting creditor's debt is alone sufficient without the concurrence of other creditors.

(5) A meeting requested under this Rule shall be held within 21 days of the energy administrator's receipt of the notice requesting the meeting.

[7.897]
24 Entitlement to vote

(1) Subject as follows, at a meeting of creditors in energy administration proceedings a person is entitled to vote only if—

(a) he has given to the energy administrator, not later than 12.00 hours on the business day before the day fixed for the meeting, details in writing of the debt which he claims to be due to him from the protected energy company;

(b) the claim has been duly admitted under the following provisions of this Rule; and

(c) there has been lodged with the energy administrator any proxy which he intends to be used on his behalf,

and details of the debt must include any calculation for the purposes of Rules 26 to 28.

(2) The chairman of the meeting may allow a creditor to vote, notwithstanding that he has failed to comply with paragraph (1)(a), if satisfied that the failure was due to circumstances beyond the creditor's control.

(3) The chairman of the meeting may call for any document or other evidence to be produced to him, where he thinks it necessary for the purpose of substantiating the whole or any part of the claim.

(4) Votes are calculated according to the amount of a creditor's claim as at the date on which the protected energy company entered energy administration, less any payments that have been made to him after that date in respect of his claim and any adjustment by way of set-off in accordance with Rule 53 as if that Rule were applied on the date that the votes are counted.

(5) A creditor shall not vote in respect of a debt for an unliquidated amount, or any debt whose value is not ascertained, except where the chairman agrees to put upon the debt an estimated minimum value for the purpose of entitlement to vote and admits the claim for that purpose.

(6) No vote shall be cast by virtue of a claim more than once on any resolution put to the meeting.

[7.898]
25 Admission and rejection of claims

(1) At any creditors' meeting the chairman has power to admit or reject a creditor's claim for the purpose of his entitlement to vote; and the power is exercisable with respect to the whole or any part of the claim.

(2) The chairman's decision under this Rule, or in respect of any matter arising under Rule 24, is subject to appeal to the court by any creditor.

(3) If the chairman is in doubt whether a claim should be admitted or rejected, he shall mark it as objected to and allow the creditor to vote, subject to his vote being subsequently declared invalid if the objection to the claim is sustained.

(4) If on appeal the chairman's decision is reversed or varied, or a creditor's vote is declared invalid, the court may order that another meeting be summoned, or make such other order as it thinks fit.

(5) Neither the energy administrator nor any person nominated by him to be chairman is personally liable for costs incurred by any person in respect of an appeal to the court under this Rule, unless the court makes an order to that effect.

[7.899]
26 Secured creditors

At a meeting of creditors a secured creditor is entitled to vote only in respect of the balance (if any) of his debt after deducting the value of his security as estimated by him.

[7.900]
27 Holders of negotiable instruments

A creditor shall not vote in respect of a debt on, or secured by, a current bill of exchange or promissory note, unless he is willing—

(a) to treat the liability to him on the bill or note of every person who is liable on it antecedently to the protected energy company, and against whom a bankruptcy order has not been made (or, in the case of a company, which has not gone into liquidation), as a security in his hands, and

(b) to estimate the value of the security and, for the purpose of his entitlement to vote, to deduct it from his claim.

[7.901]
28 Hire-purchase, conditional sale and chattel leasing agreements

(1) Subject as follows, an owner of goods under a hire-purchase or chattel leasing agreement, or a seller of goods under a conditional sale agreement, is entitled to vote in respect of the amount of the debt due and payable to him by the protected energy company on the date that the protected energy company entered energy administration.

(2) In calculating the amount of any debt for this purpose, no account shall be taken of any amount attributable to the exercise of any right under the relevant agreement, so far as the right has become exercisable solely by virtue of the making of an energy administration application or any matter arising as a consequence, or of the protected energy company entering energy administration.

[7.902]
29 Resolutions

(1) Subject as follows, at a creditors' meeting in energy administration proceedings, a resolution is passed when a majority (in value) of those present and voting, in person or by proxy, have voted in favour of it.

(2) Any resolution is invalid if those voting against it include more than half in value of the creditors to whom notice of the meeting was sent and who are not, to the best of the chairman's belief, persons connected with the protected energy company.

(3) In the case of a resolution for the nomination of a person to act as liquidator once the energy administration has ended—

(a) subject to paragraph (4), if on any vote there are two persons put forward by creditors for nomination as liquidator, the person who obtains the most support is nominated as liquidator;

(b) if there are three or more persons put forward by creditors for nomination as liquidator, and one of them has a clear majority over both or all the others together, that one is nominated as liquidator; and

(c) in any other case, the chairman of the meeting shall continue to take votes (disregarding at each vote any person who has withdrawn and, if no person has withdrawn, the person who obtained the least support last time), until a clear majority is obtained for any one person.

(4) The support referred to in paragraph (3)(a) must represent a majority in value of all those present (in person or by proxy) at the meeting and entitled to vote.

(5) Where, on such a resolution no person is nominated as liquidator, the person named as proposed liquidator in the energy administrator's proposals or revised proposals shall be the liquidator once the energy administration has ended.

(6) The chairman may at any time put to the meeting a resolution for the joint appointment of any two or more persons put forward by creditors for nomination as liquidator.

(7) In this Rule, "connected with the protected energy company" has the same meaning as the phrase "connected with a company" in section 249 of the 1986 Act.

[7.903]
30 Minutes

(1) The chairman of the meeting shall cause minutes of its proceedings to be entered in the protected energy company's minute book.

(2) The minutes shall include a list of the names and addresses of creditors who attended (personally or by proxy).

[7.904]
31 Revision of the energy administrator's proposals

(1) The energy administrator shall, as soon as reasonably practicable, under paragraph 54 of Schedule B1 of the 1986 Act, make a statement setting out the proposed revisions to his proposals which he shall attach to Form EA15 and send to all those to whom he is required to send a copy of his revised proposals.

(2) The statement of revised proposals shall include—

(a) details of the court where the proceedings are and the relevant court reference number;

(b) the full name, registered address, registered number and any other trading names of the protected energy company;

(c) details relating to his appointment as energy administrator, including the date of appointment and whether the energy administration application was made by the Secretary of State or by GEMA;

(d) the names of the directors and secretary of the protected energy company and details of any shareholdings in the protected energy company they may have;

(e) a summary of the initial proposals and the reason(s) for proposing a revision;

(f) details of the proposed revision including details of the energy administrator's assessment of the likely impact of the proposed revision upon creditors generally or upon each class of creditors (as the case may be);

(g) where a proposed revision relates to the ending of the energy administration by a creditors' voluntary liquidation and the nomination of a person to be the proposed liquidator of the protected energy company, a statement that, in accordance with paragraph 83(7) of Schedule B1 to the 1986 Act and Rule 78(3), creditors may nominate a different person as the proposed liquidator, provided that the nomination is made at a meeting of creditors called for that purpose; and

(h) any other information that the energy administrator thinks necessary.

(3) Subject to paragraph 54(4) of Schedule B1 to the 1986 Act, within 5 days of sending out the statement in paragraph (1) above, the energy administrator shall send a copy of the statement to every member of the protected energy company.

(4) When the energy administrator is acting under paragraph 54(4) of Schedule B1 to the 1986 Act, the notice shall be published once in such newspaper as he thinks most appropriate for ensuring that the notice comes to the attention of the protected energy company's members. The notice shall—

(a) state the full name of the protected energy company;

(b) state the name and address of the energy administrator;

(c) specify an address to which members can write for a copy of the statement; and

(d) be published as soon as reasonably practicable after the energy administrator sends the statement to creditors.

[7.905]
32 Reports to creditors

(1) "Progress report" means a report which includes—

(a) details of the court where the proceedings are and the relevant court reference number;

(b) full details of the protected energy company's name, address of registered office and registered number;

(c) full details of the energy administrator's name and address, date of appointment and name and address of the applicant for the energy administration application, including any changes in office-holder, and, in the case of joint energy administrators, their functions as set out in the statement made for the purposes of section 158(5) of the 2004 Act;

(d) details of progress during the period of the report, including a receipts and payments account (as detailed in paragraph (2) below);

(e) details of any assets that remain to be realised; and

(f) any other relevant information for the creditors.

(2) A receipts and payments account shall state what assets of the protected energy company have been realised, for what value, and what payments have been made to creditors or others. The account is to be in the form of an abstract showing receipts and payments during the period of the report and where the energy administrator has ceased to act, the receipts and payments account shall include a statement as to the amount paid to unsecured creditors by virtue of the application of section 176A of the 1986 Act (prescribed part).

(3) The progress report shall cover—

(a) the period of 6 months commencing on the date that the protected energy company entered energy administration, and every subsequent period of 6 months; and

(b) when the energy administrator ceases to act, any period from the date of the previous report, if any, and from the date that the protected energy company entered energy administration if there is no previous report, until the time that the energy administrator ceases to act.

(4) The energy administrator shall send a copy of the progress report, attached to Form EA16, within 1 month of the end of the period covered by the report, to—

(a) the Secretary of State;

(b) GEMA;

(c) the creditors;

(d) the court; and

(e) the registrar of companies.

(5) The court may, on the energy administrator's application, extend the period of 1 month mentioned in paragraph (4) above, or make such other order in respect of the content of the report as it thinks fit.

(6) If the energy administrator makes default in complying with this Rule, he is liable to a fine and, for continued contravention, to a daily default fine.

CHAPTER 2 COMPANY MEETINGS

[7.906]
33 Venue and conduct of company meeting

(1) Where the energy administrator summons a meeting of members of the protected energy company, he shall fix a venue for it having regard to their convenience.

(2) The chairman of the meeting shall be the energy administrator or a person nominated by him in writing to act in his place.

(3) A person so nominated must be either—

(a) one who is qualified to act as an insolvency practitioner in relation to the protected energy company, or

(b) an employee of the energy administrator or his firm who is experienced in insolvency matters.

(4) If within 30 minutes from the time fixed for commencement of the meeting there is no person present to act as chairman, the meeting stands adjourned to the same time and place in the following week or, if that day is not a business day, to the business day immediately following.

(5) Subject as above, the meeting shall be summoned and conducted as if it were a general meeting of the protected energy company summoned under the company's articles of association, and in accordance with the applicable provisions of the Companies Act.

(6) The chairman of the meeting shall cause minutes of its proceedings to be entered in the protected energy company's minute book.

PART 5
DISPOSAL OF CHARGED PROPERTY

[7.907]
34 Authority to dispose of property

(1) The following applies where the energy administrator applies to the court under paragraphs 71 or 72 of Schedule B1 to the 1986 Act for authority to dispose of property of the protected energy company which is subject to a security (other than a floating charge), or goods in the possession of the protected energy company under a hire purchase agreement.

(2) The court shall fix a venue for the hearing of the application, and the energy administrator shall as soon as reasonably practicable give notice of the venue to the person who is the holder of the security or, as the case may be, the owner under the agreement.

(3) If an order is made under paragraphs 71 or 72 of Schedule B1 to the 1986 Act the court shall send two sealed copies to the energy administrator.

(4) The energy administrator shall send one of them to that person who is the holder of the security or owner under the agreement.

(5) The energy administrator shall send a Form EA17 to the registrar of companies with a copy of the sealed order.

PART 6
EXPENSES OF THE ENERGY ADMINISTRATION

[7.908]
35 Priority of expenses of energy administration

(1) The expenses of the energy administration are payable in the following order of priority—

(a) expenses properly incurred by the energy administrator in performing his functions in the energy administration of the protected energy company;

(b) the cost of any security provided by the energy administrator in accordance with the 1986 Act or the Rules;

(c) where an energy administration order was made, the costs of the applicant and any person appearing on the hearing of the application;

(d) any amount payable to a person employed or authorised, under Part 3 of the Rules, to assist in the preparation of a statement of affairs or statement of concurrence;

(e) any allowance made, by order of the court, towards costs on an application for release from the obligation to submit a statement of affairs or statement of concurrence;

(f) any necessary disbursements by the energy administrator in the course of the energy administration (but not including any payment of corporation tax in circumstances referred to in sub-paragraph (i) below);

(g) the remuneration or emoluments of any person who has been employed by the energy administrator to perform any services for the protected energy company, as required or authorised under the 1986 Act or the 2004 Act, Schedule B1 to the 1986 Act or the Rules;

(h) the remuneration of the energy administrator agreed under Part 8 of the Rules;

(i) the amount of any corporation tax on chargeable gains accruing on the realisation of any asset of the protected energy company (without regard to whether the realisation is effected by the energy administrator, a secured creditor, or a receiver or manager appointed to deal with a security).

(2) The priorities laid down by paragraph (1) of this Rule are subject to the power of the court to make orders under paragraph (3) of this Rule where the assets are insufficient to satisfy the liabilities.

(3) The court may, in the event of the assets being insufficient to satisfy the liabilities, make an order as to the payment out of the assets of the expenses incurred in the energy administration in such order of priority as the court thinks just.

(4) For the purposes of paragraph 99(3) of Schedule B1 to the 1986 Act, the former energy administrator's remuneration and expenses shall comprise all those items set out in paragraph (1) of this Rule.

PART 7
DISTRIBUTION OF CREDITORS

CHAPTER 1 APPLICATION OF PART AND GENERAL

[7.909]
36 Distribution to creditors generally

(1) This Part applies where the energy administrator makes, or proposes to make, a distribution to any class of creditors. Where the distribution is to a particular class of creditors, references in this Part to creditors shall, in so far as the context requires, be a reference to that class of creditors only.

(2) The energy administrator shall give notice to the creditors of his intention to declare and distribute a dividend in accordance with Rule 63.

(3) Where it is intended that the distribution is to be a sole or final dividend, the energy administrator shall, after the date specified in the notice referred to in paragraph (2)—

(a) defray any items payable in accordance with the provisions of paragraph 99 of Schedule B1 to the 1986 Act;

(b) defray any amounts (including any debts or liabilities and his own remuneration and expenses) which would, if the energy administrator were to cease to be the energy administrator of the protected energy company, be payable out of the property of which he had custody or control in accordance with the provisions of paragraph 99 of Schedule B1 to the 1986 Act; and

(c) declare and distribute that dividend without regard to the claim of any person in respect of a debt not already proved.

(4) The court may, on the application of any person, postpone the date specified in the notice.

[7.910]
37 Debts of insolvent company to rank equally

Debts other than preferential debts rank equally between themselves in the energy administration and, after the preferential debts, shall be paid in full unless the assets are insufficient for meeting them, in which case they abate in equal proportions between themselves.

[7.911]
38 Supplementary provisions as to dividend

(1) In the calculation and distribution of a dividend the energy administrator shall make provision for—

(a) any debts which appear to him to be due to persons who, by reason of the distance of their place of residence, may not have had sufficient time to tender and establish their proofs;

(b) any debts which are the subject of claims which have not yet been determined; and

(c) disputed proofs and claims.

(2) A creditor who has not proved his debt before the declaration of any dividend is not entitled to disturb, by reason that he has not participated in it, the distribution of that dividend or any other dividend declared before his debt was proved, but—

(a) when he has proved that debt he is entitled to be paid, out of any money for the time being available for the payment of any further dividend, any dividend or dividends which he has failed to receive; and

(b) any dividends payable under sub-paragraph (a) shall be paid before the money is applied to the payment of any such further dividend.

(3) No action lies against the energy administrator for a dividend; but if he refuses to pay a dividend the court may, if it thinks fit, order him to pay it and also to pay, out of his own money—

(a) interest on the dividend, at the rate for the time being specified in section 17 of the Judgments Act 1838, from the time when it was withheld; and

(b) the costs of the proceedings in which the order to pay is made.

[7.912]
39 Division of unsold assets

The energy administrator may, with the permission of the creditors, divide in its existing form amongst the protected energy company's creditors, according to its estimated value, any property which from its peculiar nature or other special circumstances cannot be readily or advantageously sold.

CHAPTER 2 MACHINERY OF PROVING A DEBT

[7.913]
40 Proving a debt

(1) A person claiming to be a creditor of the protected energy company and wishing to recover his debt in whole or in part must (subject to any order of the court to the contrary) submit his claim in writing to the energy administrator.

(2) A creditor who claims is referred to as "proving" for his debt and a document by which he seeks to establish his claim is his "proof".

(3) Subject to the next paragraph, a proof must—

(a) be made out by, or under the direction of, the creditor and signed by him or a person authorised in that behalf; and

(b) state the following matters—

(i) the creditor's name and address;

(ii) the total amount of his claim as at the date on which the protected energy company entered energy administration, less any payments that have been made to him after that date in respect of his claim and any adjustment by way of set-off in accordance with Rule 53;

(iii) whether or not the claim includes outstanding uncapitalised interest;

(iv) whether or not the claim includes value added tax;

(v) whether the whole or any part of the debt falls within any, and if so, which categories of preferential debts under section 386 of the 1986 Act;

(vi) particulars of how and when the debt was incurred by the protected energy company;

(vii) particulars of any security held, the date on which it was given and the value which the creditor puts on it;

(viii) details of any reservation of title in respect of goods to which the debt refers; and

(ix) the name, address and authority of the person signing the proof (if other than the creditor himself).

(4) There shall be specified in the proof details of any documents by reference to which the debt can be substantiated; but (subject as follows) it is not essential that such document be attached to the proof or submitted with it.

(5) The energy administrator may call for any document or other evidence to be produced to him, where he thinks it necessary for the purpose of substantiating the whole or any part of the claim made in the proof.

[7.914]
41 Claim established by affidavit

(1) The energy administrator may, if he thinks it necessary, require a claim of debt to be verified by means of an affidavit in Form EA18.

(2) An affidavit may be required notwithstanding that a proof of debt has already been lodged.

[7.915]
42 Costs of proving

Unless the court otherwise orders—

(a) every creditor bears the cost of proving his own debt, including costs incurred in providing documents or evidence under Rule 40(5); and

(b) costs incurred by the energy administrator in estimating the quantum of a debt under Rule 49 are payable out of the assets as an expense of the energy administration.

[7.916]
43 Energy administrator to allow inspection of proofs

The energy administrator shall, so long as proofs lodged with him are in his hands, allow them to be inspected, at all reasonable times on any business day, by any of the following persons—

(a) any creditor who has submitted a proof of debt (unless his proof has been wholly rejected for purposes of dividend or otherwise);

(b) any contributory of the protected energy company; and

(c) any person acting on behalf of either of the above.

[7.917]
44 New energy administrator appointed

(1) If a new energy administrator is appointed in place of another, the former energy administrator shall transmit to him all proofs which he has received, together with an itemised list of them.

(2) The new energy administrator shall sign the list by way of receipt for the proofs, and return it to his predecessor.

[7.918]
45 Admission and rejection of proofs for dividend

(1) A proof may be admitted for dividend either for the whole amount claimed by the creditor, or for part of that amount.

(2) If the energy administrator rejects a proof in whole or in part, he shall prepare a written statement of his reasons for doing so, and send it as soon as reasonably practicable to the creditor.

[7.919]
46 Appeal against decision on proof

(1) If a creditor is dissatisfied with the energy administrator's decision with respect to his proof (including any decision on the question of preference), he may apply to the court for the decision to be reversed or varied. The application must be made within 21 days of his receiving the statement sent under Rule 45(2).

(2) Any other creditor may, if dissatisfied with the energy administrator's decision admitting or rejecting the whole or any part of a proof, make such an application within 21 days of becoming aware of the energy administrator's decision.

(3) Where application is made to the court under this Rule, the court shall fix a venue for the application to be heard, notice of which shall be sent by the applicant to the creditor who lodged the proof in question (if it is not himself) and the energy administrator.

(4) The energy administrator shall, on receipt of the notice, file with the court the relevant proof, together (if appropriate) with a copy of the statement sent under Rule 45(2).

(5) After the application has been heard and determined, the proof shall, unless it has been wholly disallowed, be returned by the court to the energy administrator.

(6) The energy administrator is not personally liable for costs incurred by any person in respect of an application under this Rule unless the court otherwise orders.

[7.920]
47 Withdrawal or variation of proof

A creditor's proof may at any time, by agreement between himself and the energy administrator, be withdrawn or varied as to the amount claimed.

[7.921]
48 Expunging of proof by the court

(1) The court may expunge a proof or reduce the amount claimed—

(a) on the energy administrator's application, where he thinks that the proof has been improperly admitted, or ought to be reduced; or

(b) on the application of a creditor, if the energy administrator declines to interfere in the matter.

(2) Where application is made to the court under this Rule, the court shall fix a venue for the application to be heard, notice of which shall be sent by the applicant—

(a) in the case of an application by the energy administrator, to the creditor who made the proof; and

(b) in the case of an application by a creditor, to the energy administrator and to the creditor who made the proof (if not himself).

CHAPTER 3 QUANTIFICATION OF CLAIMS

[7.922]

49 Estimate of quantum

(1) The energy administrator shall estimate the value of any debt which, by reason of its being subject to any contingency or for any other reason, does not bear a certain value; and he may revise any estimate previously made, if he thinks fit by reference to any change of circumstances or to information becoming available to him. He shall inform the creditor as to his estimate and any revision of it.

(2) Where the value of a debt is estimated under this Rule, the amount provable in the energy administration in the case of that debt is that of the estimate for the time being.

[7.923]

50 Negotiable instruments, etc

Unless the energy administrator allows, a proof in respect of money owed on a bill of exchange, promissory note, cheque or other negotiable instrument or security cannot be admitted unless there is produced the instrument or security itself or a copy of it, certified by the creditor or his authorised representative to be a true copy.

[7.924]

51 Secured creditors

(1) If a secured creditor realises his security, he may prove for the balance of his debt, after deducting the amount realised.

(2) If a secured creditor voluntarily surrenders his security for the general benefit of creditors, he may prove for his whole debt, as if it were unsecured.

[7.925]

52 Discounts

There shall in every case be deducted from the claim all trade and other discounts which would have been available to the protected energy company but for its energy administration except any discount for immediate, early or cash settlement.

[7.926]

53 Mutual credits and set-off

(1) This Rule applies where the energy administrator, being authorised to make the distribution in question, has pursuant to Rule 63, given notice that he proposes to make it.

(2) In this Rule "mutual dealings" means mutual credits, mutual debts or other mutual dealings between the protected energy company and any creditor of the protected energy company proving or claiming to prove for a debt in the energy administration but does not include any of the following—

(a) any debt arising out of an obligation incurred after the protected energy company entered energy administration;

(b) any debt arising out of an obligation incurred at a time when the creditor had notice that an application for an energy administration order was pending;

(c) any debt which has been acquired by a creditor by assignment or otherwise, pursuant to an agreement where that agreement was entered into between the creditor and any other party—

(i) after the protected energy company entered energy administration; or

(ii) at a time when the creditor had notice that an application for an energy administration order was pending.

(3) An account shall be taken as at the date of the notice referred to in paragraph (1) of what is due from each party to the other in respect of the mutual dealings and the sums due from one party shall be set off against the sums due from the other.

(4) A sum shall be regarded as being due to or from the protected energy company for the purposes of paragraph (3) whether—

(a) it is payable at present or in the future;

(b) the obligation by virtue of which it is payable is certain or contingent; or

(c) its amount is fixed or liquidated, or is capable of being ascertained by fixed rules as a matter of opinion.

(5) Rule 49 shall apply for the purposes of this Rule to an obligation to or from the protected energy company which, by virtue of its being subject to any contingency or for any other reason, does not bear a certain value.

(6) Rules 54 to 56 shall apply for the purposes of this Rule in relation to any sums due to the protected energy company which—

(a) are payable in a currency other than sterling;

(b) are of a periodical nature; or

(c) bear interest.

(7) Rule 73 shall apply for the purposes of this Rule to any sum due to or from the protected energy company which is payable in the future.

(8) Only the balance (if any) of the account owed to the creditor is provable in the energy administration. Alternatively the balance (if any) owed to the protected energy company shall be paid to the energy administrator as part of the assets except where all or part of the balance results from a contingent or prospective debt owed by the creditor and in such a case the balance (or that part of it which results from the contingent or prospective debt) shall be paid if and when the debt becomes due and payable.

(9) In this Rule "obligation" means an obligation however arising, whether by virtue of an agreement, rule of law or otherwise.

[7.927]
54 Debt in foreign currency

(1) For the purpose of proving a debt incurred or payable in a currency other than sterling, the amount of the debt shall be converted into sterling at the official exchange rate prevailing on the date when the protected energy company entered energy administration.

(2) "The official exchange rate" is the middle exchange rate on the London Foreign Exchange Market at the close of business, as published for the date in question. In the absence of any such published rate, it is such rate as the court determines.

[7.928]
55 Payments of a periodical nature

(1) In the case of rent and other payments of a periodical nature, the creditor may prove for any amounts due and unpaid up to the date when the protected energy company entered energy administration.

(2) Where at that date any payment was accruing due, the creditor may prove for so much as would have fallen due at that date, if accruing from day to day.

[7.929]
56 Interest

(1) Where a debt proved in the energy administration bears interest, that interest is provable as part of the debt except in so far as it is payable in respect of any period after the protected energy company entered energy administration.

(2) In the following circumstances the creditor's claim may include interest on the debt for periods before the protected energy company entered energy administration, although not previously reserved or agreed.

(3) If the debt is due by virtue of a written instrument, and payable at a certain time, interest may be claimed for the period from that time to the date when the protected energy company entered energy administration.

(4) If the debt is due otherwise, interest may only be claimed if, before that date, a demand for payment of the debt was made in writing by or on behalf of the creditor, and notice given that interest would be payable from the date of the demand to the date of payment.

(5) Interest under paragraph (4) may only be claimed for the period from the date of the demand to that of the protected energy company's entering energy administration and for all the purposes of the 1986 Act and the Rules shall be chargeable at a rate not exceeding that mentioned in paragraph (6).

(6) The rate of interest to be claimed under paragraphs (3) and (4) is the rate specified in section 17 of the Judgments Act 1838 on the date when the protected energy company entered energy administration.

(7) Any surplus remaining after payment of the debts proved shall, before being applied for any purpose, be applied in paying interest on those debts in respect of the periods during which they have been outstanding since the protected energy company entered energy administration.

(8) All interest payable under paragraph (7) ranks equally whether or not the debts on which it is payable rank equally.

(9) The rate of interest payable under paragraph (7) is whichever is the greater of the rate specified under paragraph (6) or the rate applicable to the debt apart from the energy administration.

[7.930]
57 Debt payable at future time

A creditor may prove for a debt of which payment was not yet due on the date when the protected energy company entered energy administration, subject to Rule 73 (adjustment of dividend where payment made before time).

[7.931]
58 Value of security

(1) A secured creditor may, with the agreement of the energy administrator or the leave of the court, at any time alter the value which he has, in his proof of debt, put upon his security.

(2) However, if a secured creditor has voted in respect of the unsecured balance of his debt he may re-value his security only with permission of the court.

[7.932]
59 Surrender for non-disclosure

(1) If a secured creditor omits to disclose his security in his proof of debt, he shall surrender his security for the general benefit of creditors, unless the court, on application by him, relieves him from the effect of this Rule on the ground that the omission was inadvertent or the result of honest mistake.

(2) If the court grants that relief, it may require or allow the creditor's proof of debt to be amended, on such terms as may be just.

[7.933]
60 Redemption by energy administrator

(1) The energy administrator may at any time give notice to a creditor whose debt is secured that he proposes, at the expiration of 28 days from the date of the notice, to redeem the security at the value put upon it in the creditor's proof.

(2) The creditor then has 21 days (or such longer period as the energy administrator may allow) in which, if he so wishes, to exercise his right to revalue his security (with the permission of the court, where Rule 58(2) applies).

If the creditor re-values his security, the energy administrator may only redeem at the new value.

(3) If the energy administrator redeems the security, the cost of transferring it is payable out of the assets.

(4) A secured creditor may at any time, by a notice in writing, call on the energy administrator to elect whether he will or will not exercise his power to redeem the security at the value then placed on it; and the energy administrator then has 3 months in which to exercise the power or determine not to exercise it.

[7.934]
61 Test of security's value

(1) Subject as follows, the energy administrator, if he is dissatisfied with the value which a secured creditor puts on his security (whether in his proof or by way of re-valuation under Rule 58), may require any property comprised in the security to be offered for sale.

(2) The terms of sale shall be such as may be agreed, or as the court may direct; and if the sale is by auction, the energy administrator on behalf of the protected energy company, and the creditor on his own behalf, may appear and bid.

[7.935]
62 Realisation of security by creditor

If a creditor who has valued his security subsequently realises it (whether or not at the instance of the energy administrator)—

(a) the net amount realised shall be substituted for the value previously put by the creditor on the security; and

(b) that amount shall be treated in all respects as an amended valuation made by him.

[7.936]
63 Notice of proposed distribution

(1) Where an energy administrator is proposing to make a distribution to creditors he shall give 28 days' notice of that fact.

(2) The notice given pursuant to paragraph (1) shall—

(a) be sent to all creditors whose addresses are known to the energy administrator;

(b) state whether the distribution is to preferential creditors or preferential creditors and unsecured creditors; and

(c) where the energy administrator proposes to make a distribution to unsecured creditors, state the value of the prescribed part, except where the court has made an order under section 176A(5) of the 1986 Act.

(3) Subject to paragraph (5), the energy administrator shall not declare a dividend unless he has by public advertisement invited creditors to prove their debts.

(4) A notice pursuant to paragraphs (1) or (3) shall—

(a) state that it is the intention of the energy administrator to make a distribution to creditors within the period of 2 months from the last date for proving;

(b) specify whether the proposed dividend is interim or final;

(c) specify a date up to which proofs may be lodged being a date which—

  (i) is the same date for all creditors; and

  (ii) is not less than 21 days from that of the notice.

(5) A notice pursuant to paragraph (1) where a dividend is to be declared for preferential creditors, need only be given to those creditors in whose case he has reason to believe that their debts are preferential and public advertisement of the intended dividend need only be given if the energy administrator thinks fit.

[7.937]
64 Admission or rejection of proofs

(1) Unless he has already dealt with them, within 7 days of the last date for proving, the energy administrator shall—

(a) admit or reject proofs submitted to him; or

(b) make such provision in respect of them as he thinks fit.

(2) The energy administrator is not obliged to deal with proofs lodged after the last date for proving, but he may do so, if he thinks fit.

(3) In the declaration of a dividend no payment shall be made more than once by virtue of the same debt.

[7.938]
65 Declaration of dividend

(1) Subject to paragraph (2), within the 2 month period referred to in Rule 63(4)(a) the energy administrator shall proceed to declare the dividend to one or more classes of creditor of which he gave notice.

(2) Except with the permission of the court, the energy administrator shall not declare a dividend so long as there is pending any application to the court to reverse or vary a decision of his on a proof, or to expunge a proof or to reduce the amount claimed.

[7.939]
66 Notice of declaration of a dividend

(1) Where the energy administrator declares a dividend he shall give notice of that fact to all creditors who have proved their debts.

(2) The notice shall include the following particulars relating to the energy administration—

(a) amounts raised from the sale of assets, indicating (so far as practicable) amounts raised by the sale of particular assets;

(b) payments made by the energy administrator when acting as such;

(c) where the energy administrator proposes to make a distribution to unsecured creditors, the value of the prescribed part, except where the court has made an order under section 176A(5) of the 1986 Act;

(d) provision (if any) made for unsettled claims, and funds (if any) retained for particular purposes;

(e) the total amount of dividend and the rate of dividend;

(f) how he proposes to distribute the dividend; and

(g) whether, and if so when, any further dividend is expected to be declared.

[7.940]
67 Payments of dividends and related matters

(1) The dividend may be distributed simultaneously with the notice declaring it.

(2) Payment of dividend may be made by post, or arrangements may be made with any creditor for it to be paid to him in another way, or held for his collection.

(3) Where a dividend is paid on a bill of exchange or other negotiable instrument, the amount of the dividend shall be endorsed on the instrument, or on a certified copy of it, if required to be produced by the holder for that purpose.

[7.941]
68 Notice of no dividend, or no further dividend

If the energy administrator gives notice to creditors that he is unable to declare any dividend or (as the case may be) any further dividend, the notice shall contain a statement to the effect either—

(a) that no funds have been realised; or

(b) that the funds realised have already been distributed or used or allocated for defraying the expenses of energy administration.

[7.942]
69 Proof altered after payment of dividend

(1) If after payment of dividend the amount claimed by a creditor in his proof is increased, the creditor is not entitled to disturb the distribution of the dividend; but he is entitled to be paid, out of any money for the time being available for the payment of any further dividend, any dividend or dividends which he has failed to receive.

(2) Any dividend or dividends payable under paragraph (1) shall be paid before the money there referred to is applied to the payment of any such further dividend.

(3) If, after a creditor's proof has been admitted, the proof is withdrawn or expunged, or the amount is reduced, the creditor is liable to repay to the energy administrator any amount overpaid by way of dividend.

[7.943]
70 Secured creditors

(1) The following applies where a creditor re-values his security at a time when a dividend has been declared.

(2) If the revaluation results in a reduction of his unsecured claim ranking for dividend, the creditor shall forthwith repay to the energy administrator, for the credit of the energy administration, any amount received by him as dividend in excess of that to which he would be entitled having regard to the revaluation of the security.

(3) If the revaluation results in an increase of his unsecured claim, the creditor is entitled to receive from the energy administrator, out of any money for the time being available for the payment of a further dividend, before any such further dividend is paid, any dividend or dividends which he has failed to receive, having regard to the revaluation of the security.

However, the creditor is not entitled to disturb any dividend declared (whether or not distributed) before the date of the revaluation.

[7.944]

71 Disqualification from dividend

If a creditor contravenes any provision of the 1986 Act or the Rules relating to the valuation of securities, the court may, on the application of the energy administrator, order that the creditor be wholly or partly disqualified from participation in any dividend.

[7.945]

72 Assignment of right to dividend

(1) If a person entitled to a dividend gives notice to the energy administrator that he wishes the dividend to be paid to another person, or that he has assigned his entitlement to another person, the energy administrator shall pay the dividend to that other accordingly.

(2) A notice given under this Rule must specify the name and address of the person to whom payment is to be made.

[7.946]

73 Debt payable at future time

(1) Where a creditor has proved for a debt of which payment is not due at the date of the declaration of dividend, he is entitled to dividend equally with other creditors, but subject as follows.

(2) For the purpose of dividend (and no other purpose), the amount of the creditor's admitted proof (or, if a distribution has previously been made to him, the amount remaining outstanding in respect of his admitted proof) shall be reduced by applying the following formula—

$$\frac{X}{1.05^n}$$

where—

(a) "X" is the value of the admitted proof; and

(b) "n" is the period beginning with the relevant date and ending with the date on which the payment of the creditor's debt would otherwise be due expressed in years and months in a decimalised form.

(3) In paragraph (2) "relevant date" means the date that the protected energy company entered energy administration.

PART 8
THE ENERGY ADMINISTRATOR

[7.947]

74 Fixing of remuneration

(1) The energy administrator is entitled to receive remuneration for his services as such.

(2) The remuneration shall be fixed by reference to the time properly given by the insolvency practitioner (as energy administrator) and his staff in attending to matters arising in the energy administration.

(3) The remuneration of the energy administrator shall be fixed by the court and the energy administrator shall make an application to court accordingly.

(4) The energy administrator shall give at least 14 days' notice of his application to the following, who may appear or be represented—

(a) the Secretary of State;
(b) GEMA; and
(c) the creditors of the protected energy company.

(5) In fixing the remuneration, the court shall have regard to the following matters—

(a) the complexity (or otherwise) of the case;
(b) any respects in which, in connection with the protected energy company's affairs, there falls on the energy administrator any responsibility of an exceptional kind or degree;
(c) the effectiveness with which the energy administrator appears to be carrying out, or to have carried out, his duties as such; and
(d) the value and nature of the property with which he has to deal.

(6) Where there are joint energy administrators, it is for them to agree between themselves as to how the remuneration payable should be apportioned. Any dispute arising between them may be referred to the court for settlement by order.

(7) If the energy administrator is a solicitor and employs his own firm, or any partner in it, to act on behalf of the protected energy company, profit costs shall not be paid unless this is authorised by the court.

PART 9
ENDING ENERGY ADMINISTRATION

[7.948]
75 Final progress reports

(1) In this Part reference to a progress report is to a report in the form specified in Rule 32.

(2) The final progress report means a progress report which includes a summary of—

(a) the energy administrator's proposals;

(b) any major amendments to, or deviations from, those proposals;

(c) the steps taken during the energy administration; and

(d) the outcome.

[7.949]
76 Application to court

(1) An application to court under paragraph 79 of Schedule B1 to the 1986 Act for an order ending an energy administration shall have attached to it a progress report for the period since the last progress report (if any) or the date the protected energy company entered energy administration and a statement indicating what the applicant thinks should be the next steps for the protected energy company (if applicable).

(2) Where such an application is made, the applicant shall—

(a) give notice in writing to the applicant for the energy administration order (unless the applicant in both cases is the same) and the creditors of the protected energy company of his intention to apply to court at least 7 days before the date that he intends to make his application; and

(b) attach to the application to court a statement that he has notified the creditors, and copies of any response from creditors to that notification.

(3) Where such an application is to be made other than by the energy administrator—

(a) the applicant shall also give notice in writing to the energy administrator of his intention to apply to court at least 7 days before the date that he intends to make his application; and

(b) upon receipt of such written notice the energy administrator shall, before the end of the 7 day notice period, provide the applicant with a progress report for the period since the last progress report (if any) or the date the protected energy company entered energy administration.

(4) Where the application is made other than by the Secretary of State, the application shall also state that it is made with the consent of the Secretary of State.

(5) Where the energy administrator applies to court under paragraph 79 of Schedule B1 to the 1986 Act in conjunction with a petition under section 124 of the 1986 Act for an order to wind up the protected energy company, he shall, in addition to the requirements of paragraphs (2) and (4), notify the creditors whether he intends to seek appointment as liquidator.

[7.950]
77 Notification by energy administrator of court order

(1) Where the court makes an order to end the energy administration, the energy administrator shall notify the registrar of companies in Form EA19, attaching a copy of the court order and a copy of the final progress report.

(2) Where the court makes such an order, it shall, where the applicant is not the energy administrator, give a copy of the order to the energy administrator.

[7.951]
78 Moving from energy administration to creditors' voluntary liquidation

(1) Where for the purposes of paragraph 83(3) of Schedule B1 to the 1986 Act, the energy administrator sends a notice of moving from energy administration to creditors' voluntary liquidation to the registrar of companies, he shall do so in Form EA20 and shall attach to that notice a final progress report which must include details of the assets to be dealt with in the liquidation.

(2) As soon as reasonably practicable the energy administrator shall send a copy of the notice and attached document to—

(a) all those who received notice of the energy administrator's appointment;

(b) where the Secretary of State did not receive notice of the energy administrator's appointment, to the Secretary of State; and

(c) where GEMA did not receive notice of the energy administrator's appointment, to GEMA.

(3) For the purposes of paragraph 83(7) of Schedule B1 to the 1986 Act, a person shall be nominated as liquidator in accordance with the provisions of Rule 20(2)(k) or Rule 31(2)(g) and his appointment takes effect—

(a) by virtue of the energy administrator's proposals or revised proposals; or

(b) where a creditors' meeting is held in accordance with Rule 23, as a consequence of such a meeting.

(4) GEMA must notify the Secretary of State before consenting to the energy administrator sending a notice of moving from energy administration to creditors' voluntary liquidation to the registrar of companies.

[7.952]
79 Moving from energy administration to dissolution

(1) Where, for the purposes of paragraph 84(1) of Schedule B1 to the 1986 Act, the energy administrator sends a notice of moving from energy administration to dissolution to the registrar of companies, he shall do so in Form EA21 and shall attach to that notice a final progress report.

(2) As soon as reasonably practicable a copy of the notice and the attached document shall be sent to—
- (a) all those who received notice of the energy administrator's appointment;
- (b) where the Secretary of State did not receive notice of the energy administrator's appointment, the Secretary of State; and
- (c) where GEMA did not receive notice of the energy administrator's appointment, to GEMA.

(3) Where a court makes an order under paragraph 84(7) of Schedule B1 to the 1986 Act, it shall, where the applicant is not the energy administrator, give a copy of the order to the energy administrator.

(4) The energy administrator shall use Form EA22 to notify the registrar of companies in accordance with paragraph 84(8) of Schedule B1 to the 1986 Act of any order made by the court under paragraph 84(7) of Schedule B1 to the 1986 Act.

(5) GEMA must notify the Secretary of State before directing the energy administrator to send a notice of moving from energy administration to dissolution to the registrar of companies.

[7.953]
80 Provision of information to the Secretary of State

Where the energy administration ends pursuant to paragraph 79, 83 or 84 of Schedule B1 to the 1986 Act, the energy administrator shall, within 5 business days from the date of the end of the energy administration, provide the Secretary of State with the following information—
- (a) a breakdown of the relevant debts (within the meaning of section 169(4) of the 2004 Act) of the protected energy company, which remain outstanding; and
- (b) details of any shortfall (within the meaning of section 169(3)(a) of the 2004 Act) in the property of the protected energy company available for meeting those relevant debts.

PART 10
REPLACING ENERGY ADMINISTRATOR

[7.954]
81 Grounds for resignation

(1) The energy administrator may give notice of his resignation on grounds of ill health or because—
- (a) he intends ceasing to be in practice as an insolvency practitioner, or
- (b) there is some conflict of interest, or change of personal circumstances, which precludes or makes impracticable the further discharge by him of the duties of energy administrator.

(2) The energy administrator may, with the permission of the court, give notice of his resignation on grounds other than those specified in paragraph (1).

[7.955]
82 Notice of intention to resign

The energy administrator shall in all cases give at least 7 days notice in Form EA23 of his intention to resign, or to apply for the court's permission to do so, to the following persons—
- (a) the Secretary of State;
- (b) GEMA;
- (c) if there is a continuing energy administrator of the protected energy company, to him; and
- (d) if there is no such energy administrator, to the protected energy company and its creditors.

[7.956]
83 Notice of resignation

(1) The notice of resignation shall be in Form EA24.

(2) The notice shall be filed with the court, and a copy sent to the registrar of companies. A copy of the notice of resignation shall be sent not more than 5 business days after it has been filed with the court to all those to whom notice of intention to resign was sent.

[7.957]
84 Application to court to remove energy administrator from office

(1) Any application under paragraph 88 of Schedule B1 to the 1986 Act shall state the grounds on which it is requested that the energy administrator should be removed from office.

(2) Service of the notice of the application shall be effected on the energy administrator, the Secretary of State, GEMA, the joint energy administrator (if any), and where there is not a joint energy administrator, to the protected energy company and all the creditors, including any floating charge holders, not less than 5 business days before the date fixed for the application to be heard.

(3) Where a court makes an order removing the energy administrator it shall give a copy of the order to the applicant who as soon as reasonably practicable shall send a copy to the energy administrator.

(4) The applicant shall also within 5 business days of the order being made send a copy of the order to all those to whom notice of the application was sent.

(5) A copy of the order shall also be sent to the registrar of companies in Form EA25 within the same time period.

[7.958]
85 Notice of vacation of office when energy administrator ceases to be qualified to act

Where the energy administrator who has ceased to be qualified to act as an insolvency practitioner in relation to the protected energy company gives notice in accordance with paragraph 89 of Schedule B1 to the 1986 Act, he shall also give notice to the registrar of companies in Form EA25.

[7.959]
86 Energy administrator deceased

(1) Subject as follows, where the energy administrator has died, it is the duty of his personal representatives to give notice of the fact to the court, specifying the date of death. This does not apply if notice has been given under either paragraph (2) or (3) of this Rule.

(2) If the deceased energy administrator was a partner in a firm, notice may be given by a partner in the firm who is qualified to act as an insolvency practitioner, or is a member of any body recognised by the Secretary of State for the authorisation of insolvency practitioners.

(3) Notice of the death may be given by any person producing to the court the relevant death certificate or a copy of it.

(4) Where a person gives notice to the court under this Rule, he shall also give notice to the registrar of companies in Form EA25.

[7.960]
87 Application to replace

(1) Where an application is made to court under paragraph 91(1) of Schedule B1 to the 1986 Act to appoint a replacement energy administrator, the application shall be accompanied by a written statement in Form EA2 by the person proposed to be the replacement energy administrator.

(2) A copy of the application shall be served, in addition to those persons listed in section 156(2) of the 2004 Act and Rule 8(3), on the person who made the application for the energy administration order.

(3) Rule 10 shall apply to the service of an application under paragraph 91(1) of Schedule B1 of the 1986 Act as it applies to service in accordance with Rule 8.

(4) Rules 11, 12 and 13(1) and 13(2) apply to an application under paragraph 91(1) of Schedule B1 to the 1986 Act.

[7.961]
88 Notification and advertisement of appointment of replacement energy administrator

Where a replacement energy administrator is appointed, the same provisions apply in respect of giving notice of, and advertising, the replacement appointment as in the case of the appointment (subject to Rule 90), and all statements, consents etc as are required shall also be required in the case of the appointment of a replacement. All forms and notices shall clearly identify that the appointment is of a replacement energy administrator.

[7.962]
89 Notification and advertisement of appointment of joint energy administrator

Where, after an initial appointment has been made, an additional person or persons are to be appointed as joint energy administrator the same Rules shall apply in respect of giving notice of and advertising the appointment as in the case of the initial appointment, subject to Rule 90.

[7.963]
90 Notification to registrar of companies

The replacement or additional energy administrator shall send notice of the appointment in Form EA26 to the registrar of companies.

[7.964]
91 Energy administrator's duties on vacating office

(1) Where the energy administrator ceases to be in office as such, in consequence of removal, resignation or cesser of qualification as an insolvency practitioner, he is under obligation as soon as reasonably practicable to deliver up to the person succeeding him as energy administrator the assets (after deduction of any expenses properly incurred and distributions made by him) and further to deliver up to that person—

- (a) the records of the energy administration, including correspondence, proofs and other related papers appertaining to the energy administration while it was within his responsibility; and
- (b) the protected energy company's books, papers and other records.

(2) If the energy administrator makes default in complying with this Rule, he is liable to a fine and, for continued contravention, to a daily default fine.

PART 11
COURT PROCEDURE AND PRACTICE

CHAPTER 1 APPLICATIONS

[7.965]
92 Preliminary

This Chapter applies to any application made to the court in energy administration proceedings, except an application for an energy administration order.

[7.966]
93 Interpretation

(1) In this Chapter, except in so far as the context otherwise requires—

"originating application" means an application to the court which is not an application in pending proceedings before the court; and

"ordinary application" means any other application to the court.

(2) Every application shall be in the form appropriate to the application concerned.

[7.967]
94 Form and contents of application

(1) Each application shall be in writing and shall state—

(a) the names of the parties;
(b) the nature of the relief or order applied for or the directions sought from the court;
(c) the names and addresses of the persons (if any) on whom it is intended to serve the application or that no person is intended to be served;
(d) where the 1986 Act, Schedule B1 to the 1986 Act or the Rules require that notice of the application is to be given to specified persons, the names and addresses of all those persons (so far as known to the applicant); and
(e) the applicant's address for service.

(2) An originating application shall set out the grounds on which the applicant claims to be entitled to the relief or order sought.

(3) The application must be signed by the applicant if he is acting in person or, when he is not so acting, by or on behalf of his solicitor.

[7.968]
95 Application under section 176A(5) of the 1986 Act to disapply section 176A of the 1986 Act

(1) An application under section 176A(5) of the 1986 Act shall be accompanied by an affidavit prepared and sworn by the energy administrator.

(2) The affidavit shall state—

(a) that the application arises in the course of an energy administration;
(b) a summary of the financial position of the protected energy company;
(c) the information substantiating the energy administrator's view that the cost of making a distribution to unsecured creditors would be disproportionate to the benefits; and
(d) whether any other insolvency practitioner is acting in relation to the protected energy company and if so his address.

[7.969]
96 Filing and service of application

(1) The application shall be filed in court, accompanied by one copy and a number of additional copies equal to the number of persons who are to be served with the application.

(2) Subject as follows in this Rule and in the next, or unless the Rule under which the application is brought provides otherwise, or the court otherwise orders, upon the presentation of the documents mentioned in paragraph (1), the court shall fix a venue for the application to be heard.

(3) Unless the court otherwise directs, the applicant shall serve a sealed copy of the application, endorsed with the venue of the hearing, on the respondent named in the application (or on each respondent if more than one).

(4) The court may give any of the following directions—

(a) that the application be served upon persons other than those specified by the relevant provision of the 1986 Act, Schedule B1 to the 1986 Act or the Rules;
(b) that the giving of notice to any person may be dispensed with;
(c) that notice be given in some way other than that specified in paragraph (3).

(5) Unless the provision of the 1986 Act, Schedule B1 to the 1986 Act or the Rules under which the application is made provides otherwise, and subject to the next paragraph, the application must be served at least 14 days before the date fixed for the hearing.

(6) Where the case is one of urgency, the court may (without prejudice to its general power to extend or abridge time limits)—

(a) hear the application immediately, either with or without notice to, or the attendance of, other parties, or
(b) authorise a shorter period of service than that provided for by paragraph (5);

and any such application may be heard on terms providing for the filing or service of documents, or the carrying out of other formalities, as the court thinks fit.

[7.970]
97 Notice of application under section 176A(5) of the 1986 Act

An application under section 176A(5) of the 1986 Act may be made without the application being served upon or notice being given to any other party.

[7.971]
98 Other hearings *ex parte*

(1) Where the relevant provisions of the 1986 Act, Schedule B1 to the 1986 Act or the Rules do not require service of the application on, or notice of it to be given to, any person, the court may hear the application *ex parte*.

(2) Where the application is properly made *ex parte*, the court may hear it forthwith, without fixing a venue as required by Rule 96(2).

(3) Alternatively, the court may fix a venue for the application to be heard, in which case Rule 96(2) applies (so far as relevant).

[7.972]
99 Hearing of application

(1) Unless allowed or authorised to be made otherwise, every application before the registrar shall, and every application before the judge may, be heard in chambers.

(2) Unless either—
 (a) the judge has given a general or special direction to the contrary, or
 (b) it is not within the registrar's power to make the order required,

the jurisdiction of the court to hear and determine the application may be exercised by the registrar, and the application shall be made to the registrar in the first instance.

(3) Where the application is made to the registrar he may refer to the judge any matter which he thinks should properly be decided by the judge, and the judge may either dispose of the matter or refer it back to the registrar with such direction as he thinks fit.

(4) Nothing in this Rule precludes an application being made directly to the judge in a proper case.

[7.973]
100 Use of affidavit evidence

(1) In any proceedings evidence may be given by affidavit unless by any provision of the Rules it is otherwise provided or the court otherwise directs; but the court may, on the application of any party, order the attendance for cross-examination of the person making the affidavit.

(2) Where, after such an order has been made, the person in question does not attend, his affidavit shall not be used in evidence without the leave of the court.

[7.974]
101 Filing and service of affidavits

(1) Unless the provisions of the 1986 Act, Schedule B1 to the 1986 Act or the Rules under which the application is made provide otherwise, or the court otherwise allows—
 (a) if the applicant intends to rely at the first hearing on affidavit evidence, he shall file the affidavit or affidavits (if more than one) in court and serve a copy or copies on the respondent, not less than 14 days before the date fixed for the hearing, and
 (b) where a respondent to an application intends to oppose it and to rely for that purpose on affidavit evidence, he shall file the affidavit or affidavits (if more than one) in court and serve a copy or copies on the applicant, not less than 7 days before the date fixed for the hearing.

(2) Any affidavit may be sworn by the applicant or by the respondent or by some other person possessing direct knowledge of the subject matter of the application.

[7.975]
102 Use of reports

(1) A report may be filed in court instead of an affidavit, unless the application involves other parties or the court otherwise orders, by the energy administrator.

(2) In any case where a report is filed instead of an affidavit, the report shall be treated for the purpose of Rule 101(1) and any hearing before the court as if it were an affidavit.

[7.976]
103 Adjournment of hearings; directions

(1) The court may adjourn the hearing of an application on such terms (if any) as it thinks fit.

(2) The court may at any time give such directions as it thinks fit as to—
 (a) service or notice of the application on or to any person, whether in connection with the venue of a resumed hearing or for any other purpose;
 (b) whether particulars of claim and defence are to be delivered and generally as to the procedure on the application;
 (c) the manner in which any evidence is to be adduced at a resumed hearing and in particular (but without prejudice to the generality of this sub-paragraph) as to—
  (i) the taking of evidence wholly or in part by affidavit or orally;

(ii) the cross-examination either before the judge or registrar on the hearing in court or in chambers, of any deponents to affidavits; and

(iii) any report to be given by the energy administrator;

(d) the matters to be dealt with in evidence.

CHAPTER 2 SHORTHAND WRITERS

[7.977]

104 Nomination and appointment of shorthand writers

(1) In the High Court the judge may in writing nominate one or more persons to be official shorthand writers to the court.

(2) The court may, at any time in the course of energy administration proceedings, appoint a shorthand writer to take down the evidence of a person examined under section 236 of the 1986 Act.

[7.978]

105 Remuneration

(1) The remuneration of a shorthand writer appointed in energy administration proceedings shall be paid by the party at whose instance the appointment was made, or out of the assets of the protected energy company, or otherwise, as the court may direct.

(2) Any question arising as to the rates of remuneration payable under this Rule shall be determined by the court in its discretion.

CHAPTER 3 ENFORCEMENT PROCEDURES

[7.979]

106 Enforcement of court orders

In any energy administration proceedings, orders of the court may be enforced in the same manner as a judgment to the same effect.

[7.980]

107 Orders enforcing compliance with the Rules

(1) The court may, on application by the energy administrator, make such orders as it thinks necessary for the enforcement of obligations falling on any person in accordance with—

(a) paragraph 47 of Schedule B1 to the 1986 Act (duty to submit statement of affairs in energy administration), or

(b) section 235 of the 1986 Act (duty of various persons to co-operate with energy administrator).

(2) An order of the court under this Rule may provide that all costs of and incidental to the application for it shall be borne by the person against whom the order is made.

[7.981]

108 Warrant under section 236 of the 1986 Act

(1) A warrant issued by the court under section 236 of the 1986 Act (inquiry into insolvent company's dealings) shall be addressed to such officer of the High Court as the warrant specifies, or to any constable.

(2) The persons referred to in section 236(5) of the 1986 Act (court's powers of enforcement) as the prescribed officer of the court are the tipstaff and his assistants of the court.

(3) In this Chapter references to property include books, papers and records.

(4) When a person is arrested under a warrant issued under section 236 of the 1986 Act, the officer arresting him shall forthwith bring him before the court issuing the warrant in order that he may be examined.

(5) If he cannot immediately be brought up for examination, the officer shall deliver him into the custody of the governor of the prison named in the warrant, who shall keep him in custody and produce him before the court as it may from time to time direct.

(6) After arresting the person named in the warrant, the officer shall forthwith report to the court the arrest or delivery into custody (as the case may be) and apply to the court to fix a venue for the person's examination.

(7) The court shall appoint the earliest practicable time for the examination, and shall—

(a) direct the governor of the prison to produce the person for examination at the time and place appointed, and

(b) forthwith give notice of the venue to the person who applied for the warrant.

(8) Any property in the arrested person's possession which may be seized shall be—

(a) lodged with, or otherwise dealt with as instructed by, whoever is specified in the warrant as authorised to receive it, or

(b) kept by the officer seizing it pending the receipt of written orders from the court as to its disposal,

as may be directed by the court.

CHAPTER 4 COURT RECORDS AND RETURNS

[7.982]
109 Title of proceedings

Every energy administration proceeding shall, with any necessary additions, be intituled "IN THE MATTER OF . . . . (naming the protected energy company to which the proceedings relate) AND IN THE MATTER OF THE INSOLVENCY ACT 1986 AND THE ENERGY ACT 2004".

[7.983]
110 Court records

The court shall keep records of all energy administration proceedings, and shall cause to be entered in the records the taking of any step in the proceedings, and such decisions of the court in relation thereto, as the court thinks fit.

[7.984]
111 Inspection of records

(1) Subject as follows, the court's records of energy administration proceedings shall be open to inspection by any person.

(2) If in the case of a person applying to inspect the records the registrar is not satisfied as to the propriety of the purpose for which inspection is required, he may refuse to allow it. That person may then apply forthwith and *ex parte* to the judge, who may refuse the inspection or allow it on such terms as he thinks fit.

(3) The decision of the judge under paragraph (2) is final.

[7.985]
112 File of court proceedings

(1) In respect of all energy administration proceedings, the court shall open and maintain a file for each case; and (subject to directions of the registrar) all documents relating to such proceedings shall be placed on the relevant file.

(2) No energy administration proceedings shall be filed in the Central office of the High Court.

[7.986]
113 Right to inspect file

(1) In the case of any energy administration proceedings, the following have the right, at all reasonable times, to inspect the court's file of the proceedings—

- (a) the Secretary of State;
- (b) GEMA;
- (c) the energy administrator;
- (d) any person stating himself in writing to be a creditor of the protected energy company to which the energy administration proceedings relate; and
- (e) every person who is, or at any time has been, a director or officer of the protected energy company to which the energy administration proceedings relate, or who is a member of the protected energy company.

(2) The right of inspection conferred as above on any person may be exercised on his behalf by a person properly authorised by him.

(3) Any person may, by leave of the court, inspect the file.

(4) The right of inspection conferred by this Rule is not exercisable in the case of documents, or parts of documents, as to which the court directs (either generally or specially) that they are not to be made open to inspection without the court's leave.

An application for a direction of the court under this paragraph may be made by the energy administrator or by any party appearing to the court to have an interest.

(5) If, for the purpose of powers conferred by the 1986 Act, Schedule B1 to the 1986 Act, the Rules or the Insolvency Rules, the Secretary of State, the Department or the official receiver wishes to inspect the file of any energy administration proceedings, and requests the transmission of the file, the court shall comply with such request (unless the file is for the time being in use for the court's purposes).

(6) Paragraphs (2) and (3) of Rule 111 apply in respect of the court's file of any energy administration proceedings as they apply in respect of court records.

[7.987]
114 Filing of Gazette notices and advertisements

(1) In any court in which energy administration proceedings are pending, an officer of the court shall file a copy of every issue of the Gazette which contains an advertisement relating to those proceedings.

(2) Where there appears in a newspaper an advertisement relating to energy administration proceedings pending in any court, the person inserting the advertisement shall file a copy of it in that court.

The copy of the advertisement shall be accompanied by, or have endorsed on it, such particulars as are necessary to identify the proceedings and the date of the advertisement's appearance.

(3) An officer of any court in which energy administration proceedings are pending shall from time to time file a memorandum giving the dates of, and other particulars relating to, any notice published in the Gazette, and any newspaper advertisements, which relate to proceedings so pending.

The officer's memorandum is prima facie evidence that any notice or advertisement mentioned in it was duly inserted in the issue of the newspaper or the Gazette which is specified in the memorandum.

CHAPTER 5 COSTS AND DETAILED ASSESSMENT

[7.988]
115 Application of CPR

Subject to provision to inconsistent effect made as follows in this Chapter, CPR Part 43 (scope of costs rules and definitions), Part 44 (general rules about costs), Part 45 (fixed costs), Part 47 (procedure for detailed assessment of costs and default provisions) and Part 48 (costs-special cases) shall apply to energy administration proceedings with any necessary modifications.

[7.989]
116 Requirement to assess costs by the detailed procedure

(1) Subject as follows, where the costs, charges or expenses of any person are payable out of the assets of the protected energy company, the amount of those costs, charges or expenses shall be decided by detailed assessment unless agreed between the energy administrator and the person entitled to payment, and in the absence of such agreement the energy administrator may serve notice in writing requiring that person to commence detailed assessment proceedings in accordance with CPR Part 47 (procedure for detailed assessment of costs and default provisions) in the court to which the energy administration proceedings are allocated or, where in relation to a protected energy company there is no such court, in any court having jurisdiction to wind up the protected energy company.

(2) Where the amount of the costs, charges or expenses of any person employed by a energy administrator in energy administration proceedings are required to be decided by detailed assessment or fixed by order of the court this does not preclude the energy administrator from making payments on account to such person on the basis of an undertaking by that person to repay immediately any money which may, when detailed assessment is made, prove to have been overpaid, with interest at the rate specified in section 17 of the Judgments Act 1838 on the date payment was made and for the period from the date of payment to that of repayment.

(3) In any proceedings before the court, the court may order costs to be decided by detailed assessment.

[7.990]
117 Procedure where detailed assessment required

(1) Before making a detailed assessment of the costs of any person employed in energy administration proceedings by an energy administrator, the costs officer shall require a certificate of employment, which shall be endorsed on the bill and signed by the energy administrator.

(2) The certificate shall include—

(a) the name and address of the person employed;

(b) details of the functions to be carried out under the employment; and

(c) a note of any special terms of remuneration which have been agreed.

(3) Every person whose costs in energy administration proceedings are required to be decided by detailed assessment shall, on being required in writing to do so by the energy administrator, commence detailed assessment proceedings in accordance with CPR Part 47 (procedure for detailed assessment of costs and default provisions).

(4) If that person does not commence detailed assessment proceedings within 3 months of the requirement under paragraph (3), or within such further time as the court, on application, may permit, the energy administrator may deal with the assets of the protected energy company without regard to any claim by that person, whose claim is forfeited by such failure to commence proceedings.

(5) Where in any such case such a claim lies additionally against an energy administrator in his personal capacity, that claim is also forfeited by such failure to commence proceedings.

[7.991]
118 Costs paid otherwise than out of the assets of the protected energy company

Where the amount of costs is decided by detailed assessment under an order of the court directing that the costs are to be paid otherwise than out of the assets of the protected energy company, the costs officer shall note on the final costs certificate by whom, or the manner in which, the costs are to be paid.

[7.992]
119 Award of costs against energy administrator

Without prejudice to any provision of the 1986 Act, Schedule B1 to the 1986 Act or the Rules by virtue of which the energy administrator is not in any event to be liable for costs and expenses, where an energy administrator is made a party to any proceedings on the application of another party to the proceedings, he shall not be personally liable for costs unless the court otherwise directs.

[7.993]
120 Application for costs

(1) This Rule applies where a party to, or person affected by, any energy administration proceedings—

(a) applies to the court for an order allowing his costs, or part of them, incidental to the proceedings, and

(b) that application is not made at the time of the proceedings.

(2) The person concerned shall serve a sealed copy of his application on the energy administrator.

(3) The energy administrator may appear on the application.

(4) No costs of or incidental to the application shall be allowed to the applicant unless the court is satisfied that the application could not have been made at the time of the proceedings.

[7.994]
121 Costs and expenses of witnesses

(1) Except as directed by the court, no allowance as a witness in any examination or other proceedings before the court shall be made to an officer of the protected energy company to which the energy administration proceedings relate.

(2) A person making any application in energy administration proceedings shall not be regarded as a witness on the hearing of the application, but the costs officer may allow his expenses of travelling and subsistence.

[7.995]
122 Final costs certificate

(1) A final costs certificate of the costs officer is final and conclusive as to all matters which have not been objected to in the manner provided for under the rules of the court.

(2) Where it is proved to the satisfaction of a costs officer that a final costs certificate has been lost or destroyed, he may issue a duplicate.

CHAPTER 6 PERSONS INCAPABLE OF MANAGING THEIR AFFAIRS

[7.996]
123 Introductory

(1) The Rules in this Chapter apply where in energy administration proceedings it appears to the court that a person affected by the proceedings is one who is incapable of managing and administering his property and affairs either—

(a) by reason of mental disorder within the meaning of the Mental Health Act 1983; or
(b) due to physical affliction or disability.

(2) The person concerned is referred to as "the incapacitated person".

[7.997]
124 Appointment of another person to act

(1) The court may appoint such person as it thinks fit to appear for, represent or act for the incapacitated person.

(2) The appointment may be made either generally or for the purpose of any particular application or proceeding, or for the exercise of particular rights or powers which the incapacitated person might have exercised but for his incapacity.

(3) The court may make the appointment either of its own motion or on application by—

(a) a person who has been appointed by a court in the United Kingdom or elsewhere to manage the affairs of, or to represent, the incapacitated person, or
(b) any relative or friend of the incapacitated person who appears to the court to be a proper person to make the application, or
(c) the energy administrator.

(4) Application under paragraph (3) may be made *ex parte*; but the court may require such notice of the application as it thinks necessary to be given to the person alleged to be incapacitated, or any other person, and may adjourn the hearing of the application to enable the notice to be given.

[7.998]
125 Affidavit in support of application

An application under Rule 124(3) shall be supported by an affidavit of a registered medical practitioner as to the mental or physical condition of the incapacitated person.

[7.999]
126 Services of notices following appointment

Any notice served on, or sent to, a person appointed under Rule 124 has the same effect as if it had been served on, or given to, the incapacitated person.

CHAPTER 7 APPEALS IN ENERGY ADMINISTRATION PROCEEDINGS

[7.1000]
127 Appeals and reviews of energy administration orders

(1) Every court having jurisdiction under the 1986 Act to wind up companies may review, rescind or vary any order made by it in the exercise of that jurisdiction.

(2) An appeal from a decision made in the exercise of that jurisdiction by a registrar of the High Court lies to a single judge of the High Court; and an appeal from a decision of that judge on such an appeal lies, with the leave of that judge or the Court of Appeal, to the Court of Appeal.

[7.1001]
128 Procedure on appeal

(1) Subject as follows, the procedure and practice of the Supreme Court relating to appeals to the Court of Appeal apply to appeals in energy administration proceedings.

(2) In relation to any appeal to a single judge of the High Court under Rule 127 above, any reference in the CPR to the Court of Appeal is replaced by a reference to that judge and any reference to the registrar of civil appeals is replaced by a reference to the registrar of the High Court who deals with energy administration proceedings.

(3) In energy administration proceedings, the procedure under CPR Part 52 (appeals to the Court of Appeal) is by ordinary application and not by application notice.

CHAPTER 8 GENERAL

[7.1002]
129 Principal court rules and practice to apply

(1) The CPR and the practice and procedure of the High Court (including any practice direction) apply to energy administration proceedings with any necessary modifications, except so far as inconsistent with the Rules.

(2) All energy administration proceedings shall be allocated to the multi-track for which CPR Part 29 (the multi-track) makes provision; accordingly those provisions of the CPR which provide for allocation questionnaires and track allocation will not apply.

[7.1003]
130 Right of audience

Rights of audience in energy administration proceedings are the same as obtain in insolvency proceedings.

[7.1004]
131 Right of attendance

(1) Subject as follows, in energy administration proceedings, any person stating himself in writing, in records kept by the court for that purpose, to be a creditor or member of the protected energy company is entitled, at his own cost, to attend in court or in chambers at any stage of the proceedings.

(2) Attendance may be by the person himself, or his solicitor.

(3) A person so entitled may request the court in writing to give him notice of any step in the energy administration proceedings; and, subject to his paying the costs involved and keeping the court informed as to his address, the court shall comply with the request.

(4) If the court is satisfied that the exercise by a person of his rights under this Rule has given rise to costs for the assets of the protected energy company which would not otherwise have been incurred and ought not, in the circumstances, to fall on that estate, it may direct that the costs be paid by the person concerned, to an amount specified.

The rights of that person under this Rule shall be in abeyance so long as those costs are not paid.

(5) The court may appoint one or more persons to represent the creditors or the members of a protected energy company, or any class of them, to have the rights conferred by this Rule, instead of the rights being exercised by any or all of them individually.

If two or more persons are appointed under this paragraph to represent the same interest, they must (if at all) instruct the same solicitor.

[7.1005]
132 Energy administrator's solicitor

Where in energy administration proceedings the attendance of the energy administrator's solicitor is required, whether in court or in chambers, the energy administrator himself need not attend, unless directed by the court.

[7.1006]
133 Formal defects

No energy administration proceedings shall be invalidated by any formal defect or by any irregularity, unless the court before which objection is made considers that substantial injustice has been caused by the defect or irregularity, and that the injustice cannot be remedied by any order of the court.

[7.1007]
134 Restriction on concurrent proceedings and remedies

Where in energy administration proceedings the court makes an order staying any action, execution or other legal process against the property of a protected energy company, service of the order may be effected by sending a sealed copy of the order to whatever is the address for service of the claimant or other party having the carriage of the proceedings to be stayed.

[7.1008]
135 Affidavits

(1) Subject to the following paragraphs of this Rule, the practice and procedure of the High Court with regard to affidavits, their form and contents, and the procedure governing their use, are to apply to all energy administration proceedings.

(2) Where in energy administration proceedings, an affidavit is made by the energy administrator he shall state the capacity in which he makes it, the position which he holds and the address at which he works.

(3) A creditor's affidavit of debt may be sworn before his own solicitor.

(4) Any officer of the court duly authorised in that behalf, may take affidavits and declarations.

(5) Subject to paragraph (6), where the Rules provide for the use of an affidavit, a witness statement verified by a statement of truth may be used as an alternative.

(6) Paragraph (5) does not apply to Rules 149 and 150.

(7) Where paragraph (5) applies, any form prescribed by Rule 160 shall be modified accordingly.

[7.1009]

136 Security in court

(1) Where security has to be given to the court (otherwise than in relation to costs), it may be given by guarantee, bond or the payment of money into court.

(2) A person proposing to give a bond as security shall give notice to the party in whose favour the security is required, and to the court, naming those who are to be sureties to the bond.

(3) The court shall forthwith give notice to the parties concerned of a venue for the execution of the bond and the making of any objection to the sureties.

(4) The sureties shall make an affidavit of their sufficiency (unless dispensed with by the party in whose favour the security is required) and shall, if required by the court, attend the court to be cross-examined.

[7.1010]

137 Payment into court

The CPR relating to payment into and out of court of money lodged in court as security for costs apply to money lodged in court under the Rules.

[7.1011]

138 Further information and disclosure

(1) Any party to energy administration proceedings may apply to the court for an order—
- (a) that any other party—
  - (i) clarify any matter which is in dispute in the proceedings, or
  - (ii) give additional information in relation to any such matter,

  in accordance with CPR Part 18 (further information); or
- (b) to obtain disclosure from any other party in accordance with CPR Part 31 (disclosure and inspection of documents).

(2) An application under this Rule may be made without notice being served on any other party.

[7.1012]

139 Office copies of documents

(1) Any person who has under the Rules the right to inspect the court file of energy administration proceedings may require the court to provide him with an office copy of any document from the file.

(2) A person's right under this Rule may be exercised on his behalf by his solicitor.

(3) An office copy provided by the court under this Rule shall be in such form as the registrar thinks appropriate, and shall bear the court's seal.

PART 12
PROXIES AND COMPANY REPRESENTATION

[7.1013]

140 Definition of proxy

(1) For the purposes of the Rules, a proxy is an authority given by a person ("the principal") to another person ("the proxy-holder") to attend a meeting and speak and vote as his representative.

(2) Proxies are for use at creditors' meetings or company meetings summoned or called under Schedule B1 to the 1986 Act or the Rules.

(3) Only one proxy may be given by a person for any one meeting at which he desires to be represented; and it may only be given to one person, being an individual aged 18 years or over. But the principal may specify one or more other such individuals to be proxy-holder in the alternative, in the order in which they are named in the proxy.

(4) Without prejudice to the generality of paragraph (3), a proxy for a particular meeting may be given to whoever is to be the chairman of the meeting; and such chairman cannot decline to be the proxy-holder in relation to that proxy.

(5) A proxy requires the holder to give the principal's vote on matters arising for determination at the meeting, or to abstain, or to propose, in the principal's name, a resolution to be voted on by the meeting, either as directed or in accordance with the holder's own discretion.

[7.1014]
141 Issue and use of forms

(1) When notice is given of a meeting to be held in energy administration proceedings and forms of proxy are sent out with the notice, no form so sent out shall have inserted in it the name or description of any person.

(2) No form of proxy shall be used at any meeting except that which is sent with the notice summoning the meeting, or a substantially similar form.

(3) A form of proxy shall be signed by the principal, or by some person authorised by him (either generally or with reference to a particular meeting). If the form is signed by a person other than the principal, the nature of the authority of that person shall be stated.

[7.1015]
142 Use of proxies at meetings

(1) A proxy given for a particular meeting may be used at any adjournment of that meeting.

(2) Where the energy administrator holds proxies to be used by him as chairman of a meeting, and some other person acts as chairman, that other person may use the energy administrator's proxies as if he were himself proxy-holder.

(3) Where a proxy directs a proxy-holder to vote for or against a resolution for the appointment of a person other than the energy administrator as proposed liquidator of the protected energy company, the proxy-holder may, unless the proxy states otherwise, vote for or against (as he thinks fit) any resolution for the appointment of that person jointly with another or others.

(4) A proxy-holder may propose any resolution which, if proposed by another, would be a resolution in favour of which by virtue of the proxy he would be entitled to vote.

(5) Where a proxy gives specific directions as to voting, this does not, unless the proxy states otherwise, preclude the proxy-holder from voting at his discretion on resolutions put to the meeting which are not dealt with in the proxy.

[7.1016]
143 Retention of proxies

(1) Subject as follows, proxies used for voting at any meeting shall be retained by the chairman of the meeting.

(2) The chairman shall deliver the proxies forthwith after the meeting to the energy administrator (where that is someone other than himself).

[7.1017]
144 Right of inspection

(1) The energy administrator shall, so long as proxies lodged with him are in his hands, allow them to be inspected, at all reasonable times on any business day, by—

- (a) the creditors, in the case of proxies used at a meeting of creditors, and
- (b) a protected energy company's members, in the case of proxies used at a meeting of the protected energy company.

(2) The reference in paragraph (1) to creditors is a reference to those persons who have submitted in writing a claim to be creditors of the protected energy company but does not include a person whose proof or claim has been wholly rejected for the purposes of voting, dividend or otherwise.

(3) The right of inspection given by this Rule is also exercisable by the directors of the protected energy company.

(4) Any person attending a meeting in energy administration proceedings is entitled, immediately before or in the course of the meeting, to inspect proxies and associated documents (including proofs) sent or given, in accordance with directions contained in any notice convening the meeting, to the chairman of that meeting or to any other person by a creditor or member for the purpose of that meeting.

[7.1018]
145 Proxy-holder with financial interest

(1) A proxy-holder shall not vote in favour of any resolution which would directly or indirectly place him, or any associate of his, in a position to receive any remuneration out of the assets of the protected energy company, unless the proxy specifically directs him to vote in that way.

(2) Where a proxy-holder has signed the proxy as being authorised to do so by his principal and the proxy specifically directs him to vote in the way mentioned in paragraph (1), he shall nevertheless not vote in that way unless he produces to the chairman of the meeting written authorisation from his principal sufficient to show that the proxy-holder was entitled so to sign the proxy.

(3) This Rule applies also to any person acting as chairman of a meeting and using proxies in that capacity under Rule 142; and in its application to him, the proxy-holder is deemed an associate of his.

(4) In this Rule "associate" shall have the same meaning as in section 435 of the 1986 Act.

[7.1019]
146 Company representation

(1) Where a person is authorised under section 375 of the Companies Act to represent a corporation at a meeting of creditors or of the protected energy company he shall produce to the chairman of the meeting a copy of the resolution from which he derives his authority.

(2) The copy resolution must be under the seal of the corporation, or certified by the secretary or a director of the corporation to be a true copy.

(3) Nothing in this Rule requires the authority of a person to sign a proxy on behalf of a principal which is a corporation to be in the form of a resolution of that corporation.

PART 13
EXAMINATION OF PERSONS IN ENERGY ADMINISTRATION PROCEEDINGS

[7.1020]
147 Preliminary

(1) The Rules in this Part relate to applications to the court, made by the energy administrator, for an order under section 236 of the 1986 Act (inquiry into protected energy company's dealings when it is, or is alleged to be, insolvent).

(2) The following definitions apply—

(a) the person in respect of whom an order is applied for is "the respondent";

(b) "section 236" means section 236 of the 1986 Act.

[7.1021]
148 Form and contents of application

(1) The application shall be in writing, and be accompanied by a brief statement of the grounds on which it is made.

(2) The respondent must be sufficiently identified in the application.

(3) It shall be stated whether the application is for the respondent—

(a) to be ordered to appear before the court, or

(b) to be ordered to clarify any matter which is in dispute in the proceedings or to give additional information in relation to any such matter and if so CPR Part 18 (further information) shall apply to any such order, or

(c) to submit affidavits (if so, particulars are to be given of the matters to which he is required to swear), or

(d) to produce books, papers or other records (if so, the items in question are to be specified),

or for any two or more of those purposes.

(4) The application may be made *ex parte*.

[7.1022]
149 Order for examination, etc

(1) The court may, whatever the purpose of the application, make any order which it has power to make under section 236.

(2) The court, if it orders the respondent to appear before it, shall specify a venue for his appearance, which shall be not less than 14 days from the date of the order.

(3) If he is ordered to submit affidavits, the order shall specify—

(a) the matters which are to be dealt with in his affidavits, and

(b) the time within which they are to be submitted to the court.

(4) If the order is to produce books, papers or other records, the time and manner of compliance shall be specified.

(5) The order must be served forthwith on the respondent; and it must be served personally, unless the court otherwise orders.

[7.1023]
150 Procedure for examination

(1) At any examination of the respondent, the energy administrator may attend in person, or be represented by a solicitor with or without counsel, and may put such questions to the respondent as the court may allow.

(2) If the respondent is ordered to clarify any matter or to give additional information, the court shall direct him as to the questions which he is required to answer, and as to whether his answers (if any) are to be made on affidavit.

(3) Where application has been made under section 236 on information provided by a creditor of the protected energy company, that creditor may, with the leave of the court and if the energy administrator does not object, attend the examination and put questions to the respondent (but only through the energy administrator).

(4) The respondent may at his own expense employ a solicitor with or without counsel, who may put to him such questions as the court may allow for the purpose of enabling him to explain or qualify any answers given by him, and may make representations on his behalf.

(5) There shall be made in writing such record of the examination as the court thinks proper. The record shall be read over either to or by the respondent and signed by him at a venue fixed by the court.

(6) The written record may, in any proceedings (whether under the 1986 Act or otherwise), be used as evidence against the respondent of any statement made by him in the course of his examination.

[7.1024]
151 Record of examination

(1) Unless the court otherwise directs, the written record of the respondent's examination, and any response given by him to any order under CPR Part 18, and any affidavits submitted by him in compliance with an order of the court under section 236, shall not be filed in court.

(2) The written record, responses and affidavits shall not be open to inspection, without an order of the court, by any person other than the energy administrator.

(3) Paragraph (2) applies also to so much of the court file as shows the grounds of the application for an order under section 236 and to any copy of any order sought under CPR Part 18.

(4) The court may from time to time give directions as to the custody and inspection of any documents to which this Rule applies, and as to the furnishing of copies of, or extracts from, such documents.

[7.1025]
152 Costs of proceedings under section 236

(1) Where the court has ordered an examination of a person under section 236, and it appears to it that the examination was made necessary because information had been unjustifiably refused by the respondent, it may order that the costs of the examination be paid by him.

(2) Where the court makes an order against a person under section 237(1) or (2) of the 1986 Act (court's enforcement powers under section 236), the costs of the application for the order may be ordered by the court to be paid by the respondent.

(3) Subject to paragraphs (1) and (2) above, the energy administrator's costs shall, unless the court otherwise orders, be paid out of the assets of the protected energy company.

(4) A person summoned to attend for examination under this Part shall be tendered a reasonable sum in respect of travelling expenses incurred in connection with his attendance. Other costs falling on him are at the court's discretion.

PART 14
MISCELLANEOUS AND GENERAL

[7.1026]
153 Power of Secretary of State to regulate certain matters

(1) Pursuant to paragraph 27 of Schedule 8 to the 1986 Act the Secretary of State may, subject to the 1986 Act, the 2004 Act, Schedule B1 to the 1986 Act and the Rules, make regulations with respect to any matter provided for in the Rules as relates to the carrying out of the functions of an energy administrator of a protected energy company, including, without prejudice to the generality of the foregoing provision, with respect to the following matters arising in an energy administration—

- (a) the preparation and keeping of books, accounts and other records, and their production to such persons as may be authorised or required to inspect them;
- (b) the auditing of an energy administrator's accounts;
- (c) the manner in which an energy administrator is to act in relation to the protected energy company's books, papers and other records, and the manner of their disposal by the energy administrator or others;
- (d) the supply by the energy administrator to creditors and members of the protected energy company of copies of documents relating to the energy administration and the affairs of the protected energy company (on payment, in such cases as may be specified by the regulations, of the specified fee).

(2) Regulations made pursuant to paragraph (1) may—

- (a) confer discretion on the court;
- (b) make non-compliance with any of the regulations a criminal offence;
- (c) make different provision for different cases, including different provision for different areas; and
- (d) contain such incidental, supplemental and transitional provisions as may appear to the Secretary of State necessary or expedient.

[7.1027]
154 Costs, expenses, etc

(1) All fees, costs, charges and other expenses incurred in the course of the energy administration proceedings are to be regarded as expenses of the energy administration.

(2) The costs associated with the prescribed part shall be paid out of the prescribed part.

[7.1028]
155 Provable debts

(1) Subject as follows, in energy administration all claims by creditors are provable as debts against the protected energy company, whether they are present or future, certain or contingent, ascertained or sounding only in damages.

(2) Any obligation arising under a confiscation order made under Parts 2, 3 or 4 of the Proceeds of Crime Act 2002 is not provable.

(3) The following are not provable except at a time when all other claims of creditors in the energy administration proceedings (other than any of a kind mentioned in this paragraph) have been paid in full with interest under Rule 56—

(a) any claim arising by virtue of section 382(1)(a) of the Financial Services and Markets Act 2000, not being a claim also arising by virtue of section 382(1)(b) of that Act;

(b) any claim which by virtue of the 1986 Act or any other enactment is a claim the payment of which is to be postponed.

(4) Nothing in this Rule prejudices any enactment or rule of law under which a particular kind of debt is not provable, whether on grounds of public policy or otherwise.

[7.1029]

156 Notices

(1) All notices required or authorised by or under the 1986 Act, the 2004 Act, Schedule B1 to the 1986 Act or the Rules to be given must be in writing, unless it is otherwise provided, or the court allows the notice to be given in some other way.

(2) Where in energy administration proceedings a notice is required to be sent or given by the energy administrator, the sending or giving of it may be proved by means of a certificate by him, or his solicitor, or a partner or an employee of either of them, that the notice was duly posted.

(3) In the case of a notice to be sent or given by a person other than the energy administrator, the sending or giving of it may be proved by means of a certificate by that person that he posted the notice, or instructed another person (naming him) to do so.

(4) A certificate under this Rule may be endorsed on a copy or specimen of the notice to which it relates.

[7.1030]

157 Quorum at meeting of creditors

(1) Any meeting of creditors in energy administration proceedings is competent to act if a quorum is present.

(2) Subject to the next paragraph, a quorum is at least one creditor entitled to vote.

(3) For the purposes of this Rule, the reference to the creditor necessary to constitute a quorum is to those persons present or represented by proxy by any person (including the chairman) and includes persons duly represented under section 375 of the Companies Act.

(4) Where at any meeting of creditors—

(a) the provisions of this Rule as to a quorum being present are satisfied by the attendance of—

(i) the chairman alone, or

(ii) one other person in addition to the chairman, and

(b) the chairman is aware, by virtue of proofs and proxies received or otherwise, that one or more additional persons would, if attending, be entitled to vote,

the meeting shall not commence until at least the expiry of 15 minutes after the time appointed for its commencement.

[7.1031]

158 Evidence of proceedings at meetings

(1) A minute of proceedings at a meeting (held under the 1986 Act, Schedule B1 to the 1986 Act or the Rules) of the creditors or of the members of a protected energy company, signed by a person describing himself as, or appearing to be, the chairman of that meeting is admissible in energy administration proceedings without further proof.

(2) The minute is prime facie evidence that—

(a) the meeting was duly convened and held,

(b) all resolutions passed at the meeting were duly passed, and

(c) all proceedings at the meeting took place.

[7.1032]

159 Documents issuing from Secretary of State

(1) Any document purporting to be, or to contain, any order, directions or certificate issued by the Secretary of State shall be received in evidence and deemed to be or (as the case may be) contain that order or certificate, or those directions, without further proof, unless the contrary is shown.

(2) Paragraph (1) applies whether the document is signed by the Secretary of State himself or an officer on his behalf.

(3) Without prejudice to the foregoing, a certificate signed by the Secretary of State or an officer on his behalf and confirming—

(a) the making of an order,

(b) the issuing of any document, or

(c) the exercise of any discretion, power or obligation arising or imposed under the 1986 Act, the 2004 Act, Schedule B1 to the 1986 Act or the Rules,

is conclusive evidence of the matters dealt with in the certificate.

[7.1033]

160 Forms for use in energy administration proceedings

(1) The forms contained in Schedule 1 to the Rules shall be used in, and in connection with, energy administration proceedings.

(2) The forms shall be used with such variations, if any, as the circumstances may require.

[7.1034]
161 Energy administrator's security

(1) Wherever under the Rules any person has to appoint a person to the office of energy administrator, he is under a duty to satisfy himself that the person appointed or to be appointed has security for the proper performance of his functions.

(2) In any energy administration proceedings the cost of the energy administrator's security shall be defrayed as an expense of the energy administration.

[7.1035]
162 Time-limits

(1) The provisions of CPR Rule 2.8 (time) apply, as regards computation of time, to anything required or authorised to be done by the Rules.

(2) The provisions of CPR rule 3.1(2)(a) (the court's general powers of management) apply so as to enable the court to extend or shorten the time for compliance with anything required or authorised to be done by the Rules.

[7.1036]
163 Service by post

(1) For a document to be properly served by post, it must be contained in an envelope addressed to the person on whom service is to be effected, and pre-paid for either first or second class post.

(2) A document to be served by post may be sent to the last known address of the person to be served.

(3) Where first class post is used, the document is treated as served on the second business day after the date of posting, unless the contrary is shown.

(4) Where second class post is used, the document is treated as served on the fourth business day after the date of posting, unless the contrary is shown.

(5) The date of posting is presumed, unless the contrary is shown, to be the date shown in the post-mark on the envelope in which the document is contained.

[7.1037]
164 General provisions as to service and notice

Subject to Rule 163 and 165, CPR Part 6 (service of documents) applies as regards any matter relating to the service of documents and the giving of notice in energy administration proceedings.

[7.1038]
165 Service outside the jurisdiction

(1) CPR Part 6, paragraphs 6.17 to 6.35 (service of process, etc, out of the jurisdiction) do not apply in energy administration proceedings.

(2) Where for the purposes of energy administration proceedings any process or order of the court, or other document, is required to be served on a person who is not in England and Wales, the court may order service to be effected within such time, on such person, at such place and in such manner as it thinks fit, and may also require such proof of service as it thinks fit.

(3) An application under this Rule shall be supported by an affidavit stating—

- (a) the grounds on which the application is made, and
- (b) in what place or country the person to be served is, or probably may be found.

[7.1039]
166 Confidentiality of documents

(1) Where in energy administration proceedings the energy administrator considers, in the case of a document forming part of the records of the proceedings, that—

- (a) it should be treated as confidential, or
- (b) it is of such a nature that its disclosure would be calculated to be injurious to the interests of the creditors or members of a protected energy company,

he may decline to allow it to be inspected by a person who would otherwise be entitled to inspect it.

(2) Where under this Rule the energy administrator determines to refuse inspection of a document, the person wishing to inspect it may apply to the court for that determination to be overruled; and the court may either overrule it altogether, or sustain it subject to such conditions (if any) as it thinks fit to impose.

(3) Nothing in this Rule entitles the energy administrator to decline to allow the inspection of any proof or proxy.

[7.1040]
167 Notices sent simultaneously to the same person

Where under the 1986 Act, the 2004 Act, Schedule B1 to the 1986 Act or the Rules, a document of any description is to be sent to a person (whether or not as a member of a class of persons to whom that same document is to be sent), it may be sent as an accompaniment to any other document or information which the person is to receive, with or without modification or adaptation of the form applicable to that document.

[7.1041]
168 Right to copy documents

Where the 1986 Act or the Rules confer a right for any person to inspect documents, the right includes that of taking copies of those documents, on payment—

(a) in the case of documents on the court's file of proceedings, of the fee chargeable under any order made under section 92 of the Courts Act 2003 and
(b) otherwise, of the appropriate fee.

[7.1042]
169 Charge for copy documents

Where the energy administrator is requested by a creditor or member to supply copies of any documents he is entitled to require the payment of the appropriate fee in respect of the supply of the documents.

[7.1043]
170 Non-receipt of notice of meeting

Where in accordance with the 1986 Act, Schedule B1 to the 1986 Act or the Rules a meeting of creditors or other persons is called or summoned by notice, the meeting is presumed to have been duly summoned and held, notwithstanding that not all those to whom the notice is to be given have received it.

[7.1044]
171 Right to have list of creditors

(1) In energy administration proceedings a creditor who under the Rules has the right to inspect documents on the court file also has the right to require the energy administrator to furnish him with a list of the creditors of the protected energy company and the amounts of their respective debts.

This does not apply if a statement of the protected energy company's affairs has been filed in court.

(2) The energy administrator, on being required by any person to furnish that list, shall send it to him, but is entitled to charge the appropriate fee for doing so.

[7.1045]
172 False claim of status as creditor

(1) Where the Rules provide for creditors or members of a protected energy company a right to inspect any documents, whether on the court's file or in the hands of the energy administrator or other person, it is an offence for a person, with the intention of obtaining a sight of documents which he has not under the Rules any right to inspect, falsely to claim a status which would entitle him to inspect them.

(2) A person guilty of an offence under this Rule is liable to imprisonment or a fine, or both.

[7.1046]
173 The Gazette

(1) A copy of the Gazette containing any notice required by the 1986 Act, Schedule B1 to the 1986 Act or the Rules to be gazetted is evidence of any fact stated in the notice.

(2) In the case of an order of the court notice of which is required by the 1986 Act, Schedule B1 to the 1986 Act or the Rules to be gazetted, a copy of the Gazette containing the notice may in any proceedings be produced as conclusive evidence that the order was made on the date specified in the notice.

(3) Where an order of the court which is gazetted has been varied, and where any matter has been erroneously or inaccurately gazetted, the person whose responsibility it was to procure the requisite entry in the Gazette shall forthwith cause the variation of the order to be gazetted or, as the case may be, a further entry to be made in the Gazette for the purpose of correcting the error or inaccuracy.

[7.1047]
174 Punishment of offences

(1) Schedule 2 to the Rules has effect with respect to the way in which contraventions of the Rules are punishable on conviction.

(2) In relation to an offence under a provision of the Rules specified in the first column of the Schedule (the general nature of the offence being described in the second column), the third column shows whether the offence is punishable on conviction on indictment, or on summary conviction, or either in the one way or the other.

(3) The fourth column shows, in relation to an offence, the maximum punishment by way of fine or imprisonment which may be imposed on a person convicted of the offence in the way specified in relation to it in the third column (that is to say, on indictment or summarily), a reference to a period of years or months being to a term of imprisonment of that duration.

(4) The fifth column shows (in relation to an offence for which there is an entry in that column) that a person convicted of the offence after continued contravention is liable to a daily default fine; that is to say, he is liable on a second or subsequent conviction of the offence to the fine specified in that column for each day on which the contravention is continued (instead of the penalty specified for the offence in the fourth column of the Schedule).

(5) Section 431 of the 1986 Act (summary proceedings), as it applies to England and Wales, has effect in relation to offences under the Rules as to offences under the 1986 Act.

[7.1048]

175 Notice of order under section 176A(5) of the 1986 Act

(1) Where the court makes an order under section 176A(5) of the 1986 Act, it shall as soon as reasonably practicable send two sealed copies of the order to the energy administrator.

(2) Where the court has made an order under section 176A(5) of the 1986 Act, the energy administrator shall, as soon as reasonably practicable, send a sealed copy of the order to the protected energy company.

(3) Where the court has made an order under section 176A(5) of the 1986 Act, the energy administrator shall, as soon as reasonably practicable, give notice to each creditor of whose claim and address he is aware.

(4) Paragraph (3) shall not apply where the court directs otherwise.

(5) The court may direct that the requirement in paragraph (3) is complied with by the energy administrator publishing a notice in such newspaper as he thinks most appropriate for ensuring that it comes to the notice of the protected energy company's unsecured creditors stating that the court has made an order disapplying the requirement to set aside the prescribed part.

(6) The energy administrator shall send a copy of the order to the registrar of companies as soon as reasonably practicable after the making of the order.

PART 15
INTERPRETATION AND APPLICATION

[7.1049]

176 Introductory

This Part of the Rules has effect for their interpretation and application; and any definition given in this Part applies except, and in so far as, the context otherwise requires.

[7.1050]

177 "The court"; "the registrar"

(1) Anything to be done in energy administration proceedings by, to or before the court may be done by, to or before a judge or the registrar.

(2) The registrar may authorise any act of a formal or administrative character which is not by statute his responsibility to be carried out by the chief clerk or any other officer of the court acting on his behalf, in accordance with directions given by the Lord Chancellor.

(3) In energy administration proceedings, "the registrar" means—

(a) subject to the following paragraph, [an Insolvency and Companies Court Judge];

(b) where the proceedings are in the District Registry of Birmingham, Bristol, Cardiff, Leeds, Liverpool, Manchester, Newcastle-upon-Tyne or Preston, the District Registrar.

NOTES

Para (3): words in square brackets substituted by the Alteration of Judicial Titles (Registrar in Bankruptcy of the High Court) Order 2018, SI 2018/130, art 3, Schedule, para 12(1)(c).

[7.1051]

178 "Give notice" etc

(1) A reference in the Rules to giving notice, or to delivering, sending or serving any document, means that the notice or document may be sent by post, unless under a particular Rule personal service is expressly required.

(2) Any form of post may be used, unless under a particular Rule a specified form is expressly required.

(3) Personal service of a document is permissible in all cases.

(4) Notice of the venue fixed for an application may be given by service of the sealed copy of the application under Rule 96(3).

[7.1052]

179 Notice, etc to solicitors

Where in energy administration proceedings a notice or other document is required or authorised to be given to a person, it may, if he has indicated that his solicitor is authorised to accept service on his behalf, be given instead to the solicitor.

[7.1053]

180 Notice to joint energy administrators

Where two or more persons are acting jointly as the energy administrator in energy administration proceedings, delivery of a document to one of them is to be treated as delivery to them all.

[7.1054]

181 "Venue"

References to the "venue" for any proceedings or attendance before the court, or for a meeting, are to the time, date and place for the proceedings, attendance or meeting.

[7.1055]
182 "Energy administration proceedings"

"Energy administration proceedings" means any proceedings under sections 154 to 171 of, and Schedules 20 and 21 to, the 2004 Act or the Rules.

[7.1056]
183 "The appropriate fee"

"The appropriate fee" means 15 pence per A4 or A5 page and 30 pence per A3 page.

[7.1057]
184 "Debt", "liability"

(1) "Debt", in relation to the energy administration of a protected energy company, means (subject to the next paragraph) any of the following—

- (a) any debt or liability to which the protected energy company is subject at the date on which it goes into energy administration;
- (b) any debt or liability to which the protected energy company may become subject after that date by reason of any obligation incurred before that date; and
- (c) any interest provable as mentioned in Rule 56(1).

(2) In determining for the purposes of any provision of the 1986 Act, section 154 to 171 of and Schedules 20 and 21 to the 2004 Act, Schedule B1 to the 1986 Act or the Rules, whether any liability in tort is a debt provable in the energy administration, the protected energy company is deemed to become subject to that liability by reason of an obligation incurred at the time when the cause of action accrued.

(3) For the purposes of references in any provision of the 1986 Act, section 154 to 171 of and Schedules 20 and 21 to the 2004 Act, Schedule B1 to the 1986 Act or the Rules, to a debt or liability, it is immaterial whether the debt or liability is present or future, whether it is certain or contingent, or whether its amount is fixed or liquidated, or is capable of being ascertained by fixed rules or as a matter of opinion; and references in any such provision to owing a debt are to be read accordingly.

(4) In any provision of the 1986 Act, section 154 to 171 of and Schedules 20 and 21 to the 2004 Act, Schedule B1 to the 1986 Act or the Rules, except in so far as the context otherwise requires, "liability" means (subject to paragraph (3) above) a liability to pay money or money's worth, including any liability under an enactment, any liability for breach of trust, any liability in contract, tort or bailment, and any liability arising out of an obligation to make restitution.

[7.1058]
185 "Authorised deposit-taker and former authorised deposit-taker"

(1) "Authorised deposit-taker" means a person with permission under Part 4 of the Financial Services and Markets Act to accept deposits.

(2) "Former authorised deposit-taker" means a person who—

- (a) is not an authorised deposit-taker,
- (b) was formerly an authorised institution under the Banking Act 1987, or a recognised bank or a licensed institution under the Banking Act 1979, and
- (c) continues to have liability in respect of any deposit for which it had a liability at a time when it was an authorised institution, recognised bank or licensed institution.

(3) Paragraphs (1) and (2) must be read with—

- (a) section 22 of the Financial Services and Markets Act 2000;
- (b) any relevant order under that section; and
- (c) Schedule 22 to that Act.

[7.1059]
186 Expressions used generally

(1) "Business day" means any day other than a Saturday, a Sunday, Christmas Day, Good Friday or a day which is a bank holiday in any part of Great Britain under or by virtue of the Banking and Financial Dealings Act 1971.

(2) "The Department" means [the Department for Business, Energy and Industrial Strategy].

(3) "File in court" and "file with the court" means deliver to the court for filing.

(4) "The Gazette" means the London Gazette.

(5) "Practice direction" means a direction as to the practice and procedure of any court within the scope of the CPR.

(6) "Prescribed part" has the same meaning as it does in section 176A(2) of the 1986 Act.

NOTES

Para (2): words in square brackets substituted by the Secretaries of State for Business, Energy and Industrial Strategy, for International Trade and for Exiting the European Union and the Transfer of Functions (Education and Skills) Order 2016, SI 2016/992, art 14, Schedule, para 33.

[7.1060]
187 Application

The Rules apply to energy administration proceedings commenced on or after the date on which the Rules come into force. Nothing contained in the Insolvency Rules shall apply to such proceedings commenced on or after that date.

SCHEDULE 1
FORMS

Rule 160

[7.1061]

NOTES

The forms themselves are not reproduced in this work, but their numbers and descriptions are listed below.

Index

Form Number	***Title***
EA1	Energy administration application
EA2	Statement of proposed energy administrator
EA3	Affidavit of service of energy administration application
EA4	Energy administration order
EA5	Notification of appointment of energy administrator (for newspaper and London Gazette)
EA6	Notice of energy administrator's appointment
EA7	Notice requiring submission of a statement of affairs
EA8	Statement of affairs
EA9	Statement of concurrence
EA10	Notice of statement of affairs
EA11	Statement of energy administrator's proposals
EA12	Notice of extension of time period
EA13	Notice of a meeting of creditors
EA14	Creditor's request for a meeting
EA15	Statement of energy administrator's revised proposals
EA16	Energy administrator's progress report
EA17	Notice of order to deal with charged property
EA18	Affidavit of debt
EA19	Notice of court order ending energy administration
EA20	Notice of move from energy administration to creditors' voluntary liquidation
EA21	Notice of move from energy administration to dissolution
EA22	Notice to registrar of companies in respect of date of dissolution
EA23	Notice of intention to resign as energy administrator
EA24	Notice of resignation by energy administrator
EA25	Notice of vacation of office by energy administrator
EA26	Notice of appointment of replacement/additional energy administrator
EA27	Originating application
EA28	Ordinary application
EA29	Declaration by official shorthand writer
EA30	Appointment of shorthand writer
EA31	Declaration by shorthand writer
EA32	Order appointing person to act for incapacitated person
EA33	Proxy
EA34	Order under section 236 of the Insolvency Act 1986 (as modified by Schedule 20 to the Energy Act 2004)
EA35	Notice to registrar of companies in respect of an order under section 176A of the Insolvency Act 1986

SCHEDULE 2
PUNISHMENT OF OFFENCES UNDER THE RULES

Rule 174

[7.1062]

Rule creating offence	***General nature of offence***	***Mode of prosecution***	***Punishment***	***Daily default fine (where applicable)***
Rule 32(6)	Energy administrator failing to send notification as to progress of energy administration	Summary	One-fifth of the statutory maximum	One-fiftieth of the statutory maximum
Rule 91(2)	Energy administrator's duties on vacating office	Summary	One-fiftieth of the statutory maximum	One-fiftieth of the statutory maximum
Rule 172(2)	False representation of status for purpose of inspecting documents	1 On indictment	2 years or a fine or both	
		2 Summary	6 months or the statutory maximum, or both	

F
ENERGY SUPPLY COMPANIES

ENERGY ACT 2011

(2011 c 16)

ARRANGEMENT OF SECTIONS

PART 2
SECURITY OF ENERGY SUPPLIES

CHAPTER 5
SPECIAL ADMINISTRATION

Special administration under this Chapter

94 Energy supply company administration orders . . . . . [7.1063]
95 Objective of an energy supply company administration . . . . . [7.1064]
96 Application of certain provisions of the Energy Act 2004 in relation to esc administration orders . . . . . [7.1065]
98 Modifications of particular or standard conditions . . . . . [7.1066]
99 Licence conditions to secure funding of energy supply company administration . . . . . [7.1067]
100 Modifications under the Enterprise Act 2002 . . . . . [7.1068]
101 Power to make further modifications of insolvency legislation . . . . . [7.1069]
102 Interpretation of Chapter 5 . . . . . [7.1070]

PART 5
MISCELLANEOUS AND GENERAL

General

120 Extent . . . . . [7.1071]
121 Commencement . . . . . [7.1072]
122 Short title . . . . . [7.1073]

An Act to make provision for the arrangement and financing of energy efficiency improvements to be made to properties by owners and occupiers; about the energy efficiency of properties in the private rented sector; about the promotion by energy companies of reductions in carbon emissions and home-heating costs; about information relating to energy consumption, efficiency and tariffs; for increasing the security of energy supplies; about access to upstream petroleum infrastructure and downstream gas processing facilities; about a special administration regime for energy supply companies; about designations under the Continental Shelf Act 1964; about licence modifications relating to offshore transmission and distribution of electricity; about the security of nuclear construction sites; about the decommissioning of nuclear sites and offshore infrastructure; for the use of pipelines for carbon capture and storage; for an annual report on contribution to carbon emissions reduction targets; for action relating to the energy efficiency of residential accommodation in England; for the generation of electricity from renewable sources; about renewable heat incentives in Northern Ireland; about the powers of the Coal Authority; for an amendment of section 137 of the Energy Act 2004; for the amendment and repeal of measures relating to home energy efficiency; and for connected purposes.

[18 October 2011]

NOTES

Note: the Insolvency Rules 1986, SI 1986/1925 are revoked and replaced (as from 6 April 2017 and subject to transitional provisions) by the Insolvency (England and Wales) Rules 2016, SI 2016/1024 at **[6.2]**, however, the Insolvency (England and Wales) Rules 2016 (Consequential Amendments and Savings) Rules 2017, SI 2017/369, r 3(g) at **[6.947]** provides that the Insolvency Rules 1986 as they had effect immediately before 6 April 2017 and insofar as they apply to proceedings under this Act, continue to have effect for the purposes of the application of this Act.

See also the Deregulation Act 2015 and Small Business, Enterprise and Employment Act 2015 (Consequential Amendments) (Savings) Regulations 2017, SI 2017/540, reg 4(1), (2)(g) and the Insolvency Amendment (EU 2015/848) Regulations 2017, SI 2017/702, reg 4 at **[2.103]**, for savings in relation to the Insolvency Act 1986 in so far as it applies to proceedings under this Act.

1–78 (*(Pt 1) outside the scope of this work.*)

PART 2
SECURITY OF ENERGY SUPPLIES

79–92 (*(Chs 1–4) outside the scope of this work.*)

CHAPTER 5 SPECIAL ADMINISTRATION

93 (*Amends the Energy Act 2004, s 166 at* **[7.861]**.)

Special administration under this Chapter

[7.1063]

94 Energy supply company administration orders

(1) An energy supply company administration order (referred to in this Chapter as an "esc administration order") is an order which—

(a) is made by the court in relation to an energy supply company; and

(b) directs that, while the order is in force, the affairs, business and property of the company are to be managed by a person appointed by the court.

(2) The person appointed in relation to a company for the purposes of an esc administration order is the energy administrator of the company.

(3) The energy administrator of a company must manage its affairs, business and property, and exercise and perform all the powers and duties of an energy administrator, so as to achieve the objective set out in section 95.

(4) In relation to an esc administration order applying to a non-GB company, references in this section to the affairs, business and property of the company are references only to its affairs and business so far as carried on in Great Britain and to its property in Great Britain.

(5) In this Chapter—

"energy supply company" means a company which is the holder of a relevant licence; and

"relevant licence" means—

(a) a licence granted under section 7A(1)(a) or (b) of the Gas Act 1986 to supply gas, or

(b) a licence granted under section 6(1)(d) of the Electricity Act 1989 to supply electricity.

[7.1064]

95 Objective of an energy supply company administration

(1) The objective of an energy supply company administration is to secure—

(a) that energy supplies are continued at the lowest cost which it is reasonably practicable to incur; and

(b) that it becomes unnecessary, by one or both of the following means, for the esc administration order to remain in force for that purpose.

(2) Those means are—

(a) the rescue as a going concern of the company subject to the esc administration order; and

(b) transfers falling within subsection (3).

(3) A transfer falls within this subsection if it is a transfer as a going concern—

(a) to another company, or

(b) as respects different parts of the undertaking of the company subject to the esc administration order, to two or more different companies,

of so much of that undertaking as it is appropriate to transfer for the purpose of achieving the objective of the energy supply company administration.

(4) The means by which transfers falling within subsection (3) may be effected include, in particular—

(a) a transfer of the undertaking of the company subject to the esc administration order, or of a part of its undertaking, to a wholly-owned subsidiary of that company; and

(b) a transfer to a company of securities of a wholly-owned subsidiary to which there has been a transfer falling within paragraph (a).

(5) The objective of an energy supply company administration may be achieved by transfers falling within subsection (3) to the extent only that—

(a) the rescue as a going concern of the company subject to the esc administration order is not reasonably practicable or is not reasonably practicable without such transfers;

(b) the rescue of that company as a going concern will not achieve that objective or will not do so without such transfers;

(c) such transfers would produce a result for the company's creditors as a whole that is better than the result that would be produced without them; or

(d) such transfers would, without prejudicing the interests of those creditors as a whole, produce a result for the company's members as a whole that is better than the result that would be produced without them.

[7.1065]

96 Application of certain provisions of the Energy Act 2004 in relation to esc administration orders

(1) Sections 156 to 167 of, and Schedules 20 and 21 to, the Energy Act 2004 (special administration regime for energy licensees) apply in relation to an esc administration order as they apply in relation to an energy administration order within the meaning given by section 154(1) of that Act, but with the modifications set out in subsections (2) to (4).

(2) In the application of those provisions generally—

(a) for "energy administration", in each place where it occurs, substitute "energy supply company administration";

(b) for "a protected energy company", in each place where it occurs, substitute "an energy supply company".

(3) In the application of Schedule 20—

(a) in paragraph 32(d), for the words from """"energy administration application"" to "Energy Act 2004" substitute """"energy supply company administration application" means an application to the court for an energy supply company administration order under Chapter 3 of Part 3 of the Energy Act 2004, as applied by section 96 of the Energy Act 2011";
(b) in paragraph 32(e), for "section 155 of the Energy Act 2004" substitute "section 95 of the Energy Act 2011";
(c) in paragraph 36, for "section 154(4) of this Act" substitute "section 94(4) of the Energy Act 2011";
(d) in paragraph 43, after "the Energy Act 2004" insert "and section 96 of the Energy Act 2011";
(e) in paragraph 44(5), after "the Energy Act 2004" insert "and section 96 of the Energy Act 2011";
(f) in paragraph 45, after "section 157(1)(e) of this Act" insert "as applied by section 96 of the Energy Act 2011";
(g) in paragraph 47, after "Part 1 of this Schedule" insert "and section 96 of the Energy Act 2011".

(4) In the application of Schedule 21—
(a) in paragraph 1(b), for "section 155(3)" substitute "section 95(3) of the Energy Act 2011";
(b) in paragraph 12, for "section 155" substitute "section 95 of the Energy Act 2011".

(5) Sections 171 and 196 of the Energy Act 2004 (interpretation) apply for the purposes of the application by subsection (1) of the provisions mentioned in that subsection, but with the modifications set out in subsection (6).

(6) In the application of section 171(1)—
(a) insert, at the appropriate places, the following definitions—

""energy supply company" has the meaning given by section 94(5) of the Energy Act 2011;";

""energy supply company administration order" has the meaning given by section 94(1) of the Energy Act 2011;";

""energy supply company administration rules" means rules made under section 411 of the 1986 Act by virtue of section 159(3) of this Act, for the purpose of giving effect to this Chapter as applied by section 96 of the Energy Act 2011;";

""objective of the energy supply company administration" is to be construed in accordance with section 95 of the Energy Act 2011;";

(b) in the definition of "energy administrator" for "section 154(2)" substitute "section 94(2) of the Energy Act 2011";
(c) in the definition of "relevant licence" for "section 154(5)" substitute "section 94(5) of the Energy Act 2011".

97 (*Amends the Energy Act 2004, s 159 at* **[7.854]**.)

[7.1066]

98 Modifications of particular or standard conditions

(1) Where the Secretary of State considers it appropriate to do so in connection with the provision made by this Chapter, the Secretary of State may make—
(a) modifications of the conditions of a gas or electricity licence held by a particular person;
(b) modifications of the standard conditions of such licences of any type.

(2) The power to make modifications under this section includes power to make incidental, consequential or transitional modifications.

(3) Before making a modification under this section, the Secretary of State must consult—
(a) the holder of any licence being modified; and
(b) such other persons as the Secretary of State considers appropriate.

(4) The Secretary of State must publish every modification made under this section.

(5) The publication must be in such manner as the Secretary of State considers appropriate.

(6) A modification under subsection (1)(a) of part of a standard condition of a licence does not prevent any other part of the condition from continuing to be regarded as a standard condition for the purposes of Part 1 of the Gas Act 1986 or Part 1 of the Electricity Act 1989.

(7) Where the Secretary of State makes modifications under subsection (1)(b) of the standard conditions of licences of any type, the Gas and Electricity Markets Authority must—
(a) make (as nearly as may be) the same modifications of those standard conditions for the purposes of their incorporation in licences of that type granted after that time; and
(b) publish the modifications in such manner as it considers appropriate.

(8) The Secretary of State's powers under this section are exercisable only during the eighteen months beginning with the commencement of this section.

(9) In section 33(1) of the Utilities Act 2000 (standard conditions of generation, distribution and supply licences under Part 1 of the Electricity Act 1989), after "76" (as inserted by section 77(5) of this Act) insert "or 98".

(10) In section 81(2) of the Utilities Act 2000 (standard conditions of transporter, supply and shipping licences under Part 1 of the Gas Act 1986), after "76" (as inserted by section 77(6) of this Act) insert "or 98".

(11) In section 146(5) of the Energy Act 2004 (standard conditions of interconnector licences under Part 1 of the Electricity Act 1989), for "or under this Act" substitute ", under this Act or under section 98 of the Energy Act 2011".

(12) In section 150(5) of the Energy Act 2004 (standard conditions of interconnector licences under Part 1 of the Gas Act 1986), for "or under this Act" substitute ", under this Act or under section 98 of the Energy Act 2011".

(13) Sections 4AA to 4B of the Gas Act 1986 (principal objective and general duties) apply in relation to the powers of the Secretary of State under this section with respect to holders of gas licences as they apply in relation to functions of the Secretary of State under Part 1 of that Act.

(14) Sections 3A to 3D of the Electricity Act 1989 (principal objective and general duties) apply in relation to the powers of the Secretary of State under this section with respect to holders of electricity licences as they apply in relation to functions of the Secretary of State under Part 1 of that Act.

(15) In this section—

(a) references to a gas licence are to a licence for the purposes of section 5 of the Gas Act 1986 (prohibition on unlicensed activities relating to gas), and

(b) references to an electricity licence are to a licence for the purposes of section 4 of the Electricity Act 1989 (prohibition on unlicensed activities relating to electricity).

[7.1067]
99 Licence conditions to secure funding of energy supply company administration

(1) The modifications that may be made under section 98 include, in particular, modifications imposing conditions requiring the holder of the licence—

(a) so to modify the charges imposed by the licence holder for anything done by the licence holder in the carrying on of the licensed activities as to raise such amounts as may be determined by or under the conditions; and

(b) to pay the amounts so raised to such persons as may be so determined for the purpose of—

(i) their applying those amounts in making good any shortfall in the property available for meeting the expenses of an energy supply company administration; or

(ii) enabling those persons to secure that those amounts are so applied.

(2) Those modifications may include modifications imposing on the licence holder an obligation to apply amounts paid to the licence holder in pursuance of conditions falling within subsection (1)(a) or (b) in making good any such shortfall.

(3) For the purposes of this section—

(a) there is a shortfall in the property available for meeting the costs of an energy supply company administration if, in a case where a company is or has been subject to an energy supply company administration order, the property available (apart from conditions falling within subsection (1) or (2)) for meeting relevant debts is insufficient for meeting them; and

(b) amounts are applied in making good that shortfall if they are paid in or towards discharging so much of a relevant debt as cannot be met out of the property otherwise available for meeting relevant debts.

(4) In this section "relevant debt" in relation to a case in which a company is or has been subject to an energy supply company administration order, means an obligation—

(a) to make payments in respect of the expenses or remuneration of any person as the energy administrator of that company;

(b) to make a payment in discharge of a debt or liability of that company arising out of a contract entered into at a time when the order was in force by the person who at that time was the energy administrator of that company;

(c) to repay the whole or a part of a grant made to that company under section 165 of the Energy Act 2004 as applied by section 96 of this Act;

(d) to repay a loan made to the company under that section as so applied, or to pay interest on such a loan;

(e) to make a payment under section 166(4) of that Act as so applied; or

(f) to make a payment under section 167(5) of that Act as so applied.

[7.1068]
100 Modifications under the Enterprise Act 2002

(1) The power to modify or apply enactments conferred on the Secretary of State by each of the sections of the Enterprise Act 2002 mentioned in subsection (2) includes power to make such consequential modifications of this Chapter as the Secretary of State considers appropriate in connection with any other provision made under that section.

(2) Those sections are—

(a) sections 248 and 277 (amendments consequential on that Act); and

(b) section 254 (power to apply insolvency law to foreign companies).

(3) . . .

NOTES

Sub-s (3): amends the Energy Act 2004, s 170 at **[7.865]**.

[7.1069]
101 Power to make further modifications of insolvency legislation

(1) The power of the Secretary of State under paragraph 46 of Schedule 20 to the Energy Act 2004 (conduct of energy administration) to make modifications includes power to make such modifications as the Secretary of State considers appropriate in relation to any provision made by or under this Chapter.

(2) . . .

NOTES

Sub-s (2): amends the Energy Act 2004, Sch 20 at **[7.872]**.

[7.1070]

102 Interpretation of Chapter 5

(1) In this Chapter—

"business", "member" and "property" have the same meanings as in the Insolvency Act 1986;

"company" means—

(a) a company registered under the Companies Act 2006, or

(b) an unregistered company;

"court", in relation to a company, means the court—

(a) having jurisdiction to wind up the company, or

(b) that would have such jurisdiction apart from section 221(2) or 441(2) of the Insolvency Act 1986 (exclusion of winding up jurisdiction in case of companies having principal place of business in, or incorporated in, Northern Ireland);

"energy administrator" has the meaning given by section 94(2) and is to be construed in accordance with subsection (2) of this section;

"energy supply company administration order" has the meaning given by section 94(1);

"energy supply company'" has the meaning given by section 94(5);

"modification" includes omission, addition or alteration, and cognate expressions are to be construed accordingly;

"non-GB company" means a company incorporated outside Great Britain;

"objective of the energy supply company administration" is to be construed in accordance with section 95;

"relevant licence" has the meaning given by section 94(5);

"subsidiary" and "wholly-owned subsidiary" have the meanings given by section 1159 of the Companies Act 2006;

"unregistered company" means a company that is not registered under the Companies Act 2006.

(2) In this Chapter references to the energy administrator of a company—

(a) include references to a person appointed under paragraph 91 or 103 of Schedule B1 to the Insolvency Act 1986, as applied by Part 1 of Schedule 20 to the Energy Act 2004 and section 96 of this Act to be the energy administrator of that company; and

(b) where two or more persons are appointed to be the energy administrator of that company, are to be construed in accordance with the provision made under section 158(5) of the Energy Act 2004, as applied by section 96 of this Act.

103–116 (*S 103 (Ch 6), ss 104–116 (Pts 3, 4) outside the scope of this work.*)

PART 5
MISCELLANEOUS AND GENERAL

117, 118 (*Outside the scope of this work.*)

General

119 (*Outside the scope of this work.*)

[7.1071]

120 Extent

(1) Subject to subsections (2) to (6), this Act extends to England and Wales and Scotland only.

(2)–(7) . . .

NOTES

Sub-ss (2)–(7): outside the scope of this work.

[7.1072]

121 Commencement

(1) The provisions of this Act come into force on such day as the Secretary of State may by order made by statutory instrument appoint, subject to subsections (2) to (5).

(2) . . .

(3) The following provisions come into force at the end of the period of two months beginning with the day on which this Act is passed—

(a)–(e) . . .

(f) sections 93 to 102 (special administration);

(g)–(n) . . .

(4) The following provisions come into force on the day on which this Act is passed—

(a)–(c) . . .

(d) sections 119 and 120, this section and section 122 (general provisions).

(5) . . .

(6) An order made by the Secretary of State or the Scottish Ministers under this section may—

(a) appoint different days for different purposes;

(b) make transitional provision and savings.

NOTES

Sub-ss (2), (5): outside the scope of this work.

Sub-s (3): paras (a)–(e), (g)–(n) outside the scope of this work.

Sub-s (4): paras (a)–(c) outside the scope of this work.

Orders: the Energy Act 2011 (Commencement No 1 and Saving) Order 2012, SI 2012/873; the Energy Act 2011 (Commencement No 2) Order 2013, SI 2013/125; the Energy Act 2011 (Commencement No 3) Order 2015, SI 2015/880.

[7.1073]

122 Short title

This Act may be cited as the Energy Act 2011.

SCHEDULES 1, 2

(*Schchs 1, 2 outside the scope of this work.*)

ENERGY SUPPLY COMPANY ADMINISTRATION RULES 2013

(SI 2013/1046)

NOTES

Made: 30 April 2013.

Authority: Insolvency Act 1986, s 411; Energy Act 2004, s 159(3) (as applied by the Energy Act 2011, s 96).

Commencement: 7 June 2013.

Note: the Insolvency Rules 1986, SI 1986/1925 are revoked and replaced (as from 6 April 2017 and subject to transitional provisions) by the Insolvency (England and Wales) Rules 2016, SI 2016/1024 at **[6.2]**, however, the Insolvency (England and Wales) Rules 2016 (Consequential Amendments and Savings) Rules 2017, SI 2017/369, r 3(i) at **[6.947]** provides that the Insolvency Rules 1986 as they had effect immediately before 6 April 2017 and insofar as they apply to proceedings under the Energy Supply Company Administration Rules 2013, continue to have effect for the purposes of the application of the 2013 Rules.

See also the Deregulation Act 2015 and Small Business, Enterprise and Employment Act 2015 (Consequential Amendments) (Savings) Regulations 2017, SI 2017/540, reg 4(1), (2)(i) and the Insolvency Amendment (EU 2015/848) Regulations 2017, SI 2017/702, reg 4 at **[2.103]**, for savings in relation to the Insolvency Act 1986 in so far as it applies to proceedings under these Rules.

ARRANGEMENT OF RULES

PART 1
INTRODUCTORY PROVISIONS

1 Citation and commencement .....[7.1074]
2 Construction and interpretation .....[7.1075]
3 Application .....[7.1076]

PART 2
APPOINTMENT OF ENERGY ADMINISTRATOR BY COURT

4 Witness statement .....[7.1077]
5 Form of application .....[7.1078]
6 Contents of application and witness statement .....[7.1079]
7 Filing of application .....[7.1080]
8 Service of application .....[7.1081]
9 Notice to officers charged with execution of writs or other process .....[7.1082]
10 Manner in which service to be effected .....[7.1083]
11 Proof of service .....[7.1084]
12 The hearing .....[7.1085]
13 Notice of esc administration order .....[7.1086]

PART 3
PROCESS OF ENERGY SUPPLY COMPANY ADMINISTRATION

14 Notification and advertisement of energy administrator's appointment .....[7.1087]
15 Notice requiring statement of affairs .....[7.1088]
16 Verification and filing .....[7.1089]
17 Limited disclosure .....[7.1090]
18 Release from duty to submit statement of affairs; extension of time .....[7.1091]
19 Expenses of statement of affairs .....[7.1092]
20 Energy administrator's proposals .....[7.1093]
21 Limited disclosure of paragraph 49 of Schedule B1 to the 1986 Act statement .....[7.1094]

PART 4
MEETINGS AND REPORTS

CHAPTER 1
CREDITORS' MEETINGS

22 Creditors' meetings generally .... [7.1095]
23 The chair at meetings .... [7.1096]
24 Creditors' meeting for nomination of alternative liquidator .... [7.1097]
25 Entitlement to vote .... [7.1098]
26 Admission and rejection of claims .... [7.1099]
27 Secured creditors .... [7.1100]
28 Holders of negotiable instruments .... [7.1101]
29 Hire-purchase, conditional sale and chattel leasing agreements .... [7.1102]
30 Resolutions .... [7.1103]
31 Minutes .... [7.1104]
32 Revision of the energy administrator's proposals .... [7.1105]
33 Reports .... [7.1106]

CHAPTER 2
COMPANY MEETINGS

34 Venue and conduct of company meeting .... [7.1107]

PART 5
DISPOSAL OF CHARGED PROPERTY

35 Authority to dispose of property .... [7.1108]

PART 6
EXPENSES OF THE ENERGY SUPPLY COMPANY ADMINISTRATION

36 Priority of expenses of energy supply company administration .... [7.1109]
37 Pre-energy supply company administration costs .... [7.1110]

PART 7
DISTRIBUTION TO CREDITORS

CHAPTER 1
APPLICATION OF PART AND GENERAL

38 Distribution to creditors generally .... [7.1111]
39 Debts of insolvent energy supply company to rank equally .... [7.1112]
40 Supplementary provisions as to dividend .... [7.1113]
41 Division of unsold assets .... [7.1114]

CHAPTER 2
MACHINERY OF PROVING A DEBT

42 Proving a debt .... [7.1115]
43 Costs of proving .... [7.1116]
44 Energy administrator to allow inspection of proofs .... [7.1117]
45 New energy administrator appointed .... [7.1118]
46 Admission and rejection of proofs for dividend .... [7.1119]
47 Appeal against decision on proof .... [7.1120]
48 Withdrawal or variation of proof .... [7.1121]
49 Expunging of proof by the court .... [7.1122]

CHAPTER 3
QUANTIFICATION OF CLAIMS

50 Estimate of quantum .... [7.1123]
51 Negotiable instruments, etc .... [7.1124]
52 Secured creditors .... [7.1125]
53 Discounts .... [7.1126]
54 Mutual credits and set off .... [7.1127]
55 Debt in foreign currency .... [7.1128]
56 Payments of a periodical nature .... [7.1129]
57 Interest .... [7.1130]
58 Debt payable at future time .... [7.1131]
59 Value of security .... [7.1132]
60 Surrender for non-disclosure .... [7.1133]
61 Redemption by energy administrator .... [7.1134]
62 Test of security's value .... [7.1135]
63 Realisation of security by creditor .... [7.1136]
64 Notice of proposed distribution .... [7.1137]

65 Admission or rejection of proofs . . . . [7.1138]
66 Postponement or cancellation of dividend . . . . [7.1139]
67 Declaration of dividend . . . . [7.1140]
68 Notice of declaration of a dividend . . . . [7.1141]
69 Payments of dividends and related matters . . . . [7.1142]
70 Notice of no dividend, or no further dividend . . . . [7.1143]
71 Proof altered after payment of dividend . . . . [7.1144]
72 Secured creditors . . . . [7.1145]
73 Disqualification from dividend . . . . [7.1146]
74 Assignment of right to dividend . . . . [7.1147]
75 Adjustment where dividend paid before time . . . . [7.1148]

PART 8
THE ENERGY ADMINISTRATOR

76 Fixing of remuneration . . . . [7.1149]
77 Remuneration of new energy administrator . . . . [7.1150]

PART 9
ENDING ENERGY SUPPLY COMPANY ADMINISTRATION

78 Final progress reports . . . . [7.1151]
79 Application to court . . . . [7.1152]
80 Notification by energy administrator of court order . . . . [7.1153]
81 Moving from energy supply company administration to creditors' voluntary liquidation . . . . [7.1154]
82 Moving from energy supply company administration to dissolution . . . . [7.1155]
83 Provision of information to the Secretary of State . . . . [7.1156]

PART 10
REPLACING ENERGY ADMINISTRATOR

84 Grounds for resignation . . . . [7.1157]
85 Notice of intention to resign . . . . [7.1158]
86 Notice of resignation . . . . [7.1159]
87 Application to court to remove energy administrator from office . . . . [7.1160]
88 Notice of vacation of office when energy administrator ceases to be qualified to act . . . . [7.1161]
89 Energy administrator deceased . . . . [7.1162]
90 Application to replace . . . . [7.1163]
91 Notification and advertisement of appointment of replacement energy administrator . . . . [7.1164]
92 Notification and advertisement of appointment of joint energy administrator . . . . [7.1165]
93 Notification to registrar of companies . . . . [7.1166]
94 Energy administrator's duties on vacating office . . . . [7.1167]

PART 11
COURT PROCEDURE AND PRACTICE

CHAPTER 1
APPLICATIONS

95 Preliminary . . . . [7.1168]
96 Form and contents of application . . . . [7.1169]
97 Application under section 176A(5) of the 1986 Act to disapply section 176A of the 1986 Act . . . . [7.1170]
98 Filing and service of application . . . . [7.1171]
99 Application under section 176A(5) of the 1986 Act . . . . [7.1172]
100 Hearings without notice . . . . [7.1173]
101 Hearing of application . . . . [7.1174]
102 Witness statements—general . . . . [7.1175]
103 Filing and service of witness statements . . . . [7.1176]
104 Use of reports . . . . [7.1177]
105 Adjournment of hearings; directions . . . . [7.1178]

CHAPTER 2
SHORTHAND WRITERS

106 Nomination and appointment of shorthand writers . . . . [7.1179]
107 Remuneration . . . . [7.1180]

CHAPTER 3
ENFORCEMENT PROCEDURES

108 Enforcement of court orders . . . . [7.1181]
109 Orders enforcing compliance with these Rules . . . . [7.1182]
110 Warrant under section 236 of the 1986 Act . . . . [7.1183]

CHAPTER 4

COURT RECORDS AND RETURNS

111 Court file . . . . . . [7.1184]

CHAPTER 5

COSTS AND DETAILED ASSESSMENT

112 Application of Chapter 8 . . . . . . [7.1185]
113 Requirement to assess costs by the detailed procedure . . . . . . [7.1186]
114 Procedure where detailed assessment required . . . . . . [7.1187]
115 Costs paid otherwise than out of the assets of the energy supply company . . . . . . [7.1188]
116 Award of costs against energy administrator . . . . . . [7.1189]
117 Application for costs . . . . . . [7.1190]
118 Costs and expenses of witnesses . . . . . . [7.1191]
119 Final costs certificate . . . . . . [7.1192]

CHAPTER 6

PERSONS WHO LACK CAPACITY TO MANAGE THEIR AFFAIRS

120 Introductory . . . . . . [7.1193]
121 Appointment of another person to act . . . . . . [7.1194]
122 Witness statement in support of application . . . . . . [7.1195]
123 Service of notices following appointment . . . . . . [7.1196]

CHAPTER 7

APPEALS IN ENERGY SUPPLY COMPANY ADMINISTRATION PROCEEDINGS

124 Appeals and reviews of esc administration orders . . . . . . [7.1197]
125 Procedure on appeal . . . . . . [7.1198]

CHAPTER 8

GENERAL

126 Principal court rules and practice to apply . . . . . . [7.1199]
127 Rights of audience . . . . . . [7.1200]
128 Formal defects . . . . . . [7.1201]
129 Service of orders staying proceedings . . . . . . [7.1202]
130 Payment into court . . . . . . [7.1203]
131 Further information and disclosure . . . . . . [7.1204]
132 Office copies of documents . . . . . . [7.1205]

PART 12

PROXIES AND ENERGY SUPPLY COMPANY REPRESENTATION

133 Definition of proxy . . . . . . [7.1206]
134 Issue and use of forms . . . . . . [7.1207]
135 Use of proxies at meetings . . . . . . [7.1208]
136 Retention of proxies . . . . . . [7.1209]
137 Right of inspection . . . . . . [7.1210]
138 Proxy holder with financial interest . . . . . . [7.1211]
139 Energy supply company representation . . . . . . [7.1212]

PART 13

EXAMINATION OF PERSONS IN ENERGY SUPPLY COMPANY ADMINISTRATION PROCEEDINGS

140 Preliminary . . . . . . [7.1213]
141 Form and contents of application . . . . . . [7.1214]
142 Order for examination, etc . . . . . . [7.1215]
143 Procedure for examination . . . . . . [7.1216]
144 Record of examination . . . . . . [7.1217]
145 Cost of proceedings under section 236 . . . . . . [7.1218]

PART 14

MISCELLANEOUS AND GENERAL

146 Power of Secretary of State to regulate certain matters . . . . . . [7.1219]
147 Costs, expenses, etc . . . . . . [7.1220]
148 Provable debts . . . . . . [7.1221]
149 False claim of status as creditor, etc . . . . . . [7.1222]
150 Punishment of offences . . . . . . [7.1223]

PART 15

PROVISIONS OF GENERAL EFFECT

CHAPTER 1

THE GIVING OF NOTICE AND THE SUPPLY OF DOCUMENTS—GENERAL

151 Application . . . . . . [7.1224]

152 Personal delivery of documents .....[7.1225]
153 Postal delivery of documents .....[7.1226]
154 Non-receipt of notice of meeting .....[7.1227]
155 Notice etc to solicitors .....[7.1228]
156 Notice of meetings by advertisement only .....[7.1229]

CHAPTER 2
THE GIVING OF NOTICE AND THE SUPPLY OF DOCUMENTS BY OR TO ENERGY ADMINISTRATORS ETC

157 Application .....[7.1230]
158 Notice to joint energy administrators .....[7.1231]
159 The form of notices and other documents .....[7.1232]
160 Proof of sending etc. .....[7.1233]
161 Authentication .....[7.1234]
162 Electronic delivery in energy supply company administration proceedings—general .....[7.1235]
163 Electronic delivery by energy administrators .....[7.1236]
164 Use of websites by energy administrator .....[7.1237]
165 Special provision on account of expense as to website use .....[7.1238]
166 Electronic delivery of energy supply company administration proceedings to courts .....[7.1239]

CHAPTER 3
SERVICE OF COURT DOCUMENTS

167 Application .....[7.1240]
168 Application of CPR Part 6 to service of court documents within the jurisdiction .....[7.1241]
169 Service of orders staying proceedings .....[7.1242]
170 Service on joint energy administrators .....[7.1243]
171 Application of CPR Part 6 to service of court documents outside the jurisdiction .....[7.1244]

CHAPTER 4
MEETINGS

172 Quorum at meeting of creditors .....[7.1245]
173 Remote attendance at meetings of creditors .....[7.1246]
174 Action where person excluded .....[7.1247]
175 Indication to excluded person .....[7.1248]
176 Complaint .....[7.1249]

CHAPTER 5
FORMS

177 Forms for use in energy supply company administration proceedings .....[7.1250]
178 Electronic submission of information instead of submission of forms to the Secretary of State, energy administrators .....[7.1251]
179 Electronic submission of information instead of submission of forms in all other cases .....[7.1252]

CHAPTER 6
GAZETTE NOTICES

180 Contents of notices to be gazetted under the 1986 Act or these Rules .....[7.1253]
181 Omission of unobtainable information .....[7.1254]
182 The Gazette—general .....[7.1255]

CHAPTER 7
NOTICE ADVERTISED OTHERWISE THAN IN THE GAZETTE

183 Notices otherwise advertised under the 1986 Act or these Rules .....[7.1256]
184 Non-Gazette notices—other provisions .....[7.1257]

CHAPTER 8
NOTIFICATIONS TO THE REGISTRAR OF COMPANIES

185 Application of this Chapter .....[7.1258]
186 Information to be contained in all notifications to the registrar .....[7.1259]
187 Notifications relating to the office of energy administrators .....[7.1260]
188 Notification relating to documents .....[7.1261]
189 Notifications relating to court orders .....[7.1262]
190 Returns or reports of meetings .....[7.1263]
191 Notifications relating to other events .....[7.1264]
192 Notifications of more than one nature .....[7.1265]
193 Notifications made to other persons at the same time .....[7.1266]

CHAPTER 9
INSPECTION OF DOCUMENTS AND THE PROVISION OF INFORMATION

194 Confidentiality of documents—grounds for refusing inspection .....[7.1267]

195 Right to copy documents . . . . [7.1268]
196 Charges for copy documents . . . . [7.1269]
197 Right to have list of creditors . . . . [7.1270]

CHAPTER 10
COMPUTATION OF TIME AND TIME LIMITS

198 Time limits . . . . [7.1271]

CHAPTER 11
SECURITY

199 Energy administrator's security . . . . [7.1272]

CHAPTER 12
NOTICE OF ORDER UNDER SECTION 176A(5) OF THE 1986 ACT

200 Notice of order under section 176A(5) of the 1986 Act . . . . [7.1273]

PART 16
INTERPRETATION AND APPLICATION

201 Introductory . . . . [7.1274]
202 "The court"; "the registrar" . . . . [7.1275]
203 "Energy supply company administration proceedings" . . . . [7.1276]
204 "The appropriate fee" . . . . [7.1277]
205 "Debt", "liability" . . . . [7.1278]
206 "Venue" . . . . [7.1279]
207 Expressions used generally . . . . [7.1280]
208 Application . . . . [7.1281]

SCHEDULES:

Schedule 1—Forms . . . . [7.1282]
Schedule 2—Punishment of Offences under these Rules . . . . [7.1283]

PART 1
INTRODUCTORY PROVISIONS

[7.1074]
1 Citation and commencement

These Rules may be cited as the Energy Supply Company Administration Rules 2013 and shall come into force on 7th June 2013.

[7.1075]
2 Construction and interpretation

(1) In these Rules—

"the 1986 Act" means the Insolvency Act 1986;

"the 2004 Act" means the Energy Act 2004;

"the 2011 Act" means the Energy Act 2011;

"administrative receiver" has the same meaning as in section 156(4) of the 2004 Act;

"the Companies Act" means the Companies Act 2006;

"CPR" means the Civil Procedure Rules 1998;

"enforcement officer" means an individual who is authorised to act as an enforcement officer under the Courts Act 2003;

"GEMA" means the Gas and Electricity Markets Authority;

"insolvency proceedings" has the same meaning as in Rule 13.7 of the Insolvency Rules;

"the Insolvency Rules" means the Insolvency Rules 1986;

"pre-energy supply company administration costs" are—

(a) fees charged, and

(b) expenses incurred,

by the energy administrator, or another person qualified to act as an insolvency practitioner, before the energy supply company entered energy supply company administration but with a view to its doing so;

"proxy", "the proxy-holder" and "the principal" have the meaning given to them in Rule 133(1);

"qualifying floating charge" has the same meaning as in paragraph 14(2) of Schedule B1 to the 1986 Act;

"registrar of companies" means the registrar of companies for England and Wales;

"unpaid pre-energy supply company administration costs" are pre-energy supply company administration costs which had not been paid when the company entered energy supply company administration.

(2) References to provisions of the 1986 Act are, where those provisions have been modified by Schedule 20 to the 2004 Act, references to those provisions as so modified.

(3) References to provisions of the 2004 Act are, where those provisions have been modified by the 2011 Act, references to those provisions as so modified.

Part 7F Special Insolvency Regimes

(4) Where the energy supply company is a non-GB company within the meaning of section 102 of the 2011 Act, references in these Rules to the affairs, business and property of the company are references only to its affairs and business so far as carried on in Great Britain and to its property in Great Britain.

(5) Where the energy supply company is an unregistered company, any requirement to deliver information to the registrar of companies applies only if the company is subject to a requirement imposed by virtue of section 1043 and 1046(1) of the Companies Act.

(6) Part 16 of these Rules has effect for their interpretation and application.

NOTES

Note: the Insolvency Rules 1986, SI 1986/1925 are revoked and replaced (as from 6 April 2017 and subject to transitional provisions) by the Insolvency (England and Wales) Rules 2016, SI 2016/1024 at **[6.2]**, however, the Insolvency (England and Wales) Rules 2016 (Consequential Amendments and Savings) Rules 2017, SI 2017/369, r 3(i) provides that the Insolvency Rules 1986 as they had effect immediately before 6 April 2017 and insofar as they apply to proceedings under the Energy Supply Company Administration Rules 2013, continue to have effect for the purposes of the application of the 2013 Rules.

[7.1076]
3 Application

These Rules apply in relation to energy supply companies which the courts in England and Wales have jurisdiction to wind up.

PART 2
APPOINTMENT OF ENERGY ADMINISTRATOR BY COURT

[7.1077]
4 Witness statement

Where it is proposed to apply to the court for an esc administration order to be made in relation to an energy supply company, the energy supply company administration application must be in Form ESCA1 and a witness statement complying with Rule 6 must be prepared with a view to it being filed with the court in support of the application.

[7.1078]
5 Form of application

(1) The application must state by whom it is made and the applicant's address for service.

(2) Where it is made by GEMA, the application must contain a statement that it is made with the consent of the Secretary of State.

(3) There must be attached to the application a written statement which must be in Form ESCA2 by each of the persons proposed to be energy administrator stating—

- (a) that the person consents to accept appointment; and
- (b) details of any prior professional relationship(s) that the person has had with the energy supply company to which that person is to be appointed as energy administrator.

[7.1079]
6 Contents of application and witness statement

(1) The energy supply company administration application must state that the company is an energy supply company.

(2) The application must state one or both of the following—

- (a) the applicant's belief that the energy supply company is, or is likely to be, unable to pay its debts;
- (b) the Secretary of State has certified that it would be appropriate to petition for the winding up of the energy supply company under section 124A of the 1986 Act (petition for winding up on grounds of public interest).

(3) There must be attached to the application a witness statement in support which must contain—

- (a) a statement of the energy supply company's financial position, specifying (to the best of the applicant's knowledge and belief) the company's assets and liabilities, including contingent and prospective liabilities;
- (b) details of any security known or believed to be held by the creditors of the energy supply company and whether in any case the security is such as to confer power on the holder to appoint an administrative receiver or to appoint an administrator under paragraph 14 of Schedule B1 to the 1986 Act; if an administrative receiver has been appointed, that fact must be stated;
- (c) details of any insolvency proceedings in relation to the energy supply company including any petition that has been presented for the winding up of the energy supply company so far as within the immediate knowledge of the applicant;
- (d) details of any notice served in accordance with section 164 of the 2004 Act by any person intending to enforce any security over the energy supply company's assets, so far as within the immediate knowledge of the applicant;
- (e) details of any step taken to enforce any such security, so far as within the immediate knowledge of the applicant;
- (f) details of any application for permission of the court to pass a resolution for the voluntary winding up of the energy supply company, so far as within the immediate knowledge of the applicant;

(g) where it is intended to appoint a number of persons as energy administrators, details of the matters set out in section 158(5) of the 2004 Act regarding the exercise of the powers and duties of the energy administrator;

(h) any other matters which, in the opinion of those intending to make the application for an esc administration order, will assist the court in deciding whether to make such an order, so far as within the knowledge or belief of the applicant.

[7.1080]

7 Filing of application

(1) The application (and all supporting documents) must be filed with the court, with a sufficient number of copies for service and use as provided by Rule 8.

(2) Each of the copies must have applied to it the seal of the court and be issued to the applicant; and on each copy there must be endorsed the date and time of filing.

(3) The court must fix a venue for the hearing of the application and this also must be endorsed on each copy of the application issued under paragraph (2).

(4) After the application is filed, it is the duty of the applicant to notify the court in writing of the existence of any insolvency proceedings, in relation to the energy supply company, as soon as the applicant becomes aware of them.

[7.1081]

8 Service of application

(1) In the following paragraphs of this Rule, references to the application are to a copy of the application issued by the court under Rule 7(2) together with the witness statement required by Rule 4 and the documents attached to the application.

(2) Notification for the purposes of section 156(2) of the 2004 Act must be by way of service in accordance with Rule 10, verified in accordance with Rule 11.

(3) The application must be served in addition to those persons referred to in section 156(2) of the 2004 Act—

(a) if an administrative receiver has been appointed, on the administrative receiver;

(b) if there is pending an administration application under Schedule B1 to the 1986 Act, without the modifications made by Schedule 20 to the 2004 Act, on the applicant;

(c) if there is pending a petition for the winding up of the energy supply company, on the petitioner (and also on the provisional liquidator, if any);

(d) on any creditor who has served notice in accordance with section 164 of the 2004 Act of the creditor's intention to enforce the creditor's security over property of the energy supply company;

(e) on the person proposed as energy administrator;

(f) on the energy supply company;

(g) if the applicant is the Secretary of State, on GEMA;

(h) if the applicant is GEMA, on the Secretary of State;

(i) if a supervisor of a voluntary arrangement under Part I of the 1986 Act has been appointed, on that person.

[7.1082]

9 Notice to officers charged with execution of writs or other process

The applicant must as soon as reasonably practicable after filing the application give notice of its being made to—

(a) any enforcement officer or other officer who to the applicant's knowledge is charged with an execution or other legal process against the energy supply company or its property; and

(b) any person who to the applicant's knowledge has distrained against the energy supply company or its property.

[7.1083]

10 Manner in which service to be effected

(1) Service of the application in accordance with Rule 8 must be effected by the applicant, or the applicant's solicitor, or by a person instructed by the applicant or the applicant's solicitor, not less than 2 business days before the date fixed for the hearing.

(2) Service must be effected as follows—

(a) on the energy supply company (subject to paragraph (3)), by delivering the documents to its registered office;

(b) on any other person (subject to paragraph (4)), by delivering the documents to that person's proper address;

(c) in either case, in such other manner as the court may direct.

(3) If delivery to an energy supply company's registered office is not practicable or if the energy supply company is an unregistered company, service may be effected by delivery to its last known principal place of business in England and Wales.

(4) Subject to paragraph (5), for the purposes of paragraph (2)(b), a person's proper address is any which that person has previously notified as the person's address for service, but if the person has not notified any such address, service may be effected by delivery to the person's usual or last known address.

(5) In the case of a person who—

(a) is an authorised deposit-taker or a former authorised deposit-taker;
(b) either—
(i) has appointed, or is or may be entitled to appoint, an administrative receiver of the energy supply company; or
(ii) is or may be entitled to appoint an administrator of the energy supply company under paragraph 14 of Schedule B1 to the 1986 Act; and
(c) has not notified an address for service,

the proper address is the address of an office of that person where, to the knowledge of the applicant, the energy supply company maintains a bank account or, where no such office is known to the applicant, the registered office of that person or, if there is no such office, that person's usual or last known address.

(6) In this Rule—
(a) "authorised deposit-taker" means a person with permission under [Part 4A of the Financial Services and Markets Act 2000] to accept deposits;
(b) "former authorised deposit-taker" means a person who—
(i) is not an authorised deposit-taker,
(ii) was formerly—
(aa) an authorised institution under the Banking Act 1987, or a recognised bank or a licensed institution under the Banking Act 1979; or
(bb) a person with permission under Part 4 [or Part 4A] of the Financial Services and Markets Act 2000; and
(iii) continues to have liability in respect of any deposit for which it had a liability at a time when it was an institution, bank or person mentioned in paragraph (ii).

(7) Paragraph (6)(a) and (b) must be read with—
(a) section 22 of the Financial Services and Markets Act 2000;
(b) any relevant order under that section; and
(c) Schedule 22 to that Act.

NOTES

Para (6): words in square brackets in sub-para (a) substituted and words in square brackets in sub-para (b) inserted by the Energy Supply Company Administration (Amendment) Rules 2013, SI 2013/2950, r 2.

[7.1084]

11 Proof of service

(1) Service of the application must be verified by a certificate of service.

(2) The certificate of service must be sufficient to identify the application served and must specify—
(a) the name and registered number of the energy supply company;
(b) the address of the registered office of the energy supply company;
(c) the name of the applicant;
(d) the court to which the application was made and the court reference number;
(e) the date of the application;
(f) whether the copy served was a sealed copy;
(g) the date on which service was effected; and
(h) the manner in which service was effected.

(3) The certificate of service must be filed with the court as soon as reasonably practicable after service, and in any event not less than 1 business day before the hearing of the application.

[7.1085]

12 The hearing

(1) At the hearing of the energy supply company administration application, any of the following may appear or be represented—
(a) the Secretary of State;
(b) GEMA;
(c) the energy supply company;
(d) one or more of the directors;
(e) if an administrative receiver has been appointed, that person;
(f) any person who has presented a petition for the winding-up of the energy supply company;
(g) the person proposed for appointment as energy administrator;
(h) any person that is the holder of a qualifying floating charge;
(i) any person who has applied to the court for an administration order under Schedule B1 to the 1986 Act, without the modifications made by Schedule 20 to the 2004 Act;
(j) any creditor who has served notice in accordance with section 164 of the 2004 Act of the creditor's intention to enforce the creditor's security over the energy supply company's property;
(k) any supervisor of a voluntary arrangement under Part I of the 1986 Act;
(l) with the permission of the court, any other person who appears to have an interest justifying the person's appearance.

(2) If the court makes an esc administration order, it must be in Form ESCA3.

(3) If the court makes an esc administration order, the costs of the applicant, and of any person whose costs are allowed by the court, are payable as an expense of the energy supply company administration.

[7.1086]
13 Notice of esc administration order

(1) If the court makes an esc administration order, it must as soon as reasonably practicable send two copies of the order to the person who made the application.

(2) The applicant must send a sealed copy of the order as soon as reasonably practicable to the person appointed as energy administrator.

(3) If the court makes an order under section 157(1)(d) of the 2004 Act or any other order under section 157(1)(f) of the 2004 Act, it must give directions as to the persons to whom, and how, notice of that order is to be given.

PART 3
PROCESS OF ENERGY SUPPLY COMPANY ADMINISTRATION

[7.1087]
14 Notification and advertisement of energy administrator's appointment

(1) The notice of appointment to be given by the energy administrator as soon as reasonably practicable after appointment must be gazetted and may be advertised in such other manner as the energy administrator thinks fit.

(2) In addition to the standard contents, the notice under paragraph (1) must state—
  (a) that an energy administrator has been appointed;
  (b) the date of the appointment; and
  (c) the nature of the business of the energy supply company.

(3) The energy administrator must, as soon as reasonably practicable after the date of the esc administration order, give notice of the appointment—
  (a) if the application for the esc administration order was made by the Secretary of State, to GEMA;
  (b) if the application for the esc administration order was made by GEMA, to the Secretary of State;
  (c) if a receiver or an administrative receiver has been appointed, to that person;
  (d) if there is pending a petition for the winding up of the energy supply company, to the petitioner (and to the provisional liquidator, if any);
  (e) to any person who has applied to the court for an administration order under Schedule B1 to the 1986 Act, without the modifications made by Schedule 20 to the 2004 Act, in relation to the energy supply company;
  (f) to any enforcement officer who, to the energy administrator's knowledge, is charged with execution or other legal process against the energy supply company;
  (g) to any person who, to the energy administrator's knowledge, has distrained against the energy supply company or its property;
  (h) to any supervisor of a voluntary arrangement under Part I of the 1986 Act;
  (i) to any holder of a qualifying floating charge who, to the energy administrator's knowledge, has served notice in accordance with section 163 of the 2004 Act that the person is seeking to appoint an administrator; and
  (j) to any creditor who, to the energy administrator's knowledge, has served notice in accordance with section 164 of the 2004 Act of that person's intention to enforce that person's security over property of the energy supply company.

(4) Where, under a provision of Schedule B1 to the 1986 Act or these Rules, the energy administrator is required to send a notice of the appointment to any person other than the registrar of companies, the energy administrator must do so in Form ESCA4.

[7.1088]
15 Notice requiring statement of affairs

(1) In this Part "relevant person" shall have the meaning given to it in paragraph 47(3) of Schedule B1 to the 1986 Act.

(2) The energy administrator must send notice in Form ESCA5 to each relevant person whom the energy administrator determines appropriate requiring that person to prepare and submit a statement of the energy supply company's affairs.

(3) The notice must inform each of the relevant persons—
  (a) of the names and addresses of all others (if any) to whom the same notice has been sent;
  (b) of the time within which the statement must be delivered;
  (c) of the effect of paragraph 48(4) of Schedule B1 to the 1986 Act (penalty for non-compliance); and
  (d) of the application to that person, and to each other relevant person, of section 235 of the 1986 Act (duty to provide information, and to attend on the energy administrator, if required).

(4) The energy administrator must furnish each relevant person to whom the energy administrator has sent notice in Form ESCA5 with the forms required for the preparation of the statement of affairs.

[7.1089]
16 Verification and filing

(1) The statement of the energy supply company's affairs must be in Form ESCA6, contain all the particulars required by that form and be verified by a statement of truth by the relevant person.

(2) The energy administrator may require any relevant person to submit a statement of concurrence in Form ESCA7 stating that the person concurs in the statement of affairs. Where the energy administrator does so, the energy administrator must inform the person making the statement of affairs of that fact.

(3) The statement of affairs must be delivered by the relevant person making the statement of truth, together with a copy, to the energy administrator. The relevant person must also deliver a copy of the statement of affairs to all those persons whom the energy administrator has required to make a statement of concurrence.

(4) A person required to submit a statement of concurrence must do so before the end of the period of 5 business days (or such other period as the energy administrator may agree) beginning with the day on which the statement of affairs being concurred with is received by that person.

(5) A statement of concurrence may be qualified in respect of matters dealt with in the statement of affairs, where the maker of the statement of concurrence is not in agreement with the relevant person, or that person considers the statement of affairs to be erroneous or misleading, or that person is without the direct knowledge necessary for concurring with it.

(6) Every statement of concurrence must be verified by a statement of truth and be delivered to the energy administrator by the person who makes it, together with a copy of it.

(7) Subject to Rule 17, the energy administrator must as soon as reasonably practicable deliver to the registrar of companies a copy of the statement of affairs and any statement of concurrence.

[7.1090]
17 Limited disclosure

(1) Where the energy administrator thinks that it would prejudice the conduct of the energy supply company administration or might reasonably be expected to lead to violence against any person for the whole or part of the statement of the energy supply company's affairs to be disclosed, the energy administrator may apply to the court for an order of limited disclosure in respect of the statement, or any specified part of it.

(2) The court may, on such application, order that the statement or, as the case may be, the specified part of it, must not be delivered to the registrar of companies.

(3) The energy administrator must as soon as reasonably practicable deliver to the registrar of companies a copy of the order and the statement of affairs (to the extent provided by the order) and any statement of concurrence.

(4) If a creditor seeks disclosure of a statement of affairs or a specified part of it in relation to which an order has been made under this Rule, the creditor may apply to the court for an order that the energy administrator disclose it or a specified part of it. The application must be supported by written evidence in the form of a witness statement.

(5) The applicant must give the energy administrator notice of the application at least 3 business days before the hearing.

(6) The court may make any order for disclosure subject to any conditions as to confidentiality, duration, the scope of the order in the event of any change of circumstances, or other matters as it sees just.

(7) If there is a material change in circumstances rendering the limit on disclosure or any part of it unnecessary, the energy administrator must, as soon as reasonably practicable after the change, apply to the court for the order or any part of it to be rescinded.

(8) The energy administrator must, as soon as reasonably practicable after the making of an order under paragraph (7), deliver to the registrar of companies a copy of the statement of affairs to the extent provided by the order.

(9) When the statement of affairs is filed in accordance with paragraph (8), the energy administrator must, where the energy administrator has sent a statement of proposals under paragraph 49 of Schedule B1 to the 1986 Act, provide the creditors with a copy of the statement of affairs as filed, or a summary thereof.

(10) The provisions of Part 31 of the CPR shall not apply to an application under this Rule.

[7.1091]
18 Release from duty to submit statement of affairs; extension of time

(1) The power of the energy administrator under paragraph 48(2) of Schedule B1 to the 1986 Act to give a release from the obligation imposed by paragraph 47(1) of Schedule B1 to the 1986 Act, or to grant an extension of time, may be exercised at the energy administrator's own discretion, or at the request of any relevant person.

(2) A relevant person may, if that person requests a release or extension of time and it is refused by the energy administrator, apply to the court for it.

(3) The court may, if it thinks that no sufficient cause is shown for the application, dismiss it without a hearing but it must not do so without giving the relevant person at least 5 business days' notice, upon receipt of which the relevant person may request the court to list the application for a without notice hearing. If the application is not dismissed, the court must fix a venue for it to be heard, and give notice to the relevant person accordingly.

(4) The relevant person must, at least 14 days before the hearing, send to the energy administrator a notice stating the venue and accompanied by a copy of the application and of any evidence which the relevant person intends to adduce in support of it.

(5) The energy administrator may appear and be heard on the application and, whether or not the energy administrator appears, the energy administrator may file a written report of any matters which the energy administrator considers ought to be drawn to the court's attention. If such a report is filed, a copy of it must be sent by the energy administrator to the relevant person, not later than 5 business days before the hearing.

(6) Sealed copies of any order made on the application must be sent by the court to the relevant person and the energy administrator.

(7) On any application under this Rule the relevant person's costs must be paid in any event by the relevant person and, unless the court otherwise orders, no allowance towards them shall be made as an expense of the energy supply company administration.

[7.1092]

19 Expenses of statement of affairs

(1) A relevant person making the statement of affairs of the energy supply company or a statement of concurrence must be allowed, and paid by the energy administrator as an expense of the energy supply company administration, any expenses incurred by the relevant person in so doing which the energy administrator considers reasonable.

(2) Any decision by the energy administrator under this Rule is subject to appeal to the court.

(3) Nothing in this Rule relieves a relevant person of any obligation with respect to the preparation, verification and submission of the statement of affairs, or to the provision of information to the energy administrator.

[7.1093]

20 Energy administrator's proposals

(1) The energy administrator must, under paragraph 49 of Schedule B1 to the 1986 Act, make a statement and deliver it to the registrar of companies.

(2) The statement must include, in addition to those matters set out in paragraph 49 of Schedule B1 to the 1986 Act—

- (a) details of the court where the proceedings are and the relevant court reference number;
- (b) the full name, registered address, registered number and any other trading names of the energy supply company;
- (c) details relating to the energy administrator's appointment, including the date of appointment and whether the application was made by the Secretary of State or GEMA and, where there are joint energy administrators, details of the matters set out in section 158(5) of the 2004 Act;
- (d) the names of the directors and secretary of the energy supply company and details of any shareholdings in the energy supply company they may have;
- (e) an account of the circumstances giving rise to the appointment of the energy administrator;
- (f) if a statement of the energy supply company's affairs has been submitted, a copy or summary of it, with the energy administrator's comments, if any;
- (g) if an order limiting the disclosure of the statement of affairs (under Rule 17) has been made, a statement of that fact, as well as—
  - (i) details of who provided the statement of affairs;
  - (ii) the date of the order of limited disclosure; and
  - (iii) the details or summary of the details that are not subject to that order;
- (h) if a full statement of affairs is not provided, the names, addresses and debts of the creditors including details of any security held;
- (i) if no statement of affairs has been submitted, details of the financial position of the energy supply company at the latest practicable date (which must, unless the court otherwise orders, be a date not earlier than that on which the energy supply company entered energy supply company administration), a list of the energy supply company's creditors including their names, addresses and details of their debts, including any security held, and an explanation as to why there is no statement of affairs;
- (j) (except where the energy administrator proposes a voluntary arrangement in relation to the energy supply company and subject to paragraph (5))—
  - (i) to the best of the energy administrator's knowledge and belief—
    - (aa) an estimate of the value of the prescribed part (whether or not the energy administrator proposes to make an application to court under section 176A(5) of the 1986 Act or section 176A(3) of the 1986 Act applies); and
    - (bb) an estimate of the value of the energy supply company's net property; and
  - (ii) whether, and if so, why, the energy administrator proposes to make an application to court under section 176A(5) of the 1986 Act;
- (k) a statement complying with paragraph (3) of any pre-energy supply company administration costs charged or incurred by the energy administrator or, to the energy administrator's knowledge, by any other person qualified to act as an insolvency practitioner;
- (l) a statement (which must comply with paragraph (4) where that paragraph applies) of how it is envisaged the objective of the energy supply company administration will be achieved and how it is proposed that the energy supply company administration shall end;
- (m) the manner in which the affairs and business of the energy supply company—
  - (i) have, since the date of the energy administrator's appointment, been managed and financed, including, where any assets have been disposed of, the reasons for such disposals and the terms upon which such disposals were made; and

(ii) will continue to be managed and financed; and

(n) such other information (if any) as the energy administrator thinks necessary.

(3) A statement of pre-energy supply company administration costs complies with this paragraph if it includes—

(a) details of any agreement under which the fees were charged and expenses incurred, including the parties to the agreement and the date on which the agreement was made;

(b) details of the work done for which the fees were charged and expenses incurred;

(c) an explanation of why the work was done before the energy supply company entered energy supply company administration and how it would further the achievement of the objective of the energy supply company administration;

(d) a statement of the amount of the pre-energy supply company administration costs, setting out separately—

(i) the fees charged by the energy administrator;

(ii) the expenses incurred by the energy administrator;

(iii) the fees charged (to the energy administrator's knowledge) by any other person qualified to act as an insolvency practitioner (and, if more than one, by each separately); and

(iv) the expenses incurred (to the energy administrator's knowledge) by any other person qualified to act as an insolvency practitioner (and, if more than one, by each separately);

(e) a statement of the amounts of pre-energy supply company administration costs which have already been paid (set out separately as under sub-paragraph (d));

(f) the identity of the person who made the payment or, if more than one person made the payment, the identity of each such person and of the amounts paid by each such person (set out separately as under sub-paragraph (d));

(g) a statement of the amounts of unpaid pre-energy supply company administration costs (set out separately as under paragraph (d)); and

(h) a statement that the payment of unpaid pre-energy supply company administration costs as an expense of the energy supply company administration is subject to approval under Rule 37.

(4) This paragraph applies where it is proposed that the energy supply company administration will end by the energy supply company moving to a creditors' voluntary liquidation; and in that case, the statement required by paragraph (2)(l) must include—

(a) details of the proposed liquidator;

(b) where applicable, the declaration required by section 231 of the 1986 Act; and

(c) a statement that the creditors may nominate a different person as liquidator in accordance with paragraph 83(7) of Schedule B1 to the Insolvency Act 1986 and Rule 81(2).

(5) Nothing in paragraph (2)(j) is to be taken as requiring any such estimate to include any information, the disclosure of which could seriously prejudice the commercial interests of the energy supply company. If such information is excluded from the calculation the estimate must be accompanied by a statement to that effect.

(6) Where the court orders, upon an application by the energy administrator under paragraph 107 of Schedule B1 to the 1986 Act, an extension of the period of time in paragraph 49(5) of Schedule B1 to the 1986 Act, the energy administrator must as soon as reasonably practicable after the making of the order—

(a) notify in Form ESCA8 every creditor of the energy supply company and every member of the energy supply company of whose address (in either case) the energy administrator is aware; and

(b) deliver a copy of the information to the registrar of companies.

(7) Where the energy administrator wishes to publish a notice under paragraph 49(6) of Schedule B1 to the 1986 Act, the notice must be advertised in such manner as the energy administrator thinks fit.

(8) In addition to the standard contents, the notice under paragraph (7) must state—

(a) that members can write for a copy of the statement of proposals for achieving the purpose of energy supply company administration; and

(b) the address to which to write.

(9) This notice must be published as soon as reasonably practicable after the energy administrator sends the statement of proposals to the energy supply company's creditors but no later than 8 weeks (or such other period as may be agreed by the creditors or as the court may order) from the date that the energy supply company entered energy supply company administration.

[7.1094]

21 Limited disclosure of paragraph 49 of Schedule B1 to the 1986 Act statement

(1) Where the energy administrator thinks that it would prejudice the conduct of the energy supply company administration or might reasonably be expected to lead to violence against any person for any of the matters specified in Rule 20(2)(h) and (i) to be disclosed, the energy administrator may apply to the court for an order of limited disclosure in respect of any specified part of the statement under paragraph 49 of Schedule B1 to the 1986 Act.

(2) The court may, on such application, order that some or all of the specified part of the statement must not be delivered to the registrar of companies or to creditors or members of the energy supply company as otherwise required by paragraph 49(4) of Schedule B1 to the 1986 Act.

(3) The energy administrator must as soon as reasonably practicable send to the persons specified in paragraph 49(4) to Schedule B1 to the 1986 Act the statement under paragraph 49 of Schedule B1 to the 1986 Act (to the extent provided by the order) and an indication of the nature of the matter in relation to which the order was made.

(4) The energy administrator must also deliver a copy of the order to the registrar of companies.

(5) A creditor who seeks disclosure of a part of a statement under paragraph 49 of Schedule B1 to the 1986 Act in relation to which an order has been made under this Rule may apply to the court for an order that the energy administrator disclose it. The application must be supported by written evidence in the form of a witness statement.

(6) The applicant must give the energy administrator notice of the application at least 3 business days before the hearing.

(7) The court may make any order for disclosure subject to any conditions as to confidentiality, duration, the scope of the order in the event of any change of circumstances, or other matters as it sees just.

(8) If there is a material change in circumstances rendering the limit on disclosure or any part of it unnecessary, the energy administrator must, as soon as reasonable practicable after the change, apply to the court for the order or any part of it to be rescinded.

(9) The energy administrator must, as soon as reasonably practicable after the making of an order under paragraph (8), send to the persons specified in paragraph 49(4) of Schedule B1 to the 1986 Act a copy of the statement under paragraph 49 of Schedule B1 to the 1986 Act to the extent provided by the order.

(10) The provisions of CPR Part 31 do not apply to an application under this Rule.

PART 4
MEETINGS AND REPORTS

CHAPTER 1 CREDITORS' MEETINGS

[7.1095]
22 Creditors' meetings generally

(1) This Rule applies to creditors' meetings summoned by the energy administrator under paragraph 62 of Schedule B1 to the 1986 Act.

(2) Notice of a creditors' meeting must be in Form ESCA9.

(3) In fixing the venue for the meeting, the energy administrator must have regard to the convenience of creditors and the meeting must be summoned for commencement between 10.00 and 16.00 on a business day, unless the court otherwise directs.

(4) Subject to paragraphs (6) and (7), at least 14 days' notice of the meeting must be given to all creditors who are known to the energy administrator and had claims against the energy supply company at the date when the energy supply company entered energy supply company administration unless that creditor has subsequently been paid in full, and the notice must—

- (a) specify the purpose of the meeting;
- (b) contain a statement of the effect of Rule 25 (entitlement to vote); and
- (c) contain the forms of proxy.

(5) As soon as reasonably practicable after notice of the meeting has been given, the energy administrator must have gazetted a notice which, in addition to the standard contents, must state—

- (a) that a creditors' meeting is to take place;
- (b) the venue fixed for the meeting;
- (c) the purpose of the meeting; and
- (d) a statement of the effect of Rule 25 (entitlement to vote).

(6) If within 30 minutes from the time fixed for the commencement of the meeting there is no person present to act as chair, the meeting stands adjourned to the same time and place in the following week or, if that is not a business day, the business day immediately following.

(7) If within 30 minutes from the time fixed for the commencement of the meeting those persons attending the meeting do not constitute a quorum, the chair may adjourn the meeting to such time and place as the chair may appoint.

(8) Once only in the course of the meeting the chair may, without an adjournment, declare the meeting suspended for a period up to 1 hour.

(9) The chair may, and must if the meeting so resolves, adjourn the meeting to such time and place as seems to the chair to be appropriate in the circumstances.

(10) An adjournment under paragraph (9) must not be for a period of more than 14 days, subject to a direction of the court.

(11) If there are subsequently further adjournments, the final adjournment must not be to a day later than 14 days after the date on which the meeting was originally held, subject to a direction of the court.

(12) Where a meeting is adjourned under this Rule, proofs and proxies may be used if lodged at any time up to 12.00 hours on the business day immediately before the adjourned meeting.

(13) Paragraph (3) applies with regard to the venue fixed for a meeting adjourned under this Rule.

[7.1096]
23 The chair at meetings

(1) At any meeting of creditors summoned by the energy administrator, either the energy administrator shall be chair, or a person nominated by the energy administrator in writing to act in the energy administrator's place.

(2) A person so nominated must be either—

(a) one who is qualified to act as an insolvency practitioner in relation to the energy supply company; or
(b) an employee of the energy administrator or the energy administrator's firm who is experienced in insolvency matters.

(3) Where the chair holds a proxy which includes a requirement to vote for a particular resolution and no other person proposes that resolution—
(a) the chair must propose it unless the chair considers that there is good reason for not doing so; and
(b) if the chair does not propose it, the chair must as soon as reasonably practicable after the meeting notify the principal of the reason why not.

[7.1097]
24 Creditors' meeting for nomination of alternative liquidator

(1) Where under Rules 20(4) or 32(2)(g) the energy administrator has proposed that the energy supply company enter creditors' voluntary liquidation once the energy supply company administration has ended, the energy administrator must, in the circumstances detailed in paragraph (2), call a meeting of creditors for the purpose of nominating a person other than the person named as proposed liquidator in the energy administrator's proposals or revised proposals.

(2) The energy administrator must call a meeting of creditors where such a meeting is requested by creditors of the energy supply company whose debts amount to at least 10 per cent of the total debts of the energy supply company.

(3) The request for a creditors' meeting for the purpose set out in paragraph (1) must be in Form ESCA10. A request for such a meeting must be made within 8 business days of the date on which the energy administrator's statement of proposals is sent out.

(4) A request under this Rule must include—
(a) a list of creditors concurring with the request, showing the amounts of the respective debts in the energy supply company administration; and
(b) from each creditor concurring, written confirmation of the creditor's concurrence,
but this paragraph does not apply if the requesting creditor's debt is alone sufficient without the concurrence of other creditors.

(5) A meeting requested under this Rule must be held within 28 days of the energy administrator's receipt of the notice requesting the meeting.

[7.1098]
25 Entitlement to vote

(1) Subject as follows, at a meeting of creditors in energy supply company administration proceedings a person is entitled to vote only if—
(a) the person has given to the energy administrator, not later than 12.00 hours on the business day before the day fixed for the meeting, details in writing of the debt which the person claims to be due to that person from the energy supply company;
(b) the claim has been duly admitted under Rule 26 or this Rule; and
(c) there has been lodged with the energy administrator any proxy which the person intends to be used on the person's behalf,
and details of the debt must include any calculation for the purposes of Rules 27 to 29.

(2) The chair of the meeting may allow a creditor to vote, notwithstanding that the creditor has failed to comply with paragraph (1)(a), if satisfied that the failure was due to circumstances beyond the creditor's control.

(3) The chair of the meeting may call for any document or other evidence to be produced to the chair, where the chair thinks it necessary for the purpose of substantiating the whole or any part of the claim.

(4) Votes are calculated according to the amount of a creditor's claim as at the date on which the energy supply company entered energy supply company administration, less any payments that have been made to the creditor after that date in respect of the claim and any adjustment by way of set-off in accordance with Rule 54 as if that Rule were applied on the date that the votes are counted.

(5) A creditor shall not vote in respect of a debt for an unliquidated amount, or any debt whose value is not ascertained, except where the chair agrees to put upon the debt an estimated minimum value for the purpose of entitlement to vote and admits the claim for that purpose.

(6) No vote shall be cast by virtue of a claim more than once on any resolution put to the meeting.

[7.1099]
26 Admission and rejection of claims

(1) At any creditors' meeting the chair has power to admit or reject a creditor's claim for the purpose of the creditor's entitlement to vote; and the power is exercisable with respect to the whole or any part of the claim.

(2) The chair's decision under this Rule, or in respect of any matter arising under Rule 25, is subject to appeal to the court by any creditor.

(3) If the chair is in doubt whether a claim should be admitted or rejected, the chair must mark it as objected to and allow the creditor to vote, subject to the creditor's vote being subsequently declared invalid if the objection to the claim is sustained.

(4) If on appeal the chair's decision is reversed or varied, or a creditor's vote is declared invalid, the court may order that another meeting be summoned, or make such other order as it thinks just.

(5) An application to the court by way of appeal under this Rule against a decision of the chair must be made not later than 21 days after the date of the meeting.

(6) Neither the energy administrator nor any person nominated by the energy administrator to be chair is personally liable for costs incurred by any person in respect of an appeal to the court under this Rule, unless the court makes an order to that effect.

[7.1100]
27 Secured creditors

At a meeting of creditors a secured creditor is entitled to vote only in respect of the balance (if any) of the creditor's debt after deducting the value of the creditor's security as estimated by the creditor.

[7.1101]
28 Holders of negotiable instruments

A creditor must not vote in respect of a debt on, or secured by, a current bill of exchange or promissory note, unless the creditor is willing—

(a) to treat the liability to the creditor on the bill or note of every person who is liable on it antecedently to the energy supply company, and against whom a bankruptcy order has not been made (or, in the case of an energy supply company, which has not gone into liquidation), as a security in the creditor's hands; and

(b) to estimate the value of the security and, for the purpose of the creditor's entitlement to vote (but not for dividend), to deduct it from the creditor's claim.

[7.1102]
29 Hire-purchase, conditional sale and chattel leasing agreements

(1) Subject as follows, an owner of goods under a hire-purchase or chattel leasing agreement, or a seller of goods under a conditional sale agreement, is entitled to vote in respect of the amount of the debt due and payable to the owner by the energy supply company on the date that the energy supply company entered energy supply company administration.

(2) In calculating the amount of any debt for this purpose, no account shall be taken of any amount attributable to the exercise of any right under the relevant agreement, so far as the right has become exercisable solely by virtue of the making of an energy supply company administration application or any matter arising as a consequence, or of the energy supply company entering energy supply company administration.

[7.1103]
30 Resolutions

(1) Subject as follows, at a creditors' meeting in energy supply company administration proceedings, a resolution is passed when a majority (in value) of those present and voting, in person or by proxy, have voted in favour of it.

(2) Any resolution is invalid if those voting against it include more than half in value of the creditors to whom notice of the meeting was sent and who are not, to the best of the chair's belief, persons connected with the energy supply company.

(3) In the case of a resolution for the nomination of a person to act as liquidator once the energy supply company administration has ended—

(a) subject to paragraph (4), if on any vote there are two persons put forward by creditors for nomination as liquidator, the person who obtains the most support is nominated as liquidator;

(b) if there are three or more persons put forward by creditors for nomination as liquidator, and one of them has a clear majority over both or all the others together, that one is nominated as liquidator;

(c) in any other case, the chair of the meeting must continue to take votes (disregarding at each vote any person who has withdrawn and, if no person has withdrawn, the person who obtained the least support last time), until a clear majority is obtained for any one person.

(4) The support referred to in paragraph (3)(a) must represent a majority in value of all those present (in person or by proxy) at the meeting and entitled to vote.

(5) Where on such a resolution no person is nominated as liquidator, the person named as proposed liquidator in the energy administrator's proposals or revised proposals shall be the liquidator once the energy supply company administration has ended.

(6) The chair may at any time put to the meeting a resolution for the joint appointment of any two or more persons put forward by creditors for nomination as liquidator.

(7) In this Rule "connected with the energy supply company" has the same meaning as "connected with a company" in section 249 of the 1986 Act.

[7.1104]
31 Minutes

(1) The chair of the meeting must cause minutes of its proceedings to be kept.

(2) The minutes must be authenticated by the chair, and be retained by the chair as part of the records of the energy supply company administration.

(3) The chair must also cause to be made up and kept a list of all the creditors who attended the meeting.

(4) The minutes must include—

(a) a list of the names of creditors who attended (personally or by proxy) and their claims; and
(b) a record of every resolution passed.

[7.1105]
32 Revision of the energy administrator's proposals

(1) The energy administrator must, as soon as reasonably practicable, under paragraph 54 of Schedule B1 to the 1986 Act, make a statement setting out the proposed revisions to the energy administrator's proposals and send it to all those to whom the energy administrator is required to send a copy of the revised proposals, attached to Form ESCA11. The energy administrator must also deliver a copy of the statement of proposed revisions to the registrar of companies.

(2) The statement of revised proposals must include—
(a) details of the court where the proceedings are and the relevant court reference number;
(b) the full name, registered address, registered number and any other trading names of the energy supply company;
(c) details relating to the energy administrator's appointment, including the date of appointment and whether the energy supply company administration application was made by the Secretary of State or GEMA;
(d) the names of the directors and secretary of the energy supply company and details of any shareholdings in the energy supply company they may have;
(e) a summary of the initial proposals and the reason(s) for proposing a revision;
(f) details of the proposed revision including details of the energy administrator's assessment of the likely impact of the proposed revision upon creditors generally or upon each class of creditors (as the case may be);
(g) where a proposed revision relates to the ending of the energy supply company administration by a creditors' voluntary liquidation and the nomination of a person to be the proposed liquidator of the energy supply company—
(i) details of the proposed liquidator;
(ii) where applicable, the declaration required by section 231 of the 1986 Act;
(iii) a statement that the creditors may nominate a different person as liquidator in accordance with paragraph 83(7)(a) of Schedule B1 to the 1986 Act and Rule 81(2); and
(h) any other information that the energy administrator thinks necessary.

(3) Subject to paragraph 54(4) of Schedule B1 to the 1986 Act, within 5 business days of sending out the statement in paragraph (1) above, the energy administrator must send a copy of the statement to every member of the energy supply company.

(4) Any notice to be published by the energy administrator acting under paragraph 54(3) of Schedule B1 to the 1986 Act must be advertised in such manner as the energy administrator thinks fit.

(5) The notice must be published as soon as reasonably practicable after the energy administrator sends the statement to the creditors and in addition to the standard contents must state—
(a) that members can write for a copy of the statement of revised proposals for the energy supply company administration; and
(b) the address to which to write.

[7.1106]
33 Reports

(1) The energy administrator must prepare a report (the "progress report") which includes—
(a) details of the court where the proceedings are and the relevant court reference number;
(b) full details of the energy supply company's name, address of registered office and registered number;
(c) full details of the energy administrator's name and address, date of appointment and name and address of the applicant for the energy supply company administration application including any changes in office-holder, and, in the case of joint energy administrators, their functions as set out in the statement made for the purposes of section 158(5) of the 2004 Act;
(d) details of progress during the period of the report, including a receipts and payments account (as detailed in paragraph (2) below);
(e) details of any assets that remain to be realised; and
(f) any other relevant information for the creditors.

(2) A receipts and payments account must state what assets of the energy supply company have been realised, for what value, and what payments have been made to creditors or others. The account is to be in the form of an abstract showing receipts and payments during the period of the report and where the energy administrator has ceased to act, the receipts and payments account must include a statement as to the amount paid to unsecured creditors by virtue of the application of section 176A of the 1986 Act (prescribed part).

(3) The progress report must cover—
(a) the period of 6 months commencing on the date that the energy supply company entered energy supply company administration, and every subsequent period of 6 months; and
(b) when the energy administrator ceases to act, any period from the date of the previous report, if any, and from the date that the energy supply company entered energy supply company administration if there is no previous report, until the time that the energy administrator ceases to act.

(4) The energy administrator must send a copy of the progress report, attached to Form ESCA12, within 1 month of the end of the period covered by the report, to—

(a) the Secretary of State;
(b) GEMA;
(c) the creditors; and
(d) the court,

and must deliver a copy to the registrar of companies, but this rule does not apply when the period covered by the report is that of a final progress report under Rule 78.

(5) The court may, on the energy administrator's application, extend the period of 1 month mentioned in paragraph (4) above, or make such other order in respect of the content of the report as it thinks fit.

(6) It is an offence for the energy administrator to fail to comply with this Rule.

CHAPTER 2 COMPANY MEETINGS

[7.1107]
34 Venue and conduct of company meeting

(1) Where the energy administrator summons a meeting of members of the energy supply company, the energy administrator must fix a venue for it having regard to their convenience.

(2) The chair of the meeting shall be the energy administrator or a person nominated by the energy administrator in writing to act in the energy administrator's place.

(3) A person so nominated must be either—
(a) one who is qualified to act as an insolvency practitioner in relation to the energy supply company, or
(b) an employee of the energy administrator or the energy administrator's firm who is experienced in insolvency matters.

(4) If within 30 minutes from the time fixed for commencement of the meeting there is no person present to act as chair, the meeting stands adjourned to the same time and place in the following week or, if that day is not a business day, to the business day immediately following.

(5) Subject to anything to the contrary in the 1986 Act and these Rules, the meeting must be summoned and conducted—
(a) in the case of an energy supply company incorporated—
(i) in England and Wales, or
(ii) outside the United Kingdom other than in an EEA state,
in accordance with the law of England and Wales, including any applicable provision in or made under the Companies Act;
(b) in the case of an energy supply company incorporated in an EEA state other than the United Kingdom, in accordance with the law of the state applicable to meetings of the company.

(6) The chair of the meeting must cause minutes of its proceedings to be entered in the energy supply company's minute book.

PART 5
DISPOSAL OF CHARGED PROPERTY

[7.1108]
35 Authority to dispose of property

(1) The following applies where the energy administrator applies to the court under paragraphs 71 or 72 of Schedule B1 to the 1986 Act for authority to dispose of property of the energy supply company which is subject to a security (other than a floating charge), or goods in the possession of the energy supply company under a hire purchase agreement.

(2) The court must fix a venue for the hearing of the application, and the energy administrator must as soon as reasonably practicable give notice of the venue to the person who is the holder of the security or, as the case may be, the owner under the agreement.

(3) If an order is made under paragraphs 71 or 72 of Schedule B1 to the 1986 Act the court must send two sealed copies to the energy administrator.

(4) The energy administrator must send one of them to that person who is the holder of the security or owner under the agreement.

(5) The energy administrator must deliver a copy of the order to the registrar of companies.

PART 6
EXPENSES OF THE ENERGY SUPPLY COMPANY ADMINISTRATION

[7.1109]
36 Priority of expenses of energy supply company administration

(1) The expenses of the energy supply company administration are payable in the following order of priority—
(a) expenses properly incurred by the energy administrator in performing the energy administrator's functions in the energy supply company administration of the energy supply company, except for those expenses referred to in sub-paragraph (g);
(b) the cost of any security provided by the energy administrator in accordance with the 1986 Act or these Rules;
(c) the costs of the applicant and any person appearing on the hearing of the application;

(d) any amount payable to a person employed or authorised, under Part 3 of these Rules, to assist in the preparation of a statement of affairs or statement of concurrence;

(e) any allowance made, by the order of the court, towards costs on an application for release from the obligation to submit a statement of affairs or statement of concurrence;

(f) any necessary disbursements by the energy administrator in the course of the energy supply company administration (but not including any payment of corporation tax in circumstances referred to in sub-paragraph (i) below);

(g) the remuneration of any person who has been employed by the energy administrator to perform any services for the energy supply company, as required or authorised under the 1986 Act, the 2004 Act or these Rules;

(h) the remuneration of the energy administrator fixed by the court under Part 8 of these Rules and unpaid pre-energy supply company administration costs approved under Rule 37;

(i) the amount of any corporation tax on chargeable gains accruing on the realisation of any asset of the energy supply company (without regard to whether the realisation is effected by the energy administrator, a secured creditor, or a receiver or manager appointed to deal with a security).

(2) The priorities laid down by paragraph (1) of this Rule are subject to the power of the court to make orders under paragraph (3) of this Rule where the assets are insufficient to satisfy the liabilities.

(3) The court may, in the event of the assets being insufficient to satisfy the liabilities, make an order as to the payment out of the assets of the expenses incurred in the energy supply company administration in such order of priority as the court thinks just.

(4) For the purposes of paragraph 99(3) of Schedule B1 to the 1986 Act, the former energy administrator's remuneration and expenses shall comprise all those items set out in paragraph (1) of this Rule.

[7.1110]
37 Pre-energy supply company administration costs

Where the energy administrator has made a statement of pre-energy supply company administration costs under Rule 20(2)(k), the energy administrator (where the costs consist of fees charged or expenses incurred by the energy administrator) or other insolvency practitioner (where the costs consist of fees charged or expenses incurred by that practitioner) must, before paying such costs, apply to the court for a determination of whether and to what extent the unpaid pre-energy supply company administration costs are approved for payment.

PART 7
DISTRIBUTION TO CREDITORS

CHAPTER 1 APPLICATION OF PART AND GENERAL

[7.1111]
38 Distribution to creditors generally

(1) This Part applies where the energy administrator makes, or proposes to make, a distribution to any class of creditors other than secured creditors. Where the distribution is to a particular class of creditors, references in this Part to creditors shall, in so far as the context requires, be a reference to that class of creditors only.

(2) The energy administrator must give notice to the creditors of the energy administrator's intention to declare and distribute a dividend in accordance with Rule 64.

(3) Where it is intended that the distribution is to be a sole or final dividend, the energy administrator must, after the date specified in the notice referred to in paragraph (2)—

(a) defray any items payable in accordance with the provisions of paragraph 99 of Schedule B1 to the 1986 Act;

(b) defray any amounts (including any debts or liabilities and the energy administrator's own remuneration and expenses) which would, if the energy administrator were to cease to be the energy administrator of the energy supply company, be payable out of the property of which the energy administrator had custody or control in accordance with the provisions of paragraph 99 of Schedule B1 to the 1986 Act; and

(c) declare and distribute that dividend without regard to the claim of any person in respect of a debt not already proved.

(4) The court may, on the application of any person, postpone the date specified in the notice.

[7.1112]
39 Debts of insolvent energy supply company to rank equally

Debts other than preferential debts rank equally between themselves in the energy supply company administration and, after the preferential debts, must be paid in full unless the assets are insufficient for meeting them, in which case they abate in equal proportions between themselves.

[7.1113]
40 Supplementary provisions as to dividend

(1) In the calculation and distribution of a dividend the energy administrator must make provision for—

(a) any debts which appear to the energy administrator to be due to persons who, by reason of the distance of their place of residence, may not have had sufficient time to tender and establish their proofs;

(b) any debts which are the subject of claims which have not yet been determined; and
(c) disputed proofs and claims.

(2) A creditor who has not proved the creditor's debt before the declaration of any dividend is not entitled to disturb, by reason that the creditor has not participated in it, the distribution of that dividend or any other dividend declared before the creditor's debt was proved, but—

(a) when the creditor has proved that debt the creditor is entitled to be paid, out of any money for the time being available for the payment of any further dividend, any dividend or dividends which the creditor has failed to receive; and
(b) any dividends payable under sub-paragraph (a) must be paid before the money is applied to the payment of any such further dividend.

(3) No action lies against the energy administrator for a dividend, but if the energy administrator refuses to pay a dividend the court may, if it thinks just, order the energy administrator to pay it and also to pay, out of the energy administrator's own money—

(a) interest on the dividend, at the rate for the time being specified in section 17 of the Judgments Act 1838, from the time when it was withheld; and
(b) the costs of the proceedings in which the order to pay is made.

[7.1114]
41 Division of unsold assets

(1) The energy administrator may, with the permission of the creditors, divide in its existing form amongst the energy supply company's creditors, according to its estimated value, any property which from its peculiar nature or other special circumstances cannot be readily or advantageously sold.

(2) The energy administrator must—

(a) in the receipts and payments account included in the final progress report under Chapter 1 of Part 4, state the estimated value of the property divided amongst the creditors of the energy supply company during the period to which the report relates, and
(b) as a note to the account, provide details of the basis of the valuation.

CHAPTER 2 MACHINERY OF PROVING A DEBT

[7.1115]
42 Proving a debt

(1) A person claiming to be a creditor of the energy supply company and wishing to recover the person's debt in whole or part must (subject to any order of the court to the contrary) submit the person's claim in writing to the energy administrator.

(2) A creditor who claims is referred to as "proving" for their debt and a document by which the creditor seeks to establish their claim is the creditor's "proof".

(3) Subject to the next paragraph, a proof must—

(a) be made out by, or under the direction of, the creditor and authenticated by the creditor or a person authorised in that behalf; and
(b) state the following matters—
    (i) the creditor's name and address;
    (ii) if the creditor is a company, its registered number;
    (iii) the total amount of the creditor's claim (including value added tax) as at the date on which the energy supply company entered energy supply company administration, less any payments made after that date in respect of the claim, any deduction under Rule 53 and any adjustment by way of set off in accordance with Rule 54;
    (iv) whether or not the claim includes outstanding uncapitalised interest;
    (v) particulars of how and when the debt was incurred by the energy supply company;
    (vi) particulars of any security held, the date on which it was given and the value which the creditor puts on it;
    (vii) details of any reservation of title in respect of goods to which the debt refers; and
    (viii) the name, address and authority of the person signing the proof (if a person other than the creditor).

(4) There must be specified in the proof details of any documents by reference to which the debt can be substantiated; but (subject as follows) it is not essential that such document be attached to the proof or submitted with it.

(5) The energy administrator may call for any document or other evidence to be produced to the energy administrator, where the energy administrator thinks it necessary for the purpose of substantiating the whole or any part of the claim made in the proof.

[7.1116]
43 Costs of proving

Unless the court otherwise orders—

(a) every creditor bears the cost of proving the creditor's own debt, including costs incurred in providing documents or evidence under Rule 42(5); and
(b) costs incurred by the energy administrator in estimating the quantum of a debt under Rule 50 are payable out of the assets as an expense of the energy supply company administration.

[7.1117]
44 Energy administrator to allow inspection of proofs

The energy administrator must, so long as proofs lodged with the energy administrator are in the energy administrator's hands, allow them to be inspected, at all reasonable times on any business day, by any of the following persons—

(a) any creditor who has submitted a proof of debt (unless the creditor's proof has been wholly rejected for purposes of dividend or otherwise);
(b) any contributory of the energy supply company; and
(c) any person acting on behalf of either of the above.

[7.1118]
45 New energy administrator appointed

(1) If a new energy administrator is appointed in place of another, the former energy administrator must as soon as reasonably practicable transmit to the new energy administrator all proofs which the former energy administrator has received, together with an itemised list of them.

(2) The new energy administrator must authenticate the list by way of receipt for the proofs, and return it to the former energy administrator.

(3) From then on, all proofs of debt must be sent to and retained by the new energy administrator.

[7.1119]
46 Admission and rejection of proofs for dividend

(1) A proof may be admitted for dividend either for the whole amount claimed by the creditor, or for part of that amount.

(2) If the energy administrator rejects a proof in whole or in part, the energy administrator must prepare a written statement of the energy administrator's reasons for doing so, and send it as soon as reasonably practicable to the creditor.

[7.1120]
47 Appeal against decision on proof

(1) If a creditor is dissatisfied with the energy administrator's decision with respect to the creditor's proof (including any decision on the question of preference), the creditor may apply to the court for the decision to be reversed or varied. The application must be made within 21 days of the creditor receiving the statement sent under Rule 46(2).

(2) A member or any other creditor may, if dissatisfied with the energy administrator's decision admitting or rejecting the whole or any part of a proof, make such an application within 21 days of becoming aware of the energy administrator's decision.

(3) Where application is made to the court under this Rule, the court must fix a venue for the application to be heard, notice of which must be sent by the applicant to the creditor who lodged the proof in question (if the applicant is not the creditor who lodged the proof) and the energy administrator.

(4) The energy administrator must, on receipt of the notice, file in court the relevant proof, together (if appropriate) with a copy of the statement sent under Rule 46(2).

(5) Where the application is made by a member, the court must not disallow the proof (in whole or in part) unless the member shows that there is (or would be but for the amount claimed in the proof), or that it is likely that there will be (or would be but for the amount claimed in the proof), a surplus of assets to which the energy supply company would be entitled.

(6) After the application has been heard and determined, the proof must, unless it has been wholly disallowed, be returned by the court to the energy administrator.

(7) The energy administrator is not personally liable for costs incurred by any person in respect of an application under this Rule unless the court otherwise orders.

[7.1121]
48 Withdrawal or variation of proof

A creditor's proof may at any time, by agreement between the creditor and the energy administrator, be withdrawn or varied as to the amount claimed.

[7.1122]
49 Expunging of proof by the court

(1) The court may expunge a proof or reduce the amount claimed—

(a) on the energy administrator's application, where the energy administrator thinks that the proof has been improperly admitted, or ought to be reduced; or
(b) on the application of a creditor, if the energy administrator declines to interfere in the matter.

(2) Where application is made to the court under this Rule, the court must fix a venue for the application to be heard, notice of which must be sent by the applicant—

(a) in the case of an application by the energy administrator, to the creditor who made the proof; and
(b) in the case of an application by a creditor, to the energy administrator and to the creditor who made the proof (if that creditor is not the applicant).

CHAPTER 3 QUANTIFICATION OF CLAIMS

[7.1123]
50 Estimate of quantum

(1) The energy administrator must estimate the value of any debt which, by reason of its being subject to any contingency or for any other reason, does not bear a certain value; and the energy administrator may revise any estimate previously made, if the energy administrator thinks fit by reference to any change of circumstances or to information becoming available.

(2) The energy administrator must inform the creditor as to the estimate under paragraph (1) and any revision of it.

(3) Where the value of a debt is estimated under this Rule, the amount provable in the energy supply company administration in the case of that debt is that of the estimate for the time being.

[7.1124]
51 Negotiable instruments, etc

Unless the energy administrator allows, a proof in respect of money owed on a bill of exchange, promissory note, cheque or other negotiable instrument or security cannot be admitted unless there is produced the instrument or security itself or a copy of it, certified by the creditor or the creditor's authorised representative to be a true copy.

[7.1125]
52 Secured creditors

(1) If a secured creditor realises the secured creditor's security, the secured creditor may prove for the balance of the secured creditor's debt, after deducting the amount realised.

(2) If a secured creditor voluntarily surrenders a security for the general benefit of creditors, the secured creditor may prove for the secured creditor's whole debt, as if it were unsecured.

[7.1126]
53 Discounts

There shall in every case be deducted from the claim all trade and other discounts which would have been available to the energy supply company but for its energy supply company administration except any discount for immediate, early or cash settlement.

[7.1127]
54 Mutual credits and set off

(1) This Rule applies where the energy administrator, being authorised to make the distribution in question, has pursuant to Rule 65, given notice that the energy administrator proposes to make it.

(2) In this Rule "mutual dealings" means mutual credits, mutual debts or other mutual dealings between the energy supply company and any creditor of the energy supply company proving or claiming to prove for a debt in the energy supply company administration but does not include—

- (a) any debt arising out of an obligation incurred after the energy supply company entered energy supply company administration;
- (b) any debt arising out of an obligation incurred at a time when the creditor had notice that—
  - (i) a meeting of creditors had been summoned under section 98 of the 1986 Act,
  - (ii) a petition for the winding up of the energy supply company was pending,
  - (iii) an application for an administration order under the 1986 Act was pending;
  - (iv) an application for an esc administration order was pending; or
  - (v) any person had given notice of intention to appoint an administrator under the 1986 Rules;
- (c) any debt which has been acquired by a creditor by assignment or otherwise, pursuant to an agreement between the creditor and any other party where that agreement was entered into—
  - (i) at a time when the creditor had notice that an application for an esc administration order was pending;
  - (ii) after the commencement of energy supply company administration,
  - (iii) at a time when the creditor had notice that a meeting of creditors had been summoned under section 98 of the 1986 Act, or
  - (iv) at a time when the creditor had notice that a winding up petition was pending, or
  - (v) at a time when the creditor had notice that an application for an administration order under the 1986 Act was pending.

(3) An account shall be taken as at the date of the notice referred to in paragraph (1) of what is due from each party to the other in respect of the mutual dealings and the sums due from one party shall be set off against the sums due from the other.

(4) A sum shall be regarded as being due to or from the energy supply company for the purposes of paragraph (3) whether—

- (a) it is payable at present or in the future;
- (b) the obligation by virtue of which it is payable is certain or contingent; or
- (c) its amount is fixed or liquidated, or is capable of being ascertained by fixed rules or as a matter of opinion.

(5) Rule 50 shall apply for the purposes of this Rule to any obligation to or from the energy supply company which, by virtue of its being subject to any contingency or for any other reason, does not bear a certain value.

(6) Rules 55 to 57 shall apply for the purposes of this Rule in relation to any sums due to the energy supply company which—

(a) are payable in a currency other than sterling;

(b) are of a periodical nature; or

(c) bear interest.

(7) Rule 75 shall apply for the purposes of this Rule to any sum due or from the energy supply company which is payable in the future.

(8) Only the balance (if any) of the account owed to the creditor is provable in the energy supply company administration.

(9) Alternatively the balance (if any) owed to the energy supply company shall be paid to the energy administrator as part of the assets except where all or part of the balance results from a contingent or prospective debt owed by the creditor and in such a case the balance (or that part of it which results from the contingent or prospective debt) must be paid if and when the debt becomes due and payable.

(10) In this Rule "obligation" means an obligation however arising, whether by virtue of an agreement, rule of law or otherwise.

[7.1128]
55 Debt in foreign currency

For the purpose of proving a debt incurred or payable in a currency other than sterling, the amount of the debt shall be converted into sterling at such rate as is agreed between the relevant creditor and the energy administrator or, where no agreement can be reached, as the court determines.

[7.1129]
56 Payments of a periodical nature

(1) In the case of rent and other payments of a periodical nature, the creditor may prove for any amounts due and unpaid up to the date when the energy supply company entered energy supply company administration.

(2) Where at that date any payment was accruing due, the creditor may prove for so much as would have fallen due at that date, if accruing from day to day.

[7.1130]
57 Interest

(1) Where a debt proved in the energy supply company administration bears interest, that interest is provable as part of the debt except in so far as it is payable in respect of any period after the energy supply company entered energy supply company administration.

(2) In the following circumstances the creditor's claim may include interest on the debt for periods before the energy supply company entered energy supply company administration, although not previously reserved or agreed.

(3) If the debt is due by virtue of a written instrument, and payable at a certain time, interest may be claimed for the period from that time to the date when the energy supply company entered energy supply company administration.

(4) If the debt is due otherwise, interest may only be claimed if, before that date, a demand for full payment of the debt was made in writing by or on behalf of the creditor, and notice given that interest would be payable from the date of the demand to the date of payment.

(5) Interest under paragraph (4) may only be claimed for the period from the date of the demand to that of the energy supply company's entering energy supply company administration and for all the purposes of the 1986 Act and these Rules shall be chargeable at a rate not exceeding that mentioned in paragraph (6).

(6) The rate of interest to be claimed under paragraphs (3) and (4) is the rate specified in section 17 of the Judgments Act 1838 on the date when the energy supply company entered energy supply company administration.

(7) Any surplus remaining after payment of the debts proved shall, before being applied for any purpose, be applied in paying interest on those debts in respect of the periods during which they have been outstanding since the energy supply company entered energy supply company administration.

(8) All interest payable under paragraph (7) ranks equally whether or not the debts on which it is payable rank equally.

(9) The rate of interest payable under paragraph (7) is whichever is the greater of the rate specified under paragraph (6) or the rate applicable to the debt apart from the energy supply company administration.

[7.1131]
58 Debt payable at future time

A creditor may prove for a debt of which payment was not yet due on the date when the energy supply company entered energy supply company administration, subject to Rule 75 (adjustment of dividend where payment made before time).

[7.1132]
59 Value of security

(1) A secured creditor may, with the agreement of the energy administrator or the permission of the court, at any time alter the value which the secured creditor's proof of debt puts upon the secured creditor's security.

(2) However, if a secured creditor has voted in respect of the unsecured balance of the secured creditor's debt the secured creditor may re-value the secured creditor's security only with permission of the court.

[7.1133]
60 Surrender for non-disclosure

(1) If a secured creditor omits to disclose a security in the secured creditor's proof of debt, the secured creditor must surrender that security for the general benefit of creditors, unless the court, on application by the secured creditor, relieves the secured creditor from the effect of this Rule on the ground that the omission was inadvertent or the result of honest mistake.

(2) If the court grants that relief, it may require or allow the creditor's proof of debt to be amended, on such terms as may be just.

(3) Nothing in this Rule or the following two Rules may affect rights in rem of creditors or third parties in respect of tangible or intangible, moveable or immoveable assets (including both specific assets and collections of indefinite assets as a whole which change from time to time) belonging to the debtor that are situated outside the United Kingdom.

[7.1134]
61 Redemption by energy administrator

(1) The energy administrator may at any time give notice to a creditor whose debt is secured that the energy administrator proposes, at the expiration of 28 days from the date of the notice, to redeem the security at the value put upon it in the creditor's proof.

(2) The creditor then has 21 days (or such longer period as the energy administrator may allow) in which, if the creditor so wishes, to exercise the right to revalue the creditor's security (with the permission of the court, where Rule 60(2) applies). If the creditor re-values the creditor's security, the energy administrator may only redeem at the new value.

(3) If the energy administrator redeems the security, the cost of transferring it is payable out of the assets.

(4) A secured creditor may at any time, by notice in writing, call on the energy administrator to elect whether the energy administrator will or will not exercise the power to redeem the security at the value then placed on it; and the energy administrator then has 3 months in which to exercise the power or determine not to exercise it.

[7.1135]
62 Test of security's value

(1) Subject as follows, the energy administrator, if dissatisfied with the value which a secured creditor puts on the creditor's security (whether in the creditor's proof or by way of revaluation under Rule 59), may require any property comprised in the security to be offered for sale.

(2) The terms of the sale shall be such as may be agreed, or as the court may direct; and if the sale is by auction, the energy administrator on behalf of the energy supply company, and the creditor on the creditor's own behalf, may appear and bid.

(3) This Rule does not apply if the security has been re-valued and the revaluation has been approved by the court.

[7.1136]
63 Realisation of security by creditor

If a creditor who has valued the creditor's security subsequently realises it (whether or not at the instance of the energy administrator)—

- (a) the net amount realised shall be substituted for the value previously put by the creditor on the security; and
- (b) that amount shall be treated in all respects as an amended valuation made by the creditor.

[7.1137]
64 Notice of proposed distribution

(1) Where an energy administrator is proposing to make a distribution to creditors the energy administrator must give notice of the fact.

(2) The notice given pursuant to paragraph (1) must—

- (a) be sent to all creditors whose addresses are known to the energy administrator;
- (b) state whether the distribution is—
  - (i) to preferential creditors; or
  - (ii) preferential creditors and unsecured creditors; and
- (c) where the energy administrator proposes to make a distribution to unsecured creditors, state the value of the prescribed part, except where the court has made an order under section 176A(5) of the 1986 Act.

(3) Subject to paragraph (5)(b), before declaring a dividend the energy administrator must by notice invite the creditors to prove their debts. Such notice—

(a) must be gazetted; and

(b) may be advertised in such other manner as the energy administrator thinks fit.

(4) A notice pursuant to paragraph (1) or (3) must, in addition to the standard contents—

(a) state that it is the intention of the energy administrator to make a distribution to creditors within the period of 2 months from the last date for proving;

(b) specify whether the proposed dividend is interim or final;

(c) specify a date up to which proofs may be lodged being a date which—

(i) is the same date for all creditors; and

(ii) is not less than 21 days from that of the notice.

(5) Where a dividend is to be declared for preferential creditors—

(a) the notice pursuant to paragraph (1) need only be given to those creditors in whose cases the energy administrator has reason to believe that their debts are preferential; and

(b) the notice pursuant to paragraph (3) need only be given if the energy administrator thinks fit.

[7.1138]

65 Admission or rejection of proofs

(1) Unless the energy administrator has already dealt with them, within 5 business days of the last date for proving, the energy administrator must—

(a) admit or reject (in whole or in part) proofs submitted to the energy administrator; or

(b) make such provision in respect of them as the energy administrator thinks fit.

(2) The energy administrator is not obliged to deal with proofs lodged after the last day for proving, but may do so, if the energy administrator thinks fit.

(3) In the declaration of a dividend no payment shall be made more than once by virtue of the same debt.

[7.1139]

66 Postponement or cancellation of dividend

If in the period of 2 months referred to in Rule 64(4)(a)—

(a) the energy administrator has rejected a proof in whole or in part and application is made to the court for that decision to be reversed or varied, or

(b) application is made to the court for the energy administrator's decision on a proof to be reversed or varied, or for a proof to be expunged, or for a reduction of the amount claimed,

the energy administrator may postpone or cancel the dividend.

[7.1140]

67 Declaration of dividend

(1) Subject to paragraph (2), within the 2 month period referred to in Rule 64(4)(a), the energy administrator must proceed to declare the dividend to one or more classes of creditor of which the energy administrator gave notice.

(2) Except with the permission of the court, the energy administrator must not declare a dividend so long as there is pending any application to the court to reverse or vary a decision of the energy administrator's on a proof, or to expunge a proof or to reduce the amount claimed.

(3) If the court gives permission under paragraph (2), the energy administrator must make such provision in respect of the proof in question as the court directs.

[7.1141]

68 Notice of declaration of a dividend

(1) Where the energy administrator declares a dividend the energy administrator must give notice of that fact to all creditors who have proved their debts.

(2) The notice must include the following particulars relating to the energy supply company administration—

(a) amounts raised from the sale of assets, indicating (so far as is practicable) amounts raised by the sale of particular assets;

(b) payments made by the energy administrator when acting as such;

(c) where the energy administrator proposed to make a distribution to unsecured creditors, the value of the prescribed part, except where the court has made an order under section 176A(5) of the 1986 Act;

(d) provision (if any) made for unsettled claims, and funds (if any) retained for particular purposes;

(e) the total amount of dividend and the rate of dividend;

(f) whether, and if so when, any further dividend is expected to be declared.

[7.1142]

69 Payments of dividends and related matters

(1) The dividend may be distributed simultaneously with the notice declaring it.

(2) Payment of the dividend may be made by post, or arrangements may be made with any creditor for it to be paid to the creditor in another way, or held for the creditor's collection.

(3) Where a dividend is paid on a bill of exchange or other negotiable instrument, the amount of the dividend shall be endorsed on the instrument, or on a certified copy of it, if required to be produced by the holder for that purpose.

[7.1143]
70 Notice of no dividend, or no further dividend

If the energy administrator gives notice to creditors that the energy administrator is unable to declare any dividend or (as the case may be) any further dividend, the notice must contain a statement to the effect either—

(a) that no funds have been realised; or
(b) that the funds realised have already been distributed or used or allocated for defraying the expenses of energy supply company administration.

[7.1144]
71 Proof altered after payment of dividend

(1) If after payment of dividend the amount claimed by a creditor in the creditor's proof is increased, the creditor is not entitled to disturb the distribution of the dividend; but the creditor is entitled to be paid, out of any money for the time being available for the payment of any further dividend, any dividend or dividends which the creditor has failed to receive.

(2) Any dividend or dividends payable under paragraph (1) must be paid before the money there referred to is applied to the payment of any such further dividend.

(3) If, after a creditor's proof has been admitted, the proof is withdrawn or expunged, or the amount is reduced, the creditor is liable to repay to the energy administrator any amount overpaid by way of dividend.

[7.1145]
72 Secured creditors

(1) The following applies where a creditor re-values the creditor's security at a time when a dividend has been declared.

(2) If the revaluation results in a reduction of the creditor's unsecured claim ranking for dividend, the creditor must as soon as reasonably practicable repay to the energy administrator, for the credit of the energy supply company administration, any amount received by the creditor as dividend in excess of that to which the creditor would be entitled having regard to the revaluation of the security.

(3) If the revaluation results in an increase of the creditor's unsecured claim, the creditor is entitled to receive from the energy administrator, out of any money for the time being available for the payment of a further dividend, before any such further dividend is paid, any dividend or dividends which the creditor has failed to receive, having regard to the revaluation of the security. However, the creditor is not entitled to disturb any dividend declared (whether or not distributed) before the date of the revaluation.

[7.1146]
73 Disqualification from dividend

If a creditor contravenes any provision of the 1986 Act or these Rules relating to the valuation of securities, the court may, on the application of the energy administrator, order that the creditor be wholly or partly disqualified from participation in any dividend.

[7.1147]
74 Assignment of right to dividend

(1) If a person entitled to a dividend gives notice to the energy administrator that the person wishes the dividend to be paid to another person, or that the person has assigned the person's entitlement to another person, the energy administrator must pay the dividend to that other accordingly.

(2) A notice under this Rule must specify the name and address of the person to whom payment is to be made.

[7.1148]
75 Adjustment where dividend paid before time

(1) Where a creditor has proved for a debt of which payment is not due at the date of the declaration of dividend, the creditor is entitled to dividend equally with other creditors, but subject as follows.

(2) For the purpose of dividend (and no other purpose), the amount of the creditor's admitted proof (or, if a distribution has previously been made to the creditor, the amount remaining outstanding in respect of the creditor's admitted proof) shall be reduced by applying the following formula—

$$\frac{X}{1.05^n}$$

where—

(a) "X" is the value of the admitted proof; and
(b) "n" is the period beginning with the date that the energy supply company entered energy supply company administration and ending with the date on which the payment of the creditor's debt would otherwise be due expressed in years and months in a decimalised form.

PART 8
THE ENERGY ADMINISTRATOR

[7.1149]
76 Fixing of remuneration

(1) The energy administrator is entitled to receive remuneration for the energy administrator's services.

(2) The remuneration shall be fixed by reference to the time properly given by the energy administrator and the energy administrator's staff in attending to matters arising in the energy supply company administration.

(3) The remuneration of the energy administrator shall be fixed by the court and the energy administrator must make an application to court accordingly.

(4) The energy administrator must give at least 14 days' notice of the energy administrator's application to the following, who may appear or be represented—

(a) the Secretary of State;
(b) GEMA; and
(c) the creditors of the energy supply company.

(5) In fixing the remuneration, the court must have regard to the following matters—

(a) the complexity (or otherwise) of the case;
(b) any respects in which, in connection with the energy supply company's affairs, there falls on the energy administrator any responsibility of an exceptional kind or degree;
(c) the effectiveness with which the energy administrator appears to be carrying out, or to have carried out, the energy administrator's duties as such; and
(d) the value and nature of the property with which the energy administrator has to deal.

(6) Where there are joint energy administrators, it is for them to agree between themselves as to how the remuneration payable should be apportioned. Any dispute arising between them may be referred to the court for settlement by order.

(7) If the energy administrator is a solicitor and employs the energy administrator's own firm, or any partner in it, to act on behalf of the energy supply company, profit costs must not be paid unless this is authorised by the court.

[7.1150]
77 Remuneration of new energy administrator

If a new energy administrator is appointed in place of another, any court order in effect under Rule 76 immediately before the former energy administrator ceased to hold office continues to apply in respect of the remuneration of the new energy administrator until a further court order is made in accordance with those provisions.

PART 9
ENDING ENERGY SUPPLY COMPANY ADMINISTRATION

[7.1151]
78 Final progress reports

(1) In this Part reference to a progress report is to a report in the form specified in Rule 33.

(2) The final progress report means a progress report which includes a summary of—

(a) the energy administrator's proposals;
(b) any major amendments to, or deviations from, those proposals;
(c) the steps taken during the energy supply company administration; and
(d) the outcome.

[7.1152]
79 Application to court

(1) An application to court under paragraph 79 of Schedule B1 to the 1986 Act for an order ending an energy supply company administration must have attached to it a progress report for the period since the last progress report (if any) or the date the energy supply company entered energy supply company administration and a statement indicating what the applicant thinks should be the next steps for the energy supply company (if applicable).

(2) Where such an application is made, the applicant must—

(a) give notice in writing to the applicant for the esc administration order (unless the applicant in both cases is the same) and the creditors of the energy supply company of the applicant's intention to apply to court at least 5 business days before the date that the applicant intends to make an application; and
(b) attach to the application to court a statement that the applicant has notified the creditors, and copies of any response from creditors to that notification.

(3) Where such an application is to be made other than by the energy administrator—

(a) the applicant must also give notice in writing to the energy administrator of the applicant's intention to apply to court at least 5 business days before the date that the applicant intends to make an application; and

(b) upon receipt of such written notice the energy administrator must, before the end of the 5 business day notice period, provide the applicant with a progress report for the period since the last progress report (if any) or the date the energy supply company entered energy supply company administration.

(4) Where the application is made other than by the Secretary of State, the application must also state that it is made with the consent of the Secretary of State.

(5) Where the energy administrator applies to court under paragraph 79 of Schedule B1 to the 1986 Act in conjunction with a petition under section 124 of the 1986 Act for an order to wind up the energy supply company, the energy administrator must, in addition to the requirements of paragraphs (2) and (4), notify the creditors whether the energy administrator intends to seek appointment as liquidator.

[7.1153]

80 Notification by energy administrator of court order

(1) Where the court makes an order to end the energy supply company administration, the energy administrator must deliver to the registrar of companies a copy of the court order and a copy of the final progress report.

(2) Where the court makes such an order, it must, where the applicant is not the energy administrator, give a copy of the order to the energy administrator.

(3) As soon as reasonably practicable, the energy administrator must send a copy of the notice and the final progress report to all other persons who received notice of the energy administrator's appointment.

[7.1154]

81 Moving from energy supply company administration to creditors' voluntary liquidation

(1) As soon as reasonably practicable after the day on which the registrar of companies registers the notice of moving from energy supply company administration to creditors' voluntary liquidation sent by the energy administrator for the purposes of paragraph 83(3) of Schedule B1 to the 1986 Act, the person who at that point ceases to be the energy administrator must (whether the energy administrator becomes the liquidator or not) send a final progress report (which must include details of the assets to be dealt with in the liquidation) to—

(a) all those who received notice of the energy administrator's appointment;

(b) where the Secretary of State did not receive notice of the energy administrator's appointment, to the Secretary of State; and

(c) where GEMA did not receive notice of the energy administrator's appointment, to GEMA,

and must deliver a copy to the registrar of companies.

(2) For the purposes of paragraph 83(7) of Schedule B1 to the 1986 Act, a person shall be nominated as liquidator in accordance with the provisions of Rule 32(2)(g) and that person's appointment takes effect, following registration under paragraph (1)—

(a) by virtue of the energy administrator's proposals or revised proposals; or

(b) where a creditors' meeting is held in accordance with Rule 24, as a consequence of such a meeting.

(3) GEMA must notify the Secretary of State before consenting to the energy administrator delivering a notice of moving from energy supply company administration to creditors' voluntary liquidation to the registrar of companies.

[7.1155]

82 Moving from energy supply company administration to dissolution

(1) Where, for the purposes of paragraph 84(1) of Schedule B1 to the 1986 Act, the energy administrator delivers a notice of moving from energy supply company administration to dissolution to the registrar of companies, the energy administrator must attach to that notice a final progress report.

(2) As soon as reasonably practicable the energy administrator must send a copy of the notice and the attached document to—

(a) all those who received notice of the energy administrator's appointment;

(b) where the Secretary of State did not receive notice of the energy administrator's appointment, the Secretary of State; and

(c) where GEMA did not receive notice of the energy administrator's appointment, to GEMA.

(3) Where a court makes an order under paragraph 84(7) of Schedule B1 to the 1986 Act, it must, where the applicant is not the energy administrator, give a copy of the order to the energy administrator.

(4) The energy administrator must notify the registrar of companies in accordance with paragraph 84(8) of Schedule B1 to the 1986 Act of any order made by the court under paragraph 84(7) of Schedule B1 to the 1986 Act.

(5) GEMA must notify the Secretary of State before directing the energy administrator to deliver a notice of moving from energy supply company administration to dissolution to the registrar of companies.

[7.1156]

83 Provision of information to the Secretary of State

Where the energy supply company administration ends pursuant to paragraph 79, 83 or 84 of Schedule B1 to the 1986 Act, the energy administrator must, at the same time as sending the final progress report under Rule 83(1), provide the Secretary of State with the following information—

(a) a breakdown of the relevant debts (within the meaning of section 98(4) of the 2011 Act) of the energy supply company, which remain outstanding; and

(b) details of any shortfall (within the meaning of section 98(3)(a) of the 2011 Act) in the property of the energy supply company available for meeting those relevant debts.

PART 10
REPLACING ENERGY ADMINISTRATOR

[7.1157]
84 Grounds for resignation

(1) The energy administrator may give notice of resignation—

(a) on the grounds of ill health; or

(b) because the energy administrator intends ceasing to be in practice as an insolvency practitioner; or

(c) because there is some conflict of interest, or a change in personal circumstances, which precludes or makes impracticable the further discharge by the energy administrator of the duties of energy administrator.

(2) The energy administrator may, with the permission of the court, give notice of the energy administrator's resignation on grounds other than those specified in paragraph (1).

[7.1158]
85 Notice of intention to resign

The energy administrator must in all cases give at least 5 business days' notice in Form ESCA13 of the energy administrator's intention to resign, or to apply for the court's permission to do so, to the following persons—

(a) the Secretary of State;

(b) GEMA;

(c) if there is a continuing energy administrator of the energy supply company, to that continuing energy administrator; and

(d) if there is no such energy administrator, to the energy supply company and its creditors.

[7.1159]
86 Notice of resignation

(1) The notice of resignation must be in Form ESCA14.

(2) The notice must be filed with the court, and a copy delivered to the registrar of companies.

(3) A copy of the notice of resignation must be sent by the energy administrator not more than 5 business days after it has been filed with the court to all those to whom notice of intention to resign was sent.

[7.1160]
87 Application to court to remove energy administrator from office

(1) Any application under paragraph 88 of Schedule B1 to the 1986 Act must state the grounds on which it is requested that the energy administrator should be removed from office.

(2) Service of the notice of the application must be effected on the energy administrator, the Secretary of State, GEMA, the joint energy administrator (if any), and where there is not a joint energy administrator, to the energy supply company and all the creditors, including any floating charge holders, not less than 5 business days before the date fixed for the application to be heard.

(3) Where a court makes an order removing the energy administrator it must give a copy of the order to the applicant who as soon as reasonably practicable must send a copy to the energy administrator.

(4) The applicant must also within 5 business days of the order being made send a copy of the order to all those to whom notice of the application was sent.

(5) A copy of the order must also be delivered to the registrar of companies within the same time period.

[7.1161]
88 Notice of vacation of office when energy administrator ceases to be qualified to act

Where the energy administrator who has ceased to be qualified to act as an insolvency practitioner in relation to the energy supply company gives notice in accordance with paragraph 89 of Schedule B1 to the 1986 Act, the energy administrator must also give notice to the registrar of companies.

[7.1162]
89 Energy administrator deceased

(1) Subject as follows, where the energy administrator has died, it is the duty of the energy administrator's personal representatives to give notice of the fact to the court, specifying the date of the death. This does not apply if notice has been given under either paragraph (2) or (3) of this Rule.

(2) If the deceased energy administrator was a partner in or an employee of a firm, notice may be given by a partner in the firm who is qualified to act as an insolvency practitioner, or is a member of any body recognised by the Secretary of State for the authorisation of insolvency practitioners.

(3) Notice of the death may be given by any person producing to the court the relevant death certificate or a copy of it.

(4) Where a person gives notice under this Rule, that person shall also give notice to the registrar of companies.

[7.1163]

90 Application to replace

(1) Where an application is made to court under paragraph 91(1) of Schedule B1 to the 1986 Act to appoint a replacement energy administrator, the application must be accompanied by a written statement in Form ESCA2 by the person proposed to be the replacement energy administrator.

(2) A copy of the application must be served, in addition to those persons listed in section 156(2) of the 2004 Act and Rule 8(3), on the person who made the application for the esc administration order.

(3) Rule 10 shall apply to the service of an application under paragraph 91(1) of Schedule B1 to the 1986 Act as it applies to service in accordance with Rule 8.

(4) Rules 11, 12 and 13(1) and 13(2) apply to an application under paragraph 91(1) of Schedule B1 to the 1986 Act.

[7.1164]

91 Notification and advertisement of appointment of replacement energy administrator

Where a replacement energy administrator is appointed, the same provisions apply in respect of giving notice of, and advertising, the replacement appointment as in the case of the appointment (subject to Rule 93), and all statements, consents etc as are required shall also be required in the case of the appointment of a replacement. All forms and notices must clearly identify that the appointment is of a replacement energy administrator.

[7.1165]

92 Notification and advertisement of appointment of joint energy administrator

Where, after an initial appointment has been made, an additional person or persons are to be appointed as joint energy administrator the same Rules shall apply in respect of giving notice of and advertising the appointment as in the case of the initial appointment, subject to Rule 93.

[7.1166]

93 Notification to registrar of companies

The replacement or additional energy administrator must deliver notice of the appointment to the registrar of companies.

[7.1167]

94 Energy administrator's duties on vacating office

(1) Where the energy administrator ceases to be in office as such, in consequence of removal, resignation or cesser of qualification as an insolvency practitioner, the energy administrator is under obligation as soon as reasonably practicable to deliver up to his or her successor the assets (after deduction of any expenses properly incurred and distributions made by the energy administrator) and further to deliver up to that person—

(a) the records of the energy supply company administration, including correspondence, proofs and other related papers appertaining to the energy supply company administration while it was within the energy administrator's responsibility; and

(b) the energy supply company's books, papers and other records.

(2) It is an offence for the energy administrator to fail to comply with this Rule.

PART 11
COURT PROCEDURE AND PRACTICE

CHAPTER 1 APPLICATIONS

[7.1168]

95 Preliminary

This Chapter applies to any application made to the court in energy supply company administration proceedings, except an application for an esc administration order.

[7.1169]

96 Form and contents of application

(1) Each application must be in writing and must state—

(a) that the application is made under the 1986 Act;

(b) the names of the parties;

(c) the name of the energy supply company which is the subject of the energy supply company administration proceedings;

(d) the court (and where applicable, the division or district registry of that court) in which the application is made;

(e) where the court has previously allocated a number to the energy supply company administration proceedings within which the application is made, that number;

(f) the nature of the remedy or order applied for or the directions sought from the court;

(g) the names and addresses of the persons (if any) on whom it is intended to serve the application or that no person is intended to be served;

(h) where the 1986 Act or these Rules require that notice of the application is to be given to specified persons, the names and addresses of all those persons (so far as known to the applicant); and

(i) the applicant's address for service.

(2) The application must be authenticated by the applicant if the applicant is acting in person or, when the applicant is not so acting, by or on behalf of the applicant's solicitor.

[7.1170]
97 Application under section 176A(5) of the 1986 Act to disapply section 176A of the 1986 Act

(1) An application under section 176A(5) of the 1986 Act must be accompanied by a witness statement by the energy administrator.

(2) The witness statement must state—

(a) that the application arises in the course of an energy supply company administration;
(b) a summary of the financial position of the energy supply company;
(c) the information substantiating the energy administrator's view that the cost of making a distribution to unsecured creditors would be disproportionate to the benefits; and
(d) whether any other office holder is acting in relation to the energy supply company and if so that office holder's address.

[7.1171]
98 Filing and service of application

(1) An application must be filed in court, accompanied by one copy and a number of additional copies equal to the number of persons who are to be served with the application.

(2) Where an application is filed with the court in accordance with paragraph (1), the court must fix a venue for the application to be heard unless—

(a) it considers it is not appropriate to do so;
(b) the Rule under which the application is brought provides otherwise; or
(c) the case is one to which Rule 100 applies.

(3) Unless the court otherwise directs, the applicant must serve a sealed copy of the application, endorsed with the venue for the hearing, on the respondent named in the application (or on each respondent if more than one).

(4) The court may give any of the following directions—

(a) that the application be served upon persons other than those specified by the relevant provision of the 1986 Act or these Rules;
(b) that the giving of notice to any person may be dispensed with;
(c) that notice be given in some way other than that specified in paragraph (3).

(5) An application must be served at least 14 days before the date fixed for its hearing unless—

(a) the provision of the 1986 Act or these Rules under which the application is made make different provision; or
(b) the case is one of urgency, to which paragraph (6) applies.

(6) Where the case is one of urgency, the court may (without prejudice to its general power to extend or abridge time limits)—

(a) hear the application immediately, either with or without notice to, or the attendance of, other parties, or
(b) authorise a shorter period of service than that provided for by paragraph (5);

and any such application may be heard on terms providing for the filing or service of documents, or the carrying out of other formalities, as the court thinks just.

[7.1172]
99 Application under section 176A(5) of the 1986 Act

An application under section 176A(5) of the 1986 Act may be made without the application being served upon or notice being given to any other party.

[7.1173]
100 Hearings without notice

Where the relevant provisions of the 1986 Act or these Rules do not require service of the application on, or notice of it to be given to, any person—

(a) the court may hear the application as soon as reasonably practicable without fixing a venue as required by Rule 98; or
(b) it may fix a venue for the application to be heard in which case Rule 98 applies to the extent that it is relevant;

but nothing in those provisions is to be taken as prohibiting the applicant from giving such notice if the applicant wishes to do so.

[7.1174]
101 Hearing of application

(1) Unless the court otherwise directs, the hearing of an application must be in open court.

(2) In a county court, the jurisdiction of the court to hear and determine an application may be exercised by the district judge (to whom any application must be made in the first instance) unless—

(a) a direction to the contrary has been given, or
(b) it is not within the district judge's power to make the order required.

(3) In the High Court, the jurisdiction of the court to hear and determine an application may be exercised by the registrar (to whom any application must be made in the first instance) unless—

(a) a direction to the contrary has been given, or

(b) it is not within the registrar's power to make the order required.

(4) Where the application is made to the district judge in the county court or to the registrar in the High Court, the district judge or the registrar may refer to the judge any matter which the district judge or registrar thinks should properly be decided by the judge, and the judge may either dispose of the matter or refer it back to the district judge or the registrar with such directions as that judge thinks just.

(5) Nothing in this Rule precludes an application being made directly to the judge in a proper case.

[7.1175]
102 Witness statements—general

(1) Subject to Rule 104, where evidence is required by the 1986 Act or these Rules as to any matter, such evidence may be provided in the form of a witness statement unless—

(a) in any specific case a Rule or the 1986 Act makes different provision; or
(b) the court otherwise directs.

(2) The court may, on the application of any party to the matter in question order the attendance for cross-examination of the person making the witness statement.

(3) Where, after such an order has been made, the person in question does not attend, that person's witness statement shall not be used in evidence without the permission of the court.

[7.1176]
103 Filing and service of witness statements

Unless the provisions of the 1986 Act or these Rules under which the application is made provide otherwise, or the court otherwise allows—

(a) if the applicant intends to rely at the first hearing on evidence in a witness statement, the applicant must file the witness statement with the court and serve a copy on the respondent, not less than 14 days before the date fixed for the hearing;
(b) where a respondent to an application intends to oppose it and rely for that purpose on evidence in a witness statement, the respondent must file the witness statement with the court and serve a copy on the applicant, not less than 5 business days before the date fixed for the hearing.

[7.1177]
104 Use of reports

(1) A report may be filed in court by the energy administrator instead of a witness statement, unless the application involves other parties or the court otherwise orders.

(2) In any case where a report is filed instead of a witness statement, the report shall be treated for the purposes of Rule 102 and any hearing before the court as if it were a witness statement.

(3) Where the witness statement is made by the energy administrator, the witness statement must state the address at which the energy administrator works.

[7.1178]
105 Adjournment of hearings; directions

(1) The court may adjourn the hearing of an application on such terms as it thinks just.

(2) The court may at any time give such directions as it thinks just as to—

(a) service or notice of the application on or to any other person;
(b) whether particulars of claim and defence are to be delivered and generally as to the procedure on the application including whether a hearing is necessary;
(c) the matters to be dealt with in evidence.

(3) The court may give directions as to the manner in which any evidence is to be adduced at a resumed hearing and in particular as to—

(a) the taking of evidence wholly or partly by witness statement or orally;
(b) the cross-examination of the maker of a witness statement; or
(c) any report to be made by the energy administrator.

CHAPTER 2 SHORTHAND WRITERS

[7.1179]
106 Nomination and appointment of shorthand writers

(1) In the High Court the judge or registrar and, in a county court, a district judge may in writing nominate one or more persons to be official shorthand writers to the court.

(2) The court may, at any time in the course of energy supply company administration proceedings, appoint a shorthand writer to take down the evidence of a person examined under section 236 of the 1986 Act.

[7.1180]
107 Remuneration

(1) The remuneration of a shorthand writer appointed in energy supply company administration proceedings must be paid by the party at whose instance the appointment was made, or out of the assets of the energy supply company, or otherwise, as the court may direct.

(2) Any question arising as to the rates of remuneration payable under this Rule shall be determined by the court in its discretion.

CHAPTER 3 ENFORCEMENT PROCEDURES

[7.1181]

108 Enforcement of court orders

(1) In energy supply company administration proceedings, orders of the court may be enforced in the same manner as a judgment to the same effect.

(2) Where a warrant for the arrest of a person is issued by the High Court, the warrant may be discharged by the county court where the person who is the subject of the warrant—

(a) has been brought before a county court exercising energy supply company administration jurisdiction; and

(b) has given to the county court an undertaking which is satisfactory to the county court to comply with the obligations that apply to that person under the provisions of the 1986 Act or these Rules.

[7.1182]

109 Orders enforcing compliance with these Rules

(1) The court may, on application by the energy administrator, make such orders as it thinks necessary for the enforcement of obligations falling on any person in accordance with—

(a) paragraph 47 of Schedule B1 to the 1986 Act (duty to submit statement of affairs in energy supply company administration), or

(b) section 235 of the 1986 Act (duty of various persons to co-operate with energy administrator).

(2) An order of the court under this Rule may provide that all costs of and incidental to the application for it shall be borne by the person against whom the order is made.

[7.1183]

110 Warrant under section 236 of the 1986 Act

(1) A warrant issued by the court under section 236 of the 1986 Act (inquiry into insolvent company's dealings) must be addressed to such officer of the High Court as the warrant specifies, or to any constable.

(2) The persons referred to in section 236(5) of the 1986 Act (court's power of enforcement) as the prescribed officer of the court are the tipstaff and the tipstaff's assistants of the court.

(3) In this Chapter references to property include books, papers and records.

(4) When a person is arrested under a warrant issued under section 236 of the 1986 Act ("the arrested person"), the officer arresting the arrested person must as soon as reasonably practicable bring the arrested person before the court issuing the warrant in order that the arrested person may be examined.

(5) If the arrested person cannot immediately be brought up for examination, the officer must deliver the arrested person into the custody of the governor of the prison named in the warrant (or where that prison is not able to accommodate the arrested person, the governor of such other prison with appropriate facilities that is able to accommodate the arrested person), who must keep the arrested person in custody and produce the arrested person before the court as it may from time to time direct.

(6) After arresting the person named in the warrant, the officer must as soon as reasonably practicable report to the court the arrest or delivery into custody (as the case may be) and apply to the court to fix a venue for the arrested person's examination.

(7) The court must appoint the earliest practicable time for the examination, and must—

(a) direct the governor of the prison to produce the person for examination at the time and place appointed, and

(b) as soon as reasonably practicable give notice of the venue to the person who applied for the warrant.

(8) Any property in the arrested person's possession which may be seized must be—

(a) lodged with, or otherwise dealt with as instructed by, whoever is specified in the warrant as authorised to receive it, or

(b) kept by the officer seizing it pending the receipt of written orders from the court as to its disposal,

as may be directed by the court.

CHAPTER 4 COURT RECORDS AND RETURNS

[7.1184]

111 Court file

(1) The court must open and maintain a file in any case (the "court file") where documents are filed with it under the 1986 Act or these Rules.

(2) Any documents which are filed with the court under the 1986 Act or these Rules must be placed on the court file.

(3) The following persons may inspect or obtain from the court a copy of, or a copy of any document or documents contained in, the court file—

(a) the energy administrator;

(b) the Secretary of State;

(c) any person who is a creditor of the energy supply company to which the proceedings relate if that person provides the court with a statement in writing by confirming that that person is a creditor; and

(d) every person who is, or at any time has been, a director or officer of the energy supply company to which the energy supply company administration proceedings relate, or who is a member of the energy supply company.

(4) The right to inspect or obtain a copy of, or a copy of any document or documents contained in, the court file may be exercised on that person's behalf by a person authorised to do so by that person.

(5) Any person who is not otherwise entitled to inspect or obtain a copy of, or a copy of any document or documents contained in, the court file may do so if that person has the permission of the court.

(6) The court may direct that the court file, a document (or part of it) or a copy of a document (or part of it) must not be made available under paragraph (3), (4) or (5) without the permission of the court.

(7) An application for a direction under paragraph (6) may be made by—

(a) the energy administrator; or

(b) any person appearing to the court to have an interest.

(8) Where any person wishes to exercise the right to inspect the court file under paragraph (3), (4) or (5), that person—

(a) if the permission of the court is required, must file in court an application notice in accordance with these Rules; or

(b) if the permission of the court is not required, may inspect the court file at any reasonable time.

(9) Where any person wishes to exercise the right to obtain a copy of a document under paragraph (3), (4) or (5), that person must pay any prescribed fee and—

(a) if the permission of the court is required, file in court an application notice in accordance with these Rules; or

(b) if the permission of the court is not required, file in court a written request for the document.

(10) An application for—

(a) permission to inspect the court file or obtain a copy of a document under paragraph (5); or

(b) a direction under paragraph (6),

may be made without notice to any other party, but the court may direct that notice must be given to any person who would be affected by its decision.

(11) If for the purposes of powers conferred by the 1986 Act or these Rules, the Secretary of State or the energy administrator requests the transmission of the file of any insolvency proceedings, the court must comply with the request (unless the file is for the time being in use for the court's own purposes).

CHAPTER 5 COSTS AND DETAILED ASSESSMENT

[7.1185]

112 Application of Chapter 8

(1) This Chapter applies in relation to costs in connection with energy supply company administration proceedings.

(2) In this Chapter a reference to costs includes charges and expenses.

[7.1186]

113 Requirement to assess costs by the detailed procedure

(1) Where the costs of any person are payable as an expense out of the assets of the energy supply company, the amount payable must be decided by detailed assessment unless agreed between the energy administrator and the person entitled to payment.

(2) In the absence of such agreement as is mentioned in paragraph (1), the energy administrator may serve notice requiring that person to commence detailed assessment proceedings in accordance with CPR Part 47.

(3) Detailed assessment proceedings must be commenced in the court to which the energy supply company administration proceedings are allocated.

(4) Where the costs of any person employed by the energy administrator in energy supply company administration proceedings are required to be decided by detailed assessment or fixed by order of the court, the energy administrator may make payments on account to such person in respect of those costs provided that person undertakes in writing—

(a) to repay as soon as reasonably practicable any money which may, when detailed assessment is made, prove to have been overpaid; and

(b) to pay interest on any such sum as is mentioned in sub-paragraph (a) at the rate specified in section 17 of the Judgments Act 1838 on the date payment was made and for the period beginning with the date of payment and ending with the date of repayment.

(5) In any proceedings before the court, the court may order costs to be decided by detailed assessment.

[7.1187]

114 Procedure where detailed assessment required

(1) Before making a detailed assessment of the costs of any person employed in energy supply company administration proceedings by the energy administrator, the costs officer must require a certificate of employment, which must be endorsed on the bill and authenticated by the energy administrator.

(2) The certificate must include—

(a) the name and address of the person employed;

(b) details of the functions to be carried out under the employment; and

(c) a note of any special terms of remuneration which have been agreed.

(3) Every person whose costs in energy supply company administration proceedings are required to be decided by detailed assessment must, on being required in writing to do so by the energy administrator, commence detailed proceedings in accordance with CPR Part 47 (procedure for detailed assessment of costs and default provisions).

(4) If that person does not commence detailed assessment proceedings within 3 months of the requirement under paragraph (3), or within such further time as the court, on application, may permit, the energy administrator may deal with the assets of the energy supply company without regard to any claim by that person, whose claim is forfeited by such failure to commence proceedings.

(5) Where in any such case such a claim lies additionally against an energy administrator in the energy administrator's personal capacity, that claim is also forfeited by such failure to commence proceedings.

(6) Where costs have been incurred in energy supply company administration proceedings in the High Court and those proceedings are subsequently transferred to a county court, all costs of those proceedings directed by the court or otherwise required to be assessed may nevertheless, on the application of the person who incurred the costs, be ordered to be decided by detailed assessment in the High Court.

[7.1188]
115 Costs paid otherwise than out of the assets of the energy supply company

Where the amount of costs is decided by detailed assessment under an order of the court directing that the costs are to be paid otherwise than out of the assets of the energy supply company, the costs officer must note on the final costs certificate by whom, or the manner in which, the costs are to be paid.

[7.1189]
116 Award of costs against energy administrator

Without prejudice to any provision of the 1986 Act or these Rules by virtue of which the energy administrator is not in any event to be liable for costs and expenses, where an energy administrator is made a party to any proceedings on the application of another party to the proceedings, the energy administrator shall not be personally liable for costs unless the court otherwise directs.

[7.1190]
117 Application for costs

(1) This Rule applies where a party, or person affected by, any energy supply company administration proceedings—

(a) applies to the court for an order allowing that party's costs, or part of them, of or incidental to the proceedings; and

(b) that application is not made at the time of the proceedings.

(2) The person concerned must serve a sealed copy of the person's application on the energy administrator.

(3) The energy administrator may appear on the application.

(4) No costs of or incidental to the application shall be allowed to the applicant unless the court is satisfied that the application could not have been made at the time of the proceedings.

[7.1191]
118 Costs and expenses of witnesses

(1) Except as directed by the court, no allowance as a witness in any examination or other proceedings before the court shall be made to an officer of the energy supply company to which the energy supply company administration proceedings relate.

(2) A person making any application in energy supply company administration proceedings shall not be regarded as a witness on the hearing of the application, but the costs officer may allow the person's expenses of travelling and subsistence.

[7.1192]
119 Final costs certificate

(1) A final costs certificate of the costs officer is final and conclusive as to all matters which have not been objected to in the manner provided for under the CPR.

(2) Where it is proved to the satisfaction of a costs officer that a final costs certificate has been lost or destroyed, the costs officer may issue a duplicate.

CHAPTER 6 PERSONS WHO LACK CAPACITY TO MANAGE THEIR AFFAIRS

[7.1193]
120 Introductory

(1) The Rules in this Chapter apply where in energy supply company administration proceedings it appears to the court that a person affected by the proceedings is one who lacks capacity within the meaning of the Mental Capacity Act 2005 to manage and administer the person's property and affairs either—

(a) by reason of lacking capacity within the meaning of the Mental Capacity Act 2005; or

(b) due to physical affliction or disability.

(2) The person concerned is referred to as "the incapacitated person".

[7.1194]
121 Appointment of another person to act

(1) The court may appoint such person as it thinks just to appear for, represent or act for the incapacitated person.

(2) The appointment may be made either generally or for the purpose of any particular application or proceeding, or for the exercise of particular rights or powers which the incapacitated person might have exercised but for the incapacitated person's incapacity.

(3) The court may make the appointment either of its own motion or on application by—

(a) a person who has been appointed by a court in the United Kingdom or elsewhere to manage the affairs of, or to represent, the incapacitated person; or

(b) any relative or friend of the incapacitated person who appears to the court to be a proper person to make the application; or

(c) the energy administrator.

(4) Application under paragraph (3) may be made without notice to any other party; but the court may require such notice of the application as it thinks necessary to be given to the person alleged to be incapacitated, or any other person, and may adjourn the hearing of the application to enable the notice to be given.

[7.1195]
122 Witness statement in support of application

An application under Rule 121(3) must be supported by a witness statement made by a registered medical practitioner as to the mental or physical condition of the incapacitated person.

[7.1196]
123 Service of notices following appointment

Any notice served on, or sent to, a person appointed under Rule 121 has the same effect as if it had been served on, or sent to, the incapacitated person.

CHAPTER 7 APPEALS IN ENERGY SUPPLY COMPANY ADMINISTRATION PROCEEDINGS

[7.1197]
124 Appeals and reviews of esc administration orders

(1) Every court having jurisdiction under the 1986 Act or these Rules may review, rescind or vary any order made by it in the exercise of that jurisdiction.

(2) Appeals in civil matters in proceedings under these Rules lie as follows—

(a) to a single judge of the High Court where the decision appealed against is made by the county court or the registrar;

(b) to the Civil Division of the Court of Appeal from a decision of a single judge of the High Court.

(3) A county court is not, in the exercise of its jurisdiction for the purposes of these Rules, subject to be restrained by the order of any other court, and no appeal lies from its decision in the exercise of that jurisdiction except as provided by this Rule.

[7.1198]
125 Procedure on appeal

(1) An appeal against a decision at first instance may only be brought with either the permission of the court which made the decision or the permission of the court which has jurisdiction to hear the appeal.

(2) An appellant must file an appellant's notice (within the meaning of CPR Part 52) within 21 days after the date of the decision of the court that the appellant wishes to appeal.

(3) The procedure set out in CPR Part 52 applies to any appeal to which this Chapter applies.

CHAPTER 8 GENERAL

[7.1199]
126 Principal court rules and practice to apply

(1) The CPR and the practice and procedure of the High Court (including any practice directions) apply to energy supply company administration proceedings with any necessary modifications, except so far as inconsistent with these Rules.

(2) All energy supply company administration proceedings shall be allocated to the multi-track for which CPR Part 29 (the multi-track) makes provision; accordingly those provisions of the CPR which provide for allocation questionnaires and track allocation will not apply.

[7.1200]
127 Rights of audience

Rights of audience in energy supply company administration proceedings are the same as in insolvency proceedings.

[7.1201]
128 Formal defects

No energy supply company administration proceedings shall be invalidated by any formal defect or by any irregularity, unless the court before which objection is made considers that substantial injustice has been caused by the defect or irregularity, and that the injustice cannot be remedied by any order of the court.

[7.1202]
129 Service of orders staying proceedings

Where in energy supply company administration proceedings the court makes an order staying any action, execution or other legal process against the property of the energy supply company, service of the order may be effected by sending a sealed copy of the order to whatever is the address for service of the claimant or other party having the carriage of the proceedings to be stayed.

[7.1203]
130 Payment into court

CPR Part 37 (miscellaneous provisions about payment into court) applies to money lodged in court under these Rules.

[7.1204]
131 Further information and disclosure

(1) Any party to energy supply company administration proceedings may apply to the court for an order—

(a) that any other party—
  (i) clarify any matter which is in dispute in the proceedings, or
  (ii) give additional information in relation to any such matter,
  in accordance with CPR Part 18 (further information); or
(b) to obtain disclosure from any other party in accordance with CPR Part 31 (disclosure and inspection of documents).

(2) An application under this Rule may be made without notice being served on any other party.

[7.1205]
132 Office copies of documents

(1) Any person who has under these Rules the right to inspect the court file of energy supply company administration proceedings may require the court to provide the person with an office copy of any document on the file.

(2) A person's rights under this Rule may be exercised on the person's behalf by the person's solicitor.

(3) An office copy provided by the court under this Rule must be in such form as the registrar thinks appropriate, and must bear the court's seal.

PART 12
PROXIES AND ENERGY SUPPLY COMPANY REPRESENTATION

[7.1206]
133 Definition of proxy

(1) For the purposes of these Rules, a proxy is an authority given by a person ("the principal") to another person ("the proxy-holder") to attend a meeting and speak and vote as the person's representative.

(2) Proxies are for use at creditors' meetings or energy supply company meetings summoned or called under Schedule B1 to the 1986 Act or these Rules.

(3) Only one proxy may be given by a person for any one meeting at which the person desires to be represented; and it may only be given to one person, being an individual aged 18 years or over. But the principal may specify one or more other such individuals to be proxy-holder in the alternative, in the order in which they are named in the proxy.

(4) Without prejudice to the generality of paragraph (3), a proxy for a particular meeting may be given to whoever is to be the chair of the meeting; and the chair cannot decline to be the proxy-holder in relation to that proxy.

(5) A proxy requires the holder to give the principal's vote on matters arising for determination at the meeting, or to abstain, or to propose, in the principal's name, a resolution to be voted on by the meeting, either as directed or in accordance with the holder's own discretion.

[7.1207]
134 Issue and use of forms

(1) When notice is given of a meeting to be held in energy supply company administration proceedings, and forms of proxy are sent out with the notice, no form so sent out shall have inserted in it the name or description of any person.

(2) No form of proxy shall be used at any meeting except that which is sent with the notice summoning the meeting, or a substantially similar form.

(3) A form of proxy must be authenticated by the principal, or by some person authorised by the principal (generally or with reference to a particular meeting). If the form is authenticated by a person other than the principal, the nature of the person's authority must be stated.

[7.1208]
135 Use of proxies at meetings

(1) A proxy given for a particular meeting may be used at any adjournment of that meeting.

(2) Where the energy administrator holds proxies to be used by the energy administrator as chair of the meeting, and some other person acts as chair, that other person may use the energy administrator's proxies as if that person were the proxy-holder.

(3) Where a proxy directs a proxy-holder to vote for or against a resolution for the appointment of a person other than the energy administrator as proposed liquidator of the energy supply company, the proxy-holder may, unless the proxy states otherwise, vote for or against (as the proxy-holder thinks fit) any resolution for the appointment of that person jointly with another or others.

(4) A proxy-holder may propose any resolution which, if proposed by another, would be a resolution in favour of which by virtue of the proxy the proxy-holder would be entitled to vote.

(5) Where a proxy gives specific directions as to voting, this does not, unless the proxy states otherwise, preclude the proxy-holder from voting at the proxy-holder's discretion on resolutions put to the meeting which are not dealt with in the proxy.

[7.1209]

136 Retention of proxies

(1) Subject as follows, proxies used for voting at any meeting must be retained by the chair of the meeting.

(2) The chair must deliver the proxies, as soon as reasonably practicable after the meeting, to the energy administrator (where the chair is not the energy administrator).

[7.1210]

137 Right of inspection

(1) The energy administrator must, so long as proxies lodged with the energy administrator are in the energy administrator's hands, allow them to be inspected, at all reasonable times on any business day by—

(a) the creditors, in the case of proxies used at a meeting of creditors, and

(b) an energy supply company's members, in the case of proxies used at a meeting of the energy supply company.

(2) The reference in paragraph (1) to creditors is a reference to those persons who have submitted in writing a claim to be creditors of the energy supply company but does not include a person whose proof or claim has been wholly rejected for the purposes of voting, dividend or otherwise.

(3) The right of inspection given by this Rule is also exercisable by the directors of the energy supply company.

(4) Any person attending a meeting in energy supply company administration proceedings is entitled, immediately before or in the course of the meeting, to inspect proxies and associated documents (including proofs) sent or given, in accordance with directions contained in any notice convening the meeting, to the chair of that meeting or to any other person by a creditor or member for the purpose of that meeting.

(5) This Rule is subject to Rule 194.

[7.1211]

138 Proxy holder with financial interest

(1) A proxy-holder must not vote in favour of any resolution which would directly or indirectly place the proxy-holder or any associate of the proxy-holder, in a position to receive any remuneration out of the assets of the energy supply company, unless the proxy specifically directs the proxy-holder to vote in that way.

(2) Where a proxy-holder has authenticated the proxy as being authorised to do so by the principal and the proxy specifically directs the proxy-holder to vote in the way mentioned in paragraph (1), the proxy-holder must nevertheless not vote in that way unless the proxy-holder produces to the chair of the meeting written authorisation from the principal sufficient to show that the proxy-holder was entitled so to authenticate the proxy.

(3) This Rule applies also to any person acting as chair of a meeting and using proxies in that capacity under Rule 135; and in its application to the chair, the proxy-holder is deemed to be an associate of the chair.

(4) In this Rule "associate" shall have the same meaning as in section 435 of the 1986 Act.

[7.1212]

139 Energy supply company representation

(1) Where a person is authorised to represent a corporation at a meeting of creditors or of the energy supply company the person must produce to the chair of the meeting a copy of the resolution from which the person derives the person's authority.

(2) The copy resolution must be under the seal of the corporation, or certified by the secretary or a director of the corporation to be a true copy.

(3) Nothing in this Rule requires the authority of a person to authenticate a proxy on behalf of a principal which is a corporation to be in the form of a resolution of that corporation.

PART 13
EXAMINATION OF PERSONS IN ENERGY SUPPLY COMPANY ADMINISTRATION PROCEEDINGS

[7.1213]
140 Preliminary

(1) The Rules in this Part apply to applications to the court, made by the energy administrator, for an order under section 236 of the 1986 Act (inquiry into energy supply company's dealings when it is, or alleged to be, insolvent).

(2) The following definitions apply—
- (a) the person in respect of whom an order is applied for is "the respondent";
- (b) "section 236" means section 236 of the 1986 Act.

[7.1214]
141 Form and contents of application

(1) The application must be in writing and specify the grounds on which it is made.

(2) The application must specify the name of the respondent.

(3) It must be stated whether the application is for the respondent—
- (a) to be ordered to appear before the court, or
- (b) to be ordered to clarify any matter which is in dispute in the proceedings or to give additional information in relation to any such matter and if so CPR Part 18 (further information) shall apply to any such order, or
- (c) to submit witness statements (if so, particulars are to be given of the matters to be included), or
- (d) to produce books, papers or other records (if so, the items in question is to be specified),

or for any two or more of those purposes.

(4) The application may be made without notice to the respondent or any other party.

[7.1215]
142 Order for examination, etc

(1) The court may, whatever the purpose of the application, make any order which it has power to make under section 236.

(2) The court, if it orders the respondent to appear before it, must specify a venue for the respondent's appearance, which must be not less than 14 days from the date of the order.

(3) If the respondent is ordered to file witness statements, the order must specify—
- (a) the matters which are to be dealt with in the respondent's witness statements, and
- (b) the time within which they are to be filed in court.

(4) If the order is to produce books, papers or other records, the time and manner of compliance must be specified.

(5) The order must be served by the energy administrator as soon as reasonably practicable on the respondent, and it must be served personally, unless the court otherwise orders.

[7.1216]
143 Procedure for examination

(1) At any examination of the respondent, the energy administrator may attend in person, or be represented by a solicitor with or without counsel, and may put such questions to the respondent as the court may allow.

(2) Any creditor who has provided information on which the application was made under section 236 may attend the examination with the permission of the court and may put questions to the respondent (but only through the energy administrator).

(3) If the respondent is ordered to clarify any matter or to give additional information, the court must direct the respondent as to the questions which the respondent is required to answer, and to whether the respondent's answers (if any) are to be made in a witness statement.

(4) The respondent may at the respondent's own expense employ a legal representative who may put to the respondent such questions as the court may allow for the purpose of enabling the respondent to explain or qualify any answers given by the respondent, and may make representations on the respondent's behalf.

(5) There shall be made in writing such record of the examination as the court thinks proper. The record shall be read over either to or by the respondent and authenticated by the respondent at a venue fixed by the court.

(6) The written record may, in any proceedings (whether under the 1986 Act or otherwise) be used as evidence against the respondent of any statement made by the respondent in the course of the respondent's examination.

[7.1217]
144 Record of examination

(1) Unless the court otherwise directs, the written record of questions put to the respondent and the respondent's answers, and any witness statements submitted by the respondent in compliance with an order of the court under section 236, are not to be filed in court.

(2) The documents set out in paragraph (3) are not open to inspection without an order of the court, by any person other than the energy administrator.

(3) The documents to which paragraph (2) applies are—

(a) the written record of the respondent's examination;

(b) copies of questions put to the respondent or proposed to be put to the respondent and answers to questions given by the respondent;

(c) any witness statement by the respondent; and

(d) any document on the court file as shows the grounds for the application for an order.

(4) The court may from time to time give directions as to the custody and inspection of any documents to which this Rule applies, and as to the furnishing of copies of, or extracts from, such documents.

[7.1218]

145 Cost of proceedings under section 236

(1) Where the court has ordered an examination of a person under section 236, and it appears to it that the examination was made necessary because information has been unjustifiably refused by the respondent, it may order that the costs of the examination by paid by the respondent.

(2) Where the court makes an order against a person under section 237(1) or (2) of the 1986 Act (court's enforcement powers under section 236), the costs of the application for the order may be ordered by the court to be paid by the respondent.

(3) Subject to paragraphs (1) and (2) above, the energy administrator's costs shall, unless the court otherwise orders, be paid out of the assets of the energy supply company.

(4) A person summoned to attend for examination under this Part shall be tendered a reasonable sum out of the assets of the energy supply company in respect of travelling expenses incurred in connection with the person's attendance. Other costs falling on the person are at the court's discretion.

PART 14
MISCELLANEOUS AND GENERAL

[7.1219]

146 Power of Secretary of State to regulate certain matters

(1) The Secretary of State may, subject to the 1986 Act and the 2004 Act, make regulations with respect to any matter provided for in these Rules as relates to the carrying out of the functions of an energy administrator of an energy supply company including, without prejudice to the generality of the foregoing provision, with respect to the following matters arising in an energy supply company administration—

(a) the preparation and keeping of books, accounts and other records, and their production to such persons as may be authorised or required to inspect them;

(b) the auditing of an energy administrator's accounts;

(c) the manner in which an energy administrator is to act in relation to the energy supply company's books, papers and other records, and the manner of their disposal by the energy administrator and others;

(d) the supply by the energy administrator to creditors and members of the energy supply company of copies of documents relating to the energy supply company administration and the affairs of the energy supply company (on payment, in such cases as may be specified by the regulations, of the specified fee).

(2) Regulations made pursuant to paragraph (1) may—

(a) confer discretion on the court;

(b) make non-compliance with any of the regulations a criminal offence;

(c) make different provision for different cases, including different provision for different areas; and

(d) contain such incidental, supplemental and transitional provisions as may appear to the Secretary of State necessary or expedient.

[7.1220]

147 Costs, expenses, etc

(1) All fees, costs, charges and other expenses incurred in the course of the energy supply company administration proceedings are to be regarded as expenses of the energy supply company administration.

(2) The costs associated with the prescribed part shall be paid out of the prescribed part.

[7.1221]

148 Provable debts

(1) Subject as follows, in energy supply company administration proceedings all claims by creditors are provable as debts against the energy supply company, whether they are present or future, certain or contingent, ascertained or sounding only in damages.

(2) Any obligation arising under a confiscation order made under Part 2, 3 or 4 of the Proceeds of Crime Act 2002 is not provable.

(3) The following are not provable except at a time when all other claims of creditors in the energy supply company administration proceedings (other than any of a kind mentioned in this paragraph) have been paid in full with interest under Rule 57—

(a) any claim arising by virtue of section 382(1)(a) of the Financial Services and Markets Act 2000, not being a claim also arising by virtue of section 382(1)(b) of that Act;

(b) any claim which by virtue of the 1986 Act or any other enactment is a claim the payment of which is to be postponed.

(4) Nothing in this Rule prejudices any enactment or rule of law under which a particular kind of debt is not provable, whether on grounds of public policy or otherwise.

[7.1222]
149 False claim of status as creditor, etc

Where these Rules provide for creditors or members of an energy supply company a right to inspect any documents, whether on the court's file or in the hands of an energy administrator or other person, it is an offence for a person, with the intention of obtaining a sight of documents which the person has not under these Rules any right to inspect, falsely to claim a status which would entitle the person to inspect them.

[7.1223]
150 Punishment of offences

(1) Schedule 2 to these Rules has effect with respect to the way in which contraventions of these Rules are punishable on conviction.

(2) In relation to an offence under a provision of the Rules specified in the first column of the Schedule (the general nature of the offence being described in the second column), the third column shows whether the offence is punishable on conviction on indictment, or on summary conviction, or either in the one way or the other.

(3) The fourth column shows, in relation to an offence, the maximum punishment by way of fine or imprisonment which may be imposed on a person convicted of the offence in the way specified in relation to it in the third column (that is to say, on indictment or summarily), a reference to a period of years or months being to a term of imprisonment of that duration.

(4) The fifth column shows (in relation to an offence for which there is an entry in that column) that a person convicted of the offence after continued contravention is liable to a daily default fine; that is to say, the person is liable on a second or subsequent conviction of the offence to the fine specified in that column for each day on which the contravention is continued (instead of the penalty specified for the offence in the fourth column of the Schedule).

(5) Section 431 of the 1986 Act (summary proceedings), as it applies to England and Wales, has effect in relation to offences under these Rules as to offences under the 1986 Act.

PART 15
PROVISIONS OF GENERAL EFFECT

CHAPTER 1 THE GIVING OF NOTICE AND THE SUPPLY OF DOCUMENTS—GENERAL

[7.1224]
151 Application

(1) Subject to paragraphs (2) and (3), this Chapter applies where a notice or other document is required to be given, delivered or sent under the 1986 Act or these Rules by any person, including an energy administrator.

(2) This Chapter does not apply to the service of—
- (a) any petition or application to the court;
- (b) any evidence in support of that petition or application; or
- (c) any order of the court.

(3) This Chapter does not apply to the delivery of documents to the registrar of companies.

[7.1225]
152 Personal delivery of documents

Personal delivery of a notice or other document is permissible in any case.

[7.1226]
153 Postal delivery of documents

Unless in any particular case some other form of delivery is required by the 1986 Act, these Rules or an order of the court, a notice or other document may be sent by post in accordance with the rules for postal service in CPR Part 6 and sending by such means has effect as specified in those rules.

[7.1227]
154 Non-receipt of notice of meeting

Where in accordance with the 1986 Act or these Rules, a meeting of creditors or other persons is summoned by notice, the meeting is presumed to have been duly summoned and held, notwithstanding that not all those to whom the notice is to be given have received it.

[7.1228]
155 Notice etc to solicitors

Where under the 1986 Act or these Rules a notice or other document is required or authorised to be given, delivered or sent to a person, it may be given, delivered or sent instead to a solicitor authorised to accept delivery on that person's behalf.

[7.1229]
156 Notice of meetings by advertisement only

(1) The court may order that notice of any meeting be given by advertisement and not by individual notice to the persons concerned.

(2) In considering whether to act under this Rule, the court must have regard to the cost of advertisement, the amount of assets available and the extent of the interest of creditors, members or any particular class of either.

CHAPTER 2 THE GIVING OF NOTICE AND THE SUPPLY OF DOCUMENTS BY OR TO ENERGY ADMINISTRATORS ETC

[7.1230]
157 Application

(1) Subject to paragraph (2) and (3), this Chapter applies where a notice or other document is to be given, delivered or sent under the 1986 Act or these Rules.

(2) This Chapter does not apply to the delivery of documents to the registrar of companies.

(3) Rules 164 to 167 do not apply to the filing of any notice or other document with the court.

[7.1231]
158 Notice to joint energy administrators

Where two or more persons are acting jointly as the energy administrator in energy supply company administration proceedings, delivery of a document to one of them is to be treated as delivery to them all.

[7.1232]
159 The form of notices and other documents

Subject to any order of the court, any notice or other document required to be given, delivered or sent must be in writing and where electronic delivery is permitted a notice or other document in electronic form is treated as being in writing if a copy of it is capable of being produced in legible form.

[7.1233]
160 Proof of sending etc

(1) Where in energy supply company administration proceedings a notice or other document is required to be given, delivered or sent by the energy administrator, the giving, delivering or sending of it may be proved by means of a certificate that the notice or other document was duly given, delivered or sent.

(2) The certificate may be given by—
- (a) the energy administrator;
- (b) the energy administrator's solicitor;
- (c) a partner or an employee of either of them.

(3) In the case of a notice or other document to be given, delivered or sent by a person other than the energy administrator, the giving delivering or sending of it may be proved by means of a certificate by that person—
- (a) that the notice or document was given, delivered or sent by that person, or
- (b) that another person (named in the certificate) was instructed to give, deliver or send it.

(4) A certificate under this Rule may be endorsed on a copy or specimen of the notice or document to which it relates.

[7.1234]
161 Authentication

(1) A document or information given, delivered or sent in hard copy form is sufficiently authenticated if it is signed by the person sending or supplying it.

(2) A document or information given, delivered or sent in electronic form is sufficiently authenticated—
- (a) if the identity of the sender is confirmed in a manner specified by the recipient, or
- (b) where no such manner has been specified by the recipient, if the communication contains or is accompanied by a statement of the identity of the sender and the recipient has no reason to doubt the truth of that statement.

[7.1235]
162 Electronic delivery in energy supply company administration proceedings—general

(1) Unless in any particular case some other form of delivery is required by the 1986 Act, these Rules or an order of the court and subject to paragraph (3), a notice or other document may be given, delivered or sent by electronic means provided that the intended recipient of the notice or other document has—
- (a) consented (whether in the specific case or generally) to electronic delivery (and has not revoked that consent); and
- (b) provided an electronic address for delivery.

(2) In the absence of evidence to the contrary, a notice or other document is presumed to have been delivered where—
- (a) the sender can produce a copy of the electronic message which—
  - (i) contained the notice or other document, or to which the notice or other document was attached, and
  - (ii) shows the time and date the message was sent; and

(b) that electronic message contains the address supplied under paragraph (1)(b).

(3) A message sent electronically is deemed to have been delivered to the recipient no later than 9.00 am on the next business day after it was sent.

[7.1236]
163 Electronic delivery by energy administrators

(1) Where an energy administrator gives, sends or delivers a notice or other document to any person by electronic means, the notice or document must contain or be accompanied by a statement that the recipient may request a hard copy of the notice or document and specifying a telephone number, e-mail address and postal address which may be used to request a hard copy.

(2) Where a hard copy of the notice or other document is requested, it must be sent within 5 business days of receipt of the request by the energy administrator.

(3) An energy administrator must not require a person making a request under paragraph (2) to pay a fee for the supply of the document.

[7.1237]
164 Use of websites by energy administrator

(1) This Rule applies for the purposes of section 246B of the 1986 Act.

(2) An energy administrator required to give, deliver or send a document to any person may (other than in a case where personal service is required) satisfy that requirement by sending that person a notice—

(a) stating that the document is available for viewing and downloading on a website;

(b) specifying the address of that website together with any password necessary to view and download the document from that site; and

(c) containing a statement that the person to whom the notice is given, delivered or sent may request a hard copy of the document and specifying a telephone number, e-mail address and postal address which may be used to request a hard copy.

(3) Where a notice to which this Rule applies is sent, the document to which it relates must—

(a) be available on the website for a period of not less than 3 months after the date on which the notice is sent; and

(b) must be in such a format as to enable it to be downloaded from the website within a reasonable time of an electronic request being made for it to be downloaded.

(4) Where a hard copy of the document is requested it must be sent within 5 business days of the receipt of the request by the energy administrator.

(5) An energy administrator must not require a person making a request under paragraph (4) to pay a fee for the supply of the document.

(6) Where a document is given, delivered or sent to a person by means of a website in accordance with this Rule, it is deemed to have been delivered—

(a) when the document was first made available on the website, or

(b) if later, when the notice under paragraph (2) was delivered to that person.

[7.1238]
165 Special provision on account of expense as to website use

(1) Where the court is satisfied that the expense of sending notices in accordance with Rule 164 would, on account of the number of persons entitled to receive them, be disproportionate to the benefit of sending notice in accordance with that Rule, it may order that the requirement to give, deliver or send a relevant document to any person may (other than in a case where personal service is required) be satisfied by the energy administrator sending each of those persons a notice—

(a) stating that all relevant documents will be made available for viewing and downloading on a website;

(b) specifying the address of that website together with any password necessary to view and download a relevant document from that site; and

(c) containing a statement that the person to whom the notice is given, delivered or sent may at any time request that hard copies of all, or specific, relevant documents are sent to that person, and specifying a telephone number, e-mail address and postal address which may be used to make that request.

(2) A document to which this Rule relates must—

(a) be available on the website for a period of not less than 12 months from the date when it was first made available on the website or, if later, from the date upon which the notice was sent, and

(b) must be in such a format as to enable it to be downloaded from the website within a reasonable time of an electronic request being made for it to be downloaded.

(3) Where hard copies of relevant documents have been requested, they must be sent by the energy administrator—

(a) within 5 business days of the receipt of the energy administrator of the request to be sent hard copies, in the case of relevant documents first appearing on the website before the request was received, or

(b) within 5 business days from the date a relevant document first appears on the website, in all other cases.

(4) An energy administrator must not require a person making a request under paragraph (3) to pay a fee for the supply of the document.

(5) Where a relevant document is given, delivered or sent to a person by means of a website in accordance with this Rule, it is deemed to have been delivered—

(a) when the relevant document was first made available on the website, or

(b) if later, when the notice under paragraph (1) was delivered to that person.

(6) In this Rule a relevant document means any document which the energy administrator is first required to give, deliver or send to any person after the court has made an order under paragraph (1).

[7.1239]

166 Electronic delivery of energy supply company administration proceedings to courts

(1) Except where paragraph (2) applies or the requirements of paragraph (3) are met, no petition, application, notice or other document may be delivered or made to a court by electronic means.

(2) This paragraph applies where electronic delivery of documents to a court is permitted by another Rule.

(3) The requirements of this paragraph are—

(a) the court provides an electronic working scheme for the proceedings to which the document relates; and

(b) the electronic communication is—

(i) delivered and authenticated in a form which complies with the requirements of the scheme;

(ii) sent to the electronic address provided by the court for electronic delivery of those proceedings; and

(iii) accompanied by any payment due to the court in respect of those proceedings made in a manner which complies with the requirements of the scheme.

(4) In this Rule "an electronic working scheme" means a scheme permitting energy supply company administration proceedings to be delivered electronically to the court set out in a practice direction.

(5) Under paragraph (3) an electronic communication is to be treated as delivered to the court at the time it is recorded by the court as having been received.

CHAPTER 3 SERVICE OF COURT DOCUMENTS

[7.1240]

167 Application

(1) Subject to paragraph (2), this Chapter applies in relation to the service of—

(a) petitions,

(b) applications,

(c) documents relating to petitions or applications, and

(d) court orders,

which are required to be served by any provision of the 1986 Act or these Rules ("court documents").

(2) For the purposes of the application by this Chapter of CPR Part 6 to the service of documents in energy supply company administration proceedings—

(a) an application commencing energy supply company administration proceedings, or

(b) an application within energy supply company administration proceedings against a respondent,

is to be treated as a claim form.

[7.1241]

168 Application of CPR Part 6 to service of court documents within the jurisdiction

Except where different provision is made in these Rules, CPR Part 6 applies in relation to the service of court documents within the jurisdiction with such modifications as the court may direct.

[7.1242]

169 Service of orders staying proceedings

(1) This Rule applies where the court makes an order staying any action, execution or other legal process against the property of the energy supply company.

(2) Service within the jurisdiction of such an order as is mentioned in paragraph (1) may be effected by sending a sealed copy of the order to the address for service of the claimant or other party having the carriage of the proceedings to be stayed.

[7.1243]

170 Service on joint energy administrators

Where there are joint energy administrators in energy supply company administration proceedings, service on one of them is to be treated as service on all of them.

[7.1244]

171 Application of CPR Part 6 to service of court documents outside the jurisdiction

CPR Part 6 applies to the service of court documents outside the jurisdiction with such modifications as the court may direct.

CHAPTER 4 MEETINGS

[7.1245]

172 Quorum at meeting of creditors

(1) Any meeting of creditors in energy supply company administration proceedings is competent to act if a quorum is present.

(2) Subject to the next paragraph, a quorum is at least one creditor entitled to vote.

(3) For the purposes of this Rule, the reference to the creditor necessary to constitute a quorum is to those persons present or represented by proxy by any person (including the chair) and in the case of any proceedings under Parts 1 to 7 of the 1986 Act includes corporations duly represented.

(4) Where at any meeting of creditors—

(a) the provisions of this Rule as to a quorum being present are satisfied by the attendance of—

(i) the chair alone, or

(ii) one other person in addition to the chair, and

(b) the chair is aware, by virtue of proofs and proxies received or otherwise, that one or more additional persons would, if attending, be entitled to vote,

the meeting must not commence until at least the expiry of 15 minutes after the time appointed for its commencement.

[7.1246]

173 Remote attendance at meetings of creditors

(1) This Rule applies to a request to the convener of a meeting under section 246A(9) of the 1986 Act to specify a place for the meeting.

(2) The request must be accompanied by—

(a) in the case of a request by creditors, a list of the creditors making or concurring with the request and the amounts of their respective debts in the energy supply company administration proceedings in question,

(b) in the case of a request by members, a list of the members making or concurring with the request and their voting rights, and

(c) from each person concurring, written confirmation of that person's concurrence.

(3) The request must be made within 7 business days of the date on which the convener sent the notice of the meeting in question.

(4) Where the convener considers that the request has been properly made in accordance with the 1986 Act and this Rule, the convener must—

(a) give notice to all those previously given notice of the meeting—

(i) that it is to be held at a specified place, and

(ii) as to whether the date and time are to remain the same or not;

(b) set a venue (including specification of a place) for the meeting, the date of which must be not later than 28 days after the original date for the meeting; and

(c) give at least 14 days' notice of that venue to all those previously given notice of the meeting;

and the notices required by sub-paragraphs (a) and (c) may be given at the same or different times.

(5) Where the convener has specified a place for the meeting in response to a request to which this Rule applies, the chair of the meeting must attend the meeting by being present in person at that place.

[7.1247]

174 Action where person excluded

(1) In this Rule and Rules 175 and 176 an "excluded person" means a person who—

(a) has taken all steps necessary to attend a meeting under the arrangements put in place to do so by the convener of the meeting under section 246A(6) of the 1986 Act; and

(b) those arrangements do not permit that person to attend the whole or part of that meeting.

(2) Where the chair becomes aware during the course of the meeting that there is an excluded person, the chair may—

(a) continue the meeting;

(b) declare the meeting void and convene the meeting again;

(c) declare the meeting valid up to the point where the person was excluded and adjourn the meeting.

(3) Where the chair continues the meeting, the meeting is valid unless—

(a) the chair decides in consequence of a complaint under Rule 176 to declare the meeting void and hold the meeting again; or

(b) the court directs otherwise.

(4) Without prejudice to paragraph (2), where the chair becomes aware during the course of the meeting that there is an excluded person, the chair may, in the chair's discretion and without an adjournment, declare the meeting suspended for any period up to 1 hour.

[7.1248]

175 Indication to excluded person

(1) A person who claims to be an excluded person may request an indication of what occurred during the period of that person's claimed exclusion (an "indication").

(2) A request under paragraph (1) must be made as soon as reasonably practicable and, in any event, no later than 4.00 pm on the business day following the day on which the exclusion is claimed to have occurred.

(3) A request under paragraph (1) must be made to—

(a) the chair, where it is made during the course of the business of the meeting; or

(b) the energy administrator where it is made after the conclusion of the business of the meeting.

(4) Where satisfied that the person making the request is an excluded person, the person to whom the request is made under paragraph (3) must give the indication as soon as reasonably practicable and, in any event, no later than 4.00 pm on the business day following the day on which the request was made under paragraph (1).

[7.1249]

176 Complaint

(1) Any person who—

(a) is, or claims to be, an excluded person; or

(b) attends the meeting (in person or by proxy) and considers that they have been adversely affected by a person's actual, apparent or claimed exclusion,

("the complainant") may make a complaint.

(2) The person to whom the complaint must be made ("the relevant person") is—

(a) the chair, where it is made during the course of the meeting; or

(b) the energy administrator, where it is made after the meeting.

(3) The relevant person must—

(a) consider whether there is an excluded person; and

(b) where satisfied that there is an excluded person, consider the complaint; and

(c) where satisfied that there has been prejudice, take such action as the relevant person considers fit to remedy the situation.

(4) Paragraph (5) applies where—

(a) the relevant person is satisfied that the complainant is an excluded person;

(b) during the period of the person's exclusion a resolution was put to the meeting and voted on; and

(c) the excluded person asserts how the excluded person intended to vote on the resolution.

(5) Subject to paragraph (6), where satisfied that the effect of the intended vote in paragraph (4), if cast, would have changed the result of the resolution, the relevant person must—

(a) count the intended vote as being cast in accordance with the complainant's stated intention;

(b) amend the record of the result of the resolution; and

(c) where those entitled to attend the meeting have been notified of the result of the resolution, notify them of the change.

(6) Where satisfied that more than one complainant in paragraph (4) is an excluded person, the relevant person must have regard to the combined effect of the intended votes.

(7) The relevant person must notify the complainant in writing of any decision.

(8) A complaint must be made as soon as reasonably practicable and, in any event, no later than 4.00 pm on the business day following—

(a) the day on which the person was, appeared or claimed to be excluded; or

(b) where an indication is sought under Rule 175, the day on which the complainant received the indication.

(9) A complainant who is not satisfied by the action of the relevant person may apply to the court for directions and any application must be made no more than 2 business days from the date of receiving the decision of the relevant person.

CHAPTER 5 FORMS

[7.1250]

177 Forms for use in energy supply company administration proceedings

(1) Subject to Rules 178 and 179, the forms contained in Schedule 1 to these Rules must be used in energy supply company administration proceedings as provided for in specific Rules.

(2) The forms must be used with such variations, if any, as the circumstances may require.

(3) The Secretary of State or the energy administrator may incorporate a barcode or other reference or recognition mark into any form in Schedule 1 to these Rules a copy of which is received by any of them or is sent to any person by any of them.

[7.1251]

178 Electronic submission of information instead of submission of forms to the Secretary of State, energy administrators

(1) This Rule applies in any case where information in a prescribed form is required by these Rules to be sent by any person to the Secretary of State or the energy administrator, or a copy of a prescribed form is to be sent to the registrar of companies.

(2) A requirement of the kind mentioned in paragraph (1) is treated as having been satisfied where—

(a) the information is submitted electronically with the agreement of the person to whom the information is sent;

(b) the form in which the electronic submission is made satisfies the requirements of the person to whom the information is sent (which may include a requirement that the information supplied can be reproduced in the format of the prescribed form);

(c) all the information required to be given in the prescribed form is provided in the electronic submission; and

(d) the person to whom the information is sent can provide in legible form the information so submitted.

(3) Where information in a prescribed form is permitted to be sent electronically under paragraph (2), any requirement in the prescribed form that the prescribed form be accompanied by a signature is taken to be satisfied—

(a) if the identity of the person who is supplying the information in the prescribed form and whose signature is required is confirmed in a manner specified by the recipient, or

(b) where no such manner has been specified by the recipient, if the communication contains or is accompanied by a statement of the identity of the person who is providing the information in the prescribed form, and the recipient has no reason to doubt the truth of that statement.

(4) Where information required in a prescribed form has been supplied to a person, whether or not it has been supplied electronically in accordance with paragraph (2), and a copy of that information is required to be supplied to another person falling within paragraph (1), the requirements contained in paragraph (2) apply in respect of the supply of the copy to that other person, as they apply in respect of the original.

[7.1252]

179 Electronic submission of information instead of submission of forms in all other cases

(1) Subject to paragraph (5), this Rule applies in any case where Rule 178 does not apply, where information in a prescribed form is required by these Rules to be sent by any person.

(2) A requirement of the kind mentioned in paragraph (1) is treated as having been satisfied where—

(a) the person to whom the information is sent has agreed—

(i) to receiving the information electronically and to the form in which it is to be sent; and

(ii) to the manner in which paragraph (3) is to be satisfied ("the specified manner");

(b) all the information required to be given in the prescribed form is provided in the electronic submission; and

(c) the person to whom the information is sent can provide in legible form the information so submitted.

(3) Any requirement in a prescribed form that it be accompanied by a signature is taken to be satisfied if the identity of the person who is supplying the information and whose signature is required, is confirmed in the specified manner.

(4) Where information required in prescribed form has been supplied to a person, whether or not it has been supplied electronically in accordance with paragraph (2), and a copy of that information is required to be supplied to another person falling within paragraph (1), the requirements contained in paragraph (2) apply in respect of the supply of the copy to that other person, as they apply in respect of the original.

CHAPTER 6 GAZETTE NOTICES

[7.1253]

180 Contents of notices to be gazetted under the 1986 Act or these Rules

(1) Where under the 1986 Act or these Rules a notice is gazetted, in addition to any content specifically required by the 1986 Act or any other provision of these Rules, the content of such a notice must be as set out in this Chapter.

(2) All notices published must specify insofar as it is applicable in relation to the particular notice—

(a) the name and postal address of the energy administrator acting in the proceedings;

(b) the capacity in which the energy administrator is acting and the date of appointment;

(c) either an e-mail address, or a telephone number, through which the energy administrator may by contacted;

(d) the name of any person other than the energy administrator (if any) who may be contacted regarding the proceedings;

(e) the number assigned to the energy administrator by the Secretary of State;

(f) the court name and any number assigned to the proceedings by the court;

(g) the registered name of the energy supply company;

(h) the energy supply company's registered number;

(i) the energy supply company's registered office, or if an unregistered company, the postal address of its principal place of business;

(j) any principal trading address of the energy supply company if this is different from its registered office;

(k) any name under which the energy supply company was registered in the 12 months prior to the date of the commencement of the proceedings which are the subject of the Gazette notice; and

(l) any name or style (other than the energy supply company's registered name) under which—

(i) the energy supply company carried on business; and

(ii) any debt owed to a creditor was incurred.

[7.1254]
181 Omission of unobtainable information

Information required under this Chapter to be included in a notice to be gazetted may be omitted if it is not reasonably practicable to obtain it.

[7.1255]
182 The Gazette—general

(1) A copy of the Gazette containing any notice required by the 1986 Act or these Rules to be gazetted is evidence of any facts stated in the notice.

(2) In the case of an order of the court notice of which is required by the 1986 Act or these Rules to be gazetted, a copy of the Gazette containing the notice may in any proceedings be produced as conclusive evidence that the order was made on the date specified in the notice.

(3) Where an order of the court which is gazetted has been varied, and where any matter has been erroneously or inaccurately gazetted, the person whose responsibility it was to procure the requisite entry in the Gazette must as soon as reasonably practicable cause the variation of the order to be gazetted or a further entry to be made in the Gazette for the purpose of correcting the error or inaccuracy.

CHAPTER 7 NOTICE ADVERTISED OTHERWISE THAN IN THE GAZETTE

[7.1256]
183 Notices otherwise advertised under the 1986 Act or these Rules

(1) Where under the 1986 Act or these Rules a notice may be advertised otherwise than in the Gazette, in addition to any content specifically required by the 1986 Act or any other provision of these Rules, the content of such a notice must be as set out in this Chapter.

(2) All notices published must specify insofar as it is applicable in relation to the particular notice—

- (a) the name and postal address of the energy administrator acting in the proceedings to which the notice relates;
- (b) the capacity in which the energy administrator is acting;
- (c) either an e-mail address, or a telephone number, through which the energy administrator may be contacted;
- (d) the registered name of the energy supply company;
- (e) the energy supply company's registered number;
- (f) any name under which the energy supply company was registered in the 12 months prior to the date of the commencement of the proceedings which are the subject of the notice; and
- (g) any name or style (other than the energy supply company's registered name) under which—
  - (i) the energy supply company carried on business; and
  - (ii) any debt owed to a creditor was incurred.

[7.1257]
184 Non-Gazette notices—other provisions

(1) The information required to be contained in a notice to which this Chapter applies must be included in the advertisement of that notice in a manner that is reasonably likely to ensure, in relation to the form of the advertising used, that a person reading, hearing or seeing the advertisement, will be able to read, hear or see that information.

(2) Information required under this Chapter to be included in a notice may be omitted if it is not reasonably practicable to obtain it.

CHAPTER 8 NOTIFICATIONS TO THE REGISTRAR OF COMPANIES

[7.1258]
185 Application of this Chapter

This Chapter applies where under the 1986 Act or these Rules information is to be delivered to the registrar of companies.

[7.1259]
186 Information to be contained in all notifications to the registrar

Where under the 1986 Act or these Rules a return, notice or any other document or information is to be delivered to the registrar of companies, that notification must—

- (a) specify—
  - (i) the registered name of the energy supply company;
  - (ii) its registered number;
  - (iii) the nature of the notification;
  - (iv) the provision of the 1986 Act or the Rule under which the notification is made;
  - (v) the date of the notification;
  - (vi) the name and postal address of the person making the notification;
  - (vii) the capacity in which that person is acting in respect of the energy supply company; and
- (b) be authenticated by the person making the notification.

Part 7F Special Insolvency Regimes

[7.1260]

187 Notifications relating to the office of energy administrators

In addition to the information required by Rule 186, a notification relating to the office of the energy administrator must also specify—

(a) the name of the energy administrator;

(b) the date of the event notified;

(c) where the notification relates to an appointment, the person, body or court making the appointment;

(d) where the notification relates to the termination of an appointment, the reason for that termination (for example, resignation); and

(e) the postal address of the energy administrator.

[7.1261]

188 Notification relating to documents

In addition to the information required by Rule 186, a notification relating to a document (for example, a statement of affairs) must also specify—

(a) the nature of the document; and

(b) either—

(i) the date of the document; or

(ii) where the document relates to a period of time (for example a report) the period of time to which the document relates.

[7.1262]

189 Notifications relating to court orders

In addition to the information required by Rule 186, a notification relating to a court order must also specify—

(a) the nature of the court order; and

(b) the date of the order.

[7.1263]

190 Returns or reports of meetings

In addition to the information required by Rule 186, the notification of a return or a report of a meeting must specify—

(a) the purpose of the meeting including the provision of the 1986 Act or the Rule under which it was convened;

(b) the venue fixed for the meeting;

(c) whether a required quorum was present for the meeting to take place; and

(d) if the meeting took place, the outcome of the meeting (including any resolutions passed at the meeting).

[7.1264]

191 Notifications relating to other events

In addition to the information required by Rule 186, a notification relating to any other event must specify—

(a) the nature of the event including the provision of the 1986 Act or Rule under which it took place; and

(b) the date the event occurred.

[7.1265]

192 Notifications of more than one nature

A notification which includes a notification of more than one nature must satisfy the requirements applying in respect of each of those notifications.

[7.1266]

193 Notifications made to other persons at the same time

(1) Where under the 1986 Act or these Rules a notice or other document is to be sent to another person at the same time that it is to be delivered to the registrar of companies, that requirement may be satisfied by sending to that other person a copy of the notification to the registrar.

(2) Paragraph (1) does not apply—

(a) where a form is prescribed for the notification to the other person; or

(b) where the notification to the registrar of companies is incomplete.

CHAPTER 9 INSPECTION OF DOCUMENTS AND THE PROVISION OF INFORMATION

[7.1267]

194 Confidentiality of documents—grounds for refusing inspection

(1) Where in energy supply company administration proceedings the energy administrator considers that a document forming part of the records of those proceedings—

(a) should be treated as confidential; or

(b) is of such a nature that its disclosure would be prejudicial to the conduct of the proceedings or might reasonably be expected to lead to violence against any person, the energy administrator may decline to allow it to be inspected by a person who would otherwise be entitled to inspect it.

(2) Where under this Rule the energy administrator determines to refuse inspection of a document, the person wishing to inspect it may apply to the court for that determination to be overruled and the court may either overrule it altogether or sustain it subject to such conditions (if any) as it thinks just.

[7.1268]
195 Right to copy documents

Where the 1986 Act or these Rules confer a right for any person to inspect documents, the right includes that of taking copies of those documents, on payment—

(a) in the case of documents on the court's file of proceedings, of the fee chargeable under any order made under section 92 of the Courts Act 2003; and
(b) in any other case, of the appropriate fee.

[7.1269]
196 Charges for copy documents

Except where prohibited by these Rules, the energy administrator is entitled to require the payment of the appropriate fee for the supply of documents requested by a creditor or member.

[7.1270]
197 Right to have list of creditors

(1) A creditor has the right to require the energy administrator to provide a list of the creditors and the amounts of their respective debts unless paragraph (4) applies.

(2) The energy administrator on being required to furnish the list under paragraph (1)—

(a) as soon as reasonably practicable must send it to the person requiring the list to be furnished; and
(b) may charge the appropriate fee for doing so.

(3) The name and address of any creditor may be omitted from the list furnished under paragraph (2) where the energy administrator is of the view that its disclosure would be prejudicial to the conduct of the proceedings or might reasonably be expected to lead to violence against any person provided that—

(a) the amount of the debt in question is shown in the list; and
(b) a statement is included in the list that the name and address of the creditor has been omitted in respect of that debt.

(4) Paragraph (1) does not apply where a statement of affairs has been delivered to the registrar of companies.

CHAPTER 10 COMPUTATION OF TIME AND TIME LIMITS

[7.1271]
198 Time limits

(1) The provisions of CPR rule 2.8 (time) apply, as regards computation of time, to anything required or authorised to be done under these Rules.

(2) The provisions of CPR rule 3.1(2)(a) (the court's general powers of management) apply so as to enable the court to extend or shorten the time for compliance with anything required or authorised to be done by these Rules.

CHAPTER 11 SECURITY

[7.1272]
199 Energy administrator's security

(1) Wherever under these Rules any person has to appoint a person to the office of energy administrator that person must, before making the appointment, be satisfied that the person appointed or to be appointed has security for the proper performance of the office of energy administrator.

(2) In any energy supply company administration proceedings the cost of the energy administrator's security shall be defrayed as an expense of the energy supply company administration.

CHAPTER 12 NOTICE OF ORDER UNDER SECTION 176A(5) OF THE 1986 ACT

[7.1273]
200 Notice of order under section 176A(5) of the 1986 Act

(1) Where the court makes an order under section 176A(5) of the 1986 Act, it must as soon as reasonably practicable send two sealed copies of the order to the energy administrator.

(2) Where the court has made an order under section 176A(5) of the 1986 Act, the energy administrator must, as soon as is reasonably practicable give notice to each creditor of whose address and claim the energy administrator is aware.

(3) Paragraph (2) does not apply where the court directs otherwise.

(4) The court may direct that the requirement in paragraph (2) is complied with if a notice has been published by the energy administrator which, in addition to containing the standard contents, states that the court has made an order disapplying the requirement to set aside the prescribed part.

(5) As soon as reasonably practicable a notice under paragraph (4)—

(a) must be gazetted; and
(b) may be advertised in such other manner as the energy administrator thinks fit.

(6) The energy administrator must deliver a copy of the order to the registrar of companies as soon as reasonably practicable after the making of the order.

PART 16
INTERPRETATION AND APPLICATION

[7.1274]
201 Introductory

This Part of these Rules has effect for their interpretation and application.

[7.1275]
202 "The court"; "the registrar"

(1) In energy supply company administration proceedings, anything to be done by, to or before the court may be done by, to or before a judge, district judge or the registrar.

(2) The registrar or district judge may authorise any act of a formal or administrative character which is not by statute the registrar's or district judge's responsibility to be carried out by the chief clerk or any other officer of the court acting on the registrar's or district judge's behalf, in accordance with directions given by the Lord Chancellor.

(3) In energy supply company administration proceedings, "the registrar" means [an Insolvency and Companies Court Judge].

NOTES

Para (3): words in square brackets substituted by the Alteration of Judicial Titles (Registrar in Bankruptcy of the High Court) Order 2018, SI 2018/130, art 3, Schedule, para 12(1)(i).

[7.1276]
203 "Energy supply company administration proceedings"

"Energy supply company administration proceedings" means any proceedings under sections 154 to 171 of, and Schedules 20 and 21 to, the 2004 Act or these Rules.

[7.1277]
204 "The appropriate fee"

"The appropriate fee" means 15 pence per A4 or A5 page and 30 pence per A3 page.

[7.1278]
205 "Debt", "liability"

(1) "Debt", in relation to the energy supply company administration of an energy supply company, means (subject to the next paragraph) any of the following—
(a) any debt or liability to which the energy supply company is subject at the date on which it goes into energy supply company administration;
(b) any debt or liability to which the energy supply company may become subject after that date by reason of any obligation incurred before that date; and
(c) any interest provable as mentioned in Rule 57(1).

(2) For the purpose of any provision of the 1986 Act, section 154 to 171 of and Schedule 20 and 21 to the 2004 Act, section 93 to 102 of the 2011 Act, or these Rules about energy supply company administration, any liability in tort is a debt provable in the energy supply company administration if either—
(a) the cause of action has accrued at the date on which the energy supply company entered energy supply company administration; or
(b) all the elements necessary to establish the cause of action exist at that date except for actionable damage.

(3) For the purposes of references in any provision of the 1986 Act, section 154 to 171 of and Schedules 20 and 21 to the 2004 Act, or these Rules, to a debt or liability, it is immaterial whether the amount is fixed or liquidated, or is capable of being ascertained by fixed rules or as a matter of opinion; and references in any such provision to owing a debt are to be read accordingly.

(4) In any provision of the 1986 Act, section 154 to 171 of and Schedule 20 and 21 to the 2004 Act, or these Rules, except in so far as the context otherwise requires, "liability" means (subject to paragraph (3) above) a liability to pay money or money's worth, including any liability under an enactment, any liability for breach of trust, any liability in contract, tort or bailment, and any liability arising out of an obligation to make restitution.

[7.1279]
206 "Venue"

References to the "venue" for any proceeding or attendance before the court, or for a meeting, are to the time, date and place for the proceeding, attendance or meeting or to the time and date for a meeting which is held in accordance with section 246A of the 1986 Act without any place being specified for it.

[7.1280]
207 Expressions used generally

(1) In these Rules expressions defined in section 102 of the 2011 Act have the meanings given to them in that section.

(2) A reference in these Rules to a numbered form is to the form so numbered in Schedule 1 to these Rules.

(3) In these Rules—

"Business day" means any day other than a Saturday, a Sunday, Christmas Day, Good Friday or a day which is a bank holiday in any part of Great Britain under or by virtue of the Banking and Financial Dealings Act 1971;

a "certificate of service" means a certificate of service verified by a statement of truth;

"costs officer" has the meaning given to it in CPR Part 43;

"File in court" means deliver to the court for filing;

"The Gazette" means the London Gazette;

"Gazetted" means advertised once in the Gazette;

"Practice direction" means a direction as to the practice and procedure of any court within the scope of the CPR;

"Prescribed part" has the same meaning as it does in section 176A(2) of the 1986 Act and the Insolvency Act 1986 (Prescribed Part) Order 2003;

"Standard contents" means—

(a) in relation to a notice to be gazetted, the contents specified in Rule 180; and

(b) in relation to a notice to be advertised in any other way, the contents specified in Rule 183;

a "statement of truth" means a statement of truth in accordance with CPR Part 22;

a "witness statement" means a witness statement verified by a statement of truth in accordance with CPR Part 22.

[7.1281]
208 Application

These Rules apply to energy supply company administration proceedings commenced on or after the date on which these Rules come into force. Nothing contained in the Insolvency Rules shall apply to such proceedings commenced on or after that date.

SCHEDULE 1
FORMS

Rule 177

NOTES

The forms themselves are not reproduced in this work, but their numbers and descriptions are listed below.

[7.1282]
Index

Form number	*Title*
ESCA1	Energy supply company administration application
ESCA2	Statement of proposed energy administrator
ESCA3	Esc administration order
ESCA4	Notice of energy administrator's appointment
ESCA5	Notice requiring submission of a statement of affairs
ESCA6	Statement of affairs
ESCA7	Statement of concurrence
ESCA8	Notice of extension of time period
ESCA9	Notice of a meeting of creditors
ESCA10	Creditor's request for a meeting
ESCA11	Statement of energy administrator's revised proposals
ESCA12	Energy administrator's progress report
ESCA13	Notice of intention to resign as energy administrator
ESCA14	Notice of resignation by energy administrator

SCHEDULE 2
PUNISHMENT OF OFFENCES UNDER THESE RULES

Rule 150

[7.1283]

Rule creating offence	*General nature of offence*	*Mode of prosecution*	*Punishment*	*Daily default fine (where applicable)*
Rule 33(6)	Energy administrator failing to send notification as to progress of energy supply company administration	Summary	One-fifth of the statutory maximum	One-fiftieth of the statutory maximum
Rule 94(2)	Energy administrator's duties on vacating office	Summary	One-fifth of the statutory maximum	One-fiftieth of the statutory maximum
Rule 149	False representation of status for purpose of inspecting documents	1 On indictment	Two years or a fine or both	
		2 Summary	Six months or the statutory maximum, or both	

G
FRIENDLY SOCIETIES

FRIENDLY SOCIETIES ACT 1992

(1992 c 40)

ARRANGEMENT OF SECTIONS

PART I
FUNCTIONS OF THE FINANCIAL CONDUCT AUTHORITY AND THE PRUDENTIAL REGULATION AUTHORITY

1 Functions of the Financial Conduct Authority and the Prudential Regulation Authority in relation to friendly societies . . . [7.1284]

PART II
INCORPORATED FRIENDLY SOCIETIES

Dissolution and winding up

19 Modes of dissolution and winding up . . . [7.1285]
20 Dissolution by consent . . . [7.1286]
21 Voluntary winding up . . . [7.1287]
22 Winding up by court: grounds and petitioners . . . [7.1288]
23 Application of winding up legislation to incorporated friendly societies . . . [7.1289]
24 Continuation of long term business . . . [7.1290]
25 Power of court to declare dissolution void . . . [7.1291]
26 Cancellation of registration . . . [7.1292]

PART X
GENERAL AND SUPPLEMENTARY

126 Short title and commencement . . . [7.1293]

SCHEDULES

Schedule 10—Application of Companies Winding Up Legislation to Incorporated Friendly Societies
Part I—General Mode of Application . . . [7.1294]
Part II—Modified Application of Insolvency Act 1986 Parts IV, 6, 7, 12 and 13 and Schedule 10 . [7.1295]
Part III—Modified Application of Insolvency (Northern Ireland) Order 1989 . . . [7.1296]
Part IV—Supplementary . . . [7.1297]

An Act to make further provision for friendly societies; to provide for the cessation of registration under the Friendly Societies Act 1974; to make provision about disputes involving friendly societies or other bodies registered under the Friendly Societies Act 1974 and about the functions of the Chief Registrar of friendly societies; and for connected purposes

[16 March 1992]

[PART I
FUNCTIONS OF THE [FINANCIAL CONDUCT AUTHORITY AND THE PRUDENTIAL REGULATION AUTHORITY]

[7.1284]

1 [Functions of the Financial Conduct Authority and the Prudential Regulation Authority in relation to friendly societies]

(1) The [Financial Conduct Authority ("the FCA")] has the following functions under this Act and the 1974 Act in relation to friendly societies—

(a) to secure that the purposes of each friendly society are in conformity with this Act and any other enactment regulating the purposes of friendly societies;

(b) to administer the system of regulation of the activities of friendly societies provided for by or under this Act and the 1974 Act; and

(c) to advise and make recommendations to the Treasury and other government departments on any matter relating to friendly societies.

[(1A) The function in subsection (1)(c) is also a function of the Prudential Regulation Authority ("the PRA").]

(2) The [FCA and the PRA also have], in relation to such societies, the other functions conferred on [them respectively] by or under this Act or any other enactment.]

NOTES

Part heading: words in square brackets substituted by the Financial Services Act 2012 (Mutual Societies) Order 2013, SI 2013/496, art 2(b), Sch 9, paras 1, 2.

Substituted, together with Part heading, for ss 1–4 as originally enacted, by the Financial Services and Markets Act 2000 (Mutual Societies) Order 2001, SI 2001/2617, art 13(1), Sch 3, Pt I, paras 53, 54.

Part 7G Special Insolvency Regimes

Section heading, sub-ss (1), (2): words in square brackets substituted by SI 2013/496, art 2(b), Sch 9, paras 1, 3(1), (2), (4), (5).
Sub-s (1A): inserted by SI 2013/496, art 2(b), Sch 9, paras 1, 3(3).

2–4 (*Substituted as noted to s 1 at* **[7.1284]**.)

PART II
INCORPORATED FRIENDLY SOCIETIES

5–18 (*Outside the scope of this work.*)

Dissolution and winding up

[7.1285]
19 Modes of dissolution and winding up

(1) An incorporated friendly society—
(a) may be dissolved by consent of the members; or
(b) may be wound up voluntarily or by the court, in accordance with this Part of this Act; and an incorporated friendly society may not, except where it is dissolved by virtue of section 85(4). 86(5) or 90(9) below, be dissolved or wound up in any other manner.

(2) An incorporated friendly society which is in the course of dissolution by consent, or is being wound up voluntarily, may be wound up by the court.

[7.1286]
20 Dissolution by consent

(1) An incorporated friendly society may be dissolved by an instrument of dissolution.
(2) An instrument of dissolution shall only have effect if it is approved by special resolution.
(3) An instrument of dissolution shall set out—
(a) the liabilities and assets of the society in detail;
(b) the number of members, and the nature of their interests in the society;
(c) the claims of creditors, and the provision to be made for their payment;
(d) the intended appropriation or division of the funds and property of the society;
(e) the names of one or more persons to be appointed as trustees for the purposes of the dissolution, and their remuneration.

(4) An instrument of dissolution may be altered, but the alteration shall only have effect if it is approved by special resolution.

(5) The provisions of this Act shall continue to apply in relation to an incorporated friendly society as if the trustees appointed under the instrument of dissolution were the committee of management of the society.

(6) The trustees shall—
(a) within 15 days of the passing of a special resolution approving an instrument of dissolution, give notice to the [FCA and, if the society is a PRA-authorised person, the PRA] of the fact and the date of commencement of the dissolution, enclosing a copy of the instrument; and
(b) within 15 days of the passing of a special resolution approving an alteration of such an instrument, give notice to the [FCA and, if the society is a PRA-authorised person, the PRA] of the fact, enclosing a copy of the altered instrument;

and if the trustees fail to comply with this subsection, they shall each be guilty of an offence and liable on summary conviction to a fine not exceeding level 3 on the standard scale.

(7) An instrument of dissolution or an alteration to such an instrument shall be binding on all members of the society as from the date on which the copy of the instrument or altered instrument, as the case may be, is placed on the public file of the society under subsection (12) below.

(8) The trustees shall, within 28 days from the termination of the dissolution, give notice to the [FCA and, if the society is a PRA-authorised person, the PRA] of the fact and the date of the termination, enclosing an account and balance sheet signed and certified by them as correct, and showing—
(a) the assets and liabilities of the society at the commencement of the dissolution; and
(b) the way in which those assets and liabilities have been applied and discharged.

(9) If the trustees fail to comply with subsection (8) above they shall each be guilty of an offence and liable on summary conviction—
(a) to a fine not exceeding level 2 on the standard scale; and
(b) in the case of a continuing offence, to an additional fine not exceeding one-tenth of that level for every day during which the offence continues.

(10) Except with the consent of the [appropriate authority], no instrument of dissolution or alteration to such an instrument shall be of any effect if the purpose of the proposed dissolution or alteration is to effect or facilitate the transfer of the society's engagements to any other friendly society or to a company.

(11) Any provision in a resolution or document that members of an incorporated friendly society proposed to be dissolved shall accept membership of some other body in or towards satisfaction of their rights in the dissolution shall be conclusive evidence of such purpose as is mentioned in subsection (10) above.

(12) The [FCA] shall keep in the public file of the society any notice or other document received by it under subsection (6) or (8) above and shall record in that file the date on which the notice or document is placed in it.

NOTES

Sub-ss (6), (8), (10), (12): words in square brackets substituted by the Financial Services Act 2012 (Mutual Societies) Order 2013, SI 2013/496, art 2(b), Sch 9, paras 1, 8.

[7.1287]
21 Voluntary winding up

(1) An incorporated friendly society may be wound up voluntarily under the applicable winding up legislation if it resolves by special resolution that it be wound up voluntarily.
(2) A copy of any special resolution passed for the voluntary winding up of an incorporated friendly society shall be sent by the society to the [FCA and, if the society is a PRA-authorised person, the PRA] within 15 days after it is passed; and the [FCA] shall keep the copy in the public file of the society.
(3) A copy of any such resolution shall be annexed to every copy of the memorandum or of the rules issued after the passing of the resolution.
(4) If an incorporated friendly society fails to comply with subsection (2) or (3) above, the society shall be guilty of an offence and liable on summary conviction to a fine not exceeding level 3 on the standard scale.
(5) For the purposes of this section, a liquidator of the society shall be treated as an officer of it.

NOTES

Sub-s (2): words in square brackets substituted by the Financial Services Act 2012 (Mutual Societies) Order 2013, SI 2013/496, art 2(b), Sch 9, paras 1, 9.

[7.1288]
22 Winding up by court: grounds and petitioners

(1) An incorporated friendly society may be wound up under the applicable winding up legislation by the court on any of the following grounds, that is to say, if—
- (a) the society has by special resolution resolved that it be wound up by the court;
- (b) the number of members is reduced below 7;
- (c) the number of members of the committee of management is reduced below 2;
- (d) the society has not commenced business within a year from its incorporation or has suspended its business for a whole year;
- (e) the society exists for an illegal purpose;
- (f) the society is unable to pay its debts; or
- (g) the court is of the opinion that it is just and equitable that the society should be wound up.

(2) Except as provided by subsection [(2A), (2B) or (3)] or the applicable winding up legislation, a petition for the winding up of an incorporated friendly society may be presented by—
- (a) the [FCA];
- [(aa) the PRA;]
- (b) the society or its committee of management;
- (c) any creditor or creditors (including any contingent or any prospective creditor); or
- (d) any contributory or contributories, or by all or any of those parties, together or separately.

[(2A) The FCA may only present a petition under subsection (2) in respect of a society which is a PRA-authorised person after consulting the PRA.
(2B) The PRA may only present a petition under subsection (2)—
- (a) in respect of a society which is a PRA-authorised person; and
- (b) after consulting the FCA.]

(3) A contributory may not present a petition unless the number of members is reduced below 7 or he has been a contributory for at least six months before the winding up.
(4) In this section "contributory" has the meaning assigned to it by paragraph 9 of Schedule 10 to this Act.

NOTES

Sub-s (2): words in square brackets substituted and para (aa) inserted by the Financial Services Act 2012 (Mutual Societies) Order 2013, SI 2013/496, art 2(b), Sch 9, paras 1, 10(1)–(4).
Sub-ss (2A), (2B): inserted by SI 2013/496, art 2(b), Sch 9, paras 1, 10(1), (5).

[7.1289]
23 Application of winding up legislation to incorporated friendly societies

(1) In this section "the companies winding up legislation" means the enactments applicable in relation to England and Wales, Scotland and Northern Ireland which are specified in paragraph 1 of Schedule 10 to this Act (including any enactment which creates an offence by any person arising out of acts or omissions occurring before the commencement of the winding up).
(2) In its application to the winding up of an incorporated friendly society, by virtue of section 21(1) or 22(I) above, the companies winding up legislation shall have effect with the modifications effected by Parts I to III of Schedule 10 to this Act; and the supplementary provisions of Part IV of that Schedule also have effect in relation to such a winding up and in relation to a dissolution by consent.
(3) In section 21 and 22 above "the applicable winding up legislation" means the companies winding up legislation as so modified.

[7.1290]

24 Continuation of long term business

(1) This section has effect in relation to the winding up of an incorporated friendly society which carries on long term business (including any reinsurance business).

(2) The liquidator shall, unless the court otherwise orders, carry on the long term business of the society with a view to its being transferred as a going concern under this Act; and, in carrying on that business, the liquidator may agree to the variation of any contracts of insurance in existence when the winding up order is made but shall not effect any new contracts of insurance.

(3) If the liquidator is satisfied that the interests of the creditors in respect of liabilities of the society attributable to its long term business require the appointment of a special manager of the society's long term business, he may apply to the court, and the court may on such application appoint a special manager of that business to act during such time as the court may direct, with such powers (including any of the powers of a receiver or manager) as may be entrusted to him by the court.

(4) Section 177(5) of the Insolvency Act 1986 or, as the case may be, Article 151 of the Insolvency (Northern Ireland) Order 1989 shall apply to a special manager appointed under subsection (3) above as it applies to a special manager appointed under that section or that Article.

(5) The court may, if it thinks fit and subject to such conditions (if any) as it may determine, reduce the amount of the contracts made by the society in the course of carrying on its long term business.

(6) The court may, on the application of the liquidator, a special manager appointed under subsection (3) above or the [FCA or the PRA] appoint an independent actuary to investigate the long term business of the society and to report to the liquidator, the special manager or the [FCA or the PRA], as the case may be, on the desirability or otherwise of that business being continued and on any reduction in the contracts made in the course of carrying on that business that may be necessary for its successful continuation.

NOTES

Sub-s (6): words in square brackets substituted by the Financial Services Act 2012 (Mutual Societies) Order 2013, SI 2013/496, art 2(b), Sch 9, paras 1, 11.

[7.1291]

25 Power of court to declare dissolution void

(1) Where an incorporated friendly society has been dissolved under section 20 above or following a winding up, the court may, at any time within 12 years after the date on which the society was dissolved, make an order under this section declaring the dissolution to have been void.

(2) An order under this section may be made, on such terms as the court thinks fit, on an application by the trustees under section 20 above or the liquidator, as the case may be, or by any other person appearing to the court to be interested.

(3) When an order under this section is made, such proceedings may be taken as might have been taken if the society had not been dissolved.

(4) The person on whose application the order is made shall, within 7 days of its being so made, or such further time as the court may allow, furnish the [FCA and, if the society is a PRA-authorised person, the PRA] with a copy of the order; and the [FCA] shall keep the copy in the public file of the society.

(5) If a person fails to comply with subsection (4) above, he shall be guilty of an offence and liable on summary conviction—

- (a) to a fine not exceeding level 3 on the standard scale; and
- (b) in the case of a continuing offence, to an additional fine not exceeding one-tenth of that level for every day during which the offence continues.

(6) In this section "the court" means—

- (a) in relation to a society whose registered office is in England and Wales, the High Court;
- (b) in relation to a society whose registered office is in Scotland, the Court of Session; and
- (c) in relation to a society whose registered office is in Northern Ireland, the High Court in Northern Ireland.

NOTES

Sub-s (4): words in square brackets substituted by the Financial Services Act 2012 (Mutual Societies) Order 2013, SI 2013/496, art 2(b), Sch 9, paras 1, 12.

[7.1292]

26 Cancellation of registration

(1) Where the [FCA] is satisfied that an incorporated friendly society has been dissolved under section 20 above or following a winding up, [it] shall cancel the society's registration under this Act.

(2) Where the [FCA] is satisfied, with respect to an incorporated friendly society—

- (a) that a certificate of incorporation has been obtained for the society by fraud or mistake; or
- (b) that the society has ceased to exist, [or
- (c) in the case of a society to which section 37(2) or (3) below applies, that the principal place of business of the society is outside the United Kingdom,]

[it] may cancel the registration of the society.

(3) Without prejudice to subsection (2) above, the [FCA] may, if it thinks fit, cancel the registration of an incorporated friendly society at the request of the society, evidenced in such manner as the [FCA] may direct.

(4) Before cancelling the registration of an incorporated friendly society under subsection (2) above, the [FCA] shall give to the society not less than two months' previous notice, specifying briefly the grounds of the proposed cancellation.

[(4A) The FCA must consult the PRA before cancelling under subsection (1), (2) or (3) the registration of a society which is a PRA-authorised person.]

(5) Where the registration of an incorporated friendly society is cancelled under subsection (2) above, the society may appeal—

(a) where the registered office of the society is situated in England and Wales, to the High Court;

(b) where that office is situated in Scotland, to the Court of Session; or

(c) where that office is situated in Northern Ireland, to the High Court in Northern Ireland;

and on any such appeal the court may, if it thinks it just to do so, set aside the cancellation.

(6) Where the registration of a society is cancelled under subsection (2) or (3) above, then, subject to the right of appeal under subsection (5) above, the society, so far as it continues to exist, shall cease to be a society incorporated under this Act.

(7) Subsection (6) above shall not affect any liability actually incurred by an incorporated friendly society; and any such liability may be enforced against the society as if the cancellation had not taken place.

(8) Any cancellation of the registration of an incorporated friendly society under this section shall be effected [by written notice given by the [FCA] to the society].

(9) As soon as practicable after the cancellation of the registration of an incorporated friendly society under this section the [FCA] shall cause notice thereof to be published in the London Gazette, the Edinburgh Gazette or the Belfast Gazette according to the situation of the society's registered office, and if it thinks fit, in one or more newspapers.

NOTES

Sub-s (1): word in first pair of square brackets substituted by the Financial Services Act 2012 (Mutual Societies) Order 2013, SI 2013/496, art 2(b), Sch 9, paras 1, 13(1), (2); word in second pair of square brackets substituted by the Financial Services and Markets Act 2000 (Mutual Societies) Order 2001, SI 2001/2617, art 13(1), Sch 3, Pt I, paras 53, 64(a).

Sub-s (2): word in first pair of square brackets substituted by SI 2013/496, art 2(b), Sch 9, paras 1, 13(1), (2); word in final pair of square brackets substituted by SI 2001/2617, art 13(1), Sch 3, Pt I, paras 53, 64(b); para (c) and word "or" immediately preceding it inserted by the Financial Institutions (Prudential Supervision) Regulations 1996, SI 1996/1669, reg 14(1).

Sub-ss (3), (4), (9): words in square brackets substituted by SI 2013/496, art 2(b), Sch 9, paras 1, 13(1), (2).

Sub-s (4A): inserted by SI 2013/496, art 2(b), Sch 9, paras 1, 13(1), (3).

Sub-s (8): words in first (outer) pair of square brackets substituted by SI 2001/2617, art 13(1), Sch 3, Pt I, paras 53, 64(d); word in second (inner) pair of square brackets substituted by SI 2013/496, art 2(b), Sch 9, paras 1, 13(1), (2).

27–101 *((Pts III–IX) outside the scope of this work.)*

PART X
GENERAL AND SUPPLEMENTARY

102–119 *(Outside the scope of this work.)*

Supplementary

120–125 *(Outside the scope of this work.)*

[7.1293]

126 Short title and commencement

(1) This Act may be cited as the Friendly Societies Act 1992.

(2) This Act shall come into force on such day as the Treasury may by order appoint and different days may be appointed for different provisions or different purposes.

(3) An order under subsection (2) above may contain such transitional provisions and savings (whether or not involving the modification of any statutory provision) as appear to the Treasury necessary or expedient in connection with the provisions brought into force.

NOTES

Orders: at present, 8 commencement orders have been made under this section. The orders relevant to provisions reproduced in this work are the Friendly Societies Act 1992 (Commencement No 1) Order 1992, SI 1992/1325 and the Friendly Societies Act 1992 (Commencement No 3 and Transitional Provisions) Order 1993, SI 1993/16.

SCHEDULES

SCHEDULES 1–9

(Schs 1–9 outside the scope of this work.)

SCHEDULE 10
APPLICATION OF COMPANIES WINDING UP LEGISLATION TO INCORPORATED FRIENDLY SOCIETIES

Section 23

PART I
GENERAL MODE OF APPLICATION

[7.1294]

1 The enactments which comprise the companies winding up legislation (referred to in this Schedule as "the enactments") are the provisions of—

(a) Parts IV, VI, VII, XII and XIII of the Insolvency Act 1986, or
(b) Parts V, VI, XI and XII of the Insolvency (Northern Ireland) Order 1989,

and, in so far as they relate to offences under any such enactment, sections 430 and 432 of, and Schedule 10 to, that Act or Article 373 of, and Schedule 7 to, that Order.

2 Subject to the following provisions of this Schedule, the enactments apply to the winding up of incorporated friendly societies as they apply to the winding up of companies registered under [the Companies Act 2006].

3 (1) Subject to the following provisions of this Schedule, the enactments shall, in their application to incorporated friendly societies, have effect with the substitution—
(a) for "company" of "incorporated friendly society";
(b) for "directors" of "committee of management";
(c) for "the registrar of companies" or "the registrar" of "the [Financial Conduct Authority]"; and
(d) for "the articles" of "the rules".

(2) Subject to the following provisions of this Schedule in the application of the enactments to incorporated friendly societies—
[(aa) every reference to a company registered in Scotland shall have effect as a reference to an incorporated friendly society whose registered office is situated in Scotland;]
(a) every reference to the officers, or to a particular officer, of a company shall have effect as a reference to the officers, or to the corresponding officer, of the incorporated friendly society and as including a person holding himself out as such an officer;
(b) every reference to a director of a company shall be construed as a reference to a member of the committee of management; and
(c) every reference to an administrator, an administration order, an administrative receiver, a shadow director or a voluntary arrangement shall be omitted.

4 (1) Where any of the enactments as applied to incorporated friendly societies requires a notice or other document to be sent to the [FCA], it shall have effect as if it required the [FCA] to keep the notice or document in the public file of the society and to record in that file the date on which the notice or document is placed in lt.

(2) Where any of the enactments, as so applied, refers to the registration, or to the date of registration, of such a notice or document, that enactment shall have effect as if it referred to the placing of the notice or document in the public file or (as the case may be) to the date on which it was placed there.

5 Any enactment which specifies a sum altered by order under section 416 of the Insolvency Act 1986 or Article 362 of the Insolvency (Northern Ireland) Order 1989 (powers to alter monetary limits) applies with the effect of the alteration.

NOTES

Para 2: words in square brackets substituted by the Companies Act 2006 (Consequential Amendments, Transitional Provisions and Savings) Order 2009, SI 2009/1941, art 2(1), Sch 1, para 133(1), (7)(a).

Para 3: words in square brackets in sub-para (1)(c) substituted by the Financial Services Act 2012 (Mutual Societies) Order 2013, SI 2013/496, art 2(b), Sch 9, paras 1, 53(1), (2); sub-para (2)(aa) inserted by the Financial Services and Markets Act 2000 (Mutual Societies) Order 2001, SI 2001/2617, art 13(1), Sch 3, Pt I, paras 53, 123(b).

Para 4: words in square brackets in sub-para (1) substituted by SI 2013/496, art 2(b), Sch 9, paras 1, 53(1), (3).

PART II
MODIFIED APPLICATION OF INSOLVENCY ACT 1986 PARTS IV[, [6, 7,] 12 AND 13] [AND SCHEDULE 10]

Preliminary

[7.1295]
6 In this Part of this Schedule, Part IV of the Insolvency Act 1986 is referred to as "Part IV"; and that Act is referred to as "the Act".

[6A Parts 4, 6, 7 and 12 of, and Schedule 10 to, the Act, in their application to incorporated friendly societies, have effect without the amendments of those Parts and that Schedule made by—
(a) section 122 of the Small Business, Enterprise and Employment Act 2015 (abolition of requirements to hold meetings: company insolvency);
(b) section 124 of that Act (ability for creditors to opt not to receive certain notices: company insolvency); and
(c) Part 1 of Schedule 9 to that Act (sections 122 to 125: further amendments).]

Members of a friendly society as contributories in winding up

7 (1) Section 74 (liability of members) of the Act is modified as follows.

(2) In subsection (1), the reference to any past member shall be omitted.

(3) Paragraphs (a) to (d) of subsection (2) shall be omitted; and so shall subsection (3).

(4) The extent of the liability of a member of an incorporated friendly society in a winding up shall not exceed the extent of his liability under paragraph 8 of Schedule 3 to this Act.

8 Sections 75 to 78 and 83 in Chapter I of Part IV (miscellaneous provisions not relevant to incorporated friendly societies) do not apply.

9 (1) Section 79 (meaning of "contributory") of the Act does not apply.

(2) In the enactments as applied to an incorporated friendly society, "contributory"—

(a) means every person liable to contribute to the assets of the society in the event of its being wound up; and

(b) for the purposes of all proceedings for determining, and all proceedings prior to the determination of, the persons who are to be deemed contributories, includes any person alleged to be a contributory; and

(c) includes persons who are liable to pay or contribute to the payment of—

(i) any debt or liability of the incorporated friendly society being wound up; or

(ii) any sum for the adjustment of rights of members among themselves; or

(iii) the expenses of the winding up;

but does not include persons liable to contribute by virtue of a declaration by the court under section 213 (imputed responsibility for fraudulent trading) or section 214 (wrongful trading) of the Act.

Voluntary winding up

10 (1) Section 84 of the Act does not apply.

(2) In the enactments as applied to an incorporated friendly society, the expression "resolution for voluntary winding up" means a resolution passed under section 21(1) above.

11 Section 88 shall have effect with the omission of the words from the beginning to "and".

12 (1) Subsection (1) of section 89 shall have effect as if for the words from the beginning to "meeting" there were substituted the words—

"(1) Where it is proposed to wind up an incorporated friendly society voluntarily, the committee of management (or, in the case of an incorporated friendly society whose committee of management has more than two members, the majority of them) may at a meeting of the committee".

(2) The reference to the directors in subsection (2) shall be construed as a reference to members of the committee of management.

13 Section 90 shall have effect as if for the words "directors' statutory declaration under section 89" there were substituted the words "statutory declaration made under section 89 by members of the committee of management".

14 Sections 95(1) and 96 shall have effect as if the word "directors" were omitted from each of them.

15 In subsection (1) of section 101 (appointment of liquidation committee) of the Act, the reference to functions conferred on a liquidation committee by or under that Act shall have effect as a reference to its functions by or under that Act as applied to incorporated friendly societies.

16 (1) Section 107 (distribution of property) of the Act does not apply; and the following applies in its place.

(2) Subject to the provisions of Part IV relating to preferential payments, an incorporated friendly society's property in a voluntary winding up shall be applied in satisfaction of the society's liabilities to creditors pari passu and, subject to that application, in accordance with the rules of the society.

17 Sections 110 and 111 (liquidator accepting shares, etc as consideration for sale of company property) of the Act do not apply.

Winding up by the court

18 In sections 117 (High Court and county court jurisdiction) and 120 (Court of Session and sheriff court jurisdiction) of the Act, each reference to a company's share capital paid up or credited as paid up shall have effect as a reference to the amount of the contribution or subscription income of an incorporated friendly society as shown by the latest balance sheet.

19 Section 122 (circumstances in which company may be wound up by the court) of the Act does not apply.

20 Section 124 (application for winding up) of the Act does not apply.

21 (1) In section 125 (powers of court on hearing of petition) of the Act, subsection (1) applies with the omission of the words from "but the court" to the end of the subsection.

(2) The conditions which the court may impose under section 125 of the Act include conditions for securing—

(a) that the incorporated friendly society be dissolved by consent of its members under section 20 above; or

(b) that the society amalgamates with, or transfers all or any of its engagements to, another friendly society under section 85 or 86 above, or

(c) that the society converts itself into a company under section 91 above,

and may also include conditions for securing that any default which occasioned the petition be made good and that the costs, or in Scotland the expenses, of the proceedings on that petition be defrayed by the person or persons responsible for the default.

22 Section 126 (power of court, between petition and winding-up order, to stay or restrain proceedings against company) of the Act has effect with the omission of subsection (2).

23 If, before the presentation of a petition for the winding up by the court of an incorporated friendly society, an instrument of dissolution under section 20 above is placed in the society's public file, section 129(1) (commencement of winding up by the court) of the Act shall also apply in relation to the date on which the notice is so placed and to any proceedings in the course of the dissolution as it applies to the commencement date for, and proceedings in, a voluntary winding up.

24 (1) Section 130 of the Act (consequences of winding-up order) shall have effect with the following modifications.

(2) Subsections (1) and (3) shall be omitted.

(3) An incorporated friendly society shall, within 15 days of a winding-up order being made in respect of it, give notice of the order to the [FCA and, if the society is a PRA-authorised person, the PRA]; and the [FCA] shall keep the notice in the public file of the society.

(4) If an incorporated friendly society fails to comply with sub-paragraph (3) above, it shall be guilty of an offence and liable on summary conviction to a fine not exceeding level 3 on the standard scale.

25 Section 140 (appointment of liquidator by court in certain circumstances) of the Act does not apply.

26 In the application of sections 141(1) and 142(1) (liquidation committees), of the Act to incorporated friendly societies, the references to functions conferred on a liquidation committee by or under that Act shall have effect as references to its functions by or under that Act as so applied.

27 The conditions which the court may impose under section 147 (power to stay or sist winding up) of the Act shall include those specified in paragraph 21(2) above.

28 Section 154 (adjustment of rights of contributories) of the Act shall have effect with the modification that any surplus is to be distributed in accordance with the rules of the society.

29 . . .

Winding up: general

30 Section 187 (power to make over assets to employees) of the Act does not apply.

31 (1) In section 201 (dissolution: voluntary winding up) of the Act, subsection (2) applies without the words from "and on the expiration" to the end of the subsection and, in subsection (3), the word "However" shall be omitted.

(2) Sections 202 to 204 (early dissolution) of the Act do not apply.

32 In section 205 (dissolution: winding up by the court) of the Act, subsection (2) applies with the omission of the words from "and, subject" to the end of the subsection; and in subsections (3) and (4) references to the Secretary of State shall have effect as references to the [FCA].

Penal provisions

33 Sections 216 and 217 of the Act (restriction on re-use of name) do not apply.

34 (1) Sections 218 and 219 (prosecution of delinquent officers) of the Act do not apply in relation to offences committed by members of an incorporated friendly society acting in that capacity.

(2) Sections 218(5) of the Act and subsections (1) and (2) of section 219 of the Act do not apply.

(3) The references in subsections (3) and (4) of section 219 of the Act to the Secretary of State shall have effect as references to the [FCA]; and the reference in subsection (3) to section 218 of the Act shall have effect as a reference to that section as supplemented by paragraph 35 below.

35 (1) Where a report is made to the prosecuting authority (within the meaning of section 218) under section 218(4) of the Act, in relation to an officer of an incorporated friendly society, he may, if he thinks fit, refer the matter to the [FCA] for further enquiry.

(2) On such a reference to it the [FCA] shall exercise its power under section 65(1) above to appoint one or more investigators to investigate and report on the matter.

(3) An answer given by a person to a question put to him, in exercise of the powers conferred by section 65 above on a person so appointed, may be used in evidence against the person giving it.

Preferential debts

36 Section 387 (meaning in Schedule 6 of "the relevant date") of the Act applies with the omission of subsections (2) and (4) to (6).

[Insolvency practitioners: their qualification and regulation

36A Section 390 of the Act (persons not qualified to act as insolvency practitioners) has effect as if for subsection (2) there were substituted—

> "(2) A person is not qualified to act as an insolvency practitioner in relation to an incorporated friendly society at any time unless at that time the person is fully authorised to act as an insolvency practitioner or partially authorised to act as an insolvency practitioner only in relation to companies.".

36B (1) In the following provisions of the Act, in a reference to authorisation or permission to act as an insolvency practitioner in relation to (or only in relation to) companies the reference to companies has effect without the modification in paragraph 3(1)(a) above—

(a) sections 390A and 390B(1) and (3) (authorisation of insolvency practitioners); and

(b) sections 391O(1)(b) and 391R(3)(b) (court sanction of insolvency practitioners in public interest cases).

(2) In sections 391Q(2)(b) (direct sanctions order: conditions) and 391S(3)(e) (power for Secretary of State to obtain information) of the Act the reference to a company has effect without the modification in paragraph 3(1)(a) above.]

NOTES

Part heading: words in first (outer) pair of square brackets substituted by the Small Business, Enterprise and Employment Act 2015 and the Insolvency (Amendment) Act (Northern Ireland) 2016 (Consequential Amendments and Transitional Provisions) Regulations 2017, SI 2017/400, reg 3(a); figures in second (inner) and words in third pairs of square brackets inserted by the Small Business, Enterprise and Employment Act 2015 (Consequential Amendments, Savings and Transitional Provisions) Regulations 2018, SI 2018/208, reg 3(a).

Para 6A: inserted by SI 2018/208, reg 3(b).

Para 24: words in square brackets substituted by the Financial Services Act 2012 (Mutual Societies) Order 2013, SI 2013/496, art 2(b), Sch 9, paras 1, 53(1), (4).

Para 29: repealed by the Companies Act 2006 (Commencement No 3, Consequential Amendments, Transitional Provisions and Savings) Order 2007, SI 2007/2194, art 10, Sch 4, Pt 3, para 71(1), Sch 5.

Paras 32, 34, 35: words in square brackets substituted by SI 2013/496, art 2(b), Sch 9, paras 1, 53(1), (5).

Paras 36A, 36B: inserted, together with preceding heading, by SI 2017/400, reg 3(b).

PART III
MODIFIED APPLICATION OF INSOLVENCY (NORTHERN IRELAND) ORDER 1989

Preliminary

[7.1296]

37 In this Part of this Schedule, Part V of the Insolvency (Northern Ireland) Order 1989 is referred to as "Part V"; and that Order is referred to as "the Order".

Members of a friendly society as contributories in winding up

38 (1) Article 61 (liability of members) of the Order is modified as follows.

(2) In paragraph (1), the reference to any past member shall be omitted.

(3) Sub-paragraphs (a) to (d) of paragraph (2) shall be omitted; and so shall paragraph (3).

(4) The extent of the liability of a member of an incorporated friendly society in a winding up shall not exceed the extent of his liability under paragraph 8 of Schedule 3 to this Act.

39 Articles 62 to 65 and 69 of the Order (miscellaneous provisions not relevant to incorporated friendly societies) do not apply.

40 (1) Article 13 (meaning of "contributory") of the Order does not apply.

(2) In the enactments as applied to an incorporated friendly society "contributory"—

(a) means every person liable to contribute to the assets of the society in the event of its being wound up; and

(b) for the purposes of all proceedings for determining, and all proceedings prior to the determination of, the persons who are to be deemed contributories, includes any person alleged to be a contributory; and

(c) includes persons who are liable to pay or contribute to the payment of—

 (i) any debt or liability of the incorporated friendly society being wound up; or

 (ii) any sum for the adjustment of rights of members among themselves; or

 (iii) the expenses of the winding up;

but does not include persons liable to contribute by virtue of a declaration by the court under Article 177 (imputed responsibility for fraudulent trading) or Article 178 (wrongful trading) of the Order.

Voluntary winding up

41 (1) Article 70 of the Order does not apply.

(2) In the enactments as applied to an incorporated friendly society, the expression "resolution for voluntary winding up" means a resolution passed under section 21(1) above.

42 Article 74 shall have effect with the omission of the words from the beginning to "and".

43 (1) Paragraph (1) of Article 75 shall have effect as if for the words from the beginning to "meeting" there were substituted the words—

> "(1) Where it is proposed to wind up an incorporated friendly society voluntarily, the committee of management (or, in the case of an incorporated friendly society whose committee of management has more than two members, the majority of them) may at a meeting of the committee".

(2) The reference to the directors in paragraph (2) shall be construed as a reference to members of the committee of management.

44 Article 76 shall have effect as if for the words "directors' statutory declaration in accordance with Article 75" there were substituted the words "statutory declaration made in accordance with Article 75 by members of the committee of management".

45 Article 81(1) and 82 shall have effect as if the word "directors" were omitted from each of them.

46 In paragraph (1) of Article 87 (appointment of liquidation committee) of the Order, the reference to functions conferred on a liquidation committee by or under that Order shall have effect as a reference to its functions by or under that Order as applied to incorporated friendly societies.

47 (1) Article 93 (distribution of property) of the Order does not apply; and the following applies in its place.

(2) Subject to the provisions of Part V relating to preferential payments, an incorporated friendly society's property in a voluntary winding up shall be applied in satisfaction of the society's liabilities to creditors pari passu and, subject to that application, in accordance with the rules of the society.

48 Articles 96 and 97 (liquidator accepting shares, etc as consideration for sale of company property) of the Order do not apply.

Winding up by the High Court

49 Article 102 (circumstances in which company may be wound up by the High Court) of the Order does not apply.

50 Article 104 (application for winding up) of the Order does not apply.

51 (1) In Article 105 (powers of High Court on hearing of petition) of the Order, paragraph (1) applies with the omission of the words from "but the Court" to the end of the paragraph.

(2) The conditions which the Court may impose under Article 105 of the Order include conditions for securing—

(a) that the incorporated friendly society be dissolved by consent of its members under section 20 above; or

(b) that the society amalgamates with, or transfers its engagements to, another friendly society under section 85 or 86 above; or

(c) that the society converts itself to a company under section 91 above,

and may also include conditions for securing that any default which occasioned the petition be made good and that the costs of the proceedings on that petition be defrayed by the person or persons responsible for the default.

52 Article 106 (power of court, between petition and winding-up order, to stay or restrain proceedings against company) of the Order has effect with the omission of paragraph (2).

53 If, before the presentation of a petition for the winding up by the High Court of an incorporated friendly society, an instrument of dissolution under section 20 is placed in the society's public file, Article 109(1) (commencement of winding up by the High Court) of the Order shall also apply in relation to the date on which the notice is so placed and to any proceedings in the course of the dissolution as it applies to the commencement date for, and proceedings in, a voluntary winding up.

54 (1) Article 110 of the Order (consequences of winding-up order) shall have effect with the following modifications.

(2) Paragraphs (1) and (3) shall be omitted.

(3) An incorporated friendly society shall, within 15 days of a winding-up order being made in respect of it, give notice of the order to the [FCA and, if the society is a PRA-authorised person, the PRA]; and the [FCA] shall keep the notice in the public file of the society.

(4) If an incorporated friendly society fails to comply with sub-paragraph (3) above, it shall be guilty of an offence and liable on summary conviction to a fine not exceeding level 3 on the standard scale.

55 Article 119 (appointment of liquidator by High Court in certain circumstances) of the Order does not apply.

56 In the application of Article 120(1) (liquidation committees), of the Order to incorporated friendly societies, the references to functions conferred on a liquidation committee by or under that Order shall have effect as references to its functions by or under that Order as so applied.

57 The conditions which the High Court may impose under Article 125 (power to stay winding up) of the Order shall include those specified in paragraph 51(2) above.

58 Article 132 (adjustment of rights of contributories) of the Order shall have effect with the modification that any surplus is to be distributed in accordance with the rules of the society.

59 . . .

Winding up: general

60 Article 158 (power to make over assets to employees) of the Order does not apply.

61 (1) In Article 166 (dissolution: voluntary winding up) of the Order, paragraph (2) applies without the words from "and on the expiration" to the end of the paragraph and, in paragraph (3), the word "However" shall be omitted.

(2) Articles 167 and 168 (early dissolution) of the Order do not apply.

62 In Article 169 (dissolution: winding up by the High Court) of the Order, paragraph (1) applies with the omission of the words from "and, subject" to the end of the paragraph; and in paragraphs (2) and (3) references to the Department shall have effect as references to the [FCA and the PRA].

Penal provisions

63 Articles 180 and 181 of the Order (restriction on re-use of name) do not apply.

64 (1) Articles 182 and 183 (prosecution of delinquent officers) of the Order do not apply in relation to offences committed by members of an incorporated friendly society acting in that capacity.

(2) Articles 182(4) and 183(1) and (2) of the Order do not apply.

(3) The references in paragraph (3) and (5) of Article 183 of the Order to the Department shall have effect as references to the [FCA]; and the reference in paragraph (3) to Article 182 of the Order shall have effect as a reference to that Article as supplemented by paragraph 65 below.

65 (1) Where a report is made to the prosecuting authority (within the meaning of Article 182) under Article 182(5) of the Order, in relation to an officer of an incorporated friendly society, he may, if he thinks fit, refer the matter to the [FCA] for further enquiry.

(2) On such a reference to it the [FCA] shall exercise its power under section 65(1) above to appoint one or more investigators to investigate and report on the matter.

(3) An answer given by a person to a question put to him in exercise of the powers conferred by section 65 above on a person so appointed may be used in evidence against the person giving it.

Preferential debts

66 Article 347 (meaning in Schedule 4 of "the relevant date") of the Order applies with the omission of paragraphs (2) and (4) to (6).

NOTES

Para 54: words in square brackets substituted by the Financial Services Act 2012 (Mutual Societies) Order 2013, SI 2013/496, art 2(b), Sch 9, paras 1, 53(1), (6).

Para 59: repealed by the Companies Act 2006 (Commencement No 3, Consequential Amendments, Transitional Provisions and Savings) Order 2007, SI 2007/2194, art 10, Sch 4, Pt 3, para 71(1), Sch 5.

Paras 62, 64, 65: words in square brackets substituted by SI 2013/496, art 2(b), Sch 9, paras 1, 53(1), (7), (8).

PART IV
SUPPLEMENTARY

Dissolution of incorporated friendly society after winding up

[7.1297]

67 (1) Where an incorporated friendly society has been wound up voluntarily, it is dissolved as from 3 months from the date of the placing in the public file of the society of the return of the final meetings of the society and its creditors made by the liquidator under—

- (a) section 94 or 106 of the Insolvency Act 1986 (as applied to incorporated friendly societies), or on such other date as is determined in accordance with section 201 of that Act; or
- (b) Article 80 or 92 of the Insolvency (Northern Ireland) Order 1989 (as so applied), or on such other date as is determined in accordance with Article 166 of that Order.

(2) Where an incorporated friendly society has been wound up by the court, it is dissolved as from 3 months from the date of the placing in the public file of the society of the liquidator's notice under—

- (a) section 172(8) of the Insolvency Act 1986 (as applied to incorporated friendly societies) or on such other date as is determined in accordance with section 205 of that Act; or
- (b) Article 146(7) of the Insolvency (Northern Ireland) Order 1989 (as so applied) or on such other date as is determined in accordance with Article 169 of that Order.

68 [(1) Sections 1012 to 1023 and 1034 of the Companies Act 2006 (property of dissolved company) apply in relation to the property of a dissolved incorporated friendly society (whether dissolved under section 20 or following its winding up) as they apply in relation to the property of a dissolved company.]

(2) Paragraph 3(1) above shall apply to those sections for the purpose of their application to incorporated friendly societies.

[(3) Any reference in those sections to restoration to the register shall be read as a reference to the effect of an order under section 25 of this Act.]

Insolvency rules and fees

69 (1) Rules may be made under—

- (a) section 411 of the Insolvency Act 1986; or
- (b) Article 359 of the Insolvency (Northern Ireland) Order 1989,

for the purpose of giving effect, in relation to incorporated friendly societies, to the provisions of the applicable winding up legislation.

(2) An order made by the competent authority under section 414 of the Insolvency Act 1986 may make provision for fees to be payable under that section in respect of proceedings under the applicable winding-up legislation and the performance by the official receiver or the Secretary of State of functions under it.

(3) An order made by the competent authority under Article 361 of the Insolvency (Northern Ireland) Order 1989 may make provisions for fees to be payable under that section in respect of proceedings under the applicable winding-up legislation and the performance by the official receiver in Northern Ireland or the Department of Economic Development in Northern Ireland of functions under it.

NOTES

Para 68: sub-para (1) substituted and sub-para (3) substituted, for original sub-paras (3), (4), by the Companies Act 2006 (Consequential Amendments, Transitional Provisions and Savings) Order 2009, SI 2009/1941, art 2(1), Sch 1, para 133(1), (7)(b).

SCHEDULES 11–22

(*Schs 11–22 outside the scope of this work.*)

H
HEALTH

NATIONAL HEALTH SERVICE ACT 2006

(2006 c 41)

ARRANGEMENT OF SECTIONS

PART 2
HEALTH SERVICE BODIES

CHAPTER 3
NHS TRUSTS

25 NHS Trusts . . . [7.1298]

CHAPTER 5
NHS FOUNDATION TRUST

Authorisation

33 Applications by NHS trusts . . . [7.1299]
35 Authorisation of NHS foundation trusts . . . [7.1300]
36 Effect of authorisation . . . [7.1301]
37 Amendments of constitution . . . [7.1302]
39 Register of NHS foundation trusts . . . [7.1303]

CHAPTER 5A
TRUST SPECIAL ADMINISTRATORS: NHS TRUSTS AND NHS FOUNDATION TRUSTS

Application

65A Application . . . [7.1304]

Appointment

65B NHS trusts: appointment of trust special administrator . . . [7.1305]
65C Suspension of directors . . . [7.1306]
65D NHS foundation trusts: appointment of trust special administrator . . . [7.1307]
65DA Objective of trust special administration . . . [7.1308]

Consultation and report

65F Draft report . . . [7.1309]
65G Consultation plan . . . [7.1310]
65H Consultation requirements . . . [7.1311]
65I Final report . . . [7.1312]
65J Power to extend time . . . [7.1313]

Action by the Secretary of State and the regulator

65K Secretary of State's decision in case of NHS trust . . . [7.1314]

Action by the regulator and the Secretary of State

65KA Regulator's decision in case of NHS foundation trust . . . [7.1315]
65KB Secretary of State's response to regulator's decision . . . [7.1316]
65KC Action following Secretary of State's rejection of final report . . . [7.1317]
65KD Secretary of State's response to re-submitted final report . . . [7.1318]
65L Trusts coming out of administration . . . [7.1319]
65LA Trusts to be dissolved . . . [7.1320]

Supplementary

65M Replacement of trust special administrator . . . [7.1321]
65N Guidance . . . [7.1322]
65O Interpretation of this Chapter . . . [7.1323]

PART 14
SUPPLEMENTARY

277 Commencement . . . [7.1324]
278 Short title, extent and application . . . [7.1325]

An Act to consolidate certain enactments relating to the health service

[8 November 2006]

1–12E (*Ss 1–12E (Pt I) outside the scope of this work.*)

PART 2
HEALTH SERVICE BODIES

13A–24A (*Ss 13A–14Z24 (Chs A1, A2) outside the scope of this work; ss 13–24A (Chs 1, 2) repealed by the Health and Social Care Act 2012, ss 33(2), 34(2).*)

CHAPTER 3 NHS TRUSTS

[7.1298]
25 NHS trusts
(1) The Secretary of State may by order establish bodies, called National Health Service trusts ("NHS trusts"), to provide goods and services for the purposes of the health service.
(2) An order under subsection (1) is referred to in this Act as "an NHS trust order".
(3) No NHS trust order may be made until after the completion of such consultation as may be prescribed.
(4) Schedule 4 makes further provision about NHS trusts.

NOTES

Repealed by the Health and Social Care Act 2012, s 179(2), as to the commencement of the 2012 Act, see s 306(1)(d), (4) thereof (at **[7.1371]**) which provides that it shall come into force on 27 March 2012 (so far as is necessary for enabling the exercise on or after that date of any power to make an order or regulations or to give directions), and as from a day to be appointed (otherwise).

Orders: orders made under this section establishing NHS trusts in specified areas are not listed in this work.

26–29 (*Ss 26, 27, and ss 28–29 (Ch 4) outside the scope of this work.*)

CHAPTER 5 NHS FOUNDATION TRUSTS

30–32 (*Outside the scope of this work.*)

Authorisation

NOTES

Heading: substituted by the words "Status etc of NHS foundation trusts" by the Health and Social Care Act 2012, s 180(5), as to the commencement of the 2012 Act, see s 306(1)(d), (4) thereof (at **[7.1371]**) which provides that it shall come into force on 27 March 2012 (so far as is necessary for enabling the exercise on or after that date of any power to make an order or regulations or to give directions), and as from a day to be appointed (otherwise).

[7.1299]
33 Applications by NHS trusts
(1) An NHS trust may make an application to the regulator for authorisation to become an NHS foundation trust, if the application is supported by the Secretary of State.
(2) The application must—
(a) . . .
(b) be accompanied by a copy of the proposed constitution of the NHS foundation trust,
and must give any further information which the regulator requires the applicant to give.
(3) The applicant may modify the application with the agreement of the regulator at any time before authorisation is given under section 35.
(4) Once an NHS trust has made the application—
(a) the provisions of the proposed constitution which give effect to paragraphs 3 to 19 of Schedule 7 have effect, but only for the purpose of establishing the initial membership of the NHS foundation trust and of the [council of governors], and the initial directors, and enabling the [council of governors] and board of directors to make preparations for the performance of their functions,
(b) the NHS trust may do anything (including the things mentioned in paragraph 14 of Schedule 4) which appears to it to be necessary or expedient for the purpose of preparing it for NHS foundation trust status.

NOTES

Repealed by the Health and Social Care Act 2012, s 180(1), as to the commencement of the 2012 Act, see s 306(1)(d), (4) thereof (at **[7.1371]**) which provides that it shall come into force on 27 March 2012 (so far as is necessary for enabling the exercise on or after that date of any power to make an order or regulations or to give directions), and as from a day to be appointed (otherwise). See also the savings in s 180(7) which provide that this section continues to have effect in the case of an NHS trust continuing in existence by virtue of s 179(3) of the 2012 Act.

Sub-s (2): para (a) repealed by the Health and Social Care Act 2012, s 159(2).

Sub-s (4): in para (a) words in square brackets substituted by the Health and Social Care Act 2012, s 151(9)(a).

34 (*Repealed by the Health and Social Care Act 2012, s 160(1), subject to savings in s 160(4), (7) thereof.*)

[7.1300]
35 Authorisation of NHS foundation trusts
(1) The regulator may give an authorisation under this section—
(a) to an NHS trust which has applied under section 33, . . .
(b) . . .
if the regulator is satisfied as to the following matters.

(2) The matters are that—

(a) the applicant's constitution will be in accordance with Schedule 7 and will otherwise be appropriate,

(b) the applicant has taken steps to secure that (taken as a whole) the actual membership of any public constituency, and (if there is one) of the patients' constituency, will be representative of those eligible for such membership,

(c) there will be a [council of governors], and a board of directors, constituted in accordance with the constitution,

(d) the steps necessary to prepare for NHS foundation trust status have been taken,

[(e) the applicant will be able to provide goods and services for the purposes of the health service in England,] and

(f) any other requirements which the regulator considers appropriate are met.

(3) In deciding whether it is satisfied as to the matters referred to in subsection (2)(e), the regulator must consider (among other things)—

(a) any report or recommendation in respect of the applicant made by [the Care Quality Commission],

(b) the financial position of the applicant.

[(3A) The regulator must not give an authorisation unless it is notified by the Care Quality Commission that it is satisfied that the applicant is complying with (so far as applicable) the requirements mentioned in section 12(2) of the Health and Social Care Act 2008 in relation to the regulated activity or activities the applicant carries on.

(3B) In subsection (3A), "regulated activity" has the same meaning as in section 8 of the Health and Social Care Act 2008.]

(4) . . .

(5) The regulator must not give an authorisation unless it is satisfied that the applicant has sought the views about the application of the following—

(a) . . .

(b) individuals who live in any area specified in the proposed constitution as the area for a public constituency,

(c) any local authority that would be authorised by the proposed constitution to appoint a member of the [council of governors],

(d) if the proposed constitution provides for a patients' constituency, individuals who would be able to apply to become members of that constituency,

(e) any prescribed persons.

(6) If regulations make provision about consultation, the regulator may not give an authorisation unless it is satisfied that the applicant has complied with the regulations.

(7) . . .

NOTES

Repealed by the Health and Social Care Act 2012, s 180(2), as to the commencement of the 2012 Act, see s 306(1)(d), (4) thereof (at **[7.1371]**) which provides that it shall come into force on 27 March 2012 (so far as is necessary for enabling the exercise on or after that date of any power to make an order or regulations or to give directions), and as from a day to be appointed (otherwise). See also the savings in s 180(7) which provide that this section continues to have effect in the case of an NHS trust continuing in existence by virtue of s 179(3) of the 2012 Act.

Sub-s (1): para (b) and word omitted immediately preceding it repealed by the Health and Social Care Act 2012, s 160(2), subject to savings in s 160(5), (7) thereof.

Sub-s (2): words in square brackets in para (c) substituted and para (e) substituted by the Health and Social Care Act 2012, s 151(3), (9)(a).

Sub-s (3): words in square brackets in para (a) substituted by the Health and Social Care Act 2008, s 95, Sch 5, Pt 3, para 83.

Sub-ss (3A), (3B): inserted by the Health and Social Care Act 2012, s 159(4), as to the commencement of the 2012 Act, see s 306(1)(d), (4) thereof (at **[7.1371]**) which provides that it shall come into force on 27 March 2012 (so far as is necessary for enabling the exercise on or after that date of any power to make an order or regulations or to give directions), and as from a day to be appointed (otherwise).

Sub-ss (4), (7): repealed by the Health and Social Care Act 2012, s 159(5).

Sub-s (5): para (a) repealed by the Local Government and Public Involvement in Health Act 2007, s 241, Sch 18, Pt 18; in para (c) words in square brackets substituted by the Health and Social Care Act 2012, s 151(9)(a).

[7.1301]

36 *Effect of authorisation*

(1) On an authorisation being given to a body corporate which is an NHS trust—

(a) it ceases to be an NHS trust and becomes an NHS foundation trust,

(b) the proposed constitution has effect, and

(c) any order under section 25(1) is revoked.

(2) . . .

(3) The authorisation is conclusive evidence that the body in question is an NHS foundation trust.

(4) Subsections (1) to (3) do not affect the continuity of the body or of its property or liabilities (including its criminal liabilities).

(5) The validity of any act of an NHS foundation trust is not affected by any vacancy among the directors or by any defect in the appointment of any director.

(6) An NHS foundation trust must not be regarded as the servant or agent of the Crown or as enjoying any status, immunity or privilege of the Crown; and an NHS foundation trust's property must not be regarded as property of, or property held on behalf of, the Crown.

NOTES

Section heading: substituted by words "Status etc of NHS foundation trusts" by the Health and Social Care Act 2012, s 180(4), as to the commencement of the 2012 Act, see s 306(1)(d), (4) thereof (at **[7.1371]**) which provides that it shall come into force on 27 March 2012 (so far as is necessary for enabling the exercise on or after that date of any power to make an order or regulations or to give directions), and as from a day to be appointed (otherwise), subject to savings in s 180(7) thereof.

Sub-ss (1), (3), (4): repealed by the Health and Social Care Act 2012, s 180(3), as to the commencement of the 2012 Act, see s 306(1)(d), (4) thereof (at **[7.1371]**) which provides that it shall come into force on 27 March 2012 (so far as is necessary for enabling the exercise on or after that date of any power to make an order or regulations or to give directions), and as from a day to be appointed (otherwise), subject to savings in s 180(7), (8) which provide (i) that those subsections continue to have effect in the case of an NHS trust continuing in existence by virtue of s 179(3) of the 2012 Act, and (ii) the repeal of sub-s (4) does not affect the continuity of anything continuing by virtue of that provision immediately before the commencement of s 180.

Sub-s (2): repealed by the Health and Social Care Act 2012, s 160(3), subject to savings in s 160(6), (7) thereof.

[7.1302]

37 Amendments of constitution

[(1)] An NHS foundation trust may make amendments of its constitution [only if—

(a) more than half of the members of the council of governors of the trust voting approve the amendments, and

(b) more than half of the members of the board of directors of the trust voting approve the amendments].

[(2) Amendments made under this section take effect as soon as the conditions in subsection (1)(a) and (b) are satisfied.

(3) But an amendment is of no effect in so far as the constitution would, as a result of the amendment, not accord with Schedule 7.

(4) The trust must inform the regulator of amendments made under this section; but the regulator's functions do not include a power or duty to determine whether or not the constitution, as a result of the amendments, accords with Schedule 7.]

NOTES

Sub-s (1): numbered as such, and words in square brackets substituted, by the Health and Social Care Act 2012, s 161(1), subject to transitional provisions in s 161(3) thereof.

Sub-ss (2)–(4): added by the Health and Social Care Act 2012, s 161(2), subject to transitional provisions in s 161(3) thereof.

38 (*Repealed by the Health and Social Care Act 2012, s 159(6).*)

[7.1303]

39 Register of NHS foundation trusts

(1) The regulator must continue to maintain a register of NHS foundation trusts.

(2) The register must contain in relation to each NHS foundation trust—

(a) a copy of the current constitution,

(b) . . .

(c) a copy of the latest annual accounts and of any report of the auditor on them,

(d) a copy of the latest annual report,

(e) . . .

(f) . . . [,

(g) a copy of any order made under section 65D, 65J, 65KC, 65L or 65LA,

(h) a copy of any report laid under section 65D,

(i) a copy of any information published under section 65D,

(j) a copy of any draft report published under section 65F,

(k) a copy of any statement provided under section 65F,

(l) a copy of any notice published under section 65F, 65G, 65H, 65J, 65KA, 65KB, 65KC or 65KD,

(m) a copy of any statement published or provided under section 65G,

(n) a copy of any final report published under section 65I,

(o) a copy of any statement published under section 65J or 65KC,

(p) a copy of any information published under section 65M].

(3) In relation to any time before an NHS foundation trust is first required to send an annual report to the regulator, the register must contain a list of the persons who were first elected or appointed as—

(a) the members of the [council of governors],

(b) the directors.

(4) Members of the public may inspect the register at any reasonable time.

(5) Any person who requests it must be provided with a copy of, or extract from, any document contained in the register on payment of a reasonable charge.

NOTES

Sub-s (2): paras (b), (e), (f) repealed, and paras (g)–(p) inserted, by the Health and Social Care Act 2012, ss 111(11)(a), 156(5), 159(7), 178(5).

Sub-s (3): in para (a) words in square brackets substituted by the Health and Social Care Act 2012, s 151(9)(a).

39A–65 (*Outside the scope of this work.*)

[CHAPTER 5A TRUST SPECIAL ADMINISTRATORS: NHS TRUSTS AND NHS FOUNDATION TRUSTS

Application

[7.1304]

65A Application

(1) This Chapter applies to—

(a) an NHS trust all or most of whose hospitals, establishments and facilities are in England;

[(b) any NHS foundation trust].

(2) . . .

NOTES

Chapter 5A (ss 65A–65O) inserted by the Health Act 2009, s 16.

Sub-s (1): para (a) repealed by the Health and Social Care Act 2012, s 179(6), Sch 14, Pt 1, paras 1, 12, as to the commencement of the 2012 Act, see s 306(1)(d), (4) thereof (at **[7.1371]**) which provides that it shall come into force on 27 March 2012 (so far as is necessary for enabling the exercise on or after that date of any power to make an order or regulations or to give directions), and as from a day to be appointed (otherwise); para (b) substituted, for original paras (b), (c), by the Health and Social Care Act 2012, s 174(1)(a).

Sub-s (2): repealed by the Health and Social Care Act 2012, s 174(1)(b).

[Appointment

[7.1305]

65B [NHS trusts: appointment of trust special administrator]

(1) The Secretary of State may make an order authorising the appointment of a trust special administrator to exercise the functions of the chairman and directors of an NHS trust to which this Chapter applies.

(2) An order may be made under subsection (1) only if the Secretary of State considers it appropriate in the interests of the health service.

(3) The order must specify the date when the appointment is to take effect, which must be within the period of 5 working days beginning with the day on which the order is made.

(4) Before making the order the Secretary of State must consult—

(a) the trust,

(b) any Strategic Health Authority in whose area the trust has hospitals, establishments or facilities, and

(c) any other person to which the trust provides goods or services under this Act and which the Secretary of State considers it appropriate to consult.

(5) The Secretary of State must lay before Parliament (with the statutory instrument containing the order) a report stating the reasons for making the order.

(6) If an order is made under subsection (1), the Secretary of State must—

(a) appoint a person as the trust special administrator with effect from the day specified in the order, and

(b) publish the name of the person appointed.

(7) A person appointed as a trust special administrator holds and vacates office in accordance with the terms of the appointment.

(8) The Secretary of State may pay remuneration and expenses to a trust special administrator.]

NOTES

Inserted as noted to s 65A at **[7.1304]**; repealed by the Health and Social Care Act 2012, s 179(6), Sch 14, Pt 1, paras 1, 13(1), as to the commencement of the 2012 Act, see s 306(1)(d), (4) thereof (at **[7.1371]**) which provides that it shall come into force on 27 March 2012 (so far as is necessary for enabling the exercise on or after that date of any power to make an order or regulations or to give directions), and as from a day to be appointed (otherwise).

Section heading: substituted by the Health and Social Care Act 2012, s 174(2).

[7.1306]

[65C Suspension of directors

(1) When the appointment of a trust special administrator takes effect, the trust's chairman and executive and non-executive directors are suspended from office.

(2) Subsection (1) does not affect the employment of the executive directors or their membership of any committee or sub-committee of the trust.]

NOTES

Inserted as noted to s 65A at **[7.1304]**; repealed by the Health and Social Care Act 2012, s 179(6), Sch 14, Pt 1, paras 1, 14, as to the commencement of the 2012 Act, see s 306(1)(d), (4) thereof (at **[7.1371]**) which provides that it shall come into force on 27 March 2012 (so far as is necessary for enabling the exercise on or after that date of any power to make an order or regulations or to give directions), and as from a day to be appointed (otherwise).

. . .

NOTES

Heading: repealed by the Health and Social Care Act 2012, s 174(7).

[7.1307]

[65D [NHS foundation trusts: appointment of trust special administrator]

[[(1) This section applies if the regulator is satisfied that[—

(a)] an NHS foundation trust is, or is likely to become, unable to pay its debts[, or
(b) there is a serious failure by an NHS foundation trust to provide services that are of sufficient quality to be provided under this Act and it is appropriate to make an order under subsection (2)].

[(1A) This section also applies if the Care Quality Commission—
(a) is satisfied that there is a serious failure by an NHS foundation trust to provide services that are of sufficient quality to be provided under this Act and that it is appropriate to make an order under subsection (2),
(b) informs the regulator that it is satisfied as mentioned in paragraph (a) and gives the regulator its reasons for being so satisfied, and
(c) requires the regulator to make an order under subsection (2).]

(2) The regulator may [or, where this section applies as a result of subsection (1A), must] make an order authorising the appointment of a trust special administrator to exercise the functions of the governors, chairman and directors of the trust.

(3) As soon as reasonably practicable after the making of an order under subsection (2), the Care Quality Commission must provide to the regulator a report on the safety and quality of the services that the trust provides under this Act.]

[(3A) Before imposing a requirement as mentioned in subsection (1A)(c), the Care Quality Commission must—
(a) consult the Secretary of State and the regulator, and
(b) having done that, consult—
(i) the trust,
(ii) the Board, and
(iii) any other person to which the trust provides services under this Act and which the Commission considers it appropriate to consult.]

(4) Before [making an order] under this section [(except where it is required to do so as a result of subsection (1A))], the regulator must consult first the Secretary of State and then—
(a) the trust,
[(aa) the Board,]
(b) . . .
(c) any other person to which the trust provides . . . services under this Act and which the regulator considers it appropriate to consult[, and
(d) the Care Quality Commission].]

[(5) An order under subsection (2) must specify the date when the appointment is to take effect, which must be within the period of 5 working days beginning with the day on which the order is made.

(6) The regulator must lay before Parliament (with the statutory instrument containing the order) a report stating the reasons for making the order.

(7) If the regulator makes an order under subsection (2), it must—
(a) appoint a person as the trust special administrator with effect from the day specified in the order, and
(b) publish the name of the person appointed.

(8) A person appointed as a trust special administrator under this section holds and vacates office in accordance with the terms of the appointment.

(9) A person appointed as a trust special administrator under this section must manage the trust's affairs, business and property, and exercise the trust special administrator's functions, so as to achieve the objective set out in section 65DA as quickly and as efficiently as is reasonably practicable.

(10) When the appointment of a trust special administrator under this section takes effect, the trust's governors, chairman and executive and non-executive directors are suspended from office; and Chapter 5 of this Part, in its application to the trust, is to be read accordingly.

(11) But subsection (10) does not affect the employment of the executive directors or their membership of any committee or sub-committee of the trust.

(12) The regulator may indemnify a trust special administrator appointed under this section in respect of such matters as the regulator may determine.]]

NOTES

Section heading: substituted by the Health and Social Care Act 2012, s 174(6).

Inserted as noted to s 65A at **[7.1304]**.

Sub-s (1): substituted, together with sub-ss (2), (3), by the Health and Social Care Act 2012, s 174(3); para (a) designated as such, and para (b) and word immediately preceding it added by the Care Act 2014, s 84(1).

Sub-ss (1A), (3A): inserted by the Care Act 2014, s 84(2), (4).

Sub-s (2): substituted, together with sub-ss (1), (3), by the Health and Social Care Act 2012, s 174(3); words in square brackets inserted by the Care Act 2014, s 84(3).

Sub-s (3): substituted, together with sub-ss (1), (2), by the Health and Social Care Act 2012, s 174(3).

Sub-s (4): words in first pair of square brackets substituted, para (aa), and para (d) and word immediately preceding it inserted, para (b) and words omitted from para (c) repealed, by the Health and Social Care Act 2012, s 174(4); words in second pair of square brackets inserted by the Care Act 2014, s 84(5).

Sub-ss (5)–(12): added by the Health and Social Care Act 2012, s 174(5).

[7.1308]

[65DA Objective of trust special administration

(1) The objective of a trust special administration is to secure—

(a) the continued provision of such of the services provided for the purposes of the NHS by the NHS foundation trust that is subject to an order under section 65D(2), at such level, as the commissioners of those services determine,

[(aa) that the services whose continuous provision is secured as mentioned in paragraph (a) are of sufficient safety and quality to be provided under this Act,] and

(b) that it becomes unnecessary for the order to remain in force for that purpose.

(2) The commissioners may determine that the objective set out in subsection (1) is to apply to a service only if they are satisfied that the criterion in subsection (3) is met.

(3) The criterion is that ceasing to provide the service under this Act would, in the absence of alternative arrangements for its provision under this Act, be likely to—

(a) have a significant adverse impact on the health of persons in need of the service or significantly increase health inequalities, or

(b) cause a failure to prevent or ameliorate either a significant adverse impact on the health of such persons or a significant increase in health inequalities.

(4) In determining whether that criterion is met, the commissioners must (in so far as they would not otherwise be required to do so) have regard to—

(a) the current and future need for the provision of the service under this Act,

(b) whether ceasing to provide the service under this Act would significantly reduce equality between those for whom the commissioner arranges for the provision of services under this Act with respect to their ability to access services so provided, and

(c) such other matters as may be specified in relation to NHS foundation trusts in guidance published by the regulator.

(5) The regulator may revise guidance under subsection (4)(c) and, if it does so, must publish the guidance as revised.

[(5A) Before publishing guidance under subsection (4)(c), the regulator must consult the Care Quality Commission.]

(6) Before publishing guidance under subsection (4)(c) or (5), the regulator must obtain the approval of—

(a) the Secretary of State;

(b) the Board.

(7) The Board must make arrangements for facilitating agreement between commissioners in determining the services provided by the trust under this Act to which the objective set out in subsection (1) is to apply.

(8) Where commissioners fail to reach agreement in pursuance of arrangements under subsection (7), the Board may make the determination (and the duty imposed by subsection (1)(a), so far as applying to the commissioners concerned, is to be regarded as discharged).

(9) In this section—

"commissioners" means the persons to which the trust provides services under this Act, and

"health inequalities" means the inequalities between persons with respect to the outcomes achieved for them by the provision of services that are provided as part of the health service.]

NOTES

Inserted by the Health and Social Care Act 2012, s 175(1).

Sub-s (1): para (aa) inserted by the Care Act 2014, s 85(1).

Sub-s (5A): inserted by the Care Act 2014, s 85(2).

65E (*Inserted as noted to s 65A at* **[7.1304]***; repealed by the Health and Social Care Act 2012, s 173(3).*)

[Consultation and report

[7.1309]

65F Draft report

(1) Within the period of [65 working days] beginning with the day on which a trust special administrator's appointment takes effect, the administrator must provide to *the Secretary of State* and publish a draft report stating the action which the administrator recommends *the Secretary of State* should take in relation to the trust.

(2) When preparing the draft report, the administrator must consult—

[(za) the Board,]

(a) . . .

(b) any other person to which the trust provides *goods or* services under this Act and which *the Secretary of State* directs the administrator to consult[, and

(c) the Care Quality Commission.]

[(2A) The administrator may not provide the draft report to the regulator under subsection (1)—

(a) without having obtained from each commissioner a statement that the commissioner considers that the recommendation in the draft report would achieve the objective set out in section 65DA, or

(b) where the administrator does not obtain a statement to that effect from one or more commissioners (other than the Board), without having obtained a statement to that effect from the Board.

(2B) Where the Board decides not to provide to the administrator a statement to that effect, the Board must—

(a) give a notice of the reasons for its decision to the administrator and to the regulator;

(b) publish the notice;

(c) lay a copy of it before Parliament.

(2C) In subsection (2A), "commissioner" means a person to which the trust provides services under this Act.]

(3) After receiving the draft report, *the Secretary of State* must lay it before Parliament.

[(4) For the purposes of this section in its application to the case of an NHS foundation trust, the references to the Secretary of State are to be read as references to the regulator.

(5) In the case of an NHS foundation trust, the administrator may not provide the draft report to the regulator under subsection (1)—

(a) without having obtained from each commissioner a statement that the commissioner considers that the recommendation in the draft report[—

(i) would achieve the objective set out in section 65DA(1)(a), and

(ii) would do so without harming essential services provided for the purposes of the NHS by any other NHS foundation trust or NHS trust that provides services under this Act to the commissioner,] or

(b) where the administrator does not obtain a statement to that effect from one or more commissioners (other than the Board), without having obtained a statement to that effect from the Board.

[(5A) Nor, in the case of an NHS foundation trust, may the administrator provide the draft report to the regulator under subsection (1) without having obtained from the Care Quality Commission a statement that it considers that the recommendation in the draft report would achieve that part of the objective set out in section 65DA(1)(aa).]

(6) Where the Board [or the Care Quality Commission] decides not to provide to the administrator a statement [to the effect mentioned in subsection (5) or (5A)], the Board [or (as the case may be) the Commission] must—

(a) give a notice of the reasons for its decision to the administrator and to the regulator;

(b) publish the notice;

(c) lay a copy of it before Parliament.

(7) In subsection (5), "commissioner" means a person to which the trust provides services under this Act.]

[(8) Where the administrator recommends taking action in relation to another NHS foundation trust or an NHS trust, the references in subsection (5) to a commissioner also include a reference to a person to which the other NHS foundation trust or the NHS trust provides services under this Act that would be affected by the action.

(9) A service provided by an NHS foundation trust or an NHS trust is an essential service for the purposes of subsection (5) if the person making the statement in question is satisfied that the criterion in section 65DA(3) is met.

(10) Section 65DA(4) applies to the person making the statement when that person is determining whether that criterion is met.]]

NOTES

Inserted as noted to s 65A at **[7.1304]**.

Sub-s (1): words in square brackets substituted by the Care Act 2014, s 120(2); for the words in italics there are substituted the words "the regulator" by the Health and Social Care Act 2012, s 179(6), Sch 14, Pt 1, paras 1, 15(1), (2), as to the commencement of the 2012 Act, see s 306(1)(d), (4) thereof (at **[7.1371]**) which provides that it shall come into force on 27 March 2012 (so far as is necessary for enabling the exercise on or after that date of any power to make an order or regulations or to give directions), and as from a day to be appointed (otherwise).

Sub-s (2): para (za) inserted, and para (a) repealed, by the Health and Social Care Act 2012, s 176(1)(a); the word "and" following para (a) was repealed, and para (c) and the word immediately preceding it was inserted, by the Care Act 2014, s 85(3); first words in italics in in para (b) repealed, and for the second words in italics in that paragraph there are substituted the words "the regulator", by the Health and Social Care Act 2012, s 179(6), Sch 14, Pt 1, paras 1, 15(1), (3), as to the commencement of the 2012 Act, see s 306(1)(d), (4) thereof (at **[7.1371]**) which provides that it shall come into force on 27 March 2012 (so far as is necessary for enabling the exercise on or after that date of any power to make an order or regulations or to give directions), and as from a day to be appointed (otherwise).

Sub-ss (2A)–(2C): inserted by the Health and Social Care Act 2012, s 179(6), Sch 14, Pt 1, paras 1, 15(1), (4), as to the commencement of the 2012 Act, see s 306(1)(d), (4) thereof (at **[7.1371]**) which provides that it shall come into force on 27 March 2012 (so far as is necessary for enabling the exercise on or after that date of any power to make an order or regulations or to give directions), and as from a day to be appointed (otherwise).

Sub-s (3): for the words in italics there are substituted the words "the regulator" by the Health and Social Care Act 2012, s 179(6), Sch 14, Pt 1, paras 1, 15(1), (5).

Sub-ss (4), (5), (6), (7): added by the Health and Social Care Act 2012, s 176(2); repealed by the Health and Social Care Act 2012, s 179(6), Sch 14, Pt 1, paras 1, 15(1), (6), as to the commencement of the 2012 Act, see s 306(1)(d), (4) thereof (at **[7.1371]**) which provides that it shall come into force on 27 March 2012 (so far as is necessary for enabling the exercise on or after that date of any power to make an order or regulations or to give directions), and as from a day to be appointed (otherwise); words in square brackets in sub-s (5)(a) substituted by the Care Act 2014, s 120(3); words in first and third pairs of square brackets in sub-s (6) inserted, and words in second pair of square brackets in that subsection substituted, by s 85(6) of the 2014 Act.

Sub-s (5A): inserted by the Care Act 2014, s 85(5).

Sub-ss (8)–(10): added by the Care Act 2014, s 120(4).

[7.1310]

[65G Consultation plan

(1) At the same time as publishing a draft report under section 65F, a trust special administrator must publish a statement setting out the means by which the administrator will seek responses to the draft report.

(2) The statement must specify a period of [40 working days] within which the administrator seeks responses (the "consultation period").

(3) The first day of the consultation period must be within the period of 5 working days beginning with the day on which the draft report is published.]

[(4) *In the case of an NHS foundation trust,* the administrator may not make a variation to the draft report following the consultation period—

(a) without having obtained from each commissioner a statement that the commissioner considers that the recommendation in the draft report as so varied[—

(i) would achieve the objective set out in section 65DA(1)(a), and

(ii) would do so without harming essential services provided for the purposes of the NHS by any other NHS foundation trust or NHS trust that provides services under this Act to the commissioner,]

(b) where the administrator does not obtain a statement to that effect from one or more commissioners (other than the Board), without having obtained a statement to that effect from the Board.

[(4A) Nor may the administrator make a variation to the draft report following the consultation period without having obtained from the Care Quality Commission a statement that it considers that the recommendation in the draft report as so varied would achieve that part of the objective set out in section 65DA(1)(aa).]

(5) Where the Board [or the Care Quality Commission] decides not to provide to the administrator a statement [to the effect mentioned in subsection (4) or (4A)], the Board [or (as the case may be) the Commission] must—

(a) give a notice of the reasons for its decision to the administrator and to the regulator;

(b) publish the notice;

(c) lay a copy of it before Parliament.

(6) In subsection (4), "commissioner" means a person to which the trust provides services under this Act.

[(7) Where the administrator recommends taking action in relation to another NHS foundation trust or an NHS trust, the references in subsection (4) to a commissioner also include a reference to a person to which the other NHS foundation trust or the NHS trust provides services under this Act that would be affected by the action.

(8) A service provided by an NHS foundation trust or an NHS trust is an essential service for the purposes of subsection (4) if the person making the statement in question is satisfied that the criterion in section 65DA(3) is met.

(9) Section 65DA(4) applies to the person making the statement when that person is determining whether that criterion is met.]]

NOTES

Inserted as noted to s 65A at **[7.1304]**.

Sub-s (2): words in square brackets substituted by the Care Act 2014, s 120(5).

Sub-s (4): added, together with sub-ss (5), (6), by the Health and Social Care Act 2012, s 176(3); words in italics repealed by the Health and Social Care Act 2012, s 179(6), Sch 14, Pt 1, paras 1, 16, as to the commencement of the 2012 Act, see s 306(1)(d), (4) thereof (at **[7.1371]**) which provides that it shall come into force on 27 March 2012 (so far as is necessary for enabling the exercise on or after that date of any power to make an order or regulations or to give directions), and as from a day to be appointed (otherwise); words in square brackets in para (a) substituted by the Care Act 2014, s 120(6).

Sub-ss (4A), (7)–(9): inserted and added respectively by the Care Act 2014, s 85(8), 120(7).

Sub-s (5): added as noted above; words in first and third pairs of square brackets inserted, and words in second pair of square brackets substituted, by the Care Act 2014, s 85(9).

Sub-(6): added as noted above.

[7.1311]

[65H Consultation requirements

(1) The following duties apply during the consultation period.

(2) The trust special administrator must publish a notice stating that the administrator is seeking responses to the draft report and describing how people can give their responses.

(3) A notice under subsection (2) must include details of how responses can be given in writing.

(4) The trust special administrator must[—

(a)] hold at least one meeting to seek responses from staff of the trust and from such persons as the trust special administrator may recognise as representing staff of the trust[, and

(b) in the case of each affected trust, hold at least one meeting to seek responses from staff of the trust and from such persons as the trust special administrator may recognise as representing staff of the trust.]

(5) The trust special administrator must hold at least one other meeting to seek responses from any person who wishes to attend, after publishing notice of the date, time and place of the meeting.

(6) Notices under subsections (2) and (5) must be published at least once in the first 5 working days of the consultation period.

(7) The trust special administrator must request a written response from—

[(za) the Board,]

(a) . . .

(b) any other person to which the trust provides *goods or* services under this Act . . . ;

[(bza) any affected trust;

(bzb) any person to which an affected trust provides goods or services under this Act that would be affected by the action recommended in the draft report;

(bzc) any local authority in whose area the trust provides goods or services under this Act;
(bzd) any local authority in whose area an affected trust provides goods or services under this Act;
(bze) any Local Healthwatch organisation for the area of a local authority mentioned in paragraph (bzc) or (bzd);]
[(ba) the Care Quality Commission;]
(c) any person within subsection (8), if required by directions given by *the Secretary of State* [;
(d) any other person specified in a direction given by *the Secretary of State*].

(8) The persons within this subsection are—
(a)–(d) . . .
[(e) . . .]
(f) the member of Parliament for any constituency.

(9) The trust special administrator must[—
(a)] hold at least one meeting to seek responses from representatives of [the Board and] each of the persons from whom the administrator must request a written response under subsection [(7)(b), [(bzb),] [(ba),] (c) or (d)]
[(b) hold at least one meeting to seek responses from representatives of each of the trusts from which the administrator must request a written response under subsection (7)(bza), and
(c) hold at least one meeting to seek responses from representatives of each of the local authorities and Local Healthwatch organisations from which the administrator must request a written response under subsection (7)(bzc), (bzd) and (bze).]

(10) *The Secretary of State* may direct an administrator to—
(a) request a written response from any person;
(b) hold a meeting to seek a response from any person.

[(10A) The Secretary of State may direct the regulator as to persons from whom it should direct the administrator under subsection (10) to request or seek a response.]

(11) In subsection (4) "staff of the trust" means persons employed by the trust or otherwise working for the trust (whether as or on behalf of a contractor, as a volunteer or otherwise).]

[(11A) In this section, "affected trust" means—
(a) where the trust in question is an NHS trust, another NHS trust, or an NHS foundation trust, which provides goods or services under this Act that would be affected by the action recommended in the draft report;
(b) where the trust in question is an NHS foundation trust, another NHS foundation trust, or an NHS trust, which provides services under this Act that would be affected by the action recommended in the draft report.]

(11B) In this section, a reference to a local authority includes a reference to the council of a district only where the district is comprised in an area for which there is no county council.]

[(12) For the purposes of this section in its application to the case of an NHS foundation trust—
(a) in subsection (7)(b)[, (bzb), (bzc) and (bzd)], the words "goods or" are to be ignored, and
(b) in subsections (7)(c) and (d) and (10), the references to the Secretary of State are to be read as references to the regulator.

(13) In the case of an NHS foundation trust, the Secretary of State may direct the regulator as to persons from whom it should direct the administrator under subsection (10) to request or seek a response.]

NOTES

Inserted as noted to s 65A at **[7.1304]**.

Sub-s (4): para (a) designated as such and para (b) and word immediately preceding it added by the Care Act 2014, s 120(8).

Sub-s (7): paras (za), (d) inserted, and para (a) and words omitted from para (b) repealed, by the Health and Social Care Act 2012, s 176(4); in para (b) words in italics repealed and in paras (c), (d) for the words in italics there are substituted the words "the regulator" by the Health and Social Care Act 2012, s 179(6), Sch 14, Pt 1, paras 1, 17(1), (2), as to the commencement of the 2012 Act, see s 306(1)(d), (4) thereof (at **[7.1371]**) which provides that it shall come into force on 27 March 2012 (so far as is necessary for enabling the exercise on or after that date of any power to make an order or regulations or to give directions), and as from a day to be appointed (otherwise); paras (bza)–(bze), (ba) inserted by the Care Act 2014, ss 85(10)(a), 120(9).

Sub-s (8): paras (a)–(d) repealed by the Health and Social Care Act 2012, ss 176(5); para (e) repealed by the Care Act 2014, s 120(10).

Sub-s (9): para (a) designated as such, references in third (inner) and final (inner) pairs of square brackets inserted, and paras (b), (c) added by the Care Act 2014, ss 85(10)(b), 120(11); in para (a) words in first pair of square brackets inserted and words in second (outer) pair of square brackets substituted by the Health and Social Care Act 2012, s 176(6).

Sub-s (10): for the words in italics there are substituted the words "the regulator" by the Health and Social Care Act 2012, s 179(6), Sch 14, Pt 1, paras 1, 17(1), (3), as to the commencement of the 2012 Act, see s 306(1)(d), (4) thereof (at **[7.1371]**) which provides that it shall come into force on 27 March 2012 (so far as is necessary for enabling the exercise on or after that date of any power to make an order or regulations or to give directions), and as from a day to be appointed (otherwise).

Sub-s (10A): inserted by the Health and Social Care Act 2012, s 179(6), Sch 14, Pt 1, paras 1, 17(1), (4), as to the commencement of the 2012 Act, see s 306(1)(d), (4) thereof (at **[7.1371]**) which provides that it shall come into force on 27 March 2012 (so far as is necessary for enabling the exercise on or after that date of any power to make an order or regulations or to give directions), and as from a day to be appointed (otherwise).

Sub-ss (11A), (11B): inserted by the Care Act 2014, s 120(12).

Sub-ss (12), (13): added by the Health and Social Care Act 2012, s 176(7); repealed by the Health and Social Care Act 2012, s 179(6), Sch 14, Pt 1, paras 1, 17(1), (5), as to the commencement of the 2012 Act, see s 306(1)(d), (4) thereof (at **[7.1371]**) which provides that it shall come into force on 27 March 2012 (so far as is necessary for enabling the exercise on or after that date of any power to make an order or regulations or to give directions), and as from a day to be appointed (otherwise); words in square brackets in sub-s (12)(a) inserted by the Care Act 2014, s 120(13).

[7.1312]

[65I Final report

(1) Within the period of 15 working days beginning with the end of the consultation period, the trust special administrator must provide to *the Secretary of State* a final report stating the action which the administrator recommends that *the Secretary of State* should take in relation to the trust.

(2) The administrator must attach to the final report a summary of all responses to the draft report which were received by the administrator in the period beginning with the publication of the draft report and ending with the last day of the consultation period.

(3) After receiving the administrator's final report, *the Secretary of State* must publish it and lay it before Parliament.

[(4) For the purposes of this section in its application to the case of an NHS foundation trust, the references to the Secretary of State are to be read as references to the regulator.]]

NOTES

Inserted as noted to s 65A at **[7.1304]**.

Sub-ss (1), (3): for the words in italics there are substituted the words "the regulator" by the Health and Social Care Act 2012, s 179(6), Sch 14, Pt 1, paras 1, 18(1)–(3), as to the commencement of the 2012 Act, see s 306(1)(d), (4) thereof (at **[7.1371]**) which provides that it shall come into force on 27 March 2012 (so far as is necessary for enabling the exercise on or after that date of any power to make an order or regulations or to give directions), and as from a day to be appointed (otherwise).

Sub-s (4): added by the Health and Social Care Act 2012, s 176(8); repealed by the Health and Social Care Act 2012, s 179(6), Sch 14, Pt 1, paras 1, 18(1), (4), as to the commencement of the 2012 Act, see s 306(1)(d), (4) thereof (at **[7.1371]**) which provides that it shall come into force on 27 March 2012 (so far as is necessary for enabling the exercise on or after that date of any power to make an order or regulations or to give directions), and as from a day to be appointed (otherwise).

[7.1313]

[65J Power to extend time

[(1) This section applies to—

(a) the duty of a trust special administrator to provide a draft report within the period specified in section 65F(1);

(b) the duty of a trust special administrator to consult in the consultation period specified under section 65G(2);

(c) the duty of a trust special administrator to provide a final report within the period specified in section 65I(1).

(2) If *the Secretary of State* thinks it is not reasonable in the circumstances for the administrator to be required to carry out the duty within the specified period, *the Secretary of State* may by order extend the period.

(3) If an order is made extending the period mentioned in subsection (1)(a) or (c) the trust special administrator must publish a notice stating the new date on which the period will expire.

(4) If an order is made extending the period mentioned in subsection (1)(b) the trust special administrator must—

(a) publish a notice stating the new date on which the period will expire, and

(b) publish a statement setting out the means by which the administrator will seek responses to the draft report during the extended consultation period.

[(5) For the purposes of this section in its application to the case of an NHS foundation trust, the references to the Secretary of State are to be read as references to the regulator.]]

NOTES

Inserted as noted to s 65A at **[7.1304]**.

Sub-s (2): for the words in italics there are substituted the words "the regulator" by the Health and Social Care Act 2012, s 179(6), Sch 14, Pt 1, paras 1, 19(1), (2), as to the commencement of the 2012 Act, see s 306(1)(d), (4) thereof (at **[7.1371]**) which provides that it shall come into force on 27 March 2012 (so far as is necessary for enabling the exercise on or after that date of any power to make an order or regulations or to give directions), and as from a day to be appointed (otherwise).

Sub-s (5): added by the Health and Social Care Act 2012, s 176(9); repealed by the Health and Social Care Act 2012, s 179(6), Sch 14, Pt 1, paras 1, 19(1), (3), as to the commencement of the 2012 Act, see s 306(1)(d), (4) thereof (at **[7.1371]**) which provides that it shall come into force on 27 March 2012 (so far as is necessary for enabling the exercise on or after that date of any power to make an order or regulations or to give directions), and as from a day to be appointed (otherwise).

[[Action by the Secretary of State and the regulator]

NOTES

Heading: substituted by the Health and Social Care Act 2012, s 177(7).

[7.1314]

65K [Secretary of State's decision in case of NHS trust]

[(1) Within the period of 20 working days beginning with the day on which the Secretary of State receives a final report under section 65I [relating to an NHS trust], the Secretary of State must decide what action to take in relation to the trust.

(2) The Secretary of State must as soon as reasonably practicable—

(a) publish a notice of the decision and of the reasons for it;

(b) lay a copy of the notice before Parliament.]

NOTES

Inserted as noted to s 65A at **[7.1304]**; repealed by the Health and Social Care Act 2012, s 179(6), Sch 14, Pt 1, paras 1, 20(1), as to the commencement of the 2012 Act, see s 306(1)(d), (4) thereof (at **[7.1371]**) which provides that it shall come into force on 27 March 2012 (so far as is necessary for enabling the exercise on or after that date of any power to make an order or regulations or to give directions), and as from a day to be appointed (otherwise).

Section heading: substituted by the Health and Social Care Act 2012, s 177(1).

Sub-s (1): words in square brackets inserted by the Health and Social Care Act 2012, s 177(1).

[Action by the regulator and the Secretary of State]

NOTES

Heading: inserted by the Health and Social Care Act 2012, s 179(6), Sch 14, Pt 1, paras 1, 21(1), (5).

[7.1315]

[65KA *Regulator's decision in case of NHS foundation trust*

(1) Within the period of 20 working days beginning with the day on which the regulator receives a final report under section 65I *relating to an NHS foundation trust*, the regulator must decide whether it is satisfied—

(a) that the action recommended in the final report would achieve the objective set out in section 65DA, and

(b) that the trust special administrator has carried out the administration duties.

(2) In subsection (1)(b), "administration duties" means the duties imposed on the administrator by—

(a) this Chapter,

(b) a direction under this Chapter, or

(c) the administrator's terms of appointment.

(3) If the regulator is satisfied as mentioned in subsection (1), it must as soon as reasonably practicable provide to the Secretary of State—

(a) the final report, and

(b) the report provided to the regulator by the Care Quality Commission under section 65D(3).

(4) If the regulator is not satisfied as mentioned in subsection (1), it must as soon as reasonably practicable give a notice of that decision to the administrator.

(5) Where the regulator gives a notice under subsection (4), sections 65F to 65J apply in relation to *the trust* to such extent, and with such modifications, as the regulator may specify in the notice.

(6) The regulator must as soon as reasonably practicable after giving a notice under subsection (4)—

(a) publish the notice;

(b) lay a copy of it before Parliament.]

NOTES

Inserted, together with ss 65KB–65KD, by the Health and Social Care Act 2012, s 177(2).

Section heading: substituted by the words "The regulator's decision" by the Health and Social Care Act 2012, s 179(6), Sch 14, Pt 1, paras 1, 21(1), (4), as to the commencement of the 2012 Act, see s 306(1)(d), (4) thereof (at **[7.1371]**) which provides that it shall come into force on 27 March 2012 (so far as is necessary for enabling the exercise on or after that date of any power to make an order or regulations or to give directions), and as from a day to be appointed (otherwise).

Sub-s (1): words in italics repealed by the Health and Social Care Act 2012, s 179(6), Sch 14, Pt 1, paras 1, 21(1), (2), as to the commencement of the 2012 Act, see s 306(1)(d), (4) thereof (at **[7.1371]**) which provides that it shall come into force on 27 March 2012 (so far as is necessary for enabling the exercise on or after that date of any power to make an order or regulations or to give directions), and as from a day to be appointed (otherwise).

Sub-s (5): for the words in italics there are substituted the words "the NHS foundation trust in question" by the Health and Social Care Act 2012, s 179(6), Sch 14, Pt 1, paras 1, 21(1), (3), as to the commencement of the 2012 Act, see s 306(1)(d), (4) thereof (at **[7.1371]**) which provides that it shall come into force on 27 March 2012 (so far as is necessary for enabling the exercise on or after that date of any power to make an order or regulations or to give directions), and as from a day to be appointed (otherwise).

[7.1316]

[65KB Secretary of State's response to regulator's decision

(1) Within the period of 30 working days beginning with the day on which the Secretary of State receives the reports referred to in section 65KA(3), the Secretary of State must decide whether the Secretary of State is satisfied—

(a) that the persons to which the NHS foundation trust in question provides services under this Act have discharged their functions for the purposes of this Chapter,

(b) that the trust special administrator has carried out the administration duties (within the meaning of section 65KA(1)(b)),

(c) that the regulator has discharged its functions for the purposes of this Chapter,

[(ca) that the Care Quality Commission has discharged its functions for the purposes of this Chapter,]

(d) that the action recommended in the final report would secure the continued provision of the services provided by the trust to which the objective set out in section 65DA applies,

(e) that the recommended action would secure the provision of services that are of sufficient safety and quality to be provided under this Act, and

(f) that the recommended action would provide good value for money.

(2) If the Secretary of State is not satisfied as mentioned in subsection (1), the Secretary of State must as soon as reasonably practicable—

(a) give the trust special administrator a notice of the decision and of the reasons for it;

(b) give a copy of the notice to the regulator [and the Care Quality Commission];

(c) publish the notice;

(d) lay a copy of it before Parliament.]

NOTES

Inserted as noted to s 65KA at [7.1316].

Sub-s (1): para (ca) inserted by the Care Act 2014, s 85(11).

Sub-s (2): in para (b) words in square brackets inserted by the Care Act 2014, s 85(12).

[7.1317]

[65KC Action following Secretary of State's rejection of final report

(1) Within the period of 20 working days beginning with the day on which the trust special administrator receives a notice under section 65KB(2), the administrator must provide to the regulator the final report varied so far as the administrator considers necessary to secure that the Secretary of State is satisfied as mentioned in section 65KB(1).

(2) Where the administrator provides to the regulator a final report under subsection (1), section 65KA applies in relation to the report as it applies in relation to a final report under section 65I; and for that purpose, that section has effect as if—

(a) in subsection (1), for "20 working days" there were substituted "10 working days", and

(b) subsection (3)(b) were omitted.

(3) If the Secretary of State thinks that, in the circumstances, it is not reasonable for the administrator to be required to carry out the duty under subsection (1) within the period mentioned in that subsection, the Secretary of State may by order extend the period.

(4) If an order is made under subsection (3), the administrator must—

(a) publish a notice stating the date on which the period will expire, and

(b) where the administrator is proposing to carry out consultation in response to the notice under section 65KB(2), publish a statement setting out the means by which the administrator will consult during the extended period.]

NOTES

Inserted as noted to s 65KA at [7.1316].

[7.1318]

[65KD Secretary of State's response to re-submitted final report

(1) Within the period of 30 working days beginning with the day on which the Secretary of State receives a final report under section 65KA(3) as applied by section 65KC(2), the Secretary of State must decide whether the Secretary of State is, in relation to the report, satisfied as to the matters in section 65KB(1)(a) to (f).

(2) If the Secretary of State is not satisfied as mentioned in subsection (1), the Secretary of State must as soon as reasonably practicable—

(a) publish a notice of the decision and the reasons for it;

(b) lay a copy of the notice before Parliament.

(3) Where the Secretary of State publishes a notice under subsection (2)(a), subsections (4) to [(8A)] apply.

(4) If the notice states that the Board has failed to discharge a function—

(a) the Board is to be treated for the purposes of this Act as having failed to discharge the function, and

(b) the failure is to be treated for those purposes as significant (and section 13Z2 applies accordingly).

(5) If the notice states that a clinical commissioning group has failed to discharge a function—

(a) the group is to be treated for the purposes of this Act as having failed to discharge the function,

(b) the Secretary of State may exercise the functions of the Board under section 14Z21(2), (3)(a) and (8)(a), and

(c) the Board may not exercise any of its functions under section 14Z21.

(6) Where, by virtue of subsection (5)(b), the Secretary of State exercises the function of the Board under subsection (3)(a) of section 14Z21, subsection (9)(a) of that section applies but with the substitution for the references to the Board of references to the Secretary of State.

(7) If the notice states that the trust special administrator has failed to discharge the administration duties (within the meaning of section 65KA(1)(b))—

(a) the administration duties are to be treated for the purposes of this Act as functions of the regulator,

(b) the regulator is to be treated for the purposes of this Act as having failed to discharge those functions, and

(c) the failure is to be treated for those purposes as significant (and section 71 of the Health and Social Care Act 2012 applies accordingly, but with the omission of subsection (3)).

(8) If the notice states that the regulator has failed to discharge a function—

(a) the regulator is to be treated for the purposes of this Act as having failed to discharge the function, and

(b) the failure is to be treated for those purposes as significant (and section 71 of the Health and Social Care Act 2012 applies accordingly, but with the omission of subsection (3)).

[(8A) If the notice states that the Care Quality Commission has failed to discharge a function—

(a) the Care Quality Commission is to be treated for the purposes of this Act as having failed to discharge the function, and

(b) the failure is to be treated for those purposes as significant (and section 82 of the Health and Social Care Act 2008 applies accordingly).]

(9) Within the period of 60 working days beginning with the day on which the Secretary of State publishes a notice under subsection (2)(a), the Secretary of State must decide what action to take in relation to the trust.
(10) The Secretary of State must as soon as reasonably practicable—
(a) publish a notice of the decision and the reasons for it;
(b) lay a copy of the notice before Parliament.]

NOTES

Inserted as noted to s 65KA at **[7.1316]**.
Sub-s (3): reference in square brackets substituted by the Care Act 2014, s 85(13).
Sub-s (8A): inserted by the Care Act 2014, s 85(14).

[7.1319]
[65L Trusts coming out of administration
(1) This section applies if the Secretary of State decides under section *65K* not to dissolve *the trust*.
(2) *The Secretary of State* must make an order specifying a date when the appointment of the trust special administrator and the suspension of the chairman *and directors* of the trust come to an end.
[(2A) For the purposes of subsection (1) in its application to the case of an NHS foundation trust, the reference to section 65K is to be read as a reference to section 65KD(9); and this section also applies in the case of an NHS foundation trust if—
(a) the Secretary of State is satisfied as mentioned in section 65KB(1) or 65KD(1) in relation to the trust, and
(b) the action recommended in the final report is to do something other than dissolve the trust.
(2B) For the purposes of subsection (2) in its application to the case of an NHS foundation trust—
(a) the reference to the Secretary of State is to be read as a reference to the regulator, and
(b) the reference to the chairman and directors of the trust is to be read as including a reference to the governors.]
(3)–(5) . . .
[(6) Subsection (7) applies in the case of an NHS foundation trust.
(7) If it appears to the regulator to be necessary in order to comply with Schedule 7, the regulator may by order—
(a) terminate the office of any governor or of any executive or non-executive director of the trust;
(b) appoint a person to be a governor or an executive or non-executive director of the trust.]]

NOTES

Inserted as noted to s 65A at **[7.1304]**.
Sub-s (1): for the number in italics there is substituted the words "65KB(2) or 65KD(2) or (9)", and for the words in italics there are substituted the words "the NHS foundation trust in question" by the Health and Social Care Act 2012, s 179(6), Sch 14, Pt 1, paras 1, 22(1), (2), as to the commencement of the 2012 Act, see s 306(1)(d), (4) thereof (at **[7.1371]**) which provides that it shall come into force on 27 March 2012 (so far as is necessary for enabling the exercise on or after that date of any power to make an order or regulations or to give directions), and as from a day to be appointed (otherwise).
Sub-s (2): for the first words in italics there are substituted the words "The regulator" and for the second words in italics there are substituted the words ", directors and governors", by the Health and Social Care Act 2012, s 179(6), Sch 14, Pt 1, paras 1, 22(1), (3), as to the commencement of the 2012 Act, see s 306(1)(d), (4) thereof (at **[7.1371]**) which provides that it shall come into force on 27 March 2012 (so far as is necessary for enabling the exercise on or after that date of any power to make an order or regulations or to give directions), and as from a day to be appointed (otherwise).
Sub-ss (2A), (2B): inserted by the Health and Social Care Act 2012, s 177(3); repealed by the Health and Social Care Act 2012, s 179(6), Sch 14, Pt 1, paras 1, 22(1), (4), as to the commencement of the 2012 Act, see s 306(1)(d), (4) thereof (at **[7.1371]**) which provides that it shall come into force on 27 March 2012 (so far as is necessary for enabling the exercise on or after that date of any power to make an order or regulations or to give directions), and as from a day to be appointed (otherwise).
Sub-ss (3)–(5): repealed by the Health and Social Care Act 2012, s 177(4).
Sub-s (6): inserted, together with sub-s (7), by the Health and Social Care Act 2012, s 177(5); repealed by the Health and Social Care Act 2012, s 179(6), Sch 14, Pt 1, paras 1, 22(1), (4), as to the commencement of the 2012 Act, see s 306(1)(d), (4) thereof (at **[7.1371]**) which provides that it shall come into force on 27 March 2012 (so far as is necessary for enabling the exercise on or after that date of any power to make an order or regulations or to give directions), and as from a day to be appointed (otherwise).
Sub-s (7): inserted as noted to sub-s (6) above.

[7.1320]
[65LA Trusts to be dissolved
(1) This section applies if—
(a) the Secretary of State is satisfied as mentioned in section 65KB(1) or 65KD(1), and
(b) the action recommended in the final report is to dissolve the NHS foundation trust in question.
(2) This section also applies if the Secretary of State decides under section 65KD(9) to dissolve the NHS foundation trust in question.
(3) The regulator may make an order—
(a) dissolving the trust, and
(b) transferring, or providing for the transfer of, the property and liabilities of the trust[—
(i) to an NHS body;
(ii) to the Secretary of State;
(iii) between more than one NHS body or between one or more NHS bodies and the Secretary of State.]
(4) An order under subsection (3) may include provision for the transfer of employees of the trust.

(5) The liabilities that may be transferred [to an NHS body] by virtue of subsection (3)(b) include criminal liabilities.]

NOTES

Inserted by the Health and Social Care Act 2012, s 177(6).

Sub-ss (3), (5): words in square brackets substituted by the Deregulation Act 2015, s 96(1), (6), (7).

[Supplementary]

[7.1321]

[65M Replacement of trust special administrator

(1) If a trust special administrator ceases to hold office for any reason before *the Secretary of State* has made either an order under section 65L(2) or an order dissolving the trust, *the Secretary of State* must—

(a) appoint another person as the trust special administrator, and

(b) publish the name of the person appointed.

(2) Where a person is appointed under subsection (1) in relation to a trust, anything done by or in relation to a previous trust special administrator has effect as if done by or in relation to that person, unless *the Secretary of State* directs otherwise.]

[(3) For the purposes of this section in its application to the case of an NHS foundation trust, the references to the Secretary of State are to be read as references to the regulator.]

NOTES

Inserted as noted to s 65A at **[7.1304]**.

Sub-ss (1), (2): for the words in italics there are substituted the words "the regulator" by the Health and Social Care Act 2012, s 179(6), Sch 14, Pt 1, paras 1, 23(1)–(3), as to the commencement of the 2012 Act, see s 306(1)(d), (4) thereof (at **[7.1371]**) which provides that it shall come into force on 27 March 2012 (so far as is necessary for enabling the exercise on or after that date of any power to make an order or regulations or to give directions), and as from a day to be appointed (otherwise).

Sub-s (3): inserted by the Health and Social Care Act 2012, s 178(1); repealed by the Health and Social Care Act 2012, s 179(6), Sch 14, Pt 1, paras 1, 23(1), (4), as to the commencement of the 2012 Act, see s 306(1)(d), (4) thereof (at **[7.1371]**) which provides that it shall come into force on 27 March 2012 (so far as is necessary for enabling the exercise on or after that date of any power to make an order or regulations or to give directions), and as from a day to be appointed (otherwise).

[7.1322]

[65N Guidance

(1) *The Secretary of State* must publish guidance for trust special administrators.

[(1A) It must, in so far as it applies to NHS trusts, include guidance about—

(a) seeking the support of commissioners for an administrator's recommendation;

(b) involving the Board in relation to finalising an administrator's report or draft report.]

(2) It must include guidance about the publication of notices under sections 65H and 65J.

[(2A) It must include guidance about the publication of—

(a) notices under section 65KC(4)(a);

(b) statements under section 65KC(4)(b).]

(3) It must include guidance about the preparation of draft reports, as to—

(a) persons to be consulted;

(b) factors to be taken into account;

(c) relevant publications.

[(3A) Before publishing guidance under this section, the Secretary of State must consult the Care Quality Commission.]

[(4) For the purposes of this section in its application to cases of NHS foundation trusts, [the references in subsections (1) and (3A) to the Secretary of State are to be read as references] to the regulator.]]

NOTES

Inserted as noted to s 65A at **[7.1304]**.

Sub-s (1): for the words in italics there are substituted the words "The regulator" by the Health and Social Care Act 2012, s 179(6), Sch 14, Pt 1, paras 1, 24(1), (2), as to the commencement of the 2012 Act, see s 306(1)(d), (4) thereof (at **[7.1371]**) which provides that it shall come into force on 27 March 2012 (so far as is necessary for enabling the exercise on or after that date of any power to make an order or regulations or to give directions), and as from a day to be appointed (otherwise).

Sub-s (1A): inserted by the Care Act 2014, s 120(14).

Sub-s (2A): inserted by the Health and Social Care Act 2012, s 178(2).

Sub-s (3A): inserted by the Care Act 2014, s 84(6).

Sub-s (4): added by the Health and Social Care Act 2012, s 178(3); repealed by the Health and Social Care Act 2012, s 179(6), Sch 14, Pt 1, paras 1, 24(1), (3), as to the commencement of the 2012 Act, see s 306(1)(d), (4) thereof (at **[7.1371]**) which provides that it shall come into force on 27 March 2012 (so far as is necessary for enabling the exercise on or after that date of any power to make an order or regulations or to give directions), and as from a day to be appointed (otherwise); words in square brackets substituted by the Care Act 2014, s 84(7).

[7.1323]

[65O Interpretation of this Chapter

[(1)] In this Chapter—

"trust special administrator" means a person appointed under section 65B(6)(a)[, section 65D(2)] or section 65M(1)(a);

"working day" means any day which is not Saturday, Sunday, Christmas Day, Good Friday or a day which is a bank holiday in England and Wales under the Banking and Financial Dealings Act 1971.]

[(2) The references in this Chapter to taking action in relation to an NHS trust include a reference to taking action, including in relation to another NHS trust or an NHS foundation trust, which is necessary for and consequential on action taken in relation to that NHS trust.
(3) The references in this Chapter to taking action in relation to an NHS foundation trust include a reference to taking action, including in relation to another NHS foundation trust or an NHS trust, which is necessary for and consequential on action taken in relation to that NHS foundation trust.]

NOTES
Inserted as noted to s 65A at **[7.1304]**.
Sub-s (1): numbered as such by the Care Act 2014, s 120(1); in definition "trust special administrator" words in square brackets inserted by the Health and Social Care Act 2012, s 178(4).
Sub-ss (2), (3): added by the Care Act 2014, s 120(1).

65P–270 (*Ss 65P–73 (Chs 5B, 6), ss 73A–270 (Pts 3–13) outside the scope of this work.*)

PART 14
SUPPLEMENTARY

271–276 (*Outside the scope of this work.*)

[7.1324]
277 Commencement
(1) Subject to this section, this Act comes into force on 1st March 2007.
(2) In this section—
"the 1977 Act" means the National Health Service Act 1977 (c 49), and
"the 2006 Act" means the Health Act 2006 (c 28).
(3) Subsection (4) applies to—
(a) sections 33 and 35 to 38 of the Health Act 1999 (c 8) (see sections 261 and 263 to 266 of this Act),
(b) subsection (7) of section 45 of the Nationality, Immigration and Asylum Act 2002 (c 41) and paragraph 2(2B) of Schedule 8 to the 1977 Act as substituted by that subsection (see paragraph 2(7) of Schedule 20 to this Act),
(c) section 21 of the Health and Social Care (Community Health and Standards) Act 2003 (c 43) (see section 50 of this Act),
(d) paragraph 3 of the Schedule to the Smoking, Health and Social Care (Scotland) Act 2005 (Consequential Modifications) (England, Wales and Northern Ireland) Order 2006 (SI 2006/1056) and section 41B(2) and (6)(b) of the 1977 Act as amended by that paragraph (see section 128 of this Act),
(e) sub-paragraphs (a) and (b) of paragraph 5 of that Schedule and section 4A(1) and (3) of the National Health Service and Community Care Act 1990 (c 19) as amended by those sub-paragraphs (see section 11 of this Act),
(f) sub-paragraph (c) of paragraph 5 of that Schedule and section 4A(4) of the National Health Service and Community Care Act 1990 as added by that sub-paragraph (see section 11 of this Act),
(g) section 34 of the 2006 Act, and section 42A of the 1977 Act as inserted by that section (see section 131 of this Act),
(h) section 35 of the 2006 Act, and subsections (2B) and (2C) of section 42 of the 1977 Act as inserted by that section (see section 129 of this Act),
(i) subsection (1) of section 36 of the 2006 Act, and section 43(2) of the 1977 Act as substituted by that subsection (see section 132 of this Act),
(j) sections 37 to 41 of, and paragraphs 7 to 9, 11, 12(a), 13(2), (5) and (6), 15, 16, 17, 21(b), 22, 29, 46 and 50 of Schedule 8 to, the 2006 Act (which relate to primary ophthalmic services) and—
(i) the 1977 Act,
(ii) section 4A of the National Health Service and Community Care Act 1990,
(iii) Schedule 1 to the Health and Social Care Act 2001 (c 15), and
(iv) section 17(1) of the National Health Service Reform and Health Care Professions Act 2002 (c 17),
to the extent that a provision mentioned in any of sub-paragraphs (i) to (iv), as amended by any of those provisions of the 2006 Act, relates to primary ophthalmic services,
(k) subsection (2) of section 42 of the 2006 Act, and paragraph 2A(1)(b) and (ba) of Schedule 12 to the 1977 Act as substituted by that subsection (see section 180 of this Act),
(l) subsection (3) of section 42 of the 2006 Act, and paragraph 2B of Schedule 12 to the 1977 Act as inserted by that subsection (see section 181 of this Act),
(m) sections 44 to 55 of the 2006 Act, and sections 76 to 78 of that Act so far as relating to those sections (see Part 10 of this Act),
(n) section 56 of, and paragraph 24(a) of Schedule 8 to, that Act and—
(i) section 98 of the 1977 Act as substituted by section 56 of that Act, and
(ii) Schedule 12B to the 1977 Act as inserted by that section,
(see section 232 of, and Schedule 15 to, this Act), and
(o) paragraphs 14, 24(b) and 25 of Schedule 8 to the 2006 Act (which relate to the substitution of "optometrist" for "ophthalmic optician") and the 1977 Act as amended by those paragraphs.
(4) To the extent that—

(a) this Act re-enacts a provision to which this subsection applies, and
(b) the provision has not come into force before the commencement of this Act,
the re-enactment by this Act of the provision does not come into force until the provision which is re-enacted comes into force; and the re-enactment comes into force immediately after, and to the extent that, the provision which is re-enacted comes into force.
(5) Accordingly, the re-enactment by this Act of the provision does not affect any power to bring the provision into force.

[7.1325]
278 Short title, extent and application
(1) This Act may be cited as the National Health Service Act 2006.
(2) Subject to this section, this Act extends to England and Wales only.
(3) (*Outside the scope of this work*).
(4) The Secretary of State may by order provide that this Act, in its application to the Isles of Scilly, has effect with such modifications as may be specified in the order.

SCHEDULES A1–22

(*Schs A1–22 outside the scope of this work.*)

HEALTH AND SOCIAL CARE ACT 2012

(2012 c 7)

ARRANGEMENT OF SECTIONS

PART 3
REGULATION OF HEALTH AND ADULT SOCIAL CARE SERVICES

CHAPTER 1
MONITOR

61 Monitor . . . [7.1326]
62 General duties . . . [7.1327]
63 Secretary of State's guidance on duty under section 62(9) . . . [7.1328]
64 General duties: supplementary . . . [7.1329]
65 Power to give Monitor functions relating to adult social care services . . . [7.1330]
66 Matters to have regard to in exercise of functions . . . [7.1331]
67 Conflicts between functions . . . [7.1332]
68 Duty to review regulatory burdens . . . [7.1333]
69 Duty to carry out impact assessments . . . [7.1334]
70 Information . . . [7.1335]
71 Failure to perform functions . . . [7.1336]

CHAPTER 3
LICENSING

Licensing requirement

81 Requirement for health service providers to be licensed . . . [7.1337]
82 Deemed breach of requirement to be licensed . . . [7.1338]
83 Exemption regulations . . . [7.1339]
84 Exemption regulations: supplementary . . . [7.1340]

Licensing procedure

85 Application for licence . . . [7.1341]
86 Licensing criteria . . . [7.1342]
87 Grant or refusal of licence . . . [7.1343]
88 Application and grant: NHS foundation trusts . . . [7.1344]
89 Revocation of licence . . . [7.1345]
90 Right to make representations . . . [7.1346]
91 Notice of decisions . . . [7.1347]
92 Appeals to the Tribunal . . . [7.1348]
93 Register of licence holders . . . [7.1349]

Licence conditions

94 Standard conditions . . . [7.1350]
95 Special conditions . . . [7.1351]
96 Limits on Monitor's functions to set or modify licence conditions . . . [7.1352]
97 Conditions: supplementary . . . [7.1353]

98 Conditions relating to the continuation of the provision of services etc . . . [7.1354]
99 Notification of commissioners where continuation of services at risk . . . [7.1355]
100 Modification of standard conditions . . . [7.1356]

CHAPTER 5
HEALTH SPECIAL ADMINISTRATION

128 Health special administration orders . . . [7.1357]
129 Objective of a health special administration . . . [7.1358]
130 Health special administration regulations . . . [7.1359]
131 Transfer schemes . . . [7.1360]
132 Indemnities . . . [7.1361]
133 Modification of this Chapter under Enterprise Act 2002 . . . [7.1362]

CHAPTER 6
FINANCIAL ASSISTANCE IN SPECIAL ADMINISTRATION CASES

Establishment of mechanisms

134 Duty to establish mechanisms for providing financial assistance . . . [7.1363]
135 Power to establish fund . . . [7.1364]

Applications for financial assistance

136 Applications . . . [7.1365]
137 Grants and loans . . . [7.1366]

CHAPTER 7
MISCELLANEOUS AND GENERAL

148 Service of documents . . . [7.1367]
149 Electronic communications . . . [7.1368]
150 Interpretation, transitional provision and consequential amendments . . . [7.1369]

PART 12
FINAL PROVISIONS

304 Regulations, orders and directions . . . [7.1370]
306 Commencement . . . [7.1371]
308 Extent . . . [7.1372]
309 Short title . . . [7.1373]

An Act to establish and make provision about a National Health Service Commissioning Board and clinical commissioning groups and to make other provision about the National Health Service in England; to make provision about public health in the United Kingdom; to make provision about regulating health and adult social care services; to make provision about public involvement in health and social care matters, scrutiny of health matters by local authorities and co-operation between local authorities and commissioners of health care services; to make provision about regulating health and social care workers; to establish and make provision about a National Institute for Health and Care Excellence; to establish and make provision about a Health and Social Care Information Centre and to make other provision about information relating to health or social care matters; to abolish certain public bodies involved in health or social care; to make other provision about health care; and for connected purposes

[27 March 2012]

1–60 *((Pts 1, 2) outside the scope of this work.)*

PART 3
REGULATION OF HEALTH AND ADULT SOCIAL CARE SERVICES

CHAPTER 1 MONITOR

[7.1326]
61 Monitor

(1) The body corporate known as the Independent Regulator of NHS Foundation Trusts—
(a) is to continue to exist, and
(b) is to be known as Monitor.

(2) Schedule 8 (which makes further provision about Monitor) has effect.

[7.1327]
62 General duties

(1) The main duty of Monitor in exercising its functions is to protect and promote the interests of people who use health care services by promoting provision of health care services which—
(a) is economic, efficient and effective, and
(b) maintains or improves the quality of the services.

(2) In carrying out its main duty, Monitor must have regard to the likely future demand for health care services.

(3) Monitor must exercise its functions with a view to preventing anti-competitive behaviour in the provision of health care services for the purposes of the NHS which is against the interests of people who use such services.

(4) Monitor must exercise its functions with a view to enabling health care services provided for the purposes of the NHS to be provided in an integrated way where it considers that this would—

(a) improve the quality of those services (including the outcomes that are achieved from their provision) or the efficiency of their provision,

(b) reduce inequalities between persons with respect to their ability to access those services, or

(c) reduce inequalities between persons with respect to the outcomes achieved for them by the provision of those services.

(5) Monitor must exercise its functions with a view to enabling the provision of health care services provided for the purposes of the NHS to be integrated with the provision of health-related services or social care services where it considers that this would—

(a) improve the quality of those health care services (including the outcomes that are achieved from their provision) or the efficiency of their provision,

(b) reduce inequalities between persons with respect to their ability to access those health care services, or

(c) reduce inequalities between persons with respect to the outcomes achieved for them by the provision of those health care services.

(6) Monitor must, in carrying out its duties under subsections (4) and (5), have regard to the way in which—

(a) the National Health Service Commissioning Board carries out its duties under section 13N of the National Health Service Act 2006, and

(b) clinical commissioning groups carry out their duties under section 14Z1 of that Act.

(7) Monitor must secure that people who use health care services, and other members of the public, are involved to an appropriate degree in decisions that Monitor makes about the exercise of its functions (other than decisions it makes about the exercise of its functions in a particular case).

(8) Monitor must obtain advice appropriate for enabling it effectively to discharge its functions from persons who (taken together) have a broad range of professional expertise in—

(a) the prevention, diagnosis or treatment of illness (within the meaning of the National Health Service Act 2006), and

(b) the protection or improvement of public health.

(9) Monitor must exercise its functions in a manner consistent with the performance by the Secretary of State of the duty under section 1(1) of the National Health Service Act 2006 (promotion of comprehensive health service).

(10) Monitor must not exercise its functions for the purpose of causing a variation in the proportion of health care services provided for the purposes of the NHS that is provided by persons of a particular description if that description is by reference to—

(a) whether the persons in question are in the public or (as the case may be) private sector, or

(b) some other aspect of their status.

(11) In this section—

"health-related services" means services that may have an effect on people's health but are not health care services or social care services;

"social care services" means services that are provided in pursuance of the social services functions of local authorities (within the meaning of the Local Authority Social Services Act 1970).

[7.1328]

63 Secretary of State's guidance on duty under section 62(9)

(1) The Secretary of State may, for the purpose of assisting Monitor to comply with its duty under section 62(9), publish guidance on—

(a) the objectives specified in the mandate published under section 13A of the National Health Service Act 2006 which the Secretary of State considers to be relevant to Monitor's exercise of its functions, and

(b) the Secretary of State's reasons for considering those objectives to be relevant to Monitor's exercise of its functions.

(2) In exercising its functions, Monitor must have regard to guidance under subsection (1).

(3) Where the Secretary of State publishes guidance under subsection (1), the Secretary of State must lay a copy of the published guidance before Parliament.

(4) The Secretary of State—

(a) may revise guidance under subsection (1), and

(b) if the Secretary of State does so, must publish the guidance as revised and lay it before Parliament.

[7.1329]

64 General duties: supplementary

(1) This section applies for the purposes of this Part.

(2) "Anti-competitive behaviour" means behaviour which would (or would be likely to) prevent, restrict or distort competition and a reference to preventing anti-competitive behaviour includes a reference to eliminating or reducing the effects (or potential effects) of the behaviour.

(3) "Health care" means all forms of health care provided for individuals, whether relating to physical or mental health, with a reference in this Part to health care services being read accordingly; and for the purposes of this Part it does not matter if a health care service is also an adult social care service (as to which, see section 65).

(4) "The NHS" means the comprehensive health service continued under section 1(1) of the National Health Service Act 2006, except the part of it that is provided in pursuance of the public health functions (within the meaning of that Act) of the Secretary of State or local authorities.
(5) A reference to the provision of health care services for the purposes of the NHS is a reference to their provision for those purposes in accordance with that Act.
(6) Nothing in section 62 requires Monitor to do anything in relation to the supply to persons who provide health care services of goods that are to be provided as part of those services.

[7.1330]
65 Power to give Monitor functions relating to adult social care services
(1) Regulations may provide for specified functions of Monitor also to be exercisable in relation to adult social care services.
(2) Any regulations under this section must apply in relation to England only.
(3) The regulations may amend this Part.
(4) "Adult social care"—
(a) includes all forms of personal care and other practical assistance provided for individuals who, by reason of age, illness, disability, pregnancy, childbirth, dependence on alcohol or drugs, or any other similar circumstances, are in need of such care or other assistance, but
(b) does not include anything provided by an establishment or agency for which Her Majesty's Chief Inspector of Education, Children's Services and Skills is the registration authority under section 5 of the Care Standards Act 2000.

[7.1331]
66 Matters to have regard to in exercise of functions
(1) In exercising its functions, Monitor must have regard, in particular, to the need to maintain the safety of people who use health care services.
(2) Monitor must, in exercising its functions, also have regard to the following matters in so far as they are consistent with the matter referred to in subsection (1)—
(a) the desirability of securing continuous improvement in the quality of health care services provided for the purposes of the NHS and in the efficiency of their provision,
(b) the need for commissioners of health care services for the purposes of the NHS to ensure that the provision of access to the services for those purposes operates fairly,
(c) the need for commissioners of health care services for the purposes of the NHS to ensure that people who require health care services for those purposes are provided with access to them,
(d) the need for commissioners of health care services for the purposes of the NHS to make the best use of resources when doing so,
(e) the desirability of persons who provide health care services for the purposes of the NHS co-operating with each other in order to improve the quality of health care services provided for those purposes,
(f) the need to promote research into matters relevant to the NHS by persons who provide health care services for the purposes of the NHS,
(g) the need for high standards in the education and training of health care professionals who provide health care services for the purposes of the NHS, and
(h) where the Secretary of State publishes a document for the purposes of section 13E of the National Health Service Act 2006 (improvement of quality of services), any guidance published by the Secretary of State on the parts of that document which the Secretary of State considers to be particularly relevant to Monitor's exercise of its functions.
(3) Where the Secretary of State publishes guidance referred to in subsection (2)(h), the Secretary of State must lay a copy of the published guidance before Parliament.
(4) The Secretary of State—
(a) may revise the guidance, and
(b) if the Secretary of State does so, must publish the guidance as revised and lay it before Parliament.

[7.1332]
67 Conflicts between functions
(1) In a case where Monitor considers that any of its general duties conflict with each other, it must secure that the conflict is resolved in the manner it considers best.
(2) Monitor must act so as to secure that there is not, and could not reasonably be regarded as being, a conflict between—
(a) its exercise of any of its functions under Chapter 5 of Part 2 of the National Health Service Act 2006 (regulation of NHS foundation trusts) *or under sections 111 and 113 of this Act (imposition of licence conditions on NHS foundation trusts during transitional period)* or under paragraph 17 of Schedule 8 to this Act (accounts of NHS foundation trusts), and
(b) its exercise of any of its other functions.
(3) Monitor must ignore the functions it has under sections 111 and 113 when exercising—
(a) its functions under Chapter 2 (competition);
(b) its functions under Chapter 4 (pricing).
(4) If Monitor secures the resolution of a conflict between its general duties in a case that comes within subsection (5), or that Monitor considers is otherwise of unusual importance, it must publish a statement setting out—
(a) the nature of the conflict,
(b) the manner in which it decided to resolve it, and

(c) its reasons for deciding to resolve it in that manner.

(5) A case comes within this subsection if it involves—

(a) a matter likely to have a significant impact on persons who provide health care services for the purposes of the NHS;

(b) a matter likely to have a significant impact on people who use health care services provided for the purposes of the NHS;

(c) a matter likely to have a significant impact on the general public in England (or in a particular part of England);

(d) a major change in the activities Monitor carries on;

(e) a major change in the standard conditions of licences under Chapter 3 (see section 94).

(6) Where Monitor is required to publish a statement under subsection (4), it must do so as soon as reasonably practicable after making its decision.

(7) The duty under subsection (4) does not apply in so far as Monitor is subject to an obligation not to publish a matter that needs to be included in the statement.

(8) Every annual report of Monitor must include—

(a) a statement of the steps it has taken in the financial year to which the report relates to comply with the duty under subsection (2), and

(b) a summary of the manner in which, in that financial year, Monitor has secured the resolution of conflicts between its general duties arising in cases of the kind referred to in subsection (5).

(9) Monitor's general duties for the purposes of this section are its duties under sections 62 and 66.

NOTES

Sub-s (2): words in italics in para (a) repealed by s 114(1)(a) of this Act, as from a day to be appointed.

Sub-s (3): repealed s 114(1)(b) of this Act, as from a day to be appointed.

[7.1333]

68 Duty to review regulatory burdens

(1) Monitor must keep the exercise of its functions under review and secure that in exercising its functions it does not—

(a) impose burdens which it considers to be unnecessary, or

(b) maintain burdens which it considers to have become unnecessary.

(2) In keeping the exercise of its functions under review, Monitor must have regard to such principles as appear to it to represent best regulatory practice.

(3) Subsection (1) does not require the removal of a burden which has become unnecessary where its removal would, having regard to all the circumstances, be impractical or disproportionate.

(4) Monitor must from time to time publish a statement setting out—

(a) what it proposes to do pursuant to subsection (1) in the period to which the statement relates,

(b) what it has done pursuant to that subsection since publishing the previous statement, and

(c) where a burden relating to the exercise of the function which has become unnecessary is maintained pursuant to subsection (3), the reasons why removal of the burden would, having regard to all the circumstances, be impractical or disproportionate.

(5) The first statement—

(a) must be published as soon as practicable after the commencement of this section, and

(b) must relate to the period of 12 months beginning with the date of publication.

(6) A subsequent statement—

(a) must be published during the period to which the previous statement related or as soon as reasonably practicable after that period, and

(b) must relate to the period of 12 months beginning with the end of the previous period.

(7) Monitor must, in exercising its functions, have regard to the statement that is in force at the time in question.

(8) Monitor may revise a statement before or during the period to which it relates; and, if it does so, it must publish the revision as soon as reasonably practicable.

[7.1334]

69 Duty to carry out impact assessments

(1) This section applies where Monitor is proposing to do something that it considers would be likely—

(a) to have a significant impact on persons who provide health care services for the purposes of the NHS;

(b) to have a significant impact on people who use health care services provided for the purposes of the NHS;

(c) to have a significant impact on the general public in England (or in a particular part of England);

(d) to involve a major change in the activities Monitor carries on;

(e) to involve a major change in the standard conditions of licences under Chapter 3 (see section 94).

(2) But this section does not apply to—

(a) the carrying out by Monitor of an analysis of how markets involving the provision of health care services are operating, or

(b) the exercise of functions under or by virtue of Chapter 2.

(3) Nor does this section apply if it appears to Monitor that the urgency of the matter makes compliance with this section impracticable or inappropriate.

(4) Before implementing the proposal, Monitor must either—

(a) carry out and publish an assessment of the likely impact of implementation, or

(b) publish a statement setting out its reasons for concluding that it does not need to carry out an assessment under paragraph (a).

(5) The assessment must set out Monitor's explanation of how the discharge of its general duties (within the meaning of section 67)—

(a) would be secured by implementation of the proposal, but

(b) would not be secured by the exercise of functions that Monitor has by virtue of section 72 or 73.

(6) The assessment may take such form, and relate to such matters, as Monitor may determine; and in determining the matters to which the assessment is to relate, Monitor must have regard to such general guidance on carrying out impact assessments as it considers appropriate.

(7) The assessment must specify the consultation period within which representations with respect to the proposal may be made to Monitor; and for that purpose the consultation period must not be less than 28 days beginning with the day after that on which the assessment is published under subsection (4).

(8) Monitor may not implement the proposal unless the consultation period has ended.

(9) Where Monitor is required (apart from this section) to consult about, or afford a person an opportunity to make representations about, a proposal that comes within subsection (1), the requirements of this section—

(a) are in addition to the other requirement, but

(b) may be met contemporaneously with it.

(10) Every annual report of Monitor must set out—

(a) a list of the assessments carried out under this section during the financial year to which the report relates, and

(b) a summary of the decisions taken during that year in relation to proposals to which assessments carried out during that year or a previous financial year relate.

[7.1335]

70 Information

(1) Information obtained by, or documents, records or other items produced to, Monitor in connection with any of its functions may be used by Monitor in connection with any of its other functions.

(2) For the purposes of exercising a function under this Part, the Secretary of State may request Monitor to provide the Secretary of State with such information as the Secretary of State may specify.

(3) Monitor must comply with a request under subsection (2).

[7.1336]

71 Failure to perform functions

(1) This section applies if the Secretary of State considers that Monitor is failing, or has failed, to perform any function of Monitor's, other than a function it has by virtue of section 72 or 73, and that the failure is significant.

(2) The Secretary of State may direct Monitor to perform such of those functions, and in such manner and within such period, as the direction specifies.

(3) But the Secretary of State may not give a direction under subsection (2) in relation to the performance of functions in a particular case.

(4) If Monitor fails to comply with a direction under subsection (2), the Secretary of State may—

(a) perform the functions to which the direction relates, or

(b) make arrangements for some other person to perform them on the Secretary of State's behalf.

(5) Where the Secretary of State exercises a power under subsection (2) or (4), the Secretary of State must publish the reasons for doing so.

(6) For the purposes of this section—

(a) a failure to perform a function includes a failure to perform it properly, and

(b) a failure to perform a function properly includes a failure to perform it consistently with what the Secretary of State considers to be the interests of the health service in England or (as the case may be) with what otherwise appears to the Secretary of State to be the purpose for which it is conferred; and "the health service" has the same meaning as in the National Health Service Act 2006.

72–80 (*(Chapter 2) outside the scope of this work.*)

CHAPTER 3 LICENSING

Licensing requirement

[7.1337]

81 Requirement for health service providers to be licensed

(1) Any person who provides a health care service for the purposes of the NHS must hold a licence under this Chapter.

(2) Regulations may make provision for the purposes of this Chapter for determining, in relation to a service provided by two or more persons acting in different capacities, which of those persons is to be regarded as the person who provides the service.

NOTES

Commencement: 27 March 2012 (in so far as is necessary for enabling the exercise of any power to make an order or regulations or to give directions that is conferred by the above section or an amendment made by it); 1 April 2013 (in relation to NHS foundation trusts); 1 April 2014 (otherwise).

Regulations: the National Health Service (Licence Exemptions, etc) Regulations 2013, SI 2013/2677.

[7.1338]
82 Deemed breach of requirement to be licensed
(1) This section applies where a licence holder—
(a) in providing a health care service for the purposes of the NHS, carries on a regulated activity (within the meaning of Part 1 of the Health and Social Care Act 2008), but
(b) is not registered under Chapter 2 of Part 1 of that Act in respect of the carrying on of that activity.
(2) The licence holder is to be regarded as providing the service in breach of the requirement under section 81 to hold a licence.

[7.1339]
83 Exemption regulations
(1) Regulations (referred to in this section and section 84 as "exemption regulations") may provide for the grant of exemptions from the requirement under section 81 in respect of—
(a) a prescribed person or persons of a prescribed description;
(b) the provision of a prescribed health care service or a health care service of a prescribed description.
(2) Exemption regulations may grant an exemption—
(a) either generally or to the extent prescribed;
(b) either unconditionally or subject to prescribed conditions;
(c) indefinitely, for a prescribed period or for a period determined by or under the exemption.
(3) Conditions subject to which an exemption may be granted include, in particular, conditions requiring any person providing a service pursuant to the exemption—
(a) to comply with any direction given by Monitor about such matters as are specified in the exemption or are of a description so specified,
(b) except to the extent that Monitor otherwise approves, to do, or not to do, such things as are specified in the exemption or are of a description so specified (or to do, or not to do, such things in a specified manner), and
(c) to refer for determination by Monitor such questions arising under the exemption as are specified in the exemption or are of a description so specified.
(4) Before making exemption regulations the Secretary of State must give notice to—
(a) Monitor,
(b) the National Health Service Commissioning Board, and
(c) the Care Quality Commission and its Healthwatch England committee.
(5) The Secretary of State must also publish a notice under subsection (4).
(6) A notice under subsection (4) must—
(a) state that the Secretary of State proposes to make exemption regulations and set out their proposed effect,
(b) set out the Secretary of State's reasons for the proposal, and
(c) specify the period ("the notice period") within which representations with respect to the proposal may be made.
(7) The notice period must be not less than 28 days beginning with the day after that on which the notice is published under subsection (5).
(8) Where an exemption is granted the Secretary of State—
(a) if the exemption is granted to a prescribed person, must give notice of it to that person, and
(b) must publish the exemption.

NOTES
Commencement: 27 March 2012 (in so far as is necessary for enabling the exercise of any power to make an order or regulations or to give directions that is conferred by the above section or an amendment made by it); 1 April 2014 (otherwise).
Regulations: the National Health Service (Licence Exemptions, etc) Regulations 2013, SI 2013/2677; the National Health Service (Licence Exemptions, etc) Amendment Regulations 2015, SI 2015/190.

[7.1340]
84 Exemption regulations: supplementary
(1) Regulations may revoke exemption regulations by which an exemption was granted to a person, or amend such regulations by which more than one exemption was so granted so as to withdraw any of the exemptions—
(a) at the person's request,
(b) in accordance with any provision of the exemption regulations by which the exemption was granted, or
(c) if the Secretary of State considers it to be inappropriate for the exemption to continue to have effect.
(2) Regulations may revoke exemption regulations by which an exemption was granted to persons of a prescribed description, or amend such regulations by which more than one exemption was so granted so as to withdraw any of the exemptions—
(a) in accordance with any provision of the exemption regulations by which the exemption was granted, or
(b) if the Secretary of State considers it to be inappropriate for the exemption to continue to have effect.
(3) The Secretary of State may by direction withdraw an exemption granted to persons of a description prescribed in exemption regulations for any person of that description—
(a) at the person's request,

(b) in accordance with any provision of the exemption regulations by which the exemption was granted, or
(c) if the Secretary of State considers it to be inappropriate for the exemption to continue to have effect in the case of the person.

(4) Subsection (5) applies where the Secretary of State proposes to—
(a) make regulations under subsection (1)(b) or (c) or (2), or
(b) give a direction under subsection (3)(b) or (c).

(5) The Secretary of State must—
(a) consult the following about the proposal—
(i) Monitor;
(ii) the National Health Service Commissioning Board;
(iii) the Care Quality Commission and its Healthwatch England committee;
(b) where the Secretary of State is proposing to make regulations under subsection (1)(b) or (c), give notice of the proposal to the person to whom the exemption was granted;
(c) where the Secretary of State is proposing to make regulations under subsection (2), publish the notice;
(d) where the Secretary of State is proposing to give a direction under subsection (3)(b) or (c), give notice of the proposal to the person from whom the Secretary of State proposes to withdraw the exemption.

(6) The notice must—
(a) state that the Secretary of State proposes to make the regulations or give the direction (as the case may be),
(b) set out the Secretary of State's reasons for the proposal, and
(c) specify the period within which representations with respect to the proposal may be made.

(7) The period so specified must be not less than 28 days beginning with the day after that on which the notice is received or (as the case may be) published.

NOTES

Commencement: 27 March 2012 (in so far as is necessary for enabling the exercise of any power to make an order or regulations or to give directions that is conferred by the above section or an amendment made by it); 1 April 2014 (otherwise).

Licensing procedure

[7.1341]

85 Application for licence

(1) A person seeking to hold a licence under this Chapter must make an application to Monitor.

(2) The application must be made in such form, and contain or be accompanied by such information, as Monitor requires.

NOTES

Commencement: 1 April 2013 (in relation to NHS foundation trusts); 1 January 2014 (otherwise).

[7.1342]

86 Licensing criteria

(1) Monitor must set and publish the criteria which must be met by a person in order for that person to be granted a licence under this Chapter.

(2) Monitor may revise the criteria and, if it does so, must publish them as revised.

(3) Monitor may not set or revise the criteria unless the Secretary of State has by order approved the criteria or (as the case may be) revised criteria.

NOTES

Commencement: 27 March 2012 (in so far as is necessary for enabling the exercise of any power to make an order or regulations or to give directions that is conferred by the above section or an amendment made by it); 1 April 2013 (in relation to NHS foundation trusts); 1 January 2014 (otherwise).

Regulations: the National Health Service (Approval of Licensing Criteria) Order 2013, SI 2013/2960.

[7.1343]

87 Grant or refusal of licence

(1) This section applies where an application for a licence has been made under section 85.

(2) If Monitor is satisfied that the applicant meets the criteria for holding a licence for the time being published under section 86 it must as soon as reasonably practicable grant the application; otherwise it must refuse it.

(3) On granting the application, Monitor must issue a licence to the applicant.

(4) A licence issued under this section is subject to—
(a) such of the standard conditions (see section 94) as are applicable to the licence,
(b) such other conditions included in the licence by virtue of section 95 (referred to in this Chapter as "the special conditions"), and
(c) any conditions included in the licence by virtue of section 111 (imposition of licence conditions on NHS foundation trusts during transitional period).

NOTES

Commencement: 1 April 2013 (in relation to NHS foundation trusts); 1 April 2014 (otherwise).

[7.1344]

88 Application and grant: NHS foundation trusts

(1) This section applies where an NHS trust becomes an NHS foundation trust pursuant to section 36 of the National Health Service Act 2006 (effect of authorisation of NHS foundation trust).

(2) The NHS foundation trust is to be treated by Monitor as having—

(a) duly made an application for a licence under section 85, and

(b) met the criteria for holding a licence for the time being published under section 86.

(3) An NHS foundation trust in existence on the day on which this section comes into force is to be treated for the purposes of this section as having become an NHS foundation trust pursuant to section 36 of the National Health Service Act 2006 on that day.

[7.1345]

89 Revocation of licence

Monitor may at any time revoke a licence under this Chapter—

(a) on the application of the licence holder, or

(b) if Monitor is satisfied that the licence holder has failed to comply with a condition of the licence.

[7.1346]

90 Right to make representations

(1) Monitor must give notice—

(a) to an applicant for a licence under this Chapter of a proposal to refuse the application;

(b) to the licence holder of a proposal to revoke a licence under section 89(b).

(2) A notice under this section must—

(a) set out Monitor's reasons for its proposal;

(b) specify the period within which representations with respect to the proposal may be made to Monitor.

(3) The period so specified must be not less than 28 days beginning with the day after that on which the notice is received.

NOTES

Commencement: 1 April 2013 (sub-ss (1)(b), (2), (3)); 1 April 2014 (otherwise).

[7.1347]

91 Notice of decisions

(1) This section applies if Monitor decides to—

(a) refuse an application for a licence under section 87, or

(b) revoke a licence under section 89(b).

(2) Monitor must give notice of its decision to the applicant or the licence holder (as the case may be).

(3) A notice under this section must explain the right of appeal conferred by section 92.

(4) A decision of Monitor to revoke a licence under section 89(b) takes effect on such day as may be specified by Monitor, being a day no earlier than—

(a) if an appeal is brought under section 92, the day on which the decision on appeal is confirmed or the appeal is abandoned,

(b) where the licence holder notifies Monitor before the end of the period for bringing an appeal under section 92 that the licence holder does not intend to appeal, the day on which Monitor receives the notification, or

(c) the day after that period.

NOTES

Commencement: 1 April 2013 (sub-s (1)(b), (2)–(4)); 1 April 2014 (otherwise).

[7.1348]

92 Appeals to the Tribunal

(1) An appeal lies to the First-tier Tribunal against a decision of Monitor to—

(a) refuse an application for a licence under section 87, or

(b) revoke a licence under section 89(b).

(2) The grounds for an appeal under this section are that the decision was—

(a) based on an error of fact,

(b) wrong in law, or

(c) unreasonable.

(3) On an appeal under this section, the First-tier Tribunal may—

(a) confirm Monitor's decision,

(b) direct that the decision is not to have effect, or

(c) remit the decision to Monitor.

NOTES

Commencement: 1 April 2013 (sub-ss (1)(b), (2), (3)); 1 April 2014 (otherwise).

[7.1349]

93 Register of licence holders

(1) Monitor must maintain and publish a register of licence holders.

(2) The register may contain such information as Monitor considers appropriate for the purpose of keeping members of the public informed about licence holders including, in particular, information about the revocation of any licence under this Chapter.
(3) Monitor must secure that copies of the register are available at its offices for inspection at all reasonable times by any person.
(4) Any person who asks Monitor for a copy of, or an extract from, the register is entitled to have one.
(5) Regulations may provide that subsections (3) and (4) do not apply—
(a) in such circumstances as may be prescribed, or
(b) to such parts of the register as may be prescribed.
(6) A fee determined by Monitor is payable for the copy or extract except—
(a) in such circumstances as may be prescribed, or
(b) in any case where Monitor considers it appropriate to provide the copy or extract free of charge.

Licence conditions

[7.1350]
94 Standard conditions
(1) Monitor must determine and publish the conditions to be included in each licence under this Chapter (referred to in this Chapter as "the standard conditions").
(2) Different standard conditions may be determined for different descriptions of licences.
(3) For the purposes of subsection (2) a description of licences may, in particular, be framed wholly or partly by reference to—
(a) the nature of the licence holder,
(b) the services provided under the licence, or
(c) the areas in which those services are provided.
(4) But different standard conditions must not be determined for different descriptions of licences to the extent that the description is framed by reference to the nature of the licence holder unless Monitor considers that at least one of requirements 1 and 2 is met.
(5) Requirement 1 is that—
(a) the standard conditions in question relate to the governance of licence holders, and
(b) it is necessary to determine different standard conditions in order to take account of differences in the status of different licence holders.
(6) Requirement 2 is that it is necessary to determine different standard conditions for the purpose of ensuring that the burdens to which different licence holders are subject as a result of holding a licence are broadly consistent.
(7) Before determining the first set of the standard conditions Monitor must consult the persons mentioned in subsection (8) on the conditions it is proposing to determine ("the draft standard conditions").
(8) Those persons are—
(a) the Secretary of State,
(b) the NHS Commissioning Board Authority,
(c) every Primary Care Trust,
(d) the Care Quality Commission, and
(e) such other persons as are likely to be affected by the inclusion of the conditions in licences under this Chapter as Monitor considers appropriate.
(9) Monitor must also publish the draft standard conditions.
(10) The Secretary of State may direct Monitor not to determine that the standard conditions will be the draft standard conditions.
(11) If, at the time Monitor discharges the function under subsection (7), the day specified by the Secretary of State for the purposes of section 14A of the National Health Service Act 2006 has passed or section 9 or 181 has come into force—
(a) in the case of section 14A of the National Health Service Act 2006, the reference in subsection (8)(c) to every Primary Care Trust is to be read as a reference to every clinical commissioning group;
(b) in the case of section 9, the reference in subsection (8)(b) to the NHS Commissioning Board Authority is to be read as a reference to the National Health Service Commissioning Board;
(c) in the case of section 181, the reference in subsection (8)(d) to the Care Quality Commission is to be read as including a reference to its Healthwatch England committee.

[7.1351]
95 Special conditions
(1) Monitor may—
(a) with the consent of the applicant, include a special condition in a licence under this Chapter, and
(b) with the consent of the licence holder, modify a special condition of a licence.
(2) Before including a special condition or making such modifications Monitor must give notice to—
(a) the applicant or the licence holder (as the case may be),
(b) the Secretary of State,
(c) the National Health Service Commissioning Board,
(d) such clinical commissioning groups as are likely to be affected by the proposed inclusion or modifications, and
(e) the Care Quality Commission and its Healthwatch England committee.
(3) Monitor must also publish the notice under subsection (2).
(4) The notice under subsection (2) must—

(a) state that Monitor proposes to include the special condition or make the modifications and set out its or their proposed effect,

(b) set out Monitor's reasons for the proposal, and

(c) specify the period ("the notice period") within which representations with respect to the proposal may be made to Monitor.

(5) The notice period must be not less than 28 days beginning with the day after that on which the notice is published under subsection (3).

(6) In this section, a reference to modifying a condition includes a reference to amending, omitting or adding a condition.

NOTES

Commencement: 1 November 2012 (for the purpose of enabling Monitor to take steps under this section to enable it to include a special condition in the licence of an NHS foundation trust from the date upon which s 81(1) comes into force in relation to NHS foundation trusts); 1 April 2013 (sub-ss (1)(a), (2)–(5), otherwise); 1 July 2013 (otherwise).

[7.1352]

96 Limits on Monitor's functions to set or modify licence conditions

(1) This section applies to the following functions of Monitor—

(a) the duty to determine the standard conditions to be included in each licence under this Chapter or in licences of a particular description (see section 94);

(b) the powers to include a special condition in a licence and to modify such a condition (see section 95);

(c) the power to modify the standard conditions applicable to all licences, or to licences of a particular description (see section 100).

(2) Monitor may only exercise a function to which this section applies—

(a) for the purpose of regulating the price payable for the provision of health care services for the purposes of the NHS;

(b) for the purpose of preventing anti-competitive behaviour in the provision of health care services for those purposes which is against the interests of people who use such services;

(c) for the purpose of protecting and promoting the right of patients to make choices with respect to treatment or other health care services provided for the purposes of the NHS;

(d) for the purpose of ensuring the continued provision of health care services for the purposes of the NHS;

(e) for the purpose of enabling health care services provided for the purposes of the NHS to be provided in an integrated way where Monitor considers that this would achieve one or more of the objectives referred to in subsection (3);

(f) for the purpose of enabling the provision of health care services provided for the purposes of the NHS to be integrated with the provision of health-related services or social care services where Monitor considers that this would achieve one or more of the objectives referred to in subsection (3);

(g) for the purpose of enabling co-operation between providers of health care services for the purposes of the NHS where Monitor considers that this would achieve one or more of the objectives referred to in subsection (3);

(h) for purposes connected with the governance of persons providing health care services for the purposes of the NHS;

(i) for purposes connected with Monitor's functions in relation to the register of NHS foundation trusts required to be maintained under section 39 of the National Health Service Act 2006;

(j) for purposes connected with the operation of the licensing regime established by this Chapter;

(k) for such purposes as may be prescribed for the purpose of enabling Monitor to discharge its duties under section 62.

(3) The objectives referred to in subsection (2)(e), (f) and (g) are—

(a) improving the quality of health care services provided for the purposes of the NHS (including the outcomes that are achieved from their provision) or the efficiency of their provision,

(b) reducing inequalities between persons with respect to their ability to access those services, and

(c) reducing inequalities between persons with respect to the outcomes achieved for them by the provision of those services.

(4) Monitor must not exercise a function to which this section applies in a way which it considers would result in a particular licence holder or holders of licences of a particular description being put at an unfair advantage or disadvantage in competing with others in the provision of health care services for the purposes of the NHS as a result of—

(a) being in the public or (as the case may be) private sector, or

(b) some other aspect of its or their status.

(5) In subsection (2)(f), "health-related services" and "social care services" each have the meaning given in section 62(11).

NOTES

Commencement: 1 November 2012 (in so far as relates to functions under sub-s (1)(a), (b), but note that sub-s (2)(a) is brought into force only for the purpose of regulating the price payable for the provision of healthcare services for the purpose of the NHS in accordance with the national tariff to be published by Monitor under s 116(1)); 1 July 2013 (sub-s (1)(c)); 1 April 2014 (otherwise).

[7.1353]
97 Conditions: supplementary
(1) The standard or special conditions of a licence under this Chapter may, in particular, include conditions—
(a) requiring the licence holder to pay to Monitor such fees of such amounts as Monitor may determine in respect of the exercise by Monitor of its functions under this Chapter,
(b) requiring the licence holder to comply with any requirement imposed on it by Monitor under Chapter 6 (financial assistance in special administration cases),
(c) requiring the licence holder to do, or not to do, specified things or things of a specified description (or to do, or not to do, any such things in a specified manner) within such period as may be specified in order to prevent anti-competitive behaviour in the provision of health care services for the purposes of the NHS which is against the interests of people who use such services,
(d) requiring the licence holder to give notice to the [CMA] before entering into an arrangement under which, or a transaction in consequence of which, the licence holder's activities, and the activities of one or more other businesses, cease to be distinct activities,
(e) requiring the licence holder to provide Monitor with such information as Monitor considers necessary for the purposes of the exercise of its functions under this Part,
(f) requiring the licence holder to publish such information as may be specified or as Monitor may direct,
(g) requiring the licence holder to charge for the provision of health care services for the purposes of the NHS in accordance with the national tariff (see section 116),
(h) requiring the licence holder to comply with other rules published by Monitor about the charging for the provision of health care services for the purposes of the NHS,
(i) requiring the licence holder—
(i) to do, or not to do, specified things or things of a specified description (or to do, or not to do, any such things in a specified manner) within such period as may be specified in order to ensure the continued provision of one or more of the health care services that the licence holder provides for the purposes of the NHS,
(ii) to give Monitor notice (of such period as may be determined by or under the licence) of the licence holder's intention to cease providing a health care service for the purposes of the NHS, and
(iii) if Monitor so directs, to continue providing that service for a period determined by Monitor,
(j) about the use or disposal by the licence holder of assets used in the provision of health care services for the purposes of the NHS in order to ensure the continued provision of one or more of the health care services that the licence holder provides for those purposes, and
(k) about the making by the licence holder of investment in relation to the provision of health care services for the purposes of the NHS in order to ensure the continued provision of one or more of the health care services that the licence holder provides for those purposes.
(2) In subsection (1) "specified" means specified in a condition.
(3) Monitor must not include a condition under subsection (1)(c) that requires the licence holder (A) to provide another licence holder with access to facilities of A.
(4) A condition under subsection (1)(d)—
(a) may be included only in the licence of an NHS foundation trust or a body which (or part of which) used to be an NHS trust established under section 25 of the National Health Service Act 2006, and
(b) ceases to have effect at the end of the period of five years beginning with the day on which it is included in the licence.
(5) The references in subsection (1)(d) to the activities of a licence holder or other business include a reference to part of the activities concerned.
(6) The references in subsections (1)(d) and (5) to the activities of a business include a reference to the activities of an NHS foundation trust in so far as its activities would not otherwise be the activities of a business.
(7) A condition of a licence under this Chapter may provide that it is to have effect, or cease to have effect, at such times and in such circumstances as may be determined by or under the conditions.

NOTES
Sub-s (1): in para (d) reference in square brackets substituted by the Enterprise and Regulatory Reform Act 2013 (Competition) (Consequential, Transitional and Saving Provisions) Order 2014, SI 2014/892, art 2, Sch 1, Pt 2, paras 187, 193.

[7.1354]
98 Conditions relating to the continuation of the provision of services etc
(1) The things which a licence holder may be required to do by a condition under section 97(1)(i)(i) include, in particular—
(a) providing information to the commissioners of services to which the condition applies and to such other persons as Monitor may direct,
(b) allowing Monitor to enter premises owned or controlled by the licence holder and to inspect the premises and anything on them, and
(c) co-operating with such persons as Monitor may appoint to assist in the management of the licence holder's affairs, business and property.

(2) A commissioner of services to which a condition under section 97(1)(i), (j) or (k) applies must co-operate with persons appointed under subsection (1)(c) in their provision of the assistance that they have been appointed to provide.

(3) Where a licence includes a condition under section 97(1)(i), (j) or (k), Monitor must carry out an ongoing assessment of the risks to the continued provision of services to which the condition applies.

(4) Monitor must publish guidance—

(a) for commissioners of a service to which a condition under section 97(1)(i), (j) or (k) applies about the exercise of their functions in connection with the licence holders who provide the service, and

(b) for such licence holders about the conduct of their affairs, business and property at a time at which such a condition applies.

(5) A commissioner of services to which a condition under section 97(1)(i), (j), or (k) applies must have regard to guidance under subsection (4)(a).

(6) Monitor may revise guidance under subsection (4) and, if it does so, must publish the guidance as revised.

(7) Before publishing guidance under subsection (4) or (6), Monitor must obtain the approval of—

(a) the Secretary of State, and

(b) the National Health Service Commissioning Board.

[7.1355]

99 Notification of commissioners where continuation of services at risk

(1) This section applies where Monitor—

(a) takes action in the case of a licence holder in reliance on a condition in the licence under section 97(1)(i), (j) or (k), and

(b) does so because it is satisfied that the continued provision for the purposes of the NHS of health care services to which that condition applies is being put at significant risk by the configuration of certain health care services provided for those purposes.

(2) In subsection (1), a reference to the provision of services is a reference to their provision by the licence holder or any other provider.

(3) Monitor must as soon as reasonably practicable notify the National Health Service Commissioning Board and such clinical commissioning groups as Monitor considers appropriate—

(a) of the action it has taken, and

(b) of its reasons for being satisfied as mentioned in subsection (1)(b).

(4) Monitor must publish for each financial year a list of the notifications under this section that it has given during that year; and the list must include for each notification a summary of Monitor's reasons for being satisfied as mentioned in subsection (1)(b).

(5) The Board and clinical commissioning groups, having received a notification under this section, must have regard to it in arranging for the provision of health care services for the purposes of the NHS.

[7.1356]

100 Modification of standard conditions

(1) Monitor may, subject to the requirements of this section, modify the standard conditions applicable to all licences under this Chapter or to licences of a particular description.

(2) Before making any such modifications Monitor must give notice to—

(a) each relevant licence holder,

(b) the Secretary of State,

(c) the National Health Service Commissioning Board,

(d) every clinical commissioning group, and

(e) the Care Quality Commission and its Healthwatch England committee.

(3) Monitor must also publish the notice under subsection (2).

(4) The notice under subsection (2) must—

(a) state that Monitor proposes to make the modifications,

(b) set out the proposed effect of the modifications,

(c) set out Monitor's reasons for the proposal, and

(d) specify the period ("the notice period") within which representations with respect to the proposal may be made to Monitor.

(5) The notice period must be not less than 28 days beginning with the day after that on which the notice is published under subsection (3).

(6) Monitor may not make any modifications under this section unless—

(a) no relevant licence holder has made an objection to Monitor about the proposal within the notice period, or

(b) subsection (7) applies to the case.

(7) This subsection applies where—

(a) one or more relevant licence holders make an objection to Monitor about the proposal within the notice period,

(b) the objection percentage is less than the percentage prescribed for the purposes of this paragraph, and

(c) the share of supply percentage is less than the percentage prescribed for the purposes of this paragraph.

(8) In subsection (7)—

(a) the "objection percentage" is the proportion (expressed as a percentage) of the relevant licence holders who objected to the proposals;

(b) the "share of supply percentage" is the proportion (expressed as a percentage) of the relevant licence holders who objected to the proposals, weighted according to their share of the supply in England of such services as may be prescribed.

(9) Regulations prescribing a percentage for the purposes of subsection (7)(c) may include provision prescribing the method to be used for determining a licence holder's share of the supply in England of the services concerned.

(10) Where Monitor modifies the standard conditions applicable to all licences or (as the case may be) to licences of a particular description under this section, Monitor—

(a) may also make such incidental or consequential modifications as it considers necessary or expedient of any other conditions of a licence which is affected by the modifications,

(b) must make (as nearly as may be) the same modifications of those conditions for the purposes of their inclusion in all licences or (as the case may be) licences of that description granted after that time, and

(c) must publish the modifications.

(11) In this section and section 101, "relevant licence holder"—

(a) in relation to proposed modifications of the standard conditions applicable to all licences, means any licence holder, and

(b) in relation to proposed modifications of the standard conditions applicable to licences of a particular description, means a holder of a licence of that description.

(12) In this section, a reference to modifying a condition includes a reference to amending, omitting or adding a condition.

NOTES

Commencement: 27 March 2012 (in so far as is necessary for enabling the exercise of any power to make an order or regulations or to give directions that is conferred by the above section or an amendment made by it); 1 July 2013 (otherwise).

Regulations: the National Health Service (Licensing and Pricing) Regulations 2013, SI 2013/2214.

101–127 (*Outside the scope of this work.*)

CHAPTER 5 HEALTH SPECIAL ADMINISTRATION

[7.1357]

128 Health special administration orders

(1) In this Chapter "health special administration order" means an order which—

(a) is made by the court in relation to a relevant provider, and

(b) directs that the affairs, business and property of the provider are to be managed by one or more persons appointed by the court.

(2) An application to the court for a health special administration order may be made only by Monitor.

(3) A person appointed as mentioned in subsection (1)(b) is referred to in this Chapter as a "health special administrator".

(4) A health special administrator of a company—

(a) is an officer of the court, and

(b) in exercising functions in relation to the company, is the company's agent.

(5) A person is not to be the health special administrator of a company unless the person is qualified to act as an insolvency practitioner in relation to the company.

(6) A health special administrator of a relevant provider must manage its affairs, business and property, and exercise the health special administrator's functions, so as to—

(a) achieve the objective set out in section 129 as quickly and as efficiently as is reasonably practicable,

(b) in seeking to achieve that objective, ensure that any regulated activity carried on in providing the services provided by the provider is carried on in accordance with any requirements or conditions imposed in respect of that activity by virtue of Chapter 2 of Part 1 of the Health and Social Care Act 2008,

(c) so far as is consistent with the objective set out in section 129, protect the interests of the creditors of the provider as a whole, and

(d) so far as is consistent with that objective and subject to those interests, protect the interests of the members of the provider as a whole.

(7) In relation to a health special administration order applying to a non-GB company, references in this Chapter to the affairs, business and property of the company are references only to its affairs and business so far as carried on in Great Britain and to its property in Great Britain.

(8) In this section—

(a) a reference to a person qualified to act as an insolvency practitioner in relation to a company is to be construed in accordance with Part 13 of the Insolvency Act 1986 (insolvency practitioners and their qualifications);

(b) "regulated activity" has the same meaning as in Part 1 of the Health and Social Care Act 2008 (see section 8 of that Act).

(9) In this Chapter—

"business" and "property" each have the same meaning as in the Insolvency Act 1986 (see section 436 of that Act);

"company" includes a company not registered under the Companies Act 2006;

"court", in relation to a company, means the court—

(a) having jurisdiction to wind up the company, or

(b) that would have such jurisdiction apart from section 221(2) or 441(2) of the Insolvency Act 1986 (exclusion of winding up jurisdiction in case of companies incorporated in, or having principal place of business in, Northern Ireland);

"member" is to be read in accordance with section 250 of the Insolvency Act 1986;

"non-GB company" means a company incorporated outside Great Britain;

"relevant provider" means a company which is providing services to which a condition included in the company's licence under section 97(1)(i), (j) or (k) applies;

"wholly-owned subsidiary" has the meaning given by section 1159 of the Companies Act 2006.

NOTES

Commencement: to be appointed.

[7.1358]

129 Objective of a health special administration

(1) The objective of a health special administration is to secure—

(a) the continued provision of such of the health care services provided for the purposes of the NHS by the company subject to the health special administration order, at such level, as the commissioners of those services determine by applying criteria specified in health special administration regulations (see section 130), and

(b) that it becomes unnecessary, by one or both of the means set out in subsection (2), for the health special administration order to remain in force for that purpose.

(2) Those means are—

(a) the rescue as a going concern of the company subject to the health special administration order, and

(b) one or more transfers falling within subsection (3).

(3) A transfer falls within this subsection if it is a transfer as a going concern—

(a) to another person, or

(b) as respects different parts of the undertaking of the company subject to the health special administration order, to two or more other persons,

of so much of that undertaking as it is appropriate to transfer for the purpose of achieving the objective of the health special administration.

(4) The means by which a transfer falling within subsection (3) may be effected include in particular—

(a) a transfer of the undertaking of the company subject to the health special administration order, or of part of its undertaking, to a wholly-owned subsidiary of that company, and

(b) a transfer to a company of securities of a wholly-owned subsidiary to which there has been a transfer falling within paragraph (a).

(5) The objective of a health special administration may be achieved by transfers to the extent only that—

(a) the rescue as a going concern of the company subject to the health special administration order is not reasonably practicable or is not reasonably practicable without such transfers,

(b) the rescue of the company as a going concern will not achieve that objective or will not do so without such transfers,

(c) such transfers would produce a result for the company's creditors as a whole that is better than the result that would be produced without them, or

(d) such transfers would, without prejudicing the interests of its creditors as a whole, produce a result for the company's members as a whole that is better than the result that would be produced without them.

NOTES

Commencement: 27 March 2012 (in so far as is necessary for enabling the exercise of any power to make an order or regulations or to give directions that is conferred by the above section or an amendment made by it); to be appointed (otherwise).

[7.1359]

130 Health special administration regulations

(1) Regulations (referred to in this Chapter as "health special administration regulations") must make further provision about health special administration orders.

(2) Health special administration regulations may apply with or without modifications—

(a) any provision of Part 2 of the Insolvency Act 1986 (administration) or any related provision of that Act, and

(b) any other enactment which relates to insolvency or administration or makes provision by reference to anything that is or may be done under that Act.

(3) Health special administration regulations may, in particular, provide that the court may make a health special administration order in relation to a relevant provider if it is satisfied, on a petition by the Secretary of State under section 124A of the Insolvency Act 1986 (petition for winding up on grounds of public interest), that it would be just and equitable (disregarding the objective of the health special administration) to wind up the provider in the public interest.

(4) Health special administration regulations may make provision about—

(a) the application of procedures under the Insolvency Act 1986 in relation to relevant providers, and

(b) the enforcement of security over property of relevant providers.

(5) Health special administration regulations may, in particular, make provision about the publication and maintenance by Monitor of a list of relevant providers.

(6) Health special administration regulations may in particular—
 (a) require Monitor to publish guidance for commissioners about the application of the criteria referred to in section 129(1)(a);
 (b) confer power on Monitor to revise guidance published by virtue of paragraph (a) and require it to publish guidance so revised;
 (c) require Monitor, before publishing guidance by virtue of paragraph (a) or (b), to obtain the approval of the Secretary of State and the National Health Service Commissioning Board;
 (d) require commissioners, when applying the criteria referred to in section 129(1)(a), to have regard to such matters as Monitor may specify in guidance published by virtue of paragraph (a) or (b);
 (e) require the National Health Service Commissioning Board to make arrangements for facilitating agreement between commissioners in their exercise of their function under section 129(1)(a);
 (f) confer power on the Board, where commissioners fail to reach agreement in pursuance of arrangements made by virtue of paragraph (e), to exercise their function under section 129(1)(a);
 (g) provide that, in consequence of the exercise of the power conferred by virtue of paragraph (f), the function under section 129(1)(a), so far as applying to the commissioners concerned, is to be regarded as discharged;
 (h) require a health special administrator to carry out in accordance with the regulations consultation on the action which the administrator recommends should be taken in relation to the provider concerned.

(7) Health special administration regulations may modify this Chapter or any enactment mentioned in subsection (8) in relation to any provision made by virtue of this Chapter.

(8) The enactments are—
 (a) the Insolvency Act 1986, and
 (b) any other enactment which relates to insolvency or administration or makes provision by reference to anything that is or may be done under that Act.

(9) The power to make rules under section 411 of the Insolvency Act 1986 (company insolvency rules) applies for the purpose of giving effect to provision made by virtue of this Chapter as it applies for the purpose of giving effect to Parts 1 to 7 of that Act.

(10) For that purpose—
 (a) the power to make rules in relation to England and Wales is exercisable by the Lord Chancellor with the concurrence of the Secretary of State and, in the case of rules that affect court procedure, with the concurrence of the Lord Chief Justice;
 (b) the power to make rules in relation to Scotland is exercisable by the Secretary of State;
 (c) references in section 411 of that Act to those Parts are to be read as including a reference to this Chapter.

(11) Before making health special administration regulations the Secretary of State must consult—
 (a) Monitor, and
 (b) such other persons as the Secretary of State considers appropriate.

NOTES

Commencement: 27 March 2012 (in so far as is necessary for enabling the exercise of any power to make an order or regulations or to give directions that is conferred by the above section or an amendment made by it); to be appointed (otherwise).

[7.1360]

131 Transfer schemes

(1) Health special administration regulations may make provision about transfer schemes to achieve the objective of a health special administration (see section 129).

(2) Health special administration regulations may, in particular, include provision—
 (a) for the making of a transfer scheme to be subject to the consent of Monitor and the person to whom the transfer is being made,
 (b) for Monitor to have power to modify a transfer scheme with the consent of parties to the transfers effected by the scheme, and
 (c) for modifications made to a transfer scheme by virtue of paragraph (b) to have effect from such time as Monitor may specify (which may be a time before the modifications were made).

(3) Health special administration regulations may, in particular, provide that a transfer scheme may include provision—
 (a) for the transfer of rights and liabilities under or in connection with a contract of employment from a company subject to a health special administration order to another person,
 (b) for the transfer of property, or rights and liabilities other than those mentioned in paragraph (a), from a company subject to a health special administration order to another person,
 (c) for the transfer of property, rights and liabilities which would not otherwise be capable of being transferred or assigned,
 (d) for the transfer of property acquired, and rights and liabilities arising, after the making of the scheme,
 (e) for the creation of interests or rights, or the imposition of liabilities, and
 (f) for the transfer, or concurrent exercise, of functions under enactments.

NOTES

Commencement: 27 March 2012 (in so far as is necessary for enabling the exercise of any power to make an order or regulations or to give directions that is conferred by the above section or an amendment made by it); to be appointed (otherwise).

[7.1361]
132 Indemnities
Health special administration regulations may make provision about the giving by Monitor of indemnities in respect of—
(a) liabilities incurred in connection with the discharge by health special administrators of their functions, and
(b) loss or damage sustained in that connection.

NOTES
Commencement: 27 March 2012 (in so far as is necessary for enabling the exercise of any power to make an order or regulations or to give directions that is conferred by the above section or an amendment made by it); to be appointed (otherwise).

[7.1362]
133 Modification of this Chapter under Enterprise Act 2002
(1) The power to modify or apply enactments conferred on the Secretary of State by each of the sections of the Enterprise Act 2002 mentioned in subsection (2) includes power to make such consequential modifications of provision made by virtue of this Chapter as the Secretary of State considers appropriate in connection with any other provision made under that section.
(2) Those sections are—
(a) sections 248 and 277 (amendments consequential on that Act), and
(b) section 254 (power to apply insolvency law to foreign companies).

NOTES
Commencement: 27 March 2012 (in so far as is necessary for enabling the exercise of any power to make an order or regulations or to give directions that is conferred by the above section or an amendment made by it); to be appointed (otherwise).

CHAPTER 6 FINANCIAL ASSISTANCE IN SPECIAL ADMINISTRATION CASES

Establishment of mechanisms

[7.1363]
134 Duty to establish mechanisms for providing financial assistance
(1) Monitor must establish, and secure the effective operation of, one or more mechanisms for providing financial assistance in cases where a provider of health care services for the purposes of the NHS (referred to in this Chapter as a "provider") is subject to—
(a) a health special administration order (within the meaning of Chapter 5), or
(b) an order under section 65D(2) of the National Health Service Act 2006 (trust special administration for NHS foundation trusts).
(2) Mechanisms that Monitor may establish under this section include, in particular—
(a) mechanisms for raising money to make grants or loans or to make payments in consequence of indemnities given by Monitor by virtue of section 132 or under section 65D(12) of the National Health Service Act 2006;
(b) mechanisms for securing that providers arrange, or are provided with, insurance facilities.
(3) Monitor may secure that a mechanism established under this section operates so as to enable it to recover the costs it incurs in establishing and operating the mechanism.
(4) Monitor may establish different mechanisms for different providers or providers of different descriptions.
(5) Monitor does not require permission under any provision of the Financial Services and Markets Act 2000 as respects activities carried out under this Chapter.
(6) An order under section 306 providing for the commencement of this Chapter may require Monitor to comply with the duty to establish under subsection (1) before such date as the order specifies.

NOTES
Commencement: 27 March 2012 (in so far as is necessary for enabling the exercise of any power to make an order or regulations or to give directions that is conferred by the above section or an amendment made by it); to be appointed (otherwise).

[7.1364]
135 Power to establish fund
(1) Monitor may, for the purposes of section 134, establish and maintain a fund.
(2) In order to raise money for investment in a fund it establishes under this section, Monitor may impose requirements on providers or commissioners.
(3) Monitor must appoint at least two managers for a fund it establishes under this section.
(4) A manager of a fund may be an individual, a firm or a body corporate.
(5) Monitor must not appoint an individual as manager of a fund unless it is satisfied that the individual has the appropriate knowledge and experience for managing investments.
(6) Monitor must not appoint a firm or body corporate as manager of a fund unless it is satisfied that arrangements are in place to secure that any individual who will exercise functions of the firm or body corporate as manager will, at the time of doing so, have the appropriate knowledge and experience for managing investments.

(7) Monitor must not appoint an individual, firm or body corporate as manager of a fund unless the individual, firm or body is an authorised or exempt person within the meaning of the Financial Services and Markets Act 2000.
(8) Monitor must secure the prudent management of any fund it establishes under this section.

NOTES
Commencement: to be appointed.

Applications for financial assistance

[7.1365]
136 Applications
(1) Monitor may, on an application by a special administrator, provide financial assistance to the special administrator by using a mechanism established under section 134.
(2) An application under this section must be in such form, and must be supported by such evidence or other information, as Monitor may require (and a requirement under this subsection may be imposed after the receipt, but before the determination, of the application).
(3) If Monitor grants an application under this section, it must notify the applicant of—
(a) the purpose for which the financial assistance is being provided, and
(b) the other conditions to which its provision is subject.
(4) The special administrator must secure that the financial assistance is used only—
(a) for the purpose notified under subsection (3)(a), and
(b) in accordance with the conditions notified under subsection (3)(b).
(5) Financial assistance under this section may be provided only in the period during which the provider in question is in special administration.
(6) If Monitor refuses an application under this section, it must notify the applicant of the reasons for the refusal.
(7) Monitor must, on a request by an applicant whose application under this section has been refused, reconsider the application; but no individual involved in the decision to refuse the application may be involved in the decision on the reconsideration of the application.
(8) For the purposes of reconsidering an application, Monitor may request information from the applicant.
(9) Monitor must notify the applicant of its decision on reconsidering the application; and—
(a) if Monitor grants the application, it must notify the applicant of the matters specified in subsection (3), and
(b) if Monitor refuses the application, it must notify the applicant of the reasons for the refusal.
(10) In this Chapter—
(a) "special administrator" means—
(i) a person appointed as a health special administrator under Chapter 5, or
(ii) a person appointed as a trust special administrator under section 65D(2) of the National Health Service Act 2006, and
(b) references to being in special administration are to be construed accordingly.

NOTES
Commencement: to be appointed.

[7.1366]
137 Grants and loans
(1) Monitor may not provide financial assistance under section 136 in the form of a grant or loan unless it is satisfied that—
(a) it is necessary for the provider—
(i) to be able to continue to provide one or more of the health care services that it provides for the purposes of the NHS, or
(ii) to be able to secure a viable business in the long term, and
(b) no other source of funding which would enable it do so and on which it would be reasonable for it to rely is likely to become available to it.
(2) The terms of a grant or loan must include a term that the whole or a specified part of the grant or loan becomes repayable in the event of a breach by the provider or special administrator of the terms of the grant or loan.
(3) Subject to that, where Monitor makes a grant or loan under section 136, it may do so in such manner and on such terms as it may determine.
(4) Monitor may take such steps as it considers appropriate (including steps to adjust the amount of future payments towards the mechanism established under section 134 to raise funds for grants or loans under section 136) to recover overpayments in the provision of a grant or loan under that section.
(5) The power to recover an overpayment under subsection (4) includes a power to recover interest, at such rate as Monitor may determine, on the amount of the overpayment for the period beginning with the making of the overpayment and ending with its recovery.

NOTES
Commencement: to be appointed.

138–146 (*Outside the scope of this work.*)

CHAPTER 7 MISCELLANEOUS AND GENERAL

147 (*Outside the scope of this work.*)

[7.1367]
148 Service of documents
(1) A notice required under this Part to be given or sent to or served on a person ("R") may be given or sent to or served on R—
(a) by being delivered personally to R,
(b) by being sent to R—
(i) by a registered post service, as defined by section 125(1) of the Postal Services Act 2000, or
(ii) by a postal service which provides for the delivery of the document to be recorded, or
(c) subject to section 149, by being sent to R by an electronic communication.
(2) Where a notice is sent as mentioned in subsection (1)(b), it is, unless the contrary is proved, to be taken to have been received on the third day after the day on which it is sent.
(3) Where a notice is sent as mentioned in subsection (1)(c) in accordance with section 149, it is, unless the contrary is proved, to be taken to have been received on the next working day after the day on which it is transmitted.
(4) In subsection (3) "working day" means a day other than—
(a) a Saturday or a Sunday;
(b) Christmas Day or Good Friday; or
(c) a day which is a bank holiday in England under the Banking and Financial Dealings Act 1971.
(5) A notice required under this Part to be given or sent to or served on a body corporate or a firm is duly given, sent or served if it is given or sent to or served on the secretary or clerk of that body or a partner of that firm.
(6) For the purposes of section 7 of the Interpretation Act 1978 in its application to this section, the proper address of a person is—
(a) in the case of a person who holds a licence under Chapter 3 who has notified Monitor of an address for service, that address, and
(b) in any other case, the address determined in accordance with subsection (7).
(7) That address is—
(a) in the case of a secretary or clerk of a body corporate, the address of the registered or principal office of the body,
(b) in the case of a partner of a firm, the address of the principal office of the firm, and
(c) in any other case, the last known address of the person.
(8) In this section and in section 149—
"electronic communication" has the same meaning as in the Electronic Communications Act 2000;
"notice" includes any other document.
(9) This section is subject to paragraph 4(3) of Schedule 8 (delivery of notice from Secretary of State of suspension of non-executive member of Monitor).

[7.1368]
149 Electronic communications
(1) If a notice required or authorised by this Part to be given or sent by or to a person or to be served on a person is sent by an electronic communication, it is to be treated as given, sent or served only if the requirements of subsection (2) or (3) are met.
(2) If the person required or authorised to give, send or serve the notice is Monitor or the [CMA]—
(a) the person to whom the notice is given or sent or on whom it is served must have indicated to Monitor or (as the case may be) [the CMA] the person's willingness to receive notices by an electronic communication and provided an address suitable for that purpose, and
(b) the notice must be sent to or given or served at the address so provided.
(3) If the person required or authorised to give, send or serve the notice is not Monitor or the [CMA], the notice must be given, sent or served in such manner as Monitor may require.
(4) An indication given for the purposes of subsection (2) may be given generally for the purposes of notices required or authorised to be given, sent or served by Monitor or (as the case may be) the [CMA] under this Part or may be limited to notices of a particular description.
(5) Monitor must publish such requirements as it imposes under subsection (3).

NOTES
Sub-ss (2)–(4): words in square brackets substituted by the Enterprise and Regulatory Reform Act 2013, s 26(4), Sch 6, Pt 1, paras 127, 136.

[7.1369]
150 Interpretation, transitional provision and consequential amendments
(1) In this Part—
"anti-competitive behaviour" has the meaning given in section 64 and references to preventing anti-competitive behaviour are to be read in accordance with subsection (2) of that section;
["the CMA" means the Competition and Markets Authority;]
"commissioner", in relation to a health care service, means the person who arranges for the provision of the service (and "commission" is to be construed accordingly);
"enactment" includes an enactment contained in subordinate legislation (within the meaning of the Interpretation Act 1978);

"facilities" has the same meaning as in the National Health Service Act 2006 (see section 275 of that Act);
"financial year" means a period of 12 months ending with 31 March;
"health care" and "health care service" each have the meaning given in section 64;
"the NHS" has the meaning given in that section;
"prescribed" means prescribed in regulations;
"service" includes facility.

(2) Until section 9 comes into force, the references in this Part to the National Health Service Commissioning Board (other than the reference in section 94(11)(b)) are to be read as references to the NHS Commissioning Board Authority.

(3) Until the day specified by Secretary of State for the purposes of section 14A of the National Health Service Act 2006, the references in this Part to a clinical commissioning group (other than the reference in section 94(11)(a)) are to be read as references to a Primary Care Trust.

(4) Until section 181 comes into force, the following provisions in this Part are to be read as if the words "and its Healthwatch England committee" were omitted—
(a) section 83(4)(c);
(b) section 84(5)(a)(iii);
(c) section 95(2)(e);
(d) section 100(2)(e).

(5) Schedule 13 (which contains minor and consequential amendments) has effect.

NOTES

Sub-s (1): definition "the CMA" inserted by the Enterprise and Regulatory Reform Act 2013, s 26(4), Sch 6, Pt 1, paras 127, 137.

Regulations: the National Health Service (Licensing and Pricing) Regulations 2013, SI 2013/2214; the National Health Service (Licence Exemptions, etc) Regulations 2013, SI 2013/2677; the National Health Service (Licence Exemptions, etc) Amendment Regulations 2015, SI 2015/190.

151–302 ((*Parts 4–11) Outside the scope of this work.*)

PART 12
FINAL PROVISIONS

303 (*Outside the scope of this work.*)

[7.1370]

304 Regulations, orders and directions

(1) A power to make regulations under this Act is exercisable by the Secretary of State.

(2) Regulations under this Act, and orders by the Secretary of State, the Welsh Ministers or the Privy Council under this Act, must be made by statutory instrument.

(3) Subject to subsections (4) to (6), a statutory instrument containing regulations under this Act, or an order by the Secretary of State or the Privy Council under this Act, is subject to annulment in pursuance of a resolution of either House of Parliament.

(4) Subsection (3) does not apply to an order under section 306 (commencement).

(5) A statutory instrument which contains (whether alone or with other provision) any of the following may not be made unless a draft of the instrument has been laid before, and approved by a resolution of, each House of Parliament—
(a) regulations under section 65 (extension of Monitor's functions to adult social care services);
(b) the first regulations under section 83 (licensing requirement: exemption regulations);
(c) the first order under section 86 (approval by Secretary of State of licensing criteria);
(d) regulations under section 100(7)(b) or (c) (percentage to be prescribed in cases of objections to proposals to modify standard licence conditions);
(e) regulations under section 105(4) (manner in which turnover to be calculated for purposes of penalty for breach of licence conditions etc);
(f) regulations under section 106(3)(d) (descriptions of action for specifying in enforcement undertaking for breach of licence conditions etc);
(g) regulations under section 120(2)(a), (b) or (c) (percentage to be prescribed in cases of objections to proposals for national tariff);
(h) regulations under section 130 (health special administration regulations);
(i) an order under section 140 (maximum amount that may be raised from levy to raise funds for special administration cases);
(j) regulations under section 142(2)(b) (percentage to be prescribed in cases of objections to proposals to impose levy);
(k) an order under section 290(4) (addition to list of bodies subject to duty co-operate);
(l) an order under section 291(5) (order prohibiting bodies subject to duty to co-operate from exercising specified functions etc);
(m) an order under section 303 (consequential provision) which includes provision that amends or repeals a provision of an Act of Parliament;
(n) regulations which, by virtue of subsection (10)(a), include provision that amends or repeals a provision of an Act of Parliament.

(6) An order by the Privy Council under this Act that includes provision which would, if included in an Act of the Scottish Parliament, fall within the legislative competence of that Parliament is subject to the negative procedure in that Parliament (in addition to the statutory instrument containing the order being subject to annulment under subsection (3)).
(7) Sections 28 and 31 of the Interpretation and Legislative Reform (Scotland) Act 2010 (negative procedure etc) apply in relation to an order of the description given in subsection (6) as they apply in relation to devolved subordinate legislation (within the meaning of Part 2 of that Act) that is subject to the negative procedure, but as if references to a Scottish statutory instrument were references to a statutory instrument.
(8) Section 32 of that Act (laying) shall apply in relation to the laying of a statutory instrument containing an order of the description given in subsection (6) before the Scottish Parliament as it applies in relation to the laying of a Scottish statutory instrument (within the meaning of Part 2 of that Act) before that Parliament.
(9) A power to make regulations under this Act, a power of the Secretary of State, the Welsh Ministers or the Privy Council to make an order under this Act, and (subject to section 71(3)) a power to give directions under or by virtue of this Act—
- (a) may be exercised either in relation to all cases to which the power extends, or in relation to those cases subject to specified exceptions, or in relation to any specified cases or descriptions of case,
- (b) may be exercised so as to make, as respects the cases in relation to which it is exercised—
  - (i) the full provision to which the power extends or any less provision (whether by way of exception or otherwise),
  - (ii) the same provision for all cases in relation to which the power is exercised, or different provision for different cases or different descriptions of case, or different provision as respects the same case or description of case for different purposes of this Act,
  - (iii) any such provision either unconditionally or subject to any specified condition, and
- (c) may, in particular, make different provision for different areas.

(10) Any such power includes—
- (a) power to make incidental, supplementary, consequential, saving, transitional or transitory provision (including, in the case of a power to make regulations, provision amending, repealing or revoking enactments), and
- (b) power to provide for a person to exercise a discretion in dealing with any matter.

(11) A power to give directions under or by virtue of this Act includes power to vary or revoke the directions by subsequent directions.
(12) A direction under this Act by a Minister of the Crown (acting alone)—
- (a) must, in the case of a direction under any of the following provisions, be given by regulations or an instrument in writing—
  - (i) section 71(2) (direction to Monitor to perform functions);
  - (ii) section 234(1) (direction to NICE to prepare quality standards);
  - (iii) section 245(1) (direction to NICE to perform functions);
  - (iv) section 249(8) (direction to Board to be transitional commissioner in relation to pre-commencement statements of quality standards);
  - (v) section 254(1) (direction to Information Centre to establish information systems);
  - (vi) section 255(5) or (6) (direction to Information Centre to comply, or not to comply, with request to establish information systems);
  - (vii) section 260(2)(d) (direction to Information Centre that information of specified description is not subject to duty to publish);
  - (viii) section 272(1) (direction to Information Centre to perform functions);
  - (ix) paragraph 7 of Schedule 6 (direction to Board to exercise functions of Secretary of State relating to Primary Care Trusts), and
- (b) must, in the case of any other direction, be given by an instrument in writing.

(13) A direction under or by virtue of this Act by any other person (or persons) must be given by an instrument in writing.

305 *(Outside the scope of this work.)*

[7.1371]
306 Commencement
(1) The following provisions come into force on the day on which this Act is passed—
- (a), (b) *(outside the scope of this work.)*
- (c) the provisions of this Part;
- (d) any other provision of this Act so far as is necessary for enabling the exercise on or after the day on which this Act is passed of any power to make an order or regulations or to give directions that is conferred by the provision or an amendment made by it.

(2), (3) *(Outside the scope of this work.)*
(4) The other provisions of this Act come into force on such day as the Secretary of State may by order appoint.
(5) Different days may be appointed under subsection (2) or (4) for different purposes (including different areas).
(6) Transitory provision in an order under subsection (2) or (4) may, in particular, modify the application of a provision of this Act pending the commencement of—
- (a) another provision of this Act, or
- (b) any other enactment (within the meaning of section 303).

(7) *(Outside the scope of this work.)*

(8) Where a provision of this Act (or an amendment made by it) requires consultation to take place, consultation undertaken before the commencement of the provision is as effective for the purposes of that provision as consultation undertaken after that commencement.

NOTES

Orders: the Health and Social Care Act 2012 (Commencement No 1 and Transitory Provision) Order 2012, SI 2012/1319; the Health and Social Care Act 2012 (Commencement No 2 and Transitional, Savings and Transitory Provisions) Order 2012, SI 2012/1831; the Health and Social Care Act 2012 (Commencement No 3, Transitional, Savings and Transitory Provisions and Amendment) Order 2012, SI 2012/2657; the Health and Social Care Act 2012 (Commencement No 4, Transitional, Savings and Transitory Provisions) Order 2013, SI 2013/160; the Health and Social Care Act 2012 (Commencement No 5, Transitional, Savings and Transitory Provisions) Order 2013, SI 2013/671; the Health and Social Care Act 2012 (Commencement No 6) Order 2013, SI 2013/2896; the Health and Social Care Act 2012 (Commencement No 7 and Transitory Provision) Order 2014, SI 2014/39; the Health and Social Care Act 2012 (Commencement No 8) Order 2014, SI 2014/1454; the Health and Social Care Act 2012 (Commencement No 9) Order 2015, SI 2015/409; the Health and Social Care Act 2012 (Commencement No 10) Order 2016, SI 2016/81.

307 (*Outside the scope of this work.*)

[7.1372]
308 Extent

(1) Subject to subsections (2) to (5), this Act extends to England and Wales only.
(2) Any amendment, repeal or revocation made by this Act has the same extent as the enactment amended, repealed or revoked.
(3) The following provisions extend to England and Wales, Scotland and Northern Ireland—
(a), (b) (*outside the scope of this work.*)
(c) section 150(2) and paragraph 1 of Schedule 13 (references to Monitor in instruments etc);
(d)–(i) (*outside the scope of this work.*)
(j) this Part.
(4) Sections 128 to 133 (health special administration) extend to England and Wales and Scotland.
(5) The Secretary of State may by order provide that specified provisions of this Act, in their application to the Isles of Scilly, have effect with such modifications as may be specified.

[7.1373]
309 Short title

This Act may be cited as the Health and Social Care Act 2012.

SCHEDULES 1–23

(*Schs 1–23 outside the scope of this work.*)

I
HOUSING

HOUSING AND PLANNING ACT 2016

(2016 c 22)

An Act to make provision about housing, estate agents, rentcharges, planning and compulsory purchase.

[12 May 2016]

1–63 *(Ss 1–63 (Pts 1–3) outside the scope of this work.)*

PART 4
SOCIAL HOUSING IN ENGLAND

64–94 *(Ss 64–94 (Chs 1–4) outside the scope of this work.)*

CHAPTER 5 INSOLVENCY OF REGISTERED PROVIDERS OF SOCIAL HOUSING

Housing administration

[7.1374]
95 Housing administration order: providers of social housing in England

(1) In this Chapter "housing administration order" means an order which—
  (a) is made by the court in relation to a private registered provider of social housing that is—
    (i) a company,
    (ii) a registered society within the meaning of the Co-operative and Community Benefit Societies Act 2014, or
    (iii) a charitable incorporated organisation within the meaning of Part 11 of the Charities Act 2011, and
  (b) directs that, while the order is in force, the provider's affairs, business and property are to be managed by a person appointed by the court.

(2) The person appointed for the purposes of the housing administration order is referred to in this Chapter as the "housing administrator".

(3) In relation to a housing administration order applying to a registered provider that is a foreign company, the reference in subsection (1)(b) to the provider's affairs, business and property is a reference to its UK affairs, business and property.

NOTES

Commencement: to be appointed.

[7.1375]
96 Objectives of housing administration

(1) A housing administrator has two objectives—
  (a) Objective 1: normal administration (see section 97), and
  (b) Objective 2: keeping social housing in the regulated sector (see section 98).

(2) Objective 1 takes priority over Objective 2 (but the housing administrator must, so far as possible, work towards both objectives).

(3) It follows that, in pursuing Objective 2, the housing administrator must not do anything that would result in a worse distribution to creditors than would be the case if the administrator did not need to pursue Objective 2.

(4) A reference in this Chapter to the objectives of a housing administration is to the objectives to be pursued by the housing administrator.

NOTES

Commencement: to be appointed.

[7.1376]
97 Objective 1: normal administration

(1) Objective 1 is to—
  (a) rescue the registered provider as a going concern,
  (b) achieve a better result for the registered provider's creditors as a whole than would be likely if the registered provider were wound up (without first being in housing administration), or
  (c) realise property in order to make a distribution to one or more secured or preferential creditors.

(2) The housing administrator must aim to achieve Objective 1(a) unless the housing administrator thinks—
  (a) that it is not reasonably practicable to achieve it, or
  (b) that Objective 1(b) would achieve a better result for the registered provider's creditors as a whole.

(3) The housing administrator may aim to achieve Objective 1(c) only if—
  (a) the housing administrator thinks that it is not reasonably practicable to achieve Objective 1(a) or (b), and

(b) the housing administrator does not unnecessarily harm the interests of the registered provider's creditors as a whole.

(4) In pursuing Objective 1(a), (b) or (c) the housing administrator must act in the interests of the registered provider's creditors as a whole so far as consistent with that Objective.

NOTES

Commencement: to be appointed.

[7.1377]

98 Objective 2: keeping social housing in the regulated sector

(1) Objective 2 is to ensure that the registered provider's social housing remains in the regulated housing sector.

(2) For this purpose, social housing remains in the regulated housing sector for so long as it is owned by a private registered provider.

NOTES

Commencement: to be appointed.

[7.1378]

99 Applications for housing administration orders

(1) An application for a housing administration order may be made only—

(a) by the Secretary of State, or

(b) with the consent of the Secretary of State, by the Regulator of Social Housing.

(2) The applicant for a housing administration order in relation to a registered provider must give notice of the application to—

(a) every person who has appointed an administrative receiver of the provider,

(b) every person who is or may be entitled to appoint an administrative receiver of the registered provider,

(c) every person who is or may be entitled to make an appointment in relation to the registered provider under paragraph 14 of Schedule B1 to the Insolvency Act 1986 (appointment of administrators by holders of floating charges), and

(d) any other persons specified by housing administration rules.

(3) The notice must be given as soon as possible after the making of the application.

(4) In this section "administrative receiver" means—

(a) an administrative receiver within the meaning given by section 251 of the Insolvency Act 1986 for the purposes of Parts 1 to 7 of that Act, or

(b) in relation to a foreign company, a person whose functions are equivalent to those of an administrative receiver and relate only to its UK affairs, business and property.

NOTES

Commencement: to be appointed.

[7.1379]

100 Powers of court

(1) On hearing an application for a housing administration order, the court has the following powers—

(a) it may make the order,

(b) it may dismiss the application,

(c) it may adjourn the hearing conditionally or unconditionally,

(d) it may make an interim order,

(e) it may treat the application as a winding-up petition and make any order the court could make under section 125 of the Insolvency Act 1986 (power of court on hearing winding-up petition), and

(f) it may make any other order which it thinks appropriate.

(2) The court may make a housing administration order in relation to a registered provider only if it is satisfied—

(a) that the registered provider is unable, or is likely to be unable, to pay its debts, or

(b) that, on a petition by the Secretary of State under section 124A of the Insolvency Act 1986, it would be just and equitable (disregarding the objectives of the housing administration) to wind up the registered provider in the public interest.

(3) The court may not make a housing administration order on the ground set out in subsection (2)(b) unless the Secretary of State has certified to the court that the case is one in which the Secretary of State considers (disregarding the objectives of the housing administration) that it would be appropriate to petition under section 124A of the Insolvency Act 1986.

(4) The court has no power to make a housing administration order in relation to a registered provider which—

(a) is in administration under Schedule B1 to the Insolvency Act 1986, or

(b) has gone into liquidation (within the meaning of section 247(2) of the Insolvency Act 1986).

(5) A housing administration order comes into force—

(a) at the time appointed by the court, or

(b) if no time is appointed by the court, when the order is made.

(6) An interim order under subsection (1)(d) may, in particular—

(a) restrict the exercise of a power of the registered provider or of its relevant officers, or

(b) make provision conferring a discretion on a person qualified to act as an insolvency practitioner in relation to the registered provider.

(7) In subsection (6)(a) "relevant officer"—

(a) in relation to a company, means a director,

(b) in relation to a registered society, means a member of the management committee or other directing body of the society, and

(c) in relation to a charitable incorporated organisation, means a charity trustee (as defined by section 177 of the Charities Act 2011).

(8) In the case of a foreign company, subsection (6)(a) is to be read as a reference to restricting the exercise of a power of the registered provider or of its directors—

(a) within the United Kingdom, or

(b) in relation to the company's UK affairs, business or property.

(9) For the purposes of this section a registered provider is unable to pay its debts if—

(a) it is deemed to be unable to pay its debts under section 123 of the Insolvency Act 1986, or

(b) it is an unregistered company which is deemed, as a result of any of sections 222 to 224 of the Insolvency Act 1986, to be so unable for the purposes of section 221 of that Act, or which would be so deemed if it were an unregistered company for the purposes of those sections.

NOTES

Commencement: to be appointed.

[7.1380]

101 Housing administrators

(1) The housing administrator of a registered provider—

(a) is an officer of the court, and

(b) in carrying out functions in relation to the registered provider, is the registered provider's agent.

(2) The housing administrator of a registered provider must aim to achieve the objectives of the housing administration as quickly and as efficiently as is reasonably practicable.

(3) A person is not to be the housing administrator of a registered provider unless qualified to act as an insolvency practitioner in relation to the registered provider.

(4) If the court appoints two or more persons as the housing administrator of a registered provider, the appointment must set out—

(a) which (if any) of the functions of a housing administrator are to be carried out only by the appointees acting jointly,

(b) the circumstances (if any) in which functions of a housing administrator are to be carried out by one of the appointees, or by particular appointees, acting alone, and

(c) the circumstances (if any) in which things done in relation to one of the appointees, or in relation to particular appointees, are to be treated as done in relation to all of them.

NOTES

Commencement: to be appointed.

[7.1381]

102 Conduct of administration etc

(1) Schedule 5 contains provision applying the provisions of Schedule B1 to the Insolvency Act 1986, and certain other legislation, to housing administration orders in relation to companies.

(2) The Secretary of State may by regulations provide for any provision of Schedule B1 to the Insolvency Act 1986 or any other insolvency legislation to apply, with or without modifications, to cases where a housing administration order is made in relation to a registered society or a charitable incorporated organisation.

(3) The Secretary of State may by regulations modify any insolvency legislation as it applies in relation to a registered society or a charitable incorporated organisation if the Secretary State considers the modifications are appropriate in connection with any provision made by or under this Chapter.

(4) In subsection (3) "insolvency legislation" means—

(a) the Insolvency Act 1986, or

(b) any other legislation (whenever passed or made) that relates to insolvency or makes provision by reference to anything that is or may be done under the Insolvency Act 1986.

(5) The power to make rules under section 411 of the Insolvency Act 1986 is to apply for the purpose of giving effect to this Chapter as it applies for the purpose of giving effect to Parts 1 to 7 of that Act (and, accordingly, as if references in that section to those Parts included references to this Chapter).

(6) Section 413(2) of the Insolvency Act 1986 (duty to consult Insolvency Rules Committee about rules) does not apply to rules made under section 411 of that Act as a result of this section.

NOTES

Commencement: 3 February 2017 (sub-ss (2)–(6)); to be appointed (otherwise).

[7.1382]

103 Housing administrator may sell land free from planning obligations

(1) If the housing administrator of a registered provider disposes of land that is the subject of a planning obligation that contains relevant terms, the relevant terms are not binding on the person to whom the land is disposed of or any successor in title.

(2) In this section—

Part 7I Special Insolvency Regimes

"disposes of", in relation to land, means sells a freehold or leasehold interest in the land or grants a lease of the land;
"planning obligation" means a planning obligation under section 106 of the Town and Country Planning Act 1990 (whether entered into before or after this section comes into force);
"relevant terms" in relation to a planning obligation, means any restrictions or requirements imposed by the planning obligation that are expressed not to apply in the event that the land is disposed of by a mortgagee.

NOTES

Commencement: to be appointed.

Restrictions on other insolvency procedures

[7.1383]
104 Winding-up orders

(1) This section applies if a person other than the Secretary of State petitions for the winding-up of a registered provider that is—
 (a) a company,
 (b) a registered society within the meaning of the Co-operative and Community Benefit Societies Act 2014, or
 (c) a charitable incorporated organisation within the meaning of Part 11 of the Charities Act 2011.
(2) The court may not exercise its powers on a winding-up petition unless—
 (a) notice of the petition has been given to the Regulator of Social Housing and a period of at least 28 days has elapsed since that notice was given, or
 (b) the Regulator of Social Housing has waived the notice requirement in paragraph (a).
(3) If an application for a housing administration order in relation to the registered provider is made to the court in accordance with section 99 before a winding-up order is made on the petition, the court may exercise its powers under section 100 (instead of exercising its powers on the petition).
(4) The Regulator of Social Housing must give the Secretary of State a copy of any notice given under subsection (2)(a).
(5) The Regulator of Social Housing may waive the notice requirement under subsection (2)(a) only with the consent of the Secretary of State.
(6) References in this section to the court's powers on a winding-up petition are to—
 (a) its powers under section 125 of the Insolvency Act 1986 (other than its power of adjournment), and
 (b) its powers under section 135 of the Insolvency Act 1986.

NOTES

Commencement: to be appointed.

[7.1384]
105 Voluntary winding up

(1) This section applies to a private registered provider that is—
 (a) a company,
 (b) a registered society within the meaning of the Co-operative and Community Benefit Societies Act 2014, or
 (c) a charitable incorporated organisation within the meaning of Part 11 of the Charities Act 2011.
(2) The registered provider has no power to pass a resolution for voluntary winding up without the permission of the court.
(3) Permission may be granted by the court only on an application made by the registered provider.
(4) The court may not grant permission unless—
 (a) notice of the application has been given to the Regulator of Social Housing and a period of at least 28 days has elapsed since that notice was given, or
 (b) the Regulator of Social Housing has waived the notice requirement in paragraph (a).
(5) If an application for a housing administration order in relation to the registered provider is made to the court in accordance with section 99 after an application for permission under this section has been made and before it is granted, the court may exercise its powers under section 100.
(6) The Regulator of Social Housing must give the Secretary of State a copy of any notice given under subsection (4)(a).
(7) The Regulator of Social Housing may waive the notice requirement under subsection (4)(a) only with the consent of the Secretary of State.
(8) In this section "a resolution for voluntary winding up" has the same meaning as in the Insolvency Act 1986.

NOTES

Commencement: to be appointed.

[7.1385]
106 Making of ordinary administration orders

(1) This section applies if a person other than the Secretary of State makes an ordinary administration application in relation to a private registered provider that is—
 (a) a company, or
 (b) a charitable incorporated organisation within the meaning of Part 11 of the Charities Act 2011.
(2) The court must dismiss the application if—

(a) a housing administration order is in force in relation to the registered provider, or
(b) a housing administration order has been made in relation to the registered provider but is not yet in force.

(3) If subsection (2) does not apply, the court, on hearing the application, must not exercise its powers under paragraph 13 of Schedule B1 to the Insolvency Act 1986 (other than its power of adjournment) unless—
(a) either—
(i) notice of the application has been given to the Regulator of Social Housing and a period of at least 28 days has elapsed since that notice was given, or
(ii) the Regulator of Social Housing has waived the notice requirement in sub-paragraph (i), and
(b) there is no application for a housing administration order which is outstanding.

(4) The Regulator of Social Housing must give the Secretary of State a copy of any notice given under subsection (3)(a).

(5) Paragraph 44 of Schedule B1 to the Insolvency Act 1986 (interim moratorium) does not prevent, or require the permission of the court for, the making of an application for a housing administration order.

(6) On the making of a housing administration order in relation to a registered provider, the court must dismiss any ordinary administration application made in relation to the registered provider which is outstanding.

(7) The Regulator of Social Housing may waive the notice requirement under subsection (3)(a)(i) only with the consent of the Secretary of State.

(8) In this section "ordinary administration application" means an application in accordance with paragraph 12 of Schedule B1 to the Insolvency Act 1986.

NOTES

Commencement: to be appointed.

[7.1386]

107 Administrator appointments by creditors

(1) Subsections (2) to (4) make provision about appointments under paragraph 14 or 22 of Schedule B1 to the Insolvency Act 1986 (powers to appoint administrators) in relation to a private registered provider that is—
(a) a company, or
(b) a charitable incorporated organisation within the meaning of Part 11 of the Charities Act 2011.

(2) If in any case—
(a) a housing administration order is in force in relation to the registered provider,
(b) a housing administration order has been made in relation to the registered provider but is not yet in force, or
(c) an application for a housing administration order in relation to the registered provider is outstanding,

a person may not take any step to make an appointment.

(3) In any other case, an appointment takes effect only if each of the following conditions are met.

(4) The conditions are—
(a) either—
(i) that notice of the appointment has been given to the Regulator of Social Housing, accompanied by a copy of every document in relation to the appointment that is filed or lodged with the court in accordance with paragraph 18 or 29 of Schedule B1 to the Insolvency Act 1986 and that a period of 28 days has elapsed since that notice was given, or
(ii) that the Regulator of Social Housing has waived the notice requirement in sub-paragraph (i),
(b) that there is no outstanding application to the court for a housing administration order in relation to the registered provider, and
(c) that the making of an application for a housing administration order in relation to the registered provider has not resulted in the making of a housing administration order which is in force or is still to come into force.

(5) The Regulator of Social Housing must give the Secretary of State a copy of any notice given under subsection (4)(a) (and a copy of the accompanying documents).

(6) The Regulator of Social Housing may waive the notice requirement under subsection (4)(a)(i) only with the consent of the Secretary of State.

(7) Paragraph 44 of Schedule B1 to the Insolvency Act 1986 (interim moratorium) does not prevent, or require the permission of the court for, the making of an application for a housing administration order at any time before the appointment takes effect.

NOTES

Commencement: to be appointed.

[7.1387]

108 Enforcement of security

(1) This section applies in relation to a private registered provider that is—
(a) a company,
(b) a registered society within the meaning of the Co-operative and Community Benefit Societies Act 2014, or

(c) a charitable incorporated organisation within the meaning of Part 11 of the Charities Act 2011

(2) A person may not take any step to enforce a security over property of the registered provider unless—

(a) notice of the intention to do so has been given to the Regulator of Social Housing and a period of at least 28 days has elapsed since the notice was given, or

(b) the Regulator of Social Housing has waived the notice requirement in paragraph (a).

(3) In the case of a company which is a foreign company, the reference to the property of the company is to its property in the United Kingdom.

(4) The Regulator of Social Housing must give the Secretary of State a copy of any notice given under subsection (2)(a).

(5) The Regulator of Social Housing may waive the notice requirement under subsection (2)(a) only with the consent of the Secretary of State.

NOTES

Commencement: to be appointed.

Financial support for registered providers in housing administration

[7.1388]

109 Grants and loans where housing administration order is made

(1) If a housing administration order has been made in relation to a registered provider, the Secretary of State may make grants or loans to the registered provider of such amounts as appear to the Secretary of State appropriate for achieving the objectives of the housing administration.

(2) A grant under this section may be made on any terms and conditions the Secretary of State considers appropriate (including provision for repayment, with or without interest).

NOTES

Commencement: to be appointed.

[7.1389]

110 Indemnities where housing administration order is made

(1) If a housing administration order has been made in relation to a registered provider, the Secretary of State may agree to indemnify persons in respect of one or both of the following—

(a) liabilities incurred in connection with the carrying out of functions by the housing administrator, and

(b) loss or damage sustained in that connection.

(2) The agreement may be made in whatever manner, and on whatever terms, the Secretary of State considers appropriate.

(3) As soon as practicable after agreeing to indemnify persons under this section, the Secretary of State must lay a statement of the agreement before Parliament.

(4) For repayment of sums paid by the Secretary of State in consequence of an indemnity agreed to under this section, see section 111.

(5) The power of the Secretary of State to agree to indemnify persons—

(a) is confined to a power to agree to indemnify persons in respect of liabilities, loss and damage incurred or sustained by them as relevant persons, but

(b) includes power to agree to indemnify persons (whether or not they are identified or identifiable at the time of the agreement) who subsequently become relevant persons.

(6) The following are relevant persons for the purposes of this section—

(a) the housing administrator,

(b) an employee of the housing administrator,

(c) a partner or employee of a firm of which the housing administrator is a partner,

(d) a partner or employee of a firm of which the housing administrator is an employee,

(e) a partner of a firm of which the housing administrator was an employee or partner at a time when the order was in force,

(f) a body corporate which is the employer of the housing administrator,

(g) an officer, employee or member of such a body corporate, and

(h) a Scottish firm which is the employer of the housing administrator or of which the housing administrator is a partner.

(7) For the purposes of subsection (6)—

(a) references to the housing administrator are to be read, where two or more persons are appointed as the housing administrator, as references to any one or more of them, and

(b) references to a firm of which a person was a partner or employee at a particular time include a firm which holds itself out to be the successor of a firm of which the person was a partner or employee at that time.

NOTES

Commencement: to be appointed.

[7.1390]

111 Indemnities: repayment by registered provider etc

(1) This section applies where a sum is paid out by the Secretary of State in consequence of an indemnity agreed to under section 110 in relation to the housing administrator of a registered provider.

(2) The registered provider must pay the Secretary of State—

(a) such amounts in or towards the repayment to the Secretary of State of that sum as the Secretary of State may direct, and

(b) interest on amounts outstanding under this subsection at such rates as the Secretary of State may direct.

(3) The payments must be made by the registered provider at such times and in such manner as the Secretary of State may determine.

(4) Subsection (2) does not apply in the case of a sum paid by the Secretary of State for indemnifying a person in respect of a liability to the registered provider.

(5) The Secretary of State must lay before Parliament a statement, relating to the sum paid out in consequence of the indemnity—

(a) as soon as practicable after the end of the financial year in which the sum is paid out, and

(b) if subsection (2) applies to the sum, as soon as practicable after the end of each subsequent financial year in relation to which the repayment condition has not been met.

(6) The repayment condition is met in relation to a financial year if—

(a) the whole of the sum has been repaid to the Secretary of State before the beginning of the year, and

(b) the registered provider was not at any time during the year liable to pay interest on amounts that became due in respect of the sum.

NOTES

Commencement: to be appointed.

[7.1391]

112 Guarantees where housing administration order is made

(1) If a housing administration order has been made in relation to a registered provider the Secretary of State may guarantee—

(a) the repayment of any sum borrowed by the registered provider while that order is in force,

(b) the payment of interest on any sum borrowed by the registered provider while that order is in force, and

(c) the discharge of any other financial obligation of the registered provider in connection with the borrowing of any sum while that order is in force.

(2) The Secretary of State may give the guarantees in whatever manner, and on whatever terms, the Secretary of State considers appropriate.

(3) As soon as practicable after giving a guarantee under this section, the Secretary of State must lay a statement of the guarantee before Parliament.

(4) For repayment of sums paid by the Secretary of State under a guarantee given under this section, see section 113.

NOTES

Commencement: to be appointed.

[7.1392]

113 Guarantees: repayment by registered provider etc

(1) This section applies where a sum is paid out by the Secretary of State under a guarantee given by the Secretary of State under section 112 in relation to a registered provider.

(2) The registered provider must pay the Secretary of State—

(a) such amounts in or towards the repayment to the Secretary of State of that sum as the Secretary of State may direct, and

(b) interest on amounts outstanding under this subsection at such rates as the Secretary of State may direct.

(3) The payments must be made by the registered provider at such times, and in such manner, as the Secretary of State may from time to time direct.

(4) The Secretary of State must lay before Parliament a statement, relating to the sum paid out under the guarantee—

(a) as soon as practicable after the end of the financial year in which the sum is paid out, and

(b) as soon as practicable after the end of each subsequent financial year in relation to which the repayment condition has not been met.

(5) The repayment condition is met in relation to a financial year if—

(a) the whole of the sum has been repaid to the Secretary of State before the beginning of the year, and

(b) the registered provider was not at any time during the year liable to pay interest on amounts that became due in respect of the sum.

NOTES

Commencement: to be appointed.

Supplementary provisions

[7.1393]

114 Modification of this Chapter under the Enterprise Act 2002

(1) The power to modify or apply enactments conferred on the Secretary of State by each of the sections of the Enterprise Act 2002 mentioned in subsection (2) includes power to make such consequential modifications of this Chapter as the Secretary of State considers appropriate in connection with any other provision made under that section.

(2) Those sections are—

(a) sections 248 and 277 of the Enterprise Act 2002 (amendments consequential on that Act), and

(b) section 254 of the Enterprise Act 2002 (power to apply insolvency law to foreign companies).

NOTES

Commencement: to be appointed.

115 (*Introduces Sch 6 (amendments which, in so far as relevant to this work, have been incorporated at the appropriate place).*)

[7.1394]

116 Interpretation of Chapter

(1) In this Chapter—

"business", "member", "property" and "security" have the same meaning as in the Insolvency Act 1986;

"charitable incorporated organisation" means a charitable incorporated organisation within the meaning of Part 11 of the Charities Act 2011;

"company" means—

(a) a company registered under the Companies Act 2006, or

(b) an unregistered company;

"the court", in relation to a company or registered society, means the court having jurisdiction to wind up the company or registered society;

"foreign company" means a company incorporated outside the United Kingdom;

"housing administration order" has the meaning given by section 95;

"housing administration rules" means rules made under section 411 of the Insolvency Act 1986 as a result of section 102 above;

"housing administrator" has the meaning given by section 95 and is to be read in accordance with subsection (2) below;

"financial year" means a period of 12 months ending with 31 March;

"legislation" includes provision made by or under—

(a) an Act,

(b) an Act of the Scottish Parliament,

(c) Northern Ireland legislation, or

(d) a Measure or Act of the National Assembly for Wales;

"objectives of the housing administration" is to be read in accordance with section 96(4);

"private registered provider" means a private registered provider of social housing (see section 80 of the Housing and Regeneration Act 2008);

"registered provider" means a registered provider of social housing (see section 80 of the Housing and Regeneration Act 2008);

"registered society" has the same meaning as in the Co-operative and Community Benefit Societies Act 2014;

"Regulator of Social Housing" has the meaning given by section 92A of the Housing and Regeneration Act 2008;

"Scottish firm" means a firm constituted under the law of Scotland;

"UK affairs, business and property", in relation to a company, means—

(a) its affairs and business so far as carried on in the United Kingdom, and

(b) its property in the United Kingdom;

"unregistered company" means a company that is not registered under the Companies Act 2006.

(2) In this Chapter references to the housing administrator of a registered provider—

(a) include a person appointed under paragraph 91 or 103 of Schedule B1 to the Insolvency Act 1986, as applied by Part 1 of Schedule 5 to this Act or regulations under section 102, to be the housing administrator of the registered provider, and

(b) if two or more persons are appointed as the housing administrator of the registered provider, are to be read in accordance with the provision made under section 101.

(3) References in this Chapter to a person qualified to act as an insolvency practitioner in relation to a registered provider are to be read in accordance with Part 13 of the Insolvency Act 1986, but as if references in that Part to a company included a company registered under the Companies Act 2006 in Northern Ireland.

(4) For the purposes of this Chapter an application made to the court is outstanding if it—

(a) has not yet been granted or dismissed, and

(b) has not been withdrawn.

(5) An application is not to be taken as having been dismissed if an appeal against the dismissal of the application, or a subsequent appeal, is pending.

(6) An appeal is to be treated as pending for this purpose if—

(a) an appeal has been brought and has not been determined or withdrawn,

(b) an application for permission to appeal has been made but has not been determined or withdrawn, or

(c) no appeal has been brought and the period for bringing one is still running.

(7) References in this Chapter to a provision of the Insolvency Act 1986 (except the references in subsection (2) above)—

(a) in relation to a company, are to that provision without the modifications made by Part 1 of Schedule 5 to this Act,

(b) in relation to a registered society, are to that provision as it applies to registered societies otherwise than by virtue of regulations under section 102 (if at all), and
(c) in relation to a charitable incorporated organisation, are to that provision as it applies to charitable incorporated organisations otherwise than by virtue of regulations under section 102 (if at all).

NOTES
Commencement: to be appointed.

[7.1395]
117 Application of Part to Northern Ireland
(1) This section makes provision about the application of this Chapter to Northern Ireland.
(2) Any reference to any provision of the Insolvency Act 1986 is to have effect as a reference to the corresponding provision of the Insolvency (Northern Ireland) Order 1989.
(3) Section 116(3) is to have effect as if the reference to Northern Ireland were to England and Wales or Scotland.

NOTES
Commencement: to be appointed.

118–211 *(Ss 118–121 (Pt 4, Ch 6), ss 122–211 (Pts 5–8) outside the scope of this work.)*

PART 9
GENERAL

212–214 (*Outside the scope of this work.*)

[7.1396]
215 Extent
(1) An amendment or repeal made by this Act has the same extent as the provision amended or repealed.
(2) Chapter 5 of Part 4 and this Part extend to—
(a) England and Wales,
(b) Scotland, and
(c) Northern Ireland.
(3) (*Outside the scope of this work.*)
(4) Subject to that, this Act extends to England and Wales only.

NOTES
Commencement: 12 May 2016.

[7.1397]
216 Commencement
(1) The following come into force on the day on which this Act is passed—
(a) this Part;
(b) (*outside the scope of this work*).
(c) (*outside the scope of this work*).
(d) (*outside the scope of this work*).
(e) (*outside the scope of this work*).
(2) (*Outside the scope of this work*).
(3) The other provisions of this Act come into force on such day as the Secretary of State may by regulations appoint.
(4) Different days may be appointed for different purposes.
(5) (*Outside the scope of this work*).

NOTES
Commencement: 12 May 2016.
Regulations: the Housing and Planning Act 2016 (Commencement No 1) Regulations 2016, SI 2016/609; the Housing and Planning Act 2016 (Commencement No 2, Transitional Provisions and Savings) Regulations 2016, SI 2016/733; the Housing and Planning Act 2016 (Commencement No 3) Regulations 2016, SI 2016/956; the Housing and Planning Act 2016 (Commencement No 4 and Transitional Provisions) Regulations 2017, SI 2017/75; the Housing and Planning Act 2016 (Commencement No 5, Transitional Provisions and Savings) Regulations 2017, SI 2017/281; the Housing and Planning Act 2016 (Commencement No 6) Regulations 2017, SI 2017/1052; the Housing and Planning Act 2016 (Commencement No 7 and Transitional Provisions) Regulations 2018, SI 2018/251; and the Housing and Planning Act 2016 (Commencement No 8) Regulations 2018, SI 2018/393.

[7.1398]
217 Short title
This Act may be cited as the Housing and Planning Act 2016.

NOTES
Commencement: 12 May 2016.

SCHEDULES 1–4

(*Schs 1–4 outside the scope of this work.*)

SCHEDULE 5
CONDUCT OF HOUSING ADMINISTRATION: COMPANIES

Section 102

PART 1
MODIFICATIONS OF SCHEDULE B1 TO THE INSOLVENCY ACT 1986

Introductory

[7.1399]

1 (1) The applicable provisions of Schedule B1 to the Insolvency Act 1986 are to have effect in relation to a housing administration order that applies to a company as they have effect in relation to an administration order under that Schedule applies to a company, but with the modifications set out in this Part of this Schedule.

(2) The applicable provisions of Schedule B1 to the Insolvency Act 1986 are—

- (a) paragraphs 1, 40 to 49, 54, 59 to 68, 70 to 79, 83 to 91, 98 to 107, 109 to 111 and 112 to 116, and
- (b) paragraph 50 (until the repeal of that paragraph by Schedule 10 to the Small Business, Enterprise and Employment Act 2015 comes into force).

General modifications of the applicable provisions

2 Those paragraphs are to have effect as if—

- (a) for "administration application", in each place, there were substituted "housing administration application",
- (b) for "administration order", in each place, there were substituted "housing administration order",
- (c) for "administrator", in each place, there were substituted "housing administrator",
- (d) for "enters administration", in each place, there were substituted "enters housing administration",
- (e) for "in administration", in each place, there were substituted "in housing administration", and
- (f) for "purpose of administration", in each place (other than in paragraph 111(1)), there were substituted "objectives of the housing administration".

Specific modifications

3 Paragraph 1 (administration) is to have effect as if—

- (a) for sub-paragraph (1) there were substituted—

  "(1) In this Schedule "housing administrator", in relation to a company, means a person appointed by the court for the purposes of a housing administration order to manage its affairs, business and property.", and

- (b) in sub-paragraph (2), for "Act" there were substituted "Schedule".

4 Paragraph 40 (dismissal of pending winding-up petition) is to have effect as if sub-paragraphs (1)(b), (2) and (3) were omitted.

5 Paragraph 42 (moratorium on insolvency proceedings) is to have effect as if sub-paragraphs (4) and (5) were omitted.

6 Paragraph 44 (interim moratorium) is to have effect as if sub-paragraphs (2) to (4), (6) and (7)(a) to (c) were omitted.

7 Paragraph 46(6) (date for notifying administrator's appointment) is to have effect as if for paragraphs (a) to (c) there were substituted "the date on which the housing administration order comes into force".

8 Paragraph 49 (administrator's proposals) is to have effect as if—

- (a) in sub-paragraph (2)(b) for "objective mentioned in paragraph 3(1)(a) or (b) cannot be achieved" there were substituted "objectives of the housing administration should be achieved by means other than just a rescue of the company as a going concern", and
- (b) in sub-paragraph (4), after paragraph (a) there were inserted—

  "(aa) to the Secretary of State and the Regulator of Social Housing,".

9 Paragraph 54 is to have effect as if the following were substituted for it—

"54 (1) The housing administrator of a company may on one or more occasions revise the proposals included in the statement made under paragraph 49 in relation to the company.

(2) If the housing administrator thinks that a revision is substantial, the housing administrator must send a copy of the revised proposals—

- (a) to the registrar of companies,
- (b) to the Secretary of State and the Regulator of Social Housing,

(c) to every creditor of the company, other than an opted-out creditor, of whose claim and address the housing administrator is aware, and
(d) to every member of the company of whose address the housing administrator is aware.

(3) A copy sent in accordance with sub-paragraph (2) must be sent within the prescribed period.

(4) The housing administrator is to be taken to have complied with sub-paragraph (2)(d) if the housing administrator publishes, in the prescribed manner, a notice undertaking to provide a copy of the revised proposals free of charge to any member of the company who applies in writing to a specified address.

(5) A housing administrator who fails without reasonable excuse to comply with this paragraph commits an offence."

10 Paragraph 60 (powers of an administrator) has effect as if after that sub-paragraph (2) there were inserted—

"(3) The housing administrator of a company has the power to act on behalf of the company for the purposes of provision contained in any legislation which confers a power on the company or imposes a duty on it.

(4) In sub-paragraph (2) "legislation" has the same meaning as in the Chapter 5 of Part 4 of the Housing and Planning Act 2016."

11 Paragraph 68 (management duties of an administrator) is to have effect as if—
(a) in sub-paragraph (1), for paragraphs (a) to (c) there were substituted "the proposals as—
(a) set out in the statement made under paragraph 49 in relation to the company, and
(b) from time to time revised under paragraph 54,
for achieving the objectives of the housing administration.", and
(b) in sub-paragraph (3), for paragraphs (a) to (d) there were substituted "the directions are consistent with the achievement of the objectives of the housing administration".

12 Paragraph 73(3) (protection for secured or preferential creditor) is to have effect as if for "or modified" there were substituted "under paragraph 54".

13 Paragraph 74 (challenge to administrator's conduct) is to have effect as if—
(a) for sub-paragraph (2) there were substituted—

"(2) If a company is in housing administration, a person mentioned in sub-paragraph (2A) may apply to the court claiming that the housing administrator is acting in a manner preventing the achievement of the objectives of the housing administration as quickly and efficiently as is reasonably practicable.

(2A) The persons who may apply to the court are—
(a) the Secretary of State;
(b) with the consent of the Secretary of State, the Regulator of Social Housing;
(c) a creditor or member of the company.",

(b) in sub-paragraph (6)—
(i) at the end of paragraph (b) there were inserted "or", and
(ii) paragraph (c) (and the "or" before it) were omitted, and
(c) after that sub-paragraph there were inserted—

"(7) In the case of a claim made otherwise than by the Secretary of State or the Regulator of Social Housing, the court may grant a remedy or relief or make an order under this paragraph only if it has given the Secretary of State or the Regulator a reasonable opportunity of making representations about the claim and the proposed remedy, relief or order.

(8) The court may grant a remedy or relief or make an order on an application under this paragraph only if it is satisfied, in relation to the matters that are the subject of the application, that the housing administrator—
(a) is acting,
(b) has acted, or
(c) is proposing to act,
in a way that is inconsistent with the achievement of the objectives of the housing administration as quickly and as efficiently as is reasonably practicable.

(9) Before the making of an order of the kind mentioned in sub-paragraph (4)(d)—
(a) the court must notify the housing administrator of the proposed order and of a period during which the housing administrator is to have the opportunity of taking steps falling within sub-paragraphs (10) to (12), and
(b) the period notified must have expired without the taking of such of those steps as the court thinks should have been taken,
and that period must be a reasonable period.

(10) In the case of a claim under sub-paragraph (1)(a), the steps referred to in sub-paragraph (9) are—
(a) ceasing to act in a manner that unfairly harms the interests to which the claim relates,
(b) remedying any harm unfairly caused to those interests, and
(c) steps for ensuring that there is no repetition of conduct unfairly causing harm to those interests.

(11) In the case of a claim under sub-paragraph (1)(b), the steps referred to in sub-paragraph (9)

are steps for ensuring that the interests to which the claim relates are not unfairly harmed.

(12) In the case of a claim under sub-paragraph (2), the steps referred to in sub-paragraph (9) are—

(a) ceasing to act in a manner preventing the achievement of the objectives of the housing administration as quickly and as efficiently as is reasonably practicable,

(b) remedying the consequences of the housing administrator having acted in such a manner, and

(c) steps for ensuring that there is no repetition of conduct preventing the achievement of the objectives of the housing administration as quickly and as efficiently as is reasonably practicable."

14 Paragraph 75(2) (misfeasance) is to have effect as if after paragraph (b) there were inserted—

"(ba) a person appointed as an administrator of the company under the provisions of this Act, as they have effect in relation to administrators other than housing administrators,".

15 Paragraph 78 (consent to extension of administrator's term of office) is to have effect as if sub-paragraph (2) were omitted.

16 Paragraph 79 (end of administration) is to have effect as if—

(a) for sub-paragraphs (1) and (2) there were substituted—

"(1) On an application made by a person mentioned in sub-paragraph (2), the court may provide for the appointment of a housing administrator of a company to cease to have effect from a specified time.

(2) An application may be made to the court under this paragraph—

(a) by the Secretary of State,

(b) with the consent of the Secretary of State, by the Regulator of Social Housing, or

(c) with the consent of the Secretary of State, by the housing administrator.", and

(b) sub-paragraph (3) were omitted.

17 Paragraph 83(3) (notice to registrar when moving to voluntary liquidation) is to have effect as if after "may" there were inserted ", with the consent of the Secretary of State or of the Regulator of Social Housing,".

18 Paragraph 84 (notice to registrar when moving to dissolution) is to have effect as if—

(a) in sub-paragraph (1), for "to the registrar of companies" there were substituted—

"(a) to the Secretary of State and the Regulator of Social Housing, and

(b) if directed to do so by either the Secretary of State or the Regulator of Social Housing, to the registrar of companies.",

(b) sub-paragraph (2) were omitted, and

(c) in sub-paragraphs (3) to (6), for "(1)", in each place, there were substituted "(1)(b)".

19 Paragraph 87(2) (resignation of administrator) is to have effect as if for paragraphs (a) to (d) there were substituted "by notice in writing to the court".

20 Paragraph 89(2) (administrator ceasing to be qualified) is to have effect as if for paragraphs (a) to (d) there were substituted "to the court".

21 Paragraph 90 (filling vacancy in office of administrator) is to have effect as if for "Paragraphs 91 to 95 apply" there were substituted "Paragraph 91 applies".

22 Paragraph 91 (vacancies in court appointments) is to have effect as if—

(a) for sub-paragraph (1) there were substituted—

"(1) The court may replace the housing administrator on an application made—

(a) by the Secretary of State,

(b) with the consent of the Secretary of State, by the Regulator of Social Housing, or

(c) where more than one person was appointed to act jointly as the housing administrator, by any of those persons who remains in office."

(b) sub-paragraph (2) were omitted.

23 Paragraph 98 (discharge from liability on vacation of office) is to have effect as if sub-paragraphs (2)(b) and (ba), (3) and (3A) were omitted.

24 Paragraph 99 (charges and liabilities upon vacation of office by administrator) is to have effect as if—

(a) in sub-paragraph (4), for the words from the beginning to "cessation", in the first place, there were substituted "A sum falling within sub-paragraph (4A)",

(b) after that sub-paragraph there were inserted—

"(4A) A sum falls within this sub-paragraph if it is—

(a) a sum payable in respect of a debt or other liability arising out of a contract that was entered into before cessation by the former housing administrator or a predecessor,

(b) a sum that must be repaid by the company in respect of a grant that was made under section 109 of the Housing and Planning Act 2016 before cessation,

(c) a sum that must be repaid by the company in respect of a loan made under that section before cessation or that must be paid by the company in respect of interest payable on such a loan,
(d) a sum payable by the company under section 111 of that Act in respect of an agreement to indemnify made before cessation, or
(e) a sum payable by the company under section 113 of that Act in respect of a guarantee given before cessation.", and"

(c) in sub-paragraph (5), for "(4)" there were substituted "(4A)(a)".

25 Paragraph 100 (joint and concurrent administrators) is to have effect as if sub-paragraph (2) were omitted.

26 Paragraph 101(3) (joint administrators) is to have effect as if after "87 to" there were inserted "91, 98 and".

27 Paragraph 103 (appointment of additional administrators) is to have effect as if—

(a) in sub-paragraph (2) the words from the beginning to "order" were omitted and for paragraph (a) there were substituted—

"(a) the Secretary of State,
(aa) the Regulator of Social Housing, or",

(b) after that sub-paragraph there were inserted—

"(2A) The consent of the Secretary of State is required for an application by the Regulator of Social Housing for the purposes of sub-paragraph (2).", and

(c) sub-paragraphs (3) to (5) were omitted.

28 Paragraph 106(2) (penalties) is to have effect as if paragraphs (a), (b), (f), (g), (i) and (l) to (n) were omitted.

29 Paragraph 109 (references to extended periods) is to have effect as if "or 108" were omitted.

30 Paragraph 111 (interpretation) is to have effect as if—

(a) in sub-paragraph (1), the definitions of "correspondence", "holder of a qualifying floating charge", "the purpose of administration" and "unable to pay its debts" were omitted,
(b) in that sub-paragraph, at the appropriate places there were inserted—

""company" and "court" have the same meaning as in Chapter 5 of Part 4 of the Housing and Planning Act 2016,",
""housing administration application" means an application to the court for a housing administration order under Chapter 5 of Part 4 of the Housing and Planning Act 2016;",
""housing administration order" has the same meaning as in Chapter 5 of Part 4 of the Housing and Planning Act 2016;",
""objectives", in relation to a housing administration, is to be read in accordance with section 96(4) of the Housing and Planning Act 2016;", and
""prescribed" means prescribed by housing administration rules within the meaning of Chapter 5 of Part 4 of the Housing and Planning Act 2016.",

(c) sub-paragraphs (1A) and (1B) were omitted, and
(d) after sub-paragraph (3) there were inserted—

"(4) For the purposes of this Schedule a reference to a housing administration order includes a reference to an appointment under paragraph 91 or 103."

NOTES
Commencement: to be appointed.

PART 2
FURTHER MODIFICATIONS OF SCHEDULE B1 TO INSOLVENCY ACT 1986: FOREIGN COMPANIES

Introductory

[7.1400]
31 (1) This Part of this Schedule applies in the case of a housing administration order applying to a foreign company.

(2) The provisions of Schedule B1 to the Insolvency Act 1986 mentioned in paragraph 1 above (as modified by Part 1 of this Schedule) have effect in relation to the company with the further modifications set out in this Part of this Schedule.

(3) The Secretary of State may by regulations amend this Part of this Schedule so as to add more modifications.

32 In paragraphs 33 to 38—

(a) the provisions of Schedule B1 to the Insolvency Act 1986 that are mentioned in paragraph 1 above are referred to as the applicable provisions, and

(b) references to those provisions, or to provisions comprised in them, are references to those provisions as modified by Part 1 of this Schedule.

Modifications

33 In the case of a foreign company—

(a) paragraphs 42(2), 83 and 84 of Schedule B1 to the Insolvency Act 1986 do not apply,
(b) paragraphs 46(4), 49(4)(a), 54(2)(a), 71(5) and (6), 72(4) and (5) and 86 of that Schedule apply only if the company is subject to a requirement imposed by regulations under section 1043 or 1046 of the Companies Act 2006 (unregistered UK companies or overseas companies), and
(c) paragraph 61 of that Schedule does not apply.

34 (1) The applicable provisions and Schedule 1 to the Insolvency Act 1986 (as applied by paragraph 60(1) of Schedule B1 to that Act) are to be read by reference to the limitation imposed on the scope of the housing administration order in question as a result of section 95(4) above.

(2) Sub-paragraph (1) has effect, in particular, so that—

(a) a power conferred, or duty imposed, on the housing administrator by or under the applicable provisions or Schedule 1 to the Insolvency Act 1986 is to be read as being conferred or imposed in relation to the company's UK affairs, business and property,
(b) references to the company's affairs, business or property are to be read as references to its UK affairs, business and property,
(c) references to goods in the company's possession are to be read as references to goods in its possession in the United Kingdom,
(d) references to premises let to the company are to be read as references to premises let to it in the United Kingdom, and
(e) references to legal process instituted or continued against the company or its property are to be read as references to such legal process relating to its UK affairs, business and property.

35 Paragraph 41 of Schedule B1 to the Insolvency Act 1986 (dismissal of receivers) is to have effect as if—

(a) for sub-paragraph (1) there were substituted—

"(1) Where a housing administration order takes effect in respect of a company—

(a) a person appointed to perform functions equivalent to those of an administrative receiver, and
(b) if the housing administrator so requires, a person appointed to perform functions equivalent to those of a receiver,

must refrain, during the period specified in sub-paragraph (1A), from performing those functions in the United Kingdom or in relation to any of the company's property in the United Kingdom.

(1A) That period is—

(a) in the case of a person mentioned in sub-paragraph (1)(a), the period while the company is in housing administration, and
(b) in the case of a person mentioned in sub-paragraph (1)(b), during so much of that period as is after the date on which the person is required by the housing administrator to refrain from performing functions.", and"

(b) sub-paragraphs (2) to (4) were omitted.

36 Paragraph 43(6A) of Schedule B1 to the Insolvency Act 1986 (moratorium on appointment to receiverships) is to have effect as if for "An administrative receiver" there were substituted "A person with functions equivalent to those of an administrative receiver".

37 Paragraph 44(7) of Schedule B1 to the Insolvency Act 1986 (proceedings to which interim moratorium does not apply) is to have effect as if for paragraph (d) there were substituted—

"(d) the carrying out of functions by a person who (whenever appointed) has functions equivalent to those of an administrative receiver of the company."

38 Paragraph 64 of Schedule B1 to the Insolvency Act 1986 (general powers of administrator) is to have effect as if—

(a) in sub-paragraph (1), after "power" there were inserted "in relation to the affairs or business of the company so far as carried on in the United Kingdom or to its property in the United Kingdom", and
(b) in sub-paragraph (2)(b), after "instrument" there were inserted "or by the law of the place where the company is incorporated".

NOTES

Commencement: to be appointed.

PART 3
OTHER MODIFICATIONS

General modifications

[7.1401]

39 (1) References within sub-paragraph (2) which are contained—

(a) in the Insolvency Act 1986 (other than Schedule B1 to that Act), or

(b) in other legislation passed or made before this Act,

include references to whatever corresponds to them for the purposes of this paragraph.

(2) The references are those (however expressed) which are or include references to—

(a) an administrator appointed by an administration order,

(b) an administration order,

(c) an application for an administration order,

(d) a company in administration,

(e) entering into administration, and

(f) Schedule B1 to the Insolvency Act 1986 or a provision of that Schedule.

(3) For the purposes of this paragraph—

(a) a housing administrator of a company corresponds to an administrator appointed by an administration order,

(b) a housing administration order in relation to a company corresponds to an administration order,

(c) an application for a housing administration order in relation to a company corresponds to an application for an administration order,

(d) a company in housing administration corresponds to a company in administration,

(e) entering into housing administration in relation to a company corresponds to entering into administration, and

(f) what corresponds to Schedule B1 to the Insolvency Act 1986 or a provision of that Schedule is that Schedule or that provision as applied by Part 1 of this Schedule.

40 (1) Paragraph 39, in its application to section 1(3) of the Insolvency Act 1986, does not entitle the housing administrator of an unregistered company to make a proposal under Part 1 of the Insolvency Act 1986 (company voluntary arrangements).

(2) Paragraph 39 does not confer any right under section 7(4) of the Insolvency Act 1986 (implementation of voluntary arrangements) for a supervisor of voluntary arrangements to apply for a housing administration order in relation to a company that is a private registered provider.

(3) Paragraph 39 does not apply to section 359 of the Financial Services and Markets Act 2000 (administration order).

Modifications of the Insolvency Act 1986

41 The following provisions of the Insolvency Act 1986 are to have effect in the case of any housing administration with the following modifications.

42 Section 5 (effect of approval of voluntary arrangements) is to have effect as if after subsection (4) there were inserted—

"(4A) Where the company is in housing administration, the court must not make an order or give a direction under subsection (3) unless—

(a) the court has given the Secretary of State or the Regulator of Social Housing a reasonable opportunity of making representations to it about the proposed order or direction, and

(b) the order or direction is consistent with the objectives of the housing administration.

(4B) In subsection (4A) "in housing administration" and "objectives of the housing administration" are to be read in accordance with Schedule B1 to this Act, as applied by Part 1 of Schedule 5 to the Housing and Planning Act 2016."

43 Section 6 (challenge of decisions in relation to voluntary arrangements) is to have effect as if—

(a) in subsection (2), for "this section" there were substituted "subsection (1)",

(b) after that subsection there were inserted—

"(2AA) Subject to this section, where a voluntary arrangement in relation to a company in housing administration is approved at the meetings summoned under section 3, an application to the court may be made—

(a) by the Secretary of State, or

(b) with the consent of the Secretary of State, by the Regulator of Social Housing,

on the ground that the voluntary arrangement is not consistent with the achievement of the objectives of the housing administration.",

(c) in subsection (4), after "subsection (1)" there were inserted "or, in the case of an application under subsection (2AA), as to the ground mentioned in that subsection", and

(d) after subsection (7) there were inserted—

"(7A) In this section "in housing administration" and "objectives of the housing administration" are to be read in accordance with Schedule B1 to this Act, as applied by Part 1 of Schedule 5 to the Housing and Planning Act 2016."

44 In section 129(1A) (commencement of winding up), the reference to paragraph 13(1)(e) of Schedule B1 is to include section 100(1)(e) of this Act.

Power to make further modifications

45 (1) The Secretary of State may by regulations amend this Part of this Schedule so as to add further modifications.

(2) The further modifications that may be made are confined to such modifications of—

(a) the Insolvency Act 1986, or

(b) other legislation passed or made before this Act that relate to insolvency or make provision by reference to anything that is or may be done under the Insolvency Act 1986,

as the Secretary of State considers appropriate in relation to any provision made by or under this Chapter.

Interpretation of Part 3 of Schedule

46 In this Part of this Schedule—

"administration order", "administrator", "enters administration" and "in administration" are to be read in accordance with Schedule B1 to the Insolvency Act 1986 (disregarding Part 1 of this Schedule), and

"enters housing administration" and "in housing administration" are to be read in accordance with Schedule B1 to the Insolvency Act 1986 (as applied by Part 1 of this Schedule).

NOTES

Commencement: to be appointed.

SCHEDULES 6–20

(*Schs 6–20 outside the scope of this work.*)

J
CO-OPERATIVE AND COMMUNITY BENEFIT SOCIETIES AND CREDIT UNIONS

ENTERPRISE ACT 2002

(2002 c 40)

NOTES

Only the section of this Act which is relevant to co-operative and community benefit societies and credit unions is reproduced here.

PART 10
INSOLVENCY

Companies, etc

[7.1402]

255 Application of law about company arrangement or administration to non-company

(1) The Treasury may with the concurrence of the Secretary of State by order provide for a company arrangement or administration provision to apply (with or without modification) in relation to—

(a) . . .

(b) a society registered under section 7(1)(b), (c), (d), (e) or (f) of the Friendly Societies Act 1974 (c 46),

(c) a friendly society within the meaning of the Friendly Societies Act 1992 (c 40), or

(d) an unregistered friendly society.

(2) In subsection (1) "company arrangement or administration provision" means—

(a) a provision of Part I of the Insolvency Act 1986 (company voluntary arrangements),

(b) a provision of Part II of that Act (administration), and

(c) [Part 26 of the Companies Act 2006] (compromise or arrangement with creditors).

(3) An order under this section may not provide for a company arrangement or administration provision to apply in relation to a society which is[—

(a) a private registered provider of social housing, or

(b)] registered as a social landlord under Part I of the Housing Act 1996 (c 52) or under [Part 2 of the Housing (Scotland) Act 2010 (asp 17)].

(4) An order under this section—

(a) may make provision generally or for a specified purpose only,

(b) may make different provision for different purposes, and

(c) may make transitional, consequential or incidental provision.

(5) Provision by virtue of subsection (4)(c) may, in particular—

(a) apply an enactment (with or without modification);

(b) amend an enactment.

(6) An order under this section—

(a) must be made by statutory instrument, and

(b) shall be subject to annulment in pursuance of a resolution of either House of Parliament.

NOTES

Sub-s (1): para (a) repealed by the Co-operative and Community Benefit Societies Act 2014, s 151(4), Sch 7.

Sub-s (2): words in square brackets substituted for original words "section 425 of the Companies Act 1985 (c 6)" by the Companies Act 2006 (Consequential Amendments etc) Order 2008, SI 2008/948, art 3(1)(b), Sch 1, Pt 2, para 225, subject to transitional provisions in arts 6, 11, 12 thereof.

Sub-s (3): words in first pair of square brackets inserted by the Housing and Regeneration Act 2008 (Consequential Provisions) Order 2010, SI 2010/866, art 5, Sch 2, Pt 2, para 119, subject to transitional provisions in art 6 of, and Sch 3, paras 1, 3, 4 to, that Order; words in second pair of square brackets substituted by the Housing (Scotland) Act 2010 (Consequential Provisions and Modifications) Order 2012, SI 2012/700, art 4, Schedule, Pt 1, para 6.

Orders: the Industrial and Provident Societies and Credit Unions (Arrangements, Reconstructions and Administration) Order 2014, SI 2014/229 at **[7.1425]**.

CO-OPERATIVE AND COMMUNITY BENEFIT SOCIETIES ACT 2014

(2014 c 14)

ARRANGEMENT OF SECTIONS

PART 1
REGISTRATION

Introduction

1 Meaning of "registered society" . . . [7.1403]

Registration

2 Societies that may be registered . . . [7.1404]

PART 5
CHARGES OVER A SOCIETY'S ASSETS

CHAPTER 3
RECEIVER OR MANAGER OF SOCIETY'S PROPERTY

65 English and Welsh societies: restriction on appointment of administrative receiver . . . [7.1405]
66 Duty to account etc of receiver or manager of a society's property . . . [7.1406]

PART 9
AMALGAMATIONS, CONVERSIONS, DISSOLUTION ETC

Voluntary arrangements and administration

118 Power to apply provisions about company arrangements and administration . . . [7.1407]

Dissolution by an instrument of dissolution

119 Dissolution of society by an instrument of dissolution . . . [7.1408]
120 Special resolutions under section 119 . . . [7.1409]
121 Instruments of dissolution: notification to FCA etc . . . [7.1410]
122 Instruments of dissolution: advertisement, dissolution etc . . . [7.1411]

Dissolution on winding up

123 Dissolution of society on winding up . . . [7.1412]
124 Liability of existing and former members in winding up . . . [7.1413]

Dissolution following administration

125 Dissolution following administration . . . [7.1414]

Restriction on dissolution etc

126 Dissolution etc to occur only after society's property dealt with . . . [7.1415]

PART 11
MISCELLANEOUS AND GENERAL

Application of company law etc

134 Power to amend this Act to assimilate to company law . . . [7.1416]
135 Power to apply company law provisions on investigations, names and dissolution etc . . . [7.1417]
136 Section 135: power to make consequential amendments . . . [7.1418]

Interpretation

149 Interpretation of Act . . . [7.1419]

PART 12
FINAL PROVISIONS

150 Pre-commencement societies . . . [7.1420]
152 Channel Islands . . . [7.1421]
153 Extent . . . [7.1422]
154 Commencement . . . [7.1423]
155 Short title . . . [7.1424]

An Act to consolidate certain enactments relating to co-operative societies, community benefit societies and other societies registered or treated as registered under the Industrial and Provident Societies Act

1965, with amendments to give effect to recommendations of the Law Commission and the Scottish Law Commission

[14 May 2014]

PART 1
REGISTRATION

Introduction

[7.1403]

1 Meaning of "registered society"

(1) In this Act "registered society" means a society registered under this Act, that is—

(a) a society registered under this Act on or after 1 August 2014 (the day this Act comes into force), or

(b) (by virtue of section 150(1)) a society that immediately before that date was registered or treated as registered under the 1965 Act.

(2) In this Act "the 1965 Act" means the Industrial and Provident Societies Act 1965.

NOTES

Commencement: 1 August 2014.

Registration

[7.1404]

2 Societies that may be registered

(1) A society for carrying on any industry, business or trade (including dealings of any kind with land) which meets the conditions in subsection (2) may be registered under this Act as—

(a) a co-operative society, or

(b) a community benefit society.

(2) The conditions are—

(a) that it is shown to the satisfaction of the FCA—

(i) in the case of registration as a co-operative society, that the society is a bona fide co-operative society, or

(ii) in the case of registration as a community benefit society, that the business of the society is being, or is intended to be, conducted for the benefit of the community,

(b) that—

(i) the society has at least 3 members, or

(ii) the society has 2 members both of which are registered societies,

(c) that the society's rules contain provision in respect of the matters mentioned in section 14, and

(d) that the place that under those rules is to be the society's registered office is in Great Britain or the Channel Islands.

(3) For the purposes of subsection (2)(a)(i) "co-operative society" does not include a society that carries on, or intends to carry on, business with the object of making profits mainly for the payment of interest, dividends or bonuses on money invested or deposited with, or lent to, the society or any other person.

(4) For registration under this Act as a credit union, see the Credit Unions Act 1979.

NOTES

Commencement: 1 August 2014.

3–58 (*Ss 3–9, 10–58 (Pts 2–4) outside the scope of this work.*)

PART 5
CHARGES OVER A SOCIETY'S ASSETS

59–64 (*(Chs 1, 2) outside the scope of this work.*)

CHAPTER 3 RECEIVER OR MANAGER OF SOCIETY'S PROPERTY

[7.1405]

65 English and Welsh societies: restriction on appointment of administrative receiver

(1) The holder of a qualifying floating charge in respect of the property of a relevant society whose registered office is situated in England and Wales may not appoint an administrative receiver of the society.

(2) This section applies to a floating charge which is created by a relevant society on or after 6th April 2014 and is either—

(a) a charge in respect of which an application under section 59 has been made; or

(b) a charge created by a debenture registered under section 9 of the Agricultural Credits Act 1928 as applied by section 14 of that Act.

(3) This section applies in spite of any provision of an agreement or instrument which purports to empower a person to appoint an administrative receiver (by whatever name).

(4) In this section—

"administrative receiver", in relation to a relevant society, means—

(a) a receiver or manager of the whole (or substantially the whole) of the society's property appointed by or on behalf of the holder of a floating charge, or by such a charge and one or more other securities, or

(b) a person who would be such a receiver or manager but for the appointment of some other person as the receiver of part of the society's property;

"holder of a qualifying floating charge in respect of the property of a relevant society" has the meaning given in paragraph 14 of Schedule B1 to the Insolvency Act 1986 as applied in relation to a relevant society by an order under section 118;

"relevant society" means a registered society which is not—

(a) a private registered provider of social housing; or

(b) registered as a social landlord under Part 1 of the Housing Act 1996 or under Part 2 of the Housing (Scotland) Act 2010.

NOTES

Commencement: 1 August 2014.

[7.1406]

66 Duty to account etc of receiver or manager of a society's property

(1) This section applies to a receiver or manager of a registered society's property who has been appointed under the powers contained in any instrument.

(2) The receiver or manager must—

(a) within one month from the date of appointment, notify the FCA of the appointment;

(b) within one month (or such longer period as the FCA may allow) after the end of each relevant period, deliver to the FCA a return showing receipts and payments in that relevant period;

(c) within one month after ceasing to act as receiver or manager, deliver to the FCA a return showing—

(i) receipts and payments in the final period, and

(ii) the total amount of payments and receipts in all preceding relevant periods.

References here to receipts and payments are to receipts and payments of the receiver or manager.

(3) For the purposes of subsection (2) the relevant periods are—

(a) the period of 6 months beginning with the date of appointment, and

(b) each subsequent period of 6 months for which the person is receiver or manager.

(4) If the society is a PRA-authorised person—

(a) the receiver or manager must send to the PRA a copy of any notification or return sent under subsection (2) to the FCA;

(b) the FCA must consult the PRA before allowing a period of more than one month under subsection (2)(b).

NOTES

Commencement: 1 August 2014.

67–108 (*(Pts 6–8) outside the scope of this work.*)

PART 9
AMALGAMATIONS, CONVERSIONS, DISSOLUTION ETC

109–117 (*Outside the scope of this work.*)

Voluntary arrangements and administration

[7.1407]

118 Power to apply provisions about company arrangements and administration

(1) The Treasury may with the concurrence of the Secretary of State by order provide for a company arrangement or administration provision to apply (with or without modifications) in relation to registered societies.

(2) "Company arrangement or administration provision" means—

(a) a provision of Part 1 of the Insolvency Act 1986 (company voluntary arrangements);

(b) a provision of Part 2 of that Act (administration);

(c) Part 26 of the Companies Act 2006 (compromise or arrangement with creditors).

(3) The order may not provide for a company arrangement or administration provision to apply in relation to a society that is—

(a) a private registered provider of social housing, or

(b) registered as a social landlord under Part 1 of the Housing Act 1996 or Part 2 of the Housing (Scotland) Act 2010 (asp 17).

(4) The order may—

(a) make provision generally or for a specified purpose only;

(b) make different provision for different purposes;

(c) make transitional, consequential or incidental provision.

(5) Provision made by virtue of subsection (4)(c) may, in particular—

(a) apply an enactment (with or without modifications);

(b) amend an enactment (including any provision of this Act except this section).

(6) Section 277 of the Enterprise Act 2002 (power of Secretary of State to make supplementary, consequential or incidental provision) has effect as if this section were part of that Act.

NOTES

Commencement: 1 August 2014.

Dissolution by an instrument of dissolution

[7.1408]

119 Dissolution of society by an instrument of dissolution

(1) A registered society may be dissolved by an instrument of dissolution that—

(a) complies with subsection (2), and

(b) is approved in a way mentioned in subsection (3).

(2) The instrument must set out—

(a) the society's assets and liabilities in detail;

(b) the number of members and the nature of their interests in the society;

(c) any creditors' claims, and the provision to be made for their payment;

(d) the intended appropriation or division of the society's funds and property (unless the instrument states that this is to be left to the award of the FCA or PRA).

(3) The ways in which the instrument may be approved are as follows—

(a) by at least 75% of the society's members consenting to it, that consent being testified by their signatures to the instrument;

(b) in the case of a dormant society that is not a credit union, by a special resolution of the society;

(c) in the case of a credit union, by a special resolution of the society that is confirmed by the appropriate authority.

(4) An alteration in an instrument of dissolution may be made—

(a) by the consent of at least 75% of the society's members, testified by their signatures to the alteration, or

(b) if the instrument was approved by a special resolution of the society, by a further special resolution.

(5) Section 120 contains provisions about special resolutions under this section.

(6) In subsection (3)(b) "dormant society" means a society—

(a) whose accounts for the current year of account and the two years of account preceding it show no accounting transactions except—

(i) fees paid to the FCA;

(ii) fees paid to the PRA;

(iii) payments of dividends;

(iv) payments of interest; and

(b) that has notified the FCA that it is dormant.

(7) For the purposes of subsection (3)(c) the appropriate authority is treated as confirming a special resolution unless it notifies the society in writing to the contrary within 21 days of the society sending a copy of the resolution to it.

NOTES

Commencement: 1 August 2014.

[7.1409]

120 Special resolutions under section 119

(1) This section supplements section 119.

(2) A resolution is a "special resolution" if—

(a) the resolution is passed at a general meeting by at least two-thirds of the eligible members who vote,

(b) notice of this meeting ("the first meeting"), specifying the intention to propose the resolution, is duly given in accordance with the society's rules,

(c) the resolution is confirmed at a subsequent general meeting by over half of the eligible members who vote,

(d) notice of this meeting ("the second meeting") is duly given, and

(e) the second meeting is held at least 14 days, and no more than one month, from the day of the first meeting.

(3) In this section—

(a) "eligible member" means a member entitled under the society's rules to vote;

(b) references to voting are to voting in person or, where the rules allow proxies, by proxy.

NOTES

Commencement: 1 August 2014.

[7.1410]

121 Instruments of dissolution: notification to FCA etc

(1) This section applies in relation to an instrument of dissolution within section 119(1).

(2) The instrument must be sent to the FCA (and, if the society is a PRA-authorised person, the PRA), accompanied by a statutory declaration that all relevant provisions of this Act have been complied with.

(3) The statutory declaration must be made by the society's secretary and—

(a) 3 members, or

(b) both members (if the society consists solely of 2 registered societies).

(4) A copy of any special resolution under section 119—

(a) signed by the chair of the second meeting, and

(b) countersigned by the society's secretary,

must be sent to the FCA (and, if the society is a PRA-authorised person, the PRA) within the period of 14 days beginning with the day of the second meeting.

(5) The FCA must register the instrument of dissolution (and any alterations to it) in the same way as an amendment of the society's rules.
But it must not register it until it has received the society's annual return for its last year of account (see section 77(8) or 78(7)).
(6) The FCA must register a copy special resolution received under subsection (4) at the same time as it registers the instrument of dissolution (and any alterations to it).
(7) The instrument of dissolution (and any alterations to it) are binding on the society's members.
(8) In this section "the second meeting" has the same meaning as in section 120.

NOTES

Commencement: 1 August 2014.

[7.1411]

122 Instruments of dissolution: advertisement, dissolution etc

(1) Where the FCA receives an instrument of dissolution of a society under section 121, it must ensure that notice of the dissolution is advertised in—
(a) the Gazette, and
(b) a newspaper circulating in or about the locality in which the society's registered office is situated.
(2) Subject to subsection (3), the society is dissolved from—
(a) the date of the advertisement, or
(b) if later, the date the certificate under section 126 is lodged with the FCA;
and the requisite consents to, or approval of, the instrument of dissolution are treated as duly obtained without proof of the signatures to it or of the special resolution (as the case may be).
(3) Subsection (2) does not apply if—
(a) within the period of 3 months from the date of the Gazette in which the advertisement appears, a member of the society or a person interested in or having a claim on its funds commences proceedings in the appropriate court to set aside the dissolution of the society, and
(b) the dissolution is accordingly set aside.
(4) The "appropriate court" means—
(a) the county court, or
(b) in Scotland, the sheriff having jurisdiction in the locality in which the society's registered office is situated.
(5) A person who takes proceedings to set aside the dissolution of a society must send the FCA (and, if the society is a PRA-authorised person, the PRA) notice of the proceedings—
(a) within 7 days after the commencement of proceedings, or
(b) if earlier, by the end of the period mentioned in subsection (3)(a).
(6) If an order setting aside the dissolution of a society is made, the society must send the FCA (and, if the society is a PRA-authorised person, the PRA) notice of the order within 7 days after the making of the order.

NOTES

Commencement: 1 August 2014.

Dissolution on winding up

[7.1412]

123 Dissolution of society on winding up

(1) A registered society may be dissolved on its being wound up in pursuance of an order or resolution made as is directed in the case of companies.
(2) The provisions relating to the winding up of companies have effect in relation to a registered society as if the society were a company, subject to the following modifications—
(a) a reference to the registrar of companies is to be read as the FCA;
(b) a reference to a company registered in Scotland is to be read as a registered society whose registered office is in Scotland;
(c) if the society is wound up in Scotland, the court having jurisdiction is the sheriff court whose jurisdiction contains the society's registered office.
(3) Where a resolution for the voluntary winding up of a registered society is passed—
(a) the society must send a copy of it to the FCA (and, if the society is a PRA-authorised person, the PRA) within 15 days after it is passed, and
(b) a copy of it must be annexed to every copy of the society's registered rules issued after it is passed.
(4) In this section "company" means a company registered under the Companies Acts.
(5) This section is subject to section 126 (dissolution to occur only after society's property has been dealt with).

NOTES

Commencement: 1 August 2014.

[7.1413]

124 Liability of existing and former members in winding up

(1) This section applies where a registered society is wound up by virtue of section 123.

(2) The liability of an existing or former member to contribute for payment of the society's debts and liabilities, the expenses of winding up, and the adjustment of the rights of contributories amongst themselves, is qualified as follows—

(a) a former member whose membership ceased at least one year before the beginning of the winding up is not liable to contribute;

(b) a former member is not liable to contribute in respect of a debt or liability contracted after the person's membership ceased;

(c) a former member is not liable to contribute unless it appears to the court that the contributions of the existing members are insufficient to satisfy the just demands on the society;

(d) the maximum contribution that a person may be required to make is the amount (if any) unpaid on the shares in respect of which the person is liable as an existing or former member;

(e) in the case of a withdrawable share that has been withdrawn, a person is treated as ceasing to be a member in respect of that share as from the date of the notice or application for withdrawal.

NOTES

Commencement: 1 August 2014.

Dissolution following administration

[7.1414]

125 Dissolution following administration

(1) A relevant society may also be dissolved under paragraph 84 of Schedule B1 to the 1986 Act as applied in relation to a relevant society by an order under section 118.

(2) In this section "relevant society" means a registered society which is not—

(a) a private registered provider of social housing, or

(b) registered as a social landlord under Part 1 of the Housing Act 1996 or under Part 2 of the Housing (Scotland) Act 2010.

NOTES

Commencement: 1 August 2014.

Restriction on dissolution etc

[7.1415]

126 Dissolution etc to occur only after society's property dealt with

(1) This section applies where—

(a) a registered society's engagements are transferred under section 110 or 112, or

(b) a registered society is to be dissolved in accordance with section 119 or 123.

(2) The society must not be dissolved, and its registration must not be cancelled, until a relevant certificate has been lodged with the FCA.

(3) "Relevant certificate" means a certificate certifying that all property vested in the society has been duly conveyed or transferred by the society to the persons entitled, signed by—

(a) the liquidator, or

(b) the secretary or some other officer of the society approved by the FCA.

NOTES

Commencement: 1 August 2014.

127–133 *((Pt 10) outside the scope of this work.)*

PART 11
MISCELLANEOUS AND GENERAL

Application of company law etc

[7.1416]

134 Power to amend this Act to assimilate to company law

(1) This section applies where, on any modification of the enactments in force relating to companies, it appears to the Treasury to be expedient to modify the relevant provisions of this Act for the purpose of assimilating the law relating to companies and the law relating to registered societies.

(2) The Treasury may by order make such modifications of the relevant provisions of this Act as they consider appropriate for that purpose.

(3) The "relevant provisions" of this Act are the provisions of this Act for the time being in force except—

(a) this section;

(b) section 2(1), (2)(a), (c) and (d), (3) and (4);

(c) sections 5 to 9;

(d) section 16(1) and (2);

(e) section 17;

(f) section 29;

(g) sections 36 to 40;

(h) sections 109 to 122;

(i) section 126;

(j) sections 135 and 136;

(k) paragraphs 2, 10 and 15 of Schedule 3.

(4) An order under this section may modify the relevant provisions of this Act so as to—

(a) confer power to make orders, regulations, rules or other subordinate legislation;
(b) create criminal offences;
(c) provide for the charging of fees, but not any charge in the nature of taxation.

(5) An order under this section may—
(a) make consequential amendments of, or repeals in, the provisions listed in subsection (3);
(b) make such transitional or saving provisions as appear to the Treasury to be necessary or expedient.

(6) In this section "modification" includes any additions.

(7) The reference in subsection (1) to modifications of the enactments relating to companies includes any modification whether effected by—
(a) an Act passed after the passing of the Industrial and Provident Societies Act 2002, or
(b) an instrument made after the passing of that Act, under an Act whenever passed.

NOTES

Commencement: 1 August 2014.

[7.1417]

135 Power to apply company law provisions on investigations, names and dissolution etc

(1) The Treasury may by regulations—
(a) make provision applying any provision mentioned in subsection (2) to registered societies, or
(b) make provision for registered societies corresponding to any such provision,

in either case, with such modifications as appear to the Treasury to be appropriate.

(2) The provisions are—
(a) Parts 14 and 15 of the Companies Act 1985 (investigations);
(b) Part 5 of the Companies Act 2006 (company names);
(c) Part 31 of that Act (dissolution and restoration to the register).

(3) Regulations made by virtue of subsection (2)(a) may amend or repeal any of sections 105 to 107 (inspections, information powers etc).

(4) Regulations made by virtue of subsection (2)(b) may amend or repeal section 10 or 11 (or both) (provisions about a society's name).

(5) Regulations made by virtue of subsection (2)(c) may amend or repeal—
(a) section 5(3)(c) (cancellation of registration: society having ceased to exist);
(b) section 126 (dissolution etc to occur only after society's property dealt with).

(6) Subsections (3) to (5) are not to be read as restricting the power conferred by section 136 (power to make consequential amendments).

(7) The regulations may—
(a) confer power to make orders, regulations and other subordinate legislation;
(b) create criminal offences, but only—
 (i) in circumstances corresponding to an offence under the Companies Acts, and
 (ii) subject to a maximum penalty no greater than is provided for in respect of the corresponding offence;
(c) provide for the charging of fees, but not any charge in the nature of taxation.

(8) The regulations may contain such supplementary, incidental and transitional provisions as appear to the Treasury to be necessary or expedient.

(9) Before making any regulations under this section the Treasury must consult such persons as appear to them to be appropriate.

NOTES

Commencement: 1 August 2014.

[7.1418]

136 Section 135: power to make consequential amendments

(1) The Treasury may by regulations make such amendments of enactments as appear to them to be appropriate in consequence of any provision made by or under section 135.

(2) This power is exercisable in relation to—
(a) this Act (except this section), and
(b) any enactment passed or made before the commencement of the relevant provision.

(3) In this section "enactment" includes—
(a) an enactment contained in subordinate legislation within the meaning of the Interpretation Act 1978,
(b) an enactment contained in, or in an instrument made under, an Act of the Scottish Parliament,
(c) an enactment contained in, or in an instrument made under, a Measure or Act of the National Assembly for Wales, and
(d) an enactment contained in, or in an instrument made under, Northern Ireland legislation within the meaning of the Interpretation Act 1978.

(4) The regulations may contain such supplementary, incidental and transitional provisions as appear to the Treasury to be necessary or expedient.

NOTES

Commencement: 1 August 2014.

137–148 (*Outside the scope of this work.*)

[7.1419]

149 Interpretation of Act

In this Act, except where the context otherwise requires—

"the 1965 Act" has the meaning given by section 1;

"amendment", in relation to a registered society's rules, includes a new rule and a resolution rescinding a rule;

"annual return" has the same meaning as in section 89;

"the appropriate authority" means—

(a) in relation to a society that is a PRA-authorised person, the PRA;

(b) in relation to any other society, the FCA;

"charitable registered society" means a registered society that is a charity;

"charity" (except in section 10)—

(a) has the meaning given by section 1(1) of the Charities Act 2011 (as modified, in the case of a society whose registered office is in Scotland, by section 7(2) of that Act);

(b) but in relation to a society whose registered office is in any of the Channel Islands, it means a society established for charitable purposes only ("charitable purposes" having the meaning given by the law of that Island);

and similar expressions are to be read accordingly;

"committee", in relation to a society, means the society's management committee or other directing body;

"the Companies Acts" means—

(a) the Companies Acts as defined in section 2(1) of the Companies Act 2006, or

(b) any law for corresponding purposes in force in any of the Channel Islands,

and includes corresponding earlier Acts or laws;

"credit union" means a registered society that is registered as a credit union;

"electronic address" means any number or address used for the purposes of sending or receiving documents or information by electronic means;

"electronic copy", "electronic form" and "electronic means" have the same meaning as in section 148;

"enactment" (except in section 136 and Schedule 5) includes—

(a) an enactment contained in subordinate legislation within the meaning of the Interpretation Act 1978,

(b) an enactment contained in, or in an instrument made under, an Act of the Scottish Parliament, and

(c) an enactment contained in, or in an instrument made under, a Measure or Act of the National Assembly for Wales;

"the FCA" means the Financial Conduct Authority;

"the Financial Ombudsman scheme" means the scheme established under Part 16 of the Financial Services and Markets Act 2000;

"Gazette", in relation to a registered society, means such one or more of the following as apply—

(a) the London Gazette, if the society's registered office is in England, Wales or the Channel Islands or it carries on business there;

(b) the Edinburgh Gazette, if the society's registered office is in Scotland or it carries on business there;

[(c) the Belfast Gazette, if a notice given by the society has been filed under section 102 (Great Britain societies carrying on business in Northern Ireland) of the Cooperative and Community Benefit Societies Act (Northern Ireland) 1969;]

"heritable security" has the same meaning as in the Conveyancing (Scotland) Act 1924 except that it includes a security constituted by ex facie absolute disposition or assignation;

"meeting", in relation to a society, includes (where the society's rules allow it) a meeting of delegates appointed by members;

"officer", in relation to a registered society—

(a) includes any treasurer, secretary, member of the committee, manager or employee of the society (except an employee appointed by the society's committee), but

(b) does not include an auditor appointed by the society in accordance with the requirements of Part 7;

"persons claiming through a member" includes the heirs, executors or administrators and assignees of a member and (where nomination is allowed) the person's nominee;

"the PRA" means the Prudential Regulation Authority;

"PRA-authorised person" has the meaning given by section 2B of the Financial Services and Markets Act 2000;

"pre-commencement society" has the meaning given by section 150;

"registered", in relation to a society's name or office, means the name or office for the time being registered under this Act in respect of the society;

"registered rules", in relation to a registered society, means the rules registered under this Act, as amended by any amendment of the rules that has been so registered;

"registered society" has the meaning given by section 1;

the FCA's "seal" means the seal provided for in regulations made under section 109(1)(b) of the Friendly Societies Act 1974 (and any reference to a document sealed by the FCA is to be read accordingly).

NOTES

Commencement: 1 August 2014.

In definition "Gazette", para (c) substituted by the Financial Services Act 2012 (Mutual Societies) Order 2018, SI 2018/223, art 2(c), Sch 4, para 2(1), (3).

PART 12
FINAL PROVISIONS

[7.1420]
150 Pre-commencement societies
(1) Any reference to a society registered under this Act includes a society that, immediately before 1 August 2014, was registered or treated as registered under the 1965 Act (a "pre-commencement society").
(2) In relation to a pre-commencement society—
- (a) any reference to an acknowledgement of the registration under this Act of a society, its rules or any amendment of its rules includes an acknowledgement of the registration under the 1965 Act of the society, its rules or an amendment (and anything treated, immediately before 1 August 2014, as such an acknowledgement);
- (b) any reference to rules or amendments of rules registered under this Act includes rules or amendments registered under the 1965 Act (and anything treated, immediately before 1 August 2014, as rules or amendments registered under that Act).

(3) In this section "reference" means a reference (expressed or implied) in this Act, another enactment or an instrument or document.
(4) Schedule 3 contain provisions applying in relation to certain pre-commencement societies.

NOTES
Commencement: 1 August 2014.

151 (*Outside the scope of this work.*)

[7.1421]
152 Channel Islands
(1) Her Majesty may by Order in Council provide for any provision of this Act, or of any instrument made under it, to extend (with or without modifications) to any of the Channel Islands.
(2) Any such Order in Council may make such transitional, incidental or supplementary provision as appears to Her Majesty to be necessary or expedient.

NOTES
Commencement: 1 August 2014.

[7.1422]
153 Extent
(1) Subject as follows, this Act extends to England and Wales and Scotland.
(2) Chapter 1 of Part 5 extends to England and Wales only.
(3) Chapter 2 of Part 5 extends to Scotland only.
(4) The following provisions also extend to Northern Ireland—
- (a) this section;
- (b) sections 136, 147, 154 and 155;
- (c) Schedule 5.

(5) Any amendment, repeal or revocation made by this Act extends to any part of the United Kingdom to which the provision amended, repealed or revoked extends.
(6) Nothing in this section applies to section 152 (and the repeals made by this Act do not affect any power by Order in Council to make provision extending to any of the Channel Islands).

NOTES
Commencement: 1 August 2014.

[7.1423]
154 Commencement
This Act comes into force on 1 August 2014, immediately after section 1 of the Co-operative and Community Benefit Societies and Credit Unions Act 2010 (registration of societies as co-operative or community benefit societies).

NOTES
Commencement: 1 August 2014.

[7.1424]
155 Short title
This Act may be cited as the Co-operative and Community Benefit Societies Act 2014.

NOTES
Commencement: 1 August 2014.

SCHEDULES 1–7

(Schs 1–7 outside the scope of this work.)

[CO-OPERATIVE AND COMMUNITY BENEFIT SOCIETIES AND CREDIT UNIONS (ARRANGEMENTS, RECONSTRUCTIONS AND ADMINISTRATION) ORDER 2014]

(SI 2014/229)

NOTES

Made: 4 February 2014.

Authority: Enterprise Act 2002, s 255(1)(a), (4), (5).

Commencement: 6 April 2014.

Title substituted by virtue of the Co-operative and Community Benefit Societies and Credit Unions Act 2010 (Consequential Amendments) Regulations 2014, SI 2014/1815, reg 2, Schedule, para 33.

ARRANGEMENT OF ARTICLES

1 Citation, commencement and interpretation . . . [7.1425]
2 Application to relevant societies of law about company arrangements and administration . . . [7.1426]
2A Application of section 176ZB of the 1986 Act . . . [7.1427]
3 Application of section 176A of the 1986 Act . . . [7.1428]
4 Application of other provisions of the 1986 Act . . . [7.1429]
5 Application of section 215 of FSMA . . . [7.1430]
6 Application of section 356 of FSMA . . . [7.1431]
7 Application of section 359 of FSMA . . . [7.1432]
8 Application of section 361 of FSMA . . . [7.1433]
9 Application of sections 362 and 362A of FSMA . . . [7.1434]
10 Application of provisions of FSMA: general provision . . . [7.1435]
11 Application of insolvency rules . . . [7.1436]
12 Application of other subordinate legislation . . . [7.1437]
13 Modified application of section 111 of the 2014 Act . . . [7.1438]
14 Modified application of section 113 of the 2014 Act . . . [7.1439]
15 Modified application of section 126 of the 2014 Act . . . [7.1440]

SCHEDULES

Schedule 1—Modified Application of Parts 1 and 2 of the Insolvency Act 1986 to Relevant Societies
Part 1—General Modifications . . . [7.1441]
Part 2—Modified Application of Part 1 of the Insolvency Act 1986 to Relevant Societies (Further Modifications) . . . [7.1442]
Part 3—Modified Application of Part 2 of the Insolvency Act 1986 to Relevant Societies (Further Modifications) . . . [7.1443]
Part 4—Modified Application of Schedule 1 to the Insolvency Act 1986 to Relevant Societies (Further Modifications) . . . [7.1444]
Schedule 2—Modified Application of Part 26 of the Companies Act 2006 to Relevant Societies . . . [7.1445]
Schedule 3—Modified Application of Other Provisions of the Insolvency Act 1986 . . . [7.1446]
Schedule 4—Modified Application of Insolvency Rules in Relation to Relevant Societies
Part 1—Interpretation . . . [7.1447]
Part 2—Modified Application of the Insolvency Rules 1986 . . . [7.1448]
Part 3—Modified Application of the Insolvency (Scotland) Rules 1986 . . . [7.1449]
Schedule 5—Application of Other Subordinate Legislation with Modifications . . . [7.1450]

[7.1425]

1 Citation, commencement and interpretation

(1) This Order may be cited as the [Co-operative and Community Benefit Societies and Credit Unions (Arrangements, Reconstructions and Administration) Order 2014], and comes into force on 6th April 2014.

(2) In this Order—

. . .

"the 1986 Act" means the Insolvency Act 1986;

"the 2006 Act" means the Companies Act 2006;

["the 2014 Act" means the Co-operative and Community Benefit Societies Act 2014;]

["the 2015 Act" means the Small Business, Enterprise and Employment Act 2015;]

"authorised person" has the meaning given in section 31(2) of FSMA;
"authorised deposit taker" has the meaning given in section 359(4) of FSMA;

. . .

"deposit" has the meaning given by article 5 of the Financial Services and Markets Act 2000 (Regulated Activities) Order 2001;

. . .

"FSMA" means the Financial Services and Markets Act 2000;
"member", in relation to a relevant society, means a person whose name is entered as a member in the register kept by the society in accordance with [section 30(1) of the 2014 Act];

. . .

"relevant person" has the meaning given in section 213(9)(a) of FSMA; and
"relevant society" means a [registered society which] is not—

(a) a private registered provider of social housing; or
(b) registered as a social landlord under Part 1 of the Housing Act 1996 or under Part 2 of the Housing (Scotland) Act 2010.

(3) The definition of "authorised deposit taker" is to be construed in accordance with—

(a) section 22 of, and Schedule 2 to, FSMA; and
(b) any relevant order under section 22.

(4) For the purposes of this Order a relevant society is "in administration" while the appointment of an administrator of the society under Schedule B1 to the 1986 Act has effect.

NOTES

Commencement: 6 April 2014.

Para (1): words in square brackets substituted by the Co-operative and Community Benefit Societies and Credit Unions Act 2010 (Consequential Amendments) Regulations 2014, SI 2014/1815, reg 2, Schedule, para 33.

Para (2): definitions "the 1965 Act", "the 1967 Act", "committee", "the FCA" and "officer" (omitted) revoked, definition "the 2014 Act" inserted, and in definitions "member" and "relevant society" words in square brackets substituted by the Co-operative and Community Benefit Societies and Credit Unions (Arrangements, Reconstructions and Administration) (Amendment) Order 2014, SI 2014/1822, arts 2, 3; definition "the 2015 Act" inserted by the Small Business, Enterprise and Employment Act 2015 (Consequential Amendments, Savings and Transitional Provisions) Regulations 2018, SI 2018/208, reg 15(1), (2).

[7.1426]

2 Application to relevant societies of law about company arrangements and administration

(1) Part 1 of the 1986 Act (company voluntary arrangements) applies in relation to a relevant society with the modifications set out in Parts 1 and 2 of Schedule 1.

(2) Part 2 of the 1986 Act (administration) applies in relation to a relevant society with the modifications set out in Parts 1, 3 and 4 of Schedule 1.

(3) Part 26 of the 2006 Act (arrangements and reconstructions) applies in relation to a relevant society with the modifications set out in Schedule 2.

NOTES

Commencement: 6 April 2014.

[7.1427]

[2A Application of section 176ZB of the 1986 Act

Section 176ZB of the 1986 Act (application of proceeds of office-holder claims) applies in relation to a relevant society which is in administration, and for that purpose—

(a) a reference to a company includes a reference to a relevant society;
(b) a reference to a section of the 1986 Act is a reference to that section as applied in relation to a relevant society; and
(c) the reference to Part 26 of the 2006 Act is a reference to that Part as applied in relation to a relevant society.]

NOTES

Commencement: 7 April 2017.

Inserted by the Small Business, Enterprise and Employment Act 2015 and the Insolvency (Amendment) Act (Northern Ireland) 2016 (Consequential Amendments and Transitional Provisions) Regulations 2017, SI 2017/400, reg 12(1), (2).

[7.1428]

3 Application of section 176A of the 1986 Act

Section 176A of the 1986 Act (share of assets for unsecured creditors) applies in relation to a relevant society which is in administration, and for that purpose—

(a) a reference to a company includes a reference to a relevant society;
(b) a reference to a receiver is to be ignored; and
(c) in subsection (4)(b) the reference to Part 26 of the 2006 Act is a reference to that Part as applied in relation to a relevant society.

NOTES

Commencement: 6 April 2014.

[7.1429]

4 Application of other provisions of the 1986 Act

The following provisions of the 1986 Act, so far as they have effect for the purposes of Part 1 or Part 2 of that Act as applied in relation to a relevant society, apply with the modifications set out in Schedule 3—

(a) Part 6 (miscellaneous provisions applying to companies which are insolvent or in liquidation);
(b) Part 7 (interpretation for first group of Parts); and
(c) Parts 12 to 19 (the third group of Parts).

NOTES

Commencement: 6 April 2014.

[7.1430]

5 Application of section 215 of FSMA

(1) Section 215 of FSMA (rights of the compensation scheme in insolvency) applies in relation to a relevant society—

(a) which is a relevant person; and
(b) in relation to which an administration application is made, an administrator is appointed or a copy of notice of intention to appoint an administrator is filed with the court under Schedule B1 to the 1986 Act.

(2) For that purpose in subsection (3) the reference to a company includes a reference to a relevant society.

NOTES

Commencement: 6 April 2014.

[7.1431]

6 Application of section 356 of FSMA

(1) Section 356 of FSMA (powers of FCA and PRA to participate in proceedings: company voluntary arrangements) applies in relation to a relevant society—

(a) which is an authorised person; and
(b) in relation to which a voluntary arrangement has effect under Part 1 of the 1986 Act.

(2) For that purpose—

(a) in subsection (1) the reference to a company includes a reference to a relevant society; and
(b) in subsection (3) the reference to an application to the court in relation to the company is a reference to an application to the court under section 6 or 7 of the 1986 Act in relation to a relevant society of the kind described in paragraph (1).

NOTES

Commencement: 6 April 2014.

[7.1432]

7 Application of section 359 of FSMA

(1) Section 359 of FSMA (administration order) applies in relation to a relevant society which—

(a) is or has been an authorised person; or
(b) is carrying on or has carried on a regulated activity in contravention of the general prohibition.

(2) For that purpose—

(a) in subsection (1) the words from "which" to the end are to be ignored; and
(b) except in the definition of "company" in subsection (4), a reference to a company is a reference to a relevant society of the kind described in paragraph (1).

NOTES

Commencement: 6 April 2014.

[7.1433]

8 Application of section 361 of FSMA

Section 361 of FSMA (administrator's duty to report to FCA and PRA) applies in relation to a relevant society, and for that purpose a reference to a company includes a reference to a relevant society.

NOTES

Commencement: 6 April 2014.

[7.1434]

9 Application of sections 362 and 362A of FSMA

(1) Section 362 of FSMA (powers of FCA and PRA to participate in proceedings) and section 362A (administrator appointed by company or directors) apply in relation to a relevant society which—

(a) is or has been an authorised person; or
(b) is carrying on or has carried on a regulated activity in contravention of the general prohibition.

(2) For that purpose—

(a) in section 362—
(i) in subsection (1) the words from "which" to the end are to be ignored;

(ii) in subsection (1A) the words "of a kind described in subsection (1)(a) to (c)" are to be ignored;

(iii) a reference to a company is a reference to a relevant society of the kind described in paragraph (1); and

(b) in section 362A—

(i) in subsection (1) the words "of a kind described in section 362(1)(a) to (c)" are to be ignored;

(ii) a reference to a company is a reference to a relevant society of the kind described in paragraph (1).

NOTES

Commencement: 6 April 2014.

[7.1435]

10 Application of provisions of FSMA: general provision

(1) In the application in relation to a relevant society of any of the provisions applied by articles 5 to 9, except sections 359(4) and 362(1B)—

(a) a reference to a provision of the 1986 Act is a reference to that provision as applied in relation to a relevant society; and

(b) a reference to Schedule B1 to the Insolvency (Northern Ireland) Order 1989 is to be ignored.

(2) In articles 5 to 9—

(a) a reference to a provision of the 1986 Act is a reference to that provision as applied in relation to a relevant society;

(b) "general prohibition" has the meaning given in section 19(2) of FSMA; and

(c) "regulated activity" has the meaning given in section 22 of FSMA.

NOTES

Commencement: 6 April 2014.

[7.1436]

11 Application of insolvency rules

(1) Part 1 (company voluntary arrangements) and, so far as applicable to voluntary arrangements, Parts 7 to 13 (the third group of Parts) of the Insolvency Rules 1986 apply where—

(a) it is intended to make, and there is made, a proposal to a relevant society and its creditors for a voluntary arrangement within the meaning given in section 1 of the 1986 Act (as applied in relation to a relevant society); and

(b) the courts in England and Wales have jurisdiction to wind up the society.

(2) Part 1 (company voluntary arrangements) and, so far as applicable to voluntary arrangements, Part 7 (provisions of general application) of the Insolvency (Scotland) Rules 1986 apply where—

(a) it is intended to make, and there is made, a proposal to a relevant society and its creditors for a voluntary arrangement within the meaning given in section 1 of the 1986 Act (as applied in relation to a relevant society); and

(b) a sheriff court in Scotland has jurisdiction to wind up the society.

(3) Part 2 (administration procedure) and, so far as applicable to administration procedure, Parts 7 to 13 of the Insolvency Rules 1986 apply in relation to the appointment of an administrator of a relevant society which the courts in England and Wales have jurisdiction to wind up.

(4) Part 2 (administration procedure) and, so far as applicable to administration procedure, Part 7 of the Insolvency (Scotland) Rules 1986 apply in relation to the appointment of an administrator of a relevant society which a sheriff court in Scotland has jurisdiction to wind up.

(5) Schedule 4 (which makes further provision about the application in relation to a relevant society of the Insolvency Rules 1986 and the Insolvency (Scotland) Rules 1986) has effect.

NOTES

Commencement: 6 April 2014.

Note that the Insolvency Rules 1986, SI 1986/1925 are revoked and replaced (as from 6 April 2017 and subject to transitional provisions) by the Insolvency (England and Wales) Rules 2016, SI 2016/1024 at **[6.2]**.

[7.1437]

12 Application of other subordinate legislation

Schedule 5 applies other subordinate legislation in relation to a relevant society with the modifications set out in that Schedule.

NOTES

Commencement: 6 April 2014.

[7.1438]

[13 Modified application of section 111 of the 2014 Act

(1) Paragraph (2) applies where, in relation to a relevant society which is in administration, the administrator's proposals under paragraph 49 or a revision to proposals under paragraph 54 include relevant provision.

(2) Section 111 of the 2014 Act (special resolutions under section 109 or 110) has effect as if—

(a) it provided that—
(i) the second meeting referred to in subsection (2) is to be treated as having been summoned by the administrator for consideration of the proposals or the revision under paragraph 53 or 54;
(ii) where that meeting confirms the resolution passed in relation to the relevant provision at the first meeting referred to in subsection (2), the relevant provision is to be treated as approved by the members of the society for the purposes of paragraph 53(1) or 54(5);
(b) in subsection (5) for the words from "Within 14 days" to "a copy of it" there were substituted "The society must send the FCA a copy of the special resolution that is"; and
(c) subsection (8) were omitted.

(3) In this article—
(a) a reference to a numbered paragraph, except the reference to paragraph (2) of this article, is a reference to the paragraph so numbered in Schedule B1 to the Insolvency Act 1986 as applied in relation to a relevant society by this Order; and
(b) "relevant provision" means provision for amalgamation in pursuance of section 109 of the 2014 Act (amalgamation of societies) or for a transfer of engagements in pursuance of section 110 of that Act (transfer of engagements between societies).]

NOTES

Commencement: 1 August 2014.

Substituted, together with arts 14, 15, for arts 13–16 as originally enacted, by the Co-operative and Community Benefit Societies and Credit Unions (Arrangements, Reconstructions and Administration) (Amendment) Order 2014, SI 2014/1822, arts 2, 4.

[7.1439]

[14 Modified application of section 113 of the 2014 Act

(1) Paragraph (2) applies where, in relation to a relevant society which is in administration, the administrator's proposals under paragraph 49 or a revision to proposals under paragraph 54 include relevant provision.

(2) Section 113 of the 2014 Act (special resolutions under section 112) has effect as if—
(a) it provided that—
(i) the second meeting referred to in subsection (2) is to be treated as having been summoned by the administrator for consideration of the proposals or the revision under paragraph 53 or 54;
(ii) where that meeting confirms the resolution passed in relation to the relevant provision at the first meeting referred to in subsection (2), the relevant provision is to be treated as approved by the members of the society for the purposes of paragraph 53(1) or 54(5);
(b) in subsection (5) the words from "Within 14 days from the day of the second meeting," were omitted; and
(c) subsection (8) were omitted.

(3) In this article—
(a) a reference to a numbered paragraph, except the reference to paragraph (2) of this article, is a reference to the paragraph so numbered in Schedule B1 to the Insolvency Act 1986 as applied in relation to a relevant society by this Order; and
(b) "relevant provision" means provision in pursuance of section 112 of the 2014 Act (conversion of society into a company, amalgamation with a company etc) for conversion into a company, amalgamation with a company or a transfer of engagements to a company.]

NOTES

Commencement: 1 August 2014.

Substituted as noted to art 13 at **[7.1438]**.

[7.1440]

[15 Modified application of section 126 of the 2014 Act

Section 126 of the 2014 Act (dissolution etc to occur only after society's property dealt with) has effect in relation to a relevant society which is in administration as if in subsection (3) the reference to the liquidator included a reference to the administrator.]

NOTES

Commencement: 1 August 2014.

Substituted as noted to art 13 at **[7.1438]**.

17 (*Inserted the Industrial and Provident Societies Act 1965, s 43A and amended ss 49, 55, 74 thereof (all repealed).*)

SCHEDULE 1
MODIFIED APPLICATION OF PARTS 1 AND 2 OF THE INSOLVENCY ACT 1986 TO RELEVANT SOCIETIES

Article 2(1) and (2)

PART 1
GENERAL MODIFICATIONS

[7.1441]

1 Unless the context otherwise requires and subject to any further modification in this Schedule, in Parts 1 and 2 of the 1986 Act—

(a) a reference to a provision of that Act or to Part 26 of the 2006 Act is a reference to that provision or that Part as applied in relation to a relevant society;

(b) an expression defined in that Act (but not an expression modified by this paragraph) has the meaning given in the Act with the modification that a reference to a company includes a reference to a relevant society;

(c) a reference to a company includes a reference to a relevant society;

(d) a reference to a company registered in England and Wales includes a reference to a relevant society whose registered office is situated in England and Wales;

(e) a reference to a company registered in Scotland includes a reference to a relevant society whose registered office is situated in Scotland;

(f) a reference to a company's creditors does not include a reference to a member of a relevant society to whom an amount is owed by the society if, but only in so far as, the amount concerned is owed in respect of the member's shares;

(g) a reference to the directors of a company is a reference to the members of the committee of a relevant society;

(h) a reference to a meeting of a company or of the members of a company is a reference to a general meeting of a relevant society and, in relation to a society whose rules allow the members to appoint delegates for meetings of the society or its members, includes a reference to a general meeting for which delegates have been appointed;

(i) a reference to a member of a company is a reference to a person whose name is entered as a member in the register kept by a relevant society in accordance with [section 30(1) of the 2014 Act] (register of members and officers);

(j) a reference to an officer of a company is a reference to an officer of a relevant society; and

(k) a reference to the registrar of companies is a reference to the FCA in its capacity as the authority responsible for the registration of a relevant society under [the 2014 Act].

NOTES

Commencement: 6 April 2014.

In sub-paras (i), (k) words in square brackets substituted by the Co-operative and Community Benefit Societies and Credit Unions (Arrangements, Reconstructions and Administration) (Amendment) Order 2014, SI 2014/1822, arts 2, 5(a).

PART 2
MODIFIED APPLICATION OF PART 1 OF THE INSOLVENCY ACT 1986 TO RELEVANT SOCIETIES (FURTHER MODIFICATIONS)

[7.1442]

2 Part 1 of the 1986 Act applies in relation to a relevant society with the further modifications set out in this Part and with any other necessary modification.

3 Part 1 (company voluntary arrangements)

Section 1 of the 1986 Act (those who may propose an arrangement) has effect as if—

(a) it required any proposal under Part 1 to be so framed as to enable a relevant society to comply with the rules of the society and the provisions of [the 2014 Act] and the Credit Unions Act 1979; and

(b) in subsection (1) the reference to debts included a reference to any amount owed by the society in respect of a member's shares where—

  (i) the society is an authorised deposit taker; and

  (ii) the amount concerned is owed in respect of a deposit.

[3A Sections 2 to 6 and 7 of, and Schedule A1 to, the 1986 Act have effect without the amendments of those provisions made by paragraphs 2 to 9 of Schedule 9 to the 2015 Act (further amendments relating to the abolition of requirements to hold meetings: company voluntary arrangements).]

4 Section 3 of the 1986 Act (summoning of meetings) has effect as if subsection (3) provided that the persons required to be summoned to a creditors' meeting included every member of the society to whom an amount is owed in respect of the member's shares where—

(a) the society is an authorised deposit taker; and

(b) the amount concerned is owed in respect of a deposit.

5 Section 7A of the 1986 Act (prosecution of delinquent officers of company) has effect as if—

(a) in subsection (2), in the definition of "the appropriate authority"—

  (i) at the end of sub-paragraph (i) there were added "or the Financial Conduct Authority ("the FCA")";

(ii) at the end of sub-paragraph (ii) there were added "or the FCA";

(b) for subsection (3) there were substituted—

"(3) Subsection (3A) applies where a report is made to the Secretary of State or the FCA under subsection (2) in relation to a relevant society (within the meaning given in [article 1(2) of the Co-operative and Community Benefit Societies and Credit Unions (Arrangements, Reconstructions and Administration) Order 2014]) whose registered office is situated in England and Wales.

(3A) The Secretary of State or the FCA may, for the purpose of investigating the matter reported and such other matters relating to the society's affairs as appear to require investigation, exercise the power to appoint inspectors which would be exercisable by the FCA under [section 106 of the Co-operative and Community Benefit Societies Act 2014] upon an application made for that purpose under subsection (1) of that section.";

(c) subsections (4) to (7) were omitted; and

(d) in subsection (8), for the definition of "prosecuting authority" there were substituted—

""prosecuting authority" means—

(a) in the case of a relevant society whose registered office is situated in England and Wales, the Director of Public Prosecutions, the Secretary of State or the FCA; and

(b) in the case of a relevant society whose registered office is situated in Scotland, the Lord Advocate.".

6 Schedule A1 (moratorium where directors propose voluntary arrangement)

In Schedule A1 to the 1986 Act paragraph 1 (interpretation) has effect as if—

(a) before the definition of "the beginning of the moratorium" there were inserted—

""administrative receiver", in relation to a relevant society whose registered office is situated in England or Wales, means—

(a) a receiver or manager of the whole (or substantially the whole) of the society's property appointed by or on behalf of the holder of a floating charge, or

(b) a person who would be such a receiver or manager but for the appointment of some other person as the receiver of part of the society's property,"; and

(b) after the definition of "the nominee" there were inserted—

""relevant society" means a [registered society (within the meaning given by section 1(1) of the Co-operative and Community Benefit Societies Act 2014) which] is not—

(a) a private registered provider of social housing; or

(b) registered as a social landlord under Part 1 of the Housing Act 1996 or under Part 2 of the Housing (Scotland) Act 2010,".

7 Schedule A1 to the 1986 Act has effect as if after paragraph 1 there were inserted—

"1A (1) In this Schedule a reference to a floating charge, in relation to a relevant society whose registered office is situated in England or Wales, is a reference to a floating charge which . . . is either—

(a) a charge in respect of which an application has been made for the purposes of [section 59 of the Co-operative and Community Benefit Societies Act 2014]; or

(b) created by a debenture registered under section 9 of the Agricultural Credits Act 1928 as applied by section 14 of that Act.

(2) In this Schedule a reference to a floating charge, in relation to a relevant society whose registered office is situated in Scotland, is a reference to a floating charge which . . . is either—

(a) a charge created by an instrument a copy of which has been delivered to the Financial Conduct Authority in pursuance of [section 63 of the Co-operative and Community Benefit Societies Act 2014]; or

(b) created and registered under Part 2 of the Agricultural Credits (Scotland) Act 1929.".

8 Schedule A1 to the 1986 Act has effect as if—

(a) in paragraph 2 (companies eligible for a moratorium) in sub-paragraph (1) the words "if it meets the requirements of paragraph 3," were omitted;

(b) paragraph 3 (requirements for eligibility for a moratorium) were omitted; and

(c) paragraph 5 (power to modify qualifications for eligibility) were omitted.

NOTES

Commencement: 6 April 2014.

Paras 3, 5–7: words in square brackets substituted by the Co-operative and Community Benefit Societies and Credit Unions (Arrangements, Reconstructions and Administration) (Amendment) Order 2014, SI 2014/1822, arts 2, 5(b)–(e).

Para 3A: inserted by the Small Business, Enterprise and Employment Act 2015 (Consequential Amendments, Savings and Transitional Provisions) Regulations 2018, SI 2018/208, reg 15(1), (3)(a).

PART 3
MODIFIED APPLICATION OF PART 2 OF THE INSOLVENCY ACT 1986 TO RELEVANT SOCIETIES (FURTHER MODIFICATIONS)

[7.1443]

9 Part 2 of the 1986 Act applies in relation to a relevant society with the further modifications set out in this Part and with any other necessary modification.

10 In this Part—

(a) a reference to a numbered paragraph is a reference to the paragraph so numbered in Schedule B1 to the 1986 Act (administration); and

(b) a reference to a sub-paragraph is a reference to a sub-paragraph of such a paragraph.

[10A Creditors' meetings and creditors' notices

Schedule B1 to the 1986 Act has effect without the amendments made by paragraph 10 of Schedule 9 to the 2015 Act (further amendments relating to the abolition of requirements to hold meetings; opted-out creditors: administration).]

11 Nature of administration

Paragraph 3 (purpose of administration) has effect as if a reference to the company's creditors as a whole included a reference to any member of the society to whom an amount is owed in respect of the member's shares where—

(a) the society is an authorised deposit taker; and

(b) the amount concerned is owed in respect of a deposit.

12 Appointment of administrator by court

Paragraph 12 (administration application) has effect as if—

(a) in sub-paragraph (1)(c) the reference to the company's creditors included a reference to any member of the society who would be entitled to petition for the winding up of the society;

(b) sub-paragraph (1) provided that—

(i) an application to the court for an administration order may also be made by the FCA in its capacity as the authority responsible for the registration of the society under [the 2014 Act]; and

(ii) in the case of a relevant society which is or has been an authorised person, such power is in addition to the power to make an administration application conferred on the FCA by section 359 of FSMA (administration order); and

(c) sub-paragraph (2) required the applicant also to notify the FCA (unless the FCA is the applicant).

13 Appointment of administrator by holder of floating charge

In paragraph 14 (power to appoint) sub-paragraph (2) has effect as if—

(a) paragraph (a) required the instrument to include the following statement—

"Paragraph 14 of Schedule B1 to the Insolvency Act 1986, as applied in relation to relevant societies by article 2(2) of the Industrial and Provident Societies and Credit Unions (Arrangements, Reconstructions and Administration) Order 2014, applies to this floating charge.";

(b) in paragraph (c) the words "within the meaning given by section 29(2)" were omitted; and

(c) paragraph (d) were omitted.

14 Paragraph 15 (restrictions on power to appoint) has effect as if for sub-paragraph (3) there were substituted—

"(3) In relation to a relevant society whose registered office is situated in Scotland, sub-paragraph (2) has effect as if the following were substituted for paragraph (a)—

"(a) it has priority of ranking in accordance with section 464(4)(b) of the Companies Act 1985 as applied in relation to a relevant society by [section 62 of the Co-operative and Community Benefit Societies Act 2014],"."

15 Effect of administration

In paragraph 41 (dismissal of administrative or other receiver), in sub-paragraph (3) ignore paragraph (b).

16 In paragraph 45 (publicity) sub-paragraph (3) has effect as if after paragraph (b) there were inserted—

"(ba) a statement of account,

(bb) an advertisement,".

17 Paragraph 46 (announcement of administrator's appointment) has effect as if sub-paragraph (2) required the administrator to send a notice of appointment also to every member of the society.

18 Process of administration

Paragraph 49 (administrator's proposals) has effect as if—

(a) after sub-paragraph (3) there were inserted—

"(3A) In the case of a relevant society, proposals under this paragraph may include provision for amending the society's rules only if the Financial Conduct Authority has issued a statement to the effect that it would register an amendment in the terms proposed if copies were [given to it for registration in accordance with section 16 of the Co-operative and Community Benefit Societies Act 2014 ("the 2014 Act")].

(3B) The proposals must not include any measure which would be contrary to the provisions of [the 2014 Act] or the Credit Unions Act 1979.

(3C) Sub-paragraph (3A) does not apply if the intended effect of the proposals is that the society will cease to be [a registered society (within the meaning given by section 1(1) of the 2014 Act)].";

(b) in sub-paragraph (4)(c) the words "of whose address he is aware" were omitted; and
(c) sub-paragraph (6) were omitted.

19 Paragraph 51 (requirement for initial creditors' meeting) has effect as if—
(a) after sub-paragraph (1) there were inserted—

"(1A) Each copy of an administrator's statement of proposals sent to a member under paragraph 49(4)(c) must be accompanied by an invitation to a members' meeting."; and

(b) in sub-paragraphs (2) and (3) the reference to an initial creditors' meeting included a reference to a members' meeting.

20 Paragraph 52 (requirement for initial creditors' meeting) has effect as if—
(a) in sub-paragraph (1) for "Paragraph 51(1)" there were substituted "Paragraph 51(1) and (1A)"; and
(b) where the administrator is required to summon an initial creditors' meeting under sub-paragraph (2), it required the administrator also to summon a members' meeting for a date within the period mentioned in sub-paragraph (3).

21 In paragraph 53 (business and result of initial creditors' meeting), in sub-paragraphs (1) and (2) the reference to an initial creditors' meeting includes a reference to a members' meeting.

22 Paragraph 54 (revision of administrator's proposals) has effect as if—
(a) in sub-paragraph (1) the reference to an initial creditors' meeting, and in sub-paragraphs (2) and (5) the reference to a creditors' meeting, included a reference to a members' meeting;
(b) after sub-paragraph (1) there were inserted—

"(1A) Where a revision is proposed in the case of a relevant society, sub-paragraphs (3A) to (3C) of paragraph 49 apply in relation to the revision.";

(c) sub-paragraph (2) required the administrator—
(i) to summon a members' meeting (as well as a creditors' meeting); and
(ii) to send a statement of the proposed revision in the prescribed form (as well as to each creditor) to every member of the society;
(d) sub-paragraphs (2)(c) and (3) were omitted; and
(e) sub-paragraph (6) required the administrator to report any decision taken at a creditors' meeting and any decision taken at a members' meeting as soon as is reasonably practicable after the conclusion of both meetings.

23 In paragraph 55 (failure to obtain approval of administrator's proposals) sub-paragraph (1) has effect as if after "an initial creditors' meeting" and "a creditors' meeting" there were inserted "or a members' meeting".

24 Paragraph 56 (further creditors' meetings) has effect as if—
(a) in sub-paragraph (1)(a) the reference to creditors of the company whose debts amount to at least 10% of the total debts of the company were a reference to at least 10% of the total number of creditors of the society or to creditors whose debts amount to at least 10% of the total debts of the society;
(b) sub-paragraph (1) also required the administrator to summon a meeting of the society's members if—
(i) a meeting is requested in the same manner prescribed for a creditors' meeting by at least 10% of the total number of those members; or
(ii) the administrator is directed to do so by the court; and
(c) in sub-paragraph (2) the reference to a creditors' meeting included a reference to a members' meeting.

25 In paragraph 58 (correspondence instead of creditors' meeting)—
(a) a reference to a creditors' meeting includes a reference to a members' meeting; and
(b) in sub-paragraph (1) the reference to correspondence between the administrator and creditors includes a reference to correspondence between the administrator and members.

26 Functions of administrator

Paragraph 59 (general powers) has effect as if it required the administrator to ensure compliance with the rules of the society and the provisions of [the 2014 Act] and the Credit Unions Act 1979.

27 Paragraph 61 (removal and appointment of director) has effect as if it required the administrator not to appoint any person to be an officer of the society unless that person is a fit and proper person to hold that position.

28 In paragraph 64 (exercise of management power), in sub-paragraph (2)(b) the reference to an instrument includes a reference to the rules of the society.

29 In paragraph 65 (distribution) sub-paragraph (1) has effect as if it provided that the administrator may make a distribution to a member of the society in relation to any amount owed by the society in respect of the member's shares where—
(a) the society is an authorised deposit taker; and
(b) the amount concerned is owed in respect of a deposit.

30 Ending administration

In paragraph 80 (termination of administration where objective achieved)—

(a) sub-paragraph (4) has effect as if it required the administrator, where the administrator sends a copy of a notice filed under sub-paragraph (2) to creditors, to send a copy also to the members of the society; and

(b) in sub-paragraph (5) a reference to a creditor includes a reference to a member of the society.

31 In paragraph 84 (moving from administration to dissolution) sub-paragraph (5) has effect as if it required the administrator, where the administrator sends a copy of a notice under sub-paragraph (1) to creditors, to send a copy also to the members of the society.

32 Replacing administrator

Paragraph 91 (supplying vacancy in office of administrator) has effect as if in sub-paragraph (1) after paragraph (c) there were inserted—

"(ca) in the case of a relevant society, the Financial Conduct Authority,

(cb) in the case of a relevant society which is or has been a PRA-authorised person (within the meaning given in section 2B(5) of the Financial Services and Markets Act 2000), the Financial Conduct Authority or the Prudential Regulation Authority,".

33 Paragraph 96 (substitution of administrator: competing floating charge-holder) has effect as if for sub-paragraph (4) there were substituted—

"(4) In relation to a relevant society whose registered office is situated in Scotland, sub-paragraph (3) has effect as if the following were substituted for paragraph (a)—

"(a) it has priority of ranking in accordance with section 464(4)(b) of the Companies Act 1985 as applied in relation to a relevant society by [section 62 of the Co-operative and Community Benefit Societies Act 2014],"."

34 General

Paragraph 111 (interpretation) has effect as if—

(a) "administrative receiver" and "floating charge" were given the same meaning as in Schedule A1 to the 1986 Act (as applied in relation to a relevant society); and

(b) there were inserted at the appropriate place—

""relevant society" means a [registered society (within the meaning given by section 1(1) of the Co-operative and Community Benefit Societies Act 2014) which] is not—

(a) a private registered provider of social housing; or

(b) registered as a social landlord under Part 1 of the Housing Act 1996 or under Part 2 of the Housing (Scotland) Act 2010,".

NOTES

Commencement: 6 April 2014.

Para 10A: inserted by the Small Business, Enterprise and Employment Act 2015 (Consequential Amendments, Savings and Transitional Provisions) Regulations 2018, SI 2018/208, reg 15(1), (3)(b).

Paras 12, 14, 18, 26, 33, 34: words in square brackets substituted by the Co-operative and Community Benefit Societies and Credit Unions (Arrangements, Reconstructions and Administration) (Amendment) Order 2014, SI 2014/1822, arts 2, 5(f)–(k).

PART 4
MODIFIED APPLICATION OF SCHEDULE 1 TO THE INSOLVENCY ACT 1986 TO RELEVANT SOCIETIES (FURTHER MODIFICATIONS)

[7.1444]

35 Schedule 1 to the 1986 Act applies in relation to a relevant society with the further modifications set out in this Part and with any other necessary modification.

36 This Part has effect without limiting paragraph 26 of this Schedule.

37 In this Part—

(a) a reference to a numbered paragraph is a reference to the paragraph so numbered in Schedule 1 to the 1986 Act;

(b) "the 1979 Act" means the Credit Unions Act 1979; and

(c) "credit union" has the meaning given in section 31(1) of the 1979 Act.

38 Paragraph 3 (power to borrow) has effect as if it provided that power to raise or borrow money and grant security over the property of the society—

(a) in the case of a credit union, is subject to—

(i) the provisions of [Chapters 1 and 2 of Part 5 of the 2014 Act (charges over a society's assets)];

(ii) section 7 (shares), section 7A (power to issue interest-bearing shares) and section 8 (general prohibition on deposit-taking) of the 1979 Act; and

(iii) the rules of the society containing provision in respect of the matters mentioned in paragraph 7 of Schedule 1 to the 1979 Act (determination of the maximum amount of the interest in the shares of the society which may be held by any member);

(b) in the case of a relevant society which is not a credit union, is subject to—

[(i) section 24 (maximum interest in a society's withdrawable shares) and section 67 (registered society with withdrawable share capital not to carry on banking etc) of the 2014 Act;

(ii) paragraphs 6 to 8 of Schedule 3 to the 2014 Act (provision about maximum shareholding and maximum deposits for certain societies registered or treated as registered before 1st August 2014);

(iii) the provisions of Chapters 1 and 2 of Part 5 of the 2014 Act (charges over a society's assets); and

(iv) the rules of the society which make provision in accordance with section 14 of the 2014 Act (content of a society's rules) about maximum shareholding and borrowing powers;] and

(c) in either such case, is subject to such other enactments and such rules of the society as govern or restrict the exercise of that power.

39 Paragraphs 15 (power to establish subsidiaries) and 16 (power to transfer property to subsidiaries) do not apply in relation to credit unions.

40 Paragraph 16 has effect in relation to a relevant society other than a credit union as if—

(a) the reference to subsidiaries were a reference to subsidiaries within the meaning given in [section 100 (meaning of company being a "subsidiary" of a society) or section 101 (meaning of society being a "subsidiary" of another society) of the 2014 Act]; and

(b) it provided that power to transfer to subsidiaries of the society the whole or any part of the business or property of the society is only exercisable in accordance with a special resolution under [section 110 (transfer of engagements between societies) or section 112 (conversion of society into a company, amalgamation with a company etc) of the 2014 Act] (as modified in relation to a relevant society by articles 14 and 15).

NOTES

Commencement: 6 April 2014.

Paras 38, 40: words in square brackets substituted by the Co-operative and Community Benefit Societies and Credit Unions (Arrangements, Reconstructions and Administration) (Amendment) Order 2014, SI 2014/1822, arts 2, 5(l), (m).

SCHEDULE 2
MODIFIED APPLICATION OF PART 26 OF THE COMPANIES ACT 2006 TO RELEVANT SOCIETIES

Article 2(3)

[7.1445]

1 Unless the context otherwise requires and subject to any further modification in this Schedule, in Part 26 of the 2006 Act—

(a) a reference to the articles of a company is a reference to the rules of a relevant society;

(b) a reference to a class of members is to be ignored;

(c) a reference to a company includes a reference to a relevant society;

(d) a reference to a company's creditors does not include a reference to a member of a relevant society to whom an amount is owed by the society if, but only in so far as, the amount concerned is owed in respect of the member's shares;

(e) a reference to the directors of a company is a reference to the members of the committee of a relevant society;

(f) a reference to a member of a company is a reference to a person whose name is entered as a member in the register kept by a relevant society in accordance with [section 30(1) of the 2014 Act];

(g) a reference to an officer of a company is a reference to an officer of a relevant society; and

(h) a reference to the registrar is a reference to the FCA in its capacity as the authority responsible for the registration of a relevant society under [the 2014 Act].

2 Part 26 of the 2006 Act applies in relation to a relevant society with the further modifications set out in the following paragraphs of this Schedule and with any other necessary modification.

3 In section 895 (application of Part 26) subsection (2) has effect as if after the definition of "company" there were inserted—

""relevant society" means a [registered society (within the meaning given by section 1(1) of the Co-operative and Community Benefit Societies Act 2014) which] is not—

(a) a private registered provider of social housing; or

(b) registered as a social landlord under Part 1 of the Housing Act 1996 or under Part 2 of the Housing (Scotland) Act 2010.".

4 In section 899 (court sanction for compromise or arrangement)—

(a) in subsection (1) the reference to a majority in number representing 75% in value of the members present and voting at the meeting summoned under section 896 is a reference to 75% of the members of a relevant society present and voting at that meeting; and

(b) in subsection (3)(b) the reference to contributories has the same meaning as it has in relation to a relevant society in the 1986 Act.

5 Section 900 (powers of court to facilitate reconstruction or amalgamation) has effect as if after subsection (4) there were inserted—

"(4A) Subsection (4B) applies where a compromise or arrangement is proposed for the purposes of, or in connection with, a scheme for the reconstruction of a relevant society or the amalgamation of a relevant society with any other relevant society or any company.

(4B) An order under this section may only be made with respect to the compromise or arrangement if the Financial Conduct Authority—

(a) is satisfied that the compromise or arrangement is not contrary to the rules of the society or the provisions of [the 2014 Act] or the Credit Unions Act 1979; and

(b) has issued a statement to that effect.".

6 Section 901 (obligations of company with respect to articles etc) has effect as if after subsection (1) there were inserted—

"(1A) Where, in the case of a relevant society, the compromise or arrangement includes provision for amending the society's rules, the order may be made only if the Financial Conduct Authority has issued a statement to the effect that it would register an amendment in the terms proposed if copies were [given to it for registration in accordance with section 16 of the Co-operative and Community Benefit Societies Act 2014].

(1B) Subsection (1A) does not apply if the intended effect of the compromise or arrangement is that the society will cease to be registered under that Act.".

7 Where a copy of any order or other document is delivered to the FCA under section 899(4), 900(6) or 901(2) (in each case as applied in relation to a relevant society by article 2(3)), that provision also has effect as if it required the document concerned to be delivered—

(a) in the case of a relevant society which is or has been an authorised person but not a PRA-authorised person, also to the FCA in its capacity as the society's regulator;

(b) in the case of a relevant society which is or has been a PRA-authorised person, also to the Prudential Regulation Authority;

(c) in the case of a relevant society which is a relevant person, also to the scheme manager.

8 In paragraph 7—

"PRA-authorised person" has the meaning given in section 2B(5) of FSMA;

"regulator" has the meaning given in section 3A of FSMA; and

"the scheme manager" means the body corporate established by the Financial Services Authority under section 212 of FSMA (the manager of the Financial Services Compensation Scheme) as originally enacted.

NOTES

Commencement: 6 April 2014.

Paras 1, 3, 5, 6: words in square brackets substituted by the Co-operative and Community Benefit Societies and Credit Unions (Arrangements, Reconstructions and Administration) (Amendment) Order 2014, SI 2014/1822, arts 2, 6.

SCHEDULE 3
MODIFIED APPLICATION OF OTHER PROVISIONS OF THE INSOLVENCY ACT 1986

Article 4

[7.1446]

1 Interpretation

In this Schedule, unless otherwise specified, a reference to a section is a reference to a section of the 1986 Act.

2 Modification of provisions applied by article 4

Unless the context otherwise requires, the provisions applied by article 4 have effect—

(a) with the modifications set out in this Schedule;

(b) subject to those modifications [and unless otherwise specified in this Schedule], with the modifications in paragraph 1 of Schedule 1; and

(c) with any other necessary modification.

3 Miscellaneous provisions applying to companies which are insolvent

For the purpose of construing the reference to an associate in subsection (3) of section 242 (gratuitous alienations (Scotland)), section 74 of the Bankruptcy (Scotland) Act 1985 (meaning of "associate") has effect as if—

(a) a reference to the directors of a company were a reference to the members of the committee of the society; and

(b) a reference to an officer of a company were a reference to an officer of the society.

4 Interpretation for first group of Parts

Section 251 (expressions used generally) has effect as if the definitions of "administrative receiver", "director", "floating charge" and "officer" were omitted.

5 [Insolvency practitioners: qualification and regulation]

Section 388 (meaning of "act as an insolvency practitioner") has effect as if in subsection (4) the definition of "company" included a reference to a relevant society.

[5A Section 390 (persons not qualified to act as insolvency practitioners) has effect as if for subsection (2) there were substituted—

"(2) A person is not qualified to act as an insolvency practitioner in relation to a relevant society (within the meaning given in article 1(2) of the Co-operative and Community Benefit Societies and Credit Unions (Arrangements, Reconstructions and Administration) Order 2014) at any time unless at that time the person is fully authorised to act as an insolvency practitioner or partially authorised to act as an insolvency practitioner only in relation to companies.".

5B (1) In the following provisions, in a reference to authorisation or permission to act as an insolvency practitioner in relation to (or only in relation to) companies the reference to companies has effect without the modification in paragraph 1(c) of Schedule 1—

(a) sections 390A and 390B(1) and (3) (authorisation of insolvency practitioners); and

(b) sections 391O(1)(b) and 391R(3)(b) (court sanction of insolvency practitioners in public interest cases).

(2) In sections 391Q(2)(b) (direct sanctions order: conditions) and 391S(3)(e) (power for Secretary of State to obtain information) the reference to a company has effect without the modification in paragraph 1(c) of Schedule 1.]

[5C Creditors' meetings

Part 6 of the 1986 Act and sections 387, 433 and 434B have effect without the amendments of those provisions made by—

(a) section 122 of the 2015 Act (abolition of requirements to hold meetings: company insolvency); and

(b) paragraphs 54 to 57 of Schedule 9 to that Act (further amendments relating to section 122).

5D Creditors' notices

Parts 6 and 7 of the 1986 Act have effect without the amendments of those Parts made by section 124 of the 2015 Act (ability for creditors to opt not to receive certain notices: company insolvency).]

6 Punishment of offences

Sections 430 (provision introducing Schedule of punishments), 431 (summary proceedings) and 432 (offences by bodies corporate) have effect as if a reference to an offence under the 1986 Act or a provision of that Act, in so far as it is a reference to an offence under a provision of that Act applied in relation to a relevant society, were a reference to the offence under that provision as so applied.

7 Schedule 10 to the 1986 Act (punishment of offences under the Act) has effect as if a reference in that Schedule to a provision which is applied in relation to a relevant society were a reference to that provision as so applied.

[8 Schedule 10 to the 1986 Act also has effect without the amendments made by paragraph 11 of Schedule 9 to the 2015 Act.]

NOTES

Commencement: 6 April 2014.

Para 2: words in square brackets in sub-para (b) inserted by the Deregulation Act 2015, the Small Business, Enterprise and Employment Act 2015 and the Insolvency (Amendment) Act (Northern Ireland) 2016 (Consequential Amendments and Transitional Provisions) Regulations 2017, SI 2017/400, reg 12(1), (3)(a).

Para 5: words in square brackets in the heading substituted by SI 2017/400, reg 12(1), (3)(b).

Paras 5A, 5B: inserted by SI 2017/400, reg 12(1), (3)(c).

Paras 5C, 5D: inserted by the Small Business, Enterprise and Employment Act 2015 (Consequential Amendments, Savings and Transitional Provisions) Regulations 2018, SI 2018/208, reg 15(1), (4)(a).

Para 8: added by SI 2018/208, reg 15(1), (4)(b).

SCHEDULE 4
MODIFIED APPLICATION OF INSOLVENCY RULES IN RELATION TO RELEVANT SOCIETIES

Article 11(5)

PART 1
INTERPRETATION

[7.1447]

1 In this Schedule—

"applied provisions"—

(a) in Part 2, means the Parts of the Insolvency Rules 1986 which are applied by article 11(1) and (3);

(b) in Part 3, means the Parts of the Insolvency (Scotland) Rules 1986 which are applied by article 11(2) and (4);

"member-depositor", in relation to a relevant society, means any member of the society to whom an amount is owed in respect of the member's shares where—

(a) the society is an authorised deposit taker; and

(b) the amount concerned is owed in respect of a deposit;

"Schedule A1" means Schedule A1 to the 1986 Act as applied in relation to a relevant society;

"Schedule B1" means Schedule B1 to the 1986 Act as applied in relation to a relevant society; and "the scheme manager" means the body corporate established by the Financial Services Authority under section 212 of FSMA (the manager of the Financial Services Compensation Scheme) as originally enacted.

2 In this Schedule—

(a) a reference to the FCA is a reference to the FCA in its capacity as the authority responsible for the registration of a relevant society under [the 2014 Act]; and

(b) a reference to the society's regulator—

(i) in relation to a relevant society which is or has been a PRA-authorised person (within the meaning given in section 2B(5) of FSMA), is a reference to—

(aa) the FCA in its capacity as regulator (within the meaning given in section 3A of FSMA) of the society; and

(bb) the Prudential Regulation Authority;

(ii) in relation to any other relevant society which is or has been an authorised person, to the FCA in its capacity as regulator of the society.

NOTES

Commencement: 6 April 2014.

Para 2: words in square brackets substituted by the Co-operative and Community Benefit Societies and Credit Unions (Arrangements, Reconstructions and Administration) (Amendment) Order 2014, SI 2014/1822, arts 2, 7(a).

Note that the Insolvency Rules 1986, SI 1986/1925 are revoked and replaced (as from 6 April 2017 and subject to transitional provisions) by the Insolvency (England and Wales) Rules 2016, SI 2016/1024 at **[6.2]**.

PART 2
MODIFIED APPLICATION OF THE INSOLVENCY RULES 1986

[7.1448]

3 This Part modifies the Parts of the Insolvency Rules 1986 which are applied by article 11(1) and (3) in relation to a relevant society which the courts in England and Wales have jurisdiction to wind up.

4 Unless the context otherwise requires and subject to any further modification in this Part, the applied provisions have effect with the following general modifications—

(a) a reference to Part 1 or any provision of Part 1, 2, 4, 6, 7 or 17 of the 1986 Act is a reference to that Part or provision as applied in relation to a relevant society;

(b) an expression defined in the 1986 Act (but not an expression modified by this paragraph) has the meaning given in that Act as read with any modification made by this Order;

(c) a reference to an administrative receiver is a reference to an administrative receiver within the meaning given in Schedule A1 in relation to a relevant society whose registered office is situated in England or Wales;

(d) a reference to the articles of a company is a reference to the rules of a relevant society;

(e) a reference to a class of creditors includes a reference to a single class of members of a relevant society that consists of the member-depositors of the society, but only in so far as the member-depositors are owed amounts in respect of deposits;

(f) a reference to a company includes a reference to a relevant society;

(g) a reference to a company's creditors, other than in a reference to a class of creditors, does not include a reference to a member of a relevant society to whom an amount is owed by the society if, but only in so far as, the amount concerned is owed in respect of the member's shares;

(h) a reference to the directors of a company is a reference to the members of the committee of a relevant society;

(i) a reference to a floating charge is a reference to a floating charge within the meaning given in Schedule A1 in relation to a relevant society whose registered office is situated in England or Wales;

(j) a reference to a meeting of a company or of the members of a company is a reference to a general meeting of a relevant society and, in relation to a society whose rules allow the members to appoint delegates for meetings of the society or its members, includes a reference to a general meeting for which delegates have been appointed;

(k) a reference to an officer of a company is a reference to an officer of a relevant society; and

(l) a reference to the registrar of companies is a reference to the FCA.

5 The applied provisions have effect as if they provided that a person appointed for the purpose by the FCA is entitled—

(a) to attend any meeting of creditors of a relevant society summoned for the purposes of Part 1 or 2 of the 1986 Act (as applied in relation to a relevant society);

(b) to attend any meeting of a committee established under paragraph 57 of Schedule B1; and

(c) to make representations as to any matter for decision at such a meeting.

6 The applied provisions have effect with the further modifications set out in this Part and with any other necessary modification.

7 Proposal by directors for company voluntary arrangement

In Rule 1.6 (additional disclosure for assistance of nominee), in paragraph (2)(a) the reference to any other company is a reference to any company or any other relevant society.

8 Consideration of proposals where moratorium obtained

In Rule 1.48 (summoning of meetings), in paragraph (3) the reference to all persons who are, to the best of the nominee's belief, members of the company is a reference to every member of the society.

9 Appointment of administrator by holder of floating charge

In Rule 2.16 (notice of appointment), in paragraph (5)(b) the reference to the date on which the floating charge was registered is a reference to the date on which—

(a) the FCA [gave an acknowledgement under section 59(4) of the 2014 Act] (charges on assets of English and Welsh societies) of the application for the recording of the charge made in accordance with [section 59(3)] of that Act; or

(b) the debenture creating the charge was registered under section 9 of the Agricultural Credits Act 1928 as applied by section 14 of that Act.

10 Process of administration

Rule 2.30 (limited disclosure) has effect as if it provided that on an application for disclosure under paragraph (4) a person appointed for the purpose by the FCA may appear and be heard, or make written representations.

11 Rule 2.31 (release from duty to submit statement of affairs; extension of time) has effect as if it provided that on an application under paragraph (2) for release or extension of time a person appointed for the purpose by the FCA (in addition to the administrator) may appear and be heard, or make written representations.

12 Meetings and reports

In the following Rules a reference to a creditors' meeting includes a reference to a members' meeting—

(a) Rule 2.34 (meetings to consider administrator's proposals);

(b) Rule 2.35 (creditors' meetings generally);

(c) Rule 2.36 (the chairman at meetings);

(d) Rule 2.43 (resolutions); and

(e) Rule 2.46 (notice to creditors).

13 Rule 2.35 has effect as if—

(a) paragraph (3) required the administrator, in fixing the venue for the meeting, to have regard to the convenience—

  (i) in the case of a members' meeting, of the members; and

  (ii) of any person appointed for the purpose of attending the meeting by the FCA, by the society's regulator or, in the case of a relevant society which is a relevant person, by the scheme manager; and

(b) paragraph (4) required 14 days' notice of a members' meeting to be given to all the members.

14 Rule 2.37 (meeting requisitioned by creditors) has effect as if it required the expenses of summoning and holding a members' meeting requested under paragraph 52(2) or 56(1) of Schedule B1 to be paid out of the assets of the society as an expense of the administration.

15 Rule 2.43 has effect as if—

(a) in paragraph (1) the words "(in value)" were omitted; and

(b) paragraph (2) were omitted.

16 In Rule 2.45 (revision of the administrator's proposals)—

(a) in paragraph (3) ignore the words "Subject to paragraph 54(3),"; and

(b) ignore paragraphs (4) and (5).

17 In Rule 2.47 (reports to creditors), in paragraphs (1)(g) and (4) the reference to the creditors includes a reference to the members of the society.

18 In Rule 2.48 (correspondence instead of creditors' meetings)—

(a) in paragraph (1)—

  (i) the reference to a resolution by the creditors includes a reference to a resolution by the members of the society;

  (ii) in the case of a members' resolution the reference to every creditor who is entitled to be notified of a creditors' meeting is a reference to every member;

(b) in paragraph (2), in relation to correspondence with the members, ignore the reference to the statement on entitlement to vote required by Rule 2.38; and

(c) in paragraphs (6) and (9) a reference to a creditors' meeting includes a reference to a members' meeting.

19 Rule 2.49 (venue and conduct of company meeting) has effect as if—

(a) paragraphs (1) to (4) and (7) were omitted; and

(b) in paragraph (5A) for sub-paragraph (a) there were substituted—

"(a) in the case of a relevant society (within the meaning given in [article 1(2) of the Co-operative and Community Benefit Societies and Credit Unions (Arrangements, Reconstructions and Administration) Order 2014]), in accordance with the law of England and Wales;".

Part 7J Special Insolvency Regimes

20 Distributions to creditors

Rule 2.68 (distributions to creditors: introduction) has effect in relation to a distribution, or a proposal to make a distribution, to member-depositors as if paragraph (2) required the administrator to give the notice referred to also to those members.

21 Rule 2.69 (debts of insolvent society to rank equally) has effect as if the first reference to debts included a reference to any amount owed by the society in respect of a member's shares where—
- (a) the society is an authorised deposit taker; and
- (b) the amount concerned is owed in respect of a deposit.

22 Rule 2.85 (mutual credits and set off) has effect as if in addition to the matters excluded from "mutual dealings" in paragraph (2) that paragraph excluded any mutual dealings between a relevant society and a member of the society to whom an amount is owed by the society if, but only in so far as, the amount concerned is owed in respect of the member's shares.

23 Rule 2.95 (notice of proposed distribution) has effect as if—
- (a) paragraph (1) required the administrator also to give notice where the administrator is proposing to make a distribution to member-depositors; and
- (b) paragraph (2)—
  - (i) required the notice to be sent also to every member-depositor and the FCA;
  - (ii) provided that for the purposes of that notice the reference to unsecured creditors included a reference to member-depositors.

24 In Rule 2.97 (declaration of dividend) member-depositors are to be regarded as a single class of creditors for the purposes of paragraph (1).

25 Rule 2.98 (notice of declaration of dividend) has effect as if—
- (a) the persons who are entitled to receive notice under paragraph (1) included—
  - (i) every member-depositor; and
  - (ii) the FCA; and
- (b) paragraph (2)—
  - (i) required that notice to give particulars of any distribution to member-depositors; and
  - (ii) provided that the member-depositors are unsecured creditors for the purpose of sub-paragraph (c).

26 In Rule 2.99 (payment of dividends and related matters), in paragraph (2) the reference to any creditor includes a reference to any member-depositor.

27 Rule 2.100 (notice of no dividend, or no further dividend) has effect as if—
- (a) it required the administrator to send a copy of any notice to the FCA, to the society's regulator and, in the case of a relevant society which is a relevant person, to the scheme manager; and
- (b) the reference to creditors included a reference to member-depositors.

28 Rule 2.103 (disqualification from dividend) has effect as if it required notice of the application and a copy of the order made on the application to be given to the FCA, to the society's regulator and, in the case of a relevant society which is a relevant person, to the scheme manager.

29 Ending administration

In Rule 2.112 (applications for extension of administration) the reference to the creditors in paragraph (4) and the second reference to the creditors in paragraph (5) include a reference to the members of the society.

30 In Rule 2.113 (notice of end of administration), in paragraphs (6) and (7) the reference to a creditor includes a reference to a member of the society.

31 Replacing administrator

Rule 2.120 (notice of intention to resign) has effect as if the persons who are entitled to receive notice of the administrator's intention to resign included the FCA, the society's regulator and, in the case of a relevant society which is a relevant person, the scheme manager.

32 (1) Rule 2.122 (application to court to remove administrator from office) and Rule 2.125 (application to replace administrator) have effect as if the persons who are entitled to receive notice of the matter concerned included the FCA, the society's regulator and, in the case of a relevant society which is a relevant person, the scheme manager.

(2) Sub-paragraph (1) does not apply in relation to—
- (a) the FCA, if the FCA made the application for the administration order; or
- (b) the society's regulator, if the society's regulator made the application.

33 Quorum at meetings

Rule 12A.21 (quorum at meeting of creditors) has effect in relation to a relevant society as if—
- (a) in paragraphs (1) and (4) the reference to any meeting of creditors included a reference to any meeting of members of the society; and
- (b) paragraph (2) provided that a quorum, in the case of a meeting of members—
  - (i) is to be determined according to the rules of the society which lay down a quorum for a general meeting of the society; or

(ii) if there are no such rules, is at least two members who are entitled to vote, or both of them if their number does not exceed two.

34 Forms

In Rule 12A.30 (forms for use in insolvency proceedings)—

(a) any form prescribed for use by paragraph (1) which is used for the purposes of Part 1 or 2 of the 1986 Act is to be read with the modifications set out in this Order (so far as applicable for the form concerned); and

(b) the requirement in paragraph (2) to use a form with such variations as the circumstances may require includes a requirement to use it with such variations as are necessary to take account of applicable modifications.

35 "Prescribed part"

In Rule 13.13 (expressions used generally in the Insolvency Rules 1986), in paragraph (15) (the definition of "prescribed part") the reference to the Insolvency Act 1986 (Prescribed Part) Order 2003 is a reference to that Order as applied in relation to a relevant society by article 12 of, and paragraph 1 of Schedule 5 to, this Order.

NOTES

Commencement: 6 April 2014.

Paras 9, 19: words in square brackets substituted by the Co-operative and Community Benefit Societies and Credit Unions (Arrangements, Reconstructions and Administration) (Amendment) Order 2014, SI 2014/1822, arts 2, 7(b), (c).

Note that the Insolvency Rules 1986, SI 1986/1925 are revoked and replaced (as from 6 April 2017 and subject to transitional provisions) by the Insolvency (England and Wales) Rules 2016, SI 2016/1024 at **[6.2]**.

PART 3
MODIFIED APPLICATION OF THE INSOLVENCY (SCOTLAND) RULES 1986

[7.1449]

36 This Part modifies the Parts of the Insolvency (Scotland) Rules 1986 which are applied by article 11(2) and (4) in relation to a relevant society which a sheriff court in Scotland has jurisdiction to wind up.

37 Unless the context otherwise requires and subject to any further modification in this Part, the applied provisions have effect with the general modifications set out in paragraphs 4 and 5 (read as if set out in this paragraph), except that—

(a) sub-paragraph (c) of paragraph 4 is omitted for this purpose; and

(b) a reference to a floating charge is a reference to a floating charge within the meaning given in Schedule A1 in relation to a relevant society whose registered office is situated in Scotland.

38 The applied provisions have effect with the further modifications set out in this Part and with any other necessary modification.

39 Proposal by directors for company voluntary arrangement

In Rule 1.6 (additional disclosure for assistance of nominee), in paragraph (2)(a) the reference to any other company is a reference to any company or any other relevant society.

40 Consideration of proposals where moratorium obtained

In Rule 1.40 (summoning of meetings; procedure at meetings etc), in paragraph (3) the reference to all persons who are, to the best of the nominee's belief, members of the company is a reference to every member of the society.

41 Appointment of administrator by holder of floating charge

In Rule 2.10 (notice of appointment), in paragraph (5)(b) the reference to the date on which the floating charge was registered is a reference to the date—

(a) stated in the FCA's acknowledgement [given under section 63(4) of the 2014 Act] (filing of information relating to charges) on which the delivery of a copy of the instrument creating the charge was effected; or

(b) on which the charge was registered under Part 2 of the Agricultural Credits (Scotland) Act 1929.

42 Process of administration

Rule 2.22 (limited disclosure) has effect as if it provided that on an application for disclosure under paragraph (4) a person appointed for the purpose by the FCA may appear and be heard, or make written representations.

43 Rule 2.23 (release from duty to submit statement of affairs; extension of time) has effect as if it provided that on an application under paragraph (2) for release or extension of time a person appointed for the purpose by the FCA may appear and be heard, or make written representations.

44 Meetings

In the following Rules a reference to a creditors' meeting includes a reference to a members' meeting—

(a) Rule 2.27 (meetings to consider administrator's proposals);

(b) Rule 2.27A (suspension and adjournment);

(c) Rule 2.28 (correspondence instead of creditors' meetings), except paragraph (9); and

(d) Rule 2.35 (notices to creditors).

45 Rule 2.27 has effect as if in paragraph (3) the reference to the creditors included a reference to the members of the society.

46 In Rule 2.28—
(a) in paragraphs (3), (4) and (10), in the case of a members' resolution, a reference to the creditors is a reference to the members of the society; and
(b) in paragraph (6), in relation to correspondence with the members ignore the reference to the statement of claim and account or voucher referred to in Rule 2.26C.

47 In Rule 2.29 (applicable law (company meetings)) ignore paragraph (a).

48 In Rule 2.34 (revision of the administrator's proposals)—
(a) in paragraph (2) ignore the words "Subject to paragraph 54(3),"; and
(b) ignore paragraphs (3) and (4).

49 In Rule 2.35, in paragraph (1)(a), in the case of a members' meeting the reference to every creditor who received notice of the meeting is a reference to every member of the society.

50 Distributions to creditors

In Rules 2.40 (distributions to creditors: introduction) and Rule 2.41A (payments of dividends) a reference to creditors includes a reference to member-depositors, but only in so far as the member-depositors are owed amounts in respect of deposits.

51 Rule 2.41 (distributions to creditors) has effect in relation to a proposal to make a distribution to member-depositors as if—
(a) for paragraph (1) there were substituted—

"(1) Subject to the modifications set out below and to any other necessary modifications, Chapter 9 of Part 4 (distribution of company's assets by liquidator), except Rule 4.67 (order of priority of expenses of liquidation), applies with regard to a proposal to make a distribution to the member-depositors of a relevant society as it applies with regard to claims to a dividend out of the assets of a company in liquidation.".

(b) for paragraph (2) there were substituted—

"(2) Subject to paragraphs (2A), (2B) and (5) below, in the application in relation to a relevant society of Chapter 9 of Part 4 or of any provision of the Bankruptcy Act as applied by Rule 4.16 or Rule 4.68 (application of the Bankruptcy Act)—
(a) a reference to the articles of a company is a reference to the rules of the society;
(b) a reference to a company is a reference to the society;
(c) a reference to a creditor does not include a reference to a member of the society to whom an amount is owed by the society if, but only in so far as, the amount concerned is owed in respect of the member's shares;
(d) a reference to the date of commencement of winding up is a reference to the date on which the society entered administration;
(e) a reference to the liquidation is a reference to the administration;
(f) a reference to the liquidation committee is a reference to the creditors' committee in the administration; and
(g) a reference to the liquidator is a reference to the administrator of the society.

(2A) In Rule 4.66 (order of priority in distribution)—
(a) in paragraph (1) a reference to ordinary debts includes a reference to any amount owed by the society in respect of a member's shares where—
(i) the society is an authorised deposit taker; and
(ii) the amount concerned is owed in respect of a deposit; and
(b) in paragraph (2) the reference to section 242 (gratuitous alienations (Scotland)) is a reference to that section as applied in relation to a relevant society by an order made under [section 118 of the Co-operative and Community Benefit Societies Act 2014].

(2B) In section 52 of the Bankruptcy Act (estate to be distributed in respect of accounting periods), in subsection (3) a reference to a creditor includes a reference to a member-depositor of a relevant society, but only in so far as the member is owed an amount in respect of deposits.";

(c) in paragraph (4) the reference to the administrator's statement of proposals, as approved by the creditors, is a reference to that statement, as approved by the creditors and members of the society; and
(d) at the end there were added—

"(6) In this Rule—
"member-depositor", in relation to a relevant society, means any member of the society to whom an amount is owed in respect of the member's shares where—
(a) the society is an authorised deposit taker; and
(b) the amount concerned is owed in respect of a deposit; and
"relevant society" has the meaning given in [article 1(2) of the Co-operative and Community Benefit Societies and Credit Unions (Arrangements, Reconstructions and Administration) Order 2014].".

52 Ending administration

In Rule 2.45 (notice of end of administration), in paragraph (4)(d) the reference to a creditor includes a reference to a member of the society.

53 Replacing administrator

Rule 2.50 (notice of intention to resign) has effect as if the persons who are entitled to receive notice of the administrator's intention to resign included the FCA, the society's regulator and, in the case of a relevant society which is a relevant person, the scheme manager.

54 (1) Rule 2.53 (application to replace administrator) and Rule 2.56 (application to court to remove administrator from office) have effect as if the persons who are entitled to receive notice of the matter concerned included the FCA, the society's regulator and, in the case of a relevant society which is a relevant person, the scheme manager.

(2) Sub-paragraph (1) does not apply in relation to—

(a) the FCA, if the FCA made the application for the administration order; or

(b) the society's regulator, if the society's regulator made the application.

55 Quorum at meetings

Rule 7.6 (meetings requisitioned) has effect as if it required the expenses of summoning and holding a members' meeting requested under paragraph 52(2) or 56(1) of Schedule B1 to be paid out of the assets of the society as an expense of the administration.

56 Rule 7.7 (quorum) has effect in relation to a relevant society as if—

(a) paragraph (1) provided that a quorum, in the case of a meeting of members of the society—

(i) is to be determined according to the rules of the society which lay down a quorum for a general meeting of the society; or

(ii) if there are no such rules, is at least two members who are entitled to vote, or both of them if their number does not exceed two; and

(b) in paragraph (3) the reference to any meeting of creditors included a reference to any meeting of members of the society.

57 Rule 7.12 (resolutions) has effect in relation to a meeting of members of the society as if the words "in value" were omitted.

58 Forms

In Rule 7.30 (forms for use in insolvency proceedings)—

(a) any form prescribed for use by this Rule which is used for the purposes of Part 1 or 2 of the 1986 Act is to be read with the modifications set out in this Order (so far as applicable for the form concerned); and

(b) the reference to the use of a form with such variations as circumstances require includes a reference to its use with such variations as are necessary to take account of applicable modifications.

NOTES

Commencement: 6 April 2014.

Paras 41, 51: words in square brackets substituted by the Co-operative and Community Benefit Societies and Credit Unions (Arrangements, Reconstructions and Administration) (Amendment) Order 2014, SI 2014/1822, arts 2, 7(d), (e).

SCHEDULE 5
APPLICATION OF OTHER SUBORDINATE LEGISLATION WITH MODIFICATIONS

Article 12

[7.1450]

1 Application of the Insolvency Act 1986 (Prescribed Part) Order 2003

The Insolvency Act 1986 (Prescribed Part) Order 2003 applies in relation to a relevant society which is in administration, and for that purpose—

(a) a reference to a company includes a reference to a relevant society; and

(b) a reference to section 176A of the 1986 Act (share of assets for unsecured creditors) is a reference to that section as applied in relation to a relevant society by article 3 of this Order.

[1A Modified application of the Insurers (Reorganisation and Winding Up) Regulations 2004

The Insurers (Reorganisation and Winding Up) Regulations 2004 have effect in relation to a relevant society as if in regulation 2(3) (interpretation of references to the law of insolvency) the reference to the Co-operative and Community Benefit Societies Act 2014 included a reference to an order made under section 118 of that Act.]

2 Modified application of the Pension Protection Fund (Entry Rules) Regulations 2005

(1) In the Pension Protection Fund (Entry Rules) Regulations 2005 regulation 6 (circumstances in which insolvency proceedings in relation to the employer are stayed or come to an end) and regulation 9 (confirmation of scheme status by insolvency practitioner) apply in relation to a relevant society, and for that purpose have effect with the following modifications.

(2) In regulation 6, in paragraph (1)(a), except paragraphs (iv), (v) and (vi)—

(a) a reference to a company includes a reference to a relevant society;

(b) a reference to a provision of the 1986 Act or the Insolvency Rules 1986 is a reference to that provision as applied in relation to a relevant society; and
(c) in paragraph (ii) the reference to the directors of the company is a reference to the members of the committee of the society.

(3) In regulation 9 a reference to a company includes a reference to a relevant society.

3 Modified application of the Financial Services and Markets Act 2000 (Administration Orders Relating to Insurers) Order 2010

(1) The Financial Services and Markets Act 2000 (Administration Orders Relating to Insurers) Order 2010 has effect in relation to a relevant society which is an insurer (within the meaning given by article 2 of the Financial Services and Markets Act 2000 (Insolvency) (Definition of "Insurer") Order 2001)—
(a) with the modifications in sub-paragraph (2); and
(b) as if article 3 (application and modification of the Insolvency Rules 1986 in relation to insurers) and article 4 (application and modification of the Insolvency (Scotland) Rules 1986 in relation to insurers) were omitted.

(2) Article 2 (application and modification of Part 2 of the 1986 Act in relation to insurers) has effect as if—
(a) before "Part 2" there were inserted "Subject to paragraph (1A),";
(b) after paragraph (1) there were inserted—

"(1A) In the case of an insurer which is a relevant society (within the meaning given in [article 1(2) of the Co-operative and Community Benefit Societies and Credit Unions (Arrangements, Reconstructions and Administration) Order 2014]), the reference in paragraph (1) to the modifications specified in the Schedule to this Order is a reference to the modifications—
(a) made by the Industrial and Provident Societies and Credit Unions (Arrangements, Reconstructions and Administration) Order 2014 in applying Part 2 of the 1986 Act in relation to a relevant society; and
(b) specified in the Schedule to this Order, except those specified in—
(i) paragraph 3 (modification of paragraph 49(4) of Schedule B1: administrator's proposals);
(ii) paragraph 4 (modification of paragraph 53(2) of Schedule B1: business and result of initial creditors' meeting);
(iii) paragraph 5 (modification of paragraph 54(2)(b) of Schedule B1: revision of administrator's proposals); and
(iv) paragraph 9 (modification of paragraph 91(1) of Schedule B1: supplying vacancy in office of administrator).".

NOTES

Commencement: 6 April 2014.

Para 1A: inserted by the Co-operative and Community Benefit Societies and Credit Unions (Arrangements, Reconstructions and Administration) (Amendment) Order 2014, SI 2014/1822, arts 2, 8(a).

Para 3: words in square brackets substituted by SI 2014/1822, arts 2, 8(b).

Note that the Insolvency Rules 1986, SI 1986/1925 are revoked and replaced (as from 6 April 2017 and subject to transitional provisions) by the Insolvency (England and Wales) Rules 2016, SI 2016/1024 at **[6.2]**.

K
FINANCIAL INFRASTRUCTURE SYSTEMS

FINANCIAL SERVICES (BANKING REFORM) ACT 2013

(2013 c 33)

ARRANGEMENT OF SECTIONS

PART 6
SPECIAL ADMINISTRATION FOR OPERATORS
OF CERTAIN INFRASTRUCTURE SYSTEMS

Introductory

111 Financial market infrastructure administration . . . [7.1451]
112 Interpretation: infrastructure companies . . . [7.1452]
113 Interpretation: other expressions . . . [7.1453]

FMI administration orders

114 FMI administration orders . . . [7.1454]
115 Objective of FMI administration . . . [7.1455]
116 Application for FMI administration order . . . [7.1456]
117 Powers of court . . . [7.1457]
118 FMI administrators . . . [7.1458]
119 Continuity of supply . . . [7.1459]
120 Power to direct FMI administrator . . . [7.1460]
121 Conduct of administration, transfer schemes etc . . . [7.1461]

Restrictions on other insolvency procedures

122 Restriction on winding-up orders and voluntary winding up . . . [7.1462]
123 Restriction on making of ordinary administration orders . . . [7.1463]
124 Restriction on enforcement of security . . . [7.1464]

Financial support for companies in FMI administration

125 Loans . . . [7.1465]
126 Indemnities . . . [7.1466]

Interpretation

127 Interpretation of Part . . . [7.1467]

Application of Part to Northern Ireland

128 Northern Ireland . . . [7.1468]

PART 8
FINAL PROVISIONS

144 Interpretation . . . [7.1469]
147 Extent . . . [7.1470]
148 Commencement and short title . . . [7.1471]

SCHEDULES

Schedule 6—Conduct of FMI Administration . . . [7.1472]
Schedule 7—Financial Market Infrastructure Transfer Schemes . . . [7.1473]

An Act to make further provision about banking and other financial services, including provision about the Financial Services Compensation Scheme; to make provision for the amounts owed in respect of certain deposits to be treated as a preferential debt on insolvency; to make further provision about payment systems and securities settlement systems; to make provision about the accounts of the Bank of England and its wholly owned subsidiaries; to make provision in relation to persons providing claims management services; and for connected purposes

[18 December 2013]

1–110 ((*Pts 1–5*) *outside the scope of this work.*)

Part 7K Special Insolvency Regimes

PART 6
SPECIAL ADMINISTRATION FOR OPERATORS OF CERTAIN INFRASTRUCTURE SYSTEMS

Introductory

[7.1451]
111 Financial market infrastructure administration

This Part—
- (a) provides for a procedure to be known as FMI administration, and
- (b) restricts the powers of persons other than the Bank of England in relation to the insolvency of infrastructure companies.

NOTES

Commencement: to be appointed.

[7.1452]
112 Interpretation: infrastructure companies

(1) In this Part "infrastructure company" has the meaning given by this section.
(2) "Infrastructure company" means a company which is—
- (a) the operator of a recognised . . . payment system, other than an operator excluded by subsection (3),
- [(b) a recognised CSD operating a securities settlement system, or]
- (c) a company designated by the Treasury under subsection (4).

(3) But a company is not an infrastructure company if it is a recognised central counterparty, as defined by section 285 of FSMA 2000.
(4) The Treasury may by order designate a company for the purposes of subsection (2)(c) if—
- (a) the company provides services to a person falling within subsection (2)(a) or (b), and
- (b) the Treasury are satisfied that an interruption in the provision of those services would have a serious adverse effect on the effective operation of the recognised . . . payment system or securities settlement system in question.

(5) An order under subsection (4) must specify the recognised . . . payment system or securities settlement system in connection with which the company is designated.
(6) Before designating a company under subsection (4), the Treasury must consult—
- (a) the company to be designated,
- (b) the person within subsection (2)(a) or (b) to whom the company provides services,
- (c) the Bank of England,
- (d) if the company is a PRA-authorised person, the PRA and the FCA, and
- (e) if the company is an authorised person other than a PRA-authorised person, the FCA.

NOTES

Commencement: to be appointed.

Words omitted repealed by the Digital Economy Act 2017, s 113, Sch 9, Pt 2, paras 35, 41.

Sub-s (2): para (b) substituted by the Central Securities Depositories Regulations 2017, SI 2017/1064, reg 10, Schedule, para 16(1), (3); for transitional provisions and savings see regs 6–9 of the 2017 Regulations. The original text read as follows:

> "(b) approved under regulations under section 785 of the Companies Act 2006 (provision enabling procedures for evidencing and transferring title) as the operator of a securities settlement system, or".

[7.1453]
113 Interpretation: other expressions

(1) In this Part—

"company" means a company registered under the Companies Act 2006;

"operator", in relation to a recognised . . . payment system, is to be read in accordance with section 183 of the Banking Act 2009;

["recognised CSD" has the meaning given by section 285 of FSMA 2000;]

"recognised . . . payment system" means [a] payment system, as defined by section 182 of the Banking Act 2009, in respect of which a recognition order under section 184 of that Act is in force;

"the relevant system" means—
- (a) in relation to an infrastructure company falling within subsection (2)(a) of section 112, the recognised . . . payment system,
- (b) in relation to an infrastructure company falling within subsection (2)(b) of that section, the securities settlement system,
- (c) in relation to a company designated under subsection (4) of that section, the recognised . . . payment system or securities settlement system falling within paragraph (b) of that subsection;

"securities settlement system" means a computer-based system, and procedures, which enable title to units of a security to be evidenced and transferred without a written instrument, and which facilitate supplementary and incidental matters.

(2) Expressions used in the definition of "securities settlement system" in subsection (1) are to be read in accordance with section 783 of the Companies Act 2006.

NOTES

Commencement: to be appointed.

Sub-s (1) is amended as follows:

Words omitted from definitions "operator" and "the relevant system" repealed, and in definition "recognised payment system" words omitted repealed, and word in square brackets substituted, by the Digital Economy Act 2017, s 113, Sch 9, Pt 2, paras 35, 42.

Definition "recognised CSD" inserted by the Central Securities Depositories Regulations 2017, SI 2017/1064, reg 10, Schedule, para 16(1), (4); for transitional provisions and savings see regs 6–9 of the 2017 Regulations.

FMI administration orders

[7.1454]

114 FMI administration orders

(1) In this Part "FMI administration order" means an order which—

(a) is made by the court in relation to an infrastructure company, and

(b) directs that, while the order is in force, the affairs, business and property of the company are to be managed by a person appointed by the court.

(2) A person appointed as mentioned in subsection (1)(b) is referred to in this Part as an FMI administrator.

(3) The FMI administrator of a company must manage its affairs, business and property, and exercise and perform the FMI administrator's functions, so as to achieve the objective in section 115.

NOTES

Commencement: to be appointed.

[7.1455]

115 Objective of FMI administration

(1) Where an FMI administrator is appointed in relation to the operator of a recognised . . . payment system . . . , the objective of the FMI administration is—

(a) to ensure that the system is and continues to be maintained and operated as an efficient and effective system,

(b) . . . and

(c) to ensure by one or both of the specified means that it becomes unnecessary for the FMI administration order to remain in force for that purpose . . . .

[(1A) Where an FMI administrator is appointed in relation to a recognised CSD operating a securities settlement system, the objective of the FMI administration is—

(a) to ensure that the system is and continues to be maintained and operated as an efficient and effective system,

(b) to ensure that the protected activities continue to be carried on, and

(c) to ensure by one or both of the specified means that it becomes unnecessary for the FMI administration order to remain in force for that purpose or those purposes.]

(2) Where an FMI administrator is appointed in relation to a company designated under subsection (4) of section 112, the objective of the FMI administration is—

(a) to ensure that services falling within that subsection continue to be provided, and

(b) to ensure by one or both of the specified means that it becomes unnecessary for the FMI administration order to remain in force for that purpose.

(3) The protected activities referred to in subsection [(1A)(b)] are such activities as the Bank of England may from time to time direct, which must be—

(a) regulated activities falling within section [285(3D)] of FSMA 2000, or

(b) related activities which are necessary for the efficient carrying on of any of those regulated activities.

(4) The specified means are—

(a) the rescue as a going concern of the company subject to the FMI administration order, and

(b) transfers falling within subsection (5).

(5) A transfer falls within this subsection if it is a transfer as a going concern—

(a) to another company, or

(b) as respects different parts of the undertaking of the company subject to the FMI administration order, to two or more different companies,

of so much of that undertaking as it is appropriate to transfer for the purpose of achieving the objective of the FMI administration.

(6) The means by which transfers falling within subsection (5) may be effected include, in particular—

(a) a transfer of the undertaking of the company subject to the FMI administration order, or of part of its undertaking, to a wholly-owned subsidiary of that company, and

(b) the transfer to a company of securities of a wholly-owned subsidiary to which there has been a transfer falling within paragraph (a).

(7) The objective of the FMI administration may be achieved by transfers falling within subsection (5) only to the extent that—

(a) the rescue as a going concern of the company subject to the FMI administration order is not reasonably practicable or is not reasonably practicable without such transfers,

(b) the rescue of that company as a going concern will not achieve that objective or will not do so without such transfers, or

(c) such transfers would produce a result for the company's creditors as a whole that is better than the result that would be produced without them.

NOTES

Commencement: to be appointed.

The first words omitted from sub-s (1) were repealed by the Digital Economy Act 2017, s 113, Sch 9, Pt 2, paras 35, 43.

The other words omitted from sub-s (1) were repealed, sub-s (1A) was inserted, and the figures in square brackets in sub-s (3) were substituted, by the Central Securities Depositories Regulations 2017, SI 2017/1064, reg 10, Schedule, para 16(1), (5); for transitional provisions and savings see regs 6–9 of the 2017 Regulations. The original sub-ss (1) and (3) read as follows:

"(1) Where an FMI administrator is appointed in relation to the operator of a recognised inter-bank payment system or a securities settlement system, the objective of the FMI administration is—

(a) to ensure that the system is and continues to be maintained and operated as an efficient and effective system,

(b) where the operator of the system is also a clearing house falling within section 285(1)(b)(ii) of FSMA 2000 (recognised clearing house that is not a recognised central counterparty), to ensure that the protected activities continue to be carried on, and

(c) to ensure by one or both of the specified means that it becomes unnecessary for the FMI administration order to remain in force for that purpose or those purposes.

(a) to ensure that services falling within that subsection continue to be provided, and

(b) to ensure by one or both of the specified means that it becomes unnecessary for the FMI administration order to remain in force for that purpose.

(3) The protected activities referred to in subsection (1)(b) are such activities as the Bank of England may from time to time direct, which must be—

(a) regulated activities falling within section 285(3)(a) or (b) of FSMA 2000, or

(b) related activities which are necessary for the efficient carrying on of any of those regulated activities.".

[7.1456]

116 Application for FMI administration order

(1) An application for an FMI administration order may be made to the court by the Bank of England.

(2) An application must nominate a person to be appointed as the FMI administrator.

(3) The infrastructure company must be given notice of an application, in accordance with rules under section 411 of the 1986 Act (as applied in relation to FMI administration).

NOTES

Commencement: to be appointed.

[7.1457]

117 Powers of court

(1) The court may make an FMI administration order in relation to an infrastructure company if satisfied—

(a) that the company is unable to pay its debts,

(b) that the company is likely to be unable to pay its debts, or

(c) that, on a petition presented by the Secretary of State under section 124A of the 1986 Act (petition for winding up on grounds of public interest), it would be just and equitable (disregarding the objective of the FMI administration) to wind up the company.

(2) The court may not make an FMI administration order on the ground set out in subsection (1)(c) unless the Secretary of State has certified to the court that the case is one in which the Secretary of State considers (disregarding the objective of the FMI administration) that it would be appropriate to petition under section 124A of the 1986 Act.

(3) On an application for an FMI administration order, the court may—

(a) grant the application;

(b) dismiss the application;

(c) adjourn the application (generally or to a specified date);

(d) make an interim order;

(e) treat the application as a winding-up petition and make any order which the court could make under section 125 of the 1986 Act;

(f) make any other order which the court thinks appropriate.

(4) An interim order under subsection (3)(d) may, in particular—

(a) restrict the exercise of a power of the company or of its directors;

(b) make provision conferring a discretion on the court or on a person qualified to act as an insolvency practitioner in relation to the company.

(5) For the purposes of this section a company is unable to pay its debts if it is treated as being so unable under section 123 of the 1986 Act (definition of inability to pay debts).

NOTES

Commencement: to be appointed.

[7.1458]

118 FMI administrators

(1) The FMI administrator of a company—

(a) is an officer of the court, and

(b) in exercising and performing powers and duties in relation to the company, is the company's agent.

(2) The management by the FMI administrator of a company of any of its affairs, business or property must be carried out for the purpose of achieving the objective of the FMI administration as quickly and efficiently as is reasonably practicable.

(3) The FMI administrator of a company must exercise and perform powers and duties in the way which, so far as it is consistent with the objective of the FMI administration to do so, best protects—
 (a) the interests of the company's creditors as a whole, and
 (b) subject to those interests, the interests of the company's members as a whole.

NOTES

Commencement: to be appointed.

[7.1459]

119 Continuity of supply

(1) This section applies where, before the commencement of FMI administration, the infrastructure company had entered into arrangements with a supplier for the provision of a supply to the infrastructure company.

(2) After the commencement of FMI administration, the supplier—
 (a) must not terminate a supply unless—
  (i) any charges in respect of the supply which relate to a supply given after the commencement of FMI administration remain unpaid for more than 28 days,
  (ii) the FMI administrator consents to the termination, or
  (iii) the supplier has the permission of the court, which may be given if the supplier can show that the continued provision of the supply would cause the supplier to suffer hardship,
 (b) must not make it a condition of a supply that any charges in respect of the supply which relate to a supply given before the commencement of FMI administration are paid, and
 (c) must not do anything which has the effect of making it a condition of the giving of a supply that any charges within paragraph (b) are paid.

(3) Where, before the commencement of FMI administration, a contractual right to terminate a supply has arisen but has not been exercised, then, for the purposes of this section, the commencement of FMI administration causes that right to lapse and the supply is only to be terminated if a ground in subsection (2)(a) applies.

(4) Any provision in a contract between the infrastructure company and the supplier that purports to terminate the agreement if any action is taken to put the infrastructure company in FMI administration is void.

(5) Any expenses incurred by the infrastructure company on the provision of a supply after the commencement of FMI administration are to be treated as necessary disbursements in the course of the FMI administration.

(6) In this section—
 "commencement of FMI administration" means the making of the FMI administration order;
 "supplier" means the person controlling the provision of a supply to the infrastructure company, and includes a company that is a group undertaking (as defined by section 1161(5) of the Companies Act 2006) in respect of the infrastructure company;
 "supply" means a supply of any of the following—
  (a) computer hardware or software used by the infrastructure company in connection with the operation of the relevant system;
  (b) financial data;
  (c) infrastructure permitting electronic communication services;
  (d) data processing;
  (e) access to secure data networks used by the infrastructure company in connection with the operation of the relevant system;
  (f) staff.

NOTES

Commencement: to be appointed.

[7.1460]

120 Power to direct FMI administrator

(1) If the Bank of England considers it necessary to do so for the purpose of achieving the objective of an FMI administration, the Bank may direct the FMI administrator to take, or refrain from taking, specified action.

(2) In deciding whether to give a direction under this section, the Bank of England must have regard to the public interest in—
 (a) the protection and enhancement of the stability of the financial system of the United Kingdom, and
 (b) the maintenance of public confidence in that system.

(3) A direction under this section must not be incompatible with a direction of the court that is in force under Schedule B1 to the 1986 Act.

(4) The Bank of England must, within a reasonable time of giving the direction, give the FMI administrator a statement of its reasons for giving the direction.

(5) A person listed in subsection (6) has immunity from liability in damages in respect of action or inaction in accordance with a direction under this section.

(6) Those persons are—
 (a) the FMI administrator;
 (b) the company in FMI administration;
 (c) the officers or staff of the company.

(7) Immunity conferred by this section does not extend to action or inaction—

(a) in bad faith, or
(b) in contravention of section 6(1) of the Human Rights Act 1998.

(8) This section does not limit the powers conferred on the Bank of England by section 191 of the Banking Act 2009 (directions) in relation to a recognised . . . payment system.

NOTES

Commencement: to be appointed.

Sub-s (8): words omitted repealed by the Digital Economy Act 2017, s 113, Sch 9, Pt 2, paras 35, 44.

[7.1461]

121 Conduct of administration, transfer schemes etc

(1) Schedule 6 (which applies the provisions of Schedule B1 to the 1986 Act about ordinary administration orders and certain other enactments to FMI administration orders) has effect.

(2) Schedule 7 (which makes provision for transfer schemes to achieve the objective of an FMI administration) has effect.

(3) The power to make rules conferred by section 411(1B) of the 1986 Act (rules relating to bank administration) is to apply for the purpose of giving effect to this Part as it applies for the purposes of giving effect to Part 3 of the Banking Act 2009 (and, accordingly, as if the reference in section 411(1B) to that Part included a reference to this Part).

NOTES

Commencement: 1 March 2014 (sub-s (1) (for the purpose of introducing Sch 6, para 6) and sub-s (3) (for the purpose of making rules)); to be appointed (otherwise).

Restrictions on other insolvency procedures

[7.1462]

122 Restriction on winding-up orders and voluntary winding up

(1) A petition by a person other than the Bank of England for a winding up order in respect of an infrastructure company may not be determined unless—
(a) the petitioner has notified the Bank of England that the petition has been presented, and
(b) the period of 14 days beginning with the day on which the notice is received by the Bank has ended.

(2) A resolution for the voluntary winding up of an infrastructure company may not be made unless—
(a) the infrastructure company has applied to the court under this section,
(b) the company has notified the Bank of England that the application has been made, and
(c) after the end of the period of 14 days beginning with the day on which the notice is received by the Bank, the court gives permission for the resolution to be made.

NOTES

Commencement: to be appointed.

[7.1463]

123 Restriction on making of ordinary administration orders

(1) This section applies where an ordinary administration application is made in relation to an infrastructure company by a person other than the Bank of England.

(2) The court must dismiss the application if—
(a) an FMI administration order is in force in relation to the company, or
(b) an FMI administration order has been made in relation to the company but is not yet in force.

(3) Where subsection (2) does not apply, the court, on hearing the application, must not exercise its powers under paragraph 13 of Schedule B1 to the 1986 Act (other than its power of adjournment) unless—
(a) the applicant has notified the Bank of England that the application has been made, and
(b) the period of 14 days beginning with the day on which the notice is received by the Bank has ended.

(4) On the making of an FMI administration order in relation to an infrastructure company, the court must dismiss any ordinary administration application made in relation to the company which is outstanding.

(5) "Ordinary administration application" means an application under paragraph 12 of Schedule B1 to the 1986 Act.

NOTES

Commencement: to be appointed.

[7.1464]

124 Restriction on enforcement of security

A person may not take any step to enforce a security over property of an infrastructure company unless—
(a) notice of the intention to do so has been given to the Bank of England, and
(b) the period of 14 days beginning with the day on which the notice was received by the Bank has ended.

NOTES

Commencement: to be appointed.

Financial support for companies in FMI administration

[7.1465]
125 Loans

(1) This section applies where an FMI administration order has been made in relation to an infrastructure company.
(2) The Treasury may, out of money provided by Parliament, make loans to the company for achieving the objective in section 115.
(3) A loan under this section may be made on such terms as the Treasury think fit.
(4) The Treasury must pay into the Consolidated Fund sums received by them as a result of this section.

NOTES
Commencement: to be appointed.

[7.1466]
126 Indemnities

(1) This section applies where an FMI administration order has been made in relation to an infrastructure company.
(2) The Treasury may agree to indemnify persons in respect of one or both of the following—
(a) liabilities incurred in connection with the exercise of powers and duties by the FMI administrator;
(b) loss or damage sustained in that connection.
(3) The agreement may be made in whatever manner, and on whatever terms, the Treasury think fit.
(4) As soon as practicable after agreeing to indemnify persons under this section, the Treasury must lay before Parliament a statement of the agreement.
(5) If sums are paid by the Treasury in consequence of an indemnity agreed to under this section, the infrastructure company must pay the Treasury—
(a) such amounts in or towards the repayment to them of those sums as the Treasury may direct, and
(b) interest, at such rates as they may direct, on amounts outstanding under this subsection.
(6) Subsection (5) does not apply in the case of a sum paid by the Treasury for indemnifying a person in respect of a liability to the infrastructure company.
(7) Where a sum has been paid out by the Treasury in consequence of an indemnity agreed to under this section, the Treasury must lay a statement relating to that sum before Parliament—
(a) as soon as practicable after the end of the financial year in which that sum is paid out, and
(b) (except where subsection (5) does not apply in the case of the sum) as soon as practicable after the end of each subsequent relevant financial year.
(8) In relation to a sum paid out in consequence of an indemnity, a financial year is a relevant financial year for the purposes of subsection (7) unless—
(a) before the beginning of that year, the whole of that sum has been repaid to the Treasury under subsection (5), and
(b) the infrastructure company is not at any time during that year subject to liability to pay interest on amounts that became due under that subsection in respect of that sum.
(9) The power of the Treasury to agree to indemnify persons—
(a) is confined to a power to agree to indemnify persons in respect of liabilities, loss and damage incurred or sustained by them as relevant persons, but
(b) includes power to agree to indemnify persons (whether or not they are identified or identifiable at the time of the agreement) who subsequently become relevant persons.
(10) For the purposes of this section each of the following is a relevant person—
(a) the FMI administrator;
(b) an employee of the FMI administrator;
(c) a member or employee of a firm of which the FMI administrator is a member;
(d) a member or employee of a firm of which the FMI administrator is an employee;
(e) a member or employee of a firm of which the FMI administrator was an employee or member at a time when the order was in force;
(f) a body corporate which is the employer of the FMI administrator;
(g) an officer, employee or member of such a body corporate.
(11) For the purposes of subsection (10)—
(a) the references to the FMI administrator are to be read, where two or more persons are appointed to act as the FMI administrator, as references to any one or more of them, and
(b) the references to a firm of which a person was a member or employee at a particular time include references to a firm which holds itself out to be the successor of a firm of which the person was a member or employee at that time.
(12) The Treasury must pay into the Consolidated Fund sums received by them as a result of subsection (5).

NOTES
Commencement: to be appointed.

Interpretation

[7.1467]
127 Interpretation of Part

(1) In this Part—
"the 1986 Act" means the Insolvency Act 1986;

"business", "member", "property" and "security" have the same meaning as in the 1986 Act;
"company" has the meaning given by section 113;
"the court" means—
(a) in England and Wales and Northern Ireland, the High Court;
(b) in Scotland, the Court of Session;
"FMI administration order" and "FMI administrator" are to be read in accordance with section 114;
"infrastructure company" has the meaning given by section 112;
"operator", in relation to a recognised . . . payment system, has the meaning given by section 113;
"recognised . . . payment system" has the meaning given by section 113;
"regulated activity" has the same meaning as in FSMA 2000;
"the relevant system" has the meaning given by section 113;
"securities settlement system" has the meaning given by section 113.

(2) In this Part references to the FMI administrator of a company include a person appointed under paragraph 91 or 103 of Schedule B1 to the 1986 Act, as applied by Schedule 6 to this Act, to be the FMI administrator of a company.

(3) In this Part references to a person qualified to act as an insolvency practitioner in relation to a company are to be read in accordance with Part 13 of the 1986 Act, but as if references in that Part to a company included a company registered under the Companies Act 2006 in Northern Ireland.

NOTES

Commencement: to be appointed.

Words omitted from the definitions "operator" and "recognised payment system" repealed by the Digital Economy Act 2017, s 113, Sch 9, Pt 2, paras 35, 45.

Application of Part to Northern Ireland

[7.1468]

128 Northern Ireland

(1) This section makes provision about this Part in its application to Northern Ireland.

(2) Any reference to any provision of the 1986 Act is to have effect as a reference to the corresponding provision of the Insolvency (Northern Ireland) Order 1989.

(3) Section 127(3) is to have effect as if the reference to Northern Ireland were a reference to England and Wales or Scotland.

NOTES

Commencement: to be appointed.

129–141 ((*Pt 7) outside the scope of this work.*)

PART 8
FINAL PROVISIONS

142, 143 (*Outside the scope of this work.*)

[7.1469]

144 Interpretation

In this Act—
"enactment" includes—
(a) an enactment contained in subordinate legislation,
(b) an enactment contained in, or in an instrument made under, an Act of the Scottish Parliament,
(c) an enactment contained in, or in an instrument made under, a Measure or Act of the National Assembly for Wales, and
(d) an enactment contained in, or in an instrument made under, Northern Ireland legislation;
"the FCA" means the Financial Conduct Authority;
"FSMA 2000" means the Financial Services and Markets Act 2000;
"the PRA" means the Prudential Regulation Authority.

NOTES

Commencement: 18 December 2013.

145, 146 (*Outside the scope of this work.*)

[7.1470]

147 Extent

(1) The provisions of this Act extend to England and Wales, Scotland and Northern Ireland. This is subject to subsection (2).

(2) . . .

NOTES

Commencement: 18 December 2013.

Sub-s (2): outside the scope of this work.

[7.1471]
148 Commencement and short title
(1) This Part comes into force on the day on which this Act is passed.
(2)–(4) . . .
(5) The remaining provisions of this Act come into force on such day as the Treasury may by order appoint.
(6) Different days may be appointed for different purposes.
(7) This Act may be cited as the Financial Services (Banking Reform) Act 2013.

NOTES
Commencement: 18 December 2013.
Sub-ss (2)-(4): outside the scope of this work.
Orders: at present, 11 commencement orders had been made under this section. The order relevant to the provisions of this Act reproduced here is the Financial Services (Banking Reform) Act 2013 (Commencement No 1) Order 2014, SI 2014/377.

SCHEDULES 1–5

(Schs 1–5 outside the scope of this work.)

SCHEDULE 6
CONDUCT OF FMI ADMINISTRATION

Section 121

[7.1472]
1. The following provisions of this Schedule provide for—
(a) the general powers and duties of FMI administrators (by application of provisions about administrators), and
(b) the general process and effects of FMI administration (by application of provisions about administration).

2. The provisions set out in the Tables apply in relation to FMI administration as in relation to administration, with—
(a) the modifications set out in paragraph 3,
(b) any other modification specified in the Tables, and
(c) any other necessary modification.

3. The modifications are that—
(a) a reference to the administrator is a reference to the FMI administrator,
(b) a reference to administration is a reference to FMI administration,
(c) a reference to an administration application is a reference to an FMI administration application,
(d) a reference to an administration order is a reference to an FMI administration order,
(e) [except where otherwise specified in Table 2,] a reference to a company is a reference to the infrastructure company, and
(f) a reference to the purpose of administration (other than the reference in paragraph 111(1) of Schedule B1) is a reference to the objective in section 115.

4. Powers conferred by this Part of this Act and by the 1986 Act (as applied) are in addition to, and not in restriction of, any existing powers of instituting proceedings against any contributory or debtor of an infrastructure company, or the estate of any contributory or debtor, for the recovery of any call or other sum.

5. A reference in an enactment or other document to anything done under a provision applied by this Part of this Act includes a reference to the provision as applied.

TABLE 1 OF APPLIED PROVISIONS: SCHEDULE B1 TO THE INSOLVENCY ACT 1986

Provision of Schedule B1	Subject	Modification
Para 40(1)(a)	Dismissal of pending winding-up petition	
Para 41	Dismissal of administrative or other receiver	
Para 42	Moratorium on insolvency proceedings	Ignore sub-paras (4) and (5).
Para 43	Moratorium on other legal process	
Para 44(1)(a) and (5)	Interim moratorium	
Para 46	Announcement of appointment	Ignore sub-para (6)(b) and (c).
Paras 47 and 48	Statement of affairs	

Part 7K Special Insolvency Regimes

Provision of Schedule B1	Subject	Modification
Para 49	Administrator's proposals	(a) The administrator must obtain the approval of the Bank of England to any proposals under sub-para (1). (b) Treat the reference in sub-para (2)(b) to the objective mentioned in Para 3(1)(a) or (b) as a reference to the objective in section 115 of this Act. (c) Ignore sub-para (3)(b).
Para 59	General powers	
Para 60 and Schedule 1	General powers	The exercise of powers under Schedule 1 is subject to section 115 of this Act.
Para 61	Directors	
Para 62	Power to call meetings of creditors	
Para 63	Application to court for directions	(a) Before making an application in reliance on this paragraph the FMI administrator must give notice to the Bank of England, which is to be entitled to participate in the proceedings. (b) In making directions the court must have regard to the objective in section 115 of this Act.
Para 64	Management powers	
Para 65	Distribution to creditors	
Para 66	Payments	
Para 67	Taking custody of property	
Para 68	Management	(a) Ignore sub-paras (1) and (3). (b) The Bank of England may apply to the court for the variation or revocation of any directions given by the court.
Para 69	Agency	
Para 70	Floating charges	
Para 71	Fixed charges	
Para 72	Hire-purchase property	
Para 73	Protection for secured and preferential creditors	
Para 74	Challenge to administrator's conduct	For sub-para (2) there is to be taken to be substituted— "(2) Where a company is in FMI administration, a creditor or member of the company may apply to the court claiming that the FMI administrator is conducting himself or herself in a manner preventing the achievement of the objective of the FMI administration as quickly and efficiently as is reasonably practicable."
Para 75	Misfeasance	In addition to applications that may anyway be made under Para 75, an application may be made by the FMI administrator or the Bank of England.
Para 79	Court ending administration on application of administrator	For sub-paras (1) to (3) there are to be taken to be substituted— "(1) On an application made by a person mentioned in sub-paragraph (2), the court may provide for the appointment of an FMI administrator of a company to cease to have effect from a specified time. (2) The persons who may apply to the court under sub-paragraph (1) are— (a) the Bank of England; (b) with the consent of the Bank, the FMI administrator."

Provision of Schedule B1	Subject	Modification
Para 84	Termination: no more assets for distribution	
Para 85	Discharge of administration order	
Para 86	Notice to Companies Registrar of end of administration	
Para 87	Resignation	An FMI administrator may not resign under Para 87 without giving 28 days' notice of the intention to do so to the Bank of England.
Para 88	Removal	An application for an order removing an FMI administrator from office may be made only by or with the consent of the Bank of England.
Para 89	Disqualification	The notice under sub-para (2) must be given to the Bank of England.
Paras 90 and 91	Replacement	(a) Para 91(1) applies as if the only person who could make an application were the Bank of England. (b) Ignore Para 91(2).
Para 98	Discharge	Ignore sub-paras (2)(b) [and (ba)][, (3) and (3A)].
Para 99	Vacation of office: charges and liabilities	In the application of sub-para (3), payments may be made only— (a) in accordance with directions of the Bank of England, and (b) if the Bank is satisfied that they will not prejudice the objective in section 115 of this Act.
Paras 100 to 103	Joint administrators	An application under Para 103 may be made only by the Bank of England.
Para 104	Validity	
Para 106 (and section 430 and Schedule 10)	Fines	
Paras 107 to 109	Extension of time limits	
Para 110	Amendment of provisions about time	An order under Para 110 may amend a provision of the Schedule as it applies by virtue of this Act (whether or not in the same way as it amends the provision as it applies otherwise).
Para 111	Interpretation	
Paras 112 to 116	Scotland	

TABLE 2 OF APPLIED PROVISIONS:
OTHER PROVISIONS OF THE INSOLVENCY ACT 1986

Section	Subject	Modification or comment
[Section 176ZB	Application of proceeds of office-holder claims]	
Section 233	Utilities	
Section 234	Getting in company's property	
Section 235	Duty to co-operate with office-holder	
Section 236	Inquiry into company's dealings	
Section 237	Section 236: enforcement by court	
Section 238	Transactions at an undervalue (England and Wales)	
Section 239	Preferences (England and Wales)	

Section	Subject	Modification or comment
Section 240	Ss 238 and 239: relevant time	
Section 241	Orders under ss 238 and 239	(a) In considering making an order in reliance on section 241 the court must have regard to the objective in section 115 of this Act. (b) Ignore subsections (2A)(a) and (3) to (3C).
Section 242	Gratuitous alienations (Scotland)	
Section 243	Unfair preferences (Scotland)	In considering the grant of a decree under subsection (5) the court must have regard to the objective in section 115 of this Act.
Section 244	Extortionate credit transactions	
Section 245	Avoidance of floating charges	
Section 246	Unenforceability of liens	
[Sections 246ZA to 246ZC	Administration: penalisation of directors etc	
Section 246ZD	Power to assign certain causes of action]	
[Sections 246ZE and 246ZF	Decisions by creditors (company insolvency)	
Section 246C	Creditors' ability to opt out of receiving certain notices	
Section 248A	Meaning of "opted-out creditor"]	
Sections 386 and 387, and Schedule 6 (and Schedule 4 to the Pension Schemes Act 1993)	Preferential debts	
Section 389	Offence of acting without being qualified	Treat references to acting as an insolvency practitioner as references to acting as an FMI administrator.
[Sections 390 to 391T	Authorisation and regulation of insolvency practitioners	(a) In section 390 treat references to acting as an insolvency practitioner as references to acting as an FMI administrator. (b) For subsection (2) of that section there is to be taken to be substituted— "(2) A person is not qualified to act as an FMI administrator at any time unless at that time the person is fully authorised to act as an insolvency practitioner or partially authorised to act as an insolvency practitioner only in relation to companies.". (c) An order under section 391 has effect in relation to any provision applied for the purposes of FMI administration. (d) In sections 390A, 390B(1) and (3), 391O(1)(b) and 391R(3)(b), in a reference to authorisation or permission to act as an insolvency practitioner in relation to (or only in relation to) companies the reference to companies has effect without the modification in paragraph 3(e) of this Schedule. (e) In sections 391Q(2)(b) and 391S(3)(e) the reference to a company has effect without the modification in paragraph 3(e) of this Schedule.]

Section	Subject	Modification or comment
Sections 423 to 425	Transactions defrauding creditors	In considering granting leave under section 424(1) or making an order in reliance on section 425, the court must have regard to the objective in section 115 of this Act.
Sections 430 to 432 and Schedule 10	Offences	

6. (1) The Treasury may by order amend this Schedule so as to make further modifications.

(2) The further modifications that may be made are confined to such modifications of—

(a) the 1986 Act, or

(b) other enactments passed or made before this Act that relate to insolvency or make provision by reference to anything that is or may be done under the 1986 Act,

as the Treasury consider appropriate in relation to any provision made by or under this Part of this Act.

(3) An order under this paragraph may also make modifications of the provisions of this Schedule.

NOTES

Commencement: 1 March 2014 (para 6); to be appointed (otherwise).

Para 3: words in square brackets in sub-para (e) inserted by the Deregulation Act 2015, the Small Business, Enterprise and Employment Act 2015 and the Insolvency (Amendment) Act (Northern Ireland) 2016 (Consequential Amendments and Transitional Provisions) Regulations 2017, SI 2017/400, reg 6(a).

Para 5 is amended as follows:

Table 1: words in first pair of square brackets in the entry relating to "Para 98" inserted by SI 2017/400, reg 6(b); words in second pair of square brackets in that entry substituted by the Small Business, Enterprise and Employment Act 2015 (Consequential Amendments, Savings and Transitional Provisions) Regulations 2018, SI 2018/208, reg 6(a).

Table 2: entries relating to "Section 176ZB", "Sections 246ZA–246ZC" and "Section 246ZD" inserted, and entries relating to "Sections 390–391T" substituted (for the original entries relating to "Sections 390 and 391"), by SI 2017/400, reg 6(c); entries relating to "Sections 246ZE and 246ZF", "Section 246C", and "Section 248A" inserted by SI 2018/208, reg 6(b).

SCHEDULE 7
FINANCIAL MARKET INFRASTRUCTURE TRANSFER SCHEMES

Section 121

Application of Schedule

[7.1473]

1. This Schedule applies where—

(a) the court has made an FMI administration order in relation to a company ("the old company"), and

(b) it is proposed that a transfer within section 115(5) be made to another company ("the new company").

Interpretation of Schedule

2. In this Schedule—

"FMI transfer scheme" has the meaning given by paragraph 4(1);

"the new company" and "the old company" are to be read in accordance with paragraph 1;

"third party", in relation to an FMI transfer scheme or a modification of such a scheme, means a person other than the old company or the new company.

FMI administrator to act on behalf of old company

3. It is for the FMI administrator, while the FMI administration order is in force, to act on behalf of the old company in the doing of anything that it is authorised or required to do by or under this Schedule.

Making of FMI transfer schemes

4. (1) The old company may—

(a) with the consent of the new company, and

(b) for the purpose of giving effect to the proposed transfer,

make a scheme under this Schedule for the transfer of property, rights and liabilities from the old company to the new company (an "FMI transfer scheme").

(2) Such a scheme may be made only at a time when the FMI administration order is in force in relation to the old company.

(3) An FMI transfer scheme may set out the property, rights and liabilities to be transferred in one or more of the following ways—

(a) by specifying or describing them in particular,

(b) by identifying them generally by reference to, or to a specified part of, the undertaking of the old company, or

(c) by specifying the manner in which they are to be determined.

Part 7K Special Insolvency Regimes

(4) An FMI transfer scheme is to take effect in accordance with paragraph 7 at the time appointed by the court.

(5) But the court must not appoint a time for a scheme to take effect unless that scheme has been approved by the Bank of England.

(6) The Bank of England may modify an FMI transfer scheme before approving it, but only modifications to which both the old company and the new company have consented may be made.

(7) In deciding whether to approve an FMI transfer scheme, the Bank of England must have regard, in particular, to—

(a) the public interest, and

(b) any effect that the scheme is likely to have on the interests of third parties.

(8) Before approving an FMI transfer scheme, the Bank of England must consult the Treasury.

(9) The old company and the new company each have a duty to provide the Bank of England with all information and other assistance that the Bank may reasonably require for the purposes of, or in connection with, the exercise of the powers conferred on it by this paragraph.

Provision that may be made by a scheme

5. (1) An FMI transfer scheme may contain provision—

(a) for the creation, in favour of the old company or the new company, of an interest or right in or in relation to property transferred in accordance with the scheme;

(b) for giving effect to a transfer to the new company by the creation, in favour of that company, of an interest or right in or in relation to property retained by the old company;

(c) for the creation of new rights and liabilities (including rights of indemnity and duties to indemnify) as between the old company and the new company;

(d) in connection with any provision made under this sub-paragraph, provision making incidental provision as to the interests, rights and liabilities of other persons with respect to the property, rights and liabilities to which the scheme relates.

(2) The property, rights and liabilities of the old company that may be transferred in accordance with an FMI transfer scheme include—

(a) property, rights and liabilities that would not otherwise be capable of being transferred or assigned by the old company;

(b) property acquired, and rights and liabilities arising, in the period after the making of the scheme but before it takes effect;

(c) rights and liabilities arising after it takes effect in respect of matters occurring before it takes effect;

(d) property situated anywhere in the United Kingdom or elsewhere;

(e) rights and liabilities under the law of a part of the United Kingdom or of a place outside the United Kingdom;

(f) rights and liabilities under an enactment, EU instrument or subordinate legislation.

(3) The transfers to which effect may be given by an FMI transfer scheme include transfers of interests and rights that are to take effect in accordance with the scheme as if there were—

(a) no such requirement to obtain a person's consent or concurrence,

(b) no such liability in respect of a contravention of any other requirement, and

(c) no such interference with any interest or right,

as there would be, in the case of a transaction apart from this Act, by reason of a provision falling within sub-paragraph (4).

(4) A provision falls within this sub-paragraph to the extent that it has effect (whether under an enactment or agreement or otherwise) in relation to the terms on which the old company is entitled, or subject, to anything to which the transfer relates.

(5) Sub-paragraph (6) applies where (apart from that sub-paragraph) a person would be entitled, in consequence of anything done or likely to be done by or under this Act in connection with an FMI transfer scheme—

(a) to terminate, modify, acquire or claim an interest or right, or

(b) to treat an interest or right as modified or terminated.

(6) That entitlement—

(a) is not enforceable in relation to that interest or right until after the transfer of the interest or right by the scheme, and

(b) is then enforceable in relation to the interest or right only in so far as the scheme contains provision for the interest or right to be transferred subject to whatever confers that entitlement.

(7) Sub-paragraphs (3) to (6) have effect where shares in a subsidiary of the old company are transferred—

(a) as if the reference in sub-paragraph (4) to the terms on which the old company is entitled or subject to anything to which the transfer relates included a reference to the terms on which the subsidiary is entitled or subject to anything immediately before the transfer takes effect, and

(b) in relation to an interest or right of the subsidiary, as if the references in sub-paragraph (6) to the transfer of the interest or right included a reference to the transfer of the shares.

(8) Sub-paragraphs (3) and (4) apply to the creation of an interest or right by an FMI transfer scheme as they apply to the transfer of an interest or right.

Further provision about transfers

6. (1) An FMI transfer scheme may make incidental, supplemental, consequential and transitional provision in connection with the other provisions of the scheme.

(2) An FMI transfer scheme may in particular make provision, in relation to a provision of the scheme—

(a) for the new company to be treated as the same person in law as the old company;

(b) for agreements made, transactions effected or other things done by or in relation to the old company to be treated, so far as may be necessary for the purposes of or in connection with a transfer in accordance with the scheme, as made, effected or done by or in relation to the new company;

(c) for references in an agreement, instrument or other document to the old company or to an employee or office holder with the old company to have effect, so far as may be necessary for the purposes of or in connection with a transfer in accordance with the scheme, with such modifications as are specified in the scheme;

(d) that the effect of any transfer in accordance with the scheme in relation to contracts of employment with the old company is not to terminate any of those contracts but is to be that periods of employment with that company are to count for all purposes as periods of employment with the new company;

(e) for proceedings commenced by or against the old company to be continued by or against the new company.

(3) Sub-paragraph (2)(c) does not apply to references in an enactment or in subordinate legislation.

(4) An FMI transfer scheme may make provision for disputes between the old company and the new company as to the effect of the scheme to be referred to such arbitration as may be specified in or determined under the scheme.

(5) Where a person is entitled, in consequence of an FMI transfer scheme, to possession of a document relating in part to the title to land or other property in England and Wales, or to the management of such land or other property—

(a) the scheme may provide for that person to be treated as having given another person an acknowledgement in writing of the right of that other person to production of the document and to delivery of copies of it, and

(b) section 64 of the Law of Property Act 1925 (production and safe custody of documents) is to have effect accordingly, and on the basis that the acknowledgement did not contain an expression of contrary intention.

(6) Where a person is entitled, in consequence of an FMI transfer scheme, to possession of a document relating in part to the title to land or other property in Scotland or to the management of such land or other property, subsections (1) and (2) of section 16 of the Land Registration (Scotland) Act 1979 (omission of certain clauses in deeds) is to have effect in relation to the transfer—

(a) as if the transfer had been effected by deed, and

(b) as if the words "unless specially qualified" were omitted from each of those subsections.

(7) Where a person is entitled, in consequence of an FMI transfer scheme, to possession of a document relating in part to the title to land or other property in Northern Ireland or to the management of such land or other property—

(a) the scheme may provide for that person to be treated as having given another person an acknowledgement in writing of the right of that other person to production of the document and to delivery of copies of it, and

(b) section 9 of the Conveyancing Act 1881 is to have effect accordingly, and on the basis that the acknowledgement does not contain an expression of contrary intention.

(8) In this paragraph references to a transfer in accordance with an FMI transfer scheme include references to the creation in accordance with such a scheme of an interest, right or liability.

Effect of scheme

7. (1) In relation to each provision of an FMI transfer scheme for the transfer of property, rights or liabilities, or for the creation of interests, rights or liabilities—

(a) the property, interests, rights or liabilities become by virtue of this Schedule the property, interests, rights or liabilities of the transferee at the time appointed by the court for the purposes of paragraph 4(4), and

(b) the provisions of that scheme in relation to that property, or those interests, rights or liabilities, have effect from that time.

(2) In this paragraph "the transferee" means—

(a) in relation to property, rights or liabilities transferred by an FMI transfer scheme, the new company;

(b) in relation to interests, rights or liabilities created by such a scheme, the person in whose favour, or in relation to whom, they are created.

Subsequent modification of scheme

8. (1) The Bank of England may by notice to the old company and the new company modify an FMI transfer scheme after it has taken effect, but only modifications to which both the old company and the new company have consented may be made.

(2) The notice must specify the time at which it is to take effect (the "modification time").

(3) Where a notice is issued under this paragraph in relation to an FMI transfer scheme, as from the modification time, the scheme is for all purposes to be treated as having taken effect, at the time appointed for the purposes of paragraph 4(4), with the modifications made by the notice.

(4) Those modifications may make—

(a) any provision that could have been included in the scheme when it took effect at the time appointed for the purposes of paragraph 4(4), and

(aa) transitional provision in connection with provision falling within paragraph (a).

(5) In deciding whether to modify an FMI transfer scheme, the Bank of England must have regard, in particular, to—

(a) the public interest, and

(b) any effect that the modification is likely to have on the interests of third parties.

(6) Before modifying an FMI transfer scheme that has taken effect, the Bank of England must consult the Treasury.

(7) The old company and the new company each have a duty to provide the Bank of England with all information and other assistance that the Bank may reasonably require for the purposes of, or in connection with, the exercise of the powers conferred on it by this paragraph.

Provision relating to foreign property

9. (1) An FMI transfer scheme may contain provision about—

(a) the transfer of foreign property, right and liabilities, and

(b) the creation of foreign property, rights and liabilities.

(2) For this purpose property, or a right, interest or liability, is "foreign" if an issue relating to it arising in any proceedings would (in accordance with the rules of private international law) be determined under the law of a country or territory outside the United Kingdom.

Application of Schedule to transfers to subsidiaries

10. Where a proposed transfer falling within subsection (5) of section 115 is a transfer of the kind mentioned in subsection (6)(a) of that section, this Schedule has effect in relation to the transfer as if—

(a) paragraph 4(1)(a) were omitted, and

(b) in paragraph 4(6), for the words from "both" onwards there were substituted "the old company has consented may be made".

NOTES

Commencement: to be appointed.

L
INSURANCE COMPANIES, INSURERS AND INSURANCE LINKED SECURITIES

INSURANCE COMPANIES ACT 1982

(1982 c 50)

ARRANGEMENT OF SECTIONS

PART II
REGULATION OF INSURANCE COMPANIES

Winding up

53 Winding up of insurance companies under Companies Acts .[7.1474]
54 Winding up on petition of Treasury .[7.1475]
55 Winding up of insurance companies with long term business .[7.1476]
56 Continuation of long term business of insurance companies in liquidation .[7.1477]
57 Subsidiary companies .[7.1478]
58 Reduction of contracts as alternative to winding up .[7.1479]
59 Winding up rules .[7.1480]

PART V
SUPPLEMENTARY PROVISIONS

Interpretation

95 Insurance business .[7.1481]
96 General interpretation .[7.1482]
96A Interpretation of expressions derived from insurance Directives .[7.1483]

An Act to consolidate the Insurance Companies Acts 1974 and 1981

[28 October 1982]

NOTES

This Act was repealed by the Financial Services and Markets Act 2000 (Consequential Amendments and Repeals) Order 2001, SI 2001/3649, art 3(1)(b), subject to transitional provisions in (i) the Financial Services and Markets Act 2000 (Transitional Provisions) (Authorised Persons etc) Order 2001, SI 2001/2636, which contains transitional arrangements for ensuring that people who have been authorised to carry on particular business under the various regulatory regimes replaced by the Financial Services and Markets Act 2000 are treated as authorised persons with the appropriate permission for the purposes of that Act, and (ii) the Financial Services and Markets Act 2000 (Miscellaneous Provisions) Order 2001, SI 2001/3650, which makes transitional provision in relation to reporting obligations and fees payable under this Act. Provisions of this Act relevant to this work are reproduced here for reference.

PART II
REGULATION OF INSURANCE COMPANIES

Winding up

[7.1474]

53 Winding up of insurance companies under Companies Acts

The court may order the winding up, in accordance with the [Insolvency Act 1986] or, as the case may be, the [Insolvency (Northern Ireland) Order 1989], of an insurance company to which this Part of this Act applies and the provisions of [that Act of 1986] or, as the case may be, [that Order of 1989] shall apply accordingly subject to the modification that the company may be ordered to be wound up on the petition of ten or more policy holders owning policies of an aggregate value of not less than £10,000.

Such a petition shall not be presented except by leave of the court, and leave shall not be granted until a prima facie case has been established to the satisfaction of the court and until security for costs for such amount as the court may think reasonable has been given.

NOTES

This section derived from the Insurance Companies Act 1974, s 45 and the Insurance Companies Act 1980, Sch 1, para 20.

Repealed as noted at the beginning of this Act.

Words in first and third pairs of square brackets substituted by the Insolvency Act 1986, s 439(2), Sch 14; words in second and fourth pairs of square brackets substituted by the Insolvency (Northern Ireland) Order 1989, SI 1989/2405, art 381(2), Sch 9, Pt II, para 33.

[7.1475]

54 Winding up on petition of [Treasury]

(1) The [Treasury] may present a petition for the winding up, in accordance with [Part IV or V of the Insolvency Act 1986], of an insurance company to which this Part of this Act applies, being a company which may be wound up by the court under the provisions of that Act, on the ground—

Part 7L Special Insolvency Regimes

(a) that the company is unable to pay its debts within the meaning of section [123 or sections 222 to 224] of that Act;
(b) that the company has failed to satisfy an obligation to which it is or was subject by virtue of this Act or any enactment repealed by this Act or by the Insurance Companies Act 1974; or
[(bb) that the company is a UK company and has failed to satisfy an obligation to which it is subject by virtue of any provision of the law of another EEA State which—
(i) gives effect to the general or long term insurance Directives; or
(ii) is otherwise applicable to the insurance activities of the company in that State;]
(c) that the company, being under the obligation imposed by [sections 221 and 222 of the Companies Act] with respect to the keeping of accounting records, has failed to satisfy that obligation or to produce records kept in satisfaction of that obligation and that the [Treasury] [are] unable to ascertain its financial position.

(2) The [Treasury] may present a petition for the winding up, in accordance with the [Part V or VI of the Insolvency (Northern Ireland) Order 1989], of an insurance company to which this Part of this Act applies, being a company which may be wound up by the court under the provisions of that Act, on the ground—
(a) that the company is unable to pay its debts within the meaning of [Article 103 or Articles 186 to 188] of that Order;
(b) that the company has failed to satisfy an obligation to which it is or was subject by virtue of this Act or any enactment repealed by this Act or by the Insurance Companies Act 1980; or
[(bb) that the company is a UK company and has failed to satisfy an obligation to which it is subject by virtue of any provision of the law of another EEA State which—
(i) gives effect to the general or long term insurance Directives; or
(ii) is otherwise applicable to the insurance activities of the company in that State;]
(c) that the company, being under an obligation imposed by [Articles 229 to 231 of the Companies (Northern Ireland) Order 1986] with respect to the keeping of accounting records, has failed to satisfy that obligation or to produce records kept in satisfaction of that obligation and that the [Treasury] [are] unable to ascertain its financial position;

and [Article 433 of the said Order of 1986] shall have effect in relation to such an insurance company as if any reference to the Department of Commerce for Northern Ireland were a reference to the [Treasury].

(3) In any proceedings on a petition to wind up an insurance company presented by the [Treasury] under subsection (1) or (2) above, evidence that the company was insolvent—
(a) at the close of the period to which—
(i) the accounts and balance sheet of the company last deposited under section 22 above; or
(ii) any statement of the company last deposited under section 25 above, relate; or
(b) at any date or time specified in a requirement under section 42 or 44 above,

shall be evidence that the company continues to be unable to pay its debts, unless the contrary is proved.

(4) If, in the case of an insurance company to which this Part of this Act applies, being a company which may be wound up by the court under the provisions of the [Insolvency Act 1986] or, as the case may be, the [Insolvency (Northern Ireland) Order 1989], it appears to the [Treasury] that it is expedient in the public interest that the company should be wound up, [the Treasury] may, unless the company is already being wound up by the court, present a petition for it to be so wound up if the court thinks it just and equitable for it to be so wound up.

[(4A) The Secretary of State may exercise the powers conferred on the Treasury by subsections (1) to (4) above, and for this purpose those subsections shall be construed as if references to the Treasury were references to the Secretary of State.]

(5) Where a petition for the winding up of an insurance company to which this Part of this Act applies is presented by a person other than the [Treasury], a copy of the petition shall be served on [the Treasury and they] shall be entitled to be heard on the petition.

NOTES

This section derived from the Insurance Companies Act 1974, s 46, the Companies Act 1976, Sch 2, the Insurance Companies Act 1980, Sch 1, para 21, and the Insurance Companies Act 1981, Sch 4, para 9.

Repealed as noted at the beginning of this Act.

Section heading: word in square brackets substituted by the Transfer of Functions (Insurance) Order 1997, SI 1997/2781, art 8, Schedule, Pt I, paras 1, 38(a).

Sub-s (1): words in first, sixth and seventh pairs of square brackets substituted by SI 1997/2781, art 8, Schedule, Pt I, paras 1, 38(a), (b); words in second and third pairs of square brackets substituted by the Insolvency Act 1986, s 439(2), Sch 14; para (bb) inserted by the Insurance Companies (Amendment) Regulations 1990, SI 1990/1333, reg 8(3), substituted by the Insurance Companies (Third Insurance Directives) Regulations 1994, SI 1994/1696, reg 31(1); words in fifth pair of square brackets substituted by the Companies Consolidation (Consequential Provisions) Act 1985, s 30, Sch 2.

Sub-s (2): words in first, sixth, seventh and ninth pairs of square brackets substituted by SI 1997/2781, art 8, Schedule, Pt I, paras 1, 38(a), (c); words in second and third pairs of square brackets substituted by the Insolvency (Northern Ireland) Order 1989, SI 1989/2405, art 381(2), Sch 9, Pt II, para 34(a); para (bb) inserted by SI 1990/1333, art 8(3), substituted by SI 1994/1696, reg 31(2); other words in square brackets substituted by the Companies Consolidation (Consequential Provisions) (Northern Ireland) Order 1986, SI 1986/1035, art 23, Sch 1, Pt II.

Sub-s (3): word in square brackets substituted by SI 1997/2781, art 8, Schedule, Pt I, paras 1, 38(a).

Sub-s (4): words in first pair of square brackets substituted by the Insolvency Act 1986, s 439(2), Sch 14; words in second pair of square brackets substituted by the Insolvency (Northern Ireland) Order 1989, SI 1989/2405, Sch 9, Pt II, para 34(b); words in third and fourth pairs of square brackets substituted by SI 1997/2781, art 8, Schedule, Pt I, paras 1, 38(a), (d).

Sub-s (4A): inserted by SI 1997/2781, art 8, Schedule, Pt I, paras 1, 38(e).

Sub-s (5): words in square brackets substituted by SI 1997/2781, art 8, Schedule, Pt I, paras 1, 38(a), (f).

Insurance Companies Act 1974, Insurance Companies Act 1980: repealed by the Statute Law (Repeals) Act 1993.

[7.1476]

55 Winding up of insurance companies with long term business

(1) No insurance company to which this Part of this Act applies which is an unincorporated body and carries on long term business shall be made the subject of bankruptcy proceedings or, in Scotland, sequestration proceedings.

(2) No insurance company to which this Part of this Act applies which carries on long term business shall be wound up voluntarily.

(3) Section 29(1) above shall not have effect in relation to the winding up of a company to which section 28(1) above applies but, subject to subsection (4) below and to rules made by virtue of section 59(2) below, in any such winding up—

- *(a) the assets representing the fund or funds maintained by the company in respect of its long term business shall be available only for meeting the liabilities of the company attributable to that business;*
- *(b) the other assets of the company shall be available only for meeting the liabilities of the company attributable to its other business.*

(4) Where the value of the assets mentioned in either paragraph of subsection (3) above exceeds the amount of the liabilities mentioned in that paragraph the restriction imposed by that subsection shall not apply to so much of those assets as represents the excess.

(5) In relation to the assets falling within either paragraph of subsection (3) above the creditors mentioned in [section 168(2) of the Insolvency Act 1986] or, as the case may be, [Article 143(2) of the Insolvency (Northern Ireland) Order 1989] shall be only those who are creditors in respect of liabilities falling within that paragraph; and any general meetings of creditors summoned for the purposes of that section shall accordingly be separate general meetings of the creditors in respect of the liabilities falling within each paragraph.

(6) Where under section [212 of the Insolvency Act 1986] or [Article 176 of the Insolvency (Northern Ireland) Order 1989] (defalcations of directors etc. disclosed in course of winding up) a court orders any money or property to be repaid or restored to a company or any sum to be contributed to its assets then, if and so far as the wrongful act which is the reason for the making of the order related to assets representing a fund or funds maintained by the company in respect of its long term business, the court shall include in the order a direction that the money, property or contribution shall be treated for the purposes of this Act as assets of that fund or those funds and this Act shall have effect accordingly.

NOTES

This section derived from the Insurance Companies Act 1974, s 47, and the Insurance Companies Act 1980, Sch 1, para 22.

Repealed as noted at the beginning of this Act.

Sub-ss (5), (6): words in first pair of square brackets substituted by the Insolvency Act 1986, s 439(2), Sch 14; words in second pair of square brackets substituted by the Insolvency (Northern Ireland) Order 1989, SI 1989/2405, art 381(2), Sch 9, Pt II, para 35.

[7.1477]

56 Continuation of long term business of insurance companies in liquidation

(1) This section has effect in relation to the winding up of an insurance company to which this Part of this Act applies, being a company carrying on long term business.

(2) The liquidator shall, unless the court otherwise orders, carry on the long term business of the company with a view to its being transferred as a going concern to another insurance company, whether an existing company or a company formed for that purpose; and, in carrying on that business as aforesaid, the liquidator may agree to the variation of any contracts of insurance in existence when the winding up order is made but shall not effect any new contracts of insurance.

(3) If the liquidator is satisfied that the interests of the creditors in respect of liabilities of the company attributable to its long term business require the appointment of a special manager of the company's long term business, he may apply to the court, and the court may on such application appoint a special manager of that business to act during such time as the court may direct, with such powers, including any of the powers of a receiver or manager, as may be entrusted to him by the court.

(4) [Section 177(5) of the Insolvency Act 1986] or, in the case of a special manager appointed in proceedings in Northern Ireland, [Article 151(5) of the Insolvency (Northern Ireland) Order 1989] (special manager to give security and receive remuneration) shall apply to a special manager appointed under subsection (3) above as they apply to a special manager appointed under [section 177 of the said Act of 1986] or, as the case may be, [Article 151 of the said Order of 1989].

(5) The court may, if it thinks fit and subject to such conditions (if any) as it may determine, reduce the amount of the contracts made by the company in the course of carrying on its long term business.

(6) The court may, on the application of the liquidator, a special manager appointed under subsection (3) above[, the Treasury] or the Secretary of State, appoint an independent actuary to investigate the long term business of the company and to report to the liquidator, the special manager[, the Treasury] or the Secretary of State, as the case may be, on the desirability or otherwise of that business being continued and on any reduction in the contracts made in the course of carrying on that business that may be necessary for its successful continuation.

(7) Notwithstanding [section 167 of, and Schedule 4 to, the Insolvency Act 1986] or, as the case may be, [Article 142 of, and Schedule 2 to, the Insolvency (Northern Ireland) Order 1989] (which requires a liquidator to obtain the sanction of the court or [a specified committee] for the bringing of legal proceedings in the name of and on behalf of the company) the liquidator may without any such sanction make an application in the name of and on behalf of the company under section 49 above.

(8) In this section "the court" means the court having jurisdiction to wind up the company.

NOTES

This section derived from the Insurance Companies Act 1974, s 48, and the Insurance Companies Act 1980, Sch 1, para 23.

Repealed as noted at the beginning of this Act.

Sub-s (4): words in first and third pairs of square brackets substituted by the Insolvency Act 1986, s 439(2), Sch 14; words in second and fourth pairs of square brackets substituted by the Insolvency (Northern Ireland) Order 1989, SI 1989/2405, art 381(2), Sch 9, Pt II, para 36(a).

Sub-s (6): words in square brackets substituted by the Transfer of Functions (Insurance) Order 1997, SI 1997/2781, art 8, Schedule, paras 1, 39.

Sub-s (7): words in first pair of square brackets substituted by the Insolvency Act 1986, s 439(2), Sch 14; words in second and third pairs of square brackets substituted by SI 1989/2405, art 381(2), Sch 9, para 36(b).

[7.1478]

57 Subsidiary companies

(1) Where the insurance business or any part of the insurance business of an insurance company has been transferred to an insurance company to which this Part of this Act applies under an arrangement in pursuance of which the first-mentioned company (in this section called the subsidiary company) or the creditors thereof has or have claims against the company to which the transfer was made (in this section called the principal company), then, if the principal company is being wound up by . . . the court, the court shall, subject to the provisions of this section, order the subsidiary company to be wound up in conjunction with the principal company, and may by the same or any subsequent order appoint the same person to be liquidator for the two companies, and make provision for such other matters as may seem to the court necessary, with a view to the companies being wound up as if they were one company.

(2) The commencement of the winding up of the principal company shall, save as otherwise ordered by the court, be the commencement of the winding up of the subsidiary company.

(3) In adjusting the rights and liabilities of the members of the several companies between themselves, the court shall have regard to the constitution of the companies, and to the arrangements entered into between the companies, in the same manner as the court has regard to the rights and liabilities of different classes of contributories in the case of the winding up of a single company, or as near thereto as circumstances admit.

(4) Where any company alleged to be subsidiary is not in process of being wound up at the same time as the principal company to which it is subsidiary, the court shall not direct the subsidiary company to be wound up unless, after hearing all objections (if any) that may be urged by or on behalf of the company against its being wound up, the court is of the opinion that the company is subsidiary to the principal company, and that the winding up of the company in conjunction with the principal company is just and equitable.

(5) An application may be made in relation to the winding up of any subsidiary company in conjunction with a principal company by any creditor of, or person interested in, the principal or subsidiary company.

(6) Where a company stands in the relation of a principal company to one company, and in the relation of a subsidiary company to some other company, or where there are several companies standing in the relation of subsidiary companies to one principal company, the court may deal with any number of such companies together or in separate groups, as it thinks most expedient, upon the principles laid down in this section.

NOTES

This section derived from the Insurance Companies Act 1974, s 49.

Repealed as noted at the beginning of this Act.

Sub-s (1): words omitted repealed by the Insolvency Act 1985, s 235(3), Sch 10, Pt II; as to transitional provisions, see the Insolvency Act 1986, s 437, Sch 11, Pt I, para 7 at **[1.561]** and **[1.596]**.

[7.1479]

58 Reduction of contracts as alternative to winding up

In the case of an insurance company which has been proved to be unable to pay its debts, the court may, if it thinks fit, reduce the amount of the contracts of the company on such terms and subject to such conditions as the court thinks just, in place of making a winding up order.

NOTES

This section derived from the Insurance Companies Act 1974, s 50.

Repealed as noted at the beginning of this Act.

[7.1480]

59 Winding up rules

(1) Rules may be made under [section [411 of the Insolvency Act 1986]] or [Article 359 of the Insolvency (Northern Ireland) Order 1989] (general rules about winding up) for determining the amount of the liabilities of an insurance company to policy holders of any class or description for the purpose of proof in a winding up and generally for carrying into effect the provisions of this Part of this Act with respect to the winding up of insurance companies.

(2) Without prejudice to the generality of subsection (1) above, rules under [section [411 of the Insolvency Act 1986]] or, as the case may be, [Article 359 of the said Order of 1989] may make provision for all or any of the following matters—

- *(a) the identification of the assets and liabilities falling within either paragraph of subsection (3) of section 55 above;*

(b) *the apportionment between the assets falling within paragraphs (a) and (b) of that subsection of the costs, charges and expenses of the winding up and of any debts of the company having priority under [sections 175 and 176 of, and Schedule 6 to, the Insolvency Act 1986], or, as the case may be, [Articles 149 and 150 of, and Schedule 4 to, the Insolvency (Northern Ireland) Order 1989];*

(c) *the determination of the amount of liabilities of any description falling within either paragraph of that subsection for the purpose of establishing whether or not there is any such excess in respect of that paragraph as is mentioned in subsection (4) of section 55 above;*

(d) *the application of assets within paragraph (a) of the said subsection (3) for meeting the liabilities within that paragraph;*

(e) *the application of assets representing any such excess as is mentioned in the said subsection (4).*

NOTES

This section derived from the Insurance Companies Act 1974, s 51 and the Insurance Companies Act 1980, Sch 1, para 24. Repealed as noted at the beginning of this Act.

Sub-s (1): words in first (outer) pair of square brackets substituted by the Insolvency Act 1985, s 235(1), Sch 8, para 37(1), (4)(a); words in second (inner) pair of square brackets substituted by the Insolvency Act 1986, s 439(2), Sch 14; words in third pair of square brackets substituted by the Insolvency (Northern Ireland) Order 1989, SI 1989/2405, art 381(2), Sch 9, Pt II, para 37(a).

Sub-s (2): words in first (outer) pair of square brackets substituted by the Insolvency Act 1985, s 235(1), Sch 8, para 37(4)(b); words in second (inner) and fourth pair of square brackets substituted by the Insolvency Act 1986, s 439(2), Sch 14; words in third and fifth pairs of square brackets substituted by SI 1989/2405, art 381(2), Sch 9, Pt II, para 37(b).

PART V
SUPPLEMENTARY PROVISIONS

Interpretation

[7.1481]

95 Insurance business

For the purposes of this Act "insurance business" includes—

(a) *the effecting and carrying out, by a person not carrying on a banking business, of contracts for fidelity bonds, performance bonds, administration bonds, bail bonds or customs bonds or similar contracts of guarantee, being contracts effected by way of business (and not merely incidentally to some other business carried on by the person effecting them) in return for the payment of one or more premiums;*

(b) *the effecting and carrying out of tontines;*

(c) *the effecting and carrying out, by a body (not being a body carrying on a banking business) that carries on business which is insurance business apart from this paragraph, of—*

(i) *capital redemption contracts;*

(ii) *contracts to manage the investments of pension funds (other than funds solely for the benefit of its own officers or employees and their dependants or, in the case of a company, partly for the benefit of officers or employees and their dependants of its subsidiary or holding company or a subsidiary of its holding company);*

(d) *the effecting and carrying out of contracts to pay annuities on human life.*

NOTES

This section derived from the Insurance Companies Act 1981, s 34.
Repealed as noted at the beginning of this Act.

[7.1482]

96 General interpretation

(1) In this Act, unless the context otherwise requires—

"actuary" means an actuary possessing the prescribed qualifications;

"annuities on human life" does not include superannuation allowances and annuities payable out of any fund applicable solely to the relief and maintenance of persons engaged or who have been engaged in any particular profession, trade or employment, or of the dependants of such persons;

["associate" shall be construed in accordance with section 96C below;]

"body corporate" does not include a corporation sole or a Scottish firm but includes a body incorporated outside the United Kingdom;

"chief executive" has the meaning given in [section 96D below];

["claims representative" has the meaning given in section 96F below;]

["commitment" means a commitment represented by insurance business of any of the classes specified in Schedule 1 to this Act;]

["the Companies Act" means the Companies Act 1985;]

"contract of insurance" includes any contract the effecting of which constitutes the carrying on of insurance business by virtue of section 95 above;

"controller" has the meaning given in [section 96C below];

["Community co-insurance operation" and, in relation to such an operation, "leading insurer" have the same meanings as in Council Directive 78/473/EEC of 30th May 1978 on the co-ordination of laws, regulations and administrative provisions relating to Community co-insurance;]

Part 7L Special Insolvency Regimes

"court" means the High Court of Justice in England or, in the case of an insurance company registered or having its head office in Scotland, the Court of Session or, in the case of an insurance company registered or having its head office in Northern Ireland, the High Court of Justice in Northern Ireland;

["criteria of sound and prudent management" means the criteria set out in Schedule 2A to this Act;]

"deed of settlement", in relation to an insurance company, includes any instrument constituting the company;

"director" includes any person occupying the position of director by whatever name called;

["EC company" has the meaning given in section 2 above;

"EEA Agreement" means the Agreement on the European Economic Area signed at Oporto on 2nd May 1992 as adjusted by the Protocol signed at Brussels on 17th March 1993;

"EEA State" means a State which is a Contracting Party to the EEA Agreement . . . ;

"EFTA company" has the meaning given by section 72B above;

"EFTA State" means an EEA State which is not a member State;]

"enactment" includes an enactment of the Parliament of Northern Ireland and a Measure of the Northern Ireland Assembly;

"financial year" means, subject to section 69 above, each period of twelve months at the end of which the balance of the accounts of the insurance company is struck or, if no such balance is struck, the calendar year;

"former Companies Acts" means the Companies Act 1929 or the Companies Act (Northern Ireland) 1932 and any enactment repealed by that Act of 1929 or, as the case may be, that Act of 1932 or by the Companies (Consolidation) Act 1908 [and the Companies Acts 1948 to 1983] [and the Companies Acts (Northern Ireland) 1960 to 1983];

"general business" has the meaning given in section 1 above;

"holding company" shall be construed in accordance with section [736] of the [Companies Act] or [Article 4] of the [Companies (Northern Ireland) Order 1986];

["home State", in relation to an EC company, means the member State in which the company's head office is situated;]

"industrial assurance business" has the meaning given in section 1(2) of the Industrial Assurance Act 1923 or Articles 2(2) and 3(1) of the Industrial Assurance (Northern Ireland) Order 1979;

"insolvent" means, in relation to an insurance company at any relevant date, that if proceedings had been taken for the winding up of the company the court could, in accordance with the provisions of sections [122 and 123 or section 221 of the Insolvency Act 1986] or, as the case may be, [Articles 102 and 103 or Article 185 of the Insolvency (Northern Ireland) Order 1989], hold or have held that the company was at that date unable to pay its debts;

"insurance company" means a person or body of persons (whether incorporated or not) carrying on insurance business;

"life policy" means any instrument by which the payment of money is assured on death (except death by accident only) or the happening of any contingency dependent on human life, or any instrument evidencing a contract which is subject to payment of premiums for a term dependent on human life;

"long term business" has the meaning given in section 1 above;

"long term policy holder" means a policy holder in respect of a policy the effecting of which by the insurer constituted the carrying on of long term business;

"main agent" has the meaning given in [section 96E below];

"manager", except in section 56, has the meaning given in [section 96D below];

"margin of solvency", "United Kingdom margin of solvency" and "Community margin of solvency" shall be construed in accordance with section 32 above;

["member State" shall be construed in accordance with section 2(7) . . . above;]

["non-EC company" has the meaning given in section 5 above;

"notifiable holding" means voting rights or shares which, if acquired by any person, will result in his becoming a 10 per cent shareholder controller, a 20 per cent shareholder controller, a 33 per cent shareholder controller, a 50 per cent shareholder controller or a majority shareholder controller;]

"mortgage", in relation to Scotland, means a heritable security within the meaning of section 9(8) of the Conveyancing and Feudal Reform (Scotland) Act 1970;

"ordinary long-term insurance business" means long term business that is not industrial assurance business;

["parent undertaking" shall be construed in accordance with section 258 of the Companies Act 1985 and Article 266 of the Companies (Northern Ireland) Order 1986;]

"policy"—

(a) in relation to ordinary long-term insurance business and industrial assurance business, includes an instrument evidencing a contract to pay an annuity upon human life;

(b) in relation to insurance business of any other class includes any policy under which there is for the time being an existing liability already accrued or under which a liability may accrue; and

(c) in relation to capital redemption business, includes any policy, bond, certificate, receipt or other instrument evidencing the contract with the company;

"policy holder" means the person who for the time being is the legal holder of the policy for securing the contract with the insurance company or, in relation to capital redemption business, means the person who for the time being is the legal holder of the policy, bond, certificate, receipt or other instrument evidencing the contract with the company, and—

(a) in relation to such ordinary long-term insurance business or industrial assurance business as consists in the granting of annuities upon human life, includes an annuitant; and

(b) in relation to insurance business of any kind other than such as is mentioned in the foregoing paragraph or capital redemption business, includes a person to whom, under a policy, a sum is due or a periodic payment is payable;

"prescribed" means prescribed by regulations under this Act; "registered society" means a society registered or deemed to be registered under the Industrial and Provident Societies Act 1965 or the Industrial and Provident Societies Act (Northern Ireland) 1969;

"registrar of companies" has [the same meaning as in] the [Companies Act] and "registrar of companies in Northern Ireland" means the registrar of companies within the meaning of [Article 2 of the Companies (Northern Ireland) Order 1986];

["relevant motor vehicle risks" means risks falling within class 10 of Schedule 2 to this Act (motor vehicle liability), but excluding carrier's liability;

"shareholder controller", "10 per cent shareholder controller", "20 per cent shareholder controller", "33 per cent shareholder controller", "50 per cent shareholder controller" and "majority shareholder controller" have the meanings given by section 96C below;

"State of the commitment", in relation to a commitment entered into at any date, means—

(a) where the policy holder is an individual, the State in which he had his habitual residence at that date;

(b) where the policy holder is not an individual, the State in which the establishment of the policy holder to which the commitment relates was situated at that date,

and "member State of the commitment" shall be construed accordingly;]

"subsidiary", except in section 57, shall be construed in accordance with section [736] of the [Companies Act] or [Article 4] of the [Companies (Northern Ireland) Order 1986];

["subsidiary undertaking" shall be construed in accordance with section 258 of the Companies Act and Article 266 of the Companies (Northern Ireland) Order 1986;]

["supervisory authority", in relation to a member State other than the United Kingdom or in relation to Switzerland, means the authority responsible in that State or country for supervising insurance companies;]

["Swiss general insurance company" has the meaning given in section 11 above;]

["UK company" has the meaning given in section 5 above;]

"underwriter" includes any person named in a policy or other contract of insurance as liable to pay or contribute towards the payment of the sum secured by the policy or contract;

"valuation regulations" means regulations under section 90 above;

"vessel" includes hovercraft.

(2) References in this Act to a fund or funds maintained in respect of long term business are references to a fund or funds maintained under section 28(1)(b) above and in sections 48(3) and 55(6) above include references to a fund or funds maintained under section 3(1) of the Insurance Companies Act 1958 or section 14(1) of the Insurance Companies Act (Northern Ireland) 1968.

(3) A person shall not be deemed to be within the meaning of any provision of this Act a person in accordance with whose directions or instructions the directors of a company or other body corporate or any of them are accustomed to act by reason only that the directors of the company or body act on advice given by him in a professional capacity.

[(2B) Any reference in this Act—

(a) to an undertaking being closely linked with any person, or being closely linked with any person by control; or

(b) to an undertaking's close links with any person,

shall be construed in accordance with regulation 2 of the Financial Institutions (Prudential Supervision) Regulations 1996).]

(4) Any reference in this Act to an enactment of the Parliament of Northern Ireland or a Measure of the Northern Ireland Assembly shall include a reference to any enactment re-enacting it with or without modifications.

[(5) Except as otherwise provided by paragraph 27 of Schedule 2F to this Act, this Act shall apply as if Gibraltar were a member State.]

NOTES

This section derived from the Insurance Companies Act 1974, s 85, the Insurance Companies Act 1980, Sch 1, para 35 and the Insurance Companies Act 1981, s 35(1), Sch 4, para 15.

Repealed as noted at the beginning of this Act.

Sub-s (1): definitions "associate", "Community co-insurance operation" and "leading insurer", "criteria of sound and prudent management", "EC company", "EEA Agreement", "EEA State", "EFTA company", "EFTA State", "home State", "relevant motor vehicle risks", "shareholder controller", "10 per cent shareholder controller", "20 per cent shareholder controller", "33 per cent shareholder controller", "50 per cent shareholder controller", "majority shareholder controller", "State of the commitment", "subsidiary undertaking", "UK company" inserted, and in definitions "chief executive", "controller", "main agent", "manager", words in square brackets substituted by the Insurance Companies (Third Insurance Directives) Regulations 1994, SI 1994/1696, reg 50(1); definition "claims representative" substituted by SI 1994/1696, reg 50(1); definition "commitment" inserted by the Insurance Companies (Amendment) Regulations 1993, SI 1993/174, reg 6(2); definition "the Companies Act" inserted by the Companies Consolidation (Consequential Provisions) Act 1985, s 30, Sch 2; in definition "EEA State" words omitted repealed by the Insurance Companies (Amendment No 2) Regulations 1996, SI 1996/944, reg 4(3)(a), subject to transitional provisions in regs 7, 8 thereof; in definition "former Companies Acts" words in first pair of square brackets inserted by the Companies Consolidation (Consequential Provisions) Act 1985, s 30, Sch 2, words in final pair of square brackets added by the Companies Consolidation (Consequential Provisions) (Northern Ireland) Order 1986, SI 1986/1035, art 23, Sch 1, Part II; in definitions "holding company", "registrar of companies" and "subsidiary" words in first and second pairs of square brackets substituted by the Companies Consolidation (Consequential Provisions) Act 1985, s 30, Sch 2, words in other pairs of square brackets substituted by SI 1986/1035, art 23, Sch 1, Part II; in definition "insolvent" words in first pair of square brackets substituted by the Insolvency Act 1986, s 439(2), Sch 14, words in second pair of square brackets substituted by the Insolvency (Northern Ireland) Order 1989, SI 1989/2405, art 381, Sch 9, Part II, para 38; definition "member State" inserted by the Insurance Companies (Amendment) Regulations 1994, SI 1994/3132, reg 3(2), words omitted repealed by SI 1996/944, reg 4(3)(b), subject to transitional provisions in regs 7, 8 thereof; definitions "non-EC company" and "notifiable holding" substituted for definition "member State of the commitment" by SI 1994/1696, reg 50(1); definition "parent undertaking" inserted by the Insurance Companies (Amendment) Regulations 1992, SI 1992/2890, reg 9(3); definitions "supervisory authority" substituted and "Swiss general insurance company" inserted by the Insurance Companies (Switzerland) Regulations 1993, SI 1993/3127, reg 4.

Sub-s (2B): inserted by the Financial Institutions (Prudential Supervision) Regulations 1996, SI 1996/1669, reg 50(2). Note: there appears to be an error in the numbering of this subsection and it is thought that it should be numbered (3A).

Sub-s (5): added by SI 1994/1696, reg 50(2).

Regulations: the Insurance (Lloyd's) Regulations 1983, SI 1983/224; the Insurance Companies (Accounts and Statements) Regulations 1996, SI 1996/943; the Insurance (Fees) Regulations 2001, SI 2001/812.

Companies Act 1929: repealed with savings by the Companies Act 1948, s 459, Sch 17.

Companies Act (Northern Ireland) 1932: repealed with savings by the Companies Act (Northern Ireland) 1960, s 403, Sch 13.

Companies (Consolidation) Act 1908: repealed by the Companies Act 1929, s 381, Sch 12.

Companies Acts 1948 to 1983: repealed by the Companies Consolidation (Consequential Provisions) Act 1985, s 29, Sch 1.

Insurance Companies Act 1958, s 3(1): repealed by the Insurance Companies Amendment Act 1973, s 54(3).

Insurance Companies Act (Northern Ireland) 1968: repealed by the Insurance Companies Act 1980, s 4(2), (3), Schs 4, 5.

Financial Institutions (Prudential Supervision) Regulations 1996: revoked by the Financial Services and Markets Act 2000 (Consequential Amendments and Repeals) Order 2001, SI 2001/3649.

[7.1483]

[96A Interpretation of expressions derived from . . . insurance Directives

(1) In this Act—

(a) "the first general insurance Directive" means Council Directive 73/239/EEC of 24 July 1973 on the coordination of laws, regulations and administrative provisions relating to the taking-up and pursuit of the business of direct insurance other than life assurance;

(b) "the second general insurance Directive" means Council Directive 88/357/EEC of 22 June 1988 on the coordination of laws, regulations and administrative provisions relating to direct insurance other than life assurance and laying down provisions to facilitate the effective exercise of freedom to provide services and amending Directive 73/239/EEC;

[(c) "the third general insurance Directive" means Council Directive 92/49/EEC of 18 June 1992 on the coordination of laws, regulations and administrative provisions relating to direct insurance other than life assurance and amending Directives 73/239/EEC and 88/357/EEC;]

and "the general insurance Directives" means those Directives as amended and such other Directives as make provision with respect to the business of direct insurance other than life assurance.

[(1A) The Directives amending the general insurance Directives referred to in subsection (1) above include Council Directive 90/618/EEC amending, particularly as regards motor vehicle liability insurance, Directive 73/239/EEC and Directive 88/357/EEC.]

[(1B) In this Act—

(a) "the first long term insurance Directive" means Council Directive 79/267/EEC of 5 March 1979 on the coordination of laws, regulations and administrative provisions relating to the taking up and pursuit of the business of direct life assurance;

(b) "the second long term insurance Directive" means Council Directive 90/619/EEC of 8 November 1990 on the coordination of laws, regulations and administrative provisions relating to direct life assurance, laying down provisions to facilitate the effective exercise of freedom to provide services and amending Directive 79/267/EEC;

[(c) "the third long term insurance Directive" means Council Directive 92/96/EEC of 10 November 1992 on the coordination of laws, regulations and administrative provisions relating to direct life assurance and amending Directives 79/267/EEC and 90/619/EEC;] and "the long term insurance Directives" means those Directives.]

[(1C) Any reference in this Act to the first or third general insurance Directive, or to the first of third long term insurance Directive, is a reference to that Directive as amended by the Prudential Supervision Directive (within the meaning of the Financial Institutions (Prudential Supervision) Regulations 1996).]

[(2) In this Act, in relation to an insurance company, "establishment" means the head office or a branch of the company; and references to a company being established in a State mean that the company has its head office or a branch there.

Any permanent presence of an insurance company in a State other than that in which it has its head office shall be regarded as a single branch, whether that presence consists of a single office which, or two or more offices each of which—

(a) is managed by the company's own staff;

(b) is an agency of the company; or

(c) is managed by a person who is independent but has permanent authority to act for the company in the same way as an agency.]

Any permanent presence of such a company in a member State shall be regarded as a branch or agency, even if that presence consists merely of an office managed by the company's own staff or by a person who is independent but has permanent authority to act for the company in the same way as an agency.

(3) References in this Act to the member State where the risk is situated are—

(a) where the insurance relates to buildings or to buildings and their contents (in so far as the contents are covered by the same policy), to the member State in which the property is situated;

(b) *where the insurance relates to vehicles of any type, to the member State of registration;*
(c) *in the case of policies of a duration of four months or less covering travel or holiday risks (whatever the class concerned), to the member State where the policy holder took out the policy;*
(d) *in a case not covered by paragraph (a) to (c)—*
(i) *where the policy holder is an individual, to the member State where he has his habitual residence [at the date when the contract is entered into];*
(ii) *otherwise, to the member State where the establishment of the policy holder to which the policy relates is situated [at that date].*

[(3A) In this Act references to the provision of insurance in the United Kingdom or any other EEA State are references to either or both of the following—
(a) *the covering (otherwise than by way of reinsurance) of a risk situated there through an establishment in another EEA State ("the provision of general insurance"); and*
(b) *the covering (otherwise than by way of reinsurance) of a commitment situated there through an establishment in another EEA State ("the provision of long term insurance").]*

(4) In this Act the "ECU" means the unit of account of that name defined in Council Regulation (EEC) No 3180/78 as amended.

The exchange rates as between the ECU and the currencies of the member States to be applied for each year beginning on 31st December shall be the rates applicable on the last day of the preceding October for which rates for the currencies of all the member States were published in the Official Journal of the Communities.]

NOTES

Inserted by the Insurance Companies (Amendment) Regulations 1990, SI 1990/1333, reg 2(1).

Repealed as noted at the beginning of this Act.

Words omitted from the section heading repealed by the Insurance Companies (Amendment) Regulations 1993, SI 1993/174, reg 6(1), (3).

Sub-s (1): para (c) inserted by the Insurance Companies (Third Insurance Directives) Regulations 1994, SI 1994/1696, reg 51(1).

Sub-s (1A): inserted, together with sub-s (1B), by the Insurance Companies (Amendment) Regulations 1992, SI 1992/2890, reg 9(1), (4).

Sub-s (1B): inserted, together with sub-s (1A), by SI 1992/2890, reg 9(1), (4); substituted by the Insurance Companies (Amendment) Regulations 1993, SI 1993/174, reg 6(1), (4); para (c) inserted by SI 1994/1696, reg 51(2).

Sub-s (1C): inserted by the Financial Institutions (Prudential Supervision) Regulations 1996, SI 1996/1669, reg 23, Sch 5, para 8.

Sub-s (2): substituted by SI 1994/1696, reg 51(3).

Sub-s (3): words in square brackets in para (d) inserted by the Insurance Companies (Amendment) Regulations 1994, SI 1994/3132, reg 10(4).

Sub-s (3A): inserted by SI 1994/1696, reg 51(4).

Financial Institutions (Prudential Supervision) Regulations 1996: revoked by the Financial Services and Markets Act 2000 (Consequential Amendments and Repeals) Order 2001, SI 2001/3649.

INSURANCE COMPANIES (WINDING-UP) RULES 1985

(SI 1985/95)

NOTES

Made: 25 January 1985.

Authority: Companies Act 1985, s 365(1) (repealed); Insurance Companies Act 1982, s 59; in so far as made under the Companies Act 1985, s 365(1) these rules now have effect as if made under the Insolvency Act 1986, s 411.

Commencement: 1 March 1985.

These Rules were revoked and replaced by the Insurers (Winding-Up) Rules 2001, SI 2001/3635 at **[7.1532]** et seq, in relation to proceedings for the winding up of an insurer which commence on or after 1 December 2001.

Official receiver: as to the contracting out of certain functions of the Official receiver conferred by or under these rules, see the Contracting Out (Functions of the Official Receiver) Order 1995, SI 1995/1386 at **[12.4]**.

ARRANGEMENT OF RULES

1 Citation and commencement . . . . . [7.1484]
2 Interpretation . . . . . [7.1485]
3 Application . . . . . [7.1486]
4 Appointment of liquidator . . . . . [7.1487]
5 Separation of long term and other business in winding-up . . . . . [7.1488]
6 Valuation of general business policies . . . . . [7.1489]
7, 8 Valuation of long term policies . . . . . [7.1490], [7.1491]
9, 10 Attribution of assets and liabilities to the long term business . . . . . [7.1492], [7.1493]
11 Excess of long term business assets . . . . . [7.1494]
12 Actuarial advice . . . . . [7.1495]
13 Utilisation of excess of assets . . . . . [7.1496]
14 Special bank account . . . . . [7.1497]
15 Custody of assets . . . . . [7.1498]
16 Maintenance of accounting, valuation and other records . . . . . [7.1499]

17 Additional powers in relation to the long term business . . . [7.1500]
18 Accounts and audit . . . [7.1501]
20 Security by liquidator and special manager . . . [7.1502]
21 Proof of debts . . . [7.1503]
22 Failure to pay premiums . . . [7.1504]
23 Notice of valuation of policy . . . [7.1505]
24 Dividends to creditors . . . [7.1506]
25 Meetings of creditors . . . [7.1507]
26 Remuneration of Liquidator carrying on long term business . . . [7.1508]
27 Appointment of costs payable out of the assets . . . [7.1509]
28 Notice of stop order . . . [7.1510]

SCHEDULES

Schedule 1—General business policies . . . [7.1511]
Schedule 2—Rules for valuing non-linked life policies, non-linked deferred annuity policies, non-linked annuities in payment and capital redemption policies . . . [7.1512]
Schedule 3—Rules for valuing life policies and deferred annuity policies which are linked policies . . . [7.1513]
Schedule 4—Rules for valuing long term policies which are not dealt with in Schedules 2 and 3 . . . [7.1514]
Schedule 5—Rules for valuing long term policies where a stop order has been made . . . [7.1515]
Schedule 6 . . . [7.1516]

[7.1484]
1 Citation and commencement

These Rules may be cited as the Insurance Companies (Winding-Up) Rules 1985 and shall come into operation on 1st March 1985.

NOTES

Revoked as noted at the beginning of these Rules.

[7.1485]
2 Interpretation

(1) In these Rules, unless the context or subject-matter otherwise requires:—

"the Act of 1923" means the Industrial Assurance Act 1923;

. . .

"the Act of 1982" means the Insurance Companies Act 1982;

["the Act of 1985" means the Companies Act 1985;

"the Act of 1986" means the Insolvency Act 1986;]

"company" means an insurance company which is being wound up;

"excess of the long term business assets" means the amount, if any, by which the value as at the date of the winding-up order of the assets representing the fund or funds maintained by the company in respect of its long term business exceeds the value as at that date of the liabilities of the company attributable to that business;

"excess of the other business assets" means the amount, if any, by which the value as at the date of the winding-up order of the assets of the company which do not represent the fund or funds maintained by the company in respect of its long term business exceeds the value as at that date of the liabilities of the company (other than liabilities in respect of share capital) which are not attributable to that business;

"general business policy" means a policy the effecting of which by the company constitutes the carrying on of general business;

["the general regulations" means the Insolvency Regulations 1986;]

"the Industrial Assurance Acts" means the Act of 1923 and the Industrial Assurance and Friendly Societies Act 1929;

"insurance company" means an insurance company to which Part II of the Act of 1982 applies;

"linked liability" means any liability under a policy the effecting of which constitutes the carrying on of long term insurance business the amount of which is determined by reference to:—

(a) the value of property of any description (whether or not specified in the policy),

(b) fluctuations in the value of such property,

(c) income from any such property, or

(d) fluctuations in an index of the value of such property;

"linked policy" means a policy which provides for linked liabilities and a policy which when made provided for linked liabilities shall be deemed to be a linked policy even if the policy holder has elected to convert his rights under the policy so that at the date of the winding-up order there are no longer linked liabilities under the policy;

"long term policy" means a policy the effecting of which by the company constitutes the carrying on of long term business;

"non-linked policy" means a policy which is not a linked policy;

"other business", in relation to a company carrying on long term business, means such of the business of the company as is not long term business;

["the principal Rules" means the Insolvency rules 1986;]

"stop order" in relation to a company means an order of the court, made under section 56(2) of the Act of 1982, ordering the Liquidator to stop carrying on the long term business of the company;

"unit" in relation to a linked policy means any unit (whether or not described as a unit in the policy) by reference to the numbers and value of which the amount of the linked liabilities under the policy at any time is measured.

(2) Unless the context otherwise requires words or expressions contained in these Rules bear the same meaning as in the principal Rules, [the general regulations], . . . the Act of 1982, [the Act of 1986] or any statutory modification thereof respectively.

NOTES

Revoked as noted at the beginning of these Rules.

Para (1): definition omitted revoked, definitions "the Act of 1985", "the Act of 1986" and "the general regulations" inserted, and definition "the principal Rules" substituted, by the Insurance Companies (Winding-up) (Amendment) Rules 1986, SI 1986/2002, r 4.

Para (2): words in square brackets inserted, and words omitted revoked, by SI 1986/2002, r 4.

Industrial Assurance Act 1923: amended and partially repealed by the Friendly Societies Act 1992, s 120(2), Sch 22, Pt I. The remainder of the Act is repealed by the Financial Services and Markets Act 2000, ss 416(1)(a), 432(3), Sch 22.

Industrial Assurance and Friendly Societies Act 1929: repealed by the Friendly Societies Act 1992, s 120(2), Sch 22, Pt I.

Insolvency Regulations 1986 (SI 1986/1994): revoked and replaced by the Insolvency Regulations 1994, SI 1994/2507.

Note that the Insolvency Rules 1986, SI 1986/1925 are revoked and replaced (as from 6 April 2017 and subject to transitional provisions) by the Insolvency (England and Wales) Rules 2016, SI 2016/1024 at **[6.2]**.

[7.1486]

3 Application

(1) These Rules apply to proceedings for the winding-up of an insurance company which commence on or after the date on which these Rules come into operation.

(2) These Rules supplement the principal Rules [and the general regulations] which continue to apply to the proceedings in the winding-up of an insurance company under [the Act of 1986] as they apply to proceedings in the winding-up of any company under that Act but in the event of conflict between these Rules and the principal Rules [or the general regulations] these Rules prevail.

NOTES

Revoked as noted at the beginning of these Rules.

Para (2): words in first and third pairs of square brackets inserted, and words in second pair of square brackets substituted, by the Insurance Companies (Winding-up) (Amendment) Rules 1986, SI 1986/2002, r 5.

[7.1487]

[4 Appointment of Liquidator

Where the court considers the appointment of a liquidator under—

(a) section 139(4) of the Act of 1986 (court appointment of liquidator where conflict between creditors and contributories), or

(b) section 140 of that Act (court appointment of liquidator following administration or voluntary arrangement),

the Policyholders Protection Board may appear on the application or (as the case may be) the petition, and make representations as to the person to be appointed.]

NOTES

Revoked as noted at the beginning of these Rules.

Substituted by the Insurance Companies (Winding-up) (Amendment) Rules 1986, SI 1986/2002, r 6.

[7.1488]

5 Separation of long term and other business in winding-up

(1) This Rule applies in the case of a company carrying on long term business.

(2) The assets of the company which in accordance with sections 55(3) and (4) of the Act of 1982 are available for meeting the liabilities of the company attributable to its long term business shall, in pursuance of [section 148 of the Act of 1986], be applied in discharge of those liabilities as though those assets and those liabilities were the assets and liabilities of a separate company.

(3) The assets of the company which in accordance with sections 55(3) and (4) of the Act of 1982 are available for meeting the liabilities of the company attributable to its other business shall, in pursuance of [section 148 of the Act of 1986], be applied in discharge of those liabilities as though those assets and those liabilities were the assets and liabilities of a separate company.

NOTES

Revoked as noted at the beginning of these Rules.

Paras (2), (3): words in square brackets substituted by the Insurance Companies (Winding-up) (Amendment) Rules 1986, SI 1986/2002, r 7.

[7.1489]

6 Valuation of general business policies

Except in relation to amounts which have fallen due for payment before the date of the winding-up order, the holder of a general business policy shall be admitted as a creditor in relation to his policy without proof for an amount equal to the value of the policy and for this purpose the value of a policy shall be determined in accordance with Schedule 1.

NOTES

Revoked as noted at the beginning of these Rules.

[7.1490]

7 Valuation of long term policies

(1) This Rule applies in relation to a company's long term business where no stop order has been made.

(2) In relation to a claim under a policy which has fallen due for payment before the date of the winding-up order, a policy holder shall be admitted as a creditor without proof for such amount as appears from the records of the company to be due in respect of that claim.

(3) In all other respects a policy holder shall be admitted as a creditor in relation to his policy without proof for an amount equal to the value of the policy and for this purpose the value of a policy of any class shall be determined in the manner applicable to policies of that class provided by Schedules 2, 3 and 4.

(4) This Rule applies in relation to a person entitled to apply for a free paid-up policy under section 24 of the Act of 1923 and to whom no such policy has been issued before the date of the winding-up order (whether or not it was applied for) as if such a policy had been issued immediately before the date of the winding-up order—

- *(a) for the minimum amount determined in accordance with section 24(2) of the Act of 1923, or*
- *(b) if the Liquidator is satisfied that it was the practice of the company during the five years immediately before the date of the winding-up order to issue policies under the said section 24 in excess of the minimum amounts so determined, for the amount determined in accordance with that practice.*

NOTES

Revoked as noted at the beginning of these Rules.

[7.1491]

8

(1) This Rule applies in relation to a company's long term business where a stop order has been made.

(2) In relation to a claim under a policy which has fallen due for payment on or after the date of the winding-up order and before the date of the stop order, a policy holder shall be admitted as a creditor without proof for such amount as appears from the records of the company and of the Liquidator to be due in respect of that claim.

(3) In all other respects a policy holder shall be admitted as a creditor in relation to his policy without proof for an amount equal to the value of the policy and for this purpose the value of a policy of any class shall be determined in the manner applicable to policies of that class provided by Schedule 5.

(4) Paragraph (4) of Rule 7 applies for the purposes of this Rule as if references to the date of the winding-up order (other than that in sub-paragraph (b) of that paragraph) were references to the date of the stop order.

NOTES

Revoked as noted at the beginning of these Rules.

[7.1492]

9 Attribution of assets and liabilities to the long term business

(1) This Rule applies in the case of a company carrying on long term business if at the date of the winding-up order there are liabilities of the company in respect of which it is not clear from the accounting and other records of the company whether they are or are not attributable to the company's long term business.

(2) The Liquidator shall, in such manner and according to such accounting principles as he shall determine, identify the liabilities referred to in paragraph (1) as attributable or not attributable to a company's long term business and those liabilities shall for the purposes of the winding-up be deemed as at the date of the winding-up order to be so attributable or not as the case may be.

(3) In making his determination under this Rule the Liquidator may determine that some liabilities are attributable to the company's long term business and that others are not or he may determine that a part of a liability is attributable to the company's long term business and that the remainder of that liability is not and he may use one method for some of the liabilities and the other method for the remainder of them.

NOTES

Revoked as noted at the beginning of these Rules.

[7.1493]

10

(1) This Rule applies in the case of a company carrying on long term business if at the date of the winding-up order there are assets of the company in respect of which—

- *(a) it is not clear from the accounting and other records of the company whether they do or do not represent the fund or funds maintained by the company in respect of its long term business, and*

(b) it cannot be inferred from the source of the income out of which those assets were provided whether they do or do not represent those funds.

(2) Subject to paragraph (6) the Liquidator shall determine which (if any) of the assets referred to in paragraph (1) are attributable to those funds and which (if any) are not and those assets shall, for the purposes of the winding-up, be deemed as at the date of the winding-up order to represent those funds or not in accordance with the Liquidator's determination.

(3) For the purposes of paragraph (2) the Liquidator may:—

(a) determine that some of those assets shall be attributable to those funds and that others of them shall not (the first method); or

(b) determine that a part of the value of one of those assets shall be attributable to those funds and that the remainder of that value shall not (the second method),

and he may use the first method for some of those assets and the second method for others of them.

(4)

(a) In making the attribution the Liquidator's objective shall in the first instance be so far as possible to reduce any deficit that may exist, at the date of the winding-up order and before any attribution is made, either in the company's long term business or in its other business.

(b) If there is a deficit in both the company's long term business and its other business the attribution shall be in the ratio that the amount of the one deficit bears to the amount of the other until the deficits are eliminated.

(c) Thereafter the attribution shall be in the ratio which the aggregate amount of the liabilities attributable to the company's long term business bears to the aggregate amount of the liabilities not so attributable.

(5) For the purpose of paragraph (4) the value of a liability of the company shall, if it falls to be valued under Rule 6 or 7, have the same value as it has under that Rule but otherwise it shall have such value as would have been included in relation to it in a balance sheet of the company prepared in pursuance of section 17 of the Act of 1982 as at the date of the winding-up order and, for the purpose of determining the ratio referred to in paragraph (4) but not for the purpose of determining the amount of any deficit therein referred to, the net balance of shareholders' funds shall be included in the liabilities not attributable to the company's long term business.

(6) Notwithstanding anything in the preceding paragraphs of this Rule the court may order that the determination of which (if any) of the assets referred to in paragraph (1) are attributable to the fund or funds maintained by the company in respect of its long term business and which (if any) are not shall be made in such manner and by such methods as the court may direct or the court may itself make the determination.

NOTES

Revoked as noted at the beginning of these Rules.

[7.1494]

11 Excess of long term business assets

Where the company is one carrying on long term business, for the purpose of determining the amount, if any, of the excess of the long term business assets, there shall be included amongst the liabilities of the company attributable to its long term business an amount determined by the Liquidator in respect of liabilities and expenses likely to be incurred in connection with the transfer of the company's long term business as a going concern to another insurance company being liabilities not included in the valuation of the long term policies made in pursuance of Rule 7.

NOTES

Revoked as noted at the beginning of these Rules.

[7.1495]

12 Actuarial advice

(1) Before determining the value of a policy in accordance with Schedules 1 to 5 (other than paragraph 2 of Schedule 1), before identifying long term assets and liabilities in accordance with Rules 9 and 10 and before determining the amount (if any) of the excess of the long term business assets in accordance with Rule 11, and before determining the terms on which he will accept payment of overdue premiums under Rule 22(1) and the amount and nature of any compensation under Rule 22(2), the Liquidator shall obtain and consider advice thereon (including an estimate of any value or amount required to be determined) from an actuary.

(2) Before seeking, for the purpose of valuing a policy, the direction of the court as to the assumption of a particular rate of interest or the employment of any rates of mortality or disability, the Liquidator shall obtain and consider advice thereon from an actuary.

NOTES

Revoked as noted at the beginning of these Rules.

[7.1496]

13 Utilisation of excess of assets

(1) Except at the direction of the court

(a) *no distribution may be made out of and no transfer to another insurance company may be made of any part of the excess of the long term business assets which has been transferred to the other business, and*

(b) *no distribution may be made out of and no transfer to another insurance company may be made of any part of the excess of the other business assets which has been transferred to the long term business.*

(2) Before giving a direction under paragraph (1) the court may require the Liquidator to advertise the proposal to make a distribution or a transfer in such manner as the court shall direct.

NOTES

Revoked as noted at the beginning of these Rules.

[7.1497]

14 Special bank account

(1) In the case of a company carrying on long term business, in whose case no stop order has been made, [Regulation 6 of the general regulations] applies only in relation to the company's other business.

(2) The Liquidator of such a company may open any [local bank account] which he is authorised to open by the Secretary of State and he may pay into such an account any moneys which form part of the assets representing the fund or funds maintained by the company in respect of its long term business.

(3) All payments out of any such [local bank account] shall be made by cheque payable to order and every cheque shall have marked or written on the face of it the name of the company and shall be signed by the Liquidator or by any special manager appointed under section 56(3) of the Act of 1982 . . .

NOTES

Revoked as noted at the beginning of these Rules.

Paras (1), (2): words in square brackets substituted by the Insurance Companies (Winding-up) (Amendment) Rules 1986, SI 1986/2002, r 8.

Para (3): words in square brackets substituted, and words omitted revoked, by SI 1986/2002, r 8.

Regulation 6 of the general regulations: this should be construed as a reference to the Insolvency Regulations 1994, SI 1994/2507, reg 6.

[7.1498]

15 Custody of assets

(1) The Secretary of State may, in the case of a company carrying on long term business in whose case no stop order has been made, require that the whole or a specified proportion of the assets representing the fund or funds maintained by the company in respect of its long term business shall be held by a person approved by him for the purpose as trustee for the company.

(2) No assets held by a person as trustee for a company in compliance with a requirement imposed under this Rule shall, so long as the requirement is in force, be released except with the consent of the Secretary of State but they may be transposed by the trustee into other assets by any transaction or series of transactions on the written instructions of the Liquidator.

(3) The Liquidator may not grant any mortgage or charge of assets which are held by a person as trustee for the company in compliance with a requirement imposed under this Rule except with the consent of the Secretary of State.

NOTES

Revoked as noted at the beginning of these Rules.

[7.1499]

16 Maintenance of accounting, valuation and other records

(1) In the case of a company carrying on long term business, in whose case no stop order has been made, [Regulation 9 of the general regulations] applies only in relation to the company's other business.

(2) The Liquidator of such a company shall, with a view to the long term business of the company being transferred to another insurance company, maintain such minute books and accounting, valuation and other records as will enable such other insurance company upon the transfer being effected to comply with the requirements of the provisions of the Act of 1982 relating to accounts and statements of insurance companies.

NOTES

Revoked as noted at the beginning of these Rules.

Para (1): words in square brackets substituted by the Insurance Companies (Winding-up) (Amendment) Rules 1986, SI 1986/2002, r 9.

Regulation 9 of the general regulations: this should be construed as a reference to the Insolvency Regulations 1994, SI 1994/2507, reg 10.

[7.1500]

17 Additional powers in relation to the long term business

(1) In the case of a company carrying on long term business, in whose case no stop order has been made, [Regulation 18 of the general regulations] applies only in relation to the company's other business.

(2) The Liquidator of a company carrying on long term business shall, so long as no stop order has been made, have power to do all such things as may be necessary to the performance of his duties under section 56(2) of the Act of 1982 but the Secretary of State may require him—

(a) not to make investments of a specified class or description,

(b) to realise, before the expiration of a specified period (or such longer period as the Secretary of State may allow), the whole or a specified proportion of investments of a specified class or description held by the Liquidator when the requirement is imposed.

NOTES

Revoked as noted at the beginning of these Rules.

Para (1): words in square brackets substituted by the Insurance Companies (Winding-up) (Amendment) Rules 1986, SI 1986/2002, r 10.

Regulation 18 of the general regulations: this should be construed as a reference to the Insolvency Regulations 1994, SI 1994/2507, reg 9.

[7.1501]

18 Accounts and audit

(1) In the case of a company carrying on long term business, in whose case no stop order has been made, [Regulations 9(2), 10, 12 and 13 of the general regulations] apply only in relation to the company's other business.

(2) The Liquidator of such a company shall supply the Secretary of State, at such times or intervals as he shall specify, with such accounts as he may specify and audited in such manner as he may require and with such information about specified matters and verified in such specified manner as he may require.

(3) The Liquidator of such a company shall, if required to do so by the Secretary of State, instruct an actuary to investigate the financial condition of the company's long term business and to report thereon in such manner as the Secretary of State may specify.

(4) The Liquidator of such a company shall, at the expiration of six months from the date of the winding-up order and at the expiration of every six months thereafter, prepare a summary of his receipts and payments in the course of carrying on the long term business of the company during that period, procure that the summary be examined and verified by [a person eligible for appointment as a company auditor under section 25 of the Companies Act 1989] and transmit to the Secretary of State two copies of the summary verified as aforesaid.

(5) The Secretary of State shall file one of these copies with the Registrar and that copy shall be open to the inspection of any person on payment of the same fee as is payable with respect to the inspection of the file of proceedings under [any order made under section 130 of the Supreme Court Act 1981 or under section 128 of the County Courts Act 1984].

NOTES

Revoked as noted at the beginning of these Rules.

Paras (1), (5): words in square brackets substituted by the Insurance Companies (Winding-up) (Amendment) Rules 1986, SI 1986/2002, r 11.

Para (4): words in square brackets substituted by the Companies Act 1989 (Eligibility for Appointment as Company Auditor) (Consequential Amendments) Regulations 1991, SI 1991/1997, reg 2, Schedule, para 61.

Regulations 9(2), 10, 12 and 13 of the general regulations: this should be construed as a reference to the Insolvency Regulations 1994, SI 1994/2507, regs 10(4), (5), 12, 14 and 15.

19 *(Revoked by the Insurance Companies (Winding-up) (Amendment) Rules 1986, SI 1986/2002, r 12.)*

[7.1502]

20 Security by liquidator and special manager

In the case of a company carrying on long term business, in whose case no stop order has been made, [Rule 4.207] of the principal Rules applies separately to the company's long term business and to its other business.

NOTES

Revoked as noted at the beginning of these Rules.

Words in square brackets substituted by the Insurance Companies (Winding-up) (Amendment) Rules 1986, SI 1986/2002, r 13.

[7.1503]

21 Proof of debts

(1) This Rule applies in the case of a company carrying on long term business.

(2) The Liquidator may in relation to the company's long term business and to its other business fix different days on or before which the creditors of the company who are required to prove their debts or claims are to prove their debts or claims and he may fix one of those days without at the same time fixing the other.

(3) In submitting a proof of any debt a creditor may claim the whole or any part of such debt as attributable to the company's long term business or to its other business or he may make no such attribution.

(4) When he admits any debt in whole or in part the Liquidator shall state in writing how much of what he admits is attributable to the company's long term business and how much to the company's other business.

NOTES

Revoked as noted at the beginning of these Rules.

[7.1504]

22 Failure to pay premiums

(1) The Liquidator may in the course of carrying on the company's long term business and on such terms as he thinks fit accept payment of a premium even though the payment is tendered after the date on which under the terms of the policy it was finally due to be paid.

(2) The Liquidator may in the course of carrying on the company's long term business, and having regard to the general practice of insurers, compensate a policy holder whose policy has lapsed in consequence of a failure to pay any premium by issuing a free paid-up policy for reduced benefits or otherwise as the Liquidator thinks fit.

NOTES

Revoked as noted at the beginning of these Rules.

[7.1505]

23 Notice of valuation of policy

(1) The Liquidator shall give notice of the value of each general business policy, as determined by him in accordance with Rule 6, to the persons appearing from the records of the company or otherwise to be entitled to an interest in that policy and he shall do so in such manner as the court may direct.

(2) In the case of a company carrying on long term business, if the Liquidator, before a stop order is made in relation to the company, summons a separate general meeting of creditors in respect of liabilities of the company attributable to its long term business in pursuance of [section 168 of the Act of 1986] as that section has effect by virtue of section 55(5) of the Act of 1982, he shall give notice in Form No 1 set out in Schedule 6 to the persons appearing from the records of the company or otherwise to be entitled to a payment under or to an interest in a long term policy of the amount of that payment or the value of that policy as determined by him in accordance with Rules 7(2) or (3) as the case may be and he shall give that notice with the notice summoning the meeting.

(3) If a stop order is made in relation to the company the Liquidator shall give notice to all the persons appearing from the records of the company or otherwise to be entitled to a payment under or to an interest in a long term policy of the amount of that payment or the value of that policy as determined by him in accordance with Rules 8(2) or (3) as the case may be and he shall give that notice in such manner as the court may direct.

(4) Any person to whom notice is so given shall be bound by the value so determined unless and until the court otherwise orders.

(5) Paragraphs (2) and (3) of this Rule have effect as though references therein to persons appearing to be entitled to an interest in a long term policy and to the value of that policy included respectively references to persons appearing to be entitled to apply for a free paid-up policy under section 24 of the Act of 1923 and to the value of that entitlement under Rule 7 (in the case of paragraph (2) of this Rule) or under Rule 8 (in the case of paragraph (3) of this Rule).

NOTES

Revoked as noted at the beginning of these Rules.

Para (2): words in square brackets substituted by the Insurance Companies (Winding-up) (Amendment) Rules 1986, SI 1986/2002, r 14.

[7.1506]

24 Dividends to creditors

(1) This Rule applies in the case of a company carrying on long term business.

(2) [Part II] of the principal Rules applies separately in relation to the two separate companies assumed for the purposes of Rule 5.

(3) The court may, at any time before the making of a stop order, permit a dividend to be declared and paid on such terms as it thinks fit in respect only of debts which fell due for payment before the date of the winding-up order or, in the case of claims under long term policies, which have fallen due for payment on or after the date of the winding-up order.

NOTES

Revoked as noted at the beginning of these Rules.

Para (2): words in square brackets substituted by the Insurance Companies (Winding-up) (Amendment) Rules 1986, SI 1986/2002, r 15.

[7.1507]

25 Meetings of creditors

(1) In the case of a company carrying on long term business, [Chapter 8 of Part 4 and Part 8 of the principal Rules (so far as relating to winding up by the court)] apply to each separate general meeting of the creditors summoned under [section 168 of the Act of 1986] as that section has effect by virtue of section 55(5) of the Act of 1982.

(2) In relation to any such separate meeting:—

(a) *[Rule 4.61(3)] of the principal Rules has effect as if the reference therein to assets of the company were a reference to the assets available under section 55 of the Act of 1982 for meeting the liabilities of the company owed to the creditors summoned to the meeting, and*

(b) *[Rule 4.63] of the principal Rules applies as if the reference therein to value in relation to a creditor who is not, by virtue of Rule 6, 7 or 8 required to prove his debt, were a reference to the value most recently notified to him under Rule 23 or, if the court has determined a different value in accordance with Rule 23(4), as if it were a reference to that different value.*

NOTES

Revoked as noted at the beginning of these Rules.

Paras (1), (2): words in square brackets substituted by the Insurance Companies (Winding-up) (Amendment) Rules 1986, SI 1986/2002, r 16.

[7.1508]

[26 Remuneration of liquidator carrying on long term business

(1) So long as no stop order has been made in relation to a company carrying on long term business, the Liquidator is entitled to receive remuneration for his services as such in relation to the carrying on of that business as provided for in this Rule.

(2) The remuneration shall be fixed by the liquidation committee by reference to the time properly given by the Liquidator and his staff in attending to matters arising in the winding up.

(3) If there is no liquidation committee, or the committee does not make the requisite determination, the Liquidator's remuneration may be fixed (in accordance with paragraph (2)) by a resolution of a meeting of creditors.

(4) If not fixed as above, the Liquidator's remuneration shall be in accordance with the scale laid down for the Official Receiver by the general regulations.

(5) If the Liquidator's remuneration has been fixed by the liquidation committee, and the Liquidator considers the amount to be insufficient, he may request that it be increased by resolution of the creditors.]

NOTES

Revoked as noted at the beginning of these Rules.

Substituted by the Insurance Companies (Winding-up) (Amendment) Rules 1986, SI 1986/2002, r 17.

[7.1509]

27 Apportionment of costs payable out of the assets

(1) [Rule 4.218] of the principal Rules applies separately to the assets of the company's long term business and to the assets of the company's other business.

(2) But where any fee, expense, cost, charge, disbursement or remuneration does not relate exclusively to the assets of the company's long term business or to the assets of the company's other business the Liquidator shall apportion it amongst those assets in such manner as he shall determine.

NOTES

Revoked as noted at the beginning of these Rules.

Para (1): words in square brackets substituted by the Insurance Companies (Winding-up) (Amendment) Rules 1986, SI 1986/2002, r 18.

[7.1510]

28 Notice of stop order

(1) When a stop order has been made in relation to the company the Registrar shall, on the same day, send to the Official Receiver a notice informing him that the stop order has been pronounced.

(2) The notice shall be in Form No 2 set out in Schedule 6 with such variation as circumstances may require.

(3) Three copies of the stop order sealed with the seal of the court shall forthwith be sent by post or otherwise by the Registrar to the Official Receiver.

(4) The Official Receiver shall cause a sealed copy of the order to be served upon the Liquidator by prepaid letter or upon such other person or persons, or in such other manner as the court may direct, and shall forward a copy of the order to the registrar of companies.

[(5) The Liquidator shall forthwith on receipt of a sealed copy of the order—

(a) *cause notice of the order in Form 3 set out in Schedule 6 to be gazetted, and*

(b) *advertise the making of the order in the newspaper in which the winding-up order was advertised by notice in Form No 4 set out in Schedule 6.]*

NOTES

Revoked as noted at the beginning of these Rules.

Para (5): substituted, for original paras (5), (6), by the Insurance Companies (Winding-up) (Amendment) Rules 1986, SI 1986/2002, r 19.

SCHEDULES

SCHEDULE 1
GENERAL BUSINESS POLICIES

Regulation 6

[7.1511]

1. (1) This paragraph applies in relation to periodic payments under a general business policy which fall due for payment after the date of the winding-up order where the event giving rise to the liability to make the payments occurred before the date of the winding-up order.

(2) The value to be attributed to such periodic payments shall be determined on such actuarial principles and assumptions in regard to all relevant factors as the court shall direct.

2. (1) This paragraph applies in relation to liabilities under a general business policy not dealt with by paragraph 1.

(2) The value to be attributed to those liabilities shall:—

(a) if the terms of the policy provide for a repayment of premium upon the early termination of the policy or the policy is expressed to run from one definite date to another or the policy may be terminated by any of the parties with effect from a definite date, be the greater of the following two amounts:—

(i) the amount (if any) which under the terms of the policy would have been repayable on early termination of the policy had the policy terminated on the date of the winding-up order, and

(ii) where the policy is expressed to run from one definite date to another or may be terminated by any of the parties with effect from a definite date, such proportion of the last premium paid as is proportionate to the unexpired portion of the period in respect of which that premium was paid; and

(b) in any other case, be a just estimate of that value.

NOTES

Revoked as noted at the beginning of these Rules.

SCHEDULE 2
RULES FOR VALUING NON-LINKED LIFE POLICIES, NON-LINKED DEFERRED ANNUITY POLICIES, NON-LINKED ANNUITIES IN PAYMENT AND CAPITAL REDEMPTION POLICIES

Regulation 7

[7.1512]

1 General

(1) In valuing a policy:—

(a) where it is necessary to calculate the present value of future payments by or to the company interest shall be assumed at such rate or rates as the court may direct;

(b) where relevant the rates of mortality and the rates of disability to be employed shall be such rates as the court may consider appropriate after taking into account:—

(i) relevant published tables of rates of mortality and rates of disability, and

(ii) the rates of mortality and the rates of disability experienced in connection with similar policies issued by the company;

(c) there shall be determined:—

(i) the present value of the ordinary benefits,

(ii) a reserve for options,

(iii) a reserve for expenses, and

(iv) if further fixed premiums fall due to be paid under the policy on or after the date of the winding-up order, the present value of the modified net premiums;

and for the purpose of this Schedule a premium is a fixed premium if the amount of it is determined by the terms of the policy and it cannot be varied.

(2) Where under the terms of the policy or on the basis of the company's established practice the policy holder has a right to receive or an expectation of receiving benefits additional to the minimum benefits guaranteed under those terms the court shall determine rates of interest, mortality and disability under paragraph (1) which will result in the inclusion in the present value of the ordinary benefits and in the present value of the modified net premiums of such margin (if any) as the court may consider appropriate to provide for that right or expectation in respect of the period after the date of the winding-up order.

2 Present value of the ordinary benefits

(1) Ordinary benefits are the benefits which will become payable to the policy holder on or after the date of the winding-up order without his having to exercise any option under the policy (including any bonus or addition to the sum assured or the amount of annuity declared before the date of the winding-up order) and for this purpose "option" includes a right to surrender the policy.

(2) The present value of the ordinary benefits shall be the value at the date of the winding-up order of the reversion in the ordinary benefits according to the contingency upon which those benefits are payable calculated on the basis of the rates of interest, mortality and disability referred to in paragraph 1.

3 Reserve for options

The amount of the reserve for options shall be the amount which, in the opinion of the Liquidator, arrived at on appropriate assumptions in regard to all relevant factors, is necessary to be provided at the date of the winding-up order (in addition to the amount of the present value of the ordinary benefits) to cover the additional liabilities likely to arise upon the exercise on or after that date by the policy holder of any option conferred upon him by the terms of the policy or, in the case of an industrial assurance policy, by the Industrial Assurance Acts other than an option whereby the policy holder can secure a guaranteed cash payment within the period of 12 months beginning with that date.

4 Reserve for expenses

(1) The amount of the reserve for expenses is the amount which, in the opinion of the Liquidator, is necessary to be provided at the date of the winding-up order for meeting future expenses.

(2) In this paragraph "future expenses" means such part of the expenses likely to be incurred after that date in the fulfilling by the Liquidator or by any transferee from the Liquidator of the company's long term business of the obligations of that business as is appropriate to the policy and which cannot be met out of the amounts (if any) by which the actual premiums payable under that policy after that date exceed the amounts of the modified net premiums which correspond to those actual premiums.

5 Net premiums

(1) For the purpose of determining the present value of the modified net premiums a net premium shall be determined in relation to each actual premium paid or payable under the policy in such a way that:—

(a) the net premiums, if they had been payable when the corresponding actual premiums were or are payable, would, on the basis of the rates of interest, mortality and disability referred to in paragraph 1, have been sufficient when the policy was issued to provide for the benefits under the policy according to the contingencies on which they are payable, exclusive of any addition for profits, expenses or other charges, and

(b) the ratio between the amounts of any two net premiums is the same as the ratio between the amounts of the two actual premiums to which they correspond (any actual premium which includes a loading for unusual risks assumed by the company in respect of part only of the term of the policy being treated for this purpose as if it did not include that loading).

(2) For the purposes of this paragraph, where at any time after the policy was issued the terms of the policy have been varied (otherwise than by the surrender of the policy in consideration of the issue of a new policy), it shall be assumed that the policy when it was issued provided for those variations to take effect at the time when they did in fact take effect.

6 Modified net premiums

(1) A modified net premium shall be determined in relation to each net premium by making an addition to each net premium such that:—

(a) the additions, if each was payable when the corresponding actual premium was or is payable, would, on the basis of the rates of interest, mortality and disability referred to in paragraph 1, have been sufficient to compensate for the acquisition expenses relating to the policy, and

(b) the ratio between the amounts of any two modified net premiums is the same as the ratio between the amounts of the two net premiums to which they correspond.

(2) For this purpose the acquisition expenses relating to the policy shall be taken to be 3.5 per cent (or the defined percentage if it be lower than 3.5 per cent) of the relevant capital sum under the contract and for this purpose:—

(a) "the defined percentage" is the percentage arrived at by taking (for all policies which in the opinion of the Liquidator have the same or similar characteristics to the policy in question, and which he considers appropriate to be taken notice of for this purpose), the average of the percentages of the relevant capital sums under those policies that represent the acquisition expenses for which, after allowing for the effects of taxation, allowance is made in the premiums actually payable; and

(b) "the relevant capital sum" in relation to any policy is:—

(i) for whole life assurances, the sum assured,

(ii) for policies where a sum is payable on maturity (including policies where a sum is also payable on earlier death), the sum payable on maturity,

(iii) for temporary assurances, the sum assured on the date of the winding-up order,

(iv) for deferred annuity policies, the capitalised value on the date on which the first payment is due to be made of the payments due to be made under the policy calculated on the basis of the rates of interest, mortality and disability referred to in paragraph 1 or, if the terms of the policy include a right on the part of the policy holder to surrender the policy on that date for a cash payment greater than the said capitalised value, the amount of that cash payment, and

(v) for capital redemption policies, the sum payable at the end of the contract period.

(3) Where the amount of a modified net premium calculated in accordance with sub-paragraphs (1) and (2) is greater than the amount of the actual premium to which it corresponds then the amount of that modified net premium shall be the amount of that actual premium and not the amount calculated in accordance with sub-paragraphs (1) and (2).

7 Present value of the modified net premiums

The present value of the modified net premiums shall be the value as at the date of the winding-up order, calculated on the basis of the rates of interest, mortality and disability referred to in paragraph 1, of the modified net premiums payable after that date on the assumption that they are payable as and when the corresponding actual premiums are payable.

8 Value of the policy

(1) Subject to sub-paragraph (2):—

(a) if no further fixed premiums fall due to be paid under the policy on or after the date of the winding-up order, the value of the policy shall be the aggregate of:—

(i) the present value of the ordinary benefits,

(ii) the reserve for options,

(iii) the reserve for expenses, and

(iv) where under the terms of the policy or on the basis of the company's established practice the policy holder has a right to receive or an expectation of receiving benefits additional to the ordinary benefits, such amount (if any) as the court may determine to reflect that right or expectation in respect of the period ending with the date of the winding-up order;

(b) if further fixed premiums fall due to be so paid and the aggregate value referred to in sub-paragraph (a) exceeds the present value of the modified net premiums, the value of the policy shall be the amount of that excess; and

(c) if further fixed premiums fall due to be so paid and that aggregate does not exceed the present value of the modified net premiums, the policy shall have no value.

(2) Where the policy holder has a right conferred upon him by the terms of the policy or by the Industrial Assurance Acts whereby the policy holder can secure a guaranteed cash payment within the period of 12 months beginning with the date of the winding-up order, the Liquidator shall determine the amount which in his opinion it is necessary to provide at that date to cover the liabilities which will accrue when that option is exercised (on the assumption that it will be exercised) and the value of the policy shall be that amount if it exceeds the value of the policy (if any) determined in accordance with sub-paragraph (1).

NOTES

Revoked as noted at the beginning of these Rules.

SCHEDULE 3
RULES FOR VALUING LIFE POLICIES AND DEFERRED ANNUITY POLICIES WHICH ARE LINKED POLICIES

Regulation 7

[7.1513]

1. *(1) Subject to sub-paragraph (2) the value of the policy shall be the aggregate of the value of the linked liabilities (calculated in accordance with paragraph 2 or 4) and the value of other than linked liabilities (calculated in accordance with paragraph 5) except where that aggregate is a negative amount in which case the policy shall have no value.*

(2) Where the terms of the policy include a right whereby the policy holder can secure a guaranteed cash payment within the period of 12 months beginning with the date of the winding-up order then, if the amount which in the opinion of the Liquidator is necessary to be provided at that date to cover any liabilities which will accrue when that option is exercised (on the assumption that it will be exercised) is greater than the value determined under sub-paragraph (1) of this paragraph, the value of the policy shall be that greater amount.

2. *(1) Where the linked liabilities are expressed in terms of units the value of those liabilities shall, subject to paragraph 3, be the amount arrived at by taking the product of the number of units of each class of units allocated to the policy on the date of the winding-up order and the value of each such unit on that date and then adding those products.*

(2) For the purposes of sub-paragraph (1):—

(i) where under the terms of the policy the value of a unit at any time falls to be determined by reference to the value at that time of the assets of a particular fund maintained by the company in relation to that and other policies, the value of a unit on the date of the winding-up order shall be determined by reference to the net realisable value of the assets credited to that fund on that date (after taking account of disposal costs, any tax liabilities resulting from the disposal of assets insofar as they have not already been provided for by the company and any other amounts which under the terms of those policies are chargeable to the fund), and

(ii) in any other case, the value of a unit on the date of the winding-up order shall be the value which would have been ascribed to each unit credited to the policy holder, after any deductions which may be made under the terms of the policy, for the purpose of determining the benefits payable under the policy on the date of the winding-up order had the policy matured on that date.

3. *(1) This paragraph applies where—*

(a) paragraph 2(2)(i) applies and the company has a right under the terms of the policy either to make periodic withdrawals from the fund referred to in that paragraph or to retain any part of the income accruing in respect of the assets of that fund, or

(b) paragraph 2(2)(ii) applies and the company has a right under the terms of the policy to receive the whole or any part of any distributions made in respect of the units referred to in that paragraph, or

(c) paragraph 2(2)(i) or paragraph 2(2)(ii) applies and the company has a right under the terms of the policy to make periodic cancellations of a proportion of the number of units credited to the policy.

(2) Where this paragraph applies the value of the linked liabilities calculated in accordance with paragraph 2(1) shall be reduced by an amount calculated in accordance with sub-paragraph (3) of this paragraph.

(3) The said amount is—

(a) where this paragraph applies by virtue of head (a) or (b) of sub-paragraph (1), the value as at the date of the winding up order, calculated on actuarial principles, of the future income of the company in respect of the units in question arising from the rights referred to in head (a) or (b) of sub-paragraph (1) as the case may be, or

(b) where this paragraph applies by virtue of head (c) of sub-paragraph (1), the value as at the date of the winding up order, calculated on actuarial principles, of the liabilities of the company in respect of the units which fall to be cancelled in the future under the right referred to in head (c) of sub-paragraph (1).

(4) In calculating any amount in accordance with sub-paragraph (3) there shall be disregarded:—

(a) such part of the rights referred to in the relevant head of sub-paragraph (1) which in the opinion of the Liquidator constitutes appropriate provision for future expenses and mortality risks, and

(b) such part of those rights (if any) which the court considers to constitute appropriate provision for any right or expectation of the policyholder to receive benefits additional to the benefits guaranteed under the terms of the policy.

(5) In determining the said amount:—

(a) interest shall be assumed at such rate or rates as the court may direct, and

(b) where relevant the rates of mortality and the rates of disability to be employed shall be such rates as the court may consider appropriate after taking into account:—

(i) relevant published tables of rates of mortality and rates of disability, and

(ii) the rates of mortality and the rates of disability experienced in connection with similar policies issued by the company,

***4.** Where the linked liabilities are not expressed in terms of units the value of those liabilities shall be the value which would have been ascribed to those liabilities had the policy matured on the date of the winding-up order.*

***5.** (1) The value of any liabilities other than linked liabilities including reserves for future expenses, options and guarantees shall be determined on actuarial principles and appropriate assumptions in regard to all relevant factors including the assumption of such rate or rates of interest, mortality and disability as the court may direct.*

(2) In valuing liabilities under this paragraph credit shall be taken for those parts of future premiums which do not fall to be applied in the allocation of further units to the policy and for any rights of the company which have been disregarded under paragraph 3(4)(a) in valuing the linked liabilities.

NOTES

Revoked as noted at the beginning of these Rules.

SCHEDULE 4

RULES FOR VALUING LONG TERM POLICIES WHICH ARE NOT DEALT WITH IN SCHEDULES 2 AND 3

Regulation 7

[7.1514]

The value of a long term policy not covered by Schedule 2 or 3 shall be determined on such actuarial principles and assumptions in regard to all relevant factors as the court shall determine.

NOTES

Revoked as noted at the beginning of these Rules.

SCHEDULE 5

RULES FOR VALUING LONG TERM POLICIES WHERE A STOP ORDER HAS BEEN MADE

Regulation 8

[7.1515]

***1.** Subject to paragraphs 2 and 3, in valuing a policy Schedules 2, 3 or 4 shall apply according to the class of that policy as if those Schedules were herein repeated but with a view to a fresh valuation of each policy on appropriate assumptions in regard to all relevant factors and subject to the following modifications:—*

(a) references to the stop order shall be substituted for references to the winding-up order,

(b) in paragraph 3 of Schedule 2 for the words "whereby the policy holder can secure a guaranteed cash payment within the period of 12 months beginning with that date" there shall be substituted the words "to surrender the policy which can be exercised on that date",

(c) *in paragraph 4(2) of Schedule 2 for the words "likely to be incurred" there shall be substituted the words "which were likely to have been incurred" and for the words "cannot be met" there shall be substituted the words "could not have been met".*
(d) *paragraph 8(2) of Schedule 2 shall be deleted, and*
(e) *paragraph 1(2) of Schedule 3 shall be deleted.*

2. *(1) This paragraph applies where the policy holder has a right conferred upon him under the terms of the policy or by the Industrial Assurance Acts to surrender the policy and that right is exercisable on the date of the stop order.*

(2) Where this paragraph applies and the amount required at the date of the stop order to provide for the benefits payable upon surrender of the policy on the assumption that the policy is surrendered on the date of the stop order is greater than the value of the policy determined in accordance with paragraph 1 the value of the policy shall, subject to paragraph 3, be the said amount so required.

(3) Where any part of the surrender value is payable after the date of the stop order sub-paragraph (2) shall apply but the value therein referred to shall be discounted at such rate of interest as the court may direct.

3. *(1) This paragraph applies in the case of a linked policy where:—*
(a) *the terms of the policy include a guarantee that the amount assured will on maturity of the policy be worth a minimum amount calculable in money terms, or*
(b) *the terms of the policy include a right on the part of the policy holder to surrender the policy and a guarantee that the payment on surrender will be worth a minimum amount calculable in money terms and that right is exercisable on or after the date of the stop order.*

(2) Where this paragraph applies the value of the policy shall be the greater of the following two amounts:—
(a) *the value the policy would have had at the date of the stop order had the policy been a non-linked policy, that is to say, had the linked liabilities provided by the policy not been so provided but the policy had otherwise been on the same terms, and*
(b) *the value the policy would have had at the date of the stop order had the policy not included any guarantees of payments on maturity or surrender worth a minimum amount calculable in money terms.*

NOTES

Revoked as noted at the beginning of these Rules.

SCHEDULE 6

[7.1516]

NOTES

This Schedule contains forms. The forms themselves are not set out in this work, but their numbers and titles are listed below.

FORM NO	*TITLE*
1	*Notice of meeting of long term business creditors*
2	*Notification to Official Receiver of Order pronounced under section 56(2) of the Insurance Companies Act 1982*
3	*Notice of Order pronounced under section 56(2) of the Insurance Companies Act 1982 for cessation of long term business*
4	*Notice for newspaper*

NOTES

Revoked as noted at the beginning of these Rules.

Forms 1, 4: amended by the Insurance Companies (Winding-up) (Amendment) Rules 1986, SI 1986/2002, r 20.

FINANCIAL SERVICES AND MARKETS ACT 2000

(2000 c 8)

An Act to make provision about the regulation of financial services and markets; to provide for the transfer of certain statutory functions relating to building societies, friendly societies, industrial and provident societies and certain other mutual societies; and for connected purposes

[14 June 2000]

NOTES

Only the sections of this Act which are relevant to insurance companies and insurers are reproduced here. Sections not reproduced are not annotated.

PART XXIV
INSOLVENCY

Administration orders

[7.1517]

360 Insurers

(1) The Treasury may by order provide that such provisions of Part II of the 1986 Act (or Part III of the 1989 Order) as may be specified are to apply in relation to insurers with such modifications as may be specified.

(2) An order under this section—

(a) may provide that such provisions of this Part as may be specified are to apply in relation to the administration of insurers in accordance with the order with such modifications as may be specified; and

(b) requires the consent of the Secretary of State.

(3) "Specified" means specified in the order.

NOTES

Orders: the Financial Services and Markets Act 2000 (Administration Orders Relating to Insurers) Order 2002, SI 2002/1242 (revoked by SI 2010/3023 and reproduced for reference at **[7.1565]**); the Financial Services and Markets Act 2000 (Administration Orders Relating to Insurers) (Amendment) Order 2003, SI 2003/2134 (which is largely revoked by SI 2010/3023); the Financial Services and Markets Act 2000 (Administration Orders Relating to Insurers) (Northern Ireland) Order 2007, SI 2007/846; the Financial Services and Markets Act 2000 (Administration Orders Relating to Insurers) Order 2010, SI 2010/3023 at **[7.1618]**.

Supplemental provisions concerning insurers

[7.1518]

376 Continuation of contracts of long-term insurance where insurer in liquidation

(1) This section applies in relation to the winding up of an insurer which effects or carries out contracts of long-term insurance.

(2) Unless the court otherwise orders, the liquidator must carry on the insurer's business so far as it consists of carrying out the insurer's contracts of long-term insurance with a view to its being transferred as a going concern to a person who may lawfully carry out those contracts.

(3) In carrying on the business, the liquidator—

(a) may agree to the variation of any contracts of insurance in existence when the winding up order is made; but

(b) must not effect any new contracts of insurance.

(4) If the liquidator is satisfied that the interests of the creditors in respect of liabilities of the insurer attributable to contracts of long-term insurance effected by it require the appointment of a special manager, he may apply to the court.

(5) On such an application, the court may appoint a special manager to act during such time as the court may direct.

(6) The special manager is to have such powers, including any of the powers of a receiver or manager, as the court may direct.

(7) Section 177(5) of the 1986 Act (or Article 151(5) of the 1989 Order) applies to a special manager appointed under subsection (5) as it applies to a special manager appointed under section 177 of the 1986 Act (or Article 151 of the 1989 Order).

(8) If the court thinks fit, it may reduce the value of one or more of the contracts of long-term insurance effected by the insurer.

(9) Any reduction is to be on such terms and subject to such conditions (if any) as the court thinks fit.

(10) The court may, on the application of an official, appoint an independent actuary to investigate the insurer's business so far as it consists of carrying out its contracts of long-term insurance and to report to the official—

(a) on the desirability or otherwise of that part of the insurer's business being continued; and

(b) on any reduction in the contracts of long-term insurance effected by the insurer that may be necessary for successful continuation of that part of the insurer's business.

(11) "Official" means—

(a) the liquidator;

(b) a special manager appointed under subsection (5); or

(c) the [PRA].

[(11A) The PRA must—

(a) consult the FCA before making an application under subsection (10), and

(b) provide the FCA with a copy of any actuary's report made to the PRA under that subsection.

(11B) In the event that the activity of effecting or carrying out long-term contracts of insurance as principal is not to any extent a [PRA-regulated] activity—

(a) the reference in subsection (11)(c) to the PRA is to be read as a reference to the FCA, and

(b) subsection (11A) does not apply.]

(12) The liquidator may make an application in the name of the insurer and on its behalf under Part VII without obtaining the permission that would otherwise be required by [Article 142 of, and Schedule 2 to, the 1989 Order.]

NOTES

Sub-s (11): word in square brackets substituted by the Financial Services Act 2012, s 44, Sch 14, paras 1, 24(1), (2).

Sub-s (11A): inserted, together with sub-s (11B), by the Financial Services Act 2012, s 44, Sch 14, paras 1, 24(1), (3); words in square brackets substituted by the Financial Services (Banking Reform) Act 2013, s 141, Sch 10, para 2.

Sub-s (11B): inserted as noted to sub-s (11A) above.

Sub-s (12): words in square brackets substituted by the Deregulation Act 2015, the Small Business, Enterprise and Employment Act 2015 and the Insolvency (Amendment) Act (Northern Ireland) 2016 (Consequential Amendments and Transitional Provisions) Regulations 2017, SI 2017/400, reg 4.

[7.1519]
377 Reducing the value of contracts instead of winding up

(1) This section applies in relation to an insurer which has been proved to be unable to pay its debts.

(2) If the court thinks fit, it may reduce the value of one or more of the insurer's contracts instead of making a winding up order.

(3) Any reduction is to be on such terms and subject to such conditions (if any) as the court thinks fit.

NOTES

See further, in relation to the disapplication of this section in relation to an EEA insurer: the Insurers (Reorganisation and Winding Up) Regulations 2004, SI 2004/353, regs 2, 4(7) at **[3.125]**, **[3.127]**.

[7.1520]
378 Treatment of assets on winding up

(1) The Treasury may by regulations provide for the treatment of the assets of an insurer on its winding up.

(2) The regulations may, in particular, provide for—

(a) assets representing a particular part of the insurer's business to be available only for meeting liabilities attributable to that part of the insurer's business;

(b) separate general meetings of the creditors to be held in respect of liabilities attributable to a particular part of the insurer's business.

NOTES

Regulations: the Financial Services and Markets Act 2000 (Treatment of Assets of Insurers on Winding Up) Regulations 2001, SI 2001/2968 (revoked by SI 2003/1102 and reproduced for reference at **[7.1528]**).

[7.1521]
379 Winding-up rules

(1) Winding-up rules may include provision—

(a) for determining the amount of the liabilities of an insurer to policyholders of any class or description for the purpose of proof in a winding up; and

(b) generally for carrying into effect the provisions of this Part with respect to the winding up of insurers.

(2) Winding-up rules may, in particular, make provision for all or any of the following matters—

(a) the identification of assets and liabilities;

(b) the apportionment, between assets of different classes or descriptions, of—

(i) the costs, charges and expenses of the winding up; and

(ii) any debts of the insurer of a specified class or description;

(c) the determination of the amount of liabilities of a specified description;

(d) the application of assets for meeting liabilities of a specified description;

(e) the application of assets representing any excess of a specified description.

(3) "Specified" means specified in winding-up rules.

(4) "Winding-up rules" means rules made under section 411 of the 1986 Act (or Article 359 of the 1989 Order).

(5) Nothing in this section affects the power to make winding-up rules under the 1986 Act or the 1989 Order.

NOTES

Rules: the Insurers (Winding Up) Rules 2001, SI 2001/3635 at **[7.1532]**; the Insurers (Winding Up) (Scotland) Rules 2001, SI 2001/4040 at **[16.147]**.

PART XXX SUPPLEMENTAL

[7.1522]
426 Consequential and supplementary provision

(1) A Minister of the Crown may by order make such incidental, consequential, transitional or supplemental provision as he considers necessary or expedient for the general purposes, or any particular purpose, of this Act or in consequence of any provision made by or under this Act or for giving full effect to this Act or any such provision.

(2)–(4) *(Outside the scope of this work.)*

[7.1523]
428 Regulations and orders

(1) Any power to make an order which is conferred on a Minister of the Crown by this Act and any power to make regulations which is conferred by this Act is exercisable by statutory instrument.

(2) The Lord Chancellor's power to make rules under section 132 is exercisable by statutory instrument.
(3) Any statutory instrument made under this Act may—
 (a) contain such incidental, supplemental, consequential and transitional provision as the person making it considers appropriate; and
 (b) make different provision for different cases.

[7.1524]
430 Extent
(1) This Act, except Chapter IV of Part XVII, extends to Northern Ireland.
(2) Except where Her Majesty by Order in Council provides otherwise, the extent of any amendment or repeal made by or under this Act is the same as the extent of the provision amended or repealed.
(3) Her Majesty may by Order in Council provide for any provision of or made under this Act relating to a matter which is the subject of other legislation which extends to any of the Channel Islands or the Isle of Man to extend there with such modifications (if any) as may be specified in the Order.

[7.1525]
431 Commencement
(1) The following provisions come into force on the passing of this Act—
 (a) this section;
 (b) sections 428, 430 and 433;
 (c) (*outside the scope of this work.*)
(2) The other provisions of this Act come into force on such day as the Treasury may by order appoint; and different days may be appointed for different purposes.

NOTES
Orders: at present 7 commencement orders have been made under this section. The ones relevant to the provisions of this Act reproduced here are the Financial Services and Markets Act 2000 (Commencement No 1) Order 2001, SI 2001/516; the Financial Services and Markets Act 2000 (Commencement No 3) Order 2001, SI 2001/1820; the Financial Services and Markets Act 2000 (Commencement No 5) Order 2001, SI 2001/2632; the Financial Services and Markets Act 2000 (Commencement No 7) Order 2001, SI 2001/3538.

FINANCIAL SERVICES AND MARKETS ACT 2000 (INSOLVENCY) (DEFINITION OF "INSURER") ORDER 2001

(SI 2001/2634)

NOTES
Made: 20 July 2001.
Authority: Financial Services and Markets Act 2000, ss 355(2), 428(3).
Commencement: 1 December 2001.

[7.1526]
1
(1) This Order may be cited as the Financial Services and Markets Act 2000 (Insolvency) (Definition of "Insurer") Order 2001 and comes into force on the day on which section 19 of the Act comes into force.
(2) In this Order, the "Regulated Activities Order" means the Financial Services and Markets Act 2000 (Regulated Activities) Order 2001.

[7.1527]
2
In Part XXIV of the Act (insolvency), . . . "insurer" means any person who is carrying on a regulated activity of the kind specified by article 10(1) or (2) of the Regulated Activities Order (effecting and carrying out contracts of insurance) but who is not—
 (a) exempt from the general prohibition in respect of that regulated activity;
 (b) a friendly society; or
 (c) a person who effects or carries out contracts of insurance all of which fall within paragraphs 14 to 18 of Part I of Schedule 1 to the Regulated Activities Order in the course of, or for the purposes of, a banking business.

NOTES
Words omitted revoked by the Financial Services and Markets Act 2000 (Administration Orders Relating to Insurers) Order 2002, SI 2002/1242, art 2.

FINANCIAL SERVICES AND MARKETS ACT 2000 (TREATMENT OF ASSETS OF INSURERS ON WINDING UP) REGULATIONS 2001

(SI 2001/2968)

NOTES

Made: 23 August 2001.
Authority: Financial Services and Markets Act 2000, ss 378, 428(3).
Commencement: 1 December 2001.
These Regulations are revoked by the Insurers (Reorganisation and Winding Up) Regulations 2003, SI 2003/1102 (noted at **[3.123]**) as from 20 April 2003 and are reproduced for reference.

[7.1528]
1 Citation, commencement and application

(1) These Regulations may be cited as the Financial Services and Markets Act 2000 (Treatment of Assets of Insurers on Winding Up) Regulations 2001 and come into force on the relevant day.

(2) These Regulations apply to the winding up of an insurer which commences on or after the relevant day.

NOTES

Revoked as noted at the beginning of these Regulations.

[7.1529]
2 Interpretation

In these Regulations—

"the Act" means the Financial Services and Markets Act 2000;

"contract of long-term insurance" has the meaning given by article 3(1) of the Financial Services and Markets Act 2000 (Regulated Activities) Order 2001;

"insurer" has the meaning given by article 2 of the Financial Services and Markets Act 2000 (Insolvency) (Definition of "Insurer") Order 2001;

"the relevant day" means the day on which section 19 of the Act comes into force.

NOTES

Revoked as noted at the beginning of these Regulations.

[7.1530]
3 Treatment of assets

(1) Where an insurer is being wound up—

(a) the assets representing the fund or funds maintained by the insurer in respect of its business of effecting or carrying out any contract of long-term insurance are to be available only for meeting the liabilities of the insurer attributable to that business; and

(b) the other assets of the insurer are to be available only for meeting the liabilities of the insurer attributable to its other business.

(2) Where the value of the assets mentioned in either sub-paragraph of paragraph (1) exceeds the amount of the liabilities mentioned in that sub-paragraph, the restriction imposed by that paragraph does not apply to so much of those assets as represents the excess.

NOTES

Revoked as noted at the beginning of these Regulations.

[7.1531]
4 General meetings of creditors

In relation to the assets falling within either sub-paragraph of regulation 3(1), the creditors mentioned in section 168(2) of the Insolvency Act 1986 or, as the case may be, Article 143(2) of the Insolvency (Northern Ireland) Order 1989 are to be only those who are creditors in respect of liabilities falling within that sub-paragraph; and, accordingly, any general meetings of creditors summoned for the purposes of that section (or, as the case may be, that Article) are to be separate general meetings of the creditors in respect of the liabilities falling within each sub-paragraph.

NOTES

Revoked as noted at the beginning of these Regulations.

INSURERS (WINDING UP) RULES 2001

(SI 2001/3635)

NOTES

Made: 9 November 2001.

Authority: Insolvency Act 1986, s 411; Financial Services and Markets Act 2000, s 379.

Commencement: 1 December 2001.

ARRANGEMENT OF RULES

1 Citation, commencement and revocation . . . [7.1532]
2 Interpretation . . . [7.1533]
3 Application . . . [7.1534]
4 Appointment of liquidator . . . [7.1535]
5 Maintenance of separate financial records for long-term and other business in winding up . . . [7.1536]
6 Valuation of general business policies . . . [7.1537]
7, 8 Valuation of long-term policies . . . [7.1538], [7.1539]
9 Attribution of liabilities to company's long-term business . . . [7.1540]
10 Attribution of assets to company's long-term business . . . [7.1541]
11 Excess of long-term business assets . . . [7.1542]
12 Actuarial advice . . . [7.1543]
13,14 Utilisation of excess of assets . . . [7.1544], [7.1545]
15 Custody of assets . . . [7.1546]
16 Maintenance of accounting, valuation and other records . . . [7.1547]
17 Additional powers in relation to long-term business . . . [7.1548]
18 Accounts and audit . . . [7.1549]
19 Security by the liquidator and special manager . . . [7.1550]
20 Proof of debts . . . [7.1551]
21 Failure to pay premiums . . . [7.1552]
22 Notice of valuation of policy . . . [7.1553]
23 Dividends to creditors . . . [7.1554]
24 Creditors' decisions . . . [7.1555]
25 Remuneration of liquidator carrying on long-term business . . . [7.1556]
26 Apportionment of costs payable out of the assets . . . [7.1557]
27 Notice of stop order . . . [7.1558]

SCHEDULES

Schedule 1—Rules for Valuing General Business Policies . . . [7.1559]
Schedule 2—Rules for Valuing Non-Linked Life Policies, Non-Linked Deferred Annuity Policies, Non-Linked Annuities in Payment, Unitised Non-Linked Policies and Capital Redemption Policies . . . [7.1560]
Schedule 3—Rules for Valuing Life Policies and Deferred Annuity Policies which are Linked Policies . . . [7.1561]
Schedule 4—Rules for Valuing Long-Term Policies which are not dealt with in Schedules 2 or 3 . . . [7.1562]
Schedule 5—Rules for Valuing Long-Term Policies where a Stop Order has been made . . . [7.1563]
Schedule 6—Forms . . . [7.1564]

[7.1532]

1 Citation, commencement and revocation

(1) These Rules may be cited as the Insurers (Winding Up) Rules 2001 and come into force on 1st December 2001.

(2) The Insurance Companies (Winding Up) Rules 1985 are revoked.

[7.1533]

2 Interpretation

(1) In these Rules, unless the context otherwise requires—

"the 1923 Act" means the Industrial Assurance Act 1923;

"the 1985 Act" means the Companies Act 1985;

"the 1986 Act" means the Insolvency Act 1986;

"the 2000 Act" means the Financial Services and Markets Act 2000;

"the Authority" means the [Financial Conduct Authority];

"company" means an insurer which is being wound up;

"contract of general insurance" and "contract of long-term insurance" have the meaning given by article 3(1) of the Financial Services and Markets Act 2000 (Regulated Activities) Order 2001;

"excess of the long-term business assets" means the amount, if any, by which the value of the assets representing the fund or funds maintained by the company in respect of its long-term business as at the liquidation date exceeds the value as at that date of the liabilities of the company attributable to that business;

"excess of the other business assets" means the amount, if any, by which the value of the assets of the company which do not represent the fund or funds maintained by the company in respect of its long-term business as at the liquidation date exceeds the value as at that date of the liabilities of the company (other than liabilities in respect of share capital) which are not attributable to that business;

"Financial Services Compensation Scheme" means the scheme established under section 213 of the 2000 Act;

"general business" means the business of effecting or carrying out a contract of general insurance;

"the general regulations" means the Insolvency Regulations 1994;

"the Industrial Assurance Acts" means the 1923 Act and the Industrial Assurance and Friendly Societies Act 1948;

"insurer" has the meaning given by article 2 of the Financial Services and Markets Act 2000 (Insolvency) (Definition of "Insurer") Order 2001;

"linked liability" means any liability under a policy the effecting of which constitutes the carrying on of long-term business the amount of which is determined by reference to—

(a) the value of property of any description (whether or not specified in the policy),

(b) fluctuations in the value of such property,

(c) income from any such property, or

(d) fluctuations in an index of the value of such property;

"linked policy" means a policy which provides for linked liabilities and a policy which when made provided for linked liabilities is deemed to be a linked policy even if the policy holder has elected to convert his rights under the policy so that at the liquidation date there are no longer linked liabilities under the policy;

"liquidation date" means the date of the winding-up order or the date on which a resolution for the winding up of the company is passed by the members of the company (or the policyholders in the case of a mutual insurance company) and, if both a winding-up order and winding-up resolution have been made, the earlier date;

"long-term business" means the business of effecting or carrying out any contract of long-term insurance;

"non-linked policy" means a policy which is not a linked policy;

"other business", in relation to a company carrying on long-term business, means such of the business of the company as is not long-term business;

"the principal rules" means [the Insolvency (England and Wales) Rules 2016];

["qualifying decision procedure" has the meaning given by section 246ZE(11) of the 1986 Act;]

"stop order", in relation to a company, means an order of the court, made under section 376(2) of the 2000 Act, ordering the liquidator to stop carrying on the long-term business of the company;

"unit" in relation to a policy means any unit (whether or not described as a unit in the policy) by reference to the numbers and value of which the amount of the liabilities under the policy at any time is measured.

(2) Unless the context otherwise requires, words or expressions contained in these Rules bear the same meaning as in the principal rules, the general regulations, the 1986 Act, the 2000 Act or any statutory modification thereof respectively.

NOTES

Words in square brackets in definition "the Authority" substituted by the Financial Services Act 2012 (Consequential Amendments and Transitional Provisions) Order 2013, SI 2013/472, art 3, Sch 2, para 69; words in square brackets in definition "the principal rules" substituted by the Insolvency (England and Wales) Rules 2016 (Consequential Amendments and Savings) Rules 2017, SI 2017/369, r 2(2), Sch 2, para 6(1), (2); definition "qualifying decision procedure" inserted by the Small Business, Enterprise and Employment Act 2015 (Consequential Amendments, Savings and Transitional Provisions) Regulations 2018, SI 2018/208, reg 7(1), (2), subject to transitional provisions in reg 18 thereof which provides that where a relevant meeting is to be held in proceedings for the winding up of an insurer (as defined above), these Rules apply in relation to the meeting without the amendments made by SI 2018/208, reg 7.

[7.1534]

3 Application

(1) These Rules apply to proceedings for the winding up of an insurer which commence on or after the date on which these Rules come into force.

(2) These Rules supplement the principal rules and the general regulations which continue to apply to the proceedings in the winding up of an insurer under the 1986 Act as they apply to proceedings in the winding up of any company under that Act; but in the event of a conflict between these Rules and the principal rules or the general regulations these Rules prevail.

[7.1535]

4 Appointment of liquidator

Where the court is considering whether to appoint a liquidator under—

(a) section 139(4) of the 1986 Act (appointment of liquidator where conflict between creditors and contributories), or

(b) section 140 of the 1986 Act (appointment of liquidator following administration or voluntary arrangement),

the manager of the Financial Services Compensation Scheme may appear and make representations to the court as to the person to be appointed.

[7.1536]

[5 Maintenance of separate financial records for long-term and other business in winding up

(1) This rule applies in the case of a company carrying on long-term business in whose case no stop order has been made.

(2) The liquidator shall prepare and keep separate financial records in respect of the long-term business and the other business of the company.

(3) Paragraphs (4) and (5) apply in the case of a company to which this rule applies which also carries on permitted general business ('a hybrid insurer').

(4) Where, before the liquidation date, a hybrid insurer has, or should properly have, apportioned the assets and liabilities attributable to its permitted general business to its long term business for the purposes of any accounts, those assets and liabilities must be apportioned to its long term business for the purposes of complying with paragraph (2) of this rule.

(5) Where, before the liquidation date, a hybrid insurer has, or should properly have, apportioned the assets and liabilities attributable to its permitted general business other than to its long term business for the purposes of any accounts, those assets and liabilities must be apportioned to its other business for the purposes of complying with paragraph (2) of this rule.

(6) Regulation 10 of the general regulations (financial records) applies only in relation to the company's other business.

(7) In relation to the long-term business, the liquidator shall, with a view to the long-term business of the company being transferred to another insurer, maintain such accounting, valuation and other records as will enable such other insurer upon the transfer being effected to comply with the requirements of any rules made by the Authority under [Part 9A] of the 2000 Act relating to accounts and statements of insurers.

(8) In paragraphs (4) and (5)—

(a) "accounts" means any accounts or statements maintained by the company in compliance with a requirement under the Companies Act 1985 or any rules made by the Authority under [Part 9A] of the 2000 Act;

(b) "permitted general business" means the business of effecting or carrying out a contract of general insurance where the risk insured against relates to either accident or sickness.]

NOTES

Substituted by the Insurers (Reorganisation and Winding Up) Regulations 2003, SI 2003/1102, regs 52, 53(1).

Paras (7), (8): words in square brackets substituted by the Financial Services Act 2012 (Consequential Amendments and Transitional Provisions) Order 2013, SI 2013/472, art 5.

[7.1537]

6 Valuation of general business policies

Except in relation to amounts which have fallen due for payment before the liquidation date and liabilities referred to in paragraph 2(1)(b) of Schedule 1, the holder of a general business policy shall be admitted as a creditor in relation to his policy without proof for an amount equal to the value of the policy and for this purpose the value of a policy shall be determined in accordance with Schedule 1.

[7.1538]

7 Valuation of long-term policies

(1) This rule applies in relation to a company's long-term business where no stop order has been made.

(2) In relation to a claim under a policy which has fallen due for payment before the liquidation date, a policy holder shall be admitted as a creditor without proof for such amount as appears from the records of the company to be due in respect of that claim.

(3) In all other respects a policy holder shall be admitted as a creditor in relation to his policy without proof for an amount equal to the value of the policy and for this purpose the value of a policy of any class shall be determined in the manner applicable to policies of that class provided by Schedules 2, 3 and 4.

(4) This rule applies in relation to a person entitled to apply for a free paid-up policy under section 24 of the 1923 Act (provisions as to forfeited policies) and to whom no such policy has been issued before the liquidation date (whether or not it was applied for) as if such a policy had been issued immediately before the liquidation date—

(a) for the minimum amount determined in accordance with section 24(2) of the 1923 Act, or

(b) if the liquidator is satisfied that it was the practice of the company during the five years immediately before the liquidation date to issue policies under that section in excess of the minimum amounts so determined, for the amount determined in accordance with that practice.

[7.1539]

8

(1) This rule applies in relation to a company's long-term business where a stop order has been made.

Part 7L Special Insolvency Regimes

(2) In relation to a claim under a policy which has fallen due for payment on or after the liquidation date and before the date of the stop order, a policy holder shall be admitted as a creditor without proof for such amount as appears from the records of the company and of the liquidator to be due in respect of that claim.

(3) In all other respects a policy holder shall be admitted as a creditor in relation to his policy without proof for an amount equal to the value of the policy and for this purpose the value of a policy of any class shall be determined in the manner applicable to policies of that class provided by Schedule 5.

(4) Paragraph (4) of rule 7 applies for the purposes of this rule as if references to the liquidation date (other than that in sub-paragraph (b) of that paragraph) were references to the date of the stop order.

[7.1540]
9 Attribution of liabilities to company's long-term business

(1) This rule applies in the case of a company carrying on long-term business if at the liquidation date there are liabilities of the company in respect of which it is not clear from the accounting and other records of the company whether they are or are not attributable to the company's long-term business.

(2) The liquidator shall, in such manner and according to such accounting principles as he shall determine, identify the liabilities referred to in paragraph (1) as attributable or not attributable to a company's long-term business and those liabilities shall for the purposes of the winding-up be deemed as at the liquidation date to be attributable or not as the case may be.

(3) For the purposes of paragraph (2) the liquidator may—
- (a) determine that some liabilities are attributable to the company's long-term business and that others are not (the first method); or
- (b) determine that a part of a liability shall be attributable to the company's long-term business and that the remainder of the liability is not (the second method),

and he may use the first method for some of the liabilities and the second method for the remainder of them.

(4) Notwithstanding anything in the preceding paragraphs of this rule, the court may order that the determination of which (if any) of the liabilities referred to in paragraph (1) are attributable to the company's long-term business and which (if any) are not shall be made in such manner and by such methods as the court may direct or the court may itself make the determination.

[7.1541]
10 Attribution of assets to company's long-term business

(1) This rule applies in the case of a company carrying on long-term business if at the liquidation date there are assets of the company in respect of which—
- (a) it is not clear from the accounting and other records of the company whether they do or do not represent the fund or funds maintained by the company in respect of its long-term business, and
- (b) it cannot be inferred from the source of the income out of which those assets were provided whether they do or do not represent those funds.

(2) Subject to paragraph (6) the liquidator shall determine which (if any) of the assets referred to in paragraph (1) are attributable to those funds and which (if any) are not and those assets shall, for the purposes of the winding up, be deemed as at the liquidation date to represent those funds or not in accordance with the liquidator's determination.

(3) For the purposes of paragraph (2) the liquidator may—
- (a) determine that some of those assets shall be attributable to those funds and that others of them shall not (the first method); or
- (b) determine that a part of the value of one of those assets shall be attributable to those funds and that the remainder of that value shall not (the second method),

and he may use the first method for some of those assets and the second method for others of them.

(4)
- (a) In making the attribution the liquidator's objective shall in the first instance be so far as possible to reduce any deficit that may exist, at the liquidation date and before any attribution is made, either in the company's long-term business or in its other business.
- (b) If there is a deficit in both the company's long-term business and its other business the attribution shall be in the ratio that the amount of the one deficit bears to the amount of the other until the deficits are eliminated.
- (c) Thereafter the attribution shall be in the ratio which the aggregate amount of the liabilities attributable to the company's long-term business bears to the aggregate amount of the liabilities not so attributable.

(5) For the purposes of paragraph (4) the value of a liability of the company shall, if it falls to be valued under rule 6 or 7, have the same value as it has under that rule but otherwise it shall have such value as would have been included in relation to it in a balance sheet of the company prepared in accordance with the 1985 Act as at the liquidation date; and, for the purpose of determining the ratio referred to in paragraph (4) but not for the purpose of determining the amount of any deficit therein referred to, the net balance of shareholders' funds shall be included in the liabilities not attributable to the company's long-term business.

(6) Notwithstanding anything in the preceding paragraphs of this rule, the court may order that the determination of which (if any) of the assets referred to in paragraph (1) are attributable to the fund or funds maintained by the company in respect of its long-term business and which (if any) are not shall be made in such manner and by such methods as the court may direct or the court may itself make the determination.

[7.1542]
11 Excess of long-term business assets

(1) Where the company is one carrying on long-term business [and in whose case no stop order has been made], for the purpose of determining the amount, if any, of the excess of the long-term business assets, there shall be included amongst the liabilities of the company attributable to its long-term business an amount determined by the liquidator in respect of liabilities and expenses likely to be incurred in connection with the transfer of the company's long-term business as a going concern to another insurance company being liabilities not included in the valuation of the long-term policies made in pursuance of rule 7.

(2) Where the liquidator is carrying on the long-term business of an insurer with a view to that business being transferred as a going concern to a person or persons ("transferee") who may lawfully carry out those contracts (or substitute policies being issued by another insurer), the liquidator may, in addition to any amounts paid by the Financial Services Compensation Scheme for the benefit of the transferee to secure such a transfer or to procure substitute policies being issued, pay to the transferee or other insurer all or part of such funds or assets as are attributable to the long-term business being transferred or substituted.

NOTES

Para (1): words in square brackets inserted by the Insurers (Reorganisation and Winding Up) Regulations 2003, SI 2003/1102, regs 52, 54.

[7.1543]
12 Actuarial advice

(1) Before doing any of the following, that is to say—
- (a) determining the value of a policy in accordance with Schedules 1 to 5 (other than paragraph 3 of Schedule 1);
- (b) identifying long-term liabilities and assets in accordance with rules 9 and 10;
- (c) determining the amount (if any) of the excess of the long-term business assets in accordance with rule 11;
- (d) determining the terms on which he will accept payment of overdue premiums under rule 21(1) or the amount and nature of any compensation under rule 21(2);

the liquidator shall obtain and consider advice thereon (including an estimate of any value or amount required to be determined) from an actuary.

(2) Before seeking, for the purpose of valuing a policy, the direction of the court as to the assumption of a particular rate of interest or the employment of any rates of mortality or disability, the liquidator shall obtain and consider advice thereon from an actuary.

[7.1544]
13 Utilisation of excess of assets

(1) Except at the direction of the court, no distribution may be made out of and no transfer to another insurer may be made of—
- (a) any part of the excess of the long-term business assets which has been transferred to the other business; or
- (b) any part of the excess of the other business assets, which has been transferred to the long-term business.

(2) Before giving a direction under paragraph (1) the court may require the liquidator to advertise the proposal to make a distribution or a transfer in such manner as the court shall direct.

[7.1545]
14

In the case of a company carrying on long-term business in whose case no stop order has been made, regulation 5 of the general regulations (payments into the Insolvency Services Account) applies only in relation to the company's other business.

[7.1546]
15 Custody of assets

(1) The Secretary of State may, in the case of a company carrying on long-term business in whose case no stop order has been made, require that the whole or a specified proportion of the assets representing the fund or funds maintained by the company in respect of its long-term business shall be held by a person approved by him for the purpose as trustee for the company.

(2) No assets held by a person as trustee for a company in compliance with a requirement imposed under this rule shall, so long as the requirement is in force, be released except with the consent of the Secretary of State but they may be transposed by the trustee into other assets by any transaction or series of transactions on the written instructions of the liquidator.

(3) The liquidator may not grant any mortgage or charge of assets which are held by a person as trustee for the company in compliance with a requirement imposed under this rule except with the consent of the Secretary of State.

[7.1547]

16 Maintenance of accounting, valuation and other records

(1) In the case of a company carrying on long-term business in whose case no stop order has been made, regulation 10 of the general regulations (financial records) applies only in relation to the company's other business.

(2) The liquidator of such company shall, with a view to the long-term business of the company being transferred to another insurer, maintain such accounting, valuation and other records as will enable such other insurer upon the transfer being effected to comply with the requirements of any rules made by the Authority under [Part 9A] of the 2000 Act relating to accounts and statements of insurers.

NOTES

Para (2): words in square brackets substituted by the Financial Services Act 2012 (Consequential Amendments and Transitional Provisions) Order 2013, SI 2013/472, art 5.

[7.1548]

17 Additional powers in relation to long-term business

(1) In the case of a company carrying on long-term business in whose case no stop order has been made, regulation 9 of the general regulations (investment or otherwise handling of funds in winding up of companies and payment of interest) applies only in relation to the company's other business.

(2) The liquidator of a company carrying on long-term business shall, so long as no stop order has been made, have power to do all such things as may be necessary to the performance of his duties under section 376(2) of the 2000 Act (continuation of contracts of long-term insurance where insurer in liquidation) but the Secretary of State may require him—

- (a) not to make investments of a specified class or description,
- (b) to realise, before the expiration of a specified period, the whole or a specified proportion of investments of a specified class or description held by the liquidator.

[7.1549]

18 Accounts and audit

(1) In the case of a company carrying on long-term business in whose case no stop order has been made, regulation 12 of the general regulations (liquidator carrying on business) applies only in relation to the company's other business.

(2) The liquidator of such a company shall supply the Secretary of State, at such times or intervals as he may specify, with such accounts as he may specify and audited in such manner as he may require and with such information about specified matters and verified in such specified manner as he may require.

(3) The liquidator of such a company shall, if required to do so by the Secretary of State, instruct at actuary to investigate the financial condition of the company's long-term business and to report thereon in such manner as the Secretary of State may specify.

[7.1550]

19 Security by the liquidator and special manager

In the case of a company carrying on long-term business in whose case no stop order has been made, [rules 5.18 (security by the liquidator and special manager in a members' voluntary winding up), 6.38 (security in a creditors' voluntary winding up) and 7.94 (winding up by the court) of the principal rules apply] separately to the company's long-term business and to its other business.

NOTES

Words in square brackets substituted by the Insolvency (England and Wales) Rules 2016 (Consequential Amendments and Savings) Rules 2017, SI 2017/369, r 2(2), Sch 2, para 6(1), (3).

[7.1551]

20 Proof of debts

(1) This rule applies in the case of a company carrying on long-term business [in whose case no stop order has been made].

(2) The liquidator may in relation to the company's long-term business and to its other business fix different days on or before which the creditors of the company who are required to prove their debts or claims are to prove their debts or claims and he may fix one of those days without at the same time fixing the other.

(3) In submitting a proof of any debt a creditor may claim the whole or any part of such debt as attributable to the company's long-term business or to its other business or he may make no such attribution.

(4) When he admits any debt, in whole or in part, the liquidator shall state in writing how much of what he admits is attributable to the company's long-term business and how much to the company's other business.

NOTES

Para (1): words in square brackets added by the Insurers (Reorganisation and Winding Up) Regulations 2003, SI 2003/1102, regs 52, 55.

[7.1552]

21 Failure to pay premiums

(1) The liquidator may in the course of carrying on the company's long-term business and on such terms as he thinks fit accept payment of a premium even though the payment is tendered after the date on which under the terms of the policy it was finally due to be paid.

(2) The liquidator may in the course of carrying on the company's long-term business, and having regard to the general practice of insurers, compensate a policy holder whose policy has lapsed in consequence of a failure to pay any premium by issuing a free paid-up policy for reduced benefits or otherwise as the liquidator thinks fit.

[7.1553]

22 Notice of valuation of policy

(1) Before paying a dividend respect of claims other than under contracts of long-term insurance, the liquidator shall give notice of the value of each general business policy, as determined by him in accordance with rule 6, to the persons appearing from the records of the company or otherwise to be entitled to an interest in that policy and he shall do so in such manner as the court may direct.

(2) Before paying a dividend in respect of claims under contracts of long-term insurance and where a stop order has not been made in relation to the company, the liquidator shall give notice to the persons appearing from the records of the company or otherwise to be entitled to a payment under or to an interest in a long-term policy of the amount of that payment or the value of that policy as determined by him in accordance with rule 7(2) or (3), as the case may be.

(3) If a stop order is made in relation to the company, the liquidator shall give notice to all the persons appearing from the records of the company or otherwise to be entitled to a payment under or to an interest in a long-term policy of the amount of that payment or the value of that policy as determined by him in accordance with rule 8(2) or (3), as the case may be, and he shall give that notice in such manner as the court may direct.

(4) Any person to whom notice is so given shall be bound by the value so determined unless and until the court otherwise orders.

(5) Paragraphs (2) and (3) of this rule have effect as though references therein to persons appearing to be entitled to an interest in a long-term policy and to the value of that policy included, respectively, references to persons appearing to be entitled to apply for a free paid-up policy under section 24 of the 1923 Act and to the value of that entitlement under rule 7 (in the case of paragraph (2) of this rule) or under rule 8 (in the case of paragraph (3) of this rule).

(6) Where the liquidator [seeks a decision] of creditors in respect of liabilities of the company [attributable to either or both] its long-term business or other business, he may adopt any valuation carried out in accordance with rules 6, 7 or 8 as the case may be or, if no such valuation has been carried out [before the date on which the liquidator seeks the decision, the liquidator may for the purposes of the qualifying decision procedure use] such estimates of the value of policies as he thinks fit.

NOTES

Para (6): words in first and third pairs of square brackets substituted for original words "summons a meeting" and "by the time of the meeting, he may conduct the meeting using" respectively, by the Small Business, Enterprise and Employment Act 2015 (Consequential Amendments, Savings and Transitional Provisions) Regulations 2018, SI 2018/208, reg 7(1), (3), subject to transitional provisions in reg 18 thereof which provides that where a relevant meeting is to be held in proceedings for the winding up of an insurer (as defined in r 2(1)), these Rules apply in relation to the meeting without the amendments made by SI 2018/208, reg 7; words in second pair of square brackets substituted by the Insurers (Reorganisation and Winding Up) Regulations 2003, SI 2003/1102, regs 52, 56.

[7.1554]

23 Dividends to creditors

(1) This rule applies in the case of a company carrying on long-term business.

(2) [Chapter 3 of Part 14] of the principal rules applies separately in relation to the two separate companies assumed for the purposes of rule 5 above.

(3) The court may, at any time before the making of a stop order, permit a dividend to be declared and paid on such terms as thinks fit in respect only of debts which fell due to payment before the liquidation date or, in the case of claims under long-term policies, which have fallen due for payment on or after the liquidation date.

NOTES

Para (2): words in square brackets substituted (for words "Part III" as substituted by the Insolvency (England and Wales) Rules 2016 (Consequential Amendments and Savings) Rules 2017, SI 2017/369, r 2(2), Sch 2, para 6(1), (4)) by the Small Business, Enterprise and Employment Act 2015 (Consequential Amendments, Savings and Transitional Provisions) Regulations 2018, SI 2018/208, reg 7(1), (4), subject to transitional provisions in reg 18 thereof which provides that where a relevant meeting is to be held in proceedings for the winding up of an insurer (as defined in r 2(1)), these Rules apply in relation to the meeting without the amendments made by SI 2018/208, reg 7.

[7.1555]

24 [Creditors' decisions]

[(1) In the case of a company carrying on long-term business in whose case no stop order has been made, the creditors entitled to participate in [a qualifying decision procedure] may be—

(a) in relation to the long-term business assets of the company, only those who are creditors in respect of liabilities attributable to the long-term business of the company; and

(b) in relation to the other business assets of the company, only those who are creditors in respect of liabilities attributable to the other business of the company.]

[(1A) For the purposes of any such separate qualifying decision procedure, rule 15.34 of the principal rules (requisite majorities) applies with the modification in paragraph (2).

(2) For the purpose of calculating the proportion (in value) of creditors voting who have voted in favour of the proposed decision, the value to be attributed to a creditor who is not, by virtue of rule 6, 7 or 8 above, required to prove for the amount of a debt or claim, is the value most recently notified to the creditor under rule 22 above, or, if the court has determined a different value in accordance with rule 22(4), that different value.]

[(3) In paragraph (1)—

"long-term business assets" means the assets representing the fund or funds maintained by the company in respect of its long-term business;

"other business assets" means any assets of the company which are not long-term business assets.]

NOTES

Rule heading: words in square brackets substituted for original words "Meetings of creditors" by the Small Business, Enterprise and Employment Act 2015 (Consequential Amendments, Savings and Transitional Provisions) Regulations 2018, SI 2018/208, reg 7(1), (5)(a), subject to transitional provisions in reg 18 thereof which provides that where a relevant meeting is to be held in proceedings for the winding up of an insurer (as defined in r 2(1)), these Rules apply in relation to the meeting without the amendments made by SI 2018/208, reg 7.

Para (1): substituted, together with para (1A), for original para (1), by the Insurers (Reorganisation and Winding Up) Regulations 2003, SI 2003/1102, regs 52, 57(1), (2); words in square brackets substituted for original words "creditors' meetings" by SI 2018/208, reg 7(1), (5)(b), subject to transitional provisions in reg 18 thereof as noted above.

Paras (1A), (2): substituted by SI 2018/208, reg 7(1), (5)(c), subject to transitional provisions in reg 18 thereof as noted above. Paras (1A), (2) previously read as follows (with para (1A) substituted, together with para (1), for original para (1), by SI 2003/1102, regs 52, 57(1), (2) and words in square brackets substituted by the Insurers (Reorganisation and Winding Up) Regulations 2004, SI 2004/353, reg 51(1), (2)):

"[(1A) In a case where separate general meetings of the creditors are summoned by the liquidator pursuant to—

(a) paragraph (1) above; or

(b) [regulation 29 of the Insurers (Reorganisation and Winding Up) Regulations 2004] (composite insurers: general meetings of creditors),

chapter 8 of Part 4 and Part 8 of the principal rules apply to each such separate meeting.]

(2) In relation to any such separate meeting—

(a) rule 4.61(3) of the principal rules (expenses of summoning meetings) has effect as if the reference therein to assets were a reference to the assets available under the above-mentioned Regulations for meeting the liabilities of the company owed to the creditors summoned to the meeting, and

(b) rule 4.63 of the principal rules (resolutions) applies as if the reference therein to value in relation to a creditor who is not, by virtue of rule 6, 7 or 8 above, required to prove his debt, were a reference to the value most recently notified to him under rule 22 above or, if the court has determined a different value in accordance with rule 22(4), as if it were a reference to that different value.".

Para (3): added by SI 2003/1102, regs 52, 57(1), (3).

[7.1556]

25 Remuneration of liquidator carrying on long-term business

(1) So long as no stop order has been made in relation to a company carrying on long-term business, the liquidator is entitled to receive remuneration for his services as such in relation to the carrying on of that business provided for in this rule.

(2) The remuneration shall be fixed by the liquidation committee by reference to the time properly given by the liquidator and his staff in attending to matters arising in the winding up.

(3) If there is no liquidation committee or the committee does not make the requisite determination, the liquidator's remuneration may be fixed (in accordance with paragraph (2)) by [decision of the creditors made by a qualifying decision procedure].

(4) If not fixed as above, the liquidator's remuneration shall be in accordance with the scale laid down for the Official Receiver by the general regulations.

(5) If the liquidator's remuneration has been fixed by the liquidation committee, and the liquidator considers the amount to be insufficient, he may request that it be increased by resolution of the creditors.

NOTES

Para (3): words in square brackets substituted for original words "a resolution of a meeting of creditors" by the Small Business, Enterprise and Employment Act 2015 (Consequential Amendments, Savings and Transitional Provisions) Regulations 2018, SI 2018/208, reg 7(1), (6), subject to transitional provisions in reg 18 thereof which provides that where a relevant meeting is to be held in proceedings for the winding up of an insurer (as defined in r 2(1)), these Rules apply in relation to the meeting without the amendments made by SI 2018/208, reg 7.

[7.1557]

26 Apportionment of costs payable out of the assets

(1) [Where no stop order has been made in relation to a company,] [rules 6.42 (general rule as to priority in a creditors' winding up) and 7.108 (general rule as to priority in a winding up by the court) of the principal rules apply] separately to the assets of the company's long-term business and to the assets of the company's other business.

(2) But where any fee, expense, cost, charge, disbursement or remuneration does not relate exclusively to the assets of the company's long-term business or to the assets of the company's other business, the liquidator shall apportion it amongst those assets in such manner as he shall determine.

NOTES

Para (1): words in first pair of square brackets substituted by the Insurers (Reorganisation and Winding Up) Regulations 2003, SI 2003/1102, regs 52, 58(1); words in second pair of square brackets substituted by the Insolvency (England and Wales) Rules 2016 (Consequential Amendments and Savings) Rules 2017, SI 2017/369, r 2(2), Sch 2, para 6(1), (5).

[7.1558]

27 Notice of stop order

(1) When a stop order has been made in relation to the company, the court shall, on the same day send to the Official Receiver a notice informing him that the stop order has been made.

(2) The notice shall be in Form No 1 set out in Schedule 6 with such variation as circumstances may require.

(3) Three copies of the stop order sealed with the seal of the court shall forthwith be sent by the court to the Official Receiver.

(4) The Official Receiver shall cause a sealed copy of the order to be served upon the liquidator by prepaid letter or upon such other person or persons, or in such other manner as the court may direct, and shall forward a copy of the order to the registrar of companies.

(5) The liquidator shall forthwith on receipt of a sealed copy of the order—
- (a) cause notice of the order in Form 2 set out in Schedule 6 to be gazetted, and
- (b) advertise the making of the order in the newspaper in which the liquidation date was advertised, by notice in Form No 3 set out in Schedule 6.

SCHEDULES

SCHEDULE 1
RULES FOR VALUING GENERAL BUSINESS POLICIES

Rule 6

[7.1559]

1. (1) This paragraph applies in relation to periodic payments under a general business policy which fall due for payment after the liquidation date where the event giving rise to the liability to make the payments occurred before the liquidation date.

(2) The value to be attributed to such periodic payments shall be determined on such actuarial principles and assumptions in regard to all relevant factors as the court shall direct.

2. (1) This paragraph applies in relation to liabilities under a general business policy which arise from events which occurred before the liquidation date but which have not—
- (a) fallen due for payment before the liquidation date; or
- (b) been notified to the company before the liquidation date.

(2) The value to be attributed to such liabilities shall be determined on such actuarial principles and assumptions in regard to all relevant factors as the court shall direct.

3. (1) This paragraph applies in relation to liabilities under a general business policy not dealt with by paragraphs 1 or 2.

(2) The value to be attributed to those liabilities shall—
- (a) if the terms of the policy provide for a repayment of premium upon the early termination of the policy or the policy is expressed to run from one definite date to another or the policy may be terminated by any of the parties with effect from a definite date, be the greater of the following two amounts—
  - (i) the amount (if any) which under the terms of the policy would have been repayable on early termination of the policy had the policy terminated on the liquidation date, and
  - (ii) where the policy is expressed to run from one definite date to another or may be terminated by any of the parties with effect from a definite date, such proportion of the last premium paid as is proportionate to the unexpired portion of the period in respect of which that premium was paid; and
- (b) in any other case, be a just estimate of that value.

Part 7L Special Insolvency Regimes

SCHEDULE 2
RULES FOR VALUING NON-LINKED LIFE POLICIES, NON-LINKED DEFERRED ANNUITY POLICIES, NON-LINKED ANNUITIES IN PAYMENT, UNITISED NON-LINKED POLICIES AND CAPITAL REDEMPTION POLICIES

Rule 7

[7.1560]

1 General

In valuing a policy—

(a) where it is necessary to calculate the present value of future payments by or to the company, interest shall be assumed at such fair and reasonable rate or rates as the court may direct;

(b) where relevant, the rates of mortality and the rates of disability to be employed shall be such rates as the court considers appropriate after taking into account—

(i) relevant published tables of rates of mortality and rates of disability, and

(ii) the rates of mortality and the rates of disability experienced in connection with similar policies issued by the company;

(c) there shall be determined—

(i) the present value of the ordinary benefits,

(ii) the present value of additional benefits;

(iii) the present value of options, and

(iv) if further premiums fall to be paid under the policy on or after the liquidation date, the present value of the premiums;

and for the purposes of this Schedule if the ordinary benefits only take into account premiums paid to date, the present value of future premiums shall be taken as nil.

2 Present value of the ordinary benefits

(1) Ordinary benefits are the benefits which will become payable to the policy holder on or after the liquidation date without his having to exercise any option under the policy (including any bonus or addition to the sum assured or the amount of annuity declared before the liquidation date) and for this purpose "option" includes a right to surrender the policy.

(2) Subject to sub-paragraph (3), the present value of the ordinary benefits shall be the value at the liquidation date of the reversion in the ordinary benefits according to the contingency upon which those benefits are payable calculated on the basis of the rates of interest, mortality and disability referred to in paragraph 1.

(3) For accumulating with profits policies—

(a) where the benefits are not expressed in the form of units in a with-profits fund, the value of the ordinary benefits is the amount that would have been payable, excluding any discretionary additions, if the policyholder had been able to exercise a right to terminate the policy at the liquidation date; and

(b) where the benefits are expressed in the form of units in a with-profits fund, the value of the ordinary benefits is the number of units held by the policy holder at the liquidation date valued at the unit price in force at that time or, if that price is not calculated on a daily basis, such price as the court may determine having regard to the last published unit price and any change in the value of assets attributable to the fund since the date of the last published unit price.

(4) Where—

(a) sub-paragraph (3) applies, and

(b) paragraph 3(1) of Schedule 3 applies to the calculation of the unit price (or as the case may be) the fund value,

the value shall be adjusted on the basis set out in paragraph 3(3) to (5) of Schedule 3.

(5) Where sub-paragraph (3) applies, the value may be further adjusted by reference to the value of the assets underlying the unit price (or as the case may be) the value of the fund, if the liquidator considers such an adjustment to be necessary.

3 Present value of additional benefits

(1) Where under the terms of the policy or on the basis of the company's established practice the policy holder has a right to receive or an expectation of receiving benefits additional to the minimum benefits guaranteed under those terms, the court shall determine rates of interest, bonus (whether reversionary, terminal or any other type of bonus used by the company), mortality and disability to provide for the present value (if any) of that right or expectation.

(2) In determining what (if any) value to attribute to any such expectations the court shall have regard to the premium payable in relation to the minimum guaranteed benefits and the amount (if any) an insurer is required to provide in respect of those expectations in any rules made by the Authority under [Part 9A] of the 2000 Act.

4 Present value of options

The amount of the present value of options shall be the amount which, in the opinion of the liquidator, is necessary to be provided at the liquidation date (in addition to the amount of the present value of the ordinary benefits) to cover the additional liabilities likely to arise upon the exercise on or after that date by the policy holder of any option conferred upon him by the terms of the policy or, in the case of an industrial assurance policy, by the Industrial Assurance Acts other than an option whereby the policy holder can secure a guaranteed cash payment within the period of 12 months beginning with that date.

5 Present value of premiums

The present value of the premiums shall be the value at the liquidation date of the premiums which fall due to be paid by the policy holder after the liquidation date calculated on the basis of the rates of interest, mortality and disability referred to in paragraph 1.

6 Value of the policy

(1) Subject to sub-paragraph (2)—

(a) if no further premiums fall due to be paid under the policy on or after the liquidation date, the value of the policy shall be the aggregate of—

(i) the present value of the ordinary benefits;

(ii) the present value of options; and

(iii) the present value of additional benefits;

(b) if further premiums fall due to be so paid and the aggregate value referred to in sub-paragraph (a) exceeds the present value of the premiums, the value of the policy shall be the amount of that excess; and

(c) if further premiums fall due to be so paid and that aggregate does not exceed the present value of the premiums, the policy shall have no value.

(2) Where the policy holder has a right conferred upon him by the terms of the policy or by the Industrial Assurance Acts whereby the policy holder can secure a guaranteed cash payment within the period of 12 months beginning with the liquidation date, the liquidator shall determine the amount which in his opinion it is necessary to provide at that date to cover the liabilities which will accrue when that option is exercised (on the assumption that it will be exercised) and the value of the policy shall be that amount if it exceeds the value of the policy (if any) determined in accordance with sub-paragraph (1).

NOTES

Para 3: words in square brackets substituted by the Financial Services Act 2012 (Consequential Amendments and Transitional Provisions) Order 2013, SI 2013/472, art 5.

SCHEDULE 3
RULES FOR VALUING LIFE POLICIES AND DEFERRED ANNUITY POLICIES WHICH ARE LINKED POLICIES

Rule 7

[7.1561]

1. (1) Subject to sub-paragraph (2) the value of the policy shall be the aggregate of the value of the linked liabilities (calculated in accordance with paragraphs 2 or 4) and the value of other than linked liabilities (calculated in accordance with paragraph 5) except where that aggregate is a negative amount it which case the policy shall have no value.

(2) Where the terms of the policy include a right whereby the policy holder can secure a guaranteed cash payment within the period of 12 months beginning with the liquidation date then, if the amount which in the opinion of the liquidator is necessary to be provided at that date to cover any liabilities which will accrue when that option is exercised (on the assumption that it will be exercised) is greater than the value determined under sub-paragraph (1) of this paragraph, the value of the policy shall be that greater amount.

2. (1) Where the linked liabilities are expressed in terms of units the value of those liabilities shall, subject to paragraph 3, be the amount arrived at by taking the product of the number of units of each class of units allocated to the policy on the liquidation date and the value of each such unit on that date and then adding those products.

(2) For the purposes of sub-paragraph (1)—

(a) where under the terms of the policy the value of a unit at any time falls to be determined by reference to the value at that time of the assets of a particular fund maintained by the company in relation to that and other policies, the value of a unit on the liquidation date shall be determined by reference to the net realisable value of the assets credited to that fund on that date (after taking account of disposal costs, any tax liabilities resulting from the disposal of assets insofar as they have not already been provided for by the company and any other amounts which under the terms of those policies are chargeable to the fund), and

(b) in any other case, the value of a unit on the liquidation date shall be the value which would have been ascribed to each unit credited to the policy holder, after any deductions which may be made under the terms of the policy, for the purpose of determining the benefits payable under the policy on the liquidation date had the policy matured on that date.

3. (1) This paragraph applies where—

(a) paragraph 2(2)(a) applies and the company has a right under the terms of the policy either to make periodic withdrawals from the fund referred to in that paragraph or to retain any part of the income accruing in respect of the assets of that fund,

(b) paragraph 2(2)(b) applies and the company has a right under the terms of the policy to receive the whole or any part of any distributions made in respect of the units referred to in that paragraph, or

(c) paragraph 2(2)(a) or paragraph 2(2)(b) applies and the company has a right under the terms of the policy to make periodic cancellations of a proportion of the number of units credited to the policy.

Part 7L Special Insolvency Regimes

(2) Where this paragraph applies, the value of the linked liabilities calculated in accordance with paragraph 2(1) shall be reduced by an amount calculated in accordance with sub-paragraph (3) of this paragraph.

(3) The said amount is—

(a) where this paragraph applies by virtue of head (a) or (b) of sub-paragraph (1), the value as at the liquidation date, calculated on actuarial principles, of the future income of the company in respect of the units in question arising from the rights referred to in head (a) or (b) of sub-paragraph (1) as the case may be, or

(b) where this paragraph applies by virtue of head (c) of sub-paragraph (1), the value as at the liquidation date, calculated on actuarial principles, of the liabilities of the company in respect of the units which fall to be cancelled in the future under the right referred to in head (c) of sub-paragraph (1).

(4) In calculating any amount in accordance with sub-paragraph (3) there shall be disregarded—

(a) such part of the rights referred to in the relevant head of sub-paragraph (1) which in the opinion of the liquidator constitutes appropriate provision for future expenses and mortality risks, and

(b) such part of those rights (if any) which the court considers to constitute appropriate provision for any right or expectation of the policy holder to receive benefits additional to the benefits guaranteed under the terms of the policy.

(5) In determining the said amount—

(a) interest shall be assumed at such rate or rates as the court may direct, and

(b) where relevant, the rates of mortality and the rates of disability to be employed shall be such rates as the court considers appropriate after taking into account—

(i) relevant published tables of rates of mortality and rates of disability, and

(ii) the rates of mortality and the rates of disability experienced in connection with similar policies issued by the company.

4. Where the linked liabilities are not expressed in terms of units the value of those liabilities shall be the value (subject to adjustment for any amounts which would have been deducted for taxation) which would have been ascribed to those liabilities had the policy matured on the liquidation date.

5. (1) The value of any liabilities other than linked liabilities including reserves for future expenses, options and guarantees shall be determined on actuarial principles and appropriate assumptions in regard to all relevant factors including the assumption of such rate or rates of interest, mortality and disability as the court may direct.

(2) In valuing liabilities under this paragraph credit shall be taken for those parts of future premiums which do not fall to be applied in the allocation of further units to the policy and for any rights of the company which have been disregarded under paragraph 3(4)(a) in valuing the linked liabilities.

SCHEDULE 4
RULES FOR VALUING LONG-TERM POLICIES WHICH ARE NOT DEALT WITH IN SCHEDULES 2 OR 3

Rule 7

[7.1562]

The value of a long-term policy not covered by Schedule 2 or 3 shall be the value of the benefits due to the policy holder determined on such actuarial principles and assumptions in regard to all relevant factors as the court shall determine.

SCHEDULE 5
RULES FOR VALUING LONG-TERM POLICIES WHERE A STOP ORDER HAS BEEN MADE

Rule 8

[7.1563]

1. Subject to paragraphs 2 and 3, in valuing a policy Schedules 2, 3 or 4 shall apply according to the class of that policy as if those Schedules were herein repeated but with a view to a fresh valuation of each policy on appropriate assumptions in regard to all relevant factors and subject to the following modifications—

(a) references to the stop order shall be substituted for references to the liquidation date,

(b) in paragraph 4 of Schedule 2 for the words "whereby the policy holder can secure a guaranteed cash payment within the period of 12 months beginning with that date" there shall be substituted the words "to surrender the policy which can be exercised on that date",

(c) paragraph 6(2) of Schedule 2 shall be deleted, and

(d) paragraph 1(2) of Schedule 3 shall be deleted.

2. (1) This paragraph applies where the policy holder has a right conferred upon him under the terms of the policy or by the Industrial Assurance Acts to surrender the policy and that right is exercisable on the date of the stop order.

(2) Where this paragraph applies and the amount required at the date of the stop order to provide for the benefits payable upon surrender of the policy (on the assumption that the policy is surrendered on the date of the stop order) is greater than the value of the policy determined in accordance with paragraph 1, the value of the policy shall, subject to paragraph 3, be the said amount so required.

(3) Where any part of the surrender value is payable after the date of the stop order, sub-paragraph (2) shall apply but the value therein referred to shall be discounted at such a rate of interest as the court may direct.

3. (1) This paragraph applies in the case of a linked policy where—

(a) the terms of the policy include a guarantee that the amount assured will on maturity of the policy be worth a minimum amount calculable in money terms, or

(b) the terms of the policy include a right on the part of the policy holder to surrender the policy and a guarantee that the payment on surrender will be worth a minimum amount calculable in money terms and that right is exercisable on or after the date of the stop order.

(2) Where this paragraph applies the value of the policy shall be the greater of the following two amounts—

(a) the value the policy would have had at the date of the stop order had the policy been a non-linked policy, that is to say, had the linked liabilities provided by the policy not been so provided but the policy had otherwise been on the same terms, and

(b) the value the policy would have had at the date of the stop order had the policy not included any guarantees of payments on maturity or surrender worth a minimum amount calculable in money terms.

SCHEDULE 6
FORMS

[7.1564]

NOTES

The forms themselves are not set out in this work, but their numbers and titles are listed below.

FORM NO	TITLE
1	Notification to Official Receiver of order made under section 376(2) of the Financial Services and Markets Act 2000
2	Notice for London Gazette
3	Notice for Newspaper

FINANCIAL SERVICES AND MARKETS ACT 2000 (ADMINISTRATION ORDERS RELATING TO INSURERS) ORDER 2002

(SI 2002/1242)

NOTES

Made: 2 May 2002.

Authority: Financial Services and Markets Act 2000, ss 355(2), 360, 426, 428(3).

Commencement: 31 May 2002.

This Order is revoked by the Financial Services and Markets Act 2000 (Administration Orders Relating to Insurers) Order 2010, SI 2010/3023, art 5, as from 1 February 2011, except in relation to the appointment of an administrator taking effect before that date: see art 6 thereof at **[7.1622]**.

[7.1565]

1 Citation, commencement and interpretation

(1) This Order may be cited as the Financial Services and Markets Act 2000 (Administration Orders Relating to Insurers) Order 2002 and comes into force on 31st May 2002.

(2) In this Order—

"the 1986 Act" means the Insolvency Act 1986;

["initial creditors' meeting" has the meaning given by paragraph 51(1) of Schedule B1;]

["Schedule B1" means Schedule B1 to the 1986 Act.]

NOTES

Revoked as noted at the beginning of this Order.

Para (2): definitions "initial creditors' meeting" and "Schedule B1" substituted for definition ""section 23 meeting" means a meeting held under section 23 of the 1986 Act" by the Financial Services and Markets Act 2000 (Administration Orders Relating to Insurers) (Amendment) Order 2003, SI 2003/2134, arts 2, 3, 8, except in relation to any case where a petition for an administration order has been presented to the court before 15 September 2003.

2 *(Amends the Financial Services and Markets Act 2000 (Insolvency) (Definition of "Insurer") Order 2001, SI 2001/2634, art 2 at* **[7.1527]***; revoked as noted at the beginning of this Order.)*

[7.1566]

3 Modification of Part II of the 1986 Act in relation to insurers

Part II of the 1986 Act (administration orders)[, other than paragraph 14 of Schedule B1 (power of holder of floating charge to appoint administrator) and paragraph 22 of Schedule B1 (power of company or directors to appoint administrator),] applies in relation to insurers with the modifications specified in the Schedule to this Order, and accordingly [paragraph 9(2) of Schedule B1] does not preclude the making of an administration order in relation to an insurer.

NOTES

Revoked as noted at the beginning of this Order.

Words in first pair of square brackets inserted by the Insurers (Reorganisation and Winding Up) Regulations 2004, SI 2004/353, reg 52; words in second pair of square brackets substituted for words "section 8(5)(a) of that Act" by the Financial Services and Markets Act 2000 (Administration Orders Relating to Insurers) (Amendment) Order 2003, SI 2003/2134, arts 2, 4, 8, except in relation to any case where a petition for an administration order has been presented to the court before 15 September 2003.

[7.1567]

4 Modification of the Insolvency Rules 1986 in relation to insurers

The Insolvency Rules 1986, so far as they give effect to Part II of the 1986 Act, have effect in relation to insurers with the modification that in [Rule 2.12(1)] of those Rules (the hearing) there is inserted after sub-paragraph (a) the following sub-paragraph—

"(aa) the Financial Services Authority;".

NOTES

Revoked as noted at the beginning of this Order.

Words in square brackets substituted for words "Rule 2.9(1)" by the Financial Services and Markets Act 2000 (Administration Orders Relating to Insurers) (Amendment) Order 2003, SI 2003/2134, arts 2, 5, 8, except in relation to any case where a petition for an administration order has been presented to the court before 15 September 2003.

[7.1568]

[5

Where an insurer, in relation to which an administration order has been made, subsequently goes into liquidation, sums due from the insurer to another party are not to be included in the account of mutual dealings rendered under rule 4.90 of the Insolvency Rules 1986 (mutual credit and set-off) if, at the time they became due—

- *(a) an administration application had been made under paragraph 12 of Schedule B1 in relation to the insurer;*
- *(b) in the case of an appointment of an administrator under paragraph 14 of Schedule B1, a notice of appointment had been filed with the court under paragraph 18 of that Schedule in relation to the insurer; or*
- *(c) in the case of an appointment of an administrator under paragraph 22 of Schedule B1, a notice of intention to appoint had been filed with the court under paragraph 27 of that Schedule in relation to the insurer.]*

NOTES

Revoked as noted at the beginning of this Order.

Substituted by the Financial Services and Markets Act 2000 (Administration Orders Relating to Insurers) (Amendment) Order 2003, SI 2003/2134, arts 2, 6, 8, except in relation to any case where a petition for an administration order was presented to the court before 15 September 2003; art 5 originally read as follows:

> **"5 Mutual credit and set-off**
>
> Where an insurer, in relation to which an administration order has been made, subsequently goes into liquidation, sums due from the insurer to another party are not to be included in the account of mutual dealings rendered under rule 4.90 of the Insolvency Rules 1986 (mutual credit and set-off) if, at the time they became due, a petition had been presented to the court under section 9 of the 1986 Act (application for an administration order) in relation to the insurer.".

SCHEDULE
MODIFICATIONS OF PART II OF THE INSOLVENCY ACT 1986 IN RELATION TO INSURERS

Article 3

[7.1569]

[1. In paragraph 49(4) of Schedule B1 (administrator's proposals), at the end of paragraph (c) add—

"and

(d) to the Financial Services Authority".

2. In paragraph 53(2) of Schedule B1 (business and result of initial creditors' meeting), at the end of paragraph (c), add—

"and

(d) the Financial Services Authority".

3. In paragraph 54(2)(b) of Schedule B1 (revision of administrator's proposals), after "creditor" insert "and to the Financial Services Authority".

4. In paragraph 76(1) of Schedule B1 (automatic end of administration), for "one year" substitute "30 months".

5. In paragraph 76(2)(b) of Schedule B1 (extension of administrator's term of office by consent) for "six" substitute "twelve".

6. In paragraph 79(1) of Schedule B1 (court ending administration on application of administrator), after the first reference to "company" insert "or the Financial Services Authority".

7. In paragraph 91(1) of Schedule B1 (supplying vacancy in office of administrator), at the end of paragraph (e) add—

"or

(f) the Financial Services Authority".]

[8]. (1) The powers of the administrator referred to in Schedule 1 to the 1986 Act (powers of administrator or administrative receiver) include the power to make—

(a) any payments due to a creditor; or

(b) any payments on account of any sum which may become due to a creditor.

(2) Any payments to a creditor made pursuant to sub-paragraph (1) must not exceed, in aggregate, the amount which the administrator reasonably considers that the creditor would be entitled to receive on a distribution of the insurer's assets in a winding up.

(3) The powers conferred by sub-paragraph (1) may be exercised until [an initial creditors' meeting] but may only be exercised thereafter—

(a) if the following conditions are met—

(i) the administrator has laid before [that meeting] or any subsequent creditors' meeting ("the relevant meeting") a statement containing the information mentioned in sub-paragraph (4); and

(ii) the powers are exercised with the consent of a majority in number representing three-fourths in value of the creditors present and voting either in person or by proxy at the relevant meeting; or

(b) with the consent of the court.

(4) The information referred to in sub-paragraph (3)(a) is an estimate of the aggregate amount of—

(a) the insurer's assets and liabilities (whether actual, contingent or prospective); and

(b) all payments which the administrator proposes to make to creditors pursuant to sub-paragraph (1);

including any assumptions which the administrator has made in calculating that estimate.

NOTES

Revoked as noted at the beginning of this Order.

Para 1–7: substituted for original paras 1–5 by the Financial Services and Markets Act 2000 (Administration Orders Relating to Insurers) (Amendment) Order 2003, SI 2003/2134, arts 2, 7(b), 8, except in relation to any case where a petition for an administration order has been presented to the court before 15 September 2003; paras 1–5 originally read as follows:

"**1.** In subsection (3) of section 13 (appointment of administrator), at the end of paragraph (c) add—

"or

(d) by the Financial Services Authority".

2. In subsection (1) of section 18 (discharge or variation of administration order), after "company" insert "or the Financial Services Authority".

3. In subsection (1)(a) of section 23 (statement of proposals), after "registrar of companies" insert ", the Financial Services Authority".

4. In subsection (4) of section 24 (consideration of proposals by creditors' meeting), after "registrar of companies" insert "; the Financial Services Authority".

5. In subsection (2)(a) of section 25 (approval of substantial revisions), after "addresses)" insert "and the Financial Services Authority"."

Para 8: renumbered as such (originally numbered as para 6), words in first pair of square brackets substituted for words "a section 23 meeting" and words in second pair of square brackets substituted for words "the section 23 meeting", by SI 2003/2134, arts 2, 7(a), (c), 8, except as noted to paras 1–7 above.

INSURERS (REORGANISATION AND WINDING UP) (LLOYD'S) REGULATIONS 2005

(SI 2005/1998)

NOTES

Made: 19 July 2005.

Authority: European Communities Act 1972, s 2(2).

Commencement: 10 August 2005.

ARRANGEMENT OF REGULATIONS

PART 1
GENERAL

1 Citation and commencement . . . [7.1570]
2 Interpretation . . . [7.1571]

PART 2
LLOYD'S MARKET REORGANISATION ORDER

3 Lloyd's market reorganisation order . . . [7.1572]
4 Condition for making order . . . [7.1573]
5 Objectives of a Lloyd's market reorganisation order . . . [7.1574]
6 Application for a Lloyd's market reorganisation order . . . [7.1575]
7 Powers of the court . . . [7.1576]
8 Moratorium . . . [7.1577]
9 Reorganisation controller . . . [7.1578]
10 Announcement of appointment of controller . . . [7.1579]
11 Market reorganisation plan . . . [7.1580]
12 Remuneration of the reorganisation controller . . . [7.1581]
13 Treatment of members . . . [7.1582]
14 Revocation of an order under regulation 13 . . . [7.1583]
15 Reorganisation controller's powers: voluntary arrangements in respect of a member . . . [7.1584]
16 Reorganisation controller's powers: individual voluntary arrangements in respect of a member . . . [7.1585]
17 Reorganisation controller's powers: trust deeds for creditors in Scotland . . . [7.1586]
18 Powers of reorganisation controller: section 899 compromise or arrangement . . . [7.1587]
19 Appointment of an administrator, receiver or interim trustee in relation to a member . . . [7.1588]
20 Reorganisation controller's powers: administration orders in respect of members . . . [7.1589]
21 Reorganisation controller's powers: receivership in relation to members . . . [7.1590]
22 Syndicate set-off . . . [7.1591]
23 Voluntary winding up of members: consent of reorganisation controller . . . [7.1592]
24 Voluntary winding up of members: powers of reorganisation controller . . . [7.1593]
25 Petition for winding up of a member by reorganisation controller . . . [7.1594]
26 Winding up of a member: powers of reorganisation controller . . . [7.1595]
27 Petition for bankruptcy of a member by reorganisation controller . . . [7.1596]
28 Bankruptcy of a member: powers of reorganisation controller . . . [7.1597]
29 Petition for winding up of the Society by reorganisation controller . . . [7.1598]
30 Winding up of the Society: service of petition etc on reorganisation controller . . . [7.1599]
31 Payments from central funds . . . [7.1600]

PART 3
MODIFICATION OF LAW OF INSOLVENCY: NOTIFICATION AND PUBLICATION

32 Application of Parts 3 and 4 . . . [7.1601]
33 Notification of relevant decision to PRA . . . [7.1602]
34 Notification of relevant decision to EEA Regulators . . . [7.1603]
35 Application of certain publication requirements in the principal Regulations to members . . . [7.1604]
36 Notification to creditors: winding up proceedings relating to members . . . [7.1605]
37 Submission of claims by EEA creditor . . . [7.1606]
38 Reports to creditors . . . [7.1607]
39 Service of notices and documents . . . [7.1608]

PART 4
APPLICATION OF PARTS 4 AND 5 OF THE PRINCIPAL REGULATIONS

40 Priority for insurance claims . . . [7.1609]
41 Treatment of liabilities arising in connection with a contract subject to reinsurance to close . . . [7.1610]
42 Assets of members . . . [7.1611]
43 Application of Part 4 of the principal Regulations: protection of settlements . . . [7.1612]
44 Challenge by reorganisation controller to conduct of insolvency practitioner . . . [7.1613]
45 Application of Part 5 of the principal Regulations . . . [7.1614]
46 Modification of provisions in Part 5 of the principal Regulations . . . [7.1615]
47 Application of Part 5 of the principal Regulations: protection of dispositions etc made before a Lloyd's market reorganisation order comes into force . . . [7.1616]
48 Non-EEA countries . . . [7.1617]

PART 1
GENERAL

[7.1570]

1 Citation and commencement

These Regulations may be cited as the Insurers (Reorganisation and Winding Up) (Lloyd's) Regulations 2005, and come into force on 10 August 2005.

[7.1571]

2 Interpretation

(1) In these Regulations—

"the Administration for Insurers Order" means the Financial Services and Markets Act 2000 (Administration Orders Relating to Insurers) Order 2002 [and the "Administration for Insurers (Northern Ireland) Order" means the Financial Services and Markets Act 2000 (Administration Relating to Insurers) (Northern Ireland) Order 2007];

"affected market participant" means any member, former member, managing agent, members' agent, Lloyd's broker, approved run-off company or coverholder to whom the Lloyd's market reorganisation order applies;

"approved run-off company" means a company with the permission of the Society to perform executive functions, insurance functions or administrative and processing functions on behalf of a managing agent;

"the association of underwriters known as Lloyd's" has the meaning it has for the purposes of [Directive 2009/138/EC of the European Parliament and of the Council of 25 November 2009 on the taking-up and pursuit of the business of Insurance and Reinsurance (Solvency II);]

"central funds" means the New Central Fund as provided for in the New Central Fund Byelaw (No 23 of 1996) and the Central Fund as provided for in the Central Fund Byelaw (No 4 of 1986);

"company" means a company within the meaning of [section 1 of the 2006 Act] or a company incorporated elsewhere than in Great Britain that is a member of Lloyd's;

"corporate member" means a company admitted to membership of Lloyd's as an underwriting member;

"coverholder" means a company or partnership authorised by a managing agent to enter into, in accordance with the terms of a binding authority, a contract or contracts of insurance to be underwritten by the members of a syndicate managed by that managing agent;

"former member" means a person who has ceased to be a member, whether by resignation or otherwise, in accordance with Lloyd's Act 1982 and any byelaw made under it or in accordance with the provisions of Lloyd's Acts 1871–1982 then in force at the time the person ceased to be a member;

["the FCA" means the Financial Conduct Authority;]

"Gazette" means the London Gazette, the Edinburgh Gazette and the Belfast Gazette;

"individual member" means a member or former member who is an individual;

"insurance market activity" has the meaning given by section 316(3) of the 2000 Act;

"insurance market debt" means an insurance debt under or in connection with a contract of insurance written at Lloyd's;

"Lloyd's Acts 1871–1982" means Lloyd's Act 1871, Lloyd's Act 1911, Lloyd's Act 1951 and Lloyd's Act 1982;

"Lloyd's broker" has the meaning given by section 2(1) of Lloyd's Act 1982;

"managing agent" has the meaning given by article 3(1) of the Financial Services and Markets Act 2000 (Regulated Activities) Order 2001;

"member" means an underwriting member of the Society;

"members' agent" means a person who carries out the activity of advising a person to become, or continue or cease to be, a member of a particular Lloyd's syndicate;

"overseas business regulatory deposit" means a deposit provided or maintained in respect of the overseas insurance and reinsurance business carried on by members in accordance with binding legal or regulatory requirements from time to time in force in the country or territory in which the deposit is held;

"overseas insurance business" means insurance business and reinsurance business transacted by members in a country or territory that is not or is not part of an EEA State;

["the PRA" means the Prudential Regulation Authority;]

"the principal Regulations" means the Insurers (Reorganisation and Winding Up) Regulations 2004;

"relevant trust fund" means any funds held on trust under a trust deed entered into by the member in accordance with the requirements of the [FCA or the PRA] and the Byelaws of the Society for the payment of an obligation arising in connection with insurance market activity carried on by the member or for the establishment of a Lloyd's deposit and includes funds held on further trusts declared by the Society or the trustee of such a trust deed in respect of any class of insurance market activity;

"the Room" has the meaning given by section 2(1) of Lloyd's Act 1982;

"the Society" means the Society incorporated by Lloyd's Act 1871;

"subsidiary of the Society" means a company that is a subsidiary of the Society within the meaning of [section 1159 of the 2006 Act];

"syndicate" has the meaning given by article 3(1) of the Financial Services and Markets Act 2000 (Regulated Activities) Order 2001.

(2) Subject to paragraph (3), words and phrases used in these Regulations have the same meaning as in the principal Regulations except where otherwise specified or where the context requires otherwise.

(3) For the purposes of these Regulations, "UK insurer" is to be treated as including a member or a former member.

(4) These Regulations have effect notwithstanding the provisions of section 360 of the 2000 Act.

NOTES

Para (1): words in square brackets in definition "the Administration for Insurers Order" inserted by the Insurers (Reorganisation and Winding Up) (Amendment) Regulations 2007, SI 2007/851, reg 3(1), (2); words in square brackets in definition "the association of underwriters known as Lloyd's" substituted by the Solvency 2 Regulations 2015, SI 2015/575, reg 60, Sch 2, para 23; words in square brackets in definitions "company" and "subsidiary of the Society" substituted by the Companies Act 2006 (Consequential Amendments and Transitional Provisions) Order 2011, SI 2011/1265, art 27(1), (2); definitions "the FCA" and "the PRA" inserted, and words in square brackets in definition "relevant trust fund" substituted, by the Financial Services Act 2012 (Consequential Amendments and Transitional Provisions) Order 2013, SI 2013/472, art 3, Sch 2, para 109(a).

PART 2
LLOYD'S MARKET REORGANISATION ORDER

[7.1572]
3 Lloyd's market reorganisation order

(1) In these Regulations "Lloyd's market reorganisation order" means an order which—
- (a) is made by the court in relation to the association of underwriters known as Lloyd's;
- (b) appoints a reorganisation controller; and
- (c) on the making of which there comes into force a moratorium on the commencement of—
  - (i) proceedings, or
  - (ii) other legal processes

  set out in regulation 8 in respect of affected market participants, the Society and subsidiaries of the Society.

(2) A Lloyd's market reorganisation order applies to—
- (a) every member, former member, managing agent, members' agent, Lloyd's broker and approved run-off company who has not been excluded from the order in accordance with regulation 7;
- (b) every coverholder who has been included in the order in accordance with regulation 7;
- (c) the Society; and
- (d) subsidiaries of the Society.

[7.1573]
4 Condition for making order

(1) The court may make a Lloyd's market reorganisation order if it is satisfied that—
- (a) any regulatory solvency requirement is not, or may not be, met; and
- (b) an order is likely to achieve one or both of the objectives in regulation 5.

(2) In paragraph (1), "regulatory solvency requirement" means a requirement to maintain adequate financial resources in respect of insurance business at Lloyd's, imposed under the 2000 Act, whether on a member or former underwriting member, either singly or together with other members or former underwriting members, or on the Society and includes a requirement to maintain a margin of solvency.

(3) In paragraph (2), "former underwriting member" has the meaning given by section 324(1) of the 2000 Act.

[7.1574]
5 Objectives of a Lloyd's market reorganisation order

The objectives of a Lloyd's market reorganisation order are—
- (a) to preserve or restore the financial situation of, or market confidence in, the association of underwriters known as Lloyd's in order to facilitate the carrying on of insurance market activities by members at Lloyd's;
- (b) to assist in achieving an outcome that is in the interests of creditors of members, and insurance creditors in particular.

[7.1575]
6 Application for a Lloyd's market reorganisation order

(1) An application for a Lloyd's market reorganisation order may be made by [the PRA] or by the Society, or by both.

[(1A) Before making an application under paragraph (1), the PRA must consult the FCA.]

(2) If the application is made by only one of those bodies it must inform the other body of its intention to make the application as soon as possible, and in any event before the application is lodged at the court.

(3) [The FCA, the PRA] and the Society are entitled to be heard at the hearing of the application, regardless of which body makes the application.

(4) An application must clearly designate—
- (a) any member, former member, managing agent, members' agent, Lloyd's broker, or approved run-off company to whom the order should not apply; and
- (b) every coverholder to whom the order should apply.

(5) The applicant must give notice of the application by—
 (a) ensuring the posting of a copy in the Room,
 (b) displaying a copy on its website, and
 (c) publishing a copy
  (i) in the Gazette, and
  (ii) in such newspaper or newspapers within the United Kingdom and elsewhere as the applicant considers appropriate to bring the application to the attention of those likely to be affected by it.

(6) The notice must be given as soon as reasonably practicable after the making of the application, unless the court orders otherwise.

NOTES

Words in square brackets in paras (1), (3) substituted, and para (1A) inserted, by the Financial Services Act 2012 (Consequential Amendments and Transitional Provisions) Order 2013, SI 2013/472, art 3, Sch 2, para 109(b).

[7.1576]

7 Powers of the court

(1) On hearing an application for a Lloyd's market reorganisation order, the court may make—
 (a) a Lloyd's market reorganisation order, and
 (b) any other order in addition to a Lloyd's market reorganisation order which the court thinks appropriate for the attainment of either or both of the objectives in regulation 5.

(2) A Lloyd's market reorganisation order comes into force—
 (a) at the time appointed by the court; or
 (b) if no time is so appointed, when the order is made

and remains in force until revoked by the court.

(3) The court may on an application made by the [PRA] or the Society at the same time as an application under regulation 6 or the reorganisation controller, the [PRA], the Society, a subsidiary of the Society or any affected market participant at any time while the Lloyd's market reorganisation order is in force, amend or vary a Lloyd's market reorganisation order so that it—
 (a) does not apply to—
  (i) particular assets, or
  (ii) particular members, former members, member's agents, managing agents, Lloyd's brokers, approved run-off companies or subsidiaries of the Society,

 specified in the order; and
 (b) does apply to any coverholder specified in the order.

(4) The court—
 (a) must appoint one or more persons to be the reorganisation controller;
 (b) must specify the powers and duties of the reorganisation controller;
 (c) may establish or approve the respective duties and functions of two or more persons appointed to be the reorganisation controller, including specifying that one of them shall have precedence; and
 (d) may from time to time vary the powers of a reorganisation controller.

(5) An application made under paragraph (3) other than at the time of the application under regulation 6 shall be served on the reorganisation controller[, the FCA and the PRA] who shall each be entitled to attend and be heard at a hearing of such an application.

NOTES

Words in square brackets in paras (3), (5) substituted by the Financial Services Act 2012 (Consequential Amendments and Transitional Provisions) Order 2013, SI 2013/472, art 3, Sch 2, para 109(c).

[7.1577]

8 Moratorium

(1) Except with the permission of the court, for the period during which a Lloyd's market reorganisation order is in force, no proceedings or other legal process may be commenced or continued against:
 (a) an affected market participant;
 (b) the Society; or
 (c) a subsidiary of the Society to which the order applies.

(2) In paragraph (1),
 (a) "court" means in England and Wales the High Court, in Northern Ireland the High Court and in Scotland the Court of Session; and
 (b) "proceedings" means proceedings of every description and includes:
  (i) [an application or] a petition under section 124 or 124A of the 1986 Act or Article 104 or 104A of the 1989 Order for the appointment of a liquidator or provisional liquidator;
  (ii) an application under section 252 of the 1986 Act or Article 226 of the 1989 Order for an interim order;
  (iii) a petition for a bankruptcy order under Part 9 of the 1986 Act or Part 9 of the 1989 Order; and
  (iv) a petition for sequestration under section 5 or 6 of the Bankruptcy (Scotland) Act, but

 does not include prosecution for a criminal offence.

Part 7L Special Insolvency Regimes

(3) Except with the permission of the court, for the period during which a Lloyd's market reorganisation order is in force, no execution may be commenced or continued, no security may be enforced, and no distress may be levied, against (or against the assets of or in the possession of):

(a) any person specified in paragraph (1);

(b) a relevant trust fund (or the trustees of a relevant trust fund); and

(c) an overseas business regulatory deposit.

(4) Paragraph (3) does not prevent the enforcement of—

(a) approved security granted to secure payment of approved debts of a member incurred in connection with an overseas regulatory deposit arrangement; or

(b) security granted by a Lloyd's broker over assets not being assets constituting or representing assets received or held by the Lloyd's broker as intermediary in respect of any contract of insurance or reinsurance written at Lloyd's or any contract of reinsurance reinsuring a member of Lloyd's in respect of a contract or contracts of insurance or reinsurance written by that member at Lloyd's.

(5) In the application of paragraph (3) to Scotland, references to execution being commenced or continued include references to diligence being carried out or continued, and references to distress being levied shall be omitted.

(6) For the period during which a Lloyd's market reorganisation order is in force, no action or step may be taken in respect of any of the persons specified in paragraph (1) by any person who is or may be entitled—

(a) under any provision in Schedule B1 [or in Schedule B1 to the 1989 Order] to appoint an administrator;

(b) to appoint an administrative receiver or receiver;

(c) under [section 899 of the 2006 Act] to propose a compromise or arrangement,

unless he has complied with paragraph (7).

(7) A person intending to take any such action or step shall give notice [in writing] to the reorganisation controller before doing so.

(8) Where a person fails to comply with paragraph (7),

(a) an appointment to which sub-paragraph (6)(a) or (b) applies shall be void, and

(b) no application under [section 899] may be entertained by the court,

except where the court, having heard the reorganisation controller, orders otherwise.

(9) Every application pursuant to paragraph (1) or paragraph (3) must be served on the reorganisation controller.

(10) For the period during which a Lloyd's market reorganisation order is in force, an affected market participant in Scotland may not grant a trust deed for his creditors without the consent of the reorganisation controller.

(11) Where a person who is subject to a Lloyd's market reorganisation order is, at the date of the order, in administration or liquidation or has been [made] bankrupt or is a person whose estate is being sequestrated or who has granted a trust deed for his creditors—

(a) any application to the court for permission to take any action that would be subject to a moratorium arising in those earlier proceedings shall be served on the reorganisation controller and the reorganisation controller shall be entitled to be heard on the application; and

(b) the court shall take into account the achievement of the objectives for which the Lloyd's market reorganisation order was made.

(12) In this regulation—

(a) "approved debt" means a debt approved by the Society at the time it is incurred;

(b) "approved security" means security approved by the Society at the time it is granted over or in respect of assets comprised in the member's premiums trust funds or liable in the future to become comprised therein;

(c) "overseas regulatory deposit arrangement" means an arrangement approved by the Society and notified to the [PRA] whose purpose is to facilitate funding of any overseas business regulatory deposit.

NOTES

Para (2): words in square brackets inserted by the Enterprise and Regulatory Reform Act 2013 (Consequential Amendments) (Bankruptcy) and the Small Business, Enterprise and Employment Act 2015 (Consequential Amendments) Regulations 2016, SI 2016/481, reg 2(2), Sch 2, Pt 1, para 9(1), (2)(a).

Para (6): words in square brackets in sub-para (a) inserted by the Insurers (Reorganisation and Winding Up) (Amendment) Regulations 2007, SI 2007/851, reg 3(1), (3)(a); words in square brackets in sub-para (c) substituted by the Companies Act 2006 (Consequential Amendments and Transitional Provisions) Order 2011, SI 2011/1265, art 27(1), (3)(a).

Para (7): words in square brackets inserted by SI 2007/851, reg 3(1), (3)(b).

Para (8): words in square brackets in sub-para (b) substituted by SI 2011/1265, art 27(1), (3)(b).

Para (11): word in square brackets substituted by SI 2016/481, reg 2(2), Sch 2, Pt 1, para 9(1), (2)(b).

Para (12): word in square brackets substituted by the Financial Services Act 2012 (Consequential Amendments and Transitional Provisions) Order 2013, SI 2013/472, art 3, Sch 2, para 109(d).

[7.1578]

9 Reorganisation controller

(1) The reorganisation controller is an officer of the court.

(2) A person may be appointed as reorganisation controller only if he is qualified [and fully authorised] to act as an insolvency practitioner under Part 13 of the 1986 Act [or under Part 12 of the 1989 Order] and the court considers that he has appropriate knowledge, expertise and experience.

(3) On an application by the reorganisation controller, the court may appoint one or more additional reorganisation controllers to act jointly or severally with the first reorganisation controller on such terms as the court sees fit.

NOTES

Para (2): words in first pair of square brackets inserted by the Deregulation Act 2015, the Small Business, Enterprise and Employment Act 2015 and the Insolvency (Amendment) Act (Northern Ireland) 2016 (Consequential Amendments and Transitional Provisions) Regulations 2017, SI 2017/400, reg 7; words in second pair of square brackets inserted by the Insurers (Reorganisation and Winding Up) (Amendment) Regulations 2007, SI 2007/851, reg 3(1), (4).

[7.1579]

10 Announcement of appointment of controller

(1) This regulation applies when the court makes a Lloyd's market reorganisation order.

(2) As soon as is practicable after the order has been made, [the PRA] must inform the EEA regulators in every EEA State—

(a) that the order has been made; and

(b) in general terms, of the possible effect of a Lloyd's market reorganisation order on—

(i) the effecting or carrying out of contracts of insurance at Lloyd's, and

(ii) the rights of policyholders under or in respect of contracts of insurance written at Lloyd's.

(3) As soon as is reasonably practicable after a person becomes the reorganisation controller, he must—

(a) procure that notice of his appointment is posted—

(i) in the Room,

(ii) on the Society's website, and

(iii) on [the PRA's] website; and

(b) publish a notice of his appointment—

(i) once in the Gazette, and

(ii) once in such newspapers as he thinks most appropriate for securing so far as possible that the Lloyd's market reorganisation order comes to the notice of those who may be affected by it.

NOTES

Words in square brackets substituted by the Financial Services Act 2012 (Consequential Amendments and Transitional Provisions) Order 2013, SI 2013/472, art 3, Sch 2, para 109(e).

[7.1580]

11 Market reorganisation plan

(1) The reorganisation controller may require any affected market participant, and any Lloyd's broker, approved run-off company, coverholder, the Society, subsidiary of the Society or trustee of a relevant trust fund—

(a) to provide him with any information he considers useful to him in the achievement of the objectives set out in regulation 5; and

(b) to carry out such work as may be necessary to prepare or organise information as the reorganisation controller may consider useful to him in the achievement of those objectives.

(2) As soon as is reasonably practicable and in any event by such date as the court may require, the reorganisation controller must prepare a plan ("the market reorganisation plan") for achieving the objectives of the Lloyd's market reorganisation order.

(3) The reorganisation controller must send a copy of the market reorganisation plan to the [PRA] and to the Society.

(4) Before the end of a period of one month beginning with the day on which it receives the market reorganisation plan, the [PRA] must notify the reorganisation controller and the Society in writing of its decision to—

(a) approve the plan;

(b) reject the plan; or

(c) approve the plan provisionally, subject to modifications set out in the notification.

(5) Where the [PRA] rejects the plan, the notification must—

(a) give reasons for its decision; and

(b) specify a date by which the reorganisation controller may submit a new market reorganisation plan.

(6) Where the reorganisation controller submits a new market reorganisation plan, he must send a copy to the [PRA] and to the Society.

(7) Before the end of a period of one month beginning with the day on which the [PRA] receives that plan, the [PRA] must—

(a) accept it;

(b) reject it; or

(c) accept it provisionally subject to modifications.

(8) Before the end of a period of one month beginning with the day on which he receives the notification from the [PRA] of the modifications required by it, the reorganisation controller must—

(a) accept the plan as modified by the [PRA]; or
(b) reject the plan as so modified.

(9) The reorganisation controller must—
(a) file with the court the market reorganisation plan that has been approved by him and the [PRA], and
(b) send a copy of it to—
(i) every member, former member, managing agent and member's agent who requests it, and
(ii) every other person who requests it, on payment of a reasonable charge.

(10) Paragraph (11) applies if—
(a) the [PRA] rejects the market reorganisation plan and the reorganisation controller decides not to submit a new market reorganisation plan;
(b) the [PRA] rejects the new market reorganisation plan submitted by the reorganisation controller; or
(c) the reorganisation controller rejects the modifications made by the [PRA] to a new market reorganisation plan.

(11) As soon as is reasonably practicable after any such rejection, the reorganisation controller must apply to the court for directions.

(12) The [PRA] or the reorganisation controller as the case may be may apply to the court for an extension of the period specified in paragraph (4), (7) or (8) by a period of not more than one month. The court may not grant more than one such extension in respect of each period.

(13) Where any person is under an obligation to publish anything under this regulation, that obligation is subject to the provisions of sections 348 and 349 of the 2000 Act.

NOTES

Word "PRA" in square brackets substituted by the Financial Services Act 2012 (Consequential Amendments and Transitional Provisions) Order 2013, SI 2013/472, art 3, Sch 2, para 109(f).

[7.1581]

12 Remuneration of the reorganisation controller

(1) The reorganisation controller shall be entitled to receive remuneration and to recover expenses properly incurred in connection with the performance of his functions under or in connection with a Lloyd's market reorganisation order.

(2) Subject to paragraph (3), the remuneration so charged is payable by—
(a) members,
(b) former members,
(c) the Society, and
(d) managing agents.

(3) The court must give directions as to the payment of the remuneration and expenses of the reorganisation controller and in particular may provide for—
(a) apportionment of the amounts so charged between the classes of persons set out in paragraph (2) and between groups of persons within those classes; and
(b) payment of such remuneration and expenses out of relevant trust funds.

(4) Amounts of such remuneration and expenses paid by any of the persons described in paragraph (2) are to be treated as payments of the expenses of a liquidator, administrator, trustee in bankruptcy or in Scotland an interim or permanent trustee.

(5) The reorganisation controller may pay the reasonable charges of those to whom he has addressed a request for assistance or information under regulation 11 or anyone else from whom he has requested assistance in the performance of his functions.

(6) The provision of such information or assistance in good faith does not constitute a breach of
(a) any duty owed by any person involved in its preparation or delivery to any company or partnership of which he is an officer, member or employee,
(b) any duty owed by an agent to his principal, or
(c) any duty of confidence, subject to sections 348 and 349 of the 2000 Act.

[7.1582]

13 Treatment of members

(1) Paragraph (2) applies where, after the making of a Lloyd's market reorganisation order, any of the following occurs pursuant to the 1986 Act, the 1989 Order or the Bankruptcy (Scotland) Act—
(a) a person seeks to exercise an entitlement to appoint an administrator,
(b) an application is made to the court for the appointment of an administrator,
(c) a petition for the winding up of a corporate member is presented to the court,
[(ca) the making of a bankruptcy application;]
(d) a petition for a bankruptcy order or sequestration is presented to the court,
in respect of a member.

(2) These Regulations, the principal Regulations[, the Administration for Insurers Order and the Administration for Insurers (Northern Ireland) Order] shall apply to the member and—
(a) for the purposes of the principal Regulations (notwithstanding regulation 3 of those Regulations), the member shall be treated as if it, he or she were a UK insurer; and

(b) for the purposes of the Administration for Insurers Order [or the Administration for Insurers (Northern Ireland) Order], a member that is a company shall be treated as if it were an insurance company.

(3) Paragraph (2) does not apply where the court so orders, on the application of the administrator, liquidator, provisional liquidator, receiver or trustee in bankruptcy, the Accountant in Bankruptcy or trustee under a trust deed for creditors or the person referred to in paragraph (1)(b) or (c) seeking the appointment or presenting the petition.

(4) A person who exercises an entitlement, makes an application or submits a petition to which paragraph (1) applies shall—

(a) if he intends to make an application under paragraph (3) make the application before doing any of those things; and

(b) include in any statement to be made under Schedule B1 [or in Schedule B1 to the 1989 Order], or in any application or petition, a statement as to whether an order under paragraph (3) has been made in respect of the member concerned.

(5) An application under paragraph (3) must be notified [in writing] to the reorganisation controller.

(6) The court must take account of any representation made by the reorganisation controller in relation to the application.

(7) The court may not make an order under paragraph (3) unless the court considers it likely that the insurance market debts of the member will be satisfied.

(8) In this regulation and regulation 14, references to a member include references to a former member.

NOTES

Para (1): sub-para (ca) inserted by the Enterprise and Regulatory Reform Act 2013 (Consequential Amendments) (Bankruptcy) and the Small Business, Enterprise and Employment Act 2015 (Consequential Amendments) Regulations 2016, SI 2016/481, reg 2(2), Sch 2, Pt 1, para 9(1), (3).

Para (2): words in first pair of square brackets substituted and words in second pair of square brackets inserted by the Insurers (Reorganisation and Winding Up) (Amendment) Regulations 2007, SI 2007/851, reg 3(1), (5)(a), (b).

Paras (4), (5): words in square brackets inserted by SI 2007/851, reg 3(1), (5)(c), (d).

[7.1583]

14 Revocation of an order under regulation 13

(1) This regulation applies in the case of a member in respect of whom an order has been made under regulation 13(3).

(2) If the Society does not meet any request for payment of a cash call made by or on behalf of such a member, it must so inform the reorganisation controller, the [PRA] and the court.

(3) If it appears to the reorganisation controller that, in respect of any such member, the insurance market debts of the member are not likely to be satisfied, he must apply to the court for the revocation of that order.

(4) If the court revokes an order made under regulation 13(3), the provisions of these Regulations, the principal Regulations and the Administration for Insurers Order [or the Administration for Insurers (Northern Ireland) Order] apply to the member and from the date of the revocation a relevant officer is to be treated as having been appointed by the court.

(5) For the purposes of paragraph (4), a relevant officer means—

(a) an administrator,

(b) a liquidator,

(c) a receiver,

(d) a trustee in bankruptcy, or

(e) in Scotland, an interim or permanent trustee,

as the case may be.

(6) For the purposes of this regulation, a "cash call" means a request or demand made by a managing agent to a member of a syndicate to make payments to the trustees of any relevant trust fund to be held for the purpose of discharging or providing for the liabilities incurred by that member as a member of the syndicate.

NOTES

Para (2): word "PRA" in square brackets substituted by the Financial Services Act 2012 (Consequential Amendments and Transitional Provisions) Order 2013, SI 2013/472, art 3, Sch 2, para 109(g).

Para (4): words in square brackets inserted by the Insurers (Reorganisation and Winding Up) (Amendment) Regulations 2007, SI 2007/851, reg 3(1), (6).

[7.1584]

15 Reorganisation controller's powers: voluntary arrangements in respect of a member

(1) The directors of a corporate member or former corporate member may make a proposal for a voluntary arrangement under Part 1 of the 1986 Act (or Part 2 of the 1989 Order) in relation to the member only if the reorganisation controller consents to the terms of that arrangement.

(2) Section 1A of that Act or Article 14A of that Order do not apply to a corporate member or former corporate member if—

(a) a Lloyd's market reorganisation order applies to it; and

(b) there is no order under regulation 13(3) in force in relation to it.

(3) The reorganisation controller is entitled to be heard at any hearing of an application relating to the arrangement.

[7.1585]

16 Reorganisation controller's powers: individual voluntary arrangements in respect of a member

(1) The reorganisation controller is entitled to be heard on an application under section 253 of the 1986 Act (or Article 227 of the 1989 Order) by an individual member or former member.

(2) When considering such an application the court shall have regard to the objectives of the Lloyd's market reorganisation order.

(3) [Paragraphs (3A)] to (7) apply if an interim order is made on the application of such a person.

[(3A) Notice of the creditors' decision procedure given under section 257(2B) of the 1986 Act must also be given to the reorganisation controller.

(3B) The reorganisation controller is entitled to participate (but not vote) in the creditors' decision procedure specified by that notice.]

(4) The reorganisation controller, or a person appointed by him for that purpose, may attend any meeting of creditors of the member or former member summoned under [Article 231 of the 1989 Order] (summoning of creditors meeting).

(5) Notice of the result of a meeting so summoned must be given [in writing] to the reorganisation controller by the chairman of the meeting.

(6) The reorganisation controller may apply to the court under section 262 (challenge of [creditors'] decision) or 263 (implementation and supervision of approved voluntary arrangement) of the 1986 Act (or Article 236 or 237 or the 1989 Order).

(7) If a person other than the reorganisation controller makes an application to the court under any provision mentioned in paragraph (6), the reorganisation controller is entitled to be heard at any hearing relating to the application.

NOTES

Para (3): words in square brackets substituted for original words "Paragraphs (4)", by the Small Business, Enterprise and Employment Act 2015 (Consequential Amendments, Savings and Transitional Provisions) Regulations 2018, SI 2018/208, reg 10(1), (2)(a), as from 13 March 2018 (for transitional provisions, see the note below).

Paras (3A), (3B): inserted by SI 2018/208, reg 10(1), (2)(b), as from 13 March 2018 (for transitional provisions, see the note below).

Para (4): words in square brackets substituted for original words "section 257 of the 1986 Act (or Article 231 of the 1989 Order)" by SI 2018/208, reg 10(1), (2)(c), as from 13 March 2018 (for transitional provisions, see the note below).

Para (5): words in square brackets inserted by the Insurers (Reorganisation and Winding Up) (Amendment) Regulations 2007, SI 2007/851, reg 3(1), (7).

Para (6): word in square brackets substituted for original word "meeting's" by SI 2018/208, reg 10(1), (2)(d), as from 13 March 2018 (for transitional provisions, see the note below).

Transitional provisions: the Small Business, Enterprise and Employment Act 2015 (Consequential Amendments, Savings and Transitional Provisions) Regulations 2018, SI 2018/208, regs 16, 21 provide as follows—

"16 Interpretation of Part 4

In this Part—

"the 1986 Act" means the Insolvency Act 1986;

"the 2000 Act" means the Financial Services and Markets Act 2000;

"the 2009 Act" means the Banking Act 2009; and

"relevant meeting" means a meeting of creditors which is to be held on or after the date on which Parts 2 and 3 of these Regulations come into force, and was—

(a) called, summoned or otherwise required before 6th April 2017 under a provision of the 1986 Act or the Insolvency Rules 1986;

(b) requisitioned by a creditor before 6th April 2017 under a provision of the 1986 Act or the Insolvency Rules 1986; or

(c) called or summoned under section 106, 146 or 331 of the 1986 Act as a result of—

(i) a final report to creditors sent before 6th April 2017 under rule 4.49D of the Insolvency Rules 1986 (final report to creditors in liquidation);

(ii) a final report to creditors and bankrupt sent before that date under rule 6.78B of those Rules (final report to creditors and bankrupt).

21 Transitional provision for regulation 10

(1) Where a relevant meeting is to be held in proceedings relating to a proposal for an individual voluntary arrangement, where the interim order under section 252 of the 1986 Act is made on the application of an individual member or former member, the Reorganisation Regulations apply in relation to the meeting without the amendments made by regulation 10(2), (8), (9) and (10)(b).

(2) Where a relevant meeting is to be held in bankruptcy proceedings under Part 9 of the 1986 Act in respect of an individual member or former member, regulation 40 of the Reorganisation Regulations applies in relation to the meeting without the amendment made by regulation 10(10)(a).

(3) In this regulation—

"former member" and "individual member" have the meaning given in regulation 2(1) of the Reorganisation Regulations; and

"the Reorganisation Regulations" means the Insurers (Reorganisation and Winding Up) (Lloyd's) Regulations 2005.".

[7.1586]

17 Reorganisation controller's powers: trust deeds for creditors in Scotland

(1) This regulation applies to the granting at any time by a debtor who is a member or former member of a trust deed for creditors.

(2) The debtor must inform the person who is or is proposed to be the trustee at or before the time that the trust deed is granted that he is a member or former member of Lloyd's.

(3) As soon as practicable after the making of the Lloyd's market reorganisation order the trustee must send to the reorganisation controller—

(a) in every case, a copy of the trust deed;

(b) where any other document or information is sent to every creditor known to the trustee in pursuance of paragraph 5(1)(c) of Schedule 5 to the Bankruptcy (Scotland) Act 1985, a copy of such document or information.

(4) If the debtor or the trustee fails without reasonable excuse to comply with any obligation in paragraph (2) or (3) he shall be guilty of an offence and shall be liable on summary conviction to a fine not exceeding level 5 on the statutory scale or to imprisonment for a term not exceeding 3 months or both.

(5) Paragraph 7 of that Schedule applies to the reorganisation controller as if he were a qualified creditor who has not been sent a copy of the notice as mentioned in paragraph 5(1)(c) of the Schedule.

(6) The reorganisation controller must be given the same notice as the creditors of any meeting of creditors held in relation to the trust deed.

(7) The reorganisation controller, or a person appointed by him for the purpose, is entitled to attend and participate in (but not to vote at) any such meeting of creditors as if the reorganisation controller were a creditor under the deed.

(8) Expressions used in this regulation and in the Bankruptcy (Scotland) Act 1985 have the same meaning in this regulation as in that Act.

[7.1587]

18 Powers of reorganisation controller: [section 899 compromise or arrangement]

(1) The reorganisation controller may apply to the court for an order that a meeting or meetings be summoned under [section 896(1) of the 2006 Act (court order for holding of meeting)] in connection with a compromise or arrangement in relation to a member or former member.

(2) Where a member, its creditors or members make an application under [section 896(1)] the reorganisation controller is entitled to attend and be heard at any hearing.

(3) Where a meeting is summoned under [section 896(1)], the reorganisation controller is entitled to attend the meeting so summoned and to participate in it (but not to vote at it).

NOTES

Regulation heading: words in square brackets substituted by the Companies Act 2006 (Consequential Amendments and Transitional Provisions) Order 2011, SI 2011/1265, art 27(1), (4).

Paras (1)–(3): words in square brackets substituted by SI 2011/1265, art 27(1), (5).

[7.1588]

19 Appointment of an administrator, receiver or interim trustee in relation to a member

(1) Where a Lloyd's market reorganisation order is in force, the following appointments may be made in relation to a member or former member only where an order has been made under regulation 13(3) and has not been revoked and shall be notified to the reorganisation controller—

(a) the appointment of an administrator under paragraph 14 of Schedule B1 [or under paragraph 15 of Schedule B1 to the 1989 Order];

(b) the appointment of an administrator under paragraph 22 of Schedule B1 [or under paragraph 23 of Schedule B1 to the 1989 Order];

(c) the appointment of an administrative receiver;

(d) the appointment of an interim receiver; and

(e) the appointment of an interim trustee, within the meaning of the Bankruptcy (Scotland) Act 1985.

(2) The notification to the reorganisation controller under paragraph (1) must be in writing.

(3) If the requirement to notify the reorganisation controller in paragraph (1) is not complied with the administrator, administrative receiver, interim receiver or interim trustee is guilty of an offence and is liable on conviction to a fine not exceeding level 3 on the standard scale.

NOTES

Para (1): words in square brackets in sub-paras (a), (b) inserted by the Insurers (Reorganisation and Winding Up) (Amendment) Regulations 2007, SI 2007/851, reg 3(1), (8).

[7.1589]

20 Reorganisation controller's powers: administration orders in respect of members

(1) The reorganisation controller may make an administration application under paragraph 12 of Schedule B1 [or under paragraph 13 of Schedule B1 to the 1989 Order] in respect of a member or former member.

(2) Paragraphs (3) to (5) apply if—

(a) a person other than the reorganisation controller makes an administration application under Schedule B1[, or under Schedule B1 to the 1989 Order,] in relation to a member or former member; and

(b) an order under regulation 13(3) is not in force in respect of that member.

(3) The reorganisation controller is entitled to be heard—

(a) at the hearing of the administration application; and

(b) at any other hearing of the court in relation to the member under Schedule B1 [or under Schedule B1 to the 1989 Order].

(4) Any notice or other document required to be sent to a creditor of the member must also be sent to the reorganisation controller.

(5) The reorganisation controller, or a person appointed by him for the purpose, may—

(a) attend any meeting of creditors of the member summoned under any enactment;

(b) attend any meeting of a committee established under paragraph 57 of Schedule B1 [or under paragraph 58 of Schedule B1 to the 1989 Order]; and

(c) make representations as to any matter for decision at such a meeting.

[(5A) The reorganisation controller is entitled to participate (but not vote) in a qualifying decision procedure (within the meaning given by section 246ZE(11) of the 1986 Act) by which a decision about any matter is sought from the creditors of the member.]

(6) If, during the course of the administration of a member, a compromise or arrangement is proposed between the member and its creditors, or any class of them, the reorganisation controller may apply to court under [section 896 of the 2006 Act].

NOTES

Paras (1), (2): words in square brackets inserted by the Insurers (Reorganisation and Winding Up) (Amendment) Regulations 2007, SI 2007/851, reg 3(1), (9)(a), (b).

Para (3): words in square brackets substituted by SI 2007/851, reg 3(1), (9)(c).

Para (5): words in square brackets inserted by SI 2007/851, reg 3(1), (9)(d).

Para (5A): inserted by the Small Business, Enterprise and Employment Act 2015 (Consequential Amendments, Savings and Transitional Provisions) Regulations 2018, SI 2018/208, reg 10(1), (3), as from 13 March 2018 and subject to transitional provisions as noted to reg 16 at **[7.1585]**.

Para (6): words in square brackets substituted by the Companies Act 2006 (Consequential Amendments and Transitional Provisions) Order 2011, SI 2011/1265, art 27(1), (6).

[7.1590]

21 Reorganisation controller's powers: receivership in relation to members

(1) This regulation applies if a receiver has been appointed in relation to a member or former member.

(2) The reorganisation controller may be heard on an application made under section 35 or 63 of the 1986 Act (or Article 45 of the 1989 Order).

(3) The reorganisation controller may make an application under section 41(1)(a) or 69(1)(a) of the 1986 Act (or Article 51(1)(a) of the 1989 Order).

(4) A report under section 48(1) or 67(1) of the 1986 Act (or Article 58(1) of the 1989 Order) must be sent by the person making it to the reorganisation controller.

(5) The reorganisation controller, or a person appointed by him for the purpose, may—

(a) attend any meeting of creditors of the member or former member summoned under any enactment;

(b) attend any meeting of a committee established under section 49 or 68 of the 1986 Act (or [Article 59] of the 1989 Order);

(c) attend any meeting of a committee of creditors of a member or former member in Scotland; and

(d) make representations as to any matter for decision at such a meeting.

(6) Where an administration application is made in respect of a member by the reorganisation controller (and there is an administrative receiver, or in Scotland a receiver, of that member), paragraph 39 of Schedule B1 [or paragraph 40 of Schedule B1 to the 1989 Order] does not require the court to dismiss the application if it thinks that—

(a) the objectives of the Lloyd's market reorganisation order are more likely to be achieved by the appointment of an administrator than by the appointment or continued appointment of a receiver in respect of that member, and

(b) the interests of the person by or on behalf of whom the receiver was appointed will be adequately protected.

NOTES

Para (5): words in square brackets in sub-para (b) substituted by the Insurers (Reorganisation and Winding Up) (Amendment) Regulations 2007, SI 2007/851, reg 3(1), (10)(a).

Para (6): words in square brackets inserted by SI 2007/851, reg 3(1), (10)(b).

[7.1591]

22 Syndicate set-off

(1) This regulation applies where—

(a) a member ("the debtor") is subject to a relevant insolvency proceeding; and

(b) no order under regulation 13(3) is in effect in relation to the debtor.

(2) In the application of section 323 of the 1986 Act or Article 296 of the 1989 Order, Rule 2.85 and Rule 4.90 of the Insolvency Rules or [Rule 2.086 and] R4.096 of the Insolvency Rules (Northern Ireland) to the debtor, the following paragraphs apply in relation to each syndicate of which the debtor is a member, and for that purpose each reference to the debtor is to the debtor as a member of that syndicate only.

(3) Subject to paragraphs (4) and (5), where there have been mutual credits, mutual debts or other mutual dealings between the debtor in the course of his business as a member of the syndicate ("syndicate A") and a creditor, an account shall be taken of what is due from the debtor to that creditor, and of what is due from that creditor to the debtor, such account to be taken in respect of business transacted by the debtor as a member of syndicate A only and the sums due from one party shall be set off against the sums due from the other.

(4) Where the creditor is a member (whether or not a member of syndicate A) and there have been mutual credits, mutual debts or other mutual dealings between the debtor as a member of syndicate A and the creditor in the course of the creditor's business as a member of syndicate A or of another syndicate of which he is a member, paragraph (5) applies.

(5) A separate account must be taken in relation to each syndicate of which the creditor is a member of what is due from the debtor to the creditor, and of what is due from the creditor to the debtor, in respect only of business transacted between the debtor as a member of syndicate A and the creditor as a member of the syndicate in question (and not in respect of business transacted by the creditor as a member of any other syndicate or otherwise), and the sums due from one party shall be set off against the sums due from the other.

(6) In this regulation—

(a) references to a member include references to a former member; and

(b) "relevant insolvency proceedings" means proceedings in respect of an application or petition referred to in regulation 13(1).

NOTES

Para (2): words in square brackets inserted by the Insurers (Reorganisation and Winding Up) (Amendment) Regulations 2007, SI 2007/851, reg 3(1), (11).

[7.1592]

23 Voluntary winding up of members: consent of reorganisation controller

(1) During any period in which a Lloyd's market reorganisation order is in force, a member or former member that is a company may not be wound up voluntarily without the consent of the reorganisation controller.

(2) Before a member or former member passes a resolution for voluntary winding up it must give written notice to the reorganisation controller.

(3) Where notice is given under paragraph (2), a resolution for voluntary winding up may be passed only—

(a) after the end of a period of five business days beginning with the day on which the notice was given, if the reorganisation controller has not refused his consent, or

(b) if the reorganisation controller has consented in writing to the passing of the resolution.

(4) A copy of a resolution for the voluntary winding up of a member forwarded to the registrar of companies in accordance with [section 30 of the 2006 Act] must be accompanied by a certificate issued by the reorganisation controller stating that he consents to the voluntary winding up of the member.

(5) If paragraph (4) is complied with, the voluntary winding up is to be treated as having commenced at the time the resolution was passed.

(6) If paragraph (4) is not complied with, the resolution has no effect.

NOTES

Para (4): words in square brackets substituted by the Companies Act 2006 (Consequential Amendments and Transitional Provisions) Order 2011, SI 2011/1265, art 27(1), (7).

[7.1593]

24 Voluntary winding up of members: powers of reorganisation controller

(1) This regulation applies in relation to a member or former member that is a company and which is being wound up voluntarily with the consent of the reorganisation controller.

(2) The reorganisation controller may apply to the court under section 112 of the 1986 Act (reference of questions to court) (or Article 98 of the 1989 Order) in respect of the member.

(3) The reorganisation controller is entitled to be heard at any hearing of the court in relation to the voluntary winding up of the member.

(4) Any notice or other document required to be sent to a creditor of the member must also be sent to the reorganisation controller.

(5) The reorganisation controller, or a person appointed by him for the purpose, is entitled—

(a) to attend any meeting of creditors of the member summoned under any enactment;

(b) to attend any meeting of a committee established under section 101 of the 1986 Act (or Article 87 of the 1989 Order); and

(c) to make representations as to any matter for decision at such a meeting.

[(5A) The reorganisation controller is entitled to participate (but not vote) in a qualifying decision procedure (within the meaning given by section 246ZE(11) of the 1986 Act) by which a decision about any matter is sought from the creditors of the member.]

(6) If, during the course of the winding up of the member, a compromise or arrangement is proposed between the member and its creditors, or any class of them, the reorganisation controller may apply to court under [section 896 of the 2006 Act].

NOTES

Para (5A): inserted by the Small Business, Enterprise and Employment Act 2015 (Consequential Amendments, Savings and Transitional Provisions) Regulations 2018, SI 2018/208, reg 10(1), (4), as from 13 March 2018 and subject to transitional provisions as noted to reg 16 at **[7.1585]**.

Para (6): words in square brackets substituted by the Companies Act 2006 (Consequential Amendments and Transitional Provisions) Order 2011, SI 2011/1265, art 27(1), (8).

[7.1594]
25 Petition for winding up of a member by reorganisation controller

(1) The reorganisation controller may present a petition to the court for the winding up of a member or former member that is a company.

(2) The petition is to be treated as made under section 124 of the 1986 Act or Article 104 of the 1989 Order.

(3) Section 122(1) of the 1986 Act, or [Article 102] of the 1989 Order must, in the case of an application made by the reorganisation controller be read as if they included the following grounds—

(a) the member is in default of an obligation to pay an insurance market debt which is due and payable; or

(b) the court considers that the member is or is likely to be unable to pay insurance market debts as they fall due; and

(c) in the case of either (a) or (b), the court thinks that the winding up of the member is necessary or desirable for achieving the objectives of the Lloyd's market reorganisation order.

NOTES

Para (3): words in square brackets substituted by the Insurers (Reorganisation and Winding Up) (Amendment) Regulations 2007, SI 2007/851, reg 3(1), (12).

[7.1595]
26 Winding up of a member: powers of reorganisation controller

(1) This regulation applies if a person other than the reorganisation controller presents a petition for the winding up of a member or former member that is a company.

(2) Any notice or other document required to be sent to a creditor of the member must also be sent to the reorganisation controller.

(3) The reorganisation controller may be heard—

(a) at the hearing of the petition; and

(b) at any other hearing of the court in relation to the member under or by virtue of Part 4 or 5 of the 1986 Act (or Part 5 or 6 of the 1989 Order).

(4) The reorganisation controller, or a person appointed by him for the purpose, may—

(a) attend any meeting of the creditors of the member;

(b) attend any meeting of a committee established for the purposes of Part 4 or 5 of the 1986 Act under section 101 of that Act or under section 141 or 142 of that Act;

(c) attend any meeting of a committee established for the purposes of Part 5 or 6 of the 1989 Order under Article 87 or Article 120 of that Order;

(d) make representations as to any matter for decision at such a meeting.

[(4A) The reorganisation controller is entitled to participate (but not vote) in a qualifying decision procedure (within the meaning given by section 246ZE(11) of the 1986 Act) by which a decision about any matter is sought from the creditors of the member.]

(5) If, during the course of the winding up of a member, a compromise or arrangement is proposed between the member and its creditors, or any class of them, the reorganisation controller may apply to the court under [section 896 of the 2006 Act].

NOTES

Para (4A): inserted by the Small Business, Enterprise and Employment Act 2015 (Consequential Amendments, Savings and Transitional Provisions) Regulations 2018, SI 2018/208, reg 10(1), (5), as from 13 March 2018 and subject to transitional provisions as noted to reg 16 at **[7.1585]**.

Para (5): words in square brackets substituted by the Companies Act 2006 (Consequential Amendments and Transitional Provisions) Order 2011, SI 2011/1265, art 27(1), (9).

[7.1596]
27 Petition for bankruptcy of a member by reorganisation controller

(1) The reorganisation controller may present a petition to the court for a bankruptcy order to be made against an individual member or, in Scotland, for the sequestration of the estate of an individual.

(2) The application shall be treated as made under section 264 of the 1986 Act (or Article 238 of the 1989 Order) or in Scotland under section 5 or 6 of the Bankruptcy (Scotland) Act 1985.

(3) On such a petition, the court may make a bankruptcy order or in Scotland an award of sequestration if (and only if)—

(a) the member is in default of an obligation to pay an insurance market debt which is due and payable; and

(b) the court thinks that the making of a bankruptcy order or award of sequestration in respect of that member is necessary or desirable for achieving the objectives of the Lloyd's market reorganisation order.

[7.1597]

28 Bankruptcy of a member: powers of reorganisation controller

(1) This regulation applies if a person other than the reorganisation controller presents a petition to the court—

(a) under section 264 of the 1986 Act (or Article 238 of the 1989 Order) for a bankruptcy order to be made against an individual member;

(b) under section 5 of the Bankruptcy (Scotland) Act 1985 for the sequestration of the estate of an individual member; or

(c) under section 6 of that Act for the sequestration of the estate belonging to or held for or jointly by the members of an entity mentioned in subsection (1) of that section.

(2) The reorganisation controller is entitled to be heard—

(a) at the hearing of the petition, and

(b) at any other hearing in relation to the individual member or entity under—

(i) Part 9 of the 1986 Act,

(ii) Part 9 of the 1989 Order; or

(iii) the Bankruptcy (Scotland) Act 1985.

[(3) In the case of a petition presented under Article 238 of the 1989 Order, a copy of the report prepared under Article 248 of that Order must also be sent to the reorganisation controller.]

(4) The reorganisation controller, or a person appointed by him for the purpose, is entitled—

(a) to attend any meeting of the creditors of the individual member or entity;

(b) to attend any meeting of a committee established under section 301 of the 1986 Act (or Article 274 of the 1989 Order);

(c) to attend any meeting of commissioners held under paragraph 17 or 18 of Schedule 6 to the Bankruptcy (Scotland) Act; and

(d) to make representations as to any matter for decision at such a meeting.

[(4A) The reorganisation controller is entitled to participate (but not vote) in a creditors' decision procedure (within the meaning given by section 379ZA(11) of the 1986 Act) by which a decision about any matter is sought from the creditors of the member.]

(5) In this regulation—

(a) references to an individual member include references to a former member who is an individual;

(b) "entity" means an entity which is a member or a former member.

NOTES

Para (3): substituted by the Enterprise and Regulatory Reform Act 2013 (Consequential Amendments) (Bankruptcy) and the Small Business, Enterprise and Employment Act 2015 (Consequential Amendments) Regulations 2016, SI 2016/481, reg 2(2), Sch 2, Pt 1, para 9(1), (4).

Para (4A): inserted by the Small Business, Enterprise and Employment Act 2015 (Consequential Amendments, Savings and Transitional Provisions) Regulations 2018, SI 2018/208, reg 10(1), (6), as from 13 March 2018 and subject to transitional provisions as noted to reg 16 at **[7.1585]**.

[7.1598]

29 Petition for winding up of the Society by reorganisation controller

(1) The reorganisation controller may present a petition to the court for the winding up of the Society in the circumstances set out in section 221(5) (winding up of unregistered companies) of the 1986 Act.

(2) Section 221(1) of that Act shall apply in respect of a petition presented by the reorganisation controller.

[7.1599]

30 Winding up of the Society: service of petition etc on reorganisation controller

(1) This regulation applies if a person other than the reorganisation controller presents a petition for the winding up of the Society.

(2) The petitioner must serve a copy of the petition on the reorganisation controller.

(3) Any notice or other document required to be sent to a creditor of the Society must also be sent to the reorganisation controller.

(4) The reorganisation controller is entitled to be heard—

(a) at the hearing of the petition; and

(b) at any other hearing of the court in relation to the Society under or by virtue of Part 5 of the 1986 Act (winding up of unregistered companies).

(5) The reorganisation controller, or a person appointed by him for the purpose, is entitled—

(a) to attend any meeting of the creditors of the Society;

(b) to attend any meeting of a committee established for the purposes of Part 5 of the 1986 Act under section 101 of that Act (appointment of liquidation committee);

(c) to make representations as to any matter for decision at such a meeting.

[(5A) The reorganisation controller is entitled to participate (but not vote) in a qualifying decision procedure (within the meaning given by section 246ZE(11) of the 1986 Act) by which a decision about any matter is sought from the creditors of the Society.]

(6) If, during the course of the winding up of the Society, a compromise or arrangement is proposed between the Society and its creditors, or any class of them, the reorganisation controller may apply to the court under [section 896 of the 2006 Act].

NOTES

Para (5A): inserted by the Small Business, Enterprise and Employment Act 2015 (Consequential Amendments, Savings and Transitional Provisions) Regulations 2018, SI 2018/208, reg 10(1), (7), as from 13 March 2018 and subject to transitional provisions as noted to reg 16 at **[7.1585]**.

Para (6): words in square brackets substituted by the Companies Act 2006 (Consequential Amendments and Transitional Provisions) Order 2011, SI 2011/1265, art 27(1), (10).

[7.1600]
31 Payments from central funds

(1) Unless otherwise agreed in writing between the Society, the reorganisation controller and the [PRA], before making a payment from central funds during the period of the Lloyd's market reorganisation order, the Society must give 5 working days [written] notice to the reorganisation controller.

(2) Notice under paragraph (1) must specify—
  (a) the amount of the proposed payment;
  (b) the purpose for which it is proposed to be made;
  (c) the recipient of the proposed payment.

(3) An agreement under paragraph (1) may in particular provide for payments—
  (a) to a specified person;
  (b) to a specified class of person;
  (c) for a specified purpose;
  (d) for a specified class of purposes,

to be made without the notice provided for in paragraph (1)

(4) If before the end of the period of 5 working days from the date on which he receives the notice under paragraph (1) the reorganisation controller considers that the payment should not be made, he must within that period—
  (a) apply to the court for a determination that the payment not be made; and
  (b) give notice [in writing] of his application to the Society and the [PRA] on or before the making of the application,

and the Society must not make payment without the permission of the court.

(5) The Society and the [PRA] may be heard at any hearing in connection with any such application.

(6) Where the reorganisation controller makes an application under paragraph (4), the Society commits an offence if it makes a payment from central funds without the permission of the court.

(7) If an offence under paragraph (6) is shown to have been committed with the consent or connivance of an officer of the Society, the officer as well as the Society is guilty of the offence.

(8) A person guilty of an offence under this regulation is liable—
  (a) on summary conviction, to a fine not exceeding the statutory maximum;
  (b) on conviction on indictment, to a fine.

(9) In this regulation "working day" means any day other than a Saturday, a Sunday, Christmas Day, Good Friday or a day which is a bank holiday under the Banking and Financial Dealings Act 1971 in any part of the United Kingdom.

(10) In paragraph (7), "officer", in relation to the Society, means the Chairman of Lloyd's, a Deputy Chairman of Lloyd's, the Chairman of the Committee established by section 5 of Lloyd's Act 1982, a deputy Chairman of the Committee, or a member of the Council established by section 3 of that Act.

NOTES

Para (1): word "PRA" in first pair of square brackets substituted by the Financial Services Act 2012 (Consequential Amendments and Transitional Provisions) Order 2013, SI 2013/472, art 3, Sch 2, para 109(h); word in second pair of square brackets inserted by the Insurers (Reorganisation and Winding Up) (Amendment) Regulations 2007, SI 2007/851, reg 3(1), (13).

Para (4): words in first pair of square brackets inserted by SI 2007/851, reg 3(1), (13); word "PRA" in second pair of square brackets substituted by SI 2013/472, art 3, Sch 2, para 109(h).

Para (5): word "PRA" in square brackets substituted by SI 2013/472, art 3, Sch 2, para 109(h).

PART 3
MODIFICATION OF LAW OF INSOLVENCY: NOTIFICATION AND PUBLICATION

[7.1601]
32 Application of Parts 3 and 4

Parts 3 and 4 of these Regulations apply where a Lloyd's market reorganisation order is in force and in respect of a member or former member in relation to whom no order under regulation 13(3) is in force.

[7.1602]

33 Notification of relevant decision to [PRA]

(1) Regulation 9 of the principal Regulations applies to a member or former member in the circumstances set out in paragraph (2) and has effect as if the modifications set out in paragraphs (3) and (4) were included in it as regards members or former members.

(2) The circumstances are where—

(a) the member or former member is subject to a Lloyd's market reorganisation order which remains in force; and

(b) no order has been made in respect of that member or former member under regulation 13(3) of these Regulations and has not been revoked.

(3) In paragraph (1) of regulation 9 of the principal Regulations, insert—

(a) after sub-paragraph (b)—

"(ba) a bankruptcy order under section 264 of the 1986 Act or under [Article 238] of the 1989 Order;

(bb) an award of sequestration under the Bankruptcy (Scotland) Act 1985;";

(b) after paragraph (c)—

"(ca) the appointment of an interim trustee under section 286 or 287 of the 1986 Act or under Article 259 or 260 of the 1989 Order;

(cb) the appointment of a trustee in bankruptcy under sections 295, 296 or 300 of that Act or under Articles 268, 269 or 273 of that Order;

(cc) the appointment of an interim or permanent trustee under the Bankruptcy (Scotland) Act 1985;".

(4) In paragraph (2) of that regulation after "voluntary arrangement", insert "or individual voluntary arrangement" and after "supervisor" insert "or nominee (as the case may be)".

(5) In paragraph (7) of that regulation, in the definition of "qualifying arrangement",

(a) after "voluntary arrangement" insert "or individual voluntary arrangement"; and

(b) for "insurer", wherever appearing substitute "member or former member".

(6) In paragraph (8), after "supervisor" insert ", nominee, trustee in bankruptcy, trustee under a trust deed for creditors".

NOTES

Regulation heading: word "PRA" in square brackets substituted by the Financial Services Act 2012 (Consequential Amendments and Transitional Provisions) Order 2013, SI 2013/472, art 3, Sch 2, para 109(i).

Para (3): words in square brackets substituted by the Insurers (Reorganisation and Winding Up) (Amendment) Regulations 2007, SI 2007/851, reg 3(1), (14).

[7.1603]

34 Notification of relevant decision to EEA Regulators

Regulation 10 of the principal Regulations applies as if—

(a) in paragraph (1)(b)(i) for "the business of an insurer" there were substituted "the insurance business of a member or former member"; and

(b) in paragraph (1)(b)(ii) for "an insurer" there were substituted "a member or former member".

[7.1604]

35 Application of certain publication requirements in the principal Regulations to members

(1) Regulation 11 of the principal Regulations (publication of voluntary arrangement, administration order, winding up order or scheme of arrangement) applies, with the following, where a qualifying decision has effect, or a qualifying order or appointment is made, in relation to a member or former member.

(2) References in regulation 11(2) to a "qualifying decision", a "qualifying order" and a "qualifying appointment" have the same meaning as in that regulation, subject to the modifications set out in paragraphs (3) and (5).

(3) Regulation 11(2)(a) has effect as if a qualifying decision included a decision with respect to the approval of a proposed individual voluntary arrangement in relation to a member in accordance with section 258 of the 1986 Act [(approval of debtor's proposal: individual voluntary arrangements)] or Article 232 of the 1989 Order (decisions of creditors' meeting: individual voluntary arrangements) or in Scotland the grant of a trust deed (within the meaning of the Bankruptcy (Scotland) Act 1985).

(4) In the case of a qualifying decision of a kind mentioned in paragraph (3) above, regulation 11(4) has effect as if the information mentioned therein included the court to which an application under sections 262 (challenge of the [creditors'] decision) and 263(3) (implementation and supervision of approved voluntary arrangement) of the 1986 Act may be made or Articles 236 (challenge of the meeting's decision) and 237(3) (implementation and supervision of approved voluntary arrangement) of the 1989 Order, or in Scotland under paragraph 12 of Schedule 5 to the Bankruptcy (Scotland) Act 1985.

(5) Regulation 11(2)(b) has effect as if a qualifying order included in relation to a member or former member a bankruptcy order under Part 9 of the 1986 Act or Part 9 of the 1989 Order, or in Scotland, an award of sequestration under the Bankruptcy (Scotland) Act.

(6) In the case of a qualifying order of the kind mentioned in paragraph (5) above, regulation 11(4) has effect as if the information mentioned therein included the court to which an application may be made under section 303 or 375 of the 1986 Act or Article 276 of the 1989 Order, or in Scotland included the court having jurisdiction to sequestrate.

(7) Regulation 11(11) has effect as if the meaning of "relevant officer" included—

(a) in the case of a voluntary arrangement under Part 9 of the 1986 Act or Part 9 of the 1989 Order, the nominee;

(b) in the case of a bankruptcy order, the trustee in bankruptcy;

(c) in Scotland,

(i) the trustee acting under a trust deed;

(ii) in the case of an award of sequestration, the interim or permanent trustee, as the case may be.

NOTES

Para (3): words in square brackets inserted by the Small Business, Enterprise and Employment Act 2015 (Consequential Amendments, Savings and Transitional Provisions) Regulations 2018, SI 2018/208, reg 10(1), (8)(a), as from 13 March 2018 and subject to transitional provisions as noted to reg 16 at **[7.1585]**.

Para (4): word in square brackets substituted for original word "meeting's", by SI 2018/208, reg 10(1), (8)(b), as from 13 March 2018 and subject to transitional provisions as noted to reg 16 at **[7.1585]**.

[7.1605]

36 Notification to creditors: winding up proceedings relating to members

(1) Regulation 12 of the principal Regulations (notification to creditors: winding up proceedings) applies, with the following modifications, where a relevant order or appointment is made, or a relevant decision is taken, in relation to a member or former member.

(2) References in paragraph (3) of that regulation to a "relevant order", a "relevant appointment" and a "relevant decision" have the meaning they have in that regulation, subject to the modifications set out in paragraphs (3) and (7).

(3) Paragraph (3) of that regulation has effect, for the purposes of this regulation, as if—

(a) a relevant order included a bankruptcy order made in relation to a member or former member under Part 9 of the 1986 Act or Part 9 of the 1989 Order or an award of sequestration under the Bankruptcy (Scotland) Act 1985; and

(b) a relevant decision included a decision as a result of which a qualifying individual voluntary arrangement in relation to a member or former member has effect in accordance with section 258 of the 1986 Act [(approval of debtor's proposal: individual voluntary arrangements)] or Article 232 of the 1989 Order (decisions of creditors' meeting: individual voluntary arrangements) or in Scotland the grant of a qualifying trust deed.

(4) Paragraph (4)(a) of that regulation has effect as if the reference to a UK insurer included a reference to a member or former member who is to be treated as a UK insurer for the purposes of the application of the principal Regulations.

(5) Paragraph (9) of that regulation has effect as if, in a case where a bankruptcy order is made in relation to a member or former member, it permitted the obligation under paragraph (1)(a)(ii) of that regulation to be discharged by sending a form of proof in accordance with rule 6.97 of the Insolvency Rules or Rule 6.095 of the Insolvency Rules (Northern Ireland) or submitting a claim in accordance with section 48 of the Bankruptcy (Scotland) Act 1985, provided that the form of proof or submission of claim complies with paragraph (7) or (8) of that regulation (whichever is applicable).

(6) Paragraph (13)(a) of that regulation has effect as if the meaning of "appointed officer" included—

(a) in the case of a qualifying individual voluntary arrangement approved in relation to a member or former member, the nominee;

(b) in the case of a bankruptcy order in relation to an individual member or former member, the trustee in bankruptcy;

(c) in Scotland in the case of a sequestration, the interim or permanent trustee; and

(d) in Scotland in the case of a relevant decision, the trustee.

(7) For the purposes of paragraph (3) of that regulation, an individual voluntary arrangement approved in relation to an individual member or former member is a qualifying individual voluntary arrangement and a trust deed within section 5(4A) of the Bankruptcy (Scotland) Act 1985 is a qualifying trust deed if its purposes or objects, as the case may be, include a realisation of some or all of the assets of that member or former member and a distribution of the proceeds to creditors, with a view to terminating the whole or any part of the business of that member carried on or formerly carried on in connection with contracts of insurance written at Lloyd's.

NOTES

Para (3): words in square brackets inserted by the Small Business, Enterprise and Employment Act 2015 (Consequential Amendments, Savings and Transitional Provisions) Regulations 2018, SI 2018/208, reg 10(1), (9), as from 13 March 2018 and subject to transitional provisions as noted to reg 16 at **[7.1585]**.

[7.1606]

37 Submission of claims by EEA creditor

(1) Regulation 13 of the principal Regulations (submission of claims by EEA creditors) applies, with the modifications set out in paragraphs (3) to (6) below, in the circumstances set out in paragraph (2) below, in the same way as it applies where an EEA creditor submits a claim or observations in the circumstances set out in paragraph (1) of that regulation.

(2) Those circumstances are where, after the date these Regulations come into force an EEA creditor submits a claim or observations relating to his claim in any relevant proceedings in respect of a member or former member (irrespective of when those proceedings were commenced or had effect).

(3) Paragraph (2) of that regulation has effect as if the "relevant proceedings" included—

(a) bankruptcy or sequestration; or

(b) a qualifying individual voluntary arrangement or in Scotland a qualifying trust deed for creditors.

(4) Paragraph (5) of that regulation has effect as if it also provided that paragraph (3) of that regulation does not apply where an EEA creditor submits his claim using—

(a) in a case of a bankruptcy or an award of sequestration of a member or former member, a form of proof in accordance with Rule 6.97 of Insolvency Rules or Rule 4.080 of the Insolvency Rules (Northern Ireland) or section 48 of the Bankruptcy (Scotland) Act 1985;

(b) in the case of a qualifying trust deed, the form prescribed by the trustee; and

(c) in the case of a qualifying individual voluntary arrangement, a form approved by the court for that purpose.

(5) For the purposes of that regulation (as applied in the circumstances set out in paragraph (2) above), an individual voluntary arrangement approved in relation to an individual member is a qualifying individual voluntary arrangement and a trust deed for creditors within section 5(4A) of the Bankruptcy (Scotland) Act 1985 is a qualifying trust deed for creditors if its purposes or objects as the case may be include a realisation of some or all of the assets of that member or former member and a distribution of the proceeds to creditors including insurance creditors, with a view to terminating the whole or any part of the business of that member carried on in connection with effecting or carrying out contracts of insurance written at Lloyd's.

[7.1607]

38 Reports to creditors

(1) Regulation 14 of the principal Regulations (reports to creditors) applies with the modifications set out in paragraphs (2) to (4) where—

(a) a liquidator is appointed in respect of a member or former member in accordance with—

(i) section 100 of the 1986 Act or Article 86 of the 1989 Order (creditors' voluntary winding up: appointment of a liquidator), or

(ii) paragraph 83 of Schedule B1 [or paragraph 84 of Schedule B1 to the 1989 Order] (moving from administration to creditors' voluntary liquidation);

(b) a winding up order is made by the court in respect of a member or former member;

(c) a provisional liquidator is appointed in respect of a member or former member;

[(d) an administrator (within the meaning given by paragraph 1(1) of Schedule B1 or paragraph 2(1) of Schedule B1 to the 1989 Order) of a member or former member includes in the statement required by Rule 2.3 of the Insolvency Rules or by Rule 2.003 of the Insolvency Rules (Northern Ireland) a statement to the effect that the objective set out in paragraph 3(1)(a) of Schedule B1 or paragraph 4(1)(a) of Schedule B1 to the 1989 Order is not reasonably likely to be achieved;] or

(e) a bankruptcy order or award of sequestration is made in respect of a member or former member.

(2) Paragraphs (2) to (5) of that regulation have effect as if they each included a reference to—

(a) an administrator who has made a statement to the effect that the objective set out in paragraph 3(1)(a) of Schedule B1 [or in paragraph 4(1)(a) of Schedule B1 to the 1989 Order] is not reasonably likely to be achieved;

(b) the official receiver or a trustee in bankruptcy; and

(c) in Scotland, an interim or permanent trustee.

(3) Paragraph (6)(a) of that regulation has effect as if the meaning of "known creditor" included—

(a) a creditor who is known to the administrator, the trustee in bankruptcy or the trustee, as the case may be;

(b) in a case where a bankruptcy order is made in respect of a member or former member, a creditor who is specified in a report submitted under section 274 of the 1986 Act or [Article 248] of the 1989 Order or a statement of affairs submitted under section 288 or Article 261 in respect of the member or former member;

(c) in a case where an administrator of a member has made a statement to the effect that the objective set out in paragraph 3(1)(a) of Schedule B1 [or in paragraph 4(1)(a) of Schedule B1 to the 1989 Order] is not reasonably likely to be achieved, a creditor who is specified in the statement of the member's affairs required by the administrator under paragraph 47(1) of [Schedule B1 or under paragraph 48(1) of Schedule B1 to the 1989 Order];

(d) in a case where a sequestration has been awarded, a creditor who is specified in a statement of assets and liabilities under section 19 of the Bankruptcy (Scotland) Act 1985.

(4) Paragraph (6)(b) of that regulation has effect as if "report" included a written report setting out the position generally as regards the progress of—

(a) the bankruptcy or sequestration; or

(b) the administration.

NOTES

Para (1): words in square brackets in sub-para (a) inserted and sub-para (d) substituted by the Insurers (Reorganisation and Winding Up) (Amendment) Regulations 2007, SI 2007/851, reg 3(1), (15)(a), (b).

Para (2): words in square brackets in sub-para (a) inserted by SI 2007/851, reg 3(1), (15)(c).

Para (3): words in square brackets in sub-para (b) and words in second pair of square brackets in sub-para (c) substituted, and words in first pair of square brackets in sub-para (c) inserted by SI 2007/851, reg 3(1), (15)(d), (e).

[7.1608]

39 Service of notices and documents

(1) Regulation 15 of the principal Regulations (service of notices and documents) applies, with the modifications set out in paragraphs (2) and (3) below, to any notification, report or other document which is required to be sent to a creditor of a member or former member by a provision of Part III of those Regulations as applied and modified by regulations 33 to 35 above.

(2) Paragraph 15(5)(a)(i) of that regulation has effect as if the reference to the UK insurer which is liable under the creditor's claim included a reference to the member or former member who or which is liable under the creditor's claim.

(3) Paragraph (7)(c) of that regulation has effect as if "relevant officer" included a trustee in bankruptcy, nominee, receiver or, in Scotland, an interim or permanent trustee under a trust deed within the meaning of section 5(4A) of the Bankruptcy (Scotland) Act who is required to send a notification to a creditor by a provision of Part III of the principal Regulations as applied and modified by regulations 33 to 37 above.

PART 4
APPLICATION OF PARTS 4 AND 5 OF THE PRINCIPAL REGULATIONS

[7.1609]

40 Priority for insurance claims

(1) Part 4 of the principal Regulations applies with the modifications set out in paragraphs (2) to (11).

(2) References, in relation to a UK insurer, to a winding up by the court have effect as if they included a reference to the bankruptcy or sequestration of a member or former member.

(3) References to the making of a winding up order in relation to a UK insurer have effect as if they included a reference to the making of a bankruptcy order or, in Scotland, an award of sequestration in relation to an individual member or a member or former member that is a Scottish limited partnership.

(4) References to an administration order in relation to a UK insurer have effect as if they included a reference to an individual voluntary arrangement in relation to an individual member and a trust deed for creditors within the meaning of section 5(4A) of the Bankruptcy (Scotland) Act.

(5) Regulation 20 (preferential debts: disapplication of section 175 of the 1986 Act or Article 149 of the 1989 Order) has effect as if the references to section 175 of the 1986 Act and Article 149 of the 1989 Order included a reference to section 328 of that Act, Article 300 of that Order and section 51(1) (d) to (h) of the Bankruptcy (Scotland) Act 1985.

(6) Regulation 21(3) (preferential debts: long term insurers and general insurers) has effect as if after the words "rank equally among themselves" there were inserted the words "after the expenses of the bankruptcy or sequestration".

(7) Regulation 27 (composite insurers: application of other assets) has effect as if the reference to section 175 of the 1986 Act or Article 149 of the 1989 Order included a reference to section 328 of that Act, Article 300 of that Order and section 51(1) (e) to (h) of the Bankruptcy (Scotland) Act.

(8) Regulation 29 (composite insurers: general meetings of creditors) has effect as if [in paragraph (1) the words from ", but only if" to the end were omitted and] after paragraph (2) there were inserted—

> ["(3) If the bankrupt's creditors propose to establish a creditors' committee pursuant to section 301(1) of the 1986 Act or if the general meeting of the bankrupt's creditors proposes to establish a creditors' committee pursuant to Article 274(1) of the 1989 Order, separate committees must be established for creditors in respect of long-term business liabilities and creditors in respect of general business liabilities."]
>
> (4) The committee of creditors in respect of long-term business liabilities may exercise the functions of a creditors' committee under the 1986 Act or the 1989 Order in relation to long term business liabilities only.
>
> (5) The committee of creditors in respect of general business liabilities may exercise the functions of a creditors' committee under the 1986 Act or the 1989 Order in relation to general business liabilities only.
>
> (6) If, in terms of section 30(1) of the Bankruptcy (Scotland) Act 1985, at the statutory meeting or any subsequent meeting of creditors it is proposed to elect one or more commissioners (or new or additional commissioners) in the sequestration, it shall elect separate commissioners in respect of the long-term business liabilities and the general business liabilities.
>
> (7) Any commissioner elected in respect of the long-term business liabilities shall exercise his functions under the Bankruptcy (Scotland) Act 1985 in respect of the long-term business liabilities only.
>
> (8) Any commissioner elected in respect of the general business liabilities shall exercise his functions under the Bankruptcy (Scotland) Act 1985 in respect of the general business liabilities only.".

(9) Regulation 30 (composite insurers: apportionment of costs payable out of the assets) has effect as if in its application to members or former members who are individuals or Scottish limited partnerships—

(a) in England and Wales, the reference to Rule 4.218 of the Insolvency Rules (general rule as to priority) included a reference to Rule 6.224 of the Insolvency Rules (general rule as to priority (bankruptcy));

(b) in Northern Ireland, the reference to Rule 4.228 of the Insolvency Rules (Northern Ireland) (general rule as to priority) included a reference to Rule 6.222 of the Insolvency Rules (Northern Ireland) (general rule as to priority (bankruptcy)); and

(c) in Scotland, the reference to Rule 4.67 of the Insolvency (Scotland) Rules includes reference to—

(i) any finally determined outlays or remuneration in a sequestration within the meaning of section 53 of the Bankruptcy (Scotland) Act 1985 and shall be calculated and applied separately in respect of the long-term business assets and the general business assets of that member; and

(ii) the remuneration and expenses of a trustee under a trust deed for creditors within the meaning of the Bankruptcy (Scotland) Act 1985,

and references to a liquidator include references to a trustee in bankruptcy, interim or permanent trustee, trustee under a trust deed for creditors, Accountant in Bankruptcy or Commissioners where appropriate.

(10) Regulation 31 (summary remedies against liquidators) has effect as if—

(a) the reference to section 212 of the 1986 Act or Article 176 of the 1989 Order included a reference to section 304 of that Act or Article 277 of that Order (liability of trustee);

(b) the references to a liquidator included a reference to a trustee in bankruptcy in respect of a qualifying insolvent member; and

(c) the reference to section 175 of the1986 Act or Article 149 of the 1989 Order included a reference to section 328 of that Act or Article 300 of that Order.

(11) Regulation 33 (voluntary arrangements: treatment of insurance debts) has effect as if after paragraph (3) there were inserted—

"(4) The modifications made by paragraph (5) apply where an individual member proposes an individual voluntary arrangement in accordance with Part 8 of the 1986 Act or Part 8 of the 1989 Order, and that arrangement includes—

(a) a composition in satisfaction of any insurance debts; and

(b) a distribution to creditors of some or all of the assets of that member in the course of, or with a view to, terminating the whole or any part of the insurance business of that member carried on at Lloyd's.

(5) Section 258 of the 1986 Act [(approval of debtor's proposal)] has effect as if—

(a) after subsection (5) there were inserted—

"(5A) [Where a Lloyd's market reorganisation order is in force and the debtor is an individual member, the debtor's creditors] shall not approve any proposal or modification under which any insurance debt of that member is to be paid otherwise than in priority to such of his debts as are not insurance debts or preferential debts.";

(b) after subsection (7) there were inserted—

"(8) For the purposes of this section—

(a) "insurance debt" has the meaning it has in the Insurers (Reorganisation and Winding Up) Regulations 2004;

(b) "Lloyd's market reorganisation order" and "individual member" have the meaning they have in the Insurers (Reorganisation and Winding Up) (Lloyd's) Regulations 2005.".

(6) Article 232 of the 1989 Order (Decisions of creditors' meeting) has effect as if—

(a) after paragraph (6) there were inserted—

"(6A) A meeting so summoned in relation to an individual member and taking place when a Lloyd's market reorganisation order is in force shall not approve any proposal or modification under which any insurance debt of that member is to be paid otherwise than in priority to such of his debts as are not insurance debts or preferential debts.";

(b) after paragraph (9) there were inserted—

"(10) For the purposes of this Article—

(a) "insurance debt" has the meaning it has in the Insurers (Reorganisation and Winding Up) Regulations 2004;

(b) "Lloyd's market reorganisation order" and "individual member" have the meaning they have in the Insurers (Reorganisation and Winding Up) (Lloyd's) Regulations 2005.".

(7) In Scotland, where a member or former member grants a trust deed for creditors, Schedule 5 to the Bankruptcy (Scotland) Act 1985 shall be read as if after paragraph 4 there were included paragraphs 4A and 4B as follows—

"**4A.** Whether or not provision is made in any trust deed, where such a trust deed includes a composition in satisfaction of any insurance debts of a member or former member and a distribution to creditors of some or all of the assets of that member or former member in the course of or with a view to meeting obligations of his insurance business carried on at Lloyd's, the trustee may not provide for any insurance debt to be paid otherwise than in priority to such of his debts as are not insurance debts or preferred debts within the meaning of section 51(2).

4B. For the purposes of paragraph 4A,

(a) "insurance debt" has the meaning it has in the Insurance (Reorganisation and Winding Up) Regulations 2004; and

(b) "member" and "former member" have the meaning given in regulation 2(1) of the Insurers (Reorganisation and Winding Up) (Lloyd's) Regulations 2005.".".

(12) The power to apply to court in section 303 of the 1986 Act or Article 276 of the 1989 Order or section 63 of the Bankruptcy (Scotland) Act (general control of trustee by court) may be exercised by the reorganisation controller if it appears to him that any act, omission or decision of a trustee of the estate of a member contravenes the provisions of Part 4 of the principal Regulations (as applied by this regulation).

NOTES

Para (8): words in first pair of square brackets inserted asnd words in second pair of square brackets substituted, by the Small Business, Enterprise and Employment Act 2015 (Consequential Amendments, Savings and Transitional Provisions) Regulations 2018, SI 2018/208, reg 10(1), (10)(a), as from 13 March 2018 and subject to transitional provisions as noted to reg 16 at **[7.1585]**.

Para (11): words in square brackets substituted by SI 2018/208, reg 10(1), (10)(b), as from 13 March 2018 and subject to transitional provisions as noted to reg 16 at **[7.1585]**.

[7.1610]

41 Treatment of liabilities arising in connection with a contract subject to reinsurance to close

(1) Where in respect of a member or former member who is subject to a Lloyd's market reorganisation order any of the events specified in paragraph (2)(a) have occurred, for the purposes of the application of Part 4 of the principal Regulations to that member (and only for those purposes), an obligation of that member under a reinsurance to close contract in respect of a debt due or treated as due under a contract of insurance written at Lloyd's is to be treated as an insurance debt.

(2) For the purposes of this regulation—

(a) The events are—

(i) in respect of a member which is a corporation the appointment of a liquidator, provisional liquidator or administrator;

(ii) in respect of an individual member, the appointment of a receiver or trustee in bankruptcy; and

(iii) in respect of a member in Scotland being either an individual or a Scottish limited partnership, the making of a sequestration order or the appointment of an interim or permanent trustee;

(b) "reinsurance to close contract" means a contract under which, in accordance with the rules or practices of Lloyd's, underwriting members ("the reinsured members") who are members of a syndicate for a year of account ("the closed year") agree with underwriting members who constitute that or another syndicate for a later year of account ("the reinsuring members") that the reinsuring members will indemnify the reinsured members against all known and unknown liabilities of the reinsured members arising out of the insurance business underwritten through that syndicate and allocated to the closed year (including liabilities under any reinsurance to close contract underwritten by the reinsured members).

[7.1611]

42 Assets of members

(1) This regulation applies where a member or former member is treated as a UK insurer in accordance with regulations 13 and 40 above.

(2) Subject to paragraphs (3) and (4), the undistributed assets of the member are to be treated as assets of the insurer for the purposes of the application of Part 4 of the principal Regulations in accordance with regulation 43 below.

(3) For the purposes of this regulation, the undistributed assets of the member so treated do not include any asset held in a relevant trust fund.

(4) But any asset released from a relevant trust fund and received by such a member is to be treated as an asset of the insurer for the purposes of the application of Part 4 of the principal Regulations.

[7.1612]

43 Application of Part 4 of the principal Regulations: protection of settlements

(1) This regulation applies where a member or former member is subject to an insolvency measure mentioned in paragraph (4) at the time that a Lloyd's market reorganisation order comes into force.

(2) Nothing in these Regulations or Part 4 of the principal Regulations affects the validity of any payment or disposition made, or any settlement agreed, by the relevant officer before the date when the Lloyd's market reorganisation order came into force.

(3) For the purposes of the application of Part 4 of the principal Regulations, the insolvent estate of the member or former member shall not include any assets which are subject to a [relevant compromise or arrangement], a relevant individual voluntary arrangement, or a relevant trust deed for creditors.

(4) In paragraph (2) "relevant officer" means—
(a) where the insolvency measure is a voluntary arrangement, the nominee;
(b) where the insolvency measure is administration, the administrator;
(c) where the insolvency measure is the appointment of a provisional liquidator, the provisional liquidator;
(d) where the insolvency measure is a winding up, the liquidator;
(e) where the insolvency measure is an individual voluntary arrangement, the nominee or supervisor;
(f) where the insolvency measure is bankruptcy, the trustee in bankruptcy;
(g) where the insolvency measure is sequestration, the interim or permanent trustee; and
(h) where the insolvency measure is a trust deed for creditors, the trustee.

(5) For the purposes of paragraph (3)—
(a) "assets" has the same meaning as "property" in section 436 of the 1986 Act or Article 2(2) of the 1989 Order;
(b) "insolvent estate" in England and Wales and Northern Ireland has the meaning given by Rule 13.8 of the Insolvency Rules or Rule 0.2 of the Insolvency Rules (Northern Ireland), and in Scotland means the whole estate of the member;
[(c) "a relevant compromise or arrangement" means—
(i) a compromise or arrangement—
(aa) sanctioned by the court under section 425 of the Companies Act 1985 (excluding a compromise or arrangement falling within section 427 or 427A of that Act),
(bb) sanctioned by the court under Article 418 of the Companies (Northern Ireland) Order 1986 (excluding a compromise or arrangement falling within Article 420 or 420A of that Order), or
(cc) which is a section 899 compromise or arrangement,
that was sanctioned by the court before the date on which an application for a Lloyd's market reorganisation order was made, or
(ii) any subsequent compromise or arrangement—
(aa) sanctioned by the court as mentioned in paragraph (i)(aa) or (bb), or
(bb) which is a section 899 compromise or arrangement,
that was sanctioned by the court to amend or replace a compromise or arrangement of the kind mentioned in paragraph (i);]
(d) "a relevant individual voluntary arrangement" and "a relevant trust deed for creditors" mean an individual voluntary arrangement or trust deed for creditors which was sanctioned by the court or entered into before the date on which an application for a Lloyd's market reorganisation order was made.

NOTES

Para (3): words in square brackets substituted by the Companies Act 2006 (Consequential Amendments and Transitional Provisions) Order 2011, SI 2011/1265, art 27(1), (11)(a).

Para (5): sub-para (c) substituted by SI 2011/1265, art 27(1), (11)(b).

[7.1613]

44 Challenge by reorganisation controller to conduct of insolvency practitioner

(1) The reorganisation controller may apply to the court claiming that a relevant officer is acting, has acted, or proposes to act in a way that fails to comply with a requirement of Part 4 of the principal Regulations.

(2) The reorganisation controller must send a copy of an application under paragraph (1) to the relevant officer in respect of whom the application is made.

(3) In the case of a relevant officer who is acting in respect of a member or former member subject to the jurisdiction of a Scottish court, the application must be made to the Court of Session.

(4) The court may—
(a) dismiss the application;
(b) make an interim order;
(c) make any other order it thinks appropriate.

(5) In particular, an order under this regulation may—
(a) regulate the relevant officer's exercise of his functions;
(b) require that officer to do or not do a specified thing;
(c) make consequential provision.

(6) An order may not be made under this regulation if it would impede or prevent the implementation of—
(a) a voluntary arrangement approved under Part 1 of the 1986 Act or Part 2 of the 1989 Order before the date when the Lloyd's market reorganisation order was made;
(b) an individual voluntary arrangement approved under Part 8 of that Act or Part 8 of that Order before the date when the Lloyd's market reorganisation order was made; or
[(c) a compromise or arrangement sanctioned by the court before the date when the Lloyd's market reorganisation order was made which is—
(i) a section 899 compromise or arrangement,

(ii) a compromise or arrangement sanctioned under section 425 of the Companies Act 1985 (excluding a compromise or arrangement falling within section 427 or 427A of that Act), or

(iii) a compromise or arrangement sanctioned under Article 418 of the Companies (Northern Ireland) Order 1986 (excluding a compromise or arrangement falling within Article 420 or 420A of that Order).]

(7) In this regulation "relevant officer" means—

(a) a liquidator,

(b) a provisional liquidator,

(c) an administrator

(d) the official receiver or a trustee in bankruptcy, or

(e) in Scotland, an interim or permanent trustee or a trustee for creditors,

who is appointed in relation to a member or former member.

NOTES

Para (6): sub-para (c) substituted by the Companies Act 2006 (Consequential Amendments and Transitional Provisions) Order 2011, SI 2011/1265, art 27(1), (12).

[7.1614]

45 Application of Part 5 of the principal Regulations

(1) Part 5 of the principal Regulations (reorganisation or winding up of UK insurers: recognition of EEA rights) applies with the modifications set out in regulation 46 where, on or after the date that a Lloyd's market reorganisation order comes into force, a member or former member is or becomes subject to a reorganisation or insolvency measure.

(2) For the purposes of this regulation a "reorganisation or insolvency measure" means—

(a) a voluntary arrangement, having a qualifying purpose, approved in accordance with section 4A of the 1986 Act or Article 17A of the 1989 Order;

(b) administration pursuant to an order under paragraph 13 of Schedule B1 [or under paragraph 14 of Schedule B1 to the 1989 Order];

(c) the reduction by the court of the value of one or more relevant contracts of insurance under section 377 of the 2000 Act or section 24(5) of the Friendly Societies Act 1992;

(d) winding up;

(e) the appointment of a provisional liquidator in accordance with section 135 of the 1986 Act or Article 115 of the 1989 Order;

(f) an individual voluntary arrangement, having a qualifying purpose, approved in accordance with section 258 of the 1986 Act or Article 232 of the 1989 Order;

(g) in Scotland a qualifying trust deed for creditors within the meaning of section 5(4A) of the Bankruptcy (Scotland) Act 1985;

(h) bankruptcy, in accordance with Part 9 of the 1986 Act or Part 9 of the1989 Order; or

(i) sequestration under the Bankruptcy (Scotland) Act 1985.

(3) A measure imposed under the law of a State or country other than the United Kingdom is not a reorganisation or insolvency measure for the purposes of this regulation.

(4) For the purposes of sub-paragraphs (a), (f) and (g) of paragraph (2), a voluntary arrangement or individual voluntary arrangement has a qualifying purpose and a trust deed is a qualifying trust deed if it—

(a) varies the rights of creditors as against the member and is intended to enable the member to continue to carry on an insurance market activity at Lloyd's; or

(b) includes a realisation of some or all of the assets of the member and the distribution of proceeds to creditors, with a view to terminating the whole or any part of that member's business at Lloyd's.

NOTES

Para (2): words in square brackets in sub-para (b) inserted by the Insurers (Reorganisation and Winding Up) (Amendment) Regulations 2007, SI 2007/851, reg 3(1), (16).

[7.1615]

46 Modification of provisions in Part 5 of the principal Regulations

(1) The modifications mentioned in regulation 45(1) are as follows.

(2) Regulation 35 is disapplied.

(3) Regulation 36 (interpretation of Part 5) has effect as if—

(a) in paragraph (1)—

(i) the meaning of "affected insurer" included a member or former member who, on or after the date that a Lloyd's market reorganisation order comes into force, is or becomes subject to a reorganisation or insolvency measure within the meaning given by regulation 44(2)of these Regulations;

(ii) the meaning of "relevant reorganisation or relevant winding up" included any reorganisation or insolvency measure, in respect of a member or former member, to which Part 5 of the principal Regulations applies by virtue of regulation 45(1) of these Regulations;

(iii) in the case of sequestration, the date of sequestration within the meaning of section 12 of the Bankruptcy (Scotland) Act 1985; and

(b) in paragraph (2) references to the opening of a relevant reorganisation or a relevant winding up meant (in addition to the meaning in the cases set out in that paragraph)—
(i) in the case of an individual voluntary arrangement, the date when a decision with respect to that arrangement has effect in accordance with section 258 of the 1986 Act or Article 232 of the 1989 Order;
(ii) in the case of bankruptcy, the date on which the bankruptcy order is made under Part 9 of the 1986 Act or Part 9 of the 1989 Order;
(iii) in the case of a trust deed for creditors under the Bankruptcy (Scotland) Act 1985 the date when the trust deed was granted.

(4) Regulation 37 of the principal Regulations (EEA rights: applicable law in the winding up of a UK insurer) has effect as if—
(a) references to a relevant winding up included (in each case) a reference to a reorganisation or insolvency measure within the meaning given by sub-paragraphs (d), (g) (h) and (i) of regulation 45(2) of these Regulations (winding up and bankruptcy) in respect of a member or former member; and
(b) the reference in paragraph (3)(c) to the liquidator included a reference to the trustee in bankruptcy or in Scotland to the interim or permanent trustee.

(5) Regulation 42 (reservation of title agreements etc) has effect as if the reference to an insurer in paragraphs (1) and (2) included a reference to a member or former member.

[7.1616]
47 Application of Part 5 of the principal Regulations: protection of dispositions etc made before a Lloyd's market reorganisation order comes into force

(1) This regulation applies where—
(a) a member or former member is subject to a reorganisation or insolvency measure on the date when a Lloyd's market reorganisation order comes into force; and
(b) Part 5 of the principal Regulations applies in relation to that reorganisation or insolvency measure by virtue of regulation 45 above.

(2) Nothing in Part 5 of the principal Regulations affects the validity of any payment or disposition made, or any settlement agreed, by the relevant officer before the date when the Lloyd's market reorganisation order came into force.

(3) For the purposes of the application of Part 5 of the principal Regulations, the insolvent estate of the member does not include any assets which are subject to a [relevant compromise or arrangement], a relevant individual voluntary arrangement, or a relevant trust deed for creditors.

(4) In paragraph (2) "relevant officer" means—
(a) where the member is subject to a voluntary arrangement in accordance with section 4A of the 1986 Act or Article 17A of the 1989 Order, the supervisor;
(b) where the member is in administration in accordance with Schedule B1 [or with Schedule B1 to the 1989 Order], the administrator;
(c) where a provisional liquidator has been appointed in relation to a member in accordance with section 135 of the 1986 Act or Article 115 of the 1989 Order, the provisional liquidator;
(d) where the member is being wound up under Part 4 of the 1986 Act or Part 5 of the 1989 Order, the liquidator;
(e) where the member has made a voluntary arrangement in accordance with Part 8 of the 1986 Act or Part 8 of the 1989 Order, the nominee;
(f) where the member is bankrupt within the meaning of Part 9 of the 1986 Act or Part 9 of the 1989 Order, the official receiver or trustee in bankruptcy;
(g) where the member is being sequestrated, the interim or permanent trustee; and
(h) where a trust deed for creditors has been granted, the trustee.

(5) For the purposes of paragraph (3)—
(a) "assets" has the same meaning as "property" in section 436 of the 1986 Act or Article 2(2) of the 1989 Order, except in relation to relevant trust deeds;
(b) "insolvent estate" in England and Wales and Northern Ireland has the meaning given by Rule 13.8 of the Insolvency Rules or Rule 0.2 of the Insolvency Rules (Northern Ireland), and in Scotland means the assets of the member;
[(c) "relevant compromise or arrangement" means—
(i) a compromise or arrangement—
(aa) sanctioned by the court under section 425 of the Companies Act 1985 (excluding a compromise or arrangement falling within section 427 or 427A of that Act),
(bb) sanctioned by the court under Article 418 of the Companies (Northern Ireland) Order 1986 (excluding a compromise or arrangement falling within Article 420 or 420A of that Order), or
(cc) which is a section 899 compromise or arrangement,
that was sanctioned by the court before the date on which an application for a Lloyd's market reorganisation order was made, or
(ii) any subsequent compromise or arrangement—
(aa) sanctioned by the court as mentioned in sub-paragraph (aa) or (bb) of paragraph (i), or
(bb) which is a section 899 compromise or arrangement,

Part 7L Special Insolvency Regimes

that was sanctioned by the court to amend or replace a compromise or arrangement of the kind mentioned in paragraph (i);]

(d) "relevant individual voluntary arrangement" means—

(i) an individual voluntary arrangement approved under Part 8 of the 1986 Act [or Part 8 of the 1989 Order] before the date when a Lloyd's market reorganisation order came in to force, and

(ii) any subsequent individual voluntary arrangement sanctioned by the court to amend or replace an arrangement of the kind mentioned in paragraph (i); and

(e) "relevant trust deed" means a trust deed granted by a member or former member before the date when the Lloyd's market reorganisation order entered into force.

NOTES

Para (3): words in square brackets substituted by the Companies Act 2006 (Consequential Amendments and Transitional Provisions) Order 2011, SI 2011/1265, art 27(1), (13)(a).

Para (4): words in square brackets in sub-para (b) inserted by the Insurers (Reorganisation and Winding Up) (Amendment) Regulations 2007, SI 2007/851, reg 3(1), (17)(a).

Para (5): sub-para (c) substituted by SI 2011/1265, art 27(1), (13)(b); words in square brackets in sub-para (d) inserted by SI 2007/851, reg 3(1), (17)(b).

[7.1617]
48 Non-EEA countries

In respect of a member or former member who is established in a country outside the EEA, the court or the [PRA] may, subject to sections 348 and 349 of the 2000 Act, make such disclosures as each considers appropriate to a court or to a regulator with a role equivalent to that of the [PRA] for the purpose of facilitating the work of the reorganisation controller.

NOTES

Word "PRA" in square brackets substituted by the Financial Services Act 2012 (Consequential Amendments and Transitional Provisions) Order 2013, SI 2013/472, art 3, Sch 2, para 109(j).

49 (*Amends the Insurers (Reorganisation and Winding Up) Regulations 2004, SI 2004/353, reg 19 at* **[3.142]**.)

FINANCIAL SERVICES AND MARKETS ACT 2000 (ADMINISTRATION ORDERS RELATING TO INSURERS) ORDER 2010

(SI 2010/3023)

NOTES

Made: 18 December 2010.

Authority: Financial Services and Markets Act 2000, ss 360, 426(1), 428(3).

Commencement: 1 February 2011.

Modification: this Order is applied with modifications in relation to a society registered under the Co-operative and Community Benefit Societies Act 2014, by the Co-operative and Community Benefit Societies and Credit Unions (Arrangements, Reconstructions and Administration) Order 2014, SI 2014/229, art 12, Sch 5, at **[7.1437]**, **[7.1450]**.

[7.1618]
1 Citation, commencement and interpretation

(1) This Order may be cited as the Financial Services and Markets Act 2000 (Administration Orders Relating to Insurers) Order 2010 and comes into force on 1st February 2011.

(2) In this Order—

"the 1986 Act" means the Insolvency Act 1986;

"Schedule B1" means Schedule B1 to the 1986 Act.

[7.1619]
2 Application and modification of Part 2 of the 1986 Act in relation to insurers

(1) Part 2 of the 1986 Act (administration), other than paragraph 14 of Schedule B1 (power of holder of floating charge to appoint administrator) and paragraph 22 of Schedule B1 (power of company or directors to appoint administrator), applies in relation to insurers with the modifications specified in the Schedule to this Order.

(2) Accordingly paragraph 9(2) of Schedule B1 does not preclude the making of an administration order in relation to an insurer.

[7.1620]
3 Application and modification of the Insolvency Rules 1986 in relation to insurers

The Insolvency Rules 1986, so far as they give effect to Part 2 of the 1986 Act, have effect in relation to insurers with the following modifications—

(a) in Rule 2.12(1) (the hearing) after sub-paragraph (a) insert—

"(aa) the [Financial Conduct Authority and, where the person is a PRA-authorised person within the meaning of the Financial Services and Markets Act 2000, the Prudential Regulation Authority];

(ab) the scheme manager of the Financial Services Compensation Scheme;".

NOTES

Words in square brackets substituted by the Financial Services Act 2012 (Consequential Amendments and Transitional Provisions) Order 2013, SI 2013/472, art 3, Sch 2, para 195(a).

[7.1621]

4 Application and modification of the Insolvency (Scotland) Rules 1986 in relation to insurers

The Insolvency (Scotland) Rules 1986, so far as they give effect to Part 2 of the 1986 Act, have effect in relation to insurers with the following modifications—

(a) in Rule 2.3(1) (service of petition) after subparagraph (a) insert—

"(aa) the [the Financial Conduct Authority and, where the person is a PRA-authorised person within the meaning of the Financial Services and Markets Act 2000, the Prudential Regulation Authority];"

(ab) the scheme manager of the Financial Services Compensation Scheme;".

NOTES

Words in square brackets substituted by the Financial Services Act 2012 (Consequential Amendments and Transitional Provisions) Order 2013, SI 2013/472, art 3, Sch 2, para 195(b).

5 *(Revokes the Financial Services and Markets Act 2000 (Administration Orders Relating to Insurers) Order 2002, SI 2002/1242 at* **[7.1565]***, the Financial Services and Markets Act 2000 (Administration Orders Relating to Insurers) (Amendment) Order 2003, SI 2003/2134, arts 2–8 and the Insurers (Reorganisation and Winding Up) Regulations 2004, SI 2004/353, reg 52.)*

[7.1622]

6 Saving

Nothing in articles 2 to 5 applies in relation to any case where the appointment of an administrator takes effect before the coming into force of this Order.

SCHEDULES

SCHEDULE
MODIFICATIONS OF PART 2 OF THE INSOLVENCY ACT 1986 IN RELATION TO INSURERS

Article 2

[7.1623]

1. (1) In paragraph 3 of Schedule B1 (purpose of administration)—

(a) at the beginning of sub-paragraph (1) insert "Subject to sub-paragraph (1A)";

(b) after sub-paragraph (1) insert—

"(1A) The administrator of an insurer which effects or carries out contracts of insurance shall, at the request of the scheme manager of the Financial Services Compensation Scheme, provide any assistance identified by the scheme manager as being necessary—

(a) to enable the scheme manager to administer the compensation scheme in relation to contracts of insurance, and

(b) to enable the scheme manager to secure continuity of insurance in relation to contracts of long-term insurance.

(1B) For the purposes of this Schedule—

(a) "compensation scheme" has the same meaning as in section 213 of the Financial Services and Markets Act 2000;

(b) "contracts of insurance" and "contracts of long-term insurance" have the same meaning as in article 3 of the Financial Services and Markets Act 2000 (Regulated Activities) Order 2001;

(c) "scheme manager" means the body corporate established by the Financial Services Authority under section 212 of the Financial Services and Markets Act 2000.".

(2) In sub-paragraph (2), for "sub-paragraph (4)," substitute "sub-paragraphs (1A) and (4) and to paragraph 3A".

2. (1) After paragraph 3 of Schedule B1, insert—

"**3A.** (1) This paragraph applies in relation to the administration of an insurer which effects or carries out contracts of long-term insurance.

(2) Unless the court orders otherwise, the administrator must carry on the insurer's business so far as that business consists of carrying out the insurer's contracts of long-term insurance ("the long-term insurance business") with a view to the business being transferred as a going concern to a person who may lawfully carry out those contracts.

(3) In carrying on the long-term insurance business, the administrator—

Part 7L Special Insolvency Regimes

(a) may agree to the variation of any contracts of insurance in existence when the administration order is made; but

(b) must not effect any new contracts of insurance without the approval of the [Prudential Regulation Authority and, if the insurer is not a PRA-authorised person within the meaning of the Financial Services and Markets Act 2000, the Financial Conduct Authority].

(4) If the administrator is satisfied that the interests of the creditors in respect of liabilities of the insurer attributable to contracts of long-term insurance effected by it require the appointment of a special manager, the administrator may apply to the court.

(5) On such an application, the court may appoint a special manager to act during such time, and to have such powers (including powers of a receiver or manager) as the court may direct.

(6) Section 177(5) of this Act (duties of special manager) applies to a special manager appointed under sub-paragraph (5) as it applies to a special manager appointed under section 177.

(7) If the court thinks fit, it may reduce the value of one or more of the contracts of long-term insurance effected by the insurer.

(8) Any reduction is to be on such terms and subject to such conditions (if any) as the court thinks fit.

(9) The court may, on the application of an official, appoint an independent actuary to investigate the insurer's long-term insurance business and to report to the official—

(a) on the desirability or otherwise of the insurer's long-term insurance business being continued; and

(b) on any reduction in the contracts of long-term insurance effected by the insurer that may be necessary for successful continuation of the insurer's long-term insurance business.

(10) "Official" means—

(a) the administrator;

(b) a special manager appointed under sub-paragraph (5); or

(c) the [Financial Conduct Authority or the Prudential Regulation Authority].".

3. In paragraph 49(4) of Schedule B1 (administrator's proposals), omit "and" at the end of paragraph (b) and at the end of paragraph (c) add—

"(d) to the [Financial Conduct Authority and the Prudential Regulation Authority], and

(e) to the scheme manager of the Financial Services Compensation Scheme.".

[**3A.** (1) For the purposes of paragraph 51 of Schedule B1 a decision of the insurer's creditors as to whether they approve the proposals set out in the administrator's statement made under paragraph 49(1) of Schedule B1 is required to be made by a qualifying decision procedure.

(2) At the time of seeking that decision the administrator must also seek a decision from the insurer's creditors as to whether they consent to the exercise by the administrator of the powers specified in Schedule 1 to the 1986 Act.

(3) That decision is also required to be made by a qualifying decision procedure.]

4. In paragraph 53(2) of Schedule B1 [(creditors' decision)], omit "and" at the end of paragraph (b) and at the end of paragraph (c), add—

"(d) the [Financial Conduct Authority and the Prudential Regulation Authority], and

(e) to the scheme manager of the Financial Services Compensation Scheme.".

5. In paragraph 54(2)(b) of Schedule B1 (revision of administrator's proposals), after ["opted-out creditor"] insert ", to the [Financial Conduct Authority and the Prudential Regulation Authority] and to the scheme manager of the Financial Services Compensation Scheme.".

6. In paragraph 76(1) of Schedule B1 (automatic end of administration), for "one year" substitute "30 months".

7. . . .

8. In paragraph 79(1) of Schedule B1 (court ending administration on application of administrator), after the first reference to "company" insert "or the [Financial Conduct Authority and the Prudential Regulation Authority]".

9. In paragraph 91(1) of Schedule B1 (supplying vacancy in office of administrator)—

(a) at the end of sub-paragraph (d), omit "or";

(b) at the end of sub-paragraph (e), insert "or";

(c) after sub-paragraph (e), insert

"(f) the [Financial Conduct Authority and the Prudential Regulation Authority]".

10. (1) The powers of the administrator specified in Schedule 1 to the 1986 Act (powers of administrator or administrative receiver) include the power to make—

(a) any payments due to a creditor; or

(b) any payments on account of any sum which may become due to a creditor.

(2) Any payments to a creditor made pursuant to sub-paragraph (1) must not exceed, in aggregate, the amount which the administrator reasonably considers that the creditor would be entitled to receive on a distribution of the insurer's assets in a winding up.

[(3) The powers conferred by sub-paragraph (1) may be exercised until the initial decision date for the decision referred to in paragraph 51(1), but may only be exercised after that date—

(a) if—

(i) the administrator, when seeking the decision referred to in paragraph 3A(2), gave the creditors a statement containing the information specified in sub-paragraph (4); and

(ii) a majority in number representing three-fourths in value of the creditors has consented to the exercise by the administrator of those powers; or

(b) with the consent of the court.]

(4) The information referred to in sub-paragraph (3)(a)(i) is an estimate of the aggregate amount of—

(a) the insurer's assets and liabilities (whether actual, contingent or prospective); and

(b) all payments which the administrator proposes to make to creditors pursuant to sub-paragraph (1);

including any assumptions which the administrator has made in calculating that estimate.

(5) In this paragraph, "initial creditors' meeting" has the meaning given by paragraph 51(1) of Schedule B1.

[**11.** Where this Schedule applies in relation to the administration of an insurer in Scotland, it is to be read with the following modifications—

(a) ignore paragraph 3A;

(b) in paragraph 4 for "(creditors' decision)" read "(business and result of initial creditors' meeting)";

(c) in paragraph 5 for ""opted-out creditor"" read ""creditor""; and

(d) read paragraph 10 as if—

(i) for sub-paragraph (3) there were substituted—

"(3) The powers conferred by sub-paragraph (1) may be exercised until an initial creditors' meeting, but may only be exercised thereafter—

(a) if the following conditions are met—

(i) the administrator has laid before that meeting or any subsequent creditors' meeting ("the relevant meeting") a statement containing the information specified in sub-paragraph (4); and

(i) the powers are exercised with the consent of a majority in number representing three-fourths in value of the creditors present and voting either in person or by proxy at the relevant meeting; or

(b) with the consent of the court.";

(ii) there were added at the end—

"(5) In this paragraph "initial creditors' meeting" has the meaning given in paragraph 51(1) of Schedule B1.".]

NOTES

Paras 2, 3, 8, 9: words in square brackets substituted by the Financial Services Act 2012 (Consequential Amendments and Transitional Provisions) Order 2013, SI 2013/472, art 3, Sch 2, para 195(c).

Paras 3A, 11: inserted by the Small Business, Enterprise and Employment Act 2015 (Consequential Amendments, Savings and Transitional Provisions) Regulations 2018, SI 2018/208, reg 12(1), (2), (6), as from 13 March 2018 (for transitional provisions, see the note below).

Para 4: words in first pair of square brackets substituted for original words "(business and result of initial creditors' meeting)", by SI 2018/208, reg 12(1), (3), as from 13 March 2018 (for transitional provisions, see the note below); words in second pair of square brackets substituted by SI 2013/472, art 3, Sch 2, para 195(c).

Para 5: words in first pair of square brackets substituted for original word "creditor", by SI 2018/208, reg 12(1), (4), as from 13 March 2018 (for transitional provisions, see the note below); words in second pair of square brackets substituted by SI 2013/472, art 3, Sch 2, para 195(c).

Para 7: revoked by the Deregulation Act 2015, the Small Business, Enterprise and Employment Act 2015 and the Insolvency (Amendment) Act (Northern Ireland) 2016 (Consequential Amendments and Transitional Provisions) Regulations 2017, SI 2017/400, reg 9.

Para 10: sub-para (3) substituted and sub-para (5) revoked, by SI 2018/208, reg 12(1), (5), as from 13 March 2018 (for transitional provisions, see the note below).

Transitional provisions: the Small Business, Enterprise and Employment Act 2015 (Consequential Amendments, Savings and Transitional Provisions) Regulations 2018, SI 2018/208, regs 16, 22 provide as follows—

"16 Interpretation of Part 4

In this Part—

"the 1986 Act" means the Insolvency Act 1986;

"the 2000 Act" means the Financial Services and Markets Act 2000;

"the 2009 Act" means the Banking Act 2009; and

"relevant meeting" means a meeting of creditors which is to be held on or after the date on which Parts 2 and 3 of these Regulations come into force, and was—

(a) called, summoned or otherwise required before 6th April 2017 under a provision of the 1986 Act or the Insolvency Rules 1986;

(b) requisitioned by a creditor before 6th April 2017 under a provision of the 1986 Act or the Insolvency Rules 1986; or

(c) called or summoned under section 106, 146 or 331 of the 1986 Act as a result of—

(i) a final report to creditors sent before 6th April 2017 under rule 4.49D of the Insolvency Rules 1986 (final report to creditors in liquidation);

Part 7L Special Insolvency Regimes

(ii) a final report to creditors and bankrupt sent before that date under rule 6.78B of those Rules (final report to creditors and bankrupt).

22 Transitional provision for regulation 12

Where a relevant meeting is to be held in proceedings for the administration under Schedule B1 to the 1986 Act of an insurer within the meaning given in the Financial Services and Markets Act 2000 (Insolvency) (Definition of "Insurer") Order 2001, the Financial Services and Markets Act 2000 (Administration Orders Relating to Insurers) Order 2010 applies in relation to the meeting without the amendments made by regulation 12, so far as those amendments relate to the abolition of requirements to hold creditors' meetings.".

RISK TRANSFORMATION REGULATIONS 2017

(SI 2017/1212)

NOTES

Made: 5 December 2017.

Authority: European Communities Act 1972, s 2(2), Financial Services and Markets Act 2000, ss 22(1), (5), 22A, 55C, 284A, 426, 428(3), Sch 2, para 25.

Commencement: 8 December 2017.

PART 1
GENERAL

[7.1624]

1 Citation and commencement

(1) These Regulations may be cited as the Risk Transformation Regulations 2017.

(2) These Regulations come into force 3 days after the day on which they are made.

NOTES

Commencement: 8 December 2017.

[7.1625]

2 Interpretation: general

(1) In these Regulations—

"alternative inspection location" means any place at which a protected cell company keeps the documents and records relating to the protected cell company, other than the protected cell company's registered office;

"appropriate registrar" means—

(a) the registrar of companies for England and Wales if a protected cell company's instrument of incorporation states that its registered office is situated in England and Wales (or Wales);

(b) the registrar of companies for Scotland if a protected cell company's instrument of incorporation states that its registered office is situated in Scotland;

(c) the registrar of companies for Northern Ireland if a protected cell company's instrument of incorporation states that its registered office is situated in Northern Ireland;

"asset" includes any interest in an asset, any right over an asset or any property;

"cell" has the meaning given in regulation 43;

"contractual arrangement" has the same meaning as in the Implementing Technical Standard;

"core" has the meaning given in regulation 42;

"counsel" means a person who is—

(a) a barrister within the meaning given in section 207 of the Legal Services Act 2007;

(b) a practising member of the faculty of advocates in Scotland; or

(c) a barrister who has been called to the bar in Northern Ireland and who holds a current practising certificate;

"creditor" incudes a contingent or prospective creditor;

"debenture" includes debenture stock, bonds and any other securities;

"FSMA" means the Financial Services and Markets Act 2000;

"general meeting" means a meeting of the persons holding voting shares issued on behalf of the core of the protected cell company;

"Implementing Technical Standard" means Commission Implementing Regulation (EU) 2015/462 of 19th March 2015 laying down implementing technical standards with regard to the procedures for supervisory approval to establish special purpose vehicles, for the cooperation and exchange of information between supervisory authorities regarding special purpose vehicles as well as to set out formats and templates for information to be reported by special purpose vehicles in accordance with Directive 2009/138/EC of the European Parliament and of the Council;

"insolvency legislation" means—

(a) the Insolvency Act 1986;

(b) the Insolvency (Northern Ireland) Order 1989;

(c) Part 24 of FSMA (insolvency);

(d) the Insolvency Act 2000;

(e) the Insolvency (Northern Ireland) Order 2002;

(f) the Bankruptcy (Scotland) Act 2016; and
(g) all subordinate legislation made under the legislation mentioned in sub-paragraphs (a) to (f);

"liability" includes a contingent or prospective liability;
"non-voting share" means a share which is not a voting share;
"officer" includes a director or manager;
"property" includes an interest in property or a right over property;
"the Regulated Activities Order" means the Financial Services and Markets Act 2000 (Regulated Activities) Order 2001;
"share" means a share in the share capital of a protected cell company or a part of a protected cell company;
"share certificate" means documentary evidence of title to a share;
"solicitor" means a person who is—

(a) a solicitor within the meaning given by section 207 of the Legal Services Act 2007;
(b) enrolled on the roll of solicitors kept under section 7 of the Solicitors (Scotland) Act 1980; or
(c) a solicitor within the meaning given by Article 3(2) of the Solicitors (Northern Ireland) Order 1976;

"voting share" means a share which confers the right to vote on a written resolution of the protected cell company or at a meeting of shareholders;
"working day" has the meaning given in section 1173(1) of the Companies Act 2006.

(2) In these Regulations—

(a) a reference to a part of a protected cell company is a reference to the core or a cell of the protected cell company (see regulations 42 and 43);
(b) a reference to enforceable arrangements between cells is a reference to arrangements between cells which—
  (i) have been made in accordance with regulations 68 and 69; and
  (ii) have not been cancelled in accordance with regulation 70; and
(c) shares are of one class if the rights attached to them are in all respects uniform.

(3) Where these Regulations refer to the Welsh equivalent of a word or expression, the Welsh equivalent of that word or expression is set out in Table 6 in Schedule 1.

NOTES

Commencement: 8 December 2017.

[7.1626]
3 Meaning of "group of cells"

(1) In these Regulations, a "group of cells" is a group of two or more cells in which each cell is linked to every other cell in the group.

(2) For the purposes of this regulation, two cells ("cell A" and "cell B") are linked if the protected cell company has made enforceable arrangements between—

(a) cell A and cell B; or
(b) cell A and another cell which is linked to cell B.

NOTES

Commencement: 8 December 2017.

4–11 *(Regs 4–9 (Pt 2), regs 10, 11 (Pt 3) outside the scope of this work.)*

PART 4
PROTECTED CELL COMPANIES

CHAPTER 1 OVERVIEW

[7.1627]
12 Overview

(1) This Part enables the creation of a type of body corporate called a protected cell company.

(2) A protected cell company is a transformer vehicle which is intended to be used as a multi-arrangement special purpose vehicle (within the meaning given by Article 2 of the Implementing Technical Standard).

(3) As a result, the protected cell company may only be used to carry out the activities mentioned in regulation 57.

(4) A protected cell company is comprised of different parts, namely the core and the cells created by the protected cell company after its registration and authorisation.

(5) The core administers the protected cell company.

(6) The cells are used for assuming risk from undertakings, issuing investments to investors to fund the protected cell company's exposure to that risk, holding the proceeds of sale of those investments and, where permitted by the protected cell company's instrument of incorporation, entering into arrangements between cells.

(7) The core and the cells do not have legal personality distinct from the protected cell company, but are nevertheless segregated from each other in accordance with the provisions of this Part.

(8) Protected cell companies are governed by the provisions of this Part rather than the Companies Act 2006, but Part 41 (business names) of that Act applies to protected cell companies and these Regulations apply certain other provisions of that Act to protected cell companies with modifications.

NOTES

Commencement: 8 December 2017.

CHAPTER 2 REGISTRATION

Section 1
Obtaining Registration

[7.1628]

13 Method of forming a protected cell company

A protected cell company is formed under this Part by a person—

(a) applying to the PRA for registration of a protected cell company in accordance with regulation 14; and

(b) complying with the requirements for registration set out in regulation 21.

NOTES

Commencement: 8 December 2017.

14–41 (*Outside the scope of this work.*)

CHAPTER 3 STRUCTURE OF A PROTECTED CELL COMPANY

[7.1629]

42 The core

(1) A protected cell company must have a core.

(2) The core—

(a) is part of the protected cell company; and

(b) does not have legal personality distinct from the protected cell company.

(3) The purpose of the core is to administer the protected cell company.

(4) For that purpose, the protected cell company may, on behalf of the core, carry out such functions as are conferred on the core by the protected cell company's instrument of incorporation.

(5) The instrument of incorporation may, amongst other things, enable the protected cell company to do the following things on behalf of the core—

(a) hold property;

(b) lease premises;

(c) enter into contracts, including contracts of employment and contracts for the provision of services;

(d) issue voting and non-voting shares;

(e) borrow money;

(f) incur liabilities.

(6) But a protected cell company may not assume a risk from an undertaking on behalf of the core.

NOTES

Commencement: 8 December 2017.

[7.1630]

43 The cells

(1) The protected cell company may have one or more cells.

(2) A cell—

(a) is part of the protected cell company; and

(b) does not have legal personality distinct from the protected cell company.

(3) The purpose of the cells is to—

(a) assume risk from undertakings;

(b) issue investments to investors to fund the protected cell company's exposure to the risks it has assumed;

(c) hold the proceeds of the sale of those investments;

(d) where permitted by the protected cell company's instrument of incorporation, enter into arrangements between cells (see regulations 68 to 74); and

(e) carry out any other functions conferred on the cells by the protected cell company's instrument of incorporation.

(4) A protected cell company may carry out the activity referred to in paragraph (3)(c) by using a trustee or nominee.

(5) Where a protected cell company uses a cell which is not a member of a group of cells to assume risk from an undertaking under a contractual arrangement, the protected cell company may not, during the time it is exposed to that risk, use that cell to assume risk from another undertaking or under a separate contractual arrangement.

(6) Where a protected cell company uses one or more cells which are members of a group of cells to assume risk from an undertaking under a contractual arrangement, the protected cell company—

- (a) may not, during the time it is exposed to that risk, use any cell in that group of cells to assume risk from another undertaking or under a separate contractual arrangement;
- (b) may use different cells in the group to carry out different activities (for example one cell may be used to assume risk and another cell may be used to issue investments to investors).

(7) A protected cell company may use different cells in a group of cells to assume risk under successive separate contractual arrangements.

NOTES

Commencement: 8 December 2017.

[7.1631]
44 Assets, liabilities and obligations

(1) Assets which are held by a protected cell company must be held on behalf of a part of the protected cell company.

(2) Liabilities or obligations incurred by a protected cell company must be incurred on behalf of a part of the protected cell company.

NOTES

Commencement: 8 December 2017.

[7.1632]
45 Liabilities and obligations which are not incurred on behalf of a part

A liability or obligation of the protected cell company which is not incurred by the protected cell company on behalf of a part of the protected cell company is to be treated as being attributable to the part of the protected cell company to which the liability or obligation is most closely related.

NOTES

Commencement: 8 December 2017.

[7.1633]
46 Records and accounts of assets, liabilities and obligations

(1) A protected cell company must at all times keep records and accounts which distinguish—

- (a) the assets held on behalf of each part of the protected cell company from the assets held on behalf of the other parts of the protected cell company; and
- (b) the liabilities and obligations which are incurred on behalf of, or which are attributable to, each part of the protected cell company from the liabilities and obligations which are incurred on behalf of, or which are attributable to, the other parts of the protected cell company.

(2) A protected cell company must ensure that the records and accounts kept by the protected cell company in accordance with paragraph (1) are accurate at all times.

NOTES

Commencement: 8 December 2017.

[7.1634]
47 Assets to be held in accordance with records and accounts

(1) A protected cell company must at all times hold its assets in accordance with the protected cell company's records and accounts kept in accordance with regulation 46.

(2) Where a protected cell company holds an asset on behalf of a part ("part A") of the protected cell company which is recorded in the records and accounts as an asset held on behalf of another part ("part B") of the protected cell company—

- (a) the protected cell company must move the asset from part A to part B; and
- (b) part A holds the asset on trust for the benefit of part B until the movement takes effect.

(3) For the purposes of the trust referred to in paragraph (2), parts A and B are to be treated as if they are distinct legal persons.

NOTES

Commencement: 8 December 2017.

[7.1635]
48 Segregation within a protected cell company

(1) The assets held by a protected cell company on behalf of a part of the protected cell company may not be used to discharge—

- (a) a liability or obligation incurred on behalf of, or attributable to, another part of the protected cell company; or

(b) a claim brought in respect of another part of the protected cell company.

(2) A liability or obligation incurred on behalf of, or attributable to, a part of a protected cell company is to be discharged solely out of the assets held by the protected cell company on behalf of that part.

(3) A claim which a person has against a protected cell company in respect of a part of the protected cell company may not be set off or netted against a claim which the protected cell company has against that person in respect of another part of the protected cell company.

(4) A provision, whether contained in the instrument of incorporation, a contract or otherwise, is void to the extent that it is inconsistent with paragraphs (1) to (3).

(5) An application of assets, or agreement to apply assets, in contravention of paragraphs (1) to (3) is void.

(6) Notwithstanding the fact that the parts of a protected cell company are not legal persons distinct from the protected cell company—

(a) the assets held by the protected cell company on behalf of a part of the protected cell company are to be treated as assets belonging exclusively to that part of the protected cell company;

(b) a liability or obligation incurred by the protected cell company on behalf of, or which is attributable to, a part of the protected cell company is to be treated as a liability or obligation of that part of the protected cell company;

(c) a creditor of a protected cell company is to be treated as a creditor of that part of the protected cell company which is treated as being indebted to the creditor by virtue of sub-paragraph (b);

(d) the property held by a protected cell company on behalf of a part of the protected cell company may be subject to orders of the court as if the part were a distinct legal person; and

(e) a protected cell company may sue or be sued in respect of a part of the protected cell company.

NOTES

Commencement: 8 December 2017.

[7.1636]

49 Third parties circumventing segregation

Where—

(a) a person has a claim against a protected cell company;

(b) the claim relates to a part of the protected cell company ("part A");

(c) the person obtains property from the protected cell company in full or partial satisfaction of the claim; and

(d) the property was held by the protected cell company on behalf of a part of the protected cell company other than part A ("part B"),

then the person holds the property on trust for the benefit of part B.

NOTES

Commencement: 8 December 2017.

[7.1637]

50 Set-off: modification of insolvency legislation

(1) This regulation applies where—

(a) a protected cell company has a liability ("liability A") to a person which was incurred on behalf of, or which is attributable to, a part of the protected cell company; and

(b) that person has a liability ("liability B") to the protected cell company in respect of a different part of the protected cell company.

(2) Nothing in the insolvency legislation enables the netting or setting off against each other of liability A and liability B.

NOTES

Commencement: 8 December 2017.

51–153 *((Chapters 4–11) outside the scope of this work.)*

CHAPTER 12 SECURITY INTERESTS

[7.1638]

154 Creation of security interests

(1) A protected cell company may only create or assert a security interest over assets held by the protected cell company on behalf of a part of the protected cell company if the security interest does not secure a liability or obligation which is incurred on behalf of, or which is attributable to, another part of the protected cell company.

(2) A protected cell company may only create or assert a security interest over the undertaking of part of the protected cell company if the security interest does not secure a liability or obligation which is incurred on behalf of, or which is attributable to, another part of the protected cell company.

(3) A security interest is void if it contravenes the requirements of paragraph (1) or (2).

(4) In this regulation, "security interest" means—

(a) a lien, pledge, charge or mortgage; or

(b) a standard security, assignation in security or any other right in security constituted under the law of Scotland, including any heritable security.

NOTES

Commencement: 8 December 2017.

155–165 *(Reg 155, regs 156–165 (Chapters 13, 14) outside the scope of this work.)*

CHAPTER 15 INSOLVENCY

[7.1639]

166 Insolvency of a cell

(1) A cell of a protected cell company may be—

(a) put into administration as if it were a company under Schedule B1 (administration) to the Insolvency Act 1986 or Schedule B1 (administration) to the Insolvency (Northern Ireland) Order 1989; or

(b) wound up as if it were an unregistered company under Part 5 (winding up of unregistered companies) of the Insolvency Act 1986 or Part 6 (winding up of unregistered companies) of the Insolvency (Northern Ireland) Order 1989.

(2) For these purposes, the insolvency legislation applies in relation to the cell with the modifications set out in Schedule 2.

(3) Where a written demand is served on a cell by a creditor in accordance with section 222(1)(a) (inability to pay debts: unpaid creditor of £750 or more) of the Insolvency Act 1986 or Article 186(1)(a) (inability to pay debts: unpaid creditor of £750 or more) of the Insolvency (Northern Ireland) Order 1989, the cell may apply to the High Court (or in Scotland the Court of Session) for an injunction restraining (or in Scotland an interdict prohibiting) the creditor from presenting or giving notice of a winding-up petition as if the cell has distinct legal personality.

(4) The entry of a cell of a protected cell company into administration or liquidation does not affect the power of the protected cell company or the directors of the protected cell company to act in relation to the core or the cells.

(5) But the protected cell company and the directors of the protected cell company may not exercise a management power in relation to a cell in administration or liquidation without the consent of the administrator or liquidator of the cell.

(6) For the purposes of paragraph (5)—

(a) "management power" means a power which could be exercised so as to interfere with the exercise of the powers of the administrator or liquidator;

(b) it is immaterial whether the power is conferred on the protected cell company or the directors by an enactment or an instrument; and

(c) consent may be general or specific.

NOTES

Commencement: 8 December 2017.

[7.1640]

167 Insolvency of the core

(1) The core of a protected cell company may be—

(a) put into administration as if it were a company under Schedule B1 (administration) to the Insolvency Act 1986 or Schedule B1 (administration) to the Insolvency (Northern Ireland) Order 1989; or

(b) wound up as if it were an unregistered company under Part 5 (winding up of unregistered companies) of the Insolvency Act 1986 or Part 6 (winding up of unregistered companies) of the Insolvency (Northern Ireland) Order 1989.

(2) For these purposes, the insolvency legislation applies in relation to the core with the modifications set out in Schedule 3.

(3) Where a written demand is served on the core by a creditor in accordance with section 222(1)(a) (inability to pay debts: unpaid creditor of £750 or more) of the Insolvency Act 1986 or Article 186(1)(a) (inability to pay debts: unpaid creditor of £750 or more) of the Insolvency (Northern Ireland) Order 1989, the core may apply to the High Court (or in Scotland the Court of Session) for an injunction restraining (or in Scotland an interdict prohibiting) the creditor from presenting or giving notice of a winding-up petition as if the core has distinct legal personality.

(4) The entry of the core of a protected cell company into administration or liquidation does not affect the powers of the protected cell company or the directors of the protected cell company to act in relation to the core or the cells.

(5) But the protected cell company and the directors of the protected cell company may not exercise a management power in relation to—

(a) the core of the protected cell company; or

(b) any cell of the protected cell company which is not in administration or liquidation,

without the consent of the administrator or liquidator of the core.

(6) For the purposes of paragraph (5)—

(a) "management power" means a power which could be exercised so as to interfere with the exercise of the powers of the administrator or liquidator;
(b) it is immaterial whether the power is conferred on the protected cell company or the directors by an enactment or an instrument; and
(c) consent may be general or specific.

NOTES

Commencement: 8 December 2017.

[7.1641]
168 Concurrent insolvency

Where two or more parts of a protected cell company are in administration or liquidation concurrently by virtue of regulation 166 or 167, then—
(a) the insolvency legislation (as applied by regulations 166(2) or 167(2)) applies in relation to each part separately; and
(b) the administrators or liquidators (as the case may be) of those parts must cooperate fully with each other in the discharge of their functions.

NOTES

Commencement: 8 December 2017.

[7.1642]
169 Disapplication of other insolvency proceedings

(1) Except to the extent provided for in this Chapter—
(a) a protected cell company may not propose a voluntary arrangement;
(b) neither a protected cell company nor a part of a protected cell company may be placed into administration;
(c) a receiver (including an administrative receiver) may not be appointed in respect of any property held by the protected cell company;
(d) a protected cell company may not pass a resolution for the winding up of the protected cell company or any part of the protected cell company;
(e) a winding-up order may not be made against the protected cell company or any part of the protected cell company;
(f) the estate of a protected cell company or any part of a protected cell company may not be sequestrated under section 6 of the Bankruptcy (Scotland) Act 2016;
(g) neither the protected cell company nor a part of the protected cell company may be subject to any other process under the insolvency legislation which applies to a person who is insolvent or who is likely to become insolvent.

(2) The reference in paragraph (1)(d) to winding up includes a reference to a members' voluntary winding up under Chapter 3 of Part 4 of the Insolvency Act 1986 or Chapter 3 of Part 5 of the Insolvency (Northern Ireland) Order 1989.

NOTES

Commencement: 8 December 2017.

170–177 ((*Chapter 16) Outside the scope of this work.*)

CHAPTER 17 DISSOLUTION

[7.1643]
178 Dissolution of a cell: procedure

(1) A protected cell company's instrument of incorporation may contain provision for the dissolution of a cell, but that provision is subject to this regulation.

(2) A protected cell company must notify the following people (the "interested persons") if it intends to dissolve a cell—
(a) any undertaking from whom the protected cell company has assumed a risk on behalf of a relevant cell;
(b) any investor who holds an investment issued on behalf of a relevant cell;
(c) any other creditor of the protected cell company in respect of a relevant cell;
(d) the FCA; and
(e) the PRA.

(3) In paragraph (2), a "relevant cell" is—
(a) the cell which the protected cell company intends to dissolve; and
(b) any other cell which has entered into enforceable arrangements with that cell.

(4) But paragraph (2) does not apply where a cell is deemed to be dissolved as a consequence of a Case 1 transfer scheme or Case 2 transfer scheme (within the meaning given by regulation 170).

(5) The notification referred to in paragraph (2) must—
(a) be in writing;
(b) identify the cell which the protected cell company intends to dissolve;
(c) state the date on which the notification is sent; and

(d) state that if the recipient intends to object to the dissolution of the cell, then any objections must be received by the protected cell company within a period of two months beginning with the date when the notification was sent.

(6) The cell may only be dissolved in the following cases—

(a) none of the interested persons object within the period referred to in paragraph (5)(d);

(b) one or more of the interested persons objects within the period referred to in paragraph (5)(d) and those objections are subsequently withdrawn;

(c) one or more of the interested persons objects within the period referred to in paragraph (5)(d) and—

(i) the FCA or PRA is not one of the interested persons who objects; and

(ii) the person or persons objecting have not commenced court proceedings against the protected cell company in respect of the cell, or put the cell into administration or liquidation, within the relevant period;

(d) the cell is deemed to be dissolved by virtue of—

(i) regulation 176(2)(a) or 176(3)(j); or

(ii) an order of the court made under regulation 175 or 177;

(e) the cell is put into administration and the cell is deemed to be dissolved at the end of administration (see paragraph 84 of Schedule B1 to the Insolvency Act 1986 and paragraph 85 of Schedule B1 to the Insolvency (Northern Ireland) Order 1989, as applied by regulation 166);

(f) the cell is put into liquidation and the cell is dissolved after winding up (see sections 202 to 205 of the Insolvency Act 1986 and Articles 167 to 169 of the Insolvency (Northern Ireland) Order 1989, as applied by regulation 166);

(g) the court directs that the cell is to be dissolved.

(7) In paragraph (6)(c), the "relevant period"—

(a) begins with the date when notification is sent in accordance with paragraph (2) or, if notifications are sent on more than one date, the date when the last such notification is sent; and

(b) lasts for a period of 12 months or, if court proceedings are brought against the protected cell company in respect of the cell or an application is made to court for the administration or winding up of the cell, such other period as may be specified by the court.

(8) For the purposes of paragraph (7)(b), the court may specify another period after the expiry of the 12 month period referred to in that paragraph, provided the cell has not been dissolved when the court specifies that period.

(9) When a protected cell company dissolves a cell, it must notify the interested persons.

(10) The notification referred to in paragraph (9) must—

(a) be in writing;

(b) identify the cell which has been dissolved; and

(c) state the time and date when it was dissolved.

NOTES

Commencement: 8 December 2017.

[7.1644]

179 Dissolution of a cell: effect on property and liabilities

(1) Where a cell of a protected cell company is dissolved in accordance with regulation 178—

(a) the protected cell company is released from all outstanding liabilities and obligations which were incurred on behalf of the cell or which are attributable to the cell;

(b) any enforceable arrangements made between the cell and any other cell are deemed to be cancelled; and

(c) any property of the protected cell company which is held on behalf of the cell is deemed to be moved to the core.

(2) A resolution of the protected cell company for the dissolution of a cell is to be treated as an instrument of transfer for the purposes of any enactment requiring the delivery of an instrument of transfer for the registration of property.

(3) Paragraph (1) is subject to regulations 181 to 185 (which are concerned with restoration).

NOTES

Commencement: 8 December 2017.

[7.1645]

180 Dissolution of a protected cell company

(1) A protected cell company may be dissolved in the following cases—

(a) the protected cell company makes an application to the FCA for its dissolution;

(b) the core of the protected cell company is put into administration and the protected cell company is dissolved at the end of administration (see paragraph 84 of Schedule B1 to the Insolvency Act 1986 and paragraph 85 of Schedule B1 to the Insolvency (Northern Ireland) Order 1989, as applied by regulation 167);

(c) the core of the protected cell company is put into liquidation and the protected cell company is dissolved after winding up (see sections 202 to 205 of the Insolvency Act 1986 and Articles 167 to 169 of the Insolvency (Northern Ireland) Order 1989 as applied by regulation 167).

(2) But a protected cell company may only be dissolved if the protected cell company has no cells.

(3) Where a protected cell company applies to the FCA for its dissolution, the application must contain, or be accompanied by, a statement made by the directors of the protected cell company, or by a majority of them, that the protected cell company has no cells.

(4) Where the FCA receives an application made under paragraph (1)(a) which contains, or is accompanied by, the statement referred to in paragraph (3), the FCA must publish a notice in the London, Edinburgh and Belfast Gazettes—

(a) identifying the protected cell company;

(b) stating that the FCA has received an application from the protected cell company for its dissolution; and

(c) inviting any person to show cause as to why the protected cell company should not be dissolved.

(5) On the expiry of a period of three months beginning with the date that the notice referred to in paragraph (4) was published in the London, Edinburgh and Belfast Gazettes, or the last such date if the notices are published on different dates, the FCA may—

(a) notify the protected cell company that it intends to strike the protected cell company off the register;

(b) record on its register of protected cell companies that the protected cell company is struck off the register; and

(c) publish notice to that effect in the London, Edinburgh and Belfast Gazettes.

(6) If the FCA is aware that the protected cell company intends to acquire or redeem shares issued on behalf of the core, the FCA may postpone publication of the notices referred to in paragraph (5)(c) for such period as appears to the FCA to be reasonable.

(7) On the publication of the notices referred to in paragraph (5)(c), or the last such notice if the notices are published on different dates, the protected cell company is dissolved.

(8) However—

(a) the liability (if any) of every director of the protected cell company continues and may be enforced as if the protected cell company had not been dissolved; and

(b) nothing in this regulation affects the power of the court to wind up the core or a cell of the protected cell company which has been struck off the register.

(9) All property and rights whatsoever vested in or held on trust for the protected cell company immediately before its dissolution (including leasehold property, but not including property held on trust for another person) are deemed to be *bona vacantia*.

(10) Sections 1012 to 1023 of the Companies Act 2006 (property of dissolved company) apply to all such property and rights as they apply to the property and rights of a company incorporated under the Companies Act 2006, with the following modifications—

(a) references to the restoration of the company are to be treated as references to the restoration of the protected cell company; and

(b) references to the registrar are to be treated as references to the FCA.

NOTES

Commencement: 8 December 2017.

[7.1646]

181 Restoration: applications to court

(1) Where a cell of a protected cell company has been dissolved, an application may be made to the court to restore the cell.

(2) Where a protected cell company has been dissolved, an application may be made to the court to restore the protected cell company to the register.

(3) Where an application is made to restore a cell of a protected cell company and the protected cell company has been dissolved, then the application must be accompanied by an application to restore the protected cell company to the register.

(4) In this regulation, "court" means the High Court or, in Scotland, the Court of Session.

NOTES

Commencement: 8 December 2017.

[7.1647]

182 Restoration: who may apply

(1) An application under regulation 181(1) may be made by—

(a) any person who would have been entitled to receive notice of the cell's dissolution under regulation 178(2);

(b) the protected cell company;

(c) a director of the protected cell company;

(d) a former administrator or liquidator of the cell; or

(e) any other person appearing to have an interest in the matter.

(2) An application under regulation 181(2) may be made by—

(a) a person who is entitled to make an application under regulation 181(1) for the restoration of a cell which formed part of the protected cell company;

(b) a former director of the protected cell company;

(c) a person who would, but for the dissolution of the protected cell company, have been—

(i) a creditor of the protected cell company; or

(ii) in a contractual relationship with the protected cell company;
(d) a person with a potential legal claim against the protected cell company;
(e) a person having an interest in land or other property—
(i) in which the protected cell company had a superior or derivative interest;
(ii) that was subject to rights vested in the protected cell company; or
(iii) that received the benefit of obligations owed by the protected cell company;
(f) a person who held shares issued on behalf of the core of the protected cell company immediately prior to the dissolution of the protected cell company;
(g) a former administrator or liquidator of the core of the protected cell company;
(h) the FCA;
(i) the PRA; or
(j) any other person appearing to have an interest in the matter.

NOTES

Commencement: 8 December 2017.

[7.1648]

183 Restoration: when an application may be made

An application to restore a cell or a protected cell company must be made within a period of six years beginning with the date when the cell or protected cell company (as the case may be) was dissolved.

NOTES

Commencement: 8 December 2017.

[7.1649]

184 Decision on application for restoration

(1) On an application under regulation 181(1), the court may order the restoration of a cell if—
(a) the requirements of regulation 178 were not complied with in relation to the dissolution of the cell; or
(b) the court considers it just to do so.

(2) On an application under regulation 181(2), the court may order the restoration of a protected cell company if—
(a) the requirements of regulation 180 were not complied with in relation to the dissolution of the protected cell company; or
(b) the court considers it just to do so.

(3) If the court orders the restoration of the cell or the protected cell company, the restoration takes effect on a copy of the court's order being delivered to the FCA.

(4) Where a protected cell company is restored to the register, the FCA must publish notice of the restoration of the protected cell company in the London, Edinburgh and Belfast Gazettes.

(5) The notices must state—
(a) the name of the protected cell company;
(b) the protected cell company's registered number; and
(c) the date on which restoration took effect.

NOTES

Commencement: 8 December 2017.

[7.1650]

185 Effect of court order for restoration

(1) The general effect of an order restoring a cell or a protected cell company is that the cell or protected cell company (as the case may be) is deemed to have continued in existence as if it had not been dissolved.

(2) The court may give directions and make such provision as seems just for placing the cell or protected cell company and all other persons in the same position (as nearly as may be) as if the cell or protected cell company had not been dissolved.

(3) In particular, the court may give directions as to—
(a) the delivery of documents to the FCA or PRA;
(b) payment of the FCA's or PRA's costs in relation to the proceedings for restoration;
(c) where property or a right previously vested in or held on trust for the protected cell company has vested as *bona vacantia*, the payment of the costs (in Scotland, the expenses) of the Crown representative—
(i) in dealing with the property during the period of dissolution; or
(ii) in connection with the proceedings on the application.

(4) In this regulation, the "Crown representative" means—
(a) in relation to property vested in the Duchy of Lancaster, the Solicitor to that Duchy;
(b) in relation to property vested in the Duke of Cornwall, the Solicitor to the Duchy of Cornwall;
(c) in relation to property in Scotland, the Queen's and Lord Treasurer's Remembrancer;
(d) in relation to other property, the Treasury Solicitor.

(5) Section 1034 of the Companies Act 2006 (effect of restoration where property has vested as *bona vacantia*) applies on the restoration of a protected cell company as it applies on the restoration of a company incorporated under the Companies Act 2006, but with the reference to section 1012 in subsection (1) being treated as a reference to regulation 180(9).

NOTES

Commencement: 8 December 2017.

186–191 (*(Chapters 18, 19) Outside the scope of this work.*)

SCHEDULE 1

(*Sch 1 outside the scope of this work.*)

SCHEDULE 2
ADMINISTRATION AND LIQUIDATION OF CELLS: MODIFICATION OF INSOLVENCY LEGISLATION

Regulation 166

Duties and powers confined to the cell

[7.1651]

1 (1) The appointment of a relevant office holder in respect of a cell, and the powers and duties of the relevant office holder, are confined to—

(a) the cell;
(b) the business and affairs of the cell; and
(c) the property held by the protected cell company on behalf of the cell.

(2) In sub-paragraph (1), a "relevant office holder" means—

(a) an administrator;
(b) a liquidator;
(c) a provisional liquidator; or
(d) a special manager.

General application of the insolvency legislation

2 The insolvency legislation applies to a cell as if—

(a) the cell is a body corporate with distinct legal personality;
(b) the cell was incorporated on its creation;
(c) the cell is registered in the part of the United Kingdom in which the protected cell company has its registered office;
(d) the registered office of the cell is the registered office of the protected cell company;
(e) the registered name of the cell is the name or number of the cell followed by "of" and the name of the protected cell company;
(f) the registrar of companies is the FCA;
(g) a person who is or was a director, shadow director, officer, employee or agent of the protected cell company is or was a director, shadow director, officer, employee or agent of the cell (as the case may be);
(h) shares issued by the protected cell company on behalf of the cell are shares issued by the cell;
(i) the cell's property, assets, liabilities, debts and creditors are determined in accordance with regulation 48(6);
(j) arrangements made between the cell and another cell in accordance with regulations 68 and 69 are contracts entered into between the cell and the protected cell company acting on behalf of that other cell;
(k) things done by the protected cell company on behalf of the cell are things done by the cell;
(l) things done to the protected cell company in respect of the cell are things done to the cell;
(m) judgments or orders made against the protected cell company in respect of the cell are judgments or orders made against the cell;
(n) the books, papers, records, registers and other documents of the protected cell company are, insofar as they relate to the cell, books, papers, records, registers and documents of the cell; and
(o) an associate of the protected cell company (within the meaning given by section 435 of the Insolvency Act 1986 or Article 4 of the Insolvency (Northern Ireland) Order 1989) is an associate of the cell.

Jurisdiction within the United Kingdom

3 (1) This paragraph specifies which court in the United Kingdom has jurisdiction in relation to the administration or winding up of a cell of a protected cell company.

(2) Her Majesty's High Court of Justice in England has jurisdiction where the registered office of a protected cell company is located in England and Wales (or Wales).

(3) The Court of Session has jurisdiction where the registered office of a protected cell company is located in Scotland.

(4) Her Majesty's High Court of Justice in Northern Ireland has jurisdiction where the registered office of a protected cell company is located in Northern Ireland.

Restrictions on applying for winding up

4 A person holding an investment issued on behalf of any cell of a protected cell company may not apply for—

(a) the winding up of a cell; or

(b) the appointment of a provisional liquidator in respect of a cell.

Appointment of administrator

5 (1) Only the court may appoint an administrator of a cell.

(2) Where a person makes an application to court for the administration of a cell, the person must file with the court notice of the existence of any insolvency proceedings in relation to the protected cell company or the cell anywhere in the world as soon as the person becomes aware of them.

(3) The duty imposed by sub-paragraph (2) ceases on the making of an administration order.

Giving of notice

6 In the insolvency legislation—

(a) a requirement that a company give notice of, or file, something is to be treated as a requirement that the protected cell company give notice of, or file, that thing on behalf of the cell; and

(b) any requirement to give notice of something on the company's website is to be ignored.

Part 24 of FSMA: references to "regulated activities" and "PRA-authorised person"

7 If the protected cell company has (or had) permission to carry on a regulated activity under Part 4A (permission to carry on regulated activities) of FSMA, then Part 24 (insolvency) of FSMA applies to the cell as if the cell has (or had) that permission.

Further modifications to specific provisions of the Insolvency Act 1986 and the Insolvency (Northern Ireland) Order 1989

8 (1) The provisions of the Insolvency Act 1986 specified in the first column of Table 7 and the provisions of the Insolvency (Northern Ireland) Order 1989 specified in the second column of Table 7 apply to a cell with the modifications specified in the fourth column of Table 7.

Table 7

Insolvency Act 1986	*Insolvency (Northern Ireland) Order 1989*	*Subject Matter*	*Modification*
Section 76	Article 63	Liability of past directors and shareholders	These provisions apply where a protected cell company has made a payment ("the relevant payment" for the purposes of these provisions) to redeem or acquire shares issued on behalf of the cell in breach of the requirements of regulation 106. The reference to the directors who signed the statement made in accordance with section 714(1) to (3) of the Companies Act 2006 for the purposes of the redemption or purchase is to be treated as a reference to the directors who authorised the redemption or purchase.
Section 103	Article 89	Cesser of directors' powers	Ignore these provisions.

Part 7L Special Insolvency Regimes

Insolvency Act 1986	*Insolvency (Northern Ireland) Order 1989*	*Subject Matter*	*Modification*
Section 124	Article 104	Application for winding up	An administrator of the cell, or an administrator or liquidator of the core, may also present a petition for the winding up of a cell.
Section 216	Article 180	Restriction on re-use of names	Ignore these provisions.
Section 221	Article 185	Winding up of unregistered companies	Where an administrator or liquidator of the core of the protected cell company applies for the winding up of a cell, the cell may be wound up if the court is satisfied that the application is made in the discharge of the duty imposed on the administrator or liquidator by paragraph 2(2)(c) of Schedule 3 to these Regulations in relation to the cell.
Section 222	Article 186	Inability to pay debts: unpaid creditor for £750 or more	The written demand must be served on the cell by leaving it at the protected cell company's registered office or in such manner as the court may approve or direct.
Section 223	Article 187	Inability to pay debts: debt remaining unsatisfied after action brought	Ignore these provisions.
Paragraph 61 of Schedule B1	Paragraph 62 of Schedule B1	Administrator's general powers (removal and appointment of directors)	Ignore these paragraphs.
Paragraph 69 of Schedule B1	Paragraph 70 of Schedule B1	Administrator as agent	An administrator of a cell acts as agent for the protected cell company (on behalf of the cell).
Paragraph 83 of Schedule B1	Paragraph 84 of Schedule B1	Moving from administration to liquidation	Ignore these paragraphs.

Further modification to subordinate legislation

9 The provisions of any subordinate legislation made under the Insolvency Act 1986 or the Insolvency (Northern Ireland) Order 1989 apply to the cell with any necessary modifications.

NOTES

Commencement: 8 December 2017.

SCHEDULE 3
ADMINISTRATION AND LIQUIDATION OF THE CORE: MODIFICATION OF INSOLVENCY LEGISLATION

Regulation 167

Meaning of "relevant office holder"

[7.1652]

1 In this Schedule, "relevant office holder" means—

(a) an administrator;
(b) a liquidator;
(c) a provisional liquidator; or
(d) a special manager.

Duties and powers of a relevant office holder appointed in respect of the core

2 (1) The appointment of a relevant office holder in respect of the core, and the powers and duties of the relevant office holder, are confined to—

(a) the core;
(b) the business and affairs of the core; and
(c) the property held by the protected cell company on behalf of the core,

except to the extent that sub-paragraphs (2) to (8) provide otherwise.

(2) An administrator or liquidator appointed in respect of the core of a protected cell company has the following duties in relation to a cell of the protected cell company which is not in administration or liquidation—

(a) a duty to ensure the protected cell company dissolves the cell in accordance with regulation 178;
(b) if the administrator or liquidator considers that there is no realistic prospect of being able to carry out the duty referred to in sub-paragraph (a) in respect of the cell, a duty to enter into a transfer scheme in respect of the cell, or the assets and liabilities held by the protected cell company on behalf of the cell and the investments issued on the cell's behalf; or
(c) if the administrator or liquidator considers that there is no realistic prospect of being able to carry out the duties referred to in sub-paragraphs (a) and (b) in respect of the cell, a duty to apply to the court for a winding-up order in respect of the cell.

(3) But sub-paragraph (2) does not apply where—

(a) the core of a protected cell company is in administration;
(b) an objective of the administration is to rescue the core as a going concern; and
(c) the administrator thinks that it is reasonably practicable to achieve that objective.

(4) An administrator or liquidator appointed in respect of the core of a protected cell company may exercise the powers mentioned in sub-paragraph (5)—

(a) in relation to a cell of the protected cell company which is not in administration or liquidation; or
(b) in relation to a cell of the protected cell company which is in administration or liquidation provided the administrator or liquidator of the cell consents to the exercise of the power.

(5) The powers referred to in sub-paragraph (4) are—

(a) a power to fulfil a requirement imposed on the protected cell company by an enactment;
(b) a power to fulfil an obligation incurred by the protected cell company on behalf of a cell or which is attributable to a cell;
(c) a power to enter into a transfer scheme in respect of a cell, or the assets and liabilities held by the protected cell company on behalf of the cell and the investments issued on the cell's behalf;
(d) a power to apply to court for a winding-up order in respect of a cell;
(e) a power to dissolve a cell in accordance with regulation 178;
(f) a power to do anything necessary or expedient to comply with a duty imposed on the administrator or liquidator by sub-paragraph (2).

(6) Where a protected cell company has no cells, an administrator or liquidator of the core also has the power to dissolve the protected cell company in accordance with regulation 180.

(7) Where this paragraph imposes a duty, or confers a power, on an administrator or liquidator, that duty or power is to be treated as if it were imposed or conferred on the administrator or liquidator by—

(a) the Insolvency Act 1986 where the protected cell company has its registered office in England and Wales (or Wales) or Scotland;
(b) the Insolvency (Northern Ireland) Order 1989 where the protected cell company has its registered office in Northern Ireland.

(8) In this paragraph, "transfer scheme" means a transfer scheme within the meaning given by regulation 170.

General application of the insolvency legislation

3 The insolvency legislation applies to the core as if—

(a) the core is a body corporate with distinct legal personality;
(b) the core was incorporated when the protected cell company was incorporated;
(c) the core is registered in the part of the United Kingdom in which the protected cell company has its registered office;
(d) the registered office of the cell is the registered office of the protected cell company;
(e) the registered name of the core is "the core of" followed by the name of the protected cell company;

Part 7L Special Insolvency Regimes

(f) the registrar of companies is the FCA;
(g) a person who is or was a director, shadow director, officer, employee or agent of the protected cell company is or was a director, shadow director, officer, employee or agent of the core (as the case may be);
(h) shares issued by the protected cell company on behalf of the core are shares issued by the core;
(i) the core's property, assets, liabilities, debts and creditors are determined in accordance with regulation 48(6);
(j) things done by the protected cell company on behalf of the core are things done by the core;
(k) things done to the protected cell company in respect of the core are things done to the core;
(l) judgments or orders made against the protected cell company in respect of the core are judgments or orders made against the core;
(m) the books, papers, records, registers and other documents of the protected cell company are, insofar as they relate to the core, books, papers, records, registers and documents of the core; and
(n) an associate of the protected cell company (within the meaning given by section 435 of the Insolvency Act 1986 or Article 4 of the Insolvency (Northern Ireland) Order 1989) is an associate of the core.

Jurisdiction within the United Kingdom

4 (1) This paragraph specifies which court in the United Kingdom has jurisdiction in relation to the administration or winding up of the core of a protected cell company.

(2) Her Majesty's High Court of Justice in England has jurisdiction where the registered office of a protected cell company is located in England and Wales (or Wales).

(3) The Court of Session has jurisdiction where the registered office of a protected cell company is located in Scotland.

(4) Her Majesty's High Court of Justice in Northern Ireland has jurisdiction where the registered office of a protected cell company is located in Northern Ireland.

Restriction on applying for winding up

5 A person holding an investment issued on behalf of a cell of a protected cell company may not apply for—
(a) the winding up of the core; or
(b) the appointment of a provisional liquidator in respect of the core.

Appointment of administrator

6 (1) Only the court may appoint an administrator of the core.

(2) Where a person makes an application to court for the administration of the core, the person must file with the court notice of the existence of any insolvency proceedings in relation to the protected cell company or the core anywhere in the world as soon as the person becomes aware of them.

(3) The duty imposed by sub-paragraph (2) ceases on the making of an administration order.

Giving notice

7 In the insolvency legislation, a requirement that a company give notice of, or file, something is to be treated as a requirement that the protected cell company give notice of, or file, that thing on behalf of the core.

Dissolution

8 References in the insolvency legislation to the dissolution of the company are to be treated as references to dissolution of the protected cell company, but a protected cell company may only be dissolved where the protected cell company has no cells.

Part 24 of FSMA: references to "regulated activities" and "PRA-authorised person"

9 If the protected cell company has (or had) permission to carry on a regulated activity under Part 4A (permission to carry on regulated activities) of FSMA, then Part 24 (insolvency) of FSMA applies to the core as if the core has (or had) that permission.

Further modification to specific provisions of the Insolvency Act 1986 and the Insolvency (Northern Ireland) Order 1989

10 (1) The provisions of the Insolvency Act 1986 specified in the first column of Table 8 and the provisions of the Insolvency (Northern Ireland) Order 1989 specified in the second column of Table 8 apply to the core with the modifications specified in the fourth column of Table 8.

Table 8

Insolvency Act 1986	*Insolvency (Northern Ireland) Order 1989*	*Subject Matter*	*Modification*
Section 76	Article 63	Liability of past directors and shareholders	These provisions apply where a protected cell company has made a payment ("the relevant payment" for the purposes of these provisions) to redeem or acquire shares issued on behalf of the core in breach of the requirements of regulation 107. The reference to the directors who signed the statement made in accordance with section 714(1) to (3) of the Companies Act 2006 for the purposes of the redemption or purchase is to be treated as a reference to the directors who authorised the redemption or purchase.
Section 103	Article 89	Cesser of directors' powers	Ignore these provisions.
Section 124	Article 104	Application for winding up	An administrator of the core may also present a petition for the winding up of the core.
Section 216	Article 180	Restriction on re-use of names	Treat references to the name of the liquidating company as references to the name of the protected cell company.
Section 222	Article 186	Inability to pay debts: unpaid creditor for £750 or more	The written demand must be served on the core by leaving it at the protected cell company's registered office or in such manner as the court may approve or direct.
Section 223	Article 187	Inability to pay debts: debt remaining unsatisfied after action brought	Ignore these provisions.
Paragraph 45 of Schedule B1	Paragraph 46 of Schedule B1	Publicity	These paragraphs apply to all business documents issued by or on behalf of the protected cell company and all of the protected cell company's websites.

Insolvency Act 1986	*Insolvency (Northern Ireland) Order 1989*	*Subject Matter*	*Modification*
Paragraph 61 of Schedule B1	Paragraph 62 of Schedule B1	Administrator's general powers (removal and appointment of directors)	Ignore these paragraphs.
Paragraph 69 of Schedule B1	Paragraph 70 of Schedule B1	Administrator as agent	An administrator of the core acts as agent for the protected cell company (on behalf of the core).
Paragraph 74 of Schedule B1	Paragraph 75 of Schedule B1	Challenge to administrator's conduct	These paragraphs apply to a person who is a creditor or shareholder in respect of the core of the protected cell company or any cell of the protected cell company to which the administrator's powers extend.
Paragraph 75 of Schedule B1	Paragraph 76 of Schedule B1	Misfeasance	In sub-paragraphs (2) to (5), references to the company are to be treated as including, where appropriate, references to a cell of the protected cell company.
Paragraph 83 of Schedule B1	Paragraph 84 of Schedule B1	Moving from administration to liquidation	Ignore these paragraphs.
Paragraph 84 of Schedule B1	Paragraph 85 of Schedule B1	Moving from administration to dissolution	The notice given under sub-paragraph (1) must also state that the protected cell company has no cells.

Further modifications to subordinate legislation

11 (1) The provisions of any subordinate legislation made under the Insolvency Act 1986 or the Insolvency (Northern Ireland) Order 1989 apply to the core with the following modifications.

(2) Any provision of subordinate legislation prescribing the circumstances in which a person may act in the ways specified in section 216(3) of the Insolvency Act 1986 or Article 180(3) of the Insolvency (Northern Ireland) Order 1989 where the whole or substantially the whole of the business of a company is acquired from that company is to be ignored.

(3) The provisions of the subordinate legislation apply with any other necessary modifications.

NOTES

Commencement: 8 December 2017.

SCHEDULE 4

(*Sch 4 contains amendments which, in so far as relevant to this work, have been incorporated at the appropriate place.*)

M
INVESTMENT BANKS

BANKING ACT 2009

(2009 c 1)

An Act to make provision about banking

[12 February 2009]

NOTES

Only the sections of this Act which are relevant to investment banks are reproduced here. Sections not reproduced are not annotated.

PART 7
MISCELLANEOUS

Investment banks

[7.1653]
232 Definition

(1) In this group of sections "investment bank" means an institution which satisfies the following conditions.

(2) Condition 1 is that the institution has permission under [Part 4A] of the Financial Services and Markets Act 2000 to carry on the regulated activity of—
- (a) safeguarding and administering investments,
- [(aa) managing an AIF or a UCITS,
- (ab) acting as trustee or depositary of an AIF or a UCITS,]
- (b) dealing in investments as principal, or
- (c) dealing in investments as agent.

[(2A) Subsection (2) must be read with section 22 of the Financial Services and Markets Act 2000, taken with Schedule 2 to that Act and any order under section 22.]

(3) Condition 2 is that the institution holds client assets.

(4) In this group of sections "client assets" means assets which an institution has undertaken to hold for a client (whether or not on trust and whether or not the undertaking has been complied with).

(5) Condition 3 is that the institution is incorporated in, or formed under the law of any part of, the United Kingdom.

[(5A) In subsection (4), "assets"—
- (a) includes money, but
- (b) does not include anything which an institution holds for the purposes of carrying on an insurance mediation activity unless—
  - (i) the activity arises in the course of carrying on an investment activity, or
  - (ii) the institution has elected, in relation to the thing, to comply with rules that would apply in relation to it if the activity were not an insurance mediation activity.

(5B) In this section—

"rules" means general rules (within the meaning of the Financial Services and Markets Act 2000) made by virtue of [section 137B(1)] of that Act;

"insurance mediation activity" has the meaning given by paragraph 2(5) of Schedule 6 to that Act (read as mentioned in paragraph 2(6) of that Schedule); and

"investment activity" means—
- (a) anything that falls within the definition of "investment services and activities" in section 417(1) of that Act; or
- (b) anything that is "designated investment business" within the meaning of the [Financial Conduct Authority Handbook or the Prudential Regulation Authority Handbook].]

(6) The Treasury may by order—
- (a) provide that a specified class of institution, which has a permission under [Part 4A] of the Financial Services and Markets Act 2000 to carry on a regulated activity, is to be treated as an investment bank for the purpose of this group of sections;
- (b) provide that a specified class of institution is not to be treated as an investment bank for the purpose of this group of sections;
- (c) provide that assets of a specified kind, or held in specified circumstances, are to be or not to be treated as client assets for the purpose of this group of sections;
- (d) amend a provision of this section in consequence of provision under paragraph (a), (b) or (c).

[(7) The Treasury may by order amend the definition of "investment activity" in subsection (5B), including by defining that term by reference to rules or guidance made by the PRA or the FCA under the Financial Services and Markets Act 2000.]

NOTES

Sub-s (2): words in first pair of square brackets substituted by the Financial Services Act 2012, s 106, Sch 17, Pt 4, paras 52, 55(1), (2); paras (aa), (ab) inserted by the Investment Bank (Amendment of Definition) and Special Administration (Amendment) Regulations 2017, SI 2017/443, reg 3(a).

Sub-s (2A): inserted by SI 2017/443, reg 3(b).

Sub-s (5A): inserted, together with sub-s (5B), by the Investment Bank (Amendment of Definition) Order 2011, SI 2011/239, art 3.

Sub-s (5B): inserted, together with sub-s (5A), by SI 2011/239, art 3; in definition "rules" words in square brackets substituted by the Financial Services Act 2012, s 106, Sch 17, Pt 4, paras 52, 55(1), (3); in definition "investment activity" words in square brackets substituted by the Financial Services Act 2012 (Consequential Amendments) Order 2013, SI 2013/636, art 2, Schedule, para 10.

Sub-s (6): words in square brackets substituted by the Financial Services Act 2012, s 106, Sch 17, Pt 4, paras 52, 55(1), (2).

Sub-s (7): added by the Financial Services Act 2012, s 106, Sch 17, Pt 4, paras 52, 55(1), (4).

Orders: the Investment Bank (Amendment of Definition) Order 2011, SI 2011/239 at **[7.1659]**.

Regulations: the Investment Bank (Amendment of Definition) and Special Administration (Amendment) Regulations 2017, SI 2017/443 at **[7.2046]**.

[7.1654]

233 Insolvency regulations

(1) The Treasury may by regulations ("investment bank insolvency regulations")—
- (a) modify the law of insolvency in its application to investment banks;
- (b) establish a new procedure for investment banks where—
  - (i) they are unable, or are likely to become unable, to pay their debts (within the meaning of section 93(4)), or
  - (ii) their winding up would be fair (within the meaning of section 93(8)).

(2) Investment bank insolvency regulations may, in particular—
- (a) apply or replicate (with or without modifications) or make provision similar to provision made by or under the Insolvency Act 1986 or Part 2 or 3 of this Act;
- (b) establish a new procedure either (i) to operate for investment banks in place of liquidation or administration (under the Insolvency Act 1986), or (ii) to operate alongside liquidation or administration in respect of a particular part of the business or affairs of investment banks.

(3) In making investment bank insolvency regulations the Treasury shall have regard to the desirability of—
- (a) identifying, protecting, and facilitating the return of, client assets,
- (b) protecting creditors' rights,
- (c) ensuring certainty for investment banks, creditors, clients, liquidators and administrators,
- (d) minimising the disruption of business and markets, and
- (e) maximising the efficiency and effectiveness of the financial services industry in the United Kingdom.

(4) A reference to returning client assets includes a reference to—
- (a) transferring assets to another institution, and
- (b) returning or transferring assets equivalent to those which an institution undertook to hold for clients.

NOTES

Regulations: the Investment Bank Special Administration Regulations 2011, SI 2011/245 at **[7.1661]**; the Investment Bank (Amendment of Definition) and Special Administration (Amendment) Regulations 2017, SI 2017/443 at **[7.2046]**.

[7.1655]

234 Regulations: details

(1) Investment bank insolvency regulations may provide for a procedure to be instituted—
- (a) by a court, or
- (b) by the action of one or more specified classes of person.

(2) Investment bank insolvency regulations may—
- (a) confer functions on persons appointed in accordance with the regulations (which may, in particular, (i) be similar to the functions of a liquidator or administrator under the Insolvency Act 1986, or (ii) involve acting as a trustee of client assets), and
- (b) specify objectives to be pursued by a person appointed in accordance with the regulations.

(3) Investment bank insolvency regulations may make the application of a provision depend—
- (a) on whether an investment bank is, or is likely to become, unable to pay its debts,
- (b) on whether the winding up of an investment bank would be fair, or
- (c) partly on those and partly on other considerations.

(4) Investment bank insolvency regulations may make provision about the relationship between a procedure established by the regulations and—
- (a) liquidation or administration under the Insolvency Act 1986,
- (b) bank insolvency or bank administration under Part 2 or 3 of this Act, and
- (c) provision made by or under any other enactment in connection with insolvency.

(5) Regulations by virtue of subsection (4) may, in particular—
- (a) include provision for temporary or permanent moratoria;
- (b) amend an enactment.

(6) Investment bank insolvency regulations may include provision—
- (a) establishing a mechanism for determining which assets are client assets (subject to section 232);

(b) establishing a mechanism for determining that assets are to be, or not to be, treated as client assets (subject to section 232);
(c) about the treatment of client assets;
(d) about the treatment of unsettled transactions (and related collateral);
(e) for the transfer to another financial institution of assets or transactions;
(f) for the creation or enforcement of rights (including rights that take preference over creditors' rights) in respect of client assets or other assets;
(g) indemnifying a person who is exercising or purporting to exercise functions under or by virtue of the regulations;
(h) for recovery of assets transferred in error.

(7) Provision may be included under subsection (6)(f) only to the extent that the Treasury think it necessary having regard to the desirability of protecting both—
(a) client assets, and
(b) creditors' rights.

(8) Investment bank insolvency regulations may confer functions on—
(a) a court or tribunal,
[(b) the Prudential Regulation Authority,
(ba) the Financial Conduct Authority,]
(c) the Financial Services Compensation Scheme (established under Part 15 of the Financial Services and Markets Act 2000),
(d) the scheme manager of that Scheme, and
(e) any other specified person.

(9) Investment bank insolvency regulations may include provision about institutions that are or were group undertakings (within the meaning of section 1161(5) of the Companies Act 2006) of an investment bank.

(10) Investment bank insolvency regulations may replicate or apply, with or without modifications, a power to make procedural rules.

(11) Investment bank insolvency regulations may include provision for assigning or apportioning responsibility for the cost of the application of a procedure established or modified by the regulations.

NOTES

Sub-s (8): paras (b), (ba) substituted, for original para (b), by the Financial Services Act 2012, s 106, Sch 17, Pt 4, paras 52, 56.

Regulations: the Investment Bank (Amendment of Definition) and Special Administration (Amendment) Regulations 2017, SI 2017/443 at **[7.2046]**.

[7.1656]

235 Regulations: procedure

(1) Investment bank insolvency regulations shall be made by statutory instrument.

(2) Investment bank insolvency regulations may not be made unless a draft has been laid before and approved by resolution of each House of Parliament.

(3) The Treasury must consult before laying draft investment bank insolvency regulations before Parliament.

(4) If the power to make investment bank insolvency regulations has not been exercised before the end of the period of 2 years beginning with the date on which this Act is passed, it lapses.

(5) An order under section 232(6)—
(a) shall be made by statutory instrument, and
(b) may not be made unless a draft has been laid before and approved by resolution of each House of Parliament.

[(6) An order under section 232(7)—
(a) is to be made by statutory instrument, and
(b) is subject to annulment in pursuance of a resolution of either House of Parliament.]

NOTES

Sub-s (6): added by the Financial Services Act 2012, s 106, Sch 17, Pt 4, paras 52, 57.

[7.1657]

236 Review

(1) The Treasury shall arrange for a review of the effect of any investment bank insolvency regulations.

(2) The review must be completed during the period of 2 years beginning with the date on which the regulations come into force.

(3) The Treasury shall appoint one or more persons to conduct the review; and a person appointed must have expertise in connection with the law of insolvency or financial services.

(4) The review must consider, in particular—
(a) how far the regulations are achieving the objectives specified in section 233(3), and
(b) whether the regulations should continue to have effect.

(5) The review must result in a report to the Treasury.

(6) The Treasury shall lay a copy of the report before Parliament.

(7) If a review recommends further reviews—
(a) the Treasury may arrange for the further reviews, and
(b) subsections (3) to (6) (and this subsection) shall apply to them.

PART 8
GENERAL

[7.1658]
259 Statutory instruments

(1) A statutory instrument under this Act—
(a) may make provision that applies generally or only for specified purposes, cases or circumstances,
(b) may make different provision for different purposes, cases or circumstances, and
(c) may include incidental, consequential or transitional provision.

(2)–(6) *(Outside the scope of this work.)*

NOTES

Regulations: the Investment Bank (Amendment of Definition) and Special Administration (Amendment) Regulations 2017, SI 2017/443 at **[7.2046]**.

INVESTMENT BANK (AMENDMENT OF DEFINITION) ORDER 2011

(SI 2011/239)

NOTES

Made: 7 February 2011.
Authority: Banking Act 2009, s 232(6).
Commencement: 8 February 2011.

[7.1659]
1 Citation, commencement and interpretation

(1) This Order may be cited as the Investment Bank (Amendment of Definition) Order 2011 and comes into force on the day after the day on which it is made.

(2) In this Order, "the Act" means the Banking Act 2009.

[7.1660]
2 Meaning of "client assets"

(1) For the purposes of sections 232 to 236 of the Act, "client assets"—
(a) includes money, but
(b) does not include anything which an institution holds for the purposes of carrying on an insurance mediation activity unless—
(i) the activity arises in the course of carrying on an investment activity, or
(ii) the institution has elected, in relation to the thing, to comply with rules that would apply in relation to it if the activity were not an insurance mediation activity.

(2) In this article, the definitions in section 232(5B) of the Act (inserted by article 3(2)) apply.

3 (*Inserts the Banking Act 2009, s 232(5A), (5B) at* **[7.76]**.)

INVESTMENT BANK SPECIAL ADMINISTRATION REGULATIONS 2011

(SI 2011/245)

NOTES

Made: 7 February 2011.
Authority: Banking Act 2009, ss 233, 234, 259(1).
Commencement: 8 February 2011.
Modification: these Regulations are applied, with modifications, in cases where a resolution instrument has been made under the Banking Act 2009, s 12A with respect to the investment bank in the relevant 3-month period, by the Financial Services (Banking Reform) Act 2013, s 17, Sch 2, Pt 2.

ARRANGEMENT OF REGULATIONS

1 Citation and commencement . . . [7.1661]
2 Interpretation . . . [7.1662]
3 Overview . . . [7.1663]
4 Special administration order . . . [7.1664]
5 Application . . . [7.1665]
6 Grounds for applying . . . [7.1666]
7 Powers of the court . . . [7.1667]
8 Notice to appropriate regulator of preliminary steps to other insolvency proceedings . . . [7.1668]

9 Application where investment bank is a deposit-taking bank . . . . [7.1669]
10 Special administration objectives . . . . [7.1670]
10A Objective 1—duty of administrator to work with the FSCS . . . . [7.1671]
10B Objective 1—transfer of client assets . . . . [7.1672]
10C Restrictions on partial property transfers—general provision . . . . [7.1673]
10D Restrictions on partial property transfers—set-off and netting arrangements . . . . [7.1674]
10E Restrictions on partial property transfers—security interests . . . . [7.1675]
10F Restrictions on partial property transfers—capital market arrangements . . . . [7.1676]
10G Restrictions on partial property transfers—financial markets . . . . [7.1677]
10H Objective 1—post-administration reconciliation of accounts and records relating to client money . . . . [7.1678]
10I Objective 1—removal of right to interest on unsecured claims for the return of client money . . . . [7.1679]
11 Objective 1—distribution of client assets . . . . [7.1680]
12 Objective 1—shortfall in client assets held in omnibus account . . . . [7.1681]
12A Objective 1—distribution of client money . . . . [7.1682]
12B Objectives 1 and 3—client assets (other than client money) which the administrator is unable to return to clients . . . . [7.1683]
12C Objectives 1 and 3—client money which the administrator is unable to return to clients . . . . [7.1684]
12D Powers of the court on application to set a hard bar date . . . . [7.1685]
12E Bar date notices—procedural requirements . . . . [7.1686]
12F Costs of making a claim . . . . [7.1687]
13 Objective 2—engaging with market infrastructure bodies and the Authorities . . . . [7.1688]
14 Continuity of supply . . . . [7.1689]
15 General powers, duties and effect . . . . [7.1690]
16 Appropriate regulator direction . . . . [7.1691]
17 Administrator's proposals in the event of Appropriate regulator direction . . . . [7.1692]
18 Revision of proposals in the event of Appropriate regulator direction . . . . [7.1693]
19 Appropriate regulator direction withdrawn . . . . [7.1694]
19A Responsibility for certain costs of the administration . . . . [7.1695]
20 Successful rescue . . . . [7.1696]
21 Dissolution or voluntary arrangement . . . . [7.1697]
22 Special administration order as an alternative order . . . . [7.1698]
23 Disqualification of directors . . . . [7.1699]
24 Limited liability partnerships . . . . [7.1700]
25 Partnerships . . . . [7.1701]
26 Northern Irish equivalent enactments . . . . [7.1702]
27 Modifications and consequential amendments to legislation . . . . [7.1703]

SCHEDULES

Schedule 1—Special Administration (Bank Insolvency) . . . . [7.1704]
Schedule 2—Special Administration (Bank Administration) . . . . [7.1705]
Schedule 3—Application of these Regulations to Limited Liability Partnerships . . . . [7.1706]
Schedule 4—Application of these Regulations to Partnerships . . . . [7.1707]
Schedule 5—Table of Enactments Referred to in these Regulations Together with the Equivalent Enactment Having Effect in Relation to Northern Ireland . . . . [7.1708]
Schedule 6—Modifications and Consequential Amendments
Part 1 . . . . [7.1709]
Part 2—Specific Modifications . . . . [7.1710]

[7.1661]
1 Citation and commencement

These Regulations may be cited as the Investment Bank Special Administration Regulations 2011 and shall come into force on the day after the day on which they are made.

[7.1662]
2 Interpretation

(1) In these Regulations, except where the context otherwise requires—

"the Act" means the Banking Act 2009;

"administrator" has the meaning set out in regulation 4;

"Authorities" means the Bank of England, the Treasury[, the FCA and the PRA];

"business day" has the meaning set out in section 251 of the Insolvency Act;

"client" means a person for whom the investment bank has undertaken to receive or hold client assets (whether or not on trust and whether or not that undertaking has been complied with);

["client money" means client assets which are money received or held by an investment bank for, or on behalf of, clients;

"client money account" means an account which the investment bank maintains in accordance with client money rules, including an account with any person which the investment bank maintains for the purpose of—
(a) any transaction with or by that person for a client's benefit; or
(b) meeting a client's obligation to provide collateral for a transaction;
"client money pool" means the pool of client money which is held on trust by the investment bank in accordance with client money rules and has been pooled in accordance with those rules for the purpose of distribution;
"client money rules" means rules made under Part 9A of FSMA (rules and guidance) which make provision relating to the handling and distribution of money held by a person who is authorised for the purposes of FSMA;]
"contributory" has the meaning set out in section 79 of the Insolvency Act;
"court" means—
(a) in England and Wales, the High Court,
(b) in Scotland, the Court of Session, and
(c) in Northern Ireland, the High Court;
"deposit-taking bank" means an investment bank to which the definition set out either in section 2 or in section 91 of the Act applies;
"the Disqualification Act" means the Company Directors Disqualification Act 1986;
["EEA central counterparty" has the meaning set out in section 285 of FSMA;]
["EEA CSD" has the meaning set out in section 285 of FSMA;]
"enactment" includes—
(a) an enactment comprised in or in an instrument made under an Act of the Scottish Parliament;
(b) Acts and Measures of the National Assembly for Wales and instruments made such an Act or Measure;
(c) Northern Ireland legislation;
and any EU Instrument (as defined in Part 2 of Schedule 1 of the European Communities Act 1972);
"fair" is to be construed in accordance with section 93(8) of the Act;
["FCA" means the Financial Conduct Authority;]
["foreign property" has the meaning given by section 39(2) of the Act;]
"FSCS" means the scheme manager of the Financial Services Compensation Scheme (established under Part 15 of FSMA);
"FSMA" means the Financial Services and Markets Act 2000;
"the Insolvency Act" means the Insolvency Act 1986;
"insolvency rules" means rules made under section 411 of the Insolvency Act as applied and modified by regulation 15;
"market charge" means a charge to which Part 7 of the Companies Act 1989 applies as a result of the operation of section 173 of that Act;
"market contract" means a contract to which Part 7 of the Companies Act 1989 applies as a result of the operation of section 155 of that Act;
"market infrastructure body" means a recognised clearing house, [recognised CSD,] recognised investment exchange[, EEA central counterparty, third country central counterparty], recognised overseas clearing house[, EEA CSD, third country CSD] or recognised overseas investment exchange in relation to which the investment bank is a counterparty in a market contract or to a market charge or is a member or participant;
"Objective 1", "Objective 2" and "Objective 3" have the meanings set out in regulation 10;
["PRA" means the Prudential Regulation Authority;
"PRA-authorised person" has the meaning given by FSMA;]
"prescribed" means prescribed by insolvency rules;
"prescribed" means prescribed by insolvency rules;
"recognised clearing house" has the meaning set out in section 285 of FSMA;
["recognised CSD" has the meaning set out in section 285 of FSMA;]
"recognised investment exchange" has the meaning set out in section 285 of FSMA;
"recognised overseas clearing house" means an overseas person in respect of whom [a recognition order has been made] under section 292 of FSMA declaring them to be a recognised clearing house;
"recognised overseas investment exchange" means an overseas person in respect of whom [a recognition order has been made] under section 292 of FSMA declaring them to be a recognised investment exchange;
["the regulators" means the FCA and the PRA, and references to a regulator are to be read accordingly;]
"Schedule B1" means Schedule B1 to the Insolvency Act;
"Schedule B1 administration" means the administration procedure set out in Schedule B1;
"securities" means financial instruments as defined in regulation 3 of the Financial Collateral Arrangements (No 2) Regulations 2003;
"security interest" means any legal or equitable interest or any other right in security (other than a title transfer financial collateral arrangement) created or otherwise arising by way of security including—
(a) a pledge,
(b) a mortgage,

(c) a fixed charge,
(d) a charge created as a floating charge, or
(e) a lien;

"special administration" has the meaning set out in regulation 3;
"special administration (bank insolvency)" has the meaning set out in paragraph 1 of Schedule 1;
"special administration (bank administration)" has the meaning set out in paragraph 1 of Schedule 2;
"special administration objectives" has the meaning set out in regulation 10;
"special administration order" has the meaning set out in regulation 4;
"statement of proposals" means the statement of proposals drawn up by the administrator in accordance with—

(a) paragraph 49 of Schedule B1 (as applied by regulation 15);
(b) where the [FCA or, where relevant, the PRA] has given a direction, regulation 17; or
(c) in relation to Schedule 2, paragraph 7 of that schedule; and

["third country central counterparty" has the meaning set out in section 285 of FSMA;]
["third country CSD" has the meaning set out in section 285 of FSMA;]
"title transfer financial collateral arrangement" has the meaning set out in regulation 3 of the Financial Collateral Arrangements (No 2) Regulations 2003.

(2) In the definition of "security interest", in sub-paragraph (c), in its application to Scotland, "fixed charge" means a fixed security within the meaning given by section 47(1) of the Bankruptcy and Diligence etc (Scotland) Act 2007.

[(2A) In these Regulations a reference to the investment bank's own bank accounts includes a reference to any account, other than a client money account, opened by the administrator for the purposes of the special administration.]

(3) References in these Regulations to a regulated activity must be read with—

(a) section 22 of FSMA (classes of regulated activity and categories of investment);
(b) any relevant order under that section; and
(c) Schedule 2 to that Act (regulated activities).

(4) For the purposes of a reference in these Regulations to inability to pay debts—

(a) an investment bank that is in default on an obligation to pay a sum due and payable under an agreement is to be treated as unable to pay its debts; and
(b) section 123 of the Insolvency Act (inability to pay debts) also applies,

and for the purposes of sub-paragraph (a), "agreement" means an agreement the making or performance of which constitutes or is part of a regulated activity carried on by the investment bank.

(5) Expressions used in these Regulations and in the Insolvency Act have the same meaning as in that Act, and the provision made by paragraphs 100 and 101 of Schedule B1 (as applied by regulation 15) in respect of the effect of the references in that Schedule also apply in respect of the same references where used in these Regulations.

(6) Expressions used in these Regulations and in the Companies Act 2006 have the same meaning as in that Act.

(7) Regulation 26 applies with respect to the application of these Regulations to Northern Ireland.

NOTES

Para (1): words in square brackets in definitions "Authorities", "recognised overseas clearing house", "recognised overseas investment exchange" and "statement of proposals" substituted, definition "FCA" substituted for original definition "FSA", and definitions "PRA", "PRA-authorised person" and "the regulators" inserted, by the Financial Services Act 2012 (Consequential Amendments and Transitional Provisions) Order 2013, SI 2013/472, art 3, Sch 2, para 198(a), subject to a transitional provision in para 199 which provides:

> **"199 Transitional provision in relation to the Investment Bank Special Administration Regulations 2011**
> For the purposes of the Investment Bank Special Administration Regulations 2011 anything done by or in relation to the Financial Services Authority under those Regulations (including, in particular, the giving of directions under regulation 16) in relation to an investment bank which is, on 1st April 2013, a PRA-authorised person within the meaning of those Regulations is to be treated as having also been done, unless the context otherwise requires, by or in relation to the Prudential Regulation Authority.";

definitions "EEA central counterparty", "third country central counterparty" inserted and words in second pair of square brackets in definition "market infrastructure body" inserted by the Financial Services and Markets Act 2000 (Over the Counter Derivatives, Central Counterparties and Trade Repositories) Regulations 2013, SI 2013/504, reg 41(1), (2);

definitions "client money", "client money account", "client money pool", "client money rules", and "foreign property" inserted by the Investment Bank (Amendment of Definition) and Special Administration (Amendment) Regulations 2017, SI 2017/443, regs 4, 5(a), as from 6 April 2017, except in relation to an investment bank which is in special administration on that date (see further reg 17 of the 2017 Regulations at **[7.2048]**);

definitions "EEA CSD", "recognised CSD" and "third country CSD" inserted, and words in first and third pairs of square brackets in definition "market infrastructure body" inserted, by the Central Securities Depositories Regulations 2017, SI 2017/1064, reg 10, Schedule, para 36(1), (2) (for transitional provisions and savings see regs 6–9 of the 2017 Regulations).

Para (2A): inserted by SI 2017/443, regs 4, 5(b), as from 6 April 2017, except in relation to an investment bank which is in special administration on that date (see further reg 17 of the 2017 Regulations at **[7.2048]**).

[7.1663]

3 Overview

(1) These Regulations provide for a procedure to be known as investment bank special administration ("special administration").

(2) The main features of special administration are that—

(a) an investment bank enters the procedure by court order;
(b) the order appoints an administrator;
(c) the administrator is to pursue the special administration objectives in accordance with the statement of proposals approved by the meeting of creditors and clients and, in certain circumstances, the [FCA or, where relevant, the PRA]; and
(d) in other respects the procedure is the same as for Schedule B1 administration under the Insolvency Act, subject to specific modifications, and the inclusion of certain liquidation provisions of the Insolvency Act.

(3) Where the investment bank is a deposit-taking bank with eligible depositors (within the meaning of section 93(3) of the Act)—
(a) regulations 4 to 8 do not apply; and
(b) in addition to the insolvency procedures established under Parts 2 and 3 of the Act, the Bank of England[, the FCA or, in certain cases, the PRA], may apply for an order to put the bank into—
[(i)] special administration (bank insolvency) as set out in Schedule 1 (as applied by regulation 9); or
[(ii)] special administration (bank administration) as set out in Schedule 2 (as applied by regulation 9).

(4) Where the investment bank is a deposit-taking bank but has no eligible depositors, the investment bank must not be put into special administration (bank insolvency); instead the investment bank may be put into either—
(a) special administration (bank administration), (in which case regulations 4 to 8 do not apply); or
(b) special administration.

NOTES

Paras (2), (3): words in square brackets substituted by the Financial Services Act 2012 (Consequential Amendments and Transitional Provisions) Order 2013, SI 2013/472, art 3, Sch 2, para 198(b), subject to a transitional provision in para 199 set out at **[7.1662]**.

The original sub-paras (c) and (d) of para (3) were renumbered as paras (i) and (ii) of sub-para (b) by the Investment Bank (Amendment of Definition) and Special Administration (Amendment) Regulations 2017, SI 2017/443, regs 4, 6, as from 6 April 2017, except in relation to an investment bank which is in special administration on that date (see further reg 17 of the 2017 Regulations at **[7.2048]**).

[7.1664]
4 Special administration order

(1) An investment bank special administration order ("special administration order") is an order appointing a person as the investment bank administrator ("administrator") of an investment bank.
(2) A person is eligible for appointment as administrator under a special administration order if qualified to act as an insolvency practitioner [in relation to the investment bank].
(3) An appointment may be made only if the person has consented to act.
(4) For the purpose of these Regulations—
(a) an investment bank is "in special administration" while the appointment of the administrator has effect;
(b) an investment bank "enters special administration" when the appointment of the administrator takes effect;
(c) an investment bank ceases to be in special administration when the appointment of the administrator ceases to have effect in accordance with these Regulations; and
(d) an investment bank does not cease to be in special administration merely because an administrator vacates office (by reason of resignation, death or otherwise) or is removed from office.

NOTES

Para (2): words in square brackets inserted by the Deregulation Act 2015, the Small Business, Enterprise and Employment Act 2015 and the Insolvency (Amendment) Act (Northern Ireland) 2016 (Consequential Amendments and Transitional Provisions) Regulations 2017, SI 2017/400, reg 10(1), (2).

[7.1665]
5 Application

(1) An application to the court for a special administration order may be made to the court by—
(a) the investment bank;
(b) the directors of the investment bank;
(c) one or more creditors of the investment bank;
(d) the designated officer for a magistrates' court in the exercise of the power conferred by section 87A of the Magistrates' Courts Act 1980 (fines imposed on companies);
(e) (subject to paragraph (7)), a contributory of the investment bank;
(f) a combination of persons listed in sub-paragraphs (a) to (e);
(g) the Secretary of State; . . .
[(h) the FCA; or
(i) if the investment bank is a PRA-authorised person, the PRA.]

(2) Where an application is made by a person other than the [FCA], the [FCA] is entitled to be heard at—
(a) the hearing of the application for special administration; and

(b) any other hearing of the court in relation to the investment bank under these Regulations.

[(2A) Where an application is made by a person other than the PRA in relation to an investment bank which is a PRA-authorised person, the PRA is entitled to be heard at—

(a) the hearing of the application for special administration; and

(b) any other hearing of the court in relation to the investment bank under these Regulations.]

(3) An application must nominate a person to be appointed as the administrator.

(4) As soon as is reasonably practicable after making the application, the applicant shall notify—

(a) a person who gave notice to the [appropriate regulator] in accordance with Condition 1 of regulation 8; and

(b) such other persons as may be prescribed.

(5) An application may not be withdrawn without the permission of the court.

(6) In sub-paragraph (1)(c), "creditor" includes a contingent creditor and a prospective creditor.

(7) A contributory ("C") is not entitled to make an application for special administration unless either—

(a) the number of members is reduced below 2; or

(b) the shares in respect of which C is a contributory, or some of them, either were originally allotted to C, or have been held by C and registered in C's name, for at least 6 months during the 18 months before the commencement of the special administration, or have devolved on C through the death of a former holder.

NOTES

Para (1): word omitted revoked, and words in square brackets substituted, by the Financial Services Act 2012 (Consequential Amendments and Transitional Provisions) Order 2013, SI 2013/472, art 3, Sch 2, para 198(c)(i), subject to a transitional provision in para 199 set out at **[7.1662]**.

Para (2): words in square brackets substituted by SI 2013/472, art 3, Sch 2, para 198(c)(ii), subject to a transitional provision in para 199 set out at **[7.1662]**.

Para (2A): inserted by SI 2013/472, art 3, Sch 2, para 198(c)(iii), subject to a transitional provision in para 199 set out at **[7.1662]**.

Para (4): words in square brackets substituted by SI 2013/472, art 3, Sch 2, para 198(c)(iv), subject to a transitional provision in para 199 set out at **[7.1662]**.

[7.1666]

6 Grounds for applying

(1) In this regulation—

(a) Ground A is that the investment bank is, or is likely to become, unable to pay its debts;

(b) Ground B is that it would be fair to put the investment bank into special administration; and

(c) Ground C is that it is expedient in the public interest to put the investment bank into special administration.

(2) The [FCA or, where relevant, the PRA] or the persons listed in regulation 5(1)(a) to (e) may apply for a special administration order only if they consider that Ground A or Ground B is met.

(3) The Secretary of State may apply for a special administration order only if it appears to the Secretary of State that Grounds B and C are met.

(4) The sources of information on the basis of which the Secretary of State may reach a decision on Ground C include those listed in section 124A(1) of the Insolvency Act (petition for winding up on grounds of public interest).

NOTES

Para (2): words in square brackets substituted by the Financial Services Act 2012 (Consequential Amendments and Transitional Provisions) Order 2013, SI 2013/472, art 3, Sch 2, para 198(d), subject to a transitional provision in para 199 set out at **[7.1662]**.

[7.1667]

7 Powers of the court

(1) On an application for a special administration order the court may—

(a) grant the application in accordance with paragraph (2);

(b) dismiss the application;

(c) adjourn the hearing (generally or to a specified date);

(d) make an interim order;

(e) on the application of the [FCA], treat the application as an administration application by the [FCA] under Schedule B1 in accordance with section 359(1) of FSMA;

[(ea) on the application of the PRA, treat the application as an administration application by the PRA under Schedule B1 in accordance with section 359(1A) of FSMA;] or

(f) make any other order which the court thinks appropriate.

(2) The court may make a special administration order if it is satisfied that the company is an investment bank and—

(a) (on the application of persons listed in regulation 5(1)(a) to (e)[, the FCA or PRA]) that Ground A or Ground B in regulation 6 is satisfied;

(b) (on the application of the Secretary of State) if satisfied that Grounds B and C in regulation 6 are satisfied.

(3) Where the application for a special administration order is made by members of the investment bank as contributories on the basis that Ground B in regulation 6 is satisfied, the court, if it is of the opinion that—

(a) the applicants are entitled to relief either by a special administration order being made in respect of the investment bank or by some other means; and

(b) in the absence of any other remedy it would be fair that the special administration order be made in respect of the investment bank,

shall make a special administration order; but this does not apply if the court is also of the opinion that an alternative remedy is available to the applicants and that they are acting unreasonably in applying for a special administration order instead of pursuing that other remedy.

(4) A special administration order takes effect in accordance with its terms.

NOTES

Para (1): words in square brackets in sub-para (e) substituted, and sub-para (ea) inserted, by the Financial Services Act 2012 (Consequential Amendments and Transitional Provisions) Order 2013, SI 2013/472, art 3, Sch 2, para 198(e)(i), subject to a transitional provision in para 199 set out at **[7.1662]**.

Para (2): words in square brackets in sub-para (a) substituted by SI 2013/472, art 3, Sch 2, para 198(e)(ii), subject to a transitional provision in para 199 set out at **[7.1662]**.

[7.1668]

8 Notice to [appropriate regulator] of preliminary steps to other insolvency proceedings

(1) An application for an administration order in respect of an investment bank may not be made unless the conditions in paragraph (5) are satisfied.

(2) A petition for a winding up order in respect of an investment bank may not be made unless the conditions in paragraph (5) are satisfied.

(3) A resolution for the voluntary winding up of an investment bank may not be made unless the conditions in paragraph (5) are satisfied.

(4) An administrator of an investment bank may not be appointed unless the conditions in paragraph (5) are satisfied.

(5) The conditions are as follows—

(a) Condition 1 is that the [appropriate regulator] has been notified of the preliminary steps taken in respect of an insolvency procedure;

(b) Condition 2 is that a copy of the notice complying with Condition 1 has been filed (in Scotland, lodged) with the court (and made available for public inspection by the court);

(c) Condition 3 is that—

(i) the period of 2 weeks, beginning with the day on which the notice is received by the [appropriate regulator], has ended, or

(ii) the [appropriate regulator] has informed the person who gave the notice that it consents to the insolvency procedure to which the notice relates going ahead; and

(d) Condition 4 is that no application for a special administration order is pending.

(6) Where the [appropriate regulator] receives notice under Condition 1, it shall inform the person who gave the notice, within the period in Condition 3—

(a) whether or not it consents to the insolvency procedure to which the notice relates going ahead;

(b) whether or not it intends to apply for that (or an alternative) insolvency procedure itself; or

(c) whether it intends to apply for a special administration order.

(7) Arranging for the giving of the notice in order to satisfy Condition 1 may be treated as a step with a view to minimising the potential loss to the investment bank's creditors for the purpose of section 214 of the Insolvency Act (as applied by regulation 15).

(8) In this regulation—

["appropriate regulator" means—

(a) in relation to an investment bank which is a PRA-authorised person, the FCA and the PRA (and any references in this regulation to the "appropriate regulator" are to be read as references to each of the FCA and PRA);

(b) in any other case, the FCA;]

"investment bank" does not include an investment bank that is a deposit-taking bank; and

"preliminary steps taken in respect of an insolvency procedure" means that—

(a) an application for an administration order has been made;

(b) a petition for a winding up order has been presented;

(c) a resolution for voluntary winding up has been proposed by the investment bank; or

(d) a resolution for the appointment of an administrator has been proposed.

NOTES

Provision heading, paras (5), (6): words in square brackets substituted by the Financial Services Act 2012 (Consequential Amendments and Transitional Provisions) Order 2013, SI 2013/472, art 3, Sch 2, para 198(f)(i), subject to a transitional provision in para 199 set out at **[7.1662]**.

Para (8): definition "appropriate regulator" inserted by SI 2013/472, art 3, Sch 2, para 198(f)(ii), subject to a transitional provision in para 199 set out at **[7.1662]**.

[7.1669]

9 Application where investment bank is a deposit-taking bank

Subject to regulation 3(4), where the investment bank is a deposit-taking bank then Schedule 1 (Special administration (bank insolvency)) and Schedule 2 (Special administration (bank administration)) apply.

[7.1670]

10 Special administration objectives

(1) The administrator has three special administration objectives ("the special administration objectives")—

(a) Objective 1 is to ensure the return of client assets as soon as is reasonably practicable;

(b) Objective 2 is to ensure timely engagement with market infrastructure bodies and the Authorities pursuant to regulation 13; and

(c) Objective 3 is to either—

(i) rescue the investment bank as a going concern, or

(ii) wind it up in the best interests of the creditors.

(2) In relation to sub-paragraph (1)(a), the administrator is entitled to deal with and return client assets in whatever order the administrator thinks best achieves Objective 1.

(3) The order in which the special administration objectives are listed in this regulation is not significant: subject to regulation 16, the administrator must—

(a) commence work on each objective immediately after appointment, prioritising the order of work on each objective as the administrator thinks fit, in order to achieve the best result overall for clients and creditors; and

(b) set out, in the statement of proposals made under paragraph 49 of Schedule B1 (as applied by regulation 15), the order in which the administrator intends to pursue the objectives once the statement has been approved.

(4) The administrator must work to achieve each objective, in accordance with the priority afforded to the objective as provided in paragraph (3), as quickly and efficiently as is reasonably practicable.

(5) For the purposes of Objective 1, "return of client assets" or where the client assets are "returned" to the client means that the investment bank relinquishes full control over the assets for the benefit of the client to the extent of—

(a) the client's beneficial entitlement to those assets (where the assets in question have been held on trust by the investment bank); or

(b) the client's right to those assets as bailor or otherwise (where the investment bank has been holding those assets as bailee (in Scotland, as custodier of those assets) or by some other means to the order of the client);

having taken into account any entitlement the investment bank might have, or a third party might have, in respect of those assets, of which the administrator is aware at the time the assets are returned to the client.

(6) In relation to paragraph (5)—

(a) where client assets are returned to a person other than the client, for "client" substitute "claimant"; and

(b) where the claimant is the investment bank, for "relinquishes control over the assets for the benefit of the client" substitute "takes full title to the assets for its benefit".

[7.1671]

[10A Objective 1—duty of administrator to work with the FSCS

(1) The administrator must—

(a) as soon as reasonably practicable after appointment as the administrator, inform the FSCS of the value of client assets held by the investment bank for each of the clients of the investment bank;

(b) keep the FSCS informed about progress towards the achievement of Objective 1;

(c) comply, as soon as reasonably practicable, with any request by the FSCS for the provision of information or the production of documents relating to the client assets held by the investment bank; and

(d) at the request of the FSCS, provide any assistance identified by the FSCS as being necessary for the purpose of enabling the FSCS to administer the compensation scheme in relation to the entitlement of clients of the investment bank to compensation.

(2) Where the administrator is required by this regulation to provide any information or produce any document, the administrator may provide the information or produce the document in hard copy or in electronic format.

(3) This regulation does not apply if the administrator is appointed under a special administration (bank insolvency) order (within the meaning given by paragraph 2 of Schedule 1).]

NOTES

Commencement: 6 April 2017.

Inserted by the Investment Bank (Amendment of Definition) and Special Administration (Amendment) Regulations 2017, SI 2017/443, regs 4, 7, as from 6 April 2017, except in relation to an investment bank which is in special administration on that date (see further reg 17 of the 2017 Regulations at **[7.2048]**).

[7.1672]

[10B Objective 1—transfer of client assets

(1) This regulation applies where—

Part 7M Special Insolvency Regimes

(a) the administrator, in pursuit of Objective 1 (whether or not also in pursuit of Objective 3) enters into a binding arrangement with another financial institution for the transfer to that institution ("the transferee") of all or some of the property, rights and liabilities of the investment bank; and
(b) for the purposes of that transfer the arrangement includes provision for a transfer of client assets to the transferee or to a person who has undertaken to receive or hold any of the assets to the order of the transferee.

(2) This regulation is subject to the restrictions on partial property transfers in regulations 10C to 10G.

(3) The transfer of client assets which the investment bank has undertaken to hold under a client contract and of relevant rights and liabilities is to have effect in spite of any—
(a) restriction affecting what can or cannot be assigned or transferred by the investment bank (whether generally or by a particular person or particular description of persons);
(b) requirement to give notice to, or obtain the consent (however referred to) of, any person who is party to the client contract; or
(c) entitlement of any person to the return of the assets otherwise than by transfer under the arrangement.

(4) For these purposes it does not matter whether a restriction, requirement or entitlement has effect by virtue of a provision contained in a contract or an enactment, or in any other way, except that in paragraph (3)(a) a restriction does not include a restriction in client money rules.

(5) To the extent that rights and liabilities under a client contract are transferred by the arrangement, the contract is to be treated for the purposes of the arrangement as if it had been made by the transferee rather than the investment bank.

(6) The transferee may vary the terms of client contracts without obtaining the agreement of persons who are party to the contracts to the extent necessary for giving effect to the transfer and ensuring that the powers, rights and obligations of the transferee acting as a trustee are exercisable.

(7) Where necessary for the purposes of the arrangement the administrator may disclose to the transferee all information which is, in the administrator's view, relevant to the transfer of client assets or rights and liabilities under client contracts.

(8) Subject to paragraph (9), paragraph (7) overrides any contractual or other requirement to keep information in confidence.

(9) Paragraphs (7) and (8) do not authorise a disclosure, in contravention of any provisions of the Data Protection Act 1998, of any personal data which are not exempt from the provisions of that Act.

(10) The arrangement must include such provision as the administrator thinks necessary to ensure that clients whose assets are to be transferred will be able to exercise their rights in relation to the assets as soon as reasonably practicable after the transfer.

(11) For the purposes of this regulation, if the arrangement purports to transfer all of the property, rights and liabilities of the investment bank, it is to be treated as having done so effectively (so that none of regulations 10C to 10G applies to it) notwithstanding the possibility that any property, right or liability purportedly transferred is foreign property and might not have been effectively transferred by the arrangement.

(12) In this regulation a reference to rights and liabilities of the investment bank or to rights and liabilities under a client contract, in relation to property held by the investment bank on trust (however arising), includes a reference to—
(a) the legal and beneficial interest of the investment bank in the property; and
(b) the powers and obligations of the investment bank acting as a trustee of the property.

(13) In this regulation—
"client assets" means client assets (within the meaning given by section 232(4) of the Act) and assets equivalent to those which the investment bank undertook to hold for clients;
"client contract" means a contract under which the investment bank undertook to—
(a) receive or hold client assets; or
(b) provide any services or enter into any transactions for the benefit of a particular client in relation to the investment bank's holding of client assets for that client;
"partial property transfer" means an arrangement of a kind referred to in paragraph (1) for the transfer of some, but not all, of the property, rights and liabilities of the investment bank; and
"relevant rights and liabilities", in relation to a client contract, means the rights and liabilities under the contract so far as they have effect in relation to any client assets which are to be transferred by the arrangement.]

NOTES

Commencement: 6 April 2017.

Inserted, together with regs 10C–10G, by the Investment Bank (Amendment of Definition) and Special Administration (Amendment) Regulations 2017, SI 2017/443, regs 4, 8, as from 6 April 2017, except in relation to an investment bank which is in special administration on that date (see further reg 17 of the 2017 Regulations at **[7.2048]**).

[7.1673]

[10C Restrictions on partial property transfers—general provision

(1) Regulation 10B has effect in relation to a partial property transfer as if paragraph (3)(b) of that regulation were omitted.

(2) Paragraph (1) does not apply in relation to the transfer of protected rights and liabilities (within the meaning given in regulation 10D(2)) or the transfer of any property, benefits, rights or liabilities to which regulation 10E, 10F or 10G applies.

(3) A partial property transfer must include such provision as the administrator thinks appropriate—

(a) to ensure that a client whose client assets are to be transferred by the arrangement will be entitled to demand a transfer back to the investment bank of assets which are transferred ("reverse transfer");

(b) for the identification of assets for the purposes of a reverse transfer; and

(c) unless the investment bank has ceased to satisfy Condition 1 in section 232 of the Act (definition of "investment bank"), to ensure that the transferee is obliged to give effect to the reverse transfer as soon as reasonably practicable after the demand is made.

(4) The administrator must take all steps necessary to give effect to the reverse transfer.

(5) A reverse transfer has effect to transfer back to the investment bank the relevant rights and liabilities transferred by the arrangement so far as they have effect in relation to the client assets which are transferred back to the investment bank.

(6) In this regulation "client assets", "partial property transfer" and "relevant rights and liabilities" have the meaning given in regulation 10B(13).]

NOTES

Commencement: 6 April 2017.

Inserted, subject to transitional provisions, as noted to reg 10B at **[7.1672]**.

[7.1674]

[10D Restrictions on partial property transfers—set-off and netting arrangements

(1) A partial property transfer may not provide for the transfer of some, but not all, of the protected rights and liabilities between a client or other person ("C") and the investment bank.

(2) Rights and liabilities between C and the investment bank are protected if—

(a) they are rights and liabilities which C or the investment bank is entitled to set off or net under a particular set-off arrangement, netting arrangement or title transfer financial collateral arrangement which C has entered into with the investment bank; and

(b) they are not excluded rights or excluded liabilities.

(3) For the purpose of paragraph (1), a partial property transfer which purports to transfer all of the protected rights and liabilities between C and the investment bank is to be treated as having done so effectively (and not in contravention of paragraph (1)) notwithstanding the possibility that any of the protected rights or liabilities are foreign property and might not have been effectively transferred by the arrangement.

(4) For the purposes of paragraph (2), it is immaterial whether or not—

(a) the arrangement which permits C or the investment bank to set off or net rights and liabilities also permits C or the investment bank to set off or net rights and liabilities with another person; or

(b) the right of C or the investment bank to set off or net is exercisable only on the occurrence of a particular event.

(5) A partial property transfer made in contravention of this regulation does not affect the exercise of the right to set off or net.

(6) In this regulation—

"excluded rights", in relation to rights between C and the investment bank, has the same meaning as it has in relation to rights between C and a banking institution by virtue of articles 1(3) and 3 of the Banking Act 2009 (Restriction of Partial Property Transfers) Order 2009, except that in article 1(3), in the definition of "excluded rights"—

(a) in sub-paragraph (e) the reference to subordinated debt is to be read as a reference to subordinated debt issued by C or by the investment bank; and

(b) in sub-paragraph (f)—

(i) the reference to a set-off arrangement, netting arrangement or title transfer financial collateral arrangement is to be read as a reference to a set-off arrangement, netting arrangement or title transfer financial collateral arrangement referred to in this regulation; and

(ii) the references to transferable securities are to be read as references to transferable securities issued by C or by the investment bank;

"excluded liabilities" means the liabilities which correspond with excluded rights;

"netting arrangement" means an arrangement under which a number of claims or obligations can be converted into a net claim or obligation and includes, in particular—

(a) a "close-out" netting arrangement, under which actual or theoretical debts are calculated during the course of a contract for the purpose of enabling them to be set off against each other or to be converted into a net debt;

(b) an arrangement which provides for netting (within the meaning given by regulation 2(1) of the Financial Markets and Insolvency (Settlement Finality) Regulations 1999); and

(c) an arrangement which includes a close-out netting provision (within the meaning given by regulation 3(1) of the Financial Collateral Arrangements (No 2) Regulations 2003);

"partial property transfer" has the same meaning as in regulation 10B(13);

"set-off arrangement" means an arrangement under which two or more debts, claims or obligations can be set off against each other; and

"title transfer financial collateral arrangement" has the meaning given by regulation 3(1) of the Financial Collateral Arrangements (No 2) Regulations 2003.]

NOTES

Commencement: 6 April 2017.

Inserted, subject to transitional provisions, as noted to reg 10B at **[7.1672]**.

[7.1675]

[10E Restrictions on partial property transfers—security interests

(1) Subject to paragraph (6), paragraphs (3), (4) and (5) apply where under any binding arrangement one party owes to the other a liability which is secured against any property or rights.

(2) For these purposes it is immaterial whether or not—

(a) the liability is secured against all or substantially all of the property or rights of a person;
(b) the liability is secured against specified property or rights; or
(c) the property or rights against which the liability is secured are owned by the person who owes the liability.

(3) A partial property transfer may not transfer the property or rights against which the liability is secured unless that liability and the benefit of the security are also transferred.

(4) A partial property transfer may not transfer the benefit of the security unless the liability which is secured is also transferred.

(5) A partial property transfer may not transfer the liability unless the benefit of the security is also transferred.

(6) Paragraphs (3), (4) and (5) do not apply if the investment bank entered into the binding arrangement in contravention of a rule prohibiting such arrangements made by the FCA or the PRA under FSMA or otherwise than in accordance with the investment bank's Part 4A permission (within the meaning given by section 55A(5) of FSMA).

(7) For the purposes of paragraphs (3), (4) and (5), a partial property transfer which purports to transfer any property, rights and liabilities is to be treated as having done so effectively (and not in contravention of any of those paragraphs) notwithstanding the possibility that any of that property, or of those rights or liabilities, is foreign property and might not have been effectively transferred by the arrangement.

(8) In this regulation "partial property transfer" has the same meaning as in regulation 10B(13).]

NOTES

Commencement: 6 April 2017.

Inserted, subject to transitional provisions, as noted to reg 10B at **[7.1672]**.

[7.1676]

[10F Restrictions on partial property transfers—capital market arrangements

(1) Subject to paragraph (2), a partial property transfer may not provide for the transfer of some, but not all, of the property, rights and liabilities which are or form part of a capital market arrangement to which the investment bank is a party.

(2) Paragraph (1) does not apply where the only property, rights and liabilities which are, or are not, transferred relate to deposits.

(3) For the purpose of paragraph (1), a partial property transfer which purports to transfer all of the property, rights and liabilities which are or form part of a capital market arrangement to which the investment bank is a party is to be treated as having done so effectively (and not in contravention of paragraph (1)) notwithstanding the possibility that any property, right or liability purportedly transferred is foreign property and might not have been effectively transferred by the arrangement.

(4) In this regulation—

"capital market arrangement" has the meaning given by paragraph 1 of Schedule 2A to the Insolvency Act;

"deposit" has the same meaning as in article 5 of the Financial Services and Markets Act 2000 (Regulated Activities) Order 2001, disregarding the exclusions in other articles of that Order; and

"partial property transfer" has the same meaning as in regulation 10B(13).]

NOTES

Commencement: 6 April 2017.

Inserted, subject to transitional provisions, as noted to reg 10B at **[7.1672]**.

[7.1677]

[10G Restrictions on partial property transfers—financial markets

(1) A partial property transfer may not transfer property, rights or liabilities to the extent that doing so would have the effect of modifying, modifying the operation of, or rendering unenforceable—

(a) a market contract;
(b) the default rules of a recognised investment exchange or recognised clearing house; or
(c) the rules of a recognised investment exchange or recognised clearing house as to the settlement of market contracts not dealt with under its default rules.

(2) A partial property transfer is void in so far as it is made in contravention of this regulation.

(3) In this regulation—

"default rules" has the meaning given in section 188 of the Companies Act 1989; and "partial property transfer" has the same meaning as in regulation 10B(13).]

NOTES

Commencement: 6 April 2017.

Inserted, subject to transitional provisions, as noted to reg 10B at **[7.1672]**.

[7.1678]

[10H Objective 1—post-administration reconciliation of accounts and records relating to client money

(1) Immediately after being appointed as the administrator, the administrator must carry out a client money reconciliation in accordance with paragraph (2) and make any transfer required by paragraph (3) or (4).

(2) The client money reconciliation must—

(a) be carried out in accordance with the method for carrying out client money reconciliations adopted by the investment bank to meet client money rules, whether or not the method adopted is in compliance with those rules;

(b) be based on records and accounts of the investment bank as they stood immediately after the last such reconciliation by the investment bank (but taking no further account of money received, or payments, transfers or transactions made, by the investment bank of which account was taken for the purposes of that reconciliation); and

(c) take account of money received, and payments, transfers and transactions made, by the investment bank after the last such reconciliation and before the appointment of the administrator.

(3) Where the client money reconciliation shows that amount A exceeds amount B, the administrator must transfer an amount equal to the difference from the investment bank's own bank accounts to any client money account other than a client transaction account.

(4) Where the client money reconciliation shows that amount B exceeds amount A, the administrator must transfer an amount equal to the difference from the client money accounts to the investment bank's own bank accounts.

(5) In this regulation—

"amount A" means the total amount of client money which the investment bank, according to its own records and accounts, is required to hold in accordance with client money rules;

"amount B" means the total amount of client money which the investment bank holds in client money accounts;

"client money reconciliation" means a reconciliation of amount A with amount B; and

"client transaction account" means an account with any person which the investment bank maintains for the purpose of—

(a) any transaction with or by that person for a client's benefit; or

(b) meeting a client's obligation to provide collateral for a transaction.]

NOTES

Commencement: 6 April 2017.

Inserted, together with reg 10I, by the Investment Bank (Amendment of Definition) and Special Administration (Amendment) Regulations 2017, SI 2017/443, regs 4, 9, as from 6 April 2017, except in relation to an investment bank which is in special administration on that date (see further reg 17 of the 2017 Regulations at **[7.2048]**).

[7.1679]

[10I Objective 1—removal of right to interest on unsecured claims for the return of client money

(1) This regulation applies where—

(a) a debt arises from a liability of the investment bank to return client money;

(b) the client has not submitted a claim for payment of the debt by way of a distribution from the client money pool; and

(c) the client makes an unsecured claim for payment of the debt.

(2) The client is not entitled to interest on the debt for the period commencing on the date on which the investment bank entered special administration, except interest on such part of the debt which remains after deduction of the total amount which the client would have received on a claim for payment of the debt by way of a distribution from the client money pool.]

NOTES

Commencement: 6 April 2017.

Inserted, subject to transitional provisions, as noted to reg 10H at **[7.1678]**.

[7.1680]

11 Objective 1—distribution of client assets

(1) If the administrator thinks it necessary in order to expedite the return of client assets, the administrator may set a bar date for the submission of—

(a) claims to the beneficial ownership, or other form of ownership, of the client assets; or

(b) claims of persons in relation to a security interest asserted over, or other entitlement to, those assets.

(2) Claims under paragraph (1) include claims that are contingent or disputed.

(3) In setting a bar date, the administrator must allow a reasonable time after notice of the special administration has been published (in accordance with insolvency rules) for persons to be able to calculate and submit their claims.

[(4) Subject to paragraph (4A), where the administrator sets a bar date—

(a) the administrator must return client assets in accordance with the prescribed procedure; but

(b) no client assets may be returned after the bar date has been set unless the court has given its approval on an application made by the administrator in accordance with the prescribed procedure.

(4A) The administrator may, at any time after setting a bar date, return client assets without the approval of the court if (and only if)—

(a) at that time the administrator has not made any application for court approval to return client assets;

(b) the administrator has identified the person who is beneficially entitled to the assets or has a right to the assets as bailor or otherwise; and

(c) the assets are not held by the investment bank in a client omnibus account (within the meaning given in regulation 12(9)).]

(5) Where the administrator, after setting a bar date, has returned client assets [with the approval of the court], if the administrator then receives a late claim of a type described in paragraph (1) in respect of assets that have been returned—

(a) there shall be no disruption to those client assets that have already been returned;

(b) the person to whom the assets have been returned acquires good title to them as against the late-claiming claimant,

and insolvency rules shall prescribe how the late claim is to be treated by the administrator.

(6) The restrictions in paragraph (5) shall not apply where—

(a) the client assets were returned to a person ("P") by the administrator in bad faith in which P was complicit; or

(b) P is later found to have made a false claim to those assets.

(7) In this regulation, "bar date" means a date by which claims as described in paragraph (1) must be submitted.

(8) This regulation does not apply to [client money].

NOTES

Paras (4), (4A): substituted (for the original para (4)) by the Investment Bank (Amendment of Definition) and Special Administration (Amendment) Regulations 2017, SI 2017/443, regs 4, 10(a), as from 6 April 2017, except in relation to an investment bank which is in special administration on that date (see further reg 17 of the 2017 Regulations at **[7.2048]**). The original text read as follows—

"(4) Where the administrator sets a bar date—

(a) the administrator shall return client assets in accordance with the procedure set down by insolvency rules; but

(b) no client assets shall be returned after the bar date has been set without the approval of the court in accordance with the procedure set down in insolvency rules.".

Para (5): words in square brackets inserted by SI 2017/443, regs 4, 10(b), as from 6 April 2017, except in relation to an investment bank which is in special administration on that date (see further reg 17 of the 2017 Regulations at **[7.2048]**).

Para (8): words in square brackets substituted by SI 2017/443, regs 4, 10(c), as from 6 April 2017, except in relation to an investment bank which is in special administration on that date (see further reg 17 of the 2017 Regulations at **[7.2048]**). The previous words (as amended by the Financial Services Act 2012 (Consequential Amendments and Transitional Provisions) Order 2013, SI 2013/472, art 3, Sch 2, para 198(g)) were "client assets received or held, or which should have been held, by the investment bank in accordance with rules made by virtue of [section 137B of FSMA (FCA general rules: clients' money, right to rescind etc)]".

[7.1681]

12 Objective 1—shortfall in client assets held in omnibus account

(1) This regulation applies if—

(a) the administrator becomes aware that there is a shortfall in the amount available for distribution of securities of a particular description held by the investment bank as client assets in a client omnibus account;

(b) the shortfall cannot be remedied following the resolution of on-going disputes; and

(c) the assets in question are not [client money].

(2) The administrator, in making the distribution, shall ensure (subject to the treatment of late claims as described in regulation 11(5)) that the shortfall referred to in paragraph (1) be borne pro rata by all clients for whom the investment bank holds securities of that particular description in that same account in proportion to their beneficial interest in those securities.

(3) A person (including the investment bank) ("a security holder") with a security interest over securities held in the client omnibus account on behalf of a particular client shall be entitled to participate in distributions and shortfall claims in respect of those securities in accordance with their entitlement as against that client (subject to the treatment of late claims as described in regulation 11(5)).

(4) Security holders shall not, at any time, be entitled to claim in aggregate in excess of the distribution which the client would have been entitled to if there had been no claim by that client.

(5) Any reduction of the client's beneficial interest as a result of the application of paragraph (2) shall limit correspondingly the rights of the security holder in respect of the distribution, (but this shall not affect the right of the security holder in respect of the client's shortfall claim as described in paragraph (7)).

(6) Where there is a dispute between persons as to their respective share of a distribution, the administrator may—

(a) make the distribution in accordance with an agreement drawn up between the parties in dispute; or

(b) lodge the securities that are the subject of the dispute with the court,

and if the administrator pursues either course of action, the administrator's obligations in respect of Objective 1 with regard to these securities shall be deemed to be discharged.

(7) The shortfall borne by a client under paragraph (2) is that client's shortfall claim against the investment bank ("shortfall claim") and shall rank as an unsecured claim.

(8) The value of a client's shortfall claim shall be based on the market price for those securities to which the shortfall claim relates on the date the investment bank entered special administration or, if that is not a business day, on the last business day prior to the investment bank entering special administration.

(9) In this regulation—

"client omnibus account" means an account held by the investment bank, or another institution in the name of the investment bank, made up of multiple accounts of clients of the investment bank;

"distribution" means the return of client assets that are securities of a particular description;

"market price" means—

(a) the value of the securities on the day in question as determined by a reputable source used by the investment bank, immediately prior to the investment bank entering special administration, for valuing or reporting in respect of those securities; or

(b) if this is not practicable, the value of those securities on the day in question as determined by the administrator which reflects, in the administrator's opinion, a fair and reasonable price for those securities; and

"securities of a particular description" means securities issued by the same issuer which are of the same class of shares or stock; or in the case of securities other than shares or stock, which are of the same currency and denomination and treated as forming part of the same issue.

NOTES

Para (1): words in square brackets substituted by the Investment Bank (Amendment of Definition) and Special Administration (Amendment) Regulations 2017, SI 2017/443, regs 4, 11, as from 6 April 2017, except in relation to an investment bank which is in special administration on that date (see further reg 17 of the 2017 Regulations at **[7.2048]**). The previous words (as amended by the Financial Services Act 2012 (Consequential Amendments and Transitional Provisions) Order 2013, SI 2013/472, art 3, Sch 2, para 198(h)) were "ones which are received or held, or should have been held, by the investment bank in accordance with rules made by virtue of [section 137B of FSMA (FCA general rules: clients' money, right to rescind etc)]".

[7.1682]

[12A Objective 1—distribution of client money

(1) If the administrator thinks it necessary in order to expedite the return of client money, the administrator may by notice set a bar date for the submission of client money claims.

(2) In setting a bar date the administrator must allow a reasonable time after notice of the special administration has been published (in accordance with insolvency rules) for persons to be able to calculate and submit client money claims.

(3) As soon as reasonably practicable after the bar date, the administrator must make a distribution of client money in accordance with client money rules to the clients or other persons who are entitled to payment under client money claims.

(4) A person who submits a client money claim after the bar date, but before the return of client money after that date, must, so far as is reasonably practicable, be included within the distribution of client money under paragraph (3).

(5) When determining the amount to be distributed under paragraph (3), the administrator must make allowance for the entitlement to the return of client money, by way of a subsequent distribution from the client money pool, of persons who have neither made a client money claim nor received any payment under a previous distribution of client money.

(6) Where the administrator has returned client money after the bar date, no payment or part of any payment made to any person under the distribution may be recovered for the purpose of meeting a late claim.

(7) The restriction in paragraph (6) does not apply where—

(a) client money was returned to a person by the administrator in bad faith in which that person was complicit; or

(b) a person to whom client money was returned is later found to have made a false claim to the money.

(8) Where the administrator determines that a client or other person who makes a late claim would have participated in the distribution of client money under paragraph (3) if the claim had been submitted before the return of client money after the bar date, the administrator must include the claimant within a subsequent distribution from the client money pool.

(9) In this regulation—

"bar date" means a date by which clients are invited to submit client money claims for the purposes of this regulation;

"client money claims" are claims for the return of client money which has been pooled in accordance with client money rules; and

"late claim" means a client money claim received after the bar date other than a claim received after that date from a person who is included within the distribution of client money under paragraph (3).]

NOTES

Commencement: 6 April 2017.

Inserted, together with regs 12B–12F, by the Investment Bank (Amendment of Definition) and Special Administration (Amendment) Regulations 2017, SI 2017/443, regs 4, 12, as from 6 April 2017, except in relation to an investment bank which is in special administration on that date (see further reg 17 of the 2017 Regulations at **[7.2048]**).

[7.1683]

[12B Objectives 1 and 3—client assets (other than client money) which the administrator is unable to return to clients

(1) This regulation applies where the administrator, after setting a soft bar date, includes in the distribution plan provision for the option of setting a hard bar date.

(2) If the administrator thinks it necessary in order to expedite the return of client assets, the administrator may by a hard bar date notice set a hard bar date.

(3) The administrator may not set a hard bar date without the approval of the court given on application by the administrator.

(4) A late claim of a type described in regulation 11(1) which is submitted in response to the setting of a bar date under that regulation on or after the date on which the administrator sets a hard bar date is to be treated as a client asset claim.

(5) Where the administrator sets a hard bar date, the administrator, after that date—

(a) must return client assets to eligible claimants;

(b) may dispose of all client assets which the investment bank still holds after the return of client assets to any eligible claimants ("residual assets"); and

(c) must transfer the proceeds of any disposal of residual assets to the investment bank's own bank accounts.

(6) A person who acquires client assets on a disposal of residual assets acquires good title to them as against all clients.

(7) Where the administrator receives a client asset claim after the hard bar date ("late claim") and—

(a) the administrator has not made any arrangements for the disposal of the residual assets, or

(b) such arrangements as the administrator has made for their disposal do not prevent the administrator from returning them,

the administrator must meet the late claim out of the residual assets.

(8) Where the administrator has returned client assets after setting a hard bar date and then receives a late claim in respect of assets that have been returned—

(a) none of those assets may be recovered for the purpose of meeting the late claim; and

(b) the person to whom the assets have been returned acquires good title to them as against the late-claiming claimant.

(9) The restrictions in paragraph (8) do not apply where—

(a) the client assets were returned to a person by the administrator in bad faith in which that person was complicit; or

(b) a person to whom client assets were returned is later found to have made a false claim to them.

(10) Where a disposal of residual assets prevents the administrator from meeting a late claim—

(a) the claim which the late-claiming claimant has against the investment bank in consequence of the disposal ranks as an unsecured claim; and

(b) the value of the unsecured claim is the value of the consideration paid to the administrator for the assets disposed of which would have been returned to that claimant if their client asset claim had been made before the hard bar date.

(11) No interest is payable on the debt for which a person makes an unsecured claim under paragraph (10).

(12) This regulation does not apply to client money.

(13) In this regulation—

"client asset claim" means a claim of a type described in regulation 11(1) which is submitted in response to the setting of a hard bar date;

"distribution plan" means the plan for the return of client assets which the administrator is required to draw up in accordance with insolvency rules after setting a soft bar date;

"eligible claimant" means—

(a) a person to whom the administrator has already returned client assets under regulation 11; or

(b) a person who—

(i) submits a client asset claim on or before the hard bar date; and

(ii) would have been eligible for a return of client assets under regulation 11 if the claim had been submitted in response to the setting of the soft bar date;

"hard bar date" means a final date (subject to provision for late claims in paragraphs (7) to (10)) for the submission of claims of a type described in regulation 11(1);

"hard bar date notice" means a notice which specifies a hard bar date and includes a statement that after the end of that day the administrator—

(a) may dispose of client assets still held by the investment bank after the administrator has returned client assets to any eligible claimants; and

(b) may, consequently, be unable to meet any further client asset claims; and

"soft bar date" means a bar date set under regulation 11.]

NOTES

Commencement: 6 April 2017.

Inserted, subject to transitional provisions, as noted to reg 12A at **[7.1682]**.

[7.1684]

[12C Objectives 1 and 3—client money which the administrator is unable to return to clients

(1) This regulation applies where the administrator, after setting a bar date under regulation 12A, thinks it is appropriate, in order to achieve Objective 1, to close the client money pool and treat any further claim for the return of client money as an unsecured claim.

(2) The administrator may by a hard bar date notice set a hard bar date.

(3) The administrator may not set a hard bar date without the approval of the court given on application by the administrator.

(4) Where the administrator sets a hard bar date, the administrator may not meet any final money claim received after the hard bar date.

(5) A final money claim received by the administrator after the hard bar date ranks as an unsecured claim.

(6) No interest is payable on the debt for which a person makes such a claim, except interest on such part of the debt which remains after deduction of the total amount which the client would have received by way of a distribution from the client money pool if the final money claim had been received by the administrator on or before the hard bar date.

(7) In this regulation—

"final money claim" means a claim for the return of client money which is submitted in response to the setting of a hard bar date;

"eligible claimant" means a person—

(a) to whom the administrator has already made a distribution of client money without receiving a claim for the return of client money to that person;

(b) who has submitted a claim for the return of client money other than a final money claim; or

(c) who submits a final money claim on or before the hard bar date;

"hard bar date" means a final date (subject to paragraph (5)) for the submission of claims for the return of client money; and

"hard bar date notice" means a notice which specifies a hard bar date and includes a statement that after the end of that day the administrator—

(a) may, in accordance with client money rules, transfer to the investment bank's own bank accounts any balance of the client money pool which the investment bank holds after the return of client money to eligible claimants; and

(b) may not meet any further final money claims.]

NOTES

Commencement: 6 April 2017.

Inserted, subject to transitional provisions, as noted to reg 12A at **[7.1682]**.

[7.1685]

[12D Powers of the court on application to set a hard bar date

(1) On an application under regulation 12B(3) or 12C(3) for the approval of the court to set a hard bar date the court may—

(a) make an order approving the setting of a hard bar date;

(b) adjourn the hearing of the application conditionally or unconditionally; or

(c) make any other order that the court thinks appropriate.

(2) The court may make an order under paragraph (1)(a) only if—

(a) it is satisfied that the administrator has taken all reasonable measures to identify and contact persons who may be entitled to the return of client assets; and

(b) it considers that if a hard bar date is set there is no reasonable prospect—

(i) that the administrator will receive claims for the return of client assets after that date; and

(ii) in the case of an application under regulation 12B(3), that the administrator will receive claims of persons in relation to a security interest asserted over, or other entitlement to, client assets which are not client money.]

NOTES

Commencement: 6 April 2017.

Inserted, subject to transitional provisions, as noted to reg 12A at **[7.1682]**.

[7.1686]

[12E Bar date notices—procedural requirements

(1) The persons to whom a bar date notice must be given are—

(a) all clients of whose claim for the return of client assets the administrator is aware;

(b) all persons whom the administrator believes have a right to assert a security interest or other entitlement over the client assets;

(c) the FCA and, where the investment bank is a PRA-authorised person, the PRA; and

(b) in a special administration (bank administration) before the Bank of England has given an Objective A Achievement Notice, the Bank of England.

(2) Paragraph (1) does not apply in relation to any such person whom the administrator has no means of contacting.

(3) A bar date notice—

(a) must be advertised once in the Gazette; and

(b) may be advertised in such other manner as the administrator thinks fit.

(4) In advertising a bar date notice under paragraph (3), the administrator must aim to ensure that the notice comes to the attention of as many persons who are eligible to submit a claim for the return of client assets as the administrator considers practicable.

(5) In this regulation—

"Gazette" means—

(a) in England and Wales, the London Gazette;

(b) in Scotland, the Edinburgh Gazette; and

(c) in Northern Ireland, the Belfast Gazette;

"bar date notice" means a notice under regulation 12A(1) or a hard bar date notice under regulation 12B or 12C; and

"Objective A Achievement Notice" has the meaning given by paragraph 3(3) of Schedule 2.]

NOTES

Commencement: 6 April 2017.

Inserted, subject to transitional provisions, as noted to reg 12A at **[7.1682]**.

[7.1687]

[12F Costs of making a claim

(1) Unless the court orders otherwise, every person who submits a relevant claim bears the cost of making the claim, including costs incurred in providing documents or evidence or responding to requests for further information.

(2) "Relevant claim" means—

(a) a claim for the return of client assets which is submitted in response to the setting of a bar date under regulation 12A, 12B or 12C; or

(b) a claim in relation to a security interest asserted over, or other entitlement to, client assets, which is submitted in response to the setting of a bar date under regulation 12B.]

NOTES

Commencement: 6 April 2017.

Inserted, subject to transitional provisions, as noted to reg 12A at **[7.1682]**.

[7.1688]

13 Objective 2—engaging with market infrastructure bodies and the Authorities

(1) The administrator shall work with—

(a) a market infrastructure body to—

(i) facilitate the operation of that body's default rules or default arrangements,

(ii) resolve issues arising from the operation of those rules or arrangements, and

(iii) facilitate the [transfer,] settlement or prompt cancellation of non-settled market contracts or, as the case may be, of unsettled settlement instructions; and

(b) the Authorities, to facilitate any actions the Authorities propose to take to minimise the disruption of businesses and the markets as a consequence of a special administration order being made in respect of the investment bank.

(2) In paragraph (1), "work with" means to—

(a) comply, as soon as reasonably practicable, with a written request from such a body or from any of the Authorities for the provision of information or the production of documents (in hard copy or in electronic format) relating to the investment bank;

(b) allow that body or any of the Authorities, on reasonable request, access to the facilities, staff and premises of the investment bank for the purposes set out in paragraph (1),

but no action need be taken in accordance with this paragraph to the extent that, in the opinion of the administrator, such action would lead to a material reduction in the value of the property of the investment bank.

(3) In the event that the administrator receives a request under paragraph (2) from a market infrastructure body based overseas, no action needs to be taken in accordance with paragraph (2) if that request conflicts with a request from any of the Authorities.

(4) Where a market infrastructure body has made a request of the type referred to in paragraph (2), that body shall provide the administrator with such information as the administrator may reasonably require in pursuit of Objective 2.

(5) Under this regulation a person or body shall not be required to provide any information—

(a) which they would be entitled to refuse to provide on grounds of legal professional privilege in proceedings in the High Court or on grounds of confidentiality of communications in the Court of Session; or

(b) if such provision by the body holding it would be prohibited by or under any enactment.

(6) In this regulation—

"default arrangements" has the meaning set out in regulation 2(1) of the Financial Markets and Insolvency (Settlement Finality) Regulations 1999; and

"default rules" has the meaning set out in section 188 of the Companies Act 1989.

NOTES

Para (1): word in square brackets inserted by the Financial Services and Markets Act 2000 (Over the Counter Derivatives, Central Counterparties and Trade Repositories) Regulations 2013, SI 2013/504, reg 41(1), (3).

[7.1689]

14 Continuity of supply

(1) This regulation applies where, before the commencement of special administration, the investment bank had entered into arrangements with a supplier for the provision of a supply to the investment bank.

(2) After the commencement of special administration, the supplier—

(a) shall not terminate a supply unless—

(i) any charges in respect of the supply, being charges for a supply given after the commencement of special administration, remain unpaid for more than 28 days,

(ii) the administrator consents to the termination, or

(iii) the supplier has the permission of the court, which may be given if the supplier can show that the continued provision of the supply shall cause the supplier to suffer hardship; and

(b) shall not make it a condition of a supply, or do anything which has the effect of making it a condition of the giving of a supply, that any outstanding charges in respect of the supply, being charges for a supply given before the commencement of special administration, are paid.

(3) Where, before the commencement of special administration, a contractual right to terminate a supply has arisen but has not been exercised, then, for the purposes of this regulation, the commencement of special administration shall cause that right to lapse and the supply shall only be terminated if a ground in paragraph (2)(a) applies.

(4) Any provision in a contract between the investment bank and the supplier that purports to terminate the agreement if any action is taken to put the investment bank into special administration is void.

(5) Any expenses incurred by the investment bank on the provision of a supply after the commencement of special administration are to be treated as necessary disbursements in the course of the special administration.

(6) In this regulation—

"accredited network provider" means a person accredited with a relevant system who operates a secure data network through which the investment bank communicates with the relevant system;

"commencement of special administration" means the making of the special administration order;

"relevant system" has the meaning set out in regulation 2(1) of the Uncertificated Securities Regulations 2001;

"sponsoring system participant" has the meaning set out in regulation 3 of the Uncertificated Securities Regulations 2001 (in the definition of "system participant");

"supplier" means the person controlling the provision of a supply to the investment bank under a licence, sub-licence or other arrangement, and includes a company that is a group undertaking (within the meaning of section 1161(5) of the Companies Act 2006) in respect of the investment bank, but does not include market infrastructure bodies; and

"supply" means a supply of—

[(za) services relating to the safeguarding or administration of client assets;]

(a) computer hardware or software or other hardware used by the investment bank in connection with the trading of securities or derivatives;

(b) financial data;

(c) infrastructure permitting electronic communication services;

(d) data processing;

(e) secure data networks provided by an accredited network provider; or

(f) access to a relevant system by a sponsoring system participant,

but does not include any services provided for in the contract between the investment bank and the supplier beyond the provision of the supply.

NOTES

Para (6): para (za) of the definition "supply" was inserted by the Investment Bank (Amendment of Definition) and Special Administration (Amendment) Regulations 2017, SI 2017/443, regs 4, 13, as from 6 April 2017, except in relation to an investment bank which is in special administration on that date (see further reg 17 of the 2017 Regulations at **[7.2048]**).

[7.1690]

15 General powers, duties and effect

(1) Without prejudice to any specific powers conferred on an administrator by these Regulations, an administrator may do anything necessary or expedient for the pursuit of the special administration objectives.

(2) The administrator is an officer of the court.

(3) The following provisions of this regulation provide for—

(a) general powers and duties of administrators (by application of provisions about administrators in Schedule B1 administration); and

(b) the general process and effect of special administration (by application of provisions about Schedule B1 administration).

(4) The provisions of Schedule B1 and other provisions of the Insolvency Act set out in the Tables apply in relation to special administration as in relation to other insolvency proceedings with the modifications set out—

(a) in paragraph (5) (in respect of the provisions listed in Table 1);

(b) in paragraph (6) (in respect of the provisions listed in Table 2),

and any other modification specified in the Tables.

(5) The modifications in respect of the provisions referred to in Table 1 are that—

(a) a reference to the administrator is a reference to the administrator appointed under a special administration order;

(b) a reference to administration is a reference to special administration;

(c) a reference to an administration order is a reference to a special administration order;

(d) a reference to a company is a reference to an investment bank;

(e) a reference to the purpose of administration is a reference to the special administration objectives; and

(f) a reference to a provision of the Insolvency Act is a reference to that provision as applied by this regulation.

(6) The modifications in respect of the provisions referred to in Table 2 are that—

(a) a reference to the liquidator is a reference to the administrator appointed under a special administration order;

(b) a reference to winding up is a reference to special administration;

(c) a reference to winding up by the court is a reference to the imposition of special administration by order of the court;

(d) a reference to being wound up under Part 4 or 5 of the Insolvency Act is a reference to an investment bank being in special administration;

(e) a reference to the commencement of winding up is a reference to the commencement of special administration;

(f) a reference to going into liquidation is a reference to entering special administration;

(g) a reference to liquidation or to insolvent liquidation is a reference to special administration;

(h) a reference to a winding up order is a reference to a special administration order;

(i) [except where otherwise specified in Table 2,] a reference to a company is a reference to an investment bank; and

(j) a reference to a provision of the Insolvency Act is a reference to that provision as applied by this regulation.

[(7) In the Tables "Schedule 9 to the 2015 Act" means Schedule 9 to the Small Business, Enterprise and Employment Act 2015 (further amendments relating to the abolition of requirements to hold meetings: company insolvency).]

Table 1: Applied provisions: Schedule B1

Schedule B1	*Subject*	*Modification or comment*
Para 40(1)(a)	Dismissal of pending winding up petition	
Para 42	Moratorium on insolvency proceedings	Sub-paragraphs (4)(a) and (4)(aa) are not applied.
Para 43	Moratorium on other legal processes	
Para 44(1) and (5)	Interim moratorium	
Para 45	Publicity	
Para 46	Announcement of administrator's appointment	(a) In sub-paragraph (3)(a), in addition to obtaining the list of creditors, the administrator shall also obtain as complete a list as possible of the clients of the investment bank. (b) In sub-paragraph (3)(b), the administrator shall send a notice of their appointment to each client of whose claim and address the administrator is aware.

Table 1: Applied provisions: Schedule B1

Schedule B1	***Subject***	***Modification or comment***
		(c) Where the special administration application has not been made by the [FCA], notice of the administrator's appointment shall also be sent under sub-paragraph (5) to the [FCA]. [(ca) Where the special administration application relates to a PRA-authorised person and has not been made by the PRA, notice of the administrator's appointment shall also be sent under sub-paragraph (5) to the PRA.] (d) Sub-paragraphs (6)(b) and (c) are not applied.
Para 47	Statement of company's affairs	In sub-paragraph (2), the statement must also include particulars (to the extent prescribed) of the client assets held by the investment bank.
Para 48	Statement of company's affairs	
Para 49	Statement of proposals	*Paragraphs 49(1) to (3), 51, 53, 54 and 55 do not apply where the [FCA or, where relevant, the PRA] gives a direction under regulation 16 and the direction has not been withdrawn: see regulations 16–19.*
Para 49		(a) Sub-paragraph (2)(b) is not applied. [(aa) Ignore the amendment made by paragraph 10(2) of Schedule 9 to the 2015 Act.] (b) Under sub-paragraph (4), the administrator shall also send a copy of the statement of proposals to— (i) every client of whose claim the administrator is aware and has a means of contacting; and (ii) the [FCA and, where the investment bank concerned is a PRA-authorised person, the PRA]. (c) The administrator shall also give notice in the prescribed manner that the statement of proposals is to be provided free of charge to a market infrastructure body who applies in writing to a specified address.
Para 50	Creditors' meeting	[(za) Ignore the repeal of Para 50 by paragraph 10(3) of Schedule 9 to the 2015 Act.] (a) In sub-paragraph (1), the administrator shall also summon the clients referred to in paragraph 49(4) to the meeting of creditors and such clients shall be given the prescribed period of notice under sub-paragraph (1)(b). (b) The [FCA and, where the investment bank concerned is a PRA-authorised person, the PRA] may appoint a person to attend a meeting of creditors and make representations as to any matter for decision.
Para 51	Requirement for initial creditors' meeting	[(za) Ignore the amendments made by paragraph 10(4) and (5) of Schedule 9 to the 2015 Act.]

Part 7M Special Insolvency Regimes

Table 1: Applied provisions: Schedule B1

Schedule B1	*Subject*	*Modification or comment*
		(a) Each copy of an administrator's proposals sent to a client under paragraph 49 shall be accompanied by an invitation to the initial creditors' meeting. (b) The administrator's proposals sent to the [FCA and, where the investment bank concerned is a PRA-authorised person, the PRA] must also be accompanied by an invitation to the initial creditors' meeting.
Para 53	Business and result of initial creditors' meeting	[(za) Ignore the amendments made by paragraph 10(8) to (10) of Schedule 9 to the 2015 Act.] (a) Insolvency rules shall prescribe how clients shall vote at meetings of creditors. (b) Under sub-paragraph (2), if the [FCA] has not appointed a person to attend the meeting, the administrator must also report any decision taken to the [FCA].
		[(c) If the investment bank concerned is a PRA-authorised person, and if the PRA has not appointed a person to attend the meeting under sub-paragraph (2), the administrator must also report any decision taken to the PRA.]
Para 54	Revision of administrator's proposals	[(za) Ignore the amendments made by paragraph 10(11) to (16) of Schedule 9 to the 2015 Act.] (a) If the revision proposed by the administrator affects both creditors and clients, then every reference in paragraph 54 to creditors includes clients. (b) If the administrator thinks that the revision proposed only affects either creditors or clients, then this paragraph only applies to the affected party, however the party not affected must be informed of the revision in a manner prescribed in insolvency rules. (c) The [FCA and, where the investment bank concerned is a PRA-authorised person, the PRA] must be invited to the creditors' meeting mentioned in sub-paragraph (2)(a). (d) The statement of the proposed revision mentioned in sub-paragraph (2)(b) must also be sent to the [FCA and, where the investment bank concerned is a PRA-authorised person, the PRA].
Para 55	Failure to obtain approval of administrator's proposals	[(za) Ignore the amendment made by paragraph 10(17) of Schedule 9 to the 2015 Act.] (a) In making an order under sub-paragraph (2) the court must have regard to the special administration objectives. (b) Sub-paragraph (2)(d) is not applied.
Para 56	Further creditors' meetings	[(a) Ignore the amendments made by paragraph 10(18) to (20) of Schedule 9 to the 2015 Act.] [(b)] The [FCA and, where the investment bank concerned is a PRA-authorised person, the PRA] must be invited to any meeting summoned under this paragraph.

Table 1: Applied provisions: Schedule B1

Schedule B1	***Subject***	***Modification or comment***
Para 57	Creditors' committee	[(za) Ignore the amendment made by paragraph 10(21) of Schedule 9 to the 2015 Act.] (a) A creditors' committee can only be established by a creditors' meeting to which creditors and clients have both been given notice. (b) The [FCA and, where the investment bank concerned is a PRA-authorised person, the PRA] may appoint a person to attend a meeting of the creditors' committee and make representations as to any matter for decision. (c) Insolvency rules shall ensure that, where a meeting of creditors resolves to establish a creditors' committee, the makeup of the creditors' committee is a reflection of all parties with an interest in the achievement of the special administration objectives.
Para 58	Correspondence instead of creditors' meeting	[Para 58 applies as it applied before its repeal by paragraph 10(22) of Schedule 9 to the 2015 Act.]
Para 59	Functions of an administrator	
Para 60 (and Schedule 1 to the Insolvency Act)	General powers	*Certain powers in Schedule 4 of the Insolvency Act are also applied (see Table 2).*
Para 61	Directors	
Para 62	Power to call meetings	[(a) Ignore the amendment made by paragraph 10(23) of Schedule 9 to the 2015 Act.] [(b)] The administrator may also call a meeting of clients or contributories.
Para 63	Application to court for directions	
Para 64	Management powers	
Para 65	Distribution to creditors	Sub-paragraph (3) is not applied [in England and Wales].
Para 66	Payments	
Para 67	Property	
Para 68	Management	In this paragraph, references to proposals approved under paragraphs 53 or 54 include— (a) proposals agreed with the [FCA or, where relevant, the PRA] under regulations 17 or 18; or (b) proposals in respect of which the court has made an order dispensing with the need for agreement in accordance with those regulations, without need for approval.
Para 69	Agency	
Para 70	Floating charge	
Para 71	Fixed charge	
Para 72	Hire purchase property	
Para 73	Protection for secured or preferential creditors	Sub-paragraph (2)(d) is not applied.
Para 74	Challenge to administrator's conduct	[(za) Ignore the amendment made by paragraph 10(24) of Schedule 9 to the 2015 Act.]

Table 1: Applied provisions: Schedule B1

Schedule B1	*Subject*	*Modification or comment*
		(a) The [FCA and, where the investment bank concerned is a PRA-authorised person, the PRA] may also make an application under this paragraph on the grounds that— (i) the administrator is acting or has acted so as unfairly to harm the interests of some or all of the members, creditors or clients; or (ii) the administrator is proposing to act in a way which would unfairly harm the interests of some or all of the members, creditors or clients. (b) A client may also make an application under sub-paragraph (1) or (2). (c) Where the [FCA or the PRA] has given a direction under regulation 16 which has not been withdrawn, an order may not be made under this paragraph if it would impede or prevent compliance with the direction. (d) Any of the following persons may make an application under this paragraph on the grounds that the administrator is not taking any action in response to a request from that person under regulation 13(2) and that the person is of the opinion that the action requested would not lead to a material reduction in the value of the property of the investment bank— (i) the Bank of England, (ii) the Treasury, (iii) the [FCA or the PRA], or (iv) a market infrastructure body. [(e) FSCS may make an application under this paragraph on the grounds that the administrator is not performing the duties set out in regulation 10A as quickly or as efficiently as is reasonably practicable. (f) Any of the following persons may make an application under this paragraph on the grounds that the administrator has made, or proposes to make, a partial property transfer (within the meaning given in regulation 10B(13)) ("relevant transfer") in contravention of regulation 10E, 10F or 10G— (i) the Bank of England; (ii) the FCA; (iii) where the investment bank is a PRA-authorised person, the PRA. (g) Any person, other than the investment bank, who is party to an arrangement of a kind referred to in regulation 10E(1) or 10F(1) may make an application under this paragraph on the grounds that the administrator has made, or proposes to make, a relevant transfer in contravention of that regulation.

Table 1: Applied provisions: Schedule B1		
Schedule B1	***Subject***	***Modification or comment***
		(h) A recognised investment exchange, a recognised clearing house[, a recognised CSD] or any person, other than the investment bank, who is party to a market contract may make an application under this paragraph on the grounds that the administrator has made, or proposes to make, a relevant transfer in contravention of regulation 10G. (i) Where an application is made under this paragraph on the grounds that the administrator has made a relevant transfer in contravention of regulation 10G— (i) sub-paragraphs (3)(a), (d) and (e) and (4) are not applied; (ii) the court may make an order declaring that the transfer was made in contravention of the regulation concerned. (j) Where an application is made under this paragraph on the grounds that the administrator has made a relevant transfer in contravention of regulation 10E or 10F, the court may make such order as it thinks fit for restoring the position to what it would have been if the transfer had been made in contravention of the regulation concerned. (k) The FCA and, where the investment bank is a PRA-authorised person, the PRA may make an application under this paragraph on the grounds that the administrator has failed to carry out a client money reconciliation in accordance with regulation 10H(2) or to transfer an amount in accordance with regulation 10H(3) or (4).]
Para 75	Misfeasance	A client and the [FCA and, where the investment bank concerned is a PRA-authorised person, the PRA] shall be included in the list of persons who may make an application under sub-paragraph (2).
Para 79	Court ending administration on application of administrator	Sub-paragraph (2) is not applied. *See regulation 20*
Para 81	Court ending administration on application of a creditor	This paragraph is not applied where the administrator was appointed by the court on the application of the [FCA or the PRA] or the Secretary of State.
Para 84	Termination: no more assets for distribution	(a) The administrator shall only send a notice under sub-paragraph (1) if the investment bank no longer holds client assets. [(aa) Ignore the amendment made by paragraph 10(33) of Schedule 9 to the 2015 Act.] (b) In sub-paragraph (5), a copy of the notice should also be sent to every client of the investment bank of whom the administrator is aware and the [FCA and, where the investment bank concerned is a PRA-authorised person, the PRA]. *See regulation 21*
Para 85	Discharge of administration order	

Part 7M Special Insolvency Regimes

Table 1: Applied provisions: Schedule B1

Schedule B1	*Subject*	*Modification or comment*
Para 86	Notice to Companies Registrar at the end of administration	
Para 87	Resignation	(a) Where the administrator was appointed by the court on the application of the [FCA or the PRA] or the Secretary of State, the notice of the resignation given in accordance with sub-paragraph (2)(a) must be also given to the applicant. (b) Sub-paragraphs (2)(b) to (d) are not applied.
Para 88	Removal	
Para 89	Disqualification	(a) Where the administrator was appointed by the court on the application of the [FCA or the PRA] or the Secretary of State, the notice given in accordance with sub-paragraph (2)(a) must be also given to the applicant. (b) Sub-paragraphs (2)(b) to (d) are not applied.
Para 90	Replacement	The reference to paragraphs 91 to 95 is to paragraph 91.
Para 91	Replacement	The [FCA and, where the investment bank concerned is a PRA-authorised person, the PRA] is added to the list of persons who may make an application to appoint an administrator but to whom the restrictions in sub-paragraph (2) apply.
Para 98	Discharge	[(a) Ignore the amendment made by paragraph 10(38) of Schedule 9 to the 2015 Act.] [(b)] Sub-paragraphs (2)(b) [and (ba)] and (3) are not applied.
Para 99	Vacation of office: charges and liabilities	(a) In sub-paragraph (3), the former administrator's remuneration and expenses incurred in respect of the pursuit of Objective 1 will be charged on and payable out of the client assets. (b) In sub-paragraph (4)(b), the reference to any charge arising under sub-paragraph (3) does not include a charge on client assets.
Para 100	Joint administrators	
Para 101	Joint administrators	In sub-paragraph (3), the reference to paragraphs 87 to 99 is to paragraphs 87 to 91 and 98 to 99.
Para 102	Joint administrators	
Para 103	Joint administrators	(a) In sub-paragraph (2), the reference to paragraph 12(1)(a) to (e) is to regulation 5(1). (b) Sub-paragraphs (3) to (5) are not applied.
Para 104	Presumption of validity	
Para 105	Majority decision of directors	
Para 106 (and section 430 of and Schedule 10 to the Insolvency Act)	Fines	[(a) Ignore the amendments made by paragraph 11 of Schedule 9 to the 2015 Act.] [(b)] Sub-paragraphs (2)(a), (2)(b) and (2)(l) to (2)(n) are not applied.

Table 1: Applied provisions: Schedule B1

Schedule B1	***Subject***	***Modification or comment***
Para 107	Extension of time limit	In considering an application under paragraph 107, the court must have regard to the special administration objectives.
Para 108	Extension of time limit	[(za) Ignore the amendments of Para 108 made by paragraph 10(39), (40), (42) and (43) of Schedule 9 to the 2015 Act.] (a) To obtain consent under this paragraph, the administrator must also obtain consent of those clients whose claims amount to more than 50% of the total amount of claims for client assets, disregarding the claims of those clients who were sent a copy of the statement of proposals but who did not respond to an invitation to give or withhold consent. (b) Sub-paragraph (3) is not applied.
Para 109	Extension of time limit	
Para 111	Interpretation	[(a) Ignore the amendment made by paragraph 10(44) of Schedule 9 to the 2015 Act.] [(b)] The definition of "administrator" and sub-paragraph (1A)(b) and (c) and sub-paragraph (1B) are not applied.
Paras 112–116	Scotland	

Table 2: Applied provisions: other provisions of the Insolvency Act

Insolvency Act	***Subject***	***Modification or comment***
Sections 74 and 76–83	Contributories	
Section 167 (and Schedule 4) [Section 176ZB	Powers of the liquidator Application of proceeds of office-holder claims]	(a) In [subsection (2) the reference] to "liquidation committee" is to "creditors' committee". (b) A client may also apply to the court under subsection (3). (c) In Schedule 4, paragraphs 4 to 10 and 12 shall not apply, and in paragraph 13, the reference to "winding up the company's affairs and distributing its assets" is to "pursuing the special administration objectives".
Section 168(4)	Discretion in managing and distributing assets	
Section 176	Preferential charges on goods distrained	
Section 176A	Unsecured creditors	
Section 178	Disclaimer of onerous property	
Section 179	Disclaimer of leaseholds	
Section 180	Land subject to rent charge	
Section 181	Disclaimer: powers of court	
Section 182	Powers of court (leaseholds)	
Section 183	Effect of execution or attachment (England and Wales)	Subsection (2)(a) is not applied.
Section 184	Duties of officers	In subsection (1), ignore the reference to a resolution having been passed for voluntary winding up.

Part 7M Special Insolvency Regimes

Table 2: Applied provisions: other provisions of the Insolvency Act		
Insolvency Act	*Subject*	*Modification or comment*
Section 185	Effect of diligence (Scotland)	In the application of section 37(1) of the Bankruptcy (Scotland) Act 1985 (c 66), the reference to an order of the court awarding winding up is a reference to the making of the special administration order.
Section 186	Rescission of contracts by the court	
Section 187	Power to make over assets to employees	
Section 193	Unclaimed dividends (Scotland)	
Section 194	Resolutions passed at adjourned meetings	[Section 194 applies as it applied before its repeal by paragraph 46 of Schedule 9 to the 2015 Act.]
Section 196	Judicial notice of court documents	
Section 197	Commission for receiving evidence	
Section 198	Court order for examination of persons in Scotland	
Section 199	Costs of application for leave to proceed (Scottish companies)	
Section 206	Fraud in anticipation of winding up	In subsection (1), omit the reference to passing a resolution for voluntary winding up.
Section 207	Transactions in fraud of creditors	In subsection (1), omit the reference to passing a resolution for voluntary winding up.
Section 208	Misconduct in course of winding up	[(a)] In subsection (1), omit "whether by the court or voluntarily". [(b) Ignore the amendment made by paragraph 52 of Schedule 9 to the 2015 Act.]
Section 209	Falsification of company's books	
Section 210	Material omissions from statement	(a) In subsection (1) omit "whether by the court or voluntarily". (b) In subsection (2), omit "or has passed a resolution for voluntary winding up".
Section 211	False representation to creditors	In subsection (1)— (a) omit "whether by the court or voluntarily"; and (b) a reference to the company's creditors includes a reference to clients of the investment bank.
Section 212	Summary remedy	
Section 213	Fraudulent trading	
Section 214	Wrongful trading	Subsection (6) is not applied.
Section 215	Proceedings under section 213 or 214	
Section 216	Restriction on re-use of company names	(a) The reference to "liquidating company" shall be to "company in special administration". (b) Subsections (7) and (8) are not applied.

Table 2: Applied provisions: other provisions of the Insolvency Act

Insolvency Act	*Subject*	*Modification or comment*
Section 217	Personal liability for debts following contravention of section 216	Subsection (6) is not applied.
Section 218	Prosecution of delinquent officers and members of company	(a) In subsection (3), ignore the first reference to the official receiver and treat the second reference as a reference to the Secretary of State. (b) In subsection (5) treat the reference to subsection (4) as a reference to subsection (3). (c) Subsections (4) and (6) are not applied.
Section 219	Obligations arising under section 218	Treat the reference to section 218(4) in subsection (1) as a reference to section 218(3).
Section 233	Utilities	
[Section 233A	Further protection of utilities]	
Section 234	Getting in the company's property	(a) Subsection (1) is not applied. (b) "Office holder" means the administrator.
Section 235	Co-operation with the administrator	(a) Subsections (1) and (4)(b) to (d) are not applied. (b) "Office holder" means the administrator.
Section 236	Inquiry into company's dealings	(a) Subsection (1) is not applied. (b) "Office holder" means the administrator.
Section 237	Enforcement by the court	
Section 238	Transactions at an undervalue (England and Wales)	
Section 239	Preferences (England and Wales)	
Section 240	Sections 238 and 239: relevant time	(a) In subsection (2)(a), the reference to being unable to pay its debts has the meaning given by regulation 2. (b) Sub-paragraphs (1)(d) and (3)(a) to (d) are not applied.
Section 241	Orders under sections 238 and 239	Subsections (3A) and (3B) are not applied.
Section 242	Gratuitous alienations (Scotland)	
Section 243	Unfair preferences (Scotland)	
Section 244	Extortionate credit transactions	
Section 245	Avoidance of floating charges	(a) In subsection (3)(c), the reference to— (i) administration application is to be read as an application for special administration, and (ii) administration order is to a special administration order. (b) In subsection (4)(a) and (b), the reference to being unable to pay its debts has the meaning given by regulation 2.

Part 7M Special Insolvency Regimes

Table 2: Applied provisions: other provisions of the Insolvency Act		
Insolvency Act	*Subject*	*Modification or comment*
		(c) Subsections (3)(d) and (5)(a) to (c) are not applied.
Section 246	Unenforceability of liens	(a) Subsection (1) is not applied. (b) "Office holder" means the administrator.
[Section 246ZD	Power to assign certain causes of action	(a) Subsection (1) is not applied. (b) "Office holder" means the administrator.]
Section 246A	Remote attendance at meetings	[(a) Ignore the amendments made by paragraph 54 of Schedule 9 to the 2015 Act.] [(b)] Treat every reference to creditors as including clients.
Section 246B	Use of websites	
Section 386 (and Schedule 6 as read with Schedule 4 to the Pensions Schemes Act 1993)	Preferential debts	
Section 387, subsections (1) and (3A).	"The relevant date"	Treat the reference to "administration" as a reference to special administration.
Section 389	Offence of acting without being qualified	(a) Treat the reference to acting as an insolvency practitioner as a reference to acting as the administrator. (b) [Subsection (2) is not applied].
[Sections 390 to 391T	Authorisation and regulation of insolvency practitioners	(a) In section 390 treat references to acting as an insolvency practitioner as references to acting as the administrator. (b) Read subsection (2) of that section (as so modified) as if after "authorised" there were inserted "to act as an insolvency practitioner". (c) An order under section 391 has effect in relation to any provision applied for the purposes of special administration. (d) In sections 390A, 390B(1) and (3), 391O(1)(b) and 391R(3)(b), in a reference to authorisation or permission to act as an insolvency practitioner in relation to (or only in relation to) companies the reference to companies has effect without the modification in paragraph (6)(i) of this regulation. (e) In sections 391Q(2)(b) and 391S(3)(e) the reference to a company has effect without the modification in paragraph (6)(i) of this regulation.]
Section 411	Insolvency rules	The reference in subsections (1A), (2C) and (3) to Part 2 of the Banking Act 2009 includes a reference to these Regulations.
Section 414	Fees orders	(a) The reference in subsection (1) to "Parts I to VII of this Act" includes these Regulations. (b) Ignore the reference to the official receiver.
Section 423	Transactions defrauding creditors	Subsection (4) is not applied.
Sections 424 and 425	Transactions defrauding creditors	
Section 426	Co-operation between courts	References to "insolvency law" includes provisions made by or under these Regulations.

Table 2: Applied provisions: other provisions of the Insolvency Act		
Insolvency Act	***Subject***	***Modification or comment***
Sections 430 and 431 (and Schedule 10)	Offences	
Section 432	Offences by bodies corporate	In subsection (4) ignore all the provisions of the Insolvency Act listed there except for sections 206 to 211.
Section 433	Statements: admissibility	In subsection (1)(a), a statement of affairs prepared "for the purposes of any provision of this Act" includes any statement made for the purposes of a provision of that Act as applied by these Regulations.
Sections 434B–434D	Supplementary provisions	[Ignore the amendments of section 434B made by paragraph 57 of Schedule 9 to the 2015 Act.]

NOTES

Para (6): words in square brackets in sub-para (i) inserted by the Deregulation Act 2015, the Small Business, Enterprise and Employment Act 2015 and the Insolvency (Amendment) Act (Northern Ireland) 2016 (Consequential Amendments and Transitional Provisions) Regulations 2017, SI 2017/400, reg 10(1), (3).

Para (7): inserted by the Small Business, Enterprise and Employment Act 2015 (Consequential Amendments, Savings and Transitional Provisions) Regulations 2018, SI 2018/208, reg 13(1), (2).

Table 1 is amended as follows:

In the second entry relating to para 49, para (aa) was inserted by SI 2018/208, reg 13(1), (3)(a).

In the entry relating to para 50, para (za) was inserted by SI 2018/208, reg 13(1), (3)(b).

In the entry relating to para 51, para (za) was inserted by SI 2018/208, reg 13(1), (3)(c).

In the entry relating to para 53, para (za) was inserted by SI 2018/208, reg 13(1), (3)(d).

In the entry relating to para 54, para (za) was inserted by SI 2018/208, reg 13(1), (3)(e).

In the entry relating to para 55, para (za) was inserted by SI 2018/208, reg 13(1), (3)(f).

In the entry relating to para 56, para (a) was inserted, and para (b) was designated as such, by SI 2018/208, reg 13(1), (3)(g).

In the entry relating to para 57, para (za) was inserted by SI 2018/208, reg 13(1), (3)(h).

In the entry relating to para 58, the words in square brackets were inserted by SI 2018/208, reg 13(1), (3)(i).

In the entry relating to para 62, para (a) was inserted, and para (b) was designated as such, by SI 2018/208, reg 13(1), (3)(j).

In the entry relating to para 65, the words "in England and Wales" in square brackets were inserted by SI 2017/400, reg 10(1), (4)(a).

In the entry relating to para 74, para (za) was inserted by SI 2018/208, reg 13(1), (3)(k); paras (e)–(k) were inserted by the Investment Bank (Amendment of Definition) and Special Administration (Amendment) Regulations 2017, SI 2017/443, regs 4, 14, as from 6 April 2017, except in relation to an investment bank which is in special administration on that date (see further reg 17 of the 2017 Regulations at **[7.2048]**]); the words ", a recognised CSD" in sub-para (h) were inserted by the Central Securities Depositories Regulations 2017, SI 2017/1064, reg 10, Schedule, para 36(1), (4) (for transitional provisions and savings see regs 6–9 of the 2017 Regulations).

In the entry relating to para 84, para (aa) was inserted by SI 2018/208, reg 13(1), (3)(l).

In the entry relating to para 98, para (a) was inserted, and para (b) was designated as such, by SI 2018/208, reg 13(1), (3)(m). The words "and (ba)" in square brackets were inserted by SI 2017/400, reg 10(1), (4)(b).

In the entry relating to para 106, para (a) was inserted, and para (b) was designated as such, by SI 2018/208, reg 13(1), (3)(n).

In the entry relating to para 108, para (za) was inserted by SI 2018/208, reg 13(1), (3)(o).

In the entry relating to para 111, para (a) was inserted, and para (b) was designated as such, by SI 2018/208, reg 13(1), (3)(p).

All other words in square brackets in Table 1 were substituted or inserted by the Financial Services Act 2012 (Consequential Amendments and Transitional Provisions) Order 2013, SI 2013/472, art 3, Sch 2, para 198(i).

Table 2 is amended as follows:

The words in square brackets in the entries relating to section 167 and section 389 were inserted by SI 2017/400, reg 10(1), (5)(a), (d).

The entries relating to section 176ZB and section 246ZD were inserted by SI 2017/400, reg 10(1), (5)(b), (c).

The words in square brackets in the entry relating to section 194 were inserted by SI 2018/208, reg 13(1), (4)(a).

In the entry relating to section 208, para (a) was designated as such and para (b) was inserted, by SI 2018/208, reg 13(1), (4)(b).

The entry relating to section 233A was inserted by the Insolvency (Protection of Essential Supplies) Order 2015, SI 2015/989, art 6, Schedule, para 5.

In the entry relating to section 246A, para (a) was inserted, and para (b) was designated as such, by SI 2018/208, reg 13(1), (4)(c).

The entries relating to sections 390–391T were substituted (for the original entries relating to section 390 and section 391) by SI 2017/400, reg 10(1), (5)(e) (subject to transitional provisions as noted to the Banking Act 2009, s 103 at **[7.40]**).

The words in square brackets in the entries relating to sections 434B–434D were inserted by SI 2018/208, reg 13(1), (4)(d).

[7.1691]

16 [Appropriate regulator] direction

(1) The [appropriate regulator] may direct the administrator to prioritise one or more special administration objectives.

(2) A direction under paragraph (1) may only be given if [that regulator] is satisfied that the giving of the direction is necessary, having regard to the public interest in—

(a) the stability of the financial systems of the United Kingdom; or

(b) the maintenance of public confidence in the stability of the financial markets of the United Kingdom.

(3) A direction under paragraph (1) must be given in writing and should set out reasons for giving the direction.

(4) Before giving such a direction the [appropriate regulator] must consult the Treasury and the Bank of England.

[(4A) Where the investment bank concerned is a PRA-authorised person, the appropriate regulator must also consult the other regulator before giving such a direction.]

(5) If the [appropriate regulator] thinks that the circumstances that gave rise to the need for it to give a direction have passed, it shall withdraw its direction.

(6) Paragraphs 49(1) to (3), 51, 53, 54 and 55 of Schedule B1 (as applied by regulation 15) shall not apply where the [appropriate regulator] has given a direction under this regulation and the direction has not been withdrawn.

[(7) In this regulation, "appropriate regulator" means—

(a) in relation to an investment bank which is a PRA-authorised person, the FCA or the PRA;

(b) in any other case, the FCA.]

NOTES

Paras (4A), (7) were inserted, and the other words in square brackets were substituted, by the Financial Services Act 2012 (Consequential Amendments and Transitional Provisions) Order 2013, SI 2013/472, art 3, Sch 2, para 198(j), subject to a transitional provision in para 199 set out at **[7.1662]**.

[7.1692]

17 Administrator's proposals in the event of [appropriate regulator] direction

(1) Where the [FCA or the PRA] has given a direction under regulation 16, the administrator shall make a statement setting out proposals for achieving the special administration objectives in accordance with the . . . direction.

(2) The statement under paragraph (1) must deal with such matters as may be prescribed and may include—

(a) a proposal for a voluntary arrangement under Part 1 of the Insolvency Act (although this regulation is without prejudice to section 4(3) of that Act); or

(b) a proposal for a compromise or arrangement to be sanctioned under Part 26 of the Companies Act 2006 (arrangements and reconstructions).

(3) The statement shall be agreed with [the regulator which has given the direction].

(4) If the administrator is unable to agree the statement with [the regulator which has given the direction], the administrator may apply to the court for directions under paragraph 63 of Schedule B1 (as applied by regulation 15).

(5) Following an application under sub-paragraph (4), the court may—

(a) make an order dispensing with the need for agreement;

(b) adjourn the hearing conditionally or unconditionally; or

(c) make any other order that the court thinks appropriate.

(6) The court may make an order under sub-paragraph (5)(a) only if it considers that the proposals set out in the statement are reasonably likely to ensure that the administrator acts in accordance with the . . . direction.

(7) Where the court makes an order, the administrator shall as soon as possible send a copy of the order to the registrar of companies.

(8) After—

(a) the statement has been agreed with [the regulator which has given the direction]; or

(b) the court has made an order dispensing with the need for agreement,

paragraph 49(4) to (8) of Schedule B1 (as applied by regulation 15) shall then apply to the statement, but the administrator need not send [the regulator which has given the direction] a copy of the statement of proposals.

(9) Where, before the [FCA or the PRA] gives its direction under regulation 16, a meeting of creditors has approved the statement of proposals in accordance with paragraph 53 of Schedule B1 (as applied by regulation 15), that statement of proposals shall be ignored for the purposes of regulation 16, this regulation and paragraph 68 of Schedule B1 (as applied by regulation 15).

NOTES

Words in square brackets substituted, and words omitted revoked, by the Financial Services Act 2012 (Consequential Amendments and Transitional Provisions) Order 2013, SI 2013/472, art 3, Sch 2, para 198(k), subject to a transitional provision in para 199 set out at **[7.1662]**.

[7.1693]

18 Revision of proposals in the event of [appropriate regulator] direction

(1) This regulation applies where—

(a) the administrator's statement of proposals under regulation 17 has been agreed with [the regulator which gave the direction under regulation 16] (or the court has made an order dispensing with the need for agreement);

(b) the administrator proposes a revision to the proposals;

(c) the administrator thinks the revision is substantial; and
(d) [that regulator] has not withdrawn its direction given under regulation 16.

(2) The administrator shall agree the revised statement with [that regulator].

(3) Regulation 17(4) to (7) shall apply where the administrator is unable to agree the revised statement with [that regulator].

(4) After the revised statement has been agreed with [that regulator] (or the court has made an order dispensing with the need for agreement) the administrator shall send the revised statement to—
(a) every creditor of the investment bank of whose claim and address the administrator is aware;
(b) every client of the investment bank of whose claim the administrator is aware and has a means of contacting;
(c) every member of the investment bank of whose address the administrator is aware.

(5) The administrator shall be taken to have complied with paragraph (4)(c) if the administrator publishes a notice undertaking to provide a copy of the revised statement free of charge to any member of the investment bank who applies in writing to a specified address.

(6) A notice under paragraph (5) shall be published in the prescribed manner and within the prescribed period.

(7) The administrator shall send a copy of the revised statement to—
(a) the court; and
(b) the registrar of companies.

NOTES

Words in square brackets substituted by the Financial Services Act 2012 (Consequential Amendments and Transitional Provisions) Order 2013, SI 2013/472, art 3, Sch 2, para 198(l), subject to a transitional provision in para 199 set out at **[7.1662]**.

[7.1694]

19 [Appropriate regulator] direction withdrawn

(1) This regulation applies if, after the administrator's statement of proposals has been agreed with the [regulator which gave the direction under regulation 16] or the court has made an order dispensing with the need for agreement under regulation 17, the . . . direction is then withdrawn.

(2) If the administrator proposes a revision to the statement of proposals and the administrator thinks that the proposed revision is substantial, then paragraphs 54 and 55 of Schedule B1 (as applied by regulation 15) apply.

NOTES

Words in square brackets substituted by the Financial Services Act 2012 (Consequential Amendments and Transitional Provisions) Order 2013, SI 2013/472, art 3, Sch 2, para 198(m), subject to a transitional provision in para 199 set out at **[7.1662]**.

[7.1695]

[19A Responsibility for certain costs of the administration

(1) Where the administrator considers that relevant costs have been incurred in consequence of a failure by the investment bank to comply with client money rules or with any relevant requirement ("a default"), the administrator—
(a) must seek the agreement of the creditors' committee established under paragraph 57 of Schedule B1 (as applied by regulation 15) to the amount incurred in consequence of the default; or
(b) if there is no creditors' committee or the administrator is unable to agree that amount with the creditors' committee, must apply to the court for an order fixing the amount.

(2) On an application under paragraph (1)(b), the court may fix the amount incurred in consequence of the default or dismiss the application on the ground that there was no default or that no relevant costs have been incurred in consequence of the default.

(3) Paragraph (4) applies where the creditors' committee agree an amount incurred in consequence of the default or the court fixes an amount by order.

(4) Notwithstanding any provision in insolvency rules prescribing how the expenses of the special administration are to be paid, responsibility for the relevant amount is assigned to the investment bank, and accordingly that amount is to be paid out of the investment bank's assets.

(5) Where the investment bank's assets are insufficient to enable the relevant amount to be met out of those assets, paragraph (4) has effect only in relation to that part of the relevant amount which can be met out of those assets.

(6) In this regulation—
"relevant amount" means the amount of relevant costs incurred in consequence of the default as agreed by the creditors' committee or fixed by the court;
"relevant costs" means costs incurred by the administrator of applying the procedure set out in Schedule B1 (as applied by regulation 15 and as prescribed) for ascertaining particulars of the client assets held by the investment bank, and of taking custody and control and distributing those assets; and
"relevant requirement" means any requirement relating to holding client assets contained in—
(a) rules made under Part 9A of FSMA (rules and guidance) which make provision relating to the handling of client assets, other than client money, held by a person who is authorised for the purposes of FSMA;

(b) Commission Delegated Regulation (EU) No 231/2013 of 19th December 2012 supplementing Directive 2011/61/EU of the European Parliament and of the Council with regard to exemptions, general operating conditions, depositaries, leverage, transparency and supervision; or

(c) Commission Delegated Regulation (EU) 2016/438 of 17th December 2015 supplementing Directive 2009/65/EC of the European Parliament and of the Council with regard to obligations of depositaries.]

NOTES

Commencement: 6 April 2017.

Inserted by the Investment Bank (Amendment of Definition) and Special Administration (Amendment) Regulations 2017, SI 2017/443, regs 4, 15, as from 6 April 2017, except in relation to an investment bank which is in special administration on that date (see further reg 17 of the 2017 Regulations at **[7.2048]**).

[7.1696]

20 Successful rescue

(1) This regulation applies if the administrator has pursued the first part of Objective 3 (as set out in regulation 10(1)(c)(i)) and thinks that it has been sufficiently achieved.

(2) The administrator shall make an application under paragraph 79 of Schedule B1 (as applied by regulation 15).

(3) An administrator who makes an application in accordance with paragraph (2) must send a copy to the [FCA and, where the investment bank concerned is a PRA-authorised person, the PRA].

NOTES

Para (3): words in square brackets substituted by the Financial Services Act 2012 (Consequential Amendments and Transitional Provisions) Order 2013, SI 2013/472, art 3, Sch 2, para 198(n), subject to a transitional provision in para 199 set out at **[7.1662]**.

[7.1697]

21 Dissolution or voluntary arrangement

(1) This section applies if—

(a) the administrator believes that Objectives 1 and 2 have been sufficiently achieved, and

(b) the administrator pursues the second part of Objective 3 (as set out in regulation 10(1)(c)(ii)).

(2) The administrator may—

(a) give a notice which is to be treated as a notice under paragraph 84 of Schedule B1 (as applied by regulation 15); or

(b) make a proposal in accordance with Part 1 of the Insolvency Act (company voluntary arrangement).

(3) Part 1 of the Insolvency Act shall apply to a proposal made by an administrator with the following modifications.

(4) In section 3 (summoning of meetings), subsection (2) (and not (1)) applies.

(5) The action that may be taken by a court under section 5(3) (effect of approval) includes suspension of the special administration order.

[(5A) Sections 2 to 6 and 7 and Schedule A1 have effect without the amendments of those provisions made by paragraphs 2 to 9 of Schedule 9 to the Small Business, Enterprise and Employment Act 2015 (further amendments relating to the abolition of requirements to hold meetings: company voluntary arrangements).]

(6) On the termination of a company voluntary arrangement the administrator may apply to the court to lift the suspension of the special administration order.

(7) For the purposes of this regulation, references in Part 1 of the Insolvency Act to "administration" include special administration.

NOTES

Para (5A): inserted by the Small Business, Enterprise and Employment Act 2015 (Consequential Amendments, Savings and Transitional Provisions) Regulations 2018, SI 2018/208, reg 13(1), (5).

[7.1698]

22 Special administration order as an alternative order

(1) On a petition for a winding up order or an application for an administration order in respect of an investment bank the court may instead make a special administration order.

(2) Paragraph (1) is subject to regulation 3.

(3) A special administration order may be made under paragraph (1) only on the application of the [FCA or, where the investment bank concerned is a PRA-authorised person, the PRA].

NOTES

Para (3): words in square brackets substituted by the Financial Services Act 2012 (Consequential Amendments and Transitional Provisions) Order 2013, SI 2013/472, art 3, Sch 2, para 198(o), subject to a transitional provision in para 199 set out at **[7.1662]**.

[7.1699]
23 Disqualification of directors

(1) In the Disqualification Act—
- (a) a reference to liquidation includes a reference to special administration;
- (b) a reference to the winding up of a company includes a reference to an investment bank being subject to a special administration order;
- (c) a reference to becoming insolvent includes a reference to becoming subject to a special administration order; and
- (d) a reference to a liquidator includes a reference to an administrator.

(2) Section 6(2) is not applied.

[(3) For the purposes of the application of section 7A of the Disqualification Act (office-holder's report on conduct of directors) to an investment bank which is in special administration—
- (a) the "office-holder" is the administrator;
- (b) the "insolvency date" means the date on which the special administration order is made; and
- (c) subsections (9) to (11) are omitted.]

(4) In section 21 of the Disqualification Act (interaction with the Insolvency Act), the references to the provisions of the Insolvency Act include those provisions as applied by these Regulations.

NOTES

Para (3): substituted by the Deregulation Act 2015, the Small Business, Enterprise and Employment Act 2015 and the Insolvency (Amendment) Act (Northern Ireland) 2016 (Consequential Amendments and Transitional Provisions) Regulations 2017, SI 2017/400, reg 10(1), (6), as from 7 April 2017.

[7.1700]
24 Limited liability partnerships

Where an investment bank is formed as a limited liability partnership, Schedule 3 (application of these Regulations to limited liability partnerships) has effect.

[7.1701]
25 Partnerships

(1) Where an investment bank is formed as a partnership, Schedule 4 (application of these Regulations to partnerships) has effect.

(2) This regulation does not apply to investment banks formed as a partnership constituted under the law of Scotland.

[7.1702]
26 Northern Irish equivalent enactments

(1) In the application of these Regulations to Northern Ireland, a reference to an enactment is to be treated as a reference to the equivalent enactment having effect in relation to Northern Ireland ("equivalent Northern Ireland enactment").

(2) The table in Schedule 5 shows the enactments referred to in these Regulations together with the equivalent Northern Ireland enactments.

(3) Where these Regulations provide for an enactment to apply with an amendment or modification, the equivalent Northern Ireland enactment is to apply with an equivalent amendment or modification (with any necessary modification being made and subject to what is said in relation to that enactment in the third column of the table in Schedule 5).

[7.1703]
27 Modifications and consequential amendments to legislation

Schedule 6 (modifications and consequential amendments) applies as follows—
- (a) Parts 1 and 2 apply in relation to a case where an investment bank which is a company is in special administration; and
- (b) Part 3 makes amendments to legislation in consequence of these Regulations.

SCHEDULES

SCHEDULE 1
SPECIAL ADMINISTRATION (BANK INSOLVENCY)

Regulation 9

[7.1704]

1. This Schedule provides for a procedure known as special administration (bank insolvency) to be used as an alternative to bank insolvency (as set out in Part 2 of the Act) where the investment bank is a deposit-taking bank.

2. A special administration (bank insolvency) order is an order appointing a person as the administrator for the purpose of this Schedule.

3. A special administration (bank insolvency) order is to be treated as a special administration order and an administrator appointed under a special administration (bank insolvency) order is to be treated as if they were appointed under a special administration order for all purposes, save that—
- (a) the modifications set out in this Schedule shall apply; and

(b) in regulation 22, the Bank of England may also make an application under paragraph (1) and the [FCA or the PRA] can only make an application with the consent of the Bank of England.

4. (1) An administrator appointed under a special administration (bank insolvency) order has the following objectives—

(a) Objective A is to work with the FSCS so as to ensure that as soon as is reasonably practicable each eligible depositor—

(i) has the relevant account transferred to another financial institution, or

(ii) receives payments from (or on behalf of) the FSCS; and

(b) the special administration objectives as set out in regulation 10.

(2) Objective A takes precedence over the special administration objectives until a full payment resolution is passed (but the administrator is to begin working towards the special administration objectives immediately on appointment, in accordance with regulation 10).

(3) The administrator must not comply with a direction of the [FCA or the PRA] given under regulation 16 in a way which prejudices the achievement of Objective A.

5. (1) The provisions of the Insolvency Act as applied by regulation 15 shall apply to special administration (bank insolvency) subject to the following additional modifications to Schedule B1—

(a) the FSCS shall be appointed as a member of the creditors' committee referred to in paragraph 57 unless it informs the administrator that it does not wish to be appointed;

(b) the Objective A committee may also make an application under paragraph 74(2));

(c) disregard paragraph 81;

(d) in the application of paragraph 87, before the Objective A committee has passed a full payment resolution, the administrator may only resign with the consent of the Bank of England and the notice of resignation shall be copied to the Bank of England;

(e) before the Objective A committee has passed a full payment resolution, only the Bank of England or the Objective A committee may make an application to remove the administrator from office under paragraph 88;

(f) the notice given under paragraph 89(2)(a) must also be copied to the Bank of England;

(g) before the passing of the full payment resolution, paragraph 91 has effect as if it provided for the Bank of England to appoint a replacement administrator as soon as is reasonably practicable;

(h) the Bank of England may also make an application under paragraph 103(2); and

(i) a reference to a provisional liquidator is to a person appointed under section 135 of the Insolvency Act as applied by paragraph 8.

(2) If any application is made to the court under these Regulations (including under the Insolvency Act as applied by these Regulations) before the Objective A committee has passed a full payment resolution, the court, in giving directions, must have regard to the achievement of Objective A.

6. (1) The provisions of Part 2 of the Act (bank insolvency) set out in the Table apply in relation to special administration (bank insolvency) with the following modifications—

(a) the modifications set out in sub-paragraph (2); and

(b) any other modification specified in the Table.

(2) The modifications are that a reference to—

(a) a bank is to a deposit-taking bank;

(b) bank insolvency is to special administration (bank insolvency);

(c) a bank insolvency order is to a special administration (bank insolvency) order;

(d) the bank liquidator is to the administrator;

(e) Objective 1 in section 99 of the Act or Objective 1 is to Objective A;

(f) the liquidation committee is to the Objective A committee;

(g) rules made under section 411 of the Insolvency Act 1986 is to insolvency rules; and

(h) section 168(5) of the Insolvency Act is to paragraph 74(2) of Schedule B1 (as applied by regulation 15).

TABLE OF APPLIED PROVISIONS

Provision of Part 2 of the Act	*Subject*	*Modification or comment*
Section 94(2) to (4)	The order	
Section 95	Application	Subsection (1)(c) is not applied.
Section 96	Grounds for applying	
Section 97	Grounds for making	In making a special administration (bank insolvency) order, the court must also be satisfied that the company is an investment bank.
Section 98	Commencement	

Provision of Part 2 of the Act	***Subject***	***Modification or comment***
Section 100	Liquidation committee	(a) This committee is established only for the purpose of ensuring that the administrator works towards the achievement of Objective A. (b) Subsections (6) and (7) are not applied.
Section 101	Liquidation committee: supplemental	(a) In subsection (2) ignore the words from "While the liquidation" to "nominated replacements)". (b) The references in subsection (5)(b) to sections 168(3) or 169(2) of the Insolvency Act are to paragraph 63 of Schedule B1 (as applied by regulation 15). (c) On the passing of the full payment resolution, the Objective A committee ceases to exist but the FSCS shall have the right to be a member of the creditors' committee. (d) Subsections (7) to (9) are not applied
Section 102	Objective 1: (a) or (b)	(a) The references to "Objective 1 (a)" and to "Objective 1(b)" are to Objective A(a) and Objective A(b) respectively. (b) The reference to Objective 2 is a reference to the special administration objectives.
Section 123	Role of the FSCS	Ignore subsection (3).
Section 124	Transfer of accounts	

7. Section 120 of the Act is applied with the following modifications—
- (a) in subsection (7)(b), the reference to a bank insolvency order includes a special administration order;
- (b) in subsection (8), the reference to bank insolvency order includes a special administration order or a special administration (bank insolvency) order;
- (c) in subsection (10)(b), the reference to bank insolvency order includes a special administration order or a special administration (bank insolvency) order; and
- (d) in subsection (10)(c), the reference to bank insolvency order includes a special administration (bank insolvency) order.

8. (1) Section 135 of the Insolvency Act is applied with the following modifications where an application is made for a special administration (bank insolvency) order—
- (a) in subsection (1), the reference to the presentation of a winding up petition is to an application for a special administration (bank insolvency) order;
- (b) in subsection (2)—
  - (i) the reference to England and Wales includes Scotland,
  - (ii) the reference to a winding up order is to a special administration order,
  - (iii) "other fit person" means a person qualified to act as an insolvency practitioner [in relation to the investment bank] and who consents to act, and
  - (iv) ignore the reference to the official receiver; and
- (c) subsection (3) is not applied.

(2) A person appointed under section 135 (as applied by this paragraph)—
- (a) must not pay dividends to creditors;
- (b) may only be removed by order of the court; and
- (c) shall vacate office if they cease to be qualified to act as a insolvency practitioner [in relation to the investment bank].

(3) The appointment of the person appointed under section 135 (as applied by this paragraph) lapses on the appointment of an administrator under a special administration (bank insolvency) order.

9. In this Schedule—
"eligible depositor" has the meaning set out in section 93(3) of the Act;

Part 7M Special Insolvency Regimes

"full payment resolution" has the meaning set out in section 100(5) of the Act as applied by paragraph 6;

"Objective A" has the meaning set out in paragraph 4; and

"Objective A committee" means the committee set up to oversee the achievement of Objective A in paragraph 4, (see paragraph 6(2) and the modification to section 100 of the Act in paragraph 6).

NOTES

Paras 3, 4: words in square brackets substituted by the Financial Services Act 2012 (Consequential Amendments and Transitional Provisions) Order 2013, SI 2013/472, art 3, Sch 2, para 198(p), subject to a transitional provision in para 199 set out at **[7.1662]**.

Para 8: words in square brackets inserted by the Deregulation Act 2015, the Small Business, Enterprise and Employment Act 2015 and the Insolvency (Amendment) Act (Northern Ireland) 2016 (Consequential Amendments and Transitional Provisions) Regulations 2017, SI 2017/400, reg 10(1), (7).

SCHEDULE 2
SPECIAL ADMINISTRATION (BANK ADMINISTRATION)

Regulation 9

General provisions

[7.1705]

1. This Schedule provides for a procedure known as special administration (bank administration) to be used as an alternative to bank administration (as set out in Part 3 of the Act) where part of the business of the [investment] bank is sold to a commercial purchaser in accordance with section 11 of the Act, or transferred to a bridge bank in accordance with section 12 (and it can also be used in certain cases of multiple transfers under Part 1 of the Act).

2. A special administration (bank administration) order is an order appointing a person as an administrator for the purposes of this Schedule.

3. (1) An administrator appointed under a special administration (bank administration) order has the following objectives—

(a) Objective A: to provide support for a private sector purchaser or bridge bank (see section 138 of the Act as applied by paragraph 6), and

(b) the special administration objectives as set out in regulation 10.

(2) Objective A takes precedence over the special administration objectives until the Bank of England notifies the administrator that the residual bank is no longer required in connection with the private sector purchaser or bridge bank, but the administrator is to begin working on the special administration objectives immediately on appointment in accordance with regulation 10.

(3) A notice under sub-paragraph (2) is referred to as an "Objective A Achievement Notice".

(4) The administrator must not comply with a direction of the [FCA or the PRA] given under regulation 16 in a way which prejudices the achievement of Objective A.

(5) In pursuing the special administration objectives following transfer to a bridge bank, the administrator may not realise any asset unless—

(a) the asset is on a list of realisable assets agreed between the administrator and the Bank of England; or

(b) the Bank of England has given an Objective A Achievement Notice.

(6) The reference to 'asset' in sub-paragraph (5) does not include client assets.

4. An administrator appointed under a special administration (bank administration) order is to be treated as if they were appointed under a special administration order subject to any modification made by this Schedule.

5. A special administration (bank administration) order is to be treated for all purposes as a special administration order save that—

(a) regulations 20 and 21 do not apply;

(b) regulation 15 does not apply except where otherwise stated;

(c) the modifications set out in this Schedule shall apply.

Application of Part 3 of the Act and the Insolvency Act

6. (1) The provisions of Part 3 of the Act (bank administration) set out in the Table apply in relation to a special administration (bank administration) with the following modifications—

(a) the modifications set out in sub-paragraph (2); and

(b) any other modification specified in the Table.

(2) The modifications are that a reference to—

(a) a bank is to a [investment] bank;

(b) bank administration is to special administration (bank administration);

(c) a bank administration order is to a special administration (bank administration) order;

(d) the bank administrator is to the administrator;

(e) Objective 1, or Objective 1 in section 137 or 138, is to Objective A in paragraph 3;

(f) the Objectives in section 137 is to Objective A and the special administration objectives;

(g) an Objective 1 Achievement Notice is to an Objective A Achievement Notice;

(h) an Objective 1 Interim Achievement Notice is to an Objective A Interim Achievement Notice (see section 150 of the Act as applied by the Table);

(i) "provisional liquidator" means a person appointed under section 135 of the Insolvency Act, as applied by this Schedule; and

(j) rules made under section 411 of the Insolvency Act 1986 is to insolvency rules.

(3) Where section 145 of the Act applies a provision of the Insolvency Act with a modification, that provision applies in relation to special administration (bank administration) with that modification unless otherwise stated in the Table.

TABLE OF APPLIED PROVISIONS

Provision of Part 3 of the Act	*Subject*	*Modification or comment*
Section 138	Objective 1: supporting private sector purchaser or bridge bank	
Section 139(2)	Objective A: duration	(a) The reference to section 145 is to that section as applied by this paragraph. (b) The reference to "notice under subsection (1) above" is to notice under paragraph 3(2).
Section 141(2) to (4)	Bank administration order	
Section 142	Application	
Section 143	Grounds for applying	
Section 144	Grounds for making	In making a special administration (bank administration) order, the court must also be satisfied that the company is an investment bank.
Section 145	General powers etc	(a) In subsection (1), the administrator may not rely on subsection (1) for the purpose of recovering property transferred by a property transfer instrument. (b) Subsection (3)(c), (5) and (6) are not applied.
Section 145	Table 1: Applied Provisions: Insolvency Act 1986, Schedule B1	In Table 1 after subsection (6)— (a) Paragraph 41 is not applied. (b) In paragraph 46— (i) in sub-paragraph (3)(a), in addition to obtaining the list of creditors, the administrator shall obtain as complete a list as possible of the clients of the investment bank, (ii) in sub-paragraph (3)(b), the administrator shall send a notice of their appointment to each client of whose claim and address the administrator is aware and to the [FCA and, where the investment bank concerned is a PRA-authorised person, the PRA]. (c) In paragraph 47, in sub-paragraph (2), the statement must also include particulars (to the extent prescribed) of the client assets held by the investment bank. (d) Paragraphs 49 to 54 are not applied: *see paragraphs 7 to 14 of this Schedule*. (e) Paragraph 55 is only applied where the Bank of England has given the Objective A Achievement Notice and— (i) sub-paragraph (1)(a) is not applied, (ii) in sub-paragraph (1)(b), the meeting referred to is one held under paragraph 12 of this Schedule,

Provision of Part 3 of the Act	*Subject*	*Modification or comment*
		(iii) in making an order under sub-paragraph (2) the court must have regard to the special administration objectives, and (iv) sub-paragraph (2)(d) is not applied. (f) In paragraph 56— (i) before the Bank of England has given an Objective A Achievement Notice, the administrator may comply with a request under sub-paragraph (1)(a) only if satisfied that it will not prejudice the achievement of Objective A, and (ii) the [FCA and, where the investment bank concerned is a PRA-authorised person, the PRA] must be invited to any meeting under this paragraph. (g) In paragraph 57— (i) a creditors' committee can only be established by a creditors' meeting of which creditors and clients have been both given notice, (ii) before the Bank of England has given an Objective A Achievement Notice, the creditors' committee, when exercising functions, must comply with any directions given to it by the Bank of England, (iii) the [FCA and, where the investment bank concerned is a PRA-authorised person, the PRA] may appoint a person to attend a meeting of the creditors' committee and make representations as to any matter for decision, (iv) the FSCS shall be appointed as a member of the creditors' committee unless it indicates to the administrator that it does not wish to be appointed, and (v) insolvency rules shall ensure that the make up of the creditors' committee is a reflection of all parties with an interest in the achievement of the special administration objectives. (h) In paragraph 60 (and Schedule 1) the exercise of powers is subject to the need to prioritise Objective A. (i) In paragraph 62, the administrator may also call a meeting of clients or contributories. (j) In paragraph 68— (i) sub-paragraph (1) includes proposals where a court order has been obtained dispensing with the need for approval in accordance with paragraph 8 or 13 of this Schedule 2, and (ii) the references to paragraphs 53 and 54 are to paragraphs 7 to 13 of this Schedule. (k) In paragraph 73— (i) the reference to the administrator's proposals under paragraph 49 is to the statement of proposals under paragraph 7 of this Schedule, and

Provision of Part 3 of the Act	*Subject*	*Modification or comment*
		(ii) sub-paragraph (2)(d) is not applied. (l) In paragraph 74— (i) the [FCA and, where the investment bank concerned is a PRA-authorised person, the PRA] may also make an application under sub-paragraph (1) on the grounds that— (aa) the administrator is acting or has acted so as unfairly to harm the interests of some or all of the members, creditors or clients, or (bb) the administrator is proposing to act in a way which would unfairly harm the interests of some or all of the members, creditors or clients, (ii) a client may also make an application under sub-paragraphs (1) and (2), but, until the Bank of England has given an Objective A Achievement Notice, an order may be made on the application of a client only if the court is satisfied that it would not prejudice pursuit of Objective A, (iii) where the [FCA or the PRA] has given a direction under regulation 16, an order may not be made on an application (by persons other than the Bank of England or the [FCA or the PRA]) under this paragraph before the direction is withdrawn if it would impede or prevent compliance with the direction, and (iv) any of the following persons may make an application under this paragraph on the grounds that the administrator is not taking any action in response to a request from that person under regulation 13(2) and that the person is of the opinion that the action requested would not lead to a material reduction in the value of the property of the investment bank— (i) the Bank of England, (ii) the Treasury, (iii) the [FCA and, where the investment bank concerned is a PRA-authorised person, the PRA], or (iv) a market infrastructure body. (m) A client and the [FCA and, where the investment bank concerned is a PRA-authorised person, the PRA] are included in the list of those persons who may make an application under paragraph 75(2). (n) Paragraph 79 is not applied: *see paragraphs 15 and 16 of this Schedule.* (o) In paragraph 91, after the Bank of England has given an Objective A Achievement Notice, the [FCA and, where the investment bank concerned is a PRA-authorised person, the PRA] may make an application to appoint an administrator but the restrictions in sub-paragraph (2) apply.

Provision of Part 3 of the Act	***Subject***	***Modification or comment***
		(p) Paragraph 96 is not applied. (q) In paragraph 98, sub-paragraph (2)(b) is not applied. (r) In paragraph 99— (i) in sub-paragraph (3), the former administrator's remuneration and expenses incurred in respect of the pursuit of Objective 1 will be charged on and payable out of client assets, and (ii) in sub-paragraph (4)(b), the reference to any charge arising under sub-paragraph (3) does not include a charge on client assets. (s) In paragraph 101, the reference to paragraphs 87 to 99 is to paragraphs 87 to 91, 98 and 99. (t) In paragraph 103(2), after the Bank of England has given the Objective A Achievement Notice, in sub-paragraph (2)(a), an application to the court under sub-paragraph (1) shall be made by a person listed in regulation 5(1). (u) In paragraph 106, sub-paragraphs (2)(a), (2)(b) and (2)(l) to (n) are not applied. (v) In paragraph 107, in considering an application the court must have regard to Objective A and the special administration objectives. (w) In paragraph 108— (i) the references in sub-paragraph (1) are to paragraphs 7 to 13 of this Schedule, and (ii) sub-paragraph (3) is not applied. (x) In paragraph 111, the definition of "administrator" and sub-paragraph (1A)(b) and (c) are not applied, and the reference in sub-paragraph (1) to paragraph 50 is to paragraph 10 of this Schedule.
Section 145	Table 2: Applied Provisions: other provisions of the Insolvency Act	In Table 2 after subsection (6)— (a) In section 135— (i) the reference in (e) to section 138(2)(a) is to that section as applied by this paragraph, and (ii) the reference in (f) to Objective 2 is to the special administration objectives. (b) In section 234— (i) subsection (1) is not applied, and (ii) "office holder" means the administrator. (c) In section 235— (i) subsections (1) and (4)(b) to (d) are not applied, and (ii) "office holder" means the administrator. (d) In section 236— (i) subsection (1) is not applied, and

Provision of Part 3 of the Act	*Subject*	*Modification or comment*
		(ii) "office holder" means the administrator. (e) In the application of section 240 to sections 238 and 239— (i) in subsection (2)(a), the reference to being unable to pay its debts has the meaning given by regulation 2, and (ii) subsections (1)(d) and (3)(b) to (e) are not applied. (f) In section 245— (i) in subsection (4)(a) the reference to being unable to pay its debts has the meaning given by regulation 2, and (ii) subsections (3)(d) and (5)(b) to (d) are not applied. (g) In section 246— (i) subsection (1) is not applied, and (ii) "office holder" means the administrator. (h) In section 387, subsections (2)(b), (2A), (3) and (4) to (6) are not applied. (i) In section 423, subsection (4) is not applied. (j) In section 432, in subsection (4) ignore all the provisions of the Insolvency Act listed there except for sections 206 to 211. (k) In section 433, subsection (4) is not applied.
Section 146	Status of administrator	
Section 147	Administrator's proposals	Section 147 is not applied.
Section 148	Sharing information	
Section 149	Multiple transfers – general application	
Section 150	Bridge bank to private sector purchaser	In subsection (5), the reference to section 139 is to paragraph 3(2) above.
Section 151	Property transfer from bridge bank	
Section 157	Other processes	The definition of an insolvency power includes regulation 5 (application for a special administration order).

(4) Where a provision of the Insolvency Act is set out in Table 2 in regulation 15(6), but is not applied by section 145 of the Act, that provision also applies to special administration (bank administration) with the modifications specified in that regulation and in sub-paragraph (2).

Statement of proposals

7. (1) In a special administration (bank administration), the proposals setting out how the purpose of the administration is to be achieved ("the statement") shall be drawn up as follows.

(2) The administrator must, as soon as is reasonably practicable after the [investment] bank enters special administration (bank administration), make a statement setting out proposals for achieving Objective A and the special administration objectives.

(3) In a case of special administration (bank administration) following transfer to a bridge bank, before making the statement the administrator must consult the Bank of England about the likelihood of a payment to the residual bank from a scheme established by a resolution fund order under section 49(3) of the Act.

8. (1) The statement is to be agreed with the Bank of England and, where [a regulator] has given a direction under regulation 16, with [that regulator].

Part 7M Special Insolvency Regimes

(2) If [neither regulator has] given a direction under regulation 16 and the administrator is unable to agree a statement with the Bank of England—

(a) the administrator may apply to the court for directions under paragraph 63 of Schedule B1 (as applied by section 145 of the Act and this Schedule); and

(b) the court may make any order it considers appropriate, including dispensing with the need for the Bank of England's agreement.

(3) If [a regulator has] given a direction under regulation 16 which has not been withdrawn and the administrator is unable to agree a statement with either the Bank of England [or that regulator], the administrator may apply to the court for directions under paragraph 63 of Schedule B1.

(4) Following an application under sub-paragraph (3), the court may—

(a) make an order dispensing with the need for agreement;

(b) adjourn the hearing conditionally or unconditionally; or

(c) make any other order that the court thinks appropriate.

(5) The court may make an order in sub-paragraph (4)(a) only if it considers that—

(i) the proposals set out in the statement are reasonably likely to ensure that the administrator acts in accordance with the . . . direction, and

(ii) the . . . direction is not likely to prejudice the achievement of Objective A.

(6) Where the court makes an order, the administrator shall as soon as reasonably practicable send the order to the registrar of companies and to such persons as may be prescribed.

9. (1) The administrator shall send the statement to—

(a) the [FCA and, where the investment bank concerned is a PRA-authorised person, the PRA];

(b) the FSCS;

(c) the registrar of companies;

(d) every creditor of the [investment] bank of whose claim and address the administrator is aware;

(e) every member of the [investment] bank of whose address the administrator is aware; and

(f) every client of the [investment bank of whose claim the administrator is aware and of whom the administrator has a means of contacting.

(2) The administrator shall comply with sub-paragraph (1) not later than 10 business days after—

(a) obtaining the agreement of the Bank of England (and where [a regulator] has given a direction, [that regulator]); or

(b) the court has made an order dispensing with the need for this agreement.

(3) The administrator shall be taken to comply with sub-paragraph (1)(d) if the administrator publishes in the prescribed manner a notice undertaking to provide a copy of the statement of proposals free of charge to any member of the [investment] bank who applies in writing to a specified address.

(4) The administrator shall also give notice in the prescribed manner that the statement of proposals is to be provided free of charge to a market infrastructure body which applies in writing to a specified address.

(5) Sub-paragraphs (7) and (8) of paragraph 49 of Schedule B1 apply with the following modifications—

(a) the reference in paragraph 49(7) to sub-paragraph (5) shall be a reference to sub-paragraph (2) of this paragraph;

(b) the reference to "this paragraph" in paragraph 49(8) means this paragraph;

(c) the reference to paragraph 107 is a reference to that paragraph as applied by section 145 of the Act and by paragraph 6(3).

Meeting of creditors and clients to approve statement

10. (1) This paragraph applies after the administrator has sent the statement of proposals to the persons listed in paragraph 9(1) unless (subject to sub-paragraph (6)) [a regulator] has given a direction under regulation 16 and the direction has not been withdrawn.

(2) Paragraph 50 of Schedule B1 applies save that—

(a) in sub-paragraph (1), the administrator shall invite the clients to the meeting of creditors and the clients shall be given the prescribed period of notice under sub-paragraph (1)(b); and

(b) the [FCA and, where the investment bank concerned is a PRA-authorised person, the PRA] may appoint a person to attend a meeting of creditors and make representations as to any matter for decision.

(3) Paragraph 51 of Schedule B1 applies save that—

(a) the reference to paragraph 49(4)(b) is to paragraph 9(1) of this Schedule; and

(b) each copy of the statement sent to a client or to [a regulator] under paragraph 9(1) of this Schedule must be accompanied by an invitation to the initial creditor's meeting.

(4) Paragraph 53 of Schedule B1 applies save that in sub-paragraph (2), if the [FCA or, where the investment bank concerned is a PRA-authorised person, the PRA] has not appointed a person to attend the meeting, the administrator must also report any decision taken to [that regulator].

(5) If the meeting of creditors is unable to approve the statement, the administrator may apply to court for an order dispensing with the need for the approval of the meeting of creditors, and paragraph 14 applies.

(6) Where, before [a regulator] gives a direction under regulation 16, a meeting of creditors has already approved the statement under this paragraph, when [that regulator] gives its direction a new statement shall be drawn up in accordance with paragraphs 7 to 9 to replace the statement that has already been approved.

[(7) For the purposes of this paragraph—

(a) paragraphs 51 and 53 of Schedule B1, as applied by this paragraph, have effect without the amendments of those paragraphs made by paragraph 10(4), (5) and (8) to (10) of Schedule 9 to the Small Business, Enterprise and Employment Act 2015 (further amendments relating to the abolition of requirements to hold meetings);

(b) ignore paragraph 10(3) of Schedule 9 to that Act (omission of paragraph 50 of Schedule B1).]

Revision to the statement of proposals (Objective A not yet achieved)

11. (1) This paragraph applies where—

(a) the administrator's statement has been—

(i) agreed with the Bank of England (or the court has made an order dispensing with the need for this agreement under paragraph 8(2)), and

(ii) approved by the meeting of creditors (or if the court has made an order dispensing with the need for this approval under paragraph 14);

(b) the administrator proposes a revision to the statement;

(c) the administrator thinks the revision is substantial; and

(d) the Bank of England has not given the Objective A Achievement Notice.

(2) The administrator shall agree the revised statement with the Bank of England and, where [a regulator] has given a direction and it has not been withdrawn, with [that regulator].

(3) Paragraph 8(2) to (6) shall apply where the administrator is unable to agree a statement with the Bank of England or (as the case may be) with the [FCA or, where relevant, the PRA].

(4) Once the revision has been approved by the Bank of England (and, as the case may be, with the [FCA or, where relevant, the PRA]) or, if the court has made an order dispensing with the need for those approvals, paragraph 54(2) to (5)(a) of Schedule B1 applies in respect of the revised statement save that—

(a) if the administrator thinks that the proposed revision affects both creditors and clients, then every reference in paragraph 54 to creditors includes clients;

(b) if the administrator thinks that the proposed revision only affects either creditors or clients, then paragraph 54 only applies in respect of the affected party,

and where sub-paragraph (b) applies, the party not affected must be informed of the proposed revision in a manner prescribed.

(5) In sub-paragraph (2) of paragraph 54, where [neither regulator has] given a direction under regulation 16, the [FCA and, where the investment bank concerned is a PRA-authorised person, the PRA shall] be sent a copy of the statement of the proposed revision and invited to appoint a representative to attend the creditors' meeting.

(6) The FSCS shall be sent a copy of the statement of the proposed revision.

(7) If the meeting of creditors is unable to approve the statement, the administrator may apply to court for an order dispensing with the need for the approval of the meeting of creditors, and paragraph 14 applies.

(8) Where the administrator makes an application under sub-paragraph (7), sub-paragraphs (6) and (7) of paragraph 54 shall apply.

[(9) In this paragraph a reference to paragraph 54 of Schedule B1 is a reference to that paragraph as applied by regulation 15.]

Revision to the statement of proposals (Objective A achieved and no [regulation 16] direction)

12. (1) This paragraph applies where—

(a) the events in paragraph 11(1)(a) to (c) have occurred;

(b) the Bank of England has given the Objective A Achievement Notice; and

(c) [no direction has been given] under regulation 16, or if it has, that direction has been withdrawn.

(2) Paragraph 54 of Schedule B1 applies in respect of that statement save that—

(a) if the administrator considers that the proposed revision affects both creditors and clients, then every reference in paragraph 54 to creditors includes clients;

(b) if the administrator considers that the proposed revision only affects either creditors or clients, then paragraph 54 only applies in respect of the affected party,

and where sub-paragraph (b) applies, the party not affected must be informed of the proposed revision in a manner prescribed.

(3) In sub-paragraph (2) of paragraph 54 the [FCA and, where the investment bank concerned is a PRA-authorised person, the PRA] shall be sent a copy of the statement of the proposed revision and be invited to appoint a representative to attend the creditors' meeting.

(4) The FSCS shall be sent a copy of the statement of the proposed revision.

[(5) In this paragraph a reference to paragraph 54 of Schedule B1 is a reference to that paragraph as applied by regulation 15.]

Revision to the statement of proposals (Objective A achieved and [regulation 16] direction has not been withdrawn)

13. (1) This paragraph applies where—

(a) the events in paragraph 11(1)(a) to (c) have occurred;

(b) the Bank of England has given the Objective A Achievement Notice; and

(c) [a regulator] has given a direction under regulation 16 and the direction has not been withdrawn.

(2) The administrator shall agree the revised statement with [that regulator].

(3) Paragraph 8(3) to (6) shall apply where the administrator is unable to agree a revision to the statement with [that regulator].

(4) After the revision to the statement has been agreed with [that regulator] or if the court makes an order under paragraph 8(4) dispensing with the need for agreement, the administrator shall send the revised statement to—

(a) every creditor of the investment bank of whose claim and address the administrator is aware;
(b) every client of the investment bank of whose claim the administrator is aware and has a means of contacting;
(c) every member of the investment bank of whose address the administrator is aware.

(5) The administrator shall be taken to have complied with paragraph (4)(c) if the administrator publishes a notice undertaking to provide a copy of the statement free of charge to any member of the investment bank who applies in writing to a specified address.

(6) A notice under paragraph (4) shall be published in the prescribed manner and within the prescribed period.

(7) The administrator shall send a copy of the revised statement to—

(a) the court; and
(b) the registrar of companies.

Powers of the court

14. (1) Where the administrator makes an application to the court under paragraph 10(5) or 11(7), the court may—

(a) make the order, if it considers that the proposals set out in the statement are likely to achieve Objective A whilst not preventing the achievement of the special administration objectives;
(b) adjourn the hearing conditionally or unconditionally; or
(c) make any other order that the court thinks appropriate.

(2) Where the court makes an order, the administrator shall as soon as reasonably practicable send the order to the registrar of companies and to such other persons as may be prescribed.

(3) Paragraph 54(7) of Schedule B1 applies as if the reference in that paragraph to sub-paragraph (6) were a reference to sub-paragraph (2) of this paragraph.

Ending of special administration (bank administration) (rescue)

15. (1) This regulation applies if—

(a) the Bank of England has given an Objective A Achievement Notice; and
(b) the administrator has pursued the first part of Objective 3 (as set out in regulation 10(1)(c)(i)) and thinks that it has been sufficiently achieved.

(2) The administrator shall make an application under paragraph 79 of Schedule B1 (as applied by regulation 15).

(3) An administrator who makes an application in accordance with sub-paragraph (2) must send a copy to the [FCA and, where the investment bank concerned is a PRA-authorised person, the PRA].

Ending of special administration (bank administration) (dissolution or voluntary arrangement

16. (1) This section applies if—

(a) the Bank of England has given an Objective A Achievement Notice;
(b) the administrator believes that Objectives 1 and 2 have been sufficiently achieved; and
(c) the administrator pursues the second part of Objective 3 (as set out in regulation 10(1)(c)(ii)).

(2) The administrator may—

(a) give a notice under paragraph 84 of Schedule B1 (as applied by regulation 15); or
(b) make a proposal in accordance with Part 1 of the Insolvency Act (company voluntary arrangement).

(3) Part 1 of the Insolvency Act shall apply to a proposal made by an administrator with the following modifications—

(a) in section 3 (summoning of meetings), subsection (2) (and not (1)) applies;
(b) the action that may be taken by a court under section 5(3) (effect of approval) includes suspension of the special administration order; . . .
[(ba) sections 2 to 6 and 7 and Schedule A1 have effect without the amendments of those provisions made by paragraphs 2 to 9 of Schedule 9 to the Small Business, Enterprise and Employment Act 2015 (further amendments relating to the abolition of requirements to hold meetings: company voluntary arrangements); and]
(c) on the termination of a company voluntary arrangement the administrator may apply to the court to lift the suspension of the special administration order.

Interpretation

17. In this Schedule—

"bridge bank" is a company wholly owned by the Bank of England to which all or part of the business of a [investment] bank may be transferred in accordance with section 12 of the Act;

"residual bank" means the non-sold or non-transferred part of the [investment] bank which remains after a power in section 11 (sale to private sector purchaser) or section 12 (transfer to bridge bank) of the Act has been exercised in respect of that bank;

"Objective A" has the meaning set out in paragraph 3(1)(a);

"Objective A Achievement Notice" has the meaning set out in paragraph 3(3);

"private sector purchaser" means a commercial purchaser to whom part of the business of the [investment] bank is sold to in accordance with section 11 of the Act; and

"statement" means the statement of proposals drawn up in accordance with paragraph 7.

NOTES

The word "investment" (in each place that it occurs) was substituted by the Financial Services Act 2012 (Consequential Amendments and Transitional Provisions) (No 3) Order 2013, SI 2013/1765, art 10.

Sub-paras 10(7), 11(9), and 12(5) were added and, in para 16, the word omitted from sub-para (3)(b) was revoked, and sub-para (3)(ba) was inserted, by the Small Business, Enterprise and Employment Act 2015 (Consequential Amendments, Savings and Transitional Provisions) Regulations 2018, SI 2018/208, reg 13(1), (6).

All other words in square brackets in paras 3, 6, 8–13, 15 were substituted, and the words omitted from para 8 were revoked, by the Financial Services Act 2012 (Consequential Amendments and Transitional Provisions) Order 2013, SI 2013/472, art 3, Sch 2, para 198(q), subject to a transitional provision in para 199 set out at **[7.1662]**.

SCHEDULE 3
APPLICATION OF THESE REGULATIONS TO LIMITED LIABILITY PARTNERSHIPS

Regulation 24

[7.1706]

1. In this Schedule, "the 2001 Regulations" means the Limited Liability Partnerships Regulations 2001.

2. These Regulations apply where the investment bank is a limited liability partnership subject to the following modifications.

3. (1) Those provisions of the Insolvency Act, as applied and modified by regulation 15 of these Regulations, shall apply in respect of an investment bank formed as a limited liability partnership subject to sub-paragraph (2).

(2) Those provisions of the Insolvency Act set out in the Table in sub-paragraph (3) shall also apply with the modifications set out in sub-paragraph (3).

(3) The modifications are—

(a) those contained in regulation 5(2) of the 2001 Regulations (not including those in regulation 5(2)(f)); and

(b) any other modification set out in the Table.

TABLE: APPLIED PROVISIONS OF THE INSOLVENCY ACT (GENERAL PROVISIONS AND SCHEDULE B1)

Provision of the Insolvency Act	*Subject*	*Modification or comment*
Section 74	Liability as contributories of present and past members	The following is substituted for section 74— "74 (1) This section applies when a limited liability partnership goes into special administration, every present and past member of the limited liability partnership is liable to contribute to its assets as follows. (2) Where a member has agreed with the other members or with the limited liability partnership, that that member be liable to contribute to the assets of the limited liability partnership in the event that that body goes into liquidation or special administration, that member is liable, to the extent that they have so agreed, to contribute— (a) to its assets to any amount sufficient for payment of its debts and liabilities; (b) to the expenses of the special administration;

Part 7M Special Insolvency Regimes

Provision of the Insolvency Act	*Subject*	*Modification or comment*
		(c) for the adjustment of the rights of the contributories among themselves. (3) A past member shall only be liable under this section if the obligation arising from such agreement in subsection (2) survived them ceasing to be a member of the limited liability partnership.".
Sections 76–78	Contributories	These sections are not applied.
Section 79	Meaning of "contributory"	(a) In subsection (1) for "every person" substitute— "every past and present member of the limited liability partnership". (b) At the end of subsection (2), insert "or section 214A (adjustment of withdrawals)". (c) Subsection (3) is not applied.
Section 83	Companies registered under the Companies Act Part XXII, Chapter II	Section 83 is not applied.
Section 183	Effect of execution or attachment	Subsection (2)(a) is not applied.
Section 187	Power to make over assets to employees	Section 187 is not applied.
Section 194	Resolutions passed at meetings	After "contributories" insert "or of the members of a limited liability partnership".
Section 214	Wrongful trading	In subsection (2), omit from "but the court shall not" to the end of the subsection.
After section 214	Adjustment of withdrawals	Insert— "214A (1) This section has effect in relation to a person, "P", who is or has been a member of a limited liability partnership where, in the course of the special administration of that limited liability partnership, it appears that subsection (2) of this section applies in relation to P. (2) This subsection applies in relation to P if— (a) within the period of two years ending with the commencement of the special administration, P was a member of the limited liability partnership who withdrew property of the limited liability partnership, whether in the form of a share of profits, salary, repayment of or payment of interest on a loan to the limited liability partnership or any other withdrawal of property; and (b) it is proved by the administrator to the satisfaction of the court that at the time of the withdrawal P knew or had reasonable ground for believing that the limited liability partnership—

Provision of the Insolvency Act	***Subject***	***Modification or comment***
		(i) was at the time of the withdrawal unable to pay its debts, or (ii) would become so unable to pay its debts after the assets of the limited liability partnership had been depleted by that withdrawal taken together with all other withdrawals (if any) made by any members contemporaneously with that withdrawal or in contemplation when that withdrawal was made. (3) Where this section has effect in relation to P, the court, on the application of the administrator, may declare that P is to be liable to make such contribution (if any) to the limited liability partnership's assets as the court thinks proper. (4) The court shall not make a declaration in relation to P the amount of which exceeds the aggregate of the amounts or values of all the withdrawals referred to in subsection (2) made by P within the period of two years referred to in that subsection. (5) The court shall not make a declaration under this section with respect to P unless P knew or ought to have concluded that after each withdrawal referred to in subsection (2) there was no reasonable prospect that the limited liability partnership would avoid going into an insolvency procedure under the Insolvency Act or special administration. (6) For the purposes of subsection (5) the facts which P ought to know or ascertain and the conclusions which P ought to reach are those which would be known, ascertained, or reached by a reasonably diligent person having both: (a) the general knowledge, skill and experience that may reasonably be expected of a person carrying out the same functions as are carried out by P in relation to the limited liability partnership; and (b) the general knowledge, skill and experience that P has. (8) In this section "member" includes a shadow member. (9) This section is without prejudice to section 214.".
Section 215	Proceedings under section 213 or 214	(a) In subsection (1) omit the word "or" between the words "213" and "214" and insert after "214" "or 214A".

Part 7M Special Insolvency Regimes

Provision of the Insolvency Act	*Subject*	*Modification or comment*
		(b) In subsection (2) substitute "any of those sections" for "either section". (c) In subsection (4) substitute "any of those sections" for "either section". (d) In subsection (5) substitute "sections 213, 214 or 214A" for "sections 213 and 214".
Section 218	Prosecution of delinquent officers and members of company	(a) In subsection (1), for "officer, or any member, of the company" substitute "member of the limited liability partnership". (b) In subsection (3) for "officer of the company, or any member of it," substitute "member of the limited liability partnership".
Section 386 of and Schedule 6 (and Schedule 4 to the Pension Schemes Act 1993)	Preferential debts	(a) In subsection (1) omit the words "or an individual". (b) In subsection (2) omit the words "or the individual".
Section 387	"The relevant date"	Subsections (5) and (6) are not applied.
Section 432	Offences by bodies corporate	In subsection (2) omit the words "secretary or".
Schedule B1 Paragraph 42	Moratorium on insolvency proceedings	For sub-paragraph (2) substitute— "(2) No determination to wind up the limited liability partnership voluntarily may be made".
Schedule B1 Paragraph 61	Directors	For paragraph 61 substitute— "**61.** The administrator has power to prevent any person from taking part in the management of the business of the limited liability partnership and to appoint any person to be a manager of that business.".
Schedule B1 Paragraph 62	Power to call meetings	At the end of the paragraph add— "The meeting shall be held in a manner provided by the Investment Bank Special Administration Regulations 2011 or by the limited liability partnership agreement or by insolvency rules (as defined in regulation 2 of those Regulations). The quorum required for a meeting of the members of the limited liability partnership shall be any quorum required by the limited liability partnership agreement for meetings of the members of the limited liability partnership and if no requirement for a quorum has been agreed upon, the quorum shall be 2 members.".
Schedule B1 Paragraph 91	Replacement	Sub-paragraph (1)(c) is not applied.
Schedule B1 Paragraph 105	Majority decision of directors	Paragraph 105 is not applied.

4. (1) The provisions of the Disqualification Act shall apply with the modifications set out in sub-paragraph (2).

(2) The modifications are—

(a) those contained in regulation 23 of these Regulations;
(b) those contained in regulation 4(2) of the 2001 Regulations; and
(c) that contained in Part 2 of Schedule 2 to the 2001 Regulations.

5. Application to Scotland

The provisions of the Insolvency Act listed in this paragraph are not applied to Scotland—

(a) section 167 (and Schedule 4);
(b) sections 185 to 187;
(c) sections 193 to 194;
(d) section 196 to the extent that that section applies to the specified devolved functions of Part 4 of the Insolvency Act;
(e) section 199;
(f) sections 206 to 215;
(g) sections 218, subsection (1);
(h) sections 242 to 243; and
(i) section 245.

6. Subordinate legislation

(1) The following subordinate legislation shall apply as from time to time in force to investment banks that are limited liability partnerships in special administration and—

(a) in case of the legislation listed in sub-paragraph (2), with such modifications as the context requires for the purpose of giving effect to the provisions of the Insolvency Act as applied by these Regulations; and
(b) in case of the legislation listed in sub-paragraph (3), with such modifications as the context requires for the purpose of giving effect to the provisions of the Companies Act 2006 and the Disqualification Act.

(2) The legislation referred to in sub-paragraph (1)(a) is—

(a) The Insolvency Practitioners Regulations 2005;
(b) The Insolvency Practitioners (Recognised Professional Bodies) Order 1986;
(c) The Insolvency Proceedings Fees Order 2004;
(d) The Insolvency Practitioners Tribunal (Conduct of Investigations) Rules 1986; and
(e) insolvency rules.

(3) The legislation referred to in sub-paragraph (1)(b) is—

(a) The Insolvent Companies (Disqualification of Unfit Directors) Proceedings Rules 1987;
(b) The Uncertificated Securities Regulations 2001;
(c) The Insolvent Companies (Reports on Conduct of Directors) Rules 1996; and
(d) The Insolvent Companies (Reports on Conduct of Directors) (Scotland) Rules 1996.

SCHEDULE 4
APPLICATION OF THESE REGULATIONS TO PARTNERSHIPS

Regulation 25

[7.1707]

1. In this Schedule, "the 1994 Order" means the Insolvent Partnerships Order 1994.

2. These Regulations apply where the investment bank is a partnership subject to the following modifications.

3. In the application of these Regulations and the Disqualification Act to partnerships, unless the contrary intention appears, the following apply—

(a) references to companies shall be construed as references to partnerships and all references to the registrar of companies shall be omitted;
(b) references to shares of a company shall be construed—
 (i) in relation to a partnership with capital, as references to rights to share in that capital, and
 (ii) in relation to a partnership without capital, as references to interests—
  (aa) conferring any right to share in the profits or liability to contribute to the losses of the partnership, or
  (bb) giving rise to an obligation to contribute to the debts or expenses of the partnership in the event of special administration; and
(c) other expressions appropriate to companies shall be construed, in relation to partnerships, as references to the corresponding persons, officers, documents or organs (as the case may be) appropriate to a partnership.

4. (1) The provisions of Schedule B1 as applied by regulation 15 apply in respect of a partnership but where a provision of Schedule B1 is listed in Table 1 below, that provision shall apply—

(a) as modified by Schedule 2 to the 1994 Order; and
(b) with the modifications set out in column 3 of Table 1,

instead of as modified in accordance with regulation 15.

(2) In the provisions referred to in the second column of Table 1, a reference to—

(a) a provision of the Insolvency Act is to that provision as applied by regulation 15 (subject to sub-paragraph (1));
(b) action includes a reference to inaction;
(c) the administrator means the administrator appointed under regulation 7;
(d) the court means the court as defined in regulation 2;
(e) the creditors' meeting has the meaning given by paragraph 50 of Schedule B1 (as applied by regulation 15);
(f) entering administration means entering special administration;

Part 7M Special Insolvency Regimes

(g) a hire purchase agreement includes a conditional sale agreement, a chattel leasing agreement and a retention of title agreement;
(h) an insolvency order is to a special administration order;
(i) an insolvency petition means an application for a special administration order;
(j) insolvency proceedings means special administration;
(k) market value means the amount which would be realised on a sale of property in the open market by a willing vendor;
(l) the purpose of administration means the pursuit of the special administration objectives;
(m) partnership is to an investment bank;
(n) the partnership being in administration is to the investment bank being in special administration;
(o) a responsible insolvency practitioner is to the administrator;
(p) a thing in writing includes a reference to a thing in electronic form; and
(q) an inability to pay its debts has the meaning given in regulation 2(4).

Table 1: Applied provisions of the 1994 Order with respect to Schedule B1

Provision of Schedule 2	*Subject*	*Modification or comment*
Para 17	Para 42: moratorium on insolvency proceedings	In the modified paragraph 42, sub-paragraph (5)(a) is not applied.
Para 18	Para 43: moratorium on other legal process	In the modified paragraph 43, sub-paragraph (6) is not applied.
Para 19	Para 47: statement of affairs	In the modified paragraph 47, in sub-paragraph (2), the statement must also include particulars (to the extent prescribed) of the client assets held by the investment bank.
Para 20	Para 49: administrator's proposals	In the modified paragraph 49— (a) sub-paragraph (2)(b) is not applied; (b) under sub-paragraph (4), the administrator shall also send a copy of the statement of proposals to— (i) every client of the investment bank of whose claim the administrator is aware and has a means of contacting, and (ii) the [FCA and, where the investment bank concerned is a PRA-authorised person, the PRA]; and (c) the administrator shall also give notice in the prescribed manner that the statement of proposals is to be provided free of charge to a market infrastructure body who applies in writing to a specified address.
Para 22	Para 61: management	
Para 23	Para 65: distribution to creditors	In the modified paragraph 61, sub-paragraph (3) is not applied.
Para 24	Para 69: agency	
Para 25	Para 73: protection for secured or preferential creditors	
Para 26	Para 74: challenge to administrator's conduct	In the modified paragraph 74— (a) the [FCA and, where the investment bank concerned is a PRA-authorised person, the PRA] may also make an application under this modified paragraph on the grounds that— (i) the administrator is acting or has acted so as unfairly to harm the interests of some or all of the members, creditors or clients; or (ii) the administrator is proposing to act in a way which would unfairly harm the interests of some or all of the members, creditors or clients;

Table 1: Applied provisions of the 1994 Order with respect to Schedule B1

Provision of Schedule 2	*Subject*	*Modification or comment*
		(b) a client may also make an application under sub-paragraph (1) or (2); (c) where the [FCA or the PRA] has given a direction under regulation 16 which has not been withdrawn, an order may not be made under this paragraph if it would impede or prevent compliance with the direction; and (d) any of the following persons may make an application under this paragraph on the grounds that the administrator is not taking any action in response to a request from that person under regulation 13(2) and that the person is of the opinion that the action requested would not lead to a material reduction in the value of the property of the investment bank— (i) the Bank of England, (ii) the Treasury, (iii) the [FCA or the PRA], or (iv) a market infrastructure body.
Para 28	Para 84: termination: no more assets for distribution	In the modified paragraph 84— (a) the administrator shall only file a notice under sub-paragraph (1) if the investment bank no longer holds client assets; and (b) in sub-paragraph (5), a copy of the notice shall be sent to every client of the investment bank of whom the administrator is aware and the [FCA and, where the investment bank concerned is a PRA-authorised person, the PRA].
Para 29	Para 87: resignation	In the modified paragraph 87— (a) where the administrator was appointed on the application of the Secretary of State[, the FCA or the PRA], the notice given in accordance with sub-paragraph (2)(a) must also be given to the applicant; and (b) sub-paragraphs (2)(b) and (c) are not applied.
Para 30	Para 89: disqualification	In the modified paragraph 89— (a) where the administrator was appointed by the Secretary of State[, the FCA or the PRA], the notice given in accordance with sub-paragraph (2)(a) must also be given to the applicant; and (b) sub-paragraphs (2)(b) and (c) are not applied.
Para 31	Para 90: replacement	In the modified paragraph 90, the reference to paragraphs 91 to 93 and 95 is to paragraph 91.
Para 32	Para 91: replacement	In the modified paragraph 91, the [FCA and, where the investment bank concerned is a PRA-authorised person, the PRA] is added to the list of persons who may make an application to appoint an administrator but to whom the restrictions in sub-paragraph (2) apply.
Para 38	Para 103: joint administrators	In the modified paragraph 103— (a) in sub-paragraph (2)(a), the reference to paragraph 12(1)(a) to (c) is to regulation 5(1); and

Part 7M Special Insolvency Regimes

Table 1: Applied provisions of the 1994 Order with respect to Schedule B1		
Provision of Schedule 2	***Subject***	***Modification or comment***
		(b) sub-paragraphs (3) and (4) are not applied.
Para 39	Para 105: majority decision of directors	Paragraph 105 is not applied.
Para 40	Para 106: fines	In the modified paragraph 106, sub-paragraphs (2)(a), (2)(b), (2)(j) and (2)(k) are not applied.
Para 42	Paras 112 to 116: Scotland	Paragraphs 112 to 116 are not applied.

5. (1) The provisions of the Insolvency Act other than those in Schedule B1 as applied by regulation 15 apply in respect of a partnership but where the provision is listed in Table 2 below, that provision shall apply subject to this paragraph.

(2) The provisions of the 1994 Order set out in Table 2 apply in relation to these Regulations, with—

(a) the modifications set out in sub-paragraph (3); and

(b) any other modification set out in Table 2.

(3) The modifications are that a reference to—

(a) the Act (the Insolvency Act) is a reference to the Regulations;

(b) a provision of the Insolvency Act is to that provision as applied and modified by regulation 15, unless the provision appears in Table 1;

(c) being wound up means that the partnership is in special administration;

(d) office-holder means the administrator; and

(e) insolvency order means a special administration order.

Table 2: Applied provisions of the 1994 Order (general)		
Provision	*Subject*	*Modification or comment*
Article 16	Application of the Disqualification Act	The reference to the partnership being wound up as an unregistered company under Part V of the Insolvency Act is a reference to it being placed in special administration under these Regulations.
Article 18	Subordinate legislation	
Schedule 2, para 43	Schedule 1 to the Insolvency Act	Paragraph 19 is not applied.
Schedule 3, para 9	Section 234 of the Insolvency Act	The reference in sub-paragraph (1) to article 7 of the 1994 Order is to be read as a reference to regulation 7.
Schedule 3, para 10	Schedule 4 to the Insolvency Act	In Schedule 4, paragraphs 4 to 10, and paragraph 12, are not applied, and in paragraph 13, the reference to "winding up the partnership's affairs and distributing its property" is a reference to "pursuing the special administration objectives."
Schedule 4, para 25	Section 211	Sub-paragraph (1) is not applied.
Schedule 8	Application of the Disqualification Act	The provisions of the Disqualification Act listed in Article 16, and applied with modification by Schedule 8, are to be read with the modifications set out in regulation 23.
Schedule 10	Subordinate legislation	(a) The reference to the Insolvency Rules 1986 is a reference to insolvency rules. (b) Ignore the reference to the following instruments— (i) The Insolvency Proceedings (Monetary Limits) Order 1986, (ii) The Administration of Insolvent Estates of Deceased Persons Order 1986, (iii) The Insolvency (Amendment of Subordinate Legislation) Order 1986, (iv) The Companies (Disqualification Orders) Regulations 2001,

Table 2: Applied provisions of the 1994 Order (general)		
		(v) The Co-operation of Insolvency Courts (Designation of Relevant Countries and Territories) Order 1986, (vi) The Insolvency Practitioners and Insolvency Services Accounts (Fees) Order 2003; and (vii) The Insolvency Proceedings (Fees) Order 2004.

NOTES

Para 4: words in square brackets in the Table substituted by the Financial Services Act 2012 (Consequential Amendments and Transitional Provisions) Order 2013, SI 2013/472, art 3, Sch 2, para 198(r), subject to a transitional provision in para 199 set out at **[7.1662]**.

Note that the Insolvency Rules 1986, SI 1986/1925 are revoked and replaced (as from 6 April 2017 and subject to transitional provisions) by the Insolvency (England and Wales) Rules 2016, SI 2016/1024 at **[6.2]**.

SCHEDULE 5
TABLE OF ENACTMENTS REFERRED TO IN THESE REGULATIONS TOGETHER WITH THE EQUIVALENT ENACTMENT HAVING EFFECT IN RELATION TO NORTHERN IRELAND

Regulation 26

[7.1708]
The enactments listed in column 2, being the equivalent Northern Ireland enactments to the enactments listed in column 1, have effect with the modifications (if any) set out in column 3.

Enactment	**Equivalent enactment in N Ireland**	**Modifications to the N Ireland enactment**
Insolvency Act	Insolvency (Northern Ireland) Order 1989 ("the Insolvency Order")	
The following provisions of the Insolvency Act	*The following provisions of the Insolvency Order*	
Part 1	Part 2	
Part 4 or 5	Part 5 or 6	
Section 3	Article 16	
Section 4	Article 17	
Section 5	Article 18	
Sections 74 and 76 to 83	Articles 61 and 63 to 69	
Section 79	Article 13	
Section 84	Article 70	
Section 123	Article 103	
Section 124(2)	Article 104(2)	
Section 124A(1)	Article 104A(1)	
Section 125	Article 105	
Section 135	Article 115	
Section 167 (and Schedule 4)	Article 142 (and Schedule 2)	[In Article 142, in paragraphs (1) and (2) the reference to the liquidation committee is a reference to the creditors' committee]
Section 168	Article 143	
Section 176	Article 150	
Section 176A	Article 150A	
Section 178	Article 152	
Section 179	Article 153	
Section 180	Article 154	
Section 181	Article 155	
Section 182	Article 156	
Section 186	Article 157	

Enactment	Equivalent enactment in N Ireland	Modifications to the N Ireland enactment
Section 187	Article 158	
Section 194	Article 163	
Section 206	Article 170	
Section 207	Article 171	
Section 208	Article 172	
Section 209	Article 173	
Section 210	Article 174	
Section 211	Article 175	
Section 212	Article 176	
Section 213	Article 177	
Section 214	Article 178	
Section 215	Article 179	
Section 216	Article 180	
Section 217	Article 181	
Section 218	Article 182	The reference to the Secretary of State in the modification to section 218 in regulation 15(6) is to be treated as a reference to the Department of Enterprise, Trade and Investment.
Section 219	Article 183	
Section 233	Article 197	
Section 234	Article 198	
Section 235	Article 199	
Section 236	Article 200	
Section 237	Article 201	
Section 238	Article 202	
Section 239	Article 203	
Section 240	Article 204	
Section 241	Article 205	
Section 244	Article 206	
Section 245	Article 207	
Section 246	Article 208	
section 247	Article 6	
Section 386 (and Schedule 6 and Schedule 4 to the Pensions Schemes Act 1993)	Article 346 (and Schedule 4 and Schedule 4 to the Social Security Pensions (Northern Ireland) Order 1975	
Section 387	Article 347	
Section 388	Article 349	
Section 389	Article 348	
[Sections 390 to 391T	Articles 349 to 350T]	
Section 411 (and Schedule 8)	Article 359 (and Schedule 5)	(a) The modifications to section 411 set out in column 3 of Table 2 in Regulation 15 are not applied. (b) Rules shall be made by the Department of Justice with the concurrence of— (i) the Department of Finance and Personnel; and

Enactment	Equivalent enactment in N Ireland	Modifications to the N Ireland enactment
		(ii) in the case of rules that affect court procedure, the Lord Chief Justice of Northern Ireland. (c) The reference to "this Order" in Article 359 includes these Regulations. (d) A reference in Schedule 5 to the Insolvency (Northern Ireland) Order 1989 to doing anything under or for the purpose of a provision in this Order includes a reference to doing anything under or for the purposes of a provision of these Regulations.
Section 414	Article 361	(a) The modifications to section 414 set out in column 3 of Table 2 in Regulation 15 are not applied. (b) The reference in this Article to "this Order" includes these Regulations. (c) Ignore the reference to the official receiver.
Section 423	Article 367	
Sections 424 and 425	Article 368 and 369	
Sections 430 and 431 (and Schedule 10)	Articles 373 and 374 (and Schedule 7)	
Section 432	Article 374	
Section 433	Article 375	(a) The modifications to section 433 set out in column 3 of Table 2 in Regulation 15 are not applied. (b) In paragraph (1)(a) a statement of affairs prepared "for the purposes of any provision of this Order" includes any statement made by a provision of that Order as applied by these Regulations. (c) In paragraph (1)(b), the reference to "this Order" includes these Regulations.
Sections 434B to 434D	Articles 384 to 386	
Schedule B1	Schedule B1	
The following provisions of Schedule B1	*The following provisions of Schedule B1*	
Para 40(1)(a)	Para 41(1)(a)	
Para 42	Para 43	
Para 43	Para 44	
Para 44	Para 45	
Para 45	Para 46	
Para 46	Para 47	
Para 47	Para 48	
Para 48	Para 49	
Para 49	Para 50	
Para 50	Para 51	

Part 7M Special Insolvency Regimes

Enactment	Equivalent enactment in N Ireland	Modifications to the N Ireland enactment
Para 51	Para 52	
Para 53	Para 54	
Para 54	Para 55	
Para 55	Para 56	
Para 56	Para 57	
Para 57	Para 58	
Para 58	Para 59	
Para 59	Para 60	
Para 60 (and Schedule 1)	Para 61 (and Schedule 1)	
Para 61	Para 62	
Para 62	Para 63	
Para 63	Para 64	
Para 64	Para 65	
Para 65	Para 66	[In Para 66, sub-paragraph (3) is not applied]
Para 66	Para 67	
Para 67	Para 68	
Para 68	Para 69	
Para 69	Para 70	
Para 70	Para 71	
Para 71	Para 72	
Para 72	Para 73	
Para 73	Para 74	
Para 74	Para 75	
Para 75	Para 76	
Para 79	Para 80	
Para 81	Para 82	
Para 84	Para 85	
Para 85	Para 86	
Para 86	Para 87	
Para 87	Para 88	
Para 88	Para 89	
Para 89	Para 90	
Para 90	Para 91	
Para 91	Para 92	
Para 98	Para 99	
Para 99	Para 100	
Para 100	Para 101	
Para 101	Para 102	
Para 102	Para 103	
Para 103	Para 104	
Para 104	Para 105	
Para 105	Para 106	
Para 106 (and section 430 and Schedule 10)	Para 107 (and Article 373 and Schedule 7)	
Para 107	Para 108	
Para 108	Para 109	
Paras 109	Para 110	
Para 111	Para 1	
[Schedule 2A, Para 1	Schedule 1A, Para 1]	

Enactment	Equivalent enactment in N Ireland	Modifications to the N Ireland enactment
Section 87A of the Magistrates' Courts Act 1980	Article 92A of the Magistrates' Courts (Northern Ireland) Order 1981	
Company Directors Disqualification Act 1986	Company Directors Disqualification (Northern Ireland) Order 2002	
Section [7A] of the Company Directors Disqualification Act 1986	Article [10A] of the Company Directors Disqualification (Northern Ireland) Order 2002	
Part 7 of the Companies Act 1989	Part 5 of the Companies (No 2) (Northern Ireland) Order 1990	
Section 155 of the Companies Act 1989	Article 80 of the Companies (No 2) (Northern Ireland) Order 1990	
Section 173 of the Companies Act 1989	Article 95 of the Companies (No 2) (Northern Ireland) Order 1990	
Section 188 of the Companies Act 1989	Article 109 of the Companies (No 2) (Northern Ireland) Order 1990	
Insolvency Practitioners (Recognised Professional Bodies) Order 1986	Insolvency Practitioners (Recognised Professional Bodies) Order (Northern Ireland) 1991	
Insolvent Companies (Disqualification of Unfit Directors) Proceedings Rules 1987	Insolvent Companies (Disqualification of Unfit Directors) Proceedings Rules (Northern Ireland) 2003	
Insolvent Partnerships Order 1994	Insolvent Partnerships Order (Northern Ireland) 1995	
Insolvent Companies (Reports on Conduct of Directors) Rules 1996	Insolvent Companies (Reports on Conduct of Directors) Rules (Northern Ireland) 2003	
Limited Liability Partnership Regulations 2001	Limited Liability Partnership Regulations (Northern Ireland) 2004	
Insolvency Proceedings Fees Order 2004	Insolvency (Fees) Order (Northern Ireland) 2006	
Insolvency Practitioners Regulations 2005	Insolvency Practitioners Regulations (Northern Ireland) 2006	
Insolvency Rules	Insolvency Rules (Northern Ireland) 1991	

NOTES

Words in square brackets in the third column of entry relating to s 167 of the Insolvency Act 1986 inserted, entry relating to ss 390 to 391T of the 1986 Act substituted (for entries relating to ss 390. 391), words in square brackets in the third column of entry relating to Sch B1, para 65 to the 1986 Act inserted and figures in square brackets in entry relating to s 7A of the Company Directors Disqualification Act 1986 substituted, by the Deregulation Act 2015, the Small Business, Enterprise and Employment Act 2015 and the Insolvency (Amendment) Act (Northern Ireland) 2016 (Consequential Amendments and Transitional Provisions) Regulations 2017, SI 2017/400, reg 10(1), (8), subject to transitional provisions as noted to the Banking Act 2009, s 103 at **[7.40]**.

Entry relating to Sch 2A, para 1 of the Insolvency Act 1986 inserted by the Investment Bank (Amendment of Definition) and Special Administration (Amendment) Regulations 2017, SI 2017/443, regs 4, 16, as from 6 April 2017, except in relation to an investment bank which is in special administration on that date (see further reg 17 of the 2017 Regulations at **[7.2048]**).

SCHEDULE 6
MODIFICATIONS AND CONSEQUENTIAL AMENDMENTS

Regulation 27

PART 1

[7.1709]

1. (1) Where this Part of this Schedule applies, the enactments set out below apply with the following modifications.

(2) References to—

(a) an administrator appointed in respect of a Schedule B1 administration include a reference to an administrator appointed under a special administration order;

(b) administration under Schedule B1 or "insolvent administration" include a reference to special administration;

(c) "administration order" include a reference to a special administration order;

(d) "insolvency legislation", the "general law of insolvency", the "enactments relating to insolvency" and similar expressions include special administration and the provisions of the Insolvency Act as applied by these Regulations;

(e) becoming insolvent, or an "insolvency event" occurring in respect of the investment bank includes being put into special administration and "insolvency proceedings" or an "insolvency procedure" include special administration;

(f) "winding up", being "wound up", "wound up by the court" "going into liquidation" or "compulsory liquidation" include being put into special administration, and a "winding-up order" include a special administration order (and, in this context, "liquidator" shall be read as "administrator");

(g) a person acting as an insolvency practitioner within the meaning of section 388 of the Insolvency Act include a person acting as an administrator under these Regulations;

(h) the provisions of the Insolvency Act include those provisions as applied and modified by these Regulations; and

(i) the provisions of the Insolvency Rules 1986, the Insolvency Rules (Northern Ireland) 1991 and the Insolvency (Scotland) Rules 1986 include the provisions of insolvency rules made under section 411 of the Insolvency Act as applied by regulation 15(6).

(3) A reference to insolvency or liquidation within the meaning of section 247 of the Insolvency Act includes a reference to special administration.

(4) A reference to the "purposes of the Insolvency Act 1986" includes a reference to the purposes of these Regulations.

Primary Legislation

Taxes Management Act 1970

Prescription and Limitation (Scotland) Act 1973

Companies Act 1985

Finance Act 1986

Companies (Northern Ireland) Order 1986

Debtors (Scotland) Act 1987

Companies Act 1989

Companies (No 2) (Northern Ireland) Order 1990

Taxation of Chargeable Gains Act 1992

Pension Schemes Act 1993

Pension Schemes (Northern Ireland) Act 1993

Pensions Act 1995

Pensions (Northern Ireland) Order 1995

Proceeds of Crime (Scotland) Act 1995

Employment Rights Act 1996

Employment Rights (Northern Ireland) Order 1996

Terrorism Act 2000

Finance Act 2000

International Criminal Court Act 2001

International Criminal Court (Scotland) Act 2001

Proceeds of Crime Act 2002

Debt Arrangement and Attachment (Scotland) Act 2002

Finance Act 2003

Pensions Act 2004

Pensions (Northern Ireland) Order 2005

Companies Act 2006 (but not including section 1078 (documents subject to Directive disclosure requirements)

Bankruptcy and Diligence (Scotland) Act 2007

Finance Act 2008

Dormant Bank and Building Society Accounts Act 2008

Corporation Tax Act 2009

Corporation Tax Act 2010

Taxation (International and other Provisions) Act 2010

Secondary Legislation

Statutory Maternity Pay (General) Regulations 1986

Statutory Maternity Pay (General) (Northern Ireland) Regulations 1987

Insolvent Companies (Disqualification of Unfit Directors) Proceedings Rules 1987

Financial Markets and Insolvency Regulations 1991

Financial Markets and Insolvency Regulations (Northern Ireland) 1991

Insolvency Regulations 1994

Non-Domestic Rating (Unoccupied Property) (Scotland) Regulations 1994

Insolvent Companies (Reports on Conduct of Directors) Rules 1996

Financial Markets and Insolvency Regulations 1996

Financial Markets and Insolvency Regulations (Northern Ireland) 1996

Individual Savings Account Regulations 1998

Corporation Tax (Simplified Arrangements for Group Relief) Regulations 1999

Financial Markets and Insolvency (Settlement Finality) Regulations 1999

Statutory Paternity Pay and Statutory Adoption Pay (General) Regulations 2002

Statutory Paternity Pay and Statutory Adoption Pay (General) (Northern Ireland) Regulations 2002

Financial Collateral Arrangements (No 2) Regulations 2003

Insolvent Companies (Reports on Conduct of Directors) Rules (Northern Ireland) 2003

Insolvent Companies (Disqualification of Unfit Directors) Proceedings Rules (Northern Ireland) 2003

Credit Institutions (Reorganisation and Winding Up) Regulations 2004

Insolvency Practitioners Regulations 2005

Pension Protection Fund (Entry Rules) Regulations 2005

Pension Protection Fund (Entry Rules) Regulations (Northern Ireland) 2005

Gender Recognition (Disclosure of Information) (England, Wales and Northern Ireland) (No 2) Order 2005

Gender Recognition (Disclosure of Information) (Scotland) Order 2005

Financial Assistance Scheme Regulations 2005

Insolvency Practitioners Regulations (Northern Ireland) 2006

Land Registration (Scotland) Rules 2006

Companies (Cross-Border Mergers) Regulations 2007

Regulated Covered Bonds Regulations 2008

[Company, Limited Liability Partnership and Business (Names and Trading Disclosures) Regulations 2015]

Land Registration (Network Access) Rules 2008

Limited Liability Partnerships (Accounts and Audit) (Application of Companies Act 2006) Regulations 2008

Registrar of Companies (Fees) (Companies, Overseas Companies and Limited Liability Partnerships) Regulations 2009

Payment Services Regulations [2017]

Companies (Disclosure of Address) Regulations 2009

Additional Statutory Paternity Pay (General) Regulations 2010

NOTES

Secondary Legislation: entry in square brackets substituted by the Company, Limited Liability Partnership and Business (Names and Trading Disclosures) Regulations 2015, SI 2015/17, reg 30, Sch 6, para 6.

Year "2017" in square brackets substituted by the Payment Services Regulations 2017, SI 2017/752, reg 156, Sch 8, Pt 3, para 11.

Note that the Insolvency Rules 1986, SI 1986/1925 are revoked and replaced (as from 6 April 2017 and subject to transitional provisions) by the Insolvency (England and Wales) Rules 2016, SI 2016/1024 at **[6.2]**.

PART 2
SPECIFIC MODIFICATIONS

[7.1710]
2. Where this Part of this Schedule applies, the enactments set out below apply with the modifications indicated.

3. Financial Services and Markets Act 2000

(1) The following provisions of the Financial Services and Markets Act 2000 apply with the modifications set out in this paragraph.

(2) In section 215 (rights of the scheme in insolvency)—
- (a) in subsection (3), the reference to making an administration application is to be read as including making an application for a special administration order; and
- (b) subsection (4) is to be read as if it provided the following—

"(4) In the case of a special administration (bank insolvency), if the scheme manager decides, pursuant to section 101 of the Banking Act 2009, as applied by paragraph 6(2) of Schedule 1 to the Investment Bank Special Administration Regulations 2011, not to be a member of the creditors' committee, the scheme manager has the same rights as are conferred on the [regulators] by section 371.".

(3) In section 220(3), the reference to an administrator is to be read as including an administrator appointed under a special administration order.

(4) In section 362(6), the reference to administration is to be read as including special administration.

(5) In section 375 ([right of FCA and PRA] to apply for an order), references to the provisions of the Insolvency Act 1986 and the Insolvency (Northern Ireland) Order 1989 are to be read as including references to those provisions as applied and modified by—
- (a) regulation 15; or
- (b) section 145 of the Banking Act 2009 (with the modifications set out in paragraph 6(3) of Schedule 2).

4. Pensions Act 2004

In section 121(3)(d) of the Pensions Act 2004 (meaning of insolvency event), the reference to "the company enters administration within the meaning of paragraph 1(2)(b) of Schedule B1 to that Act" is to be read so as to include the investment bank entering special administration.

5. Companies Act 2006

(1) The following provisions of the Companies Act 2006 apply with the modifications set out in this paragraph.

(2) In section 461 (permitted disclosure of information obtained under compulsory powers)—
- (a) subsection (4)(c) is to be read so as to include these Regulations in the list of enactments in that subsection; and
- (b) subsection (4)(g) is to be read so as to include these Regulations in the list of enactments in that subsection.

(3) Any references in Part 35 (the registrar of companies) to the Insolvency Act 1986 and the Insolvency (Northern Ireland) Order 1989 are to be read as including that legislation as applied and modified by these Regulations.

(4) Where an application is made to the court for—
- (a) a special administration order; or

(b) the appointment of a person under section 135 of the Insolvency Act 1986 or article 115 of the Insolvency (Northern Ireland) Order 1989 as applied by these Regulations,

sections 1139 and 1140 (service of documents on company, directors, secretaries and others) have effect subject to the provisions for service set out in rules made under section 411 of the Insolvency Act as applied and modified by regulation 15 of these Regulations.

(5) In Part 2 of Schedule 2 (Specified descriptions of disclosures for the purposes of section 948), under heading A—

(a) paragraph 13 is to be read so as to include these Regulations in the list of enactments in that paragraph, and

(b) paragraph 37 is to be read so as to include these Regulations in the list of enactments in that paragraph.

(6) In Part 2 of Schedule 11A (Specified descriptions of disclosures for the purposes of section 1224A)—

(a) paragraph 30 is to be read so as to include these Regulations in the list of enactments in that paragraph, and

(b) paragraph 52 is to be read so as to include these Regulations in the list of enactments in that paragraph.

6. Land Registration Rules 2003

Rule 184(1) of the Land Registration Rules 2003 is to be read as if the reference to administration included special administration.

7. Credit Institutions (Reorganisation and Winding Up) Regulations 2004

(1) The following provision of the Credit Institutions (Reorganisation and Winding Up) Regulations 2004 applies with the modification set out in this paragraph.

(2) Regulation 11(2) is to be read as if it provided the following—

"(2) The prescribed circumstances are that, after the appointment of the administrator, the administrator, in drawing up the statement of proposals in accordance with paragraph 49 of Schedule B1 (as applied by regulation 15(6) of the Investment Bank Special Administration Regulations 2011) or paragraph 7 of Schedule 2 to those Regulations has concluded that it is not possible to rescue the investment bank as a going concern.".

NOTES

Para 3: words in square brackets substituted by the Financial Services Act 2012 (Consequential Amendments and Transitional Provisions) Order 2013, SI 2013/472, art 3, Sch 2, para 198(s), subject to a transitional provision in para 199 set out at **[7.1662]**.

(Pt 3 contains amendments only.)

INVESTMENT BANK SPECIAL ADMINISTRATION (ENGLAND AND WALES) RULES 2011

(SI 2011/1301)

NOTES

Made: 15 May 2011.

Authority: Insolvency Act 1986, ss 411(1A)(a), (2), (2C), (3) (as applied by the Investment Bank Special Administration Regulations 2011, SI 2011/245 at **[7.1661]**).

Commencement: 30 June 2011.

ARRANGEMENT OF SECTIONS

PART 1
INTRODUCTORY PROVISIONS

1 Citation . . . [7.1711]
2 Commencement . . . [7.1712]
3 Extent . . . [7.1713]
4 Interpretation . . . [7.1714]
5 Application of rules . . . [7.1715]

PART 2
APPLICATION FOR ORDER

CHAPTER 1
APPLICATION FOR SPECIAL ADMINISTRATION ORDER

6 Content of application . . . [7.1716]
7 Statement of proposed administrator . . . [7.1717]
8 Witness statement in support of application . . . [7.1718]
9 Filing of application . . . [7.1719]

10 Service of application [7.1720]
11 Proof of service [7.1721]
12 Further notification [7.1722]
13 The hearing [7.1723]
14 The special administration order [7.1724]
15 Costs [7.1725]
16 Notice of special administration order [7.1726]

CHAPTER 2
APPLICATION FOR A SPECIAL ADMINISTRATION (BANK INSOLVENCY) ORDER

17 Filing of application [7.1727]
18 Service of application [7.1728]
19 Proof of service [7.1729]
20 Other persons to receive copy of application [7.1730]
21 Verification of application [7.1731]
22 Persons entitled to copy of application [7.1732]
23 Certificate of compliance [7.1733]
24 Leave for the applicant to withdraw [7.1734]
25 Witness statement in opposition [7.1735]
26 Making, transmission and advertisement of order [7.1736]
27 Special administration (bank insolvency) order [7.1737]
28 Authentication of administrator's appointment [7.1738]
29 Duties of Objective A committee [7.1739]
30 Appointment of person under section 135 [7.1740]
31 Notice of appointment [7.1741]
32 Order of appointment [7.1742]
33 Security [7.1743]
34 Failure to give or keep up security [7.1744]
35 Remuneration [7.1745]
36 Termination of appointment [7.1746]

CHAPTER 3
APPLICATION FOR A SPECIAL ADMINISTRATION (BANK ADMINISTRATION) ORDER

37 Content of application [7.1747]
38 Statement of proposed administrator [7.1748]
39 Bank of England witness statement [7.1749]
40 Filing [7.1750]
41 Service [7.1751]
42 Other notification [7.1752]
43 Venue [7.1753]
44 Hearing [7.1754]
45 Special administration (bank administration) order [7.1755]
46 Costs [7.1756]
47 Notice of order [7.1757]
48 Remuneration of the administrator [7.1758]
49 Appointment of person under section 135 [7.1759]
50 Order of appointment [7.1760]

PART 3
PROCESS OF SPECIAL ADMINISTRATION

CHAPTER 1
NOTICE OF APPOINTMENT AND STATEMENT OF AFFAIRS

51 Notification and advertisement of administrator's appointment [7.1761]
52 Notice requiring statement of affairs [7.1762]
53 Details of the client assets held by the investment bank [7.1763]
54 Verification and filing [7.1764]
55 Limited disclosure [7.1765]
56 Release from duty to submit statement of affairs [7.1766]
57 Expenses of statement of affairs [7.1767]
58 Submission of accounts [7.1768]

CHAPTER 2
STATEMENT OF PROPOSALS

59 Administrator's proposals [7.1769]
60 Limited disclosure of the statement of proposals [7.1770]

CHAPTER 3
INITIAL MEETING TO CONSIDER PROPOSALS

61 Initial meeting . . . [7.1771]
62 Notice to officers . . . [7.1772]
63 Business of the initial meeting . . . [7.1773]
64 Adjournment of meeting to approve the statement of proposals . . . [7.1774]
65 Revision of the statement of proposals . . . [7.1775]
66 Meeting to approve the revised statement of proposals . . . [7.1776]
67 Notice to creditors and clients . . . [7.1777]

CHAPTER 4
MEETINGS GENERALLY

68 Meetings generally . . . [7.1778]
69 Venue . . . [7.1779]
70 Notice of meeting by individual notice: when and where sent . . . [7.1780]
71 Notice of meeting by individual notice: content and accompanying documents . . . [7.1781]
72 Notice of meeting by advertisement only . . . [7.1782]
73 Content of notice for meetings . . . [7.1783]
74 Gazetting and advertisement of meetings . . . [7.1784]
75 Non-receipt of notice of meeting . . . [7.1785]
76 Requisition of meetings . . . [7.1786]
77 Expenses of requisitioned meetings . . . [7.1787]
78 Quorum at meetings . . . [7.1788]
79 Chair at meetings . . . [7.1789]
80 Adjournment by chair . . . [7.1790]
81 Adjournment in absence of chair . . . [7.1791]
82 Claims, proofs and proxies in adjournment . . . [7.1792]
83 Suspension . . . [7.1793]
84 Venue and conduct of company meetings . . . [7.1794]

CHAPTER 5
ENTITLEMENT TO VOTE AT MEETINGS

85 Entitlement to vote (creditors) . . . [7.1795]
86 FSCS and voting rights . . . [7.1796]
87 Calculation of voting rights (creditors) . . . [7.1797]
88 Calculation of voting rights: special cases (creditors) . . . [7.1798]
89 Procedure for admitting creditors' claims for voting . . . [7.1799]
90 Entitlement to vote (clients) . . . [7.1800]
91 Calculation of voting rights (clients) . . . [7.1801]
92 Procedure for admitting clients' claims for voting . . . [7.1802]
93 Voting at meetings of creditors and clients . . . [7.1803]
94 Requisite majorities . . . [7.1804]
95 Requisite majorities at contributories' meetings . . . [7.1805]
96 Appeals against decisions under this Chapter . . . [7.1806]

CHAPTER 6
CORRESPONDENCE AND REMOTE ATTENDANCE

97 Correspondence instead of meetings . . . [7.1807]
98 Remote attendance at meetings conducted in accordance with section 246A . . . [7.1808]
99 Action where person excluded . . . [7.1809]
100 Indication to excluded person . . . [7.1810]
101 Complaint . . . [7.1811]

CHAPTER 7
RECORDS, RETURNS AND REPORTS

102 Minutes . . . [7.1812]
103 Returns or reports of meetings . . . [7.1813]

CHAPTER 8
THE CREDITORS' COMMITTEE

104 Constitution of committee . . . [7.1814]
105 Formalities of establishment . . . [7.1815]
106 Functions and meetings of the committee . . . [7.1816]
107 The chair at meetings . . . [7.1817]
108 Quorum . . . [7.1818]
109 Committee members' representatives . . . [7.1819]
110 Resignation . . . [7.1820]

111 Termination of membership . . . . [7.1821]
112 Removal . . . . [7.1822]
113 Vacancies . . . . [7.1823]
114 Procedure at meetings . . . . [7.1824]
115 Remote attendance at meetings of creditors' committee . . . . [7.1825]
116 Procedure for requests that a place for a meeting should be specified . . . . [7.1826]
117 Resolutions of creditors' committees by post . . . . [7.1827]
118 Information from administrator . . . . [7.1828]
119 Expenses of members . . . . [7.1829]
120 Members dealing with the investment bank . . . . [7.1830]
121 Formal defects . . . . [7.1831]

CHAPTER 9
PROGRESS REPORTS

122 Content of progress report . . . . [7.1832]
123 Sending progress report . . . . [7.1833]

CHAPTER 10
PROXIES AND CORPORATE REPRESENTATION

124 Definition of proxy . . . . [7.1834]
125 Issue and use of forms . . . . [7.1835]
126 Use of proxies at meetings . . . . [7.1836]
127 Retention of proxies . . . . [7.1837]
128 Right of inspection . . . . [7.1838]
129 Proxy holder with financial interest . . . . [7.1839]
130 Company representation . . . . [7.1840]

CHAPTER 11
DISPOSAL OF CHARGED PROPERTY

131 Application to dispose of charged property . . . . [7.1841]
132 Application in a special administration (bank administration) . . . . [7.1842]

PART 4
EXPENSES OF THE SPECIAL ADMINISTRATION

133 Expenses of voluntary arrangement . . . . [7.1843]
134 Expenses to be paid out of the investment bank's assets . . . . [7.1844]
135 Expenses to be paid out of the client assets . . . . [7.1845]
136 Pre-administration costs . . . . [7.1846]
137 Allocation of expenses to be paid from client assets . . . . [7.1847]

PART 5
OBJECTIVE 1

CHAPTER 1
SETTING A BAR DATE

138 Notice of the bar date . . . . [7.1848]
139 Content of claim for client assets . . . . [7.1849]
140 Content of claim in respect of security interest . . . . [7.1850]
141 Costs of making a claim . . . . [7.1851]
142 New administrator appointed . . . . [7.1852]

CHAPTER 2
FURTHER NOTIFICATION

143 Notifying potential claimants after bar date has passed . . . . [7.1853]

CHAPTER 3
DISTRIBUTION PLAN

144 Distribution plan . . . . [7.1854]
145 Approval by the creditors' committee . . . . [7.1855]
146 Approval by the court . . . . [7.1856]
147 Treatment of late claimants . . . . [7.1857]

PART 6
DISTRIBUTIONS TO CREDITORS

CHAPTER 1
APPLICATION

148 Distribution to creditors . . . . [7.1858]
149 Debts of investment bank to rank equally . . . . [7.1859]
150 Supplementary provisions as to dividend . . . . [7.1860]

151 Division of unsold assets .... [7.1861]

CHAPTER 2
PROOFS OF DEBTS

152 Proving a debt .... [7.1862]
153 Costs of proving .... [7.1863]
154 Administrator to allow inspection of proofs .... [7.1864]
155 New administrator appointed .... [7.1865]
156 Admission and rejection of proofs for dividend .... [7.1866]
157 Appeal against decision on proof .... [7.1867]
158 Withdrawal or variation of proof .... [7.1868]
159 Expunging of proof by the court .... [7.1869]

CHAPTER 3
QUANTIFICATION OF CLAIMS

160 Estimate of quantum .... [7.1870]
161 Negotiable instruments .... [7.1871]
162 Secured creditors .... [7.1872]
163 Discounts .... [7.1873]
164 Mutual credit and set-off .... [7.1874]
165 Application of rule 164 in a special administration (bank administration) and special administration (bank insolvency) .... [7.1875]
166 Debt in a foreign currency .... [7.1876]
167 Payments of a periodical nature .... [7.1877]
168 Interest .... [7.1878]
169 Debt payable at a future time .... [7.1879]
170 Value of security .... [7.1880]
171 Surrender for non-disclosure .... [7.1881]
172 Redemption by administrator .... [7.1882]
173 Test of security's value .... [7.1883]
174 Realisation of security by creditor .... [7.1884]
175 Notice of proposed distribution .... [7.1885]
176 Admission or rejection of proofs .... [7.1886]
177 Postponement or cancellation of dividend .... [7.1887]
178 Declaration of a dividend .... [7.1888]
179 Notice of declaration of a dividend .... [7.1889]
180 Payments of dividend and related matters .... [7.1890]
181 Notice of no dividend or no further dividend .... [7.1891]
182 Proof altered after payment of dividend .... [7.1892]
183 Secured creditors .... [7.1893]
184 Disqualification from dividend .... [7.1894]
185 Assignment of right to dividend .... [7.1895]
186 Debt payable at a future time .... [7.1896]

PART 7
THE ADMINISTRATOR

CHAPTER 1
POWERS OF THE ADMINISTRATOR

187 General powers .... [7.1897]
188 Powers of disclaimer .... [7.1898]
189 Communication of disclaimer to persons interested .... [7.1899]
190 Additional notices .... [7.1900]
191 Records .... [7.1901]
192 Application by interested party .... [7.1902]
193 Interest in property to be declared on request .... [7.1903]
194 Disclaimer presumed valid and effective .... [7.1904]
195 Application for the exercise of court's powers under section 181 .... [7.1905]

CHAPTER 2
FIXING OF REMUNERATION

196 Fixing of remuneration .... [7.1906]
197 Remuneration (special administration (bank insolvency)) .... [7.1907]
198 Remuneration (special administration (bank administration) .... [7.1908]
199 Recourse to meeting of creditors and clients .... [7.1909]
200 Recourse to the court .... [7.1910]
201 Creditors' and clients' request for further information .... [7.1911]

202 Claim that remuneration is excessive . . . [7.1912]
203 Review of remuneration . . . [7.1913]
204 Remuneration of new administrator . . . [7.1914]
205 Apportionment of set fee remuneration . . . [7.1915]

CHAPTER 3
REPLACING THE ADMINISTRATOR

206 Grounds for resignation . . . [7.1916]
207 Notice of intention to resign . . . [7.1917]
208 Notice of resignation . . . [7.1918]
209 Application to court to remove administrator from office . . . [7.1919]
210 Notice of vacation of office when administrator ceases to be qualified . . . [7.1920]
211 Administrator deceased . . . [7.1921]
212 Application to replace (special administration) . . . [7.1922]
213 Application to replace (special administration (bank insolvency)) . . . [7.1923]
214 Application to replace (special administration (bank administration)) . . . [7.1924]
215 Notification and advertisement of appointment of replacement administrator . . . [7.1925]
216 Notification and advertisement of appointment of joint administrator . . . [7.1926]
217 Additional joint administrator (special administration (bank administration)) . . . [7.1927]
218 Notification of new administrator . . . [7.1928]
219 Administrator's duties on vacating office . . . [7.1929]

PART 8
END OF SPECIAL ADMINISTRATION

220 Final progress reports . . . [7.1930]
221 Application to court by administrator . . . [7.1931]
222 Application to court by creditor . . . [7.1932]
223 Notification by administrator of court order . . . [7.1933]
224 Moving from administration to dissolution . . . [7.1934]

PART 9
COURT PROCEDURE AND PRACTICE

CHAPTER 1
APPLICATION OF THE CPR

225 Principal court rules and practice to apply . . . [7.1935]

CHAPTER 2
THE COURT

226 Shorthand writers—nomination, appointment, remuneration and costs . . . [7.1936]
227 Court file . . . [7.1937]
228 Office copies of documents . . . [7.1938]
229 Payments into court . . . [7.1939]

CHAPTER 3
OBTAINING INFORMATION AND EVIDENCE

230 Further information and disclosure . . . [7.1940]
231 Witness statements—general . . . [7.1941]
232 Filing and service of witness statements . . . [7.1942]
233 Evidence provided by the administrator . . . [7.1943]

CHAPTER 4
SERVICE OF COURT DOCUMENTS

234 Application of Chapter . . . [7.1944]
235 Service of court documents within the jurisdiction . . . [7.1945]
236 Service of court documents outside jurisdiction . . . [7.1946]
237 Service of orders staying proceedings . . . [7.1947]
238 Service on joint office-holders . . . [7.1948]

CHAPTER 5
APPLICATIONS TO COURT—GENERAL

239 Application of Chapter . . . [7.1949]
240 Form and contents of application . . . [7.1950]
241 Filing and service of application . . . [7.1951]
242 Directions . . . [7.1952]
243 Hearings without notice . . . [7.1953]
244 Hearing of application . . . [7.1954]
245 Adjournment of the hearing of an application . . . [7.1955]

CHAPTER 6
APPLICATIONS TO THE COURT UNDER SECTION 176A

246 Application of Chapter . . . . [7.1956]
247 Applications under section 176A(5) to disapply section 176A . . . . [7.1957]
248 Notice of application under section 176A(5). . . . . [7.1958]
249 Notice of an order under section 176A(5) . . . . [7.1959]

CHAPTER 7
APPLICATIONS FOR AN ORDER UNDER SECTION 236

250 Application of following rules . . . . [7.1960]
251 Form and contents of application . . . . [7.1961]
252 Order for examination etc . . . . [7.1962]
253 Procedure for examination . . . . [7.1963]
254 Record of examination . . . . [7.1964]
255 Costs of proceedings under section 236 . . . . [7.1965]

CHAPTER 8
PEOPLE WHO LACK CAPACITY TO MANAGE THEIR AFFAIRS ETC

256 Application of Chapter 8 . . . . [7.1966]
257 Appointment of another person to act . . . . [7.1967]
258 Witness statement in support of application . . . . [7.1968]
259 Service of notices following appointment . . . . [7.1969]

CHAPTER 9
FORMAL DEFECTS

260 Formal defects . . . . [7.1970]

CHAPTER 10
COSTS

261 Application of Chapter 10 . . . . [7.1971]
262 Requirement to assess costs by the detailed procedure . . . . [7.1972]
263 Procedure where detailed assessment is required . . . . [7.1973]
264 Costs of officers charged with execution of writs or other process . . . . [7.1974]
265 Costs paid otherwise than out of the investment bank's estate . . . . [7.1975]
266 Award of costs against the administrator . . . . [7.1976]
267 Applications for costs . . . . [7.1977]
268 Costs and expenses of witnesses . . . . [7.1978]
269 Final costs certificate . . . . [7.1979]

CHAPTER 11
ENFORCEMENT PROCEDURES

270 Enforcement of court orders . . . . [7.1980]
271 Orders enforcing compliance with the Rules. . . . . [7.1981]
272 Warrants (general provisions) . . . . [7.1982]
273 Warrants under section 236 . . . . [7.1983]

CHAPTER 12
APPEALS

274 Application of Chapter 12 . . . . [7.1984]
275 Appeals and reviews of court orders . . . . [7.1985]
276 Procedure on appeal. . . . . [7.1986]
277 Appeal against decision of the Secretary of State . . . . [7.1987]

PART 10
PROHIBITED NAMES

278 Preliminary. . . . . [7.1988]
279 Application for permission under section 216(3) . . . . [7.1989]
280 First excepted case . . . . [7.1990]
281 Second excepted case. . . . . [7.1991]
282 Third excepted case. . . . . [7.1992]

PART 11
PROVISIONS OF GENERAL EFFECT

CHAPTER 1
MISCELLANEOUS AND GENERAL

283 Costs, expenses etc . . . . [7.1993]
284 Provable debts . . . . [7.1994]
285 False claim of status as creditor, etc . . . . [7.1995]

286 Punishment of offences . . . [7.1996]

CHAPTER 2
THE GIVING OF NOTICE AND THE SUPPLY OF DOCUMENTS

287 Application . . . [7.1997]
288 Personal delivery . . . [7.1998]
289 Postal delivery of documents . . . [7.1999]
290 Notice etc to solicitors . . . [7.2000]

CHAPTER 3
THE GIVING OF NOTICE AND THE SUPPLY OF DOCUMENTS TO OR BY THE ADMINISTRATOR

291 Application . . . [7.2001]
292 The form . . . [7.2002]
293 Proof of sending . . . [7.2003]
294 Authentication . . . [7.2004]
295 Electronic delivery – general . . . [7.2005]
296 Electronic delivery by administrator . . . [7.2006]
297 Use of websites by administrator . . . [7.2007]
298 Special provision on account of expense as to website use . . . [7.2008]
299 Electronic delivery of special administration documents to court . . . [7.2009]
300 Notice etc to joint administrators . . . [7.2010]
301 Execution overtaken by judgment debtor's insolvency . . . [7.2011]
302 Notice to enforcement officers . . . [7.2012]
303 Electronic submission of information . . . [7.2013]
304 Electronic submission of information where rule 303 does not apply . . . [7.2014]
305 Contents of notices to be gazetted . . . [7.2015]
306 Gazette notices relating to companies . . . [7.2016]
307 Omission of unobtainable information . . . [7.2017]
308 The Gazette—general . . . [7.2018]
309 Notices otherwise advertised under the Regulations or Rules . . . [7.2019]
310 Non-Gazette notices . . . [7.2020]
311 Non-Gazette notices—other provisions . . . [7.2021]

CHAPTER 4
NOTIFICATIONS TO THE REGISTRAR OF COMPANIES

312 Application of Chapter 4 . . . [7.2022]
313 Information to be contained in all notifications to the registrar . . . [7.2023]
314 Notification relating to the administrator . . . [7.2024]
315 Notifications relating to documents . . . [7.2025]
316 Notifications relating to court orders . . . [7.2026]
317 Notifications relating to other events . . . [7.2027]
318 Notifications of more than one nature . . . [7.2028]
319 Notifications made to other persons at the same time . . . [7.2029]

CHAPTER 5
FURTHER PROVISIONS CONCERNING DOCUMENTS

320 Confidentiality of documents—grounds for refusing inspection . . . [7.2030]
321 Right to copy documents . . . [7.2031]
322 Charges for copy documents . . . [7.2032]
323 Right to have list of creditors . . . [7.2033]

CHAPTER 6
TIME LIMITS AND SECURITY

324 Time limits . . . [7.2034]
325 Administrator's security . . . [7.2035]

CHAPTER 7
TRANSFER OF PROCEEDINGS

326 Proceedings commenced in the wrong court . . . [7.2036]
327 Proceedings other than special administration commenced . . . [7.2037]

PART 12
GENERAL INTERPRETATION AND APPLICATION

328 Introduction . . . [7.2038]
329 "The court"; "the registrar" . . . [7.2039]
330 Venue . . . [7.2040]
331 Insolvent estate . . . [7.2041]

332 The appropriate fee . . . .[7.2042]
333 "Debt"; "liability" . . . .[7.2043]
334 Application of the 1986 Act and the Company Directors Disqualification Act . . . .[7.2044]

SCHEDULES

Schedule—Punishment of Offences . . . .[7.2045]

PART 1
INTRODUCTORY PROVISIONS

[7.1711]
1 Citation

These Rules may be cited as the Investment Bank Special Administration (England and Wales) Rules 2011.

[7.1712]
2 Commencement

These Rules come into force on 30th June 2011.

[7.1713]
3 Extent

These Rules extend to England and Wales only.

[7.1714]
4 Interpretation

(1) In these Rules—

"the 1986 Act" means the Insolvency Act 1986;
"the 2006 Act" means the Companies Act 2006;
"the 2009 Act" means the Banking Act 2009;
"business address" means the place where a person works;
"business day" means any day other than a Saturday, a Sunday, Christmas Day, Good Friday or a day which is a bank holiday in any part of England and Wales under or by virtue of the Banking and Financial Dealings Act 1971;
"certificate of service" means a certificate of service verified by a statement of truth;
"CPR" means the Civil Procedure Rules 1998 and "CPR" followed by a Part or a rule number means the Part or rule with that number in those rules;
"file in court and file with the court" means deliver to the court for filing;
"financial contract" means a bilateral or multilateral contract entered into with the investment bank before it entered special administration, relating to transactions or positions of a financial nature, including contracts for the delivery or custody of client assets (but not including contracts which are purely administrative or contracts for services);
"the Gazette" means the London Gazette;
"gazetted" means advertised once in the Gazette;
"investment bank" has the meaning set out in section 232 of the 2009 Act;
"market price" has the meaning set out in regulation 12(9);
"means of contacting" means being able to contact that person specifically;
"person connected with the investment bank" has the same meaning in respect of the investment bank as a person connected with a company in accordance with section 249 of the 1986 Act;
"practice direction" means a direction as to the practice and procedure of any court within the scope of the CPR;
"prescribed order of priority" means the order of priority of payments laid down by rule 134;
"prescribed part" has the same meaning as it does in section 176A(2)(a) of the 1986 Act and the Insolvency Act 1986 (Prescribed Part) Order 2003;
"registered number" of the investment bank has the meaning set out in section 1066 of the 2006 Act;
"registrar of companies" means the registrar of companies for England and Wales;
"the Regulations" means the Investment Bank Special Administration Regulations 2011;
"resolution fund order" has the meaning set out in section 49(3) of the 2009 Act;
"special administration" means, unless otherwise stated, special administration, special administration (bank insolvency) or special administration (bank administration) as the case may be;
"standard contents" means—
(a) in relation to a notice to be gazetted, the contents specified in rules 300 and 301; and
(b) in relation to a notice to be advertised in any other way, the contents specified in rule 304;
"statement of truth" means a statement of truth in accordance with CPR Part 22; and
"witness statement" means a witness statement verified by a statement of truth in accordance with CPR Part 22.

(2) A fee or remuneration is charged when the work to which it relates is done.

(3) Expressions used both in these Rules and in the Regulations (including expressions used in the provisions of the 1986 Act applied by the Regulations) have, unless otherwise stated, the meaning set out in the Regulations.

(4) A reference to a numbered paragraph in these Rules shall, unless—

(a) it is a reference to a paragraph within the same rule; or
(b) otherwise stated,

be to the paragraph so numbered in Schedule B1 to the 1986 Act, as applied by regulation 15.

(5) A reference to a provision of the 1986 Act, if that provision is listed in Table 1 or 2 in regulation 15, is, unless otherwise stated and subject to paragraph (5), a reference to that provision as applied by regulation 15.

(6) A reference to a provision of the 1986 Act being applied by regulation 15 in a special administration (bank administration), means that provision as applied by section 145 of the 2009 Act, together with the modifications (if any) set out in the table in paragraph 6 of Schedule 2 to the Regulations.

(7) A reference to a numbered regulation shall, unless otherwise stated, be to the regulation so numbered in the Regulations.

[7.1715]
5 Application of rules

(1) The rules apply as follows—
(a) Part 2, Chapter 1 applies where an application is made for a special administration order;
(b) Part 2, Chapter 2 applies where an application is made for a special administration (bank insolvency) order; and
(c) Part 2, Chapter 3 applies where an application is made for a special administration (bank administration) order.

(2) Unless otherwise stated, the remaining rules apply in respect of special administration, special administration (bank insolvency) and special administration (bank administration).

PART 2
APPLICATION FOR ORDER

CHAPTER 1 APPLICATION FOR SPECIAL ADMINISTRATION ORDER

[7.1716]
6 Content of application

(1) An application for a special administration order must be made in writing and signed by the applicant.

(2) The application must state—
(a) the full name and registered number of the investment bank;
(b) any other trading names;
(c) the investment bank's date of incorporation;
(d) the investment bank's nominated capital and the amount of capital paid up;
(e) the address of the investment bank's registered office;
(f) an email address for the investment bank;
(g) the identity of the person (or persons) nominated for appointment as administrator; and
(h) a statement setting out which of the grounds in regulation 6(1) the applicant is relying on in making the application.

[7.1717]
7 Statement of proposed administrator

An application for a special administration order must be accompanied by a statement by the proposed administrator—
(a) specifying the name and business address of the person (or each person) proposed to be appointed;
(b) giving that person's (or each person's) consent to act;
(c) giving details of the person's (or each person's) qualification to act as an insolvency practitioner; and
(d) giving details of any prior professional relationship that the person (or any of them) has had with the investment bank.

[7.1718]
8 Witness statement in support of application

(1) An application for a special administration order must be accompanied by a witness statement.

(2) If the application is made by—
(a) the investment bank or one of its directors, the witness statement shall be made by one of its directors or the company secretary of the investment bank, stating that they make it on behalf of the investment bank or, as the case may be, on behalf of the directors;
(b) a creditor or a contributory of the investment bank, the witness statement shall be made by a person acting under the authority of all the creditors, or, as the case may be, all the contributories, making the application;
(c) the [FCA or, where relevant, the PRA], the witness statement must identify the person making the statement and must include the capacity in which that person makes the statement and the basis for that person's knowledge of the matters set out in the statement; or
(d) a combination of the persons listed in regulation 5(1)(a) to (e), the witness statement shall be made by a person acting under the authority of all the applicants.

(3) The witness statement shall—

(a) set out the reasons by which the applicant believes the ground in regulation 6 on which the application is based is satisfied;
(b) state the investment bank's current financial position, specifying (to the best of the applicant's knowledge and belief) the investment bank's assets and liabilities, including contingent and prospective liabilities;
(c) specify any security known or believed to be held by the creditors of the investment bank;
(d) specify the amount of client assets held by the investment bank to the best of the applicant's knowledge and belief;
(e) specify how functions are going to be allocated where more than one person is to be appointed as administrator (stating in particular whether functions are to be exercisable jointly or by any or all of the persons appointed); and
(f) specify any other matters which the applicant thinks will assist the court in deciding whether to make the special administration order.

NOTES

Para (2): words in square brackets in sub-para (c) substituted for "FSA" by the Financial Services Act 2012 (Consequential Amendments and Transitional Provisions) Order 2013, SI 2013/472, art 3, Sch 2, para 210(a), (b)(i), subject to a transitional provision in para 211 which provides:

> "**211 Transitional provision in relation to the Bank Special Administration (England and Wales) Rules 2011**
> For the purposes of the Investment Bank Special Administration (England and Wales) Rules 2011, anything done by or in relation to the Financial Services Authority under those Rules in relation to, or in connection with an investment bank which is, on 1st April 2013, a PRA-authorised person (within the meaning of those Rules) is to be treated, unless the context otherwise requires, as having also been done by or in relation to the Prudential Regulation Authority."

[7.1719]
9 Filing of application

(1) The application and its accompanying documents must be filed in court together with enough copies of the application and accompanying documents for service and proof of service under rule 10.

(2) The court shall fix a venue for the hearing of the application.

(3) In fixing the venue the court shall have regard to—
(a) the desirability of the application being heard as soon as is reasonably practicable; and
(b) the need for the investment bank's representatives to be able to reach the venue in time for the hearing.

(4) Each of the copies filed—
(a) shall have the seal of the court applied to it;
(b) shall be endorsed with the date and time of filing;
(c) shall be endorsed with the venue for the hearing of the application.

[7.1720]
10 Service of application

(1) The application shall be served on—
(a) the investment bank (if neither the investment bank nor its directors are the applicant);
(b) the person (or each of the persons) nominated for appointment as administrator;
(c) any person who has given notice to the [FCA or, where relevant, the PRA] in respect of the investment bank under regulation 8;
(d) if there is in force for the investment bank a voluntary arrangement under Part 1 of the 1986 Act, the supervisor of that arrangement.

(2) Service under paragraph (1) must be service of a sealed and endorsed copy of the application and its accompanying documents issued under rule 9.

(3) Service of the application must be effected by the applicant, or their solicitor, or by a person instructed by the applicant or the solicitor, as soon as reasonably practicable before the hearing.

(4) Service shall be effected as follows—
(a) on the investment bank (subject to paragraph (5)), by delivering the documents to its registered office; and
(b) on any other person (subject to paragraph (6)) by delivering the documents to that person's proper address.

(5) If delivery to the investment bank's registered office is not practicable, service may be effected by delivery to its last known principal place of business in England and Wales.

(6) For the purposes of paragraph (4)(b), a person's proper address is any which that person has previously notified to the applicant as their address for service, but if no address has been notified, service may be effected by delivery to that person's usual or last known address.

(7) Delivery of documents to any place or address may be made by leaving them there or by electronic delivery in accordance with rule 295 (and where the document is sent electronically, it shall be sent with a read receipt and the message shall be deemed to be delivered when the message is read).

NOTES

Para (1): words in square brackets in sub-para (c) substituted for "FSA" by the Financial Services Act 2012 (Consequential Amendments and Transitional Provisions) Order 2013, SI 2013/472, art 3, Sch 2, para 210(a), (b)(ii), subject to a transitional provision (see para 211 as noted to **[7.1718]**).

[7.1721]
11 Proof of service

(1) Service of the application shall be verified by a witness statement specifying the date and time on which, and the manner in which, service was effected.

(2) The witness statement, with a sealed copy of the application exhibited to it, shall be filed with the court—
- (a) as soon as is reasonably practicable; and
- (b) in any event, before the hearing of the application.

[7.1722]
12 Further notification

As soon as reasonably practicable after filing the application, the applicant must notify—
- (a) any enforcement officer or other officer whom the applicant knows to be charged with effecting an execution or other legal process against the investment bank or its property;
- (b) any person whom the applicant knows to have distrained against the investment bank or its property; . . .
- [(c) the FCA (if not the applicant); and
- (d) if the application relates to a PRA-authorised person, the PRA (if not the applicant).]

NOTES

Word "and" (omitted) at the end of para (b) revoked, and paras (c), (d) substituted, for original para (c), by the Financial Services Act 2012 (Consequential Amendments and Transitional Provisions) Order 2013, SI 2013/472, art 3, Sch 2, para 210(e), subject to a transitional provision (see para 211 as noted to **[7.1718]**). Para (c) originally read as follows:

"(c) (if not the applicant) the FSA.".

[7.1723]
13 The hearing

At the hearing of the application, any of the following may appear or be represented—
- (a) the applicant;
- (b) the investment bank;
- (c) one or more of the directors;
- (d) the person (or a person) nominated for appointment as administrator;
- (e) any supervisor of a voluntary arrangement under Part 1 of the 1986 Act;
- (f) any person who has given notice to the [FCA or, where relevant, the PRA] in respect of the investment bank under regulation 8;
- [(g) the FCA;
- (ga) if the investment bank concerned is a PRA-authorised person, the PRA; and]
- (h) with the permission of the court, any other person who appears to have an interest.

NOTES

Para (f): words in square brackets substituted for "FSA" by the Financial Services Act 2012 (Consequential Amendments and Transitional Provisions) Order 2013, SI 2013/472, art 3, Sch 2, para 210(a), (b)(iii), subject to a transitional provision (see para 211 as noted to **[7.1718]**).

Paras (g), (ga) substituted, for original para (g), by SI 2013/472, art 3, Sch 2, para 210(f), subject to a transitional provision (see para 211 as noted to **[7.1718]**). Para (g) originally read as follows:

"(g) the FSA; and".

[7.1724]
14 The special administration order

If the court makes a special administration order, the order shall state—
- (a) the name and address of the applicant;
- (b) the name, registered address and registered number of the investment bank to which the order refers;
- (c) details of any other parties appearing at the hearing;
- (d) the name of any administrator appointed by the order;
- (e) the date and time from which their appointment shall take effect;
- (f) the terms for costs of the application; and
- (g) any further particulars that the court thinks fit.

[7.1725]
15 Costs

If the court makes a special administration order, the following are payable as an expense of the special administration—
- (a) costs of the applicant; and
- (b) any other costs allowed by the court.

[7.1726]
16 Notice of special administration order

(1) If the court makes a special administration order, it shall, as soon as reasonably practicable, send 3 sealed copies to the applicant.

(2) The applicant shall as soon as reasonably practicable, send a sealed copy to—

(a) the administrator; . . .
[(b) the FCA (if not the applicant); and
(c) if the application relates to a PRA-authorised person, the PRA (if not the applicant).]

(3) If the court makes an order under regulation 7(1)(d), or any other order under regulation 7(1)(f), it shall give directions as to the persons to whom and how notice of that order is to be given.

NOTES

Para (2): word "and" (omitted) at the end of sub-para (a) revoked, and sub-paras (b), (c) substituted, for original sub-para (b), by the Financial Services Act 2012 (Consequential Amendments and Transitional Provisions) Order 2013, SI 2013/472, art 3, Sch 2, para 210(g), subject to a transitional provision (see para 211 as noted to **[7.1718]**). Sub-para (b) originally read as follows:

"(b) the FSA (if not the applicant).".

CHAPTER 2 APPLICATION FOR A SPECIAL ADMINISTRATION (BANK INSOLVENCY) ORDER

[7.1727]
17 Filing of application

(1) The application for a special administration (bank insolvency) order, verified by witness statement in accordance with rule 21, shall be filed in court.

(2) There shall be filed with the application—
(a) a copy for service on the investment bank;
(b) a copy to be attached to the proof of service; and
(c) further copies to be sent to the persons under rule 20.

(3) The court shall fix the venue, date and time for the hearing of the application and in doing so shall have regard to—
(a) the desirability of the application being heard as soon as is reasonably practicable; and
(b) the need to give the investment bank a reasonable opportunity to attend.

(4) Each of the copies issued to the applicant shall be sealed and be endorsed with the venue, date and time for the hearing.

(5) Any application filed in relation to an investment bank in respect of which there is in force a voluntary arrangement under Part 1 of the 1986 Act shall be filed in accordance with this rule, but a copy of that application shall also be sent to the court to which the nominee's report was submitted, if that is not the same court.

[7.1728]
18 Service of application

(1) The applicant shall serve the investment bank with a sealed copy of the application.

(2) The application shall be served on the investment bank by personal service at its registered office.

(3) In paragraph (2), "registered office" means—
(a) the place which is specified, in the investment bank's statement delivered under section 9 of the 2006 Act as the intended situation of its registered office on incorporation; or
(b) if notice has been given by the investment bank to the registrar of companies under section 87 of the 2006 Act, the place specified in that notice or, as the case may be, in the last such notice.

(4) Service of the application at the registered office may be effected in any of the following ways—
(a) it may be handed to a person who there and then acknowledges that they are, or to the best of the server's knowledge, information and belief are, a director or other officer, or employee, of the investment bank; or
(b) it may be handed to a person who there and then acknowledges that they are authorised to accept service of documents on the investment bank's behalf; or
(c) in the absence of such person as is mentioned in sub-paragraphs (a) and (b), it may be deposited at or about the registered office in such a way that it is likely to come to the notice of a person attending the office.

(5) If for any reason it is impracticable to effect service as provided by paragraph (2) or (4), the application may be served in such other manner as the court may approve or direct.

(6) Application for permission of the court under paragraph (5) may be made without notice to the investment bank, stating in a witness statement what steps have been taken to comply with paragraph (2) or (4), and the reasons why it is impracticable to effect service as there provided.

(7) If the investment bank or its legal representatives fail to attend the hearing, the court may make the bank insolvency order in its absence if satisfied that the application has been served in accordance with this rule.

[7.1729]
19 Proof of service

(1) Service of the application must be proved by a certificate of service.

(2) The certificate of service must be sufficient to identify the application served and must specify—
(a) the name and registered number of the investment bank;
(b) the address of the registered office of the investment bank;
(c) whether the applicant is the Bank of England[, the FCA or the PRA];
(d) the address of the Bank of England;

(e) whether the copy served was a sealed copy;
(f) the date on which service was effected; and
(g) the manner in which service was effected.

(3) Where substituted service has been ordered under rule 18(5), the certificate of service must have attached to it a sealed copy of the order.

(4) The certificate of service must be filed in court as soon as reasonably practicable after service.

NOTES

Para (2): words in square brackets substituted for "or the FSA" by the Financial Services Act 2012 (Consequential Amendments and Transitional Provisions) Order 2013, SI 2013/472, art 3, Sch 2, para 210(h), subject to a transitional provision (see para 211 as noted to **[7.1718]**).

[7.1730]
20 Other persons to receive copy of application

(1) The applicant shall send 2 sealed copies of the application to—
(a) the proposed administrator;
(b) the Bank of England, (if not the applicant);
[(c) the FCA (if not the applicant);
(ca) if the application relates to a PRA-authorised person, the PRA (if not the applicant);]
(d) the FSCS;
(e) any person who has given notice to the [FCA or, where relevant, the PRA] in respect of the investment bank under section 120 of the 2009 Act; and
(f) if there is in force for the investment bank a voluntary arrangement under Part 1 of the 1986 Act, the supervisor of that arrangement,

in accordance with paragraph (2).

(2) One copy shall be sent electronically as soon as practicable and the other (a sealed copy) shall be sent by first class post on the business day on which the application is served on the investment bank.

(3) Any of the persons in paragraph (1) will have the right to attend and be heard at the hearing of the application.

NOTES

Para (1): sub-paras (c), (ca) substituted, for original sub-para (c), and words in square brackets in sub-para (e) substituted for "FSA", by the Financial Services Act 2012 (Consequential Amendments and Transitional Provisions) Order 2013, SI 2013/472, art 3, Sch 2, para 210(a), (b)(iv), (i), subject to a transitional provision (see para 211 as noted to **[7.1718]**). Sub-para (c) originally read as follows:

"(c) the FSA, (if not the applicant);".

[7.1731]
21 Verification of application

(1) This rule applies where an application has been filed at the court under rule 17 above.

(2) A witness statement shall be attached to the application to state that the statements in the application are true, or are true to the best of the applicant's knowledge, information and belief.

(3) The witness statement shall identify the person making the statement and shall include the capacity in which that person makes the statement and the basis for that person's knowledge of the matters set out in the application.

[7.1732]
22 Persons entitled to copy of application

(1) Every contributory or creditor or client of the investment bank is entitled to a copy of the application on request from the applicant.

(2) The applicant shall respond to any request for a copy of the application as soon as reasonably practicable after the application has been made on payment of the appropriate fee.

[7.1733]
23 Certificate of compliance

(1) The applicant or the applicant's solicitor shall, as soon as reasonably practicable before the hearing of the application, file in court a certificate of compliance with the rules relating to service.

(2) The certificate shall show—
(a) the date of the application;
(b) the date fixed for the hearing; and
(c) the date or dates when the application was served and that notice of it was given in compliance with the Rules.

(3) A witness statement made by the proposed administrator to the effect that—
(a) the person is qualified to act as an insolvency practitioner in accordance with section 390 of the 1986 Act; and
(b) the person consents to act as the administrator,

shall be filed in court with the certificate.

[7.1734]
24 Leave for the applicant to withdraw

(1) The applicant may withdraw the application for a special administration (bank insolvency) order at any time before the hearing with the permission of the court.

(2) An application for permission under paragraph (1) may be made without notice.

(3) The court may grant permission on such terms as the court thinks fit.

[7.1735]
25 Witness statement in opposition

(1) If the investment bank intends to oppose an application, it may (but need not) file a witness statement in opposition in court.

(2) A statement under paragraph (1) must be filed before the hearing of the application and a copy must be served on the applicant, before the hearing.

(3) The statement may be served on the applicant by personal service or by electronic means.

(4) The statement should also be sent to the persons in rule 20(1) before the hearing by personal service or by electronic means.

(5) The fact that the investment bank has not filed a statement under this rule shall not prevent it being heard at the hearing.

[7.1736]
26 Making, transmission and advertisement of order

(1) The court shall not make a special administration (bank insolvency) order unless the person nominated to be appointed as the administrator in the application for the order has filed in court a witness statement under rule 23.

(2) When the order has been made, the court shall immediately send 5 sealed copies (or such larger number as the administrator may have requested) to the administrator.

(3) The court shall also, if practicable, immediately send a copy of the order to the administrator electronically.

(4) The administrator shall serve a sealed copy of the order on the investment bank at its registered office and, where the bank liquidator knows the investment bank's email address, will send an electronic copy to the investment bank.

(5) The administrator shall send 2 copies of the order—

- (a) to the Bank of England, the [FCA and, where the investment bank concerned is a PRA-authorised person, the PRA] and the FSCS; and
- (b) if there is in force for the investment bank a voluntary arrangement under Part 1 of the 1986 Act, the supervisor of that arrangement,

in accordance with paragraph (6).

(6) One copy shall be sent electronically as soon as reasonably practicable and the other (a sealed copy) shall be sent by first class post on the business day on which the order is served on the investment bank.

NOTES

Para (5): words in square brackets in sub-para (a) substituted for "FSA", by the Financial Services Act 2012 (Consequential Amendments and Transitional Provisions) Order 2013, SI 2013/472, art 3, Sch 2, para 210(c), (d)(i), subject to a transitional provision (see para 211 as noted to **[7.1718]**).

[7.1737]
27 Special administration (bank insolvency) order

If the court makes a special administration (bank insolvency) order, the order shall state—

- (a) the name and address of the applicant;
- (b) the name, registered address and registered number of the investment bank to which the order refers;
- (c) details of any other parties appearing at the hearing;
- (d) the name and business address of any administrator appointed by the order;
- (e) the date and time from which their appointment shall take effect;
- (f) the terms for costs of the application; and
- (g) any further particulars that the court thinks fit.

[7.1738]
28 Authentication of administrator's appointment

A sealed copy of the court's order may in any proceedings be adduced as proof that the person appointed is duly authorised to exercise the powers and perform the duties of the administrator in the special administration (bank insolvency).

[7.1739]
29 Duties of Objective A committee

(1) This rule applies where a special administration (bank insolvency) order has been made.

(2) As soon as reasonably practicable after the making of a special administration (bank insolvency) order, the Objective A committee shall meet the administrator for the purpose of discussing which of the objectives, or combination of objectives, mentioned in section 102(1) of the 2009 Act (as applied by paragraph 6 of Schedule 1 to the Regulations), the committee should recommend the administrator to pursue.

(3) If the administrator and every individual on the Objective A committee agree, the meeting may be held by audio or video conference.

(4) The Objective A committee shall make its recommendation to the administrator at the meeting.

(5) The Bank of England shall confirm the Objective A committee's recommendation in writing as soon as practicable after the meeting.

(6) As soon as practicable after the making of a special administration (bank insolvency) order, the Objective A committee shall also pass a resolution as to the terms on which, in accordance with rule 196, the administrator is to be remunerated in respect of—

- (a) work done by the administrator in pursuit of Objective A; and
- (b) work done by the administrator in pursuit of Objectives 2 and 3 of the special administration objectives.

(7) The Objective A committee—

- (a) shall take decisions and pass resolutions by a simple majority; and
- (b) for the purpose of taking decisions and passing resolutions, may communicate by any means that its members consider convenient.

[7.1740]
30 Appointment of person under section 135

(1) An application to the court for the appointment of a person under section 135 of the 1986 Act (as applied by paragraph 8 of Schedule 1 to the Regulations) may be made—

- (a) by the Bank of England; . . .
- [(b) by the FCA, with the consent of the Bank of England; or
- (c) if the application relates to a PRA-authorised person, by the PRA, with the consent of the Bank of England;]

(2) The application must be supported by a witness statement stating—

- (a) the grounds upon which it is proposed that the person should be appointed;
- (b) that the person to be appointed has consented to act;
- (c) that the person to be appointed is qualified to act as an insolvency practitioner;
- (d) whether to the applicant's knowledge there has been proposed or is in force for the investment bank a company voluntary arrangement under Part 1 of the 1986 Act;
- (e) the applicant's estimate of the value of the assets in respect of which the person is to be appointed; and
- (f) the functions the applicant wishes to be carried out by the person appointed under this rule in relation to the investment bank's affairs.

(3) The court may on the application, if satisfied that an application has been made for a special administration (bank insolvency) order and that sufficient grounds are shown for the appointment, make it on such terms as it thinks fit.

NOTES

Para (1): word "or" (omitted) at the end of sub-para (a) revoked, and sub-paras (b), (c) substituted, for original sub-para (b), by the Financial Services Act 2012 (Consequential Amendments and Transitional Provisions) Order 2013, SI 2013/472, art 3, Sch 2, para 210(j), subject to a transitional provision (see para 211 as noted to **[7.1718]**). Sub-para (b) originally read as follows:

"(b) by the FSA (with the consent of the Bank of England).".

[7.1741]
31 Notice of appointment

(1) Where a person has been appointed under rule 30, the court shall notify the applicant and the person appointed.

(2) Unless the court otherwise directs, on receipt of the notification under paragraph (1) the person appointed shall give notice of that appointment as soon as reasonably practicable. Such notice—

- (a) shall be gazetted; and
- (b) may be advertised in such other manner as the person appointed thinks fit.

[7.1742]
32 Order of appointment

(1) The order of appointment shall specify the functions to be carried out by the person appointed under rule 30 in relation to the investment bank's affairs.

(2) The court shall, immediately after the order is made, send 4 sealed copies of the order (or such larger number as the person appointed may have requested), to the person appointed.

(3) The court shall also, if practicable, immediately send a copy of the order to the person appointed electronically.

(4) The person appointed shall serve a sealed copy of the order on the investment bank at its registered office and, where they know the investment bank's email address, will send an electronic copy to the investment bank.

(5) The person appointed shall send 2 copies of the order—

(a) to the Bank of England, the [FCA and, where the investment bank concerned is a PRA-authorised person, the PRA], and the FSCS; and

(b) if there is in force for the investment bank a voluntary arrangement under Part 1 of the 1986 Act, the supervisor of that arrangement,

in accordance with paragraph (6).

(6) One copy shall be sent electronically as soon as reasonably practicable and the other (a sealed copy) shall be sent by first class post of the business day on which the order is served on the investment bank.

(7) The person appointed shall also send notice of the appointment to the registrar of companies.

NOTES

Para (5): words in square brackets in sub-para (a) substituted for "FSA" by the Financial Services Act 2012 (Consequential Amendments and Transitional Provisions) Order 2013, SI 2013/472, art 3, Sch 2, para 210(c), (d)(ii), subject to a transitional provision (see para 211 as noted to **[7.1718]**).

[7.1743]

33 Security

(1) The following applies where a person is appointed under rule 30.

(2) The cost of providing the security required by the 1986 Act shall be paid in the first instance by the person so appointed; but—

(a) if the special administration (bank insolvency) order is not made, the person so appointed is entitled to be reimbursed out of the estate of the investment bank, and the court may make an order on the investment bank accordingly; and

(b) if the special administration (bank insolvency) order is made, the person so appointed is entitled to be reimbursed as an expense of the administration in the prescribed order of priority.

[7.1744]

34 Failure to give or keep up security

(1) If the person appointed under rule 30 fails to give or keep up their security, that person may be removed by the court and the court make such order as it thinks just as to costs.

(2) If an order is made under this rule, the court shall give directions as to the steps to be taken for the appointment of another person under rule 30.

(3) Where another person is appointed under rule 30, that person shall send notice of their appointment to the registrar of companies.

[7.1745]

35 Remuneration

(1) The remuneration of the person appointed under rule 30 shall be fixed by the court from time to time on that person's application.

(2) In fixing the remuneration, the court shall take into account—

(a) the time properly given by the person appointed;

(b) the complexity (or otherwise) of the case;

(c) any respects in which, in connection with the investment bank's affairs, there falls on the person appointed any responsibility of an exceptional kind or degree;

(d) the effectiveness with which the person appointed appears to be carrying out, or has carried out, their duties; and

(e) the value and nature of the property with which the person appointed has to deal.

(3) Without prejudice to any order the court may make as to costs, the person appointed's remuneration shall be paid to that person and the amount of any expenses incurred by that person shall be reimbursed—

(a) if the special administration (bank insolvency) order is not made, out of the estate of the investment bank;

(b) if the special administration (bank insolvency) order is made, as an expense of the administration, in the prescribed order of priority.

(4) Unless the court otherwise directs, in a case falling within paragraph (3)(a), the person appointed may retain out of the investment bank's estate such sums or property as are, or may be, required for meeting their remuneration and expenses.

[7.1746]

36 Termination of appointment

(1) The appointment of the person appointed under rule 30 may be terminated—

(a) by the court on that person's application; or

(b) on the application of any of the persons specified in rule 30(1).

(2) The appointment of the person so appointed will be automatically terminated on the making of the special administration (bank insolvency) order.

(3) On the termination of the appointment, the court may give such directions as it thinks fit with respect to the account of that person's administration or any other matters which it thinks appropriate.

(4) Unless the court directs otherwise, where the appointment is terminated, the person who was appointed under rule 30 shall give notice of the termination. Such notice—

(a) shall be gazetted; and

(b) may be advertised in such other manner as that person thinks fit.

(5) The person who was appointed under rule 30 shall send notice of the termination of their appointment to the registrar of companies.

CHAPTER 3 APPLICATION FOR A SPECIAL ADMINISTRATION (BANK ADMINISTRATION) ORDER

[7.1747]
37 Content of application

(1) An application by the Bank of England for a special administration (bank administration) order in respect of an investment bank must specify—

(a) the full name of the investment bank;
(b) any other trading names;
(c) the address of the investment bank's registered office;
(d) an email address for the investment bank;
(e) the address of the Bank of England; and
(f) the identity of the person (or persons) nominated for appointment as administrator.

(2) If the investment bank has notified the Bank of England of an address for service which is, because of special circumstances, to be used in place of the registered office, that address shall be specified under paragraph (1)(c).

[7.1748]
38 Statement of proposed administrator

An application must be accompanied by a statement by the proposed administrator—

(a) specifying the name and business address of the person (or of each person) proposed to be appointed;
(b) giving that person's (or each person's) consent to act;
(c) giving details of the person's (or each person's) qualification to act as an insolvency practitioner; and
(d) giving details of any prior professional relationship that the person (or any of them) has had with the investment bank.

[7.1749]
39 Bank of England witness statement

(1) An application for a special administration (bank administration) order in respect of an investment bank must be accompanied by a witness statement made on behalf of the Bank of England—

(a) certifying that the conditions for applying for a special administration (bank administration) order, set out in section 143 of the 2009 Act (as applied by paragraph 6 of Schedule 2 to the Regulations), are met in respect of the investment bank;
(b) stating the investment bank's current financial position to the best of the Bank of England's knowledge and belief (including actual, contingent and prospective assets and liabilities);
(c) specifying any security which the Bank of England knows or believes to be held by a creditor of the investment bank;
(d) specify the amount of client assets held by the investment bank to the best of the applicant's knowledge and belief;
(e) specifying any insolvency proceedings which have been instituted in respect of the investment bank (including any process notified to the [FCA or, where relevant, the PRA] under section 120 of the 2009 Act);
(f) giving details of the property transfer instrument which the Bank of England has made or intends to make in respect of the investment bank;
(g) where the property transfer instrument has not yet been made, explaining what effect it is likely to have on the investment bank's financial position;
(h) specifying how functions are to be allocated where more than one person is to be appointed as administrator (stating, in particular, whether functions are to be exercisable jointly or concurrently); and
(i) including any other material which the Bank of England thinks may help the court to decide whether to make the special administration (bank administration) order.

(2) The statement must identify the person making the statement and must include the capacity in which that person makes the statement and the basis for that person's knowledge of the matters set out in the statement.

NOTES

Para (1): words in square brackets in sub-para (e) substituted for "FSA" by the Financial Services Act 2012 (Consequential Amendments and Transitional Provisions) Order 2013, SI 2013/472, art 3, Sch 2, para 210(a), (b)(v), subject to a transitional provision (see para 211 as noted to **[7.1718]**).

[7.1750]
40 Filing

(1) The application, and its accompanying documents, must be filed with the court, together with enough copies of the application and accompanying documents for service under rule 41.

(2) Each filed copy—

(a) shall have the seal of the court applied to it;

(b) shall be endorsed with the date and time of filing;
(c) shall be endorsed with the venue for the hearing of the application (fixed by the court under rule 43); and
(d) shall be issued to the Bank of England.

[7.1751]
41 Service

(1) The Bank of England shall serve the application—
(a) on the investment bank;
(b) on the person (or each of the persons) nominated for appointment as administrator;
(c) on any person who has given notice to the [FCA or, where relevant, the PRA] in respect of the investment bank under section 120 of the 2009 Act (notice of preliminary steps of other insolvency procedures); and
(d) if the property transfer instrument was made or is to be made under section 11(2)(b) of the 2009 Act, on each transferee.

(2) Service under paragraph (1) must be service of a sealed and endorsed copy of the application and its accompanying documents issued under rule 40.

(3) Service must be effected as soon as is reasonably practicable, having regard in particular to the need to give the investment bank's representatives a reasonable opportunity to attend the hearing.

(4) Service must be effected—
(a) by personal service to an address that the person has notified to the Bank of England as an address for service;
(b) by personal service to the person's registered office (where no address for service has been notified);
(c) by personal service to the person's usual or last known principal place of business in England and Wales (where there is no registered office and no address for service has been notified); or
(d) in such other manner and at such a place as the court may direct.

(5) If the Bank of England knows of an email address that is habitually used for business purposes by a person on whom service is required, the Bank must (in addition to personal service) as soon as is reasonably practicable send by email an electronic copy of a sealed and endorsed copy of the application and its accompanying documents.

(6) Service of the application shall be verified by a witness statement specifying the date on which, and the manner in which, service was effected.

(7) The witness statement, with a sealed copy of the application exhibited to it, shall be filed with the court—
(a) as soon as is reasonably practicable; and
(b) in any event, before the hearing of the application.

NOTES

Para (1): words in square brackets in sub-para (c) substituted for "FSA" by the Financial Services Act 2012 (Consequential Amendments and Transitional Provisions) Order 2013, SI 2013/472, art 3, Sch 2, para 210(a), (b)(vi), subject to a transitional provision (see para 211 as noted to **[7.1718]**).

[7.1752]
42 Other notification

As soon as is reasonably practicable after filing the application the Bank of England must notify—
(a) any enforcement officer or other officer whom the Bank of England knows to be charged with effecting an execution or other legal process against the investment bank or its property;
(b) any person whom the Bank of England knows to have distrained against the investment bank or its property; . . .
[(c) the FCA; and
(d) if the application relates to a PRA-authorised person, the PRA.]

NOTES

Word "and" (omitted) at the end of para (b) revoked, and paras (c), (d) substituted, for original para (c), by the Financial Services Act 2012 (Consequential Amendments and Transitional Provisions) Order 2013, SI 2013/472, art 3, Sch 2, para 210(k), subject to a transitional provision (see para 211 as noted to **[7.1718]**). Para (c) originally read as follows:

"(c) the FSA.".

[7.1753]
43 Venue

(1) The court shall fix the venue for the hearing when the application is filed.

(2) In fixing the venue the court shall have regard to—
(a) the desirability of the application being heard as soon as is reasonably practicable; and
(b) the need for the investment bank's representatives to be able to reach the venue in time for the hearing.

[7.1754]
44 Hearing

At the hearing of the application, any of the following may appear or be represented—

Part 7M Special Insolvency Regimes

(a) the Bank of England;
[(b) the FCA;
(ba) if the application relates to a PRA-authorised person, the PRA;]
(c) the investment bank;
(d) a director of the investment bank;
(e) the person (or a person) nominated for appointment as administrator;
(f) any person who has given notice to the [FCA or, where relevant, the PRA] in respect of the investment bank under section 120 of the 2009 Act; and
(g) with the permission of the court, any other person who appears to have an interest.

NOTES

Paras (b), (ba) substituted, for original para (b), by the Financial Services Act 2012 (Consequential Amendments and Transitional Provisions) Order 2013, SI 2013/472, art 3, Sch 2, para 210(l), subject to a transitional provision (see para 211 as noted to **[7.1718]**). Para (c) originally read as follows:

"(b) the FSA;".

Para (f): words in square brackets substituted for "FSA" by SI 2013/472, art 3, Sch 2, para 210(a), (b)(vii), subject to a transitional provision (see para 211 as noted to **[7.1718]**).

[7.1755]
45 Special administration (bank administration) order

If the court makes an special administration (bank administration) order, the order shall state—
(a) that the Bank of England is the applicant;
(b) the name, registered address and registered number of the investment bank to which the order refers;
(c) details of any other parties appearing at the hearing;
(d) the name and business address of any administrator appointed by the order;
(e) the date and time from which their appointment shall take effect;
(f) the terms for costs of the application; and
(g) any further particulars that the court thinks fit.

[7.1756]
46 Costs

If the court makes a special administration (bank administration) order, the following are payable as an expense of the bank administration—
(a) the Bank of England's costs of making the application; and
(b) any other costs allowed by the court.

[7.1757]
47 Notice of order

(1) If the court makes a special administration (bank administration) order, it shall send 4 sealed copies to the Bank of England.

(2) The Bank of England shall as soon as is reasonably practicable send—
(a) a sealed copy to the administrator;
[(b) a sealed copy to the FCA;
(ba) if the investment bank concerned is a PRA-authorised person, a sealed copy to the PRA;]
(c) a sealed copy to the FSCS.

NOTES

Para (2): sub-paras (b), (ba) substituted, for original sub-para (b), by the Financial Services Act 2012 (Consequential Amendments and Transitional Provisions) Order 2013, SI 2013/472, art 3, Sch 2, para 210(m), subject to a transitional provision (see para 211 as noted to **[7.1718]**). Sub-para (b) originally read as follows:

"(b) a sealed copy to the FSA; and".

[7.1758]
48 Remuneration of the administrator

As soon as practicable after the making of a special administration (bank administration) order, the Bank of England shall fix the terms on which, in accordance with rule 196, the administrator is to be remunerated in respect of—
(a) work done by the administrator in pursuit of Objective A; and
(b) work done by the administrator in pursuit of Objectives 2 and 3 of the special administration objectives.

[7.1759]
49 Appointment of person under section 135

(1) An application to the court for the appointment of a person under section 135 of the 1986 Act (as applied by Table 2 in section 145(6) of the 2009 Act and by paragraph 6 of Schedule 2 to the Regulations) may be made by the Bank of England.

(2) The application must be supported by a witness statement stating—
(a) why the Bank of England thinks that such a person should be appointed;
(b) that the person to be appointed has consented to act;
(c) that the person to be appointed is qualified to act as an insolvency practitioner;

(d) whether, to the Bank of England's knowledge, a company voluntary arrangement under Part 1 of the Insolvency Act 1986 has been proposed or is in force in respect of the investment bank; and
(e) the Bank of England's estimate of the value of the assets in respect of which the person is to be appointed.

(3) If satisfied that sufficient grounds are shown for the appointment, the court may make it on such terms as it thinks fit.

[7.1760]
50 Order of appointment

(1) The order appointing a person described in rule 49(1) must specify the functions to be carried out in relation to the investment bank's affairs.

(2) If the court makes an order appointing such a person, the court shall send 4 sealed copies of the order to the person appointed (and a copy by email if possible).

(3) As soon as is reasonably practicable after appointment the person appointed must send notice of the order of appointment to—
(a) the investment bank;
[(b) the FCA;
(ba) if the application relates to a PRA-authorised person, the PRA;]
(c) the FSCS; and
(d) the registrar of companies.

(4) Notice to the investment bank must be given by service in accordance with rule 41 above.

(5) Unless the court otherwise directs, on receipt of the order of appointment, as soon as reasonably practicable, the person appointed shall give notice of that appointment. Such notice—
(a) shall be gazetted; and
(b) may be advertised in such other manner as the person appointed thinks fit.

(6) The Bank of England may disclose the fact and terms of an order appointing a person under this rule to any person whom the Bank thinks has a sufficient business interest.

(7) Rules 33 to 36 shall then apply with the following modifications—
(a) a reference to "special administration (bank insolvency)" is to be read as a reference to "special administration (bank administration)"; and
(b) a reference to rule 30 is to be read as a reference to rule 49.

NOTES

Para (3): sub-paras (b), (ba) substituted, for original sub-para (b), by the Financial Services Act 2012 (Consequential Amendments and Transitional Provisions) Order 2013, SI 2013/472, art 3, Sch 2, para 210(n), subject to a transitional provision (see para 211 as noted to **[7.1718]**). Sub-para (b) originally read as follows:

"(b) the FSA;".

PART 3
PROCESS OF SPECIAL ADMINISTRATION

CHAPTER 1 NOTICE OF APPOINTMENT AND STATEMENT OF AFFAIRS

[7.1761]
51 Notification and advertisement of administrator's appointment

(1) The notice of appointment to be given by the administrator as soon as reasonably practicable after appointment under paragraph 46(2)(b)—
(a) shall be gazetted; and
(b) may be advertised in such other manner as the administrator thinks fit.

(2) In addition to the standard contents, the notice must state that an administrator has been appointed and the date of the appointment.

(3) The administrator shall as soon as practicable after appointment give notice of the appointment to—
(a) any enforcement officer who, to the administrator's knowledge, is charged with execution or other legal process against the investment bank;
(b) any person who, to the administrator's knowledge, has distrained against the investment bank; and
(c) any supervisor of a voluntary arrangement under Part 1 of the 1986 Act.

(4) The administrator shall send the notice of appointment to the registrar of companies within 7 days of the date of the order appointing them.

(5) Any notice required to be sent by the administrator under these Rules or under Schedule B1 must contain—
(a) details of the court where the proceedings are and the relevant court reference number;
(b) the full name, registered address and registered number of the investment bank; and
(c) the name and business address of the person or persons appointed as administrator and the date of their appointment.

[7.1762]
52 Notice requiring statement of affairs

(1) In this Part, "relevant person" has the meaning given to it in paragraph 47(3).

(2) The administrator shall send notice to each relevant person who the administrator deems appropriate requiring that person to prepare and submit a statement of the investment bank's affairs.

(3) The notice shall inform each of the relevant persons—

- (a) that the proceedings are being held in the High Court and the court reference number;
- (b) of the full name, registered address and registered number of the investment bank;
- (c) of the name and the business address of the administrator;
- (d) of the name and addresses of all others (if any) to whom the same notice has been sent;
- (e) that the statement must be delivered to the administrator within 11 days of receipt of the notice;
- (f) of the effect of paragraph 48(4) (penalty for non-compliance); and
- (g) of the application to that person, and to each other relevant person, of section 235 of the 1986 Act (duty to provide information and to attend on the administrator if required).

(4) The administrator shall, on request, provide details to the relevant person as to how the statement should be prepared.

[7.1763]
53 Details of the client assets held by the investment bank

(1) The statement of affairs shall include particulars of the client assets held by the investment bank.

(2) The particulars shall include—

- (a) the names and addresses of clients of the investment bank for whom the investment bank holds client assets, but where these clients are individuals, the administrator shall not disclose their names and addresses;
- (b) details as to the amount of client assets held, categorised into type and securities of a particular description;
- (c) details as to the types of ownership those clients assert over the client assets; and
- (d) details as to any security interest held by the investment bank or another person in respect of the client assets.

[7.1764]
54 Verification and filing

(1) In addition to the information required under rule 53, the statement of affairs shall be in Form 2.14B, contain all the particulars required by that form and be verified by a statement of truth by the relevant person.

(2) The administrator may require any relevant person to submit a statement of concurrence in Form 2.15B stating their concurrence in the statement of affairs and where the administrator does so, the relevant person making the statement of affairs shall be informed of that fact.

(3) The statement of affairs shall be delivered by a relevant person making the statement of truth, together with a copy, to the administrator, and the relevant person shall also deliver a copy of the statement of affairs to all those persons whom the administrator has required to make a statement of concurrence.

(4) A person required to submit a statement of concurrence shall do so before the end of the period of 5 business days (or such other period as the administrator may agree) beginning on the day on which the statement of affairs being concurred with is received by that person.

(5) A statement of concurrence may be qualified in respect of matters dealt with by the statement of affairs, where the maker of the statement of concurrence is not in agreement with the relevant person, or where they consider the statement of affairs to be erroneous or misleading, or where they are without the direct knowledge necessary for concurring with it.

(6) Every statement of concurrence shall be verified by a statement of truth and be delivered to the administrator by the person who makes it, together with a copy of it.

(7) Subject to rule 55, the administrator shall as soon as reasonably practicable send a copy of the statement of affairs and any statement of concurrence to the registrar of companies and file them with the court.

(8) In this rule, a reference to a specific form shall be to that form as prescribed in the Insolvency Rules 1986, with any modification that the person using the form thinks desirable to reflect the nature of special administration.

NOTES

Note that the Insolvency Rules 1986, SI 1986/1925 are revoked and replaced (as from 6 April 2017 and subject to transitional provisions) by the Insolvency (England and Wales) Rules 2016, SI 2016/1024 at **[6.2]**.

[7.1765]
55 Limited disclosure

(1) Where the administrator thinks that it would prejudice the conduct of the administration (or might reasonably be expected to lead to violence against any person) for the whole or part of the statement of the investment bank's affairs to be disclosed, the administrator may apply to the court for an order of limited disclosure in respect of the statement.

(2) The court may, on such application, order that the statement or, as the case may be, the specified part of it, shall not be filed with the registrar of companies.

(3) The administrator shall, as soon as reasonably practicable, send a copy of the order and the statement of affairs (to the extent provided by the order) and any statement of concurrence to the registrar of companies.

(4) If a creditor or a client seeks disclosure of a statement of affairs or a specified part of it in relation to which an order has been made under this rule, that person may apply to the court for an order that the administrator disclose it or a specified part of it.

(5) An application under paragraph (4) shall be supported by written evidence in the form of a witness statement.

(6) Where a special administration (bank administration) order has been made, and where an application has been made under paragraph (4), the Bank of England and the [FCA and, where the investment bank concerned is a PRA-authorised person, the PRA] may appear and be heard at the hearing or may make written representations.

(7) The applicant shall give the administrator notice of the application at least 3 business days before the hearing.

(8) The court may make any order for disclosure subject to any conditions as to confidentiality, duration, the scope of the order in the event of any change of circumstances, or other matters as it sees just.

(9) If there is a material change in circumstances rendering the limit on disclosure or any part of it unnecessary, the administrator shall, as soon as reasonably practicable after the change, apply to the court for the order or any part of it to be rescinded.

(10) The administrator shall, as soon as reasonably practicable after the making of an order under paragraph (9), file a copy of the statement of affairs to the extent provided by the order with the registrar of companies.

(11) When the statement of affairs is filed in accordance with paragraph (10), the administrator shall, where they have sent a statement of proposals under paragraph 49, or, in a special administration (bank administration), paragraph 9 of Schedule 2 to the Regulations, provide the creditors and clients with a copy of the statement of affairs as filed, or a summary thereof.

(12) The provisions of CPR Part 31 shall not apply to an application under this rule.

NOTES

Para (6): words in square brackets substituted by for "FSA" the Financial Services Act 2012 (Consequential Amendments and Transitional Provisions) Order 2013, SI 2013/472, art 3, Sch 2, para 210(c), (d)(iii), subject to a transitional provision (see para 211 as noted to **[7.1718]**).

[7.1766]

56 Release from duty to submit statement of affairs

(1) The power of the administrator under paragraph 48(2) to give a release from the obligation imposed by paragraph 47(1) or to grant an extension of time may be exercised at the administrator's own discretion, or at the request of any relevant person.

(2) A relevant person may, if they request a release of extension of time and it is refused by the administrator, apply to the court for it and when such an application is made, the period referred to in paragraph 48(1) is suspended pending the court's decision.

(3) The court may, if it thinks that no sufficient cause is shown for the application, dismiss it without a hearing but it shall not do so without giving the relevant person at least 5 business days' notice, upon receipt of which the relevant person may request the court to list the application for a without notice hearing.

(4) If the application is not dismissed under paragraph (3), the court shall fix a venue for it to be heard, and give notice to the relevant person and to the [FCA and, where the investment bank concerned is a PRA-authorised person, the PRA] accordingly.

(5) Where an application has been made under paragraph (2), the [FCA and, where the investment bank concerned is a PRA-authorised person, the PRA] may appear and be heard at the hearing and in a special administration (bank administration), the Bank of England may also be given notice of the hearing and may appear and be heard at the hearing or may make written representations.

(6) The relevant person shall, at least 14 days before the hearing, send to the administrator a notice stating the venue and accompanied by a copy of the application and of any evidence which the relevant person intends to adduce in support of it.

(7) The administrator may appear and be heard on the application and, whether or not they appear, the administrator may file a written report of any matters which they consider ought to be drawn to the court's attention.

(8) If a report is filed under paragraph (7), a copy of it shall be sent by the administrator to the relevant person not later than 5 business days before the hearing.

(9) Sealed copies of any order made on the application shall be sent by the court to the relevant person and the administrator.

(10) On any application under this rule, the relevant person's costs shall be paid in any event by that person and, unless the court otherwise orders, no allowance towards them shall be made as an expense of the special administration.

NOTES

Paras (4), (5): words in square brackets substituted for "FSA" by the Financial Services Act 2012 (Consequential Amendments and Transitional Provisions) Order 2013, SI 2013/472, art 3, Sch 2, para 210(c), (d)(iv), subject to a transitional provision (see para 211 as noted to **[7.1718]**).

[7.1767]
57 Expenses of statement of affairs

(1) A relevant person making the statement of the investment bank's affairs or a statement of concurrence shall be allowed, and paid by the administrator as an expense of the special administration, any expenses incurred by the relevant person in so doing which the administrator considers reasonable.

(2) Any decision by the administrator under this rule is subject to appeal to the court.

(3) Nothing in this rule relieves a relevant person from any obligation with respect to the preparation, verification and submission of the statement of affairs or to the provision of information to the administrator.

[7.1768]
58 Submission of accounts

(1) Any of the persons specified in section 235(3) of the 1986 Act shall, at the request of the administrator, provide the administrator with the investment bank's accounts as at such date and for such period as the administrator may specify.

(2) The period specified may begin from a date up to 3 years preceding the date the investment bank entered special administration, or from an earlier date to which the audited accounts of the investment bank were last prepared.

(3) The court may, on the administrator's application, require accounts for an earlier period.

(4) Rule 57 applies (with the necessary modification) in relation to the accounts to be provided under this rule as it applies to the statement of affairs.

(5) The accounts shall (if the administrator so requires) be verified by a statement of truth and (whether or not so verified) be delivered within 21 days of the request under paragraph (1) (or such longer period as the administrator may allow).

CHAPTER 2 STATEMENT OF PROPOSALS

[7.1769]
59 Administrator's proposals

(1) The administrator shall under paragraph 49 (or in the case of a special administration (bank administration) paragraph 7 of Schedule 2 to the Regulations) make a statement of proposals which shall be sent to the registrar of companies.

(2) In addition to the information required by that paragraph, the statement of proposals must include—

- (a) a statement that the proceedings are being held in the High Court and the court reference number;
- (b) the full name, any other trading names, the registered address and registered number of the investment bank;
- (c) details of the administrator's appointment (including the date of appointment);
- (d) in the case of joint administrators, details of the apportionment of functions;
- (e) the names of the directors and secretary of the investment bank and details of any shareholdings in the investment bank they have;
- (f) an account of the circumstances giving rise to the application for the appointment of the administrator;
- (g) if a statement of the investment bank's affairs has been submitted, a copy or summary of it with the administrator's comments, if any;
- (h) if an order limiting the disclosure of the statement of affairs has been made under rule 55, a statement of that fact, as well as—
  - (i) details of who provided the statement of affairs,
  - (ii) the date of the order for limited disclosure, and
  - (iii) the details or a summary of the details that are not subject to that order;
- (i) if a full statement of affairs is not provided, the names, addresses and debts of the creditors including details of any security held (or in case of any depositors of the investment bank, a single statement of their aggregate debt);
- (j) if a full statement of affairs is not provided, or if no statement of affairs is provided, the names and addresses of clients of the investment bank together with a description of the amount and type of client assets held, the type of ownership the clients have in respect of those assets and details as to any security interest held by the investment bank or another person in respect of those assets, but where those clients are individuals, their names and addresses are not to be disclosed;
- (k) if no statement of affairs is provided, details of the financial position of the investment bank at the latest practicable date (which must, unless the court otherwise orders, be a date not earlier than that on which the investment bank entered special administration), a list of the investment bank's creditors including their names, addresses and details of their debts, including any security held (or in case of any depositors of the investment bank, a single statement of their aggregate debt) and an explanation as to why there is no statement of affairs;
- (l) the basis upon which it is proposed that the administrator's remuneration should be fixed under rule 196, and, if this basis has already been set by the Objective A committee or by the Bank of England in respect of Objective A, or in respect of Objectives 2 and 3 of the special administration objectives, details as to what has been set and any proposals for this to be changed;

(m) a statement complying with paragraph (4) of any pre-administration costs charged or incurred by the administrator or, to the administrator's knowledge, by any other person qualified to act as an insolvency practitioner;
(n) details of whether (and why) the administrator proposes to apply to the court under section 176A(5) of the 1986 Act as applied by regulation 15 (unless the administrator intends to propose a company voluntary arrangement);
(o) an estimate of the value of the prescribed part for the purposes of section 176A (unless the investment bank intends to propose a company voluntary arrangement) certified as being made to the best of the administrator's knowledge and belief;
(p) an estimate of the value of the investment bank's net property (unless the administrator intends to propose a company voluntary arrangement) certified as being made to the best of the administrator's knowledge and belief;
(q) in—
(i) a special administration, an explanation of the priority that has been given since the commencement of special administration to the special administration objectives (and where the [FCA or, where relevant, the PRA] has given a direction under regulation 16, an explanation as to how this has dictated the priority given to a particular objective), and
(ii) a special administration (bank insolvency) or a special administration (bank administration)—
(aa) a summary of how Objective A is being or has been achieved and the resources devoted to the pursuit of Objective A; and
(bb) an explanation of the priority that has been given since the commencement of special administration to the special administration objectives (and where the [FCA or, where relevant, the PRA] has given a direction under regulation 16, an explanation as to how this has dictated the priority given to a particular objective);
(r) the manner in which the affairs and business of the investment bank have been managed and financed since the date of the administrator's appointment (including the reasons for and terms of any disposal of assets);
(s) details as to the order in which the administrator aims to pursue the special administration objectives and the manner in which the affairs and business of the investment bank will be managed and financed if the administrator's proposals are approved;
(t) whether the administrator expects a dividend to be paid to creditors and an estimate of the amount of this dividend;
(u) how it is proposed that the special administration shall end (winding-up or voluntary arrangement), in accordance with Objective 3 as set out in regulation 10(1)(c); and
(v) any other information which the administrator thinks necessary to enable creditors and clients to vote for the approval of the statement of proposals.

(3) In this Part—
(a) "pre-administration costs" are—
(i) fees charged, and
(ii) expenses incurred,
by the administrator, or another person qualified to act as an insolvency practitioner, before the investment bank entered special administration but with a view to its doing so; and
(b) "unpaid pre-administration costs" are pre-administration costs which had not been paid when the investment bank entered special administration.

(4) A statement of pre-administration costs complies with this paragraph if it includes—
(a) details of any agreement under which the fees were charged and expenses incurred, including the parties to the agreement and the date on which the agreement was made;
(b) details of the work done for which the fees were charged and expenses incurred;
(c) an explanation of why the work was done before the investment bank entered special administration and how it would further the achievement of the special administration objectives;
(d) a statement of the amount of the pre-administration costs, setting out separately—
(i) the fees charged by the administrator,
(ii) the expenses incurred by the administrator,
(iii) the fees charged (to the administrator's knowledge) by any other person qualified to act as an insolvency practitioner (and, if more than one, by each separately), and
(iv) the expenses incurred (to the administrator's knowledge) by any other person qualified to act as an insolvency practitioner (and, if more than one, by each separately);
(e) a statement of the amounts of pre-administration costs which have already been paid (set out separately as under sub-paragraph (d)),
(f) the identity of the person who made the payment or, if more than one person made the payment, the identity of each such person and of the amounts paid by each such person set out separately as under sub-paragraph (d),
(g) a statement of the amounts of unpaid pre-administration costs (set out separately as under sub-paragraph (d)), and
(h) a statement that the payment of unpaid pre-administration costs as an expense of the administration is—
(i) subject to approval under rule 136; and
(ii) not part of the proposals subject to approval under paragraph 53.

(5) The statement of proposals—

(a) may exclude information the disclosure of which could seriously prejudice the commercial interests of the investment bank, and
(b) must include a statement of any exclusion.

(6) In the case of special administration (bank administration) following transfer to a bridge bank under section 12(2) of the 2009 Act—
(a) the statement of proposals must state whether any payment is to be made to the investment bank from a scheme under a resolution fund order; or
(b) if that information is unavailable when the statement of proposals is made, the administrator must issue a supplemental statement when the information is available.

(7) Following an application by the administrator under paragraph 107, where the court orders an extension of the period of time in paragraph 49(5), the administrator shall notify—
(a) every creditor of the investment bank of whose address the administrator is aware;
(b) every client of the investment bank of whose claim the administrator is aware and has a means of contacting; . . .
[(c) the FCA; and
(d) if the application relates to a PRA-authorised person, the PRA,]
as soon as possible after the order is made.

(8) Where the administrator wishes to publish a notice under paragraph 49(6) or gives notice that the statement of proposals is to be provided free of charge to a market infrastructure body, either notice shall be advertised in such a manner as the administrator thinks fit.

(9) In addition to the standard contents, a notice under paragraph (7) must state—
(a) that persons can write for a copy of the statement of proposals for achieving the purpose of administration; and
(b) the address to which to write.

(10) This notice must be published as soon as reasonably practicable after the administrator sends out the statement of proposals in accordance with paragraph 49(4) (or in the case of a special administration (bank administration) under paragraph 9 of Schedule 2 to the Regulations), but no later than 8 weeks (or such other period as may be agreed by the creditors and clients or as the court may order) from the date that the investment bank entered special administration.

NOTES

Para (2): words in square brackets in sub-para (q) substituted for "FSA" by the Financial Services Act 2012 (Consequential Amendments and Transitional Provisions) Order 2013, SI 2013/472, art 3, Sch 2, para 210(a), (b)(viii), subject to a transitional provision (see para 211 as noted to **[7.1718]**).

Para (7): word "and" (omitted) at the end of sub-para (b) revoked, and sub-paras (c), (d) substituted, for original sub-para (c), by SI 2013/472, art 3, Sch 2, para 210(o), subject to a transitional provision (see para 211 as noted to **[7.1718]**). Sub-para (c) originally read as follows:

"(c) the FSA,".

[7.1770]
60 Limited disclosure of the statement of proposals

(1) Where the administrator thinks that it would prejudice the conduct of the administration (or might reasonably be expected to lead to violence against any person) for any of the matters specified in rule 59(2)(i) to (k) to be disclosed, the administrator may apply to the court for an order of limited disclosure in respect of any specified part of the statement of proposals.

(2) The court may, on such application, order that some or all of the specified part of the statement must not be sent to the registrar of companies or to creditors, clients or members of the company as otherwise required by paragraph 49(4), or, in the case of a special administration (bank administration), paragraph 9 of Schedule 2 to the Regulations.

(3) The administrator must as soon as reasonably practicable send to the persons specified in paragraph (2) the statement of proposals (to the extent provided by the order) and an indication of the nature of the matter in relation to which the order was made.

(4) The administrator must also send a copy of the order to the registrar of companies.

(5) A creditor who seeks disclosure of a part of the statement of proposals in relation to which an order has been made under this rule may apply to the court for an order that the administrator disclose it, and the application must be supported by written evidence in the form of a witness statement.

(6) Where a special administration (bank administration) order has been made and an application has been made under paragraph (5), the Bank of England and the [FCA and, where the investment bank concerned is a PRA-authorised person, the PRA] may appear and be heard at the hearing or may make written representations.

(7) The applicant must give the administrator notice of the application at least 3 business days before the hearing.

(8) The court may make any order for disclosure subject to any conditions as to confidentiality, duration, the scope of the order in the event of any change of circumstances, or other matters as it sees just.

(9) If there is a material change in circumstances rendering the limit on disclosure or any part of it unnecessary, the administrator must, as soon as reasonably practicable after the change, apply to the court for the order or any part of it to be rescinded.

(10) The administrator must, as soon as reasonably practicable after the making of an order under paragraph (9), send to the persons specified in paragraph (2) a copy of the statement of proposals to the extent provided by the order.

(11) The provisions of CPR Part 31 do not apply to an application under this rule.

NOTES

Para (6): words in square brackets substituted for "FSA" by the Financial Services Act 2012 (Consequential Amendments and Transitional Provisions) Order 2013, SI 2013/472, art 3, Sch 2, para 210(c), (d)(v), subject to a transitional provision (see para 211 as noted to **[7.1718]**).

CHAPTER 3 INITIAL MEETING TO CONSIDER PROPOSALS

[7.1771]

61 Initial meeting

(1) As soon as reasonably practicable after an invitation to the initial meeting has been sent out in accordance with paragraph 51(1) (or in a special administration (bank administration), in accordance with paragraph 10 of Schedule 2 to the Regulations), the administrator must have gazetted—

(a) that an initial meeting of creditors and clients is to take place;

(b) the venue fixed for the meeting; and

(c) the full name and business address of the administrator.

(2) The information required to be gazetted under paragraph (1) may also be advertised in such other manner as the administrator thinks fit.

(3) Where the court orders an extension to the period set out in paragraph 51(2)(b), the administrator shall notify each person who was sent notice in accordance with paragraph 49(4) (or in a special administration (bank administration), paragraph 9 to Schedule 2 to the Regulations).

(4) In a special administration (bank insolvency) or a special administration (bank administration) the Bank of England and the FSCS shall also be invited to the initial meeting, and where paragraph (3) applies, shall be notified of the extension of the period set out in paragraph 51(2)(b).

(5) This rule shall not apply where the [FCA or, where relevant, the PRA] has given a direction under regulation 16 and the direction has not been withdrawn.

NOTES

Para (5): words in square brackets substituted for "FSA" by the Financial Services Act 2012 (Consequential Amendments and Transitional Provisions) Order 2013, SI 2013/472, art 3, Sch 2, para 210(a), (b)(ix), subject to a transitional provision (see para 211 as noted to **[7.1718]**).

[7.1772]

62 Notice to officers

(1) Where rule 61 applies, notice to attend the meeting must be given to every present or former officer of the investment bank whose presence the administrator thinks is required at the same time that notice is sent to creditors and clients.

(2) That notice must contain—

(a) a statement that the proceedings are being held in the High Court and the court reference number;

(b) the full name, registered address, registered number and any other trading names of the investment bank;

(c) the full name and business address of the administrator; and

(d) details of the venue, the date and the time of the meeting.

(3) Every person who receives a notice under paragraph (1) must attend.

[7.1773]

63 Business of the initial meeting

(1) At the initial meeting of creditors and clients—

(a) a creditors' committee may be established in accordance with Chapter 8 of this Part; and

(b) the statement of proposals shall be approved as follows.

(2) The proposals shall not be approved unless both classes of voter have voted to approve them.

(3) The creditors and the clients shall vote separately on whether to approve the proposals.

(4) In a special administration (bank insolvency) (and in a special administration (bank administration) if there are depositors) the FSCS shall be entitled to vote as a creditor under this rule and rule 86 has effect with respect to its voting rights.

(5) If the proposals are approved by a class of voter subject to a modification, the proposals will not be considered approved by the other class unless that other class has approved the proposals as modified.

(6) Where the administrator is unable to get the requisite majority of a class of voter for approval of the statement of proposals (with or without any modifications), rule 64 applies.

(7) Paragraph (6) shall not apply in a special administration (bank administration).

(8) This rule shall not apply where the [FCA or, where relevant, the PRA] has given a direction under regulation 16 and the direction has not been withdrawn.

NOTES

Para (8): words in square brackets substituted for "FSA" by the Financial Services Act 2012 (Consequential Amendments and Transitional Provisions) Order 2013, SI 2013/472, art 3, Sch 2, para 210(a), (b)(x), subject to a transitional provision (see para 211 as noted to **[7.1718]**).

[7.1774]

64 Adjournment of meeting to approve the statement of proposals

(1) If, at the initial meeting of creditors and clients, there is not the requisite majority for approval of the statement of proposals (with or without any modifications), the administrator may, and shall if a resolution is passed to that effect, adjourn the meeting for not more than 14 days (subject to any direction by the court).

(2) If there are subsequently further adjournments, the final adjournment must not be to a day later than 14 days after the date on which the meeting was originally held, (subject to any direction by the court).

(3) Where a meeting is adjourned under this rule, proofs and proxies may be used if lodged at any time up to 12.00 hours on the business day immediately before the adjourned meeting.

(4) Where at the initial meeting, the proposals were approved (whether or not with modifications) by one class of voter but not the other, that approval shall no longer stand at the adjourned meeting unless the version of the proposals to be voted on has not been modified from the version that was approved.

(5) If the administrator is unable to get the requisite majority of creditors or clients for approval of the statement of proposals, the administrator may apply to the court for directions under paragraph 63.

(6) This rule shall not apply in a special administration (bank administration).

[7.1775]

65 Revision of the statement of proposals

(1) The administrator shall under paragraph 54 (or regulation 18 or paragraph 11 of Schedule 2 to the Regulations as the case may be) make a statement setting out the proposed revisions to the statement of proposals ("the revised statement").

(2) The revised statement, which shall be sent out in accordance with paragraph 54(2)(b) and (c), shall include—

- (a) a statement that the proceedings are being held in the High Court and the court reference number;
- (b) the full name, registered address, registered number and any other trading names of the investment bank;
- (c) details of the administrator's appointment (including the date of appointment);
- (d) in the case of joint administrators, details of the apportionment of functions;
- (e) the names of the directors and secretary of the investment bank and details of any shareholdings in the investment bank they have;
- (f) a summary of the initial proposals and the reasons for proposing a revision;
- (g) details of the proposed revision including details of the administrator's assessment of the likely impact of the proposed revision upon the creditors generally or upon each class of creditor or on the clients (as the case may be); and
- (h) any other information that the administrator thinks necessary to enable creditors to decide whether or not to vote for the proposed revisions.

(3) The [FCA and, where the investment bank concerned is a PRA-authorised person, the PRA] shall be sent a copy of the revised statement at the same time as the revised statement is sent out.

(4) Where the administrator considers that the revision proposed will only affect creditors or, as the case may be, clients, the notice of the meeting to consider the revised proposals shall be sent to both creditors and clients, but will state who is invited to the meeting.

(5) In a special administration (bank insolvency) or a special administration (bank administration) the Bank of England and the FSCS shall also be invited to the meeting.

(6) Subject to paragraph 54(3), within 5 business days of sending out the revised statement the administrator shall send a copy of the statement to every member of the investment bank.

(7) Any notice to be published under paragraph 54(3) shall be advertised in such a manner as the administrator thinks fit.

(8) The notice shall be published as soon as reasonably practicable after the administrator sends the revised statement in accordance with paragraph 54(2) and, in addition to the standard contents, shall—

- (a) state that members can write for a copy of the statement of revised proposals and
- (b) the address to which to write.

(9) Paragraphs (4) and (5) shall not apply—

- (a) in a special administration (bank administration) where—
  - (i) the [FCA or, where relevant, the PRA] has given a direction under regulation 16 and has not withdrawn its direction at the time that the administrator proposes a revision to the statement of proposals, and
  - (ii) Objective A has been achieved; and
- (b) in a special administration or a special administration (bank insolvency) where the [FCA or, where relevant, the PRA] has given a direction under regulation 16 and has not withdrawn its direction at the time that the administrator proposes a revision to the statement of proposals.

(10) In this rule, a reference to—

"paragraph 54(2)" also includes a reference to regulation 18(4) or paragraph 13(4) of Schedule 2 to the Regulations as the case may be; and

"paragraph 54(3)" also includes a reference to regulation 18(5) or paragraph 13(5) of Schedule 2 to the Regulations as the case may be.

NOTES

Paras (3), (9): words in square brackets substituted for "FSA" by the Financial Services Act 2012 (Consequential Amendments and Transitional Provisions) Order 2013, SI 2013/472, art 3, Sch 2, para 210(a), (b)(xi), (c), (d)(vi), subject to a transitional provision (see para 211 as noted to **[7.1718]**).

[7.1776]

66 Meeting to approve the revised statement of proposals

(1) This rule applies to a meeting of creditors, a meeting of clients or a meeting of creditors and clients to approve the revisions to the statement of proposals.

(2) Where the revisions are being approved by a meeting of creditors and clients—

(a) the creditors and the clients shall vote separately on whether to approve the revisions;

(b) the revisions shall not be approved unless both classes of voter have voted to approve them; and

(c) where the revisions are approved by a class of voter subject to a modification, the proposals will not be considered approved by the other class unless that other class has approved the proposals as modified.

(3) In a special administration (bank insolvency) (and in a special administration (bank administration) if there are depositors) the FSCS shall be entitled to vote as a creditor under this rule and rule 86 has effect with respect to its voting rights.

(4) In a special administration or a special administration (bank insolvency), where the [FCA or, where relevant, the PRA] has given a direction under regulation 16 and has not withdrawn its direction at the time that the administrator proposes a revision to the statement of proposals, this rule shall not apply.

(5) In a special administration (bank administration), where the [FCA or, where relevant, the PRA] has given a direction under regulation 16 and has not withdrawn its direction at the time that the administrator proposes a revision to the statement of proposals—

(a) if Objective A has not been achieved, paragraph (2)(c) shall not apply; and

(b) if Objective A has been achieved, this rule shall not apply.

NOTES

Paras (4), (5): words in square brackets substituted for "FSA" by the Financial Services Act 2012 (Consequential Amendments and Transitional Provisions) Order 2013, SI 2013/472, art 3, Sch 2, para 210(a), (b)(xii), subject to a transitional provision (see para 211 as noted to **[7.1718]**).

[7.1777]

67 Notice to creditors and clients

As soon as reasonably practicable after the conclusion of a meeting of creditors or clients, or of creditors and clients to consider the administrator's proposals or revised proposals, the administrator shall—

(a) send notice of the result of the meeting to every person who received a copy of the original proposals;

(b) attach a copy of the proposals considered at the meeting to the notice sent to each creditor and each client who did not receive notice of the meeting but of whose claim the administrator has subsequently become aware; and

(c) file with the court a copy of the proposals considered at the meeting and notice of the result of the meeting.

CHAPTER 4 MEETINGS GENERALLY

[7.1778]

68 Meetings generally

This chapter, except where different provision is made in the Regulations or these Rules, applies to meetings summoned by the administrator under—

(a) paragraph 51 (initial meeting);

(b) paragraph 54(2) (meeting to consider revision to the administrator's proposals);

(c) paragraph 62 (general power to summon meetings),

or following a request or a direction from the court under paragraph 56 (further creditors' meetings).

[7.1779]

69 Venue

(1) In fixing the venue for a meeting, the convener must have regard to the convenience of those attending.

(2) Meetings must be summoned for commencement between 10.00 and 16.00 hours on a business day (subject to any direction by the court).

(3) In this rule, "meeting" includes an adjourned meeting.

[7.1780]

70 Notice of meeting by individual notice: when and where sent

(1) This rule applies except where the court orders under rule 72 that notice of a meeting be given by advertisement only.

(2) Notice summoning a meeting must be delivered at least 14 days before the day fixed for the meeting as provided in paragraph (3).

(3) Notice must be sent—

(a) for a meeting involving the creditors, to all the creditors of whose address the administrator is aware and who had claims against the investment bank at the date when it entered administration (except for those who have subsequently been paid in full);

(b) for a meeting involving the clients, to all clients of whose claim the administrator is aware (except for those who have no outstanding claim to clients assets held by the investment bank) and has a means of contacting;

(c) for a meeting of contributories, to every person appearing (by the investment bank's books or otherwise) to be a contributory of the investment bank.

(4) The [FCA and, where the investment bank concerned is a PRA-authorised person, the PRA], and in a special administration (bank insolvency) or special administration (bank administration), the Bank of England and the FSCS, shall also be notified of any such meeting.

NOTES

Para (4): words in square brackets substituted for "FSA" by the Financial Services Act 2012 (Consequential Amendments and Transitional Provisions) Order 2013, SI 2013/472, art 3, Sch 2, para 210(c), (d)(vii), subject to a transitional provision (see para 211 as noted to **[7.1718]**).

[7.1781]

71 Notice of meeting by individual notice: content and accompanying documents

(1) This rule applies except where the court orders under rule 72 that notice of a meeting be given by advertisement only.

(2) Notice summoning a meeting must specify the purpose of and venue for the meeting and state that claims or proofs and (if applicable) proxies must be lodged at a specified place not later than 12.00 hours on the business day before the date fixed for the meeting in order that creditors or clients may be entitled to vote at the meeting.

(3) Forms of proxy complying with rule 125 must be sent out with every notice summoning a meeting.

[7.1782]

72 Notice of meeting by advertisement only

(1) The court may order that notice of any meeting under these Rules be given by advertisement and not by individual notice to the persons concerned.

(2) In considering whether so to order, the court must have regard to the cost of advertisement, the amount of assets available and the extent of the interest of creditors, clients, members and contributories or any particular class of them.

[7.1783]

73 Content of notice for meetings

(1) Notice of a meeting of the creditors, clients or a meeting of creditors and clients, must contain the following information—

(a) a statement that the proceedings are being held in the High Court and the court reference number;

(b) the full name, registered address, registered number and any other trading names of the investment bank;

(c) the full name and business address of the administrator;

(d) details of the venue, the date and time of the meeting;

(e) whether the meeting is—

(i) an initial creditors' and clients' meeting under paragraph 51,

(ii) to consider revisions to the administrator's proposals under paragraph 54(2),

(iii) a further creditors', or creditors and clients', or clients' meeting under paragraph 56, or

(iv) a meeting under paragraph 62,

unless the court orders that it be given by advertisement only in accordance with rule 72.

(2) Where the court orders an extension to the period set out in paragraph 51(2)(b), the administrator shall notify each person who was sent notice in accordance with paragraph 49(4) (or in a special administration (bank administration), paragraph 9 to Schedule 2 to the Regulations).

[7.1784]

74 Gazetting and advertisement of meetings

(1) The administrator, in convening a meeting under these Rules, must have gazetted a notice which, in addition to the standard contents, must state—

(a) that a creditors', clients', creditors and clients', members' or contributories' meeting is to take place;

(b) the venue fixed for the meeting;

(c) the purpose of the meeting; and

(d) the time and date by which, and place at which, those attending must lodge proxies and (in the case of a meeting of creditors, clients or both) claims or proofs in order to be entitled to vote.

(2) Notice under this Rule must be gazetted before or as soon as reasonably practicable after notice is given to those attending.

(3) Information to be gazetted under this Rule may also be advertised in such other manner as the administrator thinks fit.

[7.1785]
75 Non-receipt of notice of meeting

Where, in accordance with the Regulations or these Rules, a meeting is summoned by notice, the meeting is presumed to have been duly summoned and held, even if not all those to whom the notice is to be given have received it.

[7.1786]
76 Requisition of meetings

(1) In this Chapter, "requisitioned meeting" means a meeting requested under paragraph 56(1).

(2) A request for a meeting must contain the following information—

(a) a statement that the proceedings are being held in the High Court and the court reference number;

(b) the full name, registered address and registered number of the investment bank;

(c) the full name and address of the creditor requesting the meeting; and

(d) the full amount of that creditor's claim.

(3) The request for a requisitioned meeting must include a statement of the purpose of the proposed meeting and—

(a) either—

(i) a list of the creditors or contributories concurring with the request and of the amounts of their respective claims or values, and

(ii) written confirmation of concurrence from each creditor or contributory concurring, or

(b) a statement that the requesting creditor's debt or contributory's value alone is sufficient without the concurrence of other creditors or contributories.

(4) In the preceding paragraph, a contributory's value is the amount in respect of which the contributory may vote at any meeting.

(5) A requisitioned meeting must be held within 28 days of the date of the administrator's receipt of the notice.

(6) The administrator—

(a) shall notify the [FCA and, where the investment bank concerned is a PRA-authorised person, the PRA] of the details and purpose of the requisitioned meeting;

(b) shall—

(i) in a special administration (bank insolvency), notify the Bank of England of the details and purpose of the requisitioned meeting, or

(ii) in a special administration (bank administration) notify the Bank of England and the FSCS of the details and purpose of the requisitioned meeting, and

(c) may, if the administrator thinks appropriate, also summon the clients to the requisitioned meeting.

NOTES

Para (6): words in square brackets substituted for "FSA" by the Financial Services Act 2012 (Consequential Amendments and Transitional Provisions) Order 2013, SI 2013/472, art 3, Sch 2, para 210(c), (d)(viii), subject to a transitional provision (see para 211 as noted to **[7.1718]**).

[7.1787]
77 Expenses of requisitioned meetings

(1) The expenses of summoning and holding a requisitioned meeting shall be paid by the person who makes the request, who shall deposit with the administrator security for their payment.

(2) The sum to be deposited shall be such as the administrator may determine, and the administrator shall not act without the deposit having been made.

(3) The meeting may resolve that the expenses of summoning and holding it are to be payable out of the assets of the investment bank as an expense of the administration.

(4) To the extent that any deposit made under this rule is not required for the payment of expenses of summoning and holding the meeting, it shall be repaid to the person who made it.

[7.1788]
78 Quorum at meetings

(1) A meeting of creditors, clients, creditors and clients or contributories is not competent to act unless a quorum is present.

(2) A quorum is—

(a) in the case of a meeting of creditors, at least one creditor entitled to vote;

(b) in the case of a meeting of clients, at least one client entitled to vote;

(c) in the case of a meeting of creditors and clients, at least one creditor and one client who are each entitled to vote;

(d) in the case of a meeting of contributories, at least 2 contributories so entitled, or all the contributories, if their number does not exceed 2.

(3) Where at any meeting under paragraph (2)—

(a) the provisions of this rule as to a quorum being present are satisfied by the attendance of—

(i) the chair alone, or

(ii) one other person in addition to the chair, and

(b) the chair is aware, by virtue of claims or proofs and proxies received or otherwise, that one or more additional persons would, if attending, be entitled to vote,

the meeting must not commence until at least the expiry of 15 minutes after the time appointed for its commencement.

[7.1789]
79 Chair at meetings

(1) At any meeting of creditors, clients, or creditors and clients summoned by the administrator, either the administrator shall be the chair, or a person nominated by the administrator in writing to act in the administrator's place.

(2) A person so nominated must be either—

(a) one who is qualified to act as an insolvency practitioner in relation to the investment bank; or

(b) an employee of the administrator or the administrator's firm who is experienced in insolvency matters.

(3) Where the chair holds a proxy which includes a requirement to vote for a particular resolution and no other person proposes that resolution—

(a) the chair must propose it unless the chair considers that there is good reason for not doing so, and

(b) if the chair does not propose it, the chair must as soon as reasonably practicable after the meeting notify the principal of the reason why not.

[7.1790]
80 Adjournment by chair

(1) The chair may, and must if the meeting so resolves, adjourn the meeting to such time and place as seems to the chair to be appropriate in the circumstances.

(2) An adjournment under this paragraph must not be for a period of more than 14 days, subject to any direction by the court.

(3) If there are further adjournments, the final adjournment must not be to a day later than 14 days after the date on which the meeting was originally held.

(4) Rule 69 applies with regard to the venue fixed for a meeting adjourned under this rule.

(5) This rule does not apply to the initial meeting of creditors and clients.

[7.1791]
81 Adjournment in absence of chair

(1) If within 30 minutes from the time fixed for commencement of a meeting there is no person present to act as chair, the meeting stands adjourned to the same time and place in the following week or, if that is not a business day, to the business day immediately following.

(2) If within 30 minutes from the time fixed for the commencement of the meeting those persons attending the meeting do not constitute a quorum, the chair may adjourn the meeting to such time and place as the chair may appoint.

[7.1792]
82 Claims, proofs and proxies in adjournment

Where a meeting under these rules is adjourned, claims, proofs and proxies may be used if lodged at any time up to 12.00 hours on the business day immediately before the adjourned meeting.

[7.1793]
83 Suspension

Once only in the course of a meeting, the chair may, without an adjournment, declare it suspended for any period up to 1 hour.

[7.1794]
84 Venue and conduct of company meetings

(1) Where the administrator summons a meeting of members of the investment bank, the administrator shall fix a venue for it having regard to their convenience.

(2) The chair of the meeting shall be the administrator or a person nominated by the administrator in writing to act in the administrator's place.

(3) A person so nominated must be either—

(a) one who is qualified to act as an insolvency practitioner in relation to the investment bank; or

(b) an employee of the administrator or the administrator's firm who is experienced in insolvency matters.

(4) If within 30 minutes from the time fixed for commencement of the meeting there is no person present to act as chair, the meeting stands adjourned to the same time and place in the following week or, if that is not a business day, to the business day immediately following.

(5) Subject to anything to the contrary in the Regulations and these Rules, the meeting must be summoned and conducted in accordance with the law of England and Wales, including any applicable provision in or made under the 2006 Act.

(6) The chair of the meeting shall cause minutes of its proceedings to be entered in the company's minute book.

CHAPTER 5 ENTITLEMENT TO VOTE AT MEETINGS

[7.1795]
85 Entitlement to vote (creditors)

(1) A creditor is entitled to vote at a meeting of creditors, or at a meeting of creditors and clients, only if—

(a) the administrator has been given written details of the debt which is claimed as due to that person from the investment bank, including any calculation for the purposes of rule 87 or rule 88;

(b) the details were given to the administrator—

(i) not later than 12.00 hours on the business day before the day fixed for the meeting, or

(ii) later than that time but the chair of the meeting is satisfied that that was due to circumstances beyond that person's control; and

(c) the claim has been admitted for the purposes of entitlement to vote,

and there has been lodged with the administrator any proxy intended to be used on behalf of that person.

(2) For the purposes of this Chapter, written details of a claim, once lodged or given in accordance with this rule, need not be lodged or given again.

(3) The chair of a meeting of creditors, or at a meeting of creditors and clients, may call for any document or other evidence to be produced if the chair thinks it necessary for the purpose of substantiating the whole or any part of a claim.

[7.1796]
86 FSCS and voting rights

(1) For the purpose of voting at a meeting in a special administration (bank insolvency) (or in a special administration (bank administration) if there are depositors), the FSCS may submit, instead of giving written details, a statement containing—

(a) the names of the creditors of the investment bank in respect of whom an obligation of the FSCS has arisen or may reasonably be expected to arise;

(b) the amount of each such obligation; and

(c) the total amount of all such obligations.

(2) The FSCS may from time to time submit a further statement; and each such statement supersedes any previous statement.

(3) Any voting rights which a creditor might otherwise exercise in the special administration in respect of a claim are reduced by a sum equal to the amount of that claim in relation to which the FSCS, by virtue of its having submitted a statement under this rule, is entitled to exercise voting rights at the meeting.

[7.1797]
87 Calculation of voting rights (creditors)

(1) Votes are calculated according to the amount of each creditor's claim as at the date on which the investment bank entered special administration, less any payments that have been made to the creditor after that date in respect of the claim and any adjustment by way of set-off in accordance with rule 164 or 165 as if those rules were applied on the date on which the votes are counted.

(2) A creditor may vote in respect of a debt which is for an unliquidated amount or the value of which is not ascertained if the chair decides to put upon it an estimated minimum value for the purpose of entitlement to vote and admits the claim for that purpose.

(3) Paragraph (2) does not apply to a shortfall claim described in rule 90(4)(b).

(4) A creditor may not vote in respect of any claim or part of a claim—

(a) where the claim or part is secured, except where the vote is cast in respect of the balance (if any) of the debt after deduction of the value of the security as estimated by the creditor;

(b) where the claim is in respect of a debt wholly or partly on, or secured by, a current bill of exchange or promissory note, unless the creditor is willing—

(i) to treat as a security in the creditor's hands the liability on the bill or note of every person who is liable on it antecedently to the investment bank, and—

(aa) in the case of a company, has not gone into liquidation, or

(bb) in the case of an individual, against whom a bankruptcy order has not been made or whose estate has not been sequestrated, and

(ii) to estimate the value of the security and for the purposes of voting (but not otherwise) to deduct it from the claim.

[7.1798]
88 Calculation of voting rights: special cases (creditors)

(1) An owner of goods under a hire-purchase or chattel leasing agreement, or a seller of goods under a conditional sale agreement, is entitled to vote in respect of the amount of the debt due and payable by the investment bank on the date on which it entered special administration.

(2) In calculating the amount of any debt for the purpose of paragraph (1), no account is to be taken of any amount attributable to the exercise of any right under the relevant agreement so far as the right has become exercisable solely by virtue of—

(a) the making of a special administration application; or
(b) the investment bank entering special administration.

[7.1799]
89 Procedure for admitting creditors' claims for voting

(1) At a meeting of creditors, the chair must ascertain the entitlement of persons wishing to vote as creditors and admit or reject their claims accordingly.

(2) The chair may admit or reject a claim in whole or in part.

(3) If the chair is in any doubt whether a claim should be admitted or rejected, the claim must be marked as objected to and allow votes to be cast in respect of it, subject to such votes being subsequently declared invalid if the objection to the claim is sustained.

[7.1800]
90 Entitlement to vote (clients)

(1) A client is entitled to vote at a meeting of creditors and clients or clients only if—

(a) the administrator has been given written details of the client's claim as to the total amount of client assets over which the client asserts—
  (i) a beneficial right of ownership,
  (ii) a right of ownership as bailor, or
  (iii) another means of ownership; and
(b) the details were given to the administrator—
  (i) not later than 12.00 hours on the business day before the day fixed for the meeting, or
  (ii) later than that time but the chair of the meeting is satisfied that the delay was due to circumstances beyond that client's control; and
(c) the claim for client assets has been admitted for the purposes of entitlement to vote,

and there has been lodged with the administrator any proxy intended to be used on behalf of that person.

(2) Subject to paragraph (4), for the purposes of this Chapter, written details of a claim for client assets, once lodged or given in accordance with this rule, need not be lodged or given again.

(3) The chair may call for any document or other evidence to be produced if the chair thinks it necessary for the purpose of substantiating the whole or any part of a claim for client assets.

(4) Where at the date of the meeting the client is aware that there will be a shortfall in respect of their claim to client assets, the client shall—

(a) submit a claim under paragraph (1), subtracting the value of the shortfall of assets from that claim (as calculated, in respect of securities, in accordance with rule 91); and
(b) submit a claim under rule 85 as to the debt owed to the client by the investment bank in respect of the shortfall.

(5) If at the time that the invitation to the initial meeting, or notice of a creditors and clients' or a client's meeting, is sent out, the administrator has become aware that there will be a shortfall in respect of a client's claim to client assets, the administrator shall notify the client at the same time the invitation or notice is sent out.

(6) If after the time that the invitation to the initial meeting, or notice of a creditors and clients' or a clients' meeting, is sent out, the administrator becomes aware that there will be a shortfall in respect of a client's claim to client assets, the administrator shall notify the client as soon as reasonably practicable prior to the meeting and take this shortfall into account in calculating the client's entitlement to vote.

[7.1801]
91 Calculation of voting rights (clients)

(1) For the purposes of this Chapter, a client's voting rights are calculated according to the value of the client's claim submitted under rule 90, taking into account any shortfall identified prior to the meeting.

(2) Subject to paragraph (4), the chair is to value any securities making up the client's claim under paragraph (1) by reference to the closing or settlement price for such securities of a particular description.

(3) In paragraph (2)—

"closing or settlement price" means—

  (a) in relation to securities traded on a relevant exchange, the closing or settlement price published by that exchange; and
  (b) in relation to securities traded elsewhere, the closing or settlement price published by an appropriate pricing source on the last business day before the date the investment bank entered special administration; but where such securities are traded outside the United Kingdom, the closing or settlement price shall be the most recent closing price before that date; and

"securities of a particular description" has the meaning set out in regulation 12(9);

and in this paragraph—

"appropriate pricing source" means a reputable source used by the investment bank immediately prior to the investment bank entering special administration for valuing or reporting in respect of those securities, unless the client asserts with good reason (and the chair agrees) that an alternative source should be used; and "relevant exchange" means a recognised investment exchange or recognised overseas investment exchange used by the investment bank to trade such securities immediately prior to the investment bank entering special administration, unless the client asserts with good reason (and the chair agrees) that an alternative exchange should be used.

(4) Where the chair considers that it is not practicable to value a client asset by reference to a closing or settlement price published by a relevant exchange or an appropriate pricing source, the chair may put upon the asset an estimated minimum value for the purposes of the entitlement to vote.

(5) Where client assets are quoted in currencies other than sterling, in order to value the assets for the purposes of this chapter, the administrator shall convert the market price of the assets to sterling at the rate of exchange for that other currency as at the mean of the buying and selling spot rates prevailing in the London market as published at the close of business on the business day prior to the date the investment bank entered special administration or, in the absence of any such published rate, such rate as the court determines.

[7.1802]

92 Procedure for admitting clients' claims for voting

(1) At a meeting of creditors and clients, or clients, the chair must ascertain the entitlement of persons wishing to vote as clients and admit or reject their claims accordingly.

(2) The chair may admit or reject a claim in whole or in part.

(3) If the chair is in any doubt whether a claim should be admitted or rejected, the claim must be marked as objected to and allow votes to be cast in respect of it, subject to such votes being subsequently declared invalid if the objection to the claim is sustained.

[7.1803]

93 Voting at meetings of creditors and clients

(1) This rule applies to meetings of creditors and clients.

(2) If the administrator thinks it appropriate, the creditors and clients may vote on the same resolution at the meeting, however the creditors and the clients shall vote separately on the resolution.

(3) In a special administration (bank insolvency) the FSCS shall be entitled to vote as a creditor under this rule and rule 86 has effect with respect to its voting rights.

[7.1804]

94 Requisite majorities

(1) Subject to paragraph (2), at a meeting of creditors or clients, or of creditors and clients, a resolution is passed when a majority (in value) of those present and voting, in person or by proxy, have voted in favour of it.

(2) Any resolution is invalid if those voting against it include more than half in value of the creditors, or, as the case may be, clients, to whom notice of the meeting was sent and who are not, to the best of the chair's belief, persons connected with the investment bank.

[7.1805]

95 Requisite majorities at contributories' meetings

At a meeting of contributories, voting rights are as at a general meeting of the investment bank, subject to any provision of the articles affecting entitlement to vote, either generally or at a time when the investment bank is in liquidation.

[7.1806]

96 Appeals against decisions under this Chapter

(1) The chair's decisions under this Chapter are subject to appeal to the court by any creditor, client or contributory or member.

(2) If the chair's decision is reversed or varied, or votes are declared invalid, the court may order another meeting to be summoned or make such order as it thinks just.

(3) An appeal under this rule may not be made later than 21 days after the date of the meeting.

(4) The chair is not personally liable for costs incurred by any person in respect of an appeal under this rule unless the court makes an order to that effect.

CHAPTER 6 CORRESPONDENCE AND REMOTE ATTENDANCE

[7.1807]

97 Correspondence instead of meetings

(1) The administrator, when convening a meeting, may seek to obtain the passing by creditors, clients or contributories of a written resolution by sending a notice to that effect to every creditor, client or contributory (as the case may be) who would be entitled to be notified of (or in the case of clients, the administrator thinks it appropriate that they are summoned to) a meeting at which the resolution could be passed.

(2) Notice under paragraph (1) must contain the following information—

(a) a statement that the proceedings are being held in the High Court and the court reference number;

(b) the full name, registered address and registered number of the investment bank;

(c) the full name and business address of the administrator;

(d) the resolution to be voted on; and
(e) the closing date by which the recipient must respond to the administrator.

(3) In order to be counted, votes must—
(a) be received by the administrator by 12.00 hours on the closing date specified in the notice;
(b) in the case of a vote cast by a creditor or by a client, be accompanied by a statement of entitlement to vote on the resolution unless one has already been lodged with or given to the administrator.

(4) A statement of entitlement is written details of the creditor's claim or the client's claim in respect of client assets.

(5) The closing date is to be set at the discretion of the administrator, but must be not less than 14 days from the date of issue of the notice.

(6) Votes must be disregarded if—
(a) the requisite statement of entitlement had not accompanied them or previously been lodged with or given to the administrator, or
(b) in the application of Chapter 5 of this Part, the administrator decides that the creditor or client is not entitled to cast the votes.

(7) For the resolution to be passed, the administrator must receive at least one valid vote in favour by the closing date specified in the notice.

(8) If no valid vote is received by the closing date, the creditor must call a meeting of creditors, clients or contributories (as the case may be) to consider the resolution.

(9) Creditors the debts of whom amount to at least 10% of the total debts of the investment bank may, within 5 business days from the date of issue of the notice, require the administrator to call a meeting of creditors to consider the resolution.

(10) Clients asserting claims over at least 10% of the total value of client assets held by the investment bank may, within 5 business days from the date of issue of the notice, require the administrator to call a meeting of clients to consider the resolution.

(11) Contributories representing at least 10% of the total voting rights of all contributories having the right to vote a at meeting of contributories may, within 5 business days from the date of issue of the notice, require the administrator to call a meeting of contributories to consider the resolution.

(12) A reference in these Rules to anything done or required to be done at, or in connection with, or in consequence of, a meeting of creditors, clients or contributories extends to anything done in the course of correspondence in accordance with this rule.

[7.1808]
98 Remote attendance at meetings conducted in accordance with section 246A

(1) This Rule applies to a request to the administrator for a meeting under section 246A(9) of the 1986 Act to specify a place for the meeting.

(2) The request must be accompanied by—
(a) in the case of a request by creditors, a list of the creditors making or concurring with the request and the amounts of their respective debts in the special administration;
(b) in the case of a request by clients, a list of the clients making or concurring with the request and the amounts of their respective claims in respect of client assets in the special administration;
(c) in the case of a request by contributories, a list of the contributories making or concurring with the request and their respective values (being the amounts for which they may vote at the meeting);
(d) in the case of a request by members, a list of the members making or concurring with the request and their voting rights; and
(e) from each person concurring, written confirmation of that person's concurrence.

(3) The request must be made within 7 business days of the date on which the administrator sent the notice of the meeting in question.

(4) Where the administrator considers that the request has been properly made in accordance with the Regulations and this rule, the administrator must—
(a) give notice to all those previously given notice of the meeting—
(i) that it is to be held at a specified place, and
(ii) as to whether the date and time are to remain the same or not;
(b) set a venue (including specification of a place) for the meeting, the date of which must be not later than 28 days after the original date for the meeting; and
(c) give at least 14 days' notice of that venue to all those previously given notice of the meeting,
and the notices required by sub-paragraphs (a) and (c) may be given at the same or different times.

(5) Where the administrator has specified a place for the meeting in response to a request to which this rule applies, the chair of the meeting must attend the meeting by being present in person at that place.

(6) Rule 77 (expenses of requisitioned meetings) does not apply to the summoning and holding of a meeting at a place specified in accordance with section 246A(9).

[7.1809]
99 Action where person excluded

(1) In this rule and rules 100 and 101, an "excluded person" means a person who—
(a) has taken all steps necessary to attend a meeting under the arrangements put in place to do so by the administrator under section 246A(6) of the 1986 Act; and

(b) is not permitted by those arrangements to attend the whole or part of that meeting.

(2) Where the chair becomes aware during the course of the meeting that there is an excluded person, the chair may—

(a) continue the meeting;

(b) declare the meeting void and convene the meeting again;

(c) declare the meeting valid up to the point where the person was excluded and adjourn the meeting.

(3) Where the chair continues the meeting, the meeting is valid unless—

(a) the chair decides in consequence of a complaint under rule 101 to declare the meeting void and hold the meeting again; or

(b) the court directs otherwise.

(4) Without prejudice to paragraph (2), where the chair becomes aware during the course of the meeting that there is an excluded person, the chair may, in the chair's discretion and without an adjournment, declare the meeting suspended for any period up to 1 hour.

[7.1810]
100 Indication to excluded person

(1) A person who claims to be an excluded person may request an indication of what occurred during the period of that person's claimed exclusion (an "indication").

(2) A request under paragraph (1) must be made as soon as reasonably practicable and, in any event, no later than 16.00 hours on the business day following the day on which the exclusion is claimed to have occurred.

(3) A request under paragraph (1) must be made to—

(a) the chair, where it is made during the course of the business of the meeting; or

(b) the administrator where it is made after the conclusion of the business of the meeting.

(4) Where satisfied that the person making the request is an excluded person, the person to whom the request is made under paragraph (3) must give the indication as soon as reasonably practicable and, in any event, no later than 16.00 hours on the business day following the day on which the request was made under paragraph (1).

[7.1811]
101 Complaint

(1) Any person who—

(a) is, or claims to be, an excluded person; or

(b) attends the meeting (in person or by proxy) and considers that they have been adversely affected by a person's actual, apparent or claimed exclusion,

("the complainant") may make a complaint.

(2) The person to whom the complaint must be made ("the relevant person") is—

(a) the chair, where it is made during the course of the meeting; or

(b) the administrator where it is made after the meeting.

(3) The relevant person must—

(a) consider whether there is an excluded person; and

(b) where satisfied that there is an excluded person, consider the complaint,

and, where satisfied that there has been prejudice, take such action as the relevant person considers fit to remedy the prejudice.

(4) Paragraph (5) applies where—

(a) the relevant person is satisfied that the complainant is an excluded person;

(b) during the period of the person's exclusion, a resolution was put to the meeting and was voted on; and—

(c) the excluded person asserts how the excluded person intended to vote on the resolution.

(5) Subject to paragraph (6), where satisfied that the effect of the intended vote in paragraph (4), if cast, would have changed the result of the resolution, the relevant person must—

(a) count the intended vote as being cast in accordance with the complainant's stated intention;

(b) amend the record of the result of the resolution; and

(c) where those entitled to attend the meeting have been notified of the result of the resolution, notify them of the change.

(6) Where satisfied that more than one complainant in paragraph (4) is an excluded person, the relevant person must have regard to the combined effect of the intended votes.

(7) The relevant person must notify the complainant in writing of any decision.

(8) A complaint must be made as soon as reasonably practicable and, in any event, no later than 16.00 hours on the business day following—

(a) the day on which the person was, appeared or claimed to be excluded; or

(b) where an indication is sought under rule 100, the day on which the complainant received the indication.

(9) A complainant who is not satisfied by the action of the relevant person may apply to the court for directions and any application must be made within 2 business days of the date of receiving the decision of the relevant person.

CHAPTER 7 RECORDS, RETURNS AND REPORTS

[7.1812]
102 Minutes

(1) The chair of any meeting under the Regulations or these Rules, other than a company meeting (for which see rule 84), must cause minutes of its proceedings to be kept.

(2) The minutes must be authenticated by the chair, and be retained by the chair as part of the records of the special administration.

(3) The minutes must include—

(a) a list of the names of creditors who attended a meeting of creditors or a meeting of both creditors and clients (personally, by proxy or by corporate representative) and their claims;

(b) a list of the names of clients who attended a meeting of clients or a meeting of both creditors and clients (personally, by proxy or by corporate representative) and their claims in respect of client assets;

(c) a list of the names of contributories who attended a meeting of contributories;

(d) if a creditors' committee has been established, the names and addresses of those elected to be members of the committee; and

(e) a record of every resolution passed.

[7.1813]
103 Returns or reports of meetings

In addition to the information required by rule 308, the notification of a return or a report of a meeting must specify—

(a) the purpose of the meeting including the regulation or rule under which it was convened;

(b) the venue fixed for the meeting;

(c) whether a required quorum was present for the meeting to take place; and

(d) if the meeting took place, the outcome of the meeting (including any resolutions passed at the meeting).

CHAPTER 8 THE CREDITORS' COMMITTEE

[7.1814]
104 Constitution of committee

(1) Where it is resolved by a creditors and clients' meeting to establish a creditors' committee for the purposes of the special administration, the committee shall consist of at least 3 and not more than 5 persons elected at the meeting.

(2) In a special administration (bank insolvency), the FSCS shall be a member of the creditors' committee unless it informs the administrator prior to the meeting referred to in paragraph (1) that it does not wish to be a member.

(3) Where paragraph (1) applies, before receiving nominations for members of the committee, the administrator will set out the maximum number of members to be elected onto the committee by each class of voter so as to ensure that, subject to paragraph (2), the make-up of the committee is a reflection of all parties with an interest in the achievement of the special administration objectives.

(4) The classes of voters mentioned in paragraph (3) are—

(a) creditors; and

(b) clients.

(5) A person claiming to be a creditor is entitled to be a member of the committee provided that—

(a) that person's claim has neither been wholly disallowed for voting purposes, nor wholly rejected for the purpose of distribution or dividend; and

(b) the claim mentioned in sub-paragraph (a) is not fully secured.

(6) A person claiming to be a client is entitled to be a member of the committee provided that that person's claim in respect of client assets has neither been wholly disallowed for voting purposes, nor wholly rejected for the purpose of returning client assets.

(7) A body corporate may be a member of the committee, but it cannot act as such otherwise than by a representative appointed under rule 109.

[7.1815]
105 Formalities of establishment

(1) The creditors' committee does not come into being and accordingly cannot act until the administrator has issued a certificate of its due constitution.

(2) The certificate shall state that the creditors' committee of the investment bank has been duly constituted and shall include the following—

(a) a statement that the proceedings are being held in the High Court and the court reference number;

(b) the full name, registered address and registered number of the investment bank;

(c) the full name and business address of the administrator; and

(d) the full name and address of each member of the committee.

(3) If the chair of the creditors' meeting which resolves to establish the committee is not the administrator, the chair must as soon as reasonably practicable give notice of the resolution to the administrator and inform the administrator of the names and addresses of the persons elected to be members of the committee.

(4) No person may act as a member of the committee unless and until they have agreed to do so and, unless the relevant proxy or authorisation contains a statement to the contrary, such agreement may be given by their proxy-holder present at the meeting establishing the committee or, in the case of a corporation, by its duly appointed representative.

(5) The administrator's certificate of the committee's due constitution shall not be issued before the persons elected to be members of the committee in accordance with rule 104 have agreed to act and shall be issued as soon as reasonably practicable thereafter.

(6) If any further members are elected onto the committee at a later date, the administrator shall issue an amended certificate as and when those persons have agreed to act.

(7) The certificate, and any amended certificate, shall be sent to the registrar of companies by the administrator, as soon as reasonably practicable.

(8) If after the establishment of the committee there is any change in its membership, the administrator shall as soon as reasonably practicable report the change to the registrar of companies by filing an amended certificate.

[7.1816]

106 Functions and meetings of the committee

(1) In addition to any functions conferred on the creditors' committee by any provision of the Regulations, the creditors' committee shall assist the administrator in discharging the administrator's functions, and act in relation to the administrator in such manner as may be agreed from time to time.

(2) Subject as follows, meetings of the committee shall be held at a time and place determined by the administrator.

(3) The administrator must call a first meeting of the committee to take place within 6 weeks of the committee's establishment.

(4) After the calling of the first meeting, the administrator must call a meeting—

- (a) if so requested by a member of the committee or the member's representative (the meeting then to be held within 21 days of the request being received by the administrator); and
- (b) for a specified date, if the committee has previously resolved that a meeting be held on that date.

(5) Subject to paragraph (8), the administrator shall give 5 business days' written notice of the venue of any meeting to every member of the committee (or their representative designated for that purpose) unless in any case the requirement of notice has been waived by or on behalf of any member. Waiver may be signified either at or before the meeting.

(6) The [FCA and, where the investment bank concerned is a PRA-authorised person, the PRA] shall also be given the notice in paragraph (5).

(7) In a special administration (bank administration), if the meeting is to be held before the Bank of England has given the Objective A Achievement Notice, the Bank of England shall be given the notice in paragraph (5).

(8) Where the administrator has determined that a meeting should be conducted and held in the manner referred to in rule 115, the notice period mentioned in paragraph (5) is 7 business days.

NOTES

Para (6): words in square brackets substituted for "FSA" by the Financial Services Act 2012 (Consequential Amendments and Transitional Provisions) Order 2013, SI 2013/472, art 3, Sch 2, para 210(c), (d)(ix), subject to a transitional provision (see para 211 as noted to **[7.1718]**).

[7.1817]

107 The chair at meetings

(1) The chair at any meeting of the creditors' committee must be the administrator, or a person appointed by the administrator in writing to act.

(2) A person so appointed must be either—

- (a) one who is qualified to act as an insolvency practitioner in relation to the investment bank; or
- (b) an employee of the administrator or the administrator's firm who is experienced in insolvency matters.

[7.1818]

108 Quorum

A meeting of the committee is duly constituted if due notice of it has been given to all the members, and at least 2 members are present or represented.

[7.1819]

109 Committee members' representatives

(1) A member of the committee may, in relation to the business of the committee, be represented by another person duly authorised by the member for that purpose.

(2) A person acting as a committee-member's representative must hold a letter of authority entitling them so to act (either generally or specially) and authenticated by or on behalf of the committee-member.

(3) For the purpose of paragraph (2), any proxy in relation to any meeting of creditors, or clients, or creditors and clients shall, unless it contains a statement to the contrary, be treated as a letter of authority to act generally, authenticated by or on behalf of the committee-member.

(4) The chair at any meeting of the committee may call on a person claiming to act as a committee-member's representative to produce the letter of authority, and may exclude that person if it appears that their authority is deficient.

(5) No member may be represented by—

(a) another member of the committee;

(b) a person who is at the same time representing another committee member;

(c) a body corporate;

(d) an undischarged bankrupt;

(e) a disqualified director; or

(f) a person who is subject to a bankruptcy restrictions order (including an interim order), a bankruptcy restrictions undertaking, a debt relief restrictions order (including an interim order) or a debt relief restrictions undertaking.

(6) Where a member's representative authenticates any document on the member's behalf, the fact that the representative so authenticates must be stated below the authentication.

[7.1820]
110 Resignation

A member of the committee may resign by notice in writing delivered to the administrator.

[7.1821]
111 Termination of membership

(1) Membership of the creditors' committee is automatically terminated if the member—

(a) becomes bankrupt;

(b) at 3 consecutive meetings of the committee is neither present nor represented (unless at the third of those meetings it is resolved that this rule is not to apply in that member's case);

(c) subject to paragraph (3), if voted onto the committee under rule 104 by the creditors of the investment bank, ceases to be a creditor and a period of 3 months has elapsed from the date that that member ceased to be a creditor or is found never to have been a creditor; or

(d) subject to paragraph (4), if voted onto the committee under rule 104 by the clients of the investment bank, has had all client assets claimed for under Part 5 returned to them (subject to there being an identified shortfall in the assets to be returned to them or any assets being retained by the administrator under rule 144(1)(e)), or is found never to have been a client.

(2) However, if the cause of termination is the member's bankruptcy, their trustee in bankruptcy shall replace them as a member of the committee.

(3) A person to whom paragraph (1)(c) applies shall not have their membership terminated if—

(a) they are also a client of the investment bank; and

(b) they have not had all client assets claimed for under Part 5 returned to them (subject to there being an identified shortfall in the assets to be returned to them or any of their assets being retained by the administrator under rule 144(1)(e)),

but the administrator may require them to resign if the administrator thinks that the make-up of the committee does not reflect all parties with an interest in the achievement of the special administration objectives.

(4) A person to whom paragraph (1)(d) applies shall not have their membership terminated if they are also a creditor of the investment bank but the administrator may require them to resign if the administrator thinks that the make-up of the committee does not reflect all parties with an interest in the achievement of the special administration objectives.

[7.1822]
112 Removal

(1) A member of the committee may be removed by resolution at a meeting of creditors and clients, at least 14 days' notice having been given of the intention to move that resolution.

(2) The resolution in paragraph (1) will be voted on only by the relevant class of voter in respect of the member to be removed.

[7.1823]
113 Vacancies

(1) The following applies if there is a vacancy in the membership of the creditors' committee.

(2) The vacancy need not be filled if the administrator and a majority of the remaining members of the committee so agree, provided that—

(a) the total number of members does not fall below 3; and

(b) the administrator thinks that the make-up of the committee will continue to reflect all parties with an interest in the achievement of the special administration objectives.

(3) The administrator may appoint a person (being qualified under these Rules to be a member of the committee) from the same class of voters as the previous member to fill the vacancy, if—

(a) a majority of the other members of the committee agree to the appointment; and

(b) the person concerned consents to act.

[7.1824]
114 Procedure at meetings

(1) At any meeting of the creditors' committee, each member of it (whether present or represented) has one vote, and a resolution is passed when a majority of the members present or represented have voted in favour of it.

(2) Every resolution passed must be recorded in writing and authenticated by the chair, either separately or as part of the minutes of the meeting, and the record must be kept with the records of the proceedings.

[7.1825]
115 Remote attendance at meetings of creditors' committee

(1) This rule applies to any meeting of a creditors' committee held under these Rules.

(2) Where the administrator considers it appropriate, the meeting may be conducted and held in such a way that persons who are not present together at the same place may attend it.

(3) Where a meeting is conducted and held in the manner referred to in paragraph (2), a person attends the meeting if that person is able to exercise any rights which that person may have to speak and vote at the meeting.

(4) For the purposes of this rule—

(a) a person is able to exercise the right to speak at a meeting when that person is in a position to communicate to all those attending the meeting, during the meeting, any information or opinions which that person has on the business of the meeting; and

(b) a person is able to exercise the right to vote at a meeting when—

(i) that person is able to vote, during the meeting, on resolutions or determinations put to the vote at the meeting, and

(ii) that person's vote can be taken into account in determining whether or not such resolutions or determinations are passed at the same time as the votes of all the other persons attending the meeting.

(5) Where a meeting is to be conducted and held in the manner referred to in paragraph (2), the administrator must make whatever arrangements the administrator considers appropriate to—

(a) enable those attending the meeting to exercise their rights to speak or vote; and

(b) ensure the identification of those attending the meeting and the security of any electronic means used to enable attendance.

(6) Where in the reasonable opinion of the office-holder—

(a) a meeting will be attended by persons who will not be present together at the same place; and

(b) it is unnecessary or inexpedient to specify a place for the meeting,

any requirement under these Rules to specify a place for the meeting may be satisfied by specifying the arrangements the office-holder proposes to enable persons to exercise their rights to speak or vote.

(7) In making the arrangements referred to in paragraph (5) and in forming the opinion referred to in paragraph (6)(b), the administrator must have regard to the legitimate interests of the committee members or their representatives attending the meeting in the efficient despatch of the business of the meeting.

(8) If—

(a) the notice of a meeting does not specify a place for the meeting,

(b) the administrator is requested in accordance with rule 116 to specify a place for the meeting, and

(c) that request is made by at least one member of the committee,

the administrator must specify a place for the meeting.

[7.1826]
116 Procedure for requests that a place for a meeting should be specified

(1) This rule applies to a request to the administrator of a meeting under rule 115 to specify a place for the meeting.

(2) The request must be made within 5 business days of the date on which the administrator sent the notice of the meeting in question.

(3) Where the administrator considers that the request has been properly made in accordance with this rule, the administrator must—

(a) give notice to all those previously given notice of the meeting—

(i) that it is to be held at a specified place, and

(ii) as to whether the date and time are to remain the same or not;

(b) set a venue (including specification of a place) for the meeting, the date of which must be not later than 7 business days after the original date for the meeting; and

(c) give 5 business days' notice of the venue to all those previously given notice of the meeting;

and the notices required by sub-paragraphs (a) and (c) may be given at the same or different times.

(4) Where the administrator has specified a place for the meeting in response to a request to which this rule applies, the chair of the meeting must attend the meeting by being present in person at that place.

[7.1827]
117 Resolutions of creditors' committees by post

(1) The administrator may seek to obtain the agreement of members of the creditors' committee to a resolution by sending to every member of the committee (or designated representative) a copy of the proposed resolution.

(2) Where the administrator makes use of this procedure, the administrator shall notify each member or their representative of each proposed resolution on which a decision is sought.

(3) The [FCA and, where the investment bank concerned is a PRA-authorised person, the PRA] shall also be notified of each proposed resolution under this rule.

(4) In a special administration (bank administration), if the notification in paragraph (2) happens before the Bank of England has given the Objective A Achievement Notice, the Bank of England shall be notified of each proposed resolution under this rule.

(5) Any member of the committee may, within 7 business days of the date of the administrator notifying them of a resolution, require the administrator to summon a meeting of the committee to consider matters raised by the resolution.

(6) In the absence of such a request, the resolution is deemed to have been passed by the committee if and when the administrator is notified in writing by a majority of the members that they agree with the resolution.

(7) A copy of every resolution passed under this rule, and a note that the committee's concurrence was obtained, shall be kept with the records of the proceedings.

NOTES

Para (3): words in square brackets substituted for "FSA" by the Financial Services Act 2012 (Consequential Amendments and Transitional Provisions) Order 2013, SI 2013/472, art 3, Sch 2, para 210(c), (d)(x), subject to a transitional provision (see para 211 as noted to **[7.1718]**).

[7.1828]
118 Information from administrator

(1) Where the committee resolves to require the attendance of the administrator under paragraph 57(3)(a), the notice to the administrator shall be in writing, authenticated by the majority of the members of the committee for the time being.

(2) A member's authentication under paragraph (1) may be made by that member's representative.

(3) The meeting at which the administrator's attendance is required shall be fixed by the committee for a business day, and shall be held at such time and place as the administrator determines.

(4) The administrator shall notify the [FCA and, where the investment bank concerned is a PRA-authorised person, the PRA] of the time and place of the meeting.

(5) In a special administration (bank administration), if the meeting is to be held before the Bank of England has given the Objective A Achievement Notice, the Bank of England shall be given the notice in paragraph (4).

(6) Where the administrator so attends, the members of the committee may elect any one of their number to be chair of the meeting, in place of the administrator or the administrator's nominee.

NOTES

Para (4): words in square brackets substituted for "FSA" by the Financial Services Act 2012 (Consequential Amendments and Transitional Provisions) Order 2013, SI 2013/472, art 3, Sch 2, para 210(c), (d)(xi), subject to a transitional provision (see para 211 as noted to **[7.1718]**).

[7.1829]
119 Expenses of members

(1) Subject to paragraph (2), the administrator shall, out of the assets of the investment bank, defray, in the prescribed order of priority as set out in rule 134, any reasonable travelling expenses directly incurred by members of the creditors' committee or their representatives in relation to their attendance at the committee's meetings, or otherwise on the committee's business, as an expense of the administration.

(2) Any client members of the committee shall have their expenses referred to in paragraph (1) paid out of the client assets held by the investment bank.

(3) Paragraph (1) does not apply to any meeting of the committee held within 6 weeks of a previous meeting, unless the meeting in question is summoned at the instance of the administrator.

[7.1830]
120 Members dealing with the investment bank

(1) Membership of the committee does not prevent a person from dealing with the investment bank while it is in special administration, provided that any transactions in the course of such dealings are in good faith and for value.

(2) The court may, on the application of any person interested, set aside any transaction which appears to it to be contrary to the requirements of this rule, and may give such consequential directions as it thinks just for compensating the investment bank for any loss which it may have incurred in consequence of the transaction.

[7.1831]
121 Formal defects

The acts of the creditors' committee established for a special administration are valid despite any defect in the appointment, election or qualifications of any member of the committee or any committee-member's representative or in the formalities of its establishment.

CHAPTER 9 PROGRESS REPORTS

[7.1832]

122 Content of progress report

(1) "Progress report" means a report which includes—

(a) a statement that the proceedings are being held in the High Court and the court reference number;

(b) the full name, registered address and registered number of the investment bank;

(c) the full name and business address of the administrator;

(d) where there are joint administrators, details of the apportionment of functions;

(e) details of the basis fixed for the remuneration of the administrator under rules 29, 48 or 196 (or if not fixed at the date of the report, the steps taken during the period of the report to fix it);

(f) if the basis of remuneration has been fixed, a statement of—

(i) the remuneration charged by the administrator during the period of the report (subject to paragraph (5), and

(ii) where the report is the first to be made after the basis has been fixed, the remuneration charged by the administrator during the periods covered by the previous reports (subject to paragraph (5)), together with a description of the things done by the administrator during those periods in respect of which the remuneration was charged,

irrespective in either case of whether payment was made in respect of that remuneration during the period of the report;

(g) a statement of the expenses incurred by the administrator during the period of the report, (irrespective of whether payment was made in respect of them during that period): the statement to contain a breakdown of expenses incurred in respect of the administrator pursuing Objective 1 of the Special Administration Objectives;

(h) whether the [FCA or, where relevant, the PRA] have given a direction under regulation 16 and whether that direction has been withdrawn;

(i) details of progress during the period of the report, including a receipts and payments account (as detailed in paragraph (4) below);

(j) details of any assets of the investment bank that remain to be realised;

(k) in a special administration (bank administration), details of any amounts received from a scheme under a resolution fund order;

(l) details of whether a bar date has been set and progress made in pursuit of Objective 1 of the Special Administration Objectives;

(m) a statement of the creditors' right to request information under rule 201 and their right to challenge the administrator's remuneration and expenses under rule 202; and

(n) any other relevant information for the creditors or the clients.

(2) In a special administration (bank insolvency), before a full payment resolution has been passed, a progress report must contain details of—

(a) how Objective A (as defined in paragraph 9 of Schedule 1 to the Regulations) is being achieved;

(b) the arrangements for managing and financing the investment bank while Objective A continues to be pursued;

(c) the basis for the administrator's remuneration fixed under rule 29 and whether that has been confirmed or redetermined in accordance with rule 197.

(3) In a special administration (bank administration), before the Bank of England has given an Objective A Achievement Notice, a progress report must contain details of—

(a) the extent of the business of the investment bank that has been transferred;

(b) the property, rights and liabilities that have been transferred or which the administrator expects to be transferred, under a power in Part 1 of the 2009 Act (special resolution regime);

(c) any requirements imposed on the investment bank for the purposes of the pursuit of Objective A (as defined in paragraph 3(a) of Schedule 2 to the Regulations), under a power in Part 1 of the 2009 Act;

(d) the arrangements for managing and financing the investment bank while Objective A continues to be pursued; and

(e) the basis for the administrator's remuneration fixed under rule 48 and whether that has been confirmed or redetermined in accordance with rule 198.

(4) A receipts and payments account must be in the form of an abstract showing receipts and payments during the period of the report and, where the administrator has ceased to act, must also include a statement as to the amount paid to unsecured creditors by virtue of the application of section 176A of the 1986 Act.

(5) Where the basis for the remuneration is a set amount under rule 196(2)(c), it may be shown as that amount without any apportionment to the period of the report.

(6) Where the administrator has made a statement of pre-administration costs under rule 59(2)(m)—

(a) if they are approved under rule 136 the first progress report after the approval must include a statement setting out the date of the approval and the amounts approved;

(b) each successive report, so long as any of the costs remain unapproved, must include a statement either—

(i) of any steps taken to get approval, or

(ii) that the administrator has decided, or (as the case may be) another insolvency practitioner entitled to seek approval has told the administrator of that practitioner's decision, not to seek approval.

(7) The progress report must, except where paragraph (6) applies, cover the period of 6 months commencing on the date on which the investment bank entered special administration and every subsequent period of 6 months.

(8) The period to be covered by a progress report ends on the date when an administrator ceases to act, and the period to be covered by each subsequent progress report is each successive period of 6 months beginning immediately after that date (subject to the further application of this paragraph when another administrator ceases to act).

NOTES

Para (1): words in square brackets in sub-para (h) substituted for "FSA" by the Financial Services Act 2012 (Consequential Amendments and Transitional Provisions) Order 2013, SI 2013/472, art 3, Sch 2, para 210(a), (b)(xiii), subject to a transitional provision (see para 211 as noted to **[7.1718]**).

[7.1833]
123 Sending progress report

(1) The administrator must, within 1 month of the end of the period covered by the report, send—
- (a) a copy to the creditors and to the clients, and
- (b) a copy to the registrar of companies;

but this paragraph does not apply when the period covered by the report is that of a final progress report under rule 220.

(2) The copy sent under paragraph (1)(a) must be accompanied by a statement setting out—
- (a) that the proceedings are being held in the High Court and the court reference number;
- (b) the full name, registered address and registered number of the investment bank;
- (c) the full name and address of the administrator;
- (d) the period covered by the progress report.

(3) The court may, on the administrator's application, extend the period of 1 month mentioned in paragraph (1), or make such other order in respect of the content of the report as it thinks just.

(4) If the administrator makes default in complying with this rule, the administrator is liable to a fine and, for continued contravention, to a daily default fine.

CHAPTER 10 PROXIES AND CORPORATE REPRESENTATION

[7.1834]
124 Definition of proxy

(1) For the purposes of these Rules, a proxy is an authority given by a person ("the principal") to another person ("the proxy-holder") to attend a meeting and speak and vote as the principal's representative.

(2) Proxies are for use at creditors', creditor and clients', clients, company or contributories' meetings summoned or called under the Regulations or the Rules.

(3) Only one proxy may be given by a person for any one meeting at which that person desires to be represented; and it may only be given to one person, being an individual aged 18 or over. But the principal may specify one or more other such individuals to be proxy-holder in the alternative, in the order in which they are named in the proxy.

(4) Without prejudice to the generality of paragraph (3), a proxy for a particular meeting may be given to whoever is to be the chair of the meeting.

(5) A person given a proxy under paragraph (4) cannot decline to be the proxy-holder in relation to that proxy.

(6) A proxy requires the holder to give the principal's vote on matters arising for determination at the meeting, or to abstain, or to propose, in the principal's name, a resolution to be voted on by the meeting, either as directed or in accordance with the holder's own discretion.

[7.1835]
125 Issue and use of forms

(1) When notice is given of a meeting to be held in the course of the special administration and forms of proxy are sent out with the notice, no form so sent out shall have inserted in it the name or description of any person.

(2) No form of proxy shall be used at any meeting except that which is sent out with the notice summoning the meeting, or a substantially similar form.

(3) A form of proxy shall be authenticated by the principal, or by some person authorised by that principal (either generally or with reference to a particular meeting). If the form is authenticated by a person other than the principal, the nature of the person's authority shall be stated.

[7.1836]
126 Use of proxies at meetings

(1) A proxy given for a particular meeting may be used at any adjournment of that meeting.

(2) Where the administrator holds proxies to be used by the administrator as chair of a meeting, and some other person acts as chair, the other person may use the administrator's proxies as if that person was the proxy-holder.

(3) Where a proxy directs a proxy-holder to vote for or against a resolution for the nomination or appointment of a person as the administrator, the proxy-holder may, unless the proxy states otherwise, vote for or against (as they think fit) any resolution for the nomination or appointment of that person jointly with another or others.

(4) A proxy-holder may propose any resolution which, if proposed by another, would be a resolution in favour of which by virtue of the proxy they would be entitled to vote.

(5) Where a proxy gives specific directions as to voting, this does not, unless the proxy states otherwise, preclude the proxy-holder from voting at their discretion on resolutions put to the meeting which are not dealt with in the proxy.

[7.1837]
127 Retention of proxies

(1) Subject as follows, proxies used for voting at any meeting shall be retained by the chair of the meeting.

(2) The chair shall deliver the proxies, as soon as reasonably practicable after the meeting, to the administrator (where the administrator is someone other than the chair).

[7.1838]
128 Right of inspection

(1) So long as proxies lodged with the administrator are in the administrator's hands, the administrator shall allow them to be inspected, at all reasonable times on any business day, by—

- (a) the creditors, in the case of proxies used at a meeting of creditors, or a meeting of creditors and clients;
- (b) the clients, in the case of proxies used at a meeting of clients, or a meeting of creditors and clients; and
- (c) the investment bank's members or contributories, in the case of proxies used at a meeting of the company or of its contributories.

(2) The reference in paragraph (1) to creditors or to clients is to persons who have submitted in writing a claim to be creditors or, as the case may be, clients of the investment bank, but does not include a person whose proof or claim has been wholly rejected for purposes of voting, dividend or otherwise.

(3) The right of inspection given by this rule is also exercisable by the directors of the investment bank in special administration.

(4) Any person attending a meeting in the course of the special administration is entitled, immediately before or during the meeting, to inspect proxies and associated documents (including proofs) sent or given, in accordance with directions contained in any notice convening the meeting, to the chair of that meeting or to any other person by a creditor, client, member or contributory for the purpose of that meeting.

(5) This rule is subject to rule 320.

[7.1839]
129 Proxy holder with financial interest

(1) A proxy-holder ('P') shall not vote in favour of any resolution which would directly or indirectly place P, or any associate of P's, in a position to receive any remuneration out of the insolvent estate or the client assets, unless the proxy specifically directs P to vote in that way.

(2) Where P has authenticated the proxy as being authorised to do so by P's principal and the proxy specifically directs P to vote in the way mentioned in paragraph (1), P shall nevertheless not vote in that way unless P produces to the chair of the meeting written authorisation from P's principal sufficient to show that P was entitled so to authenticate the proxy.

(3) This rule applies also to any person acting as chair of a meeting and using proxies in that capacity under rule 124 and in its application to the chair, P is deemed an associate of that person.

[7.1840]
130 Company representation

(1) Where a person is authorised to represent a corporation at a meeting held under the Regulations or these Rules, that person shall produce to the chair of the meeting a copy of the resolution from which that person's authority is derived.

(2) The copy resolution must be under the seal of the corporation, or certified by the secretary or a director of the corporation to be a true copy.

(3) Nothing in this rule requires the authority of a person to authenticate a proxy on behalf of a principal which is a corporation to be in the form of a resolution of that corporation.

CHAPTER 11 DISPOSAL OF CHARGED PROPERTY

[7.1841]
131 Application to dispose of charged property

(1) The following applies where the administrator applies to the court under paragraph 71 or 72 for authority to dispose of property of the investment bank which is subject to a security (other than a floating charge), or goods in the possession of the investment bank under a hire purchase agreement.

(2) The court shall fix a venue for the hearing of the application, and the administrator shall as soon as reasonably practicable give notice of the venue to the person who is the holder of the security or, as the case may be, the owner under the agreement.

(3) If an order is made under paragraph 71 or 72 the court shall send 2 sealed copies to the administrator.

(4) The administrator shall send one of the copies to the person who is the holder of the security or owner under the agreement.

(5) The administrator must send notice of the order to the registrar of companies.

[7.1842]
132 Application in a special administration (bank administration)

If an application referred to in rule 131(1) is made before the Bank of England has given an Objective A Achievement Notice—

(a) the administrator must notify the Bank of England of the time and place of the hearing;
(b) the Bank of England may appear at the hearing;
(c) if an order is made, the administrator must send a copy to the Bank of England as soon as is reasonably practicable.

PART 4
EXPENSES OF THE SPECIAL ADMINISTRATION

[7.1843]
133 Expenses of voluntary arrangement

Where a special administration order, a special administration (bank insolvency) order or a special administration (bank administration) order is made and a voluntary arrangement under Part 1 of the 1986 Act is in force for the investment bank, any expenses properly incurred as expenses of the administration of the arrangement in question shall be payable in priority to any expenses in rule 134.

[7.1844]
134 Expenses to be paid out of the investment bank's assets

(1) Subject to rule 135, the expenses of the administration to be paid out of the assets of the investment bank are payable in the following order of priority—

(a) expenses properly incurred by the administrator in performing the administrator's functions in the special administration;
(b) the cost of any security provided by the administrator (and, in a special administration (bank insolvency) or a special administration (bank administration)), the cost of any security provided by a person appointed under rule 30 or 49 in accordance with the Regulations or the Rules;
(c) in a special administration (bank insolvency) or a special administration (bank administration), the remuneration of a person appointed under rule 30 or 49;
(d) in a special administration (bank insolvency) or a special administration (bank administration), any deposit lodged on the application for the appointment of a person appointed under rule 30 or 49;
(e) where an administration order was made, the costs of the applicant and any person appearing on the hearing of the application;
(f) any amount payable to a person employed or authorised, under Chapter 1 of Part 3 of the Rules, to assist in the preparation of a statement of affairs or statement of concurrence;
(g) any allowance made, by order of the court, towards costs on an application for release from the obligation to submit a statement of affairs or statement of concurrence;
(h) any necessary disbursements by the administrator in the course of the special administration (including any expenses incurred by members of the creditors' committee or their representatives and allowed for by the administrator under rule 119, but not including any payment of corporation tax in circumstances referred to in sub-paragraph (k) below);
(i) the remuneration or emoluments of any person who has been employed by the administrator to perform any services for the investment bank, as required or authorised under the Regulations or the Rules;
(j) the administrator's remuneration for services in pursuit of—
  (i) Objective A in a special administration (bank insolvency),
  (ii) Objective A in a special administration (bank administration), and
  (iii) Objectives 2 and 3,
  the basis of which has been fixed under rules 29 or 48 or Chapter 2 of Part 7 of these Rules, and
  (iv) unpaid pre-administration costs approved under rule 136 for work done in pursuit of these objectives; and
(k) the amount of any corporation tax on chargeable gains accruing on the realisation of any asset of the investment bank (without regard to who the realisation is effected by).

(2) The priorities laid down by paragraph (1) of this rule are subject to the power of the court to make orders under paragraph (3) of this rule where the assets are insufficient to satisfy the liabilities.

(3) The court may, in the event of the assets being insufficient to satisfy the liabilities, make an order as to the payment out of the assets of the expenses incurred in the administration in such order of priority as the court thinks just.

(4) For the purposes of paragraph 99(3) and subject to rule 135, the former administrator's remuneration and expenses shall comprise all those items set out in paragraph (1) of this rule.

[7.1845]

135 Expenses to be paid out of the client assets

(1) The expenses of the special administration to be paid out of the client assets held by the investment bank are payable in the following order of priority—

(a) subject to rule 136, expenses properly incurred by the administrator in pursuing Objective 1;

(b) any necessary disbursements by the administrator in the course of the special administration specific to the achievement of Objective 1 (including any expenses incurred by client members of the creditors' committee or their representatives and allowed for by the administrator under rule 119 but not including any payment of corporation tax in circumstances referred to in rule 134(1)(k));

(c) the remuneration or emoluments of any person who has been employed by the administrator to perform any services for the investment bank specific to the achievement of Objective 1, as required or authorised under the Regulations or the Rules; and

(d) the administrator's remuneration the basis of which has been fixed under rule 196 and unpaid pre-administration costs approved under rule 136 in respect of the work done in pursuance of Objective 1.

(2) The priorities laid down by paragraph (1) of this rule are subject to the power of the court to make orders under paragraph (3) of this rule where the client assets are insufficient to satisfy the liabilities.

(3) The court may, in the event of the assets being insufficient to satisfy the liabilities, make an order as to the payment out of the assets of the expenses incurred in the administration in such order of priority as the court thinks just.

(4) For the purposes of paragraph 99(3) the former administrator's remuneration and expenses incurred in respect of the pursuit of Objective 1 shall comprise all those items set out in paragraph (1) of this rule.

[7.1846]

136 Pre-administration costs

(1) Where the administrator has made a statement of pre-administration costs under rule 59(2)(m), the creditors' committee may determine whether and to what extent the unpaid pre-administration costs set out in the statement are approved for payment.

(2) But if—

(a) there is no creditors' committee; or

(b) there is but it does not make the necessary determination; or

(c) it does do so but the administrator or other insolvency practitioner who has charged fees or incurred expenses as pre-administration costs considers the amount determined to be insufficient,

paragraph (3) applies.

(3) When this paragraph applies, determination of whether and to what extent the unpaid pre-administration costs are approved for payment shall be by resolution of—

(a) where the pre-administration costs were incurred in pursuance of Objective A, or Objectives 2 and 3, a meeting of creditors;

(b) where the pre-administration costs were incurred wholly in pursuance of Objective 1, a meeting of clients; or

(c) where the pre-administration costs were incurred in pursuance of Objective 1, Objective A and Objective 2 and 3, a meeting of creditors and clients.

(4) The administrator must call a meeting of the creditors' committee or a meeting under paragraph (3) if so requested for the purposes of paragraphs (1) to (3) by another insolvency practitioner who has charged fees or incurred expenses as pre-administration costs; and the administrator must give notice of the meeting within 28 days of receipt of the request.

(5) If—

(a) there is no determination under paragraph (1) or (3); or

(b) there is such a determination but the administrator or other insolvency practitioner who has charged fees or incurred expenses as pre-administration costs considers the amount determined to be insufficient,

the administrator (where the fees were charged or expenses incurred by the administrator) or other insolvency practitioner (where the fees were charged or expenses incurred by that practitioner) may apply to the court for a determination of whether and to what extent the unpaid pre-administration costs are approved for payment.

(6) Paragraphs (2) to (4) of rule 200 apply to an application under paragraph (5) of this rule as they do to an application under paragraph (1) of that rule (references to the administrator being read as references to the insolvency practitioner who has charged fees or incurred expenses as pre-administration costs).

(7) Where the administrator fails to call a meeting of the creditors' committee or a meeting under paragraph (3) in accordance with paragraph (4), the other insolvency practitioner may apply to the court for an order requiring the administrator to do so.

[7.1847]
137 Allocation of expenses to be paid from client assets

(1) The administrator shall set out, in the distribution plan under rule 146, how the administrator proposes that the expenses of the special administration, to be paid out of the client assets in accordance with this Chapter, are to be allocated between client assets.

(2) Where paragraph (1) applies and, as a result of this, on the court approving the distribution plan in accordance with rule 146, there is a shortfall in the amount of assets to be returned to a client—
(a) that shortfall is to be treated as a debt owed to the client by the investment bank arising before the investment bank entered special administration; and
(b) where those assets are securities, the claim is to be valued in accordance with rule 91and for this purpose the references to "chair" in rule 91 shall be read as references to the administrator.

PART 5
OBJECTIVE 1

CHAPTER 1 SETTING A BAR DATE

[7.1848]
138 Notice of the bar date

(1) This Part applies where the administrator sets a bar date for the submission of claims as set out in regulation 11(1).

(2) The administrator shall give notice of the bar date—
(a) to all clients of whose claim in respect of the client assets the administrator is aware; and
(b) to all those persons whom the administrator believes have a right to assert a security interest or other entitlement over the client assets,

and whom the administrator has a means of contacting.

(3) Notice of the bar date shall also be sent to—
(a) the [FCA and, where the investment bank concerned is a PRA-authorised person, the PRA]; and
(b) in a special administration (bank administration) before the Bank of England has given an Objective A Achievement Notice, the Bank of England.

(4) Notice of the bar date—
(a) shall be gazetted; and
(b) may be advertised in such other manner as the administrator thinks fit.

(5) In advertising the date under paragraph (4), the administrator shall aim to ensure that the bar date comes to the attention of as many of those persons who are eligible to submit a claim under regulation 11(1) as the administrator considers practicable.

(6) After setting a bar date, the administrator may agree a later date for the submission of a claim under regulation 11(1) if the potential claimant submits a request to administrator before the bar date.

(7) The [FCA] may also submit a request to the administrator under paragraph (6) if the [FCA] considers that there are particular circumstances in respect of a claimant, or a class of claimants, that mean that those persons will have difficulty submitting their claim before the bar date.

[(8) If the investment bank concerned is a PRA-authorised person, the PRA may also submit a request to the administrator under paragraph (6) if the PRA considers that there are particular circumstances in respect of a claimant, or a class of claimants, that mean that those persons will have difficulty submitting their claim before the bar date.]

NOTES

Paras (3), (7): words in square brackets substituted for "FSA" by the Financial Services Act 2012 (Consequential Amendments and Transitional Provisions) Order 2013, SI 2013/472, art 3, Sch 2, para 210(c), (d)(xii), (p)(i), subject to a transitional provision (see para 211 as noted to **[7.1718]**).

Para (8): added by SI 2013/472, art 3, Sch 2, para 210(p)(ii), subject to a transitional provision (see para 211 as noted to **[7.1718]**).

[7.1849]
139 Content of claim for client assets

(1) This rule applies to the submission of claims as described in regulation 11(1)(a).

(2) A person submitting a claim must submit that claim in writing to the administrator.

(3) The claim must—
(a) be made out by, or under the direction of, the claimant and must be signed by the claimant or a person authorised in that behalf; and
(b) state the following matters—
(i) the claimant's name and address,
(ii) the total amount of client assets held or believed to be held for that claimant by the investment bank as at the time that the investment bank entered administration, categorised into type and securities of a particular description,
(iii) details as to the types of ownership the claimant asserts over those assets,
(iv) details of all financial contracts the claimant has entered into under which, at the time the claim is submitted, liabilities are still owed from either the investment bank to the claimant or vice versa, and

(v) details of any security granted by the claimant in respect of the client assets held by the investment bank; and

(c) state the name, address and authority of the person signing the claim, if not the claimant.

(4) The claim shall specify details of any documents by reference to which the claim can be substantiated; but (subject to paragraph (5)), it is not essential that such documents be attached to the claim or submitted with it.

(5) Where the administrator thinks it necessary for the purpose of substantiating the whole or any part of a claim submitted, the administrator may—

(a) call for any document or other evidence to be produced; or

(b) send a request in writing for further information from the claimant.

(6) In this rule, "securities of a particular description" has the meaning set out in regulation 12(9).

[7.1850]

140 Content of claim in respect of security interest

(1) This rule applies to the submission of claims as described in regulation 11(1)(b).

(2) A person submitting a claim must submit that claim in writing to the administrator.

(3) The claim must—

(a) be made out by, or under the direction of, the claimant and must be signed by the claimant or a person authorised in that behalf; and

(b) state the following matters—

(i) the claimant's name and address,

(ii) details of any security interest asserted by the claimant over any client assets held by the investment bank, including details of the client assets to which the security interest relates, the date on which the security interest was granted, conditions for the release of the security and the value which the claimant puts on the security interest,

(iii) details of any other parties' interest in the security interest that are known to the claimant, and

(iv) any other information relating to the security interest that the claimant considers useful to the administrator in determining the rights attached to the client assets which are the subject of the claim; and

(c) state the name, address and authority of the person signing the claim.

(4) The claim shall specify details of any documents by reference to which the claim can be substantiated; but (subject to paragraph (5)), it is not essential that such documents be attached to the claim or submitted with it.

(5) Where the administrator thinks it necessary for the purpose of substantiating the whole or any part of a claim submitted, the administrator may—

(a) call for any document or other evidence to be produced; or

(b) send a request in writing for further information from the claimant.

[7.1851]

141 Costs of making a claim

Unless the court orders otherwise, every claimant under rules 139 and 140 bears the cost of making a claim, including costs incurred in providing documents or evidence or responding to requests for further information.

[7.1852]

142 New administrator appointed

(1) If a new administrator is appointed in place of another, the former administrator must as soon as reasonably practicable transmit to the new administrator all claims received, together with an itemised list of them.

(2) The new administrator shall authenticate the list by way of receipt for the claims, and return it to the former administrator.

(3) From then on, all claims submitted under rules 139 or 140 must be sent to and retained by the new administrator.

CHAPTER 2 FURTHER NOTIFICATION

[7.1853]

143 Notifying potential claimants after bar date has passed

(1) This rule applies where, after the bar date has passed—

(a) there is evidence from either—

(i) the records of the investment bank; or

(ii) information received by the administrator under rule 139 or 140,

that there is a person ("P") who is eligible to make a claim under regulation 11(1) in respect of certain client assets, but that the administrator has not received a claim from P in respect of those clients assets; and

(b) the administrator has a means of contacting P.

(2) The administrator shall send notice to P in writing stating that the administrator believes P would have been eligible to submit a claim under regulation 11(1).

(3) Where P would have been eligible to submit a claim under rule 11(1)(a), the notice under paragraph (2) shall state that—

(a) the administrator believes that the investment bank holds client assets on behalf of P; and

(b) in making the distribution plan under rule 144, the administrator intends to calculate the amount of assets to be returned to P according to the information available to the administrator,

unless P submits a claim in accordance with rule 139 within 14 business days of receipt of the notice (or such longer period as may be agreed by the administrator).

(4) Where P would have been eligible to submit a claim under rule 11(1)(b), the notice under paragraph (2) shall state that—

(a) the administrator believes that P is able to assert a security interest over certain client assets held by the investment bank; and

(b) in making the distribution plan under rule 144, the administrator intends to take into account the security interest according to the information available to the administrator,

unless P submits a claim in accordance with rule 140 within 14 business days of receipt of the notice (or such longer period as may be agreed by the administrator).

CHAPTER 3 DISTRIBUTION PLAN

[7.1854]

144 Distribution plan

(1) This rule applies where after setting a bar date and making the notification required by rule 143, the administrator proposes to return client assets.

(2) The administrator shall draw up a distribution plan setting out—

(a) subject to paragraph (3), a schedule of dates on which the client assets are to be returned ("a distribution");

(b) the unencumbered assets to be returned and to whom;

(c) in respect of encumbered client assets, how the amount of client assets to be returned to a particular client is to be calculated ("the net asset claim"), taking into account—

(i) any liabilities owed by the client to the investment bank in respect of financial contracts;

(ii) any liabilities owed to the client by the investment bank in respect of financial contracts; and

(iii) any shortfall claim of the client (as defined under regulation 12);

(d) in respect of a client's net assets claim, whether the administrator intends to pay the client money or money's worth in lieu of returning the assets to the client (but a client cannot be paid money or money's worth out of the investment bank's estate in lieu of assets unless the estate is able to retain assets the value of which is equivalent to that paid out); and

(e) the amount and identity of client assets that are to be retained by the administrator to pay the expenses of the special administration in accordance with rules 135 and 137 and how the retention of these assets will affect the amount of client assets to be returned to clients.

(3) In setting out the schedule of dates for the return of the client assets, no date shall be sooner than the date which is 3 months after the bar date.

(4) In setting out the schedule for the return of encumbered client assets,—

(a) where a person ("P") notified under rule 143(2) has failed to respond to that notice, the administrator shall make provision in the distribution plan—

(i) for client assets to be returned to P according to the information available to the administrator in respect of the amount of client assets held for P by the investment bank; or

(ii) to take into account any security interest that according to the information available to the administrator, P is entitled to assert over certain client assets held by the investment bank,

as the case may be;

(b) the administrator shall make provision in respect of any security interest asserted over those assets by another person; and

(c) the administrator shall set out the extent to which a proportion of securities are to be held back from the initial distributions and the reasons why.

(5) The distribution plan will also set out—

(a) where any liabilities under paragraph (2)(c) are contingent, how the administrator intends to value the liability; and

(b) where any liabilities are disputed, whether the administrator intends to make an assumption as to the outcome of the dispute,

for the purpose of calculating the client's net asset claim so that the claim can be paid out (or partly paid out) or assets returned (or returned in part) before the contingency occurs or the dispute is resolved, and the arrangements by which the administrator may revise such valuations or assumptions when further information becomes known.

(6) In this rule, "encumbered client assets" means client assets over which a third party or the investment bank exerts a security interest.

[7.1855]

145 Approval by the creditors' committee

(1) Where there is a creditors' committee, the administrator shall summon a meeting of that committee to approve the distribution plan.

(2) The administrator shall send the proposed distribution plan to each member of the creditors' committee when sending out notice of the meeting.

(3) The creditors' committee may approve the distribution plan with or without modification.

[7.1856]

146 Approval by the court

(1) This rule applies where a meeting of the creditors' committee has taken place in accordance with rule 145 or where there is no creditors' committee.

(2) The administrator shall apply to the court for approval of the distribution plan.

(3) The administrator shall send a copy of the distribution plan to—

(a) all persons who have submitted a claim of the type described in regulation 11(1);

(b) all persons notified under rule 143;

(c) in a special administration (bank administration), before the Bank of England has given an Objective A Achievement Notice, the Bank of England; and

(d) the [FCA and, where the investment bank concerned is a PRA-authorised person, the PRA],

and details as to how to find out the venue for the hearing shall be sent out with the copy of the distribution plan.

(4) The court, on receiving an application under paragraph (2) shall fix the venue for the hearing and in fixing the venue shall have regard to the desirability of the application being heard as soon as is reasonably practicable subject to the persons notified under paragraph (3) and the members of the creditors' committee being able to attend and make representations at the hearing.

(5) On hearing the application under paragraph (2) the court may—

(a) make an order approving the distribution plan with or without modification if satisfied that—

(i) where rule 143 applies, the administrator has made the necessary notifications in accordance with that rule; and

(ii) where there is a creditors' committee, either that the committee has approved the distribution plan with or without modification or where the committee has been unable to approve the plan, the court has heard from the members of the committee or has given them an opportunity to explain why the committee were unable to approve the plan;

(b) dismiss the application;

(c) adjourn the hearing (generally or to a specified date); or

(d) make any other order which the court thinks appropriate.

NOTES

Para (3): words in square brackets substituted for "FSA" by the Financial Services Act 2012 (Consequential Amendments and Transitional Provisions) Order 2013, SI 2013/472, art 3, Sch 2, para 210(c), (d)(xiii), subject to a transitional provision (see para 211 as noted to **[7.1718]**).

[7.1857]

147 Treatment of late claimants

(1) This rule applies where after a distribution has taken place, the administrator receives a claim of the type described in regulation 11(1).

(2) Where the claim is not submitted in accordance with rule 139 or, as the case may be, rule 140, the administrator shall notify the claimant accordingly and ask them to resubmit their claim in accordance with the relevant rule.

(3) Where the claim is submitted in accordance with rule 139 or 140, if the administrator determines that, had the claim been submitted before the bar date, the claimant would have received client assets as part of the distribution—

(a) if enough of those assets amounting to what the client would have received in the distribution are still available to be distributed, they shall be returned to the client as soon as reasonably practicable and any remainder of the claimant's claim shall be included in the distribution plan for further distributions; and

(b) if there are insufficient assets, any assets that can be returned to the claimant shall be, but the claimant may submit a proof under rule 152 for the value of those client assets not returned.

(4) Where the claimant's proof under paragraph (3)(b) is in respect of assets that are securities, the value of those securities is to be calculated in accordance with rule 91 and for this purpose the references to "chair" in rule 91 shall be read as references to the administrator.

(5) The administrator may amend the distribution plan to reflect the return of client assets under this rule without need for the plan to be approved again by either the court or the creditors' committee.

PART 6
DISTRIBUTIONS TO CREDITORS

CHAPTER 1 APPLICATION

[7.1858]

148 Distribution to creditors

(1) This Chapter applies where the administrator makes, or proposes to make, a distribution to any class of creditors other than secured creditors.

(2) Where the distribution is to a particular class of creditors, references in this Chapter to creditors shall, in so far as the context requires, be a reference to that class of creditors only.

(3) In a special administration (bank administration), before the Bank of England has given an Objective A Achievement Notice, no distributions to creditors under this Chapter shall be made without the consent of the Bank of England.

(4) The administrator shall give notice to the creditors of his intention to declare and distribute a dividend in accordance with rule 175.

(5) Where it is intended that the distribution is to be a sole or final dividend, the administrator shall, after the date specified in the notice referred to in paragraph (4)—

- (a) defray any outstanding expenses of a voluntary arrangement that immediately preceded the special administration in accordance with rule 133;
- (b) defray any items payable in accordance with rules 134 and 136;
- (c) defray any amounts (including any debts or liabilities and the administrator's own remuneration and expenses) which would, if the administrator were to cease to be the administrator of the investment bank, be payable out of the property of which the administrator had custody or control in accordance with paragraph 99; and
- (d) declare and distribute that dividend without regard to the claim of any person in respect of a debt not already proved.

(6) The court may, on the application of any person, postpone the date specified in the notice.

[7.1859]
149 Debts of investment bank to rank equally

Debts, other than preferential debts, rank equally between themselves in the special administration and, after the preferential debts, shall be paid in full unless the assets are insufficient for meeting them, in which case they abate in equal proportions between themselves.

[7.1860]
150 Supplementary provisions as to dividend

(1) In the calculation and distribution of a dividend the administrator shall make provision for—

- (a) any debts which appear to the administrator to be due to persons who, by reason of the distance of their place of residence, may not have had sufficient time to tender and establish their proofs;
- (b) any debts which are the subject of claims which have not yet been determined; and
- (c) disputed proofs and claims.

(2) A creditor who has not proved their debt before the declaration of any dividend is not entitled to disturb, by reason that they have not participated in it, the distribution of that dividend or any other dividend declared before their debt was proved, but—

- (a) when the creditor has proved that debt, they are entitled to be paid, out of any money for the time being available for the payment of any further dividend, any dividend or dividends which the creditor has failed to receive; and
- (b) any dividends payable under sub-paragraph (a) shall be paid before the money is applied to the payment of any such further dividend.

(3) No action lies against the administrator for a dividend; but if the administrator refuses to pay a dividend the court may, if it thinks just, order the administrator to pay it and also to pay, out of the administrator's own money—

- (a) interest on the dividend, at the rate for the time being specified in section 17 of the Judgments Act 1838, from the time when it was withheld; and
- (b) the costs of the proceedings in which the order to pay is made.

[7.1861]
151 Division of unsold assets

(1) The administrator may, with the permission of the creditors' committee, or if there is no creditors' committee, the creditors, divide in its existing form amongst the investment bank's creditors, according to its estimated value, any property which from its peculiar nature or other special circumstances cannot be readily or advantageously sold.

(2) The administrator must—

- (a) in the receipts and payments account included in the final progress report under rule 220, state the estimated value of the property divided amongst the creditors of the investment during the period to which the report relates, and
- (b) as a note to the account, provide details of the basis of the valuation.

CHAPTER 2 PROOFS OF DEBTS

[7.1862]
152 Proving a debt

(1) A person claiming to be a creditor of the investment bank and wishing to recover their debt in whole or in part must (subject to any order of the court to the contrary) submit their claim in writing to the administrator.

(2) A creditor who claims is referred to as "proving" for their debt and a document by which that creditor seeks to establish their claim is their "proof".

(3) Subject to the next paragraph, a proof must—

(a) be made out by, or under the direction of, the creditor and authenticated by the creditor or a person authorised in that behalf; and
(b) state the following matters—
 (i) the creditor's name and address,
 (ii) if the creditor is a company, its registered number;
 (iii) the total amount of the creditor's claim (including value added tax) as at the date on which the investment bank entered special administration, less any payments made after that date in respect of the claim, any deduction under rule 163 and any adjustment by way of set-off in accordance with rule 164 or, as the case may be, rule 165;
 (iv) whether or not the claim includes outstanding uncapitalised interest,
 (v) particulars of how and when the debt was incurred by the investment bank,
 (vi) particulars of any security held, the date on which it was given and the value which the creditor puts on it,
 (vii) details of any reservation of title in respect of goods to which the debt refers, and
 (viii) the name, address and authority of the person authenticating the proof (if not the creditor).

(4) There shall be specified in the proof details of any documents by reference to which the debt can be substantiated; but (subject as follows) it is not essential that such document be attached to the proof or submitted with it.

(5) The administrator may call for any document or other evidence to be produced, where the administrator thinks it necessary for the purpose of substantiating the whole or any part of the claim made in the proof.

[7.1863]
153 Costs of proving

Unless the court otherwise orders—
(a) every creditor bears the cost of proving their own debt, including costs incurred in providing documents or evidence under rule 152; and
(b) costs incurred by the administrator in estimating the quantum of a debt under rule 160 are payable out of the assets as an expense of the administration.

[7.1864]
154 Administrator to allow inspection of proofs

(1) The administrator shall, so long as proofs lodged are in the administrator's hands, allow them to be inspected, at all reasonable times on any business day, by any of the following persons—
(a) any creditor who has submitted a proof of debt (unless that proof has been wholly rejected for purposes of dividend or otherwise);
(b) any contributory of the company; and
(c) any person acting on behalf of either of the above.

[7.1865]
155 New administrator appointed

(1) If a new administrator is appointed in place of another, the former administrator must as soon as reasonably practicable, transmit to the new administrator all proofs received, together with an itemised list of them.

(2) The new administrator shall authenticate the list by way of receipt for the proofs, and return it to the former administrator.

(3) From then on, all proofs of debt must be sent to and retained by the new administrator.

[7.1866]
156 Admission and rejection of proofs for dividend

(1) A proof may be admitted for dividend either for the whole amount claimed by the creditor, or for part of that amount.

(2) If the administrator rejects a proof in whole or in part, the administrator shall prepare a written statement of reasons for doing so, and send it as soon as reasonably practicable to the creditor.

[7.1867]
157 Appeal against decision on proof

(1) If a creditor is dissatisfied with the administrator's decision with respect to their proof (including any decision on the question of preference), that creditor may apply to the court for the decision to be reversed or varied and the application must be made within 21 days of the creditor receiving the statement sent under rule 156.

(2) A member or any other creditor may, if dissatisfied with the administrator's decision admitting or rejecting the whole or any part of a proof, make such an application within 21 days of becoming aware of the administrator's decision.

(3) Notice of an application under paragraph (1) or (2) shall be given by the applicant to—
(a) the [FCA and, where the investment bank concerned is a PRA-authorised person, the PRA], and
(b) in a special administration (bank administration), before the Bank of England has given an Objective A Achievement Notice, the Bank of England.

(4) Where application is made to the court under this rule, the court shall fix a venue for the application to be heard, notice of which shall be sent by the applicant to—
(a) the creditor who lodged the proof in question (if the applicant is not that creditor);

(b) the administrator;
(c) the [FCA and, where the investment bank concerned is a PRA-authorised person, the PRA]; and
(d) in a special administration (bank administration), before the Bank of England has given an Objective A Achievement Notice, the Bank of England.

(5) The administrator shall, on receipt of the notice, file with the court the relevant proof, together (if appropriate) with a copy of the statement sent under rule 156.

(6) Where the application is made by a member, the court must not disallow the proof (in whole or in part) unless the member shows that there is (or would be but for the amount claimed in the proof), or that it is likely that there will be (or would be but for the amount claimed in the proof), a surplus of assets to which the investment bank would be entitled.

(7) After the application has been heard and determined, the proof shall, unless it has been wholly disallowed, be returned by the court to the administrator.

(8) The administrator is not personally liable for costs incurred by any person in respect of an application under this rule unless the court otherwise orders.

NOTES

Paras (3), (4): words in square brackets substituted for "FSA" by the Financial Services Act 2012 (Consequential Amendments and Transitional Provisions) Order 2013, SI 2013/472, art 3, Sch 2, para 210(c), (d)(xiv), subject to a transitional provision (see para 211 as noted to **[7.1718]**).

[7.1868]
158 Withdrawal or variation of proof

A creditor's proof may at any time, by agreement with the administrator, be withdrawn or varied as to the amount claimed.

[7.1869]
159 Expunging of proof by the court

(1) The court may expunge a proof or reduce the amount claimed—
(a) on the administrator's application, where the administrator thinks that the proof has been improperly admitted, or ought to be reduced; or
(b) on the application of a creditor, if the administrator declines to interfere in the matter.

(2) Where application is made to the court under this rule, the court shall fix a venue for the application to be heard, notice of which shall be sent by the applicant—
(a) in the case of an application by the administrator, to the creditor who made the proof; and
(b) in the case of an application by a creditor, to the administrator and to the creditor who made the proof (if the applicant is not the same creditor).

CHAPTER 3 QUANTIFICATION OF CLAIMS

[7.1870]
160 Estimate of quantum

(1) The administrator shall estimate the value of any debt which, by reason of it being subject to any contingency or for any other reason, does not bear a certain value; and a previous estimation may be revised, if the administrator thinks fit, by reference to any change of circumstances or to information becoming available to the administrator.

(2) The creditors shall be informed of the estimation and any revision of it.

(3) Where the value of a debt is estimated under this rule, the amount provable in the administration in the case of that debt is that of the estimate for the time being.

[7.1871]
161 Negotiable instruments

Unless the administrator allows, a proof in respect of money owed on a bill of exchange, promissory note, cheque or other negotiable instrument or security cannot be admitted unless there is produced the instrument or security itself or a copy of it, certified by the creditor or the creditor's authorised representative to be a true copy.

[7.1872]
162 Secured creditors

(1) If a secured creditor realises their security, the creditor may prove for the balance of their debt, after deducting the amount realised.

(2) If a secured creditor voluntarily surrenders their security for the general benefit of creditors, they may prove for their whole debt, as if it were unsecured.

[7.1873]
163 Discounts

There shall in every case be deducted from the claim all trade and other discounts which would have been available to the investment bank but for it going into special administration, except any discount for immediate, early or cash settlement.

[7.1874]
164 Mutual credit and set-off

(1) This rule applies where the administrator, being authorised to make the distribution in question, has, pursuant to rule 175, given notice of a proposal to make the distribution.

(2) In this rule, "mutual dealings" means mutual credits, mutual debts or other mutual dealings between the investment bank and a creditor of the investment bank proving or claiming to prove for a debt in the special administration, but does not include any of the following—

(a) any debt arising out of an obligation incurred after the investment bank entered special administration;
(b) any debt arising out of an obligation incurred at a time when the creditor had notice that an application for a special administration order was pending;
(c) any debt which has been acquired by a creditor by assignment or otherwise, pursuant to an agreement between the creditor and any other party where that agreement was entered into—
(i) after the investment bank entered administration, or
(ii) at a time when the creditor had notice that an application for a special administration order was pending.

(3) An account shall be taken as at the date of the notice referred to in paragraph (1) of what is due from each party to the other in respect of the mutual dealings and the sums due from one party shall be set off against the sums due from the other.

(4) A sum shall be regarded as being due to or from the investment bank for the purposes of paragraph (3) whether—

(a) it is payable at present or in the future;
(b) the obligation by virtue of which it is payable is certain or contingent; or
(c) its amount is fixed or liquidated, or is capable of being ascertained by fixed rules or as a matter of opinion.

(5) Rule 160 shall apply for the purposes of this rule to any obligation to or from the investment bank which, by reason of its being subject to any contingency or for any other reason, does not bear a certain value.

(6) Rules 166 to 168 shall apply for the purposes of this rule in relation to any sums due to the investment bank which—

(a) are payable in a currency other than sterling;
(b) are of a periodical nature; or
(c) bear interest.

(7) Rule 186 shall apply for the purposes of this rule to any sum due to or from the investment bank which is payable in the future.

(8) Only the balance (if any) of the account owed to the creditor is provable in the special administration. Alternatively the balance (if any) owed to the investment bank shall be paid to the administrator as part of the assets except where all or part of the balance results from a contingent or prospective debt owed by the creditor and in such a case the balance (or that part of it which results from the contingent or prospective debt) shall be paid if and when that debt becomes due and payable.

(9) In this rule, "obligation" means an obligation however arising, whether by virtue of an agreement, rule of law or otherwise.

[7.1875]
165 Application of rule 164 in a special administration (bank administration) and special administration (bank insolvency)

(1) This rule applies—

(a) in a special administration (bank insolvency); and
(b) in a special administration (bank administration) if all or part of a creditor's claim against the investment bank is in respect of protected deposits.

(2) Rule 164 shall apply, but for the purpose of determining the sums due from the investment bank to an eligible depositor in respect of protected deposits under rule 164(3)—

(a) where the total of the sums held by the investment bank for the depositor in respect of protected deposits is no more than the amount prescribed as the maximum compensation payable in respect of protected deposits under Part 15 of the Financial Services and Markets Act 2000 ("the limit"), then paragraph (3) applies; and
(b) where the sums held exceed the limit, then paragraph (4) applies.

(3) Where this paragraph applies, there shall be deemed to have been no mutual dealings, regardless of whether there are any sums due from the depositor to the investment bank, and the sum due to the depositor from the investment bank will be the total of the sums held by the investment bank for that depositor in respect of the protected deposits.

(4) Where this paragraph applies then—

(a) any mutual dealings shall be treated as being mutual dealings only in relation to the amount by which the total of the sums due to the depositor exceeds the limit, and
(b) the sums due from the investment bank to the depositor in respect of the protected deposits will be—
(i) the amount by which that total exceeds the limit, set off against the amounts due to the investment bank from the depositor in accordance with rule 164(3); and
(ii) the sums held by the investment bank for the depositor in respect of protected deposits up to the limit.

(5) Any arrangements with regard to set-off between the investment bank and the eligible depositor in existence before the date of the notice referred to in rule 164(1) shall be subject to this rule in so far as they relate to protected deposits.

(6) In this rule—

"eligible depositor" has the meaning given to it by section 93(3) of the 2009 Act;

["the appropriate regulator rules" means the rules, as amended from time to time, made under section 213 of the Financial Services and Markets Act 2000 by the FSA or the PRA]

"protected deposit" means a protected deposit within the meaning given by [the appropriate regulator rules] held by the investment bank at the date of the notice referred to in rule 164(1).

NOTES

Para (6): definition "the appropriate regulator rules" substituted for original definition "FSA Rules", and in definition "protected deposit" words in square brackets substituted for "FSA Rules" by the Financial Services Act 2012 (Consequential Amendments and Transitional Provisions) Order 2013, SI 2013/472, art 3, Sch 2, para 210(q), subject to a transitional provision (see para 211 as noted to **[7.1718]**). Definition "FSA Rules" originally read as follows:

"FSA Rules" means the FSA's Compensation Sourcebook, as amended from time to time, made under section 213 of the Financial Services and Markets Act 2000; and".

[7.1876]
166 Debt in a foreign currency

(1) For the purpose of proving a debt incurred or payable in a currency other than sterling, the amount of the debt shall be converted into sterling at the official exchange rate prevailing on the date when the investment bank entered special administration.

(2) "The official exchange rate" means the mean of the buying and selling spot rates prevailing in the London market as published at the close of business for the date in question. In the absence of any such published rate, it is such rate as the court determines.

[7.1877]
167 Payments of a periodical nature

(1) In the case of rent and other payments of a periodical nature, the creditor may prove for any amounts due and unpaid up to the date when the investment bank entered special administration.

(2) Where at that date any payment was accruing due, the creditor may prove for so much as would have fallen due at that date, if accruing from day to day.

[7.1878]
168 Interest

(1) In this Rule, "the relevant date" means the date on which the investment bank entered special administration.

(2) Where a debt proved in the special administration bears interest, that interest is provable as part of the debt except in so far as it is payable in respect of any period after the relevant date.

(3) In the following circumstances the creditor's claim may include interest on the debt for periods before the relevant date, although not previously reserved or agreed.

(4) If the debt is due by virtue of a written instrument and payable at a certain time, interest may be claimed for the period from that time to the relevant date.

(5) If the debt is due otherwise, interest may only be claimed if, before the relevant date, a demand for payment of the debt was made in writing by or on behalf of the creditor, and notice given that interest would be payable from the date of the demand to the date of payment.

(6) Interest under paragraph (5) may only be claimed for the period from the date of the demand to the relevant date and for all the purposes of the Regulations and these Rules shall be chargeable at a rate not exceeding that mentioned in paragraph (7).

(7) The rate of interest to be claimed under paragraphs (4) and (5) is the rate specified in section 17 of the Judgments Act 1838 on the relevant date.

(8) Any surplus remaining after payment of the debts proved shall, before being applied for any purpose, be applied in paying interest on those debts in respect of the periods during which they have been outstanding since the relevant date.

(9) All interest payable under paragraph (8) ranks equally whether or not the debts on which it is payable rank equally.

(10) The rate of interest payable under paragraph (8) is whichever is the greater of the rate specified under paragraph (7) and the rate applicable to the debt apart from the special administration.

[7.1879]
169 Debt payable at a future time

A creditor may prove for a debt of which payment was not yet due on the date when the investment bank entered special administration, subject to rule 186.

[7.1880]
170 Value of security

(1) A secured creditor may, with the agreement of the administrator or the permission of the court, at any time alter the value which that creditor has, in their proof of debt, put upon their security.

(2) However, if a secured creditor—

(a) being the applicant for an special administration order, has in the application put a value on their security; or

(b) has voted in respect of the unsecured balance of their debt,

that creditor may re-value their security only with permission of the court.

[7.1881]

171 Surrender for non-disclosure

(1) If a secured creditor omits to disclose their security in their proof of debt, the creditor shall surrender their security for the general benefit of creditors, unless the court, on application by that creditor, relieves them from the effect of this rule on the ground that the omission was inadvertent or the result of honest mistake.

(2) If the court grants that relief, it may require or allow the creditor's proof of debt to be amended, on such terms as may be just.

[7.1882]

172 Redemption by administrator

(1) The administrator may at any time give notice to a creditor whose debt is secured that it is proposed, at the expiration of 28 days from the date of the notice, to redeem the security at the value put upon it in the creditor's proof.

(2) The creditor then has 21 days (or such longer period as the administrator may allow) in which, if the creditor so wishes, to exercise their right to revalue their security (with the permission of the court, where rule 170 applies). If the creditor re-values their security, the administrator may only redeem at the new value.

(3) If the administrator redeems the security, the cost of transferring it is payable out of the assets.

(4) A secured creditor may at any time, by a notice in writing, call on the administrator to elect whether the administrator will or will not exercise their power to redeem the security at the value then placed on it; and the administrator then has 3 months in which to exercise the power or determine not to exercise it.

[7.1883]

173 Test of security's value

(1) Subject as follows, the administrator, if dissatisfied with the value which a secured creditor puts on their security (whether in their proof or by way of re-valuation under rule 170), may require any property comprised in the security to be offered for sale.

(2) The terms of sale shall be such as may be agreed, or as the court may direct; and if the sale is by auction, the administrator on behalf of the investment bank, and the creditor on their own behalf, may appear and bid.

(3) This rule does not apply if the security has been revalued and the revaluation has been approved by the court.

[7.1884]

174 Realisation of security by creditor

If a creditor who has valued their security subsequently realises it (whether or not at the instance of the administrator)—

(a) the net amount realised shall be substituted for the value previously put by the creditor on the security; and

(b) that amount shall be treated in all respects as an amended valuation made by the creditor.

[7.1885]

175 Notice of proposed distribution

(1) Where an administrator is proposing to make a distribution to creditors, the administrator shall give notice of that fact.

(2) The notice in paragraph (1) shall—

(a) state whether the distribution is to preferential creditors or preferential creditors and unsecured creditors; and

(b) where the administrator proposes to make a distribution to unsecured creditors, state the value of the prescribed part, except where the court has made an order under section 176A(5) of the 1986 Act.

(3) The notice in paragraph (1) shall be given to—

(a) all creditors whose addresses are known to the administrator;

(b) the [FCA and, where the investment bank concerned is a PRA-authorised person, the PRA];

(c) in a special administration (bank administration), the FSCS; and

(d) in a special administration (bank administration), before the Bank of England has given an Objective A Achievement Notice, the Bank of England.

(4) Subject to paragraph (5)(b), before declaring a dividend the administrator shall by notice invite the creditors to prove their debts. Such notice—

(a) shall be gazetted; and

(b) may be advertised in such other manner as the administrator thinks fit.

(5) A notice pursuant to paragraph (1) must, in addition to the standard contents—

Part 7M Special Insolvency Regimes

(a) state that it is the intention of the administrator to make a distribution to creditors within the period of 2 months from the last date for proving;
(b) specify whether the proposed dividend is interim or final;
(c) specify a date up to which proofs may be lodged being a date which—
(i) is the same date for all creditors; and
(ii) is not less than 21 days from that of the notice.

(6) Where a dividend is to be declared for preferential creditors—
(a) the notice pursuant to paragraph (1) need only to be given to those creditors in whose case the administrator has reason to believe that their debts are preferential; and
(b) the notice pursuant to paragraph (3) need only be given if the administrator thinks fit.

NOTES

Para (3): words in square brackets substituted for "FSA" by the Financial Services Act 2012 (Consequential Amendments and Transitional Provisions) Order 2013, SI 2013/472, art 3, Sch 2, para 210(c), (d)(xv), subject to a transitional provision (see para 211 as noted to **[7.1718]**).

[7.1886]
176 Admission or rejection of proofs

(1) Unless the administrator has already dealt with them, within 5 business days of the last date for proving, the administrator shall—
(a) admit or reject (in whole or in part) proofs that have been submitted; or
(b) make such provision in respect of them as the administrator thinks fit.

(2) The administrator is not obliged to deal with proofs lodged after the last date for proving, but may do so, if the administrator thinks fit.

(3) In the declaration of a dividend no payment shall be made more than once by virtue of the same debt.

[7.1887]
177 Postponement or cancellation of dividend

(1) If in the period of 2 months referred to in rule 175(5)(a)—
(a) the administrator has rejected a proof in whole or in part and application is made to the court for that decision to be reversed or varied; or
(b) an application is made to the court for the administrator's decision on a proof to be reversed or varied, or for a proof to be expunged, or for a reduction of the amount claimed,

the administrator may postpone or cancel the dividend.

(2) Where in that same period the administrator considers that, due to the nature of the business of the investment bank, there is real complexity in admitting or rejecting proofs of claims submitted, or that the quantum of claims may be affected by any shortfalls in claims for client assets, the administrator may postpone the dividend.

[7.1888]
178 Declaration of a dividend

(1) Where rule 177(2) does not apply and subject to paragraph (2), within the 2 month period referred to in rule 175(5)(a) the administrator shall proceed to declare the dividend to one or more classes of creditor who have been given notice under that rule.

(2) Except with the permission of the court, the administrator shall not declare a dividend so long as there is pending any application to the court to reverse or vary the administrator's decision on a proof, or to expunge a proof or to reduce the amount claimed.

(3) If the court gives permission under paragraph (2), the administrator must make such provision in respect of the proof in question as the court directs.

[7.1889]
179 Notice of declaration of a dividend

(1) Where the administrator declares a dividend, notice of this shall be given to—
(a) all creditors who have proved their debts;
(b) the [FCA and, where the investment bank concerned is a PRA-authorised person, the PRA];
(c) in a special administration (bank administration), the FSCS; and
(d) in a special administration (bank administration), before the Bank of England has given an Objective A Achievement Notice, the Bank of England.

(2) The notice shall include the following particulars relating to the special administration—
(a) amounts raised from the sale of assets, indicating (so far as practicable) amounts raised by the sale of particular assets;
(b) payments made by the administrator when acting as such;
(c) where the administrator proposed to make a distribution to unsecured creditors, the value of the prescribed part, except where the court has made an order under section 176A(5) of the 1986 Act;
(d) provision (if any) made for unsettled claims, and funds (if any) retained for particular purposes;
(e) the total amount of dividend and the rate of dividend; and
(f) whether, and if so when, any further dividend is expected to be declared.

(3) In a special administration (bank administration) where property of the investment bank has been transferred to a bridge bank under section 12 of the 2009 Act, if the administrator declares a dividend before the Bank of England has given an Objective A Achievement Notice, the notice shall also include details of any payment made from a scheme under a resolution fund order.

NOTES

Para (1): words in square brackets substituted for "FSA" by the Financial Services Act 2012 (Consequential Amendments and Transitional Provisions) Order 2013, SI 2013/472, art 3, Sch 2, para 210(c), (d)(xvi), subject to a transitional provision (see para 211 as noted to **[7.1718]**).

[7.1890]
180 Payments of dividend and related matters

(1) The dividend may be distributed simultaneously with the notice declaring it.

(2) Payment of dividend may be made by post, or arrangements may be made with any creditor for it to be paid in another way, or held for collection.

(3) Where a dividend is paid on a bill of exchange or other negotiable instrument, the amount of the dividend shall be endorsed on the instrument, or on a certified copy of it, if required to be produced by the holder for that purpose.

[7.1891]
181 Notice of no dividend or no further dividend

(1) If the administrator gives notice to creditors that no dividend (or as the case may be, no further dividend) can be declared, the notice shall contain a statement to the effect either—

(a) that no funds have been realised; or

(b) that the funds realised have already been distributed or used or allocated for defraying the expenses of administration.

(2) The notice to creditors in paragraph (1) shall also be given to—

(a) the [FCA and, where the investment bank concerned is a PRA-authorised person, the PRA];

(b) in a special administration (bank administration), the FSCS; and

(c) in a special administration (bank administration), in a case where the Bank of England consented to a distribution, to the Bank of England.

NOTES

Para (2): words in square brackets in sub-para (a) substituted for "FSA" by the Financial Services Act 2012 (Consequential Amendments and Transitional Provisions) Order 2013, SI 2013/472, art 3, Sch 2, para 210(c), (d)(xvii), subject to a transitional provision (see para 211 as noted to **[7.1718]**).

[7.1892]
182 Proof altered after payment of dividend

(1) If after payment of dividend the amount claimed by a creditor in their proof is increased, the creditor is not entitled to disturb the distribution of the dividend; but is entitled to be paid, out of any money for the time being available for the payment of any further dividend, any dividend or dividends which that creditor has failed to receive.

(2) Any dividend or dividends payable under paragraph (1) shall be paid before the money there referred to is applied to the payment of any such further dividend.

(3) If, after a creditor's proof has been admitted, the proof is withdrawn or expunged, or the amount is reduced, the creditor is liable to repay to the administrator any amount overpaid by way of dividend.

[7.1893]
183 Secured creditors

(1) The following applies where a creditor re-values their security at a time when a dividend has been declared.

(2) If the revaluation results in a reduction of the creditor's unsecured claim ranking for dividend, the creditor shall, as soon as reasonably practicable, repay to the administrator, for the credit of the administration, any amount received by the creditor as dividend in excess of that to which that creditor would be entitled having regard to the revaluation of the security.

(3) If the revaluation results in an increase of the creditor's unsecured claim, the creditor is entitled to receive from the administrator, out of any money for the time being available for the payment of a further dividend, before any such further dividend is paid, any dividend or dividends which the creditor has failed to receive, having regard to the revaluation of the security.

(4) However, the creditor is not entitled to disturb any dividend declared (whether or not distributed) before the date of the revaluation.

[7.1894]
184 Disqualification from dividend

(1) If a creditor contravenes any provision of the Regulations or these Rules relating to the valuation of securities, the court may, on the application of the administrator, order that the creditor be wholly or partly disqualified from participation in any dividend.

(2) Notice of an application under paragraph (1) shall be given by the administrator to the [FCA] and the [FCA] shall have the right to appear and be heard at the hearing of the application.

[(3) If the investment bank concerned is a PRA-authorised person, notice of an application under paragraph (1) shall also be given by the administrator to the PRA and the PRA shall have the right to appear and be heard at the hearing of the application.]

NOTES

Para (2): word in square brackets in both places substituted for "FSA" by the Financial Services Act 2012 (Consequential Amendments and Transitional Provisions) Order 2013, SI 2013/472, art 3, Sch 2, para 210(r), subject to a transitional provision (see para 211 as noted to **[7.1718]**).

Para (3): added by SI 2013/472, art 3, Sch 2, para 210(r), subject to a transitional provision (see para 211 as noted to **[7.1718]**).

[7.1895]
185 Assignment of right to dividend

(1) If a person, entitled to a dividend, gives notice to the administrator that they wish the dividend to be paid to another person, or that they have assigned that entitlement to another person, the administrator shall pay the dividend to that other accordingly.

(2) A notice given under this rule must specify the name and address of the person to whom payment is to be made.

[7.1896]
186 Debt payable at a future time

(1) Where a creditor has proved for a debt of which payment is not due at the date of the declaration of dividend, that creditor is entitled to dividend equally with other creditors, but subject as follows.

(2) For the purpose of dividend (and no other purpose) the amount of the creditor's admitted proof (or, if a distribution has previously been made to that creditor, the amount remaining outstanding in respect of their admitted proof) shall be reduced by applying the following formula—

$$\frac{X}{1.05^{n}}$$

where—

(a) "X" is the value of the admitted proof; and
(b) "n" is the period beginning with the relevant date and ending with the date on which the payment of the creditor's debt would otherwise be due expressed in years and months in a decimalised form.

(3) In paragraph (2), "relevant date" means the date that the investment bank entered special administration.

PART 7
THE ADMINISTRATOR

CHAPTER 1 POWERS OF THE ADMINISTRATOR

[7.1897]
187 General powers

(1) Any permission given by the creditors' committee (or if there is no such committee, a meeting of the company's creditors and clients or the court under the Rules), shall not be a general permission but shall relate to a particular proposed exercise of the administrator's power in Schedule 4 to the 1986 Act.

(2) A person dealing with the administrator in good faith and for value is not concerned to enquire whether any such permission has been given.

(3) Where the administrator has done anything without that permission, the court or the creditors' committee may, for the purpose of enabling the administrator to meet the administrator's expenses out of the assets, ratify what the administrator has done; but neither shall do so unless it is satisfied that the administrator has acted in a case of urgency and has sought ratification without undue delay.

[7.1898]
188 Powers of disclaimer

(1) Where the administrator disclaims property under section 178 of the 1986 Act, the notice of disclaimer shall contain such particulars of the property disclaimed as enable it to be easily identified.

(2) The notice of disclaimer must be authenticated and dated by the administrator.

(3) As soon as reasonably practicable after authenticating the notice of disclaimer, the administrator must—

(a) send a copy of the notice to the registrar of companies; and
(b) in any case where the disclaimer is of registered land as defined in section 132(1) of the Land Registration Act 2002, send a copy of the notice to the Chief Land Registrar.

(4) For the purposes of section 178, the date of the prescribed notice is that on which the administrator authenticated it.

[7.1899]
189 Communication of disclaimer to persons interested

(1) Within 7 business days after the date of the notice of disclaimer, the administrator shall send or give copies of the notice to the persons mentioned in paragraphs (2) to (4).

(2) Where the property disclaimed is of a leasehold nature, the administrator shall send or give a copy to every person who (to the administrator's knowledge) claims under the company as underlessee or mortgagee.

(3) The administrator shall in any case send or give a copy of the notice to every person who (to the administrator's knowledge)—
  (a) claims an interest in the disclaimed property; or
  (b) is under any liability in respect of the property, not being a liability discharged by the disclaimer.

(4) If the disclaimer is of an unprofitable contract, the administrator shall send or give copies of the notice to all such persons as, to the administrator's knowledge, are parties to the contract or have interests under it.

(5) If subsequently it comes to the administrator's knowledge, in the case of any person 'P', that P has such an interest in the disclaimed property as would have entitled P to receive a copy of the notice of disclaimer in pursuance of paragraphs (2) to (4), the administrator shall then, as soon as reasonably practicable, send or give to P a copy of the notice.

(6) Compliance with paragraph (5) is not required if—
  (a) the administrator is satisfied that P has already been made aware of the disclaimer and its date, or
  (b) the court, on the administrator's application, orders that compliance is not required in that particular case.

[7.1900]
190 Additional notices

(1) The administrator disclaiming property may at any time send or give copies of the notice of the disclaimer to any persons who in the administrator's opinion ought, in the public interest or otherwise, to be informed of the disclaimer.

(2) Paragraph (1) is without prejudice to the administrator's obligations under sections 178 to 180 of the 1986 Act and rules 188 and 189.

[7.1901]
191 Records

The administrator must include in the administrator's records of the special administration a record of—
  (a) the persons to whom that administrator has sent or given copies of the notice of disclaimer under the two preceding rules, showing their names and addresses, and the nature of their respective interests;
  (b) the dates on which the copies of the notice of disclaimer were sent or given to those persons;
  (c) the date on which, as required by rule 188, a copy of the notice of disclaimer was sent to the registrar of companies; and
  (d) (where applicable) the date on which, as required by rule 188, a copy of the notice was sent to the Chief Land Registrar.

[7.1902]
192 Application by interested party

(1) The following applies where, in the case of any property, application is made to the administrator by an interested party under section 178(5) of the 1986 Act.

(2) The application must be delivered to the administrator—
  (a) personally;
  (b) by electronic means in accordance with Part 11; or
  (c) by any other means of delivery which enables proof of receipt of the application by the administrator to be provided, if requested.

[7.1903]
193 Interest in property to be declared on request

(1) If, in the case of property which the administrator has the right to disclaim, it appears to the administrator that there is some person 'P' who claims, or may claim, to have an interest in the property, the administrator may give notice to P calling on that person to declare within 14 days whether P claims any such interest and, if so, the nature and extent of it.

(2) Failing compliance with the notice, the administrator is entitled to assume that P has no such interest in the property as will prevent or impede its disclaimer.

[7.1904]
194 Disclaimer presumed valid and effective

Any disclaimer of property by the administrator is presumed valid and effective, unless it is proved that the administrator has been in breach of their duty with respect to the giving of notice of disclaimer, or otherwise, under sections 178 to 180 of the 1986 Act or under this Chapter of the Rules.

[7.1905]
195 Application for the exercise of court's powers under section 181

(1) This rule applies with respect to an application by any person under section 181 of the 1986 Act for an order of the court to vest or deliver disclaimed property.

(2) The application must be made within 3 months of the applicant becoming aware of the disclaimer, or of the applicant receiving a copy of the administrator's notice of disclaimer sent under rule 189, whichever is the earlier.

(3) The applicant shall with the application file a witness statement—
- (a) stating whether the application is made under—
  - (i) paragraph (a) of section 181(2) (claim of interest in the property), or
  - (ii) under paragraph (b) (liability not discharged);
- (b) specifying the date on which the applicant received a copy of the administrator's notice of disclaimer, or otherwise became aware of the disclaimer; and
- (c) specifying the grounds of the application and the order which the applicant desires the court to make under section 181.

(4) The court shall fix a venue for the hearing of the application; and the applicant shall, not later than 5 business days before the date fixed, give to the administrator notice of the venue, accompanied by copies of the application and the witness statement required by paragraph (3).

(5) On the hearing of the application, the court may give directions as to other persons (if any) who should be sent or given notice of the application and the grounds on which it is made.

(6) Sealed copies of any order made on the application shall be sent by the court to the applicant and the administrator.

(7) In a case where the property disclaimed is of a leasehold nature, and section 179 of the 1986 Act applies to suspend the effect of the disclaimer, there shall be included in the court's order a direction giving effect to the disclaimer.

(8) Paragraph (7) does not apply if, at the time when the order is issued, other applications under section 181 are pending in respect of the same property.

CHAPTER 2 FIXING OF REMUNERATION

[7.1906]
196 Fixing of remuneration

(1) The administrator is entitled to receive remuneration for services given in respect of—
- (a) the pursuit of—
  - (i) Objective A in a special administration (bank insolvency),
  - (ii) Objective A in a special administration (bank administration), and
  - (iii) Objectives 2 and 3,

  to be paid out of the estate of the investment bank; and
- (b) the pursuit of Objective 1 to be paid out of the client assets held by the investment bank.

(2) The basis of remuneration in both cases in paragraph (1) shall be fixed—
- (a) as a percentage of the value of the property with which the administrator has to deal; or
- (b) by reference to the time properly given by the insolvency practitioner (as administrator) and his staff in attending to matters arising in the special administration; or
- (c) as a set amount.

(3) The basis of remuneration may be fixed as any one or more of the bases set out in paragraph (2), and different bases may be fixed in respect of different things done by the administrator.

(4) Where the basis of remuneration is fixed as set out in paragraph (2)(a), different percentages may be fixed in respect of different things done by the administrator.

(5) It is for the creditors' committee (if there is one) to determine for each case—
- (a) which of the bases set out in paragraph (2) are to be fixed and (where appropriate) in what combination under paragraph (3), and
- (b) the percentage or percentages (if any) to be fixed under paragraphs (2)(a) and (4) and the amount (if any) to be set under paragraph (2)(c).

(6) In making the determinations, the committee shall have regard to the following matters—
- (a) the complexity (or otherwise) of the case;
- (b) any respects in which, in connection with the pursuit of either Objective 1, or of Objectives A, 2 and 3, there falls on the administrator any responsibility of an exceptional kind or degree;
- (c) the effectiveness with which the administrator appears to be carrying out, or to have carried out, their duties as such; and
- (d) the value and nature in each case of the property with which the administrator has to deal.

(7) If there is no creditors' committee, or the committee does not make the requisite determinations, the basis of the administrator's remuneration in each case may be fixed (in accordance with paragraphs (2) to (5)) by resolutions of a meeting of creditors and clients, or in respect of the administrator's remuneration for the purpose outlined in rule 196(1)(b), a meeting of clients and paragraph (6) applies to them as it does to the creditors' committee.

(8) If not fixed as above, the basis of the administrator's remuneration in either case shall, on the administrator's application, be fixed by the court and the provisions above apply as they do to the fixing of the basis of remuneration by the creditors' committee; but such an application may not be made by the

administrator unless the administrator has first sought fixing of the basis in accordance with paragraph (5) or (7), and in any event may not be made more than 18 months after the date of the administrator's appointment.

(9) Where there are joint administrators, it is for them to agree between themselves as to how the remuneration payable should be apportioned. Any dispute arising between them may be referred—

(a) to the court, for settlement by order; or

(b) to the creditors' committee or a meeting of creditors and clients, for settlement by resolution.

(10) If the administrator is a solicitor and employs their own firm, or any partner in it, to act on behalf of the investment bank, profit costs shall not be paid unless this is authorised by the creditors' committee, the meeting of the creditors and clients, or the court.

[7.1907]

197 Remuneration (special administration (bank insolvency))

(1) In a special administration (bank insolvency), where the basis for the administrator's remuneration for services set out in rule 196(1)(a) has been fixed in accordance with rule 29, the creditors' committee (or if there is no creditors' committee, the meeting of creditors and clients) shall resolve whether to confirm the basis for remuneration as set by the Objective A committee, or whether to redetermine the basis for remuneration in accordance with rule 196(2) to (5).

(2) Any redetermination by the creditors' committee under paragraph (1) shall apply only in respect of the administrator's remuneration as from the date of the committee's decision and shall not have retrospective effect.

[7.1908]

198 Remuneration (special administration (bank administration)

(1) In a special administration (bank administration), where the basis for the administrator's remuneration for services set out in rule 196(1)(a) has been fixed in accordance with rule 48, the creditors' committee (or if there is no creditors' committee, the meeting of creditors and clients) shall resolve whether to confirm the basis for remuneration as set by the Bank of England, or whether to redetermine the basis for remuneration in accordance with rule 196(2) to (5).

(2) Paragraph (1) only applies where the Bank of England has passed an Objective A Achievement Notice.

(3) Any redetermination by the creditors' committee under paragraph (1) shall apply only in respect of the administrator's remuneration as from the date of the committee's decision and shall not have retrospective effect.

[7.1909]

199 Recourse to meeting of creditors and clients

(1) If the basis of the administrator's remuneration for either case in rule 196(1) has been fixed by the creditors' committee or confirmed or redetermined under rules 197 or 198, and the administrator considers, in either or in both cases, the rate or amount to be insufficient, or the basis to be inappropriate, the administrator may request that the rate or amount be increased or the basis changed by resolution of the creditors and the clients.

[7.1910]

200 Recourse to the court

(1) If the administrator considers that the basis of remuneration for either case in rule 196(1) fixed for the administrator by—

(a) the creditors' committee; or

(b) by resolution of the creditors and clients, or as the case may be, a meeting of clients,

is insufficient or inappropriate, the administrator may apply to the court for an order changing it or increasing its amount or rate.

(2) If in a special administration (bank insolvency) the administrator considers that the basis for remuneration for services set out in rule 196(1)(a) fixed for the administrator by the Objective A committee or under rule 197 above is insufficient or inappropriate, the administrator may apply to the court for an order changing it or increasing its amount or rate.

(3) If in a special administration (bank administration) the administrator considers that the basis for remuneration for services set out in rule 196(1)(a) fixed for the administrator by the Bank of England or under rule 198 above is insufficient or inappropriate, the administrator may apply to the court for an order changing it or increasing its amount or rate.

(4) The administrator shall give at least 14 days' notice of the application to the members of the creditors' committee; and the committee may nominate one or more members to appear, or be represented, and to be heard on the application.

(5) If there is no creditors' committee, the notice of the application shall be sent to such one or more of the investment bank's creditors or clients as the court may direct; those creditors or clients shall nominate one or more of their number to appear or be represented.

(6) Notice of the application shall also be given to the [FCA] and the [FCA] may nominate a person to appear and be heard on the application.

[(6A) If the investment bank concerned is a PRA-authorised person, notice of the application shall also be given to the PRA and the PRA may nominate a person to appear and be heard on the application.]

(7) In a special administration (bank administration), before the Bank of England has given an Objective A Achievement Notice, the court on hearing an application under this rule shall have regard to the achievement of Objective A.

(8) The court may, if it appears to be a proper case, order the costs of the administrator's application, including the costs of any member of the creditors' committee appearing or being represented on it, or any creditor or client so appearing or being represented, to be paid as an expense of the administration.

NOTES

Para (6): words in square brackets substituted for "FSA" by the Financial Services Act 2012 (Consequential Amendments and Transitional Provisions) Order 2013, SI 2013/472, art 3, Sch 2, para 210(s)(i), subject to a transitional provision (see para 211 as noted to **[7.1718]**).

Para (6A): inserted by SI 2013/472, art 3, Sch 2, para 210(s)(ii), subject to a transitional provision (see para 211 as noted to **[7.1718]**).

[7.1911]

201 Creditors' and clients' request for further information

(1) If—

(a) within 21 days of receipt of a progress report under rule 122—
  (i) a secured creditor,
  (ii) an unsecured creditor with the concurrence of at least 5% in value of the unsecured creditors (including the creditor in question), or
  (iii) a client with the concurrence of clients claiming for at least 5% in value of the client assets (including the client in question); or

(b) with the permission of the court upon an application made within that period of 21 days, any unsecured creditor,

makes a request in writing to the administrator for further information about remuneration or expenses (other than pre-administration costs) set out in a statement required by rule 122(1)(g) or (h), the administrator must, within 14 days of receipt of the request, comply with paragraph (2).

(2) The administrator complies with this paragraph by either—

(a) providing all of the information asked for, or

(b) so far as the administrator considers that—
  (i) the time or cost of preparation of the information would be excessive, or
  (ii) disclosure of the information would be prejudicial to the conduct of the administration or might reasonably be expected to lead to violence against any person, or
  (iii) the administrator is subject to an obligation of confidentiality in respect of the information,

giving reasons for not providing all of the information.

(3) Any creditor or client, who need not be the same as the person who requested further information under paragraph (1), may apply to the court within 21 days of—

(a) the giving by the administrator of reasons for not providing all of the information asked for, or

(b) the expiry of the 14 days provided for in paragraph (1),

and the court may make such order as it thinks just.

(4) Without prejudice to the generality of paragraph (3), the order of the court under that paragraph may extend the period of 8 weeks provided for in rule 202(4) by such further period as the court thinks just.

[7.1912]

202 Claim that remuneration is excessive

(1) The following persons may apply to the court for one or more of the orders in paragraph (7) in respect of the administrator's remuneration for services set out in rule 196(1)(a)—

(a) a secured creditor;

(b) an unsecured creditor with either the concurrence of at least 10% in value of the unsecured creditors (including that creditor) or the permission of the court; or

(c) a client with the concurrence of clients representing at least 10% of the total claims in respect of client assets held by the investment bank or with the permission of the court; . . .

[(d) the FCA; or

(e) if the investment bank concerned is a PRA-authorised person, the PRA.]

(2) A client, with the concurrence of clients representing at least 10% of the total claims in respect of client assets held by the investment bank, or with the permission of the court, may apply to the court for one or more of the orders in paragraph (7) in respect of the administrator's remuneration for services set out in rule 196(1)(b).

(3) Application under paragraphs (1) and (2) may be made on the grounds that—

(a) the remuneration charged by the administrator;

(b) the basis fixed for the administrator's remuneration; or

(c) expenses incurred by the administrator,

is or are, in all the circumstances, excessive or, in the case of an application under sub-paragraph (b), inappropriate.

(4) The application must, subject to any order of the court under rule 201(4), be made no later than 8 weeks after receipt by the applicant of the progress report which first reports the charging of the remuneration or the incurring of the expenses in question ("the relevant report").

(5) The court may, if it thinks that no sufficient cause is shown for a reduction, dismiss it without a hearing but it shall not do so without giving the applicant at least 5 business days' notice, upon receipt of which the applicant may require the court to list the application for a without notice hearing. If the application is not dismissed, the court shall fix a venue for it to be heard, and give notice to the applicant accordingly.

(6) The applicant shall, at least 14 days before the hearing, send to the administrator a notice stating the venue and accompanied by a copy of the application, and of any evidence which the applicant intends to adduce in support of it.

(7) If the court considers the application to be well-founded, it must make one or more of the following orders—

- (a) an order reducing the amount of remuneration which the administrator was entitled to charge;
- (b) an order fixing the basis of remuneration at a reduced rate or amount;
- (c) an order changing the basis of remuneration;
- (d) an order that some or all of the remuneration or expenses in question be treated as not being expenses of the administration;
- (e) an order that the administrator or the administrator's personal representative pay to the investment bank the amount of the excess of remuneration or expenses or such part of the excess as the court may specify;

and may make any other order that it thinks just; but an order under sub-paragraph (b) or (c) may be made only in respect of periods after the period covered by the relevant report.

(8) Unless the court orders otherwise, the costs of the application shall be paid by the applicant, and are not payable as an expense of the special administration.

(9) In a special administration (bank administration), this rule only applies after the Bank of England has given an Objective A Achievement Notice.

NOTES

Para (1): word "or" (omitted) at the end of sub-para (c) revoked, and sub-paras (d), (e) substituted, for original sub-para (d), by the Financial Services Act 2012 (Consequential Amendments and Transitional Provisions) Order 2013, SI 2013/472, art 3, Sch 2, para 210(t), subject to a transitional provision (see para 211 as noted to **[7.1718]**). Sub-para (d) originally read as follows:

"(d) the FSA.".

[7.1913]

203 Review of remuneration

(1) Where, after the basis of the administrator's remuneration has been fixed, there is a material and substantial change in the circumstances which were taken into account in fixing it, the administrator may request that it be changed.

(2) The request must be made—

- (a) where the creditors' committee fixed the basis, to the committee;
- (b) where the creditors and clients fixed the basis, to the creditors and clients;
- (c) where the court fixed the basis, by application to the court;
- (d) where the Objective A committee fixed the basis, to that committee (unless that committee has passed a full payment resolution, in which case the request must be made to the creditors' committee, or if there is no creditors' committee, to the meeting of creditors and clients);
- (e) where the Bank of England fixed the basis, to the Bank of England (unless the Bank of England has given an Objective A Achievement Notice, in which case the request must be made to the creditors' committee, or if there is no creditors' committee, to the meeting of creditors and clients);

and this Chapter applies as appropriate.

(3) Any change in the basis for remuneration applies from the date of the request under paragraph (1) and not for any earlier period.

[7.1914]

204 Remuneration of new administrator

(1) If a new administrator is appointed in place of another, any determination, resolution or court order in effect under the preceding provisions of this Chapter immediately before the former administrator ceased to hold office continues to apply in respect of the remuneration of the new administrator until a further determination, resolution or court order is made in accordance with those provisions.

[7.1915]

205 Apportionment of set fee remuneration

(1) In a case in which the basis of the administrator's remuneration is a set amount under rule 196(2)(c) and the administrator ("the former administrator") ceases (for whatever reason) to hold office before the time has elapsed or the work has been completed in respect of which the amount was set, application may be made for determination of what portion of the amount should be paid to the former administrator or the former administrator's personal representative in respect of the time which has actually elapsed or the work which has actually been done.

(2) Application may be made—

(a) by the former administrator or the former administrator's personal representative within the period of 28 days beginning with the date upon which the former administrator ceased to hold office; or
(b) by the administrator for the time being in office if the former administrator or the former administrator's personal representative has not applied by the end of that period.

(3) Application must be made—
(a) where the creditors' committee fixed the basis, to that committee for a resolution determining the portion;
(b) where the creditors and clients fixed the basis, to the creditors and clients for a resolution determining the portion;
(c) where the court fixed the basis, to the court for an order determining the portion;
(d) where the Objective A committee fixed the basis, to that committee (unless that committee has passed a full payment resolution, in which case the request must be made to the creditors' committee, or if there is no creditors' committee, to the meeting of creditors and clients); and
(e) where the Bank of England fixed the basis, to the Bank of England (unless the Bank of England has given an Objective A Achievement Notice, in which case the request must be made to the creditors' committee, or if there is no creditors' committee, to the meeting of creditors and clients).

(4) The applicant must give a copy of the application to the administrator for the time being in office or to the former administrator or the former administrator's personal representative, as the case may be ("the recipient").

(5) The recipient may within 21 days of receipt of the copy of the application give notice of intent to make representations to the creditors' committee, or to the creditors and clients or to appear or be represented before the court, as the case may be.

(6) No determination may be made upon the application until expiry of the 21 days referred to in paragraph (5) or, if the recipient does give notice of intent in accordance with that paragraph, until the recipient has been afforded the opportunity to make representations or to appear or be represented, as the case may be.

(7) If the former administrator or the former administrator's personal representative (whether or not the original applicant) considers that the portion determined upon application to the creditors' committee or the creditors and clients is insufficient, that person may apply—
(a) in the case of a determination by the creditors' committee, to the creditors and clients for a resolution increasing the portion;
(b) in the case of a resolution of the creditors and clients (whether under paragraph (1) or under sub-paragraph (a)), to the court for an order increasing the portion;
and paragraphs (4) to (6) apply as appropriate.

CHAPTER 3 REPLACING THE ADMINISTRATOR

[7.1916]
206 Grounds for resignation

(1) The administrator may resign in the following circumstances—
(a) on grounds of ill health;
(b) that the administrator intends ceasing to be in practice as an insolvency practitioner; or
(c) that there is some conflict of interest, or change of personal circumstances, which precludes or makes impracticable the further discharge by that person of the duties of administrator.

(2) The administrator may, with the permission of the court, resign on grounds other than those specified in paragraph (1).

(3) In a special administration (bank insolvency) before the Objective A committee has passed a full payment resolution, the administrator needs the permission of the Bank of England to resign on grounds other than those specified in paragraph (1).

(4) In a special administration (bank administration) before the Bank of England has given an Objective A Achievement Notice, the administrator needs the permission of the Bank of England to resign on grounds other than those specified in paragraph (1).

[7.1917]
207 Notice of intention to resign

(1) The administrator shall in all cases give at least 5 business days' notice of their intention to resign, or their intention to apply for the court's permission to do so, to the following persons—
(a) if there is a continuing administrator of the investment bank, to that person; and
(b) if there is a creditors' committee, to it; but
(c) if there is no such administrator and no creditors' committee, to the investment bank and its creditors and clients of whose claim the administrator is aware and of whom the administrator has a means of contacting.

(2) Where the administrator was appointed on the application of the [FCA, the PRA] or the Secretary of State, notice under paragraph (1) shall also be given to the applicant.

(3) In a special administration (bank insolvency), before the Objective A committee has passed a full payment resolution, notice under paragraph (1) shall be given to the Bank of England.

(4) In a special administration (bank administration), notice under paragraph (1) shall be given to the [FCA and, where the investment bank concerned is a PRA-authorised person, the PRA] and to the Bank of England.

(5) The notice under paragraph (1) shall set out—

(a) a statement that the proceedings are being held in the High Court and the court reference number;

(b) the full name, registered address, registered number of the investment bank;

(c) the full name and business address of the administrator;

(d) either—

(i) the date on which the administrator's resignation shall take effect; or

(ii) the date upon which the administrator intends to apply to court for leave to resign.

NOTES

Paras (2), (4): words in square brackets substituted for "FSA" by the Financial Services Act 2012 (Consequential Amendments and Transitional Provisions) Order 2013, SI 2013/472, art 3, Sch 2, para 210(u), subject to a transitional provision (see para 211 as noted to **[7.1718]**).

[7.1918]

208 Notice of resignation

(1) The notice of resignation shall set out—

(a) a statement that the proceedings are being held in the High Court and the court reference number;

(b) the full name, registered address and registered number of the investment bank;

(c) the full name and business address of the administrator;

(d) whether or not the person resigning is the sole administrator of the investment bank; and

(e) a statement that either—

(i) the administrator resigns from office with effect from a specified date; or

(ii) the court gave the administrator leave to resign (and the statement shall include the date of the court's permission) and that the administrator therefore resigns with effect from a specified date.

(2) In a special administration (bank insolvency), before the Objective A committee has passed a full payment resolution, where the administrator has applied to court for leave to resign, the notice of resignation shall also contain confirmation from the Bank of England that it consents to the resignation.

(3) In a special administration (bank administration) before the Bank of England has given an Objective A Achievement Notice, where the administrator has applied to court for leave to resign, the notice of resignation shall also contain confirmation from the Bank of England that it consents to the resignation.

(4) The notice shall be filed with the court and a copy of the notice of resignation shall be sent not more than 5 business days after it has been filed with the court to all those to whom the notice of intention to resign was sent.

(5) The administrator shall notify the registrar of companies of their resignation.

[7.1919]

209 Application to court to remove administrator from office

(1) Any application under paragraph 88 shall state the grounds on which it is requested that the administrator should be removed from office.

(2) In a special administration (bank administration), the application must state that either—

(a) the Bank of England has consented to the application being made; or

(b) the Bank of England has given an Objective A Achievement Notice.

(3) Service of the notice of the application shall be effected on—

(a) the administrator;

(b) the person who made the application for the special administration order;

(c) the creditors' committee (if any);

(d) the joint administrator (if any);

(e) where there is neither a creditors' committee or joint administrator, the investment bank and all the creditors and clients of whose claim the administrator is aware and of whom they have a means of contacting;

(f) the [FCA and, where the investment bank concerned is a PRA-authorised person, the PRA]; and

(g) in a special administration (bank administration) where the Bank of England has not given an Objective A Achievement Notice, the Bank of England.

(4) Where a court makes an order removing the administrator it shall give a copy of the order to the applicant who as soon as reasonably practicable, shall send a copy to the administrator.

(5) The applicant shall also within 5 business days of the order being made send a copy of the order to all those to whom notice of the application was sent.

(6) The applicant shall send notice of the order to the registrar of companies within the same time period.

NOTES

Para (3): words in square brackets in sub-para (f) substituted for "FSA" by the Financial Services Act 2012 (Consequential Amendments and Transitional Provisions) Order 2013, SI 2013/472, art 3, Sch 2, para 210(c), (d)(xviii), subject to a transitional provision (see para 211 as noted to **[7.1718]**).

[7.1920]

210 Notice of vacation of office when administrator ceases to be qualified

Where the administrator who has ceased to be qualified to act as an insolvency practitioner in relation to the investment bank gives notice in accordance with paragraph 89, notice shall also be given—

(a) to the registrar of companies; and

(b) (where the administrator was appointed on the application of the [FCA, the PRA] or the Secretary of State) to the applicant.

NOTES

Para (b): words in square brackets substituted for "FSA" by the Financial Services Act 2012 (Consequential Amendments and Transitional Provisions) Order 2013, SI 2013/472, art 3, Sch 2, para 210(v), subject to a transitional provision (see para 211 as noted to **[7.1718]**).

[7.1921]

211 Administrator deceased

(1) Subject as follows, where the administrator has died, it is the duty of the administrator's personal representatives to give notice of the fact to the court, specifying the date of the death. This does not apply if notice has been given under either paragraph (3) or (4) of this rule.

(2) Notice of the death must also be sent to the registrar of companies.

(3) If the deceased administrator was a partner in or an employee of a firm, notice to the court may be given by a partner in the firm who is qualified to act as an insolvency practitioner, or is a member of any body recognised by the Secretary of State or the Department of Enterprise, Trade and Investment for Northern Ireland for the authorisation of insolvency practitioners.

(4) Notice of the death may be given to the court by any person producing to the court the relevant death certificate or a copy of it.

[7.1922]

212 Application to replace (special administration)

(1) Where an application is made to court under paragraph 91(1) to appoint a replacement administrator, the application shall be accompanied by a written statement by the person proposed to be the replacement administrator.

(2) The written statement shall be in accordance with rule 7.

(3) A copy of the application shall be served on—

(a) the person who made the application for a special administration order;

(b) the investment bank (if neither the investment bank nor its directors are the applicant);

(c) on the person nominated for appointment as administrator; . . .

[(d) the FCA (if not the applicant); and

(e) if the application relates to a PRA-authorised person, the PRA (if not the applicant).]

(4) Rule 10 shall apply to the service of an application under paragraph 91(1) as it applies to service of the application for a special administration order.

(5) Rules 11 and 13 apply to an application under this rule and rule 16(1) and (2) shall apply to the notice of appointment under paragraph 91(1) as it applies to notice of a special administration order.

(6) This rule does not apply—

(a) in a special administration (bank insolvency) before the Objective A committee has passed a full payment resolution; or

(b) in a special administration (bank administration) before the Bank of England has given an Objective A Achievement Notice

NOTES

Para (3): word "and" (omitted) at the end of sub-para (c) revoked, and sub-paras (d), (e) substituted, for original sub-para (d), by the Financial Services Act 2012 (Consequential Amendments and Transitional Provisions) Order 2013, SI 2013/472, art 3, Sch 2, para 210(w), subject to a transitional provision (see para 211 as noted to **[7.1718]**). Sub-para (d) originally read as follows:

"(d) on the FSA (if not the applicant).".

[7.1923]

213 Application to replace (special administration (bank insolvency))

(1) This rule applies in a special administration (bank insolvency) before the Objective A committee has passed a full payment resolution.

(2) Where there is a vacancy in office the Bank of England must appoint a replacement administrator as soon as reasonably practicable.

(3) The rules for the appointment of an administrator in Chapter 2 of Part 2 shall apply to the appointment of a replacement administrator.

[7.1924]

214 Application to replace (special administration (bank administration))

(1) This rule applies in a special administration (bank administration) before the Bank of England has given an Objective A Achievement Notice.

(2) Where there is a vacancy in office the Bank of England must appoint a replacement administrator as soon as reasonably practicable.

(3) Where an application is made by the Bank of England to remove or replace an administrator, the rules in Chapter 3 of Part 2 for the application to appoint an administrator shall apply to the service of notice of the application and of the hearing.

(4) Both the person proposed to be appointed and the existing administrator are entitled to be served and heard.

[7.1925]

215 Notification and advertisement of appointment of replacement administrator

(1) Where a replacement administrator is appointed, the same provisions apply in respect of giving notice of, and advertising, the replacement appointment as in the case of the appointment, subject to rule 218.

(2) All statements, consents etc as are required shall also be required in the case of the appointment of a replacement.

(3) All notices shall clearly identify that the appointment is of a replacement administrator.

[7.1926]

216 Notification and advertisement of appointment of joint administrator

Where, after an initial appointment has been made, an additional person or persons are to be appointed as joint administrator, the same rules shall apply in respect of giving notice of and advertising the appointment as in the case of the initial appointment, subject to rule 218.

[7.1927]

217 Additional joint administrator (special administration (bank administration))

(1) This rule applies to an application to appoint an additional joint administrator in a special administration (bank administration) before the Bank of England has given an Objective A Achievement Notice.

(2) The process for the initial appointment of an administrator under Chapter 3 of Part 2 shall apply to the appointment of an additional joint administrator.

(3) The existing administrator (or each of them) is entitled to a copy of the application and may—

- (a) file written representations; and
- (b) be heard at the hearing.

(4) An application for the appointment of an additional joint administrator under this rule may only be made by the Bank of England.

(5) Rules 216 and 218 apply in respect to the notification and advertisement of the appointment of a additional joint administrator.

[7.1928]

218 Notification of new administrator

(1) The replacement or additional administrator shall send notice of the appointment to the registrar of companies.

(2) The notice in paragraph (1) shall contain—

- (a) the name and business address of the administrator appointed;
- (b) the name, registered address and registered number of the investment bank in respect of which the appointment is made;
- (c) whether the administrator is appointed to replace an existing administrator or in addition to a previously appointed administrator; and
- (d) the date from which the administrator's appointment will take effect.

[7.1929]

219 Administrator's duties on vacating office

(1) Where the administrator ('A') ceases to be in office in consequence of this chapter, A is under obligation as soon as reasonably practicable to deliver up to the person succeeding A as administrator ('B') the assets (after deduction of any expenses properly incurred and distributions made by A) and further to deliver up to B—

- (a) the records of the administration, including correspondence, proofs and other related papers appertaining to the administration while it was within A's responsibility; and
- (b) the investment bank's books, papers and other records.

(2) If A makes default in complying with this rule, A is liable to a fine and, for continued contravention, to a daily default fine.

PART 8
END OF SPECIAL ADMINISTRATION

[7.1930]

220 Final progress reports

(1) In this Part, reference to a progress report is to a report in the form specified in rule 122.

(2) The final progress report means a progress report which includes a summary of—

(a) the administrator's proposals (including whether the [FCA or, where relevant, the PRA] has given a direction under regulation 16 and whether that direction has been withdrawn);
(b) any major amendments to, or deviations from, those proposals;
(c) the steps taken during the special administration, including in a special administration (bank insolvency) or a special administration (bank administration), the steps taken to achieve Objective A; and
(d) the outcome.

NOTES

Para (2): words in square brackets substituted for "FSA" by the Financial Services Act 2012 (Consequential Amendments and Transitional Provisions) Order 2013, SI 2013/472, art 3, Sch 2, para 210(a), (b)(xiv), subject to a transitional provision (see para 211 as noted to **[7.1718]**).

[7.1931]

221 Application to court by administrator

(1) An application to court under paragraph 79 for an order ending an administration shall have attached to it—
(a) a progress report for the period since the last progress report (if any) or the date the investment bank entered special administration; and
(b) a statement indicating what the administrator thinks should be the next steps for the investment bank (if applicable).

(2) Before making the application under paragraph (1), the administrator shall—
(a) give notice in writing to—
(i) the applicant for the special administration order under which the administrator was appointed,
(ii) the creditors and clients,
(iii) the [FCA and, where the investment bank concerned is a PRA-authorised person, the PRA],
(iv) in a special administration (bank insolvency), the Bank of England, and
(v) in a special administration (bank administration), the Bank of England and the FSCS,
of the intention to make the application; and
(b) attach to the application a statement that the creditors and clients have been notified of the application and copies of any response to that notification.

(3) Notice under paragraph (2)(a) shall be given at least 5 business days before the date that the administrator intends to makes the application.

(4) The administrator—
(a) shall send a copy of the application under paragraph (1) to the [FCA and, where the investment bank concerned is a PRA-authorised person, the PRA];
(b) must, within 5 business days of filing the application, gazette a notice undertaking to provide a copy of the application to any person who so requests it (and an address to which they can write); and
(c) advertise the notice in such other manner as the administrator thinks fit.

NOTES

Paras (2), (4): words in square brackets substituted for "FSA" by the Financial Services Act 2012 (Consequential Amendments and Transitional Provisions) Order 2013, SI 2013/472, art 3, Sch 2, para 210(c), (d)(xix), subject to a transitional provision (see para 211 as noted to **[7.1718]**).

[7.1932]

222 Application to court by creditor

(1) Where a creditor applies to the court to end the special administration a copy of the application shall be served on—
(a) the administrator;
(b) the person who made the application for the special administration order; and
(c) the [FCA and, where the investment bank concerned is a PRA-authorised person, the PRA].

(2) Service shall be effected not less than 5 business days before the date fixed for the hearing.

(3) The persons in paragraph (1) may appear at the hearing of the application.

(4) Where the court makes an order to end the special administration, the court shall send a copy of the order to the administrator.

(5) This rule does not apply in a special administration (bank insolvency) or a special administration (bank administration).

NOTES

Para (1): words in square brackets in sub-para (c) substituted for "FSA" by the Financial Services Act 2012 (Consequential Amendments and Transitional Provisions) Order 2013, SI 2013/472, art 3, Sch 2, para 210(c), (d)(xx), subject to a transitional provision (see para 211 as noted to **[7.1718]**).

[7.1933]

223 Notification by administrator of court order

(1) Where the court makes an order to end the administration, the administrator must send a copy of the court order and a copy of the final progress report to the registrar of companies.

(2) As soon as reasonably practicable, the administrator must send a copy of the notice and the final progress report to all other persons who received notice of the administrator's appointment.

[7.1934]
224 Moving from administration to dissolution

(1) Where, for the purposes of paragraph 84(1), the administrator sends a notice of moving from administration to dissolution to the registrar of companies, the administrator must attach to that notice a final progress report.

(2) As soon as reasonably practicable, a copy of the notice and the attached document shall be sent to all other persons who received notice of the administrator's appointment.

(3) Where a court makes an order under paragraph 84(7) it shall, where the applicant is not the administrator, give a copy of the order to the administrator.

PART 9
COURT PROCEDURE AND PRACTICE

CHAPTER 1 APPLICATION OF THE CPR

[7.1935]
225 Principal court rules and practice to apply

(1) The provisions of the CPR in the first column of the table in this rule (including any related practice direction) apply to special administration by virtue of the provisions of these Rules set out in the second column with any necessary modifications, except so far as inconsistent with these Rules.

Provision of CPR	*Provisions of these Rules*
CPR Part 6 (service of documents)	Chapter 4 of Part 9
CPR Part 18 (further information)	Rules 230 and 251(c)(ii)
CPR Part 31 (disclosure and inspection of documents)	Rules 230 and 251
CPR Part 37 (miscellaneous provisions about payments into court)	Rule 229
CPR Parts 44 and 47 (costs)	Chapter 10 of Part 9
CPR Part 52 (appeals)	Chapter 12 of Part 9

(2) Subject to paragraph (3), the provisions of the CPR (including any related practice direction) not referred to in the table apply to proceedings under the Regulations and Rules with any necessary modifications, except so far as inconsistent with these Rules.

(3) Proceedings in a special administration must be allocated to the multi-track for which CPR Part 29 makes provision, and accordingly those provisions of the CPR which provide for allocation questionnaires and track allocation do not apply.

(4) CPR Part 32 applies to a false statement in a document verified by a statement of truth made under these Rules as it applies to a false statement in a document verified by a statement of truth made under CPR Part 22.

CHAPTER 2 THE COURT

[7.1936]
226 Shorthand writers—nomination, appointment, remuneration and costs

(1) The judge or registrar may in writing nominate one or more persons to be official shorthand writers to the court.

(2) The court may, at any time in the course of the special administration appoint a shorthand writer to take down evidence of a person examined under section 236 of the 1986 Act.

(3) The remuneration of a shorthand writer appointed under this rule must be paid by the party at whose instance the appointment was made, or out of the insolvent estate, or otherwise, as the court may direct.

(4) Any question arising as to the rates of remuneration payable under this rule must be determined by the court.

[7.1937]
227 Court file

(1) The court must open and maintain a file in any case where documents are filed with it under the Regulations or the Rules.

(2) Any documents which are filed with the court under the Regulations or the Rules must be placed on the file opened in accordance with paragraph (1).

(3) The following persons may inspect or obtain from the court a copy of, or a copy of any document or documents contained in, the file opened in accordance with paragraph (1)—
- (a) the administrator;
- (b) the Secretary of State;
- (c) the [FCA and, where the investment bank concerned is a PRA-authorised person, the PRA];

(d) in a special administration (bank insolvency) or special administration (bank administration), the Bank of England or the FSCS;
(e) any person who is a creditor of the investment bank if that person provides the court with a statement in writing confirming that that person is a creditor; and
(f) any person who is a client of the investment bank if that person provides the court with a statement in writing confirming that that person is a client.

(4) The same right to inspect or obtain a copy of, or a copy of any document or documents contained in, the file opened in accordance with paragraph (1) is exercisable by—
(a) an officer or former officer of the investment bank in special administration; or
(b) a member of the investment bank or a contributory in the special administration.

(5) The right to inspect or obtain a copy of, or a copy of any document or documents contained in, the file opened in accordance with paragraph (1) may be exercised on that person's behalf by a person authorised to do so by that person.

(6) Any person who is not otherwise entitled to inspect or obtain a copy of, or a copy of any document or documents contained in, the file opened in accordance with paragraph (1) may do so if that person has the permission of the court.

(7) The court may direct that the file, a document (or part of it) or a copy of a document (or part of it) must not be made available under paragraph (3), (4) or (5) without the permission of the court.

(8) An application for a direction under paragraph (7) may be made by—
(a) the administrator;
(b) the [FCA and, where the investment bank concerned is a PRA-authorised person, the PRA];
(c) in a special administration (bank insolvency) or special administration (bank administration) the Bank of England; or
(d) any person appearing to the court to have an interest.

(9) Where any person wishes to exercise the right to inspect the file under paragraph (3), (4), (5) or (6), that person—
(a) if the permission of the court is required, must file with the court an application notice in accordance with these Rules; or
(b) if the permission of the court is not required, may inspect the file at any reasonable time.

(10) Where any person wishes to exercise the right to obtain a copy of a document under paragraph (3), (4), (5) or (6), that person must pay any prescribed fee and—
(a) if the permission of the court is required, file with the court an application notice in accordance with these Rules; or
(b) if the permission of the court is not required, file with the court a written request for the document.

(11) An application for—
(a) permission to inspect the file or obtain a copy of a document under paragraph (6); or
(b) a direction under paragraph (7),
may be made without notice to any other party, but the court may direct that notice must be given to any person who would be affected by its decision.

(12) If for the purposes of powers conferred by the Regulations or the Rules, the Secretary of State makes a request to inspect or requests the transmission of the file of any insolvency proceedings, the court must comply with the request (unless the file is for the time being in use for the court's own purposes).

NOTES

Paras (3), (8): words in square brackets substituted for "FSA" by the Financial Services Act 2012 (Consequential Amendments and Transitional Provisions) Order 2013, SI 2013/472, art 3, Sch 2, para 210(c), (d)(xxi), subject to a transitional provision (see para 211 as noted to **[7.1718]**).

[7.1938]
228 Office copies of documents

(1) The court must provide an office copy of any document from the court file of the special administration to any person who has under the Rules the right to inspect the court file where that person has requested such a copy.

(2) A person's rights under this rule may be exercised on that person's behalf by that person's solicitor.

(3) An office copy provided by the court under this rule must be in such form as the registrar thinks appropriate, and must bear the court's seal.

[7.1939]
229 Payments into court

CPR Part 37 (miscellaneous provisions about payments into court) apply to money lodged in court under the Rules.

CHAPTER 3 OBTAINING INFORMATION AND EVIDENCE

[7.1940]
230 Further information and disclosure

(1) Any party to the special administration may apply to court for an order—
(a) that any other party—
(i) clarify any matter that is in dispute in the proceedings, or

(ii) give additional information in relation to any such matter,
in accordance with CPR Part 18 (further information); or

(b) to obtain disclosure from any other party in accordance with CPR Part 31 (disclosure and inspection of documents).

(2) An application under this rule may be made without notice being served on any other party.

(3) In a special administration (bank insolvency), before the Objective A committee has passed a full payment resolution, the court shall only grant an order on an application under paragraph (1)(b) if satisfied that the granting of the order is unlikely to prejudice the achievement of Objective A.

[7.1941]
231 Witness statements—general

(1) Subject to rule 233 where evidence is required by the Regulations or the Rules as to any matter, such evidence may be provided in the form of a witness statement unless—

(a) in any specific case a rule or the Regulations makes different provision; or
(b) the court otherwise directs.

(2) The court may, on the application of any party to the matter in question order the attendance for cross-examination of the person making the witness statement.

(3) Where, after such an order has been made, the person in question does not attend, that person's witness statement must not be used in evidence without the leave of the court.

[7.1942]
232 Filing and service of witness statements

Unless the provision of the Regulations or Rules under which the application is made provides otherwise, or the court otherwise allows—

(a) if the applicant intends to rely at the first hearing on evidence in a witness statement, the applicant must file that witness statement with the court and serve a copy of it on the respondent not less than 14 days before the date fixed for the hearing; and

(b) where the respondent to an application intends to oppose it and rely for that purpose on evidence contained in a witness statement, the respondent must file the witness statement with the court and serve a copy on the applicant not less than 5 business days before the date fixed for the hearing.

[7.1943]
233 Evidence provided by the administrator

(1) Where in the special administration a witness statement is made by the administrator, the witness statement must state—

(a) the capacity in which that person makes the statement; and
(b) the person's business address.

(2) The administrator may file a report with the court instead of a witness statement unless the application involves other parties or the court otherwise orders.

(3) In any case where a report is filed instead of a witness statement, the report must be treated for the purpose of rule 232 and any hearing before the court as if it were a witness statement.

(4) Where this rule applies in a special administration (bank insolvency) or a special administration (bank administration), a reference to the administrator in this rule shall, for the period when a person is appointed under rules 30 or 49 be read as a reference to that person.

CHAPTER 4 SERVICE OF COURT DOCUMENTS

[7.1944]
234 Application of Chapter

(1) Subject to paragraph (2), this Chapter applies in relation to the service of—

(a) applications;
(b) documents relating to applications; and
(c) court orders,

which are required to be served by any provision of the Regulations or the Rules ("court documents").

(2) For the purpose of the application by this Chapter of CPR Part 6 to the service of court documents, an application within the special administration against a respondent is to be treated as a claim form.

[7.1945]
235 Service of court documents within the jurisdiction

Except where different provision is made in the regulations or these rules, CPR Part 6 applies in relation to the service of court documents with such modifications as the court may direct.

[7.1946]
236 Service of court documents outside jurisdiction

CPR Part 6 applies to the service of court documents outside the jurisdiction with such modifications as the court may direct.

[7.1947]
237 Service of orders staying proceedings

Where the court makes an order staying any action, execution or other legal process against the property of the investment bank, service within the jurisdiction of the order may be effected by serving a sealed copy of the order on the address for service of the claimant or other party having the carriage of the proceedings to be stayed.

[7.1948]
238 Service on joint office-holders

Where there are joint administrators, service of court documents on one of them is to be treated as service on all of them.

CHAPTER 5 APPLICATIONS TO COURT—GENERAL

[7.1949]
239 Application of Chapter

This Chapter applies to any application made to the court under the Regulations or the Rules except—

(a) an application for a special administration order under regulation 5;
(b) an application for a special administration (bank insolvency) order under section 95 of the 2009 Act (as applied by paragraph 6 of Schedule 1 to the Regulations);
(c) an application for a special administration (bank administration) order under section 143 of the 2009 Act (as applied by paragraph 6 of Schedule 2 to the Regulations).

[7.1950]
240 Form and contents of application

(1) Each application must be in writing and must state—

(a) that the application is made under the Regulations;
(b) the names of the parties;
(c) the name of the investment bank which is the subject of the insolvency proceedings to which the application relates;
(d) that the proceedings are being held in the High Court and the court reference number;
(e) where the court has previously allocated a number to the insolvency proceedings within which the application is made, that number;
(f) the nature of the remedy or order applied for or the directions sought from the court;
(g) the names and addresses of the persons on whom it is intended to serve the application or that no person is intended to be served;
(h) where the Regulations or Rules require that notice of the application is to be given to specified persons, the names and addresses of all those persons (so far as known to the applicant); and
(i) the applicant's address for service.

(2) The application must be authenticated by the applicant if the applicant is acting in person or, when the applicant is not so acting, by or on behalf of the applicant's solicitor.

[7.1951]
241 Filing and service of application

(1) An application must be filed with the court accompanied by one copy and a number of additional copies equal to the number of persons who are to be served with the application.

(2) Where an application is filed with the court in accordance with paragraph (1), the court must fix a venue for the application to be heard unless—

(a) it considers it is not appropriate to do so;
(b) the rule under which the application is brought provides otherwise; or
(c) the case is one to which rule 243 applies.

(3) Unless the court otherwise directs, the applicant must serve a sealed copy of the application, endorsed with the venue for the hearing, on the respondent named in the application (or on each respondent, if more than one).

(4) The court may give any of the following directions—

(a) that the application be served upon persons other than those specified by the relevant provision of the Regulations or Rules;
(b) that the giving of notice to any person may be dispensed with;
(c) that the notice may be given in some way other than that specified in paragraph (3).

(5) An application must be served at least 14 days before the date fixed for its hearing unless—

(a) the provision of the Regulations or the Rules under which the application is made makes different provision; or
(b) the case is one of urgency, to which paragraph (6) applies.

(6) Where the case is one of urgency, the court may (without prejudice to its general power to extend or abridge time limits)—

(a) hear the application immediately, either with or without notice to, or the attendance of, other parties; or
(b) authorise a shorter period of service than that provided for by paragraph (5),

and any such application may be heard on terms providing for the filing or service of documents, or the carrying out of other formalities, as the court thinks just.

[7.1952]
242 Directions

The court may at any time give such directions as it thinks just as to—

(a) service or notice of the application on or to any person;
(b) whether particulars of claim and defence are to be delivered and generally as to the procedure on the application including whether a hearing is necessary; and
(c) the matters to be dealt with in evidence.

[7.1953]
243 Hearings without notice

Where the relevant provisions of the Regulations or the Rules do not require service of the application on, or notice of it to be given to, any person—

(a) the court may hear the application as soon as reasonably practicable without fixing a venue as required by rule 241(2); or
(b) it may fix a venue for the application to be heard in which case rule 241 must apply to the extent that it is relevant;

but nothing in those provisions is to be taken as prohibiting the applicant from giving such notice if the applicant wishes to do so.

[7.1954]
244 Hearing of application

(1) Unless the court otherwise directs, the hearing of an application must be in open court.

(2) In the High Court, the jurisdiction of the court to hear and determine an application may be exercised by the registrar (to whom the application must be made in the first instance) unless—

(a) a direction to the contrary has been given, or
(b) it is not within the registrar's power to make the order required.

(3) Where the application is made to the registrar in the High Court, the registrar may refer to the judge any matter which the registrar thinks should properly be decided by the judge, and the judge may either dispose of the matter or refer it back to the registrar with such directions as that judge thinks just.

(4) Nothing in this rule precludes an application being made directly to the judge in a proper case.

[7.1955]
245 Adjournment of the hearing of an application

(1) The court may adjourn the hearing of an application on such terms as it thinks just.

(2) The court may give directions as to the manner in which any evidence is to be adduced at a resumed hearing and in particular as to—

(a) the taking of evidence wholly or partly by witness statement or orally;
(b) the cross-examination of the maker of a witness statement; or
(c) any report to be made by the administrator.

CHAPTER 6 APPLICATIONS TO THE COURT UNDER SECTION 176A

[7.1956]
246 Application of Chapter

The rules in this Chapter apply to applications in connection with section 176A of the 1986 Act (share of assets for unsecured creditors).

[7.1957]
247 Applications under section 176A(5) to disapply section 176A

(1) An application under section 176A(5) must be accompanied by a witness statement by the administrator.

(2) The witness statement must state—

(a) that the investment bank is in special administration;
(b) a summary of the financial position of the investment bank; and
(c) the information substantiating the administrator's view that the cost of making a distribution to unsecured creditors would be disproportionate to the benefits.

[7.1958]
248 Notice of application under section 176A(5)

An application under section 176A(5) may be made without the application being served upon, or notice being given to any other party.

[7.1959]
249 Notice of an order under section 176A(5)

(1) Where the court makes an order under section 176A(5), it must as soon as reasonably practicable deliver 2 sealed copies of the order to the applicant.

(2) Where the court has made an order under section 176A(5), the administrator must as soon as reasonably practicable give notice to each creditor of whose address the administrator is aware.

(3) Paragraph (2) does not apply where the court directs otherwise.

(4) The court may direct that the requirement in paragraph (2) is complied with if a notice has been published by the administrator which, in addition to containing the standard contents, states that the court has made an order disapplying the requirement to set aside the prescribed part. As soon as reasonably practicable the notice—

(a) must be gazetted; and
(b) may be advertised in such other manner as the administrator thinks fit.

(5) The administrator must send a copy of the order to the registrar of companies as soon as reasonably practicable after the making of the order.

CHAPTER 7 APPLICATIONS FOR AN ORDER UNDER SECTION 236

[7.1960]
250 Application of following rules

(1) This chapter applies to applications to the court for an order under section 236 of the 1986 Act (inquiry into company dealings).

(2) In this Chapter, "the respondent" means the person in respect of whom an order is applied for.

[7.1961]
251 Form and contents of application

An application to which this chapter applies—

(a) must be in writing and specify the grounds on which it is made;
(b) must specify the name of the respondent;
(c) must state whether the application is for the respondent—
  (i) to be ordered to appear before the court,
  (ii) to be ordered to clarify any matter which is in dispute in the proceedings or to give additional information in relation to any such matter (in which case CPR Part 18 (further information) shall apply to any such order),
  (iii) to submit witness statements (if so, particulars must be given of the matters to be included),
  (iv) to produce books, papers or other records (if so, the items in question must be specified), or
  (v) for any two or more of those purposes; and
(d) may be made without notice to any other party.

[7.1962]
252 Order for examination etc

(1) The court may, whatever the purpose of the application, make any order which it has power to make under section 236.

(2) The court, if it orders the respondent to appear before it, must specify a venue for the respondent's appearance, which must not be less than 14 days from the date of the order.

(3) If the respondent is ordered to submit witness statements, the order must specify—

(a) the matters which are to be dealt with in the respondent's witness statements; and
(b) the time within which they are to be submitted to the court.

(4) If the order is to produce books, papers or other records, the time and manner of compliance must be specified.

(5) The order must be served as soon as reasonably practicable on the respondent.

[7.1963]
253 Procedure for examination

(1) At any examination of the respondent, the administrator may attend in person, or be represented by a solicitor with or without counsel, and may put such questions to the respondent as the court may allow.

(2) Unless the administrator objects, the following persons may attend the examination with the permission of the court and may put questions to the respondent (but only through the administrator)—

(a) any person who could have applied for an order under section 236; and
(b) any creditor or client who has provided information on which the application was made under that section.

(3) If the respondent is ordered to clarify any matter or to give additional information, the court must direct the respondent as to the questions which the respondent is required to answer, and as to whether the respondent's answers (if any) are to be made in a witness statement.

(4) The respondent may, at the respondent's own expense, employ a solicitor with or without counsel, who may put to the respondent such questions as the court may allow for the purpose of enabling the respondent to explain or qualify any answers given by the respondent, and may make representations on the respondent's behalf.

(5) Such written record of the examination must be made as the court thinks proper and such record must be read over either to or by the respondent and authenticated by the respondent at a venue fixed by the court.

(6) The written record may, in any proceedings (whether under the Regulations, Rules or otherwise), be used as evidence against the respondent of any statement made by the respondent in the course of the respondent's examination.

[7.1964]

254 Record of examination

(1) Unless the court otherwise directs, the written record of questions put to the respondent and the respondent's answers, and any witness statements submitted by the respondent in compliance with an order of the court under section 236, are not to be filed with the court.

(2) The documents set out in paragraph (3) are not open to inspection without an order of the court, by any person other than the administrator.

(3) The documents to which paragraph (2) applies are—
- (a) the written record of the respondent's examination;
- (b) copies of questions put to the respondent or proposed to be put to the respondent and answers to questions given by the respondent;
- (c) any witness statement by the respondent; and
- (d) any document on the court file as shows grounds for the application for the order.

(4) The court may from time to time give directions as to the custody and inspection of any documents to which this rule applies, and as to the furnishing of copies of, or extracts from, such documents.

[7.1965]

255 Costs of proceedings under section 236

(1) Where the court has ordered an examination of any person under section 236 and it appears to it that the examination was made necessary because information had been unjustifiably refused by the respondent, it may order that the costs of the examination be paid by the respondent.

(2) Where the court makes an order against a person under—
- (a) section 237(1) of the 1986 Act; or
- (b) section 237(2) of the 1986 Act,

the costs of the application for the order may be ordered by the court to be paid by the respondent.

(3) Subject to paragraphs (1) and (2), the administrator's costs must, unless the court otherwise orders, be paid as an expense of the special administration.

(4) A person summoned to attend for examination under this Chapter must be tendered a reasonable sum in respect of travelling expenses incurred in connection with that person's attendance but any other costs falling on that person are at the court's discretion.

CHAPTER 8 PEOPLE WHO LACK CAPACITY TO MANAGE THEIR AFFAIRS ETC

[7.1966]

256 Application of Chapter 8

(1) The rules in this Chapter apply where in a special administration it appears to the court that a person affected by the proceedings is someone who lacks capacity to manage and administer their property and affairs either—
- (a) by reason of lacking capacity within the meaning of the Mental Capacity Act 2005; or
- (b) due to a physical affliction or disability.

(2) The person concerned is referred to in this Chapter as "the incapacitated person".

[7.1967]

257 Appointment of another person to act

(1) The court may appoint such person as it thinks just to appear for, represent or act for the incapacitated person.

(2) The appointment may be made either generally or for the purpose of any particular application or proceeding, or for the exercise of particular rights or powers which the incapacitated person might have exercised but for that person's incapacity.

(3) The court may make the appointment either of its own motion or on application by—
- (a) a person who has been appointed by a court in the United Kingdom or elsewhere to manage the affairs of, or to represent, the incapacitated person;
- (b) any relative or friend of the incapacitated person who appears to the court to be a proper person to make the application; or
- (c) the administrator.

(4) Application under paragraph (3) may be made without notice to any other party; but the court may require such notice of the application as it thinks necessary to be given to the person alleged to be incapacitated, or any other person, and may adjourn the hearing of the application to enable the notice to be given.

[7.1968]

258 Witness statement in support of application

An application under rule 257(3) must be supported by a witness statement made by a registered medical practitioner as to the mental or physical condition of the incapacitated person.

[7.1969]

259 Service of notices following appointment

Any notice served on, or sent to, a person appointed under rule 257 has the same effect as if it had been served on, or given to, the incapacitated person.

CHAPTER 9 FORMAL DEFECTS

[7.1970]
260 Formal defects

No special administration proceedings shall be invalidated by any formal defect or by any irregularity; unless the court before which an objection is made considers that substantial injustice has been caused by the defect or irregularity, and that the injustice cannot be remedied by any order of the court.

CHAPTER 10 COSTS

[7.1971]
261 Application of Chapter 10

(1) This Chapter applies in relation to costs in connection with the special administration.

(2) In this Chapter, a reference to costs includes charges and expenses.

[7.1972]
262 Requirement to assess costs by the detailed procedure

(1) Where the costs of any person are payable as an expense out of the investment bank's estate the amount payable must be decided by detailed assessment unless agreed between the administrator and the person entitled to payment.

(2) Where the costs of any person are payable as an expense out of the client assets, the amount payable must be decided by detailed assessment unless agreed between a meeting of clients and the person entitled to payment.

(3) In the absence of such agreement as is mentioned in paragraph (1) or (2), the administrator—
- (a) may serve notice requiring that person to commence detailed assessment proceedings in accordance with CPR Part 47; and
- (b) must serve such notice where the creditors' committee resolves that the amount of the costs in either case must be decided by detailed assessment.

(4) Detailed assessment proceedings must be commenced in the High Court.

(5) Where the costs of any person employed by the administrator in the special administration are required to be decided by detailed assessment or fixed by order of the court, the administrator may make payments on account to such person in respect of those costs provided that person undertakes in writing—
- (a) to repay as soon as reasonably practicable any money which may, when detailed assessment is made, prove to have been overpaid; and
- (b) to pay interest on any such sum as is mentioned in sub-paragraph (a) at the rate specified in section 17 of the Judgments Act 1838 on the date payment was made and for the period beginning with the date of payment and ending with the date of repayment.

(6) In any proceedings before the court, the court may order costs to be decided by detailed assessment.

(7) Unless otherwise directed or authorised, the costs of the administrator are to be allowed on the standard basis for which provision is made in—
- (a) CPR rule 44.4 (basis of assessment); and
- (b) CPR rule 44.5 (factors to be taken into account when deciding the amount of costs).

[7.1973]
263 Procedure where detailed assessment is required

(1) Before making a detailed assessment of the costs of any person employed in the special administration by the administrator, the costs officer must require a certificate of employment, which must be endorsed on the bill and signed by the administrator.

(2) The certificate must include—
- (a) the name and address of the person employed;
- (b) details of the functions to be carried out under the employment; and
- (c) a note of any special terms of remuneration which have been agreed.

(3) Every person whose costs in the special administration are required to be decided by detailed assessment must, on being required in writing to do so by the administrator, commence detailed assessment proceedings in accordance with CPR Part 47 (procedure for detailed assessment of costs and default provisions).

(4) If that person does not commence detailed assessment proceedings within 3 months of the requirement under paragraph (3), or within such further time as the court, on application, may permit, the administrator may deal with the investment bank's estate without regard to any claim by that person, whose claim is forfeited by such failure to commence proceedings.

(5) Where in any such case such a claim lies additionally against the administrator in the administrator's personal capacity, that claim is also forfeited by such failure to commence proceedings.

[7.1974]
264 Costs of officers charged with execution of writs or other process

(1) This rule applies where an enforcement officer, or other officer charged with execution of the writ or other person—
- (a) is required under section 184(2) of the 1986 Act to deliver up goods or money; or

(b) has under section 184(3) of the 1986 Act deducted costs from the proceeds of an execution or money paid to that officer or that person (as the case may be).

(2) The administrator may require in writing that the amount of the enforcement officer's or other officer's bill of costs be decided by detailed assessment and where such a requirement is made, rule 263(4) applies.

(3) Where, in the case of a deduction of the kind mentioned in paragraph (1)(b), any amount deducted is disallowed at the conclusion of the detailed assessment proceedings, the enforcement officer must as soon as reasonably practicable pay a sum equal to that disallowed to the administrator for the benefit of the investment bank's estate.

[7.1975]
265 Costs paid otherwise than out of the investment bank's estate

Where the amount of costs is decided by detailed assessment under an order of the court directing that those costs are to be paid otherwise than out of the investment bank's estate or out of the client assets, the costs officer must note on the final costs certificate by whom, or the manner in which, the costs are to be paid.

[7.1976]
266 Award of costs against the administrator

Without prejudice to any provision of the Regulations or Rules by virtue of which the administrator is not in any event to be liable for costs and expenses, where the administrator is made a party to any proceedings on the application of another party to the proceedings, the administrator is not to be personally liable for the costs unless the court otherwise directs.

[7.1977]
267 Applications for costs

(1) This rule applies where a party to, or person affected by, any proceedings in the special administration applies to the court for an order allowing their costs, or part of them, incidental to the proceedings, and that application is not made at the time of the proceedings.

(2) The person concerned must serve a sealed copy of the application on the administrator.

(3) The administrator may appear on an application.

(4) No costs of or incidental to the application are to be allowed to the applicant unless the court is satisfied that the application could not have been made at the time of the proceedings.

(5) The court shall specify in the order whether such costs are to be paid out of the investment bank's estate or out of the client assets.

[7.1978]
268 Costs and expenses of witnesses

Except as directed by the court, no allowance as a witness in any examination or other proceedings before the court is to be made to an officer of the investment bank to which the proceedings relate.

[7.1979]
269 Final costs certificate

(1) A final costs certificate of the costs officer is final and conclusive as to all matters which have not been objected to in the manner provided for under the rules of the court.

(2) Where it is proved to the satisfaction of a costs officer that a final costs certificate has been lost or destroyed, the costs officer may issue a duplicate.

CHAPTER 11 ENFORCEMENT PROCEDURES

[7.1980]
270 Enforcement of court orders

(1) In a special administration, orders of the court may be enforced in the same manner as a judgment to the same effect.

[7.1981]
271 Orders enforcing compliance with the Rules

(1) The court may, on application by the administrator, make such orders as it thinks necessary for the enforcement of obligations falling on any person in accordance with—

(a) paragraph 47 (duty to submit statement of affairs); or
(b) section 235 of the 1986 Act (duty of various persons to co-operate with administrator).

(2) An order of the court under this rule may provide that all costs of and incidental to the application for it shall be borne by the person against whom the order is made.

[7.1982]
272 Warrants (general provisions)

(1) A warrant issued by the court under any provision of the Regulations shall be addressed to such officer of the High Court as the warrant specifies, or to any constable.

(2) The persons referred to in section 236(5) of the 1986 Act as the prescribed officer of the court are the tipstaff and the tipstaff's assistants of the court.

(3) In this Chapter, references to property include books, papers and records.

[7.1983]
273 Warrants under section 236

(1) When a person ('P') is arrested under a warrant issued under section 236 of the 1986 Act, the officer arresting P must as soon as reasonably practicable bring P before the court issuing the warrant in order that P may be examined.

(2) If P cannot immediately be brought up for examination, the officer must deliver P into the custody of the governor of the prison named in the warrant (or where that prison is not able to accommodate P, the governor of such other prison with appropriate facilities which is able to accommodate P), who must keep that person in custody and produce P before the court as it may from time to time direct.

(3) After arresting P, the officer must as soon as reasonably practicable report to the court the arrest or delivery into custody (as the case may be) of P and apply to the court to fix a venue for P's examination.

(4) The court shall appoint the earliest practicable time for the examination, and must—

(a) direct the governor of the prison to produce P for examination at the time and place appointed; and

(b) as soon as reasonably practicable give notice of the venue to the person who applied for the warrant.

(5) Any property in P's possession which may be seized must be—

(a) lodged with, or otherwise dealt with as instructed by, whoever is specified in the warrant as authorised to receive it, or

(b) kept by the officer seizing it pending the receipt of written orders from the court as to its disposal,

as may be directed by the court.

CHAPTER 12 APPEALS

[7.1984]
274 Application of Chapter 12

This Chapter applies in relation to decisions of the court under the Regulations or the Rules.

[7.1985]
275 Appeals and reviews of court orders

(1) The court may review, rescind or vary any order made by it in the exercise of its jurisdiction under the Regulations or the Rules.

(2) Appeals in special administration proceedings are to the Civil Division of the Court of Appeal from a decision of a single judge of the High Court.

[7.1986]
276 Procedure on appeal

(1) An appeal against a decision at first instance may only be brought with either the permission of the court which made the decision or the permission of the court which has jurisdiction to hear the appeal.

(2) An appellant must file an appellant's notice (within the meaning of CPR Part 52) within 21 days after the date of the decision of the court that the appellant wishes to appeal.

(3) The procedure set out in CPR Part 52 applies to any appeal to which this Chapter applies.

[7.1987]
277 Appeal against decision of the Secretary of State

An appeal under the Regulations against a decision of the Secretary of State must be brought within 28 days of the notification of the decision.

PART 10
PROHIBITED NAMES

[7.1988]
278 Preliminary

(1) The Rules in this Part—

(a) relate to the permission required under section 216 of the 1986 Act for a person to act as mentioned in section 216(3) in relation to an investment bank with a prohibited name;

(b) prescribe the cases excepted from that provision, that is to say, those in which a person to whom the section applies may so act without that permission.

[7.1989]
279 Application for permission under section 216(3)

(1) At least 14 days notice of any application for permission to act in any of the circumstances which would otherwise be prohibited by section 216(3) must be given by the applicant to the Secretary of State, who may—

(a) appear at the hearing of the application; and

(b) whether or not appearing at the hearing, make representations.

(2) When considering an application for permission under section 216, the court may call on the administrator, or any former administrator of the investment bank for a report of the circumstances in which that investment bank became insolvent and the extent (if any) of the applicant's apparent responsibility for its doing so.

[7.1990]

280 First excepted case

(1) This rule applies where—

(a) a person ("P") was within the period mentioned in section 216(1) a director, or shadow director, of an investment bank that has gone into special administration by virtue of Ground A in regulation 6 being satisfied; and

(b) P acts in all or any of the ways specified in section 216(3) in connection with, or for the purposes of, the carrying on (or proposed carrying on) of the whole or substantially the whole of the business of the investment bank where that business (or substantially the whole of it) is (or is to be) acquired from the investment bank under arrangements—

(i) made by the administrator, or

(ii) made before the investment bank entered into special administration by an office-holder acting in relation to it as supervisor of a voluntary arrangement under Part 1 of the 1986 Act or as a person appointed under rule 30 or 49.

(2) P will not be taken to have contravened section 216 if prior to P's acting in the circumstances set out in paragraph (1) a notice is, in accordance with the requirements of paragraph (3)—

(a) given by P to every creditor of the investment bank whose name and address—

(i) is known by P, or

(ii) is ascertainable by P on the making of such enquiries as are reasonable in the circumstances; and

(b) published in the Gazette.

(3) The notice referred to in paragraph (2)—

(a) may be given and published before the completion of the arrangements referred to in paragraph (1)(b) but must be given and published no later than 28 days after that completion; and

(b) must state—

(i) the name and registered number of the investment bank,

(ii) P's name,

(iii) that it is P's intention to act in all or any of the ways specified in section 216(3) in connection with, or for the purposes of, the carrying on of the whole or substantially the whole of the business of the investment bank, and

(iv) the prohibited name.

(4) Notice may in particular be given under this rule—

(a) prior to the investment bank entering special administration where the business (or substantially the whole of the business) is, or is to be, acquired by another company under arrangements made by an office-holder acting in relation to the investment bank as supervisor of a voluntary arrangement or as a person appointed under rule 30 or 49 (whether or not at the time of the giving of the notice P is a director of that other company); or

(b) at a time where P is a director of another company where—

(i) the other company has acquired, or is to acquire, the whole, or substantially the whole, of the business of the investment bank under arrangements made by the administrator, and

(ii) it is proposed that after the giving of the notice a prohibited name should be adopted by the other company.

[7.1991]

281 Second excepted case

(1) Where a person ("P") to whom section 216 applies as having been a director or shadow director of the investment bank in special administration applies for permission of the court under that section not later than 7 business days from the date on which the investment bank went into special administration, P may, during the period specified in paragraph (2) below, act in any of the ways mentioned in section 216(3), notwithstanding that P has not the permission of the court under that section.

(2) The period referred to in paragraph (1) begins with the day on which the investment bank goes into special administration and ends either on the day falling six weeks after that date or on the day on which the court disposes of the application for permission under section 216, whichever of those days occurs first.

[7.1992]

282 Third excepted case

The court's permission under section 216(3) is not required where the investment bank there referred to, though known by a prohibited name within the meaning of the section—

(a) has been known by that name for the whole of the period of 12 months ending with the day before the investment bank went into special administration; and

(b) has not at any time in those 12 months been dormant within the meaning of section 1169(1), (2) and (3)(a) of the 2006 Act.

PART 11
PROVISIONS OF GENERAL EFFECT

CHAPTER 1 MISCELLANEOUS AND GENERAL

[7.1993]
283 Costs, expenses etc

(1) All fees, costs, charges and other expenses incurred in the course of the special administration are, unless otherwise stated, to be regarded as expenses of the special administration.

(2) In a special administration (bank insolvency), paragraph (1) does not include any money paid by the FSCS to eligible depositors in pursuance of Objective A.

(3) The costs associated with the prescribed part shall be paid out of the prescribed part.

[7.1994]
284 Provable debts

(1) Subject as follows, all claims by creditors are provable as debts against the investment bank whether they are present or future, certain or contingent, ascertained or sounding only in damages.

(2) The following are not provable—

(a) any obligation arising under Parts 2, 3 or 4 of the Proceeds of Crime Act 2002;

(b) any claim arising by virtue of section 382(1)(a) of the Financial Services and Markets Act 2000, not being a claim also arising by virtue of section 382(1)(b) of that Act; or

(c) any claim which by virtue of the 1986 Act or any other enactment is a claim the payment of which in a special administration is to be postponed.

(3) Claims under paragraphs (2)(b) and (c) are not provable except at a time when all other claims of creditors in the special administration (other than any of a kind mentioned in this paragraph) have been paid in full with interest under rule 168.

(4) Nothing in this rule prejudices any enactment or rule of law under which a particular kind of debt is not provable, whether on grounds of public policy or otherwise.

[7.1995]
285 False claim of status as creditor, etc

(1) This rule applies where the Rules provide a right for—

(a) creditors;

(b) clients;

(c) members of the investment bank; or

(d) contributories,

to inspect any documents, whether on the court's file or in the hands of the administrator or other person.

(2) It is an offence for a person ('P'), with the intention of obtaining a sight of documents which P has not under the Rules any right to inspect, falsely to claim a status which would entitle P to inspect them.

(3) A person guilty of an offence under this rule is liable to imprisonment or a fine, or both.

[7.1996]
286 Punishment of offences

(1) The Schedule to these Rules has effect with respect to the way in which contraventions of the Rules are punishable on conviction.

(2) In relation to an offence under a provision of the Rules specified in the first column of the Schedule (the general nature of the offence being described in the second column), the third column shows whether the offence is punishable on conviction on indictment, or on summary conviction, or either in the one way or the other.

(3) The fourth column shows, in relation to an offence, the maximum punishment by way of fine or imprisonment which may be imposed on a person convicted of the offence in the way specified in relation to it in the third column (that is to say, on indictment or summarily), a reference to a period of years or months being to a term of imprisonment of that duration.

(4) The fifth column shows (in relation to an offence for which there is an entry in that column) that a person convicted of the offence after continued contravention is liable to a daily default fine; that is to say, that person is liable on a second or subsequent conviction of the offence to the fine specified in that column for each day on which the contravention is continued (instead of the penalty specified for the offence in the fourth column of the Schedule).

(5) Section 431 of the 1986 Act (summary proceedings), as it is applied by the Regulations, has effect in relation to offences under the Rules as to offences under the 1986 Act.

CHAPTER 2 THE GIVING OF NOTICE AND THE SUPPLY OF DOCUMENTS

[7.1997]
287 Application

(1) Subject to paragraphs (2) and (3), this Chapter applies where a notice or other document is required to be given, delivered or sent under the Regulations or the Rules by any person, including the administrator.

(2) This Chapter does not apply to the service of—

(a) any application to the court;

(b) any evidence in support of that application; or
(c) any order of the court.

(3) This Chapter does not apply to the submission of documents to the registrar of companies.

[7.1998]
288 Personal delivery

Personal delivery of a notice or other document is permissible in any case.

[7.1999]
289 Postal delivery of documents

Unless in any particular case some other form of delivery is required by the Regulations or the Rules or an order of the court, a notice or other document may be sent by post in accordance with the rules for postal service in CPR Part 6 and sending by such means has effect as specified in those rules.

[7.2000]
290 Notice etc to solicitors

Where under the Regulations or the Rules a notice or other document is required or authorised to be given, delivered or sent to a person, it may be given, delivered or sent instead to a solicitor authorised to accept delivery on that person's behalf.

CHAPTER 3 THE GIVING OF NOTICE AND THE SUPPLY OF DOCUMENTS TO OR BY THE ADMINISTRATOR

[7.2001]
291 Application

(1) Subject to paragraphs (2) and (3), this Chapter applies where a notice or other document is required to be given, delivered or sent under the Regulations or the Rules.

(2) This Chapter does not apply to the submission of documents to the registrar of companies.

(3) Rules 295 to 298 do not apply to the filing of any notice or other document with the court.

[7.2002]
292 The form

Subject to any order of the court, any notice or other document required to be given, delivered or sent must be in writing and where electronic delivery is permitted a notice or other document in electronic form is treated as being in writing if a copy of it is capable of being produced in a legible form.

[7.2003]
293 Proof of sending

(1) Where a notice or other document is required to be given, delivered or sent by the administrator, the giving, delivering or sending of it may be proved by means of a certificate that the notice or other document was duly given, delivered or sent.

(2) In the case of the administrator the certificate may be given by—
(a) the administrator;
(b) the administrator's solicitor;
(c) a partner or an employee of either of them.

(3) In the case of a notice or other document to be given, delivered or sent by a person other than the administrator, the giving, delivering or sending of it may be proved by means of a certificate by that person—
(a) that the notice or document was given, delivered or sent by that person; or
(b) that another person (named in the certificate) was instructed to give, deliver or send it.

(4) A certificate under this rule may be endorsed on a copy or specimen of the notice or document to which it relates.

[7.2004]
294 Authentication

(1) A document or information given, delivered or sent in hard copy form is sufficiently authenticated if it is signed by the person sending or supplying it.

(2) A document or information given, delivered or sent in electronic form is sufficiently authenticated—
(a) if the identity of the sender is confirmed in a manner specified by the recipient; or
(b) where no such manner has been specified by the recipient, if the communication contains or is accompanied by a statement of the identity of the sender and the recipient has no reason to doubt the truth of that statement.

[7.2005]
295 Electronic delivery – general

(1) Unless in any particular case some other form of delivery is required by the Regulations or the Rules or an order of the court and subject to paragraph (3), a notice or other document may be given, delivered or sent by electronic means provided that the intended recipient of the notice or other document has—
(a) consented (whether in the specific case or generally) to electronic delivery (and has not revoked that consent); and

(b) provided an electronic address for delivery.

(2) In the absence of evidence to the contrary, a notice or other document is presumed to have been delivered where—

(a) the sender can produce a copy of the electronic message which—

(i) contained the notice or other document, or to which the notice or other document was attached, and

(ii) shows the time and date the message was sent; and

(b) that electronic message contains the address supplied under paragraph (1)(b).

(3) A message sent electronically is deemed to have been delivered to the recipient no later than 9.00am on the next business day after it was sent.

(4) Paragraph (3) does not apply in respect of documents sent electronically under Part 2.

[7.2006]
296 Electronic delivery by administrator

(1) Where the administrator gives, sends or delivers a notice or other document to any person by electronic means, the notice or document must contain or be accompanied by a statement that the recipient may request a hard copy of the notice or document and specifying a telephone number, e-mail address and postal address which may be used to request a hard copy.

(2) Where a hard copy of the notice or other document is requested, it must be sent within 5 business days of receipt of the request by the administrator.

(3) The administrator must not require a person making a request under paragraph (2) to pay a fee for the supply of the document.

[7.2007]
297 Use of websites by administrator

(1) This rule applies for the purposes of section 246B.

(2) Where the administrator is required to give, deliver or send a document to any person (other than in a case where personal service is required), the administrator may satisfy that requirement by sending that person a notice—

(a) stating that the document is available for viewing and downloading on a website;

(b) specifying the address of that website together with any password necessary to view and download the document from that site; and

(c) containing a statement that the person to whom the notice is given, delivered or sent may request a hard copy of the document and specifying a telephone number, e-mail address and postal address which may be used to request a hard copy.

(3) Where a notice to which this rule applies is sent, the document to which it relates must—

(a) be available on the website for a period of not less than 3 months after the date on which the notice is sent; and

(b) must be in such a format as to enable it to be downloaded from the website within a reasonable time of an electronic request being made for it to be downloaded.

(4) Where a hard copy of the document is requested it must be sent within 5 business days of the receipt of the request by the administrator.

(5) The administrator must not require a person making a request under paragraph (4) to pay a fee for the supply of the document.

(6) Where a document is given, delivered or sent to a person by means of a website in accordance with this rule, it is deemed to have been delivered—

(a) when the document was first made available on the website, or

(b) if later, when the notice under paragraph (2) was delivered to that person.

[7.2008]
298 Special provision on account of expense as to website use

(1) Where the court is satisfied that the expense of sending notices in accordance with rule 292 would, on account of the number of persons entitled to receive them, be disproportionate to the benefit of sending notices in accordance with that rule, it may order that the requirement to give, deliver or send a relevant document to any person may (other than in a case where personal service is required) be satisfied by the administrator sending each of those persons a notice—

(a) stating that all relevant documents will be made available for viewing and downloading on a website;

(b) specifying the address of that website together with any password necessary to view and download a relevant document from that site; and

(c) containing a statement that the person to whom the notice is given, delivered or sent may at any time request that hard copies of all, or specific, relevant documents are sent to that person, and specifying a telephone number, e-mail address and postal address which may be used to make that request.

(2) A document to which this rule relates must—

(a) be available on the website for a period of not less than 12 months from the date when it was first made available on the website or, if later, from the date upon which the notice was sent; and

(b) must be in such a format as to enable it to be downloaded from the website within a reasonable time of an electronic request being made for it to be downloaded.

(3) Where hard copies of relevant documents have been requested, they must be sent by the administrator—

(a) within 5 business days of the receipt by the administrator of the request to be sent hard copies, in the case of relevant documents first appearing on the website before the request was received, or

(b) within 5 business days from the date a relevant document first appears on the website, in all other cases.

(4) The administrator must not require a person making a request under paragraph (3) to pay a fee for the supply of the document.

(5) Where a relevant document is given, delivered or sent to a person by means of a website in accordance with this rule, it is deemed to have been delivered—

(a) when the relevant document was first made available on the website, or

(b) if later, when the notice under paragraph (1) was delivered to that person.

(6) In this rule, a relevant document means any document which the administrator is first required to give, deliver or send to any person after the court has made an order under paragraph (1).

[7.2009]
299 Electronic delivery of special administration documents to court

(1) Except where paragraph (2) applies or the requirements of paragraph (3) are met, no application, notice or other document may be delivered or made to a court by electronic means.

(2) This paragraph applies where electronic delivery of documents to a court is permitted by another rule.

(3) The requirements of this paragraph are—

(a) the court provides an electronic working scheme for the proceedings to which the document relates; and

(b) the electronic communication is—

(i) delivered and authenticated in a form which complies with the requirements of the scheme;

(ii) sent to the electronic address provided by the court for electronic delivery of those proceedings; and

(iii) accompanied by any payment due to the court in respect of those proceedings made in a manner which complies with the requirements of the scheme.

(4) In this rule "an electronic working scheme" means a scheme set out in a practice direction permitting insolvency proceedings to be delivered electronically to the court.

(5) Under paragraph (3) an electronic communication is to be treated as delivered to the court at the time it is recorded by the court as having been received.

[7.2010]
300 Notice etc to joint administrators

Where there are joint office-holders in a special administration, delivery of a document to one of them is to be treated as delivery to all of them.

[7.2011]
301 Execution overtaken by judgment debtor's insolvency

(1) This rule applies where execution has been taken out against property of a judgment debtor, and notice is given to the enforcement officer or other officer charged with the execution that the judgment debtor has entered special administration.

(2) Subject to rule 302, the notice must be delivered to the office of the enforcement officer or of the officer charged with the execution—

(a) by hand, or

(b) by any other means of delivery which enables proof of receipt of the document at the relevant address.

[7.2012]
302 Notice to enforcement officers

(1) This rule applies in relation to any provision of the Regulations or the Rules which makes provision for the giving of notice to an enforcement officer.

(2) Any such notice as is mentioned in paragraph (1) may be given by electronic means to any person who has been authorised to receive such notice on behalf of a specified enforcement officer or on behalf of enforcement officers generally.

[7.2013]
303 Electronic submission of information

(1) This rule applies in any case where prescribed information is required by the Rules to be sent by any person to the Secretary of State, the Chief Land Registrar or the administrator.

(2) A requirement of the kind mentioned in paragraph (1) is treated as having been satisfied where—

(a) the information is submitted electronically with the agreement of the person to whom the information is sent;

(b) the form in which the electronic submission is made satisfies the requirements of the person to whom the information is sent;

(c) that all the prescribed information is provided in the electronic submission; and
(d) the person to whom the information is sent can provide in legible form the information so submitted.

(3) Where prescribed information is permitted to be sent electronically under paragraph (2), any requirement that the information be accompanied by a signature is taken to be satisfied—
(a) if the identity of the person who is supplying the information and whose signature is required is confirmed in a manner specified by the recipient; or
(b) where no such manner has been specified by the recipient, if the communication contains or is accompanied by a statement of the identity of the person who is providing the information, and the recipient has no reason to doubt the truth of that statement.

(4) Where prescribed information has been supplied to a person, whether or not it has been supplied electronically in accordance with paragraph (2), and a copy of that information is required to be supplied to another person falling within paragraph (1), the requirements contained in paragraph (2) apply in respect of the supply of the copy to that other person, as they apply in respect of the original.

[7.2014]
304 Electronic submission of information where rule 303 does not apply

(1) This rule applies in any case where rule 303 does not apply, where prescribed information is required by the Rules to be sent by any person.

(2) A requirement of the kind mentioned in paragraph (1) is treated as having been satisfied where—
(a) the person to whom the information is sent has agreed—
(i) to receiving the information electronically and to the form in which it is to be sent, and
(ii) to the specified manner in which paragraph (3) is to be satisfied;
(b) all the prescribed information required is provided in the electronic submission; and
(c) the person to whom the information is sent can provide in legible form the information so submitted.

(3) Any requirement that the information be accompanied by a signature is taken to be satisfied if the identity of the person who is supplying the information and whose signature is required, is confirmed in the specified manner.

(4) Where prescribed information has been supplied to a person, whether or not it has been supplied electronically in accordance with paragraph (2), and a copy of that information is required to be supplied to another person falling within paragraph (1), the requirements contained in paragraph (2) apply in respect of the supply of the copy to that other person, as they apply in respect of the original.

[7.2015]
305 Contents of notices to be gazetted

(1) Where under the Regulations or the Rules a notice is gazetted, in addition to any content specifically required by the Regulations or any other provision of the Rules, the content of such a notice must be as set out in this Chapter.

(2) All notices published must specify insofar as it is applicable in relation to the particular notice—
(a) a statement that the proceedings are being held in the High Court and the court reference number;
(b) the name, postal address and date of appointment of the administrator;
(c) either an e-mail address, or a telephone number, through which the administrator may be contacted;
(d) the name of any person other than the administrator (if any) who may be contacted regarding the proceedings; and
(e) the number assigned to the office-holder by the Secretary of State.

[7.2016]
306 Gazette notices relating to companies

In addition to the information required by rule 305 a notice relating to an investment bank that is a company must specify—
(a) the registered name of the company;
(b) its registered number;
(c) its registered office;
(d) any principal trading address if this is different from its registered office;
(e) any name under which it was registered in the 12 months prior to the date the investment bank entered special administration; and
(f) any name or style (other than its registered name) under which—
(i) the investment bank carried on business;
(ii) the investment bank undertook to hold an asset on behalf of a client, or
(iii) any debt owed to a creditor was incurred.

[7.2017]
307 Omission of unobtainable information

Information required under this Chapter to be included in a notice to be gazetted may be omitted if it is not reasonably practicable to obtain it.

[7.2018]
308 The Gazette—general

(1) A copy of the Gazette containing any notice required by the Regulations or the Rules to be gazetted is evidence of any facts stated in the notice.

(2) In the case of an order of the court notice of which is required by the Regulations or the Rules to be gazetted, a copy of the Gazette containing the notice may in any proceedings be produced as conclusive evidence that the order was made on the date specified in the notice.

(3) Where an order of the court which is gazetted has been varied, and where any matter has been erroneously or inaccurately gazetted, the person whose responsibility it was to procure the requisite entry in the Gazette must as soon as is reasonably practicable cause the variation of the order to be gazetted or a further entry to be made in the Gazette for the purpose of correcting the error or inaccuracy.

[7.2019]
309 Notices otherwise advertised under the Regulations or Rules

(1) Where under the Regulations or the Rules a notice may be advertised otherwise than in the Gazette, in addition to any content specifically required by the Regulations or any other provision of the Rules, the content of such a notice must be as set out in this Chapter.

(2) All notices published must specify insofar as it is applicable in relation to the particular notice—

(a) the name and postal business address of the administrator acting in the special administration to which the notice relates; and

(b) either an e-mail address, or a telephone number, through which the administrator may be contacted.

[7.2020]
310 Non-Gazette notices

In addition to the information required by rule 309, a notice relating to an investment bank must state—

(a) the registered name of the investment bank;

(b) its registered number;

(c) any name under which it was registered in the 12 months prior to the date the investment bank entered special administration; and

(d) any name or style (other than its registered name) under which—

(i) the investment bank carried on business,

(ii) any asset was given to the investment bank to be held for a client, or

(iii) any debt owed to a creditor was incurred.

[7.2021]
311 Non-Gazette notices—other provisions

(1) The information required to be contained in a notice to which rules 309 and 310 apply must be included in the advertisement of that notice in a manner that is reasonably likely to ensure, in relation to the form of the advertising used, that a person reading, hearing or seeing the advertisement, will be able to read, hear or see that information.

(2) Information required under this Chapter to be included in a notice may be omitted if it is not reasonably practicable to obtain it.

CHAPTER 4 NOTIFICATIONS TO THE REGISTRAR OF COMPANIES

[7.2022]
312 Application of Chapter 4

This Chapter applies where under the Regulations or the Rules information is to be sent or delivered to the registrar of companies.

[7.2023]
313 Information to be contained in all notifications to the registrar

Where under the Regulations or the Rules a return, notice, or any other document or information is to be sent to the registrar of companies, that notification must specify—

(a) the registered name of the investment bank;

(b) its registered number;

(c) the nature of the notification;

(d) the regulation or the rule under which the notification is made;

(e) the date of the notification;

(f) the name and postal address of person making the notification;

(g) the capacity in which that person is acting in respect of the investment bank; and

the notification must be authenticated by the person making the notification.

[7.2024]
314 Notification relating to the administrator

In addition to the information required by rule 313, a notification relating to the office of the administrator must also specify—

(a) the name and business address of the administrator;

(b) the date of the event notified;

(c) where the notification relates to an appointment, the person, body or court making the appointment; and
(d) where the notification relates to the termination of an appointment, the reason for that termination (for example, resignation).

[7.2025]
315 Notifications relating to documents

In addition to the information required by rule 313, a notification relating to a document (for example, a statement of affairs) must also specify—
(a) the nature of the document; and
(b) the date of the document; or
(c) where the document relates to a period of time (for example a report) the period of time to which the document relates.

[7.2026]
316 Notifications relating to court orders

In addition to the information required by rule 313, a notification relating to a court order must also specify—
(a) the nature of the court order; and
(b) the date of the order.

[7.2027]
317 Notifications relating to other events

In addition to the information required by rule 313, a notification relating to any other event (for example the coming into force of a moratorium) must specify—
(a) the nature of the event including the regulation or rule under which it took place; and
(b) the date the event occurred.

[7.2028]
318 Notifications of more than one nature

A notification which includes a notification of more than one nature must satisfy the requirements applying in respect of each of those notifications.

[7.2029]
319 Notifications made to other persons at the same time

(1) Where under the Regulations or the Rules a notice or other document is to be sent to another person at the same time that it is to be sent to the registrar of companies, that requirement may be satisfied by sending to that other person a copy of the notification sent to the registrar.

(2) Paragraph (1) does not apply—
(a) where additional information is prescribed for the notification to the other person; or
(b) where the notification to the registrar of companies is incomplete.

CHAPTER 5 FURTHER PROVISIONS CONCERNING DOCUMENTS

[7.2030]
320 Confidentiality of documents—grounds for refusing inspection

(1) Where the administrator considers that a document forming part of the records of the special administration—
(a) should be treated as confidential, or
(b) is of such a nature that its disclosure would be prejudicial to the conduct of the special administration or might reasonably be expected to lead to violence against any person,

the administrator may decline to allow it to be inspected by a person who would otherwise be entitled to inspect it.

(2) The persons to whom the administrator may under this rule refuse inspection include members of the Objective A committee or the creditors' committee.

(3) Where under this rule the administrator determines to refuse inspection of a document, the person wishing to inspect it may apply to the court for that determination to be overruled and the court may either overrule it altogether or sustain it subject to such conditions (if any) as it thinks just.

[7.2031]
321 Right to copy documents

(1) Where the Regulations or the Rules confer a right for any person to inspect documents, the right includes that of taking copies of those documents, on payment—
(a) in the case of documents on the court's file of proceedings, of the fee chargeable under any order made under section 92 of the Courts Act 2003; and
(b) in any other case, of the appropriate fee.

[7.2032]
322 Charges for copy documents

Except where prohibited by the Rules, the administrator is entitled to require the payment of the appropriate fee for the supply of documents requested by a creditor, client, member, contributory or member of the creditors' committee.

[7.2033]
323 Right to have list of creditors

(1) A creditor has the right to require the administrator to provide a list of the creditors and the amounts of their respective debts unless paragraph (5) applies.

(2) The administrator on being required to furnish the list under paragraph (1)—

(a) as soon as reasonably practicable must send it to the person requiring the list to be furnished; and

(b) may charge the appropriate fee for doing so.

(3) The name and address of any creditor may be omitted from the list furnished under paragraph (2) where the administrator is of the view that its disclosure would be prejudicial to the conduct of the proceedings or might reasonably be expected to lead to violence against any person provided that—

(a) the amount of the debt in question is shown in the list; and

(b) a statement is included in the list that the name and address of the creditor has been omitted in respect of that debt.

(4) In a special administration (bank insolvency) or a special administration (bank administration), the list of creditors provided under paragraph (1) shall, in respect of creditors who are depositors, omit the names and addresses of individual depositors and shall contain a single statement of their aggregate debt.

(5) Paragraph (1) does not apply where a statement of affairs has been delivered to the registrar of companies.

CHAPTER 6 TIME LIMITS AND SECURITY

[7.2034]
324 Time limits

(1) The provisions of CPR rule 2.8 (time) apply, as regards computation of time, to anything required or authorised to be done by the Rules.

(2) The provisions of CPR rule 3.1(2)(a) (the court's general powers of management) apply so as to enable the court to extend or shorten the time for compliance with anything required or authorised to be done by the Rules.

[7.2035]
325 Administrator's security

(1) Wherever under the Rules any person has to appoint, or certify the appointment of an administrator, that person must, before making or certifying the appointment, be satisfied that the person appointed or to be appointed has security for the proper performance of that office.

(2) It is the duty of the creditors' committee to review from time to time the adequacy of the administrator's security.

(3) In a special administration (bank insolvency), before the Objective A committee have passed a full payment resolution, that committee shall have the duty in paragraph (2).

(4) In a special administration (bank administration), before the Bank of England has given a Objective A Achievement Notice, the Bank of England shall have that duty.

(5) The cost of the administrator's security shall be defrayed as an expense of the proceedings.

CHAPTER 7 TRANSFER OF PROCEEDINGS

[7.2036]
326 Proceedings commenced in the wrong court

Where a special administration is commenced in a court other than the High Court, that court may order the transfer of the proceedings to the High Court.

[7.2037]
327 Proceedings other than special administration commenced

(1) Where—

(a) a winding up order or an administration order has been made in respect of an investment bank; or

(b) a resolution has been made for the winding up of or for the appointment of an administrator of an investment bank,

the Authority may apply to the court to order that the proceedings be converted to a special administration, a special administration (bank insolvency) or a special administration (bank administration) as the case may be.

(2) In making an order under paragraph (1) the court shall give such directions as it sees fit, including directions as to the former officer-holder's remuneration and expenses.

(3) An application under paragraph (1) may be made without notice.

(4) Without prejudice to the generality of the court's power in paragraph (2), where the person ("P") appointed as office-holder under the original proceedings is not the same person as the administrator of the special administration, the court may direct that—

(a) P be sent a copy of the order under paragraph (1) by the administrator;

(b) P hand over—

(i) the records of the original proceedings, including correspondence, proofs and other related papers appertaining to those proceedings while they were within P's responsibility; and

(ii) the investment bank's books, papers and other records; and

(c) P hand over all the assets of the investment bank and the client assets held by the investment bank in P's possession.

(5) In this rule—

["the Authority" means—

(a) where the investment bank is a deposit-taker and the application under paragraph (1) is for an order to convert the proceedings to—

(i) a special administration (bank administration), the Bank of England;

(ii) a special administration (bank insolvency)—

(aa) if the investment bank is a PRA-authorised person, the Bank of England or the PRA (with the consent of the Bank of England);

(bb) in any other case, the Bank of England or the FCA (with the consent of the Bank of England);

(b) otherwise, the FCA or the PRA;]

"office-holder" means provisional liquidator, liquidator or administrator as the case may be; and

"original proceedings" means the proceedings following the making of the winding up order, the administration order or the resolution referred to in paragraph (1).

NOTES

Para (5): definition "the Authority" substituted by the Financial Services Act 2012 (Consequential Amendments and Transitional Provisions) Order 2013, SI 2013/472, art 3, Sch 2, para 210(x), subject to a transitional provision (see para 211 as noted to **[7.1718]**). Definition "the Authority" originally read as follows:

""the Authority" means—

(a) where the investment bank is a deposit-taker and the application under paragraph (1) is for an order to convert the proceedings to—

(i) a special administration (bank administration), the Bank of England; or

(ii) a special administration (bank insolvency), the Bank of England or the FSA (with the consent of the Bank of England); and

(b) otherwise, the FSA;".

PART 12
GENERAL INTERPRETATION AND APPLICATION

[7.2038]
328 Introduction

This Part of the Rules has effect for their interpretation and application; and any definition given in this Part applies except, and in so far as, the context otherwise requires.

[7.2039]
329 "The court"; "the registrar"

(1) Anything to be done under or by virtue of the Regulations or the Rules by, to or before the court may be done by, to or before a judge or the registrar.

(2) The registrar may authorise any act of a formal or administrative character which is not by statute the registrar's responsibility to be carried out by the chief clerk or any other officer of the court acting on the registrar's behalf, in accordance with directions given by the Lord Chancellor.

(3) "The registrar" means [an Insolvency and Companies Court Judge].

NOTES

Para (3): words in square brackets substituted by the Alteration of Judicial Titles (Registrar in Bankruptcy of the High Court) Order 2018, SI 2018/130, art 3, Schedule, para 12(1)(g).

[7.2040]
330 Venue

References to the "venue" for any proceeding or attendance before the court, or for a meeting, are to the time, date and place for the proceeding, attendance or meeting or to the time and date for a meeting which is held in accordance with section 246A without any place being specified for it.

[7.2041]
331 Insolvent estate

References to "the insolvent estate" are, in relation to a special administration, the investment bank's assets.

[7.2042]
332 The appropriate fee

"The appropriate fee" means 15 pence per A4 or A5 page, and 30 pence per A3 page.

[7.2043]
333 "Debt"; "liability"

(1) "Debt", in relation to the special administration means (subject to the next paragraph) any of the following—

(a) any debt or liability to which the investment bank is subject on the date when the investment bank entered special administration;
(b) any debt or liability to which the investment bank may become subject after that date by reason of any obligation incurred before that date; and
(c) any interest provable as mentioned in rule 168.

(2) In paragraph (1)(a), the reference to debt or liability includes a debt incurred by the investment bank as a result of the operation of rules 137 and 146 even if the debt is incurred after the date on which the investment bank entered special administration.

(3) For the purposes of any provision of the Regulations or the Rules, any liability in tort is a debt provable in the special administration, if either—

(a) the cause of action has accrued at the date on which the investment bank went into special administration; or
(b) all the elements necessary to establish the cause of action exist at that date except for actionable damage.

(4) For the purposes of references in any provision of the Regulations or the Rules to a debt or liability, it is immaterial whether the debt or liability is present or future, whether it is certain or contingent, or whether its amount is fixed or liquidated, or is capable of being ascertained by fixed rules or as a matter of opinion; and references in any such provision to owing a debt are to be read accordingly.

(5) In any provision of the Regulations or the Rules, except in so far as the context otherwise requires, "liability" means (subject to paragraph (4)) a liability to pay money or money's worth, including any liability under an enactment, any liability for breach of trust, any liability in contract, tort or bailment, and any liability arising out of an obligation to make restitution.

[7.2044]
334 Application of the 1986 Act and the Company Directors Disqualification Act

For the purposes of these Rules, any reference in the 1986 Act or the Company Directors Disqualification Act 1986 to "leave" of the court is to be construed as meaning "permission" of the court.

SCHEDULE
PUNISHMENT OF OFFENCES

Rule 286

[7.2045]

Note: In the fourth and fifth columns of this Schedule, "the statutory maximum" means the prescribed sum under section 32 of the Magistrates' Courts Act 1980.

Rule creating offence	*General nature of offence*	*Mode of prosecution*	*Punishment*	*Daily default fine (where applicable)*
Rule 123	Administrator failing to send a progress report	Summary	Level 3 on the standard scale	One-tenth of level 3 on the standard scale
Rule 219	Failure to comply with administrator's duties on vacating office	Summary	Level 3 on the standard scale	One-tenth of level 3 on the standard scale
Rule 285	False representation of status for purpose of inspecting documents	1 On indictment 2 Summary	2 years imprisonment or a fine, or both 6 months imprisonment or the statutory maximum, or both	

INVESTMENT BANK (AMENDMENT OF DEFINITION) AND SPECIAL ADMINISTRATION (AMENDMENT) REGULATIONS 2017

(SI 2017/443)

NOTES

Made: 16 March 2017.
Authority: Banking Act 2009, ss 232(6)(a), (d), 233, 234, 259(1).
Commencement: 6 April 2017.

PART 1
INTRODUCTORY PROVISION

[7.2046]

1 Citation and commencement

These Regulations may be cited as the Investment Bank (Amendment of Definition) and Special Administration (Amendment) Regulations 2017, and come into force on the 21st day after the day on which they are made.

NOTES

Commencement: 6 April 2017.

PART 2
DEFINITION OF "INVESTMENT BANK"

[7.2047]

2 Amendment of definition

(1) An institution of a class specified in paragraph (2) is to be treated as an investment bank for the purpose of sections 232 to 236 of the Banking Act 2009.

(2) This paragraph specifies the following classes of institution—

(a) an institution which has permission under Part 4A of the Financial Services and Markets Act 2000 to carry on the activity specified by article 51ZA of the Financial Services and Markets Act 2000 (Regulated Activities) Order 2001 (managing a UCITS) or article 51ZC of that Order (managing an AIF); and

(b) an institution which has permission under Part 4A of that Act to carry on the regulated activity specified by article 51ZB of that Order (acting as trustee or depositary of a UCITS) or article 51ZD of that Order (acting as trustee or depositary of an AIF).

NOTES

Commencement: 6 April 2017.

3 (*Amends the Banking Act 2009, s 232 at* **[7.1653]**.)

PART 3
INVESTMENT BANK INSOLVENCY REGULATIONS

4–16 (*Regs 4–16 amend the Investment Bank Special Administration Regulations 2011, SI 2011/245 at* **[7.1661]**.)

PART 4
TRANSITIONAL PROVISIONS

[7.2048]

17 Transitional provision for Part 3

(1) Part 3 of these Regulations does not have effect in relation to an investment bank which is in special administration on the date on which these Regulations come into force.

(2) For the purpose of this regulation an investment bank is in special administration on that date if the appointment of the administrator took effect before that date under—

(a) a special administration order made under regulation 7 of the Investment Bank Special Administration Regulations 2011 ("the principal Regulations");

(b) a special administration (bank insolvency) order made under section 97(1) of the Banking Act 2009 (as applied by paragraph 6 of Schedule 1 to the principal Regulations); or

(c) a special administration (bank administration) order made under section 144 of the Banking Act 2009 (as applied by paragraph 6 of Schedule 2 to the principal Regulations).

(3) Where paragraph (2)(b) or (c) applies to an investment bank which is a partnership, paragraph 6 of Schedule 1 to the principal Regulations or paragraph 6 of Schedule 2 to those Regulations (as the case may be) must be read with paragraph 3(a) of Schedule 4 to those Regulations.

NOTES

Commencement: 6 April 2017.

N
OPEN-ENDED INVESTMENT COMPANIES

FINANCIAL SERVICES AND MARKETS ACT 2000

(2000 c 8)

An Act to make provision about the regulation of financial services and markets; to provide for the transfer of certain statutory functions relating to building societies, friendly societies, industrial and provident societies and certain other mutual societies; and for connected purposes

[14 June 2000]

NOTES

Only the section of this Act relevant to open-ended investment companies is reproduced here.

PART XVII
COLLECTIVE INVESTMENT SCHEMES

CHAPTER IV OPEN-ENDED INVESTMENT COMPANIES

[7.2049]

262 Open-ended investment companies

(1) The Treasury may by regulations make provision for—

(a) facilitating the carrying on of collective investment by means of open-ended investment companies;

(b) regulating such companies.

(2) The regulations may, in particular, make provision—

(a)–(g) *(outside the scope of this work.)*

(h) as to the winding up and dissolution of such a body;

(i)–(l) *(outside the scope of this work.)*

(3)–(5) *(Outside the scope of this work.)*

NOTES

Regulations: the Open-Ended Investment Companies Regulations 2001, SI 2001/1228 at **[7.2050]**; the Undertakings for Collective Investment in Transferable Securities Regulations 2011, SI 2011/1613; the Alternative Investment Fund Managers Regulations 2013, SI 2013/1773.

OPEN-ENDED INVESTMENT COMPANIES REGULATIONS 2001

(SI 2001/1228)

NOTES

Made: 27 March 2001.
Authority: Financial Services and Markets Act 2000, ss 262, 428(3).
Commencement: see art 1(2).

ARRANGEMENT OF REGULATIONS

PART I
GENERAL

1 Citation, commencement and extent .... [7.2050]
2 Interpretation .... [7.2051]

PART II
FORMATION, SUPERVISION AND CONTROL

31 Winding up by the court .... [7.2052]
32 Dissolution on winding up by the court .... [7.2053]
33 Dissolution in other circumstances .... [7.2054]
33A Winding up of a master UCITS .... [7.2055]
33B Merger or division of a master UCITS .... [7.2056]
33C Winding up of sub-funds .... [7.2057]

PART I
GENERAL

[7.2050]

1 Citation, commencement and extent

(1) These Regulations may be cited as the Open-Ended Investment Companies Regulations 2001.

(2) These Regulations come into force—

(a) for the purpose of regulation 6, on the day on which sections 247 and 248 of the Act come into force for the purpose of making rules;

(b) for the purposes of regulations 7, 12, 13, 18(1) and (3), 74, 77 and 80 to 82, so far as relating to the making of applications for authorisation orders to be made on or after the day mentioned in sub-paragraph (c), on the day on which section 40 of the Act comes into force;

(c) for all remaining purposes, on the day on which section 19 of the Act comes into force.

[(3) Except as otherwise provided, these Regulations extend to the whole of the United Kingdom.]

NOTES

Para (3): substituted by the Companies Act 2006 (Consequential Amendments and Transitional Provisions) Order 2011, SI 2011/1265, art 15, Sch 2, paras 1, 2.

[7.2051]

2 Interpretation

(1) In these Regulations, except where the context otherwise requires—

"the Act" means the Financial Services and Markets Act 2000;

. . .

"the 1986 Act" means the Insolvency Act 1986;

["the 1989 Order" means the Insolvency (Northern Ireland) Order 1989;

"the 2006 Act" means the Companies Act 2006;]

"annual general meeting" has the meaning given in regulation 37(1);

"annual report" has the meaning given in regulation 66(1)(a);

"the appropriate registrar" means—

(a) the registrar of companies for England and Wales if the company's instrument of incorporation states that its head office is to be situated in England and Wales, or that it is to be situated in Wales;

(b) the registrar of companies for Scotland if the company's instrument of incorporation states that its head office is to be situated in Scotland;

[(c) the registrar of companies for Northern Ireland if the company's instrument of incorporation states that its head office is to be situated in Northern Ireland;]

"authorisation order" means an order made by the Authority under regulation 14;

["the Authority" means the FCA;]

"bearer shares" has the meaning given in regulation 48;

. . .

"court", in relation to any proceedings under these Regulations involving an open-ended investment company the head office of which is situated—

(a) in England and Wales [or Northern Ireland], means the High Court; and

(b) in Scotland, means the Court of Session;

"depositary", in relation to an open-ended investment company, has the meaning given in regulation 5(1);

"the designated person" means the person designated in the company's instrument of incorporation for the purposes of paragraph 4 of Schedule 4 to these Regulations;

["electronic communication" has the meaning given in section 15(1) of the Electronic Communications Act 2000;]

"[FCA rules]" means any rules made by the Authority under regulation 6(1);

"larger denomination share" has the meaning given in regulation 45(5);

"officer", in relation to an open-ended investment company, includes a director or any secretary or manager;

["open-ended investment company" means—

(a) a body incorporated by virtue of regulation 3(1), or

(b) a body treated as so incorporated by virtue of—

(i) regulation 85(3)(a) (bodies incorporated under earlier British regulations), or

(ii) Schedule 3 to the Companies Act 2006 (Consequential Amendments and Transitional Provisions) Order 2011 (transitional provisions: Northern Ireland open-ended investment companies);]

. . .

"prospectus" has the meaning given in regulation 6(2);

"relevant provision" means any requirement imposed by or under the Act;

"register of shareholders" means the register kept under paragraph 1(1) of Schedule 3 to these Regulations;

"scheme property", in relation to an open-ended investment company, means the property subject to the collective investment scheme constituted by the company;

"share certificate" has the meaning given in regulation 46(1);

"smaller denomination share" has the meaning given in regulation 45(5);

["sub-fund" means a separate part of the property of an umbrella company that is pooled separately;]

"transfer documents" has the meaning given in paragraph 5(3) [and (3A)] of Schedule 4 to these Regulations;

. . .

"umbrella company" means an open-ended investment company whose instrument of incorporation provides for such pooling as is mentioned in section 235(3)(a) of the Act (collective investment schemes) in relation to separate parts of the scheme property and whose shareholders are entitled to exchange rights in one part for rights in another; and

. . .

(2) In these Regulations any reference to a shareholder of an open-ended investment company is a reference to—

(a) the person who holds the share certificate, or other documentary evidence of title relating to that share mentioned in regulation 48; and

(b) the person whose name is entered on the company's register of shareholders in relation to any share other than a bearer share.

(3) In these Regulations, unless the contrary intention appears, expressions which are also used in [the Companies Acts (as defined in section 2 of the Companies Act 2006)] have the same meaning as in [those Acts].

NOTES

Para (1): definition "the 1985 Act" (omitted) revoked, definitions "the 1989 Order" and "the 2006 Act" inserted, words in square brackets in definitions "the appropriate registrar" and "court" inserted, and definition "open-ended investment company" substituted, by the Companies Act 2006 (Consequential Amendments and Transitional Provisions) Order 2011, SI 2011/1265, art 15, Sch 2, paras 1, 3; definition "the Authority" inserted, and in definition "FCA rules" words in square brackets substituted, by the Financial Services Act 2012 (Consequential Amendments and Transitional Provisions) Order 2013, SI 2013/472, art 3, Sch 2, para 41(1)–(3); definitions "certificated form", "participating issuer", "participating security", "uncertificated form" and "uncertificated unit of a security" (omitted) revoked by the Uncertificated Securities Regulations 2001, SI 2001/3755, reg 51, Sch 7, Pt 2, para 24(a); definition "electronic communication", and words in square brackets in definition "transfer documents" inserted, by the Open-Ended Investment Companies (Amendment) Regulations 2009, SI 2009/553, reg 2(1), (3); definition "sub-fund" inserted by the Open-Ended Investment Companies (Amendment) Regulations 2011, SI 2011/3049, reg 3(1), (2); definition "the Tribunal" (omitted) revoked by the Transfer of Tribunal Functions Order 2010, SI 2010/22, art 5(2), Sch 3, paras 16, 17, subject to transitional provisions and savings in art 5(4) thereof, and Sch 5 thereto; definition "the UCITS directive" (omitted) revoked by the Collective Investment Schemes (Miscellaneous Amendments) Regulations 2003, SI 2003/2066, reg 13(7)(a).

Para (3): words in square brackets substituted for original words "the 1985 Act" and "that Act" respectively by the Companies Act 2006 (Consequential Amendments etc) Order 2008, SI 2008/948, art 3(1)(b), Sch 1, Pt 2, para 220, subject to transitional provisions and savings in arts 6, 11, 12 thereof.

PART II
FORMATION, SUPERVISION AND CONTROL

3–30 (*Outside the scope of this work.*)

Winding up

[7.2052]

31 Winding up by the court

(1) Where an open-ended investment company is wound up as an unregistered company under Part V of the 1986 Act [or Part 6 of the 1989 Order], the provisions of that Act [or that Order] apply for the purposes of the winding up with the following modifications.

(2) A petition for the winding up of an open-ended investment company may be presented by the depositary of the company as well as by any person authorised under [section 124 of the 1986 Act or Article 104 of the 1989 Order] (application for winding up) or [section 124A of that Act or Article 104A of that Order] (petition for winding up on grounds of public interest), as those sections [or Articles] apply by virtue of Part V of that Act [or Part 6 of that Order], to present a petition for the winding up of the company.

(3) Where a petition for the winding up of an open ended investment company is presented by a person other than the Authority—

(a) that person must serve a copy of the petition on the Authority; and

(b) the Authority is entitled to be heard on the petition.

(4) If, before the presentation of a petition for the winding up by the court of an open-ended investment company as an unregistered company under Part V of the 1986 Act [or Part 6 of the 1989 Order], the affairs of the company are being wound up otherwise than by the court—

(a) [section 129(2) of that Act or Article 109(2) of that Order] (commencement of winding up by the court) is not to apply; and

(b) any winding up of the company by the court is to be deemed to have commenced—

(i) at the time at which the Authority gave its approval to a proposal mentioned in paragraph (1)(d) of regulation 21; or

(ii) in a case falling within paragraph (3)(b) of that regulation, on the day following the end of the one-month period mentioned in that paragraph.

NOTES

Para (1): words in square brackets inserted by the Companies Act 2006 (Consequential Amendments and Transitional Provisions) Order 2011, SI 2011/1265, art 15, Sch 2, paras 1, 7(a).

Part 7N Special Insolvency Regimes

Para (2): words in first and second pairs of square brackets substituted, and words in third and fourth pairs of square brackets inserted, by SI 2011/1265, art 15, Sch 2, paras 1, 7(b).

Para (4): words in first pair of square brackets inserted, and words in square brackets in sub-para (a) substituted, by SI 2011/1265, art 15, Sch 2, paras 1, 7(c).

[7.2053]

32 Dissolution on winding up by the court

(1) Section 172(8) of the 1986 Act [or Article 146(7) of the 1989 Order] (final meeting of creditors and vacation of office by liquidator), as that section applies by virtue of Part V of that Act [or Part 6 of that Order] (winding up of unregistered companies) has effect, in relation to open-ended investment companies, as if the reference to the registrar of companies was a reference to the Authority.

(2) Where, in respect of an open-ended investment company, the Authority receives—

(a) a notice given for the purposes of section 172(8) of the 1986 Act [or Article 146(7) of the 1989 Order] (as aforesaid); or

(b) a notice from the official receiver that the winding up, by the court, of the company is complete;

the Authority must, on receipt of the notice, forthwith register it and, subject to the provisions of this regulation, at the end of the period of three months beginning with the day of the registration of the notice, the company is to be dissolved.

(3) The Secretary of State may, on the application of the official receiver or any other person who appears to the Secretary of State to be interested, give a direction deferring the date at which the dissolution of the company is to take effect for such period as the Secretary of State thinks fit.

(4) An appeal to the court lies from any decision of the Secretary of State on an application for a direction under paragraph (3).

(5) Paragraph (3) does not apply to a case where the winding-up order was made by the court in Scotland, but in such a case the court may, on an application by any person appearing to the court to have an interest, order that the date at which the dissolution of the company is to take effect be deferred for such period as the court thinks fit.

(6) It is the duty of the person—

(a) on whose application a direction is given under paragraph (3);

(b) in whose favour an appeal with respect to an application for such a direction is determined; or

(c) on whose application an order is made under paragraph (5);

not later than seven days after the giving of the direction, the determination of the appeal or the making of the order, to deliver to the Authority for registration a copy of the direction or determination or, in respect of an order, a certified copy of the interlocutor.

(7) If a person without reasonable excuse fails to deliver a copy as required by paragraph (6), he is guilty of an offence.

(8) A person guilty of an offence under paragraph (7) is liable, on summary conviction—

(a) to a fine not exceeding level 1 on the standard scale; and

(b) on a second or subsequent conviction instead of the penalty set out in sub-paragraph (a), to a fine of £100 for each day on which the contravention is continued.

NOTES

Paras (1), (2): words in square brackets inserted by the Companies Act 2006 (Consequential Amendments and Transitional Provisions) Order 2011, SI 2011/1265, art 15, Sch 2, paras 1, 8.

[7.2054]

33 Dissolution in other circumstances

(1) Where the affairs of an open-ended investment company have been wound up otherwise than by the court, the Authority must, as soon as is reasonably practicable after the winding up is complete, register that fact and, subject to the provisions of this regulation, at the end of the period of three months beginning with the day of the registration, the company is to be dissolved.

(2) The court may, on the application of the Authority or the company, make an order deferring the date at which the dissolution of the company is to take effect for such period as the court thinks fit.

(3) It is the duty of the company, on whose application an order of the court under paragraph (2) is made, to deliver to the Authority, not later than seven days after the making of the order, a copy of the order for registration.

(4) Where any company, the head office of which is situated [in England and Wales (or Wales) or in Northern Ireland], is dissolved by virtue of paragraph (1), any sum of money (including unclaimed distributions) standing to the account of the company at the date of the dissolution must on such date as is determined in accordance with [FCA rules], be paid into court.

(5) Where any company, the head office of which is situated in Scotland, is dissolved by virtue of paragraph (1), any sum of money (including unclaimed dividends and unapplied or undistributable balances) standing to the account of the company at the date of the dissolution must—

(a) on such date as is determined in accordance with [FCA rules], be lodged in an appropriate bank or institution as defined in section 73(1) of the Bankruptcy (Scotland) Act 1985 (interpretation) in the name of the Accountant of the Court; and

(b) thereafter be treated as if it were a sum of money lodged in such an account by virtue of section 193 of the 1986 Act (unclaimed dividends (Scotland)), as that section applies by virtue of Part V of that Act.

NOTES

Para (4): words in first pair of square brackets substituted by the Companies Act 2006 (Consequential Amendments and Transitional Provisions) Order 2011, SI 2011/1265, art 15, Sch 2, paras 1, 9; words in second pair of square brackets substituted by the Financial Services Act 2012 (Consequential Amendments and Transitional Provisions) Order 2013, SI 2013/472, art 3, Sch 2, para 41(1), (2).

Para (5): words in square brackets substituted by SI 2013/472, art 3, Sch 2, para 41(1), (2).

[7.2055]

[33A Winding up of a master UCITS

(1) Paragraphs (2) and (3) apply if a master UCITS is wound up.

(2) If the Authority considers that an open-ended investment company which is a feeder UCITS of the master UCITS may be wound up under section 221 of the 1986 Act, the Authority must present a petition to the Court for the feeder UCITS to be wound up unless one of the conditions referred to in paragraph (4) is satisfied.

(3) If paragraph (2) does not apply, the Authority must require the directors of any open ended investment company which is a feeder UCITS of the master UCITS to submit a proposal under regulation 21 to wind up the affairs of the company unless one of the conditions referred to in paragraph (4) is satisfied.

(4) The conditions set out in paragraphs (2) and (3) are—

(a) the Authority approves under section 283A of the Act the investment by the feeder UCITS of at least 85% of its assets in units of another UCITS or master UCITS; or

(b) the Authority approves under regulation 22A an amendment of the instrument of incorporation of the company which would enable it to convert into a UCITS which is not a feeder UCITS.]

NOTES

Inserted, together with reg 33B, by the Undertakings for Collective Investment in Transferable Securities Regulations 2011, SI 2011/1613, reg 3(1), (6).

[7.2056]

[33B Merger or division of a master UCITS

(1) Paragraph (2) applies if a master UCITS—

(a) merges with another UCITS, or

(b) is divided into two or more UCITS.

(2) The Authority must require the directors of any open-ended investment company which is a feeder UCITS of the master UCITS to prepare a proposal to wind up the affairs of the feeder UCITS under regulation 21 unless—

(a) the Authority approves under section 283A of the Act the investment by the company of at least 85% of its assets in the units of—

(i) the master UCITS which results from the merger;

(ii) one of the UCITS resulting from the division; or

(iii) another UCITS or master UCITS; or

(b) the Authority approves under regulation 22A an amendment of the instrument of incorporation of the company which would enable it to convert into a UCITS which is not a feeder UCITS.]

NOTES

Inserted as noted to reg 33A at **[7.2055]**.

[7.2057]

[33C Winding up of sub-funds

(1) Save as provided in paragraphs (2) and (3), a sub-fund may be wound up as if it were an open-ended investment company in accordance with the provisions of regulations 31 to 33 provided that the appointment of the liquidator or any provisional liquidator and the powers and duties of the liquidator or any provisional liquidator shall be confined to the sub-fund which is being wound up and its affairs, business and property.

(2) Notwithstanding paragraph (1), sections 226 to 228 of the 1986 Act shall not apply where a sub-fund is wound up in accordance with the provisions of this regulation.

(3) The provisions of Part 5 of the 1986 Act with respect to staying, sisting or restraining actions and proceedings against a company at any time after the presentation of a petition for winding up and before the making of a winding-up order extend, in the case of a sub-fund, where the application to stay, sist or restrain is presented by a creditor, to actions and proceedings against the umbrella company of that sub-fund, or any of the other sub-funds of that umbrella company, in respect of a liability of that sub-fund.

(4) Notwithstanding regulation 11A(5), a sub-fund shall be treated as if it were a separate legal person for the purposes of winding up.

(5) For the purposes of paragraph (1), in regulations 31 to 33—

(a) a reference to an open-ended investment company is taken to be a reference to a sub-fund; and

(b) a reference to a company, save in relation to the term "unregistered company", is taken to be a reference to a sub-fund.

(6) For the purposes of paragraph (1), in the provisions of the 1986 Act to which reference is made in regulations 31 to 33—

(a) references to an unregistered company and to a company are taken to be references to a sub-fund;
(b) a reference to creditors is taken to be a reference to the creditors of a sub-fund; and
(c) a reference to members is taken to be a reference to the holders of the shares in a sub-fund.

(7) Subject to paragraph (8), regulation 11A(6) shall not apply after the appointment of a liquidator or a provisional liquidator.

(8) Where an order has been made for the winding-up of a sub-fund, no action or proceedings shall be commenced or proceeded with against the umbrella company or the sub-fund in respect of any liability of the sub-fund, except by leave of the court and subject to such terms as the court may impose.]

NOTES

Inserted by the Open-Ended Investment Companies (Amendment) Regulations 2011, SI 2011/3049, reg 3(1), (5), subject to transitional provisions in regs 4–10 thereof.

34–85 *((Pts III–V) outside the scope of this work.)*

SCHEDULES 1–7

(Schs 1–7 outside the scope of this work.)

O
POSTAL

POSTAL SERVICES ACT 2011

(2011 c 5)

ARRANGEMENT OF SECTIONS

PART 4
SPECIAL ADMINISTRATION REGIME

Postal administration orders

68 Postal administration orders . . . . . [7.2058]
69 Objective of a postal administration order . . . . . [7.2059]
70 Applications for postal administration orders . . . . . [7.2060]
71 Powers of court . . . . . [7.2061]
72 Postal administrators . . . . . [7.2062]
73 Conduct of administration, transfer schemes etc . . . . . [7.2063]

Restrictions on other insolvency procedures

74 Winding-up orders . . . . . [7.2064]
75 Voluntary winding up . . . . . [7.2065]
76 Making of ordinary administration orders . . . . . [7.2066]
77 Administrator appointments by creditors etc . . . . . [7.2067]
78 Enforcement of security . . . . . [7.2068]

Financial support for companies in administration

79 Grants and loans . . . . . [7.2069]
80 Indemnities . . . . . [7.2070]
81 Guarantees where postal administration order is made. . . . . [7.2071]

Modifications of regulatory conditions etc

82 Regulatory powers exercisable during postal administration . . . . . [7.2072]
83 Regulatory conditions to secure funding of postal administration order . . . . . [7.2073]

Supplementary provisions

84 Modification of Part 4 under Enterprise Act 2002 . . . . . [7.2074]
85 Interpretation of Part 4. . . . . [7.2075]
86 Partnerships . . . . . [7.2076]
87 Northern Ireland . . . . . [7.2077]
88 Review of Part 4 . . . . . [7.2078]

PART 5
GENERAL

89 Orders and regulations made by Ministers of Crown. . . . . [7.2079]
90 Minor definitions . . . . . [7.2080]
93 Short title, commencement and extent . . . . . [7.2081]

SCHEDULES

Schedule 10—Conduct of postal administration
Part 1—Modifications of Schedule B1 to 1986 Act. . . . . [7.2082]
Part 2—Further modifications of Schedule B1 to 1986 Act: foreign companies. . . . . [7.2083]
Part 3—Other modifications . . . . . [7.2084]
Schedule 11—Postal transfer schemes. . . . . [7.2085]

An Act to make provision for the restructuring of the Royal Mail group and about the Royal Mail Pension Plan; to make new provision about the regulation of postal services, including provision for a special administration regime; and for connected purposes.

[13 June 2011]

1–67 ((*Pts 1–3) outside the scope of this work.*)

PART 4
SPECIAL ADMINISTRATION REGIME

Postal administration orders

[7.2058]

68 Postal administration orders

(1) In this Part "postal administration order" means an order which—

(a) is made by the court in relation to a company which is a universal service provider, and

(b) directs that, while the order is in force, the company's affairs, business and property are to be managed by a person appointed by the court.

(2) The person appointed in relation to a company for the purposes of a postal administration order is referred to in this Part as the postal administrator of the company.

(3) The postal administrator of a company must—

(a) manage the company's affairs, business and property, and

(b) exercise and perform all the powers and duties conferred or imposed on the postal administrator of the company,

so as to achieve the objective set out in section 69.

(4) In relation to a postal administration order applying to a foreign company, references in this section to the company's affairs, business and property are references to its UK affairs, business and property.

[7.2059]

69 Objective of a postal administration

(1) The objective of a postal administration is to secure—

(a) that a universal postal service is provided in accordance with the standards set out in the universal postal service order, and

(b) that it becomes unnecessary, by one or both of the following means, for the postal administration order to remain in force for that purpose.

(2) Those means are—

(a) the rescue as a going concern of the company subject to the order, and

(b) relevant transfers.

(3) A transfer is a "relevant" transfer if it is a transfer as a going concern—

(a) to another company, or

(b) as respects different parts of the undertaking of the company subject to the order, to two or more different companies,

of so much of that undertaking as it is appropriate to transfer for the purpose of achieving the objective of the postal administration.

(4) The means by which relevant transfers may be effected include, in particular—

(a) a transfer of the undertaking of the company subject to the order, or of a part of its undertaking, to a wholly-owned subsidiary of that company, and

(b) a transfer to a company of securities of a wholly-owned subsidiary to which there has been a transfer within paragraph (a).

In this subsection "wholly-owned subsidiary" has the meaning given by section 1159 of the Companies Act 2006.

(5) The objective of a postal administration may be achieved by relevant transfers to the extent only that—

(a) the rescue as a going concern of the company is not reasonably practicable or is not reasonably practicable without the transfers,

(b) the rescue of the company as a going concern will not achieve the objective of the postal administration or will not do so without the transfers,

(c) the transfers would produce a result for the company's creditors as a whole that is better than the result that would be produced without them, or

(d) the transfers would, without prejudicing the interests of the company's creditors as a whole, produce a result for the company's members as a whole that is better than the result that would be produced without them.

[7.2060]

70 Applications for postal administration orders

(1) An application for a postal administration order in relation to a company may be made only—

(a) by the Secretary of State, or

(b) with the consent of the Secretary of State, by OFCOM.

(2) The applicant for a postal administration order in relation to a company must give notice of the application to—

(a) every person who has appointed an administrative receiver of the company,

(b) every person who is or may be entitled to appoint an administrative receiver of the company,

(c) every person who is or may be entitled to make an appointment in relation to the company under paragraph 14 of Schedule B1 to the 1986 Act (appointment of administrators by holders of floating charges), and

(d) such other persons as may be prescribed by postal administration rules.

(3) The notice must be given as soon as reasonably practicable after the making of the application.

(4) In this section "administrative receiver" means—

(a) an administrative receiver within the meaning given by section 251 of the 1986 Act for the purposes of Parts 1 to 7 of that Act, or

(b) a person whose functions in relation to a foreign company are equivalent to those of an administrative receiver and relate only to its UK affairs, business and property.

[7.2061]
71 Powers of court

(1) On hearing an application for a postal administration order, the court has the following powers—
- (a) it may make the order,
- (b) it may dismiss the application,
- (c) it may adjourn the hearing conditionally or unconditionally,
- (d) it may make an interim order,
- (e) it may treat the application as a winding-up petition and make any order the court could make under section 125 of the 1986 Act (power of court on hearing winding-up petition), and
- (f) it may make any other order which it thinks appropriate.

(2) The court may make a postal administration order in relation to a company only if it is satisfied—
- (a) that the company is unable, or is likely to be unable, to pay its debts, or
- (b) that, on a petition by the Secretary of State under section 124A of the 1986 Act, it would be just and equitable (disregarding the objective of the postal administration) to wind up the company in the public interest.

(3) The court may not make a postal administration order on the ground set out in subsection (2)(b) unless the Secretary of State has certified to the court that the case is one in which the Secretary of State considers (disregarding the objective of the postal administration) that it would be appropriate to petition under section 124A of the 1986 Act.

(4) The court has no power to make a postal administration order in relation to a company which—
- (a) is in administration under Schedule B1 to the 1986 Act, or
- (b) has gone into liquidation (within the meaning of section 247(2) of the 1986 Act).

(5) A postal administration order comes into force—
- (a) at the time appointed by the court, or
- (b) if no time is appointed by the court, when the order is made.

(6) An interim order under subsection (1)(d) may, in particular—
- (a) restrict the exercise of a power of the company or of its directors, or
- (b) make provision conferring a discretion on a person qualified to act as an insolvency practitioner in relation to the company.

(7) In the case of a foreign company, subsection (6)(a) is to be read as a reference to restricting the exercise of a power of the company or of its directors—
- (a) within the United Kingdom, or
- (b) in relation to the company's UK affairs, business or property.

(8) For the purposes of this section a company is unable to pay its debts if—
- (a) it is a company which is deemed to be unable to pay its debts under section 123 of the 1986 Act, or
- (b) it is an unregistered company which is deemed, as a result of any of sections 222 to 224 of the 1986 Act, to be so unable for the purposes of section 221 of the 1986 Act, or which would be so deemed if it were an unregistered company for the purposes of those sections.

[7.2062]
72 Postal administrators

(1) The postal administrator of a company—
- (a) is an officer of the court, and
- (b) in exercising and performing powers and duties in relation to the company, is the company's agent.

(2) The management by the postal administrator of a company of any of its affairs, business or property must be carried out for the purpose of achieving the objective of the postal administration as quickly and as efficiently as is reasonably practicable.

(3) The postal administrator of a company must exercise and perform powers and duties in the way which, so far as it is consistent with the objective of the postal administration to do so, best protects—
- (a) the interests of the company's creditors as a whole, and
- (b) subject to those interests, the interests of the company's members as a whole.

(4) A person is not to be the postal administrator of a company unless qualified to act as an insolvency practitioner in relation to the company.

(5) If the court appoints two or more persons as the postal administrator of a company, the appointment must set out—
- (a) which (if any) of the powers and duties of a postal administrator are to be exercisable or performed only by the appointees acting jointly,
- (b) the circumstances (if any) in which powers and duties of a postal administrator are to be exercisable, or may be performed, by one of the appointees, or by particular appointees, acting alone, and
- (c) the circumstances (if any) in which things done in relation to one of the appointees, or in relation to particular appointees, are to be treated as done in relation to all of them.

[7.2063]
73 Conduct of administration, transfer schemes etc

(1) Schedule 10 contains provision applying the provisions of Schedule B1 to the 1986 Act, and certain other enactments, to postal administration orders.

(2) Schedule 11 contains provision for transfer schemes to achieve the objective of a postal administration.
(3) The power to make rules under section 411 of the 1986 Act is to apply for the purpose of giving effect to this Part as it applies for the purpose of giving effect to Parts 1 to 7 of that Act (and, accordingly, as if references in that section to those Parts included references to this Part).
(4) Section 413(2) of the 1986 Act (duty to consult Insolvency Rules Committee about rules) is not to apply to rules made under section 411 of the 1986 Act as a result of this section.

NOTES

Rules: the Postal Administration Rules 2013, SI 2013/3208 at **[7.2086]**.

Restrictions on other insolvency procedures

[7.2064]
74 Winding-up orders
(1) This section applies if a person other than the Secretary of State petitions for the winding-up of a company which is a universal service provider.
(2) The court is not to exercise its powers on a winding-up petition unless—
- (a) notice of the petition has been served on the Secretary of State and OFCOM, and
- (b) a period of at least 14 days has elapsed since the service of the last of those notices to be served.

(3) If an application for a postal administration order in relation to the company is made to the court in accordance with section 70(1) before a winding-up order is made on the petition, the court may exercise its powers under section 71 (instead of exercising its powers on the petition).
(4) References in this section to the court's powers on a winding-up petition are to—
- (a) its powers under section 125 of the 1986 Act (other than its power of adjournment), and
- (b) its powers under section 135 of the 1986 Act.

[7.2065]
75 Voluntary winding up
(1) A company which is a universal service provider has no power to pass a resolution for voluntary winding up without the permission of the court.
(2) Permission may be granted by the court only on an application made by the company.
(3) The court is not to grant permission unless—
- (a) notice of the application has been served on the Secretary of State and OFCOM, and
- (b) a period of at least 14 days has elapsed since the service of the last of those notices to be served.

(4) If an application for a postal administration order in relation to the company is made to the court in accordance with section 70(1) after an application for permission under this section has been made and before it is granted, the court may exercise its powers under section 71 (instead of granting permission).
(5) In this section "a resolution for voluntary winding up" has the same meaning as in the 1986 Act.

[7.2066]
76 Making of ordinary administration orders
(1) This section applies if a person other than the Secretary of State makes an ordinary administration application in relation to a company which is a universal service provider.
(2) The court must dismiss the application if—
- (a) a postal administration order is in force in relation to the company, or
- (b) a postal administration order has been made in relation to the company but is not yet in force.

(3) If subsection (2) does not apply, the court, on hearing the application, must not exercise its powers under paragraph 13 of Schedule B1 to the 1986 Act (other than its power of adjournment) unless—
- (a) notice of the application has been served on the Secretary of State and OFCOM,
- (b) a period of at least 14 days has elapsed since the service of the last of those notices to be served, and
- (c) there is no application for a postal administration order which is outstanding.

(4) Paragraph 44 of Schedule B1 to the 1986 Act (interim moratorium) does not prevent, or require the permission of the court for, the making of an application for a postal administration order.
(5) On the making of a postal administration order in relation to a company, the court must dismiss any ordinary administration application made in relation to the company which is outstanding.
(6) In this section "ordinary administration application" means an application in accordance with paragraph 12 of Schedule B1 to the 1986 Act.

[7.2067]
77 Administrator appointments by creditors etc
(1) Subsections (2) to (4) make provision about appointments under paragraph 14 or 22 of Schedule B1 to the 1986 Act (powers to appoint administrators) in relation to a company which is a universal service provider.
(2) If in any case—
- (a) a postal administration order is in force in relation to the company,
- (b) a postal administration order has been made in relation to the company but is not yet in force, or
- (c) an application for a postal administration order in relation to the company is outstanding,

a person may not take any step to make an appointment.
(3) In any other case, an appointment takes effect only if each of the following conditions are met.
(4) The conditions are—

(a) that a copy of every document in relation to the appointment that is filed or lodged with the court in accordance with paragraph 18 or 29 of Schedule B1 to the 1986 Act has been served on the Secretary of State and OFCOM,

(b) that a period of 14 days has elapsed since the service of the last of those copies to be served,

(c) that there is no outstanding application to the court for a postal administration order in relation to the company, and

(d) that the making of an application for a postal administration order in relation to the company has not resulted in the making of a postal administration order which is in force or is still to come into force.

(5) Paragraph 44 of Schedule B1 to the 1986 Act (interim moratorium) does not prevent, or require the permission of the court for, the making of an application for a postal administration order at any time before the appointment takes effect.

[7.2068]

78 Enforcement of security

(1) A person may not take any step to enforce a security over property of a company which is a universal service provider unless—

(a) notice of the intention to do so has been served on the Secretary of State and OFCOM, and

(b) a period of at least 14 days has elapsed since the service of the last of those notices to be served.

(2) In the case of a foreign company which is a universal service provider, the reference to the property of the company is to its property in the United Kingdom.

Financial support for companies in administration

[7.2069]

79 Grants and loans

(1) This section applies if a postal administration order has been made in relation to a company.

(2) The Secretary of State may, with the consent of the Treasury, make grants or loans to the company of such amounts as it appears to the Secretary of State appropriate for achieving the objective of the postal administration.

(3) The grants or loans may be made in whatever manner, and on whatever terms, the Secretary of State considers appropriate.

(4) The terms on which the grants may be made include, in particular, terms requiring the whole or a part of the grants to be repaid to the Secretary of State if there is a contravention of the other terms on which they are made.

(5) The terms on which loans may be made include, in particular, terms requiring—

(a) the loans to be repaid at such times and by such methods as the Secretary of State may, with the consent of the Treasury, from time to time direct, and

(b) interest to be paid on the loans at such rates and at such times as the Secretary of State may, with the consent of the Treasury, from time to time direct.

(6) The Secretary of State must pay sums received as a result of this section into the Consolidated Fund.

[7.2070]

80 Indemnities

(1) This section applies if a postal administration order has been made in relation to a company.

(2) The Secretary of State may, with the consent of the Treasury, agree to indemnify persons in respect of one or both of the following—

(a) liabilities incurred in connection with the exercise and performance of powers and duties by the postal administrator, and

(b) loss or damage sustained in that connection.

(3) The agreement may be made in whatever manner, and on whatever terms, the Secretary of State considers appropriate.

(4) As soon as practicable after agreeing to indemnify persons under this section, the Secretary of State must lay a statement of the agreement before Parliament.

(5) If sums are paid by the Secretary of State in consequence of an indemnity agreed to under this section, the company must pay the Secretary of State—

(a) such amounts in or towards the repayment to the Secretary of State of those sums as the Secretary of State may, with the consent of the Treasury, direct, and

(b) interest on amounts outstanding under this subsection at such rates as the Secretary of State may, with the consent of the Treasury, direct.

(6) The payments must be made by the company at such times and in such manner as the Secretary of State may, with the consent of the Treasury, determine.

(7) Subsection (5) does not apply in the case of a sum paid by the Secretary of State for indemnifying a person in respect of a liability to the company.

(8) If a sum has been paid out in consequence of an indemnity agreed to under this section, the Secretary of State must lay a statement relating to that sum before Parliament—

(a) as soon as practicable after the end of the financial year in which the sum is paid out, and

(b) if subsection (5) applies to the sum, as soon as practicable after the end of each subsequent financial year in relation to which the repayment condition has not been met.

(9) The repayment condition is met in relation to a financial year if—

(a) the whole of the sum has been repaid to the Secretary of State before the beginning of the year, and

(b) the company was not at any time during the year liable to pay interest on amounts that became due in respect of the sum.

(10) The power of the Secretary of State to agree to indemnify persons—

(a) is confined to a power to agree to indemnify persons in respect of liabilities, loss and damage incurred or sustained by them as relevant persons, but

(b) includes power to agree to indemnify persons (whether or not they are identified or identifiable at the time of the agreement) who subsequently become relevant persons.

(11) The following are relevant persons for the purposes of this section—

(a) the postal administrator,

(b) an employee of the postal administrator,

(c) a partner or employee of a firm of which the postal administrator is a partner,

(d) a partner or employee of a firm of which the postal administrator is an employee,

(e) a partner of a firm of which the postal administrator was an employee or partner at a time when the order was in force,

(f) a body corporate which is the employer of the postal administrator,

(g) an officer, employee or member of such a body corporate, and

(h) a Scottish firm which is the employer of the postal administrator or of which the postal administrator is a partner.

(12) For the purposes of subsection (11)—

(a) references to the postal administrator are to be read, where two or more persons are appointed as the postal administrator, as references to any one or more of them, and

(b) references to a firm of which a person was a partner or employee at a particular time include a firm which holds itself out to be the successor of a firm of which the person was a partner or employee at that time.

(13) The Secretary of State must pay sums received as a result of subsection (5) into the Consolidated Fund.

[7.2071]

81 Guarantees where postal administration order is made

(1) This section applies if a postal administration order has been made in relation to a company.

(2) The Secretary of State may, with the consent of the Treasury, guarantee—

(a) the repayment of any sum borrowed by the company while that order is in force,

(b) the payment of interest on any sum borrowed by the company while that order is in force, and

(c) the discharge of any other financial obligation of the company in connection with the borrowing of any sum while that order is in force.

(3) The Secretary of State may give the guarantees in such manner, and on such terms, as the Secretary of State considers appropriate.

(4) As soon as practicable after giving a guarantee under this section, the Secretary of State must lay a statement of the guarantee before Parliament.

(5) If sums are paid out by the Secretary of State under a guarantee given under this section, the company must pay the Secretary of State—

(a) such amounts in or towards the repayment to the Secretary of State of those sums as the Secretary of State may, with the consent of the Treasury, direct, and

(b) interest on amounts outstanding under this subsection at such rates as the Secretary of State may, with the consent of the Treasury, direct.

(6) The payments must be made by the company at such times, and in such manner, as the Secretary of State may, with the consent of the Treasury, from time to time direct.

(7) If a sum has been paid out under a guarantee given under this section, the Secretary of State must lay a statement relating to that sum before Parliament—

(a) as soon as practicable after the end of the financial year in which the sum is paid out, and

(b) as soon as practicable after the end of each subsequent financial year in relation to which the repayment condition has not been met.

(8) The repayment condition is met in relation to a financial year if—

(a) the whole of the sum has been repaid to the Secretary of State before the beginning of the year, and

(b) the company was not at any time during the year liable to pay interest on amounts that became due in respect of the sum.

(9) The Secretary of State must pay sums received as a result of subsection (5) into the Consolidated Fund.

(10) In this section "financial year" means a period of 12 months ending with 31 March.

Modifications of regulatory conditions etc

[7.2072]

82 Regulatory powers exercisable during postal administration

(1) This section applies if a postal administration order has been made.

(2) The Secretary of State may by order modify the universal postal service order made by OFCOM under section 30.

An order under this subsection is subject to negative resolution procedure.

(3) Before modifying that order, the Secretary of State must consult—

(a) OFCOM, and

(b) such other persons as the Secretary of State considers appropriate.

(4) If the Secretary of State modifies that order, it is for the Secretary of State (rather than OFCOM) to notify the European Commission of the modification.

(5) The Secretary of State may by order amend section 31.
(6) An order under subsection (5)—
(a) is subject to approval after being made, and
(b) may include such amendments of Part 3 as the Secretary of State considers necessary or expedient in consequence of any provision made by the order.
(7) The Secretary of State may modify or revoke any regulatory condition if the Secretary of State considers it appropriate to do so for, or in connection with, achieving the objective of the postal administration.
(8) The Secretary of State's power to make modifications includes power to make incidental, supplementary, consequential, transitional or transitory modifications.
(9) Before modifying or revoking a regulatory condition, the Secretary of State must consult—
(a) OFCOM,
(b) the person whose condition is being modified or revoked, and
(c) such other persons as the Secretary of State considers appropriate.
(10) The Secretary of State must publish every modification or revocation of a regulatory condition made under this section.
(11) The publication must be in such manner as the Secretary of State considers appropriate.
(12) The provisions of Part 3 (including section 29) other than—
(a) sections 57 to 60 (appeals), and
(b) paragraph 3 of Schedule 6 (procedure for modifying or revoking regulatory conditions),
apply in relation to the modification or revocation by the Secretary of State of regulatory conditions as they apply in relation to the modification or revocation by OFCOM of regulatory conditions.
(13) The power conferred by subsection (2) or (5) may not be exercised at any time after the postal administration order has ceased to be in force.
(14) Any duty to consult under this section may be met by consultation before the making of the postal administration order.

[7.2073]
83 Regulatory conditions to secure funding of postal administration order
(1) The modifications that may be made under section 82 include, in particular, modifications of any price control provision contained in a regulatory condition for the purpose of raising such amounts as may be determined by the Secretary of State.
(2) The modified condition may require the person on whom it is imposed to pay those amounts to such persons as may be so determined for the purpose of—
(a) their applying those amounts in making good any shortfall in the property available for meeting the expenses of the postal administration, or
(b) enabling those persons to secure that those amounts are so applied.
(3) The modified condition may require the person on whom it is imposed to apply amounts paid to it as result of this section in making good any shortfall in the property available for meeting the expenses of the postal administration.
(4) For the purposes of this section "price control provision" means—
(a) provision as to the tariffs that are to be used as mentioned in section 36(4) (designated USP condition: tariffs), or
(b) provision as to prices that may be charged for the giving of access under an access condition (within the meaning of Part 3).
(5) For the purposes of this section—
(a) there is a shortfall in the property available for meeting the costs of a postal administration if the property available (apart from this section) for meeting relevant debts is insufficient for meeting them, and
(b) amounts are applied in making good that shortfall if they are paid in or towards discharging so much of a relevant debt as cannot be met out of the property otherwise available for meeting relevant debts.
(6) In this section "relevant debt", in relation to a case in which a company is or has been subject to a postal administration order, means an obligation—
(a) to make payments in respect of the expenses or remuneration of any person as the postal administrator of the company,
(b) to make a payment in discharge of a debt or other liability of the company arising out of a contract entered into at a time when the order was in force by the person who at that time was the postal administrator of the company,
(c) to repay the whole or a part of a grant made to the company under section 79,
(d) to repay a loan made to the company under section 79 or to pay interest on such a loan,
(e) to make a payment under section 80(5), or
(f) to make a payment under section 81(5).

Supplementary provisions

[7.2074]
84 Modification of Part 4 under Enterprise Act 2002
The power to modify or apply enactments conferred on the Secretary of State by—
(a) sections 248 and 277 of the Enterprise Act 2002 (amendments consequential on that Act), and
(b) section 254 of that Act (power to apply insolvency law to foreign companies),
includes power to make such consequential modifications of this Part as the Secretary of State considers appropriate in connection with any other provision made under any of those sections.

[7.2075]

85 Interpretation of Part 4

(1) In this Part—

"the 1986 Act" means the Insolvency Act 1986,

"business", "member", "property" and "security" have the same meaning as in the 1986 Act,

"company" means—

(a) a company registered under the Companies Act 2006, or

(b) an unregistered company,

"the court", in relation to a company, means the court having jurisdiction to wind up the company,

"foreign company" means a company incorporated outside the United Kingdom,

"objective of the postal administration" is to be read in accordance with section 69,

"postal administration order" has the meaning given by section 68(1),

"postal administration rules" means rules made under section 411 of the 1986 Act as a result of section 73 above,

"postal administrator" has the meaning given by section 68(2) and is to be read in accordance with subsection (3) below,

"Scottish firm" means a firm constituted under the law of Scotland,

"UK affairs, business and property", in relation to a company, means—

(a) its affairs and business so far as carried on in the United Kingdom, and

(b) its property in the United Kingdom, and

"unregistered company" means a company that is not registered under the Companies Act 2006.

(2) Any expression which is used in this Part and in Part 3 has the same meaning in this Part as in that Part.

(3) In this Part references to the postal administrator of a company—

(a) include a person appointed under paragraph 91 or 103 of Schedule B1 to the 1986 Act, as applied by Part 1 of Schedule 10 to this Act, to be the postal administrator of the company, and

(b) if two or more persons are appointed as the postal administrator of the company, are to be read in accordance with the provision made under section 72(5).

(4) References in this Part to a person qualified to act as an insolvency practitioner in relation to a company are to be read in accordance with Part 13 of the 1986 Act, but as if references in that Part to a company included a company registered under the Companies Act 2006 in Northern Ireland.

(5) For the purposes of this Part an application made to the court is outstanding if it—

(a) has not yet been granted or dismissed, and

(b) has not been withdrawn.

(6) An application is not to be taken as having been dismissed if an appeal against the dismissal of the application, or a subsequent appeal, is pending.

(7) An appeal is to be treated as pending for this purpose if—

(a) an appeal has been brought and has not been determined or withdrawn,

(b) an application for permission to appeal has been made but has not been determined or withdrawn, or

(c) no appeal has been brought and the period for bringing one is still running.

(8) References in this Part to Schedule B1 to the 1986 Act, or to a provision of that Schedule (except the references in subsection (2) above), are to that Schedule or that provision without the modifications made by Part 1 of Schedule 10 to this Act.

[7.2076]

86 Partnerships

(1) The Lord Chancellor may, by order made with the concurrence of the Secretary of State and the Lord Chief Justice, apply (with or without modifications) any provision of this Part in relation to partnerships.

(2) An order under subsection (1) is subject to negative resolution procedure.

(3) Subsection (1) does not apply in relation to Scottish firms.

(4) The Lord Chief Justice may nominate a judicial office holder (as defined in section 109(4) of the Constitutional Reform Act 2005) to exercise the function of the Lord Chief Justice under subsection (1).

(5) The Secretary of State may by order apply (with or without modifications) any provision of this Part in relation to Scottish firms.

(6) An order under subsection (5) is subject to negative resolution procedure.

[7.2077]

87 Northern Ireland

(1) This section makes provision about the application of this Part to Northern Ireland.

(2) Any reference to any provision of the 1986 Act is to have effect as a reference to the corresponding provision of the Insolvency (Northern Ireland) Order 1989.

(3) Section 85(4) is to have effect as if the reference to Northern Ireland were to England and Wales or Scotland.

(4) Section 86 is to have effect as if—

(a) in subsection (1)—

(i) the reference to the Secretary of State were to the Department of Enterprise, Trade and Investment, and

(ii) the reference to the Lord Chief Justice were to the Lord Chief Justice of Northern Ireland, and

(b) for subsection (4) there were substituted—

"(4) The Lord Chief Justice of Northern Ireland may nominate—
(a) the holder of one of the offices listed in Schedule 1 to the Justice (Northern Ireland) Act 2002, or
(b) a Lord Justice of Appeal (as defined in section 88 of that Act),
to exercise the function of the Lord Chief Justice of Northern Ireland under subsection (1)."

[7.2078]
88 Review of Part 4
(1) As soon as reasonably practicable after the end of the review period, the Secretary of State must—
(a) carry out a review of the provisions of this Part, and
(b) set out the conclusions of the review in a report.
(2) The report must, in particular—
(a) set out the objectives intended to be achieved by the regulatory system established by those provisions,
(b) assess the extent to which those objectives have been achieved, and
(c) assess whether those objectives remain appropriate and, if so, the extent to which they could be achieved with a system that imposed less regulation.
(3) The review period is the period of 5 years beginning with the day on which the provisions of this Part come generally into force.
(4) The Secretary of State must lay the report before Parliament.

PART 5
GENERAL

[7.2079]
89 Orders and regulations made by Ministers of Crown
(1) This section applies to orders and regulations under this Act made by the Secretary of State, [the Minister for the Civil Service,] the Treasury or the Lord Chancellor.
(2) Any order or regulations may—
(a) contain incidental, supplementary, consequential, transitional, transitory or saving provision, and
(b) make different provision for different cases or circumstances or for different areas.
(3) Any order or regulations are to be made by statutory instrument.
(4) Where any order or regulations are subject to "affirmative resolution procedure" the order or regulations may not be made unless a draft of the statutory instrument containing the order or regulations has been laid before, and approved by a resolution of, each House of Parliament.
(5) Where any order is subject to "approval after being made", the order—
(a) must be laid before Parliament after being made, and
(b) ceases to have effect at the end of the period of 28 days beginning with the day on which it was made unless, during that period, it is approved by a resolution of each House of Parliament.
(6) In reckoning the period of 28 days no account is to be taken of any time—
(a) during which Parliament is dissolved or adjourned, or
(b) during which both Houses are adjourned for more than 4 days.
(7) The order ceasing to have effect does not affect—
(a) anything previously done under it, or
(b) the making of a new order.
(8) Where any order or regulations are subject to "negative resolution procedure" the statutory instrument containing the order or regulations is subject to annulment in pursuance of a resolution of either House of Parliament.
(9) Any provision that may be made by any order or regulations subject to negative resolution procedure may be included in an order or regulations subject to affirmative resolution procedure (in which case negative resolution procedure does not apply to the order or regulations).

NOTES
Sub-s (1): words in square brackets inserted by the Transfer of Functions (Royal Mail Pension Plan) Order 2014, SI 2014/500, art 5(1), (8).

[7.2080]
90 Minor definitions
In this Act—
"enactment" includes—
(a) an enactment contained in subordinate legislation within the meaning of the Interpretation Act 1978,
(b) an enactment contained in, or in an instrument made under, an Act of the Scottish Parliament,
(c) an enactment contained in, or in an instrument made under, Northern Ireland legislation, and
(d) an enactment contained in, or in an instrument made under, a Measure or Act of the National Assembly for Wales, and
"OFCOM" means the Office of Communications.

91, 92 (*Outside the scope of this work.*)

[7.2081]

93 Short title, commencement and extent

(1) This Act may be cited as the Postal Services Act 2011.

(2) The following provisions of this Act come into force on the day on which this Act is passed—

(a) . . .

(b) . . .

(c) sections 89 and 90,

(d) . . .

(e) . . .

(f) this section, and

(g) any other provisions of this Act so far as necessary for the purposes of any of the provisions mentioned above.

(3) The remaining provisions of this Act come into force on such day as the Secretary of State may by order appoint (and different days may be appointed for different purposes).

(4) The Secretary of State may by order make such transitional provision and savings as the Secretary of State considers necessary or expedient in connection with the commencement of any provision made by this Act.

(5) Any amendment or repeal made by this Act has the same extent as the enactment to which it relates.

(6) Subject to that, this Act extends to England and Wales, Scotland and Northern Ireland.

NOTES

Sub-s (2): paras (a), (b), (d), (e) outside the scope of this work.

Orders: the Postal Services Act 2011 (Commencement No 1 and Transitional Provisions) Order 2011, SI 2011/2329; the Postal Services Act 2011 (Commencement No 2) Order 2011, SI 2011/3044; the Postal Services Act 2011 (Commencement No 3 and Saving Provisions) Order 2012, SI 2012/1095.

SCHEDULES 1–9

(*Schs 1–9 outside the scope of this work.*)

SCHEDULE 10
CONDUCT OF POSTAL ADMINISTRATION

Section 73

PART 1
MODIFICATIONS OF SCHEDULE B1 TO 1986 ACT

Introductory

[7.2082]

1 Paragraphs 1, 40 to 50, 54, 59 to 68, 70 to 75, 79, 83 to 91, 98 to 107, 109 to 111 and 112 to 116 of Schedule B1 to the 1986 Act are to have effect in relation to postal administration orders as they have effect in relation to administration orders under that Schedule, but with the modifications set out in this Part of this Schedule.

General modifications of the applicable provisions

2 Those paragraphs are to have effect as if—

(a) for "administration application", in each place, there were substituted "postal administration application",

(b) for "administration order", in each place, there were substituted "postal administration order",

(c) for "administrator", in each place, there were substituted "postal administrator",

(d) for "enters administration", in each place, there were substituted "enters postal administration",

(e) for "in administration", in each place, there were substituted "in postal administration", and

(f) for "purpose of administration", in each place (other than in paragraph 111(1)), there were substituted "objective of the postal administration".

Specific modifications

3 Paragraph 1 (administration) is to have effect as if—

(a) for sub-paragraph (1) there were substituted—

"(1) In this Schedule "postal administrator", in relation to a company, means a person appointed by the court for the purposes of a postal administration order to manage its affairs, business and property.", and

(b) in sub-paragraph (2), for "Act" there were substituted "Schedule".

4 Paragraph 40 (dismissal of pending winding-up petition) is to have effect as if sub-paragraphs (1)(b), (2) and (3) were omitted.

5 Paragraph 42 (moratorium on insolvency proceedings) is to have effect as if sub-paragraphs (4) and (5) were omitted.

6 Paragraph 44 (interim moratorium) is to have effect as if sub-paragraphs (2) to (4), (6) and (7)(a) to (c) were omitted.

7 Paragraph 46(6) (date for notifying administrator's appointment) is to have effect as if for paragraphs (a) to (c) there were substituted "the date on which the postal administration order comes into force".

8 Paragraph 49 (administrator's proposals) is to have effect as if—

(a) in sub-paragraph (2)(b) for "objective mentioned in paragraph 3(1)(a) or (b) cannot be achieved" there were substituted "objective of the postal administration should be achieved by means other than just a rescue of the company as a going concern", and

(b) in sub-paragraph (4), after paragraph (a) there were inserted—

"(aa) to the Secretary of State and OFCOM,".

9 Paragraph 54 is to have effect as if the following were substituted for it—

"**54** (1) The postal administrator of a company may on one or more occasions revise the proposals included in the statement made under paragraph 49 in relation to the company.

(2) If the postal administrator thinks that a revision is substantial, the postal administrator must send a copy of the revised proposals—

(a) to the registrar of companies,

(b) to the Secretary of State and OFCOM,

(c) to every creditor of the company of whose claim and address the postal administrator is aware, and

(d) to every member of the company of whose address the postal administrator is aware [other than an opted-out creditor].

(3) A copy sent in accordance with sub-paragraph (2) must be sent within the prescribed period.

(4) The postal administrator is to be taken to have complied with sub-paragraph (2)(d) if the postal administrator publishes, in the prescribed manner, a notice undertaking to provide a copy of the revised proposals free of charge to any member of the company who applies in writing to a specified address.

(5) The postal administrator who fails without reasonable excuse to comply with this paragraph commits an offence."

10 Paragraph 60 (powers of an administrator) is to have effect as if the existing text were to become sub-paragraph (1) and as if after that sub-paragraph there were inserted—

"(2) The postal administrator of a company has the power to act on behalf of the company for the purposes of any enactment which confers a power on the company or imposes a duty on it.

(3) In sub-paragraph (2) "enactment" has the same meaning as in the Postal Services Act 2011 (see section 90)."

11 Paragraph 68 (management duties of an administrator) is to have effect as if—

(a) in sub-paragraph (1), for paragraphs (a) to (c) there were substituted—

"the proposals as—

(a) set out in the statement made under paragraph 49 in relation to the company, and

(b) from time to time revised under paragraph 54,

for achieving the objective of the postal administration." and

(b) in sub-paragraph (3), for paragraphs (a) to (d) there were substituted "the directions are consistent with the achievement of the objective of the postal administration".

12 Paragraph 71(3)(b) (charged property: non-floating charge) is to have effect as if for "market" there were substituted "the appropriate".

13 Paragraph 72(3)(b) (hire-purchase property) is to have effect as if for "market" there were substituted "the appropriate".

14 Paragraph 73(3) (protection for secured or preferential creditor) is to have effect as if for "or modified" there were substituted "under paragraph 54".

15 Paragraph 74 (challenge to administrator's conduct) is to have effect as if—

(a) for sub-paragraph (2) there were substituted—

"(2) If a company is in postal administration, a person mentioned in sub-paragraph (2A) may apply to the court claiming that the postal administrator is acting in a manner preventing the achievement of the objective of the postal administration as quickly and efficiently as is reasonably practicable.

(2A) The persons who may apply to the court are—

(a) the Secretary of State,

(b) with the consent of the Secretary of State, OFCOM,

(c) a creditor or member of the company.",

(b) in sub-paragraph (6)—

(i) at the end of paragraph (b) there were inserted "or", and

(ii) paragraph (c) (and the "or" before it) were omitted, and

(c) after that sub-paragraph there were inserted—

"(7) In the case of a claim made otherwise than by the Secretary of State or OFCOM, the court may grant a remedy or relief or make an order under this paragraph only if it has given the Secretary of State or OFCOM a reasonable opportunity of making representations about the claim and the proposed remedy, relief or order.

(8) The court may grant a remedy or relief or make an order on an application under this paragraph only if it is satisfied, in relation to the matters that are the subject of the application, that the postal administrator—

(a) is acting,
(b) has acted, or
(c) is proposing to act,

in a way that is inconsistent with the achievement of the objective of the postal administration as quickly and as efficiently as is reasonably practicable.

(9) Before the making of an order of the kind mentioned in sub-paragraph (4)(d)—

(a) the court must notify the postal administrator of the proposed order and of a period during which the postal administrator is to have the opportunity of taking steps falling within sub-paragraphs (10) to (12), and
(b) the period notified must have expired without the taking of such of those steps as the court thinks should have been taken,

and that period must be a reasonable period.

(10) In the case of a claim under sub-paragraph (1)(a), the steps referred to in sub-paragraph (9) are—

(a) ceasing to act in a manner that unfairly harms the interests to which the claim relates,
(b) remedying any harm unfairly caused to those interests, and
(c) steps for ensuring that there is no repetition of conduct unfairly causing harm to those interests.

(11) In the case of a claim under sub-paragraph (1)(b), the steps referred to in sub-paragraph (9) are steps for ensuring that the interests to which the claim relates are not unfairly harmed.

(12) In the case of a claim under sub-paragraph (2), the steps referred to in sub-paragraph (9) are—

(a) ceasing to act in a manner preventing the achievement of the objective of the postal administration as quickly and as efficiently as is reasonably practicable,
(b) remedying the consequences of the postal administrator having acted in such a manner, and
(c) steps for ensuring that there is no repetition of conduct preventing the achievement of the objective of the postal administration as quickly and as efficiently as is reasonably practicable."

16 Paragraph 75(2) (misfeasance) is to have effect as if after paragraph (b) there were inserted—

"(ba) a person appointed as an administrator of the company under the provisions of this Act, as they have effect in relation to administrators other than postal administrators,".

17 Paragraph 79 (end of administration) is to have effect as if—

(a) for sub-paragraphs (1) and (2) there were substituted—

"(1) On an application made by a person mentioned in sub-paragraph (2), the court may provide for the appointment of a postal administrator of a company to cease to have effect from a specified time.

(2) An application may be made to the court under this paragraph—

(a) by the Secretary of State,
(b) with the consent of the Secretary of State, by OFCOM, or
(c) with the consent of the Secretary of State, by the postal administrator.", and

(b) sub-paragraph (3) were omitted.

18 Paragraph 83(3) (notice to registrar when moving to voluntary liquidation) is to have effect as if after "may" there were inserted ", with the consent of the Secretary of State or of OFCOM,".

19 (1) Paragraph 84 (notice to registrar when moving to dissolution) is to have effect as if—

(a) in sub-paragraph (1), for "to the registrar of companies" there were substituted—

"(a) to the Secretary of State and OFCOM, and
(b) if directed to do so by either the Secretary of State or OFCOM, to the registrar of companies.",

(b) sub-paragraph (2) were omitted, and
(c) in sub-paragraphs (3) to (6), for "(1)", in each place, there were substituted "(1)(b)".

20 Paragraph 87(2) (resignation of administrator) is to have effect as if for paragraphs (a) to (d) there were substituted "by notice in writing to the court".

21 Paragraph 89(2) (administrator ceasing to be qualified) is to have effect as if for paragraphs (a) to (d) there were substituted "to the court".

22 Paragraph 90 (filling vacancy in office of administrator) is to have effect as if for "Paragraphs 91 to 95 apply" there were substituted "Paragraph 91 applies".

23 Paragraph 91 (vacancies in court appointments) is to have effect as if—

(a) for sub-paragraph (1) there were substituted—

"(1) The court may replace the postal administrator on an application made—

(a) by the Secretary of State,

(b) with the consent of the Secretary of State, by OFCOM, or

(c) where more than one person was appointed to act jointly as the postal administrator, by any of those persons who remains in office.", and

(b) sub-paragraph (2) were omitted.

24 Paragraph 98 (discharge from liability on vacation of office) is to have effect as if sub-paragraphs (2)(b) and (3) were omitted.

25 Paragraph 99 (charges and liabilities upon vacation of office by administrator) is to have effect as if—

(a) in sub-paragraph (4), for the words from the beginning to "cessation", in the first place, there were substituted "A sum falling within sub-paragraph (4A)",

(b) after that sub-paragraph there were inserted—

"(4A) A sum falls within this sub-paragraph if it is—

(a) a sum payable in respect of a debt or other liability arising out of a contract that was entered into before cessation by the former postal administrator or a predecessor,

(b) a sum that must be repaid by the company in respect of a grant that was made before cessation under section 79 of the Postal Services Act 2011 as is mentioned in subsection (4) of that section,

(c) a sum that must be repaid by the company in respect of a loan made before cessation under that section or that must be paid by the company in respect of interest payable on such a loan,

(d) a sum payable by the company under subsection (5) of section 80 of that Act in respect of an agreement to indemnify made before cessation, or

(e) a sum payable by the company under subsection (5) of section 81 of that Act in respect of a guarantee given before cessation.", and

(c) in sub-paragraph (5), for "(4)" there were substituted "(4A)(a)".

26 Paragraph 100 (joint and concurrent administrators) is to have effect as if sub-paragraph (2) were omitted.

27 Paragraph 101(3) (joint administrators) is to have effect as if after "87 to" there were inserted "91, 98 and".

28 Paragraph 103 (appointment of additional administrators) is to have effect as if—

(a) in sub-paragraph (2) the words from the beginning to "order" were omitted and for paragraph (a) there were substituted—

"(a) the Secretary of State,

(aa) OFCOM, or",

(b) after that sub-paragraph there were inserted—

"(2A) The consent of the Secretary of State is required for an application by OFCOM for the purposes of sub-paragraph (2).", and

(c) sub-paragraphs (3) to (5) were omitted.

29 Paragraph 106(2) (penalties) is to have effect as if paragraphs (a), (b), (f), (g), (i) and (l) to (n) were omitted.

30 Paragraph 109 (references to extended periods) is to have effect as if "or 108" were omitted.

31 Paragraph 111 (interpretation) is to have effect as if—

(a) in sub-paragraph (1), the definitions of "correspondence", "holder of a qualifying floating charge", "market value", "the purpose of administration" and "unable to pay its debts" were omitted,

(b) in that sub-paragraph, after the definition of "administrator" (as modified as a result of paragraph 2 above) there were inserted—

""appropriate value" means the best price which would be reasonably available on a sale which is consistent with the achievement of the objective of the postal administration,",

(c) in that sub-paragraph, before the definition of "creditors' meeting" there were inserted—

""company" and "court" have the same meaning as in Part 4 of the Postal Services Act 2011,",

(d) in that sub-paragraph, after the definition of "hire purchase agreement" there were inserted—

""objective", in relation to a postal administration, is to be read in accordance with section 69 of the Postal Services Act 2011,

"OFCOM" means the Office of Communications,

"postal administration application" means an application to the court for a postal administration order under Part 4 of the Postal Services Act 2011,

"postal administration order" has the same meaning as in Part 4 of the Postal Services Act 2011,

"prescribed" means prescribed by postal administration rules within the meaning of Part 4 of the Postal Services Act 2011.",

(e) sub-paragraphs (1A) and (1B) were omitted, and
(f) after sub-paragraph (3) there were inserted—

"(4) For the purposes of this Schedule a reference to a postal administration order includes a reference to an appointment under paragraph 91 or 103."

NOTES

Para 9: words in square brackets in the substituted paragraph 54(2)(d) inserted by the Deregulation Act 2015 and Small Business, Enterprise and Employment Act 2015 (Consequential Amendments) (Savings) Regulations 2017, SI 2017/540, reg 2, Sch 1, para 6.

PART 2
FURTHER MODIFICATIONS OF SCHEDULE B1 TO 1986 ACT: FOREIGN COMPANIES

Introductory

[7.2083]

32 (1) This Part of this Schedule applies in the case of a postal administration order applying to a foreign company.

(2) The provisions of Schedule B1 to the 1986 Act mentioned in paragraph 1 above (as modified by Part 1 of this Schedule) have effect in relation to the company with the further modifications set out in this Part of this Schedule.

(3) The Secretary of State may by order amend this Part of this Schedule so as to add more modifications.

(4) An order under this paragraph is subject to negative resolution procedure.

33 In paragraphs 34 to 39—
(a) the provisions of Schedule B1 to the 1986 Act that are mentioned in paragraph 1 above are referred to as the applicable provisions, and
(b) references to those provisions, or to provisions comprised in them, are references to those provisions as modified by Part 1 of this Schedule.

Modifications

34 In the case of a foreign company—
(a) paragraphs 42(2), 83 and 84 of Schedule B1 to the 1986 Act do not apply,
(b) paragraphs 46(4), 49(4)(a), 54(2)(a), 71(5) and (6), 72(4) and (5) and 86 of that Schedule apply only if the company is subject to a requirement imposed by regulations under section 1043 or 1046 of the Companies Act 2006 (unregistered UK companies or overseas companies), and
(c) paragraph 61 of that Schedule does not apply.

35 (1) The applicable provisions and Schedule 1 to the 1986 Act (as applied by paragraph 60(1) of Schedule B1 to that Act) are to be read by reference to the limitation imposed on the scope of the postal administration order in question as a result of section 68(4) above.

(2) Sub-paragraph (1) has effect, in particular, so that—
(a) a power conferred, or duty imposed, on the postal administrator by or under the applicable provisions or Schedule 1 to the 1986 Act is to be read as being conferred or imposed in relation to the company's UK affairs, business and property,
(b) references to the company's affairs, business or property are to be read as references to its UK affairs, business and property,
(c) references to goods in the company's possession are to be read as references to goods in its possession in the United Kingdom,
(d) references to premises let to the company are to be read as references to premises let to it in the United Kingdom, and
(e) references to legal process instituted or continued against the company or its property are to be read as references to such legal process relating to its UK affairs, business and property.

36 Paragraph 41 of Schedule B1 to the 1986 Act (dismissal of receivers) is to have effect as if—
(a) for sub-paragraph (1) there were substituted—

"(1) Where a postal administration order takes effect in respect of a company—
(a) a person appointed to perform functions equivalent to those of an administrative receiver, and
(b) if the postal administrator so requires, a person appointed to perform functions equivalent to those of a receiver,

must refrain, during the period specified in sub-paragraph (1A), from performing those functions in the United Kingdom or in relation to any of the company's property in the United Kingdom.

(1A) That period is—

(a) in the case of a person mentioned in sub-paragraph (1)(a), the period while the company is in postal administration, and

(b) in the case of a person mentioned in sub-paragraph (1)(b), during so much of that period as is after the date on which the person is required by the postal administrator to refrain from performing functions.", and

(b) sub-paragraphs (2) to (4) were omitted.

37 Paragraph 43(6A) of Schedule B1 to the 1986 Act (moratorium on appointment to receiverships) is to have effect as if for "An administrative receiver" there were substituted "A person with functions equivalent to those of an administrative receiver".

38 Paragraph 44(7) of Schedule B1 to the 1986 Act (proceedings to which interim moratorium does not apply) is to have effect as if for paragraph (d) there were substituted—

"(d) the carrying out of functions by a person who (whenever appointed) has functions equivalent to those of an administrative receiver of the company."

39 Paragraph 64 of Schedule B1 to the 1986 Act (general powers of administrator) is to have effect as if—

(a) in sub-paragraph (1), after "power" there were inserted "in relation to the affairs or business of the company so far as carried on in the United Kingdom or to its property in the United Kingdom", and

(b) in sub-paragraph (2)(b), after "instrument" there were inserted "or by the law of the place where the company is incorporated".

PART 3
OTHER MODIFICATIONS

General modifications

[7.2084]

40 (1) References within sub-paragraph (2) which are contained—

(a) in the 1986 Act (other than Schedule B1 to that Act), or

(b) in other enactments passed or made before this Act,

include references to whatever corresponds to them for the purposes of this paragraph.

(2) The references are those (however expressed) which are or include references to—

(a) an administrator appointed by an administration order,

(b) an administration order,

(c) an application for an administration order,

(d) a company in administration,

(e) entering into administration, and

(f) Schedule B1 to the 1986 Act or a provision of that Schedule.

(3) For the purposes of this paragraph—

(a) a postal administrator corresponds to an administrator appointed by an administration order,

(b) a postal administration order corresponds to an administration order,

(c) an application for a postal administration order corresponds to an application for an administration order,

(d) a company in postal administration corresponds to a company in administration,

(e) entering into postal administration corresponds to entering into administration, and

(f) what corresponds to Schedule B1 to the 1986 Act or a provision of that Schedule is that Schedule or that provision as applied by Part 1 of this Schedule.

41 (1) Paragraph 40, in its application to section 1(3) of the 1986 Act, does not entitle the postal administrator of an unregistered company to make a proposal under Part 1 of the 1986 Act (company voluntary arrangements).

(2) Paragraph 40 does not confer any right under section 7(4) of the 1986 Act (implementation of voluntary arrangements) for a supervisor of voluntary arrangements to apply for a postal administration order in relation to a company which is a universal service provider.

(3) Paragraph 40 does not apply to section 359 of the Financial Services and Markets Act 2000 ([administration order]).

Modifications of 1986 Act

42 The following provisions of the 1986 Act are to have effect in the case of any postal administration with the following modifications.

43 Section 5 (effect of approval of voluntary arrangements) is to have effect as if after subsection (4) there were inserted—

"(4A) Where the company is in postal administration, the court must not make an order or give a direction under subsection (3) unless—

(a) the court has given the Secretary of State or the Office of Communications a reasonable opportunity of making representations to it about the proposed order or direction, and

(b) the order or direction is consistent with the objective of the postal administration.

(4B) In subsection (4A) "in postal administration" and "objective of the postal administration" are to be read in accordance with Schedule B1 to this Act, as applied by Part 1 of Schedule 10 to the Postal Services Act 2011."

44 Section 6 (challenge of decisions in relation to voluntary arrangements) is to have effect as if—

(a) in subsection (2), for "this section" there were substituted "subsection (1)",

(b) after that subsection there were inserted—

"(2AA) Subject to this section, where a voluntary arrangement in relation to a company in postal administration is approved at the meetings summoned under section 3, an application to the court may be made—

(a) by the Secretary of State, or

(b) with the consent of the Secretary of State, by the Office of Communications,

on the ground that the voluntary arrangement is not consistent with the achievement of the objective of the postal administration.",

(c) in subsection (4), after "subsection (1)" there were inserted "or, in the case of an application under subsection (2AA), as to the ground mentioned in that subsection", and

(d) after subsection (7) there were inserted—

"(7A) In this section "in postal administration" and "objective of the postal administration" are to be read in accordance with Schedule B1 to this Act, as applied by Part 1 of Schedule 10 to the Postal Services Act 2011."

45 In section 129(1A) (commencement of winding up), the reference to paragraph 13(1)(e) of Schedule B1 is to include section 71(1)(e) of this Act.

Power to make further modifications

46 (1) The Secretary of State may by order amend this Part of this Schedule so as to add further modifications.

(2) The further modifications that may be made are confined to such modifications of—

(a) the 1986 Act, or

(b) other enactments passed or made before this Act that relate to insolvency or make provision by reference to anything that is or may be done under the 1986 Act,

as the Secretary of State considers appropriate in relation to any provision made by or under this Part of this Act.

(3) An order under this paragraph is subject to affirmative resolution procedure.

Interpretation of Part 3 of Schedule

47 In this Part of this Schedule—

"administration order", "administrator", "enters administration" and "in administration" are to be read in accordance with Schedule B1 to the 1986 Act (disregarding Part 1 of this Schedule), and

"enters postal administration" and "in postal administration" are to be read in accordance with Schedule B1 to the 1986 Act (as applied by Part 1 of this Schedule).

NOTES

Para 41: words in square brackets substituted by the Financial Services Act 2012, s 114(1), Sch 18, Pt 2, para 133.

SCHEDULE 11
POSTAL TRANSFER SCHEMES

Section 73

Application of Schedule

[7.2085]

1 This Schedule applies if—

(a) the court has made a postal administration order in relation to a company (the "old company"), and

(b) it is proposed that a relevant transfer (within the meaning of section 69(3)) be made to another company (or companies) (a "new company").

2 While the order is in force, the postal administrator is to act on behalf of the old company in doing anything that it is authorised or required to do by or under this Schedule.

Making of postal transfer schemes

3 (1) The old company may for the purpose of giving effect to the proposed transfer make a scheme (a "postal transfer scheme") for the transfer of property, rights and liabilities from it to the new company (or companies).

(2) A postal transfer scheme has effect only if—

(a) the new company (or companies) have consented to the making of the scheme, and

(b) the Secretary of State has approved the scheme.

(3) A postal transfer scheme may be made only at a time when the postal administration order is in force in relation to the old company.

(4) A postal transfer scheme takes effect at the time specified in the scheme.

(5) In the case of a proposed transfer falling within section 69(4)(a) (transfer to wholly-owned subsidiary), sub-paragraph (2)(a) does not apply.

Approval and modification of scheme by Secretary of State

4 (1) The Secretary of State may modify a postal transfer scheme before approving it.

(2) After a postal transfer scheme has taken effect—

(a) the Secretary of State may by notice to the old company and the new company (or companies) modify the scheme, and

(b) the scheme as modified is to be treated for all purposes as having come into force at the time specified under paragraph 3(4).

(3) The only modifications that may be made by the Secretary of State under this paragraph are ones—

(a) to which the old company and the new company (or companies) have consented, or

(b) in the case of a proposed transfer falling within section 69(4)(a), to which the old company has consented.

(4) In connection with giving effect to modifications under sub-paragraph (2), the Secretary of State may make incidental, supplementary, consequential, transitional, transitory or saving provision (and different provision may be made for different cases or circumstances).

(5) In deciding whether to approve or modify a postal transfer scheme, the Secretary of State must have regard to—

(a) the public interest, and

(b) any effect the scheme or modification is likely to have on the interests of persons other than the old company and a new company.

(6) Before approving or modifying a postal transfer scheme, the Secretary of State must consult OFCOM.

(7) The old company and the new company (or companies) each have a duty to provide the Secretary of State with any information or other assistance that the Secretary of State may reasonably require for the purposes of, or in connection with, the exercise of any power under this paragraph.

(8) That duty overrides a contractual or other requirement to keep information in confidence.

(9) That duty is enforceable in civil proceedings by the Secretary of State—

(a) for an injunction,

(b) for specific performance of a statutory duty under section 45 of the Court of Session Act 1988, or

(c) for any other appropriate remedy or relief.

Identification of property etc to be transferred

5 (1) A postal transfer scheme may identify the property, rights and liabilities to be transferred by specifying or describing them.

(2) A postal transfer scheme may provide for the way in which property, rights or liabilities of any description are to be identified.

Property, rights and liabilities that may be transferred

6 (1) A postal transfer scheme may transfer—

(a) property situated in any part of the world, and

(b) rights and liabilities arising (in any way) under the law of any country or territory.

(2) The property, rights and liabilities that may be transferred by a postal transfer scheme include—

(a) property, rights and liabilities acquired or arising after the scheme has been made but before the time at which it takes effect,

(b) rights and liabilities arising after that time in respect of matters occurring before that time, and

(c) property, rights and liabilities that would not otherwise be capable of being transferred or assigned.

(3) The transfers to which effect may be given by a postal transfer scheme include ones that are to take effect as if there were no such contravention, liability or interference with any interest or right as there would otherwise be by reason of any provision having effect in relation to the terms on which the old company is entitled or subject to anything to which the transfer relates.

(4) In sub-paragraph (3) the reference to any provision is a reference to any provision, whether under an enactment or agreement or otherwise.

(5) Sub-paragraph (3) has effect where shares in a subsidiary of the old company are transferred as if the reference to the terms on which that company is entitled or subject to anything to which the transfer relates included a reference to the terms on which the subsidiary is entitled or subject to anything immediately before the transfer takes effect.

Dividing and modifying the old company's property, rights and liabilities

7 (1) A postal transfer scheme may contain provision—

(a) for the creation, in favour of the old company or a new company, of an interest or right in or in relation to property or rights transferred in accordance with the scheme,

(b) for giving effect to a transfer by the creation, in favour of a new company, of an interest or right in or in relation to property or rights retained by the old company, and

(c) for the creation of new rights and liabilities (including rights of indemnity and duties to indemnify) as between the old company and a new company.

(2) A postal transfer scheme may contain provision for the creation of rights and liabilities for the purpose of converting arrangements between different parts of the old company's undertaking into a contract—

(a) between different new companies, or
(b) between a new company and the old company.

(3) A postal transfer scheme may contain provision—

(a) for rights and liabilities to be transferred so as to be enforceable by or against more than one new company or by or against both the new company and the old company, and
(b) for rights and liabilities enforceable against more than one person in accordance with provision falling within paragraph (a) to be enforceable in different or modified respects by or against each or any of them.

(4) A postal transfer scheme may contain provision for interests, rights or liabilities of third parties in relation to anything to which the scheme relates to be modified in the manner set out in the scheme.

(5) The reference here to third parties is to persons other than the old company and a new company.

(6) Paragraph 6(2)(c) and (3) apply to the creation of interests and rights as they apply to the transfer of interests and rights.

Transfer of regulatory conditions etc

8 (1) A postal transfer scheme may contain provision—

(a) for a new company to be treated for all purposes as having been designated by OFCOM under section 35 as a universal service provider, and
(b) for the transfer to a new company of the whole or part of any obligation contained in a regulatory condition to which the old company was subject.

(2) The reference to the transfer of a part of any obligation includes the transfer of any obligation so far as relating to an area specified or described in provision made by the scheme.

(3) A postal transfer scheme may, in consequence of provision made under sub-paragraph (1), make modifications of regulatory conditions to which the old company or new company are subject.

Transfer etc of statutory functions

9 (1) A postal transfer scheme may contain provision—

(a) for the transfer of relevant statutory functions to a new company, or
(b) for relevant statutory functions to be exercisable concurrently by the old company and a new company (or companies).

(2) For this purpose "relevant statutory functions" means powers and duties conferred or imposed on the old company by or under an enactment so far as they are connected with—

(a) the undertaking of the old company to which the postal transfer scheme relates, or
(b) property, rights or liabilities transferred in accordance with the scheme.

(3) Provision within sub-paragraph (1) may apply to relevant statutory functions so far as exercisable in an area specified or described in the provision.

Effect of postal transfer scheme: general

10 (1) At the time at which a postal transfer scheme takes effect—

(a) the property, rights and liabilities to be transferred in accordance with the scheme, and
(b) the interests, rights and liabilities to be created in accordance with the scheme,

are, as a result of this paragraph, to vest in the appropriate person.

(2) For this purpose "the appropriate person" means—

(a) in the case of property, rights and liabilities to be transferred, the new company (or companies), and
(b) in the case of interests, right and liabilities to be created, the person in whose favour, or in relation to whom, they are to be created.

Effect of postal transfer scheme on right to terminate or modify interest etc

11 (1) This paragraph applies where a person would otherwise be entitled, in consequence of anything done or likely to be done by or under this Act in connection with a postal transfer scheme—

(a) to terminate, modify, acquire or claim an interest or right, or
(b) to treat an interest or right as modified or terminated.

(2) The entitlement—

(a) is not enforceable in relation to the interest or right until after the transfer of the interest or right by the scheme, and
(b) after that transfer, is enforceable in relation to the interest or right only in so far as the scheme contains provision for the interest or right to be transferred subject to whatever confers the entitlement.

(3) Where shares in a subsidiary of the old company are transferred, sub-paragraph (2) has effect in relation to an interest or right of the subsidiary as if the references to the transfer of the interest or right included a reference to the transfer of the shares.

Supplementary provisions of postal transfer schemes

12 (1) A postal transfer scheme may—
(a) contain incidental, supplementary, consequential, transitional, transitory or saving provision, and
(b) make different provision for different cases or circumstances.

(2) Nothing in paragraphs 13 to 17 limits sub-paragraph (1).

(3) In those paragraphs any reference to a transfer in accordance with a postal transfer scheme includes the creation in accordance with a postal transfer scheme of an interest, right or liability.

13 (1) A postal transfer scheme may provide, in relation to transfers in accordance with the scheme—
(a) for a new company to be treated as the same person in law as the old company,
(b) for agreements made, transactions effected or other things done by or in relation to the old company to be treated, so far as may be necessary for the purposes of or in connection with the transfers, as made, effected or done by or in relation to a new company,
(c) for references in any document to the old company, or to an employee or office holder of it, to have effect, so far as may be necessary for the purposes of or in connection with any of the transfers, with such modifications as are specified in the scheme, and
(d) for proceedings commenced by or against the old company to be continued by or against a new company.

(2) In sub-paragraph (1)(c) "document" includes an agreement or instrument, but does not include an enactment.

14 (1) A postal transfer scheme may contain provision about—
(a) the transfer of foreign property, rights and liabilities, and
(b) the creation of foreign rights, interests and liabilities.

(2) For this purpose property, or a right, interest or liability, is "foreign" if an issue relating to it arising in any proceedings would (in accordance with the rules of private international law) be determined under the law of a country or territory outside the United Kingdom.

15 (1) A postal transfer scheme may contain provision for and in connection with the payment of compensation to persons other than the old company and a new company if their property, rights, interests or liabilities have been affected by (or as a result of) a postal transfer scheme.

(2) The provision may provide for the appointment of an arbitrator to determine disputes about compensation.

16 A postal transfer scheme may make provision for disputes as to the effect of the scheme—
(a) between different new companies, or
(b) between the old company and a new company,
to be referred to such arbitration as may be specified in or determined under the scheme.

17 (1) This paragraph applies if, in consequence of a postal transfer scheme, a person ("P") is entitled to possession of a document relating in part to the title to, or to the management of, land or other property.

(2) If the land or other property is in England and Wales—
(a) the scheme may provide for P to be treated as having given another person an acknowledgement in writing of the other person's right to production of the document and to delivery of copies of it, and
(b) section 64 of the Law of Property Act 1925 (production and safe custody of documents) is to apply to the acknowledgement and is to apply on the basis that the acknowledgement does not contain an expression of contrary intention.

(3) If the land or other property is in Scotland, section 16(1) of the Land Registration (Scotland) Act 1979 (omission of certain clauses in deeds) has effect in relation to the transfer as if—
(a) the transfer had been effected by deed, and
(b) the words "unless specially qualified" were omitted from that subsection.

(4) If the land or other property is in Northern Ireland—
(a) the scheme may provide for P to be treated as having given another person an acknowledgement in writing of the other person's right to production of the document and to delivery of copies of it, and
(b) section 9 of the Conveyancing Act 1881 (which corresponds to section 64 of the 1925 Act) is to apply to the acknowledgement and is to apply on the basis that the acknowledgement does not contain an expression of contrary intention.

Proof of title by certificate

18 A certificate issued by the Secretary of State to the effect that any property, interest, right or liability vested (in accordance with a postal transfer scheme) in a person specified in the certificate at a time so specified is conclusive evidence of the matters so specified.

Staff

19 The Transfer of Undertakings (Protection of Employment) Regulations 2006 apply to a transfer (under a postal transfer scheme) of rights and liabilities under a contract of employment (whether or not the transfer would otherwise be a relevant transfer for the purposes of those regulations).

20 If an employee of the old company becomes an employee of a new company as a result of a postal transfer scheme—

(a) a period of employment with the old company is to be treated as a period of employment with the new company, and

(b) the transfer to the new company is not to be treated as a break in service.

Transfers in case of foreign companies

21 (1) This paragraph applies if the old company is a foreign company.

(2) The property, rights and liabilities which may be transferred by a postal transfer scheme, or in or in relation to which interests, rights or liabilities may be created by a postal transfer scheme, are confined to—

(a) property of the old company in the United Kingdom,

(b) rights and liabilities arising in relation to its property in the United Kingdom, and

(c) rights and liabilities arising in connection with its affairs and business so far as carried on in the United Kingdom.

Transfers by two or more postal transfer schemes

22 (1) This paragraph applies if there are two or more postal transfer schemes making transfers to new companies.

(2) Paragraph 7 has effect as if—

(a) in sub-paragraph (1)(a) the reference to property or rights transferred in accordance with a postal transfer scheme included property or rights transferred in accordance with another postal transfer scheme, and

(b) in sub-paragraphs (2)(a) and (3) references to a new company included a company that is a new company for the purposes of another postal transfer scheme.

(3) Accordingly, in relation to anything done by a postal transfer scheme as a result of this paragraph, any reference to a new company in paragraphs 13 to 16 includes a company that is a new company for the purposes of another postal transfer scheme.

SCHEDULE 12

(*Sch 12 contains amendments which, in so far as relevant to this work, have been incorporated at the appropriate place.*)

POSTAL ADMINISTRATION RULES 2013

(SI 2013/3208)

NOTES

Made: 18 December 2013.

Authority: Insolvency Act 1986, s 411; Postal Services Act 2011, s 73(3), (4).

Commencement: 31 January 2014.

Note: the Insolvency Rules 1986, SI 1986/1925 are revoked and replaced (as from 6 April 2017 and subject to transitional provisions) by the Insolvency (England and Wales) Rules 2016, SI 2016/1024 at **[6.2]**, however, the Insolvency (England and Wales) Rules 2016 (Consequential Amendments and Savings) Rules 2017, SI 2017/369, r 3(j) at **[6.947]** provides that the Insolvency Rules 1986 as they had effect immediately before 6 April 2017 and insofar as they apply to proceedings under the Postal Administration Rules 2013, continue to have effect for the purposes of the application of the 2013 Rules.

See also the Deregulation Act 2015 and Small Business, Enterprise and Employment Act 2015 (Consequential Amendments) (Savings) Regulations 2017, SI 2017/540, reg 4(1), (2)(j) and the Insolvency Amendment (EU 2015/848) Regulations 2017, SI 2017/702, reg 4 at **[2.103]**, for savings in relation to the Insolvency Act 1986 in so far as it applies to proceedings under these Rules.

ARRANGEMENT OF RULES

PART 1
INTRODUCTORY PROVISIONS

1 Citation and commencement . . . [7.2086]
2 Construction and Interpretation . . . [7.2087]
3 Extent . . . [7.2088]

PART 2
APPOINTMENT OF POSTAL ADMINISTRATOR BY COURT

4 Witness statement . . . [7.2089]
5 Form of application . . . [7.2090]
6 Contents of application and witness statement . . . [7.2091]
7 Filing of application . . . [7.2092]
8 Service of application . . . [7.2093]
9 Notice to officers charged with execution of writs or other process . . . [7.2094]
10 Manner in which service to be effected . . . [7.2095]

11 Proof of service . . . [7.2096]
12 The hearing . . . [7.2097]
13 Notice of postal administration order . . . [7.2098]

PART 3
PROCESS OF POSTAL ADMINISTRATION

14 Notification and advertisement of postal administrator's appointment . . . [7.2099]
15 Notice requiring statement of affairs . . . [7.2100]
16 Verification and filing . . . [7.2101]
17 Limited disclosure . . . [7.2102]
18 Release from duty to submit statement of affairs; extension of time . . . [7.2103]
19 Expenses of statement of affairs . . . [7.2104]
20 Postal administrator's proposals . . . [7.2105]
21 Limited disclosure of paragraph 49 statement . . . [7.2106]

PART 4
MEETINGS AND REPORTS

CHAPTER 1
CREDITORS MEETINGS

22 Creditors' meetings generally . . . [7.2107]
23 The chair at meetings . . . [7.2108]
24 Creditors' meeting for nomination of alternative liquidator . . . [7.2109]
25 Notice of meetings by advertisement only . . . [7.2110]
26 Entitlement to vote . . . [7.2111]
27 Admission and rejection of claims . . . [7.2112]
28 Secured creditors . . . [7.2113]
29 Holders of negotiable instruments . . . [7.2114]
30 Hire-purchase, conditional sale and chattel leasing agreements . . . [7.2115]
31 Resolutions . . . [7.2116]
32 Minutes . . . [7.2117]
33 Revision of the postal administrator's proposals . . . [7.2118]
34 Reports to creditors . . . [7.2119]

CHAPTER 2
COMPANY MEETINGS

35 Venue and conduct of company meeting . . . [7.2120]

PART 5
DISPOSAL OF CHARGED PROPERTY

36 Authority to dispose of property . . . [7.2121]

PART 6
EXPENSES OF THE POSTAL ADMINISTRATION

37 Priority of expenses of postal administration . . . [7.2122]
38 Pre-postal administration costs . . . [7.2123]

PART 7
DISTRIBUTION TO CREDITORS

CHAPTER 1
APPLICATION OF PART AND GENERAL

39 Distribution to creditors generally . . . [7.2124]
40 Debts of insolvent company to rank equally . . . [7.2125]
41 Supplementary provisions as to dividend . . . [7.2126]
42 Division of unsold assets . . . [7.2127]

CHAPTER 2
MACHINERY OF PROVING A DEBT

43 Proving a debt . . . [7.2128]
44 Costs of proving . . . [7.2129]
45 Postal administrator to allow inspection of proofs . . . [7.2130]
46 New postal administrator appointed . . . [7.2131]
47 Admission and rejection of proofs for dividend . . . [7.2132]
48 Appeal against decision on proof . . . [7.2133]
49 Withdrawal or variation of proof . . . [7.2134]
50 Expunging of proof by the court . . . [7.2135]

CHAPTER 3
QUANTIFICATION OF CLAIMS

51 Estimate of quantum . . . [7.2136]

52 Negotiable instruments, etc .....[7.2137]
53 Secured creditors .....[7.2138]
54 Discounts .....[7.2139]
55 Mutual credits and set-off .....[7.2140]
56 Debt in foreign currency.....[7.2141]
57 Payments of a periodical nature.....[7.2142]
58 Interest.....[7.2143]
59 Debt payable at future time .....[7.2144]
60 Value of security .....[7.2145]
61 Surrender for non-disclosure .....[7.2146]
62 Redemption by postal administrator .....[7.2147]
63 Test of security's value.....[7.2148]
64 Realisation of security by creditor .....[7.2149]
65 Notice of proposed distribution .....[7.2150]
66 Admission or rejection of proofs .....[7.2151]
67 Postponement or cancellation of dividend .....[7.2152]
68 Declaration of dividend .....[7.2153]
69 Notice of declaration of a dividend.....[7.2154]
70 Payments of dividends and related matters.....[7.2155]
71 Notice of no dividend, or no further dividend .....[7.2156]
72 Proof altered after payment of dividend .....[7.2157]
73 Secured creditors .....[7.2158]
74 Disqualification from dividend .....[7.2159]
75 Assignment of right to dividend .....[7.2160]
76 Debt payable at future time .....[7.2161]

PART 8
THE POSTAL ADMINISTRATOR

77 Fixing of remuneration.....[7.2162]

PART 9
ENDING POSTAL ADMINISTRATION

78 Final progress reports .....[7.2163]
79 Application to court .....[7.2164]
80 Notification by postal administrator of court order .....[7.2165]
81 Moving from postal administration to creditors' voluntary liquidation.....[7.2166]
82 Moving from postal administration to dissolution .....[7.2167]
83 Provision of information to the Secretary of State .....[7.2168]

PART 10
REPLACING POSTAL ADMINISTRATOR

84 Grounds for resignation .....[7.2169]
85 Notice of intention to resign.....[7.2170]
86 Notice of resignation.....[7.2171]
87 Application to court to remove postal administrator from office .....[7.2172]
88 Notice of vacation of office when postal administrator ceases to be qualified to act.....[7.2173]
89 Postal administrator deceased .....[7.2174]
90 Application to replace .....[7.2175]
91 Notification and advertisement of appointment of replacement postal administrator .....[7.2176]
92 Notification and advertisement of appointment of joint postal administrator .....[7.2177]
93 Notification to Registrar of Companies .....[7.2178]
94 Postal administrator's duties on vacating office.....[7.2179]

PART 11
COURT PROCEDURE AND PRACTICE

CHAPTER 1
APPLICATIONS

95 Preliminary .....[7.2180]
96 Form and contents of application.....[7.2181]
97 Application under section 1765) of the 1986 Act to disapply section 176A of the 1986 Act. . .[7.2182]
98 Filing and service of application .....[7.2183]
99 Notice of application under section 1765) of the 1986 Act .....[7.2184]
100 Hearings without notice .....[7.2185]
101 Hearing of application .....[7.2186]
102 Witness statements—general.....[7.2187]
103 Filing and service of witness statements .....[7.2188]

104 Use of reports . . . [7.2189]
105 Adjournment of hearing; directions . . . [7.2190]
106 General power of transfer . . . [7.2191]
107 Proceedings commenced in wrong court . . . [7.2192]
108 Applications for transfer . . . [7.2193]
109 Procedure following order for transfer . . . [7.2194]

CHAPTER 2
SHORTHAND WRITERS

110 Nomination and appointment of shorthand writers . . . [7.2195]
111 Remuneration . . . [7.2196]

CHAPTER 3
ENFORCEMENT PROCEDURES

112 Enforcement of court orders . . . [7.2197]
113 Orders enforcing compliance with the Rules . . . [7.2198]
114 Warrants under section 236 of the 1986 Act . . . [7.2199]

CHAPTER 4
COURT RECORDS AND RETURNS

115 Court file . . . [7.2200]

CHAPTER 5
COSTS AND DETAILED ASSESSMENT

116 Application of Chapter 5 . . . [7.2201]
117 Requirement to assess costs by the detailed procedure . . . [7.2202]
118 Procedure where detailed assessment required . . . [7.2203]
119 Costs paid otherwise than out of the assets of the company . . . [7.2204]
120 Award of costs against postal administrator . . . [7.2205]
121 Applications for costs . . . [7.2206]
122 Costs and expenses of witnesses . . . [7.2207]
123 Final costs certificate . . . [7.2208]

CHAPTER 6
PERSONS WHO LACK CAPACITY TO MANAGE THEIR AFFAIRS

124 Introductory . . . [7.2209]
125 Appointment of another person to act . . . [7.2210]
126 Witness statement in support of application . . . [7.2211]
127 Service of notices following appointment . . . [7.2212]

CHAPTER 7
APPEALS IN POSTAL ADMINISTRATION PROCEEDINGS

128 Appeals and reviews of postal administration orders . . . [7.2213]
129 Procedure on appeal . . . [7.2214]

CHAPTER 8
GENERAL

130 Principal court rules and practice to apply . . . [7.2215]
131 Right of audience . . . [7.2216]
132 Formal defects . . . [7.2217]
133 Service of orders staying proceedings . . . [7.2218]
134 Payment into court . . . [7.2219]
135 Further Information and Disclosure . . . [7.2220]
136 Office copies of documents . . . [7.2221]

PART 12
PROXIES AND COMPANY REPRESENTATION

137 Definition of "proxy" . . . [7.2222]
138 Issue and use of forms . . . [7.2223]
139 Use of proxies at meetings . . . [7.2224]
140 Retention of proxies . . . [7.2225]
141 Right of inspection . . . [7.2226]
142 Proxy-holder with financial interest . . . [7.2227]
143 Company representation . . . [7.2228]

PART 13
EXAMINATION OF PERSONS IN POSTAL ADMINISTRATION PROCEEDINGS

144 Preliminary . . . [7.2229]
145 Form and contents of application . . . [7.2230]

146 Order for examination, etc . . . [7.2231]
147 Procedure for examination . . . [7.2232]
148 Record of examination . . . [7.2233]
149 Costs of proceedings under section 236 . . . [7.2234]

PART 14
MISCELLANEOUS AND GENERAL

150 Power of Secretary of State to regulate certain matters . . . [7.2235]
151 Costs, expenses, etc . . . [7.2236]
152 Provable debts . . . [7.2237]
153 False claim of status as creditor, etc . . . [7.2238]
154 Punishment of offences . . . [7.2239]

PART 15
PROVISIONS OF GENERAL EFFECT

CHAPTER 1
THE GIVING OF NOTICE AND THE SUPPLY OF DOCUMENTS—GENERAL

155 Application . . . [7.2240]
156 Personal delivery of documents . . . [7.2241]
157 Postal delivery of documents . . . [7.2242]
158 Non-receipt of notice of meeting . . . [7.2243]
159 Notice etc to solicitors . . . [7.2244]

CHAPTER 2
THE GIVING OF NOTICE AND THE SUPPLY OF DOCUMENTS
BY OR TO A POSTAL ADMINISTRATOR ETC

160 Application . . . [7.2245]
161 The form of notices and other documents . . . [7.2246]
162 Proof of sending etc . . . [7.2247]
163 Authentication . . . [7.2248]
164 Electronic delivery in postal administration proceedings—general . . . [7.2249]
165 Electronic delivery by postal administrator . . . [7.2250]
166 Use of websites by postal administrator . . . [7.2251]
167 Special provision on account of expense as to website use . . . [7.2252]
168 Electronic delivery of postal administration proceedings to courts . . . [7.2253]
169 Notice etc to joint postal administrators . . . [7.2254]

CHAPTER 3
SERVICE OF COURT DOCUMENTS

170 Application of CPR Part 6 to service of court documents within the jurisdiction . . . [7.2255]
171 Service on joint postal administrators . . . [7.2256]
172 Application of CPR Part 6 to service of court documents outside the jurisdiction . . . [7.2257]

CHAPTER 4
MEETINGS

173 Quorum at meeting of creditors . . . [7.2258]
174 Remote attendance at meetings of creditors . . . [7.2259]
175 Action where person excluded . . . [7.2260]
176 Indication to excluded person . . . [7.2261]
177 Complaint . . . [7.2262]

CHAPTER 5
FORMS

178 Forms for use in postal administration proceedings . . . [7.2263]
179 Electronic submission of information instead of submission of forms to the Secretary of State, postal administrators, and of copies to the registrar of companies . . . [7.2264]
180 Electronic submission of information instead of submission of forms in all other cases . . . [7.2265]

CHAPTER 6
GAZETTE NOTICES

181 Contents of notices to be gazetted under the 1986 Act or the Rules . . . [7.2266]
182 Omission of unobtainable information . . . [7.2267]
183 The Gazette—general . . . [7.2268]

CHAPTER 7
NOTICES ADVERTISED OTHERWISE THAN IN THE GAZETTE

184 Notices otherwise advertised under the 1986 Act or the Rules . . . [7.2269]
185 Non-Gazette notices—other provisions . . . [7.2270]

CHAPTER 8
NOTIFICATIONS TO THE REGISTRAR OF COMPANIES
186 Application of this Chapter . . . [7.2271]
187 Information to be contained in all notifications to the registrar . . . [7.2272]
188 Notifications relating to the office of postal administrator . . . [7.2273]
189 Notifications relating to documents . . . [7.2274]
190 Notifications relating to court orders . . . [7.2275]
191 Returns or reports of meetings . . . [7.2276]
192 Notifications relating to other events . . . [7.2277]
193 Notifications of more than one nature . . . [7.2278]
194 Notifications made to other persons at the same time . . . [7.2279]

CHAPTER 9
INSPECTION OF DOCUMENTS AND THE PROVISION OF INFORMATION
195 Confidentiality of documents—grounds for refusing inspection . . . [7.2280]
196 Right to copy documents . . . [7.2281]
197 Charges for copy documents . . . [7.2282]
198 Right to have list of creditors . . . [7.2283]

CHAPTER 10
COMPUTATION OF TIME AND TIME LIMITS
199 Time limits . . . [7.2284]

CHAPTER 11
SECURITY
200 Postal administrator's security . . . [7.2285]

CHAPTER 12
NOTICE OF ORDER UNDER SECTION 1765) OF THE 1986 ACT
201 Notice of order under section 1765) of the 1986 Act . . . [7.2286]

PART 16
INTERPRETATION AND APPLICATION
202 Introductory . . . [7.2287]
203 "The appropriate fee" . . . [7.2288]
204 "Authorised deposit-taker and former authorised deposit-taker" . . . [7.2289]
205 "The court"; "the registrar" . . . [7.2290]
206 "Debt", "liability" . . . [7.2291]
207 "Petitioner" . . . [7.2292]
208 "Venue" . . . [7.2293]
209 Expressions used generally . . . [7.2294]
210 Application . . . [7.2295]
211 Application of the 1986 Act . . . [7.2296]

SCHEDULES

Schedule 1—Forms . . . [7.2297]
Schedule 2—Punishment of Offences under these Rules . . . [7.2298]

PART 1
INTRODUCTORY PROVISIONS

[7.2086]
1 Citation and Commencement

These Rules may be cited as the Postal Administration Rules 2013 and shall come into force on 31st January 2014.

NOTES

Commencement: 31 January 2014.

[7.2087]
2 Construction and Interpretation

(1) In these Rules—

"the 1986 Act" means the Insolvency Act 1986;

"the 2011 Act" means the Postal Services Act 2011;

"administrative receiver" has the same meaning as in section 70(4) of the 2011 Act;

"the appropriate fee" has the meaning given in Rule 203 of these Rules;

"authorised deposit-taker and former authorised deposit-taker" has the meaning given in Rule 204 of these Rules;

"the Companies Act" means the Companies Act 2006;
"CPR" means the Civil Procedure Rules 1998 and "CPR" followed by a Part or rule number means the Part or rule with that number in those Rules;
"debt" has the meaning given in Rule 206 of these Rules;
"enforcement officer" means an individual who is authorised to act as an enforcement officer under the Courts Act 2003;
"insolvency proceedings" has the same meaning as in Rule 13.7 of the Insolvency Rules;
"the Insolvency Rules" means the Insolvency Rules 1986;
"OFCOM" means the Office of Communications;
"petitioner" has the meaning given in Rule 207 of these Rules;
"pre-postal administration costs" are—
(a) fees charged, and
(b) expenses incurred,
by the postal administrator, or another person qualified to act as an insolvency practitioner, before the company entered postal administration but with a view to its doing so;
"the registrar" has the meaning given in Rule 205 of these Rules;
"registrar of companies" means the registrar of companies for England and Wales;
"the Rules" means the Postal Administration Rules 2013;
"unpaid pre-postal administration costs" are pre-postal administration costs which had not been paid when the company entered postal administration; and
"venue" has the meaning given in Rule 208 of these Rules.

(2) References in the Rules to ex parte hearings shall be construed as references to hearings without notice being served on any other party; references to applications made ex parte as references to applications made without notice being served on any other party and other references which include the expression "ex parte" shall be similarly construed.

(3) References to a numbered paragraph shall, unless otherwise stated, be to the paragraph so numbered in Schedule B1 to the 1986 Act as modified and applied by Schedule 10 to the 2011 Act.

(4) References to other provisions of the 1986 Act are, where those provisions have been modified by Schedule 10 to the 2011 Act, references to those provisions as so modified.

(5) Where the universal service provider is a foreign company within the meaning of section 85 of the 2011 Act, references in the Rules to the affairs, business and property of the company are references only to its affairs and business so far as carried on in the United Kingdom and to its property in the United Kingdom unless otherwise stated.

(6) Where the universal service provider is an unregistered company, any requirement to send information to the registrar of companies applies only if the company is subject to a requirement imposed by virtue of section 1043 or 1046 of the Companies Act.

(7) Subject to paragraphs (1) to (6) of this Rule, Part 16 of the Rules has effect for their interpretation and application.

NOTES

Commencement: 31 January 2014.

Note: the Insolvency Rules 1986, SI 1986/1925 are revoked and replaced (as from 6 April 2017 and subject to transitional provisions) by the Insolvency (England and Wales) Rules 2016, SI 2016/1024 at **[6.2]**, however, the Insolvency (England and Wales) Rules 2016 (Consequential Amendments and Savings) Rules 2017, SI 2017/369, r 3(j) provides that the Insolvency Rules 1986 as they had effect immediately before 6 April 2017 and insofar as they apply to proceedings under the Postal Administration Rules 2013, continue to have effect for the purposes of the application of the 2013 Rules.

[7.2088]
3 Extent

The Rules apply in relation to a company which is a universal service provider which the courts in England and Wales have jurisdiction to wind up.

NOTES

Commencement: 31 January 2014.

PART 2
APPOINTMENT OF POSTAL ADMINISTRATOR BY COURT

[7.2089]
4 Witness statement

Where it is proposed to apply to the court for a postal administration order to be made in relation to a company, the administration application shall be in Form PA1 and a witness statement complying with Rule 6 must be prepared with a view to its being filed with the court in support of the application.

NOTES

Commencement: 31 January 2014.

[7.2090]
5 Form of application

(1) The application shall state whether it is made by OFCOM or the Secretary of State and the applicant's address for service.

(2) Where it is made by OFCOM, the application shall contain a statement that it is made with the consent of the Secretary of State.

(3) There shall be attached to the application a written statement which shall be in Form PA2 made by each of the persons proposed to be postal administrator stating—

(a) that the person consents to accept the appointment; and

(b) details of any prior professional relationshis) that the person has had with the company to which that person is to be appointed as postal administrator.

NOTES

Commencement: 31 January 2014.

[7.2091]

6 Contents of application and witness statement

(1) The postal administration application shall state that the company is a universal service provider.

(2) The application shall state one or both of the following—

(a) the applicant's belief that the company is unable, or is likely to be unable, to pay its debts;

(b) the Secretary of State has certified that it would be appropriate to petition for the winding up of the universal service provider under section 124A of the 1986 Act (petition for winding up on grounds of public interest).

(3) There shall be attached to the application a witness statement in support which shall contain—

(a) a statement of the company's financial position, specifying (to the best of the applicant's knowledge and belief) its assets and liabilities, including contingent and prospective liabilities;

(b) details of any security known or believed to be held by creditors of the company, and whether in any case the security is such as to confer power on the holder to appoint an administrative receiver or to appoint an administrator under paragraph 14. If an administrative receiver has been appointed, that fact shall be stated;

(c) details of any insolvency proceedings in relation to the company including any petition that has been presented for the winding up of the company so far as within the immediate knowledge of the applicant;

(d) details of any notice served in accordance with section 78 of the 2011 Act by any person intending to enforce any security over the company's assets, so far as within the immediate knowledge of the applicant;

(e) details of any step taken to enforce any such security, so far as within the immediate knowledge of the applicant;

(f) details of any application for permission of the court to pass a resolution for the voluntary winding up of the company, so far as within the immediate knowledge of the applicant;

(g) where it is intended to appoint a number of persons as postal administrators, details of the matters set out in section 72(5) of the 2011 Act regarding the exercise of the powers and duties of the postal administrators; and

(h) any other matters which, in the opinion of those intending to make the application for a postal administration order, will assist the court in deciding whether to make such an order, so far as lying within the knowledge or belief of the applicant.

NOTES

Commencement: 31 January 2014.

[7.2092]

7 Filing of application

(1) The application (and all supporting documents) shall be filed with the court, with a sufficient number of copies for service and use as provided by Rule 8.

(2) Each of the copies filed shall have applied to it the seal of the court and be issued to the applicant; and on each copy there shall be endorsed the date and time of filing.

(3) The court shall fix a venue for the hearing of the application and this also shall be endorsed on each copy of the application issued under paragraph (2) of this Rule.

(4) After the application is filed, it is the duty of the applicant to notify the court in writing of the existence of any insolvency proceedings in relation to the company, as soon as the applicant becomes aware of them.

NOTES

Commencement: 31 January 2014.

[7.2093]

8 Service of application

(1) In the following paragraphs of this Rule, references to the application are to a copy of the application issued by the court under Rule 7(2) together with the witness statement required by Rule 6 and the documents attached to the application.

(2) Notification for the purposes of section 70(2) of the 2011 Act shall be by way of service in accordance with Rule 10, verified in accordance with Rule 11.

(3) The application shall be served, in addition to those persons referred to in section 70(2) of the 2011 Act—

- (a) on any administrative receiver that has been appointed;
- (b) if there is pending an administration application under Schedule B1 to the 1986 Act, without the modifications made by Schedule 10 to the 2011 Act, on the applicant;
- (c) if there is pending a petition for the winding-up of the company, on the petitioner (and also on the provisional liquidator, if any);
- (d) on any creditor who has served notice in accordance with section 78(1) of the 2011 Act of their intention to enforce their security over property of the company;
- (e) on the person proposed as postal administrator;
- (f) on the company;
- (g) if the applicant is the Secretary of State, on OFCOM;
- (h) if the applicant is OFCOM, on the Secretary of State;
- (i) on any supervisor of a voluntary arrangement under Part I of the 1986 Act who has been appointed.

NOTES

Commencement: 31 January 2014.

[7.2094]

9 Notice to officers charged with execution of writs or other process

The applicant shall as soon as reasonably practicable after filing the application give notice of its being made to—

- (a) any enforcement officer or other officer who to the applicant's knowledge is charged with an execution or other legal process against the company or its property; and
- (b) any person who to the applicant's knowledge has distrained against the company or its property.

NOTES

Commencement: 31 January 2014.

[7.2095]

10 Manner in which service to be effected

(1) Service of the application in accordance with Rule 8 shall be effected by the applicant, or the applicant's solicitor, or by a person instructed by the applicant or the applicant's solicitor, not less than 5 business days before the date fixed for the hearing.

(2) Service shall be effected as follows—

- (a) on the company (subject to paragraph (3) of this Rule), by delivering the documents to its registered office;
- (b) on any other person (subject to paragraph (4) of this Rule), by delivering the documents to their proper address;
- (c) in either case, in such other manner as the court may direct.

(3) If delivery to the company's registered office is not practicable or if the company is an unregistered company, service may be effected by delivery to its last known principal place of business in England and Wales.

(4) Subject to paragraph (5) of this Rule, for the purposes of paragraph (2)(b) of this Rule, a person's proper address is any which they have previously notified as their address for service; but if they have not notified any such address, service may be effected by delivery to their usual or last known address.

(5) In the case of a person who—

- (a) is an authorised deposit-taker or former authorised deposit-taker;
- (b) either-
  - (i) has appointed, or is or may be entitled to appoint, an administrative receiver of the company, or
  - (ii) is, or may be, entitled to appoint an administrator of the company under paragraph 14; and
- (c) has not notified an address for service,

the proper address is the address of an office of that person where, to the knowledge of the applicant, the company maintains a bank account or, where no such office is known to the applicant, the registered office of that person, or, if there is no such office, their usual or last known address.

NOTES

Commencement: 31 January 2014.

[7.2096]

11 Proof of service

(1) Service of the application must be verified by a certificate of service.

(2) The certificate of service must be sufficient to identify the application served and must specify—

- (a) the name and registered number of the company;
- (b) the address of the registered office of the company;
- (c) the name of the applicant;
- (d) the court to which the application was made and the court reference number;
- (e) the date of the application;

(f) whether the copy served was a sealed copy;
(g) the date on which service was effected; and
(h) the manner in which service was effected.

(3) The certificate of service shall be filed with the court as soon as reasonably practicable after service, and in any event not less than 1 business day before the hearing of the application.

NOTES

Commencement: 31 January 2014.

[7.2097]
12 The hearing

(1) At the hearing of the postal administration application, any of the following may appear or be represented—

(a) The Secretary of State;
(b) OFCOM;
(c) the company;
(d) one or more of the directors;
(e) if an administrative receiver has been appointed, that person;
(f) any person who has presented a petition for the winding-up of the company;
(g) the person proposed for appointment as postal administrator;
(h) any person that is the holder of a qualifying floating charge;
(i) any person who has applied to the court for an administration order under Schedule B1 to the 1986 Act, without the modifications made by Schedule 10 to the 2011 Act;
(j) any creditor who has served notice in accordance with section 78(1) of the 2011 Act of their intention to enforce their security over property of the company;
(k) any supervisor of a voluntary arrangement under Part I of the 1986 Act;
(l) with the permission of the court, any other person who appears to have an interest justifying their appearance.

(2) If the court makes a postal administration order, it shall be in Form PA3.

(3) If the court makes a postal administration order, the costs of the applicant, and of any person whose costs are allowed by the court, are payable as an expense of the postal administration.

NOTES

Commencement: 31 January 2014.

[7.2098]
13 Notice of postal administration order

(1) If the court makes a postal administration order, it shall as soon as reasonably practicable send two sealed copies of the order to the person who made the application.

(2) The applicant shall send a sealed copy of the order as soon as reasonably practicable to the person appointed as postal administrator.

(3) If the court makes an order under section 71(1)(d) of the 2011 Act or any other order under section 71(1)(f) of the 2011 Act, it shall give directions as to the persons to whom, and how, notice of that order is to be given.

NOTES

Commencement: 31 January 2014.

PART 3
PROCESS OF POSTAL ADMINISTRATION

[7.2099]
14 Notification and advertisement of postal administrator's appointment

(1) The notice of appointment to be given by the postal administrator as soon as reasonably practicable after appointment under paragraph 46(2)(b) shall be gazetted and may be advertised in such other manner as the postal administrator thinks fit.

(2) In addition to the standard contents, the notice under paragraph (1) of this Rule must state—

(a) that a postal administrator has been appointed; and
(b) the date of the appointment.

(3) The postal administrator shall, as soon as reasonably practicable after the date specified in paragraph 46(6), give notice of their appointment—

(a) if the application for the postal administration order was made by the Secretary of State, to OFCOM;
(b) if the application for the postal administration order was made by OFCOM, to the Secretary of State;
(c) to any receiver or administrative receiver that has been appointed;
(d) if there is pending a petition for the winding up of the company, to the petitioner (and also to the provisional liquidator, if any);

(e) to any person who has applied to the court for an administration order under Schedule B1 to the 1986 Act, without the modifications made by Schedule 10 to the 2011 Act, in relation to the company;
(f) to any enforcement officer who, to the postal administrator's knowledge, is charged with execution or other legal process against the company;
(g) to any person who, to the postal administrator's knowledge, has distrained against the company or its property; and
(h) any supervisor of a voluntary arrangement under Part I of the 1986 Act.

(4) Where, under a provision of Schedule B1 to the 1986 Act or the Rules, the postal administrator is required to send a notice of their appointment to any person other than the registrar of companies they shall do so in Form PA4.

NOTES

Commencement: 31 January 2014.

[7.2100]
15 Notice requiring statement of affairs

(1) In this Part "relevant person" shall have the meaning given to it in paragraph 47(3).

(2) The postal administrator shall send notice in Form PA5 to each relevant person whom the postal administrator determines appropriate requiring them to prepare and submit a statement of the company's affairs.

(3) The notice shall inform each of the relevant persons—
(a) of the names and addresses of all others (if any) to whom the same notice has been sent;
(b) of the time within which the statement must be delivered;
(c) of the effect of paragraph 48(4) (penalty for non-compliance); and
(d) of the application to the relevant person, and to each other relevant person, of section 235 of the 1986 Act (duty to provide information, and to attend on the administrator, if required).

(4) The postal administrator shall furnish each relevant person to whom the postal administrator has sent notice in Form PA5 with the forms required for the preparation of the statement of affairs.

NOTES

Commencement: 31 January 2014.

[7.2101]
16 Verification and filing

(1) The statement of the company's affairs shall be in Form PA6, contain all the particulars required by that form and be verified by a statement of truth by the relevant person.

(2) The postal administrator may require any relevant person to submit a statement of concurrence in Form PA7 stating that they concur in the statement of affairs. Where the postal administrator does so, the postal administrator shall inform the person making the statement of affairs of that fact.

(3) The statement of affairs shall be delivered by the relevant person making the statement of truth, together with a copy, to the postal administrator. The relevant person shall also deliver a copy of the statement of affairs to all those persons whom the postal administrator has required to make a statement of concurrence.

(4) A person required to submit a statement of concurrence shall do so before the end of the period of 5 business days (or such other period as the postal administrator may agree) beginning with the day on which the statement of affairs being concurred with is received by them.

(5) A statement of concurrence may be qualified in respect of matters dealt with in the statement of affairs, where the maker of the statement of concurrence is not in agreement with the relevant person, or the maker of the statement considers the statement of affairs to be erroneous or misleading, or the maker of the statement is without the direct knowledge necessary for concurring with it.

(6) Every statement of concurrence shall be verified by a statement of truth and be delivered to the postal administrator by the person who makes it, together with a copy of it.

(7) Subject to Rule 17, the postal administrator shall as soon as reasonably practicable send to the registrar of companies a copy of the statement of affairs and any statement of concurrence.

NOTES

Commencement: 31 January 2014.

[7.2102]
17 Limited disclosure

(1) Where the postal administrator thinks that it would prejudice the conduct of the postal administration or might reasonably be expected to lead to violence against any person for the whole or part of the statement of the company's affairs to be disclosed, the postal administrator may apply to the court for an order of limited disclosure in respect of the statement, or any specified part of it.

(2) The court may, on such application, order that the statement or, as the case may be, the specified part of it, shall not be filed with the registrar of companies.

(3) The postal administrator shall as soon as reasonably practicable send to the registrar of companies a copy of the order and the statement of affairs (to the extent provided by the order) and any statement of concurrence.

(4) If a creditor seeks disclosure of a statement of affairs or a specified part of it in relation to which an order has been made under this Rule, they may apply to the court for an order that the postal administrator disclose it or a specified part of it. The application shall be supported by written evidence in the form of a witness statement.

(5) The applicant shall give the postal administrator notice of their application at least 3 business days before the hearing.

(6) The court may make any order for disclosure subject to any conditions as to confidentiality, duration, the scope of the order in the event of any change of circumstances, or other matters as it sees just.

(7) If there is a material change in circumstances rendering the limit on disclosure or any part of it unnecessary, the postal administrator shall, as soon as reasonably practicable after the change, apply to the court for the order or any part of it to be rescinded.

(8) The postal administrator shall, as soon as reasonably practicable after the making of an order under paragraph (7) of this Rule, file with the registrar of companies a copy of the statement of affairs to the extent provided by the order.

(9) When the statement of affairs is filed in accordance with paragraph (8) of this Rule, the postal administrator shall, where the postal administrator has sent a statement of proposals under paragraph 49, provide the creditors with a copy of the statement of affairs as filed, or a summary thereof.

(10) The provisions of Part 31 of the CPR shall not apply to an application under this Rule.

NOTES

Commencement: 31 January 2014.

[7.2103]

18 Release from duty to submit statement of affairs; extension of time

(1) The power of the postal administrator under paragraph 48(2) to give a release from the obligation imposed by paragraph 47(1), or to grant an extension of time, may be exercised at the postal administrator's own discretion, or at the request of any relevant person.

(2) A relevant person may, if they request a release or extension of time and it is refused by the postal administrator, apply to the court for it.

(3) The court may, if it thinks that no sufficient cause is shown for the application, dismiss it without a hearing but it shall not do so without giving the relevant person at least 5 business days' notice, upon receipt of which the relevant person may request the court to list the application for a without notice hearing. If the application is not dismissed the court shall fix a venue for it to be heard, and give notice to the relevant person accordingly.

(4) The relevant person shall, at least 14 days before the hearing, send to the postal administrator a notice stating the venue and accompanied by a copy of the application and of any evidence which the relevant person intends to adduce in support of it.

(5) The postal administrator may appear and be heard on the application and, whether or not they appear, they may file a written report of any matters which they consider ought to be drawn to the court's attention. If such a report is filed, a copy of it shall be sent by the postal administrator to the relevant person, not later than 5 business days before the hearing.

(6) Sealed copies of any order made on the application shall be sent by the court to the relevant person and the postal administrator.

(7) On any application under this Rule the relevant person's costs shall be paid in any event by the relevant person and, unless the court otherwise orders, no allowance towards them shall be made as an expense of the postal administration.

NOTES

Commencement: 31 January 2014.

[7.2104]

19 Expenses of statement of affairs

(1) A relevant person making the statement of affairs of the company or statement of concurrence shall be allowed, and paid by the postal administrator as an expense of the postal administration, any expenses incurred by the relevant person in so doing which the postal administrator considers reasonable.

(2) Any decision by the postal administrator under this Rule is subject to appeal to the court.

(3) Nothing in this Rule relieves a relevant person from any obligation with respect to the preparation, verification and submission of the statement of affairs, or to the provision of information to the postal administrator.

NOTES

Commencement: 31 January 2014.

[7.2105]
20 Postal administrator's proposals

(1) The postal administrator shall, under paragraph 49, make a statement which the postal administrator shall send to the registrar of companies.

(2) The statement shall include, in addition to those matters set out in paragraph 49—

(a) details of the court where the proceedings are and the relevant court reference number;

(b) the full name, registered address, registered number and any other trading names of the company;

(c) details relating to their appointment as postal administrator, including the date of appointment and whether the postal administration application was made by OFCOM or the Secretary of State and, where there are joint postal administrators, details of the matters set out in section 72(5) of the 2011 Act;

(d) the names of the directors and secretary of the company and details of any shareholdings in the company they may have;

(e) an account of the circumstances giving rise to the appointment of the postal administrator;

(f) if a statement of the company's affairs has been submitted, a copy or summary of it, with the postal administrator's comments, if any;

(g) if an order limiting the disclosure of the statement of affairs (under Rule 17) has been made, a statement of that fact, as well as—

(i) details of who provided the statement of affairs;

(ii) the date of the order of limited disclosure; and

(iii) the details or a summary of the details that are not subject to that order;

(h) if a full statement of affairs is not provided, the names, addresses and debts of the creditors including details of any security held;

(i) if no statement of affairs has been submitted, details of the financial position of the company at the latest practicable date (which must, unless the court otherwise orders, be a date not earlier than that on which the company entered postal administration), a list of the company's creditors including their names, addresses and details of their debts, including any security held, and an explanation as to why there is no statement of affairs;

(j) except where the postal administrator proposes a voluntary arrangement in relation to the company and subject to paragraph (5) of this Rule—

(i) to the best of the postal administrator's knowledge and belief—

(aa) an estimate of the value of the prescribed part (whether or not they propose to make an application to court under section 1765) or section 1763) of the 1986 Act applies); and

(bb) an estimate of the value of the company's net property; and

(ii) whether, and, if so, why, the postal administrator proposes to make an application to court under section 1765) of the 1986 Act;

(k) a statement complying with paragraph (3) of this Rule of any pre-postal administration costs charged or incurred by the postal administrator or, to the postal administrator's knowledge, by any other person qualified to act as an insolvency practitioner.

(l) a statement (which must comply with paragraph (4) of this Rule where that paragraph applies) of how it is envisaged the purpose of the postal administration will be achieved and how it is proposed that the postal administration shall end;

(m) the manner in which the affairs and business of the company—

(i) have, since the date of the postal administrator's appointment, been managed and financed, including, where any assets have been disposed of, the reasons for such disposals and the terms upon which such disposals were made; and

(ii) will continue to be managed and financed; and

(n) such other information (if any) as the postal administrator thinks necessary to enable creditors to decide whether or not to vote for the adoption of the proposals.

(3) A statement of pre-postal administration costs complies with this paragraph if it includes—

(a) details of any agreement under which the fees were charged and expenses incurred, including the parties to the agreement and the date on which the agreement was made;

(b) details of the work done for which the fees were charged and expenses incurred;

(c) an explanation of why the work was done before the company entered postal administration and how it would further the achievement of the objective of the postal administration;

(d) a statement of the amount of the pre-postal administration costs, setting out separately—

(i) the fees charged by the postal administrator;

(ii) the expenses incurred by the postal administrator;

(iii) the fees charged (to the postal administrator's knowledge) by any other person qualified to act as an insolvency practitioner (and, if more than one, by each separately); and

(iv) the expenses incurred (to the postal administrator's knowledge) by any other person qualified to act as an insolvency practitioner (and, if more than one, by each separately);

(e) a statement of the amounts of pre-postal administration costs which have already been paid (set out separately as under sub-paragraph (d));

(f) the identity of the person who made the payment or, if more than one person made the payment, the identity of each such person and of the amounts paid by each such person set out separately as under sub-paragraph (d);

(g) a statement of the amounts of unpaid pre-postal administration costs (set out separately as under paragraph (d)); and

(h) a statement that the payment of unpaid pre-postal administration costs as an expense of the postal administration is subject to approval under Rule 38.

(4) This paragraph applies where it is proposed that the postal administration will end by the company moving to a creditors' voluntary liquidation; and in that case, the statement required by paragraph (2)(l) of this Rule must include—

(a) details of the proposed liquidator;

(b) where applicable, the declaration required by section 231 of the 1986 Act; and

(c) a statement that the creditors may nominate a different person as liquidator in accordance with paragraph 83(7)(a) and Rule 81(3).

(5) Nothing in paragraph (2)(j) of this Rule is to be taken as requiring any such estimate to include any information, the disclosure of which could seriously prejudice the commercial interests of the company. If such information is excluded from the calculation the estimate shall be accompanied by a statement to that effect.

(6) Where the court orders, upon an application by the postal administrator under paragraph 107, an extension of the period of time in paragraph 49(5), the postal administrator must as soon as reasonably practicable after the making of the order—

(a) notify in Form PA8 every creditor of the company and every member of the company of whose address (in either case) the postal administrator is aware, and

(b) send a copy of the notification to the registrar of companies.

(7) Where the postal administrator wishes to publish a notice under paragraph 49(6), the notice shall be advertised in such manner as the postal administrator thinks fit.

(8) In addition to the standard contents, the notice under paragraph (7) of this Rule must state—

(a) that members can write for a copy of the statement of proposals for achieving the purpose of postal administration; and

(b) the address to which to write.

(9) This notice must be published as soon as reasonably practicable after the postal administrator sends their statement of proposals to the company's creditors but no later than 8 weeks (or such other period as may be agreed by the creditors or as the court may order) from the date that the company entered postal administration.

NOTES

Commencement: 31 January 2014.

[7.2106]

21 Limited disclosure of paragraph 49 statement

(1) Where the postal administrator thinks that it would prejudice the conduct of the postal administration or might reasonably be expected to lead to violence against any person for any of the matters specified in Rule 20(2)(h) and (i) to be disclosed, the postal administrator may apply to the court for an order of limited disclosure in respect of any specified part of the statement under paragraph 49.

(2) The court may, on such application, order that some or all of the specified part of the statement must not be sent to the registrar of companies or to creditors or members of the company as otherwise required by paragraph 49(4).

(3) The postal administrator must as soon as reasonably practicable send to the persons specified in paragraph 49(4) the statement under paragraph 49 (to the extent provided by the order) and an indication of the nature of the matter in relation to which the order was made.

(4) The postal administrator must also send a copy of the order to the registrar of companies.

(5) A creditor who seeks disclosure of a part of a statement under paragraph 49 in relation to which an order has been made under this Rule may apply to the court for an order that the postal administrator disclose it. The application must be supported by written evidence in the form of a witness statement.

(6) The applicant must give the postal administrator notice of the application at least 3 business days before the hearing.

(7) The court may make any order for disclosure subject to any conditions as to confidentiality, duration, the scope of the order in the event of any change of circumstances, or other matters as it sees just.

(8) If there is a material change in circumstances rendering the limit on disclosure or any part of it unnecessary, the postal administrator must, as soon as reasonably practicable after the change, apply to the court for the order or any part of it to be rescinded.

(9) The postal administrator must, as soon as reasonably practicable after the making of an order under paragraph (8) of this Rule, send to the persons specified in paragraph 49(4) a copy of the statement under paragraph 49 to the extent provided by the order.

(10) The provisions of CPR Part 31 do not apply to an application under this Rule.

NOTES

Commencement: 31 January 2014.

PART 4
MEETINGS AND REPORTS

CHAPTER 1 CREDITORS MEETINGS

[7.2107]
22 Creditors' meetings generally

(1) This Rule applies to creditors' meetings summoned by the postal administrator under paragraph 62 (general power to summon meetings of creditors).

(2) Notice of any meeting referred to in paragraph (1) of this Rule shall be in Form PA9.

(3) In fixing the venue for the meeting, the postal administrator shall have regard to the convenience of creditors and the meeting shall be summoned for commencement between 10.00 and 16.00 hours on a business day, unless the court otherwise directs.

(4) Subject to paragraphs (6) and (7) of this Rule, at least 14 days' notice of the meeting shall be given to all creditors who are known to the postal administrator and had claims against the company at the date when the company entered postal administration unless that creditor has subsequently been paid in full; and the notice shall—

- (a) specify the purpose of the meeting;
- (b) contain a statement of the effect of Rule 26 (entitlement to vote); and
- (c) contain the forms of proxy.

(5) As soon as reasonably practicable after notice of the meeting has been given, the postal administrator must have gazetted a notice which, in addition to the standard contents, must state—

- (a) that a creditors' meeting is to take place;
- (b) the venue fixed for the meeting;
- (c) the purpose of the meeting; and
- (d) a statement of the effect of Rule 26 (entitlement to vote).

(6) If within 30 minutes from the time fixed for commencement of the meeting there is no person present to act as chair, the meeting stands adjourned to the same time and place in the following week or, if that is not a business day, to the business day immediately following.

(7) If within 30 minutes from the time fixed for the commencement of the meeting those persons attending the meeting do not constitute a quorum, the chair may adjourn the meeting to such time and place as the chair may appoint.

(8) Once only in the course of the meeting the chair may, without an adjournment, declare the meeting suspended for any period up to 1 hour.

(9) The chair may, and must if the meeting so resolves, adjourn the meeting to such time and place as seems to the chair to be appropriate in the circumstances. An adjournment under this paragraph must not be for a period of more than 14 days, subject to the direction of the court.

(10) If there are subsequently further adjournments, the final adjournment must not be to a day later than 14 days after the date on which the meeting was originally held.

(11) Where a meeting is adjourned under this Rule, proofs and proxies may be used if lodged at any time up to 12.00 hours on the business day immediately before the adjourned meeting.

(12) Paragraph (3) of this Rule applies with regard to the venue fixed for a meeting adjourned under this Rule.

NOTES

Commencement: 31 January 2014.

[7.2108]
23 The chair at meetings

(1) At any meeting of creditors summoned by the postal administrator, either the postal administrator shall be chair, or a person nominated by the postal administrator in writing to act in their place.

(2) A person so nominated must be either—

- (a) one who is qualified to act as an insolvency practitioner in relation to the company; or
- (b) an employee of the postal administrator or the postal administrator's firm who is experienced in insolvency matters.

(3) Where the chair holds a proxy which includes a requirement to vote for a particular resolution and no other person proposes that resolution—

- (a) the chair must propose it unless the chair considers that there is good reason for not doing so, and
- (b) if the chair does not propose it, the chair must as soon as reasonably practicable after the meeting notify the principal of the reason why not.

NOTES

Commencement: 31 January 2014.

[7.2109]

24 Creditors' meeting for nomination of alternative liquidator

(1) Where under Rules 20(4) or 33(2)(g) the postal administrator has proposed that the company enter creditors' voluntary liquidation once the postal administration has ended, the postal administrator must, in the circumstances detailed in paragraph (2) of this Rule, call a meeting of creditors for the purpose of nominating a person other than the person named as proposed liquidator in the postal administrator's proposals or revised proposals.

(2) The postal administrator must call a meeting of creditors where such a meeting is requested by creditors of the company whose debts amount to at least 10 per cent of the total debts of the company.

(3) The request for a creditors' meeting for the purpose set out in paragraph (1) of this Rule must be in Form PA10. A request for such a meeting must be made within 8 business days of the date on which the postal administrator's statement of proposals is sent out.

(4) A request under this Rule must include—

(a) a list of creditors concurring with the request, showing the amounts of the respective debts in the postal administration; and

(b) from each creditor concurring, written confirmation of the creditor's concurrence;

but this paragraph does not apply if the requesting creditor's debt is alone sufficient without the concurrence of other creditors.

(5) A meeting requested under this Rule must be held within 28 days of the postal administrator's receipt of the notice requesting the meeting.

NOTES

Commencement: 31 January 2014.

[7.2110]

25 Notice of meetings by advertisement only

(1) The court may order that notice of any meeting be given by advertisement and not by individual notice to the persons concerned.

(2) In considering whether to act under this Rule, the court must have regard to the cost of advertisement, the amount of assets available and the extent of the interest of creditors, members or any particular class of either.

NOTES

Commencement: 31 January 2014.

[7.2111]

26 Entitlement to vote

(1) Subject as follows, at a meeting of creditors in postal administration proceedings a person is entitled to vote only if—

(a) they have given to the postal administrator, not later than 12.00 hours on the business day before the day fixed for the meeting, details in writing of the debt which they claim to be due to them from the company;

(b) the claim has been duly admitted under Rule 27 or this Rule; and

(c) there has been lodged with the postal administrator any proxy which they intend to be used on their behalf,

and details of the debt must include any calculation for the purposes of Rules 28 to 30.

(2) The chair of the meeting may allow a creditor to vote, notwithstanding that the creditor has failed to comply with paragraph (1)(a) of this Rule, if satisfied that the failure was due to circumstances beyond the creditor's control.

(3) The chair of the meeting may call for any document or other evidence to be produced to them, where the chair thinks it necessary for the purpose of substantiating the whole or any part of the claim.

(4) Votes are calculated according to the amount of a creditor's claim as at the date on which the company entered postal administration, less any payments that have been made to them after that date in respect of their claim and any adjustment by way of set-off in accordance with Rule 55 as if that Rule were applied on the date that the votes are counted.

(5) A creditor shall not vote in respect of a debt for an unliquidated amount, or any debt whose value is not ascertained, except where the chair agrees to put upon the debt an estimated minimum value for the purpose of entitlement to vote and admits the claim for that purpose.

(6) No vote shall be cast by virtue of a claim more than once on any resolution put to the meeting.

NOTES

Commencement: 31 January 2014.

[7.2112]

27 Admission and rejection of claims

(1) At any creditors' meeting the chair has power to admit or reject a creditor's claim for the purpose of their entitlement to vote; and the power is exercisable with respect to the whole or any part of the claim.

Part 70 Special Insolvency Regimes

(2) The chair's decision under this Rule, or in respect of any matter arising under Rule 26, is subject to appeal to the court by any creditor.

(3) If the chair is in doubt whether a claim should be admitted or rejected, the chair shall mark it as objected to and allow the creditor to vote, subject to their vote being subsequently declared invalid if the objection to the claim is sustained.

(4) If on an appeal the chair's decision is reversed or varied, or a creditor's vote is declared invalid, the court may order that another meeting be summoned, or make such other order as it thinks just.

(5) An application to the court by way of appeal under this Rule against a decision of the chair must be made not later than 21 days after the date of the meeting.

(6) Neither the postal administrator nor any person nominated by the postal administrator to be chair is personally liable for costs incurred by any person in respect of an appeal to the court under this Rule, unless the court makes an order to that effect.

NOTES

Commencement: 31 January 2014.

[7.2113]
28 Secured creditors

At a meeting of creditors a secured creditor is entitled to vote only in respect of the balance (if any) of their debt after deducting the value of their security as estimated by them.

NOTES

Commencement: 31 January 2014.

[7.2114]
29 Holders of negotiable instruments

A creditor shall not vote in respect of a debt on, or secured by, a current bill of exchange or promissory note, unless the creditor is willing—

(a) to treat the liability to them on the bill or note of every person who is liable on it antecedently to the company, and against whom a bankruptcy order has not been made (or, in the case of a company, which has not gone into liquidation), as a security in their hands; and

(b) to estimate the value of the security and, for the purpose of their entitlement to vote (but not for dividend), to deduct it from their claim.

NOTES

Commencement: 31 January 2014.

[7.2115]
30 Hire-purchase, conditional sale and chattel leasing agreements

(1) Subject as follows, an owner of goods under a hire-purchase or chattel leasing agreement, or a seller of goods under a conditional sale agreement, is entitled to vote in respect of the amount of the debt due and payable to them by the company on the date that the company entered postal administration.

(2) In calculating the amount of any debt for this purpose, no account shall be taken of any amount attributable to the exercise of any right under the relevant agreement, so far as the right has become exercisable solely by virtue of the making of a postal administration application or any matter arising as a consequence, or of the company entering postal administration.

NOTES

Commencement: 31 January 2014.

[7.2116]
31 Resolutions

(1) Subject to paragraph (2) of this Rule, at a creditors' meeting in postal administration proceedings, a resolution is passed when a majority (in value) of those present and voting, in person or by proxy, have voted in favour of it.

(2) Any resolution is invalid if those voting against it include more than half in value of the creditors to whom notice of the meeting was sent and who are not, to the best of the chair's belief, persons connected with the company.

(3) In the case of a resolution for the nomination of a person to act as liquidator once the postal administration has ended—

(a) subject to paragraph (4) of this Rule, if on any vote there are two persons put forward by creditors for nomination as liquidator, the person who obtains the most support is nominated as liquidator;

(b) if there are three or more persons put forward by creditors for nomination as liquidator, and one of them has a clear majority over both or all the others together, that one is nominated as liquidator;

(c) in any other case, the chair of the meeting must continue to take votes (disregarding at each vote any person who has withdrawn and, if no person has withdrawn, the person who obtained the least support last time), until a clear majority is obtained for any one person.

(4) The support referred to in paragraph (3)(a) of this Rule must represent a majority in value of all those present (in person or by proxy) at the meeting and entitled to vote.

(5) Where on such a resolution no person is nominated as liquidator, the person named as proposed liquidator in the postal administrator's proposals or revised proposals shall be the liquidator once the postal administration has ended.

(6) The chair may at any time put to the meeting a resolution for the joint appointment of any two or more persons put forward by creditors for nomination as liquidator.

(7) In this Rule "connected with the company" has the same meaning as "connected with a company" in section 249 of the 1986 Act.

NOTES

Commencement: 31 January 2014.

[7.2117]

32 Minutes

(1) The chair of the meeting must cause minutes of its proceedings to be kept.

(2) The minutes must be authenticated by the chair, and be retained by the chair as part of the records of the postal administration.

(3) The minutes must include—

(a) a list of the names of creditors who attended (personally or by proxy) and their claims; and

(b) a record of every resolution passed.

NOTES

Commencement: 31 January 2014.

[7.2118]

33 Revision of the postal administrator's proposals

(1) The postal administrator shall, as soon as reasonably practicable, under paragraph 54, make a statement setting out the proposed revisions to their proposals which they shall send to all those to whom they are required to send a copy of their revised proposals and to the registrar of companies.

(2) The statement of revised proposals shall include—

(a) details of the court where the proceedings are and the relevant court reference number;

(b) the full name, registered address, registered number and any other trading names of the company;

(c) details relating to their appointment as postal administrator, including the date of appointment and whether the postal administration application was made by the Secretary of State or OFCOM;

(d) the names of the directors and secretary of the company and details of any shareholdings in the company they may have;

(e) a summary of the initial proposals and the reasos) for proposing a revision;

(f) details of the proposed revision including details of the postal administrator's assessment of the likely impact of the proposed revision upon creditors generally or upon each class of creditors (as the case may be);

(g) where a proposed revision relates to the ending of the postal administration by a creditors' voluntary liquidation and the nomination of a person to be the proposed liquidator of the company—

(i) details of the proposed liquidator,

(ii) where applicable, the declaration required by section 231 of the 1986 Act, and

(iii) a statement that the creditors may nominate a different person as liquidator in accordance with paragraph 83(7)(a) and Rule 81(3); and

(h) any other information that the postal administrator thinks necessary to enable creditors to decide whether or not to vote for the proposed revisions.

(3) Subject to paragraph 54(4), within 5 business days of sending out the statement in paragraph (1) of this Rule, the postal administrator shall send a copy of the statement to every member of the company.

(4) Any notice to be published by the postal administrator acting under paragraph 54(4) shall be advertised in such manner as the postal administrator thinks fit.

(5) The notice must be published as soon as reasonably practicable after the postal administrator sends the statement to the creditors and in addition to the standard contents must state—

(a) that members can write for a copy of the statement of revised proposals for the postal administration; and

(b) the address to which to write.

NOTES

Commencement: 31 January 2014.

[7.2119]

34 Reports to creditors

(1) The postal administrator must prepare a report ("the progress report") which includes—

(a) details of the court where the proceedings are and the relevant court reference number;

(b) full details of the company's name, address of registered office and registered number;

(c) full details of the postal administrator's name and address, date of appointment and name and address of applicant for the postal administration application, including any changes in the postal administrator, and, in the case of joint postal administrators, their functions as set out in the statement made for the purposes of section 72(5) of the 2011 Act;
(d) details of progress during the period of the report, including a receipts and payments account (as detailed in paragraph (2) of this Rule);
(e) details of any assets that remain to be realised; and
(f) any other relevant information for the creditors.

(2) A receipts and payments account must be in the form of an abstract showing receipts and payments during the period of the report and, where the postal administrator has ceased to act, must also include a statement as to the amount paid to unsecured creditors by virtue of the application of section 176A of the 1986 Act.

(3) The progress report must, except where paragraph (4) of this Rule applies, cover the period of 6 months commencing on the date on which the company entered postal administration and every subsequent period of 6 months.

(4) The period to be covered by a progress report ends on the date when a postal administrator ceases to act, and the period to be covered by each subsequent progress report of a new postal administrator is each successive period of 6 months beginning immediately after that date (subject to the further application of this paragraph when another postal administrator ceases to act).

(5) The postal administrator must send a copy of the progress report within 1 month of the end of the period covered by the report, to—
(a) the Secretary of State;
(b) OFCOM;
(c) the creditors, and
(d) the registrar of companies;

(6) The court may, on the postal administrator's application, extend the period of 1 month mentioned in paragraph (5) of this Rule, or make such other order in respect of the content of the report as it thinks just.

(7) If the postal administrator makes default in complying with this Rule, the postal administrator is liable to a fine and, for continued contravention, to a daily default fine.

NOTES
Commencement: 31 January 2014.

CHAPTER 2 COMPANY MEETINGS

[7.2120]
35 Venue and conduct of company meeting

(1) Where the postal administrator summons a meeting of members of the company, the postal administrator shall fix a venue for it having regard to the postal administrator's convenience.

(2) The chair of the meeting shall be the postal administrator or a person nominated by the postal administrator in writing to act in the postal administrator's place.

(3) A person so nominated must be either—
(a) one who is qualified to act as an insolvency practitioner in relation to the company; or
(b) an employee of the postal administrator or the postal administrator's firm who is experienced in insolvency matters.

(4) If within 30 minutes from the time fixed for commencement of the meeting there is no person present to act as chair, the meeting stands adjourned to the same time and place in the following week or, if that is not a business day, to the business day immediately following.

(5) Subject to anything to the contrary in the 1986 Act and the Rules, the meeting must be summoned and conducted—
(a) in the case of a company incorporated—
(i) in England and Wales, or in Wales, or
(ii) outside the United Kingdom other than in an EEA state,

in accordance with the law of England and Wales, including any applicable provision in or made under the Companies Act;
(b) in the case of a company incorporated in an EEA state other than the United Kingdom, in accordance with the law of that state applicable to meetings of the company.

(6) The chair of the meeting shall cause minutes of its proceedings to be entered in the company's minute book.

NOTES
Commencement: 31 January 2014.

PART 5
DISPOSAL OF CHARGED PROPERTY

[7.2121]
36 Authority to dispose of property

(1) The following applies where the postal administrator applies to the court under paragraphs 71 or 72 for authority to dispose of property of the company which is subject to a security (other than a floating charge), or goods in the possession of the company under a hire purchase agreement.

(2) The court shall fix a venue for the hearing of the application, and the postal administrator shall as soon as reasonably practicable give notice of the venue to the person who is the holder of the security or, as the case may be, the owner under the agreement.

(3) If an order is made under paragraphs 71 or 72 the court shall send two sealed copies to the postal administrator.

(4) The postal administrator shall send one of them to that person who is the holder of the security or owner under the agreement.

(5) The postal administrator must send a copy of the sealed order to the registrar of companies.

NOTES

Commencement: 31 January 2014.

PART 6
EXPENSES OF THE POSTAL ADMINISTRATION

[7.2122]
37 Priority of expenses of postal administration

(1) The expenses of the postal administration are payable in the following order of priority—

(a) expenses properly incurred by the postal administrator in performing the postal administrator's functions in the administration of the company;

(b) the cost of any security provided by the postal administrator in accordance with the 1986 Act or the Rules;

(c) where a postal administration order was made, the costs of the applicant and any person appearing on the hearing of the application;

(d) any amount payable to a person employed or authorised, under Part 3 of the Rules, to assist in the preparation of a statement of affairs or statement of concurrence;

(e) any allowance made, by order of the court, towards costs on an application for release from the obligation to submit a statement of affairs or statement of concurrence;

(f) any necessary disbursements by the postal administrator in the course of the postal administration (but not including any payment of corporation tax in circumstances referred to in sub-paragraph (i) below);

(g) the remuneration or emoluments of any person who has been employed by the postal administrator to perform any services for the company, as required or authorised under the 1986 Act or the Rules;

(h) the remuneration of the postal administrator fixed by the court under Part 8 of the Rules and unpaid pre-postal administration costs approved under Rule 38;

(i) the amount of any corporation tax on chargeable gains accruing on the realisation of any asset of the company (without regard to whether the realisation is effected by the postal administrator, a secured creditor, or a receiver or manager appointed to deal with a security).

(2) The priorities laid down by paragraph (1) of this Rule are subject to the power of the court to make orders under paragraph (3) of this Rule where the assets are insufficient to satisfy the liabilities.

(3) The court may, in the event of the assets being insufficient to satisfy the liabilities, make an order as to the payment out of the assets of the expenses incurred in the postal administration in such order of priority as the court thinks just.

(4) For the purposes of paragraph 99(3), the former postal administrator's remuneration and expenses shall comprise all those items set out in paragraph (1) of this Rule.

NOTES

Commencement: 31 January 2014.

[7.2123]
38 Pre-postal administration costs

Where the postal administrator has made a statement of pre-postal administration costs under Rule 20(2)(k), the postal administrator (where the costs consist of fees charged or expenses incurred by the postal administrator) or other insolvency practitioner (where the costs consist of fees charged or expenses incurred by that practitioner) must, before paying such costs, apply to the court for a determination of whether and to what extent the unpaid pre-postal administration costs are approved for payment.

NOTES

Commencement: 31 January 2014.

PART 7
DISTRIBUTION TO CREDITORS

CHAPTER 1 APPLICATION OF PART AND GENERAL

[7.2124]
39 Distribution to creditors generally

(1) This Part applies where the postal administrator makes, or proposes to make, a distribution to any class of creditors other than secured creditors. Where the distribution is to a particular class of creditors, references in this Part to creditors shall, in so far as the context requires, be a reference to that class of creditors only.

(2) The postal administrator shall give notice to the creditors of the postal administrator's intention to declare and distribute a dividend in accordance with Rule 65.

(3) Where it is intended that the distribution is to be a sole or final dividend, the postal administrator shall, after the date specified in the notice referred to in paragraph (2) of this Rule—

(a) defray any items payable in accordance with the provisions of paragraph 99;
(b) defray any amounts (including any debts or liabilities and the postal administrator's own remuneration and expenses) which would, if the postal administrator were to cease to be the postal administrator of the company, be payable out of the property of which the postal administrator had custody or control in accordance with the provisions of paragraph 99; and
(c) declare and distribute that dividend without regard to the claim of any person in respect of a debt not already proved.

(4) The court may, on the application of any person, postpone the date specified in the notice.

NOTES

Commencement: 31 January 2014.

[7.2125]
40 Debts of insolvent company to rank equally

Debts other than preferential debts rank equally between themselves in the postal administration and, after the preferential debts, shall be paid in full unless the assets are insufficient for meeting them, in which case they abate in equal proportions between themselves.

NOTES

Commencement: 31 January 2014.

[7.2126]
41 Supplementary provisions as to dividend

(1) In the calculation and distribution of a dividend the postal administrator shall make provision for—

(a) any debts which appear to the postal administrator to be due to persons who, by reason of the distance of their place of residence, may not have had sufficient time to tender and establish their proofs;
(b) any debts which are the subject of claims which have not yet been determined; and
(c) disputed proofs and claims.

(2) A creditor who has not proved their debt before the declaration of any dividend is not entitled to disturb, by reason that they have not participated in it, the distribution of that dividend or any other dividend declared before their debt was proved, but—

(a) when they have proved that debt they are entitled to be paid, out of any money for the time being available for the payment of any further dividend, any dividend or dividends which they have failed to receive; and
(b) any dividends payable under sub-paragraph (a) of this paragraph shall be paid before the money is applied to the payment of any such further dividend.

(3) No action lies against the postal administrator for a dividend; but if the postal administrator refuses to pay a dividend the court may, if it thinks just, order the postal administrator to pay it and also to pay, out of the postal administrator's own money—

(a) interest on the dividend, at the rate for the time being specified in section 17 of the Judgments Act 1838, from the time when it was withheld; and
(b) the costs of the proceedings in which the order to pay is made.

NOTES

Commencement: 31 January 2014.

[7.2127]
42 Division of unsold assets

(1) The postal administrator may, with the permission of the creditors, divide in its existing form amongst the company's creditors, according to its estimated value, any property which from its peculiar nature or other special circumstances cannot be readily or advantageously sold.

(2) The postal administrator must—

(a) in the receipts and payments account included in the final progress report under Part 9 of the Rules, state the estimated value of the property divided amongst the creditors of the company during the period to which the report relates, and

(b) as a note to the account, provide details of the basis of the valuation.

NOTES

Commencement: 31 January 2014.

CHAPTER 2 MACHINERY OF PROVING A DEBT

[7.2128]

43 Proving a debt

(1) A person claiming to be a creditor of the company and wishing to recover their debt in whole or in part must (subject to any order of the court to the contrary) submit their claim in writing to the postal administrator.

(2) A creditor who claims is referred to as "proving" for their debt and a document by which they seek to establish their claim is their "proof".

(3) Subject to the next paragraph, a proof must—

(a) be made out by, or under the direction of, the creditor and authenticated by them or a person authorised in that behalf; and

(b) state the following matters—

(i) the creditor's name and address;

(ii) if the creditor is a company, its registered number;

(iii) the total amount of the creditor's claim (including value added tax) as at the date on which the company entered postal administration less any payments made after that date in respect of the claim, any deduction under Rule 54 and any adjustment by way of set-off in accordance with Rule 55;

(iv) whether or not the claim includes outstanding uncapitalised interest;

(v) particulars of how and when the debt was incurred by the company;

(vi) particulars of any security held, the date on which it was given and the value which the creditor puts on it;

(vii) details of any reservation of title in respect of goods to which the debt refers; and

(viii) the name, address and authority of the person authenticating the proof (if other than the creditor themselves).

(4) There shall be specified in the proof details of any documents by reference to which the debt can be substantiated; but (subject as follows) it is not essential that such document be attached to the proof or submitted with it.

(5) The postal administrator may call for any document or other evidence to be produced to the postal administrator, where the postal administrator thinks it necessary for the purpose of substantiating the whole or any part of the claim made in the proof.

NOTES

Commencement: 31 January 2014.

[7.2129]

44 Costs of proving

Unless the court otherwise orders—

(a) every creditor bears the cost of proving their own debt, including costs incurred in providing documents or evidence under Rule 43(5); and

(b) costs incurred by the postal administrator in estimating the quantum of a debt under Rule 51 are payable out of the assets as an expense of the postal administration.

NOTES

Commencement: 31 January 2014.

[7.2130]

45 Postal administrator to allow inspection of proofs

The postal administrator shall, so long as proofs lodged with the postal administrator are in the postal administrator's hands, allow them to be inspected, at all reasonable times on any business day, by any of the following persons—

(a) any creditor who has submitted a proof of debt (unless their proof has been wholly rejected for purposes of dividend or otherwise);

(b) any contributory of the company; and

(c) any person acting on behalf of either of the above.

NOTES

Commencement: 31 January 2014.

[7.2131]

46 New postal administrator appointed

(1) If a new postal administrator is appointed in place of another, the former postal administrator must as soon as reasonably practicable transmit to the new postal administrator all proofs which the former postal administrator has received, together with an itemised list of them.

(2) The new postal administrator shall authenticate the list by way of receipt for the proofs, and return it to the new postal administrator's predecessor.

(3) From then on, all proofs of debt must be sent to and retained by the new postal administrator.

NOTES

Commencement: 31 January 2014.

[7.2132]

47 Admission and rejection of proofs for dividend

(1) A proof may be admitted for dividend either for the whole amount claimed by the creditor, or for part of that amount.

(2) If the postal administrator rejects a proof in whole or in part, the postal administrator shall prepare a written statement of their reasons for doing so, and send it as soon as reasonably practicable to the creditor.

NOTES

Commencement: 31 January 2014.

[7.2133]

48 Appeal against decision on proof

(1) If a creditor is dissatisfied with the postal administrator's decision with respect to their proof (including any decision on the question of preference), the creditor may apply to the court for the decision to be reversed or varied. The application must be made within 21 days of the creditor receiving the statement sent under Rule 47(2).

(2) A member or any other creditor may, if dissatisfied with the postal administrator's decision admitting or rejecting the whole or any part of a proof, make such an application within 21 days of becoming aware of the postal administrator's decision.

(3) Where application is made to the court under this Rule, the court shall fix a venue for the application to be heard, notice of which shall be sent by the applicant to the creditor who lodged the proof in question (if it is not themselves) and the postal administrator.

(4) The postal administrator shall, on receipt of the notice, file with the court the relevant proof, together (if appropriate) with a copy of the statement sent under Rule 47(2).

(5) Where the application is made by a member, the court must not disallow the proof (in whole or in part) unless the member shows that there is (or would be but for the amount claimed in the proof), or that it is likely that there will be (or would be but for the amount claimed in the proof), a surplus of assets to which the company would be entitled.

(6) After the application has been heard and determined, the proof shall, unless it has been wholly disallowed, be returned by the court to the postal administrator.

(7) The postal administrator is not personally liable for costs incurred by any person in respect of an application under this Rule unless the court otherwise orders.

NOTES

Commencement: 31 January 2014.

[7.2134]

49 Withdrawal or variation of proof

A creditor's proof may at any time, by agreement between themselves and the postal administrator, be withdrawn or varied as to the amount claimed.

NOTES

Commencement: 31 January 2014.

[7.2135]

50 Expunging of proof by the court

(1) The court may expunge a proof or reduce the amount claimed—

(a) on the postal administrator's application, where the postal administrator thinks that the proof has been improperly admitted, or ought to be reduced; or

(b) on the application of a creditor, if the postal administrator declines to interfere in the matter.

(2) Where application is made to the court under this Rule, the court shall fix a venue for the application to be heard, notice of which shall be sent by the applicant—

(a) in the case of an application by the postal administrator, to the creditor who made the proof; and

(b) in the case of an application by a creditor, to the postal administrator and to the creditor who made the proof (if not themselves).

NOTES

Commencement: 31 January 2014.

CHAPTER 3 QUANTIFICATION OF CLAIMS

[7.2136]

51 Estimate of quantum

(1) The postal administrator shall estimate the value of any debt which, by reason of its being subject to any contingency or for any other reason, does not bear a certain value; and the postal administrator may revise any estimate previously made, if the postal administrator thinks fit by reference to any change of circumstances or to information becoming available to the postal administrator. The postal administrator shall inform the creditor as to the postal administrator's estimate and any revision of it.

(2) Where the value of a debt is estimated under this Rule, the amount provable in the postal administration in the case of that debt is that of the estimate for the time being.

NOTES

Commencement: 31 January 2014.

[7.2137]

52 Negotiable instruments, etc

Unless the postal administrator allows, a proof in respect of money owed on a bill of exchange, promissory note, cheque or other negotiable instrument or security cannot be admitted unless there is produced the instrument or security itself or a copy of it, certified by the creditor or the creditor's authorised representative to be a true copy.

NOTES

Commencement: 31 January 2014.

[7.2138]

53 Secured creditors

(1) If a secured creditor realises their security, they may prove for the balance of their debt, after deducting the amount realised.

(2) If a secured creditor voluntarily surrenders their security for the general benefit of creditors, they may prove for their whole debt, as if it were unsecured.

NOTES

Commencement: 31 January 2014.

[7.2139]

54 Discounts

There shall in every case be deducted from the claim all trade and other discounts which would have been available to the company but for its postal administration except any discount for immediate, early or cash settlement.

NOTES

Commencement: 31 January 2014.

[7.2140]

55 Mutual credits and set-off

(1) This Rule applies where the postal administrator, being authorised to make the distribution in question, has, pursuant to Rule 65 given notice that the postal administrator proposes to make it.

(2) In this Rule "mutual dealings" means mutual credits, mutual debts or other mutual dealings between the company and any creditor of the company proving or claiming to prove for a debt in the postal administration but does not include any of the following—

(a) any debt arising out of an obligation incurred at a time when the creditor had notice that—
  (i) a meeting of creditors had been summoned under section 98 of the 1986 Act,
  (ii) a petition for the winding up of the company was pending,
  (iii) an application for an administration order under the 1986 Act was pending;
  (iv) an application for a postal administration order was pending; or
  (v) any person had given notice of intention to appoint an administrator under the 1986 Rules;

(b) any debt which has been acquired by a creditor by assignment or otherwise, pursuant to an agreement between the creditor and any other party where that agreement was entered into—
  (i) at a time when the creditor had notice that an application for a postal administration order was pending;
  (ii) after the commencement of postal administration,
  (iii) at a time when the creditor had notice that a meeting of creditors had been summoned under section 98 of the 1986 Act, or
  (iv) at a time when the creditor had notice that a winding up petition was pending, or
  (v) at a time when the creditor had notice that an application for an administration order under the 1986 Act was pending; or

(c) any debt arising out of an obligation incurred after the company entered administration.

Part 7O Special Insolvency Regimes

(3) An account shall be taken as at the date of the notice referred to in paragraph (1) of this Rule of what is due from each party to the other in respect of the mutual dealings and the sums due from one party shall be set off against the sums due from the other.

(4) A sum shall be regarded as being due to or from the company for the purposes of paragraph (3) of this Rule whether—

(a) it is payable at present or in the future;
(b) the obligation by virtue of which it is payable is certain or contingent; or
(c) its amount is fixed or liquidated, or is capable of being ascertained by fixed rules or as a matter of opinion.

(5) Rule 51 shall apply for the purposes of this Rule to any obligation to or from the company which, by reason of its being subject to any contingency or for any other reason, does not bear a certain value;

(6) Rules 56 to 58 shall apply for the purposes of this Rule in relation to any sums due to the company which—

(a) are payable in a currency other than sterling;
(b) are of a periodical nature; or
(c) bear interest.

(7) Rule 76 shall apply for the purposes of this Rule to any sum due to or from the company which is payable in the future.

(8) Only the balance (if any) of the account owed to the creditor is provable in the postal administration. Alternatively the balance (if any) owed to the company shall be paid to the postal administrator as part of the assets except where all or part of the balance results from a contingent or prospective debt owed by the creditor and in such a case the balance (or that part of it which results from the contingent or prospective debt) shall be paid if and when that debt becomes due and payable.

(9) In this Rule "obligation" means an obligation however arising, whether by virtue of an agreement, rule of law or otherwise.

NOTES

Commencement: 31 January 2014.

[7.2141]
56 Debt in foreign currency

(1) For the purpose of proving any debt incurred or payable in a currency other than sterling, the amount of those debts shall be converted into sterling at a single rate for that currency determined by the postal administrator with reference to the exchange rates prevailing on the relevant date.

(2) If the postal administrator receives any objections from the creditors to that rate the postal administrator must apply to the court to determine the rate.

(3) In this Rule, and Rule 58, "the relevant date" means the date on which the company entered postal administration.

NOTES

Commencement: 31 January 2014.

[7.2142]
57 Payments of a periodical nature

(1) In the case of rent and other payments of a periodical nature, the creditor may prove for any amounts due and unpaid up to the date when the company entered postal administration.

(2) Where at that date any payment was accruing due, the creditor may prove for so much as would have fallen due at that date, if accruing from day to day.

NOTES

Commencement: 31 January 2014.

[7.2143]
58 Interest

(1) Where a debt proved in the postal administration bears interest, that interest is provable as part of the debt except in so far as it is payable in respect of any period after the relevant date.

(2) In the following circumstances the creditor's claim may include interest on the debt for periods before the relevant date, although not previously reserved or agreed.

(3) If the debt is due by virtue of a written instrument, and payable at a certain time, interest may be claimed for the period from that time to the relevant date.

(4) If the debt is due otherwise, interest may only be claimed if, before the relevant date, a demand for payment of the debt was made in writing by or on behalf of the creditor, and notice given that interest would be payable from the date of the demand to the date of payment.

(5) Interest under paragraph (4) of this Rule may only be claimed for the period from the date of the demand to the relevant date and for all the purposes of the 1986 Act and the Rules shall be chargeable at a rate not exceeding that mentioned in paragraph (6) of this Rule.

(6) The rate of interest to be claimed under paragraphs (3) and (4) of this Rule is the rate specified in section 17 of the Judgments Act 1838 on the relevant date.

(7) Any surplus remaining after payment of the debts proved shall, before being applied for any purpose, be applied in paying interest on those debts in respect of the periods during which they have been outstanding since the relevant date.

(8) All interest payable under paragraph (7) of this Rule ranks equally whether or not the debts on which it is payable rank equally.

(9) The rate of interest payable under paragraph (7) of this Rule is whichever is the greater of the rate specified under paragraph (6) of this Rule and the rate applicable to the debt apart from the postal administration.

NOTES

Commencement: 31 January 2014.

[7.2144]

59 Debt payable at future time

A creditor may prove for a debt of which payment was not yet due on the date when the company entered postal administration subject to Rule 76 (adjustment of dividend where payment made before time).

NOTES

Commencement: 31 January 2014.

[7.2145]

60 Value of security

(1) A secured creditor may, with the agreement of the postal administrator or the permission of the court, at any time alter the value which they have, in their proof of debt, put upon their security.

(2) However, if a secured creditor has voted in respect of the unsecured balance of their debt, they may re-value their security only with permission of the court.

NOTES

Commencement: 31 January 2014.

[7.2146]

61 Surrender for non-disclosure

(1) If a secured creditor omits to disclose their security in their proof of debt, they shall surrender their security for the general benefit of creditors, unless the court, on application by them, relieves them from the effect of this Rule on the ground that the omission was inadvertent or the result of honest mistake.

(2) If the court grants that relief, it may require or allow the creditor's proof of debt to be amended, on such terms as may be just.

NOTES

Commencement: 31 January 2014.

[7.2147]

62 Redemption by postal administrator

(1) The postal administrator may at any time give notice to a creditor whose debt is secured that the postal administrator proposes, at the expiration of 28 days from the date of the notice, to redeem the security at the value put upon it in the creditor's proof.

(2) The creditor then has 21 days (or such longer period as the postal administrator may allow) in which, if they so wish, to exercise their right to revalue their security (with the permission of the court, where Rule 60(2) applies). If the creditor re-values their security, the postal administrator may only redeem at the new value.

(3) If the postal administrator redeems the security, the cost of transferring it is payable out of the assets.

(4) A secured creditor may at any time, by a notice in writing, call on the postal administrator to elect whether the postal administrator will or will not exercise the postal administrator's power to redeem the security at the value then placed on it; and the postal administrator then has 3 months in which to exercise the power or determine not to exercise it.

NOTES

Commencement: 31 January 2014.

[7.2148]

63 Test of security's value

(1) Subject as follows, if the postal administrator is dissatisfied with the value which a secured creditor puts on their security (whether in their proof or by way of re-valuation under Rule 60) the postal administrator may require any property comprised in the security to be offered for sale.

(2) The terms of sale shall be such as may be agreed, or as the court may direct; and if the sale is by auction, the postal administrator on behalf of the company, and the creditor on his own behalf, may appear and bid.

(3) This Rule does not apply if the security has been re-valued and the revaluation has been approved by the court.

NOTES

Commencement: 31 January 2014.

[7.2149]

64 Realisation of security by creditor

(1) If a creditor who has valued their security subsequently realises it (whether or not at the instance of the postal administrator)—

(a) the net amount realised shall be substituted for the value previously put by the creditor on the security; and

(b) that amount shall be treated in all respects as an amended valuation made by them.

NOTES

Commencement: 31 January 2014.

[7.2150]

65 Notice of proposed distribution

(1) Where a postal administrator is proposing to make a distribution to creditors the postal administrator shall give notice of that fact.

(2) The notice given pursuant to paragraph (1) of this Rule shall—

(a) be sent to all creditors whose addresses are known to the postal administrator;

(b) state whether the distribution is to preferential creditors or preferential creditors and unsecured creditors; and

(c) where the postal administrator proposes to make a distribution to unsecured creditors, state the value of the prescribed part, except where the court has made an order under section 1765) of the 1986 Act.

(3) Subject to paragraph (5)(b) of this Rule, before declaring a dividend the postal administrator shall by notice invite the creditors to prove their debts. Such notice—

(a) shall be gazetted; and

(b) may be advertised in such other manner as the postal administrator thinks fit.

(4) A notice pursuant to paragraph (1) or (3) of this Rule must, in addition to the standard contents—

(a) state that it is the intention of the postal administrator to make a distribution to creditors within the period of 2 months from the last date for proving;

(b) specify whether the proposed dividend is interim or final;

(c) specify a date up to which proofs may be lodged being a date which—

(i) is the same date for all creditors; and

(ii) is not less than 21 days from that of the notice.

(5) Where a dividend is to be declared for preferential creditors—

(a) the notice pursuant to paragraph (1) of this Rule need only to be given to those creditors in whose case the postal administrator has reason to believe that their debts are preferential; and

(b) the notice pursuant to paragraph (3) of this Rule need only be given if the postal administrator thinks fit.

NOTES

Commencement: 31 January 2014.

[7.2151]

66 Admission or rejection of proofs

(1) Unless the postal administrator has already dealt with them, within 5 business days of the last date for proving, the postal administrator shall—

(a) admit or reject (in whole or in part) proofs submitted to the postal administrator; or

(b) make such provision in respect of them as the postal administrator thinks fit.

(2) The postal administrator is not obliged to deal with proofs lodged after the last date for proving, but may do so, if the postal administrator thinks fit.

(3) In the declaration of a dividend no payment shall be made more than once by virtue of the same debt.

NOTES

Commencement: 31 January 2014.

[7.2152]

67 Postponement or cancellation of dividend

If in the period of 2 months referred to in Rule 65(4)(a)—

(a) the postal administrator has rejected a proof in whole or in part and application is made to the court for that decision to be reversed or varied, or

(b) application is made to the court for the postal administrator's decision on a proof to be reversed or varied, or for a proof to be expunged, or for a reduction of the amount claimed,

the postal administrator may postpone or cancel the dividend.

NOTES

Commencement: 31 January 2014.

[7.2153]

68 Declaration of dividend

(1) Subject to paragraph (2) of this Rule, within the 2 month period referred to in Rule 65(4)(a) the postal administrator shall proceed to declare the dividend to one or more classes of creditor of which the postal administrator gave notice.

(2) Except with the permission of the court, the postal administrator shall not declare a dividend so long as there is pending any application to the court to reverse or vary a decision of the postal administrator on a proof, or to expunge a proof or to reduce the amount claimed.

(3) If the court gives permission under paragraph (2) of this Rule, the postal administrator must make such provision in respect of the proof in question as the court directs.

NOTES

Commencement: 31 January 2014.

[7.2154]

69 Notice of declaration of a dividend

(1) Where the postal administrator declares a dividend the postal administrator shall give notice of that fact to all creditors who have proved their debts.

(2) The notice shall include the following particulars relating to the administration—

- (a) amounts raised from the sale of assets, indicating (so far as practicable) amounts raised by the sale of particular assets;
- (b) payments made by the postal administrator when acting as such;
- (c) where the postal administrator proposed to make a distribution to unsecured creditors, the value of the prescribed part, except where the court has made an order under section 1765) of the 1986 Act;
- (d) provision (if any) made for unsettled claims, and funds (if any) retained for particular purposes;
- (e) the total amount of dividend and the rate of dividend; and
- (f) whether, and if so when, any further dividend is expected to be declared.

NOTES

Commencement: 31 January 2014.

[7.2155]

70 Payments of dividends and related matters

(1) The dividend may be distributed simultaneously with the notice declaring it.

(2) Payment of dividend may be made by post, or arrangements may be made with any creditor for it to be paid to them in another way, or held for their collection.

(3) Where a dividend is paid on a bill of exchange or other negotiable instrument, the amount of the dividend shall be endorsed on the instrument, or on a certified copy of it, if required to be produced by the holder for that purpose.

NOTES

Commencement: 31 January 2014.

[7.2156]

71 Notice of no dividend, or no further dividend

If the postal administrator gives notice to creditors that the postal administrator is unable to declare any dividend or (as the case may be) any further dividend, the notice shall contain a statement to the effect either—

- (a) that no funds have been realised; or
- (b) that the funds realised have already been distributed or used or allocated for defraying the expenses of the postal administration.

NOTES

Commencement: 31 January 2014.

[7.2157]

72 Proof altered after payment of dividend

(1) If after payment of dividend the amount claimed by a creditor in their proof is increased, the creditor is not entitled to disturb the distribution of the dividend; but they are entitled to be paid, out of any money for the time being available for the payment of any further dividend, any dividend or dividends which they have failed to receive.

(2) Any dividend or dividends payable under paragraph (1) of this Rule shall be paid before the money there referred to is applied to the payment of any such further dividend.

(3) If, after a creditor's proof has been admitted, the proof is withdrawn or expunged, or the amount is reduced, the creditor is liable to repay to the postal administrator any amount overpaid by way of dividend.

NOTES

Commencement: 31 January 2014.

[7.2158]
73 Secured creditors

(1) The following applies where a creditor re-values their security at a time when a dividend has been declared.

(2) If the revaluation results in a reduction of their unsecured claim ranking for dividend, the creditor shall as soon as reasonably practicable repay to the postal administrator, for the credit of the postal administration, any amount received by them as dividend in excess of that to which they would be entitled having regard to the revaluation of the security.

(3) If the revaluation results in an increase of their unsecured claim, the creditor is entitled to receive from the postal administrator, out of any money for the time being available for the payment of a further dividend, before any such further dividend is paid, any dividend or dividends which they have failed to receive, having regard to the revaluation of the security. However, the creditor is not entitled to disturb any dividend declared (whether or not distributed) before the date of the revaluation.

NOTES

Commencement: 31 January 2014.

[7.2159]
74 Disqualification from dividend

If a creditor contravenes any provision of the 1986 Act or the Rules relating to the valuation of securities, the court may, on the application of the postal administrator, order that the creditor be wholly or partly disqualified from participation in any dividend.

NOTES

Commencement: 31 January 2014.

[7.2160]
75 Assignment of right to dividend

(1) If a person entitled to a dividend gives notice to the postal administrator that they wish the dividend to be paid to another person, or that they have assigned their entitlement to another person, the postal administrator shall pay the dividend to that other accordingly.

(2) A notice given under this Rule must specify the name and address of the person to whom payment is to be made.

NOTES

Commencement: 31 January 2014.

[7.2161]
76 Debt payable at future time

(1) Where a creditor has proved for a debt of which payment is not due at the date of the declaration of dividend, they are entitled to dividend equally with other creditors, but subject as follows.

(2) For the purpose of dividend (and no other purpose) the amount of the creditor's admitted proof (or, if a distribution has previously been made to them, the amount remaining outstanding in respect of their admitted proof) shall be reduced by applying the following formula—

$$\frac{X}{1.05^n}$$

where—

(a) "X" is the value of the admitted proof; and
(b) "n" is the period beginning with the date the company entered postal administration and ending with the date on which the payment of the creditor's debt would otherwise be due expressed in years and months in a decimalised form.

NOTES

Commencement: 31 January 2014.

PART 8
THE POSTAL ADMINISTRATOR

[7.2162]
77 Fixing of remuneration

(1) The postal administrator is entitled to receive remuneration for their services as such.

(2) The basis of remuneration shall be fixed by reference to the time properly given by the insolvency practitioner (as postal administrator) and their staff in attending to matters arising in the postal administration.

(3) The postal administrator's remuneration shall, on the postal administrator's application, be fixed by the court.

(4) The postal administrator shall give at least 14 days notice of their application to the following who may appear or be represented—

- (a) the Secretary of State;
- (b) OFCOM; and
- (c) the creditors of the company.

(5) In fixing the remuneration, the court shall have regard to the following matters—

- (a) the complexity (or otherwise) of the case;
- (b) any respects in which, in connection with the company's affairs, there falls on the postal administrator any responsibility of an exceptional kind or degree;
- (c) the effectiveness with which the postal administrator appears to be carrying out, or to have carried out, the postal administrator's duties as such; and
- (d) the value and nature of the property with which the postal administrator has had to deal.

(6) Where there are joint postal administrators, it is for them to agree between themselves as to how the remuneration payable should be apportioned. Any dispute arising between them may be referred to the court, for settlement by order.

(7) If the postal administrator is a solicitor and employs their own firm, or any partner in it, to act on behalf of the company, profit costs shall not be paid unless this is authorised by the court.

NOTES

Commencement: 31 January 2014.

PART 9
ENDING POSTAL ADMINISTRATION

[7.2163]
78 Final progress reports

(1) In this Part reference to a progress report is to a report in the form specified in Rule 34.

(2) The final progress report means a progress report which includes a summary of—

- (a) the postal administrator's proposals;
- (b) any major amendments to, or deviations from, those proposals;
- (c) the steps taken during the postal administration; and
- (d) the outcome.

NOTES

Commencement: 31 January 2014.

[7.2164]
79 Application to court

(1) An application to court under paragraph 79 for an order ending a postal administration shall have attached to it a progress report for the period since the last progress report (if any) or the date the company entered postal administration and a statement indicating what the postal administrator thinks should be the next steps for the company (if applicable).

(2) Where such an application is made the applicant shall—

- (a) give notice in writing to the applicant for the postal administration order (unless the applicant in both cases is the same) and the creditors of their intention to apply to court at least 5 business days before the date that they intend to make their application; and
- (b) attach to the application to court a statement that they have notified the creditors, and copies of any response from creditors to that notification.

(3) Where the application is made otherwise than by the postal administrator—

- (a) the applicant shall also give notice in writing to the postal administrator of their intention to apply to court at least 5 business days before the date that the applicant intends to make their application; and
- (b) upon receipt of such written notice the postal administrator shall, before the end of the 5 day period, provide the applicant with a progress report for the period since the last progress report (if any) or the date the company entered postal administration.

(4) Where the postal administrator applies to court under paragraph 79 in conjunction with a petition under section 124 of the 1986 Act for an order to wind up the company, the postal administrator shall, in addition to the requirements of paragraph (3) of this Rule, notify the creditors whether the postal administrator intends to seek appointment as liquidator.

NOTES

Commencement: 31 January 2014.

[7.2165]
80 Notification by postal administrator of court order

(1) Where the court makes an order to end the postal administration, the postal administrator must send to the registrar of companies a copy of the court order and a copy of the postal administrator's final progress report.

(2) As soon as reasonably practicable, the postal administrator must send a copy of the order and the final progress report to all other persons who received notice of the postal administrator's appointment.

NOTES

Commencement: 31 January 2014.

[7.2166]
81 Moving from postal administration to creditors' voluntary liquidation

(1) As soon as reasonably practicable after the day on which the registrar of companies registers the notice of moving from postal administration to creditors' voluntary liquidation (sent by the postal administrator for the purposes of paragraph 83(3)), the person who at that point ceases to be the postal administrator must send a final progress report to—

(a) the registrar of companies; and
(b) all those who received notice of the postal administrator's appointment.

(2) The postal administrator must comply with the requirement in paragraph (1) of this Rule whether they are the liquidator or not, and the final progress report must include details of the assets to be dealt with in the liquidation.

(3) For the purposes of paragraph 83(7)(a), a person shall be nominated as liquidator in accordance with the provisions of Rule 20(2)(l) or Rule 33(2)(g) and that person's appointment takes effect, following registration under paragraph (1) of this Rule—

(a) by virtue of the postal administrator's proposals or revised proposals; or
(b) where a creditors' meeting is held in accordance with Rule 24, as a consequence of such a meeting.

(4) OFCOM must notify the Secretary of State before consenting to the postal administrator delivering a notice of moving from postal administration to creditors' voluntary liquidation to the registrar of companies.

NOTES

Commencement: 31 January 2014.

[7.2167]
82 Moving from postal administration to dissolution

(1) Where, for the purposes of paragraph 84(1), the postal administrator sends a notice of moving from postal administration to dissolution to the registrar of companies, the postal administrator must attach to that notice a final progress report.

(2) As soon as reasonably practicable a copy of the notice and the attached document shall be sent to all other persons who received notice of the postal administrator's appointment.

(3) Where a court makes an order under paragraph 84(7) it shall, where the applicant is not the postal administrator, give a copy of the order to the postal administrator.

(4) OFCOM must notify the Secretary of State before directing the postal administrator to deliver a notice of moving from postal administration to dissolution to the registrar of companies.

NOTES

Commencement: 31 January 2014.

[7.2168]
83 Provision of information to the Secretary of State

Where the postal administration ends pursuant to paragraph 79, 83 or 84 the postal administrator shall, within 5 business days from the date of the end of the postal administration, provide the Secretary of State with the following information—

(a) a breakdown of the relevant debts (within the meaning of section 83(6) of the 2011 Act) of the company which remain outstanding; and
(b) details of any shortfall (within the meaning of section 83(5) of the 2011 Act) in the property of the company available for meeting those relevant debts.

NOTES

Commencement: 31 January 2014.

PART 10
REPLACING POSTAL ADMINISTRATOR

[7.2169]
84 Grounds for resignation

(1) The postal administrator may give notice of their resignation on grounds of ill health or because—

(a) the postal administrator intends ceasing to be in practice as an insolvency practitioner; or

(b) there is some conflict of interest, or change of personal circumstances, which precludes or makes impracticable the further discharge by the postal administrator of the duties of postal administrator.

(2) The postal administrator may, with the permission of the court, give notice of their resignation on grounds other than those specified in paragraph (1) of this Rule.

NOTES

Commencement: 31 January 2014.

[7.2170]

85 Notice of intention to resign

The postal administrator shall in all cases give at least 5 business days' notice in Form PA11 of their intention to resign, or to apply for the court's permission to do so, to the following persons—

(a) the Secretary of State;
(b) OFCOM;
(c) if there is a continuing postal administrator of the company, to them; and
(d) if there is no such postal administrator, to the company and its creditors.

NOTES

Commencement: 31 January 2014.

[7.2171]

86 Notice of resignation

The notice shall be filed with the court, and a copy sent to the registrar of companies. A copy of the notice of resignation shall be sent not more than 5 business days after it has been filed with the court to all those to whom notice of intention to resign was sent.

NOTES

Commencement: 31 January 2014.

[7.2172]

87 Application to court to remove postal administrator from office

(1) Any application under paragraph 88 shall state the grounds on which it is requested that the postal administrator should be removed from office.

(2) Service of the notice of the application shall be effected on the postal administrator, the Secretary of State, OFCOM, the joint postal administrator (if any), and where there is not a joint postal administrator, to the company and all the creditors, including any floating charge holders, not less than 5 business days before the date fixed for the application to be heard.

(3) Where a court makes an order removing the postal administrator it shall give a copy of the order to the applicant who as soon as reasonably practicable shall send a copy to the postal administrator.

(4) The applicant shall also within 5 business days of the order being made send a copy of the order to all those to whom notice of the application was sent.

(5) A copy of the order shall also be sent to the registrar of companies within the same time period.

NOTES

Commencement: 31 January 2014.

[7.2173]

88 Notice of vacation of office when postal administrator ceases to be qualified to act

Where the postal administrator who has ceased to be qualified to act as an insolvency practitioner in relation to the company gives notice in accordance with paragraph 89, the postal administrator shall also give notice to the registrar of companies.

NOTES

Commencement: 31 January 2014.

[7.2174]

89 Postal administrator deceased

(1) Subject as follows, where the postal administrator has died, it is the duty of the postal administrator's personal representatives to give notice of the fact to the court, specifying the date of the death. This does not apply if notice has been given under either paragraph (2) or (3) of this Rule.

(2) If the deceased postal administrator was a partner in or an employee of a firm, notice may be given by a partner in the firm who is qualified to act as an insolvency practitioner, or is a member of any body recognised by the Secretary of State for the authorisation of insolvency practitioners.

(3) Notice of the death may be given by any person producing to the court the relevant death certificate or a copy of it.

(4) Where a person gives notice to the court under this Rule, they shall also give notice to the registrar of companies.

NOTES

Commencement: 31 January 2014.

[7.2175]

90 Application to replace

(1) Where an application is made to court under paragraph 91(1) to appoint a replacement postal administrator, the application shall be accompanied by a written statement made in Form PA2 by the person proposed to be the replacement postal administrator.

(2) A copy of the application shall be served, in addition to those persons listed in section 70(2) of the 2011 Act and Rule 8(3), on the person who made the application for the postal administration order.

(3) Rule 10 shall apply to the service of an application under paragraph 91(1) as it applies to service in accordance with Rule 8.

(4) Rules 11, 12, 13(1) and (2) apply to an application under paragraph 91(1).

NOTES

Commencement: 31 January 2014.

[7.2176]

91 Notification and advertisement of appointment of replacement postal administrator

Where a replacement postal administrator is appointed, the same provisions apply in respect of giving notice of, and advertising, the replacement appointment as in the case of the appointment (subject to Rule 93), and all statements, consents etc as are required shall also be required in the case of the appointment of a replacement. All forms and notices shall clearly identify that the appointment is of a replacement postal administrator.

NOTES

Commencement: 31 January 2014.

[7.2177]

92 Notification and advertisement of appointment of joint postal administrator

Where, after an initial appointment has been made, an additional person or persons are to be appointed as joint postal administrator the same Rules shall apply in respect of giving notice of and advertising the appointment as in the case of the initial appointment, subject to Rule 93.

NOTES

Commencement: 31 January 2014.

[7.2178]

93 Notification to Registrar of Companies

The replacement or additional postal administrator shall send notice of the appointment to the registrar of companies.

NOTES

Commencement: 31 January 2014.

[7.2179]

94 Postal administrator's duties on vacating office

(1) Where the postal administrator ceases to be in office as such, in consequence of removal, resignation or cesser of qualification as an insolvency practitioner, the postal administrator is under obligation as soon as reasonably practicable to deliver up to the person succeeding them as postal administrator the assets (after deduction of any expenses properly incurred and distributions made by the postal administrator) and further to deliver up to that person—

(a) the records of the postal administration, including correspondence, proofs and other related papers appertaining to the postal administration while it was within the postal administrator's responsibility; and

(b) the company's books, papers and other records.

(2) If the postal administrator makes default in complying with this Rule, the postal administrator is liable to a fine and, for continued contravention, to a daily default fine.

NOTES

Commencement: 31 January 2014.

PART 11
COURT PROCEDURE AND PRACTICE
CHAPTER 1 APPLICATIONS

[7.2180]
95 Preliminary

This Chapter applies to any application made to the court in postal administration proceedings under the Rules, except an application for a postal administration order.

NOTES
Commencement: 31 January 2014.

[7.2181]
96 Form and contents of application

(1) Each application shall be in writing and shall state—
- (a) the names of the parties;
- (b) the name of company which is the subject of the postal administration proceedings to which the application relates;
- (c) the court (and where applicable, the division or district registry of that court) in which the application is made;
- (d) where the court has previously allocated a number to the postal administration proceedings within which the application is made, that number;
- (e) the nature of the remedy or order applied for or the directions sought from the court;
- (f) the names and addresses of the persons (if any) on whom it is intended to serve the application or that no person is intended to be served;
- (g) where the 1986 Act or Rules require that notice of the application is to be given to specified persons, the names and addresses of all those persons (so far as known to the applicant); and
- (h) the applicant's address for service.

(2) The application must be authenticated by the applicant if they are acting in person or, when they are not so acting, by or on behalf of their solicitor.

NOTES
Commencement: 31 January 2014.

[7.2182]
97 Application under section 1765) of the 1986 Act to disapply section 176A of the 1986 Act

(1) An application under section 1765) of the 1986 Act shall be accompanied by a witness statement by the postal administrator.

(2) The witness statement shall state—
- (a) that the application arises in the course of a postal administration under the 2011 Act;
- (b) a summary of the financial position of the company;
- (c) the information substantiating the postal administrator's view that the cost of making a distribution to unsecured creditors would be disproportionate to the benefits; and
- (d) whether any other postal administrator is acting in relation to the company and if so their address.

NOTES
Commencement: 31 January 2014.

[7.2183]
98 Filing and service of application

(1) An application must be filed with the court, accompanied by one copy and a number of additional copies equal to the number of persons who are to be served with the application.

(2) Where an application is filed with the court in accordance with paragraph (1) of this Rule, the court must fix a venue for the application to be heard unless—
- (a) it considers it is not appropriate to do so;
- (b) the Rule under which the application is brought provides otherwise; or
- (c) the case is one to which Rule 100 applies.

(3) Unless the court otherwise directs, the applicant shall serve a sealed copy of the application, endorsed with the venue for the hearing, on the respondent named in the application (or on each respondent if more than one).

(4) The court may give any of the following directions—
- (a) that the application be served upon persons other than those specified by the relevant provision of the 1986 Act or the Rules;
- (b) that the giving of notice to any person may be dispensed with;
- (c) that notice be given in some way other than that specified in paragraph (3) of this Rule.

(5) An application must be served at least 14 days before the date fixed for its hearing unless—
- (a) the provision of the 1986 Act or the Rules under which the application is made makes different provision; or
- (b) the case is one of urgency, to which paragraph (6) of this Rule applies.

(6) Where the case is one of urgency, the court may (without prejudice to its general power to extend or abridge time limits)—

(a) hear the application immediately, either with or without notice to, or the attendance of, other parties, or

(b) authorise a shorter period of service than that provided for by paragraph (5) of this Rule;

and any such application may be heard on terms providing for the filing or service of documents, or the carrying out of other formalities, as the court thinks just.

NOTES

Commencement: 31 January 2014.

[7.2184]
99 Notice of application under section 1765) of the 1986 Act

An application under section 1765) of the 1986 Act may be made without the application being served upon or notice being given to any other party.

NOTES

Commencement: 31 January 2014.

[7.2185]
100 Hearings without notice

Where the relevant provisions of the 1986 Act or the Rules do not require service of the application on, or notice of it to be given to, any person—

(a) the court may hear the application as soon as reasonably practicable without fixing a venue as required by Rule 98(2); or

(b) it may fix a venue for the application to be heard in which case Rule 98 will apply to the extent that it is relevant;

but nothing in those provisions is to be taken as prohibiting the applicant from giving such notice if the applicant wishes to do so.

NOTES

Commencement: 31 January 2014.

[7.2186]
101 Hearing of application

(1) Unless the court otherwise directs, the hearing of an application must be in open court.

(2) In a county court, the jurisdiction of the court to hear and determine an application may be exercised by the district judge (to whom any application must be made in the first instance) unless—

(a) a direction to the contrary has been given, or

(b) it is not within the district judge's power to make the order required.

(3) In the High Court the jurisdiction of the court to hear and determine an application may be exercised by the registrar (to whom the application must be made in the first instance) unless—

(a) a direction to the contrary has been given, or

(b) it is not within the registrar's power to make the order required.

(4) Where the application is made to the district judge in the county court or to the registrar in the High Court, the district judge or the registrar may refer to the judge any matter which the district judge or the registrar thinks should properly be decided by the judge, and the judge may either dispose of the matter or refer it back to the district judge or the registrar with such directions as that judge thinks just.

(5) Nothing in this Rule precludes an application being made directly to the judge in a proper case.

NOTES

Commencement: 31 January 2014.

[7.2187]
102 Witness statements—general

(1) Subject to Rule 104, where evidence is required by the 1986 Act or the Rules as to any matter, such evidence may be provided in the form of a witness statement unless—

(a) in any specific case a Rule or the 1986 Act makes different provision; or

(b) the court otherwise directs.

(2) The court may, on the application of any party to the matter in question order the attendance for cross-examination of the person making the witness statement.

(3) Where, after such an order has been made, the person in question does not attend, that person's witness statement must not be used in evidence without the permission of the court.

NOTES

Commencement: 31 January 2014.

[7.2188]
103 Filing and service of witness statements

Unless the provision of the 1986 Act or the Rules under which the application is made provides otherwise, or the court otherwise allows—

(a) if the applicant intends to rely at the first hearing on evidence in a witness statement, the applicant shall file the witness statement with the court and serve a copy on the respondent, not less than 14 days before the date fixed for the hearing, and
(b) where a respondent to an application intends to oppose it and to rely for that purpose on evidence in a witness statement, the respondent shall file the witness statement with the court and serve a copy on the applicant, not less than 5 business days before the date fixed for the hearing.

NOTES
Commencement: 31 January 2014.

[7.2189]
104 Use of reports

(1) A report may be filed in court by the postal administrator instead of a witness statement, unless the application involves other parties or the court otherwise orders.

(2) In any case where a report is filed instead of a witness statement, the report shall be treated for the purposes of Rule 103 and any hearing before the court as if it were a witness statement.

(3) Where the witness statement is made by the postal administrator, the witness statement must state the address at which the postal administrator works.

NOTES
Commencement: 31 January 2014.

[7.2190]
105 Adjournment of hearing; directions

(1) The court may adjourn the hearing of an application on such terms as it thinks just.

(2) The court may at any time give such directions as it thinks just as to—
(a) service or notice of the application on or to any person;
(b) whether particulars of claim and defence are to be delivered and generally as to the procedure on the application including whether a hearing is necessary;
(c) the matters to be dealt with in evidence.

(3) The court may give directions as to the manner in which any evidence is to be adduced at a resumed hearing and in particular as to—
(a) the taking of evidence wholly or partly by witness statement or orally;
(b) the cross-examination of the maker of a witness statement; or
(c) any report to be made by the postal administrator.

NOTES
Commencement: 31 January 2014.

[7.2191]
106 General power of transfer

(1) Where postal administration proceedings are pending in the High Court, the court may order them to be transferred to a specified county court.

(2) Where postal administration proceedings are pending in a county court, the court may order them to be transferred either to the High Court or to another county court.

(3) In any case where proceedings are transferred to a county court, the transfer must be to a court which has jurisdiction to wind up companies.

(4) A transfer of proceedings under this Rule may be ordered—
(a) by the court of its own motion, or
(b) on the application of the postal administrator, or
(c) on the application of a person appearing to the court to have an interest in the proceedings.

NOTES
Commencement: 31 January 2014.

[7.2192]
107 Proceedings commenced in wrong court

Where postal administration proceedings are commenced in a court which is, in relation to those proceedings, the wrong court, that court may—
(a) order the transfer of the proceedings to the court in which they ought to have been commenced;
(b) order that the proceedings be continued in the court in which they have been commenced; or
(c) order the proceedings to be struck out.

NOTES
Commencement: 31 January 2014.

[7.2193]
108 Applications for transfer

(1) An application by the postal administrator for proceedings to be transferred shall be made with a report by the postal administrator—

(a) setting out the reasons for the transfer, and
(b) including a statement that the applicant for the postal administration order consents to the transfer, or that the applicant has been given at least 14 days' notice of the postal administrator's application.

(2) If the court is satisfied from the postal administrator's report that the proceedings can be conducted more conveniently in another court, the proceedings shall be transferred to that court.

NOTES
Commencement: 31 January 2014.

[7.2194]
109 Procedure following order for transfer

(1) Subject as follows, the court making an order under Rule 106 shall as soon as reasonably practicable send to the transferee court a sealed copy of the order, and the file of the proceedings.

(2) On receipt of these, the transferee court shall as soon as reasonably practicable send notice of the transfer to the transferor court.

NOTES
Commencement: 31 January 2014.

CHAPTER 2 SHORTHAND WRITERS

[7.2195]
110 Nomination and appointment of shorthand writers

(1) In the High Court the judge or registrar and, in a county court, a district judge may in writing nominate one or more persons to be official shorthand writers to the court.

(2) The court may, at any time in the course of the postal administration proceedings, appoint a shorthand writer to take down the evidence of a person examined under section 236 of the 1986 Act.

NOTES
Commencement: 31 January 2014.

[7.2196]
111 Remuneration

(1) The remuneration of a shorthand writer appointed in postal administration proceedings shall be paid by the party at whose instance the appointment was made, or out of the assets of the company, or otherwise, as the court may direct.

(2) Any question arising as to the rates of remuneration payable under this Rule shall be determined by the court in its discretion.

NOTES
Commencement: 31 January 2014.

CHAPTER 3 ENFORCEMENT PROCEDURES

[7.2197]
112 Enforcement of court orders

(1) In any postal administration proceedings under the Rules, orders of the court may be enforced in the same manner as a judgment to the same effect.

(2) Where a warrant for the arrest of a person is issued by the High Court, the warrant may be discharged by the county court where the person who is the subject of the warrant—

(a) has been brought before a county court exercising postal administration jurisdiction; and
(b) has given to the county court an undertaking which is satisfactory to the county court to comply with the obligations that apply to that person under the provisions of the 1986 Act or the Rules.

NOTES
Commencement: 31 January 2014.

[7.2198]
113 Orders enforcing compliance with the Rules

(1) The court may, on application by the postal administrator, make such orders as it thinks necessary for the enforcement of obligations falling on any person in accordance with—

(a) paragraph 47 (duty to submit statement of affairs in postal administration), or
(b) section 235 of the 1986 Act (duty of various persons to co-operate with postal administrator).

(2) An order of the court under this Rule may provide that all costs of and incidental to the application for it shall be borne by the person against whom the order is made.

NOTES

Commencement: 31 January 2014.

[7.2199]

114 Warrants under section 236 of the 1986 Act

(1) A warrant issued by the court under section 236 of the 1986 Act (inquiry into insolvent company's dealings) shall be addressed to such officer of the High Court as the warrant specifies, or to any constable.

(2) The persons referred to in section 236(5) of the 1986 Act (court's powers of enforcement) as the prescribed officer of the court are the tipstaff and the tipstaff's assistants of the court.

(3) In this Chapter references to property include books, papers and records.

(4) When a person is arrested under a warrant issued under section 236 of the 1986 Act, the officer arresting them shall as soon as reasonably practicable bring them before the court issuing the warrant in order that they may be examined.

(5) If they cannot immediately be brought up for examination, the officer shall deliver them into the custody of the governor of the prison named in the warrant (or where that prison is not able to accommodate the arrested person, the governor of such other prison with appropriate facilities which is able to accommodate the arrested person), who shall keep them in custody and produce them before the court as it may from time to time direct.

(6) After arresting the person named in the warrant, the officer shall as soon as reasonably practicable report to the court the arrest or delivery into custody (as the case may be) and apply to the court to fix a venue for the person's examination.

(7) The court shall appoint the earliest practicable time for the examination, and shall—

(a) direct the governor of the prison to produce the person for examination at the time and place appointed, and

(b) as soon as reasonably practicable give notice of the venue to the person who applied for the warrant.

(8) Any property in the arrested person's possession which may be seized shall be—

(a) lodged with, or otherwise dealt with as instructed by, whoever is specified in the warrant as authorised to receive it, or

(b) kept by the officer seizing it pending the receipt of written orders from the court as to its disposal,

as may be directed by the court.

NOTES

Commencement: 31 January 2014.

CHAPTER 4 COURT RECORDS AND RETURNS

[7.2200]

115 Court file

(1) The court must open and maintain a file in any case where documents are filed with it under the 1986 Act or the Rules.

(2) Any documents which are filed with the court under the 1986 Act or the Rules must be placed on the file opened in accordance with paragraph (1) of this Rule.

(3) The following persons may inspect or obtain from the court a copy of, or a copy of any document or documents contained in, the file opened in accordance with paragraph (1) of this Rule—

(a) the postal administrator;

(b) the Secretary of State;

(c) OFCOM;

(d) any person who is a creditor of the company to which the proceedings relate if that person provides the court with a statement in writing confirming that that person is a creditor; and

(e) any person who is, or at any time has been, a director or officer of the company to which the postal administration proceedings relate, or who is a member of that company.

(4) The right to inspect or obtain a copy of, or a copy of any document or documents contained in, the file opened in accordance with paragraph (1) of this Rule may be exercised on that person's behalf by a person authorised to do so by that person.

(5) Any person who is not otherwise entitled to inspect or obtain a copy of, or a copy of any document or documents contained in, the file opened in accordance with paragraph (1) of this Rule may do so if that person has the permission of the court.

(6) The court may direct that the file, a document (or part of it) or a copy of a document (or part of it) must not be made available under paragraph (3) or (4) of this Rule without the permission of the court.

(7) An application for a direction under paragraph (6) of this Rule may be made by—

(a) the postal administrator; or

(b) any person appearing to the court to have an interest.

(8) Where any person wishes to exercise the right to inspect the file under paragraph (3), (4) or (5) of this Rule that person—

(a) if the permission of the court is required, must file with the court an application notice in accordance with the Rules; or
(b) if the permission of the court is not required, may inspect the file at any reasonable time.

(9) Where any person wishes to exercise the right to obtain a copy of a document under paragraph (3), (4) or (5) of this Rule that person must pay any prescribed fee and—
(a) if the permission of the court is required, file with the court an application notice in accordance with the Rules; or
(b) if the permission of the court is not required, file with the court a written request for the document.

(10) An application for—
(a) permission to inspect the file or obtain a copy of a document under paragraph (5) of this Rule; or
(b) a direction under paragraph (6) of this Rule,
may be made without notice to any other party, but the court may direct that notice must be given to any person who would be affected by its decision.

(11) If for the purposes of powers conferred by the 1986 Act or the Rules, the Secretary of State or the postal administrator requests the transmission of the file of any postal administration proceedings, the court must comply with the request (unless the file is for the time being in use for the court's own purposes).

NOTES

Commencement: 31 January 2014.

CHAPTER 5 COSTS AND DETAILED ASSESSMENT

[7.2201]

116 Application of Chapter 5

(1) This Chapter applies in relation to costs in connection with postal administration proceedings under the Rules.

(2) In this Chapter a reference to costs includes charges and expenses.

NOTES

Commencement: 31 January 2014.

[7.2202]

117 Requirement to assess costs by the detailed procedure

(1) Where the costs of any person are payable as an expense out of the assets of the company, the amount payable must be decided by detailed assessment unless agreed between the postal administrator and the person entitled to payment.

(2) In the absence of such agreement as is mentioned in paragraph (1) of this Rule, the postal administrator may serve notice requiring that person to commence detailed assessment proceedings in accordance with CPR Part 47 (procedure for detailed assessment of costs and default provisions).

(3) Where the costs of any person employed by a postal administrator in postal administration proceedings are required to be decided by detailed assessment or fixed by order of the court, the postal administrator may make payments on account to such person in respect of those costs provided that person undertakes in writing—
(a) to repay as soon as reasonably practicable any money which may, when detailed assessment is made, prove to have been overpaid; and
(b) to pay interest on any such sum as is mentioned in sub-paragraph (a) at the rate specified in section 17 of the Judgments Act 1838 on the date payment was made and for the period beginning with the date of payment and ending with the date of repayment.

(4) In any proceedings before the court, the court may order costs to be decided by detailed assessment.

NOTES

Commencement: 31 January 2014.

[7.2203]

118 Procedure where detailed assessment required

(1) Before making a detailed assessment of the costs of any person employed in postal administration proceedings by the postal administrator, the costs officer shall require a certificate of employment, which shall be endorsed on the bill and authenticated by the postal administrator.

(2) The certificate shall include—
(a) the name and address of the person employed,
(b) details of the functions to be carried out under the employment, and
(c) a note of any special terms of remuneration which have been agreed.

(3) Every person whose costs in postal administration proceedings are required to be decided by detailed assessment shall, on being required in writing to do so by the postal administrator, commence detailed assessment proceedings in accordance with CPR Part 47 (procedure for detailed assessment of costs and default provisions).

(4) If that person does not commence detailed assessment proceedings within 3 months of the requirement under paragraph (3) of this Rule, or within such further time as the court, on application, may permit, the postal administrator may deal with the assets of the company without regard to any claim by that person, whose claim is forfeited by such failure to commence proceedings.

(5) Where in any such case such a claim lies additionally against a postal administrator in their personal capacity, that claim is also forfeited by such failure to commence proceedings.

(6) Where costs have been incurred in postal administration proceedings in the High Court and those proceedings are subsequently transferred to a county court, all costs of those proceedings directed by the court or otherwise required to be assessed may nevertheless, on the application of the person who incurred the costs, be ordered to be decided by detailed assessment in the High Court.

NOTES

Commencement: 31 January 2014.

[7.2204]

119 Costs paid otherwise than out of the assets of the company

Where the amount of costs is decided by detailed assessment under an order of the court directing that those costs are to be paid otherwise than out of the assets of the company, the costs officer shall note on the final costs certificate by whom, or the manner in which, the costs are to be paid.

NOTES

Commencement: 31 January 2014.

[7.2205]

120 Award of costs against postal administrator

Without prejudice to any provision of the 1986 Act or the Rules by virtue of which the postal administrator is not in any event to be liable for costs and expenses, where a postal administrator is made a party to any proceedings on the application of another party to the proceedings, the postal administrator shall not be personally liable for costs unless the court otherwise directs.

NOTES

Commencement: 31 January 2014.

[7.2206]

121 Applications for costs

(1) This Rule applies where a party to, or person affected by, any proceedings under the Rules—

(a) applies to the court for an order allowing their costs, or part of them, incidental to the proceedings; and

(b) that application is not made at the time of the proceedings.

(2) The person concerned shall serve a sealed copy of their application on the postal administrator.

(3) The postal administrator may appear on any such application.

(4) No costs of or incidental to the application shall be allowed to the applicant unless the court is satisfied that the application could not have been made at the time of the proceedings.

NOTES

Commencement: 31 January 2014.

[7.2207]

122 Costs and expenses of witnesses

(1) Except as directed by the court, no allowance as a witness in any examination or other proceedings before the court shall be made to an officer of the company to which the proceedings relate.

(2) A person making any application in postal administration proceedings shall not be regarded as a witness on the hearing of the application, but the costs officer may allow their expenses of travelling and subsistence.

NOTES

Commencement: 31 January 2014.

[7.2208]

123 Final costs certificate

(1) A final costs certificate of the costs officer is final and conclusive as to all matters which have not been objected to in the manner provided for under the rules of the court.

(2) Where it is proved to the satisfaction of a costs officer that a final costs certificate has been lost or destroyed, they may issue a duplicate.

NOTES

Commencement: 31 January 2014.

CHAPTER 6 PERSONS WHO LACK CAPACITY TO MANAGE THEIR AFFAIRS

[7.2209]

124 Introductory

(1) The Rules in this Chapter apply where in postal administration proceedings it appears to the court that a person affected by the proceedings is one who lacks capacity within the meaning of the Mental Capacity Act 2005 to manage and administer their property and affairs either—

(a) by reason of lacking capacity within the meaning of the Mental Capacity Act 2005, or

(b) due to physical affliction or disability.

(2) The person concerned is referred to as "the incapacitated person".

NOTES

Commencement: 31 January 2014.

[7.2210]

125 Appointment of another person to act

(1) The court may appoint such person as it thinks just to appear for, represent or act for the incapacitated person.

(2) The appointment may be made either generally or for the purpose of any particular application or proceeding, or for the exercise of particular rights or powers which the incapacitated person might have exercised but for their incapacity.

(3) The court may make the appointment either of its own motion or on application by—

(a) a person who has been appointed by a court in the United Kingdom or elsewhere to manage the affairs of, or to represent, the incapacitated person, or

(b) any relative or friend of the incapacitated person who appears to the court to be a proper person to make the application, or

(c) the postal administrator.

(4) Application under paragraph (3) of this Rule may be made without notice to any other party; but the court may require such notice of the application as it thinks necessary to be given to the person alleged to be incapacitated, or any other person, and may adjourn the hearing of the application to enable the notice to be given.

NOTES

Commencement: 31 January 2014.

[7.2211]

126 Witness statement in support of application

An application under Rule 125(3) must be supported by a witness statement made by a registered medical practitioner as to the mental or physical condition of the incapacitated person.

NOTES

Commencement: 31 January 2014.

[7.2212]

127 Service of notices following appointment

Any notice served on, or sent to, a person appointed under Rule 125 has the same effect as if it had been served on, or given to, the incapacitated person.

NOTES

Commencement: 31 January 2014.

CHAPTER 7 APPEALS IN POSTAL ADMINISTRATION PROCEEDINGS

[7.2213]

128 Appeals and reviews of postal administration orders

(1) The High Court may review, rescind or vary any order made by it in the exercise of its jurisdiction as regards postal administration proceedings.

(2) Appeals from decisions made in the exercise of that jurisdiction lie as follows—

(a) to a single judge of the High Court where the decision appealed against is made by the county court or the registrar;

(b) to the Civil Division of the Court of Appeal from a decision of a single judge of the High Court.

(3) A county court is not, in the exercise of its jurisdiction for the purposes of the Rules, subject to be restrained by the order of any other court, and no appeal lies from its decision in the exercise of that jurisdiction except as provided by this Rule.

NOTES

Commencement: 31 January 2014.

[7.2214]
129 Procedure on appeal

(1) An appeal against a decision at first instance may only be brought with either the permission of the court which made the decision or the permission of the court which has jurisdiction to hear the appeal.

(2) An appellant must file an appellant's notice (within the meaning of CPR Part 52) within 21 days after the date of the decision of the court that the appellant wishes to appeal.

(3) The procedure set out in CPR Part 52 applies to any appeal to which this Chapter applies.

NOTES

Commencement: 31 January 2014.

CHAPTER 8 GENERAL

[7.2215]
130 Principal court rules and practice to apply

(1) The provisions of the CPR (including any related practice direction) apply to postal administration proceedings with any necessary modifications, except so far as inconsistent with the Rules.

(2) All postal administration proceedings must be allocated to the multi-track for which CPR Part 29 makes provision, and accordingly those provisions of the CPR which provide for allocation questionnaires and track allocation do not apply.

(3) CPR Part 32 applies to a false statement in a document verified by a statement of truth made under the Rules as it applies to a false statement in a document verified by a statement of truth made under CPR Part 22.

NOTES

Commencement: 31 January 2014.

[7.2216]
131 Right of audience

Rights of audience in postal administration proceedings are the same as in insolvency proceedings.

NOTES

Commencement: 31 January 2014.

[7.2217]
132 Formal defects

No postal administration proceedings shall be invalidated by any formal defect or by any irregularity, unless the court before which objection is made considers that substantial injustice has been caused by the defect or irregularity, and that the injustice cannot be remedied by any order of the court.

NOTES

Commencement: 31 January 2014.

[7.2218]
133 Service of orders staying proceedings

Where in postal administration proceedings the court makes an order staying any action, execution or other legal process against the property of the company, service of the order may be effected by sending a sealed copy of the order to whatever is the address for service of the claimant or other party having the carriage of the proceedings to be stayed.

NOTES

Commencement: 31 January 2014.

[7.2219]
134 Payment into court

CPR Part 37 (miscellaneous provisions about payment into court) applies to money lodged in court under the Rules.

NOTES

Commencement: 31 January 2014.

[7.2220]
135 Further Information and Disclosure

(1) Any party to postal administration proceedings may apply to the court for an order—
- (a) that any other party
  - (i) clarify any matter which is in dispute in the proceedings, or
  - (ii) give additional information in relation to any such matter;

  in accordance with CPR Part 18 (further information); or
- (b) to obtain disclosure from any other party in accordance with CPR Part 31 (disclosure and inspection of documents), except so far as is otherwise provided by the Rules.

(2) An application under this Rule may be made without notice being served on any other party.

NOTES

Commencement: 31 January 2014.

[7.2221]

136 Office copies of documents

(1) Any person who has under the Rules the right to inspect the court file of postal administration proceedings may require the court to provide them with an office copy of any document from the file.

(2) A person's rights under this Rule may be exercised on their behalf by their solicitor.

(3) An office copy provided by the court under this Rule shall be in such form as the registrar thinks appropriate, and shall bear the court's seal.

NOTES

Commencement: 31 January 2014.

PART 12
PROXIES AND COMPANY REPRESENTATION

[7.2222]

137 Definition of "proxy"

(1) For the purposes of the Rules, a proxy is an authority given by a person ("the principal") to another person ("the proxy-holder") to attend a meeting and speak and vote as their representative.

(2) Proxies are for use at creditors' or company meetings summoned or called under the 1986 Act or the Rules.

(3) Only one proxy may be given by a person for any one meeting at which they desire to be represented; and it may only be given to one person, being an individual aged 18 or over. But the principal may specify one or more other such individuals to be proxy-holder in the alternative, in the order in which they are named in the proxy.

(4) Without prejudice to the generality of paragraph (3) of this Rule, a proxy for a particular meeting may be given to whoever is to be the chair of the meeting.

(5) A person given a proxy under paragraph (4) of this Rule cannot decline to be the proxy-holder in relation to that proxy.

(6) A proxy requires the holder to give the principal's vote on matters arising for determination at the meeting, or to abstain, or to propose, in the principal's name, a resolution to be voted on by the meeting, either as directed or in accordance with the holder's own discretion.

NOTES

Commencement: 31 January 2014.

[7.2223]

138 Issue and use of forms

(1) When notice is given of a meeting to be held in postal administration proceedings, and forms of proxy are sent out with the notice, no form so sent out shall have inserted in it the name or description of any person.

(2) No form of proxy shall be used at any meeting except that which is sent out with the notice summoning the meeting, or a substantially similar form.

(3) A form of proxy shall be authenticated by the principal, or by some person authorised by the principal (either generally or with reference to a particular meeting). If the form is authenticated by a person other than the principal, the nature of the person's authority shall be stated.

NOTES

Commencement: 31 January 2014.

[7.2224]

139 Use of proxies at meetings

(1) A proxy given for a particular meeting may be used at any adjournment of that meeting.

(2) Where the postal administrator holds proxies to be used by the postal administrator as chair of a meeting, and some other person acts as chair, the other person may use the postal administrator's proxies as if that person were themselves proxy-holder.

(3) Where a proxy directs a proxy-holder to vote for or against a resolution for the appointment of a person other than the postal administrator as proposed liquidator of the company, the proxy-holder may, unless the proxy states otherwise, vote for or against (as the proxy-holder thinks fit) any resolution for the nomination or appointment of that person jointly with another or others.

(4) A proxy-holder may propose any resolution which, if proposed by another, would be a resolution in favour of which by virtue of the proxy they would be entitled to vote.

(5) Where a proxy gives specific directions as to voting, this does not, unless the proxy states otherwise, preclude the proxy-holder from voting at their discretion on resolutions put to the meeting which are not dealt with in the proxy.

NOTES
Commencement: 31 January 2014.

[7.2225]
140 Retention of proxies

(1) Subject as follows, proxies used for voting at any meeting shall be retained by the chair of the meeting.

(2) The chair shall deliver the proxies, as soon as reasonably practicable after the meeting, to the postal administrator (where that is someone other than the chair).

NOTES
Commencement: 31 January 2014.

[7.2226]
141 Right of inspection

(1) The postal administrator shall, so long as proxies lodged with the postal administrator are in the postal administrator's hands, allow them to be inspected, at all reasonable times on any business day, by—

(a) the creditors, in the case of proxies used at a meeting of creditors, and

(b) the company's members, in the case of proxies used at a meeting of the company.

(2) The reference in paragraph (1) of this Rule to creditors is to those persons who have submitted in writing a claim to be creditors of the company but does not include a person whose proof or claim has been wholly rejected for purposes of voting, dividend or otherwise.

(3) The right of inspection given by this Rule is also exercisable by the directors of the company.

(4) Any person attending a meeting in postal administration proceedings is entitled, immediately before or in the course of the meeting, to inspect proxies and associated documents (including proofs) sent or given, in accordance with directions contained in any notice convening the meeting, to the chair of that meeting or to any other person by a creditor, member or contributory for the purpose of that meeting.

(5) This Rule is subject to Rule 195 (confidentiality of documents—grounds for refusing inspection).

NOTES
Commencement: 31 January 2014.

[7.2227]
142 Proxy-holder with financial interest

(1) A proxy-holder shall not vote in favour of any resolution which would directly or indirectly place them, or any associate of theirs, in a position to receive any remuneration out of the assets of the company, unless the proxy specifically directs them to vote in that way.

(2) Where a proxy-holder has authenticated the proxy as being authorised to do so by their principal and the proxy specifically directs the proxy-holder to vote in the way mentioned in paragraph (1) of this Rule, they shall nevertheless not vote in that way unless they produce to the chair of the meeting written authorisation from their principal sufficient to show that the proxy-holder was entitled so to authenticate the proxy.

(3) This Rule applies also to any person acting as chair of a meeting and using proxies in that capacity under Rule 139; and in its application to them, the proxy-holder is deemed an associate of theirs.

(4) In this Rule "associate" shall have the same meaning as in section 435 of the 1986 Act.

NOTES
Commencement: 31 January 2014.

[7.2228]
143 Company representation

(1) Where a person is authorised to represent a corporation at a meeting of creditors or of the company, they shall produce to the chair of the meeting a copy of the resolution from which they derive their authority.

(2) The copy resolution must be under the seal of the corporation, or certified by the secretary or a director of the corporation to be a true copy.

(3) Nothing in this Rule requires the authority of a person to authenticate a proxy on behalf of a principal which is a corporation to be in the form of a resolution of that corporation.

NOTES
Commencement: 31 January 2014.

PART 13
EXAMINATION OF PERSONS IN POSTAL ADMINISTRATION PROCEEDINGS

[7.2229]
144 Preliminary

(1) The Rules in this Part apply to applications to the court, made by the postal administrator, for an order under section 236 of the 1986 Act (inquiry into company's dealings),
(2) The following definitions apply—
(a) the person in respect of whom an order is applied for is "the respondent";
(b) "section 236" means section 236 of the 1986 Act;

NOTES
Commencement: 31 January 2014.

[7.2230]
145 Form and contents of application

(1) The application shall be in writing and specify the grounds on which it is made.
(2) The application must specify the name of the respondent.
(3) It shall be stated whether the application is for the respondent—
(a) to be ordered to appear before the court, or
(b) to be ordered to clarify any matter which is in dispute in the proceedings or to give additional information in relation to any such matter (in which case CPR Part 18 (further information) applies to any such order), or
(c) to submit witness statements (if so, particulars to be given of the matters to be included), or
(d) to produce books, papers or other records (if so, the items in question to be specified),
or for any two or more of those purposes.
(4) The application may be made without notice to any other party.

NOTES
Commencement: 31 January 2014.

[7.2231]
146 Order for examination, etc

(1) The court may, whatever the purpose of the application, make any order which it has power to make under section 236.
(2) The court, if it orders the respondent to appear before it, shall specify a venue for their appearance, which shall be not less than 14 days from the date of the order.
(3) If the respondent is ordered to submit witness statements, the order shall specify—
(a) the matters which are to be dealt with in their witness statements, and
(b) the time within which they are to be submitted to the court.
(4) If the order is to produce books, papers or other records, the time and manner of compliance shall be specified.
(5) The order must be served as soon as reasonably practicable on the respondent; and it must be served personally, unless the court otherwise orders.

NOTES
Commencement: 31 January 2014.

[7.2232]
147 Procedure for examination

(1) At any examination of the respondent, the postal administrator may attend in person, or be represented by a solicitor with or without counsel, and may put such questions to the respondent as the court may allow.
(2) Where application has been made under section 236 on information provided by a creditor of the company, that creditor may, with the permission of the court and if the postal administrator does not object, attend the examination and put questions to the respondent (but only through the postal administrator).
(3) If the respondent is ordered to clarify any matter or to give additional information, the court shall direct them as to the questions which they are required to answer, and as to whether their answers (if any) are to be made in a witness statement.
(4) The respondent may at their own expense employ a solicitor with or without counsel, who may put to them such questions as the court may allow for the purpose of enabling them to explain or qualify any answers given by them, and may make representations on their behalf.
(5) There shall be made in writing such record of the examination as the court thinks proper. The record shall be read over either to or by the respondent and authenticated by them at a venue fixed by the court.
(6) The written record may, in any proceedings (whether under the 1986 Act or otherwise), be used as evidence against the respondent of any statement made by them in the course of their examination.

NOTES

Commencement: 31 January 2014.

[7.2233]
148 Record of examination

(1) Unless the court otherwise directs, the written record of questions put to the respondent and the respondent's answers, and any witness statements submitted by the respondent in compliance with an order of the court under the section 236, are not to be filed with the court.

(2) The documents set out in paragraph (3) of this Rule are not open to inspection without an order of the court, by any person other than the postal administrator.

(3) The documents to which paragraph (2) of this Rule applies are—

(a) the written record of the respondent's examination;

(b) copies of questions put to the respondent or proposed to be put to the respondent and answers to questions given by the respondent;

(c) any witness statement by the respondent; and

(d) any document on the court file as shows the grounds for the application for an order.

(4) The court may from time to time give directions as to the custody and inspection of any documents to which this Rule applies, and as to the furnishing of copies of, or extracts from, such documents.

NOTES

Commencement: 31 January 2014.

[7.2234]
149 Costs of proceedings under section 236

(1) Where the court has ordered an examination of any person under section 236, and it appears to it that the examination was made necessary because information had been unjustifiably refused by the respondent, it may order that the costs of the examination be paid by the respondent.

(2) Where the court makes an order against a person under section 237(1) or (2) of the 1986 Act (court's enforcement powers under section 236) the costs of the application for the order may be ordered by the court to be paid by the respondent.

(3) Subject to paragraphs (1) and (2) of this Rule, the postal administrator's costs shall, unless the court otherwise orders, be paid out of the assets of the company.

(4) A person summoned to attend for examination under this Part shall be tendered a reasonable sum in respect of travelling expenses incurred in connection with their attendance. Other costs falling on them are at the court's discretion.

NOTES

Commencement: 31 January 2014.

PART 14
MISCELLANEOUS AND GENERAL

[7.2235]
150 Power of Secretary of State to regulate certain matters

(1) Pursuant to paragraph 27 of Schedule 8 to the 1986 Act, the Secretary of State may, subject to the 1986 Act, the 2011 Act and the Rules, make regulations with respect to any matter provided for in the Rules as relates to the carrying out of the functions of a postal administrator of a company, including, without prejudice to the generality of the foregoing, provision with respect to the following matters arising in a postal administration—

(a) the preparation and keeping of books, accounts and other records, and their production to such persons as may be authorised or required to inspect them;

(b) the auditing of a postal administrator's accounts;

(c) the manner in which a postal administrator is to act in relation to the company's books, papers and other records, and the manner of their disposal by the postal administrator or others;

(d) the supply by the postal administrator to creditors and members of the company of copies of documents relating to the postal administration and the affairs of the company (on payment, in such cases as may be specified by the regulations, of the specified fee);

(2) Regulations made pursuant to paragraph (1) of this Rule may—

(a) confer a discretion on the court;

(b) make non-compliance with any of the regulations a criminal offence;

(c) make different provision for different cases, including different provision for different areas; and

(d) contain such incidental, supplemental and transitional provisions as may appear to the Secretary of State necessary or expedient.

NOTES

Commencement: 31 January 2014.

[7.2236]

151 Costs, expenses, etc

(1) All fees, costs, charges and other expenses incurred in the course of the postal administration are to be regarded as expenses of the postal administration.

(2) The costs associated with the prescribed part shall be paid out of the prescribed part.

NOTES

Commencement: 31 January 2014.

[7.2237]

152 Provable debts

(1) Subject as follows, in postal administration all claims by creditors are provable as debts against the company whether they are present or future, certain or contingent, ascertained or sounding only in damages.

(2) Any obligation arising under a confiscation order made under Parts 2, 3 or 4 of the Proceeds of Crime Act 2002 is not provable.

(3) The following are not provable except at a time when all other claims of creditors in the postal administration proceedings (other than any of a kind mentioned in this paragraph) have been paid in full with interest under Rule 58—

(a) any claim arising by virtue of section 382(1)(a) of the Financial Services and Markets Act 2000, not being a claim also arising by virtue of section 382(1)(b) of that Act;

(b) any claim which by virtue of the 1986 Act or any other enactment is a claim the payment of which is to be postponed.

(4) Nothing in this Rule prejudices any enactment or rule of law under which a particular kind of debt is not provable, whether on grounds of public policy or otherwise.

NOTES

Commencement: 31 January 2014.

[7.2238]

153 False claim of status as creditor, etc

(1) Where the Rules provide for creditors or members of a company a right to inspect any documents, whether on the court's file or in the hands of a postal administrator or other person, it is an offence for a person, with the intention of obtaining a sight of documents which the person has not under the Rules any right to inspect, falsely to claim a status which would entitle the person to inspect them.

(2) A person guilty of an offence under this Rule is liable to imprisonment, or a fine, or both.

NOTES

Commencement: 31 January 2014.

[7.2239]

154 Punishment of offences

(1) Schedule 2 to the Rules has effect with respect to the way in which contraventions of the Rules are punishable on conviction.

(2) In relation to an offence under a provision of the Rules specified in the first column of the Schedule (the general nature of the offence being described in the second column), the third column shows whether the offence is punishable on conviction on indictment, or on summary conviction, or either in the one way or the other.

(3) The fourth column shows, in relation to an offence, the maximum punishment by way of fine or imprisonment which may be imposed on a person convicted of the offence in the way specified in relation to it in the third column (that is to say, on indictment or summarily), a reference to a period of years or months being to a term of imprisonment of that duration.

(4) The fifth column shows (in relation to an offence for which there is an entry in that column) that a person convicted of the offence after continued contravention is liable to a daily default fine; that is to say, the person is liable on a second or subsequent conviction of the offence to the fine specified in that column for each day on which the contravention is continued (instead of the penalty specified for the offence in the fourth column of the Schedule).

(5) Section 431 of the 1986 Act (summary proceedings), as it applies to England and Wales, has effect in relation to offences under the Rules as to offences under the 1986 Act.

NOTES

Commencement: 31 January 2014.

PART 15
PROVISIONS OF GENERAL EFFECT

CHAPTER 1 THE GIVING OF NOTICE AND THE SUPPLY OF DOCUMENTS—GENERAL

[7.2240]
155 Application

(1) Subject to paragraphs (2) and (3) of this Rule, this Chapter applies where a notice or other document is required to be given, delivered or sent under the 1986 Act or the Rules by any person, including a postal administrator.

(2) This Chapter does not apply to the service of—
- (a) any application to the court;
- (b) any evidence in support of that application; or
- (c) any order of the court.

(3) This Chapter does not apply to the delivery of documents to the registrar of companies.

NOTES

Commencement: 31 January 2014.

[7.2241]
156 Personal delivery of documents

Personal delivery of a notice or other document is permissible in any case.

NOTES

Commencement: 31 January 2014.

[7.2242]
157 Postal delivery of documents

Unless in any particular case some other form of delivery is required by the 1986 Act, the Rules or an order of the court, a notice or other document may be sent by post in accordance with the rules for postal service in CPR Part 6 and sending by such means has effect as specified in those rules.

NOTES

Commencement: 31 January 2014.

[7.2243]
158 Non-receipt of notice of meeting

Where in accordance with the 1986 Act or the Rules, a meeting of creditors or other persons is summoned by notice, the meeting is presumed to have been duly summoned and held, notwithstanding that not all those to whom the notice is to be given have received it.

NOTES

Commencement: 31 January 2014.

[7.2244]
159 Notice etc to solicitors

Where under the 1986 Act or the Rules a notice or other document is required or authorised to be given, delivered or sent to a person, it may be given, delivered or sent instead to a solicitor authorised to accept delivery on that person's behalf.

NOTES

Commencement: 31 January 2014.

CHAPTER 2 THE GIVING OF NOTICE AND THE SUPPLY OF DOCUMENTS BY OR TO A POSTAL ADMINISTRATOR ETC

[7.2245]
160 Application

(1) Subject to paragraphs (2) to (3) of this Rule, this Chapter applies where a notice or other document is required to be given, delivered or sent under the 1986 Act or the Rules.

(2) This Chapter does not apply to the submission of documents to the registrar of companies.

(3) Rules 164 to 167 do not apply to the filing of any notice or other document with the court.

NOTES

Commencement: 31 January 2014.

[7.2246]
161 The form of notices and other documents

Subject to any order of the court, any notice or other document required to be given, delivered or sent must be in writing and where electronic delivery is permitted a notice or other document in electronic form is treated as being in writing if a copy of it is capable of being produced in a legible form.

NOTES

Commencement: 31 January 2014.

[7.2247]

162 Proof of sending etc

(1) Where in any postal administration proceedings a notice or other document is required to be given, delivered or sent by the postal administrator, the giving, delivering or sending of it may be proved by means of a certificate by them, or their solicitor, or a partner or employee of either of them, that the notice or other document was duly given, delivered or sent.

(2) A certificate under this Rule may be endorsed on a copy or specimen of the notice or document to which it relates.

NOTES

Commencement: 31 January 2014.

[7.2248]

163 Authentication

(1) A document or information given, delivered or sent in hard copy form is sufficiently authenticated if it is signed by the person sending or supplying it.

(2) A document or information given, delivered or sent in electronic form is sufficiently authenticated—

(a) if the identity of the sender is confirmed in a manner specified by the recipient, or

(b) where no such manner has been specified by the recipient, if the communication contains or is accompanied by a statement of the identity of the sender and the recipient has no reason to doubt the truth of that statement.

NOTES

Commencement: 31 January 2014.

[7.2249]

164 Electronic delivery in postal administration proceedings—general

(1) Unless in any particular case some other form of delivery is required by the 1986 Act or the Rules or an order of the court and subject to paragraph (3) of this Rule, a notice or other document may be given, delivered or sent by electronic means provided that the intended recipient of the notice or other document has—

(a) consented (whether in the specific case or generally) to electronic delivery (and has not revoked that consent); and

(b) provided an electronic address for delivery.

(2) In the absence of evidence to the contrary, a notice or other document is presumed to have been delivered where—

(a) the sender can produce a copy of the electronic message which—

(i) contained the notice or other document, or to which the notice or other document was attached, and

(ii) shows the time and date the message was sent; and

(b) that electronic message contains the address supplied under paragraph (1)(b) of this Rule.

(3) A message sent electronically is deemed to have been delivered to the recipient no later than 9.00am on the next business day after it was sent.

NOTES

Commencement: 31 January 2014.

[7.2250]

165 Electronic delivery by postal administrator

(1) Where a postal administrator gives, sends or delivers a notice or other document to any person by electronic means, the notice or document must contain or be accompanied by a statement that the recipient may request a hard copy of the notice or document and specifying a telephone number, e-mail address and postal address which may be used to request a hard copy.

(2) Where a hard copy of the notice or other document is requested, it must be sent within 5 business days of receipt of the request by the postal administrator.

(3) A postal administrator must not require a person making a request under paragraph (2) of this Rule to pay a fee for the supply of the document.

NOTES

Commencement: 31 January 2014.

[7.2251]

166 Use of websites by postal administrator

(1) This Rule applies for the purposes of sections 246B (use of websites) of the 1986 Act.

(2) A postal administrator required to give, deliver or send a document to any person may (other than in a case where personal service is required) satisfy that requirement by sending that person a notice—

(a) stating that the document is available for viewing and downloading on a website;
(b) specifying the address of that website together with any password necessary to view and download the document from that site; and
(c) containing a statement that the person to whom the notice is given, delivered or sent may request a hard copy of the document and specifying a telephone number, e-mail address and postal address which may be used to request a hard copy.

(3) Where a notice to which this Rule applies is sent, the document to which it relates must—
(a) be available on the website for a period of not less than 3 months after the date on which the notice is sent; and
(b) must be in such a format as to enable it to be downloaded from the website within a reasonable time of an electronic request bcing made for it to be downloaded.

(4) Where a hard copy of the document is requested it must be sent within 5 business days of the receipt of the request by the postal administrator.

(5) A postal administrator must not require a person making a request under paragraph (4) of this Rule to pay a fee for the supply of the document.

(6) Where a document is given, delivered or sent to a person by means of a website in accordance with this Rule, it is deemed to have been delivered—
(a) when the document was first made available on the website, or
(b) if later, when the notice under paragraph (2) of this Rule was delivered to that person.

NOTES

Commencement: 31 January 2014.

[7.2252]

167 Special provision on account of expense as to website use

(1) Where the court is satisfied that the expense of sending notices in accordance with Rule 166 would, on account of the number of persons entitled to receive them, be disproportionate to the benefit of sending notices in accordance with that Rule, it may order that the requirement to give, deliver or send a relevant document to any person may (other than in a case where personal service is required) be satisfied by the postal administrator sending each of those persons a notice—
(a) stating that all relevant documents will be made available for viewing and downloading on a website;
(b) specifying the address of that website together with any password necessary to view and download a relevant document from that site; and
(c) containing a statement that the person to whom the notice is given, delivered or sent may at any time request that hard copies of all, or specific, relevant documents are sent to that person, and specifying a telephone number, e-mail address and postal address which may be used to make that request.

(2) A document to which this Rule relates must—
(a) be available on the website for a period of not less than 12 months from the date when it was first made available on the website or, if later, from the date upon which the notice was sent, and
(b) must be in such a format as to enable it to be downloaded from the website within a reasonable time of an electronic request being made for it to be downloaded.

(3) Where hard copies of relevant documents have been requested, they must be sent by the postal administrator—
(a) within 5 business days of the receipt by the postal administrator of the request to be sent hard copies, in the case of relevant documents first appearing on the website before the request was received, or
(b) within 5 business days from the date a relevant document first appears on the website, in all other cases.

(4) A postal administrator must not require a person making a request under paragraph (3) of this Rule to pay a fee for the supply of the document.

(5) Where a relevant document is given, delivered or sent to a person by means of a website in accordance with this Rule, it is deemed to have been delivered—
(a) when the relevant document was first made available on the website, or
(b) if later, when the notice under paragraph (1) of this Rule was delivered to that person.

(6) In this Rule a relevant document means any document which the postal administrator is first required to give, deliver or send to any person after the court has made an order under paragraph (1) of this Rule.

NOTES

Commencement: 31 January 2014.

[7.2253]

168 Electronic delivery of postal administration proceedings to courts

(1) Except where paragraph (2) of this Rule applies or the requirements of paragraph (3) of this Rule are met, no application, notice or other document may be delivered or made to a court by electronic means.

(2) This paragraph applies where electronic delivery of documents to a court is permitted by another Rule.

(3) The requirements of this paragraph are—
  (a) the court provides an electronic working scheme for the proceedings to which the document relates; and
  (b) the electronic communication is—
    (i) delivered and authenticated in a form which complies with the requirements of the scheme;
    (ii) sent to the electronic address provided by the court for electronic delivery of those proceedings; and
    (iii) accompanied by any payment due to the court in respect of those proceedings made in a manner which complies with the requirements of the scheme.

(4) In this Rule "an electronic working scheme" means a scheme permitting insolvency proceedings to be delivered electronically to the court set out in a practice direction.

(5) Under paragraph (3) of this Rule an electronic communication is to be treated as delivered to the court at the time it is recorded by the court as having been received.

NOTES

Commencement: 31 January 2014.

[7.2254]
169 Notice etc to joint postal administrators

Where there are joint postal administrators, delivery of a document to one of them is to be treated as delivery to all of them.

NOTES

Commencement: 31 January 2014.

CHAPTER 3 SERVICE OF COURT DOCUMENTS

[7.2255]
170 Application of CPR Part 6 to service of court documents within the jurisdiction

(1) Except where different provision is made in the Rules, CPR Part 6 applies in relation to the service of court documents within the jurisdiction with such modifications as the court may direct.

(2) For the purpose of the application by this Chapter of CPR Part 6 to the service of documents in postal administration proceedings, an application commencing those proceedings is to be treated as a claim form.

NOTES

Commencement: 31 January 2014.

[7.2256]
171 Service on joint postal administrators

Where there are joint postal administrators, service on one of them is to be treated as service on all of them.

NOTES

Commencement: 31 January 2014.

[7.2257]
172 Application of CPR Part 6 to service of court documents outside the jurisdiction

CPR Part 6 applies to the service of court documents outside the jurisdiction with such modifications as the court may direct.

NOTES

Commencement: 31 January 2014.

CHAPTER 4 MEETINGS

[7.2258]
173 Quorum at meeting of creditors

(1) Any meeting of creditors in postal administration proceedings is competent to act if a quorum is present.

(2) Subject to the next paragraph, a quorum is at least one creditor entitled to vote.

(3) For the purposes of this Rule, the reference to the creditor necessary to constitute a quorum is to those persons present or represented by proxy by any person (including the chair) and includes corporations duly represented.

(4) Where at any meeting of creditors—
  (a) the provisions of this Rule as to a quorum being present are satisfied by the attendance of—
    (i) the chair alone, or
    (ii) one other person in addition to the chair, and

(b) the chair is aware, by virtue of proofs and proxies received or otherwise, that one or more additional persons would, if attending, be entitled to vote,

the meeting must not commence until at least the expiry of 15 minutes after the time appointed for its commencement.

NOTES

Commencement: 31 January 2014.

[7.2259]

174 Remote attendance at meetings of creditors

(1) This Rule applies to a request to the convener of a meeting under section 2469) of the 1986 Act to specify a place for the meeting.

(2) The request must be accompanied by—

- (a) in the case of a request by creditors, a list of the creditors making or concurring with the request and the amounts of their respective debts in the postal administration proceedings in question,
- (b) in the case of a request by members, a list of the members making or concurring with the request and their voting rights, and
- (c) from each person concurring, written confirmation of that person's concurrence.

(3) The request must be made within 7 business days of the date on which the convener sent the notice of the meeting in question.

(4) Where the convener considers that the request has been properly made in accordance with the 1986 Act and this Rule, the convener must—

- (a) give notice to all those previously given notice of the meeting—
  - (i) that it is to be held at a specified place, and
  - (ii) as to whether the date and time are to remain the same or not;
- (b) set a venue (including specification of a place) for the meeting, the date of which must be not later than 28 days after the original date for the meeting; and
- (c) give at least 14 days' notice of that venue to all those previously given notice of the meeting;

and the notices required by sub-paragraphs (a) and (c) may be given at the same or different times.

(5) Where the convener has specified a place for the meeting in response to a request to which this Rule applies, the chair of the meeting must attend the meeting by being present in person at that place.

NOTES

Commencement: 31 January 2014.

[7.2260]

175 Action where person excluded

(1) In this Rule and Rules 176 and 177 an "excluded person" means a person who—

- (a) has taken all steps necessary to attend a meeting under the arrangements put in place to do so by the convener of the meeting under section 2466) of the 1986 Act; and
- (b) those arrangements do not permit that person to attend the whole or part of that meeting.

(2) Where the chair becomes aware during the course of the meeting that there is an excluded person, the chair may—

- (a) continue the meeting;
- (b) declare the meeting void and convene the meeting again;
- (c) declare the meeting valid up to the point where the person was excluded and adjourn the meeting.

(3) Where the chair continues the meeting, the meeting is valid unless—

- (a) the chair decides in consequence of a complaint under Rule 177 to declare the meeting void and hold the meeting again; or
- (b) the court directs otherwise.

(4) Without prejudice to paragraph (2) of this Rule, where the chair becomes aware during the course of the meeting that there is an excluded person, the chair may, in the chair's discretion and without an adjournment, declare the meeting suspended for any period up to 1 hour.

NOTES

Commencement: 31 January 2014.

[7.2261]

176 Indication to excluded person

(1) A person who claims to be an excluded person may request an indication of what occurred during the period of that person's claimed exclusion (an "indication").

(2) A request under paragraph (1) of this Rule must be made as soon as reasonably practicable and, in any event, no later than 4.00 pm on the business day following the day on which the exclusion is claimed to have occurred.

(3) A request under paragraph (1) of this Rule must be made to—

- (a) the chair, where it is made during the course of the business of the meeting; or
- (b) the postal administrator where it is made after the conclusion of the business of the meeting.

Part 7O Special Insolvency Regimes

(4) Where satisfied that the person making the request is an excluded person, the person to whom the request is made under paragraph (3) of this Rule must give the indication as soon as reasonably practicable and, in any event, no later than 4.00 pm on the business day following the day on which the request was made under paragraph (1) of this Rule.

NOTES

Commencement: 31 January 2014.

[7.2262]
177 Complaint

(1) Any person who—
 (a) is, or claims to be, an excluded person; or
 (b) attends the meeting (in person or by proxy) and considers that they have been adversely affected by a person's actual, apparent or claimed exclusion,

("the complainant") may make a complaint.

(2) The person to whom the complaint must be made ("the relevant person") is—
 (a) the chair, where it is made during the course of the meeting; or
 (b) the postal administrator, where it is made after the meeting.

(3) The relevant person must—
 (a) consider whether there is an excluded person; and
 (b) where satisfied that there is an excluded person, consider the complaint; and
 (c) where satisfied that there has been prejudice, take such action as the relevant person considers fit to remedy the prejudice.

(4) Paragraph (5) of this Rule applies where—
 (a) the relevant person is satisfied that the complainant is an excluded person;
 (b) during the period of the person's exclusion—
  (i) a resolution was put to the meeting; and
  (ii) voted on; and
 (c) the excluded person asserts how the excluded person intended to vote on the resolution.

(5) Subject to paragraph (6) of this Rule, where satisfied that the effect of the intended vote in paragraph (4) of this Rule, if cast, would have changed the result of the resolution, the relevant person must—
 (a) count the intended vote as being cast in accordance with the complainant's stated intention;
 (b) amend the record of the result of the resolution; and
 (c) where those entitled to attend the meeting have been notified of the result of the resolution, notify them of the change.

(6) Where satisfied that more than one complainant in paragraph (4) of this Rule is an excluded person, the relevant person must have regard to the combined effect of the intended votes.

(7) The relevant person must notify the complainant in writing of any decision.

(8) A complaint must be made as soon as reasonably practicable and, in any event, no later than 4 pm on the business day following—
 (a) the day on which the person was, appeared or claimed to be excluded; or
 (b) where an indication is sought under Rule 176, the day on which the complainant received the indication.

(9) A complainant who is not satisfied by the action of the relevant person may apply to the court for directions and any application must be made no more than 2 business days from the date of receiving the decision of the relevant person.

NOTES

Commencement: 31 January 2014.

CHAPTER 5 FORMS

[7.2263]
178 Forms for use in postal administration proceedings

(1) Subject to the next Rule, the forms contained in Schedule 1 to the Rules must be used in postal administration proceedings as provided for in specific Rules.

(2) The forms must be used with such variations, if any, as the circumstances may require.

(3) The Secretary of State or a postal administrator may incorporate a barcode or other reference or recognition mark into any form in Schedule 1 to the Rules a copy of which is received by any of them or is sent to any person by any of them.

NOTES

Commencement: 31 January 2014.

[7.2264]
179 Electronic submission of information instead of submission of forms to the Secretary of State, postal administrators, and of copies to the registrar of companies

(1) This Rule applies in any case where information in a prescribed form is required by the Rules to be sent by any person to the Secretary of State or a postal administrator, or a copy of a prescribed form is to be sent to the registrar of companies.

(2) A requirement of the kind mentioned in paragraph (1) of this Rule is treated as having been satisfied where—

(a) the information is submitted electronically with the agreement of the person to whom the information is sent;

(b) the form in which the electronic submission is made satisfies thc requirements of the person to whom the information is sent (which may include a requirement that the information supplied can be reproduced in the format of the prescribed form);

(c) that all the information required to be given in the prescribed form is provided in the electronic submission; and

(d) the person to whom the information is sent can provide in legible form the information so submitted.

(3) Where information in a prescribed form is permitted to be sent electronically under paragraph (2) of this Rule, any requirement in the prescribed form that the prescribed form be accompanied by a signature is taken to be satisfied—

(a) if the identity of the person who is supplying the information in the prescribed form and whose signature is required is confirmed in a manner specified by the recipient, or

(b) where no such manner has been specified by the recipient, if the communication contains or is accompanied by a statement of the identity of the person who is providing the information in the prescribed form, and the recipient has no reason to doubt the truth of that statement.

(4) Where information required in prescribed form has been supplied to a person, whether or not it has been supplied electronically in accordance with paragraph (2) of this Rule, and a copy of that information is required to be supplied to another person falling within paragraph (1) of this Rule, the requirements contained in paragraph (2) of this Rule apply in respect of the supply of the copy to that other person, as they apply in respect of the original.

NOTES

Commencement: 31 January 2014.

[7.2265]
180 Electronic submission of information instead of submission of forms in all other cases

(1) This Rule applies in any case where Rule 179 does not apply, where information in a prescribed form is required by the Rules to be sent by any person.

(2) A requirement of the kind mentioned in paragraph (1) of this Rule is treated as having been satisfied where—

(a) the person to whom the information is sent has agreed—

(i) to receiving the information electronically and to the form in which it is to be sent; and

(ii) to the specified manner in which paragraph (3) of this Rule is to be satisfied.

(b) all the information required to be given in the prescribed form is provided in the electronic submission; and

(c) the person to whom the information is sent can provide in legible form the information so submitted.

(3) Any requirement in a prescribed form that it be accompanied by a signature is taken to be satisfied if the identity of the person who is supplying the information and whose signature is required, is confirmed in the specified manner.

(4) Where information required in a prescribed form has been supplied to a person, whether or not it has been supplied electronically in accordance with paragraph (2) of this Rule, and a copy of that information is required to be supplied to another person falling within paragraph (1) of this Rule, the requirements contained in paragraph (2) of this Rule apply in respect of the supply of the copy to that other person, as they apply in respect of the original.

NOTES

Commencement: 31 January 2014.

CHAPTER 6 GAZETTE NOTICES

[7.2266]
181 Contents of notices to be gazetted under the 1986 Act or the Rules

(1) Where under the 1986 Act or the Rules a notice is gazetted, in addition to any content specifically required by the 1986 Act or any other provision of the Rules, the content of such a notice must be as set out in this Chapter.

(2) All notices published must specify insofar as it is applicable in relation to the particular notice—

(a) the name and postal address of the postal administrator acting in the proceedings;

(b) the date of the postal administrator's appointment;

(c) either an e-mail address, or a telephone number, through which the postal administrator may be contacted;
(d) the name of any person other than the postal administrator (if any) who may be contacted regarding the proceedings;
(e) the number assigned to the postal administrator by the Secretary of State;
(f) the court name and any number assigned to the proceedings by the court;
(g) the registered name of the company;
(h) its registered number;
(i) its registered office, or if an unregistered company, the postal address of its principal place of business;
(j) any principal trading address if this is different from its registered office;
(k) any name under which it was registered in the 12 months prior to the date of the commencement of the proceedings which are the subject of the Gazette notice; and
(l) any name or style (other than its registered name) under which—
  (i) the company carried on business; and
  (ii) any debt owed to a creditor was incurred.

NOTES

Commencement: 31 January 2014.

[7.2267]
182 Omission of unobtainable information

Information required under this Chapter to be included in a notice to be gazetted may be omitted if it is not reasonably practicable to obtain it.

NOTES

Commencement: 31 January 2014.

[7.2268]
183 The Gazette—general

(1) A copy of the Gazette containing any notice required by the 1986 Act or the Rules to be gazetted is evidence of any facts stated in the notice.

(2) In the case of an order of the court notice of which is required by the 1986 Act or the Rules to be gazetted, a copy of the Gazette containing the notice may in any proceedings be produced as conclusive evidence that the order was made on the date specified in the notice.

(3) Where an order of the court which is gazetted has been varied, and where any matter has been erroneously or inaccurately gazetted, the person whose responsibility it was to procure the requisite entry in the Gazette must as soon as is reasonably practicable cause the variation of the order to be gazetted or a further entry to be made in the Gazette for the purpose of correcting the error or inaccuracy.

NOTES

Commencement: 31 January 2014.

CHAPTER 7 NOTICES ADVERTISED OTHERWISE THAN IN THE GAZETTE

[7.2269]
184 Notices otherwise advertised under the 1986 Act or the Rules

(1) Where under the 1986 Act or the Rules a notice may be advertised otherwise than in the Gazette, in addition to any content specifically required by the 1986 Act or any other provision of the Rules, the content of such a notice must be as set out in this Chapter.

(2) All notices published must specify insofar as it is applicable in relation to the particular notice—
(a) the name and postal address of the postal administrator acting in the proceedings to which the notice relates;
(b) either an e-mail address, or a telephone number, through which the postal administrator may be contacted;
(c) the registered name of the company;
(d) its registered number;
(e) any name under which it was registered in the 12 months prior to the date of the commencement of the proceedings which are the subject of the notice; and
(f) any name or style (other than its registered name) under which—
  (i) the company carried on business; and
  (ii) any debt owed to a creditor was incurred.

NOTES

Commencement: 31 January 2014.

[7.2270]
185 Non-Gazette notices—other provisions

(1) The information required to be contained in a notice to which this Chapter applies must be included in the advertisement of that notice in a manner that is reasonably likely to ensure, in relation to the form of the advertising used, that a person reading, hearing or seeing the advertisement, will be able to read, hear or see that information.

(2) Information required under this Chapter to be included in a notice may be omitted if it is not reasonably practicable to obtain it.

NOTES

Commencement: 31 January 2014.

CHAPTER 8 NOTIFICATIONS TO THE REGISTRAR OF COMPANIES

[7.2271]
186 Application of this Chapter

This Chapter applies where under the 1986 Act or the Rules information is to be sent or delivered to the registrar of companies.

NOTES

Commencement: 31 January 2014.

[7.2272]
187 Information to be contained in all notifications to the registrar

Where under the 1986 Act or the Rules a return, notice, or any other document or information is to be sent to the registrar of companies, that notification must specify—

(a) the registered name of the company;
(b) its registered number;
(c) the nature of the notification;
(d) the section of the 1986 Act or the Rule under which the notification is made;
(e) the date of the notification;
(f) the name and postal address of person making the notification;
(g) the capacity in which that person is acting in respect of the company; and

the notification must be authenticated by the person making the notification.

NOTES

Commencement: 31 January 2014.

[7.2273]
188 Notifications relating to the office of postal administrator

In addition to the information required by Rule 187, a notification relating to the office of the postal administrator must also specify—

(a) the name of the postal administrator;
(b) the date of the event notified;
(c) where the notification relates to an appointment, the person, body or court making the appointment;
(d) where the notification relates to the termination of an appointment, the reason for that termination (for example, resignation); and
(e) the postal address of the postal administrator.

NOTES

Commencement: 31 January 2014.

[7.2274]
189 Notifications relating to documents

In addition to the information required by Rule 187 notification relating to a document (for example, a statement of affairs) must also specify—

(a) the nature of the document; and
(b) the date of the document; or
(c) where the document relates to a period of time (for example a report) the period of time to which the document relates.

NOTES

Commencement: 31 January 2014.

[7.2275]
190 Notifications relating to court orders

In addition to the information required by Rule 187, a notification relating to a court order must also specify—

(a) the nature of the court order; and
(b) the date of the order.

NOTES

Commencement: 31 January 2014.

[7.2276]

191 Returns or reports of meetings

In addition to the information required by Rule 187, the notification of a return or a report of a meeting must specify—

(a) the purpose of the meeting including the section of the 1986 Act or Rule under which it was convened;

(b) the venue fixed for the meeting;

(c) whether a required quorum was present for the meeting to take place; and

(d) if the meeting took place, the outcome of the meeting (including any resolutions passed at the meeting).

NOTES

Commencement: 31 January 2014.

[7.2277]

192 Notifications relating to other events

In addition to the information required by Rule 187, a notification relating to any other event (for example the coming in to force of a moratorium) must specify—

(a) the nature of the event including the section of the 1986 Act or Rule under which it took place; and

(b) the date the event occurred.

NOTES

Commencement: 31 January 2014.

[7.2278]

193 Notifications of more than one nature

A notification which includes a notification of more than one nature must satisfy the requirements applying in respect of each of those notifications.

NOTES

Commencement: 31 January 2014.

[7.2279]

194 Notifications made to other persons at the same time

(1) Where under the 1986 Act or the Rules a notice or other document is to be sent to another person at the same time that it is to be sent to the registrar of companies, that requirement may be satisfied by sending to that other person a copy of the notification sent to the registrar of companies.

(2) Paragraph (1) of this Rule does not apply—

(a) where a form is prescribed for the notification to the other person; or

(b) where the notification to the registrar of companies is incomplete.

NOTES

Commencement: 31 January 2014.

CHAPTER 9 INSPECTION OF DOCUMENTS AND THE PROVISION OF INFORMATION

[7.2280]

195 Confidentiality of documents—grounds for refusing inspection

(1) Where in postal administration proceedings the postal administrator considers that a document forming part of the records of those proceedings—

(a) should be treated as confidential, or

(b) is of such a nature that its disclosure would be prejudicial to the conduct of the proceedings or might reasonably be expected to lead to violence against any person,

the postal administrator may decline to allow it to be inspected by a person who would otherwise be entitled to inspect it.

(2) Where under this rule the postal administrator determines to refuse inspection of a document, the person wishing to inspect it may apply to the court for that determination to be overruled and the court may either overrule it altogether or sustain it subject to such conditions (if any) as it thinks just.

NOTES

Commencement: 31 January 2014.

[7.2281]

196 Right to copy documents

Where the 1986 Act or the Rules confer a right for any person to inspect documents, the right includes that of taking copies of those documents, on payment—

(a) in the case of documents on the court's file of proceedings, of the fee chargeable under any order made under section 92 of the Courts Act 2003, and
(b) in any other case, of the appropriate fee.

NOTES

Commencement: 31 January 2014.

[7.2282]
197 Charges for copy documents

Except where prohibited by the Rules, a postal administrator is entitled to require the payment of the appropriate fee for the supply of documents requested by a creditor or member.

NOTES

Commencement: 31 January 2014.

[7.2283]
198 Right to have list of creditors

(1) In postal administration proceedings a creditor has the right to require the postal administrator to provide a list of the creditors and the amounts of their respective debts unless paragraph (4) of this Rule applies.

(2) The postal administrator on being required to furnish the list under paragraph (1) of this Rule—
(a) as soon as reasonably practicable must send it to the person requiring the list to be furnished; and
(b) may charge the appropriate fee for doing so.

(3) The name and address of any creditor may be omitted from the list furnished under paragraph (2) of this Rule where the postal administrator is of the view that its disclosure would be prejudicial to the conduct of the proceedings or might reasonably be expected to lead to violence against any person provided that—
(a) the amount of the debt in question is shown in the list; and
(b) a statement is included in the list that the name and address of the creditor has been omitted in respect of that debt.

(4) Paragraph (1) of this Rule does not apply where a statement of affairs has been delivered to the registrar of companies.

NOTES

Commencement: 31 January 2014.

CHAPTER 10 COMPUTATION OF TIME AND TIME LIMITS

[7.2284]
199 Time limits

(1) The provisions of CPR rule 2.8 (time) apply, as regards computation of time, to anything required or authorised to be done by the Rules.

(2) The provisions of CPR rule 3.1(2)(a) (the court's general powers of management) apply so as to enable the court to extend or shorten the time for compliance with anything required or authorised to be done by the Rules.

NOTES

Commencement: 31 January 2014.

CHAPTER 11 SECURITY

[7.2285]
200 Postal administrator's security

(1) Wherever under the Rules any person has to appoint a person to the office of postal administrator that person must, before making the appointment, be satisfied that the person appointed or to be appointed has security for the proper performance of the office of postal administrator.

(2) In any postal administration proceedings the cost of the postal administrator's security shall be defrayed as an expense of the postal administration.

NOTES

Commencement: 31 January 2014.

CHAPTER 12 NOTICE OF ORDER UNDER SECTION 1765) OF THE 1986 ACT

[7.2286]
201 Notice of order under section 1765) of the 1986 Act

(1) Where the court makes an order under section 1765) of the 1986 Act, it must as soon as reasonably practicable send two sealed copies of the order to the applicant and a sealed copy to the postal administrator.

(2) Where the court has made an order under section 1765) of the 1986 Act, the postal administrator must as soon as reasonably practicable, give notice to each creditor of whose address and claim they are aware.

(3) Paragraph (2) of this Rule does not apply where the court directs otherwise.

(4) The court may direct that the requirement in paragraph (2) of this Rule is complied with if a notice has been published by the postal administrator which, in addition to containing the standard contents, states that the court has made an order disapplying the requirement to set aside the prescribed part.

(5) As soon as reasonably practicable the notice—
 (a) must be gazetted; and
 (b) may be advertised in such other manner as the postal administrator thinks fit.

(6) The postal administrator must send a copy of the order to the registrar of companies as soon as reasonably practicable after the making of the order.

NOTES

Commencement: 31 January 2014.

PART 16
INTERPRETATION AND APPLICATION

[7.2287]
202 Introductory

This Part of the Rules has effect for their interpretation and application; and any definition given in this Part applies except, and in so far as, the context otherwise requires.

NOTES

Commencement: 31 January 2014.

[7.2288]
203 "The appropriate fee"

"The appropriate fee" means 15 pence per A4 or A5 page, and 30 pence per A3 page.

NOTES

Commencement: 31 January 2014.

[7.2289]
204 "Authorised deposit-taker and former authorised deposit-taker"

(1) "Authorised deposit-taker" means a person with permission under Part 4A of the Financial Services and Markets Act 2000 to accept deposits.

(2) "Former authorised deposit-taker" means a person who—
 (a) is not an authorised deposit-taker,
 (b) was formerly an authorised institution under the Banking Act 1987, or a recognised bank or a licensed institution under the Banking Act 1979, and
 (c) continues to have liability in respect of any deposit for which it had a liability at a time when it was an authorised institution, recognised bank or licensed institution.

(3) Paragraphs (1) and (2) of this Rule must be read with—
 (a) section 22 of the Financial Services and Markets Act 2000;
 (b) any relevant order under that section; and
 (c) Schedule 2 to that Act.

NOTES

Commencement: 31 January 2014.

[7.2290]
205 "The court"; "the registrar"

(1) Anything to be done under or by virtue of the 1986 Act or the Rules by, to or before the court may be done by, to or before a judge, district judge or the registrar.

(2) The registrar or district judge may authorise any act of a formal or administrative character which is not by statute the registrar's or district judge's responsibility to be carried out by the chief clerk or any other officer of the court acting on the registrar's behalf, in accordance with directions given by the Lord Chancellor.

(3) "the registrar" means—
 (a) [an Insolvency and Companies Court Judge];
 (b) where the proceedings are in the District Registry of Birmingham, Bristol, Caernarfon, Cardiff, Leeds, Liverpool, Manchester, Mold, Newcastle-upon-Tyne or Preston, a district judge attached to the District Registry in question.

NOTES

Commencement: 31 January 2014.

Para (3): words in square brackets substituted by the Alteration of Judicial Titles (Registrar in Bankruptcy of the High Court) Order 2018, SI 2018/130, art 3, Schedule, para 12(1)(h).

[7.2291]
206 "Debt", "liability"

(1) "Debt", in relation to the postal administration of a company, means (subject to the next paragraph) any of the following—

(a) any debt or liability to which the company is subject at the date on which the company entered postal administration;

(b) any debt or liability to which the company may become subject after that date by reason of any obligation incurred before that date; and

(c) any interest provable as mentioned in Rule 58.

(2) For the purposes of any provision of the 1986 Act or the Rules about postal administration, any liability in tort is a debt provable in the postal administration, if either—

(a) the cause of action has accrued at the date on which the company entered postal administration; or

(b) all the elements necessary to establish the cause of action exist at that date except for actionable damage.

(3) For the purposes of references in any provision of the 1986 Act or the Rules about postal administration to a debt or liability, it is immaterial whether the debt or liability is present or future, whether it is certain or contingent, or whether its amount is fixed or liquidated, or is capable of being ascertained by fixed rules or as a matter of opinion; and references in any such provision to owing a debt are to be read accordingly.

(4) In any provision of the 1986 Act or the Rules about postal administration, except in so far as the context otherwise requires, "liability" means (subject to paragraph (3) of this Rule) a liability to pay money or money's worth, including any liability under an enactment, any liability for breach of trust, any liability in contract, tort or bailment, and any liability arising out of an obligation to make restitution.

NOTES
Commencement: 31 January 2014.

[7.2292]
207 "Petitioner"

In winding-up, references to "the petitioner" include any person who has been substituted as such.

NOTES
Commencement: 31 January 2014.

[7.2293]
208 "Venue"

References to the "venue" for any proceeding or attendance before the court, or for a meeting, are to the time, date and place for the proceeding, attendance or meeting.

NOTES
Commencement: 31 January 2014.

[7.2294]
209 Expressions used generally

(1) "Business day" means any day other than a Saturday, a Sunday, Christmas Day, Good Friday or a day which is a bank holiday in any part of England and Wales under or by virtue of the Banking and Financial Dealings Act 1971.

(2) "File in court" and "file with the court" means deliver to the court for filing.

(3) "The Gazette" means the London Gazette.

(4) "Gazetted" means advertised once in the Gazette.

(5) "Practice direction" means a direction as to the practice and procedure of any court within the scope of the CPR.

(6) "Prescribed part" has the same meaning as it does in section 1762)(a) of the 1986 Act and the Insolvency Act 1986 (Prescribed Part) Order 2003.

(7) "Standard contents" means—

(a) in relation to a notice to be gazetted, the contents specified in Rule 181; and

(b) in relation to a notice to be advertised in any other way, the contents specified in Rule 184.

(8) A "certificate of service" means a certificate of service verified by a statement of truth.

(9) A "statement of truth" means a statement of truth in accordance with CPR Part 22.

(10) A "witness statement" means a witness statement verified by a statement of truth in accordance with CPR Part 22.

NOTES
Commencement: 31 January 2014.

[7.2295]

210 Application

The Rules apply to postal administration proceedings commenced on or after the date on which the Rules come into force. Nothing in the Insolvency Rules shall apply to such proceedings commenced on or after that date.

NOTES

Commencement: 31 January 2014.

[7.2296]

211 Application of the 1986 Act

For the purposes of the Rules, any reference in the 1986 Act to "leave" of the court is to be construed as meaning "permission" of the court.

NOTES

Commencement: 31 January 2014.

SCHEDULE 1
FORMS

Rule 178

NOTES

The forms themselves are not reproduced in this work, but their numbers and descriptions are listed below.

[7.2297]

Index

Form number	Title
PA1	Company administration application
PA2	Statement of proposed postal administrator
PA3	Postal administration order
PA4	Notice of postal administrator's appointment
PA5	Notice requiring submission of a statement of affairs
PA6	Statement of affairs
PA7	Statement of concurrence
PA8	Notice of extension of time period
PA9	Notice of a meeting of creditors
PA10	Creditor's request for a meeting
PA11	Notice of intention to resign as postal administrator

NOTES

Commencement: 31 January 2014.

SCHEDULE 2
PUNISHMENT OF OFFENCES UNDER THESE RULES

Rule 154

[7.2298]

Rule creating offence	General nature of offence	Mode of prosecution	Punishment	Daily default fine (where applicable)
Rule 34(7)	Postal administrator failing to send notification as to progress of energy administration	Summary	One-fifth of the statutory maximum	One-fiftieth of the statutory maximum
Rule 94(2)	Postal administrator's duties on vacating office	Summary	One-fifth of the statutory maximum	One-fiftieth of the statutory maximum

Rule creating offence	General nature of offence	Mode of prosecution	Punishment	Daily default fine (where applicable)
Rule 153(1)	False representation of status for purpose of inspecting documents	1 On indictment 2 Summary	Two years or a fine or both Six months or the statutory maximum, or both	

NOTES

Commencement: 31 January 2014.

P
PUBLIC PRIVATE PARTNERSHIP

GREATER LONDON AUTHORITY ACT 1999

(1999 c 29)

ARRANGEMENT OF SECTIONS

PART IV
TRANSPORT

CHAPTER VII
PUBLIC-PRIVATE PARTNERSHIP AGREEMENTS

Introductory

210 PPP agreements .....[7.2299]

Insolvency

220 Meaning and effect of PPP administration orders .....[7.2300]
221 PPP administration orders made on special petitions .....[7.2301]
222 Restriction on making winding-up order .....[7.2302]
223 Restrictions on voluntary winding-up etc. .....[7.2303]
224 Meaning of "company" and application of provisions to unregistered, foreign and other companies .....[7.2304]

PART XII
SUPPLEMENTARY PROVISIONS

Miscellaneous and supplemental

424 Interpretation.....[7.2305]
425 Short title, commencement and extent .....[7.2306]

SCHEDULES

Schedule 14—PPP administration orders
Part I—Modifications of the 1986 Act .....[7.2307]
Part II—Further modifications of the 1986 Act: Application in relation to foreign companies .....[7.2308]
Part III—Supplemental .....[7.2309]
Schedule 15—Transfer of relevant activities in connection with PPP administration orders .....[7.2310]

An Act to establish and make provision about the Greater London Authority, the Mayor of London and the London Assembly; to make provision in relation to London borough councils and the Common Council of the City of London with respect to matters consequential on the establishment of the Greater London Authority; to make provision with respect to the functions of other local authorities and statutory bodies exercising functions in Greater London; to make provision about transport and road traffic in and around Greater London; to make provision about policing in Greater London and to make an adjustment of the metropolitan police district; and for connected purposes

[11 November 1999]

1–140 ((*Pts I–III) outside the scope of this work.*)

PART IV
TRANSPORT

141–209 ((*Chs I–VI) outside the scope of this work.*)

CHAPTER VII PUBLIC-PRIVATE PARTNERSHIP AGREEMENTS

Introductory

[7.2299]
210 PPP agreements

(1) For the purposes of this Chapter a public-private partnership agreement (referred to as a "PPP agreement") is a contract in the case of which the conditions set out in the following provisions of this section are satisfied.

(2) At least one of the parties to the contract must be a relevant body for the purposes of this Chapter, that is to say—

(a) London Regional Transport;
(b) Transport for London; or
(c) a subsidiary of London Regional Transport or Transport for London.

(3) The contract must be one which involves—

(a) the provision, construction, renewal, or improvement, and

Part 7P Special Insolvency Regimes

(b) the maintenance,

of a railway or proposed railway and, if or to the extent that the contract so provides, of any stations, rolling stock or depots used or to be used in connection with that railway.

(4) The railway or proposed railway must be one which—

(a) belongs or will belong to, or to a subsidiary of, London Regional Transport or Transport for London, or

(b) is being provided, constructed, renewed or improved under the contract for, or for a subsidiary of, London Regional Transport or Transport for London.

(5) If a party who undertakes to carry out or secure the carrying out of any or all of the work mentioned in subsection (3) above (a "PPP company") is a public sector operator at the time when the contract is made, that party must no longer be a public sector operator on the day following the expiration of the period of six weeks beginning with the day on which the condition in subsection (6) below is satisfied.

(6) The contract must be one which is, or is of a description which is, designated as a PPP agreement.

211–219 (*Outside the scope of this work.*)

Insolvency

[7.2300]

220 Meaning and effect of PPP administration orders

(1) A "PPP administration order" is an order of the court made in accordance with section 221, 222 or 223 below in relation to a PPP company and directing that, during the period for which the order is in force, the affairs, business and property of the company shall be managed, by a person appointed by the court,—

(a) for the achievement of the purposes of such an order; and

(b) in a manner which protects the respective interests of the members and creditors of the company.

(2) The purposes of a PPP administration order made in relation to any company shall be—

(a) the transfer to another company, or (as respects different parts of its undertaking) to two or more different companies, as a going concern, of so much of the company's undertaking as it is necessary to transfer in order to ensure that the relevant activities may be properly carried on; and

(b) the carrying on of those relevant activities pending the making of the transfer.

(3) Schedule 14 to this Act shall have effect for applying provisions of the Insolvency Act 1986 where a PPP administration order is made.

(4) Schedule 15 to this Act shall have effect for enabling provision to be made with respect to cases in which, in pursuance of a PPP administration order, another company is to carry on all or any of the relevant activities of a PPP company in place of that company.

(5) Without prejudice to paragraph 20 of Schedule 14 to this Act, the power conferred by section 411 of the Insolvency Act 1986 to make rules shall apply for the purpose of giving effect to the PPP administration order provisions of this Act as it applies for the purpose of giving effect to Parts I to VII of that Act, but taking any reference in that section to those Parts as a reference to those provisions.

(6) For the purposes of this Chapter, the "relevant activities", in relation to a PPP company, are the activities carried out, or to be carried out, by that company in performing its obligations under the PPP agreement to which it is party.

(7) In this section—

"business" and "property" have the same meaning as they have in the Insolvency Act 1986;

["the court", in relation to a PPP company, means the court—

(a) having jurisdiction to wind up the company, or

(b) that would have such jurisdiction apart from section 221(2) or 441(2) of the Insolvency Act 1986 (exclusion of winding up jurisdiction in case of companies having principal place of business in, or incorporated in, Northern Ireland);]

"the PPP administration order provisions of this Act" means this section, sections 221 to 224 below and Schedules 14 and 15 to this Act.

NOTES

Sub-s (7): definition "the court" substituted by the Companies Act 2006 (Consequential Amendments, Transitional Provisions and Savings) Order 2009, SI 2009/1941, art 2(1), Sch 1, para 178(1), (4).

Rules: the PPP Administration Order Rules 2007, SI 2007/3141 at **[7.2311]**.

[7.2301]

221 PPP administration orders made on special petitions

(1) If, on an application made to the court by petition presented by the Mayor, the court is satisfied that either or both of the grounds specified in subsection (2) below is satisfied in relation to that PPP company, the court may make a PPP administration order in relation to that company.

(2) The grounds mentioned in subsection (1) above are, in relation to any company,—

(a) that the company is or is likely to be unable to pay its debts;

(b) that, in a case in which the Secretary of State has certified that it would be appropriate for him to petition for the winding up of the company under section 124A of the 1986 Act (petition by the Secretary of State following inspectors' report etc), it would be just and equitable, as mentioned in that section, for the company to be wound up.

(3) Notice of any petition under this section for a PPP administration order shall be given forthwith to such persons and in such manner as may be prescribed by rules made under section 411 of the 1986 Act; and no such petition shall be withdrawn except with the leave of the court.

(4) Subsections (4) and (5) of section 9 of the 1986 Act (powers on application for administration order) shall apply on the hearing of the petition for a PPP administration order in relation to any company as they apply on the hearing of a petition for an administration order.

(5) Subsections (1), (2), (4) and (5) of section 10 of the 1986 Act (effect of petition) shall apply in the case of a petition for a PPP administration order in relation to any company as if—

(a) the reference in subsection (1) to an administration order were a reference to a PPP administration order; and

(b) paragraph (b) of that subsection did require the leave of the court for the taking of any of the steps mentioned in paragraphs (b) and (c) of subsection (2) (appointment of, and exercise of functions by, administrative receiver).

(6) For the purposes of this section a company is unable to pay its debts if—

(a) it is a company which is deemed to be so unable under section 123 of the 1986 Act (definition of inability to pay debts); or

(b) it is an unregistered company, within the meaning of Part V of the 1986 Act, which is deemed, by virtue of any of sections 222 to 224 of that Act, to be so unable for the purposes of section 221 of that Act (winding up of unregistered companies).

(7) The functions of the Mayor under this section may be exercised by Transport for London acting as his agent, and where Transport for London so acts references to the Mayor shall be construed accordingly.

(8) In this section—

"the 1986 Act" means the Insolvency Act 1986;

"the court" has the same meaning as in section 220 above.

[7.2302]

222 Restriction on making winding-up order

(1) Where a petition for the winding up of a PPP company is presented by a person other than the Mayor, the court shall not make a winding-up order in relation to that company on that petition unless—

(a) notice of the petition has been served on the Mayor; and

(b) a period of at least fourteen days has elapsed since the service of that notice.

(2) Where a petition for the winding up of a PPP company has been presented, the Mayor may, at any time before a winding-up order is made on the petition, make an application to the court for a PPP administration order in relation to that company; and where such an application is made the court may, if it is satisfied as mentioned in section 221(1) above, make a PPP administration order instead of a winding-up order.

(3) Where, on a petition for the winding up of a PPP company, the court makes, or proposes to make, a PPP administration order by virtue of subsection (2) above, subsections (4) and (5) of section 9 of the Insolvency Act 1986 (powers on application for administration order) shall apply on the hearing of that petition as they apply on the hearing of a petition for an administration order.

(4) In this section "the court" has the same meaning as in section 220 above.

[7.2303]

223 Restrictions on voluntary winding-up etc

(1) No resolution for voluntary winding up shall be passed by a PPP company without leave of the court granted on an application made for the purpose by the company.

(2) No such leave shall be granted unless—

(a) notice of the application has been served on the Mayor; and

(b) a period of at least fourteen days has elapsed since the service of that notice.

(3) Where an application for leave under subsection (1) above has been made by a PPP company, the Mayor may, at any time before leave has been granted under subsection (1) above, make an application to the court for a PPP administration order in relation to that company; and where such an application is made the court may, if it is satisfied as mentioned in section 221(1) above, make a PPP administration order instead of granting leave under subsection (1) above.

(4) Where, on an application for leave under subsection (1) above, the court makes, or proposes to make, a PPP administration order by virtue of subsection (3) above, subsections (4) and (5) of section 9 of the Insolvency Act 1986 (powers on application for administration order) shall apply on the hearing of that application as they apply on the hearing of a petition for an administration order.

(5) No administration order under Part II of the Insolvency Act 1986 shall be made in relation to a PPP company unless—

(a) notice of the application for the order has been served on the Mayor; and

(b) a period of at least fourteen days has elapsed since the service of that notice.

(6) Where an application for an administration order under Part II of the Insolvency Act 1986 has been made in the case of a PPP company, the Mayor may, at any time before such an order has been made on that application, make an application to the court for a PPP administration order in relation to that company; and where such an application is made the court may, if it is satisfied as mentioned in section 221(1) above, make a PPP administration order instead of an administration order under Part II of the Insolvency Act 1986.

(7) No step shall be taken by any person to enforce any security over a PPP company's property, except where that person has served fourteen days' notice of his intention to take that step on the Mayor.

(8) In this section—

"the court" has the same meaning as in section 220 above;

"resolution for voluntary winding up" has the same meaning as in the Insolvency Act 1986;

"security" and "property" have the same meaning as in the Insolvency Act 1986.

[7.2304]

224 Meaning of "company" and application of provisions to unregistered, foreign and other companies

[(1) In the PPP administration order provisions of this Act—

"company" means—

(a) a company registered under the Companies Act 2006, or

(b) an unregistered company; and

"unregistered company" means a company that is not registered under that Act.]

(2) In the application of section 220(1) above in a case where the PPP company there mentioned is a foreign company, the reference to the affairs, business and property of the company shall be taken as a reference to the affairs and business of the company, so far as carried on in Great Britain, and the property of the company within Great Britain.

(3) In the application of section 9(5) of the 1986 Act by virtue of subsection (4) of section 221 above or subsection (3) of section 222 above where the petition mentioned in the subsection in question relates to a company which is a foreign company, the reference to restricting the exercise of any powers of the directors or of the company shall be taken as a reference to restricting—

(a) the exercise within Great Britain of the powers of the directors or of the company; or

(b) any exercise of those powers so far as relating to the affairs, business or property of the company in Great Britain.

(4) In the application of provisions in section 10 of the 1986 Act by virtue of subsection (5) of section 221 above where the company mentioned in that subsection is a foreign company—

(a) paragraph (a) of subsection (1) shall be omitted;

(b) any reference in paragraph (b) or (c) of that subsection to property or goods shall be taken as a reference to property or (as the case may be) goods for the time being situated within Great Britain;

(c) in paragraph (c) of that subsection—

(i) the reference to the commencement or continuation of proceedings shall be taken as a reference to the commencement or continuation of proceedings in Great Britain; and

(ii) the reference to the levying of distress against the company shall be taken as a reference to the levying of distress against the foreign company to the extent of its property in England and Wales; and

(d) any reference in subsection (2) to an administrative receiver shall be taken to include a reference to any person performing, in relation to the foreign company, functions equivalent to those of an administrative receiver, within the meaning of section 251 of the 1986 Act.

(5) Subsections (1) to (4) of section 223 above shall not have effect in relation to a PPP company which is a foreign company.

(6) In the application of subsection (7) of that section where the PPP company there mentioned is a foreign company, the reference to the company's property shall be taken as a reference to such of its property as is for the time being situated in Great Britain.

(7) In this section—

"the 1986 Act" means the Insolvency Act 1986;

"foreign company" means a company incorporated outside Great Britain;

"the PPP administration order provisions of this Act" means sections 220 to 223 above, this section and Schedules 14 and 15 to this Act.

NOTES

Sub-s (1): substituted by the Companies Act 2006 (Consequential Amendments, Transitional Provisions and Savings) Order 2009, SI 2009/1941, art 2(1), Sch 1, para 178(1), (5).

225–404 *(Ss 225–303 (Chs VIII–XVI), ss 304–404 (Pts V–XI) outside the scope of this work.)*

PART XII
SUPPLEMENTARY PROVISIONS

405–419 *(Outside the scope of this work.)*

Miscellaneous and supplemental

420–423 *(Outside the scope of this work.)*

[7.2305]

424 Interpretation

(1) In this Act, unless the context otherwise requires,—

. . .

"Mayor" means Mayor of London [(but see also section 85(3A) above)];

. . .

"Minister of the Crown" has the same meaning as in the Ministers of the Crown Act 1975;

. . .

"notice" means notice in writing;

. . .

"subsidiary" has the meaning given [by section 1159 of the Companies Act 2006];

. . .

(2)–(5) *(Outside the scope of this work.)*

NOTES

Sub-s (1): definitions omitted outside the scope of this work; words in square brackets in definition "Mayor" inserted by the Greater London Authority Act 2007, s 12(16)(b), with effect in relation to financial years beginning on or after 30 October 2007; words in square brackets in definition "subsidiary" substituted by the Companies Act 2006 (Consequential Amendments, Transitional Provisions and Savings) Order 2009, SI 2009/1941, art 2(1), Sch 1, para 178(1), (6).

[7.2306]

425 Short title, commencement and extent

(1) This Act may be cited as the Greater London Authority Act 1999.

(2) Apart from this section, section 420 above and any power of a Minister of the Crown to make regulations or an order (which accordingly come into force on the day on which this Act is passed) the provisions of this Act shall come into force on such day as the Secretary of State may by order appoint; and different days may be appointed for different purposes.

(3) . . .

(4) Any order under this section may make such transitional provision as appears to the Secretary of State to be necessary or expedient in connection with the provisions brought into force by the order.

(5) Any such order may include such adaptations of—

(a) the provisions which it brings into force, or

(b) any other provisions of this Act then in force,

as appear to the Secretary of State to be necessary or expedient for the purpose or in consequence of the operation of any provision of this Act (including, in particular, the provisions which the order brings into force) before the coming into force of any other provision.

(6)–(8) (*Outside the scope of this work.*)

NOTES

Sub-s (3): repealed by the Railways and Transport Safety Act 2003, ss 114(6), 118, Sch 8.

Orders: at present, 11 commencement orders have been made under this section. The orders relevant to the provisions of the Act reproduced here are the Greater London Authority Act 1999 (Commencement No 3 and Transitional Finance Provisions) Order 1999, SI 1999/3434; the Greater London Authority Act 1999 (Commencement No 11) Order 2003, SI 2003/1920.

SCHEDULES

SCHEDULES 1–13

(*Schs 1–13 outside the scope of this work.*)

SCHEDULE 14
PPP ADMINISTRATION ORDERS

Section 220

PART I
MODIFICATIONS OF THE 1986 ACT

General application of provisions of 1986 Act

[7.2307]

1. Where a PPP administration order has been made, sections 11 to 23 and 27 of the 1986 Act (which relate to administration orders under Part II of that Act) shall apply, with the modifications specified in the following provisions of this Part of this Schedule—

(a) as if references in those sections to an administration order were references to a PPP administration order and references to an administrator were references to a special PPP administrator; and

(b) where the company in relation to which the order has been made is a PPP company which [is not a company registered under the Companies Act 2006 in England and Wales or Scotland], as if references in those sections to a company included references to such a company.

Effect of order

2. In section 11 of the 1986 Act (effect of order), as applied by this Part of this Schedule, the requirement in subsection (1)(a) that any petition for the winding up of the company shall be dismissed shall be without prejudice to the PPP administration order in a case where the order is made by virtue of section 222 of this Act.

Appointment of special PPP administrator

3. In section 13 of the 1986 Act (appointment of administrator), as applied by this Part of this Schedule, for subsection (3) there shall be substituted the following subsection—

"(3) An application for an order under subsection (2) may be made—

(a) by the Mayor of London;

(b) by any continuing special PPP administrator of the company or, where there is no such special PPP administrator, by the company, the directors or any creditor or creditors of the company."

General powers of special PPP administrator

4. In section 14 of the 1986 Act (general powers of administrator), as applied by this Part of this Schedule,—

(a) in subsection (1)(b), the reference to the powers specified in Schedule 1 to that Act shall be taken to include a reference to a power to act on behalf of the company for the purposes of Chapter VII of Part IV of this Act or any provision of a local or private Act which confers any power, or imposes any duty or obligation, on the company; and

(b) in subsection (4), the reference to a power conferred by the company's [articles of association]—

(i) shall be taken to include a reference to any power conferred by any provision of a local or private Act which confers any power, or imposes any duty or obligation, on the company; and

(ii) in the case of a company which is an unregistered company, shall be taken also to include a reference to any power conferred by the company's constitution.

Power to deal with charged property

5. (1) Section 15 of the 1986 Act (power to deal with charged property), as applied by this Part of this Schedule, shall have effect as follows.

(2) In subsection (5)(b) (amount to be paid to chargeholder not to be less than open market value), for the words "in the open market by a willing vendor" there shall be substituted the words "for the best price which is reasonably available on a sale which is consistent with the purposes of the PPP administration order".

Duties of special PPP administrator

6. (1) Section 17 of the 1986 Act (duties of administrator), as applied by this Part of this Schedule, shall have effect in accordance with the following provisions of this paragraph.

(2) For subsection (2) there shall be substituted the following subsection—

"(2) Subject to any directions of the court, it shall be the duty of the special PPP administrator to manage the affairs, business and property of the company in accordance with proposals, as for the time being revised under section 23, which have been prepared for the purposes of that section by him or any predecessor of his."

(3) In subsection (3), paragraph (a) (right of creditors to require the holding of a creditors' meeting) shall be omitted.

Discharge of order

7. (1) Section 18 of the 1986 Act (discharge and variation of administration order), as applied by this Part of this Schedule, shall have effect as follows.

(2) For subsections (1) and (2) there shall be substituted the following subsection—

"(1) An application for a PPP administration order to be discharged may be made—

(a) by the special PPP administrator, on the ground that the purposes of the order have been achieved; or

(b) by the Mayor of London, on the ground that it is no longer necessary that the purposes of the order are achieved."

(3) In subsection (3), the words "or vary" shall be omitted.

(4) In subsection (4), the words "or varied" and "or variation" shall be omitted and for the words "to the registrar of companies" there shall be substituted—

["(a) where the company—

(i) is registered under the Companies Act 2006, or

(ii) is subject to a requirement imposed by regulations under section 1043 or 1046 of the Companies Act 2006 (unregistered UK companies or overseas companies) to deliver any documents to the registrar of companies,

the words "to the Mayor of London and the registrar of companies"; and

(b) where paragraph (a) above does not apply, the words "to the Mayor of London"."]

Notice of making of order

8. In section 21(2) of the 1986 Act (notice of order to be given by administrator), as applied by this Part of this Schedule, for the words "to the registrar of companies" there shall be substituted—

["(a) where the company—

(i) is registered under the Companies Act 2006, or

(ii) is subject to a requirement imposed by regulations under section 1043 or 1046 of the Companies Act 2006 (unregistered UK companies or overseas companies) to deliver any documents to the registrar of companies,

the words "to the Mayor of London and the registrar of companies"; and

(b) where paragraph (a) above does not apply, the words "to the Mayor of London"."]

Statement of proposals

9. In section 23 of the 1986 Act (statement of proposals), as applied by this Part of this Schedule, for subsections (1) and (2) there shall be substituted the following subsections—

"(1) Where a PPP administration order has been made, the special PPP administrator shall, within 3 months (or such longer period as the court may allow) after the making of the order, send a statement of his proposals for achieving the purposes of the order—

(a) to the Mayor of London;

(b) so far as he is aware of their addresses, to all creditors of the company; and

(c) except where the company is an unregistered company which is not subject to a requirement imposed under or by virtue of section 691(1) or 718 of the Companies Act 1985 to deliver any documents to the registrar of companies, to the registrar of companies;

and may from time to time revise those proposals.

(2) If at any time—

(a) the special PPP administrator proposes to make revisions of the proposals for achieving the purposes of the PPP administration order, and

(b) those revisions appear to him to be substantial,

the special PPP administrator shall, before making those revisions, send a statement of the proposed revisions to the persons specified in subsection (2A).

(2A) The persons mentioned in subsection (2) are—

(a) the Mayor of London;

(b) all creditors of the company, so far as the special PPP administrator is aware of their addresses; and

[(c) where the company—

(i) is registered under the Companies Act 2006, or

(ii) is subject to a requirement imposed by regulations under section 1043 or 1046 of the Companies Act 2006 (unregistered UK companies or overseas companies) to deliver any documents to the registrar of companies,

the registrar of companies.]

(2B) Where the special PPP administrator is required by subsection (1) or (2) to send any person a statement before the end of any period or before making any revision of any proposals, he shall also, before the end of that period or, as the case may be, before making those revisions either—

(a) send a copy of the statement (so far as he is aware of their addresses) to all members of the company; or

(b) publish in the prescribed manner a notice stating an address to which members should write for copies of the statement to be sent to them free of charge."

Applications to court

10. (1) Section 27 of the 1986 Act (protection of interests of creditors and members), as applied by this Part of this Schedule, shall have effect as follows.

(2) After subsection (1) there shall be inserted the following subsections—

"(1A) At any time when a PPP administration order is in force the Mayor of London may apply to the High Court by petition for an order under this section on the ground specified in subsection (1B).

(1B) The ground mentioned in subsection (1A) is that the special PPP administrator has exercised or is exercising, or proposing to exercise, his powers in relation to the company in a manner which will not best ensure the achievement of the purposes of the order.

(1C) Where an application is made under subsection (1) in respect of a company in relation to which a PPP administration order is in force—

(a) notice of the application shall be given to the Mayor of London; and

(b) he shall be entitled to be heard by the court in connection with that application."

(3) Subsection (3) (order not to prejudice or prevent voluntary arrangements or administrator's proposals) shall be omitted.

(4) In subsection (4) (provision that may be made in an order), the words "Subject as above" shall be omitted and for paragraph (d) there shall be substituted—

"(d) without prejudice to the powers exercisable by the court in making a PPP administration order—

(i) provide that the PPP administration order is to be discharged as from such date as may be specified in the order unless, before that date, such measures are taken as the court thinks fit for the purpose of protecting the interests of creditors; and

(ii) make such consequential provision as the court thinks fit."

(5) For subsection (6) there shall be substituted—

"(6) Where a PPP administration order is discharged in consequence of such provision in an order under this section as is mentioned in subsection (4)(d)(i), the special PPP administrator shall, within 14 days after the date on which the discharge takes effect, send [a copy] of the order under this section—

(a) to the Mayor of London; and

[(b) where the company—
(i) is registered under the Companies Act 2006, or
(ii) is subject to a requirement imposed by regulations under section 1043 or 1046 of the Companies Act 2006 (unregistered UK companies or overseas companies) to deliver any documents to the registrar of companies,

to the registrar of companies];

and if, without reasonable excuse, the special PPP administrator fails to comply with this subsection, he is liable to a fine and, for continued contravention, to a daily default fine."

Particular powers of special PPP administrator

11. In the application of Schedule 1 to the 1986 Act (which sets out certain powers of the administrator) by virtue of section 14 of that Act, as applied by this Part of this Schedule in relation to a company which is an unregistered company, paragraph 22 shall be omitted.

NOTES

Paras 1, 4, 7–10: words in square brackets substituted by the Companies Act 2006 (Consequential Amendments, Transitional Provisions and Savings) Order 2009, SI 2009/1941, art 2(1), Sch 1, para 178(1), (8).

Note that the Insolvency Act 1986, Pt II (ss 8–27) is substituted by the Enterprise Act 2002, s 248(1), subject to savings and transitional provisions (i) in a case where a petition for an administration order has been presented before 15 September 2003 (see the Enterprise Act 2002 (Commencement No 4 and Transitional Provisions and Savings) Order 2003, SI 2003/2093, art 3 at **[2.26]**), and (ii) in relation to special administration regimes (see s 249 of the 2002 Act at **[2.10]**). The administration of companies is now dealt with in Sch B1 to the 1986 Act at **[1.575]**.

PART II
FURTHER MODIFICATIONS OF THE 1986 ACT: APPLICATION IN RELATION TO FOREIGN COMPANIES

Introductory

[7.2308]

12. (1) Where a PPP administration order has been made in relation to a company which is a foreign company, sections 11 to 23 and 27 of the 1986 Act (as applied by Part I of this Schedule) shall apply in relation to that foreign company with the further modifications set out in the following provisions of this Part of this Schedule.

(2) In this Part of this Schedule, "foreign company" means a company incorporated outside Great Britain.

Effect of order

13. (1) Section 11 of the 1986 Act (effect of administration order), as applied by this Part of this Schedule in relation to a foreign company, shall have effect as follows.

(2) In subsection (1), paragraph (b) shall be omitted.

(3) Subsection (2) shall be omitted.

(4) In subsection (3)—
(a) paragraphs (a) and (b) shall be omitted; and
(b) in paragraph (d)—
(i) the reference to the commencement or continuation of proceedings shall be taken as a reference to the commencement or continuation of proceedings in Great Britain; and
(ii) the reference to the levying of distress against the company shall be taken as a reference to the levying of distress against the foreign company to the extent of its property in England and Wales;

and any reference to property or goods shall be taken as a reference to property or (as the case may be) goods for the time being situated within Great Britain.

(5) Subsections (4) and (5) shall be omitted.

(6) At the end of that section there shall be added—

"(6) Where a PPP administration order is in force in relation to a company which is a foreign company within the meaning of section 224 of the Greater London Authority Act 1999—
(a) any person appointed to perform functions equivalent to those of an administrative receiver, and
(b) if the special PPP administrator so requires, any person appointed to perform functions equivalent to those of a receiver,

shall refrain from performing those functions in Great Britain in relation to the foreign company and any of the company's property for the time being situated in Great Britain, during the period for which that order is in force or, in the case of such a person as is mentioned in paragraph (b) above, during so much of that period as falls after the date on which he is required to do so."

Notification of order

14. In section 12 of the 1986 Act (notification of order), as applied by this Part of this Schedule in relation to a foreign company, the reference to a statement that the affairs, business and property of the company are being managed by the administrator shall be taken as a reference to a statement that—
(a) the affairs and business of the foreign company so far as carried on in Great Britain, and

(b) the property of the foreign company so far as that property is for the time being situated within Great Britain,

are being managed by the special PPP administrator.

General powers of special PPP administrator

15. (1) Section 14 of the 1986 Act (general powers of administrator), as applied by this Part of this Schedule in relation to a foreign company, shall have effect as follows.

(2) In subsection (1)(a), the reference to the affairs, business and property of the company shall be taken as a reference to—

(a) the affairs and business of the foreign company so far as carried on in Great Britain, and

(b) the property of that company so far as that property is for the time being situated within Great Britain.

(3) Subsection (2)(a) shall be omitted.

(4) In subsection (4)—

(a) the reference to any power conferred on the company or its officers shall be taken to include any power conferred on the foreign company or its officers under the law under which the foreign company is incorporated; and

(b) any reference (however expressed) to the exercise of any power conferred on the company or its officers shall be taken as a reference to the exercise of that power so far as it relates to—

(i) the affairs and business of the foreign company so far as carried on in Great Britain, or

(ii) the property of that company so far as that property is for the time being situated within Great Britain.

Power to deal with charged property

16. In section 15 of the 1986 Act (power of administrator to deal with charged property etc), as applied by this Part of this Schedule in relation to a foreign company, any reference to property or goods shall be taken as a reference to property or (as the case may be) goods for the time being situated within Great Britain.

Duties of special PPP administrator

17. In section 17 of the 1986 Act (general duties of administrator), as applied by this Part of this Schedule in relation to a foreign company,—

(a) in subsection (1), the reference to property shall be taken as a reference to property for the time being situated within Great Britain; and

(b) in subsection (2), the reference to the affairs, business and property of the company shall be taken as a reference to—

(i) the affairs and business of the foreign company so far as carried on in Great Britain, and

(ii) the property of that company so far as that property is for the time being situated within Great Britain.

Statement as to company's affairs

18. In section 22(1) of the 1986 Act (power of administrator to require certain persons to provide him with a statement as to company's affairs), as applied by this Part of this Schedule in relation to a foreign company, the reference to the affairs of the company shall be taken as a reference to the affairs of the foreign company so far as they are carried on in Great Britain, or relate to property of that company for the time being situated within Great Britain.

Particular powers of special PPP administrator

19. (1) The powers conferred on a special PPP administrator by virtue of Schedule 1 to the 1986 Act (which sets out certain powers of an administrator), as that Schedule applies by virtue of section 14 of that Act, as applied by this Part of this Schedule in relation to a foreign company, shall be exercisable only in relation to—

(a) the affairs and business of that company, so far as carried on in Great Britain; and

(b) the property of that company, so far as that property is for the time being situated within Great Britain.

(2) In that Schedule, as it so applies,—

(a) without prejudice to sub-paragraph (1) above, references to the property of that company shall be taken as references to that property, so far as that property is for the time being situated within Great Britain; and

(b) paragraph 19 shall be omitted.

NOTES

Note that the Insolvency Act 1986, Pt II (ss 8–27) is substituted by the Enterprise Act 2002, s 248(1), subject to savings and transitional provisions (i) in a case where a petition for an administration order has been presented before 15 September 2003 (see the Enterprise Act 2002 (Commencement No 4 and Transitional Provisions and Savings) Order 2003, SI 2003/2093, art 3 at **[2.26]**), and (ii) in relation to special administration regimes (see s 249 of the 2002 Act at **[2.10]**). The administration of companies is now dealt with in Sch B1 to the 1986 Act at **[1.575]**.

PART III
SUPPLEMENTAL

General adaptations and saving

[7.2309]

20. (1) Subject to the preceding provisions of this Schedule, references in the 1986 Act (except in sections 8 to 10 and 24 to 26), or in any other enactment passed before this Act, to an administration order under Part II of that Act, to an application for such an order and to an administrator shall include references, respectively, to a PPP administration order, to an application for a PPP administration order and to a special PPP administrator.

(2) Subject as aforesaid and to sub-paragraph (3) below, references in the 1986 Act, or in any other enactment passed before this Act, to an enactment contained in Part II of that Act shall include references to that enactment as applied by section 221, 222, 223 or 224 of this Act or Part I or II of this Schedule.

(3) Sub-paragraphs (1) and (2) above shall apply in relation to a reference in an enactment contained in Part II of the 1986 Act only so far as necessary for the purposes of the operation of the provisions of that Part as so applied.

(4) The provisions of this Schedule shall be without prejudice to the power conferred by section 411 of the 1986 Act (company insolvency rules), as modified by sub-paragraphs (1) and (2) above.

Interpretation

21. (1) In this Schedule "the 1986 Act" means the Insolvency Act 1986.

(2) In this Schedule, and in any modification of the 1986 Act made by this Schedule, "special PPP administrator", in relation to a PPP administration order, means any person appointed in relation to that order for the purposes of section 220(1) of this Act; and in any such modification "PPP administration order" has the same meaning as in Chapter VII of Part IV of this Act.

NOTES

Note that the Insolvency Act 1986, Pt II (ss 8–27) is substituted by the Enterprise Act 2002, s 248(1), subject to savings and transitional provisions (i) in a case where a petition for an administration order has been presented before 15 September 2003 (see the Enterprise Act 2002 (Commencement No 4 and Transitional Provisions and Savings) Order 2003, SI 2003/2093, art 3 at **[2.26]**), and (ii) in relation to special administration regimes (see s 249 of the 2002 Act at **[2.10]**). The administration of companies is now dealt with in Sch B1 to the 1986 Act at **[1.575]**.

SCHEDULE 15
TRANSFER OF RELEVANT ACTIVITIES IN CONNECTION WITH PPP ADMINISTRATION ORDERS

Section 220

Application of Schedule

[7.2310]

1. (1) This Schedule shall apply in any case where—
- (a) the court has made a PPP administration order in relation to a PPP company ("the existing appointee"); and
- (b) it is proposed that, on and after a date appointed by the court, another company ("the new appointee") should carry on the relevant activities of the existing appointee, in place of the existing appointee.

(2) In this Schedule—

"the court", in the case of any PPP company, means the court having jurisdiction to wind up the company;

"other appointee" means any company, other than the existing appointee or the new appointee, which may be affected by the proposal mentioned in sub-paragraph (1)(b) above;

"the relevant date" means such day, being a day before the discharge of the PPP administration order takes effect, as the court may appoint for the purposes of this Schedule; and

"special PPP administrator", in relation to a company in relation to which a PPP administration order has been made, means the person for the time being holding office for the purposes of section 220(1) of this Act.

Making and modification of transfer schemes

2. (1) The existing appointee, acting with the consent of the new appointee and, in relation to the matters affecting them, of any other appointees, may make a scheme under this Schedule for the transfer of property, rights and liabilities from the existing appointee to the new appointee.

(2) A scheme under this Schedule shall not take effect unless it is approved by the Mayor.

(3) Where a scheme under this Schedule is submitted to the Mayor for his approval, he may, with the consent of the new appointee, of the existing appointee and, in relation to the matters affecting them, of any other appointees, modify the scheme before approving it.

(4) If at any time after a scheme under this Schedule has come into force in relation to the property, rights and liabilities of any company the Mayor considers it appropriate to do so and the existing appointee, the new appointee and, in relation to the provisions of the order which affect them, any other appointees consent to the making of the order, the Mayor may by order provide that that scheme shall for all purposes be deemed to have come into force with such modifications as may be specified in the order.

(5) An order under sub-paragraph (4) above may make, with effect from the coming into force of the scheme to which it relates, any such provision as could have been made by the scheme and, in connection with giving effect to that provision from that time, may contain such supplemental, consequential and transitional provision as the Mayor considers appropriate.

(6) In determining, in accordance with the duties imposed upon him by or under this Act or any other enactment (whenever passed or made), whether and in what manner to exercise any power conferred on him by this paragraph, the Mayor shall have regard to the need to ensure that any provision for the transfer of property, rights and liabilities in accordance with a scheme under this Schedule allocates property, rights and liabilities to the different companies affected by the scheme in such proportions as appear to him to be appropriate in the context of the different relevant activities of the existing appointee which will, by virtue of this Act, be carried out at different times on and after the relevant date by the new appointee, by the existing appointee and by any other appointees.

(7) It shall be the duty of the new appointee, of the existing appointee and of any other appointees to provide the Mayor with all such information and other assistance as he may reasonably require for the purposes of, or in connection with, the exercise of any power conferred on him by this paragraph.

(8) Without prejudice to the other provisions of this Act relating to the special PPP administrator of a company, anything which is required by this paragraph to be done by a company shall, where that company is a company in relation to which a PPP administration order is in force, be effective only if it is done on the company's behalf by its special PPP administrator.

Transfers by scheme

3. (1) A scheme under this Schedule for the transfer of the existing appointee's property, rights and liabilities shall come into force on the relevant date and, on coming into force, shall have effect, in accordance with its provisions and without further assurance, so as to transfer the property, rights and liabilities to which the scheme relates to the new appointee.

(2) For the purpose of making any division of property, rights or liabilities which it is considered appropriate to make in connection with the transfer of property, rights and liabilities in accordance with a scheme under this Schedule, the provisions of that scheme may—

- (a) create for the existing appointee, the new appointee or any other appointees an interest in or right over any property to which the scheme relates;
- (b) create new rights and liabilities as between any two or more of those companies; and
- (c) in connection with any provision made by virtue of paragraph (a) or (b) above, make incidental provision as to the interests, rights and liabilities of other persons with respect to the subject-matter of the scheme.

(3) The property, rights and liabilities of the existing appointee that shall be capable of being transferred in accordance with a scheme under this Schedule shall include—

- (a) property, rights and liabilities that would not otherwise be capable of being transferred or assigned by the existing appointee;
- (b) such property, rights and liabilities to which the existing appointee may become entitled or subject after the making of the scheme and before the relevant date as may be described in the scheme;
- (c) property situated anywhere in the United Kingdom or elsewhere;
- (d) rights and liabilities under the law of any part of the United Kingdom or of any country or territory outside the United Kingdom.

(4) The provision that may be made by virtue of sub-paragraph (2)(b) above includes—

- (a) provision for treating any person who is entitled by virtue of a scheme under this Schedule to possession of a document as having given another person an acknowledgement in writing of the right of that other person to the production of the document and to delivery of copies thereof; and
- (b) provision applying section 64 of the Law of Property Act 1925 (production and safe custody of documents) in relation to any case in relation to which provision falling within paragraph (a) above has effect.

(5) For the avoidance of doubt, it is hereby declared that the transfers authorised by paragraph (a) of sub-paragraph (3) above include transfers which, by virtue of that paragraph, are to take effect as if there were no such contravention, liability or interference with any interest or right as there would be, in the case of a transfer or assignment otherwise than in accordance with a scheme under this Schedule, by reason of any provision having effect (whether under any enactment or agreement or otherwise) in relation to the terms on which the existing appointee is entitled or subject to the property, right or liability in question.

Transfer of licences

4. (1) A scheme under this Schedule may provide for a licence held by the existing appointee to have effect as if it had been granted to the new appointee.

(2) Different schemes under this Schedule may provide for a licence held by the same existing appointee to have effect as if it had been granted as a separate licence to each of the new appointees under those schemes.

(3) In this paragraph "licence" means a licence under section 8 of the Railways Act 1993.

Supplemental provisions of schemes

5. (1) A scheme under this Schedule may contain supplemental, consequential and transitional provision for the purposes of, or in connection with, the provision for the transfers or any other provision made by the scheme.

(2) Without prejudice to the generality of sub-paragraph (1) above, a scheme under this Schedule may provide—

(a) that for purposes connected with any transfers made in accordance with the scheme (including the transfer of rights and liabilities under an enactment) the new appointee is to be treated as the same person in law as the existing appointee;

(b) that, so far as may be necessary for the purposes of or in connection with any such transfers, agreements made, transactions effected and other things done by or in relation to the existing appointee are to be treated as made, effected or done by or in relation to the new appointee;

(c) that, so far as may be necessary for the purposes of or in connection with any such transfers, references in any agreement (whether or not in writing) or in any deed, bond, instrument or other document to, or to any officer of, the existing appointee are to have effect with such modifications as are specified in the scheme;

(d) that proceedings commenced by or against the existing appointee are to be continued by or against the new appointee;

(e) that the effect of any transfer under the scheme in relation to contracts of employment with the existing appointee is not to be to terminate any of those contracts but is to be that periods of employment with the existing appointee are to count for all purposes as periods of employment with the new appointee;

(f) that disputes as to the effect of the scheme between the existing appointee and the new appointee, between either of them and any other appointee or between different companies which are other appointees are to be referred to such arbitration as may be specified in or determined under the scheme;

(g) that determinations on such arbitrations and certificates given jointly by two or more such appointees as are mentioned in paragraph (f) above as to the effect of the scheme as between the companies giving the certificates are to be conclusive for all purposes.

Duties of existing appointee after the scheme comes into force

6. (1) A scheme under this Schedule may provide for the imposition of duties on the existing appointee and on the new appointee to take all such steps as may be requisite to secure that the vesting in the new appointee, by virtue of the scheme, of any foreign property, right or liability is effective under the relevant foreign law.

(2) The provisions of a scheme under this Schedule may require the existing appointee to comply with any directions of the new appointee in performing any duty imposed on the existing appointee by virtue of a provision included in the scheme under sub-paragraph (1) above.

(3) A scheme under this Schedule may provide that, until the vesting of any foreign property, right or liability of the existing appointee in the new appointee is effective under the relevant foreign law, it shall be the duty of the existing appointee to hold that property or right for the benefit of, or to discharge that liability on behalf of, the new appointee.

(4) Nothing in any provision included by virtue of this paragraph in a scheme under this Schedule shall be taken as prejudicing the effect under the law of any part of the United Kingdom of the vesting by virtue of the scheme in the new appointee of any foreign property, right or liability.

(5) A scheme under this Schedule may provide that, in specified cases, foreign property, rights or liabilities that are acquired or incurred by an existing appointee after the scheme comes into force are immediately to become property, rights or liabilities of the new appointee; and such a scheme may make the same provision in relation to any such property, rights or liabilities as can be made, by virtue of the preceding provisions of this paragraph, in relation to foreign property, rights and liabilities vested in the existing appointee when the scheme comes into force.

(6) References in this paragraph to any foreign property, right or liability are references to any property, right or liability as respects which any issue arising in any proceedings would have to be determined (in accordance with the rules of private international law) by reference to the law of a country or territory outside the United Kingdom.

(7) Any expenses incurred by an existing appointee in consequence of any provision included by virtue of this paragraph in a scheme under this Schedule shall be met by the new appointee.

(8) Duties imposed on a company by virtue of this paragraph shall be enforceable in the same way as if they were imposed by a contract between the existing appointee and the new appointee.

Functions exercisable by virtue of PPP agreements

7. (1) A scheme under this Schedule may provide that any functions exercisable by the existing appointee by virtue of a PPP agreement shall instead be—

(a) exercisable by the new appointee or any of the other appointees;

(b) concurrently exercisable by two or more companies falling within paragraph (a) above; or

(c) concurrently exercisable by the existing appointee and one or more companies falling within paragraph (a) above;

and different schemes under this Schedule may provide for any such functions exercisable by the same existing appointee to have effect as mentioned in paragraphs (a) to (c) above in relation to each of the new appointees under those schemes or of all or any of the other appointees.

(2) Sub-paragraph (1) above applies in relation to any function under a statutory provision if and to the extent that the statutory provision—

(a) relates to any part of the existing appointee's undertaking, or to any property, which is to be transferred by the scheme; or

(b) authorises the carrying out of works designed to be used in connection with any such part of the existing appointee's undertaking or the acquisition of land for the purpose of carrying out any such works.

(3) A scheme under this Schedule may define any functions exercisable by the existing appointee which are instead to be made exercisable or concurrently exercisable by the scheme in accordance with sub-paragraph (1) above—

(a) by specifying the statutory provisions in question;

(b) by referring to all the statutory provisions which—

(i) relate to any part of the existing appointee's undertaking, or to any property, which is to be transferred by the scheme, or

(ii) authorise the carrying out of works designed to be used in connection with any such part of the existing appointee's undertaking or the acquisition of land for the purpose of carrying out any such works; or

(c) by referring to all the statutory provisions within paragraph (b) above, but specifying certain excepted provisions.

(4) In this paragraph "statutory provision" means a provision whether of a general or of a special nature contained in, or in any document made or issued under, any Act, whether of a general or a special nature.

SCHEDULES 16–34

(*Schs 16–34 outside the scope of this work.*)

PPP ADMINISTRATION ORDER RULES 2007

(SI 2007/3141)

NOTES

Made: 31 October 2007.

Authority: Insolvency Act 1986, s 411; Greater London Authority Act 1999, s 220(5).

Commencement: 30 November 2007.

Note: the Insolvency Rules 1986, SI 1986/1925 are revoked and replaced (as from 6 April 2017 and subject to transitional provisions) by the Insolvency (England and Wales) Rules 2016, SI 2016/1024 at **[6.2]**, however, the Insolvency (England and Wales) Rules 2016 (Consequential Amendments and Savings) Rules 2017, SI 2017/369, r 3(e) at **[6.947]** provides that the Insolvency Rules 1986 as they had effect immediately before 6 April 2017 and insofar as they apply to proceedings under the PPP Administration Order Rules 2007, continue to have effect for the purposes of the application of the 2007 Rules.

See also the Deregulation Act 2015 and Small Business, Enterprise and Employment Act 2015 (Consequential Amendments) (Savings) Regulations 2017, SI 2017/540, reg 4(1), (2)(e) and the Insolvency Amendment (EU 2015/848) Regulations 2017, SI 2017/702, reg 4 at **[2.103]**, for savings in relation to the Insolvency Act 1986 in so far as it applies to proceedings under these Rules.

ARRANGEMENT OF RULES

PART 1
INTRODUCTORY PROVISIONS

1 Citation and commencement . . . [7.2311]
2 Construction and interpretation . . . [7.2312]
3 Extent . . . [7.2313]

PART 2
PPP ADMINISTRATION PROCEDURE

4 Affidavit to support petition . . . [7.2314]
5 Contents of affidavit . . . [7.2315]
6 Form of petition . . . [7.2316]
7 Filing of petition . . . [7.2317]
8 Service of petition . . . [7.2318]
9 Notice to enforcement officer, etc . . . [7.2319]
10 Manner in which service of petition is to be effected . . . [7.2320]
11 Proof of service . . . [7.2321]
12 The hearing . . . [7.2322]
13 Notice and advertisement of PPP administration order . . . [7.2323]
14 Discharge of PPP administration order . . . [7.2324]

PART 3
STATEMENT OF AFFAIRS AND PROPOSALS TO CREDITORS

15 Notice requiring statement of affairs . . . [7.2325]

16 Verification and filing . . . [7.2326]
17 Limited disclosure . . . [7.2327]
18 Release from duty to submit statement of affairs; extension of time . . . [7.2328]
19 Expenses of statement of affairs . . . [7.2329]
20 Statement to be annexed to proposals . . . [7.2330]
21 Notice to members of proposals to creditors . . . [7.2331]

PART 4
MEETINGS

22 Creditors' meetings generally . . . [7.2332]
23 The chairman at meetings . . . [7.2333]
24 Entitlement to vote . . . [7.2334]
25 Admission and rejection of claims . . . [7.2335]
26 Secured creditors . . . [7.2336]
27 Holders of negotiable instruments . . . [7.2337]
28 Retention of title creditors . . . [7.2338]
29 Hire-purchase, conditional sale and chattel leasing agreements . . . [7.2339]
30 Resolutions and minutes . . . [7.2340]
31 Report to creditors . . . [7.2341]
32 Venue and conduct of members' meeting . . . [7.2342]

PART 5
THE SPECIAL PPP ADMINISTRATOR

33 Fixing of remuneration . . . [7.2343]
34 Disposal of charged property, etc . . . [7.2344]
35 Abstract of receipts and payments . . . [7.2345]
36 Resignation . . . [7.2346]
37 Special PPP Administrator deceased . . . [7.2347]
38 Order filling vacancy . . . [7.2348]

PART 6
COURT PROCEDURE AND PRACTICE

CHAPTER 1
APPLICATIONS

39 Preliminary . . . [7.2349]
40 Form and contents of application . . . [7.2350]
41 Filing and service of application . . . [7.2351]
42 Other hearings without notice . . . [7.2352]
43 Hearing of application . . . [7.2353]
44 Use of affidavit evidence . . . [7.2354]
45 Filing and service of affidavits . . . [7.2355]
46 Use of reports . . . [7.2356]
47 Adjournment of hearing: directions . . . [7.2357]

CHAPTER 2
SHORTHAND WRITERS

48 Appointment and remuneration of shorthand writers . . . [7.2358]

CHAPTER 3
ENFORCEMENT PROCEDURES

49 Enforcement of court orders . . . [7.2359]
50 Orders enforcing compliance with these Rules . . . [7.2360]
51 Warrants under section 236 of the 1986 Act . . . [7.2361]

CHAPTER 4
COURT RECORDS AND RETURNS

52 Title of proceedings . . . [7.2362]
53 Court records . . . [7.2363]
54 Inspection of records . . . [7.2364]
55 File of court proceedings . . . [7.2365]
56 Right to inspect the file . . . [7.2366]
57 Filing of Gazette notices and advertisements . . . [7.2367]

CHAPTER 5
COSTS AND DETAILED ASSESSMENT

58 Application of the Civil Procedure Rules . . . [7.2368]
59 Requirement to assess costs by the detailed procedure . . . [7.2369]
60 Procedure where detailed assessment required . . . [7.2370]

61 Costs paid otherwise than out of the assets of the PPP company . . . . [7.2371]
62 Award of costs against special PPP administrator . . . . [7.2372]
63 Applications for costs . . . . [7.2373]
64 Costs and expenses of witnesses . . . . [7.2374]
65 Final costs certificate . . . . [7.2375]

CHAPTER 6
PERSONS INCAPABLE OF MANAGING THEIR AFFAIRS

66 Introductory . . . . [7.2376]
67 Appointment of another person to act . . . . [7.2377]
68 Affidavit in support of application . . . . [7.2378]
69 Service of notices following appointment . . . . [7.2379]

CHAPTER 7
APPEALS IN PPP ADMINISTRATION PROCEEDINGS

70 Appeals and reviews of PPP administration orders . . . . [7.2380]
71 Procedure on appeal . . . . [7.2381]

CHAPTER 8
GENERAL

72 Principal court rules and practice to apply . . . . [7.2382]
73 Right of audience . . . . [7.2383]
74 Right of attendance . . . . [7.2384]
75 Special PPP administrator's solicitor . . . . [7.2385]
76 Formal defects . . . . [7.2386]
77 Affidavits . . . . [7.2387]
78 Security in court . . . . [7.2388]
79 Payment into court . . . . [7.2389]
80 Further information and disclosure . . . . [7.2390]
81 Office copies of documents . . . . [7.2391]

PART 7
PROXIES AND COMPANY REPRESENTATION

82 Definition of proxy . . . . [7.2392]
83 Issue and use of forms of proxy . . . . [7.2393]
84 Use of proxies at meetings . . . . [7.2394]
85 Retention of proxies . . . . [7.2395]
86 Right of inspection . . . . [7.2396]
87 Proxy-holder with financial interest . . . . [7.2397]
88 Company representation . . . . [7.2398]

PART 8
EXAMINATION OF PERSONS IN PPP ADMINISTRATION PROCEEDINGS

89 Application . . . . [7.2399]
90 Form and contents of application . . . . [7.2400]
91 Order for examination, etc . . . . [7.2401]
92 Procedure for examination . . . . [7.2402]
93 Record of examination . . . . [7.2403]
94 Costs of proceedings under section 236 . . . . [7.2404]

PART 9
MISCELLANEOUS AND GENERAL

95 Power of Secretary of State to regulate certain matters . . . . [7.2405]
96 Notices . . . . [7.2406]
97 Quorum at creditors' meetings . . . . [7.2407]
98 Evidence of proceedings at meeting . . . . [7.2408]
99 Documents issuing from Secretary of State . . . . [7.2409]
100 Forms for use in PPP administration proceedings . . . . [7.2410]
101 Special PPP administrator's security . . . . [7.2411]
102 Time-limits . . . . [7.2412]
103 Service by post . . . . [7.2413]
104 General provisions as to service and notice . . . . [7.2414]
105 Service outside the jurisdiction . . . . [7.2415]
106 Confidentiality of documents . . . . [7.2416]
107 Notices sent simultaneously to the same person . . . . [7.2417]
108 Right to copy documents . . . . [7.2418]
109 Charge for copy documents . . . . [7.2419]
110 Non-receipt of notice of meeting . . . . [7.2420]

111 Right to have list of creditors . . . . . [7.2421]
112 False claim of status as creditor or member. . . . . [7.2422]
113 The Gazette . . . . . [7.2423]
114 Punishment of offences . . . . . [7.2424]

PART 10
INTERPRETATION AND APPLICATION

115 Introductory . . . . . [7.2425]
116 "The court"; "the registrar" . . . . . [7.2426]
117 "Give notice" etc . . . . . [7.2427]
118 Notice, etc to solicitors . . . . . [7.2428]
119 Notice to joint special PPP administrators. . . . . . [7.2429]
120 "Petition" . . . . . [7.2430]
121 "Venue" . . . . . [7.2431]
122 "PPP administration proceedings" . . . . . [7.2432]
123 "The appropriate fee" . . . . . [7.2433]
124 Expressions used generally . . . . . [7.2434]
125 Application and transitional provision . . . . . [7.2435]

SCHEDULES

Schedule—Forms . . . . . [7.2436]

PART 1
INTRODUCTORY PROVISIONS

[7.2311]
1 Citation and commencement

These Rules may be cited as the PPP Administration Order Rules 2007 and shall come into force on 30th November 2007.

[7.2312]
2 Construction and interpretation

(1) In these Rules—

"the 1985 Act" means the Companies Act 1985;

"the 1986 Act" means the Insolvency Act 1986;

"the 1999 Act" means the Greater London Authority Act 1999;

"the 2006 Act" means the Companies Act 2006;

"CPR" means the Civil Procedure Rules 1998 and "CPR" followed by a Part or rule number means the Part or rule with that number in those Rules;

"insolvency proceedings" means any proceedings under the 1986 Act or the Insolvency Rules;

"the Insolvency Rules" means the Insolvency Rules 1986;

"the PPP Arbiter" means the person for the time being appointed to the office of the Public-Private Partnership Agreement Arbiter under section 225 of the 1999 Act; and

"PPP company" shall be construed in accordance with section 210(5) of the 1999 Act.

(2) Except where the context requires otherwise, references to provisions of the 1986 Act are references to those provisions as applied by section 220 to 224 of, and Schedule 14 to, the 1999 Act, construed in accordance with section 249 of the Enterprise Act 2002.

(3) Where the PPP company is an unregistered company, any requirement to send information to the registrar of companies applies only if the company is subject to a requirement imposed by virtue of section 691(1) or 718 of the 1985 Act.

(4) Subject to paragraphs (1), (2) and (3), Part 10 of these Rules has effect for their interpretation and application.

NOTES

Note: the Insolvency Rules 1986, SI 1986/1925 are revoked and replaced (as from 6 April 2017 and subject to transitional provisions) by the Insolvency (England and Wales) Rules 2016, SI 2016/1024 at **[6.2]**, however, the Insolvency (England and Wales) Rules 2016 (Consequential Amendments and Savings) Rules 2017, SI 2017/369, r 3(e) provides that the Insolvency Rules 1986 as they had effect immediately before 6 April 2017 and insofar as they apply to proceedings under the PPP Administration Order Rules 2007, continue to have effect for the purposes of the application of the 2007 Rules.

[7.2313]
3 Extent

These Rules apply in relation to PPP companies which the courts in England and Wales have jurisdiction to wind up.

PART 2
PPP ADMINISTRATION PROCEDURE

[7.2314]
4 Affidavit to support petition

Where it is proposed to apply to the court by petition for a PPP administration order to be made in relation to a PPP company, an affidavit complying with rule 5 below must be prepared and sworn by or with the authority of the Mayor (or Transport for London if it acts as his agent) with a view to its being filed in court in support of the petition.

[7.2315]
5 Contents of affidavit

(1) The affidavit shall state that the company is a PPP company within the meaning of Part 4 of the 1999 Act.

(2) The affidavit shall state one or both of the following—
- (a) the deponent's belief that the PPP company is, or is likely to become, unable to pay its debts and the grounds for that belief;
- (b) that the Secretary of State has certified that it would be appropriate for him to petition for the winding up of the PPP company under section 124A (petition for winding up on grounds of public interest) of the 1986 Act and that in his view it would be just and equitable, as mentioned in that section, for the company to be wound up.

(3) There shall, in the affidavit, be provided a statement of the PPP company's financial position, specifying (to the best of the deponent's knowledge and belief) the assets and liabilities of the company, including contingent and prospective liabilities.

(4) Details shall be given of any security known or believed to be held by creditors of the PPP company, and whether in any case the security is such as to confer power on the holder to appoint an administrative receiver. If an administrative receiver has been appointed, that fact shall be stated.

(5) So far as within the immediate knowledge of the deponent, the affidavit shall contain details of—
- (a) any petition which has been presented for the winding up of the PPP company;
- (b) any application for the permission of the court to pass a resolution for the voluntary winding up of the PPP company;
- (c) any application for an administration order under Part 2 of the 1986 Act in relation to the PPP company;
- (d) any notice served in accordance with section 223(7) of the 1999 Act by any person intending to enforce any security over a PPP company's property; and
- (e) any step taken to enforce any such security.

(6) If there are other matters which, in the opinion of the person intending to present the petition for a PPP administration order, will assist the court in deciding whether to make such an order, those matters shall also be stated in the affidavit.

[7.2316]
6 Form of petition

(1) The petition shall be in Form PPP1 and shall state by whom it is presented and the address for service.

(2) The petition shall specify the name and address of the person proposed to be appointed as special PPP administrator; and it shall be stated that, to the best of the petitioner's knowledge and belief, the person proposed to be appointed as special PPP administrator is qualified to act as an insolvency practitioner in relation to the PPP company.

(3) There shall be exhibited to the affidavit in support of the petition—
- (a) a copy of the petition;
- (b) the written consent, in Form PPP2, of the proposed special PPP administrator accepting the appointment.

[7.2317]
7 Filing of petition

(1) The petition and affidavit shall be filed in court, with a sufficient number of copies for service and use as provided by rules 8 and 10.

(2) Each of the copies delivered shall have applied to it the seal of the court and be issued to the petitioner; and on each copy there shall be endorsed the date and time of filing.

(3) The court shall fix a venue for the hearing of the petition and this also shall be endorsed on each copy of the petition issued under paragraph (2).

(4) After the petition is filed, it is the duty of the petitioner to notify the court in writing of any insolvency proceedings affecting the PPP company, as soon as he becomes aware of them.

[7.2318]
8 Service of petition

(1) In this rule and rules 9, 10 and 11, references to the petition are to a copy of the petition issued by the court under rule 7(2) together with the affidavit in support of it and the documents (other than the copy of the petition) exhibited to the affidavit.

(2) The petition shall be served—

(a) on any person who has appointed or is or may be entitled to appoint an administrative receiver of the PPP company;
(b) on any person who has applied to the court for an administration order under Part 2 of the 1986 Act in relation to the PPP company;
(c) if an administrative receiver has been appointed, on him;
(d) if there is pending a petition for the winding up of the PPP company, on the petitioner (and also on the provisional liquidator, if any);
(e) on the person proposed for appointment as special PPP administrator;
(f) on the PPP company;
(g) on the Secretary of State.

[7.2319]
9 Notice to enforcement officer, etc

(1) The petitioner shall forthwith after filing the petition give notice of its presentation to—
(a) any enforcement officer or other officer who to his knowledge is charged with an execution or other legal process against the PPP company or its property; and
(b) any person who to his knowledge has distrained against the PPP company or its property.

(2) In the application of paragraph (1) in a case where the PPP company is a foreign company, within the meaning of paragraph 12(2) of Part 2 of Schedule 14 to the 1999 Act, the reference to property shall be taken as a reference to property situated within Great Britain.

[7.2320]
10 Manner in which service of petition is to be effected

(1) Service of the petition in accordance with rule 8 shall be effected by the petitioner, or his solicitor, or by a person instructed by him or his solicitor, not less than two days before the date fixed for the hearing.
(2) Service shall be effected as follows—
(a) on the PPP company (subject to paragraph (3)), by delivering the documents to its registered office; and
(b) on any other person (subject to paragraph (4)), by delivering the documents to his proper address,

or, in either case, in such manner as the court may direct.
(3) If delivery to the PPP company's registered office is not practicable or if the PPP company is an unregistered company, service may be effected by delivery to the company's last known principal place of business in England and Wales.
(4) Subject to paragraph (5), for the purposes of paragraph (2)(b), a person's proper address is any which he has previously notified as his address for service; but if he has not notified any such address, service may be effected by delivery to his usual or last known address.
(5) In the case of a person who—
(a) is an authorised deposit taker or a former authorised institution;
(b) has appointed, or is or may be entitled to appoint, an administrative receiver of the PPP company; and
(c) has not notified an address for service,

the proper address is the address of an office of that person where, to the knowledge of the petitioner, the PPP company maintains a bank account or, where no such office is known to the petitioner, the registered office of that person, or, if there is no such office, his usual or last known address.
(6) For the purposes of paragraph (5)—
"authorised deposit taker" means a person who has permission under Part 4 of the Financial Services and Markets Act 2000 to accept deposits; and
"former authorised institution" means an institution which continues to have a liability in respect of a deposit which was held in accordance with the Banking Act 1979 or the Banking Act 1987, but is not an authorised deposit taker.
(7) References in paragraph (6) to deposits and their acceptance must be read with—
(a) section 22 of the Financial Services and Markets Act 2000;
(b) any relevant order under that section; and
(c) Schedule 2 to that Act.

[7.2321]
11 Proof of service

(1) Service of the petition shall be verified by affidavit in Form PPP3, specifying the date on which, and the manner in which, service was effected.

(2) The affidavit, with a sealed copy of the petition exhibited to it, shall be filed in court forthwith after service, and in any event not less than one day before the hearing of the petition.

[7.2322]
12 The hearing

(1) At the hearing of the petition, any of the following may appear or be represented—
(a) the Mayor;
(b) Transport for London;
(c) any person who has appointed, or is or may be entitled to appoint, an administrative receiver of the PPP company;

(d) any person who has applied to the court for an administration order under Part 2 of the 1986 Act in relation to the PPP company;
(e) if an administrative receiver has been appointed, that administrative receiver;
(f) any person who has presented a petition for the winding up of the PPP company (and the provisional liquidator, if any);
(g) the person proposed for appointment as special PPP administrator;
(h) the PPP company; and
(i) with the permission of the court, any other person who appears to have an interest justifying his appearance.

(2) If the court makes a PPP administration order, it shall be in Form PPP4.

(3) If the court makes a PPP administration order, the costs of the petitioner, and of any person appearing whose costs are allowed by the court, are payable as an expense of the administration.

[7.2323]
13 Notice and advertisement of PPP administration order

(1) If the court makes a PPP administration order, it shall forthwith give notice to the person appointed as special PPP administrator in Form PPP5.

(2) After the order is made, the special PPP administrator shall forthwith advertise its making once in the Gazette, and once in such newspaper as he thinks most appropriate for ensuring that the order comes to the notice of the PPP company's creditors in Form PPP6.

(3) Subject to paragraph (5), the special PPP administrator shall also forthwith give notice in Form PPP7 of the making of the order—
(a) to the Mayor;
(b) to Transport for London;
(c) to any person who has appointed, or is or may be entitled to appoint, an administrative receiver of the PPP company;
(d) if an administrative receiver has been appointed, to him;
(e) if there is pending a petition for the winding up of the PPP company, to the petitioner (and to the provisional liquidator, if any);
(f) to any person who has applied to the court for an administration order under Part 2 of the 1986 Act in relation to the PPP company;
(g) to the registrar of companies; and
(h) to the Secretary of State.

(4) The court shall send two sealed copies of the order to the special PPP administrator, who shall send one of those copies accompanied by Form PPP8 to the registrar of companies in accordance with section 21(2) of the 1986 Act.

(5) If under section 9(4) of the 1986 Act the court makes any other order, it shall give directions as to the persons to whom, and how, notice of it is to be given.

[7.2324]
14 Discharge of PPP administration order

Where the PPP administration order is discharged, the special PPP administrator shall send an office copy of the order effecting the discharge to the registrar of companies in accordance with section 18(4) of the 1986 Act accompanied by Form PPP9.

PART 3
STATEMENT OF AFFAIRS AND PROPOSALS TO CREDITORS

[7.2325]
15 Notice requiring statement of affairs

(1) Where the special PPP administrator decides to require a statement of the PPP company's affairs to be made out and submitted to him in accordance with section 22 of the 1986 Act, he shall send notice in Form PPP10 to each of the persons whom he considers should be made responsible under that section, requiring them to prepare and submit the statement.

(2) The persons to whom the notice is sent are referred to in this Part as "the deponents".

(3) The notice shall inform each of the deponents—
(a) of the names and addresses of all others (if any) to whom the same notice has been sent;
(b) of the time within which the statement must be delivered;
(c) of the effect of section 22(6) (penalty for non-compliance) of the 1986 Act; and
(d) of the application to him, and to each of the other deponents, of section 235 (duty to co-operate with office-holder) of the 1986 Act.

(4) The special PPP administrator shall, on request, furnish each deponent with copies of Form PPP11 for the preparation of the statement of affairs.

[7.2326]
16 Verification and filing

(1) The statement of affairs shall be in Form PPP11, shall contain all the particulars required by that form and shall be verified by affidavit by the deponents (using the same form).

(2) The special PPP administrator may require any of the persons mentioned in section 22(3) of the 1986 Act to submit to him an affidavit of concurrence in Form PPP12, stating that he concurs in the statement of affairs. Where the special PPP administrator does so, he shall inform the person making the statement of affairs of that fact.

(3) An affidavit of concurrence may be qualified in respect of matters dealt with in the statement of affairs, where the maker of the affidavit is not in agreement with the deponents, or he considers the statement to be erroneous or misleading, or he is without the direct knowledge necessary for concurring with it.

(4) The statement of affairs shall be delivered to the special PPP administrator by the deponent making the affidavit (or by one of them, if more than one), together with a copy.

(5) Every affidavit of concurrence shall be delivered to the special PPP administrator by the person who makes it, together with a copy.

(6) The special PPP administrator shall file the verified copy of the statement of affairs and the affidavits of concurrence (if any) in court as soon as is reasonably practicable.

[7.2327]
17 Limited disclosure

(1) Where the special PPP administrator thinks that it would prejudice the conduct of the PPP administration for the whole or part of the statement of affairs to be disclosed, he may apply to the court for an order of limited disclosure in respect of the statement, or any specified part of it.

(2) The court may on the application order that the statement or, as the case may be, the specified part of it, be not filed in court, or that it is to be filed separately and not be open to inspection otherwise than with the permission of the court.

(3) The court's order may include directions as to the delivery of documents to the registrar of companies and the disclosure of relevant information to other persons.

[7.2328]
18 Release from duty to submit statement of affairs; extension of time

(1) The power of the special PPP administrator under section 22(5) of the 1986 Act to give a release from the obligation imposed by that section, or to grant an extension of time, may be exercised at the special PPP administrator's own discretion, or at the request of any deponent.

(2) A deponent may, if he requests a release or extension of time and it is refused by the special PPP administrator, apply to the court for it.

(3) The court may, if it thinks that no sufficient cause is shown for the application, dismiss it; but it shall not do so unless the deponent has had an opportunity to attend the court for a hearing without notice being served on any other party, of which he has been given at least 7 days' notice.

(4) If the application is not dismissed under paragraph (3), the court shall fix a venue for it to be heard, and give notice to the deponent accordingly.

(5) The deponent shall, at least 14 days before the hearing, send to the special PPP administrator a notice stating the venue and accompanied by a copy of the application, and of any evidence which he (the deponent) intends to adduce in support of it.

(6) The special PPP administrator may appear and be heard on the application; and whether or not he appears, he may file a written report of any matters which he considers ought to be drawn to the attention of the court.

(7) If such a report is filed, a copy of it shall be sent by the special PPP administrator to the deponent, no later than five days before the hearing.

(8) Sealed copies of any order made on the application shall be sent by the court to the deponent and to the special PPP administrator.

(9) On any application under this rule, the applicant's costs shall be paid in any event by him and, unless the court otherwise orders, no allowance towards them shall be made out of the assets of the PPP company.

[7.2329]
19 Expenses of statement of affairs

(1) A deponent making the statement of affairs and an affidavit in support of it shall be allowed, and paid by the special PPP administrator out of his receipts, any expenses incurred by the deponent in so doing which the special PPP administrator considers reasonable.

(2) Any decision by the special PPP administrator under this rule is subject to appeal to the court.

(3) Nothing in this rule relieves a deponent of any obligation with respect to the preparation, verification and submission of the statement of affairs, or to the provision of information to the special PPP administrator.

[7.2330]
20 Statement to be annexed to proposals

(1) Subject to paragraph (5), a statement shall be annexed by the special PPP administrator to his proposals sent under section 23(1) of the 1986 Act in Form PPP13 to the relevant persons showing—

(a) details relating to his appointment as special PPP administrator;
(b) the names of the directors and secretary of the PPP company;
(c) an account of the circumstances giving rise to the application for a PPP administration order;

(d) if a statement of affairs has been submitted, a copy or summary of it, with the special PPP administrator's comments, if any;
(e) if no statement of affairs has been submitted, details of the financial position of the PPP company at the latest practicable date (which must, unless the court otherwise orders, be a date not earlier than that of the PPP administration order);
(f) the manner in which the affairs and business of the PPP company—
  (i) have since the date of the special PPP administrator's appointment, been managed and financed, and
  (ii) will continue to be managed and financed; and
(g) such other information (if any) as the special PPP administrator thinks necessary.

(2) Subject to paragraph (3), where the special PPP administrator has cause to amend or alter his proposals, he shall send in Form PPP14 details of these revisions and the reasons for them to the relevant persons.

(3) Where the Mayor or the special PPP administrator intends to apply to the court under section 18 of the 1986 Act for a PPP administration order to be discharged at a time before the special PPP administrator has sent a statement of his proposals to the relevant persons, he shall, at least 10 days before he makes such an application, send to the relevant persons (so far as he is aware of their addresses) and to the Mayor or the special PPP administrator (as appropriate) a report containing the information required by paragraph (1)(a) to (g) of this rule.

(4) In this rule, "the relevant persons" are the members of the company and the persons referred to in section 23(2A) of the 1986 Act.

(5) Where the special PPP administrator publishes a notice in accordance with section 23(2B)(b) of the 1986 Act stating an address to which members of the PPP company should write for copies of the relevant statement to be sent to them free of charge, the special PPP administrator is not required to send a copy of the relevant statement nor such further information as this rule requires to a member of the PPP company unless that member has written to request a copy.

[7.2331]
21 Notice to members of proposals to creditors

For the purposes of section 23(2B)(b) of the 1986 Act, the notice shall be published once in the Gazette and once in the newspaper in which the making of the PPP administration order was advertised.

PART 4
MEETINGS

[7.2332]
22 Creditors' meetings generally

(1) This rule applies to creditors' meetings summoned by the special PPP administrator under section 14(2)(b) of the 1986 Act or pursuant to a direction of the court under section 17(3)(b) of that Act.

(2) In fixing the venue for the meeting, the special PPP administrator shall have regard to the convenience of creditors.

(3) The meeting shall be summoned for commencement between 10.00 and 16.00 hours on a business day, unless the court otherwise directs.

(4) At least 21 days' notice of the meeting shall be given to all creditors who are known to the special PPP administrator and who had claims against the PPP company at the date of the PPP administration order. The notice in Form PPP15 shall specify the purpose of the meeting and contain a statement of the effect of rule 24(1) (entitlement to vote).

(5) With the notice summoning the meeting there shall be sent forms of proxy in Form PPP24.

(6) If within 30 minutes from the time fixed for the commencement of the meeting there is no person present to act as chairman, the meeting shall stand adjourned to the same time and place in the following week or, if that day is not a business day, to the business day immediately following.

(7) The meeting may from time to time be adjourned, if the chairman thinks fit, but not for more than 14 days from the date on which it was fixed to commence, subject to the direction of the court.

(8) If a meeting is adjourned, the special PPP administrator shall as soon as reasonably practicable notify the creditors of the venue of the adjourned meeting.

[7.2333]
23 The chairman at meetings

(1) At any meeting of creditors summoned by the special PPP administrator, the chairman shall either be the special PPP administrator or a person nominated by him in writing to act in his place.

(2) A person so nominated must be either—
(a) one who is qualified to act as an insolvency practitioner in relation to the PPP company; or
(b) an employee of the special PPP administrator or his firm who is experienced in insolvency matters.

[7.2334]
24 Entitlement to vote

(1) Subject to paragraphs (2) and (5), at a meeting of creditors in PPP administration proceedings a person is entitled to vote only if—

(a) he has given to the special PPP administrator not later than 12.00 hours on the business day before the day fixed for the meeting, details in writing of the debt which he claims to be due to him from the PPP company, and the claim has been duly admitted under the provisions of this Part; and

(b) there has been lodged with the special PPP administrator any proxy which he intends to be used on his behalf.

Details of the debt must include any calculation for the purposes of rules 26 to 29.

(2) The chairman of the meeting may allow a creditor to vote, notwithstanding that he has failed to comply with paragraph (1)(a), if satisfied that the failure was due to circumstances beyond the creditor's control.

(3) The special PPP administrator or, if other, the chairman of the meeting may call for any document or other evidence to be produced to him, where he thinks it necessary for the purpose of substantiating the whole or any part of the claim.

(4) Votes are calculated according to the amount of a creditor's debt as at the date of the PPP administration order, deducting any amounts paid in respect of the debt after that date.

(5) A creditor shall not vote in respect of a debt for an unliquidated amount, or any debt whose value is not ascertained, except where the chairman agrees to put upon the debt an estimated minimum value for the purpose of entitlement to vote and admits the claim for that purpose.

(6) No vote shall be cast by virtue of a claim more than once on any resolution put to the meeting.

[7.2335]
25 Admission and rejection of claims

(1) At any creditors' meeting the chairman has power to admit or reject a creditor's claim for the purpose of his entitlement to vote; and the power is exercisable with respect to the whole or any part of the claim.

(2) The chairman's decision under this rule, or in respect of any matter arising under rule 24, is subject to appeal to the court by any creditor.

(3) If the chairman is in doubt whether a claim should be admitted or rejected, he shall mark it as objected to and allow the creditor to vote, subject to his vote being subsequently declared invalid if the objection to the claim is sustained.

(4) If on appeal the chairman's decision is reversed or varied, or a creditor's vote is declared invalid, the court may order that another meeting be summoned, or make such other order as it thinks just.

(5) Neither the special PPP administrator nor any person nominated by him to be chairman is personally liable for costs incurred by any person in respect of an appeal to the court under this rule, unless the court makes an order to that effect.

[7.2336]
26 Secured creditors

At a meeting of creditors, a secured creditor is entitled to vote only in respect of the balance (if any) of his debt after deducting the value of his security as estimated by him.

[7.2337]
27 Holders of negotiable instruments

A creditor shall not vote in respect of a debt on, or secured by, a current bill of exchange or promissory note, unless he is willing—

(a) to treat the liability to him on the bill or note of every person who is liable on it antecedent to the PPP company, and against whom a bankruptcy order has not been made (or, in the case of a company, which has not gone into liquidation), as a security in his hands; and

(b) to estimate the value of the security and, for the purpose of his entitlement to vote, to deduct it from his claim.

[7.2338]
28 Retention of title creditors

For the purpose of entitlement to vote at a creditors' meeting in PPP administration proceedings, a seller of goods to the PPP company under a retention of title agreement shall deduct from his claim the value, as estimated by him, of any rights arising under that agreement in respect of goods in the possession of the PPP company.

[7.2339]
29 Hire-purchase, conditional sale and chattel leasing agreements

(1) Subject to paragraph (2), an owner of goods under a hire-purchase or chattel leasing agreement, or a seller of goods under a conditional sale agreement, is entitled to vote in respect of the amount of the debt due and payable to him by the PPP company as at the date of the PPP administration order.

(2) In calculating the amount of any debt for this purpose, no account shall be taken of any amount attributable to the exercise of any right under the relevant agreement in so far as the right has become exercisable solely by virtue of the presentation of the petition for a PPP administration order or any matter arising in consequence of that, or the making of the order.

[7.2340]
30 Resolutions and minutes

(1) Subject to paragraph (2), at a creditors' meeting in PPP administration proceedings, a resolution is passed when a majority (in value) of those present and voting, in person or by proxy, have voted in favour of it.

(2) Any resolution is invalid if those voting against it include more than half in value of the creditors to whom notice of the meeting was sent and who are not, to the best of the chairman's belief, persons connected with the PPP company.

(3) The chairman of the meeting shall cause minutes of its proceedings to be entered in the PPP company's minute book.

(4) The minutes shall include a list of the creditors who attended (personally or by proxy).

(5) In this rule, "connected with the PPP company" has the same meaning as the phrase "connected with a company" in section 249 of the 1986 Act.

[7.2341]
31 Report to creditors

(1) Within 14 days of the end of every period of 6 months beginning with the date of appointment of the special PPP administrator the special PPP administrator shall send to all creditors of the PPP company a report on the progress of the administration until he vacates office.

(2) On vacating office the special PPP administrator shall send to creditors a report on the administration up to that time.

(3) Paragraph (2) does not apply where the PPP administration is immediately followed by the PPP company going into liquidation, nor when the special PPP administrator is removed from office by the court or ceases to be qualified as an insolvency practitioner.

[7.2342]
32 Venue and conduct of members' meeting

(1) Where the special PPP administrator summons a meeting of members of the PPP company, he shall fix a venue for it having regard to their convenience.

(2) The chairman of the meeting shall be the special PPP administrator or a person nominated by him in writing to act in his place.

(3) A person so nominated must be either—
- (a) one who is qualified to act as an insolvency practitioner in relation to the PPP company; or
- (b) an employee of the special PPP administrator or his firm who is experienced in insolvency matters.

(4) If within 30 minutes from the time fixed for commencement of the meeting there is no person present to act as chairman, the meeting shall stand adjourned to the same time and place in the following week or, if that day is not a business day, to the business day immediately following.

(5) Subject to the above, the meeting shall be summoned and conducted as if it were a general meeting of the PPP company summoned under the company's articles of association, and in accordance with the applicable provisions of the 1985 Act or the 2006 Act.

(6) The chairman of the meeting shall cause minutes of its proceedings to be entered in the PPP company's minute book.

PART 5
THE SPECIAL PPP ADMINISTRATOR

[7.2343]
33 Fixing of remuneration

(1) The special PPP administrator is entitled to receive remuneration for his services as such.

(2) The remuneration shall be fixed by reference to the time properly given by the insolvency practitioner (as special PPP administrator) and his staff in attending to matters arising in the PPP administration.

(3) The remuneration of the special PPP administrator shall be fixed by the court and the special PPP administrator shall make an application to court accordingly.

(4) The special PPP administrator shall give at least 14 days' notice of his application to the following, who may appear or be represented—
- (a) the Mayor;
- (b) Transport for London;
- (c) the creditors of the PPP company; and
- (d) the Secretary of State.

(5) In fixing the remuneration, the court shall have regard to the following matters—
- (a) the complexity (or otherwise) of the case;
- (b) any respects in which, in connection with the PPP company's affairs, there falls on the special PPP administrator any responsibility of an exceptional kind or degree;
- (c) the effectiveness with which the special PPP administrator appears to be carrying out, or to have carried out, his duties as such; and
- (d) the value and nature of the property with which he has to deal.

(6) Where there are joint special PPP administrators, it is for them to agree between themselves as to how the remuneration payable should be apportioned. Any dispute arising between them may be referred to the court for settlement by order.

(7) If the special PPP administrator is a solicitor and employs his own firm, or any partner of that firm, to act on behalf of the PPP company, profit costs shall not be paid unless this is authorised by the court.

[7.2344]
34 Disposal of charged property, etc

(1) The following applies where the special PPP administrator applies to the court under section 15(2) of the 1986 Act for authority to dispose of property of the PPP company which is subject to a security, or goods in the possession of the PPP company under an agreement, to which that subsection relates.

(2) The court shall fix a venue for the hearing of the application, and the special PPP administrator shall forthwith give notice of the venue to the person who is the holder of the security or, as the case may be, the owner under the agreement.

(3) If an order is made under the said section 15(2), the special PPP administrator shall forthwith give notice of it to that person or owner and to the registrar of companies in Form PPP16.

(4) The court shall send two sealed copies of the order to the special PPP administrator, who shall send one of them to that person or owner.

[7.2345]
35 Abstract of receipts and payments

(1) The special PPP administrator shall—
- (a) within 2 months after the end of 6 months from the date of his appointment, and of every subsequent period of 6 months; and
- (b) within 2 months after he ceases to act as special PPP administrator,

send the requisite accounts of the receipts and payments of the PPP company to the court, and to the registrar of companies.

(2) The court may, on the application of the special PPP administrator, extend the period of two months mentioned above.

(3) The accounts are to be in the form of an abstract in Form PPP17 showing—
- (a) receipts and payments during the relevant period of 6 months; or
- (b) where the special PPP administrator has ceased to act, receipts and payments during the period from the end of the last 6 month period to the time when he so ceased (alternatively if there has been no previous abstract, receipts and payments in the period since his appointment as special PPP administrator).

(4) The special PPP administrator is guilty of an offence if he makes default in complying with this rule and is liable on summary conviction to a fine not exceeding [one-fifth of the greater of £5,000 or the amount corresponding to level 4 on the standard scale for summary offences] and, for continued contravention, to a daily default fine not exceeding [one-fiftieth of the greater of those amounts].

NOTES

Para (4): words in square brackets substituted by the Legal Aid, Sentencing and Punishment of Offenders Act 2012 (Fines on Summary Conviction) Regulations 2015, SI 2015/664, reg 3(1), Sch 3, Pt 1, para 12.

[7.2346]
36 Resignation

(1) The special PPP administrator may give notice to the court and to the registrar of companies in Form PPP18 of his resignation on grounds of ill health or because—
- (a) he intends ceasing to be in practice as an insolvency practitioner; or
- (b) there is some conflict of interest, or change of personal circumstances, which precludes or makes impracticable the further discharge by him of the duties of special PPP administrator.

(2) The special PPP administrator may, with the permission of the court, give notice to the court and to the registrar of companies in Form PPP19 of his resignation on grounds other than those specified in paragraph (1).

(3) The special PPP administrator must give at least 7 days' notice of his intention to resign, or to apply for the court's permission to do so, to—
- (a) the Mayor;
- (b) any continuing special PPP administrator of the PPP company; and
- (c) if there is no such continuing special PPP administrator, to the PPP company and its creditors.

[7.2347]
37 Special PPP Administrator deceased

(1) Subject to paragraph (2), where the special PPP administrator has died, it is the duty of his personal representative to give notice of the fact to the court and to the registrar of companies, specifying the date of death.

(2) In the alternative, notice of the death may be given to the court and to the registrar of companies:
- (a) if the deceased special PPP administrator was a partner in a firm, by a partner in the firm who is qualified to act as an insolvency practitioner, or is a member of any body recognised by the Secretary of State for the authorisation of insolvency practitioners; or
- (b) by any person, if he delivers with the notice a copy of the relevant death certificate.

[7.2348]
38 Order filling vacancy

Where the court makes an order filling a vacancy in the office of special PPP administrator, the same provisions apply in respect of giving notice of, and advertising, the order as in the case of the PPP administration order under rule 13(2) and (3) (disregarding all references to forms in those paragraphs).

PART 6
COURT PROCEDURE AND PRACTICE

CHAPTER 1 APPLICATIONS

[7.2349]
39 Preliminary

This Chapter applies to any application made to the court in PPP administration proceedings, except a petition for a PPP administration order.

[7.2350]
40 Form and contents of application

(1) Each application shall be in writing in Form PPP20 and shall state—
  (a) the names of the parties;
  (b) the nature of the relief or order applied for or the directions sought from the court;
  (c) the names and addresses of the persons (if any) on whom it is intended to serve the application or that no person is intended to be served;
  (d) where the 1986 Act or these Rules require that notice of the application is to be given to specified persons, the names and addresses of all those persons (so far as known to the applicant); and
  (e) the applicant's address for service.

(2) The application must be signed by the applicant if he is acting in person or, when he is not so acting, by or on behalf of his solicitor.

[7.2351]
41 Filing and service of application

(1) The application shall be filed in court, accompanied by one copy and a number of additional copies equal to the number of persons who are to be served with the application.

(2) Subject as follows in this rule and in the next, or unless the rule under which the application is brought provides otherwise, or the court otherwise orders, upon the presentation of the documents mentioned in paragraph (1), the court shall fix a venue for the application to be heard.

(3) Unless the court otherwise directs, the applicant shall serve a sealed copy of the application, endorsed with the venue of the hearing, on the respondent named in the application (or on each respondent if more than one).

(4) The court may give any of the following directions—
  (a) that the application be served upon persons other than those specified by the relevant provision of the 1986 Act or these Rules;
  (b) that the giving of notice to any person be dispensed with;
  (c) that notice be given in some way other than that specified in paragraph (3).

(5) Unless the provision of the 1986 Act or these Rules under which the application is made provides otherwise, and subject to paragraph (6), the application must be served at least 14 days before the date fixed for the hearing.

(6) Where the case is one of urgency, the court may (without prejudice to its general power to extend or abridge time limits)—
  (a) hear the application immediately, either with or without notice to or the attendance of, other parties; or
  (b) authorise a shorter period of service than that provided for by paragraph (5),

and any such application may be heard on terms providing for the filing or service of documents, or the carrying out of other formalities, as the court thinks fit.

[7.2352]
42 Other hearings without notice

(1) Where the relevant provisions of the 1986 Act or these Rules do not require service of the application on, or notice of it to be given to, any person, the court may hear the application without notice being served on any other party.

(2) Where the application is properly made without notice being served on any other party, the court may hear it forthwith, without fixing a venue as required by rule 41(2).

(3) Alternatively, the court may fix a venue for the application to be heard, in which case rule 41 applies (so far as relevant).

[7.2353]
43 Hearing of application

(1) Unless allowed or authorised to be made otherwise, every application before the registrar shall, and every application before the judge may, be heard in chambers.

(2) Unless either—

(a) the judge has given a general or special direction to the contrary; or

(b) it is not within the registrar's power to make the order required,

the jurisdiction of the court to hear and determine the application may be exercised by the registrar, and the application shall be made to the registrar in the first instance.

(3) Where the application is made to the registrar he may refer to the judge any matter which he thinks should properly be decided by the judge, and the judge may either dispose of the matter or refer it back to the registrar with such direction as he thinks fit.

(4) Nothing in this rule precludes an application being made directly to the judge in a proper case.

[7.2354]
44 Use of affidavit evidence

(1) In any proceedings evidence may be given by affidavit unless by any provision of these Rules it is otherwise provided or the court otherwise directs; but the court may, on the application of any party, order the attendance for cross-examination of the person making the affidavit.

(2) Where, after such an order has been made, the person in question does not attend, his affidavit shall not be used in evidence without the permission of the court.

[7.2355]
45 Filing and service of affidavits

(1) Unless the provisions of the 1986 Act or these Rules under which the application is made provide otherwise, or the court otherwise allows—

(a) if the applicant intends to rely at the first hearing on affidavit evidence, he shall file the affidavit or affidavits (if more than one) in court and serve a copy or copies on the respondent, not less than 14 days before the date fixed for the hearing; and

(b) where a respondent to an application intends to oppose it and to rely for that purpose on affidavit evidence, he shall file the affidavit or affidavits (if more than one) in court and serve a copy or copies on the applicant, not less than 7 days before the date fixed for the hearing.

(2) Any affidavit may be sworn by the applicant or by the respondent or by some other person possessing direct knowledge of the subject matter of the application.

[7.2356]
46 Use of reports

(1) The special PPP administrator may file a report in court instead of an affidavit, unless the application involves other parties or the court otherwise orders.

(2) In any case where a report is filed instead of an affidavit the report shall be treated for the purpose of rule 45(1) and any hearing before the court as if it were an affidavit.

[7.2357]
47 Adjournment of hearing: directions

(1) The court may adjourn the hearing of an application on such terms (if any) as it thinks fit.

(2) The court may at any time give such directions as it thinks fit as to—

(a) service or notice of the application on or to any person, whether in connection with the venue of a resumed hearing or for any other purpose;

(b) whether particulars of claims and defence are to be delivered and generally as to the procedure on the application;

(c) the manner in which any evidence is to be adduced at a resumed hearing and in particular (but without prejudice to the generality of this sub-paragraph) as to—

  (i) the taking of evidence wholly or in part by affidavit or orally;

  (ii) the cross-examination either before the judge or registrar on the hearing in court or in chambers, of any deponents to affidavits; and

  (iii) any report to be given by the special PPP administrator; and

(d) the matters to be dealt with in evidence.

CHAPTER 2 SHORTHAND WRITERS

[7.2358]
48 Appointment and remuneration of shorthand writers

(1) The court may, at any time in the course of PPP administration proceedings, appoint a shorthand writer to take down the evidence of a person examined in the course of those proceedings in Form PPP21. Any shorthand writer so appointed shall complete a declaration in Form PPP22.

(2) The remuneration of a shorthand writer appointed in PPP administration proceedings shall be paid by the party who requested that the court make such an appointment, or out of the assets of the PPP company, or otherwise, as the court may direct.

(3) Any question arising as to the rates of remuneration payable under this rule shall be determined by the court in its discretion.

CHAPTER 3 ENFORCEMENT PROCEDURES

[7.2359]
49 Enforcement of court orders

In any PPP administration proceedings, orders of the court may be enforced in the same manner as a judgment to the same effect.

[7.2360]
50 Orders enforcing compliance with these Rules

(1) The court may, on application by the special PPP administrator, make such orders as it thinks necessary for the enforcement of obligations falling on any person in accordance with section 22 (statement of affairs to be submitted to administrator) or section 235 (duty to co-operate with office-holder) of the 1986 Act.

(2) An order of the court under this rule may provide that all costs of and incidental to the application for it shall be borne by the person against whom the order is made.

[7.2361]
51 Warrants under section 236 of the 1986 Act

(1) A warrant issued by the court under section 236 (inquiry into company's dealings, etc) of the 1986 Act shall be addressed to such officer of the High Court as the warrant specifies, or to any constable.

(2) The persons referred to in section 236(5) of the 1986 Act as the prescribed officer of the court are the tipstaff of the court and his assistants.

(3) When a person is arrested under a warrant issued under section 236 of the 1986 Act, the officer arresting him shall forthwith bring him before the court issuing the warrant in order that he may be examined.

(4) If he cannot immediately be brought up for examination, the officer shall deliver him into the custody of the governor of the prison named in the warrant, who shall keep him in custody and produce him before the court as it may from time to time direct.

(5) The court shall appoint the earliest practicable time for the examination, and shall—
- (a) direct the governor of the prison to produce the person for examination at the time and place appointed; and
- (b) forthwith give notice of the venue to the person who applied for the warrant.

(6) Any property in the arrested person's possession which may be seized shall be—
- (a) lodged with, or otherwise dealt with as instructed by, whoever is specified in the warrant as authorised to receive it; or
- (b) kept by the officer seizing it pending the receipt of written orders from the court as to its disposal,

as may be directed by the court.

(7) In this rule references to property include books, papers and records.

CHAPTER 4 COURT RECORDS AND RETURNS

[7.2362]
52 Title of proceedings

Every PPP administration proceeding shall, with any necessary additions, name the PPP company to which the proceedings relate and be entitled "IN THE MATTER OF THE INSOLVENCY ACT 1986 AND THE GREATER LONDON AUTHORITY ACT 1999".

[7.2363]
53 Court records

The court shall keep records of all PPP administration proceedings, and shall cause to be entered in the records the taking of any step in the proceedings, and such decisions of the court in relation thereto, as the court thinks fit.

[7.2364]
54 Inspection of records

(1) Subject to paragraphs (2) and (3), the court's records of PPP administration proceedings shall be open to inspection by any person.

(2) If, in the case of a person applying to inspect the records, the registrar is not satisfied as to the propriety of the purpose for which inspection is required, he may refuse to allow it. That person may then apply forthwith and without notice being served on any other party to the judge, who may refuse the inspection or allow it on such terms as he thinks fit.

(3) The decision of the judge under paragraph (2) is final.

[7.2365]
55 File of court proceedings

(1) In respect of all PPP administration proceedings, the court shall open and maintain a file for each case; and (subject to directions of the registrar) all documents relating to such proceedings shall be placed on the relevant file.

(2) No PPP administration proceedings shall be filed in the Central Office of the High Court.

[7.2366]
56 Right to inspect the file

(1) In the case of any PPP administration proceedings, the following persons have the right, at all reasonable times, to inspect the court's file of the proceedings—

(a) the Mayor;
(b) Transport for London;
(c) the special PPP administrator;
(d) the PPP Arbiter;
(e) any person stating himself in writing to be a creditor of the PPP company to which the PPP administration proceedings relate;
(f) every person who is, or at any time has been, a director or officer of the PPP company to which the PPP administration proceedings relate and every person who is a member of that company; and
(g) the Secretary of State.

(2) The right of inspection conferred on any person by paragraph (1) may be exercised on his behalf by a person properly authorised by him.

(3) Any person may, with the special permission of the court, inspect the file.

(4) The right of inspection conferred by this rule is not exercisable in the case of documents, or parts of documents, as to which the court directs, either generally or specially, that they are not to be made open to inspection without the court's permission.

(5) An application under paragraph (4) for a direction of the court may be made by the special PPP administrator or by any party appearing to the court to have an interest.

(6) If, for the purpose of powers conferred by the 1986 Act, these Rules or the Insolvency Rules, the Secretary of State wishes to inspect the file of any PPP administration proceedings and requests the transmission of the file, the court shall comply with such request (unless the file is for the time being in use for the court's purposes).

(7) Paragraphs (2) and (3) of rule 54 apply in respect of the court's file of any proceedings as they apply in respect of court records.

[7.2367]
57 Filing of Gazette notices and advertisements

(1) In any court in which PPP administration proceedings are pending, an officer of the court shall file a copy of every issue of the Gazette which contains an advertisement relating to those proceedings.

(2) Where there appears in a newspaper an advertisement relating to PPP administration proceedings pending in any court, the person inserting the advertisement shall file a copy of it in that court.

(3) The copy of the advertisement shall be accompanied by, or have endorsed on it, such particulars as are necessary to identify the proceedings and the date of the advertisement's appearance.

(4) An officer of any court in which PPP administration proceedings are pending shall from time to time file a memorandum giving the dates of, and other particulars relating to, any notice published in the Gazette, and any newspaper advertisements, which relate to proceedings so pending.

(5) The officer's memorandum shall be prime facie evidence that any notice or advertisement mentioned in it was duly inserted in the issue of the newspaper or the Gazette which is specified in the memorandum.

CHAPTER 5 COSTS AND DETAILED ASSESSMENT

[7.2368]
58 Application of the Civil Procedure Rules

Subject to provision to inconsistent effect made as follows in this Chapter, CPR Part 43 (scope of costs rules and definitions), Part 44 (general rules about costs), Part 45 (fixed costs), Part 47 (procedure for detailed assessment of costs and default provisions) and Part 48 (costs – special cases) shall apply to PPP administration proceedings with any necessary modifications.

[7.2369]
59 Requirement to assess costs by the detailed procedure

(1) The amount of any costs, charges or expenses of any person which are payable out of the assets of the PPP company shall be decided by detailed assessment unless the special PPP administrator and the person entitled to payment agree to the contrary.

(2) In the absence of such agreement, the special PPP administrator may serve notice in writing requiring the person entitled to payment to commence detailed assessment proceedings in accordance with CPR Part 47 (procedure for detailed assessment of costs and default provisions) in the court to which the PPP administration proceedings are allocated.

(3) In any proceedings before the court, including proceedings on a petition, the court may order costs to be decided by detailed assessment.

(4) Nothing in this rule prevents the special PPP administrator from making payments on account to any person on the basis of an undertaking by that person to repay immediately any money which may, when detailed assessment is made, prove to have been overpaid, with interest at the rate specified in section 17 of the Judgments Act 1838 on the date payment was made and for the period from the date of payment to that of repayment.

[7.2370]

60 Procedure where detailed assessment required

(1) Before making a detailed assessment of the costs of any person employed in PPP administration proceedings by a special PPP administrator, the costs officer shall require a certificate of employment, which shall be endorsed on the bill and signed by the special PPP administrator.

(2) The certificate shall include—

(a) the name and address of the person employed;

(b) details of the functions to be carried out under the employment; and

(c) a note of any special terms of remuneration which have been agreed.

(3) Every person whose costs in PPP administration proceedings are required to be decided by detailed assessment shall, on being required in writing to do so by the special PPP administrator, commence detailed assessment proceedings in accordance with CPR Part 47 (procedure for detailed assessment of costs and default provisions).

(4) If that person does not commence detailed assessment proceedings within 3 months of the requirement under paragraph (3), or within such further time as the court, on application, may permit, the special PPP administrator may deal with the assets of the PPP company without regard to any claim by that person, whose claim is forfeited by such failure to commence proceedings.

(5) Where in any such case such a claim lies additionally against a special PPP administrator in his personal capacity, that claim is also forfeited by such failure to commence proceedings.

[7.2371]

61 Costs paid otherwise than out of the assets of the PPP company

Where the amount of costs is decided by detailed assessment under an order of the court directing that the costs are to be paid otherwise than out of the assets of the PPP company, the costs officer shall note on the final costs certificate by whom, or the manner in which, the costs are to be paid.

[7.2372]

62 Award of costs against special PPP administrator

Without prejudice to any provision of the 1986 Act, the 1999 Act, the Insolvency Rules or these Rules by virtue of which the special PPP administrator is not in any event to be liable for costs and expenses, where a special PPP administrator is made a party to any proceedings on the application of another party to the proceedings, he shall not be personally liable for costs unless the court otherwise directs.

[7.2373]

63 Applications for costs

(1) This rule applies where a party to, or person affected by, any PPP administration proceedings—

(a) applies to the court for an order allowing his costs, or part of them, incidental to the proceedings, and

(b) that application is not made at the time of the proceedings.

(2) The person concerned shall serve a sealed copy of his application on the special PPP administrator.

(3) The special PPP administrator may appear on the application.

(4) No costs of or incidental to the application shall be allowed to the applicant unless the court is satisfied that the application could not have been made at the time of the proceedings.

[7.2374]

64 Costs and expenses of witnesses

(1) Except as directed by the court, no allowance as a witness in any examination or other proceedings before the court shall be made to an officer of the PPP company to which the PPP administration proceedings relate.

(2) A person presenting a petition in PPP administration proceedings shall not be regarded as a witness on the hearing of the petition, but the costs officer may allow his expenses of travelling and subsistence.

[7.2375]

65 Final costs certificate

(1) A final costs certificate of the costs officer is final and conclusive as to all matters which have not been objected to in the manner provided for under the rules of the court.

(2) Where it is proved to the satisfaction of a costs officer that a costs certificate has been lost or destroyed, he may issue a duplicate.

CHAPTER 6 PERSONS INCAPABLE OF MANAGING THEIR AFFAIRS

[7.2376]

66 Introductory

(1) The rules in this Chapter apply where in PPP administration proceedings it appears to the court that a person affected by the proceedings is one who is incapable of managing and administering his property and affairs either—

(a) by reason of a lack of capacity (within the meaning of the Mental Capacity Act 2005); or

(b) due to physical affliction or disability.

(2) The person concerned is referred to as "the incapacitated person".

[7.2377]
67 Appointment of another person to act

(1) The court may appoint such person as it thinks fit to appear for, represent or act for the incapacitated person in Form PPP23.

(2) The appointment may be made either generally or for the purpose of any particular application or proceeding, or for the exercise of particular rights or powers which the incapacitated person might have exercised but for his incapacity.

(3) The court may make the appointment either of its own motion or on application by—

(a) a person who has been appointed by a court in the United Kingdom or elsewhere to manage the affairs of, or to represent, the incapacitated person; or

(b) any relative or friend of the incapacitated person who appears to the court to be a proper person to make the application; or

(c) the special PPP administrator.

(4) Application under paragraph (3) may be made without notice being served on any other party, but the court may require such notice of the application as it thinks necessary to be given to the person alleged to be incapacitated, or any other person, and may adjourn the hearing of the application to enable the notice to be given.

[7.2378]
68 Affidavit in support of application

An application under rule 67(3) shall be supported by an affidavit of a registered medical practitioner as to the mental or physical condition of the incapacitated person.

[7.2379]
69 Service of notices following appointment

Any notice served on, or sent to, a person appointed under rule 67 has the same effect as if it had been served on, or given to, the incapacitated person.

CHAPTER 7 APPEALS IN PPP ADMINISTRATION PROCEEDINGS

[7.2380]
70 Appeals and reviews of PPP administration orders

(1) Every court having jurisdiction under the 1986 Act to wind up companies may review, rescind or vary any order made by it in the exercise of that jurisdiction.

(2) An appeal from a decision made in the exercise of that jurisdiction by a registrar of the High Court lies to a single judge of the High Court; and an appeal from a decision of that judge on such an appeal lies to the Court of Appeal.

[7.2381]
71 Procedure on appeal

(1) Subject to paragraphs (2) and (3), the procedure and practice of the Supreme Court relating to appeals to the Court of Appeal apply to appeals in PPP administration proceedings.

(2) In relation to any appeal to a single judge of the High Court under Rule 70 above, any reference in the CPR to the Court of Appeal is replaced by a reference to that judge and any reference to the registrar of civil appeals is replaced by a reference to the registrar of the High Court who deals with PPP administration proceedings.

(3) In PPP administration proceedings, the procedure under CPR Part 52 (appeals to the Court of Appeal) is by an application in Form PPP20 and not by application notice.

CHAPTER 8 GENERAL

[7.2382]
72 Principal court rules and practice to apply

(1) The CPR and the practice and procedure of the High Court (including any practice direction) apply to PPP administration proceedings, with necessary modifications, except so far as inconsistent with these Rules.

(2) All PPP administration proceedings shall be allocated to the multi-track for which CPR Part 29 (the multi-track) makes provision, accordingly those provisions of the CPR which provide for allocation questionnaires and track allocation will not apply.

[7.2383]
73 Right of audience

Rights of audience in PPP administration proceedings are the same as obtain in insolvency proceedings.

[7.2384]
74 Right of attendance

(1) Subject as follows, in PPP administration proceedings, any person stating himself in writing, in records kept by the court for that purpose, to be a creditor or member of the PPP company is entitled, at his own cost, to attend in court or in chambers at any stage of the proceedings.

(2) Attendance may be by the person himself, or his solicitor.

(3) A person so entitled to attend may request the court in writing to give him notice of any step in the PPP administration proceedings; and, subject to his paying the costs involved and keeping the court informed as to his address, the court shall comply with the request.

(4) If the court is satisfied that the exercise by a person of his rights under this rule has given rise to costs for the assets of the PPP company which would not otherwise have been incurred and ought not, in the circumstances, to be paid out of those assets, the court may direct that the costs be paid by the person concerned, to an amount specified.

(5) Where the court makes a direction under paragraph (4) in relation to a person, the rights of that person under this rule shall be in abeyance so long as those costs are not paid.

(6) The court may appoint one or more persons to represent the creditors or the members of a PPP company, or any class of them, to have the rights conferred by this rule, instead of the rights being exercised by any or all of them individually.

(7) If two or more persons are appointed under paragraph (6) to represent the same interest, they must (if at all) instruct the same solicitor.

[7.2385]
75 Special PPP administrator's solicitor

Where in PPP administration proceedings the attendance of the special PPP administrator's solicitor is required, whether in court or in chambers, the special PPP administrator himself need not attend, unless directed by the court.

[7.2386]
76 Formal defects

No PPP administration proceedings shall be invalidated by any formal defect or by any irregularity, unless the court before which objection is made considers that substantial injustice has been caused by the defect or irregularity, and that the injustice cannot be remedied by any order of the court.

[7.2387]
77 Affidavits

(1) Subject to the following paragraphs of this rule, the practice and procedure of the High Court with regard to affidavits, their form and contents, and the procedure governing their use, are to apply to all PPP administration proceedings.

(2) Where in PPP administration proceedings an affidavit is made by the special PPP administrator, the deponent shall state the capacity in which he makes it, the position which he holds and the address at which he works.

(3) Subject to paragraph (4), where these Rules provide for the use of an affidavit, a witness statement verified by a statement of truth may be used as an alternative.

(4) Paragraph (3) does not apply to rules 91 and 92.

(5) Where paragraph (3) applies, any form prescribed by rule 100 shall be modified accordingly.

[7.2388]
78 Security in court

(1) Where security has to be given to the court (otherwise than in relation to costs), it may be given by guarantee, bond or the payment of money into court.

(2) A person proposing to give a bond as security shall give notice to the party in whose favour the security is required, and to the court, naming those who are to be sureties to the bond.

(3) The court shall forthwith give notice to the parties concerned of a venue for the execution of the bond and the making of any objection to the sureties.

(4) The sureties shall make an affidavit of their sufficiency (unless dispensed with by the party in whose favour the security is required) and shall, if required by the court, attend the court to be cross-examined.

[7.2389]
79 Payment into court

The CPR relating to payment into and out of court of money lodged in court as security for costs apply to money lodged in court under these Rules.

[7.2390]
80 Further information and disclosure

(1) Any party to PPP administration proceedings may apply to the court for an order—

- (a) that any other party—
  - (i) clarify any matter which is in dispute in the proceedings; or
  - (ii) give additional information in relation to any such matter,

  in accordance with CPR Part 18 (further information); or
- (b) to obtain disclosure from any other party in accordance with CPR Part 31 (disclosure and inspection of documents).

(2) An application under this rule may be made without notice being served on any other party.

[7.2391]
81 Office copies of documents

(1) Any person who has under these Rules the right to inspect the court file of PPP administration proceedings may require the court to provide him with an office copy of any document from the file.

(2) A person's right under this rule may be exercised on his behalf by his solicitor.

(3) An office copy provided by the court under this rule shall be in such form as the registrar thinks appropriate, and shall bear the court's seal.

PART 7
PROXIES AND COMPANY REPRESENTATION

[7.2392]
82 Definition of proxy

(1) For the purposes of these Rules, a proxy is an authority given by a person ("the principal") to another person ("the proxy-holder") to attend a meeting and speak and vote as his representative.

(2) Proxies are for use at creditors' or members' meetings summoned or called by the special PPP administrator under section 14(2)(b) of the 1986 Act or summoned by him pursuant to a direction made by the court under section 17(3)(b) of that Act.

(3) Only one proxy may be given by a person for any one meeting at which he desires to be represented; and it may only be given to one person, being an individual aged 18 years or over. But the principal may specify one or more other such individuals to be proxy-holder in the alternative, in the order in which they are named in the proxy.

(4) Without prejudice to the generality of paragraph (3), a proxy for a particular meeting may be given to whoever is to be the chairman of the meeting, and such chairman cannot decline to be the proxy-holder in relation to that proxy.

(5) A proxy requires the holder to give the principal's vote on matters arising for determination at the meeting, or to abstain, or to propose, in the principal's name, a resolution to be voted on by the meeting, either as directed or in accordance with the holder's own discretion.

[7.2393]
83 Issue and use of forms of proxy

(1) When a notice is given of a meeting to be held in PPP administration proceedings and forms of proxy are sent out with the notice, no form so sent out with the notice shall have inserted in it the name or description of any person.

(2) No form of proxy shall be used at any meeting except that which is sent with the notice summoning the meeting, or a substantially similar form.

(3) A form of proxy in Form PPP24 shall be signed by the principal, or by some person authorised by him (either generally or with reference to a particular meeting).

(4) If the form of proxy is signed by a person other than the principal, the nature of the authority of that person shall be stated.

[7.2394]
84 Use of proxies at meetings

(1) A proxy given for a particular meeting may be used at any adjournment of that meeting.

(2) Where the special PPP administrator holds proxies for use by him as chairman of a meeting, and some other person acts as chairman, that other person may use the proxies of the special PPP administrator as if he were himself proxy-holder.

(3) A proxy-holder may propose any resolution which, if proposed by another, would be a resolution in favour of which by virtue of the proxy he would be entitled to vote.

(4) Where a proxy gives specific directions as to voting, this does not, unless the proxy states otherwise, preclude the proxy-holder from voting at his discretion on resolutions put to the meeting which are not dealt with in the proxy.

[7.2395]
85 Retention of proxies

(1) Subject to paragraph (2), proxies used for voting at any meeting shall be retained by the chairman of the meeting.

(2) The chairman shall deliver the proxies forthwith after the meeting to the special PPP administrator, where that is someone other than himself.

[7.2396]
86 Right of inspection

(1) The special PPP administrator shall, so long as proxies lodged with him are in his hands, allow them to be inspected, at all reasonable times on any business day by—

- (a) all creditors who have submitted in writing a claim to be creditors of the PPP company;
- (b) that company's members, in the case of proxies used at a meeting of that company; and
- (c) the directors of that company.

(2) The reference in paragraph (1) to creditors does not include a person whose claim has been wholly rejected for the purposes of voting, dividend or otherwise.

(3) Any person attending a meeting in PPP administration proceedings is entitled, immediately before or in the course of the meeting, to inspect proxies and associated documents (including proofs) sent or given, in accordance with directions contained in any notice convening the meeting, to the chairman of that meeting or to any other person by a creditor or member of the PPP company for the purpose of that meeting.

[7.2397]
87 Proxy-holder with financial interest

(1) A proxy-holder shall not vote in favour of any resolution which would directly or indirectly place him, or any associate of his, in a position to receive any remuneration out of the assets of the PPP company, unless the proxy specifically directs him to vote in that way.

(2) Where a proxy-holder has signed the proxy as being authorised to do so by his principal and the proxy specifically directs him to vote in the way mentioned in paragraph (1), he shall nevertheless not vote in that way unless he produces to the chairman of the meeting written authorisation from his principal sufficient to show that the proxy-holder was entitled so to sign the proxy.

(3) This rule applies also to any person acting as chairman of a meeting and using proxies in that capacity under rule 84, and in its application to him, the proxy-holder is deemed an associate of his.

(4) In this rule "associate" shall have the same meaning as in section 435 of the 1986 Act.

[7.2398]
88 Company representation

(1) Section 323 of the 2006 Act (representation of corporations at meetings) applies to a meeting of creditors called in PPP administration proceedings as to a meeting of the company (references to a member of the company being read as references to a creditor).

(2) Where a person is authorised under section 323 of the 2006 Act to represent a corporation at a meeting of creditors called in PPP administration proceedings, he shall produce to the chairman of the meeting a copy of the resolution from which he derives his authority.

(3) The copy resolution must be under the seal of the corporation, or certified by the secretary or a director of the corporation to be a true copy.

(4) Nothing in this rule requires the authority of a person to sign a proxy on behalf of a principal which is a corporation to be in the form of a resolution of that corporation.

PART 8
EXAMINATION OF PERSONS IN PPP ADMINISTRATION PROCEEDINGS

[7.2399]
89 Application

The rules in this Part relate to applications to the court, made by the special PPP administrator, for an order under section 236 (inquiry into company's dealings, etc) of the 1986 Act.

[7.2400]
90 Form and contents of application

(1) The application shall be in writing, and be accompanied by a brief statement of the grounds on which it is made.

(2) The respondent must be sufficiently identified in the application.

(3) It shall be stated whether the application is for the respondent—

- (a) to be ordered to appear before the court; or
- (b) to be ordered to clarify any matter which is in dispute in the proceedings or to give additional information in relation to any such matter and if so CPR Part 18 (further information) shall apply to any such order; or
- (c) to submit an affidavit (if so, particulars are to be given of the matters to which he is required to swear); or
- (d) to produce books, papers or other records (if so, the items in question are to be specified),

or for any two or more of those purposes.

(4) The application may be made without notice being served on any other party.

[7.2401]
91 Order for examination, etc

(1) The court may, whatever the purpose of the application, make any order which it has power to make under section 236.

(2) The court, if it orders the respondent to appear before it, shall specify a venue for his appearance, which shall be not less than 14 days from the date of the order.

(3) If he is ordered to submit affidavits, the order shall specify—

- (a) the matters which are to be dealt with in his affidavits; and
- (b) the time within which they are to be submitted to the court.

(4) If the order is to produce books, papers or other records, the time and manner of compliance shall be specified.

(5) The order must be served forthwith on the respondent; and it must be served personally, unless the court otherwise orders.

[7.2402]
92 Procedure for examination

(1) At any examination of the respondent, the special PPP administrator may attend in person, or be represented by a solicitor with or without counsel, and may put such questions to the respondent as the court may allow.

(2) If the respondent is ordered to clarify any matter or to give additional information, the court shall direct him as to the questions which he is required to answer, and as to whether his answers (if any) are to be made on affidavit.

(3) Where an application has been made under section 236 on information provided by a creditor of the PPP company, that creditor may, with the permission of the court and if the special PPP administrator does not object, attend the examination and put questions to the respondent (but only through the special PPP administrator).

(4) The respondent may at his own expense employ a solicitor with or without counsel, who may put to him such questions as the court may allow for the purpose of enabling him to explain or qualify any answers given by him, and may make representations on his behalf.

(5) There shall be made in writing such record of the examination as the court thinks proper. The record shall be read over either to or by the respondent and signed by him at a venue fixed by the court.

(6) The written record may, in any proceedings (whether under the 1986 Act or otherwise), be used as evidence against the respondent of any statement made by him in the course of his examination.

[7.2403]
93 Record of examination

(1) Unless the court otherwise directs, the written record of the respondent's examination, and any response given by him to any order under CPR Part 18 (further information), and any affidavits submitted by him in compliance with an order of the court under section 236, shall not be filed in court.

(2) The written record, responses and affidavits shall not be open to inspection, without an order of the court, by any person other than the special PPP administrator.

(3) Paragraph (2) applies also to so much of the court file as shows the grounds of the application for an order under section 236 and to any copy of any order sought under CPR Part 18.

(4) The court may from time to time give directions as to the custody and inspection of any documents to which this rule applies, and as to the furnishing of copies of, or extracts from, such documents.

[7.2404]
94 Costs of proceedings under section 236

(1) Where the court has ordered an examination of a person under section 236, and it appears to it that the examination was made necessary because information had been unjustifiably refused by the respondent, it may order that the costs of the examination be paid by him.

(2) Where the court makes an order against a person under section 237(1) or section 237(2) (court's enforcement powers under section 236) of the 1986 Act, the costs of the application for the order may be ordered by the court to be paid by the respondent.

(3) Subject to paragraphs (1) and (2), the special PPP administrator's costs shall, unless the court otherwise orders, be paid out of the assets of the PPP company.

(4) A person summoned to attend for examination under this Part shall be tendered a reasonable sum in respect of travelling expenses incurred in connection with his attendance. Other costs falling on him are at the court's discretion.

PART 9
MISCELLANEOUS AND GENERAL

[7.2405]
95 Power of Secretary of State to regulate certain matters

(1) Pursuant to paragraph 27 of Schedule 8 to the 1986 Act, the Secretary of State may, subject to the 1986 Act, the 1999 Act and these Rules, make regulations with respect to any matter provided for in these Rules as relates to the carrying out of the functions of a special PPP administrator of a PPP company.

(2) Regulations made pursuant to paragraph (1) may—

(a) confer discretion on the court;
(b) make non-compliance with any of the regulations a criminal offence;
(c) make different provision for different cases, including different provision for different areas; and
(d) contain such incidental, supplemental and transitional provisions as may appear to the Secretary of State necessary or expedient.

[7.2406]
96 Notices

(1) All notices required or authorised by or under the 1986 Act or these Rules to be given must be in writing, unless it is otherwise provided, or the court allows the notice to be given in some other way.

(2) Where in any PPP administration proceedings a notice is required to be sent or given by the special PPP administrator, the sending or giving of it may be proved by means of a certificate by him, or his solicitor, or a partner or an employee of either of them, that the notice was duly posted.

(3) In the case of a notice to be sent or given by a person other than the special PPP administrator, the sending or giving of it may be proved by means of a certificate by that person that he posted the notice, or instructed another person (naming him) to do so.

(4) A certificate under this rule may be endorsed on a copy or specimen of the notice to which it relates.

[7.2407]
97 Quorum at creditors' meetings

(1) Any meeting of creditors called or summoned by a special PPP administrator is competent to act if a quorum is present.

(2) Subject to paragraph (3), a quorum is at least one creditor entitled to vote.

(3) For the purposes of this rule, the reference to the creditor necessary to constitute a quorum is to those persons present or represented by proxy by any person (including the chairman) and includes persons duly represented under section 323 (representation of corporations at meetings) of the 2006 Act as applied by rule 88(1).

(4) Where at any meeting of creditors—
- (a) the provisions of this rule as to a quorum being present are satisfied by the attendance of—
  - (i) the chairman alone; or
  - (ii) one other person in addition to the chairman; and
- (b) the chairman is aware, by virtue of proofs and proxies received or otherwise, that one or more additional persons would, if attending, be entitled to vote,

the meeting shall not commence until at least the expiry of 15 minutes after the time appointed for its commencement.

[7.2408]
98 Evidence of proceedings at meeting

(1) A minute of proceedings at a meeting (held under the 1986 Act or these Rules) of the creditors or the members of a PPP company called or summoned by the special PPP administrator, signed by a person describing himself as, or appearing to be, the chairman of that meeting is admissible in PPP administration proceedings without further proof.

(2) The minute is prime facie evidence that—
- (a) the meeting was duly convened and held;
- (b) all resolutions passed at the meeting were duly passed; and
- (c) all proceedings at the meeting duly took place.

[7.2409]
99 Documents issuing from Secretary of State

(1) Any document purporting to be, or to contain, any order, directions or certificate issued by the Secretary of State shall be received in evidence and deemed to be or (as the case may be) contain that order or certificate, or those directions, without further proof, unless the contrary is shown.

(2) Paragraph (1) applies whether the document is signed by the Secretary of State himself or an officer on his behalf.

(3) Without prejudice to the foregoing, a certificate signed by the Secretary of State or an officer on his behalf and confirming—
- (a) the making of an order;
- (b) the issuing of any document; or
- (c) the exercise of any discretion, power or obligation arising or imposed under the 1986 Act, the 1999 Act or these Rules,

is conclusive evidence of the matters dealt with in the certificate.

[7.2410]
100 Forms for use in PPP administration proceedings

(1) The forms contained in the Schedule to these Rules shall be used in, and in connection with, PPP administration proceedings.

(2) The forms shall be used with such variations, if any, as the circumstances may require.

[7.2411]
101 Special PPP administrator's security

(1) Wherever under the 1999 Act or these Rules any person has to appoint, or proposes the appointment of, a person to the office of special PPP administrator, he is under a duty to satisfy himself that the person appointed or to be appointed has security for the proper performance of his functions.

(2) In any PPP administration proceedings the cost of the special PPP administrator's security shall be defrayed as an expense of the proceedings.

[7.2412]
102 Time-limits

(1) The provisions of CPR rule 2.8 (time) apply, as regards computation of time, to anything required or authorised to be done by these Rules.

(2) The provisions of CPR rule 3.1(2)(a) (the court's general powers of management) apply so as to enable the court to extend or shorten the time for compliance with anything required or authorised to be done by these Rules.

[7.2413]
103 Service by post

(1) For a document to be properly served by post, it must be contained in an envelope addressed to the person on whom service is to be effected, and pre-paid for first class post.

(2) A document to be served by post may be sent to the last known address of the person to be served.

(3) Where a document is served by post, the document is treated as served on the second business day after the date of posting unless the contrary is shown.

(4) The date of posting is presumed, unless the contrary is shown, to be the date shown in the post-mark on the envelope in which the document is contained.

[7.2414]
104 General provisions as to service and notice

Subject to rules 103, 105(1) and 117, CPR Part 6 (service of documents) applies as regards any matter relating to the service of documents and the giving of notice in PPP administration proceedings.

[7.2415]
105 Service outside the jurisdiction

(1) Section 3 of CPR Part 6 (special provisions about service out of the jurisdiction) does not apply in PPP administration proceedings.

(2) Where for the purposes of PPP administration proceedings any process or order of the court, or other document, is required to be served on a person who is not in England and Wales, the court may order service to be effected within such time, on such person, at such place and in such manner as it thinks fit, and may also require such proof of service as it thinks fit.

(3) An application under this rule shall be supported by an affidavit stating—
- (a) the grounds on which the application is made; and
- (b) in what place or country the person to be served is, or probably may be found.

[7.2416]
106 Confidentiality of documents

(1) Where in PPP administration proceedings the special PPP administrator considers, in the case of a document forming part of the records of the proceedings, that—
- (a) it should be treated as confidential; or
- (b) it is of such a nature that its disclosure would be calculated to be injurious to the interests of the creditors or members of a PPP company,

he may decline to allow it to be inspected by a person who would otherwise be entitled to inspect it.

(2) Where under this rule the special PPP administrator determines to refuse inspection of a document, the person wishing to inspect it may apply to the court for that determination to be overruled; and the court may either overrule it altogether, or sustain it subject to such conditions (if any) as it thinks fit to impose.

(3) Nothing in this rule entitles the special PPP administrator to decline to allow the inspection of any claim or proxy.

[7.2417]
107 Notices sent simultaneously to the same person

Where under the 1986 Act, the 1999 Act or these Rules a document of any description is to be sent to a person (whether or not as a member of a class of persons to whom that same document is to be sent), it may be sent as an accompaniment to any other document or information which the person is to receive, with or without modification or adaptation of the form applicable to that document.

[7.2418]
108 Right to copy documents

(1) Where under the 1986 Act or these Rules a person has a right to inspect documents, the right includes that of taking copies of those documents, on payment—
- (a) in the case of documents on the court's file of proceedings, of the fee chargeable under any order made under section 92 of the Courts Act 2003; and
- (b) otherwise, of the appropriate fee.

[7.2419]
109 Charge for copy documents

Where in PPP administration proceedings the special PPP administrator is requested by a creditor or member to supply copies of any documents, he is entitled to require the payment of the appropriate fee in respect of the supply of the documents.

[7.2420]
110 Non-receipt of notice of meeting

Where in accordance with the 1986 Act or these Rules a meeting of creditors is called or summoned by notice, the meeting is presumed to have been duly summoned and held, notwithstanding that not all those to whom the notice is to be given have received it.

[7.2421]
111 Right to have list of creditors

(1) In any PPP administration proceedings a creditor who under these Rules has the right to inspect documents on the court file also has the right to require the special PPP administrator to furnish him with a list of the creditors of the PPP company and the amounts of their respective debts.

This does not apply if a statement of the PPP company's affairs has been filed in court.

(2) The special PPP administrator, on being required by any person to furnish that list, shall send it to him, but is entitled to charge the appropriate fee for doing so.

[7.2422]
112 False claim of status as creditor or member

(1) Where these Rules provide for creditors or members of a PPP company a right to inspect any documents, whether on the court's file or in the hands of the special PPP administrator or other person, it is an offence for a person, with the intention of obtaining a sight of documents which he has not under these Rules any right to inspect, falsely to claim a status which would entitle him to inspect them.

(2) A person guilty of an offence under this rule is liable—
- (a) in summary proceedings, to a maximum of six months' imprisonment or a fine of the statutory maximum, or both;
- (b) on indictment, to two years' imprisonment or a fine, or both.

[7.2423]
113 The Gazette

(1) A copy of the Gazette containing any notice required by the 1986 Act or these Rules to be gazetted is evidence of any fact stated in the notice.

(2) In the case of an order of the court notice of which is required by the 1986 Act or these Rules to be gazetted, a copy of the Gazette containing the notice may in any proceedings be produced as conclusive evidence that the order was made on the date specified in the notice.

(3) Where an order of the court which is gazetted has been varied, and where any matter has been erroneously or inaccurately gazetted, the person whose responsibility it was to procure the requisite entry in the Gazette shall forthwith cause the variation of the order to be gazetted or, as the case may be, a further entry to be made in the Gazette for the purpose of correcting the error or inaccuracy.

[7.2424]
114 Punishment of offences

Section 431 (summary proceedings) of the 1986 Act, as it applies to England and Wales, has effect in relation to offences under these Rules as to offences under that Act.

PART 10
INTERPRETATION AND APPLICATION

[7.2425]
115 Introductory

This Part of these Rules has effect for their interpretation and application; and any definition given in this Part applies except in so far as the context otherwise requires.

[7.2426]
116 "The court"; "the registrar"

(1) Anything to be done in PPP administration proceedings by, to or before the court may be done by, to or before a judge or the registrar.

(2) The registrar may authorise any act of a formal or administrative character which is not by statute his responsibility to be carried out by the chief clerk or any other officer of the court acting on his behalf, in accordance with directions given by the Lord Chancellor.

(3) In PPP administration proceedings, "the registrar" means—
- (a) where the proceedings are in the District Registry of Birmingham, Bristol, Caernarfon, Cardiff, Leeds, Liverpool, Manchester, Mold, Newcastle-upon-Tyne or Preston, the District Judge; and
- (b) in all other cases, [an Insolvency and Companies Court Judge].

NOTES

Para (3): words in square brackets substituted by the Alteration of Judicial Titles (Registrar in Bankruptcy of the High Court) Order 2018, SI 2018/130, art 3, Schedule, para 12(1)(e).

[7.2427]
117 "Give notice" etc

(1) A reference in these Rules to giving notice means that the notice may be sent by post or by any means of electronic communication that is received, or readily accessible by the person to whom it is sent, in legible form.

(2) A reference in these Rules to delivering, sending or serving any document means that the document may be sent by post, unless under a particular rule personal service is expressly required.

(3) Personal service of a document is permissible in all cases.

(4) Notice of the venue fixed for an application may be given by service of the sealed copy of the application under rule 41(3).

[7.2428]
118 Notice, etc to solicitors

Where in PPP administration proceedings a notice or other document is required or authorised to be given to a person, it may, if he has indicated that his solicitor is authorised to accept service on his behalf, be given instead to the solicitor.

[7.2429]
119 Notice to joint special PPP administrators

Where 2 or more persons are acting jointly as the special PPP administrator in any proceedings, delivery of a document to one of them is to be treated as delivery to them all.

[7.2430]
120 "Petition"

"Petition" means a petition for a PPP administration order to be made in relation to a PPP company.

[7.2431]
121 "Venue"

References to the "venue" for any proceedings or attendance before the court, or for a meeting, are to the time, date and place for the proceedings, attendance or meeting.

[7.2432]
122 "PPP administration proceedings"

"PPP administration proceedings" means any proceedings under sections 220 to 224 of, and Schedule 14 to, the 1999 Act.

[7.2433]
123 "The appropriate fee"

"The appropriate fee" means 15 pence per A4 or A5 page and 30 pence per A3 page.

[7.2434]
124 Expressions used generally

(1) "File in court" means deliver to the court for filing.

(2) "The Gazette" means The London Gazette.

(3) "Business day" means any day other than a Saturday, a Sunday, Christmas Day, Good Friday or a day which is a bank holiday in any part of Great Britain under or by virtue of the Banking and Financial Dealings Act 1971.

[7.2435]
125 Application and transitional provision

(1) These Rules apply to PPP administration proceedings which—
- (a) commenced on or after the date on which these Rules come into force; or
- (b) commenced before that date but which are still in progress on that date, insofar as anything falling to be done under these Rules can be done under them on or after that date.

(2) Except as provided for in these Rules, nothing contained in the Insolvency Rules shall apply to such proceedings.

(3) Where, in relation to PPP administration proceedings to which paragraph (1)(b) applies, an act has been performed before the date on which these Rules come into force which, had it been performed on or after that date, would satisfy a requirement of these Rules, that act may be taken to satisfy that requirement.

SCHEDULE
FORMS

Rule 100

[7.2436]

NOTES

The forms themselves are not reproduced in this work, but their numbers and descriptions are listed below.

FORM NO	TITLE
PPP1	Petition for PPP administration order
PPP2	Consent of special PPP administrator
PPP3	Affidavit of service of petition for PPP administration order
PPP4	PPP administration order
PPP5	Notice to special PPP administrator of PPP administration order
PPP6	Notice of PPP administration order (for newspaper and London Gazette)

FORM NO	TITLE
PPP7	Notice of PPP administration order
PPP8	Notice of PPP administration order to the registrar of companies
PPP9	Notice of PPP discharge of PPP administration order
PPP10	Notice requiring preparation and submission of PPP administration statement of affairs
PPP11	Statement of affairs
PPP12	Affidavit of concurrence
PPP13	Statement of special PPP administrator's proposals
PPP14	Statement of special PPP administrator's revised proposals
PPP15	Notice of meetings in PPP administration proceedings
PPP16	Notice of order to deal with charged property
PPP17	Special PPP administrator's abstract of receipts and payments
PPP18	Notice to court of special PPP administrator's resignation under rule 36(1)
PPP19	Notice to court of special PPP administrator's resignation under rule 36(2)
PPP20	Application
PPP21	Appointment of shorthand writer
PPP22	Declaration by shorthand writer
PPP23	Order appointing person to act for incapacitated person
PPP24	Proxy

Q
RAILWAYS

RAILWAYS ACT 1993

(1993 c 43)

ARRANGEMENT OF SECTIONS

PART I
THE PROVISION OF RAILWAY SERVICES

59 Meaning and effect of railway administration order . . . . . . [7.2437]
60 Railway administration orders made on special petitions . . . . . . [7.2438]
61 Restriction on making winding-up order in respect of protected railway company. . . . . . . [7.2439]
62 Restrictions on voluntary winding up and insolvency proceedings in the case of protected railway companies . . . . . . [7.2440]
63 Government financial assistance where railway administration orders made . . . . . . [7.2441]
64 Guarantees under section 63. . . . . . [7.2442]
64A Financial assistance by Scottish Ministers . . . . . . [7.2443]
65 Meaning of "company" and application of provisions to unregistered, foreign and other companies . . . . . . [7.2444]

Interpretation

83 Interpretation of Part I . . . . . . [7.2445]

PART III
MISCELLANEOUS, GENERAL AND SUPPLEMENTAL PROVISIONS

Supplemental

151 General interpretation. . . . . . [7.2446]
154 Short title, commencement and extent . . . . . . [7.2447]

SCHEDULES

Schedule 6—Railway Administration Orders
Part I—Modifications of the 1986 Act . . . . . . [7.2448]
Part II—Further Modifications of the 1986 Act: Application in Relation to Foreign Companies . . . . . . [7.2449]
Part III—Supplemental . . . . . . [7.2450]
Schedule 7—Transfer of Relevant Activities in Connection with Railway Administration Orders. . . . [7.2451]

An Act to provide for the appointment and functions of a Rail Regulator and a Director of Passenger Rail Franchising and of users' consultative committees for the railway industry and for certain ferry services; to make new provision with respect to the provision of railway services and the persons by whom they are to be provided or who are to secure their provision; to make provision for and in connection with the grant and acquisition of rights over, and the disposal or other transfer and vesting of, any property, rights or liabilities by means of which railway services are, or are to be, provided; to amend the functions of the British Railways Board; to make provision with respect to the safety of railways and the protection of railway employees and members of the public from personal injury and other risks arising from the construction or operation of railways; to make further provision with respect to transport police; to make provision with respect to certain railway pension schemes; to make provision for and in connection with the payment of grants and subsidies in connection with railways and in connection with the provision of facilities for freight haulage by inland waterway; to make provision in relation to tramways and other guided transport systems; and for connected purposes

[5 November 1993]

PART I
THE PROVISION OF RAILWAY SERVICES

1–58 (*In so far as unrepealed, outside the scope of this work.*)

Railway administration orders, winding up and insolvency

[7.2437]
59 Meaning and effect of railway administration order
(1) A "railway administration order" is an order of the court made in accordance with section 60, 61 or 62 below in relation to a protected railway company and directing that, during the period for which the order is in force, the affairs, business and property of the company shall be managed, by a person appointed by the court—

(a) for the achievement of the purposes of such an order; and

Part 7Q Special Insolvency Regimes

(b) in a manner which protects the respective interests of the members and creditors of the company.

(2) The purposes of a railway administration order made in relation to any company shall be—

(a) the transfer to another company, or (as respects different parts of its undertaking) to two or more different companies, as a going concern, of so much of the company's undertaking as it is necessary to transfer in order to ensure that the relevant activities may be properly carried on; and

(b) the carrying on of those relevant activities pending the making of the transfer.

(3) Schedule 6 to this Act shall have effect for applying provisions of the Insolvency Act 1986 where a railway administration order is made.

(4) Schedule 7 to this Act shall have effect for enabling provision to be made with respect to cases in which, in pursuance of a railway administration order, another company is to carry on all or any of the relevant activities of a protected railway company in place of that company.

(5) Without prejudice to paragraph 20 of Schedule 6 to this Act, the power conferred by section 411 of the Insolvency Act 1986 to make rules shall apply for the purpose of giving effect to the railway administration order provisions of this Act as it applies for the purpose of giving effect to Parts I to VII of that Act, but taking any reference in that section to those Parts as a reference to those provisions.

(6) For the purposes of this Part—

[(za) "appropriate national authority"—

(i) in relation to a Scottish protected railway company or a company subject to a railway administration order that was such a company when the order was made, means the Scottish Ministers; and

(ii) in relation to any other protected railway company or company subject to a railway administration order, means the Secretary of State;]

(a) "protected railway company" means a company which is both a private sector operator and the holder of—

(i) a passenger licence [or a European licence which authorises the carriage of passengers by railway (or both)]; or

(ii) a network licence, a station licence or a light maintenance depot licence; . . .

(b) the "relevant activities", in relation to a protected railway company, are—

(i) in the case of a company which is the holder of a passenger licence [or a European licence which authorises the carriage of passengers by railway (or both)], the carriage of passengers by railway; or

(ii) in the case of a company which is the holder of a network licence, a station licence or a light maintenance depot licence, the management of a network, a station or a light maintenance depot, according to the description of licence in question.

[(c) "Scottish protected railway company" means a protected railway company that is such a company only in respect of activities carried on by it as franchise operator in relation to a Scottish franchise agreement].

(7) In this section—

"business" and "property" have the same meaning as they have in the Insolvency Act 1986;

["the court", in relation to a protected railway company, means the court—

(a) having jurisdiction to wind up the company, or

(b) that would have such jurisdiction apart from section 221(2) or 441(2) of the Insolvency Act 1986 (exclusion of winding up jurisdiction in case of companies having principal place of business in, or incorporated in, Northern Ireland);]

"the railway administration order provisions of this Act" means this section, sections 60 to 65 below and Schedules 6 and 7 to this Act.

NOTES

Sub-s (6): paras (za), (c) inserted, and word omitted from para (a) repealed, by the Railways Act 2005, ss 49(1), 59(6), Sch 13, Pt 1, for effect see s 49(10), (11) of that Act; words in square brackets in paras (a), (b) inserted by the Railway (Licensing of Railway Undertakings) Regulations 2005, SI 2005/3050, reg 3, Sch 1, para 3(1), (5), subject to transitional provisions in reg 20, Sch 4, paras 1–4, 8–14 thereto.

Sub-s (7): definition "the court" substituted by the Companies Act 2006 (Consequential Amendments, Transitional Provisions and Savings) Order 2009, SI 2009/1941, art 2(1), Sch 1, para 143(1), (3).

Rules: the Railway Administration Order Rules 2001, SI 2001/3352 at **[7.2452]**.

[7.2438]

60 Railway administration orders made on special petitions

[(1) If, on an application relating to a protected railway company] the court is satisfied that either or both of the grounds specified in subsection (2) below is satisfied in relation to that protected railway company, the court may make a railway administration order in relation to that company.

[(1A) An application under subsection (1) for the making of a railway administration order may be made—

(a) in the case of an application on the ground specified in paragraph (a) of subsection (2), only by the appropriate national authority; and

(b) in the case of an application on the ground specified in paragraph (b) of that subsection, only by the Secretary of State.]

(2) The grounds mentioned in subsection (1) above are, in relation to any company—

(a) that the company is or is likely to be unable to pay its debts;

(b) that, in a case in which the Secretary of State has certified that it would be appropriate for him to petition for the winding up of the company under section 124A of the 1986 Act (petition by the Secretary of State following inspectors' report etc), it would be just and equitable, as mentioned in that section, for the company to be wound up.

(3) Notice of any petition under this section for a railway administration order shall be given forthwith to such persons and in such manner as may be prescribed by rules made under section 411 of the 1986 Act; and no such petition shall be withdrawn except with the leave of the court.

(4) Subsections (4) and (5) of section 9 of the 1986 Act (powers on application for administration order) shall apply on the hearing of the petition for a railway administration order in relation to any company as they apply on the hearing of a petition for an administration order.

(5) Subsections (1), (2), (4) and (5) of section 10 of the 1986 Act (effect of petition) shall apply in the case of a petition for a railway administration order in relation to any company as if—

(a) the reference in subsection (1) to an administration order were a reference to a railway administration order;

(b) paragraph (b) of that subsection did require the leave of the court for the taking of any of the steps mentioned in paragraphs (b) and (c) of subsection (2) (appointment of, and exercise of functions by, administrative receiver); and

(c) the reference in paragraph (c) of subsection (1) to proceedings included a reference to any proceedings under or for the purposes of section 55 [or 57A] above.

(6) For the purposes of this section a company is unable to pay its debts if—

(a) it is a company which is deemed to be so unable under section 123 of the 1986 Act (definition of inability to pay debts); or

(b) it is an unregistered company, within the meaning of Part V of the 1986 Act, which is deemed, by virtue of any of sections 222 to 224 of that Act, to be so unable for the purposes of section 221 of that Act (winding up of unregistered companies).

(7) In this section—

"the 1986 Act" means the Insolvency Act 1986;

"the court" has the same meaning as in section 59 above.

NOTES

Sub-s (1): words in square brackets substituted by the Railways Act 2005, s 49(2), for effect see s 49(10), (11) of that Act.

Sub-s (1A): inserted by the Railways Act 2005, s 49(3), for effect see s 49(10), (11) of that Act.

Sub-s (5): words in square brackets in para (c) inserted by the Transport Act 2000, s 252, Sch 27, paras 17, 34.

[7.2439]

61 Restriction on making winding-up order in respect of protected railway company

(1) Where a petition for the winding up of a protected railway company is presented by a person other than the Secretary of State, the court shall not make a winding-up order in relation to that company on that petition unless—

(a) notice of the petition has been served on—

(i) the [appropriate national authority]; and

(ii) . . .

(b) a period of at least fourteen days has elapsed since the service of that notice.

(2) Where a petition for the winding up of a protected railway company has been presented—

(a) the [appropriate national authority], . . .

(b) . . .

may, at any time before a winding-up order is made on the petition, make an application to the court for a railway administration order in relation to that company; and where such an application is made the court may, if it is satisfied as mentioned in section 60(1) above, make a railway administration order instead of a winding-up order.

(3) Where, on a petition for the winding up of a protected railway company, the court makes, or proposes to make, a railway administration order by virtue of subsection (2) above, subsections (4) and (5) of section 9 of the Insolvency Act 1986 (powers on application for administration order) shall apply on the hearing of that petition as they apply on the hearing of a petition for an administration order.

(4) In this section "the court" has the same meaning as in section 59 above.

NOTES

Sub-s (1): words in square brackets in para (a)(i) substituted, and para (a)(ii) repealed, by the Railways Act 2005, ss 1(1), 49(4)(a), 59(6), Sch 1, Pt 1, para 27(1)(a), Sch 13, Pt 1, for effect see s 49(10), (11) of that Act.

Sub-s (2): words in square brackets substituted, and para (b) and word immediately preceding it repealed, by the Railways Act 2005, ss 1(1), 49(4)(a), 59(6), Sch 1, Pt 1, para 27(1)(a), Sch 13, Pt 1, for effect see s 49(10), (11) of that Act.

[7.2440]

62 Restrictions on voluntary winding up and insolvency proceedings in the case of protected railway companies

(1) No resolution for voluntary winding up shall be passed by a protected railway company without leave of the court granted on an application made for the purpose by the company.

(2) No such leave shall be granted unless—

(a) notice of the application has been served on—

(i) the [appropriate national authority]; and

(ii) . . .

(b) a period of at least fourteen days has elapsed since the service of that notice.

(3) Where an application for leave under subsection (1) above has been made by a protected railway company—

(a) the [appropriate national authority], . . .

(b) . . .

may, at any time before leave has been granted under subsection (1) above, make an application to the court for a railway administration order in relation to that company; and where such an application is made the court may, if it is satisfied as mentioned in section 60(1) above, make a railway administration order instead of granting leave under subsection (1) above.

(4) Where, on an application for leave under subsection (1) above, the court makes, or proposes to make, a railway administration order by virtue of subsection (3) above, subsections (4) and (5) of section 9 of the Insolvency Act 1986 (powers on application for administration order) shall apply on the hearing of that application as they apply on the hearing of a petition for an administration order.

(5) No administration order under Part II of the Insolvency Act 1986 shall be made in relation to a protected railway company unless—

(a) notice of the application for the order has been served on—

(i) the [appropriate national authority]; and

(ii) . . .

(b) a period of at least fourteen days has elapsed since the service of that notice.

(6) Where an application for an administration order under Part II of the Insolvency Act 1986 has been made in the case of a protected railway company—

(a) the [appropriate national authority], . . .

(b) . . .

may, at any time before such an order has been made on that application, make an application to the court for a railway administration order in relation to that company; and where such an application is made the court may, if it is satisfied as mentioned in section 60(1) above, make a railway administration order instead of an administration order under Part II of the Insolvency Act 1986.

(7) No step shall be taken by any person to enforce any security over a protected railway company's property, except where that person has served fourteen days' notice of his intention to take that step on—

(a) the [appropriate national authority]; . . .

(b) . . .

(8) In this section—

"the court" has the same meaning as in section 59 above;

"resolution for voluntary winding up" has the same meaning as in the Insolvency Act 1986;

"security" and "property" have the same meaning as in the Insolvency Act 1986.

NOTES

Sub-s (2): words in square brackets in para (a)(i) substituted, and para (a)(ii) repealed, by the Railways Act 2005, ss 1(1), 49(4)(b), 59(6), Sch 1, Pt 1, para 27(1)(b), Sch 13, Pt 1, for effect see s 49(10), (11) of that Act.

Sub-s (3): words in square brackets in para (a) substituted, and para (b) and word immediately preceding it repealed, by the Railways Act 2005, ss 1(1), 49(4)(b), 59(6), Sch 1, Pt 1, para 27(1)(b), Sch 13, Pt 1, for effect see s 49(10), (11) of that Act.

Sub-s (5): words in square brackets in para (a)(i) substituted, and para (a)(ii) repealed, by the Railways Act 2005, ss 1(1), 49(4)(b), 59(6), Sch 1, Pt 1, para 27(1)(b), Sch 13, Pt 1, for effect see s 49(10), (11) of that Act.

Sub-s (6): words in square brackets in para (a) substituted, and para (b) and word immediately preceding it repealed, by the Railways Act 2005, ss 1(1), 49(4)(b), 59(6), Sch 1, Pt 1, para 27(1)(b), Sch 13, Pt 1, for effect see s 49(10), (11) of that Act.

Sub-s (7): words in square brackets in para (a) substituted, and para (b) and word immediately preceding it repealed, by the Railways Act 2005, ss 1(1), 49(4)(b), 59(6), Sch 1, Pt 1, para 27(1)(b), Sch 13, Pt 1, for effect see s 49(10), (11) of that Act.

[7.2441]

63 Government financial assistance where railway administration orders made

(1) Where a railway administration order is for the time being in force in relation to a company [other than a Scottish protected railway company], the Secretary of State may, with the consent of the Treasury—

(a) make to the company grants or loans of such sums as appear to him to be appropriate for the purpose of facilitating the achievement of the purposes of the order;

[(b) agree to indemnify a relevant person in respect of—

(i) liabilities incurred by that person in connection with the carrying out by the railway administrator of his functions under the order; and

(ii) loss or damage incurred by that person in that connection.]

(2) The Secretary of State may, with the consent of the Treasury, guarantee, . . . , the repayment of the principal of, the payment of interest on and the discharge of any other financial obligation in connection with any sum which is borrowed from any person by a company [where that company—

(a) is a company in relation to which a railway administration order is in force at the time when the guarantee is given; and

(b) is not a Scottish protected railway company.]

[(2A) A grant, loan, indemnity or guarantee under this section may be made or given in whatever manner, and on whatever terms and subject to whatever conditions, the Secretary of State considers appropriate.]

(3) Without prejudice to any provision applied in relation to the company by Schedule 6 to this Act—

(a) the terms and conditions on which a grant is made to any company under this section may require the whole or a part of the grant to be repaid to the Secretary of State if there is a contravention of the other terms and conditions on which the grant is made; and

(b) any loans which the Secretary of State makes to a company under this section shall be repaid to him at such times and by such methods, and interest on the loans shall be paid to him at such rates and at such times, as he may, with the consent of the Treasury, from time to time direct.

[(3A) The power of the Secretary of State under this section to agree to indemnify a relevant person—

(a) is confined to a power to agree to indemnify that person in respect of liabilities, loss and damage incurred or sustained by him as a relevant person; but

(b) includes power to agree to indemnify persons (whether or not they are identified or identifiable at the time of the agreement) who subsequently become relevant persons.

(3B) A person is a relevant person for the purposes of this section if he is—

(a) the railway administrator;

(b) an employee of the railway administrator;

(c) a member or employee of a firm of which the railway administrator is a member;

(d) a member or employee of a firm of which the railway administrator is an employee;

(e) a member of a firm of which the railway administrator was an employee or member at a time when the order was in force;

(f) a body corporate which is the employer of the railway administrator; or

(g) an officer, employee or member of such a body corporate.

(3C) For the purposes of this section—

(a) the references in this section to the railway administrator, in relation to a railway administration order, are references to the person appointed to achieve the purposes of the order and, where two or more persons are so appointed, are to be construed as references to any one or more of them; and

(b) the references to a firm of which a person was a member or employee at a particular time include references to a firm which holds itself out to be the successor of a firm of which he was a member or employee at that time.]

(4) Any grant or loan made under this section and any sums required to be paid by the Secretary of State in respect of an indemnity given under this section shall be paid out of money provided by Parliament.

[(4A) If sums are paid by the Secretary of State in consequence of an indemnity agreed to under this section in the case of a company in relation to which a railway administration order is in force, the company must pay him—

(a) such amounts in or towards the repayment to him of those sums as he may direct; and

(b) interest, at such rates as he may direct, on amounts outstanding under this subsection.

(4B) Payments to the Secretary of State under subsection (4A) must be made at such times and in such manner as he may determine.

(4C) Subsection (4A) does not apply in the case of a sum paid by the Secretary of State for indemnifying a person in respect of a liability to the company in relation to which the railway administration order in question was made.

(4D) The consent of the Treasury is required for the giving of a direction under subsection (4A) and for the making of a determination under subsection (4B).]

(5) Any sums received under subsection (3) above by the Secretary of State shall be paid into the Consolidated Fund.

NOTES

Sub-s (1): words in square brackets inserted, and para (b) substituted, by the Railways Act 2005, ss 50(1)(a), 54(4), Sch 11, paras 1, 9(1).

Sub-s (2): words omitted repealed, and words in square brackets substituted, by the Railways Act 2005, ss 50(1)(b), 59(6), Sch 13, Pt 1.

Sub-ss (2A), (3A)–(3C), (4A)–(4D): inserted by the Railways Act 2005, s 54(4), Sch 11, paras 1, 9(2)–(4).

[7.2442]

64 Guarantees under section 63

(1) This section applies in relation to any guarantee given by the Secretary of State under section 63 above.

(2) Immediately after a guarantee to which this section applies is given, the Secretary of State shall lay a statement of the guarantee before each House of Parliament.

(3) Where any sum is paid out for fulfilling a guarantee to which this section applies, the Secretary of State shall, as soon as possible after the end of each financial year (beginning with that in which the sum is paid out and ending with that in which all liability in respect of the principal of the sum and in respect of the interest thereon is finally discharged), lay before each House of Parliament a statement relating to that sum.

(4) Any sums required by the Secretary of State for fulfilling a guarantee to which this section applies shall be paid out of money provided by Parliament.

(5) Without prejudice to any provision applied in relation to the relevant company by Schedule 6 to this Act, if any sums are paid out in fulfilment of a guarantee to which this section applies, the relevant company shall make to the Secretary of State, at such times and in such manner as the Secretary of State may from time to time direct—

(a) payments of such amounts as the Secretary of State may so direct in or towards repayment of the sums so paid out; and

(b) payments of interest, at such rate as the Secretary of State may so direct, on what is outstanding for the time being in respect of sums so paid out;

and the consent of the Treasury shall be required for the giving of a direction under this subsection.

(6) Any sums received by the Secretary of State under subsection (5) above shall be paid into the Consolidated Fund.

(7) In subsection (5) above "the relevant company" in relation to a guarantee, means the company which borrowed the sums in respect of which the guarantee was given.

[7.2443]

[64A Financial assistance by Scottish Ministers

(1) Where a railway administration order is for the time being in force in relation to a Scottish protected railway company, the Scottish Ministers may—

(a) make grants or loans to the company of such sums as appear to them to be appropriate for the purpose of facilitating the achievement of the purposes of the order; or

(b) agree to indemnify a relevant person in respect of—

(i) liabilities incurred by that person in connection with the carrying out by the railway administrator of his functions under the order; and

(ii) loss or damage incurred by that person in that connection.

(2) The Scottish Ministers may guarantee—

(a) the repayment of the principal of any sum borrowed by a Scottish protected railway company in relation to which a railway administration order is in force when the guarantee is given;

(b) the payment of interest on a sum so borrowed; and

(c) the discharge of any other financial obligation in relation to a sum so borrowed.

(3) A grant, loan, indemnity or guarantee under this section may be made or given in whatever manner, and on whatever terms and subject to whatever conditions, the Scottish Ministers consider appropriate.

(4) The terms on which a grant may be made under this section include, in particular, terms requiring the whole or a part of the grant to be repaid to the Scottish Ministers if there is a contravention of the other terms on which the grant is made.

(5) The terms on which a loan may be made under this section include, in particular, terms requiring—

(a) the loan to be repaid at such times and by such methods, and

(b) interest to be paid on the loan at such rates and at such times,

as the Scottish Ministers may from time to time direct.

(6) The power of the Scottish Ministers under this section to agree to indemnify a relevant person—

(a) is confined to a power to agree to indemnify that person in respect of liabilities, loss and damage incurred or sustained by him as a relevant person; but

(b) includes power to agree to indemnify persons (whether or not they are identified or identifiable at the time of the agreement) who subsequently become relevant persons.

(7) A person is a relevant person for the purposes of this section if he is—

(a) the railway administrator;

(b) an employee of the railway administrator;

(c) a member or employee of a firm of which the railway administrator is a member;

(d) a member or employee of a firm of which the railway administrator is an employee;

(e) a member of a firm of which the railway administrator was an employee or member at a time when the order was in force;

(f) a body corporate which is the employer of the railway administrator; or

(g) an officer, employee or member of such a body corporate.

(8) In this section—

(a) references to the railway administrator, in relation to a railway administration order, are references to the person appointed to achieve the purposes of the order and, where two or more persons are so appointed, are to be construed as references to any one or more of them; and

(b) the references to a firm of which a person was a member or employee at a particular time include references to a firm which holds itself out to be the successor of a firm of which he was a member or employee at that time.

(9) If sums are paid out by the Scottish Ministers in respect of an indemnity or guarantee under this section, the company in relation to which the indemnity or guarantee was given must pay them—

(a) such amounts in or towards the repayment to them of those sums as they may direct; and

(b) interest, at such rates as they may direct, on amounts outstanding under this subsection.

(10) Payments to the Scottish Ministers under subsection (9) must be made at such times and in such manner as they may determine.

(11) Subsection (9) does not apply in the case of a sum paid by the Scottish Ministers for indemnifying a person in respect of a liability to the company in relation to which the railway administration order in question was made.]

NOTES

Inserted by the Railways Act 2005, s 50(2).

[7.2444]

65 Meaning of "company" and application of provisions to unregistered, foreign and other companies

[(1) In the railway administration order provisions of this Act—

"company" means—

(a) a company registered under the Companies Act 2006, or

(b) an unregistered company; and

"unregistered company" means a company that is not registered under that Act.]

(2) In the application of section 59(1) above in a case where the protected railway company there mentioned is a foreign company, the reference to the affairs, business and property of the company shall be taken as a reference to the affairs and business of the company, so far as carried on in Great Britain, and the property of the company within Great Britain.

(3) In the application of section 9(5) of the 1986 Act by virtue of subsection (4) of section 60 above or subsection (3) of section 61 above where the petition mentioned in the subsection in question relates to a company which is a foreign company, the reference to restricting the exercise of any powers of the directors or of the company shall be taken as a reference to restricting—

(a) the exercise within Great Britain of the powers of the directors or of the company; or

(b) any exercise of those powers so far as relating to the affairs, business or property of the company in Great Britain.

(4) In the application of provisions in section 10 of the 1986 Act by virtue of subsection (5) of section 60 above where the company mentioned in that subsection is a foreign company—

(a) paragraph (a) of subsection (1) shall be omitted;

(b) any reference in paragraph (b) or (c) of that subsection to property or goods shall be taken as a reference to property or (as the case may be) goods for the time being situated within Great Britain;

(c) in paragraph (c) of that subsection—

(i) the reference to the commencement or continuation of proceedings shall be taken as a reference to the commencement or continuation of proceedings in Great Britain; and

(ii) the reference to the levying of distress against the company shall be taken as a reference to the levying of distress against the foreign company to the extent of its property in England and Wales; and

(d) any reference in subsection (2) to an administrative receiver shall be taken to include a reference to any person performing, in relation to the foreign company, functions equivalent to those of an administrative receiver, within the meaning of section 251 of the 1986 Act.

(5) Subsections (1) to (4) of section 62 above shall not have effect in relation to a protected railway company which is a foreign company.

(6) In the application of subsection (7) of that section where the protected railway company there mentioned is a foreign company, the reference to the company's property shall be taken as a reference to such of its property as is for the time being situated in Great Britain.

(7) In this section—

"the 1986 Act" means the Insolvency Act 1986;

"foreign company" means a company incorporated outside Great Britain;

"the railway administration order provisions of this Act" means sections 59 to 64 above, this section and Schedules 6 and 7 to this Act.

NOTES

Sub-s (1): substituted by the Companies Act 2006 (Consequential Amendments, Transitional Provisions and Savings) Order 2009, SI 2009/1941, art 2(1), Sch 1, para 143(1), (4).

66–80 *(In so far as unrepealed, outside the scope of this work.)*

Interpretation

81, 82 *(Outside the scope of this work.)*

[7.2445]

83 Interpretation of Part I

(1) In this Part, unless the context otherwise requires—

. . .

["appropriate national authority" has the meaning given by section 59(6)(za) above;]

. . .

"goods" includes mail, parcels, animals, plants and any other creature, substance or thing capable of being transported, but does not include passengers;

. . .

"light maintenance depot" means any land or other property which is normally used for or in connection with the provision of light maintenance services, whether or not it is also used for other purposes;

"light maintenance depot licence" means a licence authorising a person—

(a) to be the operator of a light maintenance depot; and

(b) to be the operator of a train being used on a network for a purpose preparatory or incidental to, or consequential on, the provision of light maintenance services;

. . .

"network" means—

(a) any railway line, or combination of two or more railway lines, and

(b) any installations associated with any of the track comprised in that line or those lines,

together constituting a system of track and other installations which is used for and in connection with the support, guidance and operation of trains;

"network licence" means a licence authorising a person—

(a) to be the operator of a network;

(b) to be the operator of a train being used on a network for any purpose comprised in the operation of that network; and

(c) to be the operator of a train being used on a network for a purpose preparatory or incidental to, or consequential on, using a train as mentioned in paragraph (b) above;

. . .

"passenger licence" means a licence authorising a person—

(a) to be the operator of a train being used on a network for the purpose of carrying passengers by railway; and

(b) to be the operator of a train being used on a network for a purpose preparatory or incidental to, or consequential on, using a train as mentioned in paragraph (a) above;

. . .

"private sector operator" means any body or person other than a public sector operator;

. . .

"station" means any land or other property which consists of premises used as, or for the purposes of, or otherwise in connection with, a railway passenger station or railway passenger terminal (including any approaches, forecourt, cycle store or car park), whether or not the land or other property is, or the premises are, also used for other purposes;

"station licence" means a licence authorising a person to be the operator of a station;

. . .

[(1A)], (2), [(3)] (*Outside the scope of this work.*)

NOTES

Sub-s (1): definition "appropriate national authority" inserted by the Railways Act 2005, s 54(4), Sch 11, paras 1, 13(a); definitions omitted outside the scope of this work.

84–116 ((*Pt II*) *outside the scope of this work.*)

PART III
MISCELLANEOUS, GENERAL AND SUPPLEMENTAL PROVISIONS

117–142 (*In so far as unrepealed, outside the scope of this work.*)

Supplemental

143–150 (*Outside the scope of this work.*)

[7.2446]

151 General interpretation

(1) In this Act, unless the context otherwise requires—

[. . .]

. . .

"contravention", in relation to any direction, condition, requirement, regulation or order, includes any failure to comply with it and cognate expressions shall be construed accordingly;

. . .

"functions" includes powers, duties and obligations;

. . .

"notice" means notice in writing;

. . .

(2)–(9) (*Outside the scope of this work.*)

NOTES

Sub-s (1): definition "the Authority" (omitted) inserted by the Transport Act 2000, s 252, Sch 27, paras 17, 43 and repealed by the Railways Act 2005, s 59(6), Sch 13, Pt 1; other definitions omitted outside the scope of this work.

152, 153 (*Outside the scope of this work.*)

[7.2447]

154 Short title, commencement and extent

(1) This Act may be cited as the Railways Act 1993.

(2) Except for section 1 and Schedule 1 (which come into force on the passing of this Act), this Act shall come into force on such day as may be specified in an order made by the Secretary of State; and different days may be so specified—

(a) for different provisions;

(b) for different purposes of the same provision; and

(c) for different areas within the United Kingdom.

(3), (4) (*Outside the scope of this work.*)

NOTES

Orders: at present 4 commencement orders have been made under this section. The orders relevant to the provisions of this Act reproduced in this work are the Railways Act 1993 (Commencement No 1) Order 1993, SI 1993/3237; the Railways Act 1993 (Commencement No 3) Order 1994, SI 1994/447; the Railways Act 1993 (Commencement No 4 and Transitional Provision) Order 1994, SI 1994/571.

SCHEDULES

SCHEDULES 1–5

(Schs 1–5 in so far as unrepealed, outside the scope of this work.)

SCHEDULE 6
RAILWAY ADMINISTRATION ORDERS

Section 59

PART I
MODIFICATIONS OF THE 1986 ACT

General application of provisions of 1986 Act

[7.2448]
1. Where a railway administration order has been made, sections 11 to 23 and 27 of the 1986 Act (which relate to administration orders under Part II of that Act) shall apply, with the modifications specified in the following provisions of this Part of this Schedule—

(a) as if references in those sections to an administration order were references to a railway administration order and references to an administrator were references to a special railway administrator;

[(aa) as if references in those sections to the appropriate national authority were to be construed in accordance with section 59(6)(za) of this Act;] and

(b) where the company in relation to which the order has been made is a protected railway company which [is not a company registered under the Companies Act 2006 in England and Wales or Scotland], as if references in those sections to a company included references to such a company.

Effect of order

2. In section 11 of the 1986 Act (effect of order), as applied by this Part of this Schedule—

(a) the requirement in subsection (1)(a) that any petition for the winding up of the company shall be dismissed shall be without prejudice to the railway administration order in a case where the order is made by virtue of section 61 of this Act; and

(b) the reference in subsection (3)(d) to proceedings shall include a reference to any proceedings under or for the purposes of section 55 [or 57A] of this Act.

Appointment of special railway administrator

3. In section 13 of the 1986 Act (appointment of administrator), as applied by this Part of this Schedule, for subsection (3) there shall be substituted the following subsection—

"(3) An application for an order under subsection (2) may be made—

(a) by the [appropriate national authority];

(b) . . .

(c) by any continuing special railway administrator of the company or, where there is no such special railway administrator, by the company, the directors or any creditor or creditors of the company."

General powers of special railway administrator

4. In section 14 of the 1986 Act (general powers of administrator), as applied by this Part of this Schedule—

(a) in subsection (1)(b), the reference to the powers specified in Schedule 1 to that Act shall be taken to include a reference to a power to act on behalf of the company for the purposes of this Act or any provision of a local or private Act which confers any power, or imposes any duty or obligation, on the company; and

(b) in subsection (4), the reference to a power conferred by the company's [articles of association]—

(i) shall be taken to include a reference to any power conferred by any provision of a local or private Act which confers any power, or imposes any duty or obligation, on the company; and

(ii) in the case of a company which is an unregistered company, shall be taken also to include a reference to any power conferred by the company's constitution.

Power to deal with charged property

5. (1) Section 15 of the 1986 Act (power to deal with charged property), as applied by this Part of this Schedule, shall have effect as follows.

(2) In subsection (5)(b) (amount to be paid to chargeholder not to be less than open market value), for the words "in the open market by a willing vendor" there shall be substituted the words "for the best price which is reasonably available on a sale which is consistent with the purposes of the railway administration order".

Duties of special railway administrator

6. (1) Section 17 of the 1986 Act (duties of administrator), as applied by this Part of this Schedule, shall have effect in accordance with the following provisions of this paragraph.

(2) For subsection (2) there shall be substituted the following subsection—

"(2) Subject to any directions of the court, it shall be the duty of the special railway administrator to manage the affairs, business and property of the company in accordance with proposals, as for the time being revised under section 23, which have been prepared for the purposes of that section by him or any predecessor of his."

(3) In subsection (3), paragraph (a) (right of creditors to require the holding of a creditors' meeting) shall be omitted.

Discharge of order

7. (1) Section 18 of the 1986 Act (discharge and variation of administration order), as applied by this Part of this Schedule, shall have effect as follows.

(2) For subsections (1) and (2) there shall be substituted the following subsection—

"(1) An application for a railway administration order to be discharged may be made—

(a) by the special railway administrator, on the ground that the purposes of the order have been achieved; or

(b) by the [appropriate national authority] . . . , on the ground that it is no longer necessary that the purposes of the order are achieved."

(3) In subsection (3), the words "or vary" shall be omitted.

(4) In subsection (4), the words "or varied" and "or variation" shall be omitted and for the words "to the registrar of companies" there shall be substituted—

["(a) where the company—

(i) is registered under the Companies Act 2006, or

(ii) is subject to a requirement imposed by regulations under section 1043 or 1046 of the Companies Act 2006 (unregistered UK companies or overseas companies) to deliver any documents to the registrar of companies,

the words "to [the Office of Rail and Road], the appropriate national authority and the registrar of companies"; and

(b) where paragraph (a) above does not apply, the words "to [the Office of Rail and Road] and the appropriate national authority"."]

Notice of making of order

8. In section 21(2) of the 1986 Act (notice of order to be given by administrator), as applied by this Part of this Schedule, for the words "to the registrar of companies" there shall be substituted—

["(a) where the company—

(i) is registered under the Companies Act 2006, or

(ii) is subject to a requirement imposed by regulations under section 1043 or 1046 of the Companies Act 2006 (unregistered UK companies or overseas companies) to deliver any documents to the registrar of companies,

the words "to [the Office of Rail and Road], the appropriate national authority and the registrar of companies"; and

(b) where paragraph (a) above does not apply, the words "to [the Office of Rail and Road] and the appropriate national authority"."]

Statement of proposals

9. In section 23 of the 1986 Act (statement of proposals), as applied by this Part of this Schedule, for subsections (1) and (2) there shall be substituted the following subsections—

"(1) Where a railway administration order has been made, the special railway administrator shall, within 3 months (or such longer period as the court may allow) after the making of the order, send a statement of his proposals for achieving the purposes of the order—

(a) to the [appropriate national authority];

(b) to [the Office of Rail and Road];

(c) . . .

(d) so far as he is aware of their addresses, to all creditors of the company; and

(e) except where the company is an unregistered company which is not subject to a requirement imposed under or by virtue of section 691(1) or 718 of the Companies Act 1985 to deliver any documents to the registrar of companies, to the registrar of companies;

and may from time to time revise those proposals.

(2) If at any time—

(a) the special railway administrator proposes to make revisions of the proposals for achieving the purposes of the railway administration order, and

(b) those revisions appear to him to be substantial,

the special railway administrator shall, before making those revisions, send a statement of the proposed revisions to the persons specified in subsection (2A).

(2A) The persons mentioned in subsection (2) are—

(a) the Secretary of State;

(b) [the Office of Rail and Road];

(c) . . .

(d) all creditors of the company, so far as the special railway administrator is aware of their addresses; and

[(e) where the company—

(i) is registered under the Companies Act 2006, or

(ii) is subject to a requirement imposed by regulations under section 1043 or 1046 of the Companies Act 2006 (unregistered UK companies or overseas companies) to deliver any documents to the registrar of companies,

the registrar of companies.]

(2B) Where the special railway administrator is required by subsection (1) or (2) to send any person a statement before the end of any period or before making any revision of any proposals, he shall also, before the end of that period or, as the case may be, before making those revisions either—

(a) send a copy of the statement (so far as he is aware of their addresses) to all members of the company; or

(b) publish in the prescribed manner a notice stating an address to which members should write for copies of the statement to be sent to them free of charge."

Applications to court

10. (1) Section 27 of the 1986 Act (protection of interests of creditors and members), as applied by this Part of this Schedule, shall have effect as follows.

(2) After subsection (1) there shall be inserted the following subsections—

"(1A) At any time when a railway administration order is in force the [appropriate national authority] . . . may apply to the High Court or the Court of Session by petition for an order under this section on the ground specified in subsection (1B).

(1B) The ground mentioned in subsection (1A) is that the special railway administrator has exercised or is exercising, or proposing to exercise, his powers in relation to the company in a manner which—

(a) will not best ensure the achievement of the purposes of the order; or

(b) without prejudice to paragraph (a) above, involves a contravention of any of the conditions of any licence under Part I of the Railways Act 1993 held by the company.

(1C) Where an application is made under subsection (1) in respect of a company in relation to which a railway administration order is in force—

(a) notice of the application shall be given to the [appropriate national authority]; and

(b) he shall be entitled to be heard by the court in connection with that application."

(3) Subsection (3) (order not to prejudice or prevent voluntary arrangements or administrator's proposals) shall be omitted.

(4) In subsection (4) (provision that may be made in an order), the words "Subject as above" shall be omitted and for paragraph (d) there shall be substituted—

"(d) without prejudice to the powers exercisable by the court in making a railway administration order—

(i) provide that the railway administration order is to be discharged as from such date as may be specified in the order unless, before that date, such measures are taken as the court thinks fit for the purpose of protecting the interests of creditors; and

(ii) make such consequential provision as the court thinks fit."

(5) For subsection (6) there shall be substituted—

"(6) Where a railway administration order is discharged in consequence of such provision in an order under this section as is mentioned in subsection (4)(d)(i), the special railway administrator shall, within 14 days after the date on which the discharge takes effect, send [a copy] of the order under this section—

(a) to [the Office of Rail and Road];

(b) to the [Strategic Rail Authority]; and

[(c) where the company—

(i) is registered under the Companies Act 2006, or

(ii) is subject to a requirement imposed by regulations under section 1043 or 1046 of the Companies Act 2006 (unregistered UK companies or overseas companies) to deliver any documents to the registrar of companies,

to the registrar of companies.]

and if, without reasonable excuse, the special railway administrator fails to comply with this subsection, he is liable to a fine and, for continued contravention, to a daily default fine."

Particular powers of special railway administrator

11. In the application of Schedule 1 to the 1986 Act (which sets out certain powers of the administrator) by virtue of section 14 of that Act, as applied by this Part of this Schedule in relation to a company which is an unregistered company, paragraph 22 shall be omitted.

NOTES

Para 1: sub-para (aa) inserted by the Railways Act 2005, s 49(5), for effect see s 49(10), (11) of that Act; words in square brackets in sub-para (b) substituted by the Companies Act 2006 (Consequential Amendments, Transitional Provisions and Savings) Order 2009, SI 2009/1941, art 2(1), Sch 1, para 143(1), (7)(a).

Para 2: words in square brackets in sub-para (b) inserted by the Transport Act 2000, s 252, Sch 27, paras 17, 48.

Para 3: in the Insolvency Act 1986, s 13(3), as set out, words in square brackets in para (a) substituted, and para (b) repealed, by the Railways Act 2005, ss 49(4)(c), 59(6), Sch 13, Pt 1, for effect see ss 1(1), 49(10), (11) of, and Sch 1, para 27(2) to, that Act.

Para 4: words in square brackets in sub-para (b) substituted by SI 2009/1941, art 2(1), Sch 1, para 143(1), (7)(b).

Para 7: in the Insolvency Act 1986, s 18(1), as set out, words in square brackets substituted, and words omitted repealed, by the Railways Act 2005, ss 49(4)(c), 59(6), Sch 13, Pt 1, for effect see ss 1(1), 49(10), (11) of, and Sch 1, para 27(2) to, that Act; in s 18(4), as set out, words in square brackets substituted by SI 2009/1941, art 2(1), Sch 1, para 143(1), (7)(c). In sub-para (4) words "the Office of Rail and Road" in square brackets in each place substituted by the Office of Rail Regulation (Change of Name) Regulations 2015, SI 2015/1682, reg 2(2), Schedule, Pt 1, para 1(ddd).

Para 8: in the Insolvency Act 1986, s 21(2), as set out, sub-paras (a), (b) in square brackets substituted by SI 2009/1941, art 2(1), Sch 1, para 143(1), (7)(c); words "the Office of Rail and Road" in square brackets substituted by SI 2015/1682, reg 2(2), Schedule, Pt 1, para 1(ddd).

Para 9: in the Insolvency Act 1986, s 23(1), as set out, words in square brackets in para (a) substituted, and para (c) repealed, by the Railways Act 2005, ss 49(4)(c), 59(6), Sch 13, Pt 1, for effect see ss 1(1), 49(10), (11) of, and Sch 1, para 27(2) to, that Act, words "the Office of Rail and Road" in square brackets substituted by SI 2015/1682, reg 2(2), Schedule, Pt 1, para 1(ddd); in s 23(2A), as set out, words "the Office of Rail and Road" in square brackets substituted by SI 2015/1682, reg 2(2), Schedule, Pt 1, para 1(ddd), para (c) repealed by the Railways Act 2005, s 59(6), Sch 13, Pt 1, for effect see s 1(1) of, and Sch 1, para 27(2) to, that Act, and para (e) substituted by SI 2009/1941, art 2(1), Sch 1, para 143(1), (7)(d).

Para 10: in the Insolvency Act 1986, s 27(1A), as set out, words in square brackets substituted, and words omitted repealed, by the Railways Act 2005, ss 49(4)(c), 59(6), Sch 13, Pt 1, for effect see ss 1(1), 49(10), (11) of, and Sch 1, para 27(2) to, that Act; in s 27(1C), as set out, words in square brackets substituted by the Railways Act 2005, s 49(4)(c), for effect see s 49(1), (11) of that Act; in s 27(6), as set out above, words in first pair of square brackets and sub-para (c) substituted by SI 2009/1941, art 2(1), Sch 1, para 143(1), (7)(e), words in square brackets in sub-para (a) substituted by the Railways and Transport Safety Act 2003, s 16(5), Sch 2, Pt 1, paras 1, 18, for savings see Sch 3 to that Act, and words in square brackets in sub-para (b) substituted by the Transport Act 2000, s 215(1), Sch 16, paras 2, 7; words "the Office of Rail and Road" in square brackets substituted by SI 2015/1682, reg 2(2), Schedule, Pt 1, para 1(ddd).

Note that the Insolvency Act 1986, Pt II (ss 8–27) is substituted by the Enterprise Act 2002, s 248(1), subject to savings and transitional provisions (i) in a case where a petition for an administration order has been presented before 15 September 2003 (see the Enterprise Act 2002 (Commencement No 4 and Transitional Provisions and Savings) Order 2003, SI 2003/2093, art 3 at **[2.26]**), and (ii) in relation to special administration regimes (see s 249 of the 2002 Act at **[2.10]**). The administration of companies is now dealt with in Sch B1 to the 1986 Act at **[1.575]**.

PART II
FURTHER MODIFICATIONS OF THE 1986 ACT: APPLICATION IN RELATION TO FOREIGN COMPANIES

Introductory

[7.2449]

12. (1) Where a railway administration order has been made in relation to a company which is a foreign company, sections 11 to 23 and 27 of the 1986 Act (as applied by Part I of this Schedule) shall apply in relation to that foreign company with the further modifications set out in the following provisions of this Part of this Schedule.

(2) In this Part of this Schedule, "foreign company" means a company incorporated outside Great Britain.

Effect of order

13. (1) Section 11 of the 1986 Act (effect of administration order), as applied by this Part of this Schedule in relation to a foreign company, shall have effect as follows.

(2) In subsection (1), paragraph (b) shall be omitted.

(3) Subsection (2) shall be omitted.

(4) In subsection (3)—

(a) paragraphs (a) and (b) shall be omitted; and

(b) in paragraph (d)—

(i) the reference to the commencement or continuation of proceedings shall be taken as a reference to the commencement or continuation of proceedings in Great Britain; and

(ii) the reference to the levying of distress against the company shall be taken as a reference to the levying of distress against the foreign company to the extent of its property in England and Wales;

and any reference to property or goods shall be taken as a reference to property or (as the case may be) goods for the time being situated within Great Britain.

(5) Subsections (4) and (5) shall be omitted.

(6) At the end of that section there shall be added—

"(6) Where a railway administration order is in force in relation to a company which is a foreign company within the meaning of section 65 of the Railways Act 1993—

(a) any person appointed to perform functions equivalent to those of an administrative receiver, and

(b) if the special railway administrator so requires, any person appointed to perform functions equivalent to those of a receiver,

shall refrain from performing those functions in Great Britain in relation to the foreign company and any of the company's property for the time being situated in Great Britain, during the period for which that order is in force or, in the case of such a person as is mentioned in paragraph (b) above, during so much of that period as falls after the date on which he is required to do so.".

Notification of order

14. In section 12 of the 1986 Act (notification of order), as applied by this Part of this Schedule in relation to a foreign company, the reference to a statement that the affairs, business and property of the company are being managed by the administrator shall be taken as a reference to a statement that—

(a) the affairs and business of the foreign company so far as carried on in Great Britain, and

(b) the property of the foreign company so far as that property is for the time being situated within Great Britain,

are being managed by the special railway administrator.

General powers of special railway administrator

15. (1) Section 14 of the 1986 Act (general powers of administrator), as applied by this Part of this Schedule in relation to a foreign company, shall have effect as follows.

(2) In subsection (1)(a), the reference to the affairs, business and property of the company shall be taken as a reference to—

(a) the affairs and business of the foreign company so far as carried on in Great Britain, and

(b) the property of that company so far as that property is for the time being situated within Great Britain.

(3) Subsection (2)(a) shall be omitted.

(4) In subsection (4)—

(a) the reference to any power conferred on the company or its officers shall be taken to include any power conferred on the foreign company or its officers under the law under which the foreign company is incorporated; and

(b) any reference (however expressed) to the exercise of any power conferred on the company or its officers shall be taken as a reference to the exercise of that power so far as it relates to—

(i) the affairs and business of the foreign company so far as carried on in Great Britain, or

(ii) the property of that company so far as that property is for the time being situated within Great Britain.

Power to deal with charged property

16. In section 15 of the 1986 Act (power of administrator to deal with charged property etc), as applied by this Part of this Schedule in relation to a foreign company, any reference to property or goods shall be taken as a reference to property or (as the case may be) goods for the time being situated within Great Britain.

Duties of special railway administrator

17. In section 17 of the 1986 Act (general duties of administrator), as applied by this Part of this Schedule in relation to a foreign company—

(a) in subsection (1), the reference to property shall be taken as a reference to property for the time being situated within Great Britain; and

(b) in subsection (2), the reference to the affairs, business and property of the company shall be taken as a reference to—

(i) the affairs and business of the foreign company so far as carried on in Great Britain, and

(ii) the property of that company so far as that property is for the time being situated within Great Britain.

Statement as to company's affairs

18. In section 22(1) of the 1986 Act (power of administrator to require certain persons to provide him with a statement as to company's affairs), as applied by this Part of this Schedule in relation to a foreign company, the reference to the affairs of the company shall be taken as a reference to the affairs of the foreign company so far as they are carried on in Great Britain, or relate to property of that company for the time being situated within Great Britain.

Particular powers of special railway administrator

19. (1) The powers conferred on a special railway administrator by virtue of Schedule 1 to the 1986 Act (which sets out certain powers of an administrator), as that Schedule applies by virtue of section 14 of that Act, as applied by this Part of this Schedule in relation to a foreign company, shall be exercisable only in relation to—

(a) the affairs and business of that company, so far as carried on in Great Britain; and

(b) the property of that company, so far as that property is for the time being situated within Great Britain.

(2) In that Schedule, as it so applies—

(a) without prejudice to sub-paragraph (1) above, references to the property of that company shall be taken as references to that property, so far as that property is for the time being situated within Great Britain; and

(b) paragraph 19 shall be omitted.

NOTES

Note that the Insolvency Act 1986, Pt II (ss 8–27) is substituted by the Enterprise Act 2002, s 248(1), subject to savings and transitional provisions (i) in a case where a petition for an administration order has been presented before 15 September 2003 (see the Enterprise Act 2002 (Commencement No 4 and Transitional Provisions and Savings) Order 2003, SI 2003/2093, art 3 at **[2.26]**), and (ii) in relation to special administration regimes (see s 249 of the 2002 Act at **[2.10]**). The administration of companies is now dealt with in Sch B1 to the 1986 Act at **[1.575]**.

PART III
SUPPLEMENTAL

General adaptations and saving

[7.2450]

20. (1) Subject to the preceding provisions of this Schedule, references in the 1986 Act (except in sections 8 to 10 and 24 to 26), or in any other enactment passed before this Act, to an administration order under Part II of that Act, to an application for such an order and to an administrator shall include references, respectively, to a railway administration order, to an application for a railway administration order and to a special railway administrator.

(2) Subject as aforesaid and to sub-paragraph (3) below, references in the 1986 Act, or in any other enactment passed before this Act, to an enactment contained in Part II of that Act shall include references to that enactment as applied by section 60, 61, 62 or 65 of this Act or Part I or II of this Schedule.

(3) Sub-paragraphs (1) and (2) above shall apply in relation to a reference in an enactment contained in Part II of the 1986 Act only so far as necessary for the purposes of the operation of the provisions of that Part as so applied.

(4) The provisions of this Schedule shall be without prejudice to the power conferred by section 411 of the 1986 Act (company insolvency rules), as modified by sub-paragraphs (1) and (2) above.

Interpretation

21. (1) In this Schedule "the 1986 Act" means the Insolvency Act 1986.

(2) In this Schedule, and in any modification of the 1986 Act made by this Schedule, "special railway administrator", in relation to a railway administration order, means any person appointed in relation to that order for the purposes of section 59(1) of this Act; and in any such modification "railway administration order" has the same meaning as in this Act.

NOTES

Note that the Insolvency Act 1986, Pt II (ss 8–27) is substituted by the Enterprise Act 2002, s 248(1), subject to savings and transitional provisions (i) in a case where a petition for an administration order has been presented before 15 September 2003 (see the Enterprise Act 2002 (Commencement No 4 and Transitional Provisions and Savings) Order 2003, SI 2003/2093, art 3 at **[2.26]**), and (ii) in relation to special administration regimes (see s 249 of the 2002 Act at **[2.10]**). The administration of companies is now dealt with in Sch B1 to the 1986 Act at **[1.575]**.

SCHEDULE 7
TRANSFER OF RELEVANT ACTIVITIES IN CONNECTION WITH RAILWAY ADMINISTRATION ORDERS

Section 59

Application of Schedule

[7.2451]

1. (1) This Schedule shall apply in any case where—

(a) the court has made a railway administration order in relation to a protected railway company ("the existing appointee"); and

(b) it is proposed that, on and after a date appointed by the court, another company ("the new appointee") should carry on the relevant activities of the existing appointee, in place of the existing appointee.

(2) In this Schedule—

"the court", in the case of any protected railway company, means the court having jurisdiction to wind up the company;

"other appointee" means any company, other than the existing appointee or the new appointee, which is the holder of a licence under section 8 of this Act [or of a European licence] and which may be affected by the proposal mentioned in sub-paragraph (1)(b) above;

"the relevant date" means such day, being a day before the discharge of the railway administration order takes effect, as the court may appoint for the purposes of this Schedule; and "special railway administrator", in relation to a company in relation to which a railway administration order has been made, means the person for the time being holding office for the purposes of section 59(1) of this Act.

(3) Any reference in this Schedule to "assignment" shall be construed in Scotland as a reference to assignation.

Making and modification of transfer schemes

2. (1) The existing appointee, acting with the consent of the new appointee and, in relation to the matters affecting them, of any other appointees, may make a scheme under this Schedule for the transfer of property, rights and liabilities from the existing appointee to the new appointee.

(2) A scheme under this Schedule shall not take effect unless it is approved by [the appropriate national authority].

(3) Where a scheme under this Schedule is submitted to [the appropriate national authority, it] may, with the consent of the new appointee, of the existing appointee and, in relation to the matters affecting them, of any other appointees, modify the scheme before approving it.

(4) If at any time after a scheme under this Schedule has come into force in relation to the property, rights and liabilities of any company [the appropriate national authority] considers it appropriate to do so and the existing appointee, the new appointee and, in relation to the provisions of the order which affect them, any other appointees consent to the making of the order, [the appropriate national authority] may by order provide that that scheme shall for all purposes be deemed to have come into force with such modifications as may be specified in the order.

(5) An order under sub-paragraph (4) above may make, with effect from the coming into force of the scheme to which it relates, any such provision as could have been made by the scheme and, in connection with giving effect to that provision from that time, may contain such supplemental, consequential and transitional provision as [the appropriate national authority] considers appropriate.

(6) In determining, in accordance with [the appropriate national authority's] duties under Part I of this Act, whether and in what manner to exercise any power conferred on [the appropriate national authority] by this paragraph [the appropriate national authority], shall have regard to the need to ensure that any provision for the transfer of property, rights and liabilities in accordance with a scheme under this Schedule allocates property, rights and liabilities to the different companies affected by the scheme in such proportions as appear to [the appropriate national authority] to be appropriate in the context of the different relevant activities of the existing appointee which will, by virtue of this Act, be carried out at different times on and after the relevant date by the new appointee, by the existing appointee and by any other appointees.

(7) It shall be the duty of the new appointee, of the existing appointee and of any other appointees to provide [the appropriate national authority] with all such information and other assistance as [the appropriate national authority] may reasonably require for the purposes of, or in connection with, the exercise of any power conferred . . . by this paragraph.

(8) Without prejudice to the other provisions of this Act relating to the special railway administrator of a company, anything which is required by this paragraph to be done by a company shall, where that company is a company in relation to which a railway administration order is in force, be effective only if it is done on the company's behalf by its special railway administrator.

[(9) A statutory instrument containing an order under this paragraph by the Scottish Ministers is subject to annulment in pursuance of a resolution of the Scottish Parliament.]

Transfers by scheme

3. (1) A scheme under this Schedule for the transfer of the existing appointee's property, rights and liabilities shall come into force on the relevant date and, on coming into force, shall have effect, in accordance with its provisions and without further assurance, so as to transfer the property, rights and liabilities to which the scheme relates to the new appointee.

(2) For the purpose of making any division of property, rights or liabilities which it is considered appropriate to make in connection with the transfer of property, rights and liabilities in accordance with a scheme under this Schedule, the provisions of that scheme may—

- (a) create for the existing appointee, the new appointee or any other appointees an interest in or right over any property to which the scheme relates;
- (b) create new rights and liabilities as between any two or more of those companies; and
- (c) in connection with any provision made by virtue of paragraph (a) or (b) above, make incidental provision as to the interests, rights and liabilities of other persons with respect to the subject-matter of the scheme.

(3) The property, rights and liabilities of the existing appointee that shall be capable of being transferred in accordance with a scheme under this Schedule shall include—

- (a) property, rights and liabilities that would not otherwise be capable of being transferred or assigned by the existing appointee;
- (b) such property, rights and liabilities to which the existing appointee may become entitled or subject after the making of the scheme and before the relevant date as may be described in the scheme;
- (c) property situated anywhere in the United Kingdom or elsewhere;
- (d) rights and liabilities under the law of any part of the United Kingdom or of any country or territory outside the United Kingdom.

(4) The provision that may be made by virtue of sub-paragraph (2)(b) above includes—

(a) provision for treating any person who is entitled by virtue of a scheme under this Schedule to possession of a document as having given another person an acknowledgement in writing of the right of that other person to the production of the document and to delivery of copies thereof;

(b) provision applying section 64 of the Law of Property Act 1925 (production and safe custody of documents) in relation to any case in relation to which provision falling within paragraph (a) above has effect; and

(c) provision that where a scheme under this Schedule transfers any interest in land or other property situated in Scotland, subsections (1) and (2) of section 16 of the Land Registration (Scotland) Act 1979 (omission of certain clauses in deeds) shall have effect in relation to the transfer as if the transfer had been effected by deed and as if from each of those subsections the words "unless specially qualified" were omitted.

(5) For the avoidance of doubt, it is hereby declared that the transfers authorised by paragraph (a) of sub-paragraph (3) above include transfers which, by virtue of that paragraph, are to take effect as if there were no such contravention, liability or interference with any interest or right as there would be, in the case of a transfer or assignment otherwise than in accordance with a scheme under this Schedule, by reason of any provision having effect (whether under any enactment or agreement or otherwise) in relation to the terms on which the existing appointee is entitled or subject to the property, right or liability in question.

Transfer of licences

4. (1) A scheme under this Schedule may provide for a licence held by the existing appointee to have effect as if it had been granted to the new appointee.

(2) Different schemes under this Schedule may provide for a licence held by the same existing appointee to have effect as if it had been granted as a separate licence to each of the new appointees under those schemes.

[(3) Sub-paragraphs (1) and (2) have effect in relation to a European licence as they have effect in relation to a licence.]

Supplemental provisions of schemes

5. (1) A scheme under this Schedule may contain supplemental, consequential and transitional provision for the purposes of, or in connection with, the provision for the transfers or any other provision made by the scheme.

(2) Without prejudice to the generality of sub-paragraph (1) above, a scheme under this Schedule may provide—

(a) that for purposes connected with any transfers made in accordance with the scheme (including the transfer of rights and liabilities under an enactment) the new appointee is to be treated as the same person in law as the existing appointee;

(b) that, so far as may be necessary for the purposes of or in connection with any such transfers, agreements made, transactions effected and other things done by or in relation to the existing appointee are to be treated as made, effected or done by or in relation to the new appointee;

(c) that, so far as may be necessary for the purposes of or in connection with any such transfers, references in any agreement (whether or not in writing) or in any deed, bond, instrument or other document to, or to any officer of, the existing appointee are to have effect with such modifications as are specified in the scheme;

(d) that proceedings commenced by or against the existing appointee are to be continued by or against the new appointee;

(e) that the effect of any transfer under the scheme in relation to contracts of employment with the existing appointee is not to be to terminate any of those contracts but is to be that periods of employment with the existing appointee are to count for all purposes as periods of employment with the new appointee;

(f) that disputes as to the effect of the scheme between the existing appointee and the new appointee, between either of them and any other appointee or between different companies which are other appointees are to be referred to such arbitration as may be specified in or determined under the scheme;

(g) that determinations on such arbitrations and certificates given jointly by two or more such appointees as are mentioned in paragraph (f) above as to the effect of the scheme as between the companies giving the certificates are to be conclusive for all purposes.

Duties of existing appointee after the scheme comes into force

6. (1) A scheme under this Schedule may provide for the imposition of duties on the existing appointee and on the new appointee to take all such steps as may be requisite to secure that the vesting in the new appointee, by virtue of the scheme, of any foreign property, right or liability is effective under the relevant foreign law.

(2) The provisions of a scheme under this Schedule may require the existing appointee to comply with any directions of the new appointee in performing any duty imposed on the existing appointee by virtue of a provision included in the scheme under sub-paragraph (1) above.

(3) A scheme under this Schedule may provide that, until the vesting of any foreign property, right or liability of the existing appointee in the new appointee is effective under the relevant foreign law, it shall be the duty of the existing appointee to hold that property or right for the benefit of, or to discharge that liability on behalf of, the new appointee.

(4) Nothing in any provision included by virtue of this paragraph in a scheme under this Schedule shall be taken as prejudicing the effect under the law of any part of the United Kingdom of the vesting by virtue of the scheme in the new appointee of any foreign property, right or liability.

(5) A scheme under this Schedule may provide that, in specified cases, foreign property, rights or liabilities that are acquired or incurred by an existing appointee after the scheme comes into force are immediately to become property, rights or liabilities of the new appointee; and such a scheme may make the same provision in relation to any such property, rights or liabilities as can be made, by virtue of the preceding provisions of this paragraph, in relation to foreign property, rights and liabilities vested in the existing appointee when the scheme comes into force.

(6) References in this paragraph to any foreign property, right or liability are references to any property, right or liability as respects which any issue arising in any proceedings would have to be determined (in accordance with the rules of private international law) by reference to the law of a country or territory outside the United Kingdom.

(7) Any expenses incurred by an existing appointee in consequence of any provision included by virtue of this paragraph in a scheme under this Schedule shall be met by the new appointee.

(8) Duties imposed on a company by virtue of this paragraph shall be enforceable in the same way as if they were imposed by a contract between the existing appointee and the new appointee.

Functions under private and local legislation etc

7. (1) A scheme under this Schedule may provide that any functions of the existing appointee under a statutory provision—

- (a) shall be transferred to the new appointee or any of the other appointees;
- (b) shall be concurrently exercisable by two or more companies falling within paragraph (a) above; or
- (c) shall be concurrently exercisable by the existing appointee and one or more companies falling within paragraph (a) above;

and different schemes under this Schedule may provide for any such functions of the same existing appointee to have effect as mentioned in paragraphs (a) to (c) above in relation to each of the new appointees under those schemes or of all or any of the other appointees.

(2) Sub-paragraph (1) above applies in relation to any function under a statutory provision if and to the extent that the statutory provision—

- (a) relates to any part of the existing appointee's undertaking, or to any property, which is to be transferred by the scheme; or
- (b) authorises the carrying out of works designed to be used in connection with any such part of the existing appointee's undertaking or the acquisition of land for the purpose of carrying out any such works.

(3) Sub-paragraph (1) above does not apply to any function of the Board or of any of the Board's subsidiaries under any provision of this Act or of—

- *(a) the Transport Act 1962;*
- *(b) the Transport Act 1968;*
- *(c) section 4 of the Railways Act 1974; or*
- *(d) sections 119 to 124 of the Transport Act 1985.*

(4) A scheme under this Schedule may define any functions of the existing appointee to be transferred or made concurrently exercisable by the scheme in accordance with sub-paragraph (1) above—

- (a) by specifying the statutory provisions in question;
- (b) by referring to all the statutory provisions *(except those specified in sub-paragraph (3) above)* which—
  - (i) relate to any part of the existing appointee's undertaking, or to any property, which is to be transferred by the scheme, or
  - (ii) authorise the carrying out of works designed to be used in connection with any such part of the existing appointee's undertaking or the acquisition of land for the purpose of carrying out any such works; or
- (c) by referring to all the statutory provisions within paragraph (b) above, but specifying certain excepted provisions.

(5) In this paragraph "statutory provision" means a provision whether of a general or of a special nature contained in, or in any document made or issued under, any Act, whether of a general or a special nature.

NOTES

Para 1: words in square brackets in definition "other appointee" inserted by the Railway (Licensing of Railway Undertakings) Regulations 2005, SI 2005/3050, reg 3, Sch 1, Pt 1, para 3(1), (10)(a), subject to transitional provisions in reg 20, Sch 4, paras 1–4, 8–14 thereto.

Para 2: words in square brackets in sub-paras (2)–(6) substituted by the Railways Act 2005, s 49(7)(a)–(c), (8), for effect see s 49(10), (11) of that Act; in sub-para (7), words in square brackets substituted by the Railways Act 2005, s 49(7)(d), for effect see s 49(10), (11) of that Act, and words omitted repealed by the Transport Act 2000, ss 215, 274, Sch 16, paras 8, 54(1), (5)(c), Sch 31, Pt IV; sub-para (9) added by the Railways Act 2005, s 49(9), for effect see s 49(10), (11) of that Act.

Para 4: sub-para (3) added by SI 2005/3050, reg 3, Sch 1, Pt 1, para 3(1), (10)(b), subject to transitional provisions in reg 20, Sch 4, paras 1–4, 8–14 thereto.

Para 7: sub-para (3) and words in italics in sub-para (4) repealed by the Transport Act 2000, s 274, Sch 31, Pt IV, as from a day to be appointed.

SCHEDULES 8–14

(*Schs 8–14 outside the scope of this work.*)

RAILWAY ADMINISTRATION ORDER RULES 2001

(SI 2001/3352)

NOTES

Made: 6 October 2001.

Authority: Insolvency Act 1986, s 411; Railways Act 1993, s 59(5).

Commencement: 7 October 2001.

Note: the Insolvency Rules 1986, SI 1986/1925 are revoked and replaced (as from 6 April 2017 and subject to transitional provisions) by the Insolvency (England and Wales) Rules 2016, SI 2016/1024 at **[6.2]**, however, the Insolvency (England and Wales) Rules 2016 (Consequential Amendments and Savings) Rules 2017, SI 2017/369, r 3(a) at **[6.947]** provides that the Insolvency Rules 1986 as they had effect immediately before 6 April 2017 and insofar as they apply to proceedings under the Railway Administration Order Rules 2001, continue to have effect for the purposes of the application of the 2001 Rules.

See also the Deregulation Act 2015 and Small Business, Enterprise and Employment Act 2015 (Consequential Amendments) (Savings) Regulations 2017, SI 2017/540, reg 4(1), (2)(a) and the Insolvency Amendment (EU 2015/848) Regulations 2017, SI 2017/702, reg 4 at **[2.103]**, for savings in relation to the Insolvency Act 1986 in so far as it applies to proceedings under these Rules.

ARRANGEMENT OF RULES

PART 1
INTRODUCTORY PROVISIONS

1.1 Citation and commencement .....[7.2452]
1.2 Construction and interpretation .....[7.2453]
1.3 Extent .....[7.2454]

PART 2
RAILWAY ADMINISTRATION PROCEDURE

2.1 Affidavit to support petition .....[7.2455]
2.2 Independent report on company's affairs .....[7.2456]
2.3 Contents of affidavit .....[7.2457]
2.4 Form of petition .....[7.2458]
2.5 Filing of petition .....[7.2459]
2.6 Service of petition .....[7.2460]
2.7 Notice to sheriff, etc .....[7.2461]
2.8 Manner in which service of petition is to be effected .....[7.2462]
2.9 Proof of service .....[7.2463]
2.10 The hearing .....[7.2464]
2.11 Notice and advertisement of railway administration order .....[7.2465]

PART 3
STATEMENT OF AFFAIRS AND PROPOSALS TO CREDITORS

3.1 Notice requiring statement of affairs .....[7.2466]
3.2 Verification and filing .....[7.2467]
3.3 Limited disclosure .....[7.2468]
3.4 Release from duty to submit statement of affairs; extension of time .....[7.2469]
3.5 Expenses of statement of affairs .....[7.2470]
3.6 Statement to be annexed to proposals .....[7.2471]
3.7 Notice to members of proposals to creditors .....[7.2472]

PART 4
MEETINGS

4.1 Creditors' meetings generally .....[7.2473]
4.2 The chairman at meetings .....[7.2474]
4.3 Entitlement to vote .....[7.2475]
4.4 Admission and rejection of claims .....[7.2476]
4.5 Secured creditors .....[7.2477]
4.6 Holders of negotiable instruments .....[7.2478]
4.7 Retention of title creditors .....[7.2479]
4.8 Hire-purchase, conditional sale and chattel leasing agreements .....[7.2480]
4.9 Resolutions and minutes .....[7.2481]

4.10 Report to creditors .....[7.2482]
4.11 Venue and conduct of members' meeting .....[7.2483]

PART 5
THE SPECIAL RAILWAY ADMINISTRATOR

5.1 Fixing of remuneration .....[7.2484]
5.2 Recourse to the court .....[7.2485]
5.3 Creditors' claim that remuneration is excessive .....[7.2486]
5.4 Disposal of charged property, etc .....[7.2487]
5.5 Abstract of receipts and payments .....[7.2488]
5.6 Resignation .....[7.2489]
5.7 Special Railway Administrator deceased .....[7.2490]
5.8 Order filling vacancy .....[7.2491]

PART 6
COURT PROCEDURE AND PRACTICE

CHAPTER 1
APPLICATIONS

6.1 Preliminary .....[7.2492]
6.2 Interpretation .....[7.2493]
6.3 Form and contents of application .....[7.2494]
6.4 Filing and service of application .....[7.2495]
6.5 Other hearings *ex parte* .....[7.2496]
6.6 Hearing of application .....[7.2497]
6.7 Use of affidavit evidence .....[7.2498]
6.8 Filing and service of affidavits .....[7.2499]
6.9 Use of reports .....[7.2500]
6.10 Adjournment of hearing: directions .....[7.2501]

CHAPTER 2
SHORTHAND WRITERS

6.11 Appointment and remuneration of shorthand writers .....[7.2502]

CHAPTER 3
ENFORCEMENT PROCEDURES

6.12 Enforcement of court orders .....[7.2503]
6.13 Orders enforcing compliance with the Rules .....[7.2504]
6.14 Warrants under section 236 of the 1986 Act .....[7.2505]

CHAPTER 4
COURT RECORDS AND RETURNS

6.15 Title of proceedings .....[7.2506]
6.16 Court records .....[7.2507]
6.17 Inspection of records .....[7.2508]
6.18 File of court proceedings .....[7.2509]
6.19 Right to inspect the file .....[7.2510]
6.20 Filing of Gazette notices and advertisements .....[7.2511]

CHAPTER 5
COSTS AND DETAILED ASSESSMENT

6.21 Application of the Civil Procedure Rules .....[7.2512]
6.22 Requirement to assess costs by the detailed procedure .....[7.2513]
6.23 Procedure where detailed assessment required .....[7.2514]
6.24 Costs paid otherwise than out of the assets of the protected railway company .....[7.2515]
6.25 Award of costs against special railway administrator .....[7.2516]
6.26 Applications for costs .....[7.2517]
6.27 Costs and expenses of witnesses .....[7.2518]
6.28 Final costs certificate .....[7.2519]

CHAPTER 6
PERSONS INCAPABLE OF MANAGING THEIR AFFAIRS

6.29 Introductory .....[7.2520]
6.30 Appointment of another person to act .....[7.2521]
6.31 Affidavit in support of application .....[7.2522]
6.32 Service of notices following appointment .....[7.2523]

CHAPTER 7
GENERAL

6.33 Principal court rules and practice to apply .....[7.2524]

6.34 Right of audience [7.2525]
6.35 Right of attendance [7.2526]
6.36 Special railway administrator's solicitor [7.2527]
6.37 Formal defects [7.2528]
6.38 Restriction on concurrent proceedings and remedies [7.2529]
6.39 Affidavits [7.2530]
6.40 Security in court [7.2531]
6.41 Payment into court [7.2532]
6.42 Further information and disclosure [7.2533]
6.43 Office copies of documents [7.2534]

PART 7
PROXIES AND COMPANY REPRESENTATION

7.1 Definition of Proxy [7.2535]
7.2 Issue and use of forms of proxy [7.2536]
7.3 Use of proxies at meetings [7.2537]
7.4 Retention of proxies [7.2538]
7.5 Right of inspection [7.2539]
7.6 Proxy-holder with financial interest [7.2540]
7.7 Company representation [7.2541]

PART 8
EXAMINATION OF PERSONS IN RAILWAY ADMINISTRATION PROCEEDINGS

8.1 Interpretation and Application [7.2542]
8.2 Form and contents of application [7.2543]
8.3 Order for examination, etc [7.2544]
8.4 Procedure for examination [7.2545]
8.5 Record of examination [7.2546]
8.6 Costs of proceedings under section 236 [7.2547]

PART 9
MISCELLANEOUS AND GENERAL

9.1 Power of Secretary of State to regulate certain matters [7.2548]
9.2 Notices [7.2549]
9.3 Quorum at creditors' meetings [7.2550]
9.4 Evidence of proceedings at meeting [7.2551]
9.5 Documents issuing from Secretary of State [7.2552]
9.6 Forms for use in railway administration proceedings [7.2553]
9.7 Special railway administrator's security [7.2554]
9.8 Time-limits [7.2555]
9.9 Service by post [7.2556]
9.10 General provisions as to service and notice [7.2557]
9.11 Service outside the jurisdiction [7.2558]
9.12 Confidentiality of documents [7.2559]
9.13 Notices sent simultaneously to the same person [7.2560]
9.14 Right to copy documents [7.2561]
9.15 Charge for copy documents [7.2562]
9.16 Non-receipt of notice of meeting [7.2563]
9.17 Right to have list of creditors [7.2564]
9.18 False claim of status as creditor [7.2565]
9.19 The Gazette [7.2566]
9.20 Punishment of offences [7.2567]

PART 10
INTERPRETATION AND APPLICATION

10.1 Introductory [7.2568]
10.2 "The court"; "the registrar" [7.2569]
10.3 "Give notice" etc [7.2570]
10.4 Notice, etc to solicitors [7.2571]
10.5 Notice to joint special railway administrators [7.2572]
10.6 "Petition" [7.2573]
10.7 "Venue" [7.2574]
10.8 "Railway administration proceedings" [7.2575]
10.9 "The appropriate fee" [7.2576]
10.10 Expressions used generally [7.2577]
10.11 Application [7.2578]

SCHEDULES

Schedule—Forms . . . .[7.2579]

PART 1
INTRODUCTORY PROVISIONS

[7.2452]
1.1 Citation and commencement

These Rules may be cited as the Railway Administration Order Rules 2001 and shall come into force on 7th October 2001.

[7.2453]
1.2 Construction and interpretation

(1) In these Rules—

"the 1986 Act" means the Insolvency Act 1986;

"the 1993 Act" means the Railways Act 1993;

"the Companies Act" means the Companies Act 1985;

"CPR" means the Civil Procedure Rules 1998 and "CPR" followed by a Part or rule number means the Part or rule with that number in those Rules;

"the Department" means [the Department for Business, Energy and Industrial Strategy];

"the Insolvency Rules" mean the Insolvency Rules 1986

"RSC" followed by an Order and number means the Order with that number set out in Schedule 1 to the CPR; and

"the Rules" means the Railway Administration Order Rules 2001.

(2) References in the Rules to *ex parte* hearings shall be construed as references to hearings without notice being served on any other party; references to applications made *ex parte* as references to applications made without notice being served on any other party and other references which include the expression "*ex parte*" shall be similarly construed.

(3) References to provisions of the 1986 Act are references to those provisions as applied by sections 59 to 62 and 65 of, and Schedule 6 to, the 1993 Act.

(4) Subject to paragraphs (1), (2) and (3), Part 10 of the Rules has effect for their interpretation and application.

NOTES

Para (1): words in square brackets in definition "the Department" substituted by the Secretaries of State for Business, Energy and Industrial Strategy, for International Trade and for Exiting the European Union and the Transfer of Functions (Education and Skills) Order 2016, SI 2016/992, art 14, Schedule, para 25.

Note: the Insolvency Rules 1986, SI 1986/1925 are revoked and replaced (as from 6 April 2017 and subject to transitional provisions) by the Insolvency (England and Wales) Rules 2016, SI 2016/1024 at **[6.2]**, however, the Insolvency (England and Wales) Rules 2016 (Consequential Amendments and Savings) Rules 2017, SI 2017/369, r 3(a) provides that the Insolvency Rules 1986 as they had effect immediately before 6 April 2017 and insofar as they apply to proceedings under the Railway Administration Order Rules 2001, continue to have effect for the purposes of the application of the 2001 Rules.

[7.2454]
1.3 Extent

The Rules apply in relation to protected railway companies which the courts in England and Wales have jurisdiction to wind up.

PART 2
RAILWAY ADMINISTRATION PROCEDURE

[7.2455]
2.1 Affidavit to support petition

Where it is proposed to apply to the court by petition for a railway administration order to be made in relation to a protected railway company, an affidavit complying with Rule 2.3 below must be prepared and sworn, with a view to its being filed in court in support of the petition.

[7.2456]
2.2 Independent report on company's affairs

(1) There may be prepared, with a view to its being exhibited to the affidavit in support of the petition, a report by an independent person to the effect that the appointment of a special railway administrator for the protected railway company is expedient.

(2) The report may be by the person proposed as special railway administrator, or by any other person having adequate knowledge of the affairs of the protected railway company, not being a director, secretary, manager, member, or employee of the company.

[7.2457]
2.3 Contents of affidavit

(1) The affidavit shall state that the company is a protected railway company within the meaning of Part I of the 1993 Act.

Part 7Q Special Insolvency Regimes

(2) The affidavit shall state one or more of the following—

(a) the deponent's belief that the protected railway company is, or is likely to become, unable to pay its debts and the grounds of that belief;

(b) that the Secretary of State has certified that it would be appropriate for him to petition for the winding up of the protected railway company under section 124A of the 1986 Act (petition for winding up on grounds of public interest) and that it would be just and equitable, as mentioned in that section, for the company to be wound up;

(c) that an agreement between the Secretary of State and a relevant rail link undertaker has been determined.

(3) There shall in the affidavit be provided a statement of the protected railway company's financial position, specifying (to the best of the deponent's knowledge and belief) assets and liabilities of the company, including contingent and prospective liabilities.

(4) Details shall be given of any security known or believed to be held by creditors of the protected railway company, and whether in any case the security is such as to confer power on the holder to appoint an administrative receiver. If an administrative receiver has been appointed, that fact shall be stated.

(5) So far as within the immediate knowledge of the deponent, the affidavit shall contain details of—

(a) any petition which has been presented for the winding up of the protected railway company;

(b) any application for leave of the court to pass a resolution for the voluntary winding up of the protected railway company;

(c) any application for an administration order under Part II of the 1986 Act in relation to the protected railway company;

(d) any notice served in accordance with section 62(7) of the 1993 Act by any person intending to enforce any security over a protected railway company's property; and

(e) any step taken to enforce any such security.

(6) If there are other matters which, in the opinion of the person intending to present the petition for a railway administration order, will assist the court in deciding whether to make such an order, those matters (so far as lying within the knowledge or belief of the deponent) shall also be stated.

(7) If a report has been prepared for the protected railway company under Rule 2.2, that fact shall be stated.

[7.2458]

2.4 Form of petition

[Form 1]

(1) The petition shall state by whom it is presented and the address for service.

(2) Where it is presented by the Authority, the petition shall contain a statement that it relates to a protected railway company which is the holder of a passenger licence and is presented with the consent of the Secretary of State.

[Form 1]

(3) The petition shall specify the name and address of the person proposed to be appointed as special railway administrator; and it shall be stated that, to the best of the petitioner's knowledge and belief, the person proposed to be appointed as special railway administrator is qualified to act as an insolvency practitioner in relation to the protected railway company.

(4) There shall be exhibited to the affidavit in support of the petition—

(a) a copy of the petition;

[Form 2]

(b) a written consent by the proposed special railway administrator to accept appointment, if a railway administration order is made; and

(c) if a report has been prepared under Rule 2.2, a copy of it.

[7.2459]

2.5 Filing of petition

(1) The petition and affidavit shall be filed in court, with a sufficient number of copies for service and use as provided by Rule 2.6.

(2) Each of the copies delivered shall have applied to it the seal of the court and be issued to the petitioner; and on each copy there shall be endorsed the date and time of filing.

(3) The court shall fix a venue for the hearing of the petition and this also shall be endorsed on each copy of the petition issued under paragraph (2).

(4) After the petition is filed, it is the duty of the petitioner to notify the court in writing of any winding-up petition presented against the protected railway company, as soon as he becomes aware of it.

[7.2460]

2.6 Service of petition

(1) In the following paragraphs of this Rule, references to the petition are to a copy of the petition issued by the court under Rule 2.5(2) together with the affidavit in support of it and the documents (other than the copy petition) exhibited to the affidavit.

(2) The petition shall be served—

(a) on any person who has appointed an administrative receiver of, or who has applied to the court for an administration order under Part II of the 1986 Act in relation to, the protected railway company;

(b) if an administrative receiver has been appointed, on him;
(c) if there is pending a petition for the winding up of the protected railway company, on the petitioner (and also on the provisional liquidator, if any);
(d) on the person proposed as special railway administrator;
(e) on the protected railway company;
(f) where the petitioner is the Secretary of State, on the Authority; and
(g) where the petitioner is the Authority, on the Secretary of State.

[7.2461]
2.7 Notice to sheriff, etc

(1) The petitioner shall forthwith after filing the petition give notice of its presentation to—
(a) any sheriff or other officer who to his knowledge is charged with an execution or other legal process against the protected railway company or its property, and
(b) any person who to his knowledge has distrained against the protected railway company or its property.

(2) In the application of paragraph (1) of this Rule in a case where the protected railway company is a foreign company, within the meaning of Part II of Schedule 6 to the 1993 Act, the reference to property shall be taken as a reference to property situated within England and Wales.

[7.2462]
2.8 Manner in which service of petition is to be effected

(1) Service of the petition in accordance with Rule 2.6 shall be effected by the petitioner, or his solicitor, or by a person instructed by him or his solicitor, not less than two days before the date fixed for the hearing.

(2) Service shall be effected as follows—
(a) on the protected railway company (subject to paragraph (3) below), by delivering the documents to its registered office;
(b) on any other person (subject to paragraph (4)), by delivering the documents to his proper address;
(c) in either case, in such manner as the court may direct.

(3) If delivery to the protected railway company's registered office is not practicable or if the protected railway company is an unregistered company, service may be effected by delivery to the company's last known principal place of business in England and Wales.

(4) Subject to paragraph (5), for the purposes of paragraph (2)(b), a person's proper address is any which he has previously notified as his address for service; but if he has not notified any such address, service may be effected by delivery to his usual or last known address.

(5) In the case of a person who—
[(a) is an authorised deposit taker or a former authorised institution,]
(b) has appointed, or is or may be entitled to appoint, an administrative receiver of the protected railway company, and
(c) has not notified an address for service,

the proper address is the address of an office of that person where, to the knowledge of the petitioner, the protected railway company maintains a bank account or, where no such office is known to the petitioner, the registered office of that person, or, if there is no such office, his usual or last known address.

(6) Delivery of the documents to any place or address may be made by leaving them there, or sending them by first class post.

[(6A) For the purposes of paragraph (5)—
(a) "authorised deposit taker" means a person who has permission under Part 4 of the Financial Services and Markets Act 2000 to accept deposits; and
(b) "former authorised institution" means an institution which continues to have a liability in respect of a deposit which was held by it in accordance with the Banking Act 1979 or the Banking Act 1987, but is not an authorised deposit taker.

(6B) References in paragraph (6A) to deposits and their acceptance must be read with—
(a) section 22 of the Financial Services and Markets Act 2000;
(b) any relevant order under that section; and
(c) Schedule 2 to that Act.]

NOTES

Para (5): sub-para (a) substituted by the Financial Services and Markets Act 2000 (Consequential Amendments) Order 2002, SI 2002/1555, art 46(1), (2).

Paras (6A), (6B): added by SI 2002/1555, art 46(1), (3).

[7.2463]
2.9 Proof of service

[Form 3]

(1) Service of the petition shall be verified by affidavit, specifying the date on which, and the manner in which, service was effected.

(2) The affidavit, with a sealed copy of the petition exhibited to it, shall be filed in court forthwith after service, and in any event not less than one day before the hearing of the petition.

[7.2464]
2.10 The hearing

(1) At the hearing of the petition, any of the following may appear or be represented—
- (a) the Secretary of State;
- (b) the Authority;
- (c) the protected railway company;
- (d) any person who has appointed, or is or may be entitled to appoint, an administrative receiver of the protected railway company;
- (e) if an administrative receiver has been appointed, that administrative receiver;
- (f) any person who has presented a petition for the winding up of the protected railway company;
- (g) any person who has applied to the court for an administration order under Part II of the 1986 Act in relation to the protected railway company;
- (h) the person proposed for appointment as special railway administrator; and
- (i) with the leave of the court, any other person who appears to have an interest justifying his appearance.

[Form 4]

(2) If the court makes a railway administration order, the costs of the petitioner, and of any person appearing whose costs are allowed by the court, are payable as an expense of the administration.

[7.2465]
2.11 Notice and advertisement of railway administration order

[Form 5]

(1) If the court makes a railway administration order, it shall forthwith give notice to the person appointed as special railway administrator.

[Form 6]

(2) Forthwith after the order is made, the special railway administrator shall advertise its making once in the Gazette, and once in such newspaper as he thinks most appropriate for ensuring that the order comes to the notice of the protected railway company's creditors.

(3) The special railway administrator shall also forthwith give notice of the making of the order—
- (a) to the Secretary of State;
- (b) to [the Office of Rail Regulation];
- (c) to the Authority;
- (d) to any person who has appointed, or is or may be entitled to appoint, an administrative receiver of the protected railway company;
- (e) if an administrative receiver has been appointed, to him;
- (f) if there is pending a petition for the winding up of the protected railway company, to the petitioner (and to the provisional liquidator, if any);
- (g) to any person who has applied to the court for an administration order under Part II of the 1986 Act in relation to the protected railway company; and

[Form 7]
- (h) to the registrar of companies.

[Form 8]

(4) Two sealed copies of the order shall be sent by the court to the special railway administrator, one of which shall be sent by him to the registrar of companies in accordance with section 21(2) of the 1986 Act.

(5) Paragraphs 3(h) and (4) shall not apply where the protected railway company is an unregistered company which is not subject to a requirement imposed under or by virtue of section 691(1) or 718 of the Companies Act to deliver any documents to the registrar of companies.

(6) If under section 9(4) of the 1986 Act the court makes any other order, it shall give directions as to the persons to whom, and how, notice of it is to be given.

NOTES

Para (3): words in square brackets substituted for original words "the Rail Regulator" by virtue of the Railways and Transport Safety Act 2003, s16(4), (5), Sch 3, para 4, for savings see s 16, Sch 3 thereto.

PART 3
STATEMENT OF AFFAIRS AND PROPOSALS TO CREDITORS

[7.2466]
3.1 Notice requiring statement of affairs

[Form 9]

(1) Where the special railway administrator determines to require a statement of the protected railway company's affairs to be made out and submitted to him in accordance with section 22 of the 1986 Act, he shall send notice to each of the persons whom he considers should be made responsible under that section, requiring them to prepare and submit the statement.

(2) The persons to whom the notice is sent are referred to in this Part as "the deponents".

(3) The notice shall inform each of the deponents—
- (a) of the names and addresses of all others (if any) to whom the same notice has been sent;
- (b) of the time within which the statement must be delivered; and
- (c) of the effect of section 22(6) of the 1986 Act (penalty for non-compliance); and

(d) of the application to him, and to each of the other deponents, of section 235 of the 1986 Act (duty to provide information, and to attend on the special railway administrator if required).

(4) The special railway administrator shall, on request, furnish each deponent with the forms required for the preparation of the statement of affairs.

[7.2467]
3.2 Verification and filing
[Form 10]

(1) The statement of affairs shall be in Form 10, shall contain all the particulars required by that form and shall be verified by affidavit by the deponents (using the same form).

(2) The special railway administrator may require any of the persons mentioned in section 22(3) of the 1986 Act to submit an affidavit of concurrence, stating that he concurs in the statement of affairs.

(3) An affidavit of concurrence may be qualified in respect of matters dealt with in the statement of affairs, where the maker of the affidavit is not in agreement with the deponents, or he considers the statement to be erroneous or misleading, or he is without the direct knowledge necessary for concurring with it.

(4) The statement of affairs shall be delivered to the special railway administrator by the deponent making the affidavit of verification (or by one of them, if more than one), together with a copy of the verified statement.

(5) Every affidavit of concurrence shall be delivered by the person who makes it, together with a copy.

(6) The special railway administrator shall file the verified copy of the statement, and the affidavits of concurrence (if any) in court.

[7.2468]
3.3 Limited disclosure

(1) Where the special railway administrator thinks that it would prejudice the conduct of the railway administration for the whole or part of the statement of affairs to be disclosed, he may apply to the court for an order of limited disclosure in respect of the statement, or any specified part of it.

(2) The court may on the application order that the statement or, as the case may be, the specified part of it, be not filed in court, or that it is to be filed separately and not be open to inspection otherwise than with leave of the court.

(3) The court's order may include directions as to the delivery of documents to the registrar of companies and the disclosure of relevant information to other persons.

[7.2469]
3.4 Release from duty to submit statement of affairs; extension of time

(1) The power of the special railway administrator under section 22(5) of the 1986 Act to give a release from the obligation imposed by that section, or to grant an extension of time, may be exercised at the special railway administrator's own discretion, or at the request of any deponent.

(2) A deponent may, if he requests a release or extension of time and it is refused by the special railway administrator, apply to the court for it.

(3) The court may, if it thinks that no sufficient cause is shown for the application, dismiss it; but it shall not do so unless the deponent has had an opportunity to attend the court for an *ex parte* hearing, of which he has been given at least 7 days' notice.

If the application is not dismissed under this paragraph, the court shall fix a venue for it to be heard, and give notice to the deponent accordingly.

(4) The deponent shall, at least 14 days before the hearing, send to the special railway administrator a notice stating the venue and accompanied by a copy of the application, and of any evidence which he (the deponent) intends to adduce in support of it.

(5) The special railway administrator may appear and be heard on the application; and whether or not he appears, he may file a written report of any matters which he considers ought to be drawn to the attention of the court.

If such a report is filed, a copy of it shall be sent by the special railway administrator to the deponent, no later than five days before the hearing.

(6) Sealed copies of any order made on the application shall be sent by the court to the deponent and to the special railway administrator.

(7) On any application under this Rule, the applicant's costs shall be paid in any event by him and, unless the court otherwise orders, no allowance towards them shall be made out of the assets of the protected railway company.

[7.2470]
3.5 Expenses of statement of affairs

(1) A deponent making the statement of affairs and affidavit shall be allowed, and paid by the special railway administrator out of his receipts, any expenses incurred by the deponent in so doing which the special railway administrator considers reasonable.

(2) Any decision by the special railway administrator under this Rule is subject to appeal to the court.

(3) Nothing in this Rule relieves a deponent of any obligation with respect to the preparation, verification and submission of the statement of affairs, or to the provision of information to the special railway administrator.

[7.2471]
3.6 Statement to be annexed to proposals

(1) There shall be annexed to the special railway administrator's proposals sent, under section 23 of the 1986 Act, to the relevant persons a statement by him showing—

(a) details relating to his appointment as special railway administrator;
(b) the names of the directors and secretary of the protected railway company;
(c) an account of the circumstances giving rise to the application for a railway administration order;
(d) if a statement of affairs has been submitted, a copy or summary of it, with the special railway administrator's comments, if any;
(e) if no statement of affairs has been submitted, details of the financial position of the protected railway company at the latest practicable date (which must, unless the court otherwise orders, be a date not earlier than that of the railway administration order);
(f) the manner in which the affairs and business of the protected railway company—
  (i) have, since the date of the special railway administrator's appointment, been managed and financed, and
  (ii) will continue to be managed and financed; and
(g) such other information (if any) as the special railway administrator thinks necessary.

(2) Where the Secretary of State, the Authority or the special railway administrator intends to apply to the court under section 18 of the 1986 Act for a railway administration order to be discharged at a time before the special railway administrator has sent a statement of his proposals to the relevant persons, he shall, at least 10 days before he makes such an application, send to the relevant persons (so far as he is aware of their addresses) a report containing the information required by paragraph (1)(a)–(f)(i) of this Rule.

(3) In this Rule "the relevant persons" means the persons referred to in paragraphs (a) to (e) of section 23(1) of the 1986 Act.

[7.2472]
3.7 Notice to members of proposals to creditors

For the purposes of section 23(2)(b) of the 1986 Act, the notice shall be published once in the Gazette and once in the newspaper in which the making of the railway administration order was advertised.

PART 4
MEETINGS

[7.2473]
4.1 Creditors' meetings generally

(1) This Rule applies to creditors' meetings summoned by the special railway administrator under section 14(2)(b) of the 1986 Act or pursuant to a direction of the court under section 17(3)(b) of that Act.

(2) In fixing the venue for the meeting, the special railway administrator shall have regard to the convenience of creditors.

(3) The meeting shall be summoned for commencement between 10.00 and 16.00 hours on a business day, unless the court otherwise directs.

[Form 11]

(4) At least 21 days' notice of the meeting shall be given to all creditors who are known to the special railway administrator and who had claims against the protected railway company at the date of the railway administration order. The notice shall specify the purpose of the meeting and contain a statement of the effect of Rule 4.3 (entitlement to vote).

[Form 23]

(5) With the notice summoning the meeting there shall be sent forms of proxy.

(6) If within 30 minutes from the time fixed for the commencement of the meeting there is no person present to act as chairman, the meeting shall stand adjourned to the same time and place in the following week or, if that day is not a business day, to the business day immediately following.

(7) The meeting may from time to time be adjourned, if the chairman thinks fit, but not for more than 14 days from the date on which it was fixed to commence.

[7.2474]
4.2 The chairman at meetings

(1) At any meeting of creditors summoned by the special railway administrator, either he shall be chairman, or a person nominated by him in writing to act in his place.

(2) A person so nominated must be either—

(a) one who is qualified to act as an insolvency practitioner in relation to the protected railway company, or
(b) an employee of the special railway administrator or his firm who is experienced in insolvency matters.

[7.2475]
4.3 Entitlement to vote

(1) Subject as follows, at a meeting of creditors in railway administration proceedings a person is entitled to vote only if—

(a) he has given to the special railway administrator not later than 12.00 hours on the business day before the day fixed for the meeting, details in writing of the debt which he claims to be due to him from the protected railway company, and the claim has been duly admitted under the following provisions of this Rule, and
(b) there has been lodged with the special railway administrator any proxy which he intends to be used on his behalf.

Details of the debt must include any calculation for the purposes of Rules 4.5 to 4.8.

(2) The chairman of the meeting may allow a creditor to vote, notwithstanding that he has failed to comply with paragraph (1)(a), if satisfied that the failure was due to circumstances beyond the creditor's control.

(3) The special railway administrator or, if other, the chairman of the meeting may call for any document or other evidence to be produced to him, where he thinks it necessary for the purpose of substantiating the whole or any part of the claim.

(4) Votes are calculated according to the amount of a creditor's debt as at the date of the railway administration order, deducting any amounts paid in respect of the debt after that date.

(5) A creditor shall not vote in respect of a debt for an unliquidated amount, or any debt whose value is not ascertained, except where the chairman agrees to put upon the debt an estimated minimum value for the purpose of entitlement to vote and admits the claim for that purpose.

[7.2476]
4.4 Admission and rejection of claims

(1) At any creditors' meeting the chairman has power to admit or reject a creditor's claim for the purpose of his entitlement to vote; and the power is exercisable with respect to the whole or any part of the claim.

(2) The chairman's decision under this Rule, or in respect of any matter arising under Rule 4.3, is subject to appeal to the court by any creditor.

(3) If the chairman is in doubt whether a claim should be admitted or rejected, he shall mark it as objected to and allow the creditor to vote, subject to his vote being subsequently declared invalid if the objection to the claim is sustained.

(4) If on appeal the chairman's decision is reversed or varied, or a creditor's vote is declared invalid, the court may order that another meeting be summoned, or make such other order as it thinks just.

(5) Neither the special railway administrator nor any person nominated by him to be chairman is personally liable for costs incurred by any person in respect of an appeal to the court under this Rule, unless the court makes an order to that effect.

[7.2477]
4.5 Secured creditors

At a meeting of creditors, a secured creditor is entitled to vote only in respect of the balance (if any) of his debt after deducting the value of his security as estimated by him.

[7.2478]
4.6 Holders of negotiable instruments

A creditor shall not vote in respect of a debt on, or secured by, a current bill of exchange or promissory note, unless he is willing—
(a) to treat the liability to him on the bill or note of every person who is liable on it antecedently to the protected railway company, and against whom a bankruptcy order has not been made (or, in the case of a company, which has not gone into liquidation), as a security in his hands, and
(b) to estimate the value of the security and, for the purpose of his entitlement to vote, to deduct it from his claim.

[7.2479]
4.7 Retention of title creditors

For the purpose of entitlement to vote at a creditors' meeting in railway administration proceedings, a seller of goods to the protected railway company under a retention of title agreement shall deduct from his claim the value, as estimated by him, of any rights arising under that agreement in respect of goods in the possession of the protected railway company.

[7.2480]
4.8 Hire-purchase, conditional sale and chattel leasing agreements

(1) Subject as follows, an owner of goods under a hire-purchase or chattel leasing agreement, or a seller of goods under a conditional sale agreement, is entitled to vote in respect of the amount of the debt due and payable to him by the protected railway company as at the date of the railway administration order.

(2) In calculating the amount of any debt for this purpose, no account shall be taken of any amount attributable to the exercise of any right under the relevant agreement, so far as the right has become exercisable solely by virtue of the presentation of the petition for a railway administration order or any matter arising in consequence of that, or of the making of the order.

[7.2481]
4.9 Resolutions and minutes

(1) Subject to paragraph (2), at a creditors' meeting in railway administration proceedings, a resolution is passed when a majority (in value) of those present and voting, in person or by proxy, have voted in favour of it.

(2) Any resolution is invalid if those voting against it include more than half in value of the creditors to whom notice of the meeting was sent and who are not, to the best of the chairman's belief, persons connected with the protected railway company.

(3) The chairman of the meeting shall cause minutes of its proceedings to be entered in the protected railway company's minute book.

(4) The minutes shall include a list of the creditors who attended (personally or by proxy).

[7.2482]
4.10 Report to creditors

(1) Within 14 days of the end of every period of 6 months beginning with the date of appointment of the special railway administrator the special railway administrator shall send to all creditors of the protected railway company a report on the progress of the administration.

(2) On vacating office the special railway administrator shall send to creditors a report on the administration up to that time.

This does not apply where the railway administration is immediately followed by the protected railway company going into liquidation, nor when the special railway administrator is removed from office by the court or ceases to be qualified as an insolvency practitioner.

[7.2483]
4.11 Venue and conduct of members' meeting

(1) Where the special railway administrator summons a meeting of members of the protected railway company, he shall fix a venue for it having regard to their convenience.

(2) The chairman of the meeting shall be the special railway administrator or a person nominated by him in writing to act in his place.

(3) A person so nominated must be either—

(a) one who is qualified to act as an insolvency practitioner in relation to the protected railway company, or

(b) an employee of the special railway administrator or his firm who is experienced in insolvency matters.

(4) If within 30 minutes from the time fixed for commencement of the meeting there is no person present to act as chairman, the meeting stands adjourned to the same time and place in the following week or, if that day is not a business day, to the business day immediately following.

(5) Subject as above, the meeting shall be summoned and conducted as if it were a general meeting of the protected railway company summoned under the company's articles of association, and in accordance with the applicable provisions of the Companies Act.

(6) The chairman of the meeting shall cause minutes of its proceedings to be entered in the protected railway company's minute book.

PART 5
THE SPECIAL RAILWAY ADMINISTRATOR

[7.2484]
5.1 Fixing of remuneration

(1) The special railway administrator is entitled to receive remuneration for his services as such.

(2) The remuneration shall be fixed either—

(a) as a percentage of the value of the property with which he has to deal, or

(b) by reference to the time properly given by the insolvency practitioner (as special railway administrator) and his staff in attending to matters arising in the administration.

(3) The remuneration of the special railway administrator may be fixed by a resolution of a meeting of creditors, determining both whether the remuneration is to be fixed under paragraph (2)(a) or (b) and, if under paragraph (2)(a), any percentage to be applied as there mentioned.

(4) In arriving at that determination, the meeting of creditors shall have regard to the following matters—

(a) the complexity (or otherwise) of the case,

(b) any respects in which, in connection with the protected railway company's affairs, there falls on the special railway administrator any responsibility of an exceptional kind or degree,

(c) the effectiveness with which the special railway administrator appears to be carrying out, or to have carried out, his duties as such, and

(d) the value and nature of the property with which he has to deal.

(6) If not fixed as above, the special railway administrator's remuneration shall, on his application, be fixed by the court.

(7) The court may, if it appears to be a proper case, order the costs of the special railway administrator's application to be paid as an expense of the railway administration.

(8) Where there are joint special railway administrators, it is for them to agree between themselves as to how the remuneration payable should be apportioned. Any dispute arising between them may be referred to the court for settlement by order.

(9) If the special railway administrator is a solicitor and employs his own firm, or any partner of that firm, to act on behalf of the protected railway company, profit costs shall not be paid unless this is authorised by the court.

[7.2485]
5.2 Recourse to the court

(1) If the special railway administrator considers that the remuneration fixed for him by resolution of the creditors is insufficient, he may apply to the court for an order increasing its amount or rate.

(2) The special railway administrator shall give at least 14 days' notice of his application to such one or more of the company's creditors as the court may direct, which creditors may nominate one or more of their number to appear or be represented, and to be heard, on the application.

(3) The court may, if it appears to be a proper case, order the costs of the special railway administrator's application, including the costs of any creditors appearing or being represented, to be paid as an expense of the railway administration.

[7.2486]
5.3 Creditors' claim that remuneration is excessive

(1) Any creditor of the protected railway company may, with the concurrence of at least 25 per cent in value of the creditors (including himself), apply to the court for an order that the special railway administrator's remuneration be reduced, on the grounds that it is, in all the circumstances, excessive.

(2) The court may, if it thinks that no sufficient cause is shown for a reduction, dismiss the application; but it shall not do so unless the applicant has had an opportunity to attend the court for an *ex parte* hearing, of which he has been given at least seven days' notice.

If the application is not dismissed under this paragraph, the court shall fix a venue for it to be heard, and give notice to the applicant accordingly.

(3) The applicant shall, at least 14 days before the hearing, send to the special railway administrator a notice stating the venue and accompanied by a copy of the application, and of any evidence which the applicant intends to adduce in support of it.

(4) If the court considers the application to be well-founded, it shall make an order fixing the remuneration at a reduced amount or rate.

(5) Unless the court orders otherwise, the costs of the application shall be paid by the applicant, and are not payable as an expense of the administration.

[7.2487]
5.4 Disposal of charged property, etc

(1) The following applies where the special railway administrator applies to the court under section 15(2) of the 1986 Act for authority to dispose of property of the protected railway company which is subject to a security, or goods in the possession of the protected railway company under an agreement, to which that subsection relates.

(2) The court shall fix a venue for the hearing of the application, and the special railway administrator shall forthwith give notice of the venue to the person who is the holder of the security or, as the case may be, the owner under the agreement.

(3) If an order is made under the said section 15(2), the special railway administrator shall forthwith give notice of it to that person or owner.

(4) The court shall send two sealed copies of the order to the special railway administrator, who shall send one of them to that person or owner.

[7.2488]
5.5 Abstract of receipts and payments

(1) The special railway administrator shall—

(a) within 2 months after the end of 6 months from the date of his appointment, and of every subsequent period of 6 months, and

(b) within 2 months after he ceases to act as special railway administrator,

send the requisite accounts of the receipts and payments of the protected railway company to the court, and to the registrar of companies except where the protected railway company is an unregistered company which is not subject to a requirement imposed under or by virtue of section 691(1) or 718 of the Companies Act to deliver any documents to the registrar of companies.

(2) The court may, on the application of the special railway administrator, extend the period of two months mentioned above.

(3) The accounts are to be in the form of an abstract showing—

(a) receipts and payments during the relevant period of 6 months, or

[Form 12]

(b) where the special railway administrator has ceased to act, receipts and payments during the period from the end of the last 6 month period to the time when he so ceased (alternatively if there has been no previous abstract, receipts and payments in the period since his appointment as special railway administrator).

(4) The special railway administrator is guilty of an offence if he makes default in complying with this Rule and is liable on summary conviction to a fine not exceeding [one-fifth of the greater of £5,000 or the amount corresponding to level 4 on the standard scale for summary offences] and, for continued contravention, to a daily default fine not exceeding [one-fiftieth of the greater of those amounts].

(5) . . .

NOTES

Para (4): words in square brackets substituted by the Legal Aid, Sentencing and Punishment of Offenders Act 2012 (Fines on Summary Conviction) Regulations 2015, SI 2015/664, reg 3(1), Sch 3, Pt 1, para 11(a), (b).

Para (5): revoked by SI 2015/664, reg 3(1), Sch 3, Pt 1, para 11(c).

[7.2489]
5.6 Resignation

[Form 13]

(1) The special railway administrator may give notice of his resignation on grounds of ill health or because—

(a) he intends ceasing to be in practice as an insolvency practitioner, or

(b) there is some conflict of interest, or change of personal circumstances, which precludes or makes impracticable the further discharge by him of the duties of special railway administrator.

[Form 14]

(2) The special railway administrator may, with the leave of the court, give notice of his resignation on grounds other than those specified in paragraph (1).

(3) The special railway administrator must give to the persons specified below at least 7 days' notice of his intention to resign, or to apply for the court's leave to do so,—

(a) the Secretary of State;

(b) the Authority;

(c) any continuing special railway administrator of the protected railway company, and

(d) if there is no such continuing special railway administrator, to the protected railway company and its creditors.

[7.2490]
5.7 Special Railway Administrator deceased

(1) Subject as follows, where the special railway administrator has died, it is the duty of his personal representative to give notice of the fact to the court, specifying the date of death.

This does not apply if notice has been given under any of the following paragraphs of this Rule.

(2) If the deceased special railway administrator was a partner in a firm, notice of the death may be given by a partner in the firm who is qualified to act as an insolvency practitioner, or is a member of any body recognised by the Secretary of State for the authorisation of insolvency practitioners.

(3) Notice of the death may be given by any person producing to the court the relevant death certificate or a copy of it.

[7.2491]
5.8 Order filling vacancy

Where the court makes an order filling a vacancy in the office of special railway administrator, the same provisions apply in respect of giving notice of, and advertising, the order as in the case of the railway administration order.

PART 6
COURT PROCEDURE AND PRACTICE

CHAPTER 1 APPLICATIONS

[7.2492]
6.1 Preliminary

This Chapter applies to any application made to the court in railway administration proceedings, except a petition for a railway administration order.

[7.2493]
6.2 Interpretation

(1) In this Chapter, except in so far as the context otherwise requires—

"originating application" means an application to the court which is not an application in pending proceedings before the court; and

"ordinary application" means any other application to the court.

[Forms 19 and 20]

(2) Every application shall be in the form appropriate to the application concerned.

[7.2494]
6.3 Form and contents of application

(1) Each application shall be in writing and shall state—

(a) the names of the parties;

(b) the nature of the relief or order applied for or the directions sought from the court;
(c) the names and addresses of the persons (if any) on whom it is intended to serve the application or that no person is intended to be served;
(d) where the 1986 Act, the 1993 Act or the Rules require that notice of the application is to be given to specified persons, the names and addresses of all those persons (so far as known to the applicant); and
(e) the applicant's address for service.

(2) An originating application shall set out the grounds on which the applicant claims to be entitled to the relief or order sought.

(3) The application must be signed by the applicant if he is acting in person or, when he is not so acting, by or on behalf of his solicitor.

[7.2495]
6.4 Filing and service of application

(1) The application shall be filed in court, accompanied by one copy and a number of additional copies equal to the number of persons who are to be served with the application.

(2) Subject as follows in this Rule and in the next, or unless the Rule under which the application is brought provides otherwise, or the court otherwise orders, upon the presentation of the documents mentioned in paragraph (1), the court shall fix a venue for the application to be heard.

(3) Unless the court otherwise directs, the applicant shall serve a sealed copy of the application, endorsed with the venue of the hearing, on the respondent named in the application (or on each respondent if more than one).

(4) The court may give any of the following directions—
(a) that the application be served upon persons other than those specified by the relevant provision of the 1986 Act, the 1993 Act or the Rules;
(b) that the giving of notice to any person be dispensed with;
(c) that notice be given in some way other than that specified in paragraph (3).

(5) Unless the provision of the 1986 Act, the 1993 Act or the Rules under which the application is made provides otherwise, and subject to the next paragraph, the application must be served at least 14 days before the date fixed for the hearing.

(6) Where the case is one of urgency, the court may (without prejudice to its general power to extend or abridge time limits)—
(a) hear the application immediately, either with or without notice to or the attendance of, other parties, or
(b) authorise a shorter period of service than that provided for by paragraph (5);
and any such application may be heard on terms providing for the filing or service of documents, or the carrying out of other formalities, as the court thinks fit.

[7.2496]
6.5 Other hearings ex parte

(1) Where the relevant provisions of the 1986 Act, the 1993 Act or the Rules do not require service of the application on, or notice of it to be given to, any person, the court may hear the application *ex parte*.

(2) Where the application is properly made *ex parte*, the court may hear it forthwith, without fixing a venue as required by Rule 6.4(2).

(3) Alternatively, the court may fix a venue for the application to be heard, in which case Rule 6.4 applies (so far as relevant).

[7.2497]
6.6 Hearing of application

(1) Unless allowed or authorised to be made otherwise, every application before the registrar shall, and every application before the judge may, be heard in chambers.

(2) Unless either—
(a) the judge has given a general or special direction to the contrary, or
(b) it is not within the registrar's power to make the order required,
the jurisdiction of the court to hear and determine the application may be exercised by the registrar, and the application shall be made to the registrar in the first instance.

(3) Where the application is made to the registrar he may refer to the judge any matter which he thinks should properly be decided by the judge, and the judge may either dispose of the matter or refer it back to the registrar with such direction as he thinks fit.

(4) Nothing in this Rule precludes an application being made directly to the judge in a proper case.

[7.2498]
6.7 Use of affidavit evidence

(1) In any proceedings evidence may be given by affidavit unless by any provision of the Rules it is otherwise provided or the court otherwise directs; but the court may, on the application of any party, order the attendance for cross-examination of the person making the affidavit.

(2) Where, after such an order has been made, the person in question does not attend, his affidavit shall not be used in evidence without the leave of the court.

[7.2499]

6.8 Filing and service of affidavits

(1) Unless the provisions of the 1986 Act, the 1993 Act or the Rules under which the application is made provide otherwise, or the court otherwise allows—

(a) if the applicant intends to rely at the first hearing on affidavit evidence, he shall file the affidavit or affidavits (if more than one) in court and serve a copy or copies on the respondent, not less than 14 days before the date fixed for the hearing, and

(b) where a respondent to an application intends to oppose it and to rely for that purpose on affidavit evidence, he shall file the affidavit or affidavits (if more than one) in court and serve a copy or copies on the applicant, not less than 7 days before the date fixed for the hearing.

(2) Any affidavit may be sworn by the applicant or by the respondent or by some other person possessing direct knowledge of the subject matter of the application.

[7.2500]

6.9 Use of reports

(1) A report may be filed in court instead of an affidavit, unless the application involves other parties or the court otherwise orders, by the special railway administrator.

(2) In any case where a report is filed instead of an affidavit, the report shall be treated for the purpose of Rule 6.8(1) and any hearing before the court as if it were an affidavit.

[7.2501]

6.10 Adjournment of hearing: directions

(1) The court may adjourn the hearing of an application on such terms (if any) as it thinks fit.

(2) The court may at any time give such directions as it thinks fit as to—

(a) service or notice of the application on or to any person, whether in connection with the venue of a resumed hearing or for any other purpose;

(b) whether particulars of claims and defence are to be delivered and generally as to the procedure on the application;

(c) the manner in which any evidence is to be adduced at a resumed hearing and in particular (but without prejudice to the generality of this sub-paragraph) as to—

(i) the taking of evidence wholly or in part by affidavit or orally;

(ii) the cross-examination either before the judge or registrar on the hearing in court or in chambers, of any deponents to affidavits; and

(iii) any report to be given by the special railway administrator; and

(d) the matters to be dealt with in evidence.

CHAPTER 2 SHORTHAND WRITERS

[7.2502]

6.11 Appointment and remuneration of shorthand writers

[Form 21]

(1) In the High Court the judge may in writing nominate one or more persons to be official shorthand writers to the court.

[Forms 21 and 22]

(2) The court may, at any time in the course of railway administration proceedings, appoint a shorthand writer to take down the evidence of a person examined in the course of those proceedings.

(3) The remuneration of a shorthand writer appointed in railway administration proceedings shall be paid by the party at whose instance the appointment was made, or out of the assets of the protected railway company, or otherwise, as the court may direct.

(4) Any question arising as to the rates of remuneration payable under this Rule shall be determined by the court in its discretion.

CHAPTER 3 ENFORCEMENT PROCEDURES

[7.2503]

6.12 Enforcement of court orders

In any railway administration proceedings, orders of the court may be enforced in the same manner as a judgment to the same effect.

[7.2504]

6.13 Orders enforcing compliance with the Rules

(1) The court may, on application by the special railway administrator, make such orders as it thinks necessary for the enforcement of obligations falling on any person in accordance with section 22 (statement of affairs to be submitted to the administrator) or section 235 (duty to co-operate with office-holder) of the 1986 Act.

(2) An order of the court under this Rule may provide that all costs of and incidental to the application for it shall be borne by the person against whom the order is made.

[7.2505]
6.14 Warrants under section 236 of the 1986 Act

(1) A warrant issued by the court under section 236 of the 1986 Act shall be addressed to such officer of the High Court as the warrant specifies, or to any constable.

(2) The persons referred to in section 236(5) of the 1986 Act as the prescribed officer of the court are the tipstaff and his assistants of the court.

(3) In this Chapter references to property include books, papers and records.

(4) When a person is arrested under a warrant issued under section 236 (inquiry into insolvent company's dealings) of the 1986 Act, the officer arresting him shall forthwith bring him before the court issuing the warrant in order that he may be examined.

(5) If he cannot immediately be brought up for examination, the officer shall deliver him into the custody of the governor of the prison named in the warrant, who shall keep him in custody and produce him before the court as it may from time to time direct.

(6) After arresting the person named in the warrant, the officer shall forthwith report to the court the arrest or delivery into custody (as the case may be) and apply to the court to fix a venue for the person's examination.

(7) The court shall appoint the earliest practicable time for the examination, and shall—
- (a) direct the governor of the prison to produce the person for examination at the time and place appointed, and
- (b) forthwith give notice of the venue to the person who applied for the warrant.

(8) Any property in the arrested person's possession which may be seized shall be—
- (a) lodged with, or otherwise dealt with as instructed by, whoever is specified in the warrant as authorised to receive it, or
- (b) kept by the officer seizing it pending the receipt of written orders from the court as to its disposal,

as may be directed by the court.

CHAPTER 4 COURT RECORDS AND RETURNS

[7.2506]
6.15 Title of proceedings

Every railway administration proceeding shall, with any necessary additions, be intituled "IN THE MATTER OF . . . (naming the protected railway company to which the proceedings relate) AND IN THE MATTER OF THE INSOLVENCY ACT 1986 AND THE RAILWAYS ACT 1993".

[7.2507]
6.16 Court records

The court shall keep records of all railway administration proceedings, and shall cause to be entered in the records the taking of any step in the proceedings, and such decisions of the court in relation thereto, as the court thinks fit.

[7.2508]
6.17 Inspection of records

(1) Subject to paragraphs (2) and (3), the court's records of railway administration proceedings shall be open to inspection by any person.

(2) If in the case of a person applying to inspect the records the registrar is not satisfied as to the propriety of the purpose for which inspection is required, he may refuse to allow it. That person may then apply forthwith and *ex parte* to the judge, who may refuse the inspection or allow it on such terms as he thinks fit.

(3) The decision of the judge under paragraph (2) is final.

[7.2509]
6.18 File of court proceedings

(1) In respect of all railway administration proceedings, the court shall open and maintain a file for each case; and (subject to directions of the registrar) all documents relating to such proceedings shall be placed on the relevant file.

(2) No railway administration proceedings shall be filed in the Central Office of the High Court.

[7.2510]
6.19 Right to inspect the file

(1) In the case of any railway administration proceedings, the following persons have the right, at all reasonable times, to inspect the court's file of the proceedings—
- (a) the Secretary of State;
- (b) the Authority;
- (c) the special railway administrator;
- (d) any person stating himself in writing to be a creditor of the protected railway company to which the railway administration proceedings relate; and
- (e) every person who is, or at any time has been, a director or officer of the protected railway company to which the railway administration proceedings relate and every person who is a member of that company.

(2) The right of inspection conferred on any person by paragraph (1) may be exercised on his behalf by a person properly authorised by him.

(3) Any person may, by special leave of the court, inspect the file.

(4) The right of inspection conferred by this Rule is not exercisable in the case of documents, or parts of documents, as to which the court directs, either generally or specially, that they are not to be made open to inspection without the court's leave.

(5) An application under paragraph (4) for a direction of the court may be made by the special railway administrator or by any party appearing to the court to have an interest.

(6) If, for the purpose of powers conferred by the 1986 Act or the Rules or the Insolvency Rules the Secretary of State, the Department or the official receiver wishes to inspect the file of any railway administration proceedings, and requests the transmission of the file, the court shall comply with such request (unless the file is for the time being in use for the court's purposes).

(7) Paragraphs (2) and (3) of Rule 6.17 apply in respect of the court's file of any proceedings as they apply in respect of court records.

[7.2511]
6.20 Filing of Gazette notices and advertisements

(1) In any court in which railway administration proceedings are pending, an officer of the court shall file a copy of every issue of the Gazette which contains an advertisement relating to those proceedings.

(2) Where there appears in a newspaper an advertisement relating to railway administration proceedings pending in any court, the person inserting the advertisement shall file a copy of it in that court.

The copy of the advertisement shall be accompanied by, or have endorsed on it, such particulars as are necessary to identify the proceedings and the date of the advertisement's appearance.

(3) An officer of any court in which railway administration proceedings are pending shall from time to time file a memorandum giving the dates of, and other particulars relating to, any notice published in the Gazette, and any newspaper advertisements, which relate to proceedings so pending.

The officer's memorandum shall be prime facie evidence that any notice or advertisement mentioned in it was duly inserted in the issue of the newspaper or the Gazette which is specified in the memorandum.

CHAPTER 5 COSTS AND DETAILED ASSESSMENT

[7.2512]
6.21 Application of the Civil Procedure Rules

Subject to provision to inconsistent effect made as follows in this Chapter CPR Part 43 (scope of costs rules and definitions), Part 44 (general rules about costs), Part 45 (fixed costs), Part 47 (procedure for detailed assessment of costs and default provisions) and Part 48 (costs—special cases) shall apply to railway administration proceedings with any necessary modifications.

[7.2513]
6.22 Requirement to assess costs by the detailed procedure

(1) Subject as follows, where the costs, charges or expenses of any person are payable out of the assets of the protected railway company, the amount of those costs, charges or expenses shall be decided by detailed assessment unless agreed between the special railway administrator and the person entitled to payment, and in the absence of such agreement the special railway administrator may serve notice in writing requiring that person to commence detailed assessment proceedings in accordance with CPR Part 47 (procedure for detailed assessment of costs and default provisions) in the court to which the railway administration proceedings are allocated or, where in relation to a protected railway company there is no such court, in any court having jurisdiction to wind up the protected railway company.

(2) Where the amount of the costs, charges or expenses of any person employed by a special railway administrator in railway administration proceedings are required to be decided by detailed assessment or fixed by order of the court this does not preclude the special railway administrator from making payments on account to such person on the basis of an undertaking by that person to repay immediately any money which may, when detailed assessment is made, prove to have been overpaid, with interest at the rate specified in section 17 of the Judgments Act 1838 on the date payment was made and for the period from the date of payment to that of repayment.

(3) In any proceedings before the court, including proceedings on a petition, the court may order costs to be decided by detailed assessment.

[7.2514]
6.23 Procedure where detailed assessment required

(1) Before making a detailed assessment of the costs of any person employed in railway administration proceedings by a special railway administrator, the costs officer shall require a certificate of employment, which shall be endorsed on the bill and signed by the special railway administrator.

(2) The certificate shall include—
- (a) the name and address of the person employed;
- (b) details of the functions to be carried out under the employment; and
- (c) a note of any special terms of remuneration which have been agreed.

(3) Every person whose costs in railway administration proceedings are required to be decided by detailed assessment shall, on being required in writing to do so by the special railway administrator, commence detailed assessment proceedings in accordance with CPR Part 47 (procedure for detailed assessment of costs and default provisions).

(4) If that person does not commence detailed assessment proceedings within three months of the requirement under paragraph (3), or within such further time as the court, on application, may permit, the special railway administrator may deal with the assets of the protected railway company without regard to any claim by that person, whose claim is forfeited by such failure to commence proceedings.

(5) Where in any such case such a claim lies additionally against a special railway administrator in his personal capacity, that claim is also forfeited by such failure to commence proceedings.

[7.2515]

6.24 Costs paid otherwise than out of the assets of the protected railway company

Where the amount of costs is decided by detailed assessment under an order of the court directing that the costs are to be paid otherwise than out of the assets of the protected railway company, the costs officer shall note on the final costs certificate by whom, or the manner in which, the costs are to be paid.

[7.2516]

6.25 Award of costs against special railway administrator

Without prejudice to any provision of the 1986 Act, the 1993 Act, the Insolvency Rules or the Rules by virtue of which the special railway administrator is not in any event to be liable for costs and expenses, where a special railway administrator is made a party to any proceedings on the application of another party to the proceedings, he shall not be personally liable for costs unless the court otherwise directs.

[7.2517]

6.26 Applications for costs

(1) This Rule applies where a party to, or person affected by, any railway administration proceedings—

(a) applies to the court for an order allowing his costs, or part of them, incidental to the proceedings, and

(b) that application is not made at the time of the proceedings.

(2) The person concerned shall serve a sealed copy of his application on the special railway administrator.

(3) The special railway administrator may appear on the application.

(4) No costs of or incidental to the application shall be allowed to the applicant unless the court is satisfied that the application could not have been made at the time of the proceedings.

[7.2518]

6.27 Costs and expenses of witnesses

(1) Except as directed by the court, no allowance as a witness in any examination or other proceedings before the court shall be made to an officer of the protected railway company to which the railway administration proceedings relate.

(2) A person presenting a petition in railway administration proceedings shall not be regarded as a witness on the hearing of the petition, but the costs officer may allow his expenses of travelling and subsistence.

[7.2519]

6.28 Final costs certificate

(1) A final costs certificate of the costs officer is final and conclusive as to all matters which have not been objected to in the manner provided for under the rules of the court.

(2) Where it is proved to the satisfaction of a costs officer that a certificate of taxation has been lost or destroyed, he may issue a duplicate.

CHAPTER 6 PERSONS INCAPABLE OF MANAGING THEIR AFFAIRS

[7.2520]

6.29 Introductory

(1) The Rules in this Chapter apply where in railway administration proceedings it appears to the court that a person affected by the proceedings is one who is incapable of managing and administering his property and affairs either—

(a) by reason of mental disorder within the meaning of the Mental Health Act 1983, or

(b) due to physical affliction or disability.

(2) The person concerned is referred to as "the incapacitated person".

[7.2521]

6.30 Appointment of another person to act

[Form 24]

(1) The court may appoint such person as it thinks fit to appear for, represent or act for the incapacitated person.

(2) The appointment may be made either generally or for the purpose of any particular application or proceeding, or for the exercise of particular rights or powers which the incapacitated person might have exercised but for his incapacity.

(3) The court may make the appointment either of its own motion or on application by—

(a) a person who has been appointed by a court in the United Kingdom or elsewhere to manage the affairs of, or to represent, the incapacitated person, or

(b) any relative or friend of the incapacitated person who appears to the court to be a proper person to make the application, or

(c) the official receiver, or

(d) the special railway administrator.

(4) Application under paragraph (3) may be made *ex parte*, but the court may require such notice of the application as it thinks necessary to be given to the person alleged to be incapacitated, or any other person, and may adjourn the hearing of the application to enable the notice to be given.

[7.2522]
6.31 Affidavit in support of application

(1) Except where made by the official receiver, an application under Rule 6.30(3) shall be supported by an affidavit of a registered medical practitioner as to the mental or physical condition of the incapacitated person.

(2) In the excepted case, a report made by the official receiver is sufficient.

[7.2523]
6.32 Service of notices following appointment

Any notice served on, or sent to, a person appointed under Rule 6.30 has the same effect as if it had been served on, or given to, the incapacitated person.

CHAPTER 7 GENERAL

[7.2524]
6.33 Principal court rules and practice to apply

(1) The CPR and the practice and procedure of the High Court (including any practice direction) apply to railway administration proceedings, with necessary modifications, except so far as inconsistent with the Rules.

(2) All railway administration proceedings shall be allocated to the multi-track for which CPR Part 29 (the multi-track) makes provision, accordingly those provisions of the CPR which provide for allocation questionnaires and track allocation will not apply.

[7.2525]
6.34 Right of audience

(1) Official receivers and deputy official receivers have right of audience in railway administration proceedings.

(2) Subject as above, rights of audience in railway administration proceedings are the same as obtain in insolvency proceedings.

(3) In this Rule "insolvency proceedings" has the same meaning as in the Insolvency Rules.

[7.2526]
6.35 Right of attendance

(1) Subject as follows, in railway administration proceedings, any person stating himself in writing, in records kept by the court for that purpose, to be a creditor or member of the protected railway company is entitled, at his own cost, to attend in court or in chambers at any stage of the proceedings.

(2) Attendance may be by the person himself, or his solicitor.

(3) A person so entitled to attend may request the court in writing to give him notice of any step in the railway administration proceedings; and, subject to his paying the costs involved and keeping the court informed as to his address, the court shall comply with the request.

(4) If the court is satisfied that the exercise by a person of his rights under this Rule has given rise to costs for the assets of the protected railway company which would not otherwise have been incurred and ought not, in the circumstances, to be paid out of those assets, the court may direct that the costs be paid by the person concerned, to an amount specified.

The rights of that person under this Rule shall be in abeyance so long as those costs are not paid.

(5) The court may appoint one or more persons to represent the creditors or the members of a protected railway company, or any class of them, to have the rights conferred by this Rule, instead of the rights being exercised by any or all of them individually.

If two or more persons are appointed under this paragraph to represent the same interest, they must (if at all) instruct the same solicitor.

[7.2527]
6.36 Special railway administrator's solicitor

Where in railway administration proceedings the attendance of the special railway administrator's solicitor is required, whether in court or in chambers, the special railway administrator himself need not attend, unless directed by the court.

[7.2528]
6.37 Formal defects

No railway administration proceedings shall be invalidated by any formal defect or by any irregularity, unless the court before which objection is made considers that substantial injustice has been caused by the defect or irregularity, and that the injustice cannot be remedied by any order of the court.

[7.2529]
6.38 Restriction on concurrent proceedings and remedies

Where in railway administration proceedings the court makes an order staying any action, execution or other legal process against the property of a protected railway company, service of the order may be effected by sending a sealed copy of the order to whatever is the address for service of the claimant or other party having the carriage of the proceedings to be stayed.

[7.2530]
6.39 Affidavits

(1) Subject to the following paragraphs of this Rule, the practice and procedure of the High Court with regard to affidavits, their form and contents, and the procedure governing their use, are to apply to all railway administration proceedings.

(2) Where in railway administration proceedings an affidavit is made by the official receiver or the special railway administrator, the deponent shall state the capacity in which he makes it, the position which he holds and the address at which he works.

(3) A creditor's affidavit of debt may be sworn before his own solicitor.

(4) The official receiver, any deputy official receiver, or any officer of the court duly authorised in that behalf, may take affidavits and declarations.

(5) Subject to paragraph (6), where the Rules provide for the use of an affidavit, a witness statement verified by a statement of truth may be used as an alternative.

(6) Paragraph (5) does not apply to Rules 3.2, 8.3 and 8.4.

(7) Where paragraph (5) applies, any form prescribed by Rule 9.6 shall be modified accordingly.

[7.2531]
6.40 Security in court

(1) Where security has to be given to the court (otherwise than in relation to costs), it may be given by guarantee, bond or the payment of money into court.

(2) A person proposing to give a bond as security shall give notice to the party in whose favour the security is required, and to the court, naming those who are to be sureties to the bond.

(3) The court shall forthwith give notice to the parties concerned of a venue for the execution of the bond and the making of any objection to the sureties.

(4) The sureties shall make an affidavit of their sufficiency (unless dispensed with by the party in whose favour the security is required) and shall, if required by the court, attend the court to be cross-examined.

[7.2532]
6.41 Payment into court

The CPR relating to payment into and out of court of money lodged in court as security for costs apply to money lodged in court under the Rules.

[7.2533]
6.42 Further information and disclosure

(1) Any party to railway administration proceedings may apply to the court for an order—
- (a) that any other party
  - (i) clarify any matter which is in dispute in the proceedings, or
  - (ii) give additional information in relation to any such matter,

  in accordance with CPR Part 18 (further information); or
- (b) to obtain disclosure from any other party in accordance with CPR Part 31 (disclosure and inspection of documents).

(2) An application under this Rule may be made *ex parte*.

[7.2534]
6.43 Office copies of documents

(1) Any person who has under the Rules the right to inspect the court file of railway administration proceedings may require the court to provide him with an office copy of any document from the file.

(2) A person's right under this Rule may be exercised on his behalf by his solicitor.

(3) An office copy provided by the court under this Rule shall be in such form as the registrar thinks appropriate, and shall bear the court's seal.

PART 7
PROXIES AND COMPANY REPRESENTATION

[7.2535]
7.1 Definition of Proxy

(1) For the purposes of the Rules, a proxy is an authority given by a person ("the principal") to another person ("the proxy-holder") to attend a meeting and speak and vote as his representative.

(2) Proxies are for use at creditors' meetings summoned or called by the special railway administrator under section 14(2)(b) of the 1986 Act or summoned by him pursuant to a direction made by the court under section 17(3)(b) of that Act.

(3) Only one proxy may be given by a person for any one meeting at which he desires to be represented; and it may only be given to one person, being an individual aged 18 years or over. But the principal may specify one or more other such individuals to be proxy-holder in the alternative, in the order in which they are named in the proxy.

(4) Without prejudice to the generality of paragraph (3), a proxy for a particular meeting may be given to whoever is to be the chairman of the meeting, and such chairman cannot decline to be the proxy-holder in relation to that proxy.

(5) A proxy requires the holder to give the principal's vote on matters arising for determination at the meeting, or to abstain, or to propose, in the principal's name, a resolution to be voted on by the meeting, either as directed or in accordance with the holder's own discretion.

[7.2536]
7.2 Issue and use of forms of proxy

(1) When a notice is given of a meeting to be held in railway administration proceedings and forms of proxy are sent out with the notice, no form so sent out with the notice shall have inserted in it the name or description of any person.

(2) No form of proxy shall be used at any meeting except that which is sent with the notice summoning the meeting, or a substantially similar form.
[Form 23]

(3) A form of proxy shall be signed by the principal, or by some person authorised by him (either generally or with reference to a particular meeting). If the form is signed by a person other than the principal, the nature of the authority of that person shall be stated.

[7.2537]
7.3 Use of proxies at meetings

(1) A proxy given for a particular meeting may be used at any adjournment of that meeting.

(2) Where the special railway administrator holds proxies for use by him as chairman of a meeting, and some other person acts as chairman, that other person may use the proxies of the special railway administrator as if he were himself proxy-holder.

(3) A proxy-holder may propose any resolution which, if proposed by another, would be a resolution in favour of which by virtue of the proxy he would be entitled to vote.

(4) Where a proxy gives specific directions as to voting, this does not, unless the proxy states otherwise, preclude the proxy-holder from voting at his discretion on resolutions put to the meeting which are not dealt with in the proxy.

[7.2538]
7.4 Retention of proxies

(1) Subject as follows, proxies used for voting at any meeting shall be retained by the chairman of the meeting.

(2) The chairman shall deliver the proxies forthwith after the meeting to the special railway administrator, where that is someone other than himself.

[7.2539]
7.5 Right of inspection

(1) The special railway administrator shall, so long as proxies lodged with him are in his hands, allow them to be inspected, at all reasonable times on any business day by—
- (a) all creditors who have submitted in writing a claim to be creditors of the protected railway company,
- (b) that company's members, in the case of proxies used at a meeting of that company, and
- (c) the directors of that company.

(2) The reference in paragraph (1) to creditors does not include a person whose claim has been wholly rejected for the purposes of voting, dividend or otherwise.

(3) Any person attending a meeting in railway administration proceedings is entitled, immediately before or in the course of the meeting, to inspect proxies and associated documents (including proofs) sent or given, in accordance with directions contained in any notice convening the meeting, to the chairman of that meeting or to any other person by a creditor or member of the protected railway company for the purpose of that meeting.

[7.2540]

7.6 Proxy-holder with financial interest

(1) A proxy-holder shall not vote in favour of any resolution which would directly or indirectly place him, or any associate of his, in a position to receive any remuneration out of the assets of the protected railway company, unless the proxy specifically directs him to vote in that way.

(2) Where a proxy-holder has signed the proxy as being authorised to do so by his principal and the proxy specifically directs him to vote in the way mentioned in paragraph (1), he shall nevertheless not vote in that way unless he produces to the chairman of the meeting written authorisation from his principal sufficient to show that the proxy-holder was entitled so to sign the proxy.

(3) This Rule applies also to any person acting as chairman of a meeting and using proxies in that capacity under Rule 7.3, and in its application to him, the proxy-holder is deemed an associate of his.

(4) In this Rule "associate" shall have the same meaning as in section 435 of the 1986 Act.

[7.2541]

7.7 Company representation

(1) Where a person is authorised under section 375 of the Companies Act to represent a corporation at a meeting of creditors called in railway administration proceedings, he shall produce to the chairman of the meeting a copy of the resolution from which he derives his authority.

(2) The copy resolution must be under the seal of the corporation, or certified by the secretary or a director of the corporation to be a true copy.

(3) Nothing in this Rule requires the authority of a person to sign a proxy on behalf of a principal which is a corporation to be in the form of a resolution of that corporation.

PART 8
EXAMINATION OF PERSONS IN RAILWAY ADMINISTRATION PROCEEDINGS

[7.2542]

8.1 Interpretation and Application

(1) The Rules in this Part relate to applications to the court, made by the special railway administrator, for an order under section 236 of the 1986 Act (inquiry into protected railway company's dealings when it is, or is alleged to be, insolvent).

(2) The following definitions apply—

(a) the person in respect of whom an order is applied for is "the respondent";

(b) "section 236" means section 236 of the 1986 Act.

[7.2543]

8.2 Form and contents of application

(1) The application shall be in writing, and be accompanied by a brief statement of the grounds on which it is made.

(2) The respondent must be sufficiently identified in the application.

(3) It shall be stated whether the application is for the respondent—

(a) to be ordered to appear before the court, or

(b) to be ordered to clarify any matter which is in dispute in the proceedings or to give additional information in relation to any such matter and if so CPR Part 18 (further information) shall apply to any such order, or

(c) to submit an affidavit (if so, particulars are to be given of the matters to which he is required to swear), or

(d) to produce books, papers or other records (if so, the items in question are to be specified),

or for any two or more of those purposes.

(4) The application may be made *ex parte*.

[7.2544]

8.3 Order for examination, etc

(1) The court may, whatever the purpose of the application, make any order which it has power to make under section 236.

(2) The court, if it orders the respondent to appear before it, shall specify a venue for his appearance, which shall be not less than 14 days from the date of the order.

(3) If he is ordered to submit affidavits, the order shall specify—

(a) the matters which are to be dealt with in his affidavits, and

(b) the time within which they are to be submitted to the court.

(4) If the order is to produce books, papers or other records, the time and manner of compliance shall be specified.

(5) The order must be served forthwith on the respondent; and it must be served personally, unless the court otherwise orders.

[7.2545]
8.4 Procedure for examination

(1) At any examination of the respondent, the special railway administrator may attend in person, or be represented by a solicitor with or without counsel, and may put such questions to the respondent as the court may allow.

(2) If the respondent is ordered to clarify any matter or to give additional information, the court shall direct him as to the questions which he is required to answer, and as to whether his answers (if any) are to be made on affidavit.

(3) Where an application has been made under section 236 on information provided by a creditor of the protected railway company, that creditor may, with the leave of the court and if the special railway administrator does not object, attend the examination and put questions to the respondent (but only through the special railway administrator).

(4) The respondent may at his own expense employ a solicitor with or without counsel, who may put to him such questions as the court may allow for the purpose of enabling him to explain or qualify any answers given by him, and may make representations on his behalf.

(5) There shall be made in writing such record of the examination as the court thinks proper. The record shall be read over either to or by the respondent and signed by him at a venue fixed by the court.

(6) The written record may, in any proceedings (whether under the 1986 Act or otherwise), be used as evidence against the respondent of any statement made by him in the course of his examination.

[7.2546]
8.5 Record of examination

(1) Unless the court otherwise directs, the written record of the respondent's examination, and any response given by him to any order under CPR Part 18, and any affidavits submitted by him in compliance with an order of the court under section 236, shall not be filed in court.

(2) The written record, responses and affidavits shall not be open to inspection, without an order of the court, by any person other than the special railway administrator.

(3) Paragraph (2) applies also to so much of the court file as shows the grounds of the application for an order under section 236 and to any copy of any order sought under CPR Part 18.

(4) The court may from time to time give directions as to the custody and inspection of any documents to which this Rule applies, and as to the furnishing of copies of, or extracts from, such documents.

[7.2547]
8.6 Costs of proceedings under section 236

(1) Where the court has ordered an examination of a person under section 236, and it appears to it that the examination was made necessary because information had been unjustifiably refused by the respondent, it may order that the costs of the examination be paid by him.

(2) Where the court makes an order against a person under section 237(1) or section 237(2) of the 1986 Act (court's enforcement powers under section 236), the costs of the application for the order may be ordered by the court to be paid by the respondent.

(3) Subject to paragraphs (1) and (2), the special railway administrator's costs shall, unless the court otherwise orders, be paid out of the assets of the protected railway company.

(4) A person summoned to attend for examination under this Part shall be tendered a reasonable sum in respect of travelling expenses incurred in connection with his attendance. Other costs falling on him are at the court's discretion.

PART 9
MISCELLANEOUS AND GENERAL

[7.2548]
9.1 Power of Secretary of State to regulate certain matters

(1) Pursuant to paragraph 27 of Schedule 8 to the 1986 Act the Secretary of State may, subject to the 1986 Act, the 1993 Act and the Rules, make regulations with respect to any matter provided for in the Rules as relates to the carrying out of the functions of a special railway administrator of a protected railway company.

(2) Regulations made pursuant to paragraph (1) may—

- (a) confer discretion on the court;
- (b) make non-compliance with any of the regulations a criminal offence;
- (c) make different provision for different cases, including different provision for different areas; and
- (d) contain such incidental, supplemental and transitional provisions as may appear to the Secretary of State necessary or expedient.

[7.2549]
9.2 Notices

(1) All notices required or authorised by or under the 1986 Act or the Rules to be given must be in writing, unless it is otherwise provided, or the court allows the notice to be given in some other way.

(2) Where in any railway administration proceedings a notice is required to be sent or given by the special railway administrator, the sending or giving of it may be proved by means of a certificate by him, or his solicitor, or a partner or an employee of either of them, that the notice was duly posted.

(3) In the case of a notice to be sent or given by a person other than the special railway administrator, the sending or giving of it may be proved by means of a certificate by that person that he posted the notice, or instructed another person (naming him) to do so.

(4) A certificate under this Rule may be endorsed on a copy or specimen of the notice to which it relates.

(5) This Rule is without prejudice to the provisions of section 149 of the 1993 Act.

[7.2550]
9.3 Quorum at creditors' meetings

(1) Any meeting of creditors called or summoned by a special railway administrator is competent to act if a quorum is present.

(2) Subject to the next paragraph, a quorum is at least one creditor entitled to vote.

(3) For the purposes of this Rule, the reference to the creditor necessary to constitute a quorum is to those persons present or represented by proxy by any person (including the chairman) and includes persons duly represented under section 375 of the Companies Act.

(4) Where at any meeting of creditors—
- (a) the provisions of this Rule as to a quorum being present are satisfied by the attendance of—
  - (i) the chairman alone, or
  - (ii) one other person in addition to the chairman, and
- (b) the chairman is aware, by virtue of proofs and proxies received or otherwise, that one or more additional persons would, if attending, be entitled to vote,

the meeting shall not commence until at least the expiry of 15 minutes after the time appointed for its commencement.

[7.2551]
9.4 Evidence of proceedings at meeting

(1) A minute of proceedings at a meeting (held under the 1986 Act or the Rules) of the creditors or the members of a protected railway company called or summoned by the special railway administrator, signed by a person describing himself as, or appearing to be, the chairman of that meeting is admissible in railway administration proceedings without further proof.

(2) The minute is prime facie evidence that—
- (a) the meeting was duly convened and held,
- (b) all resolutions passed at the meeting were duly passed, and
- (c) all proceedings at the meeting duly took place.

[7.2552]
9.5 Documents issuing from Secretary of State

(1) Any document purporting to be, or to contain, any order, directions or certificate issued by the Secretary of State shall be received in evidence and deemed to be or (as the case may be) contain that order or certificate, or those directions, without further proof, unless the contrary is shown.

(2) Paragraph (1) applies whether the document is signed by the Secretary of State himself or an officer on his behalf.

(3) Without prejudice to the foregoing, a certificate signed by the Secretary of State or an officer on his behalf and confirming—
- (a) the making of an order,
- (b) the issuing of any document, or
- (c) the exercise of any discretion, power or obligation arising or imposed under the 1986 Act, the 1993 Act or the Rules,

is conclusive evidence of the matters dealt with in the certificate.

[7.2553]
9.6 Forms for use in railway administration proceedings

(1) The forms contained in the Schedule to the Rules shall be used in, and in connection with, railway administration proceedings.

(2) The forms shall be used with such variations, if any, as the circumstances may require.

[7.2554]
9.7 Special railway administrator's security

(1) Wherever under the Rules any person has to appoint, or proposes the appointment of, a person to the office of special railway administrator, he is under a duty to satisfy himself that the person appointed or to be appointed has security for the proper performance of his functions.

(2) In any railway administration proceedings the cost of the special railway administrator's security shall be defrayed as an expense of the proceedings.

[7.2555]
9.8 Time-limits

(1) The provisions of CPR rule 2.8 (time) apply, as regards computation of time, to anything required or authorised to be done by the Rules.

(2) The provisions of CPR rule 3.1(2)(a) (the court's general powers of management) apply so as to enable the court to extend or shorten the time for compliance with anything required or authorised to be done by the Rules.

[7.2556]
9.9 Service by post

(1) Section 149 of the 1993 Act applies as regards the service of documents in railway administration proceedings.

(2) Where a document is served by post, the document is treated as served, where first class post is used on the second business day after the date of posting, and where second class post is used on the fourth business day after the date of posting, unless the contrary is shown.

(3) The date of posting is presumed, unless the contrary is shown, to be the date shown in the post-mark on the envelope in which the document is contained.

[7.2557]
9.10 General provisions as to service and notice

Subject to section 149 of the 1993 Act, Rule 9.9 and (subject to Rule 9.11(1)) CPR Part 6 (service of documents) applies as regards any matter relating to the service of documents and the giving of notice in railway administration proceedings.

[7.2558]
9.11 Service outside the jurisdiction

(1) Section III of CPR Part 6 (special provisions about service out of the jurisdiction) does not apply in railway administration proceedings.

(2) Where for the purposes of railway administration proceedings any process or order of the court, or other document, is required to be served on a person who is not in England and Wales, the court may order service to be effected within such time, on such person, at such place and in such manner as it thinks fit, and may also require such proof of service as it thinks fit.

(3) An application under this Rule shall be supported by an affidavit stating—

- (a) the grounds on which the application is made, and
- (b) in what place or country the person to be served is, or probably may be found.

[7.2559]
9.12 Confidentiality of documents

(1) Where in railway administration proceedings the special railway administrator considers, in the case of a document forming part of the records of the proceedings, that—

- (a) it should be treated as confidential, or
- (b) it is of such a nature that its disclosure would be calculated to be injurious to the interests of the creditors or members of a protected railway company,

he may decline to allow it to be inspected by a person who would otherwise be entitled to inspect it.

(2) Where under this Rule the special railway administrator determines to refuse inspection of a document, the person wishing to inspect it may apply to the court for that determination to be overruled; and the court may either overrule it altogether, or sustain it subject to such conditions (if any), as it thinks fit to impose.

(3) Nothing in this Rule entitles the special railway administrator to decline to allow the inspection of any claim or proxy.

[7.2560]
9.13 Notices sent simultaneously to the same person

Where under the 1986 Act, the 1993 Act or the Rules a document of any description is to be sent to a person (whether or not as a member of a class of persons to whom that same document is to be sent), it may be sent as an accompaniment to any other document or information which the person is to receive, with or without modification or adaptation of the form applicable to that document.

[7.2561]
9.14 Right to copy documents

Where under the 1986 Act or the Rules a person has a right to inspect documents, the right includes that of taking copies of those documents, on payment—

- (a) in the case of documents on the court's file of proceedings, of the fee chargeable under any order made under [section 92 of the Courts Act 2003,] and
- (b) otherwise, of the appropriate fee.

NOTES

Words in square brackets substituted by the Courts Act 2003 (Transitional Provisions, Savings and Consequential Provisions) Order 2005, SI 2005/911, art 15.

[7.2562]
9.15 Charge for copy documents

Where in railway administration proceedings the special railway administrator is requested by a creditor or member to supply copies of any documents, he is entitled to require the payment of the appropriate fee in respect of the supply of the documents.

[7.2563]

9.16 Non-receipt of notice of meeting

Where in accordance with the 1986 Act or the Rules a meeting of creditors is called or summoned by notice, the meeting is presumed to have been duly summoned and held, notwithstanding that not all those to whom the notice is to be given have received it.

[7.2564]

9.17 Right to have list of creditors

(1) In any railway administration proceedings a creditor who under the Rules has the right to inspect documents on the court file also has the right to require the special railway administrator to furnish him with a list of the creditors of the protected railway company and the amounts of their respective debts.

This does not apply if a statement of the protected railway company's affairs has been filed in court.

(2) The special railway administrator, on being required by any person to furnish that list, shall send it to him, but is entitled to charge the appropriate fee for doing so.

[7.2565]

9.18 False claim of status as creditor

(1) Where the Rules provide for creditors of a protected railway company a right to inspect any documents, whether on the court's file or in the hands of the special railway administrator or other person, it is an offence for a person, with the intention of obtaining a sight of documents which he has not under the Rules any right to inspect, falsely to claim a status which would entitle him to inspect them.

(2) A person guilty of an offence under this Rule is liable—

(a) in summary proceedings, to a maximum of six months' imprisonment or a fine of the statutory maximum, or both;

(b) on indictment, to two years' imprisonment or a fine, or both.

[7.2566]

9.19 The Gazette

(1) A copy of the Gazette containing any notice required by the 1986 Act or the Rules to be gazetted is evidence of any fact stated in the notice.

(2) In the case of an order of the court notice of which is required by the 1986 Act or the Rules to be gazetted, a copy of the Gazette containing the notice may in any proceedings be produced as conclusive evidence that the order was made on the date specified in the notice.

(3) Where an order of the court which is gazetted has been varied, and where any matter has been erroneously or inaccurately gazetted, the person whose responsibility it was to procure the requisite entry in the Gazette shall forthwith cause the variation of the order to be gazetted or, as the case may be, a further entry to be made in the Gazette for the purpose of correcting the error or inaccuracy.

[7.2567]

9.20 Punishment of offences

Section 431 (summary proceedings) of the 1986 Act, as it applies to England and Wales, has effect in relation to offences under the Rules as to offences under that Act.

PART 10
INTERPRETATION AND APPLICATION

[7.2568]

10.1 Introductory

This Part of the Rules has effect for their interpretation and application; and any definition given in this Part applies except, and in so far as, the context otherwise requires.

[7.2569]

10.2 "The court"; "the registrar"

(1) Anything to be done in railway administration proceedings by, to or before the court may be done by, to or before a judge or the registrar.

(2) The registrar may authorise any act of a formal or administrative character which is not by statute his responsibility to be carried out by the chief clerk or any other officer of the court acting on his behalf, in accordance with directions given by the Lord Chancellor [after consulting the Lord Chief Justice].

(3) In railway administration proceedings, "the registrar" means—

(a) subject to the following paragraph, [an Insolvency and Companies Court Judge];

(b) where the proceedings are in the District Registry of Birmingham, Bristol, Cardiff, Leeds, Liverpool, Manchester, Newcastle-upon-Tyne or Preston, the District Registrar.

[(4) The Lord Chief Justice may nominate a judicial office holder (as defined in section 109(4) of the Constitutional Reform Act 2005) to exercise his functions under paragraph (2).]

NOTES

Para (2): words in square brackets added by the Lord Chancellor (Transfer of Functions and Supplementary Provisions) Order 2006, SI 2006/680, art 2, Sch 1, para 63(1), (2).

Para (3): words in square brackets substituted by the Alteration of Judicial Titles (Registrar in Bankruptcy of the High Court) Order 2018, SI 2018/130, art 3, Schedule, para 12(1)(b).

Para (4): added by SI 2006/680, art 2, Sch 1, para 63(1), (3).

[7.2570]
10.3 "Give notice" etc

(1) A reference in the Rules to giving notice, or to delivering, sending or serving any document, means that the notice or document may be sent by post, unless under a particular Rule personal service is expressly required.

(2) Any form of post may be used, unless under a particular Rule a specified form is expressly required.

(3) Personal service of a document is permissible in all cases.

(4) Notice of the venue fixed for an application may be given by service of the sealed copy of the application under Rule 6.4(3).

[7.2571]
10.4 Notice, etc to solicitors

Where in railway administration proceedings a notice or other document is required or authorised to be given to a person, it may, if he has indicated that his solicitor is authorised to accept service on his behalf, be given instead to the solicitor.

[7.2572]
10.5 Notice to joint special railway administrators

Where two or more persons are acting jointly as the special railway administrator in any proceedings, delivery of a document to one of them is to be treated as delivery to them all.

[7.2573]
10.6 "Petition"

References to "petition" means petition for a railway administration order to be made in relation to a protected railway company.

[7.2574]
10.7 "Venue"

References to the "venue" for any proceedings or attendance before the court, or for a meeting, are to the time, date and place for the proceedings, attendance or meeting.

[7.2575]
10.8 "Railway administration proceedings"

"Railway administration proceedings" means any proceedings under sections 59 to 62 of, and Schedule 6 to, the 1993 Act.

[7.2576]
10.9 "The appropriate fee"

"The appropriate fee" means 15 pence per A4 or A5 page and 30 pence per A3 page.

[7.2577]
10.10 Expressions used generally

(1) "File in court" means deliver to the court for filing.

(2) "The Gazette" means The London Gazette.

(3) "Business day" means any day other than a Saturday, a Sunday, Christmas Day, Good Friday or a day which is a bank holiday in any part of Great Britain under or by virtue of the Banking and Financial Dealings Act 1971.

[7.2578]
10.11 Application

The Rules apply to railway administration proceedings commenced on or after the date on which the Rules come into force. Nothing contained in the Insolvency Rules 1986 shall apply to such proceedings commenced on or after that date.

SCHEDULE
FORMS

Rule 9.6

[7.2579]

NOTES

The forms themselves are not set out in this work, but their numbers and titles are listed below.

FORM NO	TITLE
1	Petition for railway administration order
2	Consent of special railway administrator(s) to act
3	Affidavit of service of petition for railway administration order
4	Railway administration order
5	Notice to special railway administrator of railway administration order

FORM NO	TITLE
6	Notice of railway administration order for newspaper or London Gazette
7	Notice of railway administration order
8	Notice of railway administration order to registrar of companies
9	Notice requiring preparation and submission of railway administration statement of affairs
10	Statement of affairs
11	Notice of meetings in railway administration proceedings
12	Special railway administrator's abstract of receipt and payments
13	Notice to court of special railway administrator's resignation under rule 5.6(1)
14	Notice to court of special railway administrator's resignation under rule 5.6(2)
15	Notice of order to deal with charged property
16	Notice of discharge of railway administration order
17	Statement of special railway administrator's proposals
18	Statement of revised proposals
19	Originating application
20	Ordinary application
21	Appointment of shorthand writer to take examination
22	Declaration by shorthand writer
23	Proxy (railway administration)
24	Order appointing person to act for incapacitated person

R
TECHNICAL AND FURTHER EDUCATION

TECHNICAL AND FURTHER EDUCATION ACT 2017

(2017 c 19)

An Act to make provision about technical and further education.

[27 April 2017]

1, 2 *((Pt 1) Outside the scope of this work.)*

PART 2
FURTHER EDUCATION BODIES: INSOLVENCY ETC

CHAPTER 1 INTRODUCTION

[7.2580]
3 Overview
This Part is mainly about the insolvency of further education bodies—
(a) Chapter 2 ensures that normal insolvency procedures apply to further education bodies that are statutory corporations;
(b) Chapter 3 restricts the use of normal insolvency procedures;
(c) Chapter 4 creates a special administration regime;
(d) Chapter 5 is about the treatment of trust property held by certain bodies;
(e) Chapter 6 imposes restrictions on existing procedures for dissolution;
(f) Chapter 7 confers power to make provision about the disqualification of members of further education bodies.

NOTES
Commencement: to be appointed.

[7.2581]
4 "Further education body"
(1) In this Part "further education body" means—
(a) a further education body in England, or
(b) a further education body in Wales.
(2) In this Part "further education body in England" means—
(a) a further education corporation in England,
(b) a sixth form college corporation, or
(c) a company conducting a designated further education institution in England.
(3) In this Part "further education body in Wales" means—
(a) a further education corporation in Wales, or
(b) a company conducting a designated further education institution in Wales.

NOTES
Commencement: to be appointed.

[7.2582]
5 Other key definitions
In this Part—
"appropriate national authority"—
(a) in relation to a further education body in England, means the Secretary of State;
(b) in relation to a further education body in Wales, means the Welsh Ministers;
"company" means a company within the meaning of the Companies Act 2006;
"designated further education institution" means an institution that—
(a) is designated under section 28 of the Further and Higher Education Act 1992, and
(b) is principally concerned with the provision of further education;
"further education corporation" means a body corporate that—
(a) is established under section 15 or 16 of the Further and Higher Education Act 1992, or
(b) has become a further education corporation by virtue of section 33D or 47 of that Act;
"further education corporation in England" means a further education corporation established to conduct an institution in England;
"further education corporation in Wales" means a further education corporation established to conduct an institution in Wales;
"sixth form college corporation" means a body corporate—
(a) designated as a sixth form college corporation under section 33A or 33B of the Further and Higher Education Act 1992, or
(b) established under section 33C of that Act.

NOTES

Commencement: to be appointed.

CHAPTER 2 APPLICATION OF NORMAL INSOLVENCY TO STATUTORY CORPORATIONS

[7.2583]

6 Application of normal insolvency procedures

(1) The purpose of this section is to make the following insolvency procedures available in relation to further education bodies that are statutory corporations—

(a) voluntary arrangements,
(b) administration,
(c) creditors' voluntary winding up, and
(d) winding up by the court,

and to make provision about receivers and managers of property.

(2) For that purpose, the relevant insolvency legislation applies in relation to further education bodies that are statutory corporations as it applies in relation to companies, subject to—

(a) any modifications or omissions specified in regulations made by the Secretary of State, and
(b) sections 9 to 12 (restrictions on normal insolvency procedures to facilitate special administration).

(3) The "relevant insolvency legislation" means any provision made by or under the following provisions of the Insolvency Act 1986—

(a) Part 1 (company voluntary arrangements);
(b) Part 2 (administration);
(c) Part 3 (receivership);
(d) Part 4 (winding up);
(e) Parts 6, 7 and 12 to 18 (supplementary provision).

(4) The modifications or omissions that may be made under subsection (2)(a) include modifications or omissions in connection with the interaction between the insolvency procedures made available in relation to further education bodies by this section and education administration under Chapter 4 of this Part.

(5) Regulations under this section that modify or omit a provision of an Act as it applies by virtue of this section are subject to the affirmative resolution procedure.

(6) Any other regulations under this section are subject to the negative resolution procedure.

NOTES

Commencement: to be appointed.

[7.2584]

7 Application of other insolvency law

(1) The Secretary of State may make regulations, in consequence of section 6 or regulations made under it—

(a) providing for any legislation about insolvency to apply in relation to a further education body that is a statutory corporation (with or without modifications);
(b) amending, or modifying, any legislation about insolvency as it applies in relation to a further education body that is a statutory corporation.

(2) In subsection (1) "legislation about insolvency" includes any legislation that makes provision by reference to anything that is or may be done under any provision of the Insolvency Act 1986, or under any provision of subordinate legislation made under that Act, as applied by section 6.

(3) Regulations under this section that apply, amend or modify a provision of an Act are subject to the affirmative resolution procedure.

(4) Any other regulations under this section are subject to the negative resolution procedure.

(5) In this section "legislation" means provision made by Schedule 3 to this Act or provision made by or under any other Act passed before or in the same session as this Act.

NOTES

Commencement: to be appointed.

[7.2585]

8 Records etc

(1) The Secretary of State may by regulations make provision for or in connection with—

(a) the delivery to the registrar of companies of documents that relate to the insolvency of further education bodies;
(b) the registrar's function of keeping records of information contained in such documents under section 1080(1) of the Companies Act 2006;
(c) the publication of, or access to, those records or related information.

(2) The regulations may, in particular, provide for any provision made by or under the following sections of the Companies Act 2006 to apply (with or without modifications) in relation to those documents or records.

Provision of Companies Act 2006	*Description*

sections 29 and 30	copies of resolutions etc to be forwarded to the registrar
section 859K	registration of enforcement of security
sections 1077 and 1079	public notice of receipt of certain documents
sections 1081, 1084 and 1085 to 1091	keeping and inspection of register of companies
sections 1093 to 1097	correction or removal of material on companies register
section 1104	documents relating to Welsh companies
sections 1112 to 1113	supplementary provisions

(3) The power under subsection (1) includes power—

(a) to impose requirements on a person who delivers a document to the registrar in relation to the insolvency of a further education body to provide supplementary information;

(b) to confer power on the registrar to make rules in accordance with section 1117 of the Companies Act 2006 imposing such requirements.

(4) Provision made under this section is in addition to any applicable provision made by Part 35 of the Companies Act 2006 or elsewhere.

(5) Regulations under this section are subject to the affirmative resolution procedure.

(6) Section 1114(1) of the Companies Act 2006 (meaning of document etc) applies for the purposes of this section.

NOTES

Commencement: to be appointed.

CHAPTER 3 RESTRICTIONS ON USE OF NORMAL INSOLVENCY PROCEDURES

[7.2586]

9 Making of ordinary administration orders

(1) This section applies if a person other than the appropriate national authority makes an ordinary administration application in relation to a further education body.

(2) The court must dismiss the application if—

(a) an education administration order is in force in relation to the further education body, or

(b) an education administration order has been made in relation to the further education body but is not yet in force.

(3) If subsection (2) does not apply, the court, on hearing the application, must not exercise its powers under paragraph 13 of Schedule B1 to the Insolvency Act 1986 (other than its power of adjournment) unless—

(a) notice of the application has been given to the appropriate national authority,

(b) a period of at least 14 days has elapsed since that notice was given, and

(c) there is no outstanding education administration application.

(4) Paragraph 44 of Schedule B1 to the Insolvency Act 1986 (interim moratorium) does not prevent, or require the permission of the court for, the making of an education administration application.

(5) In this section "ordinary administration application" means an application in accordance with paragraph 12 of Schedule B1 to the Insolvency Act 1986.

NOTES

Commencement: to be appointed.

[7.2587]

10 Administrator appointments by creditors etc

(1) Subsections (2) to (4) make provision about the appointment of an administrator under—

(a) paragraph 14 of Schedule B1 to the Insolvency Act 1986, in relation to a further education body that is a company, or

(b) paragraph 22 of Schedule B1 to the Insolvency Act 1986, in relation to any further education body.

(2) If in any case—

(a) an education administration order is in force in relation to the further education body,

(b) an education administration order has been made in relation to the further education body but is not yet in force, or

(c) an education administration application in relation to the further education body is outstanding,

a person may not take any step to make an appointment.

(3) In any other case, an appointment takes effect only if each of the following conditions are met.

(4) The conditions are—

(a) that notice of the appointment has been given to the appropriate national authority, accompanied by a copy of every document in relation to the appointment that is filed or lodged with the court in accordance with paragraph 18 or 29 of Schedule B1 to the Insolvency Act 1986,

(b) that a period of at least 14 days has elapsed since that notice was given,

(c) that there is no outstanding education administration application in relation to the further education body, and
(d) that the making of an education administration application in relation to the further education body has not resulted in the making of an education administration order which is in force or is still to come into force.

(5) Paragraph 44 of Schedule B1 to the Insolvency Act 1986 (interim moratorium) does not prevent, or require the permission of the court for, the making of an education administration application at any time before the appointment takes effect.

NOTES

Commencement: to be appointed.

[7.2588]
11 Winding-up order

(1) This section applies if a person other than the appropriate national authority petitions for the winding up of a further education body.
(2) The court is not to exercise its powers on a winding-up petition unless—
(a) notice of the petition has been given to the appropriate national authority, and
(b) a period of at least 14 days has elapsed since that notice was given.
(3) If an education administration application is made in relation to the further education body before a winding-up order is made on the petition, the court may exercise its powers under sections 19 and 20 (instead of exercising its powers on the petition).
(4) References in this section to the court's powers on a winding-up petition are to—
(a) its powers under section 125 of the Insolvency Act 1986 (other than its power of adjournment), and
(b) its powers under section 135 of the Insolvency Act 1986.

NOTES

Commencement: to be appointed.

[7.2589]
12 Voluntary winding up

(1) A further education body has no power to pass a resolution for voluntary winding up without the permission of the court.
(2) Permission may be granted by the court only on an application made by the further education body.
(3) The court may not grant permission unless—
(a) notice of the application has been given to the appropriate national authority, and
(b) a period of at least 14 days has elapsed since that notice was given.
(4) If an education administration application is made in relation to the further education body after an application for permission under this section has been made but before it is granted, the court may exercise its powers under sections 19 and 20 (instead of granting permission).
(5) In this section "a resolution for voluntary winding up" has the same meaning as in the Insolvency Act 1986.

NOTES

Commencement: to be appointed.

[7.2590]
13 Enforcement of security

A person may not take any step to enforce a security over property of a further education body unless—
(a) notice of the intention to do so has been given to the appropriate national authority, and
(b) a period of at least 14 days has elapsed since the notice was given.

NOTES

Commencement: to be appointed.

[7.2591]
14 Interpretation of Chapter

(1) In this Chapter—
"the court", in relation to a further education body, means the court having jurisdiction to wind up the body;
"education administration application" has the meaning given by section 18;
"education administration order" has the meaning given by section 17.
(2) For the purposes of this Chapter an application made to the court is outstanding if it—
(a) has not yet been granted or dismissed, and
(b) has not been withdrawn.
(3) An application is not to be taken as having been dismissed if an appeal against the dismissal of the application, or a subsequent appeal, is pending.
(4) An appeal is to be treated as pending for this purpose if—
(a) an appeal has been brought and has not been determined or withdrawn,
(b) an application for permission to appeal has been made but has not been determined or withdrawn, or
(c) no appeal has been brought and the period for bringing one is still running.

(5) In relation to a further education body that is a statutory corporation, a reference in this Chapter to a provision of the Insolvency Act 1986 is to that provision as it applies to the body by virtue of section 6.

NOTES

Commencement: to be appointed.

CHAPTER 4 FURTHER EDUCATION BODIES: SPECIAL ADMINISTRATION

Introduction to education administration

[7.2592]

15 Overview of Chapter

(1) This Chapter creates a procedure to be known as education administration.

(2) The main features of an education administration are that—

(a) it can be used where a further education body is unable to pay its debts or is likely to become unable to pay its debts,

(b) the court appoints an education administrator on the application of the appropriate national authority, and

(c) the education administrator manages the body's affairs, business and property with a view to avoiding or minimising disruption to the studies of existing students.

NOTES

Commencement: to be appointed.

[7.2593]

16 Objective of education administration

(1) The objective of an education administration is to—

(a) avoid or minimise disruption to the studies of the existing students of the further education body as a whole, and

(b) ensure that it becomes unnecessary for the body to remain in education administration for that purpose.

(2) The means by which the education administrator may achieve that objective include—

(a) rescuing the further education body as a going concern,

(b) transferring some or all of its undertaking to another body,

(c) keeping it going until existing students have completed their studies, or

(d) making arrangements for existing students to complete their studies at another institution.

NOTES

Commencement: to be appointed.

Process

[7.2594]

17 Education administration order

(1) An education administration order is an order of the court appointing a person as the education administrator of a further education body.

(2) A person is eligible for appointment as an education administrator only if the person would be qualified to act as an insolvency practitioner in relation to the further education body.

(3) While an education administration order is in force the further education body may be described as being "in education administration".

NOTES

Commencement: to be appointed.

[7.2595]

18 Application for education administration order

(1) An education administration order may be made only on an application by the appropriate national authority.

(2) The appropriate national authority must give notice of an application—

(a) to the further education body to which the application relates, and

(b) to any person specified in education administration rules (for those rules, see section 32).

(3) An application for an education administration order is referred to in this Chapter as an "education administration application".

NOTES

Commencement: to be appointed.

[7.2596]

19 Grounds for making an education administration order

(1) The court may make an education administration order on an application only if satisfied that the further education body—

(a) is unable to pay its debts, or

(b) is likely to become unable to pay its debts.

(2) The court has no power to make an education administration order in relation to a further education body which—

(a) is in administration under Schedule B1 to the Insolvency Act 1986, or
(b) has gone into liquidation (within the meaning of section 247(2) of the Insolvency Act 1986).

(3) For the purposes of this section a further education body is unable to pay its debts if it is deemed to be unable to pay its debts under section 123 of the Insolvency Act 1986.

NOTES

Commencement: to be appointed.

[7.2597]

20 Powers of the court on hearing an application

(1) On hearing an education administration application the court may—
(a) grant the application,
(b) adjourn the application conditionally or unconditionally,
(c) dismiss the application,
(d) make an interim order,
(e) treat that application as a winding-up petition and make any order the court could make under section 125 of the Insolvency Act 1986 (power of court on hearing winding-up petition), or
(f) make any other order that it thinks appropriate.

(2) An interim order under subsection (1)(d) may, in particular—
(a) restrict the exercise of a power of the further education body,
(b) in the case of a further education body that is a statutory corporation, restrict the exercise of a power of its members,
(c) in the case of a further education body that is a company, restrict the exercise of a power of its directors, and
(d) make provision conferring a discretion on a person who would be qualified to act as an insolvency practitioner in relation to the further education body.

(3) An education administration order comes into force—
(a) at the time appointed by the court, or
(b) if no time is appointed by the court, when the order is made.

NOTES

Commencement: to be appointed.

[7.2598]

21 Appointment of two or more education administrators

If an education administration order appoints two or more persons as the education administrator of a further education body, the order must set out—
(a) which (if any) of the functions of the education administrator are to be carried out only by the appointees acting jointly,
(b) the circumstances (if any) in which the functions of an education administrator are to be carried out by one of the appointees, or by particular appointees, acting alone, and
(c) the circumstances (if any) in which things done in relation to one of the appointees, or in relation to particular appointees, are to be treated as done in relation to all of them.

NOTES

Commencement: to be appointed.

[7.2599]

22 Duty to dismiss ordinary administration application

(1) On the making of an education administration order in relation to a further education body, the court must dismiss any ordinary administration application made in relation to the body which is outstanding.

(2) In this section "ordinary administration application" means an application in accordance with paragraph 12 of Schedule B1 to the Insolvency Act 1986.

(3) Subsections (2) to (4) of section 14 (meaning of "outstanding") apply for the purposes of this section.

NOTES

Commencement: to be appointed.

[7.2600]

23 Status of education administrator

(1) An education administrator is an officer of the court.

(2) In carrying out functions in relation to a further education body an education administrator acts as its agent.

NOTES

Commencement: to be appointed.

Functions of administrator and conduct of administration

[7.2601]

24 General functions of education administrator

(1) Where an education administration order is in force in relation to a further education body, the body's affairs, business and property are to be managed by the education administrator.

(2) The education administrator must carry out his or her functions for the purpose of achieving the objective of the education administration.
(3) In pursuing the objective of the education administration set out in section 16(1)(a) the education administrator must, in particular, take into account the needs of existing students who have special educational needs.
(4) The education administrator of a further education body that is a statutory corporation must, so far as is consistent with the objective of the education administration, carry out his or her functions in a way that achieves the best result for the further education body's creditors as a whole.
(5) The education administrator of a further education body that is a company must, so far as is consistent with the objective of the education administration, carry out his or her functions in a way that achieves the best result for—
(a) the company's creditors as a whole, and
(b) subject to that, the company's members as a whole.
(6) For the purposes of this section an existing student has "special educational needs" if he or she has a learning difficulty which calls for special educational provision to be made for him or her.
(7) In subsection (6)—
"special educational provision", in relation to an existing student, means provision for education or training that is additional to, or different from, that made generally for other students of the same age;
"learning difficulty" is to be read in accordance with section 19(6) and (7) of the Further and Higher Education Act 1992.

NOTES
Commencement: to be appointed.

[7.2602]
25 Transfer schemes
Schedule 2 gives an education administrator the power to make transfer schemes.

NOTES
Commencement: to be appointed.

[7.2603]
26 Conduct of administration
(1) Schedule 3 applies provisions of the Insolvency Act 1986, with modifications, in relation to the education administration of a further education body that is a statutory corporation.
(2) Schedule 4 makes similar provision in relation to the education administration of a further education body that is a company.

NOTES
Commencement: to be appointed.

Financial support for bodies in education administration

[7.2604]
27 Grants and loans where education administration order is made
(1) If an education administration order has been made in relation to a further education body, the appropriate national authority may make grants or loans to the body for the purpose of achieving the objective of the education administration.
(2) A grant or loan under this section may be made on whatever terms the appropriate national authority considers appropriate (including terms relating to repayment of the grant or loan, with or without interest).
(3) In the case of a loan, the terms must provide for paragraph 99(7)(a), (b) or (c) of Schedule B1 to the Insolvency Act 1986 (vacation of office: charges and liabilities) to apply in relation to any sum that must be paid by the further education body in respect of the loan or interest on it.
(4) In subsection (3) the reference to paragraph 99 of Schedule B1 to the Insolvency Act 1986 is to that Schedule as applied by Schedule 3 or 4 to this Act.

NOTES
Commencement: to be appointed.

[7.2605]
28 Indemnities where education administration order is made
(1) If an education administration order has been made in relation to a further education body, the appropriate national authority may agree to indemnify persons in respect of one or both of the following—
(a) liabilities incurred in connection with the carrying out of functions by the education administrator, and
(b) loss or damage sustained in that connection.
(2) The agreement may be made in whatever manner, and on whatever terms, the appropriate national authority considers appropriate.
(3) As soon as possible after agreeing to indemnify persons under this section, the appropriate national authority must lay a statement of the agreement before Parliament or the National Assembly for Wales (as appropriate).

(4) For repayment of sums paid by the appropriate national authority in consequence of an indemnity agreed to under this section, see section 29.

(5) The power of the appropriate national authority to agree to indemnify persons—

(a) is confined to a power to agree to indemnify persons in respect of liabilities, loss and damage incurred or sustained by them as relevant persons, but

(b) includes power to agree to indemnify persons (whether or not they are identified or identifiable at the time of the agreement) who subsequently become relevant persons.

(6) The following are relevant persons for the purposes of this section—

(a) the education administrator;

(b) an employee of the education administrator;

(c) a partner or employee of a firm of which the education administrator is a partner or employee;

(d) a partner of a firm of which the education administrator was an employee or partner at a time when the order was in force;

(e) a body corporate which is the employer of the education administrator;

(f) an officer, employee or member of such a body corporate;

(g) a Scottish firm which is the employer of the education administrator or of which the education administrator is a partner.

(7) For the purposes of subsection (6)—

(a) references to the education administrator are to be read, where two or more persons are appointed as the education administrator, as references to any one or more of them, and

(b) references to a firm of which a person was a partner or employee at a particular time include a firm which holds itself out to be the successor of a firm of which the person was a partner or employee at that time.

NOTES

Commencement: to be appointed.

[7.2606]

29 Indemnities: repayment by further education bodies etc

(1) This section applies where a sum is paid out by the appropriate national authority in consequence of an indemnity agreed to under section 28 in relation to the education administration of a further education body.

(2) The further education body must pay the appropriate national authority—

(a) any amounts in or towards the repayment of that sum that the appropriate national authority directs, and

(b) interest on amounts outstanding under this subsection at whatever rates the appropriate national authority directs.

(3) The payments must be made by the further education body at times, and in a manner, determined by the appropriate national authority

(4) Subsection (2) does not apply in the case of a sum paid by the appropriate national authority for indemnifying a person in respect of a liability to the further education body.

(5) The appropriate national authority must lay before Parliament or the National Assembly for Wales (as appropriate) a statement relating to the sum paid out in consequence of the indemnity—

(a) as soon as possible after the end of the financial year in which the sum is paid out, and

(b) if subsection (2) applies to the sum, as soon as possible after the end of each subsequent financial year in relation to which the repayment condition has not been met.

(6) The repayment condition is met in relation to a financial year if—

(a) the whole of the sum has been repaid to the appropriate national authority before the beginning of the year, and

(b) the further education body was not at any time during the year liable to pay interest on amounts that became due in respect of the sum.

NOTES

Commencement: to be appointed.

[7.2607]

30 Guarantees where education administration order is made

(1) If an education administration order has been made in relation to a further education body the appropriate national authority may guarantee—

(a) the repayment of any sum borrowed by the body while that order is in force,

(b) the payment of interest on any sum borrowed by the body while that order is in force, and

(c) the discharge of any other financial obligation of the body in connection with the borrowing of any sum while that order is in force.

(2) The appropriate national authority may give the guarantees in whatever manner, and on whatever terms, the appropriate national authority considers appropriate.

(3) As soon as possible after giving a guarantee under this section, the appropriate national authority must lay a statement of the guarantee before Parliament or the National Assembly for Wales (as appropriate).

(4) For repayment of sums paid by the appropriate national authority under a guarantee given under this section, see section 31.

NOTES

Commencement: to be appointed.

[7.2608]

31 Guarantees: repayment by further education body etc

(1) This section applies where a sum is paid out by the appropriate national authority under a guarantee given by the appropriate national authority under section 30 in relation to a further education body.

(2) The further education body must pay the appropriate national authority—

(a) any amounts in or towards the repayment of that sum that the appropriate national authority directs, and

(b) interest on amounts outstanding under this subsection at whatever rates the appropriate national authority directs.

(3) The payments must be made by the further education body at times, and in a manner, determined by the appropriate national authority.

(4) The appropriate national authority must lay before Parliament or the National Assembly for Wales (as appropriate) a statement relating to the sum paid out under the guarantee—

(a) as soon as possible after the end of the financial year in which the sum is paid out, and

(b) as soon as possible after the end of each subsequent financial year in relation to which the repayment condition has not been met.

(5) The repayment condition is met in relation to a financial year if—

(a) the whole of the sum has been repaid to the appropriate national authority before the beginning of the year, and

(b) the further education body was not at any time during the year liable to pay interest on amounts that became due in respect of the sum.

NOTES

Commencement: to be appointed.

Supplementary

[7.2609]

32 Education administration rules

(1) The power to make rules under section 411 of the Insolvency Act 1986 is to apply for the purpose of giving effect to this Chapter as it applies for the purpose of giving effect to Parts 1 to 7 of that Act (and, accordingly, as if references in that section to those Parts included references to this Chapter).

(2) Section 413(2) of the Insolvency Act 1986 (duty to consult Insolvency Rules Committee about rules) does not to apply to rules made under section 411 of the Insolvency Act 1986 as a result of this section.

NOTES

Commencement: to be appointed.

[7.2610]

33 Application of other insolvency law

(1) The Secretary of State may make regulations, in consequence of this Chapter or subordinate legislation made under it—

(a) providing for any legislation about insolvency to apply in relation to a further education body (with or without modifications);

(b) amending, or modifying, any legislation about insolvency as it applies in relation to a further education body.

(2) In subsection (1) "legislation about insolvency" includes any legislation that makes provision by reference to anything that is or may be done under any provision of the Insolvency Act 1986, or under any provision of subordinate legislation made under that Act, as applied by this Chapter.

(3) Regulations under this section that apply, amend or modify a provision of an Act are subject to the affirmative resolution procedure.

(4) Any other regulations under this section are subject to the negative resolution procedure.

(5) In this section "legislation" means any provision made by or under an Act passed before or in the same session as this Act.

NOTES

Commencement: to be appointed.

[7.2611]

34 Modification of this Chapter under the Enterprise Act 2002

A power to modify or apply enactments conferred on the Secretary of State by section 248 or 277 of the Enterprise Act 2002 includes power to make such consequential modifications of this Chapter as the Secretary of State considers appropriate in connection with any other provision made under that section.

NOTES

Commencement: to be appointed.

[7.2612]

35 Interpretation of Chapter

(1) In this Chapter—

"business", "property" and "security" have the same meaning as in the Insolvency Act 1986;

"the court", in relation to a further education body, means the court having jurisdiction to wind up the body;

"education administration application" has the meaning given by section 18;
"education administration order" has the meaning given by section 17;
"education administration rules" means rules made under section 411 of the Insolvency Act 1986 as a result of section 32 above;
"education administrator" means a person appointed by an education administration order and is to be read in accordance with subsection (2) below;
"existing student", in relation to a further education body that is in education administration, means a person who—
(a) is a student at the relevant institution when the administration order is made, or
(b) has accepted a place on a course at the relevant institution when the administration order is made;
"financial year" means a period of 12 months ending with 31 March;
"member", in relation to a further education body that is a company, has the same meaning as in the Insolvency Act 1986;
"objective of the education administration" is to be read in accordance with section 16;
"the relevant institution"—
(a) in relation to a further education corporation, means the institution which the corporation is established to conduct;
(b) in relation to a sixth form college corporation, means the relevant sixth form college as defined by section 90(1) of the Further and Higher Education Act 1992;
(c) in relation to a company conducting a designated further education institution, means that designated further education institution;
"Scottish firm" means a firm constituted under the law of Scotland.

(2) In this Chapter references to the education administrator of a further education body—
(a) include a person appointed under paragraph 91 or 103 of Schedule B1 to the Insolvency Act 1986, as applied by Schedule 3 or 4 to this Act, to be the education administrator of the further education body, and
(b) if two or more persons are appointed as the education administrator of the further education body, are to be read in accordance with the provision made under section 21.

(3) References in this Chapter to a person qualified to act as an insolvency practitioner in relation to a further education body are to be read in accordance with Part 13 of the Insolvency Act 1986.

(4) In relation to a further education body that is a statutory corporation, references in this Chapter to a provision of the Insolvency Act 1986 (except the references in sections 27, 32 and 33 and Schedule 3 and in subsection (2) above) are to that provision as it applies to further education bodies by virtue of section 6.

NOTES

Commencement: to be appointed.

CHAPTER 5 TRUST PROPERTY HELD BY SIXTH FORM COLLEGE CORPORATIONS

[7.2613]

36 Trust property held by sixth form college corporations

If a sixth form college corporation to which section 33J of the Further and Higher Education Act 1992 applies is being wound up under the Insolvency Act 1986, any property held by the corporation on trust for the purposes of the relevant sixth form college must be transferred to the trustees of the relevant sixth form college (as defined by section 90(1) of that Act).

NOTES

Commencement: to be appointed.

37–41 *(Ss 37, 38 (Chapter 6) outside the scope of this work; s 39 (Chapter 7) inserts the Company Directors Disqualification Act 1986, s 22G at* **[4.49]***; ss 40, 42 (Pt 3) outside the scope of this work.)*

PART 4
GENERAL

42–45 *(Outside the scope of this work.)*

[7.2614]

46 Extent

(1) Any amendment or repeal made by this Act has the same extent as the enactment amended or repealed.

(2) This Part and section 6 so far as it relates to section 426 of the Insolvency Act 1986 extend to—
(a) England and Wales,
(b) Scotland, and
(c) Northern Ireland.

(3) Except as mentioned above, this Act extends to England and Wales only.

NOTES

Commencement: 27 April 2017.

[7.2615]
47 Commencement
(1) This Part and paragraph 35 of Schedule 1 come into force on the day on which this Act is passed.
(2) The other provisions of this Act come into force on such day as the Secretary of State may by regulations appoint.
(3) Different days may be appointed for different purposes.

NOTES
Commencement: 27 April 2017.
Orders: the Technical and Further Education Act 2017 (Commencement No 1 and Transitional Provision) Regulations 2017, SI 2017/844; the Technical and Further Education Act 2017 (Commencement No 2 and Transitional Provision) Regulations 2017, SI 2017/1055.

[7.2616]
48 Short title
This Act may be cited as the Technical and Further Education Act 2017.

NOTES
Commencement: 27 April 2017.

SCHEDULE 1

(*Schs 1, 2 outside the scope of this work.*)

SCHEDULE 3
CONDUCT OF EDUCATION ADMINISTRATION: STATUTORY CORPORATIONS

Section 26

Introductory

[7.2617]
1 (1) The provisions of the Insolvency Act 1986 mentioned in sub-paragraph (2) apply in relation to the education administration of a further education body that is a statutory corporation as they apply in relation to a company administration, but with the modifications set out in this Schedule.
(2) The provisions are—
(a) sections 233 to 237 (management by administrators, liquidators etc);
(b) sections 238 to 241 (transactions at an undervalue and preferences);
(c) section 244 (extortionate credit bargains);
(d) section 246 (unenforceability of liens on books, etc);
(e) section 246ZA to 246ZC (fraudulent and wrongful trading);
(f) section 246ZD (power to assign certain causes of action);
(g) section 246B (use of websites);
(h) section 246C (creditors' ability to opt out of receiving certain notices);
(i) sections 247, 248(b), 249 and 251 (interpretation);
(j) the applicable provisions of Schedule B1 (conduct of administration).
(3) The applicable provisions of Schedule B1 are—
(a) paragraphs 1, 40 to 49, 54, 59, 60, 61 to 68, 71 to 75, 79, 83 to 91, 98 to 104, 106 and 107 and 109 to 111, and
(b) paragraph 50 (until the repeal of that paragraph by Schedule 10 to the Small Business, Enterprise and Employment Act 2015 comes into force).

General modifications

2 The provisions of the Insolvency Act 1986 applied by paragraph 1 are to have effect as if for any term specified in column 1 of the table there were substituted the term specified in column 2.

Term	*Modification*
company	further education body
administration application	education administration application
administration order	education administration order
administrator	education administrator
director	(a) member of the further education body, (b) principal of the relevant institution, or (c) if the context requires, both of the above.
enters administration	enters education administration
in administration	in education administration

Part 7R Special Insolvency Regimes

officer (in relation to a company)	(a) a member of the further education body, (b) the clerk to the further education body, (c) the chief executive of the relevant institution, (d) any senior post holder or principal of the relevant institution, or (e) if the context requires, all of the above.
purpose of administration	objective of the education administration
the rules	the education administration rules

Specific modifications to Schedule B1 to the Insolvency Act 1986

3 Paragraphs 4 to 37 set out modifications to the applicable provisions of Schedule B1 to the Insolvency Act 1986 as applied by paragraph 1 above.

4 Paragraph 1 (administration) is to have effect as if—
(a) for sub-paragraph (1) there were substituted—

"(1) In this Schedule "education administrator", in relation to a further education body, means a person appointed by the court for the purposes of an education administration order to manage its affairs, business and property.", and

(b) in sub-paragraph (2), for "Act" there were substituted "Schedule".

5 Paragraph 40 (dismissal of pending winding-up petition) is to have effect as if sub-paragraphs (1)(b), (2) and (3) were omitted.

6 Paragraph 41 (dismissal of administrative or other receiver) is to have effect as if—
(a) sub-paragraph (1) were omitted;
(b) in sub-paragraph (3), "administrative receiver or" and "(1) or" were omitted;
(c) in sub-paragraph (4)(a) and (b), "administrative receiver or" were omitted.

7 Paragraph 42 (moratorium on insolvency proceedings) is to have effect as if sub-paragraphs (4) and (5) were omitted.

8 Paragraph 43 (moratorium on other legal process) is to have effect as if sub-paragraphs (5) and (6A) were omitted.

9 Paragraph 44 (interim moratorium) is to have effect as if sub-paragraphs (2) to (4), (6) and (7) were omitted.

10 Paragraph 45(2) (publicity) is to have effect as if for paragraph (b) there were substituted—

"(b) a member of the further education body,
(ba) the clerk to the further education body,
(bb) the chief executive of the relevant institution,
(bc) any senior post holder or principal of the relevant institution, and".

11 Paragraph 46(6) (date for notifying administrator's appointment) is to have effect as if for paragraphs (a) to (c) there were substituted "the date on which the education administration order comes into force".

12 Paragraph 47 (statement of affairs) is to have effect as if—
(a) for sub-paragraph (3)(a) there were substituted—

"(a) a person who is or has been a member of the further education body,
(aa) a person who is or has been the clerk to the further education body,
(ab) a person who is or has been chief executive of the relevant institution,
(ac) a person who is or has been a senior post holder or principal of the relevant institution, and",

(b) in sub-paragraph (3), paragraph (d) were omitted, and
(c) sub-paragraph (5) were omitted.

13 Paragraph 49 (administrator's proposals) is to have effect as if—
(a) sub-paragraphs (2)(b) and (3) were omitted,
(b) in sub-paragraph (4), after paragraph (a) there were inserted—

"(aa) to the appropriate national authority,
(ab) to the director of children's services at the local authority or combined authority in whose area the relevant institution is based, and to any other director of children's services that the education administrator thinks appropriate,", and

(c) sub-paragraphs (5)(b) and (6) were omitted.

14 Paragraph 54 is to have effect as if the following were substituted for it—

"**54** (1) The education administrator of a further education body may on one or more occasions revise the proposals included in the statement made under paragraph 49 in relation to the body.

(2) If the education administrator thinks that a revision is substantial, the education administrator must send a copy of the revised proposals—

(a) to the registrar of companies,

(b) to the appropriate national authority,

(c) to any director of children's services to whom the statement of proposals was sent under paragraph 49,

(d) to every creditor of the further education body, other than an opted-out creditor, of whose claim and address the education administrator is aware, and

(e) to every member of the further education body of whose address the education administrator is aware.

(3) A copy sent in accordance with sub-paragraph (2) must be sent within the prescribed period.

(4) An education administrator who fails without reasonable excuse to comply with this paragraph commits an offence."

15 Paragraph 60 is to have effect as if the following were substituted for it—

"**60** (1) The education administrator of a further education body has the powers specified in Schedule 1 to this Act (reading references in that Schedule to the company as references to the further education body).

(2) The education administrator of a further education body has the power to act on behalf of the further education body for the purposes of provision contained in any legislation which confers a power on the further education body or imposes a duty on it.

(3) In sub-paragraph (2) "legislation" means provision made by or under any Act."

16 Paragraph 61 is to have effect as if the following were substituted for it—

"**61** The education administrator—

(a) may appoint or remove the clerk to the further education body,

(b) may appoint or remove the chief executive of the relevant institution, and

(c) may appoint or remove the principal of the relevant institution."

17 Paragraph 64 (management powers may not be exercised without consent of the administrator) is to have effect as if in sub-paragraph (1) for "an officer of a company in administration" there were substituted "the clerk to the further education body or chief executive of the relevant institution".

18 Paragraph 68 (management duties of an administrator) is to have effect as if—

(a) in sub-paragraph (1), for paragraphs (a) to (c) there were substituted "the proposals as—

"(a) set out in the statement made under paragraph 49 in relation to the further education body, and

(b) from time to time revised under paragraph 54,for achieving the objective of the education administration.", and

(b) in sub-paragraph (3), for paragraphs (a) to (d) there were substituted "the directions are consistent with the achievement of the objective of the education administration".

19 Paragraph 71 (charged property: non-floating charge), is to have effect as if, in sub-paragraph (1), the words "(other than a floating charge)" were omitted.

20 Paragraph 73 (protection for secured or preferential creditor) is to have effect as if—

(a) in sub-paragraph (2), paragraphs (c) and (d) were omitted, and

(b) in sub-paragraph (3), for "or modified" there were substituted "under paragraph 54".

21 Paragraph 74 (challenge to administrator's conduct) is to have effect as if—

(a) sub-paragraph (1) were omitted,

(b) for sub-paragraph (2) there were substituted—

"(2) Where a further education body is in education administration the appropriate national authority or a creditor may apply to the court claiming that the education administrator is not carrying out his or her functions in accordance with section 24(2) or (4) of the Technical and Further Education Act 2017 (general functions of education administrator).",

(c) in sub-paragraph (6), paragraphs (b) to (c) were omitted, and

(d) after that sub-paragraph there were inserted—

"(7) In the case of a claim made by a creditor, the court may grant a remedy or relief or make an order under this paragraph only if it has given the appropriate national authority a reasonable opportunity of making representations about the claim and the proposed remedy, relief or order.

(8) Before the making of an order of the kind mentioned in sub-paragraph (4)(d)—

(a) the court must notify the education administrator of the proposed order and of a period during which the education administrator is to have the opportunity of taking steps falling within sub-paragraph (9), and

(b) the period notified must have expired without the taking of such of those steps as the court thinks should have been taken, and that period must be a reasonable period.

(9) The steps referred to in sub-paragraph (8) are steps for—

(a) remedying the failure to carry out functions in accordance with section 24(2) or (4) of the Technical and Further Education Act 2017, and

(b) ensuring that the failure is not repeated."

22 Paragraph 75(2) (misfeasance) is to have effect as if—

(a) after paragraph (b) there were inserted—

"(ba) a person appointed as an administrator of the further education body under the provisions of this Act as they have effect in relation to administrators other than education administrators,",

(b) at the end of paragraph (c) there were inserted "or", and

(c) paragraph (e) (and the "or" before it) were omitted.

23 Paragraph 79 (end of administration) is to have effect as if—

(a) for sub-paragraphs (1) and (2) there were substituted—

"(1) On an application made by a person mentioned in sub-paragraph (2), the court may provide for the appointment of an education administrator of a further education body to cease to have effect from a specified time.

(2) An application may be made to the court under this paragraph—

(a) by the appropriate national authority, or

(b) with the consent of the appropriate national authority, by the education administrator.", and

(b) sub-paragraph (3) were omitted.

24 Paragraph 83 (notice to registrar when moving to voluntary liquidation) is to have effect as if—

(a) sub-paragraph (2) were omitted, and

(b) in sub-paragraph (3) after "may" there were inserted ", with the consent of the appropriate national authority,".

25 Paragraph 84 (notice to registrar when moving to dissolution) is to have effect as if—

(a) in sub-paragraph (1), for "to the registrar of companies" there were substituted—

"(a) to the appropriate national authority, and

(b) if directed to do so by the appropriate national authority, to the registrar of companies",

(b) sub-paragraph (2) were omitted, and

(c) in sub-paragraphs (3) to (6), for "(1)", in each place, there were substituted "(1)(b)".

26 Paragraph 87(2) (resignation of administrator) is to have effect as if for paragraphs (a) to (d) there were substituted "by notice in writing to the court".

27 Paragraph 89(2) (administrator ceasing to be qualified) is to have effect as if for paragraphs (a) to (d) there were substituted "to the court".

28 Paragraph 90 (filling vacancy in office of administrator) is to have effect as if for "Paragraphs 91 to 95 apply" there were substituted "Paragraph 91 applies".

29 Paragraph 91 (vacancies in court appointments) is to have effect as if—

(a) for sub-paragraph (1) there were substituted—

"(1) The court may replace the education administrator on an application made—

(a) by the appropriate national authority, or

(b) where more than one person was appointed to act jointly as the education administrator, by any of those persons who remains in office.", and

(b) sub-paragraph (2) were omitted.

30 Paragraph 98 (discharge from liability on vacation of office) is to have effect as if sub-paragraphs (2)(b) and (ba), (3) and (3A) were omitted.

31 Paragraph 99 (charges and liabilities upon vacation of office by administrator) is to have effect as if—

(a) in sub-paragraph (3), paragraph (b) were omitted, and

(b) after sub-paragraph (6) there were inserted—

"(7) Where a loan is made under section 27 of the Technical and Further Education Act 2017 before cessation, sub-paragraph (4) does not apply in relation to the loan or interest on it and—

(a) if the terms of the loan provide for this paragraph to apply, any sum that must be paid by the further education body in respect of the loan or interest shall be—

(i) charged on and payable out of property of which the education administrator had custody or control immediately before cessation, and

(ii) payable in priority to any charge arising under sub-paragraph (3);

(b) if the terms of the loan provide for this paragraph to apply, any sum that must be paid by the further education body in respect of the loan or interest shall be treated as an unsecured debt that is not a preferential debt;

(c) if the terms of the loan provide for this paragraph to apply, any sum that must be paid by the further education body in respect of the loan or interest shall be payable after all other creditors have been paid in full."

32 Paragraph 100 (joint and concurrent administrators) is to have effect as if sub-paragraph (2) were omitted.

33 Paragraph 101(3) (joint administrators) is to have effect as if after "87 to" there were inserted "91, 98 and".

34 Paragraph 103 (appointment of additional administrators) is to have effect as if—

(a) in sub-paragraph (2) the words from the beginning to "order" were omitted,
(b) in sub-paragraph (2), for paragraph (a) there were substituted—

"(a) the appropriate national authority, or", and

(c) sub-paragraphs (3) to (5) were omitted.

35 Paragraph 106(2) (penalties) is to have effect as if paragraphs (a), (b), (f), (g), (i) and (l) to (n) were omitted.

36 Paragraph 109 (references to extended periods) is to have effect as if "or 108" were omitted.

37 Paragraph 111 (interpretation) is to have effect as if the following were substituted for it—

"**111** (1) In this Schedule—

"education administrator" includes a reference to a former education administrator, where the context requires;

"enters education administration" has the meaning given by paragraph 1;

"hire-purchase agreement" includes a conditional sale agreement, a chattel leasing agreement and a retention of title agreement;

"in education administration" has the meaning given by paragraph 1;

"market value" means the amount which would be realised on a sale of property in the open market by a willing vendor.

(2) For the purposes of this Schedule a reference to an education administration order includes a reference to an appointment under paragraph 91 or 103.

(3) In this Schedule a reference to a provision of this Act other than this Schedule is to the provision as it applies to a further education body by virtue of section 6 of the Technical and Further Education Act 2017.

(4) In this Schedule a reference to action includes a reference to inaction."

Specific modifications to section 251 of the Insolvency Act 1986

38 Section 251 of the Insolvency Act 1986 (definitions) as applied by paragraph 1 above is to have effect as if—

(a) for the definition of "prescribed" there were substituted—

""prescribed" means prescribed by rules made under section 411 of the Insolvency Act 1986 as a result of section 32 of the Technical and Further Education Act 2017;",

(b) the definitions of "officer" and "the rules" were omitted, and
(c) at the appropriate places, there were inserted—

""appropriate national authority"—

(a) in relation to a further education body in England, means the Secretary of State;
(b) in relation to a further education body in Wales, means the Welsh Ministers;",

""combined authority" means an authority established under section 103(1) of the Local Democracy, Economic Development and Construction Act 2009;",

""director of children's services" means—

(a) in respect of a local authority, a person appointed under section 18 of the Children Act 2004;
(b) in respect of a combined authority, a person appointed to discharge functions corresponding to those of a person appointed under section 18 of the Children Act 2004;",

""education administration application" has the meaning given by section 18 of the Technical and Further Education Act 2017;",

""education administration order" has the meaning given by section 17 of the Technical and Further Education Act 2017;",

""education administration rules" has the meaning given by section 35 of the Technical and Further Education Act 2017;",

""education administrator" has the meaning given by section 35 of the Technical and Further Education Act 2017;",

""further education body" has the meaning given by section 4 of the Technical and Further Education Act 2017;",

""further education body in England" has the meaning given by section 4 of the Technical and Further Education Act 2017;", ""further education body in Wales" has the meaning given by section 4 of the Technical and Further Education Act 2017;",

""local authority" has the meaning given in section 65 of the Children Act 2004;",

""the principal", in relation to a relevant institution, means a principal appointed under the further education body's instrument of government;",

""objective", in relation to an education administration, is to be read in accordance with section 16 of the Technical and Further Education Act 2017;",

""the relevant institution"—

(a) in relation to a further education corporation, means the institution which the corporation is established to conduct, and

(b) in relation to a sixth form college corporation, means the relevant sixth form college as defined by section 90(1) of the Further and Higher Education Act 1992;",

""senior post holder", in relation to a relevant institution, means a person appointed as a senior post holder by the further education body;".".

Power to add modifications

39 (1) The Secretary of State may by regulations—

(a) amend paragraph 1(3)(a) so as to add further provisions to the list of applicable provisions in Schedule B1 to the Insolvency Act 1986;

(b) amend this Schedule so as to add further modifications to that Schedule.

(2) Regulations under this paragraph are subject to the affirmative resolution procedure.

NOTES

Commencement: to be appointed.

SCHEDULE 4
CONDUCT OF EDUCATION ADMINISTRATION: COMPANIES

Section 26

Introductory

[7.2618]

1 (1) The provisions of the Insolvency Act 1986 mentioned in sub-paragraph (2) apply in relation to an education administration of a further education body that is a company as they apply in relation to administration under that Act, but with the modifications set out in this Schedule.

(2) The provisions are—

(a) sections 233 to 237 (management by administrators, liquidators etc);
(b) sections 238 to 241 (transactions at an undervalue and preferences);
(c) section 244 (extortionate credit bargains);
(d) section 246 (unenforceability of liens on books, etc);
(e) section 246ZA to 246ZC (fraudulent and wrongful trading);
(f) section 246ZD (power to assign certain causes of action);
(g) section 246B (use of websites);
(h) section 246C (creditors' ability to opt out of receiving certain notices);
(i) sections 247, 248(b), 249 and 251 (interpretation);
(j) the applicable provisions of Schedule B1 (conduct of administration).

(3) The applicable provisions of Schedule B1 are—

(a) paragraphs 1, 40 to 49, 54, 59, 60, 61 to 68, 70 to 75, 79, 83 to 91, 98 to 104, 106 and 107 and 109 to 111, and

(b) paragraph 50 (until the repeal of that paragraph by Schedule 10 to the Small Business, Enterprise and Employment Act 2015 comes into force).

General modifications

2 The provisions of the Insolvency Act 1986 applied by paragraph 1 are to have effect as if for any term specified in column 1 of the table there were substituted the term specified in column 2.

Term	*Modification*
administration application	education administration application
administration order	education administration order
administrator	education administrator
enters administration	enters education administration
in administration	in education administration
purpose of administration	objective of the education administration
the rules	the education administration rules

Specific modifications to Schedule B1 to the Insolvency Act 1986

3 Paragraphs 4 to 35 set out modifications to the applicable provisions of Schedule B1 to the Insolvency Act 1986 as applied by paragraph 1 above.

4 Paragraph 1 (administration) is to have effect as if—

(a) for sub-paragraph (1) there were substituted—

"(1) In this Schedule "education administrator", in relation to a company, means a person appointed by the court for the purposes of an education administration order to manage its affairs, business and property.", and

(b) in sub-paragraph (2), for "Act" there were substituted "Schedule".

5 Paragraph 40 (dismissal of pending winding-up petition) is to have effect as if sub-paragraphs (1)(b), (2) and (3) were omitted.

6 Paragraph 42 (moratorium on insolvency proceedings) is to have effect as if sub-paragraphs (4) and (5) were omitted.

7 Paragraph 43 (moratorium on other legal process) is to have effect as if sub-paragraphs (5) and (6A) were omitted.

8 Paragraph 44 (interim moratorium) is to have effect as if sub-paragraphs (2) to (4), (6) and (7)(a) to (c) were omitted.

9 Paragraph 45(2) (publicity) is to have effect as if after paragraph (b) there were inserted—

"(ba) a member of the governing body of the relevant institution,
(bb) any senior post holder or principal of the relevant institution,".

10 Paragraph 46(6) (date for notifying administrator's appointment) is to have effect as if for paragraphs (a) to (c) there were substituted "the date on which the education administration order comes into force".

11 Paragraph 47 (statement of affairs) is to have effect as if—

(a) in sub-paragraph (3), after paragraph (a) there were inserted—

"(aa) a member of the governing body of the relevant institution,
(ab) any senior post holder or principal of the relevant institution, and", and

(b) sub-paragraph (5) were omitted.

12 Paragraph 49 (administrator's proposals) is to have effect as if—

(a) sub-paragraphs (2)(b) and, (3) were omitted,
(b) in sub-paragraph (4), after paragraph (a) there were inserted—

"(aa) to the appropriate national authority,
(ab) to the director of children's services at the local authority or combined authority in whose area the relevant institution is based, and to any other director of children's services that the education administrator thinks appropriate,", and

(c) sub-paragraph (5)(b) and (6) were omitted.

13 Paragraph 54 is to have effect as if the following were substituted for it—

"**54** (1) The education administrator of a company may on one or more occasions revise the proposals included in the statement made under paragraph 49 in relation to the company.
(2) If the education administrator thinks that a revision is substantial, the education administrator must send a copy of the revised proposals—
(a) to the registrar of companies,
(b) to the appropriate national authority,
(c) to any director of children's services to whom the statement of proposals was sent under paragraph 49,
(d) to every creditor of the company, other than an opted-out creditor, of whose claim and address the education administrator is aware, and
(e) to every member of the company of whose address the education administrator is aware.
(3) A copy sent in accordance with sub-paragraph (2) must be sent within the prescribed period.
(4) The education administrator is to be taken to have complied with sub-paragraph (2)(d) if the education administrator publishes, in the prescribed manner, a notice undertaking to provide a copy of the revised proposals free of charge to any member of the company who applies in writing to a specified address.
(5) An education administrator who fails without reasonable excuse to comply with this paragraph commits an offence."

14 Paragraph 60 (powers of an administrator) is to have effect as if the following were substituted for it—

"**60** (1) The education administrator of a company has the powers specified in Schedule 1 to this Act.
(2) The education administrator of a company has the power to act on behalf of the company for the purposes of provision contained in any legislation which confers a power on the company or imposes a duty on it.
(3) In sub-paragraph (2) "legislation" means provision made by or under any Act."

15 Paragraph 61 is to have effect as if the following were substituted for it—

"**61** The education administrator—
(a) may appoint or remove a director of the company,
(b) may appoint or remove a member of the governing body of the relevant institution,
(c) may appoint or remove the chief executive of the relevant institution, and
(d) may appoint or remove the principal of the relevant institution."

16 Paragraph 64 (management powers may not be exercised without consent of the administrator) is to have effect as if in sub-subparagraph (1) after "an officer of a company in administration" there were inserted "or the chief executive of the relevant institution".

17 Paragraph 68 (management duties of an administrator) is to have effect as if—
(a) in sub-paragraph (1), for paragraphs (a) to (c) there were substituted "the proposals as—
"(a) set out in the statement made under paragraph 49 in relation to the company, and
(b) from time to time revised under paragraph 54,for achieving the objective of the education administration.", and
(b) in sub-paragraph (3), for paragraphs (a) to (d) there were substituted "the directions are consistent with the achievement of the objective of the education administration".

18 Paragraph 73 (protection for secured or preferential creditor) is to have effect as if in sub-paragraph (3) for "or modified" there were substituted "under paragraph 54".

19 Paragraph 74 (challenge to administrator's conduct) is to have effect as if—
(a) for sub-paragraph (2) there were substituted—

"(2) Where a company is in education administration, the appropriate national authority, a creditor or member may apply to the court claiming that the education administrator is not carrying out his or her functions in accordance with section 24(2) or (5) of the Technical and Further Education Act 2017 (general functions of education administrator).",

(b) sub-paragraph (6)—
(i) at the end of paragraph (b) there were inserted "or", and
(ii) paragraph (c) (and the "or" before it) were omitted, and
(c) after that sub-paragraph there were inserted—

"(7) In the case of a claim made by a creditor or member, the court may grant a remedy or relief or make an order under this paragraph only if it has given the appropriate national authority a reasonable opportunity of making representations about the claim and the proposed remedy, relief or order.
(8) Before the making of an order of the kind mentioned in sub-paragraph (4)(d)—
(a) the court must notify the education administrator of the proposed order and of a period during which the education administrator is to have the opportunity of taking steps falling within sub-paragraph (9), and
(b) the period notified must have expired without the taking of such of those steps as the court thinks should have been taken,

and that period must be a reasonable period.
(9) The steps referred to in sub-paragraph (8) are—
(a) remedying the failure to carry out functions in accordance with section 24(2) or (5) of the Technical and Further Education Act 2017, and
(b) ensuring that the failure is not repeated."

20 Paragraph 75(2) (misfeasance) is to have effect as if after paragraph (b) there were inserted—

"(ba) a person appointed as an administrator of the company under the provisions of this Act as they have effect in relation to administrators other than education administrators,".

21 Paragraph 79 (end of administration) is to have effect as if—
(a) for sub-paragraphs (1) and (2) there were substituted—

"(1) On an application made by a person mentioned in sub-paragraph (2), the court may provide for the appointment of an education administrator of a company to cease to have effect from a specified time.
(2) An application may be made to the court under this paragraph—
(a) by the appropriate national authority, or
(b) with the consent of the appropriate national authority, by the education administrator.", and

(b) sub-paragraph (3) were omitted.

22 Paragraph 83 (notice to registrar when moving to voluntary liquidation) is to have effect as if—
(a) sub-paragraph (2) were omitted, and
(b) in sub-paragraph (3) after "may" there were inserted ", with the consent of the appropriate national authority,".

23 Paragraph 84 (notice to registrar when moving to dissolution) is to have effect as if—
(a) in sub-paragraph (1), for "to the registrar of companies" there were substituted—

"(a) to the appropriate national authority, and
(b) if directed to do so by the appropriate national authority, to the registrar of companies",

(b) sub-paragraph (2) were omitted, and
(c) in sub-paragraphs (3) to (6), for "(1)", in each place, there were substituted "(1)(b)".

24 Paragraph 87(2) (resignation of administrator) is to have effect as if for paragraphs (a) to (d) there were substituted "by notice in writing to the court".

25 Paragraph 89(2) (administrator ceasing to be qualified) is to have effect as if for paragraphs (a) to (d) there were substituted "to the court".

26 Paragraph 90 (filling vacancy in office of administrator) is to have effect as if for "Paragraphs 91 to 95 apply" there were substituted "Paragraph 91 applies".

27 Paragraph 91 (vacancies in court appointments) is to have effect as if—
(a) for sub-paragraph (1) there were substituted—

"(1) The court may replace the education administrator on an application made—
(a) by the appropriate national authority, or
(b) where more than one person was appointed to act jointly as the education administrator, by any of those persons who remains in office.", and

(b) sub-paragraph (2) were omitted.

28 Paragraph 98 (discharge from liability on vacation of office) is to have effect as if sub-paragraphs (2)(b) and (ba), (3) and (3A) were omitted.

29 Paragraph 99 (charges and liabilities upon vacation of office by administrator) is to have effect as if after sub-paragraph (6) there were inserted—

"(7) Where a loan is made under section 27 of the Technical and Further Education Act 2017 before cessation, sub-paragraph (4) does not apply in relation to the loan or interest on it and—
(a) if the terms of the loan provide for this paragraph to apply, any sum that must be paid by the company in respect of the loan or interest shall be—
(i) charged on and payable out of property of which the education administrator had custody or control immediately before cessation, and
(ii) payable in priority to any charge arising under sub-paragraph (3);
(b) if the terms of the loan provide for this paragraph to apply, any sum that must be paid by the company in respect of the loan or interest shall be treated as an unsecured debt that is not a preferential debt,
(c) if the terms of the loan provide for this paragraph to apply, any sum that must be paid by the company in respect of the loan or interest shall be payable after all other creditors have been paid in full."

30 Paragraph 100 (joint and concurrent administrators) is to have effect as if sub-paragraph (2) were omitted.

31 Paragraph 101(3) (joint administrators) is to have effect as if after "87 to" there were inserted "91, 98 and".

32 Paragraph 103 (appointment of additional administrators) is to have effect as if—
(a) in sub-paragraph (2) the words from the beginning to "order" were omitted,
(b) for paragraph (a) there were substituted—

"(a) the appropriate national authority, or", and

(c) sub-paragraphs (3) to (5) were omitted.

34 Paragraph 109 (references to extended periods) is to have effect as if "or 108" were omitted.

35 Paragraph 111 (interpretation) is to have effect as if the following were substituted for it—

"**111** (1) In this Schedule—
"administrative receiver" has the meaning given by section 251,
""appropriate national authority"—
(a) in relation to a company conducting a designated further education institution in England, means the Secretary of State;
(b) in relation to a company conducting a designated further education institution in Wales, means the Welsh Ministers;
"designated further education institution" has the meaning given by section 5;
"education administrator" includes a reference to a former education administrator, where the context requires;
"enters education administration" has the meaning given by paragraph 1;
"floating charge" means a charge which is a floating charge on its creation;
"governing body", in relation to a designated further education institution, means any board of governors of the institution or any persons responsible for the management of the institution, whether or not formally constituted as a governing body or board of governors;

"hire-purchase agreement" includes a conditional sale agreement, a chattel leasing agreement and a retention of title agreement;

"in education administration" has the meaning given by paragraph 1;

"market value" means the amount which would be realised on a sale of property in the open market by a willing vendor;

"the relevant institution" in relation to company, means the institution which the company is established to conduct;

"senior post holder", in relation to a relevant institution, means a person appointed as a senior post holder at the institution.

(2) For the purposes of this Schedule a reference to an education administration order includes a reference to an appointment under paragraph 91 or 103.

(3) In this Schedule a reference to action includes a reference to inaction."

Specific modifications to section 251 of the Insolvency Act 1986

36 Section 251 of the Insolvency Act 1986 (definitions) as applied by paragraph 1 above is to have effect as if—

(a) for the definition of "prescribed" there were substituted—

""prescribed" means prescribed by rules made under section 411 of the Insolvency Act 1986 as a result of section 32 of the Technical and Further Education Act 2017;",

(b) the definition of "the rules" were omitted, and

(c) at the appropriate places, there were inserted—

""combined authority" means an authority established under section 103(1) of the Local Democracy, Economic Development and Construction Act 2009;",

""director of children's services" means—

(a) in respect of a local authority, a person appointed under section 18 of the Children Act 2004;

(b) in respect of a combined authority, a person appointed to discharge functions corresponding to those of a person appointed under section 18 of the Children Act 2004;",

""education administration application" has the meaning given by section 18 of the Technical and Further Education Act 2017;",

""education administration order" has the meaning given by section 17 of the Technical and Further Education Act 2017;",

""education administration rules" has the meaning given by section 35 of the Technical and Further Education Act 2017;",

""education administrator" has the meaning given by section 35 of the Technical and Further Education Act 2017;",

""local authority" has the meaning given in section 65 of the Children Act 2004;",

""objective", in relation to an education administration, is to be read in accordance with section 16 of the Technical and Further Education Act 2017;".

Power to add modifications

37 (1) The Secretary of State may by regulations—

(a) amend paragraph 1(3)(a) so as to add further provisions to the list of applicable provisions in Schedule B1 to the Insolvency Act 1986;

(b) amend this Schedule so as to add further modifications to that Schedule.

(2) Regulations under this paragraph are subject to the affirmative resolution procedure.

NOTES

Commencement: to be appointed.

S
WATER INDUSTRY

WATER INDUSTRY ACT 1991

(1991 c 56)

ARRANGEMENT OF SECTIONS

PART II
APPOINTMENT AND REGULATION OF UNDERTAKERS

CHAPTER II
ENFORCEMENT AND INSOLVENCY

Special administration orders

23 Meaning and effect of special administration order . . . . [7.2619]
24 Special administration orders made on special petitions . . . . [7.2620]
25 Power to make special administration order on winding-up petition . . . . [7.2621]

Restrictions on voluntary winding up and insolvency proceedings

26 Restrictions on voluntary winding up and insolvency proceedings . . . . [7.2622]

PART VIII
MISCELLANEOUS AND SUPPLEMENTAL

Construction of Act

219 General interpretation . . . . [7.2623]

Other supplemental provisions

223 Short title, commencement and extent . . . . [7.2624]

SCHEDULES

Schedule 3—Special administration orders
Part I—Modifications of the 1986 Act . . . . [7.2625]
Part II—Supplemental . . . . [7.2626]

An Act to consolidate enactments relating to the supply of water and the provision of sewerage services, with amendments to give effect to recommendations of the Law Commission

[25 July 1991]

NOTES

Transfer of functions in relation to Wales: as to the transfer of functions under this Act from Ministers of the Crown to the National Assembly for Wales, see the National Assembly for Wales (Transfer of Functions) Order 1999, SI 1999/672, and the National Assembly for Wales (Transfer of Functions) Order 2000, SI 2000/253.

1–5 *((Pt I) outside the scope of this work.)*

PART II
APPOINTMENT AND REGULATION OF UNDERTAKERS

6–17R *((Ch I) outside the scope of this work.)*

CHAPTER II ENFORCEMENT AND INSOLVENCY

18–22F *(Outside the scope of this work.)*

Special administration orders

[7.2619]
23 Meaning and effect of special administration order

(1) A special administration order is an order of the High Court made in accordance with section 24 or 25 below in relation to a company holding an appointment under Chapter I of this Part [or which is *a qualifying licensed water supplier*] and directing that, during the period for which the order is in force, the affairs, business and property of the company shall be managed, by a person appointed by the High Court—

(a) for the achievement of the purposes of such an order; and
(b) in a manner which protects the respective interests of the members and creditors of the company.

(2) The purposes of a special administration order made in relation to any company [holding an appointment under Chapter 1 of this Part] shall be—

(a) the transfer to another company, or (as respects different parts of the area to which the company's appointment relates, or different parts of its undertaking) to two or more different companies, as a going concern, of so much of the company's undertaking as it is necessary to transfer in order to ensure that the functions which have been vested in the company by virtue of its appointment may be properly carried out; and

(b) the carrying out of those functions pending the making of the transfer and the vesting of those functions in the other company or companies (whether by virtue of the transfer or of an appointment or variation which replaces the former company as a relevant undertaker).

[(2A) The purposes of a special administration order made in relation to any company which is [a qualifying water supply licensee] shall be—

(a) the transfer to another company or companies, as a going concern, of so much of the company's undertaking as it is necessary to transfer in order to ensure that activities relating to the introduction or introductions of water mentioned in [subsection (7)] below may be properly carried on; and

(b) the carrying on of those activities pending the making of the transfer.]

[(2AA) The purposes of a special administration order made in relation to a company which is a qualifying sewerage licensee must be—

(a) the transfer to another company or companies, as a going concern, of so much of the company's undertaking as it is necessary to transfer in order to secure that the activities relating to the removal or removals of matter mentioned in subsection (9) may be properly carried on, and

(b) the carrying on of those activities pending the making of the transfer.]

[(2B) Where a company is in special administration as a result of an order made on the grounds that the company is or is likely to be unable to pay its debts—

(a) a purpose of the special administration order is to rescue the company as a going concern, and

(b) the transfer purpose under subsection (2)(a) *or (2A)(a)* applies only if the special administrator thinks that—

(i) it is not likely to be possible to rescue the company as a going concern, or

(ii) transfer is likely to secure more effective performance of the functions or activities mentioned in subsection (2)(a) *or (2A)(a)*.

(2C) Where subsection (2B) applies, subsections (2)(b) *and (2A)(b)* have effect as if they referred to carrying out functions, or carrying on activities, pending rescue or transfer.

(2D) For the purpose of rescuing the company as a going concern a special administrator may propose—

(a) a company voluntary arrangement under Part 1 of the Insolvency Act 1986, or

(b) a compromise or arrangement in accordance with Part 26 of the Companies Act 2006.

(2E) The Secretary of State may by regulations made by statutory instrument—

(a) modify a provision of the Insolvency Act 1986 or the Companies Act 2006 in respect of the arrangements and compromises mentioned in subsection (2D) in so far as they apply to a company which is or has been in special administration;

(b) make other supplemental provision about those arrangements and compromises (which may, in particular, apply or modify the effect of an enactment about insolvency or companies).

(2F) Provision under subsection (2E)(a) or (b) may, in particular, confer a function on—

(a) the Secretary of State,

(b) the Welsh Ministers, or

(c) the Authority.

(2G) Regulations under subsection (2E) may not be made unless—

(a) the Welsh Ministers have consented to the making of the regulations, and

(b) a draft has been laid before and approved by resolution of each House of Parliament (and section 213(1) shall not apply).]

[(2H) A transfer under subsection (2) or (2A) may be effected by—

(a) transferring all or part of the company's undertaking to a wholly-owned subsidiary of the company, and

(b) then transferring securities in the subsidiary to another company.]

(3) Schedule 3 to this Act shall have effect for applying provisions of the Insolvency Act 1986 where a special administration order is made.

(4) Schedule 2 to this Act shall have effect for enabling provision to be made with respect to cases in which—

[(a) a company is replaced by another as a relevant undertaker without an appointment or variation under Chapter 1 of this Part; or

(b) a company carries on activities relating to the introduction or introductions of water mentioned in subsection (6)(b) below formerly carried on by another company,

in pursuance of a special administration order.]

(5) In this section "business" and "property" have the same meanings as in the Insolvency Act 1986.

[(6) For the purposes of this section, sections 24 to 26 below and Schedule 2 to this Act, a [water supply licensee] is a [qualifying water supply licensee] if—

[(a) it is the holder of a water supply licence giving it a wholesale *or supplementary* authorisation (within the meaning of Chapter 1A of this Part), and

(b) the condition in subsection (7) is satisfied in relation to it.]]

[(7) The condition in this subsection is that—

(a) the introduction of water by the licence holder which is permitted under section 66B or 66C is designated as a strategic supply under section 66G, or

(b) the introductions of water by the licence holder which are permitted under section 66B or 66C are designated as a collective strategic supply under section 66H.]

[(8) For the purposes of this section, sections 24 to 26 and Schedule 2, a sewerage licensee is a qualifying sewerage licensee if—

(a) it is the holder of a sewerage licence giving it a wholesale or disposal authorisation (within the meaning of Chapter 1A of this Part), and

(b) the condition in subsection (9) is satisfied in relation to it.

(9) The condition in this subsection is that—

(a) the removal of matter by the licence holder which is permitted under section 117C or 117D is designated as strategic sewerage provision under section 117N, or

(b) the removals of matter by the licence holder which are permitted under section 117C or 117D are designated as collective strategic sewerage provision under section 117O.]

NOTES

Sub-s (1): words in square brackets inserted by the Water Act 2003, s 101(1), Sch 8, paras 2, 8(1), (2); for the words in italics therein there are substituted the words "a qualifying water supply licensee or a qualifying sewerage licensee" by the Water Act 2014, s 56, Sch 7, paras 2, 35(1), (2), as from 1 April 2017 (in relation to a qualifying water supply licensee) and as from a day to be appointed (otherwise).

Sub-s, (2): words in square brackets inserted by the Water Act 2003, s 101(1), Sch 8, paras 2, 8(1), (3).

Sub-s (2A): inserted by the Water Act 2003, s 101(1), Sch 8, paras 2, 8(1), (4); words in square brackets substituted by the Water Act 2014, s 56, Sch 7, paras 2, 35(1), (3).

Sub-s (2AA): inserted by the Water Act 2014, s 56, Sch 7, paras 2, 35(1), (4), as from a day to be appointed.

Sub-ss (2B)–(2G): inserted by the Flood and Water Management Act 2010, s 34, Sch 5, para 3, as from 1 October 2010 for the purpose of making regulations under sub-s (2E), and as from a day to be appointed otherwise; in sub-s (2B) for the words in italics in both places there are substituted the words ", (2A)(a) or (2AA)(a)", and in sub-s (2C) for the words in italics there are substituted the words ", (2A)(b) and (2AA)(b)", by the Water Act 2014, s 56, Sch 7, paras 2, 35(1), (5), (6), as from a day to be appointed.

Sub-s (2H): inserted by the Flood and Water Management Act 2010, s 34, Sch 5, para 5(1), as from a day to be appointed.

Sub-s (3): substituted by new sub-ss (3), (3A)–(3D) by the Flood and Water Management Act 2010, s 34, Sch 5, para 6(1), as from 1 October 2010 for the purpose of making regulations under sub-s (3A), and as from a day to be appointed for remaining purposes, as follows:

"(3) Schedule B1 to the Insolvency Act 1986 (administration) applies to special administration (subject to regulations under subsection (3A)).

(3A) The Secretary of State may make regulations about special administration which—

(a) apply (with or without modification) an insolvency provision;

(b) disapply an insolvency provision;

(c) modify the effect of an insolvency provision;

(d) make provision similar to, and in place of, an insolvency provision.

(3B) In subsection (3A) "insolvency provision" means a provision of the Insolvency Act 1986 or another enactment about insolvency (including (i) a provision about administration, (ii) a provision about consequences of insolvency, and (iii) a provision conferring power to make rules).

(3C) A reference in an enactment to Part II of the Insolvency Act 1986 includes a reference to that Part as applied by or under this section (subject to regulations under subsection (3A)).

(3D) Regulations under subsection (3A) shall be made by statutory instrument and may not be made unless—

(a) the Welsh Ministers have consented to the making of the regulations, and

(b) a draft has been laid before and approved by resolution of each House of Parliament (and section 213(1) shall not apply).".

Sub-s (4): words in square brackets substituted by the Water Act 2003, s 101(1), Sch 8, paras 2, 8(1), (5); para (b) substituted as follows by the Water Act 2014, s 56, Sch 7, paras 2, 35(1), (7), as from a day to be appointed:

"(b) a company carries on activities relating to—

(i) the introduction or introductions of water mentioned in subsection (7) formerly carried on by another company; or

(ii) the removal or removals of matter mentioned in subsection (9) formerly carried on by another company,".

Sub-s (6): added by the Water Act 2003, s 101(1), Sch 8, paras 2, 8(1), (6); words in square brackets substituted by the Water Act 2014, s 56, Sch 7, paras 2, 35(1), (8); in para (a) words "or supplementary" in italics repealed by the Water Act 2014, s 5, Sch 5, paras 1, 23, in relation to Wales, as from a day to be appointed.

Sub-s (7): added by the Water Act 2014, s 56, Sch 7, paras 2, 35(1), (9).

Sub-ss (8), (9): added by the Water Act 2014, s 56, Sch 7, paras 2, 35(1), (10), as from a day to be appointed.

Special administration order: the substitution of the Insolvency Act 1986, Pt II (administration orders) by the Enterprise Act 2002, s 248(1), (2), Sch 16, does not affect water and sewerage undertakers for which special arrangements for the administration procedure have been made by this section, ss 24, 25 of and Sch 3 to this Act at **[7.2620]**, **[7.2621]**, **[7.2625]** by applying Pt II of the 1986 Act with modifications; see s 249 of the 2002 Act at **[2.10]**.

See further, in relation to the application of this section, with modifications, for the purposes of the regulation of specified infrastructure projects: the Water Industry (Specified Infrastructure Projects) (English Undertakers) Regulations 2013, SI 2013/1582, reg 3(1), Sch 1, paras 1, 7(2).

[7.2620]

24 Special administration orders made on special petitions

(1) If, on an application made to the High Court by petition presented—

(a) by the Secretary of State; or

(b) with the consent of the Secretary of State, by [the Authority],

that Court is satisfied in relation to any company which holds an appointment under Chapter I of this Part that any one or more of the grounds specified in subsection (2) below is satisfied in relation to that company, that Court may make a special administration order in relation to that company.

[(1A) If on an application made to the High Court by petition presented—

(a) by the Secretary of State *(after consulting the Assembly)*; or

(b) with the consent of the Secretary of State *(after consulting the Assembly)*, [by] the Authority, the Court is satisfied in relation to any company which is a *qualifying licensed water supplier* that any one or more of the grounds specified in subsection (2) below is satisfied in relation to that company, that Court may make a special administration order in relation to that company.]

[(1B) Before presenting a petition under subsection (1A) *in relation to a qualifying water supply licensee whose licence gives it a supplementary authorisation,* the Secretary of State or the Authority (as the case may be) must consult the Welsh Ministers.]

(2) The grounds mentioned in [subsections (1) and (1A)] above are, in relation to any company—

(a) that there has been, is or is likely to be such a contravention by the company of any principal duty, not being a contravention in respect of which a notice has been served under subsection (3) of section 19 above, as is serious enough to make it inappropriate for the company to continue to hold its appointment [or licence];

(b) that there has been, is or is likely to be such a contravention by the company of the provisions of any enforcement order which—

(i) is not for the time being the subject-matter of proceedings brought by virtue of section 21(1) above; and

(ii) if it is a provisional enforcement order, has been confirmed,

as is serious enough to make it inappropriate for the company to continue to hold its appointment [or licence];

[(bb) in the case of a company which is a *qualifying licensed water supplier*, that—

(i) action taken by the company has caused a contravention by a water undertaker of any principal duty; and

(ii) that action is serious enough to make it inappropriate for the company to continue to hold its licence;]

[(bc) in the case of a company which is a qualifying sewerage licensee, that—

(i) action taken by the company has caused a contravention by a sewerage undertaker of any principal duty; and

(ii) that action is serious enough to make it inappropriate for the company to continue to hold its licence;]

(c) that the company is or is likely to be unable to pay its debts;

(d) that, in a case in which the Secretary of State has certified that it would be appropriate, but for section 25 below, for him to petition for the winding up of the company under *section 440 of the Companies Act 1985* (petition by the Secretary of State following inspectors' report etc.), it would be just and equitable, as mentioned in that section, for the company to be wound up if it did not hold an appointment under Chapter I of this Part [or was not a *qualifying licensed water supplier*]; or

(e) [in the case of a company holding an appointment under Chapter 1 of this Part,] that the company is unable or unwilling adequately to participate in arrangements certified by the Secretary of State or [the Authority] to be necessary by reason of or in connection with, a proposal for the making by virtue of section 7(4)(c) above of any appointment or variation replacing a company as a relevant undertaker.

(3) Notice of any petition under this section for a special administration order shall be given forthwith to such persons and in such manner as may be prescribed by rules made under section 411 of the Insolvency Act 1986 ("the 1986 Act"); and no such petition shall be withdrawn except with the leave of the High Court.

(4) Subsections (4) and (5) of section 9 of the 1986 Act (powers on application for administration order) shall apply on the hearing of the petition for a special administration order in relation to any company as they apply on the hearing of a petition for an administration order.

(5) Subsections (1), (2) and (4) of section 10 of the 1986 Act (effect of petition) shall apply in the case of a petition for a special administration order in relation to any company as if—

(a) the reference in subsection (1) to an administration order were a reference to a special administration order;

(b) paragraph (b) of that subsection did require the leave of the court for the taking of any of the steps mentioned in paragraphs (b) and (c) of subsection (2) (appointment of and exercise of functions by, administrative receiver); and

(c) the reference in paragraph (c) of subsection (1) to proceedings included a reference to any proceedings under or for the purposes of section 18 above.

(6) For the purposes of this section a company is unable to pay its debts if—

(a) it is a limited company which is deemed to be so unable under section 123 of the 1986 Act (definition of inability to pay debts); or

(b) it is an unregistered company which is deemed, by virtue of any of sections 222 to 224 of that Act, to be so unable for the purposes of section 221 of that Act (winding up of unregistered companies).

[(7) In this section "principal duty" means—

(a) in relation to a company holding an appointment under Chapter 1 of this Part, a requirement imposed on the company by section 37 or 94 below;

(b) in relation to a company which is a *qualifying licensed water supplier*, any condition of its licence or any statutory requirement imposed on it in consequence of its licence.]

NOTES

Sub-s (1): words in square brackets substituted by virtue of the Water Act 2003, s 36(2).

Sub-s (1A): inserted by the Water Act 2003, s 101(1), Sch 8, paras 2, 9(1), (2); words in italics in paras (a), (b) repealed, word in square brackets in para (b) inserted, and for the final words in italics there are substituted the words "qualifying water supply licensee or qualifying sewerage licensee" by the Water Act 2014, s 56, Sch 7, paras 2, 36(1), (2), as from 1 April 2017 (except in relation to qualifying sewerage licensees) and as from a day to be appointed (exception noted above).

Sub-s (1B): inserted by the Water Act 2014, s 56, Sch 7, paras 2, 36(1), (3); words in italics repealed in relation to Wales by the Water Act 2014, s 5, Sch 5, paras 1, 24, as from a day to be appointed.

Sub-s (2): words in first pair of square brackets substituted, words in square brackets in paras (a), (b), (d), the whole of para (bb), and words in first pair of square brackets in para (e), inserted by the Water Act 2003, s 101(1), Sch 8, paras 2, 9(1), (3); for the words in italics in para (bb) there are substituted the words "qualifying water supply licensee", para (bc) inserted, and for the second words in italics in para (d) there are substituted the words "qualifying water supply licensee or a qualifying sewerage licensee", by the Water Act 2014, s 56, Sch 7, paras 2, 36(1), (4), as from 1 April 2017 (except in relation to qualifying sewerage licensees) and as from a day to be appointed (exception noted above); words in second pair of square brackets in para (e) substituted by virtue of the Water Act 2003, s 36(2); for the first words in italics in para (d) there are substituted the words "section 124A of the Insolvency Act 1986" by the Flood and Water Management Act 2010, s 34, Sch 5, para 6(4), as from a day to be appointed.

Sub-ss (4), (5): repealed by the Flood and Water Management Act 2010, s 34, Sch 5, para 6(2), as from a day to be appointed.

Sub-s (7): substituted by the Water Act 2003, s 101(1), Sch 8, paras 2, 9(1), (4); for the words in italics in para (b) there are substituted the words "qualifying water supply licensee or a qualifying sewerage licensee" by the Water Act 2014, s 56, Sch 7, paras 2, 36(1), (5), as from 1 April 2017 (except in relation to qualifying sewerage licensees) and as from a day to be appointed (exception noted above).

Special administration order: see the note to s 23 at **[7.2619]**.

See further, in relation to the application of this section, with modifications, for the purposes of the regulation of specified infrastructure projects: the Water Industry (Specified Infrastructure Projects) (English Undertakers) Regulations 2013, SI 2013/1582, reg 3(1), Sch 1, paras 1, 7(3).

Companies Act 1985, s 440: repealed by the Companies Act 1989, ss 60(1), 212, Sch 24; see now the Insolvency Act 1986, s 124A at **[1.123]**.

[7.2621]

25 Power to make special administration order on winding-up petition

On an application made to any court for the winding up of a company which holds an appointment under Chapter I of this Part [or is a *qualifying licensed water supplier*]—

(a) the court shall not make a winding-up order in relation to the company; but

(b) if the court is satisfied that it would be appropriate to make such an order if the company were not a company holding such an appointment [or a *qualifying licensed water supplier*], it shall, instead, make a special administration order in relation to the company.

NOTES

Words in square brackets inserted by the Water Act 2003, s 101(1), Sch 8, paras 2, 10; for the words in italics in both places there are substituted the words "qualifying water supply licensee or a qualifying sewerage licensee" by the Water Act 2014, s 56, Sch 7, paras 2, 37, as from 1 April 2017 (except in relation to qualifying sewerage licensees) and as from a day to be appointed (exception noted above).

Special administration order: see the note to s 23 at **[7.2619]**.

See further, in relation to the application of this section, with modifications, for the purposes of the regulation of specified infrastructure projects: the Water Industry (Specified Infrastructure Projects) (English Undertakers) Regulations 2013, SI 2013/1582, reg 3(1), Sch 1, paras 1, 7(5).

Restrictions on voluntary winding up and insolvency proceedings

[7.2622]

26 Restrictions on voluntary winding up and insolvency proceedings

(1) Where a company holds an appointment under Chapter I of this Part [or is a *qualifying licensed water supplier*]—

(a) the company shall not be wound up voluntarily;

(b) no administration order shall be made in relation to the company under Part II of the Insolvency Act 1986; and

(c) no step shall be taken by any person to enforce any security over the company's property except where that person has served fourteen days' notice of his intention to take that step on the Secretary of State and on [the Authority].

(2) In this section "security" and "property" have the same meanings as in Parts I to VII of the Insolvency Act 1986.

NOTES

Sub-s (1): words in first pair of square brackets inserted by the Water Act 2003, s 101(1), Sch 8, paras 2, 11; for the words in italics therein there are substituted the words "qualifying water supply licensee or a qualifying sewerage licensee" by the Water Act 2014, s 56, Sch 7, paras 2, 38, as from 1 April 2017 (except in relation to qualifying sewerage licensees) and as from a day to be appointed (exception noted above); words in second pair of square brackets substituted by virtue of the Water Act 2003, s 36(2).

See further, in relation to the application of this section, with modifications, for the purposes of the regulation of specified infrastructure projects: the Water Industry (Specified Infrastructure Projects) (English Undertakers) Regulations 2013, SI 2013/1582, reg 3(1), Sch 1, paras 1, 7(6).

27–207 *(Ss 27–36 (Chs III, IV) ss 36A–207 (Pts 2A–VII) outside the scope of this work.)*

PART VIII
MISCELLANEOUS AND SUPPLEMENTAL

208–215 (*Outside the scope of this work.*)

Construction of Act

216–218 (*Outside the scope of this work.*)

[7.2623]

219 General interpretation

(1) In this Act, except in so far as the context otherwise requires—

. . .

["the Authority" means the Water Services Regulation Authority;]

. . .

"contravention" includes a failure to comply, and cognate expressions shall be construed accordingly;

. . .

"enactment" includes an enactment contained in this Act or in any Act passed after this Act;

. . .

"functions", in relation to a relevant undertaker, means the functions of the undertaker under or by virtue of any enactment and shall be construed subject to section 217 above;

[. . .]

["limited company" means a company (as defined in section 1(1) of the Companies Act 2006) that—

(a) is registered in England and Wales or Scotland, and

(b) is limited by shares.]

"local statutory provision" means—

(a) a provision of a local Act (including an Act confirming a provisional order);

(b) a provision of so much of any public general Act as has effect with respect to a particular area, with respect to particular persons or works or with respect to particular provisions falling within any paragraph of this definition;

(c) a provision of an instrument made under any provision falling within paragraph (a) or (b) above; or

(d) a provision of any other instrument which is in the nature of a local enactment;

"modifications" includes additions, alterations and omissions, and cognate expressions shall be construed accordingly;

. . .

"notice" means notice in writing;

. . .

"prescribed" means prescribed by regulations made by the Secretary of State;

. . .

"relevant undertaker" means a water undertaker or sewerage undertaker;

. . .

["sewerage licensee" is to be construed in accordance with section 17BA(6);]

. . .

"special administration order" has the meaning given by section 23 above;

"statutory water company" means any company which was a statutory water company for the purposes of the Water Act 1973 immediately before 1st September 1989;

. . .

["water supply licensee" is to be construed in accordance with section 17A(7);]

. . .

(2)–(10) (*Outside the scope of this work.*)

NOTES

Sub-s (1): definitions "the Authority" and "licensed water supplier" inserted by the Water Act 2003, s 101(1), Sch 7, Pt 2, para 27(1), (7)(a), Sch 8, paras 2, 50(1), (2)(c); definition "licensed water supplier" repealed, and definitions "sewerage licensee" and "water supply licensee" inserted, by the Water Act 2014, s 56, Sch 7, paras 2, 120(1), (2)(f), (g); definition "limited company" substituted by the Companies Act 2006 (Consequential Amendments, Transitional Provisions and Savings) Order 2009, SI 2009/1941, art 2(1), Sch 1, para 126(1), (3); definitions omitted outside the scope of this work.

220 (*Outside the scope of this work.*)

Other supplemental provisions

221, 222 (*Outside the scope of this work.*)

[7.2624]

223 Short title, commencement and extent

(1) This Act may be cited as the Water Industry Act 1991.

(2) This Act shall come into force on 1st December 1991.

(3) Except for the purpose of giving effect to any scheme under Schedule 2 to this Act, this Act extends to England and Wales only.

SCHEDULES

SCHEDULES 1–2

(Schs 1, 1A, 2 outside the scope of this work.)

SCHEDULE 3
SPECIAL ADMINISTRATION ORDERS

Section 23

PART I
MODIFICATIONS OF THE 1986 ACT

General application of provisions of 1986 Act

[7.2625]

1. Where a special administration order has been made, sections 11 to 15, 17 to 23 and 27 of the 1986 Act (which relate to administration orders under Part II of that Act) shall apply, with the modifications specified in the following provisions of this Part of this Schedule—

(a) as if references in those sections to an administration order were references to a special administration order and references to an administrator were references to a special administrator; . . .

(b) . . .

Effect of order

2. In section 11 of the 1986 Act (effect of order), as applied by this Part of this Schedule—

(a) the requirement in subsection (1)(a) that any petition for the winding up of the company shall be dismissed shall be without prejudice to the special administration order in a case where the order is made by virtue of section 25 of this Act;

(b) . . . and

(c) the reference in subsection (3)(d) to proceedings shall include a reference to any proceedings under or for the purposes of section 18 of this Act.

Appointment of special administrator

3. In section 13 of the 1986 Act (appointment of administrator), as applied by this Part of this Schedule, for subsection (3) there shall be substituted the following subsection—

"(3) An application for an order under subsection (2) may be made—

(a) by the Secretary of State;

(b) with the consent of the Secretary of State, by [the Water Services Regulation Authority];

(c) by any continuing special administrator of the company or, where there is no such special administrator, by the company, the directors or any creditor or creditors of the company."

General powers of special administrator

4. In section 14 of the 1986 Act (general powers of administrator), as applied by this Part of this Schedule—

(a) in subsection (1)(b), the reference to the powers specified in Schedule 1 to that Act shall be deemed to include a reference to a power to act on behalf of the company for the purposes of this Act, any local statutory provision or the exercise or performance of any power or duty which is conferred or imposed on the company by virtue of its holding an appointment under Chapter I of Part II of this Act [or a licence under Chapter 1A of that Part]; and

(b) in subsection (4), the reference to a power conferred by the company's [articles of association] shall be deemed to include a reference to a power conferred by a local statutory provision or by virtue of the company's holding such an appointment [or licence].

Power to deal with charged property

5. (1) Section 15 of the 1986 Act (power to deal with charged property), as applied by this Part of this Schedule, shall have effect as follows.

(2) In subsection (5)(b) (amount to be paid to chargeholder not to be less than open market value), for the words "in the open market by a willing vendor" there shall be substituted the words "for the best price which is reasonably available on a sale which is consistent with the purposes of the special administration order".

(3) . . .

Duties of special administrator

6. (1) Section 17 of the 1986 Act (duties of administrator), as applied by this Part of this Schedule, shall have effect as follows.

(2) For subsection (2) there shall be substituted the following subsection—

"(2) Subject to any directions of the court, it shall be the duty of the special administrator to manage the affairs, business and property of the company in accordance with proposals, as for the time being revised under section 23, which have been prepared for the purposes of that section by him or any predecessor of his."

(3) In subsection (3), paragraph (a) (right of creditors to require the holding of a creditors' meeting) shall be omitted.

Discharge of order

7. (1) Section 18 of the 1986 Act (discharge and variation of administration order), as applied by this Part of this Schedule, shall have effect as follows.

(2) For subsections (1) and (2) there shall be substituted the following subsection—

"(1) An application for a special administration order to be discharged may be made—

(a) by the special administrator, on the ground that the purposes of the order have been achieved; or

(b) by the Secretary of State or, with the consent of the Secretary of State, [the Water Services Regulation Authority], on the ground that it is no longer necessary that those purposes are achieved."

(3) In subsection (3), the words "or vary" shall be omitted.

(4) In subsection (4), the words "or varied" and "or variation" shall be omitted and for the words "to the registrar of companies" there shall be substituted—

(a) . . .

(b) . . . the words "to the registrar of companies and to [the Water Services Regulation Authority]".

Notice of making of order

8. In section 21(2) of the 1986 Act (notice of order to be given by administrator), as applied by this Part of this Schedule, for the words "to the registrar of companies" there shall be substituted—

(a) . . .

(b) . . . the words "to the registrar of companies, to [the Water Services Regulation Authority]".

Statement of proposals

9. In section 23 of the 1986 Act (statement of proposals), as applied by this Part of this Schedule, for subsections (1) and (2) there shall be substituted the following subsections—

"(1) Where a special administration order has been made, the special administrator shall, within 3 months (or such longer period as the court may allow) after the making of the order, send a statement of his proposals for achieving the purposes of the order—

(a) to the Secretary of State and to [the Water Services Regulation Authority];

(b) so far as he is aware of their addresses, to all creditors of the company; and

(c) . . . to the registrar of companies;

and may from time to time revise those proposals.

(2) If at any time—

(a) the special administrator proposes to make revisions of the proposals for achieving the purposes of the special administration order; and

(b) those revisions appear to him to be substantial,

the special administrator shall, before making those revisions, send a statement of the proposed revisions to the Secretary of State, to [the Water Services Regulation Authority], (so far as he is aware of their addresses) to all creditors of the company and . . . to the registrar of companies.

(2A) Where the special administrator is required by subsection (1) or (2) to send any person a statement before the end of any period or before making any revision of any proposals, he shall also, before the end of that period or, as the case may be, before making those revisions either—

(a) send a copy of the statement (so far as he is aware of their addresses) to all members of the company; or

(b) publish in the prescribed manner a notice stating an address to which members should write for copies of the statement to be sent to them free of charge."

Applications to court

10. (1) Section 27 of the 1986 Act (protection of interests of creditors and members), as applied by this Part of this Schedule, shall have effect as follows.

(2) After subsection (1) there shall be inserted the following subsection—

"(1A) At any time when a special administration order is in force the Secretary of State or, with the consent of the Secretary of State, [the Water Services Regulation Authority] may apply to the High Court by petition for an order under this section on the ground that the special administrator has exercised or is exercising, or proposing to exercise, his powers in relation to the company in a manner which—

(a) will not best ensure the achievement of the purposes of the order; or

(b) without prejudice to paragraph (a) above, involves either a contravention of the conditions of the company's appointment under Chapter I of Part II of the Water Industry Act 1991 [or its licence under Chapter 1A of that Part] or of any statutory or other requirement imposed on the company in consequence of that appointment [or licence]."

(3) In subsection (3) (order not to prejudice or prevent voluntary arrangements or administrator's proposals), for paragraphs (a) and (b) there shall be substituted the words "the achievement of the purposes of the order".

(4) Subsections (4)(d) and (6) (power of court to order discharge) shall be omitted.

NOTES

Para 1: sub-para (b) and word omitted immediately preceding it repealed by the Deregulation Act 2015, s 107, Sch 23, Pt 5, para 28(1), (4)(e)(i).

Para 2: sub-para (b) repealed by the Deregulation Act 2015, s 107, Sch 23, Pt 5, para 28(1), (4)(e)(ii).

Para 3: words in square brackets substituted by virtue of the Water Act 2003, s 36(2).

Para 4: words in first and third pairs of square brackets inserted by the Water Act 2003, s 101(1), Sch 8, paras 2, 52(1), (2); words in second pair of square brackets substituted by the Companies Act 2006 (Consequential Amendments, Transitional Provisions and Savings) Order 2009, SI 2009/1941, art 2(1), Sch 1, para 126(1), (4).

Para 5: sub-para (3) repealed by the Deregulation Act 2015, s 107, Sch 23, Pt 5, para 28(1), (4)(e)(iii).

Para 7: words in square brackets substituted by virtue of the Water Act 2003, s 36(2); sub-para (4)(a) and words omitted from sub-para (4)(b) repealed by the Deregulation Act 2015, s 107, Sch 23, Pt 5, para 28(1), (4)(e)(iv), (v).

Para 8: words in square brackets substituted by virtue of the Water Act 2003, s 36(2); sub-para (a) and words omitted from sub-para (b) repealed by the Deregulation Act 2015, s 107, Sch 23, Pt 5, para 28(1), (4)(e)(vi), (vii).

Para 9: words in square brackets substituted by virtue of the Water Act 2003, s 36(2); words omitted repealed by the Deregulation Act 2015, s 107, Sch 23, Pt 5, para 28(1), (4)(e)(viii), (ix).

Para 10: words in first pair of square brackets substituted by virtue of the Water Act 2003, s 36(2); words in second and third pairs of square brackets inserted by the Water Act 2003, s 101(1), Sch 8, paras 2, 52(1), (3).

Special administration order: see the note to s 23 at **[7.2619]**.

PART II
SUPPLEMENTAL

General adaptations and saving

[7.2626]

11. (1) Subject to the preceding provisions of this Schedule, references in the 1986 Act (except in sections 8 to 10 and 24 to 26), or in any other enactment passed before 6th July 1989, to an administration order under Part II of that Act, to an application for such an order and to an administrator shall include references, respectively, to a special administration order, to an application for a special administration order and to a special administrator.

(2) Subject as aforesaid and to sub-paragraph (3) below, references in the 1986 Act, or in any other enactment passed before 6th July 1989, to an enactment contained in Part II of that Act shall include references to that enactment as applied by section 24 of this Act or Part I of this Schedule.

(3) Sub-paragraphs (1) and (2) above shall apply in relation to a reference in an enactment contained in Part II of the 1986 Act only so far as necessary for the purposes of the operation of the provisions of that Part as so applied.

(4) The provisions of this Schedule shall be without prejudice to the power conferred by section 411 of the 1986 Act (company insolvency rules), as modified by sub-paragraphs (1) and (2) above.

Interpretation

12. (1) In this Schedule "the 1986 Act" means the Insolvency Act 1986.

(2) In this Schedule, and in any modification of the 1986 Act made by this Schedule, "special administrator", in relation to a special administration order, means any person appointed in relation to that order for the purposes of section 23(1) of this Act; and in any such modification "special administration order" has the same meaning as in this Act.

NOTES

Special administration order: see the note to s 23 at **[7.2619]**.

SCHEDULES 3A–15

(Schs 3A–15 outside the scope of this work.)

WATER INDUSTRY (SPECIAL ADMINISTRATION) RULES 2009

(SI 2009/2477)

NOTES

Made: 8 September 2009.

Authority: Insolvency Act 1986, s 411 (as applied by the Water Industry Act 1991, ss 23, 24, Sch 3).

Commencement: 1 November 2009.

Regulation of specified infrastructure projects: for the application of these rules in relation to specified infrastructure projects, see the Water Industry (Specified Infrastructure Projects) (English Undertakers) Regulations 2013, SI 2013/1582, reg 3(1), Sch 1, paras 1, 7(7).

Note: the Insolvency Rules 1986, SI 1986/1925 are revoked and replaced (as from 6 April 2017 and subject to transitional provisions) by the Insolvency (England and Wales) Rules 2016, SI 2016/1024 at **[6.2]**, however, the Insolvency (England and Wales) Rules 2016 (Consequential Amendments and Savings) Rules 2017, SI 2017/369, r 3(f) at **[6.947]** provides that the Insolvency Rules 1986 as they had effect immediately before 6 April 2017 and insofar as they apply to proceedings under the Water Industry (Special Administration) Rules 2009, continue to have effect for the purposes of the application of the 2009 Rules.

See also the Deregulation Act 2015 and Small Business, Enterprise and Employment Act 2015 (Consequential Amendments) (Savings) Regulations 2017, SI 2017/540, reg 4(1), (2)(f) and the Insolvency Amendment (EU 2015/848) Regulations 2017, SI 2017/702, reg 4 at **[2.103]**, for savings in relation to the Insolvency Act 1986 in so far as it applies to proceedings under these Rules.

ARRANGEMENT OF RULES

PART 1
INTRODUCTION

1 Citation . . . [7.2627]
2 Commencement . . . [7.2628]
3 Definitions and interpretation . . . [7.2629]
4 Application: general . . . [7.2630]
5 Application of Insolvency Rules 1986 . . . [7.2631]
6 Forms for use in special administration proceedings . . . [7.2632]

PART 2
THE PETITION AND THE SPECIAL ADMINISTRATION ORDER

7 Form of petition . . . [7.2633]
8 Contents of affidavit . . . [7.2634]
9 Filing of petition . . . [7.2635]
10 Notice to enforcement officer, etc . . . [7.2636]
11 Service of petition . . . [7.2637]
12 Proof of service . . . [7.2638]
13 Insolvency proceedings brought after petition presented . . . [7.2639]
14 The hearing: right of appearance . . . [7.2640]
15 Form of special administration order . . . [7.2641]
16 Costs of petitioner etc . . . [7.2642]
17 Notice and advertisement of special administration order . . . [7.2643]
18 Notice of discharge of special administration order . . . [7.2644]

PART 3
THE SPECIAL ADMINISTRATOR

19 Special administrator's remuneration . . . [7.2645]
20 Fixing of remuneration by court . . . [7.2646]
21 Remuneration: joint special administrators . . . [7.2647]
22 Remuneration: special administrator a solicitor . . . [7.2648]
23 Resignation of special administrator . . . [7.2649]
24 Special administrator's death in office . . . [7.2650]
25 Order filling vacancy . . . [7.2651]

PART 4
CONDUCT OF THE SPECIAL ADMINISTRATION

CHAPTER 1
STATEMENT OF AFFAIRS AND PROPOSALS TO CREDITORS

26 Meaning of "responsible person" . . . [7.2652]
27 Notice requiring statement of affairs . . . [7.2653]
28 Verification of statement of affairs . . . [7.2654]
29 Filing the statement of affairs . . . [7.2655]
30 Limiting disclosure of statement of affairs . . . [7.2656]
31 Release from obligation or extension of time . . . [7.2657]
32 Expenses of statement of affairs . . . [7.2658]
33 Statement to be annexed to proposals . . . [7.2659]
34 Form of statement of revised proposals . . . [7.2660]
35 Statement if special administration order to be discharged before statement of proposals . . . [7.2661]
36 Notice to members of proposals to creditors . . . [7.2662]

CHAPTER 2
DISPOSAL OF PROPERTY

37 Disposal of charged property, etc . . . [7.2663]

CHAPTER 3
ACCOUNTS

38 Abstract of receipts and payments . . . . . [7.2664]

CHAPTER 4
ACCESS TO DOCUMENTS

39 Confidentiality of documents . . . . . [7.2665]
40 Right to copy documents . . . . . [7.2666]
41 Right to have list of creditors . . . . . [7.2667]
42 False claim of status as creditor or member etc . . . . . [7.2668]

PART 5
MEETINGS

CHAPTER 1
CREDITORS' MEETINGS

43 Application of Chapter . . . . . [7.2669]
44 Venue and notice of creditors' meetings . . . . . [7.2670]
45 Non-receipt of notice of meeting . . . . . [7.2671]
46 Who presides at meetings . . . . . [7.2672]
47 Adjournment . . . . . [7.2673]
48 Entitlement to vote: meetings of creditors . . . . . [7.2674]
49 Admission and rejection of claims . . . . . [7.2675]
50 Voting by secured creditors . . . . . [7.2676]
51 Voting by holders of negotiable instruments . . . . . [7.2677]
52 Voting by retention of title creditors . . . . . [7.2678]
53 Voting by creditors under hire-purchase, conditional sale and chattel leasing agreements . . . . [7.2679]
54 Quorum at meetings . . . . . [7.2680]
55 Resolutions . . . . . [7.2681]
56 Minutes . . . . . [7.2682]
57 Report to creditors . . . . . [7.2683]

CHAPTER 2
MEMBERS' MEETINGS

58 Venue and conduct of members' meeting . . . . . [7.2684]

CHAPTER 3
MEETINGS GENERALLY

59 Evidence of proceedings at meeting . . . . . [7.2685]

PART 6
PROXIES AND COMPANY REPRESENTATION

60 Application of this Part . . . . . [7.2686]
61 Definition and grant of proxy . . . . . [7.2687]
62 Issue and use of forms of proxy . . . . . [7.2688]
63 Use of proxies at meetings . . . . . [7.2689]
64 Retention of proxies . . . . . [7.2690]
65 Right of inspection of proxies . . . . . [7.2691]
66 Proxy-holder with financial interest . . . . . [7.2692]
67 Company representation . . . . . [7.2693]

PART 7
COURT PROCEDURE AND PRACTICE

CHAPTER 1
APPLICATIONS

68 Preliminary . . . . . [7.2694]
69 Interpretation . . . . . [7.2695]
70 Form and contents of applications . . . . . [7.2696]
71 Filing and service of applications . . . . . [7.2697]
72 Hearings without notice . . . . . [7.2698]
73 Hearing of applications in private . . . . . [7.2699]
74 Exercise of court's jurisdiction by registrar . . . . . [7.2700]
75 Use of witness statements . . . . . [7.2701]
76 Filing and service of witness statements . . . . . [7.2702]
77 Use of reports . . . . . [7.2703]
78 Adjournment of hearing: directions . . . . . [7.2704]

CHAPTER 2
ENFORCEMENT

79 Enforcement of court orders . . . . . [7.2705]

80 Orders enforcing compliance with these Rules . . . [7.2706]

CHAPTER 3
ACCESS TO COURT RECORDS

81 CPR rules not to apply . . . [7.2707]
82 Certain persons' right to inspect the court file . . . [7.2708]
83 Right to copy documents . . . [7.2709]
84 Official copies of documents on court file . . . [7.2710]
85 False claim of status as creditor or member . . . [7.2711]
86 Filing of copies of London Gazette notices and advertisements . . . [7.2712]

CHAPTER 4
COSTS AND DETAILED ASSESSMENT

87 Application of the Civil Procedure Rules . . . [7.2713]
88 Costs to be assessed by detailed assessment . . . [7.2714]
89 Procedures for detailed assessment: employees of the special administrator . . . [7.2715]
90 Procedures for detailed assessment: time limit to bring proceedings . . . [7.2716]
91 Costs paid otherwise than out of the assets of the water company . . . [7.2717]
92 Award of costs against special administrator . . . [7.2718]
93 Applications for costs . . . [7.2719]
94 Costs and expenses of witnesses . . . [7.2720]
95 Final costs certificate . . . [7.2721]
96 Replacement of lost or destroyed costs certificate . . . [7.2722]

CHAPTER 5
PERSONS WHO LACK CAPACITY

97 Children and patients . . . [7.2723]

CHAPTER 6
APPEALS

98 Appeal and review of orders . . . [7.2724]
99 Procedure on appeal . . . [7.2725]

CHAPTER 7
GENERAL

100 Principal court rules and practice to apply . . . [7.2726]
101 Title of proceedings . . . [7.2727]
102 Right of audience . . . [7.2728]
103 Special administrator's solicitor . . . [7.2729]
104 Formal defects . . . [7.2730]
105 Affidavits . . . [7.2731]
106 Giving of security to the court . . . [7.2732]
107 Payment into court . . . [7.2733]
108 Further information and disclosure . . . [7.2734]

PART 8
EXAMINATION OF PERSONS IN SPECIAL ADMINISTRATION PROCEEDINGS

109 Application . . . [7.2735]
110 Interpretation . . . [7.2736]
111 Form and contents of application . . . [7.2737]
112 Order for examination, etc . . . [7.2738]
113 Procedure for examination . . . [7.2739]
114 Recording of proceedings . . . [7.2740]
115 Warrants under section 236 of the Insolvency Act . . . [7.2741]
116 Filing of record of examination . . . [7.2742]
117 Costs of proceedings under section 236 of the Insolvency Act . . . [7.2743]

PART 9
MISCELLANEOUS AND GENERAL

118 Special administrator's security . . . [7.2744]
119 Power of Secretary of State to regulate certain matters . . . [7.2745]
120 Evidence of orders, directions or certificates issued by Secretary of State or Welsh Ministers . [7.2746]
121 Time limits . . . [7.2747]
122 General provisions as to service and notice . . . [7.2748]
123 Service outside the jurisdiction . . . [7.2749]
124 Notice, etc to solicitors . . . [7.2750]
125 Notice to joint special administrators . . . [7.2751]
126 Notices sent simultaneously to the same person . . . [7.2752]

127 The London Gazette as evidence . . . . [7.2753]
128 Punishment of offences . . . . [7.2754]
129 Powers of the court and the registrar . . . . [7.2755]

SCHEDULES

Schedule—Forms . . . . [7.2756]

PART 1
INTRODUCTION

[7.2627]
1 Citation

These Rules may be cited as the Water Industry (Special Administration) Rules 2009.

[7.2628]
2 Commencement

These Rules come into force on 1st November 2009.

[7.2629]
3 Definitions and interpretation

(1) In these Rules—

"the Authority" means the Water Services Regulation Authority;

"business day" means any day other than a Saturday, a Sunday, Christmas Day, Good Friday or a day that is a bank holiday in any part of England and Wales;

"the CPR" means the Civil Procedure Rules 1998 and "CPR" followed by a Part or rule number means the Part or rule with that number in those Rules;

"court" means the High Court;

"file" means file in court;

"Form WAT" followed by a number means the form with that number in the Schedule;

"the Insolvency Act" means, subject to paragraph (2), the Insolvency Act 1986;

"proxy" has the meaning given in rule 61;

"the registrar" means—

(a) in the case of proceedings in a district registry of the Chancery Division of the High Court, the district judge; and

(b) in any other case, [an Insolvency and Companies Court Judge];

"solicitor" (except in relation to witnessing an affidavit) includes any person who has, under or pursuant to an enactment, the right to conduct litigation in relation to special administration proceedings;

"special administration order" has the meaning given by section 23 of the Water Industry Act 1991;

"special administration proceedings" means proceedings under sections 23 to 25 of, and Schedule 3 to, the Water Industry Act 1991;

"special administrator" has the meaning given in paragraph 12 of Schedule 3 to the Water Industry Act 1991;

"statement of affairs" has the meaning given in section 22 of the Insolvency Act;

"water company" means a relevant undertaker or a qualifying [water supply licensee] within the meaning of the Water Industry Act 1991.

(2) A reference to the Insolvency Act or a provision of that Act is a reference to that Act or provision as applied, substituted or modified by sections 23 to 26 of, and Schedule 3 to, the Water Industry Act 1991, construed in accordance with section 249 of the Enterprise Act 2002.

(3) A reference to the Insolvency Rules 1986 is a reference to those Rules as in force immediately before 15th September 2003.

(4) A reference to the venue for proceedings, for an attendance before the court, or for a meeting, is to the time, date and place for the proceedings, attendance or meeting.

NOTES

Para (1): words in square brackets in definition "the registrar" substituted by the Alteration of Judicial Titles (Registrar in Bankruptcy of the High Court) Order 2018, SI 2018/130, art 3, Schedule, para 12(1)(f); in definition "water company" words in square brackets substituted by the Water Act 2014 (Consequential Amendments etc) Order 2017, SI 2017/506, art 25.

Note: the Insolvency Rules 1986, SI 1986/1925 are revoked and replaced (as from 6 April 2017 and subject to transitional provisions) by the Insolvency (England and Wales) Rules 2016, SI 2016/1024 at **[6.2]**, however, the Insolvency (England and Wales) Rules 2016 (Consequential Amendments and Savings) Rules 2017, SI 2017/369, r 3(f) at **[6.947]** provides that the Insolvency Rules 1986 as they had effect immediately before 6 April 2017 and insofar as they apply to proceedings under the Water Industry (Special Administration) Rules 2009, continue to have effect for the purposes of the application of the 2009 Rules.

[7.2630]
4 Application: general

(1) These Rules apply to special administration proceedings that commence, in relation to a water company, on or after the date on which these Rules come into force.

(2) For special administration proceedings that commenced before that date, these Rules apply to steps taken in those proceedings on or after that date.

[7.2631]

5 Application of Insolvency Rules 1986

(1) These Rules apply the Insolvency Rules 1986, with modifications.

(2) Except as provided for in these Rules, nothing in the Insolvency Rules 1986 applies to—

(a) special administration proceedings commenced, in relation to a water company, on or after the date on which these Rules come into force; or

(b) any step taken on or after that date in special administration proceedings that commenced before that date.

NOTES

Note: the Insolvency Rules 1986, SI 1986/1925 are revoked and replaced (as from 6 April 2017 and subject to transitional provisions) by the Insolvency (England and Wales) Rules 2016, SI 2016/1024 at **[6.2]**, however, the Insolvency (England and Wales) Rules 2016 (Consequential Amendments and Savings) Rules 2017, SI 2017/369, r 3(f) at **[6.947]** provides that the Insolvency Rules 1986 as they had effect immediately before 6 April 2017 and insofar as they apply to proceedings under the Water Industry (Special Administration) Rules 2009, continue to have effect for the purposes of the application of the 2009 Rules.

[7.2632]

6 Forms for use in special administration proceedings

(1) The forms in the Schedule must be used in, and in connection with, special administration proceedings.

(2) A form may be used with any variations that the circumstances require.

PART 2
THE PETITION AND THE SPECIAL ADMINISTRATION ORDER

[7.2633]

7 Form of petition

(1) A petition for an order for special administration in relation to a water company must be in Form WAT1.

(2) The petition must state the petitioner's name and address for service.

(3) If the petitioner is the Secretary of State, and the water company is a qualifying [water supply licensee] (within the meaning of the Water Industry Act 1991) the petition must state that the Secretary of State has consulted the Welsh Ministers before presenting it.

(4) If the petitioner is the Authority, the petition must state—

(a) that it is presented with the consent of—

(i) if the water company is a relevant undertaker (within the meaning of the Water Industry Act 1991) whose area is wholly or mainly in Wales, the Welsh Ministers; or

(ii) the Secretary of State; and

(b) if the water company is a qualifying [water supply licensee] (within the meaning of the Water Industry Act 1991), that the Secretary of State has consulted the Welsh Ministers before consenting.

(5) The petition—

(a) must specify the name and address of the person, or each person, proposed to be appointed as special administrator; and

(b) must state that, to the best of the petitioner's knowledge and belief, the person, or each person, proposed is qualified to act as an insolvency practitioner in relation to the water company.

(6) The petitioner, or another person on the petitioner's behalf, must prepare and swear an affidavit complying with rule 8.

(7) There must be exhibited to the affidavit—

(a) a copy of the petition;

(b) the proposed special administrator's written consent, in Form WAT2, to being appointed.

NOTES

Paras (3), (4): words in square brackets substituted by the Water Act 2014 (Consequential Amendments etc) Order 2017, SI 2017/506, art 25.

[7.2634]

8 Contents of affidavit

(1) The affidavit must state—

(a) whether the water company that is the subject of the petition is a relevant undertaker or a qualifying [water supply licensee] (within the meaning of the Water Industry Act 1991);

(b) which of the grounds set out in section 24(2) of the Water Industry Act 1991 the petitioner believes are satisfied in relation to the water company; and

(c) the reasons for that belief.

(2) The affidavit must contain a statement of the water company's financial position, setting out (so far as the deponent knows) the assets and liabilities of the company, including contingent and prospective liabilities.

(3) The affidavit must set out details (to the best of the deponent's knowledge and belief) of—

(a) any security held by creditors of the water company; and

(b) whether any such security gives its holder power to appoint an administrative receiver.

(4) If the deponent knows or believes that an administrative receiver has been appointed, the affidavit must state that fact.

(5) The affidavit must contain details (to the best of the deponent's knowledge and belief) of—

(a) any petition that has been presented for the winding up of the water company;

(b) any notice served in accordance with section 26(1)(c) of the Water Industry Act 1991 by any person intending to enforce a security over the water company's property; and

(c) any step taken to enforce such a security.

(6) If there are other matters that, in the opinion of the person intending to present the petition for a special administration order, will assist the court in deciding whether to make such an order, those matters must also be stated in the affidavit.

NOTES

Para (1): words in square brackets substituted by the Water Act 2014 (Consequential Amendments etc) Order 2017, SI 2017/506, art 25.

[7.2635]

9 Filing of petition

(1) The petitioner must file as many copies of the petition and affidavit as are required to be served in accordance with rule 11.

(2) The court must—

(a) seal each filed copy; and

(b) endorse it with the date and time of filing.

(3) The court must also—

(a) fix a venue for the hearing of the petition; and

(b) endorse the details of the venue on each copy of the petition.

(4) The court must then issue each copy to the petitioner.

[7.2636]

10 Notice to enforcement officer, etc

As soon as reasonably practicable after filing the petition, the petitioner must give notice of its presentation—

(a) to any enforcement officer or other officer who, to the petitioner's knowledge, is charged with an execution or other legal process against the water company or its property; and

(b) to any person who, to the petitioner's knowledge, has distrained against the water company or its property.

[7.2637]

11 Service of petition

(1) Not less than 2 days before the hearing the petitioner must serve on each person specified in paragraph (2)—

(a) a copy of the petition issued by the court,

(b) a copy of the affidavit and exhibits in support of it.

(2) The following must be served—

(a) the water company;

(b) any person who has appointed, or is or may be entitled to appoint, an administrative receiver of the water company;

(c) if an administrative receiver has been appointed, the administrative receiver;

(d) any person who has applied to the court for an administration order under Part II of the Insolvency Act in relation to the water company;

(e) if a petition is pending for the winding up of the water company, the petitioner and any provisional liquidator;

(f) the person, or each person, proposed for appointment as special administrator;

(g) the Environment Agency;

(h) the Consumer Council for Water;

(i) the Chief Inspector of Drinking Water;

(j) if the petitioner is the Secretary of State, the Welsh Ministers and the Authority;

(k) if the petitioner is the Welsh Ministers, the Secretary of State and the Authority;

(l) if the petitioner is the Authority, the Secretary of State and the Welsh Ministers.

(3) Service is in any way that the court directs or by delivering documents in accordance with the following table.

Person served	*Method of delivery*
The water company	(a) Delivery to its registered office or, if this is not practicable, to its last known principal place of business in England and Wales; (b) any other way permitted by any enactment relating to companies
Any other company	Any way permitted by any enactment relating to companies
Any person—	
who is an authorised deposit taker or a former authorised institution;	(a) The address of an office of the person, if the petitioner knows that the water company maintains a bank account;
who has appointed, or is or may be entitled to appoint, an administrative receiver of the water company, or	(b) if the petitioner knows of no such office, the person's registered office; or
who has not notified an address for service	(c) if the person has no registered office, the person's usual or last known address
Any other person	(a) If the person has previously notified an address as the person's address for service, that address; (b) the address at which the person lives or carries on business; or (c) the person's usual or last known address

(4) In the table—

"authorised deposit taker" means a person who has permission under Part 4 of the Financial Services and Markets Act 2000 to accept deposits;

"former authorised institution" means an institution that—

(a) continues to have a liability in respect of a deposit which was held in accordance with the Banking Act 1979 or the Banking Act 1987; but

(b) is not an authorised deposit taker.

(5) References in this rule to deposits and their acceptance must be read with—

(a) section 22 of the Financial Services and Markets Act 2000;

(b) any relevant order under that section; and

(c) Schedule 2 to that Act.

[7.2638]

12 Proof of service

(1) The person, or each person, who served the petition and annexed documents must swear and file an affidavit in Form WAT3, specifying the date on which, and the manner in which, service was effected.

(2) The affidavit of service must be filed as soon as reasonably practicable after service, and in any event not less than one day before the hearing of the petition.

[7.2639]

13 Insolvency proceedings brought after petition presented

If after the petition is presented the petitioner becomes aware of any other insolvency proceedings affecting the water company concerned, the petitioner must notify the court in writing of those proceedings.

[7.2640]

14 The hearing: right of appearance

At the hearing of the petition, the following may appear or be represented—

(a) any person on whom the petition was served;

(b) with the leave of the court, any other person who appears to have an interest justifying the appearance.

[7.2641]

15 Form of special administration order

A special administration order must be in Form WAT4.

[7.2642]

16 Costs of petitioner etc

(1) If the court makes a special administration order, the petitioner's costs are payable as an expense of the administration.

(2) The court may direct that the costs of any other person appearing are also payable as an expense of the administration.

[7.2643]
17 Notice and advertisement of special administration order

(1) If the court makes a special administration order the petitioner must, as soon as reasonably practicable, give notice, in Form WAT5, to the person or each person appointed as special administrator.

(2) The special administrator must, as soon as reasonably practicable, give notice, in Form WAT6, of the making of the order, by advertising—

(a) in the London Gazette; and

(b) in such newspaper as the administrator thinks most appropriate for ensuring that the order comes to the notice of the water company's creditors.

(3) The special administrator must also, as soon as reasonably practicable—

(a) give notice, in Form WAT7, of the order to each person (other than the water company) on whom the petition was served; and

(b) send a sealed copy of that form to the registrar of companies.

(4) The special administrator must send a sealed copy of the order to whichever of the Secretary of State, the Welsh Ministers and the Authority were not the petitioner.

(5) The special administrator, when sending to the registrar of companies a copy of the order in accordance with section 21(2) of the Insolvency Act, must also send to the registrar a completed Form WAT8.

(6) If the court makes any other order, it will give directions as to—

(a) whom notice of the order is to be given; and

(b) how that notice is to be given.

[7.2644]
18 Notice of discharge of special administration order

If a special administration order is discharged, the special administrator must send a copy of the order effecting the discharge and a completed Form WAT9 to each of the Secretary of State, the Welsh Ministers, the Authority and the registrar of companies.

PART 3
THE SPECIAL ADMINISTRATOR

[7.2645]
19 Special administrator's remuneration

(1) The special administrator is entitled to receive remuneration for work done in acting as special administrator.

(2) The remuneration is determined either—

(a) as a percentage of the value of the property with which the special administrator has to deal; or

(b) by reference to the time properly given by the special administrator and the special administrator's staff in attending to matters arising in the administration.

[7.2646]
20 Fixing of remuneration by court

(1) The special administrator must apply to the court to rule—

(a) whether the remuneration will be under rule 19(2)(a) or rule 19 (2)(b), and

(b) if it is under rule 19(2)(a), the percentage to be applied.

(2) The special administrator must give at least 14 days' notice of the application to the following, who may appear or be represented—

(a) the Authority (whether or not it is the petitioner);

(b) any creditors that the special administrator knows about.

(3) In determining the remuneration, the court must have regard to—

(a) any oral or written representations made by the Authority;

(b) the complexity (or otherwise) of the case;

(c) any respects in which, in connection with the water company's affairs, an exceptional kind or degree of responsibility falls or may fall on the special administrator;

(d) how effectively the special administrator appears to be carrying out, or to have carried out, the duties of special administrator; and

(e) the value and nature of the property with which the special administrator has to deal.

(4) The court may in its discretion order the costs of the special administrator's application to be paid as an expense of the special administration.

[7.2647]
21 Remuneration: joint special administrators

(1) If there are joint special administrators, they may agree as to how their remuneration should be apportioned.

(2) The court may settle, by order, any dispute between joint special administrators about the apportionment of their remuneration.

[7.2648]
22 Remuneration: special administrator a solicitor

If the special administrator is a solicitor and employs, to act on behalf of the water company, a firm or a partner of a firm of which the special administrator is a member, profit costs must not be paid unless authorised by the court.

[7.2649]
23 Resignation of special administrator

(1) The special administrator may resign, by giving a notice of intention to resign to the court—
(a) on grounds of ill health;
(b) because the special administrator intends to cease practice as an insolvency practitioner; or
(c) because a conflict of interest or change of personal circumstances precludes or makes impracticable the continued discharge of the duties of special administrator.

(2) In any other circumstance, the special administrator may resign with the permission of the court.

(3) The special administrator must give at least 7 days' written notice of intention to resign to—
(a) the Secretary of State or the Welsh Ministers, as appropriate;
(b) the Authority;
(c) any continuing special administrator of the water company; and
(d) if there is no continuing special administrator, the water company and each creditor.

(4) The special administrator must, as soon as reasonably practicable—
(a) give notice to the court—
(i) in Form WAT10 of resignation under paragraph (1), or
(ii) in Form WAT11 of resignation under paragraph (2); and
(b) send a completed copy of Form WAT10 or Form WAT11 to the registrar of companies.

[7.2650]
24 Special administrator's death in office

(1) If a special administrator dies while in office, the special administrator's personal representative must give notice of the fact, specifying the date of death, to the court.

(2) The personal representative must send a copy of the notice to—
(a) the Secretary of State or the Welsh Ministers, as appropriate;
(b) the Authority; and
(c) the registrar of companies.

(3) Paragraph (1) is taken to have been complied with—
(a) if the deceased special administrator was a partner in a firm, if the notice is given by another partner in the firm who—
(i) is qualified to act as an insolvency practitioner, or
(ii) is a member of a body recognised by order under section 391 of the Insolvency Act for the authorisation of insolvency practitioners; or
(b) in any other case, if a person gives the court a copy of the relevant death certificate.

[7.2651]
25 Order filling vacancy

If the court makes an order filling a vacancy in the office of special administrator, the person so appointed must give notice of the appointment—
(a) once in the London Gazette;
(b) in such other way as the person thinks most appropriate to ensure that the appointment comes to the notice of the water company's creditors;
(c) to the Secretary of State or the Welsh Ministers, as appropriate;
(d) to any person (other than the water company) on whom the petition was served; and
(e) to the registrar of companies.

PART 4
CONDUCT OF THE SPECIAL ADMINISTRATION

CHAPTER 1 STATEMENT OF AFFAIRS AND PROPOSALS TO CREDITORS

[7.2652]
26 Meaning of "responsible person"

In this Chapter, a reference to a responsible person is a reference to a person to whom the special administrator of a water company has sent a notice of the kind referred to in rule 27.

[7.2653]
27 Notice requiring statement of affairs

(1) If the special administrator determines that a person should be required to prepare and submit a statement of affairs in accordance with section 22 of the 1986 Act, the special administrator must send notice in WAT 12 to each of the persons whom the special administrator considers should be made responsible under that section, requiring them to prepare and submit the statement.

(2) The notice must set out—
(a) the names and addresses of every other responsible person (if any);
(b) the period within which the statement must be delivered;

(c) the effect of section 22(6) (penalty for non-compliance) of the Insolvency Act; and
(d) the effect of section 235 (duty to co-operate with office-holder) of that Act.

[7.2654]
28 Verification of statement of affairs

(1) The statement of affairs shall be in Form WAT13, must contain all the particulars required by that form and must be verified by affidavit by the deponents (using the same form).

(2) The special administrator may require any of the persons mentioned in section 22(3) of the 1986 Act to submit to the special administrator an affidavit of concurrence in Form WAT14, stating that that person concurs in the statement of affairs.

(3) A special administrator who does so must inform the person making the statement of affairs of that fact.

(4) An affidavit of concurrence may be qualified in respect of matters dealt with in the statement of affairs, where the maker of the affidavit is not in agreement with the deponents, or he considers the statement to be erroneous or misleading, or he is without the direct knowledge necessary for concurring with it.

(5) The statement of affairs must be delivered to the special administrator by the deponent making the affidavit (or by one of them, if more than one), together with a copy.

(6) Every affidavit of concurrence must be delivered to the special administrator by the person who makes it, together with a copy.

[7.2655]
29 Filing the statement of affairs

The special administrator must file the verified copy of the statement of affairs and the affidavits of concurrence (if any) in court as soon as is reasonably practicable.

[7.2656]
30 Limiting disclosure of statement of affairs

(1) If the special administrator thinks that it would prejudice the conduct of the special administration if the whole or a part of the statement of affairs were disclosed, the special administrator may apply to the court for an order limiting disclosure of the statement or any specified part of it.

(2) The court may in its discretion order that the statement or specified part—
(a) is not to be filed; or
(b) is to be filed separately and is not to be open to inspection otherwise than with the permission of the court.

(3) The court may also give directions as to the delivery of documents to the registrar of companies and the disclosure of relevant information to other persons.

[7.2657]
31 Release from obligation or extension of time

(1) This rule applies if—
(a) the special administrator refuses to exercise the power given it under section 22(5) of the Insolvency Act to—
(i) release a responsible person from the obligation to submit a statement of affairs, or
(ii) extend the period within which the statement must be submitted; and
(b) the responsible person applies to the court.

(2) The court may dismiss the application if it considers that the applicant has not shown sufficient cause for the release or extension.

(3) However, the court must not do so unless it first—
(a) gives the applicant 7 days' notice that it proposes to do so; and
(b) invites the applicant to make oral representations to the court at a "preliminary hearing".

(4) No notice need be given to any other person of the preliminary hearing.

(5) If the court does not dismiss the application at the preliminary hearing, the court must fix a venue for it to be heard, and give notice to the applicant accordingly.

(6) The applicant must, at least 14 days before the hearing of the application, send the special administrator—
(a) a notice of the hearing stating the venue;
(b) a copy of the application; and
(c) copies of any evidence that the applicant intends to rely on.

(7) The special administrator may appear and be heard on the application.

(8) The special administrator may file a written report of any matter that the special administrator considers should be drawn to the court's attention (whether or not the special administrator appears at the hearing of the application).

(9) If the special administrator files such a report, the special administrator must also send a copy of it to the applicant no later than 5 days before the hearing.

(10) The court must send sealed copies of the order made on the application to the applicant and to the special administrator.

(11) On any application under this Rule, the applicant's costs shall be paid in any event by the applicant and, unless the court otherwise orders, no allowance towards them shall be made out of the assets of the water company.

[7.2658]
32 Expenses of statement of affairs

(1) A responsible person who makes a statement of affairs or an affidavit of concurrence must be allowed, and must be paid by the special administrator out of the receipts of the administration, any expenses that the responsible person reasonably incurs in doing so.

(2) Any decision by the special administrator under this rule relating to expenses is subject to appeal to the court.

(3) Nothing in this rule relieves a responsible person of any obligation with respect to the preparation, verification and submission of the statement of affairs, or to the provision of information to the special administrator.

[7.2659]
33 Statement to be annexed to proposals

(1) The statement of the special administrator's proposals required by section 23(1) of the Insolvency Act must be in form WAT15.

(2) The special administrator must annex to that statement a further statement setting out—
- (a) details of the appointment of the special administrator;
- (b) the names of the directors and any secretary of the water company;
- (c) an account of the circumstances that gave rise to the application for a special administration order;
- (d) if a statement of affairs has been submitted, a copy or summary of it, with the special administrator's comments, if any;
- (e) if no statement of affairs has been submitted, details of the financial position of the water company at the latest practicable date (which must, unless the court otherwise orders, be a date not earlier than that of the special administration order);
- (f) the manner in which the special administrator—
  - (i) has managed and financed the affairs and business of the water company since the date of the special administrator's appointment; and
  - (ii) will continue to manage and finance those affairs and that business; and
- (g) any other information that the special administrator thinks necessary.

[7.2660]
34 Form of statement of revised proposals

(1) A statement of the special administrator's revised proposals required by section 25(2) of the Insolvency Act to be sent to creditors must be in form WAT16.

(2) The special administrator must, when sending form WAT16 to the creditors, send a copy of form WAT16 to the registrar of companies.

[7.2661]
35 Statement if special administration order to be discharged before statement of proposals

If the special administrator, the Secretary of State, the Welsh Ministers or the Authority intends to apply to the court under section 18 of the Insolvency Act for the special administration order to be discharged but the special administrator has not yet sent to the authorities and persons mentioned in section 23(1) of that Act ("the relevant persons")—
- (a) the statement of proposals mentioned in rule 33(1), and
- (b) the further statement mentioned in rule 33(2),

the special administrator, must, at least 10 days before the application to the court is made, send to the relevant persons the further statement mentioned in rule 33(2).

[7.2662]
36 Notice to members of proposals to creditors

(1) For the purposes of section 23(2A)(b) of the Insolvency Act, the prescribed manner is that the notice must be published—
- (a) once in the London Gazette; and
- (b) in such other manner as the special administrator thinks most appropriate to ensure that the appointment comes to the notice of the relevant water company's creditors.

CHAPTER 2 DISPOSAL OF PROPERTY

[7.2663]
37 Disposal of charged property, etc

(1) This rule applies if the special administrator of a water company applies to the court under section 15(2) of the Insolvency Act for an order authorising the disposal of—
- (a) property of the water company that is subject to a security to which section 15(2) applies; or
- (b) goods in the possession of the water company under a hire-purchase agreement (within the meaning given by section 15(9) of that Act).

(2) The court will fix a venue for the hearing of the application, and the special administrator must, as soon as reasonably practicable, give notice of the venue to the person who is the holder of the security or the owner under the agreement, as the case may be.

(3) If the court makes an order under section 15(2) of that Act the special administrator must, as soon as reasonably practicable, give notice of the order by sending a copy of the order and a completed Form WAT17, to the holder or owner.

CHAPTER 3 ACCOUNTS

[7.2664]

38 Abstract of receipts and payments

(1) The special administrator of a water company must send accounts of the receipts and payments of the water company to the court and to the registrar of companies—

- (a) within 2 months after the end of—
  - (i) 6 months from the date of appointment; and
  - (ii) each subsequent 6-month period; and
- (b) within 2 months after ceasing to act as special administrator.

(2) The court may, on the application of the special administrator, extend either 2-month period mentioned in paragraph (1).

(3) The accounts must be in the form of an abstract, in Form WAT18, showing—

- (a) receipts and payments during the relevant 6-month period; or
- (b) if the special administrator has ceased to act—
  - (i) receipts and payments during the period from the end of the last 6-month period to the time of ceasing to act; or
  - (ii) if there has been no previous abstract, receipts and payments in the period since the special administrator's appointment.

(4) It is an offence for the special administrator to fail to comply with this rule, punishable—

- (a) on summary conviction, to a fine not exceeding level 3 on the standard scale; and
- (b) for continued contravention, to a daily fine not exceeding one-tenth of that amount.

CHAPTER 4 ACCESS TO DOCUMENTS

[7.2665]

39 Confidentiality of documents

(1) If in the course of a special administration the special administrator considers that a document forming part of the records of the special administration—

- (a) should be treated as confidential, or
- (b) is of such a nature that its disclosure would be injurious to the interests of the creditors or members of the water company in special administration,

the special administrator may refuse to allow the document to be inspected by a person who would otherwise be entitled to do so.

(2) If the special administrator decides to refuse to allow a person to inspect a document, the person may apply to the court to overrule that refusal.

(3) The court may overrule or confirm the refusal it, and may confirm it subject to conditions.

(4) Nothing in this rule entitles the special administrator to refuse to allow the inspection of a claim or proxy.

[7.2666]

40 Right to copy documents

(1) If under the Insolvency Act or these Rules a person has a right to inspect a document, the person may also take a copy of it, on payment of the appropriate fee.

(2) If a creditor or member of a water company asks a special administrator of the company to supply a copy of a document, the special administrator is entitled to require the payment of the appropriate fee for the supply of the copy.

(3) For this rule, the appropriate fee is 15 pence for each A4 or A5 page or 30 pence for each A3 page.

[7.2667]

41 Right to have list of creditors

(1) A creditor who, under these Rules, has the right to inspect documents on the court file also has the right to require the special administrator to give the creditor, on payment of the appropriate fee, a list of the creditors of the water company and the amounts that each of them is owed.

(2) This does not apply if a statement of the water company's affairs has been filed.

(3) For this rule, the appropriate fee is 15 pence for each A4 or A5 page or 30 pence for each A3 page.

[7.2668]

42 False claim of status as creditor or member etc

(1) It is an offence for a person falsely to claim, with the intention of obtaining a sight of documents that the person has, under these Rules, no right to inspect, a status that would entitle the person to inspect them.

(2) A person guilty of an offence under this rule is liable—

(a) on summary conviction, to a fine not exceeding the statutory maximum or to imprisonment for a term not exceeding six months, or to both; or
(b) on conviction on indictment, to a fine or to imprisonment for a term not exceeding two years, or to both.

PART 5
MEETINGS

CHAPTER 1 CREDITORS' MEETINGS

[7.2669]
43 Application of Chapter

This Chapter applies to a meeting of the creditors of a water company summoned by the special administrator of the company, whether under section 14(2)(b) of the Insolvency Act or by direction of the court under section 17(3)(b) of that Act.

[7.2670]
44 Venue and notice of creditors' meetings

(1) In fixing the venue for a meeting, the special administrator must have regard to the convenience of creditors.

(2) The time fixed for the start of a meeting must be between 10.00 am and 4.00 pm on a business day, unless the court directs otherwise.

(3) The special administrator must give at least 21 days' written notice of a meeting to each creditor known to the special administrator who had a claim against the water company at the date of the special administration order.

(4) The notice of a meeting—
(a) must be in Form WAT19;
(b) must specify the purpose of the meeting; and
(c) must contain a statement of the effect of rule 48 (entitlement to vote).

(5) A form of proxy must be sent with each notice.

[7.2671]
45 Non-receipt of notice of meeting

If in accordance with the Insolvency Act or these Rules a meeting of creditors is called or summoned by notice, the meeting is taken to have been properly summoned and held, even if not all those to whom the notice is to be given have received it.

[7.2672]
46 Who presides at meetings

(1) At a meeting, the chair is either the special administrator, or a person nominated by the special administrator in writing to act as the chair.

(2) Any person nominated must be—
(a) a person who is qualified to act as an insolvency practitioner in relation to the water company; or
(b) an employee of the special administrator or a member of the special administrator's firm who is experienced in insolvency matters.

[7.2673]
47 Adjournment

(1) If within 30 minutes from the time fixed for the commencement of a meeting neither the special administrator nor a person nominated under rule 46 to preside is present, the meeting stands adjourned to the same time and place in the following week or, if that day is not a business day, to the business day immediately after it.

(2) A meeting may be adjourned from time to time, if the person presiding thinks fit, but not for more than 14 days from the date on which it was fixed to commence, unless the court directs otherwise.

(3) If a meeting is adjourned, the special administrator must, as soon as reasonably practicable, notify the creditors of the venue of the adjourned meeting.

[7.2674]
48 Entitlement to vote: meetings of creditors

(1) Subject to paragraphs (3) and (6), a person may only vote at a meeting if—
(a) the person has given the special administrator, not later than noon on the business day before the day fixed for the meeting, details in writing of the debt that the person claims is due to the person from the water company;
(b) the claim has been admitted under this Part; and
(c) any proxy to be used on the person's behalf has been lodged with the special administrator.

(2) The details of the debt must set out any calculation for the purposes of rules 49 to 53.

(3) The person presiding at the meeting may allow a creditor to vote even if the creditor has failed to comply with paragraph (1)(a), if the person presiding is satisfied that the failure was due to circumstances beyond the creditor's control.

(4) The person presiding may require the production of any document or other evidence necessary for the purpose of substantiating the whole or any part of the claim.

(5) Votes are to be calculated according to the amount of each creditor's debt as at the date of the special administration order, deducting any amounts paid in respect of the debt after that date.

(6) A creditor must not vote in respect of a debt for an unliquidated amount, or a debt whose value is not ascertained, unless the person presiding agrees to put an estimated minimum value on the debt for the purpose of entitlement to vote and admits the claim for that purpose.

(7) A creditor is not entitled to vote more than once on any resolution put to the meeting.

(8) A creditor may appeal to the court against a decision, under this rule, of the person presiding.

[7.2675]
49 Admission and rejection of claims

(1) At a creditors' meeting the person presiding may admit or reject a creditor's claim for the purpose of the creditor's entitlement to vote, and may do so with respect to the whole or any part of the claim.

(2) If the person presiding is in doubt whether a creditor's claim should be admitted or rejected, the person presiding must mark it as objected to and allow the creditor to vote.

(3) However, the creditor's vote is invalid if the objection to the claim is sustained.

(4) A creditor may appeal to the court against a decision, under this rule, of the person presiding.

(5) If on appeal the decision is reversed or varied, or a creditor's vote is declared invalid, the court may order that another meeting be summoned, or make such other order as it thinks just.

(6) Neither the special administrator nor a person nominated by the special administrator to preside at a meeting is personally liable for costs incurred by a person in respect of an appeal to the court under this rule, unless the court so orders.

[7.2676]
50 Voting by secured creditors

At a meeting of creditors, a secured creditor is entitled to vote only in respect of the balance (if any) of the creditor's debt after deducting the value of the creditor's security as estimated by the creditor.

[7.2677]
51 Voting by holders of negotiable instruments

A creditor must not vote in respect of a debt on, or secured by, a current bill of exchange or promissory note, unless the creditor agrees—

(a) to treat the liability to the creditor on the bill or note of every person who is liable on it antecedent to the water company, and against whom a bankruptcy order has not been made (or, in the case of a company, which has not gone into liquidation), as a security in the creditor's hands; and

(b) to estimate the value of that security and, for the purpose of calculating the creditor's entitlement to vote, to deduct it from the creditor's claim.

[7.2678]
52 Voting by retention of title creditors

For the purpose of calculating entitlement to vote at a creditors' meeting, a creditor of the water company who is a seller of goods to the water company under a retention of title agreement must deduct from the claim the value, as estimated by the creditor, of any rights arising under that agreement in respect of goods in the possession of the water company.

[7.2679]
53 Voting by creditors under hire-purchase, conditional sale and chattel leasing agreements

(1) Subject to paragraph (2), a creditor of the water company who is an owner of goods under a hire-purchase or chattel leasing agreement, or a seller of goods under a conditional sale agreement, is entitled to vote in respect of the amount of the debt due and payable to the creditor by the water company as at the date of the special administration order.

(2) In calculating the amount of a debt for this purpose, no account is to be taken of any amount attributable to the exercise of any right under the relevant agreement in so far as the right has become exercisable solely because of the presentation of the petition for a special administration order or any matter arising in consequence of that presentation, or the making of the order.

[7.2680]
54 Quorum at meetings

(1) A meeting of creditors called or summoned by a special administrator is competent to act if a quorum is present.

(2) One creditor entitled to vote is a quorum.

(3) For the purposes of this rule, the reference to the creditor necessary to constitute a quorum is to those persons present or represented by proxy by any person (including the chair) and includes persons duly represented under section 323 (representation of corporations at meetings) of the Companies Act 2006 as applied by rule 67.

(4) If at a meeting of creditors—

(a) a quorum is present because only the person presiding at the meeting, or that person and one other person, are present, and
(b) the person presiding is aware, because of proofs and proxies received or otherwise, that an additional person or persons would, if attending, be entitled to vote,

the meeting must not commence until at least 15 minutes after the time appointed for its commencement.

(5) In this rule "proof" means a document in which a creditor seeks to establish a claim.

[7.2681]
55 Resolutions

(1) Subject to paragraph (2), at a creditors' meeting a resolution is passed when a majority (in value) of those present and voting, in person or by proxy, have voted in favour of it.

(2) A resolution is invalid if those voting against it include more than half in value of the creditors—
(a) to whom notice of the meeting was sent; and
(b) who are not, so far as the person presiding knows, connected with the water company (within the meaning given by section 249 of the Insolvency Act).

[7.2682]
56 Minutes

(1) The person presiding at a meeting must ensure that minutes of its proceedings are entered in the water company's minute book.

(2) The minutes must include a list of the creditors who attended (personally or by proxy).

[7.2683]
57 Report to creditors

(1) Within 14 days of the end of every period of 6 months beginning with the date of a special administrator's appointment, the special administrator must send each creditor of the water company concerned a report on the progress of the administration.

(2) On vacating office, the special administrator must send each creditor a report on the administration up to that time.

(3) Paragraph (2) does not apply if—
(a) the water company goes into liquidation immediately after the special administration ends; or
(b) the special administrator is removed from office by the court or ceases to be qualified as an insolvency practitioner.

CHAPTER 2 MEMBERS' MEETINGS

[7.2684]
58 Venue and conduct of members' meeting

(1) If the special administrator of a water company summons a meeting of members of the company, the special administrator must have regard to their convenience in fixing a venue for it.

(2) Subject to paragraphs (2) to (5) and Part 6, the meeting must be summoned and conducted—
(a) as if it were a general meeting of the water company summoned under the company's articles of association; and
(b) in accordance with the Companies Act 2006.

(3) The special administrator, or a person nominated by the special administrator in writing, is to preside at the meeting.

(4) To be eligible for nomination, a person must be—
(a) qualified to act as an insolvency practitioner in relation to the water company; or
(b) an employee of the special administrator or the special administrator's firm and experienced in insolvency matters.

(5) If within 30 minutes from the time fixed for the start of the meeting there is no person present to preside, the meeting stands adjourned to the same time and place in the following week or, if that day is not a business day, to the next business day after it.

(6) The person presiding at the meeting must ensure that minutes of its proceedings are entered in the water company's minute book.

CHAPTER 3 MEETINGS GENERALLY

[7.2685]
59 Evidence of proceedings at meeting

(1) A minute of proceedings at a meeting of the creditors or members of a water company called or summoned by the special administrator, and signed by a person described as having, or appearing to have, presided at the meeting (for example, by being described as chair or chairman of the meeting), is admissible in special administration proceedings without further proof.

(2) The minute is prima facie evidence that—
(a) the meeting was duly convened and held;
(b) resolutions passed at the meeting were properly passed; and
(c) the proceedings recorded in the minutes took place.

PART 6
PROXIES AND COMPANY REPRESENTATION

[7.2686]
60 Application of this Part

This Part applies to any meeting of the creditors or members of a water company that is called or summoned under the Insolvency Act or under these Rules.

[7.2687]
61 Definition and grant of proxy

(1) For the purposes of these Rules, a proxy is a written authority in form WAT20 given by a person ("the principal") to another person ("the proxy-holder")—
- (a) to attend a meeting; and
- (b) to speak and vote at the meeting as the principal's representative.

(2) A proxy-holder must be an individual aged 18 years or over.

(3) A proxy requires the proxy-holder to give the principal's vote on matters arising for determination at the meeting, or to abstain, or to propose, in the principal's name, a resolution to be voted on by the meeting, either as directed or, if not directed, in accordance with the proxy-holder's own discretion.

(4) A principal may give only one proxy for any one meeting, and must give it to only one proxy-holder.

(5) However, the principal may specify one or more other individuals to be the proxy-holder in the alternative (if more than one, in the order in which they are named in the proxy).

(6) Without affecting the generality of paragraphs (4) and (5), a proxy for a particular meeting may be given to the person who presides at the meeting, and that person cannot decline to be the proxy-holder for that proxy.

[7.2688]
62 Issue and use of forms of proxy

(1) A form of proxy sent out with the notice of a meeting must not have a person's name or description inserted in it.

(2) The only form of proxy that may be used at a meeting is one sent with the notice summoning the meeting.

(3) A form of proxy must be signed by the principal, or by a person authorised by the principal to do so (either generally or with reference to a particular meeting).

(4) If a form of proxy is signed by a person other than the principal, the nature of that person's authority must be stated.

(5) A form of proxy is invalid if it does not comply with any part of this rule.

[7.2689]
63 Use of proxies at meetings

(1) A form of proxy given for a particular meeting may be used at an adjournment of that meeting.

(2) If the special administrator holds forms of proxy for use as chair of a meeting, and another person acts as chair, that other person may use the forms of proxy of the special administrator as if the other person were the proxy-holder.

(3) A proxy-holder may propose any resolution that, if it were proposed by another person, would be a resolution in favour of which, by virtue of the proxy, the proxy-holder would be entitled to vote.

(4) If a form of proxy gives specific directions as to voting, the proxy-holder is not, unless the form of proxy states otherwise, prevented from voting at the proxy-holder's discretion on any resolution put to the meeting but not dealt with in the proxy.

[7.2690]
64 Retention of proxies

(1) Subject to paragraph (2), the person presiding at a meeting must retain all forms of proxy used for voting at the meeting.

(2) If the chair is not the special administrator of the water company concerned, that person must deliver the forms of proxy to the special administrator as soon as reasonably practicable after the meeting.

[7.2691]
65 Right of inspection of proxies

(1) The special administrator of a water company who holds forms of proxy must allow them to be inspected, at any reasonable time on any business day, by any of the following—
- (a) a creditor who has submitted a written claim to be a creditor of the water company, if that claim has been admitted, in whole or in part, for the purpose of voting, dividend or otherwise;
- (b) in the case of forms of proxy used at a meeting of that company, that company's members;
- (c) the directors of that company;
- (d) the Secretary of State;
- (e) the Welsh Ministers;
- (f) the Authority.

(2) In paragraph (1)(a), "creditor" does not include a person whose claim has been wholly rejected for the purposes of voting, dividend or otherwise.

(3) Any person who attends a meeting is entitled, immediately before or during the meeting, to inspect forms of proxy and associated documents (including proofs as defined in rule 54(5)) sent or given, in accordance with directions contained in any notice summoning the meeting, by a creditor or member of the water company for the purpose of that meeting to—

(a) the person presiding at the meeting; or
(b) any other person.

[7.2692]
66 Proxy-holder with financial interest

(1) In this rule, subject to paragraph (4), "associate" has the same meaning as in section 435 of the Insolvency Act.

(2) A proxy-holder must not vote in favour of a resolution that would directly or indirectly place the proxy-holder, or an associate of the proxy-holder, in a position to receive remuneration out of the assets of the water company concerned, unless the form of proxy specifically directs the proxy-holder to vote in that way.

(3) If a proxy-holder holds a form of proxy that has been signed by that proxy-holder on behalf of the principal under an authority given by the principal under rule 63(4), and the form of proxy specifically directs the proxy-holder to vote in the way referred to in paragraph (2), the proxy-holder must nevertheless not vote in that way unless the proxy-holder shows the person presiding at the meeting the principal's written authorisation for the proxy-holder to have signed the form of proxy.

(4) For the purposes of paragraph (2), if a person other than the special administrator presides at a meeting, and uses forms of proxy of the special administrator in the circumstances set out in rule 63(2), the special administrator is taken to be an associate of the person presiding at the meeting.

[7.2693]
67 Company representation

(1) Section 323 of the Companies Act 2006 (representation of corporations at meetings) applies to a meeting of creditors under these Rules as to a meeting of the company (references to a member of the company being read as references to a creditor).

(2) A person is authorised under section 323 of the 2006 Act to represent a corporation at a meeting of creditors, must produce to the chair of the meeting a copy of the resolution from which he derives the authority to do so is derived.

(3) The copy resolution must be under the seal of the corporation, or certified by the secretary or a director of the corporation to be a true copy.

(4) Nothing in this rule requires the authority of a person to sign a proxy on behalf of a principal which is a corporation to be in the form of a resolution of that corporation.

PART 7
COURT PROCEDURE AND PRACTICE

CHAPTER 1 APPLICATIONS

[7.2694]
68 Preliminary

This Chapter applies to all applications made to the court in special administration proceedings, except a petition for a special administration order.

[7.2695]
69 Interpretation

In this Chapter—

"originating application" means an application to the court that is not made in pending proceedings before the court; and

"ordinary application" means any other application to the court.

[7.2696]
70 Form and contents of applications

(1) An application must be in writing and must state—

(a) the names of the parties;
(b) the nature of the relief or order applied for or the directions sought from the court;
(c) if the application is to be served on any other person, the name and address of each person on whom the applicant will serve the application;
(d) if the Insolvency Act or these Rules require that notice of the application is to be given to a particular person, the name and address of that person (so far as the applicant knows); and
(e) the applicant's address for service.

(2) If the application is not to be served on any other person, it must contain a statement to that effect.

(3) An originating application must set out the grounds on which the applicant claims the relief or order sought.

(4) An originating application must be in Form WAT21.

(5) An ordinary application must be in Form WAT22.

(6) The application must be signed—

(a) by the applicant;

(b) if the applicant is a child or a protected party (within the meaning of CPR rule 21), by a litigation friend of the applicant; or

(c) by the applicant's solicitor.

[7.2697]

71 Filing and service of applications

(1) An application must be filed, with as many extra copies as there are persons to be served with the application, plus one more copy.

(2) Subject to paragraphs (3) to (6) and rule 72(3), or unless the rule under which the application is made provides otherwise, or the court otherwise orders, the court will fix a venue for the hearing of the application.

(3) Unless the court otherwise directs, the applicant must serve a sealed copy of the application, endorsed with the venue of the hearing, on the respondent or each respondent.

(4) Subject to any direction of the court under paragraph (5)(c), service on a person of a sealed copy of the application is sufficient notice of the venue for the application.

(5) The court may give any of the following directions—

(a) that the application be served upon a person other than one specified by the relevant provision of the Insolvency Act or these Rules;

(b) that the giving of notice to a particular person or persons be dispensed with; or

(c) that notice be given in some way other than that specified in paragraph (3).

(6) Subject to any provision of the Insolvency Act or these Rules, and subject to any direction under paragraph (5)(b), the application must be served at least 14 days before the date fixed for the hearing.

[7.2698]

72 Hearings without notice

(1) In an urgent case, the court may—

(a) hear the application immediately, either with or without notice to, or with or without the attendance of, other parties; or

(b) authorise a shorter period of service than required by rule 71(6).

(2) The court may hear an application referred to in paragraph (1) on terms providing for the filing or service of documents, or the carrying out of other formalities, as the court thinks fit.

(3) If hearing an application without service on any other party is permitted, the court may hear it as soon as reasonably practicable, without fixing a venue.

(4) However, if the court fixes a venue for the application to be heard, rule 71 applies (so far as relevant).

[7.2699]

73 Hearing of applications in private

Unless the court orders otherwise—

(a) an application before a registrar must be heard in private; and

(b) an application before a judge may be heard in private.

[7.2700]

74 Exercise of court's jurisdiction by registrar

(1) The registrar may exercise the jurisdiction of the court to hear and determine an application made to the registrar in the first instance, unless—

(a) a judge has given a general or special direction to the contrary; or

(b) it is not within the registrar's power to make an order sought by the application.

(2) If the application is made to the registrar, the registrar may refer to a judge any matter that the registrar thinks should properly be decided by a judge, and the judge may either dispose of the matter or refer it back to the registrar with such direction as the judge thinks fit.

(3) Nothing in this rule prevents an application being made directly to the judge.

[7.2701]

75 Use of witness statements

(1) Evidence may be given by witness statement supported by a statement of truth unless the court otherwise directs.

(2) CPR Part 32 applies to the use of witness statements in special administration proceedings.

[7.2702]

76 Filing and service of witness statements

(1) Unless the provision of the Insolvency Act or these Rules under which an application is made provides otherwise, or the court allows otherwise—

(a) if the applicant intends to rely on a witness statement, the applicant must file the statement and serve a copy on the respondent not less than 14 days before the date fixed for the hearing; and

(b) if a respondent to an application intends to oppose it and to rely for that purpose on a witness statement, the respondent must file the statement and serve a copy on the applicant not less than 7 days before the date fixed for the hearing.

[7.2703]

77 Use of reports

(1) The special administrator may file a report instead of an affidavit or witness statement, unless the application involves other parties or the court otherwise orders.

(2) If the special administrator files a report instead of an affidavit or witness statement, the report must be treated as if it were a witness statement.

(3) In particular, the court may order the special administrator to attend for cross-examination on the report.

[7.2704]

78 Adjournment of hearing: directions

(1) The court may adjourn the hearing of an application on such terms (if any) as it thinks fit.

(2) The court may give directions generally as to the procedure on the application and in particular as to—

(a) service on, or notice of the application to, a person, whether in connection with the venue of a resumed hearing or for any other purpose;
(b) whether particulars of claim and defence are to be delivered;
(c) the manner in which evidence is to be adduced, and in particular as to—
  (i) the taking of evidence wholly or in part by affidavit or witness statement or orally;
  (ii) the cross-examination of deponents to affidavits or persons who have made witness statements; and
  (iii) any report to be given by the special administrator; and
(d) the matters to be dealt with in evidence.

CHAPTER 2 ENFORCEMENT

[7.2705]

79 Enforcement of court orders

In special administration proceedings, an order of the court may be enforced in the same manner as a judgment.

[7.2706]

80 Orders enforcing compliance with these Rules

(1) The court may, on application by the special administrator, make such orders as it thinks necessary for the enforcement of obligations falling on a person in accordance with section 22 (statement of affairs to be submitted to administrator) or section 235 of the Insolvency Act (duty to co-operate with office-holder).

(2) An order of the court under this rule may provide that all costs of and incidental to the application for it must be borne by the person against whom the order is made.

CHAPTER 3 ACCESS TO COURT RECORDS

[7.2707]

81 CPR rules not to apply

CPR Part 5 (other than rules 5.4B and 5.4C) does not apply to documents filed in special administration proceedings.

[7.2708]

82 Certain persons' right to inspect the court file

(1) The following may, at a reasonable time, inspect the court's file in relation to any special administration proceedings—

(a) the special administrator;
(b) the Authority;
(c) the Secretary of State;
(d) the Welsh Ministers;
(e) the Chief Inspector of Drinking Water;
(f) the Environment Agency;
(g) the Consumer Council for Water;
(h) subject to paragraph (2), a creditor of the water company to which the special administration proceedings relate;
(i) a person who is, or at any time has been, a director or officer of that company;
(j) a member of that company.

(2) A person who claims to be a creditor of the water company must make a written statement as to being such a creditor.

(3) A person's right of inspection may be exercised on the person's behalf by another person authorised by the first person.

(4) Any other person may inspect the file with the court's permission.

(5) However, the court may declare that the right of inspection under this rule is not exercisable in relation to a particular document, or a part of a document, without the court's permission.

(6) An application for a declaration under paragraph (5) may be made by the special administrator or by any other person who has an interest.

[7.2709]
83 Right to copy documents

If a person has a right to inspect a document on the court's file, the person may also take a copy of the document, on payment of the fee prescribed under section 92 of the Courts Act 2003.

[7.2710]
84 Official copies of documents on court file

(1) A person who has the right to inspect the court file of special administration proceedings may request the court for an official copy of any document from the file.

(2) A person's solicitor may exercise the person's right under this rule.

(3) An official copy provided under this rule will be in the form that the registrar thinks appropriate, and will bear the court's seal.

[7.2711]
85 False claim of status as creditor or member

(1) It is an offence for a person falsely to claim, with the intention of obtaining a sight of documents on the court file that the person has no right to inspect, a status that would entitle the person to inspect such a document.

(2) A person guilty of an offence under this rule is liable—

(a) on summary conviction, to a fine not exceeding the statutory maximum or to imprisonment for a term not exceeding six months, or to both; or

(b) on conviction on indictment, to a fine or to imprisonment for a term not exceeding two years, or to both.

[7.2712]
86 Filing of copies of London Gazette notices and advertisements

(1) If a person causes a notice to be published in the London Gazette in relation to special administration proceedings, the person must file a copy of the notice.

(2) If a person causes an advertisement to be published in a newspaper in relation to special administration proceedings, the person must file a copy of the advertisement.

(3) The copy of the notice or advertisement must be accompanied by, or have endorsed on it, sufficient particulars to identify the proceedings and the date of the notice's or advertisement's appearance.

CHAPTER 4 COSTS AND DETAILED ASSESSMENT

[7.2713]
87 Application of the Civil Procedure Rules

Subject to any inconsistent provision in this Chapter, CPR Parts 43 (scope of costs rules and definitions), 44 (general rules about costs), 45 (fixed costs), 47 (procedure for detailed assessment of costs and default provisions) and 48 (costs—special cases) apply to special administration proceedings.

[7.2714]
88 Costs to be assessed by detailed assessment

(1) The amount of any costs, charges or expenses of a person that are payable out of the assets of a water company must be decided by detailed assessment unless the special administrator and the person entitled to payment agree to the contrary.

(2) In the absence of such an agreement, the special administrator may serve notice in writing on the person to commence detailed assessment proceedings in accordance with CPR Part 47 (procedure for detailed assessment of costs and default provisions).

(3) In any proceedings before the court, including proceedings on a petition, the court may order costs to be decided by detailed assessment.

(4) Nothing in this rule prevents the special administrator from making payments on account to a person on the basis of an undertaking by the person to repay immediately any money that may, when detailed assessment is made, prove to have been overpaid, with interest at the rate specified in section 17 of the Judgments Act 1838 on the date payment was made and for the period from the date of payment to that of repayment.

[7.2715]
89 Procedures for detailed assessment: employees of the special administrator

(1) Before making a detailed assessment of the costs of a person employed, in special administration proceedings, by a special administrator, the costs officer will require from the special administrator a certificate of the person's employment in accordance with paragraphs (2) and (3).

(2) The special administrator must endorse the certificate on the person's bill and must sign it.

(3) The certificate must set out—

(a) the person's name and address;

(b) details of the functions that the person carried out under the employment; and
(c) a note of any special terms of remuneration that have been agreed.

[7.2716]
90 Procedures for detailed assessment: time limit to bring proceedings

(1) A person whose costs in special administration proceedings are required to be decided by detailed assessment must, on being required in writing to do so by the special administrator, commence detailed assessment proceedings in accordance with CPR Part 47 (procedure for detailed assessment of costs and default provisions).

(2) If the person does not commence detailed assessment proceedings within 3 months of the requirement under paragraph (1), or within such further time as the court, on application, may permit, the special administrator may deal with the assets of the water company without regard to the person's claim for costs.

(3) The person's claim for costs is forfeited by that failure to commence detailed assessment proceedings.

(4) If in such a case the person also has such a claim against a special administrator personally, that claim is also forfeited by the person's failure to commence detailed assessment proceedings.

[7.2717]
91 Costs paid otherwise than out of the assets of the water company

If the amount of costs is decided by detailed assessment under an order of the court directing that the costs are to be paid otherwise than out of the assets of the water company, the costs officer will note, on the final costs certificate, whom the costs are to be paid by or how they are to be paid.

[7.2718]
92 Award of costs against special administrator

(1) If a special administrator is made a party to proceedings on the application of another party, the special administrator is not personally liable for costs unless the court so directs.

(2) Paragraph (1) is subject to any provision of the Insolvency Act, the Water Industry Act 1991 or the Insolvency Rules 1986, or any other provision of these Rules, under which the special administrator is not in any event to be liable for costs and expenses.

[7.2719]
93 Applications for costs

(1) This rule applies if a party to, or a person affected by, special administration proceedings—
(a) applies to the court for an order allowing the person's costs, or part of them, incidental to the proceedings; and
(b) that application was not made at the time of the proceedings.

(2) The party or person must serve a sealed copy of the application on the special administrator.

(3) The special administrator may oppose, or make submissions to the court orally or in writing about, the application.

(4) The court will not allow the applicant any costs in relation to the application unless the court is satisfied that the application could not have been made at the time of the proceedings.

[7.2720]
94 Costs and expenses of witnesses

(1) An officer of the water company concerned in special administration proceedings is not entitled to any allowance as a witness in any examination or other proceedings before the court unless the court so orders.

(2) A person presenting a petition in special administration proceedings is not taken to be a witness on the hearing of the petition, but the costs officer may allow the person's expenses of travelling and subsistence.

[7.2721]
95 Final costs certificate

A final costs certificate of the costs officer is final and conclusive as to all matters that have not been objected to in the manner provided for under the CPR.

[7.2722]
96 Replacement of lost or destroyed costs certificate

If a costs officer is satisfied that a costs certificate has been lost or destroyed, the costs officer may issue a duplicate certificate.

CHAPTER 5 PERSONS WHO LACK CAPACITY

[7.2723]
97 Children and patients

If a party to proceedings to which these Rules apply lacks capacity (within the meaning given by the Mental Capacity Act 2005) in relation to the proceedings, CPR Part 21 applies to—
(a) the conduct of those proceedings by or on behalf of the party;
(b) the appointment of a litigation friend for the party; and

(c) any compromise or settlement of the proceedings.

CHAPTER 6 APPEALS

[7.2724]
98 Appeal and review of orders

(1) The court may review, rescind or vary any order that it makes in proceedings to which these Rules apply.

(2) An appeal from a decision of a registrar in such proceedings lies to a single judge of the High Court.

(3) An appeal from a decision of that judge on such an appeal lies, with the permission of that judge or the Court of Appeal, to the Court of Appeal.

[7.2725]
99 Procedure on appeal

(1) Subject to paragraph (2), CPR Part 52 (appeals) applies to appeals in special administration proceedings.

(2) In relation to an appeal to a single judge of the High Court under rule 98(2)—

(a) a reference in the CPR to the Court of Appeal is taken to be a reference to that judge; and
(b) a reference in the CPR to the registrar of civil appeals is taken to be a reference to the registrar of the High Court who deals with special administration proceedings.

CHAPTER 7 GENERAL

[7.2726]
100 Principal court rules and practice to apply

(1) The CPR and the practice and procedure of the High Court (including any practice direction) apply to special administration proceedings, with necessary modifications, except so far as inconsistent with these Rules.

(2) All special administration proceedings shall be allocated to the multi-track for which CPR Part 29 (the multi-track) makes provision, accordingly those provisions of the CPR that provide for allocation questionnaires and track allocation do not apply.

[7.2727]
101 Title of proceedings

A document that is filed in special administration proceedings—

(a) must name the water company to which the proceedings relate; and
(b) must be entitled "In the matter of the Insolvency Act 1986 and the Water Industry Act 1991".

[7.2728]
102 Right of audience

Rights of audience in special administration proceedings are the same as in insolvency proceedings under the Insolvency Act or the Insolvency Rules 1986.

[7.2729]
103 Special administrator's solicitor

If the attendance of the special administrator's solicitor is required in special administration proceedings, the special administrator need not attend in person unless the court so directs.

[7.2730]
104 Formal defects

Special administration proceedings are not invalidated by any formal defect or by any irregularity, unless the court considers that substantial injustice has been caused by the defect or irregularity, and that the injustice cannot be remedied by any order of the court.

[7.2731]
105 Affidavits

(1) Subject to paragraphs (2) to (5), the practice and procedure of the High Court with regard to affidavits, their form and contents, and the procedure governing their use, apply to special administration proceedings.

(2) If the special administrator makes an affidavit in special administration proceedings, the deponent must state—

(a) the capacity in which the deponent makes the affidavit;
(b) the position that the deponent holds; and
(c) the address at which the deponent works.

(3) Subject to paragraph (4), where these Rules provide for the use of an affidavit, a witness statement verified by a statement of truth may be used instead.

(4) If the court has ordered a person to submit an affidavit the person must not substitute a witness statement.

(5) If a witness statement is used instead of an affidavit, in any form filed in the proceedings references to a witness statement must be substituted for references to an affidavit, and references to the maker of the statement must be substituted for references to the deponent.

[7.2732]
106 Giving of security to the court

(1) If security has to be given to the court (otherwise than in relation to costs), it may be given by guarantee, bond or the payment of money into court.

(2) A person proposing to give a bond as security must give notice to the party in whose favour the security is required, and to the court, naming the persons who are to be sureties to the bond.

(3) The court will give notice to the parties concerned of a venue for the execution of the bond and the making of any objection to the sureties.

(4) The sureties must make an affidavit of their sufficiency (unless dispensed with by the party in whose favour the security is required) and must, if required by the court, attend the court to be cross-examined.

[7.2733]
107 Payment into court

CPR Part 37 applies to money paid into court in proceedings to which these Rules apply.

[7.2734]
108 Further information and disclosure

(1) A party to special administration proceedings may apply to the court for an order—
- (a) that any other party—
  - (i) clarify a matter in dispute in the proceedings, or
  - (ii) give additional information in relation to such a matter,

  in accordance with CPR Part 18 (further information); or
- (b) to obtain disclosure from any other party in accordance with CPR Part 31 (disclosure and inspection of documents).

(2) An application under this rule may be made without notice being served on any other party.

PART 8
EXAMINATION OF PERSONS IN SPECIAL ADMINISTRATION PROCEEDINGS

[7.2735]
109 Application

The rules in this Part relate to applications to the court by a special administrator for an order under section 236 (inquiry into company's dealings, etc) of the Insolvency Act.

[7.2736]
110 Interpretation

In this Part "respondent" means the person in respect of whom an order is applied for.

[7.2737]
111 Form and contents of application

(1) An application must be in writing, and must be accompanied by a brief statement of the grounds on which it is made.

(2) The application must sufficiently identify the respondent and what the application is for.

(3) The applicant may apply for the respondent to be ordered—
- (a) to appear before the court;
- (b) to clarify a matter in dispute in the proceedings or to give additional information in relation to such a matter;
- (c) to submit an affidavit; or
- (d) to produce books, papers or other records.

(4) If the application is for an order for the respondent to submit a witness statement or an affidavit, the application must specify the matters about which the respondent is to be required to make the statement, or to which the respondent is to be required to swear.

(5) If the application is for an order for the respondent to produce books, papers or other records, the application must specify the items that the respondent is to be required to produce.

(6) The application may be made without notice being served on any other party.

[7.2738]
112 Order for examination, etc

(1) In an application under this Part, the court may make any order that it has power to make under section 236 of the Insolvency Act.

(2) If the court orders the respondent to appear before it, it will specify a venue for that appearance.

(3) The date and time specified will be at least 14 days after the date of the order.

(4) If the respondent is ordered to submit an affidavit or witness statement, the order will specify—
- (a) the matters that the affidavit or witness statement must deal with; and
- (b) the time within which the affidavit or witness statement is to be submitted to the court.

(5) If the order is to produce books, papers or other records, the order will specify the time, place and manner of compliance.

(6) The special administrator must serve the order on the respondent as soon as reasonably practicable.

(7) It must be served on the respondent personally, unless the court otherwise orders.

[7.2739]
113 Procedure for examination

(1) At the examination of the respondent, the special administrator may attend in person, or be represented by a solicitor, and may put any question to the respondent that the court allows.

(2) If the respondent is ordered to clarify a matter or to give additional information, the court will direct the respondent as to the questions that the respondent is required to answer, and as to whether the answers (if any) are to be made on affidavit.

(3) If the relevant application under section 236 was made on information provided by a creditor of the water company, that creditor may, with the permission of the court and if the special administrator does not object, attend the examination and put questions to the respondent (but only through the special administrator).

(4) The respondent may at the respondent's own expense employ a solicitor.

(5) The respondent's solicitor—

(a) may put to the respondent any question that the court allows for the purpose of enabling the respondent to explain or qualify an answer; and

(b) may make representations on the respondent's behalf.

[7.2740]
114 Recording of proceedings

(1) A written record must be made of the examination.

(2) The record must be read over by or to the respondent and signed by the respondent at a venue fixed by the court.

(3) The written record may be used in any proceedings (whether under the Insolvency Act or otherwise) against the respondent as evidence of any statement made by the respondent in the course of the examination.

(4) The court may appoint, in Form WAT23, a shorthand writer to take down the evidence of a person examined in the course of special administration proceedings.

(5) A shorthand writer so appointed must make a declaration in Form WAT24.

(6) The remuneration of a shorthand writer in special administration proceedings is payable by the party who requested the appointment, or out of the assets of the water company concerned, or otherwise, as the court may direct.

(7) Any question arising as to the rates of remuneration payable must be determined by the court in its discretion.

[7.2741]
115 Warrants under section 236 of the Insolvency Act

(1) The tipstaff and any assistant of the tipstaff are prescribed officers of the court for the purposes of section 236(5) of the Insolvency Act.

(2) If a person is arrested under a warrant issued under that section, the officer or constable who arrests the person must, as soon as reasonably practicable, bring the person before the court so that the person can be examined.

(3) If the person cannot immediately be brought up for examination, the officer or constable must deliver the person into the custody of the governor of the prison specified in the warrant, who must keep the person in custody and produce the person before the court as the court directs.

(4) After arresting the person, the officer or constable must immediately—

(a) report to the court the arrest or delivery into custody; and

(b) apply to the court to fix a venue for the person's examination.

(5) The court must appoint the earliest practicable time for the examination, and must—

(a) direct the governor of the prison to produce the person for examination at the time and place appointed; and

(b) give notice of the venue to the person who applied for the warrant.

(6) Any property in the arrested person's possession that has been seized must, in accordance with any direction of the court—

(a) be lodged with, or otherwise dealt with as instructed by, whoever is specified in the warrant as authorised to receive it; or

(b) be kept by the officer or constable seizing it pending the receipt of written orders from the court as to its disposal.

[7.2742]
116 Filing of record of examination

(1) The written record of the respondent's examination, and any response the respondent gives to, and any affidavit or witness statement submitted in compliance with, an order of the court under section 236 of the Insolvency Act, must not be filed unless the court directs.

(2) The written record, responses and affidavits or witness statements are not open to inspection, without an order of the court, by any person other than the special administrator.

(3) Paragraph (2) applies also to so much of the court file as shows the grounds of the application for an order under that section and to any copy of any order.

(4) The court may from time to time give directions as to the custody and inspection of documents to which this rule applies, and as to the furnishing of copies of, or extracts from, such documents.

[7.2743]
117 Costs of proceedings under section 236 of the Insolvency Act

(1) Subject to paragraphs (2) and (3), the special administrator's costs must be paid out of the assets of the water company unless the court otherwise orders.

(2) If the court orders an examination of a person under section 236 of the Insolvency Act because the respondent unjustifiably refused to provide information, it may order the respondent to pay the costs of the examination.

(3) If the court makes an order against a person under section 237(1) or section 237(2) (court's enforcement powers under section 236) of the Insolvency Act, the court may order the respondent to pay the costs of the application for the order.

(4) A person summoned to attend for examination under this Part must be tendered a reasonable sum in respect of travelling expenses incurred in connection with that attendance.

(5) Other costs incurred by that person are at the court's discretion.

PART 9
MISCELLANEOUS AND GENERAL

[7.2744]
118 Special administrator's security

(1) Wherever under these Rules any person has to appoint, or proposes the appointment of, a person to the office of special administrator, that person must be satisfied that the person appointed or to be appointed has security for the proper performance of his functions.

(2) In any administration proceedings the cost of the special administrator's security must be defrayed as an expense of the proceedings.

[7.2745]
119 Power of Secretary of State to regulate certain matters

(1) Pursuant to paragraph 27 of Schedule 8 to the Insolvency Act the Secretary of State may make regulations, not inconsistent with the Insolvency Act, the Water Industry Act 1991 or these Rules, with respect to any matter provided for in these Rules that relates to the carrying out of the functions of a special administrator of a water company.

(2) Those Regulations may—
- (a) confer discretion on the court;
- (b) make non-compliance with any of the regulations a criminal offence;
- (c) make different provision for different cases, including different provision for different areas; and
- (d) contain such incidental, supplemental and transitional provisions as may appear to the Secretary of State necessary or expedient.

[7.2746]
120 Evidence of orders, directions or certificates issued by Secretary of State or Welsh Ministers

(1) A document purporting to be, or to contain, an order, direction or certificate issued by the Secretary of State or the Welsh Ministers must be received in evidence and taken to be or to contain (as the case may be) that order, direction or certificate without further proof, unless the contrary is shown.

(2) Paragraph (1) applies whether the document is signed by—
- (a) the Secretary of State personally or on behalf of the Secretary of State; or
- (b) a Welsh Minister personally or on behalf of a Welsh Minister.

(3) Without prejudice to paragraph (1), a certificate signed by or on behalf of the Secretary of State or the Welsh Ministers confirming—
- (a) the making of an order,
- (b) the issuing of a document, or
- (c) the exercise of a discretion, power or obligation arising or imposed under the Insolvency Act, the Water Industry Act 1991 or these Rules,

is conclusive evidence of the matters dealt with in the certificate.

[7.2747]
121 Time limits

(1) CPR rule 2.8 (time) applies as regards computation of the period of time within which anything is required or authorised to be done by these Rules.

(2) CPR rule 3.1(2)(a) applies so as to enable the court to extend or shorten the period within which compliance with anything is required or authorised to be done by these Rules (even if the period has ended).

[7.2748]
122 General provisions as to service and notice

CPR Part 6 (service of documents) applies in relation to the service of documents and the giving of notice in special administration proceedings except for service outside the jurisdiction.

[7.2749]
123 Service outside the jurisdiction

(1) If for the purposes of special administration proceedings a document is required to be served on a person who is not in England and Wales, the court—

(a) may order service to be effected within the time, on the person, at the place and in the manner it thinks fit; and

(b) may require proof of service as it thinks fit.

(2) However, paragraph (1) does not apply if Regulation (EC) No 1393/2007 of the European Parliament and of the Council on the service in the Member States of judicial and extrajudicial documents in civil or commercial matters (service of documents) applies to the document.

(3) An application for an order under paragraph (1) must be supported by an affidavit stating—

(a) the grounds on which the application is made; and

(b) in what place or country the person to be served is, or probably may be found.

[7.2750]
124 Notice, etc to solicitors

If in special administration proceedings a notice or other document is required or authorised to be given to a person who has indicated that the person's solicitor is authorised to accept service on the person's behalf, the notice or document is sufficiently served if given to the solicitor.

[7.2751]
125 Notice to joint special administrators

If two or more persons are acting jointly as the special administrator in any proceedings, delivery of a document to one of them is to be treated as delivery to them all.

[7.2752]
126 Notices sent simultaneously to the same person

If under the Insolvency Act, the Water Industry Act 1991 or these Rules a document is to be sent to a person (whether or not as a member of a class of persons to whom the document is to be sent), it may be sent with any other document or information that the person is to receive, with or without modification or adaptation of the form applicable to it.

[7.2753]
127 The London Gazette as evidence

(1) A copy of the London Gazette containing a notice required by the Insolvency Act or these Rules to be published in the London Gazette is evidence of any fact stated in the notice.

(2) In the case of an order of the court notice of which is required, by the Insolvency Act or these Rules, to be gazetted, a copy of the London Gazette containing the notice is conclusive evidence that the order was made on the date specified in the notice.

(3) If—

(a) an order of the court that has been gazetted has been varied, or

(b) a matter has been erroneously or inaccurately gazetted,

the person whose responsibility it was to procure the requisite entry in the London Gazette must, as soon as reasonably practicable, cause the variation of the order to be gazetted or, as the case may be, a further entry to be made in the London Gazette for the purpose of correcting the error or inaccuracy.

[7.2754]
128 Punishment of offences

Section 431 (summary proceedings) of the Insolvency Act, as it applies to England and Wales, has effect in relation to offences under these Rules as to offences under that Act.

[7.2755]
129 Powers of the court and the registrar

(1) Anything to be done in special administration proceedings by, to or before the court may be done by, to or before a judge or the registrar.

(2) The registrar may authorise any formal or administrative act that is not by statute the registrar's responsibility to be carried out by an officer of the court on the registrar's behalf, in accordance with directions given by the Lord Chancellor.

SCHEDULE
FORMS

Rule 6

[7.2756]

NOTES

The forms themselves are not reproduced in this work, but their numbers and descriptions are listed below.

Form No	*Title*
WAT1	Petition for special administration order

Form No	*Title*
WAT2	Consent of special administrator(s) to act
WAT3	Affidavit of service of petition for special administration order
WAT4	Special administration order
WAT5	Notice to special administrator of special administration order
WAT6	Notice of special administration order (for newspaper or London Gazette)
WAT7	Notice of special administration order
WAT8	Notice of special administration order to registrar of companies and Water Services Regulation Authority
WAT9	Notice of discharge of special administration order
WAT10	Notice of special administrator's resignation on grounds of [ill health]/[cessation of practice as an insolvency practitioner]/[conflict of interest]/[change of personal circumstances]
WAT11	Notice of special administrator's resignation with permission of the court
WAT12	Notice to prepare and submit special administration statement of affairs
WAT13	Statement of affairs
WAT14	Affidavit of concurrence with statement of affairs
WAT15	Statement of special administrator's proposals
WAT16	Statement of special administrator's revised proposals
WAT17	Notice of order to deal with charged property
WAT18	Special administrator's abstract of receipts and payments
WAT19	Notice of meeting in special administration proceedings
WAT20	Proxy (special administration)
WAT21	Originating application
WAT22	Ordinary application
WAT23	Appointment of shorthand writer (special administration proceedings)
WAT24	Declaration of shorthand writer (special administration proceedings)

PART 8
GENERAL INSOLVENCY STATUTORY INSTRUMENTS—ENGLAND AND WALES

INSOLVENCY PROCEEDINGS (MONETARY LIMITS) ORDER 1986

(SI 1986/1996)

NOTES

Made: 20 November 1986.

Authority: Insolvency Act 1986, ss 416, 418, Sch 6, paras 9, 12.

Commencement: 29 December 1986.

Application: this Order is applied, with such modifications as the context requires for the purpose of giving effect to the provisions of the Insolvency Act 1986, by the Limited Liability Partnerships Regulations 2001, SI 2001/1090, reg 10, Sch 6, Pt II at **[10.38]**, **[10.43]**.

Application to Charitable Incorporated Organisations: as to the application of this Order in relation to CIOs, see the Charitable Incorporated Organisations (Insolvency and Dissolution) Regulations 2012, SI 2012/3013 at **[18.221]**.

ARRANGEMENT OF ARTICLES

1 . . . .[8.1]
2 . . . .[8.2]
3 . . . .[8.3]
4 . . . .[8.4]
5 . . . .[8.5]

SCHEDULES

Schedule
Part II—Monetary Amounts for Purposes of Second Group of Parts of Insolvency Act 1986 . . . . . .[8.6]

[8.1]
1

(1) This Order may be cited as the Insolvency Proceedings (Monetary Limits) Order 1986 and shall come into operation on 29th December 1986.

(2) In this Order "the Act" means the Insolvency Act 1986.

[8.2]
2

(1) The provisions in the first Group of Parts of the Act (companies winding up) set out in column 1 of Part 1 of the Schedule to this Order (shortly described in column 2) are hereby amended by substituting for the amounts specified in column 3 in relation to those provisions the amounts specified in column 4.

(2) The sum specified in column 4 of Part I of the Schedule in relation to section 184(3) of the Act is not to affect any case where the goods are sold or payment to avoid sale is made, before the coming into force of the increase.

[8.3]
3

The amounts prescribed for the purposes of the provisions in the second Group of Parts of the Act [(bankruptcy and debt relief orders)] set out in column 1 of Part II of the Schedule to this Order (shortly described in column 2) are the amounts specified in column 3 in relation to those provisions.

NOTES

Words in square brackets substituted by the Insolvency Proceedings (Monetary Limits) (Amendment) Order 2009, SI 2009/465, art 2.

[8.4]
4

The amount prescribed for the purposes of paragraphs 9 and 12 of Schedule 6 to the Act (maximum amount for preferential status of employees' claims for remuneration and under the Reserve Forces (Safeguard of Employment) Act 1985) is £800.

[8.5]
[5

The court shall, in determining the value of the bankrupt's interest for the purposes of section 313A(2), disregard that part of the value of the property in which the bankrupt's interest subsists which is equal to the value of—

(a) any loans secured by mortgage or other charge against the property;
(b) any other third party interest; and
(c) the reasonable costs of sale.]

NOTES

Added by the Insolvency Proceedings (Monetary Limits) (Amendment) Order 2004, SI 2004/547, art 3.

Part 8 SIs: General

SCHEDULE

(*Pt I amends the Insolvency Act 1986, ss 184, 206 at* **[1.188]**, **[1.210]**.)

[PART II
MONETARY AMOUNTS FOR PURPOSES OF SECOND GROUP OF PARTS OF INSOLVENCY ACT 1986

[8.6]
Article 3

Section of the Act (1)	Short Description (2)	Monetary Amount (3)
[251S(4)	Maximum amount of credit which a person in respect of whom a debt relief order is made may obtain without disclosure of his status	£500]
273(1)(a)	Maximum level of unsecured bankruptcy debts on debtor's petition for case to be referred to insolvency practitioner to assess possibility of voluntary arrangement with creditors.	£40,000
273(1)(b)	Minimum potential value of bankrupt's estate for case to be referred as described above.	£4,000
313A(2)	Minimum value of interests in a dwelling-house for application by trustee for order for sale, possession or an order under section 313.	£1,000
346(3)	Minimum amount of judgment, determining whether amount recovered on sale of debtor's goods is to be treated as part of his estate in bankruptcy.	£1,000
354(1) and (2)	Minimum amount of concealed debt, or value of property concealed or removed, determining criminal liability under the section.	£1,000
358	Minimum value of property taken by a bankrupt out of England and Wales, determining his criminal liability.	£1,000
360(1)	Maximum amount of credit which bankrupt may obtain without disclosure of his status.	£500
364(2)(d)	Minimum value of goods removed by the bankrupt, determining his liability to arrest.	£1,000
[Schedule 4ZA—	Monetary conditions which must be satisfied for a debt relief order to be made—	
(a) paragraph 6(1)	(a) maximum amount of a person's debts:	[£20,000]
(b) paragraph 7(1)	(b) maximum amount of monthly surplus income:	£50
(c) paragraph 8(1)	(c) maximum total value of property:	[£1,000]]]

NOTES

Substituted by the Insolvency Proceedings (Monetary Limits) (Amendment) Order 2004, SI 2004/547, art 2, Schedule.

Entries in square brackets relating to s 251S(4) and Sch 4ZA inserted by the Insolvency Proceedings (Monetary Limits) (Amendment) Order 2009, SI 2009/465, art 3.

In entry relating to Sch 4ZA in column (3) first and second sums in square brackets substituted for original sums "£15,000" and "£300" respectively, by the Insolvency Proceedings (Monetary Limits) (Amendment) Order 2015, SI 2015/26, arts 2, 3, in relation to applications made under s 251B(1) on or after 1 October 2015.

INSOLVENCY FEES ORDER 1986

(SI 1986/2030)

NOTES

Made: 24 November 1986.

Authority: Bankruptcy Act 1914, s 133 (repealed); Insolvency Act 1986, ss 414, 415; Public Offices Fees Act 1879, s 2.

Commencement: 29 December 1986.

Application: this Order is applied, with such modifications as the context requires for the purpose of giving effect to the provisions of the Insolvency Act 1986, by the Limited Liability Partnerships Regulations 2001, SI 2001/1090, reg 10, Sch 6, Pt II at **[10.38]**, **[10.43]**.

This Order is revoked by the Insolvency Proceedings (Fees) Order 2004, SI 2004/593, art 3, Sch 1 (as amended by SI 2006/561, art 3), as from 1 April 2004, subject to transitional provisions in Sch 1 thereto at **[8.80]**. Further revoked by the Insolvency Proceedings (Fees) (Amendment) Order 2007, SI 2007/521, art 3(a), Schedule, also in relation to any case where a winding-up or bankruptcy order was made under the Insolvency Act 1986 before 1 April 2004, subject to transitional provisions in art 4(1), (10) thereof at **[2.46]**.

ARRANGEMENT OF ARTICLES

1 Citation, Commencement and Application . . . . . [8.7]
2 Interpretation . . . . . [8.8]
3, 4 Fees payable in company and individual insolvency proceedings . . . . . [8.9], [8.10]
4A Limits on certain fees . . . . . [8.11]
5 . . . . . [8.12]
6 . . . . . [8.13]
7–11 Deposits on presentation of bankruptcy or winding-up petition . . . . . [8.14]–[8.18]
12 Fees payable to insolvency practitioner appointed under section 273 . . . . . [8.19]

SCHEDULES

Schedule—Fees Payable under Insolvency Act 1986
Part I—Company Insolvency, Companies Winding-Up . . . . . [8.20]
Part II—Insolvency of Individuals; Bankruptcy . . . . . [8.21]

[8.7]

1 Citation, Commencement and Application

(1) This Order may be cited as the Insolvency Fees Order 1986 and shall come into force on 29th December 1986.

(2) This Order applies to proceedings under the Insolvency Act 1986 and the Insolvency Rules 1986 where—

- *(a) in the case of bankruptcy proceedings, the petition was presented on or after the day on which this Order comes into force, and*
- *(b) in the case of any other proceedings, those proceedings commenced on or after that day.*

(3) This Order extends to England and Wales only.

NOTES

Revoked as noted at the beginning of this Order.

[8.8]

2 Interpretation

In this Order, unless the context otherwise requires—

- *(a) "the Act" means the Insolvency Act 1986 (any reference to a numbered section being to a section of that Act);*
- *(b) "the Rules" means the Insolvency Rules 1986 (any reference to a numbered rule being to a rule so numbered in the Rules);*
- *(c) "the Regulations" means [the Insolvency Regulations 1994] (any reference to a numbered regulation being to a regulation so numbered in the Regulations).*

NOTES

Revoked as noted at the beginning of this Order.

Words in square brackets substituted by the Insolvency Fees (Amendment) Order 1994, SI 1994/2541, art 3(a).

[8.9]

3 Fees payable in company and individual insolvency proceedings

The fees to be charged in respect of proceedings under Parts I to VII of the Act (Company Insolvency; Companies Winding Up), and the performance by the official receiver or Secretary of State of functions under those Parts, shall be those set out in Part I of the Schedule to this Order.

NOTES

Revoked as noted at the beginning of this Order.

[8.10]
4

[Subject to article 4A below,] the fees to be charged in respect of proceedings under Parts VIII to XI of the Act (Insolvency of Individuals; Bankruptcy) and the performance by the official receiver or Secretary of State of functions under those Parts, shall be those set out in Part II of the Schedule to this Order.

NOTES

Revoked as noted at the beginning of this Order.
Words in square brackets inserted by the Insolvency Fees (Amendment) Order 1994, SI 1994/2541, art 3(b).

[8.11]
[4A Limits on certain fees

(1) Fee No 5 listed in Part II of the Schedule to this Order shall not exceed the sum which is arrived at by applying the scale by which that fee is calculated to such part of the payments made by the official receiver into the Insolvency Services Account as a result of the performance of his functions as receiver and manager under section 287 as is required to pay the maximum amount.

(2) Fee No 13 listed in Part II of the Schedule to this Order shall not exceed the sum which is arrived at by applying the scale by which that fee is calculated to such part of the amounts paid into the Insolvency Services Account by trustees under regulation 20 and by the official receiver as receiver and manager under section 287 as is required to pay the maximum amount.

(3) In paragraphs (1) and (2) above, "the maximum amount" means the total sum of—
- *(a) the bankruptcy debts to the extent required to be paid by the Rules (ignoring those debts paid otherwise than out of the proceeds of the realisation of the bankrupt's assets or which have been secured to the satisfaction of the court);*
- *(b) the expenses of the bankruptcy other than:*
  - *(i) fees or the remuneration of the official receiver;*
  - *(ii) for the purposes of paragraph (1) above, any sums spent in carrying on the business of the debtor;*
  - *(iii) for the purposes of paragraph (2) above, any sums spent out of money received in carrying on the business of the debtor;*
- *(c) fees payable under this Order other than Fee No 5 and Fee No 13 in Part II of the Schedule to this Order; and*
- *(d) the remuneration of the official receiver, other than remuneration calculated pursuant to regulation 33 by reference to the realisation scale in Table 1 of Schedule 2 to the Regulations.*

(4) For the purposes of this article—
- *(a) the expression "bankruptcy debts" shall include any interest payable by virtue of section 328(4); and*
- *(b) the expression "the expenses of the bankruptcy" shall have the meaning which it bears in the Rules.]*

NOTES

Revoked as noted at the beginning of this Order.
Inserted by the Insolvency Fees (Amendment) Order 1994, SI 1994/2541, art 3(c).

[8.12]
5

(1) All fees shall be taken in cash.

(2) When a fee is paid to an officer of a court the person paying the fee shall inform the officer whether the fee relates to a company insolvency proceeding or an individual insolvency proceeding.

NOTES

Revoked as noted at the beginning of this Order.

[8.13]
6

Where Value Added Tax is chargeable in respect of the provision of a service for which a fee is prescribed in the Schedule, there shall be payable in addition to that fee the amount of the Value Added Tax.

NOTES

Revoked as noted at the beginning of this Order.

[8.14]
7 Deposits on presentation of bankruptcy or winding-up petition

The following 5 Articles apply where it is intended to present to the court a winding-up or bankruptcy petition under the Act.

NOTES

Revoked as noted at the beginning of this Order.

[8.15]
8

(1) Before a winding-up or bankruptcy petition can be presented the appropriate deposit (as specified in Article 9 below) must be paid to the court in which the petition is to be presented.

(2) That deposit is security—

(a) for Fee No 1 listed in Part I of the Schedule 10 to this Order or Fee No 2 listed in Part II of that Schedule, as the case may be (each such fee being referred to in this Order as "the administration fee"), or

(b) where an insolvency practitioner is appointed under section 273, for the payment of his fee under Article 12 below.

NOTES

Revoked as noted at the beginning of this Order.

[8.16]
9

The appropriate deposit referred to in Article 8 is—

(a) in relation to a winding-up petition to be presented under the Act, [£500];

(b) in relation to a bankruptcy petition to be presented under section 264(1)(b), [£250];

(c) in relation to a bankruptcy petition to be presented under section 264(1)(a), (c) or (d), [£300].

NOTES

Revoked as noted at the beginning of this Order.

Sums in square brackets substituted by the Insolvency Fees (Amendment) Order 1994, SI 1994/2541, art 3(d).

[8.17]
10

The court shall (except in a case falling within Article 12 below) transmit the deposit paid to the official receiver attached to the court.

NOTES

Revoked as noted at the beginning of this Order.

[8.18]
11

(1) In the circumstances specified in this Article a deposit made under Article 8 above is to be repaid to the person who made it.

(2) Where a winding-up or bankruptcy petition under the Act is dismissed or withdrawn the deposit shall be repaid in full, unless—

(a) a winding-up or bankruptcy order has been made, or

(b) a fee has become payable to an insolvency practitioner under Article 12 below.

(3) If the assets of the company being wound up are, or (as the case may be) the bankrupt's estate is, sufficient to pay the whole or part of the relevant administration fee, then the deposit shall be repaid to the extent that it is not required for payment of that fee.

(4) Where a winding-up or bankruptcy order is annulled, rescinded or recalled, the deposit shall be repaid to the extent that it is not required for payment of the relevant administration fee, unless a fee has become payable to an insolvency practitioner under Article 12 below.

NOTES

Revoked as noted at the beginning of this Order.

[8.19]
12 Fees payable to insolvency practitioner appointed under section 273

Where the court appoints an insolvency practitioner under section 273(2) to prepare and submit a report under section 274 the court shall, on submission of that report, pay to the practitioner a fee of [£250] (that sum being inclusive of Value Added Tax).

NOTES

Revoked as noted at the beginning of this Order.

Sum in square brackets substituted by the Insolvency Fees (Amendment) Order 1994, SI 1994/2541, art 3(e).

13 (*Revokes the Bankruptcy Fees Order 1984, SI 1984/880, Schedule, Table B, Fee No 6.*)

SCHEDULE
FEES PAYABLE UNDER INSOLVENCY ACT 1986

Article 3

PART I
COMPANY INSOLVENCY, COMPANIES WINDING-UP

[8.20]

No of Fee	*Description of Proceeding*	*Amount £*
1	*For the performance by the official receiver of his general duties as official receiver on the making of a winding-up order*	*[640.00]*
2	*For all official stationery, printing, postage and telephone charges, including notices to creditors and contributories in respect of the first meeting of creditors and contributories and of sittings of the court—*	
	(i) for a number of creditors and contributories not exceeding 25	*[175.00]*
	(ii) for every additional 10 creditors and contributories or part thereof	*[40.00]*
3	*(a) Where the official receiver decides to summon meetings of creditors and contributories under section 136(4), for the holding of those meetings*	*[65.00]*
	(b) Where any other meetings of creditors and contributories are held by the official receiver, for summoning and holding the meetings—	
	(i) for a number of creditors and contributories not exceeding 25	*[155.00]*
	(ii) for every additional 10 creditors and contributories or part thereof	*[20.00]*
4	*On any application to the court for the rescission or recall of a winding-up order [or a stay of the winding-up proceedings under section 147] where the official receiver attends or makes a report to the court*	*[90.00]*
	for each further attendance or report	*[45.00]*
5	*Where the official receiver supervises a special manager or the carrying on of a company's business-for each week or part thereof*	*[90.00]*
6	*For taking an affidavit, affirmation or declaration, except affidavits of debt—*	
	(i) for each person making the same	*[4.00]*
	(ii) for each exhibit or schedule to be marked	*[1.00]*
7		
8	*On each application by a liquidator to the Secretary of State or to the official receiver to exercise the powers of a [liquidation] committee by virtue of section [141(4) or (5)] or rule 4.172*	*[27.00]*
9	*On an application to the Secretary of State under [regulations 7 and 8] for a payment from the Insolvency Services Account or for the re-issue of a cheque, money order or payable order in respect of moneys standing to the credit of the Insolvency Services Account, for each cheque, money order or payable order issued or re-issued*	*[0.65]*
10	*For the performance by the Secretary of State of his general duties under the Act, the Rules and the Regulations in relation to the administration of the affairs of companies which are being wound-up by the court, a fee in accordance with the following scale, calculated on the amount paid into the Insolvency Services Account by liquidators under [regulations 5(1) and 18] (after deducting any sums paid to secured creditors in respect of their securities and any sums spent out of money received in carrying on the business of the company):—*	

No of Fee	Description of Proceeding	Amount £
	(i) on the first £50,000 or fraction thereof	[per cent 15.00]
	(ii) on the next £50,000 or fraction thereof	[per cent 11.25]
	(iii) on the next £400,000 or fraction thereof	[per cent 9.75]
	(iv) on the next £500,000 or fraction thereof	[per cent 5.625]
	(v) on the next £4,000,000 or fraction thereof	[per cent 3.00]
	[(vi) on the next £15,000,000 or fraction thereof	per cent 1.50
	(vii) on the next £30,000,000 or fraction thereof	per cent 0.25
	(viii) on all further amounts	per cent 0.10]
11	For the performance by the Secretary of State of his general duties under the Act, the Rules and the Regulations in relation to the administration of the affairs of companies which are being wound-up voluntarily, the following fees calculated on payments into the Insolvency Services Account by liquidators under [regulations 5(2) and 18]:—	
	(1) Where the money consists of unclaimed dividends . . .	[per cent 1.75]
	(2) Where the money consists of undistributed funds or balances:—	
	(i) on the first £50,000 or fraction thereof	[per cent 1.75]
	(ii) on all further amounts	[per cent 1.25]
	but so that the total fee payable under this sub-paragraph (2) shall not exceed [£12,500]	
12	On the amount expended on any purchase of Government securities (including the renewal of Treasury Bills) pursuant to a request made under [regulation 9]	[per cent 0.625]

NOTES

Revoked as noted at the beginning of this Order.

Fee Nos 1–8: fees in square brackets substituted, words in square brackets in para 4 inserted, words in square brackets in para 8 substituted, and para 7 revoked, by the Insolvency Fees (Amendment) Order 1991, SI 1991/496, art 3(c).

Fee No 9: words in first pair of square brackets substituted by the Insolvency Fees (Amendment) Order 1994, SI 1994/2541, art 3(f)(i); fees in second pair of square brackets substituted by SI 1991/496, art 3(c).

Fee No 10: words in first pair of square brackets substituted by SI 1994/2541, art 3(f)(ii); fees in square brackets in sub-paras (i)–(v) substituted by the Insolvency Fees (Amendment) Order 1988, SI 1988/95, art 2; sub-paras (vi)–(viii) substituted, for original sub-para (vi), by the Insolvency Fees (Amendment) Order 1992, SI 1992/34, art 2(a).

Fee No 11: words in first pair of square brackets substituted by SI 1994/2541, art 3(f)(iii); figure in second pair of square brackets and fees in square brackets substituted by SI 1988/95, art 2.

Fee No 12: words in first pair of square brackets substituted by SI 1994/254, art 3(f)(iv); fees in second pair of square brackets substituted by SI 1988/95, art 2.

PART II
INSOLVENCY OF INDIVIDUALS: BANKRUPTCY

[8.21]

No of fee	Description of Proceeding	Amount £
1	On registration with the Secretary of State of an individual voluntary arrangement under Part VIII of the Act	[35.00]
2	For the performance by the official receiver of his general duties as official receiver on the making of a bankruptcy order	[320.00]
3	For all official stationery, printing, postage and telephone charges, including notices to creditors in respect of the first meeting of creditors and of sittings of the court—	
	(i) for a number of creditors not exceeding 25 . .	[175.00]
	(ii) for every additional 10 creditors or part thereof	[40.00]

No of fee	Description of Proceeding	Amount £
4	(a) Where the official receiver decides to summon a meeting of creditors under section 293(1), for the holding of that meeting.	[65.00]
	(b) Where any other meeting of creditors is held by the official receiver, for summoning and holding the meeting—	
	(i) for a number of creditors not exceeding 25. .	[155.00]
	(ii) for every additional 10 creditors or part thereof	[20.00]
5	On the payments made by the official receiver into the Insolvency Services Account as a result of the performance of his functions as receiver and manager under section 287 (after deducting any sums paid to secured creditors in respect of their securities and any sums spent in carrying on the business of the debtor) a fee in accordance with the following scale—	
	(i) on the first £5,000 or fraction thereof	per cent 20.00
	(ii) on the next £5,000 or fraction thereof	per cent 15.00
	(iii) on the next £90,000 or fraction thereof	per cent 10.00
	(iv) on all further sums	per cent 5.00
6	Where the official receiver, acting as receiver and manager under section 287, makes any payment to creditors, a fee of one-half the scale fee calculated under Fee No 5 on the amount of the payment.	
7	On any application to the court for the rescission or annulment of a bankruptcy order or relating to the discharge of a bankrupt, where the official receiver attends or makes a report to the court	[90.00]
	for each further attendance or report.	[45.00]
8	Where the official receiver supervises a special manager or the carrying on of a debtor's business—for each week or part thereof	[90.00]
9	For taking an affidavit, affirmation or declaration, except affidavits of debt—	
	(i) for each person making the same	[4.00]
	(ii) for each exhibit or schedule to be marked . .	[1.00]
10	. . .	
11	On each application by a trustee to the Secretary of State or to the official receiver to exercise the powers of a creditors' committee by virtue of section 302 or rule 6.166	[27.00]
12	On each application to the Secretary of State under [regulations 22 and 23] for a payment from the Insolvency Services Account or for the re-issue of a cheque, money order or payable order in respect of moneys standing to the credit of the Insolvency Services Account, for each cheque, money order or payable order issued or re-issued	[0.65]
13	For the performance by the Secretary of State of his general duties under the Act, the Rules and the Regulations in relation to the administration of the estates of individuals, a fee in accordance with the following scale, calculated on the amount paid into the Insolvency Service Account by trustees under [regulation 20] and by the official receiver as receiver and manager under section 287 (after deducting any sums paid to secured creditors in respect of their securities and any sums spent out of money received in carrying on the business of the debtor):—	
	(a) on the first £50,000 or fraction thereof	[per cent 15.00]

No of fee	Description of Proceeding		Amount £
	(b)	*on the next £50,000 or fraction thereof*	*[per cent 11.25]*
	(c)	*on the next £400,000 or fraction thereof* . . .	*[per cent 9.75]*
	(d)	*on the next £500,000 or fraction thereof* . . .	*[per cent 5.625]*
	(e)	*on the next £4,000,000 or fraction thereof* . .	*[per cent 3.00]*
	[(f)	*on the next £15,000,000 or fraction thereof* .	*per cent 1.50*
	(g)	*on the next £30,000,000 or fraction thereof* .	*per cent 0.25*
	(h)	*on all further amounts*	*per cent 0.10]*
[14	*On the amount expended on any purchase of Government securities (including the renewal of Treasury Bills) pursuant to a request made under regulation 23A*		*per cent 0.625]*

NOTES

Revoked as noted at the beginning of this Order.

Fee Nos 1–11: fees in square brackets substituted, and Fee No 10 revoked, by the Insolvency Fees (Amendment) Order 1991, SI 1991/496, art 3(c).

Fee No 12: words in first pair of square brackets substituted by the Insolvency Fees (Amendment) Order 1994, SI 1994/2541, art 3(f)(v); fees in second pair of square brackets substituted by SI 1991/496, art 3(c).

Fee No 13: words in first pair of square brackets substituted by SI 1994/2541, art 3(f)(vi); fees in square brackets in sub-paras (a)–(e) substituted by the Insolvency Fees (Amendment) Order 1988, SI 1988/95, art 2; sub-paras (f)–(h) substituted, for original sub-para (f), by the Insolvency Fees (Amendment) Order 1992, SI 1992/34, art 2(b).

Fee No 14: added by the Insolvency Fees (Amendment) Order 2001, SI 2001/761, art 2.

INSOLVENCY REGULATIONS 1994

(SI 1994/2507)

NOTES

Made: 26 September 1994.

Authority: Insolvency Rules 1986, SI 1986/1925, r 12.1; Insolvency Act 1986, ss 411, 412, Sch 8, para 27, Sch 9, para 30.

Commencement: 24 October 1994.

Application: these Regulations are applied to limited liability partnerships with such modifications as the context requires for the purpose of giving effect to the provisions of the Insolvency Act 1986, by the Limited Liability Partnerships Regulations 2001, SI 2001/1090, reg 10, Sch 6, Pt II at **[10.38]**, **[10.43]**.

Modification: these Regulations are applied, with modifications, in so far as they relate to bank insolvency or administration under the Banking Act 2009, Pts 2, 3, by the Banking Act 2009 (Parts 2 and 3 Consequential Amendments) Order 2009, SI 2009/317, art 3, Schedule at **[7.86]**, **[7.92]**.

Official receiver: as to the contracting out of certain functions of the Official receiver conferred by or under these regulations, see the Contracting Out (Functions of the Official Receiver) Order 1995, SI 1995/1386 at **[12.4]**.

Application to Charitable Incorporated Organisations: as to the application of these Regulations in relation to CIOs, see the Charitable Incorporated Organisations (Insolvency and Dissolution) Regulations 2012, SI 2012/3013 at **[18.221]**.

ARRANGEMENT OF REGULATIONS

PART 1
GENERAL

1 Citation and commencement . . . . [8.22]
2 Revocations . . . . [8.23]
3 Interpretation and application . . . . [8.24]

PART 1A
ADMINISTRATION

3A Disposal of company's records and provision of information to the Secretary of State . . . . . . [8.25]
3B Payment of unclaimed dividends or other money . . . . [8.26]

PART 1B
ADMINISTRATIVE RECEIVERSHIP

3C Payment of unclaimed dividends or other money . . . . [8.27]

PART 2
WINDING UP

4 Introductory . . . . [8.28]

Payment into and out of the Insolvency Services Account

5 Payments into the Insolvency Services Account . . . . [8.29]
6 Local bank account and handling of funds not belonging to the company . . . . [8.30]

7 Payment of disbursements etc out of the Insolvency Services Account . . . . [8.31]

Dividends to creditors and returns of capital to contributories of a company

8 Payment . . . . [8.32]

Investment or otherwise handling of funds in winding up of companies and payment of interest

9 . . . . [8.33]

Records to be maintained by liquidators and the provision of information

10 Financial records. . . . . [8.34]
11 Provision of information by liquidator . . . . [8.35]
12 Liquidator carrying on business . . . . [8.36]
13 Retention and delivery of records . . . . [8.37]
14 Provision of accounts by liquidator and audit of accounts. [8.38]
15 Production and inspection of records . . . . [8.39]
16 Disposal of company's books, papers and other records . . . . [8.40]
17 Voluntary liquidator to provide information to Secretary of State. . . . . [8.41]
18 Payment of unclaimed dividends or other money . . . . [8.42]

PART 3
BANKRUPTCY

19 Introductory . . . . [8.43]

Payments into and out of the Insolvency Services Account

20 Payments into the Insolvency Services Account. . . . . [8.44]
21 Local bank account and handling of funds not forming part of the bankrupt's estate. . . . . [8.45]
22 Payment of disbursements etc out of the Insolvency Services Account. . . . . [8.46]

Dividends to creditors

23 Payment. . . . . [8.47]
23A Investment or otherwise handling of funds in bankruptcy and payment of interest . . . . [8.48]

Records to be maintained by trustees and the provision of information

24 Financial records. . . . . [8.49]
25 Provision of information by trustee . . . . [8.50]
26 Trustee carrying on business . . . . [8.51]
27 Retention and delivery of records . . . . [8.52]
28 Provision of accounts by trustee and audit of accounts. . . . . [8.53]
29 Production and inspection of records . . . . [8.54]
30 Disposal of bankrupt's books, papers and other records . . . . [8.55]
31 Payment of unclaimed or undistributed assets, dividends or other money . . . . [8.56]

PART 4
CLAIMING MONEY PAID INTO THE INSOLVENCY SERVICES ACCOUNT

32 . . . . [8.57]

PART 5
REMUNERATION OF OFFICIAL RECEIVER

33 Official receiver's remuneration while acting as liquidator or trustee calculated as a percentage of the value of assets realised or distributed. . . . . [8.58]
34 Limits on official receiver's remuneration as trustee . . . . [8.59]
35 Official receiver's general remuneration while acting as interim receiver, provisional liquidator, liquidator or trustee . . . . [8.60]
36 Official receiver's remuneration while acting as liquidator or provisional liquidator in respect of the realisation of property charged. . . . . [8.61]

PART 5A
INFORMATION ABOUT TIME SPENT ON A CASE TO BE PROVIDED BY INSOLVENCY PRACTITIONER TO CREDITORS ETC

36A . . . . [8.62]

PART 6
TRANSITIONAL AND SAVING PROVISIONS

37 . . . . [8.63]

SCHEDULES

Schedule 2. . . . . [8.64]
Schedule 3. . . . . [8.65]

PART 1
GENERAL

[8.22]
1 Citation and commencement

These Regulations may be cited as the Insolvency Regulations 1994 and shall come into force on 24th October 1994.

[8.23]
2 Revocations

Subject to regulation 37 below, the Regulations listed in Schedule 1 to these Regulations are hereby revoked.

[8.24]
3 Interpretation and application

(1) In these Regulations, except where the context otherwise requires—

["bank" means—

(a) a person who has permission under Part 4 of the Financial Services and Markets Act 2000 to accept deposits, or

(b) an EEA firm of the kind mentioned in paragraph 5(b) of Schedule 3 to that Act, which has permission under paragraph 15 of that Schedule (as a result of qualifying for authorisation under paragraph 12(1) of that Schedule) to accept deposits;]

"bankrupt" means the bankrupt or his estate;

"company" means the company which is being wound up;

"creditors' committee" means any committee established under section 301;

["electronic transfer" means transmission by any electronic means;] "liquidation committee" means, in the case of a winding up by the court, any committee established under section 141 and, in the case of a creditors' voluntary winding up, any committee established under section 101;

"liquidator" includes, in the case of a company being wound up by the court, the official receiver when so acting;

"local bank" means any bank in, or in the neighbourhood of, the insolvency district, or the district in respect of which the court has winding-up jurisdiction, in which the proceedings are taken, or in the locality in which any business of the company or, as the case may be, the bankrupt is carried on;

"local bank account" means, in the case of a winding up by the court, a current account opened with a local bank under regulation 6(2) below and, in the case of a bankruptcy, a current account opened with a local bank under regulation 21(1) below;

"payment instrument" means a cheque or payable order;

"the Rules" means [The Insolvency (England and Wales) Rules 2016]; and

"trustee", subject to regulation 19(2) below, means trustee of a bankrupt's estate including the official receiver when so acting;

and other expressions used in these Regulations and defined by the Rules have the meanings which they bear in the Rules.

(2) A Rule referred to in these Regulations by number means the Rule so numbered in the Rules.

(3) Any application to be made to the Secretary of State or to the Department or anything required to be sent to the Secretary of State or to the Department under these Regulations shall be addressed to [the Department for Business, Energy and Industrial Strategy], The Insolvency Service, PO Box 3690, Birmingham B2 4UY.

(4) Where a regulation makes provision for the use of a form obtainable from the Department, the Department may provide different forms for different cases arising under that regulation.

(5) Subject to regulation 37 below, these Regulations [(except for regulations 3A and 36A)] apply—

(a) to winding-up proceedings commenced on or after 29th December 1986; and

(b) to bankruptcy proceedings where the bankruptcy petition is or was presented on or after that day.

[(6) Regulation 3A applies in any case where a company entered into administration on or after 15th September 2003 other than a case where the company entered into administration by virtue of a petition presented before that date.

(7) Regulation 36A applies in any case where an insolvency practitioner is appointed on or after 1st April 2005.]

NOTES

Para (1): definition "bank" substituted by the Financial Services and Markets Act 2000 (Consequential Amendments and Repeals) Order 2001, SI 2001/3649, art 471; definition "electronic transfer" inserted by the Insolvency (Amendment) Regulations 2000, SI 2000/485, reg 3, Schedule, para 1; words in square brackets in definition "the Rules" substituted by the Insolvency (England and Wales) Rules 2016 (Consequential Amendments and Savings) Rules 2017, SI 2017/369, r 2(2), Sch 2, para 4(1), (2).

Para (3): words in square brackets substituted by the Secretaries of State for Business, Energy and Industrial Strategy, for International Trade and for Exiting the European Union and the Transfer of Functions (Education and Skills) Order 2016, SI 2016/992, art 14, Schedule, para 19.

Para (5): words in square brackets inserted by the Insolvency (Amendment) Regulations 2005, SI 2005/512, reg 5(1), (2).

Paras (6), (7): added by SI 2005/512, reg 5(1), (3).

[PART 1A ADMINISTRATION

[8.25]

3A Disposal of company's records and provision of information to the Secretary of State

(1) The person who was the last administrator of a company which has been dissolved may, at any time after the expiration of a period of one year from the date of dissolution, destroy or otherwise dispose of the books, papers and other records of the company.

(2) An administrator or former administrator shall within 14 days of a request by the Secretary of State give the Secretary of State particulars of any money in his hands or under his control representing unclaimed or undistributed assets of the company or dividends or other sums due to any person as a member or former member of the company.]

NOTES

Inserted, together with proceeding Part heading, by the Insolvency (Amendment) Regulations 2005, SI 2005/512, reg 6.

[8.26]

[3B Payment of unclaimed dividends or other money

(1) This regulation applies to monies which—

(a) are held by the former administrator of a dissolved company, and
(b) represent either or both of the following—
(i) unclaimed dividends due to creditors, or
(ii) sums held by the company in trust in respect of dividends or other sums due to any person as a member or former member of the company.

(2) Any monies to which this regulation applies may be paid into the Insolvency Services Account.

(3) Where under this regulation the former administrator pays any sums into the Insolvency Services Account, he shall at the same time give notice to the Secretary of State of—

(a) the name of the company,
(b) the name and address of the person to whom the dividend or other sum is payable,
(c) the amount of the dividend or other sum, and
(d) the date on which it was paid.

(4) Where a dividend or other sum is paid to a person by way of a payment instrument, any payment into the Insolvency Services Account in respect of that dividend or sum pursuant to paragraph (2) may not be made earlier than on or after the expiry of 6 months from the date of the payment instrument.]

NOTES

Inserted by the Insolvency (Amendment) Regulations 2008, SI 2008/670, reg 3(1), (2).

[PART 1B ADMINISTRATIVE RECEIVERSHIP

[8.27]

3C Payment of unclaimed dividends or other money

(1) This regulation applies to monies which—

(a) are held by the former administrative receiver of a dissolved company, and
(b) represent either or both of the following—
(i) unclaimed dividends due to creditors, or
(ii) sums held by the company in trust in respect of dividends or other sums due to any person as a member or former member of the company.

(2) Any monies to which this regulation applies may be paid into the Insolvency Services Account.

(3) Where under this regulation the former administrative receiver pays any sums into the Insolvency Services Account, he shall at the same time give notice to the Secretary of State of—

(a) the name of the company,
(b) the name and address of the person to whom the dividend or other sum is payable,
(c) the amount of the dividend or other sum, and
(d) the date on which it was paid.

(3) Where a dividend or other sum is paid to a person by way of a payment instrument, any payment in respect of that dividend or sum into the Insolvency Services Account pursuant to paragraph (2) may not be made earlier than on or after the expiry of 6 months from the date of the payment instrument.]

NOTES

Inserted, together with proceeding Part heading, by the Insolvency (Amendment) Regulations 2008, SI 2008/670, reg 3(1), (2). (Note the second para (3) above has been reproduced in accordance with the Queen's Printer's copy of SI 2008/670.)

PART 2 WINDING UP

[8.28]

4 Introductory

This Part of these Regulations relates to—

(a) voluntary winding up and
(b) winding up by the court

of companies which the courts in England and Wales have jurisdiction to wind up.

Payments Into and Out of the Insolvency Services Account

[8.29]

5 Payments into the Insolvency Services Account

(1) In the case of a winding up by the court, subject to regulation 6 below, the liquidator shall pay all money received by him in the course of carrying out his functions as such without any deduction into the Insolvency Services Account kept by the Secretary of State with the Bank of England to the credit of the company once every 14 days or forthwith if £5,000 or more has been received.

[(2) . . .]

[(3) Every payment of money into the Insolvency Services Account under this regulation shall be—
(a) made through the Bank Giro system; or
(b) sent direct to the Bank of England, Threadneedle Street, London EC2R 8AH by cheque drawn in favour of the "Insolvency Services Account" and crossed "A/c payee only" "Bank of England"; or
(c) made by electronic transfer,

and the liquidator shall on request be given by the Department a receipt for the money so paid.]

(4) Every payment of money [made under sub-paragraph (a) or (b) of paragraph (3) above] shall be accompanied by a form obtainable from the Department for that purpose or by a form that is substantially similar. [Every payment of money made under sub-paragraph (c) of paragraph (3) above shall specify the name of the liquidator making the payment and the name of the company to whose credit such payment is made.]

(5) Where in a voluntary winding up a liquidator pays any unclaimed dividend into the Insolvency Services Account, he shall at the same time give notice to the Secretary of State, on a form obtainable from the Department or on one that is substantially similar, of the name and address of the person to whom the dividend is payable and the amount of the dividend.

NOTES

Para (2): revoked by the Insolvency (Amendment) Regulations 2011, SI 2011/2203, regs 3, 4, Schedule, para 1, except in relation to any voluntary winding up where a payment has been made into the Insolvency Services Account in relation to that winding up before 1 October 2011. Para (2) (as substituted by the Insolvency (Amendment) Regulations 2004, SI 2004/472, reg 2, Schedule, para 1) previously read as follows:

"(2) In the case of a voluntary winding up, the liquidator may make payments into the Insolvency Services Account to the credit of the company.".

Para (3): substituted by the Insolvency (Amendment) Regulations 2000, SI 2000/485, reg 3, Schedule, para 2.

Para (4): words in first pair of square brackets substituted, and words in second pair of square brackets inserted, by SI 2000/485, reg 3, Schedule, para 3.

[8.30]

6 Local bank account and handling of funds not belonging to the company

(1) This regulation does not apply in the case of a voluntary winding up.

(2) Where the liquidator intends to exercise his power to carry on the business of the company, he may apply to the Secretary of State for authorisation to open a local bank account, and the Secretary of State may authorise him to make his payments into and out of a specified bank, subject to a limit, instead of into and out of the Insolvency Services Account if satisfied that an administrative advantage will be derived from having such an account.

(3) Money received by the liquidator relating to the purpose for which the account was opened may be paid into the local bank account to the credit of the company to which the account relates.

(4) Where the liquidator opens a local bank account pursuant to an authorisation granted under paragraph (2) above, he shall open and maintain the account in the name of the company.

(5) Where money which is not an asset of the company is provided to the liquidator for a specific purpose, it shall be clearly identifiable in a separate account.

(6) The liquidator shall keep proper records, including documentary evidence of all money paid into and out of every local bank account opened and maintained under this regulation.

(7) The liquidator shall pay without deduction any surplus over any limit imposed by an authorisation granted under paragraph (2) above into the Insolvency Services Account in accordance with regulation 5 above as that regulation applies in the case of a winding up by the court.

(8) As soon as the liquidator ceases to carry on the business of the company or vacates office or an authorisation given in pursuance of an application under paragraph (2) above is withdrawn, he shall close the account and pay any balance into the Insolvency Services Account in accordance with regulation 5 above as that regulation applies in the case of a winding up by the court.

[8.31]

7 Payment of disbursements etc out of the Insolvency Services Account

[(A1) Paragraphs (1) [and (2)] of this regulation are subject to paragraph (3A).]

(1) In the case of a winding up by the court, on application to the Department, the liquidator shall be repaid all necessary disbursements made by him, and expenses properly incurred by him, in the course of his administration to the date of his vacation of office out of any money standing to the credit of the company in the Insolvency Services Account.

(2) In the case of a winding up by the court, the liquidator shall on application to the Department obtain payment instruments to the order of the payee for sums which become payable on account of the company for delivery by the liquidator to the persons to whom the payments are to be made.

(3) . . .

[(3A) In respect of an application made by the liquidator under [paragraph (1) or (2)] above, the Secretary of State, if requested to do so by the liquidator, may, at his discretion,

(a) make the payment which is the subject of the application to the liquidator by electronic transfer; or

(b) as an alternative to the issue of payment instruments, make payment by electronic transfer to the persons to whom the liquidator would otherwise deliver payment instruments.]

(4) Any application under this regulation shall be made by the liquidator on a form obtainable from the Department for the purpose or on a form that is substantially similar.

(5) In the case of a winding up by the court, on the liquidator vacating office, he shall be repaid by any succeeding liquidator out of any funds available for the purpose any necessary disbursements made by him and any expenses properly incurred by him but not repaid before he vacates office.

NOTES

Para (A1): inserted by the Insolvency (Amendment) Regulations 2000, SI 2000/485, reg 3, Schedule, para 4; words in square brackets substituted for original words "to (3)" by the Insolvency (Amendment) Regulations 2011, SI 2011/2203, regs 3, 4, Schedule, para 2, except in relation to any voluntary winding up where a payment has been made into the Insolvency Services Account in relation to that winding up before 1 October 2011.

Para (3): revoked by SI 2011/2203, regs 3, 4, Schedule, para 3, except in relation to any voluntary winding up where a payment has been made into the Insolvency Services Account in relation to that winding up before 1 October 2011. Para (3) originally read as follows:

> "(3) In the case of a voluntary winding up, where the liquidator requires to make payments out of any money standing to the credit of the company in the Insolvency Services Account in respect of the expenses of the winding up, he shall apply to the Secretary of State who may either authorise payment to the liquidator of the sum required by him, or may direct payment instruments to be issued to the liquidator for delivery by him to the persons to whom the payments are to be made.".

Para (3A): inserted by SI 2000/485, reg 3, Schedule, para 5; words in square brackets substituted for original words "paragraphs (1) to (3)" by SI 2011/2203, regs 3, 4, Schedule, para 4, except in relation to any voluntary winding up where a payment has been made into the Insolvency Services Account in relation to that winding up before 1 October 2011.

Dividends to Creditors and Returns of Capital to Contributories of a Company

[8.32]
8 Payment

[(A1) Paragraphs (1) [and (2)] of this regulation are subject to paragraph (3A).]

(1) In the case of a winding up by the court, the liquidator shall pay every dividend by payment instruments which shall be prepared by the Department on the application of the liquidator and transmitted to him for distribution amongst the creditors.

(2) In the case of a winding up by the court, the liquidator shall pay every return of capital to contributories by payment instruments which shall be prepared by the Department on application.

(3) . . .

[(3A) In respect of an application made by the liquidator under [paragraphs (1) or (2)] above, the Secretary of State, if requested to do so by the liquidator, may, at his discretion,

(a) as an alternative to the issue of payment instruments, make payment by electronic transfer to the persons to whom the liquidator would otherwise deliver payment instruments; or

(b) make the payment which is the subject of the application to the liquidator by electronic transfer.]

(4) Any application under this regulation for a payment instrument [or payment by electronic transfer] shall be made by the liquidator on a form obtainable from the Department for the purpose or on a form which is substantially similar.

(5) In the case of a winding up by the court, the liquidator shall enter the total amount of every dividend and of every return to contributories that he desires to pay under this regulation in the records to be kept under regulation 10 below in one sum.

(6) On the liquidator vacating office, he shall send to the Department any valid unclaimed or undelivered payment instruments for dividends or returns to contributories after endorsing them with the word "cancelled".

NOTES

Para (A1): inserted by the Insolvency (Amendment) Regulations 2000, SI 2000/485, reg 3, Schedule, para 6; words in square brackets substituted for original words "to (3)" by the Insolvency (Amendment) Regulations 2011, SI 2011/2203, regs 3, 4, Schedule, para 5, except in relation to any voluntary winding up where a payment has been made into the Insolvency Services Account in relation to that winding up before 1 October 2011.

Para (3): revoked by SI 2011/2203, regs 3, 4, Schedule, para 6, except in relation to any voluntary winding up where a payment has been made into the Insolvency Services Account in relation to that winding up before 1 October 2011. Para (3) originally read as follows:

"(3) In the case of a voluntary winding up, where the liquidator requires to make payments out of any money standing to the credit of the company in the Insolvency Services Account by way of distribution, he shall apply in writing to the Secretary of State who may either authorise payment to the liquidator of the sum required by him, or may direct payment instruments to be issued to the liquidator for delivery by him to the persons to whom the payments are to be made.".

Para (3A): inserted by SI 2000/485, reg 3, Schedule, para 7; words in square brackets substituted for original words "paragraphs (1) to (3)" by SI 2011/2203, regs 3, 4, Schedule, para 7, except in relation to any voluntary winding up where a payment has been made into the Insolvency Services Account in relation to that winding up before 1 October 2011.

Para (4): words in square brackets inserted by SI 2000/485, reg 3, Schedule, para 8.

Investment or Otherwise Handling of Funds in Winding up of Companies and Payment of Interest

[8.33]

9

(1) When the cash balance standing to the credit of the company in the account in respect of that company kept by the Secretary of State is in excess of the amount which, in the opinion of the liquidator, is required for the immediate purposes of the winding up and should be invested, he may request the Secretary of State to invest the amount not so required in Government securities, to be placed to the credit of that account for the company's benefit.

(2) When any of the money so invested is, in the opinion of the liquidator, required for the immediate purposes of the winding up, he may request the Secretary of State to raise such sum as may be required by the sale of such of those securities as may be necessary.

(3) In cases where investments have been made at the request of the liquidator in pursuance of paragraph (1) above and additional sums to the amounts so invested, including money received under paragraph (7) below, are paid into the Insolvency Services Account to the credit of the company, a request shall be made to the Secretary of State by the liquidator if it is desired that these additional sums should be invested.

(4) Any request relating to the investment in, or sale of, as the case may be, Treasury Bills made under paragraphs (1), (2) or (3) above shall be made on a form obtainable from the Department or on one that is substantially similar and any request relating to the purchase or sale, as the case may be, of any other type of Government security made under the provisions of those paragraphs shall be made in writing.

(5) Any request made under paragraphs (1), (2) or (3) above shall be sufficient authority to the Secretary of State for the investment or sale as the case may be.

[(6) Subject to paragraphs (6A) and (6B), at any time after 1st April 2004 whenever there are any monies standing to the credit of the company in the Insolvency Services Account the company shall be entitled to interest on those monies at the rate of 4.25 per cent per annum.

(6A) Interest shall cease to accrue pursuant to paragraph (6) from the date of receipt by the Secretary of State of a notice in writing from the liquidator that in the opinion of the liquidator it is necessary or expedient in order to facilitate the conclusion of the winding up that interest should cease to accrue but interest shall start to accrue again pursuant to paragraph (6) where the liquidator gives a further notice in writing to the Secretary of State requesting that interest should start to accrue again.

(6B) The Secretary of State may by notice published in the London Gazette vary the rate of interest prescribed by paragraph (6) and such variation shall have effect from the day after the date of publication of the notice in the London Gazette or such later date as may be specified in the notice.]

(7) All money received in respect of investments and interest earned under this regulation shall be paid into the Insolvency Services Account to the credit of the company.

(8) . . .

NOTES

Paras (6), (6A), (6B): substituted, for original para (6), by the Insolvency (Amendment) Regulations 2004, SI 2004/472, reg 2, Schedule, para 2(1), subject to para 2(2) of the Schedule thereto, which provides that where a notice that interest should cease is given pursuant to para (6)(a) as it stood immediately before 1 April 2004, that notice shall be treated as having been given for the purposes of para (6A). Para (6) originally read as follows:

"(6) Whenever the amount standing to the credit of a company in the Insolvency Services Account on or after 24th October 1994 exceeds £2,000, the company shall be entitled to interest on the excess at the rate of 3½ per cent per annum provided that:

(a) where, in the opinion of the liquidator, it is necessary or expedient in order to facilitate the conclusion of the winding up that interest should cease to accrue, he may give notice in writing to the Secretary of State to that effect and interest shall cease to accrue from the date of receipt of that notice by the Secretary of State; and

(b) at any time after receipt by the Secretary of State of a notice under sub-paragraph (a) above, provided that the balance standing to the credit of the company exceeds £2,000, the liquidator may give notice in writing to the Secretary of State requesting that interest should accrue on the excess and interest shall start to accrue on the excess at the rate of 3½ per cent per annum from the date of receipt of the notice by the Secretary of State.".

Para (8): revoked by the Insolvency (Amendment) Regulations 2011, SI 2011/2203, regs 3, 4, Schedule, para 8, except in relation to any voluntary winding up where a payment has been made into the Insolvency Services Account in relation to that winding up before 1 October 2011. Para (8) originally read as follows:

"(8) In addition to the application of paragraphs (1) to (7) above, in a voluntary winding up:

(a) any money invested or deposited at interest by the liquidator shall be deemed to be money under his control, and when such money forms part of the balance of funds in his hands or under his control relating to the company required to be paid into the Insolvency Services Account under regulation 5 above, the liquidator shall realise the investment or withdraw the deposit and shall pay the proceeds into that Account: Provided that where the money is invested in Government securities, such securities may, with the permission of the Secretary of State, be transferred to the control of the Secretary of State instead of being forthwith realised and the proceeds paid into the Insolvency Services Account; and

(b) where any of the money represented by securities transferred to the control of the Secretary of State pursuant to sub-paragraph (a) above is, in the opinion of the liquidator, required for the immediate purposes of the winding up he may request the Secretary of State to raise such sums as may be required by the sale of such of those securities as may be necessary and such request shall be sufficient authority to the Secretary of State for the sale and the Secretary of State shall pay the proceeds of the realisation into the Insolvency Services Account in accordance with paragraph (7) above and deal with them in the same way as other money paid into that Account may be dealt with.".

Para (4): the reference to Treasury Bills includes a reference to uncertificated units of eligible Treasury bills; see the Uncertificated Securities (Amendment) (Eligible Debt Securities) Regulations 2003, SI 2003/1633, reg 15(1), Sch 2, para 2(h).

Records to be Maintained by Liquidators and the Provision of Information

[8.34]

10 Financial records

(1) This regulation does not apply in the case of a members' voluntary winding up.

(2) The liquidator shall prepare and keep—

(a) separate financial records in respect of each company; and

(b) such other financial records as are required to explain the receipts and payments entered in the records described in sub-paragraph (a) above or regulation 12(2) below, including an explanation of the source of any receipts and the destination of any payments;

and shall, subject to regulation 12(2) below as to trading accounts, from day to day enter in those records all the receipts and payments . . . made by him.

(3) In the case of a winding up by the court, the liquidator shall obtain and keep bank statements relating to any local bank account in the name of the company.

(4) The liquidator shall submit financial records to the liquidation committee when required for inspection.

(5) In the case of a winding up by the court, if the liquidation committee is not satisfied with the contents of the financial records submitted under paragraph (4) above it may so inform the Secretary of State, giving the reasons for its dissatisfaction, and the Secretary of State may take such action as he thinks fit.

NOTES

Para (2): words "(including, in the case of a voluntary winding up, those relating to the Insolvency Services Account)" (omitted) revoked by the Insolvency (Amendment) Regulations 2011, SI 2011/2203, regs 3, 4, Schedule, para 9, except in relation to any voluntary winding up where a payment has been made into the Insolvency Services Account in relation to that winding up before 1 October 2011.

[8.35]

11 Provision of information by liquidator

(1) In the case of a winding up by the court, the liquidator shall, within 14 days of the receipt of a request for a statement of his receipts and payments as liquidator from any creditor, contributory or director of the company, supply free of charge to the person making the request, a statement of his receipts and payments as liquidator during the period of one year ending on the most recent anniversary of his becoming liquidator which preceded the request.

(2) In the case of a voluntary winding up, the liquidator shall, on request from any creditor, contributory or director of the company for a copy of a statement for any period, including future periods, sent to the registrar of companies under section 192, send such copy free of charge to the person making the request and the copy of the statement shall be sent within 14 days of the liquidator sending the statement to the registrar or the receipt of the request whichever is the later.

[8.36]

12 Liquidator carrying on business

(1) This regulation does not apply in the case of a members' voluntary winding up.

(2) Where the liquidator carries on any business of the company, he shall—

(a) keep a separate and distinct account of the trading, including, where appropriate, in the case of a winding up by the court, particulars of all local bank account transactions; and

(b) incorporate in the financial records required to be kept under regulation 10 above the total weekly amounts of the receipts and payments made by him in relation to the account kept under sub-paragraph (a) above.

[8.37]

13 Retention and delivery of records

(1) All records kept by the liquidator under regulations 10 and 12(2) and any such records received by him from a predecessor in that office shall be retained by him for a period of 6 years following—

(a) his vacation of office, or

(b) in the case of the official receiver, his release as liquidator under section 174,

unless he delivers them to another liquidator who succeeds him in office.

(2) Where the liquidator is succeeded in office by another liquidator, the records referred to in paragraph (1) above shall be delivered to that successor forthwith, unless, in the case of a winding up by the court, the winding up is for practical purposes complete and the successor is the official receiver, in which case the records are only to be delivered to the official receiver if the latter so requests.

[8.38]

14 Provision of accounts by liquidator and audit of accounts

(1) The liquidator shall, if required by the Secretary of State at any time, send to the Secretary of State an account in relation to the company of the liquidator's receipts and payments covering such period as the Secretary of State may direct and such account shall, if so required by the Secretary of State, be certified by the liquidator.

(2) Where the liquidator in a winding up by the court vacates office prior to [sending the final account to creditors] under section 146, he shall within 14 days of vacating office send to the Secretary of State an account of his receipts and payments as liquidator for any period not covered by an account previously so sent by him or if no such account has been sent, an account of his receipts and payments in respect of the whole period of his office.

[(3) In the case of a winding up by the court, where an account has been sent pursuant to section 146(3)(a), the liquidator shall, within 14 days of sending the account, send to the Secretary of State an account of his receipts and payments as liquidator which are not covered by any previous account so sent by him, or if no such account has been sent an account of his receipts and payments in respect of the whole period of his office.]

(4) In the case of a winding up by the court, where a statement of affairs has been submitted under the Act, any account sent under this regulation shall be accompanied by a summary of that statement of affairs and shall show the amount of any assets realised and explain the reasons for any non-realisation of any assets not realised.

(5) In the case of a winding up by the court, where a statement of affairs has not been submitted under the Act, any account sent under this regulation shall be accompanied by a summary of all known assets and their estimated values and shall show the amounts actually realised and explain the reasons for any non-realisation of any assets not realised.

(6) Any account sent to the Secretary of State shall, if he so requires, be audited, but whether or not the Secretary of State requires the account to be audited, the liquidator shall send to the Secretary of State on demand any documents (including vouchers and bank statements) and any information relating to the account.

NOTES

Para (2): words in square brackets substituted by the Insolvency (England and Wales) and Insolvency (Scotland) (Miscellaneous and Consequential Amendments) Rules 2017, SI 2017/1115, rr 15, 16(1), (2).

Para (3): substituted by SI 2017/1115, rr 15, 16(1), (3).

[8.39]

15 Production and inspection of records

(1) The liquidator shall produce on demand to the Secretary of State, and allow him to inspect, any accounts, books and other records kept by him (including any passed to him by a predecessor in office), and this duty to produce and allow inspection shall extend—

(a) to producing and allowing inspection at the premises of the liquidator; and
(b) to producing and allowing inspection of any financial records of the kind described in regulation 10(2)(b) above prepared by the liquidator (or any predecessor in office of his) before 24th October 1994 and kept by the liquidator;

and any such demand may—

(i) require the liquidator to produce any such accounts, books or other records to the Secretary of State, and allow him to inspect them—
  (A) at the same time as any account is sent to the Secretary of State under regulation 14 above; or
  (B) at any time after such account is sent to the Secretary of State;
  whether or not the Secretary of State requires the account to be audited; or
(ii) where it is made for the purpose of ascertaining whether the provisions of these Regulations relating to the handling of money received by the liquidator in the course of carrying out his functions have been or are likely to be complied with, be made at any time, whether or not an account has been sent or should have been sent to the Secretary of State under regulation 14 above and whether or not the Secretary of State has required any account to be audited.

(2) The liquidator shall allow the Secretary of State on demand to remove and take copies of any accounts, books and other records kept by the liquidator (including any passed to him by a predecessor in office), whether or not they are kept at the premises of the liquidator.

[8.40]

16 Disposal of company's books, papers and other records

(1) The liquidator in a winding up by the court, on the authorisation of the official receiver, during his tenure of office or on vacating office, or the official receiver while acting as liquidator, may at any time sell, destroy or otherwise dispose of the books, papers and other records of the company.

(2) In the case of a voluntary winding up, the person who was the last liquidator of a company which has been dissolved may, at any time after the expiration of a period of one year from the date of dissolution, destroy or otherwise dispose of the books, papers and other records of the company.

[8.41]

17 Voluntary liquidator to provide information to Secretary of State

(1) In the case of a voluntary winding up, a liquidator or former liquidator, . . . shall, within 14 days of a request by the Secretary of State, give the Secretary of State particulars of any money in his hands or under his control representing unclaimed or undistributed assets of the company or dividends or other sums due to any person as a member or former member of the company . . .

(2) . . .

NOTES

Para (1): first words omitted revoked by the Insolvency (England and Wales) Rules 2016 (Consequential Amendments and Savings) Rules 2017, SI 2017/369, r 2(2), Sch 2, para 4(1), (4); words "and such other particulars as the Secretary of State may require for the purpose of ascertaining or getting in any money payable into the Insolvency Services Account" (omitted in the second place) revoked by the Insolvency (Amendment) Regulations 2011, SI 2011/2203, regs 3, 4, Schedule, para 10, except in relation to any voluntary winding up where a payment has been made into the Insolvency Services Account in relation to that winding up before 1 October 2011.

Para (2): revoked by SI 2011/2203, regs 3, 4, Schedule, para 11, except in relation to any voluntary winding up where a payment has been made into the Insolvency Services Account in relation to that winding up before 1 October 2011. Para (2) originally read as follows:

"(2) The particulars referred to in paragraph (1) above shall, if the Secretary of State so requires, be certified by the liquidator, or former liquidator, as the case may be.".

[8.42]

[18 Payment of unclaimed dividends or other money

(1) This regulation applies to monies which—

(a) are held by the former liquidator of a dissolved company, and

(b) represent either or both of the following—

(i) unclaimed dividends due to creditors, or

(ii) sums held by the company in trust in respect of dividends or other sums due to any person as a member or former member of the company.

(2) Monies to which this regulation applies—

(a) may in the case of a voluntary winding up,

(b) must in the case of a winding up by the court,

be paid into the Insolvency Services Account.

(3) Where the former liquidator pays any sums into the Insolvency Services Account pursuant to paragraph (2), he shall at the same time give notice to the Secretary of State of—

(a) the name of the company,

(b) the name and address of the person to whom the dividend or other sum is payable,

(c) the amount of the dividend, and

(d) the date on which it was paid.

(4) Where a dividend or other sum is paid to a person by way of a payment instrument, any payment into the Insolvency Services Account in respect of that dividend or sum pursuant to paragraph (2) may not be made earlier than on or after the expiry of 6 months from the date of the payment instrument.]

NOTES

Substituted by the Insolvency (Amendment) Regulations 2008, SI 2008/670, reg 3(1), (3).

PART 3
BANKRUPTCY

[8.43]

19 Introductory

(1) This Part of these Regulations relates to bankruptcy and extends to England and Wales only.

(2) In addition to the application of the provisions of this Part to the official receiver when acting as trustee, the provisions of this Part (other than regulations 30 and 31) shall also apply to him when acting as receiver or manager under section 287 and the term "trustee" shall be construed accordingly.

Payments Into and Out of the Insolvency Services Account

[8.44]

20 Payments into the Insolvency Services Account

(1) Subject to regulation 21 below, the trustee shall pay all money received by him in the course of carrying out his functions as such without any deduction into the Insolvency Services Account kept by the Secretary of State with the Bank of England to the credit of the bankrupt once every 14 days or forthwith if £5,000 or more has been received.

[(2) Every payment of money into the Insolvency Services Account under this regulation shall be—

(a) made through the Bank Giro system; or

(b) sent direct to the Bank of England, Threadneedle Street, London EC2R 8AH by cheque drawn in favour of the "Insolvency Services Account" and crossed "A/c payee only" "Bank of England"; or

(c) made by electronic transfer,

and the trustee shall on request be given by the Department a receipt for the money so paid.]

(3) Every payment of money [made under sub-paragraph (a) or (b) of paragraph (2) above] shall be accompanied by a form obtainable from the Department for that purpose or by a form that is substantially similar. [Every payment of money made under sub-paragraph (c) of paragraph (2) above shall specify the name of the trustee making the payment and the name of the bankrupt to whose credit such payment is made.]

NOTES

Para (2): substituted by the Insolvency (Amendment) Regulations 2000, SI 2000/485, reg 3, Schedule, para 9.

Para (3): words in first pair of square brackets substituted, and words in second pair of square brackets inserted, by SI 2000/485, reg 3, Schedule, para 10.

[8.45]

21 Local bank account and handling of funds not forming part of the bankrupt's estate

(1) Where the trustee intends to exercise his power to carry on the business of the bankrupt, he may apply to the Secretary of State for authorisation to open a local bank account, and the Secretary of State may authorise him to make his payments into and out of a specified bank, subject to a limit, instead of into and out of the Insolvency Services Account if satisfied that an administrative advantage will be derived from having such an account.

(2) Money received by the trustee relating to the purpose for which the account was opened may be paid into the local bank account to the credit of the bankrupt to whom the account relates.

(3) Where the trustee opens a local bank account pursuant to an authorisation granted under paragraph (1) above he shall open and maintain the account in the name of the bankrupt.

(4) Where money which does not form part of the bankrupt's estate is provided to the trustee for a specific purpose it shall be clearly identifiable in a separate account.

(5) The trustee shall keep proper records, including documentary evidence of all money paid into and out of every local bank account opened and maintained under this regulation.

(6) The trustee shall pay without deduction any surplus over any limit imposed by an authorisation granted under paragraph (1) above into the Insolvency Services Account in accordance with regulation 20(1) above.

(7) As soon as the trustee ceases to carry on the business of the bankrupt or vacates office or an authorisation given in pursuance of an application under paragraph (1) above is withdrawn, he shall close the account and pay any balance into the Insolvency Services Account in accordance with regulation 20(1) above.

[8.46]

22 Payment of disbursements etc out of the Insolvency Services Account

[(A1) Paragraphs (1) and (2) of this regulation are subject to paragraph (2A).]

(1) On application to the Department, the trustee shall be repaid all necessary disbursements made by him, and expenses properly incurred by him, in the course of his administration to the date of his vacation of office out of any money standing to the credit of the bankrupt in the Insolvency Services Account.

(2) The trustee shall on application to the Department obtain payment instruments to the order of the payee for sums which become payable on account of the bankrupt for delivery by the trustee to the persons to whom the payments are to be made.

[(2A) In respect of an application made by the trustee under paragraph (1) or (2) above, the Secretary of State, if requested to do so by the trustee, may, at his discretion,

(a) make the payment which is the subject of the application to the trustee by electronic transfer; or

(b) as an alternative to the issue of payment instruments, make payment by electronic transfer to the persons to whom the trustee would otherwise deliver payment instruments.]

(3) Any application under this regulation shall be made on a form obtainable from the Department or on one that is substantially similar.

(4) On the trustee vacating office, he shall be repaid by any succeeding trustee out of any funds available for the purpose any necessary disbursements made by him and any expenses properly incurred by him but not repaid before he vacates office.

NOTES

Paras (A1), (2A): inserted by the Insolvency (Amendment) Regulations 2000, SI 2000/485, reg 3, Schedule, paras 11, 12.

Dividends to Creditors

[8.47]

23 Payment

(1) [Subject to paragraph (1A),] the trustee shall pay every dividend by payment instruments which shall be prepared by the Department on the application of the trustee and transmitted to him for distribution amongst the creditors.

[(1A) In respect of an application made by the trustee under paragraph (1) above, the Secretary of State, if requested to do so by the trustee, may, at his discretion, as an alternative to the issue of payment instruments, make payment by electronic transfer to the persons to whom the trustee would otherwise deliver payment instruments.]

(2) Any application under this regulation for a payment instrument [or payment by electronic transfer] shall be made by the trustee on a form obtainable from the Department for the purpose or on a form which is substantially similar.

(3) The trustee shall enter the total amount of every dividend that he desires to pay under this regulation in the records to be kept under regulation 24 below in one sum.

(4) On the trustee vacating office, he shall send to the Department any valid unclaimed or undelivered payment instruments for dividends after endorsing them with the word "cancelled".

NOTES

Paras (1), (2): words in square brackets inserted by the Insolvency (Amendment) Regulations 2000, SI 2000/485, reg 3, Schedule, paras 13, 15.

Para (1A): inserted by SI 2000/485, reg 3, Schedule, para 14.

[8.48]
[23A Investment or otherwise handling of funds in bankruptcy and payment of interest

(1) When the cash balance standing to the credit of the bankrupt in the account in respect of that bankrupt kept by the Secretary of State is in excess of the amount which, in the opinion of the trustee, is required for the immediate purposes of the bankruptcy and should be invested, he may request the Secretary of State to invest the amount not so required in Government securities, to be placed to the credit of that account for the benefit of the bankrupt.

(2) When any of the money so invested is, in the opinion of the trustee, required for the immediate purposes of the bankruptcy, he may request the Secretary of State to raise such sum as may be required by the sale of such of those securities as may be necessary.

(3) In cases where investments have been made at the request of the trustee in pursuance of paragraph (1) above and additional sums to the amounts so invested, including money received under paragraph (7) below, are paid into the Insolvency Services Account to the credit of the bankrupt, a request shall be made to the Secretary of State by the trustee if it is desired that these additional funds should be invested.

(4) Any request relating to the investment in, or sale of, as the case may be, Treasury Bills under paragraphs (1), (2) or (3) above shall be made on a form obtainable from the Department or on one that is substantially similar and any request relating to the purchase or sale, as the case may be, of any other type of Government security made under the provisions of those paragraphs shall be made in writing.

(5) Any request made under paragraphs (1), (2) or (3) above shall be sufficient authority to the Secretary of State for the investment or sale as the case may be.

[(6) Subject to paragraphs (6A) and (6B), at any time after 1st April 2004 whenever there are any monies standing to the credit of the estate of the bankrupt in the Insolvency Services Account the estate shall be entitled to interest on those monies at the rate of 4.25 per cent per annum.

(6A) Interest shall cease to accrue pursuant to paragraph (6) from the date of receipt by the Secretary of State of a notice in writing from the trustee that in the opinion of the trustee it is necessary or expedient in order to facilitate the conclusion of the bankruptcy that interest should cease to accrue but interest shall start to accrue again pursuant to paragraph (6) where the trustee gives a further notice in writing to the Secretary of State requesting that interest should start to accrue again.

(6B) The Secretary of State may by notice published in the London Gazette vary the rate of interest prescribed by paragraph (6) and such variation shall have effect from the day after the date of publication of the notice in the London Gazette or such later date as may be specified in the notice.]

(7) All money received in respect of investments and interest earned under this regulation shall be paid into the Insolvency Services Account to the credit of the bankrupt.]

NOTES

Inserted by the Insolvency (Amendment) Regulations 2001, SI 2001/762, reg 3, Schedule.

Paras (6), (6A), (6B): substituted, for original para (6), by the Insolvency (Amendment) Regulations 2004, SI 2004/472, reg 2, Schedule, para 3(1), subject to para 3(2) of the Schedule thereto, which provides that where a notice that interest should cease is given pursuant to para (6)(a) as it stood immediately before 1 April 2004, that notice shall be treated as having been given for the purposes of para (6A). Para (6) originally read as follows:

"(6) Whenever the amount standing to the credit of a bankrupt in the Insolvency Services Account on or after 2nd April 2001 exceeds £2,000, the bankrupt shall be entitled to interest on the excess at the rate of 3½ per cent per annum provided that:

(a) where, in the opinion of the trustee, it is necessary or expedient in order to facilitate the conclusion of the bankruptcy that interest should cease to accrue, he may give notice in writing to the Secretary of State to that effect and interest shall cease to accrue from the date of receipt of that notice by the Secretary of State, and

(b) at any time after receipt by the Secretary of State of a notice under sub-paragraph (a) above, provided that the balance standing to the credit of the bankrupt exceeds £2,000, the trustee may give notice in writing to the Secretary of State requesting that interest should accrue on the excess and interest shall start to accrue on the excess at the rate of 3½ per cent per annum from the date of receipt of the notice by the Secretary of State.".

Para (4): the reference to Treasury Bills includes a reference to uncertificated units of eligible Treasury bills; see the Uncertificated Securities (Amendment) (Eligible Debt Securities) Regulations 2003, SI 2003/1633, reg 15(1), Sch 2, para 2(h).

See further, the rate of interest prescribed by para (6) above is varied from 1.25% to 0.5% with effect from 13 May 2009; the London Gazette, 12 May 2009.

Records to be Maintained by Trustees and the Provision of Information

[8.49]

24 Financial records

(1) The trustee shall prepare and keep—

(a) separate financial records in respect of each bankrupt; and

(b) such other financial records as are required to explain the receipts and payments entered in the records described in sub-paragraph (a) above or regulation 26 below, including an explanation of the source of any receipts and the destination of any payments;

and shall, subject to regulation 26 below as to trading accounts, from day to day enter in those records all the receipts and payments made by him.

(2) The trustee shall obtain and keep bank statements relating to any local bank account in the name of the bankrupt.

(3) The trustee shall submit financial records to the creditors' committee when required for inspection.

(4) If the creditors' committee is not satisfied with the contents of the financial records submitted under paragraph (3) above it may so inform the Secretary of State, giving the reasons for its dissatisfaction and the Secretary of State may take such action as he thinks fit.

[8.50]

25 Provision of information by trustee

The trustee shall, within 14 days of the receipt of a request from any creditor or the bankrupt for a statement of his receipts and payments as trustee, supply free of charge to the person making the request, a statement of his receipts and payments as trustee during the period of one year ending on the most recent anniversary of his becoming trustee which preceded the request.

[8.51]

26 Trustee carrying on business

Subject to paragraph (2) below, where the trustee carries on any business of the bankrupt, he shall—

(a) keep a separate and distinct account of the trading, including, where appropriate, particulars of all local bank account transactions; and

(b) incorporate in the financial records required to be kept under regulation 24 above the total weekly amounts of the receipts and payments made by him in relation to the account kept under paragraph (a) above.

[8.52]

27 Retention and delivery of records

(1) All records kept by the trustee under regulations 24 and 26 and any such records received by him from a predecessor in that office shall be retained by him for a period of 6 years following—

(a) his vacation of office, or

(b) in the case of the official receiver, his release as trustee under section 299,

unless he delivers them to another trustee who succeeds him in office.

(2) Where the trustee is succeeded in office by another trustee, the records referred to in paragraph (1) above shall be delivered to that successor forthwith, unless the bankruptcy is for practical purposes complete and the successor is the official receiver, in which case the records are only to be delivered to the official receiver if the latter so requests.

[8.53]

28 Provision of accounts by trustee and audit of accounts

(1) The trustee shall, if required by the Secretary of State at any time, send to the Secretary of State an account of his receipts and payments as trustee of the bankrupt covering such period as the Secretary of State may direct and such account shall, if so required by the Secretary of State, be certified by the trustee.

(2) Where the trustee vacates office prior to [sending the final report to creditors] under section 331, he shall within 14 days of vacating office send to the Secretary of State an account of his receipts and payments as trustee for any period not covered by an account previously so sent by him, or if no such account has been sent, an account of his receipts and payments in respect of the whole period of his office.

[(3) Where a report has been sent pursuant to section 331(2A)(a), the trustee shall, within 14 days of sending the report, send to the Secretary of State an account of his receipts and payments as trustee which are not covered by any previous account so sent by him, or if no such account has been sent, an account of his receipts and payments in respect of the whole period of his office.]

(4) Where a statement of affairs has been submitted under the Act, any account sent under this regulation shall be accompanied by a summary of that statement of affairs and shall show the amount of any assets realised and explain the reasons for any non-realisation of any assets not realised.

(5) Where a statement of affairs has not been submitted under the Act, any account sent under this regulation shall be accompanied by a summary of all known assets and their estimated values and shall show the amounts actually realised and explain the reasons for any non-realisation of any assets not realised.

(6) Any account sent to the Secretary of State shall, if he so requires, be audited, but whether or not the Secretary of State requires the account to be audited, the trustee shall send to the Secretary of State on demand any documents (including vouchers and bank statements) and any information relating to the account.

NOTES

Para (2): words in square brackets substituted by the Insolvency (England and Wales) and Insolvency (Scotland) (Miscellaneous and Consequential Amendments) Rules 2017, SI 2017/1115, rr 15, 17(1), (2).

Para (3): substituted by SI 2017/1115, rr 15, 17(1), (3).

[8.54]

29 Production and inspection of records

(1) The trustee shall produce on demand to the Secretary of State, and allow him to inspect, any accounts, books and other records kept by him (including any passed to him by a predecessor in office), and this duty to produce and allow inspection shall extend—

(a) to producing and allowing inspection at the premises of the trustee; and

(b) to producing and allowing inspection of any financial records of the kind described in regulation 24(1)(b) above prepared by the trustee before 24th October 1994 and kept by him;

and any such demand may—

(i) require the trustee to produce any such accounts, books or other records to the Secretary of State, and allow him to inspect them—

(A) at the same time as any account is sent to the Secretary of State under regulation 28 above; or

(B) at any time after such account is sent to the Secretary of State;

whether or not the Secretary of State requires the account to be audited; or

(ii) where it is made for the purpose of ascertaining whether the provisions of these Regulations relating to the handling of money received by the trustee in the course of carrying out his functions have been or are likely to be complied with, be made at any time, whether or not an account has been sent or should have been sent to the Secretary of State under regulation 28 above and whether or not the Secretary of State has required any account to be audited.

(2) The trustee shall allow the Secretary of State on demand to remove and take copies of any accounts, books and other records kept by the trustee (including any passed to him by a predecessor in office), whether or not they are kept at the premises of the trustee.

[8.55]

30 Disposal of bankrupt's books, papers and other records

The trustee, on the authorisation of the official receiver, during his tenure of office or on vacating office, or the official receiver while acting as trustee, may at any time sell, destroy or otherwise dispose of the books, papers and other records of the bankrupt.

[8.56]

31 Payment of unclaimed or undistributed assets, dividends or other money

Notwithstanding anything in these Regulations, any money—

(a) in the hands of the trustee at the date of his vacation of office, or

(b) which comes into the hands of any former trustee at any time after his vacation of office,

representing, in either case, unclaimed or undistributed assets of the bankrupt or dividends, shall forthwith be paid by him into the Insolvency Services Account.

PART 4
CLAIMING MONEY PAID INTO THE INSOLVENCY SERVICES ACCOUNT

[8.57]

32

(1) Any person claiming to be entitled to any money paid into the Insolvency Services Account may apply to the Secretary of State for payment and shall provide such evidence of his claim as the Secretary of State may require.

(2) Any person dissatisfied with the decision of the Secretary of State in respect of his claim made under this regulation may appeal to the court.

PART 5
REMUNERATION OF OFFICIAL RECEIVER

[8.58]

33 Official receiver's remuneration while acting as liquidator or trustee calculated as a percentage of the value of assets realised or distributed

Subject to regulations 34, 35 and 36 below, when he is the liquidator of a company or trustee, the official receiver's remuneration for his services as such shall be calculated on the scales in Table 1 of Schedule 2 to these Regulations, as a percentage of the money received by him from the realisation of the assets of the company or the bankrupt, as the case may be, (including any Value Added Tax received on the realisation but after deducting any sums paid to secured creditors in respect of their securities and any sums spent out of money received in carrying on the business of the company or the bankrupt, as the case may be) and a percentage of the value of assets distributed to the creditors of the company or the bankrupt, as the case may be, (including payments made in respect of preferential debts) and, in the case of a company, to contributories.

NOTES

Revoked, together with regs 34, 36, by the Insolvency (Amendment) Regulations 2004, SI 2004/472, reg 2, Schedule, para 4, as from 1 April 2004, and reproduced for reference.

[8.59]

34 Limits on official receiver's remuneration as trustee

(1) That part of the official receiver's remuneration for his services as trustee which is calculated on the realisation scale set out in Table 1 of Schedule 2 to these Regulations shall not exceed such sum as is arrived at by:

(a) applying that scale to such part of the proceeds of the realisation of the bankrupt's assets as is required to pay:

(i) the bankruptcy debts to the extent required to be paid by the Rules (ignoring those debts paid otherwise than out of the proceeds of the realisation of the bankrupt's assets or which have been secured to the satisfaction of the court);

(ii) the expenses of the bankruptcy other than:

(A) fees or the remuneration of the official receiver;

(B) any sums spent out of money received in carrying on the business of the bankrupt;

(iii) fees payable under the Insolvency Fees Order 1986 other than Fee No 5 and Fee No 13 in Part II of the Schedule to that Order; and

(iv) the remuneration of the official receiver other than remuneration calculated pursuant to regulation 33 by reference to the realisation scale in Table 1 of Schedule 2 to these Regulations; and

(b) deducting from the sum arrived at under sub-paragraph (a) above any sum paid in respect of Fee No 5 in Part II of the Schedule to the Insolvency Fees Order 1986.

(2) For the purposes of this regulation the expression "bankruptcy debts" shall include any interest payable by virtue of section 328(4).

NOTES

Revoked as noted to reg 33 at **[8.58]**.

[8.60]

[35 Official receiver's general remuneration while acting as interim receiver, provisional liquidator, liquidator or trustee

(1) The official receiver shall be entitled to remuneration calculated in accordance with the applicable hourly rates set out in paragraph (2) for services provided by him (or any of his officers) in relation to—

(a) a distribution made by him when acting as liquidator or trustee to creditors (including preferential or secured creditors or both such classes of creditor);

(b) the realisation of assets on behalf of the holder of a fixed or floating charge or both types of those charges;

(c) the supervision of a special manager;

(d) the performance by him of any functions where he acts as provisional liquidator; or

(e) the performance by him of any functions where he acts as an interim receiver.

(2) The applicable hourly rates referred to in paragraph (1) are—

(a) in relation to the official receiver of the London insolvency district, those set out in Table 2 in Schedule 2; and

(b) in relation to any other official receiver, those set out in Table 3 in Schedule 2.]

NOTES

Substituted by the Insolvency (Amendment) Regulations 2005, SI 2005/512, reg 7, subject to transitional provisions in reg 3 thereof, which provide that this substitution only applies in relation to services provided by the official receiver (or any of his officers) in relation to: (a) a company in respect of which a winding-up order is made on or after 1 April 2005; (b) a bankruptcy where the bankruptcy order is made on or after 1 April 2005; or (c) his appointment as an interim receiver or provisional liquidator where he is appointed on or after 1 April 2005.

Before the substitution noted above, reg 35 (as amended by SI 2004/472) read as follows:

"35 Official receiver's general remuneration while acting as interim receiver, provisional liquidator, liquidator or trustee

(1) When [the official receiver acting as liquidator or trustee makes a distribution to creditors, supervises a special manager or] he is an interim receiver appointed under section 286 or the provisional liquidator of a company being wound up or where as official receiver he performs any duty as liquidator or trustee for which . . . a fee is not provided under any order made under section 414 or 415, the official receiver's remuneration for the services provided by himself and his officers in that capacity shall be calculated on the total hourly rate as specified in Table 2 or, as the case may be, Table 3 in Schedule 2 to these Regulations.

(2) Table 2 shall be used when calculating the remuneration of the official receiver of the London insolvency district and Table 3 shall be used when calculating the remuneration of the official receiver of any other district.".

[8.61]

36 Official receiver's remuneration while acting as liquidator or provisional liquidator in respect of the realisation of property charged

When he is a liquidator or provisional liquidator, the official receiver's remuneration in respect of the realisation of property of the company—

(a) for secured creditors (other than a creditor who holds a floating charge on the company's undertaking or property) shall be calculated on the realisation scale set out in Table 1 in Schedule 2 to these Regulations in the manner set out in regulation 33; and

(b) for creditors who hold a floating charge on the company's undertaking or property shall be calculated on both the scales set out in Table 1 in Schedule 2 and in the manner set out in regulation 33.

NOTES

Revoked as noted to reg 33 at **[8.58]**.

[PART 5A
INFORMATION ABOUT TIME SPENT ON A CASE TO BE PROVIDED BY INSOLVENCY PRACTITIONER TO CREDITORS ETC

[8.62]

36A

(1) Subject as set out in this regulation, in respect of any case in which he acts, an insolvency practitioner shall on request in writing made by any person mentioned in paragraph (2), supply free of charge to that person a statement of the kind described in paragraph (3).

(2) The persons referred to in paragraph (1) are—

(a) any creditor in the case;

(b) where the case relates to a company, any director or contributory of that company; and

(c) where the case relates to an individual, that individual.

(3) The statement referred to in paragraph (1) shall comprise in relation to the period beginning with the date of the insolvency practitioner's appointment and ending with the relevant date the following details—

(a) the total number of hours spent on the case by the insolvency practitioner and any staff assigned to the case during that period;

(b) for each grade of individual so engaged, the average hourly rate at which any work carried out by individuals in that grade is charged; and

(c) the number of hours spent by each grade of staff during that period.

(4) In relation to paragraph (3) the "relevant date" means the date next before the date of the making of the request on which the insolvency practitioner has completed any period in office which is a multiple of six months or, where the insolvency practitioner has vacated office, the date that he vacated office.

(5) Where an insolvency practitioner has vacated office, an obligation to provide information under this regulation shall only arise in relation to a request that is made within 2 years of the date he vacates office.

(6) Any statement required to be provided to any person under this regulation shall be supplied within 28 days of the date of the receipt of the request by the insolvency practitioner.

(7) In this regulation the expression "insolvency practitioner" shall be construed in accordance with section 388 of the Insolvency Act 1986.]

NOTES

Inserted, together with proceeding Part heading, by the Insolvency (Amendment) Regulations 2005, SI 2005/512, reg 8.

PART 6
TRANSITIONAL AND SAVING PROVISIONS

[8.63]

37

The Regulations shall have effect subject to the transitional and saving provisions set out in Schedule 3 to these Regulations.

SCHEDULES

SCHEDULE 1

(Sch 1 revokes the Insolvency Regulations 1986, SI 1986/1994, and the amending SI 1987/1959, SI 1988/1739 and SI 1991/380.)

SCHEDULE 2

Regulations 33 to 36

TABLE 1

[8.64]

The realisation scale

i	*on the first £5,000 or fraction thereof*	*20%*
ii	*on the next £5,000 or fraction thereof*	*15%*
iii	*on the next £90,000 or fraction thereof*	*10%*
iv	*on all further sums realised*	*5%*

The distribution scale

i	*on the first £5,000 or fraction thereof*	*10%*
ii	*on the next £5,000 or fraction thereof*	*7½%*
iii	*on the next £90,000 or fraction thereof*	*5%*
iv	*on all further sums distributed*	*2½%*

[TABLE 2 LONDON RATES

Grade according to the Insolvency Service grading structure/ Status of Official	***Total hourly rate £***
D2/Official Receiver	75
C2/Deputy or Assistant Official Receiver	63
C1/Senior Examiner	58
L3/Examiner	46
L2 Examiner	42
B2/Administrator	46
L1/Examiner	40
B1/Administrator	46
A2/Administrator	40
A1/Administrator	35

TABLE 3 PROVINCIAL RATES

Grade according to the Insolvency Service grading structure/ Status of Official	***Total hourly rate £***
D2/Official Receiver	69
C2/Deputy or Assistant Official Receiver	58
C1/Senior Examiner	52
L3/Examiner	46
L2 Examiner	40
B2/Administrator	43
L1/Examiner	38
B1/Administrator	42
A2/Administrator	36
A1/Administrator	31]

NOTES

Table 1: revoked by the Insolvency (Amendment) Regulations 2004, SI 2004/472, reg 2, Schedule, para 6, as from 1 April 2004, and reproduced for reference.

Tables 2, 3: substituted by the Insolvency (Amendment) Regulations 2009, SI 2009/482, reg 2.

SCHEDULE 3

Regulation 37

[8.65]

1 Interpretation

In this Schedule the expression "the former Regulations" means the Insolvency Regulations 1986 as amended by the Insolvency (Amendment) Regulations 1987, the Insolvency (Amendment) Regulations 1988 and the Insolvency (Amendment) Regulations 1991.

2 Requests pursuant to regulation 13(1) of the former Regulations

Any request made pursuant to regulation 13(1) of the former Regulations which has not been complied with prior to 24th October 1994 shall be treated, in the case of a company that is being wound up by the court, as a request made pursuant to regulation 11(1) of these Regulations and, in the case of a bankruptcy, as a request made pursuant to regulation 25 of these Regulations and in each case the request shall be treated as if it had been made on 24th October 1994.

3 Things done under the provisions of the former Regulations

So far as anything done under, or for the purposes of, any provision of the former Regulations could have been done under, or for the purposes of, the corresponding provision of these Regulations, it is not invalidated by the revocation of that provision but has effect as if done under, or for the purposes of, the corresponding provision.

4 Time periods

Where any period of time specified in a provision of the former Regulations is current immediately before 24th October 1994, these Regulations have effect as if the corresponding provision of these Regulations had been in force when the period began to run; and (without prejudice to the foregoing) any period of time so specified and current is deemed for the purposes of these Regulations—

(a) to run from the date or event from which it was running immediately before 24th October 1994, and

(b) to expire whenever it would have expired if these Regulations had not been made;

and any rights, obligations, requirements, powers or duties dependent on the beginning, duration or end of such period as above-mentioned shall be under these Regulations as they were or would have been under the former Regulations.

5 References to other provisions

Where in any provision of these Regulations there is reference to another provision of these Regulations, and the first-mentioned provision operates, or is capable of operating, in relation to things done or omitted, or events occurring or not occurring, in the past (including in particular past acts of compliance with the former Regulations), the reference to that other provision is to be read as including a reference to the corresponding provision of the former Regulations.

6 Provisions of Schedule to be without prejudice to the operation of sections 16 and 17 of the Interpretation Act 1978

The provisions of this Schedule are to be without prejudice to the operation of sections 16 and 17 of the Interpretation Act 1978 (saving from, and effect of, repeals) as they are applied by section 23 of that Act.

7 Meaning of "corresponding provision"

(1) A provision in the former Regulations, except regulation 13(1) of those Regulations, is to be regarded as the corresponding provision of a provision in these Regulations notwithstanding any modifications made to the provision as it appears in these Regulations.

(2) Without prejudice to the generality of the term "corresponding provision" the following table shall, subject to sub-paragraph (3) below, have effect in the interpretation of that expression with a provision of these Regulations listed in the left hand column being regarded as the corresponding provision of a provision of the former Regulations listed opposite it in the right hand column and that latter provision being regarded as the corresponding provision of the first-mentioned provision:

TABLE

Provision in these Regulations	*Provision in the former Regulations*
5(1), 5(3), 5(4)	4
5(2), 5(3), 5(4)	24
6	6
7(1), 7(2), 7(4), 7(5)	5
7(3), 7(4)	25
8(1), 8(2), 8(4), 8(5), 8(6)	15
8(3), 8(4)	25
9	18, 34
10	9, 27
11(2)	31
12	10, 28
13	10A, 28A
15	12A, 30A
16(1)	14
16(2)	32
17	35
18	16, 33

Provision in these Regulations	***Provision in the former Regulations***
20	4
21	6
22	5
23	15
24	9
26	10
27	10A
29	12A
30	14
31	16A
32	17, 33
33, Table 1 in Schedule 2	19
35, Tables 2 and 3 in Schedule 2	20
36, Table 1 in Schedule 2	22

(3) Where a provision of the former Regulations is expressed in the Table in sub-paragraph (2) above to be the corresponding provision of a provision in these Regulations and the provision in the former Regulations was capable of applying to other proceedings in addition to those to which the provision in these Regulations is capable of applying, the provision in the former Regulations shall be construed as the corresponding provision of the provision in these Regulations only to the extent that they are both capable of applying to the same type of proceedings.

INSOLVENCY ACT 1986, SECTION 72A (APPOINTED DATE) ORDER 2003

(SI 2003/2095)

NOTES

Made: 8 August 2003.
Authority: Insolvency Act 1986, s 72A.
Commencement: 8 August 2003.

[8.66]
1 Citation and commencement

This Order may be cited as the Insolvency Act 1986, Section 72A (Appointed Date) Order 2003.

[8.67]
2 Appointed date

The date appointed under section 72A(4)(a) of the Insolvency Act 1986 is 15th September 2003.

INSOLVENCY ACT 1986 (PRESCRIBED PART) ORDER 2003

(SI 2003/2097)

NOTES

Made: 8 August 2003.
Authority: Insolvency Act 1986, s 176A.
Commencement: 15 September 2003.

Application to Charitable Incorporated Organisations: as to the application of this Order in relation to CIOs, see the Charitable Incorporated Organisations (Insolvency and Dissolution) Regulations 2012, SI 2012/3013 at **[18.221]**.

Application to Co-operative and Community Benefit Societies and Credit Unions: as to the application of this Order in relation to a society registered under the Co-operative and Community Benefit Societies Act 2014, see the Co-operative and Community Benefit Societies and Credit Unions (Arrangements, Reconstructions and Administration) Order 2014, SI 2014/229, art 12, Sch 5, at **[7.1437]**, **[7.1450]**.

[8.68]
1 Citation, Commencement and Interpretation

(1) This Order may be cited as the Insolvency Act 1986 (Prescribed Part) Order 2003 and shall come into force on 15th September 2003.

(2) In this order "the 1986 Act" means the Insolvency Act 1986.

[8.69]
2 Minimum value of the company's net property

For the purposes of section 176A(3)(a) of the 1986 Act the minimum value of the company's net property is £10,000.

[8.70]
3 Calculation of prescribed part

(1) The prescribed part of the company's net property to be made available for the satisfaction of unsecured debts of the company pursuant to section 176A of the 1986 Act shall be calculated as follows—

- (a) where the company's net property does not exceed £10,000 in value, 50% of that property;
- (b) subject to paragraph (2), where the company's net property exceeds £10,000 in value the sum of—
  - (i) 50% of the first £10,000 in value; and
  - (ii) 20% of that part of the company's net property which exceeds £10,000 in value.

(2) The value of the prescribed part of the company's net property to be made available for the satisfaction of unsecured debts of the company pursuant to section 176A shall not exceed £600,000.

INSOLVENCY PROCEEDINGS (FEES) ORDER 2004

(SI 2004/593)

NOTES

Made: 4 March 2004.

Authority: Insolvency Act 1986, ss 414, 415; Bankruptcy Act 1914, s 133; Companies Act 1985, s 663(4).

Commencement: 1 April 2004.

Revocation: this Order is revoked (as from 21 July 2016) by the Insolvency Proceedings (Fees) Order 2016, SI 2016/692, art 6, Sch 2, subject to transitional provisions and savings in art 7 thereof at **[8.88]**.

Application to Charitable Incorporated Organisations: as to the application of this Order in relation to CIOs, see the Charitable Incorporated Organisations (Insolvency and Dissolution) Regulations 2012, SI 2012/3013 at **[18.221]**.

ARRANGEMENT OF ARTICLES

1 Citation and commencement . . . [8.71]
2 Interpretation . . . [8.72]
3 Revocations and Transitional Provisions . . . [8.73]
4 Fees payable in connection with bankruptcies, debt relief orders, individual voluntary arrangements and winding up . . . [8.74]
5 Fees payable to an insolvency practitioner appointed under section 273 . . . [8.75]
6 Deposits—winding up by the court and bankruptcy . . . [8.76]
7 Deposits—official receiver acting as nominee in individual voluntary arrangement . . . [8.77]
8 Reduction and refund of fees—individual voluntary arrangement following bankruptcy . . . [8.78]
9 Value Added Tax . . . [8.79]

SCHEDULES

Schedule 1: Revocations . . . [8.80]
Schedule 2: Fees Payable in Insolvency Proceedings . . . [8.81]

[8.71]
1 Citation and commencement

This Order may be cited as the Insolvency Proceedings (Fees) Order 2004 and shall come into force on 1st April 2004.

NOTES

Revoked as noted at the beginning of this Order.

[8.72]
2 Interpretation

(1) In this Order—

"the Act" means the Insolvency Act 1986 (any reference to a numbered section being to the section so numbered in that Act);

"the commencement date" is the date referred to in Article 1;

"individual voluntary arrangement" means a voluntary arrangement pursuant to Part VIII of the Act; and

"the Rules" means the Insolvency Rules 1986 (any reference to a numbered Rule being to the Rule so numbered in the Rules).

(2) A reference to a fee by a means of letters and a number is a reference to the fee so designated in the table in Schedule 2.

NOTES

Revoked as noted at the beginning of this Order.

[8.73]

3 Revocations and Transitional Provisions

The instruments listed in the Schedule 1 to this Order are revoked to the extent set out in that Schedule.

NOTES

Revoked as noted at the beginning of this Order.

[8.74]

4 Fees payable in connection with bankruptcies, [debt relief orders,] individual voluntary arrangements and winding up

(1) Subject to paragraphs (2) and (3) and article 8, the fees payable to the Secretary of State in respect of [the costs of persons acting as approved intermediaries under Part 7A of the Act,] proceedings under Parts I to XI of the Act and the performance by the [adjudicator,] official receiver or Secretary of State of functions under those Parts shall be determined in accordance with the provisions of Schedule 2 to this Order.

(2) Paragraph (1) and the provisions of Schedule 2 shall not apply to a bankruptcy where the bankruptcy order was made before the commencement date except insofar as is necessary to enable the charging of—

(a) fee INV1; or

(b) as regards an individual voluntary arrangement proposed by, or entered into by, the bankrupt, fees IVA1, IVA2 or IVA3.

(3) Paragraph (1) and the provisions of Schedule 2 shall not apply to a winding up by the court where the winding-up order was made before the commencement date except insofar as is necessary to enable the charging of fee INV1.

(4) Each request for the purchase of any government securities made by a trustee in bankruptcy under the Bankruptcy Act 1914 or a liquidator in a winding up under the provisions of the Companies Act 1985 shall be accompanied by [the appropriate amount of fee INV1].

NOTES

Revoked as noted at the beginning of this Order.

Section heading: words in square brackets inserted by the Insolvency Proceedings (Fees) (Amendment) Order 2009, SI 2009/645, arts 3, 4(1)(a).

Para (1): words in first pair of square brackets inserted by SI 2009/645, arts 3, 4(1)(b); word in second pair of square brackets inserted by the Insolvency Proceedings (Fees) (Amendment) Order 2016, SI 2016/184, arts 2, 3.

Para (4): words in square brackets substituted for original words "a fee of £50" by SI 2009/645, arts 3, 4(1)(c), where the request to purchase or sell securities was made on or after 6 April 2009; see art 7(1), (2) thereof at **[2.67]**.

[8.75]

5 Fees payable to an insolvency practitioner appointed under section 273

Where a court appoints an insolvency practitioner under section 273(2) to prepare and submit a report under section 274 the court shall, on submission of the report, pay to the practitioner a fee of [£450] (that sum being inclusive of Value Added Tax).

NOTES

Revoked as noted at the beginning of this Order.

Revoked by the Insolvency Proceedings (Fees) (Amendment) Order 2016, SI 2016/184, arts 2, 4, 7, except in relation to petitions presented before 6 April 2016.

Sum in square brackets substituted for previous sum "£360" by the Insolvency Proceedings (Fees) (Amendment) Order 2010, SI 2010/732, arts 3, 4, in relation to reports submitted to the court in respect of debtors' petitions presented on or after 6 April 2010; see art 8(1), (2) thereof at **[2.85]**.

Note: the previous sum "£360" was substituted for the sum "£345" by the Insolvency Proceedings (Fees) (Amendment) Order 2009, SI 2009/645, arts 3, 4(2), in relation to reports submitted to the court in respect of debtors' petitions presented on or after 6 April 2009; see art 7(1)–(3) thereof at **[2.67]**. The previous sum "£345" was substituted for sum "£335", by the Insolvency Proceedings (Fees) (Amendment) Order 2008, SI 2008/714, art 2(1), (2), in relation to reports submitted to the court in respect of debtors' petitions presented on or after 6 April 2008; see art 3(1), (2) thereof at **[2.48]**. The previous sum of £335 was substituted for original sum £310, by the Insolvency Proceedings (Fees) (Amendment) Order 2007, SI 2007/521, art 2(1), (2), in relation to reports submitted to the court in respect of debtors' petitions presented on or after 1 April 2007; see art 4(1), (2) thereof at **[2.46]**.

[8.76]

6 Deposits—winding up by the court and bankruptcy

(1) In this Article—

"appropriate deposit" means—

(a) in relation to a winding-up petition to be presented under the Act[, other than a winding-up petition to be presented under section 124A, the sum of [£1,350]];

[(aa) in relation to a winding-up petition to be presented under section 124A the sum of £5,000]

(b) in relation to a bankruptcy petition to be presented [by the personal representative of a deceased debtor] the sum of [£525]; . . .

[(ba) in relation to a bankruptcy application to be made under section 263H(c) the sum of £525; or]

(c) in relation to a bankruptcy petition to be presented under sections 264(1)(a), [(ba), (bb),] (c) or (d) the sum of [£825];

"order" means a winding-up, or as the case may be, bankruptcy order;

"petition" means a winding-up, or as the case may be, bankruptcy petition;

"relevant assets" means the assets of the company or, as the case may be the assets comprised in the estate of the bankrupt; and

"relevant fees" means in relation to winding-up proceedings fee W1 and in relation to bankruptcy proceedings fee B1 together with any fees payable under section 273.

(2) [Where [a bankruptcy application is made or] a bankruptcy or winding-up petition is presented the appropriate deposit is payable by [the applicant or (as the case may be)] the petitioner and the deposit] shall be security for the payment of the relevant fees and shall be used to discharge those fees to the extent that the relevant assets are insufficient for that purpose.

(3) Where a deposit is paid to the court, the court shall (except to the extent that a fee is payable by virtue of Article 5) transmit the deposit paid to the official receiver attached to the court.

(4) A deposit shall be repaid to the person who made it in a case where a petition is dismissed or withdrawn . . .

[(4A) The deposit will be repaid to the debtor where—

(a) the adjudicator has refused to make a bankruptcy order,

(b) 14 days have elapsed from the date of delivery of the notice of refusal, and

(c) the debtor has not made a request to the adjudicator to review the decision.

(4B) Where the debtor has made a request to the adjudicator to review the decision to refuse to make a bankruptcy order the deposit will be repaid to the debtor where—

(a) the adjudicator has confirmed the refusal to make a bankruptcy order,

(b) 28 days have elapsed from the date of delivery of the confirmation of the notice of refusal, and

(c) the debtor has not appealed to the court against the refusal to make a bankruptcy order.

(4C) Where the debtor has appealed to the court against the refusal to make a bankruptcy order the deposit will be repaid to the debtor where the appeal is dismissed or withdrawn.]

(5) In any case where an order is made (including any case where the order is subsequently annulled, rescinded or recalled), any deposit made shall be returned to the person who made it save to the extent that the relevant assets are insufficient to discharge the fees for which the deposit is security.

NOTES

Revoked as noted at the beginning of this Order.

Para (1): in sub-para (a) words in first (outer) pair of square brackets substituted and sub-para (aa) inserted, by the Insolvency Proceedings (Fees) (Amendment) Order 2014, SI 2014/583, arts 2(a), (b), 4, in relation to petitions presented on or after 6 April 2014; sum in second (inner) pair of square brackets in sub-para (a) substituted for sum "£1,250" by the Insolvency Proceedings (Fees) (Amendment) Order 2015, SI 2015/1819, arts 2(a), 4(1), in relation to petitions presented on or after 16 November 2015.

In sub-para (b) words in square brackets substituted and word omitted revoked by the Insolvency Proceedings (Fees) (Amendment) Order 2016, SI 2016/184, arts 2, 5(a); sum in square brackets substituted for sum "£450" by the Insolvency Proceedings (Fees) (Amendment) Order 2011, SI 2011/1167, arts 2(b), 3, in relation to petitions presented on or after 1 June 2011.

Sub-para (ba) inserted by SI 2016/184, arts 2, 5(a)(ii).

The previous sum of "£1, 250" in para (a) was substituted for the sum "£1,165" by SI 2014/583, arts 2(a), 4, in relation to petitions presented on or after 6 April 2014. The previous sum of "£1,165" in sub-para (a) was substituted for the sum "£1,000" by SI 2011/1167, arts 2(a), 3, in relation to petitions presented on or after 1 June 2011. The previous sums of "£1,000" and "£450" in sub-paras (a), (b) were substituted for sums "£715" and "£360" respectively by the Insolvency Proceedings (Fees) (Amendment) Order 2010, SI 2010/732, arts 3, 5(a), (b), in relation to petitions presented on or after 6 April 2010; see art 8(1), (3) thereof at **[2.85]**. The previous sums of "£715" and "£360" were substituted for sums "£690" and "£345" respectively by the Insolvency Proceedings (Fees) (Amendment) Order 2009, SI 2009/645, arts 3, 4(3)(a), (b), in relation to petitions presented on or after 6 April 2009; see art 7(1)–(4) thereof at **[2.67]**. The previous sums of "£690" and "£345" were substituted for sums "£670" and "£335" respectively (as previously substituted by SI 2007/521, art 2(1), (3)(a), (b), in relation to petitions presented on or after 1 April 2007; see art 4(1), (3) thereof at **[2.46]**) by the Insolvency Proceedings (Fees) (Amendment) Order 2008, SI 2008/714, art 2(1), (3)(a), (b), in relation to petitions presented on or after 6 April 2008; see art 3(1), (3) thereof at **[2.48]**.

In sub-para (c), words in first pair of square brackets inserted by the Insolvency Proceedings Fees (Amendment) Order 2005, SI 2005/544, arts 4, 5(a); sum in square brackets substituted for previous sum "£750" by SI 2015/1819, arts 2(b), 4(1), in relation to petitions presented on or after 16 November 2015.

The previous sum of "£750" was substituted for the sum "£700" by SI 2014/583, arts 2(c), 4, in relation to petitions presented on or after 6 April 2014. The previous sum of "£700" was substituted for sum "£600" by SI 2011/1167, arts 2(c), 3, in relation to petitions presented on or after 1 June 2011. The previous sum of "£600" was substituted for sum "£430" by SI 2010/732, arts 3, 5(c), in relation to petitions presented on or after 6 April 2010; see art 8(1), (3) thereof at **[2.85]**. The previous sum of "£430" was substituted for sum "£415" by SI 2009/645, arts 3, 4(3)(c), in relation to petitions presented on or after 6 April 2009; see art 7(1)–(4) thereof at **[2.67]**. The previous sum of "£415" was substituted for sum "£400" (as previously substituted by SI 2007/521, art 2(1), (3)(c), in relation to petitions presented on or after 1 April 2007; see art 4(1), (3) thereof at **[2.46]**) by SI 2008/714, art 2(1), (3)(c), in relation to petitions presented on or after 6 April 2008; see art 3(1), (3) thereof at **[2.48]**.

Para (2): words in first (outer) pair of square brackets substituted by SI 2005/544, arts 4, 5(b); words in second and third (inner) pairs of square brackets inserted by SI 2016/184, arts 2, 5(b).

Para (4): words omitted revoked by SI 2016/184, arts 2, 5(c).

Paras (4A)–(4C): inserted by SI 2016/184, arts 2, 5(d).

[8.77]
7 Deposits—official receiver acting as nominee in individual voluntary arrangement

(1) Where a proposal for an individual voluntary arrangement with the official receiver acting as nominee is notified to the official receiver, the notification shall be accompanied by a deposit of [£315] as security for fee IVA1 and fee IVA2.

(2) The deposit shall be used to discharge fee IVA1 and fee IVA2.

(3) Where the official receiver declines to act in relation to a proposal of the kind mentioned in paragraph (1) the deposit mentioned in that paragraph shall be refunded to the person entitled to it.

(4) Where the official receiver agrees to act as nominee in relation to a proposal of the kind mentioned in paragraph (1) but the proposal is rejected by the bankrupt's creditors, any balance of the deposit after deducting fee IVA2 shall be returned to the person who is entitled to it.

NOTES

Revoked as noted at the beginning of this Order.

Para (1): sum in square brackets substituted for previous sum "£310" by the Insolvency Proceedings (Fees) (Amendment) Order 2009, SI 2009/645, arts 3, 4(4), in relation to notifications sent to the official receiver on or after 6 April 2009; see art 7(1)–(3), (5) thereof at **[2.67]**.

Note: the previous sum "£310" was substituted for sum "£315" (as previously substituted by the Insolvency Proceedings (Fees) (Amendment) Order 2006, SI 2006/561, art 2(1), (3), subject to transitional provisions in art 6(2) thereof at **[2.39]**) by the Insolvency Proceedings (Fees) (Amendment) Order 2007, SI 2007/521, art 2(1), (4), in relation to notifications sent to the official receiver on or after 1 April 2007; see art 4(1), (4) thereof at **[2.46]**.

[8.78]
8 Reduction and refund of fees—individual voluntary arrangement following bankruptcy

Where proposals made by a bankrupt for an individual voluntary arrangement with the official receiver acting as supervisor are approved by the bankrupt's creditors, fee B1 shall be reduced to [£857.50] and any payments made in respect of fee B1 which exceed that amount shall be refunded to the credit of the estate of the bankrupt.

NOTES

Revoked as noted at the beginning of this Order.

Sum in square brackets substituted for original sum "£812.50" by the Insolvency Proceedings (Fees) (Amendment) Order 2007, SI 2007/521, art 2(1), (5), in relation to cases in which the bankruptcy order relating to the bankrupt was made on or after 1 April 2007; see art 4(1), (5) thereof at **[2.46]**.

[8.79]
9 Value Added Tax

Where Valued Added Tax is chargeable in respect of the provision of a service for which a fee is prescribed by virtue of any provision of this Order (other than Article 5), there shall be payable in addition to that fee the amount of the Value Added Tax.

NOTES

Revoked as noted at the beginning of this Order.

SCHEDULES

SCHEDULE 1
REVOCATIONS

Article 3

[8.80]

Reference	*Extent of revocation*
The Bankruptcy Fees Order 1984	*All the entries in the Schedule to that Order except for the entry relating to Fee 13 in Table B.*
The Bankruptcy Fees (Amendment) Order 1985	*The whole Order.*
The Companies (Department of Trade and Industry) Fees Order 1985	*The entries in the Schedule to that Order except for the entry relating to Fee 3.*
The Insolvency Fees Order 1986	*The whole Order is revoked except in relation to any case where a winding-up or bankruptcy order is made under the Act before the commencement date but in such a case the Order shall continue to have effect with the deletion of all the entries in the Schedule to the Order except, in relation to a winding up by the court, that relating to Fee 10 in Part 1 of the Schedule and, in relation to a bankruptcy, that relating to Fee 13 in Part 2 of the Schedule.*

Reference	Extent of revocation
The Insolvency Fees (Amendment) Order 1988	*The whole Order.*
The Bankruptcy and Companies (Department of Trade and Industry) Fees (Amendment) Order 1990	*The whole Order.*
The Insolvency Fees (Amendment) Order 1990	*The whole Order.*
The Bankruptcy and Companies (Department of Trade and Industry) Fees (Amendment) Order 1991	*The whole Order.*
The Insolvency Fees (Amendment) Order 1991	*The whole Order.*
The Insolvency Fees (Amendment) Order 1992	*The whole Order.*
The Insolvency Fees (Amendment) Order 1994	*The whole Order.*
The Insolvency Fees (Amendment) Order 2001	*The whole Order.*

NOTES

Revoked as noted at the beginning of this Order.

Entries relating to "The Bankruptcy Fees Order 1984", "The Companies (Department of Trade and Industry) Fees Order 1985" and "The Insolvency Fees Order 1986" revoked by the Insolvency Proceedings (Fees) (Amendment) Order 2007, SI 2007/521, art 3(b), Schedule, subject to transitional provisions in art 4(1), (10) thereof at **[2.46]**.

SCHEDULE 2
FEES PAYABLE IN INSOLVENCY PROCEEDINGS

Article 4

[8.81]

1. *(1) In this Schedule—*

"the bankruptcy ceiling" means in relation to a bankruptcy, the sum which is arrived at by adding together—

(a) the bankruptcy debts required to be paid under the Rules

[(b) any interest payable by virtue of sections 328(4) and 329(2)(b); and]

(c) the expenses of the bankruptcy as set out in Rule 6.224 other than—

(i) any sums spent out of money received in carrying on the business of the bankrupt; and

(ii) fee B2 in the Table set out in paragraph 2;

"chargeable receipts" means those sums which are paid into the Insolvency Services Account after first deducting any amounts paid into the Insolvency Services Account which are subsequently paid out to secured creditors in respect of their securities or in carrying on the business of the company or the bankrupt;

[. . .] and

"the insolvency legislation" means the Insolvency Act 1986, the Insolvency Rules 1986 and the Insolvency Regulations 1994.

(2) In this Schedule, references to the performance of the "general duties" of the official receiver on the making of a winding-up or bankruptcy order—

(a) include the payment by the official receiver of any fees, costs or disbursements except for those associated with the realisation of assets or the distribution of funds to creditors; but

[(b) does not include anything done by the official receiver in connection with or for the purposes of—

(i) the appointment of agents for the purposes of, or in connection with, the realisation of assets;

(ii) the making of a distribution to creditors (including preferential or secured creditors or both such classes of creditor);

(iii) the realisation of assets on behalf of the holder of a fixed or floating charge or both types of those charges; or

(iv) the supervision of a special manager.]

2. *Fees payable to the Secretary of State in respect of proceedings under Parts I to XI of the Act and the performance by the official receiver and the Secretary of State of functions under those Parts shall be determined in accordance with the provisions of the Table of Fees set out below—*

Table of Fees

Fees payable in respect of individual voluntary arrangements only

Designation of Fee	*Description of fee and circumstances in which it is charged*	*Amount of fee or applicable %*
IVA1	***Individual voluntary arrangement registration fee*** *On the registration of an individual voluntary arrangement by the Secretary of State there is payable a fee of—*	*[£15]*
IVA2	***Individual voluntary arrangement—official receiver's nominee fee*** *For the performance by the official receiver in relation to an individual voluntary arrangement of the functions of nominee there shall be payable on the agreement of the official receiver so to act a fee of—*	*£300*
IVA3	***Individual voluntary arrangement—official receiver's supervisor fee*** *For the performance by the official receiver in relation to an individual voluntary arrangement of the functions of supervisor, there shall be payable, a fee calculated as a percentage of any monies realised whilst he acts as supervisor at the rate of—*	*15%*

Fees payable in bankruptcies only

Designation of Fee	*Description of fee and circumstances in which it is charged*	*Amount of fee or applicable %*
[BAF1	***Application for a bankruptcy order – adjudicator's administration fee*** *On the application to the adjudicator for a bankruptcy order, for the performance of the adjudicator functions, there is payable the fee of—*	*£130]*
B1	***[Bankruptcy—Official receiver's administration fee*** *For the performance by the official receiver of his general duties as official receiver on the making of a bankruptcy order, including his duty to investigate and report upon the affairs of bankrupts, there shall be payable a fee of—*	*[£1,990]]*
[B2	***Bankruptcy—Secretary of State's administration fee applicable to bankruptcy orders made on or after 6 April 2010*** *For the performance of the Secretary of State's general duties under the insolvency legislation in relation to the administration of the estate of each bankrupt, there shall be payable a fee calculated in accordance with the following scale as a percentage of chargeable receipts relating to the bankruptcy (but ignoring that part of the chargeable receipts which exceeds the bankruptcy ceiling) at the rate of—*	*0% of the first £2,000* *[75%] of the next £1,700* *[50%] of the next £1,500* *15% of the next £396,000* *1% of the remainder, subject to a maximum of £80,000.]*

[Fees payable in relation to debt relief orders

Designation of Fee	*Description of fee and circumstances in which it is charged*	*Amount of fee*

Table of Fees		
DRO1	***Application for a debt relief order—official receiver's administration fee and costs of persons acting as approved intermediaries***	
	For the performance by the official receiver of his functions, and for the payment of an amount not exceeding £10 in respect of the costs of persons acting as approved intermediaries, under Part 7A of the Act, there shall be payable in connection with an application for a debt relief order, a fee of—	*£90]*
Fees payable in relation to winding up by the court only		
Designation of Fee	*Description of fee and circumstances in which it is charged*	*Amount of fee or applicable %*
[W1	***Winding up by the court other than a winding up on a petition presented under section 124A—official receiver's administration fee***	
	For the performance by the official receiver of his general duties as official receiver on the making of a winding-up order other than on a petition presented under section 124A, including his duty to investigate and report upon the affairs of bodies in liquidation, there shall be payable a fee of—	*[£2,520]*
W1A	***Winding up by the court on a petition presented under section 124A—official receiver's administration fee***	
	For the performance by the official receiver of his general duties as official receiver on the making of a winding-up order on a petition presented under section 124A, including his duty to investigate and report upon the affairs of bodies in liquidation, there shall be payable a fee of—	*£5,000]*
[W2	***Winding up by the court—Secretary of State's administration fee applicable to winding up orders made on or after 6 April 2010***	
	For the performance of the Secretary of State's general duties under the insolvency legislation in relation to the administration of the affairs of each company which is being wound up by the court, there shall be payable a fee calculated in accordance with the following scale as a percentage of chargeable receipts relating to the company at the rate of—	
		0% of the first £2,500
		[75%] of the next £1,700
		[50%] of the next £1,500
		15% of the next £396,000
		1% of the remainder, subject to a maximum of £80,000.]
Fees payable in bankruptcies and both types of winding up		
Designation of Fee	*Description of fee and circumstances in which it is charged*	*Amount of fee or applicable %*
[INV1	***Investment fee on purchase or sale of government securities—***	
	For each purchase or sale of any government securities made at the request of a trustee in bankruptcy or a liquidator in a compulsory or voluntary winding up—	
	(a) in respect of a purchase, where the cost of the securities (including accrued interest, if any)—	
	(i) does not exceed £5,000, a fee of—	*£50*

Table of Fees

	(ii) exceeds £5,000, a fee of—	*£50 plus 0.3% of the cost in excess of £5,000*
	(b) in respect of a sale, where the proceeds of sale of the securities (including accrued interest, if any) exceed £5,000, a fee of—	*£50 plus 0.3% of the proceeds in excess of £5,000]*

NOTES

Revoked as noted at the beginning of this Order.

Para 1: in definition "the bankruptcy ceiling", sub-para (b) substituted by the Insolvency Proceedings (Fees) (Amendment) Order 2007, SI 2007/521, art 2(1), (6), in relation to bankruptcy orders made on or after 1 April 2007; see art 4(1), (6) thereof at **[2.46]**, and previously read as follows:

"(b) any interest payable by virtue of section 328(4); and";

definitions "excepted bankruptcy" and "excepted winding-up" (omitted) inserted by the Insolvency Proceedings (Fees) (Amendment) Order 2009, SI 2009/645, arts 3, 5; revoked by the Insolvency Proceedings (Fees) (Amendment) Order 2010, SI 2010/732, art 7, in respect of bankruptcy and winding-up orders made on or after 6th April 2010; see art 8(1), (5) thereof at **[2.85]**; and originally read as follows:

"["excepted bankruptcy" means a bankruptcy where the bankruptcy order was made on or before 31st March 2005; "excepted winding-up" means a winding up by the court of a company where the winding up order was made on or before 31st March 2005;]".

Para 1(2)(b): substituted by the Insolvency Proceedings Fees (Amendment) Order 2005, SI 2005/544, arts 3, 4, 6, in relation to any case where a winding-up or a bankruptcy order is made on or after 1 April 2005, and originally read as follows:

"(b) does not include anything done by the official receiver—

(i) in connection with the appointment of agents for the purposes of, or in connection with, the realisation of assets or

(ii) anything done in connection with or, for the purposes of, distributing assets to creditors.".

Para 2: the Table of Fees is amended as follows:

sum in square brackets in entry relating to fee IVA1 substituted for sum "£10" by the Insolvency Proceedings (Fees) (Amendment) Order 2009, SI 2009/645, arts 3, 6(1), (2), subject to transitional provisions in art 7(1), (6) thereof at **[2.67]** (the previous sum of "£10" was substituted for sum "£15" (as previously substituted by the Insolvency Proceedings (Fees) (Amendment) Order 2006, SI 2006/561, art 2(1), (4), subject to transitional provisions in art 6(3) thereof at **[2.39]**) by the Insolvency Proceedings (Fees) (Amendment) Order 2007, SI 2007/521, art 2(1), (7)(a), subject to transitional provisions in art 4(1), (7) thereof at **[2.46]**);

entry relating to fee BAF1 inserted by the Insolvency Proceedings (Fees) (Amendment) Order 2016, SI 2016/184, arts 2, 6;

entry relating to fee B1 substituted by SI 2007/521, art 2(1), (7)(b), in relation to bankruptcy orders made on or after 1 April 2007; see art 4(1), (8) thereof at **[2.46]**; sum in square brackets substituted for previous sum "£1,850" by the Insolvency Proceedings (Fees) (Amendment) Order 2015, SI 2015/1819, arts 3(1), (2), 4(2), in respect of bankruptcy and winding-up orders made on or after 16 November 2015. The previous sum "£1,850" was substituted for the sum "£1,715" by the Insolvency Proceedings (Fees) (Amendment) Order 2014, SI 2014/583, arts 3(1), (2), 4, in relation to petitions presented on or after 6 April 2014;

entry relating to fee B2 substituted by SI 2010/732, arts 3, 6(1), (3), in respect of bankruptcy and winding-up orders made on or after 6 April 2010;

in entry relating to fee B2, percentages in first and second square brackets substituted for percentages "100%" and "75%" respectively, by SI 2015/1819, arts 3(1), (4), 4(2), in respect of bankruptcy and winding-up orders made on or after 16 November 2015;

entry relating to fee DR01 inserted by SI 2009/645, arts 3, 6(1), (4);

entries relating to fees W1 and W1A substituted for entry relating to fee W1 by SI 2014/583, arts 3(1), (3), 4, in relation to petitions presented on or after 6 April 2014, and entry relating to fee W1 previously (as amended by SI 2010/732, arts 3, 6(1), (2)) read as follows:

"W1 **[Winding up by the court—official receiver's administration fee**

For the performance by the official receiver of his general duties as official receiver on the making of a winding-up order, including his duty to investigate and report upon the affairs of bodies in liquidation, there shall be payable a fee of— [£2,235]]";

in entry relating to fee W1, sum in square brackets substituted for sum "£2,400" by SI 2015/1819, arts 3(1), (3), 4(2), in respect of bankruptcy and winding-up orders made on or after 16 November 2015.

Entry relating to fee W2 substituted by SI 2010/732, arts 3, 6(1), (4), in respect of bankruptcy and winding-up orders made on or after 6 April 2010. Entry relating to fee W2 (as amended by SI 2008/714, art 2(1), (4)(c), subject to transitional provisions in art 3(1), (4), (5) thereof at **[2.48]**, and by SI 2009/645, arts 3, 6(1), (5)) previously read as follows:

"W2 **Winding up by the court—Secretary of State's administration fee**

For the performance by the Secretary of State of her general duties under the insolvency legislation in relation to the administration of the affairs of each company which is being wound up by the court, there shall be payable a fee (up to a maximum of [£80,000]) calculated as a percentage of total chargeable receipts relating to the company (but ignoring the first £2000 [and receipts which on or after 6th April 2009 relate to an excepted winding up]) at the rate of— 17%

in entry relating to fee W2, percentages in first and second square brackets substituted for percentages "100%" and "75%" respectively, by SI 2015/1819, arts 3(1), (4), 4(2), in respect of bankruptcy and winding-up orders made on or after 16 November 2015.

Entry relating to fee INV1 substituted by SI 2009/645, arts 3, 6(1), (6), subject to transitional provisions in art 7(1), (7) thereof at **[2.67]** and previously read as follows:

"INV1 **Investment fee—all cases**

Each request made by a trustee in bankruptcy or a liquidator in a compulsory or a voluntary winding up for the purchase of any government securities shall be accompanied by a fee of— £50".

INSOLVENCY PROCEEDINGS (FEES) ORDER 2016

(SI 2016/692)

NOTES

Made: 29 June 2016.
Authority: Insolvency Act 1986, ss 414, 415.
Commencement: 21 July 2016.

[8.82]

1 Citation and commencement

This Order may be cited as the Insolvency Proceedings (Fees) Order 2016 and comes into force twenty-one days after the day on which it is laid.

NOTES

Commencement: 21 July 2016.

[8.83]

2 Interpretation

In this Order—

"the Act" means the Insolvency Act 1986;

"chargeable receipts" means the sums which are paid into the Insolvency Services Account after deducting any amounts which are paid out to secured creditors or paid out in carrying on the business of the bankrupt or the company;

"the commencement date" means the date this Order comes into force;

"deposit" means—

(a) on the making of a bankruptcy application, the sum of £550,
(b) on the presentation of a bankruptcy petition, the sum of £990,
(c) on the presentation of a winding up petition, other than a petition presented under section 124A of the Act, the sum of £1,600,
(d) on the presentation of a winding-up petition under section 124A of the Act, the sum of £5,000;

"official receiver's administration fee" means the fee payable to the official receiver on the making of a bankruptcy or winding up order out of the chargeable receipts of the estate of the bankrupt or, as the case may be, the assets of the insolvent company for the performance of the official receiver's functions under the Act.

NOTES

Commencement: 21 July 2016.

[8.84]

3 Fees payable in connection with individual voluntary arrangements, debt relief orders and bankruptcy and winding up

The fees payable to the Secretary of State in respect of the matters specified in column 1 of the Table of Fees in Schedule 1 (Fees payable in insolvency proceedings) are the fees specified in column 2 to that Table.

NOTES

Commencement: 21 July 2016.

[8.85]

4 Deposit

(1) On the making of a bankruptcy application, the debtor will pay a deposit to the adjudicator as security for the payment of the official receiver's administration fee.

(2) On the presentation of a bankruptcy petition or a winding-up petition, the petitioner will pay a deposit to the court as security for the payment of the official receiver's administration fee.

(3) Where a deposit is paid to the court, the court will transmit the deposit paid to the official receiver attached to the court.

(4) The deposit will be used to discharge the official receiver's administration fee to the extent that the assets comprised in the estate of the bankrupt or, as the case may be, the assets of the company are insufficient to discharge the official receiver's administration fee.

(5) Where a bankruptcy order or a winding up order is made (including any case where a bankruptcy order or a winding up is subsequently annulled, rescinded or recalled), the deposit will be returned to the person who paid it save to the extent that the assets comprised in the estate of the bankrupt or, as the case may be, the assets of the company are insufficient to discharge the official receiver's administration fee.

(6) The deposit will be repaid to the debtor where—

(a) the adjudicator has refused to make a bankruptcy order,
(b) 14 days have elapsed from the date of delivery of the notice of refusal, and
(c) the debtor has not made a request to the adjudicator to review the decision.

(7) Where the debtor has made a request to the adjudicator to review the decision to refuse to make a bankruptcy order the deposit will be repaid to the debtor where—

(a) the adjudicator has confirmed the refusal to make a bankruptcy order,
(b) 28 days have elapsed from the date of delivery of the confirmation of the notice of refusal, and
(c) the debtor has not appealed to the court against the refusal to make a bankruptcy order.

(8) Where the debtor has appealed to the court against the refusal to make a bankruptcy order the deposit will be repaid to the debtor where the appeal is dismissed or withdrawn.

(9) Where—

(a) a deposit was paid by the petitioner to the court, and
(b) the petition is withdrawn or dismissed by the court

that deposit, less an administration fee of £50, will be repaid to the petitioner.

NOTES

Commencement: 21 July 2016.

[8.86]

5 Value Added Tax

Where Value Added Tax is chargeable in respect of the provision of a service for which a fee is payable by virtue of any provision of this Order, Value Added Tax must be paid on that fee.

NOTES

Commencement: 21 July 2016.

[8.87]

6 Revocation

The enactments listed in Schedule 2 are revoked.

NOTES

Commencement: 21 July 2016.

[8.88]

7 Transitional and saving provisions

(1) This Order has no effect in respect of any fees payable in respect of—

(a) the preparation and submission of a report under section 274 (action on report of insolvency practitioner) of the Act; and
(b) bankruptcy orders and winding-up orders made following the making of a bankruptcy application or presentation of a petition before the commencement date.

(2) This Order has no effect in respect of any deposit paid on the making of a bankruptcy application or the presentation of a petition for bankruptcy or winding up before the commencement date.

NOTES

Commencement: 21 July 2016.

SCHEDULE 1
FEES PAYABLE IN INSOLVENCY PROCEEDINGS

Article 3

[8.89]
Table of Fees

Description of fee and circumstances in which it is charged	*Amount of fee or applicable %*
Individual voluntary arrangement registration fee On the registration by the Secretary of State of an individual voluntary arrangement made under Part 8 of the Act, the fee of—	£15
Application for a debt relief order—official receiver's administration fee and costs of persons acting as approved intermediaries On the application for a debt relief order, for the performance of the official receiver's functions and for the payment of an amount not exceeding £10 in respect of the costs of persons acting as approved intermediaries under Part 7A of the Act, the fee of—	£90
Application for a bankruptcy order—adjudicator's administration fee On the application to the adjudicator for a bankruptcy order, for the performance of the adjudicator functions, the fee of—	£130
Bankruptcy—official receiver's administration fee following debtor's application On the making of a bankruptcy order on a debtor's application, for the performance of the official receiver's duties as official receiver the fee of—	£1,990
Bankruptcy—official receiver's administration fee following creditor's petition On the making of a bankruptcy order on a creditor's petition, for the performance of the official receiver's duties as official receiver the fee of—	£2,775
Bankruptcy—trustee in bankruptcy fee For the performance of the official receiver's duties while acting as trustee in bankruptcy of the bankrupt's estate a fee calculated as a percentage of chargeable receipts realised by the official receiver in the capacity of trustee in bankruptcy at the rate of—	15%
Bankruptcy—income payments agreement fee On entering into an income payments agreement with the official receiver under section 310A of the Act, the fee of—	£150
Bankruptcy—income payments order fee On the making of an income payments order by the court under section 310 of the Act, the fee of—	£150
Winding up by the court other than a winding up on a petition presented under section 124A—official receiver's administration fee On the making of a winding-up order, other than on a petition presented under section 124A, for the performance of the official receiver's duties as official receiver, including the duty to investigate and report on the affairs of bodies in liquidation, the fee of—	£5,000
Winding up by the court on a petition presented under section 124A—official receiver's administration fee On the making of a winding-up order on a petition presented under section 124A, for the performance of the official receiver's duties as official receiver, including the duty to investigate and report on the affairs of bodies in liquidation, the fee of—	£7,500
Winding up—liquidator fee For the performance of the official receiver's duties while acting as liquidator of the insolvent estate a fee calculated as a percentage of chargeable receipts realised by the official receiver in the capacity of liquidator at the rate of—	15%

Official receiver's general fee On the making of a bankruptcy order or the making of a winding up order by the court for the costs not recovered out of the official receiver's administration fee of administering— (a) bankruptcy orders, (b) winding up orders made by the court the fee of—	£6,000

NOTES

Commencement: 21 July 2016.

SCHEDULE 2

(Sch 2 lists the instruments revoked by art 6; SI 2004/593 and the amending SI 2005/544, SI 2006/561, SI 2007/521, SI 2008/714, SI 2009/645, SI 2010/732, SI 2011/1167, SI 2014/583, SI 2015/1819, SI 2016/184, are revoked.)

ALTERATION OF JUDICIAL TITLES (REGISTRAR IN BANKRUPTCY OF THE HIGH COURT) ORDER 2018

(SI 2018/130)

NOTES

Made: 31 January 2018.
Authority: Courts Act 2003, s 64.
Commencement: 26 February 2018.

[8.90]
1 Citation and commencement

This Order may be cited as the Alteration of Judicial Titles (Registrar in Bankruptcy of the High Court) Order 2018 and comes into force on 26th February 2018.

NOTES

Commencement: 26 February 2018.

[8.91]
2 Alteration of judicial titles

(1) The name of the office of "Registrar in Bankruptcy of the High Court" is changed to "Insolvency and Companies Court Judge".

(2) A person appointed to act as a deputy or as a temporary additional officer for a person holding the office referred to in paragraph (1) is to be styled as a "Deputy Insolvency and Companies Court Judge".

NOTES

Commencement: 26 February 2018.

[8.92]
3 Amendments consequential on article 2

The Schedule, which makes provision in consequence of article 2, has effect.

NOTES

Commencement: 26 February 2018.

SCHEDULE

(The Schedule contains amendments to primary and secondary legislation; in so far as they are relevant to this work they have been incorporated at the appropriate place.)

Official receiver's general fee On the making of a bankruptcy order or the making of a winding-up order by the court for the costs not recovered out of the official receiver's administration fee of administering— (a) bankruptcy orders; (b) winding-up orders made by the court the fee of—	£6,000

Made: 1 February 2018.

[5.90]

[5.91]

[5.92]

PART 9
STATUTORY INSTRUMENTS RELATING TO CORPORATE INSOLVENCY—ENGLAND AND WALES

FINANCIAL MARKETS AND INSOLVENCY REGULATIONS 1991

(SI 1991/880)

NOTES

Made: 27 March 1991.

Authority: Companies Act 1989, ss 155(4), (5), 158(4), (5), 160(5), 173(4), (5), 174(2)–(4), 185, 186, 187(3).

Commencement: 25 April 1991.

Modification: these Regulations are applied, with modifications, in so far as they relate to bank insolvency or administration under the Banking Act 2009, Pts 2, 3, by the Banking Act 2009 (Parts 2 and 3 Consequential Amendments) Order 2009, SI 2009/317, art 3, Schedule at **[7.86]**, **[7.92]**.

ARRANGEMENT OF REGULATIONS

PART I
GENERAL

1 Citation and commencement . . . [9.1]
2 Interpretation: general . . . [9.2]

PART V
MARKET CHARGES

7 Interpretation of Part V . . . [9.3]
8 Charges on land or any interest in land not to be treated as market charges . . . [9.4]
10 Extent to which charge granted in favour of recognised investment exchange to be treated as market charge . . . [9.5]
11 Extent to which charge granted in favour of recognised clearing house to be treated as market charge . . . [9.6]
11A Extent to which charge granted in favour of recognised CSD to be treated as market charge . . . [9.7]
12 Circumstances in which CGO Service charge to be treated as market charge . . . [9.8]
13 Extent to which CGO Service charge to be treated as market charge . . . [9.9]
14 Limitation on disapplication of moratorium on certain legal processes under Schedule B1 to the Insolvency Act 1986 (administration) in relation to CGO Service charges . . . [9.10]
15 Ability of administrator or receiver to recover assets in case of property subject to CGO Service charge or Talisman charge . . . [9.11]

PART VI
CONSTRUCTION OF REFERENCES TO PARTIES TO MARKET CONTRACTS

16 Circumstances in which member or designated non-member dealing as principal to be treated as acting in different capacities . . . [9.12]

PART VIII
LEGAL PROCEEDINGS

19 Court having jurisdiction in respect of proceedings under Part VII of the Act . . . [9.13]

PART I
GENERAL

[9.1]

1 Citation and commencement

These Regulations may be cited as the Financial Markets and Insolvency Regulations 1991 and shall come into force on 25th April 1991.

[9.2]

2 Interpretation: general

(1) In these Regulations "the Act" means the Companies Act 1989.

[(1A) In these Regulations "the Recognition Requirements Regulations" means the Financial Services and Markets Act 2000 (Recognition Requirements for Investment Exchanges[, Clearing Houses and Central Securities Depositories]) Regulations 2001.]

(2) A reference in any of these Regulations to a numbered regulation shall be construed as a reference to the regulation bearing that number in these Regulations.

(3) A reference in any of these Regulations to a numbered paragraph shall, unless the reference is to a paragraph of a specified regulation, be construed as a reference to the paragraph bearing that number in the regulation in which the reference is made.

NOTES

Para (1A): inserted by the Financial Markets and Insolvency Regulations 2009, SI 2009/853, reg 3(1), (2); words in square brackets substituted by the Central Securities Depositories Regulations 2017, SI 2017/1064, reg 10, Schedule, para 20(1), (2) (for transitional provisions and savings see regs 6–9 of the 2017 Regulations).

3–6 *(Reg 3 (Pt II) amends the Companies Act 1989, s 155(2) at* **[17.58]**; *regs 4, 5 (Pt III) amend the Companies Act 1989, ss 159, 160 at* **[17.62]**, **[17.63]**; *reg 6 (Pt IV) amends the Companies Act 1989, s 162 at* **[17.65]**.)

PART V
MARKET CHARGES

[9.3]

7 Interpretation of Part V

In this Part of these Regulations, unless the context otherwise requires—

"the Bank" means the Bank of England;

"business day" has the same meaning as in section 167(3) of the Act;

. . .

"CGO Service" means the computer-based system established by the Bank and The Stock Exchange to facilitate the transfer of specified securities;

"CGO Service charge" means a charge of the kind described in section 173(1)(c) of the Act;

"CGO Service member" means a person who is entitled by contract with [CRESTCo Limited (which is now responsible for operating the CGO Service)] to use the CGO Service;

["clearing member" has the same meaning as in section 190(1) of the Act;

"client" has the same meaning as in section 190(1) of the Act;]

["default fund contribution" has the same meaning as in section 188(3A) of the Act;]

["EEA CSD" has the same meaning as in section 190(1) of the Act;]

"former CGO Service member" means a person whose entitlement . . . to use the CGO Service has been terminated or suspended;

["indirect client" has the same meaning as in section 190(1) of the Act;]

"market charge" means a charge which is a market charge for the purposes of Part VII of the Act;

["recognised body" has the same meaning as in section 190(1) of the Act;]

["recognised central counterparty" has the same meaning as in section 190(1) of the Act;]

["recognised CSD" has the same meaning as in section 190(1) of the Act;]

"settlement bank" means a person who has agreed under a contract with [CRESTCo Limited (which is now responsible for operating the CGO Service)] to make payments of the kind mentioned in section 173(1)(c) of the Act;

"specified securities" has the meaning given in section 173(3) of the Act;

"Talisman" means The Stock Exchange settlement system known as Talisman;

"Talisman charge" means a charge granted in favour of The Stock Exchange over property credited to an account within Talisman maintained in the name of the chargor in respect of certain property beneficially owned by the chargor; . . .

["third country CSD" has the same meaning as in section 190(1) of the Act; and]

"transfer" when used in relation to specified securities has the meaning given in section 173(3) of the Act.

NOTES

Definition "CGO" (omitted) revoked, words in square brackets in definitions "CGO Service member" and "settlement bank" substituted, and words omitted from definition "former CGO Service member" revoked, by the Financial Markets and Insolvency (CGO Service) Regulations 1999, SI 1999/1209, reg 3(1).

Definitions "clearing member", "client", "indirect client", and "recognised central counterparty" inserted by the Financial Services and Markets Act 2000 (Over the Counter Derivatives, Central Counterparties and Trade Repositories) Regulations 2013, SI 2013/504, reg 30(1), (2).

Definition "default fund contribution" inserted by the Financial Markets and Insolvency Regulations 2009, SI 2009/853, reg 3(1), (3).

Definitions "EEA CSD", "recognised body", "recognised CSD", and "third country CSD" inserted, and word omitted from the definition "Talisman Charge" revoked, by the Central Securities Depositories Regulations 2017, SI 2017/1064, reg 10, Schedule, para 20(1), (3) (for transitional provisions and savings see regs 6–9 of the 2017 Regulations).

[9.4]

8 Charges on land or any interest in land not to be treated as market charges

(1) No charge, whether fixed or floating, shall be treated as a market charge to the extent that it is a charge on land or any interest in land.

(2) For the purposes of paragraph (1), a charge on a debenture forming part of an issue or series shall not be treated as a charge on land or any interest in land by reason of the fact that the debenture is secured by a charge on land or any interest in land.

9 (*Amends the Companies Act 1989, s 173 at* **[17.76]**.)

[9.5]

10 Extent to which charge granted in favour of recognised investment exchange to be treated as market charge

(1) A charge granted in favour of a recognised investment exchange other than The Stock Exchange shall be treated as a market charge only to the extent that—

(a) it is a charge over property provided as margin in respect of market contracts entered into by the exchange for the purposes of or in connection with the provision of clearing services [or over property provided as a default fund contribution to the exchange];

(b) in the case of a recognised UK investment exchange, it secures the obligation to pay to the exchange [any sum due to the exchange from a member or designated non-member of the exchange or from a recognised clearing house [or from a recognised CSD] or from another recognised investment exchange in respect of unsettled market contracts to which the member, designated non-member [or recognised body] is a party under the rules referred to in paragraph 12 of the Schedule to the Recognition Requirements Regulations]; and

(c) in the case of a recognised overseas investment exchange, it secures the obligation to reimburse the cost (other than fees and other incidental expenses) incurred by the exchange in settling unsettled market contracts in respect of which the charged property is provided as margin.

(2) A charge granted in favour of The Stock Exchange shall be treated as a market charge only to the extent that—

(a) it is a charge of the kind described in paragraph (1); or

(b) it is a Talisman charge and secures an obligation of either or both of the kinds mentioned in paragraph (3).

(3) The obligations mentioned in this paragraph are—

(a) the obligation of the chargor to reimburse The Stock Exchange for payments (including stamp duty and taxes but excluding Stock Exchange fees and incidental expenses arising from the operation by The Stock Exchange of settlement arrangements) made by The Stock Exchange in settling, through Talisman, market contracts entered into by the chargor; and

(b) the obligation of the chargor to reimburse The Stock Exchange the amount of any payment it has made pursuant to a short term certificate.

(4) In paragraph (3), "short term certificate" means an instrument issued by The Stock Exchange undertaking to procure the transfer of property of a value and description specified in the instrument to or to the order of the person to whom the instrument is issued or his endorsee or to a person acting on behalf of either of them and also undertaking to make appropriate payments in cash, in the event that the obligation to procure the transfer of property cannot be discharged in whole or in part.

NOTES

Para (1): words in square brackets in sub-para (a) inserted, and words in first (outer) pair of square brackets in sub-para (b) substituted, by the Financial Markets and Insolvency Regulations 2009, SI 2009/853, reg 3(1), (4). Words in second (inner) pair of square brackets in sub-para (b) inserted, and words in third (inner) pair of square brackets substituted, by the Central Securities Depositories Regulations 2017, SI 2017/1064, reg 10, Schedule, para 20(1), (4) (for transitional provisions and savings see regs 6–9 of the 2017 Regulations).

[9.6]

11 Extent to which charge granted in favour of recognised clearing house to be treated as market charge

A charge granted in favour of a recognised clearing house shall be treated as a market charge only to the extent that—

(a) it is a charge over property provided as margin in respect of market contracts entered into by the clearing house [or over property provided as a default fund contribution to the clearing house];

[(aa) in the case of a recognised central counterparty, it secures the obligation to pay to the recognised central counterparty any sum due to it from a clearing member, a client, an indirect client, a recognised investment exchange[, a recognised CSD] or recognised clearing house in respect of unsettled market contracts to which the clearing member, client, indirect client [or recognised body] is a party;]

(b) [in the case of a recognised clearing house which is not a recognised central counterparty], it secures the obligation to pay to the clearing house [any sum due to the clearing house from a member of the clearing house or from a recognised investment exchange [or from a recognised CSD] or from another recognised clearing house in respect of unsettled market contracts to which the member [or recognised body] is a party under the rules referred to in paragraph 25 of the Schedule to the Recognition Requirements Regulations]; and

(c) in the case of a recognised overseas clearing house, it secures the obligation to reimburse the cost (other than fees or other incidental expenses) incurred by the clearing house in settling unsettled market contracts in respect of which the charged property is provided as margin.

NOTES

Words in square brackets in para (a) inserted, and words in second (outer) pair of square brackets in para (b) substituted, by the Financial Markets and Insolvency Regulations 2009, SI 2009/853, reg 3(1), (5).

Para (aa) inserted, and words in first pair of square brackets in para (b) substituted, by the Financial Services and Markets Act 2000 (Over the Counter Derivatives, Central Counterparties and Trade Repositories) Regulations 2013, SI 2013/504, reg 30(1), (3).

Words in first pair of square brackets in para (aa) inserted, words in second pair of square brackets in that sub-paragraph substituted, words in third (inner) pair of square brackets in sub-para (b) inserted, and words in fourth (inner) pair of square brackets substituted, by the Central Securities Depositories Regulations 2017, SI 2017/1064, reg 10, Schedule, para 20(1), (5) (for transitional provisions and savings see regs 6–9 of the 2017 Regulations).

[9.7]

[11A Extent to which charge granted in favour of recognised CSD to be treated as market charge

(1) A charge granted in favour of a recognised CSD shall be treated as a market charge only to the extent that—

(a) it is a charge over property provided as margin in respect of market contracts entered into by the recognised CSD or over property provided as a default fund contribution to the recognised CSD; and

(b) it secures the obligation to pay to the recognised CSD any sum due to it from a member of the recognised CSD or from a recognised clearing house or from a recognised investment exchange or from another recognised CSD in respect of unsettled market contracts to which the member or recognised body is a party.

(2) A charge granted in favour of an EEA CSD or third country CSD shall be treated as a market charge only to the extent that—

(a) it is a charge over property provided as margin in respect of market contracts entered into by the EEA CSD or third country CSD or over property provided as a default fund contribution to the EEA CSD or third country CSD; and

(b) it secures the obligation to reimburse the cost (other than fees or other incidental expenses) incurred by the EEA CSD or third country CSD in settling unsettled market contracts in respect of which the charged property is provided as margin.]

NOTES

Commencement: 28 November 2017.

Inserted by the Central Securities Depositories Regulations 2017, SI 2017/1064, reg 10, Schedule, para 20(1), (6) (for transitional provisions and savings see regs 6–9 of the 2017 Regulations).

[9.8]

12 Circumstances in which CGO Service charge to be treated as market charge

A CGO Service charge shall be treated as a market charge only if—

(a) it is granted to a settlement bank by a person for the purpose of securing debts or liabilities of the kind mentioned in section 173(1)(c) of the Act incurred by that person through his use of the CGO Service as a CGO Service member; and

(b) it contains provisions which refer expressly to the [CGO Service].

NOTES

Words in square brackets substituted by the Financial Markets and Insolvency (CGO Service) Regulations 1999, SI 1999/1209, reg 3(2).

[9.9]

13 Extent to which CGO Service charge to be treated as market charge

A CGO Service charge shall be treated as a market charge only to the extent that—

(a) it is a charge over any one or more of the following—

(i) specified securities held within the CGO Service to the account of a CGO Service member or a former CGO Service member;

(ii) specified securities which were held as mentioned in sub-paragraph (i) above immediately prior to their being removed from the CGO Service consequent upon the person in question becoming a former CGO Service member;

(iii) sums receivable by a CGO Service member or former CGO Service member representing interest accrued on specified securities held within the CGO Service to his account or which were so held immediately prior to their being removed from the CGO Service consequent upon his becoming a former CGO Service member;

(iv) sums receivable by a CGO Service member or former CGO Service member in respect of the redemption or conversion of specified securities which were held within the CGO Service to his account at the time that the relevant securities were redeemed or converted or which were so held immediately prior to their being removed from the CGO Service consequent upon his becoming a former CGO Service member; and

(v) sums receivable by a CGO Service member or former CGO Service member in respect of the transfer by him of specified securities through the medium of the CGO Service; and

(b) it secures the obligation of a CGO Service member or former CGO Service member to reimburse a settlement bank for the amount due from him to the settlement bank as a result of the settlement bank having discharged or become obliged to discharge payment obligations in respect of transfers or allotments of specified securities made to him through the medium of the CGO Service.

[9.10]

14 [Limitation on disapplication of moratorium on certain legal processes under Schedule B1 to the Insolvency Act 1986 (administration) in relation to CGO Service charges]

(1) In this regulation "qualifying period" means the period beginning with the fifth business day before the day on which [an application] for the making of an administration order in relation to the relevant CGO Service member or former CGO Service member is presented and ending with the second business day after the day on which an administration order is made in relation to the relevant CGO Service member or former CGO Service member pursuant to the petition.

[(1A) A reference in paragraph (1) to an application for an administration order shall be treated as including a reference to—

(a) appointing an administrator under paragraph 14 or 22 of Schedule B1 to the Insolvency Act 1986, or

(b) filing with the court a notice of intention to appoint an administrator under either of those paragraphs,

and a reference to "an administration order" shall include the appointment of an administrator under paragraph 14 or 22 of Schedule B1 to the Insolvency Act 1986.]

(2) [The disapplication of paragraph 43(2) of Schedule B1 to the Insolvency Act 1986 (including that provision as applied by paragraph 44 of that Schedule)] by section 175(1)(a) of the Act shall be limited in respect of a CGO Service charge so that it has effect only to the extent necessary to enable there to be realised, whether through the sale of specified securities or otherwise, a sum equal to whichever is less of the following—

(a) the total amount of payment obligations discharged by the settlement bank in respect of transfers and allotments of specified securities made during the qualifying period to the relevant CGO Service member or former CGO Service member through the medium of the CGO Service less the total amount of payment obligations discharged to the settlement bank in respect of transfers of specified securities made during the qualifying period by the relevant CGO Service member or former CGO Service member through the medium of the CGO Service; and

(b) the amount (if any) described in regulation 13(b) due to the settlement bank from the relevant CGO Service member or former CGO Service member.

NOTES

Regulation heading: substituted for original heading "Limitation on disapplication of sections 10(1)(b) and 11(3)(c) of Insolvency Act 1986 in relation to CGO Service charges" by the Enterprise Act 2002 (Insolvency) Order 2003, SI 2003/2096, arts 5, 6, Schedule, paras 47, 48(a), except in any case where a petition for an administration order was presented before 15 September 2003.

Para (1): words in square brackets substituted for words "a petition" by SI 2003/2096, arts 5, 6, Schedule, paras 47, 48(b), except in any case where a petition for an administration order was presented before 15 September 2003.

Para (1A): inserted by SI 2003/2096, arts 5, 6, Schedule, paras 47, 48(c), except in any case where a petition for an administration order was presented before 15 September 2003.

Para (2): words in square brackets substituted for words "The disapplication of section 10(1)(b) and 11(3)(c) of Insolvency Act 1986" by SI 2003/2096, arts 5, 6, Schedule, paras 47, 48(d), except in any case where a petition for an administration order was presented before 15 September 2003.

[9.11]

15 Ability of administrator or receiver to recover assets in case of property subject to CGO Service charge or Talisman charge

(1) [The disapplication—

(a) by section 175(1)(b) of the Act, of paragraphs 70, 71 and 72 of Schedule B1 to the Insolvency Act 1986, and

(b) by section 175(3) of the Act, of sections 43 and 61 of the 1986 Act,

shall cease to have effect] in respect of a charge which is either a CGO Service charge or a Talisman charge after the end of the second business day after the day on which an administration order is made or, as the case may be, an administrative receiver or a receiver is appointed, in relation to the grantor of the charge, in relation to property subject to it which—

(a) in the case of a CGO Service charge, is not, on the basis of a valuation in accordance with paragraph (2), required for the realisation of whichever is the less of the sum referred to in regulation 14(2)(a) and the amount referred to in regulation 14(2)(b) due to the settlement bank at the close of business on the second business day referred to above; and

(b) in the case of a Talisman charge is not, on the basis of a valuation in accordance with paragraph (2), required to enable The Stock Exchange to reimburse itself for any payment it has made of the kind referred to in regulation 10(3).

[(1A) A reference in paragraph (1) to "an administration order" shall include the appointment of an administrator under paragraph 14 or 22 of Schedule B1 to the Insolvency Act 1986.]

(2) For the purposes of paragraph (1) the value of property shall, except in a case falling within paragraph (3), be such as may be agreed between whichever is relevant of the administrator, administrative receiver or receiver on the one hand and the settlement back or The Stock Exchange on the other.

(3) For the purposes of paragraph (1), the value of any investment for which a price for the second business day referred to above is quoted in the Daily Official List of The Stock Exchange shall—

(a) in a case in which two prices are so quoted, be an amount equal to the average of those two prices, adjusted where appropriate to take account of any accrued interest; and

(b) in a case in which one price is so quoted, be an amount equal to that price, adjusted where appropriate to take account of any accrued interest.

NOTES

Para (1): words in square brackets substituted for words "The disapplication of sections 15(1) and (2), 43 and 61 of the Insolvency Act 1986 by section 175(1)(b) and 175(3) of the Act shall cease to have effect" by the Enterprise Act 2002 (Insolvency) Order 2003, SI 2003/2096, arts 5, 6, Schedule, paras 47, 49(a), except in any case where a petition for an administration order was presented before 15 September 2003.

Para (1A): inserted by SI 2003/2096, arts 5, 6, Schedule, paras 47, 49(b), except in any case where a petition for an administration order was presented before 15 September 2003.

PART VI
CONSTRUCTION OF REFERENCES TO PARTIES TO MARKET CONTRACTS

[9.12]

16 Circumstances in which member or designated non-member dealing as principal to be treated as acting in different capacities

(1) In this regulation "relevant transaction" means—

[(a) a market contract, effected as principal by a member or designated non-member of a recognised investment exchange or a member of a recognised clearing house [or a member of a recognised CSD], in relation to which money received by the member or designated non-member is—

(i) clients' money for the purposes of rules relating to clients' money, or

(ii) would be clients' money for the purposes of those rules were it not money which, in accordance with those rules, may be regarded as immediately due and payable to the member or designated non-member for its own account; and]

(b) a market contract which would be regarded as a relevant transaction by virtue of sub-paragraph (a) above were it not for the fact that no money is received by the member or designated non-member in relation to the contract

[(1A) In addition "relevant transaction" means a market contract entered into by a recognised clearing house effected as principal in relation to which money is received by the recognised clearing house from a recognised investment exchange [or from a recognised CSD] or from another recognised clearing house.

(1B) In addition "relevant transaction" means a market contract entered into by a recognised investment exchange effected as principal in relation to which money is received by the recognised investment exchange from a recognised clearing house [or from a recognised CSD] or from another recognised investment exchange.

[(1BA) In addition "relevant transaction" means a market contract entered into by a recognised CSD effected as principal in relation to which money is received by the recognised CSD from a recognised clearing house or from a recognised investment exchange or from another recognised CSD.]

[(1C) Where paragraph (1A), (1B) or (1BA) applies, paragraph (1) applies to the recognised clearing house, recognised investment exchange or recognised CSD as it does to a member of the recognised clearing house, recognised investment exchange or recognised CSD, and as if the recognised clearing house, recognised investment exchange or recognised CSD were subject to the rules referred to in paragraph (1)(a)(i).]

[(1D) In paragraph (1), "rules relating to clients' money" are rules made by the Financial Conduct Authority under sections 137A and 137B of the Financial Services and Markets Act 2000.]]

[(2) For the purposes of section 187(1) of the Act (construction of references to parties to market contracts)—

(a) a recognised investment exchange or a member or designated non-member of a recognised investment exchange, . . .

(b) a recognised clearing house or a member of a recognised clearing house, [or

(c) a recognised CSD or a member of a recognised CSD].

shall be treated as effecting relevant transactions in a different capacity from other market contracts it has effected as principal.]

[(3), (4) . . .]

NOTES

Para (1): sub-para (a) substituted by the Financial Markets and Insolvency Regulations 2009, SI 2009/853, reg 3(1), (6)(a). Words in square brackets in sub-para (a) inserted by the Central Securities Depositories Regulations 2017, SI 2017/1064, reg 10, Schedule, para 20(1), (7)(a) (for transitional provisions and savings see regs 6–9 of the 2017 Regulations).

Paras (1A), (1B), (1C), (1D): inserted by SI 2009/853, reg 3(1), (6)(b). Words in square brackets in paras (1A), (1B) inserted, and para (1C) substituted, by SI 2017/1064, reg 10, Schedule, para 20(1), (7)(b), (c), (e) (for transitional provisions and savings see regs 6–9 of the 2017 Regulations). Para (1D) subsequently substituted by the Financial Services Act 2012 (Consequential Amendments and Transitional Provisions) Order 2013, SI 2013/472, art 3, Sch 2, para 9.

Para (1BA): inserted by SI 2017/1064, reg 10, Schedule, para 20(1), (7)(d) (for transitional provisions and savings see regs 6–9 of the 2017 Regulations).

Para (2): substituted by SI 2009/853, reg 3(1), (6)(c). Word omitted from sub-para (a) revoked, and sub-para (c) (and the preceding word) inserted, by SI 2017/1064, reg 10, Schedule, para 20(1), (7)(f) (for transitional provisions and savings see regs 6–9 of the 2017 Regulations).

Paras (3), (4): originally added by the Financial Services and Markets Act 2000 (Consequential Amendments and Repeals) Order 2001, SI 2001/3649, art 415(1), (3), and subsequently revoked by SI 2009/853, reg 3(1), (6)(d).

17 *((Pt VII) amends the Companies Act 1989, Sch 21.)*

PART VIII
LEGAL PROCEEDINGS

18 (*Amends the Companies Act 1989, s 175(2) at* **[17.78]**.)

[9.13]

19 Court having jurisdiction in respect of proceedings under Part VII of Act

(1) For the purposes of sections 161, 163, 164, 175(5) and 182 of the Act (various legal proceedings under Part VII of Act) "the court" shall be the court which has last heard an application in the proceedings under the Insolvency Act 1986 or the Bankruptcy (Scotland) Act 1985 in which the relevant office-holder is acting or, as the case may be, any court having jurisdiction to hear applications in those proceedings.

(2) For the purposes of subsection (2) [and (2A)] of section 175 of the Act (administration orders etc), "the court" shall be the court which has made the administration order or, as the case may be, to which the [application] for an administration order has been presented [or the notice of intention to appoint has been filed].

(3) The rules regulating the practice and procedure of the court in relation to applications to the court in England and Wales under sections 161, 163, 164, 175 and 182 of the Act shall be the rules applying in relation to applications to that court under the Insolvency Act 1986.

NOTES

Para (2): words in first pair of square brackets inserted, word in second pair of square brackets substituted for word "petition", and words in third pair of square brackets added, by the Enterprise Act 2002 (Insolvency) Order 2003, SI 2003/2096, arts 5, 6, Schedule, paras 47, 50, except in any case where a petition for an administration order was presented before 15 September 2003.

FINANCIAL MARKETS AND INSOLVENCY REGULATIONS 1996

(SI 1996/1469)

NOTES

Made: 5 June 1996.

Authority: Companies Act 1989, ss 185, 186.

Commencement: 15 July 1996.

Modification: these Regulations are applied, with modifications, in so far as they relate to bank insolvency or administration under the Banking Act 2009, Pts 2, 3, by the Banking Act 2009 (Parts 2 and 3 Consequential Amendments) Order 2009, SI 2009/317, art 3, Schedule at **[7.86]**, **[7.92]**.

ARRANGEMENT OF REGULATIONS

PART I
GENERAL

1 Citation and commencement . . . [9.14]
2 Interpretation . . . [9.15]

PART II
SYSTEM-CHARGES

3 Application of Part VII of the Act in relation to system-charges . . . [9.16]
4 Circumstances in which Part VII applies in relation to system-charge . . . [9.17]
5 Extent to which Part VII applies to a system-charge . . . [9.18]
6 Limitation on disapplication of moratorium on certain legal processes under Schedule B1 to the Insolvency Act 1986 (administration) in relation to system-charges . . . [9.19]
7 Limitation on disapplication of moratorium on certain legal processes under Schedule B1 to the Insolvency Act 1986 (administration) in relation to system-charges granted by a system-beneficiary . . . [9.20]
8 Ability of administrator or receiver to recover assets in case of property subject to system-charge . . . [9.21]

PART I
GENERAL

[9.14]

1 Citation and commencement

These Regulations may be cited as the Financial Markets and Insolvency Regulations 1996 and shall come into force on 15th July 1996.

[9.15]

2 Interpretation

(1) In these Regulations—

"the Act" means the Companies Act 1989;

"business day" means any day which is not a Saturday or Sunday, Christmas Day, Good Friday or a bank holiday in any part of the United Kingdom under the Banking and Financial Dealings Act 1971;

"issue", in relation to an uncertificated unit of a security, means to confer on a person title to a new unit;

"register of securities"—

(a) in relation to shares, means a register of members; and

(b) in relation to units of a security other than shares, means [a register, whether maintained by virtue of the Uncertificated Securities Regulations 2001 or otherwise], of persons holding the units;

"relevant nominee" means a system-member who is a subsidiary undertaking of the Operator designated by him as such in accordance with such rules and practices as are mentioned in [paragraph 25(f) of Schedule 1 to the Uncertificated Securities Regulations 2001];

"settlement bank" means a person who has contracted with an Operator to make payments in connection with transfers, by means of a relevant system, of title to uncertificated units of a security and of interests of system-beneficiaries in relation to such units;

"system-beneficiary" means a person on whose behalf a system-member or former system-member holds or held uncertificated units of a security;

"system-charge" means a charge of a kind to which regulation 3(2) applies;

"system-member" means a person who is permitted by an Operator to transfer by means of a relevant system title to uncertificated units of a security held by him; and "former system-member" means a person whose participation in the relevant system is terminated or suspended;

"transfer", in relation to title to uncertificated units of a security, means [the registration of a transfer of title to those units in the relevant Operator register of securities;] and in relation to an interest of a system-beneficiary in relation to uncertificated units of a security, means the transfer of the interest to another system-beneficiary by means of a relevant system; and

other expressions used in these Regulations which are also used in [the Uncertificated Securities Regulations 2001] have the same meanings as in those Regulations.

(2) For the purposes of these Regulations, a person holds a unit of a security if—

(a) in the case of an uncertificated unit, he is entered on a register of securities in relation to the unit in accordance with [regulation 20, 21 or 22 of the Uncertificated Securities Regulations 2001]; and

(b) in the case of a certificated unit, he has title to the unit.

(3) A reference in any of these Regulations to a numbered regulation shall be construed as a reference to the regulation bearing that number in these Regulations.

(4) A reference in any of these Regulations to a numbered paragraph shall, unless the reference is to a paragraph of a specified regulation, be construed as a reference to the paragraph bearing that number in the regulation in which the reference is made.

NOTES

Para (1): words in square brackets substituted, and definition "the 1995 Regulations" (omitted) revoked, by the Uncertificated Securities Regulations 2001, SI 2001/3755, reg 51, Sch 7, Pt 2, para 20(a).

Para (2): words in square brackets substituted by SI 2001/3755, reg 51, Sch 7, Pt 2, para 20(b).

PART II
SYSTEM-CHARGES

[9.16]

3 Application of Part VII of the Act in relation to system-charges

(1) Subject to the provisions of these Regulations, Part VII of the Act shall apply in relation to—

(a) a charge to which paragraph (2) applies ("a system-charge") and any action taken to enforce such a charge; and

(b) any property subject to a system-charge,

in the same way as it applies in relation to a market charge, any action taken to enforce a market charge and any property subject to a market charge.

(2) This paragraph applies in relation to a charge granted in favour of a settlement bank for the purpose of securing debts or liabilities arising in connection with any of the following—

(a) a transfer of uncertificated units of a security to a system-member by means of a relevant system whether the system-member is acting for himself or on behalf of a system-beneficiary;

(b) a transfer, by one system-beneficiary to another and by means of a relevant system, of his interests in relation to uncertificated units of a security held by a relevant nominee where the relevant nominee will continue to hold the units;

(c) an agreement to make a transfer of the kind specified in paragraph (a);

(d) an agreement to make a transfer of the kind specified in paragraph (b); and

(e) an issue of uncertificated units of a security to a system-member by means of a relevant system whether the system-member is acting for himself or on behalf of a system-beneficiary.

(3) In its application, by virtue of these Regulations, in relation to a system-charge, section 173(2) of the Act shall have effect as if the references to "purposes specified" and "specified purposes" were references to any one or more of the purposes specified in paragraph (2).

[9.17]

4 Circumstances in which Part VII applies in relation to system-charge

(1) Part VII of the Act shall apply in relation to a system-charge granted by a system-member and in relation to property subject to such a charge only if—

(a) it is granted to a settlement bank by a system-member for the purpose of securing debts or liabilities arising in connection with any of the transactions specified in regulation 3(2), being debts or liabilities incurred by that system-member or by a system-beneficiary on whose behalf he holds uncertificated units of a security; and

(b) it contains provisions which refer expressly to the relevant system in relation to which the grantor is a system-member.

(2) Part VII of the Act shall apply in relation to a system-charge granted by a system-beneficiary and in relation to property subject to such a charge only if—

(a) it is granted to a settlement bank by a system-beneficiary for the purpose of securing debts or liabilities arising in connection with any of the transactions specified in regulation 3(2), incurred by that system-beneficiary or by a system-member who holds uncertificated units of a security on his behalf; and

(b) it contains provisions which refer expressly to the relevant system in relation to which the system-member who holds the uncertificated units of a security in relation to which the system-beneficiary has the interest is a system-member.

[9.18]

5 Extent to which Part VII applies to a system-charge

Part VII of the Act shall apply in relation to a system-charge only to the extent that—

(a) it is a charge over any one or more of the following—

(i) uncertificated units of a security held by a system-member or a former system-member;

(ii) interests of a kind specified in [regulation 31(2)(b) or 31(4)(b) of the Uncertificated Securities Regulations 2001] in uncertificated units of a security in favour of a system member or a former system-member;

(iii) interests of a system-beneficiary in relation to uncertificated units of a security;

(iv) units of a security which are no longer in uncertificated form because the person holding the units has become a former system-member;

(v) sums or other benefits receivable by a system-member or former system-member by reason of his holding uncertificated units of a security, or units which are no longer in uncertificated form because the person holding the units has become a former system-member;

(vi) sums or other benefits receivable by a system-beneficiary by reason of his having an interest in relation to uncertificated units of a security or in relation to units which are no longer in uncertificated form because the person holding the units has become a former system-member;

(vii) sums or other benefits receivable by a system-member or former system-member by way of repayment, bonus, preference, redemption, conversion or accruing or offered in respect of uncertificated units of a security, or units which are no longer in uncertificated form because the person holding the units has become a former system-member;

(viii) sums or other benefits receivable by a system-beneficiary by way of repayment, bonus, preference, redemption, conversion or accruing or offered in respect of uncertificated units of a security in relation to which he has an interest or in respect of units in relation to which the system-beneficiary has an interest and which are no longer in uncertificated form because the person holding the units has become a former system-member;

(ix) sums or other benefits receivable by a system-member or former system-member in respect of the transfer of uncertificated units of a security by or to him by means of a relevant system;

(x) sums or other benefits receivable by a system-member or former system-member in respect of an agreement to transfer uncertificated units of a security by or to him by means of a relevant system;

(xi) sums or other benefits receivable by a system-beneficiary in respect of the transfer of the interest of a system-beneficiary in relation to uncertificated units of a security by or to him by means of a relevant system or in respect of the transfer of uncertificated units of a security by or to a system-member acting on his behalf by means of a relevant system;

(xii) sums or other benefits receivable by a system-beneficiary in respect of an agreement to transfer the interest of a system-beneficiary in relation to uncertificated units of a security by or to him by means of a relevant system, or in respect of an agreement to transfer uncertificated units of a security by or to a system-member acting on his behalf by means of a relevant system; and

(b) it secures—

(i) the obligation of a system-member or former system-member to reimburse a settlement bank, being an obligation which arises in connection with any of the transactions specified in regulation 3(2) and whether the obligation was incurred by the system-member when acting for himself or when acting on behalf of a system-beneficiary; or

(ii) the obligation of a system-beneficiary to reimburse a settlement bank, being an obligation which arises in connection with any of the transactions specified in regulation 3(2) and whether the obligation was incurred by the system-beneficiary when acting for himself or by reason of a system-member acting on his behalf.

NOTES

Para (a): words in square brackets in sub-para (ii) substituted by the Uncertificated Securities Regulations 2001, SI 2001/3755, reg 51, Sch 7, Pt 2, para 20(c).

[9.19]

6 [Limitation on disapplication of moratorium on certain legal processes under Schedule B1 to the Insolvency Act 1986 (administration) in relation to system-charges]

(1) This regulation applies where an administration order is made in relation to a system-member or former system-member.

[(1A) A reference in paragraph (1) to "an administration order" shall include the appointment of an administrator under paragraph 14 or 22 of Schedule B1 to the Insolvency Act 1986.]

(2) [The disapplication of paragraph 43(2) of Schedule B1 to the Insolvency Act 1986 (including that provision as applied by paragraph 44 of that Schedule)] by section 175(1)(a) of the Act shall have effect, in relation to a system-charge granted by a system-member or former system-member, only to the extent necessary to enable there to be realised, whether through the sale of uncertificated units of a security or otherwise, the lesser of the two sums specified in paragraphs (3) and (4).

(3) The first sum of the two sums referred to in paragraph (2) is the net sum of—

(a) all payment obligations discharged by the settlement bank in connection with—

(i) transfers of uncertificated units of a security by means of a relevant system made during the qualifying period to or by the relevant system-member or former system-member, whether acting for himself or on behalf of a system-beneficiary;

(ii) agreements made during the qualifying period to transfer uncertificated units of a security by means of a relevant system to or from the relevant system-member or former system-member, whether acting for himself or on behalf of a system-beneficiary; and

(iii) issues of uncertificated units of a security by means of a relevant system made during the qualifying period to the relevant system-member or former system-member, whether acting for himself or on behalf of a system-beneficiary; less

(b) all payment obligations discharged to the settlement bank in connection with transactions of any kind described in paragraph (3)(a)(i) and (ii).

(4) The second of the two sums referred to in paragraph (2) is the sum (if any) due to the settlement bank from the relevant system-member or former system-member by reason of an obligation of the kind described in regulation 5(b)(i).

(5) In this regulation and regulation 7, "qualifying period" means the period—

(a) beginning with the fifth business day before the day on which [the application] for the making of the administration order was presented; and

(b) ending with the second business day after the day on which the administration order is made.

[(5A) A reference in paragraph (5) to an application for an administration order shall be treated as including a reference to—

(a) appointing an administrator under [paragraph 14] or 22 of Schedule B1 to the Insolvency Act 1986, or

(b) filing with the court a notice of intention to appoint an administrator under either of those paragraphs,

and a reference to "an administration order" shall include the appointment of an administrator under paragraph 14 or 22 of Schedule B1 to the Insolvency Act 1986.]

NOTES

Regulation heading: substituted for original heading "Limitation on disapplication of sections 10(1)(b) and 11(3)(c) of Insolvency Act 1986 in relation to system-charges" by the Enterprise Act 2002 (Insolvency) Order 2003, SI 2003/2096, arts 5, 6, Schedule, paras 61, 62(a), except in any case where a petition for an administration order was presented before 15 September 2003.

Para (1A): inserted by SI 2003/2096, arts 5, 6, Schedule, paras 61, 62(b), except in any case where a petition for an administration order was presented before 15 September 2003.

Para (2): words in square brackets substituted for words "The disapplication of section 10(1)(b) and 11(3)(c) of Insolvency Act 1986" by SI 2003/2096, arts 5, 6, Schedule, paras 61, 62(c), except in any case where a petition for an administration order was presented before 15 September 2003.

Para (5): words in square brackets substituted for words "the petition" by SI 2003/2096, arts 5, 6, Schedule, paras 61, 62(d), except in any case where a petition for an administration order was presented before 15 September 2003. (Note that para 62(d) of the Schedule to SI 2003/2096 actually substitutes the words "*a* petition" with the words "an application".)

Para (5A): inserted by SI 2003/2096, arts 5, 6, Schedule, paras 61, 62(e), except in any case where a petition for an administration order was presented before 15 September 2003; words in square brackets substituted by the Enterprise Act (Insolvency) Order 2004, SI 2004/2312, art 3.

[9.20]

7 [Limitation on disapplication of moratorium on certain legal processes under Schedule B1 to the Insolvency Act 1986 (administration) in relation to system-charges granted by a system-beneficiary]

(1) This regulation applies where an administration order is made in relation to a system-beneficiary.

[(1A) A reference in paragraph (1) to "an administration order" shall include the appointment of an administrator under paragraph 14 or 22 of Schedule B1 to the Insolvency Act 1986.]

(2) [The disapplication of paragraph 43(2) of Schedule B1 to the Insolvency Act 1986 (including that provision as applied by paragraph 44 of that Schedule)] by section 175(1)(a) of the Act shall have effect, in relation to a system-charge granted by a system-beneficiary, only to the extent necessary to enable there to be realised, whether through the sale of interests of a system-beneficiary in relation to uncertificated units of a security or otherwise, the lesser of the two sums specified in paragraphs (3) and (4).

(3) The first of the two sums referred to in paragraph (2) is the net sum of—

(a) all payment obligations discharged by the settlement bank in connection with—

(i) transfers, to or by the relevant system-beneficiary by means of a relevant system made during the qualifying period, of interests of the system-beneficiary in relation to uncertificated units of a security held by a relevant nominee, where the relevant nominee has continued to hold the units;

(ii) agreements made during the qualifying period to transfer, to or from the relevant system-beneficiary by means of a relevant system, interests of the system-beneficiary in relation to uncertificated units of a security held by a relevant nominee, where the relevant nominee will continue to hold the units;

(iii) transfers, during the qualifying period and by means of a relevant system, of uncertificated units of a security, being transfers made to or by a system-member acting on behalf of the relevant system-beneficiary;

(iv) agreements made during the qualifying period to transfer uncertificated units of a security by means of a relevant system to or from a system-member acting on behalf of the relevant system-beneficiary; and

(v) issues of uncertificated units of a security made during the qualifying period and by means of a relevant system, being issues to a system-member acting on behalf of the relevant system-beneficiary; less

(b) all payment obligations discharged to the settlement bank in connection with transactions of any kind described in paragraph (3)(a)(i) to (iv).

(4) The second of the two sums referred to in paragraph (2) is the sum (if any) due to the settlement bank from the relevant system-beneficiary by reason of an obligation of the kind described in regulation 5(b)(ii).

NOTES

Regulation heading: substituted for original heading "Limitation on disapplication of sections 10(1)(b) and 11(3)(c) of Insolvency Act 1986 in relation to system-charges granted by a system-beneficiary" by the Enterprise Act 2002 (Insolvency) Order 2003, SI 2003/2096, arts 5, 6, Schedule, paras 61, 63(a), except in any case where a petition for an administration order was presented before 15 September 2003.

Para (1A): inserted by SI 2003/2096, arts 5, 6, Schedule, paras 61, 63(b), except in any case where a petition for an administration order was presented before 15 September 2003.

Para (2): words in square brackets substituted for words "The disapplication of section 10(1)(b) and 11(3)(c) of Insolvency Act 1986" by SI 2003/2096, arts 5, 6, Schedule, paras 61, 63(c), except in any case where a petition for an administration order was presented before 15 September 2003.

[9.21]

8 Ability of administrator or receiver to recover assets in case of property subject to system-charge

(1) This regulation applies where an administration order is made or an administrator or an administrative receiver or a receiver is appointed, in relation to a system-member, former system-member or system-beneficiary.

[(1A) A reference in paragraph (1) to "an administration order" shall include the appointment of an administrator under paragraph 14 or 22 of Schedule B1 to the Insolvency Act 1986.]

(2) [The disapplication—

(a) by section 175(1)(b) of the Act, of paragraphs 70, 71 and 72 of Schedule B1 to the Insolvency Act 1986, and

(b) by section 175(3) of the Act, of sections 43 and 61 of the 1986 Act,

shall cease to have effect] after the end of the relevant day in respect of any property which is subject to a system-charge granted by the system-member, former system-member or system-beneficiary if on the basis of a valuation in accordance with paragraph (3), the charge is not required for the realisation of the sum specified in paragraph (4) or (5).

(3) For the purposes of paragraph (2), the value of property shall, except in a case falling within paragraph (6), be such as may be agreed between the administrator, administrative receiver or receiver on the one hand and the settlement bank on the other.

(4) Where the system-charge has been granted by a system-member or former system-member, the sum referred to in paragraph (2) is whichever is the lesser of—

(a) the sum referred to in regulation 6(3);

(b) the sum referred to in regulation 6(4) due to the settlement bank at the close of business on the relevant day.

(5) Where the system-charge has been granted by a system-beneficiary, the sum referred to in paragraph (2) is whichever is the lesser of—

(a) the sum referred to in regulation 7(3);

(b) the sum referred to in regulation 7(4) due to the settlement bank at the close of business on the relevant day.

(6) For the purposes of paragraph (2), the value of any property for which a price for the relevant day is quoted in the Daily Official List of The London Stock Exchange Limited shall—

(a) in a case in which two prices are so quoted, be an amount equal to the average of those two prices, adjusted where appropriate to take account of any accrued dividend or interest; and

(b) in a case in which one price is so quoted, be an amount equal to that price, adjusted where appropriate to take account of any accrued dividend or interest.

(7) In this regulation "the relevant day" means the second business day after the day on which the [company enters administration], or the administrative receiver or receiver is appointed.

NOTES

Para (1A): inserted by the Enterprise Act 2002 (Insolvency) Order 2003, SI 2003/2096, arts 5, 6, Schedule, paras 61, 64(a), except in any case where a petition for an administration order was presented before 15 September 2003.

Para (2): words in square brackets substituted for words "The disapplication, by section 175(1)(b) and (3) of the Act, of sections 15(1) and (2), 43 and 61 of the Insolvency Act 1986 shall cease to have effect" by SI 2003/2096, arts 5, 6, Schedule, paras 61, 64(b), except in any case where a petition for an administration order was presented before 15 September 2003.

Para (7): words in square brackets substituted for words "administration order is made" by SI 2003/2096, arts 5, 6, Schedule, paras 61, 64(c), except in any case where a petition for an administration order was presented before 15 September 2003.

9 *((Pt III) spent; amended the Companies Act 1989, s 156 (repealed).)*

OCCUPATIONAL PENSION SCHEMES (DEFICIENCY ON WINDING UP ETC) REGULATIONS 1996

(SI 1996/3128)

NOTES

Made: 11 December 1996.

Authority: Pensions Act 1995, ss 68(2)(e), 75(5), (9), (10), 89(2), 118(1)(a), (b), 119, 124(1), 125(2), (3), (4)(a), 174(2), (3).

Commencement: see reg 1(2)–(6).

ARRANGEMENT OF REGULATIONS

Preliminary

1 Citation and commencement . . . . . [9.22]
2 Interpretation . . . . . [9.23]

Schemes which are not money purchase schemes

3 Calculation of the value of scheme liabilities and assets . . . . . [9.24]
3A Valuation of liabilities where employer not insolvent and where winding up commences before 11th June 2003 . . . . . [9.25]
3B Valuation of liabilities where employer not insolvent and where winding up commences on or after 11th June 2003 . . . . . [9.26]
3C Valuation of liabilities where winding up commences, and date of calculation falls, on or after 15 February 2005 . . . . . [9.27]
3D Valuation of liabilities where there is more than one employer . . . . . [9.28]
4 Multi-employer schemes . . . . . [9.29]
5 Former employers . . . . . [9.30]
6 Ceasing to participate: transitional provision . . . . . [9.31]

Money purchase schemes

7 Money purchase schemes: deficiency owing to fraud etc . . . . . [9.32]
8 Multi-employer money purchase schemes . . . . . [9.33]
9 Former employers of money purchase schemes . . . . . [9.34]

General and supplementary

10 Disapplication of section 75 . . . . . [9.35]
11 Minor modifications . . . . . [9.36]
12 Modification of schemes: apportionment of section 75 debts . . . . . [9.37]
13 Revocations and savings . . . . . [9.38]

SCHEDULES

Schedule 2—Minor modifications . . . . . [9.39]

Preliminary

[9.22]

1 Citation and commencement

(1) These Regulations may be cited as the Occupational Pension Schemes (Deficiency on Winding Up etc) Regulations 1996.

(2) This regulation shall come into force on 19th December 1996.

(3) Subject to paragraphs (2) and (4) to (6) and regulation 6(1) (in so far as it relates to the period there mentioned), these Regulations shall come into force on 6th April 1997.

(4) Regulations 3 to 6 shall not apply where the applicable time falls before that date.

(5) Regulations 3 to 6 shall not apply to any scheme which began to be wound up earlier than 19th December 1996.

(6) Regulations 7 to 9 shall only apply where the act or omission to which the reduction in value is attributable occurred after 5th April 1997.

[9.23]
2 Interpretation

(1) For the purposes of these Regulations the time when a scheme begins to be wound up shall be determined in accordance with regulation 2 of the Occupational Pension Schemes (Winding Up) Regulations 1996.

(2) In these Regulations, unless the context otherwise requires—

["the actuary" means the actuary appointed for the scheme in pursuance of section 47(1)(b) or, in the case of a scheme to which that provision does not apply by virtue of regulations made under subsection (5) of that section, an actuary otherwise authorised by the trustees or managers to provide such valuations or certifications as may be required under these Regulations;]

"the applicable time" has the same meaning as in section 75 (but see the modifications in regulations 4(3), 6(3) and 7(2));

[. . .]

"employer" has the same meaning as in section 75 (but see paragraph (4) and regulations 5, 6 and 9);

"the MFR Regulations" means the Occupational Pension Schemes (Minimum Funding Requirement and Actuarial Valuations) Regulations 1996;

["money purchase scheme" means an occupational pension scheme under which all the benefits that may be provided other than death benefits are money purchase benefits]

"the Taxes Act" means the Income and Corporation Taxes Act 1988.

(3) References in these Regulations to a relevant insolvency event occurring in relation to an employer have the same meaning as in section 75.

(4) In these Regulations "scheme" must be construed in appropriate cases in accordance with subsections (1B) and (1C) of section 75 (as inserted by regulation 4(2) or, as the case may be, regulation 8) and Schedule 2 (and "employer" and "member" must be construed accordingly).

[(5) References in these Regulations to the guidance in GN 19 are to the guidelines on winding up and scheme asset deficiency (GN 19), adopted or prepared, and from time to time revised, by [the Financial Reporting Council Limited][, with any such revisions at the applicable time].]

(6) References in these Regulations to the guidance in GN 27 are to the guidelines on minimum funding requirement (GN 27), [published by the Institute and Faculty of Actuaries] and approved for the purposes of the MFR Regulations by the Secretary of State, with such revisions as have been so approved at the applicable time.

(7) Subject to the previous provisions of this regulation and unless the context otherwise requires—

(a) expressions used in these Regulations have the same meaning as if they were used in Part I of the Pensions Act 1995; and

(b) in these Regulations any reference to a section shall be construed as a reference to a section of that Act.

NOTES

Para (2): definition "the actuary" inserted by the Personal and Occupational Pension Schemes (Miscellaneous Amendments) (No 2) Regulations 1997, SI 1997/3038, reg 5; definition omitted inserted by the Occupational and Personal Pension Schemes (Prescribed Bodies) Regulations 2007, SI 2007/60, reg 2, Schedule, para 8(a)(i), revoked by the Occupational and Personal Pension Schemes (Prescribed Bodies) Regulations 2012, SI 2012/1817, reg 2, Schedule, para 4(1)(a)(i); definition "money purchase scheme" substituted by the Personal and Occupational Pension Schemes (Miscellaneous Amendments) Regulations 1997, SI 1997/786, reg 3, Sch 1, para 19(2).

Para (5): substituted by SI 2007/60, reg 2, Schedule, para 8(a)(ii); words in first pair of square brackets substituted by SI 2012/1817, reg 2, Schedule, para 4(1)(a)(ii); words in second pair of square brackets substituted by the Pensions Act 2007 (Actuarial Guidance) (Consequential Provisions) Order 2008, SI 2008/2301, art 2, Schedule, para 4.

Para (6): words in square brackets substituted by the Pensions (Institute and Faculty of Actuaries and Consultation by Employers—Amendment) Regulations 2012, SI 2012/692, reg 6.

Schemes which are not money purchase schemes

[9.24]
3 Calculation of the value of scheme liabilities and assets

(1) [[Subject to [regulations 3A to 3D]], the liabilities] and assets of a scheme which are to be taken into account for the purposes of section 75(1) and their amount or value shall be determined, calculated and verified by the actuary—

(a) on the general assumptions specified in paragraphs (2) and (3) of regulation 3 of the MFR Regulations;

(b) subject to paragraphs (3) and (4), in accordance with regulations 4 to 8 of the MFR Regulations;

(c) subject to sub-paragraph (d), in so far as the guidance given in GN 27 applies as respects regulations 3(2) and (3) and 4 to 8 of the MFR Regulations, in accordance with that guidance; and

(d) in accordance with the guidance given in GN 19 so far as that guidance applies for the purposes of these Regulations;

and where in these Regulations (or in the MFR Regulations as applied by this paragraph) there is a reference to the value of any asset or the amount of any liability being calculated or verified in accordance with the opinion of the actuary or as he thinks appropriate, he shall comply with any relevant provision in the guidance given in GN 27 or, as the case may be, GN 19 in making that calculation or verification.

(2) The value of the assets and the amount of the liabilities of a scheme which are to be taken into account for the purposes of section 75(1) must be certified by the actuary in the form set out in Schedule 1 to these Regulations, but if the scheme is being wound up on the date as at which the valuation is made, the actuary must modify the note at the end of the certificate by omitting the words from "if the scheme" onwards.

(3) For the purposes of this regulation—

(a) references in regulations 3(2), 4, 5, 7 and 8 of the MFR Regulations to the relevant date shall be taken as references to the applicable time;

(b) regulations 4(1), 7(1) and 8(2) of the MFR Regulations shall have effect with the substitution for the words "the minimum funding requirement is met" of the words "the value of the assets of the scheme is less than the amount of the liabilities of the scheme";

(c) regulation 6(1)(b) of the MFR Regulations shall have effect with the addition at the end of the words "(and any amount treated as a debt due to the trustees or managers of the scheme under section 75(1) by virtue of the valuation in question)".

(4) In its application for the purposes of this regulation in a case where the applicable time falls after the scheme has begun to be wound up, regulation 6(1) of the MFR Regulations has effect with the addition after sub-paragraph (c) of the words—

"and for the purposes of sub-paragraph (a), regulation 5(1)(a) of the Occupational Pension Schemes (Investment) Regulations 1996 (exclusion of employer-related investments over 5 per cent of current market value) shall be disregarded.".

NOTES

Para (1): words in first (outer) pair of square brackets substituted by the Occupational Pension Schemes (Minimum Funding Requirement and Miscellaneous Amendments) Regulations 2002, SI 2002/380, reg 4(1), (2); words in second (inner) pair of square brackets substituted by the Occupational Pension Schemes (Winding Up and Deficiency on Winding Up etc) (Amendment) Regulations 2004, SI 2004/403, reg 3(1), (2); words in third (inner) pair of square brackets substituted by the Occupational Pension Schemes (Winding Up, Deficiency on Winding Up and Transfer Values) (Amendment) Regulations 2005, SI 2005/72, reg 3(1), (2).

Application: in relation to the continued application of the reference "minimum funding requirement" to a scheme on or after 6 April 2007, notwithstanding the repeal of that definition by the Pensions Act 2004, s 320, Sch 13, Pt I, see the Pensions Act 2004 (Commencement No 10 and Saving Provision) Order 2006, SI 2006/2272, arts 2, 3.

[9.25]

[3A Valuation of liabilities where employer not insolvent [and where winding up commences before 11th June 2003]

(1) Where a scheme (including a section of a scheme in relation to which there is more than one employer which is treated as a separate scheme for the purposes of section 75) is being wound up and the employer was not insolvent immediately before the winding up of the scheme commenced, regulation 3 shall have effect as if—

(a) in paragraph (1)—

(i) at the beginning of subparagraph (a), there were inserted the words "except to the extent that the liabilities are in respect of any entitlement to a pension or other benefit that has arisen under the scheme and in respect of which paragraph (1B) below applies,";

(ii) for the words "paragraphs (2) and (3)" in subparagraph (a), there were substituted the words "paragraphs (2)(a) to (c) and (3)";

(iii) for the words "paragraphs (3) and (4)" in subparagraph (b), there were substituted the words "paragraphs (1B), (3) and (4)";

(iv) for the words "regulations 3(2) and (3)" in subparagraph (c), there were substituted the words "regulations 3(2)(a) to (c) and (3)"; and

(v) after the words "and 4 to 8 of the MFR Regulations" in subparagraph (c), there were inserted the words "or as respects paragraphs (1A) and (1B) below"; and

(b) after paragraph (1) there were inserted the following paragraphs:

"(1A) The liabilities of a scheme which are to be taken into account under paragraph (1) above shall include all expenses (except the cost of annuities taken into account by virtue of paragraph (1B) below) which, in the opinion of the trustees or managers of the scheme, are likely to be incurred in connection with the winding up of the scheme."; and

"(1B) When calculating the liabilities of the scheme in respect of any entitlement to the payment of any pension or other benefit (including any increase in a pension) that has arisen under the scheme on or before the applicable time, it shall be assumed that all such liabilities will be discharged by the purchase of annuities of a kind described in section 74(3)(c) (discharge of liabilities by insurance—annuity purchase) and, for the purposes of the calculation, the actuary shall estimate the cost of purchasing any such annuities.".

(2) Where a scheme to which regulation 4 (multi-employer schemes) applies (including a section of a scheme in relation to which there is more than one employer which is treated as a separate scheme for the purposes of section 75) is being wound up in circumstances where—

(a) an employer in relation to the scheme ceases to employ persons in the description or category of employment to which the scheme relates at a time when there are no other employers in relation to the scheme continuing to employ such persons; and

(b) that employer was not insolvent immediately before the winding up commenced,
regulation 3 shall have effect with the modifications set out in paragraph (1)(a) and (b) of this regulation.

(3) For the purposes of paragraphs (1) and (2) above, an employer is insolvent if a relevant insolvency event has occurred in relation to that employer.

(4) In the Note at the end of the form of certificate set out in Schedule 1 (form of actuary's certificate), after the word "securing" there shall be inserted the words "all of".]

NOTES

Inserted by the Occupational Pension Schemes (Minimum Funding Requirement and Miscellaneous Amendments) Regulations 2002, SI 2002/380, reg 4(1), (3).

Regulation heading: words in square brackets inserted by the Occupational Pension Schemes (Winding Up and Deficiency on Winding Up etc) (Amendment) Regulations 2004, SI 2004/403, reg 3(1), (3).

[9.26]

[3B Valuation of liabilities where employer not insolvent and where winding up commences on or after 11th June 2003

(1) [Subject to regulation 3C,] this regulation shall apply in the case of a scheme to which regulation 4B of the Occupational Pension Schemes (Winding Up) Regulations 1996 (calculation of liabilities where employer not insolvent and where winding up commences on or after 11th June 2003) applies.

(2) In the case of a scheme to which this regulation applies, paragraph (1)(b) of regulation 3A (valuation of the liabilities where employer not insolvent) shall have effect as if for paragraph (1B) in quotation marks there were substituted the following paragraph—

"(1B) When calculating the liabilities of the scheme for any—

(a) accrued rights that exist on or before the applicable time to the payment of any pension or other benefit under the scheme (including any increase to a pension);

(b) future pensions, or other future benefits, attributable (directly or indirectly) to pension credits (including any increase to a pension) which have arisen on or before the applicable time; and

(c) entitlement to the payment of a pension or other benefit (including any increase in a pension) that has arisen on or before the applicable time,

it shall be assumed that all such liabilities will be discharged by the purchase of annuities of the type described in section 74(3)(c) (discharge of liabilities by insurance – annuity purchase) and, for the purposes of the calculation, the actuary shall estimate the costs of purchasing any such annuities.".]

NOTES

Inserted by the Occupational Pension Schemes (Winding Up and Deficiency on Winding Up etc) (Amendment) Regulations 2004, SI 2004/403, reg 3(1), (4).

Para (1): words in square brackets inserted by the Occupational Pension Schemes (Winding Up, Deficiency on Winding Up and Transfer Values) (Amendment) Regulations 2005, SI 2005/72, reg 3(1), (3).

[9.27]

[3C Valuation of liabilities where winding up commences, and date of calculation falls, on or after 15 February 2005

[(1) This regulation shall apply in the case of a scheme which begins to wind up on or after 15 February 2005 ("the commencement date"), and the date by reference to which the liabilities and assets of the scheme are determined, calculated and verified for the purposes of section 75 is a date falling on or after the commencement date.

(2) In the case of a scheme to which this regulation applies, regulation 3 shall have effect as if—

(a) in paragraph (1)—

(i) at the beginning of sub-paragraph (a), there were inserted the words "except to the extent that the liabilities are in respect of any entitlement to a pension or other benefit that has arisen under the scheme and in respect of which paragraph (1B) applies,";

(ii) for the words "paragraphs (2) and (3)" in sub-paragraph (a), there were substituted the words "paragraphs (2)(a) to (c) and (3)";

(iii) for the words "paragraphs (3) and (4)" in sub-paragraph (b), there were substituted the words "paragraphs (1B), (3) and (4)";

(iv) for the words "regulations 3(2) and (3)" in sub-paragraph (c), there were substituted the words "regulations 3(2)(a) to (c) and (3)"; and

(v) after the words "and 4 to 8 of the MFR Regulations" in sub-paragraph (c), there were inserted the words "or as respects paragraphs (1A) and (1B)"; and

(b) after paragraph (1) there were inserted the following paragraphs:

"(1A) The liabilities of a scheme which are to be taken into account under paragraph (1) above shall include all expenses (except the cost of annuities taken into account by virtue of paragraph (1B)) which, in the opinion of the trustees or managers of the scheme, are likely to be incurred in connection with the winding up of the scheme.

(1B) When calculating the liabilities of the scheme for any—

(a) accrued rights that exist on or before the applicable time to the payment of any pension or other benefit under the scheme (including any increase to a pension);

(b) future pensions, or other future benefits, attributable (directly or indirectly) to pension credits (including any increase to a pension) which have arisen on or before the applicable time; and

(c) entitlement to the payment of a pension or other benefit (including any increase in a pension) that has arisen on or before the applicable time,

it shall be assumed that all such liabilities will be discharged by the purchase of annuities of the type described in section 74(3)(c) and, for the purposes of the calculation, the actuary shall estimate the costs of purchasing any such annuities.".]

NOTES

Inserted, together with reg 3D, by the Occupational Pension Schemes (Winding Up, Deficiency on Winding Up and Transfer Values) (Amendment) Regulations 2005, SI 2005/72, reg 3(1), (4).

[9.28]

[3D Valuation of liabilities where there is more than one employer

(1) This regulation shall apply where there is a scheme to which regulation 4 (multi-employer schemes) applies (including a section of a scheme in relation to which there is more than one employer which is treated as a separate scheme for the purposes of section 75) and the circumstances described in paragraph (2) apply.

(2) The circumstances are that—

(a) the scheme is not being wound up;

(b) a relevant insolvency event occurs in relation to an employer in relation to the scheme; and

(c) the applicable time is on or after 15 February 2005.

(3) In the case of a scheme to which this regulation applies, regulation 3 shall have effect with the modifications set out in regulation 3C(2)(a) and (b).]

NOTES

Inserted as noted to reg 3C at **[9.27]**.

[9.29]

4 Multi-employer schemes

(1) In its application to a scheme in relation to which there is more than one employer, section 75 has effect with the following modifications.

(2) After subsection (1) insert—

"(1A) In the case of a scheme in relation to which there is more than one employer, the amount of the debt due from each employer shall, unless the scheme provides for the total amount of the debt due under subsection (1) to be otherwise apportioned amongst the employers, be such proportion of that total amount as, in the opinion of the actuary after consultation with the trustees or managers, the amount of the scheme's liabilities attributable to employment with that employer bears to the total amount of the scheme's liabilities attributable to employment with any of the employers.

(1B) Where a scheme in relation to which there is more than one employer is divided into two or more sections and the provisions of the scheme are such that—

(a) different sections of the scheme apply to different employers or groups of employers (whether or not more than one section applies to any particular employer or groups including any particular employer);

(b) contributions payable to the scheme by an employer, or by a member in employment under that employer, are allocated to that employer's section (or, if more than one section applies to the employer, to the section which is appropriate in respect of the employment in question); and

(c) a specified part or proportion of the assets of the scheme is attributable to each section and cannot be used for the purposes of any other section,

each section of the scheme shall be treated as a separate scheme for the purposes of this section.

(1C) Where—

(a) a scheme which has been such a scheme as is mentioned in subsection (1B) is divided into two or more sections, some or all of which apply only to members who are not in pensionable service under the section; and

(b) the provisions of the scheme have not been amended so as to prevent the conditions mentioned in subsection (1B)(a) to (c) being satisfied in relation to two or more sections; but

(c) those conditions have ceased to be satisfied in relation to one or more sections (whether before or after this section came into force) by reason only of there being no members in pensionable service under the section and no contributions which are to be allocated to it,

the section in relation to which those conditions have ceased to be satisfied shall be treated as a separate scheme for the purposes of this section.

[(1D) For the purposes of subsections (1B) and (1C), there shall be disregarded any provisions of the scheme by virtue of which contributions or transfers of assets may be made to make provision for death benefits; and where subsection (1B) or (1C) applies and contributions or transfers are so made to a section ("the death benefits section") the assets of which may only be applied for the provision of death benefits, the death benefits section shall also be treated as if it were a separate scheme for the purposes of this section.

(1E) For the purposes of subsections (1B), (1C) and (1D), there shall be disregarded any provisions of the scheme by virtue of which on the winding up of the scheme assets attributable to one section may be used for the purposes of another section.]".

(3) For subsection (3) substitute—

"(3) In this section "the applicable time" means—

(a) in relation to a scheme which is being wound up, any time—

(i) after the commencement of the winding up, and

(ii) before a relevant insolvency event has occurred in relation to each of the employers to whom the scheme relates; and

(b) in relation to a scheme which is not being wound up—

(i) in relation only to any employer who ceases to be a person employing persons in the description or category of employment to which the scheme relates at a time when at least one other person continues to employ such persons, immediately before he so ceases, and

(ii) in relation only to any employer in relation to whom a relevant insolvency event occurs, immediately before that event occurs.".

(4) Where (apart from this paragraph) paragraph (1) does not apply to a scheme by reason of its not being a scheme in relation to which there is more than one employer but, if it did so, subsection (1C) of section 75 (as inserted by paragraph (2)) would apply to the scheme, that section shall have effect with the modifications made by paragraphs (2) and (3).

(5) For the purposes of section 75(1A) (as inserted by paragraph (2))—

(a) the total amount of the scheme's liabilities which are attributable to employment with any of the employers; and

(b) the amount of the liabilities attributable to employment with any one employer,

shall be such amount as is determined, calculated and verified by the actuary in accordance with the guidance given in GN 19; and a determination under this paragraph must be certified by the actuary as being in accordance with that guidance.

NOTES

Para (2): words in square brackets added by the Personal and Occupational Pension Schemes (Miscellaneous Amendments) Regulations 1997, SI 1997/786, reg 3, Sch 1, para 19(3).

[9.30]

5 Former employers

(1) In the application of section 75 and these Regulations to a scheme which has no active members, "the employer" includes every person who employed persons in the description or category of employment to which the scheme relates immediately before the occurrence of the event after which the scheme ceased to have any active members.

(2) In the application of section 75 and these Regulations to a scheme, "the employer" includes any person who has ceased on or after 6th April 1997 and before the applicable time to be a person employing persons in the description or category of employment to which the scheme relates, unless—

(a) when he so ceased the scheme was not being wound up and continued to have active members, and

(b) one of the conditions in paragraph (3) is met.

(3) Those conditions are—

(a) that no debt was treated as becoming due from him under section 75(1) by virtue of his so ceasing;

(b) that such a debt was treated as becoming due from him [and—

(i) has been paid before the applicable time, or

(ii) if not so paid, was not so paid solely because he was not notified of the debt, and of the amount of it, sufficiently in advance of the applicable time for it to be paid before the applicable time;]

(c) that such a debt was treated as becoming due from him but at the applicable time it is excluded from the value of the assets of the scheme by virtue of regulation 6(1)(b) of the MFR Regulations (exclusion of debts unlikely to be recovered).

NOTES

Para (3): in sub-para (b) words in square brackets substituted by the Personal and Occupational Pension Schemes (Miscellaneous Amendments) Regulations 1999, SI 1999/3198, reg 4(1), (2).

[9.31]

6 Ceasing to participate: transitional provision

(1) This regulation applies to a scheme if a person ceased to be a person employing persons in the description or category of employment to which the scheme relates during the period beginning with 19th December 1996 and ending with 5th April 1997 and at a time when the scheme was not being wound up and continued to have active members; and in this regulation "former participator" means a person who so ceased.

(2) In the application of section 75 and these Regulations to a scheme to which this regulation applies, "employer" includes a former participator, unless before the applicable time a time which was the applicable time in relation to the former participator by virtue of paragraph (3) below has occurred and—

(a) no debt was then treated as due from him under section 75(1), or

(b) such a debt was then treated as becoming due from him [and—

(i) has been paid before the applicable time, or

(ii) if not so paid, was not so paid solely because he was not notified of the debt, and of the amount of it, sufficiently in advance of the applicable time for it to be paid before the applicable time;] or

(c) such a debt was then treated as becoming due from him but at the applicable time it is excluded from the value of the assets of the scheme by virtue of regulation 6(1)(b) of the MFR Regulations (exclusion of debts unlikely to be recovered).

(3) In the application of section 75 and these Regulations to a scheme to which this regulation applies which is not being wound up, "the applicable time", in relation to a former participator only, includes—

(a) the date by reference to which the earliest minimum funding valuation required by section 57(1)(a) for the scheme is made, or

(b) the earliest time when a debt is treated under section 75(1) as becoming due from another person by virtue of section 75(3)(b)(i) or (ii) (as substituted by regulation 4(3)),

whichever is the earlier.

NOTES

Para (2): in sub-para (b) words in square brackets substituted by the Personal and Occupational Pension Schemes (Miscellaneous Amendments) Regulations 1999, SI 1999/3198, reg 4(1), (3).

Money purchase schemes

[9.32]

7 Money purchase schemes: deficiency owing to fraud etc

(1) Subject to regulation 10, section 75 shall apply to money purchase schemes with the following modifications.

(2) For subsections (1) and (2) substitute—

"(1) If, in the case of an occupational pension scheme which is a money purchase scheme, the value at the applicable time of the unallocated assets of the scheme is less than the amount of any criminal reduction in the aggregate value of the allocated assets of the scheme, then an amount equal to the difference shall be treated as a debt due from the employer to the trustees or managers of the scheme.

(2) In this section—

"allocated assets", in relation to a scheme, means assets which have been specifically allocated for the provision of benefits to or in respect of members (whether generally or individually) or for the payment of the scheme's expenses (and "unallocated" shall be construed accordingly);

"the applicable time" means the time immediately after the act or omission to which the criminal reduction is attributable occurs or, if that time cannot be determined, the earliest time when the auditor of the scheme knows that the reduction has occurred;

"criminal reduction" means a reduction which is attributable to an act or omission which constitutes an offence prescribed for the purposes of section 81(1)(c) (or, in the case of an act or omission which occurred outside England and Wales or Scotland, would constitute such an offence if it occurred in England and Wales or in Scotland).".

(3) Omit subsections (3), (4) and (6).

(4) For the purpose of section 75(1) (as substituted by paragraph (2)), paragraphs (5) to (9) apply instead of regulation 3.

(5) In the case of a scheme other than an ear-marked scheme—

(a) the value at the applicable time of the unallocated assets of the scheme shall be taken to be the value of those assets as certified in a statement by the scheme's auditor; and

(b) the amount of the criminal reduction in the aggregate value of the allocated assets of the scheme is to be calculated by subtracting the actual aggregate value of those assets at the applicable time from the notional aggregate value of those assets.

(6) The notional aggregate value mentioned in paragraph (5)(b) shall be taken to be the sum of the values of the assets—

(a) as stated in the audited accounts which most immediately precede the relevant act or omission, or

(b) if there are none, as certified in a statement by the scheme's auditor,

adjusted appropriately to take account of any alteration in their values (other than any alteration attributable to that act or omission) between the date as at which those accounts are prepared or, as the case may be, as at which that statement is given and the applicable time.

(7) The actual aggregate value mentioned in paragraph (5)(b) shall be calculated in the same manner as it was calculated for the purposes of the accounts mentioned in paragraph (6)(a) or, as the case may be, the statement mentioned in paragraph (6)(b).

(8) In the case of an ear-marked scheme, the value at the applicable time of the unallocated assets of the scheme and the amount of the criminal reduction in the aggregate value of the allocated assets of the scheme are the amounts certified in a statement by the relevant insurer.

(9) In this regulation—

"ear-marked scheme" means a scheme under which all the benefits are secured by one or more policies of insurance or annuity contracts, being policies or contracts specifically allocated to the provision of benefits for individual members or any other person who has a right to benefits under the scheme; and

"the relevant insurer", in relation to such a scheme, is the insurer with whom the insurance contract or annuity contract is made.

[9.33]

8 Multi-employer money purchase schemes

(1) Regulation 4(1) and (3) to (5) does not apply to a money purchase scheme, but in its application to such a scheme in relation to which there is more than one employer, section 75 (as modified by regulation 7) applies with the insertion after subsection (1) of the same subsections as are inserted by regulation 4(2), omitting from subsection (1A) the words "in the opinion of the actuary after consultation with the trustees or managers".

(2) Where (apart from this paragraph) section 75 does not apply to a money purchase scheme with the modification made by paragraph (1) but, if it did so, subsection (1C) of that section would apply to the scheme, that section shall have effect with the modification made by paragraph (1).

[9.34]

9 Former employers of money purchase schemes

Regulations 5 and 6 shall not apply to a money purchase scheme, but in the application of section 75 and these regulations to such a scheme which has no active members at the applicable time "the employer" includes every person who employed persons in the description or category of employment to which the scheme relates immediately before the occurrence of the event after which the scheme ceased to have any active members.

General and supplementary

[9.35]

10 Disapplication of section 75

(1) Section 75 does not apply—

(a) to a public service pension scheme—

(i) under the provisions of which there is no requirement for assets related to the intended rate or amount of benefit under the scheme to be set aside in advance (disregarding requirements relating to additional voluntary contributions); or

(ii) which is made under section 7 of the Superannuation Act 1972 (superannuation of persons employed in local government service etc) or section 2 of the Parliamentary and other Pensions Act 1987 (power to provide for pensions for Members of the House of Commons etc);

(b) to any occupational pension scheme in respect of which any Minister of the Crown has given a guarantee or made any other arrangements for the purpose of securing that the assets of the scheme are sufficient to meet its liabilities;

(c) to an occupational pension scheme which provides relevant benefits, but is neither an approved scheme nor a relevant statutory scheme;

(d) to a section 615(6) scheme;

(e) to a scheme with less than two members;

(f) to a scheme—

(i) the only benefits provided by which are death benefits, and

(ii) under the provisions of which no member has accrued rights;

(g) to a relevant lump sum retirement benefits scheme; or

(h) to the scheme established by the Salvation Army Act 1963.

(2) In this regulation—

"approved scheme" means a scheme which is approved or was formerly approved under section 590 or 591 of the Taxes Act or in respect of which an application for such approval has been duly made which has not been determined;

["contracted-out" is to be construed in accordance with section 7B(2) (meaning of "contracted-out scheme" etc) of the Pension Schemes Act 1993;]

"lump sum benefits" does not include benefits paid by way of commuted retirement pension;

"relevant benefits" has the meaning given in section 612(1) of the Taxes Act;

"relevant lump sum retirement benefits scheme" means an approved scheme—

(a) which has been categorised by the Commissioners of Inland Revenue for the purposes of its approval as a centralised scheme for non-associated employers;

(b) which [was not contracted-out at any time before the second abolition date]; and

(c) under the provisions of which the only benefits which may be provided on or after retirement (other than money purchase benefits derived from the payment of additional contributions by any person) are lump sum benefits which are not calculated by reference to any member's salary;

"relevant statutory scheme" has the meaning given in section 611A of the Taxes Act;

["the second abolition date" has the meaning given in section 181(1) (general interpretation) of the Pension Schemes Act 1993;]

"section 615(6) scheme" means a scheme with such a superannuation fund as is mentioned in section 615(6) of the Taxes Act.

(3) For the purposes of paragraph (1)(e) "scheme" shall be construed as if subsections (1B) and (1C) of section 75 (as inserted by regulation 4(2) or, as the case may be, regulation 8) were omitted.

NOTES

Para (2): definitions "contracted-out" and "the second abolition date" inserted and words in square brackets in definition "relevant lump sum retirement benefits scheme" substituted, by the Pensions Act 2014 (Abolition of Contracting-out for Salary Related Pension Schemes) (Consequential Amendments and Savings) Order 2016, SI 2016/200, reg 10.

[9.36]

11 Minor modifications

Schedule 2 to these Regulations shall have effect for the purpose of modifying section 75 and these Regulations.

[9.37]

12 Modification of schemes: apportionment of section 75 debts

In the case of a trust scheme (whether or not a money purchase scheme) which apart from this regulation could not be modified for the purpose of making provision for the total amount of a debt due under section 75(1) to be apportioned amongst the employers in different proportions from those which would otherwise apply by virtue of section 75(1A) (as inserted by regulation 4(2) or, as the case may be, regulation 8), for the purposes of section 68(2)(e), such a modification of the scheme is a modification for a prescribed purpose.

[9.38]

13 Revocations and savings

(1) The Occupational Pension Schemes (Deficiency on Winding Up etc) Regulations 1994 are hereby revoked, except in their application in any case in which section 144 of the Pension Schemes Act 1993 continues to apply (schemes which began winding up before 19th December 1996 and debts treated as due by virtue of valuations as at applicable times falling before 6th April 1997).

(2) Where before 6th April 1997 such arrangements have been made as are mentioned in subsection (1C) of section 144 of the Pension Schemes Act 1993 (as inserted by regulation 4 of those Regulations), then—

- (a) the revocation of those Regulations shall not affect—
  - (i) the recoverability of any debt or part of a debt, the recoverability of which is affected by subsections (1C) to (1G) of that section immediately before that date, or
  - (ii) the power of assignment conferred by subsection (1G) of that section; and
- (b) the making of, or failure to make, contributions in accordance with the arrangements, and any relevant insolvency event occurring on or after that date shall have the same effect as they would have had before that date.

(3) Paragraph (2) is without prejudice to the generality of paragraph (1).

SCHEDULES

SCHEDULE 1

(Sch 1 sets out the form of the actuary's certificate in accordance with reg 3(2).)

SCHEDULE 2
MINOR MODIFICATIONS

Regulation 11

[9.39]

1 Schemes covering United Kingdom and foreign employment

(1) This paragraph applies where a scheme which applies to members in employment in the United Kingdom and members in employment outside the United Kingdom is divided into two or more sections and the provisions of the scheme are such that—

- (a) different sections of the scheme apply to members in employment in the United Kingdom and to members in employment outside the United Kingdom ("the United Kingdom section" and "the foreign section"),
- (b) contributions payable to the scheme in respect of a member are allocated to the section applying to that member's employment,
- (c) a specified part or proportion of the assets of the scheme is attributable to each section and cannot be used for the purposes of any other section,
- (d) the United Kingdom section is approved and the foreign section is not approved.

(2) In sub-paragraph (1)(d) "approved" means approved or formerly approved under section 590 or 591 of the Taxes Act.

(3) Where this paragraph applies, section 75 and these Regulations shall apply as if each section of the scheme were a separate scheme, and the reference to the scheme in the form set out in Schedule 1 may be modified appropriately.

2 (1) This paragraph applies in any case where a scheme which applies to members in employment in the United Kingdom and members in employment outside the United Kingdom does not fall within paragraph 1 and part of the scheme is approved under section 590 or 591 of the Taxes Act by virtue of section 611(3) of that Act.

(2) Where this paragraph applies, section 75 and these Regulations shall apply as if the approved and unapproved parts of the scheme were separate schemes, and the reference to the scheme in the form set out in Schedule 1 may be modified appropriately.

3 Schemes with partial government guarantee

Where such a guarantee has been given or such arrangements have been made as are mentioned in regulation 10(1)(b) in respect of part only of a scheme, section 75 and these Regulations shall apply as if that part and the other part of the scheme were separate schemes, and the reference to the scheme in the form set out in Schedule 1 may be modified appropriately.

4 . . .

NOTES

Para 4: revoked by the Personal and Occupational Pension Schemes (Miscellaneous Amendments) Regulations 1997, SI 1997/786, regs 3, 4, Sch 1, para 19(4), Sch 2.

FINANCIAL MARKETS AND INSOLVENCY (SETTLEMENT FINALITY) REGULATIONS 1999

(SI 1999/2979)

NOTES

Made: 2 November 1999.

Authority: European Communities Act 1972, s 2(2).

Commencement: 11 December 1999.

Modification: these Regulations are applied, with modifications, in so far as they relate to bank insolvency or administration under the Banking Act 2009, Pts 2, 3, by the Banking Act 2009 (Parts 2 and 3 Consequential Amendments) Order 2009, SI 2009/317, art 3, Schedule at **[7.86]**, **[7.92]**.

ARRANGEMENT OF REGULATIONS

PART I
GENERAL

1 Citation, commencement and extent . . . [9.40]
2 Interpretation . . . [9.41]

PART II
DESIGNATED SYSTEMS

3 Application for designation . . . [9.42]
4 Grant and refusal of designation . . . [9.43]
5 Fees . . . [9.44]
6 Certain bodies deemed to satisfy requirements for designation . . . [9.45]
7 Revocation of designation . . . [9.46]
8 Undertakings treated as institutions . . . [9.47]
9 Indirect participants treated as participants . . . [9.48]
10 Provision of information by designated systems . . . [9.49]
11 Exemption from liability in damages . . . [9.50]
12 Publication of information and advice . . . [9.51]

PART III
TRANSFER ORDERS EFFECTED THROUGH A DESIGNATED SYSTEM AND COLLATERAL SECURITY

13 Modifications of the law of insolvency . . . [9.52]
14 Proceedings of designated system take precedence over insolvency proceedings . . . [9.53]
15 Net sum payable on completion of action taken under default arrangements . . . [9.54]
16 Disclaimer of property, rescission of contracts, &c . . . [9.55]
17 Adjustment of prior transactions . . . [9.56]

Collateral security charges

18 Modifications of the law of insolvency . . . [9.57]
19 Administration orders, &c . . . [9.58]

General

20 Transfer order entered into designated system following insolvency . . . [9.59]
21 Disapplication of certain provisions of Part VII and Part V . . . [9.60]

22 Notification of insolvency order or passing of resolution for creditors' voluntary winding up . . . . [9.61]
23 Applicable law relating to securities held as collateral security . . . . [9.62]
24 Applicable law where insolvency proceedings are brought. . . . . [9.63]
25 Insolvency proceedings in other jurisdictions . . . . [9.64]
26 Systems designated in other EEA States and Gibraltar . . . . [9.65]

SCHEDULES

Schedule—Requirements for Designation of System. . . . . [9.66]

PART I
GENERAL

[9.40]
1 Citation, commencement and extent

(1) These Regulations may be cited as the Financial Markets and Insolvency (Settlement Finality) Regulations 1999 and shall come into force on 11th December 1999.

(2) . . .

NOTES

Para (2): revoked by the Financial Markets and Insolvency (Settlement Finality) (Amendment) Regulations 2006, SI 2006/50, reg 2(1), (2).

[9.41]
2 Interpretation

(1) In these Regulations—

["administration" and "administrator" shall be interpreted in accordance with the modifications made by the enactments mentioned in paragraph (5);]

["the 2000 Act" means the Financial Services and Markets Act 2000;]

["business day" shall cover both day and night-time settlements and shall encompass all events happening during the business cycle of a system;]

"central bank" means a central bank of an EEA State or the European Central Bank;

"central counterparty" means a body corporate or unincorporated association interposed between the institutions in a . . . system and which acts as the exclusive counterparty of those institutions with regard to transfer orders;

"charge" means any form of security, including a mortgage and, in Scotland, a heritable security;

"clearing house" means a body corporate or unincorporated association which is responsible for the calculation of the net positions of institutions and any central counterparty or settlement agent in a . . . system;

"collateral security" means any realisable assets provided under a charge or a repurchase or similar agreement, or otherwise (including [credit claims and] money provided under a charge)—

(a) for the purpose of securing rights and obligations potentially arising in connection with a . . . system ("collateral security in connection with participation in a . . . system"); or

(b) to a central bank for the purpose of securing rights and obligations in connection with its operations in carrying out its functions as a central bank ("collateral security in connection with the functions of a central bank");

"collateral security charge" means, where collateral security consists of realisable assets (including money) provided under a charge, that charge;

["credit claims" means pecuniary claims arising out of an agreement whereby a credit institution grants credit in the form of a loan;]

["credit institution" means a credit institution as defined in Article 4(1)(1) of Regulation (EU) No 575/2013 of the European Parliament and of the Council of 26 June 2013 on prudential requirements for credit institutions and investment firms and amending Regulation (EU) No 648/2012;]

"creditors' voluntary winding-up resolution" means a resolution for voluntary winding up (within the meaning of the Insolvency Act 1986 [or the Insolvency (Northern Ireland) Order 1989]) where the winding up is a creditors' winding up (within the meaning of that Act [or that Order]);

"default arrangements" means the arrangements put in place by a designated system [or by a system which is an interoperable system in relation to that system] to limit systemic and other types of risk which arise in the event of a participant [or a system operator of an interoperable system] appearing to be unable, or likely to become unable, to meet its obligations in respect of a transfer order, including, for example, any default rules within the meaning of Part VII [or Part V] or any other arrangements for—

(a) netting,

(b) the closing out of open positions, . . .

(c) the application or transfer of collateral security; [or]

[(d) the transfer of assets or positions on the default of a participant in the system;]

"defaulter" means a person in respect of whom action has been taken by a designated system under its default arrangements;

"designated system" means a system which is declared by a designation order for the time being in force to be a designated system for the purposes of these Regulations;

["designating authority" means—

(a) in the case of a system which is, or the operator of which is, a recognised investment exchange for the purposes of the 2000 Act, the FCA;

(b) in any other case, the Bank of England;]

"designation order" has the meaning given by regulation 4;

["EEA State" has the meaning given by Schedule 1 to the Interpretation Act 1978;]

["ESMA" means the European Securities and Markets Authority established by Regulation (EU) No 1095/2010 of the European Parliament and of the Council of 24th November 2010 establishing a European Supervisory Authority (European Securities and Markets Authority);]

"guidance", in relation to a designated system, means guidance issued or any recommendation made by it which is intended to have continuing effect and is issued in writing or other legible form to all or any class of its participants or users or persons seeking to participate in the system or to use its facilities and which would, if it were a rule, come within the definition of a rule;

["the FCA" means the Financial Conduct Authority;]

["indirect participant" means an institution, central counterparty, settlement agent, clearing house or system operator—

(a) which has a contractual relationship with a participant in a designated system that enables the indirect participant to effect transfer orders through that system, and

(b) the identity of which is known to the system operator;]

"institution" means—

(a) a credit institution;

[(aa) an electronic money institution within the meaning of Article 2.1 of Directive 2009/110/EC of the European Parliament and of the Council of 16 September 2009 on the taking up, pursuit and prudential supervision of the business of electronic money institutions amending Directives 2005/60/EC and 2006/48/EC and repealing Directive 2000/46/EC;]

[(ab) an authorised payment institution or small payment institution as defined in regulation 2(1) of the Payment Services Regulations 2017, or a person whose head office, registered office or place of residence, as the case may be, is outside the United Kingdom and whose functions correspond to those of such an institution;]

(b) an investment firm as defined in [Article 4.1.1 of Directive [2014/65/EU of the European Parliament and of the Council of 15 May 2014] on markets in financial instruments, other than a person to whom Article 2 applies];

(c) a public authority or publicly guaranteed undertaking;

(d) any undertaking whose head office is outside the European Community and whose functions correspond to those of a credit institution or investment firm as defined in (a) and (b) above; or

(e) any undertaking which is treated by the designating authority as an institution in accordance with regulation 8(1),

which participates in a . . . system and which is responsible for discharging the financial obligations arising from transfer orders which are effected through the system;

["interoperable system" in relation to a system ("the first system"), means a second system whose system operator has entered into an arrangement with the system operator of the first system that involves cross-system execution of transfer orders;]

"netting" means the conversion into one net claim or obligation of different claims or obligations between participants resulting from the issue and receipt of transfer orders between them, whether on a bilateral or multilateral basis and whether through the interposition of a clearing house, central counterparty or settlement agent or otherwise;

["Part V" means Part V of the Companies (No 2) (Northern Ireland) Order 1990;]

"Part VII" means Part VII of the Companies Act 1989;

"participant" means—

(a) an institution,

[(aa) a system operator;]

(b) a body corporate or unincorporated association which carries out any combination of the functions of a central counterparty, a settlement agent or a clearing house, with respect to a system, or

(c) an indirect participant which is treated as a participant, or is a member of a class of indirect participants which are treated as participants, in accordance with regulation 9;

["the PRA" means the Prudential Regulation Authority;]

"protected trust deed" and "trust deed" shall be construed in accordance with section 73(1) of the Bankruptcy (Scotland) Act 1985 (interpretation);

"relevant office-holder" means—

(a) the official receiver;

(b) any person acting in relation to a company as its liquidator, provisional liquidator, or administrator;

(c) any person acting in relation to an individual (or, in Scotland, any debtor within the meaning of the Bankruptcy (Scotland) Act 1985) as his trustee in bankruptcy or interim receiver of his property or as permanent or interim trustee in the sequestration of his estate or as his trustee under a protected trust deed; . . .

(d) any person acting as administrator of an insolvent estate of a deceased person; [or]

[(e) any person appointed pursuant to insolvency proceedings of a country or territory outside the United Kingdom;]

and in sub-paragraph (b), "company" means any company, society, association, partnership or other body which may be wound up under the Insolvency Act 1986 [or the Insolvency (Northern Ireland) Order 1989];

"rules", in relation to a designated system, means rules or conditions governing the system with respect to the matters dealt with in these Regulations;

"securities" means (except for the purposes of the definition of "charge") any instruments referred to in section [C of Annex I to Directive [2014/65/EU of the European Parliament and of the Council of 15 May 2014] on markets in financial instruments];

"settlement account" means an account at a central bank, a settlement agent or a central counterparty used to hold funds or securities (or both) and to settle transactions between participants in a . . . system;

"settlement agent" means a body corporate or unincorporated association providing settlement accounts to the institutions and any central counterparty in a . . . system for the settlement of transfer orders within the system and, as the case may be, for extending credit to such institutions and any such central counterparty for settlement purposes;

["system operator" means the entity or entities legally responsible for the operation of a system. A system operator may also act as a settlement agent, central counterparty or clearing house;]

"the Settlement Finality Directive" means Directive 98/26/EC of the European Parliament and of the Council of 19th May 1998 on settlement finality in payment and securities settlement systems[, as last amended by Regulation (EU) No 909/2014 of the European Parliament and of the Council of 23rd July 2014 on improving securities settlement in the European Union and on central securities depositories];

"transfer order" means—

(a) an instruction by a participant to place at the disposal of a recipient an amount of money by means of a book entry on the accounts of a credit institution, a central bank[, a central counterparty] or a settlement agent, or an instruction which results in the assumption or discharge of a payment obligation as defined by the rules of a designated system ("a payment transfer order"); or

(b) an instruction by a participant to transfer the title to, or interest in, securities by means of a book entry on a register, or otherwise ("a securities transfer order");

["winding-up" means—

(a) winding up by the court or creditors' voluntary winding up within the meaning of the Insolvency Act 1986 or the Insolvency (Northern Ireland) Order 1989 (but does not include members' voluntary winding up within the meaning of that Act or that Order);

(b) sequestration of a Scottish partnership under the Bankruptcy (Scotland) Act 1985;

(c) . . .]

[and shall be interpreted in accordance with the modifications made by the enactments mentioned in paragraph (5); and "liquidator" shall be construed accordingly.]

(2) In these Regulations—

[(za) references to the Bank of England do not include the Bank acting in its capacity as the Prudential Regulation Authority;]

[(a) references to the law of insolvency—

(i) include references to every provision made by or under the Bankruptcy (Scotland) Act 1985, Part 10 of the Building Societies Act 1986, the Insolvency Act 1986, the Insolvency (Northern Ireland) Order 1989 and in relation to a building society references to insolvency law or to any provision of the Insolvency Act 1986 or the Insolvency (Northern Ireland) Order 1989 are to that law or provision as modified by the Building Societies Act 1986;

(ii) shall also be interpreted in accordance with the modifications made by the enactments mentioned in paragraph (5);]

(b) in relation to Scotland, references to—

(i) sequestration include references to the administration by a judicial factor of the insolvent estate of a deceased person,

(ii) an interim or permanent trustee include references to a judicial factor on the insolvent estate of a deceased person, and

(iii) "set off" include compensation.

[(2A) For the purposes of these regulations, references to insolvency proceedings do not include crisis prevention measures or crisis management measures taken in relation to an undertaking under the recovery and resolution directive unless—

(a) express provision is made in a contract to which that undertaking is a party that crisis prevention measures or crisis management measures taken in relation to the undertaking are to be treated as insolvency proceedings; and

(b) the substantive obligations provided for in the contract containing that provision (including payment and delivery obligations and provision of collateral) are no longer being performed.

(2B) For the purposes of paragraph (2A)—

(a) "crisis prevention measure" and "crisis management measure" have the meaning given in section 48Z of the Banking Act 2009; and

(b) "recovery and resolution directive" means Directive 2014/59/EU of the European Parliament and of the Council of 15th May 2014 establishing a framework for the recovery and resolution of credit institutions and investment firms.]

(3) Subject to paragraph (1), expressions used in these Regulations which are also used in the Settlement Finality Directive have the same meaning in these Regulations as they have in the Settlement Finality Directive.

(4) References in these Regulations to things done, or required to be done, by or in relation to a designated system shall, in the case of a designated system which is neither a body corporate nor an unincorporated association, be treated as references to things done, or required to be done, by or in relation to the operator of that system.

[(5) The enactments referred to in the definitions of "administration", "administrator", "liquidator" and "winding up" in paragraph (1), and in paragraph (2)(a)(ii), are—

(a) article 3 of, and the Schedule to, the Banking Act 2009 (Parts 2 and 3 Consequential Amendments) Order 2009;

(b) article 18 of, and paragraphs (1)(a), (2) and (3) of Schedule 2 to, the Building Societies (Insolvency and Special Administration) Order 2009;

(c) regulation 27 of, and Schedule 6 to, the Investment Bank Special Administration Regulations 2011.]

NOTES

Para (1): definition relating to "administration" and "administrator" inserted, in definition "default arrangements" word omitted from para (b) revoked and para (d) and word immediately preceding it added, in definition "winding-up" para (c) revoked and final words in square brackets added by the Financial Services and Markets Act 2000 (Over the Counter Derivatives, Central Counterparties and Trade Repositories) Regulations 2013, SI 2013/504, reg 32(1), (2)(a);

definition "the 2000 Act" substituted (for original definition "the 1986 Act") by the Financial Services and Markets Act 2000 (Consequential Amendments) Order 2002, SI 2002/1555, art 39(1), (2)(a);

definitions "business day", "credit claims", "interoperable system" and "system operator" inserted, in definitions "central counterparty", "clearing house", "settlement account", "settlement agent", word "designated" (omitted) revoked, in definition "collateral security", words in square brackets inserted and word "designated" (omitted in both places) revoked, in definition "default arrangements" first and second words in square brackets inserted, definitions "indirect participant", "winding up" substituted, in definition "institution" sub-para (aa) inserted and word "designated" (omitted) revoked, in definition "participant" sub-para (aa) inserted, in definition "relevant office-holder" word "or" (omitted) revoked and words in square brackets inserted, in definition "transfer order" words in square brackets inserted by the Financial Markets and Insolvency (Settlement Finality and Financial Collateral Arrangements) (Amendment) Regulations 2010, SI 2010/2993, reg 2(1), (2)(a)–(d), (f)–(l), (n)–(o) (see also reg 3 of the 2010 Regulations which provides that nothing in the Regulations affects any existing designation order, and no system operator shall be required to apply for an amended designation order in consequence only of the 2010 Regulations);

definition "credit institution" substituted by the Capital Requirements Regulations 2013, SI 2013/3115, reg 46(1), Sch 2, Pt 3, para 48;

definition "designating authority" substituted, and definitions "the FCA" and "the PRA" inserted, by the Financial Services Act 2012 (Consequential Amendments and Transitional Provisions) Order 2013, SI 2013/472, art 3, Sch 2, para 27(a);

definition "EEA State" substituted by the Financial Services (EEA State) Regulations 2007, SI 2007/108, reg 5;

definition "ESMA" inserted by the Financial Services and Markets (Disclosure of Information to the European Securities and Markets Authority etc and Other Provisions) Regulations 2016, SI 2016/1095, reg 2(1), (2);

sub-para (aa) of the definition "institution" inserted, and word omitted from that definition revoked, by SI 2010/2993, reg 2(1), (2)(h). Sub-para (ab) of that definition inserted by the Payment Systems and Services and Electronic Money (Miscellaneous Amendments) Regulations 2017, SI 2017/1173, reg 2. Words in first (outer) pair of square brackets in sub-para (b) of that definition substituted by the Financial Services and Markets Act 2000 (Markets in Financial Instruments) Regulations 2007, SI 2007/126, reg 3(6), Sch 6, Pt 2, para 14. Words in second (inner) pair of square brackets substituted by the Financial Services and Markets Act 2000 (Markets in Financial Instruments) Regulations 2017, SI 2017/701, reg 50(4), Sch 5, para 2(a);

words in square brackets in definition "creditors' voluntary winding up resolution", definition "Part V", and third words in square brackets in definitions "default arrangements", "relevant office-holder" inserted by SI 2006/50, reg 2(1), (3)(a)–(d);

words in first (outer) pair of square brackets in the definition "securities" substituted by SI 2007/126, reg 3(6), Sch 6, Pt 2, para 14 and words in second (inner) pair of square brackets substituted by SI 2017/701, reg 50(4), Sch 5, para 2(b);

in definition "the Settlement Finality Directive" words in square brackets inserted by SI 2010/2993, reg 2(1), (2)(m), and substituted by the Financial Markets and Insolvency (Settlement Finality) (Amendment) Regulations 2015, SI 2015/347, reg 2(1), (2).

Para (2): sub-para (za) inserted by the Bank of England and Financial Services (Consequential Amendments) Regulations 2017, SI 2017/80, reg 2, Schedule, para 23; sub-para (a) substituted by SI 2013/504, reg 32(1), (2)(b).

Paras (2A), (2B): inserted by the Bank Recovery and Resolution (No 2) Order 2014, SI 2014/3348, art 226, Sch 3, Pt 3, paras 1, 7.

Para (5): added by SI 2013/504, reg 32(1), (2)(c).

PART II
DESIGNATED SYSTEMS

[9.42]

3 Application for designation

(1) Any body corporate or unincorporated association may apply to the designating authority for an order declaring it, or any system of which it is the operator, to be a designated system for the purposes of these Regulations.

(2) Any such application—

(a) shall be made in such manner as the designating authority may direct; and

(b) shall be accompanied by such information as the designating authority may reasonably require for the purpose of determining the application.

(3) At any time after receiving an application and before determining it, the designating authority may require the applicant to furnish additional information.

(4) The directions and requirements given or imposed under paragraphs (2) and (3) may differ as between different applications.

(5) Any information to be furnished to the designating authority under this regulation shall be in such form or verified in such manner as it may specify.

(6) Every application shall be accompanied by copies of the rules of the system to which the application relates and any guidance relating to that system.

[9.43]
4 Grant and refusal of designation

(1) Where—

(a) an application has been duly made under regulation 3;
(b) the applicant has paid any fee charged by virtue of regulation 5(1); and
(c) the designating authority is satisfied that the requirements of the Schedule are satisfied with respect to the system to which the application relates;

the designating authority may make an order (a "designation order") declaring the system to be a designated system [and identifying the system operator of that system] for the purposes of these Regulations.

(2) In determining whether to make a designation order, the designating authority shall have regard to systemic risks.

(3) Where an application has been made to the [FCA] under regulation 3 in relation to a system through which both securities transfer orders and payment transfer orders are effected, the Authority shall consult the Bank of England before deciding whether to make a designation order.

(4) A designation order shall state the date on which it takes effect.

(5) Where the designating authority refuses an application for a designation order it shall give the applicant a written notice to that effect stating the reasons for the refusal.

[(6) The designating authority must notify [ESMA] of a designation order made by it.]

NOTES

Para (1): words in square brackets inserted by the Financial Markets and Insolvency (Settlement Finality and Financial Collateral Arrangements) (Amendment) Regulations 2010, SI 2010/2993, reg 2(1), (3) (see also reg 3 of the 2010 Regulations which provides that nothing in the Regulations affects any existing designation order, and no system operator shall be required to apply for an amended designation order in consequence only of the 2010 Regulations).

Para (3): word in square brackets substituted by the Financial Services Act 2012 (Consequential Amendments and Transitional Provisions) Order 2013, SI 2013/472, art 3, Sch 2, para 27(b).

Para (6): added by the Financial Markets and Insolvency (Settlement Finality) (Amendment) Regulations 2015, SI 2015/347, reg 2(1), (3); word in square brackets substituted by the Financial Services and Markets (Disclosure of Information to the European Securities and Markets Authority etc and Other Provisions) Regulations 2016, SI 2016/1095, reg 2(1), (3).

[9.44]
5 Fees

(1) The designating authority may charge a fee to an applicant for a designation order.

(2) The designating authority may charge [the system operator of] a designated system a periodical fee.

(3) Fees chargeable by the designating authority under this regulation shall not exceed an amount which reasonably represents the amount of costs incurred or likely to be incurred—

(a) in the case of a fee charged to an applicant for a designation order, in determining whether the designation order should be made; and
(b) in the case of a periodical fee, in satisfying itself that the designated [system and its system operator continue] to meet the requirements of the Schedule and [are complying] with any obligations to which [they are subject] by virtue of these Regulations.

NOTES

Para (2): words in square brackets inserted by the Financial Markets and Insolvency (Settlement Finality and Financial Collateral Arrangements) (Amendment) Regulations 2010, SI 2010/2993, reg 2(1), (4)(a) (see also reg 3 of the 2010 Regulations which provides that nothing in the Regulations affects any existing designation order, and no system operator shall be required to apply for an amended designation order in consequence only of the 2010 Regulations).

Para (3): first words in square brackets substituted for the words "system continues", second words in square brackets substituted for the words "is complying" and third words in square brackets substituted for the words "it is subject" by SI 2010/2993, reg 2(1), (4)(b) (see also reg 3 of the 2010 Regulations which provides that nothing in the Regulations affects any existing designation order, and no system operator shall be required to apply for an amended designation order in consequence only of the 2010 Regulations).

[9.45]
6 Certain bodies deemed to satisfy requirements for designation

[(1) Subject to paragraph (2), a recognised body, an EEA central counterparty, a third country central counterparty, an EEA CSD and a third country CSD shall be deemed to satisfy the requirements in paragraphs 2 and 3 of the Schedule.]

(2) Paragraph (1) does not apply to overseas investment exchanges or overseas clearing houses within the meaning of [the 2000 Act].

[(3) "EEA central counterparty", "third country central counterparty", "EEA CSD" and "third country CSD" have the meanings given by section 285 of the 2000 Act.

(4) "recognised body" has the meaning given by section 313 of the 2000 Act.]

NOTES

Para (1): substituted by the Central Securities Depositories Regulations 2017, SI 2017/1064, reg 10, Schedule, para 22(1), (2)(a) (for transitional provisions and savings see regs 6–9 of the 2017 Regulations).

Para (2): words in square brackets substituted by the Financial Markets and Insolvency (Settlement Finality) (Amendment) Regulations 2009, SI 2009/1972, regs 2, 3.

Paras (3), (4): substituted (for para (3) as originally added by SI 2013/504, reg 32(1), (3)(b)) by SI 2017/1064, reg 10, Schedule, para 22(1), (2)(b) (for transitional provisions and savings see regs 6–9 of the 2017 Regulations).

[9.46]

7 Revocation of designation

(1) A designation order may be revoked by a further order made by the designating authority if at any time it appears to the designating authority—

(a) that any requirement of the Schedule is not satisfied in the case of the system to which the designation order relates; or

(b) that the system [or the system operator of that system] has failed to comply with any obligation to which [they are subject] by virtue of these Regulations.

(2) [[Subsections (1) to (6)] of section 298 of the 2000 Act] shall apply in relation to the revocation of a designation order under paragraph (1) as they apply in relation to the revocation of a recognition order under [section 297(2) of that Act]; and in those subsections as they so apply—

[(a) any reference to a recognised body shall be taken to be a reference to a designated system;

(b) any reference to members of a recognised body shall be taken to be a reference to participants in a designated system;

[(ba) any reference to the appropriate regulator shall be taken to be a reference to the designating authority;]

(c) . . .

[(d) subsection (4) has effect as if the period for making representations specified in the notice must be at least three months.]]

[(3) An order revoking a designation order—

(a) shall state the date on which it takes effect, being no earlier than three months after the day on which the revocation order is made; and

(b) may contain such transitional provisions as the designating authority thinks necessary or expedient.

(4) A designation order may be revoked at the request or with the consent of the [system operator of the] designated system, and any such revocation shall not be subject to the restriction imposed by paragraph (3)(a), or to the requirements imposed by subsections (1) to (6) of section 298 of the 2000 Act.]

NOTES

Para (1): first words in square brackets inserted, and second words in square brackets substituted for the words "it is subject", by the Financial Markets and Insolvency (Settlement Finality and Financial Collateral Arrangements) (Amendment) Regulations 2010, SI 2010/2993, reg 2(1), (5) (see also reg 3 of the 2010 Regulations which provides that nothing in the Regulations affects any existing designation order, and no system operator shall be required to apply for an amended designation order in consequence only of the 2010 Regulations).

Para (2) is amended as follows:

Words "Subsections (1) to (6)" in square brackets substituted, sub-para (ba) inserted, and sub-para (d) substituted, by the Central Securities Depositories Regulations 2017, SI 2017/1064, reg 10, Schedule, para 22(1), (3) (for transitional provisions and savings see regs 6–9 of the 2017 Regulations).

Sub-para (c) revoked by the Financial Services Act 2012 (Consequential Amendments and Transitional Provisions) Order 2013, SI 2013/472, art 3, Sch 2, para 27(c) (subject to a transitional provision; see below); other words in square brackets substituted by the Financial Services and Markets Act 2000 (Consequential Amendments) Order 2002, SI 2002/1555, art 39(1), (4). Note that art 39(4)(b) of the 2002 Order actually provides—

"for "*under* subsection (1) of that section" substitute "section 297(2) of that Act"";

It is believed that this is an error and that the word "under" should not be removed from para (2).

Para (3): added, together with para (4), by SI 2002/1555, art 39(1), (5).

Para (4): added as noted to para (3); words in square brackets inserted by SI 2010/2993, reg 2(1), (6) (see also reg 3 of the 2010 Regulations which provides that nothing in the Regulations affects any existing designation order, and no system operator shall be required to apply for an amended designation order in consequence only of the 2010 Regulations).

Transitional provisions: see the Financial Services Act 2012 (Consequential Amendments and Transitional Provisions) Order 2013, SI 2013/472, art 3, Sch 2, para 28 which provides that for the purposes of this regulation, the Bank of England may exercise the power to revoke a designation order where (a) the designation order was made before 1 April 2013, and (b) if an application for the designation order had been made on 1 April 2013, it would have been made to the Bank of England as the designating authority.

[9.47]
8 Undertakings treated as institutions

(1) A designating authority may treat as an institution any undertaking which participates in a designated system and which is responsible for discharging financial obligations arising from transfer orders effected through that system, provided that—

(a) the designating authority considers such treatment to be required on grounds of systemic risk, and

(b) the designated system is one in which at least three institutions (other than any undertaking treated as an institution by virtue of this paragraph) participate and through which securities transfer orders are effected.

(2) Where a designating authority decides to treat an undertaking as an institution in accordance with paragraph (1), it shall give written notice of that decision to the designated system in which the undertaking is to be treated as a participant [and to the system operator of that system].

NOTES

Para (2): words in square brackets added by the Financial Markets and Insolvency (Settlement Finality and Financial Collateral Arrangements) (Amendment) Regulations 2010, SI 2010/2993, reg 2(1), (7) (see also reg 3 of the 2010 Regulations which provides that nothing in the Regulations affects any existing designation order, and no system operator shall be required to apply for an amended designation order in consequence only of the 2010 Regulations).

[9.48]
9 Indirect participants treated as participants

(1) A designating authority may treat—

(a) an indirect participant as a participant in a designated system, or

(b) a class of indirect participants as participants in a designated system,

where it considers this to be required on grounds of systemic risk, and shall give written notice of any decision to that effect to the designated system [and to the system operator of that system].

[(2) Where a designating authority, in accordance with paragraph (1), treats an indirect participant as a participant in a designated system, the liability of the participant through which that indirect participant passes transfer orders to the designated system is not affected.]

NOTES

Para (1): words in square brackets added by the Financial Markets and Insolvency (Settlement Finality and Financial Collateral Arrangements) (Amendment) Regulations 2010, SI 2010/2993, reg 2(1), (8)(a) (see also reg 3 of the 2010 Regulations which provides that nothing in the Regulations affects any existing designation order, and no system operator shall be required to apply for an amended designation order in consequence only of the 2010 Regulations).

Para (2): added by SI 2010/2993, reg 2(1), (8)(b) (see also reg 3 of the 2010 Regulations which provides that nothing in the Regulations affects any existing designation order, and no system operator shall be required to apply for an amended designation order in consequence only of the 2010 Regulations).

Note: this regulation did not have a para (2) in the original Queen's Printer's copy of these Regulations.

[9.49]
10 Provision of information by designated systems

[(1) The system operator of a designated system shall, when that system is declared to be a designated system, provide to the designating authority in writing a list of the participants (including the indirect participants) in the designated system and shall give written notice to the designating authority of any amendment to the list within seven days of such amendment.]

(2) The designating authority may, in writing, require [the system operator of a designated system] to furnish to it such other information relating to that designated system as it reasonably requires for the exercise of its functions under these Regulations, within such time, in such form, at such intervals and verified in such manner as the designating authority may specify.

(3) When [the system operator of a designated system] amends, revokes or adds to its rules or its guidance, it shall within fourteen days give written notice to the designating authority of the amendment, revocation or addition.

(4) [The system operator of a designated system] shall give the designating authority at least [three months]' written notice of any proposal to amend, revoke or add to its default arrangements.

[(4A) The designating authority may, if it considers it appropriate, agree a shorter period of notice.]

(5) Nothing in this regulation shall require [the system operator of a designated system] to give any notice or furnish any information to [the FCA or the Bank of England where the notice or information has already been given or furnished to the FCA or the Bank of England (as the case may be)] pursuant to any requirement imposed by or under [section 293 of the 2000 Act] (notification requirements) or any other enactment.

NOTES

Para (1): substituted by the Financial Markets and Insolvency (Settlement Finality and Financial Collateral Arrangements) (Amendment) Regulations 2010, SI 2010/2993, reg 2(1), (9)(a) (see also reg 3 of the 2010 Regulations which provides that nothing in the Regulations affects any existing designation order, and no system operator shall be required to apply for an amended designation order in consequence only of the 2010 Regulations). Para (1) previously read as follows:

"(1) A designated system shall, on being declared to be a designated system, provide to the designating authority in writing a list of its participants and shall give written notice to the designating authority of any amendment to the list within seven days of such amendment.".

Paras (2)–(4): words in square brackets substituted for the words "a designated system" by SI 2010/2993, reg 2(1), (9)(b) (see also reg 3 of the 2010 Regulations which provides that nothing in the Regulations affects any existing designation order, and no system operator shall be required to apply for an amended designation order in consequence only of the 2010 Regulations).

Para (4): words in square brackets substituted by the Financial Services and Markets Act 2000 (Over the Counter Derivatives, Central Counterparties and Trade Repositories) Regulations 2013, SI 2013/504, reg 32(1), (4)(a).

Para (4A): inserted by SI 2013/504, reg 32(1), (4)(b).

Para (5): first words in square brackets substituted for the words "a designated system" by SI 2010/2993, reg 2(1), (9)(b) (see also reg 3 of the 2010 Regulations which provides that nothing in the Regulations affects any existing designation order, and no system operator shall be required to apply for an amended designation order in consequence only of the 2010 Regulations); second words in square brackets substituted by the Financial Services Act 2012 (Consequential Amendments and Transitional Provisions) Order 2013, SI 2013/472, art 3, Sch 2, para 27(d); third words in square brackets substituted by the Financial Services and Markets Act 2000 (Consequential Amendments) Order 2002, SI 2002/1555, art 39(1), (6).

[9.50]

11 Exemption from liability in damages

(1) Neither the designating authority nor any person who is, or is acting as, a member, officer or member of staff of the designating authority shall be liable in damages for anything done or omitted in the discharge, or purported discharge, of the designating authority's functions under these Regulations.

(2) Paragraph (1) does not apply—

(a) if the act or omission is shown to have been in bad faith; or

(b) so as to prevent an award of damages made in respect of an act or omission on the ground that the act or omission was unlawful as a result of section 6(1) of the Human Rights Act 1998 (acts of public authorities).

[9.51]

12 Publication of information and advice

A designating authority may publish information or give advice, or arrange for the publication of information or the giving of advice, in such form and manner as it considers appropriate with respect to any matter dealt with in these Regulations.

PART III
TRANSFER ORDERS EFFECTED THROUGH A DESIGNATED SYSTEM AND COLLATERAL SECURITY

[9.52]

13 Modifications of the law of insolvency

(1) The general law of insolvency has effect in relation to—

(a) transfer orders effected through a designated system and action taken under the rules of a designated system with respect to such orders; and

(b) collateral security,

subject to the provisions of this Part.

(2) Those provisions apply in relation to—

[(a) insolvency proceedings in respect of a participant in a designated system, or of a participant in a system which is an interoperable system in relation to that designated system;]

(b) insolvency proceedings in respect of a provider of collateral security in connection with the functions of a central bank, in so far as the proceedings affect the rights of the central bank to the collateral security; [and

(c) insolvency proceedings in respect of a system operator of a designated system or of a system which is an interoperable system in relation to that designated system;]

but not in relation to any other insolvency proceedings, notwithstanding that rights or liabilities arising from transfer orders or collateral security fall to be dealt with in the proceedings.

(3) Subject to regulation 21, nothing in this Part shall have the effect of disapplying Part VII [or Part V].

[(4) References in this Part to "insolvency proceedings" shall [include winding up and administration.]

(a), (b) . . .]

NOTES

Para (2): sub-para (a) substituted, and sub-para (c) inserted, together with word immediately preceding it, by the Financial Markets and Insolvency (Settlement Finality and Financial Collateral Arrangements) (Amendment) Regulations 2010, SI 2010/2993, reg 2(1), (10)(a)–(c) (see also reg 3 of the 2010 Regulations which provides that nothing in the Regulations affects any existing designation order, and no system operator shall be required to apply for an amended designation order in consequence only of the 2010 Regulations). Para (2)(a) previously read as follows:

"(a) insolvency proceedings in respect of a participant in a designated system; and".

Para (3): words in square brackets added by the Financial Markets and Insolvency (Settlement Finality) (Amendment) Regulations 2006, SI 2006/50, reg 2(1), (5).

Para (4): added by SI 2010/2993, reg 2(1), (10)(d) (see also reg 3 of the 2010 Regulations which provides that nothing in the Regulations affects any existing designation order, and no system operator shall be required to apply for an amended designation order in consequence only of the 2010 Regulations); words in square brackets substituted, and sub-paras (a), (b) revoked, by the Financial Services and Markets Act 2000 (Over the Counter Derivatives, Central Counterparties and Trade Repositories) Regulations 2013, SI 2013/504, reg 32(1), (5).

[9.53]

14 Proceedings of designated system take precedence over insolvency proceedings

(1) None of the following shall be regarded as to any extent invalid at law on the ground of inconsistency with the law relating to the distribution of the assets of a person on bankruptcy, winding up, [administration,] sequestration or under a protected trust deed, or in the administration of an insolvent estate [or with the law relating to other insolvency proceedings of a country or territory outside the United Kingdom]—

(a) a transfer order;
(b) the default arrangements of a designated system;
(c) the rules of a designated system [or in a system which is an interoperable system in relation to that designated system] as to the settlement of transfer orders not dealt with under its default arrangements;
(d) a contract for the purpose of realising collateral security in connection with participation in a designated system [or in a system which is an interoperable system in relation to that designated system] otherwise than pursuant to its default arrangements; or
(e) a contract for the purpose of realising collateral security in connection with the functions of a central bank.

(2) The powers of a relevant office-holder in his capacity as such, and the powers of the court under the Insolvency Act 1986[, the Insolvency (Northern Ireland) Order 1989] or the Bankruptcy (Scotland) Act 1985, shall not be exercised in such a way as to prevent or interfere with—

(a) the settlement in accordance with the rules of a designated system of a transfer order not dealt with under its default arrangements;
(b) any action taken under [the default arrangements of a designated system];
(c) any action taken to realise collateral security in connection with participation in a designated system [or in a system which is an interoperable system in relation to that designated system] otherwise than pursuant to its default arrangements; or
(d) any action taken to realise collateral security in connection with the functions of a central bank.

. . .

(3) Nothing in the following provisions of this Part shall be construed as affecting the generality of the above provisions.

(4) A debt or other liability arising out of a transfer order which is the subject of action taken under default arrangements may not be proved in a winding up[, bankruptcy or administration,] or in Scotland claimed in a winding up, sequestration or under a protected trust deed, until the completion of the action taken under default arrangements.

A debt or other liability which by virtue of this paragraph may not be proved or claimed shall not be taken into account for the purposes of any set-off until the completion of the action taken under default arrangements.

(5) Paragraph (1) has the effect that the following provisions (which relate to preferential debts and the payment of expenses etc) apply subject to paragraph (6), namely—

(a) in the case of collateral security provided by a company (within the meaning of [section 1 of the Companies Act 2006) or by a building society (within the meaning of section 119 of the Building Societies Act 1986)])—
  [(i) sections 175, 176ZA and 176A of, and paragraph 65(2) of Schedule B1 to, the Insolvency Act 1986 or Articles 149, 150ZA, and 150A of, and paragraph 66(2) of Schedule B1 to, the Insolvency (Northern Ireland) Order 1989;
  (ii) Rules 4.30(3) and 4.218(2)(b) of the Insolvency Rules 1986, Rules 4.033(3) and 4.228(2)(b) of the Insolvency Rules (Northern Ireland) 1991 and rule 4.5(3) of the Insolvency (Scotland) Rules 1986;]
  [(iii) section 40 (or in Scotland, section 59 and 60(1)(e)) of the Insolvency Act 1986, paragraph 99(3) of Schedule B1 to that Act and section 19(4) of that Act as that section has effect by virtue of section 249(1) of the Enterprise Act 2002;
  [(iv) paragraph 100(3) of Schedule B1 to the Insolvency (Northern Ireland) Order 1989, Article 31(4) of that Order, as it has effect by virtue of Article 4(1) of the Insolvency (Northern Ireland) Order 2005, and Article 50 of the Insolvency (Northern Ireland) Order 1989; and]
  (v) section 754 of the Companies Act 2006 [(including that section as applied or modified by any enactment made under the Banking Act 2009)]; and]
(b) in the case of collateral security provided by an individual, section 328(1) and (2) of the Insolvency Act 1986 [or, in Northern Ireland, Article 300(1) and (2) of the Insolvency (Northern Ireland) Order 1989] or, in Scotland, in the case of collateral security provided by an individual or a partnership, section 51 of the Bankruptcy (Scotland) Act 1985 and any like provision or rule of law affecting a protected trust deed.

(6) The claim of a participant[, system operator] or central bank to collateral security shall be paid in priority to—

(a) the expenses of the winding up mentioned in sections 115 and 156 of the Insolvency Act 1986 [or Articles 100 and 134 of the Insolvency (Northern Ireland) Order 1989], the expenses of the bankruptcy within the meaning of that Act [or that Order] or, as the case may be, the remuneration and expenses of the administrator mentioned in [paragraph 99(3) of Schedule B1 to that Act] [and in section 19(4) of that Act as that section has effect by virtue of section 249(1) of the Enterprise Act 2002] [or in paragraph 100(3) to Schedule B1 to that Order] [and Article 31(4) of that Order, as that Article has effect by virtue of Article 4(1) of the Insolvency (Northern Ireland) Order 2005], and

(b) the preferential debts of the company or the individual (as the case may be) within the meaning given by section 386 of that Act [or Article 346 of that Order], [and

(c) the debts or liabilities arising or incurred under contracts mentioned in—

(i) paragraph 99(4) of Schedule B1 to the Insolvency Act 1986 and section 19(5) of that Act, as that section has effect by virtue of section 249(1) of the Enterprise Act 2002, or

(ii) paragraph 100(4) of Schedule B1 to, the Insolvency (Northern Ireland) Order 1989 and Article 31(5) of that Order as that article has effect by virtue of Article 4(1) of the Insolvency (Northern Ireland) Order 2005,]

unless the terms on which the collateral security was provided expressly provide that such expenses, remuneration or preferential debts are to have priority.

(7) As respects Scotland—

(a) the reference in paragraph (6)(a) to the expenses of bankruptcy shall be taken to be a reference to the matters mentioned in paragraphs (a) to (d) of section 51(1) of the Bankruptcy (Scotland) Act 1985, or any like provision or rule of law affecting a protected trust deed; and

(b) the reference in paragraph (6)(b) to the preferential debts of the individual shall be taken to be a reference to the preferred debts of the debtor within the meaning of the Bankruptcy (Scotland) Act 1985, or any like definition applying with respect to a protected trust deed by virtue of any provision or rule of law affecting it.

NOTES

Para (1): first word in square brackets inserted by the Financial Markets and Insolvency (Settlement Finality) (Amendment) Regulations 2009, SI 2009/1972, regs 2, 4(a); second and third words in square brackets inserted by the Financial Markets and Insolvency (Settlement Finality and Financial Collateral Arrangements) (Amendment) Regulations 2010, SI 2010/2993, reg 2(1), (11)(a), (b) (see also reg 3 of the 2010 Regulations which provides that nothing in the Regulations affects any existing designation order, and no system operator shall be required to apply for an amended designation order in consequence only of the 2010 Regulations).

Para (2): first words in square brackets inserted by the Financial Markets and Insolvency (Settlement Finality) (Amendment) Regulations 2006, SI 2006/50, reg 2(1), (6)(a); in sub-para (b) words in square brackets substituted for the words "its default arrangements" and in sub-para (c) words in square brackets inserted by SI 2010/2993, reg 2(1), (11)(c), (d) (see also reg 3 of the 2010 Regulations which provides that nothing in the Regulations affects any existing designation order, and no system operator shall be required to apply for an amended designation order in consequence only of the 2010 Regulations); words omitted revoked by SI 2009/1972, regs 2, 4(b).

Para (4): words in square brackets substituted by SI 2009/1972, regs 2, 4(c).

Para (5): in sub-para (a) first, second and third words in square brackets substituted by SI 2009/1972, regs 2, 4(d); sub-para (a)(iv) substituted and words in square brackets in sub-para (a)(v) inserted by SI 2010/2993, reg 2(1), (11)(e), (f) (see also reg 3 of the 2010 Regulations which provides that nothing in the Regulations affects any existing designation order, and no system operator shall be required to apply for an amended designation order in consequence only of the 2010 Regulations); in sub-para (b) words in square brackets inserted by SI 2006/50, reg 2(1), (6)(e). Sub-para (a)(iv) previously read as follows:

> "(iv) paragraph 100(3) of Schedule B1 to, and Article 31(4) of that Order, as that Article has effect by virtue of Article 4(1) of the Insolvency (Northern Ireland) Order 2005; and".

Para (6): first words in square brackets inserted by SI 2010/2993, reg 2(1), (11)(g) (see also reg 3 of the 2010 Regulations which provides that nothing in the Regulations affects any existing designation order, and no system operator shall be required to apply for an amended designation order in consequence only of the 2010 Regulations); in sub-para (a), first and second words in square brackets inserted by SI 2006/50, reg 2(1), (6)(f), third words in square brackets substituted for words "section 19(4) of that Act" by SI 2003/2096, arts 5, 6, Schedule, paras 74, 75(b), except in any case where a petition for an administration order was presented before 15 September 2003, fourth and sixth words in square brackets inserted by SI 2009/1972, regs 2, 4(e)(i), fifth words in square brackets (originally inserted by SI 2006/50, reg 2(1), (6)(f)) substituted by SI 2007/832, reg 2(1), (3); in sub-para (b), words in square brackets inserted by SI 2006/50, reg 2(1), (6)(g); sub-para (c), and word immediately preceding it, inserted by SI 2009/1972, regs 2, 4(e)(ii).

[9.54]

15 Net sum payable on completion of action taken under default arrangements

(1) The following provisions apply with respect to any sum which is owed on completion of action taken under default arrangements [of a designated system] by or to a defaulter but do not apply to any sum which (or to the extent that it) arises from a transfer order which is also a market contract within the meaning of Part VII [or Part V], in which case sections 162 and 163 of the Companies Act 1989 [or Articles 85 and 86 of the Companies (No 2) (Northern Ireland) Order 1990] apply subject to the modification made by regulation 21.

(2) If, in England and Wales [or Northern Ireland], a bankruptcy[, winding-up or administration] order has been made or a creditors' voluntary winding-up resolution has been passed, the debt—

(a) is provable in the bankruptcy[, winding-up or administration] or, as the case may be, is payable to the relevant office-holder; and

(b) shall be taken into account, where appropriate, under section 323 of the Insolvency Act 1986 [or Article 296 of the Insolvency (Northern Ireland) Order 1989] [or Rule 2.85 of the Insolvency Rules 1986 or Rule 2.086 of the Insolvency Rules (Northern Ireland) 1991] (mutual dealings and set-off) or the corresponding provision applicable in the case of winding up [or administration];

in the same way as a debt due before the commencement of bankruptcy, the date on which the body corporate goes into liquidation (within the meaning of section 247 of the Insolvency Act 1986 [or Article 6 of the Insolvency (Northern Ireland) Order 1989]) or [enters into administration (within the meaning of paragraph 1 of Schedule B1 to the Insolvency Act 1986 or paragraph 2 of Schedule B1 to the Insolvency (Northern Ireland) Order 1989) or], in the case of a partnership, the date of the winding-up order.

(3) If, in Scotland, an award of sequestration or a winding-up order has been made, or a creditors' voluntary winding-up resolution has been passed, or a trust deed has been granted and it has become a protected trust deed, the debt—

(a) may be claimed in the sequestration or winding up or under the protected trust deed or, as the case may be, is payable to the relevant office-holder; and

(b) shall be taken into account for the purposes of any rule of law relating to set-off applicable in sequestration, winding up or in respect of a protected trust deed;

in the same way as a debt due before the date of sequestration (within the meaning of section 73(1) of the Bankruptcy (Scotland) Act 1985) or the commencement of the winding up (within the meaning of section 129 of the Insolvency Act 1986) or the grant of the trust deed.

[(4) A reference in this regulation to "administration order" shall include—

(a) the appointment of an administrator under paragraph 14 or 22 of Schedule B1 to the Insolvency Act 1986 or under paragraph 15 or 23 of Schedule B1 to the Insolvency (Northern Ireland) Order 1989;

(b) the making of an order under section 8 of that Act as it has effect by virtue of section 249(1) of the Enterprise Act 2002; and

(c) the making of an order under Article 21 of that Order as it has effect by virtue of Article 4(1) of the Insolvency (Northern Ireland) Order 2005;

and "administration" shall be construed accordingly.]

NOTES

Para (1): first words in square brackets inserted by the Financial Markets and Insolvency (Settlement Finality and Financial Collateral Arrangements) (Amendment) Regulations 2010, SI 2010/2993, reg 2(1), (12) (see also reg 3 of the 2010 Regulations which provides that nothing in the Regulations affects any existing designation order, and no system operator shall be required to apply for an amended designation order in consequence only of the 2010 Regulations); second and third words in square brackets inserted by the Financial Markets and Insolvency (Settlement Finality) (Amendment) Regulations 2006, SI 2006/50, reg 2(1), (7)(a).

Para (2): first, fourth and seventh words in square brackets inserted by SI 2006/50, reg 2(1), (7)(b)–(d); second and third words in square brackets substituted, and fifth, sixth and eighth words in square brackets inserted, by the Financial Markets and Insolvency (Settlement Finality) (Amendment) Regulations 2009, SI 2009/1972, regs 2, 5(a).

Para (4): added by SI 2009/1972, regs 2, 5(b).

[9.55]

16 Disclaimer of property, rescission of contracts, &c

(1) Sections 178, 186, 315 and 345 of the Insolvency Act 1986 [or Articles 152, 157, 288 and 318 of the Insolvency (Northern Ireland) Order 1989] (power to disclaim onerous property and court's power to order rescission of contracts, &c) do not apply in relation to—

(a) a transfer order; or

(b) a contract for the purpose of realising collateral security.

In the application of this paragraph in Scotland, the reference to sections 178, 315 and 345 shall be construed as a reference to any rule of law having the like effect as those sections.

(2) In Scotland, a permanent trustee on the sequestrated estate of a defaulter or a liquidator or a trustee under a protected trust deed granted by a defaulter is bound by any transfer order given by that defaulter and by any such contract as is mentioned in paragraph (1)(b) notwithstanding section 42 of the Bankruptcy (Scotland) Act 1985 or any rule of law having the like effect applying in liquidations or any like provision or rule of law affecting the protected trust deed.

(3) [Sections 88, 127, 245 and 284 of the Insolvency Act 1986] [or [Articles 74, 107, 207 and 257 of the Insolvency (Northern Ireland) Order 1989]] (avoidance of property dispositions effected after commencement of winding up or presentation of bankruptcy petition), section 32(8) of the Bankruptcy (Scotland) Act 1985 (effect of dealing with debtor relating to estate vested in permanent trustee) and any like provision or rule of law affecting a protected trust deed, do not apply to—

(a) a transfer order, or any disposition of property in pursuance of such an order;

(b) the provision of collateral security;

(c) a contract for the purpose of realising collateral security or any disposition of property in pursuance of such a contract; or

(d) any disposition of property in accordance with the rules of a designated system as to the application of collateral security.

NOTES

Para (1): words in square brackets inserted by the Financial Markets and Insolvency (Settlement Finality) (Amendment) Regulations 2006, SI 2006/50, reg 2(1), (8)(a).

Para (3): first and third (inner) words in square brackets substituted by the Financial Markets and Insolvency (Settlement Finality) (Amendment) Regulations 2009, SI 2009/1972, regs 2, 6; second (outer) words in square brackets inserted by SI 2006/50, reg 2(1), (8)(b).

[9.56]

17 Adjustment of prior transactions

(1) No order shall be made in relation to a transaction to which this regulation applies under—

(a) section 238 or 339 of the Insolvency Act 1986 [or Article 202 or 312 of the Insolvency (Northern Ireland) Order 1989] (transactions at an undervalue);
(b) section 239 or 340 of that Act [or Article 203 or 313 of that Order] (preferences); or
(c) section 423 of that Act [or Article 367 of that Order] (transactions defrauding creditors).

(2) As respects Scotland, no decree shall be granted in relation to any such transaction—
(a) under section 34 or 36 of the Bankruptcy (Scotland) Act 1985 or section 242 or 243 of the Insolvency Act 1986 (gratuitous alienations and unfair preferences); or
(b) at common law on grounds of gratuitous alienations or fraudulent preferences.

(3) This regulation applies to—
(a) a transfer order, or any disposition of property in pursuance of such an order;
(b) the provision of collateral security;
(c) a contract for the purpose of realising collateral security or any disposition of property in pursuance of such a contract; or
(d) any disposition of property in accordance with the rules of a designated system as to the application of collateral security.

NOTES

Para (1): words in square brackets inserted by the Financial Markets and Insolvency (Settlement Finality) (Amendment) Regulations 2006, SI 2006/50, reg 2(1), (9).

Collateral security charges

[9.57]
18 Modifications of the law of insolvency

The general law of insolvency has effect in relation to a collateral security charge and the action taken to enforce such a charge, subject to the provisions of regulation 19.

[9.58]
19 Administration orders, &c

(1) The following provisions of [Schedule B1 to] the Insolvency Act 1986 (which relate to administration orders and administrators) do not apply in relation to a collateral security charge—
[(a) paragraph 43(2) including that provision as applied by paragraph 44; and
(b) paragraphs 70, 71 and 72 of that Schedule;]
and [paragraph 41(2) of that Schedule] (receiver to vacate office when so required by administrator) does not apply to a receiver appointed under such a charge.

[(1ZA) The following provisions of the Insolvency Act 1986 (which relate to administration orders and administrators), as they have effect by virtue of section 249(1) of the Enterprise Act 2002, do not apply in relation to a collateral security charge—
(a) sections 10(1)(b) and 11(3)(c) (restriction on enforcement of security while petition for administration order pending or order in force); and
(b) sections 15(1) and (2) (power of administrator to deal with charged property);
and section 11(2) (receiver to vacate office when so required by administrator) does not apply to a receiver appointed under such a charge.]

[(1A) The following provisions of [Schedule B1 to] the Insolvency (Northern Ireland) Order 1989 (which relate to administration orders and administrators) do not apply in relation to a collateral security charge—
[(a) paragraph 44(2), including that provision as applied by paragraph 45 (restrictions on enforcement of security where company in administration or where administration application has been made); and
(b) paragraphs 71, 72 and 73 (charged and hire purchase property);]
and [paragraph 42(2)] (receiver to vacate office when so required by administrator) does not apply to a receiver appointed under such a charge.]

[(1B) The following provisions of the Insolvency (Northern Ireland) Order 1989 (administration), as they have effect by virtue of Article 4(1) of the Insolvency (Northern Ireland) Order 2005, do not apply in relation to a collateral security charge—
(a) Article 23(1)(b) and Article 24(3)(c) (restriction on enforcement of security while petition for administration order pending or order in force); and
(b) Article 28(1) and (2) (power of administrator to deal with charged property);
and Article 24(2) of that Order (receiver to vacate office at request of administrator) shall not apply to a receiver appointed under such a charge.]

(2) However, where a collateral security charge falls to be enforced after an administration order has been made or a petition for an administration order has been presented, and there exists another charge over some or all of the same property ranking in priority to or *pari passu* with the collateral security charge, on the application of any person interested, the court may order that there shall be taken after enforcement of the collateral security charge such steps as the court may direct for the purpose of ensuring that the chargee under the other charge is not prejudiced by the enforcement of the collateral security charge.

[(2A) A reference in paragraph (2) to "an administration order" shall include the appointment of an administrator under paragraph 14 or 22 of Schedule B1 to the Insolvency Act 1986 [or under paragraph 15 or 23 of Schedule B1 to the Insolvency (Northern Ireland) Order 1989].]

(3) Sections 127 and 284 of the Insolvency Act 1986 [or Articles 107 and 257 of the Insolvency (Northern Ireland) Order 1989] (avoidance of property dispositions effected after commencement of winding up or presentation of bankruptcy petition), section 32(8) of the Bankruptcy (Scotland) Act 1985 (effect of dealing with debtor relating to estate vested in permanent trustee) and any like provision or rule of law affecting a protected trust deed, do not apply to a disposition of property as a result of which the property becomes subject to a collateral security charge or any transactions pursuant to which that disposition is made.

[(4) Paragraph 20 and paragraph 12(1)(g) of Schedule A1 to the Insolvency Act 1986, and paragraph 31 and paragraph 23(1)(g) of Schedule A1 to the Insolvency (Northern Ireland) Order 1989 (effect of moratorium on creditors) shall not apply (if they would otherwise do so) to any collateral security charge.]

NOTES

Para (1): first words in square brackets inserted, sub-paras (a), (b) substituted, for original sub-paras (a), (b), and third words in square brackets substituted for words "section 11(2) of that Act", by the Enterprise Act 2002 (Insolvency) Order 2003, SI 2003/2096, arts 5, 6, Schedule, paras 74, 76(a), except in any case where a petition for an administration order was presented before 15 September 2003. Sub-paras (a), (b) originally read as follows:

"(a) sections 10(1)(b) and 11(3)(c) (restriction on enforcement of security while petition for administration order pending or order in force); and

(b) section 15(1) and (2) (power of administrator to deal with charged property);".

Para (1ZA): inserted by the Financial Markets and Insolvency (Settlement Finality) (Amendment) Regulations 2009, SI 2009/1972, regs 2, 7(a).

Para (1A): inserted by the Financial Markets and Insolvency (Settlement Finality) (Amendment) Regulations 2006, SI 2006/50, reg 2(1), (10)(a); first words in square brackets inserted, and sub-paras (a), (b) and final words in square brackets substituted by the Financial Markets and Insolvency (Settlement Finality) (Amendment) Regulations 2007, SI 2007/832, reg 2(1), (4).

Para (1B): inserted by SI 2009/1972, regs 2, 7(b).

Para (2A): inserted by SI 2003/2096, arts 5, 6, Schedule, paras 74, 76(b), except in any case where a petition for an administration order was presented before 15 September 2003; words in square brackets inserted by SI 2007/832, reg 2(1), (5).

Para (3): words in square brackets inserted by SI 2006/50, reg 2(1), (10)(b).

Para (4): added by SI 2009/1972, regs 2, 7(c).

General

[9.59]

20 Transfer order entered into designated system following insolvency

(1) This Part does not apply in relation to any transfer order given by a participant which is entered into a designated system after—

(a) a court has made an order of a type referred to in regulation 22 [in respect of—

(i) that participant;

(ii) a participant in a system which is an interoperable system in relation to the designated system; or

(iii) a system operator which is not a participant in the designated system, or]

(b) that participant[, a participant in a system which is an interoperable system in relation to the designated system or a system operator of that designated system] has passed a creditors' voluntary winding-up resolution, or

(c) a trust deed granted by that participant[, a participant in a system which is an interoperable system in relation to the designated system or a system operator of that designated system] has become a protected trust deed,

unless the [conditions mentioned in either paragraph (2) or paragraph (4)] are satisfied.

(2) [The conditions referred to in this paragraph] are that—

(a) the transfer order is carried out on the [same business day of the designated system] that the event specified in paragraph (1)(a), (b) or (c) occurs, and

(b) [the system operator] can show that it did not have notice of that event at [the time the transfer order became irrevocable].

(3) For the purposes of paragraph (2)(b), [the relevant system operator] shall be taken to have notice of an event specified in paragraph (1)(a), (b) or (c) if it deliberately failed to make enquiries as to that matter in circumstances in which a reasonable and honest person would have done so.

[(4) The conditions referred to in this paragraph are that—

(a) a recognised central counterparty, EEA central counterparty or third country central counterparty is the system operator;

(b) a clearing member of that central counterparty has defaulted; and

(c) the transfer order has been entered into the system pursuant to the provisions of the default rules of the central counterparty that provide for the transfer of the positions or assets of a clearing member on its default.

(5) In paragraph (4)—

(a) "recognised central counterparty", "EEA central counterparty" and "third country central counterparty" have the meanings given by section 285 of the 2000 Act; and

(b) "clearing member" has the meaning given by section 190(1) of the Companies Act 1989.]

NOTES

Para (1): in sub-para (a) words in square brackets substituted for the words "in respect of that participant" and in sub-paras (b), (c) words in square brackets inserted by the Financial Markets and Insolvency (Settlement Finality and

Financial Collateral Arrangements) (Amendment) Regulations 2010, SI 2010/2993, reg 2(1), (13)(i), (b) (see also reg 3 of the 2010 Regulations which provides that nothing in the Regulations affects any existing designation order, and no system operator shall be required to apply for an amended designation order in consequence only of the 2010 Regulations); final words in square brackets substituted by the Financial Services and Markets Act 2000 (Over the Counter Derivatives, Central Counterparties and Trade Repositories) Regulations 2013, SI 2013/504, reg 32(1), (6)(a).

Para (2): first words in square brackets substituted by SI 2013/504, reg 32(1), (6)(b); in sub-para (a) words in square brackets substituted for the words "same day", and in sub-para (b) first words in square brackets substituted for the words "the settlement agent, the central counterparty or the clearing house" and second words in square brackets substituted for the words "the time of settlement of the transfer order" by SI 2010/2993, reg 2(1), (13)(c) (see also reg 3 of the 2010 Regulations which provides that nothing in the Regulations affects any existing designation order, and no system operator shall be required to apply for an amended designation order in consequence only of the 2010 Regulations).

Para (3): words in square brackets substituted for the words "the relevant settlement agent, central counterparty or clearing house" by SI 2010/2993, reg 2(1), (13)(d) (see also reg 3 of the 2010 Regulations which provides that nothing in the Regulations affects any existing designation order, and no system operator shall be required to apply for an amended designation order in consequence only of the 2010 Regulations).

Paras (4), (5): added by SI 2013/504, reg 32(1), (6)(c).

[9.60]

21 Disapplication of certain provisions of Part VII [and Part V]

(1) The provisions of the Companies Act 1989 [or the Companies (No 2) (Northern Ireland) Order 1990] mentioned in paragraph (2) do not apply in relation to—

(a) a market contract which is also a transfer order effected through a designated system; or

(b) a market charge which is also a collateral security charge.

(2) The provisions referred to in paragraph (1) are as follows—

(a) section 163(4) to (6) [and Article 86(3) to (5)] (net sum payable on completion of default proceedings);

(b) section 164(4) to (6) [and Article 87(3) to (5)] (disclaimer of property, rescission of contracts, &c); and

(c) section 175(5) and (6) [and Article 97(5) and (6)] (administration orders, &c).

NOTES

Words in square brackets inserted by the Financial Markets and Insolvency (Settlement Finality) (Amendment) Regulations 2006, SI 2006/50, reg 2(1), (11).

[9.61]

22 Notification of insolvency order or passing of resolution for creditors' voluntary winding up

(1) Upon the making of an order for bankruptcy, sequestration, administration or winding up in respect of a participant in a designated system, the court shall forthwith notify both [the system operator of that designated system] and the designating authority that such an order has been made.

(2) Following receipt of—

(a) such notification from the court, or

(b) notification from a participant of the passing of a creditors' voluntary winding-up resolution or of a trust deed becoming a protected trust deed, pursuant to paragraph 5(4) of the Schedule,

the designating authority shall forthwith inform the Treasury[, the Board, ESMA and other EEA States] of the notification.

[(3) In paragraph (2) "the Board" means the European Systemic Risk Board established by Regulation (EU) No 1092/2010 of the European Parliament and of the Council of 24th November 2010 on European Union macro-prudential oversight of the financial system and establishing a European Systemic Risk Board.]

NOTES

Para (1): words in square brackets substituted for the words "the system" by the Financial Markets and Insolvency (Settlement Finality and Financial Collateral Arrangements) (Amendment) Regulations 2010, SI 2010/2993, reg 2(1), (14) (see also reg 3 of the 2010 Regulations which provides that nothing in the Regulations affects any existing designation order, and no system operator shall be required to apply for an amended designation order in consequence only of the 2010 Regulations).

Para (2): words in square brackets inserted by the Financial Services and Markets (Disclosure of Information to the European Securities and Markets Authority etc and Other Provisions) Regulations 2016, SI 2016/1095, reg 2(1), (4)(a).

Para (3): added by SI 2016/1095, reg 2(1), (4)(b).

[9.62]

23 Applicable law relating to securities held as collateral security

Where—

(a) securities (including rights in securities) are provided as collateral security to a participant[, a system operator] or a central bank (including any nominee, agent or third party acting on behalf of the participant[, the system operator] or the central bank), and

(b) a register, account or centralised deposit system located in an EEA State legally records the entitlement of that person to the collateral security,

the rights of that person as a holder of collateral security in relation to those securities shall be governed by the law of the EEA State or, where appropriate, the law of the part of the EEA State, where the register, account, or centralised deposit system is located.

NOTES

Words in square brackets inserted by the Financial Markets and Insolvency (Settlement Finality and Financial Collateral Arrangements) (Amendment) Regulations 2010, SI 2010/2993, reg 2(1), (15) (see also reg 3 of the 2010 Regulations which provides that nothing in the Regulations affects any existing designation order, and no system operator shall be required to apply for an amended designation order in consequence only of the 2010 Regulations).

[9.63]
24 Applicable law where insolvency proceedings are brought

Where insolvency proceedings are brought in any jurisdiction against a person who participates, or has participated, in a system designated for the purposes of the Settlement Finality Directive, any question relating to the rights and obligations arising from, or in connection with, that participation and falling to be determined by a court in England and Wales[, the High Court in Northern Ireland] or in Scotland shall (subject to regulation 23) be determined in accordance with the law governing that system.

NOTES

Words in square brackets inserted by the Financial Markets and Insolvency (Settlement Finality) (Amendment) Regulations 2006, SI 2006/50, reg 2(1), (12).

[9.64]
25 Insolvency proceedings in other jurisdictions

(1) The references to insolvency law in section 426 of the Insolvency Act 1986 (co-operation between courts exercising jurisdiction in relation to insolvency) include, in relation to a part of the United Kingdom, this Part and, in relation to a relevant country or territory within the meaning of that section, so much of the law of that country or territory as corresponds to this Part.

(2) A court shall not, in pursuance of that section or any other enactment or rule of law, recognise or give effect to—

(a) any order of a court exercising jurisdiction in relation to insolvency law in a country or territory outside the United Kingdom, or
(b) any act of a person appointed in such a country or territory to discharge any functions under insolvency law,

in so far as the making of the order or the doing of the act would be prohibited in the case of a court in England and Wales or Scotland[, the High Court in Northern Ireland] or a relevant office-holder by this Part.

(3) Paragraph (2) does not affect the recognition or enforcement of a judgment required to be recognised or enforced under or by virtue of the Civil Jurisdiction and Judgments Act 1982 [or *Council Regulation (EC) No 44/2001 of 22nd December 2000 on jurisdiction and the recognition and enforcement of judgments in civil and commercial matters*][*, as amended from time to time and as applied by the Agreement made on 19th October 2005 between the European Community and the Kingdom of Denmark on jurisdiction and the recognition and enforcement of judgments in civil and commercial matters*].

NOTES

Para (2): words in square brackets inserted by the Financial Markets and Insolvency (Settlement Finality) (Amendment) Regulations 2006, SI 2006/50, reg 2(1), (13).

Para (3): words in first pair of square brackets added by the Civil Jurisdiction and Judgments Order 2001, SI 2001/3929, art 5, Sch 3, para 27; words in second pair of square brackets added by the Civil Jurisdiction and Judgments Regulations 2007, SI 2007/1655, reg 5, Schedule, Pt 2, para 32; for the words in italics there are substituted the words "Regulation (EU) No 1215/2012 of the European Parliament and of the Council of 12 December 2012 on jurisdiction and the recognition and enforcement of judgments in civil and commercial matters (recast), as amended from time to time and as applied by virtue of the Agreement made on 19 October 2005 between the European Community and the Kingdom of Denmark on jurisdiction and the recognition and enforcement of judgments in civil and commercial matters (OJ No L299, 16.11.2005, p 62; OJ No L79, 21.3.2013, p 4)" by the Civil Jurisdiction and Judgments (Amendment) Regulations 2014, SI 2014/2947, reg 5, Sch 4, para 5 (note that for the purposes of proceedings, judgments and authentic instruments and court settlements to which, by virtue of Article 66(2) of Regulation 1215/2012/EU (transitional provisions), Regulation 44/2001/EC continues to apply (a) the amendments made by the 2014 Regulations do not apply; and (b) the enactments amended by the 2014 Regulations continue to have effect as if those amendments had not been made).

[9.65]
26 Systems designated in other EEA States . . . and Gibraltar

(1) Where an equivalent overseas order or equivalent overseas security is subject to the insolvency law of England and Wales or Scotland [or Northern Ireland], this Part shall apply—

(a) in relation to the equivalent overseas order as it applies in relation to a transfer order; and
(b) in relation to the equivalent overseas security as it applies in relation to collateral security . . .

(2) In paragraph (1)—

(a) "equivalent overseas order" means an order having the like effect as a transfer order which is effected through a system designated for the purposes of the Settlement Finality Directive in another EEA State . . . or Gibraltar; and
[(b) "equivalent overseas security" means any realisable assets provided under a charge or a repurchase or similar agreement, or otherwise (including credit claims and money provided under a charge)—

(i) for the purpose of securing rights and obligations potentially arising in connection with such a system, or

(ii) to a central bank for the purpose of securing rights and obligations in connection with its operations in carrying out its functions as a central bank.]

NOTES

Provision heading: words omitted revoked by the Financial Markets and Insolvency (Settlement Finality) (Amendment) Regulations 2006, SI 2006/50, reg 2(1), (14)(a).

Para (1): words in square brackets inserted by SI 2006/50, reg 2(1), (14)(b); words "in connection with a designated system" (omitted) revoked by the Financial Markets and Insolvency (Settlement Finality and Financial Collateral Arrangements) (Amendment) Regulations 2010, SI 2010/2993, reg 2(1), (16)(a) (see also reg 3 of the 2010 Regulations which provides that nothing in the Regulations affects any existing designation order, and no system operator shall be required to apply for an amended designation order in consequence only of the 2010 Regulations).

Para (2): words omitted revoked by SI 2006/50, reg 2(1), (14)(c); sub-para (b) substituted by SI 2010/2993, reg 2(1), (16)(b) (see also reg 3 of the 2010 Regulations which provides that nothing in the Regulations affects any existing designation order, and no system operator shall be required to apply for an amended designation order in consequence only of the 2010 Regulations), and previously read as follows:

"(b) "equivalent overseas security" means any realisable assets provided under a charge or a repurchase or similar agreement, or otherwise (including money provided under a charge) for the purpose of securing rights and obligations potentially arising in connection with such a system.".

SCHEDULES

SCHEDULE
REQUIREMENTS FOR DESIGNATION OF SYSTEM

Regulation 4(1)

[9.66]

1 Establishment, participation and governing law

(1) The head office of at least one of the participants in the system must be in . . . [the United Kingdom] and the law of England and Wales[, Northern Ireland] or Scotland must be the governing law of the system.

(2) There must be not less than three institutions participating in the system, unless otherwise determined by the designating authority in any case where—

(a) there are two institutions participating in a system; and

(b) the designating authority considers that designation is required on the grounds of systemic risk.

(3) The system must be a system through which transfer orders are effected.

(4) Where orders relating to financial instruments other than securities are effected through the system—

(a) the system must primarily be a system through which securities transfer orders are effected; and

(b) the designating authority must consider that designation is required on grounds of systemic risk.

[(5) An arrangement entered into between interoperable systems shall not constitute a system.]

2 Arrangements and resources

The system must have adequate arrangements and resources for the effective monitoring and enforcement of compliance with its rules or, as respects monitoring, arrangements providing for that function to be performed on its behalf (and without affecting its responsibility) by another body or person who is able and willing to perform it.

3 Financial resources

The [system operator] must have financial resources sufficient for the proper performance of its functions as a [system operator].

4 Co-operation with other authorities

[The system operator] must be able and willing to co-operate, by the sharing of information and otherwise, with—

(a) the [FCA],

(b) the Bank of England,

[(ba) the PRA,]

(c) any relevant office-holder, and

(d) any authority, body or person having responsibility for any matter arising out of, or connected with, the default of a participant.

5 Specific provision in the rules

(1) The rules of the system must—

(a) specify the point at which a transfer order takes effect as having been entered into the system,

(b) specify the point after which a transfer order may not be revoked by a participant or any other party, and

(c) prohibit the revocation by a participant or any other party of a transfer order from the point specified in accordance with paragraph (b).

[(1A) Where the system has one or more interoperable systems, the rules required under paragraph (1)(a) and (b) shall, as far as possible, be co-ordinated with the rules of those interoperable systems.

(1B) The rules of the system which are referred to in paragraph (1)(a) and (b) shall not be affected by any rules of that system's interoperable systems in the absence of express provision in the rules of the system and all of those interoperable systems.]

(2) The rules of the system must require each institution which participates in the system to provide upon payment of a reasonable charge the information mentioned in sub-paragraph (3) to any person who requests it, save where the request is frivolous or vexatious. The rules must require the information to be provided within fourteen days of the request being made.

(3) The information referred to in sub-paragraph (2) is as follows—
- (a) details of the systems which are designated for the purposes of the Settlement Finality Directive in which the institution participates, and
- (b) information about the main rules governing the functioning of those systems.

(4) The rules of the system must require each participant upon—
- (a) the passing of a creditors' voluntary winding up resolution, or
- (b) a trust deed granted by him becoming a protected trust deed,

to notify forthwith both the system and the designating authority that such a resolution has been passed, or, as the case may be, that such a trust deed has become a protected trust deed.

6 Default arrangements

The system must have default arrangements which are appropriate for that system in all the circumstances.

NOTES

Para 1: in sub-para (1) words omitted revoked and words in square brackets inserted by the Financial Markets and Insolvency (Settlement Finality) (Amendment) Regulations 2006, SI 2006/50, reg 2(1), (15); sub-para (5) added by the Financial Markets and Insolvency (Settlement Finality and Financial Collateral Arrangements) (Amendment) Regulations 2010, SI 2010/2993, reg 2(1), (17)(a) (see also reg 3 of the 2010 Regulations which provides that nothing in the Regulations affects any existing designation order, and no system operator shall be required to apply for an amended designation order in consequence only of the 2010 Regulations).

Para 3: words in square brackets substituted in both places for the word "system" by SI 2010/2993, reg 2(1), (17)(b) (see also reg 3 of the 2010 Regulations which provides that nothing in the Regulations affects any existing designation order, and no system operator shall be required to apply for an amended designation order in consequence only of the 2010 Regulations).

Para 4: first words in square brackets substituted for the words "the system" by SI 2010/2993, reg 2(1), (17)(c) (see also reg 3 of the 2010 Regulations which provides that nothing in the Regulations affects any existing designation order, and no system operator shall be required to apply for an amended designation order in consequence only of the 2010 Regulations); word in square brackets in sub-para (a) substituted, and sub-para (ba) inserted, by the Financial Services Act 2012 (Consequential Amendments and Transitional Provisions) Order 2013, SI 2013/472, art 3, Sch 2, para 27(e).

Para 5: sub-paras (1A), (1B) inserted by SI 2010/2993, reg 2(1), (17)(d) (see also reg 3 of the 2010 Regulations which provides that nothing in the Regulations affects any existing designation order, and no system operator shall be required to apply for an amended designation order in consequence only of the 2010 Regulations).

OCCUPATIONAL PENSION SCHEMES (WINDING UP NOTICES AND REPORTS ETC) REGULATIONS 2002

(SI 2002/459)

NOTES

Made: 4 March 2002.

Authority: Pension Schemes Act 1993, s 113(1); Pensions Act 1995, ss 10(2)(b), (3), 23(2), 26B(3)(b), 26C(2), (3), 49A(2)(b), (3), 71A(4), 72A(1)(b), (2), (7), (8)(a), 72B(2)(c)(iii), (3), (5)(c), (6)(c), (8)(b), 118(2), 124(3E), 174(2), (3)

Commencement: 1 April 2002.

Application: the Royal Mail Statutory Pension Scheme is to be treated as an occupational pension scheme for the purposes of these Regulations: see the Postal Services Act 2011 (Transfer of Accrued Pension Rights) Order 2012, SI 2012/687, arts 2, 9, Sch 4, Pt I, paras 1, 5(c).

ARRANGEMENT OF REGULATIONS

1 Citation and commencement and interpretation . . . [9.67]
5 Persons exempted from obligations to give notices to the Authority under section 26A or section 26B of the 1995 Act . . . [9.68]
6 Schemes excluded from sections 26A and 26B of the 1995 Act . . . [9.69]
7 Penalties for failing to give notice to the Authority under section 26A or section 26B of the 1995 Act . . . [9.70]
8 Applications to the Authority to modify schemes to secure winding up . . . [9.71]
9 Reports to the Authority about winding up: time limits . . . [9.72]
10 Contents of reports to the Authority about winding up . . . [9.73]
11 Exemption from requirement to make reports to the Authority about winding up . . . [9.74]
12 Time when winding up taken to begin . . . [9.75]

13 Records of decisions about winding up . . . . [9.76]
14 Directions by the Authority for facilitating winding up . . . . [9.77]

[9.67]
1 Citation and commencement and interpretation

(1) These Regulations may be cited as the Occupational Pension Schemes (Winding Up Notices and Reports etc) Regulations 2002 and come into force on 1st April 2002.

(2) In these Regulations—

"the 1993 Act" means the Pension Schemes Act 1993,

"the 1995 Act" means the Pensions Act 1995,

"member", "deferred member" and "pensioner member" have the meanings given in section 124(1) of the 1995 Act, subject to the provision made by regulations 6(3) and 11(3), and

"small self-administered scheme" has the meaning given in regulation 2(1) of the Retirement Benefits Schemes (Restriction on Discretion to Approve) (Small Self-administered Schemes) Regulations 1991.

2–4 (*Reg 2 amends the Occupational Pension Schemes (Disclosure of Information) Regulations 1996, SI 1996/1655, reg 5; regs 3, 4 revoked by the Occupational Pension Schemes (Independent Trustee) Regulations 2005, SI 2005/703, reg 14(3).*)

[9.68]
5 Persons exempted from obligations to give notices to the Authority under section 26A or section 26B of the 1995 Act

In section 26C of the 1995 Act (construction of sections 26A and 26B) references, in relation to a scheme, to a person involved in the administration of the scheme do not include any person whose only involvement with the scheme is in connection with—

(a) underwriting policies of insurance that are specifically allocated to the provision of benefits for individual members or other persons with rights to benefits under the scheme or annuity contracts, or

(b) providing advice about the management of investments.

[9.69]
6 Schemes excluded from sections 26A and 26B of the 1995 Act

(1) Section 26A of the 1995 Act does not apply to any scheme within paragraph (2)(a) or (b) and 26B of that Act does not apply to any scheme within paragraph (2).

(2) A scheme is within this paragraph if it is—

(a) a scheme of which there is only one member,

(b) a small self-administered scheme,

(c) a scheme of which each member is a trustee, or

(d) a scheme—

(i) the only benefits provided by which are death benefits, and

(ii) under the provisions of which no member has accrued rights.

(3) In this regulation "member" means a deferred member or a pensioner member.

[9.70]
7 Penalties for failing to give notice to the Authority under section 26A or section 26B of the 1995 Act

(1) This regulation applies for the purpose of prescribing the meaning of "the maximum amount" in section 10 of the 1995 Act (civil penalties) in cases where that section applies to any person by virtue of section 26A(7) or (8) or 26B(4) of that Act (failure to give certain notices to the Authority).

(2) Where that person is an individual, the maximum amount is £1,000.

(3) Where that person is not an individual, the maximum amount is £10,000.

[9.71]
8 Applications to the Authority to modify schemes to secure winding up

(1) This regulation applies where an application is made to the Authority under section 71A of the 1995 Act (modification by the Authority to secure winding up) to make an order modifying a scheme with a view to ensuring that it is properly wound up.

(2) The application must—

(a) set out the modification requested,

(b) specify the effects, if any, which the modification would or might have—

(i) on benefits under the scheme that are in payment at the time of the application, and

(ii) on benefits under it which are or may be payable at a later time,

(c) specify the reason for requesting the modification,

(d) specify whether any previous application has been made to the court or to the Authority for an order to make the modification requested by the application or any similar modification,

(e) confirm that at the time the application is made the employer in relation to the scheme is subject to an insolvency procedure (within the meaning given by section 71A(8) of the 1995 Act),

(f) specify whether the modification would reduce the value of the assets, if any, which might otherwise be distributed to that employer on the winding up, and

(g) contain a statement that the notices required by paragraph (3) have been given.

(3) Before making the application the trustees or managers of the scheme must give notice in writing that the application is being made—

(a) to all members of the scheme [(except a member mentioned in paragraph (3A)) in accordance with regulations 26 to 28 of the Occupational and Personal Pension Schemes (Disclosure of Information) Regulations 2013 (giving information and documents), and]

(b) if the modification would reduce the value of the assets which might otherwise be distributed to the employer on the winding up, to the person acting as an insolvency practitioner in relation to the employer or, as the case may be, the official receiver;

and the references in sub-paragraph (b) to "acting as an insolvency practitioner" and "official receiver" are to be construed in accordance with sections 388 and 399 of the Insolvency Act 1986.

[(3A) A member referred to in paragraph (3)(a) is a member—

(a) whose present postal address and electronic address is not known to the trustees or managers of the scheme, and

(b) in respect of whom the trustees or managers of the scheme have sent correspondence to their last known—

(i) postal address and that correspondence has been returned, or

(ii) electronic address and the trustees or managers of the scheme are satisfied that that correspondence has not been delivered.]

(4) A notice under paragraph (3) must—

(a) in the case of a notice under paragraph (3)(a), specify the information referred to in paragraph (2)(a), (b), (c) and (f),

(b) in the case of a notice under paragraph (3)(b), specify the information referred to in paragraph (2)(a) to (d) and (f),

(c) specify the date on which it is given, and

(d) contain a statement about the recipient's rights under paragraph (5).

(5) A member of the scheme in respect of which the application is made or a person to whom a notice is to be given under paragraph (3)(b) may make representations to the Authority about the modification requested by the application during the period of one month beginning with the date specified under paragraph (4)(c).

(6) Before determining the application, the Authority must consider any representations duly made to them under paragraph (5).

(7) The application must be accompanied by the following documents—

(a) a copy of—

(i) the documents constituting the scheme or, if any of those documents have been consolidated, the consolidated version of them,

(ii) if the documents mentioned in sub-paragraph (a)(i) do not set out the rules of the scheme, those rules, and

(iii) any document which amends or supplements or wholly or partly supersedes any document within sub-paragraph (a)(i) or (ii),

(b) if an actuary is required to be appointed under section 47(1)(b) of the 1995 Act, a copy of any advice given by the actuary so appointed to the trustees or managers concerning the effects, if any, that the modification requested by the application would or might have on the assets of, or the benefits provided by, the scheme,

(c) subject to paragraph (9), a copy of any legal advice given to the trustees or managers in relation to the modification requested by the application,

(d) a copy of any determination by a court concerning the modification requested or any similar modification, and

(e) if a record is required to be kept under section 49A(1) of the 1995 Act of the trustees' or managers' determination that the scheme be wound up, a copy of that record.

(8) Subject to paragraph (9), if in dealing with the application it appears to the Authority necessary or desirable that any information or document which is not required to be given to them under paragraph (2) or (7) be given to them before they determine the application, they may require the trustees or managers to provide it.

(9) Nothing in paragraph (7)(c) or (8) requires a person to produce a document if he would be entitled to refuse to produce it in any proceedings in any court on the grounds that it was the subject of legal professional privilege or, in Scotland, that it contained a confidential communication made by or to an advocate or solicitor in that capacity.

NOTES

Para (3): words in square brackets in sub-para (a) substituted by the Occupational and Personal Pension Schemes (Disclosure of Information) Regulations 2013, SI 2013/2734, reg 1(4), Sch 9, para 11(a).

Para (3A): inserted by SI 2013/2734, reg 1(4), Sch 9, para 11(b).

[9.72]

9 Reports to the Authority about winding up: time limits

(1) Section 72A of the 1995 Act (reports to Authority while schemes are being wound up) applies to a winding up beginning on or after 1st April 1973.

(2) In the case of a winding up which began before 1st April 2002, the first report to be made under section 72A must be made before the relevant date.

(3) The "relevant date" in relation to a winding up, means—
- (a) if the winding up began before 1st January 1990, 1st June 2002,
- (b) if the winding up began on or after 1st January 1990 but before 1st January 1993, 1st April 2003,
- (c) if the winding up began on or after 1st January 1993 but before 1st January 1996, 1st April 2004,
- (d) if the winding up began on or after 1st January 1996 but before 1st January 1999, 1st April 2005,
- (e) if the winding up began on or after 1st January 1999 but before 1st April 2002, 1st April 2006.

(4) In the case of a winding up which begins on or after 1st April 2002 but before 1st April 2003, the first report to be made under section 72A must be made—
- (a) after the end of the period of three years beginning with the day on which the winding up begins, and
- (b) before the end of the period of one year beginning with the end of the period that applies under sub-paragraph (a).

(5) In the case of a winding up which begins on or after 1st April 2003 [but before 1st October 2007], the first report to be made under section 72A must be made—
- (a) after the end of the period of three years beginning with the day on which the winding up begins, and
- (b) before the end of the period of three months beginning with the end of the period that applies under sub-paragraph (a).

[(6) In the case of a winding-up which begins on or after 1st October 2007, the first report to be made under section 72A must be made—
- (a) after the end of the period of two years beginning with the day on which the winding up begins, and
- (b) before the end of the period of three months beginning with the end of the period that applies under sub-paragraph (a).]

NOTES

Para (5): words in square brackets inserted by the Occupational Pension Schemes (Winding Up, Winding Up Notices and Reports etc) (Amendment) Regulations 2007, SI 2007/1930, reg 4(a).

Para (6): added by SI 2007/1930, reg 4(b).

[9.73]

10 Contents of reports to the Authority about winding up

(1) In the case of each winding up, the first report to the Authority under section 72A(1) of the 1995 Act must contain—
- (a) the name by which the scheme is known,
- (b) the date on which the winding up began,
- (c) the number allotted to the scheme by the Registrar of Occupational and Personal Pension Schemes for the purposes of the register kept under section 6 of the 1993 Act,
- (d) a statement as to the nature of the benefits provided by the scheme,
- (e) a statement as to whether an appointment has been made under section 23(1)(b) of the 1995 Act (appointment of independent trustee by insolvency practitioner or official receiver), and if such an appointment has been made and the report is not being made by the person appointed, that person's name and address,
- (f) if an actuary is required to be appointed under section 47(1)(b) of the 1995 Act, his name and address,
- (g) a statement as to whether any of the administration of the scheme is being carried out by a person other than the trustees or managers and, if so, the person's name and address,
- (h) a statement as to when the person making the report estimates that the winding up will be completed,
- (i) a statement as to—
  - (i) what steps in the winding up have been completed,
  - (ii) what steps remain to be completed, and
  - (iii) when the person making the report estimates that each of those steps will be completed, and
- (j) a statement as to whether any particular difficulties are hindering or delaying completion of the winding up.

(2) In the case of each winding up, a second or subsequent report to the Authority under section 72A(1) of the 1995 Act ("the later report") must contain—
- (a) the name by which the scheme is known,
- (b) the date on which the winding up began,
- (c) a statement as to whether any of the administration of the scheme is being carried out by a person other than the trustees or managers and, if so, the person's name and address,
- (d) if the person making the later report estimates that the winding up will be completed at a different time from that stated in the previous report under section 72A(1), a statement as to that time,
- (e) a statement as to—
  - (i) the steps in the winding up that have been completed since the previous report was made,
  - (ii) if steps stated in that report to be due for completion before the date when the later report is made have not been so completed, the reasons why they have not,
  - (iii) what steps remain to be completed, and
  - (iv) when the person making the later report estimates that each of those steps will be completed, and

(f) a statement as to whether any particular difficulties are hindering or delaying completion of the winding up.

[9.74]

11 Exemption from requirement to make reports to the Authority about winding up

(1) There is no obligation to make a report to the Authority under section 72A(1) of the 1995 Act if on the latest date for the making of the report the scheme is within paragraph (2).

(2) A scheme is within this paragraph if it is—

(a) a scheme of which there is only one member,
(b) a small self-administered scheme,
(c) a scheme of which each member is a trustee, or
(d) a scheme—
(i) the only benefits provided by which are death benefits, and
(ii) under the provisions of which no member has accrued rights.

(3) In this regulation "member" means a deferred member or a pensioner member.

[9.75]

12 Time when winding up taken to begin

Section 124(3A) to (3D) of the 1995 Act (time when winding up of a scheme is to be taken to begin) does not apply for the purposes of—

(a) sections 73 and 74 of that Act (preferential liabilities on winding up and discharge of liabilities by insurance, etc), or
(b) the Occupational Pension Schemes (Winding Up) Regulations 1996.

NOTES

Disapplication: in respect of a scheme that begins to wind up on or after 6 April 2005, see the Occupational Pension Schemes (Winding up etc) Regulations 2005, SI 2005/706, regs 1(3), 12.

[9.76]

13 Records of decisions about winding up

(1) The obligations imposed on trustees, managers and other persons by section 49A of the 1995 Act and this regulation do not apply in relation to determinations and decisions made before 1st April 2002.

(2) A record of a determination for the winding up of a scheme that is required to be kept under section 49A(1)(a) of the 1995 Act must specify—

(a) the names of the persons making the determination, and
(b) the date on which it is made.

(3) A record of a decision as to the time from which steps for the purposes of the winding up of the scheme are to be taken that is required to be kept under section 49A(1)(b) of that Act must specify the date on which the first steps for winding it up are to be taken.

(4) A record of a determination that is required to be kept under section 49A(1)(c) or (d) of that Act (determinations to defer winding up) must—

(a) if a date on which it is proposed to wind up the scheme is determined, specify that date, and
(b) if no such date is determined but a date on which the determination of that date will be considered is determined, specify that date.

(5) Where such a determination or decision as is mentioned in paragraph (a), (b), (c) or (d) of section 49A(1) of that Act is made by persons who—

(a) are not trustees or managers of the scheme, but
(b) are entitled in accordance with the scheme's rules to make a determination for its winding up,

the obligation under that section applies to those persons.

(6) Paragraph (5) applies whether or not the determination or decision in question is also made by persons who are trustees or managers of the scheme, and—

(a) in a case where it is also made by the trustees or managers, the obligation under section 49A(1) applies to the persons on whom it is imposed by paragraph (5) as well as the trustees or managers, but
(b) in a case where it is not also made by the trustees or managers, the obligation under section 49A(1) applies to the persons on whom it is imposed by paragraph (5) instead of the trustees or managers.

(7) A person who fails to take all such steps as are reasonable to comply with an obligation imposed by paragraph (5) is liable to pay a penalty under section 10 of that Act of such amount not exceeding—

(a) £5,000 in the case of an individual, and
(b) £50,000 in any other case,

as is specified in a notice in writing from the Authority requiring him to pay the penalty under that section.

(8) Such a penalty must be paid within 28 days beginning with the date on which the notice is given.

[9.77]

14 Directions by the Authority for facilitating winding up

(1) For the purposes of section 72B(2)(c)(iii) of the 1995 Act (by virtue of which the Authority may give directions during the winding up of a scheme if they consider that it is being obstructed or delayed by the failure of any person to provide information to a person of a prescribed description), the following persons are prescribed.

(2) They are—

(a) any person who has exercised or is exercising functions in relation to the scheme by or under an enactment,

(b) any person acting as the custodian of any investments on behalf of the trustees or managers of the scheme,

(c) any person holding—

(i) documents relating to the payroll for pensions payable under the scheme or their payment,

(ii) payroll records relating to employment to which the scheme relates,

(iii) personnel pension records in respect of those who are or have been in such employment, or

(iv) other information relating to the past or present membership of the scheme,

(d) any person holding, or involved in the production or issue of, scheme documentation, announcements or written materials,

(e) any person who is obliged under a contract with a person falling within any of sub-paragraphs (a) to (d) above to carry out on his behalf any function by virtue of the performance of which the other person falls or would fall within the sub-paragraph in question, and

(f) any person appearing to the Authority to hold information or documents relating to the functioning of the scheme.

(3) For the purposes of section 72B(3) of that Act (under which, except in prescribed circumstances, the Authority's power to give directions under section 72B is limited to cases where periodic reports are required to be made under section 72A of that Act and the first report has been made or is due), the following circumstances are prescribed.

(4) They are that—

(a) the trustees or managers of the scheme have applied for the Authority to give directions under section 72B of that Act, or

(b) the circumstances of the scheme are such that its winding up is unlikely to be completed within a reasonable period unless the Authority give such directions, or

(c) the winding up began before 1st April 2006.

(5) For the purposes of section 72B(5)(c) of that Act (by virtue of which a direction under section 72B may impose a requirement on a person of a prescribed description), any person formerly involved in the administration of the scheme is prescribed.

(6) For the purposes of section 72B(6)(c) of that Act (by virtue of which a direction under section 72B may impose a requirement to provide information to a person of a prescribed description), any person exercising functions in relation to the scheme by or under an enactment is prescribed.

(7) An application under section 72B(7) of that Act for the extension (or further extension) of a period within which steps required by a direction under section 72B are to be taken must be made in writing no later than two months before the date on which, apart from any extension (or further extension) as a result of the application, the period would end.

PETROLEUM LICENSING (EXPLORATION AND PRODUCTION) (SEAWARD AND LANDWARD AREAS) REGULATIONS 2004

(SI 2004/352)

NOTES

Made: 11 February 2004.
Authority: Petroleum Act 1998, s 4.
Commencement: 5 March 2004.

ARRANGEMENT OF REGULATIONS

1 Citation and Commencement . . . . . . [9.78]

SCHEDULES

Schedule 1—Model Clauses for Exploration Licences . . . . . . [9.79]
Schedule 2—Model Clauses for Production Licences Relating to Frontier Areas—No Break Clause. . . . . . [9.80]
Schedule 3—Model Clauses for Production Licences Relating to Frontier Areas—Including Break Clause . . . . . . [9.81]
Schedule 4—Model Clauses for Standard Production Licences . . . . . . [9.82]
Schedule 6—Model Clauses for Petroleum Exploration and Development Licences . . . . . . [9.83]

[9.78]

1 Citation and Commencement

These Regulations may be cited as the Petroleum Licensing (Exploration and Production) (Seaward and Landward Areas) Regulations 2004 and shall come into force on 5th March 2004.

2, 3 (*Outside the scope of this work.*)

SCHEDULE 1
MODEL CLAUSES FOR EXPLORATION LICENCES

Regulation 3(2)

[9.79]

1 Interpretation

(1) In the following clauses the following expressions have the meanings hereby respectively assigned to them, that is to say—

. . .

"the Licensee" means the person or persons to whom this licence is granted, his personal representatives and any person or persons to whom the rights conferred by this licence may lawfully have been assigned;

"the Minister" means [the Secretary of State for Energy and Climate Change];

. . .

(2) (*Outside the scope of this work.*)

2–19 (*Outside the scope of this work.*)

20 Power of revocation

(1) If any of the events specified in the following paragraph shall occur then and in any such case the Minister may revoke this licence and thereupon the same and all the rights hereby granted shall cease and determine but subject nevertheless and without prejudice to any obligation or liability incurred by the Licensee or imposed upon him by or under the terms and conditions hereof.

(2) The events referred to in the foregoing paragraph are—

(a) any consideration specified in Schedule 1 hereto or any part thereof being in arrear or unpaid for two months next after any of the days whereon the same ought to have been paid;

(b) any breach or non-observance by the Licensee of any of the terms and conditions of this licence;

(c) [in Great Britain,] the bankruptcy [or sequestration] of the Licensee;

(d) [in Great Britain,] the making by the Licensee of any arrangement or composition with his creditors;

(e) [in Great Britain,] if the Licensee is a company, the appointment of a receiver or administrator or any liquidation whether compulsory or voluntary;

[(ee) in a jurisdiction other than Great Britain, the commencement of any procedure or the making of any arrangement or appointment substantially corresponding to any of those mentioned in sub-paragraphs (c) to (e) of this paragraph;]

(f) if the Licensee is a company, the Licensee's ceasing to direct and control either—

(i) its operations under the licence; or

(ii) any commercial activities in connection with those operations from a fixed place within the United Kingdom;

and where two or more persons are the Licensee any reference to the Licensee in sub-paragraphs (b) to (f) of this paragraph is a reference to any of those persons.

20A–23 (*Outside the scope of this work.*)

NOTES

Para 1: definitions omitted from sub-para (1) outside the scope of this work; words in square brackets in definition "the Minister" in sub-para (1) substituted by the Secretary of State for Energy and Climate Change Order 2009, SI 2009/229, art 9, Sch 2, Pt 2, para 14(1).

Para 20: words in square brackets in sub-paras (2)(c)–(e), and sub-para (2)(ee) inserted by the Petroleum Licensing (Exploration and Production) (Seaward and Landward Areas) (Amendment) Regulations 2006, SI 2006/784, reg 3(1), (5)(a), (6)(a), (7)(a).

Disapplication: in relation to the disapplication of this Schedule, to any licence granted after 13 November 2009, see the Offshore Exploration (Petroleum, and Gas Storage and Unloading) (Model Clauses) Regulations 2009, SI 2009/2814, reg 3.

SCHEDULE 2
MODEL CLAUSES FOR PRODUCTION LICENCES RELATING TO FRONTIER AREAS—NO BREAK CLAUSE

Regulation 3(3)

[9.80]

1 Interpretation, etc

(1) In the following clauses, the following expressions have the meanings hereby respectively assigned to them, that is to say—

. . .

"the Licensee" means the person or persons to whom this licence is granted, his personal representatives and any person or persons to whom the rights conferred by this licence may lawfully have been assigned;

"the Minister" means [the Secretary of State for Business, Enterprise and Regulatory Reform];

. . .

(2) *(Outside the scope of this work.)*

2–37 *(Outside the scope of this work.)*

38 Power of revocation

(1) If any of the events specified in the following paragraph shall occur then and in any such case the Minister may revoke this licence and thereupon the same and all the rights hereby granted shall cease and determine but subject nevertheless and without prejudice to any obligation or liability incurred by the Licensee or imposed upon him by or under the terms and conditions hereof.

(2) The events referred to in the foregoing paragraph are—

(a), (b) *(outside the scope of this work.)*

(c) [in Great Britain,] the bankruptcy [or sequestration] of the Licensee;

(d)–(i) *(outside the scope of this work.)*

and where two or more persons are the Licensee any reference to the Licensee in sub-paragraphs (c) to (g) of this paragraph is a reference to any of those persons.

(3)–(5) *(Outside the scope of this work.)*

38A–41 *(Outside the scope of this work.)*

NOTES

Para 1: definitions omitted from sub-para (1) outside the scope of this work; words in square brackets in definition "the Minister" in sub-para (1) substituted by the Secretaries of State for Children, Schools and Families, for Innovation, Universities and Skills and for Business, Enterprise and Regulatory Reform Order 2007, SI 2007/3224, art 15, Schedule, Pt 2, para 41(2)(b).

Para 38: words in square brackets in sub-para (2)(c) inserted by the Petroleum Licensing (Exploration and Production) (Seaward and Landward Areas) (Amendment) Regulations 2006, SI 2006/784, reg 3(1), (5)(b), (6)(b).

Disapplication: in relation to the disapplication of this Schedule and Schs 3, 4, to any licence granted after 6 April 2008, see the Petroleum Licensing (Production) (Seaward Areas) Regulations 2008, SI 2008/225, reg 2(2).

SCHEDULE 3
MODEL CLAUSES FOR PRODUCTION LICENCES RELATING TO FRONTIER AREAS—INCLUDING BREAK CLAUSE

Regulation 3(4)

[9.81]

1 Interpretation, etc

(1) In the following clauses, the following expressions have the meanings hereby respectively assigned to them, that is to say—

. . .

"the Licensee" means the person or persons to whom this licence is granted, his personal representatives and any person or persons to whom the rights conferred by this licence may lawfully have been assigned;

"the Minister" means [the Secretary of State for Business, Enterprise and Regulatory Reform];

. . .

(2) *(Outside the scope of this work.)*

2–38 *(Outside the scope of this work.)*

39 Power of revocation

(1) If any of the events specified in the following paragraph shall occur then and in any such case the Minister may revoke this licence and thereupon the same and all the rights hereby granted shall cease and determine but subject nevertheless and without prejudice to any obligation or liability incurred by the Licensee or imposed upon him by or under the terms and conditions hereof.

(2) The events referred to in the foregoing paragraph are—

(a), (b) *(outside the scope of this work.)*

(c) [in Great Britain,] the bankruptcy [or sequestration] of the Licensee;

(d)–(i) *(outside the scope of this work.)*

and where two or more persons are the Licensee any reference to the Licensee in sub-paragraphs (c) to (g) of this paragraph is a reference to any of those persons.

(3)–(5) *(Outside the scope of this work.)*

39A–42 *(Outside the scope of this work.)*

NOTES

Para 1: definitions omitted from sub-para (1) outside the scope of this work; words in square brackets in definition "the Minister" in sub-para (1) substituted by the Secretaries of State for Children, Schools and Families, for Innovation, Universities and Skills and for Business, Enterprise and Regulatory Reform Order 2007, SI 2007/3224, art 15, Schedule, Pt 2, para 41(2)(b).

Para 39: words in square brackets in sub-para (2)(c) inserted by the Petroleum Licensing (Exploration and Production) (Seaward and Landward Areas) (Amendment) Regulations 2006, SI 2006/784, reg 3(1), (5)(c), (6)(c).

Disapplication: see the note to Sch 2 at **[9.80]**.

SCHEDULE 4
MODEL CLAUSES FOR STANDARD PRODUCTION LICENCES

Regulation 3(5)

[9.82]

1 Interpretation, etc

(1) In the following clauses, the following expressions have the meanings hereby respectively assigned to them, that is to say—

. . .

"the Licensee" means the person or persons to whom this licence is granted, his personal representatives and any person or persons to whom the rights conferred by this licence may lawfully have been assigned;

"the Minister" means [the Secretary of State for Business, Enterprise and Regulatory Reform];

. . .

(2) (*Outside the scope of this work.*)

2–36 (*Outside the scope of this work.*)

37 Power of revocation

(1) If any of the events specified in the following paragraph shall occur then and in any such case the Minister may revoke this licence and thereupon the same and all the rights hereby granted shall cease and determine but subject nevertheless and without prejudice to any obligation or liability incurred by the Licensee or imposed upon him by or under the terms and conditions hereof.

(2) The events referred to in the foregoing paragraph are—

(a), (b) (*outside the scope of this work.*)

(c) [in Great Britain,] the bankruptcy [or sequestration] of the Licensee;

(d)–(i) (*outside the scope of this work.*)

and where two or more persons are the Licensee any reference to the Licensee in sub-paragraphs (c) to (g) of this paragraph is a reference to any of those persons.

(3)–(5) (*Outside the scope of this work.*)

37A–40 (*Outside the scope of this work.*)

NOTES

Para 1: definitions omitted from sub-para (1) outside the scope of this work; words in square brackets in definition "the Minister" in sub-para (1) substituted by the Secretaries of State for Children, Schools and Families, for Innovation, Universities and Skills and for Business, Enterprise and Regulatory Reform Order 2007, SI 2007/3224, art 15, Schedule, Pt 2, para 41(3)(b).

Para 37: words in square brackets in sub-para (2)(c) inserted by the Petroleum Licensing (Exploration and Production) (Seaward and Landward Areas) (Amendment) Regulations 2006, SI 2006/784, reg 3(1), (5)(d), (6)(d).

Disapplication: see the note to Sch 2 at **[9.80]**.

SCHEDULE 5

(*Sch 5 outside the scope of this work.*)

SCHEDULE 6
MODEL CLAUSES FOR PETROLEUM EXPLORATION AND DEVELOPMENT LICENCES

Regulation 3(7)

[9.83]

1 Interpretation

(1) In the following clauses, the following expressions have the meanings hereby respectively assigned to them, that is to say—

. . .

"the Licensee" means the person or persons to whom this licence is granted, his personal representatives and any person or persons to whom the rights conferred by this licence may lawfully have been assigned;

"the Minister" means [the Secretary of State for Energy and Climate Change];

. . .

(2) (*Outside the scope of this work.*)

2–35 (*Outside the scope of this work.*)

36 Power of revocation

(1) If any of the events specified in the following paragraph shall occur then and in any such case the Minister may revoke this licence and thereupon the same and all the rights hereby granted shall cease and determine but subject nevertheless and without prejudice to any obligation or liability incurred by the Licensee or imposed upon him by or under the terms and conditions hereof.

(2) The events referred to in the foregoing paragraph are—

(a), (b) (*outside the scope of this work.*)

(c) [in Great Britain,] the bankruptcy [or sequestration] of the Licensee;
(d)–(i) *(outside the scope of this work.)*
and where two or more persons are the Licensee any reference to the Licensee in sub-paragraphs (c) to (g) of this paragraph is a reference to any of those persons.
(3)–(5) *(Outside the scope of this work.)*

36A, 37 *(Outside the scope of this work.)*

NOTES

Para 1: definitions omitted from sub-para (1) outside the scope of this work; words in square brackets in definition "the Minister" in sub-para (1) substituted by the Secretary of State for Energy and Climate Change Order 2009, SI 2009/229, art 9, Sch 2, Pt 2, para 14(2)(b).

Para 36: words in square brackets in sub-para (2)(c) inserted by the Petroleum Licensing (Exploration and Production) (Seaward and Landward Areas) (Amendment) Regulations 2006, SI 2006/784, reg 3(1), (5)(e), (6)(e).

SCHEDULE 7

(Sch 7 outside the scope of this work.)

BANKING ACT 2009 (THIRD PARTY COMPENSATION ARRANGEMENTS FOR PARTIAL PROPERTY TRANSFERS) REGULATIONS 2009

(SI 2009/319)

NOTES

Made: 19 February 2009.
Authority: Banking Act 2009, ss 60, 259(1).
Commencement: 21 February 2009.

ARRANGEMENT OF REGULATIONS

1 Citation, commencement and interpretation . . . [9.84]
2 Application of these Regulations . . . [9.85]
3 Requirement to include a third party compensation order . . . [9.86]
4 Mandatory provisions—appointment of independent valuer . . . [9.87]
5 Mandatory provisions—assessment of insolvency treatment . . . [9.88]
6 Mandatory provisions—choice of insolvency process . . . [9.89]
7 Mandatory provisions—valuation principles . . . [9.90]
8 Mandatory provisions—interim payments . . . [9.91]
9 Mandatory provisions—valuations provided by creditors . . . [9.92]
10 Optional provisions—valuation principles . . . [9.93]

[9.84]

1 Citation, commencement and interpretation

(1) These Regulations may be cited as the Banking Act 2009 (Third Party Compensation Arrangements for Partial Property Transfers) Regulations 2009.

(2) These Regulations come into force on 21st February 2009.

(3) In these Regulations—

"the Act" means the Banking Act 2009;

"the Bank" means the Bank of England;

"banking institution" means—

(a) a bank (within the meaning of Part 1 of the Act);

[(aa) an investment firm;]

(b) a building society (within the meaning of section 119 of the Building Societies Act 1986); . . .

[(c) a banking group company;] [or

(d) a third-country institution (within the meaning of section 89JA of the Act (resolution of UK branches of third-country institutions));]

"relevant time" means—

(a) in relation to Case 1 (as specified in regulation 2(2)), the time at which the partial property transfer took effect;

(b) in relation to Case 2 (as specified in regulation 2(3)), the time at which the property transfer instrument made in accordance with section 11(2) or 12(2) of the Act took effect;

(c) in relation to Case 3 (as specified in regulation 2(4)), the time at which the share transfer order made in accordance with section 13(2) of the Act . . . took effect;

[(d) in relation to Case 4 (as specified in regulation 2(4A)), the time at which the resolution instrument made in accordance with section 12A(2) of the Act took effect;

(e) in relation to Case 5 (as specified in regulation 2(4B)), the time at which the third-country instrument made in section 89H(2)(a) or (c) of the Act took effect;]

[(f) in relation to Case 6 (as specified in regulation 2(4C)), the time at which the share transfer instrument made in accordance with section 12(2) of the Act took effect;]

"third party compensation order in relation to a partial property transfer" has the meaning given in regulation 3(2).

[(4) References in this Order to sections of the Banking Act 2009 include, as the context requires, references to those provisions as applied with or without modifications by that Act, as that Act has effect on the day on which the Bank Recovery and Resolution Order 2016 comes into force.]

NOTES

Para (3) is amended as follows:

In the definition "banking institution", para (aa) was inserted by the Banking Act 2009 (Third Party Compensation Arrangements for Partial Property Transfers) (Amendment) Regulations 2014, SI 2014/1830, reg 2.

Word omitted from para (b) of the definition "banking institution" revoked, and para (d) of that definition (and the preceding word) added, by the Bank Recovery and Resolution Order 2016, SI 2016/1239, art 38(1), (2)(a).

In the definition "banking institution" para (c) substituted, and paras (d), (e) of the definition "relevant time" added, by the Bank Recovery and Resolution Order 2014, SI 2014/3329, art 126(1), (2).

Word omitted from para (c) of the definition "relevant time" revoked, and para (f) of that definition added, by SI 2016/1239, art 38(1), (2)(b).

Para (4): added by SI 2016/1239, art 38(1), (2)(c).

[9.85]

2 Application of these Regulations

(1) These Regulations apply in the following cases.

(2) Case 1 is where a partial property transfer has been made by the Bank in accordance with section 11(2)[, 12(2) or 12ZA(3)] of the Act.

(3) Case 2 is where—

(a) the Bank has made a property transfer instrument in accordance with section 11(2)[, 12(2) or 12ZA(3)] of the Act which is not a partial property transfer; but

(b) an onward property transfer instrument has been made by the Bank in accordance with section 43 of the Act which is a partial property transfer.

(4) Case 3 is where—

(a) the Treasury have made a share transfer order in accordance with section 13(2) of the Act . . . ; and

(b) a property transfer order has been made by the Treasury in accordance with section 45(2) of the Act . . . which by virtue of section 45(5)(b) of the Act is to be treated as a partial property transfer.

[(4A) Case 4 is where—

(a) the Bank has made a resolution instrument (or, where more than one resolution instrument has been made, the first resolution instrument) in accordance with section 12A(2) of the Act (bail-in option), and

(b) a property transfer instrument has been made under section 41A(2) (transfer of property subsequent to resolution instrument), 42 (supplemental instruments) or 44A (bail in: reverse property transfer) of the Act which is a partial property transfer.

(4B) Case 5 is where—

(a) the Bank has made a third-country instrument in accordance with section 89H of the Act (recognition of third-country resolution actions),

(b) either—

(i) that third-country instrument or

(ii) any further third-country instrument made under section 89I(4)(b),

makes provision which would otherwise be made in a property transfer instrument and which, if made in a property transfer instrument, would be a partial property transfer.]

[(4C) Case 6 is where—

(a) the Bank has made a share transfer instrument in accordance with section 12(2) of the Act; and

(b) a property transfer instrument has been made by the Bank in accordance with section 44D(2) (bridge bank: supplemental property transfer powers) or section 44E(2) (bridge bank: supplemental reverse property transfer powers) of the Act which is a partial property transfer.]

(5) For the purposes of these Regulations, a property transfer instrument or property transfer order which purports to transfer all property, rights and liabilities of an undertaking shall be treated as having done so effectively (and so shall not be treated as a partial property transfer), notwithstanding the possibility that any of the property, rights or liabilities are foreign property and may not have been effectively transferred by the property transfer instrument or order or by virtue of steps taken under section 39 of the Act.

NOTES

Paras (2), (3): words in square brackets substituted by the Bank Recovery and Resolution Order 2014, SI 2014/3329, art 126(1), (3)(a), (b).

Para (4): words omitted revoked by the Bank Recovery and Resolution Order 2016, SI 2016/1239, art 38(1), (3)(a).

Paras (4A), (4B): inserted by SI 2014/3329, art 126(1), (3)(c).

Para (4C): inserted by SI 2016/1239, art 38(1), (3)(b).

[9.86]
3 Requirement to include a third party compensation order

(1) A compensation scheme order or a resolution fund order made in the cases in which these Regulations apply must include a third party compensation order.

(2) Regulations 4 to 9 set out provisions which must be included in a such a third party compensation order ("a third party compensation order in relation to a partial property transfer"); regulation 10 sets out provisions which may be included in such an order.

[9.87]
4 Mandatory provisions—appointment of independent valuer

[(1)] A third party compensation order in relation to a partial property transfer must include provision for a person ("an independent valuer") to be appointed to determine—

[(a) whether all relevant persons, a class of relevant persons or a particular relevant person should be paid compensation; and]

(b) if compensation should be paid, what amount is to be paid,

(and, by virtue of section 59(3)(a) of the Act, sections 54 to 56 (appointment etc of independent valuer) apply to the independent valuer appointed in accordance with this regulation).

[(2) In these Regulations, "relevant persons" means the pre-resolution shareholders and creditors (within the meaning of section 60B(3) of the Act).]

NOTES

Para (1): numbered as such, and sub-para (a) substituted, by the Bank Recovery and Resolution Order 2014, SI 2014/3329, art 126(1), (4)(a).

Para (2): added by SI 2014/3329, art 126(1), (4)(b).

[9.88]
5 Mandatory provisions—assessment of insolvency treatment

(1) A third party compensation order in relation to a partial property transfer must include the following provisions (subject to any necessary modifications).

(2) The independent valuer must assess the treatment ("the insolvency treatment") which [relevant persons] would have received had the banking institution in relation to which or in connection with which the partial property transfer has been made entered insolvency immediately before the relevant time.

(3) The independent valuer must assess the treatment ("the actual treatment") which [relevant persons] have received, are receiving or are likely to receive (as specified in the order) if no (or no further) compensation is paid.

(4) If the independent valuer considers that, in relation to any [relevant person], the actual treatment assessed under paragraph (3) is less favourable than the insolvency treatment assessed under paragraph (2), the independent valuer must determine that compensation be paid to that [relevant person].

(5) The amount of compensation payable by virtue of paragraph (4) must be determined by the independent valuer by reference to the difference in treatment assessed under paragraph (4) and on the basis of the fair and equitable value of that difference in treatment.

NOTES

Paras (2)–(4): words in square brackets substituted by the Bank Recovery and Resolution Order 2014, SI 2014/3329, art 126(1), (5).

[9.89]
6 Mandatory provisions—choice of insolvency process

A third party compensation order in relation to a partial property transfer must include either—

(a) a provision specifying that the independent valuer must assess the insolvency treatment as required under regulation 5(2) on the basis that the banking institution had entered a particular insolvency process specified in the order; or

(b) a provision specifying that the independent valuer must determine what insolvency process it is likely that the banking institution would have entered, had the following instrument or order not been made—

(i) in the case of Case 1 (as specified in regulation 2(2)), the partial property transfer;

(ii) in the case of Case 2 (as specified in regulation 2(3)), the property transfer instrument made in accordance with section 11(2)[, 12(2) or 12ZA(3)] of the Act;

(iii) in the case of Case 3 (as specified in regulation 2(4)), the share transfer order made in accordance with section 13(2) of the Act . . . ;

[(iv) in the case of Case 4 (as specified in regulation 2(4A)), the resolution instrument made in accordance with section 12A(2) of the Act (or if more than one instrument has been made, the first resolution instrument made in accordance with that section);

(v) in the case of Case 5 (as specified in regulation 2(4B)), the third-country instrument made in accordance with 89H(2)(a) or (c)];

[(vi) in the case of Case 6 (as specified in regulation 2(4C), the share transfer instrument made in accordance with section 12(2).]

NOTES

In para (b)(ii) words in square brackets substituted, and para (b)(iv), (v) added, by the Bank Recovery and Resolution Order 2014, SI 2014/3329, art 126(1), (6).

Words omitted from sub-para (b)(iii) revoked, and sub-para (b)(vi) inserted, by the Bank Recovery and Resolution Order 2016, SI 2016/1239, art 38(1), (4).

[9.90]

7 Mandatory provisions—valuation principles

(1) A third party compensation order in relation to a partial property transfer must include the following provisions (subject to any necessary modifications).

(2) In making the assessment of the insolvency treatment as required under regulation 5(2), the independent valuer must determine the amount of compensation in accordance with the following principles (in addition to the principle which applies by virtue of section 57(3) of the Act)—

(a) that the banking institution in relation to which or in connection with which the partial property transfer has been made would have entered insolvency immediately before the relevant time;

(b) that the partial property transfer has not been made and that no other order or instrument under Part 1 of the Act would have been made in relation to or in connection with the banking institution (or, in appropriate cases, any of the banking institutions);

(c) that no financial assistance would have, after the relevant time, been provided by the Bank or the Treasury.

[9.91]

8 Mandatory provisions—interim payments

(1) A third party compensation order in relation to a partial property transfer must include the following provisions (subject to any necessary modifications).

(2) The independent valuer may determine that payments should be made to a [relevant person], a class of [relevant persons] or all [relevant persons] on account of compensation to be payable under the third party compensation order ("payments on account").

(3) The independent valuer may make such a determination at any time before the determination required by regulation 5(5) has been made.

(4) Once the determination required by regulation 5(5) has been made, the independent valuer must determine what balancing payments are appropriate to ensure that the [relevant person] receives the amount of compensation determined under regulation 5(5) (and no more than that amount).

(5) Subject to paragraph (6), the independent valuer may make such provision as to payments on account as he thinks fit (including a requirement that payments be made in instalments).

(6) Payments on account must be made subject to the following conditions—

(a) that the acceptance of such a payment by the [relevant person] reduces any obligation (whether in existence at the time of the payment or not) on the Treasury, the Financial Services Compensation Scheme or any other person (as the case may be) to pay compensation to the [relevant person] by the amount of the payment on account;

(b) that, where the independent valuer, in accordance with paragraph (4) determines that the [relevant person] should make a balancing payment to the Treasury, the Financial Services Compensation Scheme or any other person (as the case may be), the [relevant person] is liable to pay that amount.

(7) In considering whether to require payments on account to be made in accordance with this regulation, the independent valuer must have regard to the merits of ensuring that pre-transfer creditors receive compensation in a timely manner.

NOTES

Paras (2), (4), (6): words in square brackets substituted by the Bank Recovery and Resolution Order 2014, SI 2014/3329, art 126(1), (7).

[9.92]

9 Mandatory provisions—valuations provided by creditors

A third party compensation order in relation to a partial property transfer must make provision requiring the independent valuer to have regard to any information provided by a [relevant person] which is relevant to the exercise of the independent valuer's functions under the order; in particular, the independent valuer must have regard to any information which relates to the assessment of the insolvency treatment required by regulation 5(2) or the assessment of the actual treatment required by regulation 5(3).

NOTES

Words in square brackets substituted by the Bank Recovery and Resolution Order 2014, SI 2014/3329, art 126(1), (8).

[9.93]

10 Optional provisions—valuation principles

(1) A third party compensation order in relation to a partial property transfer may make any of the following provisions (subject to any necessary modifications).

(2) In making the assessment of the insolvency treatment required by regulation 5(2), the independent valuer must assume that property specified in the order (or property of a class specified in the order) would have been sold for the price specified in the order or calculated by reference to criteria specified in the order.

(3) In making the assessment of the insolvency treatment required by regulation 5(2), the independent valuer must assume that property specified in the order (or property of a class specified in the order) would have been treated in the manner specified in order.

PART 10

STATUTORY INSTRUMENTS RELATING TO PARTNERSHIP INSOLVENCY—ENGLAND AND WALES

INSOLVENT PARTNERSHIPS ORDER 1994

(SI 1994/2421)

NOTES

Made: 13 September 1994.
Authority: Insolvency Act 1986, s 420(1), (2); Company Directors Disqualification Act 1986, s 21(2).
Commencement: 1 December 1994.

ARRANGEMENT OF ARTICLES

PART I
GENERAL

1 Citation, commencement and extent . . . . [10.1]
2 Interpretation: definitions . . . . [10.2]
3 Interpretation: expressions appropriate to companies . . . . [10.3]

PART II
VOLUNTARY ARRANGEMENTS

4 Voluntary arrangement of insolvent partnership . . . . [10.4]
5 Voluntary arrangements of members of insolvent partnership . . . . [10.5]

PART III
ADMINISTRATION

6 Administration in relation to insolvent partnership . . . . [10.6]

PART IV
CREDITORS' ETC WINDING-UP PETITIONS

7 Winding up of insolvent partnership as unregistered company on petition of creditor etc where no concurrent petition presented against member . . . . [10.7]
8 Winding up of insolvent partnership as unregistered company on the petition of creditor etc where concurrent petitions presented against one or more members . . . . [10.8]

PART V
MEMBERS' PETITIONS

9 Winding up of insolvent partnership as unregistered company on member's petition where no concurrent petition presented against member . . . . [10.9]
10 Winding up of insolvent partnership as unregistered company on member's petition where concurrent petitions presented against all members . . . . [10.10]
11 Insolvency proceedings not involving winding up of insolvent partnership as unregistered company where individual members present joint bankruptcy petition . . . . [10.11]

PART VI
PROVISIONS APPLYING IN INSOLVENCY PROCEEDINGS IN RELATION TO INSOLVENT PARTNERSHIPS

11A Decision procedure in insolvency proceedings in relation to insolvent partnerships . . . . [10.12]
12 Winding up of unregistered company which is member of insolvent partnership being wound up by virtue of this Order . . . . [10.13]
13 Deposit on petitions . . . . [10.14]

PART VII
DISQUALIFICATION

16 Application of Company Directors Disqualification Act 1986 . . . . [10.15]

PART VIII
MISCELLANEOUS

17 Forms . . . . [10.16]
18 Application of subordinate legislation . . . . [10.17]
19 Supplemental and transitional provisions . . . . [10.18]

SCHEDULES

Schedule 1—Modified provisions of Part I of, and Schedule A1 to, the Act (company voluntary arrangements) as applied by article 4
Part I—Modified provisions of sections 1 to 7B of the Act . . . . [10.19]
Part II—Modified provisions of Schedule A1 to the Act . . . . [10.20]
Schedule 2—Modified provisions of Part II of, and Schedule B1 to, the Act (administration) as applied by article 6 . . . . [10.21]
Schedule 3—Provisions of the Act which apply with modifications for the purposes of article 7 to winding up of insolvent partnership on petition of creditor etc where no concurrent petition presented against member
Part I—Modified provisions of Part V of the Act . . . . [10.22]
Part II—Other modified provisions of the Act about winding up by the court . . . . [10.23]

Schedule 4—Provisions of the Act which apply with modifications for the purposes of article 8 to winding up of insolvent partnership on creditor's petition where concurrent petitions are presented against one or more members
Part I—Modified provisions of Part V of the Act . . . [10.24]
Part II—Other modified provisions of the Act about winding up by the court and bankruptcy of individuals . . . [10.25]
Schedule 5—Provisions of the Act which apply with modifications for the purposes of article 9 to winding up of insolvent partnership on member's petition where no concurrent petition presented against member . . . [10.26]
Schedule 6—Provisions of the Act which apply with modifications for the purposes of article 10 to winding up of insolvent partnership on member's petition where concurrent petitions are presented against all the members . . . [10.27]
Schedule 7—Provisions of the Act which apply with modifications for the purposes of article 11 where joint bankruptcy petition presented by individual members without winding up partnership as unregistered company . . . [10.28]
Schedule 7A—Decisions of creditors of the partnership and of the members of the partnership . . . [10.29]
Schedule 8—Modified provisions of Company Directors Disqualification Act 1986 for the purposes of article 16 . . . [10.30]
Schedule 9—Forms . . . [10.31]
Schedule 10—Subordinate legislation applied . . . [10.32]

PART I
GENERAL

[10.1]

1 Citation, commencement and extent

(1) This Order may be cited as the Insolvent Partnerships Order 1994 and shall come into force on 1st December 1994.

(2) This Order—

(a) in the case of insolvency proceedings in relation to companies and partnerships, relates to companies and partnerships which the courts in England and Wales have jurisdiction to wind up; and

(b) in the case of insolvency proceedings in relation to individuals, extends to England and Wales only.

(3) In paragraph (2) the term "insolvency proceedings" has the meaning ascribed to it by article 2 below.

[10.2]

2 Interpretation: definitions

(1) In this Order, except in so far as the context otherwise requires—

"the Act" means the Insolvency Act 1986;

"agricultural charge" has the same meaning as in the Agricultural Credits Act 1928;

"agricultural receiver" means a receiver appointed under an agricultural charge;

"corporate member" means an insolvent member which is a company;

"the court", in relation to an insolvent partnership, means the court which has jurisdiction to wind up the partnership;

"individual member" means an insolvent member who is an individual;

"insolvency order" means—

(a) in the case of an insolvent partnership or a corporate member, a winding-up order; and

(b) in the case of an individual member, a bankruptcy order;

"insolvency petition" means, in the case of a petition presented to the court—

(a) against a corporate member, a petition for its winding up by the court;

(b) against an individual member, a petition for a bankruptcy order to be made against that individual,

where the petition is presented in conjunction with a petition for the winding up of the partnership by the court as an unregistered company under the Act;

"insolvency proceedings" means any proceedings under the Act, this Order or the [Insolvency (England and Wales) Rules 2016];

"insolvent member" means a member of an insolvent partnership, against whom an insolvency petition is being or has been presented;

"joint bankruptcy petition" means a petition by virtue of article 11 of this Order;

"joint debt" means a debt of an insolvent partnership in respect of which an order is made by virtue of Part IV or V of this Order;

"joint estate" means the partnership property of an insolvent partnership in respect of which an order is made by virtue of Part IV or V of this Order;

"joint expenses" means expenses incurred in the winding up of an insolvent partnership or in the winding up of the business of an insolvent partnership and the administration of its property;

"limited partner" has the same meaning as in the Limited Partnerships Act 1907;

"member" means a member of a partnership and any person who is liable as a partner within the meaning of section 14 of the Partnership Act 1890;

"officer", in relation to an insolvent partnership, means—

(a) a member; or

(b) a person who has management or control of the partnership business;

"partnership property" has the same meaning as in the Partnership Act 1890;

"postponed debt" means a debt the payment of which is postponed by or under any provision of the Act or of any other enactment;

"responsible insolvency practitioner" means—

(a) in winding up, the liquidator of an insolvent partnership or corporate member; and

(b) in bankruptcy, the trustee of the estate of an individual member,

and in either case includes the official receiver when so acting;

"separate debt" means a debt for which a member of a partnership is liable, other than a joint debt;

"separate estate" means the property of an insolvent member against whom an insolvency order has been made;

"separate expenses" means expenses incurred in the winding up of a corporate member, or in the bankruptcy of an individual member; and

"trustee of the partnership" means a person authorised by order made by virtue of article 11 of this Order to wind up the business of an insolvent partnership and to administer its property.

(2) The definitions in paragraph (1), other than the first definition, shall be added to those in section 436 of the Act.

(3) References in provisions of the Act applied by this Order to any provision of the Act so applied shall, unless the context otherwise requires, be construed as references to the provision as so applied.

(4) Where, in any Schedule to this Order, all or any of the provisions of two or more sections of the Act are expressed to be modified by a single paragraph of the Schedule, the modification includes the combination of the provisions of those sections into the one or more sections set out in that paragraph.

NOTES

Para (1): in definition "insolvency proceedings" words in square brackets substituted for original words "Insolvency Rules 1986", in relation to England and Wales, by the Insolvency (Miscellaneous Amendments) Regulations 2017, SI 2017/1119, reg 2, Sch 2, paras 1, 2, as from 8 December 2017, subject to transitional and savings provisions in Sch 2, para 10 thereto which provides as follows:

"10 Transitional and savings provisions

(1) This Schedule does not apply in relation to any case in which a winding-up or a bankruptcy order was made in relation to a partnership or an insolvent member of a partnership before this Schedule came into force, and where this Schedule does not apply the law in force immediately before this Schedule came into force continues to have effect.

(2) Where winding-up or bankruptcy proceedings, commenced under the provisions of the law in force immediately before this Schedule came into force, were pending in relation to a partnership or an insolvent member of a partnership immediately before this Schedule came into force, either—

(a) those proceedings shall be continued, after the coming into force of this Schedule, in accordance with the provisions of this Schedule; or

(b) if the court so directs, they shall be continued under the provisions of the law in force immediately before this Schedule came into force.

(3) For the purpose of sub-paragraph (2) above, winding-up or bankruptcy proceedings are pending if a statutory or written demand has been served or a winding-up or bankruptcy petition has been presented.".

[10.3]

3 Interpretation: expressions appropriate to companies

(1) This article applies for the interpretation in relation to insolvent partnerships of expressions appropriate to companies in provisions of the Act and of the Company Directors Disqualification Act 1986 applied by this Order, unless the contrary intention appears.

(2) References to companies shall be construed as references to insolvent partnerships and all references to the registrar of companies shall be omitted.

(3) References to shares of a company shall be construed—

(a) in relation to an insolvent partnership with capital, as references to rights to share in that capital; and

(b) in relation to an insolvent partnership without capital, as references to interests—

(i) conferring any right to share in the profits or liability to contribute to the losses of the partnership, or

(ii) giving rise to an obligation to contribute to the debts or expenses of the partnership in the event of a winding up.

(4) Other expressions appropriate to companies shall be construed, in relation to an insolvent partnership, as references to the corresponding persons, officers, documents or organs (as the case may be) appropriate to a partnership.

PART II
VOLUNTARY ARRANGEMENTS

[10.4]

4 Voluntary arrangement of insolvent partnership

[(1) The provisions of Part I of, and Schedule A1 to, the Act shall apply in relation to an insolvent partnership, certain of those provisions being modified in such manner that, after modification, they are as set out in Schedule 1 to this Order.]

(2) For the purposes of the provisions of the Act applied by paragraph (1), the provisions of the Act specified in paragraph (3) below, insofar as they relate to company voluntary arrangements, shall also apply in relation to insolvent partnerships.

(3) The provisions referred to in paragraph (2) are—

(a) section 233 [and section 233A] in Part VI,

(b) Part VII, with the exception of section 250,

(c) Part XII,

(d) Part XIII,

(e) sections 411, 413, 414 and 419 in Part XV, and

(f) Parts XVI to XIX.

NOTES

Para (1): substituted by the Insolvent Partnerships (Amendment) (No 2) Order 2002, SI 2002/2708, art 4, subject to transitional provisions in art 11(1), (3) thereof, as noted below. Para (1) originally read as follows:

"(1) The provisions of Part I of the Act shall apply in relation to an insolvent partnership, those provisions being modified in such manner that, after modification, they are as set out in Schedule 1 to this Order.".

Transitional Provisions: SI 2002/2708, art 11 provides as follows:

"11 Transitional provisions

(1) The amendments to the 1994 Order set out in articles 3, 4, 5, 6, 8, 9 and 10 of, and Schedules 1 and 2 to, this Order do not apply where, in relation to a voluntary arrangement under Part I of the Act, as the case may be, a proposal is made by—

(a) the members of a partnership and before this Order comes into force the intended nominee has endorsed a copy of the written notice of the proposal under rule 1.4(3),

(b) the liquidator or the administrator (acting as nominee) and before this Order comes into force the liquidator or administrator (as the case may be) has sent out a notice summoning the meetings under section 3 of the Act as required by rule 1.11, or

(c) the liquidator or the administrator of a partnership (not acting as the nominee) and before this Order comes into force the intended nominee has endorsed a copy of the written notice of the proposal under rule 1.12(2).

(2) The amendments to the 1994 Order set out in article 7 of this Order do not apply where a petition for an administration order in relation to an insolvent partnership has been presented before this Order comes into force.

(3) Where, by virtue of the 1994 Order, provisions of the Act apply in a case falling within paragraph (1) or (2), those provisions shall continue to have effect as if this Order had not been made.".

Para (3): words in square brackets inserted by the Insolvency (Protection of Essential Supplies) Order 2015, SI 2015/989, art 6, Schedule, para 1.

[10.5]

5 Voluntary arrangements of members of insolvent partnership

(1) Where insolvency orders are made against an insolvent partnership and an insolvent member of that partnership in his capacity as such, Part I of the Act shall apply to corporate members and Part VIII to individual members of that partnership, with the modification that any reference to the creditors of the company or of the debtor, as the case may be, includes a reference to the creditors of the partnership.

(2) Paragraph (1) is not to be construed as preventing the application of Part I or (as the case may be) Part VIII of the Act to any person who is a member of an insolvent partnership (whether or not a winding-up order has been made against that partnership) and against whom an insolvency order has not been made under this Order or under the Act.

[PART III
ADMINISTRATION

[10.6]

6 Administration in relation to insolvent partnership

(1) The provisions of Part II of, and Schedule B1 to, the Act shall apply in relation to an insolvent partnership, certain of those provisions being modified in such manner that, after modification, they are as set out in Schedule 2 to this Order.

(2) In its application to insolvent partnerships, Part II of, and Schedule B1 to, the Act (as modified as set out in Schedule 2 to this Order) shall be read subject to paragraph (3).

(3) For every reference to—

(a) "administrative receiver" there shall be substituted "agricultural receiver"; and

(b) "floating charge" there shall be substituted "agricultural floating charge".

(4) For the purposes of the provisions of the Act applied by paragraph (1), the provisions of the Act specified in paragraph (5) below, insofar as they relate to the appointment of an administrator, shall also apply in relation to insolvent partnerships.

(5) The provisions referred to in paragraph (4) are—

(a) Part VI,

(b) Part VII (with the exception of section 250),

(c) Part XII,

(d) Part XIII,

(e) sections 411, 413, 414 and 419 in Part XV, and

(f) Parts XVI to XIX.

(6) For the purposes of this Article and the provisions of the Act applied by paragraph (1), "agricultural floating charge" shall be construed as a reference to a floating charge created under section 5 of the Agricultural Credits Act 1928.]

NOTES

Substituted, together with preceding Part heading, by the Insolvent Partnerships (Amendment) Order 2005, SI 2005/1516, arts 2, 3, except where a petition for an administration order has been presented in relation to an insolvent partnership before 1 July 2005. Part III previously read as follows:

"PART III
ADMINISTRATION ORDERS

6 Administration order in relation to insolvent partnership

(1) The provisions of Part II of the Act shall apply in relation to an insolvent partnership, certain of those provisions being modified in such manner that, after modification, they are as set out in Schedule 2 to this Order.

(2) For the purposes of the provisions of the Act applied by paragraph (1), the provisions of the Act specified in paragraph (3) below, insofar as they relate to administration orders, shall also apply in relation to insolvent partnerships.

(3) The provisions referred to in paragraph (2) are—

(a) section 212 in Part IV,
(b) Part VI,
(c) Part VII, with the exception of section 250,
(d) Part XIII,
(e) sections 411, 413, 414 and 419 in Part XV, and
(f) Parts XVI to XIX.".

PART IV
CREDITORS' ETC WINDING-UP PETITIONS

[10.7]

7 Winding up of insolvent partnership as unregistered company on petition of creditor etc where no concurrent petition presented against member

(1) Subject to paragraph (2) below, the provisions of Part V of the Act shall apply in relation to the winding up of an insolvent partnership as an unregistered company on the petition of a creditor, [of a liquidator (within the meaning of Article 2(b) of the EC Regulation) appointed in proceedings by virtue of Article 3(1) of the EC Regulation, of a temporary administrator (within the meaning of Article 38 of the EC Regulation),] of a responsible insolvency practitioner[, of the Secretary of State or of any other person other than a member,] where no insolvency petition is presented by the petitioner against a member or former member of that partnership in his capacity as such.

(2) Certain of the provisions referred to in paragraph (1) are modified in their application in relation to insolvent partnerships which are being wound up by virtue of that paragraph in such manner that, after modification, they are as set out in Part I of Schedule 3 to this Order.

(3) The provisions of the Act specified in Part II of Schedule 3 to this Order shall apply as set out in that Part for the purposes of section 221(5) of the Act, as modified by Part I of that Schedule.

NOTES

Para (1): first words in square brackets inserted by the Insolvent Partnerships (Amendment) Order 2002, SI 2002/1308, arts 2, 3; second words in square brackets substituted by the Insolvent Partnerships (Amendment) Order 1996, SI 1996/1308, art 2.

[10.8]

8 [Winding up of insolvent partnership as unregistered company on the petition of creditor etc where concurrent petitions presented against one or more members]

(1) Subject to paragraph (2) below, the provisions of Part V of the Act (other than sections 223 and 224), shall apply in relation to the winding up of an insolvent partnership as an unregistered company on [the petition of a creditor, of a liquidator (within the meaning of Article 2(b) of the EC Regulation) appointed in proceedings by virtue of Article 3(1) of the EC Regulation, or of a temporary administrator (within the meaning of Article 38 of the EC Regulation)] where insolvency petitions are presented by the petitioner against the partnership and against one or more members or former members of the partnership in their capacity as such.

(2) Certain of the provisions referred to in paragraph (1) are modified in their application in relation to insolvent partnerships which are being wound up by virtue of that paragraph in such manner that, after modification, they are as set out in Part I of Schedule 4 to this Order.

(3) The provisions of the Act specified in Part II of Schedule 4 to this Order shall apply as set out in that Part for the purposes of section 221(5) of the Act, as modified by Part I of that Schedule.

(4) The provisions of the Act specified in paragraph (5) below, insofar as they relate to winding up of companies by the court in England and Wales on a creditor's petition, shall apply in relation to the winding up of a corporate member or former corporate member (in its capacity as such) of an insolvent partnership which is being wound up by virtue of paragraph (1).

(5) The provisions referred to in paragraph (4) are—

(a) Part IV [. . .],
(b) Part VI,
(c) Part VII, and
(d) Parts XII to XIX.

(6) The provisions of the Act specified in paragraph (7) below, insofar as they relate to the bankruptcy of individuals in England and Wales on a petition presented by a creditor, shall apply in relation to the bankruptcy of an individual member or former individual member (in his capacity as such) of an insolvent partnership which is being wound up by virtue of paragraph (1).

(7) The provisions referred to in paragraph (6) are—

(a) Part IX (other than sections 269, 270, 287 and 297), and
(b) Parts X to XIX.

(8) Certain of the provisions referred to in paragraphs (4) and (6) are modified in their application in relation to the corporate or individual members or former corporate or individual members of insolvent partnerships in such manner that, after modification, they are as set out in Part II of Schedule 4 to this Order.

(9) The provisions of the Act applied by this Article shall further be modified so that references to a corporate or individual member include any former such member against whom an insolvency petition is being or has been presented by virtue of this Article.

NOTES

Article heading: substituted by the Insolvent Partnerships (Amendment) Order 2002, SI 2002/1308, arts 2, 4(2).

Para (1): words in square brackets substituted by SI 2002/1308, arts 2, 4(1).

Para (5): words "(other than section 176A)" omitted (originally inserted by the Insolvent Partnerships (Amendment) Order 2005, SI 2005/1516, art 4) revoked by the Insolvent Partnerships (Amendment) Order 2006, SI 2006/622, art 3, except in respect of any insolvency proceedings in relation to an insolvent partnership commenced before 6 April 2006; see SI 2006/622, art 2 at **[2.41]**.

PART V
MEMBERS' PETITIONS

[10.9]

9 Winding up of insolvent partnership as unregistered company on member's petition where no concurrent petition presented against member

The following provisions of the Act shall apply in relation to the winding up of an insolvent partnership as an unregistered company on the petition of a member where no insolvency petition is presented by the petitioner against a member of that partnership in his capacity as such—

(a) sections 117 and 221, modified in such manner that, after modification, they are as set out in Schedule 5 to this Order; and
(b) the other provisions of Part V of the Act, certain of those provisions being modified in such manner that, after modification, they are as set out in Part I of Schedule 3 to this Order.

[10.10]

10 Winding up of insolvent partnership as unregistered company on member's petition where concurrent petitions presented against all members

(1) The following provisions of the Act shall apply in relation to the winding up of an insolvent partnership as an unregistered company on a member's petition where insolvency petitions are presented by the petitioner against the partnership and against all its members in their capacity as such—

(a) sections 117, 124, 125, 221, 264, [265 and 271] of the Act, modified in such manner that, after modification, they are as set out in Schedule 6 to this Order; and
(b) sections 220, 225 and 227 to 229 in Part V of the Act, section 220 being modified in such manner that, after modification, it is as set out in Part I of Schedule 4 to this Order.

(2) The provisions of the Act specified in paragraph (3) below, insofar as they relate to winding up of companies by the court in England and Wales on a member's petition, shall apply in relation to the winding up of a corporate member (in its capacity as such) of an insolvent partnership which is wound up by virtue of paragraph (1).

(3) The provisions referred to in paragraph (2) are—

(a) Part IV [. . .],
(b) Part VI,
(c) Part VII, and
(d) Parts XII to XIX.

(4) The provisions of the Act specified in paragraph (5) below, insofar as they relate to the bankruptcy of individuals in England and Wales where [a bankruptcy application is made] by a debtor, shall apply in relation to the bankruptcy of an individual member (in his capacity as such) of an insolvent partnership which is being wound up by virtue of paragraph (1).

(5) The provisions referred to in paragraph (4) are—

(a) Part IX (other than sections . . . 287 and 297), and
(b) Parts X to XIX.

[(6) Certain of the provisions referred to in paragraphs (2) and (4) are modified in their application in relation to the corporate or individual members of insolvent partnerships in such manner that, after modification, they are as set out in Part II of Schedule 4 to this Order.]

NOTES

Para (1): words in square brackets substituted for original words "265, 271 and 272", in relation to England and Wales, by the Insolvency (Miscellaneous Amendments) Regulations 2017, SI 2017/1119, reg 2, Sch 2, paras 1, 3, as from 8 December 2017, subject to transitional and savings provisions in Sch 2, para 10 thereto as noted to art 2 at **[10.2]**.

Para (3): words "(other than section 176A)" omitted (originally inserted by the Insolvent Partnerships (Amendment) Order 2005, SI 2005/1516, art 5(a)) revoked by the Insolvent Partnerships (Amendment) Order 2006, SI 2006/622, art 4, except in respect of any insolvency proceedings in relation to an insolvent partnership commenced before 6 April 2006; see SI 2006/622, art 2 at **[2.41]**.

Para (4): words in square brackets substituted by the Enterprise and Regulatory Reform Act 2013 (Consequential Amendments) (Bankruptcy) and the Small Business, Enterprise and Employment Act 2015 (Consequential Amendments) Regulations 2016, SI 2016/481, reg 2(2), Sch 2, para 5(1), (2)(a).

Para (5): words omitted revoked by SI 2016/481, reg 2(2), Sch 2, para 5(1), (2)(b).

Para (6): substituted by SI 2005/1516, art 5(b).

[10.11]

11 Insolvency proceedings not involving winding up of insolvent partnership as unregistered company where individual members present joint bankruptcy petition

(1) The provisions of the Act specified in paragraph (2) below shall apply in relation to the bankruptcy of the individual members of an insolvent partnership where those members jointly present a petition to the court for orders to be made for the bankruptcy of each of them in his capacity as a member of the partnership, and the winding up of the partnership business and administration of its property, without the partnership being wound up as an unregistered company under Part V of the Act.

(2) The provisions referred to in paragraph (1) are—

(a) Part IX (other than [section] 287), and

(b) Parts X to XIX,

insofar as they relate to the insolvency of individuals in England and Wales where [a bankruptcy application is made] by a debtor.

(3) Certain of the provisions referred to in paragraph (1) are modified in their application in relation to the individual members of insolvent partnerships in such manner that, after modification, they are as set out in Schedule 7 to this Order.

NOTES

Para (2): words in square brackets substituted by the Enterprise and Regulatory Reform Act 2013 (Consequential Amendments) (Bankruptcy) and the Small Business, Enterprise and Employment Act 2015 (Consequential Amendments) Regulations 2016, SI 2016/481, reg 2(2), Sch 2, para 5(1), (3).

PART VI
PROVISIONS APPLYING IN INSOLVENCY PROCEEDINGS IN RELATION TO INSOLVENT PARTNERSHIPS

[10.12]

[11A Decision procedure in insolvency proceedings in relation to insolvent partnerships

Sections 246ZE, 246ZF, 379ZA and 379ZB of the Act apply in insolvency proceedings in relation to insolvent partnerships with the modifications set out in Schedule 7A to this Order.]

NOTES

Commencement: 6 April 2017.

Inserted by the Deregulation Act 2015 and Small Business, Enterprise and Employment Act 2015 (Consequential Amendments) (Savings) Regulations 2017, SI 2017/540, reg 3, Sch 2, paras 2, 3.

[10.13]

12 Winding up of unregistered company which is a member of insolvent partnership being wound up by virtue of this Order

Where an insolvent partnership or other body which may be wound up under Part V of the Act as an unregistered company is itself a member of an insolvent partnership being so wound up, articles 8 and 10 above shall apply in relation to the latter insolvent partnership as though the former body were a corporate member of that partnership.

[10.14]

13 Deposit on petitions

(1) Where an order under section 414(4) or 415(3) of the Act (security for fees) provides for any sum to be deposited on presentation of a winding-up or bankruptcy petition, that sum shall, in the case of petitions presented by virtue of articles 8 and 10 above, only be required to be deposited in respect of the petition for winding up the partnership, but shall be treated as a deposit in respect of all those petitions.

(2) Production of evidence as to the sum deposited on presentation of the petition for winding up the partnership shall suffice for the filing in court of an insolvency petition against an insolvent member.

14, 15 (*Art 14 amends the Insolvency Act 1986, ss 168, 303, at* **[1.169]**, **[1.366]**; *art 15 amends s 388 of that Act at* **[1.475]**.)

Part 10 SIs: Partnership Insolvency

PART VII
DISQUALIFICATION

[10.15]

16 Application of Company Directors Disqualification Act 1986

Where an insolvent partnership is wound up as an unregistered company under Part V of the Act, the provisions of [sections 1, 1A, 5A, 6 to 10, 12C, 13 to 15C, 17, 19(c) and 20 of, and Schedule 1 to], the Company Directors Disqualification Act 1986 shall apply, certain of those provisions being modified in such manner that, after modification, they are as set out in Schedule 8 to this Order.

NOTES

Words in square brackets substituted for words "[sections 1, 1A, 6 to 10, 13 to 15, 17], 19(c) and 20 of, and Schedule 1 to" (as amended by the Insolvent Partnerships (Amendment) Order 2001, SI 2001/767, art 2), in relation to England and Wales, by the Insolvency (Miscellaneous Amendments) Regulations 2017, SI 2017/1119, reg 2, Sch 2, paras 1, 4, as from 8 December 2017, subject to transitional and savings provisions in Sch 2, para 10 thereto as noted to art 2 at **[10.2]**.

PART VIII
MISCELLANEOUS

[10.16]

17 Forms

(1) The forms contained in Schedule 9 to this Order shall be used in and in connection with proceedings by virtue of this Order, whether in the High Court or a county court.

(2) The forms shall be used with such variations, if any, as the circumstances may require.

[10.17]

18 Application of subordinate legislation

(1) The subordinate legislation specified in Schedule 10 to this Order shall apply as from time to time in force and with such modifications as the context requires for the purpose of giving effect to the provisions of the Act and of the Company Directors Disqualification Act 1986 which are applied by this Order.

(2) In the case of any conflict between any provision of the subordinate legislation applied by paragraph (1) and any provision of this Order, the latter provision shall prevail.

[10.18]

19 Supplemental and transitional provisions

(1) This Order does not apply in relation to any case in which a winding-up or a bankruptcy order was made under the Insolvent Partnerships Order 1986 in relation to a partnership or an insolvent member of a partnership, and where this Order does not apply the law in force immediately before this Order came into force continues to have effect.

(2) Where winding-up or bankruptcy proceedings commenced under the provisions of the Insolvent Partnerships Order 1986 were pending in relation to a partnership or an insolvent member of a partnership immediately before this Order came into force, either—

- (a) those proceedings shall be continued, after the coming into force of this Order, in accordance with the provisions of this Order, or
- (b) if the court so directs, they shall be continued under the provisions of the 1986 Order, in which case the law in force immediately before this Order came into force continues to have effect.

(3) For the purpose of paragraph (2) above, winding-up or bankruptcy proceedings are pending if a statutory or written demand has been served or a winding-up or bankruptcy petition has been presented.

[(4) Nothing in this Order is to be taken as preventing a petition being presented against an insolvent partnership under section 367 of the Financial Services and Markets Act 2000, or any other enactment [except where paragraph 12 of Schedule A1 to the Act, as applied by this Order, has the effect of preventing a petition being so presented].]

(5) Nothing in this Order is to be taken as preventing any creditor or creditors owed one or more debts by an insolvent partnership from presenting a petition under the Act against one or more members of the partnership liable for that debt or those debts (as the case may be) without including the others and without presenting a petition for the winding up of the partnership as an unregistered company.

(6) Bankruptcy proceedings may be consolidated by virtue of article 14(2) above irrespective of whether they were commenced under the Bankruptcy Act 1914 or the Insolvency Act 1986 or by virtue of the Insolvent Partnerships Order 1986 or this Order, and the court shall, in the case of proceedings commenced under or by virtue of different enactments, make provision for the manner in which the consolidated proceedings are to be conducted.

NOTES

Para (4): substituted by the Financial Services and Markets Act 2000 (Consequential Amendments and Repeals) Order 2001, SI 2001/3649, art 467; words in square brackets added by the Insolvent Partnerships (Amendment) (No 2) Order 2002, SI 2002/2708, art 5, subject to transitional provisions in art 11(1), (3) thereof (see further the note to art 4 at **[10.4]**).

20 (*Revokes the Insolvent Partnerships Order 1986, SI 1986/2142.*)

SCHEDULES

[SCHEDULE 1

MODIFIED PROVISIONS OF PART I OF, AND SCHEDULE A1 TO, THE ACT (COMPANY VOLUNTARY ARRANGEMENTS) AS APPLIED BY ARTICLE 4

Article 4

PART I

MODIFIED PROVISIONS OF SECTIONS 1 TO 7B OF THE ACT

[10.19]

For sections 1 to 7B of the Act there shall be substituted:—

"PART I

PARTNERSHIP VOLUNTARY ARRANGEMENTS

The proposal

1 Those who may propose an arrangement

(1) The members of an insolvent partnership (other than one [which is in administration], or which is being wound up as an unregistered company, or in respect of which an order has been made by virtue of article 11 of the Insolvent Partnerships Order 1994) may make a proposal under this Part to the partnership's creditors for a composition in satisfaction of the debts of the partnership or a scheme of arrangement of its affairs (from here on referred to, in either case, as a "voluntary arrangement").

(2) A proposal under this Part is one which provides for some person ("the nominee") to act in relation to the voluntary arrangement either as trustee or otherwise for the purpose of supervising its implementation; and the nominee must be a person who is qualified to act as an insolvency practitioner . . . in relation to the voluntary arrangement.

(3) Such a proposal may also be made—

(a) where [the partnership is in administration], by the administrator,

(b) where the partnership is being wound up as an unregistered company, by the liquidator, and

(c) where an order has been made by virtue of article 11 of the Insolvent Partnerships Order 1994, by the trustee of the partnership.

(4) . . .

1A Moratorium

(1) Where the members of an eligible insolvent partnership intend to make a proposal for a voluntary arrangement, they may take steps to obtain a moratorium for the insolvent partnership.

(2) Subject to subsections (3), (4), (5), (6) and (7), the provisions of Schedule A1 to this Act have effect with respect to—

(a) insolvent partnerships eligible for a moratorium under this section,

(b) the procedure for obtaining such a moratorium,

(c) the effects of such a moratorium, and

(d) the procedure applicable (in place of sections 2 to 6 and 7) in relation to the approval and implementation of a voluntary arrangement where such a moratorium is or has been in force.

(3) Certain of the provisions applied in relation to insolvent partnerships by virtue of subsection (2) are modified in their application in relation to insolvent partnerships in such manner that, after modification, they are as set out in Part II of Schedule 1 to the Insolvent Partnerships Order 1994.

(4) Paragraphs 4A, 4B, 4C, 4D, 4E, 4F, 4G, 4H, 4I, 4J, 4K, 5, 7(4), 8(8), 32(7), 34(2), 41(5) and 45 of Schedule A1 to this Act shall not apply.

(5) An insolvent partnership is not liable to a fine under paragraphs 16(2), 17(3), 18(3), 19(3), 22 or 23(1) of Schedule A1 to the Act.

(6) Notwithstanding subsection (5) an officer of an insolvent partnership may be liable to imprisonment or a fine under the paragraphs referred to in that subsection in the same manner as an officer of a company.

(7) In the application of Schedule A1, and the application of the entries in Schedule 10 relating to offences under Schedule A1, to insolvent partnerships—

(a) references to the directors or members of a company shall be construed as references to the members of an insolvent partnership,

(b) references to officers of a company shall be construed as references to the officers of an insolvent partnership,

(c) references to a meeting of a company shall be construed as references to a meeting of the members of an insolvent partnership, and

(d) references to a floating charge shall be construed as references to a floating charge created under section 5 of the Agricultural Credits Act 1928.

2 Procedure where nominee is not the liquidator, administrator or trustee

(1) This section applies where the nominee under section 1 is not the liquidator, administrator or trustee of the insolvent partnership and the members of the partnership do not propose to take steps to obtain a moratorium under section 1A for the insolvent partnership.

(2) The nominee shall, within 28 days (or such longer period as the court may allow) after he is given notice of the proposal for a voluntary arrangement, submit a report to the court stating—

(a) whether, in his opinion, the proposed voluntary arrangement has a reasonable prospect of being approved and implemented,

[(b) whether, in his opinion, the proposal should be considered by a meeting of the members of the partnership and by the partnership's creditors, and

(c) if in his opinion it should, the date on which, and time and place at which, he proposes a meeting should be held.]

(3) The nominee shall also state in his report whether there are in existence any insolvency proceedings in respect of the insolvent partnership or any of its members.

(4) For the purposes of enabling the nominee to prepare his report, the person intending to make the proposal shall submit to the nominee—

(a) a document setting out the terms of the proposed voluntary arrangement, and

(b) a statement of the partnership's affairs containing—

(i) such particulars of the partnership's creditors and of the partnership's debts and other liabilities and of the partnership property as may be prescribed, and

(ii) such other information as may be prescribed.

(5) The court may—

(a) on an application made by the person intending to make the proposal, in a case where the nominee has failed to submit the report required by this section or has died, or

(b) on an application made by that person or the nominee, in a case where it is impracticable or inappropriate for the nominee to continue to act as such,

direct that the nominee be replaced as such by another person qualified to act as an insolvency practitioner . . . in relation to the voluntary arrangement.

3 Summoning of meetings

(1) Where the nominee under section 1 is not the liquidator, administrator or trustee of the insolvent partnership, and it has been reported to the court [under section 2(2) that the proposal should be considered by a meeting of the members of the partnership and by the partnership's creditors], the person making the report shall (unless the court otherwise [directs)—

(a) summon a meeting of the members of the partnership to consider the proposal for the time, date and place proposed in the report, and

(b) seek a decision from the partnership's creditors as to whether they approve the proposal.]

(2) Where the nominee is the liquidator, administrator or trustee of the insolvent partnership, he [must—

(a) summon a meeting of the members of the partnership to consider the proposal for such time, date and place as he thinks fit, and

(b) seek a decision from the partnership's creditors as to whether they approve the proposal.]

[(3) A decision of the partnership's creditors as to whether they approve the proposal is to be made by a qualifying decision procedure.

(4) Notice of the qualifying decision procedure must be given to every creditor of the partnership of whose claim and address the person summoning the meeting is aware.]

Consideration and implementation of proposal

4 Decisions of [the members of the partnership and its creditors]

[(1) This section applies where, under section 3—

(a) a meeting of the members of the partnership is summoned to consider the proposed voluntary arrangement, and

(b) the partnership's creditors are asked to decide whether to approve the proposed voluntary arrangement.

(1A) The members of the partnership and its creditors may approve the proposed voluntary arrangement with or without modifications.]

(2) The modifications may include one conferring the functions proposed to be conferred on the nominee on another person qualified to act as an insolvency practitioner . . . in relation to the voluntary arrangement.

But they shall not include any modification by virtue of which the proposal ceases to be a proposal such as is mentioned in section 1.

(3) [Neither the members of the partnership nor its creditors may] approve any proposal or modification which affects the right of a secured creditor of the partnership to enforce his security, except with the concurrence of the creditor concerned.

(4) Subject as follows, [neither the members of the partnership nor its creditors may] approve any proposal or modification under which—

(a) any preferential debt of the partnership is to be paid otherwise than in priority to such of its debts as are not preferential debts, . . .

[(aa) any ordinary preferential debt of the partnership is to be paid otherwise than in priority to any secondary preferential debts that it may have,]

(b) a preferential creditor of the partnership is to be paid an amount in respect of [an ordinary preferential debt] that bears to that debt a smaller proportion than is borne to [another ordinary] preferential debt by the amount that is to be paid in respect of that other debt [or

(c) a preferential creditor of the partnership is to be paid an amount in respect of a secondary preferential debt that bears to that debt a smaller proportion than is borne to another secondary preferential debt by the amount that is to be paid in respect of that other debt.]

However, [such a proposal or modification may be approved] with the concurrence of the preferential creditor concerned.

(5) Subject as above, [the meeting of the members of the partnership and the qualifying decision procedure] shall be conducted in accordance with the rules.

(6) After the conclusion of [the meeting of the members of the partnership] in accordance with the rules, the chairman of the meeting shall report the result of the meeting to the court, and, immediately after reporting to the court, shall give notice of the result of the meeting to all those who were sent notice of the meeting in accordance with the rules.

[(6A) After the partnership's creditors have decided whether to approve the proposed voluntary arrangement the person who sought the decision must—

(a) report the creditors' decision to the court, and

(b) immediately after reporting to the court, give notice of the creditors' decision to everyone who was invited to consider the proposal or to whom notice of a decision procedure or meeting was delivered.]

(7) References in this section to preferential debts[, ordinary preferential debts, secondary preferential debts] and preferential creditors are to be read in accordance with section 386 in Part XII of this Act.

4A Approval of arrangement

(1) This section applies to a decision, under section 4, with respect to the approval of a proposed voluntary arrangement.

(2) The decision has effect if, in accordance with the rules—

(a) it has been taken by [the meeting of the members of the partnership summoned under section 3 and by the partnership's creditors pursuant to that section], or

(b) (subject to any order made under subsection (6)) it has been taken by the [partnership's creditors pursuant to] that section.

(3) If the decision taken by the [partnership's creditors] differs from that taken by the meeting of the members of the partnership, a member of the partnership may apply to court.

(4) An application under subsection (3) shall not be made after the end of the period of 28 days beginning with—

(a) the day on which the decision was taken by the [partnership's creditors], or

(b) where the decision of the meeting of the members of the partnership was taken on a later day, that day.

[(5) Where a member of an insolvent partnership which is regulated applies to the court under subsection (3), the appropriate regulator is entitled to be heard on the application.

(5A) "The appropriate regulator" means—

(a) where the partnership is a PRA-regulated partnership, the Prudential Regulation Authority and the Financial Conduct Authority;

(b) in any other case the Financial Conduct Authority.

(5B) For the purposes of subsection (5A), a "PRA-regulated partnership" means a partnership which—

(a) is or has been, a PRA-authorised person (within the meaning of the Financial Services and Markets Act 2000),

(b) is, or has been, an appointed representative within the meaning given by section 39 of that Act, whose principal (or one of whose principals) is, or was, a PRA-authorised person, or

(c) is carrying on, or has carried on, a PRA-regulated activity (within the meaning of that Act) in contravention of the general prohibition under section 19 of that Act.]

(6) On an application under subsection (3), the court may—

(a) order the decision of the meeting of the members of the partnership to have effect instead of the decision of the [partnership's creditors], or

(b) make such other order as it thinks fit.

(7) In this section "regulated" in relation to an insolvent partnership means a person who—

(a) is, or has been, an authorised person within the meaning given by section 31 of the Financial Services and Markets Act 2000,

(b) is, or has been, an appointed representative within the meaning given by section 39 of that Act, or

(c) is carrying on, or has carried on, a regulated activity, within the meaning given by section 22 of that Act, in contravention of the general prohibition within the meaning given by section 19 of that Act.

5 Effect of approval

(1) This section applies where a decision approving a voluntary arrangement has effect under section 4A.

(2) The voluntary arrangement—

(a) takes effect as if made by the members of the partnership at the [time the creditors decided to approve the voluntary arrangement], and

(b) binds every person who in accordance with the rules—

(i) was entitled to vote [in the qualifying decision procedure by which the creditors' decision to approve the voluntary arrangement was made], or

(ii) would have been so entitled if he had had notice of [the procedure],

as if he were a party to the voluntary arrangement.

(2A) If—

(a) when the arrangement ceases to have effect any amount payable under the arrangement to a person bound by virtue of subsection 2(b)(ii) has not been paid, and

(b) the arrangement did not come to an end prematurely,

the insolvent partnership shall at that time become liable to pay to that person the amount payable under the arrangement.

(3) Subject as follows, if the partnership is being wound up as an unregistered company, or [is in administration] or an order by virtue of article 11 of the Insolvent Partnerships Order 1994 is in force, the court may do one or both of the following, namely—

(a) by order—

(i) stay all proceedings in the winding up or in the proceedings under the order made by virtue of the said article 11 (as the case may be), including any related insolvency proceedings of a member of the partnership in his capacity as such, or

(ii) [provide for the appointment of the administrator to cease to have effect];

(b) give such directions as it thinks appropriate for facilitating the implementation of the voluntary arrangement with respect to—

(i) the conduct of the winding up, the proceedings by virtue of the said article 11 or the administration (as the case may be), and

(ii) the conduct of any related insolvency proceedings as referred to in paragraph (a)(i) above.

(4) The court shall not make an order under subsection (3)(a)—

(a) at any time before the end of the period of 28 days beginning with the first day on which each of the reports required by section 4(6) [and (6A)] has been made to the court, or

(b) at any time when an application under the next section or an appeal in respect of such an application is pending, or at any time in the period within which such an appeal may be brought.

6 Challenge of decisions

(1) Subject to this section, an application to the court may be made, by any of the persons specified below, on one or both of the following grounds, namely—

(a) that a voluntary arrangement which has effect under section 4A unfairly prejudices the interests of a creditor, member or contributory of the partnership;

(b) that there has been some material irregularity at or in relation to [the meeting of the members of the partnership or in the relevant qualifying decision procedure].

(2) The persons who may apply under this section are—

(a) a person entitled, in accordance with the rules, to vote at [the meeting of the members of the partnership or in the relevant qualifying decision procedure];

(b) a person who would have been entitled, in accordance with the rules, to vote [in the relevant qualifying decision procedure] if he had had notice of it;

(c) the nominee or any person who has replaced him under section 2(5) or 4(2); and

(d) if the partnership is being wound up as an unregistered company or [is in administration or an] order by virtue of article 11 of the Insolvent Partnerships Order 1994 is in force, the liquidator, administrator or trustee of the partnership.

(3) An application under this section shall not be made—

(a) after the end of the period of 28 days beginning with the first day on which each of the reports required by section 4(6) [and (6A)] has been made to the court, or

(b) in the case of a person who was not given notice of the [relevant qualifying decision procedure], after the end of the period of 28 days beginning with the day on which he became aware that [the relevant qualifying decision procedure] had taken place,

but (subject to that) an application made by a person within subsection (2)(b) on the ground that the voluntary arrangement prejudices his interests may be made after the voluntary arrangement has ceased to have effect, unless it came to an end prematurely.

(4) Where on such an application the court is satisfied as to either of the grounds mentioned in subsection (1), it may do [any] of the following, namely—

(a) revoke or suspend any decision approving the voluntary arrangement which has effect under section 4A or, in a case falling within subsection (1)(b), any decision taken by the meeting [of the members of the partnership, or in the relevant qualifying decision procedure,] which has effect under that section;

(b) give a direction to any person for the summoning of [a further meeting of the members of the partnership] to consider any revised proposal the person who made the original proposal may make or, in a case falling within subsection (1)(b) [and relating to the meeting of the members of the partnership, a further meeting of the members of the partnership] to reconsider the original proposal;

[(c) direct any person—

(i) to seek a decision from the partnership's creditors (using a qualifying decision procedure) as to whether they approve any revised proposal the person who made the original proposal may make, or

(ii) in a case falling within subsection (1)(b) and relating to the relevant qualifying decision procedure, to seek a decision from the partnership's creditors (using a qualifying decision procedure) as to whether they approve the original proposal.]

(5) Where at any time after giving a direction under subsection (4)(b) [or (c) in relation to] a revised proposal the court is satisfied that the person who made the original proposal does not intend to submit a revised proposal, the court shall revoke the direction and revoke or suspend any decision approving the voluntary arrangement which has effect under section 4A.

(6) In a case where the court, on an application under this section with respect to any meeting [or relevant qualifying decision procedure]—

(a) gives a direction under subsection (4)(b) [or (c)], or

(b) revokes or suspends an approval under subsection (4)(a) or (5),

the court may give such supplemental directions as it thinks fit, and, in particular, directions with respect to things done under the voluntary arrangement since it took effect.

(7) Except in pursuance of the preceding provisions of this section,

[(a)] a decision taken at a meeting [of the members of the partnership] summoned under section 3 is not invalidated by any irregularity at or in relation to the meeting[, and

(b) a decision of the creditors of the partnership made in the relevant qualifying decision procedure is not invalidated by any irregularity in relation to the relevant qualifying decision procedure.]

6A False representations, etc

(1) If, for the purpose of obtaining the approval of the members or creditors of an insolvent partnership or of the members or creditors of any of its members to a proposal for a voluntary arrangement in relation to the partnership or any of its members, a person who is an officer of the partnership or an officer (which for this purpose includes a shadow director) of a corporate member in relation to which a voluntary arrangement is proposed—

(a) makes a false representation, or

(b) fraudulently does, or omits to do, anything,

he commits an offence.

(2) Subsection (1) applies even if the proposal is not approved.

(3) A person guilty of an offence under this section is liable to imprisonment or a fine, or both.

7 Implementation of proposal

(1) This section applies where a voluntary arrangement has effect under section 4A.

(2) The person who is for the time being carrying out in relation to the voluntary arrangement the functions conferred—

(a) on the nominee by virtue of the approval [of the voluntary arrangement by the members of the partnership or its creditors (or both) pursuant to] section 3, or

(b) by virtue of section 2(5) or 4(2) on a person other than the nominee,

shall be known as the supervisor of the voluntary arrangement.

(3) If any of the partnership's creditors or any other person is dissatisfied by any act, omission or decision of the supervisor, he may apply to the court; and on the application the court may—

(a) confirm, reverse or modify any act or decision of the supervisor,

(b) give him directions, or

(c) make such other order as it thinks fit.

(4) The supervisor—

(a) may apply to the court for directions in relation to any particular matter arising under the voluntary arrangement, and

(b) is included among the persons who may apply to the court for the winding up of the partnership as an unregistered company or for an administration order to be made in relation to it.

(5) The court may, whenever—

(a) it is expedient to appoint a person to carry out the functions of the supervisor, and

(b) it is inexpedient, difficult or impracticable for an appointment to be made without the assistance of the court,

make an order appointing a person who is qualified to act as an insolvency practitioner . . . in relation to the voluntary arrangement, either in substitution for the existing supervisor or to fill a vacancy.

(6) The power conferred by subsection (5) is exercisable so as to increase the number of persons exercising the functions of supervisor or, where there is more than one person exercising those functions, so as to replace one or more of those persons.

7A Prosecution of delinquent officers of partnership

(1) This section applies where a moratorium under section 1A has been obtained for an insolvent partnership or the approval of a voluntary arrangement in relation to an insolvent partnership has taken effect under section 4A or paragraph 36 of Schedule A1.

(2) If it appears to the nominee or supervisor that any past or present officer of the insolvent partnership has been guilty of any offence in connection with the moratorium or, as the case may be, voluntary arrangement for which such officer is criminally liable, the nominee or supervisor shall forthwith—

(a) report the matter to the Secretary of State, and

(b) provide the Secretary of State with such information and give him such access to and facilities for inspecting and taking copies of documents (being information or documents in the possession or under the control of the nominee or supervisor and relating to the matter in question) as the Secretary of State requires.

(3) Where a prosecuting authority institutes criminal proceedings following any report under subsection (2), the nominee or supervisor, and every officer and agent of the insolvent partnership past or present (other than the defendant), shall give the authority all assistance in connection with the prosecution which he is reasonably able to give.

For this purpose—

"agent" includes any banker or solicitor of the insolvent partnership and any person employed by the insolvent partnership as auditor, whether that person is or is not an officer of the insolvent partnership,

"prosecuting authority" means the Director of Public Prosecutions or the Secretary of State.

(4) The court may, on the application of the prosecuting authority, direct any person referred to in subsection (3) to comply with that subsection if he has failed to do so.

7B Arrangements coming to an end prematurely

For the purposes of this Part, a voluntary arrangement the approval of which has taken effect under section 4A or paragraph 36 of Schedule A1 comes to an end prematurely if, when it ceases to have effect, it has not been fully implemented in respect of all persons bound by the arrangement by virtue of section 5(2)(b)(i) or, as the case may be, paragraph 37(2)(b)(i) of Schedule A1.".]

NOTES

Substituted by the Insolvent Partnerships (Amendment) (No 2) Order 2002, SI 2002/2708, art 6, Sch 1, subject to transitional provisions in art 11(1), (3) thereof (see further the note to art 4 at **[10.4]**). The previous text is set out below.

In s 1 of the Act (as set out above) words in square brackets substituted and sub-s (4) revoked by the Insolvent Partnerships (Amendment) Order 2005, SI 2005/1516, art 6(1), (2); words omitted from sub-s (2) revoked by the Deregulation Act 2015 (Insolvency) (Consequential Amendments and Transitional and Savings Provisions) Order 2015, SI 2015/1641, art 5, Sch 2, para 1(1), (2)(a).

In s 2 of the Act (as set out above). sub-s (2)(b), (c) substituted by the Deregulation Act 2015 and Small Business, Enterprise and Employment Act 2015 (Consequential Amendments) (Savings) Regulations 2017, SI 2017/540, reg 3, Sch 2, paras 2, 4(1), (2); words omitted from sub-s (5) revoked by SI 2015/1641, art 5, Sch 2, para 1(1), (2)(b).

In s 3 of the Act (as set out above) words in square brackets substituted by SI 2017/540, reg 3, Sch 2, paras 2, 4(1), (3).

In s 4 of the Act (as set out above) words in square brackets in the heading and sub-ss (3), (5), (6) substituted, sub-ss (1), (1A) substituted for original sub-s (1), words in first and final pairs of square brackets in sub-s (4) substituted and sub-s (6A) inserted by SI 2017/540, reg 3, Sch 2, paras 2, 4(1), (4); words omitted from sub-s (2) revoked by SI 2015/1641, art 5, Sch 2, para 1(1), (2)(c); word omitted from sub-s (4)(a) revoked, sub-s (4)(aa) inserted, in sub-para (4)(b) first words in square brackets substituted, and sub-para (c) and word immediately preceding it added, and in sub-s (7) words in square brackets inserted, by the Banks and Building Societies (Depositor Preference and Priorities) Order 2014, SI 2014/3486, art 12.

In s 4A of the Act (as set out above) words in square brackets in sub-ss (2), (3), (4), (6) substituted by SI 2017/540, reg 3, Sch 2, paras 2, 4(1), (5); sub-ss (5)–(5B) substituted by the Financial Services Act 2012 (Consequential Amendments and Transitional Provisions) Order 2013, SI 2013/472, art 3, Sch 2, para 11.

In s 5 of the Act (as set out above) words in square brackets in sub-s (2) substituted and words in square brackets in sub-s (4) inserted, by SI 2017/540, reg 3, Sch 2, paras 2, 4(1), (6); words in square brackets in sub-s (3) substituted by SI 2005/1516, art 6(1), (3).

In s 6 of the Act (as set out above) words in square brackets in sub-s (2)(d) substituted by SI 2005/1516, art 6(1), (4); all other words in square brackets substituted or inserted by SI 2017/540, reg 3, Sch 2, paras 2, 4(1), (7).

In s 7 of the Act (as set out above) words in square brackets in sub-s (2) substituted by SI 2017/540, reg 3, Sch 2, paras 2, 4(1), (8); words omitted from sub-s (5) revoked by SI 2015/1641, art 5, Sch 2, para 1(1), (2)(d).

[PART II
MODIFIED PROVISIONS OF SCHEDULE A1 TO THE ACT

[10.20]

The following provisions of Schedule A1 to the Act are modified so as to read as follows:

"**3.** (1) An insolvent partnership meets the requirements of this paragraph if the qualifying conditions are met—

(a) in the year ending with the date of filing, or

(b) in the tax year of the insolvent partnership which ended last before that date.

(2) For the purposes of sub-paragraph (1) the qualifying conditions are met by an insolvent partnership in a period if, in that period, it satisfies two or more of the requirements set out in sub-paragraph (3).

(3) The qualifying conditions referred to in this paragraph are—

(a) turnover of not more than [£5.6] million,

(b) assets of not more than [£2.8] million, and

(c) no more than 50 employees.

(4) For the purposes of sub-paragraph (3)—

(a) the total of turnover is the amount which is or would be, as the case may be, entered as turnover in the partnership's tax return,

(b) the total of assets is the amount which—

(i) in the case of the period referred to in paragraph 3(1)(a), is entered in the partnership's statement of affairs which must be filed with the court under paragraph 7(1)(b), or

(ii) in the case of the period referred to in paragraph 3(1)(b), would be entered in the partnership's statement of affairs had it prepared such a statement on the last day of the period to which the amount for turnover is calculated for the purposes of paragraph 3(4)(a),

(c) the number of employees is the average number of persons employed by the insolvent partnership—

(i) in the case of the period referred to in paragraph 3(1)(a), in the period ending with the date of filing,

(ii) in the case of the period referred to in paragraph 3(1)(b), in the period to which the amount for turnover is calculated for the purposes of paragraph 3(4)(a).

(5) Where the period covered by the qualifying conditions in respect of the insolvent partnership is not a year the total of turnover referred to in paragraph 3(3)(a) shall be proportionately adjusted.

(6) The average number of persons employed by the insolvent partnership shall be calculated as follows—

(a) by ascertaining the number of persons employed by it under contracts of service for each month of the year (whether throughout the month or not),

(b) by adding those figures together, and

(c) by dividing the resulting figure by the number of months during which persons were so employed by it during the year.

(7) In this paragraph—

"tax return" means a return under section 12AA of the Taxes Management Act 1970,

"tax year" means the 12 months beginning with 6th April in any year.

4. (1) An insolvent partnership is excluded from being eligible for a moratorium if, on the date of filing—

(a) [the partnership is in administration],

(b) the insolvent partnership is being wound up as an unregistered company,

(c) there is an agricultural receiver of the insolvent partnership,

(d) a voluntary arrangement has effect in relation to the insolvent partnership,

(e) there is a provisional liquidator of the insolvent partnership,

(f) a moratorium has been in force for the insolvent partnership at any time during the period of 12 months ending with the date of filing and—

(i) no voluntary arrangement had effect at the time at which the moratorium came to an end, or

(ii) a voluntary arrangement which had effect at any time in that period has come to an end prematurely,

(g) a voluntary arrangement in relation to the insolvent partnership which had effect in pursuance of a proposal under section 1(3) has come to an end prematurely and, during the period of 12 months ending with the date of filing, an order under section 5(3)(a) has been made, or

(h) an order has been made by virtue of article 11 of the Insolvent Partnerships Order 1994.

(2) Sub-paragraph (1)(b) does not apply to an insolvent partnership which, by reason of a winding-up order made after the date of filing, is treated as being wound up on that date.

Effect on creditors, etc

12. (1) During the period for which a moratorium is in force for an insolvent partnership—

(a) no petition may be presented for the winding-up of the insolvent partnership as an unregistered company,

(b) no meeting of the members of the partnership may be called or requisitioned except with the consent of the nominee or the leave of the court and subject (where the court gives leave) to such terms as the court may impose,

(c) no order may be made for the winding-up of the insolvent partnership as an unregistered company,

[(d) no administration application may be made in respect of the partnership,

(da) no administrator of the partnership may be appointed under paragraph 14 or 22 of Schedule B1,]

(e) no agricultural receiver of the partnership may be appointed except with the leave of the court and subject to such terms as the court may impose,

(f) no landlord or other person to whom rent is payable may exercise any rights of forfeiture by peaceable re-entry in relation to premises forming part of the partnership property or let to one or more officers of the partnership in their capacity as such in respect of a failure by the partnership or one or more officers of the partnership to comply with any term or condition of the tenancy of such premises, except with the leave of the court and subject to such terms as the court may impose,

(g) no other steps may be taken to enforce any security over the partnership property, or to repossess goods in the possession, under any hire-purchase agreement, of one or more officers of the partnership in their capacity as such, except with the leave of the court and subject to such terms as the court may impose,

(h) no other proceedings and no execution or other legal process may be commenced or continued, and no distress may be levied, against the insolvent partnership or the partnership property except with the leave of the court and subject to such terms as the court may impose,

(i) no petition may be presented, and no order may be made, by virtue of article 11 of the Insolvent Partnerships Order 1994, and

(j) no application or order may be made under section 35 of the Partnership Act 1890 in respect of the insolvent partnership.

(2) Where a petition, other than an excepted petition, for the winding-up of the insolvent partnership has been presented before the beginning of the moratorium, section 127 shall not apply in relation to any disposition of partnership property, any transfer of an interest in the insolvent partnership or alteration in status of a member of the partnership made during the moratorium or at a time mentioned in paragraph 37(5)(a).

(3) Paragraph (a) of sub-paragraph (1) does not apply to an excepted petition and, where such a petition has been presented before the beginning of the moratorium or is presented during the moratorium, paragraphs (b) and (c) of that sub-paragraph do not apply in relation to proceedings on the petition.

(4) For the purposes of this paragraph, "excepted petition" means a petition under—

(a) article 7(1) of the Insolvent Partnerships Order 1994 presented by the Secretary of State on the grounds mentioned in subsections (b), (c) and (d) of section 124A of this Act,

(b) section 72 of the Financial Services Act 1986 on the ground mentioned in subsection (1)(b) of that section,

(c) section 92 of the Banking Act 1987 on the ground mentioned in subsection (1)(b) of that section, or

(d) section 367 of the Financial Services and Markets Act 2000 on the ground mentioned in subsection (3)(b) of that section.

Disposal of charged property, etc

20. (1) This paragraph applies where—

(a) any partnership property of the insolvent partnership is subject to a security, or

(b) any goods are in possession of one or more officers of the partnership in their capacity as such under a hire-purchase agreement.

(2) If the holder of the security consents, or the court gives leave, the insolvent partnership may dispose of the property as if it were not subject to the security.

(3) If the owner of the goods consents, or the court gives leave, the insolvent partnership may dispose of the goods as if all rights of the owner under the hire-purchase agreement were vested in the members of the partnership.

(4) Where property subject to a security which, as created, was a floating charge is disposed of under sub-paragraph (2), the holder of the security has the same priority in respect of any partnership property directly or indirectly representing the property disposed of as he would have had in respect of the property subject to the security.

(5) Sub-paragraph (6) applies to the disposal under sub-paragraph (2) or (as the case may be) sub-paragraph (3) of—

(a) any property subject to a security other than a security which, as created, was a floating charge, or

(b) any goods in the possession of one or more officers of the partnership in their capacity as such under a hire-purchase agreement.

(6) It shall be a condition of any consent or leave under sub-paragraph (2) or (as the case may be) sub-paragraph (3) that—

(a) the net proceeds of the disposal, and

(b) where those proceeds are less than such amount as may be agreed, or determined by the court, to be the net amount which would be realised on a sale of the property or goods in the open market by a willing vendor, such sums as may be required to make good the deficiency,

shall be applied towards discharging the sums secured by the security or payable under the hire-purchase agreement.

(7) Where a condition imposed in pursuance of sub-paragraph (6) relates to two or more securities, that condition requires—

(a) the net proceeds of the disposal, and

(b) where paragraph (b) of sub-paragraph (6) applies, the sums mentioned in that paragraph,

to be applied towards discharging the sums secured by those securities in the order of their priorities.

(8) In this paragraph "floating charge" means a floating charge created under section 5 of the Agricultural Credits Act 1928.

Effect of approval of voluntary arrangement

37. (1) This paragraph applies where a decision approving a voluntary arrangement has effect under paragraph 36.

(2) The approved voluntary arrangement—

(a) takes effect as if made by the members of the partnership at the [time the creditors decided to approve the voluntary arrangement], and

(b) binds every person who in accordance with the rules—

(i) was entitled to vote [in the qualifying decision procedure by which the creditors' decision to approve the voluntary arrangement was made], or

(ii) would have been so entitled if he had had notice of [the procedure],

as if he were a party to the voluntary arrangement.

(3) If—

(a) when the arrangement ceases to have effect any amount payable under the arrangement to a person bound by virtue of sub-paragraph (2)(b)(ii) has not been paid, and

(b) the arrangement did not come to an end prematurely,

the insolvent partnership shall at that time become liable to pay to that person the amount payable under the arrangement.

(4) Where a petition for the winding-up of the insolvent partnership as an unregistered company or a petition by virtue of article 11 of the Insolvent Partnerships Order 1994, other than an excepted petition within the meaning of paragraph 12, was presented before the beginning of the moratorium, the court shall dismiss the petition.

(5) The court shall not dismiss a petition under sub-paragraph (4)—

(a) at any time before the end of the period of 28 days beginning with the first day on which each of the reports . . . required by paragraph 30(3) [and (4)] has been made to the court, or

(b) at any time when an application under paragraph 38 or an appeal in respect of such an application is pending, or at any time in the period within which such an appeal may be brought.

Challenge of actions of officers of insolvent partnership

40. (1) This paragraph applies in relation to acts or omissions of the officers of a partnership during a moratorium.

(2) A creditor or member of the insolvent partnership may apply to the court for an order under this paragraph on the ground—

(a) that the partnership's affairs and business and partnership property are being or have been managed by the officers of the partnership in a manner which is unfairly prejudicial to the interests of its creditors or members generally, or of some part of its creditors or members (including at least the petitioner), or

(b) that any actual or proposed act or omission of the officers of the partnership is or would be so prejudicial.

(3) An application for an order under this paragraph may be made during or after the moratorium.

(4) On an application for an order under this paragraph the court may—

(a) make such order as it thinks fit for giving relief in respect of the matters complained of,

(b) adjourn the hearing conditionally or unconditionally, or

(c) make an interim order or any other order that it thinks fit.

(5) An order under this paragraph may in particular—

(a) regulate the management by the officers of the partnership of the partnership's affairs and business and partnership property during the remainder of the moratorium,

(b) require the officers of the partnership to refrain from doing or continuing an act complained of by the petitioner, or to do an act which the petitioner has complained they have omitted to do,

(c) require the summoning of a meeting of . . . members of the partnership for the purpose of considering such matters as the court may direct,

[(ca) require a decision of the partnership's creditors to be sought (using a qualifying decision procedure) on such matters as the court may direct,]

(d) bring the moratorium to an end and make such consequential provision as the court thinks fit.

(6) In making an order under this paragraph the court shall have regard to the need to safeguard the interests of persons who have dealt with the insolvent partnership in good faith and for value.

[(7) Sub-paragraph (8) applies where—

(a) the appointment of an administrator has effect in relation to the insolvent partnership and the appointment took effect before the moratorium came into force, or

(b) the insolvent partnership is being wound up as an unregistered company or an order by virtue of article 11 of the Insolvent Partnerships Order 1994 has been made, in pursuance of a petition presented before the moratorium came into force.

(8) No application for an order under this paragraph may be made by a creditor or member of the insolvent partnership; but such an application may be made instead by the administrator (or as the case may be) the liquidator.]

42. (1) If, for the purpose of obtaining a moratorium, or an extension of a moratorium, for an insolvent partnership or any of its members (a moratorium meaning in the case of an individual the effect of an application for, or the making of, an interim order under Part VIII of the Act), a person who is an officer of an insolvent partnership or an officer (which for this purpose includes a shadow director) of a corporate member in relation to which a voluntary arrangement is proposed—

(a) makes any false representation, or

(b) fraudulently does, or omits to do, anything,

he commits an offence.

(2) Sub-paragraph (1) applies even if no moratorium or extension is obtained.

(3) A person guilty of an offence under this paragraph is liable to imprisonment or a fine, or both.".]

NOTES

Substituted, subject to transitional provisions, as noted to Pt I of this Schedule at **[10.19]**.

In Sch A1, paras 3, 4, 12 to the Act (as set out above) words in square brackets substituted by the Insolvent Partnerships (Amendment) Order 2005, SI 2005/1516, art 6(1), (5)–(7).

In Sch A1, para 37 to the Act (as set out above) words in square brackets substituted or inserted and words omitted revoked by the Deregulation Act 2015 and Small Business, Enterprise and Employment Act 2015 (Consequential Amendments) (Savings) Regulations 2017, SI 2017/540, reg 3, Sch 2, paras 2, 5(1), (2).

In Sch A1, para 40 to the Act (as set out above) words omitted from sub-para (5)(c) revoked and sub-para (5)(ca) inserted by SI 2017/540, reg 3, Sch 2, paras 2, 5(1), (3); sub-paras (7), (8) substituted (for original sub-para (7)) by SI 2005/1516, art 6(1), (8).

[SCHEDULE 2
MODIFIED PROVISIONS OF PART II OF, AND SCHEDULE B1 TO, THE ACT (ADMINISTRATION) AS APPLIED BY ARTICLE 6

Article 6

[10.21]

1. The following provisions of Schedule B1 and Schedule 1 to the Act are modified as follows.

2. Paragraph 2 is modified so as to read as follows—

"**2.** A person may be appointed as administrator of a partnership—
(a) by administration order of the court under paragraph 10,
(b) by the holder of an agricultural floating charge under paragraph 14, or
(c) by the members of the insolvent partnership in their capacity as such under paragraph 22.".

3. Paragraph 7 is modified so as to read as follows—

"**7.** A person may not be appointed as administrator of a partnership which is in administration (subject to the provisions of paragraphs 90 to 93, 95 to 97, and 100 to 103 about replacement and additional administrators).".

4. Paragraph 8 is modified so as to read as follows—

"**8.** (1) A person may not be appointed as administrator of a partnership after—
(a) an order has been made in relation to it by virtue of Article 11 of the Insolvent Partnerships Order 1994; or
(b) an order has been made for it to be wound up by the court as an unregistered company.
(2) Sub-paragraph (1)(a) is subject to paragraph 38.
(3) Sub-paragraph (1)(b) is subject to paragraphs 37 and 38.".

5. Paragraph 11 is modified so as to read as follows—

"**11.** The court may make an administration order in relation to a partnership only if satisfied—
(a) that the partnership is unable to pay its debts, and
(b) that the administration order is reasonably likely to achieve the purpose of administration.".

6. Paragraph 12 is modified so as to read as follows—

"**12.** (1) An application to the court for an administration order in respect of a partnership ("an administration application") shall be by application in Form 1 in Schedule 9 to the Insolvent Partnerships Order 1994 and may be made only by—
(a) the members of the insolvent partnership in their capacity as such;
(b) one or more creditors of the partnership; or
(c) a combination of persons listed in paragraphs (a) and (b).
(2) As soon as is reasonably practicable after the making of an administration application the applicant shall notify—
(a) any person who has appointed an agricultural receiver of the partnership;
(b) any person who is or may be entitled to appoint an agricultural receiver of the partnership;
(c) any person who is or may be entitled to appoint an administrator of the partnership under paragraph 14; and
(d) such other persons as may be prescribed.
(3) An administration application may not be withdrawn without the permission of the court.
(4) In sub-paragraph (1) "creditor" includes a contingent creditor and a prospective creditor.
(5) Sub-paragraph (1) is without prejudice to section 7(4)(b).".

7. Paragraph 14 is modified so as to read as follows—

"**14.** (1) The holder of a qualifying agricultural floating charge in respect of partnership property may appoint an administrator of the partnership.
(2) For the purposes of sub-paragraph (1) an agricultural floating charge qualifies if created by an instrument which—
(a) states that this paragraph applies to the agricultural floating charge,
(b) purports to empower the holder of the agricultural floating charge to appoint an administrator of the partnership, [or]
(c) purports to empower the holder of the agricultural floating charge to make an

appointment which would be the appointment of an agricultural receiver.

(3) For the purposes of sub-paragraph (1) a person is the holder of a qualifying agricultural floating charge in respect of partnership property if he holds one or more charges of the partnership secured—

(a) by a qualifying agricultural floating charge which relates to the whole or substantially the whole of the partnership property,

(b) by a number of qualifying agricultural floating charges which together relate to the whole or substantially the whole of the partnership property, or

(c) by charges and other forms of security which together relate to the whole or substantially the whole of the partnership property and at least one of which is a qualifying agricultural floating charge.".

8. Paragraph 15 is modified so as to read as follows—

"**15.** (1) A person may not appoint an administrator under paragraph 14 unless—

(a) he has given at least two business days' written notice to the holder of any prior agricultural floating charge which satisfies paragraph 14(2); or

(b) the holder of any prior agricultural floating charge which satisfies paragraph 14(2) has consented in writing to the making of the appointment.

[(2) For the purposes of this paragraph, one agricultural floating charge is prior to another in accordance with the provisions of section 8(2) of the Agricultural Credits Act 1928.]".

9. Paragraph 22 is modified so as to read as follows—

"**22.** The members of the insolvent partnership may appoint an administrator.".

10. Paragraph 23 is modified so as to read as follows—

"**23.** (1) This paragraph applies where an administrator of a partnership is appointed—

(a) under paragraph 22, or

(b) on an administration application made by the members of the partnership.

(2) An administrator of the partnership may not be appointed under paragraph 22 during the period of 12 months beginning with the date on which the appointment referred to in sub-paragraph (1) ceases to have effect.".

11. Paragraph 26 is modified so as to read as follows—

"**26.** (1) A person who proposes to make an appointment under paragraph 22 shall give at least five business days' written notice to—

(a) any person who is or may be entitled to appoint an agricultural receiver of the partnership, and

(b) any person who is or may be entitled to appoint an administrator of the partnership under paragraph 14.

(2) A person who proposes to make an appointment under paragraph 22 shall also give such notice as may be prescribed to such other persons as may be prescribed.

(3) A notice under this paragraph must—

(a) identify the proposed administrator, and

(b) be in Form 1A in Schedule 9 to the Insolvent Partnerships Order 1994.".

12. Paragraph 27 is modified so as to read as follows—

"**27.** (1) A person who gives notice of intention to appoint under paragraph 26 shall file with the court as soon as is reasonably practicable a copy of—

(a) the notice, and

(b) any document accompanying it.

(2) The copy filed under sub-paragraph (1) must be accompanied by a statutory declaration made by or on behalf of the person who proposes to make the appointment—

(a) that the partnership is unable to pay its debts,

(b) that the partnership is not in liquidation, and

(c) that, so far as the person making the statement is able to ascertain, the appointment is not prevented by paragraphs 23 to 25, and

(d) to such additional effect, and giving such information, as may be prescribed.

(3) A statutory declaration under sub-paragraph (2) must—

(a) be in the prescribed form, and

(b) be made during the prescribed period.

(4) A person commits an offence if in a statutory declaration under sub-paragraph (2) he makes a statement—

(a) which is false, and

(b) which he does not reasonably believe to be true.".

13. Paragraph 29 is modified so as to read as follows—

"**29.** (1) A person who appoints an administrator of a partnership under paragraph 22 shall file with the court—

(a) a notice of appointment, and

(b) such other documents as may be prescribed.

(2) The notice of appointment must include a statutory declaration by or on behalf of the person who makes the appointment—

(a) that the person is entitled to make an appointment under paragraph 22,

(b) that the appointment is in accordance with this Schedule, and

(c) that, so far as the person making the statement is able to ascertain, the statements made, and information given in the statutory declaration filed with the notice of intention to appoint remain accurate.

(3) The notice of appointment must identify the administrator and must be accompanied by a statement by the administrator—

(a) that he consents to the appointment,

(b) that in his opinion the purpose of administration is reasonably likely to be achieved, and

(c) giving such other information and opinions as may be prescribed.

(4) For the purpose of a statement under sub-paragraph (3) an administrator may rely on information supplied by members of the partnership (unless he has reason to doubt its accuracy).

(5) The notice of appointment must be in Form 1B in Schedule 9 to the Insolvent Partnerships Order 1994 and any document accompanying it must be in the prescribed form.

(6) A statutory declaration under sub-paragraph (2) must be made during the prescribed period.

(7) A person commits an offence if in a statutory declaration under sub-paragraph (2) he makes a statement—

(a) which is false, and

(b) which he does not reasonably believe to be true.".

14. Paragraph 35 is modified so as to read as follows—

"**35.** (1) This paragraph applies where an administration application in respect of a partnership—

(a) is made by the holder of a qualifying agricultural floating charge in respect of the partnership property, and

(b) includes a statement that the application is made in reliance on this paragraph.

(2) The court may make an administration order—

(a) whether or not satisfied that the partnership is unable to pay its debts; but

(b) only if satisfied that the applicant could appoint an administrator under paragraph 14.".

15. Paragraph 39 is modified so as to read as follows—

"**39.** (1) Where there is an agricultural receiver of a partnership the court must dismiss an administration application in respect of the partnership unless—

(a) the person by or on behalf of whom the agricultural receiver was appointed consents to the making of the administration order,

(b) the court thinks that the security by virtue of which the agricultural receiver was appointed would be liable to be released or discharged under sections 238 to 240 (transaction at undervalue and preference) if an administration order were made, or

(c) the court thinks that the security by virtue of which the agricultural receiver was appointed would be avoided under section 245 (avoidance of floating charge) if an administration order were made.

(2) Sub-paragraph (1) applies whether the agricultural receiver is appointed before or after the making of the administration application.".

16. Paragraph 41 is modified so as to read as follows—

"**41.** (1) When an administration order takes effect in respect of a partnership any agricultural receiver of the partnership shall vacate office.

(2) Where a partnership is in administration, any receiver of part of the partnership property shall vacate office if the administrator requires him to.

(3) Where an agricultural receiver vacates office under sub-paragraph (1) or (2), his remuneration shall be charged on and paid out of any partnership property which was in his custody or under his control immediately before he vacated office.

(4) In the application of sub-paragraph (3)—

(a) "remuneration" includes expenses properly incurred and any indemnity to which the agricultural receiver is entitled out of the partnership property,

(b) the charge imposed takes priority over security held by the person by whom or on whose behalf the agricultural receiver was appointed, and

(c) the provision for payment is subject to paragraph 43.".

17. Paragraph 42 is modified so as to read as follows—

"**42.** (1) This paragraph applies to a partnership in administration.

(2) No order may be made for the winding up of the partnership.

(3) No order may be made by virtue of Article 11 of the Insolvent Partnerships Order 1994 in respect of the partnership.

(4) No order may be made under section 35 of the Partnership Act 1890 in respect of the partnership.

(5) Sub-paragraph (2) does not apply to an order made on a petition presented under—

(a) section 124A (public interest); or

(b) section 367 of the Financial Services and Markets Act 2000 (c 8) [(winding-up petitions)].

(6) If a petition presented under a provision referred to in sub-paragraph (5) comes to the attention of the administrator, he shall apply to the court for directions under paragraph 63.".

18. Paragraph 43 is modified so as to read as follows—

"**43.** (1) This paragraph applies to a partnership in administration.

(2) No step may be taken to enforce security over the partnership property except—

(a) with the consent of the administrator, or

(b) with the permission of the court.

(3) No step may be taken to repossess goods in the partnership's possession under a hire-purchase agreement except—

(a) with the consent of the administrator, or

(b) with the permission of the court.

(4) A landlord may not exercise a right of forfeiture by peaceable re-entry in relation to premises forming part of the partnership property or let to one or more officers of the partnership in their capacity as such except—

(a) with the consent of the administrator, or

(b) with the permission of the court.

(5) No legal process (including legal proceedings, execution, distress and diligence) may be instituted or continued against the partnership or partnership property except—

(a) with the consent of the administrator, or

(b) with the permission of the court.

(6) An agricultural receiver of the partnership may not be appointed.

(7) Where the court gives permission for a transaction under this paragraph it may impose a condition on or a requirement in connection with the transaction.

(8) In this paragraph "landlord" includes a person to whom rent is payable.".

19. Paragraph 47 is modified so as to read as follows—

"**47.** (1) As soon as is reasonably practicable after appointment the administrator of a partnership shall by notice in the prescribed form require one or more relevant persons to provide the administrator with a statement of the affairs of the partnership.

(2) The statement must—

(a) be verified by a statement of truth in accordance with Civil Procedure Rules,

(b) be in the prescribed form,

(c) give particulars of the partnership property, debts and liabilities,

(d) give the names and addresses of the creditors of the partnership,

(e) specify the security held by each creditor,

(f) give the date on which each security was granted, and

(g) contain such other information as may be prescribed.

(3) In sub-paragraph (1) "relevant person" means—

(a) a person who is or has been an officer of the partnership,

(b) a person who took part in the formation of the partnership during the period of one year ending with the date on which the partnership enters administration,

(c) a person employed by the partnership during that period, and

(d) a person who is or has been during that period an officer or employee of a partnership which is or has been during that year an officer of the partnership.

(4) For the purpose of sub-paragraph (3) a reference to employment is a reference to employment through a contract of employment or a contract for services.".

20. Paragraph 49 is modified so as to read as follows—

"**49.** (1) The administrator of a partnership shall make a statement setting out proposals for achieving the purpose of administration.

(2) A statement under sub-paragraph (1) must, in particular—

(a) deal with such matters as may be prescribed, and

(b) where applicable, explain why the administrator thinks that the objective mentioned in paragraph 3(1)(a) or (b) cannot be achieved.

(3) Proposals under this paragraph may include a proposal for a voluntary arrangement under Part I of this Act (although this paragraph is without prejudice to section 4(3)).

(4) The administrator shall send a copy of the statement of his proposals—

(a) to the court,

(b) to every creditor of the partnership[, other than an opted-out creditor,] of whose claim and address he is aware, and

(c) to every member of the partnership of whose address he is aware.

(5) The administrator shall comply with sub-paragraph (4)—

(a) as soon as is reasonably practicable after the partnership enters administration, and

(b) in any event, before the end of the period of eight weeks beginning with the day on which the partnership enters administration.

(6) The administrator shall be taken to comply with sub-paragraph (4)(c) if he publishes in the prescribed manner a notice undertaking to provide a copy of the statement of proposals free of charge to any member of the partnership who applies in writing to a specified address.

(7) An administrator commits an offence if he fails without reasonable excuse to comply with sub-paragraph (5).

(8) A period specified in this paragraph may be varied in accordance with paragraph 107.".

21. Paragraph 52 is modified so as to read as follows—

"**52.** (1) Paragraph 51(1) shall not apply where the statement of proposals states that the administrator thinks—

(a) that the partnership has sufficient property to enable each creditor of the partnership to be paid in full,

(b) that the partnership has insufficient property to enable a distribution to be made to unsecured creditors, or

(c) that neither of the objectives specified in paragraph 3(1)(a) and (b) can be achieved.

(2) But the administrator shall [seek a decision from the partnership's creditors as to whether they approve the proposals set out in the statement made under paragraph 49(1) if requested to do so]—

(a) by creditors of the partnership whose debts amount to at least 10 per cent of the total debts of the partnership,

(b) in the prescribed manner, and

(c) in the prescribed period.

[(3) Where a decision is sought by virtue of sub-paragraph (2) the initial decision date (as defined in paragraph 51(3)) must be within the prescribed period.]

(4) The period prescribed under sub-paragraph (3) may be varied in accordance with paragraph 107.".

22. Paragraph 61 is modified so as to read as follows—

"**61.** The administrator of a partnership—

(a) may prevent any person from taking part in the management of the partnership business, and

(b) may appoint any person to be a manager of that business.".

23. Paragraph 65 is modified so as to read as follows—

"**65.** (1) The administrator of a partnership may make a distribution to a creditor of the partnership.

(2) Section 175(1) and (2)(a) shall apply in relation to a distribution under this paragraph as it applies in relation to a winding up.

(3) A payment may not be made by way of distribution under this paragraph to a creditor of the partnership who is neither secured nor preferential unless the court gives permission.".

24. Paragraph 69 is modified so as to read as follows:—

"**69.** (1) Subject to sub-paragraph (2) below, in exercising his function under this Schedule the administrator of a partnership acts as the agent of the members of the partnership in their capacity as such.

(2) An officer of the partnership shall not, unless he otherwise consents, be personally liable for the debts and obligations of the partnership incurred during the period when the partnership is in administration.".

25. Paragraph 73 is modified so as to read as follows—

"**73.** (1) An administrator's statement of proposals under paragraph 49 may not include any action which—

(a) affects the right of a secured creditor of the partnership to enforce his security,

(b) would result in a preferential debt of the partnership being paid otherwise than in priority to its non-preferential debts, . . .

[(bb) would result in an ordinary preferential debt of the partnership being paid otherwise than in priority to any secondary preferential debts that it may have,]

(c) would result in one preferential creditor of the partnership being paid a smaller proportion of [an ordinary preferential debt] than another [or

(d) would result in one preferential creditor of the partnership being paid a smaller proportion of a secondary preferential debt than another.]

(2) Sub-paragraph (1) does not apply to—

(a) action to which the relevant creditor consents, or

(b) a proposal for a voluntary arrangement under Part I of this Act (although this sub-paragraph is without prejudice to section 4(3)).

(3) The reference to a statement of proposals in sub-paragraph (1) includes a reference to a statement as revised or modified.".

26. Paragraph 74 is modified so as to read as follows—

"**74.** (1) A creditor or member of a partnership in administration may apply to the court claiming that—

(a) the administrator is acting or has acted so as unfairly to harm the interests of the applicant (whether alone or in common with some or all other members or creditors), or

(b) the administrator proposes to act in a way which would unfairly harm the interests of the applicant (whether alone or in common with some or all other members or creditors).

(2) A creditor or member of a partnership in administration may apply to the court claiming that the administrator is not performing his functions as quickly or as efficiently as is reasonably practicable.
(3) The court may—
(a) grant relief;
(b) dismiss the application;
(c) adjourn the hearing conditionally or unconditionally;
(d) make an interim order;
(e) make any other order it thinks appropriate.
(4) In particular, an order under this paragraph may—
(a) regulate the administrator's exercise of his functions;
(b) require the administrator to do or not do a specified thing;
[(c) require a decision of the partnership's creditors to be sought on a matter;]
(d) provide for the appointment of an administrator to cease to have effect;
(e) make consequential provision.
(5) An order may be made on a claim under sub-paragraph (1) whether or not the action complained of—
(a) is within the administrator's powers under that Schedule;
(b) was taken in reliance on an order under paragraph 71 or 72.
(6) An order may not be made under this paragraph if it would impede or prevent the implementation of—
(a) a voluntary arrangement approved under Part I, or
(b) proposals or a revision approved under paragraph 53 or 54 more than 28 days before the day on which the application for the order under this paragraph is made.".

27. Omit paragraph 83.

28. Paragraph 84 is modified so as to read as follows—

"**84.** (1) If the administrator of a partnership thinks that the partnership has no property which might permit a distribution to its creditors, he shall file a notice to that effect with the court.
(2) The court may on the application of the administrator of a partnership disapply sub-paragraph (1) in respect of the partnership.
(3) On the filing of a notice in respect of a partnership under sub-paragraph (1) the appointment of an administrator of the partnership shall cease to have effect.
(4) If an administrator files a notice under sub-paragraph (1) he shall as soon as is reasonably practicable send a copy of the notice to each creditor of whose claim and address he is aware.
(5) At the end of the period of three months beginning with the date of filing of a notice in respect of a partnership under sub-paragraph (1) the partnership is deemed to be dissolved.
(6) On an application in respect of a partnership by the administrator or another interested person the court may—
(a) extend the period specified in sub-paragraph (5);
(b) suspend that period; or
(c) disapply sub-paragraph (5).
(7) An administrator commits an offence if he fails without reasonable excuse to comply with sub-paragraph (4).".

29. Paragraph 87 is modified to read as follows—

"**87.** (1) An administrator may resign only in prescribed circumstances.
(2) Where an administrator may resign he may do so only—
(a) in the case of an administrator appointed by administration order, by notice in writing to the court,
(b) in the case of an administrator appointed under paragraph 14, by notice in writing to the holder of the agricultural floating charge by virtue of which the appointment was made, or
(c) in the case of an administrator appointed under paragraph 22, by notice in writing to the members of the insolvent partnership.".

30. Paragraph 89 is modified so as to read as follows—

"**89.** (1) The administrator of a partnership shall vacate office if he ceases to be qualified to act as an insolvency practitioner in relation to the partnership.
(2) Where an administrator vacates office by virtue of sub-paragraph (1) he shall give notice in writing—
(a) in the case of an administrator appointed by administration order, to the court,
(b) in the case of an administrator appointed under paragraph 14, to the holder of the agricultural floating charge by virtue of which the appointment was made, or
(c) in the case of an administrator appointed under paragraph 22, to the members of the insolvent partnership.
(3) An administrator who fails without reasonable excuse to comply with sub-paragraph (2) commits an offence.".

31. Paragraph 90 is modified so as to read as follows—

"**90.** Paragraphs 91 to 93 and 95 apply where an administrator—

(a) dies
(b) resigns
(c) is removed from office under paragraph 88, or
(d) vacates office under paragraph 89.".

32. Paragraph 91 is modified so as to read as follows—

"91. (1) Where the administrator was appointed by administration order, the court may replace the administrator on an application under this sub-paragraph made by—
(a) a creditors' committee of the partnership,
(b) the members of the partnership,
(c) one or more creditors of the partnership, or
(d) where more than one person was appointed to act jointly or concurrently as the administrator, any of those persons who remains in office.
(2) But an application may be made in reliance on sub-paragraph (1)(b) and (c) only where—
(a) there is no creditors' committee of the partnership,
(b) the court is satisfied that the creditors' committee or a remaining administrator is not taking reasonable steps to make a replacement, or
(c) the court is satisfied that for another reason it is right for the application to be made.".

33. Paragraph 93 is modified so as to read as follows—

"93. (1) Where the administrator was appointed under paragraph 22 by the members of the partnership they may replace the administrator.
(2) A replacement under this paragraph may be made only—
(a) with the consent of each person who is the holder of a qualifying agricultural floating charge in respect of the partnership property, or
(b) where consent is withheld, with the permission of the court.".

34. Omit paragraph 94.

35. Paragraph 95 is modified so as to read as follows—

"95. The court may replace an administrator on the application of a person listed in paragraph 91(1) if the court—
(a) is satisfied that a person who is entitled to replace the administrator under any of paragraphs 92 and 93 is not taking reasonable steps to make a replacement, or
(b) that for another reason it is right for the court to make the replacement.".

36. Paragraph 96 is modified so as to read as follows—

"96. (1) This paragraph applies where an administrator of a partnership is appointed under paragraph 14 by the holder of a qualifying agricultural floating charge in respect of the partnership property.
(2) The holder of a prior qualifying agricultural floating charge in respect of the partnership property may apply to the court for the administrator to be replaced by an administrator nominated by the holder of the prior agricultural floating charge.
(3) One agricultural floating charge is prior to another for the purposes of this paragraph if—
(a) it was created first, or
(b) it is to be treated as having priority in accordance with an agreement to which the holder of each agricultural floating charge was party.".

37. Paragraph 97 is modified so as to read as follows—

"97. (1) This paragraph applies where—
(a) an administrator of a partnership is appointed by the members of the partnership under paragraph 22, and
(b) there is no holder of a qualifying agricultural floating charge in respect of the partnership property.
[(2) The administrator may be replaced by a decision of the creditors made by a qualifying decision procedure.
(3) The decision has effect only if, before the decision is made, the new administrator has consented to act in writing.]".

38. Paragraph 103 is modified so as to read as follows—

"103. (1) Where a partnership is in administration, a person may be appointed to act as administrator jointly or concurrently with the person or persons acting as the administrator of the partnership.
(2) Where a partnership entered administration by administration order, an appointment under sub-paragraph (1) must be made by the court on the application of—
(a) a person or group listed in paragraph 12(1)(a) to (c), or
(b) the person or persons acting as the administrator of the partnership.
(3) Where a partnership entered administration by virtue of an appointment under paragraph 14, an appointment under sub-paragraph (1) must be made by—
(a) the holder of the agricultural floating charge by virtue of which the appointment was made, or

(b) the court on the application of the person or persons acting as the administrator of the partnership.

(4) Where a partnership entered administration by virtue of an appointment under paragraph 22, an appointment under sub-paragraph (1) above must be made either by the court on the application of the person or persons acting as the administrator of the partnership or—

(a) by the members of the partnership, and

(b) with the consent of each person who is the holder of a qualifying agricultural floating charge in respect of the partnership property or, where consent is withheld, with the permission of the court.

(5) An appointment under sub-paragraph (1) may be made only with the consent of the person or persons acting as the administrator of the partnership.".

39. Omit paragraph 105.

40. Paragraph 106 is modified so as to read as follows—

"**106.** (1) A person who is guilty of an offence under this Schedule is liable to a fine (in accordance with section 430 and Schedule 10).

(2) A person who is guilty of an offence under any of the following paragraphs of this Schedule is liable to a daily default fine (in accordance with section 430 and Schedule 10)—

(a) paragraph 20,
(b) paragraph 32,
(c) paragraph 46,
(d) paragraph 48,
(e) paragraph 49,
(f) paragraph 51,
(g) paragraph 53,
(h) paragraph 54,
(i) paragraph 56,
(j) paragraph 78,
(k) paragraph 80,
(l) paragraph 84, and
(m) paragraph 89.".

41. Paragraph 111 is modified so as to read as follows—

"**111.** (1) In this Schedule—

"administrator" has the meaning given by paragraph 1 and, where the context requires, includes a reference to a former administrator,

"agricultural floating charge" means a charge which is an agricultural floating charge on its creation,

. . .

. . .

"enters administration" has the meaning given by paragraph 1,

"in administration" has the meaning given by paragraph 1,

"hire-purchase agreement" includes a conditional sale agreement, a chattel leasing agreement and a retention of title agreement,

"holder of a qualifying agricultural floating charge" in respect of partnership property has the meaning given by paragraph 14,

"market value" means the amount which would be realised on a sale of property in the open market by a willing vendor,

"the purpose of administration" means an objective specified in paragraph 3, and

"unable to pay its debts" has the meaning given by sections 222, 223, and 224.

(2) A reference in this Schedule to a thing in writing includes a reference to a thing in electronic form.

(3) In this Schedule a reference to action includes a reference to inaction.".

42. Omit paragraphs 112–116.

43. Schedule 1 is modified to read as follows:—

"SCHEDULE 1
POWERS OF ADMINISTRATOR

Paragraph 60 of Schedule B1

1.

Power to take possession of, collect and get in the partnership property and, for that purpose, to take such proceedings as may seem to him expedient.

2.

Power to sell or otherwise dispose of the partnership property by public auction or private auction or private contract or, in Scotland, to sell, feu, hire out or otherwise dispose of the partnership property by public roup or private bargain.

Part 10 SIs: Partnership Insolvency

3.

Power to raise or borrow money and grant security therefor over the partnership property.

4.

Power to appoint a solicitor or accountant or other professionally qualified person to assist him in the performance of his functions.

5.

Power to bring or defend any action or other legal proceedings in the name and on behalf of any member of the partnership in his capacity as such or of the partnership.

6.

Power to refer to arbitration any question affecting the partnership.

7.

Power to effect and maintain insurances in respect of the partnership business and property.

8.

Power to do all acts and execute, in the name and on behalf of the partnership or of any member of the partnership in his capacity as such, any deed, receipt or other document.

9.

Power to draw, accept, make and endorse any bill of exchange or promissory note in the name and on behalf of any member of the partnership in his capacity as such or of the partnership.

10.

Power to appoint any agent to do any business which he is unable to do himself or which can more conveniently be done by an agent and power to employ and dismiss employees.

11.

Power to do all such things (including the carrying out of works) as may be necessary for the realisation of the partnership property.

12.

Power to make any payment which is necessary or incidental to the performance of his functions.

13.

Power to carry on the business of the partnership.

14.

Power to establish subsidiary undertakings of the partnership.

15.

Power to transfer to subsidiary undertakings of the partnership the whole or any part of the business of the partnership or of the partnership property.

16.

Power to grant or accept a surrender of a lease or tenancy of any of the partnership property, and to take a lease or tenancy of any property required or convenient for the business of the partnership.

17.

Power to make any arrangement or compromise on behalf of the partnership or of its members in their capacity as such.

18.

Power to rank and claim in the bankruptcy, insolvency, sequestration or liquidation of any person indebted to the partnership and to receive dividends, and to accede to trust deeds for the creditors of any such person.

19.

Power to present or defend a petition for the winding up of the partnership under the Insolvent Partnerships Order 1994.

20.

Power to do all other things incidental to the exercise of the foregoing powers.".]

NOTES

Substituted by the Insolvent Partnerships (Amendment) Order 2005, SI 2005/1516, arts 2, 7, Sch 1, except where a petition for an administration order has been presented in relation to an insolvent partnership before 1 July 2005.

Para 7: in modified para 14 (as set out above) word in square brackets inserted by the Insolvent Partnerships (Amendment) Order 2006, SI 2006/622, art 5(1), (2)(a), except in respect of any insolvency proceedings in relation to an insolvent partnership commenced before 6 April 2006; see SI 2006/622, art 2 at **[2.41]**.

Para 8: in modified para 15 (as set out above) sub-para (2) substituted by SI 2006/622, art 5(1), (2)(b), except in respect of any insolvency proceedings in relation to an insolvent partnership commenced before 6 April 2006; see SI 2006/622, art 2 at **[2.41]**.

Para 17: in modified para 42 (as set out above) words in square brackets substituted by the Financial Services Act 2012 (Consequential Amendments and Transitional Provisions) Order 2013, SI 2013/472, art 3, Sch 2, para 11.

Para 20: in modified para 49 (as set out above) words in square brackets inserted by the Deregulation Act 2015 and Small Business, Enterprise and Employment Act 2015 (Consequential Amendments) (Savings) Regulations 2017, SI 2017/540, reg 3, Sch 2, paras 2, 6(1), (2).

Para 21: in modified para 52 (as set out above) words in square brackets substituted by SI 2017/540, reg 3, Sch 2, paras 2, 6(1), (3).

Para 25: in modified para 73 (as set out above) word omitted from sub-para (1)(b) revoked, sub-para (bb) inserted, in sub-para (c) first words in square brackets substituted, and sub-para (d) and word immediately preceding it added, by the Banks and Building Societies (Depositor Preference and Priorities) Order 2014, SI 2014/3486, art 13.

Para 26: in modified para 74 (as set out above) words in square brackets substituted by SI 2017/540, reg 3, Sch 2, paras 2, 6(1), (4).

Para 37: in modified para 97 (as set out above) words in square brackets substituted by SI 2017/540, reg 3, Sch 2, paras 2, 6(1), (5).

Para 41: in modified para 111 (as set out above) words omitted revoked by SI 2017/540, reg 3, Sch 2, paras 2, 6(1), (6).

SCHEDULE 3
PROVISIONS OF THE ACT WHICH APPLY WITH MODIFICATIONS FOR THE PURPOSES OF ARTICLE 7 TO WINDING UP OF INSOLVENT PARTNERSHIP ON PETITION OF CREDITOR ETC WHERE NO CONCURRENT PETITION PRESENTED AGAINST MEMBER

Article 7

PART I
MODIFIED PROVISIONS OF PART V OF THE ACT

[10.22]

1 Sections 220 to 223 of the Act are set out as modified in Part I of this Schedule, and sections 117, 131, 133, 234 and Schedule 4 are set out as modified in Part II.

2 Section 220: Meaning of "unregistered company"

Section 220 is modified so as to read as follows:—

"220 For the purposes of this Part, the expression "unregistered company" includes any insolvent partnership.".

3 Section 221: Winding up of unregistered companies

Section 221 is modified so as to read as follows:—

"221 (1) Subject to subsections (2) and (3) below and to the provisions of this Part, any insolvent partnership may be wound up under this Act if it has, or at any time had, in England and Wales either—

(a) a principal place of business, or

(b) a place of business at which business is or has been carried on in the course of which the debt (or part of the debt) arose which forms the basis of the petition for winding up the partnership.

(2) Subject to subsection (3) below, an insolvent partnership shall not be wound up under this Act if the business of the partnership has not been carried on in England and Wales at any time in the period of 3 years ending with the day on which the winding-up petition is presented.

(3) If an insolvent partnership has a principal place of business situated in Scotland or in Northern Ireland, the court shall not have jurisdiction to wind up the partnership unless it had a principal place of business in England and Wales—

(a) in the case of a partnership with a principal place of business in Scotland, at any time in the period of 1 year, or

(b) in the case of a partnership with a principal place of business in Northern Ireland, at any time in the period of 3 years,

ending with the day on which the winding-up petition is presented.

[(3A) The preceding subsections are subject to Article 3 of the EC Regulation (jurisdiction under the EC Regulation).]

(4) No insolvent partnership shall be wound up under this Act voluntarily.

(5) To the extent that they are applicable to the winding up of a company by the court in England and Wales on the petition of a creditor or of the Secretary of State, all the provisions of this Act and the Companies Act about winding up apply to the winding up of an insolvent partnership as an unregistered company—

(a) with the exceptions and additions mentioned in the following subsections of this section and in section 221A, and

(b) with the modifications specified in Part II of Schedule 3 to the Insolvent Partnerships Order 1994.

(6) Sections 73(1), 74(2)(a) to (d) and (3), 75 to 78, 83, 122, 123, [176A,] 202, 203, 205 and 250 shall not apply.

(7) The circumstances in which an insolvent partnership may be wound up as an unregistered company are as follows—

(a) if the partnership is dissolved, or has ceased to carry on business, or is carrying on business only for the purpose of winding up its affairs;

(b) if the partnership is unable to pay its debts;

(c) if the court is of the opinion that it is just and equitable that the partnership should be wound up;

[(d) at the time at which a moratorium for the insolvent partnership under section 1A comes to an end, no voluntary arrangement approved under Part I of this Act has effect in relation to the insolvent partnership.

(7A) A winding-up petition on the ground set out in section 221(7)(d) may only be presented by one or more creditors.]

(8) Every petition for the winding up of an insolvent partnership under Part V of this Act shall be verified by affidavit in Form 2 in Schedule 9 to the Insolvent Partnerships Order 1994.

221A Petition by liquidator, administrator, trustee or supervisor to wind up insolvent partnership as unregistered company

(1) A petition in Form 3 in Schedule 9 to the Insolvent Partnerships Order 1994 for winding up an insolvent partnership may be presented by—

(a) the liquidator or administrator of a corporate member or of a former corporate member, or

(b) the administrator of the partnership, or

(c) the trustee of an individual member's, or of a former individual member's, estate, or

(d) the supervisor of a voluntary arrangement approved under Part I of this Act in relation to a corporate member or the partnership, or under Part VIII of this Act in relation to an individual member,

if the ground of the petition is one of the circumstances set out in section 221(7).

(2) In this section "petitioning insolvency practitioner" means a person who has presented a petition under subsection (1).

(3) If the ground of the petition presented under subsection (1) is that the partnership is unable to pay its debts and the petitioning insolvency practitioner is able to satisfy the court that an insolvency order has been made against the member whose liquidator or trustee he is because of that member's inability to pay a joint debt, that order shall, unless it is proved otherwise to the satisfaction of the court, be proof for the purposes of section 221(7) that the partnership is unable to pay its debts.

(4) Where a winding-up petition is presented under subsection (1), the court may appoint the petitioning insolvency practitioner as provisional liquidator of the partnership under section 135 (appointment and powers of provisional liquidator).

(5) Where a winding-up order is made against an insolvent partnership after the presentation of a petition under subsection (1), the court may appoint the petitioning insolvency practitioner as liquidator of the partnership; and where the court makes an appointment under this subsection, section 140(3) (official receiver not to become liquidator) applies as if an appointment had been made under that section.

(6) Where a winding-up petition is presented under subsection (1), in the event of the partnership property being insufficient to satisfy the costs of the petitioning insolvency practitioner the costs may be paid out of the assets of the corporate or individual member, as the case may be, as part of the expenses of the liquidation, administration, bankruptcy or voluntary arrangement of that member, in the same order of priority as expenses properly chargeable or incurred by the practitioner in getting in any of the assets of the member.".

4 Section 222: Inability to pay debts: unpaid creditor for £750 or more

Section 222 is modified so as to read as follows:—

"**222** (1) An insolvent partnership is deemed (for the purposes of section 221) unable to pay its debts if there is a creditor, by assignment or otherwise, to whom the partnership is indebted in a sum exceeding £750 then due and—

(a) the creditor has served on the partnership, in the manner specified in subsection (2) below, a written demand in the prescribed form requiring the partnership to pay the sum so due, and

(b) the partnership has for 3 weeks after the service of the demand neglected to pay the sum or to secure or compound for it to the creditor's satisfaction.

(2) Service of the demand referred to in subsection (1)(a) shall be effected—

(a) by leaving it at a principal place of business of the partnership in England and Wales, or

(b) by leaving it at a place of business of the partnership in England and Wales at which business is carried on in the course of which the debt (or part of the debt) referred to in subsection (1) arose, or

(c) by delivering it to an officer of the partnership, or

(d) by otherwise serving it in such manner as the court may approve or direct.

(3) The money sum for the time being specified in subsection (1) is subject to increase or reduction by regulations under section 417 in Part XV; but no increase in the sum so specified affects any case in which the winding-up petition was presented before the coming into force of the increase.".

5 Section 223: Inability to pay debts: debt remaining unsatisfied after action brought

Section 223 is modified so as to read as follows:—

"223 (1) An insolvent partnership is deemed (for the purposes of section 221) unable to pay its debts if an action or other proceeding has been instituted against any member for any debt or demand due, or claimed to be due, from the partnership, or from him in his character of member, and—

(a) notice in writing of the institution of the action or proceeding has been served on the partnership in the manner specified in subsection (2) below, and

(b) the partnership has not within 3 weeks after service of the notice paid, secured or compounded for the debt or demand, or procured the action or proceeding to be stayed or sisted, or indemnified the defendant or defender to his reasonable satisfaction against the action or proceeding, and against all costs, damages and expenses to be incurred by him because of it.

(2) Service of the notice referred to in subsection (1)(a) shall be effected—

(a) by leaving it at a principal place of business of the partnership in England and Wales, or

(b) by leaving it at a place of business of the partnership in England and Wales at which business is carried on in the course of which the debt or demand (or part of the debt or demand) referred to in subsection (1) arose, or

(c) by delivering it to an officer of the partnership, or

(d) by otherwise serving it in such manner as the court may approve or direct.".

NOTES

Para 3: in s 221 of the Act (as set out above) sub-s (3A) inserted by the Insolvent Partnerships (Amendment) Order 2002, SI 2002/1308, arts 2, 5(1); figure in square brackets in sub-s (6) inserted by the Insolvent Partnerships (Amendment) Order 2006, SI 2006/622, art 6, except in respect of any insolvency proceedings in relation to an insolvent partnership commenced before 6 April 2006; see SI 2006/622, art 2 at **[2.41]**; sub-s (7)(d) and sub-s (7A) inserted by the Insolvent Partnerships (Amendment) (No 2) Order 2002, SI 2002/2708, art 8, subject to transitional provisions in art 11(1), (3) thereof (see further the note to art 4 at **[10.4]**).

PART II
OTHER MODIFIED PROVISIONS OF THE ACT ABOUT WINDING UP BY THE COURT

[10.23]

6 Section 117: High Court and county court jurisdiction

Section 117 is modified so as to read as follows:—

"117 (1) Subject to subsections (3) and (4) below, the High Court has jurisdiction to wind up any insolvent partnership as an unregistered company by virtue of article 7 of the Insolvent Partnerships Order 1994 if the partnership has, or at any time had, in England and Wales either—

(a) a principal place of business, or

(b) a place of business at which business is or has been carried on in the course of which the debt (or part of the debt) arose which forms the basis of the petition for winding up the partnership.

(2) Subject to subsections (3) and (4) below, a petition for the winding up of an insolvent partnership by virtue of the said article 7 may be presented to a county court in England and Wales if the partnership has, or at any time had, within the insolvency district of that court either—

(a) a principal place of business, or

(b) a place of business at which business is or has been carried on in the course of which the debt (or part of the debt) arose which forms the basis of the winding-up petition.

(3) Subject to subsection (4) below, the court only has jurisdiction to wind up an insolvent partnership if the business of the partnership has been carried on in England and Wales at any time in the period of 3 years ending with the day on which the petition for winding it up is presented.

(4) If an insolvent partnership has a principal place of business situated in Scotland or in Northern Ireland, the court shall not have jurisdiction to wind up the partnership unless it had a principal place of business in England and Wales—

(a) in the case of a partnership with a principal place of business in Scotland, at any time in the period of 1 year, or

(b) in the case of a partnership with a principal place of business in Northern Ireland, at any time in the period of 3 years,

ending with the day on which the petition for winding it up is presented.

(5) The Lord Chancellor [may, with the concurrence of the Lord Chief Justice, by order] in a statutory instrument exclude a county court from having winding-up jurisdiction, and for the purposes of that jurisdiction may attach its district, or any part thereof, to any other county court, and may by statutory instrument revoke or vary any such order.

In exercising the powers of this section, the Lord Chancellor shall provide that a county court is not to have winding-up jurisdiction unless it has for the time being jurisdiction for the purposes of Parts VIII to XI of this Act (individual insolvency).

(6) Every court in England and Wales having winding-up jurisdiction has for the purposes of that jurisdiction all the powers of the High Court; and every prescribed officer of the court shall perform any duties which an officer of the High Court may discharge by order of a judge of that court or otherwise in relation to winding up.

[(7) This section is subject to Article 3 of the EC Regulation (jurisdiction under the EC Regulation).]

[(8) The Lord Chief Justice may nominate a judicial office holder (as defined in section 109(4) of the Constitutional Reform Act 2005) to exercise his functions under this section.]".

7 Section 131: Statement of affairs of insolvent partnership

Section 131 is modified so as to read as follows:—

"**131** (1) Where the court has, by virtue of article 7 of the Insolvent Partnerships Order 1994, made a winding-up order or appointed a provisional liquidator in respect of an insolvent partnership, the official receiver may require some or all of the persons mentioned in subsection (3) below to make out and submit to him a statement in the prescribed form as to the affairs of the partnership.

(2) The statement shall be verified by affidavit by the persons required to submit it and shall show—

(a) particulars of the debts and liabilities of the partnership and of the partnership property;

(b) the names and addresses of the partnership's creditors;

(c) the securities held by them respectively;

(d) the dates when the securities were respectively given; and

(e) such further or other information as may be prescribed or as the official receiver may require.

(3) The persons referred to in subsection (1) are—

(a) those who are or have been officers of the partnership;

(b) those who have taken part in the formation of the partnership at any time within one year before the relevant date;

(c) those who are in the employment of the partnership, or have been in its employment within that year, and are in the official receiver's opinion capable of giving the information required;

(d) those who are or have been within that year officers of, or in the employment of, a company which is, or within that year was, an officer of the partnership.

(4) Where any persons are required under this section to submit a statement of affairs to the official receiver, they shall do so (subject to the next subsection) before the end of the period of 21 days beginning with the day after that on which the prescribed notice of the requirement is given to them by the official receiver.

(5) The official receiver, if he thinks fit, may—

(a) at any time release a person from an obligation imposed on him under subsection (1) or (2) above; or

(b) either when giving the notice mentioned in subsection (4) or subsequently, extend the period so mentioned;

and where the official receiver has refused to exercise a power conferred by this subsection, the court, if it thinks fit, may exercise it.

(6) In this section—

"employment" includes employment under a contract for services; and

"the relevant date" means—

(a) in a case where a provisional liquidator is appointed, the date of his appointment; and

(b) in a case where no such appointment is made, the date of the winding-up order.

(7) If a person without reasonable excuse fails to comply with any obligation imposed under this section, he is liable to a fine and, for continued contravention, to a daily default fine.".

8 Section 133: Public examination of officers of insolvent partnerships

Section 133 is modified so as to read as follows:—

"**133** (1) Where an insolvent partnership is being wound up by virtue of article 7 of the Insolvent Partnerships Order 1994, the official receiver may at any time before the winding up is complete apply to the court for the public examination of any person who—

(a) is or has been an officer of the partnership; or

(b) has acted as liquidator or administrator of the partnership or as receiver or manager or, in Scotland, receiver of its property; or

(c) not being a person falling within paragraph (a) or (b), is or has been concerned, or has taken part, in the formation of the partnership.

(2) Unless the court otherwise orders, the official receiver shall make an application under subsection (1) if he is requested in accordance with the rules to do so by one-half, in value, of the creditors of the partnership.

(3) On an application under subsection (1), the court shall direct that a public examination of the person to whom the application relates shall be held on a day appointed by the court; and that person shall attend on that day and be publicly examined as to the formation or management of the partnership or as to the conduct of its business and affairs, or his conduct or dealings in relation to the partnership.

(4) The following may take part in the public examination of a person under this section and may question that person concerning the matters mentioned in subsection (3), namely—

(a) the official receiver;

(b) the liquidator of the partnership;

(c) any person who has been appointed as special manager of the partnership's property or business;

(d) any creditor of the partnership who has tendered a proof in the winding up.".

[8A Sections 165 and 167

(1) Section 165(2) has effect as if for "Parts 1 to 3" there were substituted "Parts 1 and 2".

(2) Section 167(1) has effect as if for "Parts 1 to 3" there were substituted "Parts 1 and 2".]

9 Section 234: Getting in the partnership property

Section 234 is modified so as to read as follows:—

"234 (1) This section applies where, by virtue of article 7 of the Insolvent Partnerships Order 1994—

(a) an insolvent partnership is being wound up, or

(b) a provisional liquidator of an insolvent partnership is appointed;

and "the office-holder" means the liquidator or the provisional liquidator, as the case may be.

(2) Any person who is or has been an officer of the partnership, or who is an executor or administrator of the estate of a deceased officer of the partnership, shall deliver up to the office-holder, for the purposes of the exercise of the office-holder's functions under this Act and (where applicable) the Company Directors Disqualification Act 1986, possession of any partnership property which he holds for the purposes of the partnership.

(3) Where any person has in his possession or control any property, books, papers or records to which the partnership appears to be entitled, the court may require that person forthwith (or within such period as the court may direct) to pay, deliver, convey, surrender or transfer the property, books, papers or records to the office-holder or as the court may direct.

(4) Where the office-holder—

(a) seizes or disposes of any property which is not partnership property, and

(b) at the time of seizure or disposal believes, and has reasonable grounds for believing, that he is entitled (whether in pursuance of an order of the court or otherwise) to seize or dispose of that property,

the next subsection has effect.

(5) In that case the office-holder—

(a) is not liable to any person in respect of any loss or damage resulting from the seizure or disposal except in so far as that loss or damage is caused by the office-holder's own negligence, and

(b) has a lien on the property, or the proceeds of its sale, for such expenses as were incurred in connection with the seizure or disposal.".

10 Schedule 4 is modified so as to read as follows:—

"SCHEDULE 4

POWERS OF LIQUIDATOR IN A WINDING UP

Section 167

PART I

. . .

1.

Power to pay any class of creditors in full.

2.

Power to make any compromise or arrangement with creditors or persons claiming to be creditors, or having or alleging themselves to have any claim (present or future, certain or contingent, ascertained or sounding only in damages) against the partnership, or whereby the partnership may be rendered liable.

3.

Power to compromise, on such terms as may be agreed—

(a) all debts and liabilities capable of resulting in debts, and all claims (present or future, certain or contingent, ascertained or sounding only in damages) subsisting or supposed to subsist between the partnership and a contributory or alleged contributory or other debtor or person apprehending liability to the partnership, and

(b) all questions in any way relating to or affecting the partnership property or the winding up of the partnership,

and take any security for the discharge of any such debt, liability or claim and give a complete discharge in respect of it.

[3A.

Power to bring legal proceedings under section 213, 214, 238, 239 or 423.]

4.

Power to bring or defend any action or other legal proceeding in the name and on behalf of any member of the partnership in his capacity as such or of the partnership.

Part 10 SIs: Partnership Insolvency

5.

Power to carry on the business of the partnership so far as may be necessary for its beneficial winding up.

PART II

. . .

6.

Power to sell any of the partnership property by public auction or private contract, with power to transfer the whole of it to any person or to sell the same in parcels.

7.

Power to do all acts and execute, in the name and on behalf of the partnership or of any member of the partnership in his capacity as such, all deeds, receipts and other documents.

8.

Power to prove, rank and claim in the bankruptcy, insolvency or sequestration of any contributory for any balance against his estate, and to receive dividends in the bankruptcy, insolvency or sequestration in respect of that balance, as a separate debt due from the bankrupt or insolvent, and rateably with the other separate creditors.

9.

Power to draw, accept, make and endorse any bill of exchange or promissory note in the name and on behalf of any member of the partnership in his capacity as such or of the partnership, with the same effect with respect to the liability of the partnership or of any member of the partnership in his capacity as such as if the bill or note had been drawn, accepted, made or endorsed in the course of the partnership's business.

10.

Power to raise on the security of the partnership property any money requisite.

11.

Power to take out in his official name letters of administration to any deceased contributory, and to do in his official name any other act necessary for obtaining payment of any money due from a contributory or his estate which cannot conveniently be done in the name of the partnership.

In all such cases the money due is deemed, for the purpose of enabling the liquidator to take out the letters of administration or recover the money, to be due to the liquidator himself.

12.

Power to appoint an agent to do any business which the liquidator is unable to do himself.

13.

Power to do all such other things as may be necessary for winding up the partnership's affairs and distributing its property.".

NOTES

Para 6: in s 117 of the Act (as set out above) words in square brackets in sub-s (5) substituted and sub-s (8) added by the Lord Chancellor (Transfer of Functions and Supplementary Provisions) Order 2006, SI 2006/680, art 3, Sch 2, paras 5, 6(1)(a), (2), (3); sub-s (7) added by the Insolvent Partnerships (Amendment) Order 2002, SI 2002/1308, arts 2, 5(2).

Para 8A: inserted by the Deregulation Act 2015 and Small Business, Enterprise and Employment Act 2015 (Consequential Amendments) (Savings) Regulations 2017, SI 2017/540, reg 3, Sch 2, paras 2, 7(1), (2).

Para 10: in Sch 4 to the Act (as set out above) words omitted from Part headings revoked by SI 2017/540, reg 3, Sch 2, paras 2, 7(1), (3), (4); para 3A inserted by the Insolvent Partnerships (Amendment) Order 2005, SI 2005/1516, art 8.

SCHEDULE 4
PROVISIONS OF THE ACT WHICH APPLY WITH MODIFICATIONS FOR THE PURPOSES OF ARTICLE 8 TO WINDING UP OF INSOLVENT PARTNERSHIP ON CREDITOR'S PETITION WHERE CONCURRENT PETITIONS ARE PRESENTED AGAINST ONE OR MORE MEMBERS

Article 8

PART I
MODIFIED PROVISIONS OF PART V OF THE ACT

[10.24]

1 (1) Sections 220 to 222 of the Act are set out as modified in Part I of this Schedule, and the provisions of the Act specified in sub-paragraph (2) below are set out as modified in Part II.

(2) The provisions referred to in sub-paragraph (1) are sections 117, 122 to 125, 131, 133, 136, 137, 139 to 141, 143, 146, 147, 168, 172, 174, 175, 189, 211, 230, 231, 234, 264, 265, 267, 268, 271, 283, [283A,] 284, 288, 292 to 296, 298 to 303, 305, [313A,] 314, 328, 331 and 356, and Schedule 4.

2 Section 220: Meaning of "unregistered company"

Section 220 is modified so as to read as follows:—

"220 For the purposes of this Part, the expression "unregistered company" includes any insolvent partnership.".

3 Section 221: Winding up of unregistered companies

Section 221 is modified so as to read as follows:—

"221 (1) Subject to subsections (2) and (3) below and to the provisions of this Part, any insolvent partnership may be wound up under this Act if it has, or at any time had, in England and Wales either—

(a) a principal place of business, or

(b) a place of business at which business is or has been carried on in the course of which the debt (or part of the debt) arose which forms the basis of the petition for winding up the partnership.

(2) Subject to subsection (3) below, an insolvent partnership shall not be wound up under this Act if the business of the partnership has not been carried on in England and Wales at any time in the period of 3 years ending with the day on which the winding-up petition is presented.

(3) If an insolvent partnership has a principal place of business situated in Scotland or in Northern Ireland, the court shall not have jurisdiction to wind up the partnership unless it had a principal place of business in England and Wales—

(a) in the case of a partnership with a principal place of business in Scotland, at any time in the period of 1 year, or

(b) in the case of a partnership with a principal place of business in Northern Ireland, at any time in the period of 3 years,

ending with the day on which the winding-up petition is presented.

[(3A) The preceding subsections are subject to Article 3 of the EC Regulation (jurisdiction under the EC Regulation).]

(4) No insolvent partnership shall be wound up under this Act voluntarily.

(5) To the extent that they are applicable to the winding up of a company by the court in England and Wales on a creditor's petition, all the provisions of this Act and the Companies Act about winding up apply to the winding up of an insolvent partnership as an unregistered company—

(a) with the exceptions and additions mentioned in the following subsections of this section, and

(b) with the modifications specified in Part II of Schedule 4 to the Insolvent Partnerships Order 1994.

(6) Sections 73(1), 74(2)(a) to (d) and (3), 75 to 78, 83, 154, [176A,] 202, 203, 205 and 250 shall not apply.

(7) Unless the contrary intention appears, a member of a partnership against whom an insolvency order has been made by virtue of article 8 of the Insolvent Partnerships Order 1994 shall not be treated as a contributory for the purposes of this Act.

[(8) The circumstances in which an insolvent partnership may be wound up as an unregistered company are as follows—

(a) the partnership is unable to pay its debts,

(b) at the time at which a moratorium for the insolvent partnership under section 1A comes to an end, no voluntary arrangement approved under Part I of this Act has effect in relation to the insolvent partnership.]

(9) Every petition for the winding up of an insolvent partnership under Part V of this Act shall be verified by affidavit in Form 2 in Schedule 9 to the Insolvent Partnerships Order 1994.".

4 Section 222: Inability to pay debts: unpaid creditor for £750 or more

Section 222 is modified so as to read as follows:—

"222 (1) An insolvent partnership is deemed (for the purposes of section 221) unable to pay its debts if there is a creditor, by assignment or otherwise, to whom the partnership is indebted in a sum exceeding £750 then due and—

(a) the creditor has served on the partnership, in the manner specified in subsection (2) below, a written demand in Form 4 in Schedule 9 to the Insolvent Partnerships Order 1994 requiring the partnership to pay the sum so due,

(b) the creditor has also served on any one or more members or former members of the partnership liable to pay the sum due (in the case of a corporate member by leaving it at its registered office and in the case of an individual member by serving it in accordance with the rules) a demand in Form 4 in Schedule 9 to that Order, requiring that member or those members to pay the sum so due, and

(c) the partnership and its members have for 3 weeks after the service of the demands, or the service of the last of them if served at different times, neglected to pay the sum or to secure or compound for it to the creditor's satisfaction.

(2) Service of the demand referred to in subsection (1)(a) shall be effected—

(a) by leaving it at a principal place of business of the partnership in England and Wales, or

(b) by leaving it at a place of business of the partnership in England and Wales at which business is carried on in the course of which the debt (or part of the debt) referred to in subsection (1) arose, or

(c) by delivering it to an officer of the partnership, or

(d) by otherwise serving it in such manner as the court may approve or direct.

(3) The money sum for the time being specified in subsection (1) is subject to increase or reduction by regulations under section 417 in Part XV; but no increase in the sum so specified affects any case in which the winding-up petition was presented before the coming into force of the increase.".

NOTES

Para 1: figures in square brackets inserted by the Insolvent Partnerships (Amendment) Order 2005, SI 2005/1516, art 9(1), (2).

Para 3: in s 221 of the Act (as set out above) sub-s (3A) inserted by the Insolvent Partnerships (Amendment) Order 2002, SI 2002/1308, arts 2, 5(1); figure in square brackets in sub-s (6) inserted by the Insolvent Partnerships (Amendment) Order 2006, SI 2006/622, art 7, except in respect of any insolvency proceedings in relation to an insolvent partnership commenced before 6 April 2006; see SI 2006/622, art 2 at **[2.41]**; sub-s (8) substituted by the Insolvent Partnerships (Amendment) (No 2) Order 2002, SI 2002/2708, art 9(1), (2), subject to transitional provisions in art 11(1), (3) thereof (see further the note to art 4 at **[10.4]**), and previously read as follows:

"(8) The circumstance in which an insolvent partnership may be wound up as an unregistered company is that the partnership is unable to pay its debts.".

PART II
OTHER MODIFIED PROVISIONS OF THE ACT ABOUT WINDING UP BY THE COURT AND BANKRUPTCY OF INDIVIDUALS

[10.25]

5 Sections 117 and 265: High Court and county court jurisdiction

Sections 117 and 265 are modified so as to read as follows:—

"**117** (1) Subject to the provisions of this section, the High Court has jurisdiction to wind up any insolvent partnership as an unregistered company by virtue of article 8 of the Insolvent Partnerships Order 1994 if the partnership has, or at any time had, in England and Wales either—

(a) a principal place of business, or

(b) a place of business at which business is or has been carried on in the course of which the debt (or part of the debt) arose which forms the basis of the petition for winding up the partnership.

(2) Subject to subsections (3) and (4) below, a petition for the winding up of an insolvent partnership by virtue of the said article 8 may be presented to a county court in England and Wales if the partnership has, or at any time had, within the insolvency district of that court either—

(a) a principal place of business, or

(b) a place of business at which business is or has been carried on in the course of which the debt (or part of the debt) arose which forms the basis of the winding-up petition.

(3) Subject to subsection (4) below, the court only has jurisdiction to wind up an insolvent partnership if the business of the partnership has been carried on in England and Wales at any time in the period of 3 years ending with the day on which the petition for winding it up is presented.

(4) If an insolvent partnership has a principal place of business situated in Scotland or in Northern Ireland, the court shall not have jurisdiction to wind up the partnership unless it had a principal place of business in England and Wales—

(a) in the case of a partnership with a principal place of business in Scotland, at any time in the period of 1 year, or

(b) in the case of a partnership with a principal place of business in Northern Ireland, at any time in the period of 3 years,

ending with the day on which the petition for winding it up is presented.

(5) Subject to subsection (6) below, the court has jurisdiction to wind up a corporate member or former corporate member, or make a bankruptcy order against an individual member or former individual member, of a partnership against which a petition has been presented by virtue of article 8 of the Insolvent Partnerships Order 1994 if it has jurisdiction in respect of the partnership.

(6) Petitions by virtue of the said article 8 for the winding up of an insolvent partnership and the bankruptcy of one or more members or former members of that partnership may not be presented to a district registry of the High Court.

(7) The Lord Chancellor [may, with the concurrence of the Lord Chief Justice, by order] in a statutory instrument exclude a county court from having winding-up jurisdiction, and for the purposes of that jurisdiction may attach its district, or any part thereof, to any other county court, and may by statutory instrument revoke or vary any such order.

In exercising the powers of this section, the Lord Chancellor shall provide that a county court is not to have winding-up jurisdiction unless it has for the time being jurisdiction for the purposes of Parts VIII to XI of this Act (individual insolvency).

(8) Every court in England and Wales having winding-up jurisdiction has for the purposes of that jurisdiction all the powers of the High Court; and every prescribed officer of the court shall perform any duties which an officer of the High Court may discharge by order of a judge of that court or otherwise in relation to winding up.

[(9) This section is subject to Article 3 of the EC Regulation (jurisdiction under the EC Regulation).]

[(10) The Lord Chief Justice may nominate a judicial office holder (as defined in section 109(4) of the Constitutional Reform Act 2005) to exercise his functions under this section.]".

6 Circumstances in which members of insolvent partnerships may be wound up or made bankrupt by the court: Section 122—corporate member; Section 267—individual member

(a) Section 122 is modified so as to read as follows:—

[“122 A corporate member or former corporate member of an insolvent partnership may be wound up by the court if—

(a) it is unable to pay its debts,

(b) there is a creditor, by assignment or otherwise, to whom the insolvent partnership is indebted and the corporate member or former corporate member is liable in relation to that debt and at the time at which a moratorium for the insolvent partnership under section 1A comes to an end, no voluntary arrangement approved under Part I of this Act has effect in relation to the insolvent partnership.”].

(b) Section 267 is modified so as to read as follows:—

“267 (1) Where a petition for the winding up of an insolvent partnership has been presented to the court by virtue of article 8 of the Insolvent Partnerships Order 1994, a creditor’s petition against any individual member or former individual member of that partnership by virtue of that article must be in respect of one or more joint debts owed by the insolvent partnership, and the petitioning creditor or each of the petitioning creditors must be a person to whom the debt or (as the case may be) at least one of the debts is owed.

(2) Subject to [subsection (2A) below and] section 268, a creditor’s petition may be presented to the court in respect of a joint debt or debts only if, at the time the petition is presented—

(a) the amount of the debt, or the aggregate amount of the debts, is equal to or exceeds the bankruptcy level,

(b) the debt, or each of the debts, is for a liquidated sum payable to the petitioning creditor, or one or more of the petitioning creditors, immediately, and is unsecured,

(c) the debt, or each of the debts, is a debt for which the individual member or former member is liable and which he appears to be unable to pay, and

(d) there is no outstanding application to set aside a statutory demand served (under section 268 below) in respect of the debt or any of the debts.

[(2A) A creditor’s petition may be presented to the court in respect of a joint debt or debts if at the time at which a moratorium for the insolvent partnership under section 1A comes to an end, no voluntary arrangement approved under Part I of this Act has effect in relation to the insolvent partnership.]

(3) “The bankruptcy level” is [£5,000]; but the Secretary of State may by order in a statutory instrument substitute any amount specified in the order for that amount or (as the case may be) for the amount which by virtue of such an order is for the time being the amount of the bankruptcy level.

(4) An order shall not be made under subsection (3) unless a draft of it has been laid before, and approved by a resolution of, each House of Parliament.”.

7 Definition of inability to pay debts: Section 123—corporate member; Section 268—individual member

(a) Section 123 is modified so as to read as follows:—

“123 (1) A corporate member or former member is deemed unable to pay its debts if there is a creditor, by assignment or otherwise, to whom the partnership is indebted in a sum exceeding £750 then due for which the member or former member is liable and—

(a) the creditor has served on that member or former member and the partnership, in the manner specified in subsection (2) below, a written demand in Form 4 in Schedule 9 to the Insolvent Partnerships Order 1994 requiring that member or former member and the partnership to pay the sum so due, and

(b) the corporate member or former member and the partnership have for 3 weeks after the service of the demands, or the service of the last of them if served at different times, neglected to pay the sum or to secure or compound for it to the creditor’s satisfaction.

(2) Service of the demand referred to in subsection (1)(a) shall be effected, in the case of the corporate member or former corporate member, by leaving it at its registered office, and, in the case of the partnership—

(a) by leaving it at a principal place of business of the partnership in England and Wales, or

(b) by leaving it at a place of business of the partnership in England and Wales at which business is carried on in the course of which the debt (or part of the debt) referred to in subsection (1) arose, or

(c) by delivering it to an officer of the partnership, or

(d) by otherwise serving it in such manner as the court may approve or direct.

(3) The money sum for the time being specified in subsection (1) is subject to increase or reduction by order under section 416 in Part XV.”.

(b) Section 268 is modified so as to read as follows:—

“268 (1) For the purposes of section 267(2)(c), an individual member or former individual member appears to be unable to pay a joint debt for which he is liable if the debt is payable immediately and the petitioning creditor to whom the insolvent partnership owes the joint debt has served—

(a) on the individual member or former individual member in accordance with the rules a demand (known as "the statutory demand"), in Form 4 in Schedule 9 to the Insolvent Partnerships Order 1994, and

(b) on the partnership in the manner specified in subsection (2) below a demand (known as "the written demand") in the same form,

requiring the member or former member and the partnership to pay the debt or to secure or compound for it to the creditor's satisfaction, and at least 3 weeks have elapsed since the service of the demands, or the service of the last of them if served at different times, and neither demand has been complied with nor the demand against the member set aside in accordance with the rules.

(2) Service of the demand referred to in subsection (1)(b) shall be effected—

(a) by leaving it at a principal place of business of the partnership in England and Wales, or

(b) by leaving it at a place of business of the partnership in England and Wales at which business is carried on in the course of which the debt (or part of the debt) referred to in subsection (1) arose, or

(c) by delivering it to an officer of the partnership, or

(d) by otherwise serving it in such manner as the court may approve or direct.".

8 Sections 124 and 264: Applications to wind up insolvent partnership and to wind up or bankrupt insolvent member

Sections 124 and 264 are modified so as to read as follows:—

"**124** (1) An application to the court by virtue of article 8 of the Insolvent Partnerships Order 1994 for the winding up of an insolvent partnership as an unregistered company and the winding up or bankruptcy (as the case may be) of at least one of its members or former members shall—

(a) in the case of the partnership, be by petition in Form 5 in Schedule 9 to that Order,

(b) in the case of a corporate member or former corporate member, be by petition in Form 6 in that Schedule, and

(c) in the case of an individual member or former individual member, be by petition in Form 7 in that Schedule.

(2) Each of the petitions mentioned in subsection (1) may be presented by [a liquidator (within the meaning of Article 2(b) of the EC Regulation) appointed in proceedings by virtue of Article 3(1) of the EC Regulation, a temporary administrator (within the meaning of Article 38 of the EC Regulation) or] any creditor or creditors to whom the partnership and the member or former member in question is indebted in respect of a liquidated sum payable immediately.

(3) The petitions mentioned in subsection (1)—

(a) shall all be presented to the same court and, except as the court otherwise permits or directs, on the same day, and

(b) except in the case of the petition mentioned in subsection (1)(c), shall be advertised in Form 8 in the said Schedule 9.

(4) At any time after presentation of a petition under this section the petitioner may, with the leave of the court obtained on application and on such terms as it thinks just, add other members or former members of the partnership as parties to the proceedings in relation to the insolvent partnership.

(5) Each petition presented under this section shall contain particulars of other petitions being presented in relation to the partnership, identifying the partnership and members concerned.

(6) The hearing of the petition against the partnership fixed by the court shall be in advance of the hearing of any petition against an insolvent member.

(7) On the day appointed for the hearing of the petition against the partnership, the petitioner shall, before the commencement of the hearing, hand to the court Form 9 in Schedule 9 to the Insolvent Partnerships Order 1994, duly completed.

(8) Any member of the partnership or any person against whom a winding-up or bankruptcy petition has been presented in relation to the insolvent partnership is entitled to appear and to be heard on any petition for the winding up of the partnership.

(9) A petitioner under this section may at the hearing withdraw a petition if—

(a) subject to subsection (10) below, he withdraws at the same time every other petition which he has presented under this section; and

(b) he gives notice to the court at least 3 days before the date appointed for the hearing of the relevant petition of his intention to withdraw the petition.

(10) A petitioner need not comply with the provisions of subsection (9)(a) in the case of a petition against an insolvent member if the court is satisfied on application made to it by the petitioner that, because of difficulties in serving the petition or for any other reason, the continuance of that petition would be likely to prejudice or delay the proceedings on the petition which he has presented against the partnership or on any petition which he has presented against any other insolvent member.

(11) Where notice is given under subsection (9)(b), the court may, on such terms as it thinks just, substitute as petitioner, both in respect of the partnership and in respect of each insolvent member against whom a petition has been presented, any creditor of the partnership who in its opinion would have a right to present the petitions, and if the court makes such a substitution the petitions in question will not be withdrawn.

(12) Reference in subsection (11) to substitution of a petitioner includes reference to change of carriage of the petition in accordance with the rules.".

9 Sections 125 and 271: Powers of court on hearing of petitions against insolvent partnership and members

Sections 125 and 271 are modified so as to read as follows:—

"125 (1) Subject to the provisions of section 125A, on hearing a petition under section 124 against an insolvent partnership or any of its insolvent members, the court may dismiss it, or adjourn the hearing conditionally or unconditionally or make any other order that it thinks fit; but the court shall not refuse to make a winding-up order against the partnership or a corporate member on the ground only that the partnership property or (as the case may be) the member's assets have been mortgaged to an amount equal to or in excess of that property or those assets, or that the partnership has no property or the member no assets.

(2) An order under subsection (1) in respect of an insolvent partnership may contain directions as to the future conduct of any insolvency proceedings in existence against any insolvent member in respect of whom an insolvency order has been made.

125A Hearing of petitions against members

(1) On the hearing of a petition against an insolvent member the petitioner shall draw the court's attention to the result of the hearing of the winding-up petition against the partnership and the following subsections of this section shall apply.

(2) If the court has neither made a winding-up order, nor dismissed the winding-up petition, against the partnership the court may adjourn the hearing of the petition against the member until either event has occurred.

(3) Subject to subsection (4) below, if a winding-up order has been made against the partnership, the court may make a winding-up order against the corporate member in respect of which, or (as the case may be) a bankruptcy order against the individual member in respect of whom, the insolvency petition was presented.

(4) If no insolvency order is made under subsection (3) against any member within 28 days of the making of the winding-up order against the partnership, the proceedings against the partnership shall be conducted as if the winding-up petition against the partnership had been presented by virtue of article 7 of the Insolvent Partnerships Order 1994 and the proceedings against any member shall be conducted under this Act without the modifications made by that Order (other than the modifications made to sections 168 and 303 by article 14).

(5) If the court has dismissed the winding-up petition against the partnership, the court may dismiss the winding-up petition against the corporate member or (as the case may be) the bankruptcy petition against the individual member. However, if an insolvency order is made against a member, the proceedings against that member shall be conducted under this Act without the modifications made by the Insolvent Partnerships Order 1994 (other than the modifications made to sections 168 and 303 of this Act by article 14 of that Order).

(6) The court may dismiss a petition against an insolvent member if it considers it just to do so because of a change in circumstances since the making of the winding-up order against the partnership.

(7) The court may dismiss a petition against an insolvent member who is a limited partner, if—

(a) the member lodges in court for the benefit of the creditors of the partnership sufficient money or security to the court's satisfaction to meet his liability for the debts and obligations of the partnership; or

(b) the member satisfies the court that he is no longer under any liability in respect of the debts and obligations of the partnership.

(8) Nothing in sections 125 and 125A or in sections 267 and 268 prejudices the power of the court, in accordance with the rules, to authorise a creditor's petition to be amended by the omission of any creditor or debt and to be proceeded with as if things done for the purposes of those sections had been done only by or in relation to the remaining creditors or debts.".

10 Sections 131 and 288: Statements of affairs—Insolvent partnerships; corporate members; individual members

Sections 131 and 288 are modified so as to read as follows:—

"131 (1) This section applies where the court has, by virtue of article 8 of the Insolvent Partnerships Order 1994—

(a) made a winding-up order or appointed a provisional liquidator in respect of an insolvent partnership, or

(b) made a winding-up order or appointed a provisional liquidator in respect of any corporate member of that partnership, or

(c) made a bankruptcy order in respect of any individual member of that partnership.

(2) The official receiver may require some or all of the persons mentioned in subsection (4) below to make out and submit to him a statement as to the affairs of the partnership or member in the prescribed form.

(3) The statement shall be verified by affidavit by the persons required to submit it and shall show—

(a) particulars of the debts and liabilities of the partnership or of the member (as the case may be), and of the partnership property and member's assets;

(b) the names and addresses of the creditors of the partnership or of the member (as the case may be);

(c) the securities held by them respectively;

(d) the dates when the securities were respectively given; and

Part 10 SIs: Partnership Insolvency

(e) such further or other information as may be prescribed or as the official receiver may require.

(4) The persons referred to in subsection (2) are—

(a) those who are or have been officers of the partnership;

(b) those who are or have been officers of the corporate member;

(c) those who have taken part in the formation of the partnership or of the corporate member at any time within one year before the relevant date;

(d) those who are in the employment of the partnership or of the corporate member, or have been in such employment within that year, and are in the official receiver's opinion capable of giving the information required;

(e) those who are or have been within that year officers of, or in the employment of, a company which is, or within that year was, an officer of the partnership or an officer of the corporate member.

(5) Where any persons are required under this section to submit a statement of affairs to the official receiver, they shall do so (subject to the next subsection) before the end of the period of 21 days beginning with the day after that on which the prescribed notice of the requirement is given to them by the official receiver.

(6) The official receiver, if he thinks fit, may—

(a) at any time release a person from an obligation imposed on him under subsection (2) or (3) above; or

(b) either when giving the notice mentioned in subsection (5) or subsequently, extend the period so mentioned;

and where the official receiver has refused to exercise a power conferred by this subsection, the court, if it thinks fit, may exercise it.

(7) In this section—

"employment" includes employment under a contract for services; and

"the relevant date" means—

(a) in a case where a provisional liquidator is appointed, the date of his appointment; and

(b) in a case where no such appointment is made, the date of the winding-up order.

(8) Any person who without reasonable excuse fails to comply with any obligation imposed under this section (other than, in the case of an individual member, an obligation in respect of his own statement of affairs), is liable to a fine and, for continued contravention, to a daily default fine.

(9) An individual member who without reasonable excuse fails to comply with any obligation imposed under this section in respect of his own statement of affairs, is guilty of a contempt of court and liable to be punished accordingly (in addition to any other punishment to which he may be subject).".

11 Section 133: Public examination of officers of insolvent partnerships

Section 133 is modified so far as insolvent partnerships are concerned so as to read as follows:—

"133 (1) Where an insolvent partnership is being wound up by virtue of article 8 of the Insolvent Partnerships Order 1994, the official receiver may at any time before the winding up is complete apply to the court for the public examination of any person who—

(a) is or has been an officer of the partnership; or

(b) has acted as liquidator or administrator of the partnership or as receiver or manager or, in Scotland, receiver of its property;

(c) not being a person falling within paragraph (a) or (b), is or has been concerned, or has taken part, in the formation of the partnership.

(2) Unless the court otherwise orders, the official receiver shall make an application under subsection (1) if he is requested in accordance with the rules to do so by one-half, in value, of the creditors of the partnership.

(3) On an application under subsection (1), the court shall direct that a public examination of the person to whom the application relates shall be held on a day appointed by the court; and that person shall attend on that day and be publicly examined as to the formation or management of the partnership or as to the conduct of its business and affairs, or his conduct or dealings in relation to the partnership.

(4) The following may take part in the public examination of a person under this section and may question that person concerning the matters mentioned in subsection (3), namely—

(a) the official receiver;

(b) the liquidator of the partnership;

(c) any person who has been appointed as special manager of the partnership's property or business;

(d) any creditor of the partnership who has tendered a proof in the winding up.

(5) On an application under subsection (1), the court may direct that the public examination of any person under this section in relation to the affairs of an insolvent partnership be combined with the public examination of any person under this Act in relation to the affairs of a corporate member of that partnership against which, or an individual member of the partnership against whom, an insolvency order has been made.".

12 Sections 136, 293 and 294: Functions of official receiver in relation to office of responsible insolvency practitioner

Sections 136, 293 and 294 are modified so as to read as follows:—

"136 (1) The following provisions of this section . . . have effect, subject to section 140 below, where insolvency orders are made in respect of an insolvent partnership and one or more of its insolvent members by virtue of article 8 of the Insolvent Partnerships Order 1994.

(2) The official receiver, by virtue of his office, becomes the responsible insolvency practitioner of the partnership and of any insolvent member and continues in office until another person becomes responsible insolvency practitioner under the provisions of this Part.

(3) The official receiver is, by virtue of his office, the responsible insolvency practitioner of the partnership and of any insolvent member during any vacancy.

(4) At any time when he is the responsible insolvency practitioner of the insolvent partnership and of any insolvent member, the official receiver may [in accordance with the rules seek nominations from] the creditors of the partnership and the creditors of such member, for the purpose of choosing a person to be responsible insolvency practitioner in place of the official receiver.

[(5) It is the duty of the official receiver—

(a) as soon as practicable in the period of 12 weeks beginning with the day on which the insolvency order was made, to decide whether to exercise his power under subsection (4), and

(b) if in pursuance of paragraph (a) he decides not to exercise that power, to give notice of his decision, before the end of that period, to the court and to the creditors of the partnership and of the creditors of any insolvent member against whom an insolvency order has been made, and

(c) (whether or not he has decided to exercise that power) to exercise his power under subsection (4) if he is at any time requested, in accordance with the rules, to do so by one-quarter, in value, of either—

(i) the partnership's creditors, or

(ii) the creditors of any insolvent member against whom an insolvency order has been made,

and accordingly, where the duty imposed by paragraph (c) arises before the official receiver has performed a duty imposed by paragraph (a) or (b), he is not required to perform the latter duty.

(6) A notice given under subsection (5)(b) to the creditors must contain an explanation of the creditors' power under subsection (5)(c) to require the official receiver to seek nominations from the creditors of the partnership and of any insolvent member.]

. . .

13 Sections 137, 295, 296 and 300: Appointment of responsible insolvency practitioner by Secretary of State

Sections 137, 295, 296 and 300 are modified so as to read as follows:—

"137 (1) This section and the next apply where the court has made insolvency orders in respect of an insolvent partnership and one or more of its insolvent members by virtue of article 8 of the Insolvent Partnerships Order 1994.

(2) The official receiver may, at any time when he is the responsible insolvency practitioner of the partnership and of any insolvent member, apply to the Secretary of State for the appointment of a person as responsible insolvency practitioner of both the partnership and of such member in his place.

(3) If [a nomination is sought from the creditors of the partnership and of any insolvent member], but no person is chosen to be responsible insolvency practitioner [by the creditors], it is the duty of the official receiver to decide whether to refer the need for an appointment to the Secretary of State.

137A Consequences of section 137 application

(1) On an application under section 137(2), or a reference made in pursuance of a decision under section 137(3), the Secretary of State shall either make an appointment or decline to make one.

(2) If on an application under section 137(2), or a reference made in pursuance of a decision under section 137(3), no appointment is made, the official receiver shall continue to be responsible insolvency practitioner of the partnership and its insolvent member or members, but without prejudice to his power to make a further application or reference.

(3) Where a responsible insolvency practitioner has been appointed by the Secretary of State under subsection (1) of this section, and an insolvency order is subsequently made against a further insolvent member by virtue of article 8 of the Insolvent Partnerships Order 1994, then the practitioner so appointed shall also be the responsible insolvency practitioner of the member against whom the subsequent order is made.

(4) Where a responsible insolvency practitioner has been appointed by the Secretary of State under subsection (1), or has become responsible insolvency practitioner of a further insolvent member under subsection (3), that practitioner shall give notice of his appointment or further appointment (as the case may be) to the creditors of the insolvent partnership and the creditors of the insolvent member or members against whom insolvency orders have been made or, if the court so allows, shall advertise his appointment in accordance with the directions of the court.

(5) Subject to subsection (6) below, in that notice or advertisement the responsible insolvency practitioner [must explain the procedure for establishing a liquidation committee under section 141.]

[(6) In a case where subsection (3) applies, in the notice or advertisement the responsible insolvency practitioner must—

(a) if a liquidation committee has already been established under section 141, state whether he proposes to appoint additional members of the committee under section 141A(3); or

(b) if such a committee has not been established, explain the procedure for establishing a liquidation committee under section 141.]".

14 Section 139: Rules applicable to [decision making]

Section 139 is modified so as to read as follows:—

"**139** (1) This section applies where the court has made insolvency orders against an insolvent partnership and one or more of its insolvent members by virtue of article 8 of the Insolvent Partnerships Order 1994.

[(2) Subject to subsection (4) below, the rules relating to decision making on the winding up of a company are to apply (with the necessary modifications) to decisions sought from creditors of the partnership, of any corporate members against which an insolvency order has been made or of any insolvent member, where the decision is one to be made with creditors of the partnership.

(3) Subject to subsection (4) below, the rules relating to decision making on the bankruptcy of an individual are to apply (with the necessary modifications) to decisions sought from creditors of any individual member against whom an insolvency order has been made.

(4) Any decision to be made by the creditors of the partnership and of the insolvent member or members must be conducted as if there were a single set of creditors.]".

15 Section 140: Appointment by the court following administration or voluntary arrangement

Section 140 is modified so as to read as follows:—

"**140** (1) This section applies where insolvency orders are made in respect of an insolvent partnership and one or more of its insolvent members by virtue of article 8 of the Insolvent Partnerships Order 1994.

(2) Where the orders referred to in subsection (1) are made immediately upon the [appointment of an administrator in respect of the partnership ceasing to have effect], the court may appoint as responsible insolvency practitioner the person [whose appointment as administrator has ceased to have effect].

(3) Where the orders referred to in subsection (1) are made at a time when there is a supervisor of a voluntary arrangement approved in relation to the partnership under Part I, the court may appoint as responsible insolvency practitioner the person who is the supervisor at the time when the winding-up order against the partnership is made.

(4) Where the court makes an appointment under this section, the official receiver does not become the responsible insolvency practitioner as otherwise provided by section 136(2), and [section 136(5)(a) and (b) does not apply.]".

16 Sections 141, 301 and 302: Creditors' Committee: Insolvent partnership and members

Sections 141, 301 and 302 are modified so as to read as follows:—

"[**141** (1) This section applies where insolvency orders are made in respect of an insolvent partnership and one or more of its insolvent members by virtue of article 8 of the Insolvent Partnerships Order 1994.

(2) If both the creditors of the partnership and the creditors of any insolvent members decide that a liquidation committee should be established, a liquidation committee is to be established in accordance with the rules.

(3) A "liquidation committee" is a committee having such functions as are conferred on it by or under this Act.

(4) The responsible insolvency practitioner must seek a decision from the creditors of the partnership and of any insolvent members as to whether a liquidation committee should be established if requested, in accordance with the rules, to do so by one-tenth in value of the creditors.]

141A Functions and membership of creditors' committee

(1) The committee established under section 141 shall act as liquidation committee for the partnership and for any corporate member against which an insolvency order has been made, and as creditors' committee for any individual member against whom an insolvency order has been made, and shall as appropriate exercise the functions conferred on liquidation and creditors' committees in a winding up or bankruptcy by or under this Act.

(2) The rules relating to liquidation committees are to apply (with the necessary modifications and with the exclusion of all references to contributories) to a committee established under section 141.

(3) Where the appointment of the responsible insolvency practitioner also takes effect in relation to a further insolvent member under section 136A(5) or 137A(3), the practitioner may appoint any creditor of that member (being qualified under the rules to be a member of the committee) to be an additional member of any creditors' committee already established under section 141, provided that the creditor concerned consents to act.

(4) The court may at any time, on application by a creditor of the partnership or of any insolvent member against whom an insolvency order has been made, appoint additional members of the creditors' committee.

(5) If additional members of the creditors' committee are appointed under subsection (3) or (4), the limit on the maximum number of members of the committee specified in the rules shall be

increased by the number of additional members so appointed.

(6) The creditors' committee is not to be able or required to carry out its functions at any time when the official receiver is responsible insolvency practitioner of the partnership and of its insolvent member or members; but at any such time its functions are vested in the Secretary of State except to the extent that the rules otherwise provide.

(7) Where there is for the time being no creditors' committee, and the responsible insolvency practitioner is a person other than the official receiver, the functions of such a committee are vested in the Secretary of State except to the extent that the rules otherwise provide.".

17 Sections 143, 168(4) and 305: General functions of responsible insolvency practitioner

Sections 143, 168(4) and 305 are modified so as to read as follows:—

"143 (1) The functions of the responsible insolvency practitioner of an insolvent partnership and of its insolvent member or members against whom insolvency orders have been made by virtue of article 8 of the Insolvent Partnerships Order 1994, are to secure that the partnership property and the assets of any such corporate member, and the estate of any such individual member, are got in, realised and distributed to their respective creditors and, if there is a surplus of such property or assets or in such estate, to the persons entitled to it.

(2) In the carrying out of those functions, and in the management of the partnership property and of the assets of any corporate member and of the estate of any individual member, the responsible insolvency practitioner is entitled, subject to the provisions of this Act, to use his own discretion.

(3) It is the duty of the responsible insolvency practitioner, if he is not the official receiver—

(a) to furnish the official receiver with such information,

(b) to produce to the official receiver, and permit inspection by the official receiver of, such books, papers and other records, and

(c) to give the official receiver such other assistance,

as the official receiver may reasonably require for the purposes of carrying out his functions in relation to the winding up of the partnership and any corporate member or the bankruptcy of any individual member.

(4) The official name of the responsible insolvency practitioner in his capacity as trustee of an individual member shall be "the trustee of the estate of . . . ., a bankrupt" (inserting the name of the individual member); but he may be referred to as "the trustee in bankruptcy" of the particular member.".

18 Sections 146 and 331: Duty to summon final meeting of creditors

Sections 146 and 331 are modified so as to read as follows:—

["146 Final Account

(1) This section applies if it appears to the responsible insolvency practitioner of an insolvent partnership which is being wound up by virtue of article 8 of the Insolvent Partnerships Order 1994 and of its insolvent member or members that the winding up of the partnership or of any corporate member, or the administration of any individual member's estate is for practical purposes complete and the practitioner is not the official receiver.

(2) The responsible insolvency practitioner must make up an account of the winding up or administration, showing how it has been conducted and the property disposed of.

(3) The responsible insolvency practitioner must—

(a) send a copy of the account to the creditors of the partnership (other than opted-out creditors), and

(b) give the partnership's creditors (other than opted-out creditors) a notice explaining the effect of section 174(4)(d) and how they may object to the liquidator's release.

(4) The liquidator must during the relevant period send to the court and, in the case of a corporate member, send to the registrar of companies—

(a) a copy of the account, and

(b) a statement of whether any of the partnership's creditors objected to the liquidator's release.

(5) The relevant period is the period of 7 days beginning with the day after the last day of the period prescribed by the rules as the period within which the creditors may object to the responsible insolvency practitioner's release."]

19 Section 147: Power of court to stay proceedings

Section 147 is modified, so far as insolvent partnerships are concerned, so as to read as follows:—

"147 (1) The court may, at any time after an order has been made by virtue of article 8 of the Insolvent Partnerships Order 1994 for winding up an insolvent partnership, on the application either of the responsible insolvency practitioner or the official receiver or any creditor or contributory, and on proof to the satisfaction of the court that all proceedings in the winding up of the partnership ought to be stayed, make an order staying the proceedings, either altogether or for a limited time, on such terms and conditions as the court thinks fit.

(2) If, in the course of hearing an insolvency petition presented against a member of an insolvent partnership, the court is satisfied that an application has been or will be made under subsection (1) in respect of a winding-up order made against the partnership, the court may adjourn the petition against the insolvent member, either conditionally or unconditionally.

(3) Where the court makes an order under subsection (1) staying all proceedings on the order for winding up an insolvent partnership—

(a) the court may, on hearing any insolvency petition presented against an insolvent member of the partnership, dismiss that petition; and

(b) if any insolvency order has already been made by virtue of article 8 of the Insolvent Partnerships Order 1994 in relation to an insolvent member of the partnership, the court may make an order annulling or rescinding that insolvency order, or may make any other order that it thinks fit.

(4) The court may, before making any order under this section, require the official receiver to furnish to it a report with respect to any facts or matters which are in his opinion relevant to the application.".

[19A Sections 165 and 167

(1) Section 165(2) has effect as if for "Parts 1 to 3" there were substituted "Parts 1 and 2".

(2) Section 167(1) has effect as if for "Parts 1 to 3" there were substituted "Parts 1 and 2".]

20 Sections 168, 303 and 314(7): Supplementary powers of responsible insolvency practitioner

Sections 168(1) to (3) and (5), 303 and 314(7) are modified so as to read as follows:—

"**168** (1) This section applies where the court has made insolvency orders in respect of an insolvent partnership and one or more of its insolvent members by virtue of article 8 of the Insolvent Partnerships Order 1994.

[(2) The responsible insolvency practitioner may seek a decision on any matter from the creditors of the partnership or of any insolvent member; and must seek a decision on a matter if requested to do so by one-tenth in value of the creditors.]

(3) . . .

(4) The responsible insolvency practitioner may apply to the court (in the prescribed manner) for directions in relation to any particular matter arising in the winding up of the insolvent partnership or in the winding up or bankruptcy of an insolvent member.

(5) If any person is aggrieved by an act or decision of the responsible insolvency practitioner, that person may apply to the court; and the court may confirm, reverse or modify the act or decision complained of, and make such order in the case as it thinks just.".

21 Sections 172 and 298: Removal etc of responsible insolvency practitioner or of provisional liquidator

Sections 172 and 298 are modified so as to read as follows:—

"**172** (1) This section applies with respect to the removal from office and vacation of office of—

(a) the responsible insolvency practitioner of an insolvent partnership which is being wound up by virtue of article 8 of the Insolvent Partnerships Order 1994 and of its insolvent member or members against whom insolvency orders have been made, or

(b) a provisional liquidator of an insolvent partnership, and of any corporate member of that partnership, against which a winding-up petition is presented by virtue of that article,

and, subject to subsections (6) and (7) below, any removal from or vacation of office under this section relates to all offices held in the proceedings relating to the partnership.

(2) Subject as follows, the responsible insolvency practitioner or provisional liquidator may be removed from office only by an order of the court.

(3) If appointed by the Secretary of State, the responsible insolvency practitioner may be removed from office by a direction of the Secretary of State.

(4) A responsible insolvency practitioner or provisional liquidator, not being the official receiver, shall vacate office if he ceases to be a person who is qualified to act as an insolvency practitioner in relation to the insolvent partnership or any insolvent member of it against whom an insolvency order has been made.

(5) The responsible insolvency practitioner may, with the leave of the court (or, if appointed by the Secretary of State, with the leave of the court or the Secretary of State), resign his office by giving notice of his resignation to the court.

[(6) A responsible insolvency practitioner who has produced an account of the winding up or administration under section 146 must vacate office immediately upon complying with the requirements of section 146(3).]

(7) The responsible insolvency practitioner shall vacate office as trustee of the estate of an individual member if the insolvency order against that member is annulled.".

22 Sections 174 and 299: Release of responsible insolvency practitioner or of provisional liquidator

Sections 174 and 299 are modified so as to read as follows:—

"**174** (1) This section applies with respect to the release of—

(a) the responsible insolvency practitioner of an insolvent partnership which is being wound up by virtue of article 8 of the Insolvent Partnerships Order 1994 and of its insolvent member or members against whom insolvency orders have been made, or

(b) a provisional liquidator of an insolvent partnership, and of any corporate member of that partnership, against which a winding-up petition is presented by virtue of that article.

(2) Where the official receiver has ceased to be the responsible insolvency practitioner and a person is appointed in his stead, the official receiver has his release with effect from the following time, that is to say—

(a) in a case where that person was nominated by [the] creditors of the partnership and of any insolvent member or members, or was appointed by the Secretary of State, the time at which the official receiver gives notice to the court that he has been replaced;

(b) in a case where that person is appointed by the court, such time as the court may determine.

(3) If the official receiver while he is a responsible insolvency practitioner gives notice to the Secretary of State that the winding up of the partnership or of any corporate member or the administration of the estate of any individual member is for practical purposes complete, he has his release as liquidator or trustee (as the case may be) with effect from such time as the Secretary of State may determine.

(4) A person other than the official receiver who has ceased to be a responsible insolvency practitioner has his release with effect from the following time, that is to say—

(a) in the case of a person who has died, the time at which notice is given to the court in accordance with the rules that that person has ceased to hold office;

(b) in the case of a person who has been removed from office by the court or by the Secretary of State, or who has vacated office under section 172(4), such time as the Secretary of State may, on an application by that person, determine;

(c) in the case of a person who has resigned, such time as may be directed by the court (or, if he was appointed by the Secretary of State, such time as may be directed by the court or as the Secretary of State may, on an application by that person, determine);

[(d) in the case of a person who has vacated office under section 172(6)—

(i) if any of the creditors of the partnership or of any insolvent member objected to the person's release before the end of the period for so objecting prescribed by the rules, such time as the Secretary of State may, on an application by that person, determine, and

(ii) otherwise, the time at which the person vacated office.]

(5) A person who has ceased to hold office as a provisional liquidator has his release with effect from such time as the court may, on an application by him, determine.

(6) Where a bankruptcy order in respect of an individual member is annulled, the responsible insolvency practitioner at the time of the annulment has his release with effect from such time as the court may determine.

(7) Where the responsible insolvency practitioner or provisional liquidator (including in both cases the official receiver when so acting) has his release under this section, he is, with effect from the time specified in the preceding provisions of this section, discharged from all liability both in respect of acts or omissions of his in the winding up of the insolvent partnership or any corporate member or the administration of the estate of any individual member (as the case may be) and otherwise in relation to his conduct as responsible insolvency practitioner or provisional liquidator.

But nothing in this section prevents the exercise, in relation to a person who has had his release under this section, of the court's powers under section 212 (summary remedy against delinquent directors, liquidators, etc) or section 304 (liability of trustee).".

23 Sections 175 and 328: Priority of expenses and debts

Sections 175 and 328(1) to (3) and (6) are modified so as to read as follows:—

"175 Priority of expenses

(1) The provisions of this section shall apply in a case where article 8 of the Insolvent Partnerships Order 1994 applies, as regards priority of expenses incurred by a responsible insolvency practitioner of an insolvent partnership, and of any insolvent member of that partnership against whom an insolvency order has been made.

(2) The joint estate of the partnership shall be applicable in the first instance in payment of the joint expenses and the separate estate of each insolvent member shall be applicable in the first instance in payment of the separate expenses relating to that member.

(3) Where the joint estate is insufficient for the payment in full of the joint expenses, the unpaid balance shall be apportioned equally between the separate estates of the insolvent members against whom insolvency orders have been made and shall form part of the expenses to be paid out of those estates.

(4) Where any separate estate of an insolvent member is insufficient for the payment in full of the separate expenses to be paid out of that estate, the unpaid balance shall form part of the expenses to be paid out of the joint estate.

(5) Where after the transfer of any unpaid balance in accordance with subsection (3) or (4) any estate is insufficient for the payment in full of the expenses to be paid out of that estate, the balance then remaining unpaid shall be apportioned equally between the other estates.

(6) Where after an apportionment under subsection (5) one or more estates are insufficient for the payment in full of the expenses to be paid out of those estates, the total of the unpaid balances of the expenses to be paid out of those estates shall continue to be apportioned equally between the other estates until provision is made for the payment in full of the expenses or there is no estate available for the payment of the balance finally remaining unpaid, in which case it abates in equal proportions between all the estates.

(7) Without prejudice to subsections (3) to (6) above, the responsible insolvency practitioner may, with the sanction of any creditors' committee established under section 141 or with the leave of the court obtained on application—

(a) pay out of the joint estate as part of the expenses to be paid out of that estate any expenses incurred for any separate estate of an insolvent member; or

(b) pay out of any separate estate of an insolvent member any part of the expenses incurred for the joint estate which affects that separate estate.

175A Priority of debts in joint estate

(1) The provisions of this section and the next (which are subject to the provisions of section 9 of the Partnership Act 1890 as respects the liability of the estate of a deceased member) shall apply as regards priority of debts in a case where article 8 of the Insolvent Partnerships Order 1994 applies.

(2) After payment of expenses in accordance with section 175 and subject to section 175C(2), the joint debts of the partnership shall be paid out of its joint estate in the following order of priority—

[(a) the ordinary preferential debts;

(aa) the secondary preferential debts;]

(b) the debts which are neither preferential debts nor postponed debts;

(c) interest under section 189 on the joint debts (other than postponed debts);

(d) the postponed debts;

(e) interest under section 189 on the postponed debts.

(3) The responsible insolvency practitioner shall adjust the rights among themselves of the members of the partnership as contributories and shall distribute any surplus to the members or, where applicable, to the separate estates of the members, according to their respective rights and interests in it.

(4) The debts referred to in each of [paragraphs (a), (aa) and (b)] of subsection (2) rank equally between themselves, and in each case if the joint estate is insufficient for meeting them, they abate in equal proportions between themselves.

(5) Where the joint estate is not sufficient for the payment of the joint debts in accordance with [paragraphs (a), (aa) and (b)] of subsection (2), the responsible insolvency practitioner shall aggregate the value of those debts to the extent that they have not been satisfied or are not capable of being satisfied, and that aggregate amount shall be a claim against the separate estate of each member of the partnership against whom an insolvency order has been made which—

(a) shall be a debt provable by the responsible insolvency practitioner in each such estate, and

(b) shall rank equally with the debts of the member referred to in section 175B(1)(b) below.

(6) Where the joint estate is sufficient for the payment of the joint debts in accordance with [paragraphs (a), (aa) and (b)] of subsection (2) but not for the payment of interest under paragraph (c) of that subsection, the responsible insolvency practitioner shall aggregate the value of that interest to the extent that it has not been satisfied or is not capable of being satisfied, and that aggregate amount shall be a claim against the separate estate of each member of the partnership against whom an insolvency order has been made which—

(a) shall be a debt provable by the responsible insolvency practitioner in each such estate, and

(b) shall rank equally with the interest on the separate debts referred to in section 175B(1)(c) below.

(7) Where the joint estate is not sufficient for the payment of the postponed joint debts in accordance with paragraph (d) of subsection (2), the responsible insolvency practitioner shall aggregate the value of those debts to the extent that they have not been satisfied or are not capable of being satisfied, and that aggregate amount shall be a claim against the separate estate of each member of the partnership against whom an insolvency order has been made which—

(a) shall be a debt provable by the responsible insolvency practitioner in each such estate, and

(b) shall rank equally with the postponed debts of the member referred to in section 175B(1)(d) below.

(8) Where the joint estate is sufficient for the payment of the postponed joint debts in accordance with paragraph (d) of subsection (2) but not for the payment of interest under paragraph (e) of that subsection, the responsible insolvency practitioner shall aggregate the value of that interest to the extent that it has not been satisfied or is not capable of being satisfied, and that aggregate amount shall be a claim against the separate estate of each member of the partnership against whom an insolvency order has been made which—

(a) shall be a debt provable by the responsible insolvency practitioner in each such estate, and

(b) shall rank equally with the interest on the postponed debts referred to in section 175B(1)(e) below.

(9) Where the responsible insolvency practitioner receives any distribution from the separate estate of a member in respect of a debt referred to in paragraph (a) of subsection (5), (6), (7) or (8) above, that distribution shall become part of the joint estate and shall be distributed in accordance with the order of priority set out in subsection (2) above.

175B Priority of debts in separate estate

(1) The separate estate of each member of the partnership against whom an insolvency order has been made shall be applicable, after payment of expenses in accordance with section 175 and subject to section 175C(2) below, in payment of the separate debts of that member in the following order of priority—

[(a) the ordinary preferential debts;

(aa) the secondary preferential debts;]

(b) the debts which are neither preferential debts nor postponed debts (including any debt referred to in section 175A(5)(a));

(c) interest under section 189 on the separate debts and under section 175A(6);

(d) the postponed debts of the member (including any debt referred to in section 175A(7)(a));

(e) interest under section 189 on the postponed debts of the member and under section 175A(8).

(2) The debts referred to in each of [paragraphs (a), (aa) and (b)] of subsection (1) rank equally between themselves, and in each case if the separate estate is insufficient for meeting them, they abate in equal proportions between themselves.

(3) Where the responsible insolvency practitioner receives any distribution from the joint estate or from the separate estate of another member of the partnership against whom an insolvency order has been made, that distribution shall become part of the separate estate and shall be distributed in accordance with the order of priority set out in subsection (1) of this section.

175C Provisions generally applicable in distribution of joint and separate estates

(1) Distinct accounts shall be kept of the joint estate of the partnership and of the separate estate of each member of that partnership against whom an insolvency order is made.

(2) No member of the partnership shall prove for a joint or separate debt in competition with the joint creditors, unless the debt has arisen—

(a) as a result of fraud, or

(b) in the ordinary course of a business carried on separately from the partnership business.

(3) For the purpose of establishing the value of any debt referred to in section 175A(5)(a) or (7)(a), that value may be estimated by the responsible insolvency practitioner in accordance with section 322 or (as the case may be) in accordance with the rules.

(4) Interest under section 189 on preferential debts ranks equally with interest on debts which are neither preferential debts nor postponed debts.

(5) Sections 175A and 175B are without prejudice to any provision of this Act or of any other enactment concerning the ranking between themselves of postponed debts and interest thereon, but in the absence of any such provision postponed debts and interest thereon rank equally between themselves.

(6) If any two or more members of an insolvent partnership constitute a separate partnership, the creditors of such separate partnership shall be deemed to be a separate set of creditors and subject to the same statutory provisions as the separate creditors of any member of the insolvent partnership.

(7) Where any surplus remains after the administration of the estate of a separate partnership, the surplus shall be distributed to the members or, where applicable, to the separate estates of the members of that partnership according to their respective rights and interests in it.

(8) Neither the official receiver, the Secretary of State nor a responsible insolvency practitioner shall be entitled to remuneration or fees under the [Insolvency (England and Wales) Rules 2016], the Insolvency Regulations 1986 or the Insolvency Fees Order 1986 for his services in connection with—

(a) the transfer of a surplus from the joint estate to a separate estate under section 175A(3),

(b) a distribution from a separate estate to the joint estate in respect of a claim referred to in section 175A(5), (6), (7) or (8), or

(c) a distribution from the estate of a separate partnership to the separate estates of the members of that partnership under subsection (7) above.".

24 Sections 189 and 328: Interest on debts

Sections 189 and 328(4) and (5) are modified so as to read as follows:—

"189 (1) In the winding up of an insolvent partnership or the winding up or bankruptcy (as the case may be) of any of its insolvent members interest is payable in accordance with this section, in the order of priority laid down by sections 175A and 175B, on any debt proved in the winding up or bankruptcy, including so much of any such debt as represents interest on the remainder.

(2) Interest under this section is payable on the debts in question in respect of the periods during which they have been outstanding since the winding-up order was made against the partnership or any corporate member (as the case may be) or the bankruptcy order was made against any individual member.

(3) The rate of interest payable under this section in respect of any debt ("the official rate" for the purposes of any provision of this Act in which that expression is used) is whichever is the greater of—

(a) the rate specified in section 17 of the Judgments Act 1838 on the day on which the winding-up or bankruptcy order (as the case may be) was made, and

(b) the rate applicable to that debt apart from the winding up or bankruptcy.".

25 Sections 211 and 356: False representations to creditors

Sections 211 and 356(2)(d) are modified so as to read as follows:—

"211 (1) This section applies where insolvency orders are made against an insolvent partnership and any insolvent member or members of it by virtue of article 8 of the Insolvent Partnerships Order 1994.

(2) Any person, being a past or present officer of the partnership or a past or present officer (which for these purposes includes a shadow director) of a corporate member against which an insolvency order has been made—

(a) commits an offence if he makes any false representation or commits any other fraud for the purpose of obtaining the consent of the creditors of the partnership (or any of them) or of the creditors of any of its members (or any of such creditors) to an agreement with reference to the affairs of the partnership or of any of its members or to the winding up of the partnership or of a corporate member, or the bankruptcy of an individual member, and

(b) is deemed to have committed that offence if, prior to the winding up or bankruptcy (as the case may be), he has made any false representation, or committed any other fraud, for that purpose.

(3) A person guilty of an offence under this section is liable to imprisonment or a fine, or both.".

26 Sections 230, 231 and 292: Appointment to office of responsible insolvency practitioner or provisional liquidator

Sections 230, 231 and 292 are modified so as to read as follows:—

"230 (1) This section applies with respect to the appointment of—

(a) the responsible insolvency practitioner of an insolvent partnership which is being wound up by virtue of article 8 of the Insolvent Partnerships Order 1994 and of one or more of its insolvent members, or

(b) a provisional liquidator of an insolvent partnership, or of any of its corporate members, against which a winding-up petition is presented by virtue of that article,

but is without prejudice to any enactment under which the official receiver is to be, or may be, responsible insolvency practitioner or provisional liquidator.

(2) No person may be appointed as responsible insolvency practitioner unless he is, at the time of the appointment, qualified to act as an insolvency practitioner both in relation to the insolvent partnership and to the insolvent member or members.

(3) No person may be appointed as provisional liquidator unless he is, at the time of the appointment, qualified to act as an insolvency practitioner both in relation to the insolvent partnership and to any corporate member in respect of which he is appointed.

(4) If the appointment or nomination of any person to the office of responsible insolvency practitioner or provisional liquidator relates to more than one person, or has the effect that the office is to be held by more than one person, then subsection (5) below applies.

(5) The appointment or nomination shall declare whether any act required or authorised under any enactment to be done by the responsible insolvency practitioner or by the provisional liquidator is to be done by all or any one or more of the persons for the time being holding the office in question.

(6) The appointment of any person as responsible insolvency practitioner takes effect only if that person accepts the appointment in accordance with the rules. Subject to this, the appointment of any person as responsible insolvency practitioner takes effect at the time specified in his certificate of appointment.

230A Conflicts of interest

(1) If the responsible insolvency practitioner of an insolvent partnership being wound up by virtue of article 8 of the Insolvent Partnerships Order 1994 and of one or more of its insolvent members is of the opinion at any time that there is a conflict of interest between his functions as liquidator of the partnership and his functions as responsible insolvency practitioner of any insolvent member, or between his functions as responsible insolvency practitioner of two or more insolvent members, he may apply to the court for directions.

(2) On an application under subsection (1), the court may, without prejudice to the generality of its power to give directions, appoint one or more insolvency practitioners either in place of the applicant to act as responsible insolvency practitioner of both the partnership and its insolvent member or members or to act as joint responsible insolvency practitioner with the applicant.".

27 Section 234: Getting in the partnership property

Section 234 is modified, so far as insolvent partnerships are concerned, so as to read as follows:—

"234 (1) This section applies where—

(a) insolvency orders are made by virtue of article 8 of the Insolvent Partnerships Order 1994 in respect of an insolvent partnership and its insolvent member or members, or

(b) a provisional liquidator of an insolvent partnership and any of its corporate members is appointed by virtue of that article;

and "the office-holder" means the liquidator or the provisional liquidator, as the case may be.

(2) Any person who is or has been an officer of the partnership, or who is an executor or administrator of the estate of a deceased officer of the partnership, shall deliver up to the office-holder, for the purposes of the exercise of the office-holder's functions under this Act and (where applicable) the Company Directors Disqualification Act 1986, possession of any partnership property which he holds for the purposes of the partnership.

(3) Where any person has in his possession or control any property, books, papers or records to which the partnership appears to be entitled, the court may require that person forthwith (or within such period as the court may direct) to pay, deliver, convey, surrender or transfer the property, books, papers or records to the office-holder or as the court may direct.

(4) Where the office-holder—

(a) seizes or disposes of any property which is not partnership property, and

(b) at the time of seizure or disposal believes, and has reasonable grounds for believing, that he is entitled (whether in pursuance of an order of the court or otherwise) to seize or dispose of that property,

the next subsection has effect.

(5) In that case the office-holder—

(a) is not liable to any person in respect of any loss or damage resulting from the seizure or disposal except in so far as that loss or damage is caused by the office-holder's own negligence, and

(b) has a lien on the property, or the proceeds of its sale, for such expenses as were incurred in connection with the seizure or disposal.".

28 Section 283: Definition of individual member's estate

Section 283 is modified so as to read as follows:—

"283 (1) Subject as follows, the estate of an individual member for the purposes of this Act comprises—

(a) all property belonging to or vested in the individual member at the commencement of the bankruptcy, and

(b) any property which by virtue of any of the provisions of this Act is comprised in that estate or is treated as falling within the preceding paragraph.

(2) Subsection (1) does not apply to—

(a) such tools, books, vehicles and other items of equipment as are not partnership property and as are necessary to the individual member for use personally by him in his employment, business or vocation;

(b) such clothing, bedding, furniture, household equipment and provisions as are not partnership property and as are necessary for satisfying the basic domestic needs of the individual member and his family.

This subsection is subject to section 308 in Chapter IV (certain excluded property reclaimable by trustee).

(3) Subsection (1) does not apply to—

(a) property held by the individual member on trust for any other person, or

(b) the right of nomination to a vacant ecclesiastical benefice.

(4) References in any provision of this Act to property, in relation to an individual member, include references to any power exercisable by him over or in respect of property except in so far as the power is exercisable over or in respect of property not for the time being comprised in the estate of the individual member and—

(a) is so exercisable at a time after either the official receiver has had his release in respect of that estate under section 174(3) or [the trustee of that estate has vacated office under section 298(6)], or

(b) cannot be so exercised for the benefit of the individual member;

and a power exercisable over or in respect of property is deemed for the purposes of any provision of this Act to vest in the person entitled to exercise it at the time of the transaction or event by virtue of which it is exercisable by that person (whether or not it becomes so exercisable at that time).

(5) For the purposes of any such provision of this Act, property comprised in an individual member's estate is so comprised subject to the rights of any person other than the individual member (whether as a secured creditor of the individual member or otherwise) in relation thereto, but disregarding any rights which have been given up in accordance with the rules.

(6) This section has effect subject to the provisions of any enactment not contained in this Act under which any property is to be excluded from a bankrupt's estate.".

[28A Section 283A: Individual member's home ceasing to form part of estate

Section 283A is modified so as to read as follows:—

"283A (1) This section applies where property comprised in the estate of an individual member consists of an interest in a dwelling-house which at the date of the bankruptcy was the sole or principal residence of—

(a) the individual member;

(b) the individual member's spouse [or civil partner], or

(c) a former spouse [or former civil partner] of the individual member.

(2) At the end of the period of three years beginning with the date of the bankruptcy the interest mentioned in subsection (1) shall—

(a) cease to be comprised in the individual member's estate, and

Part 10 SIs: Partnership Insolvency

(b) vest in the individual member (without conveyance, assignment or transfer).

(3) Subsection (2) shall not apply if during the period mentioned in that subsection—

(a) the trustee realises the interest mentioned in subsection (1),

(b) the trustee applies for an order for sale in respect of the dwelling-house,

(c) the trustee applies for an order for possession of the dwelling-house,

(d) the trustee applies for an order under section 313 in Chapter IV in respect of that interest, or

(e) the trustee and the individual member agree that the individual member shall incur a specified liability to his estate (with or without the addition of interest from the date of the agreement) in consideration of which the interest mentioned in subsection (1) shall cease to form part of the estate.

(4) Where an application of a kind described in subsection (3)(b) to (d) is made during the period mentioned in subsection (2) and is dismissed, unless the court orders otherwise the interest to which the application relates shall on the dismissal of the application—

(a) cease to be comprised in the individual member's estate, and

(b) vest in the individual member (without conveyance, assignment or transfer).

(5) If the individual member does not inform the trustee or the official receiver of his interest in a property before the end of the period of three months beginning with the date of the bankruptcy, the period of three years mentioned in subsection (2)—

(a) shall not begin with the date of the bankruptcy, but

(b) shall begin with the date on which the trustee or official receiver becomes aware of the individual member's interest.

(6) The court may substitute for the period of three years mentioned in subsection (2) a longer period—

(a) in prescribed circumstances, and

(b) in such other circumstances as the court thinks appropriate.

(7) The rules may make provision for this section to have effect with the substitution of a shorter period for the period of three years mentioned in subsection (2) in specified circumstances (which may be described by reference to action to be taken by a trustee in bankruptcy).

(8) The rules may also, in particular, make provision—

(a) requiring or enabling the trustee of an individual member's estate to give notice that this section applies or does not apply;

(b) about the effect of a notice under paragraph (a);

(c) requiring the trustee of an individual member's estate to make an application to the Chief Land Registrar.

(9) Rules under subsection (8)(b) may, in particular—

(a) disapply this section;

(b) enable a court to disapply this section;

(c) make provision in consequence of a disapplication of this section;

(d) enable a court to make provision in consequence of a disapplication of this section;

(e) make provision (which may include provision conferring jurisdiction on a court or tribunal) about compensation.".]

29 Section 284: Individual member: Restrictions on dispositions of property

Section 284 is modified so as to read as follows:—

"284 (1) Where an individual member is adjudged bankrupt by virtue of article 8 of the Insolvent Partnerships Order 1994, any disposition of property made by that member in the period to which this section applies is void except to the extent that it is or was made with the consent of the court, or is or was subsequently ratified by the court.

(2) Subsection (1) applies to a payment (whether in cash or otherwise) as it applies to a disposition of property and, accordingly, where any payment is void by virtue of that subsection, the person paid shall hold the sum paid for the individual member as part of his estate.

(3) This section applies to the period beginning with the day of the presentation of the petition for the bankruptcy order and ending with the vesting, under Chapter IV of this Part, of the individual member's estate in a trustee.

(4) The preceding provisions of this section do not give a remedy against any person—

(a) in respect of any property or payment which he received before the commencement of the bankruptcy in good faith, for value and without notice that the petition had been presented, or

(b) in respect of any interest in property which derives from an interest in respect of which there is, by virtue of this subsection, no remedy.

(5) Where after the commencement of his bankruptcy the individual member has incurred a debt to a banker or other person by reason of the making of a payment which is void under this section, that debt is deemed for the purposes of any provision of this Act to have been incurred before the commencement of the bankruptcy unless—

(a) that banker or person had notice of the bankruptcy before the debt was incurred, or

(b) it is not reasonably practicable for the amount of the payment to be recovered from the person to whom it was made.

(6) A disposition of property is void under this section notwithstanding that the property is not or, as the case may be, would not be comprised in the individual member's estate; but nothing in this section affects any disposition made by a person of property held by him on trust for any other person other than a disposition made by an individual member of property held by him on trust for the partnership.".

[29A Section 313A: Low value home: application for sale, possession or charge

Section 313A is modified so as to read as follows:—

"313A (1) This section applies where—

(a) property comprised in the individual member's estate consists of an interest in a dwelling-house which at the date of the bankruptcy was the sole or principal residence of—

(i) the individual member,

(ii) the individual member's spouse [or civil partner], or

(iii) a former spouse [or former civil partner] of the individual member, and

(b) the trustee applies for an order for the sale of the property, for an order for possession of the property or for an order under section 313 in respect of the property.

(2) The court shall dismiss the application if the value of the interest is below the amount prescribed for the purposes of this subsection.

(3) In determining the value of an interest for the purposes of this section the court shall disregard any matter which it is required to disregard by the order which prescribes the amount for the purposes of subsection (2).".]

30 Schedule 4 is modified so as to read as follows:—

"SCHEDULE 4

POWERS OF LIQUIDATOR IN A WINDING UP

Section 167

PART I

. . .

1.

Power to pay any class of creditors in full.

2.

Power to make any compromise or arrangement with creditors or persons claiming to be creditors, or having or alleging themselves to have any claim (present or future, certain or contingent, ascertained or sounding only in damages) against the partnership, or whereby the partnership may be rendered liable.

3.

Power to compromise, on such terms as may be agreed—

(a) all debts and liabilities capable of resulting in debts, and all claims (present or future, certain or contingent, ascertained or sounding only in damages) subsisting or supposed to subsist between the partnership and a contributory or alleged contributory or other debtor or person apprehending liability to the partnership, and

(b) all questions in any way relating to or affecting the partnership property or the winding up of the partnership,

and take any security for the discharge of any such debt, liability or claim and give a complete discharge in respect of it.

[3A.

Power to bring legal proceedings under section 213, 214, 238, 239 or 423.]

4.

Power to bring or defend any action or other legal proceeding in the name and on behalf of any member of the partnership in his capacity as such or of the partnership.

5.

Power to carry on the business of the partnership so far as may be necessary for its beneficial winding up.

PART II

. . .

6.

Power to sell any of the partnership property by public auction or private contract, with power to transfer the whole of it to any person or to sell the same in parcels.

7.

Power to do all acts and execute, in the name and on behalf of the partnership or of any member of the partnership in his capacity as such, all deeds, receipts and other documents.

8.

Power to prove, rank and claim in the bankruptcy, insolvency or sequestration of any contributory for any balance against his estate, and to receive dividends in the bankruptcy, insolvency or sequestration in respect of that balance, as a separate debt due from the bankrupt or insolvent, and rateably with the other separate creditors.

9.

Power to draw, accept, make and endorse any bill of exchange or promissory note in the name and on behalf of any member of the partnership in his capacity as such or of the partnership, with the same effect with respect to the liability of the partnership or of any member of the partnership in his capacity as such as if the bill or note had been drawn, accepted, made or endorsed in the course of the partnership's business.

10.

Power to raise on the security of the partnership property any money requisite.

11.

Power to take out in his official name letters of administration to any deceased contributory, and to do in his official name any other act necessary for obtaining payment of any money due from a contributory or his estate which cannot conveniently be done in the name of the partnership.

In all such cases the money due is deemed, for the purpose of enabling the liquidator to take out the letters of administration or recover the money, to be due to the liquidator himself.

12.

Power to appoint an agent to do any business which the liquidator is unable to do himself.

13.

Power to do all such other things as may be necessary for winding up the partnership's affairs and distributing its property.".

NOTES

Except as noted below, all words in square brackets were substituted or inserted, and the words omitted were revoked by the Deregulation Act 2015 and Small Business, Enterprise and Employment Act 2015 (Consequential Amendments) (Savings) Regulations 2017, SI 2017/540, reg 3, Sch 2, paras 2, 8.

Para 5: in s 117 of the Act (as set out above) words in square brackets in sub-s (7) substituted and sub-s (10) added by the Lord Chancellor (Transfer of Functions and Supplementary Provisions) Order 2006, SI 2006/680, art 3, Sch 2, paras 5, 7(1)(a), (2), (3); sub-s (9) added by the Insolvent Partnerships (Amendment) Order 2002, SI 2002/1308, arts 2, 5(3).

Para 6: s 122 of the Act (as set out above) substituted by the Insolvent Partnerships (Amendment) (No 2) Order 2002, SI 2002/2708, art 9(1), (3), subject to transitional provisions in art 11(1), (3) thereof (see further the note to art 4 at **[10.4]**); the previous text read as follows:

"122

A corporate member or former corporate member may be wound up by the court if it is unable to pay its debts.";

in s 267 of the Act (as set out above) words in square brackets in sub-s (2) and the whole of sub-s (2A) inserted by SI 2002/2708, art 9(1), (4), subject to transitional provisions in art 11(1), (3) thereof (see further the note to art 4 at **[10.4]**) and in sub-s (3), sum in square brackets substituted for original sum "£750", in relation to England and Wales, by the Insolvency (Miscellaneous Amendments) Regulations 2017, SI 2017/1119, reg 2, Sch 2, paras 1, 5(1), (2), as from 8 December 2017, subject to transitional and savings provisions in Sch 2, para 10 thereto as noted to art 2 at **[10.2]**.

Para 8: in s 124(2) of the Act (as set out above) words in square brackets inserted by SI 2002/1308, arts 2, 5(4).

Para 15: in s 140(2) of the Act (as set out above) words in square brackets substituted by the Insolvent Partnerships (Amendment) Order 2005, SI 2005/1516, art 9(1), (3).

Para 23: in s 175A of the Act (as set out above) sub-para (2)(a), (aa) substituted, for sub-para (2)(a) as originally enacted, and in sub-paras (4)–(6) words in square brackets substituted, in s 175B of the Act (as set out above) sub-para (1)(a), (aa) substituted, for sub-para (1)(a) as originally enacted, and in sub-para (2) words in square brackets substituted, by the Banks and Building Societies (Depositor Preference and Priorities) Order 2014, SI 2014/3486, art 14;

in s 175C of the Act (as set out above) words in square brackets in sub-s (8) substituted for original words "Insolvency Rules 1986", in relation to England and Wales, by SI 2017/1119, reg 2, Sch 2, paras 1, 5(1), (3), as from 8 December 2017, subject to transitional and savings provisions in Sch 2, para 10 thereto as noted to art 2 at **[10.2]**.

Para 28A: inserted by SI 2005/1516, art 9(1), (4); words in square brackets in s 283A of the Act (as set out above) inserted by the Civil Partnership Act 2004 (Amendments to Subordinate Legislation) Order 2005, SI 2005/2114, art 2(18), Sch 18, Pt 1, para 2(1), (2).

Para 29A: inserted by SI 2005/1516, art 9(1), (5); words in square brackets in s 313A of the Act (as set out above) inserted by SI 2005/2114, art 2(18), Sch 18, Pt 1, para 2(1), (3).

Para 30: in Sch 4 to the Act (as set out above) para 3A inserted by SI 2005/1516, art 9(1), (6).

SCHEDULE 5
PROVISIONS OF THE ACT WHICH APPLY WITH MODIFICATIONS FOR THE PURPOSES OF ARTICLE 9 TO WINDING UP OF INSOLVENT PARTNERSHIP ON MEMBER'S PETITION WHERE NO CONCURRENT PETITION PRESENTED AGAINST MEMBER

Article 9

[10.26]

1 Section 117: High Court and county court jurisdiction

Section 117 is modified so as to read as follows:—

"117 (1) Subject to subsections (3) and (4) below, the High Court has jurisdiction to wind up any insolvent partnership as an unregistered company by virtue of article 9 of the Insolvent Partnerships Order 1994 if the partnership has, or at any time had, a principal place of business in England and Wales.

(2) Subject to subsections (3) and (4) below, a petition for the winding up of an insolvent partnership by virtue of the said article 9 may be presented to a county court in England and Wales if the partnership has, or at any time had, a principal place of business within the insolvency district of that court.

(3) Subject to subsection (4) below, the court only has jurisdiction to wind up an insolvent partnership if the business of the partnership has been carried on in England and Wales at any time in the period of 3 years ending with the day on which the petition for winding it up is presented.

(4) If an insolvent partnership has a principal place of business situated in Scotland or in Northern Ireland, the court shall not have jurisdiction to wind up the partnership unless it had a principal place of business in England and Wales—

(a) in the case of a partnership with a principal place of business in Scotland, at any time in the period of 1 year, or

(b) in the case of a partnership with a principal place of business in Northern Ireland, at any time in the period of 3 years,

ending with the day on which the petition for winding it up is presented.

(5) The Lord Chancellor [may, with the concurrence of the Lord Chief Justice, by order] in a statutory instrument exclude a county court from having winding-up jurisdiction, and for the purposes of that jurisdiction may attach its district, or any part thereof, to any other county court, and may by statutory instrument revoke or vary any such order.

In exercising the powers of this section, the Lord Chancellor shall provide that a county court is not to have winding-up jurisdiction unless it has for the time being jurisdiction for the purposes of Parts VIII to XI of this Act (individual insolvency).

(6) Every court in England and Wales having winding-up jurisdiction has for the purposes of that jurisdiction all the powers of the High Court; and every prescribed officer of the court shall perform any duties which an officer of the High Court may discharge by order of a judge of that court or otherwise in relation to winding up.

[(7) This section is subject to Article 3 of the EC Regulation (jurisdiction under the EC Regulation).]

[(8) The Lord Chief Justice may nominate a judicial office holder (as defined in section 109(4) of the Constitutional Reform Act 2005) to exercise his functions under this section.]".

2 Section 221: Winding up of unregistered companies

Section 221 is modified so as to read as follows:—

"221 (1) Subject to subsections (2) and (3) below and to the provisions of this Part, any insolvent partnership which has, or at any time had, a principal place of business in England and Wales may be wound up under this Act.

(2) Subject to subsection (3) below an insolvent partnership shall not be wound up under this Act if the business of the partnership has not been carried on in England and Wales at any time in the period of 3 years ending with the day on which the winding-up petition is presented.

(3) If an insolvent partnership has a principal place of business situated in Scotland or in Northern Ireland, the court shall not have jurisdiction to wind up the partnership unless it had a principal place of business in England and Wales—

(a) in the case of a partnership with a principal place of business in Scotland, at any time in the period of 1 year, or

(b) in the case of a partnership with a principal place of business in Northern Ireland, at any time in the period of 3 years,

ending with the day on which the winding-up petition is presented.

[(3A) The preceding subsections are subject to Article 3 of the EC Regulation (jurisdiction under the EC Regulation).]

(4) No insolvent partnership shall be wound up under this Act voluntarily.

(5) To the extent that they are applicable to the winding up of a company by the court in England and Wales on a member's petition or on a petition by the company, all the provisions of this Act and the Companies Act about winding up apply to the winding up of an insolvent partnership as an unregistered company—

(a) with the exceptions and additions mentioned in the following subsections of this section and in section 221A, and

(b) with the modifications specified in Part II of Schedule 3 to the Insolvent Partnerships Order 1994.

(6) Sections 73(1), 74(2)(a) to (d) and (3), 75 to 78, 83, 122, 123, 124(2) and (3), [176A,] 202, 203, 205 and 250 shall not apply.

(7) The circumstances in which an insolvent partnership may be wound up as an unregistered company are as follows—

(a) if the partnership is dissolved, or has ceased to carry on business, or is carrying on business only for the purpose of winding up its affairs;

(b) if the partnership is unable to pay its debts;

(c) if the court is of the opinion that it is just and equitable that the partnership should be wound up.

(8) Every petition for the winding up of an insolvent partnership under Part V of this Act shall be verified by affidavit in Form 2 in Schedule 9 to the Insolvent Partnerships Order 1994.

221A Who may present petition

(1) A petition for winding up an insolvent partnership may be presented by any member of the partnership if the partnership consists of not less than 8 members.

(2) A petition for winding up an insolvent partnership may also be presented by any member of it with the leave of the court (obtained on his application) if the court is satisfied that—

(a) the member has served on the partnership, by leaving at a principal place of business of the partnership in England and Wales, or by delivering to an officer of the partnership, or by otherwise serving in such manner as the court may approve or direct, a written demand in Form 10 in Schedule 9 to the Insolvent Partnerships Order 1994 in respect of a joint debt or debts exceeding £750 then due from the partnership but paid by the member, other than out of partnership property;

(b) the partnership has for 3 weeks after the service of the demand neglected to pay the sum or to secure or compound for it to the member's satisfaction; and

(c) the member has obtained a judgment, decree or order of any court against the partnership for reimbursement to him of the amount of the joint debt or debts so paid and all reasonable steps (other than insolvency proceedings) have been taken by the member to enforce that judgment, decree or order.

(3) Subsection (2)(a) above is deemed included in the list of provisions specified in subsection (1) of section 416 of this Act for the purposes of the Secretary of State's order-making power under that section.".

NOTES

Para 1: in s 117 of the Act (as set out above) words in square brackets in sub-s (5) substituted and sub-s (8) added by the Lord Chancellor (Transfer of Functions and Supplementary Provisions) Order 2006, SI 2006/680, art 3, Sch 2, paras 5, 6(1)(b), (2), (3); sub-s (7) added by the Insolvent Partnerships (Amendment) Order 2002, SI 2002/1308, arts 2, 5(2).

Para 2: in s 221 of the Act (as set out above) sub-s (3A) inserted by SI 2002/1308, arts 2, 5(1); figure in square brackets in sub-s (6) inserted by the Insolvent Partnerships (Amendment) Order 2006, SI 2006/622, art 8, except in respect of any insolvency proceedings in relation to an insolvent partnership commenced before 6 April 2006; see SI 2006/622, art 2 at **[2.41]**.

SCHEDULE 6
PROVISIONS OF THE ACT WHICH APPLY WITH MODIFICATIONS FOR THE PURPOSES OF ARTICLE 10 TO WINDING UP OF INSOLVENT PARTNERSHIP ON MEMBER'S PETITION WHERE CONCURRENT PETITIONS ARE PRESENTED AGAINST ALL THE MEMBERS

Article 10

[10.27]

1 Sections 117 and 265: High Court and county court jurisdiction

Sections 117 and 265 are modified so as to read as follows:—

"117 (1) Subject to the provisions of this section, the High Court has jurisdiction to wind up any insolvent partnership as an unregistered company by virtue of article 10 of the Insolvent Partnerships Order 1994 if the partnership has, or at any time had, a principal place of business in England and Wales.

(2) Subject to the provisions of this section, a petition for the winding up of an insolvent partnership by virtue of the said article 10 may be presented to a county court in England and Wales if the partnership has, or at any time had, a principal place of business within the insolvency district of that court.

(3) Subject to subsection (4) below, the court only has jurisdiction to wind up an insolvent partnership if the business of the partnership has been carried on in England and Wales at any time in the period of 3 years ending with the day on which the petition for winding it up is presented.

(4) If an insolvent partnership has a principal place of business situated in Scotland or in Northern Ireland, the court shall not have jurisdiction to wind up the partnership unless it had a principal place of business in England and Wales—

(a) in the case of a partnership with a principal place of business in Scotland, at any time in the period of 1 year, or

(b) in the case of a partnership with a principal place of business in Northern Ireland, at any time in the period of 3 years,

ending with the day on which the petition for winding it up is presented.

(5) Subject to subsection (6) below, the court has jurisdiction to wind up a corporate member, or make a bankruptcy order against an individual member, of a partnership against which a petition has been presented by virtue of article 10 of the Insolvent Partnerships Order 1994 if it has jurisdiction in respect of the partnership.

(6) Petitions by virtue of the said article 10 for the winding up of an insolvent partnership and the bankruptcy of one or more members of that partnership may not be presented to a district registry of the High Court.

(7) The Lord Chancellor [may, with the concurrence of the Lord Chief Justice, by order] in a statutory instrument exclude a county court from having winding-up jurisdiction, and for the purposes of that jurisdiction may attach its district, or any part thereof, to any other county court, and may by statutory instrument revoke or vary any such order.

In exercising the powers of this section, the Lord Chancellor shall provide that a county court is not to have winding-up jurisdiction unless it has for the time being jurisdiction for the purposes of Parts VIII to XI of this Act (individual insolvency).

(8) Every court in England and Wales having winding-up jurisdiction has for the purposes of that jurisdiction all the powers of the High Court; and every prescribed officer of the court shall perform any duties which an officer of the High Court may discharge by order of a judge of that court or otherwise in relation to winding up.

[(9) This section is subject to Article 3 of the EC Regulation (jurisdiction under the EC Regulation).]

[(10) The Lord Chief Justice may nominate a judicial office holder (as defined in section 109(4) of the Constitutional Reform Act 2005) to exercise his functions under this section.]".

2 Sections [124 and 264]: Applications to wind up insolvent partnership and to wind up or bankrupt insolvent members

Sections [124 and 264] are modified so as to read as follows:—

"124 (1) An application to the court by a member of an insolvent partnership by virtue of article 10 of the Insolvent Partnerships Order 1994 for the winding up of the partnership as an unregistered company and the winding up or bankruptcy (as the case may be) of all its members shall—

(a) in the case of the partnership, be by petition in Form 11 in Schedule 9 to that Order,

(b) in the case of a corporate member, be by petition in Form 12 in that Schedule, and

(c) in the case of an individual member, be by petition in Form 13 in that Schedule.

(2) Subject to subsection (3) below, a petition under subsection (1)(a) may only be presented by a member of the partnership on the grounds that the partnership is unable to pay its debts and if—

(a) petitions are at the same time presented by that member for insolvency orders against every member of the partnership (including himself or itself); and

(b) each member is willing for an insolvency order to be made against him or it and the petition against him or it contains a statement to this effect.

(3) If the court is satisfied, on application by any member of an insolvent partnership, that presentation of petitions under subsection (1) against the partnership and every member of it would be impracticable, the court may direct that petitions be presented against the partnership and such member or members of it as are specified by the court.

(4) The petitions mentioned in subsection (1)—

(a) shall all be presented to the same court and, except as the court otherwise permits or directs, on the same day, and

(b) except in the case of the petition mentioned in subsection (1)(c) shall be advertised in Form 8 in the said Schedule 9.

(5) Each petition presented under this section shall contain particulars of the other petitions being presented in relation to the partnership, identifying the partnership and members concerned.

(6) The hearing of the petition against the partnership fixed by the court shall be in advance of the hearing of the petitions against the insolvent members.

(7) On the day appointed for the hearing of the petition against the partnership, the petitioner shall, before the commencement of the hearing, hand to the court Form 9 in Schedule 9 to the Insolvent Partnerships Order 1994, duly completed.

(8) Any person against whom a winding-up or bankruptcy petition has been presented in relation to the insolvent partnership is entitled to appear and to be heard on any petition for the winding up of the partnership.

(9) A petitioner under this section may at the hearing withdraw the petition if—

(a) subject to subsection (10) below, he withdraws at the same time every other petition which he has presented under this section; and

(b) he gives notice to the court at least 3 days before the date appointed for the hearing of the relevant petition of his intention to withdraw the petition.

(10) A petitioner need not comply with the provisions of subsection (9)(a) in the case of a petition against a member, if the court is satisfied on application made to it by the petitioner that, because of difficulties in serving the petition or for any other reason, the continuance of that petition would be likely to prejudice or delay the proceedings on the petition which he has presented against the partnership or on any petition which he has presented against any other insolvent member.".

3 Sections 125 and 271: Powers of court on hearing of petitions against insolvent partnership and members

Sections 125 and 271 are modified so as to read as follows:—

"125 (1) Subject to the provisions of section 125A, on hearing a petition under section 124 against an insolvent partnership or any of its insolvent members, the court may dismiss it, or adjourn the hearing conditionally or unconditionally or make any other order that it thinks fit; but the court shall not refuse to make a winding-up order against the partnership or a corporate member on the ground only that the partnership property or (as the case may be) the member's assets have been mortgaged to an amount equal to or in excess of that property or those assets, or that the partnership has no property or the member no assets.

(2) An order under subsection (1) in respect of an insolvent partnership may contain directions as to the future conduct of any insolvency proceedings in existence against any insolvent member in respect of whom an insolvency order has been made.

125A Hearing of petitions against members

(1) On the hearing of a petition against an insolvent member the petitioner shall draw the court's attention to the result of the hearing of the winding-up petition against the partnership and the following subsections of this section shall apply.

(2) If the court has neither made a winding-up order, nor dismissed the winding-up petition, against the partnership the court may adjourn the hearing of the petition against the member until either event has occurred.

(3) Subject to subsection (4) below, if a winding-up order has been made against the partnership, the court may make a winding-up order against the corporate member in respect of which, or (as the case may be) a bankruptcy order against the individual member in respect of whom, the insolvency petition was presented.

(4) If no insolvency order is made under subsection (3) against any member within 28 days of the making of the winding-up order against the partnership, the proceedings against the partnership shall be conducted as if the winding-up petition against the partnership had been presented by virtue of article 7 of the Insolvent Partnerships Order 1994, and the proceedings against any member shall be conducted under this Act without the modifications made by that Order (other than the modifications made to sections 168 and 303 by article 14).

(5) If the court has dismissed the winding-up petition against the partnership, the court may dismiss the winding-up petition against the corporate member or (as the case may be) the bankruptcy petition against the individual member. However, if an insolvency order is made against a member, the proceedings against that member shall be conducted under this Act without the modifications made by the Insolvent Partnerships Order 1994 (other than the modifications made to sections 168 and 303 of this Act by article 14 of that Order).

(6) The court may dismiss a petition against an insolvent member if it considers it just to do so because of a change in circumstances since the making of the winding-up order against the partnership.

(7) The court may dismiss a petition against an insolvent member who is a limited partner, if—

(a) the member lodges in court for the benefit of the creditors of the partnership sufficient money or security to the court's satisfaction to meet his liability for the debts and obligations of the partnership; or

(b) the member satisfies the court that he is no longer under any liability in respect of the debts and obligations of the partnership.".

4 Section 221: Winding up of unregistered companies

Section 221 is modified so as to read as follows:—

"221 (1) Subject to subsections (2) and (3) below and to the provisions of this Part, any insolvent partnership which has, or at any time had, a principal place of business in England and Wales may be wound up under this Act.

(2) Subject to subsection (3) below, an insolvent partnership shall not be wound up under this Act if the business of the partnership has not been carried on in England and Wales at any time in the period of 3 years ending with the day on which the winding-up petition is presented.

(3) If an insolvent partnership has a principal place of business situated in Scotland or in Northern Ireland, the court shall not have jurisdiction to wind up the partnership unless it had a principal place of business in England and Wales—

(a) in the case of a partnership with a principal place of business in Scotland, at any time in the period of 1 year, or

(b) in the case of a partnership with a principal place of business in Northern Ireland, at any time in the period of 3 years,

ending with the day on which the winding-up petition is presented.

[(3A) The preceding subsections are subject to Article 3 of the EC Regulation (jurisdiction under the EC Regulation).]

(4) No insolvent partnership shall be wound up under this Act voluntarily.

(5) To the extent that they are applicable to the winding up of a company by the court in England and Wales on a member's petition, all the provisions of this Act and the Companies Act about winding up apply to the winding up of an insolvent partnership as an unregistered company—

(a) with the exceptions and additions mentioned in the following subsections of this section, and

(b) with the modifications specified in Part II of Schedule 4 to the Insolvent Partnerships Order 1994.

(6) Sections 73(1), 74(2)(a) to (d) and (3), 75 to 78, 83, 124(2) and (3), 154, [176A,] 202, 203, 205 and 250 shall not apply.

(7) Unless the contrary intention appears, the members of the partnership against whom insolvency orders are made by virtue of article 10 of the Insolvent Partnerships Order 1994 shall not be treated as contributories for the purposes of this Act.

(8) The circumstances in which an insolvent partnership may be wound up as an unregistered company are that the partnership is unable to pay its debts.

(9) Every petition for the winding up of an insolvent partnership under Part V of this Act shall be verified by affidavit in Form 2 in Schedule 9 to the Insolvent Partnerships Order 1994.".

NOTES

Para 1: in s 117 of the Act (as set out above) words in square brackets in sub-s (7) substituted and sub-s (10) added by the Lord Chancellor (Transfer of Functions and Supplementary Provisions) Order 2006, SI 2006/680, art 3, Sch 2, paras 5, 7(1)(b), (2), (3); sub-s (9) added by the Insolvent Partnerships (Amendment) Order 2002, SI 2002/1308, arts 2, 5(3).

Para 2: words in square brackets in both places substituted for original words "124, 264 and 272", in relation to England and Wales, by the Insolvency (Miscellaneous Amendments) Regulations 2017, SI 2017/1119, reg 2, Sch 2, paras 1, 6, as from 8 December 2017, subject to transitional and savings provisions in Sch 2, para 10 thereto as noted to art 2 at **[10.2]**.

Para 4: in s 221 of the Act (as set out above) sub-s (3A) inserted by SI 2002/1308, arts 2, 5(1); figure in square brackets in sub-s (6) inserted by the Insolvent Partnerships (Amendment) Order 2006, SI 2006/622, art 9, except in respect of any insolvency proceedings in relation to an insolvent partnership commenced before 6 April 2006; see SI 2006/622, art 2 at **[2.41]**.

SCHEDULE 7
PROVISIONS OF THE ACT WHICH APPLY WITH MODIFICATIONS FOR THE PURPOSES OF ARTICLE 11 WHERE JOINT BANKRUPTCY PETITION PRESENTED BY INDIVIDUAL MEMBERS WITHOUT WINDING UP PARTNERSHIP AS UNREGISTERED COMPANY

Article 11

[10.28]

1 (1) The provisions of the Act specified in sub-paragraph (2) below, are set out as modified in this Schedule.

(2) The provisions referred to in sub-paragraph (1) above are sections 264 to 266, . . . , . . . 283, 284, 290, 292 to 301, 305, 312, 328, 331 and 387.

2 Section 264: Presentation of joint bankruptcy petition

Section 264 is modified so as to read as follows:—

"**264** (1) Subject to section 266(1) below, a joint bankruptcy petition may be presented to the court by virtue of article 11 of the Insolvent Partnerships Order 1994 by all the members of an insolvent partnership in their capacity as such provided that all the members are individuals and none of them is a limited partner.

(2) A petition may not be presented under paragraph (1) by the members of an insolvent partnership [if the partnership—

(a) has permission under Part 4 of the Financial Services and Markets Act 2000 to accept deposits, other than such a permission only for the purpose of carrying on another regulated activity in accordance with that permission, or

(b) continues to have a liability in respect of a deposit which was held by it in accordance with the Banking Act 1979 or the Banking Act 1987].

[(2A) Subsection 2(a) must be read with—

(a) section 22 of the Financial Services and Markets Act 2000;

(b) any relevant order under that section; and

(c) Schedule 2 to that Act.]

(3) The petition—

(a) shall be in Form 14 in Schedule 9 to the Insolvent Partnerships Order 1994; and

(b) shall contain a request that the trustee shall wind up the partnership business and administer the partnership property without the partnership being wound up as an unregistered company under Part V of this Act.

(4) The petition shall either—

(a) be accompanied by an affidavit in Form 15 in Schedule 9 to the Insolvent Partnerships Order 1994 made by the member who signs the petition, showing that all the members are individual members (and that none of them is a limited partner) and concur in the presentation of the petition, or

(b) contain a statement that all the members are individual members and be signed by all the members.

(5) On presentation of a petition under this section, the court may make orders in Form 16 in Schedule 9 to the Insolvent Partnerships Order 1994 for the bankruptcy of the members and the winding up of the partnership business and administration of its property.".

3 Section 265: Conditions to be satisfied in respect of members

Section 265 is modified so as to read as follows:—

"**265** (1) Subject to the provisions of this section, a joint bankruptcy petition by virtue of article 11 of the Insolvent Partnerships Order 1994 may be presented—

(a) to the High Court (other than to a district registry of that Court) if the partnership has, or at any time had, a principal place of business in England and Wales, or

(b) to a county court in England and Wales if the partnership has, or at any time had, a principal place of business within the insolvency district of that court.

(2) A joint bankruptcy petition shall not be presented to the court by virtue of article 11 unless the business of the partnership has been carried on in England and Wales at any time in the period of 3 years ending with the day on which the joint bankruptcy petition is presented.

[(3) A joint bankruptcy petition may be presented to the court by the members of a partnership only on the grounds that the partnership is unable to pay its debts.

(4) A petition under subsection (3) must be accompanied by—

(a) a statement of each member's affairs in Form 17 in Schedule 9 to the Insolvent Partnerships Order 1994, and

(b) a statement of the affairs of the partnership in Form 18 in that Schedule, sworn by one or more members of the partnership.

(5) The statements of affairs required by subsection (4) must contain—

(a) particulars of the member's or (as the case may be) partnership's creditors, debts and other liabilities and of their assets, and

(b) such other information as is required by the relevant form.]".

4 Section 266: Other preliminary conditions

Section 266 is modified so as to read as follows:—

"266 (1) If the court is satisfied, on application by any member of an insolvent partnership, that the presentation of the petition under section 264(1) by all the members of the partnership would be impracticable, the court may direct that the petition be presented by such member or members as are specified by the court.

(2) A joint bankruptcy petition shall not be withdrawn without the leave of the court.

(3) The court has a general power, if it appears to it appropriate to do so on the grounds that there has been a contravention of the rules or for any other reason, to dismiss a joint bankruptcy petition or to stay proceedings on such a petition; and, where it stays proceedings on a petition, it may do so on such terms and conditions as it thinks fit.".

5 . . .

6 . . .

7 Section 283: Definition of member's estate

Section 283 is modified so as to read as follows:—

"283 (1) Subject as follows, a member's estate for the purposes of this Act comprises—

(a) all property belonging to or vested in the member at the commencement of the bankruptcy, and

(b) any property which by virtue of any of the provisions of this Act is comprised in that estate or is treated as falling within the preceding paragraph.

(2) Subsection (1) does not apply to—

(a) such tools, books, vehicles and other items of equipment as are not partnership property and as are necessary to the member for use personally by him in his employment, business or vocation;

(b) such clothing, bedding, furniture, household equipment and provisions as are not partnership property and as are necessary for satisfying the basic domestic needs of the member and his family.

This subsection is subject to section 308 in Chapter IV (certain excluded property reclaimable by trustee).

(3) Subsection (1) does not apply to—

(a) property held by the member on trust for any other person, or

(b) the right of nomination to a vacant ecclesiastical benefice.

(4) References in any provision of this Act to property, in relation to a member, include references to any power exercisable by him over or in respect of property except insofar as the power is exercisable over or in respect of property not for the time being comprised in the member's estate and—

(a) is so exercisable at a time after either the official receiver has had his release in respect of that estate under section 299(2) in Chapter III or [the trustee of that estate has vacated office under section 298(6)], or

(b) cannot be so exercised for the benefit of the member;

and a power exercisable over or in respect of property is deemed for the purposes of any provision of this Act to vest in the person entitled to exercise it at the time of the transaction or event by virtue of which it is exercisable by that person (whether or not it becomes so exercisable at that time).

(5) For the purposes of any such provision of this Act, property comprised in a member's estate is so comprised subject to the rights of any person other than the member (whether as a secured creditor of the member or otherwise) in relation thereto, but disregarding any rights which have been given up in accordance with the rules.

(6) This section has effect subject to the provisions of any enactment not contained in this Act under which any property is to be excluded from a bankrupt's estate.".

[7A Section 283A: Bankrupt's home ceasing to form part of estate

Section 283A is modified so as to read as follows:—

"283A (1) This section applies where property comprised in the estate of an individual member consists of an interest in a dwelling-house which at the date of the bankruptcy was the sole or principal residence of—

(a) the individual member;

(b) the individual member's spouse [or civil partner], or

(c) a former spouse [or former civil partner] of the individual member.

(2) At the end of the period of three years beginning with the date of the bankruptcy the interest mentioned in subsection (1) shall—
(a) cease to be comprised in the individual member's estate, and
(b) vest in the individual member (without conveyance, assignment or transfer).
(3) Subsection (2) shall not apply if during the period mentioned in that subsection—
(a) the trustee realises the interest mentioned in subsection (1),
(b) the trustee applies for an order for sale in respect of the dwelling-house,
(c) the trustee applies for an order for possession of the dwelling-house,
(d) the trustee applies for an order under section 313 in Chapter IV in respect of that interest, or
(e) the trustee and the individual member agree that the individual member shall incur a specified liability to his estate (with or without the addition of interest from the date of the agreement) in consideration of which the interest mentioned in subsection (1) shall cease to form part of the estate.
(4) Where an application of a kind described in subsection (3)(b) to (d) is made during the period mentioned in subsection (2) and is dismissed, unless the court orders otherwise the interest to which the application relates shall on the dismissal of the application—
(a) cease to be comprised in the individual member's estate, and
(b) vest in the individual member (without conveyance, assignment or transfer).
(5) If the individual member does not inform the trustee or the official receiver of his interest in a property before the end of the period of three months beginning with the date of the bankruptcy, the period of three years mentioned in subsection (2)—
(a) shall not begin with the date of the bankruptcy, but
(b) shall begin with the date on which the trustee or official receiver becomes aware of the individual member's interest.
(6) The court may substitute for the period of three years mentioned in subsection (2) a longer period—
(a) in prescribed circumstances, and
(b) in such other circumstances as the court thinks appropriate.
(7) The rules may make provision for this section to have effect with the substitution of a shorter period for the period of three years mentioned in subsection (2) in specified circumstances (which may be described by reference to action to be taken by a trustee in bankruptcy).
(8) The rules may also, in particular, make provision—
(a) requiring or enabling the trustee of an individual member's estate to give notice that this section applies or does not apply;
(b) about the effect of a notice under paragraph (a);
(c) requiring the trustee of an individual member's estate to make an application to the Chief Land Registrar.
(9) Rules under subsection (8)(b) may, in particular—
(a) disapply this section;
(b) enable a court to disapply this section;
(c) make provision in consequence of a disapplication of this section;
(d) enable a court to make provision in consequence of a disapplication of this section;
(e) make provision (which may include provision conferring jurisdiction on a court or tribunal) about compensation.".]

8 Section 284: Restrictions on dispositions of property

Section 284 is modified so as to read as follows:—

"**284** (1) Where a member is adjudged bankrupt on a joint bankruptcy petition, any disposition of property made by that member in the period to which this section applies is void except to the extent that it is or was made with the consent of the court, or is or was subsequently ratified by the court.
(2) Subsection (1) applies to a payment (whether in cash or otherwise) as it applies to a disposition of property and, accordingly, where any payment is void by virtue of that subsection, the person paid shall hold the sum paid for the member as part of his estate.
(3) This section applies to the period beginning with the day of the presentation of the joint bankruptcy petition and ending with the vesting, under Chapter IV of this Part, of the member's estate in a trustee.
(4) The preceding provisions of this section do not give a remedy against any person—
(a) in respect of any property or payment which he received before the commencement of the bankruptcy in good faith, for value, and without notice that the petition had been presented, or
(b) in respect of any interest in property which derives from an interest in respect of which there is, by virtue of this subsection, no remedy.
(5) Where after the commencement of his bankruptcy the member has incurred a debt to a banker or other person by reason of the making of a payment which is void under this section, that debt is deemed for the purposes of any provision of this Act to have been incurred before the commencement of the bankruptcy unless—
(a) that banker or person had notice of the bankruptcy before the debt was incurred, or
(b) it is not reasonably practicable for the amount of the payment to be recovered from the person to whom it was made.

(6) A disposition of property is void under this section notwithstanding that the property is not or, as the case may be, would not be comprised in the member's estate; but nothing in this section affects any disposition made by a person of property held by him on trust for any other person other than a disposition made by a member of property held by him on trust for the partnership.".

9 Section 290: Public examination of member

Section 290 is modified so as to read as follows:—

"**290** (1) Where orders have been made against the members of an insolvent partnership on a joint bankruptcy petition, the official receiver may at any time before the discharge of any such member apply to the court for the public examination of that member.

(2) Unless the court otherwise orders, the official receiver shall make an application under subsection (1) if notice requiring him to do so is given to him, in accordance with the rules, by one of the creditors of the member concerned with the concurrence of not less than one-half, in value, of those creditors (including the creditor giving notice).

(3) On an application under subsection (1), the court shall direct that a public examination of the member shall be held on a day appointed by the court; and the member shall attend on that day and be publicly examined as to his affairs, dealings and property and as to those of the partnership.

(4) The following may take part in the public examination of the member and may question him concerning the matters mentioned in subsection (3), namely—

(a) the official receiver,

(b) the trustee of the member's estate, if his appointment has taken effect,

(c) any person who has been appointed as special manager of the member's estate or business or of the partnership property or business,

(d) any creditor of the member who has tendered a proof in the bankruptcy.

(5) On an application under subsection (1), the court may direct that the public examination of a member under this section be combined with the public examination of any other person.

(6) If a member without reasonable excuse fails at any time to attend his public examination under this section he is guilty of a contempt of court and liable to be punished accordingly (in addition to any other punishment to which he may be subject).".

10 Section 292: Power to appoint trustee

Section 292 is modified so as to read as follows:—

"**292** [(1) This section applies to any appointment of a person (other than the official receiver) as trustee of a bankrupt's estate.]

(2) No person may be appointed as trustee of the members' estates and as trustee of the partnership unless he is, at the time of the appointment, qualified to act as an insolvency practitioner both in relation to the insolvent partnership and to each of the members.

(3) Any power to appoint a person as trustee of the members' estates and of the partnership includes power to appoint two or more persons as joint trustees; but such an appointment must make provision as to the circumstances in which the trustees must act together and the circumstances in which one or more of them may act for the others.

(4) The appointment of any person as trustee of the members' estates and of the partnership takes effect only if that person accepts the appointment in accordance with the rules. Subject to this, the appointment of any person as trustee takes effect at the time specified in his certificate of appointment.

(5) . . .

292A Conflicts of interest

(1) If the trustee of the members' estates and of the partnership is of the opinion at any time that there is a conflict of interest between his functions as trustee of the members' estates and his functions as trustee of the partnership, or between his functions as trustee of the estates of two or more members, he may apply to the court for directions.

(2) On an application under subsection (1), the court may, without prejudice to the generality of its power to give directions, appoint one or more insolvency practitioners either in place of the applicant to act both as trustee of the members' estates and as trustee of the partnership, or to act as joint trustee with the applicant.".

11 . . .

12 . . .

13 Section 296: Appointment of trustee by Secretary of State

Section 296 is modified so as to read as follows:—

"**296** (1) At any time when the official receiver is the trustee of the members' estates and of the partnership by virtue of any provision of this Chapter he may apply to the Secretary of State for the appointment of a person as trustee instead of the official receiver.

(2) On an application under subsection (1) the Secretary of State shall either make an appointment or decline to make one.

(3) Such an application may be made notwithstanding that the Secretary of State has declined to make an appointment either on a previous application under subsection (1) or on a reference under section 295 or under section 300(2) below.

(4) Where a trustee has been appointed by the Secretary of State under subsection (2) of this section, and an insolvency order is subsequently made against a further insolvent member by virtue of article 11 of the Insolvent Partnerships Order 1994, then the trustee so appointed shall also be the trustee of the member against whom the subsequent order is made.

(5) Where the trustee of the members' estates and of the partnership has been appointed by the Secretary of State (whether under this section or otherwise) or has become trustee of a further insolvent member under subsection (4), the trustee shall give notice of his appointment or further appointment (as the case may be) to the creditors of the members and the creditors of the partnership or, if the court so allows, shall advertise his appointment in accordance with the court's directions.

[(6) In that notice or advertisement the trustee must explain the procedure for establishing a creditors' committee under section 301, except in a case where such a committee has already been formed, in which case the trustee must state whether he proposes to appoint additional members of the committee under section 301A(3).]".

14 . . .

15 Section 298: Removal of trustee; vacation of office

Section 298 is modified so as to read as follows:—

[**"298** (1) Subject as follows, the trustee of the estates of the members and of the partnership may be removed from office only by an order of the court or by a decision of the creditors of the members and the partnership made by a creditors' decision procedure instigated specially for that purpose in accordance with the rules.

(1A) Where the official receiver is trustee or a trustee is appointed by the Secretary of State or by the court, a creditors' decision procedure may be instigated for the purpose of removing the trustee only if—

(a) the trustee thinks fit;

(b) the court so directs; or

(c) one of the creditors of the members or the partnership so requests, with the concurrence of not less than one-quarter, in value, of the creditors (including the creditor making the request).

(1B) Where the creditors of the members and the partnership decide to remove a trustee, they may in accordance with the rules appoint another person as trustee in his place.

(1C) Where the decision to remove a trustee is made under subsection (1A), the decision does not take effect until the creditors of the members and the partnership appoint another person as trustee in his place.

(2) If the trustee was appointed by the Secretary of State, he may be removed by a direction of the Secretary of State.

(3) The trustee (not being the official receiver) shall vacate office if he ceases to be a person who is for the time being qualified to act as an insolvency practitioner in relation to any member or to the partnership.

(4) The trustee may, with the leave of the court (or, if appointed by the Secretary of State, with the leave of the court or the Secretary of State), resign his office by giving notice of his resignation to the court.

(5) Subject to subsection (7), any removal from or vacation of office under this section relates to all offices held in the proceedings by virtue of article 11 of the Insolvent Partnerships Order 1994.

(6) A trustee who has produced an account of the winding up or administration under section 331 vacates office immediately upon complying with the requirements of section 331(3).

(7) The trustee must vacate office as trustee of a member if the order made by virtue of article 11 of the Insolvent Partnerships Order 1994 in relation to that member is annulled."]

16 Section 299: Release of trustee

Section 299 is modified so as to read as follows:—

"299 (1) Where the official receiver has ceased to be the trustee of the members' estates and of the partnership and a person is appointed in his stead, the official receiver shall have his release with effect from the following time, that is to say—

(a) where that person is appointed by [the] creditors of the members and of the partnership or by the Secretary of State, the time at which the official receiver gives notice [under this paragraph to the prescribed person] that he has been replaced, and

(b) where that person is appointed by the court, such time as the court may determine.

(2) If the official receiver while he is the trustee gives notice to the Secretary of State that the administration of the estate of any member, or the winding up of the partnership business and administration of its affairs, is for practical purposes complete, he shall have his release as trustee of any member or as trustee of the partnership (as the case may be) with effect from such time as the Secretary of State may determine.

(3) A person other than the official receiver who has ceased to be the trustee of the estate of any member or of the partnership shall have his release with effect from the following time, that is to say—

(a) in the case of a person who has died, the time at which notice is given to the court in accordance with the rules that that person has ceased to hold office;

(b) in the case of a person who has been removed from office by the court or by the Secretary of State, or who has vacated office under section 298(3), such time as the Secretary of State may, on an application by that person, determine;

(c) in the case of a person who has resigned, such time as may be directed by the court (or, if he was appointed by the Secretary of State, such time as may be directed by the court or as the Secretary of State may, on an application by that person, determine);

[(d) in the case of a person who has vacated office under section 298(6)—

(i) if any of the creditors of the members and of the partnership objected to the person's release before the end of the period for so objecting prescribed by the rules, such time as the Secretary of State may, on an application by that person, determine, and

(ii) otherwise, the time at which the person vacated office.]

(4) Where an order by virtue of article 11 of the Insolvent Partnerships Order 1994 is annulled in so far as it relates to any member, the trustee at the time of the annulment has his release in respect of that member with effect from such time as the court may determine.

(5) Where the trustee (including the official receiver when so acting) has his release under this section, he shall, with effect from the time specified in the preceding provisions of this section, be discharged from all liability both in respect of acts or omissions of his in the administration of the estates of the members and in the winding up of the partnership business and administration of its affairs and otherwise in relation to his conduct as trustee.

But nothing in this section prevents the exercise, in relation to a person who has had his release under this section, of the court's powers under section 304 (liability of trustee).".

17 Section 300: Vacancy in office of trustee

Section 300 is modified so as to read as follows:—

"300 (1) This section applies where the appointment of any person as trustee of the members' estates and of the partnership fails to take effect or, such an appointment having taken effect, there is otherwise a vacancy in the office of trustee.

(2) The official receiver may refer the need for an appointment to the Secretary of State and shall be trustee until the vacancy is filled.

(3) On a reference to the Secretary of State under subsection (2) the Secretary of State shall either make an appointment or decline to make one.

(4) If on a reference under subsection (2) no appointment is made, the official receiver shall continue to be trustee, but without prejudice to his power to make a further reference.

(5) References in this section to a vacancy include a case where it is necessary, in relation to any property which is or may be comprised in a member's estate, to revive the trusteeship of that estate after the [vacation of office by the trustee under section 298(6)] or the giving by the official receiver of notice under section 299(2).".

18 Section 301: Creditors' committee

Section 301 is modified so as to read as follows:—

"301 (1) Subject as follows, [the creditors of the members and of the partnership] may establish a committee (known as "the creditors' committee") to exercise the functions conferred on it by or under this Act.

(2) [The] creditors of the members and of the partnership shall not establish such a committee, or confer any functions on such a committee, at any time when the official receiver is the trustee, except in connection with [the appointment] of a person to be trustee instead of the official receiver.

301A Functions and membership of creditors' committee

(1) The committee established under section 301 shall act as creditors' committee for each member and as liquidation committee for the partnership, and shall as appropriate exercise the functions conferred on creditors' and liquidation committees in a bankruptcy or winding up by or under this Act.

(2) The rules relating to liquidation committees are to apply (with the necessary modifications and with the exclusion of all references to contributories) to a committee established under section 301.

(3) Where the appointment of the trustee also takes effect in relation to a further insolvent member under section 293(8) or 296(4), the trustee may appoint any creditor of that member (being qualified under the rules to be a member of the committee) to be an additional member of any creditors' committee already established under section 301, provided that the creditor concerned consents to act.

(4) The court may at any time, on application by a creditor of any member or of the partnership, appoint additional members of the creditors' committee.

(5) If additional members of the creditors' committee are appointed under subsection (3) or (4), the limit on the maximum number of members of the committee specified in the rules shall be increased by the number of additional members so appointed.".

19 Section 305: General functions and powers of trustee

Section 305 is modified so as to read as follows:—

"305 (1) The function of the trustee of the estates of the members and of the partnership is to get in, realise and distribute the estates of the members and the partnership property in accordance with the following provisions of this Chapter.

(2) The trustee shall have all the functions and powers in relation to the partnership and the partnership property that he has in relation to the members and their estates.

(3) In the carrying out of his functions and in the management of the members' estates and the partnership property the trustee is entitled, subject to the following provisions of this Chapter, to use his own discretion.

(4) It is the duty of the trustee, if he is not the official receiver—

(a) to furnish the official receiver with such information,

(b) to produce to the official receiver, and permit inspection by the official receiver of, such books, papers and other records, and

(c) to give the official receiver such other assistance,

as the official receiver may reasonably require for the purpose of enabling him to carry out his functions in relation to the bankruptcy of the members and the winding up of the partnership business and administration of its property.

(5) The official name of the trustee in his capacity as trustee of a member shall be "the trustee of the estate of . . . . , a bankrupt" (inserting the name of the member concerned); but he may be referred to as "the trustee in bankruptcy" of the particular member.

(6) The official name of the trustee in his capacity as trustee of the partnership shall be "the trustee of a partnership" (inserting the name of the partnership concerned).".

20 Section 312: Obligation to surrender control to trustee

Section 312 is modified so as to read as follows:—

"312 (1) This section applies where orders are made by virtue of article 11 of the Insolvent Partnerships Order 1994 and a trustee is appointed.

(2) Any person who is or has been an officer of the partnership in question, or who is an executor or administrator of the estate of a deceased officer of the partnership, shall deliver up to the trustee of the partnership, for the purposes of the exercise of the trustee's functions under this Act, possession of any partnership property which he holds for the purposes of the partnership.

(3) Each member shall deliver up to the trustee possession of any property, books, papers or other records of which he has possession or control and of which the trustee is required to take possession.

This is without prejudice to the general duties of the members as bankrupts under section 333 in this Chapter.

(4) If any of the following is in possession of any property, books, papers or other records of which the trustee is required to take possession, namely—

(a) the official receiver,

(b) a person who has ceased to be trustee of a member's estate,

(c) a person who has been the administrator of the partnership or supervisor of a voluntary arrangement approved in relation to the partnership under Part I,

(d) a person who has been the supervisor of a voluntary arrangement approved in relation to a member under Part VIII,

the official receiver or, as the case may be, that person shall deliver up possession of the property, books, papers or records to the trustee.

(5) Any banker or agent of a member or of the partnership, or any other person who holds any property to the account of, or for, a member or the partnership shall pay or deliver to the trustee all property in his possession or under his control which forms part of the member's estate or which is partnership property and which he is not by law entitled to retain as against the member, the partnership or the trustee.

(6) If any person without reasonable excuse fails to comply with any obligation imposed by this section, he is guilty of a contempt of court and liable to be punished accordingly (in addition to any other punishment to which he may be subject).".

[20A Section 313A: Low value home: application for sale, possession or charge

Section 313A is modified so as to read as follows:—

"313A (1) This section applies where—

(a) property comprised in the individual member's estate consists of an interest in a dwelling-house which at the date of the bankruptcy was the sole or principal residence of—

(i) the individual member,

(ii) the individual member's spouse [or civil partner], or

(iii) a former spouse [or former civil partner] of the individual member, and

(b) the trustee applies for an order for the sale of the property, for an order for possession of the property or for an order under section 313 in respect of the property.

(2) The court shall dismiss the application if the value of the interest is below the amount prescribed for the purposes of this subsection.

(3) In determining the value of an interest for the purposes of this section the court shall disregard any matter which it is required to disregard by the order which prescribes the amount for the purposes of subsection (2).".]

21 Section 328: Priority of expenses and debts

Section 328 is modified so as to read as follows:—

"328 Priority of expenses

(1) The provisions of this section shall apply in a case where article 11 of the Insolvent Partnerships Order 1994 applies, as regards priority of expenses incurred by a person acting as trustee of the estates of the members of an insolvent partnership and as trustee of that partnership.
(2) The joint estate of the partnership shall be applicable in the first instance in payment of the joint expenses and the separate estate of each insolvent member shall be applicable in the first instance in payment of the separate expenses relating to that member.
(3) Where the joint estate is insufficient for the payment in full of the joint expenses, the unpaid balance shall be apportioned equally between the separate estates of the insolvent members against whom insolvency orders have been made and shall form part of the expenses to be paid out of those estates.
(4) Where any separate estate of an insolvent member is insufficient for the payment in full of the separate expenses to be paid out of that estate, the unpaid balance shall form part of the expenses to be paid out of the joint estate.
(5) Where after the transfer of any unpaid balance in accordance with subsection (3) or (4) any estate is insufficient for the payment in full of the expenses to be paid out of that estate, the balance then remaining unpaid shall be apportioned equally between the other estates.
(6) Where after an apportionment under subsection (5) one or more estates are insufficient for the payment in full of the expenses to be paid out of those estates, the total of the unpaid balances of the expenses to be paid out of those estates shall continue to be apportioned equally between the other estates until provision is made for the payment in full of the expenses or there is no estate available for the payment of the balance finally remaining unpaid, in which case it abates in equal proportions between all the estates.
(7) Without prejudice to subsections (3) to (6) above, the trustee may, with the sanction of any creditors' committee established under section 301 or with the leave of the court obtained on application—
(a) pay out of the joint estate as part of the expenses to be paid out of that estate any expenses incurred for any separate estate of an insolvent member; or
(b) pay out of any separate estate of an insolvent member any part of the expenses incurred for the joint estate which affects that separate estate.

328A Priority of debts in joint estate

(1) The provisions of this section and the next (which are subject to the provisions of section 9 of the Partnership Act 1890 as respects the liability of the estate of a deceased member) shall apply as regards priority of debts in a case where article 11 of the Insolvent Partnerships Order 1994 applies.
(2) After payment of expenses in accordance with section 328 and subject to section 328C(2), the joint debts of the partnership shall be paid out of its joint estate in the following order of priority—
[(a) the ordinary preferential debts;
(aa) the secondary preferential debts;]
(b) the debts which are neither preferential debts nor postponed debts;
(c) interest under section 328D on the joint debts (other than postponed debts);
(d) the postponed debts;
(e) interest under section 328D on the postponed debts.
(3) The responsible insolvency practitioner shall adjust the rights among themselves of the members of the partnership as contributories and shall distribute any surplus to the members or, where applicable, to the separate estates of the members, according to their respective rights and interests in it.
(4) The debts referred to in each of [paragraphs (a), (aa) and (b)] of subsection (2) rank equally between themselves, and in each case if the joint estate is insufficient for meeting them, they abate in equal proportions between themselves.
(5) Where the joint estate is not sufficient for the payment of the joint debts in accordance with [paragraphs (a), (aa) and (b)] of subsection (2), the responsible insolvency practitioner shall aggregate the value of those debts to the extent that they have not been satisfied or are not capable of being satisfied, and that aggregate amount shall be a claim against the separate estate of each member of the partnership against whom an insolvency order has been made which—
(a) shall be a debt provable by the responsible insolvency practitioner in each such estate, and
(b) shall rank equally with the debts of the member referred to in section 328B(1)(b) below.
(6) Where the joint estate is sufficient for the payment of the joint debts in accordance with [paragraphs (a), (aa) and (b)] of subsection (2) but not for the payment of interest under paragraph (c) of that subsection, the responsible insolvency practitioner shall aggregate the value of that interest to the extent that it has not been satisfied or is not capable of being satisfied, and that aggregate amount shall be a claim against the separate estate of each member of the partnership against whom an insolvency order has been made which—
(a) shall be a debt provable by the responsible insolvency practitioner in each such estate, and
(b) shall rank equally with the interest on the separate debts referred to in section 328B(1)(c) below.
(7) Where the joint estate is not sufficient for the payment of the postponed joint debts in accordance with paragraph (d) of subsection (2), the responsible insolvency practitioner shall aggregate the value of those debts to the extent that they have not been satisfied or are not capable of being satisfied, and that aggregate amount shall be a claim against the separate estate of each member of the partnership against whom an insolvency order has been made which—

(a) shall be a debt provable by the responsible insolvency practitioner in each such estate, and
(b) shall rank equally with the postponed debts of the member referred to in section 328B(1)(d) below.

(8) Where the joint estate is sufficient for the payment of the postponed joint debts in accordance with paragraph (d) of subsection (2) but not for the payment of interest under paragraph (e) of that subsection, the responsible insolvency practitioner shall aggregate the value of that interest to the extent that it has not been satisfied or is not capable of being satisfied, and that aggregate amount shall be a claim against the separate estate of each member of the partnership against whom an insolvency order has been made which—
(a) shall be a debt provable by the responsible insolvency practitioner in each such estate, and
(b) shall rank equally with the interest on the postponed debts referred to in section 328B(1)(e) below.

(9) Where the responsible insolvency practitioner receives any distribution from the separate estate of a member in respect of a debt referred to in paragraph (a) of subsection (5), (6), (7) or (8) above, that distribution shall become part of the joint estate and shall be distributed in accordance with the order of priority set out in subsection (2) above.

328B Priority of debts in separate estate

(1) The separate estate of each member of the partnership against whom an insolvency order has been made shall be applicable, after payment of expenses in accordance with section 328 and subject to section 328C(2) below, in payment of the separate debts of that member in the following order of priority—
[(a) the ordinary preferential debts;
(aa) the secondary preferential debts;]
(b) the debts which are neither preferential debts nor postponed debts (including any debt referred to in section 328A(5)(a));
(c) interest under section 328D on the separate debts and under section 328A(6);
(d) the postponed debts of the member (including any debt referred to in section 328A(7)(a));
(e) interest under section 328D on the postponed debts of the member and under section 328A(8).

(2) The debts referred to in each of [paragraphs (a), (aa) and (b)] of subsection (1) rank equally between themselves, and in each case if the separate estate is insufficient for meeting them, they abate in equal proportions between themselves.

(3) Where the responsible insolvency practitioner receives any distribution from the joint estate or from the separate estate of another member of the partnership against whom an insolvency order has been made, that distribution shall become part of the separate estate and shall be distributed in accordance with the order of priority set out in subsection (1) of this section.

328C Provisions generally applicable in distribution of joint and separate estates

(1) Distinct accounts shall be kept of the joint estate of the partnership and of the separate estate of each member of that partnership against whom an insolvency order is made.

(2) No member of the partnership shall prove for a joint or separate debt in competition with the joint creditors, unless the debt has arisen—
(a) as a result of fraud, or
(b) in the ordinary course of a business carried on separately from the partnership business.

(3) For the purpose of establishing the value of any debt referred to in section 328A(5)(a) or (7)(a), that value may be estimated by the responsible insolvency practitioner in accordance with section 322.

(4) Interest under section 328D on preferential debts ranks equally with interest on debts which are neither preferential debts nor postponed debts.

(5) Sections 328A and 328B are without prejudice to any provision of this Act or of any other enactment concerning the ranking between themselves of postponed debts and interest thereon, but in the absence of any such provision postponed debts and interest thereon rank equally between themselves.

(6) If any two or more members of an insolvent partnership constitute a separate partnership, the creditors of such separate partnership shall be deemed to be a separate set of creditors and subject to the same statutory provisions as the separate creditors of any member of the insolvent partnership.

(7) Where any surplus remains after the administration of the estate of a separate partnership, the surplus shall be distributed to the members or, where applicable, to the separate estates of the members of that partnership according to their respective rights and interests in it.

(8) Neither the official receiver, the Secretary of State nor a responsible insolvency practitioner shall be entitled to remuneration or fees under the [Insolvency (England and Wales) Rules 2016], the Insolvency Regulations 1986 or the Insolvency Fees Order 1986 for his services in connection with—
(a) the transfer of a surplus from the joint estate to a separate estate under section 328A(3),
(b) a distribution from a separate estate to the joint estate in respect of a claim referred to in section 328A(5), (6), (7) or (8), or

(c) a distribution from the estate of a separate partnership to the separate estates of the members of that partnership under subsection (7) above.

328D Interest on debts

(1) In the bankruptcy of each of the members of an insolvent partnership and in the winding up of that partnership's business and administration of its property, interest is payable in accordance with this section, in the order of priority laid down by sections 328A and 328B, on any debt proved in the bankruptcy including so much of any such debt as represents interest on the remainder.

(2) Interest under this section is payable on the debts in question in respect of the periods during which they have been outstanding since the relevant order was made by virtue of article 11 of the Insolvent Partnerships Order 1994.

(3) The rate of interest payable under this section in respect of any debt ("the official rate" for the purposes of any provision of this Act in which that expression is used) is whichever is the greater of—

(a) the rate specified in section 17 of the Judgments Act 1838 on the day on which the relevant order was made, and

(b) the rate applicable to that debt apart from the bankruptcy or winding up.".

[22 Section 331: Final account

Section 331 is modified so as to read as follows:—

"331 (1) Subject as follows in this section and the next, this section applies where—

(a) it appears to the trustee of the estates of the members and of the partnership that the administration of any member's estate or the winding up of the partnership business and administration of the partnership property is for practical purposes complete, and

(b) the trustee is not the official receiver.

(2) The trustee must—

(a) give the creditors of the members and of the partnership (other than opted-out creditors) notice that it appears to the trustee that the administration of the member's estate or the winding up of the partnership business and administration of the partnership property is for practical purposes complete,

(b) make up an account of the administration or winding up, showing how it has been conducted and the property disposed of,

(c) send a copy of the account to the creditors of the members and of the partnership (other than opted-out creditors), and

(d) give the creditors of the members and of the partnership (other than opted-out creditors) a notice explaining the effect of section 299(3)(d) and how they may object to the trustee's release.

(3) The trustee must during the relevant period send to the court and, in the case of a corporate member, send to the registrar of companies—

(a) a copy of the account, and

(b) a statement of whether any of the creditors of the members and of the partnership objected to the trustee's release.

(4) The relevant period is the period of 7 days beginning with the day after the last day of the period prescribed by the rules as the period within which the creditors may object to the trustee's release."].

23 Section 387: The "relevant date"

Section 387 is modified so as to read as follows:—

"387 Where an order has been made in respect of an insolvent partnership by virtue of article 11 of the Insolvent Partnerships Order 1994, references in Schedule 6 to this Act to the relevant date (being the date which determines the existence and amount of a preferential debt) are to the date on which the said order was made.".

NOTES

Para 1: figure "272" (omitted in the first place) revoked, in relation to England and Wales, by the Insolvency (Miscellaneous Amendments) Regulations 2017, SI 2017/1119, reg 2, Sch 2, paras 1, 7(1), (2), as from 8 December 2017, subject to transitional and savings provisions in Sch 2, para 10 thereto as noted to art 2 at **[10.2]**; figure omitted in second place revoked by the Insolvent Partnerships (Amendment) Order 2005, SI 2005/1516, art 10(1), (2).

Para 2: in s 264 of the Act (as set out above) words in square brackets in sub-s (2) substituted, and the whole of sub-s (2A) inserted, by the Financial Services and Markets Act 2000 (Consequential Amendments and Repeals) Order 2001, SI 2001/3649, art 469.

Para 3: in s 265 of the Act (as set out above) sub-ss (3)–(5) inserted by the Deregulation Act 2015 and Small Business, Enterprise and Employment Act 2015 (Consequential Amendments) (Savings) Regulations 2017, SI 2017/540, reg 3, Sch 2, paras 2, 9(1), (2).

Paras 5, 11, 12, 14: revoked by SI 2017/540, reg 3, Sch 2, paras 2, 9(1), (3), (6), (8).

Para 6: revoked by SI 2005/1516, art 10(1), (3).

Para 7: in s 283 of the Act (as set out above) words in square brackets substituted by SI 2017/540, reg 3, Sch 2, paras 2, 9(1), (4).

Para 7A: inserted by SI 2005/1516, art 10(1), (4); words in square brackets in s 283A of the Act (as set out above) inserted by the Civil Partnership Act 2004 (Amendments to Subordinate Legislation) Order 2005, SI 2005/2114, art 2(18), Sch 18, Pt 1, para 2(1), (4).

Para 10: in s 292 of the Act (as set out above) sub-s (1) substituted and sub-s (5) revoked by SI 2017/540, reg 3, Sch 2, paras 2, 9(1), (5).

Para 13: in s 296 of the Act (as set out above) sub-s (6) substituted by SI 2017/540, reg 3, Sch 2, paras 2, 9(1), (7).

Para 15: s 298 of the Act (as set out above) substituted in relation to England and Wales, by the Insolvency (Miscellaneous Amendments) Regulations 2017, SI 2017/1119, reg 2, Sch 2, paras 1, 7(1), (3), as from 8 December 2017, subject to transitional and savings provisions in Sch 2, para 10 thereto as noted to art 2 at **[10.2]**, and previously read as follows (with sub-s (6) substituted by SI 2017/540, reg 3, Sch 2, paras 2, 9(1), (9)):

> **"298** (1) Subject as follows, the trustee of the estates of the members and of the partnership may be removed from office only by an order of the court.
>
> (2) If the trustee was appointed by the Secretary of State, he may be removed by a direction of the Secretary of State.
>
> (3) The trustee (not being the official receiver) shall vacate office if he ceases to be a person who is for the time being qualified to act as an insolvency practitioner in relation to any member or to the partnership.
>
> (4) The trustee may, with the leave of the court (or, if appointed by the Secretary of State, with the leave of the court or the Secretary of State), resign his office by giving notice of his resignation to the court.
>
> (5) Subject to subsections (6) and (7) below, any removal from or vacation of office under this section relates to all offices held in the proceedings by virtue of article 11 of the Insolvent Partnerships Order 1994.
>
> [(6) A trustee who has produced an account of the winding up or administration under section 331 must vacate office immediately upon complying with the requirements of section 331(3).]
>
> (7) The trustee shall vacate office as trustee of a member if the order made by virtue of article 11 of the Insolvent Partnerships Order 1994 in relation to that member is annulled.".

Para 16: in s 299 of the Act (as set out above) words in square brackets substituted by SI 2017/540, reg 3, Sch 2, paras 2, 9(1), (10).

Para 17: in s 300 of the Act (as set out above) words in square brackets substituted by SI 2017/540, reg 3, Sch 2, paras 2, 9(1), (11).

Para 18: in s 301 of the Act (as set out above) words in square brackets substituted by SI 2017/540, reg 3, Sch 2, paras 2, 9(1), (12).

Para 20A: inserted by SI 2005/1516, art 10(1), (5); words in square brackets in s 313A of the Act (as set out above) inserted by SI 2005/2114, art 2(18), Sch 18, Pt 1, para 2(1), (5).

Para 21: in s 328A of the Act (as set out above) sub-para (2)(a), (aa) substituted, for sub-para (2)(a) as originally enacted, and in sub-paras (4)–(6) words in square brackets substituted, in s 328B of the Act (as set out above) sub-para (1)(a), (aa) substituted, for sub-para (1)(a) as originally enacted, and in sub-para (2) words in square brackets substituted, by the Banks and Building Societies (Depositor Preference and Priorities) Order 2014, SI 2014/3486, art 15;

in s 328C of the Act (as set out above) words in square brackets in sub-s (8) substituted for original words "Insolvency Rules 1986" by the Insolvency (Miscellaneous Amendments) Regulations 2017, SI 2017/1119, reg 2, Sch 2, paras 1, 7(1), (4), as from 8 December 2017, subject to transitional and savings provisions in Sch 2, para 10 thereto as noted to art 2 at **[10.2]**.

Para 22: substituted by SI 2017/540, reg 3, Sch 2, paras 2, 9(1), (13).

[SCHEDULE 7A

Article 11A

Decisions of Creditors of the Partnership and of the Members of the Partnership

[10.29]

1 Sections 246ZE, 246ZF, 379ZA and 379ZB of the Act are set out as modified in this Schedule.

2 Sections 246ZE and 246ZF are modified so as to read as follows—

> **"246ZE Creditors' decisions: general**
>
> (1) This section applies where, for the purposes of this Group of Parts, a person ("P") seeks a decision about any matter from the creditors of the partnership and the creditors of any insolvent members.
>
> (2) The decision may be made by any qualifying decision procedure P thinks fit, except that it may not be made by a meeting of the creditors of the partnership and the creditors of any insolvent members unless subsection (3) applies.
>
> (3) This subsection applies if at least the minimum number of creditors make a request to P in writing that the decision be made by a meeting.
>
> (4) If subsection (3) applies P must summon a meeting of the creditors of the partnership and the creditors of any insolvent members.
>
> (5) Subsection (2) is subject to any provision of this Act, the rules or any other legislation, or any order of the court—
>
> (a) requiring a decision to be made, or prohibiting a decision from being made, by a particular qualifying decision procedure (other than a meeting);
>
> (b) permitting or requiring a decision to be made by a meeting.
>
> (6) Section 246ZF provides that in certain cases the deemed consent procedure may be used instead of a qualifying decision procedure.
>
> (7) For the purposes of subsection (3) the "minimum number" of creditors is any of the following—
>
> (a) 10% in value of the creditors;
>
> (b) 10% in number of the creditors;
>
> (c) 10 creditors.
>
> (8) The references in subsection (7) to creditors are to creditors of any class, even where a decision is sought only from creditors of a particular class.
>
> (9) In this section references to a meeting are to a meeting where the creditors are invited to be present together at the same place (whether or not it is possible to attend the meeting without being present at that place).
>
> (10) Except as provided by subsection (8), references in this section to creditors include creditors

of a particular class.

(11) In this Group of Parts "qualifying decision procedure" means a procedure prescribed or authorised under paragraph 8A of Schedule 8.

246ZF Deemed consent procedure

(1) The deemed consent procedure may be used instead of a qualifying decision procedure where the creditors of the partnership and the creditors of any insolvent members are to make a decision about any matter, unless—

(a) a decision about the matter is required by virtue of this Act, the rules, or any other legislation to be made by a qualifying decision procedure, or

(b) the court orders that a decision about the matter is to be made by a qualifying decision procedure.

(2) If the rules provide for the creditors of the partnership and the creditors of any insolvent members to make a decision about the remuneration of any person, they must provide that the decision is to be made by a qualifying decision procedure.

(3) The deemed consent procedure is that the relevant creditors (other than opted-out creditors) are given notice of—

(a) the matter about which they are to make a decision,

(b) the decision that the person giving the notice proposes should be made (the "proposed decision"),

(c) the effect of subsections (4) and (5), and

(d) the procedure for objecting to the proposed decision.

(4) If less than the appropriate number of relevant creditors object to the proposed decision in accordance with the procedure set out in the notice, the creditors are to be treated as having made the proposed decision.

(5) Otherwise—

(a) the creditors are to be treated as not having made a decision about the matter in question, and

(b) if a decision about that matter is again sought from the creditors it must be sought using a qualifying decision procedure.

(6) For the purposes of subsection (4) the "appropriate number" of relevant creditors or is 10% in value of those creditors.

(7) "Relevant creditors" means the creditors who, if the decision were to be made by a qualifying decision procedure, would be entitled to vote in the procedure.

(8) In this section references to creditors include creditors of a particular class.".

3 Sections 379ZA and 379ZB are modified so as to read as follows—

"379ZA Creditors' decisions: general

(1) This section applies where, for the purposes of this Group of Parts, a person ("P") seeks a decision from the creditors of the partnership and the creditors of any insolvent members about any matter.

(2) The decision may be made by any creditors' decision procedure P thinks fit, except that it may not be made by a meeting of the creditors of the partnership and the creditors of any insolvent members unless subsection (3) applies.

(3) This subsection applies if at least the minimum number of creditors request in writing that the decision be made by a creditors' meeting.

(4) If subsection (3) applies, P must summon a meeting of the creditors of the partnership and the creditors of any insolvent member.

(5) Subsection (2) is subject to any provision of this Act, the rules or any other legislation, or any order of the court—

(a) requiring a decision to be made, or prohibiting a decision from being made, by a particular creditors' decision procedure (other than a meeting);

(b) permitting or requiring a decision to be made by a meeting.

(6) Section 379ZB provides that in certain cases the deemed consent procedure may be used instead of a creditors' decision procedure.

(7) For the purposes of subsection (3) the "minimum number" of creditors is any of the following—

(a) 10% in value of the creditors;

(b) 10% in number of the creditors;

(c) 10 creditors.

(8) The references in subsection (7) to creditors are to creditors of any class, even where a decision is sought only from creditors of a particular class.

(9) In this section references to a meeting are to a meeting where the creditors are invited to be present together at the same place (whether or not it is possible to attend the meeting without being present at that place).

(10) Except as provided by subsection (8), references in this section to creditors include creditors of a particular class.

(11) In this Group of Parts "creditors' decision procedure" means a procedure prescribed or authorised under paragraph 11A of Schedule 9.

379ZB Deemed consent procedure

(1) The deemed consent procedure may be used instead of a creditors' decision procedure where the creditors of the partnership and the creditors of any insolvent members are to make a decision about any matter, unless—

(a) a decision about the matter is required by virtue of this Act, the rules or any other legislation to be made by a creditors' decision procedure, or

(b) the court orders that a decision about the matter is to be made by a creditors' decision procedure.

(2) If the rules provide for the creditors of the partnership and the creditors of any insolvent members to make a decision about the remuneration of any person, they must provide that the decision is to be made by a creditors' decision procedure.

(3) The deemed consent procedure is that the relevant creditors (other than opted-out creditors) are given notice of—

(a) the matter about which the creditors are to make a decision,

(b) the decision the person giving the notice proposes should be made (the "proposed decision"),

(c) the effect of subsections (4) and (5), and

(d) the procedure for objecting to the proposed decision.

(4) If less than the appropriate number of relevant creditors object to the proposed decision in accordance with the procedure set out in the notice, the creditors are to be treated as having made the proposed decision.

(5) Otherwise—

(a) the creditors are to be treated as not having made a decision about the matter in question, and

(b) if a decision about that matter is again sought from the creditors, it must be sought using a creditors' decision procedure.

(6) For the purposes of subsection (4) the "appropriate number" of relevant creditors is 10% in value of those creditors.

(7) "Relevant creditors" means the creditors who, if the decision were to be made by a creditors' decision procedure, would be entitled to vote in the procedure.

(8) In this section references to creditors include creditors of a particular class.

(9) The rules may make further provision about the deemed consent procedure.".]

NOTES

Commencement: 6 April 2017.

Inserted by the Deregulation Act 2015 and Small Business, Enterprise and Employment Act 2015 (Consequential Amendments) (Savings) Regulations 2017, SI 2017/540, reg 3, Sch 2, paras 2, 10.

SCHEDULE 8
MODIFIED PROVISIONS OF COMPANY DIRECTORS DISQUALIFICATION ACT 1986 FOR THE PURPOSES OF ARTICLE 16

Article 16

[10.30]

The following provisions of the Company Directors Disqualification Act 1986 are modified so as to read as follows:—

[5A Section 5A: Disqualification for certain convictions abroad

(1) If it appears to the Secretary of State that it is expedient in the public interest that a disqualification order under this section should be made against a person, the Secretary of State may apply to the court for such an order.

(2) The court may, on an application under subsection (1), make a disqualification order against a person who has been convicted of a relevant foreign offence.

(3) A "relevant foreign offence" is an offence committed outside Great Britain in connection with the promotion, formation, management or liquidation of a partnership (or any similar procedure) which corresponds to an indictable offence under the law of England and Wales.

(4) Where it appears to the Secretary of State that, in the case of a person who has offered to give a disqualification undertaking—

(a) the person has been convicted of a relevant foreign offence; and

(b) it is expedient in the public interest that the Secretary of State should accept the undertaking (instead of applying, or proceeding with an application, for a disqualification order),

the Secretary of State may accept the undertaking.

(5) In this section—

"partnership" includes an overseas partnership;

"the court" means the High Court.

(6) The maximum period of disqualification under an order under this section is 15 years.]

[6 Section 6: Duty of court to disqualify unfit officers of certain partnerships

(1) The court shall make a disqualification order against a person in any case where, on an application under this section, it is satisfied—

(a) that he is or has been an officer of a partnership which has at any time become insolvent (whether while he was an officer or subsequently); and

(b) that his conduct as an officer of that partnership (either taken alone or taken together with his conduct as an officer of one or more other partnerships or overseas partnerships, or as a director of one or more companies or overseas companies) makes him unfit to be concerned in the management of a company.

(1A) In this section references to a person's conduct as an officer of any partnership or overseas partnership, or as a director of any company or overseas company include, where that partnership or overseas partnership, or company or overseas company, has become insolvent, references to that person's conduct in relation to any matter connected with or arising out of the insolvency.

(2) For the purposes of this section—

(a) a partnership becomes insolvent if—

(i) the court makes an order for it to be wound up as an unregistered company at a time when its assets are insufficient for the payment of its debts and other liabilities and the expenses of the winding up; or

(ii) the partnership enters administration; and

(b) a company becomes insolvent if—

(i) the company goes into liquidation at a time when its assets are insufficient for the payment of its debts and other liabilities and the expenses of the winding up;

(ii) the company enters administration; or

(iii) an administrative receiver of the company is appointed.

(2A) For the purposes of this section, an overseas company or partnership becomes insolvent if the company or partnership enters into insolvency proceedings of any description (including interim proceedings) in any jurisdiction.

(3) In this section and section 7(2), "the court" means—

(a) where the partnership in question is being or has been wound up as an unregistered company by the court, that court;

(b) where paragraph (a) does not apply but an administrator has at any time been appointed in relation to the partnership in question, any court which has jurisdiction to wind it up.

(3A) Section 117 of the Insolvency Act 1986 (High Court and county court jurisdiction), as modified and set out in Schedule 5 to the 1994 Order, shall apply for the purposes of subsection (3) as if in a case within paragraph (b) of that subsection the references to the presentation of the petition for winding up in sections 117(3) and 117(4) of the Insolvency Act 1986, as modified and set out in that Schedule, were references to the making of the administration order.

(3B) Nothing in subsection (3) invalidates any proceedings by reason of their being taken in the wrong court; and proceedings—

(a) for or in connection with a disqualification order under this section; or

(b) in connection with a disqualification undertaking accepted under section 7,

may be retained in the court in which the proceedings were commenced, although it may not be the court in which they ought to have been commenced.

(3C) In this section and section 7, "director" includes a shadow director.

(4) Under this section the minimum period of disqualification is 2 years, and the maximum period is 15 years.]

[7 Section 7: Disqualification order or undertaking; applications and acceptance of undertakings

(1) If it appears to the Secretary of State that it is expedient in the public interest that a disqualification order under section 6 should be made against any person, an application for the making of such an order against that person may be made—

(a) by the Secretary of State; or

(b) if the Secretary of State so directs in the case of a person who is or has been an officer of a partnership which is being or has been wound up by the court as an unregistered company, by the official receiver.

(2) Except with the leave of the court, an application for the making under that section of a disqualification order against any person shall not be made after the end of the period of 3 years beginning with the day on which the partnership of which that person is or has been an officer became insolvent.

(2A) If it appears to the Secretary of State that the conditions mentioned in section 6(1) are satisfied as respects any person who has offered to give him a disqualification undertaking, he may accept the undertaking if it appears to him that it is expedient in the public interest that he should do so (instead of applying, or proceeding with an application, for a disqualification order).

(4) The Secretary of State or the official receiver may require any person—

(a) to furnish him with such information with respect to that person's or another person's conduct as an officer of a partnership, or as a director of a company which has at any time become insolvent (whether while the person was an officer or director or subsequently); and

(b) to produce and permit inspection of such books, papers and other records as are considered by the Secretary of State or (as the case may be) the official receiver to be relevant to that person's or another person's conduct as such an officer or director,

as the Secretary of State or the official receiver may reasonably require for the purpose of determining whether to exercise, or of exercising, any function of his under this section.

(5) Subsections (1A) and (2) of section 6 apply for the purposes of this section as they apply for the purposes of that section.]

[7A Section 7A: Office-holder's report on conduct of officers of the partnership

(1) The office-holder in respect of a partnership which is insolvent must prepare a report (a "conduct report") about the conduct of each person who was an officer of the partnership—

(a) on the insolvency date; or

(b) at any time during the period of 3 years ending with that date.

(2) For the purposes of this section a partnership is insolvent if—

(a) the partnership is in liquidation and at the time it went into liquidation its assets were insufficient for the payment of its debts and other liabilities and the expenses of the winding up; or

(b) the partnership enters administration,

and subsection (1A) of section 6 applies for the purposes of this section as it applies for the purpose of that section.

(3) A conduct report must, in relation to each person, describe any conduct of the person which may assist the Secretary of State in deciding whether to exercise the power under section 7(1) or (2A) in relation to the person.

(4) The office-holder must send the conduct report to the Secretary of State before the end of—

(a) the period of 3 months beginning with the insolvency date; or

(b) such other longer period as the Secretary of State considers appropriate in the particular circumstances.

(5) If new information comes to the attention of an office-holder, the office-holder must send that information to the Secretary of State as soon as reasonably practicable.

(6) "New information" is information which an office-holder considers should have been included in a conduct report prepared in relation to the partnership, or would have been so included had it been available before the report was sent.

(7) If there is more than one office-holder in respect of a partnership at any particular time, subsection (1) applies only to the first of the office-holders to be appointed.

(9) The "office-holder" in respect of a partnership which is insolvent is—

(a) in the case of a partnership being wound up by the court in England and Wales, the official receiver;

(b) in the case of a partnership being wound up otherwise, the liquidator;

(c) in the case of a partnership in administration, the administrator.

(10) The "insolvency date"—

(a) in the case of a partnership being wound up by the court, means the date on which the court makes the winding-up order (see section 125 of the Insolvency Act 1986);

(b) in the case of a partnership being wound up by way of a members' voluntary winding up, means the date on which the liquidator forms the opinion that the partnership will be unable to pay its debts in full (together with interest at the official rate) within the period stated in the declaration of solvency under section 89 of the Insolvency Act 1986;

(c) in the case of a partnership being wound up by way of a creditors' voluntary winding up where no such declaration under section 89 of that Act has been made, means the date of the passing of the resolution for voluntary winding up;

(d) in the case of a company which has entered administration, means the date the company did so.

(12) In this section "court" has the same meaning as in section 6.]

[8 Section 8: Disqualification of officer on finding of unfitness

(1) If it appears to the Secretary of State that it is expedient in the public interest that a disqualification order should be made against a person who is or has been an officer of an insolvent partnership, he may apply to the court for such an order.

(2) The court may make a disqualification order against a person where, on an application under this section, it is satisfied that his conduct in relation to the partnership (either taken alone or taken together with his conduct as an officer of one or more other partnerships or overseas partnerships, or as a director of one or more companies or overseas companies) makes him unfit to be concerned in the management of a company.

(2A) Where it appears to the Secretary of State that, in the case of a person who has offered to give him a disqualification undertaking—

(a) the conduct of the person in relation to an insolvent partnership of which the person is or has been an officer (either taken alone or taken together with his conduct as an officer of one or more other partnerships or overseas partnerships, or as a director of one or more companies or overseas companies) makes him unfit to be concerned in the management of a company; and

(b) it is expedient in the public interest that he should accept the undertaking (instead of applying, or proceeding with an application, for a disqualification order),

he may accept the undertaking.

(2B) Subsection (1A) of section 6 applies for the purposes of this section as it applies for the purposes of that section.

(3) In this section "the court" means the High Court.

(4) The maximum period of disqualification under this section is 15 years.]

[8ZA Section 8ZA: Persons instructing unfit officers

(1) The court may make a disqualification order against a person ("P") if, on an application under section 8ZB, it is satisfied—

(a) either—

(i) that a disqualification order under section 6 has been made against a person who is or has been an officer of a partnership; or

(ii) that the Secretary of State has accepted a disqualification undertaking from such a person under section 7(2A); and

(b) that P exercised the requisite amount of influence over the person.

That person is referred to in this section as "the main transgressor".

(2) For the purposes of this section, P exercised the requisite amount of influence over the main transgressor if any of the conduct—

(a) for which the main transgressor is subject to the order made under section 6; or

(b) in relation to which the undertaking was accepted from the main transgressor under section 7(2A),

was the result of the main transgressor acting in accordance with P's directions or instructions.

(3) But P does not exercise the requisite amount of influence over the main transgressor by reason only that the main transgressor acts on advice given by P in a professional capacity.

(4) Under this section the minimum period of disqualification is 2 years and the maximum period is 15 years.

(5) In this section and section 8ZB "the court" has the same meaning as in section 6; and subsection (3B) of section 6 applies in relation to proceedings mentioned in subsection (6) below as it applies in relation to proceedings mentioned in section 6(3B)(a) and (b).

(6) The proceedings are proceedings—

(a) for or in connection with a disqualification order under this section; or

(b) in connection with a disqualification undertaking accepted under section 8ZC.

8ZB Section 8ZB: Application for order under section 8ZA

(1) If it appears to the Secretary of State that it is expedient in the public interest that a disqualification order should be made against a person under section 8ZA, the Secretary of State may—

(a) make an application to the court for such an order; or

(b) in a case where an application for an order under section 6 against the main transgressor has been made by the official receiver, direct the official receiver to make such an application.

(2) Except with the leave of the court, an application for a disqualification order under section 8ZA must not be made after the end of the period of 3 years beginning with the day on which the partnership in question became insolvent (within the meaning given by section 6(2)).

(3) Subsection (4) of section 7 applies for the purposes of this section as it applies for the purposes of that section.

8ZC Section 8ZC: Disqualification undertaking instead of an order under section 8ZA

(1) If it appears to the Secretary of State that it is expedient in the public interest to do so, the Secretary of State may accept a disqualification undertaking from a person ("P") if—

(a) any of the following is the case—

(i) a disqualification order under section 6 has been made against a person who is or has been an officer of a partnership;

(ii) the Secretary of State has accepted a disqualification undertaking from such a person under section 7(2A); or

(iii) it appears to the Secretary of State that such an undertaking could be accepted from such a person (if one were offered); and

(b) it appears to the Secretary of State that P exercised the requisite amount of influence over the person.

That person is referred to in this section as "the main transgressor".

(2) For the purposes of this section, P exercised the requisite amount of influence over the main transgressor if any of the conduct—

(a) for which the main transgressor is subject to the disqualification order made under section 6;

(b) in relation to which the disqualification undertaking was accepted from the main transgressor under section 7(2A); or

(c) which led the Secretary of State to the conclusion set out in subsection (1)(a)(iii),

was the result of the main transgressor acting in accordance with P's directions or instructions.

(3) But P does not exercise the requisite amount of influence over the main transgressor by reason only that the main transgressor acts on advice given by P in a professional capacity.

(4) Subsection (4) of section 7 applies for the purposes of this section as it applies for the purposes of that section.

8ZD Section 8ZD: Order disqualifying person instructing unfit director; other cases

(1) The court may make a disqualification order against a person ("P") if, on an application under this section, it is satisfied—

(a) either—

(i) that a disqualification order under section 8 has been made against a person who is or has been an officer of a partnership; or

(ii) that the Secretary of State has accepted a disqualification undertaking from such a person under section 8(2A); and

(b) that P exercised the requisite amount of influence over the person.

That person is referred to in this section as "the main transgressor".

(2) The Secretary of State may make an application to the court for a disqualification order against P under this section if it appears to the Secretary of State that it is expedient in the public interest for such an order to be made.
(3) For the purposes of this section, P exercised the requisite amount of influence over the main transgressor if any of the conduct—
(a) for which the main transgressor is subject to the order made under section 8; or
(b) in relation to which the undertaking was accepted from the main transgressor under section 8(2A),
was the result of the main transgressor acting in accordance with P's directions or instructions.
(4) But P does not exercise the requisite amount of influence over the main transgressor by reason only that the main transgressor acts on advice given by P in a professional capacity.
(5) Under this section the maximum period of disqualification is 15 years.
(6) In this section "the court" means the High Court.

8ZE Section 8ZE: Disqualification undertaking instead of an order under section 8ZD
(1) If it appears to the Secretary of State that it is expedient in the public interest to do so, the Secretary of State may accept a disqualification undertaking from a person ("P") if—
(a) any of the following is the case—
(i) a disqualification order under section 8 has been made against a person who is or has been an officer of a partnership;
(ii) the Secretary of State has accepted a disqualification undertaking from such a person under section 8(2A); or
(iii) it appears to the Secretary of State that such an undertaking could be accepted from such a person (if one were offered); and
(b) it appears to the Secretary of State that P exercised the requisite amount of influence over the person.
That person is referred to in this section as "the main transgressor".
(2) For the purposes of this section, P exercised the requisite amount of influence over the main transgressor if any of the conduct—
(a) for which the main transgressor is subject to the disqualification order made under section 8;
(b) in relation to which the disqualification undertaking was accepted from the main transgressor under section 8(2A); or
(c) which led the Secretary of State to the conclusion set out in subsection (1)(a)(iii),
was the result of the main transgressor acting in accordance with P's directions or instructions.
(3) But P does not exercise the requisite amount of influence over the main transgressor by reason only that the main transgressor acts on advice given by P in a professional capacity.]

9 . . .

[12C Section 12C: Determining unfitness etc: matters to be taken into account
(1) This section applies where a court must determine—
(a) whether a person's conduct as an officer of a partnership (either taken alone or taken together with his conduct as an officer of one or more other partnerships or overseas partnerships, or as a director of one or more companies or overseas companies) makes the person unfit to be concerned in the management of a company;
(b) whether to exercise any discretion it has to make a disqualification order under any of sections 5A or 8;
(c) where the court has decided to make a disqualification order under any of those sections or is required to make an order under section 6, what the period of disqualification should be.
(3) This section also applies where the Secretary of State must determine—
(a) whether a person's conduct as an officer of a partnership (either taken alone or taken together with his conduct as an officer of one or more other partnerships or overseas partnerships, or as a director of one or more companies or overseas companies) makes the person unfit to be concerned in the management of a company;
(b) whether to exercise any discretion the Secretary of State has to accept a disqualification undertaking under section 5A, 7 or 8.
(4) In making any such determination in relation to a person, the court or the Secretary of State must—
(a) in every case, have regard in particular to the matters set out in paragraphs 1 to 4 of Schedule 1;
(b) in a case where the person concerned is or has been an officer of a partnership or overseas partnership, or director of a company or overseas company, also have regard in particular to the matters set out in paragraphs 5 to 7 of that Schedule.
(6) Subsection (1A) of section 6 applies for the purposes of this section as it applies for the purposes of that section.]

[13 Section 13: Criminal penalties
If a person acts in contravention of a disqualification order or disqualification undertaking he is liable—
(a) on conviction on indictment, to imprisonment for not more than 2 years or a fine or both; and

(b) on summary conviction, to imprisonment for not more than 6 months or a fine not exceeding the statutory maximum, or both.

14 Section 14: Offences by body corporate

(1) Where a body corporate is guilty of an offence of acting in contravention of a disqualification order or disqualification undertaking and it is proved that the offence occurred with the consent or connivance of, or was attributable to any neglect on the part of any director, manager, secretary or other similar officer of the body corporate, or any person who was purporting to act in any such capacity he, as well as the body corporate, is guilty of the offence and liable to be proceeded against and punished accordingly.

(2) Where the affairs of a body corporate are managed by its members, subsection (1) applies in relation to the acts and defaults of a member in connection with his functions of management as if he were a director of the body corporate.

15 Section 15: Personal liability for company's debts where person acts while disqualified

(1) A person is personally responsible for all the relevant debts of a company if at any time—

(a) in contravention of a disqualification order or disqualification undertaking he is involved in the management of the company, or

(b) as a person who is involved in the management of the company, he acts or is willing to act on instructions given without the leave of the court by a person whom he knows at that time to be the subject of a disqualification order or disqualification undertaking or a disqualification order under Part II of the Companies (Northern Ireland) Order 1989 or to be an undischarged bankrupt.

(2) Where a person is personally responsible under this section for the relevant debts of a company, he is jointly and severally liable in respect of those debts with the company and any other person who, whether under this section or otherwise, is so liable.

(3) For the purposes of this section the relevant debts of a company are—

(a) in relation to a person who is personally responsible under paragraph (a) of subsection (1), such debts and other liabilities of the company as are incurred at a time when that person was involved in the management of the company, and

(b) in relation to a person who is personally responsible under paragraph (b) of that subsection, such debts and other liabilities of the company as are incurred at a time when that person was acting or was willing to act on instructions given as mentioned in that paragraph.

(4) For the purposes of this section, a person is involved in the management of a company if he is a director of the company or if he is concerned, whether directly or indirectly, or takes part, in the management of the company.

(5) For the purposes of this section a person who, as a person involved in the management of a company, has at any time acted on instructions given without the leave of the court by a person whom he knew at that time to be the subject of a disqualification order or disqualification undertaking or a disqualification order under Part II of the Companies (Northern Ireland) Order 1989 or to be an undischarged bankrupt is presumed, unless the contrary is shown, to have been willing at any time thereafter to act on any instructions given by that person.

[15A Section 15A: Compensation orders and undertakings

(1) The court may make a compensation order against a person on the application of the Secretary of State if it is satisfied that the conditions mentioned in subsection (3) are met.

(2) If it appears to the Secretary of State that the conditions mentioned in subsection (3) are met in respect of a person who has offered to give the Secretary of State a compensation undertaking, the Secretary of State may accept the undertaking instead of applying, or proceeding with an application, for a compensation order.

(3) The conditions are that—

(a) the person is subject to a disqualification order or disqualification undertaking under this Act; and

(b) conduct for which the person is subject to the order or undertaking has caused loss to one or more creditors of an insolvent partnership of which the person has at any time been an officer.

(4) An "insolvent partnership" is a partnership that is or has been insolvent and a partnership becomes insolvent if the partnership goes into liquidation at a time when its assets are insufficient for the payment of its debts and other liabilities and the expenses of the winding up.

(5) The Secretary of State may apply for a compensation order at any time before the end of the period of two years beginning with the date on which the disqualification order referred to in paragraph (a) of subsection (3) was made, or the disqualification undertaking referred to in that paragraph was accepted.

(6) In the case of a person subject to a disqualification order under section 8ZA or 8ZD, or a disqualification undertaking under section 8ZC or 8ZE, the reference in subsection (3)(b) to conduct is a reference to the conduct of the main transgressor in relation to which the person has exercised the requisite amount of influence.

(7) In this section and sections 15B and 15C "the court" means—

(a) in a case where a disqualification order has been made, the court that made the order;

(b) in any other case, the High Court.

15B Section 15B: Amounts payable under compensation orders and undertakings

(1) A compensation order is an order requiring the person against whom it is made to pay an amount specified in the order—

(a) to the Secretary of State for the benefit of—

(i) a creditor or creditors specified in the order;

(ii) a class or classes of creditor so specified;

(b) as a contribution to the assets of a partnership so specified.

(2) A compensation undertaking is an undertaking to pay an amount specified in the undertaking—

(a) to the Secretary of State for the benefit of—

(i) a creditor or creditors specified in the undertaking;

(ii) a class or classes of creditor so specified;

(b) as a contribution to the assets of a partnership so specified.

(3) When specifying an amount the court (in the case of an order) and the Secretary of State (in the case of an undertaking) must in particular have regard to—

(a) the amount of the loss caused;

(b) the nature of the conduct mentioned in section 15A(3)(b);

(c) whether the person has made any other financial contribution in recompense for the conduct (whether under a statutory provision or otherwise).

(4) An amount payable by virtue of subsection (2) under a compensation undertaking is recoverable as if payable under a court order.

(5) An amount payable under a compensation order or compensation undertaking is provable as a bankruptcy debt.]

[17 Section 17: Application for leave under an order or undertaking

(1) Where a person is subject to a disqualification order made by a court having jurisdiction to wind up partnerships, any application for leave for the purposes of section 1(1)(a) shall be made to that court.

(3) Where a person is subject to a disqualification undertaking accepted at any time under section 5A, 7 or 8, any application for leave for the purposes of section 1A(1)(a) shall be made to any court to which, if the Secretary of State had applied for a disqualification order under the section in question at that time, his application could have been made.

(3ZA) Where a person is subject to a disqualification undertaking accepted at any time under section 8ZC, any application for leave for the purposes of section 1A(1)(a) must be made to any court to which, if the Secretary of State had applied for a disqualification order under section 8ZA at that time, that application could have been made.

(3ZB) Where a person is subject to a disqualification undertaking accepted at any time under section 8ZE, any application for leave for the purposes of section 1A(1)(a) must be made to the High Court.

(3A) Where a person is subject to a disqualification undertaking accepted at any time under section 9B any application for leave for the purposes of section 9B(4) must be made to the High Court.

(4) But where a person is subject to two or more disqualification orders or undertakings (or to one or more disqualification orders and to one or more disqualification undertakings), any application for leave for the purposes of sections 1(1)(a) or 1A(1)(a) shall be made to any court to which any such application relating to the latest order to be made, or undertaking to be accepted, could be made.

(5) On the hearing of an application for leave for the purposes of section 1(1)(a) or 1A(1)(a), the Secretary of State shall appear and call the attention of the court to any matters which seem to him to be relevant, and may himself give evidence or call witnesses.]

[SCHEDULE 1

DETERMINING UNFITNESS ETC: MATTERS TO BE TAKEN INTO ACCOUNT.

Section 12C

Matters to be taken into account in all cases

1 The extent to which the person was responsible for the causes of any material contravention by a partnership or overseas partnership, or a company or overseas company, of any applicable legislative or other requirement.

2 Where applicable, the extent to which the person was responsible for the causes of a partnership or overseas partnership, or company or overseas company, becoming insolvent.

3 The frequency of conduct of the person which falls within paragraph 1 or 2.

4 The nature and extent of any loss or harm caused, or any potential loss or harm which could have been caused, by the person's conduct as an officer of any partnership or overseas partnership or as a director of any company or overseas company.

Additional matters to be taken into account where person is or has been an officer of a partnership or a director

5 Any misfeasance or breach of any fiduciary or other duty by the person in relation to a partnership or overseas partnership or a company or overseas company.

6 Any material breach of any legislative or other obligation of the person which applies as a result of being—

(a) an officer of a partnership or overseas partnership; or
(b) a director of a company or overseas company.

7 The frequency of conduct of the person which falls within paragraph 5 or 6.

Interpretation

8 Subsections (1A) to (2A) of section 6 apply for the purposes of this Schedule as they apply for the purposes of that section.

9 In this Schedule "director" includes a shadow director.]

NOTES

Sections 5A, 7A, 8ZA–8ZE, 12C, 15A, 15B of the Act (as set out above) inserted in relation to England and Wales, by the Insolvency (Miscellaneous Amendments) Regulations 2017, SI 2017/1119, reg 2, Sch 2, paras 1, 8(1), (2), (4), (6), (8), (9), as from 8 December 2017, subject to transitional and savings provisions in Sch 2, para 10 thereto as noted to art 2 at **[10.2]**.

Sections 6, 7, 8 of the Act (as set out above) substituted by SI 2017/1119, reg 2, Sch 2, paras 1, 8(1), (3), (5), as from 8 December 2017, subject to transitional and savings provisions in Sch 2, para 10 thereto as noted to art 2 at **[10.2]**.

Section 9 of the Act (as set out above) revoked by SI 2017/1119, reg 2, Sch 2, paras 1, 8(1), (7), as from 8 December 2017, subject to transitional and savings provisions in Sch 2, para 10 thereto as noted to art 2 at **[10.2]**.

Sections 13–15 of the Act (as set out above) inserted by SI 2001/767, art 3(1), (6).

Section 17 of the Act (as set out above) substituted by SI 2017/1119, reg 2, Sch 2, paras 1, 8(1), (10), as from 8 December 2017, subject to transitional and savings provisions in Sch 2, para 10 thereto as noted to art 2 at **[10.2]**.

Sch 1 to the Act (as set out above) substituted by SI 2017/1119, reg 2, Sch 2, paras 1, 8(1), (11), as from 8 December 2017, subject to transitional and savings provisions in Sch 2, para 10 thereto as noted to art 2 at **[10.2]**.

Prior to amendment by SI 2017/1119 as noted above, ss 6, 7, 8, 9, 17 and Sch 1 (and the notes relating to those provisions) read as follows:

"6 Section 6: Duty of court to disqualify unfit officers of insolvent partnerships

(1) The court shall make a disqualification order against a person in any case where, on an application under this section, it is satisfied—

(a) that he is or has been an officer of a partnership which has at any time become insolvent (whether while he was an officer or subsequently), and
(b) that his conduct as an officer of that partnership (either taken alone or taken together with his conduct as an officer of any other partnership or partnerships, or as a director of any company or companies) makes him unfit to be concerned in the management of a company.

(2) For the purposes of this section and the next—

(a) a partnership becomes insolvent if—
  (i) the court makes an order for it to be wound up as an unregistered company at a time when its assets are insufficient for the payment of its debts and other liabilities and the expenses of the winding up; or
  (ii) [the partnership enters administration]; and
(b) a company becomes insolvent if—
  (i) the company goes into liquidation at a time when its assets are insufficient for the payment of its debts and other liabilities and the expenses of the winding up,
  (ii) [the company enters administration], or
  (iii) an administrative receiver of the company is appointed.

(3) For the purposes of this section and the next, references to a person's conduct as an officer of any partnership or partnerships, or as a director of any company or companies, include, where the partnership or company concerned or any of the partnerships or companies concerned has become insolvent, that person's conduct in relation to any matter connected with or arising out of the insolvency of that partnership or company.

[(4) In this section and section 7(2), "the court" means—

(a) where the partnership in question is being or has been wound up as an unregistered company by the court, that court,
(b) where the preceding paragraph does not apply but [an administrator has at any time been appointed] in relation to the partnership in question, any court which has jurisdiction to wind it up.

(4A) Section 117 of the Insolvency Act 1986 (High Court and county court jurisdiction), as modified and set out in Schedule 5 to the 1994 Order, shall apply for the purposes of subsection (4) as if in a case within paragraph (b) of that subsection the references to the presentation of the petition for winding up in sections 117(3) and 117(4) of the Insolvency Act 1986, as modified and set out in that Schedule, were references to the making of the administration order.

(4B) Nothing in subsection (4) invalidates any proceedings by reason of their being taken in the wrong court; and proceedings—

(a) for or in connection with a disqualification order under this section, or
(b) in connection with a disqualification undertaking accepted under section 7,

may be retained in the court in which the proceedings were commenced, although it may not be the court in which they ought to have been commenced.

(4C) In this section and section 7, "director" includes a shadow director.]

(5) Under this section the minimum period of disqualification is 2 years, and the maximum period is 15 years.

[7 Section 7: Disqualification order or undertaking; and reporting provisions]

(1) If it appears to the Secretary of State that it is expedient in the public interest that a disqualification order under section 6 should be made against any person, an application for the making of such an order against that person may be made—

(a) by the Secretary of State, or
(b) if the Secretary of State so directs in the case of a person who is or has been an officer of a partnership which is being [or has been] wound up by the court as an unregistered company, by the official receiver.

(2) Except with the leave of the court, an application for the making under that section of a disqualification order against any person shall not be made after the end of the period of 2 years beginning with the day on which the partnership of which that person is or has been an officer became insolvent.

[(2A) If it appears to the Secretary of State that the conditions mentioned in section 6(1) are satisfied as respects any person who has offered to give him a disqualification undertaking, he may accept the undertaking if it appears to him that it is expedient in the public interest that he should do so (instead of applying, or proceeding with an application, for a disqualification order).]

(3) If it appears to the office-holder responsible under this section, that is to say—

(a) in the case of a partnership which is being wound up by the court as an unregistered company, the official receiver, or

(b) in the case of a partnership [which is in administration], the administrator,

that the conditions mentioned in section 6(1) are satisfied as respects a person who is or has been an officer of that partnership, the office-holder shall forthwith report the matter to the Secretary of State.

(4) The Secretary of State or the official receiver may require any of the persons mentioned in subsection (5) below—

(a) to furnish him with such information with respect to any person's conduct as an officer of a partnership or as a director of a company, and

(b) to produce and permit inspection of such books, papers and other records relevant to that person's conduct as such an officer or director,

as the Secretary of State or the official receiver may reasonably require for the purpose of determining whether to exercise, or of exercising, any function of his under this section.

(5) The persons referred to in subsection (4) are—

(a) the liquidator or administrator, or former liquidator or administrator of the partnership,

(b) the liquidator, administrator or administrative receiver, or former liquidator, administrator or administrative receiver, of the company.

8 Section 8: Disqualification after investigation

[(1) If it appears to the Secretary of State from—

(a) a report made by an inspector or person appointed to conduct an investigation under a provision mentioned in subsection (1A), or

(b) information or documents obtained under a provision mentioned in subsection (1B),

that it is expedient in the public interest that a disqualification order should be made against any person who is or has been an officer of an insolvent partnership, he may apply to the court for such an order to be made against that person.

(1A) The provisions are—

(a) section 437 of the Companies Act,

(b) section 167, 168, 169(1)(b) or 284 of the Financial Services and Markets Act 2000, or

(c) regulations made as a result of section 262(2)(k) of that Act.

(1B) The provisions are—

(a) section 447 or 448 of the Companies Act,

(b) section 2 of the Criminal Justice Act 1987,

(c) section 52 of the Criminal Justice (Scotland) Act 1987,

(d) section 83 of the Companies Act 1989, or

(e) section 171 or 173 of the Financial Services and Markets Act 2000.]

(2) The court may make a disqualification order against a person where, on an application under this section, it is satisfied that his conduct in relation to the partnership makes him unfit to be concerned in the management of a company.

[(2A) Where it appears to the Secretary of State from such report, information or documents that, in the case of a person who has offered to give him a disqualification undertaking—

(a) the conduct of the person in relation to an insolvent partnership of which the person is or has been an officer makes him unfit to be concerned in the management of a company, and

(b) it is expedient in the public interest that he should accept the undertaking (instead of applying, or proceeding with an application, for a disqualification order),

he may accept the undertaking.]

(3) In this section "the court" means the High Court.

(4) The maximum period of disqualification under this section is 15 years.

9 Section 9: Matters for determining unfitness of officers of partnerships

(1) This section applies where it falls to a court to determine whether a person's conduct as an officer of a partnership (either taken alone or taken together with his conduct as an officer of any other partnership or partnerships or as a director . . . of any company or companies) makes him unfit to be concerned in the management of a company.

[(1A) In determining whether he may accept a disqualification undertaking from any person the Secretary of State shall, as respects the person's conduct as an officer of any partnership or a director of any company concerned, have regard in particular—

(a) to the matters mentioned in Part I of Schedule 1 to this Act, and

(b) where the partnership or the company (as the case may be) has become insolvent, to the matters mentioned in Part II of that Schedule;

and references in that Schedule to the officer and the partnership or, as the case may be, to the director and the company are to be read accordingly.]

(2) The court shall, as respects that person's conduct as an officer of that partnership or each of those partnerships or as a director of that company or each of those companies, have regard in particular—

(a) to the matters mentioned in Part I of Schedule 1 to this Act, and

(b) where the partnership or company (as the case may be) has become insolvent, to the matters mentioned in Part II of that Schedule;

and references in that Schedule to the officer and the partnership or, as the case may be, to the director and the company, are to be read accordingly [and in this section and that Schedule "director" includes a shadow director].

(3) Subsections (2) and (3) of section 6 apply for the purposes of this section and Schedule 1 as they apply for the purposes of sections 6 and 7.

(4) Subject to the next subsection, any reference in Schedule 1 to an enactment contained in the Companies Act or the Insolvency Act includes, in relation to any time before the coming into force of that enactment, the corresponding enactment

in force at that time.
(5) The Secretary of State may by order modify any of the provisions of Schedule 1; and such an order may contain such transitional provisions as may appear to the Secretary of State necessary or expedient.
(6) The power to make orders under this section is exercisable by statutory instrument subject to annulment in pursuance of a resolution of either House of Parliament.

17 Section 17: Application for leave under an order or undertaking
(1) Where a person is subject to a disqualification order made by a court having jurisdiction to wind up partnerships, any application for leave for the purposes of section 1(1)(a) shall be made to that court.
(2) Where a person is subject to a disqualification undertaking accepted at any time under section 7 or 8, any application for leave for the purposes of section 1A(1)(a) shall be made to any court to which, if the Secretary of State had applied for a disqualification order under the section in question at that time, his application could have been made.
(3) But where a person is subject to two or more disqualification orders or undertakings (or to one or more disqualification orders and to one or more disqualification undertakings), any application for leave for the purposes of section 1(1)(a) or 1A(1)(a) shall be made to any court to which any such application relating to the latest order to be made, or undertaking to be accepted, could be made.
(4) On the hearing of an application for leave for the purposes of section 1(1)(a) or 1A(1)(a), the Secretary of State shall appear and call the attention of the court to any matters which seem to him to be relevant, and may himself give evidence or call witnesses.]

SCHEDULE 1
MATTERS FOR DETERMINING UNFITNESS OF OFFICERS OF PARTNERSHIPS

Section 9

PART I
MATTERS APPLICABLE IN ALL CASES

1. Any misfeasance or breach of any fiduciary or other duty by the officer in relation to the partnership or, as the case may be, by the director in relation to the company.
2. Any misapplication or retention by the officer or the director of, or any conduct by the officer or the director giving rise to an obligation to account for, any money or other property of the partnership or, as the case may be, of the company.
3. The extent of the officer's or the director's responsibility for the partnership or, as the case may be, the company entering into any transaction liable to be set aside under Part XVI of the Insolvency Act (provisions against debt avoidance).
4. The extent of the director's responsibility for any failure by the company to comply with any of the following provisions of the Companies Act, namely—
(a) section 221 (companies to keep accounting records);
(b) section 222 (where and for how long records to be kept);
(c) section 288 (register of directors and secretaries);
(d) section 352 (obligation to keep and enter up register of members);
(e) section 353 (location of register of members);
(f) section 363 (duty of company to make annual returns); and
(g) sections 399 and 415 (company's duty to register charges it creates).
5. The extent of the director's responsibility for any failure by the directors of the company to comply with—
(a) section 226 or 227 of the Companies Act (duty to prepare annual accounts), or
(b) section 233 of that Act (approval and signature of accounts).
6. Any failure by the officer to comply with any obligation imposed on him by or under any of the following provisions of the Limited Partnerships Act 1907—
(a) section 8 (registration of particulars of limited partnership);
(b) section 9 (registration of changes in particulars);
(c) section 10 (advertisement of general partner becoming limited partner and of assignment of share of limited partner).

PART II
MATTERS APPLICABLE WHERE PARTNERSHIP OR COMPANY HAS BECOME INSOLVENT

7. The extent of the officer's or the director's responsibility for the causes of the partnership or (as the case may be) the company becoming insolvent.
8. The extent of the officer's or the director's responsibility for any failure by the partnership or (as the case may be) the company to supply any goods or services which have been paid for (in whole or in part).
9. The extent of the officer's or the director's responsibility for the partnership or (as the case may be) the company entering into any transaction or giving any preference, being a transaction or preference—
(a) liable to be set aside under section 127 or sections 238 to 240 of the Insolvency Act, or
(b) challengeable under section 242 or 243 of that Act or under any rule of law in Scotland.
10. . . .
11. Any failure by the director to comply with any obligation imposed on him by or under any of the following provisions of the Insolvency Act—
(a) section 47 (statement of affairs to administrative receiver);
(b) section 66 (statement of affairs in Scottish receivership);
(c) section 99 ([directors to lay statement of affairs before creditors]).
12. Any failure by the officer or the director to comply with any obligation imposed on him by or under any of the following provisions of the Insolvency Act (both as they apply in relation to companies and as they apply in relation to insolvent partnerships by virtue of the provisions of the Insolvent Partnerships Order 1994)—
(a) [paragraph 48 of Schedule B1] (statement of affairs in administration);
(b) section 131 (statement of affairs in winding up by the court);
(c) section 234 (duty of any one with property to deliver it up);
(d) section 235 (duty to co-operate with liquidator, etc).

In s 6 of the Act (as set out above) words in square brackets in sub-ss (2), (4) substituted by the Insolvent Partnerships (Amendment) Order 2005, SI 2005/1516, art 11(1), (2); sub-ss (4)–(4C) substituted, for original sub-s (4), by the Insolvent Partnerships (Amendment) Order 2001, SI 2001/767, art 3(1), (2).

In s 7 of the Act (as set out above) heading substituted, and words in square brackets in sub-s (1) and the whole of sub-s (2A) inserted, by SI 2001/767, art 3(1), (3); words in square brackets in sub-s (3) substituted by SI 2005/1516, art 11(1), (3).

In s 8 of the Act (as set out above) sub-ss (1)–(1B) substituted, for original sub-s (1), by the Financial Services and Markets Act 2000 (Consequential Amendments and Repeals) Order 2001, SI 2001/3649, art 470; sub-s (2A) inserted by SI 2001/767, art 3(1), (4).

In s 9 of the Act (as set out above) words omitted from sub-s (1) revoked and the whole of sub-s (1A) and words in square brackets in sub-s (2) inserted, by SI 2001/767, art 3(1), (5).

S 17 of the Act (as set out above) inserted by SI 2001/767, art 3(1), (6).

In Sch 1 to the Act (as set out above) para 10 (omitted) revoked and words in square brackets in para 11 substituted by the Deregulation Act 2015 and Small Business, Enterprise and Employment Act 2015 (Consequential Amendments) (Savings) Regulations 2017, SI 2017/540, reg 3, Sch 2, paras 2, 11; words in square brackets in para 12 substituted by SI 2005/1516, art 11(1), (4).".

SCHEDULE 9
FORMS

Article 17

[10.31]

NOTES

This Schedule contains forms. The forms themselves are not set out in this work, but their numbers and titles are listed below.

FORM NO	*TITLE*
1	Administration application
1A	Notice of intention to appoint an administrator by the members of the partnership
1B	Notice of appointment of an administrator by the members of the partnership (where a notice of intention to appoint has not been issued)
2	Affidavit Verifying Petition to Wind Up Partnership
3	Petition to Wind Up Partnership by Liquidator, Administrator, Trustee or Supervisor
4	Written/Statutory Demand by Creditor
5	Creditor's Petition to Wind Up Partnership (Presented in Conjunction with Petitions against Members)
6	Creditor's Petition to Wind Up Corporate Member (Presented in Conjunction with Petition against Partnership)
7	Creditor's Bankruptcy Petition against Individual Member (Presented in Conjunction with Petition against Partnership)
8	Advertisement of Winding Up Petition(s) against Partnership (and any Corporate Members)
9	Notice to Court of Progress on Petitions Presented
10	Demand by Member
11	Members' Petition to Wind Up Partnership (Presented in Conjunction with Petitions Against Members)
12	Members' Petition to Wind Up Corporate Member (Presented in Conjunction with Petitions Against Partnership)
13	Members' Bankruptcy Petition Against Individual Member (Presented in Conjunction with Petition Against Partnership)
14	Joint Bankruptcy Petition Against Individual Members
15	Affidavit of Individual Member(s) as to Concurrence of All Members in Presentation of Joint Bankruptcy Petition against Individual Members
16	Bankruptcy Orders on Joint Bankruptcy Petition Presented by Individual Members
17	Statement of Affairs of Member of Partnership
18	Statement of Affairs of Partnership

NOTES

Forms 1, 3, 11–14, 16: substituted by the Insolvent Partnerships (Amendment) Order 2002, SI 2002/1308, arts 2, 6, Schedule.

Forms 1, 16 further substituted, forms 1A, 1B inserted, and form 4 substituted by the Insolvent Partnerships (Amendment) Order 2005, SI 2005/1516, arts 2, 12, Sch 2, except where a petition for an administration order has been presented in relation to an insolvent partnership before 1 July 2005.

Forms 1A, 1B: substituted by the Insolvent Partnerships (Amendment) Order 2006, SI 2006/622, art 10, Schedule, except in respect of any insolvency proceedings in relation to an insolvent partnership commenced before 6 April 2006; see SI 2006/622, art 2 at **[2.41]**.

Forms 5–7: substituted by the Insolvent Partnerships (Amendment) (No 2) Order 2002, SI 2002/2708, arts 10, Schedule, subject to transitional provisions in art 11(1), (3) thereof (see further the note to art 4 at **[10.4]**).

SCHEDULE 10
SUBORDINATE LEGISLATION APPLIED

Article 18

[10.32]

The Insolvency Practitioners Tribunal (Conduct of Investigations) Rules 1986

The Insolvency Practitioners (Recognised Professional Bodies) Order 1986

[The Insolvency (England and Wales) Rules 2016]

[The Insolvency Regulations 1994]

The Insolvency Proceedings (Monetary Limits) Order 1986

The Administration of Insolvent Estates of Deceased Persons Order 1986

The Insolvency (Amendment of Subordinate Legislation) Order 1986

. . .

[The Companies (Disqualification Orders) Regulations 2001]

The Co-operation of Insolvency Courts (Designation of Relevant Countries and Territories) Order 1986

[The Insolvent Companies (Reports on Conduct of Directors) Rules 1996]

The Insolvent Companies (Disqualification of Unfit Directors) Proceedings Rules 1987

[The Insolvency Practitioners Regulations 2005]

[The Insolvency Practitioners and Insolvency Services Accounts (Fees) Order 2003

The Insolvency Proceedings (Fees) Order 2004]

NOTES

Entry "The Insolvency (England and Wales) Rules 2016" substituted for original words "The Insolvency Rules 1986", in relation to England and Wales, by the Insolvency (Miscellaneous Amendments) Regulations 2017, SI 2017/1119, reg 2, Sch 2, paras 1, 9, as from 8 December 2017, subject to transitional and savings provisions in Sch 2, para 10 thereto as noted to art 2 at **[10.2]**.

Other words in square brackets substituted or inserted by the Insolvent Partnerships (Amendment) Order 2005, SI 2005/1516, art 13.

LIMITED LIABILITY PARTNERSHIPS REGULATIONS 2001

(SI 2001/1090)

NOTES

Made: 19 March 2001.

Authority: Limited Liability Partnerships Act 2000, ss 14–17.

Commencement: 6 April 2001.

Note: the Insolvency Rules 1986, SI 1986/1925 are revoked and replaced (as from 6 April 2017 and subject to transitional provisions) by the Insolvency (England and Wales) Rules 2016, SI 2016/1024 at **[6.2]**, however, the Insolvency (England and Wales) Rules 2016 (Consequential Amendments and Savings) Rules 2017, SI 2017/369, r 3(b) at **[6.947]** provides that the Insolvency Rules 1986 as they had effect immediately before 6 April 2017 and insofar as they apply to proceedings under the Limited Liability Partnerships Regulations 2001, continue to have effect for the purposes of the application of the 2001 Regulations.

See also the Deregulation Act 2015 and Small Business, Enterprise and Employment Act 2015 (Consequential Amendments) (Savings) Regulations 2017, SI 2017/540, reg 4(1), (2)(b) and the Insolvency Amendment (EU 2015/848) Regulations 2017, SI 2017/702, reg 4 at **[2.103]**, for savings in relation to the Insolvency Act 1986 in so far as it applies to proceedings under these Regulations.

ARRANGEMENT OF REGULATIONS

PART I
CITATION, COMMENCEMENT AND INTERPRETATION

1 Citation and commencement . . . . [10.33]
2 Interpretation . . . . [10.34]
2A Application of provisions . . . . [10.35]

PART III
COMPANIES ACT 1985 AND COMPANY DIRECTORS
DISQUALIFICATION ACT 1986

4 Application of certain provisions of the 1985 Act and of the provisions of the Company Directors Disqualification Act 1986 to limited liability partnerships . . . . [10.36]

PART IV
WINDING UP AND INSOLVENCY

5 Application of the Insolvency Act 1986 to limited liability partnerships . . . . [10.37]

PART VII
MISCELLANEOUS

10 Application of subordinate legislation . . . . [10.38]

SCHEDULES

Schedule 2
Part I—Modifications to provisions of the Companies Act 1985 applied to limited liability partnerships . . . . [10.39]
Part II—Modifications to the Company Directors Disqualification Act 1986 . . . . [10.40]
Schedule 3—Modifications to the Insolvency Act 1986 . . . . [10.41]
Schedule 4—Application of provisions to Scotland . . . . [10.42]
Schedule 6—Application of subordinate legislation
Part II—Regulations made under the 1986 Act . . . . [10.43]
Part III—Regulations made under other legislation . . . . [10.44]
Schedule 7—Transitional and Savings Provisions . . . . [10.45]

PART I
CITATION, COMMENCEMENT AND INTERPRETATION

[10.33]
1 Citation and commencement

These Regulations may be cited as the Limited Liability Partnerships Regulations 2001 and shall come into force on 6th April 2001.

[10.34]
2 Interpretation

In these Regulations—

"the 1985 Act" means the Companies Act 1985; "the 1986 Act" means the Insolvency Act 1986;

"the 2000 Act" means the Financial Services and Markets Act 2000;

"devolved", in relation to the provisions of the 1986 Act, means the provisions of the 1986 Act which are listed in Schedule 4 and, in their application to Scotland, concern wholly or partly, matters which are set out in Section C 2 of Schedule 5 to the Scotland Act 1998 as being exceptions to the reservations made in that Act in the field of insolvency;

"limited liability partnership agreement", in relation to a limited liability partnership, means any agreement express or implied between the members of the limited liability partnership or between the limited liability partnership and the members of the limited liability partnership which determines the mutual rights and duties of the members, and their rights and duties in relation to the limited liability partnership;

"the principal Act" means the Limited Liability Partnerships Act 2000; and

"shadow member", in relation to limited liability partnerships, means a person in accordance with whose directions or instructions the members of the limited liability partnership are accustomed to act (but so that a person is not deemed a shadow member by reason only that the members of the limited partnership act on advice given by him in a professional capacity).

[10.35]
[2A Application of provisions

(1) The provisions of these Regulations applying—
 (a) the Company Directors Disqualification Act 1986, or
 (b) provisions of the Insolvency Act 1986,
have effect only in relation to limited liability partnerships registered in Great Britain.

(2) The other provisions of these Regulations have effect in relation to limited liability partnerships registered in any part of the United Kingdom.]

NOTES

Inserted by the Limited Liability Partnerships (Application of Companies Act 2006) Regulations 2009, SI 2009/1804, reg 85, Sch 3, Pt 2, para 13(1), (2).

3 *((Pt II) outside the scope of this work.)*

Part 10 SIs: Partnership Insolvency

PART III
COMPANIES ACT 1985 AND COMPANY DIRECTORS DISQUALIFICATION ACT 1986

[10.36]

4 Application of [certain provisions] of the 1985 Act and of the provisions of the Company Directors Disqualification Act 1986 to limited liability partnerships

(1) The provisions of the 1985 Act specified in the first column of Part I of Schedule 2 to these Regulations shall apply to limited liability partnerships, except where the context otherwise requires, with the following modifications—

(a) references to a company shall include references to a limited liability partnership;
(b) . . .
(c) references to the Insolvency Act 1986 shall include references to that Act as it applies to limited liability partnerships by virtue of Part IV of these Regulations;
[(d) references in a provision of the 1985 Act to—
(i) other provisions of that Act, or
(ii) provisions of the Companies Act 2006,
shall include references to those provisions as they apply to limited liability partnerships.]
(e) . . .
(f) . . .
(g) references to a director of a company or to an officer of a company shall include references to a member of a limited liability partnership;
(h) the modifications, if any, specified in the second column of Part I of Schedule 2 opposite the provision specified in the first column; and
(i) such further modifications as the context requires for the purpose of giving effect to that legislation as applied by these Regulations.

(2) The provisions of the Company Director Disqualification Act 1986 shall apply to limited liability partnerships, except where the context otherwise requires, with the following modifications—

(a) references to a company shall include references to a limited liability partnership;
(b) references to the Companies Acts shall include references to the principal Act and regulations made thereunder and references to the companies legislation shall include references to the principal Act, regulations made thereunder and to any enactment applied by regulations to limited liability partnerships;
(d) references to the Insolvency Act 1986 shall include references to that Act as it applies to limited liability partnerships by virtue of Part IV of these Regulations;
(e) . . .
(f) references to a shadow director shall include references to a shadow member;
(g) references to a director of a company or to an officer of a company shall include references to a member of a limited liability partnership;
(h) the modifications, if any, specified in the second column of Part II of Schedule 2 opposite the provision specified in the first column; and
(i) such further modifications as the context requires for the purpose of giving effect to that legislation as applied by these Regulations.

NOTES

Regulation heading: words in square brackets substituted by the Limited Liability Partnerships (Application of Companies Act 2006) Regulations 2009, SI 2009/1804, reg 85, Sch 3, Pt 2, para 13(1), (3)(a).

Para (1): sub-paras (b), (e), (f) revoked and sub-para (d) substituted by SI 2009/1804, reg 85, Sch 3, Pt 2, para 13(1), (3)(b).

Para (2): sub-para (e) revoked by the Companies Act 2006 (Consequential Amendments, Transitional Provisions and Savings) Order 2009, SI 2009/1941, art 2(1), Sch 1, para 192(1), (2).

See further: the following commencement orders for the Companies Act 2006 do not affect the application of provisions of the 1985 Act by these Regulations; see SI 2006/3428, art 8(2), SI 2007/1093, art 11(1), SI 2007/2194, art 12(2), SI 2007/3495, art 12(1), SI 2008/674, art 6(1), SI 2008/948, art 11, and SI 2008/1886, art 7(4).

PART IV
WINDING UP AND INSOLVENCY

[10.37]

5 Application of the 1986 Act to limited liability partnerships

(1) Subject to paragraphs (2) and (3), the following provisions of the 1986 Act, shall apply to limited liability partnerships—

(a) Parts I, II, III, IV, VI and VII of the First Group of Parts (company insolvency; companies winding up),
(b) the Third Group of Parts (miscellaneous matters bearing on both company and individual insolvency; general interpretation; final provisions).

(2) The provisions of the 1986 Act referred to in paragraph (1) shall apply to limited liability partnerships, except where the context otherwise requires, with the following modifications—

(a) references to a company shall include references to a limited liability partnership;
(b) references to a director or to an officer of a company shall include references to a member of a limited liability partnership;
(c) references to a shadow director shall include references to a shadow member;

(d) references to [the Companies Acts], the Company Directors Disqualification Act 1986, the Companies Act 1989 or to any provisions of those Acts or to any provisions of the 1986 Act shall include references to those Acts or provisions as they apply to limited liability partnerships by virtue of the principal Act;

(e) references . . . to the articles of association of a company shall include references to the limited liability partnership agreement of a limited liability partnership;

(f) the modifications set out in Schedule 3 to these Regulations; and

(g) such further modifications as the context requires for the purpose of giving effect to that legislation as applied by these Regulations.

(3) In the application of this regulation to Scotland, the provisions of the 1986 Act referred to in paragraph (1) shall not include the provisions listed in Schedule 4 to the extent specified in that Schedule.

NOTES

Para (2): words in square brackets in sub-para (d) substituted and words omitted from sub-para (e) revoked by the Companies Act 2006 (Consequential Amendments, Transitional Provisions and Savings) Order 2009, SI 2009/1941, art 2(1), Sch 1, para 192(1), (3).

6–8 *((Pts V, VI) outside the scope of this work.)*

PART VII
MISCELLANEOUS

9 *(Outside the scope of this work.)*

[10.38]

10 Application of subordinate legislation

(1) The subordinate legislation specified in Schedule 6 shall apply as from time to time in force to limited liability partnerships and—

(a) in the case of the subordinate legislation listed in Part I of that Schedule with such modifications as the context requires for the purpose of giving effect to the provisions of the Companies Act 1985 which are applied by these Regulations;

(b) in the case of the subordinate legislation listed in Part II of that Schedule with such modifications as the context requires for the purpose of giving effect to the provisions of the Insolvency Act 1986 which are applied by these Regulations; and

(c) in the case of the subordinate legislation listed in Part III of that Schedule with such modifications as the context requires for the purpose of giving effect to the provisions of . . . the Company Directors Disqualification Act 1986 which are applied by these Regulations.

(2) In the case of any conflict between any provision of the subordinate legislation applied by paragraph (1) and any provision of these Regulations, the latter shall prevail.

NOTES

Para (1): words omitted from para (c) revoked by the Limited Liability Partnerships (Application of Companies Act 2006) Regulations 2009, SI 2009/1804, reg 85, Sch 3, Pt 2, para 13(1), (4).

SCHEDULES

SCHEDULE 1

(Sch 1 outside the scope of this work.)

SCHEDULE 2

Regulation 4

PART I
MODIFICATIONS TO PROVISIONS OF THE 1985 ACT APPLIED TO LIMITED LIABILITY PARTNERSHIPS

[10.39]

Provisions	**Modification**
Floating charges and Receivers (Scotland)	
464 (ranking of floating charges)	In subsection (1), for the words “section 462” substitute “the law of Scotland”.
466 (alteration of floating charges)	Omit subsections (1), (2), (3) and (6).
486 (interpretation for Part XVIII generally)	For the current definition of “company” substitute ““company” means a limited liability partnership;” Omit the definition of “Register of Sasines”.
487 (extent of Part XVIII)	

NOTES

Note: only parts of this table relevant to this work have been reproduced.

Part 10 SIs: Partnership Insolvency

See further: the following commencement orders for the Companies Act 2006 do not affect the application of provisions of the 1985 Act by these Regulations; see SI 2006/3428, art 8(2), SI 2007/1093, art 11(1), SI 2007/2194, art 12(2), SI 2007/3495, art 12(1), SI 2008/674, art 6(1), SI 2008/948, art 11, and SI 2008/1886, art 7(4).

PART II
MODIFICATIONS TO THE COMPANY DIRECTORS DISQUALIFICATION ACT 1986

[10.40]

Part II of Schedule I	*After paragraph 8 insert—* *"8A The extent of the member's and shadow members' responsibility for events leading to a member or shadow member, whether himself or some other member or shadow member, being declared by the court to be liable to make a contribution to the assets of the limited liability partnership under section 214A of the Insolvency Act 1986."*

NOTES

Revoked, in relation to England and Wales, by the Insolvency (Miscellaneous Amendments) Regulations 2017, SI 2017/1119, reg 2, Sch 1, Pt 2, paras 4, 5, as from 8 December 2017.

SCHEDULE 3
MODIFICATIONS TO THE 1986 ACT

Regulation 5

[10.41]

Provisions	**Modifications**
Section 1 (those who may propose an arrangement)	
subsection (1)	For "The directors of a company" substitute "A limited liability partnership" and delete "to the company and".
subsection (3)	At the end add "but where a proposal is so made it must also be made to the limited liability partnership".
[Section 1A (moratorium)	
subsection (1)	For "the directors of an eligible company intend" substitute "an eligible limited liability partnership intends". For "they" substitute "it".]
The following modifications to sections 2 to 7 apply where a proposal under section 1 has been made by the limited liability partnership.	
Section 2 (procedure where the nominee is not the liquidator or administrator)	
[subsection (1)	[For "the directors do" substitute "the limited liability partnership does".
[subsection (2)	In paragraph (b) omit "a meeting of the company and by". Omit paragraph (c).]
subsection (3)	For "the person intending to make the proposal" substitute "the designated members of the limited liability partnership".
subsection (4)	[In paragraph (a)] for "the person intending to make the proposal" substitute "the designated members of the limited liability partnership". [In paragraph (b) for "that person" substitute "those designated members".]
Section 3 (summoning of meetings)	
[subsection (1)	For subsection (1) substitute— "(1) Where the nominee under section 1 is not the liquidator or administrator, and it has been reported to the court under section 2(2) that the proposal should be considered by the creditors of the limited liability partnership, the person making the report shall (unless the court otherwise directs) seek a decision from the creditors of the limited liability partnership as to whether they approve the proposal.".
subsection (2)	Omit paragraph (a).]
Section 4 (decisions of meetings)	
[subsection (1)	Omit paragraph (a).]

Provisions	**Modifications**
[subsection (1A)	For "The company and its creditors" substitute "The creditors of the limited liability partnership".
subsection (3)	For "Neither the company nor its creditors" substitute "The creditors of the limited liability partnership may not".
subsection (4)	For "Neither the company nor its creditors" substitute "The creditors of the limited liability partnership may not".]
[subsection (5)	Omit "the meeting of the company and".]
[new subsection (5A)	Insert a new subsection (5A) as follows—
	"(5A) If modifications to the proposal are proposed by creditors, the nominee under section 1(2) must, before the date on which the creditors are to be asked whether to approve the proposed voluntary arrangement, ascertain from the limited liability partnership whether or not it agrees to the proposed modifications; and if at that date the limited liability partnership has failed to respond to a proposed modification, it shall be presumed not to have agreed to it."]
[subsection (6)	Omit.]
[subsection (6A)	In paragraph (a) after "creditors' decision" insert "(including, where modifications to the proposal were proposed, the response of the limited liability partnership)". In paragraph (b) after "be prescribed" insert "and to the limited liability partnership".
[Section 4A (approval of arrangement)	
[subsection (2)	In paragraph (a) for "meeting of the company summoned under section 3 and by the company's creditors pursuant to that section, or", substitute "the creditors of the limited liability partnership pursuant to section 3";
	Omit paragraph (b).]
subsection (3)	Omit.
subsection (4)	Omit.
subsection (5)	Omit.
[subsection (5A)	Omit.]
subsection (6)	Omit.]
Section 5 (effect of approval)	
. . .	. . .
[subsection (4)	In paragraph (a) for "each of the reports required by section 4(6) and (6A)" substitute "the report required by section 4(6A)".]
Section 6 (challenge of decisions)	
[subsection (1)	In paragraph (b) omit "the meeting of the company, or in relation to".
subsection (2)	In paragraph (a) omit "at the meeting of the company or".
	After paragraph (aa) insert a new paragraph as follows—
	"(ab) any member of the limited liability partnership; and".
	Omit the word "and" at the end of paragraph (b).
	Omit paragraph (c).]
subsection (3)	In paragraph (a) for "each for the reports required by section 4(6) and (6A)" substitute "the report required by section 4(6A)".
subsection (4)	For subsection (4) substitute the following—
	"(4) Where on such an application the court is satisfied as to either of the grounds mentioned in subsection (1), it may do either of the following, namely—
	(a) revoke or suspend any decision approving the voluntary arrangement which has effect under section 4A or, in a case falling within subsection (1)(b) any decision taken in the relevant qualifying decision procedure which has effect under that section;

Part 10 SIs: Partnership Insolvency

Provisions	Modifications
	(b) direct any person— (i) to seek a decision from the creditors of the limited liability partnership, using a qualifying decision procedure, as to whether they approve any revised proposal the person who made the original proposal may make; or (ii) in a case falling within subsection (1)(b) and relating to the relevant qualifying decision procedure, to seek a decision from the creditors of the limited liability partnership, using a qualifying decision procedure, as to whether they approve the original proposal."
subsection (5)	Omit "or (c)".]
[subsection (7)	Omit paragraph (a).]
[Section 6A (false representations, etc)	
subsection (1)	Omit "members or".]
Section 7 (implementation of proposal)	
. . .	. . .
[subsection (2)	In paragraph (a) for "company or its creditors (or both)" substitute "creditors of the limited liability partnership".]

The following modifications to sections 2 and 3 apply where a proposal under section 1 has been made, where [the limited liability partnership is in administration], by the administrator or, where the limited liability partnership is being wound up, by the liquidator.

Provisions	Modifications
[Section 2	
subsection (2)	In paragraph (b) for "the company" substitute "members of the limited liability partnership".]
Section 3 (summoning of meetings)	
[subsection (2)	In paragraph (a) for "the company" substitute "members of the limited liability partnership".]
. . .	. . .
. . .	. . .
. . .	. . .
. . .	. . .
. . .	. . .
. . .	. . .
. . .	. . .
Section 74 (liability as contributories of present and past members)	For section 74 there shall be substituted the following— "74. When a limited liability partnership is wound up every present and past member of the limited liability partnership who has agreed with the other members or with the limited liability partnership that he will, in circumstances which have arisen, be liable to contribute to the assets of the limited liability partnership in the event that the limited liability partnership goes into liquidation is liable, to the extent that he has so agreed, to contribute to its assets to any amount sufficient for payment of its debts and liabilities, and the expenses of the winding up, and for the adjustment of the rights of the contributories among themselves. However, a past member shall only be liable if the obligation arising from such agreement survived his ceasing to be a member of the limited liability partnership."
Section 75 to 78	Delete sections 75 to 78.
Section 79 (meaning of "contributory")	
subsection (1)	In subsection (1) for "every person" substitute "(a) every present member of the limited liability partnership and (b) every past member of the limited liability partnership".
subsection (2)	After "section 214 (wrongful trading)" insert "or 214A (adjustment of withdrawals)".
subsection (3)	Delete subsection (3).
Section 83 (companies registered under Companies Act, Part XXII, Chapter II)	

Provisions	**Modifications**
	Delete section 83.
Section 84 (circumstances in which company may be wound up voluntarily)	
subsection (1)	For subsection (1) substitute the following— "(1) A limited liability partnership may be wound up voluntarily when it determines that it is to be wound up voluntarily."
subsection (2)	Omit subsection (2).
[subsection (2A)	For "company passes a resolution for voluntary winding up" substitute "limited liability partnership determines that it is to be wound up voluntarily" and for "resolution" where it appears for the second time substitute "determination".
subsection (2B)	For "resolution for voluntary winding up may be passed only" substitute "determination to wind up voluntarily may only be made" and in sub-paragraph (b), for "passing of the resolution" substitute "making of the determination".]
subsection (3)	For subsection (3) substitute the following— "(3) Within 15 days after a limited liability partnership has determined that it be wound up there shall be forwarded to the registrar of companies either a printed copy or else a copy in some other form approved by the registrar of the determination."
subsection [(5)]	After subsection [(4)] insert a new subsection [(5)]— "[(5)] If a limited liability partnership fails to comply with this regulation the limited liability partnership and every designated member of it who is in default is liable on summary conviction to a fine not exceeding level 3 on the standard scale."
Section 85 (notice of resolution to wind up)	
subsection (1)	For subsection (1) substitute the following— "(1) When a limited liability partnership has determined that it shall be wound up voluntarily, it shall within 14 days after the making of the determination give notice of the determination by advertisement in the Gazette."
Section 86 (commencement of winding up)	Substitute the following new section— "86. A voluntary winding up is deemed to commence at the time when the limited liability partnership determines that it be wound up voluntarily.".
Section 87 (effect on business and status of company)	
subsection (2)	In subsection (2), for "articles" substitute "limited liability partnership agreement".
Section 88 (avoidance of share transfers, etc after winding-up resolution)	For "shares" substitute "the interest of any member in the property of the limited liability partnership".
Section 89 (statutory declaration of solvency)	For "director(s)" wherever it appears in section 89 substitute "designated member(s)";
subsection (2)	For paragraph (a) substitute the following— "(a) it is made within the 5 weeks immediately preceding the date when the limited liability partnership determined that it be wound up voluntarily or on that date but before the making of the determination, and".
subsection (3)	For "the resolution for winding up is passed" substitute "the limited liability partnership determined that it be wound up voluntarily".
subsection (5)	For "in pursuance of a resolution passed" substitute "voluntarily".

Provisions	Modifications
Section 90 (distinction between "members" and "creditors" voluntary winding up)	For "directors'" substitute "designated members'".
Section 91 (appointment of liquidator)	
subsection (1)	Delete "in general meeting".
subsection (2)	For the existing wording substitute— "(2) On the appointment of a liquidator the powers of the members of the limited liability partnership shall cease except to the extent that a meeting of the members of the limited liability partnership summoned for the purpose or the liquidator sanctions their continuance." After subsection (2) insert— "(3) Subsections (3) and (4) of section 92 shall apply for the purposes of this section as they apply for the purposes of that section."
Section 92 (power to fill vacancy in office of liquidator)	
subsection (1)	For "the company in general meeting" substitute "a meeting of the members of the limited liability partnership summoned for the purpose".
subsection (2)	For "a general meeting" substitute "a meeting of the members of the limited liability partnership".
subsection (3)	In subsection (3), for "articles" substitute "limited liability partnership agreement".
new subsection (4)	Add a new subsection (4) as follows— "(4) The quorum required for a meeting of the members of the limited liability partnership shall be any quorum required by the limited liability partnership agreement for meetings of the members of the limited liability partnership and if no requirement for a quorum has been agreed upon the quorum shall be 2 members."
Section 93 (general company meeting at each year's end)	
subsection (1)	*For "a general meeting of the company" substitute "a meeting of the members of the limited liability partnership".*
new subsection (4)	*Add a new subsection (4) as follows—* *"(4) subsections (3) and (4) of section 92 shall apply for the purposes of this section as they apply for the purposes of that section."*
. . .	. . .
Section 95 (effect of company's insolvency)	
subsection (1)	For "directors'" substitute "designated members'".
. . .	. . .
Section 96 (conversion to creditors' voluntary winding up)	
[subsection (2)	For "directors" substitute "designated members".]
. . .	. . .
. . .	. . .
Section 99 (directors to lay statement of affairs before creditors)	
[subsection (1)	For "directors of the company" substitute "designated members".
subsection (2A)	For "directors" substitute "designated members".
subsection (3)	For "directors" substitute "designated members".]
Section 100 (appointment of liquidator)	
[subsection (1)	For subsection (1) substitute the following— "(1) The members of the limited liability partnership may nominate a person to be liquidator at the meeting at which the resolution for voluntary winding up is passed."

Provisions	**Modifications**
[subsection (1B)	For "directors of the company" substitute "designated members".]
subsection (3)	Delete "director,".
Section 101 (appointment of liquidation committee)	
subsection (2)	For subsection (2) substitute the following— "(2) If such a committee is appointed, the limited liability partnership may, when it determines that it be wound up voluntarily or at any time thereafter, appoint such number of persons as they think fit to act as members of the committee, not exceeding 5."
Section 105 (meetings of company and creditors at each year's end)	
subsection (1)	*For "a general meeting of the company" substitute "a meeting of the members of the limited liability partnership".*
new subsection (5)	*Add a new subsection (5) as follows— "(5) Subsections (3) and (4) of section 92 shall apply for the purposes of this section as they apply for the purposes of that section."*
. . .	
Section 110 (acceptance of shares, etc, as consideration for sale of company property)	For the existing section substitute the following— "(1) This section applies, in the case of a limited liability partnership proposed to be, or being, wound up voluntarily, where the whole or part of the limited liability partnership's business or property is proposed to be transferred or sold to another company whether or not it is a company within the meaning of the Companies Act ("the transferee company") or to a limited liability partnership ("the transferee limited liability partnership"). (2) With the requisite sanction, the liquidator of the limited liability partnership being, or proposed to be, wound up ("the transferor limited liability partnership") may receive, in compensation or part compensation for the transfer or sale, shares, policies or other like interests in the transferee company or the transferee limited liability partnership for distribution among the members of the transferor limited liability partnership. (3) The sanction required under subsection (2) is— (a) in the case of a members' voluntary winding up, that of a determination of the limited liability partnership at a meeting of the members of the limited liability partnership conferring either a general authority on the liquidator or an authority in respect of any particular arrangement, (subsections (3) and (4) of section 92 to apply for this purpose as they apply for the purposes of that section), and (b) in the case of a creditor's voluntary winding up, that of either court or the liquidation committee. (4) Alternatively to subsection (2), the liquidator may (with the sanction) enter into any other arrangement whereby the members of the transferor limited liability partnership may, in lieu of receiving cash, shares, policies or other like interests (or in addition thereto), participate in the profits, or receive any other benefit from the transferee company or the transferee limited liability partnership. (5) A sale or arrangement in pursuance of this section is binding on members of the transferor limited liability partnership.

Provisions	Modifications
	(6) A determination by the limited liability partnership is not invalid for the purposes of this section by reason that it is made before or concurrently with a determination by the limited liability partnership that it be wound up voluntarily or for appointing liquidators; but, if an order is made within a year for winding up the limited liability partnership by the court, the determination by the limited liability partnership is not valid unless sanctioned by the court."
Section 111 (dissent from arrangement under section 110)	
subsections (1)–(3)	For subsections (1)–(3) substitute the following— "(1) This section applies in the case of a voluntary winding up where, for the purposes of section 110(2) or (4), a determination of the limited liability partnership has provided the sanction requisite for the liquidator under that section. (2) If a member of the transferor limited liability partnership who did not vote in favour of providing the sanction required for the liquidator under section 110 expresses his dissent from it in writing addressed to the liquidator and left at the registered office of the limited liability partnership within 7 days after the date on which that sanction was given, he may require the liquidator either to abstain from carrying the arrangement so sanctioned into effect or to purchase his interest at a price to be determined by agreement or arbitration under this section. (3) If the liquidator elects to purchase the member's interest, the purchase money must be paid before the limited liability partnership is dissolved and be raised by the liquidator in such manner as may be determined by the limited liability partnership."
subsection (4)	Omit subsection (4).
Section 117 (high court and county court jurisdiction)	
subsection (2)	Delete "Where the amount of a company's share capital paid up or credited as paid up does not exceed £120,000, then (subject to this section)".
subsection (3)	Delete subsection (3).
Section 120 (court of session and sheriff court jurisdiction)	
subsection (3)	Delete "Where the amount of a company's share capital paid up or credited as paid up does not exceed £120,000,".
subsection (5)	Delete subsection (5).
Section 122 (circumstances in which company may be wound up by the court)	
subsection (1)	For subsection (1) substitute the following— "(1) A limited liability partnership may be wound up by the court if— (a) the limited liability partnership has determined that the limited liability partnership be wound up by the court, (b) the limited liability partnership does not commence its business within a year from its incorporation or suspends its business for a whole year, (c) the number of members is reduced below two, (d) the limited liability partnership is unable to pay its debts . . . [(da) at the time at which a moratorium for the limited liability partnership under section 1A comes to an end, no voluntary arrangement approved under Part I has effect in relation to the limited liability partnership,] (e) the court is of the opinion that it is just and equitable that the limited liability partnership should be wound up."
Section 124 (application for winding up)	

Provisions	**Modifications**
subsections (2), (3) and (4)(a)	Delete these subsections.
[subsection (3A)	For "122(1)(fa)" substitute "122(1)(da)".]
Section 124A (petition for winding-up on grounds of public interest)	
subsection (1)	[Omit paragraphs (b) and (bb).]
Section 126 (power to stay or restrain proceedings against company)	
subsection (2)	Delete subsection (2).
Section 127 (avoidance of property dispositions, etc)	
[subsection (1)]	For "any transfer of shares" substitute "any transfer by a member of the limited liability partnership of his interest in the property of the limited liability partnership".
Section 129 (commencement of winding up by the court)	
subsection (1)	For "a resolution has been passed by the company" substitute "a determination has been made" and for "at the time of the passing of the resolution" substitute "at the time of that determination".
Section 130 (consequences of winding-up order)	
subsection (3)	Delete subsection (3).
Section 148 (settlement of list of contributories and application of assets)	
subsection (1)	Delete ", with power to rectify the register of members in all cases where rectification is required in pursuance of the Companies Act or this Act,".
Section 149 (debts due from contributory to company)	
subsection (1)	Delete "the Companies Act or".
subsection (2)	Delete subsection (2).
subsection (3)	Delete ", whether limited or unlimited,".
Section 160 (delegation of powers to liquidator (England and Wales))	
subsection (1)	In subsection (1)(b) delete "and the rectifying of the register of members".
subsection (2)	For subsection (2) substitute the following— "(2) But the liquidator shall not make any call without the special leave of the court or the sanction of the liquidation committee."
Section 165 (voluntary winding up)	
. . .	. . .
subsection (4)	For paragraph (c) substitute the following— "(c) summon meetings of the members of the limited liability partnership for the purpose of obtaining their sanction or for any other purpose he may think fit."
new subsection (4A)	Insert a new subsection (4A) as follows— "(4A) Subsections (3) and (4) of section 92 shall apply for the purposes of this section as they apply for the purposes of that section."
Section 166 (creditors' voluntary winding up)	
[subsection (5)	For "directors" substitute "designated members".]
Section 171 (removal, etc (voluntary winding up))	
subsection (2)	For paragraph (a) substitute the following— "(a) in the case of a members' voluntary winding up, by a meeting of the members of the limited liability partnership summoned specially for that purpose, or".
[new subsection (8)	Insert a new subsection (8) as follows—

Part 10 SIs: Partnership Insolvency

Provisions	Modifications
	"(8) subsections (3) and (4) of section 92 are to apply for the purposes of this section as they apply for the purposes of that section."]
Section 173 (release (voluntary winding up))	
[subsection (2)	In paragraph (a)(i) for "a general meeting of the company" substitute "a meeting of the members of the limited liability partnership".]
Section 183 (effect of execution or attachment (England and Wales))	
subsection (2)	Delete paragraph (a).
Section 184 (duties of sheriff (England and Wales))	
subsection (1)	For "a resolution for voluntary winding up has been passed" substitute "the limited liability partnership has determined that it be wound up voluntarily".
subsection (4)	Delete "or of a meeting having been called at which there is to be proposed a resolution for voluntary winding up," and "or a resolution is passed (as the case may be)".
Section 187 (power to make over assets to employees)	
	Delete section 187.
. . .	. . .
Section 195 (meetings to ascertain wishes of creditors or contributories)	
subsection (3)	Delete "the Companies Act or".
Section 206 (fraud, etc in anticipation of winding up)	
subsection (1)	For "passes a resolution for voluntary winding up" substitute "makes a determination that it be wound up voluntarily".
Section 207 (transactions in fraud of creditors)	
subsection (1)	For "passes a resolution for voluntary winding up" substitute "makes a determination that it be wound up voluntarily".
Section 210 (material omissions from statement relating to company's affairs)	
subsection (2)	For "passed a resolution for voluntary winding up" substitute "made a determination that it be wound up voluntarily".
Section 214 (wrongful trading)	
subsection (2)	Delete from "but the court shall not" to the end of the subsection.
After section 214	
	Insert the following new section 214A—
	"214A Adjustment of withdrawals
	(1) This section has effect in relation to a person who is or has been a member of a limited liability partnership where, in the course of the winding up of that limited liability partnership, it appears that subsection (2) of this section applies in relation to that person.
	(2) This subsection applies in relation to a person if—
	(a) within the period of two years ending with the commencement of the winding up, he was a member of the limited liability partnership who withdrew property of the limited liability partnership, whether in the form of a share of profits, salary, repayment of or payment of interest on a loan to the limited liability partnership or any other withdrawal of property, and

Provisions	**Modifications**
	(b) it is proved by the liquidator to the satisfaction of the court that at the time of the withdrawal he knew or had reasonable ground for believing that the limited liability partnership—
	(i) was at the time of the withdrawal unable to pay its debts within the meaning of section 123, or
	(ii) would become so unable to pay its debts after the assets of the limited liability partnership had been depleted by that withdrawal taken together with all other withdrawals (if any) made by any members contemporaneously with that withdrawal or in contemplation when that withdrawal was made.
	(3) Where this section has effect in relation to any person the court, on the application of the liquidator, may declare that that person is to be liable to make such contribution (if any) to the limited liability partnership's assets as the court thinks proper.
	(4) The court shall not make a declaration in relation to any person the amount of which exceeds the aggregate of the amounts or values of all the withdrawals referred to in subsection (2) made by that person within the period of two years referred to in that subsection.
	(5) The court shall not make a declaration under this section with respect to any person unless that person knew or ought to have concluded that after each withdrawal referred to in subsection (2) there was no reasonable prospect that the limited liability partnership would avoid going into insolvent liquidation.
	(6) For the purposes of subsection (5) the facts which a member ought to know or ascertain and the conclusions which he ought to reach are those which would be known, ascertained, or reached by a reasonably diligent person having both:
	(a) the general knowledge, skill and experience that may reasonably be expected of a person carrying out the same functions as are carried out by that member in relation to the limited liability partnership, and
	(b) the general knowledge, skill and experience that that member has.
	(7) For the purposes of this section a limited liability partnership goes into insolvent liquidation if it goes into liquidation at a time when its assets are insufficient for the payment of its debts and other liabilities and the expenses of the winding up.
	(8) In this section "member" includes a shadow member.
	(9) This section is without prejudice to section 214."
Section 215 (proceedings under ss 213, 214)	
subsection (1)	Omit the word "or" between the words "213" and "214" and insert after "214" "or 214A".
subsection (2)	For "either section" substitute "any of those sections".
subsection (4)	For "either section" substitute "any of those sections".
subsection (5)	For "Sections 213 and 214" substitute "Sections 213, 214 or 214A".
Section 218 (prosecution of delinquent officers and members of company)	
subsection (1)	For "officer, or any member, of the company" substitute "member of the limited liability partnership".
subsections (3), (4) and (6)	For "officer of the company, or any member of it," substitute "officer or member of the limited liability partnership".
. . .	. . .
Section 247 ("insolvency" and "go into liquidation")	

Part 10 SIs: Partnership Insolvency

Provisions	Modifications
subsection (2)	For "passes a resolution for voluntary winding up" substitute "makes a determination that it be wound up voluntarily" and for "passing such a resolution" substitute "making such a determination".
[subsection (3)	For "resolution for voluntary winding up" substitute "determination to wind up voluntarily".]
Section 249 ("connected with a company")	For the existing words substitute— "For the purposes of any provision in this Group of Parts, a person is connected with a company (including a limited liability partnership) if— (a) he is a director or shadow director of a company or an associate of such a director or shadow director (including a member or a shadow member of a limited liability partnership or an associate of such a member or shadow member); or (b) he is an associate of the company or of the limited liability partnership."
Section 250 ("member" of a company)	Delete section 250.
Section 251 (expressions used generally)	Delete the word "and" appearing after the definition of "the rules" and insert the word "and" after the definition of "shadow director". After the definition of "shadow director" insert the following— ""shadow member", in relation to a limited liability partnership, means a person in accordance with whose directions or instructions the members of the limited liability partnership are accustomed to act (but so that a person is not deemed a shadow member by reason only that the members of the limited liability partnership act on advice given by him in a professional capacity);".
Section 386 (categories of preferential debts)	
subsection (1)	In subsection (1), omit the words "or an individual".
subsection (2)	In subsection (2), omit the words "or the individual".
Section 387 ("the relevant date")	
subsection (3)	[In paragraph (ab) for "passed a resolution for voluntary winding up" substitute "made a determination that it be wound up voluntarily".] In paragraph (c) for "passing of the resolution for the winding up of the company" substitute "making of the determination by the limited liability partnership that it be wound up voluntarily".
subsection (5)	Omit subsection (5).
subsection (6)	Omit subsection (6).
Section 388 (meaning of "act as insolvency practitioner")	
subsection (2)	Omit subsection (2).
subsection (3)	Omit subsection (3).
subsection (4)	Delete ""company" means a company within the meaning given by section 735(1) of the Companies Act or a company which may be wound up under Part V of this Act (unregistered companies);" and delete ""interim trustee" and "permanent trustee" mean the same as the Bankruptcy (Scotland) Act 1985".
Section 389 (acting without qualification an offence)	
subsection (1)	Omit the words "or an individual".
. . .	. . .
Section 402 (official petitioner)	Delete section 402.

Provisions	**Modifications**
Section 412 (individual insolvency rules (England and Wales))	Delete section 412.
Section 415 (Fees orders (individual insolvency proceedings in England and Wales))	Delete section 415.
Section 416 (monetary limits (companies winding up))	
subsection (1)	In subsection (1), omit the words "section 117(2) (amount of company's share capital determining whether county court has jurisdiction to wind it up);" and the words "section 120(3) (the equivalent as respects sheriff court jurisdiction in Scotland);".
subsection (3)	In subsection (3), omit the words "117(2), 120(3) or".
Section 418 (monetary limits (bankruptcy))	Delete section 418.
Section 420 (insolvent partnerships)	Delete section 420.
Section 421 (insolvent estates of deceased persons)	Delete section 421.
Section 422 (recognised banks, etc)	Delete section 422.
[Section 426A (disqualification from Parliament (England and Wales))	Omit.
Section 426B (devolution)	Omit.
Section 426C (irrelevance of privilege)	Omit.]
Section 427 (parliamentary disqualification)	Delete section 427.
Section 429 (disabilities on revocation or administration order against an individual)	Delete section 429.
Section 432 (offences by bodies corporate)	
subsection (2)	Delete "secretary or".
Section 435 (meaning of "associate")	
new subsection (3A)	Insert a new subsection (3A) as follows— "(3A) A member of a limited liability partnership is an associate of that limited liability partnership and of every other member of that limited liability partnership and of the husband or wife [or civil partner] or relative of every other member of that limited liability partnership.".
subsection (11)	For subsection (11) there shall be substituted— "(11) In this section "company" includes any body corporate (whether incorporated in Great Britain or elsewhere); and references to directors and other officers of a company and to voting power at any general meeting of a company have effect with any necessary modifications.".
Section 436 (expressions used generally)	The following expressions and definitions shall be added to the section— ""designated member" has the same meaning as it has in the Limited Liability Partnerships Act 2000; "limited liability partnership" means a limited liability partnership formed and registered under the Limited Liability Partnerships Act 2000;

Part 10 SIs: Partnership Insolvency

Provisions	Modifications
	"limited liability partnership agreement", in relation to a limited liability partnership, means any agreement, express or implied, made between the members of the limited liability partnership or between the limited liability partnership and the members of the limited liability partnership which determines the mutual rights and duties of the members, and their rights and duties in relation to the limited liability partnership.".
Section 437 (transitional provisions, and savings)	Delete section 437.
Section 440 (extent (Scotland))	
subsection (2)	In subsection (2), omit paragraph (b).
Section 441 (extent (Northern Ireland))	
	Delete section 441.
Section 442 (extent (other territories))	
	Delete section 442.
[**Schedule A1**	
Paragraph 6	
sub-paragraph (1)	For "directors of a company wish" substitute "limited liability partnership wishes".
	For "they" substitute "the designated members of the limited liability partnership".
[sub-paragraph (2)	For "directors" substitute "designated members of the limited liability partnership".
	In sub-paragraph (c) for "company and by the company's creditors" substitute "creditors of the limited liability partnership".]
Paragraph 7	
[sub-paragraph (1)	For "directors of a company" substitute "designated members of the limited liability partnership".
	In sub-paragraph (e)(iii) for "company and by the company's creditors" substitute "creditors of the limited liability partnership".]
Paragraph 8	
[sub-paragraph (2)(a)	Omit.
sub-paragraph (3A)	Omit.
sub-paragraph (4)(a)	Omit.
sub-paragraph (6)(c)(i)	Omit.]
Paragraph 9	
sub-paragraph (1)	For "directors" substitute "designated members of the limited liability partnership".
sub-paragraph (2)	For "directors" substitute "designated members of the limited liability partnership".
Paragraph 12	
sub-paragraph (1)(b)	Omit.
sub-paragraph (1)(c)	For "resolution may be passed" substitute "determination that it may be wound up may be made".
sub-paragraph (2)	For "transfer of shares" substitute "any transfer by a member of the limited liability partnership of his interest in the property of the limited liability partnership".
Paragraph 20	
sub-paragraph (8)	For "directors" substitute "designated members of the limited liability partnership".
sub-paragraph (9)	For "directors" substitute "designated members of the limited liability partnership".
Paragraph 24	
sub-paragraph (2)	For "directors" substitute "designated members of the limited liability partnership".
Paragraph 25	

Provisions	**Modifications**
sub-paragraph (2)(c)	For "directors" substitute "designated members of the limited liability partnership".
Paragraph 26	
sub-paragraph (1)	Omit ", director".
Paragraph 29	
[sub-paragraph (1)(a)	Omit.]
Paragraph 30	
[sub-paragraph (1)	Omit "the company meeting summoned under paragraph 29 and". For "that paragraph" substitute "paragraph 29".
new sub-paragraph (1A)	"If modifications to the proposal are proposed by creditors, the nominee must, before the date on which the creditors are to be asked whether to approve the proposed voluntary arrangement, ascertain from the limited liability partnership whether or not it agrees to the proposed modifications; and if at that date the limited liability partnership has failed to respond to a proposed modification, it shall be presumed not to have agreed to it.".]
[sub-paragraph (2)	Omit.]
. . .	. . .
[sub-paragraph (3)	Omit.]
Paragraph 31	
[sub-paragraph (1)(a)	Omit.
sub-paragraph (1A)	For "The company and its creditors" substitute "The creditors of the limited liability partnership".
sub-paragraph (4)	For "Neither the company nor its creditors may" substitute "The creditors of the limited liability partnership may not".
sub-paragraph (5)	For "neither the company nor its creditors may" substitute "the creditors of the limited liability partnership may not".
sub-paragraph (7)	For sub-paragraph (7) substitute the following— "(7) The designated members of the limited liability partnership may, before the beginning of the relevant period, give notice to the nominee of any modifications of the proposal for which the designated members intend to seek the approval of the creditors.".
sub-paragraph (7A)(a)	Omit.]
Paragraph 32	
[sub-paragraph (1)	Omit.
sub-paragraph (3)	Omit "the meeting of the company or (as the case may be) inform".
sub-paragraph (4)	For sub-paragraph (4) substitute— "(4) Where, in accordance with sub-paragraph (3)(b) the nominee informs the creditors of the limited liability partnership, of the expected cost of his intended actions, the creditors by a qualifying decision procedure shall decide whether or not to approve that expected cost.".
sub-paragraph (6)	For "A meeting of the company may resolve, and the creditors by a qualifying decision procedure may decide," substitute "The creditors by a qualifying decision procedure may decide".]
[Paragraph 35	
sub-paragraph (1)	Omit "a meeting of the company resolves, or".
sub-paragraph (1A)	Omit "meeting may resolve, and the". Omit "by the meeting or (as the case may be)".
sub-paragraph (2)	Omit.]
Paragraph 36	
sub-paragraph (2)	For sub-paragraph (2) substitute— "(2) The decision has effect if, in accordance with the rules, it has been taken by the creditors' meeting summoned under paragraph 29.".

Provisions	**Modifications**
sub-paragraph (3)	Omit.
sub-paragraph (4)	Omit.
sub-paragraph (5)	Omit.
. . .	. . .
Paragraph 38	
[sub-paragraph (1)(b)	Omit "at or in relation to the meeting of the company summoned under paragraph 29, or".
sub-paragraph (2)(a)	Omit "at the meeting of the company or".
sub-paragraph (3)(a)	For "30(3) and (4)" substitute "30(4)".
sub-paragraph (4)(a)(ii)	Omit "by the meeting of the company, or".
sub-paragraph (4)(b)	Omit.
sub-paragraph (5)	Omit "(b)(i) or".
sub-paragraph (6)	For "(4)(b) or (c)" substitute "(4)(c)".
sub-paragraph (7)(a)	Omit "(b) or".]
. . .	. . .
Schedule B1	
Paragraph 2	
sub-paragraph (c)	For "company or its directors" substitute "limited liability partnership".
Paragraph 8	
sub-paragraph (1)(a)	For "resolution for voluntary winding up" substitute "determination to wind up voluntarily".
Paragraph 9	Omit.
Paragraph 12	
sub-paragraph (1)(b)	Omit.
Paragraph 22	For sub-paragraph (1) substitute— "(1) A limited liability partnership may appoint an administrator.". Omit sub-paragraph (2).
Paragraph 23	
sub-paragraph (1)(b)	Omit "or its directors".
Paragraph 42	
sub-paragraph (2)	For "resolution may be passed for the winding up of' substitute "determination to wind up voluntarily may be made by".
[Paragraph 60A	
sub-paragraph (3)(b)	For "a company connected with the company." substitute "a company or limited liability partnership connected with the limited liability partnership.".]
Paragraph 61	For paragraph 61 substitute—" "61. The administrator has power to prevent any person from taking part in the management of the business of the limited liability partnership and to appoint any person to be a manager of that business.".
Paragraph 62	At the end add the following— "Subsections (3) and (4) of section 92 shall apply for the purposes of this paragraph as they apply for the purposes of that section.".
Paragraph 83	
sub-paragraph (6)(b)	For "resolution for voluntary winding up" substitute "determination to wind up voluntarily".
sub-paragraph (8)(b)	For "passing of the resolution for voluntary winding up" substitute "determination to wind up voluntarily".
sub-paragraph (8)(e)	For "passing of the resolution for voluntary winding up" substitute "determination to wind up voluntarily".
Paragraph 87	
sub-paragraph (2)(b)	Insert at the end "or".
sub-paragraph (2)(c)	Omit ", or".

Provisions	**Modifications**
sub-paragraph (2)(d)	Omit the words from "(d)" to "company".
Paragraph 89	
sub-paragraph (2)(b)	Insert at the end "or".
sub-paragraph (2)(c)	Omit ", or".
sub-paragraph (2)(d)	Omit the words from "(d)" to "company".
Paragraph 91	
sub-paragraph (1)(c)	Omit.
Paragraph 94	Omit.
Paragraph 95	For "to 94" substitute "and 93".
Paragraph 97	
sub-paragraph (1)(a)	Omit "or directors".
Paragraph 103	
sub-paragraph (5)	Omit.
Paragraph 105	Omit.]
Schedule 1	
Paragraph 19	For paragraph 19 substitute the following— "19. Power to enforce any rights the limited liability partnership has against the members under the terms of the limited liability partnership agreement."
Schedule 10	
[Section 6A(1)	In the entry relating to section 6A omit "members' or".]
Section 85(2)	In the entry relating to section 85(2) for "resolution for voluntary winding up" substitute "making of determination for voluntary winding up".
Section 89(4)	In the entry relating to section 89(4) for "Director" substitute "Designated member".
Section 93(3)	In the entry relating to section 93(3) for "general meeting of the company" substitute "meeting of members of the limited liability partnership".
Section 99(3)	In the entries relating to section 99(3) for "director" and "directors" where they appear substitute "designated member" or "designated members" as appropriate.
Section 105(3)	In the entry relating to section 105(3) for "company general meeting" substitute "meeting of the members of the limited liability partnership".
. . .	. . .
Sections 353(1) to 362	Delete the entries relating to sections 353(1) to 362 inclusive.
Section 429(5)	Delete the entry relating to section 429(5).
[Schedule A1, paragraph 9(2)	For "Directors" substitute "Designated Members".
Schedule A1, paragraph 20(9)	For "Directors" substitute "Designated Members".
Schedule B1, paragraph 27(4)	Omit "or directors".
Schedule B1, paragraph 29(7)	Omit "or directors".
Schedule B1, paragraph 32	Omit "or directors".]

NOTES

Entries relating to sections 1A, 4A, 6A, 389A, 426A–426C inserted by the Limited Liability Partnerships (Amendment) Regulations 2005, SI 2005/1989, reg 3, Sch 2, paras 1, 2, 3(b), (e), 12, 13, as from 1 October 2005, except in relation to a case where a petition for an administration order has been presented before that date; entry relating to s 389A (omitted) revoked by the Deregulation Act 2015 (Insolvency) (Consequential Amendments and Transitional and Savings Provisions) Order 2015, SI 2015/1641, art 4, Sch 1, para 3(1), (2), subject to savings in arts 7–9 thereof.

In the entry relating to section 2, the entry for sub-s (2) was substituted by the Insolvency (Miscellaneous Amendments) Regulations 2017, SI 2017/1119, reg 2, Sch 1, Pt 2, paras 6, 7, as from 8 December 2017 (note that Sch 1, Pt 2 to the 2017 Regulations applies to England and Wales only, and this entry, as it had effect before the amendments made by the 2017 Regulations, is set out below). Other words in square brackets inserted by SI 2005/1989, reg 3, Sch 2, paras 1, 3(a), as from 1 October 2005, except in relation to a case where a petition for an administration order has been presented before that date.

Entries relating to sub-ss (1) and (2) of section 3 substituted by SI 2017/1119, reg 2, Sch 1, Pt 2, paras 6, 8, as from 8 December 2017 (note that Sch 1, Pt 2 to the 2017 Regulations applies to England and Wales only, and this entry, as it had effect before the amendments made by the 2017 Regulations, is set out below).

Entries relating to sub-ss (1), (5), (5A), (6) of section 4 substituted, and entries relating to sub-ss (1A), (3), (4), (6A) inserted, by SI 2017/1119, reg 2, Sch 1, Pt 2, paras 6, 9–14, as from 8 December 2017 (note that Sch 1, Pt 2 to the 2017 Regulations applies to England and Wales only, and this entry, as it had effect before the amendments made by the 2017 Regulations, is set out below).

Entry relating to sub-s (2) of section 4A substituted, and entry relating to sub-s (5A) inserted, by SI 2017/1119, reg 2, Sch 1, Pt 2, paras 6, 15, 16, as from 8 December 2017 (note that Sch 1, Pt 2 to the 2017 Regulations applies to England and Wales only, and this entry, as it had effect before the amendments made by the 2017 Regulations, is set out below).

Entry relating to sub-s (4) of section 5 substituted, by SI 2017/1119, reg 2, Sch 1, Pt 2, paras 6, 17, as from 8 December 2017 (note that Sch 1, Pt 2 to the 2017 Regulations applies to England and Wales only, and this entry, as it had effect before the amendments made by the 2017 Regulations, is set out below). Words omitted from entry relating to section 5 revoked by SI 2005/1989, reg 3, Sch 2, paras 1, 3(c), as from 1 October 2005, except in relation to a case where a petition for an administration order has been presented before that date.

Entries relating to sub-ss (1)–(5) of section 6 substituted, and entry relating to sub-s (7) inserted, by SI 2017/1119, reg 2, Sch 1, Pt 2, paras 6, 18, 19, as from 8 December 2017 (note that Sch 1, Pt 2 to the 2017 Regulations applies to England and Wales only, and this entry, as it had effect before the amendments made by the 2017 Regulations, is set out below).

Entry relating to sub-s (1) of section 7 revoked, and entry relating to sub-s (2) originally inserted, by SI 2005/1989, reg 3, Sch 2, paras 1, 3(f), as from 1 October 2005, except in relation to a case where a petition for an administration order has been presented before that date. Entry relating to sub-s (2) subsequently substituted by SI 2017/1119, reg 2, Sch 1, Pt 2, paras 6, 20, as from 8 December 2017 (note that Sch 1, Pt 2 to the 2017 Regulations applies to England and Wales only, and this entry, as it had effect before the amendments made by the 2017 Regulations, is set out below).

In the paragraph following the entry for section 7, words in square brackets substituted by SI 2005/1989, reg 3, Sch 2, paras 1, 3(g), as from 1 October 2005, except in relation to a case where a petition for an administration order has been presented before that date.

Entry relating to sub-s (2) of section 2 substituted by SI 2017/1119, reg 2, Sch 1, Pt 2, paras 6, 21(1), (2), as from 8 December 2017 (note that Sch 1, Pt 2 to the 2017 Regulations applies to England and Wales only, and this entry, as it had effect before the amendments made by the 2017 Regulations, is set out below).

Entry relating to sub-s (2) of section 3 substituted by SI 2017/1119, reg 2, Sch 1, Pt 2, paras 6, 21(1), (3), as from 8 December 2017 (note that Sch 1, Pt 2 to the 2017 Regulations applies to England and Wales only, and this entry, as it had effect before the amendments made by the 2017 Regulations, is set out below).

Entry relating to s 8: revoked by SI 2005/1989, regs 3, 4, Sch 2, paras 1, 4, except where a petition for an administration order has been presented before 1 October 2005, and previously (as amended by SI 2004/355) read as follows:

"Section 8 (power of court to make order)	
. . .	. . .
subsection (4)	Omit subsection (4).
[subsection (5)	Omit subsection (5).
subsection (6)	Omit subsection (6).]".

Entries relating to ss 9–11, 13, 14: revoked by SI 2005/1989, regs 3, 4, Sch 2, paras 1, 4, except where a petition for an administration order has been presented before 1 October 2005, and previously read as follows:

"Section 9 (application for order)	
subsection (1)	Delete ", or the directors".
Section 10 (effect of application)	
subsection (1)	In paragraph (a) for "no resolution may be passed" to the end of the subsection substitute "no determination may be made or order made for the winding up of the limited liability partnership.".
Section 11 (effect of order)	
subsection (3)	In paragraph (a) for "no resolution may be passed" to the end of the subsection substitute "no determination may be made or order made for the winding up of the limited liability partnership.".
Section 13 (appointment of administrator)	
subsection (3)	In paragraph (c) delete "or the directors".
Section 14 (general powers)	
subsection (2)	For paragraph (a) substitute— "(a) to prevent any person from taking part in the management of the business of the limited liability partnership and to appoint any person to be a manager of that business, and"; and at the end add the following— "Subsections (3) and (4) of section 92 shall apply for the purposes of this subsection as they apply for the purposes of that section."".

Entries relating to sections 73, 94, 98, 194 revoked by SI 2017/1119, reg 2, Sch 1, Pt 2, paras 6, 22, 23, 27, 36, as from 8 December 2017 (note that Sch 1, Pt 2 to the 2017 Regulations applies to England and Wales only, and these entries, as they had effect before the amendments made by the 2017 Regulations, are set out below).

Entries relating to sub-s (2A), (2B) of section 84 inserted, and in the entry relating to sub-s (5) the figures in square brackets were substituted, by SI 2005/1989, reg 3, Sch 2, paras 1, 5, as from 1 October 2005, except in relation to a case where a petition for an administration order has been presented before that date.

Entries relating to sections 93 and 105 revoked by the Public Services Reform (Insolvency) (Scotland) Order 2016, SSI 2016/141, art 7(3)(a), as from a day to be appointed (being the day that the Small Business, Enterprise and Employment Act 2015, s 122(2) comes into force for all remaining purposes in Scotland). For savings, see the note to the Insolvency Act 1986, s 66 at **[1.52]**).

Entry relating to sub-s (7) of section 95 revoked by SI 2017/1119, reg 2, Sch 1, Pt 2, paras 6, 24, as from 8 December 2017 (note that Sch 1, Pt 2 to the 2017 Regulations applies to England and Wales only, and this entry, as it had effect before the amendments made by the 2017 Regulations, is set out below).

Entry relating to sub-s (2) of section 96 substituted, and words omitted revoked, by SI 2017/1119, reg 2, Sch 1, Pt 2, paras 6, 25, 26, as from 8 December 2017 (note that Sch 1, Pt 2 to the 2017 Regulations applies to England and Wales only, and this entry, as it had effect before the amendments made by the 2017 Regulations, is set out below).

Entries relating to sub-ss (1), (2A), (3) of section 99 substituted by SI 2017/1119, reg 2, Sch 1, Pt 2, paras 6, 28, as from 8 December 2017 (note that Sch 1, Pt 2 to the 2017 Regulations applies to England and Wales only, and this entry, as it had effect before the amendments made by the 2017 Regulations, is set out below).

Entry relating to sub-s (1) of section 100 substituted, and entry relating to sub-s (1B) inserted, by SI 2017/1119, reg 2, Sch 1, Pt 2, paras 6, 29, 30, as from 8 December 2017 (note that Sch 1, Pt 2 to the 2017 Regulations applies to England and Wales only, and this entry, as it had effect before the amendments made by the 2017 Regulations, is set out below).

Entry relating to section 106: revoked by SI 2017/1119, reg 2, Sch 1, Pt 2, paras 6, 31, as from 8 December 2017 (note that Sch 1, Pt 2 to the 2017 Regulations applies to England and Wales only, and this entry, as it had effect before the amendments made by the 2017 Regulations, is set out below). Note that para 31 provides that the entry relating to "subsection (1) of section 106 (including the heading)" should be omitted. On a strict interpretation of this wording, that would leave the entries for sub-ss (5A) and (6) of section 106 in the table (without a heading above them). BEIS have subsequently confirmed that the intention was to omit the entire entry.

Words in square brackets in entries relating to sections 122, 124, 127, 247, 387 inserted by SI 2005/1989, reg 3, Sch 2, paras 1, 6–8, 10, 11, as from 1 October 2005, except in relation to a case where a petition for an administration order has been presented before that date.

In entry relating to section 124A, words in square brackets substituted by the Financial Services and Markets Act 2000 (Consequential Amendments) Order 2004, SI 2004/355, art 10(1), (3), as from 4 March 2004.

Entry relating to sub-s (2) of section 165 revoked by SI 2017/1119, reg 2, Sch 1, Pt 2, paras 6, 32, as from 8 December 2017 (note that Sch 1, Pt 2 to the 2017 Regulations applies to England and Wales only, and this entry, as it had effect before the amendments made by the 2017 Regulations, is set out below).

Entry relating to sub-s (5) of section 166 substituted by SI 2017/1119, reg 2, Sch 1, Pt 2, paras 6, 33, as from 8 December 2017 (note that Sch 1, Pt 2 to the 2017 Regulations applies to England and Wales only, and this entry, as it had effect before the amendments made by the 2017 Regulations, is set out below).

Entry relating to sub-s (8) of section 171 substituted by SI 2017/1119, reg 2, Sch 1, Pt 2, paras 6, 34, as from 8 December 2017 (note that Sch 1, Pt 2 to the 2017 Regulations applies to England and Wales only, and this entry, as it had effect before the amendments made by the 2017 Regulations, is set out below).

Entry relating to sub-s (2) of section 173 substituted by SI 2017/1119, reg 2, Sch 1, Pt 2, paras 6, 35, as from 8 December 2017 (note that Sch 1, Pt 2 to the 2017 Regulations applies to England and Wales only, and this entry, as it had effect before the amendments made by the 2017 Regulations, is set out below).

Entry relating to s 233 revoked by SI 2005/1989, regs 3, 4, Sch 2, paras 1, 9, except where a petition for an administration order has been presented before 1 October 2005, and previously read as follows:

"Section 233 (supplies of gas, water, electricity etc)

subsection (1)	For paragraph (c) substitute the following— "(c) a voluntary arrangement under Part I has taken effect in accordance with section 5".
subsection (4)	For paragraph (c) substitute the following— "(c) the date on which the voluntary arrangement took effect in accordance with section 5"."

In entry relating to section 435, words in square brackets inserted by the Civil Partnership Act 2004 (Amendments to Subordinate Legislation) Order 2005, SI 2005/2114, art 2(18), Sch 18, Pt 1, para 3, as from 5 December 2005.

Entries relating to Sch A1 and Sch B1 inserted by SI 2005/1989, reg 3, Sch 2, paras 1, 14, as from 1 October 2005, except in relation to a case where a petition for an administration order has been presented before that date. All amendments in the entries relating to Sch A1 and Sch B1 were made by SI 2017/1119, reg 2, Sch 1, Pt 2, paras 6, 37–53, as from 8 December 2017 (note that Sch 1, Pt 2 to the 2017 Regulations applies to England and Wales only, and the relevant entries, as they had effect before the amendments made by the 2017 Regulations, are set out below).

Entries in square brackets in entry relating to Sch 10 inserted by SI 2005/1989, reg 3, Sch 2, paras 1, 15, as from 1 October 2005, except in relation to a case where a petition for an administration order has been presented before that date. Entry omitted revoked by SI 2017/1119, reg 2, Sch 1, Pt 2, paras 6, 54, as from 8 December 2017 (note that Sch 1, Pt 2 to the 2017 Regulations applies to England and Wales only, and this entry, as it had effect before the amendments made by the 2017 Regulations, is set out below).

Transitional provisions and savings: see further Sch 7 at **[10.45]**.

Note: the Insolvency (Miscellaneous Amendments) Regulations 2017, SI 2017/1119, Sch 1, Pt 2 applies to England and Wales only. The entries amended by those Regulations (as they had effect before those amendments were made) read as follows—

Provisions	Modifications
The following modifications to sections 2 to 7 apply where a proposal under section 1 has been made by the limited liability partnership.	
Section 2 (procedure where the nominee is not the liquidator or administrator)	
[subsection (1)	[For "the directors do" substitute "the limited liability partnership does".
subsection (2)	In paragraph [(aa)] for "meetings of the company and of it creditors" substitute "a meeting of the creditors of the limited liability partnership";
	In paragraph (b) for the first "meetings" substitute "a meeting" and for the second "meetings" substitute "meeting".
subsection (3)	For "the person intending to make the proposal" substitute "the designated members of the limited liability partnership".

Provisions	Modifications
subsection (4)	[In paragraph (a)] for "the person intending to make the proposal" substitute "the designated members of the limited liability partnership". [In paragraph (b) for "that person" substitute "those designated members".]
Section 3 (summoning of meetings)	
subsection (1)	For "such meetings as are mentioned in section 2(2)" substitute "a meeting of creditors" and for "those meetings" substitute "that meeting".
subsection (2)	Delete subsection (2).
Section 4 (decisions of meetings)	
subsection (1)	For "meetings" substitute "meeting".
subsection (5)	For "each of the meetings" substitute "the meeting".
new subsection (5A)	Insert a new subsection (5A) as follows—
	"(5A) If modifications to the proposal are proposed at the meeting the chairman of the meeting shall, before the conclusion of the meeting, ascertain from the limited liability partnership whether or not it accepts the proposed modifications; and if at that conclusion the limited liability partnership has failed to respond to a proposed modification it shall be presumed not to have agreed to it."
subsection (6)	For "either" substitute "the"; after "the result of the meeting", in the first place where it occurs, insert "(including, where modifications to the proposal were proposed at the meeting, the response to those proposed modifications made by the limited liability partnership)"; and at the end add "and to the limited liability partnership".
[Section 4A (approval of arrangement)	
subsection (2)	Omit "—(a)".
	For "both meetings" substitute "the meeting".
	Omit the words from ", or" to "that section".
subsection (3)	Omit.
subsection (4)	Omit.
subsection (5)	Omit.
subsection (6)	Omit.]
Section 5 (effect of approval)	
. . .	. . .
subsection (4)	For "each of the reports" substitute "the report".
Section 6 (challenge of decisions)	
subsection (1)	For . . . "either of the meetings" substitute "the meeting".
subsection (2)	For "either of the meetings" substitute "the meeting" and after paragraph [(aa)] add a new paragraph [(ab) as follows—
	"(ab)] any member of the limited liability partnership; and".
	Omit the word "and" at the end of paragraph (b) and omit paragraph (c).
subsection (3)	For "each of the reports" substitute "the report".
subsection (4)	For subsection (4) substitute the following—
	"(4) Where on such an application the court is satisfied as to either of the grounds mentioned in subsection (1), it may do one or both of the following, namely—
	(a) revoke or suspend [any decision approving the voluntary arrangement which has effect under section 4A];
	(b) give a direction to any person for the summoning of a further meeting to consider any revised proposal the limited liability partnership may make or, in a case falling within subsection (1)(b), a further meeting to consider the original proposal."
subsection (5)	For . . . "meetings" substitute "a meeting", for . . . and for "person who made the original proposal" substitute "limited liability partnership".
Section 7 (implementation of proposal)	
. . .	. . .
[subsection (2)	In paragraph (a) omit "one or both of" and for "meetings" substitute "meeting".]

Provisions	**Modifications**
The following modifications to sections 2 and 3 apply where a proposal under section 1 has been made, where [the limited liability partnership is in administration], by the administrator or, where the limited liability partnership is being wound up, by the liquidator.	
Section 2 (procedure where the nominee is not the liquidator or administrator)	
subsection (2)	In paragraph (a) for "meetings of the company" substitute "meetings of the members of the limited liability partnership".
Section 3 (summoning of meetings)	
subsection (2)	For "meetings of the company" substitute "a meeting of the members of the limited liability partnership".
Section 73 (alternative modes of winding up)	
subsection (1)	Delete ", within the meaning given to that expression by section 735 of the Companies Act,".
Section 94 (final meeting prior to dissolution)	
subsection (1)	For "a general meeting of the company" substitute "a meeting of the members of the limited liability partnership".
new subsection (5A)	Add a new subsection (5A) as follows "(5A) Subsections (3) and (4) of section 92 shall apply for the purposes of this section as they apply for the purposes of that section."
subsection (6)	For "a general meeting of the company" substitute "a meeting of the members of the limited liability partnership".
Section 95 (effect of company's insolvency)	
subsection (1)	For "directors'" substitute "designated members'".
subsection (7)	For subsection (7) substitute the following— "(7) In this section "the relevant period" means the period of 6 months immediately preceding the date on which the limited liability partnership determined that it be wound up voluntarily."
Section 96 (conversion to creditors' voluntary winding up)	
paragraph (a)	For "directors'" substitute "designated members'".
paragraph (b)	Substitute a new paragraph (b) as follows— "(b) the creditors' meeting was the meeting mentioned in section 98 in the next Chapter;".
Section 98 (meeting of creditors)	
subsection (1)	For paragraph (a) substitute the following— "(a) cause a meeting of its creditors to be summoned for a day not later than the 14th day after the day on which the limited liability partnership determines that it be wound up voluntarily;".
subsection (5)	For "were sent the notices summoning the company meeting at which it was resolved that the company be wound up voluntarily" substitute "the limited liability partnership determined that it be wound up voluntarily".
Section 99 (directors to lay statement of affairs before creditors)	
subsection (1)	For "the directors of the company" substitute "the designated members" and for "the director so appointed" substitute "the designated member so appointed".
subsection (2)	For "directors" substitute "designated members".
subsection (3)	For "directors" substitute "designated members" and for "director" substitute "designated member".
Section 100 (appointment of liquidator)	
subsection (1)	For "The creditors and the company at their respective meetings mentioned in section 98" substitute "The creditors at their meeting mentioned in section 98 and the limited liability partnership".
subsection (3)	Delete "director,".
Section 106 (final meeting prior to dissolution)	
subsection (1)	For "a general meeting of the company" substitute "a meeting of the members of the limited liability partnership".
new subsection (5A)	After subsection (5) insert a new subsection (5A) as follows— "(5A) Subsections (3) and (4) of section 92 shall apply for the purposes of this section as they apply for the purposes of that section."
subsection (6)	For "a general meeting of the company" substitute "a meeting of the members of the limited liability partnership".

Provisions	Modifications
Section 165 (voluntary winding up)	
subsection (2)	In paragraph (a) for "an extraordinary resolution of the company" substitute "a determination by a meeting of the members of the limited liability partnership".
subsection (4)	For paragraph (c) substitute the following— "(c) summon meetings of the members of the limited liability partnership for the purpose of obtaining their sanction or for any other purpose he may think fit."
new subsection (4A)	Insert a new subsection (4A) as follows— "(4A) Subsections (3) and (4) of section 92 shall apply for the purposes of this section as they apply for the purposes of that section."
Section 166 (creditors' voluntary winding up)	
subsection (5)	In paragraph (b) for "directors" substitute "designated members".
Section 171 (removal, etc (voluntary winding up))	
subsection (2)	For paragraph (a) substitute the following— "(a) in the case of a members' voluntary winding up, by a meeting of the members of the limited liability partnership summoned specially for that purpose, or".
subsection (6)	In paragraph (a) for "final meeting of the company" substitute "final meeting of the members of the limited liability partnership" and in paragraph (b) for "final meetings of the company" substitute "final meetings of the members of the limited liability partnership".
new subsection (7)	Insert a new subsection (7) as follows— "(7) Subsections (3) and (4) of section 92 are to apply for the purposes of this section as they apply for the purposes of that section."
Section 173 (release (voluntary winding up))	
subsection (2)	In paragraph (a) for "a general meeting of the company" substitute "a meeting of the members of the limited liability partnership".
Section 194 (resolutions passed at adjourned meetings)	After "contributories" insert "or of the members of a limited liability partnership".
[Schedule A1	
Paragraph 6	
sub-paragraph (1)	For "directors of a company wish" substitute "limited liability partnership wishes". For "they" substitute "the designated members of the limited liability partnership".
sub-paragraph (2)	For "directors" substitute "the designated members of the limited liability partnership". In sub-paragraph (c), for "meetings of the company and" substitute "a meeting of".
Paragraph 7	
sub-paragraph (1)	For "directors of a company" substitute "designated members of the limited liability partnership". In sub-paragraph (e)(iii), for "meetings of the company and" substitute "a meeting of".
Paragraph 8	
sub-paragraph (2)	For "meetings" substitute "meeting". For "are" substitute "is". Omit the words in parenthesis.
sub-paragraph (3)	For "either of those meetings" substitute "the meeting". For "those meetings were" substitute "that meeting was". Omit the words in parenthesis.
sub-paragraph (4)	For "either" substitute "the".
sub-paragraph (6)(c)	For "one or both of the meetings" substitute "the meeting".
Paragraph 29	
sub-paragraph (1)	For "meetings of the company and its creditors" substitute "a meeting of the creditors of the limited liability partnership".
Paragraph 30	
sub-paragraph (1)	For "meetings" substitute "meeting".

Provisions	Modifications
new sub-paragraph (2A)	Insert new sub-paragraph (2A) as follows—
	"(2A) If modifications to the proposal are proposed at the meeting the chairman of the meeting shall, before the conclusion of the meeting, ascertain from the limited liability partnership whether or not it accepts the proposed modifications; and if at that conclusion the limited liability partnership has failed to respond to a proposed modification it shall be presumed not to have agreed to it.".
sub-paragraph (3)	For "either" substitute "the".
	After "the result of the meeting" in the first place where it occurs insert "(including, where modifications to the proposal were proposed at the meeting, the response to those proposed modifications made by the limited liability partnership)".
	At the end add "and to the limited liability partnership".
Paragraph 31	
sub-paragraph (1)	For "meetings" substitute "meeting".
sub-paragraph (7)	For "directors of the company" substitute "designated members of the limited liability partnership".
	For "meetings (or either of them)" substitute "meeting".
	For "directors" substitute "limited liability partnership".
	For "those meetings" substitute "that meeting".
Paragraph 32	
sub-paragraph (2)	For sub-paragraphs (a) and (b) substitute "with the day on which the meeting summoned under paragraph 29 is first held.".
Paragraph 37	
sub-paragraph (5)	For "each of the reports of the meetings" substitute "the report of the meeting".
Paragraph 38	
sub-paragraph (1)(a)	For "one or both of the meetings" substitute "the meeting".
sub-paragraph (1)(b)	For "either of those meetings" substitute "the meeting".
sub-paragraph (2)(a)	For "either of the meetings" substitute "the meeting".
	After sub-paragraph (2)(a) insert new (aa) as follows— "(aa) any member of the limited liability partnership;".
sub-paragraph (2)(b)	Omit "creditors'".
sub-paragraph (3)(a)	For "each of the reports" substitute "the report".
sub-paragraph (3)(b)	Omit "creditors'".
sub-paragraph (4)(a)(ii)	Omit "in question".
sub-paragraph (4)(b)(i)	For "further meetings" substitute "a further meeting" and for "directors" substitute "limited liability partnership".
sub-paragraph (4)(b)(ii)	Omit "company or (as the case may be) creditors'".
sub-paragraph (5)	For "directors do" substitute "limited liability partnerships does".
Paragraph 39	
sub-paragraph (1)	For "one or both of the meetings" substitute "the meeting".
Schedule 10	
Section 106(6)	In the entry relating to section 106(6) for "final meeting of the company" substitute "final meeting of the members of the limited liability partnership".

SCHEDULE 4

Regulation 5(3)

[10.42]
The provisions listed in this Schedule are not applied to Scotland to the extent specified below—

Sections 50 to 52;

Section 53(1) and (2), to the extent that those subsections do not relate to the requirement for a copy of the instrument and notice being forwarded to the registrar of companies;

Section 53(4) (6) and (7);

Section 54(1), (2), (3) (to the extent that that subsection does not relate to the requirement for a copy of the interlocutor to be sent to the registrar of companies), and subsections (5), (6) and (7);

Sections 55 to 58;

Section 60, other than subsection (1);

Section 61, including subsections (6) and (7) to the extent that those subsections do not relate to anything to be done or which may be done to or by the registrar of companies;

Part 10 SIs: Partnership Insolvency

Section 62, including subsection (5) to the extent that that subsection does not relate to anything to be done or which may be done to or by the registrar of companies;
Sections 63 to 66;
Section 67, including subsections (1) and (8) to the extent that those subsections do not relate to anything to be done or which may be done to the registrar of companies;
Section 68;
Section 69, including subsections (1) and (2) to the extent that those subsections do not relate to anything to be done or which may be done by the registrar of companies;
Sections 70 and 71;
Subsection 84(3), to the extent that it does not concern the copy of the resolution being forwarded to the registrar of companies within 15 days;
Sections 91 to [92A];
Section 94, including subsections (3) and (4) to the extent that those subsections do not relate to the liquidator being required to send to the registrar of companies a copy of the account and a return of the final meeting;
Section 95;
Section 97;
Sections 100 to 102;
Sections 104 to [104A];
Section 106, including subsections [(3) to (7)] to the extent that those subsections do not relate to the liquidator being required to send to the registrar of companies a copy of the account of winding up and a return of the final meeting/quorum [or a statement about a member State liquidator];
Sections 109 to 111;
Section 112, including subsection (3) to the extent that that subsection does not relate to the liquidator being required to send to the registrar a copy of the order made by the court;
Sections 113 to 115;
Sections 126 to 128;
Section 130(1) to the extent that that subsection does not relate to a copy of the order being forwarded by the court to the registrar;
Section 131;
Sections 133 to 135;
Sections 138 to 140;
Sections 142 to 146;
Section 147, including subsection (3) to the extent that that subsection does not relate to a copy of the order being forwarded by the company to the registrar;
Section 162 to the extent that that section concerns the matters set out in Section C.2 of Schedule 5 to the Scotland Act 1998 as being exceptions to the insolvency reservation;
Sections 163 to 167;
Section 169;
Section 170, including subsection (2) to the extent that that subsection does not relate to an application being made by the registrar to make good the default;
Section 171;
Section 172, including [subsections (8) to (10) to the extent that those subsections do] not relate to the liquidator being required to give notice to the registrar [or a statement about a member State liquidator];
Sections 173 and 174;
Section 177;
Sections 185 to 189;
Sections 191 to 194;
Section 196 to the extent that that section applies to the specified devolved functions of Part IV of the Insolvency Act 1986;
Section 199;
Section 200 to the extent that it applies to the specified devolved functions of Part IV of the First Group of Parts of the 1986 Act;
Sections 206 to 215;
Section 218 subsections (1), (2), (4) and (6);
Section 231 to 232 to the extent that the sections apply to administrative receivers, liquidators and provisional liquidators;
Section 233, to the extent that that section applies in the case of the appointment of an administrative receiver, of a voluntary arrangement taking effect, of a company going into liquidation or where a provisional liquidator is appointed;
[Section 233A to the extent that that section applies in the case of a voluntary arrangement taking effect]
Section 234 to the extent that that section applies to situations other than those where an administration order applies;
Section 235 to the extent that that section applies to situations other than those where an administration order applies;
Sections 236 to 237 to the extent that those sections apply to situations other than administration orders and winding up;
Sections 242 to 243;
Section 244 to the extent that that section applies in circumstances other than a company which is subject to an administration order;

Section 245;
Section 251, to the extent that that section contains definitions which apply only to devolved matters;
Section 416(1) and (4), to the extent that those subsections apply to section 206(1)(a) and (b) in connection with the offence provision relating to the winding up of a limited liability partnership;
Schedule 2;
Schedule 3;
Schedule 4;
Schedule 8, to the extent that that Schedule does not apply to voluntary arrangements or administrations within the meaning of Parts I and II of the 1986 Act.
In addition, Schedule 10, which concerns punishment of offences under the Insolvency Act 1986, lists various sections of the Insolvency Act 1986 which create an offence. The following sections, which are listed in Schedule 10, are devolved in their application to Scotland:
Section 51(4);
Section 51(5);
Sections 53(2) to 62(5) to the extent that those subsections relate to matters other than delivery to the registrar of companies;
Section 64(2);
Section 65(4);
Section 66(6);
Section 67(8) to the extent that that subsection relates to matters other than delivery to the registrar of companies;
Section 93(3);
Section 94(4) to the extent that that subsection relates to matters other than delivery to the registrar of companies;
Section 94(6);
Section 95(8);
Section 105(3);
Section 106(4) to the extent that that subsection relates to matters other than delivery to the registrar of companies;
Section 106(6);
Section 109(2);
Section 114(4);
Section 131(7);
Section 164;
Section 166(7);
Section 188(2);
Section 192(2);
Sections 206 to 211; and
Section 235(5) to the extent that it relates to matters other than administration orders.

NOTES

The figure "92A" in square brackets was substituted (for the original figure "93"), and the figure "104A" in square brackets was substituted (for the original figure "105"), by the Public Services Reform (Insolvency) (Scotland) Order 2016, SSI 2016/141, art 7(3)(b) (for savings, see the note to the Insolvency Act 1986, s 66 at **[1.52]**).

In the entries relating to sections 106 and 172, the words in the first pair of square brackets were substituted, and the words in the final pair of square brackets were inserted, by the Insolvency (Miscellaneous Amendments) Regulations 2017, SI 2017/1119, reg 2, Sch 1, Pt 3, para 56, as from 8 December 2017.

Entry relating to "section 233A" inserted by the Insolvency (Protection of Essential Supplies) Order 2015, SI 2015/989, art 6, Schedule, para 2.

SCHEDULE 5

(Sch 5 (General and consequential amendments in other legislation) in so far as relevant to this work, the amendments contained in this Schedule have been incorporated at the appropriate place.)

SCHEDULE 6
APPLICATION OF SUBORDINATE LEGISLATION

Regulation 10

(Pt I outside the scope of this work.)

PART II
REGULATIONS MADE UNDER THE 1986 ACT

[10.43]

1. Insolvency Practitioners Regulations 1990

2. The Insolvency Practitioners (Recognised Professional Bodies) Order 1986

3. The Insolvency Rules 1986 and the Insolvency (Scotland) Rules 1986 (except in so far as they relate to the exceptions to the reserved matters specified in section C 2 of Part II of Schedule 5 to the Scotland Act 1998)

4. The Insolvency Fees Order 1986

5. The Co-operation of Insolvency Courts (Designation of Relevant Countries and Territories) Order 1986

6. The Co-operation of Insolvency Courts (Designation of Relevant Countries and Territories) Order 1996

7. The Co-operation of Insolvency Courts (Designation of Relevant Country) Order 1998

8. Insolvency Proceedings (Monetary Limits) Order 1986

9. Insolvency Practitioners Tribunal (Conduct of Investigations) Rules 1986

10. Insolvency Regulations 1994

11. Insolvency (Amendment) Regulations 2000

NOTES

Para 9: revoked by the Deregulation Act 2015 (Insolvency) (Consequential Amendments and Transitional and Savings Provisions) Order 2015, SI 2015/1641, art 4, Sch 1, para 3(1), (3), subject to savings in arts 7–9 thereof.

PART III
REGULATIONS MADE UNDER OTHER LEGISLATION

[10.44]

1. . . .

2. The Companies (Disqualification Orders) Regulations 1986

3. The Insolvent Companies (Disqualification of Unfit Directors) Proceedings Rules 1987

4. The Contracting Out (Functions of the Official Receiver) Order 1995

5. The Uncertificated Securities Regulations 1995

[**6.** The Insolvent Companies (Reports on Conduct of Directors) (England and Wales) Rules 2016

7. The Insolvent Companies (Reports on Conduct of Directors) (Scotland) Rules 2016]

NOTES

Para 1: revoked by the Limited Liability Partnerships (Application of Companies Act 2006) Regulations 2009, SI 2009/1804, reg 85, Sch 3, Pt 2, para 13(1), (7)(b).

Paras 6, 7: substituted by the Enterprise and Regulatory Reform Act 2013 (Consequential Amendments) (Bankruptcy) and the Small Business, Enterprise and Employment Act 2015 (Consequential Amendments) Regulations 2016, SI 2016/481, reg 4.

[SCHEDULE 7
TRANSITIONAL AND SAVINGS PROVISIONS

[10.45]

1 Interpretation

In this Schedule—

"the 1986 Act" means the Insolvency Act 1986, as applied to limited liability partnerships;

"the 1986 Rules" means the Insolvency Rules 1986 as they had effect immediately before the 6th April 2017 in their application to limited liability partnerships;

"the 2016 Rules" means the Insolvency (England and Wales) Rules 2016, as applied to limited liability partnerships; and

"the commencement date" means the date this Schedule comes into force.

2 Amendments to the 2016 Rules made by the Insolvency Amendment (EU 2015/848) Regulations 2017 do not apply where proceedings opened before commencement date

(1) The amendments made by the Insolvency Amendment (EU 2015/848) Regulations 2017 to the 2016 Rules do not apply where proceedings in relation to a limited liability partnership opened before the commencement date.

(2) The time at which proceedings are opened is to be determined for the purpose of this paragraph in accordance with Article 2(8) of Regulation (EU) 2015/848 of the European Parliament and of the Council of 20th May 2015.

3 Requirement for office-holder to provide information to creditors on opting out

(1) Rule 1.39 of the 2016 Rules (which requires an office-holder to inform a creditor in the first communication that the creditor may elect to opt out of receiving further documents relating to the proceedings) does not apply to an office-holder in relation to a limited liability partnership who delivers the first communication before the commencement date.

(2) However, if such an office-holder informs a creditor in a communication that the creditor may elect to opt out as mentioned in sub-paragraph (1), the communication must contain the information required by rule 1.39(2) of the 2016 Rules.

4 Electronic communication

(1) Where proceedings in relation to a limited liability partnership commence before the commencement date, Rule 1.45(4) of the 2016 Rules does not apply.

(2) For the purposes of this paragraph proceedings "commence" on—
- (a) the delivery of a proposal for a voluntary arrangement to the intended nominee;
- (b) the appointment of an administrator under paragraph 14 or 22 of Schedule B1 to the 1986 Act;
- (c) the making of an administration order;
- (d) the appointment of an administrative receiver;
- (e) the passing or deemed passing of a resolution to wind up a limited liability partnership; or
- (f) the making of a winding-up order.

5 Statements of affairs

(1) Where proceedings in relation to a limited liability partnership commence before the commencement date and a person is required to provide a statement of affairs, the provisions of the 2016 Rules relating to statements of affairs in administration, administrative receivership and winding up do not apply and the following rules in the 1986 Rules continue to apply—
- (a) rules 2.28 to 2.32 (administration);
- (b) rules 3.3 to 3.8 (administrative receivership); and
- (c) rules 4.32 to 4.42 (winding up).

(2) For the purposes of this paragraph proceedings "commence" on—
- (a) the appointment of an administrator under paragraph 14 or 22 of Schedule B1;
- (b) the making of an administration order;
- (c) the appointment of an administrative receiver
- (d) the passing or deemed passing of a resolution to wind up a limited liability partnership; or
- (e) the making of a winding-up order.

6 Savings in respect of meetings taking place on or after the commencement date and resolutions by correspondence

(1) This paragraph applies where in relation to a limited liability partnership on or after the commencement date—
- (a) a creditors' or contributories' meeting is to be held as a result of a notice issued before that date in relation to a meeting for which provision is made by the 1986 Rules or the 1986 Act;
- (b) a meeting is to be held as a result of a requisition by a creditor or contributory made before that date;
- (c) a meeting is to be held as a result of a statement made under paragraph 52(1)(b) of Schedule B1 to the 1986 Act and a request is made before that date which obliges the administrator to summon an initial creditors' meeting; or
- (d) a meeting is required by sections 93 or 105 of the 1986 Act in the winding up of a limited liability partnership where the resolution to wind up was passed before 6th April 2010.

(2) Where a meeting referred to in sub-paragraph (1)(a) to (d) is held in relation to a limited liability partnership, Part 15 of the 2016 Rules does not apply and the provisions of the 1986 Rules relating to the following continue to apply—
- (a) the requirement to hold the meeting;
- (b) notice and advertisement of the meeting;
- (c) governance of the meeting;
- (d) recording and taking minutes of the meeting;
- (e) the report or return of the meeting;
- (f) membership and formalities of establishment of liquidation and creditors' committees where a resolution to form the committee is passed at the meeting;
- (g) the office-holder's resignation or removal at the meeting;
- (h) the office-holder's release;
- (i) fixing the office-holder's remuneration;
- (j) hand-over of assets to a supervisor of a voluntary arrangement where the proposal is approved at the meeting;
- (k) the notice of the appointment of a supervisor of a voluntary arrangement where the appointment is made at the meeting;
- (l) claims that remuneration is or that other expenses are excessive; and
- (m) complaints about exclusion at the meeting.

(3) Where in relation to a limited liability partnership, before the commencement date, the office-holder seeks to obtain the passing of a resolution by correspondence under rule 2.48, 4.63A or 6.88A of the 1986 Rules—
- (a) the relevant provisions of the 2016 Rules do not apply;
- (b) the provisions of the 1986 Rules relating to resolutions by correspondence continue to apply; and
- (c) the provisions of the 1986 Rules referred to in sub-paragraph (2) of this paragraph apply in relation to any meeting that those provisions require the office-holder to summon.

(4) However, any application to the court in respect of a meeting or vote to which this paragraph applies is to be made in accordance with Part 12 of the 2016 Rules.

7 Savings in respect of final meetings taking place on or after the commencement date

(1) This paragraph applies where—

(a) before the commencement date—
  (i) a final report to creditors is sent under rule 4.49D of the 1986 Rules (final report to creditors in liquidation),
  (ii) a final report to creditors and bankrupt is sent under rule 6.78B of the 1986 Rules (final report to creditors and bankrupt), or
  (iii) a meeting is called under sections 94, 106, 146 or 331 of the 1986 Act (final meeting); and
(b) a meeting under section 94, 106, 146 or 331 of the 1986 Act is held on or after the commencement date.

(2) Where this paragraph applies, Part 15 of the 2016 Rules does not apply and the provisions of the 1986 Rules relating to the following continue to apply—
(a) the requirement to hold the meeting;
(b) notice and advertisement of the meeting;
(c) governance of the meeting;
(d) recording and taking minutes of the meeting;
(e) the form and content of the final report;
(f) the office-holder's resignation or removal;
(g) the office-holder's release;
(h) fixing the office-holder's remuneration;
(i) requests for further information from creditors;
(j) claims that remuneration is or other expenses are excessive; and
(k) complaints about exclusion at the meeting.

(3) However, any application to the court in respect of such a meeting is to be made in accordance with Part 12 of the 2016 Rules.

8 Progress reports and statements to the registrar of companies

(1) Where in relation to a limited liability partnership an obligation to prepare a progress report arises but is not fulfilled before the commencement date the following provisions of the 1986 Rules continue to apply—
(a) rule 2.47 (reports to creditors in administration); and
(b) rules 4.49B and 4.49C (progress reports—winding up).

(2) Where before the commencement date, a notice under paragraph 83(3) of Schedule B1 to the 1986 Act is sent to the registrar of companies, rule 2.117A(1) of the 1986 Rules continues to apply.

(3) The provisions of the 2016 Rules relating to progress reporting do not apply in the case of the winding up of a limited liability partnership, where the winding-up order was made on a petition presented before 6th April 2010.

(4) Where the voluntary winding up of a limited liability partnership commenced before 6th April 2010, rule 4.223-CVL of the 1986 Rules as it had effect immediately before that date in its application to limited liability partnerships, continues to apply

(5) Where, in relation to a limited liability partnership, before the commencement date an office-holder ceases to act, or an administrator sends a progress report to creditors in support of a request for their consent to an extension of the administration, resulting in a change in reporting period under rule 2.47(3A), 2.47(3B), 4.49B(5), 4.49C(3), or 6.78A(4) of the 1986 Rules, the period for which reports must be made is the period for which reports were required to be made under the 1986 Rules immediately before the commencement date.

9 Foreign currency

(1) Where, in relation to a limited liability partnership, before the commencement date an amount stated in a foreign currency on an application, claim or proof of debt is converted into sterling by the office-holder under rules 2.86, 4.91, 5A.3 or 6.111 of the 1986 Rules, the office-holder and any successor to the office-holder must continue to use the same exchange rate for subsequent conversions of that currency into sterling for the purpose of distributing any assets of the limited liability partnership.

(2) However when, in relation to a limited liability partnership, an office-holder, convener, appointed person or chair uses an exchange rate to convert an application, claim or proof in a foreign currency into sterling solely for voting purposes before the commencement date, sub-paragraph (1) does not prevent the office-holder from using an alternative rate for subsequent conversions.

10 CVA moratoria

Where, before the commencement date, the designated members of a limited liability partnership submit to the nominee the document, statement and information required under paragraph 6(1) of Schedule A1 to the 1986 Act, the provisions of the 1986 Rules relating to moratoria continue to apply to the proposed voluntary arrangement.

11 Priority of expenses of voluntary arrangements

Rule 4.21A of the 1986 Rules (expenses of voluntary arrangement) continues to apply in relation to a limited liability partnership where a winding up petition is presented before the commencement date.

12 General powers of liquidator

Rule 4.184 of the 1986 Rules (general powers of liquidator) continues to apply in relation to a limited liability partnership as regards a person dealing in good faith and for value with a liquidator and in respect of the power of the court or the liquidation committee to ratify anything done by the liquidator without permission before the commencement date.

13 Applications before the court

(1) Where, in relation to a limited liability partnership, an application to court is filed or a petition for winding up is presented under the 1986 Act or under the 1986 Rules before the commencement date and the court remains seised of that application or petition on the commencement date, the 1986 Rules continue to apply to that application or petition.

(2) For the purpose of sub-paragraph (1), the court is no longer seised of an application or petition for winding up when—

(a) in relation to an application, it makes an order having the effect of determining of the application; or

(b) in relation to a petition for winding up—

(i) the court makes a winding up order,

(ii) the court dismisses the petition, or

(iii) the petition is withdrawn.

14 Forms

A form contained in Schedule 4 to the 1986 Rules may be used in relation to a limited liability partnership on or after the commencement date if—

(a) the form is used to provide a statement of affairs in proceedings where pursuant to paragraph 5 of this Schedule the provisions of the 1986 Rules set out in that paragraph continue to apply;

(b) the form relates to a meeting held under the 1986 Rules as described in paragraph 6(1) of this Schedule;

(c) the form is required because before the commencement date, the office-holder seeks to obtain the passing of a resolution by correspondence; or

(d) the form relates to any application to the court or petition for winding up presented before the commencement date.

15 Administrations commenced before 15th September 2003

The 1986 Rules continue to apply to administrations of limited liability partnerships where the petition for an administration order was presented before 15th September 2003.

16 Set-off in insolvency proceedings commenced before 1st April 2005

Where before 1st April 2005 a limited liability partnership entered administration or went into liquidation, the office-holder calculating any set-off must apply the 1986 Rules as they had effect in their application to limited liability partnerships immediately before 1st April 2005.

17 Calculating the value of future debts in insolvency proceedings commenced before 1st April 2005

Where before 1st April 2005 a limited liability partnership entered administration or went into liquidation the office-holder calculating the value of a future debt for the purpose of dividend (and no other purpose) must apply the 1986 Rules as they had effect in their application to limited liability partnerships immediately before 1st April 2005.

18 Insolvency practitioner fees and expenses estimates

(1) Rules 18.4(1)(e), 18.16(4) to (10), and 18.30 of the 2016 Rules do not apply in relation to limited liability partnerships where before 1st October 2015—

(a) the appointment of an administrator took effect;

(b) a liquidator was nominated under section 100(2), or 139(3) of the 1986 Act;

(c) a liquidator was appointed under section 139(4) or 140 of the 1986 Act;

(d) a person was directed by the court or appointed to be a liquidator under section 100(3) of the 1986 Act; or

(e) a liquidator was nominated or the administrator became the liquidator under paragraph 83(7) of Schedule B1 to the 1986 Act.

(2) Rule 18.20(4) and (5) of the 2016 Rules do not apply in relation to a limited liability partnership where an administrator was appointed before 1st October 2015 and—

(a) the limited liability partnership is wound up under paragraph 83 of Schedule B1 to the 1986 Act on or after the commencement date and the administrator becomes the liquidator; or

(b) a winding-up order is made upon the appointment of an administrator ceasing to have effect on or after the commencement date and the court under section 140(1) of the 1986 Act appoints as liquidator the person whose appointment as administrator has ceased to have effect.

19 Transitional provision for limited liability partnerships entering administration before 6th April 2010 and moving to voluntary liquidation between 6th April 2010 and commencement (inclusive of those dates)

Where—

(a) a limited liability partnership went into administration before 6th April 2010, and

(b) the limited liability partnership goes into voluntary liquidation under paragraph 83 of Schedule B1 between 6th April 2010 and commencement (inclusive of those dates),

the 1986 Rules as amended by the Insolvency (Amendment) Rules 2010 apply to the extent necessary to give effect to section 104A of the Act notwithstanding that by virtue of paragraph 1(6)(a) or (b) of Schedule 4 to the Insolvency (Amendment) Rules 2010 those amendments to the Insolvency Rules 1986 would otherwise not apply.]

NOTES

Commencement: 8 December 2017.

Added by the Insolvency (Miscellaneous Amendments) Regulations 2017, SI 2017/1119, reg 2, Sch 1, Pt 2, paras 6, 55.

PART 11
STATUTORY INSTRUMENTS RELATING TO PERSONAL INSOLVENCY—ENGLAND AND WALES

ADMINISTRATION OF INSOLVENT ESTATES OF DECEASED PERSONS ORDER 1986

(SI 1986/1999)

NOTES

Made: 21 November 1986.
Authority: Insolvency Act 1986, s 421.
Commencement: 29 December 1986.

ARRANGEMENT OF ARTICLES

1 . . . . [11.1]
2 . . . . [11.2]
3 . . . . [11.3]
4 . . . . [11.4]
5 . . . . [11.5]

SCHEDULES

Schedule 1—Provisions of the Act applying with relevant modifications to the administration in bankruptcy of insolvent estates of deceased persons dying before making of a bankruptcy application or presentation of a bankruptcy petition
Part I—General modifications of provisions of the Act . . . . . [11.6]
Part II—Provisions of the Act not included in Part III of this Schedule. . . . . [11.7]
Part III—Provisions of Part VIII of the Act relating to individual voluntary arrangements . . . . . [11.8]
Schedule 2—Death of debtor after making of a bankruptcy application or presentation of a bankruptcy petition. . . . . [11.9]
Schedule 3—Forms relating to administration in bankruptcy of insolvent estates of deceased debtors. . [11.10]

[11.1]
1

This Order may be cited as the Administration of Insolvent Estates of Deceased Persons Order 1986 and shall come into force on 29th December 1986.

[11.2]
2

In this Order—

"the Act" means the Insolvency Act 1986;

"insolvency administration order" means an order for the administration in bankruptcy of the insolvent estate of a deceased debtor (being an individual at the date of his death);

"insolvency administration petition" means a petition for an insolvency administration order; and

"the Rules" means [the Insolvency (England and Wales) Rules 2016].

NOTES

In definition "the Rules" words in square brackets substituted by the Insolvency (Miscellaneous Amendments) Regulations 2017, SI 2017/1119, reg 2, Sch 3, para 1(1), (2), subject to transitional provisions and savings in Sch 3, para 3 thereto.

[11.3]
3

(1) The provisions of the Act specified in Parts II and III of Schedule 1 to this Order shall apply to the administration in bankruptcy of the insolvent estates of deceased persons dying before [the making of a bankruptcy application or] presentation of a bankruptcy petition with the modifications specified in those Parts and with any further such modifications as may be necessary to render them applicable to the estate of a deceased person and in particular with the modifications specified in Part I of that Schedule, and the provisions of the Rules, the Insolvency Regulations 1986 and any order made under section 415 of the Act (fees and deposits) shall apply accordingly.

(2) In the case of any conflict between any provision of the Rules and any provision of this Order, the latter provision shall prevail.

NOTES

Para (1): words in square brackets inserted by the Enterprise and Regulatory Reform Act 2013 (Consequential Amendments) (Bankruptcy) and the Small Business, Enterprise and Employment Act 2015 (Consequential Amendments) Regulations 2016, SI 2016/481, reg 2(2), Sch 2, Pt 1, para 2(1), (2).

[11.4]
4

(1) Where the estate of a deceased person is insolvent and is being administered otherwise than in bankruptcy, subject to paragraphs (2) and (3) below, the same provisions as may be in force for the time being under the law of bankruptcy with respect to the assets of individuals [made] bankrupt shall apply

to the administration of the estate with respect to the respective rights of secured and unsecured creditors, to debts and liabilities provable, to the valuation of future and contingent liabilities and to the priorities of debts and other payments.

(2) The reasonable funeral, testamentary and administration expenses have priority over the preferential debts listed in Schedule 6 to the Act.

(3) Section 292(2) of the Act shall not apply.

NOTES

Para (1): word in square brackets substituted by the Enterprise and Regulatory Reform Act 2013 (Consequential Amendments) (Bankruptcy) and the Small Business, Enterprise and Employment Act 2015 (Consequential Amendments) Regulations 2016, SI 2016/481, reg 2(2), Sch 2, Pt 1, para 2(1), (3).

[11.5]
5

[(A1) If a debtor dies after making a bankruptcy application, the proceedings will continue as if the deceased debtor were alive, with the modifications specified in Schedule 2 to this Order.]

(1) If a debtor . . . against whom a bankruptcy petition has been presented dies, the proceedings in the matter shall, unless the court otherwise orders, be continued as if he were alive, with the modifications specified in Schedule 2 to this Order.

(2) The reasonable funeral and testamentary expenses have priority over the preferential debts listed in Schedule 6 to the Act.

(3) If a debtor dies after presentation of a bankruptcy petition but before service, the court may order service to be effected on his personal representative or such other person as it thinks fit.

NOTES

Para (A1): inserted by the Enterprise and Regulatory Reform Act 2013 (Consequential Amendments) (Bankruptcy) and the Small Business, Enterprise and Employment Act 2015 (Consequential Amendments) Regulations 2016, SI 2016/481, reg 2(2), Sch 2, Pt 1, para 2(1), (4)(a).

Para (1): words omitted revoked by SI 2016/481, reg 2(2), Sch 2, Pt 1, para 2(1), (4)(b).

6 (*Amends the Insolvency Act 1986, s 385 at* **[1.472]**.)

SCHEDULES

SCHEDULE 1
PROVISIONS OF THE ACT APPLYING WITH RELEVANT MODIFICATIONS TO THE ADMINISTRATION IN BANKRUPTCY OF INSOLVENT ESTATES OF DECEASED PERSONS DYING BEFORE [MAKING OF A BANKRUPTCY APPLICATION OR] PRESENTATION OF A BANKRUPTCY PETITION

Article 3

NOTES

Schedule heading: words in square brackets inserted by the Enterprise and Regulatory Reform Act 2013 (Consequential Amendments) (Bankruptcy) and the Small Business, Enterprise and Employment Act 2015 (Consequential Amendments) Regulations 2016, SI 2016/481, reg 2(2), Sch 2, Pt 1, para 2(1), (5).

PART I
GENERAL MODIFICATIONS OF PROVISIONS OF THE ACT

[11.6]

Except in so far as the context otherwise requires, for any such reference as is specified in column 1 of the Table set out below there shall be substituted the reference specified in column 2.

TABLE

Reference in provision of the Act specified in Part II of this Schedule	Substituted references
(1)	(2)
the bankrupt; the debtor	the deceased debtor or his personal representative (or if there is no personal representative such person as the court may order) as the case may require.
the bankrupt's estate	the deceased debtor's estate.
the commencement of the bankruptcy	the date of the insolvency administration order.
a bankruptcy order	an insolvency administration order.
an individual being [made] bankrupt	an insolvency administration order being made.

Reference in provision of the Act specified in Part II of this Schedule	**Substituted references**
(1)	(2)
[a bankruptcy application]	a petition by the personal representative of a deceased debtor for an insolvency administration order.

NOTES

Table: words in square brackets substituted by the Enterprise and Regulatory Reform Act 2013 (Consequential Amendments) (Bankruptcy) and thc Small Business, Enterprise and Employment Act 2015 (Consequential Amendments) Regulations 2016, SI 2016/481, reg 2(2), Sch 2, Pt 1, para 2(1), (6).

PART II
PROVISIONS OF THE ACT NOT INCLUDED IN PART III OF THIS SCHEDULE

[11.7]

The following provisions of the Act shall apply:—

1. Section 264 with the following modifications:—

(a) the words "against an individual" shall be omitted;

(b) at the end of paragraph 1(a) there shall be added the words "in Form 1 set out in Schedule 3 to the Administration of Insolvent Estates of Deceased Persons Order 1986";

[(ba) after subsection (1)(a) there shall be added—

"(aa) by the personal representative of the deceased debtor,".]

(c) . . .

[(ca) at the end of paragraph 1(ba) there shall be added the words "in Form 1, with such variations as the case requires (if any), set out in Schedule 3 to the Administration of Insolvent Estates of Deceased Persons Order 1986";

(cb) at the end of paragraph 1(bb) there shall be added the words "in Form 1, with such variations as the case requires (if any), set out in Schedule 3 to the Administration of Insolvent Estates of Deceased Persons Order 1986";]

(d) in paragraph 1(c) after the words "Part VIII" there shall be added the words "in Form 2 set out in the said Schedule 3";

(e) at the end of paragraph 1(d) there shall be added the words "in Form 3 set out in the said Schedule 3 in any case where a creditor could present such a petition under paragraph (a) above"; and

(f) at the end of subsection (2) there shall be added the words "in Form 4 set out in the said Schedule 3".

[**1A.** Section 265 with the modification that after subsection (4) there shall be inserted—

"(5) A petition by the personal representative of a deceased debtor for an insolvency administration order in Form 6 set out in Schedule 3 to the Administration of Insolvent Estates of Deceased Persons Order 1986 may be presented to the court only on the grounds that the estate of a deceased debtor is insolvent.

(6) A petition under subsection (5) must be accompanied by a statement of the deceased debtor's affairs containing—

(a) such particulars of the debtor's creditors and of his debts and other liabilities and of his assets as may be prescribed; and

(b) such other information as is required by Form 7 set out in Schedule 3 to the Administration of Insolvent Estates of Deceased Persons Order 1986."]

2. Section 266 with the following modifications:—

[(a) for subsection (1) there shall be substituted the following:—

"(1) An insolvency administration petition shall—

(a) if a liquidator (within the meaning of Article 2(b) of the EC Regulation) has been appointed in proceedings by virtue of Article 3(1) of the EC Regulation in relation to the deceased debtor, be served on him;

(b) unless the court directs otherwise, be served on the personal representative; and

(c) be served on such other persons as the court may direct."]; and

(b) in subsection (3) for the words "bankruptcy petition" there shall be substituted the words "petition to the court for an insolvency administration order with or without costs".

3. Section 267 with the following modifications to subsection (2):—

(a) before the words "at the time" there shall be inserted the words "had the debtor been alive"; and

(b) for paragraphs (a) to (d) there shall be substituted the following:—

"(a) the amount of the debt, or the aggregate amount of the debts, owed by the debtor would have been equal to or exceeded the bankruptcy level, or

(b) the debt, or each of the debts, owed by the debtor would have been for a liquidated sum payable to the petitioning creditor, or one or more of the petitioning creditors, either immediately or at some certain future time, and would have been unsecured.".

4. Section 269 with the modification that in subsection (2) for the words "sections 267 to 270" there shall be substituted the words "section 267 and this section".

5. Section 271 as if for that section there were substituted the following—

"271 (1) The court may make an insolvency administration order on a petition for such an order under section 264(1) if it is satisfied—

(a) that the debt, or one of the debts, in respect of which the petition was presented is a debt which,

(i) having been payable at the date of the petition or having since become payable, has neither been paid nor secured or compounded for; or

(ii) has no reasonable prospect of being able to be paid when it falls due; and

(b) that there is a reasonable probability that the estate will be insolvent.

(2) A petition for an insolvency administration order shall not be presented to the court after proceedings have been commenced in any court of justice for the administration of the deceased debtor's estate.

(3) Where proceedings have been commenced in any such court for the administration of the deceased debtor's estate, that court may, if satisfied that the estate is insolvent, transfer the proceedings to the court exercising jurisdiction for the purposes of the Parts in the second Group of Parts.

(4) Where proceedings have been transferred to the court exercising jurisdiction for the purposes of the Parts in the second Group of Parts, that court may make an insolvency administration order in Form 5 set out in Schedule 3 to the Administration of Insolvent Estates of Deceased Persons Order 1986 as if a petition for such an order had been presented under section 264.

(5) Nothing in sections 264, 266, 267, 269 or 271 or 273 shall invalidate any payment made or any act or thing done in good faith by the personal representative before the date of the insolvency administration order.

[(6) The court must make an insolvency administration order in Form 4 set out in Schedule 3 to the Administration of Insolvent Estates of Deceased Persons Order 1986 on the hearing of a petition presented under section 265(5) if it is satisfied that the deceased debtor's estate is insolvent.".]

6. . . .

7. . . .

8. Section 276(2).

9. Section 277.

10. Section 278 except paragraph (b) as if for paragraph (a) there were substituted the following:—

"(a) commences with the day on which the insolvency administration order is made;".

11. Section 282(1) and (4).

12. Sections 283 to 285 with the modification that they shall have effect as if the petition had been presented and the insolvency administration order had been made on the date of death of the deceased debtor, and with the following modifications to section 283:—

(a) in subsection (2)(b), for the words "bankrupt and his family" there shall be substituted the words "family of the deceased debtor"; and

(b) after subsection (4) there shall be added the following subsection:—

"(4A) References in any of this Group of Parts to property, in relation to a deceased debtor, include the capacity to exercise and take proceedings for exercising all such powers over or in respect of property as might have been exercised by his personal representative for the benefit of the estate on the date of the insolvency administration order and as are specified in subsection (4) above.".

13. Section 286(1) and (3) to (8).

14. Section 287.

[15. Section 288 with the modification that for subsections (1) to (3) there shall be substituted the following—

"(1) Where an insolvency administration order has been made, the official receiver may at any time require the personal representative, or if there is no personal representative such person as the court may on the application of the official receiver direct, to submit to the official receiver a statement of the deceased debtor's affairs.

(2) The statement of affairs must contain—

(a) particulars of the assets and liabilities of the estate as at the date of the insolvency administration order, and

(b) other particulars of the affairs of the deceased debtor in Form 7 set out in Schedule 3 to the Administration of Insolvent Estates of Deceased Persons Order 1986, or as the official receiver may require.

(3) Where the personal representative or such person as the court may direct is required under subsection (1) to submit a statement of affairs to the official receiver, the statement must be submitted before the end of the period of 56 days beginning with the date on which notice of the requirement under subsection (1) is given by the official receiver, or such longer period as he or the court may allow.".]

16. Section 289 as if for that section there were substituted the following:—

"**289** The official receiver is not under any duty to investigate the conduct and affairs of the deceased debtor unless he thinks fit but may make such report (if any) to the court as he thinks fit.".

17. Section 291.

[**17A.** Section 291A.]

[**18.** Sections 292 to 302.]

19. Sections 303 and 304.

20. Section 305 with the modification that after subsection (4) there shall be added the following subsection:—

"(5) In the exercise of his functions under this section where an insolvency administration order has been made, the trustee shall have regard to any claim by the personal representative to payment of reasonable funeral, testamentary and administration expenses incurred by him in respect of the deceased debtor's estate or, if there is no such personal representative, to any claim by any other person to payment of any such expenses incurred by him in respect of the estate provided that the trustee has sufficient funds in hand for the purpose, and such claims shall have priority over the preferential debts listed in Schedule 6 to this Act.".

21. Section 306.

22. Section 307 with the modification that in subsection (1) for the words "commencement of the bankruptcy" there shall be substituted the words "date of death of the deceased debtor".

23. Sections 308 to 327.

24. Sections 328 and 329 with the modification that for the words "commencement of the bankruptcy", wherever they occur, there shall be substituted the words "date of death of the deceased debtor".

[**25.** Section 330 with the following modifications:—

(a) in subsection (5) for the words "the bankrupt is entitled to the surplus" there shall be substituted the words "the surplus shall be paid to the personal representative unless the court otherwise orders", and

(b) after subsection (5) there shall be added:—

"(6) Subsection (5) is subject to Article 35 of the EC Regulation (surplus in secondary proceedings to be transferred to main proceedings).".]

26. Sections 331 to 340.

[**27.** Section 341 with the modification that in subsection (1)(a) for the words from "day of the making" to "made bankrupt" there shall be substituted the words "date of death of the deceased debtor".]

[**28.** Sections 342 to 349 and 350(1), (2), and (4) to (6).]

29. Section 359 with the following modifications:—

(a) subsection (1), and the reference to that subsection in subsection (3), shall be omitted; and

[(b) in subsection (2), for the words from "the making" to "initial period" there shall be substituted the words "the date of death of the deceased debtor".]

30. Sections 363 and 365 to 381.

31. Section 382 with the modification that in the definition of "bankruptcy debt" for the words "commencement of the bankruptcy", wherever they occur, there shall be substituted the words "date of death of the deceased debtor".

[**32.** Sections 383 to 384.]

33. Section 385 with the modification that at the end of the definition of "the court" there shall be added the words "and subject thereto "the court" means the court within the jurisdiction of which the debtor resided or carried on business for the greater part of the six months immediately prior to his death".

34. Section 386.

35. Section 387(1), (5) and (6) with the modification that in subsection (6)(*a*) and (*b*) for the reference to the making of the bankruptcy order there shall be substituted a reference to the date of death of the deceased debtor.

36. Sections 388 to 410, 412, 413, 415, 418 to 420, 423 to 426, 428, 430 to 436 and 437 so far as it relates to Parts II, except paragraph 13, IV and V of Schedule 11 to the Act.

NOTES

Para 1: sub-para (ba) inserted by the Insolvency (Miscellaneous Amendments) Regulations 2017, SI 2017/1119, reg 2, Sch 3, para 1(1), (3)(a), (b), subject to transitional provisions and savings in Sch 3, para 3 thereto; sub-para (c) revoked by the Enterprise and Regulatory Reform Act 2013 (Consequential Amendments) (Bankruptcy) and the Small Business, Enterprise and Employment Act 2015 (Consequential Amendments) Regulations 2016, SI 2016/481, reg 2(2), Sch 2, Pt 1, para 2(1), (7)(a); sub-paras (ca), (cb) inserted by the Administration of Insolvent Estates of Deceased Persons (Amendment) Order 2002, SI 2002/1309, arts 2(1), 3(1).

Para 1A: inserted by SI 2017/1119, reg 2, Sch 3, para 1(1), (3)(c), subject to transitional provisions and savings in Sch 3, para 3 thereto.

Para 2: sub-para (a) substituted by SI 2002/1309, arts 2(1), 3(2).

Para 5: in the Insolvency Act 1986, s 271 (as set out) sub-s (6) in square brackets inserted by SI 2017/1119, reg 2, Sch 3, para 1(1), (3)(d), subject to transitional provisions and savings in Sch 3, para 3 thereto.

Paras 6, 7: revoked by SI 2017/1119, reg 2, Sch 3, para 1(1), (3)(e), (f), subject to transitional provisions and savings in Sch 3, para 3 thereto.

Para 15: substituted by the Deregulation Act 2015 and Small Business, Enterprise and Employment Act 2015 (Consequential Amendments) (Savings) Regulations 2017, SI 2017/540, reg 3, Sch 2, para 1(1), (3).

Para 17A: inserted by SI 2017/540, reg 3, Sch 2, para 1(1), (4).

Para 18: substituted by SI 2017/540, reg 3, Sch 2, para 1(1), (5).

Para 25: substituted by SI 2002/1309, arts 2(1), 3(3).

Para 27: substituted by SI 2016/481, reg 2(2), Sch 2, Pt 1, para 2(1), (7)(d).

Para 28: substituted by SI 2017/540, reg 3, Sch 2, para 1(1), (6).

Para 29: sub-para (b) substituted by SI 2016/481, reg 2(2), Sch 2, Pt 1, para 2(1), (7)(e).

Para 32: substituted by SI 2017/540, reg 3, Sch 2, para 1(1), (7).

PART III
PROVISIONS OF PART VIII OF THE ACT RELATING TO INDIVIDUAL VOLUNTARY ARRANGEMENTS

[11.8]

The following provisions of the Act shall apply where court has made an interim order under section 252 of the Act in respect of an individual who subsequently dies:—

1. Section 256 with the modification that where the individual dies before he has submitted the document and statement referred to in subsection (2), after subsection (1) there shall be added the following subsections:—

> "(1A) The nominee shall after the death of the individual comes to his knowledge give notice to the court that the individual has died.
>
> (1B) After receiving such a notice the court shall discharge the order mentioned in subsection (1) above.".

[**2.** Section 257 with the modification that where the individual dies before the individual's creditors have decided whether to approve the proposed voluntary arrangement, the creditors must not approve the proposal and, if the individual was at the date of his death an undischarged bankrupt, the personal representative shall give notice of the death to the deceased debtor's creditors, the trustee of his estate and the official receiver.]

[**3.** Section 258.]

[**3A.** Section 259 with the modification that after subsection (1) there shall be added—

> "(1A) Where the individual's creditors considered the debtor's proposal pursuant to a report to the court under section 256(1)(aa) but the individual has died before the creditors have decided whether to approve the proposed voluntary arrangement—
>
> (a) the creditors must not approve the proposal;
>
> (b) the personal representative must report to the court that the proposal has not been approved; and
>
> (c) if the individual was at the date of his death an undischarged bankrupt, the personal representative must give notice of the death to the deceased debtor's creditors, the trustee of his estate and the official receiver.".]

4. Sections 260 to 262 with the modification that they shall cease to apply on or after the death of the individual.

5. Section 263 with the modification that where the individual dies after a voluntary arrangement has been approved, then—

(a) in subsection (3), for the words "debtor, any of his" there shall be substituted the words "personal representative of the deceased debtor, any of the deceased debtor's"; and

(b) the supervisor shall give notice to the court that the individual has died.

NOTES

Para 2: substituted by the Deregulation Act 2015 and Small Business, Enterprise and Employment Act 2015 (Consequential Amendments) (Savings) Regulations 2017, SI 2017/540, reg 3, Sch 2, para 1(1), (8).

Paras 3, 3A: substituted (for original para 3) by SI 2017/540, reg 3, Sch 2, para 1(1), (9).

SCHEDULE 2
DEATH OF DEBTOR AFTER [MAKING OF A BANKRUPTCY APPLICATION OR] PRESENTATION OF A BANKRUPTCY PETITION

Article 5

NOTES

Schedule heading: words in square brackets inserted by the Enterprise and Regulatory Reform Act 2013 (Consequential Amendments) (Bankruptcy) and the Small Business, Enterprise and Employment Act 2015 (Consequential Amendments) Regulations 2016, SI 2016/481, reg 2(2), Sch 2, Pt 1, para 2(1), (8)(a).

[11.9]

1. Modifications

For subsections (1) and (2) of section 288 of the Act there shall be substituted the following:—

"(1) Where a bankruptcy order has been made otherwise than on a [bankruptcy application] and the debtor has subsequently died without submitting a statement of his affairs to the official receiver, the personal representative or such other person as the court, on the application of the official receiver, may direct shall submit to the official receiver a statement of the deceased debtor's affairs containing particulars of the assets and liabilities of the estate as at the date of the order together with other particulars of the affairs of the deceased debtor in Form 7 set out in Schedule 3 to the Administration of Insolvent Estates of Deceased Persons Order 1986 or as the official receiver may require, and the Rules shall apply to such a statement as they apply to an ordinary statement of affairs of a debtor.

(2) The statement shall be submitted before the end of the period of fifty-six days beginning with the date of a request by the official receiver for the statement or such longer period as he or the court may allow.".

2. At the end of section 330(4)(b) of the Act there shall be added the words "and of the personal representative of a debtor dying after [the making of a bankruptcy application, or (as the case may be)] the presentation of a bankruptcy petition in respect of reasonable funeral and testamentary expenses of which notice has not already been given to the trustee".

NOTES

Para 1: words in square brackets substituted by the Enterprise and Regulatory Reform Act 2013 (Consequential Amendments) (Bankruptcy) and the Small Business, Enterprise and Employment Act 2015 (Consequential Amendments) Regulations 2016, SI 2016/481, reg 2(2), Sch 2, Pt 1, para 2(1), (8)(b).

Para 2: words in square brackets inserted by SI 2016/481, reg 2(2), Sch 2, Pt 1, para 2(1), (8)(c).

SCHEDULE 3
FORMS RELATING TO ADMINISTRATION IN BANKRUPTCY OF INSOLVENT ESTATES OF DECEASED DEBTORS

Schedule 1, Pt II, paras 1, 5–7, 15, Schedule 2, para 1

[11.10]

NOTES

This Schedule contains forms. The forms themselves are not set out in this work, but their numbers and titles are listed below.

FORM NO	*TITLE*
1	Creditor's Petition for Insolvency Administration Order
2	Petition for Insolvency Administration Order by Supervisor of Voluntary Arrangement or Person Bound by it
3	Criminal Bankruptcy Petition for an Insolvency Administration Order
4	Insolvency Administration Order
5	Insolvency Administration Order on Transfer of Proceedings
6	Petition by Personal Representative for Insolvency Administration Order
7	Statement of Affairs (Deceased Insolvent)

NOTES

Forms 1, 2, 4–6: substituted by the Administration of Insolvent Estates of Deceased Persons (Amendment) Order 2002, SI 2002/1309, arts 2(1), 3(4), Schedule.

NATIONAL HEALTH SERVICE PENSION SCHEME (ADDITIONAL VOLUNTARY CONTRIBUTIONS) REGULATIONS 2000

(SI 2000/619)

NOTES

Made: 16 March 2000.

Authority: Superannuation Act 1972, ss 10(1), (2), (2A), (3), 12(1), Sch 3.

Commencement: 10 April 2000.

PART I
PRELIMINARY

[11.11]
1 Citation, commencement and retrospective effect

(1) These Regulations may be cited as the National Health Service Pension Scheme (Additional Voluntary Contributions) Regulations 2000.

(2) These Regulations shall come into force on 10th April 2000.

(3) The following regulations shall have effect from 1st February 1991—
- (a) regulations 1 to 10;
- (b) regulations 11(1) to (5), (7) and (8);
- (c) regulations 12 to 18; and
- (d) regulation 21.

(4) Regulation 11(6) shall have effect from 1st December 1999.

2–13 (*Outside the scope of this work.*)

PART IV
MISCELLANEOUS PROVISIONS

14–17A (*Outside the scope of this work.*)

[11.12]
18 Benefits not assignable on bankruptcy

(1) On the bankruptcy of a person entitled to benefit under these Regulations, no part of the benefit shall be paid to any trustee or other person acting on behalf of creditors, except as provided for in paragraph (2).

(2) Where, following the bankruptcy of any person entitled to benefit under these Regulations, the court makes an order under section 310 of the Insolvency Act 1986 that requires the Secretary of State to pay all or part of the benefit to the person's trustee in bankruptcy the Secretary of State shall comply with that order.

19–22 (*Outside the scope of this work.*)

SCHEDULES 1 AND 2

(*Sch 1 revoked by the National Health Service (Pension Scheme, Injury Benefits and Additional Voluntary Contributions) Amendment Regulations 2006, SI 2006/600, reg 39; Sch 2 outside the scope of this work.*)

PRIVATE HIRE VEHICLES (LONDON) (OPERATORS' LICENCES) REGULATIONS 2000

(SI 2000/3146)

NOTES

Made: 28 November 2000.
Authority: Private Hire Vehicles (London) Act 1998, ss 3(4), 4(3), (4), 20(1), (2), 23(1), 32, 37.
Commencement: 22 January 2001.

PART I
GENERAL

[11.13]
1 Citation and commencement

These Regulations may be cited as the Private Hire Vehicles (London) (Operators' Licences) Regulations 2000 and shall come into force on 22nd January 2001.

[11.14]
2 Interpretation

In these Regulations, unless the context otherwise requires—

"the 1998 Act" means the Private Hire Vehicles (London) Act 1998;

. . .

"licence" means a London PHV operator's licence;

"licensing authority" means the person appointed under section 24(1) of the 1998 Act for the purpose of exercising the functions of the Secretary of State under that Act or, where no such appointment has been made, the Secretary of State;

. . .

"operator" means a London PHV operator and in relation to a licence means the operator to whom the licence was granted;

. . .

NOTES

Definitions omitted outside the scope of this work.

3–16 *((Pts II–IV) outside the scope of this work.)*

PART V
OTHER MATTERS

17, 18 *(Outside the scope of this work.)*

[11.15]

19 Continuance of licence on death, bankruptcy etc

(1) This regulation applies in relation to a licence granted in the sole name of an individual in the event of—

(a) the death of that individual;

(b) the bankruptcy of that individual; or

(c) that individual becoming a patient under Part VII of the Mental Health Act 1983.

(2) After the happening of the event mentioned in paragraph (1)(a) the licensing authority may direct that the licence shall not be treated as terminated when the individual died but suspended until the date when a direction under paragraph (3) comes into force.

(3) After the happening of any of the events mentioned in paragraph (1) the licensing authority may direct that a person carrying on the business of the operator is to be treated for the purposes of the 1998 Act as if he were the operator for such purpose and to such extent as is specified in the direction for a period not exceeding—

(a) six months from the date of the coming into force of that direction; or

(b) if less, the remainder of the period of the licence.

20 *(Outside the scope of this work.)*

BANKRUPTCY (FINANCIAL SERVICES AND MARKETS ACT 2000) RULES 2001

(SI 2001/3634)

NOTES

Made: 9 November 2001.

Authority: Insolvency Act 1986, s 412.

Commencement: 1 December 2001.

These Rules modify the Insolvency Rules 1986, SI 1986/1925, which are revoked and replaced by the Insolvency (England and Wales) Rules 2016, SI 2016/1024, r 2, Sch 1, as from 6 April 2017, subject to transitional provisions in Sch 2 thereto at **[6.935]**. See further the notes at **[6.1]** in relation to the 1986 Rules.

ARRANGEMENT OF RULES

1 Citation and commencement . . . . [11.16]
2 Interpretation . . . . [11.17]
3 Modification of the 1986 Rules . . . . [11.18]
4 Rule 6.1. . . . . [11.19]
5 Rule 6.2. . . . . [11.20]
6 Rules 6.3, 6.5, 6.11 and 6.25. . . . . [11.21]
7 Rule 6.4. . . . . [11.22]
8 Rule 6.9. . . . . [11.23]

[11.16]

1 Citation and commencement

These Rules may be cited as the Bankruptcy (Financial Services and Markets Act 2000) Rules 2001 and come into force on 1st December 2001.

Part 11 SIs: Personal Insolvency

[11.17]
2 Interpretation

In these Rules—

"the Act" means the Financial Services and Markets Act 2000;

["the Authority" in relation to an individual means—

(a) if the individual is a PRA-authorised person or was carrying on a PRA-regulated activity in contravention of the general prohibition, the FCA or the PRA,

(b) in any other case, the FCA,

and terms used in this definition which are defined in the Act have the meaning given in the Act;]

"debt" means the sum referred to in section 372(4)(a) of the Act;

"demand" means a demand made under section 372(4)(a) of the Act;

"individual" has the meaning given by section 372(7) of the Act;

"person" excludes a body of persons corporate or unincorporate;

"the 1986 Rules" means the Insolvency Rules 1986.

NOTES

Definition "the Authority" substituted by the Financial Services Act 2012 (Consequential Amendments and Transitional Provisions) Order 2013, SI 2013/472, art 3, Sch 2, para 68.

[11.18]
3 Modification of the 1986 Rules

The 1986 Rules apply in relation to a demand with the following modifications.

[11.19]
4 Rule 6.1

(1) Rule 6.1 (form and content of statutory demand) is disapplied.

(2) A demand must be dated and signed by a member of the Authority's staff authorised by it for that purpose.

(3) A demand must specify that it is made under section 372(4)(a) of the Act.

(4) A demand must state the amount of the debt, to whom it is owed and the consideration for it or, if there is no consideration, the way in which it arises; but if the person to whom the debt is owed holds any security in respect of the debt of which the Authority is aware—

(a) the demand must specify the nature of the security and the value which the Authority puts upon it as at the date of the demand; and

(b) the amount of which payment is claimed by the demand must be the full amount of the debt less the amount specified as the value of the security.

(5) A demand must state the grounds on which it is alleged that the individual appears to have no reasonable prospect of paying the debt.

[11.20]
5 Rule 6.2

(1) Rule 6.2 (information to be given in statutory demand) is disapplied—

(2) The demand must include an explanation to the individual of the following matters—

(a) the purpose of the demand and the fact that, if the individual does not comply with the demand, bankruptcy proceedings may be commenced against him;

(b) the time within which the demand must be complied with, if that consequence is to be avoided;

(c) the methods of compliance which are open to the individual; and

(d) the individual's right to apply to the court for the demand to be set aside.

(3) The demand must specify the name and address (and telephone number, if any) of one or more persons with whom the individual may, if he wishes, enter into communication with a view to establishing to the Authority's satisfaction that there is a reasonable prospect that the debt will be paid when it falls due or (as the case may be) that the debt will be scoured or compounded.

[11.21]
6 Rules 6.3, 6.5, 6.11 and 6.25

(1) Rules 6.3 (requirements as to service), 6.5 (hearing of application to set aside), 6.11, (proof of service of statutory demand) and 6.25 (decision on the hearing) apply as if—

(a) references to the debtor were references to an individual;

(b) references (other than in rule 6.5(2) and (4)(c)) to the creditor were references to the Authority; and

(c) references to the creditor in rule 6.5(2) and (4)(c) were references to the person to whom the debt is owed.

(2) Rule 6.5(2) applies as if the reference to the creditor also included a reference to the Authority.

(3) Rule 6.5(5) is disapplied and there is substituted the following—

"Where the person to whom the debt is owed holds some security in respect of his debt, and rule 4(4) of the Bankruptcy (Financial Services and Markets Act 2000) Rules 2001 is complied with in respect of it but the court is satisfied that the security is undervalued in the demand, the Authority may be required to amend the demand accordingly (but without prejudice to its right to present a bankruptcy by reference to the original demand)."

[11.22]
7 Rule 6.4

Rule 6.4 (application to set aside statutory demand) applies as if—

(a) references to the debtor were references to an individual;
(b) the words in paragraph (2), "the creditor issuing the statutory demand is a Minister of the Crown or a Government Department, and" were omitted; and
(c) the reference to the creditor in paragraph (2)(b) was a reference to the Authority.

[11.23]
8 Rule 6.9

Rule 6.9 (court in which petition to be presented) applies as if, for paragraph (1)(a), there were substituted—

"(a) if in any demand on which the petition is based the Authority has indicated the intention to present a bankruptcy petition to that Court,".

OCCUPATIONAL AND PERSONAL PENSION SCHEMES (BANKRUPTCY) (NO 2) REGULATIONS 2002

(SI 2002/836)

NOTES

Made: 26 March 2002.

Authority: Bankruptcy (Scotland) Act 1985, ss 36C(4)(a), (7), (8), 36F(3)(a), (6)–(8); Insolvency Act 1986, ss 342C(4)(a), (7)–(9), 342F(6)(a), (9)–(11); Welfare Reform and Pensions Act 1999, ss 11(2)(h), 12(1)–(3), 83(1), (2), (4), (6).

Commencement: 6 April 2002.

Application: the Royal Mail Statutory Pension Scheme is to be treated as an occupational pension scheme for the purposes of these Regulations: see the Postal Services Act 2011 (Transfer of Accrued Pension Rights) Order 2012, SI 2012/687, arts 2, 9, Sch 4, Pt I, paras 1, 7(a).

ARRANGEMENT OF REGULATIONS

PART I
GENERAL

1 Citation, commencement, extent and interpretation . . . [11.24]

PART II
ENGLAND AND WALES

2 Prescribed pension arrangements . . . [11.25]
3 Unapproved pension arrangements . . . [11.26]
4 Exclusion of rights under unapproved pension arrangements . . . [11.27]
5 Exclusion orders . . . [11.28]
6 Qualifying agreements . . . [11.29]
7 Calculation and verification of rights under pension arrangements . . . [11.30]
8 Time for compliance with restoration order . . . [11.31]
9 Calculation and verification of rights under destination arrangements . . . [11.32]
10 Time for compliance with request for information . . . [11.33]

PART III
SCOTLAND

11 Prescribed pension arrangements . . . [11.34]
12 Unapproved pension arrangements . . . [11.35]
13 Exclusion of rights under unapproved pension arrangements . . . [11.36]
14 Exclusion orders . . . [11.37]
15 Qualifying agreements . . . [11.38]
16 Calculation and verification of rights under pension arrangements . . . [11.39]
17 Time for compliance with restoration order . . . [11.40]
18 Calculation and verification of transferee's rights under a pension arrangement derived from a pension-sharing transaction . . . [11.41]
19 Time for compliance with request for information . . . [11.42]

PART I
GENERAL

[11.24]

1 Citation, commencement, extent and interpretation

(1) These Regulations, which supersede the Occupational and Personal Pension Schemes (Bankruptcy) Regulations 2002, may be cited as the Occupational and Personal Pension Schemes (Bankruptcy) (No 2) Regulations 2002 and shall come into force on 6th April 2002.

(2) Part II of these Regulations applies to England and Wales.

(3) Part III, and (by virtue of regulation 11 of that Part) regulation 2 of Part II, of these Regulations apply to Scotland.

(4) In this paragraph and—

(a) Parts II and III of these Regulations—

"the 1999 Act" means the Welfare Reform and Pensions Act 1999;

["the 2003 Act" means the Income Tax (Earnings and Pensions) Act 2003;]

"income-related benefit" has the meaning given in section 123(1) of the Social Security Contributions and Benefits Act 1992;

["relevant benefits" means any pension, lump sum, gratuity or other like benefit which is, or is to be, provided—

(a) by reason, or in anticipation, of retirement,

(b) by reason of death,

(c) by reason of a pension sharing order or provision,

(d) in connection with past service,

(e) after retirement or death,

(f) in anticipation of, or in connection with, any change in the nature of the service of the employee in question,

but does not include any benefit which is to be provided solely by reason of the disablement or death due to an accident suffered by a person during his pensionable service;]

"the Taxes Act" means the Income and Corporation Taxes Act 1988;

"week" means a period of seven days;

(b) Part II of these Regulations—

"the 1986 Act" means the Insolvency Act 1986;

"court" means the court which made the bankruptcy order against the bankrupt;

"destination arrangement" has the meaning given in section 342E(1)(b) of the 1986 Act;

["employer-financed retirement benefits scheme" has the same meaning given by section 393A of the 2003 Act (employer-financed retirement benefits scheme);]

"pension-sharing transaction" has the meaning given in section 342D(9) of the 1986 Act;

"responsible person" means the person responsible for a pension arrangement within the meaning of section 342C(6) of the 1986 Act;

"restoration order" means an order made under section 342A of the 1986 Act;

"transferee" has the meaning given in section 342D(9) of the 1986 Act;

"transferor" has the meaning given in section 342D(9) of the 1986 Act;

(c) Part III of these Regulations—

"the 1980 Act" means the Solicitors (Scotland) Act 1980;

"the 1985 Act" means the Bankruptcy (Scotland) Act 1985;

"court" means the sheriff before whom the sequestration is depending or to whom it has been transferred or remitted in terms of section 15 of the 1985 Act or, where a judicial factor has been appointed, the court which appointed the judicial factor;

"debtor" has the meaning given in section 73 of the 1985 Act, and in relation to regulations 12 to 15 and 19 also includes a solicitor on whose estate a judicial factor has been appointed;

"judicial factor" means a judicial factor appointed under section 41 of the 1980 Act;

"pension-sharing transaction" has the meaning given in section 36D(10) of the 1985 Act;

"permanent trustee" shall be construed in accordance with section 3 of the 1985 Act;

"responsible person" means the person responsible for a pension arrangement within the meaning of section 36C(6) of the 1985 Act;

"restoration order" means an order made under section 36A of the 1985 Act;

"transferee" has the meaning given in section 36D(10) of the 1985 Act;

"transferor" has the meaning given in section 36D(10) of the 1985 Act.

NOTES

Para (4): in sub-para (a), definition "the 2003 Act" inserted and definition "relevant benefits" substituted, and in sub-para (b), definition "employer-financed retirement benefits scheme" inserted, by the Taxation of Pension Schemes (Consequential Amendments of Occupational and Personal Pension Schemes Legislation) Order 2006, SI 2006/744, art 21(1), (2).

PART II
ENGLAND AND WALES

[11.25]

2 Prescribed pension arrangements

(1) The arrangements prescribed for the purposes of section 11(2)(h) of the 1999 Act (pension arrangements which are "approved pension arrangements") are arrangements (including an annuity purchased for the purpose of giving effect to rights under any such arrangement)—

(a) to which—

(i) the holder of an office or employment has contributed by way of payments out of [earnings which have been allowed as a deduction under paragraph 51 of Schedule 36 to the Finance Act 2004 (individuals with pre-commencement entitlement to corresponding relief),]

(ii) Article 17A of the Convention set out in the Schedule to the Double Taxation Relief (Taxes on Income) (Republic of Ireland) Order 1976 (pension scheme contributions) applies;

[(b) made with a scheme which is an occupational pension scheme—

(i) registered under section 153 of the Finance Act 2004, or

(ii) which is to be treated as becoming a registered pension scheme under section 153(9) of the Finance Act 2004 in accordance with Part 1 of Schedule 36 to that Act,]

[(c) to which section 308A of the 2003 Act (exemption of contributions to overseas pension scheme) applies;]

(d) which are exempt or qualify for relief from, or are not liable to charge to, income tax by virtue of [section 614 or 615 of the Taxes Act (exemptions and reliefs in respect of income from investments etc of certain pension schemes and other overseas pensions), or section 629, 630 or 643 of the 2003 Act (pre-1973 pensions paid under the Overseas Pensions Act 1973 and Malawi, Trinidad and Tobago and Zambia government pensions);]

(e) made with—

(i) a public service pension scheme, or

(ii) an occupational pension scheme established under the auspices of a government department or by any person acting on behalf of the Crown;

(f) . . .

[(2) Paragraph (1)(e) above does not apply to any employer-financed retirement benefits scheme arrangement which has been provided to an employee as part of or in addition to any pension arrangement referred to in paragraph (1)(e) above.]

(3) For the purposes of this regulation—

(a) . . .

(b) "occupational pension scheme" has the meaning given in section 1 of the Pension Schemes Act 1993;

(c) "public service pension scheme" has the meaning given in section 1 of the Pension Schemes Act 1993;

(d) . . .

NOTES

Para (1): sub-paras (b), (c), and words in square brackets in sub-paras (a)(i), (d) substituted, and sub-para (f) revoked, by the Taxation of Pension Schemes (Consequential Amendments of Occupational and Personal Pension Schemes Legislation) Order 2006, SI 2006/744, art 21(1), (3)(a).

Para (2): substituted by SI 2006/744, art 21(1), (3)(b).

Para (3): sub-paras (a), (d) revoked by SI 2006/744, art 21(1), (3)(c).

[11.26]

3 Unapproved pension arrangements

[(1) For the purposes of section 12 of the 1999 Act (effect of bankruptcy on pension rights: unapproved arrangements), a pension arrangement falling within—

(a) section 157 of the Finance Act 2004 (de-registration);

(b) paragraphs 52 to 57 of Schedule 36 to that Act; or

(c) section 393A of the 2003 Act,

shall be an "unapproved pension arrangement" if it satisfies the conditions specified in paragraph (2) below.]

(2) The conditions referred to in paragraph (1) above are that the pension arrangement—

(a) is established under—

(i) an irrevocable trust, or

(ii) a contract, agreement or arrangement made with the bankrupt;

(b) has as its primary purpose the provision of relevant benefits; and

(c) is the bankrupt's sole pension arrangement or his main means of pension provision (other than a pension under Part II of the Social Security Contributions and Benefits Act 1992 (contributory benefits) or Part II of the Social Security Contributions and Benefits (Northern Ireland) Act 1992 (contributory benefits)).

(3) For the purposes of section 12(2)(c) of the 1999 Act, the prescribed person shall be the responsible person.

NOTES

Para (1): substituted by the Taxation of Pension Schemes (Consequential Amendments of Occupational and Personal Pension Schemes Legislation) Order 2006, SI 2006/744, art 21(1), (4).

[11.27]

4 Exclusion of rights under unapproved pension arrangements

For the purpose of excluding his rights under an unapproved pension arrangement from his estate for the purposes of Parts VIII to XI of the 1986 Act (which cover individual voluntary arrangements, bankruptcy and individual insolvency), a bankrupt may—

(a) make an application to the court for an exclusion order in accordance with the provisions of regulation 5 below;

(b) enter into a qualifying agreement with the trustee in bankruptcy in accordance with the provisions of regulation 6 below.

[11.28]

5 Exclusion orders

(1) Subject to paragraph (2) below, an application for an exclusion order shall be made to the court within a period of—

(a) thirteen weeks beginning with—

(i) the date on which the bankrupt's estate vests in the trustee in bankruptcy in accordance with the provisions of section 306 of the 1986 Act (vesting of bankrupt's estate in trustee), or

(ii) in the case of a scheme referred to in regulation [3(1)(a) above, the date, if later than that referred to in head (i) above, on which any rights of the bankrupt vest in the trustee in bankruptcy on the de-registration of the scheme by Her Majesty's Revenue and Customs by virtue of section 157 of the Finance Act 2004; or]

(b) thirty days beginning with the date on which a qualifying agreement is revoked in accordance with the provisions of regulation 6 below.

(2) The court may, either before or after it has expired and where good cause is shown, extend the period referred to in paragraph (1)(a) or, as the case may be, (1)(b) above.

(3) In deciding whether to make an exclusion order and, if so, whether to make it in respect of part or all (but not exceeding the total amount) of the excludable rights, the court shall have reference to—

(a) the future likely needs of the bankrupt and his family;

(b) whether any benefits by way of pension or otherwise (other than a pension under Part II of the Social Security Contributions and Benefits Act 1992 or Part II of the Social Security Contributions and Benefits (Northern Ireland) Act 1992 (contributory benefits) or an income-related benefit [or universal credit under Part 1 of the Welfare Reform Act 2012]) are likely to be received by virtue of rights of the bankrupt which have already accrued under any other pension arrangements at the date on which the application for an exclusion order is made and the extent to which they appear likely to be adequate for meeting any such needs.

NOTES

Para (1): words in square brackets in sub-para (a)(ii) substituted by the Taxation of Pension Schemes (Consequential Amendments of Occupational and Personal Pension Schemes Legislation) Order 2006, SI 2006/744, art 21(1), (5).

Para (3): words in square brackets in sub-para (b) inserted by the Universal Credit (Consequential, Supplementary, Incidental and Miscellaneous Provisions) Regulations 2013, SI 2013/630, reg 32(1), (2).

[11.29]

6 Qualifying agreements

(1) A qualifying agreement shall be made within a period of nine weeks beginning with the later of the following—

(a) the date on which the bankrupt's estate vests in the trustee in bankruptcy in accordance with the provisions of section 306 of the 1986 Act (vesting of bankrupt's estate in trustee); or

(b) in the case of a scheme referred to in regulation [3(1)(a) above, the date, if later than that referred to in sub-paragraph (a) above, on which any rights of the bankrupt vest in the trustee in bankruptcy on the de-registration of the scheme by Her Majesty's Revenue and Customs by virtue of section 157 of the Finance Act 2004.]

(2) A qualifying agreement made between the bankrupt and the trustee in bankruptcy shall be by deed and incorporate all the terms which they have expressly agreed.

(3) Where—

(a) the bankrupt has failed to make full disclosure of all material facts in respect of any pension arrangement which is the subject of a qualifying agreement; and

(b) has failed to do so for the purpose of enabling his rights under such an arrangement to be excluded from his estate for the purposes of Parts VIII to XI of the 1986 Act where they would not have otherwise been excluded,

the trustee in bankruptcy may revoke that agreement by giving the bankrupt notice of revocation.

(4) A notice of revocation shall—

(a) be dated;

(b) be in writing;

(c) specify the reasons for revocation of the qualifying agreement;

(d) specify the date on which the agreement shall be revoked, such date not being one falling within a period of thirty days beginning with the date of the notice; and

(e) inform the bankrupt that he has the right to apply for an exclusion order within a period of thirty days beginning with the date referred to in sub-paragraph (d) above.

(5) Where a qualifying agreement has been made or revoked in accordance with the provisions of this regulation, the trustee in bankruptcy shall, within a period of thirty days beginning with the date on which that agreement was made or, in the case of a notice of revocation, the date required under paragraph (4)(a) above, notify the responsible person in writing of that fact.

NOTES

Para (1): words in square brackets in sub-para (b) substituted by the Taxation of Pension Schemes (Consequential Amendments of Occupational and Personal Pension Schemes Legislation) Order 2006, SI 2006/744, art 21(1), (6).

[11.30]

7 Calculation and verification of rights under pension arrangements

(1) For the purposes of section 342B(4)(b) of the 1986 Act, the value of the individual's ("the bankrupt's") rights under an approved pension arrangement, or of his excluded rights under an unapproved pension arrangement, shall be the cash equivalent of those rights as calculated and verified in accordance with paragraph (2) below.

(2) In calculating and verifying the cash equivalent of the rights referred to in paragraph (1) above, regulation 3 of the Pensions on Divorce etc (Provision of Information) Regulations 2000 (information about pensions and divorce [and dissolution of a civil partnership]: valuation of pension benefits) shall have effect for the purposes of this regulation in like manner to that in which it has effect for the valuation of benefits in connection with the supply of information in connection with domestic and overseas divorce etc [and dissolution of a civil partnership] in England, Wales and Northern Ireland for the purposes of those Regulations; and for these purposes "the date on which the request for the valuation was received" in that regulation shall be read as "the date on which the trustee in bankruptcy's request for the valuation was received".

NOTES

Para (2): words in square brackets inserted by the Civil Partnership (Pensions, Social Security and Child Support) (Consequential, etc Provisions) Order 2005, SI 2005/2877, art 2(2), Sch 2, para 9.

[11.31]

8 Time for compliance with restoration order

The responsible person shall comply with the restoration order before the end of a period of seventeen weeks beginning with the date of service of that order.

[11.32]

9 Calculation and verification of rights under destination arrangements

(1) Where section 342E of the 1986 Act applies, the value of a transferee's rights under a destination arrangement, derived directly or indirectly from a pension-sharing transaction, shall be—

(a) the cash equivalent of those rights at the date on which the trustee in bankruptcy's request for that valuation is received by the responsible person; and

(b) calculated and verified in accordance with paragraph (2) below.

(2) In calculating and verifying the cash equivalent of the transferee's rights referred to in paragraph (1) above, regulation 24 of the Pension Sharing (Pension Credit Benefit) Regulations 2000 shall have effect for the purposes of this regulation in like manner to that in which it has effect for the calculation and verification of pension credit for the purposes of those Regulations.

[11.33]

10 Time for compliance with request for information

(1) Subject to paragraph (2) below, where a request for information has been made to the responsible person by—

(a) the trustee in bankruptcy or the bankrupt in connection with the making of an application for an exclusion order;

(b) the bankrupt for, or in connection with, the making of a qualifying agreement referred to in regulation 6 above; or

(c) the trustee in bankruptcy—

(i) pursuant to section 342C(1) of the 1986 Act (which enables the trustee in bankruptcy to request the responsible person to provide information which he may reasonably need for the making of an application for a restoration order) and relating to the cash equivalent of a bankrupt's rights or excluded rights,

(ii) pursuant to section 342F(1) to (3) of the 1986 Act (which enables the transferor's trustee in bankruptcy to request the responsible person to provide information which he may reasonably need for the making of an application under sections 339 and 340 of the 1986 Act) and relating to the cash equivalent of a transferee's rights under a destination arrangement,

he shall comply with that request within a period of nine weeks beginning with the day on which it is received.

Part 11 SIs: Personal Insolvency

(2) In the case of a request for information falling within sub-paragraph (a) of paragraph (1) above, the court may, either before or after it has expired and where good cause is shown, extend the period referred to in that paragraph.

PART III
SCOTLAND

[11.34]
11 Prescribed pension arrangements

For the purposes of section 11(2)(h) of the 1999 Act, regulation 2 above shall apply to Scotland in like manner to that in which it applies to England and Wales.

[11.35]
12 Unapproved pension arrangements

[(1) For the purposes of section 12 of the 1999 Act, a pension arrangement falling within—
- (a) section 157 of the Finance Act 2004;
- (b) paragraphs 52 to 57 of Schedule 36 to that Act; or
- (c) section 393A of the 2003 Act,

shall be an "unapproved pension arrangement" if it satisfies the conditions specified in paragraph (2) below.]

(2) The conditions referred to in paragraph (1) above are that the pension arrangement—
- (a) is established under—
  - (i) an irrevocable trust, or
  - (ii) a contract, agreement or arrangement made with the debtor;
- (b) has as its primary purpose the provision of relevant benefits; and
- (c) is the debtor's sole pension arrangement or his main means of pension provision (other than a pension under Part II of the Social Security Contributions and Benefits Act 1992 (contributory benefits) or Part II of the Social Security Contributions and Benefits (Northern Ireland) Act 1992 (contributory benefits)).

(3) For the purposes of section 12(2)(c) of the 1999 Act, the prescribed person shall be the responsible person.

NOTES

Para (1): substituted by the Taxation of Pension Schemes (Consequential Amendments of Occupational and Personal Pension Schemes Legislation) Order 2006, SI 2006/744, art 21(1), (7).

[11.36]
13 Exclusion of rights under unapproved pension arrangements

For the purpose of excluding his rights under an unapproved pension arrangement from his estate for the purposes of the 1980 Act or the 1985 Act, as the case may be, a debtor may—
- (a) make an application to the court for an exclusion order in accordance with the provisions of regulation 14 below;
- (b) enter into a qualifying agreement with the permanent trustee or judicial factor in accordance with the provisions of regulation 15 below.

[11.37]
14 Exclusion orders

(1) Subject to paragraph (2) below, an application to the court for an exclusion order shall be made within a period of—
- (a) thirteen weeks beginning with—
  - (i) the date on which the act and warrant is issued on confirmation of the permanent trustee's appointment in accordance with the provisions of the 1985 Act or the date of the appointment of a judicial factor, or
  - (ii) in the case of a scheme referred to in regulation [12(1)(a) above, the date, if later than that referred to in head (i) above, on which any rights of the debtor vest in the permanent trustee or judicial factor on the de-registration of the scheme by Her Majesty's Revenue and Customs by virtue of section 157 of the Finance Act 2004; or]
- (b) thirty days beginning with the date on which a qualifying agreement is revoked in accordance with the provisions of regulation 15 below.

(2) The court may, either before or after it has expired and on cause shown, extend the period referred to in paragraph (1)(a) or, as the case may be, (1)(b) above.

(3) In deciding whether to make an exclusion order and, if so, whether to make it in respect of part or all (but not exceeding the total amount) of the excludable rights, the court shall have reference to—
- (a) the future likely needs of the debtor and his family;
- (b) whether any benefits by way of pension or otherwise (other than a pension under Part II of the Social Security Contributions and Benefits Act 1992 or Part II of the Social Security Contributions and Benefits (Northern Ireland) Act 1992 (contributory benefits) or an income-related benefit [or universal credit under Part 1 of the Welfare Reform Act 2012]) are likely to be received by virtue of rights of the debtor which have already accrued under any other pension arrangements at the date on which the application for an exclusion order is made and the extent to which they appear likely to be adequate for meeting any such needs.

NOTES

Para (1): words in square brackets in sub-para (a)(ii) substituted by the Taxation of Pension Schemes (Consequential Amendments of Occupational and Personal Pension Schemes Legislation) Order 2006, SI 2006/744, art 21(1), (8).

Para (3): words in square brackets in sub-para (b) inserted by the Universal Credit (Consequential, Supplementary, Incidental and Miscellaneous Provisions) Regulations 2013, SI 2013/630, reg 32(1), (2).

[11.38]

15 Qualifying agreements

(1) A qualifying agreement shall be made within a period of nine weeks beginning with the later of the following dates—

(a) the date on which the act and warrant is issued on confirmation of the permanent trustee's appointment in accordance with the provisions of the 1985 Act or the date of the appointment of a judicial factor; or

(b) in the case of a scheme referred to in regulation [12(1)(a) above, the date, if later than that referred to in sub-paragraph (a) above, on which any rights of the debtor vest in the permanent trustee or judicial factor on the de-registration of the scheme by Her Majesty's Revenue and Customs by virtue of section 157 of the Finance Act 2004.]

(2) A qualifying agreement shall—

(a) be in writing;

(b) incorporate all the terms which the debtor and the permanent trustee or judicial factor have expressly agreed; and

(c) be subscribed by the debtor and the permanent trustee or judicial factor, in each case in accordance with section 3(1) of the Requirements of Writing (Scotland) Act 1995.

(3) Where—

(a) the debtor has failed to make full disclosure of all material facts in respect of any pension arrangement which is the subject of a qualifying agreement; and

(b) has failed to do so for the purpose of enabling his rights under such an arrangement to be excluded from his estate for the purposes of the 1980 Act or the 1985 Act where they would not have otherwise been excluded,

the permanent trustee or judicial factor may revoke that agreement by giving the debtor notice of revocation.

(4) A notice of revocation shall—

(a) be dated;

(b) be in writing;

(c) specify the reasons for revocation of the qualifying agreement;

(d) specify the date on which that agreement shall be revoked, such date not being one falling within a period of thirty days beginning with the date of the notice; and

(e) inform the debtor that he has the right to apply for an exclusion order within a period of thirty days beginning with the date on which the agreement falls to be revoked in accordance with that notice.

(5) Where a qualifying agreement has been made or revoked in accordance with the provisions of this regulation, the permanent trustee or judicial factor shall, within a period of thirty days beginning with the date on which the agreement was made or, in the case of a notice of revocation, the date required under paragraph (4)(a) above, notify the responsible person in writing of that fact.

NOTES

Para (1): words in square brackets in sub-para (b) substituted by the Taxation of Pension Schemes (Consequential Amendments of Occupational and Personal Pension Schemes Legislation) Order 2006, SI 2006/744, art 21(1), (9).

[11.39]

16 Calculation and verification of rights under pension arrangements

(1) For the purposes of section 36B(4)(b) of the 1985 Act, the value of the debtor's rights under an approved pension arrangement, or of his excluded rights under an unapproved pension arrangement, shall be the cash equivalent of those rights as calculated and verified in accordance with paragraph (2) below.

(2) In calculating and verifying the cash equivalent of the rights referred to in paragraph (1) above, regulation 3 of the Divorce etc (Pensions) (Scotland) Regulations 2000 (valuation), except paragraph (11) thereof, shall have effect for the purposes of this regulation in like manner to that in which it has effect for the valuation of benefits in connection with the supply of information in connection with divorce in Scotland for the purposes of those Regulations; and for these purposes "the relevant date" in that regulation shall be read as "the date on which the permanent trustee's request for the valuation was received".

[11.40]

17 Time for compliance with restoration order

The responsible person shall comply with the restoration order before the end of a period of seventeen weeks beginning with the date of service of that order.

[11.41]

18 Calculation and verification of transferee's rights under a pension arrangement derived from a pension-sharing transaction

(1) Where section 36E of the 1985 Act applies, the value of a transferee's rights under a pension arrangement derived directly or indirectly from a pension-sharing transaction, shall be—

(a) the cash equivalent of those rights at the date on which the permanent trustee's request for that valuation is received by the responsible person; and

(b) calculated and verified in accordance with paragraph (2) below.

(2) In calculating and verifying the cash equivalent of the transferee's rights referred to in paragraph (1) above, regulation 24 of the Pension Sharing (Pension Credit Benefit) Regulations 2000 shall have effect for the purposes of this regulation in like manner to that in which it has effect for the calculation and verification of pension credit for the purposes of those Regulations.

[11.42]

19 Time for compliance with request for information

(1) Subject to paragraph (2) below, where a request for information has been made to the responsible person by—

(a) the permanent trustee, judicial factor or the debtor in connection with the making of an application for an exclusion order;

(b) the debtor for, or in connection with, the making of a qualifying agreement referred to in regulation 15 above; or

(c) the permanent trustee—

(i) pursuant to section 36C(1) of the 1985 Act (which enables the permanent trustee to request the responsible person to provide information which he may reasonably need for the making of an application for a restoration order) and relating to the cash equivalent of a debtor's rights or excluded rights,

(ii) pursuant to section 36F(1) of the 1985 Act (which enables the transferor's permanent trustee to request the responsible person to provide information which he may reasonably need for the making of an application under sections 34 to 36 of the 1985 Act) and relating to the cash equivalent of a transferee's rights under a pension arrangement referred to in regulation 18(1) above,

he shall comply with that request within a period of nine weeks beginning with the day on which it is received.

(2) In the case of a request for information falling within sub-paragraph (a) of paragraph (1) above, the court may, either before or after it has expired and on cause shown, extend the period referred to in that paragraph.

20 (*Revokes the Occupational and Personal Pension Schemes (Bankruptcy) Regulations 2002, SI 2002/427.*)

NATIONAL HEALTH SERVICE (COMPENSATION FOR PREMATURE RETIREMENT) REGULATIONS 2002

(SI 2002/1311)

NOTES

Made: 10 May 2002.

Authority: Superannuation Act 1972, s 24(1), (3), (4), Sch 3, paras 8, 9, 13.

Commencement: 31 May 2002.

[11.43]

1 Citation and commencement

These Regulations may be cited as the National Health Service (Compensation for Premature Retirement) Regulations 2002 and shall come into force on 31st May 2002.

2–12 (*Outside the scope of this work.*)

[11.44]

13 Compensation not assignable

(1) Any assignment of, or charge on, or any agreement to assign or charge, any right to compensation under these Regulations is void.

(2) On the bankruptcy of an entitled officer, no part of the compensation shall be paid to any trustee or other person acting on behalf of the creditors, except as provided for in paragraph (3).

(3) Where, following the bankruptcy of an entitled officer, the court makes an income payments order under section 310 of the Insolvency Act 1986 that requires the Secretary of State to pay all or part of the compensation to the entitled officer's trustee in bankruptcy, the Secretary of State shall comply with that order.

14–16 (*Outside the scope of this work.*)

SCHEDULES 1, 2 (*Schs 1, 2 outside the scope of this work.*)

COUNCIL FOR HEALTHCARE REGULATORY EXCELLENCE (APPOINTMENT, PROCEDURE ETC) REGULATIONS 2008

(SI 2008/2927)

NOTES

Made: 10 November 2008.

Authority: National Health Service Reform and Health Care Professions Act 2002, s 38(5), (7), Sch 7, para 6.

Commencement: 1 January 2009.

[11.45]

1 Citation, commencement and interpretation

(1) These Regulations may be cited as the Council for Healthcare Regulatory Excellence (Appointment, Procedure etc) Regulations 2008 and come into force on 1st January 2009.

(2) In these Regulations—

"the 2002 Act" means the National Health Service Reform and Health Care Professions Act 2002;

"the appointor" means —

(a) in the case of the appointment of the chair, the Privy Council; and

(b) in the case of the appointment of a non-executive member, the person who appoints that member under paragraph 4 of Schedule 7 to the 2002 Act;

"the chair" means the chair of the Council;

["the Council" means the Professional Standards Authority for Health and Social Care];

"final outcome", in relation to any proceedings where there are rights of appeal, means the outcome of the proceedings—

(a) once the period for bringing an appeal has expired without an appeal being brought; or

(b) if an appeal is brought in accordance with those rights, once those rights have been exhausted;

"licensing body" means any body anywhere in the world that licenses or regulates any profession;

"non-executive member" means a non-executive member of the Council;

"spent conviction" means—

(a) in relation to a conviction by a court in Great Britain, a conviction that is a spent conviction for the purposes of the Rehabilitation of Offenders Act 1974; or

(b) in relation to a conviction by a court in Northern Ireland, a conviction that is a spent conviction for the purposes of the Rehabilitation of Offenders (Northern Ireland) Order 1978.

NOTES

Para (1): definition "the Council" substituted by the Health and Social Care Act 2012 (Consequential Amendments—the Professional Standards Authority for Health and Social Care) Order 2012, SI 2012/2672, art 4.

[11.46]

2 Conditions of appointment for chair and non-executive members of the Council

(1) It is a condition for the appointment as the chair or a non-executive member that that person—

(a) lives or works wholly or mainly in the United Kingdom; and

(b) does not fall within paragraph (2).

(2) A person falls within this paragraph if that person—

(a) has at any time been convicted—

(i) of an offence involving dishonesty or deception in the United Kingdom, or

(ii) of an offence in the United Kingdom, and the final outcome of the proceedings was a sentence of imprisonment or detention (whether suspended or not) of over three months, and

the conviction is not a spent conviction;

(b) has at any time been convicted of an offence elsewhere than in the United Kingdom and the appointor is satisfied that the person's membership of the Council would be liable to undermine public confidence in the Council;

(c) has at any time—

(i) been adjudged bankrupt or had a sequestration of his estate awarded unless (in either case) that person has been discharged or the bankruptcy order has been annulled,

(ii) been made the subject of a bankruptcy restrictions order or an interim bankruptcy restrictions order under Schedule 4A to the Insolvency Act 1986 or Schedule 2A to the Insolvency (Northern Ireland) Order 1989, unless that order has ceased to have effect or has been annulled, or

(iii) made a composition or arrangement with, or granted a trust deed for, the person's creditors unless that person has been discharged in respect of it;

(d) has at any time been removed from office as a chair, member, convenor or director of any public body on the grounds, in terms, that it was not in the interests, or conducive to the good management, of that body that the person should continue to hold that office;

(e) has at any time been, or is currently the subject of, any investigation or proceedings concerning the person's professional conduct by any licensing body and the appointor is satisfied that it would not to be appropriate for the person to be a member of the Council given that investigation or those proceedings;

(f) is subject to—

(i) a disqualification order or disqualification undertaking under the Company Directors Disqualification Act 1986,

(ii) a disqualification order under Part II of the Companies (Northern Ireland) Order 1989,

(iii) a disqualification order or disqualification undertaking under the Company Directors Disqualification (Northern Ireland) Order 2002,

(iv) an order made under section 429(2) of the Insolvency Act 1986 (disabilities on revocation of a county court administration order);

(g) has at any time been removed—

(i) from the office of charity trustee or trustee for a charity by an order made by the Charity Commissioners, the Charity Commission for Northern Ireland or the High Court on the grounds of any misconduct or mismanagement in the administration of the charity—

(aa) for which the person was responsible or to which the person was privy, or

(bb) which the person by their conduct contributed to or facilitated, or

(ii) under—

(aa) section 7 of the Law Reform (Miscellaneous Provisions) (Scotland) Act 1990 (powers of the court of Session to deal with management of charities), or

(bb) section 34(5)(e) of the Charities and Trustees Investment (Scotland) Act 2005 (powers of Court of Session),

from being concerned with the management or control of any body;

(h) has been included by—

(i) the [Disclosure and Barring Service] in a barred list (within the meaning of the Safeguarding Vulnerable Groups Act 2006 or the Safeguarding Vulnerable Groups (Northern Ireland) Order 2007, or

(ii) the Scottish Ministers in the children's list or the adults' list (within the meaning of the Protection of Vulnerable Groups (Scotland) Act 2007);

(i) is a member of the Council of, or a Council that is, a regulatory body mentioned in section 25(3) of the 2002 Act; or

(j) is or has been a member of a profession regulated by the—

(i) Chiropractors Act 1994,

(ii) Dentists Act 1984,

[(iii) Health and Social Work Professions Order 2001,]

(iv) Nursing and Midwifery Order 2001,

(v) Medical Act 1983,

(vi) Osteopaths Act 1993,

(vii) Opticians Act 1989,

[(viii) Pharmacy Order 2010], and

(ix) Pharmacy (Northern Ireland) Order 1976.

NOTES

Para (2): words in square brackets in sub-para (h)(i) substituted by the Protection of Freedoms Act 2012 (Disclosure and Barring Service Transfer of Functions) Order 2012, SI 2012/3006, art 13(1), (3)(j); sub-para (j)(iii) substituted by the Health and Social Care Act 2012 (Consequential Provision—Social Workers) Order 2012, SI 2012/1479, art 11, Schedule, Pt 1, para 56; sub-para (j)(viii) substituted by the Pharmacy Order 2010, SI 2010/231, art 68, Sch 4, Pt 2, para 67.

3–9 (*Outside the scope of this work.*)

EDUCATION (STUDENT LOANS) (REPAYMENT) REGULATIONS 2009

(SI 2009/470)

NOTES

Made: 1 March 2009.

Authority: Education (Scotland) Act 1980, ss 73(f), 73B; Teaching and Higher Education Act 1998, ss 22, 42; Sale of Student Loans Act 2008, ss 5, 6.

Commencement: see reg 1(1)–(3) at **[11.47]**.

Previous Regulations:

The Education (Student Support) (No 2) Regulations 2002, SI 2002/3200 were revoked by the Education (Student Support) Regulations 2005, SI 2005/52, reg 3(1), Sch 1, as from 1 September 2005, subject to transitional provisions in reg 3(2), (3) thereof.

The Education (Student Support) Regulations 2005, SI 2005/52 were revoked as from 1 September 2006, by the Education (Student Support) Regulations 2006, SI 2006/119, reg 3(1)(a), in relation to England, subject to transitional provisions and savings in reg 3(2), (3) thereof, and by the Assembly Learning Grants and Loans (Higher Education) (Wales) Regulations 2006, SI 2006/126, reg 3(1)(a), in relation to Wales, subject to transitional provisions and savings in reg 3(2)–(4) thereof.

The Education (Student Support) Regulations 2006, SI 2006/119, were revoked by the Education (Student Support) Regulations 2007, SI 2007/176, reg 4(1)(a), as from 1 September 2007, subject to savings and transitional provisions in reg 4(2)–(4) thereof.

The Education (Student Support) Regulations 2007, SI 2007/176, were revoked by the Education (Student Support) Regulations 2008, SI 2008/529, reg 3(1)(a), as from 1 September 2008, subject to savings and transitional provisions in reg 3(2), (3) thereof.

The Education (Student Support) Regulations 2008, SI 2008/529 were revoked by the Education (Student Support) (No 2) Regulations 2008, SI 2008/1582, reg 4(1)(a), as from 1 September 2008, subject to savings and transitional provisions in reg 4(2)–(6) thereof.

The Education (Student Support) (No 2) Regulations 2008, SI 2008/1582 were revoked by the Education (Student Support) Regulations 2009, SI 2009/1555, reg 4(2)(a), as from 1 September 2010, subject to savings and transitional provisions in reg 4(3)–(6) thereof.

PART 1
GENERAL

[11.47]

1 Citation, commencement and extent

(1) These Regulations may be cited as the Education (Student Loans) (Repayment) Regulations 2009 and, subject to paragraphs (2) and (3), come into force on 6 April 2009.

(2) Regulations 2(2), 21 and Part 6 come into force on 1 September 2009.

(3) (*Outside the scope of this work.*)

(4) Subject to paragraphs (5) and (6), these Regulations extend to England and Wales only.

(5) Regulation 80(3) extends to Northern Ireland.

(6) These Regulations extend to all of the United Kingdom in so far as they impose any obligation or confer any power on HMRC, an employer or a borrower in relation to repayments under Parts 3 or 4 or on any other person in relation to the retention or production of information or records.

2–79 *(Regs 2–8, 9–79 (Pts 2–5) outside the scope of this work.)*

PART 6
INSOLVENCY

[11.48]

80 Effect of borrower insolvency on student loans [and postgraduate master's degree loans]

(1) In this Part, "eligible student" means any person who is an eligible student—

- (a) in England, for the purposes of the Education (Student Support) (No 2) Regulations 2008 or any subsequent Regulations made under section 22 of the 1998 Act;
- (b) in Wales, for the purposes of the Assembly Learning Grants and Loans (Higher Education) (Wales) Regulations 2008 or any subsequent Regulations made under section 22 of the 1998 Act; or
- (c) In Northern Ireland, for the purposes of the Education (Student Support) Regulations (Northern Ireland) 2008 or any subsequent Regulations made under the Education (Student Support) (Northern Ireland) Order 1998.

(2) In England and Wales—

- (a) any sum payable to an eligible student by way of a student loan [or postgraduate master's degree loan] which the eligible student receives or is entitled to receive after the commencement of that person's bankruptcy, will not be treated as part of the bankrupt's estate or claimed for the bankrupt's estate under [section 307, 310 or 310A] of the Insolvency Act 1986, whether the entitlement arises before or after the commencement of the bankruptcy; . . .
- (b) any debt or liability to which that person is or may become subject in respect of any sum payable to an eligible student by way of a student loan [or postgraduate master's degree loan] will not be included in that person's bankruptcy debts when the person receives or is entitled to receive that sum—
  - (i) in the case of a bankruptcy commencing before 1 September 2004, after the commencement of the bankruptcy; or
  - (ii) in the case of a bankruptcy commencing on or after 1 September 2004, before or after the commencement of the bankruptcy.
- [(c) any sum payable to an eligible student by way of student loan [or postgraduate master's degree loan] which the eligible student receives or is entitled to receive before or after the approval of that person's individual voluntary arrangement under Part 8 of the Insolvency Act 1986 will not be treated as part of any arrangement approved under section 258 or 263D of that Act, whether the entitlement arises before or after the approval of the arrangement; and
- (d) any debt or liability to which that person is or may become subject in respect of any sum payable to an eligible student by way of student loan [or postgraduate master's degree loan] will not be included in that person's individual voluntary arrangement when that person receives or is entitled to receive that sum—
  - (i) in the case of an individual voluntary arrangement approved before 6 April 2010, after the approval of that arrangement; or

(ii) in the case of an individual voluntary arrangement approved on or after 6 April 2010, before or after the approval of that arrangement.]

(3) In Northern Ireland—

(a) any sum payable to an eligible student by way of a student loan [or postgraduate master's degree loan] which the eligible student receives or is entitled to receive after the commencement of that person's bankruptcy, will not be treated as part of the bankrupt's estate or claimed for the bankrupt's estate under [Article 280, 283 or 283A] of the Insolvency (Northern Ireland) Order 1989, whether the entitlement arises before or after the commencement of the bankruptcy;

. . .

(b) any debt or liability to which that person is or may become subject in respect of any sum payable to an eligible student by way of a student loan [or postgraduate master's degree loan] will not be included in that person's bankruptcy debts when the person receives or is entitled to receive that sum—

(i) in the case of a bankruptcy commencing before 1 March 2005, after the commencement of the bankruptcy; or

(ii) in the case of a bankruptcy commencing on or after 1 March 2005, before or after the commencement of the bankruptcy.

[(c) any sum payable to an eligible student by way of a student loan [or postgraduate master's degree loan] which the eligible student receives or is entitled to receive before or after the approval of that person's individual voluntary arrangement under Part 8 of the Insolvency (Northern Ireland) Order 1989 will not be treated as part of the individual voluntary arrangement approved under articles 232 or 237D of that Order, whether the entitlement arises before or after the approval of the arrangement; and

(d) any debt or liability to which that person is or may become subject in respect of any sum payable to an eligible student by way of a student loan [or postgraduate master's degree loan] will not be included in that person's individual voluntary arrangement when that person receives or is entitled to receive that sum—

(i) in the case of an individual voluntary arrangement approved before 6 April 2010, after the approval of the arrangement; or

(ii) in the case of an individual voluntary arrangement approved on or after 6 April 2010, before or after the approval of the arrangement.]

NOTES

Heading: words in square brackets inserted by the Repayment of Student Loans and Postgraduate Master's Degree Loans (Amendment) Regulations 2017, SI 2017/831, regs 2, 40(1), (2).

Para (2): in sub-para (a) words in second pair of square brackets substituted, and word omitted revoked, and sub-paras (c), (d) added, by the Education (Student Loans) (Repayment) (Amendment) Regulations 2010, SI 2010/661, regs 2, 8(a), (b); all other words in square brackets inserted by SI 2017/831, regs 2, 40(1), (3).

Para (3): in sub-para (a) words in second pair of square brackets substituted, and word omitted revoked, and sub-paras (c), (d) added, by SI 2010/661, regs 2, 8(c), (d); all other words in square brackets inserted by SI 2017/831, regs 2, 40(1), (3).

SCHEDULES 1, 2

(Schs 1, 2 outside the scope of this work.)

TEACHERS' PENSIONS REGULATIONS 2010

(SI 2010/990)

NOTES

Made: 24 March 2010.
Authority: Superannuation Act 1972, ss 9, 12, 24, Sch 3.
Commencement: 1 September 2010.

PART 1
PRELIMINARY

[11.49]
1 Citation and commencement

These Regulations may be cited as the Teachers' Pensions Regulations 2010 and come into force on 1st September 2010.

2–106 *(Regs 2–4, 5–106 (Pts 2–10) outside the scope of this work.)*

PART 11
GENERAL

107–121 *(Outside the scope of this work.)*

[11.50]
122 Benefits not assignable

(1) Where a benefit is payable to a person or a person has a right to a future benefit, the benefit or the right to the benefit cannot be assigned in favour of the person's widow, widower, surviving civil partner or dependant and an agreement to this effect is void.
(2) Section 91 of PA 1995 (inalienability of occupational pensions) prevents assignment in other circumstances.

NOTES
Pensions Act 1995, s 91: see **[17.126]**.

123–137 *(Regs 123, 124, 125–137 (Pts 12, 13) outside the scope of this work.)*

SCHEDULES 1–13

(Schedules 1–13 outside the scope of this work.)

LONDON INSOLVENCY DISTRICT (COUNTY COURT AT CENTRAL LONDON) ORDER 2014

(SI 2014/818)

NOTES
Made: 31 March 2014.
Authority: Insolvency Act 1986, s 374.
Commencement: 22 April 2014.

[11.51]
1 Citation and commencement

This Order may be cited as the London Insolvency District (County Court at Central London) Order 2014 and comes into force on 22nd April 2014.

NOTES
Commencement: 22 April 2014.

2 *(Revokes the London Insolvency District (Central London County Court) Order 2011, SI 2011/761.)*

[11.52]
3 Insolvency Districts

The London insolvency district comprises the areas served by the following hearing centres of the county court—
(a) Barnet;
(b) Bow;
(c) Brentford;
(d) The County Court at Central London;
(e) Clerkenwell and Shoreditch;
(f) Edmonton;
(g) Lambeth;
(h) Mayor's and City of London Court;
(i) Wandsworth;
(j) West London; and
(k) Willesden.

NOTES
Commencement: 22 April 2014.

TEACHERS (COMPENSATION FOR REDUNDANCY AND PREMATURE RETIREMENT) REGULATIONS 2015

(SI 2015/601)

NOTES
Made: 5 March 2015.
Authority: Public Service Pensions Act 2013, ss 1, 3, Sch 3.
Commencement: 1 April 2015.

PART 1
GENERAL

[11.53]

1 Citation and commencement

These Regulations may be cited as the Teachers (Compensation for Redundancy and Premature Retirement) Regulations 2015 and come into force on 1st April 2015.

NOTES

Commencement: 1 April 2015.

2–32 (*Regs 2–4, regs 5–32 (Pts 2–7) outside the scope of this work.*)

PART 8
MISCELLANEOUS

33–39 (*Outside the scope of this work.*)

[11.54]

40 Compensation not assignable

(1) Any assignment of, or charge on, or agreement to assign or charge, any compensation payable under these Regulations is void.

(2) On the bankruptcy of a person eligible for such compensation no part of the compensation is to pass to any trustee or other person acting on behalf of the creditors except in accordance with an income payments order made by a court under section 310 of the Insolvency Act 1986.

NOTES

Commencement: 1 April 2015.

41 (*Outside the scope of this work.*)

PART 9
CONSEQUENTIAL AMENDMENTS, REVOCATION AND TRANSITIONAL PROVISIONS

42, 43 (*Outside the scope of this work.*)

[11.55]

44 Revocation and transitional provisions

(1) (*Outside the scope of this work.*)

(2) Anything done or having effect as if done under or for the purposes of a provision of the Teachers (Compensation for Redundancy and Premature Retirement) Regulations 1997 has effect, if it could have been done under or for the purpose of the corresponding provision of these Regulations, as if done under or for the purposes of that corresponding provision.

(3) If a period of time specified in, or applying by virtue of, a provision of the Teachers (Compensation for Redundancy and Premature Retirement) Regulations 1997 is current at the commencement of these Regulations, these Regulations have effect as if the corresponding provision of these Regulations had been in force when that period began to run.

NOTES

Commencement: 1 April 2015.

SCHEDULES 1–4

(*Schs 1–4 outside the scope of this work.*)

PART 12
STATUTORY INSTRUMENTS RELATING TO OFFICIAL RECEIVERS AND INSOLVENCY PRACTITIONERS—ENGLAND AND WALES

INSOLVENCY PRACTITIONERS (RECOGNISED PROFESSIONAL BODIES) ORDER 1986

(SI 1986/1764)

NOTES

Made: 10 October 1986.

Authority: Insolvency Act 1985, ss 3(2), (10) (repealed); this Order now has effect as if made under the Insolvency Act 1986, ss 391(1), (4).

Commencement: 10 November 1986.

Application: this Order is applied to limited liability partnerships with such modifications as the context requires for the purpose of giving effect to the provisions of the Insolvency Act 1986, by the Limited Liability Partnerships Regulations 2001, SI 2001/1090, reg 10, Sch 6, Pt II at **[10.38]**, **[10.43]**.

Application to Charitable Incorporated Organisations: as to the application of this Order in relation to CIOs, see the Charitable Incorporated Organisations (Insolvency and Dissolution) Regulations 2012, SI 2012/3013 at **[18.221]**.

[12.1]
1

This Order may be cited as the Insolvency Practitioners (Recognised Professional Bodies) Order 1986 and shall come into force on 10th November 1986.

[12.2]
2

The bodies specified in the Schedule to this Order are hereby declared to be recognised professional bodies for the purposes of section 3 of the Insolvency Act 1985.

NOTES

Insolvency Act 1985, s 3: see now the Insolvency Act 1986, ss 390(2), 391, at **[1.478]**, **[1.481]**.

SCHEDULE
RECOGNISED PROFESSIONAL BODIES

Article 2

[12.3]
The Chartered Association of Certified Accountants

The Insolvency Practitioners Association

The Institute of Chartered Accountants in England and Wales

The Institute of Chartered Accountants in Ireland

The Institute of Chartered Accountants of Scotland

. . .

. . .

NOTES

Entry "The Law Society" (omitted) revoked by the Insolvency Practitioners (Recognised Professional Bodies) (Revocation of Recognition) Order 2016, SI 2016/403, art 2.

Entry "The Law Society of Scotland" (omitted) revoked by the Insolvency Practitioners (Recognised Professional Bodies) (Revocation of Recognition) Order 2015, SI 2015/2067, art 2.

CONTRACTING OUT (FUNCTIONS OF THE OFFICIAL RECEIVER) ORDER 1995

(SI 1995/1386)

NOTES

Made: 29 May 1995.

Authority: Deregulation and Contracting Out Act 1994, s 69.

Commencement: 30 May 1995.

Application: this Order is applied to limited liability partnerships with such modifications as the context requires for the purpose of giving effect to the provisions of the Insolvency Act 1986, by the Limited Liability Partnerships Regulations 2001, SI 2001/1090, reg 10, Sch 6, Pt III at **[10.38]**, **[10.44]**.

[12.4]
1 Citation and commencement

(1) This Order may be cited as the Contracting Out (Functions of the Official Receiver) Order 1995.

(2) This Order shall come into force on the day after the day on which it is made.

[12.5]
2 Interpretation

(1) In this Order—

"the 1986 Act" means the Insolvency Act 1986;

"the insolvency legislation" means the Insolvency Act 1986, the Companies Act 1985, the Company Directors Disqualification Act 1986, any subordinate legislation made under any of those Acts and any regulations made under [Introductory Rule 5] of the Rules;

["the Rules" means the Insolvency (England and Wales) Rules 2016]; and

"right of audience" has the meaning given to it by section 119(1) of the Courts and Legal Services Act 1990.

(2) Any expression used in this Order other than one referred to in paragraph (1) above shall bear the same meaning as it bears in the 1986 Act.

(3) In this Order a rule referred to by number means the rule so numbered in the Rules and, except where otherwise expressly provided, a section referred to by number means the section so numbered in the 1986 Act.

NOTES

Para (1): words in square brackets in definition "the insolvency legislation" substituted and definition "the Rules" substituted, by the Insolvency (England and Wales) Rules 2016 (Consequential Amendments and Savings) Rules 2017, SI 2017/369, r 2(2), Sch 2, para 5(1), (2).

[12.6]
3 Contracting out of functions

(1) Subject to paragraph (2) below, any function of the official receiver which is conferred by or under the insolvency legislation, except one which is listed in the Schedule to this Order, may be exercised by, or by employees of, such person (if any) as may be authorised in that behalf by the official receiver.

(2) A function to which paragraph (1) above applies, and which involves the exercise of a right of audience in relation to any proceedings before a court, may only be exercised subject to the fulfilment of the condition specified in paragraph (3) below.

(3) Such right of audience as is mentioned in paragraph (2) shall not be exercised by any person other than a person who has a right of audience in relation to the proceedings in question by virtue of the provisions of Part II of the Courts and Legal Services Act 1990.

NOTES

Part II of the Courts and Legal Services Act 1990: the relevant provisions of Part II have been repealed; see now Part 3 of the Legal Services Act 2007.

SCHEDULE

Article 3

[12.7]
1. The functions of the official receiver as—

(a) a receiver appointed pursuant to section 32 (power for court to appoint official receiver);

(b) a provisional liquidator appointed pursuant to section 135 (appointment and powers of provisional liquidator); or

(c) an interim receiver appointed pursuant to section 286 (power to appoint interim receiver).

2. The receipt of any deposit which relates to a [bankruptcy application or] bankruptcy or winding-up petition.

3. . . .

4. The making of an application to the Secretary of State—

(a) under section 137(1) for the appointment of another person as liquidator in the place of the official receiver; or

(b) under section 296(1) for the appointment of a person as trustee instead of the official receiver.

5. The taking of a decision—

(a) pursuant to section 137(2), whether or not to refer to the Secretary of State the need for an appointment of a liquidator in any case where at meetings held in pursuance of a decision under section 136(5)(a) no person is chosen to be liquidator;

(b) pursuant to section 295(1), whether or not to refer to the Secretary of State the need for an appointment of a trustee in any case where at a meeting summoned under section 293 or 294 no appointment of a person as trustee is made.

6. The making of a reference to the Secretary of State under section 300(4) of the need for an appointment of a trustee by the Secretary of State in the circumstances referred to in that sub-section.

7. The making of a reference to the court or the Secretary of State, as the case may be, under section 300(5) of the need to fill any vacancy in the circumstances referred to in that sub-section.

[**8.** The functions of the official receiver—
 (a) exercisable under rule 17.28(2) (functions of committee in winding up by court or bankruptcy exercisable by official receiver); or
 (b) in relation to the hearing of an application made under—
  (i) section 280 (discharge by order of the court);
  (ii) rule 7.44(2) (application to court for a release or extension of time in respect of statement of affairs in a winding up by the court); or
  (iii) rule 10.58(2) (application to court by bankrupt for a release or extension of time in respect of statement of affairs).]

9. The bringing or the conduct of proceedings under the Company Directors Disqualification Act 1986.

10. The giving of notice to the Secretary of State pursuant to section 174(3) (release of official receiver in winding up by the court) or section 299(2) (release of official receiver as trustee).

11. . . .

12. The making or conduct of any application to the court—
 (a) to commit a bankrupt for contempt of court for failure to comply with an obligation imposed on him by—
  (i) section 288 (statement of affairs);
  (ii) section 291 (duties of bankrupt in relation to official receiver);
  (iii) section 312 (obligation to surrender control to trustee);
  (iv) section 333 (duties of bankrupt in relation to trustee); or
  (v) section 363 (general control of court); or
 (b) pursuant to section 279(3) (suspension of discharge on application by official receiver).

13. The making or conduct of any application to the court to commit for contempt of court—
 (a) a person who has failed to attend his public examination under section 133 (public examination of officers, etc); or
 (b) a bankrupt who has failed to attend his public examination under section 290 (public examination of bankrupt).

14. The making of a report to the court pursuant to—
 (a) section 132(1) (investigation by official receiver);
 (b) section 289(1) (investigatory duties of official receiver);
 (c) section 289(2) (report to the court on application by bankrupt for discharge from bankruptcy);
 (d) [rule 7.44(6)(a)] (report to court, etc on application by officers of company, etc for release from duty to submit statement of affairs or for extension of time);
 (e) [rule 10.58(6)(a)] (report to court, etc on application by bankrupt for release from duty to submit statement of affairs or for extension of time); or
 (f) [rule 10.142(2)] (report in support of application for suspension of discharge).

15. The making or conduct of an application to the court for a public examination under section 133(1) or section 290(1) and the making or conduct of any application in relation to any public examination.

16. The making or conduct of an application to the court to relieve the official receiver from an obligation to make an application for a public examination requested pursuant to section 133(2) or required pursuant to section 290(2).

17. The taking part in a public examination or the questioning of a person pursuant to section 133(4)(a) or the taking part in a public examination or the questioning of a bankrupt pursuant to section 290(4)(a).

18. The making or conduct of an application to the court—
 (a) pursuant to section 134(2) for the issue of a warrant for the arrest of a person and for the seizure of any books, papers, records, money or goods in that person's possession; or
 (b) pursuant to section 364, for the issue of a warrant for the arrest of a debtor, an undischarged bankrupt or a discharged bankrupt, and for the seizure of any books, papers, records, money or goods in the debtor's or the bankrupt's possession, as the case may be.

19. The making or conduct of an application to the court pursuant to section 158 for the arrest of a contributory and for the seizure of his books, papers and movable personal property.

20. The making or conduct of an application to the court for the transfer of winding-up or bankruptcy proceedings from one court to another.

21. . . .

22. Any function of the official receiver in relation to the hearing of—
 (a) an application by a bankrupt for leave to act as a director of, or directly or indirectly to take part in or be concerned in the promotion, formation or management of, a company; or
 (b) an application by a director in respect of whom a disqualification order made under the Company Directors Disqualification Act 1986 is in force, for leave—
  (a) to be a director of a company,

(b) to be a liquidator or administrator of a company,
(c) to be a receiver or manager of a company's property, or
(d) to be concerned or to take part in the promotion, formation or management of a company in any way, whether directly or indirectly.

23. The making of a report to the Secretary of State pursuant to section 7(3) of the Company Directors Disqualification Act 1986.

24. Any function corresponding to one referred to in paragraphs 1 to 23 above which is exercisable by the official receiver by virtue of the application (with or without modifications) of any provision of the insolvency legislation to insolvent partnerships or unregistered companies.

25. The presentation of a winding-up petition pursuant to section 124(5) (application by official receiver for winding up of company being wound up voluntarily).

NOTES

Para 2: words in square brackets inserted by SI 2016/481, reg 2(2), Sch 2, Pt 1, para 6.

Paras 3, 11, 21 revoked, para 8 substituted and words in square brackets in para 14 substituted by the Insolvency (England and Wales) Rules 2016 (Consequential Amendments and Savings) Rules 2017, SI 2017/369, r 2(2), Sch 2, para 5(1), (3)–(6).

TRANSNATIONAL INFORMATION AND CONSULTATION OF EMPLOYEES REGULATIONS 1999

(SI 1999/3323)

NOTES

Made: 12 December 1999.
Authority: European Communities Act 1972, s 2(2).
Commencement: 15 January 2000.

PART I
GENERAL

[12.8]
1 Citation, commencement and extent

(1) These Regulations may be cited as the Transnational Information and Consultation of Employees Regulations 1999 and shall come into force on 15th January 2000.

(2) These Regulations extend to Northern Ireland.

2 (*Outside the scope of this work.*)

[12.9]
3 Controlled and Controlling Undertaking

(1) In these Regulations "controlling undertaking" means an undertaking which can exercise a dominant influence over another undertaking by virtue, for example, of ownership, financial participation or the rules which govern it and "controlled undertaking" means an undertaking over which such a dominant influence can be exercised.

(2) The ability of an undertaking to exercise a dominant influence over another undertaking shall be presumed, unless the contrary is proved, when in relation to another undertaking it directly or indirectly—
(a) can appoint more than half of the members of that undertaking's administrative, management or supervisory body;
(b) controls a majority of the votes attached to that undertaking's issued share capital; or
(c) holds a majority of that undertaking's subscribed capital.

(3) In applying the criteria in paragraph (2), a controlling undertaking's rights as regards voting and appointment shall include—
(a) the rights of its other controlled undertakings; and
(b) the rights of any person or body acting in his or its own name but on behalf of the controlling undertaking or of any other of the controlling undertaking's controlled undertakings.

(4) Notwithstanding paragraphs (1) and (2) an undertaking shall not be a controlling undertaking of another undertaking in which it has holdings where the first undertaking is a company referred to in Article 3(5)(a) or (c) of Council Regulation [(EC) No 139/2004 of 20 January 2004] on the control of concentrations between undertakings.

(5) A dominant influence shall not be presumed to be exercised solely by virtue of the fact that an office holder is exercising functions, according to the law of a Member State, relating to liquidation, winding-up, insolvency, cessation of payments, compositions of creditors or analogous proceedings.

(6) Where the law governing an undertaking is the law of a Member State, the law applicable in order to determine whether an undertaking is a controlling undertaking shall be the law of that Member State.

(7) Where the law governing an undertaking is not that of a Member State the law applicable shall be the law of the Member State within whose territory—

(a) the representative of the undertaking is situated; or

(b) in the absence of such a representative, the management of the group undertaking which employs the greatest number of employees is situated.

(8) If two or more undertakings (whether situated in the same or in different Member States) meet one or more of the criteria in paragraph (2) in relation to another undertaking, the criteria shall be applied in the order listed in relation to each of the first-mentioned undertakings and that which meets the criterion that is highest in the order listed shall be presumed, unless the contrary is proved, to exercise a dominant influence over the undertaking in question.

NOTES

Para (4): words in square brackets substituted by the EC Merger Control (Consequential Amendments) Regulations 2004, SI 2004/1079, reg 2, Schedule, para 4.

4–48 (*Regs 4, 5, 6–48 (Pts II–X) outside the scope of this work.*)

SCHEDULE

(*Schedule outside the scope of this work.*)

FINANCIAL SERVICES AND MARKETS ACT 2000 (EXEMPTION) ORDER 2001

(SI 2001/1201)

NOTES

Made: 26 March 2001.
Authority: Financial Services and Markets Act 2000, ss 38, 428(3).
Commencement: 1 December 2001.

1–4 (*Outside the scope of this work.*)

[12.10]

5 Persons exempt in respect of particular regulated activities

(1) Subject to the limitation, if any, expressed in relation to him, each of the persons listed in Part III of the Schedule is exempt from the general prohibition in respect of any regulated activity of the kind specified by any of the following provisions of the Regulated Activities Order, or article 64 of that Order (agreeing to carry on specified kinds of activity) so far as relevant to any such activity—

(a) article 14 (dealing in investments as principal);
(b) article 21 (dealing in investments as agent);
(c) article 25 (arranging deals in investments);
[(ca) article 25D (operating a multilateral trading facility);]
[(cb) article 25DA (operating an organised trading facility);]
(d) article 37 (managing investments);
[(da) article 39A (assisting in the administration and performance of a contract of insurance);]
(e) article 40 (safeguarding and administering investments);
(f) article 45 (sending dematerialised instructions);
[(ga) article 51ZA (managing a UCITS);
(gb) article 51ZB (acting as a trustee or depositary of a UCITS);
(gc) article 51ZC (managing an AIF);
(gd) article 51ZD (acting as a trustee or depositary of an AIF);
(ge) article 51ZE (establishing etc a collective investment scheme);]
(h) article 52 (establishing etc a . . . pension scheme);
(i) article 53 (advising on investments).

(2) Subject to the limitation, if any, expressed in relation to him, each of the persons listed in Part IV of the Schedule is exempt from the general prohibition in respect of any regulated activity of the kind referred to in relation to him, or an activity of the kind specified by article 64 of the Regulated Activities Order so far as relevant to any such activity.

NOTES

Para (1): sub-para (ca) inserted by the Financial Services and Markets Act 2000 (Exemption) (Amendment) Order 2007, SI 2007/125, arts 2, 4; sub-para (cb) inserted by the Financial Services and Markets Act 2000 (Regulated Activities) (Amendment) Order 2017, SI 2017/488, art 14, Schedule, para 6(1), (2); sub-para (da) inserted by the Financial Services and Markets Act 2000 (Exemption) (Amendment) (No 2) Order 2003, SI 2003/1675, art 2(1), (3); sub-paras (ga)–(ge) substituted for original sub-para (g), by the Alternative Investment Fund Managers Regulations 2013, SI 2013/1773, reg 81(1), Sch 2, Pt 2, para 8(1), (2); word omitted from sub-para (h) revoked by the Financial Services and Markets Act 2000 (Regulated Activities) (Amendment) Order 2006, SI 2006/1969, art 10.

[12.11]

[5A Persons exempt in respect of administering a benchmark

Part 1 of the Schedule does not apply to the regulated activity specified in article 63S of the Regulated Activities Order (administering a benchmark). The persons exempt in respect of the regulated activity of administering a benchmark are those listed, or carrying out an activity listed, in Article 2(2) of Regulation EU 2016/1011 of the European Parliament and of the Council of 8 June 2016 on indices used as benchmarks in financial instruments and financial contracts or to measure the performance of investment funds and amending Directives 2008/48/EC and 2014/17/EU and Regulation (EU) No 596/2014.]

NOTES

Commencement: 27 February 2018.

Inserted by the Financial Services and Markets Act 2000 (Benchmarks) Regulations 2018, SI 2018/135, reg 54.

6 (*Outside the scope of this work.*)

SCHEDULE

Articles 3 to 5

(*Pts I, II outside the scope of this work.*)

PART III
PERSONS EXEMPT IN RESPECT OF ANY REGULATED ACTIVITY MENTIONED IN ARTICLE 5(1)

[12.12]

26–34C. (*Outside the scope of this work.*)

35. A person acting as an official receiver within the meaning of section 399 of the Insolvency Act 1986 or article 2 of the Insolvency (Northern Ireland) Order 1989.

36–39. (*Outside the scope of this work.*)

(*Pt IV outside the scope of this work.*)

FINANCIAL SERVICES AND MARKETS ACT 2000 (DISCLOSURE OF CONFIDENTIAL INFORMATION) REGULATIONS 2001

(SI 2001/2188)

NOTES

Made: 15 June 2001.

Authority: Financial Services and Markets Act 2000, ss 349(1)(b), (2), (3), 417(1), 426, 427, 428(3).

Commencement: 18 June 2001.

ARRANGEMENT OF REGULATIONS

PART I
PRELIMINARY

1 Citation and Commencement . . . . . [12.13]

PART II
DISCLOSURE OF CONFIDENTIAL INFORMATION GENERALLY

5 Disclosure for the purposes of certain other proceedings . . . . . [12.14]

PART III
DISCLOSURE OF SINGLE MARKET INFORMATION

10 Disclosure by Schedule 1 person . . . . . [12.15]
10A Disclosure of recovery and resolution directive information . . . . . [12.16]
10B Assessment of effects of disclosure . . . . . [12.17]

PART IV
DISCLOSURE OF CONFIDENTIAL INFORMATION
NOT SUBJECT TO SINGLE MARKET RESTRICTIONS

11 Application of this Part . . . . . [12.18]
12 Disclosure by and to a Schedule 1 or 2 person or disciplinary proceedings authority . . . . . [12.19]

SCHEDULES

Schedule 1—Disclosure of Confidential Information whether or not subject to Single Market Restrictions

Part 1 . . . . [12.20]
Part 5 . . . . [12.21]
Schedule 3—Prescribed Disciplinary Proceedings. . . . . [12.22]

PART I
PRELIMINARY

[12.13]
1 Citation and Commencement

These Regulations may be cited as the Financial Services and Markets Act 2000 (Disclosure of Confidential Information) Regulations 2001 and come into force on 18th June 2001.

2 (*Outside the scope of this work.*)

PART II
DISCLOSURE OF CONFIDENTIAL INFORMATION GENERALLY

3, 4 (*Outside the scope of this work.*)

[12.14]
5 Disclosure for the purposes of certain other proceedings

(1) Subject to paragraphs (4) and (5), a primary recipient of confidential information, or a person obtaining such information directly or indirectly from a primary recipient, is permitted to disclose such information to—

(a) a person mentioned in paragraph (3) for the purpose of initiating proceedings to which this regulation applies, or of facilitating a determination of whether they should be initiated; or

(b) any person for the purposes of proceedings to which this regulation applies and which have been initiated, or for the purpose of bringing to an end such proceedings, or of facilitating a determination of whether they should be brought to an end.

(2) A person mentioned in paragraph (3) (or a person who is employed by [one of the regulators] or the Secretary of State) is permitted to disclose confidential information to any person for a purpose mentioned in paragraph (1)(a).

(3) The persons referred to in paragraphs (1)(a) and (2) are—

(a) [the regulators];

(b) the Secretary of State; and

(c) the Department of Enterprise, Trade and Investment in Northern Ireland.

(4) This regulation does not permit the disclosure of information with a view to the institution of, or in connection with, proceedings of the kind referred to in paragraph (6)(e) to the extent that—

(a) the information relates to an authorised person, former authorised person or former regulated person ("A");

(b) the information also relates to another person ("B") who, to the knowledge of the primary recipient (or person obtaining confidential information directly or indirectly from him), is or has been involved in an attempt to rescue A, or A's business, from insolvency or impending insolvency; and

(c) B is not a director, controller or manager of A.

(5) This regulation does not permit disclosure in contravention of any of the [single market restrictions].

(6) The proceedings to which this regulation applies are—

(a) civil proceedings arising under or by virtue of the Act, an enactment referred to in section 338 of the Act, the Banking Act 1979, the Friendly Societies Act 1974, the Insurance Companies Act 1982, the Financial Services Act 1986, the Building Societies Act 1986, the Banking Act 1987, the Friendly Societies Act 1992 or the Investment Services Regulations 1995;

(b) proceedings before the Tribunal;

(c) any other civil proceedings to which [one of the regulators] is, or is proposed to be, a party;

(d) proceedings under section 7 or 8 of the Company Directors Disqualification Act 1986 or article 10 or 11 of the Companies (Northern Ireland) Order 1989 in respect of a director or former director of an authorised person, former authorised person or former regulated person; or

(e) proceedings under Parts I to VI or IX to X of the Insolvency Act 1986, the Bankruptcy (Scotland) Act 1985 or Parts II to VII or IX or X of the Insolvency (Northern Ireland) Order 1989 in respect of an authorised person, former authorised person or former regulated person.

NOTES

Paras (2), (3), (6): words in square brackets substituted by the Financial Services Act 2012 (Consequential Amendments and Transitional Provisions) Order 2013, SI 2013/472, art 3, Sch 2, para 47(4).

Para (5): words in square brackets substituted by the Financial Services (Omnibus 1 Directive) Regulations 2012, SI 2012/916, reg 3(1), (4).

Modifications: this provision is applied, with modifications, in respect of the Financial Conduct Authority's functions under the Payment Services Regulations 2009, SI 2009/209, by SI 2009/209, reg 95, Sch 5, Pt 2, para 10(b), (c); in respect of the exercise of the Financial Conduct Authority's functions under the Electronic Money Regulations 2011, SI 2011/99, by SI 2011/99, reg 62, Sch 3, Pt 2, para 11(b); in respect of the Financial Conduct Authority's functions under the Payments in Euro

(Credit Transfers and Direct Debits) Regulations 2012, SI 2012/3122, by SI 2012/3122, reg 21, Schedule, Pt 3, para 9(b), (c); and for the purposes of the Legal Aid, Sentencing and Punishment of Offenders Act 2012 Referral Fees) Regulations 2013, SI 2013/1635, by SI 2013/1635, reg 12(1), (3).

Insurance Companies Act 1982: repealed by the Financial Services and Markets Act 2000 (Consequential Amendments and Repeals) Order 2001, SI 2001/3649.

Financial Services Act 1986: repealed by SI 2001/3649.

Banking Act 1987: repealed by SI 2001/3649.

Investment Services Regulations 1995: repealed by SI 2001/3649.

6, 7 (*Outside the scope of this work.*)

PART III
DISCLOSURE OF [SINGLE MARKET INFORMATION] . . .

NOTES

Words in square brackets in Part heading substituted by the Financial Services (Omnibus 1 Directive) Regulations 2012, SI 2012/916, reg 3(1), (5).

Words omitted from Part heading revoked by the Collective Investment Schemes (Miscellaneous Amendments) Regulations 2003, SI 2003/2066, reg 12(b).

8, 9 (*Outside the scope of this work.*)

[12.15]
10 Disclosure by Schedule 1 person

A person specified in the first column in Schedule 1 is permitted to disclose information to which this Part applies for the purpose of enabling or assisting him to discharge any of the functions listed beside him in that Schedule.

[12.16]
[10A Disclosure of recovery and resolution directive information

(1) The Bank of England may disclose recovery and resolution directive information to any person for the purpose of enabling the Bank to prepare for and carry out the functions given to it under—

(a) Parts 1, 2 and 3 of the Banking Act 2009, or

(b) the Investment Bank Special Administration Regulations 2011,

provided that any such disclosure is made subject to the conditions in paragraph (2), and following the assessment required in regulation 10B.

(2) A disclosure made by the Bank of England under paragraph (1) must be made subject to—

(a) a requirement that the information disclosed is kept confidential and not disclosed to any other person without the consent of the Bank; and

(b) restrictions imposed by the Bank as to the way in which the information may be used.

(3) A resolution administrator appointed under section 62B of the Banking Act 2009 may disclose recovery and resolution directive information to a regulator.]

NOTES

Commencement: 10 January 2015.

Inserted, together with reg 10B, by the Bank Recovery and Resolution (No 2) Order 2014, SI 2014/3348, art 226, Sch 3, Pt 3, para 8(1), (5).

Recovery and resolution directive: European Parliament and Council Directive 2014/59/EU at **[3.418]**.

[12.17]
[10B Assessment of effects of disclosure

(1) Before any disclosure is made of recovery and resolution directive information the person disclosing that information must—

(a) assess the possible effects of disclosing the information in question on—

(i) the public interest in relation to financial, monetary or economic policy;

(ii) the commercial interests of natural and legal persons;

(iii) the purpose of any investigation, inspection or audit to which the information is relevant; and

(b) where the information in question relates to the recovery plan or resolution plan of any undertaking, assess the effects of the disclosure of any part of that recovery plan or resolution plan.

(2) In this regulation—

"recovery plan" means a recovery plan drawn up and maintained in accordance with Article 5 of the recovery and resolution directive or a group recovery plan drawn up and maintained in accordance with Article 7 of that directive; and

"resolution plan" means a resolution plan drawn up in accordance with Article 10 of the recovery and resolution directive or a group recovery plan drawn up in accordance with Articles 12 and 13 of that directive.]

NOTES

Commencement: 10 January 2015.

Inserted as noted to reg 10A at **[12.16]**.

Recovery and resolution directive: European Parliament and Council Directive 2014/59/EU at **[3.418]**.

PART IV
DISCLOSURE OF CONFIDENTIAL INFORMATION NOT SUBJECT TO [SINGLE MARKET RESTRICTIONS]

NOTES

Words in square brackets in Part heading substituted by the Financial Services (Omnibus 1 Directive) Regulations 2012, SI 2012/916, reg 3(1), (8).

[12.18]

11 Application of this Part

This Part applies to confidential information other than—

(a) [single market information];

(b) . . .

(c) . . .

[(d) markets in financial instruments directive information, where that information has been received from—

(i) an overseas regulatory authority under a cooperation agreement referred to in [article 88] of the markets in financial instruments directive; or

(ii) an EEA competent [authority] under [article 81.1] of the markets in financial instruments directive,

unless that authority has given its express consent for disclosure that is covered by this Part].

[(e) UCITS directive information, where that information has been received from—

(i) an overseas regulatory authority under a cooperation agreement referred to in Article 102 of the UCITS directive; or

(ii) an EEA competent authority under Article 101.2 of the UCITS directive,

unless that authority has given its express consent for disclosure that is covered by this Part];

[(f) EMIR information, where that information has been received from the competent authority of an EEA State other than the United Kingdom under the EMIR regulation, unless that authority has given its express consent for disclosure that is covered by this Part];

[(fa) SFTR information where that information has been received from the competent authority of an EEA State other than the United Kingdom under the SFT regulation, unless that authority has given its express consent for disclosure that is covered by this Part;]

[(g) recovery and resolution directive information];

[(h) . . .].

NOTES

Para (a): words in square brackets substituted by the Financial Services (Omnibus 1 Directive) Regulations 2012, SI 2012/916, reg 3(1), (9).

Para (b): revoked by the Collective Investment Schemes (Miscellaneous Amendments) Regulations 2003, SI 2003/2066, reg 12(d).

Para (c): revoked by the Financial Services and Markets Act 2000 (Disclosure of Confidential Information) (Amendment) Regulations 2006, SI 2006/3413, regs 2, 6(a).

Para (d): added by SI 2006/3413, regs 2, 6(b); words in first and third pairs of square brackets substituted by the Financial Services and Markets Act 2000 (Markets in Financial Instruments) Regulations 2017, SI 2017/701, reg 50(2), Sch 3, para 4(1), (5)(a); word in second pair of square brackets inserted by the Undertakings for Collective Investment in Transferable Securities Regulations 2011, SI 2011/1613, reg 5(1), (4)(a).

Para (e): added by SI 2011/1613, reg 5(1), (4)(b).

Para (f): added by the Financial Services and Markets Act 2000 (Over the Counter Derivatives, Central Counterparties and Trade Repositories) Regulations 2013, SI 2013/504, reg 35(1), (5).

Para (fa): added by the Financial Services and Markets Act 2000 (Transparency of Securities Financing Transactions and of Reuse) Regulations 2016, SI 2016/715, reg 30, Sch 2, para 2(1), (5).

Para (g): added by the Bank Recovery and Resolution (No 2) Order 2014, SI 2014/3348, art 226, Sch 3, Pt 3, para 8(1), (6).

Para (h): added by the Financial Services and Markets Act 2000 (Market Abuse) Regulations 2016, SI 2016/680, reg 18(1), (5); revoked by SI 2017/701, reg 50(2), Sch 3, para 4(1), (5)(b).

Modifications: this provision is applied, with modifications, in respect of the Financial Conduct Authority's functions under the Payment Services Regulations 2009, SI 2009/209, by SI 2009/209, reg 95, Sch 5, Pt 2, para 10(f); in respect of the Financial Conduct Authority's functions under the Electronic Money Regulations 2011, SI 2011/99, by SI 2011/99, reg 62, Sch 3, Pt 2, para 11(e); and in respect of the Financial Conduct Authority's functions under the Payments in Euro (Credit Transfers and Direct Debits) Regulations 2012, SI 2012/3122, reg 21, Schedule, Pt 3, para 9(f).

[12.19]

12 Disclosure by and to a Schedule 1 or 2 person or disciplinary proceedings authority

(1) A primary recipient of information to which this Part applies, or a person obtaining such information directly or indirectly from a primary recipient, is permitted to disclose such information to—

(a) a person specified in the first column in Schedule 1 or 2 for the purpose of enabling or assisting that person to discharge any function listed beside him in the second column in Schedule 1 or 2; or

(b) a disciplinary proceedings authority for the purposes of any prescribed disciplinary proceedings which have been or may be initiated, or for the purpose of initiating or bringing to an end any such proceedings, or of facilitating a determination of whether they should be initiated or brought to an end.

(2) A person specified in the first column in Schedule 1 or 2 is permitted to disclose information to which this Part applies to any person for the purpose of enabling or assisting the person making the disclosure to discharge any function listed beside him in the second column in Schedule 1 or 2.

(3) A disciplinary proceedings authority is permitted to disclose information to which this Part applies to any person for any of the purposes mentioned in paragraph (1)(b).

[(4) This regulation does not permit disclosure of short selling regulation information to a person specified in the first column in Part 3 of Schedule 1 unless the disclosure is in accordance with article 40 of the short selling regulation or a cooperation arrangement of the kind referred to in article 38 of the short selling regulation.]

[(5) This regulation does not permit the disclosure of information if—

(a) the information is confidential information received by the FCA in the course of discharging its functions as a competent authority under the market abuse regulation or any directly applicable EU regulation made under the market abuse regulation; and

(b) the disclosure of the information contravenes the market abuse regulation.]

[(6) This regulation does not permit disclosure of the EU Benchmarks Regulation 2016 information which has been received from another competent authority unless the disclosure is in accordance with Article 38 of the EU Benchmarks Regulation 2016.]

NOTES

Para (4): added by the Financial Services and Markets Act 2000 (Short Selling) Regulations 2012, SI 2012/2554, reg 3(1), (3).

Para (5): added by the Financial Services and Markets Act 2000 (Markets in Financial Instruments) Regulations 2017, SI 2017/701, reg 50(2), Sch 3, para 4(1), (6).

Para (6): added by the Financial Services and Markets Act 2000 (Benchmarks) Regulations 2018, SI 2018/135, reg 56(1), (3).

12A–17 (*Outside the scope of this work.*)

SCHEDULES

SCHEDULE 1
DISCLOSURE OF CONFIDENTIAL INFORMATION WHETHER OR NOT SUBJECT TO [SINGLE MARKET RESTRICTIONS]

Regulations 9, 10 and 12

PART 1

[12.20]

Person	*Functions*
. . .	. . .
An official receiver appointed under section 399 of the Insolvency Act 1986, or an official receiver for Northern Ireland appointed under article 355 of the Insolvency (Northern Ireland) Order 1989	His functions under enactments relating to insolvency, in so far as they relate to— (i) former authorised persons or persons who have carried on former regulated activities; or (ii) persons carrying on, or who have carried on, regulated activities [or (ii) banking group companies (as defined in section 81D of the Banking Act 2009)]
. . .	. . .
A recognised professional body within the meaning of section 391 of the Insolvency Act 1986 or article 350 of the Insolvency (Northern Ireland) Order 1989	(a) Its functions as such a body under that Act or that Order (b) Its functions in relation to disciplinary proceedings against insolvency practitioners
. . .	. . .

NOTES

Entries omitted outside the scope of this work.

Heading: words in square brackets substituted by the Financial Services (Omnibus 1 Directive) Regulations 2012, SI 2012/916, reg 3(1), (10).

In entry beginning with the words "An official receiver appointed under section 399 of the Insolvency Act 1986" in column 2 para (iii) and word immediately preceding it inserted by the Bank Recovery and Resolution (No 2) Order 2014, SI 2014/3348, art 226, Sch 3, Pt 3, paras 1, 8(1), (7)(a)(ii).

Modifications: this Schedule is applied, with modifications, in respect of the Financial Conduct Authority's functions under the Payment Services Regulations 2009, SI 2009/209, by SI 2009/209, reg 95, Sch 5, Pt 2, para 10(g); in respect of the Financial Conduct Authority's functions under the Electronic Money Regulations 2011, SI 2011/99, by SI 2011/99, reg 62, Sch 3, Pt 2, para 11; and in respect of the Financial Conduct Authority's functions under the Payments in Euro (Credit Transfers and Direct Debits) Regulations 2012, SI 2012/3122, reg 21, Schedule, Pt 3, para 9(g).

(Sch 1, Pts 2–4, outside the scope of this work.)

[PART 5

[12.21]

Person	*Functions*
A central government department in another EEA state, responsible for legislation on the supervision of credit institutions, financial institutions, investment services and insurance companies	Its functions as such]

NOTES

Added by the Capital Requirements (Amendment) Regulations 2010, SI 2010/2628, reg 14, Sch 2, para 3(1), (4)(c).

SCHEDULE 2

(Sch 2 outside the scope of this work.)

SCHEDULE 3
PRESCRIBED DISCIPLINARY PROCEEDINGS

Regulation 2

[12.22]
The following disciplinary proceedings are prescribed for the purposes of section 349(5)(d) of the Act—

(a) disciplinary proceedings relating to the exercise by a barrister, solicitor, auditor, accountant, valuer or actuary of his professional duties;
(b) disciplinary proceedings relating to the discharge of his duties by an officer or servant of—
 (i) the Crown;
 (ii) [any of the regulators];
 (iii) the body known as the Panel on Takeovers and Mergers;
 (iv) the Charity Commissioners for England and Wales;
 (v) . . .
 (vi) the [Competition and Markets Authority];
 (vii) the Insolvency Practitioners Tribunal in relation to its functions under the Insolvency Act 1986;
 (viii) the Occupational Pensions Board in relation to its functions under the Social Security Act 1973 and the Social Security Acts 1975 to 1986;
 (ix) the organs of the Society of Lloyd's being organs constituted by or under Lloyd's Act 1982 in relation to their functions under Lloyd's Acts 1871–1982 and the byelaws made thereunder of the Society of Lloyd's;
 (x) the [Gambling Commission] in relation to [its] functions under the National Lottery etc Act 1993.

NOTES

Words in square brackets in para (b)(ii) substituted by the Financial Services Act 2012 (Consequential Amendments and Transitional Provisions) Order 2013, SI 2013/472, art 3, Sch 2, para 47(1), (10); para (b)(v) revoked and words in square brackets in para (b)(vi) substituted by the Enterprise and Regulatory Reform Act 2013 (Competition) (Consequential, Transitional and Saving Provisions) (No 2) Order 2014, SI 2014/549, art 2, Sch 1, Pt 2, para 30(1), (4); words in square brackets in para (b)(x) substituted by the Public Bodies (Merger of the Gambling Commission and the National Lottery Commission) Order 2013, SI 2013/2329, art 4(2), Schedule, para 34(c).

INSOLVENCY PRACTITIONERS AND INSOLVENCY SERVICES ACCOUNT (FEES) ORDER 2003

(SI 2003/3363)

NOTES

Made: 30 December 2003.
Authority: Insolvency Act 1986, s 415A.
Commencement: 30 January 2004 (art 2(3)); 1 April 2004 (remaining provisions).
Modification: these Regulations are applied, with modifications, in so far as they relate to bank insolvency or administration under the Banking Act 2009, Pts 2, 3, by the Banking Act 2009 (Parts 2 and 3 Consequential Amendments) Order 2009, SI 2009/317, art 3, Schedule at **[7.86]**, **[7.92]**.

ARRANGEMENT OF ARTICLES

1 Citation, Commencement, Interpretation and Extent . . . . . [12.23]
2 Fees payable in connection with the recognition of professional bodies pursuant to section 391 . . . . . [12.24]
3 Fees payable in connection with authorisations by the Secretary of State under section 393 . . . . . [12.25]
4 Transitional cases—early applications for authorisation . . . . . [12.26]
5 Fees payable in connection with the operation of the Insolvency Services Account . . . . . [12.27]
6 Value Added Tax. . . . . [12.28]

SCHEDULE

Schedule—Fees Payable in Connection with the Operation of the Insolvency Services Account . . . . . [12.29]

[12.23]
1 Citation, Commencement, Interpretation and Extent

(1) This Order may be cited as the Insolvency Practitioners and Insolvency Services Account (Fees) Order 2003 and shall come into force on 1st April 2004 ("the principal commencement date") except for Article 2(3) which shall come into force on 30th January 2004.

(2) In this Order any reference to a numbered section is to the section so numbered in the Insolvency Act 1986.

(3) All the provisions of this Order except Article 5 and the Schedule to this Order extend to England and Wales and Scotland and Article 5 and the Schedule to this Order extend only to England and Wales.

[12.24]
2 Fees payable in connection with the recognition of professional bodies pursuant to section 391

(1) Every application by a body for recognition pursuant to section 391 shall be accompanied by a fee of [£12,000].

[(2) On or before 6th April 2009 and on or before 6th April in each subsequent year, there shall be paid to the Secretary of State by each body recognised pursuant to section 391 in respect of the maintenance of that body's recognition pursuant to that section, a fee calculated by multiplying [£360] by the number of persons who as at the 1st January in that year were authorised to act as insolvency practitioners by virtue of membership of that body.]

(3) Each body recognised pursuant to section 391 shall on or before 31st January in each year submit to the Secretary of State a list of its members who as at 1st January in that year were authorised to act as insolvency practitioners by virtue of membership of that body.

NOTES

Para (1): sum in square brackets substituted by the Insolvency Practitioners and Insolvency Services Account (Fees) (Amendment) Order 2015, SI 2015/1977, art 2(a).

Para (2): substituted by the Insolvency Practitioners and Insolvency Services Account (Fees) (Amendment) Order 2009, SI 2009/487, arts 2, 3, subject to transitional provisions in art 4 thereof, which provides as follows:

"**4**

(1) This article applies to a body recognised pursuant to section 391 of the Insolvency Act 1986 that—

(a) pursuant to article 2(2) of the principal Order (as it stood before the coming into force of this Order) makes a payment by reference to the number of persons who as at 1st January 2009 were authorised to act as insolvency practitioners by virtue of membership of that body; and

(b) makes that payment in the period commencing on 1st January 2009 and ending immediately before 6th April 2009.

(2) The substitution of article 2(2) of the principal Order by article 3 of this Order shall not require a body to which this article applies to make any further payment by reference to the number of persons who as at 1st January 2009 were authorised to act as insolvency practitioners by virtue of membership of that body.".

Prior to this substitution, para (2) (as substituted for paras (2), (2A), (2B) by SI 2008/3, arts 2, 3, subject to transitional provisions in art 4 thereof (with paras (2), (2A), (2B) being previously substituted for original para (2) by SI 2005/3524, arts 2, 3(1), subject to art 4 thereof)), read as follows:

"[(2) On or before 6th April 2008 and on or before 6th April in each subsequent year, there shall be paid to the Secretary of State by each body recognised pursuant to section 391 in respect of the maintenance of that body's recognition pursuant to that section, a fee calculated by multiplying £207 by the number of persons who as at the preceding 1st January in that year were authorised to act as insolvency practitioners by virtue of membership of that body.]";

sum in square brackets substituted for original sum "£300" by SI 2015/1977, arts 2(b), 3, in respect of such persons who are so authorised as at 1 January 2016 and each subsequent 1st January.

[12.25]
3 Fees payable in connection with authorisations by the Secretary of State under section 393

(1) [Subject to paragraph (1A), every person] who on the principal commencement date is the holder of an authorisation to act as an insolvency practitioner granted by the Secretary of State pursuant to section 393 shall within 7 days of that date pay to the Secretary of State a fee in respect of the maintenance of that authorisation calculated in accordance with paragraph (2).

[(1A) Paragraph (1) does not apply to—

(a) any authorisation granted on the principal commencement date; or

(b) any authorisation granted on the 1st April in any year prior to the year 2004.]

(2) The fee payable by virtue of paragraph (1) shall be calculated by multiplying [£2,100] by the number of days in the period starting with the principal commencement date and ending with the date immediately before the next anniversary of the granting of the authorisation or the date of expiry of the authorisation (whichever occurs first) and dividing the result by 365.

(3) Every application made to the Secretary of State pursuant to section 392 for authorisation to act as an insolvency practitioner shall be accompanied by a fee of [£850, in connection with the grant of the application.

(3A) Where the application is granted, the individual to whom authorisation has been granted must pay to the Secretary of State as soon as reasonably practicable a fee of £2,400 in connection with the maintenance of the authorisation for the period of 12 months commencing with the date of the grant of the authorisation.]

(4) Subject to paragraph (5), every person who holds an authorisation granted by the Secretary of State pursuant to section 393 to act as an insolvency practitioner shall, on each anniversary of the granting of that authorisation when it is in force, pay to the Secretary of State in connection with the maintenance of that authorisation a fee of [£3,250].

(5) Where on the relevant anniversary the authorisation mentioned in paragraph (4) has less than a year to run, the fee shall be calculated by multiplying [£3,250] by the number of days that the authorisation has to run (starting with the day of the anniversary) and dividing the result by 365.

NOTES

Para (1): words in square brackets substituted by the Insolvency Practitioners and Insolvency Services Account (Fees) (Amendment) Order 2004, SI 2004/476, art 2(1), (2); revoked by the Deregulation Act 2015 (Insolvency) (Consequential Amendments and Transitional and Savings Provisions) Order 2015, SI 2015/1641, art 4, Sch 1, para 4(1), (2), subject to savings in arts 7–9 thereof (see the note "Savings" below).

Para (1A): inserted by SI 2004/476, art 2(1), (3); revoked by SI 2015/1641, art 4, Sch 1, para 4(1), (2), subject to savings in arts 7–9 thereof (see the note "Savings" below).

Para (2): sum in square brackets substituted by the Insolvency Practitioners and Insolvency Services Account (Fees) (Amendment) (No 2) Order 2005, SI 2005/3524, arts 2, 3(2); revoked by SI 2015/1641, art 4, Sch 1, para 4(1), (2), subject to savings in arts 7–9 thereof (see the note "Savings" below).

Para (3): words beginning "£850, in connection with" substituted, together with para (3A) for sum "£3,250" by the Provision of Services (Insolvency Practitioners) Regulations 2009, SI 2009/3081, regs 3, 5, except in relation to an application for authorisation to act as an insolvency practitioner under the Insolvency Act 1986, s 393 made or granted before 28 December 2009; revoked by SI 2015/1641, art 4, Sch 1, para 4(1), (2), subject to savings in arts 7–9 thereof (see the note "Savings" below).

Para (3A): substituted as noted to para (3); revoked by SI 2015/1641, art 4, Sch 1, para 4(1), (3), subject to savings in arts 7–9 thereof (see the note "Savings" below).

Paras (4), (5): sums in square brackets substituted by the Insolvency Practitioners and Insolvency Services Account (Fees) (Amendment) Order 2009, SI 2009/487, arts 2, 5; revoked by SI 2015/1641, art 4, Sch 1, para 4(1), (2), subject to savings in arts 7–9 thereof (see the note "Savings" below).

Savings: the Deregulation Act 2015 (Insolvency) (Consequential Amendments and Transitional and Savings Provisions) Order 2015, SI 2015/1641, arts 7–9 provide as follows—

> "7
>
> (1) Where, during the transitional period, the Secretary of State grants an application made, before 1st October 2015, by an individual for authorisation to act as an insolvency practitioner pursuant to section 393 of the 1986 Act, the individual to whom authorisation is granted must, as soon as reasonably practicable, pay to the Secretary of State a fee in connection with the maintenance of the authorisation.
>
> (2) The fee shall be calculated by multiplying £2400 by the number of days the authorisation has to run (starting with the date of authorisation and ending on 30th September 2016) and dividing the result by 365.
>
> **8** (1) Subject to paragraph (2), the amendments made by article 4 of, and Schedule 1 to, this Order have no effect for the duration of the transitional period in relation to an individual who before the 1st October 2015—
>
> (a) has applied for authorisation to act as an insolvency practitioner under section 392 of the 1986 Act and that application has not been granted, refused or withdrawn; or
>
> (b) holds an authorisation so to act granted under section 393 of the 1986 Act.
>
> (2) The reference in paragraph (1) to Schedule 1 to this Order does not include paragraphs 3(2), 4(3), 5(3) and 5(5) of that Schedule.
>
> **9** (1) Where during the transitional period section 393(3A) of the Insolvency 1986 Act applies to an authorisation to act as an insolvency practitioner by virtue of paragraph 23(2) of Schedule 6 to the Act, and the insolvency practitioner has not requested or consented to a withdrawal of the authorisation, the revocation of regulation 11 of the Insolvency Practitioners Regulations 2005 by article 4 of, and paragraphs 5(1) and (5) of Schedule 1 to, this Order shall have no effect.
>
> (2) During the transitional period the Secretary of State may request that the holder of an authorisation granted by the Secretary of State to act as an insolvency practitioner provide any information relating to any matters of the kind referred to in paragraph (1) of regulation 11 of the Insolvency Practitioners Regulations 2005 and any such request must be complied with within one month of its receipt or within such longer period as the Secretary of State may allow.".

Note that "the transitional period" mentioned in SI 2015/1641, arts 7–9 is defined by art 2 thereof as the period of one year beginning on 1 October 2015.

[12.26]

4 Transitional cases—early applications for authorisation

(1) This article applies to an application made to the Secretary of State pursuant to section 392 for the granting of an authorisation to act as an insolvency practitioner—

(a) *where the applicant was as at the date of its making the holder of an authorisation granted pursuant to section 393;*

(b) *where the application was made—*

(i) *after the date of the making of this Order but before the principal commencement date; and*

(ii) *more than three months before the expiry of the authorisation mentioned in sub-paragraph (a); and*

(c) *in respect of which as at the principal commencement date no decision as to whether to grant or refuse it has been taken.*

(2) In respect of an application to which this article applies, there shall be paid to the Secretary of State by the applicant within 7 days of the principal commencement date a fee of £1,500.

NOTES

Revoked by the Deregulation Act 2015 (Insolvency) (Consequential Amendments and Transitional and Savings Provisions) Order 2015, SI 2015/1641, art 4, Sch 1, para 4(1), (4), subject to savings in arts 7–9 thereof (see the note "Savings" at **[12.25]**).

[12.27]

5 Fees payable in connection with the operation of the Insolvency Services Account

There shall be payable in connection with the operation of the Insolvency Services Account fees as provided for in the Schedule to this Order.

[12.28]

6 Value Added Tax

Where Value Added Tax is chargeable in respect of the provision of a service for which a fee is prescribed by any provision of this Order, there shall be payable in addition to that fee the amount of the Value Added Tax.

SCHEDULE
FEES PAYABLE IN CONNECTION WITH THE OPERATION OF THE INSOLVENCY SERVICES ACCOUNT

Article 5

[12.29]

1 Interpretation for the purposes of the Schedule

(1) In this Schedule a reference to a numbered regulation is to the regulation so numbered in the Insolvency Regulations 1994.

(2) In this Schedule "payment date" means any of the following dates in any year—

(a) 1st January;

(b) 1st April;

(c) 1st July; and

(d) 1st October.

[(2A) In this Schedule "working day" means any day other than a Saturday, a Sunday, Good Friday, Christmas Day or a Bank Holiday in England and Wales in accordance with the Banking and Financial Dealings Act 1971.]

(3) Subject to paragraphs (4) and (5), for the purposes of this Schedule an account is "maintained with the Secretary of State in respect of monies which may from time to time be paid into the Insolvency Services Account" where—

(a) in a winding up by the court or a bankruptcy the Secretary of State creates a record in relation to the winding up or, as the case may be, the bankruptcy for the purpose of recording payments into and out of the Insolvency Services Account relating to the winding up or, as the case may be, the bankruptcy; and

(b) in a voluntary winding up on the request of the liquidator the Secretary of State creates a record in relation to the winding up for the purposes of recording payments into and out of the Insolvency Services Account relating to the winding up.

[(4) An account ceases to be maintained with the Secretary of State in the case of a winding up by the court or a bankruptcy where—

(a) the liquidator or the trustee has filed a receipts and payments account with the Secretary of State pursuant to regulation 14 or regulation 28;

(b) the account contains, or is accompanied by, a statement that it is a final receipts and payments account; and

(c) four working days have elapsed since the requirements of paragraphs (a) and (b) have been met,

but an account is revived in the circumstances mentioned in paragraph (5).

(4A) An account ceases to be maintained with the Secretary of State in the case of a voluntary winding up where—

(a) no monies to which that account relates are held in the Insolvency Services Account (other than any unclaimed dividends or any amount that it is impracticable to distribute to creditors or is required for the payment of fees that are or will become payable while the account is maintained); and

(b) notice in writing has been given to the Secretary of State that the account is no longer required and four working days have elapsed since the receipt of that notice by the Secretary of State,

but an account is revived in the circumstances mentioned in paragraph (5).]

(5) The circumstances referred to in [paragraphs (4) and (4A)] are—

(a) the receipt by the Secretary of State of notice in writing given by the trustee or liquidator for the revival of the account; or

(b) the payment into the Insolvency Services Account of any sums to the credit of the company or, as the case may be, the estate of the bankrupt,

and on the occurrence of either of the circumstances mentioned above, an account is "maintained with the Secretary of State in respect of monies which may from time to time be paid into the Insolvency Services Account".

(6) References to a bankruptcy include a bankruptcy under the Bankruptcy Act 1914 and references to a winding up include a winding up under the provisions of the Companies Act 1985.

2 Fees payable in connection with the operation of the Insolvency Services Account

Fees shall be payable in relation to the operation of the Insolvency Services Account (including payments into and out of that account) in the circumstances set out in the table below—

No of fee	*Description of fee and circumstances in which it is payable*	*Amount*
1	**Banking fee; winding up by the court and bankruptcy** Where in any bankruptcy or winding up by the court an account is maintained with the Secretary of State in respect of monies which may from time to time be paid into the Insolvency Services Account, there shall be payable out of the estate of the bankrupt or, as the case may be, the assets of the company on each payment date where the liquidator or the trustee is not the official receiver, a fee of—	[£22]
2	**Banking fee; voluntary winding up** Where in a voluntary winding up an account is maintained with the Secretary of State in respect of monies which may from time to time be paid into the Insolvency Services Account there shall be payable out of the assets of the company on each payment date a fee of—	[£25]
[2A	**Payment of unclaimed dividends or other money—administration** Where any money is paid into the Insolvency Services Account pursuant to regulation 3B, that payment shall be accompanied by a fee in respect of each company to which it relates of—	[£25.75]
2B	**Payment of unclaimed dividends or other money—administrative receivership** Where any money is paid into the Insolvency Services Account pursuant to regulation 3C, that payment shall be accompanied by a fee in respect of each company to which it relates of—	[£25.75]]
[2C	**Payment of unclaimed dividends or other money—voluntary winding up** Where any money is paid into the Insolvency Services Account pursuant to regulation 18(2)(a), that payment shall be accompanied by a fee in respect of each company to which it relates of—	[£25.75]]
3	**Cheque etc issue fee** Where a cheque, money order or payable order in respect of monies in the Insolvency Services Account is issued or reissued on the application of— (a) a liquidator pursuant to regulations 7 or 8; (b) a trustee pursuant to regulations 22 or 23; or (c) any person claiming any monies in that account pursuant to regulation 32, there shall be payable out of the assets of the company, the estate of the bankrupt or, as the case may be, by the claimant— (i) where the application is made before principal commencement date, a fee in respect of that cheque, money order or payable order of—	£0.65
	(ii) where the application is made on or after the principal commencement date, a fee in respect of that cheque, money order or payable order of—	[£1.10]
[4	**Electronic funds systems (CHAPs and BACs etc) fees** On the making or remaking of a transfer in respect of funds held in the Insolvency Services Account on an application made by—	

No of fee	Description of fee and circumstances in which it is payable	Amount
	(a) a liquidator pursuant to regulations 7 or 8;	
	(b) a trustee pursuant to regulations 22 or 23; or	
	(c) any person claiming pursuant to regulation 32, any monies held in the Insolvency Services Account,	
	there shall be payable out of the assets of the company, the estate of the bankrupt or, as the case may be, by the claimant, a fee in respect of that transfer as follows—	
	(i) where it is made through the Clearing House Automated Payments System (CHAPs), a fee of	[£10.30]
	(ii) where it is made through the Bankers' Clearing System (BACs) or any electronic funds transfer system other than CHAPs, a fee of	£0.15.]

NOTES

Para 1: sub-para (2A) inserted, sub-paras (4), (4A) substituted for original sub-para (4), and words in square brackets in sub-para (5) substituted by the Insolvency Practitioners and Insolvency Services Account (Fees) (Amendment) Order 2005, SI 2005/523, art 2.

Para 2: sums in square brackets in Fees 1, 2, 3 substituted by the Insolvency Practitioners and Insolvency Services Account (Fees) (Amendment) Order 2012, SI 2012/2264, art 2(a), (b), (d); Fees 2A, 2B inserted by the Insolvency Practitioners and Insolvency Services Account (Fees) (Amendment) (No 2) Order 2008, SI 2008/672, arts 2, 4, sums in square brackets substituted by SI 2012/2264, art 2(c); Fee 2C inserted by the Insolvency Practitioners and Insolvency Services Account (Fees) (Amendment) Order 2009, SI 2009/487, arts 2, 6, sum in square brackets substituted by SI 2012/2264, art 2(c); Fee 4 substituted by the Insolvency Practitioners and Insolvency Services Account (Fees) (Amendment) Order 2007, SI 2007/133, arts 2, 4, sum in square brackets substituted by SI 2012/2264, art 2(e).

INSOLVENCY PRACTITIONERS REGULATIONS 2005

(SI 2005/524)

NOTES

Made: 8 March 2005.

Authority: Insolvency Act 1986, ss 390, 392, 393, 419.

Commencement: 1 April 2005.

Modification: these Regulations are applied, with modifications, in so far as they relate to bank insolvency or administration under the Banking Act 2009, Pts 2, 3, by the Banking Act 2009 (Parts 2 and 3 Consequential Amendments) Order 2009, SI 2009/317, art 3, Schedule at **[7.86]**, **[7.92]**.

Application to Charitable Incorporated Organisations: as to the application of these Regulations in relation to CIOs, see the Charitable Incorporated Organisations (Insolvency and Dissolution) Regulations 2012, SI 2012/3013 at **[18.221]**.

ARRANGEMENT OF REGULATIONS

PART 1
INTRODUCTORY

1 Citation and commencement .....[12.30]
2 Interpretation: general .....[12.31]
3 Interpretation—meaning of initial and subsequent capacity .....[12.32]
4 Revocations and transitional and saving provisions .....[12.33]

PART 2
AUTHORISATION OF INSOLVENCY PRACTITIONERS BY COMPETENT AUTHORITIES

5 Interpretation of Part .....[12.34]
6 Matters for determining whether an applicant for an authorisation is a fit and proper person .....[12.35]
7 Requirements as to education and training—applicants who have never previously been authorised to act as insolvency practitioners .....[12.36]
8 Requirements relating to education and training etc—applicants previously authorised to act as insolvency practitioners .....[12.37]
8A Requirements relating to education and training etc—further authorisation to act as insolvency practitioners .....[12.38]
9 Records of continuing professional development activities .....[12.39]
10 Maximum period of authorisation .....[12.40]
11 Returns by insolvency practitioners authorised by the Secretary of State .....[12.41]

PART 3
THE REQUIREMENTS FOR SECURITY AND CAUTION FOR THE PROPER PERFORMANCE OF THE FUNCTIONS OF AN INSOLVENCY PRACTITIONER ETC

12 . . . . . [12.42]

PART 4
RECORDS TO BE MAINTAINED BY INSOLVENCY PRACTITIONERS: INSPECTION OF RECORDS

13 Records to be maintained by insolvency practitioners . . . . . [12.43]
14 Notification of whereabouts of records . . . . . [12.44]
15 Inspection of records. . . . . . [12.45]
16 Inspection of practice records. . . . . . [12.46]
17 Inspection of records in administration and administrative receiverships . . . . . [12.47]

SCHEDULES

Schedule 2—Requirements for Security or Caution and Related Matters . . . . . [12.48]

PART 1
INTRODUCTORY

[12.30]

1 Citation and commencement

These Regulations may be cited as the Insolvency Practitioners Regulations 2005 and shall come into force on 1st April 2005.

[12.31]

2 Interpretation: general

(1) In these Regulations—

"the Act" means the Insolvency Act 1986;

"commencement date" means the date on which these Regulations come into force;

"initial capacity" shall be construed in accordance with regulation 3;

"insolvency practitioner" means [a person who is authorised to act as an insolvency practitioner under section 390A of the Act].

"insolvent" means a person in respect of whom an insolvency practitioner is acting;

"interim trustee", "permanent trustee" and "trust deed for creditors" have the same meanings as in the Bankruptcy (Scotland) Act 1985;

"subsequent capacity" shall be construed in accordance with regulation 3.

(2) In these Regulations a reference to the date of release or discharge of an insolvency practitioner includes—

(a) where the insolvency practitioner acts as nominee in relation to proposals for a voluntary arrangement under Part I or VIII of the Act, whichever is the earlier of the date on which—
  (i) the proposals are rejected by creditors;
  (ii) he is replaced as nominee by another insolvency practitioner; or
  (iii) the arrangement takes effect without his becoming supervisor in relation to it; and

(b) where an insolvency practitioner acts as supervisor of a voluntary arrangement, whichever is the earlier of the date on which—
  (i) the arrangement is completed or terminated; or
  (ii) the insolvency practitioner otherwise ceases to act as supervisor in relation to the arrangement.

NOTES

Para (1): words in square brackets in definition "insolvency practitioner" substituted for the following original words, by the Deregulation Act 2015 (Insolvency) (Consequential Amendments and Transitional and Savings Provisions) Order 2015, SI 2015/1641, art 4, Sch 1, para 5(1), (2), subject to savings in arts 7–9 thereof (see the note "Savings" at **[12.25]**)—

"means a person who is authorised to act as an insolvency practitioner by virtue of—
(a) membership of a body recognised pursuant to section 391 of the Act; or
(b) an authorisation granted pursuant to section 393 of the Act;".

[12.32]

3 Interpretation—meaning of initial and subsequent capacity

(1) In these Regulations an insolvency practitioner holds office in relation to an insolvent in a "subsequent capacity" where he holds office in relation to that insolvent in one of the capacities referred to in paragraph (3) and immediately prior to his holding office in that capacity, he held office in relation to that insolvent in another of the capacities referred to in that paragraph.

(2) The first office held by the insolvency practitioner in the circumstances referred to in paragraph (1) is referred to in these Regulations as the "initial capacity".

(3) The capacities referred to in paragraph (1) are, nominee in relation to proposals for a voluntary arrangement under Part I of the Act, supervisor of a voluntary arrangement under Part I of the Act, administrator, provisional liquidator, liquidator, nominee in relation to proposals for a voluntary arrangement under Part VIII of the Act, supervisor of a voluntary arrangement under Part VIII of the Act, trustee, interim trustee and permanent trustee.

[12.33]
4 Revocations and transitional and saving provisions

(1) Subject to paragraphs (2), (3) and (4), the Regulations listed in Schedule 1 are revoked.

(2) Parts I and II of the Insolvency Practitioners Regulations 1990 shall continue to apply in relation to an application for authorisation under section 393 of the Act to act as an insolvency practitioner made to the Secretary of State before the commencement date and accordingly nothing in these Regulations shall apply to such an application.

(3) Parts I, III and IV of the Insolvency Practitioners Regulations 1990 shall continue to apply in relation to any case in respect of which an insolvency practitioner is appointed—

(a) before the commencement date; or

(b) in a subsequent capacity and he was appointed in an initial capacity in that case before the commencement date.

(4) Only regulations 16 and 17 of these Regulations shall apply in relation to the cases mentioned in paragraph (3).

NOTES

Para (2): revoked by the Deregulation Act 2015 (Insolvency) (Consequential Amendments and Transitional and Savings Provisions) Order 2015, SI 2015/1641, art 4, Sch 1, para 5(1), (3), subject to savings in arts 7–9 thereof (see the note "Savings" at **[12.25]**).

PART 2
AUTHORISATION OF INSOLVENCY PRACTITIONERS BY COMPETENT AUTHORITIES

[12.34]
5 Interpretation of Part

In this Part—

"advisory work experience" means experience obtained in providing advice to the office-holder in insolvency proceedings or anyone who is a party to, or whose interests are affected by, those proceedings;

"application" means an application made by an individual to the competent authority for authorisation under section 393 of the Act to act as an insolvency practitioner and "applicant" shall be construed accordingly;

"authorisation" means an authorisation to act as an insolvency practitioner granted under section 393 of the Act;

"continuing professional development" has the meaning given to it by regulation 8(3);

"higher insolvency work experience" means engagement in work in relation to insolvency proceedings where the work involves the management or supervision of the conduct of those proceedings on behalf of the office-holder acting in relation to them;

"insolvency legislation" means the provisions of, or any provision made under, the Act, the Bankruptcy (Scotland) Act 1985 or the Deeds of Arrangement Act 1914 and any other enactment past or present applying to Great Britain (or any part of it) that relates to the insolvency of any person;

"insolvency practice" means the carrying on of the business of acting as an insolvency practitioner or in a corresponding capacity under the law of any country or territory outside Great Britain, and for this purpose acting as an insolvency practitioner shall include acting as a judicial factor on the bankrupt estate of a deceased person;

"insolvency proceedings" means any proceedings in which an office-holder acts under any provision of insolvency legislation or the corresponding provision of the law of any country or territory outside Great Britain;

"insolvency work experience" means engagement in work related to the administration of insolvency proceedings—

(a) as the office-holder in those proceedings;

(b) in the employment of a firm or body whose members or employees act as insolvency practitioners; or

(c) in the course of employment in the Insolvency Service of the Department of Trade and Industry[, of the Department for Business, Enterprise and Regulatory Reform or of the Department for Business, Innovation and Skills].

"office-holder" means a person who acts as an insolvency practitioner or a judicial factor on the bankrupt estate of a deceased person or in a corresponding capacity under the law of any country or territory outside Great Britain and includes the official receiver acting as liquidator, provisional liquidator, trustee, interim receiver or nominee or supervisor of a voluntary arrangement; and

"regulatory work experience" means experience of work relating to the regulation of insolvency practitioners for or on behalf of a competent authority or a body recognised pursuant to section 391 of the Act or experience of work in connection with any function of the Secretary of State under that section.

NOTES

Revoked by the Deregulation Act 2015 (Insolvency) (Consequential Amendments and Transitional and Savings Provisions) Order 2015, SI 2015/1641, art 4, Sch 1, para 5(1), (4), subject to savings in arts 7–9 thereof (see the note "Savings" at **[12.25]**).

Words in square brackets in definition "insolvency work experience" inserted by the Secretaries of State for Children, Schools and Families, for Innovation, Universities and Skills and for Business, Enterprise and Regulatory Reform Order 2007, SI 2007/3224, art 15, Schedule, Pt 2, para 53, and substituted by the Secretary of State for Business, Innovation and Skills Order 2009, SI 2009/2748, art 8, Schedule, Pt 2, para 31.

[12.35]

6 Matters for determining whether an applicant for an authorisation is a fit and proper person

The matters to be taken into account by a competent authority in deciding whether an individual is a fit and proper person to act as an insolvency practitioner for the purpose of section 393(2)(a) or 393(4)(a) shall include—

- *(a) whether the applicant has been convicted of any offence involving fraud or other dishonesty or violence;*
- *(b) whether the applicant has contravened any provision in any enactment contained in insolvency legislation;*
- *(c) whether the applicant has engaged in any practices in the course of carrying on any trade, profession or vocation or in the course of the discharge of any functions relating to any office or employment appearing to be deceitful or oppressive or otherwise unfair or improper, whether unlawful or not, or which otherwise cast doubt upon his probity or competence for discharging the duties of an insolvency practitioner;*
- *(d) whether in respect of any insolvency practice carried on by the applicant at the date of or at any time prior to the making of the application, there were established adequate systems of control of the practice and adequate records relating to the practice, including accounting records, and whether such systems of control and records have been or were maintained on an adequate basis;*
- *(e) whether the insolvency practice of the applicant is, has been or, where the applicant is not yet carrying on such a practice, will be, carried on with the independence, integrity and the professional skills appropriate to the range and scale of the practice and the proper performance of the duties of an insolvency practitioner and in accordance with generally accepted professional standards, practices and principles;*
- *(f) whether the applicant, in any case where he has acted as an insolvency practitioner, has failed to disclose fully to such persons as might reasonably be expected to be affected thereby circumstances where there is or appears to be a conflict of interest between his so acting and any interest of his own, whether personal, financial or otherwise, without having received such consent as might be appropriate to his acting or continuing to act despite the existence of such circumstances.*

NOTES

Revoked by the Deregulation Act 2015 (Insolvency) (Consequential Amendments and Transitional and Savings Provisions) Order 2015, SI 2015/1641, art 4, Sch 1, para 5(1), (4), subject to savings in arts 7–9 thereof (see the note "Savings" at **[12.25]**).

[12.36]

7 Requirements as to education and training—applicants who have never previously been authorised to act as insolvency practitioners

(1) The requirements as to education, training and practical experience prescribed for the purposes of section 393(2)(b) of the Act in relation to an applicant who has never previously been authorised to act as an insolvency practitioner (whether by virtue of membership of a body recognised under section 391 of the Act or by virtue of an authorisation granted by a competent authority under section 393 of the Act) shall be as set out in this regulation.

(2) An applicant must at the date of the making of his application have passed the Joint Insolvency Examination set by the Joint Insolvency Examination Board or have acquired in, or been awarded in, a country or territory outside Great Britain professional or vocational qualifications which indicate that the applicant has the knowledge and competence that is attested by a pass in that examination.

(3) An applicant must either—

- *(a) have held office as an office-holder in not less than 30 cases during the period of 10 years immediately preceding the date on which he made his application for authorisation; or*
- *(b) have acquired not less than [2000] hours of insolvency work experience of which no less than 1400 hours must have been acquired within the period of two years immediately prior to the date of the making of his application and show that he satisfies one of the three requirements set out in paragraph (4).*

(4) The three requirements referred to in paragraph (3)(b) are—

- *(a) the applicant has become an office-holder in at least 5 cases within the period of 5 years immediately prior to the date of the making of his application;*
- *(b) the applicant has acquired 1,000 hours or more of higher insolvency work experience or experience as an office-holder within the period referred to in sub-paragraph (a); and*
- *(c) the applicant can show that within the period referred to in sub-paragraph (a) he has achieved one of the following combinations of positions as an office-holder and hours acquired of higher insolvency work experience—*
  - *(i) 4 cases and 200 hours;*

Part 12 SIs: ORs & Insolvency Practitioners

(ii) 3 cases and 400 hours;
(iii) 2 cases and 600 hours; or
(iv) 1 case and 800 hours.

(5) Where in order to satisfy all or any of the requirements set out in paragraphs (3) and (4) an applicant relies on appointment as an office-holder or the acquisition of insolvency work experience or higher insolvency work experience in relation to cases under the laws of a country or territory outside the United Kingdom, he shall demonstrate that he has no less than 1,400 hours of insolvency work experience in cases under the law of any part of the United Kingdom acquired within the period of two years immediately prior to the date of the making of his application.

(6) In ascertaining whether an applicant meets all or any of the requirements of paragraphs (3) and (4)—

(a) no account shall be taken of any case where—
(i) he was appointed to the office of receiver (or to a corresponding office under the law of a country or territory outside Great Britain) by or on behalf of a creditor who at the time of the appointment was an associate of the applicant; or
(ii) in a members' voluntary winding up or in a corresponding procedure under the laws of a country or territory outside Great Britain he was appointed liquidator at a general meeting where his associates were entitled to exercise or control the exercise of one third or more of the voting power at that general meeting;

(b) where the applicant has been an office-holder in relation to—
(i) two or more companies which were associates at the time of appointment; or
(ii) two or more individuals who were carrying on business in partnership with each other at the time of appointment,

he shall be treated as having held office in only one case in respect of all offices held in relation to the companies which were associates or in respect of all offices held in relation to the individuals who were in partnership, as the case may be.

(7) An applicant must have a good command of the English language.

NOTES

Revoked by the Deregulation Act 2015 (Insolvency) (Consequential Amendments and Transitional and Savings Provisions) Order 2015, SI 2015/1641, art 4, Sch 1, para 5(1), (4), subject to savings in arts 7–9 thereof (see the note "Savings" at **[12.25]**).

Para (3): number in square brackets substituted for original number "7000" by the Provision of Services (Insolvency Practitioners) Regulations 2009, SI 2009/3081, regs 4, 5, Schedule, paras 2, 3, except in relation to an application for authorisation to act as an insolvency practitioner under the Insolvency Act 1986, s 393 made or granted before 28 December 2009.

[12.37]

8 Requirements relating to education and training etc—applicants previously authorised to act as insolvency practitioners

(1) The requirements prescribed for the purposes of section 393(2)(b) of the Act in relation to an applicant who has at any time been authorised to act as an insolvency practitioner (whether by virtue of membership of a body recognised under section 391 of the Act or an authorisation granted by a competent authority under section 393 of the Act) shall be as set out in this regulation.

(2) The applicant must—

(a) satisfy the requirements set out in regulation 7(3) to (5) or have acquired within the period of three years preceding the date of the making of his application [450] hours of any combination of the following types of experience—
(i) experience as an office-holder;
(ii) higher insolvency work experience;
(iii) regulatory work experience; or
(iv) advisory work experience; and

(b) subject to paragraph (4), have completed at least 108 hours of continuing professional development in the period of three years ending on the day before the date of the making of his application of which—
(i) a minimum of 12 hours must be completed in each of those years; and
(ii) 54 hours must fall into the categories in paragraphs (3)(b)(i) to (v).

(3) "Continuing professional development" means any activities which—

(a) relate to insolvency law or practice or the management of the practice of an insolvency practitioner; and

(b) fall into any of the following categories—
(i) the production of written material for publication;
(ii) attendance at courses, seminars or conferences;
(iii) the viewing of any recording of a course, seminar or conference;
(iv) the giving of lectures or the presentation of papers at courses, seminars or conferences;
(v) the completion of on-line tests; and
(vi) the reading of books or periodical publications (including any on-line publication).

(4) The requirement in paragraph (2)(b) shall only apply in relation to any application made on or after the third anniversary of the commencement date.

(5) For the purposes of paragraph (3)(b)(i), "publication" includes making material available to a body recognised in pursuance of section 391 of the Act or any association or body representing the interests of those who act as insolvency practitioners.

NOTES

Revoked by the Deregulation Act 2015 (Insolvency) (Consequential Amendments and Transitional and Savings Provisions) Order 2015, SI 2015/1641, art 4, Sch 1, para 5(1), (4), subject to savings in arts 7–9 thereof (see the note "Savings" at **[12.25]**).

Para (2): number in square brackets in sub-para (a) substituted for original number "500" by the Provision of Services (Insolvency Practitioners) Regulations 2009, SI 2009/3081, regs 4, 5, Schedule, paras 2, 4(1), (2), except in relation to an application for authorisation to act as an insolvency practitioner under the Insolvency Act 1986, s 393 made or granted before 28 December 2009.

[12.38]

[8A Requirements relating to education and training etc—further authorisation to act as insolvency practitioners

(1) The requirements prescribed under section 393(2)(b) of the Act in relation to further authorisation under section 393(3A) of the Act are as set out in this regulation.

(2) The individual must—

(a) have acquired within the period in regulation 11(1A) 150 hours of any combination of the following types of experience—

(i) experience as an office-holder;

(ii) higher insolvency work experience;

(iii) regulatory work experience; or

(iv) advisory work experience; and

(b) have completed within the period in regulation 11(1A) at least 36 hours of continuing professional development of which 18 hours must fall into the categories in regulation 8(3)(b)(i) to (v).

(3) In the first period after the grant of an authorisation an individual must comply with—

(a) paragraph (2)(a) where the number of hours is 125; and

(b) paragraph (2)(b) where the number of hours are 30 and 15 respectively.]

NOTES

Inserted by the Provision of Services (Insolvency Practitioners) Regulations 2009, SI 2009/3081, regs 4, 5, Schedule, paras 2, 4(1), (3), except in relation to an application for authorisation to act as an insolvency practitioner under the Insolvency Act 1986, s 393 made or granted before 28 December 2009.

Revoked by the Deregulation Act 2015 (Insolvency) (Consequential Amendments and Transitional and Savings Provisions) Order 2015, SI 2015/1641, art 4, Sch 1, para 5(1), (4), subject to savings in arts 7–9 thereof (see the note "Savings" at **[12.25]**).

[12.39]

9 Records of continuing professional development activities

(1) Every holder of an authorisation granted by the Secretary of State shall maintain a record of each continuing professional development activity undertaken by him for a period of six years from the date on which the activity was completed.

(2) The record shall contain details of—

(a) which of the categories in regulation 8(3)(b) the activity comes within;

(b) the date that the activity was undertaken;

(c) the duration of the activity; and

(d) the topics covered by the activity.

(3) Where the continuing professional development comprises—

(a) attendance at a course, seminar or conference; or

(b) the giving of a lecture or presentation of a paper at a course, seminar or conference,

the holder of the authorisation shall keep with the record evidence from the organiser of the course, seminar or conference of the attendance of the holder at the course, seminar or conference.

(4) The Secretary of State may, on the giving of reasonable notice, inspect and take copies of any records or evidence maintained pursuant to this regulation.

NOTES

Revoked by the Deregulation Act 2015 (Insolvency) (Consequential Amendments and Transitional and Savings Provisions) Order 2015, SI 2015/1641, art 4, Sch 1, para 5(1), (4), subject to savings in arts 7–9 thereof (see the note "Savings" at **[12.25]**).

[12.40]

10 Maximum period of authorisation

For the purposes of section 393(3) of the Act, the maximum period that an authorisation may continue in force shall be three years.

NOTES

Revoked by the Provision of Services (Insolvency Practitioners) Regulations 2009, SI 2009/3081, regs 4, 5, Schedule, paras 2, 5, except in relation to an application for authorisation to act as an insolvency practitioner under the Insolvency Act 1986, s 393 made or granted before 28 December 2009.

[12.41]

11 Returns by insolvency practitioners authorised by the Secretary of State

(1) Every holder of an authorisation granted by the Secretary of State shall make a return to the Secretary of State in respect of each period [in paragraph (1A)] during the whole or any part of which he held an authorisation granted by the Secretary of State containing the following information—

(a) the number of cases in respect of whom the holder of the authorisation has acted as an insolvency practitioner during the period;

(b) in respect of each case where the holder of the authorisation has acted as an insolvency practitioner—

(i) the name of the person in respect of whom the insolvency practitioner is acting,

(ii) the date of the appointment of the holder of the authorisation,

(iii) the type of proceedings involved, and

(iv) the number of hours worked in relation to the case by the holder of the authorisation and any person assigned to assist him in the case; . . .

(c) the following details of any continuing professional development undertaken activity during the period by the holder of the authorisation—

(i) the nature of the activity;

(ii) the date that the activity was undertaken;

(iii) the duration of the activity; and

(iv) the topics covered by the activity[; and

(d) the number of hours of any experience of the types in regulation 8A(2)(a)(i) to (iv).

(1A) The period is the period of 12 months ending two months before the anniversary of the grant of the authorisation or the last further authorisation.]

(2) Every return required to be submitted pursuant to this regulation shall be submitted within one month of the end of the period to which it relates.

(3) The Secretary of State may at any time request the holder of an authorisation to provide any information relating to any matters of the kind referred to in paragraph (1) and any such request shall be complied with by the holder of the authorisation [no later than 6 weeks before] its receipt or such longer period as the Secretary of State may allow.

NOTES

Revoked by the Deregulation Act 2015 (Insolvency) (Consequential Amendments and Transitional and Savings Provisions) Order 2015, SI 2015/1641, art 4, Sch 1, para 5(1), (5), subject to savings in arts 7–9 thereof (see the note "Savings" at **[12.25]**).

Para (1): words in first pair of square brackets substituted for original words "of 12 months ending on 31st December", word "and" (omitted) revoked, and sub-para (d), word "and" immediately preceding it inserted, together with para (1A), by the Provision of Services (Insolvency Practitioners) Regulations 2009, SI 2009/3081, regs 4, 5, Schedule, paras 2, 6(1), (2), except in relation to an application for authorisation to act as an insolvency practitioner under the Insolvency Act 1986, s 393 made or granted before 28 December 2009.

Para (1A): inserted as noted to para (1) above.

Para (2): words in square brackets substituted for original words "within one month of" by SI 2009/3081, regs 4, 5, Schedule, paras 2, 6(1), (3), except in relation to an application for authorisation to act as an insolvency practitioner under the Insolvency Act 1986, s 393 made or granted before 28 December 2009.

PART 3
THE REQUIREMENTS FOR SECURITY AND CAUTION FOR THE PROPER PERFORMANCE OF THE FUNCTIONS OF AN INSOLVENCY PRACTITIONER ETC

[12.42]

12

(1) Schedule 2 shall have effect in respect of the requirements prescribed for the purposes of section 390(3)(b) in relation to security or caution for the proper performance of the functions of an insolvency practitioner and for related matters.

(2) Where two or more persons are appointed jointly to act as insolvency practitioners in relation to any person, the provisions of this regulation shall apply to each of them individually.

[(3) Where, in accordance with sections 390(2) and 390A(2)(b) of the Act a person is qualified to act as an insolvency practitioner by virtue of an authorisation granted by the Department of Enterprise, Trade and Investment for Northern Ireland under Article 352 of the Insolvency (Northern Ireland) Order 1989, this Part applies in relation to that person as if that authorisation had been granted pursuant to section 393 of the Act immediately before 1st October 2015.]

NOTES

Para (3): substituted by the Deregulation Act 2015 (Insolvency) (Consequential Amendments and Transitional and Savings Provisions) Order 2015, SI 2015/1641, art 4, Sch 1, para 5(1), (6), subject to savings in arts 7–9 thereof (see the note "Savings" at **[12.25]**). Para (3) was originally added by the Provision of Services (Insolvency Practitioners) Regulations 2009, SI 2009/3081, regs 4, 5, Schedule, paras 2, 7, except in relation to an application for authorisation to act as an insolvency practitioner under the Insolvency Act 1986, s 393 made or granted before 28 December 2009, and previously read as follows—

> "[(3) Where, in accordance with section 390(2)(c) of the Act a person is qualified to act as an insolvency practitioner by virtue of an authorisation granted by the Department of Enterprise, Trade and Investment for Northern Ireland under Article 352 of the Insolvency (Northern Ireland) Order 1989, this Part applies in relation to that person as if that authorisation had been granted pursuant to section 393 of the Act.]".

PART 4
RECORDS TO BE MAINTAINED BY INSOLVENCY PRACTITIONERS—INSPECTION OF RECORDS

[12.43]

13 Records to be maintained by insolvency practitioners

[(1) In respect of each case in which an insolvency practitioner acts, the insolvency practitioner shall maintain records containing information sufficient to show and explain—

(a) the administration of that case by the insolvency practitioner and the insolvency practitioner's staff; and

(b) any decisions made by the insolvency practitioner which materially affect that case.]

(2) Where at any time the records referred to in paragraph (1) do not contain all the information referred to in [paragraph (1)], the insolvency practitioner shall forthwith make such changes to the records as are necessary to ensure that the records contains all such information.

(3) . . .

(4) . . .

(5) Any records created in relation to a case pursuant to this regulation shall be preserved by the insolvency practitioner until whichever is the later of—

(a) the sixth anniversary of the date of the grant to the insolvency practitioner of his release or discharge in that case; or

(b) the sixth anniversary of the date on which any security or caution maintained in that case expires or otherwise ceases to have effect.

NOTES

Para (1): substituted by the Insolvency Practitioners (Amendment) Regulations 2015, SI 2015/391, reg 3(1).

Para (2): words in square brackets substituted by SI 2015/391, reg 3(2).

Paras (3), (4): revoked by SI 2015/391, reg 3(3).

[12.44]

14 Notification of whereabouts of records

The insolvency practitioner shall notify the [person] referred to in regulation . . . 15(1)(b) of the place where the records required to be maintained under this Part are so maintained and the place (if different) where they may be inspected pursuant to regulation 15.

NOTES

Revoked by the Deregulation Act 2015 (Insolvency) (Consequential Amendments and Transitional and Savings Provisions) Order 2015, SI 2015/1641, art 4, Sch 1, para 5(1), (7), subject to savings in arts 7–9 thereof (see the note "Savings" at **[12.25]**).

Word in square brackets substituted and words omitted revoked by the Insolvency Practitioners (Amendment) Regulations 2015, SI 2015/391, reg 4.

[12.45]

15 Inspection of records

(1) Any records maintained by an insolvency practitioner pursuant to this Part shall on the giving of reasonable notice be made available by him for inspection by—

(a) any professional body recognised under section 391 of the Act of which he is a member and the rules of membership of which entitle him to act as an insolvency practitioner;

(b) any competent authority by whom the insolvency practitioner is authorised to act pursuant to section 393 of the Act; and

(c) the Secretary of State.

(2) Any person who is entitled to inspect any record pursuant to paragraph (1) shall also be entitled to take a copy of those records.

NOTES

Para (1): sub-para (b) revoked by the Deregulation Act 2015 (Insolvency) (Consequential Amendments and Transitional and Savings Provisions) Order 2015, SI 2015/1641, art 4, Sch 1, para 5(1), (8), subject to savings in arts 7–9 thereof (see the note "Savings" at **[12.25]**).

[12.46]

16 Inspection of practice records

(1) This regulation applies to any relevant records which are held by—

(a) the holder of an authorisation to act as an insolvency practitioner granted by the Secretary of State pursuant to section 393 of the Act;

(b) his employer or former employer; or

(c) any firm or other body of which he is or was a member or partner.

(2) In this regulation "relevant records" mean any records which relate to any case where the holder of the authorisation mentioned in paragraph (1) has acted as an insolvency practitioner and which—

(a) record receipts and payments made in relation to, or in connection with, that case;

(b) record time spent on that case by the holder of the authorisation or any person assigned to assist the holder;

(c) relate to any business carried on in the case by or at the direction of the holder of the authorisation; or

(d) otherwise relate to the management of that case.

(3) The Secretary of State may, on the giving of reasonable notice to their holder, inspect and take copies of any records to which this regulation applies.

NOTES

Revoked by the Deregulation Act 2015 (Insolvency) (Consequential Amendments and Transitional and Savings Provisions) Order 2015, SI 2015/1641, art 4, Sch 1, para 5(1), (9), subject to savings in arts 7–9 thereof (see the note "Savings" at **[12.25]**).

[12.47]

17 Inspection of records in administration and administrative receiverships

On the giving of reasonable notice to the insolvency practitioner, the Secretary of State shall be entitled to inspect and take copies of any records in the possession or control of that insolvency practitioner which—

(a) were required to be created by or under any provision of the Act (or any provision made under the Act); and

(b) relate to an administration or an administrative receivership.

SCHEDULE 1

(Sch 1 revokes the Insolvency Practitioners Regulations 1990, SI 1990/439 (subject to transitional provisions and savings), the Insolvency Practitioners (Amendment) Regulations 1993, SI 1993/221, the Insolvency Practitioners (Amendment) Regulations 2002, SI 2002/2710, the Insolvency Practitioners (Amendment) (No 2) Regulations 2002, SI 2002/2748, the Insolvency Practitioners (Amendment) Regulations 2004, SI 2004/473.)

SCHEDULE 2
REQUIREMENTS FOR SECURITY OR CAUTION AND RELATED MATTERS

Regulation 12

PART 1
INTERPRETATION

[12.48]

1 Interpretation

In this Schedule—

"cover schedule" means the schedule referred to in paragraph 3(2)(c);

"the insolvent" means the individual or company in relation to which an insolvency practitioner is acting;

"general penalty sum" shall be construed in accordance with paragraph 3(2)(b);

"insolvent's assets" means all assets comprised in the insolvent's estate together with any monies provided by a third party for the payment of the insolvent's debts or the costs and expenses of administering the insolvent's estate;

["professional liability insurance" means insurance taken out by the insolvency practitioner in respect of potential liabilities to the insolvent and third parties arising out of acting as an insolvency practitioner;]

"specific penalty sum" shall be construed in accordance with paragraph 3(2)(a).

PART 2
REQUIREMENTS RELATING TO SECURITY AND CAUTION

2 Requirements in respect of security or caution

The requirements in respect of security or caution for the proper performance of the duties of insolvency practitioners prescribed for the purposes of section 390(3)(b) shall be as set out in this Part.

[2A Requirement for bond or professional liability insurance

Where an insolvency practitioner is appointed to act in respect of an insolvent there must be in force—

(a) a bond in a form approved by the Secretary of State which complies with paragraph 3; or

(b) where the insolvency practitioner is already established in another EEA state and is already covered in that state by professional liability insurance or a guarantee, professional liability insurance or a guarantee which complies with paragraph 8A.]

3 [Terms of the Bond]

[(1) The bond must—

(a) be in writing or in electronic form;

(b) contain provision whereby a surety or cautioner undertakes to be jointly and severally liable for losses in relation to the insolvent caused by—

(i) the fraud or dishonesty of the insolvency practitioner whether acting alone or in collusion with one or more persons; or

(ii) the fraud or dishonesty of any person committed with the connivance of the insolvency practitioner; and

(c) otherwise conform to the requirements of this paragraph and paragraphs 4 to 8.]

(2) The terms of the bond shall provide—

(a) for the payment, in respect of each case where the insolvency practitioner acts, of claims in respect of liabilities for losses of the kind mentioned in sub-paragraph (1) up to an aggregate maximum sum in respect of that case ("the specific penalty sum") calculated in accordance with the provisions of this Schedule;
(b) in the event that any amounts payable under (a) are insufficient to meet all claims arising out of any case, for a further sum of £250,000 ("the general penalty sum") out of which any such claims are to be met;
(c) for a schedule containing the name of the insolvent and the value of the insolvent's assets to be submitted to the surety or cautioner within such period as may be specified in the bond;
(d) that where at any time before the insolvency practitioner obtains his release or discharge in respect of his acting in relation to an insolvent, he forms the opinion that the value of that insolvent's assets is greater than the current specific penalty sum, a revised specific penalty sum shall be applicable on the submission within such time as may be specified in the bond of a cover schedule containing a revised value of the insolvent's assets;
(e) for the payment of losses of the kind mentioned in sub-paragraph (1), whether they arise during the period in which the insolvency practitioner holds office in the capacity in which he was initially appointed or a subsequent period where he holds office in a subsequent capacity;

(3) The terms of the bond may provide—
(a) that total claims in respect of the acts of the insolvency practitioner under all bonds relating to him are to be limited to a maximum aggregate sum (which shall not be less than £25,000,000); and
(b) for a time limit within which claims must be made.

4 Subject to paragraphs 5, 6 and 7, the amount of the specific penalty in respect of a case in which the insolvency practitioner acts, shall equal at least the value of the insolvent's assets as estimated by the insolvency practitioner as at the date of his appointment but ignoring the value of any assets—
(a) charged to a third party to the extent of any amount which would be payable to that third party; or
(b) held on trust by the insolvent to the extent that any beneficial interest in those assets does not belong to the insolvent.

5 In a case where an insolvency practitioner acts as a nominee or supervisor of a voluntary arrangement under Part I or Part VIII of the Act, the amount of the specific penalty shall be equal to at least the value of those assets subject to the terms of the arrangement (whether or not those assets are in his possession) including, where under the terms of the arrangement the debtor or a third party is to make payments, the aggregate of any payments to be made.

6 Where the value of the insolvent's assets is less than £5,000, the specific penalty sum shall be £5,000.

7 Where the value of the insolvent's assets is more than £5,000,000 the specific penalty sum shall be £5,000,000.

8 In estimating the value of an insolvent's assets, unless he has reason to doubt their accuracy, the insolvency practitioner may rely upon—
(a) any statement of affairs produced in relation to that insolvent pursuant to any provision of the Act; and
(b) in the case of a sequestration—
  (i) the debtor's list of assets and liabilities under section 19 of the Bankruptcy (Scotland) Act 1985;
  (ii) the preliminary statement under that Act; or
  (iii) the final statement of the debtor's affairs by the interim trustee under section 23 of the Bankruptcy (Scotland) Act 1985.

[8A Compliance of professional liability insurance cover in another EEA state

Where paragraph 2A(b) applies to an insolvency practitioner, the professional liability insurance or guarantee complies with this paragraph if the Secretary of State determines that it is equivalent or essentially comparable to the bond referred to in paragraph 3 as regards—
(a) its purpose, and
(b) the cover it provides in terms of—
  (i) the risk covered,
  (ii) the amount covered, and
  (iii) exclusions from the cover.

8B Procedure for determining compliance of professional liability insurance or guarantee

(1) Where an insolvency practitioner seeks a determination under paragraph 8A, the insolvency practitioner must send to the Secretary of State—
(a) a copy of the document providing the professional liability insurance or guarantee cover in the EEA state in which the insolvency practitioner is established;
(b) where the document in sub-paragraph (a) is not in English, a translation of it into English; and
(c) a notice—
  (i) where the insolvency practitioner intends to act in respect of an insolvent, specifying—
    (aa) the name of the insolvent; and
    (bb) the time and date when the insolvency practitioner intends to consent to be appointed to act; or

(ii) that the insolvency practitioner seeks a determination without reference to a specific appointment.

(2) Where there is a notice sent under sub-paragraph (1)(c)(i), the documents sent under sub-paragraph (1) must be sent to the Secretary of State such that the Secretary of State receives them no later than 5 business days before the date in the notice.

(3) Where the Secretary of State receives the documents sent under sub-paragraph (1), the Secretary of State must—

(a) as soon as is reasonably practicable, notify the insolvency practitioner whether they were received in accordance with sub-paragraph (2);

(b) consider them; and

(c) determine whether the document sent under sub-paragraph (1)(a) complies with paragraph 8A.

(4) Where the Secretary of State determines that the document sent under sub-paragraph (1)(a) complies with paragraph 8A, the Secretary of State must—

(a) notify the insolvency practitioner that it complies with paragraph 8A; and

(b) determine whether it contains a term equivalent or essentially comparable to a requirement to provide—

(i) a specific penalty sum; or

(ii) a cover schedule.

(5) Where the Secretary of State determines under sub-paragraph (4)(b) that the document sent under sub-paragraph (1)(a)—

(a) contains a term equivalent or essentially comparable to a requirement to provide a specific penalty sum or a cover schedule, the notice sent under paragraph (4)(a) must specify—

(i) the term equivalent or essentially comparable to a requirement to provide a specific penalty sum or a cover schedule; and

(ii) the thing in the term in sub-paragraph (i) which is equivalent or essentially comparable to a specific penalty sum or a cover schedule; or

(b) does not contain a term equivalent or essentially comparable to a requirement to provide a specific penalty sum or a cover schedule, the notice sent under paragraph (4)(a) must state that determination.

(6) Where the Secretary of State determines that the document sent under sub-paragraph (1)(a) does not comply with paragraph 8A, the Secretary of State must notify the insolvency practitioner and—

(a) give reasons for the determination; and

(b) specify any terms which, if included in a supplementary guarantee, will cause the Secretary of State to make a determination in accordance with paragraph 8A.

(7) In this paragraph a "business day" means any day other than a Saturday, a Sunday, Christmas Day, Good Friday or a day which is a bank holiday in England and Wales under or by virtue of the Banking and Financial Dealings Act 1971.

(8) Any documents in this paragraph or paragraph 8C or 8D may be sent electronically.

8C Procedure for determining compliance of supplementary guarantee

(1) Where the Secretary of State has made a determination under paragraph 8B(6), the insolvency practitioner may send to the Secretary of State—

(a) a supplementary guarantee purporting to provide for the matters specified in paragraph 8B(6)(b); and

(b) where the supplementary guarantee is not in English, a translation of it into English.

(2) Where the Secretary of State receives the documents sent under sub-paragraph (1), the Secretary of State must—

(a) as soon as is reasonably practicable, notify the insolvency practitioner of the date and time of their receipt;

(b) consider them; and

(c) determine whether the document sent under sub-paragraph (1)(a) provides for the matters specified in paragraph 8B(6)(b).

(3) Where the Secretary of State determines that the document sent under sub-paragraph (1)(a)—

(a) provides for the matters in specified in paragraph 8B(6)(b); and

(b) together with the document in paragraph 8B(1)(a) complies with paragraph 8A,

the Secretary of State must notify the insolvency practitioner that the documents sent under sub-paragraph (1)(a) and paragraph 8B(1)(a) together comply with paragraph 8A.

(4) Where the Secretary of State determines in accordance with sub-paragraph (3), the Secretary of State must also determine whether the document sent under sub-paragraph (1)(a) or paragraph 8B(1)(a) contains a term equivalent or essentially comparable to a requirement to provide—

(a) a specific penalty sum; or

(b) a cover schedule.

(5) Where the Secretary of State determines under sub-paragraph (4) that the document sent under sub-paragraph (1)(a) or paragraph 8B(1)(a)—

(a) contains a term equivalent or essentially comparable to a requirement to provide a specific penalty sum or a cover schedule, the notice sent under sub-paragraph (3) must specify—

(i) the term equivalent or essentially comparable to a requirement to provide a specific penalty sum or a cover schedule;

(ii) the thing in the term in sub-paragraph (i) which is equivalent or essentially comparable to a requirement to a specific penalty sum or a cover schedule; and

(iii) the document in which the term in sub-paragraph (i) and the thing in sub-paragraph (ii) are to be found; or

(b) does not contain a term equivalent or essentially comparable to a requirement to provide a specific penalty sum or a cover schedule, the notice sent under sub-paragraph (3) must state that determination.

(6) Where the Secretary of State determines that the document sent under sub-paragraph (1)(a)—

(a) does not provide for the matters specified in paragraph 8B(6)(b), or

(b) together with the document sent under paragraph 8B(1)(a) does not comply with paragraph 8A,

the Secretary of State must notify the insolvency practitioner that the documents sent under sub-paragraphs (1)(a) and paragraph 8B(1)(a) together do not comply with paragraph 8A.

8D Time for notification of determinations

(1) The Secretary of State must notify the insolvency practitioner of the determinations under paragraph 8B or 8C in the periods set out in this paragraph.

(2) The Secretary of State must notify the insolvency practitioner—

(a) where a notice under paragraph 8B(1)(c)(i) is received by the Secretary of State in accordance with paragraph 8B(2) and the determination is under—

(i) paragraph 8B(4), (5) or (6), such that the insolvency practitioner receives the notice sent under paragraph 8B(4) or (6) or before the time and date in the notice sent under paragraph 8B(1)(c)(i); or

(ii) paragraph 8C(4), (5) or (6), as soon as is reasonably practicable after receipt of the documents sent under paragraph 8C(1);

(b) where a notice sent under paragraph 8B(1)(c)(i) is received by the Secretary of State but not in accordance with paragraph 8B(2), and the determination is under—

(i) paragraph 8B(4), (5) or (6), as soon as is reasonably practicable after receipt of the documents sent under paragraph 8B(1); or

(ii) paragraph 8C(3), (5) or (6), as soon as is reasonably practicable after receipt of the documents sent under paragraph 8C(1); or

(c) where the notice is sent under paragraph 8B(1)(c)(ii), and the determination is under—

(i) paragraph 8B(4), (5) or (6), within 28 days of receipt of the documents sent under paragraph 8B(1); or

(ii) paragraph 8C(3), (5) or (6), within 14 days of receipt of the documents sent under paragraph 8C(1).

8E Notification of determination out of time

(1) This paragraph applies where the insolvency practitioner—

(a) sends a notice under paragraph 8B(1)(c)(i);

(b) receives notification sent under paragraph 8B(3)(a) that the Secretary of State received the documents in paragraph 8B(1) in accordance with paragraph 8B(2); and

(c) does not receive the notifications in the time in paragraph 8D(2)(a)(i).

(2) The insolvency practitioner is qualified to act as an insolvency practitioner in respect of the insolvent specified in the notice under paragraph 8B(1)(c)(i) until the Secretary of State notifies the insolvency practitioner of the determination under paragraph 8B or 8C.

(3) Subject to sub-paragraph (4), where the Secretary of State notifies the insolvency practitioner of the determination under paragraph 8B or 8C—

(a) the determination applies; and

(b) the insolvency practitioner ceases to be qualified to act as an insolvency practitioner under sub-paragraph (2).

(4) Where—

(a) the Secretary of State gives notice under paragraph 8B(6); and

(b) the insolvency practitioner sends the documents in paragraph 8C(1),

the insolvency practitioner is qualified to act as an insolvency practitioner under sub-paragraph (2) until the Secretary of State determines in accordance with paragraph 8C(4) or (6).]

PART 3
RECORDS RELATING TO BONDING AND CONNECTED MATTERS

9 Record of specific penalty sums to be maintained by insolvency practitioner

(1) An insolvency practitioner shall maintain a record of all specific penalty sums that are applicable in relation to any case where he is acting and such record shall contain the name of each person to whom the specific penalty sum relates and the amount of each penalty sum that is in force.

(2) Any record maintained by an insolvency practitioner pursuant to this paragraph shall, on the giving of reasonable notice, be made available for inspection by—

(a) any professional body recognised under section 391 of the Act of which he is or was a member and the rules of membership of which entitle or entitled him to act as an insolvency practitioner;

(b) any competent authority by whom the insolvency practitioner is or was authorised to act pursuant to section 393 of the Act; and

(c) the Secretary of State.

[(3) Subject to sub-paragraph (4), where the Secretary of State has notified the insolvency practitioner in accordance with paragraph 8B(5)(a) or 8C(5)(a) in relation to a specific penalty sum, the thing notified under paragraph 8B(5)(a)(ii) or 8C(5)(a)(ii) is construed as a specific penalty sum for the purposes of this paragraph . . . .

(4) Where the Secretary of State has notified the insolvency practitioner in accordance with paragraph 8B(5)(b) or 8C(5)(b) in relation to a specific penalty sum, this paragraph does not apply.]

10 Retention of bond by recognised professional body or competent authority

[(1) The documents in sub-paragraph (2) or a copy must] be sent by the insolvency practitioner to—

(a) any professional body recognised under section 391 of the Act of which he is a member and the rules of membership of which entitle him to act as an insolvency practitioner; or

(b) any competent authority by whom the insolvency practitioner is authorised to act pursuant to section 393 of the Act.

[(2) The documents in this sub-paragraph are—

(a) the bond referred to in paragraph 3;

(b) where the Secretary of State has determined under paragraph 8B(4)—

(i) the document in paragraph 8B(1)(a) and (b); and

(ii) the notice under paragraph 8B(4);

(c) where the Secretary of State has determined under paragraph 8C(4)

(i) the documents in paragraphs 8B(1)(a) and (b) and 8C(1)(a) and (b); and

(ii) the notice under paragraph 8C(3).

(3) The document in sub-paragraph (2) or a copy of it may be sent electronically.]

11 Inspection and retention requirements relating to cover schedule—England and Wales

(1) This regulation applies to an insolvency practitioner appointed in insolvency proceedings under the Act to act—

(a) in relation to a company which the courts in England and Wales have jurisdiction to wind up; or

(b) in respect of an individual.

(2) The insolvency practitioner shall retain a copy of the cover schedule submitted by him in respect of his acting in relation to the company or, as the case may be, individual until the second anniversary of the date on which he is granted his release or discharge in relation to that company or, as the case may be, that individual.

(3) The copy of a schedule kept by an insolvency practitioner in pursuance of sub-paragraph (2) shall be produced by him on demand for inspection by—

(a) any creditor of the person to whom the schedule relates;

(b) where the schedule relates to an insolvent who is an individual, that individual;

(c) where the schedule relates to an insolvent which is a company, any contributory or director or other officer of the company; and

(d) the Secretary of State.

[(4) Subject to sub-paragraph (5), where the Secretary of State has notified the insolvency practitioner tin accordance with paragraph 8B(5)(a) or 8C(5)(a) in relation to a cover schedule, the thing notified under paragraph 8B(5)(a)(ii) or 8C(5)(a)(ii) is construed as a cover schedule for the purposes of this paragraph, paragraph 12 [and] paragraph 13 . . . .

(5) Where the Secretary of State has notified the insolvency practitioner in accordance with paragraph 8B(5)(b) or 8C(5)(b) in relation to a cover schedule, this paragraph, paragraph 12 and paragraph 13 do not apply.]

12 Inspection and retention requirements relating to the cover schedule—Scotland

(1) Where an insolvency practitioner is appointed to act in relation to a company which the courts in Scotland have jurisdiction to wind up, he shall retain in the sederunt book kept under rule 7.33 of the Insolvency (Scotland) Rules 1986, the principal copy of any cover schedule containing entries in relation to his so acting.

(2) Where an insolvency practitioner is appointed to act as interim trustee or permanent trustee or as a trustee under a trust deed for creditors, he shall retain in the sederunt book kept for those proceedings, the principal copy of any cover schedule containing entries in relation to his so acting.

13 Requirements to submit cover schedule to authorising body

(1) Every insolvency practitioner shall submit to his authorising body not later than 20 days after the end of each month during which he holds office in a case—

(a) the information submitted to a surety or cautioner in any cover schedule related to that month;

(b) where no cover schedule is submitted in relation to the month, a statement either that there are no relevant particulars to be supplied or, as the case may be, that it is not practicable to supply particulars in relation to any appointments taken in that month; and

(c) a statement identifying any case in respect of which he has been granted his release or discharge.

(2) In this regulation "authorising body" means in relation to an insolvency practitioner—

(a) any professional body recognised under section 391 of the Act of which he is a member and the rules of membership of which entitle him to act as an insolvency practitioner; or

(b) any competent authority by whom he is authorised to act as an insolvency practitioner pursuant to section 393 of the Act.

NOTES

Para 1: definition "professional liability insurance" inserted by the Provision of Services (Insolvency Practitioners) Regulations 2009, SI 2009/3081, regs 4, 5, Schedule, paras 2, 8(1), (2), except in relation to an application for authorisation to act as an insolvency practitioner under the Insolvency Act 1986, s 393 made or granted before 28 December 2009.

Para 2A: inserted by SI 2009/3081, regs 4, 5, Schedule, paras 2, 8(1), (3), except in relation to an application for authorisation to act as an insolvency practitioner under the Insolvency Act 1986, s 393 made or granted before 28 December 2009.

Para 3: heading substituted for original heading "Requirement for Bonding—Terms of the Bond" and sub-para (1) substituted by SI 2009/3081, regs 4, 5, Schedule, paras 2, 8(1), (4), except in relation to an application for authorisation to act as an insolvency practitioner under the Insolvency Act 1986, s 393 made or granted before 28 December 2009. Previous sub-para (1) read as follows:

"(1) Where an insolvency practitioner is appointed to act in respect of an insolvent there shall be in force a bond in a form approved by the Secretary of State which—

(a) contains provision whereby a surety or cautioner undertakes to be jointly and severally liable for losses in relation to the insolvent caused by—

(i) the fraud or dishonesty of the insolvency practitioner whether acting alone or in collusion with one or more persons; or

(ii) the fraud or dishonesty of any person committed with the connivance of the insolvency practitioner and

(b) otherwise conforms to the requirements of this Part.".

Paras 8A–8E: added by SI 2009/3081, regs 4, 5, Schedule, paras 2, 8(1), (5), except in relation to an application for authorisation to act as an insolvency practitioner under the Insolvency Act 1986, s 393 made or granted before 28 December 2009.

Para 9: sub-para (2)(b) revoked by the Deregulation Act 2015 (Insolvency) (Consequential Amendments and Transitional and Savings Provisions) Order 2015, SI 2015/1641, art 4, Sch 1, para 5(1), (10), subject to savings in arts 7–9 thereof (see the note "Savings" at **[12.25]**); sub-paras (3), (4) added by SI 2009/3081, regs 4, 5, Schedule, paras 2, 8(1), (6), except in relation to an application for authorisation to act as an insolvency practitioner under the Insolvency Act 1986, s 393 made or granted before 28 December 2009; words omitted from sub-para (3) revoked by the Insolvency Practitioners (Amendment) Regulations 2015, SI 2015/391, reg 5.

Para 10: sub-para (1) numbered as such, words in square brackets in sub-para (1) substituted for original words "The bond referred to in paragraph 3 shall" and sub-paras (2), (3) added by SI 2009/3081, regs 4, 5, Schedule, paras 2, 8(1), (7), except in relation to an application for authorisation to act as an insolvency practitioner under the Insolvency Act 1986, s 393 made or granted before 28 December 2009; sub-para (1)(b) revoked by SI 2015/1641, art 4, Sch 1, para 5(1), (11), subject to savings in arts 7–9 thereof (see the note "Savings" at **[12.25]**).

Para 11: sub-paras (4), (5) added by SI 2009/3081, regs 4, 5, Schedule, paras 2, 8(1), (8), except in relation to an application for authorisation to act as an insolvency practitioner under the Insolvency Act 1986, s 393 made or granted before 28 December 2009; in sub-para (4), word in square brackets substituted and words omitted revoked, by SI 2015/391, reg 6.

Para 13: sub-para (2)(b) revoked by SI 2015/1641, art 4, Sch 1, para 5(1), (12), subject to savings in arts 7–9 thereof (see the note "Savings" at **[12.25]**).

SCHEDULE 3

(Sch 3 revoked by the Insolvency Practitioners (Amendment) Regulations 2015, SI 2015/391, reg 7.)

PROCEEDS OF CRIME ACT 2002 (EXTERNAL REQUESTS AND ORDERS) ORDER 2005

(SI 2005/3181)

NOTES

Made: 15 November 2005.
Authority: Proceeds of Crime Act 2002, ss 444, 459(2).
Commencement: 1 January 2006.

ARRANGEMENT OF ARTICLES

PART 1
GENERAL PROVISIONS

1 Title and commencement . . . [12.49]
2 Interpretation . . . [12.50]
3 Insolvency practitioners . . . [12.51]
4 Insolvency practitioners: interpretation . . . [12.52]

PART 2
GIVING EFFECT IN ENGLAND AND WALES TO EXTERNAL REQUESTS IN CONNECTION WITH CRIMINAL INVESTIGATIONS OR PROCEEDINGS AND TO EXTERNAL ORDERS ARISING FROM SUCH PROCEEDINGS

CHAPTER 2
EXTERNAL ORDERS

33 Application of sums by enforcement receivers . . . [12.53]
34 Sums received by relevant Director . . . [12.54]

PART 3
GIVING EFFECT IN SCOTLAND TO EXTERNAL REQUESTS IN CONNECTION WITH CRIMINAL INVESTIGATIONS OR PROCEEDINGS AND TO EXTERNAL ORDERS ARISING FROM SUCH PROCEEDINGS

CHAPTER 2
EXTERNAL ORDERS

77 Application of sums by enforcement administrator . . . . . [12.55]
78 Sums received by clerk of court . . . . . [12.56]

PART 4
GIVING EFFECT IN NORTHERN IRELAND TO EXTERNAL REQUESTS IN CONNECTION WITH CRIMINAL INVESTIGATIONS OR PROCEEDINGS AND TO EXTERNAL ORDERS ARISING FROM SUCH PROCEEDINGS

CHAPTER 2
EXTERNAL ORDERS

119 Application of sums by enforcement receivers . . . . . [12.57]
120 Sums received by appropriate chief clerk . . . . . [12.58]

PART 5
GIVING EFFECT IN THE UNITED KINGDOM TO EXTERNAL ORDERS BY MEANS OF CIVIL RECOVERY

CHAPTER 2
CIVIL RECOVERY IN THE HIGH COURT OR COURT OF SESSION

191 Applying realised proceeds . . . . . [12.59]

PART 1
GENERAL PROVISIONS

[12.49]
1 Title and commencement

This Order may be cited as the Proceeds of Crime Act 2002 (External Requests and Orders) Order 2005 and shall come into force on 1st January 2006.

[12.50]
2 Interpretation

In this Order—

"the Act" means the Proceeds of Crime Act 2002;

["the 2014 Regulations" means the Criminal Justice and Data Protection (Protocol No 36) Regulations 2014;]

. . .

"country" includes territory;

"external order" has the meaning set out in section 447(2) of the Act;

"external request" has the meaning set out in section 447(1) of the Act;

["overseas confiscation order" has the same meaning as in the 2014 Regulations;]

"a relevant officer of Revenue and Customs" means such an officer exercising functions by virtue of section 6 of the Commissioners for Revenue and Customs Act 2005.

NOTES

Definitions "the 2014 Regulations" and "overseas confiscation order" inserted by the Proceeds of Crime Act 2002 (External Requests and Orders) (Amendment) Order 2016, SI 2016/662, arts 3, 4.

Definition omitted revoked by the Proceeds of Crime Act 2002 (External Requests and Orders) (Amendment) Order 2008, SI 2008/302, art 2(1), (2).

[12.51]
3 Insolvency practitioners

(1) Paragraphs (2) and (3) apply if a person acting as an insolvency practitioner seizes or disposes of any property in relation to which his functions are not exercisable because—

(a) it is for the time being subject to a restraint order made under article 8, 58 or 95; or

(b) it is for the time being subject to a property freezing order made under article 147, an interim receiving order made under article 151, a prohibitory property order made under article 161 or an interim administration order made under article 167,

and at the time of the seizure or disposal he believes on reasonable grounds that he is entitled (whether in pursuance of an order of a court or otherwise) to seize or dispose of the property.

(2) He is not liable to any person in respect of any loss or damage resulting from the seizure or disposal, except so far as the loss or damage is caused by his negligence.

(3) He has a lien on the property or the proceeds of its sale—

(a) for such of his expenses as were incurred in connection with the liquidation, bankruptcy, sequestration or other proceedings in relation to which he purported to make the seizure or disposal, and

(b) for so much of his remuneration as may reasonably be assigned to his acting in connection with those proceedings.

(4) Paragraph (2) does not prejudice the generality of any provision of . . . the 1986 Act, [the 2016 Act,] the 1989 Order or any Act or Order which confers a protection from liability on him.

(5) Paragraph (7) applies if—

(a) property is subject to a restraint order made under article 8, 58 or 95,

(b) a person acting as an insolvency practitioner incurs expenses in respect of property subject to the restraint order, and

(c) he does not know (and has no reasonable grounds to believe) that the property is subject to the restraint order.

(6) Paragraph (7) also applies if—

(a) property is subject to a restraint order made under article 8, 58 or 95,

(b) a person acting as an insolvency practitioner incurs expenses which are not ones in respect of property subject to the restraint order, and

(c) the expenses are ones which (but for the effect of the restraint order) might have been met by taking possession of and realising property subject to it.

[(6A) Paragraph (7) also applies if—

(a) property is detained under or by virtue of article 11A, 17I, 17J, 60A, 65I[, 65J, 98A, 103I or 103J];

(b) a person acting as an insolvency practitioner incurs expenses which are not ones in respect of the detained property; and

(c) the expenses are ones which (but for the effect of the detention of the property) might have been met by taking possession of and realising the property.]

[(7) Whether or not the insolvency practitioner has seized or disposed of any property, the insolvency practitioner is entitled to payment of the expenses under—

(a) article 33(2), 34(3) or 48D(2) if the restraint order was made under article 8 or the property was detained under or by virtue of article 11A, 17I or 17J;

(b) article 77(2), 78(3) or 86D(2) if the restraint order was made under article 58 or the property was detained under or by virtue of article 60A, 65I or 65J;

[(c) article 119(2), 120(3) or 134D(2) if the restraint order was made under article 95 or the property was detained under or by virtue of article 98A, 103I or 103J.]]

(8) Paragraph (10) applies if—

(a) property is subject to a property freezing order made under article 147, an interim receiving order made under article 151, a prohibitory property order made under article 161 or an interim administration order made under article 167,

(b) a person acting as an insolvency practitioner incurs expenses in respect of property subject to the order, and

(c) he does not know (and has no reasonable grounds to believe) that the property is subject to the order.

(9) Paragraph (10) also applies if—

(a) property is subject to a property freezing order made under article 147, an interim receiving order made under article 151, a prohibitory property order made under article 161 or an interim administration order made under article 167,

(b) a person acting as an insolvency practitioner incurs expenses which are not ones in respect of property subject to the order, and

(c) the expenses are ones which (but for the effect of the order) might have been met by taking possession of and realising property subject to it.

(10) Whether or not he has seized or disposed of any property, he is entitled to payment of the expenses under article 191.

NOTES

Para (4): words "the 1985 Act," (omitted) revoked and words in square brackets inserted by the Bankruptcy (Scotland) Act 2016 (Consequential Provisions and Modifications) Order 2016, SI 2016/1034, art 7(1), (3), Sch 1, para 39(1), (2), as from 30 November 2016 (except in relation to (i) a sequestration as regards which the petition is presented, or the debtor application is made before that date; or (ii) a trust deed executed before that date).

Para (6A): inserted by the Proceeds of Crime Act 2002 (External Requests and Orders) (Amendment) Order 2015, SI 2015/1750, arts 3, 4(1), (2); words in square brackets in sub-para (a) substituted by the Proceeds of Crime Act 2002 (External Requests and Orders) (Amendment) Order 2016, SI 2016/662, arts 3, 5(a).

Para (7): substituted by SI 2015/1750, arts 3, 4(1), (3); sub-para (c) added by SI 2016/662, arts 3, 5(b).

[12.52]

4 Insolvency practitioners: interpretation

(1) This article applies for the purposes of article 3.

(2) A person acts as an insolvency practitioner if he so acts within the meaning given by section 388 of the 1986 Act or Article 3 of the 1989 Order; but this is subject to paragraphs (3) to (5).

(3) The expression "person acting as an insolvency practitioner" includes the official receiver acting as receiver or manager of the property concerned.

(4) In applying section 388 of the 1986 Act under paragraph (2) above—

(a) the reference in section 388(2)(a) to a permanent or interim trustee in sequestration must be taken to include a reference to a trustee in sequestration;

(b) section 388(5) (which includes provision that nothing in the section applies to anything done by the official receiver or the Accountant in Bankruptcy) must be ignored.

(5) In applying Article 3 of the 1989 Order under paragraph (2) above, paragraph (5) (which includes provision that nothing in the Article applies to anything done by the official receiver) must be ignored.

(6) The following sub-paragraphs apply to references to Acts or Orders—

(a) the 1913 Act is the Bankruptcy (Scotland) Act 1913;

(b) the 1914 Act is the Bankruptcy Act 1914;

(c) the 1985 Act is the Bankruptcy (Scotland) Act 1985;

(d) the 1986 Act is the Insolvency Act 1986;

[(da) the 2016 Act is the Bankruptcy (Scotland) Act 2016;]

(e) the 1989 Order is the Insolvency (Northern Ireland) Order 1989.

(7) An award of sequestration is made on the date of sequestration within the meaning of section 12(4) of the 1985 Act.

NOTES

Para (6): sub-para (c) revoked and sub-para (da) inserted by the Bankruptcy (Scotland) Act 2016 (Consequential Provisions and Modifications) Order 2016, SI 2016/1034, art 7(1), (3), Sch 1, para 39(1), (3), as from 30 November 2016 (except in relation to (i) a sequestration as regards which the petition is presented, or the debtor application is made before that date; or (ii) a trust deed executed before that date).

5 (*Outside the scope of this work.*)

PART 2
GIVING EFFECT IN ENGLAND AND WALES TO EXTERNAL REQUESTS IN CONNECTION WITH CRIMINAL INVESTIGATIONS OR PROCEEDINGS AND TO EXTERNAL ORDERS ARISING FROM SUCH PROCEEDINGS

6–17L (*(Chs 1, 1A) outside the scope of this work.*)

CHAPTER 2 EXTERNAL ORDERS

18–32 (*Arts 18–29 outside the scope of this work; arts 30–32 revoked by the Proceeds of Crime Act 2002 (External Requests and Orders) (Amendment) Order 2008, SI 2008/302, art 2(1), (11).*)

[12.53]

33 Application of sums by enforcement receivers

(1) This article applies to sums which are in the hands of a receiver appointed under article 27 if they are—

(a) the proceeds of the realisation of property under article 28 or 29;

(b) where article 28 applies, sums (other than those mentioned in sub-paragraph (a)) in which the defendant holds an interest.

(2) The sums must be applied as follows—

(a) first, they must be applied in payment of such expenses incurred by a person acting as an insolvency practitioner as are payable under this paragraph by virtue of article 3;

(b) second, they must be applied in making any payments directed by the Crown Court;

(c) third, they must be applied on the defendant's behalf towards satisfaction of the external order.

(3) If the amount payable under the external order has been fully paid and any sums remain in the receiver's hands he must distribute them—

(a) among such persons who held (or hold) interests in the property concerned as the Crown Court directs; and

(b) in such proportions as it directs.

(4) Before making a direction under paragraph (3) the court must give persons who held (or hold) interests in the property concerned a reasonable opportunity to make representations to it.

(5) For the purposes of paragraphs (3) and (4) the property concerned is—

(a) the property represented by the proceeds mentioned in paragraph (1)(a);

(b) the sums mentioned in paragraph (1)(b).

(6) The receiver applies sums as mentioned in paragraph (2)(c) by paying them to the relevant Director on account of the amount payable under the order.

[12.54]

34 Sums received by relevant Director

(1) This article applies if a relevant Director receives sums on account of the amount payable under a registered external order or the value of the property specified in the order.

(2) The relevant Director's receipt of the sums reduces the amount payable under the order, but he must apply the sums received as follows.

(3) First he must apply them in payment of such expenses incurred by a person acting as an insolvency practitioner as—

(a) are payable under this paragraph by virtue of article 3, but

(b) are not already paid under article 33(2)(a).

(4) He must next apply them—

(a) first, in payment of the remuneration and expenses of a receiver appointed under article 15 to the extent that they have not been met by virtue of the exercise by that receiver of a power conferred under article 16(2)(d);
(b) second, in payment of the remuneration and expenses of the receiver appointed under article 27;
[(c) third, in payment to an appropriate officer of any amount to which the officer is entitled by virtue of article 48B(3).]

(5) Any sums which remain after the relevant Director has made any payments required by the preceding provisions of this article must be paid into the Consolidated Fund.

(6) Paragraph (4) does not apply if the receiver is a member of the staff of [the Crown Prosecution Service or the Serious Fraud Office]; and it is immaterial whether he is a permanent or temporary member or he is on secondment from elsewhere.

NOTES

Para (4): sub-para (c) inserted by the Proceeds of Crime Act 2002 (External Requests and Orders) (Amendment) Order 2015, SI 2015/1750, arts 5, 14.

Para (6): words in square brackets substituted by the Public Bodies (Merger of the Director of Public Prosecutions and the Director of Revenue and Customs Prosecutions) Order 2014, SI 2014/834, art 3(3)(c), Sch 3, paras 14, 17.

35–55 (*Arts 35, 36, 39 revoked by the Proceeds of Crime Act 2002 (External Requests and Orders) (Amendment) Order 2008, SI 2008/302, art 2(1), (12), (14); arts 37, 38, 40–55 (Chs 3–4) outside the scope of this work.*)

PART 3
GIVING EFFECT IN SCOTLAND TO EXTERNAL REQUESTS IN CONNECTION WITH CRIMINAL INVESTIGATIONS OR PROCEEDINGS AND TO EXTERNAL ORDERS ARISING FROM SUCH PROCEEDINGS

56–65L (*(Chs 1, 1A) outside the scope of this work.*)

CHAPTER 2 EXTERNAL ORDERS

66–76 (*Outside the scope of this work.*)

[12.55]
77 Application of sums by enforcement administrator

(1) This article applies to sums which are in the hands of an administrator appointed under article 73 if they are—
(a) the proceeds of the realisation of property under article 74 or 75;
(b) where article 74 applies, sums (other than those mentioned in sub-paragraph (a)) in which the offender holds an interest.

(2) The sums must be applied as follows—
(a) first, they must be applied in payment of such expenses incurred by a person acting as an insolvency practitioner as are payable under this paragraph by virtue of article 3;
(b) second, they must be applied in making any payments as directed by the court;
(c) third, they must be applied on the offender's behalf towards satisfaction of the external order.

(3) If the amount payable under the external order has been fully paid and any sums remain in the administrator's hands he must distribute them—
(a) among such persons who held (or hold) interests in the property concerned as the court directs; and
(b) in such proportions as it directs.

(4) Before making a direction under paragraph (3) the court must give persons who held (or hold) interests in the property concerned a reasonable opportunity to make representations to it.

(5) For the purposes mentioned in paragraphs (3) and (4) the property concerned is—
(a) the property represented by the proceeds mentioned in paragraph (1)(a);
(b) the sums mentioned in paragraph (1)(b).

(6) The administrator applies sums as mentioned in paragraph (2)(c) by paying them to the appropriate clerk of court on account of the amount payable under the order.

(7) The appropriate clerk of court is the sheriff clerk appointed [under] article 69(1).

NOTES

Para (7): word in square brackets inserted by the Proceeds of Crime Act 2002 (External Requests and Orders) (Amendment) Order 2016, SI 2016/662, arts 10, 18.

[12.56]
78 Sums received by clerk of court

(1) This section applies if a clerk of court receives sums on account of the amount payable under a registered external order or the value of the property specified in the order.

(2) The clerk of court's receipt of the sums reduces the amount payable under the order, but he must apply the sums received as follows.

(3) First he must apply them in payment of such expenses incurred by a person acting as an insolvency practitioner as—

(a) are payable under this paragraph by virtue of article 3; but
(b) are not already paid under article 77(2)(a) [or 86D(2)(a)].

(4) If the Lord Advocate has reimbursed the administrator in respect of remuneration or expenses under article 80 the clerk of court must next apply the sums in reimbursing the Lord Advocate.

(5) If the clerk of court received the sums under article 77 he must next apply them in payment of the administrator's remuneration and expenses.

[(5A) If the clerk of court received the sums from an appropriate officer under article 77 or 86D, the clerk of court must next apply them in payment to an appropriate officer of any amount to which the officer is entitled by virtue of article 86B.]

(6) If any amount remains after the clerk of court makes any payments required by the preceding paragraphs of this article, the amount must be disposed of in accordance with [section 211(6)] of the Criminal Procedure (Scotland) Act 1995 as if it were a fine imposed [under that Act].

NOTES

Para (3): words in square brackets in sub-para (b) inserted by the Proceeds of Crime Act 2002 (External Requests and Orders) (Amendment) Order 2015, SI 2015/1750, arts 21, 27(1), (2).

Para (5A): inserted by SI 2015/1750, arts 21, 27(1), (3).

Para (6): words in square brackets substituted by the Proceeds of Crime Act 2002 (External Requests and Orders) (Amendment) Order 2016, SI 2016/662, arts 10, 19.

79–92 *(Art 79, arts 80–92 (Chs 3–4) outside the scope of this work.)*

PART 4
GIVING EFFECT IN NORTHERN IRELAND TO EXTERNAL REQUESTS IN CONNECTION WITH CRIMINAL INVESTIGATIONS OR PROCEEDINGS AND TO EXTERNAL ORDERS ARISING FROM SUCH PROCEEDINGS

93–103L *((Chs 1, 1A) outside the scope of this work.)*

CHAPTER 2 EXTERNAL ORDERS

104–118 *(Arts 104–115 outside the scope of this work; arts 116–118 revoked by the Proceeds of Crime Act 2002 (External Requests and Orders) (Amendment) Order 2008, SI 2008/302, art 2(1), (27).)*

[12.57]
119 Application of sums by enforcement receivers

(1) This article applies to sums which are in the hands of a receiver appointed under article 113 if they are—
(a) the proceeds of the realisation of property under article 114 or 115;
(b) where article 114 applies, sums (other than those mentioned in sub-paragraph (a)) in which the defendant holds an interest.

(2) The sums must be applied as follows—
(a) first, they must be applied in payment of such expenses incurred by a person acting as an insolvency practitioner as are payable under this paragraph by virtue of article 3;
(b) second, they must be applied in making any payments directed by the Crown Court;
(c) third, they must be applied on the defendant's behalf towards satisfaction of the external order.

(3) If the amount payable under the external order has been fully paid and any sums remain in the receiver's hands he must distribute them—
(a) among such persons who held (or hold) interests in the property concerned as the Crown Court directs; and
(b) in such proportions as it directs.

(4) Before making a direction under paragraph (3) the court must give persons who held (or hold) interests in the property concerned a reasonable opportunity to make representations to it.

(5) For the purposes of paragraphs (3) and (4) the property concerned is—
(a) the property represented by the proceeds mentioned in paragraph (1)(a);
(b) the sums mentioned in paragraph (1)(b).

(6) The receiver applies sums as mentioned in paragraph (2)(c) by paying them to the appropriate chief clerk on account of the amount payable under the order.

(7) The appropriate chief clerk is the chief clerk of the court at the place where the external order was registered.

[12.58]
120 Sums received by appropriate chief clerk

(1) This article applies if the appropriate chief clerk receives sums on account of the amount payable under a registered external order or the value of the property specified in the order.

(2) The appropriate chief clerk's receipt of the sums reduces the amount payable under the order, but he must apply the sums received as follows.

(3) First he must apply them in payment of such expenses incurred by a person acting as an insolvency practitioner as—
(a) are payable under this paragraph by virtue of article 3, but
(b) are not already paid under article 119(2)(a).

(4) He must next apply them—

(a) first, in payment of the remuneration and expenses of a receiver appointed under article 101 to the extent that they have not been met by virtue of the exercise by that receiver of a power conferred under article 102(2)(d);

(b) second, in payment of the remuneration and expenses of the receiver appointed under article 113;

[(c) third, in payment to an appropriate officer of any amount to which the officer is entitled by virtue of article 134B(3).]

(5) If any amount remains after the appropriate chief clerk makes any payments required by the preceding provisions of this article, the amount must be treated for the purposes of section 20 of the Administration of Justice Act (Northern Ireland) 1954 (application of fines) as if it were a fine.

(6) Paragraph (4) does not apply if the receiver is a member of the staff of the Public Prosecution Service for Northern Ireland, or the Serious Fraud Office; and it is immaterial whether he is a permanent or temporary member or he is on secondment from elsewhere.

NOTES

Para (4): sub-para (c) added by the Proceeds of Crime Act 2002 (External Requests and Orders) (Amendment) Order 2016, SI 2016/662, arts 20, 30.

121–141ZN (*Arts 121, 122, 125 revoked by the Proceeds of Crime Act 2002 (External Requests and Orders) (Amendment) Order 2008, SI 2008/302, art 2(1), (28), (30); arts 123, 124, arts 126–141 (Chs 3, 3A, 4), arts 141A–141ZN (Pts 4A, 4B) outside the scope of this work.*)

PART 5
GIVING EFFECT IN THE UNITED KINGDOM TO EXTERNAL ORDERS BY MEANS OF CIVIL RECOVERY

142 (*(Ch 1) outside the scope of this work.*)

CHAPTER 2 CIVIL RECOVERY IN THE HIGH COURT OR COURT OF SESSION

143–190 (*Outside the scope of this work.*)

Vesting and realisation of recoverable property

[12.59]

191 Applying realised proceeds

(1) This article applies to—

(a) sums which represent the realised proceeds of property which was vested in the trustee for civil recovery by a recovery order or which he obtained in pursuance of a recovery order,

(b) sums vested in the trustee by a recovery order or obtained by him in pursuance of a recovery order.

(2) The trustee is to make out of the sums—

(a) first, any payment required to be made by him by virtue of article 183,

(b) next, any payment of legal expenses which, after giving effect to article 177(11), are payable under this paragraph in pursuance of provision under article 177(10) contained in the recovery order,

(c) next, any payment of expenses incurred by a person acting as an insolvency practitioner which are payable under this paragraph by virtue of article 3(10),

and any sum which remains is to be paid to the enforcement authority.

(3) The [enforcement authority (unless it is the Scottish Ministers)] may apply a sum received by [it] under paragraph (2) in making payment of the remuneration and expenses of—

(a) the trustee, or

(b) any interim receiver appointed in, or in anticipation of, the proceedings for the recovery order.

(4) Paragraph (3)(a) does not apply in relation to the remuneration of the trustee if the trustee is a member of the staff of the [enforcement authority concerned].

NOTES

Paras (3), (4): words in square brackets substituted by the Proceeds of Crime Act 2002 (External Requests and Orders) (Amendment) Order 2008, SI 2008/302, art 2(1), (39).

192–213 (*Arts 192–201, arts 202–209 and 211–213 (Ch 3) outside the scope of this work; art 210 revoked by the Proceeds of Crime Act 2002 (External Requests and Orders) (Amendment) Order 2008, SI 2008/302, art 2(1), (41).*)

SCHEDULES 1–5

(*Schs 1–5 outside the scope of this work.*)

EUROPEAN UNION (RECOGNITION OF PROFESSIONAL QUALIFICATIONS) REGULATIONS 2015

(SI 2015/2059)

NOTES

Made: 17 December 2015.
Authority: European Communities Act 1972, s 2(2).
Commencement: 18 January 2016.

ARRANGEMENT OF REGULATIONS

PART 1
GENERAL PROVISIONS

1 Citation and commencement .... [12.60]
4 Competent authorities .... [12.61]
8 Regulated profession, regulated education and training and applicants .... [12.62]

PART 3
FREEDOM OF ESTABLISHMENT

34 .... [12.63]

SCHEDULES

Schedule 1—Regulated professions
Part 1—Professions regulated by law or public authority .... [12.64]
Schedule 3—Professions in respect of which the right of the applicant to choose between an adaptation period and an aptitude test is displaced
Part 1—Professions under regulation 34(a) .... [12.65]

PART 1
GENERAL PROVISIONS

[12.60]
1 Citation and commencement

These Regulations may be cited as the European Union (Recognition of Professional Qualifications) Regulations 2015 and come into force on 18th January 2016.

NOTES

Commencement: 18 January 2016.

2, 3 (*Outside the scope of this work.*)

[12.61]
4 Competent authorities

(1) In the case of a regulated profession listed in any of Parts 1 to 3 of Schedule 1, the competent authority in the United Kingdom for the purposes of the Directive so far as relating to that profession is the body or authority specified in relation to that profession in that Part of that Schedule.

(2) In the case of a regulated profession that is regulated in the United Kingdom but is not listed in Schedule 1, the competent authority in the United Kingdom for the purposes of the Directive so far as relating to that profession is the governing body of that profession in the United Kingdom.

(3) In these Regulations "competent authority", in relation to a profession listed in Part 4 of Schedule 1, means the body or authority specified in relation to that profession in that Part of that Schedule.

(4) In regulations 8 and 9, and in Parts 4 and 5 of these Regulations, "competent authority" includes the assistance centre.

(5) For the purposes of these Regulations, the competent authority in another relevant European State in relation to—

(a) any document, certificate, attestation of competence, diploma or qualification,
(b) any period of professional experience, or
(c) any application, action or decision,

is the authority, body or person who under laws, regulations or administrative provisions is authorised in that State to issue, award or recognise the document or information concerned or (as the case may be) to certify the period of professional experience, to receive the application or to take the action or decision.

NOTES

Commencement: 18 January 2016.

5–7 (*Outside the scope of this work.*)

[12.62]

8 Regulated profession, regulated education and training and applicants

(1) In these Regulations, "regulated profession" means—

(a) in relation to the United Kingdom—

(i) a profession listed in any of Parts 1, 3 and 4 of Schedule 1;

(ii) a profession practised by members of a professional association who have a title or designation set out in Part 2 of Schedule 1;

(iii) a professional activity or group of activities access to which, the pursuit of which or one of the modes of pursuit of which is subject (directly or indirectly) by virtue of legislative, regulatory or administrative provisions to the possession of specific professional qualifications; or

(iv) a professional activity or group of activities pursuit of which is by persons using a professional title limited by legislative, regulatory or administrative provisions to holders of a given professional qualification;

(b) in relation to another relevant European State, a professional activity, or group of professional activities, which constitutes a profession if and in so far as the activity, or group of activities, is regulated in that State as a professional activity.

(2) "Regulated education and training" means education and training which is directly geared to the practice of a profession in a relevant European State, and comprises a course or courses complemented where appropriate by professional training or probationary or professional practice, the structure and level of which are determined by the laws, regulations or administrative provisions of that relevant European State or which are monitored or approved by the competent authority in a relevant European State.

(3) For the purposes of Part 2, and of any other provision of these Regulations so far as relating to Part 2, including Part 4, "applicant" means an individual—

(a) who wishes to access and pursue a regulated profession in the United Kingdom on a temporary and occasional basis, whether in an employed or self-employed capacity;

(b) who is a national of a relevant European State or who, although not a national of such a State, is by virtue of any enforceable EU right entitled to be treated, for the purposes of access to and pursuit of a regulated profession, no less favourably than a national of such a State;

(c) whose qualifications were obtained in a relevant European State or a third country;

(d) who is legally established in their home State for the purpose of pursuing the same profession there; and

(e) who, if neither that profession nor the education and training leading to it is regulated in their home State, has pursued that profession in that State for at least one year during the ten years preceding the provision of services.

(4) For the purposes of Chapters 1, 2 and 4 of Part 3, and of any other provision of these Regulations so far as relating to those Chapters, including Part 4, "applicant" means an individual—

(a) who wishes to access and pursue a regulated profession in the United Kingdom on a permanent basis, whether in an employed or self-employed capacity;

(b) who is a national of a relevant European State or who, although not a national of such a State, is by virtue of any enforceable Community right entitled to be treated, for the purposes of access to and pursuit of a regulated profession, no less favourably than a national of such a State;

(c) whose qualifications were obtained in a relevant European State or a third country; and

(d) who, if his qualifications were obtained in a third country, has three years' professional experience in the profession concerned—

(i) on the territory of a relevant European State which recognised the formal qualifications obtained in the third country by permitting the individual to pursue the profession on its territory in accordance with its rules, and

(ii) certified by that State.

NOTES

Commencement: 18 January 2016.

9–26 (*Regs 9–11, regs 12–26 (Pt 2) outside the scope of this work.*)

PART 3
FREEDOM OF ESTABLISHMENT

27–33 (*Outside the scope of this work.*)

[12.63]

34

Where a requirement is imposed under regulation 32(1), the choice between an adaptation period and aptitude test must be that of the applicant except—

(a) in the regulated professions set out in the first column of the table in Part 1 of Schedule 3, whose pursuit requires precise knowledge of national law and in respect of which the provision of advice or assistance or both concerning national law is an essential and constant aspect of the professional activity, where the requirements set out in the second column of that table in respect of each profession shall apply, or

(b) in cases specified in—

(i) regulation 3(8)(a) (except for nurses responsible for general care and midwives) and (b);

(ii) regulation 3(8)(c) concerning only doctors and dental practitioners;

(iii) regulation 3(8)(d), where the applicant is a specialist nurse without training as a general nurse and seeks recognition in the United Kingdom where the relevant professional activities are pursued by nurses responsible for general care or specialised nurses holding evidence of formal qualifications as a specialist which follows the training leading to the possession of the titles listed in Annex V, point 5.2.2 of the Directive; or

(iv) regulation 3(8)(e);

where for each of the professions set out in the first column of the table in Part 2 of Schedule 3, the requirements set out in the second column of that table shall apply;

(c) in the case of a holder of a professional qualification referred to in regulation 27(a) who applies for recognition of that holder's professional qualifications where the national professional qualification required is classified under regulation 27(c), where the Secretary of State may, in respect of a particular profession, either require an aptitude test or require an adaptation period;

(d) in the case of a holder of a professional qualification referred to in regulation 27(b) who applies for recognition of that holder's professional qualification where the national professional qualification required is classified under regulation 27(d) or (e), where the Secretary of State may, in respect of a particular profession, either require an aptitude test or require an adaptation period;

(e) in the case of a holder of a professional qualification referred to in regulation 27(a) who applies for recognition of the qualification where the national professional qualification required is classified under regulation 27(d), where the Secretary of State may, in respect of a particular profession, require both an adaptation period and an aptitude test.

NOTES

Commencement: 18 January 2016.

35–80 (*Regs 35–43, regs 44–80 (Pts 4–6) outside the scope of this work.*)

SCHEDULE 1
REGULATED PROFESSIONS

Regulations 3 and 8

PART 1
PROFESSIONS REGULATED BY LAW OR PUBLIC AUTHORITY

[12.64]

Profession	*Competent authority*
. . .	
Insolvency Practitioner	The Insolvency Practitioners Association Department of Enterprise, Trade and Investment in Northern Ireland The Association of Chartered Certified Accountants The Institute of Chartered Accountants in England and Wales The Institute of Chartered Accountants in Ireland The Institute of Chartered Accountants of Scotland The Law Society of Northern Ireland
. . .	. . .

NOTES

Commencement: 18 January 2016.

Entries omitted outside the scope of this work.

PARTS 2–4

(*Sch 1, Pts 2–4 outside the scope of this work.*)

SCHEDULE 2

(*Sch 2 outside the scope of this work.*)

SCHEDULE 3
PROFESSIONS IN RESPECT OF WHICH THE RIGHT OF THE APPLICANT TO CHOOSE BETWEEN AN ADAPTATION PERIOD AND AN APTITUDE TEST IS DISPLACED

Regulation 34

PART 1
PROFESSIONS UNDER REGULATION 34(A)

[12.65]

Profession	***Requirement***
. . .	. . .
Insolvency Practitioner	Aptitude test
. . .	. . .

NOTES

Commencement: 18 January 2016.

Entries omitted outside the scope of this work.

PART 2

(*Sch 3, Pt 2 outside the scope of this work.*)

SCHEDULES 4–6

(*Schs 4–6 outside the scope of this work.*)

PART 13
STATUTORY INSTRUMENTS RELATING TO CROSS-BORDER INSOLVENCY—ENGLAND AND WALES

CO-OPERATION OF INSOLVENCY COURTS (DESIGNATION OF RELEVANT COUNTRIES AND TERRITORIES) ORDER 1986

(SI 1986/2123)

NOTES

Made: 2 December 1986.

Authority: Insolvency Act 1986, s 426(11).

Commencement: 29 December 1986.

Application: this Order is applied, with such modifications as the context requires for the purpose of giving effect to the provisions of the Insolvency Act 1986, by the Limited Liability Partnerships Regulations 2001, SI 2001/1090, reg 10, Sch 6, Pt II at **[10.38]**, **[10.43]**.

[13.1]
1

This Order may be cited as the Co-operation of Insolvency Courts (Designation of Relevant Countries and Territories) Order 1986 and shall come into force on 29th December 1986.

[13.2]
2

The countries and territories specified in the Schedule to this Order are hereby designated relevant countries and territories for the purposes of section 426 of the Insolvency Act 1986.

SCHEDULE
RELEVANT COUNTRIES AND TERRITORIES

Article 2

[13.3]
ANGUILLA

AUSTRALIA

THE BAHAMAS

BERMUDA

BOTSWANA

CANADA

CAYMAN ISLANDS

FALKLAND ISLANDS

GIBRALTAR

HONG KONG

REPUBLIC OF IRELAND

MONTSERRAT

NEW ZEALAND

ST HELENA

TURKS AND CAICOS ISLANDS

TUVALU

VIRGIN ISLANDS

EUROPEAN ECONOMIC INTEREST GROUPING REGULATIONS 1989

(SI 1989/638)

NOTES

Made: 10 April 1989.

Authority: European Communities Act 1972, s 2.

Commencement: 1 July 1989.

ARRANGEMENT OF REGULATIONS

PART I
GENERAL

1 Citation, commencement and extent . . . .[13.4]
2 Interpretation . . . .[13.5]

PART II
PROVISIONS RELATING TO ARTICLES 1–38 OF THE EC REGULATION
6 Cessation of membership (Article 28(1) of the EC Regulation). . . . .[13.6]
7 Competent authority (Articles 32(1) and (3) and 38 of the EC Regulation) . . . .[13.7]
8 Winding up and conclusion of liquidation (Articles 35 and 36 of the EC Regulation). . . . .[13.8]

PART IV
SUPPLEMENTAL PROVISIONS
18 Application of provisions of the Companies Acts . . . .[13.9]
19 Application of insolvency legislation . . . .[13.10]
20 Application of legislation relating to disqualification of directors . . . .[13.11]
21 Penalties. . . . .[13.12]

SCHEDULES

Schedule 1—Council Regulation (EEC) No 2137/85 of 25th July 1985 on the European Economic Interest Grouping (EEIG) . . . .[13.13]
Schedule 4—Provisions of Companies Acts applying to EEIGS and their establishments
Part 1—Provisions of Companies Act 1985 . . . .[13.14]
Part 2—Provisions of Companies Act 2006 . . . .[13.15]

PART I
GENERAL

[13.4]
1 Citation, commencement and extent

These Regulations, which extend to [the whole of the United Kingdom], may be cited as the European Economic Interest Grouping Regulations 1989 and shall come into force on 1st July 1989.

NOTES

Words in square brackets substituted by the European Economic Interest Grouping (Amendment) Regulations 2009, SI 2009/2399, regs 3, 4.

[13.5]
2 Interpretation

(1) In these Regulations—

"the 1985 Act" means the Companies Act 1985;

["the 2006 Act" means the Companies Act 2006;]

["the Companies Acts" has the meaning given by section 2 of [the 2006 Act];]

"the contract" means the contract for the formation of an EEIG;

"the EC Regulation" means Council Regulation (EEC) No 2137/85 set out in Schedule 1 to these Regulations;

"EEIG" means a European Economic Interest Grouping being a grouping formed in pursuance of article 1 of the EC Regulation;

"officer", in relation to an EEIG, includes a manager, or any other person provided for in the contract as an organ of the EEIG; and

["the registrar" has the same meaning as in the Companies Acts (see section 1060 of the 2006 Act);]

and other expressions used in these Regulations and defined [for the purposes of the Companies Acts] or in relation to insolvency and winding up by the Insolvency Act 1986 [or, as regards Northern Ireland, by the Insolvency (Northern Ireland) Order 1989] have the meanings assigned to them by those provisions as if any reference to a company in any such definition were a reference to an EEIG.

[(2) . . .]

(3) In these Regulations, "certified translation" means a translation certified to be a correct translation—

(a) if the translation was made in the United Kingdom, by
  (i) a notary public in any part of the United Kingdom;
  (ii) a solicitor (if the translation was made in Scotland), a solicitor of the Supreme Court of Judicature of England and Wales (if it was made in England or Wales), or a [solicitor of the Court of Judicature of Northern Ireland] (if it was made in Northern Ireland); or
  (iii) a person certified by a person mentioned above to be known to him to be competent to translate the document into English; or

(b) if the translation was made outside the United Kingdom, by—
  (i) a notary public;
  (ii) a person authorised in the place where the translation was made to administer an oath;

(iii) any of the British officials mentioned in section 6 of the Commissioners for Oaths Act 1889;

(iv) a person certified by a person mentioned in sub-paragraph (i), (ii) or (iii) of this paragraph to be known to him to be competent to translate the document into English.

NOTES

Para (1): definition "the Companies Acts" inserted, and words in the penultimate pair of square brackets substituted, by the Companies Act 2006 (Consequential Amendments etc) Order 2008, SI 2008/948, art 3(1), Sch 1, Pt 2, para 161; definition "the 2006 Act" inserted, words in square brackets in definition "the Companies Acts" substituted, definition "the registrar" substituted, and words in final pair of square brackets inserted, by the European Economic Interest Grouping (Amendment) Regulations 2009, SI 2009/2399, regs 3, 5(1), (2).

Para (2): revoked by the European Economic Interest Grouping and European Public Limited-Liability Company (Amendment) Regulations 2014, SI 2014/2382, regs 2, 3; it had previously been substituted by SI 2009/2399, regs 3, 5(1), (3).

Para (3): words in square brackets substituted by the Constitutional Reform Act 2005, s 59, Sch 11, Pt 2, para 5.

Supreme Court of England and Wales: the Supreme Court of England and Wales is renamed the Senior Courts of England and Wales; see the Constitutional Reform Act 2005, s 59(1) (as from 1 October 2009).

PART II
PROVISIONS RELATING TO ARTICLES 1–38 OF THE EC REGULATION

3–5 (*Outside the scope of this work.*)

[13.6]

6 Cessation of membership (Article 28(1) of the EC Regulation)

For the purposes of national law on liquidation, winding up, insolvency or cessation of payments, a member of an EEIG registered under these Regulations shall cease to be a member if—

(a) in the case of an individual—

(i) a bankruptcy order has been made against him in England and Wales [or Northern Ireland]; or

(ii) sequestration of his estate has been awarded by the court in Scotland under the Bankruptcy (Scotland) Act 1985;

(b) in the case of a partnership—

(i) a winding up order has been made against the partnership in England and Wales [or Northern Ireland];

[(ii) a bankruptcy order has been made against each of the partnership's members in England and Wales on a bankruptcy petition presented under Article 11(1) of the Insolvent Partnerships Order 1994;

(iia) a bankruptcy order has been made against each of the partnership's members in Northern Ireland on a bankruptcy petition presented under Article 11(1) of the Insolvent Partnerships Order (Northern Ireland) 1995; or]

(iii) sequestration of the estate of the partnership has been awarded by the court in Scotland under the Bankruptcy (Scotland) Act 1985;

(c) in the case of a company, the company goes into liquidation in [the United Kingdom]; or

(d) in the case of any legal person or partnership, it is otherwise wound up or otherwise ceases to exist after the conclusion of winding up or insolvency.

NOTES

Words in first and second pairs of square brackets inserted, and other words in square brackets substituted, by the European Economic Interest Grouping (Amendment) Regulations 2009, SI 2009/2399, regs 3, 9.

[13.7]

7 Competent authority (Articles 32(1) and (3) and 38 of the EC Regulation)

[(1) The competent authority for the purposes of making an application to the court under Article 32(1) of the EC Regulation (winding up of EEIG in certain circumstances) shall be—

(a) in the case of an EEIG whose official address is in Northern Ireland, the Department of Enterprise, Trade and Investment in Northern Ireland;

(b) in any other case, the Secretary of State.]

(2) The court may, on an application by [the appropriate authority], order the winding up of an EEIG which has its official address in [the United Kingdom], if the EEIG acts contrary to the public interest and it is expedient in the public interest that the EEIG should be wound up and the court is of the opinion that it is just and equitable for it to be so.

[(2A) In paragraph (2) above "the appropriate authority" means—

(a) in the case of an EEIG whose official address is in Great Britain, the Secretary of State;

(b) in the case of an EEIG whose official address is in Northern Ireland, the Department of Enterprise, Trade and Investment in Northern Ireland.]

(3) The court, on an application by [the appropriate authority], shall be the competent authority for the purposes of prohibiting under article 38 of the EC Regulation any activity carried on in [the United Kingdom] by an EEIG where such an activity is in contravention of the public interest there.

[(4) In paragraph (3) above "the appropriate authority" means—

(a) in the case of any activity carried on in Great Britain, the Secretary of State;

(b) in the case of any activity carried on in Northern Ireland, the Department of Enterprise, Trade and Investment in Northern Ireland.]

NOTES

Para (1): substituted by the European Economic Interest Grouping (Amendment) Regulations 2009, SI 2009/2399, regs 3, 10(1), (2).

Paras (2), (3): words in square brackets substituted by SI 2009/2399, regs 3, 10(1), (3), (5).

Paras (2A), (4): inserted and added respectively by SI 2009/2399, regs 3, 10(1), (4), (6).

[13.8]

8 Winding up and conclusion of liquidation (Articles 35 and 36 of the EC Regulation)

(1) Where an EEIG is wound up as an unregistered company under Part V of the Insolvency Act 1986, the provisions of Part V shall apply in relation to the EEIG as if any reference in that Act . . . to a director or past director of a company included a reference to a manager of the EEIG and any other person who has or has had control or management of the EEIG's business and with the modification that in section 221(1) after the words "all the provisions" there shall be added the words "of Council Regulation (EEC) No 2137/85 and".

[(1A) Where an EEIG is wound up as an unregistered company under Part 6 of the Insolvency (Northern Ireland) Order 1989, the provisions of Part 6 shall apply in relation to the EEIG as if—

(a) any reference in that Order to a director or past director of a company included a reference to a manager of the EEIG and any other person who has or has had control or management of the EEIG's business; and

(b) in Article 185(1) after "all the provisions" there were inserted "of Council Regulation (EEC) No 2137/85 and".]

(2) At the end of the period of three months beginning with the day of receipt by the registrar of a notice of the conclusion of the liquidation of an EEIG, the EEIG shall be dissolved.

NOTES

Para (1): words omitted revoked by the Companies Act 2006 (Consequential Amendments etc) Order 2008, SI 2008/948, art 3(1), Sch 1, Pt 2, para 162.

Para (1A): inserted by the European Economic Interest Grouping (Amendment) Regulations 2009, SI 2009/2399, regs 3, 11.

9–16 *((Pt III) outside the scope of this work.)*

PART IV
SUPPLEMENTAL PROVISIONS

17 *(Revoked by the European Economic Interest Grouping (Amendment) Regulations 2009, SI 2009/2399, regs 3, 18.)*

[13.9]

[18 Application of provisions of the Companies Acts

(1) The provisions of the Companies Acts specified in Schedule 4 to these Regulations apply to EEIGs, and their establishments, registered or in the process of being registered under these Regulations, as if they were companies formed and registered or in the process of being registered under [the 2006 Act].

(2) The provisions applied have effect with the following adaptations—

(a) any reference to the 1985 Act[, the 2006 Act] or the Companies Acts includes a reference to these Regulations;

(b) any reference to a registered office includes a reference to an official address;

[(ba) any reference to the register is to be read as a reference to the EEIG register;

(bb) any reference to an officer of a company is to be read as a reference to an officer of an EEIG, within the meaning of these Regulations;]

(c) any reference to a daily default fine shall be omitted.

(3) The provisions applied also have effect subject to any limitations mentioned in relation to those provisions in that Schedule.]

[(4) In this regulation "the EEIG register" means—

(a) the documents and particulars required to be kept by the registrar under these Regulations; and

(b) the records falling within section 1080(1) of the 2006 Act which relate to EEIGs or their establishments.

(5) This regulation does not affect the application of provisions of the Companies Acts to EEIGs or their establishments otherwise than by virtue of this regulation.]

NOTES

Substituted by the Companies Act 2006 (Consequential Amendments etc) Order 2008, SI 2008/948, art 3(1), Sch 1, Pt 2, para 163.

Para (1): words in square brackets substituted by the European Economic Interest Grouping (Amendment) Regulations 2009, SI 2009/2399, regs 3, 19(1), (2).

Para (2): words in square brackets inserted by SI 2009/2399, regs 3, 19(1), (3).

Paras (4), (5): added by SI 2009/2399, regs 3, 19(1), (4).

[13.10]

19 [Application of insolvency legislation]

(1) Part III of the Insolvency Act 1986 shall apply to EEIGs, and their establishments, registered under these Regulations [in England and Wales or Scotland], as if they were companies registered under [the 2006 Act].

[(1A) Part 4 of the Insolvency (Northern Ireland) Order 1989 shall apply to EEIGs, and their establishments, registered under these Regulations in Northern Ireland, as if they were companies registered under the 2006 Act.]

(2) Section 120 of the Insolvency Act 1986 shall apply to an EEIG, and its establishments, registered under these Regulations in Scotland, as if it were a company registered in Scotland the paid-up or credited as paid-up share capital of which did not exceed £120,000 and as if in that section any reference to the Company's registered office were a reference to the official address of the EEIG.

NOTES

Regulation heading: substituted by the European Economic Interest Grouping (Amendment) Regulations 2009, SI 2009/2399, regs 3, 20(1), (4).

Para (1): words in first pair of square brackets inserted, and words in second pair of square brackets substituted, by SI 2009/2399, regs 3, 20(1), (2).

Para (1A): inserted by SI 2009/2399, regs 3, 20(1), (3).

[13.11]

20 [Application of legislation relating to disqualification of directors]

[(1)] Where an EEIG is wound up as an unregistered company under Part V of the Insolvency Act 1986, the provisions of sections 1, 2, [4 to 7, 8, 9, 10, 11], 12(2), 15 to 17, 20 and 22 of, and Schedule 1 to, the Company Directors Disqualification Act 1986 shall apply in relation to the EEIG as if any reference to a director or past director of a company included a reference to a manager of the EEIG and any other person who has or has had control or management of the EEIG's business and the EEIG were a company as defined by section 22(2)(b) of that Act.

[(2) Where an EEIG is wound up as an unregistered company under Part 6 of the Insolvency (Northern Ireland) Order 1989 the provisions of Articles 2(2) to (6), 3, 5, 7 to 11, 13, 14, 15, 16(2), 19 to 21 and 23 of, and Schedule 1 to, the Company Directors Disqualification (Northern Ireland) Order 2002 shall apply in relation to the EEIG as if—

(a) any reference to a director or past director of a company included a reference to a manager of the EEIG and any other person who has or has had control or management of the EEIG's business; and

(b) the EEIG were a company as defined by Article 2(2) of that Order.]

NOTES

Regulation heading: substituted by the European Economic Interest Grouping (Amendment) Regulations 2009, SI 2009/2399, regs 3, 21(1), (5).

Para (1): numbered as such, and words in square brackets substituted, by SI 2009/2399, regs 3, 21(1)–(3).

Para (2): added by SI 2009/2399, regs 3, 21(1), (4).

[13.12]

21 Penalties

Nothing in these Regulations shall create any new criminal offence punishable to a greater extent than is permitted under paragraph 1(1)(d) of Schedule 2 to the European Communities Act 1972.

SCHEDULES

SCHEDULE 1
COUNCIL REGULATION (EEC) NO 2137/85 OF 25TH JULY 1985 ON THE EUROPEAN ECONOMIC INTEREST GROUPING (EEIG)

[13.13]

Articles 1–14 . . .

Article 15 1. Where the law applicable to a grouping by virtue of Article 2 provides for the nullity of that grouping, such nullity must be established or declared by judicial decision. However, the court to which the matter is referred must, where it is possible for the affairs of the grouping to be put in order, allow time to permit that to be done.

2. The nullity of a grouping shall entail its liquidation in accordance with the conditions laid down in Article 35.

3. A decision establishing or declaring the nullity of a grouping may be relied on as against third parties in accordance with the conditions laid down in Article 9(1).

Such a decision shall not of itself affect the validity of liabilities, owed by or to a grouping, which originated before it could be relied on as against third parties in accordance with the conditions laid down in the previous subparagraph.

Articles 16–23 . . .

Article 24 1. The members of a grouping shall have unlimited joint and several liability for its debts and other liabilities of whatever nature. National law shall determine the consequences of such liability.

2. Creditors may not proceed against a member for payment in respect of debts and other liabilities, in accordance with the conditions laid down in paragraph 1, before the liquidation of a grouping is concluded, unless they have first requested the grouping to pay and payment has not been made within an appropriate period.

Articles 25–27 . . .

Article 28 1. A member of a grouping shall cease to belong to it on death or when he no longer complies with the conditions laid down in Article 4(1).

In addition, a Member State may provide, for the purposes of its liquidation, winding up, insolvency or cessation of payments laws, that a member shall cease to be a member of any grouping at the moment determined by those laws.

2. In the event of the death of a natural person who is a member of a grouping, no person may become a member in his place except under the conditions laid down in the contract for the formation of the grouping or, failing that, with the unanimous agreement of the remaining members.

Article 29 As soon as a member ceases to belong to a grouping, the manager or managers must inform the other members of that fact; they must also take the steps required as listed in Articles 7 and 8. In addition, any person concerned may take those steps.

Article 30 Except where the contract for the formation of a grouping provides otherwise and without prejudice to the rights acquired by a person under Articles 22(1) or 28(2), a grouping shall continue to exist for the remaining members after a member has ceased to belong to it, in accordance with the conditions laid down in the contract for the formation of the grouping or determined by unanimous decision of the members in question.

Article 31 1. A grouping may be wound up by a decision of its members ordering its winding up. Such a decision shall be taken unanimously, unless otherwise laid down in the contract for the formation of the grouping.

2. A grouping must be wound up by a decision of its members—

(a) noting the expiry of the period fixed in the contract for the formation of the grouping or the existence of any other cause for winding up provided for in the contract, or

(b) noting the accomplishment of the grouping's purpose or the impossibility of pursuing it further.

Where, three months after one of the situations referred to in the first subparagraph has occurred, a members' decision establishing the winding up of the grouping has not been taken, any member may petition the court to order winding up.

3. A grouping must also be wound up by a decision of its members or of the remaining member when the conditions laid down in Article 4(2) are no longer fulfilled.

4. After a grouping has been wound up by decision of its members, the manager or managers must take the steps required as listed in Articles 7 and 8. In addition, any person concerned may take those steps.

Article 32 1. On application by any person concerned or by a competent authority, in the event of the infringement of Articles 3, 12 or 31(3), the court must order a grouping to be wound up, unless its affairs can be and are put in order before the court has delivered a substantive ruling.

2. On application by a member, the court may order a grouping to be wound up on just and proper grounds.

3. A Member State may provide that the court may, on application by a competent authority, order the winding up of a grouping which has its official address in the State to which that authority belongs, wherever the grouping acts in contravention of that State's public interest, if the law of that State provides for such a possibility in respect of registered companies or other legal bodies subject to it.

Article 33 When a member ceases to belong to a grouping for any reason other than the assignment of his rights in accordance with the conditions laid down in Article 22(1), the value of his rights and obligations shall be determined taking into account the assets and liabilities of the grouping as they stand when he ceases to belong to it.

The value of the rights and obligations of a departing member may not be fixed in advance.

Article 34 Without prejudice to Article 37(1), any member who ceases to belong to a grouping shall remain answerable, in accordance with the conditions laid down in Article 24, for the debts and other liabilities arising out of the grouping's activities before he ceased to be a member.

Article 35 1. The winding up of a grouping shall entail its liquidation.

2. The liquidation of a grouping and the conclusion of its liquidation shall be governed by national law.

3. A grouping shall retain its capacity, within the meaning of Article 1(2), until its liquidation is concluded.

4. The liquidator or liquidators shall take the steps required as listed in Articles 7 and 8.

Article 36 Groupings shall be subject to national laws governing insolvency and cessation of payments. The commencement of proceedings against a grouping on grounds of its insolvency or cessation of payments shall not by itself cause the commencement of such proceedings against its members.

Article 37 1. A period of limitation of five years after the publication, pursuant to Article 8, of notice of a member's ceasing to belong to a grouping shall be substituted for any longer period which may be laid down by the relevant national law for actions against that member in connection with debts and other liabilities arising out of the grouping's activities before he ceased to be a member.

2. A period of limitation of five years after the publication, pursuant to Article 8, of notice of the conclusion of the liquidation of a grouping shall be substituted for any longer period which may be laid down by the relevant national law for actions against a member of the grouping in connection with debts and other liabilities arising out of the grouping's activities.

Articles 38, 39 . . .

Article 40 The profits or losses resulting from the activities of a grouping shall be taxable only in the hands of its members.

Articles 41, 42 . . .

Article 43 This Regulation shall enter into force on the third day following its publication in the *Official Journal of the European Communities*.

It shall apply from 1 July 1989, with the exception of Articles 39, 41 and 42 which shall apply as from the entry into force of the Regulation.

This Regulation shall be binding in its entirety and directly applicable in all Member States.

NOTES

Arts 1–14, 16–23, 25–27, 38, 39, 41, 42: outside the scope of this work.

SCHEDULES 2, 3

(*Sch 2 revoked by the European Economic Interest Grouping and European Public Limited-Liability Company (Amendment) Regulations 2014, SI 2014/2382, regs 2, 10; Sch 3 outside the scope of this work.*)

SCHEDULE 4
PROVISIONS OF [COMPANIES ACTS] APPLYING TO EEIGS AND THEIR ESTABLISHMENTS

Regulation 18

[PART 1
PROVISIONS OF COMPANIES ACT 1985]

[13.14]

1–12. . . .

13. Part XVIII relating to floating charges and receivers (Scotland).

14–24. . . .

NOTES

Schedule heading: words in square brackets substituted by the Companies Act 2006 (Consequential Amendments etc) Order 2008, SI 2008/948, art 3(1), Sch 1, Pt 2, para 164(1), (2).

Part heading: inserted by SI 2008/948, art 3(1), Sch 1, Pt 2, para 164(1), (3).

Paras 1–12, 14–24: insofar as unrevoked, outside the scope of this work.

[PART 2
PROVISIONS OF COMPANIES ACT 2006

[13.15]

[25. . . .

26. Part 25 (company charges).

27. Section 993 (offence of fraudulent trading).

28–30. . . .

31. Section 1084 (records relating to companies that have been dissolved etc), as if subsection (4) were omitted.

32–36. . . .

37. Section 1112 (general false statement offence).

38–40. . . .]]

NOTES

Part 2 inserted by the Companies Act 2006 (Consequential Amendments etc) Order 2008, SI 2008/948, art 3(1), Sch 1, Pt 2, para 164(1), (5).

Paras 25–40: substituted for original paras 1, 2 by the European Economic Interest Grouping (Amendment) Regulations 2009, SI 2009/2399, regs 3, 23(1), (3).
Paras 25, 28–30, 32–36, 38–40: outside the scope of this work.

INSOLVENCY ACT 1986 (GUERNSEY) ORDER 1989

(SI 1989/2409)

NOTES

Made: 19 December 1989.
Authority: Insolvency Act 1986, s 442.
Commencement: 1 February 1990.

[13.16]
1
This Order may be cited as the Insolvency Act 1986 (Guernsey) Order 1989 and shall come into force on 1st February 1990.

[13.17]
2
Subsections (4), (5), (10) and (11) of section 426 of the Insolvency Act 1986 shall extend to the Bailiwick of Guernsey with the modifications specified in the Schedule to this Order.

SCHEDULE
MODIFICATIONS IN THE EXTENSION OF PROVISIONS OF THE INSOLVENCY ACT 1986 TO THE BAILIWICK OF GUERNSEY

Article 2

[13.18]
1. Any reference to any provision of section 426 of the Insolvency Act 1986 shall be construed as a reference to that provision as it has effect in the Bailiwick of Guernsey.

2. In subsections (4) and (5), for "United Kingdom" there shall be substituted "Bailiwick of Guernsey".

3. For paragraphs (a), (b) and (c) of subsection (10) there shall be substituted the following paragraphs:

"(a) in relation to Guernsey:
(i) Titres II to V of the Law entitled "Loi ayant rapport aux Débiteurs et à la Renonciation" of 1929;
(ii) the Ordinance entitled "Ordonnance relative à la Renonciation" of 1929;
(iii) articles LXXI to LXXXI of the Law entitled "Loi relative aux Sociétés Anonymes ou à Responsabilité Limitée" of 1908;
(iv) sections 1, 3(3) and 4(2) of the Law of Property (Miscellaneous Provisions) (Guernsey) Law 1979;
(v) the Preferred Debts (Guernsey) Law 1983;
(vi) sections 12 and 32 to 39 of the Insurance Business (Guernsey) Law 1986;
(vii) the rules of the customary law of Guernsey concerning persons who are unable to pay their judgment debts;
(viii) any enactment for the time being in force in Guernsey which amends, modifies, supplements or replaces any of those rules or provisions;

(b) in relation to Alderney:
(i) Part I of the Companies (Amendment) (Alderney) Law 1962;
(ii) the Preferred Debts (Guernsey) Law 1983;
(iii) sections 12, 32 to 39, 68(2) and 68(5) of the Insurance Business (Guernsey) Law 1986;
(iv) the rules of the customary law of Alderney concerning persons who are unable to pay their judgment debts;
(v) any enactment for the time being in force in Alderney which amends, modifies, supplements or replaces any of those rules or provisions;

(c) in relation to Sark:
(i) the rules of the customary law of Sark concerning persons who are unable to pay their judgment debts;
(ii) any enactment for the time being in force in Sark which amends, modifies, supplements or replaces any of those rules;".

4. For paragraphs (a) and (b) of subsection (11) there shall be substituted "the United Kingdom, the Bailiwick of Jersey or the Isle of Man".

CO-OPERATION OF INSOLVENCY COURTS (DESIGNATION OF RELEVANT COUNTRIES) ORDER 1996

(SI 1996/253)

NOTES

Made: 8 February 1996.

Authority: Insolvency Act 1986, s 426(11).

Commencement: 1 March 1996.

Application: this Order is applied to limited liability partnerships with such modifications as the context requires for the purpose of giving effect to the provisions of the Insolvency Act 1986, by the Limited Liability Partnerships Regulations 2001, SI 2001/1090, reg 10, Sch 6, Pt II at **[10.38]**, **[10.43]**.

[13.19]
1

This Order may be cited as the Co-operation of Insolvency Courts (Designation of Relevant Countries) Order 1996 and shall come into force on 1st March 1996.

[13.20]
2

The countries specified in the Schedule to this Order are hereby designated relevant countries for the purposes of section 426 of the Insolvency Act 1986.

SCHEDULE
RELEVANT COUNTRIES

Article 2

[13.21]
Malaysia

Republic of South Africa

CO-OPERATION OF INSOLVENCY COURTS (DESIGNATION OF RELEVANT COUNTRY) ORDER 1998

(SI 1998/2766)

NOTES

Made: 11 November 1998.

Authority: Insolvency Act 1986, s 426(11).

Commencement: 11 December 1998.

Application: this Order is applied to limited liability partnerships with such modifications as the context requires for the purpose of giving effect to the provisions of the Insolvency Act 1986, by the Limited Liability Partnerships Regulations 2001, SI 2001/1090, reg 10, Sch 6, Pt II at **[10.38]**, **[10.43]**.

[13.22]
1

This Order may be cited as the Co-operation of Insolvency Courts (Designation of Relevant Country) Order 1998 and shall come into force on 11th December 1998.

[13.23]
2

Brunei Darussalam is hereby designated a relevant country for the purposes of section 426 of the Insolvency Act 1986.

PART 14
STATUTORY INSTRUMENTS RELATING TO DIRECTORS DISQUALIFICATION—ENGLAND AND WALES

COMPANIES (DISQUALIFICATION ORDERS) REGULATIONS 1986

(SI 1986/2067)

NOTES

Made: 27 November 1986.

Authority: Companies Act 1985, s 301; Company Directors Disqualification Act 1986, s 18.

Commencement: 29 December 1986.

Revoked by the Companies (Disqualification Orders) Regulations 2001, SI 2001/967, regs 3, 4, as from 6 April 2001, in relation to (i) any disqualification order made after that date, (ii) any grant of leave made after that date, or (iii) any action taken by a court after that date in consequence of which a disqualification order or undertaking is varied or ceases to be in force (whether the disqualification order or undertaking to which the grant of leave or the action relates was made by the court or accepted by the Secretary of State before or after that date) and reproduced here for reference.

Application: these regulations are applied, with such modifications as the context requires for the purpose of giving effect to the provisions of the Insolvency Act 1986, by the Limited Liability Partnerships Regulations 2001, SI 2001/1090, reg 10, Sch 6, Pt II at **[10.38]**, **[10.43]**.

[14.1]

1 Citation, commencement and interpretation

(1) These Regulations may be cited as the Companies (Disqualification Orders) Regulations 1986 and shall come into operation on 29th December 1986.

(2) In these Regulations—

"the Act" means the Company Directors Disqualification Act 1986;

"disqualification order" means an order of the court under any of sections 2 to 6, 8 and 10 of the Act;

"grant of leave" means a grant by the court of leave under section 17 of the Act to any person in relation to a disqualification order.

NOTES

Revoked as noted at the beginning of these Regulations.

2 (Revokes the Companies (Register of Disqualification Orders) (Fee) Regulations 1977, SI 1977/776, and the Companies (Disqualification Orders) Regulations 1985, SI 1985/829.)

[14.2]

3 Particulars to be furnished by officers of the court

These Regulations apply in relation to a disqualification order made after the coming into operation of these Regulations and to a grant of leave, or any action taken by a court in consequence of which a disqualification order is varied or ceases to be in force, made or taken after that date, in relation to a disqualification order made before, on or after that date.

NOTES

Revoked as noted at the beginning of these Regulations.

[14.3]

4

(1) The following officers of the court shall furnish to the Secretary of State the particulars specified in Regulation 5(a) to (c) below in the form and manner there specified—

- *(a) where a disqualification order is made by the Crown Court, the Chief Clerk;*
- *(b) where a disqualification order or grant of leave is made by the High Court, the Chief Clerk;*
- *(c) where a disqualification order or grant of leave is made by a county court, the Chief Clerk;*
- *(d) where a disqualification order is made by a magistrates' court, the Clerk to the Justices;*
- *(e) where a disqualification order is made by the High Court of Justiciary, the Deputy Principal Clerk of Justiciary;*
- *(f) where a disqualification order or grant of leave is made by a sheriff court, the sheriff clerk; and*
- *(g) where a disqualification order or grant of leave is made by the Court of Session, the Deputy Principal Clerk of Session.*

(2) Where a disqualification order made by any of the courts mentioned in paragraph (1) above and subsequently any action is taken by a court in consequence of which that order is varied or ceases to be in force, the officer of the first-mentioned court specified in paragraph (1) above shall furnish to the Secretary of State the particulars specified in Regulation 5(d) below in the form and manner there specified.

NOTES

Revoked as noted at the beginning of these Regulations.

[14.4]

5

The form in which the particulars are to be furnished is—

- *(a) that set out in Schedule 1 to these Regulations with such variations as circumstances require when the person against whom the disqualification order is made is an individual, and the particulars contained therein are the particulars specified for that purpose;*

(b) *that set out in Schedule 2 to these Regulations with such variations as circumstances require when the person against whom the disqualification order is made is a body corporate, and the particulars contained therein are the particulars specified for that purpose;*

(c) *that set out in Schedule 3 to these Regulations with such variations as circumstances require when a grant of leave is made by the court, and the particulars contained therein are the particulars specified for that purpose;*

(d) *that set out in Schedule 4 to these Regulations with such variations as circumstances require when any action is taken by a court in consequence of which a disqualification order is varied or ceases to be in force, and the particulars contained therein are the particulars specified for that purpose.*

NOTES

Revoked as noted at the beginning of these Regulations.

[14.5]

6

The time within which a prescribed officer is to furnish the Secretary of State with the said particulars shall be a period of fourteen days beginning with the day on which the disqualification order or grant of leave is made, or any action is taken by a court in consequence of which the disqualification order is varied or ceases to be in force, as the case may be.

NOTES

Revoked as noted at the beginning of these Regulations.

SCHEDULES 1–4

NOTES

Schs 1–4 contain forms. The forms themselves are not set out in this work, but their numbers and titles are listed below.

[14.6]

FORM NO	*TITLE*
[DO1	*Disqualification order against an individual*
[DO1	*Disqualification order against an individual (alternative form)]*
DO2	*Disqualification order against a body corporate*
DO3	*Grant of leave in relation to a disqualification order*
DO4	*Variation or cessation of a disqualification order]*

NOTES

Revoked as noted at the beginning of these Regulations.

Forms DO1–DO4 substituted by the Companies (Disqualification Orders) (Amendment) Regulations 1995, SI 1995/1509, reg 3, Schedule; Form DO1 (alternative form) inserted by the Companies (Disqualification Orders) (Amendment) Regulations 2002, SI 2002/689, reg 3, Schedule.

INSOLVENT COMPANIES (DISQUALIFICATION OF UNFIT DIRECTORS) PROCEEDINGS RULES 1987

(SI 1987/2023)

NOTES

Made: 25 November 1987.

Authority: Insolvency Act 1986, s 411; Company Directors Disqualification Act 1986, s 21.

Commencement: 11 January 1988.

Application: these Rules are applied to limited liability partnerships with such modifications as the context requires for the purpose of giving effect to the provisions of the Insolvency Act 1986, by the Limited Liability Partnerships Regulations 2001, SI 2001/1090, reg 10, Sch 6, Pt III at **[10.38]**, **[10.44]**, and applied, with modifications, in so far as they relate to bank insolvency or administration under the Banking Act 2009, Pts 2, 3, by the Banking Act 2009 (Parts 2 and 3 Consequential Amendments) Order 2009, SI 2009/317, art 3, Schedule at **[7.86]**, **[7.92]**.

ARRANGEMENT OF RULES

1 Citation, commencement and interpretation . . . . . [14.7]
2 Form and conduct of applications . . . . . [14.8]
2A Application of Rules 3 to 8 . . . . . [14.9]
3 The case against the defendant . . . . . [14.10]
4 Endorsement on claim form . . . . . [14.11]
5 Service and acknowledgement . . . . . [14.12]
6 Evidence . . . . . [14.13]
7 The hearing of the application . . . . . [14.14]

8 Making and setting aside of disqualification order . . . .[14.15]
10 Right of audience . . . .[14.16]
11 Revocation and saving. . . . .[14.17]

[14.7]

1 Citation, commencement and interpretation

(1) These Rules may be cited as the Insolvent Companies (Disqualification of Unfit Directors) Proceedings Rules 1987 and shall come into force on 11th January 1988.

[(2) In these Rules—

(a) "the Companies Act" means the Companies Act 1985,

(b) "the Company Directors Disqualification Act" means the Company Directors Disqualification Act 1986,

(c) "CPR" followed by a Part or rule by number means that Part or rule with that number in the Civil Procedure Rules 1998,

(d) "practice direction" means a direction as to the practice and procedure of any court within the scope of the Civil Procedure Rules,

[(e) "registrar" has the same meaning as in rule 1.2(2) of the Insolvency (England and Wales) Rules 2016, and]

(f) "file in court" means deliver to the court for filing.]

[(3) These Rules apply to an application made under the Company Directors Disqualification Act on or after 6th August 2007—

(a) for leave to commence proceedings for a disqualification order after the end of the period mentioned in section 7(2) of that Act;

(b) to enforce any duty arising under section 7(4) of that Act;

(c) for a disqualification order where made—

(i) by the Secretary of State or the official receiver under section 7(1) of that Act (disqualification of unfit directors of insolvent companies);

[(ii) by the Secretary of State under section 5A (disqualification for certain convictions abroad), 8 (disqualification of director on finding of unfitness), 8ZB (Application for order under section 8ZA) or 8ZD (order disqualifying person instructing unfit director: other cases) of that Act;]

(iii) by the [Competition and Markets Authority] or a specified regulator under section 9A of that Act (competition disqualification order);

(d) under section 8A of that Act (variation etc. of disqualification undertaking); or—

(e) for leave to act under—

(i) section 1A(1) or 9B(4) of that Act (and section 17 of that Act as it applies for the purposes of either of those sections); or

(ii) sections 1 and 17 as they apply for the purposes of section [5A,] 6, 7(1), 8, [8ZA, 8ZC, 8ZD, 8ZE,] 9A or 10 of that Act.]

NOTES

Para (2): substituted by the Insolvent Companies (Disqualification of Unfit Directors) Proceedings (Amendment) Rules 1999, SI 1999/1023, r 3, Schedule, para 2; sub-para (e) substituted by the Insolvency (England and Wales) Rules 2016 (Consequential Amendments and Savings) Rules 2017, SI 2017/369, r 2(2), Sch 2, para 3(1), (2).

Para (3): substituted by the Insolvent Companies (Disqualification of Unfit Directors) Proceedings (Amendment) Rules 2007, SI 2007/1906, r 2, except in relation to any application made before 6 August 2007. Before substitution, para (3) (as amended by SI 1999/1023, SI 2003/1367) read as follows:

"(3) These Rules apply with respect to an application for a disqualification order against any person ("the [defendant]"), where made—

(a) by the Secretary of State or the official receiver under section 7(1) of the Company Directors Disqualification Act (on the grounds of the person's unfitness to be concerned in the management of a company), or

(b) by the Secretary of State under section 8 of that Act (alleged expedient in the public interest, following report of inspectors under section 437 of the Companies Act, or information or documents obtained under section 447 or 448 of that Act), [or

(c) by the Office of Fair Trading or (as the case may be) a specified regulator under section 9A of that Act (breach of competition law by undertaking and unfitness to be concerned in the management of a company),]

on or after the date on which these Rules come into force.";

sub-para (c)(ii) substituted and figures in square brackets in sub-para (e)(ii) inserted by the Small Business, Enterprise and Employment Act 2015 (Consequential Amendments) (Insolvency and Company Directors Disqualification) Regulations 2015, SI 2015/1651, reg 2(1)–(3); words in square brackets in sub-para (c)(iii) substituted by the Enterprise and Regulatory Reform Act 2013 (Competition) (Consequential, Transitional and Saving Provisions) (No 2) Order 2014, SI 2014/549, art 2, Sch 1, Pt 2, para 24 (for transitional provisions in relation to the continuity of functions, etc, see art 3 of the 2014 Order).

[14.8]

[2 Form and conduct of applications

(1) The Civil Procedure Rules 1998, and any relevant practice direction, apply in respect of any application to which these Rules apply, except where these Rules make provision to inconsistent effect.

[(2) Subject to paragraph (5), an application shall be made either—

(a) by claim form as provided by the relevant practice direction and the claimant must use the CPR Part 8 (alternative procedure for claims) procedure, or

(b) by application notice as provided for by the relevant practice direction.]

(3) CPR rule 8.1(3) (power of the court to order the claim to continue as if the claimant had not used the Part 8 procedure), CPR rule 8.2 (contents of the claim form) and CPR rule 8.7 (Part 20 claims) do not apply.

[(4) Rule 12.59 (appeals and reviews of court orders in corporate insolvency) and rule 12.62 (procedure on appeal) of the Insolvency (England and Wales) Rules 2016 apply.]

[(5) [The Insolvency (England and Wales) Rules 2016] shall apply to an application to enforce any duty arising under section 7(4) of the Company Directors Disqualification Act . . .]]

NOTES

Substituted by the Insolvent Companies (Disqualification of Unfit Directors) Proceedings (Amendment) Rules 1999, SI 1999/1023, r 3, Schedule, para 3.

Para (2): substituted by the Insolvent Companies (Disqualification of Unfit Directors) Proceedings (Amendment) Rules 2007, SI 2007/1906, r 3(1), (2), except in relation to any application made before 6 August 2007, and previously read as follows:

"(2) An application shall be made by claim form as provided by the relevant practice direction and the claimant must use the CPR Part 8 (alternative procedure for claims) procedure.".

Para (4): substituted by the Insolvency (England and Wales) Rules 2016 (Consequential Amendments and Savings) Rules 2017, SI 2017/369, r 2(2), Sch 2, para 3(1), (3)(a).

Para (5): added by SI 2007/1906, r 3(1), (3), except in relation to any application made before 6 August 2007; words in square brackets substituted by SI 2017/369, r 2(2), Sch 2, para 3(1), (3)(b); words omitted revoked by the Deregulation Act 2015 (Insolvency) (Consequential Amendments and Transitional and Savings Provisions) Order 2015, SI 2015/1641, art 6, Sch 3, para 4.

[14.9]

[2A Application of Rules 3 to 8

Rules 3 to 8 only apply to the types of application referred to in Rule 1(3)(c).]

NOTES

Inserted by the Insolvent Companies (Disqualification of Unfit Directors) Proceedings (Amendment) Rules 2007, SI 2007/1906, r 4, except in relation to any application made before 6 August 2007.

[14.10]

3 The case against the [defendant]

(1) There shall, at the time when the [claim form] is issued, be filed in court evidence in support of the application for a disqualification order; and copies of the evidence shall be served with the [claim form] on the [defendant].

(2) The evidence shall be by one or more affidavits, except where the [claimant] is the official receiver, in which case it may be in the form of a written report (with or without affidavits by other persons) which shall be treated as if it had been verified by affidavit by him and shall be prima facie evidence of any matter contained in it.

(3) There shall in the affidavit or affidavits or (as the case may be) the official receiver's report be included a statement of the matters by reference to which the [defendant] is alleged to be unfit to be concerned in the management of a company.

NOTES

Words in square brackets substituted by the Insolvent Companies (Disqualification of Unfit Directors) Proceedings (Amendment) Rules 1999, SI 1999/1023, r 3, Schedule, para 1.

[14.11]

4 Endorsement on [claim form]

There shall on the [claim form] be endorsed information to the [defendant] as follows—

(a) that the application is made in accordance with these Rules;

(b) that, in accordance with the relevant enactments, the court has power to impose disqualifications as follows—

(i) where the application is under section 7 [or 8ZB] of the Company Directors Disqualification Act, for a period of not less than 2, and up to 15, years; and

(ii) where the application is [under section [5A,] 8[, 8ZD] or 9A of that Act], for a period of up to 15 years;

(c) that the application for a disqualification order may, in accordance with these Rules, be heard and determined summarily, without further or other notice to the [defendant], and that, if it is so heard and determined, the court may impose disqualification for a period of up to 5 years;

(d) that if at the hearing of the application the court, on the evidence then before it, is minded to impose, in the [defendant's] case, disqualification for any period longer than 5 years, it will not make a disqualification order on that occasion but will adjourn the application to be heard (with further evidence, if any) at a later date to be notified; and

(e) that any evidence which the [defendant] wishes to be taken into consideration by the court must be filed in court in accordance with the time limits imposed under Rule 6 (the provisions of which shall be set out on the [claim form]).

NOTES

Words in square brackets in para (b)(i) inserted and figures in second and third (inner) pairs of square brackets in para (b)(ii) inserted, by the Small Business, Enterprise and Employment Act 2015 (Consequential Amendments) (Insolvency and Company Directors Disqualification) Regulations 2015, SI 2015/1651, reg 2(1), (4), (5).

Words in first (outer) pair of square brackets in para (b)(ii) substituted by the Insolvent Companies (Disqualification of Unfit Directors) Proceedings (Amendment) Rules 2003, SI 2003/1367, r 3, Schedule, para 2.

All other words in square brackets substituted by the Insolvent Companies (Disqualification of Unfit Directors) Proceedings (Amendment) Rules 1999, SI 1999/1023, r 3, Schedule, para 1.

[14.12]

5 Service and acknowledgement

(1) The [claim form] shall be served on the [defendant] by sending it by first class post to his last known address; and the date of service shall, unless the contrary is shown, be deemed to be the 7th day next following that on which the [claim form] was posted.

(2) Where any process or order of the court or other document is required under proceedings subject to these Rules to be served on any person who is not in England and Wales, the court may order service on him of that process or order or other document to be effected within such time and in such manner as it thinks fit, and may also require such proof of service as it thinks fit.

[(3) The claim form served on the defendant shall be accompanied by an acknowledgment of service as provided for by practice direction and CPR rule 8.3(2) (dealing with the contents of an acknowledgment of service) does not apply.]

(4) The . . . acknowledgement of service shall state that the [defendant] should indicate—

- (a) whether he contests the application on the grounds that, in the case of any particular company—
  - (i) he was not a director or shadow director of the company at a time when conduct of his, or of other persons, in relation to that company is in question, or
  - (ii) his conduct as director or shadow director of that company was not as alleged in support of the application for a disqualification order,
- (b) whether, in the case of any conduct of his, he disputes the allegation that such conduct makes him unfit to be concerned in the management of a company, and
- (c) whether he, while not resisting the application for a disqualification order, intends to adduce mitigating factors with a view to justifying only a short period of disqualification.

NOTES

Para (1): words in square brackets substituted by the Insolvent Companies (Disqualification of Unfit Directors) Proceedings (Amendment) Rules 1999, SI 1999/1023, r 3, Schedule, para 1.

Para (3): substituted by SI 1999/1023, r 3, Schedule, para 4(1).

Para (4): words omitted revoked, and word in square brackets substituted, by SI 1999/1023, r 3, Schedule, paras 1, 4(2).

[14.13]

6 Evidence

(1) The [defendant] shall, within 28 days from the date of service of the [claim form], file in court any affidavit evidence in opposition to the application he wishes the court to take into consideration and shall forthwith serve upon the [claimant] a copy of such evidence.

(2) The [claimant] shall, within 14 days from receiving the copy of the [defendant's] evidence, file in court any further evidence in reply he wishes the court to take into consideration and shall forthwith serve a copy of that evidence upon the [defendant].

[(3) CPR rules 8.5 (filing and serving written evidence) and 8.6(1) (requirements where written evidence is to be relied on) do not apply.]

NOTES

Paras (1), (2): words in square brackets substituted by the Insolvent Companies (Disqualification of Unfit Directors) Proceedings (Amendment) Rules 1999, SI 1999/1023, r 3, Schedule, para 1.

Para (3): added by SI 1999/1023, r 3, Schedule, para 5.

[14.14]

7 The hearing of the application

[(1) When the claim form is issued, the court will fix a date for the first hearing of the claim which shall not be less than 8 weeks from the date of issue of the claim form.]

(2) The hearing shall in the first instance be before the registrar in open court.

(3) The registrar shall either determine the case on the date fixed or adjourn it.

(4) The registrar shall adjourn the case for further consideration if—

- (a) he forms the provisional opinion that a disqualification order ought to be made, and that a period of disqualification longer than 5 years is appropriate, or
- (b) he is of opinion that questions of law or fact arise which are not suitable for summary determination.

(5) If the registrar adjourns the case for further consideration he shall—

- (a) direct whether the case is to be heard by a registrar or, if he thinks it appropriate, by the judge, for determination by him;
- (b) state the reasons for the adjournment; and

(c) give directions as to the following matters—
  (i) the manner in which and the time within which notice of the adjournment and the reasons for it are to be given to the [defendant],
  (ii) the filing in court and the service of further evidence (if any) by the parties,
  (iii) such other matters as the registrar thinks necessary or expedient with a view to an expeditious disposal of the application, and
  (v) the time and place of the adjourned hearing.

(6) Where a case is adjourned other than to the judge, it may be heard by the registrar who originally dealt with the case or by another registrar.

NOTES

Para (1): substituted by the Insolvent Companies (Disqualification of Unfit Directors) Proceedings (Amendment) Rules 1999, SI 1999/1023, r 3, Schedule, para 6.

Para (5): word in square brackets substituted by SI 1999/1023, r 3, Schedule, para 1.

[14.15]

8 Making and setting aside of disqualification order

(1) The court may make a disqualification order against the [defendant], whether or not the latter appears, and whether or not he has completed and returned the acknowledgement of service of the [claim form], or filed evidence in accordance with Rule 6.

(2) Any disqualification order made in the absence of the [defendant] may be set aside or varied by the court on such terms as it thinks just.

NOTES

Words in square brackets substituted by the Insolvent Companies (Disqualification of Unfit Directors) Proceedings (Amendment) Rules 1999, SI 1999/1023, r 3, Schedule, para 1.

9 (*Revoked by the Insolvent Companies (Disqualification of Unfit Directors) Proceedings (Amendment) Rules 2001, SI 2001/765, r 2.*)

[14.16]

10 Right of audience

Official receivers and deputy official receivers have right of audience in any proceedings to which these Rules apply, whether the application is made by the Secretary of State or by the official receiver at his direction, and whether made in the High Court or a county court.

[14.17]

11 Revocation and saving

(1) . . .

(2) Notwithstanding paragraph (1) the former Rules shall continue to apply and have effect in relation to any application described in paragraph 3(a) or (b) of Rule 1 of these Rules made before the date on which these Rules come into force.

NOTES

Para (1): revokes the Insolvent Companies (Disqualification of Unfit Directors) Proceedings Rules 1986, SI 1986/612.

INSOLVENT COMPANIES (REPORTS ON CONDUCT OF DIRECTORS) RULES 1996

(SI 1996/1909)

NOTES

Made: 22 July 1996.

Authority: Insolvency Act 1986, s 411; Company Directors Disqualification Act 1986, s 21(2).

Commencement: 30 September 1996.

Revocation: these Rules are revoked by the Insolvent Companies (Reports on Conduct of Directors) (England and Wales) Rules 2016, SI 2016/180, r 2(a), as from 6 April 2016, subject to transitional and savings provisions in r 10 thereof at **[14.50]**.

Application: these Rules are applied to limited liability partnerships with such modifications as the context requires for the purpose of giving effect to the provisions of the Insolvency Act 1986, by the Limited Liability Partnerships Regulations 2001, SI 2001/1090, reg 10, Sch 6, Pt III at **[10.38]**, **[10.44]**, and applied, with modifications, in so far as they relate to bank insolvency or administration under the Banking Act 2009, Pts 2, 3, by the Banking Act 2009 (Parts 2 and 3 Consequential Amendments) Order 2009, SI 2009/317, art 3, Schedule at **[7.86]**, **[7.92]**.

ARRANGEMENT OF RULES

1 Citation and commencement and interpretation . . . [14.18]
3 Reports required under section 7(3) of the Act . . . [14.19]
4 Return by office-holder . . . [14.20]
5 Forms . . . [14.21]
6 Enforcement of section 7(4) . . . [14.22]
7 Transitional and saving provisions . . . [14.23]

SCHEDULES

Schedule—Forms . . . .[14.24]

[14.18]

1 Citation, commencement and interpretation

(1) These Rules may be cited as the Insolvent Companies (Reports on Conduct of Directors) Rules 1996.

(2) These Rules shall come into force on 30th September 1996.

(3) In these Rules—

"the Act" means the Company Directors Disqualification Act 1986;

"the former Rules" means the Insolvent Companies (Reports on Conduct of Directors) No 2 Rules 1986; and

"the commencement date" means 30th September 1996.

NOTES

Revoked as noted at the beginning of these Rules.

2 (Revokes (subject to r 7 below) the Insolvent Companies (Reports on Conduct of Directors) No 2 Rules 1986, SI 1986/2134.)

[14.19]

3 Reports required under section 7(3) of the Act

(1) This rule applies to any report made to the Secretary of State under section 7(3) of the Act by—

(a) the liquidator of a company which the courts in England and Wales have jurisdiction to wind up which passes a resolution for voluntary winding up on or after the commencement date;

(b) an administrative receiver of a company appointed otherwise than under section 51 of the Insolvency Act 1986 (power to appoint receiver under the law of Scotland) on or after the commencement date; or

(c) the administrator of a company which the courts in England and Wales have jurisdiction to wind up [which enters administration] on or after the commencement date.

(2) Such a report shall be made in the Form D1 set out in the Schedule hereto, or in a form which is substantially similar, and in the manner and to the extent required by the Form D1.

NOTES

Revoked as noted at the beginning of these Rules.

Para (1): words in square brackets substituted for words "in relation to which the court makes an administration order" by the Enterprise Act 2002 (Insolvency) Order 2003, SI 2003/2096, arts 5, 6, Schedule, paras 68, 69, except in any case where a petition for an administration order was presented before 15 September 2003.

[14.20]

4 Return by office-holder

(1) This rule applies where it appears to a liquidator of a company as mentioned in rule 3(1)(a), to an administrative receiver as mentioned in rule 3(1)(b), or to an administrator as mentioned in rule 3(1)(c) (each of whom is referred to hereinafter as "an office-holder") that the company has at any time become insolvent within the meaning of section 6(2) of the Act.

(2) Subject as follows there may be furnished to the Secretary of State by an office-holder at any time during the period of 6 months from the relevant date (defined in paragraph (4) below) a return with respect to every person who—

(a) was, on the relevant date, a director or shadow director of the company, or

(b) had been a director or shadow director of the company at any time in the 3 years immediately preceding that date.

(3) The return shall be made in the Form D2 set out in the Schedule hereto, or in a form which is substantially similar, and in the manner and to the extent required by the Form D2.

(4) For the purposes of this rule, "the relevant date" means—

(a) in the case of a company in creditors' voluntary winding up (there having been no declaration of solvency by the directors under section 89 of the Insolvency Act 1986), the date of the passing of the resolution for voluntary winding up,

(b) in the case of a company in members' voluntary winding up, the date on which the liquidator forms the opinion that, at the time when the company went into liquidation, its assets were insufficient for the payment of its debts and other liabilities and the expenses of winding up,

(c) in the case of the administrative receiver, the date of his appointment,

(d) in the case of the administrator, the date [that the company enters administration],

and for the purposes of sub-paragraph (c) above the only appointment of an administrative receiver to be taken into account in determining the relevant date shall be that appointment which is not that of a successor in office to an administrative receiver who has vacated office either by death or pursuant to section 45 of the Insolvency Act 1986.

(5) Subject to paragraph (6) below, it shall be the duty of an office-holder to furnish a return complying with the provisions of paragraphs (3) and (4) of this rule to the Secretary of State—

(a) where he is in office in relation to the company on the day one week before the expiry of the period of 6 months from the relevant date, not later than the expiry of such period;

(b) where he vacates office (otherwise than by death) before the day one week before the expiry of the period of 6 months from the relevant date, within 14 days after his vacation of office except where he has furnished such a return on or prior to the day one week before the expiry of such period.

(6) A return need not be provided under this rule by an office-holder if he has, whilst holding that office in relation to the company, since the relevant date, made a report under rule 3 with respect to all persons falling within paragraph (2) of this rule and (apart from this paragraph) required to be the subject of a return.

(7) If an office-holder without reasonable excuse fails to comply with the duty imposed by paragraph (5) of this rule, he is guilty of an offence and—

(a) on summary conviction of the offence, is liable to a fine not exceeding level 3 on the standard scale, and

(b) after continued contravention, is liable to a daily default fine; that is to say, he is liable on a second or subsequent summary conviction of the offence to a fine of one-tenth of level 3 on the standard scale for each day on which the contravention is continued (instead of the penalty specified in sub-paragraph (a)).

(8) Section 431 of the Insolvency Act 1986 (summary proceedings), as it applies to England and Wales, has effect in relation to an offence under this rule as to offences under Parts I to VII of that Act.

NOTES

Revoked as noted at the beginning of these Rules.

Para (4): words in square brackets substituted for words "of the administration order made in relation to the company" by the Enterprise Act 2002 (Insolvency) Order 2003, SI 2003/2096, arts 5, 6, Schedule, paras 68, 70, except in any case where a petition for an administration order was presented before 15 September 2003.

[14.21]
5 Forms

The forms referred to in rule 3(2) and rule 4(3) shall be used with such variations, if any, as the circumstances may require.

NOTES

Revoked as noted at the beginning of these Rules.

[14.22]
6 Enforcement of section 7(4)

(1) This rule applies where under section 7(4) of the Act (power to call on liquidators, former liquidators and others to provide information) the Secretary of State or the official receiver requires or has required a person—

(a) to furnish him with information with respect to a person's conduct as director or shadow director of a company, and

(b) to produce and permit inspection of relevant books, papers and other records.

(2) On the application of the Secretary of State or (as the case may be) the official receiver, the court may make an order directing compliance within such period as may be specified.

(3) The court's order may provide that all costs of and incidental to the application shall be borne by the person to whom the order is directed.

NOTES

Revoked as noted at the beginning of these Rules.

[14.23]
7 Transitional and saving provisions

(1) Subject to paragraph (2) below, rules 3 and 4 of the former Rules shall continue to apply as if the former Rules had not been revoked when any of the events mentioned in sub-paragraphs (a), (b) or (c) of rule 3(1) of the former Rules (passing of resolution for voluntary winding up, appointment of administrative receiver, making of administration order) occurred on or after 29th December 1986 but before the commencement date.

(2) Until 31st December 1996—

(a) the forms contained in the Schedule to the former Rules which were required to be used for the purpose of complying with those Rules, or

(b) the Form D1 or D2 as set out in the Schedule to these Rules, as appropriate, or a form which is substantially similar thereto, with such variations, if any, as the circumstances may require,

may be used for the purpose of complying with rules 3 and 4 of the former Rules as applied by paragraph (1) above; but after that date the forms mentioned in sub-paragraph (b) of this paragraph shall be used for that purpose.

(3) When a period referred to in rule 5(2) of the former Rules is current immediately before the commencement date, these Rules have effect as if rule 6(2) of these Rules had been in force when the period began and the period is deemed to expire whenever it would have expired if these Rules had not been made and any right, obligation or power dependent on the beginning, duration or end of such period shall be under rule 6(2) of these Rules as it was or would have been under the said rule 5(2).

(4) The provisions of this rule are to be without prejudice to the operation of section 16 of the Interpretation Act 1978 (saving from repeals) as it is applied by section 23 of that Act.

NOTES

Revoked as noted at the beginning of these Rules.

SCHEDULE
FORMS

[14.24]

NOTES

This Schedule contains forms. The forms themselves are not reproduced in this work, but their numbers and titles are listed below.

FORM NO	*TITLE*
[D1	*Report under section 7(3) of the Company Directors Disqualification Act 1986*
D2	*Return by Office-Holder under rule 4 of the Insolvent Companies (Reports on Conduct of Directors) Rules 1996]*

NOTES

Revoked as noted at the beginning of these Rules.

Substituted by the Insolvent Companies (Reports on Conduct of Directors) (Amendment) Rules 2001, SI 2001/764, r 2, Schedule.

COMPANIES (DISQUALIFICATION ORDERS) REGULATIONS 2001

(SI 2001/967)

NOTES

Made: 13 March 2001.

Authority: Company Directors Disqualification Act 1986, s 18.

Commencement: 6 April 2001.

These Regulations are revoked by the Companies (Disqualification Orders) Regulations 2009, SI 2009/2471, reg 3(a), as from 1 October 2009, subject to transitional provisions in reg 4 thereof at **[14.35]**.

ARRANGEMENT OF REGULATIONS

1 Citation and commencement . . . . . [14.25]
2 Definitions . . . . . [14.26]
4 Transitional provisions . . . . . [14.27]
5 . . . . . [14.28]
6–8 Particulars to be furnished by officers of the court . . . . . [14.29]–[14.31]
9 Extension of certain of the provisions of section 18 of the Act to orders made and leave granted in Northern Ireland . . . . . [14.32]

[14.25]

1 Citation and commencement

These Regulations may be cited as the Companies (Disqualification Orders) Regulations 2001 and shall come into force on 6th April 2001.

NOTES

Revoked as noted at the beginning of these Regulations.

[14.26]

2 Definitions

In these Regulations:

"the Act" means the Company Directors Disqualification Act 1986;

"disqualification order" means an order of the court under any of sections 2 to 6, 8, and 10 of the Act;

"disqualification undertaking" means an undertaking accepted by the Secretary of State under section 7 or 8 of the Act;

"grant of leave" means a grant by the court of leave under section 17 of the Act to any person in relation to a disqualification order or a disqualification undertaking.

NOTES

Revoked as noted at the beginning of these Regulations.

3 (Revokes the Companies (Disqualification Orders) Regulations 1986, SI 1986/2067.)

[14.27]
4 Transitional provisions

Other than regulation 9, these regulations apply in relation to:

- *(a) a disqualification order made after the coming into force of these Regulations; and*
- *(b)*
  - *(i) a grant of leave made after the coming into force of these Regulations; or*
  - *(ii) any action taken by a court after the coming into force of these Regulations in consequence of which a disqualification order or a disqualification undertaking is varied or ceases to be in force,*

whether the disqualification order or disqualification undertaking to which, as the case may be, the grant of leave or the action relates was made by the court or accepted by the Secretary of State before or after the coming into force of these Regulations.

NOTES

Revoked as noted at the beginning of these Regulations.

[14.28]
5

Regulation 9 applies to particulars of orders made and leave granted under Part II of the Companies (Northern Ireland) Order 1989 received by the Secretary of State after the coming into force of these Regulations other than particulars of orders made and leave granted under that Order which relate to disqualification orders made by the courts of Northern Ireland before 2 April 2001.

NOTES

Revoked as noted at the beginning of these Regulations.

[14.29]
6 Particulars to be furnished by officers of the court

(1) The following officers of the court shall furnish to the Secretary of State the particulars specified in Regulation 7(a) to (c) below in the form and manner there specified:

- *(a) where a disqualification order is made by the Crown Court, the Court Manager;*
- *(b) where a disqualification order or grant of leave is made by the High Court, the Court Manager;*
- *(c) where a disqualification order or grant of leave is made by a County Court, the Court Manager;*
- *(d) where a disqualification order is made by a Magistrates' Court, the Chief Executive to the Justices;*
- *(e) where a disqualification order is made by the High Court of Justiciary, the Deputy Principal Clerk of Justiciary;*
- *(f) where a disqualification order or grant of leave is made by a Sheriff Court, the Sheriff Clerk;*
- *(g) where a disqualification order or grant of leave is made by the Court of Session, the Deputy Principal Clerk of Session;*
- *(h) where a disqualification order or grant of leave is made by the Court of Appeal, the Court Manager; and*
- *(i) where a disqualification order or grant of leave is made by the House of Lords, the Judicial Clerk.*

(2) Where a disqualification order has been made by any of the courts mentioned in paragraph (1) above or a disqualification undertaking has been accepted by the Secretary of State, and subsequently any action is taken by a court in consequence of which, as the case may be, that order or that undertaking is varied or ceases to be in force, the officer specified in paragraph (1) above of the court which takes such action shall furnish to the Secretary of State the particulars specified in Regulation 7(d) below in the form and manner there specified.

NOTES

Revoked as noted at the beginning of these Regulations.

[14.30]
7

The form in which the particulars are to be furnished is:

- *(a) that set out in Schedule 1 to these Regulations with such variations as circumstances require when the person against whom the disqualification order is made is an individual, and the particulars contained therein are the particulars specified for that purpose;*
- *(b) that set out in Schedule 2 to these Regulations with such variations as circumstances require when the person against whom the disqualification order is made is a body corporate, and the particulars contained therein are the particulars specified for that purpose;*
- *(c) that set out in Schedule 3 to these Regulations with such variations as circumstances require when a grant of leave is made by the court, and the particulars contained therein are the particulars specified for that purpose;*
- *(d) that set out in Schedule 4 to these Regulations with such variations as circumstances require when any action is taken by a court in consequence of which a disqualification order or a disqualification undertaking is varied or ceases to be in force, and the particulars contained therein are the particulars specified for that purpose.*

NOTES

Revoked as noted at the beginning of these Regulations.

[14.31]

8

The time within which the officer specified in regulation 6(1) is to furnish the Secretary of State with the said particulars shall be a period of fourteen days beginning with the day on which the disqualification order or grant of leave is made, or any action is taken by a court in consequence of which the disqualification order or disqualification undertaking is varied or ceases to be in force, as the case may be.

NOTES

Revoked as noted at the beginning of these Regulations.

[14.32]

9 Extension of certain of the provisions of section 18 of the Act to orders made and leave granted in Northern Ireland

(1) Section 18(2) of the Act is hereby extended to the particulars furnished to the Secretary of State of orders made and leave granted under Part II of the Companies (Northern Ireland) Order 1989.

[(1A) Section 18(2A) is hereby extended to the particulars of disqualification undertakings accepted under and orders made and leave granted in relation to disqualification undertakings under the Company Directors Disqualification (Northern Ireland) Order 2002.]

(2) Section 18(3) of the Act is hereby extended to all entries in the register and particulars relating to them furnished to the Secretary of State in respect of orders made under Part II of the Companies (Northern Ireland) Order 1989 [or disqualification undertakings accepted under the Company Directors Disqualification (Northern Ireland) Order 2002].

NOTES

Revoked as noted at the beginning of these Regulations.

Para (1A): inserted by the Companies (Disqualification Orders) (Amendment) Regulations 2004, SI 2004/1940, reg 3(a).

Para (2): words in square brackets inserted by SI 2004/1940, reg 3(b).

SCHEDULES 1–4

(Schs 1–4 revoked as noted at the beginning of these Regulations. Sch 1, as amended by the Companies (Disqualification Orders) (Amendment No 2) Regulations 2002, SI 2002/1834, sets out two alternative forms of form DO1 containing particulars of a disqualification order made against an individual; Sch 2 sets out form DO2 containing particulars of a disqualification order made against a body corporate; Sch 3 sets out form DO3 containing particulars of the grant of leave in relation to a disqualification order or disqualification undertaking; Sch 4 sets out form DO4 containing particulars of the variation or cessation of a disqualification order or disqualification undertaking.)

COMPANIES (DISQUALIFICATION ORDERS) REGULATIONS 2009

(SI 2009/2471)

NOTES

Made: 8 September 2009.

Authority: Company Directors Disqualification Act 1986, s 18.

Commencement: 1 October 2009.

ARRANGEMENT OF REGULATIONS

1 Citation and commencement . . . . . [14.33]
2 Definitions . . . . . [14.34]
4 Transitional provisions . . . . . [14.35]
5 . . . . . [14.36]
6–8 Particulars to be furnished by officers of the court . . . . . [14.37]–[14.39]
9 Extension of certain of the provisions of section 18 of the Act to orders made, undertakings accepted and leave granted in Northern Ireland . . . . . [14.40]

[14.33]

1 Citation and commencement

These Regulations may be cited as the Companies (Disqualification Orders) Regulations 2009 and come into force on 1st October 2009.

Part 14 SIs: Directors Disqualification

[14.34]
2 Definitions

(1) In these Regulations—

"the Act" means the Company Directors Disqualification Act 1986;

["disqualification order" means an order of the court under any of sections 2 to 5, 5A, 6, 8, 8ZA, 8ZD, 9A and 10 of the Act;]

["disqualification undertaking" means an undertaking accepted by the Secretary of State under section 5A, 7, 8, 8ZC, 8ZE or 9B of the Act;]

"grant of leave" means a grant by the court of leave under section 17 of the Act to any person in relation to a disqualification order or a disqualification undertaking.

(2) For the purposes of regulations 5 and 9, "leave granted"—

(a) in relation to a disqualification order granted under Part 2 of the Companies (Northern Ireland) Order 1989 means leave granted by a court for a person subject to such an order to do anything which otherwise the order prohibits that person from doing; and

(b) in relation to a disqualification undertaking accepted under the Company Directors Disqualification (Northern Ireland) Order 2002 means leave granted by a court for a person subject to such an undertaking to do anything which otherwise the undertaking prohibits that person from doing.

NOTES

Para (1): definitions "disqualification order" and "disqualification undertaking" substituted by the Small Business, Enterprise and Employment Act 2015 (Consequential Amendments) (Insolvency and Company Directors Disqualification) Regulations 2015, SI 2015/1651, reg 4(1), (2).

3 *(Revokes the Companies (Disqualification Orders) Regulations 2001, SI 2001/967 at* **[14.25]***, the Companies (Disqualification Orders) (Amendment No 2) Regulations 2002, SI 2002/1834, and the Companies (Disqualification Orders) (Amendment) Regulations 2004, SI 2004/1940.)*

[14.35]
4 Transitional provisions

Other than regulation 9, these Regulations apply—

(a) in relation to a disqualification order made after the coming into force of these Regulations; and

(b) in relation to—

(i) a grant of leave made after the coming into force of these Regulations; or

(ii) any action taken by a court after the coming into force of these Regulations in consequence of which a disqualification order or a disqualification undertaking is varied or ceases to be in force,

whether the disqualification order or disqualification undertaking to which the grant of leave or the action relates was made by the court or accepted by the Secretary of State before or after the coming into force of these Regulations.

[14.36]
5

Regulation 9 applies to—

(a) particulars of disqualification orders made and leave granted under Part 2 of the Companies (Northern Ireland) Order 1989 received by the Secretary of State on or after 1st October 2009 other than particulars of disqualification orders made and leave granted under that Order which relate to disqualification orders made by the courts of Northern Ireland before 2nd April 2001; and

(b) particulars of undertakings accepted under the Company Directors Disqualification (Northern Ireland) Order 2002 on or after 1st October 2009, and to leave granted under that Order in relation to such undertakings.

[14.37]
6 Particulars to be furnished by officers of the court

(1) The following officers of the court must furnish to the Secretary of State the particulars specified in regulation 7(a) to (c) in the form and manner there specified—

(a) where a disqualification order is made by the Crown Court, the Court Manager;

(b) where a disqualification order or grant of leave is made by the High Court, the Court Manager;

(c) where a disqualification order or grant of leave is made by a County Court, the Court Manager;

(d) where a disqualification order is made by a Magistrates' Court, the designated officer for a Magistrates' Court;

(e) where a disqualification order is made by the High Court of Justiciary, the Deputy Principal Clerk of Justiciary;

(f) where a disqualification order or grant of leave is made by a Sheriff Court, the Sheriff Clerk;

(g) where a disqualification order or grant of leave is made by the Court of Session, the Deputy Principal Clerk of Session;

(h) where a disqualification order or grant of leave is made by the Court of Appeal, the Court Manager; and

(i) where a disqualification order or grant of leave is made by the Supreme Court, the Registrar of the Supreme Court.

(2) Where—

(a) a disqualification order has been made by any of the courts mentioned in paragraph (1), or
(b) a disqualification undertaking has been accepted by the Secretary of State,

and subsequently any action is taken by a court in consequence of which that order or that undertaking is varied or ceases to be in force, the officer specified in paragraph (1) of the court which takes such action must furnish to the Secretary of State the particulars specified in regulation 7(d) in the form and manner there specified.

[14.38]
7

The form in which the particulars are to be furnished is—

(a) that set out in Schedule 1 to these Regulations with such variations as circumstances require when the person against whom the disqualification order is made is an individual, and the particulars contained therein are the particulars specified for that purpose;
(b) that set out in Schedule 2 to these Regulations with such variations as circumstances require when the person against whom the disqualification order is made is a body corporate, and the particulars contained therein are the particulars specified for that purpose;
(c) that set out in Schedule 3 to these Regulations with such variations as circumstances require when a grant of leave is made by the court in relation to a disqualification order or a disqualification undertaking, and the particulars contained therein are the particulars specified for that purpose;
(d) that set out in Schedule 4 to these Regulations with such variations as circumstances require when any action is taken by a court in consequence of which a disqualification order or a disqualification undertaking is varied or ceases to be in force, and the particulars contained therein are the particulars specified for that purpose.

[14.39]
8

The time within which the officer specified in regulation 6(1) is to furnish the Secretary of State with the said particulars is the period of 14 days beginning with the day on which the disqualification order or grant of leave is made or on which action is taken by a court in consequence of which the disqualification order or disqualification undertaking is varied or ceases to be in force.

[14.40]
9 Extension of certain of the provisions of section 18 of the Act to orders made, undertakings accepted and leave granted in Northern Ireland

(1) Section 18(2) of the Act is extended to the particulars furnished to the Secretary of State of disqualification orders made and leave granted under Part 2 of the Companies (Northern Ireland) Order 1989.

(2) Section 18(2A) of the Act is extended to the particulars of disqualification undertakings accepted under and leave granted in relation to disqualification undertakings under the Company Directors Disqualification (Northern Ireland) Order 2002.

(3) Section 18(3) of the Act is extended to all entries in the register and particulars relating to them furnished to the Secretary of State in respect of orders made under Part 2 of the Companies (Northern Ireland) Order 1989 or disqualification undertakings accepted under the Company Directors Disqualification (Northern Ireland) Order 2002.

SCHEDULES 1–4

(Sch 1 sets out form DQO1 containing particulars of a disqualification order made against an individual; Sch 2 sets out form DQO2 containing particulars of a disqualification order made against a corporate body or firm; Sch 3 sets out form DQO3 containing particulars of the grant of leave in relation to a disqualification order or disqualification undertaking; Sch 4 sets out form DQO4 containing particulars of the variation or cessation of a disqualification order or disqualification undertaking. Note that forms DQ01 and DQ02 were substituted by the Small Business, Enterprise and Employment Act 2015 (Consequential Amendments) (Insolvency and Company Directors Disqualification) Regulations 2015, SI 2015/1651, reg 4(1), (3), (4).)

INSOLVENT COMPANIES (REPORTS ON CONDUCT OF DIRECTORS) (ENGLAND AND WALES) RULES 2016

(SI 2016/180)

NOTES

Made: 11 February 2016.
Authority: Insolvency Act 1986, s 411(1)(a); Company Directors Disqualification Act 1986, s 21(2).
Commencement: 6 April 2016.

ARRANGEMENT OF RULES

1 Citation, extent, commencement and interpretation . . . [14.41]
2 Revocations . . . [14.42]
3 Enforcement of section 7(4) of the Act . . . [14.43]
4 Conduct reports required to be sent under section 7A(4) of the Act . . . [14.44]
5 Applications for a longer period under section 7A(4)(b) of the Act . . . [14.45]
6 New information required to be sent under section 7A(5) of the Act . . . [14.46]
7 Unavailability of the portal . . . [14.47]
8 Enforcement of rules 4 to 6 . . . [14.48]
9 Review . . . [14.49]
10 Transitional and savings provisions . . . [14.50]

[14.41]
1 Citation, extent, commencement and interpretation

(1) These Rules may be cited as the Insolvent Companies (Reports on Conduct of Directors) (England and Wales) Rules 2016, and extend to England and Wales only.

(2) These Rules come into force on 6th April 2016.

(3) In these Rules—

"by electronic means" means sent initially and received at its destination by means of electronic equipment for the processing (which expression includes digital compression) or storage of data, and entirely transmitted, conveyed and received by wire, by radio, by optical means or by other electromagnetic means;

"the Act" means the Company Directors Disqualification Act 1986;

"the former Rules" means the Insolvent Companies (Reports on Conduct of Directors) Rules 1996; and

"the portal" means a digital service provided by the Secretary of State for the functions of both the sending and acknowledgement of receipt, by electronic means, of reports, applications, information and notifications in accordance with these Rules.

NOTES

Commencement: 6 April 2016.

[14.42]
2 Revocations

Subject to rule 10, the following are revoked—

(a) the former Rules;
(b) the Insolvent Companies (Reports on Conduct of Directors) (Amendment) Rules 2001; and
(c) the Enterprise Act 2002 (Insolvency) Order 2003, paragraphs 68 to 70 of the Schedule.

NOTES

Commencement: 6 April 2016.

[14.43]
3 Enforcement of section 7(4) of the Act

(1) This rule applies where, for the purpose of determining whether to exercise any function under section 7 of the Act (disqualification orders under section 6: applications and acceptance of undertakings), the Secretary of State or the official receiver requires or has required a person to—

(a) furnish the Secretary of State or (as the case may be) the official receiver with information under section 7(4)(a), or
(b) produce and permit inspection of books, papers and other records in accordance with section 7(4)(b).

(2) On the application of the Secretary of State or (as the case may be) the official receiver, the court may make an order directing compliance within such period as may be specified.

(3) The court's order may provide that all costs of and incidental to the application are to be borne by the person to whom the order is directed.

NOTES

Commencement: 6 April 2016.

[14.44]
4 Conduct reports required to be sent under section 7A(4) of the Act

(1) This rule is subject to rule 7.

(2) A conduct report required to be sent under section 7A(4) of the Act must be sent by the office-holder to the Secretary of State by electronic means via the portal.

(3) The Secretary of State must as soon as reasonably practicable acknowledge receipt, by electronic means via the portal, of a conduct report sent in accordance with this rule.

NOTES
Commencement: 6 April 2016.

[14.45]
5 Applications for a longer period under section 7A(4)(b) of the Act

(1) This rule is subject to rule 7.

(2) This rule applies where the particular circumstances of a case may require a period longer than that provided for by section 7A(4)(a) of the Act for the sending of a conduct report to the Secretary of State.

(3) The office-holder may apply to the Secretary of State for a longer period in which to send the report.

(4) The application must be sent by electronic means via the portal before the expiry of the period specified in section 7A(4)(a) of the Act.

(5) The application must explain the particular circumstances for the making of the application.

(6) The Secretary of State must as soon as reasonably practicable acknowledge receipt, by electronic means via the portal, of an application sent in accordance with this rule.

(7) The Secretary of State must, as soon as is reasonably practicable, notify the office-holder, by electronic means via the portal,—

(a) of the outcome of the application; and
(b) if the application is successful, of the longer period considered appropriate in the particular circumstances for the sending of the report to the Secretary of State under section 7A(4)(b) of the Act.

NOTES
Commencement: 6 April 2016.

[14.46]
6 New information required to be sent under section 7A(5) of the Act

(1) This rule is subject to rule 7.

(2) New information required to be sent under section 7A(5) of the Act must be sent by the office-holder to the Secretary of State by electronic means via the portal.

(3) The Secretary of State must as soon as reasonably practicable acknowledge receipt, by electronic means via the portal, of new information sent in accordance with this rule.

NOTES
Commencement: 6 April 2016.

[14.47]
7 Unavailability of the portal

(1) The Secretary of State—

(a) may at any time when the portal is unable to carry out one or more of its functions, and
(b) must, where the portal has been unable to carry out one or more of its functions for a period of 7 business days,

provide alternative means for complying with a requirement under rules 4, 5 or 6.

(2) The Secretary of State must give notice to office-holders specifying the means provided for the purposes of paragraph (1) and the period of time for which those means are made available.

(3) The Secretary of State may by notice vary the means provided under paragraph (1) or the period of time for which those means are made available.

(4) A notice under paragraph (3) must give office-holders at least 1 business day's notice before any variation takes effect.

(5) The time within which an office-holder must comply with rules 4, 5 or 6 does not include any day the whole or part of which forms part of a suspension period.

(6) For the purpose of paragraph (5) a suspension period is a period of time during which—

(a) the portal is unable to receive reports, applications or information;
(b) no notice under paragraph (2) or (3) is in force; and
(c) the office-holder has attempted to and been prevented from sending a report, application or information at least once during that period on the basis of sub-paragraph (a).

(7) In this rule, "business day" means any day other than a Saturday, a Sunday, Christmas Day, Good Friday or a day which is a bank holiday in any part of Great Britain.

NOTES
Commencement: 6 April 2016.

[14.48]
8 Enforcement of rules 4 to 6

(1) An office-holder who without reasonable excuse fails to comply with any of the obligations imposed by section 7A(4) or 7A(5) of the Act is guilty of an offence and—

(a) on summary conviction of the offence, is liable to a fine not exceeding level 3 on the standard scale, and

(b) for continued contravention, is liable to a daily default fine; that is to say, the office-holder is liable on a second or subsequent summary conviction of the offence to a fine not exceeding one-tenth of level 3 on the standard scale for each day on which the contravention is continued (instead of the penalty specified in sub-paragraph (a)).

(2) Section 431 of the Insolvency Act 1986 (summary proceedings), as it applies to England and Wales, has effect in relation to an offence under this rule as to offences under Parts 1 to 7 of that Act.

NOTES

Commencement: 6 April 2016.

[14.49]
9 Review

(1) The Secretary of State must from time to time—
(a) carry out a review of these Rules,
(b) set out the conclusions of the review in a report, and
(c) publish the report.

(2) The report must in particular—
(a) set out the objectives intended to be achieved by the regulatory system established by these Rules,
(b) assess the extent to which those objectives are achieved, and
(c) assess whether those objectives remain appropriate and, if so, the extent to which they could be achieved with a system that imposes less regulation.

(3) The first report under this rule must be published before the end of the period of 5 years beginning on 6th April 2016.

(4) Reports under this rule are afterwards to be published at intervals not exceeding 5 years.

NOTES

Commencement: 6 April 2016.

[14.50]
10 Transitional and savings provisions

(1) Rule 6 of the former Rules continues to apply when a period referred to in rule 6(2) of the former Rules has not expired by 6th April 2016.

(2) Until 6th October 2016 rules 3 to 5 of the former Rules continue to apply as if the former Rules had not been revoked when the relevant date for the purposes of rule 4 of the former Rules occurred before 6th April 2016.

(3) Until 6th October 2016 the forms contained in the Schedule to the former Rules must be used for the purpose of complying with rules 3 to 5 of the former Rules.

NOTES

Commencement: 6 April 2016.

COMPENSATION ORDERS (DISQUALIFIED DIRECTORS) PROCEEDINGS (ENGLAND AND WALES) RULES 2016

(SI 2016/890)

NOTES

Made: 7 September 2016.
Authority: Insolvency Act 1986, s 411(1).
Commencement: 1 October 2016.

ARRANGEMENT OF RULES

1 Citation, commencement and interpretation . . . . [14.51]
2 Application . . . . [14.52]
3 Form and conduct of applications . . . . [14.53]
4 The claimant's case . . . . [14.54]
5 Endorsements etc on claim form. . . . . [14.55]
6 Acknowledgment of service . . . . [14.56]
7 Evidence . . . . [14.57]
8 The hearing of the application . . . . [14.58]
9 Compensation orders: making and setting aside of an order . . . . [14.59]

[14.51]

1 Citation, commencement and interpretation

(1) These Rules may be cited as the Compensation Orders (Disqualified Directors) Proceedings (England and Wales) Rules 2016.

(2) These Rules come into force on 1st October 2016.

(3) In these Rules—

"the Act" means the Company Directors Disqualification Act 1986 and a reference to a numbered section is to that section of that Act;

"CPR" followed by a Part or rule by number means that Part or rule with that number in the Civil Procedure Rules 1998;

"practice direction" means a direction as to the practice and procedure of any court within the scope of the Civil Procedure Rules 1998;

["registrar" has the same meaning as in rule 1.2(2) of the Insolvency (England and Wales) Rules 2016];

"relevant party" means—

(a) the defendant (in the case of an application under section 15A(1)); or

(b) the Secretary of State (in the case of an application under section 15C(1)).

NOTES

Commencement: 1 October 2016.

Para (3): definition "registrar" substituted by the Insolvency (England and Wales) Rules 2016 (Consequential Amendments and Savings) Rules 2017, SI 2017/369, r 2(2), Sch 2, para 12(1), (2).

[14.52]

2 Application

(1) Subject to paragraph (2), these Rules apply to an application under the Act made on or after 1st October 2016—

(a) by the Secretary of State for a compensation order against a person under section 15A(1); and

(b) by a person who is subject to a compensation undertaking under section 15A(2) for variation or revocation of that undertaking under section 15C(1).

(2) These Rules apply to applications where the courts in England and Wales—

(a) have made a disqualification order against the person;

(b) have jurisdiction to make a disqualification order against the person (in a case where proceedings for a disqualification order have or are being commenced); or

(c) would have had jurisdiction to make a disqualification order against the person (in a case where the person is subject to disqualification undertaking).

NOTES

Commencement: 1 October 2016.

[14.53]

3 Form and conduct of applications

(1) The Civil Procedure Rules 1998, and any relevant practice direction, apply in respect of applications under these Rules, except where these Rules make different provision.

(2) An application must be made by claim form and the claimant must use the CPR Part 8 (alternative procedure for claims) procedure.

(3) In the case of an application under section 15C(1), the Secretary of State is the defendant for the purposes of the Civil Procedure Rules 1998.

(4) CPR rule 8.1(3) (power of the court to order the claim to continue as if the claimant had not used the Part 8 procedure), CPR rule 8.2 (contents of the claim form) and CPR rule 8.7 (Part 20 claims) do not apply to applications under these Rules.

[(5) Rule 12.49 (appeals and reviews of court orders in corporate insolvency) and rule 12.61 (procedure on appeal) of the Insolvency (England and Wales) Rules 2016 apply to applications under these rules.]

NOTES

Commencement: 1 October 2016.

Para (5): substituted by the Insolvency (England and Wales) Rules 2016 (Consequential Amendments and Savings) Rules 2017, SI 2017/369, r 2(2), Sch 2, para 12(1), (3).

[14.54]

4 The claimant's case

(1) The claimant must, at the time when the claim form is issued, file in court evidence in support of the application.

(2) The claimant must serve on the relevant party with the claim form copies of the evidence under paragraph (1).

(3) The evidence must be by one or more affidavits or witness statements, which must include—

(a) in the case of an application under section 15A(1), a statement—

(i) of the disqualification order or undertaking in respect of which the application is being brought, or of the proceedings for a disqualification order either commenced or being commenced alongside the application;

(ii) of the loss it is alleged has been caused by the conduct in respect of which—
(aa) the defendant is subject to the disqualification order or undertaking, or
(bb) proceedings for a disqualification order have been or are being commenced;
(iii) identifying the creditor or creditors to whom it is alleged loss has been caused;
(iv) identifying particulars of the order the claimant is seeking under section 15B(1); and
(v) of any other matters considered to be of relevance to the application; and
(b) in the case of an application under section 15C(1), the compensation undertaking (or a copy).

(4) In the case of an application under section 15A(1), where the insolvent company as referred to in section 15A(3)(b) is in administration or liquidation, or there is an administrative receiver of that company, the claimant must also give notice of the claim to the administrator, liquidator or administrative receiver within 14 days of the claim form being issued.

(5) The notice under paragraph (4) must identify particulars of the order the claimant is seeking under section 15B(1).

NOTES

Commencement: 1 October 2016.

[14.55]
5 Endorsements etc on claim form

(1) The following information must be endorsed on the claim form—
(a) that the application is made in accordance with these Rules;
(b) in the case of an application under section 15A(1), that the court has the power to make such an order in respect of loss it is alleged has been caused by the defendant's conduct;
(c) in the case of an application under 15C(1), that the court has the power to reduce the amount of a compensation undertaking offered and accepted under section 15A(2) or to provide that such an undertaking is not to have effect; and
(d) that any evidence which the relevant party wishes the court to take into consideration must be filed in court in accordance with the time limit under rule 7(1).

(2) The time limit referred to in paragraph (1)(d) must be set out in the claim form.

NOTES

Commencement: 1 October 2016.

[14.56]
6 Acknowledgment of service

(1) The claim form served on the relevant party must be accompanied by an acknowledgment of service and CPR rule 8.3(2) (dealing with the contents of an acknowledgment of service) does not apply.

(2) In the case of an application under section 15A(1), the acknowledgment of service must state that the defendant should indicate—
(a) whether the defendant is contesting the disqualification on which the application is based by—
(i) contesting the making of a disqualification order (either before it has been made or by way of an appeal), or
(ii) applying for a disqualification undertaking to cease to be in force;
(b) whether the defendant disputes that the conduct on which the application is based caused the loss alleged in the application; or
(c) whether the defendant, while not resisting the application, intends to adduce mitigating factors with a view to justifying a reduced level of compensation.

(3) In the case of an application under section 15C(1)—
(a) the acknowledgment of service must state whether or not the Secretary of State intends to file any evidence relating to the application; and
(b) CPR rule 8.4 (consequence of not filing an acknowledgment of service) does not apply.

NOTES

Commencement: 1 October 2016.

[14.57]
7 Evidence

(1) The relevant party must, within 28 days from the date of service of the claim form, file in court any evidence relating to the application which the relevant party wishes the court to take into consideration.

(2) The relevant party must, at the same time, serve on the claimant a copy of any such evidence.

(3) The claimant must, within 14 days of receiving the copy of the relevant party's evidence, file in court any further evidence in reply which the claimant wishes the court to take into consideration.

(4) The claimant must, at the same time, serve a copy of any such further evidence on the relevant party.

(5) Any evidence filed and served under this rule must be by either affidavit or witness statement.

(6) CPR rules 8.5 (filing and serving written evidence) and 8.6(1) (requirements where written evidence is to be relied on) do not apply.

NOTES

Commencement: 1 October 2016.

[14.58]

8 The hearing of the application

(1) When the claim form is issued, the court must fix a date for the first hearing of the claim for a date not less than 8 weeks from the date of issue of the claim form.

(2) The hearing must in the first instance be before the registrar in open court.

(3) Without prejudice to the Secretary of State's rights and obligations under sections 15C(2) and 16(3) on the hearing of an application, subject to the direction of the court, any of the parties may give evidence, call and cross-examine witnesses at the hearing.

(4) The registrar must either determine the case on the date fixed or adjourn it.

(5) If the registrar adjourns the case for further consideration the registrar must—

- (a) direct whether the case is to be heard by a registrar or, if the registrar thinks it appropriate, for determination by the judge;
- (b) state the reasons for the adjournment; and
- (c) give directions as to the following matters—
  - (i) the manner in which and the time within which notice of the adjournment and the reasons for it are to be given to the relevant party,
  - (ii) any order for the provision of further information or for disclosure by the parties,
  - (iii) the filing in court and the service of further evidence (if any) by the parties,
  - (iv) such other matters as the registrar thinks necessary or expedient with a view to an expeditious disposal of the application, and
  - (v) the time and place of the adjourned hearing.

(6) Where a case is adjourned other than to the judge, it may be heard by the registrar who originally dealt with the case or by another registrar.

NOTES

Commencement: 1 October 2016.

[14.59]

9 Compensation orders: making and setting aside of an order

(1) The court may make a compensation order under section 15A(1) against the defendant whether or not the defendant—

- (a) appears,
- (b) has completed and returned the acknowledgment of service of the claim form, or
- (c) has filed evidence in accordance with rule 7.

(2) Any compensation order made in the absence of the defendant may be set aside or varied by the court on such terms as it thinks just.

NOTES

Commencement: 1 October 2016.

DISQUALIFIED DIRECTORS COMPENSATION ORDERS (FEES) (ENGLAND AND WALES) ORDER 2016

(SI 2016/1047)

NOTES

Made: 31 October 2016.
Authority: Insolvency Act 1986, s 414(1)(b).
Commencement: 30 November 2016.

[14.60]

1 Citation, commencement and interpretation

(1) This Order may be cited as the Disqualified Directors Compensation Orders (Fees) (England and Wales) Order 2016 and comes into force on 30th November 2016.

(2) In this Order—

"compensation order" means a court order under section 15A(1) of the Company Directors Disqualification Act 1986; and

"compensation undertaking" means an undertaking accepted by the Secretary of State under section 15A(2) of the Company Directors Disqualification Act 1986.

NOTES

Commencement: 30 November 2016.

[14.61]
2 Application

This Order applies in relation to—

(a) compensation orders made by the courts in England and Wales; and
(b) compensation undertakings accepted in cases where the courts in England and Wales would have had jurisdiction to make a compensation order.

NOTES
Commencement: 30 November 2016.

[14.62]
3 Fees payable in connection with compensation orders and compensation undertakings

(1) The Secretary of State is to be paid a fee for performing the function of distributing to a creditor an amount received by the Secretary of State in respect of a compensation order or a compensation undertaking to which this Order applies.

(2) The fee is to be paid out of the amount received before such a distribution is made to a creditor.

(3) The fee means the aggregate of—

(a) the time spent by the appropriate officials carrying out the Secretary of State's function under paragraph (1) in relation to all creditors specified in a compensation order or a compensation undertaking, multiplied by the hourly rate in accordance with the table in the Schedule; and
(b) any necessary disbursements or expenses properly incurred in carrying out that function,

divided equally between the total number of creditors specified in the compensation order or the compensation undertaking.

NOTES
Commencement: 30 November 2016.

[14.63]
4 Value Added Tax

Where Value Added Tax is chargeable in respect of the provision of a service for which a fee is payable by virtue of this Order, the amount of the Value Added Tax must be paid in addition to the fee.

NOTES
Commencement: 30 November 2016.

SCHEDULE
HOURLY RATES FOR SECRETARY OF STATE'S FEE

Article 3

[14.64]

Grade according to the Insolvency Service grading structure	Total hourly rate £
D2/Section Head	69
C2/Deputy Section Head	58
C1/Senior Examiner	52
L3/Examiner	46
L2/Examiner	40
B2/Administrator	43
L1/Examiner	38
B1/Administrator	42
A2/Administrator	36
A1/Administrator	31

NOTES
Commencement: 30 November 2016.

PART 15
INSOLVENCY (SCOTLAND) RULES 1986

INSOLVENCY (SCOTLAND) RULES 1986

(SI 1986/1915 (S 139))

NOTES

Made: 10 November 1986.

Authority: Insolvency Act 1986, s 411.

Commencement: 29 December 1986.

Application: these Rules are applied to limited liability partnerships with such modifications as the context requires for the purpose of giving effect to the provisions of the Insolvency Act 1986, by the Limited Liability Partnerships Regulations 2001, SI 2001/1090, reg 10, Sch 6, Pt II at **[10.38]**, **[10.43]** (except in so far as they relate to the exceptions to the reserved matters specified in section C2 of Pt II of Sch 5 to the Scotland Act 1998), and by the Limited Liability Partnerships (Scotland) Regulations 2001, SSI 2001/128, reg 6 at **[16.133]**.

Modifications: these Rules are extensively applied and modified in respect of bank and building society insolvency and administration, by the Bank Administration (Scotland) Rules 2009, SI 2009/350; the Bank Insolvency (Scotland) Rules 2009, SI 2009/351; the Building Society Special Administration (Scotland) Rules 2009, SI 2009/806; the Building Society Insolvency (Scotland) Rules 2010, SI 2010/2584.

These Rules are applied with modifications in relation to an authorised bank in Scotland and Northern Ireland (other than the Bank of England) so that any reference to "asset", "property", "estate", "sum" or "fund" does not include a reference to the backing assets; see the Scottish and Northern Ireland Banknote Regulations 2009, SI 2009/3056, reg 29, Sch 1, Pt 2, para 5.

In so far as they apply to the winding up of an unregistered company, these Rules are applied with modifications, by the Collective Investment in Transferable Securities (Contractual Scheme) Regulations 2013, SI 2013/1388, reg 17, Sch 4 at **[7.835]**, **[7.843]**.

These Rules are applied with modifications in relation to a society registered under the Industrial and Provident Societies Act 1965 (other than a society which is a private registered provider of social housing or is registered as a social landlord) by the Industrial and Provident Societies and Credit Unions (Arrangements, Reconstructions and Administration) Order 2014, SI 2014/229, art 11, Sch 4, at **[7.1436]**, **[7.1447]**.

ARRANGEMENT OF THE RULES

INTRODUCTORY PROVISIONS

0.1 Citation and commencement .... [15.1]
0.2 Interpretation .... [15.2]
0.3 Application .... [15.3]

PART 1
COMPANY VOLUNTARY ARRANGEMENTS

CHAPTER 1
PRELIMINARY

1.1 Scope of this Part; interpretation .... [15.4]

CHAPTER 1A
THE GIVING OF NOTICE AND THE SUPPLY OF DOCUMENTS

1.1A Application .... [15.5]
1.1B Electronic delivery .... [15.6]
1.1C Use of websites by nominee or supervisor .... [15.7]
1.1D Special provision on account of expense as to website use .... [15.8]

CHAPTER 2
PROPOSAL BY DIRECTORS

1.3 Contents of proposal .... [15.9]
1.4 Notice to intended nominee .... [15.10]
1.5 Statement of affairs .... [15.11]
1.6 Additional disclosure for assistance of nominee .... [15.12]
1.7 Nominee's report on the proposal .... [15.13]
1.8 Replacement of nominee .... [15.14]
1.9 Summoning of meetings under section 3 .... [15.15]

CHAPTER 3
PROPOSAL BY ADMINISTRATOR OR LIQUIDATOR
WHERE HE IS THE NOMINEE

1.10 Preparation of proposal .... [15.16]
1.11 Summoning of meetings under section 3 .... [15.17]

CHAPTER 4
PROPOSAL BY ADMINISTRATOR OR LIQUIDATOR WHERE ANOTHER
INSOLVENCY PRACTITIONER IS THE NOMINEE

1.12 Preparation of proposal and notice to nominee .... [15.18]

CHAPTER 5
MEETINGS

1.13 General .... [15.19]

1.14 Summoning of meetings . . . . . [15.20]
1.14ZA Remote Attendance at Meetings . . . . . [15.21]
1.14A The Chairman at meetings . . . . . [15.22]
1.14AA Chairman of meeting as proxy holder . . . . . [15.23]
1.15 Attendance by company officers . . . . . [15.24]
1.15A Entitlement to vote (creditors) . . . . . [15.25]
1.15AA Entitlement to vote (members) . . . . . [15.26]
1.15B Procedure for admission of creditors' claims for voting purposes . . . . . [15.27]
1.16 . . . . . [15.28]
1.16A Requisite majorities at creditors' meetings . . . . . [15.29]
1.16B Requisite majorities at company meetings . . . . . [15.30]
1.16C Action where person excluded . . . . . [15.31]
1.16D Indication to excluded person . . . . . [15.32]
1.16E Complaint . . . . . [15.33]
1.17 Report of meetings . . . . . [15.34]

CHAPTER 6
IMPLEMENTATION OF THE VOLUNTARY ARRANGEMENT

1.18 Resolutions to follow approval . . . . . [15.35]
1.18A Notice of order made under section 4A(6) . . . . . [15.36]
1.19 Hand-over of property, etc to supervisor . . . . . [15.37]
1.20 Revocation or suspension of the arrangement . . . . . [15.38]
1.21 Supervisor's accounts and reports . . . . . [15.39]
1.21A Supervisor's reports . . . . . [15.39]
1.22 Fees, costs, charges and expenses . . . . . [15.41]
1.23 Completion or termination of the arrangement . . . . . [15.42]
1.24 False representations, etc . . . . . [15.43]

CHAPTER 7
OBTAINING A MORATORIUM
PROCEEDINGS DURING A MORATORIUM
NOMINEES
CONSIDERATION OF PROPOSALS WHERE MORATORIUM OBTAINED

SECTION A: OBTAINING A MORATORIUM

1.25 Preparation of proposal by directors and submission to nominee . . . . . [15.44]
1.26 Delivery of documents to the intended nominee etc . . . . . [15.45]
1.27 Statement of affairs . . . . . [15.46]
1.28 The nominee's statement . . . . . [15.47]
1.29 Documents submitted to the court to obtain moratorium . . . . . [15.48]
1.30 Notice and advertisement of beginning of a moratorium . . . . . [15.49]
1.31 Notice of extension of moratorium . . . . . [15.50]
1.32 Notice and advertisement of end of moratorium . . . . . [15.51]
1.33 Inspection of court file . . . . . [15.52]

SECTION B: PROCEEDINGS DURING A MORATORIUM

1.34 Disposal of charged property etc during a moratorium . . . . . [15.53]

SECTION C: NOMINEES

1.35 Withdrawal of nominee's consent to act . . . . . [15.54]
1.36 Replacement of nominee by the court . . . . . [15.55]
1.37 Notification of appointment of a replacement nominee . . . . . [15.56]
1.38 Applications to court under paragraphs 26 or 27 of Schedule A1 to the Act . . . . . [15.57]

SECTION D: CONSIDERATION OF PROPOSALS
WHERE MORATORIUM OBTAINED

1.39 General . . . . . [15.58]
1.40 Summoning of meetings; procedure at meetings etc . . . . . [15.59]
1.41 Entitlement to vote (creditors) . . . . . [15.60]
1.42 Procedure for admission of creditors' claims for voting purposes . . . . . [15.61]
1.43 Requisite majorities (creditors) . . . . . [15.62]
1.44 Proceedings to obtain agreement on the proposal . . . . . [15.63]
1.45 Implementation of the arrangement . . . . . [15.64]

CHAPTER 8
EU REGULATION—CONVERSION OF VOLUNTARY
ARRANGEMENT INTO WINDING UP

1.46 Application for conversion into winding up . . . . . [15.65]

1.47 Contents of affidavit .... [15.66]
1.48 Power of court .... [15.67]

CHAPTER 9
EU REGULATION—MEMBER STATE LIQUIDATOR
1.49 Notice to member State liquidator .... [15.68]

CHAPTER 10
1.50 Omission of Information from Statement of Affairs .... [15.69]

PART 2
ADMINISTRATION PROCEDURE

CHAPTER 1
PRELIMINARY
2.1 Introductory and interpretation .... [15.70]

CHAPTER 2
APPOINTMENT OF ADMINISTRATOR BY COURT
2.2 Form of application .... [15.71]
2.3 Service of petition .... [15.72]
2.4 Application to appoint specified person as administrator by holder of qualifying floating charge .... [15.73]
2.5 Application where company in liquidation .... [15.74]
2.6 Expenses .... [15.75]
2.7 Administration orders where company in liquidation .... [15.76]
2.8 Notice of dismissal of application for an administration order .... [15.77]

CHAPTER 3
APPOINTMENT OF ADMINISTRATOR BY
HOLDER OF FLOATING CHARGE
2.9 Notice of intention to appoint .... [15.78]
2.10 Notice of appointment .... [15.79]
2.11 Notice to administrator .... [15.80]
2.12 Appointment taking place out of court business hours .... [15.81]

CHAPTER 4
APPOINTMENT OF ADMINISTRATOR BY COMPANY OR DIRECTORS
2.13 Notice of intention to appoint .... [15.82]
2.14 Timing of statutory declaration .... [15.83]
2.15 Resolution or decision to appoint .... [15.84]
2.16 Notice of appointment .... [15.85]
2.17 Appointment where no notice of intention to appoint has been given .... [15.86]
2.18 Notice to administrator .... [15.87]

CHAPTER 5
PROCESS OF ADMINISTRATION
2.19 Notification and advertisement of administrator's appointment .... [15.88]
2.20 Notice requiring statement of affairs .... [15.89]
2.21 Statements of affairs and statements of concurrence .... [15.90]
2.22 Limited disclosure .... [15.91]
2.23 Release from duty to submit statement of affairs; extension of time .... [15.92]
2.24 Expenses of statement of affairs .... [15.93]
2.25 Administrator's proposal .... [15.94]
2.25A Limited disclosure of paragraph 49 statement .... [15.95]

CHAPTER 5A
THE GIVING OF NOTICE AND SUPPLY OF DOCUMENTS
2.25B Application .... [15.96]
2.25C Electronic delivery .... [15.97]
2.25D Use of websites by administrator .... [15.98]
2.25E Special provision on account of expense as to website use .... [15.99]

CHAPTER 6
MEETINGS
2.26 General .... [15.100]
2.26A Notice of meetings .... [15.101]
2.26B Remote attendance at meetings .... [15.102]
2.26C Entitlement to vote and draw dividend .... [15.103]
2.27 Meetings to consider administrator's proposals .... [15.104]

2.27A Suspension and adjournment . . . . [15.105]
2.28 Correspondence instead of creditors' meetings . . . . [15.106]
2.29 Applicable law (company meetings) . . . . [15.107]
2.30 Entitlement to vote—member State liquidators . . . . [15.108]
2.31 Meeting requisitioned by creditors . . . . [15.109]
2.32 . . . . [15.110]
2.32A Notice of meetings by advertisement only . . . . [15.111]
2.33 Hire-purchase, conditional sale and hiring agreements . . . . [15.112]
2.34 Revision of the administrator's proposals . . . . [15.113]
2.35 Notices to creditors . . . . [15.114]
2.35A Action where person excluded . . . . [15.115]
2.35B Indication to excluded person . . . . [15.116]
2.35C Complaint . . . . [15.117]

CHAPTER 7
THE CREDITORS' COMMITTEE

2.36 Constitution of committee . . . . [15.118]
2.36A Functions of the committee . . . . [15.119]
2.36B Formalities of establishment . . . . [15.120]
2.36C Meetings of the committee . . . . [15.121]
2.36D Remote attendance at meetings of creditors' committees . . . . [15.122]
2.36E Procedure for requests that a place for a meeting should be specified under Rule 2.36D . . . . [15.123]
2.36F The chairman at meetings . . . . [15.124]
2.36G Quorum . . . . [15.125]
2.36H Committee members' representatives . . . . [15.126]
2.36I Resignation . . . . [15.127]
2.36J Termination of membership . . . . [15.128]
2.36K Removal . . . . [15.129]
2.36L Vacancies . . . . [15.130]
2.36M Voting rights and resolutions . . . . [15.131]
2.36N Resolutions otherwise than at a meeting . . . . [15.132]
2.36O Expenses of members, etc . . . . [15.133]
2.36P Formal defects . . . . [15.134]
2.36Q Information from administrator . . . . [15.135]
2.36R Members' dealings with the company . . . . [15.136]

CHAPTER 8
FUNCTIONS AND REMUNERATION OF ADMINISTRATOR

2.37 Disposal of secured property, etc . . . . [15.137]
2.38 Progress reports . . . . [15.138]
2.39 Determination of outlays and remuneration . . . . [15.139]
2.39A Appeal against fixing of remuneration . . . . [15.140]

CHAPTER 8A
EXPENSES OF THE ADMINISTRATION

2.39B Expenses of the administration . . . . [15.141]
2.39C Pre-administration costs . . . . [15.142]

CHAPTER 9
DISTRIBUTIONS TO CREDITORS

2.40 . . . . [15.143]
2.41 . . . . [15.144]
2.41A Payments of Dividends . . . . [15.145]
2.41B New administrator appointed . . . . [15.146]

CHAPTER 10
ENDING ADMINISTRATION

2.42 Final progress reports . . . . [15.147]
2.43 Notice of automatic end of administration . . . . [15.148]
2.44 Applications for extension of administration . . . . [15.149]
2.45 Notice of end of administration . . . . [15.150]
2.46 Application to court . . . . [15.151]
2.47 Moving from administration to creditors' voluntary liquidation . . . . [15.152]
2.48 Moving from administration to dissolution . . . . [15.153]

CHAPTER 11
REPLACING ADMINISTRATOR

2.49 Grounds for resignation . . . . [15.154]

2.50 Notice of intention to resign .... [15.155]
2.51 Notice of resignation .... [15.156]
2.52 Administrator deceased .... [15.157]
2.53 Application to replace .... [15.158]
2.54 .... [15.159]
2.55 Joint or concurrent appointments .... [15.160]
2.56 Application to court to remove administrator from office .... [15.161]

CHAPTER 12
EU REGULATION—CONVERSION OF ADMINISTRATION TO WINDING UP

2.57 Application for conversion .... [15.162]
2.58 Contents of affidavit .... [15.163]
2.59 Power of court .... [15.164]

CHAPTER 13
EU REGULATION—MEMBER STATE LIQUIDATOR

2.60 Interpretation of creditor and notice to member State liquidator .... [15.165]

PART 3
RECEIVERS

CHAPTER 1
APPOINTMENT

3.1 Acceptance of appointment .... [15.166]

CHAPTER 2
STATEMENT OF AFFAIRS

3.2 Notice requiring statement of affairs .... [15.167]
3.2A Limited disclosure of the statement of affairs .... [15.168]
3.3 Expenses of statement of affairs .... [15.169]

CHAPTER 3
THE CREDITORS' COMMITTEE

3.4 Constitution of committee .... [15.170]
3.5 Functions of the committee .... [15.171]
3.6 Application of provisions relating to liquidation committee .... [15.172]
3.7 Information from receiver .... [15.173]
3.8 Members' dealings with the company .... [15.174]
3.8A Prescribed Part .... [15.175]

CHAPTER 4
MISCELLANEOUS

3.9 Abstract of receipts and payments .... [15.176]
3.9A Electronic measures–application .... [15.177]
3.9B Electronic delivery .... [15.178]
3.9C Electronic delivery by receivers etc .... [15.179]
3.10 Receiver deceased .... [15.180]
3.11 Vacation of office .... [15.181]

CHAPTER 5
VAT BAD DEBT RELIEF

3.12 Issue of certificate of insolvency .... [15.182]
3.13 Notice to creditors .... [15.183]
3.14 Preservation of certificate with company's records .... [15.184]

PART 4
WINDING UP BY THE COURT

CHAPTER 1
PROVISIONAL LIQUIDATOR

4.1 Appointment of provisional liquidator .... [15.185]
4.2 Order of appointment .... [15.186]
4.3 Caution .... [15.187]
4.4 Failure to find or to maintain caution .... [15.188]
4.5 Remuneration .... [15.189]
4.6 Termination of appointment .... [15.190]

CHAPTER 2
STATEMENT OF AFFAIRS

4.7 Notice requiring statement of affairs .... [15.191]

4.8 Form of the statement of affairs . . . . . [15.192]
4.8A Limited disclosure of the statement of affairs . . . . . [15.193]
4.9 Expenses of statement of affairs . . . . . [15.194]

CHAPTER 3
INFORMATION

4.10 Information to creditors and contributories . . . . . [15.195]
4.11 Information to registrar of companies . . . . . [15.196]

CHAPTER 4
MEETINGS OF CREDITORS AND CONTRIBUTORIES

4.12 First meetings in the liquidation . . . . . [15.197]
4.13 Other meetings . . . . . [15.198]
4.14 Attendance at meetings of company's personnel . . . . . [15.199]

CHAPTER 5
CLAIMS IN LIQUIDATION

4.15 Submission of claims. . . . . . [15.200]
4.16 False claims or evidence. . . . . . [15.201]
4.16A Evidence of Claims. . . . . . [15.202]
4.16B Adjudication of claims . . . . . [15.203]
4.16C Entitlement to vote and draw a dividend . . . . . [15.204]
4.16D Liabilities and rights of co-obligants. . . . . . [15.205]
4.16E Amount which may be claimed generally . . . . . [15.206]
4.16F Debts depending on contingency . . . . . [15.207]
4.16G Secured debts . . . . . [15.208]
4.17 Claims in foreign currency . . . . . [15.209]

CHAPTER 6
THE LIQUIDATOR

SECTION A: APPOINTMENT AND FUNCTIONS OF LIQUIDATOR

4.18 Appointment of liquidator by the court . . . . . [15.210]
4.19 Appointment by creditors or contributories . . . . . [15.211]
4.20 Authentication of liquidator's appointment . . . . . [15.212]
4.21 Hand-over of assets to liquidator. . . . . . [15.213]
4.22 Taking possession and realisation of the company's assets . . . . . [15.214]
4.22A Realisation of the company's heritable property . . . . . [15.215]

SECTION B: REMOVAL AND RESIGNATION; VACATION OF OFFICE

4.23 Summoning of meeting for removal of liquidator . . . . . [15.216]
4.24 Procedure on liquidator's removal . . . . . [15.217]
4.25 Release of liquidator on removal. . . . . . [15.218]
4.26 Removal of liquidator by the court. . . . . . [15.219]
4.26A Power to make a block transfer of cases . . . . . [15.220]
4.26B Application for block transfer order . . . . . [15.221]
4.26C Action following application for a block transfer order . . . . . [15.222]
4.27 Advertisement of removal. . . . . . [15.223]
4.28 Resignation of liquidator. . . . . . [15.224]
4.29 Action following acceptance of liquidator's resignation . . . . . [15.225]
4.30 Leave to resign granted by the court. . . . . . [15.226]

SECTION C: RELEASE ON COMPLETION OF WINDING UP

4.31 Final meeting . . . . . [15.227]

SECTION D: OUTLAYS AND REMUNERATION

4.32 Determination of amount of outlays and remuneration . . . . . [15.228]
4.33 Recourse of liquidator to meeting of creditors . . . . . [15.229]
4.34 Recourse to the court. . . . . . [15.230]
4.35 Creditors' claim that remuneration is excessive. . . . . . [15.231]

SECTION E: SUPPLEMENTARY PROVISIONS

4.36 Liquidator deceased . . . . . [15.232]
4.37 Loss of qualification as insolvency practitioner. . . . . . [15.233]
4.38 Power of court to set aside certain transactions. . . . . . [15.234]
4.39 Rule against solicitation . . . . . [15.235]

CHAPTER 7
THE LIQUIDATION COMMITTEE

4.40 Preliminary . . . . . [15.236]

4.41 Membership of committee . . . [15.237]
4.42 Formalities of establishment . . . [15.238]
4.43 Committee established by contributories . . . [15.239]
4.44 Obligations of liquidator to committee . . . [15.240]
4.45 Meetings of the committee . . . [15.241]
4.46 The chairman at meetings . . . [15.242]
4.47 Quorum . . . [15.243]
4.48 Committee members' representatives . . . [15.244]
4.49 Resignation . . . [15.245]
4.50 Termination of membership . . . [15.246]
4.51 Removal . . . [15.247]
4.52 Vacancy (creditor members) . . . [15.248]
4.53 Vacancy (contributory members) . . . [15.249]
4.54 Voting rights and resolutions . . . [15.250]
4.55 Resolutions by post . . . [15.251]
4.56 Liquidator's reports . . . [15.252]
4.57 Expenses of members, etc . . . [15.253]
4.58 Dealings by committee-members and others . . . [15.254]
4.59 Composition of committee when creditors paid in full . . . [15.255]
4.59A Formal defects . . . [15.256]

CHAPTER 8
THE LIQUIDATION COMMITTEE WHERE WINDING UP FOLLOWS IMMEDIATELY ON ADMINISTRATION

4.60 Preliminary . . . [15.257]
4.61 Continuation of creditors' committee . . . [15.258]
4.62 Membership of committee . . . [15.259]
4.63 Liquidator's certificate . . . [15.260]
4.64 Obligations of liquidator to committee . . . [15.261]
4.65 Application of Chapter 7 . . . [15.262]

CHAPTER 9
DISTRIBUTION OF COMPANY'S ASSETS BY LIQUIDATOR

4.66 Order of priority in distribution . . . [15.263]
4.67 Order of priority of expenses of liquidation . . . [15.264]
4.68 Estate to be distributed in respect of the accounting periods . . . [15.265]
4.68A Payment of dividends . . . [15.266]
4.68B Unclaimed dividends . . . [15.267]

CHAPTER 10
SPECIAL MANAGER

4.69 Appointment and remuneration . . . [15.268]
4.70 Caution . . . [15.269]
4.71 Failure to find or to maintain caution . . . [15.270]
4.72 Accounting . . . [15.271]
4.73 Termination of appointment . . . [15.272]

CHAPTER 11
PUBLIC EXAMINATION OF COMPANY OFFICERS AND OTHERS

4.74 Notice of order for public examination . . . [15.273]
4.75 Order on request by creditors or contributories . . . [15.274]

CHAPTER 12
MISCELLANEOUS

4.75A Electronic measures – application . . . [15.275]
4.75B Electronic delivery . . . [15.276]
4.75C Electronic delivery by liquidators etc . . . [15.277]
4.76 Limitation . . . [15.278]
4.77 Dissolution after winding up . . . [15.279]

CHAPTER 13
COMPANY WITH PROHIBITED NAME

4.78 Preliminary . . . [15.280]
4.79 Application for leave under section 216(3) . . . [15.281]
4.80 First excepted case . . . [15.282]
4.81 Second excepted case . . . [15.283]
4.82 Third excepted case . . . [15.284]

CHAPTER 14
EU REGULATION—MEMBER STATE LIQUIDATOR

4.83 Interpretation of creditor and notice to member State liquidator . . . . . [15.285]

CHAPTER 15
EU REGULATION—CREDITOR'S VOLUNTARY WINDING UP: CONFIRMATION BY THE COURT

4.84 Application for confirmation . . . . . [15.286]
4.85 Notice to member State liquidator and creditors in member States . . . . . [15.287]

PART 5
CREDITORS' VOLUNTARY WINDING UP

5 Application of Part 4 . . . . . [15.288]

PART 6
MEMBERS' VOLUNTARY WINDING UP

6 Application of Part 4 . . . . . [15.289]

PART 7
PROVISIONS OF GENERAL APPLICATION

CHAPTER 1
MEETINGS

7.1 Scope of Chapter 1 . . . . . [15.290]
7.2 Summoning of meetings . . . . . [15.291]
7.3 Notice of meeting . . . . . [15.292]
7.4 Additional notices in certain cases . . . . . [15.293]
7.5 Chairman of meetings . . . . . [15.294]
7.6 Meetings requisitioned . . . . . [15.295]
7.7 Quorum . . . . . [15.296]
7.8 Adjournment . . . . . [15.297]
7.9 Entitlement to vote (creditors) . . . . . [15.298]
7.10 Entitlement to vote (members and contributories) . . . . . [15.299]
7.11 Chairman of meeting as proxy holder . . . . . [15.300]
7.12 Resolutions . . . . . [15.301]
7.13 Report of meeting . . . . . [15.302]
7.13A Application under section 176A(5) to disapply section 176A . . . . . [15.303]
7.13B Notice of order under section 176A(5) . . . . . [15.304]

CHAPTER 2
PROXIES AND COMPANY REPRESENTATION

7.14 Definition of "proxy" . . . . . [15.305]
7.15 Form of proxy . . . . . [15.306]
7.16 Use of proxy at meeting . . . . . [15.307]
7.17 Retention of proxies . . . . . [15.308]
7.18 Right of inspection . . . . . [15.309]
7.19 Proxy-holder with financial interest . . . . . [15.310]
7.20 Representation of corporations . . . . . [15.311]
7.20A Interpretation of creditor . . . . . [15.312]

CHAPTER 2A
THE EU REGULATION

7.20B Main proceedings in Scotland: undertaking by office-holder in respect of assets in another member State (Article 36 of the EU Regulation) . . . . . [15.313]
7.20C Main proceedings in another member State: approval of undertaking offered by the member State liquidator to local creditors in the UK . . . . . [15.314]
7.20D Powers of an office-holder or member State liquidator in proceedings concerning members of a group of companies (Article 60 of the EU Regulation) . . . . . [15.315]
7.20E Group coordination proceedings (Section 2 of Chapter 5 of the EU Regulation) . . . . . [15.316]
7.20F Group coordination order (Article 68 EU Regulation) . . . . . [15.317]
7.20G Delivery of group coordination order to registrar of companies . . . . . [15.318]
7.20H Office holder's report . . . . . [15.319]
7.20I Publication of opening of proceedings by a member State liquidator . . . . . [15.320]
7.20J Statement by member State liquidator that insolvency proceedings in another member State are closed etc . . . . . [15.321]

CHAPTER 3
MISCELLANEOUS

7.21 Giving of notices, etc . . . . . [15.322]

7.21A Contents of notices to be published in the Edinburgh Gazette under the Act or Rules . . . [15.323]
7.21B Notices otherwise advertised under the Act or Rules . . . [15.324]
7.21C Notices otherwise advertised—other additional provision . . . [15.325]
7.21D Omission of unobtainable information . . . [15.326]
7.22 Sending by post . . . [15.327]
7.23 Certificate of giving notice, etc . . . [15.328]
7.24 Validity of proceedings . . . [15.329]
7.25 Evidence of proceedings at meetings . . . [15.330]
7.26 Right to list of creditors and copy documents . . . [15.331]
7.27 Confidentiality of documents . . . [15.332]
7.28 Insolvency practitioner's caution . . . [15.333]
7.29 Punishment of offences . . . [15.334]
7.30 Forms for use in insolvency proceedings . . . [15.335]
7.30A Electronic submission of information instead of submission of forms to the Secretary of State, office-holders, and of copies to the registrar of companies . . . [15.336]
7.30B Electronic submission of information instead of submission of forms in all other cases . . . [15.337]
7.30C Electronic submission: exceptions . . . [15.338]
7.31 Fees, expenses, etc . . . [15.339]
7.32 Power of court to cure defects in procedure . . . [15.340]
7.33 Sederunt book . . . [15.341]
7.34 Disposal of company's books, papers and other records . . . [15.342]
7.35 Information about time spent on a case: administration and company voluntary arrangements . . . [15.343]
7.36 Information about time spent on a case . . . [15.344]

SCHEDULES

Schedule 1—Modifications of Part 4 in relation to creditors' voluntary winding up . . . [15.345]
Schedule 2—Application of Part 4 in relation to members' voluntary winding up . . . [15.346]
Schedule 3—Deposit Protection Board's voting rights . . . [15.347]
Schedule 4—Punishment of offences under the Rules . . . [15.348]
Schedule 5—List of Forms . . . [15.349]

INTRODUCTORY PROVISIONS

[15.1]

0.1 Citation and commencement

These Rules may be cited as the Insolvency (Scotland) Rules 1986 and shall come into operation on 29th December 1986.

[15.2]

0.2 Interpretation

(1) In these Rules—

"the Act" means the Insolvency Act 1986;

"the Companies Act" means the Companies Act 1985;

["the Banking Act" means the Banking Act 1987;]

"the Bankruptcy Act" means the Bankruptcy (Scotland) Act 1985;

"the Rules" means the Insolvency (Scotland) Rules 1986;

"accounting period" in relation to the winding up of a company, shall be construed in accordance with [Rule 4.68(1) to (3)];

["authorised person" is a reference to a person who is authorised pursuant to section 389A of the Act to act as nominee or supervisor of a voluntary arrangement proposed or approved under Part I or Part VIII of the Act.]

"business day" means any day other than a Saturday, a Sunday, Christmas Day, Good Friday or a day which is a bank holiday in any part of Great Britain;

["centre of main interests" has the same meaning as in the [EU] Regulation;]

"company" means a company which the courts in Scotland have jurisdiction to wind up;

["EU Regulation" means Regulation (EU) 2015/848 of the European Parliament and of the Council on insolvency proceedings;]

["establishment" has the meaning given by Article 2(10) of the EU Regulation;]

"insolvency proceedings" means any proceedings under the first group of Parts in the Act or under these Rules;

["main proceedings" means "proceedings opened in accordance with Article 3(1) of the EU Regulation and falling within the definition of insolvency proceedings in Article 2(4) of the EU Regulation and which—

(a) in relation to Scotland are set out in Annex A to the EU Regulation under the heading "United Kingdom"; and

(b) in relation to another member State, are set out under the heading relating to that member State;]

["member State liquidator" means a person falling within the definition of "insolvency practitioner" in Article 2(5) of the EU Regulation appointed in proceedings to which the EU Regulation applies in a member State other than the United Kingdom;]

["prescribed part" has the same meaning as it does in section 176A(2)(a) of the Act]

["proxy-holder" shall be construed in accordance with Rule 7.14;]

"receiver" means a receiver appointed under section 51 (Receivers (Scotland)); and

"responsible insolvency practitioner" means, in relation to any insolvency proceedings, the person acting as supervisor of a voluntary arrangement under Part I of the Act, or as administrator, receiver, liquidator or provisional liquidator.

["secondary proceedings" means proceedings opened in accordance with Article 3(2) and (3) of the EU Regulation and falling within the definition of insolvency proceedings in Article 2(4) of that Regulation and which—

(a) in relation to Scotland are set out in Annex A to that Regulation under the heading "United Kingdom";

(b) and in relation to another member State are set out under the heading relating to that member State;]

["Standard content" means—

(a) in relation to a notice to be published or advertised in the Edinburgh Gazette, the contents specified in Rule 7.21A; and

(b) in relation to a notice to be advertised in any other way, the contents specified in Rule 7.21B;]

["statutory demand" means a written demand served by a creditor on a company under section 123(1)(a) or 222(1)(a);]

["territorial proceedings" means proceedings opened in accordance with Article 3(2) and (4) of the EU Regulation and falling within the definition of insolvency proceedings in Article 2(4) of the EU Regulation and which—

(a) in relation to Scotland are set out in Annex A to that Regulation under the heading "United Kingdom";

(b) and in relation to another member State are set out under the heading relating to that member State].

(2) In these Rules, unless the context otherwise requires, any reference—

(a) to a section is a reference to a section of the Act;

(b) to a Rule is a reference to a Rule of the Rules;

(c) to a Part or a Schedule is a reference to a Part of, or Schedule to, the Rules;

(d) to a Chapter is a reference to a Chapter of the Part in which that reference is made.

[(3) A document or information given, delivered or sent in hard copy form under any Rule in Parts 1 [to 6, or any other Rule applied by any of those parts], is sufficiently authenticated if it is signed by the person sending or supplying it.

(4) A document or information given, delivered or sent in electronic form under any Rule in Parts 1 [to 6, or any other Rule applied by any of those parts], is sufficiently authenticated—

(a) if the identity of the sender is confirmed in a manner specified by the recipient, or

(b) where no such manner has been specified by the recipient, if the communication contains or is accompanied by a statement of the identity of the sender and the recipient has no reason to doubt the truth of that statement.]

NOTES

Para (1): in the definition "accounting period", words in square brackets substituted for original words "section 52(1) and (6) of the Bankruptcy Act as applied by Rule 4.68" and definition "statutory demand" inserted, by the Insolvency (Scotland) Amendment Rules 2014, SSI 2014/114, rr 2, 3, subject to savings in r 29 thereof (see the note "Savings" below); definitions "the Banking Act" and "proxy-holder" inserted by the Insolvency (Scotland) Amendment Rules 1987, SI 1987/1921, r 3(1), Schedule, Pt I, para 1; definition "authorised person" inserted by the Insolvency (Scotland) Amendment Rules 2002, SI 2002/2709, r 3; definition "the Bankruptcy Act" revoked by the Bankruptcy (Scotland) Act 2016 (Consequential Provisions and Modifications) Order 2016, SI 2016/1034, art 7(1), (3), Sch 1, para 36(1), (2), as from 30 November 2016 (except in relation to (i) a sequestration as regards which the petition is presented, or the debtor application is made before that date; or (ii) a trust deed executed before that date); definitions "centre of main interests", "EC Regulation", "establishment", "main proceedings", "member State liquidator", "secondary proceedings" and "territorial proceedings" inserted by the Insolvency (Scotland) Regulations 2003, SI 2003/2109, regs 23, 24, subject to the saving that anything done under or for the purposes of any provision of these Rules before 8 September 2003 has effect as if done under or for the purposes of the provision as amended; definition "prescribed part" inserted by the Enterprise Act 2002 (Consequential Amendments) (Prescribed Part) (Scotland) Order 2003, SI 2003/2108, art 3; definition "Standard content" inserted by the Insolvency (Scotland) Amendment Rules 2010, SI 2010/688, r 3, Sch 1, para 1, subject to transitional provisions in r 4 thereof at **[2.80]**.

Word in square brackets in definition "centre of main interests" substituted for original word "EC", definitions "establishment", "main proceedings", "member State liquidator", "secondary proceedings", "territorial proceedings" substituted and definition "EU Regulation" substituted for original definition "EC Regulation", by the Insolvency Amendment (EU 2015/848) Regulations 2017, SI 2017/702, regs 2, 3, Schedule, Pt 5, paras 61, 62, as from 26 June 2017, except in relation to proceedings opened before that date. The substituted definitions previously read as follows:

""EC Regulation" means Council Regulation (EC) No 1346/2000 of 29th May 2000 on insolvency proceedings;

"establishment" has the meaning given by Article 2(h) of the EC Regulation;

"main proceedings" means proceedings opened in accordance with Article 3(1) of the EC Regulation and falling within the definition of insolvency proceedings in Article 2(a) of the EC Regulation, and

(2) Where a nominee or supervisor gives, sends or delivers a notice or other document to any person by electronic means, it must contain or be accompanied by a statement that the recipient may request a hard copy of the notice or document, and specify a telephone number, e-mail address and postal address that may be used to make such a request.

(3) Where a hard copy of the notice or other document is requested it must be sent within 5 business days of receipt of the request by the nominee or supervisor, who may not make a charge for sending it in that form.

(4) In the absence of evidence to the contrary, a notice or other document shall be presumed to have been delivered where—

(a) the sender can produce a copy of the electronic message which—

(i) contained the notice or other document, or to which the notice or other document was attached; and

(ii) shows the time and date the message was sent; and

(b) that electronic message was sent to the address supplied under paragraph (1)(b).

(5) A message sent electronically is deemed to have been delivered to the recipient no later than 9.00 am on the next business day after it was sent.]

NOTES

Inserted as noted to r 1.1A at **[15.5]**.

[15.7]

[1.1C Use of websites by nominee or supervisor

(1) This Rule applies for the purpose of section 246B.

(2) A nominee or supervisor required to give, deliver or send a document to any person may (other than in a case where personal service is required) satisfy that requirement by sending that person a notice—

(a) stating that the document is available for viewing and downloading on a website;

(b) specifying the address of that website together with any password necessary to view and download the document from that website; and

(c) containing a statement that the recipient of the notice may request a hard copy of the document, and specifying a telephone number, e-mail address and postal address which may be used to make such a request.

(3) Where a notice to which this Rule applies is sent, the document to which it relates must—

(a) be available on the website for a period of not less than 3 months after the date on which the notice is sent; and

(b) be in such a format as to enable it to be downloaded from the website within a reasonable time of an electronic request being made for it to be downloaded.

(4) Where a hard copy of the document is requested it must be sent within 5 business days of the receipt of the request by the nominee or supervisor, who may not make a charge for sending it in that form.

(5) Where a document is given, delivered or sent to a person by means of a website in accordance with this Rule, it is deemed to have been delivered—

(a) when the document was first made available on the website, or

(b) if later, when the notice under paragraph (2) was delivered to that person.]

NOTES

Inserted as noted to r 1.1A at **[15.5]**.

[15.8]

[1.1D Special provision on account of expense as to website use

(1) Where the court is satisfied that the expense of sending notices in accordance with Rule 1.1C would, on account of the number of persons entitled to receive them, be disproportionate to the benefit of sending notices in accordance with that Rule, it may order that the requirement to give, deliver or send a relevant document to any person may (other than in a case where personal service is required) be satisfied by the nominee or supervisor sending each of those persons a notice—

(a) stating that all relevant documents will be made available for viewing and downloading on a website;

(b) specifying the address of that website together with any password necessary to view and download a relevant document from that site; and

(c) containing a statement that the person to whom the notice is given, delivered or sent may at any time request that hard copies of all, or specific, relevant documents are sent to that person, and specifying a telephone number, e-mail address and postal address which may be used to make that request.

(2) A document to which this Rule relates must—

(a) be available on the website for a period of not less than 12 months from the date when it was first made available on the website or, if later, from the date upon which the notice was sent, and

(b) be in such a format as to enable it to be downloaded from the website within a reasonable time of an electronic request being made for it to be downloaded.

(3) Where hard copies of relevant documents have been requested, they must be sent by the nominee or supervisor—

(a) within 5 business days of the receipt by the nominee or supervisor of the request to be sent hard copies, in the case of relevant documents first appearing on the website before the request was received, or

(b) within 5 business days from the date a relevant document first appears on the website, in all other cases.

(4) A nominee or supervisor must not require a person making a request under paragraph (3) to pay a fee for the supply of the document.

(5) Where a relevant document is given, delivered or sent to a person by means of a website in accordance with this Rule, it is deemed to have been delivered—

(a) when the relevant document was first made available on the website, or

(b) if later, when the notice under paragraph (1) was delivered to that person.

(6) In this Rule a relevant document means any document which the nominee or supervisor is first required to give, deliver or send to any person after the court has made an order under paragraph (1).]

NOTES

Inserted as noted to r 1.1A at **[15.5]**.

CHAPTER 2 PROPOSAL BY DIRECTORS

1.2 (*Revoked by the Insolvency (Scotland) Amendment Rules 2010, SI 2010/688, r 3, Sch 1, para 4, subject to transitional provisions in rr 4, 5 thereof at* **[2.80]**, **[2.81]**.)

[15.9]

1.3 Contents of proposal

(1) The directors' proposal shall provide a short explanation why, in their opinion, a voluntary arrangement under Part I of the Act is desirable, and give reasons why the company's creditors may be expected to concur with such an arrangement.

(2) The following matters shall be stated, or otherwise dealt with, in the directors' proposal—

(a) the following matters, so far as within the directors' immediate knowledge—

(i) the company's assets, with an estimate of their respective values;

(ii) the extent (if any) to which the assets are subject to any security in favour of any creditors;

(iii) the extent (if any) to which particular assets of the company are to be excluded from the voluntary arrangement;

(b) particulars of any property other than assets of the company itself, which is proposed to be included in the arrangement, the source of such property and the terms on which it is to be made available for inclusion;

(c) the nature and amount of the company's liabilities (so far as within the directors' immediate knowledge), the manner in which they are proposed to be met, modified, postponed or otherwise dealt with by means of the arrangement, and (in particular)—

(i) how it is proposed to deal with preferential creditors (defined in section 386) and creditors who are, or claim to be, secured;

(ii) how persons connected with the company (being creditors) are proposed to be treated under the arrangement; and

(iii) whether there are, to the directors' knowledge, any circumstances giving rise to the possibility, in the event that the company should go into liquidation, of claims under—

section 242 (gratuitous alienations),

section 243 (unfair preferences),

section 244 (extortionate credit transactions), or

section 245 (floating charges invalid);

and, where any such circumstances are present, whether, and if so how, it is proposed under the voluntary arrangement to make provision for wholly or partly indemnifying the company in respect of such claims;

[(ca) to the best of the directors' knowledge and belief—

(i) an estimate of the value of the prescribed part, should the company go into liquidation if the proposal for the voluntary arrangement is not accepted, whether or not section 176A is to be disapplied, and

(ii) an estimate of the value of the company's net property on the date that the estimate is made,

provided that such estimates shall not be required to include any information the disclosure of which could seriously prejudice the commercial interests of the company, but if such information is excluded the estimates shall be accompanied by a statement to that effect;]

(d) whether any, and if so what, cautionary obligations (including guarantees) have been given of the company's debts by other persons, specifying which (if any) of the cautioners are persons connected with the company;

(e) the proposed duration of the voluntary arrangement;

(f) the proposed dates of distributions to creditors, with estimates of their amounts;

[(fa) how it is proposed to deal with the claim of any person who is bound by the arrangement by virtue of section 5(2)(b)(ii);]

(g) the amount proposed to be paid to the nominee (as such) by way of remuneration and expenses;

(h) the manner in which it is proposed that the supervisor of the arrangement should be remunerated and his expenses defrayed;
(i) whether, for the purposes of the arrangement, any cautionary obligations (including guarantees) are to be offered by directors, or other persons, and whether (if so) any security is to be given or sought;
(j) the manner in which funds held for the purposes of the arrangement are to be banked, invested or otherwise dealt with pending distribution to creditors;
(k) the manner in which funds held for the purpose of payment to creditors, and not so paid on the termination of the arrangement, are to be dealt with;
(l) the manner in which the business of the company is being and is proposed to be conducted during the course of the arrangement;
(m) details of any further credit facilities which it is intended to arrange for the company and how the debts so arising are to be paid;
(n) the functions which are to be undertaken by the supervisor of the arrangement;
[(o) the name, address and qualification of the person proposed as supervisor of the voluntary arrangement, and confirmation that he is either qualified to act as an insolvency practitioner in relation to the company or is an authorised person in relation to the company][; . . .
(p) whether the [EU Regulation] will apply and, if so, whether the proceedings will be main proceedings or territorial proceedings][; and
(q) such other matters (if any) as the directors consider appropriate for ensuring that members and creditors are enabled to reach an informed decision on the proposal.]

(3) With the agreement in writing of the nominee, the directors' proposal may be amended at any time up to delivery of the [nominee's] report to the court under section 2(2).

NOTES

Para (2): sub-para (ca) inserted by the Enterprise Act 2002 (Consequential Amendments) (Prescribed Part) (Scotland) Order 2003, SI 2003/2108, art 4(1); sub-para (fa) inserted and sub-para (o) substituted by the Insolvency (Scotland) Amendment Rules 2002, SI 2002/2709, r 4(1), Schedule, Pt 1, para 2, subject to savings contained in r 4(2) as noted to r 1.1 at **[15.4]**. Sub-para (o) originally read as follows:

"(o) the name, address and qualification of the person proposed as supervisor of the voluntary arrangement, and confirmation that he is (so far as the directors are aware) qualified to act as an insolvency practitioner in relation to the company.";

sub-para (p) and word "and" (omitted) immediately preceding it substituted by the Insolvency (Scotland) Regulations 2003, SI 2003/2109, regs 23, 25(2), subject to the saving that anything done under or for the purposes of any provision of these Rules before 8 September 2003 has effect as if done under or for the purposes of the provision as amended. (Note that reg 25(2) purports to substitute sub-para (p) and the word "and" immediately preceding it for "; and."); word omitted from sub-para (o) revoked, and sub-para (q) and word "and" immediately preceding it added, by the Insolvency (Scotland) Amendment Rules 2010, SI 2010/688, r 3, Sch 1, para 5, subject to transitional provisions in r 6 thereof at **[2.82]**; words in square brackets in sub-para (p) substituted for original words "EC Regulation" by the Insolvency Amendment (EU 2015/848) Regulations 2017, SI 2017/702, regs 2, 3, Schedule, Pt 5, paras 61, 63, as from 26 June 2017, except in relation to proceedings opened before that date.

Para (3): word in square brackets substituted for original word "former's" by SI 2010/688, r 3, Sch 1, para 6, subject to transitional provisions in r 4 thereof at **[2.80]**.

[15.10]
1.4 Notice to intended nominee

(1) The directors shall give to the intended nominee written notice of their proposal.

(2) The notice, accompanied by a copy of the proposal, shall be delivered either to the nominee himself, or to a person authorised to take delivery of documents on his behalf.

(3) If the intended nominee agrees to act, he shall cause a copy of the notice to be endorsed to the effect that it has been received by him on a specified date; and the period of 28 days referred to in section 2(2) then runs from that date.

(4) The copy of the notice so endorsed shall be returned by the nominee [as soon as is reasonably practicable] to the directors at an address specified by them in the notice for that purpose.

NOTES

Para (4): words in square brackets substituted for original word "forthwith" by the Insolvency (Scotland) Amendment Rules 2009, SI 2009/662, r 2, Schedule, para 1, subject to transitional provisions in r 3 thereof which provides as follows:

"The amendments to the principal Rules contained in the Schedule shall not apply—
(a) where a moratorium under a company voluntary arrangement comes into force; or
(b) in an administration, where the company enters administration;
before 6th April 2009.".

[15.11]
1.5 Statement of affairs

[(1) The directors shall, at the same time as the proposal is delivered to the nominee, deliver to the nominee a statement of the company's affairs.]

(2) The statement shall comprise the following particulars (supplementing or amplifying, so far as is necessary for clarifying the state of the company's affairs, those already given in the directors' proposal)—

(a) a list of the company's assets, divided into such categories as are appropriate for easy identification, with estimated values assigned to each category;
(b) in the case of any property on which a claim against the company is wholly or partly secured, particulars of the claim and its amount and of how and when the security was created;
(c) the names and addresses of the company's preferential creditors (defined in section 386), with the amounts of their respective claims;
(d) the names and addresses of the company's unsecured creditors, with the amounts of their respective claims;
(e) particulars of any debts owed by or to the company to or by persons connected with it;
(f) the names and addresses of the company's members and details of their respective shareholdings; and
(g) such other particulars (if any) as the nominee may in writing require to be furnished for the purposes of making his report to the court on the directors' proposal.

(3) The statement of affairs shall be made up to a date not earlier than 2 weeks before the date of the notice given by the directors to the nominee under Rule 1.4. However the nominee may allow an extension of that period to the nearest practicable date (not earlier than 2 months before the date of the notice under Rule 1.4); and if he does so, he shall give his reasons in his report to the court on the directors' proposal.

(4) The statement shall be certified as correct, to the best of [the relevant director's] knowledge and belief, by [one director].

NOTES

Para (1): substituted by the Insolvency (Scotland) Amendment Rules 2010, SI 2010/688, r 3, Sch 1, para 7, subject to transitional provisions in r 4 thereof at **[2.80]**, and previously read as follows:

"(1) The directors shall, within 7 days after their proposal is delivered to the nominee, or within such longer time as he may allow, deliver to him a statement of the company's affairs.".

Para (4): words in first pair of square brackets substituted for original word "their" and words in second pair of square brackets substituted for original words "two or more directors of the company or by the company secretary and at least one director (other than the secretary himself)" by SI 2010/688, r 3, Sch 1, para 8, subject to transitional provisions in r 4 thereof at **[2.80]**.

[15.12]
1.6 Additional disclosure for assistance of nominee

(1) If it appears to the nominee that he cannot properly prepare his report on the basis of information in the directors' proposal and statement of affairs, he may call on the directors to provide him with—
(a) further and better particulars as to the circumstances in which, and the reasons why, the company is insolvent or (as the case may be) threatened with insolvency;
(b) particulars of any previous proposals which have been made in respect of the company under Part I of the Act;
(c) any further information with respect to the company's affairs which the nominee thinks necessary for the purposes of his report.

(2) The nominee may call on the directors to inform him, with respect to any person who is, or at any time in the 2 years preceding the notice under Rule 1.4 has been, a director or officer of the company, whether and in what circumstances (in those 2 years or previously) that person—
(a) has been concerned in the affairs of any other company (whether or not incorporated in Scotland) which has become insolvent, or
(b) has had his estate sequestrated, granted a trust deed for his creditors, been adjudged bankrupt or compounded or entered into an arrangement with his creditors [or had a debt relief order made in respect of him (under Part 7A of the Insolvency Act 1986)].

(3) For the purpose of enabling the nominee to consider their proposal and prepare his report on it, the directors must give [the nominee such access to the company's accounts and records as the nominee may require].

NOTES

Para (2): words in square brackets in sub-para (b) added, in relation to a debt relief order the application for which is made after 1 October 2012, by the Tribunals, Courts and Enforcement Act 2007 (Consequential Amendments) Order 2012, SI 2012/2404, arts 3(3), 7, Sch 3, para 4(1), (2).

Para (3): words in square brackets substituted for original words "him access to the company's accounts and records" by the Insolvency (Scotland) Amendment Rules 2010, SI 2010/688, r 3, Sch 1, para 9, subject to transitional provisions in r 4 thereof at **[2.80]**.

[15.13]
1.7 Nominee's report on the proposal

(1) With his report to the court under section 2 the nominee shall lodge—
(a) a copy of the directors' proposal (with amendments, if any, authorised under Rule 1.3(3));
(b) a copy or summary of the company's statement of affairs.

(2) If the nominee makes known his opinion [that the directors' proposal has a reasonable prospect of being approved and implemented and] that meetings of the company and its creditors should be summoned under section 3, his report shall have annexed to it his comments on the proposal. If his opinion is otherwise, he shall give his reasons for that opinion.

[(2A) The nominee must examine whether there is jurisdiction to open the proceedings and must specify in the nominee's comments on the proposal required by paragraph (2) whether the EU Regulation will apply and, if so, whether the proceedings will be main proceedings, territorial proceedings or secondary with the reasons for so stating.]

(3) The nominee shall send a copy of his report and of his comments (if any) to the company. Any director, member or creditor of the company is entitled, at all reasonable times on any business day, to inspect the report and comments.

NOTES

Para (2): words in square brackets inserted by the Insolvency (Scotland) Amendment Rules 2002, SI 2002/2709, r 4(1), Schedule, Pt 1, para 3, subject to savings contained in r 4(2) as noted to r 1.1 at **[15.4]**.

Para (2A): inserted by the Insolvency Amendment (EU 2015/848) Regulations 2017, SI 2017/702, regs 2, 3, Schedule, Pt 5, paras 61, 64, as from 26 June 2017, except in relation to proceedings opened before that date.

[15.14]

[1.8 Replacement of nominee

(1) Where a person other than the nominee intends to apply to the court under section 2(4) for the nominee to be replaced (except in any case where the nominee has died), he shall give to the nominee at least [5 business] days' notice of his application.

(2) Where the nominee intends to apply to the court under section 2(4) to be replaced, he shall give at least [5 business] days' notice of his application to the person intending to make the proposal.

(3) No appointment of a replacement nominee shall be made by the court unless there is lodged in court a statement by the replacement nominee—

(a) indicating his consent to act; and

(b) that he is qualified to act as an insolvency practitioner in relation to the company or is an authorised person in relation to the company.]

NOTES

Substituted by the Insolvency (Scotland) Amendment Rules 2002, SI 2002/2709, r 4(1), Schedule, Pt 1, para 4, subject to savings contained in r 4(2) as noted to r 1.1 at **[15.4]**, and originally read as follows:

"**1.8 Replacement of nominee**

Where any person intends to apply to the court under section 2(4) for the nominee to be replaced he shall give to the nominee at least 7 days' notice of his application.".

Paras (1), (2): words in square brackets substituted for original number "7" by the Insolvency (Scotland) Amendment Rules 2010, SI 2010/688, r 3, Sch 1, para 10, subject to transitional provisions in r 4 thereof at **[2.80]**.

Para (3): see Sch 5, Form 1.8 (Scot) at **[15.349]**.

[15.15]

1.9 Summoning of meetings under section 3

(1) If in his report the nominee states that in his opinion meetings of the company and its creditors should be summoned to consider the directors' proposal, the date on which the meetings are to be held shall be not . . . more than 28 days from the date on which he lodged his report in court under section 2.

(2) The notice summoning the meeting shall specify the court in which the nominee's report under section 2 has been lodged [and shall state the effect of Rule 1.16A(2) to (4),] and with each notice there shall be sent—

(a) a copy of the directors' proposal;

(b) a copy of the statement of affairs or, if the nominee thinks fit, a summary of it (the summary to include a list of creditors and the amount of their debts); . . .

(c) the nominee's comments on the proposal[; and

(d) forms of proxy.]

[(3) Notices calling the meetings shall be sent by the nominee at least 14 days before the day fixed for them to be held—

(a) in the case of the creditors' meeting, to all the creditors specified in the statement of affairs, and any other creditors of the company of whose address the nominee is aware; and

(b) in the case of the meeting of members of the company, to all persons who are, to the best of the nominee's belief, members of it.]

NOTES

Para (1): words "less than 14, nor" (omitted) revoked by the Insolvency (Scotland) Amendment Rules 2010, SI 2010/688, r 3, Sch 1, para 11, subject to transitional provisions in rr 4, 6 thereof at **[2.80]**, **[2.82]**.

Para (2): words in first pair of square brackets inserted, word "and" omitted from sub-para (b) revoked and sub-para (d) and word "and" immediately preceding it added by SI 2010/688, r 3, Sch 1, paras 12, 13, subject to transitional provisions in r 4 thereof at **[2.80]**.

Para (3): added by SI 2010/688, r 3, Sch 1, para 14, subject to transitional provisions in r 4 thereof at **[2.80]**.

CHAPTER 3 PROPOSAL BY ADMINISTRATOR OR LIQUIDATOR WHERE HE IS THE NOMINEE

[15.16]

1.10 Preparation of proposal

The responsible insolvency practitioner's proposal shall specify—

(a) all such matters as under Rule 1.3 [(subject to paragraph (c) below)] in Chapter 2 the directors of the company would be required to include in a proposal by them [with, in addition, where the company is [in administration] [or liquidation], the names and addresses of the company's preferential creditors (defined in section 386), with the amounts of their respective claims,] and

(b) . . .

[(c) the administrator or liquidator shall include, in place of the estimate referred to in Rule 1.3(2)(ca), a statement which contains—

(i) to the best of his knowledge and belief—

(aa) an estimate of the value of the prescribed part (whether or not he proposes to make an application under section 176A(5) or section 176A(3) applies), and

(bb) an estimate of the value of the company's net property, provided that such estimates shall not be required to include any information the disclosure of which could seriously prejudice the commercial interests of the company, but if such information is excluded the estimates shall be accompanied by a statement to that effect; and

(ii) whether, and, if so, why, he proposes to make an application under section 176A(5).]

[(d) the reasons for stating whether the EU Regulation will apply and, if so, whether the proceedings will be main proceedings, territorial proceedings or secondary proceedings].

NOTES

Para (a): words in first pair of square brackets inserted by the Enterprise Act 2002 (Consequential Amendments) (Prescribed Part) (Scotland) Order 2003, SI 2003/2108, art 4(2)(a); words in second (outer) pair of square brackets inserted by the Insolvency (Scotland) Amendment Rules 1987, SI 1987/1921, r 3(1), Schedule, Pt I, para 2; words in third (inner) pair of square brackets substituted for words "subject to an administration order" by the Insolvency (Scotland) Amendment Rules 2003, SI 2003/2111, r 6, Sch 2, para 2, subject to savings in r 7 thereof at **[2.34]**; words in fourth (inner) pair of square brackets inserted by the Insolvency (Scotland) Amendment Rules 2010, SI 2010/688, r 3, Sch 1, para 15(a), subject to transitional provisions in r 6 thereof at **[2.82]**.

Para (b): revoked by SI 2010/688, r 3, Sch 1, para 15(b), subject to transitional provisions in r 6 thereof at **[2.82]**, and previously read as follows:

"(b) such other matters (if any) as the insolvency practitioner considers appropriate for ensuring that members and creditors of the company are enabled to reach an informed decision on the proposal.".

Para (c): added by SI 2003/2108, art 4(2)(b).

Para (d): added by the Insolvency Amendment (EU 2015/848) Regulations 2017, SI 2017/702, regs 2, 3, Schedule, Pt 5, paras 61, 65, as from 26 June 2017, except in relation to proceedings opened before that date.

[15.17]

1.11 Summoning of meetings under section 3

[(1) Notices calling meetings under section 3(2) shall be sent by the responsible insolvency practitioner at least 14 days before the day fixed for them to be held—

(a) in the case of the creditors' meeting, to all the creditors specified in the statement of affairs, and any other creditors of the company of whose address the responsible insolvency practitioner is aware; and

(b) in the case of the meeting of members of the company, to all persons who are, to the best of the responsible insolvency practitioner's belief, members of it.]

(2) With each notice summoning the meeting, there shall be sent—

(a) a copy of the responsible insolvency practitioner's proposal; . . .

(b) a copy of the company's statement of affairs or, if he thinks fit, a summary of it (the summary to include a list of the creditors and the amount of their debts);

[(c) a statement of the effect of Rule 1.16A(2) to (4); and

(d) forms of proxy.]

NOTES

Para (1): substituted by the Insolvency (Scotland) Amendment Rules 2010, SI 2010/688, r 3, Sch 1, para 16, subject to transitional provisions in r 4 thereof at **[2.80]**, and previously read as follows:

"(1) The responsible insolvency practitioner shall give at least 14 days' notice of the meetings of the company and of its creditors under section 3(2).".

Para (2): word "and" (omitted) revoked and sub-paras (c), (d) added by SI 2010/688, r 3, Sch 1, para 17, subject to transitional provisions in r 4 thereof at **[2.80]**.

CHAPTER 4 PROPOSAL BY ADMINISTRATOR OR LIQUIDATOR WHERE ANOTHER INSOLVENCY PRACTITIONER IS THE NOMINEE

[15.18]

1.12 Preparation of proposal and notice to nominee

(1) The responsible insolvency practitioner shall give notice to the intended nominee, and prepare his proposal for a voluntary arrangement, in the same manner as is required of the directors in the case of a proposal by them, under Chapter 2.

(2) Rule 1.2 applies to the responsible insolvency practitioner as it applies to the directors; and Rule 1.4 applies as regards the action to be taken by the nominee.

(3) The content of the proposal shall be as required by [Rule 1.10], reading references to the directors as referring to the responsible insolvency practitioner.

(4) Rule 1.6 applies, in respect of the information to be provided to the nominee, reading references to the directors as referring to the responsible insolvency practitioner.

(5) With the proposal the responsible insolvency practitioner shall provide a copy of the company's statement of affairs.

(6) Rules 1.7 to 1.9 apply as regards a proposal under this Chapter as they apply to a proposal under Chapter 2.

NOTES

Para (3): words in square brackets substituted by the Insolvency (Scotland) Amendment Rules 1987, SI 1987/1921, r 3(1), Schedule, Pt I, para 3.

CHAPTER 5 MEETINGS

[15.19]

1.13 General

The provisions of Chapter 1 of Part 7 (Meetings) shall apply with regard to the meetings of the company and of the creditors which are summoned under section 3, subject to Rules 1.9, 1.11 and 1.12(6) and the provisions in this Chapter.

NOTES

Revoked by the Insolvency (Scotland) Amendment Rules 2010, SI 2010/688, r 3, Sch 1, para 18, subject to transitional provisions in r 4 thereof at **[2.80]**.

[15.20]

1.14 Summoning of meetings

(1) In fixing the date, time and place for the creditors' meeting and the company meeting, the [nominee must] have regard primarily to the convenience of the creditors.

[(2) The meetings may be held on the same day or on different days. If held on the same day, the meetings shall be held in the same place, but in either case the creditors' meeting shall be fixed for a time in advance of the company meeting.

(3) Where the meetings are not held on the same day, they shall be held within [5 business] days of each other.]

[(4) Meetings shall, in all cases, be summoned for commencement between 10.00 and 16.00 hours on a business day.]

NOTES

Para (1): words in square brackets substituted for original words "person summoning the meetings ("the convenor") shall" by the Insolvency (Scotland) Amendment Rules 2010, SI 2010/688, r 3, Sch 1, para 19, subject to transitional provisions in r 4 thereof at **[2.80]**.

Para (2): substituted, together with para (3), for para (2) by the Insolvency (Scotland) Amendment Rules 2002, SI 2002/2709, r 4(1), Schedule, Pt 1, para 5, subject to savings contained in r 4(2) as noted to r 1.1 at **[15.4]**. Para (2) originally read as follows:

> "(2) The meetings shall be held on the same day and in the same place, but the creditors' meeting shall be fixed for a time in advance of the company meeting.".

Para (3): substituted as noted to para (2); words in square brackets substituted for original number "7" by SI 2010/688, r 3, Sch 1, para 20, subject to transitional provisions in r 4 thereof at **[2.80]**.

Para (4): added by SI 2010/688, r 3, Sch 1, para 21, subject to transitional provisions in r 4 thereof at **[2.80]**.

[15.21]

[1.14ZA Remote Attendance at Meetings

(1) This Rule applies to a request to the nominee of a meeting under section 246A(9) to specify a place for the meeting.

(2) The request must be accompanied by—

- (a) in the case of a request by creditors, a list of the creditors making (or concurring with) the request and the amounts of those creditors' respective debts in the insolvency proceedings in question,
- (b) in the case of a request by members, a list of the members making (or concurring with) the request and those members' voting rights, and
- (c) from each person concurring, written confirmation of that person's concurrence.

(3) The request must be made within 7 business days of the date on which the nominee sent the notice of the meeting in question.

(4) Where the nominee considers that the request has been properly made in accordance with the Act and these Rules, the nominee must—

(a) give notice (to all those previously given notice of the meeting)—

(i) that the meeting is to be held at a specified place, and

(ii) whether the date and time of the meeting are to remain the same or not;

(b) specify a time, date and place for the meeting, the date of which must not be more than 28 days after the original date for the meeting; and

(c) give at least 14 days notice of the time, date and place of the meeting (to all those previously given notice of the meeting),

and the notices required by subparagraphs (a) and (c) may be given at the same or different times.

(5) Where the nominee has specified a place for the meeting in response to a request to which this Rule applies, the chairman of the meeting must attend the meeting by being present in person at that place.]

NOTES

Inserted by the Insolvency (Scotland) Amendment Rules 2010, SI 2010/688, r 3, Sch 1, para 22, subject to transitional provisions in rr 4, 5 thereof at **[2.80]**, **[2.81]**.

[15.22]
[1.14A The Chairman at meetings

(1) Subject as follows, at both the creditors' meeting and the company meeting, and at any combined meeting, the convenor shall be chairman.

(2) If for any reason he is unable to attend, he may nominate another person to act as chairman in his place; but a person so nominated must be—

(a) a person qualified to act as an insolvency practitioner in relation to the company;

(b) an authorised person in relation to the company; or

(c) an employee of the convenor or his firm who is experienced in insolvency matters.]

NOTES

Inserted by the Insolvency (Scotland) Amendment Rules 2002, SI 2002/2709, r 4(1), Schedule, Pt 1, para 6, subject to savings contained in r 4(2) as noted to r 1.1 at **[15.4]**.

[15.23]
[1.14AA Chairman of meeting as proxy holder

At any meeting, the chairman shall not, by virtue of any proxy held by him, vote to increase or reduce the amount of the remuneration or expenses of the nominee or the supervisor of the proposed arrangement, unless the proxy specifically directs him to vote in that way.]

NOTES

Inserted by the Insolvency (Scotland) Amendment Rules 2010, SI 2010/688, r 3, Sch 1, para 23, subject to transitional provisions in r 4 thereof at **[2.80]**.

[15.24]
1.15 Attendance by company officers

(1) At least 14 days' notice to attend the meetings shall be given by the convenor to—

(a) all directors of the company, and

(b) any persons in whose case the convenor thinks that their presence is required as being officers of the company or as having been directors or officers of it at any time in the 2 years immediately preceding the date of the notice.

(2) The chairman may, if he thinks fit, exclude any present or former director or officer from attendance at a meeting, either completely or for any part of it; and this applies whether or not a notice under this Rule has been sent to the person excluded.

[15.25]
[1.15A Entitlement to vote (creditors)

(1) Subject as follows, every creditor who has notice of the creditors' meeting is entitled to vote at the meeting or any adjournment of it.

(2) Votes are calculated according to the amount of the creditor's debt as at the date of the meeting or, where the company is being wound up or is subject to an administration order, the date of its going into liquidation or (as the case may be) of the administration order.

(3) A creditor may vote in respect of a debt for an unliquidated amount or any debt whose value is not ascertained and for the purposes of voting (but not otherwise) his debt shall be valued at £1 unless the chairman agrees to put a higher value on it.

[(4) A creditor is entitled to vote at any meeting if the creditor, either at the meeting or before it, has submitted the creditor's claim to the responsible insolvency practitioner and the creditor's claim has been accepted in whole or in part.]]

NOTES

Inserted, together with r 1.15B, by the Insolvency (Scotland) Amendment Rules 2002, SI 2002/2709, r 4(1), Schedule, Pt 1, para 7, subject to savings contained in r 4(2) as noted to r 1.1 at **[15.4]**.

Para (4): added by the Insolvency (Scotland) Amendment Rules 2010, SI 2010/688, r 3, Sch 1, para 24, subject to transitional provisions in r 4 thereof at **[2.80]**.

[15.26]
[1.15AA Entitlement to vote (members)

(1) Members of a company at their meeting shall vote according to the rights attaching to their shares in accordance with the company's articles of association.

(2) Reference in this Rule to a person's shares include any other interests which that person may have as a member of the company.]

NOTES

Inserted by the Insolvency (Scotland) Amendment Rules 2010, SI 2010/688, r 3, Sch 1, para 25, subject to transitional provisions in r 4 thereof at **[2.80]**.

[15.27]
[1.15B Procedure for admission of creditors' claims for voting purposes

(1) Subject as follows, at any creditors' meeting the chairman shall ascertain the entitlement of persons wishing to vote and shall admit or reject their claims accordingly.

(2) The chairman may admit or reject a claim in whole or in part.

(3) The chairman's decision on any matter under this Rule or under paragraph (3) of Rule 1.15A is subject to appeal to the court by any creditor or member of the company.

(4) If the chairman is in doubt whether a claim should be admitted or rejected, he shall mark it as objected to and allow votes to be cast in respect of it, subject to such votes being subsequently declared invalid if the objection to the claim is sustained.

(5) If on an appeal the chairman's decision is reversed or varied, or votes are declared invalid, the court may order another meeting to be summoned, or make such order as it thinks just.

The court's power to make an order under this paragraph is exercisable only if it considers that the circumstances giving rise to the appeal give rise to unfair prejudice or material irregularity.

(6) An application to the court by way of appeal against the chairman's decision shall not be made after the end of the period of 28 days beginning with the first day on which the report required by section 4(6) has been made to the court.

(7) The chairman is not personally liable for any expenses incurred by any person in respect of an appeal under this Rule.]

NOTES

Inserted as noted to r 1.15A at **[15.25]**.

[15.28]
[1.16

(1) If the chairman thinks fit, the creditors' meeting and the company meeting may be held together.

(2) The chairman may, and shall if it is so resolved at the meeting in question, adjourn that meeting for not more than 14 days.

(3) If there are subsequently further adjournments, the final adjournment shall not be to a day later than 14 days after the date on which the meeting in question was originally held.

(4) In the case of a proposal by the directors, if the meetings are adjourned under paragraph (2), notice of the fact shall be given by the nominee [as soon as is reasonably practicable] to the court.

(5) If following the final adjournment of the creditors' meeting the proposal (with or without modifications) has not been approved by the creditors it is deemed rejected.

[(6) During a meeting, the chairman may, in the chairman's discretion and without an adjournment, declare the meeting suspended for any period up to one hour.]]

NOTES

Substituted by the Insolvency (Scotland) Amendment Rules 2002, SI 2002/2709, r 4(1), Schedule, Pt 1, para 8, subject to savings contained in r 4(2) as noted to r 1.1 at **[15.4]**, and originally read as follows:

"1.16 Adjournments

(1) On the day on which the meetings are held, they may from time to time be adjourned; and, if the chairman thinks fit for the purpose of obtaining the simultaneous agreement of the meetings to the proposal (with the same modifications, if any), the meetings may be held together.

(2) If on that day the requisite majority for the approval of the voluntary arrangement (with the same modifications, if any) has not been obtained from both creditors and members of the company, the chairman may, and shall, if it is so resolved, adjourn the meetings for not more than 14 days.

(3) If there are subsequently further adjournments, the final adjournment shall not be to a day later than 14 days after the date on which the meetings were originally held.

(4) There shall be no adjournment of either meeting unless the other is also adjourned to the same business day.

(5) In the case of a proposal by the directors, if the meetings are adjourned under paragraph (2), notice of the fact shall be given by the nominee forthwith to the court.

(6) If following any final adjournment of the meetings the proposal (with the same modifications, if any) is not agreed by both meetings, it is deemed rejected.".

Para (4): words in square brackets substituted for original word "forthwith" by the Insolvency (Scotland) Amendment Rules 2009, SI 2009/662, r 2, Schedule, para 1, subject to transitional provisions in r 3 thereof as noted to r 1.4 at **[15.10]**.

Para (6): added by the Insolvency (Scotland) Amendment Rules 2010, SI 2010/688, r 3, Sch 1, para 26, subject to transitional provisions in r 4 thereof at **[2.80]**.

[15.29]

[1.16A Requisite majorities at creditors' meetings

(1) Subject to paragraph (2), a resolution is passed at a creditors' meeting when a majority (in value) of those present and voting in person or by proxy have voted in favour of it.

(2) A resolution to approve the proposal or a modification is passed when a majority of three quarters or more (in value) of those present and voting in person or by proxy have voted in favour of it.

(3) There is to be left out of account a creditor's vote in respect of any claim or part of a claim—

(a) where written notice of the claim was not given, either at the meeting or before it, to the chairman or nominee;

(b) where the claim or part is secured;

(c) where the claim is in respect of a debt wholly or partly on, or secured by, a current bill of exchange or promissory note, unless the creditor is willing—

(i) to treat the liability to the creditor on the bill or note of every person who is liable on it antecedently to the company, and who has not been made bankrupt or had their estate sequestrated (or in the case of a company, which has not gone into liquidation), as a security in the creditor's hands; and

(ii) to estimate the value of the security and (for the purpose of entitlement to vote, but not of any distribution under the arrangement) to deduct it from the creditor's claim.

(4) Any resolution is invalid if those voting against it include more than half in value of the creditors—

(a) to whom notice of the meeting was sent;

(b) whose votes are not to be left out of account under paragraph (3); and

(c) who are not, to the best of the chairman's belief, persons connected with the company.

(5) It is for the chairman of the meeting to decide whether under this Rule—

(a) a vote is to be left out of account in accordance with paragraph (3), and

(b) a person is a connected person for the purpose of paragraph (4)(c),

and in relation to the second of these two cases the chairman is entitled to rely on the information provided by the company's statement of affairs or otherwise in accordance with this Part of the Rules.

(6) If the chairman uses a proxy contrary to Rule 1.14AA the chairman's vote with that proxy does not count towards any majority under this Rule.

(7) The chairman's decision on any matter under the Rule is subject to appeal to the court by any creditor and paragraphs (5) to (7) of Rule 1.15B apply as regards such an appeal.]

NOTES

Inserted, together with rr 1.16B–1.16E, by the Insolvency (Scotland) Amendment Rules 2010, SI 2010/688, r 3, Sch 1, para 27, subject to transitional provisions in rr 4, 5 thereof at **[2.80]**, **[2.81]**.

[15.30]

[1.16B Requisite majorities at company meetings

(1) Subject as follows and to any express provision made in the articles of association of the company, at a meeting of the members of the company any resolution is to be regarded as passed if voted for by more than one-half in value of the members present in person or by proxy and voting on the resolution.

(2) The value of members is determined by reference to the number of votes conferred on each member by the company's articles.

(3) If the chairman uses a proxy contrary to Rule 1.14AA, the chairman's vote with that proxy does not count towards any majority under this Rule.]

NOTES

Inserted as noted to r 1.16A at **[15.29]**.

[15.31]

[1.16C Action where person excluded

(1) In this Rule and Rules 1.16D and 1.16E an "excluded person" means a person who—

(a) has taken all steps necessary to attend a meeting under the arrangements put in place to do so by the convener of the meeting under section 246A(6); and

(b) those arrangements do not permit that person to attend the whole or part of that meeting.

(2) Where the chairman becomes aware during the course of the meeting that there is an excluded person, the chairman may—

(a) continue the meeting;

(b) declare the meeting void and convene the meeting again; or

(c) declare the meeting valid up to the point where the person was excluded and adjourn the meeting.

(3) Where the chairman continues the meeting, the meeting is valid unless—

(a) the chairman decides in consequence of a complaint under Rule 1.16E to declare the meeting void and hold the meeting again; or

(b) the court directs otherwise.

(4) Without prejudice to paragraph (2), where the chairman becomes aware during the course of the meeting of an excluded person, the chairman may, in the chairman's discretion and without an adjournment, declare the meeting suspended for any period up to one hour.]

NOTES

Inserted as noted to r 1.16A at **[15.29]**.

[15.32]

[1.16D Indication to excluded person

(1) A person who claims to be an excluded person may request an indication of what occurred during the period of that person's claimed exclusion (the "indication").

(2) A request under paragraph (1) must be made as soon as reasonably practicable, and, in any event, no later than 4 pm on the business day following the day on which the exclusion is claimed to have occurred.

(3) A request under paragraph (1) must be made to—

(a) the chairman, where it is made during the course of the business of the meeting; or

(b) the nominee or supervisor where it is made after the conclusion of the business of the meeting.

(4) Where satisfied that the person making the request is an excluded person, the person to whom the request is made must give the indication as soon as reasonably practicable and, in any event, no later than 4. pm on the day following the request in paragraph (1).]

NOTES

Inserted as noted to r 1.16A at **[15.29]**.

[15.33]

[1.16E Complaint

(1) Any person who—

(a) is, or claims to be, an excluded person; or

(b) attends the meeting (in person or by proxy) and considers that they have been adversely affected by a person's actual, apparent or claimed exclusion,

("the complainant") may make a complaint.

(2) The person to whom the complaint must be made ("the relevant person") is—

(a) the chairman, where it is made during the course of the meeting; or

(b) the nominee or supervisor, where it is made after the meeting.

(3) The relevant person must—

(a) consider whether there is an excluded person;

(b) where satisfied that there is an excluded person, consider the complaint; and

(c) where satisfied that there has been prejudice, take such action as the relevant person considers fit to remedy the prejudice.

(4) Paragraph (5) applies where—

(a) the relevant person is satisfied that the complainant is an excluded person;

(b) during the period of the person's exclusion—

(i) a resolution was put to the meeting; and

(ii) voted on; and

(c) the excluded person asserts how the excluded person intended to vote on the resolution.

(5) Subject to paragraph (6), where satisfied that the effect of the intended vote in paragraph (4), if cast, would have changed the result of the resolution, the relevant person must—

(a) count the intended vote as being cast in accordance with the complainant's stated intention;

(b) amend the record of the result of the resolution; and

(c) where those entitled to attend the meeting have been notified of the result of the resolution, notify them of the change.

(6) Where satisfied that more than one complainant in paragraph (4) is an excluded person, the relevant person must have regard to the combined effect of the intended votes.

(7) A complaint must be made as soon as reasonably practicable and, in any event, by 4 pm on the business day following—

(a) the day on which the person was excluded; or

(b) where an indication is requested under Rule 1.16D, the day on which the complainant received the indication.

(8) The relevant person must notify the complainant in writing of any decision.

(9) A complainant who is not satisfied by the action of the relevant person may apply to the court for a direction to be given to the relevant person as to the action to be taken in respect of the complaint, and any application must be made no more than 2 business days from the date of receiving the decision of the relevant person.]

NOTES

Inserted as noted to r 1.16A at **[15.29]**.

[15.34]
1.17 Report of meetings

(1) A report of the meetings shall be prepared by the person who was chairman of them.

(2) The report shall—

[(a) state whether the proposal for a voluntary arrangement was approved by the creditors of the company alone or by both the creditors and members of the company and in either case whether such approval was with any modifications;]

(b) set out the resolutions which were taken at each meeting, and the decision on each one;

(c) list the creditors and members of the company (with their respective values) who were present or represented at the meeting, and how they voted on each resolution; . . .

[(ca) state whether, in the opinion of the supervisor—

(i) the [EU Regulation] applies to the voluntary arrangement; and

(ii) if so, whether the proceedings are main proceedings or territorial proceedings [or secondary proceedings]; and]

(d) include such further information (if any) as the chairman thinks it appropriate to make known to the court.

(3) A copy of the chairman's report shall, within 4 [business] days of the meetings being held, be lodged in court.

(4) In respect of each of the meetings the persons to whom notice of the result of the meetings is to be sent under section 4(6) are all those who were sent notice of the meeting. The notice shall be sent [as soon as reasonably practicable] after a copy of the chairman's report is lodged in court under paragraph (3).

(5) [If the decision approving the voluntary arrangement has effect under section 4A] (whether or not in the form proposed) the chairman shall [as soon as is reasonably practicable] send a copy of the report to the registrar of companies.

NOTES

Para (2): sub-para (a) substituted by the Insolvency (Scotland) Amendment Rules 2002, SI 2002/2709, r 4(1), Schedule, Pt 1, para 9(a), subject to the savings contained in r 4(2) as noted to r 1.1 at **[15.4]**. Sub-para (a) originally read as follows:

> "(a) state whether the proposal for a voluntary arrangement was approved or rejected and, if approved, with what (if any) modifications;";

word omitted from sub-para (c) revoked and sub-para (ca) inserted by the Insolvency (Scotland) Regulations 2003, SI 2003/2109, regs 23, 25(3), subject to the saving that anything done under or for the purposes of any provision of these Rules before 8 September 2003 has effect as if done under or for the purposes of the provision as amended; words in square brackets in sub-para (ca)(i) substituted for original words "EC Regulation" and words in square brackets in sub-para (ca)(ii) inserted by the Insolvency Amendment (EU 2015/848) Regulations 2017, SI 2017/702, regs 2, 3, Schedule, Pt 5, paras 61, 66, as from 26 June 2017, except in relation to proceedings opened before that date.

Para (3): word in square brackets inserted by the Insolvency (Scotland) Amendment Rules 2010, SI 2010/688, r 3, Sch 1, para 28, subject to transitional provisions in r 4 thereof at **[2.80]**.

Para (4): words in square brackets substituted for original word "immediately" by SI 2010/688, r 3, Sch 1, para 29, subject to transitional provisions in r 4 thereof at **[2.80]**.

Para (5): words in first pair of square brackets substituted for original words "If the voluntary arrangement has been approved by the meetings" by SI 2002/2709, r 4(1), Schedule, Pt 1, para 9(b), subject to savings contained in r 4(2) as noted to r 1.1 at **[15.4]**; words in second pair of square brackets substituted for original word "forthwith" by the Insolvency (Scotland) Amendment Rules 2009, SI 2009/662, r 2, Schedule, para 1, subject to transitional provisions in r 3 thereof as noted to r 1.4 at **[15.10]**.

Para (5): see Sch 5, Form 1.1 (Scot) at **[15.349]**, and the notes to that Schedule.

CHAPTER 6 IMPLEMENTATION OF THE VOLUNTARY ARRANGEMENT

[15.35]
1.18 Resolutions to follow approval

[(1) If the voluntary arrangement is approved (with or without modifications) by the creditors' meeting, a resolution [must] be taken by the creditors, where two or more supervisors are appointed, on the question whether acts to be done in connection with the arrangement may be done by any one or more of them, or must be done by all of them.]

(2) . . .

(3) If at either meeting a resolution is moved for the appointment of some person other than the nominee to be supervisor of the arrangement, there must be produced to the chairman, at or before the meeting—

(a) that person's written consent to act (unless the person is present and then and there signifies his consent), and

(b) his written confirmation that he is qualified to act as an insolvency practitioner in relation to the company [or is an authorised person in relation to the company].

NOTES

Para (1): substituted by the Insolvency (Scotland) Amendment Rules 2002, SI 2002/2709, r 4(1), Schedule, Pt 1, para 10(a), subject to savings contained in r 4(2) as noted to r 1.1 at **[15.4]**. Para (1) originally read as follows:

> "(1) If the voluntary arrangement is approved (with or without modifications) by the two meetings, a resolution may be taken by the creditors, where two or more insolvency practitioners are appointed to act as supervisor, on the question whether acts to be done in connection with the arrangement may be done by one of them or are to be done by both or all.".

Word in square brackets substituted for original word "may" by the Insolvency (Scotland) Amendment Rules 2010, SI 2010/688, r 3, Sch 1, para 30, subject to transitional provisions in r 4 thereof at **[2.80]**.

Para (2): revoked by SI 2002/2709, r 4(1), Schedule, Pt 1, para 10(b), subject to savings contained in r 4(2) as noted to r 1.1 at **[15.4]**. Para (2) originally read as follows:

"(2) A resolution under paragraph (1) may be passed in anticipation of the approval of the voluntary arrangement by the company meeting if such meeting has not at that time been concluded.".

Para (3): words in square brackets added by SI 2002/2709, r 4(1), Schedule, Pt 1, para 10(c), subject to savings contained in r 4(2) as noted to r 1.1 at **[15.4]**.

[15.36]

[1.18A Notice of order made under section 4A(6)

(1) This Rule applies where the court makes an order under section 4A(6).

(2) The member of the company who applied for the order shall serve certified copies of it on—

(a) the supervisor of the voluntary arrangement; and

(b) the directors of the company.

(3) Service on the directors may be effected by service of a single copy on the company at its registered office.

(4) The directors or (as the case may be) the supervisor shall [as soon as is reasonably practicable] after receiving a copy of the court's order, give notice of it to all persons who were sent notice of the creditors' or company meetings or who, not having been sent such notice, are affected by the order.

(5) The person on whose application the order of the court was made shall, within [5 business] days of the order, deliver a certified copy interlocutor to the registrar of companies.]

NOTES

Inserted by the Insolvency (Scotland) Amendment Rules 2002, SI 2002/2709, r 4(1), Schedule, Pt 1, para 11, subject to savings contained in r 4(2) as noted to r 1.1 at **[15.4]**.

Para (4): words in square brackets substituted for original word "forthwith" by the Insolvency (Scotland) Amendment Rules 2009, SI 2009/662, r 2, Schedule, para 1, subject to transitional provisions in r 3 thereof as noted to r 1.4 at **[15.10]**.

Para (5): words in square brackets substituted for original number "7" by the Insolvency (Scotland) Amendment Rules 2010, SI 2010/688, r 3, Sch 1, para 31, subject to transitional provisions in r 4 thereof at **[2.80]**.

[15.37]

1.19 Hand-over of property, etc to supervisor

(1) [Where the decision approving the voluntary arrangement has effect under section 4A], the directors or, where—

(a) the company is in liquidation or is [in administration], and

(b) a person other than the responsible insolvency practitioner is appointed as supervisor of the voluntary arrangement,

the responsible insolvency practitioner, shall [as soon as is reasonably practicable] do all that is required for putting the supervisor into possession of the assets included in the arrangement.

(2) Where paragraph (1)(a) and (b) applies, the supervisor shall, on taking possession of the assets, discharge any balance due to the responsible insolvency practitioner by way of remuneration or on account of—

(a) fees, costs, charges and expenses properly incurred and payable under the Act or the Rules, and

(b) any advances made in respect of the company, together with interest on such advances at the official rate (within the meaning of Rule 4.66(2)(b)) ruling at the date on which the company went into liquidation or (as the case may be) [entered administration].

(3) Alternatively, the supervisor shall, before taking possession, give the responsible insolvency practitioner a written undertaking to discharge any such balance out of the first realisation of assets.

(4) The sums due to the responsible insolvency practitioner as above shall be paid out of the assets included in the arrangement in priority to all other sums payable out of those assets, subject only to the deduction from realisations by the supervisor of the proper costs and expenses of such realisations.

(5) The supervisor shall from time to time out of the realisation of assets discharge all cautionary obligations (including guarantees) properly given by the responsible insolvency practitioner for the benefit of the company and shall pay all the responsible insolvency practitioner's expenses.

NOTES

Para (1): words in first pair of square brackets substituted for original words "After the approval of the voluntary arrangement" by the Insolvency (Scotland) Amendment Rules 2002, SI 2002/2709, r 4(1), Schedule, Pt 1, para 12, subject to savings contained in r 4(2) as noted to r 1.1 at **[15.4]**; words in second pair of square brackets substituted for words "subject to an administration order" by the Insolvency (Scotland) Amendment Rules 2003, SI 2003/2111, r 6, Sch 2, para 3(a), subject to savings in r 7 thereof at **[2.34]**; words in third pair of square brackets substituted for original word "forthwith" by the Insolvency (Scotland) Amendment Rules 2009, SI 2009/662, r 2, Schedule, para 1, subject to transitional provisions in r 3 thereof as noted to r 1.4 at **[15.10]**.

Para (2): words in square brackets substituted for words "became subject to the administration order" by SI 2003/2111, r 6, Sch 2, para 3(b), subject to savings in r 7 thereof at **[2.34]**.

[15.38]

1.20 Revocation or suspension of the arrangement

(1) This Rule applies where the court makes an order of revocation or suspension under section 6.

(2) The person who applied for the order shall serve copies of it—

(a) on the supervisor of the voluntary arrangement, and

(b) on the directors of the company or the administrator or liquidator (according to who made the proposal for the arrangement).

Service on the directors may be effected by service of a single copy of the order on the company at its registered office.

(3) If the order includes a direction given by the court, under section 6(4)(b), for any further meetings to be summoned, notice shall also be given by the person who applied for the order to whoever is, in accordance with the direction, required to summon the meetings.

(4) The directors or (as the case may be) the administrator or liquidator shall—

(a) [as soon as is reasonably practicable] after receiving a copy of the court's order, give notice of it to all persons who were sent notice of the creditors' and the company meetings or who, not having been sent that notice, appear to be affected by the order; and

(b) within [5 business] days of their receiving a copy of the order (or within such longer period as the court may allow), give notice to the court whether it is intended to make a revised proposal to the company and its creditors, or to invite re-consideration of the original proposal.

(5) The person on whose application the order of revocation or suspension was made shall, within [5 business] days after the making of the order, deliver a copy of the order to the registrar of companies.

NOTES

Para (4): words in square brackets in sub-para (a) substituted for original word "forthwith" by the Insolvency (Scotland) Amendment Rules 2009, SI 2009/662, r 2, Schedule, para 1, subject to transitional provisions in r 3 thereof as noted to r 1.4 at **[15.10]**; words in square brackets in sub-para (b) substituted for original words number "7" by the Insolvency (Scotland) Amendment Rules 2010, SI 2010/688, r 3, Sch 1, para 32, subject to transitional provisions in r 4 thereof at **[2.80]**.

Para (5): words in square brackets substituted for original words number "7" by SI 2010/688, r 3, Sch 1, para 32, subject to transitional provisions in r 4 thereof at **[2.80]**.

Para (5): see Sch 5, Form 1.2 (Scot) at **[15.349]**, and the notes to that Schedule.

[15.39]

[1.21 Supervisor's accounts

(1) This Rule applies where the voluntary arrangement authorises or requires the supervisor—

(a) to carry on the business of the company or trade on its behalf or in its name;

(b) to realise assets of the company; or

(c) otherwise to administer or dispose of any of its funds.

(2) The supervisor must keep accounts and records of the supervisor's acts and dealings in, and in connection with, the arrangement, including in particular records of all receipts and payments of money.

(3) The supervisor must preserve any accounts and records in paragraph (2) which—

(a) were kept by any other person who has acted as supervisor of the arrangement; and

(b) are in the supervisor's possession.]

NOTES

Substituted, together with r 1.21A, for r 1.21, by the Insolvency (Scotland) Amendment Rules 2010, SI 2010/688, r 3, Sch 1, para 33, subject to transitional provisions in r 4 thereof at **[2.80]**. Rule 1.21 previously read as follows:

"1.21 Supervisor's accounts and reports

(1) Where the voluntary arrangement authorises or requires the supervisor—

(a) to carry on the business of the company, or to trade on its behalf or in its name, or

(b) to realise assets of the company, or

(c) otherwise to administer or dispose of any of its funds,

he shall keep accounts and records of his acts and dealings in and in connection with the arrangement, including in particular records of all receipts and payments of money.

(2) The supervisor shall, not less often than once in every 12 months beginning with the date of his appointment, prepare an abstract of such receipts and payments and send copies of it, accompanied by his comments on the progress and efficacy of the arrangement, to—

(a) the court,

(b) the registrar of companies,

(c) the company,

(d) all those of the company's creditors who are bound by the arrangement,

(e) subject to paragraph (5) below, the members of the company who are so bound, and

(f) where the company is not in liquidation, the company's auditors for the time being.

If in any period of 12 months he has made no payments and had no receipts, he shall at the end of that period send a statement to that effect to all those specified in sub-paragraphs (a) to (f) above.

(3) An abstract provided under paragraph (2) shall relate to a period beginning with the date of the supervisor's appointment or (as the case may be) the day following the end of the last period for which an abstract was prepared under this Rule; and copies of the abstract shall be sent out, as required by paragraph (2), within the two months following the end of the period to which the abstract relates.

(4) If the supervisor is not authorised as mentioned in paragraph (1), he shall, not less often than once in every 12 months beginning with the date of his appointment, send to all those specified in paragraphs 2(a) to (f) a report on the progress and efficacy of the voluntary arrangement.

(5) The court may, on application by the supervisor—

(a) dispense with the sending under this Rule of abstracts or reports to members of the company, either altogether or on the basis that the availability of the abstract or report to members on request is to be advertised by the supervisor in a specified manner;

(b) vary the dates on which the obligation to send abstracts or reports arises.".

[15.40]

[1.21A Supervisor's reports

(1) Subject to paragraph (2), the supervisor must, in respect of each period of 12 months ending with the anniversary of the commencement of the arrangement, send within 2 months of the end of that period a report on the progress and prospects for the full implementation of the voluntary arrangement to—

(a) the registrar of companies;

(b) the company;

(c) all of the company's creditors who are bound by the voluntary arrangement of whose address the supervisor is aware;

(d) subject to paragraph (4) below, the members of the company; and

(e) if the company is not in liquidation, the company's auditors (if any) for the time being.

(2) The supervisor is not required to send a report under paragraph (1), if an obligation to send a final report under Rule 1.23 arises in the period of 2 months mentioned in paragraph (1).

(3) Where the supervisor is authorised or required to do any of the things mentioned in Rule 1.21(1)(a) to (c), the report required to be sent pursuant to paragraph (1), must include or be accompanied by—

(a) an abstract of receipts and payments required to be recorded by virtue of Rule 1.21(2); or

(b) where there have been no such receipts and payments, a statement to that effect.

(4) The court may, on application by the supervisor, dispense with the sending under this Rule of abstracts or reports to members of the company, either altogether or on the basis that the availability of the abstract or report to members is to be advertised by the supervisor in a specified manner.]

NOTES

Substituted as noted to r 1.21 at **[15.39]**.

[15.41]

1.22 Fees, costs, charges and expenses

The fees, costs, charges and expenses that may be incurred for any of the purposes of a voluntary arrangement are—

(a) any disbursements made by the nominee prior to the [decision approving the arrangement taking effect under section 4A], and any remuneration for his services as is agreed between himself and the company (or, as the case may be, the administrator or liquidator);

(b) any fees, costs, charges or expenses which—

(i) are sanctioned by the terms of the arrangement, or

(ii) would be payable, or correspond to those which would be payable, in an administration or winding up.

NOTES

Words in square brackets in para (a) substituted for original words "approval of the arrangement" by the Insolvency (Scotland) Amendment Rules 2002, SI 2002/2709, r 4(1), Schedule, Pt 1, para 13, subject to savings contained in r 4(2) as noted to r 1.1 at **[15.4]**.

[15.42]

[1.23 Completion or termination of the arrangement

(1) Not more than 28 days after the final completion or termination of the voluntary arrangement, the supervisor shall send to creditors and members of the company who are bound by it a notice that the voluntary arrangement has been fully implemented or (as the case may be) has terminated.

(2) With the notice there shall be sent to each creditor and member a copy of a report by the supervisor summarising all receipts and payments made by him in pursuance of the arrangement, and explaining in relation to implementation of the arrangement any departure from the proposals as they originally took effect, or (in the case of termination of the arrangement) explaining the reasons why the arrangement has terminated.

[(2A) In the report under paragraph (2), the supervisor shall include a statement as to the amount paid, if any, to unsecured creditors by virtue of the application of section 176A (prescribed part).]

(3) The supervisor shall, within the 28 days mentioned above, send to the registrar of companies and to the court a copy of the notice to creditors and members under paragraph (1), together with a copy of the report under paragraph (2), and the supervisor shall not vacate office until after such copies have been sent.]

NOTES

Substituted by the Insolvency (Scotland) Amendment Rules 2002, SI 2002/2709, r 4(1), Schedule, Pt 1, para 14, subject to savings contained in r 4(2) as noted to r 1.1 at **[15.4]**, and originally read as follows:

"1.23 Completion of the arrangement

(1) Not more than 28 days after the final completion of the voluntary arrangement, the supervisor shall send to all creditors and members of the company who are bound by it a notice that the voluntary arrangement has been fully implemented.

(2) With the notice there shall be sent to each creditor and member a copy of a report by the supervisor, summarising all receipts and payments made by him in pursuance of the arrangement, and explaining any difference in the actual implementation of it as compared with the proposal approved by the creditors' and company meetings.

(3) The supervisor shall, within the 28 days mentioned above, send to the registrar of companies and to the court a copy of the notice to creditors and members under paragraph (1), together with a copy of the report under paragraph (2).

(4) The court may, on application by the supervisor, extend the period of 28 days under paragraphs (1) or (3)."

Para (2A): inserted by the Enterprise Act 2002 (Consequential Amendments) (Prescribed Part) (Scotland) Order 2003, SI 2003/2108, art 4(3).

Para (3): see Sch 5, Form 1.4 (Scot) at **[15.349]**, and the notes to that Schedule.

[15.43]
1.24 False representations, etc

(1) A person being a past or present officer of a company commits an offence if he make any false representation or commits any other fraud for the purpose of obtaining the approval of the company's members or creditors to a proposal for a voluntary arrangement under Part I of the Act.

(2) For this purpose "officer" includes a shadow director.

(3) A person guilty of an offence under this Rule is liable to imprisonment or a fine, or both.

NOTES

Revoked by the Insolvency (Scotland) Amendment Rules 2002, SI 2002/2709, r 4(1), Schedule, Pt 1, para 15, subject to savings contained in r 4(2) as noted to r 1.1 at **[15.4]**.

[CHAPTER 7 OBTAINING A MORATORIUM PROCEEDINGS DURING A MORATORIUM NOMINEES CONSIDERATION OF PROPOSALS WHERE MORATORIUM OBTAINED

Section A: Obtaining a Moratorium

[15.44]
1.25 Preparation of proposal by directors and submission to nominee

(1) The document containing the proposal referred to in paragraph 6(1)(a) of Schedule A1 to the Act shall—

- (a) be prepared by the directors;
- (b) comply with the requirements of paragraphs (1) and (2) of Rule 1.3 (save that the reference to preferential creditors shall be to preferential creditors within the meaning of paragraph 31(8) of Schedule A1 to the Act); and
- (c) state the address to which notice of the consent of the nominee to act and the documents referred to in Rule 1.28 shall be sent.

(2) With the agreement in writing of the nominee, the directors may amend the proposal at any time before submission to them by the nominee of the statement required by paragraph 6(2) of Schedule A1 to the Act.]

NOTES

Chapter 7 (rr 1.25–1.45) inserted by the Insolvency (Scotland) Amendment Rules 2002, SI 2002/2709, r 4(1), Schedule, Pt 1, para 16, as from 1 January 2003, subject to savings contained in r 4(2) as noted to r 1.1 at **[15.4]**.

[15.45]
[1.26 Delivery of documents to the intended nominee etc

(1) The documents required to be delivered to the nominee pursuant to paragraph 6(1) of Schedule A1 to the Act shall be delivered to the nominee himself or to a person authorised to take delivery of documents on his behalf.

(2) On receipt of the documents, the nominee shall [as soon as is reasonably practicable] issue an acknowledgement of receipt of the documents to the directors which shall indicate the date on which the documents were received.]

NOTES

Inserted as noted to r 1.25 at **[15.44]**.

Para (2): words in square brackets substituted for original word "forthwith" by the Insolvency (Scotland) Amendment Rules 2009, SI 2009/662, r 2, Schedule, para 1, subject to transitional provisions in r 3 thereof as noted to r 1.4 at **[15.10]**.

[15.46]
[1.27 Statement of affairs

(1) The statement of the company's affairs required to be delivered to the nominee pursuant to paragraph 6(1)(b) of Schedule A1 to the Act shall be delivered to the nominee [at the same time as] the delivery to him of the document setting out the terms of the proposed voluntary arrangement . . .

(2) The statement of affairs shall comprise the same particulars as required by Rule 1.5(2) (supplementing or amplifying, so far as is necessary for clarifying the state of the company's affairs, those already given in the directors' proposal).

(3) The statement of affairs shall be made up to a date not earlier than 2 weeks before the date of the delivery of the document containing the proposal for the voluntary arrangement to the nominee under Rule 1.26(1).

However, the nominee may allow an extension of that period to the nearest practicable date (not earlier than 2 months before the date of delivery of the documents referred to in Rule 1.26(1)) and if he does so, he shall give a statement of his reasons in writing to the directors.

(4) The statement of affairs shall be certified as correct, to the best of [the relevant director's] knowledge and belief, by [one director].]

NOTES

Inserted as noted to r 1.25 at **[15.44]**.

Para (1): words in square brackets substituted for original words "no later than 7 days after" and words "or such longer time as he may allow" (omitted) revoked by the Insolvency (Scotland) Amendment Rules 2010, SI 2010/688, r 3, Sch 1, para 34, subject to transitional provisions in r 4 thereof at **[2.80]**.

Para (4): words in first pair of square brackets substituted for original word "their" and words in second pair of square brackets substituted for original words "two or more directors of the company, or by the company secretary and at least one director (other than the secretary himself)" by SI 2010/688, r 3, Sch 1, para 35, subject to transitional provisions in r 4 thereof at **[2.80]**.

Para (1): see Sch 5, Form 1.6 (Scot) at **[15.349]**, and the notes to that Schedule.

[15.47]
[1.28 The nominee's statement

(1) The nominee shall submit to the directors the statement required by paragraph 6(2) of Schedule A1 to the Act within 28 days of the submission to him of the document setting out the terms of the proposed voluntary arrangement.

(2) The statement shall have annexed to it—

(a) the nominee's comments on the proposal, unless the statement contains an opinion in the negative on any of the matters referred to in paragraph 6(2)(a) and (b) of Schedule A1 to the Act, in which case he shall instead give his reasons for that opinion, and

(b) where he is willing to act in relation to the proposed arrangement, a statement of his consent to act.]

[(2A) The nominee must examine whether there is jurisdiction to open the proceedings and must specify in the nominee's comments on the proposal required by paragraph (2) whether the EU Regulation will apply and, if so, whether the proceedings will be main proceedings, territorial proceedings, or secondary proceedings with the reasons for so stating.]

NOTES

Inserted as noted to r 1.25 at **[15.44]**.

Para (1): see Sch 5, Form 1.5 (Scot), Form 1.8 (Scot) at **[15.349]**, and the notes to that Schedule.

Para (2A): inserted by the Insolvency Amendment (EU 2015/848) Regulations 2017, SI 2017/702, regs 2, 3, Schedule, Pt 5, paras 61, 67, as from 26 June 2017, except in relation to proceedings opened before that date.

[15.48]
[1.29 Documents submitted to the court to obtain moratorium

(1) Where pursuant to paragraph 7 of Schedule A1 to the Act the directors lodge the document and statements referred to in that paragraph in court those documents shall be delivered together with 4 copies of a schedule listing them within 3 working days of the date of the submission to them of the nominee's statement under paragraph 6(2) of Schedule A1 to the Act.

(2) When the directors lodge the document and statements referred to in paragraph (1), they shall also lodge—

(a) a copy of any statement of reasons made by the nominee pursuant to Rule 1.27(3); and

(b) a copy of the nominee's comments on the proposal submitted to them pursuant to Rule 1.28(2).

[(c) a statement from the nominee whether the proceedings will be main, secondary, territorial or non-EU proceedings with the reasons for so stating must also be filed with the court].

(3) The copies of the schedule shall be endorsed by the court with the date on which the documents were lodged in court and 3 copies of the schedule certified by the court shall be returned by the court to the person who lodged the documents in court.

(4) The statement of affairs required to be lodged under paragraph 7(1)(b) of Schedule A1 to the Act shall comprise the same particulars as required by Rule 1.5(2).]

NOTES

Inserted as noted to r 1.25 at **[15.44]**.

Para (2): sub-para (c) inserted by the Insolvency Amendment (EU 2015/848) Regulations 2017, SI 2017/702, regs 2, 3, Schedule, Pt 5, paras 61, 68, as from 26 June 2017, except in relation to proceedings opened before that date.

Para (1): see Sch 5, Form 1.7 (Scot), Form 1.8 (Scot), Form 1.9 (Scot) at **[15.349]**, and the notes to that Schedule.

[15.49]
[1.30 Notice and advertisement of beginning of a moratorium

(1) After receiving the copies of the schedule endorsed by the court under Rule 1.29(3), the directors shall [as soon as is reasonably practicable] serve two of them on the nominee and one on the company.

[(2) On receipt of the copies of the schedule pursuant to paragraph (1), the nominee—

(a) as soon as is reasonably practicable, shall advertise the coming into force of the moratorium once in the Edinburgh Gazette; and

(b) may advertise the coming into force of the moratorium in such other manner as the nominee thinks fit.]

[(2A) In addition to the standard content, notices published under paragraph (2) must state—

(a) the nature of the business of the company;

(b) that a moratorium under section 1A has come into force; and

(c) the date upon which the moratorium came into force.]

(3) The nominee shall [as soon as is reasonably practicable] notify the registrar of companies, the keeper of the register of inhibitions and adjudications, the company and any petitioning creditor of the company of whose claim [and address the nominee] is aware of the coming into force of the moratorium and such notification shall specify the date on which the moratorium came into force.

(4) The nominee shall give notice of the coming into force of the moratorium specifying the date on which it came into force to any messenger-at-arms or sheriff officer who, to his knowledge, is instructed to execute diligence or other legal process against the company or its property.]

NOTES

Inserted as noted to r 1.25 at **[15.44]**.

Para (1): words in square brackets substituted for original word "forthwith" by the Insolvency (Scotland) Amendment Rules 2009, SI 2009/662, r 2, Schedule, para 1, subject to transitional provisions in r 3 thereof as noted to r 1.4 at **[15.10]**.

Para (2): substituted by SI 2009/662, r 2, Schedule, para 2, subject to transitional provisions in r 3 thereof as noted to r 1.4 at **[15.10]**, and originally read as follows:

"(2) Forthwith after receiving the copies of the schedule pursuant to paragraph (1) the nominee shall advertise the coming into force of the moratorium once in the Edinburgh Gazette, and once in such newspaper as he thinks most appropriate for ensuring that its coming into force comes to the notice of the company's creditors.".

Para (2A): inserted by the Insolvency (Scotland) Amendment Rules 2010, SI 2010/688, r 3, Sch 1, para 36, subject to transitional provisions in r 4 thereof at **[2.80]**.

Para (3): words in first pair of square brackets substituted for original word "forthwith" by SI 2009/662, r 2, Schedule, para 1, subject to transitional provisions in r 3 thereof as noted to r 1.4 at **[15.10]**; words in second pair of square brackets substituted for original word "he" by SI 2010/688, r 3, Sch 1, para 37, subject to transitional provisions in r 4 thereof at **[2.80]**.

Para (2): see Sch 5, Form 1.10 (Scot) at **[15.349]**, and the notes to that Schedule.

[15.50]

[1.31 Notice of extension of moratorium

(1) The nominee shall [as soon as is reasonably practicable] notify the registrar of companies, the keeper of the register of inhibitions and adjudications and the court of a decision taking effect pursuant to paragraph 36 of Schedule A1 to the Act to extend or further extend the moratorium and such notice shall specify the new expiry date of the moratorium.

(2) Where an order is made by the court extending or further extending or renewing or continuing a moratorium, the nominee shall [as soon as is reasonably practicable] after receiving a copy of the same give notice to the registrar of companies and the keeper of the register of inhibitions and adjudications and together with the notice shall send a [copy] to the registrar of companies.]

NOTES

Inserted as noted to r 1.25 at **[15.44]**.

Para (1): words in square brackets substituted for original word "forthwith" by the Insolvency (Scotland) Amendment Rules 2009, SI 2009/662, r 2, Schedule, para 1, subject to transitional provisions in r 3 thereof as noted to r 1.4 at **[15.10]**.

Para (2): words in first pair of square brackets substituted for original word "forthwith" by SI 2009/662, r 2, Schedule, para 1, subject to transitional provisions in r 3 thereof as noted to r 1.4 at **[15.10]**; word in second pair of square brackets substituted for original words "certified copy interlocutor" by the Insolvency (Scotland) Amendment Rules 2010, SI 2010/688, r 3, Sch 1, para 38, subject to transitional provisions in r 4 thereof at **[2.80]**.

Para (1): see Sch 5, Form 1.12 (Scot), Form 1.13 (Scot) at **[15.349]**, and the notes to that Schedule.

[15.51]

[1.32 Notice and advertisement of end of moratorium

[(1) After the moratorium comes to an end, the nominee—

(a) as soon as is reasonably practicable, shall advertise its coming to an end once in the Edinburgh Gazette; and

(b) may advertise its coming to an end in such other manner as the nominee thinks fit;

and such notice shall specify the date on which the moratorium came to an end.]

[(1A) In addition to the standard content, notices published under paragraph (2) must state—

(a) the nature of the business of the company;

(b) that a moratorium under section 1A has come to an end; and

(c) the date upon which the moratorium came to an end.]

(2) The nominee shall [as soon as is reasonably practicable] give notice of the ending of the moratorium to the registrar of companies, the court, the keeper of the register of inhibitions and adjudications, the company and any creditor of the company of whose claim [and address the nominee] is aware and such notice shall specify the date on which the moratorium came to an end.]

NOTES

Inserted as noted to r 1.25 at **[15.44]**.

Para (1): substituted by the Insolvency (Scotland) Amendment Rules 2009, SI 2009/662, r 2, Schedule, para 3, subject to transitional provisions in r 3 thereof as noted to r 1.4 at **[15.10]**, and originally read as follows:

"(1) After the moratorium comes to an end, the nominee shall forthwith advertise its coming to an end once in the Edinburgh Gazette, and once in such newspaper as he thinks most appropriate for ensuring that its coming to an end comes to the notice of the company's creditors, and such notice shall specify the date on which the moratorium came to an end.".

Para (1A): inserted by the Insolvency (Scotland) Amendment Rules 2010, SI 2010/688, r 3, Sch 1, para 39, subject to transitional provisions in r 4 thereof at **[2.80]**.

Para (2): words in first pair of square brackets substituted for original word "forthwith" by SI 2009/662, r 2, Schedule, para 1, subject to transitional provisions in r 3 thereof as noted to r 1.4 at **[15.10]**; words in square brackets substituted for original word "he" by SI 2010/688, r 3, Sch 1, para 40, subject to transitional provisions in r 4 thereof at **[2.80]**.

Para (1): see Sch 5, Form 1.10 (Scot) at **[15.349]**, and the notes to that Schedule.

Para (2): see Sch 5, Form 1.14 (Scot), Form 1.15 (Scot) at **[15.349]**, and the notes to that Schedule.

[15.52]
[1.33 Inspection of court file

Any director, member or creditor of the company is entitled, at all reasonable times on any business day, to inspect the court file.]

NOTES

Inserted as noted to r 1.25 at **[15.44]**.

[SECTION B: PROCEEDINGS DURING A MORATORIUM

[15.53]
1.34 Disposal of charged property etc during a moratorium

(1) This Rule applies in any case where the company makes an application to the court under paragraph 20 of Schedule A1 to the Act for leave to dispose of property of the company which is subject to a security, or goods in possession of the company under an agreement to which that paragraph relates.

(2) The court shall fix a venue for the hearing of the application and the company shall [as soon as is reasonably practicable] give notice of the venue to the person who is the holder of the security or, as the case may be, the owner under the agreement.

(3) If an order is made, the company shall [as soon as is reasonably practicable] give notice of it to that person or owner.

(4) The court shall send two certified copies of the order to the company, who shall send one of them to that person or owner.]

NOTES

Inserted as noted to r 1.25 at **[15.44]**.

Paras (2), (3): words in square brackets substituted for original word "forthwith" by the Insolvency (Scotland) Amendment Rules 2009, SI 2009/662, r 2, Schedule, para 1, subject to transitional provisions in r 3 thereof as noted to r 1.4 at **[15.10]**.

[SECTION C: NOMINEES

[15.54]
1.35 Withdrawal of nominee's consent to act

Where the nominee withdraws his consent to act, he shall, pursuant to paragraph 25(5) of Schedule A1 to the Act, [as soon as is reasonably practicable] give notice of his withdrawal and the reason for withdrawing his consent to act to—

(a) the registrar of companies;
(b) the court;
(c) the company; and
(d) any creditor of the company of whose claim [and address the nominee] is aware.]

NOTES

Inserted as noted to r 1.25 at **[15.44]**.

Words in first pair of square brackets substituted for original word "forthwith" by the Insolvency (Scotland) Amendment Rules 2009, SI 2009/662, r 2, Schedule, para 1, subject to transitional provisions in r 3 thereof as noted to r 1.4 at **[15.10]**; words in square brackets in para (d) substituted for original word "he" by the Insolvency (Scotland) Amendment Rules 2010, SI 2010/688, r 3, Sch 1, para 41, subject to transitional provisions in r 4 thereof at **[2.80]**.

See Sch 5, Form 1.16 (Scot), Form 1.17 (Scot) at **[15.349]**, and the notes to that Schedule.

[15.55]
[1.36 Replacement of nominee by the court

(1) Where the directors intend to make an application to the court under paragraph 28 of Schedule A1 to the Act for the nominee to be replaced, they shall give to the nominee at least [5 business] days' notice of their application.

(2) Where the nominee intends to make an application to the court under that paragraph to be replaced, he shall give to the directors at least [5 business] days' notice of his application.

(3) No appointment of a replacement nominee shall be made by the court unless there is lodged in court a statement by the replacement nominee indicating [that the replacement nominee—

(a) consents to act; and
(b) is qualified to act as an insolvency practitioner in relation to the company or is an authorised person in relation to the company.]

NOTES

Inserted as noted to r 1.25 at **[15.44]**.

Paras (1), (2): words in square brackets substituted for original number "7" by the Insolvency (Scotland) Amendment Rules 2010, SI 2010/688, r 3, Sch 1, para 42, subject to transitional provisions in r 4 thereof at **[2.80]**.

Para (3): words in square brackets substituted for original words "his consent to act" by SI 2010/688, r 3, Sch 1, para 43, subject to transitional provisions in r 4 thereof at **[2.80]**.

Para (3): see Sch 5, Form 1.8 (Scot) at **[15.349]**, and the notes to that Schedule.

[15.56]

[1.37 Notification of appointment of a replacement nominee

Where a person is appointed as a replacement nominee he shall [as soon as is reasonably practicable] give notice of his appointment to—

(a) the registrar of companies;

(b) the court (in any case where he was not appointed by the court); and

(c) the person whom he has replaced as nominee.]

NOTES

Inserted as noted to r 1.25 at **[15.44]**.

Words in square brackets substituted for original word "forthwith" by the Insolvency (Scotland) Amendment Rules 2009, SI 2009/662, r 2, Schedule, para 1, subject to transitional provisions in r 3 thereof as noted to r 1.4 at **[15.10]**.

See Sch 5, Form 1.18 (Scot), Form 1.19 (Scot) at **[15.349]**, and the notes to that Schedule.

[15.57]

[1.38 Applications to court under paragraphs 26 or 27 of Schedule A1 to the Act

Where any person intends to make an application to the court pursuant to paragraph 26 or 27 of Schedule A1 to the Act, he shall give to the nominee at least [5 business] days' notice of his application.]

NOTES

Inserted as noted to r 1.25 at **[15.44]**.

Words in square brackets substituted for original number "7" by the Insolvency (Scotland) Amendment Rules 2010, SI 2010/688, r 3, Sch 1, para 44, subject to transitional provisions in r 4 thereof at **[2.80]**.

[SECTION D: CONSIDERATION OF PROPOSALS WHERE MORATORIUM OBTAINED

[15.58]

1.39 General

(1) . . .

[(2) Subject to the provisions in this section of this Chapter, Rules 1.14, 1.14ZA, 1.14A, 1.14AA, 1.15, 1.15AA, 1.16A(3) to (7) and 1.16B to 1.16E shall apply with regard to meetings summoned pursuant to paragraph 29(1) of Schedule A1 to the Act as they apply to meetings of the company and creditors which are summoned under section 3 of the Act.]]

NOTES

Inserted as noted to r 1.25 at **[15.44]**.

Para (1): revoked by the Insolvency (Scotland) Amendment Rules 2010, SI 2010/688, r 3, Sch 1, para 45, subject to transitional provisions in r 4 thereof at **[2.80]**, and previously read as follows:

> "(1) The provisions of Chapter 1 of Part 7 (Meetings) shall apply with regard to the meetings of the company and of the creditors which are summoned pursuant to paragraph 29(1) of Schedule A1 to the Act, subject to the provisions in this section of this Chapter.".

Para (2): substituted by SI 2010/688, r 3, Sch 1, para 46, subject to transitional provisions in r 4 thereof at **[2.80]**, and previously read as follows:

> "(2) The provisions of Rules 1.14, 1.14A and 1.15 shall apply with regard to meetings as mentioned in paragraph (1) above as they apply to meetings of the company and of creditors which are summoned under section 3.".

[15.59]

[1.40 Summoning of meetings; procedure at meetings etc

(1) Where the nominee summons meetings of creditors and the company pursuant to paragraph 29(1) of Schedule A1 to the Act, each of those meetings shall be summoned for a date that is not more than 28 days from the date on which the moratorium came into force.

(2) Notices calling the creditors' meetings shall be sent by the nominee to all creditors specified in the statement of affairs and any other creditors of the company of whose address [the nominee] is aware at least 14 days before the day fixed for the meeting.

(3) Notices calling the company meeting shall be sent by the nominee to all persons who are, to the best of the nominee's belief, members of the company at least 14 days before the day fixed for the meeting.

[(4) Each notice sent under this Rule must—

(a) in addition to the standard content, specify—

(i) the court in which the documents relating to the obtaining of the moratorium were lodged; and

(ii) the court reference; and

(b) state the effect of Rule 1.43.

(4A) With each notice there must be sent—
(a) a copy of the directors' proposal;
(b) a copy of the statement of the company's affairs or, if the nominee thinks fit, a summary of it (the summary to include a list of creditors and the amount of their debts);
(c) the nominee's comments on the proposal; and
(d) forms of proxy.]

NOTES

Inserted as noted to r 1.25 at **[15.44]**.

Para (2): words in square brackets substituted for original word "he" by the Insolvency (Scotland) Amendment Rules 2010, SI 2010/688, r 3, Sch 1, para 47, subject to transitional provisions in r 4 thereof at **[2.80]**.

Paras (4), (4A): substituted for para (4) by SI 2010/688, r 3, Sch 1, para 48, subject to transitional provisions in r 4 thereof at **[2.80]**. Para (4) previously read as follows:

"(4) Each notice sent under this Rule shall specify the court in which the documents relating to the obtaining of the moratorium were lodged and state the effect of paragraphs (1), (2) and (3) of Rule 1.43 (requisite majorities (creditors)); and with each notice there shall be sent—
(a) a copy of the directors' proposal;
(b) a copy of the statement of the company's affairs or, if the nominee thinks fit, a summary of it (the summary to include a list of creditors and the amount of their debts); and
(c) the nominee's comments on the proposal.".

[15.60]
[1.41 Entitlement to vote (creditors)

(1) Subject as follows, every creditor who has notice of the creditors' meeting is entitled to vote at the meeting or any adjournment of it.

(2) Votes are calculated according to the amount of the creditor's debt as at the beginning of the moratorium, after deducting any amounts paid in respect of that debt after that date.

(3) A creditor may vote in respect of a debt for an unliquidated amount or any debt whose value is not ascertained and for the purposes of voting (but not otherwise) his debt shall be valued at £1 unless the chairman agrees to put a higher value on it.]

NOTES

Inserted as noted to r 1.25 at **[15.44]**.

[15.61]
[1.42 Procedure for admission of creditors' claims for voting purposes

(1) Subject as follows, at any creditors' meeting the chairman shall ascertain the entitlement of persons wishing to vote and shall admit or reject their claims accordingly.

(2) The chairman may admit or reject a claim in whole or in part.

(3) The chairman's decision on any matter under this Rule or under paragraph (3) of Rule 1.41 is subject to appeal to the court by any creditor or member of the company.

(4) If the chairman is in doubt whether a claim should be admitted or rejected, he shall mark it as objected to and allow votes to be cast in respect of it, subject to such votes being subsequently declared invalid if the objection to the claim is sustained.

(5) If on an appeal the chairman's decision is reversed or varied, or votes are declared invalid, the court may order another meeting to be summoned, or make such order as it thinks just.

The court's power to make an order under this paragraph is exercisable only if it considers that the circumstances giving rise to the appeal give rise to unfair prejudice or material irregularity.

(6) An application to the court by way of appeal against the chairman's decision shall not be made after the end of the period of 28 days beginning with the first day on which the report required by paragraph 30(3) of Schedule A1 to the Act has been made to the court.

(7) The chairman is not personally liable for any expenses incurred by any person in respect of an appeal under this Rule.]

NOTES

Inserted as noted to r 1.25 at **[15.44]**.

[15.62]
[1.43 Requisite majorities (creditors)

[(1) Subject as follows, a resolution is passed at a creditors' meeting when a majority (in value) of those present and voting in person or by proxy have voted in favour of it.

(2) A resolution to approve the proposal or a modification is passed when a majority of three quarters or more (in value) of those present and voting in person or by proxy have voted in favour of it.]

(3) At a meeting of the creditors for any resolution to pass extending (or further extending) a moratorium, or to bring a moratorium to an end before the end of the period of any extension, there must be a majority in excess of three-quarters in value of the creditors present in person or by proxy and voting on the resolution. For this purpose a secured creditor is entitled to vote in respect of the amount of his claim without deducting the value of his security.]

NOTES

Inserted as noted to r 1.25 at **[15.44]**.

Paras (1), (2): substituted by the Insolvency (Scotland) Amendment Rules 2010, SI 2010/688, r 3, Sch 1, para 49, subject to transitional provisions in r 4 thereof at **[2.80]**, and previously read as follows:

> "(1) Subject as follows, at the creditors' meeting for any resolution to pass approving any proposal or modification there must be a majority in excess of three-quarters in value of the creditors present in person or by proxy and voting on the resolution.
>
> (2) The same applies in respect of any other resolution proposed at the meeting, but substituting one-half for three-quarters.".

[15.63]

[1.44 Proceedings to obtain agreement on the proposal

(1) If the chairman thinks fit, the creditors' meeting and the company meeting may be held together.

[(1A) During a meeting, the chairman may, in the chairman's discretion and without an adjournment, declare the meeting suspended for any period up to one hour.]

(2) The chairman may, and shall if it is so resolved at the meeting in question, adjourn that meeting, but any adjournment shall not be to a day which is more than 14 days after the date on which the moratorium (including any extension) ends.

(3) If the meetings are adjourned under paragraph (2), notice of the fact shall be given by the nominee [as soon as is reasonably practicable] to the court.

(4) If following the final adjournment of the creditors' meeting the proposal (with or without modifications) has not been approved by the creditors, it is deemed rejected.]

NOTES

Inserted as noted to r 1.25 at **[15.44]**.

Para (1A): inserted by the Insolvency (Scotland) Amendment Rules 2010, SI 2010/688, r 3, Sch 1, para 50, subject to transitional provisions in r 4 thereof at **[2.80]**.

Para (3): words in square brackets substituted for original word "forthwith" by the Insolvency (Scotland) Amendment Rules 2009, SI 2009/662, r 2, Schedule, para 1, subject to transitional provisions in r 3 thereof as noted to r 1.4 at **[15.10]**.

[15.64]

[1.45 Implementation of the arrangement

(1) Where a decision approving the arrangement has effect under paragraph 36 of Schedule A1 to the Act, the directors shall [as soon as is reasonably practicable] do all that is required for putting the supervisor into possession of the assets included in the arrangement.

(2) Subject to paragraph (3), Rules 1.17, 1.18, 1.18A and 1.20 to 1.23 apply.

(3) The provisions referred to in paragraph (2) are modified as follows—

(a) in paragraph (4) of Rule 1.17 the reference to section 4(6) is to be read as a reference to paragraph 30(3) of Schedule A1 to the Act;

(b) in paragraph (5) of Rule 1.17 the reference to section 4A is to be read as a reference to paragraph 36 of Schedule A1 to the Act;

(c) in paragraph (1) of Rule 1.18A the reference to section 4A(6) is to be read as a reference to paragraph 36(5) of Schedule A1 to the Act;

(d) in paragraph (1) of Rule 1.20 the reference to section 6 is to be read as a reference to paragraph 38 of Schedule A1 to the Act and the references in paragraphs (2) and (4) to the administrator or liquidator shall be ignored;

(e) in paragraph (3) of Rule 1.20 the reference to section 6(4)(b) is to be read as a reference to paragraph 38 (4)(b) of Schedule A1 to the Act; and

(f) in sub-paragraph (a) of paragraph (1) of Rule 1.22 the reference to section 4A is to be read as a reference to paragraph 36 of Schedule A1 to the Act.]

NOTES

Inserted as noted to r 1.25 at **[15.44]**.

Para (1): words in square brackets substituted for original word "forthwith" by the Insolvency (Scotland) Amendment Rules 2009, SI 2009/662, r 2, Schedule, para 1, subject to transitional provisions in r 3 thereof as noted to r 1.4 at **[15.10]**.

[CHAPTER 8 [EU REGULATION]—CONVERSION OF VOLUNTARY ARRANGEMENT INTO WINDING UP

[15.65]

1.46 Application for conversion into winding up

[(1) Where a member State liquidator proposes to apply to the court for conversion of a voluntary arrangement into winding-up proceedings, an affidavit complying with Rule 1.47 must be prepared and filed in court in support of the application.

(1A) In this Rule, and in Rules 1.47 and 1.48, "conversion into winding-up proceedings" means an order under [Article 51 of the EU Regulation (conversion of secondary insolvency proceedings] that the voluntary arrangement is converted into—

(a) administration proceedings . . . ;

(b) a creditors' voluntary winding up; or

(c) a winding up by the court.]

(2) The application and the affidavit required under this Rule shall be served upon—

(a) the company; and

(b) the supervisor.]

NOTES

Chapter heading preceding this Rule, and this Rule, together with rr 1.47–1.49, inserted by the Insolvency (Scotland) Regulations 2003, SI 2003/2109, regs 23, 25(4), as from 8 September 2003, subject to the saving that anything done under or for the purposes of any provision of these Rules before 8 September 2003 has effect as if done under or for the purposes of the provision as amended.

Words in square brackets in Chapter heading substituted for original words "EC Regulation" by the Insolvency Amendment (EU 2015/848) Regulations 2017, SI 2017/702, regs 2, 3, Schedule, Pt 5, paras 61, 69, as from 26 June 2017, except in relation to proceedings opened before that date.

Para (1): substituted (together with para (1A)) for original para (1) by the Insolvency (Scotland) Amendment Rules 2010, SI 2010/688, r 3, Sch 1, para 51, subject to transitional provisions in r 4 thereof at **[2.80]**. Para (1) previously read as follows:

> "(1) Where a member State liquidator proposes to apply to the court for the conversion under Article 37 of the EC Regulation (conversion of earlier proceedings) of a voluntary arrangement into a winding up, an affidavit complying with Rule 1.47 must be prepared and sworn, and lodged in court in support of the application.".

Para (1A): substituted as noted to para (1) above; words in square brackets substituted for original words "Article 37 of the EC Regulation (conversion of earlier proceedings)" and words "whose purposes are limited to the winding up of the company through administration and are to exclude the purpose contained in paragraph 3(1)(a) of Schedule B1 to the Act" omitted from sub-para (a) revoked, by SI 2017/702, regs 2, 3, Schedule, Pt 5, paras 61, 70, as from 26 June 2017, except in relation to proceedings opened before that date.

[15.66]

[1.47 Contents of affidavit

(1) The affidavit shall state—

(a) that main proceedings have been opened in relation to the company in a member State other than the United Kingdom;

(b) the [belief of the person making the statement] that the conversion of the voluntary arrangement into [winding-up proceedings] [would be most appropriate as regards the interests of the local creditors and coherence between the main and secondary insolvency proceedings];

[(c) the opinion of the person making the statement as to whether the company ought to enter [administration,] voluntary winding up or be wound up by the court; and]

(d) all other matters that, in the opinion of the member State liquidator, would assist the court—

(i) in deciding whether to make such an order, and

(ii) if the court were to do so, in considering the need for any consequential provision that would be necessary or desirable.

(2) An affidavit under this Rule shall be sworn by, or on behalf of, the member State liquidator.]

NOTES

Inserted as noted to r 1.46 at **[15.65]**.

Para (1): in sub-para (b), words in first pair of square brackets substituted for original words "deponent's belief" and words in second pair of square brackets substituted for original words "a winding up", and sub-para (c) substituted by the Insolvency (Scotland) Amendment Rules 2010, SI 2010/688, r 3, Sch 1, paras 52, 53, subject to transitional provisions in r 4 thereof at **[2.80]**. Sub-para (c) previously read as follows:

> "(c) the deponent's opinion as to whether the company ought to enter voluntary winding up or be wound up by the court; and";

words in third pair of square brackets in sub-para (b) substituted for original words "would prove to be in the interests of the creditors in the main proceedings" and word in square brackets in sub-para (c) inserted by the Insolvency Amendment (EU 2015/848) Regulations 2017, SI 2017/702, regs 2, 3, Schedule, Pt 5, paras 61, 71, as from 26 June 2017, except in relation to proceedings opened before that date.

[15.67]

[1.48 Power of court

(1) On hearing the application for conversion into [winding-up proceedings], the court may make such order as it thinks fit.

(2) If the court makes an order for conversion into [winding-up proceedings], the order may contain all such consequential provisions as the court deems necessary or desirable.

(3) Without prejudice to the generality of paragraph (1), an order under that paragraph may provide that the company be wound up as if a resolution for voluntary winding up under section 84 were passed on the day on which the order is made.

(4) Where the court makes an order for conversion into [winding-up proceedings] under paragraph (1), any expenses properly incurred as expenses of the administration of the voluntary arrangement in question shall be a first charge on the company's assets.]

NOTES

Inserted as noted to r 1.46 at **[15.65]**.

Paras (1), (2), (4): words in square brackets substituted for original words "winding up" by the Insolvency (Scotland) Amendment Rules 2010, SI 2010/688, r 3, Sch 1, para 54, subject to transitional provisions in r 4 thereof at **[2.80]**.

[CHAPTER 9 [EU REGULATION]—MEMBER STATE LIQUIDATOR

[15.68]

1.49 Notice to member State liquidator

(1) This Rule applies where a member State liquidator has been appointed in relation to the company.

(2) Where the supervisor is obliged to give notice to, or provide a copy of a document (including an order of court) to, the court or the registrar of companies, the supervisor shall give notice or provide a copy, as appropriate, to[—

(a) any member State liquidator; or

(b) where the supervisor knows that an application has been made to commence insolvency proceedings in another member State, but a member State liquidator has not yet been appointed, to the court to which that application has been made].

(3) Paragraph (2) is without prejudice to the generality of the obligations imposed by [Article 41 of the EU Regulation (cooperation and communication between insolvency practitioners)].]

NOTES

Inserted, together with chapter heading preceding this Rule, as noted to r 1.46 at **[15.65]**.

Words in square brackets in Chapter heading substituted for original words "EC Regulation" by the Insolvency Amendment (EU 2015/848) Regulations 2017, SI 2017/702, regs 2, 3, Schedule, Pt 5, paras 61, 72, as from 26 June 2017, except in relation to proceedings opened before that date.

Para (2): words in square brackets substituted for original words "the member State liquidator" by SI 2017/702, regs 2, 3, Schedule, Pt 5, paras 61, 73(1), (2), as from 26 June 2017, except in relation to proceedings opened before that date.

Para (3): words in square brackets substituted for original words "Article 31 of the EC Regulation (duty to co operate and communicate information)" by SI 2017/702, regs 2, 3, Schedule, Pt 5, paras 61, 73(1), (3), as from 26 June 2017, except in relation to proceedings opened before that date.

[CHAPTER 10

[15.69]

1.50 Omission of Information from Statement of Affairs

The court, on the application of the nominee, the directors or any person appearing to it to have an interest, may direct that specified information may be omitted from any statement of affairs required to be sent to the creditors where the disclosure of such information would be likely to prejudice the conduct of the voluntary arrangement or might reasonably be expected to lead to violence against any person.]

NOTES

Inserted, together with chapter heading preceding this Rule, by the Insolvency (Scotland) Amendment Rules 2010, SI 2010/688, r 3, Sch 1, para 55, subject to transitional provisions in r 4 thereof at **[2.80]**.

[PART 2
ADMINISTRATION PROCEDURE

CHAPTER 1 PRELIMINARY

[15.70]

2.1 Introductory and interpretation

(1) In this Part—

(a) Chapter 2 applies in relation to the appointment of an administrator by the court;

(b) Chapter 3 applies in relation to the appointment of an administrator by the holder of a qualifying floating charge under paragraph 14;

(c) Chapter 4 applies in relation to the appointment of an administrator by the company or the directors under paragraph 22;

(d) The following Chapters apply in all the cases mentioned in sub paragraphs (a) to (c) above:

— Chapter 5: Process of administration;

[— Chapter 5A The Giving of Notice and Supply of Documents;]

— Chapter 6: Meetings;

— Chapter 7: The creditors' committee;

— Chapter 8: Functions and remuneration of administrator;

[— Chapter 8A: Expenses of the administration;]

— Chapter 9: Distributions to creditors;

— Chapter 10: Ending administration;

— Chapter 11: Replacing administrator;

— Chapter 12: [EU Regulation]—conversion of administration to winding up;

— Chapter 13: [EU Regulation]—member State liquidator.

(2) In this Part of these Rules a reference to a numbered paragraph shall, unless the context otherwise requires, be to the paragraph so numbered in Schedule B1 to the Act.]

NOTES

This Part (Pt 2 (rr 2.1–2.60)) substituted for existing Pt 2 (rr 2.1–2.25) by the Insolvency (Scotland) Amendment Rules 2003, SI 2003/2111, r 3, Sch 1, Pt 1, as from 15 September 2003, subject to savings in r 7 thereof at **[2.34]**.

Para (1): words in first pair of square brackets inserted by the Insolvency (Scotland) Amendment Rules 2010, SI 2010/688, r 3, Sch 1, para 56, subject to transitional provisions in r 4 thereof at **[2.80]**; words in second pair of square brackets inserted by the Insolvency (Scotland) Amendment Rules 2008, SI 2008/662, rr 2–4, except in relation to any case where a company has entered administration before 6 April 2008.

Words in square brackets in entries relating to Chapters 12 and 13 substituted for original words "EC Regulation" by the Insolvency Amendment (EU 2015/848) Regulations 2017, SI 2017/702, regs 2, 3, Schedule, Pt 5, paras 61, 74, as from 26 June 2017, except in relation to proceedings opened before that date.

This Part and related notes prior to the substitution by SI 2003/2111 as noted above read as follows:

"CHAPTER 1
APPLICATION FOR, AND MAKING OF, THE ORDER

2.1 Independent report on company's affairs

(1) Where it is proposed to apply to the court by way of petition for an administration order to be made under section 8 in relation to a company, there may be prepared in support of the petition a report by an independent person to the effect that the appointment of an administrator for the company is expedient.

(2) The report may be by the person proposed as administrator, or by any other person having adequate knowledge of the company's affairs, not being a director, secretary, manager, member or employee of the company.

(3) The report shall specify which of the purposes specified in section 8(3) may, in the opinion of the person preparing it, be achieved for the company by the making of an administration order in relation to it.

2.2 Notice of petition

(1) Under section 9(2)(a), notice of the petition shall forthwith be given by the petitioner [to any person] who has appointed, or is or may be entitled to appoint, an administrative receiver, and to the following persons—

(a) an administrative receiver, if appointed;

(b) if a petition for the winding up of the company has been presented but no order for winding up has yet been made, the petitioner under that petition;

(c) a provisional liquidator, if appointed;

(d) the person proposed in the petition to be the administrator;

(e) the registrar of companies;

(f) the Keeper of the Register of Inhibitions and Adjudications for recording in that register; and

(g) the company, if the petition for the making of an administration order is presented by the directors or by a creditor or creditors of the company.

(2) Notice of the petition shall also be given to the persons upon whom the court orders that the petition be served.

NOTES

Para (1): words in square brackets substituted by the Insolvency (Scotland) Amendment Rules 1987, SI 1987/1921, r 3(1), Schedule, Pt I, para 4.

Para (1): see Sch 5, Form 2.1 (Scot).

2.3 Notice and advertisement of administration order

(1) If the court makes an administration order, it shall forthwith give notice of the order to the person appointed as administrator.

(2) Under section 21(1)(a) the administrator shall forthwith after the order is made, advertise the making of the order once in the Edinburgh Gazette and once in a newspaper circulating in the area where the company has its principal place of business or in such newspaper as he thinks most appropriate for ensuring that the order comes to the notice of the company's creditors.

(3) Under section 21(2), the administrator shall send a notice with a copy of the court's order certified by the clerk of court to the registrar of companies, and in addition shall send a copy of the order to the following persons—

[(a) any person who has appointed, or is or may be entitled to appoint, an administrative receiver;]

(b) an administrative receiver, if appointed;

(c) a petitioner in a petition for the winding up of the company, if that petition is pending;

(d) any provisional liquidator of the company, if appointed; and

(e) the Keeper of the Register of Inhibitions and Adjudications for recording in that register.

(4) If the court dismisses the petition under section 9(4) or discharges the administration order under section 18(3) or 24(5), the petitioner or, as the case may be, the administrator shall—

(a) forthwith send a copy of the court's order dismissing the petition or effecting the discharge to the Keeper of the Register of Inhibitions and Adjudications for recording in that register; and

(b) within 14 days after the date of making of the order, send a notice with a copy, certified by the clerk of court, of the court's order dismissing the petition or effecting the discharge to the registrar of companies.

(5) Paragraph (4) is without prejudice to any order of the court as to the persons by and to whom, and how, notice of any order made by the court under section 9(4), 18 or 24 is to be given and to section 18(4) or 24(6) (notice by administrator of court's order discharging administration order).

NOTES

Para (3): sub-para (a) substituted by the Insolvency (Scotland) Amendment Rules 1987, SI 1987/1921, r 3(1), Schedule, Pt I, para 5.

Para (3): see Sch 5, Form 2.2 (Scot).

Para (4): see Sch 5, Forms 2.3 (Scot), 2.4 (Scot).

CHAPTER 2
STATEMENT OF AFFAIRS AND PROPOSALS TO CREDITORS

2.4 Notice requiring statement of affairs

(1) This Rule and Rules 2.5 and 2.6 apply where the administrator decides to require a statement as to the affairs of the company to be made out and submitted to him in accordance with section 22.

(2) The administrator shall send to each of the persons upon whom he decides to make such a requirement under section 22, a notice in the form required by Rule 7.30 and Schedule 5 requiring him to make out and submit a statement of affairs.

(3) Any person to whom a notice is sent under this Rule is referred to in this Chapter as "a deponent".

NOTES

Para (2): see Sch 5, Form 2.5 (Scot).

2.5 Form of the statement of affairs

(1) The statement of affairs shall be in the form required by Rule 7.30 and Schedule 5.

(2) The administrator shall insert any statement of affairs submitted to him in the sederunt book.

NOTES

Para (1): see Sch 5, Form 2.6 (Scot).

2.6 Expenses of statement of affairs

(1) A deponent who makes up and submits to the administrator a statement of affairs shall be allowed and be paid by the administrator out of his receipts, any expenses incurred by the deponent in so doing which the administrator considers to be reasonable.

(2) Any decision by the administrator under this Rule is subject to appeal to the court.

(3) Nothing in this Rule relieves a deponent from any obligation to make up and submit a statement of affairs, or to provide information to the administrator.

2.7 Statement to be annexed to proposals

[(1)] There shall be annexed to the administrator's proposals, when sent to the registrar of companies under section 23 and laid before the creditors' meeting to be summoned under that section, a statement by him showing—

(a) details relating to his appointment as administrator, the purposes for which an administration order was applied for and made, and any subsequent variation of those purposes;

(b) the names of the directors and secretary of the company;

(c) an account of the circumstances giving rise to the application for an administration order;

(d) if a statement of affairs has been submitted, a copy or summary of it with the administrator's comments, if any;

(e) if no statement of affairs has been submitted, details of the financial position of the company at the latest practicable date (which must, unless the court otherwise orders, be a date not earlier than that of the administration order);

[(f) the manner in which the affairs and business of the company—

(i) have, since the date of the administrator's appointment, been managed and financed, and

(ii) will, if the administrator's proposals are approved, continue to be managed and financed; . . .]

[(fa) whether—

(i) the EC Regulation applies; and

(ii) if so, whether the proceedings are main proceedings or territorial proceedings; and]

(g) such other information (if any) as the administrator thinks necessary to enable creditors to decide whether or not to vote for the adoption of the proposals.

[(2) Where the administrator intends to apply to the court under section 18 for the administration order to be discharged at a time before he has sent a statement of his proposals to creditors, in accordance with section 23(1), he shall, at least 10 days before he makes such an application, send to all creditors of the company of whom he is aware, a report containing the information required by paragraph (1)(a) to (f)(i) of this Rule.]

NOTES

Para (1): numbered as such, and sub-para (f) substituted, by the Insolvency (Scotland) Amendment Rules 1987, SI 1987/1921, r 3(1), Schedule Pt I, para 6(1), (2); word omitted from sub-para (f) revoked, and sub-para (fa) inserted, by the Insolvency (Scotland) Regulations 2003, SI 2003/2109, regs 23, 26(1), subject to the saving that anything done under or for the purposes of any provision of these Rules before 8 September 2003 has effect as if done under or for the purposes of the provision as amended.

Para (2): added by SI 1987/1921, r 3(1), Schedule, Pt I, para 6(1), (3).

Para (1): see Sch 5, Form 2.7 (Scot).

2.8 Notices of proposals to members

Any notice required to be published by the administrator—

(a) under section 23(2)(b) (notice of address for members of the company to write for a copy of the administrator's statement of proposals), and

(b) under section 25(3)(b) (notice of address for members of the company to write for a copy of the administrator's statement of proposed revisions to the proposals),

shall be inserted once in the Edinburgh Gazette and once in the newspaper in which the administrator's appointment was advertised.

CHAPTER 3
MEETINGS AND NOTICES

2.9 General

The provisions of Chapter 1 of Part 7 (Meetings) shall apply with regard to meetings of the company's creditors or members which are summoned by the administrator, subject to the provisions in this Chapter.

[2.9A Applicable law

(1) Rule 2.9 does not apply where the laws of a member State (and not the law of Scotland) apply in relation to the conduct of the meeting.

(2) Where this Rule applies, subject as above, the meeting shall be summoned and conducted in accordance with the constitution of the company and the laws of the member State referred to in paragraph (1) above shall apply to the conduct of the meeting.]

NOTES

Inserted, together with r 2.9B, by the Insolvency (Scotland) Regulations 2003, SI 2003/2109, regs 23, 26(2), subject to the saving that anything done under or for the purposes of any provision of these Rules before 8 September 2003 has effect as if done under or for the purposes of the provision as amended.

[2.9B Entitlement to vote

(1) No vote shall be cast by virtue of a claim more than once on any resolution put to the meeting.

(2) Where—

(a) a creditor is entitled to vote under this Rule,

(b) has lodged his claim in one or more sets of other proceedings; and

(c) votes (either in person or by proxy) on a resolution put to the meeting,

only the creditor's vote shall be counted.

(3) Where—

(a) a creditor has lodged his claim in more than one set of other proceedings, and

(b) more than one member State liquidator seeks to vote by virtue of that claim,

the entitlement to vote by virtue of that claim is exercisable by the member State liquidator in main proceedings, whether or not the creditor has lodged his claim in the main proceedings.

(4) For the purposes of paragraph (1), the claim of a creditor and of any member State liquidator in relation to the same debt are a single claim.

(5) For the purposes of paragraphs (2) and (3), "other proceedings" mean main proceedings or territorial proceedings in another member State.]

NOTES

Inserted as noted to r 2.9A.

2.10 Meeting to consider administrator's proposals

(1) The administrator shall give at least 14 days' notice to attend the meeting of the creditors under section 23(1) to any directors or officers of the company (including persons who have been directors or officers in the past) whose presence at the meeting is, in the administrator's opinion, required.

(2) If at the meeting there is not the requisite majority for approval of the administrator's proposals (with modifications, if any), the chairman may, and shall if a resolution is passed to that effect, adjourn the meeting for not more than 14 days.

2.11 Retention of title creditors

For the purpose of entitlement to vote at a creditors' meeting in administration proceedings, a seller of goods to the company under a retention of title agreement shall deduct from his claim the value, as estimated by him, of any rights arising under that agreement in respect of goods in the possession of the company.

2.12 Hire-purchase, conditional sale and hiring agreements

(1) Subject as follows, an owner of goods under a hire-purchase agreement or under an agreement for the hire of goods for more than 3 months, or a seller of goods under a conditional sale agreement, is entitled to vote in respect of the amount of the debt due and payable to him by the company as at the date of the administration order.

(2) In calculating the amount of any debt for this purpose, no account shall be taken of any amount attributable to the exercise of any right under the relevant agreement, so far as the right has become exercisable solely by virtue of the presentation of the petition for an administration order or any matter arising in consequence of that or of the making of the order.

[2.13 Report and notice of meetings

Any report or notice by the administrator of the result of creditors' meetings held under section 23(1) or 25(2) shall have annexed to it details of the proposals which were considered by the meeting in question and of any revisions and modifications to the proposals which were also considered.]

NOTES

Substituted by the Insolvency (Scotland) Amendment Rules 1987, SI 1987/1921, r 3(1), Schedule, Pt I, para 7.

2.14 Notices to creditors

(1) Within 14 days after the conclusion of a meeting of creditors to consider the administrator's proposals or proposed revisions under section 23(1) or 25(2), the administrator shall send notice of the result of the meeting (including, where appropriate, details of the proposals as approved) to every creditor to whom notice of the meeting was sent and to any other creditor of whom the administrator has become aware since the notice was sent.

(2) Within 14 days after the end of every period of 6 months beginning with the date of approval of the administrator's proposals or proposed revisions, the administrator shall send to all creditors of the company a report on the progress of the administration.

(3) On vacating office, the administrator shall send to creditors a report on the administration up to that time. This does not apply where the administration is immediately followed by the company going into liquidation, nor where the administrator is removed from office by the court or ceases to be qualified to act as an insolvency practitioner.

CHAPTER 4
THE CREDITORS' COMMITTEE

2.15 Application of provisions in Part 3 (Receivers)

(1) Chapter 3 of Part 3 (The creditors' committee) shall apply with regard to the creditors' committee in the administration as it applies to the creditors' committee in receivership, subject to the modifications specified below and to any other necessary modifications.

(2) For any reference in the said Chapter 3, or in any provision of Chapter 7 of Part 4 as applied by Rule 3.6, to the receiver, receivership or the creditors' committee in receivership, there shall be substituted a reference to the administrator, the administration and the creditors' committee in the administration.

(3) In Rule 3.4(1) and 3.7(1), for the reference to section 68 or 68(2), there shall be substituted a reference to section 26 or 26(2).

(4) For Rule 3.5 there shall be substituted the following rule—

"3.5 Functions of the Committee

The creditors' committee shall assist the administrator in discharging his functions and shall act in relation to him in such manner as may be agreed from time to time.".

CHAPTER 5
THE ADMINISTRATOR

2.16 Remuneration

(1) The administrator's remuneration shall be determined from time to time by the creditors' committee or, if there is no creditors' committee, by the court, and shall be paid out of the assets as an expense of the administration.

(2) The basis for determining the amount of the remuneration payable to the administrator may be a commission calculated by reference to the value of the company's property with which he has to deal, but there shall in any event be taken into account—

(a) the work which, having regard to that value, was reasonably undertaken by him; and

(b) the extent of his responsibilities in administering the company's assets.

(3) Rules 4.32 to 4.34 of Chapter 6 of Part 4 shall apply to an administration as they apply to a liquidation but as if for any reference to the liquidator or the liquidation committee there was substituted a reference to the administrator or the creditors committee.

2.17 Abstract of receipts and payments

(1) The administrator shall—

(a) within 2 months after the end of 6 months from the date of his appointment, and of every subsequent period of 6 months, and

(b) within 2 months after he ceases to act as administrator,

send to the court, and to the registrar of companies, and to each member of the creditors' committee, the requisite accounts of the receipts and payments of the company.

(2) The court may, on the administrator's application, extend the period of 2 months mentioned in paragraph (1).

(3) The amounts are to be in the form of an abstract showing—

(a) receipts and payments during the relevant period of 6 months, or

(b) where the administrator has ceased to act, receipts and payments during the period from the end of the last 6 month period to the time when he so ceased (alternatively, if there has been no previous abstract, receipts and payments in the period since his appointment as administrator).

(4) If the administrator makes default in complying with this Rule, he is liable to a fine and, for continued contravention, to a daily default fine.

NOTES

Paras (1), (3): see Sch 5, Form 2.9 (Scot).

2.18 Resignation from office

(1) The administrator may give notice of his resignation on grounds of ill health or because—

(a) he intends ceasing to be in practice as an insolvency practitioner, or

(b) there is some conflict of interest or change of personal circumstances, which precludes or makes impracticable the further discharge by him of the duties of administrator.

(2) The administrator may, with the leave of the court, give notice of his resignation on grounds other than those specified in paragraph (1).

(3) The administrator must give to the persons specified below at least 7 days' notice of his intention to resign, or to apply for the court's leave to do so—

(a) if there is a continuing administrator of the company, to him;

(b) if there is no such administrator, to the creditors' committee; and

(c) if there is no such administrator and no creditors' committee, to the company and its creditors.

[(4) Where the administrator gives notice under paragraph (3), he must also give notice to a member State liquidator, if such a person has been appointed in relation to the company.]

NOTES

Para (4): inserted by the Insolvency (Scotland) Regulations 2003, SI 2003/2109, regs 23, 26(3), subject to the saving that anything done under or for the purposes of any provision of these Rules before 8 September 2003 has effect as if done under or for the purposes of the provision as amended.

Para (1): see Sch 5, Form 2.13 (Scot).

2.19 Administrator deceased

(1) Subject to the following paragraph, where the administrator has died, it is the duty of his executors or, where the deceased administrator was a partner in a firm, of a partner of that firm to give notice of that fact to the court, specifying the date of the death. This does not apply if notice has been given under the following paragraph.

(2) Notice of the death may also be given by any person producing to the court a copy of the death certificate.

2.20 Order filling vacancy

Where the court makes an order filling a vacancy in the office of administrator, the same provisions apply in respect of giving notice of, and advertising, the appointment as in the case of the [administration order].

NOTES

Words in square brackets substituted by the Insolvency (Scotland) Amendment Rules 1987, SI 1987/1921, r 3(1), Schedule, Pt I, para 8.

CHAPTER 6
VAT BAD DEBT RELIEF

2.21 Application of provisions in Part 3 (Receivers)

Chapter 5 of Part 3 (VAT bad debt relief) shall apply to an administrator as it applies to an administrative receiver, subject to the modification that, for any reference to the administrative receiver, there shall be substituted a reference to the administrator.

[CHAPTER 7
EC REGULATION—CONVERSION OF ADMINISTRATION INTO WINDING UP

2.22 Application for conversion into winding up

(1) Where a member State liquidator proposes to apply to the court for the conversion under Article 37 of the EC Regulation (conversion of earlier proceedings) of an administration into a winding up, an affidavit complying with Rule 2.23 must be prepared and sworn, and lodged in court in support of the application.

(2) The application and the affidavit required under this Rule shall be served upon—

(a) the company; and

(b) the administrator.]

NOTES

Inserted, together with the Chapter heading preceding this Rule and rr 2.23–2.25, by the Insolvency (Scotland) Regulations 2003, SI 2003/2109, regs 23, 26(4), as from 8 September 2003, subject to the saving that anything done under or for the purposes of any provision of these Rules before 8 September 2003 has effect as if done under or for the purposes of the provision as amended.

[2.23 Contents of affidavit

(1) The affidavit shall state—

(a) that main proceedings have been opened in relation to the company in a member State other than the United Kingdom;

(b) the deponent's belief that the conversion of the administration into a winding up would prove to be in the interests of the creditors in the main proceedings;

(c) the deponent's opinion as to whether the company ought to enter voluntary winding up or be wound up by the court; and

(d) all other matters that, in the opinion of the member State liquidator, would assist the court—

(i) in deciding whether to make such an order, and

(ii) if the court were to do so, in considering the need for any consequential provision that would be necessary or desirable.

(2) An affidavit under this Rule shall be sworn by, or on behalf of, the member State liquidator.]

NOTES

Inserted as noted to r 2.22.

[2.24 Power of court

(1) On hearing the application for conversion into winding up, the court may make such order as it thinks fit.

(2) If the court makes an order for conversion into winding up, the order may contain all such consequential provisions as the court deems necessary or desirable.

(3) Without prejudice to the generality of paragraph (1), an order under that paragraph may provide that the company be wound up as if a resolution for voluntary winding up under section 84 were passed on the day on which the order is made.]

NOTES

Inserted as noted to r 2.22.

[CHAPTER 8
EC REGULATION—MEMBER STATE LIQUIDATOR

2.25 Interpretation of creditor and notice to member State liquidator

(1) This Rule applies where a member State liquidator has been appointed in relation to the company.

(2) For the purposes of the Rules referred to in paragraph (3) the member State liquidator is deemed to be a creditor.

(3) The Rules referred to in paragraph (2) are—

(a) Rule 2.10(1);

(b) Rule 2.11;

(c) Rule 2.12; and

(d) Rule 2.14.

(4) For the purposes of the application by Rule 2.15 of Rule 3.4 with regard to a creditors' committee in an administration, the member State liquidator is deemed to be a creditor.

(5) For the purposes of the application by Rule 2.9 of Rule 7.9(3) insofar as—

(a) Rule 7.9(3) applies Rules 4.15 and 4.16; and

(b) by virtue of its application by Rule 7.9(3), Rule 4.16 applies section 49 of the Bankruptcy Act,

the member State liquidator is deemed to be a creditor.

(6) For the purposes of the application by Rule 2.15 of Chapter 3 of Part 3 and the application by Rule 3.6 of Rules 4.50(b) and 4.52(3), the member State liquidator is deemed to be a creditor.

(7) For the purposes of the application by Rule 2.16 of Rule 4.34(3), the member State liquidator is deemed to be a creditor.

(8) Paragraphs (2) to (7) are without prejudice to the generality of the right to participate referred to in paragraph 3 of Article 32 of the EC Regulation (exercise of creditors' rights).

(9) Where the administrator is obliged to give notice to, or provide a copy of a document (including an order of court) to, the court or the registrar of companies, the administrator shall give notice or provide copies, as the case may be, to the member State liquidator.

(10) Paragraph (9) is without prejudice to the generality of the obligations imposed by Article 31 of the EC Regulation (duty to co operate and communicate information).]

NOTES

Inserted, together with the Chapter heading preceding this Rule, as noted to r 2.22.".

[CHAPTER 2 APPOINTMENT OF ADMINISTRATOR BY COURT

[15.71]

2.2 Form of application

(1) Where an application is made by way of petition for an administration order to be made in relation to a company, there shall be lodged together with the petition a Statement of the Proposed Administrator.

(2) In this Part, references to a Statement of the Proposed Administrator are to a statement by each of the persons proposed to be administrator of a company, in the form required by Rule 7.30 and Schedule 5, stating—

- (a) that he consents to accept appointment as administrator of that company;
- (b) details of any prior professional relationship that he has had with that company; and
- (c) his opinion that it is reasonably likely that the purpose of administration will be achieved.

(3) The petition shall state whether, in the opinion of the petitioner, (i) [the EU Regulation] will apply and (ii) if so, whether the proceedings will be [main, secondary or territorial proceedings].]

NOTES

Substitution: see the note to r 2.1 at **[15.70]**.

Para (3): words in first pair of square brackets substituted for original words "the EC Regulation" by the Insolvency Amendment (EU 2015/848) Regulations 2017, SI 2017/702, regs 2, 3, Schedule, Pt 5, paras 61, 75, as from 26 June 2017, except in relation to proceedings opened before that date; words in second pair of square brackets substituted for original words "main proceedings or territorial proceedings" by the Insolvency (Scotland) Amendment Rules 2006, SI 2006/734, r 5, subject to transitional provisions in r 2(1) thereof at **[2.43]**.

Para (2): see Sch 5, Form 2.1B (Scot) at **[15.349]**, and the notes to that Schedule.

[15.72]

[2.3 Service of petition

(1) Notice of a petition under paragraph 12 shall be given by the petitioner to any holder of a qualifying floating charge, and to the following persons

- (a) an administrative receiver, if appointed;
- (b) a member State liquidator, if one has been appointed in main proceedings in relation to the company;
- (c) if a petition for the winding up of the company has been presented but no order for winding up has yet been made, the petitioner under that petition;
- (d) a provisional liquidator, if appointed;
- (e) the person proposed in the petition to be the administrator;
- (f) the registrar of companies;
- (g) the Keeper of the Register of Inhibitions and Adjudications for recording in that register;
- (h) the company, if the application is made by anyone other than the company; and
- (i) the supervisor of a voluntary arrangement under Part I of the Act, if such has been appointed.

(2) Notice of the petition shall also be given to the persons upon whom the court orders that the petition be served.]

NOTES

Substitution: see the note to r 2.1 at **[15.70]**.

Modification: para (1) modified, in relation to insurers, in so far as these Rules give effect to the Insolvency Act 1986, Pta 2, except where the appointment of an administrator took effect before 1 February 2011, by the Financial Services and Markets Act 2000 (Administration Orders Relating to Insurers) Order 2010, SI 2010/3023, arts 4, 6 at **[7.1621]**, **[7.1622]**.

Para (1): see further Sch 5, Form 2.2B (Scot) at **[15.349]**, and the notes to that Schedule.

[15.73]

[2.4 Application to appoint specified person as administrator by holder of qualifying floating charge

(1) This Rule applies where the holder of a qualifying floating charge, who has been given notice of an administration application, applies under paragraph 36(1)(b) to have a specified person appointed as administrator in place of the person proposed in the application.

(2) An application under paragraph 36(1)(b) shall include averments as to the basis upon which the applicant is entitled to make an appointment under paragraph 14, and shall be accompanied by—

- (a) the written consent, in accordance with Rule 2.10(5), of all holders of a prior qualifying floating charge;
- (b) the Statement of the Proposed Administrator
- (c) a copy of the instrument or instruments by which the relevant floating charge was created, including any relevant instrument of alteration; and
- (d) such other documents as the applicant considers might assist the court in determining the application.

(3) If an administration order is made appointing the specified person, the expenses of the original petitioner and of the applicant under this Rule shall, unless the court orders otherwise, be paid as an expense of the administration.]

NOTES

Substitution: see the note to r 2.1 at **[15.70]**.

Para (2): see further Sch 5, Form 2.1B (Scot) at **[15.349]**, and the notes to that Schedule.

[15.74]
[2.5 Application where company in liquidation

(1) Where an administration application is made under paragraph 37 or 38, the petition shall contain, in addition to those averments required in an application under paragraph 12, averments in relation to—

(a) the full details of the existing insolvency proceedings, including the name and address of the liquidator, the date he was appointed and by whom; and

(b) the reasons why administration has subsequently been considered appropriate,

and shall be accompanied by a copy of the order or certificate by which the liquidator was appointed and by such other documents as the petitioner considers might assist the court in determining the application.

(2) Where an administration application is made under paragraph 37, the petition shall contain, in addition to the averments required by paragraph (1) above, averments as to the basis upon which the petitioner is qualified to make an appointment under paragraph 14, and shall be accompanied by a copy of the instrument or instruments by which the relevant floating charge was created, including any relevant instrument of alteration, and by such other documents as the petitioner considers might assist the court in determining the application.]

NOTES

Substitution: see the note to r 2.1 at **[15.70]**.

[15.75]
[2.6 Expenses

If the court makes an administration order, the expenses of the petitioner, and of any other party whose expenses are allowed by the court, shall be regarded as expenses of the administration.]

NOTES

Substitution: see the note to r 2.1 at **[15.70]**.

[15.76]
[2.7 Administration orders where company in liquidation

Where the court makes an administration order in relation to a company which is in liquidation, the administration order shall contain consequential provisions, including—

(a) in the case of a liquidator in a voluntary winding up, his removal from office;

(b) provisions concerning the release of the liquidator, including his entitlement to recover expenses and to be paid his remuneration;

(c) provision for payment of the costs of the petitioning creditor in the winding-up;

(d) provisions regarding any indemnity given to the liquidator;

(e) provisions regarding the handling or realisation of any of the company's assets under the control of the liquidator; and

(f) such other provisions as the court shall think fit.]

NOTES

Substitution: see the note to r 2.1 at **[15.70]**.

[15.77]
[2.8 Notice of dismissal of application for an administration order

If the court dismisses the petition under paragraph 13(1)(b), the petitioner shall as soon as reasonably practicable send notice of the court's order dismissing the petition to all those to whom the petition was notified under Rule 2.3.]

NOTES

Substitution: see the note to r 2.1 at **[15.70]**.
See further Sch 5, Form 2.3B (Scot) at **[15.349]**, and the notes to that Schedule.

[CHAPTER 3 APPOINTMENT OF ADMINISTRATOR BY HOLDER OF FLOATING CHARGE

[15.78]
2.9 Notice of intention to appoint

For the purposes of paragraph 44(2), a notice of intention to appoint shall be in the form required by Rule 7.30 and Schedule 5, and shall be lodged in court at the same time as it is sent in accordance with paragraph 15(1) to the holder of any prior qualifying floating charge.]

NOTES

Substitution: see the note to r 2.1 at **[15.70]**.
See further Sch 5, Form 2.4B (Scot) at **[15.349]**, and the notes to that Schedule.

[15.79]
[2.10 Notice of appointment

(1) The notice of appointment under paragraph 14 shall be in the form required by Rule 7.30 and Schedule 5.

(2) Subject to Rule 2.12, there shall be lodged together with the notice of appointment—

(a) the Statement of the Proposed Administrator; and

(b) either—
   (i) evidence that the person making the appointment has fulfilled the requirements of paragraph 15(1)(a); or
   (ii) copies of the written consent of all those required to give consent in accordance with paragraph 15(1)(b).

(3) The statutory declaration required by paragraph 18(2) shall be made no earlier than 5 days before the notice of appointment is lodged.

(4) The holder of a prior floating charge may indicate his consent by completing the section provided on the form of notice of intention to appoint and returning to the person making the appointment a copy of that form.

(5) Where the holder of a prior floating charge does not choose to use the form of notice of intention to appoint to indicate his consent or no such form has been sent to him, his written consent shall include—
(a) details of the name, registered address and registered number of the company in respect of which the appointment is proposed to be made;
(b) details of the charge held including the date it was registered and, where applicable, any financial limit and any deeds of priority;
(c) the name and address of the floating charge holder consenting to the proposed appointment;
(d) the name and address of the holder of the qualifying floating charge who is proposing to make the appointment;
(e) the date that notice of intention to appoint was given;
(f) the name of the proposed administrator; and
(g) a statement of consent to the proposed appointment.

(6) Where the holder of a qualifying floating charge receives notice of an administration application and makes an appointment under paragraph 14, he shall as soon as reasonably practicable send a copy of the notice of appointment to the petitioner and to the court in which the petition has been lodged.]

NOTES

Substitution: see the note to r 2.1 at **[15.70]**.
Para (1): see further Sch 5, Form 2.5B (Scot) at **[15.349]**, and the notes to that Schedule.
Para (2): see further Sch 5, Form 2.1B (Scot) at **[15.349]**, and the notes to that Schedule.

[15.80]
[2.11 Notice to administrator

The person making the appointment shall, as soon as reasonably practicable, send to the administrator a copy of the notice of appointment, certified by the clerk of court and endorsed with the date and time of presentation of the principal notice.]

NOTES

Substitution: see the note to r 2.1 at **[15.70]**.

[15.81]
[2.12 Appointment taking place out of court business hours

(1) The holder of a qualifying floating charge may lodge a notice of appointment under paragraph 14 in court in accordance with this Rule when (and only when) the court is not open for public business.

(2) A notice of appointment lodged under this Rule shall be in the form required by Rule 7.30 and Schedule 5.

(3) The person making the appointment shall lodge the notice by sending it by fax to the court, and shall ensure that a fax transmission report is produced by the sending machine which records the date and time of the fax transmission.

(4) The person making the appointment shall send to the administrator, as soon as reasonably practicable, a copy of the notice of appointment and of the fax transmission report.

(5) The appointment shall take effect from the date and time of the fax transmission.

(6) The person making the appointment shall lodge in court, on the next day that the court is open for public business, the principal notice of appointment together with the documents required by Rule 2.10(2) and—
(a) the fax transmission report showing the date and time at which the notice was sent; and
(b) a statement of the full reasons for the out of hours lodging of the notice of appointment, including why it would have been damaging to the company or its creditors not to have so acted.

(7) The administrator's appointment shall cease to have effect if the requirements of paragraph (6) of this Rule are not met within the time set out in that paragraph.

(8) Where any question arises in respect of the date and time that the notice of appointment was lodged in court it shall be a presumption capable of rebuttal that the date and time shown on the fax transmission report is the date and time at which the notice was so lodged.]

NOTES

Substitution: see the note to r 2.1 at **[15.70]**.
Para (2): see further Sch 5, Form 2.6B (Scot) at **[15.349]**, and the notes to that Schedule.

[CHAPTER 4 APPOINTMENT OF ADMINISTRATOR BY COMPANY OR DIRECTORS

[15.82]
2.13 Notice of intention to appoint

(1) A notice of intention to appoint given under paragraph 26 shall be in the form required by Rule 7.30 and Schedule 5 and shall be given by the company or the directors, as the case may be, to any holder of a qualifying floating charge.

(2) A copy of the notice of intention to appoint shall at the same time be sent—

(a) to the supervisor of any voluntary arrangement under Part I of the Act; and

(b) where the notice is given by the directors (other than as agents of the company), to the company.]

NOTES

Substitution: see the note to r 2.1 at **[15.70]**.

Para (2): see further Sch 5, Form 2.7B (Scot) at **[15.349]**, and the notes to that Schedule.

[15.83]
[2.14 Timing of statutory declaration

The statutory declaration required by paragraph 27(2) shall be made not more than 5 business days before the notice is lodged in court.]

NOTES

Substitution: see the note to r 2.1 at **[15.70]**.

[15.84]
[2.15 Resolution or decision to appoint

The person making the appointment shall lodge together with the notice of intention to appoint either a copy of the resolution of the company to appoint an administrator (where the company proposes to make the appointment) or a record of the decision of the directors (where the directors propose to make the appointment).]

NOTES

Substitution: see the note to r 2.1 at **[15.70]**.

[15.85]
[2.16 Notice of appointment

(1) The notice of appointment referred to in paragraph 29 shall be in the form required by Rule 7.30 and Schedule 5.

(2) The statutory declaration required by paragraph 29(2) shall be made no earlier than 5 days before the notice is lodged.

(3) There shall be lodged together with the notice of appointment the Statement of the Proposed Administrator and, unless the period of notice set out in paragraph 26(1) has expired, the written consent of all those persons to whom notice was given in accordance with that paragraph.]

NOTES

Substitution: see the note to r 2.1 at **[15.70]**.

Para (1): see further Sch 5, Form 2.8B (Scot), Form 2.9B (Scot) at **[15.349]**, and the notes to that Schedule.

Para (3): see further Sch 5, Form 2.1B (Scot) at **[15.349]**, and the notes to that Schedule.

[15.86]
[2.17 Appointment where no notice of intention to appoint has been given

Where a notice of intention to appoint an administrator has not been given, there shall be lodged together with the notice of appointment either a copy of the resolution of the company to appoint an administrator (where the company proposes to make the appointment) or a record of the decision of the directors (where the directors propose to make the appointment).]

NOTES

Substitution: see the note to r 2.1 at **[15.70]**.

[15.87]
[2.18 Notice to administrator

The person making the appointment shall, as soon as reasonably practicable, send to the administrator a copy of the notice of appointment, certified by the clerk of court and endorsed with the date and time of presentation of the principal notice.]

NOTES

Substitution: see the note to r 2.1 at **[15.70]**.

[CHAPTER 5 PROCESS OF ADMINISTRATION

[15.88]

2.19 Notification and advertisement of administrator's appointment

[(1) The notice of appointment, which an administrator must publish as soon as is reasonably practicable after his appointment by virtue of paragraph 46(2)(b), shall be advertised in the Edinburgh Gazette and may be advertised in such other manner as the administrator thinks fit.]

[(1A) In addition to the standard content, notices published under paragraph (1) must state—
(a) that an administrator has been appointed,
(b) the date of the appointment; and
(c) the nature of the business of the company.]

(2) The administrator shall at the same time give notice of his appointment to the following persons—
(a) a receiver, if appointed;
(b) a petitioner in a petition for the winding up of the company, if that petition is pending;
(c) any provisional liquidator of the company, if appointed;
(d) any supervisor of a voluntary arrangement under Part 1 of the Act; and
(e) the Keeper of the Register of Inhibitions and Adjudications for recording in that register.

(3) Where, by virtue of a provision of Schedule B1 to the Act or of these Rules, the administrator is required to send a notice of his appointment to any person, he shall satisfy that requirement by sending to that person a notice in the form required by Rule 7.30 and Schedule 5.]

NOTES

Substitution: see the note to r 2.1 at **[15.70]**.

Para (1): substituted by the Insolvency (Scotland) Amendment Rules 2009, SI 2009/662, r 2, Schedule, para 4, subject to transitional provisions in r 3 thereof as noted to r 1.4 at **[15.10]**, and originally read as follows:

"(1) As soon as is reasonably practicable, the administrator shall advertise his appointment once in the Edinburgh Gazette and once in a newspaper circulating in the area where the company has its principal place of business or in such newspaper as he thinks appropriate for ensuring that the order comes to the notice of the company's creditors.".

Para (1A): inserted by the Insolvency (Scotland) Amendment Rules 2010, SI 2010/688, r 3, Sch 1, para 57, subject to transitional provisions in r 4 thereof at **[2.80]**.

Para (1): see further Sch 5, Form 2.10B (Scot) at **[15.349]**, and the notes to that Schedule.

Para (3): see further Sch 5, Form 2.11B (Scot) at **[15.349]**, and the notes to that Schedule.

[15.89]

[2.20 Notice requiring statement of affairs

(1) In this Chapter "relevant person" has the meaning given to it in paragraph 47(3).

(2) Subject to Rule 2.21, the administrator shall send to each relevant person upon whom he decides to make a requirement under paragraph 47 a notice in the form required by Rule 7.30 and Schedule 5 requiring him to provide a statement of the company's affairs

(3) The notice shall inform each of the relevant persons—
(a) of the names and addresses of all others (if any) to whom the same notice has been sent;
(b) of the time within which the statement must be delivered;
(c) of the effect of paragraph 48(4) (penalty for non-compliance); and
(d) of the application to him, and to each other relevant person, of section 235 (duty to provide information, and to attend on the administrator, if required).

(4) The administrator shall furnish each relevant person upon whom he decides to make a requirement under paragraph 47 with the forms required for the preparation of the statement of affairs.]

NOTES

Substitution: see the note to r 2.1 at **[15.70]**.

Para (2): see further Sch 5, Form 2.12B (Scot) at **[15.349]**, and the notes to that Schedule.

[15.90]

[2.21 Statements of affairs and statements of concurrence

(1) The statement of the company's affairs shall be in the form required by Rule 7.30 and Schedule 5.

(2) Where more than one relevant person is required to submit a statement of affairs the administrator may require one or more such persons to submit, in place of a statement of affairs, a statement of concurrence in the form required by Rule 7.30 and Schedule 5; and where the administrator does so, he shall inform the person making the statement of affairs of that fact.

(3) The person making the statutory declaration in support of a statement of affairs shall send the statement, together with one copy thereof, to the administrator, and a copy of the statement to each of those persons whom the administrator has required to submit a statement of concurrence.

(4) A person required to submit a statement of concurrence shall deliver to the administrator the statement of concurrence, together with one copy thereof, before the end of the period of 5 business days (or such other period as the administrator may agree) beginning with the day on which the statement of affairs being concurred with is received by him.

(5) A statement of concurrence may be qualified in respect of matters dealt with in the statement of affairs, where the maker of the statement of concurrence is not in agreement with the statement of affairs, he considers that statement to be erroneous or misleading, or he is without the direct knowledge necessary for concurring with it.

(6) Subject to Rule 2.22, the administrator shall, as soon as is reasonably practicable, file a copy of the statement of affairs and any statement of concurrence with the registrar of companies

(7) Subject to Rule 2.22, the administrator shall insert any statement of affairs submitted to him, together with any statement of concurrence, in the sederunt book.]

NOTES

Substitution: see the note to r 2.1 at **[15.70]**.

Para (1): see further Sch 5, Form 2.13B (Scot) at **[15.349]**, and the notes to that Schedule.

Para (2): see further Sch 5, Form 2.14B (Scot) at **[15.349]**, and the notes to that Schedule.

Para (6): see further Sch 5, Form 2.15B (Scot) at **[15.349]**, and the notes to that Schedule.

[15.91]

[2.22 Limited disclosure

(1) Where the administrator thinks that it would prejudice the conduct of the administration [or might be reasonably expected to lead to violence against any person] for the whole or part of the statement of the company's affairs to be disclosed, he may apply to the court for an order of limited disclosure in respect of the statement, or any specified part of it.

(2) The court may order that the statement or, as the case may be, the specified part of it, shall not be filed with the registrar of companies or entered in the sederunt book.

(3) The administrator shall as soon as reasonably practicable file a copy of that order with the registrar of companies, and shall place a copy of the order in the sederunt book.

(4) If a creditor seeks disclosure of the statement of affairs or a specified part of it in relation to which an order has been made under this Rule, he may apply to the court for an order that the administrator disclose it or a specified part of it.

(5) The court may attach to an order for disclosure any conditions as to confidentiality, duration and scope of the order in any material change of circumstances, and other matters as it sees fit.

(6) If there is a material change in circumstances rendering the limit on disclosure unnecessary, the administrator shall, as soon as reasonably practicable after the change, apply to the court for the order to be discharged or varied; and upon the discharge or variation of the order the administrator shall, as soon as reasonably practicable—

- (a) file a copy of the full statement of affairs (or so much of the statement of affairs as is no longer subject to the order) with the registrar of companies;
- (b) where he has previously sent a copy of his proposals to the creditors in accordance with paragraph 49, provide the creditors with a copy of the full statement of affairs (or so much of the statement as is no longer subject to the order) or a summary thereof; and
- (c) place a copy of the full statement of affairs (or so much of the statement as is no longer subject to the order) in the sederunt book.]

NOTES

Substitution: see the note to r 2.1 at **[15.70]**.

Para (1): words in square brackets inserted by the Insolvency (Scotland) Amendment Rules 2010, SI 2010/688, r 3, Sch 1, para 58, subject to transitional provisions in r 4 thereof at **[2.80]**.

[15.92]

[2.23 Release from duty to submit statement of affairs; extension of time

(1) The power of the administrator under paragraph 48(2) to revoke a requirement under paragraph 47(1), or to grant an extension of time, may be exercised at the administrator's own instance, or at the request of any relevant person.

(2) A relevant person whose request under this Rule has been refused by the administrator may apply to the court for a release or extension of time.

(3) An applicant under this Rule shall bear his own expenses in the application and, unless the court otherwise orders, no allowance towards such expenses shall be made [as an expense of the administration] of the company.]

NOTES

Substitution: see the note to r 2.1 at **[15.70]**.

Para (3): words in square brackets substituted for original words "out of the assets" by the Insolvency (Scotland) Amendment Rules 2010, SI 2010/688, r 3, Sch 1, para 59, subject to transitional provisions in r 4 thereof at **[2.80]**.

[15.93]

[2.24 Expenses of statement of affairs

(1) A relevant person who provides to the administrator a statement of [affairs of the company] or statement of concurrence shall be allowed, and paid by the administrator [as an expense of the administration], any expenses incurred by the relevant person in so doing which the administrator considers reasonable.

(2) Any decision by the administrator under this Rule is subject to appeal to the court.

(3) Nothing in this Rule relieves a relevant person from any obligation to provide a statement of affairs or statement of concurrence, or to provide information to the administrator.]

NOTES

Substitution: see the note to r 2.1 at **[15.70]**.

Para (1): words in first pair of square brackets substituted for original words "the company's affairs" and words in second pair of square brackets substituted for original words "out of his receipts" by the Insolvency (Scotland) Amendment Rules 2010, SI 2010/688, r 3, Sch 1, para 60, subject to transitional provisions in r 4 thereof at **[2.80]**.

[15.94]
[2.25 Administrator's proposals

(1) The statement required to be made by the administrator under paragraph 49 shall include, in addition to the matters set out in that paragraph—

(a) details of the court which granted the administration order or in which the notice of appointment was lodged, and the relevant court reference number (if any);

(b) the full name, registered address, registered number and any other trading names of the company;

(c) details relating to his appointment as administrator, including the date of appointment and the person making the application or appointment, and, where there are joint administrators, a statement of the matters referred to in paragraph 100(2);

(d) the names of the directors and secretary of the company and details of any shareholdings which they have in the company;

(e) an account of the circumstances giving rise to the appointment of the administrator;

(f) if a statement of the company's affairs has been submitted, a copy or summary of it, with the administrator's comments, if any;

(g) if an order limiting the disclosure of the statement of affairs has been made, a statement of that fact, as well as—

  (i) details of who provided the statement of affairs;
  (ii) the date of the order of limited disclosure; and
  (iii) the details or a summary of the details that are not subject to that order;

(h) if a full statement of affairs is not provided, the names and addresses of the creditors, and details of the debts owed to, and security held by, each of them;

(i) if no statement of affairs has been submitted—

  (i) details of the financial position of the company at the latest practicable date (which must, unless the court otherwise orders, be a date not earlier than that on which the company entered administration);
  (ii) the names and addresses of the creditors, and details of the debts owed to, and security held by, each of them; and
  (iii) an explanation as to why there is no statement of affairs;

(j) the basis upon which it is proposed that the administrator's remuneration should be fixed;

[(ka) a statement complying with paragraph (1B) of any pre-administration costs charged or incurred by the administrator or, to the administrator's knowledge, by any other person qualified to act as an insolvency practitioner;]

(k) except where the administrator proposes a voluntary arrangement in relation to the company—

  (i) to the best of the administrator's knowledge and belief—

    (aa) an estimate of the value of the prescribed part (whether or not he proposes to make an application to the court under section 176A(5) and whether or not section 176A(3) applies); and
    (bb) an estimate of the value of the company's net property, provided that such estimates shall not be required to include any information the disclosure of which could serious prejudice the commercial interests of the company, but if such information is excluded the estimates shall be accompanied by a statement to that effect; and

  (ii) whether and, if so, why the administrator proposes to make an application to the court under section 176A(5);

[(l) a statement (which must comply with paragraph (1C) where that paragraph applies) of how it is envisaged the purpose of the administration will be achieved and how it is proposed that the administration shall end;]

(m) . . .

(n) where it is proposed to make distributions to creditors in accordance with Chapter 9, the classes of creditors to whom it is proposed that distributions be made and whether or not the administrator intends to make an application to the court under paragraph 65(3);

(o) where the administrator has decided not to call a meeting of creditors, his reasons;

(p) the manner in which the affairs and business of the company—

  (i) have, since the date of the administrator's appointment, been managed and financed; and
  (ii) will, if the administrator's proposals are approved, continue to be managed and financed;

(q) whether—

  (i) [the EU Regulation] applies; and
  (ii) if so, whether the proceedings are [main, secondary or territorial proceedings]; and

(r) such other information (if any) as the administrator thinks necessary to enable creditors to decide whether or not to vote for the adoption of the proposals.

[(1A) In this Part—

(a) "pre-administration costs" are—

  (i) fees charged, and
  (ii) expenses incurred,

by the administrator, or another person qualified to act as an insolvency practitioner, before the company entered administration but with a view to its doing so; and

(b) "unpaid pre-administration costs" are pre-administration costs which had not been paid when the company entered administration.

(1B) A statement of pre-administration costs complies with this paragraph if it includes—

(a) details of any agreement under which the fees were charged and expenses incurred, including the parties to the agreement and the date on which the agreement was made,

(b) details of the work done for which the fees were charged and expenses incurred,

(c) an explanation of why the work was done before the company entered administration and how it would further the achievement of an objective in sub-paragraph (1) of paragraph 3 in accordance with sub-paragraphs (2) to (4) of that paragraph,

(d) a statement of the amount of the pre-administration costs, setting out separately—

(i) the fees charged by the administrator,

(ii) the expenses incurred by the administrator,

(iii) the fees charged (to the administrator's knowledge) by any other person qualified to act as an insolvency practitioner (and, if more than one, by each separately), and

(iv) the expenses incurred (to the administrator's knowledge) by any other person qualified to act as an insolvency practitioner (and, if more than one, by each separately),

(e) a statement of the amounts of unpaid pre-administration costs (set out separately as under sub-paragraph (d),

(f) the identity of the person who made the payment or, if more than one person made the payment, the identity of each such person and of the amounts paid by each such person set out separately as under sub-paragraph (d),

(g) a statement of the amounts of unpaid pre-administration costs (set out separately as under sub-paragraph (d)), and

(h) a statement that the payment of unpaid pre-administration costs as an expense of the administration is—

(i) subject to approval under Rule 2.39C, and

(ii) not part of the proposals subject to approval under paragraph 53.

(1C) This paragraph applies where it is proposed that the administration will end by the company moving to a creditors' voluntary liquidation; and in that case, the statement required by Rule 2.25(1)(l) must include—

(a) details of the proposed liquidator;

(b) where applicable, the declaration required by section 231 (appointment to office of two or more persons); and

(c) a statement that the creditors may, before the proposals are approved, nominate a different person as liquidator in accordance with paragraph 83(7)(a) and Rule 2.47.]

(2) A copy of the administrator's statement of his proposals shall be sent to the registrar of companies together with a notice in the form required by Rule 7.30 and Schedule 5.

(3) Where the statement of proposals states that the administrator thinks—

(a) that the company has sufficient property to enable each creditor of the company to be paid in full;

(b) that the company has insufficient property to make a distribution to unsecured creditors other than by virtue of section 176A(2)(a); or

(c) that neither of the objectives specified in paragraph 3(1)(a) and (b) can be achieved,

and no meeting has been requisitioned under paragraph 52(2), the administrator's proposals shall be deemed to have been approved by the creditors upon the expiry of the period set out in Rule 2.31.

[(3A) Where proposals are deemed under paragraph (3) to have been approved, the administrator must, as soon as reasonably practicable after the expiry of the period set out in Rule 2.31, give notice of the date on which they were deemed to have been approved to the registrar of companies, the court and the creditors in the form required by Rule 7.30 and Schedule 5; and a copy of the proposals must be attached to the notice given to the court and to creditors who have not previously received them.]

(4) The administrator shall give notice to the creditors of any order varying the period referred to in paragraph 49(5) (which sets out the period during which the administrator shall send out a copy of his statement of proposals).

(5) Where the administrator intends to apply to the court (or to lodge a notice under paragraph 80(2)) for the administration to cease at a time before he has sent a statement of his proposals to creditors in accordance with paragraph 49, he shall, at least [7 business] days before he makes such an application or lodges such a notice, send to all creditors of the company (so far as he is aware of their addresses) a report containing the information required by paragraph (1)(a) to (q) of this Rule.

[(6) Where the administrator wishes to publish a notice under paragraph 49(6), the notice shall be advertised in such manner as the administrator thinks fit.]

[(6A) A notice published under Rule 2.25(6) must include the standard content and must state—

(a) that members can write to request that a copy of the statement of proposals be provided free of charge; and

(b) the address to which to write.]

(7) A notice under paragraph 49(6) must be published as soon as reasonably practicable after the administrator sends his statement of proposals to the company's creditors and in any case no later than 8 weeks (or such other period as may be agreed by the creditors or ordered by the court) from the date upon which the company entered administration.]

NOTES

Substitution: see the note to r 2.1 at **[15.70]**.

Para (1): sub-para (ka) inserted, sub-para (l) substituted and sub-para (m) revoked by the Insolvency (Scotland) Amendment Rules 2010, SI 2010/688, r 3, Sch 1, paras 61–63, subject to transitional provisions in r 4 thereof at **[2.80]**. Sub-paras (l), (m) previously read as follows:

"(l) how it is envisaged the purpose of the administration will be achieved and how it is proposed that the administration shall end;" and

"(m) where a creditors' voluntary liquidation is proposed—

(i) details of the proposed liquidator; and

(ii) a statement that, in accordance with paragraph 83(7) and Rule 2.47, creditors may nominate another person to act as liquidator;".

Words in square brackets in sub-para (q)(i) substituted for original words "the EC Regulation" by the Insolvency Amendment (EU 2015/848) Regulations 2017, SI 2017/702, regs 2, 3, Schedule, Pt 5, paras 61, 76, as from 26 June 2017, except in relation to proceedings opened before that date.

Words in square brackets in sub-para (q)(ii) substituted for original words "main proceedings or territorial proceedings" by the Insolvency (Scotland) Amendment Rules 2006, SI 2006/734, r 6, subject to transitional provisions in r 2(1) thereof at **[2.43]**.

Paras (1A)–(1C): inserted by SI 2010/688, r 3, Sch 1, para 64, subject to transitional provisions in r 4 thereof at **[2.80]**.

Para (3A): inserted by SI 2010/688, r 3, Sch 1, para 65, subject to transitional provisions in r 4 thereof at **[2.80]**.

Para (5): words in square brackets substituted for original number "10" by SI 2010/688, r 3, Sch 1, para 66, subject to transitional provisions in r 4 thereof at **[2.80]**.

Para (6): substituted by the Insolvency (Scotland) Amendment Rules 2009, SI 2009/662, r 2, Schedule, para 5, subject to transitional provisions in r 3 thereof as noted to r 1.4 at **[15.10]**, and originally read as follows:

"(6) Where the administrator wishes to publish a notice under paragraph 49(6) he shall publish the notice once in the Edinburgh Gazette and once in the newspaper in which the administrator's appointment was advertised. The notice shall—

(a) state the full name of the company;

(b) state the full name and address of the administrator;

(c) give details of the administrator's appointment; and

(d) specify an address to which any member of the company may apply in writing for a copy of the statement of proposals to be provide free of charge.".

Para (6A): inserted by SI 2009/662, r 2, Schedule, para 6, subject to transitional provisions in r 3 thereof as noted to r 1.4 at **[15.10]**; substituted by SI 2010/688, r 3, Sch 1, para 67, subject to transitional provisions in r 4 thereof at **[2.80]**, and previously read as follows:

"(6A) A notice published under Rule 2.25(6) shall—

(a) state the full name of the company;

(b) state the full name and address of the administrator;

(c) give details of the administrator's appointment; and

(d) specify an address to which any member of the company can write to request that a copy of the statement of proposals be provided free of charge.".

Para (6): see further Sch 5, Form 2.16B (Scot) at **[15.349]**, and the notes to that Schedule.

[15.95]

[2.25A Limited disclosure of paragraph 49 statement

(1) Where the administrator thinks that it would prejudice the conduct of the administration or might reasonably be expected to lead to violence against any person for any of the matters specified in Rule 2.25(1)(h) and (i) to be disclosed, the administrator may apply to the court for an order of limited disclosure in respect of any specified part of the statement under paragraph 49 containing such matter.

(2) The court may, on such application, order that some or all of the specified part of the statement must not be sent to the registrar of companies or to creditors or members of the company as otherwise required by paragraph 49(4).

(3) The administrator must as soon as reasonably practicable send to the persons specified in paragraph 49(4) the statement under paragraph 49 (to the extent provided by the order) and an indication of the nature of the matter in relation to which the order was made.

(4) The administrator must also send a copy of the order to the registrar of companies.

(5) A creditor who seeks disclosure of a part of a statement under paragraph 49 in relation to which an order has been made under this Rule may apply to the court for an order that the administrator disclose it. The application must be supported by written evidence in the form of an affidavit.

(6) The court may make any order for disclosure subject to any conditions as to confidentiality, duration and scope of the order in the event of any change of circumstances, or other matters as it sees just.

(7) If there is a material change in circumstances rendering the limit on disclosure or any part of it unnecessary, the administrator must, as soon as reasonably practicable after the change, apply to the court for the order or any part of it to be discharged or varied.

(8) The administrator must, as soon as reasonably practicable after the making of an order under paragraph (7), send to the persons specified in paragraph 49(4) a copy of the statement under paragraph 49 to the extent provided by the order.]

NOTES

Inserted, together with rr 2.25B–2.25E and related Chapter heading, by the Insolvency (Scotland) Amendment Rules 2010, SI 2010/688, r 3, Sch 1, para 68, subject to transitional provisions in rr 4, 5 thereof at **[2.80]**, **[2.81]**.

[CHAPTER 5A THE GIVING OF NOTICE AND SUPPLY OF DOCUMENTS

[15.96]
2.25B Application

(1) Subject to paragraph (2), this Chapter applies where a notice or other document is required to be given, delivered or sent under this Part of these Rules.

(2) This Chapter does not apply to—
- (a) the lodging of any application, or other document, with the court;
- (b) the service of any application, or other document, lodged with the court;
- (c) the service of any order of the court; or
- (d) the submission of documents to the registrar of companies.]

NOTES

Inserted as noted to r 2.25A at **[15.95]**.

[15.97]
[2.25C Electronic delivery

(1) Unless in any particular case some other form of delivery is required by the Act or these Rules or any order of the court, a notice or other document may be given, delivered or sent by electronic means provided that the intended recipient of the notice or other document has—
- (a) consented (whether in the specific case or generally) to electronic delivery (and has not revoked that consent); and
- (b) provided an electronic address for delivery.

(2) Where an administrator gives, sends or delivers a notice or other document to any person by electronic means, it must contain or be accompanied by a statement that the recipient may request a hard copy of the notice or document, and specify a telephone number, e-mail address and postal address which may be used to make such a request.

(3) Where a hard copy of the notice or other document is requested it must be sent within 5 business days of receipt of the request by the administrator, who may not make a charge for sending it in that form.

(4) In the absence of evidence to the contrary, a notice or other document shall be presumed to have been delivered where—
- (a) the sender can produce a copy of the electronic message which—
  - (i) contained the notice or other document, or to which the notice or other document was attached; and
  - (ii) shows the time and date the message was sent; and
- (b) that electronic message was sent to the address supplied under paragraph (1)(b).

(5) A message delivered electronically shall be deemed to have been delivered to the recipient at 9.00 am on the next business day after it was sent.]

NOTES

Inserted as noted to r 2.25A at **[15.95]**.

[15.98]
[2.25D Use of websites by administrator

(1) This Rule applies for the purpose of section 246B.

(2) An administrator required to give, deliver or send a document to any person may (other than in a case where personal service is required) satisfy that requirement by sending that person a notice—
- (a) stating that the document is available for viewing and downloading on a website;
- (b) specifying the address of that website together with any password necessary to view and download the document from that website; and
- (c) containing a statement that the recipient of the notice may request a hard copy of the document, and specifying a telephone number, e-mail address and postal address which may be used to make such a request.

(3) Where a notice to which this Rule applies is sent, the document to which it relates must—
- (a) be available on the website for a period of not less than 3 months after the date on which the notice is sent; and
- (b) be in such a format as to enable it to be downloaded from the website within a reasonable time of an electronic request being made for it to be downloaded.

(4) Where a hard copy of the document is requested it must be sent within 5 business days of the receipt of the request by the administrator, who may not make a charge for sending it in that form.

(5) Where a document is given, delivered or sent to a person by means of a website in accordance with this Rule, it is deemed to have been delivered—
- (a) when the document was first made available on the website, or
- (b) if later, when the notice under paragraph (2) was delivered to that person.]

NOTES

Inserted as noted to r 2.25A at **[15.95]**.

[15.99]
[2.25E Special provision on account of expense as to website use

(1) Where the court is satisfied that the expense of sending notices in accordance with Rule 2.25D would, on account of the number of persons entitled to receive them, be disproportionate to the benefit of sending notices in accordance with that Rule, it may order that the requirement to give, deliver or send a relevant document to any person may (other than in a case where personal service is required) be satisfied by the administrator sending each of those persons a notice—

(a) stating that all relevant documents will be made available for viewing and downloading on a website;

(b) specifying the address of that website together with any password necessary to view and download the document from that site; and

(c) containing a statement that the person to whom the notice is given, delivered or sent may at any time request that hard copies of all, or specific, relevant documents are sent to that person, and specifying a telephone number, e-mail address and postal address which may be used to make that request.

(2) A document to which this Rule relates must—

(a) be available on the website for a period of not less than 12 months from the date when it was first made available on the website or, if later, from the date upon which the notice was sent, and

(b) be in such a format as to enable it to be downloaded from the website within a reasonable time of an electronic request being made for it to be downloaded.

(3) Where hard copies of relevant documents have been requested, they must be sent by the administrator—

(a) within 5 business days of the receipt by the administrator of the request to be sent hard copies, in the case of relevant documents first appearing on the website before the request was received, or

(b) within 5 business days from the date a relevant document first appears on the website, in all other cases.

(4) An administrator must not require a person making a request under paragraph (3) to pay a fee for the supply of the document.

(5) Where a relevant document is given, delivered or sent to a person by means of a website in accordance with this Rule, it is deemed to have been delivered—

(a) when the relevant document was first made available on the website, or

(b) if later, when the notice under paragraph (1) was delivered to that person.

(6) In this Rule a relevant document means any document which the administrator is first required to give, deliver or send to any person after the court has made an order under paragraph (1).]

NOTES

Inserted as noted to r 2.25A at **[15.95]**.

[CHAPTER 6 MEETINGS

[15.100]
2.26 General

The provisions of Chapter 1 of Part 7 (Meetings) shall apply with regard to meetings of the company's creditors or members which are summoned by the administrator, subject to the provisions in this chapter.]

NOTES

Substitution: see the note to r 2.1 at **[15.70]**.

[15.101]
[2.26A Notice of meetings

[(1) The administrator shall publish notice of all meetings of the company's creditors or members in the Edinburgh Gazette and in such other manner as the administrator thinks fit to ensure the meeting comes to the notice of any persons who are entitled to attend.]

(3) A notice published under [paragraph (1)] shall include—

(a) the name, registered number and address of the registered office of the company in administration;

(b) the venue fixed for the meeting;

(c) the date and time of the meeting; and

(d) the full name and address of the administrator.

(4) Rule 7.3(3) (notice of meeting) shall not apply to a meeting of creditors summoned by the administrator.]

NOTES

Inserted by the Insolvency (Scotland) Amendment Rules 2009, SI 2009/662, r 2, Schedule, para 7, subject to transitional provisions in r 3 thereof as noted to r 1.4 at **[15.10]**.

Para (1): substituted for paras (1), (2) by the Insolvency (Scotland) Amendment Rules 2010, SI 2010/688, r 3, Sch 1, para 69, subject to transitional provisions in r 4 thereof at **[2.80]**. Paras (1), (2) previously read as follows:

"(1) The administrator shall publish notice of an initial creditors' meeting under paragraph 51 in the Edinburgh Gazette and the notice may be advertised in such other manner as the administrator thinks fit.

(2) An administrator may publish notice of any other meeting, in such manner as the administrator thinks fit to ensure the meeting comes to the notice of any persons who are entitled to attend.".

Para (3): words in square brackets substituted for original words "paragraphs (1) or (2)" by SI 2010/688, r 3, Sch 1, para 69, subject to transitional provisions in r 4 thereof at **[2.80]**.

[15.102]
[2.26B Remote attendance at meetings

(1) This Rule applies to a request to the administrator under section 246A(9) to specify a place for the meeting.

(2) The request must be accompanied by—

- (a) in the case of a request by creditors, a list of the creditors making (or concurring with) the request and the amounts of those creditors' respective debts in the insolvency proceedings in question,
- (b) in the case of a request by members, a list of the members making (or concurring with) the request and those members' voting rights, and
- (c) from each person concurring, written confirmation of that person's concurrence.

(3) The request must be made within 7 business days of the date on which the administrator sent the notice of the meeting in question.

(4) Where the administrator considers that the request has been properly made in accordance with the Act and these Rules, the administrator must—

- (a) give notice (to all those previously given notice of the meeting)—
  - (i) that the meeting is to be held at a specified place, and
  - (ii) whether the date and time of the meeting are to remain the same or not;
- (b) specify a time, date and place for the meeting, the date of which must not be more than 28 days after the original date for the meeting; and
- (c) give at least 14 days' notice of the time, date and place of the meeting to all those previously given notice of the meeting,

and the notices required by subparagraphs (a) and (c) may be given at the same or different times.

(5) Where the administrator has specified a place for the meeting in response to a request to which this Rule applies, the chairman of the meeting must attend the meeting by being present in person at that place.

(6) Rule 7.6 (4), (5), (6) and (7) (expenses of summoning meetings) as applied by Rule 2.26, do not apply to the summoning and holding of a meeting at a place specified in accordance with section 246A(9).]

NOTES

Inserted, together with r 2.26C, by the Insolvency (Scotland) Amendment Rules 2010, SI 2010/688, r 3, Sch 1, para 70, subject to transitional provisions in rr 4, 5 thereof at **[2.80]**, **[2.81]**.

[15.103]
[2.26C Entitlement to vote and draw dividend

(1) A creditor, in order to obtain an adjudication as to entitlement—

- (a) to vote at any meeting of the creditors in the administration; or
- (b) to a dividend (so far as funds are available) out of the assets of the company in respect of any accounting period,

must submit a claim to the administrator.

(2) A creditor's claim must be submitted—

- (a) at or before the meeting; or, as the case may be,
- (b) not later than 8 weeks before the end of the accounting period.

(3) A creditor's claim must—

- (a) be made out by, or under the direction of, the creditor;
- (b) have attached an account or voucher (according to the nature of the debt claimed) which constitutes *prima facie* evidence of the debt; and
- (c) state the following matters—
  - (i) the creditor's name and address;
  - (ii) if the creditor is a company, its registered number;
  - (iii) the total amount of the creditor's claim (including value added tax) as at the date on which the company entered administration, (or if the company was in liquidation when it entered administration, the date on which it went into liquidation) less any payments that have been made to the creditor after that date in respect of that claim;
  - (iv) whether or not the claim includes outstanding uncapitalised interest;
  - (v) particulars of how and when the debt was incurred by the company;
  - (vi) particulars of any security held, the date on which it was given and the value which the creditor puts on it;
  - (vii) details of any reservation of title in respect of goods to which the debt refers; and
  - (viii) the name, address and authority of the person making out the proof, if other than the creditor.

(4) The administrator may dispense with any requirement in paragraph (3)(b) in respect of any debt or any class of debt.

(5) A claim submitted by a creditor, which has been accepted in whole or in part by the administrator for the purpose of voting at a meeting, or of drawing a dividend in respect of any accounting period, shall be deemed to have been resubmitted for the purpose of obtaining an adjudication as to the creditor's entitlement both to vote at any subsequent meeting and (so far as funds are available) to a dividend in respect of an accounting period or, as the case may be, any subsequent accounting period.

(6) A creditor who has submitted a claim, may at any time submit a further claim specifying a different amount for that creditor's claim, provided that a secured creditor shall not be entitled to produce a further claim specifying a different value for the security at any time after the administrator has required the creditor to discharge, convey or assign the security.

(7) Where an administration is immediately preceded by a winding up, a creditor who has proved a debt in the winding up is deemed to have proved it in the administration.]

NOTES

Inserted as noted to r 2.26B at **[15.102]**.

[15.104]

[2.27 Meetings to consider administrator's proposals

(1) The administrator may, upon giving at least 14 days' notice, require the attendance at a creditors' meeting of any directors or officers of the company (including persons who have been directors or officers in the past) whose presence at the meeting is, in the administrator's opinion, appropriate.

(2) If at the meeting there is not the requisite majority for approval of the administrator's proposals (with modifications, if any), the chairman may, and shall if a resolution is passed to that effect, adjourn the meeting . . . for not more than 14 days.

(3) The administrator shall give notice to the creditors of any order varying the period referred to in paragraph 51(2) (which sets out the period during which the administrator must set the date for an initial creditors' meeting).

(4) . . .]

NOTES

Substitution: see the note to r 2.1 at **[15.70]**.

Para (2): words "once only and" (omitted) revoked by the Insolvency (Scotland) Amendment Rules 2010, SI 2010/688, r 3, Sch 1, para 71, subject to transitional provisions in r 4 thereof at **[2.80]**.

Para (4): revoked by SI 2010/688, r 3, Sch 1, para 72, subject to transitional provisions in r 4 thereof at **[2.80]**, and previously read as follows:

"(4) Rule 7.8 (adjournment), with the exception of Rule 7.8(6), shall not apply in relation to initial creditors' meetings in administration.".

[15.105]

[2.27A Suspension and adjournment

(1) This Rule applies to all meetings of creditors, and Rule 7.8 does not apply.

(2) If within 30 minutes from the time fixed for the commencement of the meeting those persons attending the meeting do not constitute a quorum, the chairman may adjourn the meeting to such time and place as the chairman may appoint.

(3) Once only in the course of the meeting the chairman may, without an adjournment, declare the meeting suspended for any period up to one hour.

(4) In the course of any meeting, the chairman may, in the chairman's discretion, and shall, if the meeting so resolves, adjourn it to such date, time and place as seems to the chairman to be appropriate in the circumstances.

(5) An adjournment under paragraph (4) must not be for a period of more than 14 days, subject to a direction from the court.

(6) If there are subsequent further adjournments, the final adjournment must not be to a day later than 14 days after the date on which the meeting was originally held.

(7) Where a meeting is adjourned under this Rule, proxies may be used if lodged at or before the adjourned meeting.

(8) Where a meeting is adjourned under this Rule, any proxies given for the original meeting may be used at the adjourned meeting.]

NOTES

Inserted by the Insolvency (Scotland) Amendment Rules 2010, SI 2010/688, r 3, Sch 1, para 73, subject to transitional provisions in r 4 thereof at **[2.80]**.

[15.106]

[2.28 Correspondence instead of creditors' meetings

(1) This Rule applies where an administrator proposes to conduct the business of a creditors' meeting by correspondence in accordance with paragraph 58.

(2) Notice of the business to be conducted shall be given to all who are entitled to be notified of a creditors' meeting by virtue of paragraph 51.

(3) The administrator may seek to obtain the agreement of the creditors to a resolution by sending to every creditor a copy of the proposed resolution.

(4) The administrator shall send to the creditors a copy of any proposed resolution on which a decision is sought, which shall be set out in such a way that agreement with or dissent from each separate resolution may be indicated by the recipient on the copy so sent.

(5) The administrator shall set a closing date for receipt of votes and comments. The closing date shall be set at the discretion of the administrator, but shall not be less than 14 days from the date of issue of the notice under paragraph (1) of this Rule.

(6) In order to be considered, votes and comments must be received by the administrator by the closing date and must be accompanied by the statement of claim and account or voucher referred to in Rule [2.26C, except where the statement of claim and account or voucher have already been submitted by the creditor to the administrator].

(7) For the conduct of business to proceed, the administrator must receive at least one response which satisfies the requirements of paragraph (6) of this Rule.

(8) If no responses are received by the closing date then the administrator shall summon a creditors' meeting.

(9) Any single creditor, or a group of creditors, of the company whose debt(s) amount to at least 10% of the total debts of the company may, within 5 business days from the date of the administrator sending out a resolution or proposals, require him to summon a creditors' meeting to consider the matters raised therein.

(10) If the administrator's proposals or revised proposals are rejected by the creditors pursuant to this Rule, the administrator may summon a creditors' meeting.

(11) A reference in this Part to anything done at a creditors' meeting includes a reference to anything done in the course of correspondence in accordance with this Rule; and Rule 2.35 shall apply to the business of a creditors' meeting conducted by correspondence as it applies to a creditors' meeting.]

NOTES

Substitution: see the note to r 2.1 at **[15.70]**.

Para (6): words in square brackets substituted for original words "4.15 as applied by this Part" by the Insolvency (Scotland) Amendment Rules 2010, SI 2010/688, r 3, Sch 1, para 74, subject to transitional provisions in r 4 thereof at **[2.80]**.

[15.107]

[2.29 Applicable Law (Company Meetings)

Subject to anything to the contrary in the Act and these Rules, a meeting of the members of the company must be summoned and conducted—

(a) in the case of a company incorporated in a part of the United Kingdom in accordance with the law of that part including any applicable provision in or made under the Companies Act 2006;

(b) in the case of a company incorporated in an EEA state other than the United Kingdom, in accordance with the law of that state applicable to meetings of the company; or

(c) in any other case, in accordance with the law of Scotland, including any provision in or made under the Companies Act 2006 applicable to the company as an overseas company.]

NOTES

Substituted by the Insolvency (Scotland) Amendment Rules 2010, SI 2010/688, r 3, Sch 1, para 75, subject to transitional provisions in r 4 thereof at **[2.80]**, and previously read as follows:

"**2.29 Applicable law**

(1) This Rule applies where the laws of a member State and not the law of Scotland applies in relation to the conduct of the meeting.

(2) Where this Rule applies, subject as above, the meeting shall be summoned and conducted in accordance with the constitution of the company and the laws of the member State referred to in paragraph (1) of this Rule shall apply to the conduct of the meeting.".

[15.108]

[2.30 Entitlement to vote—member State liquidators

(1) Where—

(a) a creditor is entitled to vote at a creditors' meeting;

(b) has lodged his claim in one or more sets of other proceedings;

(c) votes (either in person or by proxy) on a resolution put to the meeting; and

(d) a member State liquidator casts a vote in respect of the same claim,

only the creditor's vote shall be counted.

(2) Where—

(a) a creditor has lodged his claim in more than one set of other proceedings; and

(b) more than one member State liquidator seeks to vote by virtue of that claim,

the entitlement to vote by virtue of that claim is exercisable by the member State liquidator in main proceedings, whether or not the creditor has lodged his claim in the main proceedings.

(3) For the purposes of this Rule, "other proceedings" means [main, secondary or territorial proceedings] in another member State.]

NOTES

Substitution: see the note to r 2.1 at **[15.70]**.

Para (3): words in square brackets substituted for original words "main proceedings or territorial proceedings" by the Insolvency (Scotland) Amendment Rules 2006, SI 2006/734, r 7, subject to transitional provisions in r 2(1) thereof at **[2.43]**.

[15.109]
[2.31 Meeting requisitioned by creditors

The request for an initial creditors' meeting under paragraph 52(2) must be made within [8 business] days of the date upon which the administrator sends out his statement of proposals.]

NOTES

Substitution: see the note to r 2.1 at **[15.70]**.

Words in square brackets substituted for original number "12" by the Insolvency (Scotland) Amendment Rules 2010, SI 2010/688, r 3, Sch 1, para 76, subject to transitional provisions in r 4 thereof at **[2.80]**.

[15.110]
[2.32

(1) Rule 7.6(2)(a) [and (b) do] not apply if the requisitioning creditor's debt alone is sufficient to meet the requirement of paragraph 52(2)(a) or, as the case may be, paragraph 56(1)(a), without the concurrence of other creditors.

(2) In its application to initial creditors' meetings in administration, for the period of 35 days referred to in Rule 7.6(3) there is substituted a period of 28 days.]

NOTES

Substitution: see the note to r 2.1 at **[15.70]**.

Para (1): words in square brackets substituted for original word "does" by the Insolvency (Scotland) Amendment Rules 2010, SI 2010/688, r 3, Sch 1, para 77, subject to transitional provisions in r 4 thereof at **[2.80]**.

[15.111]
[2.32A Notice of meetings by advertisement only

(1) The court may order that notice of any meeting be given by advertisement and not by individual notice to the persons concerned.

(2) In considering whether to act under this Rule, the court must have regard to the cost of advertisement, the amount of assets available and the extent of the interest of creditors, members or any particular class of either.]

NOTES

Inserted by the Insolvency (Scotland) Amendment Rules 2010, SI 2010/688, r 3, Sch 1, para 78, subject to transitional provisions in r 4 thereof at **[2.80]**.

[15.112]
[2.33 Hire-purchase, conditional sale and hiring agreements

(1) Subject as follows, an owner of goods under a hire-purchase agreement or under an agreement for the hire of goods for more than 3 months, or a seller of goods under a conditional sale agreement, is entitled to vote in respect of the amount of the debt due and payable to him by the company on the date that the company entered administration.

(2) In calculating the amount of any debt for this purpose, no account shall be taken of any amount attributable to the exercise of any right under the relevant agreement, so far as the right has become exercisable solely by virtue of the making of an administration application, a notice of intention to appoint an administrator or any matter arising as a consequence, or of the company entering administration.]

NOTES

Substitution: see the note to r 2.1 at **[15.70]**.

[15.113]
[2.34 Revision of the administrator's proposals

(1) A statement of revised proposals under paragraph 54 shall include

(a) details of the court which granted the administration order or in which the notice of appointment was lodged and the relevant court reference number (if any);

(b) the full name, registered address, registered number and any other trading names of the company;

(c) details relating to the appointment of the administrator, including the date of appointment and the person making the administration application or appointment;

(d) the names of the directors and secretary of the company and details of any shareholdings which they have in the company;

(e) a summary of the initial proposals and the reason or reasons for proposing a revision;

(f) details of the proposed revision including details of the administrator's assessment of the likely impact of the proposed revision upon creditors generally or upon each class of creditors (as the case may be);

(g) where it is proposed, by virtue of the revision, to make distributions to creditors in accordance with Chapter 9, the classes of creditors to whom it is proposed that distributions be made and whether or not the administrator intends to make an application to the court under paragraph 65(3);

(h) where the revision includes a proposal to move from administration to a creditors' voluntary liquidation—

(i) details of the proposed liquidator;
(ii) a statement that, in accordance with paragraph 83(7) and Rule 2.47, creditors may nominate another person to act as liquidator; and
(iii) any other information that the administrator thinks necessary to enable creditors to decide whether or not to vote for the proposed revisions[; and
(iv) where applicable, the declaration required by section 231].

(2) Subject to paragraph 54(3), within 5 [business] days of sending out the statement mentioned in paragraph (1) above, the administrator shall send a copy of the statement to every member of the company.

[(3) Where the administrator wishes to publish a notice under paragraph 54(3), the notice shall be advertised in such manner as the administrator thinks fit.]

[(4) The notice referred to in paragraph (3) shall—
(a) state the full name of the company;
(b) state the name and address of the administrator;
(c) specify an address to which any member of the company can write to request that a copy of the statement be provided free of charge; and
(d) be published as soon as is reasonably practicable after the administrator sends the statement to the creditors.]]

NOTES

Substitution: see the note to r 2.1 at **[15.70]**.

Para (1): sub-para (h)(iv) and word "and" immediately preceding it added by the Insolvency (Scotland) Amendment Rules 2010, SI 2010/688, r 3, Sch 1, para 79, subject to transitional provisions in r 4 thereof at **[2.80]**.

Para (2): word in square brackets inserted by SI 2010/688, r 3, Sch 1, para 80, subject to transitional provisions in r 4 thereof at **[2.80]**.

Para (3): substituted by the Insolvency (Scotland) Amendment Rules 2009, SI 2009/662, r 2, Schedule, para 8, subject to transitional provisions in r 3 thereof as noted to r 1.4 at **[15.10]**, and originally read as follows:

"(3) A notice under paragraph 54(3) shall be published once in the Edinburgh Gazette and once in the newspaper in which the administrator's appointment was advertised, and shall—
(a) state the full name of the company;
(b) state the name and address of the administrator;
(c) specify an address to which any member of the company may apply in writing for a copy of the statement to be provided free of charge; and
(d) be published as soon as reasonably practicable after the administrator sends the statement to creditors.".

Para (4): inserted by SI 2009/662, r 2, Schedule, para 9, subject to transitional provisions in r 3 thereof as noted to r 1.4 at **[15.10]**.

Para (1): see further Sch 5, Form 2.17B (Scot) at **[15.349]**, and the notes to that Schedule.

[15.114]
[2.35 Notices to creditors

(1) As soon as reasonably practicable after the conclusion of a meeting of creditors to consider the administrator's proposals or revised proposals, or of the conclusion of the business of such a meeting by correspondence in accordance with these Rules, the administrator shall—
(a) send notice of the result of the meeting in the form required by Rule 7.30 and Schedule 5 (including details of any modifications to the proposals that were approved) to every creditor who received notice of the meeting [and to the registrar of companies;]
(b) lodge in court, and send . . . to any creditors who did not receive notice of the meeting and of whose claim he has become subsequently aware, a copy of the notice of the result of the meeting along with a copy of the proposals which were considered at that meeting; and
(c) place a copy of the notice of the result of the meeting in the sederunt book.

(2) Where the business of a creditors' meeting has been carried out by correspondence in accordance with Rule 2.28, for the references in the foregoing paragraph of this Rule to the result of the meeting and notice of the meeting there shall be substituted references to the result of the correspondence and to the correspondence.]

NOTES

Substitution: see the note to r 2.1 at **[15.70]**.

Para (1): words in square brackets in sub-para (a) added and words "to the registrar of companies and" (omitted) revoked by the Insolvency (Scotland) Amendment Rules 2010, SI 2010/688, r 3, Sch 1, paras 81, 82, subject to transitional provisions in r 4 thereof at **[2.80]**.

Para (1): see further Sch 5, Form 2.18B (Scot) at **[15.349]**, and the notes to that Schedule.

[15.115]
[2.35A Action where person excluded

(1) In this Rule and Rules 2.35B and 2.35C an "excluded person" means a person who—
(a) has taken all steps necessary to attend a meeting under the arrangements put in place to do so by the convener of the meeting under section 246A(6); and
(b) those arrangements do not permit that person to attend the whole or part of that meeting.

(2) Where the chairman becomes aware during the course of the meeting that there is an excluded person, the chairman may—
(a) continue the meeting;

(b) declare the meeting void and convene the meeting again;
(c) declare the meeting valid up to the point where the person was excluded and adjourn the meeting.

(3) Where the chairman continues the meeting, the meeting is valid unless—
(a) the chairman decides in consequence of a complaint under Rule 2.35C to declare the meeting void and hold the meeting again; or
(b) the court directs otherwise.

(4) Without prejudice to paragraph (2), where the chairman becomes aware during the course of the meeting of an excluded person, the chairman may, in the chairman's discretion and without an adjournment, declare the meeting suspended for any period up to one hour.]

NOTES

Inserted, together with rr 2.35B, 2.35C, by the Insolvency (Scotland) Amendment Rules 2010, SI 2010/688, r 3, Sch 1, para 83, subject to transitional provisions in rr 4, 5 thereof at **[2.80]**, **[2.81]**.

[15.116]
[2.35B Indication to excluded person

(1) A person who claims to be an excluded person may request an indication of what occurred during the period of that person's claimed exclusion (the "indication").

(2) A request under paragraph (1) must be made as soon as reasonably practicable, and, in any event, no later than 4 pm on the business day following the day on which the exclusion is claimed to have occurred.

(3) A request under paragraph (1) must be made to—
(a) the chairman, where it is made during the course of the business of the meeting; or
(b) the administrator where it is made after the conclusion of the business of the meeting.

(4) Where satisfied that the person making the request is an excluded person, the person to whom the request is made must give the indication as soon as reasonably practicable and, in any event, no later than 4. pm on the day following the request in paragraph (1).]

NOTES

Inserted as noted to r 2.35A at **[15.115]**.

[15.117]
[2.35C Complaint

(1) Any person who—
(a) is, or claims to be, an excluded person; or
(b) attends the meeting (in person or by proxy) and considers that they have been adversely affected by a person's actual, apparent or claimed exclusion,

("the complainant") may make a complaint.

(2) The person to whom the complaint must be made ("the relevant person") is—
(a) the chairman, where it is made during the course of the meeting; or
(b) the administrator, where it is made after the meeting.

(3) The relevant person must—
(a) consider whether there is an excluded person;
(b) where satisfied that there is an excluded person, consider the complaint; and
(c) where satisfied that there has been prejudice, take such action as the relevant person considers fit to remedy the prejudice.

(4) Paragraph (5) applies where—
(a) the relevant person is satisfied that the complainant is an excluded person;
(b) during the period of the person's exclusion—
(i) a resolution was put to the meeting; and
(ii) voted on; and
(c) the excluded person asserts how the excluded person intended to vote on the resolution.

(5) Subject to paragraph (6), where satisfied that the effect of the intended vote in paragraph (4), if cast, would have changed the result of the resolution, the relevant person must—
(a) count the intended vote as being cast in accordance with the complainant's stated intention;
(b) amend the record of the result of the resolution; and
(c) where those entitled to attend the meeting have been notified of the result of the resolution, notify them of the change.

(6) Where satisfied that more than one complainant in paragraph (4) is an excluded person, the relevant person must have regard to the combined effect of the intended votes.

(7) A complaint must be made as soon as reasonably practicable and, in any event, by 4 pm on the business day following—
(a) the day on which the person was excluded; or
(b) where an indication is requested under Rule 2.35B, the day on which the complainant received the indication.

(8) The relevant person must notify the complainant in writing of any decision.

(9) A complainant who is not satisfied by the action of the relevant person may apply to the court for a direction to be given to the relevant person as to the action to be taken in respect of the complaint, and any application must be made no more than 2 business days from the date of receiving the decision of the relevant person.]

NOTES

Inserted as noted to r 2.35A at **[15.115]**.

[CHAPTER 7 THE CREDITORS' COMMITTEE]

NOTES

Substitution: see the note to r 2.1 at **[15.70]**.

[15.118]

[2.36 Constitution of committee

(1) Where it is resolved by the creditors' meeting to establish a creditors' committee under paragraph 57, the committee shall consist of at least 3 and not more than 5 creditors of the company elected at the meeting.

(2) A person claiming to be a creditor is entitled to be a member of the committee provided that—

(a) that person's claim has neither been wholly disallowed for voting purposes, nor wholly rejected for the purpose of distribution or dividend; and

(b) the claim mentioned in sub-paragraph (a) is not fully secured.

(3) A body corporate or a partnership may be a member of the committee, but it cannot act as such otherwise than by a representative appointed under Rule 2.36H.]

NOTES

Substituted, together with rr 2.36A–2.36R, for r 2.36, by the Insolvency (Scotland) Amendment Rules 2010, SI 2010/688, r 3, Sch 1, para 84, subject to transitional provisions in r 4 thereof at **[2.80]**. Rule 2.36 previously read as follows:

> **"2.36 Application of provisions in Part 3 (Receivers)**
>
> (1) Chapter 3 of Part 3 (the creditors' committee) shall apply with regard to the creditors' committee in administration as it applies to the creditors' committee in receivership, subject to the modifications specified below and to any other necessary modifications.
>
> (2) For any reference in the said Chapter 3, or in any provision of Chapter 7 of Part 4 as applied by Rule 3.6, to the receiver, receivership or the creditors' committee in receivership, there shall be substituted a reference to the administrator, the administration and the creditors' committee in the administration.
>
> (3) In Rules 3.4(1) and 3.7(1), for the reference to section 68 or 68(2), there shall be substituted a reference to paragraph 57 or 57(2).
>
> (4) For Rule 3.5 there shall be substituted the following Rule—
>
> **"3.5 Functions of the Committee**
>
> The creditors' committee shall assist the administrator in discharging his functions and shall act in relation to him in such manner as may be agreed from time to time."."

[15.119]

[2.36A Functions of the committee

In addition to any functions conferred on the creditors' committee by any provisions of the Act, the creditors' committee shall assist the administrator in discharging the administrator's functions and shall act in relation to the administrator in such manner as may be agreed from time to time.]

NOTES

Substituted as noted to r 2.36 at **[15.118]**.

[15.120]

[2.36B Formalities of establishment

(1) The creditors' committee shall not come into being, and accordingly cannot act, until the administrator has issued a certificate of its due constitution.

(2) If the chairman of the meeting which resolves to establish the committee is not the administrator, the chairman shall, as soon as reasonably practicable, give notice of the resolution to the administrator (or, as the case may be, the person appointed as administrator by the same meeting), and inform the administrator of the names and addresses of the persons elected to be members of the committee.

(3) No person may act as a member of the committee unless and until that person has agreed to do so and, unless the relevant proxy or authorisation contains a statement to the contrary, such agreement may be given on behalf of the member by that member's proxy-holder who is present at the meeting at which the committee is established or, in the case of a body corporate or partnership, by its duly appointed representative.

(4) The administrator's certificate of the committee's due constitution shall not be issued before the minimum number of members set out in Rule 2.36(1) elected to be members of the committee have agreed to act, but shall be issued as soon as reasonably practicable thereafter.

(5) As and when the others elected to be members of the committee (if any) agree to act, the administrator shall issue an amended certificate.

(6) The certificate (and any amended certificate) shall be sent by the administrator to the registrar of companies.

(7) If after the first establishment of the committee there is any change in its membership, the administrator shall, as soon as reasonably practicable report the change to the registrar of companies.]

NOTES

Substituted as noted to r 2.36 at **[15.118]**.

[15.121]

[2.36C Meetings of the committee

(1) Subject as follows, meetings of the creditors' committee shall be held when and where determined by the administrator.

(2) The administrator shall call a first meeting of the committee to take place within 6 weeks of the committee's establishment.

(3) After the calling of the first meeting, the administrator must call a meeting—

(a) if so requested by a member of the committee or a member's representative (the meeting then to be held within 21 days of the request being received by the administrator), and

(b) for a specified date, if the committee has previously resolved that a meeting be held on that date.

(4) Subject to paragraph (5) the administrator shall give 5 business days written notice of the time and place of any meeting to every member of the committee (or a member's representative, if designated for that purpose), unless in any case the requirement of the notice has been waived by or on behalf of any member. Waiver may be signified either at or before the meeting.

(5) Where the administrator has determined that a meeting should be conducted and held in the manner referred to in Rule 2.36D, the notice period mentioned in paragraph (4) is 7 business days.]

NOTES

Substituted as noted to r 2.36 at **[15.118]**.

[15.122]

[2.36D Remote attendance at meetings of creditors' committees

(1) This Rule applies to any meeting of a creditors' committee held under this Part.

(2) Where the administrator considers it appropriate, the meeting may be conducted and held in such a way that persons who are not present together at the same place may attend it.

(3) Where a meeting is conducted and held in the manner referred to in paragraph (2), a person attends the meeting if that person is able to exercise any rights which that person may have to speak and vote at the meeting.

(4) For the purposes of this Rule—

(a) a person is able to exercise the right to speak at a meeting when that person is in a position to communicate to all those attending the meeting, during the meeting, any information or opinions which that person has on the business of the meeting; and

(b) a person is able to exercise the right to vote at a meeting when—

(i) that person is able to vote, during the meeting, on resolutions or determinations put to the vote at the meeting, and

(ii) that person's vote can be taken into account in determining whether or not such resolutions or determinations are passed at the same time as the votes of all the other persons attending the meeting.

(5) Where a meeting is to be conducted and held in the manner referred to in paragraph (2), the administrator must make whatever arrangements the administrator considers appropriate to—

(a) enable those attending the meeting to exercise their rights to speak or vote, and

(b) ensure the identification of those attending the meeting and the security of any electronic means used to enable attendance.

(6) Where in the reasonable opinion of the administrator—

(a) a meeting will be attended by persons who will not be present together at the same place, and

(b) it is unnecessary or inexpedient to specify a place for the meeting,

any requirement under these Rules to specify a place for the meeting may be satisfied by specifying the arrangements the administrator proposes to enable persons to exercise their rights to speak or vote.

(7) In making the arrangements referred to in paragraph (5) and in forming the opinion referred to in paragraph (6)(b), the administrator must have regard to the legitimate interests of the committee members or their representatives attending the meeting in the efficient despatch of the business of the meeting.

(8) If—

(a) the notice of a meeting does not specify a place for the meeting,

(b) the administrator is requested in accordance with Rule 2.36E to specify a place for the meeting, and

(c) that request is made by at least one member of the committee,

the administrator must specify a place for the meeting.]

NOTES

Substituted as noted to r 2.36 at **[15.118]**.

[15.123]
[2.36E Procedure for requests that a place for a meeting should be specified under Rule 2.36D

(1) This Rule applies to a request to the administrator of a meeting under Rule 2.36D to specify a place for the meeting.

(2) The request must be made within 5 business days of the date on which the administrator sent the notice of the meeting in question.

(3) Where the administrator considers that the request has been properly made in accordance with this Rule, the administrator must—

(a) give notice to all those previously given notice of the meeting—
(i) that it is to be held at a specified place, and
(ii) whether the date and time are to remain the same or not;

(b) specify a time, date and place for the meeting, the date of which must be not later than 7 business days after the original date for the meeting; and

(c) give 5 business days' notice of the time, date and place to all those previously given notice of the meeting,

and the notices required by sub-paragraphs (a) and (c) may be given at the same or different times.

(4) Where the administrator has specified a place for the meeting in response to a request to which this Rule applies, the chairman of the meeting must attend the meeting by being present in person at that place.]

NOTES

Substituted as noted to r 2.36 at **[15.118]**.

[15.124]
[2.36F The chairman at meetings

(1) The chairman at any meeting of the creditors' committee must be the administrator, or a person appointed by the administrator in writing to act.

(2) A person so appointed must be either—

(a) a person who is qualified to act as an insolvency practitioner in relation to the company, or

(b) an employee of the administrator or the administrator's firm who is experienced in insolvency matters.]

NOTES

Substituted as noted to r 2.36 at **[15.118]**.

[15.125]
[2.36G Quorum

A meeting of the committee is duly constituted if due notice of it has been given to all the members, and at least 2 members are present or represented.]

NOTES

Substituted as noted to r 2.36 at **[15.118]**.

[15.126]
[2.36H Committee members' representatives

(1) A member of the creditors' committee may, in relation to the business of the committee, be represented by another person duly authorised by the creditor for that purpose.

(2) A person acting as a committee member's representative must hold a mandate entitling that person so to act (either generally or specially) and authenticated by or on behalf of the committee member, and for this purpose any proxy in relation to any meeting of creditors of the company shall, unless it contains a statement to the contrary, be treated as such a mandate to act generally authenticated by or on behalf of the committee member.

(3) The chairman at any meeting of the committee may call on a person claiming to act as a committee member's representative to produce a mandate and may exclude that person if it appears that the mandate is deficient.

(4) No member may be represented by—

(a) another member of the committee;
(b) a person who is at the same time representing another committee member;
(c) a body corporate;
(d) a partnership;
(e) a person whose estate is currently sequestrated;
(f) an undischarged bankrupt [or a person in relation to whom a moratorium period under a debt relief order applies (under Part 7A of the Insolvency Act 1986)];
(g) a person who is subject to a bankruptcy restrictions order, bankruptcy restrictions undertaking or interim bankruptcy restrictions order; . . .
[(ga) a person who is subject to a debt relief restrictions order, a debt relief restrictions undertaking or interim debt relief restrictions order (under Schedule 4ZB to the Insolvency Act 1986); or]
(h) a disqualified director.

(5) Where a member's representative authenticates any document on the member's behalf, the fact that the representative so authenticates must be stated below the representative's signature.]

NOTES

Substituted as noted to r 2.36 at **[15.118]**.

Para (4): in sub-para (f) words in square brackets added, sub-para (ga) inserted, and word immediately preceding it revoked, in relation to a debt relief order the application for which is made after 1 October 2012, by the Tribunals, Courts and Enforcement Act 2007 (Consequential Amendments) Order 2012, SI 2012/2404, arts 3(3), 7, Sch 3, para 4(1), (3).

[15.127]

[2.36I Resignation

A member of the creditors' committee may resign by notice in writing delivered to the administrator.]

NOTES

Substituted as noted to r 2.36 at **[15.118]**.

[15.128]

[2.36J Termination of membership

Membership of the creditors' committee of any person is automatically terminated if—

(a) the member's estate is sequestrated or the member becomes bankrupt [or has a debt relief order made in respect of him (under Part 7A of the Insolvency Act 1986)] or grants a trust deed for the benefit of, or makes a composition with, creditors,

(b) at 3 consecutive meetings of the committee the member is neither present nor represented (unless at the third of those meetings it is resolved that this Rule is not to apply in the member's case), or

(c) the member ceases to be a creditor and a period of 3 months has elapsed from the date that that member ceased to be a creditor, or the member is found never to have been a creditor.]

NOTES

Substituted as noted to r 2.36 at **[15.118]**.

In para (a) words in square brackets inserted, in relation to a debt relief order the application for which is made after 1 October 2012, by the Tribunals, Courts and Enforcement Act 2007 (Consequential Amendments) Order 2012, SI 2012/2404, arts 3(3), 7, Sch 3, para 4(1), (4).

[15.129]

[2.36K Removal

A member of the creditors' committee may be removed by resolution at a meeting of creditors. At least 14 days notice must be given of the intention to move such a resolution.]

NOTES

Substituted as noted to r 2.36 at **[15.118]**.

[15.130]

[2.36L Vacancies

(1) The following applies if there is a vacancy among the members of the creditors' committee.

(2) The vacancy need not be filled if the administrator and a majority of the remaining members so agree, provided that the total number of members does not fall below 3.

(3) The administrator may appoint any creditor, who is qualified under the Rules to be a member of the committee, to fill the vacancy, if a majority of the other members agree to the appointment, and the creditor concerned consents to act.

(4) Alternatively, a meeting of creditors may resolve that a creditor be appointed (with that creditor's consent) to fill the vacancy.

(5) Where the vacancy is filled by an appointment made by a creditors' meeting at which the administrator is not present, the chairman of the meeting must report to the administrator the appointment which has been made.]

NOTES

Substituted as noted to r 2.36 at **[15.118]**.

[15.131]

[2.36M Voting rights and resolutions

(1) At any meeting of the creditors' committee, each member of it (whether present in person or by a member's representative) has one vote; and a resolution is passed when a majority of the members present or represented have voted in favour of it.

(2) Every resolution passed must be recorded in writing and authenticated by the chairman, either separately or as part of the minutes of the meeting, and the record must be kept as part of the sederunt book.]

NOTES

Substituted as noted to r 2.36 at **[15.118]**.

[15.132]
[2.36N Resolutions otherwise than at a meeting

(1) In accordance with this Rule, the administrator may seek to obtain the agreement of members of the creditors' committee to a resolution by sending to every member (or a member's representative designated for the purpose) a copy of the proposed resolution.

(2) Where the administrator makes use of the procedure allowed by this Rule, the administrator shall send out to members of the committee or their representatives (as the case may be) a statement incorporating a copy of any proposed resolution on which a decision is sought, which shall be set out in such a way that agreement with or dissent from each separate resolution may be indicated by the recipient on the copy so sent.

(3) Any member of the committee may, within 7 business days from the date of the administrator sending out a resolution, require the administrator to summon a meeting of the committee to consider the matters raised by the resolution.

(4) In the absence of such a requirement, the resolution is deemed to have been passed by the committee if and when the administrator is notified in writing by a majority of the members that they concur with it.

(5) A copy of every resolution passed under this Rule, and a note that the committee's concurrence was obtained, shall be kept in the sederunt book.]

NOTES

Substituted as noted to r 2.36 at **[15.118]**.

[15.133]
[2.36O Expenses of members, etc

(1) The administrator shall defray any reasonable travelling expenses directly incurred by members of the creditors' committee or their representatives in respect of their attendance at the committee's meetings, or otherwise on the committee's business, as an expense of the administration.

(2) Paragraph (1) does not apply to any meeting of the committee held within 6 weeks of a previous meeting, unless the meeting in question is summoned at the instance of the administrator.]

NOTES

Substituted as noted to r 2.36 at **[15.118]**.

[15.134]
[2.36P Formal defects

The acts of the creditors' committee established for any administration are valid notwithstanding any defect in the appointment, election or qualifications of any member of the committee or any committee member's representative or in the formalities of its establishment.]

NOTES

Substituted as noted to r 2.36 at **[15.118]**.

[15.135]
[2.36Q Information from administrator

(1) Where the creditors' committee resolves to require the attendance of the administrator under paragraph 57(3), the notice to the administrator shall be in writing and authenticated by the majority of the members of the committee for the time being or their representatives.

(2) The meeting at which the administrator's attendance is required shall be fixed by the committee for a business day, and shall be held at such time and place as the administrator determines.

(3) Where the administrator so attends, the members of the committee may elect any one of their number to be chairman of the meeting, in place of the administrator or any nominee of the administrator.]

NOTES

Substituted as noted to r 2.36 at **[15.118]**.

[15.136]
[2.36R Members' dealings with the company

(1) This Rule applies to—
- (a) any member of a creditors' committee;
- (b) any committee member's representative;
- (c) any person who is an associate of—
  - (i) a member of the committee, or
  - (ii) a committee member's representative; and
- (d) any person who has been a member of the committee at any time in the last 12 months or who is an associate of such a member.

(2) A person to whom this Rule applies may deal with the company provided that any transactions in the course of such dealings are in good faith and for value.]

NOTES

Substituted as noted to r 2.36 at **[15.118]**.

[CHAPTER 8 FUNCTIONS AND REMUNERATION OF ADMINISTRATOR

[15.137]
2.37 Disposal of secured property, etc

(1) This Rule applies where the administrator applies to the court under paragraph 71 or 72 for authority to dispose of property of the company which is subject to a security (other than a floating charge), or goods in the possession of the company under a hire purchase agreement.

(2) If an order is made under paragraph 71 or 72 the administrator shall as soon as reasonably practicable give notice of it to that person or owner and shall send to that person or owner a copy of the order, certified by the clerk of court

(3) The administrator shall place in the sederunt book a copy of any order granted under paragraph 71 or 72.]

NOTES

Substitution: see the note to r 2.1 at **[15.70]**.

Para (3): see further Sch 5, Form 2.19B (Scot) at **[15.349]**, and the notes to that Schedule.

[15.138]
[2.38 Progress reports

(1) The administrator shall

(a) within six weeks after the end of each accounting period; and
(b) within six weeks after he ceases to act as administrator,

send to the court and to the registrar of companies, and to each creditor, a progress report.

[(2) For the purposes of this Part, including Rules contained elsewhere in these Rules but applied by this Part, "accounting period" in relation to an administration shall be construed as follows:

(a) the first accounting period is the period of 6 months beginning with the date on which the company entered administration; and
(b) any subsequent accounting period is the period of 6 months beginning with the end of the last accounting period.]

(3) For the purposes of this Part, "progress report" means a report which includes—

(a) the name of the court which granted the administration order or in which the notice of appointment was lodged, and the court reference number (if any);
(b) details of the company's name, address and registration number;
(c) details of the administrator's name and address, date of appointment and, where the administrator was appointed under paragraph 14 or 22, the name and address of the person who made the appointment;
(d) details of any extensions to the initial period of appointment;
(e) details of progress to date, including a receipts and payments account which states what assets of the company have been realised, for what value, and what payments have been made to creditors. The account is to be in the form of an abstract showing—
  (i) receipts and payments during the relevant accounting period; or
  (ii) where the administrator has ceased to act, receipts and payments during the period from the end of the last accounting period to the time when he so ceased (or, where he has made no previous progress report, receipts and payments in the period since his appointment as administrator);
(f) details of what assets remain to be realised;
(g) where a distribution is to be made in accordance with Chapter 9 in respect of an accounting period, the scheme of division; and
(h) any other relevant information for the creditors.

(4) In a receipts and payments account falling within paragraph (3)(e)(ii) above, the administrator shall include a statement as to the amount paid to unsecured creditors by virtue of the application of section 176A (prescribed part).

(5) The court may, on the application of the administrator, extend the period of six weeks referred to in paragraph (1) of this Rule.

(6) If the administrator makes default in complying with this Rule, he is liable to a fine and, for continued contravention, to a daily default fine.

(7) This Rule is without prejudice to the requirements of Chapter 9 (distributions to creditors).]

NOTES

Substitution: see the note to r 2.1 at **[15.70]**.

Para (2): substituted by the Insolvency (Scotland) Amendment Rules 2010, SI 2010/688, r 3, Sch 1, para 85, subject to transitional provisions in rr 4, 5 thereof at **[2.80]**, **[2.81]**, and previously read as follows:

> "(2) For the purposes of this Part, "accounting period", in relation to an administration, shall be construed in accordance with section 52(1) and (6) of the Bankruptcy Act as applied by virtue of Rule 2.41.".

Para (1): see further Sch 5, Form 2.20B (Scot) at **[15.349]**, and the notes to that Schedule.

[15.139]

[2.39 Determination of outlays and remuneration

(1) Within 2 weeks after the end of an accounting period, the administrator shall in respect of that period submit to the creditors' committee or, if there is no creditors' committee, to a meeting of creditors—

(a) his accounts of his intromissions with the company's assets for audit and, where funds are available after making allowance for contingencies, a scheme of division of the divisible funds; and

(b) a claim for the outlays reasonably incurred by him and for his remuneration.

(2) The administrator may, at any time before the end of an accounting period, submit to the creditors' committee or, if there is no creditors' committee, a meeting of creditors an interim claim in respect of that period for the outlays reasonably incurred by him and for his remuneration and the creditors' committee or meeting of creditors, as the case may be, may make an interim determination in relation to the amount of the outlays and remuneration payable to the administrator and, where they do so, they shall take into account that interim determination when making their determination under paragraph (3)(a)(ii).

(3) Within 6 weeks after the end of an accounting period—

(a) the creditors' committee or, as the case may be, a meeting of creditors—

(i) may audit the accounts; and

(ii) shall issue a determination fixing the amount of the outlays and the remuneration payable to the administrator; and

(b) the administrator shall make the audited accounts, scheme of division and the said determination available for inspection by the members of the company and the creditors.

(4) The basis for fixing the amount of the remuneration payable to the administrator may be a commission calculated by reference to the value of the company's assets which have been realised by the administrator, but there shall in any event be taken into account—

(a) the work which, having regard to that value, was reasonably undertaken by him; and

(b) the extent of his responsibilities in administering the company's assets.

(5) If the administrator's remuneration and outlays have been fixed by determination of the creditors' committee in accordance with paragraph (3)(a)(ii) and he considers the amount to be insufficient, he may request that it be increased by resolution of the creditors.

(6) If the creditors' committee fails to issue a determination in accordance with paragraph (3)(a)(ii), the administrator shall submit his claim to a meeting of creditors and they shall issue a determination in accordance with paragraph (3)(a)(ii).

(7) If the meeting of creditors fails to issue a determination in accordance with paragraph (6) then the administrator shall submit his claim to the court and it shall issue a determination.

(8) In a case where the administrator has made a statement under paragraph 52(1)(b), a resolution under paragraph (5) or Rule 2.39A(8) shall be taken to be passed if (and only if) passed with the approval of—

(a) each secured creditor of the company; or

(b) if the administrator has made, or proposes to make, a distribution to preferential creditors—

(i) each secured creditor of the company; and

(ii) preferential creditors whose debts amount to more than 50% of the preferential debts of the company, disregarding debts of any creditor who does not respond to an invitation to give or withhold approval.

(9) In a case where the administrator has made a statement under paragraph 52(1)(b), if there is no creditor's committee, or the committee does not make the requisite determination in accordance with paragraphs (2) or (3)(a)(ii), the administrator's remuneration and outlays may be fixed (in accordance with this Rule) by the approval of—

(a) each secured creditor of the company; or

(b) if the administrator has made, or proposes to make, a distribution to preferential creditors—

(i) each secured creditor of the company; and

(ii) preferential creditors whose debts amount to more than 50% of the preferential debts of the company, disregarding debts of any creditor who does not respond to an invitation to give or withhold approval.

(10) In fixing the amount of the administrator's remuneration and outlays in respect of any accounting period, the creditors' committee or, as the case may be, a meeting of creditors may take into account any adjustment which the creditors' committee or meeting of creditors may wish to make in the amount of the remuneration and outlays fixed in respect of any earlier accounting period.]

NOTES

Substituted together with r 2.39A, for original r 2.39, by the Insolvency (Scotland) Amendment Rules 2006, SI 2006/734, r 8, subject to transitional provisions in r 2(1) thereof at **[2.43]**. This rule and the related notes previously read as follows:

"**[2.39 Determination of outlays and remuneration**

(1) Rules 4.32 to 4.35 and Rule 4.76 shall apply to an administration as they apply to a liquidation, subject to the modifications specified in the following paragraph of this Rule and to any other necessary modifications.

(2) For any references in the said Rules 4.32 to 4.35 and 4.76 or in the provisions of the Bankruptcy Act as applied by Rule 4.32 to the liquidator, the liquidation and the liquidation committee, there shall be substituted a reference to the administrator, the administration and the creditors' committee in the administration.

(3) Where the administrator has made a statement under paragraph 52(1)(b), a resolution under Rule 4.33, as applied by this Rule, or a resolution under paragraph (4)(b) of this Rule, shall be taken to be passed if (and only if) passed with the approval of—

(a) each secured creditor of the company; or

(b) if the administrator has made, or proposes to make, a distribution to preferential creditors—
  (i) each secured creditor of the company; and
  (ii) preferential creditors whose debts amount to more than 50% of the preferential debts of the company, disregarding debts of any creditor who does not respond to an invitation to give or withhold approval.

(4)
(a) Where there are joint administrators, it is for them to agree between themselves as to how the remuneration payable should be apportioned.
(b) Where joint administrators cannot agree as to how the remuneration payable should be apportioned, any one of them may refer the issue for determination—
  (i) by the court; or
  (ii) by resolution of the creditors' committee or a meeting of creditors.]

NOTES

Substitution: see the note to r 2.1.".

[15.140]
[2.39A Appeal against fixing of remuneration

(1) If the administrator considers that the remuneration [or outlays] fixed for him by the creditors' committee, or by resolution of the creditors is insufficient, he may apply to the court for an order increasing [their] amount or rate.

(2) The administrator shall give at least 14 days' notice of his application to the members of the creditors' committee; and the committee may nominate one or more members to appear or be represented, and to be heard, on the application.

(3) If there is no creditors' committee, the administrator's notice of his application shall be sent to such one or more of the company's creditors as the court may direct, which creditors may nominate one or more of their number to appear or be represented and be heard.

(4) The court may, if it appears to be a proper case, order the expenses of the administrator's application, including the expenses of any member of the creditors' committee appearing or being represented on it, or any creditor so appearing or being represented, to be paid as an expense of the administration.

(5) If the administrator's remuneration [and outlays have] been fixed by the creditors' committee or by the creditors, any creditor or creditors of the company representing in value at least 25 per cent of the creditors may apply to the court not later than 8 weeks after the end of an accounting period for an order that the administrator's remuneration [or outlays be reduced on the grounds that they are, in all the circumstances, excessive].

(6) If the court considers the application to be well-founded, it shall make an order fixing the remuneration at a reduced amount or rate.

(7) The court may, if it appears to be a proper case, order the expenses of the creditor making the application to be paid as an expense of the administration.

(8) Where there are joint administrators—
  (a) it is for them to agree between themselves as to how the remuneration payable should be apportioned;
  (b) if they cannot agree as to how the remuneration payable should be apportioned, any one of them may refer the issue for determination—
    (i) by the court; or
    (ii) by resolution of the creditors' committee or a meeting of creditors.]

NOTES

Substituted as noted to r 2.39 at **[15.139]**.

Para (1): words in first pair of square brackets inserted and word in square brackets substituted for original word "its" by the Insolvency (Scotland) Amendment Rules 2010, SI 2010/688, r 3, Sch 1, para 86, subject to transitional provisions in r 4 thereof at **[2.80]**.

Para (5): words in first pair of square brackets substituted for original word "has" and words in second pair of square brackets substituted for original words "be reduced, on the grounds that it is, in all the circumstances, excessive" by SI 2010/688, r 3, Sch 1, para 87, subject to transitional provisions in r 4 thereof at **[2.80]**.

[CHAPTER 8A EXPENSES OF THE ADMINISTRATION

[15.141]
2.39B Expenses of the administration

(1) This Rule applies for the purposes of determining the order of priority of the expenses of the administration.

(2) Paragraphs (1) and (3) of Rule 4.67 shall apply with regard to the expenses of the administration as they do to a company in liquidation, subject to the modifications specified below.

(3) In Rule 4.67(1) and (3) as applied by paragraph (2)—
  (a) in paragraph (1)—
    (i) omit the words "Subject to section 156 and paragraph (2),";
    (ii) for any reference to liquidator there is substituted a reference to administrator;
    (iii) for any reference to liquidation there is substituted a reference to administration;
    (iv) omit the words "provisional liquidator or" in sub-paragraph (a) and the words "provisional liquidator," in sub-paragraph (b);
    (v) omit the words "or special manager" in sub-paragraph (b);

(vi) omit sub-paragraphs (c) and (e);
(vii) for the words "Rule 4.9(1)" in sub-paragraph (f) there is substituted "Rule 2.24(1)"; and
(viii) for the words "Rule 4.32" in sub-paragraph (h) there is substituted "Rule 2.39" [and unpaid pre-administration costs approved under Rule 2.39C]; and

(b) in paragraph (3) for the reference to liquidator there is substituted a reference to administrator.

(4) The priorities laid down by virtue of paragraph (2) are subject to the power of the court to make orders under paragraph (5) where the assets are insufficient to satisfy the liabilities.

(5) The court may, in the event of the assets being insufficient to satisfy the liabilities, make an order as to the payment out of the assets of the expenses incurred in the administration in such order of priority as the court thinks just.

(6) For the purposes of paragraph 99(3), the former administrator's remuneration and expenses shall comprise all those items set out in Rule 4.67(1) as applied by paragraph (2).]

NOTES

Inserted, together with preceding Chapter heading, by the Insolvency (Scotland) Amendment Rules 2008, SI 2008/662, rr 2, 3, 5, except in relation to any case where a company has entered administration before 6 April 2008.

Para (3): words in square brackets inserted by the Insolvency (Scotland) Amendment Rules 2010, SI 2010/688, r 3, Sch 1, para 88, subject to transitional provisions in r 4 thereof at **[2.80]**.

Modification: see the Regulated Covered Bonds Regulations 2008, SI 2008/346, reg 46, Schedule, Pt 2, para 8 at **[18.178]**, **[18.180]**.

[15.142]

[2.39C Pre-administration costs

(1) Where the administrator has made a statement of pre-administration costs under Rule 2.25(1)(ka), the creditors' committee may determine whether and to what extent the unpaid pre-administration costs set out in the statement are approved for payment.

(2) But paragraph (3) applies if—

(a) there is no creditors' committee,
(b) there is, but it does not make the necessary determination, or
(c) it does do so, but the administrator or other insolvency practitioner who has charged fees or incurred expenses as pre-administration costs considers the amount determined to be insufficient.

(3) When this paragraph applies, determination of whether and to what extent the unpaid pre-administration costs are approved for payment shall be—

(a) by resolution of a meeting of creditors other than in a case falling in sub-paragraph (b), or
(b) in a case where the administrator has made a statement under paragraph 52(1)(b)—
(i) by the approval of each secured creditor of the company, or
(ii) if the administrator has made, or intends to make, a distribution to preferential creditors, by the approval of each secured creditor of the company and preferential creditors whose debts amount to more than 50% of the preferential debts of the company, disregarding debts of any creditor who does not respond to an invitation to give or withhold approval.

(4) The administrator must call a meeting of the creditors' committee or of creditors if so requested for the purposes of paragraphs (1) to (3) by another insolvency practitioner who has charged fees or incurred expenses as pre-administration costs; and the administrator must give notice of the meeting within 28 days of receipt of the request.

(5) If—

(a) there is no determination under paragraph (1) or (3), or
(b) there is such a determination but the administrator or other insolvency practitioner who has charged fees or incurred expenses as pre-administration costs considers the amount determined to be insufficient,

the administrator (where the fees were charged or expenses incurred by the administrator) or other insolvency practitioner (where the fees were charged or expenses incurred by that practitioner) may apply to the court for a determination of whether and to what extent the unpaid pre-administration costs are approved for payment.

(6) Paragraphs (2) to (4) of Rule 2.39A apply to an application under paragraph (5) of this Rule as they do to an application under paragraph (1) of that Rule (references to the administrator being read as references to the insolvency practitioner who has charged fees or incurred expenses as pre-administration costs).

(7) Where the administrator fails to call a meeting of the creditors' committee or of creditors in accordance with paragraph (4), the other insolvency practitioner may apply to the court for an order requiring the administrator to do so.]

NOTES

Inserted by the Insolvency (Scotland) Amendment Rules 2010, SI 2010/688, r 3, Sch 1, para 89, subject to transitional provisions in r 4 thereof at **[2.80]**.

[CHAPTER 9 DISTRIBUTIONS TO CREDITORS

[15.143]
2.40

(1) This Chapter applies in any case where the administrator proposes to make a distribution to creditors or any class of them.

(2) Where the distribution is to a particular class of creditors, references in this Chapter (except Rule 2.41(4)(c)) to creditors shall, so far as the context requires, be references to that class of creditors only.]

NOTES

Substitution: see the note to r 2.1 at **[15.70]**.

[15.144]
[2.41

(1) Chapter 5 of Part 4 (claims in liquidation) and Chapter 9 of that Part (distribution of company's assets by liquidator) [(except Rule 4.67)] shall apply with regard to claims to a dividend out of the assets of a company in administration as they do to a company in liquidation, subject to the modifications specified below and to any other necessary modifications.

[(1A) Rule 4.68A shall not apply for the purposes of this Rule.]

(2) [Subject to paragraph (5) below,] in the said Chapters 5 and 9 . . . —

(a) for any reference to the liquidator, liquidation, and liquidation committee there shall be substituted a reference to the administrator, the administration and the creditors' committee in the administration; and

(b) for any reference to the date of commencement of winding up there shall be substituted a reference to the date on which the company entered administration.

[(3) Rule 4.68(4) shall apply subject to paragraph (4) of this Rule.]

(4) The administrator may make a distribution to secured or preferential creditors or, where he has the permission of the court, to unsecured creditors only if—

(a) he has sufficient funds for the purpose;

(b) he does not intend to give notice pursuant to paragraph 83;

(c) his statement of proposals, as approved by the creditors under paragraph 53(1) or 54(5), contains a proposal to make a distribution to the class of creditors in question; and

(d) the payment of a dividend is consistent with the functions and duties of the administrator and any proposals made by him or which he intends to make.]

[(5) Where the administration was immediately preceded by a winding up—

(a) in Rule 4.17(2) the reference to administration and the date on which the company entered administration existing but for the application of this Rule shall be construed as a reference to liquidation and the date of commencement of winding up respectively;

[(b) in Rule 4.16E, the reference to the date on which the company entered administration in paragraph (1) and the second reference to that date in paragraph (2) shall be construed as references to the date of commencement of winding up within the meaning of section 129;][and

(c) in Rule 4.66(1)(d) the reference to "date of commencement of the administration" shall be construed as a reference to the date of commencement of winding up.]]

NOTES

Substitution: see the note to r 2.1 at **[15.70]**.

Para (1): words in square brackets inserted by the Insolvency (Scotland) Amendment Rules 2008, SI 2008/662, rr 2, 3, 6, except in relation to any case where a company has entered administration before 6 April 2008.

Para (1A): inserted by the Insolvency (Scotland) Amendment Rules 2006, SI 2006/734, r 9(1)(a) and substituted by the Insolvency (Scotland) Amendment Rules 2014, SSI 2014/114, rr 2, 4(a), subject to savings in r 29 thereof as noted to r 0.2 at **[15.2]**. Para (1A) previously read as follows—

"[(1A) Section 53 of the Bankruptcy Act, as applied by Rule 4.68, shall not apply for the purposes of this Rule.]".

Para (2): words in square brackets inserted by SI 2006/734, r 9(1)(b); words ", or in any provision of the Bankruptcy Act as applied by Rule 4.16 or 4.68" (omitted) revoked by SSI 2014/114, rr 2, 4(b), subject to savings in r 29 thereof as noted to r 0.2 at **[15.2]**.

Para (3): substituted by SSI 2014/114, rr 2, 4(c), subject to savings in r 29 thereof as noted to r 0.2 at **[15.2]**, and previously read as follows (with words in square brackets substituted by SI 2006/734, r 9(1)(c))—

"(3) [Section 52(3)] of the Bankruptcy Act, as applied by Rule 4.68, shall apply subject to paragraph (4) of this Rule.".

Para (5): added by SI 2006/734, r 9(1)(d); sub-para (c) and word "and" immediately preceding it added by the Insolvency (Scotland) Amendment Rules 2010, SI 2010/688, r 3, Sch 1, para 90, subject to transitional provisions in r 4 thereof at **[2.80]**; para (b) substituted by SSI 2014/114, rr 2, 4(d), subject to savings in r 29 thereof as noted to r 0.2 at **[15.2]**, and previously read as follows

"(b) in Schedule 1 to the Bankruptcy Act, as applied by Rule 4.16, the reference to the date on which the company entered administration in paragraph 1(1) and the second reference to that date in paragraph 1(2) shall be construed as a reference to the date of commencement of winding up within the meaning of section 129".

[15.145]

[2.41A Payments of Dividends

(1) On the final determination of the remuneration under Rules 2.39 and 2.39A, the administrator shall, subject to Rule 2.41, pay to the creditors their dividends in accordance with the scheme of division.

(2) Any dividend—

(a) allocated to a creditor which is not cashed or uplifted; or

(b) dependent on a claim in respect of which an amount has been set aside under [Rule 4.68(7) or (8) as applied by Rule 2.41];

shall be deposited by the administrator in an appropriate bank or institution.

(3) If a creditor's claim is revalued, the administrator may—

(a) in paying any dividend to that creditor, make such adjustment to it as he considers necessary to take account of that revaluation; or

(b) require the creditor to repay to him the whole or part of a dividend already paid to him.

(4) The administrator shall insert in the sederunt book the audited accounts, the scheme of division and the final determination in relation to the administrator's outlays and remuneration.

(5) For the purposes of paragraph 99(3), the former administrator's remuneration and expenses shall comprise all those items set out in Rule 4.67(1) as applied by Rule 2.41.]

NOTES

Inserted by the Insolvency (Scotland) Amendment Rules 2006, SI 2006/734, r 10, subject to transitional provisions in r 2(1) thereof at **[2.43]**.

Para (2): words in square brackets in sub-para (b) substituted for original words "subsection (7) or (8) of section 52 of the Bankruptcy Act as applied by Rules 2.41 and 4.68", by the Insolvency (Scotland) Amendment Rules 2014, SSI 2014/114, rr 2, 5, subject to savings in r 29 thereof as noted to r 0.2 at **[15.2]**.

[15.146]

[2.41B New administrator appointed

(1) If a new administrator is appointed in place of another, the former administrator must, as soon as reasonably practicable, transmit to the new administrator all the creditors' claims which the former administrator has received, together with an itemised list of them.

(2) The new administrator must authenticate the list by way of receipt for the creditors' claims and return it to the former administrator.

(3) From then on, all creditors' claims must be sent to and retained by the new administrator.]

NOTES

Inserted by the Insolvency (Scotland) Amendment Rules 2010, SI 2010/688, r 3, Sch 1, para 91, subject to transitional provisions in r 4 thereof at **[2.80]**.

[CHAPTER 10 ENDING ADMINISTRATION

[15.147]

2.42 Final progress reports

"Final progress report" means a progress report which includes a summary account of—

(a) the administrator's original proposals;

(b) any major changes to, or deviations from, those proposals in the course of the administration;

(c) the steps taken during the administration; and

(d) the outcome.]

NOTES

Substitution: see the note to r 2.1 at **[15.70]**.

[15.148]

[2.43 Notice of automatic end of administration

(1) Where the appointment of an administrator has ceased to have effect, and the administrator is not required by any other Rule to give notice of that fact, he shall, as soon as reasonably practicable, and in any event within 5 business days of the date when the appointment has ceased, lodge in court a notice of automatic end of administration in the form required by Rule 7.30 and Schedule 5, together with a final progress report.

(2) The administrator shall, as soon as reasonably practicable, send a copy of the notice and accompanying report to the registrar of companies, and to all [other] persons who received a copy of the administrator's proposals.

(3) If the administrator makes default in complying with this Rule, he is liable to a fine and, for continued contravention, to a daily default fine.]

NOTES

Substitution: see the note to r 2.1 at **[15.70]**.

Para (2): word in square brackets inserted by the Insolvency (Scotland) Amendment Rules 2010, SI 2010/688, r 3, Sch 1, para 92, subject to transitional provisions in rr 4, 5 thereof at **[2.80]**, **[2.81]**.

[15.149]
[2.44 Applications for extension of administration

(1) An application to court for an extension of administration shall be accompanied by a progress report for the period since the last progress report (if any).

(2) A request for an extension of administration by consent of creditors shall be accompanied by a progress report for the period since the administrator's last progress report (if any).

(3) The administrator shall use the notice of extension of period of administration in the form required by Rule 7.30 and Schedule 5 in all circumstances where he is required to give such notice.]

NOTES

Substitution: see the note to r 2.1 at **[15.70]**.

Para (3): see further Sch 5, Form 2.22B (Scot) at **[15.349]**, and the notes to that Schedule.

[15.150]
[2.45 Notice of end of administration[—other than by a creditors' voluntary liquidation under paragraph 83 or by dissolution under paragraph 84]

(1) A notice by the administrator

(a) that the purpose of administration has been sufficiently achieved; or

(b) that the court has ordered that the appointment shall cease to have effect,

shall be in the form required by Rule 7.30 and Schedule 5, and shall be accompanied by a final progress report.

(2) The administrator shall, as soon as reasonably practicable, and (in the case of a notice under paragraph 80(2)) within 5 business days of satisfying the requirements of paragraph 80(2)(a), send a copy of the notice to every creditor of the company of whose claim and address he is aware, to all [other] persons who were notified of his appointment, and to the company.

[(3) Where the administrator wishes to publish a notice under paragraph 80(5), the notice

(a) shall be published in the Edinburgh Gazette; and

(b) may be advertised in such other manner as the administrator thinks fit.

(4) A notice published under Rule 2.45(3) shall—

(a) state the full name of the company;

(b) state the name and address of the administrator;

(c) state the date when the administrator's appointment ceased to have effect;

(d) specify an address to which any creditor of the company can write to request that a copy of the notice be provided; and

(e) be published within five business days of filing the notice of the end of administration with the court.]]

NOTES

Substitution: see the note to r 2.1 at **[15.70]**.

Rule heading: words in square brackets inserted by the Insolvency (Scotland) Amendment Rules 2010, SI 2010/688, r 3, Sch 1, para 93, subject to transitional provisions in r 4 thereof at **[2.80]**.

Para (2): word in square brackets substituted for original word "those" by SI 2010/688, r 3, Sch 1, para 94, subject to transitional provisions in rr 4, 5 thereof at **[2.80]**, **[2.81]**.

Paras (3), (4): substituted by the Insolvency (Scotland) Amendment Rules 2009, SI 2009/662, r 2, Schedule, paras 10, 11, subject to transitional provisions in r 3 thereof as noted to r 1.4 at **[15.10]**, and originally read as follows:

"(3) The administrator shall be taken to have complied with the requirements of paragraph 80(5) if, within 5 business days of satisfying the requirements of paragraph 80(2)(a), he publishes, once in the Edinburgh Gazette and once in the newspaper in which his appointment was advertised, a notice undertaking to provide a copy of the notice of end of administration to any creditor of the company.

(4) The notice referred to in paragraph (3) above must—

(a) state the full name of the company;

(b) state the name and address of the administrator;

(c) state the date upon which the administrator's appointment ceased to have effect; and

(d) specify an address to which any creditor may apply in writing for a copy of the notice of end of administration to be provided to him.".

Para (1): see further Sch 5, Form 2.23B (Scot), Form 2.24B (Scot) at **[15.349]**, and the notes to that Schedule.

[15.151]
[2.46 Application to court

(1) An application under paragraph 79 for an order providing for the appointment of an administrator of the company to cease to have effect shall be accompanied by a progress report for the period since the last such report (if any) and a statement indicating what the administrator thinks should be the next steps for the company.

(2) Where the administrator applies to the court because the creditors' meeting has required him to, his application shall be accompanied by a statement in which he shall indicate (giving reasons) whether or not he agrees with the creditors' requirement that he make the application.

(3) Where the administrator applies to the court other than at the request of a creditors' meeting, he shall give to—

(a) the applicant for the administration order under which he was appointed;

(b) the person by whom he was appointed or to the holder of the floating charge by virtue of which he was appointed (as the case may be); and

(c) the creditors,
at least [5 business] days' written notice of his intention so to apply.

(4) Where the administrator applies to court under paragraph 79 in conjunction with a petition under section 124 for an order to wind up the company, he shall, in addition to the requirements of paragraph (3), notify the creditors of whether he intends to seek appointment as liquidator.]

NOTES

Substitution: see the note to r 2.1 at **[15.70]**.

Para (3): words in square brackets substituted for original number "7" by the Insolvency (Scotland) Amendment Rules 2010, SI 2010/688, r 3, Sch 1, para 95, subject to transitional provisions in r 4 thereof at **[2.80]**.

Para (5): see further Sch 5, Form 2.24B (Scot) at **[15.349]**, and the notes to that Schedule.

[15.152]
[2.47 Moving from administration to creditors' voluntary liquidation

(1) A notice pursuant to paragraph 83(3) shall be in the form required by Rule 7.30 and Schedule 5.

(2) As soon as reasonably practicable after the day on which the registrar registers that notice, the person who has ceased to be the administrator (whether or not that person becomes the liquidator) must send a final progress report (which must include details of the assets to be dealt with in the liquidation) to the registrar and to all other persons who received notice of the administrator's appointment.

(3) For the purposes of paragraph 83(7)(a) a person is nominated by the creditors as liquidator by—
(a) the creditors' approval of the statement of the proposed liquidator in the administrator's proposals or revised proposals, or
(b) the nomination by the creditors of a different person before the creditors' approval of the administrator's proposals or revised proposals.

(4) Where the creditors nominate a different person, the nomination must, where applicable, include the declaration required by section 231 (appointment to office of two or more persons).]

NOTES

Substituted by the Insolvency (Scotland) Amendment Rules 2010, SI 2010/688, r 3, Sch 1, para 96, subject to transitional provisions in r 4 thereof at **[2.80]**. Rule 2.47 and related note previously read as follows:

"2.47 Moving from administration to creditors' voluntary liquidation

(1) A notice pursuant to paragraph 83(3) shall be in the form required by Rule 7.30 and Schedule 5, and shall be accompanied by a final progress report which includes details of the assets to be dealt with in the liquidation

(2) As soon as reasonably practicable, the administrator shall send a copy of the notice and accompanying documents to all those who received notice of the administrator's appointment.

(3) For the purposes of paragraph 83(7), a person shall be nominated by the creditors either—
(a) by the approval by the creditors of the administrator's statement of proposals under paragraph 49(1) or his statement of revised proposals under paragraph 54(2) in which that person is proposed to be nominated as liquidator; or
(b) where the creditors wish to nominate a person other than that proposed by the administrator, at the meeting held to consider the statement of proposals, or of revised proposals (as the case may be) in which the move from administration to creditors' voluntary liquidation is proposed.

NOTES

Para (1): see further Sch 5, Form 2.25B (Scot) at **[15.349]**, and the notes to that Schedule.".

[15.153]
[2.48 Moving from administration to dissolution

(1) The notice required by paragraph 84(1) shall be in the form required by Rule 7.30 and Schedule 5, and shall be accompanied by a final progress report.

(2) As soon as reasonably practicable a copy of the notice and accompanying documents shall be sent to all [other persons] who received notice of the administrator's appointment.

(3) Where the court makes an order under paragraph 84(7) it shall, where the applicant is not the administrator, give a copy of the order to the administrator.

(4) The notice required by paragraph 84(8) shall be in the form required by Rule 7.30 and Schedule 5.]

NOTES

Substitution: see the note to r 2.1 at **[15.70]**.

Para (2): words in square brackets substituted for original word "those" by the Insolvency (Scotland) Amendment Rules 2010, SI 2010/688, r 3, Sch 1, para 97, subject to transitional provisions in r 4 thereof at **[2.80]**.

Para (1): see further Sch 5, Form 2.26B (Scot) at **[15.349]**, and the notes to that Schedule.

Para (4): see further Sch 5, Form 2.27B (Scot) at **[15.349]**, and the notes to that Schedule.

[CHAPTER 11 REPLACING ADMINISTRATOR

[15.154]
2.49 Grounds for resignation

(1) The administrator may give notice of his resignation on grounds of ill health or because—
(a) he intends ceasing to be in practice as an insolvency practitioner; or
(b) there is some conflict of interest, or change of personal circumstances, which precludes or makes impracticable the further discharge by him of the duties of administrator.

(2) The administrator may, with the leave of the court, give notice of his resignation on grounds other than those specified in paragraph (1).]

NOTES

Substitution: see the note to r 2.1 at **[15.70]**.

[15.155]
[2.50 Notice of intention to resign

(1) The administrator must give to the persons specified below at least [5 business] days' notice of his intention to resign, or to apply for the court's leave to do so

(a) if there is a continuing administrator of the company, to him;
(b) if there is a creditors' committee, to it; and
(c) if there is no such administrator and no creditors' committee, to the company and its creditors.

(2) Where the administrator gives notice under paragraph (1), he shall also give notice to a member State liquidator, if such a person has been appointed in relation to the company.

(3) Where the administrator was appointed by the holder of a qualifying floating charge under paragraph 14, the notice of intention to resign shall also be sent to all holders of a qualifying floating charge.

(4) Where the administrator was appointed by the company or the directors of the company under paragraph 22, a copy of the notice of intention to resign shall also be sent to the company and to all holders of a qualifying floating charge.]

NOTES

Substitution: see the note to r 2.1 at **[15.70]**.

Para (1): words in square brackets substituted for original words number "7" by the Insolvency (Scotland) Amendment Rules 2010, SI 2010/688, r 3, Sch 1, para 98, subject to transitional provisions in r 4 thereof at **[2.80]**.

Para (1): see further Sch 5, Form 2.28B (Scot) at **[15.349]**, and the notes to that Schedule.

[15.156]
[2.51 Notice of resignation

(1) Where the administrator was appointed under an administration order, the notice of resignation shall be lodged in court, and a copy sent to the registrar of companies.

(2) A copy of the notice of resignation shall be sent, not more than 5 business days after it has been lodged in court, to all [other persons] to whom notice of intention to resign was sent.

(3) Where the administrator was appointed by the holder of a qualifying floating charge, a copy of the notice of resignation shall be lodged in court and sent to the registrar of companies, and to anyone else who received notice of intention to resign, within 5 business days of the notice of resignation being sent to the holder of the floating charge by virtue of which the appointment was made.

(4) Where the administrator was appointed by the company or the directors, a copy of the notice of resignation shall be lodged in court and sent to the registrar of companies, and to anyone else who received the notice of intention to resign, within 5 business days of the notice of resignation being sent to either the company or the directors that made the appointment.]

NOTES

Substitution: see the note to r 2.1 at **[15.70]**.

Para (2): words in square brackets substituted for original word "those" by the Insolvency (Scotland) Amendment Rules 2010, SI 2010/688, r 3, Sch 1, para 99, subject to transitional provisions in r 4 thereof at **[2.80]**.

Para (1): see further Sch 5, Form 2.29B (Scot) at **[15.349]**, and the notes to that Schedule.

[15.157]
[2.52 Administrator deceased

(1) Subject to the following paragraph of this Rule, where the administrator has died, it is the duty of his executors . . . to give notice of that fact to the court and to the registrar of companies, specifying the date of death

[(1A) If the deceased administrator was a partner in or an employee of a firm, notice may be given by a partner in the firm who is qualified to act as an insolvency practitioner, or is a member of any body recognised by the Secretary of State for the authorisation of insolvency practitioners.]

(2) Notice of the death may also be given by any person.

(3) Where an administrator who has ceased to be qualified to act as an insolvency practitioner in relation to the company gives notice in accordance with paragraph 89(2), he shall also give notice to the registrar of companies.]

NOTES

Substitution: see the note to r 2.1 at **[15.70]**.

Para (1): words "or, where the deceased administrator was a partner in a firm, of a partner of that firm" (omitted) revoked by the Insolvency (Scotland) Amendment Rules 2010, SI 2010/688, r 3, Sch 1, para 100, subject to transitional provisions in r 4 thereof at **[2.80]**.

Para (1A): inserted by SI 2010/688, r 3, Sch 1, para 101, subject to transitional provisions in r 4 thereof at **[2.80]**.

Para (1): see further Sch 5, Form 2.30B (Scot) at **[15.349]**, and the notes to that Schedule.

[15.158]
[2.53 Application to replace

(1) Where an application is made to the court under paragraph 91 or 95 to appoint a replacement administrator, the application shall be accompanied by a Statement of the Proposed Administrator.

(2) Where the original administrator was appointed under an administration order, a copy of the application shall be served on the person who made the application for the administration order.

(3) Where the court makes an order filling a vacancy in the office of administrator, the same provisions shall apply, subject to such modification as may be necessary, in respect of giving notice of, and advertising, the appointment as in the case of the original appointment of an administrator.]

NOTES

Substitution: see the note to r 2.1 at **[15.70]**.

Para (1): see further Sch 5, Form 2.1B (Scot) at **[15.349]**, and the notes to that Schedule.

[15.159]
[2.54

(1) This Rule applies where any person has appointed an administrator by notice in accordance with these Rules and a replacement administrator is appointed.

(2) The same provisions apply in respect of giving notice of, and advertising, the replacement appointment as in the case of an initial appointment, and all statements, consents and other documents as required shall also be required in this case.

(3) All forms and notices shall clearly identify that the appointment is of a replacement administrator.]

NOTES

Substitution: see the note to r 2.1 at **[15.70]**.

Para (1): see further Sch 5, Form 2.31B (Scot) at **[15.349]**, and the notes to that Schedule.

[15.160]
[2.55 Joint or concurrent appointments

(1) Where a person is appointed in accordance with paragraph 103 to act as administrator jointly or concurrently with the person or persons then acting, the same provisions shall apply, subject to this Rule and to such other modification as may be necessary, in respect of the making of this appointment as in the case of the original appointment of an administrator.

(2) An appointment made under paragraph 103 shall be notified to the registrar of companies in the form required by Rule 7.30 and Schedule 5.]

NOTES

Substitution: see the note to r 2.1 at **[15.70]**.

Para (2): see further Sch 5, Form 2.31B (Scot) at **[15.349]**, and the notes to that Schedule.

[15.161]
[2.56 Application to court to remove administrator from office

(1) An application to the court to remove an administrator from office shall be served upon—

(a) the administrator;

(b) where the administrator was appointed by the court, the person who made the application for the administration order;

(c) where the appointment was made by the holder of a qualifying floating charge, the holder of the floating charge by virtue of which the appointment was made;

(d) where the appointment was made by the directors or by the company, the person who made the appointment;

(e) the creditors' committee (if any);

(f) the joint administrator (if any); and

(g) where there is neither a creditor's committee nor a joint administrator, upon the company and the creditors.

(2) An applicant under this Rule shall, within 5 business days of the order being made, send a copy of the order to all those to whom notice of the application was sent, and a notice to the registrar of companies in the form required by Rule 7.30 and Schedule 5.]

NOTES

Substitution: see the note to r 2.1 at **[15.70]**.

Para (2): see further Sch 5, Form 2.30B (Scot) at **[15.349]**, and the notes to that Schedule.

[CHAPTER 12 [EU REGULATION]—CONVERSION OF ADMINISTRATION TO WINDING UP

[15.162]
2.57 Application for conversion . . .

[(1) Where a member State liquidator proposes to apply to the court for the conversion into winding-up proceedings of an administration, an affidavit complying with Rule 2.58 must be prepared and lodged in court in support of the application.

(1A) In this Rule, and in Rules 2.58 and 2.59, "conversion into winding-up proceedings" means an order under [Article 51 of the EU Regulation (conversion of secondary insolvency proceedings)] that—

(a) *the purposes of the administration are to be limited to the winding up of the company through administration and are to exclude the purpose contained in sub-paragraph (a) of paragraph 3(1);*

[(aa) the administration is converted into a company voluntary arrangement;]

(b) the administration is converted into a creditors' voluntary winding up; or

(c) the administration is converted into a winding up by the court.]

(2) The application and the affidavit required under this Rule shall be served upon—

(a) the company; and

(b) the administrator.]

NOTES

Words in square brackets in Chapter heading substituted for original words "EC Regulation" by the Insolvency Amendment (EU 2015/848) Regulations 2017, SI 2017/702, regs 2, 3, Schedule, Pt 5, paras 61, 77, as from 26 June 2017, except in relation to proceedings opened before that date.

Substitution: see the note to r 2.1 at **[15.70]**.

Rule heading: words "into winding up" (omitted) revoked by SI 2017/702, regs 2, 3, Schedule, Pt 5, paras 61, 78(1), as from 26 June 2017, except in relation to proceedings opened before that date.

Para (1): substituted (together with para (1A)) for para (1) by the Insolvency (Scotland) Amendment Rules 2010, SI 2010/688, r 3, Sch 1, para 102, subject to transitional provisions in r 4 thereof at **[2.80]**. Para (1) previously read as follows (with words in square brackets inserted by the Insolvency (Scotland) Amendment Rules 2006, SI 2006/734, r 11:

> "(1) Where a member State liquidator proposes to apply to the court for the conversion under Article 37 of the EC Regulation (conversion of earlier proceedings) of an administration into a winding up[, whether by entering voluntary winding up, being wound up by the court or wound up through the administration], there shall be lodged in support of his application an affidavit complying with Rule 2.58.

Para (1A): substituted as noted to para (1) above; words in square brackets substituted for original words "Article 37 of the EC Regulation (conversion of earlier proceedings)", sub-para (a) revoked and sub-para (aa) inserted by SI 2017/702, regs 2, 3, Schedule, Pt 5, paras 61, 78(2), as from 26 June 2017, except in relation to proceedings opened before that date.

[15.163]

[2.58 Contents of affidavit

(1) The affidavit shall state—

(a) that main proceedings have been opened in relation to the company in a member State other than the United Kingdom;

(b) the deponent's belief that the conversion of the administration into [winding-up proceedings] [would be most appropriate as regards the interests of the local creditors and coherence between the main and secondary insolvency proceedings;]

(c) the deponent's opinion as to whether the company ought to enter voluntary winding up[, be wound up by the court or be wound up through the administration]; and

(d) all other matters that, in the opinion of the member State liquidator, would assist the court—

 (i) in deciding whether to make such an order; and

 (ii) if the court were to do so, in considering the need for any consequential provision that would be necessary or desirable.

(2) An affidavit under this rule shall be sworn by, or on behalf of, the member State liquidator.]

NOTES

Substitution: see the note to r 2.1 at **[15.70]**.

Para (1): words in first pair of square brackets in sub-para (b) substituted for original words "a winding up" by the Insolvency (Scotland) Amendment Rules 2010, SI 2010/688, r 3, Sch 1, para 103, subject to transitional provisions in r 4 thereof at **[2.80]**; words in second pair of square brackets substituted for original words "would prove to be in the interests of the creditors in the main proceedings" by the Insolvency Amendment (EU 2015/848) Regulations 2017, SI 2017/702, regs 2, 3, Schedule, Pt 5, paras 61, 79, as from 26 June 2017, except in relation to proceedings opened before that date; words in square brackets in sub-para (c) substituted by the Insolvency (Scotland) Amendment Rules 2006, SI 2006/734, r 12.

Para (1): see further Sch 5, Form 2.30B (Scot) at **[15.349]**, and the notes to that Schedule.

[15.164]

[2.59 Power of court

(1) On hearing the application for conversion into [winding-up proceedings] the court may make such order as it thinks fit.

(2) If the court makes an order for conversion into [winding-up proceedings] the order may contain all such consequential provisions as the court deems necessary or desirable.

(3) Without prejudice to the generality of paragraph (1) of this Rule, an order under that paragraph may provide that the company be wound up as if a resolution for voluntary winding up under section 84 were passed on the day on which the order is made.]

NOTES

Substitution: see the note to r 2.1 at **[15.70]**.

Paras (1), (2): words in square brackets substituted for original words "winding up" by the Insolvency (Scotland) Amendment Rules 2010, SI 2010/688, r 3, Sch 1, para 104, subject to transitional provisions in r 4 thereof at **[2.80]**.

[CHAPTER 13 [EU REGULATION]—MEMBER STATE LIQUIDATOR

[15.165]

2.60 Interpretation of creditor and notice to member State liquidator

(1) This Rule applies where a member State liquidator has been appointed in relation to the company.

(2) For the purposes of Chapters 6, 7 and 8 of these Rules, (and except where the context otherwise requires) the member State liquidator is deemed to be a creditor.

(3) Paragraph (2) of this Rule is without prejudice to the generality of the right to participate referred to in paragraph 3 of [Article 45 of the EU Regulation] (exercise of creditor's rights).

(4) Where the administrator is obliged to give notice to, or provide a copy of a document (including an order of court) to, the court, the registrar of companies, or a provisional liquidator or liquidator, the administrator shall also give notice or provide copies, as the case may be, to the member State liquidator.

(5) Paragraph (4) is without prejudice to the generality of the obligations imposed by [Article 41 of the EU Regulation (cooperation and communication between insolvency practitioners)].]

NOTES

Substitution: see the note to r 2.1 at **[15.70]**.

Words in square brackets in Chapter heading substituted for original words "EC Regulation" by the Insolvency Amendment (EU 2015/848) Regulations 2017, SI 2017/702, regs 2, 3, Schedule, Pt 5, paras 61, 80, as from 26 June 2017, except in relation to proceedings opened before that date.

Para (3): words in square brackets substituted for original words "Article 32 of the EC Regulation" by SI 2017/702, regs 2, 3, Schedule, Pt 5, paras 61, 81(a), as from 26 June 2017, except in relation to proceedings opened before that date.

Para (5): words in square brackets substituted for original words "Article 31 of the EC Regulation (duty to co-operate and communicate information)" by SI 2017/702, regs 2, 3, Schedule, Pt 5, paras 61, 81(b), as from 26 June 2017, except in relation to proceedings opened before that date.

PART 3
RECEIVERS

CHAPTER 1 APPOINTMENT

[15.166]

3.1 Acceptance of appointment

(1) Where a person has been appointed a receiver by the holder of a floating charge under section 53, his acceptance (which need not be in writing) of that appointment for the purposes of paragraph (a) of section 53(6) shall be intimated by him to the holder of the floating charge or his agent within the period specified in that paragraph and he shall, as soon as possible after his acceptance, endorse a written docquet to that effect on the instrument of appointment.

(2) The written docquet evidencing receipt of the instrument of appointment, which is required by section 53(6)(b), shall also be endorsed on the instrument of appointment.

(3) The receiver shall, as soon as possible after his acceptance of the appointment, deliver a copy of the endorsed instrument of appointment to the holder of the floating charge or his agent.

(4) This Rule shall apply in the case of the appointment of joint receivers as it applies to the appointment of a receiver, except that, where the docquet of acceptance required by paragraph (1) is endorsed by each of the joint receivers, or two or more of them, on the same instrument of appointment, it is the joint receiver who last endorses his docquet of acceptance who is required to send a copy of the instrument of appointment to the holder of the floating charge or his agent under paragraph (3).

CHAPTER 2 STATEMENT OF AFFAIRS

[15.167]

3.2 Notice requiring statement of affairs

(1) Where the receiver decides to require from any person or persons a statement as to the affairs of the company to be made out and submitted to him in accordance with section 66, he shall send to each of those persons a notice in the form required by Rule 7.30 and Schedule 5 requiring him to make out and submit a statement of affairs in the form prescribed by the Receivers (Scotland) Regulations 1986.

(2) Any person to whom a notice is sent under this Rule is referred to in this Chapter as "a deponent".

(3) [Subject to Rule 3.2A,] the receiver shall insert any statement of affairs submitted to him in the sederunt book.

NOTES

Para (3): words in square brackets inserted by the Insolvency (Scotland) Amendment Rules 2014, SSI 2014/114, rr 2, 24(1), subject to savings in r 29 thereof as noted to r 0.2 at **[15.2]**.

Para (1): see Sch 5, Form 3.1 (Scot) at **[15.349]**, and the notes to that Schedule.

[15.168]

[3.2A Limited disclosure of the statement of affairs

(1) Where the receiver thinks it would prejudice the conduct of the receivership or might reasonably be expected to lead to violence against any person for the whole or part of the statement of affairs to be disclosed, the receiver may apply to the court for an order of limited disclosure in respect of the statement, or a specified part of it.

(2) The court may order that the statement or, as the case may be, the specified part of it shall not be entered in the sederunt book.

(3) The receiver shall as soon as reasonably practicable place a copy of the order in the sederunt book.

(4) A creditor who seeks disclosure of the statement of affairs or a specified part of it in relation to which an order has been made under this Rule may apply to the court for an order that the receiver disclose that statement or specified part.

(5) The court may attach to an order for disclosure any conditions as to confidentiality, duration and scope of the order in any material change of circumstances, and other matters as it sees fit.

(6) If there is a material change in circumstances rendering the limit on disclosure unnecessary, the receiver shall, as soon as reasonably practicable after the change, apply to the court for the order to be discharged or varied; and upon the discharge or variation of the order the receiver shall, as soon as reasonably practicable place a copy of the full statement of affairs (or so much of the statement as is no longer subject to the order) in the sederunt book.]

NOTES

Commencement: 30 May 2014.

Inserted by the Insolvency (Scotland) Amendment Rules 2014, SSI 2014/114, rr 2, 24(2), subject to savings in r 29 thereof as noted to r 0.2 at **[15.2]**.

[15.169]
3.3 Expenses of statement of affairs

(1) A deponent who makes up and submits to the receiver a statement of affairs shall be allowed and be paid by the receiver, as an expense of the receivership, any expenses incurred by the deponent in so doing which the receiver considers to be reasonable.

(2) Any decision by the receiver under this Rule is subject to appeal to the court.

(3) Nothing in this Rule relieves a deponent from any obligation to make up and submit a statement of affairs, or to provide information to the receiver.

CHAPTER 3 THE CREDITORS' COMMITTEE

[15.170]
3.4 Constitution of committee

(1) Where it is resolved by the creditors' meeting to establish a creditors' committee under section 68, the committee shall consist of at least 3 and not more than 5 creditors of the company elected at the meeting.

(2) Any creditor of the company who has lodged a claim is eligible to be a member of the committee, so long as his claim has not been rejected for the purpose of his entitlement to vote.

(3) A body corporate or a partnership may be a member of the committee, but it cannot act as such otherwise than by a representative appointed under Rule 7.20, as applied by Rule 3.6.

[15.171]
3.5 Functions of the committee

In addition to the functions conferred on it by the Act, the creditors' committee shall represent to the receiver the views of the unsecured creditors and shall act in relation to him in such manner as may be agreed from time to time.

[15.172]
3.6 Application of provisions relating to liquidation committee

(1) Chapter 7 of Part 4 (The liquidation committee) shall apply with regard to the creditors' committee in the receivership and its members as it applies to the liquidation committee and the creditor members thereof, subject to the modifications specified below and to any other necessary modifications.

(2) For any reference in the said Chapter 7 to—

(a) the liquidator or the liquidation committee, there shall be substituted a reference to the receiver or to the creditors' committee;

(b) to the creditor member, there shall be substituted a reference to a creditor, and any reference to a contributory member shall be disregarded.

(3) In Rule 4.42(3) and 4.52(2), for the reference to Rule 4.41(1), there shall be substituted a reference to Rule 3.4(1).

(4) In Rule 4.57,

(a) for the reference to an expense of the liquidation, there shall be substituted a reference to an expense of the receivership;

(b) at the end of that Rule there shall be inserted the following—

"This does not apply to any meeting of the committee held within 3 months of a previous meeting, unless the meeting in question is summoned at the instance of the receiver.".

(5) The following Rules shall not apply, namely—
Rules 4.40, 4.41, 4.43 to 4.44, 4.53, 4.56, 4.58 and 4.59.

[15.173]
3.7 Information from receiver

(1) Where the committee resolves to require the attendance of the receiver under section 68(2), the notice to him shall be in writing signed by the majority of the members of the committee for the time being or their representatives.

(2) The meeting at which the receiver's attendance is required shall be fixed by the committee for a business day, and shall be held at such time and place as he determines.

(3) Where the receiver so attends, the members of the committee may elect any one of their number to be chairman of the meeting, in place of the receiver or any nominee of his.

[15.174]
3.8 Members' dealings with the company

(1) Membership of the committee does not prevent a person from dealing with the company while the receiver is acting, provided that any transactions in the course of such dealings are entered into on normal commercial terms.

(2) The court may, on the application of any person interested, set aside a transaction which appears to it to be contrary to the requirements of this Rule, and may give such consequential directions as it thinks fit for compensating the company for any loss which it may have incurred in consequence of the transaction.

[15.175]
[3.8A Prescribed Part

Where a receiver is appointed over the whole or any part of the property of a company and section 176A(2) applies, the receiver shall—
- (a) where the company is in liquidation or administration, make available to the liquidator or administrator for distribution to unsecured creditors the sums representing the prescribed part, or
- (b) in any other case (save where the receiver petitions for the winding up of the company), apply to the court for directions as to the disposal of the prescribed part.]

NOTES

Inserted by the Enterprise Act 2002 (Consequential Amendments) (Prescribed Part) (Scotland) Order 2003, SI 2003/2108, art 5.

CHAPTER 4 MISCELLANEOUS

[15.176]
3.9 Abstract of receipts and payments

(1) The receiver shall—
- (a) within 2 months after the end of 12 months from the date of his appointment, and of every subsequent period of 12 months, and
- (b) within 2 months after he ceases to act as receiver,

send the requisite accounts of his receipts and payments as receiver to—
- [(i) the Accountant in Bankruptcy]
- (ii) the holder of the floating charge by virtue of which he was appointed,
- (iii) the members of the creditors' committee (if any),
- (iv) the company or, if it is in liquidation, the liquidator.

(2) The court may, on the receiver's application, extend the period of 2 months referred to in paragraph (1).

(3) The accounts are to be in the form of an abstract showing—
- (a) receipts and payments during the relevant period of 12 months, or
- (b) where the receiver has ceased to act, receipts and payments during the period from the end of the last 12-month period to the time when he so ceased (alternatively, if there has been no previous abstract, receipts and payments in the period since his appointment as receiver).

(4) This Rule is without prejudice to the receiver's duty to render proper accounts required otherwise than as above.

(5) If the receiver makes default in complying with this Rule, he is liable to a fine and, for continued contravention, to a daily default fine.

NOTES

Para (1): sub-para (b)(i) substituted by the Scotland Act 1998 (Consequential Modifications) (No 2) Order 1999, SI 1999/1820, art 4, Sch 2, Pt II, para 141(1), (2).

Para (3): see Sch 5, Form 3.2 (Scot) at **[15.349]**, and the notes to that Schedule.

[15.177]
[3.9A Electronic measures – application

(1) Subject to paragraph (2), this Rule and Rules 3.9B and 3.9C apply where a notice or other document is required to be given, delivered or sent under this Part or Part III of the Act.

(2) This Rule and Rules 3.9B and 3.9C do not apply to—
- (a) lodging any application or other document with the court;
- (b) service of any application, or other document lodged with the court;

Part 15 Insolvency (Scotland) Rules 1986

(c) service of any order of the court; or
(d) submission of documents to the registrar of companies.]

NOTES

Commencement: 30 May 2014.

Inserted, together with rr 3.9B, 3.9C, by the Insolvency (Scotland) Amendment Rules 2014, SSI 2014/114, rr 2, 26(1), subject to savings in r 29 thereof as noted to r 0.2 at **[15.2]**.

[15.178]
[3.9B Electronic delivery

(1) Unless in any particular case some other form of delivery is required by the Act or the Rules or an order of the court, a notice or other document may be given, delivered or sent by electronic means provided that the intended recipient of the notice or other document has—
(a) consented (whether in the specific case or generally) to electronic delivery (and has not revoked that consent); and
(b) provided an electronic address for delivery.

(2) In the absence of evidence to the contrary, a notice or other document is presumed to have been delivered where—
(a) the sender can produce a copy of the electronic message which—
(i) contained the notice or other document, or to which the notice or other document was attached; and
(ii) shows the time and date the message was sent; and
(b) that electronic message contains the address supplied under paragraph (1)(b).

(3) A message sent electronically is deemed to have been delivered to the recipient no later than 9.00am on the next business day after it was sent.]

NOTES

Commencement: 30 May 2014.

Inserted as noted to r 3.9A at **[15.177]**.

[15.179]
[3.9C Electronic delivery by receivers etc

(1) Where an office-holder gives, sends or delivers a notice or other document to any person by electronic means, the notice or document must contain or be accompanied by a statement that the recipient may request a hard copy of the notice or document and specifying a telephone number, e-mail address and postal address which may be used to request a hard copy.

(2) Where a hard copy of the notice or other document is requested, it must be sent within 5 business days of receipt of the request by the office-holder.

(3) An office-holder must not require a person making a request under paragraph (2) to pay a fee for the supply of the document.]

NOTES

Commencement: 30 May 2014.

Inserted as noted to r 3.9A at **[15.177]**.

[15.180]
3.10 Receiver deceased

If the receiver dies, the holder of the floating charge by virtue of which he was appointed shall, forthwith on his becoming aware of the death, give notice of it to—
(a) the registrar of companies,
(b) the members of the creditors' committee (if any),
(c) the company or, if it is in liquidation, the liquidator,
(d) the holder of any other floating charge and any receiver appointed by him,
[(e) the Accountant in Bankruptcy.]

NOTES

Para (e): added by the Scotland Act 1998 (Consequential Modifications) (No 2) Order 1999, SI 1999/1820, art 4, Sch 2, Pt II, para 141(1), (3).

See Sch 5, Form 3.3 (Scot) at **[15.349]**, and the notes to that Schedule.

[15.181]
3.11 Vacation of office

The receiver, on vacating office on completion of the receivership or in consequence of his ceasing to be qualified as an insolvency practitioner, shall, in addition to giving notice to the registrar of companies [and the Accountant in Bankruptcy] under section 62(5), give notice of his vacating office, within 14 days thereof, to—
(a) the holder of the floating charge by virtue of which he was appointed,
(b) the members of the creditors' committee (if any),
(c) the company of, if it is in liquidation, the liquidator,
(d) the holder of any other floating charge and any receiver appointed by him.

NOTES

Words in square brackets inserted by the Scotland Act 1998 (Consequential Modifications) (No 2) Order 1999, SI 1999/1820, art 4, Sch 2, Pt II, para 141(1), (4).

CHAPTER 5 VAT BAD DEBT RELIEF

[15.182]

3.12 Issue of certificate of insolvency

(1) In accordance with this Rule, it is the duty of the administrative receiver to issue a certificate in the terms of paragraph (b) of section 22(3) of the Value Added Tax Act 1983 (which specifies the circumstances in which a company is deemed insolvent for the purposes of that section) forthwith upon his forming the opinion described in that paragraph.

(2) There shall in the certificate be specified—

(a) the name of the company and its registered number;
(b) the name of the administrative receiver and the date of his appointment; and
(c) the date on which the certificate is issued.

(3) The certificate shall be entitled "CERTIFICATE OF INSOLVENCY FOR THE PURPOSES OF SECTION 22(3)(b) OF THE VALUE ADDED TAX ACT 1983".

[15.183]

3.13 Notice to creditors

(1) Notice of the issue of the certificate shall be given by the administrative receiver within 3 months of his appointment or within 2 months of issuing the certificate, whichever is the later, to all of the company's unsecured creditors of whose address he is then aware and who have, to his knowledge, made supplies to the company, with a charge to value added tax, at any time before his appointment.

(2) Thereafter, he shall give the notice to any such creditor of whose address and supplies to the company he becomes aware.

(3) He is not under obligation to provide any creditor with a copy of the certificate.

[15.184]

3.14 Preservation of certificate with company's records

(1) The certificate shall be retained with the company's accounting records, and section 222 of the Companies Act (where and for how long records are to be kept) shall apply to the certificate as it applies to those records.

(2) It is the duty of the administrative receiver, on vacating office, to bring this Rule to the attention of the directors or (as the case may be) any successor of his as receiver.

PART 4
WINDING UP BY THE COURT

CHAPTER 1 PROVISIONAL LIQUIDATOR

[15.185]

4.1 Appointment of provisional liquidator

[(1)] An application to the court for the appointment of a provisional liquidator under section 135 may be made by the petitioner in the winding up, or by a creditor of the company, or by a contributory, or by the company itself, or by any person who under any enactment would be entitled to present a petition for the winding up of the company.

[(2) The court shall be satisfied that a person has caution for the proper performance of his functions as provisional liquidator if a statement is lodged in court or it is averred in the winding-up petition that the person to be appointed is an insolvency practitioner, duly qualified under the Act to act as liquidator, and that he consents so to act.]

NOTES

Para (1): numbered as such by the Insolvency (Scotland) Amendment Rules 1987, SI 1987/1921, r 3(1), Schedule, Pt I, para 9.

Para (2): added by SI 1987/1921, r 3(1), Schedule, Pt I, para 9.

[15.186]

4.2 Order of appointment

(1) The provisional liquidator shall forthwith after the order appointing him is made, give notice of his appointment to—

(a) the registrar of companies;
[(aa) the Accountant in Bankruptcy;]
(b) the company; and
(c) any receiver of the whole or any part of the property of the company.

(2) The provisional liquidator shall advertise his appointment in accordance with any directions of the court.

NOTES

Para (1): sub-para (aa) inserted by the Scotland Act 1998 (Consequential Modifications) (No 2) Order 1999, SI 1999/1820, art 4, Sch 2, Pt II, para 141(1), (5).

See Sch 5, Form 4.9 (Scot) at **[15.349]**, and the notes to that Schedule.

[15.187]
4.3 Caution

The cost of providing the caution required by the provisional liquidator under the Act shall unless the court otherwise directs be—

(a) if a winding up order is not made, reimbursed to him out of the property of the company, and the court may make an order against the company accordingly, and

(b) if a winding up order is made, reimbursed to him as an expense of the liquidation.

[15.188]
4.4 Failure to find or to maintain caution

(1) If the provisional liquidator fails to find or to maintain his caution, the court may remove him and make such order as it thinks fit as to expenses.

(2) If an order is made under this Rule removing the provisional liquidator, or discharging the order appointing him, the court shall give directions as to whether any, and if so what, steps should be taken for the appointment of another person in his place.

[15.189]
4.5 Remuneration

(1) The remuneration of the provisional liquidator shall be fixed by the court from time to time.

[(2) The basis for the court fixing the amount of the remuneration payable to the provisional liquidator may be a commission calculated by reference to the value of the company's assets with which the provisional liquidator has had to deal but there shall in any event be taken into account—

(a) the work which, having regard to that value, was reasonably undertaken by the provisional liquidator; and

(b) the extent of the provisional liquidator's responsibilities in administering the company's assets.]

[(3) Without prejudice to any order of the court as to expenses, the provisional liquidator's remuneration shall be paid to him, and the amount of any expenses incurred by him (including the remuneration and expenses of any special manager appointed under section 177) reimbursed—

(a) if a winding up order is not made, out of the property of the company], and

(b) if a winding up order is made, as an expense of the liquidation.

[(4) Unless the court otherwise directs, in a case falling within paragraph (3)(a) above, the provisional liquidator may retain out of the company's property such sums or property as are or may be required for meeting his remuneration and expenses.

NOTES

Para (2): substituted by the Insolvency (Scotland) Amendment Rules 2014, SSI 2014/114, rr 2, 6, subject to savings in r 29 thereof as noted to r 0.2 at **[15.2]**, and previously read as follows—

"(2) Section 53(4) of the Bankruptcy Act shall apply to determine the basis for fixing the amount of the remuneration of the provisional liquidator, subject to the modifications specified in Rule 4.16(2) and to any other necessary modifications.".

Para (3): substituted by the Insolvency (Scotland) Amendment Rules 1987, SI 1987/1921, r 3(1), Schedule, Pt I, para 10(1).
Para (4): added by SI 1987/1921, r 3(1), Schedule, Pt I, para 10(2).

[15.190]
4.6 Termination of appointment

(1) [Except in relation to winding-up petitions under section 124A,] the appointment of the provisional liquidator may be terminated by the court on his application, or on that of any of the persons entitled to make application for his appointment under Rule 4.1.

(2) If the provisional liquidator's appointment terminates, in consequence of the dismissal of the winding up petition or otherwise, the court may give such directions as it thinks fit with respect to—

(a) the accounts of his administration;

(b) the expenses properly incurred by the provisional liquidator; or

(c) any other matters which it thinks appropriate, . . .

[(3) In winding-up petitions under section 124A, the appointment of the provisional liquidator may be terminated by the court on his application, or on that of the Secretary of State.]

NOTES

Para (1): words in square brackets inserted by the Insolvency (Scotland) Amendment Rules 2006, SI 2006/734, r 13(a).
Para (2): words omitted revoked by the Insolvency (Scotland) Amendment Rules 1987, SI 1987/1921, r 3(1), Schedule, Pt I, para 11.
Para (3): added by SI 2006/734, r 13(b).

CHAPTER 2 STATEMENT OF AFFAIRS

[15.191]
4.7 Notice requiring statement of affairs

(1) This Chapter applies where the liquidator or, in a case where a provisional liquidator is appointed, the provisional liquidator decides to require a statement as to the affairs of the company to be made out and submitted to him in accordance with section 131.

(2) In this Chapter [(except for Rule 4.8A)] the expression "liquidator" includes "provisional liquidator".

(3) The liquidator shall send to each of the persons upon whom he decides to make such a requirement under section 131, a notice in the form required by Rule 7.30 and Schedule 5 requiring him to make out and submit a statement of affairs.

(4) Any person to whom a notice is sent under this Rule is referred to in this Chapter as "a deponent".

NOTES

Para (2): words in square brackets inserted by the Insolvency (Scotland) Amendment Rules 2014, SSI 2014/114, rr 2, 25(1), subject to savings in r 29 thereof as noted to r 0.2 at **[15.2]**.

Para (3): see Sch 5, Form 4.3 (Scot), Form 4.4 (Scot) at **[15.349]**, and the notes to that Schedule.

[15.192]
4.8 Form of the statement of affairs

(1) The statement of affairs shall be in the form required by Rule 7.30 and Schedule 5.

(2) [Subject to Rule 4.8A,] the liquidator shall insert any statement of affairs submitted to him in the sederunt book.

NOTES

Para (2): words in square brackets inserted by the Insolvency (Scotland) Amendment Rules 2014, SSI 2014/114, rr 2, 25(2), subject to savings in r 29 thereof as noted to r 0.2 at **[15.2]**.

[15.193]
[4.8A Limited disclosure of the statement of affairs

(1) Where the liquidator thinks that it would prejudice the conduct of the winding up or might reasonably be expected to lead to violence against any person for the whole or part of the statement of affairs to be disclosed, the liquidator may apply to the court for an order of limited disclosure in respect of the statement, or any specified part of it.

(2) The court may order that the statement or, as the case may be, the specified part of it shall not be entered in the sederunt book.

(3) The liquidator shall as soon as reasonably practicable place a copy of the order in the sederunt book.

(4) A creditor who seeks disclosure of a statement or specified part of it in relation to which an order has been made under this Rule may apply to the court for an order that the liquidator disclose that statement or specified part.

(5) The court may attach to an order for disclosure any conditions as to confidentiality, duration and scope of the order in any material change of circumstances, and other matters as it sees fit.

(6) If there is a material change in circumstances rendering the limit on disclosure unnecessary, the liquidator shall, as soon as reasonably practicable after the change, apply to the court for the order to be discharged or varied; and upon the discharge or variation of the order the liquidator shall, as soon as reasonably practicable place a copy of the full statement of affairs (or so much of the statement as is no longer subject to the order) in the sederunt book.]

NOTES

Commencement: 30 May 2014.

Inserted by the Insolvency (Scotland) Amendment Rules 2014, SSI 2014/114, rr 2, 25(3), subject to savings in r 29 thereof as noted to r 0.2 at **[15.2]**.

[15.194]
4.9 Expenses of statement of affairs

(1) At the request of any deponent, made on the grounds that he cannot himself prepare a proper statement of affairs, the liquidator may authorise an allowance towards expenses to be incurred by the deponent in employing some person or persons to be approved by the liquidator to assist the deponent in preparing it.

(2) Any such request by the deponent shall be accompanied by an estimate of the expenses involved.

(3) An authorisation given by the liquidator under this Rule shall be subject to such conditions (if any) as he thinks fit to impose with respect to the manner in which any person may obtain access to relevant books and papers.

(4) Nothing in this Rule relieves a deponent from any obligation to make up and submit a statement of affairs, or to provide information to the liquidator.

(5) Any allowance by the liquidator under this Rule shall be an expense of the liquidation.

(6) The liquidator shall intimate to the deponent whether he grants or refuses his request for an allowance under this Rule and where such request is refused the deponent affected by the refusal may appeal to the court not later than 14 days from the date intimation of such refusal is made to him.

CHAPTER 3 INFORMATION

[15.195]
4.10 Information to creditors and contributories

(1) The liquidator shall report to the creditors, and, except where he considers it would be inappropriate to do so, the contributories with respect to the proceedings in the winding up within six weeks after the end of each accounting period or he may submit such a report to a meeting of creditors or of contributories held within such period.

[(1A) The report under paragraph (1) shall include—

(a) to the best of the liquidator's knowledge and belief—

(i) an estimate of the value of the prescribed part (whether or not he proposes to make an application to the court under section 176A(5) or section 176A(3) applies), and

(ii) an estimate of the value of the company's net property,

provided that such estimates shall not be required to include any information the disclosure of which could seriously prejudice the commercial interests of the company, but if such information is excluded the estimates shall be accompanied by a statement to that effect, and

(b) whether, and, if so, why, the liquidator proposes to make an application to the court under section 176A(5).]

(2) Any reference in this Rule to creditors is to persons known to the liquidator to be creditors of the company.

(3) Where a statement of affairs has been submitted to him, the liquidator may send out to creditors and contributories with the next convenient report to be made under paragraph (1) a summary of the statement and such observations (if any) as he thinks fit to make with respect to it.

[(4) Any person appointed as liquidator of a company under section 140(1) who, following such appointment becomes aware of creditors of the company of whom he was not aware when he was acting as the administrator of the company, shall send to such creditors a copy of any statement or report which was sent by him to creditors under [Rule 2.25], with a note to the effect that it is being sent under this Rule.]

NOTES

Para (1A): inserted by the Enterprise Act 2002 (Consequential Amendments) (Prescribed Part) (Scotland) Order 2003, SI 2003/2108, art 6(1).

Para (4): added by the Insolvency (Scotland) Amendment Rules 1987, SI 1987/1921, r 3(1), Schedule, Pt I, para 12; rule reference in square brackets substituted for original rule reference "Rule 2.7" by the Insolvency (Scotland) Amendment Rules 2003, SI 2003/2111, r 6, Sch 2, para 4, subject to savings in r 7 thereof at **[2.34]**.

[15.196]
4.11 Information to registrar of companies

The statement which section 192 requires the liquidator to send to [the Accountant in Bankruptcy] if the winding up is not concluded within one year from its commencement, shall be sent not more than 30 days after the expiration of that year and thereafter [not more than 30 days after the end of each accounting period which ends after that year] until the winding up is concluded in the form required by Rule 7.30 and Schedule 5 and shall contain the particulars specified therein.

NOTES

Words in first pair of square brackets substituted by the Scotland Act 1998 (Consequential Modifications) (No 2) Order 1999, SI 1999/1820, art 4, Sch 2, Pt II, para 141(1), (6); words in second pair of square brackets substituted by the Insolvency (Scotland) Amendment Rules 1987, SI 1987/1921, r 3(1), Schedule, Pt I, para 13.

See Sch 5, Forms 4.5 (Scot), 4.6 (Scot) at **[15.349]**, and the notes to that Schedule.

CHAPTER 4 MEETING OF CREDITORS AND CONTRIBUTORIES

[15.197]
4.12 First meetings in the liquidation

(1) This Rule applies where under [section 138(3) or (4)] the interim liquidator summons meetings of the creditors and the contributories of the company [or, as the case may be, a meeting of the creditors] for the purpose of choosing a person to be liquidator of the company in place of the interim liquidator.

(2) Meetings summoned by the interim liquidator under that section are known respectively as "the first meeting of creditors" and "the first meeting of contributories", and jointly as "the first meetings in the liquidation".

[(2A) Any meetings of creditors or contributories under section 138(3) or (4) shall be summoned for a date not later than 42 days after the date of the winding up order or such longer period as the court may allow.]

(3) Subject as follows, no resolutions shall be taken at the first meeting of creditors other than the following—

(a) a resolution to appoint one or more named insolvency practitioners to be liquidator or, as the case may be, joint liquidators and, in the case of joint liquidators, whether any act required or authorised to be done by the liquidator is to be done by both or all of them, or by any one or more;

(b) a resolution to establish a liquidation committee under section 142(1);

(c) unless a liquidation committee is to be established, a resolution specifying the terms on which the liquidator is to be remunerated, or to defer consideration of that matter;

(d) a resolution to adjourn the meeting for not more than 3 weeks;

(e) any other resolution which the chairman considers it right to allow for special reason.

(4) This rule also applies with respect to the first meeting of contributories except that that meeting shall not pass any resolution to the effect of paragraph (3)(c).

NOTES

Para (1): words in first pair of square brackets substituted and words in second pair of square brackets inserted by the Insolvency (Scotland) Amendment Rules 1987, SI 1987/1921, r 3(1), Schedule, Pt I, para 14(1).

Para (2A): inserted by SI 1987/1921, r 3(1), Schedule, Pt I, para 14(2).

[15.198]

4.13 Other meetings

(1) The liquidator shall summon a meeting of the creditors in each year during which the liquidation is in force.

(2) Subject to the above provision, the liquidator may summon a meeting of the creditors or of the contributories at any time for the purpose of ascertaining their wishes in all matters relating to the liquidation.

[15.199]

4.14 Attendance at meetings of company's personnel

(1) This Rule applies to meetings of creditors and to meetings of contributories.

(2) Whenever a meeting is summoned, the liquidator may, if he thinks fit, give at least 21 days' notice to any one or more of the company's personnel that he is or they are required to be present at the meeting or be in attendance.

(3) In this Rule, "the company's personnel" means the persons referred to in paragraphs (a) to (d) of section 253(3) (present and past officers, employees, etc).

(4) The liquidator may authorise payment to any person whose attendance is requested at a meeting under this Rule of his reasonable expenses incurred in travelling to the meeting and any payment so authorised shall be an expense of the liquidation.

(5) In the case of any meeting, any of the company's personnel may, if he has given reasonable notice of his wish to be present, be admitted to take part; but this is at the discretion of the chairman of the meeting, whose decision as to what (if any) intervention may be made by any of them is final.

(6) If it is desired to put questions to any of the company's personnel who are not present, the meeting may be adjourned with a view to obtaining his attendance.

(7) Where one of the company's personnel is present at a meeting, only such questions may be put to him as the chairman may in his discretion allow.

CHAPTER 5 CLAIMS IN LIQUIDATION

[15.200]

4.15 Submission of claims

(1) A creditor, in order to obtain an adjudication as to his entitlement—

(a) to vote at any meeting of the creditors in the liquidation; or

(b) to a dividend (so far as funds are available) out of the assets of the company in respect of any accounting period,

shall submit his claim to the liquidator—

(a) at or before the meeting; or, as the case may be,

(b) not later than 8 weeks before the end of the accounting period.

(2) A creditor shall submit his claim by producing to the liquidator—

(a) a statement of claim in the form required by Rule 7.30 and Schedule 5; and

(b) an account or voucher (according to the nature of the debt claimed) which constitutes *prima facie* evidence of the debt,

but the liquidator may dispense with any requirement of this paragraph in respect of any debt or any class of debt.

(3) A claim submitted by a creditor, which has been accepted in whole or in part by the liquidator for the purpose of voting at a meeting or of drawing a dividend in respect of any accounting period, shall be deemed to have been resubmitted for the purpose of obtaining an adjudication as to his entitlement both to vote at any subsequent meeting and (so far as funds are available) to a dividend in respect of an accounting period or, as the case may be, any subsequent accounting period.

(4) A creditor, who has submitted a claim, may at any time submit a further claim specifying a different amount for his claim—

Provided that a secured creditor shall not be entitled to produce a further claim specifying a different value for the security at any time after the liquidator has required the creditor to discharge, or convey or assign, the security under [Rule 4.16G(2)].

[(5) Votes are calculated according to the amount of—

(a) a creditor's debt as at the date of the commencement of the winding up within the meaning of section 129, deducting any amount paid in respect of that debt after that date; or

(b) in relation to a member State liquidator, the debt claimed to be due to creditors in proceedings in relation to which he holds office.]

[(5A) No vote shall be cast by virtue of a debt more than once on any resolution put to the meeting.

(5B) Where a creditor—

(a) is entitled to vote under this Rule (as read with Rule 7.9);

(b) has lodged his claim in one or more sets of other proceedings; and

(c) votes (either in person or by proxy) on a resolution put to the meeting,

only the creditor's vote shall be counted.

(5C) Where—

(a) a creditor has lodged his claim in more than one set of other proceedings; and

(b) more than one member State liquidator seeks to vote by virtue of that claim,

the entitlement to vote by virtue of that claim is exercisable by the member State liquidator in main proceedings, whether or not the creditor has lodged his claim in the main proceedings.

(5D) For the purposes of paragraphs (5B) and (5C), "other proceedings" means main proceedings, secondary proceedings or territorial proceedings in another member State.]

[(6) In this Rule and in Rules 4.16 to 4.16G, any reference to the liquidator includes a reference to the chairman of the meeting (construed in accordance with Rule 7.5).]

NOTES

Para (4): words in square brackets substituted for original words "paragraph 5(2) of Schedule 1 to the Bankruptcy Act, as applied by the following Rule", by the Insolvency (Scotland) Amendment Rules 2014, SSI 2014/114, rr 2, 7(a), subject to savings in r 29 thereof as noted to r 0.2 at **[15.2]**.

Para (5): substituted by the Insolvency (Scotland) Regulations 2003, SI 2003/2109, regs 23, 27(1)(a), subject to the saving that anything done under or for the purposes of any provision of these Rules before 8 September 2003 has effect as if done under or for the purposes of the provision as amended.

Paras (5A)–(5D): inserted by SI 2003/2109, regs 23, 27(1)(b), subject to the saving noted to para (5) above.

Para (6): substituted by SSI 2014/114, rr 2, 7(b), subject to savings in r 29 thereof as noted to r 0.2 at **[15.2]**, and previously read as follows—

"(6) In this Rule and in Rule 4.16, including the provisions of the Bankruptcy Act applied by that Rule, any reference to the liquidator includes a reference to the chairman of the meeting.".

See Sch 5, Form 4.7 (Scot) at **[15.349]**, and the notes to that Schedule.

[15.201]
[4.16 False claims or evidence

(1) If a creditor produces under Rule 4.15 a statement of claim, account, voucher or other evidence which is false—

(a) the creditor shall be guilty of an offence unless the creditor shows that the creditor neither knew nor had reason to believe that the statement of claim, account, voucher or other evidence was false;

(b) the company shall be guilty of an offence if the company—

(i) knew or became aware that the statement of claim, account, voucher or other evidence was false; and

(ii) failed as soon as practicable after acquiring such knowledge to report it to the liquidator.

(2) A person convicted of an offence under paragraph (1) shall be liable—

(a) on summary conviction—

(i) to a fine not exceeding the statutory maximum;

(ii) to imprisonment for a term not exceeding three months or, if the person has previously been convicted of an offence inferring dishonest appropriation of property or an attempt at such appropriation, to imprisonment for a term not exceeding six months; or

(iii) to both such a fine and such imprisonment; or

(b) on conviction on indictment to a fine or to imprisonment for a term not exceeding two years or to both.]

NOTES

Commencement: 30 May 2014.

Substituted, together with rr 4.16A–4.16G for original r 4.16, by the Insolvency (Scotland) Amendment Rules 2014, SSI 2014/114, rr 2, 8, subject to savings in r 29 thereof as noted to r 0.2 at **[15.2]**. This rule (and the notes relating to it) previously read as follows—

"4.16 Application of the Bankruptcy Act

(1) Subject to the provisions in this Chapter, the following provisions of the Bankruptcy Act shall apply in relation to a liquidation of a company in like manner as they apply in a sequestration of a debtor's estate, subject to the modifications specified in [paragraphs (2) and (3)] and to any other necessary modifications—

(a) section 22(5) and (10) (criminal offence in relation to producing false claims or evidence);

(b) section 48(5), (6) and (8), together with sections 44(2) and (3) and 47(1) as applied by those sections (further evidence in relation to claims);

(c) section 49 (adjudication of claim);
(d) section 50 (entitlement to vote and draw dividend);
(e) section 60 (liabilities and rights of co-obligants); and
(f) Schedule 1 except paragraphs 2, 4 and 6 (determination of amount of creditor's claim).

(2) [Subject to paragraph (3) below,] for any reference in the provisions of the Bankruptcy Act, as applied by these rules, to any expression in column 1 below, there shall be substituted a reference to the expression in column 2 opposite thereto—

Column 1	*Column 2*
Interim trustee	Liquidator
Permanent trustee	Liquidator
Sequestration	Liquidation
Date of sequestration	Date of commencement of winding up within the meaning of section 129
Debtor	[The company or, in the application of section 49(6) of the Bankruptcy Act, any member or contributory of the company]
[Debtor's estate]	Company's assets
Accountant in Bankruptcy	The court
Commissioners	Liquidation committee
Sheriff	The court
Preferred debts	Preferential debts within the meaning of section 386

[(3) Where the winding up was immediately preceded by an administration, the references to the date of sequestration in paragraph 1(1) of Schedule 1 to the Bankruptcy Act and the second reference to that date in paragraph 1(2) shall be construed as references to the date on which the company entered administration.]

NOTES

Para (1): words in square brackets substituted for original words "paragraph (2)" by the Insolvency (Scotland) Rules 1986 Amendment Rules 2008, SSI 2008/393, rr 2, 3(a), 7(1), except where a company commenced liquidation before 20 December 2008.

Para (2): words in first pair of square brackets inserted by SSI 2008/393, rr 2, 3(b), 7(1), except where a company commenced liquidation before 20 December 2008; in the table words in square brackets substituted by the Insolvency (Scotland) Amendment Rules 1987, SI 1987/1921, r 3(1), Schedule, Pt I, para 15.

Para (3): added by SSI 2008/393, rr 2, 3(c), 7(1), except where a company commenced liquidation before 20 December 2008.

Modification: see the Financial Collateral Arrangements (No 2) Regulations 2003, SI 2003/3226, reg 15 at **[3.295]**.".

[15.202]

[4.16A Evidence of Claims

(1) The liquidator, for the purpose of being satisfied as to the validity or amount of a claim submitted by a creditor under Rule 4.15, may require—

(a) the creditor to produce further evidence; or
(b) any other person who the liquidator believes can produce relevant evidence, to produce such evidence,

and, if the creditor or other person refuses or delays to do so, the liquidator may apply to the court for an order requiring the creditor or other person to attend for private examination before the court.

(2) Subject to paragraph (3), on an application to it under paragraph (1) above the court may make an order requiring the creditor or other person to attend for private examination before it on a date (being not earlier than 8 days nor later than 16 days after the date of the order) and at a time specified in the order.

(3) If a creditor or other person is for any good reason prevented from attending for examination, the court may grant a commission to take the examination (the commissioner being in this Rule as an "examining commissioner").

(4) At any private examination under paragraph (2), a solicitor or counsel may act on behalf of the liquidator, or the liquidator may appear.

(5) The examination, whether before the court or an examining commissioner, shall be taken on oath.

(6) A person who fails without reasonable excuse to comply with an order made under paragraph (2) above shall be guilty of an offence and liable on summary conviction to a fine not exceeding level 5 on the standard scale or to imprisonment for a term not exceeding three months or to both.

(7) References in this Rule to a creditor in a case where the creditor is one of the following entities—

(a) a trust;
(b) a partnership (including a dissolved partnership);
(c) a body corporate or an unincorporated body;
(d) a limited partnership (including a dissolved partnership) within the meaning of the Limited Partnerships Act 1907,

shall be construed, unless the context otherwise requires, as references to a person representing the entity.]

NOTES

Commencement: 30 May 2014.
Substituted as noted to r 4.16 at **[15.201]**.

[15.203]

[4.16B Adjudication of claims

(1) At the commencement of every meeting of creditors, the liquidator shall, for the purposes of Rule 4.15 so far as it relates to voting at that meeting, accept or reject the claim of each creditor.

(2) Where funds are available for payment of a dividend out of the company's assets in respect of an accounting period, the liquidator for the purpose of determining who is entitled to such a dividend shall—

(a) not later than 4 weeks before the end of the period, accept or reject every claim submitted or deemed to have been re-submitted under Rule 4.15; and

(b) at the same time make a decision on any matter requiring to be specified under paragraph (5)(a) or (b) below.

(3) On accepting or rejecting, under paragraph (2) above, every claim submitted or deemed to have been re-submitted, the liquidator shall, as soon as is reasonably practicable, send a list of every claim so accepted or rejected (including the amount of each claim and whether it has been accepted or rejected) to every creditor known to the liquidator.

(4) Where the liquidator rejects a claim, the liquidator shall without delay notify the creditor giving reasons for the rejection.

(5) Where the liquidator accepts or rejects a claim, the liquidator shall record in the sederunt book the decision on the claim specifying—

(a) the amount of the claim accepted;

(b) the category of debt, and the value of any security, as decided by the liquidator; and

(c) if rejecting the claim, the reasons therefor.

(6) Any member or contributory of the company or any creditor may, if dissatisfied with the acceptance or rejection of any claim (or, in relation to such acceptance or rejection, with a decision in respect of any matter requiring to be specified under paragraph (5)(a) or (b) above), appeal therefrom to the court—

(a) if the acceptance or rejection is under paragraph (1) above, within 2 weeks of that acceptance or rejection;

(b) if the acceptance or rejection is under paragraph (2) above, not later than 2 weeks before the end of the accounting period,

and the liquidator shall record the court's decision in the sederunt book.

(7) Any reference in this Rule to the acceptance or rejection of a claim shall be construed as a reference to the acceptance or rejection of the claim in whole or in part.]

NOTES

Commencement: 30 May 2014.

Substituted as noted to r 4.16 at **[15.201]**.

[15.204]

[4.16C Entitlement to vote and draw a dividend

(1) A creditor who has had that creditor's claim accepted in whole or in part by the liquidator or on appeal under Rule 4.16B(6) shall be entitled—

(a) in a case where the acceptance is under (or on appeal arising from) Rule 4.16B(1), to vote on any matter at the meeting of creditors for the purpose of voting at which the claim is accepted; and

(b) in a case where the acceptance is under (or on appeal arising from) Rule 4.16B(2), to payment out of the company's assets of a dividend in respect of the accounting period for the purposes of which the claim is accepted; but such entitlement to payment shall arise only in so far as the company has funds available to make that payment, having regard to Rule 4.66.

(2) No vote shall be cast by virtue of a debt more than once on any resolution put to a meeting of creditors.

(3) Where a creditor—

(a) is entitled to vote under this Rule;

(b) has lodged the creditor's claim in one or more sets of other proceedings; and

(c) votes (either in person or by proxy) on a resolution put to the meeting,

only the creditor's vote shall be counted.

(4) Where—

(a) a creditor has lodged the creditor's claim in more than one set of other proceedings; and

(b) more than one member State liquidator seeks to vote by virtue of that claim,

the entitlement to vote by virtue of that claim is exercisable by the member State liquidator in main proceedings, whether or not the creditor has lodged the claim in the main proceedings.

(5) For the purposes of paragraphs (3) and (4) above, "other proceedings" means main proceedings, secondary proceedings or territorial proceedings in a member State other than the United Kingdom.]

NOTES

Commencement: 30 May 2014.

Substituted as noted to r 4.16 at **[15.201]**.

[15.205]
[4.16D Liabilities and rights of co-obligants

(1) Where a creditor has an obligant (the "co-obligant") bound to the creditor along with the company for the whole or part of the debt, the co-obligant is not freed or discharged from liability for the debt by reason of the dissolution of the company or the creditor's voting or drawing a dividend or assenting to or not opposing—

(a) the dissolution of the company; or
(b) any composition.

(2) Where—

(a) a creditor has had a claim accepted in whole or in part; and
(b) a co-obligant holds a security over any part of the company's assets,

the co-obligant shall account to the liquidator so as to put the estate in the same position as if the co-obligant had paid the debt to the creditor and thereafter had had the co-obligant's claim accepted in whole or in part in the liquidation after deduction of the value of the security.

(3) Without prejudice to any right under any rule of law of a co-obligant who has paid the debt, the co-obligant may require and obtain at the co-obligant's own expense from the creditor an assignation of the debt on payment of the amount thereof, and thereafter may in respect of that debt submit a claim, and vote and draw a dividend, if otherwise legally entitled to do so.

(4) In this Rule a "co-obligant" includes a cautioner.]

NOTES

Commencement: 30 May 2014.
Substituted as noted to r 4.16 at **[15.201]**.

[15.206]
[4.16E Amount which may be claimed generally

(1) Subject to the provisions of this Rule and Rules 4.16F and 4.16G, the amount in respect of which a creditor shall be entitled to claim shall be the accumulated sum of principal and any interest which is due on the debt as at the date of commencement of winding up.

(2) If a debt does not depend on a contingency but would not be payable but for the liquidation until after the date of commencement of winding up, the amount of the claim shall be calculated as if the debt were payable on the date of commencement of winding up but subject to the deduction of interest at the rate specified in paragraph (4) from that date until the date for payment of the debt.

(3) In calculating the amount of a creditor's claim, the creditor shall deduct any discount (other than any discount for payment in cash) which is allowable by contract or course of dealing between the creditor and the company or by the usage of trade.

(4) The rate of interest referred to in paragraph (2) shall be whichever is the greater of—

(a) the prescribed rate at the date of commencement of winding up; and
(b) the rate applicable to that debt apart from the liquidation.

(5) Subject to paragraph (6), in this Rule, "date of commencement of winding up" means the date on which the winding up is deemed to commence by virtue of section 129.

(6) Where the winding up was immediately preceded by an administration, the reference to the date of commencement of winding up in paragraph (1) and the second reference to that date in paragraph (2) shall be construed as references to the date on which the company entered administration.]

NOTES

Commencement: 30 May 2014.
Substituted as noted to r 4.16 at **[15.201]**.

[15.207]
[4.16F Debts depending on contingency

(1) Subject to paragraph (2) below, the amount which a creditor shall be entitled to claim shall not include a debt in so far as its existence or amount depends upon a contingency.

(2) On an application by the creditor—

(a) to the liquidator; or
(b) if there is no liquidator, to the court,

the liquidator or court shall put a value on the debt in so far as it is contingent, and the amount in respect of which the creditor shall then be entitled to claim shall be that value but no more; and, where the contingent debt is an annuity, a cautioner may not then be sued for more than that value.

(3) Any interested person may appeal to the court against a valuation under sub-paragraph (2) above by the liquidator, and the court may affirm or vary that valuation.]

NOTES

Commencement: 30 May 2014.
Substituted as noted to r 4.16 at **[15.201]**.

[15.208]
[4.16G Secured debts

(1) In calculating the amount of a secured creditor's claim—

(a) the secured creditor is to deduct the value of any security as estimated by the secured creditor;

(b) but if the secured creditor surrenders, or undertakes in writing to surrender, a security for the benefit of the company's assets, the secured creditor is not required to deduct the value of that security.

(2) The liquidator may, at any time after the expiry of 12 weeks from the date of commencement of winding up within the meaning of section 129, require a secured creditor at the expense of the company's assets to discharge the security or convey or assign it to the liquidator on payment to the creditor of the value specified by the creditor; and the amount in respect of which the creditor shall then be entitled to claim shall be any balance of the creditor's debt remaining after receipt of such payment.

(3) In calculating the amount of the claim of a creditor whose security has been realised the creditor shall deduct the amount (less the expenses of realisation) which the creditor has received, or is entitled to receive, from the realisation.]

NOTES

Commencement: 30 May 2014.

Substituted as noted to r 4.16 at **[15.201]**.

[15.209]

4.17 Claims in foreign currency

(1) A creditor may state the amount of his claim in a currency other than sterling where—

(a) his claim is constituted by decree or other order made by a court ordering the company to pay to the creditor a sum expressed in a currency other than sterling, or

(b) where it is not so constituted, his claim arises from a contract or bill of exchange in terms of which payment is or may be required to be made by the company to the creditor in a currency other than sterling.

(2) Where a claim is stated in currency other than sterling for the purpose of the preceding paragraph, it shall be converted into sterling at the rate of exchange for that other currency at the mean of the buying and selling spot rates prevailing in the London market at the close of business on the date of commencement of winding up [or, if the liquidation was immediately preceded by an administration, on the date on which the company entered administration].

NOTES

Para (2): words in square brackets added by the Insolvency (Scotland) Rules 1986 Amendment Rules 2008, SSI 2008/393, rr 2, 4, 7(1), except where a company commenced liquidation before 20 December 2008.

Modification: see the Financial Collateral Arrangements (No 2) Regulations 2003, SI 2003/3226, reg 15 at **[3.295]**.

CHAPTER 6 THE LIQUIDATOR

SECTION A: APPOINTMENT AND FUNCTIONS OF LIQUIDATOR

[15.210]

4.18 Appointment of liquidator by the court

(1) This Rule applies where a liquidator is appointed by the court under section 138(1) (appointment of interim liquidator), 138(5) (no person appointed or nominated by the meetings of creditors and contributories), 139(4) (different persons nominated by creditors and contributories) or 140(1) or (2) (liquidation following administration or voluntary arrangement).

(2) The court shall not make the appointment unless and until there is lodged in court a statement to the effect that the person to be appointed is an insolvency practitioner, duly qualified under the Act to be the liquidator, and that he consents so to act.

(3) Thereafter the courts shall send a copy of the order to the liquidator, whose appointment takes effect from the date of the order.

(4) The liquidator shall—

(a) within 7 days of his appointment, give notice of it to [the Accountant in Bankruptcy]; and

(b) within 28 days of his appointment, give notice of it to the creditors and contributories or, if the court so permits, he shall advertise his appointment in accordance with the directions of the court.

(5) In any notice or advertisement to be given by him under this Rule, the liquidator shall [state whether a liquidation committee has been established by a meeting of creditors or contributories, and, if this is not the case, he shall]—

(a) state whether he intends to summon meetings of creditors and contributories for the purpose of establishing a liquidation committee or whether he proposes to summon only a meeting of creditors for that purpose; and

(b) if he does not propose to summon any meeting, set out the powers of the creditors under section 142(3) to require him to summon such a meeting.

NOTES

Para (4): in sub-para (a) words in square brackets substituted by the Scotland Act 1998 (Consequential Modifications) (No 2) Order 1999, SI 1999/1820, art 4, Sch 2, Pt II, para 141(1), (7).

Para (5): words in square brackets inserted by the Insolvency (Scotland) Amendment Rules 1987, SI 1987/1921, r 3(1), Schedule, Pt I, para 16.

See Sch 5, Form 4.9 (Scot) at **[15.349]**, and the notes to that Schedule.

[15.211]
4.19 Appointment by creditors or contributories

(1) This Rule applies where a person is nominated for appointment as liquidator under section 139(2) either by a meeting of creditors or by a meeting of contributories.

(2) Subject to section 139(4) the interim liquidator, as chairman of the meeting, or, where the interim liquidator is nominated as liquidator, the chairman of the meeting, shall certify the appointment of a person as liquidator by the meeting but not until and unless the person to be appointed has provided him with a written statement to the effect that he is an insolvency practitioner, duly qualified under the Act to be the liquidator and that he consents so to act.

(3) The appointment of the liquidator [takes effect upon the passing of the resolution for his appointment] and [the date of his appointment] shall be stated in the certificate.

(4) The liquidator shall—

(a) within 7 days of his appointment, give notice of his appointment to the court and to [the Accountant in Bankruptcy]; and

(b) within 28 days of his appointment, give notice of it in a newspaper circulating in the area where the company has its principal place of business, or in such newspaper as he thinks most appropriate for ensuring that it comes to the notice of the company's creditors and contributories.

(5) The provisions of Rule 4.18(5) shall apply to any notice given by the liquidator under this Rule.

(6) Paragraphs (4) and (5) need not be complied with in the case of a liquidator appointed by [a meeting of contributories] and replaced by another liquidator appointed on the same day by a creditors' meeting.

NOTES

Paras (3), (6): words in square brackets substituted by the Insolvency (Scotland) Amendment Rules 1987, SI 1987/1921, r 3(1), Schedule, Pt I, para 17.

Para (4): words in square brackets substituted by the Scotland Act 1998 (Consequential Modifications) (No 2) Order 1999, SI 1999/1820, art 4, Sch 2, Pt II, para 141(1), (8).

Para (2): see Sch 5, Form 4.8 (Scot) at **[15.349]**, and the notes to that Schedule.

Para (4): see Sch 5, Form 4.9 (Scot) at **[15.349]**, and the notes to that Schedule.

[15.212]
4.20 Authentication of liquidator's appointment

A copy certified by the clerk of the court of any order of court appointing the liquidator or, as the case may be, a copy, certified by the chairman of the meeting which appointed the liquidator, of the certificate of the liquidator's appointment under Rule 4.19(2), shall be sufficient evidence for all purposes and in any proceedings that he has been appointed to exercise the powers and perform the duties of liquidator in the winding up of the company.

[15.213]
4.21 Hand-over of assets to liquidator

(1) This Rule applies where a person appointed as liquidator ("the succeeding liquidator") succeeds a previous liquidator ("the former liquidator") as the liquidator.

(2) When the succeeding liquidator's appointment takes effect, the former liquidator shall forthwith do all that is required for putting the succeeding liquidator into possession of the assets.

(3) The former liquidator shall give to the succeeding liquidator all such information, relating to the affairs of the company and the course of the winding up, as the succeeding liquidator considers to be reasonably required for the effective discharge by him of his duties as such and shall hand over all books, accounts, statements of affairs, statements of claim and other records and documents in his possession relating to the affairs of the company and its winding up.

[15.214]
[4.22 Taking possession and realisation of the company's assets

(1) The liquidator shall—

(a) as soon as may be after his appointment take possession of the whole assets of the company and any property, books, papers or records in the possession or control of the company or to which the company appears to be entitled; and

(b) make up and maintain an inventory and valuation of the assets which he shall retain in the sederunt book.

(2) The liquidator shall be entitled to have access to all documents or records relating to the assets or the property or the business or financial affairs of the company sent by or on behalf of the company to a third party and in that third party's hands and to make copies of any such documents or records.

(3) If any person obstructs a liquidator who is exercising, or attempting to exercise, a power conferred by subsection (2) above, the court, on the application of the liquidator, may order that person to cease so to obstruct the liquidator.

(4) The liquidator may require delivery to him of any title deed or other document or record of the company, notwithstanding that a right of lien is claimed over the title deed or document or record, but this paragraph is without prejudice to any preference of the holder of the lien.

(5) . . .]

NOTES

Substituted by the Insolvency (Scotland) Amendment Rules 1987, SI 1987/1921, r 3(1), Schedule, Pt I, para 18.

Para (5): revoked by the Insolvency (Scotland) Amendment Rules 2014, SSI 2014/114, rr 2, 9, subject to savings in r 29 thereof as noted to r 0.2 at **[15.2]** and previously read as follows—

"(5) Section 39(4) and (7) of the Bankruptcy Act shall apply in relation to a liquidation of a company as it applies in relation to a sequestration of a debtor's estate, subject to the modifications specified in Rule 4.16(2) and to any other necessary modifications.".

[15.215]
[4.22A Realisation of the company's heritable property

(1) In the case of the sale of any part of the company's heritable property over which a heritable security is held by a creditor or creditors if the rights of the secured creditor or creditors are preferable to those of the liquidator—

(a) the liquidator may sell that part only with the concurrence of every such creditor unless the liquidator obtains a sufficiently high price to discharge every such security;

(b) subject to sub-paragraph (c) below, the following acts shall be precluded—

(i) the taking of steps by a creditor to enforce the creditor's security over that part after the liquidator has intimated to the creditor an intention to sell it;

(ii) the commencement by the liquidator of the procedure for the sale of that part after a creditor has intimated to the liquidator that the creditor intends to commence the procedure for its sale;

(c) where the liquidator or a creditor has given intimation under paragraph (b) above, but has unduly delayed in proceeding with the sale, then, if authorised by the court in the case of intimation under—

(i) sub-paragraph (b)(i), any creditor to whom intimation has been given may enforce the creditor's security; or

(ii) sub-paragraph (b)(ii), the liquidator may sell that part.

(2) The validity of the title of any purchaser shall not be challengeable on the ground that there has been a failure to comply with a requirement of this Rule.]

NOTES

Commencement: 30 May 2014.

Inserted by the Insolvency (Scotland) Amendment Rules 2014, SSI 2014/114, rr 2, 10(1), subject to savings in r 29 thereof as noted to r 0.2 at **[15.2]**.

SECTION B: REMOVAL AND RESIGNATION; VACATION OF OFFICE

[15.216]
4.23 Summoning of meeting for removal of liquidator

(1) Subject to section 172(3) and without prejudice to any other method of summoning the meeting, a meeting of creditors for the removal of the liquidator in accordance with section 172(2) shall be summoned by the liquidator if requested to do so by not less than one quarter in value of the creditors.

(2) Where a meeting of creditors is summoned especially for the purpose of removing the liquidator in accordance with section 172(2), the notice summoning it shall draw attention to section 174(4)(a) or (b) with respect to the liquidator's release.

(3) At the meeting, a person other than the liquidator or his nominee may be elected to act as chairman; but if the liquidator or his nominee is chairman and a resolution has been proposed for the liquidator's removal, the chairman shall not adjourn the meeting without the consent of at least one-half (in value) of the creditors present (in person or by proxy) and entitled to vote.

(4) Where a meeting is to be held or is proposed to be summoned under this Rule, the court may, on the application of any creditor, give directions as to the mode of summoning it, the sending out and return of forms of proxy, the conduct of the meeting, and any other matter which appears to the court to require regulation or control under this Rule.

[15.217]
4.24 Procedure on liquidator's removal

(1) Where the creditors have resolved that the liquidator be removed, the chairman of the creditors' meeting shall forthwith—

(a) if, at the meeting, another liquidator was not appointed, send a certificate of the liquidator's removal to the court and [a copy of the certificate] to [the Accountant in Bankruptcy], and

(b) otherwise, deliver the certificate to the new liquidator, who shall forthwith send [a copy of the certificate] to the court and to [the Accountant in Bankruptcy].

(2) The liquidator's removal is effective as from such date as the meeting of the creditors shall determine, and this shall be stated in the certificate of removal.

NOTES

Para (1): words in first pair of square brackets inserted and words in third pair of square brackets substituted by the Insolvency (Scotland) Amendment Rules 1987, SI 1987/1921, r 3(1), Schedule, Pt I, para 19; words in second and final pairs of square brackets substituted by the Scotland Act 1998 (Consequential Modifications) (No 2) Order 1999, SI 1999/1820, art 4, Sch 2, Pt II, para 141(1), (9).

Para (1): see Sch 5, Form 4.10 (Scot) at **[15.349]**, and the notes to that Schedule.

[15.218]
4.25 Release of liquidator on removal

(1) Where the liquidator has been removed by a creditors' meeting which has not resolved against his release, the date on which he has his release in terms of section 174(4)(a) shall be stated in the certificate of removal before a copy of it is sent to the court and to [the Accountant in Bankruptcy] under Rule 4.24(1).

(2) Where the liquidator is removed by a creditors' meeting which has resolved against his release, or is removed by the court, he must apply to the Accountant of Court for his release.

(3) When the Accountant of Court releases the former liquidator, he shall—
- (a) issue a certificate of release to the new liquidator who shall send a copy of it to the court and to [the Accountant in Bankruptcy], and
- (b) send a copy of the certificate to the former liquidator,

and in this case release of the former liquidator is effective from the date of the certificate.

NOTES

Paras (1), (3): words in square brackets substituted by the Scotland Act 1998 (Consequential Modifications) (No 2) Order 1999, SI 1999/1820, art 4, Sch 2, Pt II, para 141(1), (10).

Para (2): see Sch 5, Form 4.12 (Scot) at **[15.349]**, and the notes to that Schedule.

Para (3): see Sch 5, Forms 4.13 (Scot), 4.14 (Scot) at **[15.349]**, and the notes to that Schedule.

[15.219]
4.26 Removal of liquidator by the court

(1) This Rule applies where application is made to the court for the removal of the liquidator, or for an order directing the liquidator to summon a meeting of creditors for the purpose of removing him.

(2) The court may require the applicant to make a deposit or give caution for the expenses to be incurred by the liquidator on the application.

(3) The applicant shall, at least 14 days before the hearing, send to the liquidator a notice stating its date, time and place and accompanied by a copy of the application, and of any evidence which he intends to adduce in support of it.

(4) Subject to any contrary order of the court, the expenses of the application are not payable as an expense of the liquidation.

(5) Where the court removes the liquidator—
- (a) it shall send two copies of the order of removal to him;
- (b) the order may include such provision as the court thinks fit with respect to matters arising in connection with the removal; and
- (c) if the court appoints a new liquidator, Rule 4.18 applies,

and the liquidator, on receipt of the two court orders under sub-paragraph (a), shall send one copy of the order to [the Accountant in Bankruptcy], together with a notice of his ceasing to act as a liquidator.

NOTES

Para (5): words in square brackets substituted by the Scotland Act 1998 (Consequential Modifications) (No 2) Order 1999, SI 1999/1820, art 4, Sch 2, Pt II, para 141(1), (11).

Para (5): see Sch 5, Form 4.11 (Scot) at **[15.349]**, and the notes to that Schedule.

[15.220]
[4.26A Power to make a block transfer of cases

(1) This Rule applies where a person appointed as a liquidator ("the outgoing liquidator")—
- (a) dies;
- (b) retires from practice; or
- (c) is otherwise unable or unwilling to continue in office,

and it is expedient to transfer some or all of the cases in which the outgoing liquidator holds office to one or more liquidators ("the replacement liquidator") in a single transaction.

(2) In a case to which this Rule applies the Court of Session may make an order ("a block transfer order") appointing a replacement liquidator in the place of the outgoing liquidator.

(3) The replacement liquidator must be qualified to act as an insolvency practitioner.]

NOTES

Commencement: 30 May 2014.

Inserted, together with rr 4.26B, 4.26C, by the Insolvency (Scotland) Amendment Rules 2014, SSI 2014/114, rr 2, 11(1), subject to savings in r 29 thereof as noted to r 0.2 at **[15.2]**.

[15.221]
[4.26B Application for block transfer order

(1) A single application may be made to the Court of Session for a block transfer order seeking—
- (a) the removal of the outgoing liquidator by the exercise of any of the powers in—
  - (i) section 172(2) and Rule 4.26A(2); and
  - (ii) section 108(2);

(b) the appointment of a replacement liquidator by the exercise of any of the powers in—
(i) Rule 4.26A(2); and
(ii) section 108(2);
(c) such other order or direction as may be necessary or expedient in connection with the matters referred to in sub-paragraphs (a) and (b).

(2) An application may be made by—
(a) the outgoing liquidator;
(b) any person who holds the office of liquidator jointly with the outgoing liquidator;
(c) any person who is proposed to be appointed as the replacement liquidator; or
(d) the recognised professional body by which the outgoing liquidator is or was authorised.

(3) The application must include—
(a) evidence of the circumstances which gave rise to it being expedient to appoint a replacement liquidator;
(b) a statement that the replacement liquidator is an insolvency practitioner duly qualified under the Act to be a replacement liquidator and consents to act as replacement liquidator; and
(c) the name of each case, the case number (if any) and, where relevant, the name of the sheriff court which has jurisdiction for each case.

(4) The application must be served on—
(a) the outgoing liquidator (if not the applicant or deceased);
(b) every person who holds office jointly with the outgoing liquidator; and
(c) any person the Court of Session directs.]

NOTES

Commencement: 30 May 2014.
Inserted as noted to r 4.26A at **[15.220]**.

[15.222]
[4.26C Action following application for a block transfer order

(1) In determining to what extent (if any) the costs of making an application under Rule 4.26B should be paid as an expense of the case to which the application relates, the Court of Session must take into account—
(a) the reasons for making the application;
(b) the number of cases to which the application relates;
(c) the value of the assets comprised in those cases;
(d) the nature and extent of costs involved.

(2) Where an appointment under Rule 4.26A(2) is made—
(a) the replacement liquidator must—
(i) as soon as reasonably practicable give notice of the appointment to the Accountant in Bankruptcy;
(ii) within 28 days give notice of the appointment to the creditors and contributories, or if the court so permits, advertise the appointment in accordance with the directions of the court; and
(iii) give notice to such other persons, and in such form, as the Court of Session may direct; and
(b) Rule 4.26(5)(c) does not apply.

(3) In any notice given by the replacement liquidator under this Rule the replacement liquidator must state—
(a) that the outgoing liquidator has been removed; and
(b) whether the outgoing liquidator has been released.]

NOTES

Commencement: 30 May 2014.
Inserted as noted to r 4.26A at **[15.220]**.

[15.223]
4.27 Advertisement of removal

Where a new liquidator is appointed in place of the one removed, Rules 4.19 to 4.21 shall apply to the appointment of the new liquidator except that the notice to be given by the new liquidator under Rule 4.19(4) shall also state—
(a) that his predecessor as liquidator has been removed; and
(b) whether his predecessor has been released.

NOTES

See Sch 5, Form 4.9 (Scot) at **[15.349]**, and the notes to that Schedule.

[15.224]
4.28 Resignation of liquidator

(1) Before resigning his office under section 172(6) the liquidator shall call a meeting of creditors for the purpose of receiving his resignation.

(2) The notice summoning the meeting shall draw attention to section 174(4)(c) and Rule 4.29(4) with respect of the liquidator's release and shall also be accompanied by an account of the liquidator's administration of the winding up, including a summary of his receipts and payments [and a statement as to the amount paid to unsecured creditors by virtue of the application of section 176A (prescribed part)].

(3) Subject to paragraph (4), the liquidator may only proceed under this Rule on the grounds of ill health or because—

(a) he intends ceasing to be in practice as an insolvency practitioner; or

(b) there has been some conflict of interest or change of personal circumstances which precludes or makes impracticable the further discharge by him of the duties of the liquidator.

(4) Where two or more persons are acting as liquidator jointly, any one of them may resign (without prejudice to the continuation in office of the other or others) on the ground that, in his opinion and that of the other or others, it is no longer expedient that there should continue to be the present number of joint liquidators.

NOTES

Para (2): words in square brackets inserted by the Enterprise Act 2002 (Consequential Amendments) (Prescribed Part) (Scotland) Order 2003, SI 2003/2108, art 6(2).

[15.225]

4.29 Action following acceptance of liquidator's resignation

(1) This Rule applies where a meeting is summoned to receive the liquidator's resignation.

(2) If the liquidator's resignation is accepted, it is effective as from such date as the meeting of the creditors may determine and that date shall be stated in the notice given by the liquidator under paragraph (3).

(3) The liquidator, whose resignation is accepted, shall forthwith after the meeting give notice of his resignation to the court as required by section 172(6) and shall send a copy of it to [the Accountant in Bankruptcy].

(4) The meeting of the creditors may grant the liquidator his release from such date as they may determine. If the meeting resolves against the liquidator having his release, Rule 4.25(2) and (3) shall apply.

(5) Where the creditors have resolved to appoint a new liquidator in place of the one who has resigned, Rules 4.19 to 4.21 shall apply to the appointment of the new liquidator, except that the notice to be given by the new liquidator under Rule 4.19(4) shall also state that his predecessor as liquidator has resigned and whether he has been released.

[(6) If there is no quorum present at the meeting summoned to receive the liquidator's resignation, the meeting is deemed to have been held, a resolution is deemed to have been passed that the liquidator's resignation be accepted, and the creditors are deemed not to have resolved against the liquidator having his release.

(7) Where paragraph (6) applies—

(a) the liquidator's resignation is effective as from the date for which the meeting was summoned and that date shall be stated in the notice given by the liquidator under paragraph (3), and

(b) the liquidator is deemed to have been released as from that date.]

NOTES

Para (3): words in square brackets substituted by the Scotland Act 1998 (Consequential Modifications) (No 2) Order 1999, SI 1999/1820, art 4, Sch 2, Pt II, para 141(1), (12).

Paras (6), (7): added by the Insolvency (Scotland) Amendment Rules 1987, SI 1987/1921, r 3(1), Schedule, Pt I, para 20.

Para (3): see Sch 5, Form 4.15 (Scot), Form 4.16 (Scot) at **[15.349]**, and the notes to that Schedule.

[15.226]

4.30 Leave to resign granted by the court

(1) If at a creditors' meeting summoned to receive the liquidator's resignation, it is resolved that it be not accepted, the court may, on the liquidator's application, make an order giving him leave to resign.

(2) The court's order under this Rule may include such provision as it thinks fit with respect to matters arising in connection with the resignation including the notices to be given to the creditors and [the Accountant in Bankruptcy] and shall determine the date from which the liquidator's release is effective.

NOTES

Para (2): words in square brackets substituted by the Scotland Act 1998 (Consequential Modifications) (No 2) Order 1999, SI 1999/1820, art 4, Sch 2, Pt II, para 141(1), (13).

SECTION C: RELEASE ON COMPLETION OF WINDING UP

[15.227]

4.31 Final meeting

(1) The liquidator shall give at least 28 days' notice of the final meeting of creditors to be held under section 146. The notice shall be sent to all creditors whose claims in the liquidation have been accepted.

(2) The liquidator's report laid before the meeting shall contain an account of his administration of the winding up, including a summary of his receipts and payments [and a statement as to the amount paid to unsecured creditors by virtue of the application of section 176A (prescribed part)].

(3) At the final meeting, the creditors may question the liquidator with respect to any matter contained in his report, and may resolve against the liquidator having his release.

(4) The liquidator shall within 7 days of the meeting give notice to the court and to the registrar of companies [and the Accountant in Bankruptcy] under section 172(8) that the final meeting has been held and the notice shall state whether or not he has been released, and be accompanied by a copy of the report laid before the meeting.

(5) If there is no quorum present at the final meeting, the liquidator shall report to the court that a final meeting was summoned in accordance with the Rules, but that there was no quorum present; and the final meeting is then deemed to have been held and the creditors not to have resolved against the liquidator being released.

(6) If the creditors at the final meeting have not resolved against the liquidator having his release, he is released in terms of section 174(4)(d)(ii) when he vacates office under section 172(8). If they have so resolved he shall apply for his release to the Accountant of Court, and Rules 4.25(2) and (3) shall apply accordingly [subject to the modifications that in Rule 4.25(3) sub-paragraph (a) shall apply with the word "new" replaced by the word "former" and sub-paragraph (b) shall not apply].

NOTES

Para (2): words in square brackets inserted by the Enterprise Act 2002 (Consequential Amendments) (Prescribed Part) (Scotland) Order 2003, SI 2003/2108, art 6(3).

Para (4): words in square brackets inserted by the Scotland Act 1998 (Consequential Modifications) (No 2) Order 1999, SI 1999/1820, art 4, Sch 2, Pt II, para 141(1), (14).

Para (6): words in square brackets added by the Insolvency (Scotland) Amendment Rules 1987, SI 1987/1921, r 3(1), Schedule, Pt I, para 21.

Para (4): see Sch 5, Form 4.17 (Scot) at **[15.349]**, and the notes to that Schedule.

SECTION D: OUTLAYS AND REMUNERATION

[15.228]
[4.32 Determination of amount of outlays and remuneration

(1) Subject to the provision of Rules 4.33 to 4.35, claims by the liquidator for the outlays reasonably incurred and for the liquidator's remuneration shall be made in accordance with this Rule.

(2) Within 14 days after the end of an accounting period, the liquidator shall in respect of that period submit to the liquidation committee or, if there is no liquidation committee, to the court—

- (a) accounts of the liquidator's intromissions with the company's assets for audit and, where funds are available after making allowance for contingencies, a scheme of division of the divisible funds; and
- (b) a claim for the outlays reasonably incurred by the liquidator and for the liquidator's remuneration.

(3) Where the documents mentioned in paragraph (2) are submitted to the liquidation committee, the liquidator shall send a copy of them to the court.

(4) The liquidator may, at any time before the end of the accounting period, submit to the liquidation committee (if any) an interim claim in respect of that period for the outlays reasonably incurred by the liquidator and for the liquidator's remuneration and the liquidation committee may make an interim determination in relation to the amount of the outlays and remuneration payable to the liquidator and, where they do so, they shall take into account that interim determination when making their determination under paragraph (7)(a)(ii).

(5) Subject to paragraph (6) below, all accounts in respect of legal services incurred by the liquidator shall, before payment thereof, be submitted for taxation to the auditor of the court before which the liquidation is pending.

(6) Where—

- (a) any such account has been agreed between the liquidator and the person entitled to payment in respect of that account (in this paragraph referred to as "the payee");
- (b) the liquidator is not an associate of the payee; and
- (c) the liquidation committee or, if there is no liquidation committee, the court, have determined that the account need not be submitted for taxation,

the liquidator may pay such account without submitting it for taxation.

(7) Within 6 weeks after the end of an accounting period—

- (a) the liquidation committee or, as the case may be, the court—
  - (i) may audit the accounts; and
  - (ii) shall issue a determination fixing the amount of the outlays and the remuneration payable to the liquidator; and
- (b) the liquidator shall make the audited accounts, scheme of division and the said determination available for inspection by the creditors and the contributories.

(8) The basis of remuneration must be fixed—

- (a) as a percentage of the value of the company's assets which are realised by the liquidator;
- (b) by reference to the work which was reasonably undertaken by the liquidator and the liquidator's staff in attending to matters arising in the winding up; or

(c) as a set amount.

(9) The basis of remuneration may be fixed as any one or more of the bases set out in paragraph (8)(a) to (c), and different bases may be fixed in respect of different things done by the liquidator.

(10) In fixing the amount of such remuneration in respect of any accounting period, the liquidation committee or, as the case may be, the court may take into account any adjustment which the liquidation committee or the court may wish to make in the amount of the remuneration fixed in respect of any earlier accounting period.

(11) Not later than 14 days after the issue of the determination, the liquidator, any creditor or contributory may appeal against a determination issued under paragraph (4) or (7)(a)(ii) above, where it is a determination of the liquidation committee, to the court.

(12) An appeal may only be made against a determination issued under paragraph (7)(a) by a creditor or a contributory if notice is given to the liquidator of intention to appeal.]

NOTES

Commencement: 30 May 2014.

Substituted by the Insolvency (Scotland) Amendment Rules 2014, SSI 2014/114, rr 2, 12, subject to savings in r 29 thereof as noted to r 0.2 at **[15.2]**. This rule previously read as follows—

"**4.32 Determination of amount of outlays and remuneration**

(1) Subject to the provisions of Rules 4.33 to 4.35, claims by the liquidator for the outlays reasonably incurred by him and for his remuneration shall be made in accordance with section 53 of the Bankruptcy Act as applied by Rule 4.68 and as further modified by paragraphs (2) and (3) below.

(2) After section 53(1) of the Bankruptcy Act, there shall be inserted the following subsection—

"(1A) The liquidator may, at any time before the end of an accounting period, submit to the liquidation committee (if any) an interim claim in respect of that period for the outlays reasonably incurred by him and for his remuneration and the liquidation committee may make an interim determination in relation to the amount of the outlays and remuneration payable to the liquidator and, where they do so, they shall take into account that interim determination when making their determination under subsection (3)(a)(ii).".

(3) In section 53(6) of the Bankruptcy Act, for the reference to "subsection (3)(a)(ii)" there shall be substituted a reference to "subsection (1A) or (3)(a)(ii)".".

[15.229]

4.33 Recourse of liquidator to meeting of creditors

If the liquidator's remuneration has been fixed by the liquidation committee and he considers the amount to be insufficient, he may request that it be increased by resolution of the creditors.

[15.230]

4.34 Recourse to the court

(1) If the liquidator considers that the remuneration fixed for him by the liquidation committee, or by resolution of the creditors, is insufficient, he may apply to the court for an order increasing its amount or rate.

(2) The liquidator shall give at least 14 days' notice of his application to the members of the liquidation committee; and the committee may nominate one or more members to appear or be represented, and to be heard, on the application.

(3) If there is no liquidation committee, the liquidator's notice of his application shall be sent to such one or more of the company's creditors as the court may direct, which creditors may nominate one or more of their number to appear or be represented.

(4) The court may, if it appears to be a proper case, order the expenses of the liquidator's application, including the expenses of any member of the liquidation committee appearing [or being represented] on it, or any creditor so appearing [or being represented], to be paid as an expense for the liquidation.

NOTES

Para (4): words in square brackets inserted by the Insolvency (Scotland) Amendment Rules 1987, SI 1987/1921, r 3(1), Schedule, Pt I, para 22.

[15.231]

4.35 Creditors' claim that remuneration is excessive

(1) If the liquidator's remuneration has been fixed by the liquidation committee or by the creditors, any creditor or creditors of the company representing in value at least 25 per cent of the creditors may apply to the court for an order that the liquidator's remuneration be reduced, on the grounds that it is, in all the circumstances, excessive.

(2) If the court considers the application to be well-founded, it shall make an order fixing the remuneration at a reduced amount or rate.

(3) Unless the court orders otherwise, the expenses of the application shall be paid by the applicant, and are not payable as an expense of the liquidation.

Section E: Supplementary Provisions

[15.232]
4.36 Liquidator deceased

(1) Subject to the following paragraph, where the liquidator has died, it is the duty of his executors or, where the deceased liquidator was a partner in a firm, of a partner in that firm to give notice of that fact to the court and to [the Accountant in Bankruptcy], specifying the date of death. This does not apply if notice has been given under the following paragraph.

(2) Notice of the death may also be given by any person producing to the court and to [the Accountant in Bankruptcy] a copy of the death certificate.

NOTES

Paras (1), (2): words in square brackets substituted by the Scotland Act 1998 (Consequential Modifications) (No 2) Order 1999, SI 1999/1820, art 4, Sch 2, Pt II, para 141(1), (15).

Para (1): see Sch 5, Form 4.18 (Scot) at **[15.349]**, and the notes to that Schedule.

[15.233]
4.37 Loss of qualification as insolvency practitioner

(1) This Rule applies where the liquidator vacates office on ceasing to be qualified to act as an insolvency practitioner in relation to the company.

(2) He shall forthwith give notice of his doing so to the court and to [the Accountant in Bankruptcy].

(3) Rule 4.25(2) and (3) apply as regards the liquidator obtaining his release, as if he had been removed by the court.

NOTES

Para (2): words in square brackets substituted by the Scotland Act 1998 (Consequential Modifications) (No 2) Order 1999, SI 1999/1820, art 4, Sch 2, Pt II, para 141(1), (16).

Para (2): see Sch 5, Form 4.19 (Scot) at **[15.349]**, and the notes to that Schedule.

[15.234]
4.38 Power of court to set aside certain transactions

(1) If in the course of the liquidation the liquidator enters into any transaction with a person who is an associate of his, the court may, on the application of any person interested, set the transaction aside and order the liquidator to compensate the company for any loss suffered in consequence of it.

(2) This does not apply if either—
- (a) the transaction was entered into with the prior consent of the court, or
- (b) it is shown to the court's satisfaction that the transaction was for value, and that it was entered into by the liquidator without knowing, or having any reason to suppose, that the person concerned was an associate.

(3) Nothing in this Rule is to be taken as prejudicing the operation of any rule of law with respect to a trustee's dealings with trust property, or the fiduciary obligations of any person.

[15.235]
4.39 Rule against solicitation

(1) Where the court is satisfied that any improper solicitation has been used by or on behalf of the liquidator in obtaining proxies or procuring his appointment, it may order that no remuneration be allowed as an expense of the liquidation to any person by whom, or on whose behalf, the solicitation was exercised.

(2) An order of the court under this Rule overrides any resolution of the liquidation committee or the creditors, or any other provision of the Rules relating to the liquidator's remuneration.

CHAPTER 7 THE LIQUIDATION COMMITTEE

[15.236]
4.40 Preliminary

For the purposes of this Chapter—
- (a) an "insolvent winding up" takes place where a company is being wound up on grounds which include its inability to pay its debts, and
- (b) a "solvent winding up" takes place where a company is being wound up on grounds which do not include that one.

[15.237]
4.41 Membership of committee

(1) Subject to Rule 4.43 below, the liquidation committee shall consist as follows—
- (a) in the case of any winding up, of at least 3 and not more than 5 creditors of the company, elected by the meeting of creditors held under section 138 or 142 of the Act, and also
- (b) in the case of a solvent winding up where the contributories' meeting held under either of those sections so decides, [of] up to 3 contributories, elected by that meeting.

(2) Any creditor of the company (other than one whose debt is fully secured and who has not agreed to surrender his security to the liquidator) is eligible to be a member of the committee, so long as—
- (a) he has lodged a claim of his debt in the liquidation, and

(b) his claim has neither been wholly rejected for voting purposes, nor wholly rejected for the purposes of his entitlement so far as funds are available to a dividend.

(3) No person can be a member as both a creditor and a contributory.

(4) A body corporate or a partnership may be a member of the committee, but it cannot act as such otherwise than by a member's representative appointed under Rule 4.48 below.

(5) In this Chapter, members of the committee elected or appointed by a creditors' meeting are called "creditor members", and those elected or appointed by contributories' meeting are called "contributory members".

(6) Where the Deposit Protection Board exercises the right (under [section 58 of the Banking Act]) to be a member of the committee, the Board is to be regarded as an additional creditor member.

NOTES

Para (1): word in square brackets inserted by the Insolvency (Scotland) Amendment Rules 1987, SI 1987/1921, r 3(1), Schedule, Pt I, para 23.

Para (6): words in square brackets substituted by SI 1987/1921, r 3(1), Schedule, Pt I, para 23.

[15.238]

4.42 Formalities of establishment

(1) The liquidation committee shall not come into being, and accordingly cannot act, until the liquidator has issued a certificate of its due constitution.

(2) If the chairman of the meeting which resolves to establish the committee is not the liquidator, he shall [without delay] give notice of the resolution to the liquidator (or, as the case may be, the person appointed as liquidator by the same meeting), and inform him of the names and addresses of the persons elected to be members of the committee.

(3) No person may act as a member of the committee unless and until he has agreed to do so [and, unless the relevant proxy or authorisation contains a statement to the contrary, such agreement may be given on behalf of the member by his proxy-holder or[, in the case of a corporation, by its duly authorised representative] who is present at the meeting at which the committee is established]; and the liquidator's certificate of the committee's due constitution shall not be issued until at least the minimum number of persons in accordance with Rule 4.41 who are to be members of it have agreed to act, but shall be issued [without delay] thereafter.

(4) As and when the others (if any) agree to act, the liquidator shall issue an amended certificate.

(5) The certificate (and any amended certificate) shall be sent by the liquidator to [the Accountant in Bankruptcy].

(6) If after the first establishment of the committee there is any change in its membership, the liquidator shall report the change to [the Accountant in Bankruptcy].

NOTES

Para (2): words in square brackets substituted for original word "forthwith" by the Insolvency (Scotland) Amendment Rules 2014, SSI 2014/114, rr 2, 13(a), subject to savings in r 29 thereof as noted to r 0.2 at **[15.2]**.

Para (3): words in first (outer) pair of square brackets inserted by the Insolvency (Scotland) Amendment Rules 1987, SI 1987/1921, r 3(1), Schedule, Pt I, para 24; words in second (inner) and third pairs of square brackets substituted for original words "any representative under section 375 of the Companies Act" and "forthwith" respectively, by SSI 2014/114, rr 2, 13, subject to savings in r 29 thereof as noted to r 0.2 at **[15.2]**.

Paras (5), (6): words in square brackets substituted by the Scotland Act 1998 (Consequential Modifications) (No 2) Order 1999, SI 1999/1820, art 4, Sch 2, Pt II, para 141(1), (17).

Paras (3), (4): see Sch 5, Form 4.20 (Scot) at **[15.349]**, and the notes to that Schedule.

Paras (5), (6): see Sch 5, Form 4.22 (Scot) at **[15.349]**, and the notes to that Schedule.

[15.239]

4.43 Committee established by contributories

(1) The following applies where the creditors' meeting under section 138 or 142 of the Act does not decide that a liquidation committee should be established or decides that a liquidation committee should not be established.

(2) A meeting of contributories under section 138 or 142 may appoint one of their number to make application to the court for an order to the liquidator that a further creditors' meeting be summoned for the purpose of establishing a liquidation committee; and

(a) the court may, if it thinks that there are special circumstances to justify it, make that order, and

(b) the creditors' meeting summoned by the liquidator in compliance with the order is deemed to have been summoned under section 142.

(3) If the creditors' meeting so summoned does not establish a liquidation committee, a meeting of contributories may do so.

(4) The committee shall then consist of at least 3, and not more than 5, contributories elected by that meeting; and Rule 4.42 shall apply to such a committee [with the substitution of the reference to Rule 4.41 in paragraph (3) of that Rule by a reference to this paragraph].

NOTES

Para (4): words in square brackets substituted by the Insolvency (Scotland) Amendment Rules 1987, SI 1987/1921, r 3(1), Schedule, Pt I, para 25.

[15.240]

4.44 Obligations of liquidator to committee

(1) Subject as follows, it is the duty of the liquidator to report to the members of the liquidation committee all such matters as appear to him to be, or as they have indicated to him as being, of concern to them with respect to the winding up.

(2) In the case of matters so indicated to him by the committee, the liquidator need not comply with any request for information where it appears to him that—

(a) the request is frivolous or unreasonable, or

(b) the cost of complying would be excessive, having regard to the relative importance of the information, or

(c) there are not sufficient assets to enable him to comply.

(3) Where the committee has come into being more than 28 days after the appointment of the liquidator, he shall report to them, in summary form, what actions he has taken since his appointment, and shall answer all such questions as they may put to him regarding his conduct of the winding up hitherto.

(4) A person who becomes a member of the committee at any time after its first establishment is not entitled to require a report to him by the liquidator, otherwise than in summary form, of any matters previously arising.

(5) Nothing in this Rule disentitles the committee, or any member of it, from having access to the liquidator's cash book and sederunt book, or from seeking an explanation of any matter within the committee's responsibility.

[15.241]

4.45 Meetings of the committee

(1) Subject as follows, meetings of the liquidation committee shall be held when and where determined by the liquidator.

(2) The liquidator shall call a first meeting of the committee to take place within [6 weeks] of his appointment or of the committee's establishment (whichever is the later); and thereafter he shall call a meeting—

(a) if so requested by a creditor member of the committee or his representative (the meeting then to be held within 21 days of the request being received by the liquidator), and

(b) for a specified date, if the committee has previously resolved that a meeting be held on that day.

(3) The liquidator shall give 7 days' written notice of the time and place of any meeting to every member of the committee (or his representative, if designated for that purpose), unless in any case the requirement of the notice has been waived by or on behalf of any member. Waiver may be signified either at or before the meeting.

NOTES

Para (2): words in square brackets substituted for original words "3 months", by the Insolvency (Scotland) Amendment Rules 2014, SSI 2014/114, rr 2, 14, subject to savings in r 29 thereof as noted to r 0.2 at **[15.2]**.

[15.242]

4.46 The chairman at meetings

(1) The chairman at any meeting of the liquidation committee shall be the liquidator, or a person nominated by him to act.

(2) A person so nominated must be either—

(a) a person who is qualified to act as an insolvency practitioner in relation to the company, or

(b) an employee of the liquidator or his firm who is experienced in insolvency matters.

[15.243]

4.47 Quorum

A meeting of the committee is duly constituted if due notice of it has been given to all the members, and at least 2 creditor members or, in the case of a committee of contributories, 2 contributory members are present or represented.

[15.244]

4.48 Committee members' representatives

(1) A member of the liquidation committee may, in relation to the business of the committee, be represented by another person duly authorised by him for that purpose.

(2) A person acting as a committee-member's representative must hold a mandate entitling him so to act (either generally or specially) and signed by or on behalf of the committee member[, and for this purpose any proxy or [authorisation given by a corporation] in relation to any meeting of creditors (or, as the case may be, members or contributories) of the company shall, unless it contains a statement to the contrary, be treated as such a mandate to act generally signed by or on behalf of the committee-member].

(3) The chairman at any meeting of the committee may call on a person claiming to act as a committee-member's representative to produce his mandate and may exclude him if it appears that his mandate is deficient.

(4) No member may be represented by a body corporate or by a partnership, or by an undischarged bankrupt [or by a person in relation to whom a moratorium period under a debt relief order applies (under Part 7A of the Insolvency Act 1986)].

(5) No person shall—

(a) on the same committee, act at one and the same time as representative of more than one committee-member, or

(b) act both as a member of the committee and as representative of another member.

(6) Where a member's representative signs any document on the member's behalf, the fact that he so signs must be stated below his signature.

NOTES

Para (2): words in first (outer) pair of square brackets added by the Insolvency (Scotland) Amendment Rules 1987, SI 1987/1921, r 3(1), Schedule, Pt I, para 26; words in second (inner) pair of square brackets substituted for original words "authorisation under section 375 of the Companies Act", by the Insolvency (Scotland) Amendment Rules 2014, SSI 2014/114, rr 2, 15, subject to savings in r 29 thereof as noted to r 0.2 at **[15.2]**.

Para (4): words in square brackets added, in relation to a debt relief order the application for which is made after 1 October 2012, by the Tribunals, Courts and Enforcement Act 2007 (Consequential Amendments) Order 2012, SI 2012/2404, arts 3(3), 7, Sch 3, para 4(1), (5).

[15.245]
4.49 Resignation

A member of the liquidation committee may resign by notice in writing delivered to the liquidator.

[15.246]
[4.50 Termination of membership

(1) A person's membership of the liquidation committee is automatically terminated if—

(a) that person's estate is sequestrated or the person becomes bankrupt or is made subject to a debt relief order (under Part 7A of the Act) or grants a trust deed for the benefit of or makes a composition with creditors;

(b) at 3 consecutive meetings of the committee the person is neither present nor represented (unless at the third of those meetings it is resolved that this Rule is not to apply in the case of the person); or

(c) the person is deceased.

(2) The membership of a creditor member who ceases to be, or is found never to have been, a creditor is also automatically terminated.

(3) The membership of a body corporate member or partnership member of the liquidation committee is also automatically terminated if the body corporate or partnership is dissolved.]

NOTES

Commencement: 30 May 2014.

Substituted by the Insolvency (Scotland) Amendment Rules 2014, SSI 2014/114, rr 2, 16, subject to savings in r 29 thereof as noted to r 0.2 at **[15.2]**. This rule previously read as follows (with words in square brackets inserted by the Tribunals, Courts and Enforcement Act 2007 (Consequential Amendments) Order 2012, SI 2012/2404, arts 3(3), 7, Sch 3, para 4(1), (6))—

"**4.50 Termination of membership**

Membership of the liquidation committee of any person is automatically terminated if—

(a) his estate is sequestrated or becomes bankrupt [or has a debt relief order made in respect of him (under Part 7A of the Insolvency Act 1986)] or grants a trust deed for the benefit of or makes a composition with his creditors, or

(b) at 3 consecutive meetings of the committee he is neither present nor represented (unless at the third of those meetings it is resolved that this Rule is not to apply in his case), or

(c) that creditor being a creditor member, he ceases to be, or is found never to have been a creditor.".

[15.247]
4.51 Removal

A creditor member of the committee may be removed by resolution at a meeting of creditors; and a contributory member may be removed by a resolution of a meeting of contributories.

[15.248]
4.52 Vacancy (creditor members)

(1) The following applies if there is a vacancy among the creditor members of the committee.

(2) The vacancy need not be filled if the liquidator and a majority of the remaining creditor members so agree, provided that the total number of members does not fall below the minimum required by Rule 4.41(1).

(3) The liquidator may appoint any creditor, who is qualified under the Rules to be a member of the committee, to fill the vacancy, if a majority of the other creditor members agrees to the appointment, and the creditor concerned consents to act.

(4) Alternatively, a meeting of creditors may resolve that a creditor be appointed (with his consent) to fill the vacancy. In this case, at least 14 days' notice must have been given of the resolution to make such an appointment (whether or not of a person named in the notice).

(5) Where the vacancy is filled by an appointment made by a creditors' meeting at which the liquidator is not present, the chairman of the meeting shall report to the liquidator the appointment which has been made.

[15.249]

4.53 Vacancy (contributory members)

(1) The following applies if there is a vacancy among the contributory members of the committee.

(2) The vacancy need not be filled if the liquidator and the majority of the remaining contributory members so agree, provided that, in the case of a committee of contributory members only, the total number of members does not fall below the minimum required by [Rule 4.43(4)] or, as the case may be, 4.59(4).

(3) The liquidator may appoint any contributory member (being qualified under the Rules to be a member of the committee) to fill the vacancy, if a majority of the other contributory members agree to the appointment, and the contributory concerned consents to act.

(4) Alternatively, a meeting of contributories may resolve that a contributory be appointed (with his consent) to fill the vacancy. In this case, at least 14 days' notice must have been given of the resolution to make such an appointment (whether or not of a person named in the notice).

(5) Where the vacancy is filled by an appointment made by a contributories' meeting at which the liquidator is not present, the chairman of the meeting shall report to the liquidator the appointment which has been made.

NOTES

Para (2): words in square brackets substituted by the Insolvency (Scotland) Amendment Rules 1987, SI 1987/1921, r 3(1), Schedule, Pt I, para 27.

[15.250]

4.54 Voting rights and resolutions

(1) At any meeting of the committee, each member of it (whether present himself, or by his representative) has one vote; and a resolution is passed when a majority of the creditor members present or represented have voted in favour of it.

(2) Subject to the next paragraph, the votes of contributory members do not count towards the number required for passing a resolution, but the way in which they vote on any resolution shall be recorded.

(3) Paragraph (2) does not apply where, by virtue of Rule 4.43(4) or 4.59, the only members of the committee are contributories. In that case the committee is to be treated for voting purposes as if all its members were creditors.

(4) Every resolution passed shall be recorded in writing, either separately or as part of the minutes of the meeting. The record shall be signed by the chairman and kept as part of the sederunt book.

[15.251]

4.55 Resolutions by post

(1) In accordance with this Rule, the liquidator may seek to obtain the agreement of members of the liquidation committee to a resolution by sending to every member (or his representative designated for the purpose) a copy of the proposed resolution.

(2) Where the liquidator makes use of the procedure allowed by this Rule, he shall send out to members of the committee or their representatives (as the case may be) [a copy of any proposed resolution on which a decision is sought, which shall be set out in such a way that agreement with or dissent from each separate resolution may be indicated by the recipient on the copy so sent].

(3) Any creditor member of the committee may, within 7 business days from the date of the liquidator sending out a resolution, require him to summon a meeting of the committee to consider the matters raised by the resolution.

(4) In the absence of such a request, the resolution is deemed to have been passed by the committee if and when the liquidator is notified in writing by a majority of the creditor members that they concur with it.

(5) A copy of every resolution passed under this Rule, and a note that the committee's concurrence was obtained, shall be kept in the sederunt book.

NOTES

Para (2): words in square brackets substituted by the Insolvency (Scotland) Amendment Rules 1987, SI 1987/1921, r 3(1), Schedule, Pt I, para 28.

[15.252]

4.56 Liquidator's reports

(1) The liquidator shall, as and when directed by the liquidation committee (but not more often than once in any period of 2 months), send a written report to every member of the committee setting out the position generally as regards the progress of the winding up and matters arising in connection with it, to which the liquidator considers the committee's attention should be drawn.

(2) In the absence of such directions by the committee, the liquidator shall send such a report not less often than once in every period of 6 months.

(3) The obligations of the liquidator under this Rule are without prejudice to those imposed by Rule 4.44.

[15.253]
4.57 Expenses of members, etc

(1) The liquidator shall defray any reasonable travelling expenses directly incurred by members of the liquidation committee or their representatives in respect of their attendance at the committee's meetings, or otherwise on the committee's business, as an expense of the liquidation.

(2) Paragraph (1) does not apply to any meeting of the committee held within 3 months of a previous meeting.

[15.254]
4.58 Dealings by committee-members and others

(1) This Rule applies to—
- (a) any member of the liquidation committee;
- (b) any committee-member's representative;
- (c) any person who is an associate of a member of the committee or of a committee-member's representative; and
- (d) any person who has been a member of the committee at any time in the last 12 months.

(2) Subject as follows, a person to whom this Rule applies shall not enter into any transaction whereby he—
- (a) receives out of the company's assets any payment for services given or goods supplied in connection with the liquidation, or
- (b) obtains any profit from the liquidation, or
- (c) acquires any part of the company's assets.

(3) Such a transaction may be entered into by a person to whom this Rule applies—
- (a) with the prior leave of the court, or
- (b) if he does so as a matter of urgency, or by way of performance of a contract in force before the date on which the company went into liquidation, and obtains the court's leave for the transaction, having applied for it without undue delay, or
- (c) with the prior sanction of the liquidation committee, where it is satisfied (after full disclosure of the circumstances) that the transaction will be on normal commercial terms.

(4) Where in the committee a resolution is proposed that sanction be accorded for a transaction to be entered into which, without that sanction or the leave of the court, would be in contravention of this Rule, no member of the committee, and no representative of a member, shall vote if he is to participate directly or indirectly in the transaction.

(5) The court may, on the application of any person interested—
- (a) set aside a transaction on the ground that it has been entered into in contravention of this Rule, and
- (b) make with respect to it such other order as it thinks fit, including (subject to the following paragraph) an order requiring a person to whom this Rule applies to account for any profit obtained from the transaction and compensate the company's assets for any resultant loss.

(6) In the case of a person to whom this Rule applies as an associate of a member of the committee or of a committee-member's representative, the court shall not make any order under paragraph (5), if satisfied that he entered into the relevant transaction without having any reason to suppose that in doing so he would contravene this Rule.

(7) The expenses of an application to the court for leave under this Rule are not payable as an expense of the liquidation, unless the court so orders.

[15.255]
[4.59 Composition of committee when creditors paid in full

(1) Where the creditors have been paid in full together with interest in accordance with section 189, the liquidator must, without delay—
- (a) issue a certificate to that effect by sending a copy to each member of the liquidation committee; and
- (b) send a notice to that effect, together with a copy of the certificate to the Accountant in Bankruptcy.

(2) On the issue of a certificate the creditor members of the liquidation committee cease to be members of the committee.

(3) The committee continues to exist unless—
- (a) it is abolished by a decision of a meeting of contributories; or
- (b) the number of members is less than 3 and 28 days have elapsed since the issue of the liquidator's certificate.

(4) At any time in the period referred to in paragraph (3)(b) where the committee consists of less than 3 contributory members it is suspended and cannot act.

(5) The certificate issued under paragraph (1)(a) must—
- (a) identify the liquidator;
- (b) contain a statement by the liquidator certifying that the creditors of the company have been paid in full with interest in accordance with section 189; and
- (c) be authenticated and dated by the liquidator.]

NOTES

Commencement: 30 May 2014.

Substituted by the Insolvency (Scotland) Amendment Rules 2014, SSI 2014/114, rr 2, 17, subject to savings in r 29 thereof as noted to r 0.2 at **[15.2]**. This rule (as amended by the Scotland Act 1998 (Consequential Modifications) (No 2) Order 1999, SI 1999/1820, art 4, Sch 2, Pt II, para 141(1), (18)) previously read as follows—

"4.59 Composition of committee when creditors paid in full

(1) This Rule applies if the liquidator issues a certificate that the creditors have been paid in full, with interest in accordance with section 189.

(2) The liquidator shall forthwith send a copy of the certificate to [the Accountant in Bankruptcy].

(3) The creditor members of the liquidation committee shall cease to be members of the committee.

(4) The committee continues in being unless and until abolished by decision of a meeting of contributories, and (subject to the next paragraph) so long as it consists of at least 2 contributory members.

(5) The committee does not cease to exist on account of the number of contributory members falling below 2, unless and until 28 days have elapsed since the issue of the liquidator's certificate under paragraph (1), but at any time when the committee consists of less than 2 contributory members, it is suspended and cannot act.

(6) Contributories may be co-opted by the liquidator, or appointed by a contributories' meeting, to be members of the committee; but the maximum number of members is 5.

(7) The foregoing Rules in this Chapter continue to apply to the liquidation committee (with any necessary modifications) as if all the members of the committee were creditor members.".

[15.256]
[4.59A Formal defects

The Acts of the liquidation committee established for any winding up are valid notwithstanding any defect in the appointment, election or qualifications of any member of the committee or any committee-member's representative or in the formalities of its establishment.]

NOTES

Inserted by the Insolvency (Scotland) Amendment Rules 1987, SI 1987/1921, r 3(1), Schedule, Pt I, para 29.

CHAPTER 8 THE LIQUIDATION COMMITTEE WHERE WINDING UP FOLLOWS IMMEDIATELY ON ADMINISTRATION

[15.257]
4.60 Preliminary

(1) The Rules in this Chapter apply where—
- (a) the winding up order has been made immediately upon the [ending of administration] under Part II of the Act, and
- (b) the court makes an order under section 140(1) appointing as liquidator the person who was previously the administrator.

(2) In this Chapter the expressions "insolvent winding up", "solvent winding up", "creditor member", and "contributory member" each have the same meaning as in Chapter 7.

NOTES

Para (1): words in square brackets substituted for words "discharge of an administration order" by the Insolvency (Scotland) Amendment Rules 2003, SI 2003/2111, r 6, Sch 2, para 5, subject to savings in r 7 thereof at **[2.34]**.

[15.258]
4.61 Continuation of creditors' committee

(1) If under [Schedule B1 to the Act] a creditors' committee has been established for the purposes of the administration, then (subject as follows in this Chapter) that committee continues in being as the liquidation committee for the purposes of the winding up, and—
- (a) it is deemed to be a committee established as such under section 142, and
- (b) no action shall be taken under subsections (1) to (4) of that section to establish any other.

(2) This Rule does not apply if, at the time when the court's order under section 140(1) is made, the committee under [Schedule B1 to the Act] consists of less than 3 members; and a creditor who was, immediately before the date of that order, a member of such a committee ceases to be a member on the making of the order if his debt is fully secured (and he has not agreed to surrender his security to the liquidator).

NOTES

Words in square brackets substituted for words "section 26" by the Insolvency (Scotland) Amendment Rules 2003, SI 2003/2111, r 6, Sch 2, para 6, subject to savings in r 7 thereof at **[2.34]**.

[15.259]
4.62 Membership of committee

(1) Subject as follows, the liquidation committee shall consist of at least 3, and not more than 5, creditors of the company, elected by the creditors' meeting held under [Schedule B1 to the Act] or (in order to make up numbers or fill vacancies) by a creditors' meeting summoned by the liquidator after the company goes into liquidation.

(2) In the case of a solvent winding up, the liquidator shall, on not less than 21 days' notice, summon a meeting of contributories, in order to elect (if it so wishes) contributory members of the liquidation committee, up to 3 in number.

NOTES

Para (1): words in square brackets substituted for words "section 26" by the Insolvency (Scotland) Amendment Rules 2003, SI 2003/2111, r 6, Sch 2, para 6, subject to savings in r 7 thereof at **[2.34]**.

[15.260]
4.63 Liquidator's certificate

(1) The liquidator shall issue a certificate of the liquidation committee's continuance specifying the persons who are, or are to be, members of it.

(2) It shall be stated in the certificate whether or not the liquidator has summoned a meeting of contributories under Rule 4.62(2), and whether (if so) the meeting has elected contributories to be members of the committee.

(3) Pending the issue of the liquidator's certificate, the committee is suspended and cannot act.

(4) No person may act, or continue to act, as a member of the committee unless and until he has agreed to do so; and the liquidator's certificate shall not be issued until at least the minimum number of persons required under Rule 4.62 to form a committee elected, whether under Rule 4.62 above or under [Schedule B1 to the Act], have signified their agreement.

(5) As and when the others signify their agreement, the liquidator shall issue an amended certificate.

(6) The liquidator's certificate (or, as the case may be, the amended certificate) shall be sent by him to [the Accountant in Bankruptcy].

(7) If subsequently there is any change in the committee's membership, the liquidator shall report the change to [the Accountant in Bankruptcy].

NOTES

Para (4): words in square brackets substituted for words "section 26" by the Insolvency (Scotland) Amendment Rules 2003, SI 2003/2111, r 6, Sch 2, para 6, subject to savings in r 7 thereof at **[2.34]**.

Paras (6), (7): words in square brackets substituted by the Scotland Act 1998 (Consequential Modifications) (No 2) Order 1999, SI 1999/1820, art 4, Sch 2, Pt II, para 141(1), (19).

Para (5): see Sch 5, Form 4.21 (Scot) at **[15.349]**, and the notes to that Schedule.

Paras (6), (7): see Sch 5, Form 4.22 (Scot) at **[15.349]**, and the notes to that Schedule.

[15.261]
4.64 Obligations of liquidator to committee

(1) As soon as may be after the issue of the liquidator's certificate under Rule 4.63, the liquidator shall report to the liquidation committee what actions he has taken since the date on which the company went into liquidation.

(2) A person who becomes a member of the committee after that date is not entitled to require a report to him by the liquidator, otherwise than in a summary form, of any matters previously arising.

(3) Nothing in this Rule disentitles the committee, or any member of it, from having access to the sederunt book (whether relating to the period when he was administrator, or to any subsequent period), or from seeking an explanation of any matter within the committee's responsibility.

[15.262]
4.65 Application of Chapter 7

Except as provided elsewhere in this Chapter, [Rules 4.44 to 4.59A] of Chapter 7 shall apply to a liquidation committee established under this Chapter from the date of issue of the certificate under Rule 4.63 as if it had been established under section 142.

NOTES

Words in square brackets substituted by the Insolvency (Scotland) Amendment Rules 1987, SI 1987/1921, r 3(1), Schedule, Pt I, para 30.

See Sch 5, Form 4.21 (Scot) at **[15.349]**, and the notes to that Schedule.

CHAPTER 9 DISTRIBUTION OF COMPANY'S ASSETS BY LIQUIDATOR

[15.263]
4.66 Order of priority in distribution

(1) The funds of the company's assets shall be distributed by the liquidator to meet the following expenses and debts in the order in which they are mentioned—

(a) the expenses of the liquidation;

[(aa) Where the court makes a winding up order in relation to a company and, at the time when the petition for winding up was first presented to the court, there was in force in relation to the company a voluntary arrangement under Part 1 of the Act, any expenses properly incurred as expenses of the administration of that arrangement;]

(b) any preferential debts within the meaning of section 386 (excluding any interest which has been accrued thereon to the date of commencement of the winding up within the meaning of section 129);

(c) ordinary debts, that is to say a debt which is neither a secured debt nor a debt mentioned in any other sub-paragraph of this paragraph;

(d) interest at the official rate on—

(i) the preferential debts, and
(ii) the ordinary debts,
between the said date of commencement of the winding up and the date of payment of the debt; and

(e) any postponed debt.

(2) In the above paragraph—

(a) "postponed debt" means a creditor's right to any alienation which has been reduced or restored to the company's assets under section 242 or to the proceeds of sale of such an alienation; and

(b) "official rate" shall be construed in accordance with subsection (4) of section 189 and, for the purposes of paragraph (a) of that subsection, as applied to Scotland by subsection (5), the rate specified in the Rules shall be 15 per centum per annum.

(3) The expenses of the liquidation mentioned in sub-paragraph (a) of paragraph (1) are payable in the order of priority mentioned in Rule 4.67.

(4) Subject to the provisions of section 175, any debt falling within any of sub-paragraphs (b) to (e) of paragraph (1) shall have the same priority as any other debt falling within the same sub-paragraph and, where the funds of the company's assets are inadequate to enable the debts mentioned in this sub-paragraph to be paid in full, they shall abate in equal proportions.

(5) Any surplus remaining, after all expenses and debts mentioned in paragraph (1) have been paid in full, shall (unless the articles of the company otherwise provide) be distributed among the members according to their rights and interests in the company.

(6) Nothing in this Rule shall affect—

(a) the right of a secured creditor which is preferable to the rights of the liquidator; or

(b) any preference of the holder of a lien over a title deed or other document which has been delivered to [the liquidator] in accordance with a requirement under [Rule 4.22(4)].

NOTES

Para (1): sub-para (aa) inserted by the Insolvency (Scotland) Amendment Rules 1987, SI 1987/1921, r 3(1), Schedule, Pt I, para 31.

Para (6): words in square brackets substituted by SI 1987/1921, r 3(1), Schedule, Pt I, para 31.

[15.264]

4.67 Order of priority of expenses of liquidation

(1) Subject to section 156 and paragraph (2), the expenses of the liquidation are payable out of the assets in the following order of priority—

(a) any outlays properly chargeable or incurred by the provisional liquidator or liquidator in carrying out his functions in the liquidation [including any costs referred to in Article 30 and 59 of the EU Regulation], except those outlays specifically mentioned in the following sub-paragraphs;

(b) the cost, or proportionate cost, of any caution provided by a provisional liquidator, liquidator or special manager in accordance with the Act or the Rules;

(c) the remuneration of the provisional liquidator (if any);

(d) the expenses of the petitioner in the liquidation, and of any person appearing in the petition whose expenses are allowed by the court;

(e) the remuneration of the special manager (if any);

(f) any allowance made by the liquidator under Rule 4.9(1) (expenses of statement of affairs);

(g) the remuneration or emoluments of any person who has been employed by the liquidator to perform any services for the company, as required or authorised by or under the Act or the Rules;

(h) the remuneration of the liquidator determined in accordance with Rule 4.32;

(i) the amount of any [corporation] tax on chargeable gains accruing on the realisation of any asset of the company (without regard to whether the realisation is effected by the liquidator, a secured creditor or otherwise).

(2) In any winding up by the court which follows immediately on a voluntary winding up (whether members' voluntary or creditors' voluntary), such outlays and remuneration of the voluntary liquidator as the court may allow, shall have the same priority as the outlays mentioned in sub-paragraph (a) of paragraph (1).

(3) Nothing in this Rule applies to or affects the power of any court, in proceedings by or against the company, to order expenses to be paid by the company, or the liquidator; nor does it affect the rights of any person to whom such expenses are ordered to be paid.

NOTES

Para (1): words in square brackets in sub-para (a) inserted by the Insolvency Amendment (EU 2015/848) Regulations 2017, SI 2017/702, regs 2, 3, Schedule, Pt 5, paras 61, 82, as from 26 June 2017, except in relation to proceedings opened before that date; word in square brackets in sub-para (i) substituted by the Insolvency (Scotland) Amendment Rules 1987, SI 1987/1921, r 3(1), Schedule, Pt I, para 32.

Modification: see the Regulated Covered Bonds Regulations 2008, SI 2008/346, reg 46, Schedule, Pt 2, para 8 at **[18.178]**, **[18.180]**.

[15.265]
[4.68 Estate to be distributed in respect of the accounting periods

(1) The liquidator shall make up accounts of the liquidator's intromissions with the company's assets in respect of each accounting period.

(2) In this Rule "accounting period" shall be construed as follows—

(a) the first accounting period shall be the period of 6 months beginning with the date of commencement of winding up within the meaning of section 129; and

(b) any subsequent accounting period shall be the period of 6 months beginning with the end of the last accounting period; except that—

(i) where the liquidator and the liquidation committee agree; or

(ii) where there is no liquidation committee, the court determines,

that the accounting period shall be such other period beginning with the end of the last accounting period as may be agreed or, as the case may be determined, it shall be that other period.

(3) An agreement or determination under paragraph (2)(b)(i) or (ii) above—

(a) may be made in respect of one or more than one accounting period;

(b) may be made before the beginning of the accounting period in relation to which it has effect and, in any event, shall not have effect unless made before the day on which such accounting period would, but for the agreement or determination, have ended;

(c) may provide for different accounting periods to be of different durations,

and shall be recorded in the sederunt book by the liquidator.

(4) Subject to the following provisions of this Rule, the liquidator shall, if the funds of the company's assets are sufficient and after making allowance for future contingencies, pay under Rule 4.68A(1) a dividend out of the company's assets to the creditors in respect of each accounting period.

(5) The liquidator may pay—

(a) the expenses of the winding up mentioned in Rule 4.67(1)(a), other than the liquidator's own remuneration, at any time;

(b) the preferential debts within the meaning of section 386 at any time but only with the consent of the liquidation committee or, if there is no liquidation committee, of the court.

(6) If the liquidator—

(a) is not ready to pay a dividend in respect of an accounting period; or

(b) considers it would be inappropriate to pay such a dividend because the expense of doing so would be disproportionate to the amount of the dividend,

the liquidator may postpone such payment to a date not later than the time for payment of a dividend in respect of the next accounting period.

(7) Where an appeal is taken under Rule 4.16B against the acceptance or rejection of a creditor's claim, the liquidator shall, at the time of payment of dividends and until the appeal is determined, set aside an amount which would be sufficient, if the determination in the appeal were to provide for the claim being accepted in full, to pay a dividend in respect of that claim.

(8) Where a creditor—

(a) has failed to produce evidence in support of a claim earlier than 8 weeks before the end of an accounting period on being required by the liquidator to do so under Rule 4.16A(1); and

(b) has given a reason for such failure which is acceptable to the liquidator,

the liquidator shall set aside, for such time as is reasonable to enable the creditor to produce that evidence or any other evidence that will enable the liquidator to be satisfied under Rule 4.16A(1), an amount which would be sufficient, if the claim were accepted in full, to pay a dividend in respect of that claim.

(9) Where a creditor submits a claim to the liquidator later than 8 weeks before the end of an accounting period but more than 8 weeks before the end of a subsequent accounting period in respect of which, after making allowance for contingencies, funds are available for the payment of a dividend, the liquidator shall, if accepting the claim in whole or in part, pay to the creditor—

(a) the same dividend or dividends as has or have already been paid to creditors of the same class in respect of any accounting period or periods; and

(b) whatever dividend may be payable to that creditor in respect of the said subsequent accounting period:

Provided that paragraph (a) above shall be without prejudice to any dividend which has already been paid.

(10) In the declaration of and payment of a dividend, no payments shall be made more than once by virtue of the same debt.

(11) Subject to any notification by the person entitled to a dividend given to the liquidator that the person wishes the dividend to be paid to another person, or has assigned that entitlement to another person, where both a creditor and a member State liquidator have had a claim accepted in relation to the same debt, payment shall only be made to the creditor.]

NOTES

Commencement: 30 May 2014.

Substituted, together with rr 4.68A, 4.68B for original r 4.68, by the Insolvency (Scotland) Amendment Rules 2014, SSI 2014/114, rr 2, 18, subject to savings in r 29 thereof as noted to r 0.2 at **[15.2]**. This rule and the notes relating to it previously read as follows—

"4.68 Application of the Bankruptcy Act

(1) Sections 52, 53 and 58 of the Bankruptcy Act shall apply in relation to the liquidation of a company as they apply in relation to a sequestration of a debtor's estate, subject to the modifications specified in Rules 4.16(2) and 4.32(2) and (3) and the following paragraph and to any other necessary modifications.

(2) In section 52, the following modifications shall be made—

(a) in subsection (4)(a) for the reference to "the debts mentioned in subsection (1)(a) to (d)", there shall be substituted a reference to the expenses of the winding up mentioned in Rule 4.67(1)(a);

(b) in subsection (5), the words "with the consent of the commissioners or if there are no commissioners of the Accountant in Bankruptcy" should be deleted; . . .

(c) in subsection (7) and (8) for the references to section 48(5) and 49(6)(b) there should be substituted a reference to those sections as applied by Rule 4.16(1)[; and

(d) for subsection (11) substitute—

"(11) Subject to any notification by the person entitled to a dividend given to the liquidator that he wishes the dividend to be paid to another person, or that he has assigned his entitlement to another person, where both a creditor and a member State liquidator have had a claim accepted in relation to the same debt, payment shall only be made to the creditor.".]

NOTES

Para (2): word omitted from sub-para (b) revoked, and sub-para (d) and word "and" immediately preceding it added, by the Insolvency (Scotland) Regulations 2003, SI 2003/2109, regs 23, 27(2), subject to the saving that anything done under or for the purposes of any provision of these Rules before 8 September 2003 has effect as if done under or for the purposes of the provision as amended.".

[15.266]

[4.68A Payment of dividends

(1) On the expiry of the period within which an appeal may be taken under Rule 4.32(11) or, if an appeal is so taken, on the final determination of the last such appeal, the liquidator shall pay to the creditors their dividends in accordance with the scheme of division.

(2) Any dividend—

(a) allocated to a creditor which is not cashed or uplifted; or

(b) dependent on a claim in respect of which an amount has been set aside under Rule 4.68(7) or (8),

shall be deposited by the liquidator in an appropriate bank or institution.

(3) If a creditor's claim is revalued, the liquidator may—

(a) in paying any dividend to that creditor, make such adjustment to it as is considered necessary to take account of that revaluation; or

(b) require the creditor to repay the whole or part of a dividend already paid to that creditor.

(4) The liquidator shall insert in the sederunt book the audited accounts, the scheme of division and the final determination in relation to the liquidator's outlays and remuneration.]

NOTES

Commencement: 30 May 2014.

Substituted as noted to r 4.68 at **[15.265]**.

[15.267]

[4.68B Unclaimed dividends

(1) Any person, producing evidence of that person's right, may apply to the court to receive a dividend deposited under section 193(2), if the application is made not later than seven years after the date of such deposit.

(2) If the court is satisfied of the applicant's right to the dividend, it shall authorise the appropriate bank or institution to pay to the applicant the amount of that dividend and of any interest which has accrued thereon.

(3) The liquidator shall, at the expiry of 7 years from the date of deposit of any unclaimed dividend or unapplied balance under section 193(2), hand over the deposit receipt or other voucher relating to such dividend or balance to the Secretary of State, who shall thereupon be entitled to payment of the amount due, principal and interest, from the bank or institution in which the deposit was made.]

NOTES

Commencement: 30 May 2014.

Substituted as noted to r 4.68 at **[15.265]**.

CHAPTER 10 SPECIAL MANAGER

[15.268]

4.69 Appointment and remuneration

(1) This Chapter applies to an application under section 177 by the liquidator or, where one has been appointed, by the provisional liquidator for the appointment of a person to be special manager (references in this Chapter to the liquidator shall be read as including the provisional liquidator).

(2) An application shall be supported by a report setting out the reasons for the appointment. the report shall include the applicant's estimate of the value of the assets in respect of which the special manager is to be appointed.

(3) The order of the court appointing the special manager shall specify the duration of his appointment, which may be for a period of time or until the occurrence of a specified event. Alternatively the order may specify that the duration of the appointment is to be subject to a further order of the court.

(4) The appointment of a special manager may be renewed by order of the court.

(5) The special manager's remuneration shall be fixed from time to time by the court.

(6) The acts of the special manager are valid notwithstanding any defect in his appointment or qualifications.

[15.269]
4.70 Caution

(1) The appointment of the special manager does not take effect until the person appointed has found (or, being allowed by the court to do so, has undertaken to find) caution to the person who applies for him to be appointed.

(2) It is not necessary that caution be found for each separate company liquidation; but it may be found either specially for a particular liquidation, or generally for any liquidation in relation to which the special manager may be employed as such.

(3) The amount of the caution shall be not less than the value of the assets in respect of which he is appointed, as estimated by the applicant in his report under Rule 4.69.

(4) When the special manager has found caution to the person applying for his appointment, that person shall certify the adequacy of the security and notify the court accordingly.

(5) The cost of finding caution shall be paid in the first instance by the special manager; but—

- (a) where a winding up order is not made, he is entitled to be reimbursed out of the property of the company, and the court may make an order on the company accordingly, and
- (b) where a winding up order has been or is subsequently made, he is entitled to be reimbursed as an expense of the liquidation.

[15.270]
4.71 Failure to find or to maintain caution

(1) If the special manager fails to find the required caution within the time stated for that purpose by the order appointing him, or any extension of that time that may be allowed, the liquidator shall report the failure to the court, which may thereupon discharge the order appointing the special manager.

(2) If the special manager fails to maintain his caution the liquidator shall report his failure to the court, which may thereupon remove the special manager and make such order as it thinks fit as to expenses.

(3) If an order is made under this Rule removing the special manager, or recalling the order appointing him, the court shall give directions as to whether any, and if so what, steps should be taken to appoint another special manager in his place.

[15.271]
4.72 Accounting

(1) The special manager shall produce accounts containing details of his receipts and payments for the approval of the liquidator.

(2) The accounts shall be in respect of 3-month periods for the duration of the special manager's appointment (or for a lesser period if his appointment terminates less than 3 months from its date, or from the date to which the last accounts were made up).

(3) When the accounts have been approved, the special manager's receipts and payments shall be added to those of the liquidator.

[15.272]
4.73 Termination of appointment

(1) The special manager's appointment terminates if the winding up petition is dismissed or, if a provisional liquidator having been appointed, he is discharged without a winding up order having been made.

(2) If the liquidator is of opinion that the employment of the special manager is no longer necessary or profitable for the company, he shall apply to the court for directions, and the court may order the special manager's appointment to be terminated.

(3) The liquidator shall make the same application if a resolution of the creditors is passed, requesting that the appointment be terminated.

CHAPTER 11 PUBLIC EXAMINATION OF COMPANY OFFICERS AND OTHERS

[15.273]
4.74 Notice of order for public examination

Where the court orders the public examination of any person under section 133(1), then, unless the court otherwise directs, the liquidator shall give at least 14 days' notice of the time and place of the examination to the persons specified in paragraphs (c) to (e) of section 133(4) and the liquidator may, if he thinks fit, cause notice of the order to be given, by public advertisement in one or more newspapers circulating in the area of the principal place of business of the company, at least 14 days before the date fixed for the examination but there shall be no such advertisement before at least 7 days have elapsed from the date when the person to be examined was served with the order.

[15.274]
4.75 Order on request by creditors or contributories

(1) A request to the liquidator by a creditor or creditors or contributory or contributories under section 133(2) shall be made in writing and be accompanied by—

(a) a list of the creditors (if any) concurring with the request and the amounts of their respective claims in the liquidation, or (as the case may be) of the contributories (if any) so concurring, with their respective values, and

(b) from each creditor or contributory concurring, written confirmation of his concurrence.

(2) The request must specify the name of the proposed examinee, the relationship which he has, or has had, to the company and the reasons why his examination is requested.

(3) Before an application to the court is made on the request, the requisitionists shall deposit with the liquidator such sum as the latter may determine to be appropriate by way of caution for the expenses of the hearing of a public examination, if ordered.

(4) Subject as follows, the liquidator shall, within 28 days of receiving the request, make the application to the court required by section 133(2).

(5) If the liquidator is of opinion that the request is an unreasonable one in the circumstances, he may apply to the court for an order relieving him from the obligation to make the application required by that subsection.

(6) If the court so orders, and the application for the order was made ex parte, notice of the order shall be given forthwith by the liquidator to the requisitionists. If the application for an order is dismissed, the liquidator's application under section 133(2) shall be made forthwith on conclusion of the hearing of the application first mentioned.

(7) Where a public examination of the examinee has been ordered by the court on a creditors' or contributories' requisition under this Rule the court may order that the expenses of the examination are to be paid, as to a specified proportion, out of the caution under paragraph (3), instead of out of the assets.

CHAPTER 12 MISCELLANEOUS

[15.275]
[4.75A Electronic measures – application

(1) Subject to paragraph (2), this Rule and Rules 4.75B and 4.75C apply where a notice or other document is required to be given, delivered or sent under this Part or Parts IV or V of the Act or Part VI of the Act so far as it applies where a company goes into liquidation.

(2) This Rule and Rules 4.75B and 4.75C do not apply to—

(a) lodging any application, or other document with the court;

(b) service of any application, or other document lodged with the court;

(c) service of any order of the court;

(d) submission of documents to the registrar of companies;

(e) service of a statutory demand;

(f) a notice or other document to be given, delivered or sent to or by a provisional liquidator appointed under section 135; or

(g) a notice or other document to be given, delivered or sent under section 233.

(3) For the purposes of paragraph (1) a company goes into liquidation if it passes a resolution for voluntary winding up or a winding-up order is made by the court at a time when it has not already gone into liquidation by passing such a resolution.

(4) The reference to a resolution for voluntary winding up in paragraph (3) includes a reference to a resolution which is deemed to occur by virtue of—

(a) paragraph 83(6)(b) of Schedule B1 to the Act; or

(b) an order made following conversion of administration or a voluntary arrangement into winding up by virtue of [Article 51 of the EU Regulation].]

NOTES

Commencement: 30 May 2014.

Inserted, together with rr 4.75B. 4.75C, by the Insolvency (Scotland) Amendment Rules 2014, SSI 2014/114, rr 2, 26(2), subject to savings in r 29 thereof as noted to r 0.2 at **[15.2]**.

Para (4): words in square brackets in sub-para (b) substituted for original words "Article 37 of the EC Regulation" by the Insolvency Amendment (EU 2015/848) Regulations 2017, SI 2017/702, regs 2, 3, Schedule, Pt 5, paras 61, 83, as from 26 June 2017, except in relation to proceedings opened before that date.

[15.276]
[4.75B Electronic delivery

(1) Unless in any particular case some other form of delivery is required by the Act or the Rules or an order of the court, a notice or other document may be given, delivered or sent by electronic means provided that the intended recipient of the notice or other document has—

(a) consented (whether in the specific case or generally) to electronic delivery (and has not revoked that consent); and

(b) provided an electronic address for delivery.

(2) In the absence of evidence to the contrary, a notice or other document is presumed to have been delivered where—

(a) the sender can produce a copy of the electronic message which—

(i) contained the notice or other document, or to which the notice or other document was attached; and

(ii) shows the time and date the message was sent; and

(b) that electronic message contains the address supplied under paragraph (1)(b).

(3) A message sent electronically is deemed to have been delivered to the recipient no later than 9.00am on the next business day after it was sent.]

NOTES

Commencement: 30 May 2014.

Inserted as noted to r 4.75A at **[15.275]**.

[15.277]

[4.75C Electronic delivery by liquidators etc

(1) Where an office-holder gives, sends or delivers a notice or other document to any person by electronic means, the notice or document must contain or be accompanied by a statement that the recipient may request a hard copy of the notice or document and specifying a telephone number, e-mail address and postal address which may be used to request a hard copy.

(2) Where a hard copy of the notice or other document is requested, it must be sent within 5 business days of receipt of the request by the office-holder.

(3) An office-holder must not require a person making a request under paragraph (2) to pay a fee for the supply of the document.]

NOTES

Commencement: 30 May 2014.

Inserted as noted to r 4.75A at **[15.275]**.

[15.278]

[4.76 Limitation

(1) The provisions in paragraph (2) apply in relation to the liquidation as they apply in relation to a sequestration subject to the substitution of "petition for winding up" for references to "petition for sequestration" and to any other necessary modifications.

(2) The provisions are—

(a) sections 13(5) and 46(8), as read with section 228(8) to (10), of the Bankruptcy (Scotland) Act 2016;

(b) article 6(1)(a) and (b), (2) and (3) of the Bankruptcy (Scotland) Act 2016 (Consequential Provisions and Modifications) Order 2016.]

NOTES

Commencement: 30 November 2016.

Substituted by the Bankruptcy (Scotland) Act 2016 (Consequential Provisions and Modifications) Order 2016, SI 2016/1034, art 7(1), (3), Sch 1, para 36(1), (3), as from 30 November 2016 (except in relation to (i) a sequestration as regards which the petition is presented, or the debtor application is made before that date; or (ii) a trust deed executed before that date). Rule 4.76 originally read as follows (with words in square brackets substituted for original words "modifications specified in Rule 4.16(2)", by SSI 2014/114, rr 2, 19, subject to savings in r 29 thereof as noted to r 0.2 at **[15.2]**)—

> **"4.76 Limitation**
> The provisions of section 8(5) and 22(8), as read with section 73(5), of the Bankruptcy (Scotland) Act 1985 (presentation of petition or submission of claim to bar effect of limitation of actions) shall apply in relation to the liquidation as they apply in relation to a sequestration, subject to the [substitution of "petition for winding up" for references to "petition for sequestration"] and to any other necessary modifications.".

[15.279]

4.77 Dissolution after winding up

Where the court makes an order under section 204(5) or 205(5), the person on whose application the order was made shall deliver to the registrar of companies a copy of the order.

NOTES

See Sch 5, Form 4.28 (Scot) at **[15.349]**, and the notes to that Schedule.

CHAPTER 13 COMPANY WITH PROHIBITED NAME

[15.280]

4.78 Preliminary

The rules of this Chapter—

(a) relate to the leave required under section 216 (restriction on re-use of name of company in insolvent liquidation) for a person to act as mentioned in section 216(3) in relation to a company with a prohibited name, and

(b) prescribe the cases excepted from that provision, that is to say, those in which a person to whom the section applies may so act without that leave[, and

(c) apply to all windings up to which section 216 applies, whether or not the winding up commenced before or after the coming into force of the Insolvency (Scotland) Amendment Rules 1987].

NOTES

Para (c) and word "and" immediately preceding it added by the Insolvency (Scotland) Amendment Rules 1987, SI 1987/1921, r 3(1), Schedule, Pt I, para 33.

[15.281]
4.79 Application for leave under section 216(3)

When considering an application for leave under section 216, the court may call on the liquidator, or any former liquidator, of the liquidating company for a report of the circumstances in which that company became insolvent, and the extent (if any) of the applicant's apparent responsibility for its doing so.

[15.282]
[4.80 First excepted case

(1) This Rule applies where—

(a) a person ("the person") was within the period mentioned in section 216(1) a director, or shadow director, of an insolvent company that has gone into insolvent liquidation;

(b) the person acts in all or any of the ways specified in section 216(3) in connection with, or for the purposes of, the carrying on (or proposed carrying on) of the whole or substantially the whole of the business of the insolvent company where that business (or substantially the whole of it) is (or is to be) acquired from the insolvent company under arrangements—

(i) made by its liquidator; or

(ii) made before the insolvent company entered into insolvent liquidation by an office-holder acting in relation to it as administrator, receiver or supervisor of a voluntary arrangement under Part 1 of the Act.

(2) The person will not be taken to have contravened section 216 if prior to his acting in the circumstances set out in paragraph (1) a notice is, in accordance with the requirements of paragraph (3)—

(a) given by the person to every creditor of the insolvent company whose name and address—

(i) is known by him; or

(ii) is ascertainable by him on the making of such enquiries as are reasonable in the circumstances; and

(b) published in the Edinburgh Gazette.

(3) The notice referred to in paragraph (2)—

(a) may be given and published before the completion of the arrangements referred to in paragraph (1)(b) but must be given and published no later than 28 days after that completion;

(b) must state—

(i) the name and registered number of the insolvent company;

(ii) the name of the person;

(iii) that it is his intention to act (or, where the insolvent company has not entered insolvent liquidation, to act or continue to act) in all or any of the ways specified in section 216(3) in connection with, or for the purposes of, the carrying on of the whole, or substantially the whole, of the business of the insolvent company; and

(iv) the prohibited name or, where the company has not entered insolvent liquidation, the name under which the business is being, or is to be, carried on which would be a prohibited name in respect of the person in the event of the insolvent company entering insolvent liquidation; and

(c) must in the case of notice given to each creditor of the company be given using Form 4.32(Scot).

(4) Notice may in particular be given under this Rule—

(a) prior to the insolvent company entering insolvent liquidation where the business (or substantially the whole of the business) is, or is to be, acquired by another company under arrangements made by an office-holder acting in relation to the insolvent company as administrator, receiver or supervisor of a voluntary arrangement (whether or not at the time of the giving of the notice the director is a director of that other company); or

(b) at a time where the person is a director of another company where—

(i) the other company has acquired, or is to acquire, the whole, or substantially the whole, of the business of the insolvent company under arrangements made by its liquidator; and

(ii) it is proposed that after the giving of the notice a prohibited name should be adopted by the other company.]

NOTES

Substituted by the Insolvency (Scotland) Amendment Rules 2007, SI 2007/2537, r 3(1), (2), subject to transitional provisions in r 2 thereof, which provides that r 4.80 as it stands before 1 October 2007 shall, in relation to any arrangements referred to in para (1) of that Rule (see below) which have been completed before that date, continue to apply to a person who was a director or shadow director of the insolvent company the whole, or substantially the whole, of whose business is acquired.

Prior to substitution, r 4.80 read as follows:

"4.80 First excepted case

(1) Where a company ("the successor company") acquires the whole, or substantially the whole, of the business of an insolvent company, under arrangements made by an insolvency practitioner acting as its liquidator, administrator or receiver, or as supervisor of a voluntary arrangement under Part I of the Act, the successor company may for the purposes of section 216 give notice under this Rule to the insolvent company's creditors.

(2) To be effective, the notice must be given within 28 days from the completion of the arrangements to all creditors of the insolvent company of whose addresses the successor is aware in that period; and it must specify—

(a) the name and registered number of the insolvent company and the circumstances in which its business has been acquired by the successor company,

(b) the name which the successor company has assumed, or proposes to assume for the purpose of carrying on the business, if that name is or will be a prohibited name under section 216, and

(c) any change of name which it has made, or proposes to make, for that purpose under section 28 of the Companies Act.

(3) The notice may name a person to whom section 216 may apply as having been a director or shadow director of the insolvent company, and give particulars as to the nature and duration of that directorship, with a view to his being a director of the successor company or being otherwise associated with its management.

(4) If the successor company has effectively given notice under this Rule to the insolvent company's creditors, a person who is so named in the notice may act in relation to the successor company in any of the ways mentioned in section 216(3), notwithstanding that he has not the leave of the court under that section.".

[15.283]
[4.81 Second excepted case

(1) Where a person to whom section 216 applies as having been a director or shadow director of the liquidating company applies for leave of the court under that section not later than 7 days from the date on which the company went into liquidation, he may, during the period specified in paragraph (2) below, act in any of the ways mentioned in section 216(3), notwithstanding that he has not the leave of the court under that section.

(2) The period referred to in paragraph (1) begins with the day in which the company goes into liquidation and ends either on the day falling 6 weeks after that date or on the day on which the court disposes of the application for leave under section 216, whichever of those days occurs first.]

NOTES

Substituted by the Insolvency (Scotland) Amendment Rules 1987, SI 1987/1921, r 3(1), Schedule, Pt I, para 34.

[15.284]
4.82 Third excepted case

The court's leave under section 216(3) is not required where the company there referred to, though known by a prohibited name within the meaning of the section,

(a) has been known by that name for the whole of the period of 12 months ending with the day before the liquidating company went into liquidation, and

(b) has not at any time in those 12 months been dormant within the meaning of section 252(5) of the Companies Act.

[CHAPTER 14 [EU REGULATION]—MEMBER STATE LIQUIDATOR

[15.285]
4.83 Interpretation of creditor and notice to member State liquidator

(1) This Rule applies where a member State liquidator has been appointed in relation to the company.

(2) For the purposes of the provisions referred to in paragraph (3) the member State liquidator is deemed to be a creditor.

(3) The provisions referred to in paragraph (2) are—

(a) Rules 4.10(1) (report to creditors and contributories), 4.10(3) (summary of statement of affairs), 4.13 (other meetings of creditors), 4.15 (submission of claims), [4.16A (evidence of claims), 4.16B (adjudication of claims),] 4.17 (claims in foreign currency), 4.18(4) (appointment of liquidator by court), 4.23(2) and (4) (summoning of meeting for removal of liquidator), 4.31 (final meeting), 4.35 (creditors' claim that remuneration is excessive), 4.41(1), (2) and (3) (membership of liquidation committee), 4.52(3) (vacancy (creditor members)), 4.62(1) (membership of committee), [4.68(4) (estate to be distributed in respect of the accounting periods),] 4.74 (notice of order for public examination), 7.3 (notice of meeting) (insofar as it applies to a notice of meeting of creditors under section 138(3) or (4) for the purposes of rule 4.12 and to a meeting requisitioned under rule 7.6 insofar as it applies in a winding up by the court), 7.6(2) (meetings requisitioned) (insofar as it applies in a winding up by the court) and 7.9 (entitlement to vote (creditors)) (insofar as it applies in a winding up by the court); *and*

(b) sections 48(5), (6) and (8) and 49 of the Bankruptcy Act as applied by Rule 4.16 and section 52(3) of that Act as applied by rule 4.68(1).

(4) Paragraphs (2) and (3) are without prejudice to the generality of the right to participate referred to in paragraph 3 of [Article 45 of the EU Regulation] (exercise of creditors' rights).

(5) Where the liquidator is obliged to give notice to, or provide a copy of a document (including an order of court) to, the court or the registrar of companies, the liquidator shall give notice or provide copies, as the case may be, to the member State liquidator.

(6) Paragraph (5) is without prejudice to the generality of the obligations imposed by [Article 41 of the EU Regulation (cooperation and communication between insolvency practitioners)].]

NOTES

Inserted, together with the Chapter heading preceding this Rule and rr 4.84, 4.85, by the Insolvency (Scotland) Regulations 2003, SI 2003/2109, regs 23, 27(3), as from 8 September 2003, subject to the saving that anything done under or

Part 15 Insolvency (Scotland) Rules 1986

for the purposes of any provision of these Rules before 8 September 2003 has effect as if done under or for the purposes of the provision as amended.

Words in square brackets in Chapter heading substituted for original words "EC Regulation" by the Insolvency Amendment (EU 2015/848) Regulations 2017, SI 2017/702, regs 2, 3, Schedule, Pt 5, paras 61, 84, as from 26 June 2017, except in relation to proceedings opened before that date.

Para (3): words in square brackets in sub-para (a) inserted and sub-para (b) revoked, together with word immediately preceding it, by the Insolvency (Scotland) Amendment Rules 2014, SSI 2014/114, rr 2, 20, subject to savings in r 29 thereof as noted to r 0.2 at **[15.2]**.

Para (4): words in square brackets substituted for original words "Article 32 of the EC Regulation" by SI 2017/702, regs 2, 3, Schedule, Pt 5, paras 61, 85(a), as from 26 June 2017, except in relation to proceedings opened before that date.

Para (6): words in square brackets substituted for original words "Article 31 of the EC Regulation (duty to co operate and communicate information)" by SI 2017/702, regs 2, 3, Schedule, Pt 5, paras 61, 85(b), as from 26 June 2017, except in relation to proceedings opened before that date.

[CHAPTER 15 [EU REGULATION]—CREDITORS' VOLUNTARY WINDING UP—CONFIRMATION BY THE COURT

[15.286]

4.84 Application for confirmation

(1) Where a company has passed a resolution for voluntary winding up, and no declaration under section 89 has been made, the liquidator may apply to the court for an order confirming the creditors' voluntary winding up for the purposes of the [EU Regulation].

(2) The application shall be in writing in the form required by Rule 7.30 and Schedule 5 and verified by affidavit by the liquidator (using the same form) and shall state—

(a) the name of the applicant;
(b) the name of the company and its registered number;
(c) the date on which the resolution for voluntary winding up was passed;
(d) that the application is accompanied by all of the documents required under paragraph (3) which are true copies of the documents required; and
[(e) that the EU Regulation will apply to the company and whether the proceedings will be main proceedings, territorial proceedings or secondary proceedings and the reasons for so stating].

(3) The liquidator shall lodge in court two copies of the application, together with one copy of the following—

(a) the resolution for voluntary winding up referred to by section 84(3);
(b) evidence of his appointment as liquidator of the company; and
(c) the statement of affairs required under section 99.

(4) It shall not be necessary to serve the application on, or give notice of it to, any person.

(5) On an application under this Rule the court may confirm the creditors' voluntary winding up.

(6) If the court confirms the creditor's voluntary winding up it may do so without a hearing.

(7) This Rule applies in relation to a UK insurer (within the meaning of the Insurers (Reorganisation and Winding Up) Regulations 2003) with the modification specified in paragraph (8) below.

(8) For the purposes of paragraph (7), this Rule has effect as if there were substituted for paragraph (1) above—

"(1) Where a UK Insurer (within the meaning of the Insurers (Reorganisation and Winding Up) Regulations 2003) has passed a resolution for voluntary winding up, and no declaration under section 89 has been made, the liquidator may apply to court for an order confirming the creditors' voluntary winding up for the purposes of [Articles 274 and 293 of Directive 2009/138/EC of the European Parliament and of the Council of 25 November 2009 on the taking-up and pursuit of the business of Insurance and Reinsurance (Solvency II)].".]

NOTES

Inserted, together with the Chapter heading preceding this Rule, as noted to r 4.83 at **[15.285]**.

Words in square brackets in Chapter heading substituted for original words "EC Regulation" by the Insolvency Amendment (EU 2015/848) Regulations 2017, SI 2017/702, regs 2, 3, Schedule, Pt 5, paras 61, 86, as from 26 June 2017, except in relation to proceedings opened before that date.

Para (1): words in square brackets substituted for original words "EC Regulation" by SI 2017/702, regs 2, 3, Schedule, Pt 5, paras 61, 87(a), as from 26 June 2017, except in relation to proceedings opened before that date.

Para (2): sub-para (e) substituted by SI 2017/702, regs 2, 3, Schedule, Pt 5, paras 61, 87(b), as from 26 June 2017, except in relation to proceedings opened before that date, and previously read as follows:

"(e) that the EC Regulation will apply to the company and whether the proceedings will be main proceedings, territorial proceedings or secondary proceedings.".

Para (8): words in square brackets substituted by the Solvency 2 Regulations 2015, SI 2015/575, reg 60, Sch 2, para 1.

Para (2): see Sch 5, Form 4.30 (Scot) at **[15.349]**, and the notes to that Schedule.

[15.287]

[4.85 Notice to member State liquidator and creditors in member States

Where the court has confirmed the creditors' voluntary winding up, the liquidator shall forthwith give notice—

(a) if there is a member State liquidator in relation to the company, to[—
(i) any member State liquidator; or

(ii) where the liquidator knows that an application has been made to commence insolvency proceedings in another member State but a member State liquidator has not yet been appointed, to the court to which that application has been made];

(b) in accordance with [Article 54 of the EU Regulation] (duty to inform creditors).]

NOTES

Inserted as noted to r 4.83 at [15.285].

Words in square brackets in para (a) substituted for original words "the member State liquidator" and words in square brackets in para (b) substituted for original words "Article 40 of the EC Regulation" by the Insolvency Amendment (EU 2015/848) Regulations 2017, SI 2017/702, regs 2, 3, Schedule, Pt 5, paras 61, 88, as from 26 June 2017, except in relation to proceedings opened before that date.

PART 5
CREDITORS' VOLUNTARY WINDING UP

[15.288]
5 Application of Part 4

The provisions of Part 4 shall apply in a creditors' voluntary winding up of a company as they apply in a winding up by the court subject to the modifications specified in Schedule 1 and to any other necessary modifications.

PART 6
MEMBERS' VOLUNTARY WINDING UP

[15.289]
6 Application of Part 4

The provisions of Part 4, which are specified in Schedule 2, shall apply in relation to a members' voluntary winding up of a company as they apply in a winding up by the court, subject to the modifications specified in Schedule 2 and to any other necessary modifications.

PART 7
PROVISIONS OF GENERAL APPLICATION

CHAPTER 1 MEETINGS

[15.290]
7.1 Scope of Chapter 1

(1) This Chapter applies to any meetings held in insolvency proceedings other than meetings of a creditors' committee in administration or receivership, or of a liquidation committee.

(2) The Rules in this Chapter shall apply to any such meeting subject to any contrary provision in the Act or in the Rules, or to any direction of the court.

[15.291]
7.2 Summoning of meetings

(1) In fixing the date, time and place for a meeting, the person summoning the meeting ("the convenor") shall have regard to the convenience of the persons who are to attend.

(2) Meetings shall in all cases be summoned for commencement between 10.00 and 16.00 hours on a business day, unless the court otherwise directs.

[15.292]
7.3 Notice of meeting

(1) The convenor shall give not less than 21 days' notice of the date, time and place of the meeting to every person known to him as being entitled to attend the meeting.

(2) In paragraph (1), for the reference to 21 days, there shall be substituted a reference to 14 days in the following cases—

[(a) any meeting of the company or of its creditors under paragraph 52, 56 or 62 of Schedule B1 to the Act;]

(b) a meeting of the creditors under [paragraph 51 or 54(2)] (to consider administrator's proposals or proposed revisions); . . .

(c) a meeting of creditors under section 67(2) (meeting of unsecured creditors in receivership)[; and

(d) a meeting of creditors or contributories under section 138(3) or (4).]

(3) The convenor may also publish notice of the date, time and place of the meeting in a newspaper circulating in the area of the principal place of business of the company or in such other newspaper as he thinks most appropriate for ensuring that it comes to the notice of the persons who are entitled to attend the meeting. . . .

[(3A) Any notice under this paragraph [or Rule 2.26A(1) or (2)] shall be published not less than 21 days or, in cases to which paragraph (2) above applies, 14 days before the meeting.]

(4) Any notice under this Rule shall state—

(a) the purpose of the meeting;

(b) the persons who are entitled to attend and vote at the meeting;

(c) the effects of Rule 7.9 or, as the case may be, 7.10 (Entitlement to Vote) and of the relevant provisions of Rule 7.12 (Resolutions);

(d) in the case of a meeting of creditors or contributories, that proxies may be lodged at or before the meeting and the place where they may be lodged; and

(e) in the case of a meeting of creditors, that claims may be lodged by those who have not already done so at or before the meeting and the place where they may be lodged.

Where a meeting of creditors is summoned specially for the purpose of removing the liquidator in accordance with section 171(2) or 172(2), or of receiving his resignation under Rule 4.28, the notice summoning it shall also include the information required by Rule 4.23(2) or, as the case may be, 4.28(2).

(5) With the notice given under paragraph (1), the convenor shall also send out a proxy form.

(6) In the case of any meeting of creditors or contributories, the court may order that notice of the meeting be given by public advertisement in such form as may be specified in the order and not by individual notice to the persons concerned. In considering whether to make such an order, the court shall have regard to the cost of the public advertisement, to the amount of the assets available and to the extent of the interest of creditors or contributories or any particular class of either.

[(7) The provisions of this Rule shall not apply to a meeting of creditors summoned under section 95 or 98 but any notice advertised in accordance with section 95(2)(c) or 98(1)(c) shall give not less than 7 days' notice of the meeting.]

NOTES

Para (2): sub-para (a) substituted by the Insolvency (Scotland) Amendment Rules 2010, SI 2010/688, r 3, Sch 1, para 105, subject to transitional provisions in r 4 thereof at **[2.80]**, and previously read as follows:

"(a) any meeting of the company or of its creditors summoned under section 3 (to consider directors' proposals for voluntary arrangement);";

words in square brackets in sub-para (b) substituted for words "section 23(1)(b) or 25(2)(b)" by the Insolvency (Scotland) Amendment Rules 2003, SI 2003/2111, r 6, Sch 2, para 7(a), subject to savings in r 7 thereof at **[2.34]**; word omitted revoked and words in second pair of square brackets added by the Insolvency (Scotland) Amendment Rules 1987, SI 1987/1921, r 3(1), Schedule, Pt I, para 35(1).

Para (3): words "In the case of a creditors' meeting summoned by the administrator under [paragraph 51], the administrator shall publish such a notice." (as amended by SI 2003/2111, r 6, Sch 2, para 7(b)) revoked by the Insolvency (Scotland) Amendment Rules 2009, SI 2009/662, r 2, Schedule, para 12, subject to transitional provisions in r 3 thereof as noted to r 1.4 at **[15.10]**.

Para (3A): inserted by SI 1987/1921, r 3(1), Schedule, Pt I, para 35(2); words in square brackets inserted by SI 2009/662, r 2, Schedule, para 13, subject to transitional provisions in r 3 thereof as noted to r 1.4 at **[15.10]**.

Para (7): added by SI 1987/1921, r 3(1), Schedule, Pt I, para 35(3).

[15.293]

7.4 Additional notices in certain cases

[(1) This Rule applies where a company goes, or proposes to go, into liquidation and it is an authorised institution or a former authorised institution within the meaning of the Banking Act.]

(2) Notice of any meeting of the company at which it is intended to propose a resolution for its voluntary winding up shall be given by the directors to the Bank of England ("the Bank") and to the Deposit Protection Board ("the Board") as such notice is given to members of the company.

(3) Where a creditors' meeting is summoned by the liquidator under section 95 or 98, the same notice of meeting must be given to the Bank and Board as is given to the creditors under this Chapter.

(4) Where the company is being wound up by the court, notice of the first meetings of creditors and contributories within the meaning of Rule 4.12 shall be given to the Bank and the Board by the liquidator.

(5) Where in any winding up a meeting of creditors or contributories is summoned for the purpose of—

(a) receiving the liquidator's resignation or

(b) removing the liquidator, or

(c) appointing a new liquidator,

the person summoning the meeting and giving notice of it shall also give notice to the Bank and the Board.

(6) The Board is entitled to be represented at any meeting of which it is required by this Rule to be given notice; and Schedule 3 has effect with respect to the voting rights of the Board at such a meeting.

NOTES

Para (1): substituted by the Insolvency (Scotland) Amendment Rules 1987, SI 1987/1921, r 3(1), Schedule, Pt I, para 36.

[15.294]

7.5 Chairman of meetings

(1) The chairman at any meeting of creditors in insolvency proceedings[, other than at a meeting of creditors summoned under section 98,] shall be the responsible practitioner, or [except at a meeting of creditors summoned under section 95] a person nominated by him in writing.

(2) A person nominated under this Rule must be either—

(a) a person who is qualified to act as an insolvency practitioner in relation to the company, or

(b) an employee of the administrator, receiver or liquidator, as the case may be, or his firm who is experienced in insolvency matters.

(3) This Rule also applies to meetings of contributories in a liquidation.

(4) At the first meeting of creditors or contributories in a winding up by the court, the interim liquidator shall be the chairman except that, where a resolution is proposed to appoint the interim liquidator to be the liquidator, another person may be elected to act as chairman for the purpose of choosing the liquidator.

(5) The Rule is subject to Rule 4.23(3) (meeting for removal of liquidator).

NOTES

Para (1): words in square brackets inserted by the Insolvency (Scotland) Amendment Rules 1987, SI 1987/1921, r 3(1), Schedule, Pt I, para 37.

[15.295]

7.6 Meetings requisitioned

[(1) Subject to paragraph (8), this Rule applies to any request by a creditor or creditors—

(a) to—

(i) an administrator under [paragraph 52(2) or 56(1)], or

(ii) a liquidator under section 171(3) or 172(3),

for a meeting of creditors; or

(b) to a liquidator under section 142(3) for separate meetings of creditors and contributories, or for any other meeting under any other provision of the Act or the Rules.]

(2) Any such request shall be accompanied by—

(a) a list of any creditors concurring with the request, showing the amounts of the respective claims against the company of the creditor making the request and the concurring creditors;

(b) from each creditor concurring, written confirmation of his concurrence; and

(c) a statement of the purpose of the proposed meeting.

(3) If the administrator or, as the case may be, the liquidator considers the request to be properly made in accordance with the Act or the Rules, he shall summon a meeting of the creditors to be held on a date not more than 35 days from the date of his receipt of the request.

(4) Expenses of summoning and holding a meeting under this Rule shall be paid by the creditor making the request, who shall deposit with the administrator [or, as the case may be, the liquidator] caution for their payment.

(5) The sum to be deposited shall be such as the administrator or, as the case may be, the liquidator may determine and he shall not act without the deposit having been made.

(6) The meeting may resolve that the expenses of summoning and holding it are to be payable out of the assets of the company as an expense of the administration or, as the case may be, the liquidation.

(7) To the extent that any caution deposited under this Rule is not required for the payment of expenses of summoning and holding the meeting, it shall be repaid to the person or persons who made it.

(8) This Rule applies to requests by a contributory or contributories for a meeting of contributories, with the modification that, for the reference in paragraph (2) to the creditors' respective claims, there shall be substituted a reference to the contributories' respective values (being the amounts for which they may vote at any meeting).

(9) This Rule is without prejudice to the powers of the court under Rule 4.67(2) (voluntary winding up succeeded by winding up by the court).

NOTES

Para (1): substituted by the Insolvency (Scotland) Amendment Rules 1987, SI 1987/1921, r 3(1), Schedule, Pt I, para 38(1); words in square brackets substituted for words "section 17(3)" by the Insolvency (Scotland) Amendment Rules 2003, SI 2003/2111, r 6, Sch 2, para 8, subject to savings in r 7 thereof at **[2.34]**.

Para (4): words in square brackets inserted by SI 1987/1921, r 3(1), Schedule, Pt I, para 38(2).

[15.296]

7.7 Quorum

(1) Subject to the next paragraph, a quorum is—

(a) in the case of a creditors' meeting, at least one creditor entitled to vote;

(b) in the case of a meeting of contributories, at least 2 contributories so entitled, or all the contributories, if their number does not exceed 2.

(2) For the purposes of this Rule, the reference to the creditor or contributories necessary to constitute a quorum is not confined to those persons present or duly represented under section 375 of the Companies Act but includes those represented by proxy by any person (including the chairman).

[(3) Where at any meeting of creditors or contributories—

(a) the provisions of this Rule as to a quorum being present are satisfied by the attendance of—

(i) the chairman alone, or

(ii) one other person in addition to the chairman, and

(b) the chairman is aware, by virtue of claims and proxies received or otherwise, that one or more additional persons would, if attending, be entitled to vote,

the meeting shall not commence until at least the expiry of 15 minutes after the time appointed for its commencement.]

NOTES

Para (3): added by the Insolvency (Scotland) Amendment Rules 1987, SI 1987/1921, r 3(1), Schedule, Pt I, para 39.

[15.297]
7.8 Adjournment

(1) This Rule applies to meetings of creditors and to meetings of contributories.

(2) If, within a period of 30 minutes from the time appointed for the commencement of a meeting, a quorum is not present, then, unless the chairman otherwise decides, the meeting shall be adjourned to the same time and place in the following week or, if that is not a business day, to the business day immediately following.

(3) In the course of any meeting, the chairman may, in his discretion, and shall, if the meeting so resolves, adjourn it to such date, time and place as seems to him to be appropriate in the circumstances.

(4) Paragraph (3) is subject to Rule 4.23(3) where the liquidator or his nominee is chairman and a resolution has been proposed for the liquidator's removal.

(5) An adjournment under paragraph [(2) or (3)] shall not be for a period of more than 21 days [and notice of the adjourned meeting may be given by the chairman].

(6) Where a meeting is adjourned, any proxies given for the original meeting may be used at the adjourned meeting.

[(7) Where a company meeting at which a resolution for voluntary winding up is to be proposed is adjourned without that resolution having been passed, any resolution passed at a meeting under section 98 held before the holding of the adjourned company meeting only has effect on and from the passing by the company of a resolution for winding up.]

NOTES

Para (5): words in first pair of square brackets substituted and words in second pair of square brackets inserted by the Insolvency (Scotland) Amendment Rules 1987, SI 1987/1921, r 3(1), Schedule, Pt I, para 40(1).

Para (7): added by SI 1987/1921, r 3(1), Schedule, Pt I, para 40(2).

[15.298]
7.9 Entitlement to vote (creditors)

(1) This Rule applies to a creditors' meeting in any insolvency proceedings.

(2) A creditor is entitled to vote at any meeting if he has submitted his claim to the responsible insolvency practitioner and his claim has been accepted in whole or in part.

(3) Chapter 5 of Part 4 (claims in liquidation) shall apply for the purpose of determining a creditor's entitlement to vote at any creditors' meeting in any insolvency proceedings as it applies for the purpose of determining a creditor's entitlement to vote at a meeting of creditors in a liquidation, subject to the modifications specified in the following paragraphs and to any other necessary modification.

(4) For any reference in the said Chapter 5 . . . to—

(a) the liquidator, there shall be substituted a reference to the . . . administrator or receiver, as the case may be;

(b) the liquidation, there shall be substituted a reference to the . . . administration or receivership as the case may be;

(c) the date of commencement of winding up, there shall be substituted a reference—

(i) . . .

(ii) in the case of a meeting in the administration or receivership, to [the date upon which the company entered administration] or, as the case may be, the date of appointment of the receiver;

(5) In the application to meetings of creditors other than in liquidation proceedings of [Rules 4.16E to 4.16G, Rule 4.16G(2) and (3)] (secured creditors) shall not apply.

(6) This Rule is subject to Rule 7.4(6) and Schedule 3.

NOTES

Para (4): words ", or in any provision of the Bankruptcy Act as applied by Rule 4.16(1)," omitted in the first place revoked by the Insolvency (Scotland) Amendment Rules 2014, SSI 2014/114, rr 2, 21(a), subject to savings in r 29 thereof as noted to r 0.2 at **[15.2]**; in para (a) word "supervisor" and in sub-para (b) words "voluntary arrangement" (omitted) revoked and sub-para (c)(i) revoked by the Insolvency (Scotland) Amendment Rules 2010, SI 2010/688, r 3, Sch 1, paras 106–108, subject to transitional provisions in r 4 thereof at **[2.80]**. Sub-para (c)(i) (as amended by the Insolvency (Scotland) Amendment Rules 2003, SI 2003/2111, r 6, Sch 2, para 9(a), subject to savings in r 7 thereof at **[2.34]**) previously read as follows:

"(i) in the case of a meeting in a voluntary arrangement, to the date of the meeting or, where the company is being wound up or is in administration, the date of its going into liquidation or, as the case may be, entering administration; and".

In sub-para (c)(ii), words in square brackets substituted for words "the date of the administration order" by SI 2003/2111, r 6, Sch 2, para 9(b), subject to savings in r 7 thereof at **[2.34]**.

Para (5): words in square brackets substituted for original words "Schedule 1 to the Bankruptcy Act, paragraph 5(2) and (3)", by SSI 2014/114, rr 2, 21(b), subject to savings in r 29 thereof as noted to r 0.2 at **[15.2]**.

[15.299]
7.10 Entitlement to vote (members and contributories)

(1) Members of a company or contributories at their meetings shall vote according to their rights attaching to their shares respectively in accordance with the articles of association.

(2) . . .

(3) Reference in this Rule to a person's share include any other interests which he may have as a member of the company.

NOTES

Para (2): revoked by the Insolvency (Scotland) Amendment Rules 2002, SI 2002/2709, r 4(1), Schedule, Pt 2, para 17, subject to savings contained in r 4(2) as noted to r 1.1 at **[15.4]**. Para (2) originally read as follows:

> "(2) In the case of a meeting of members of the company in a voluntary arrangement, where no voting rights attach to a member's share, he is nevertheless entitled to vote either for or against the proposal or any modification of it.".

[15.300]

7.11 Chairman of meeting as proxy holder

(1) Where the chairman at a meeting of creditors or contributories holds a proxy which requires him to vote for a particular resolution and no other person proposes that resolution—

- (a) he shall propose it himself, unless he considers that there is good reason for not doing so, and
- (b) if he does not propose it, he shall forthwith after the meeting notify the person who granted him the proxy of the reason why he did not do so.

(2) . . .

NOTES

Para (2): revoked by the Insolvency (Scotland) Amendment Rules 2010, SI 2010/688, r 3, Sch 1, para 109, subject to transitional provisions in r 4 thereof at **[2.80]**, and previously read as follows:

> "(2) At any meeting in a voluntary arrangement, the chairman shall not, by virtue of any proxy by him, vote to increase or reduce the amount of the remuneration or expenses of the nominee or the supervisor of the proposed arrangement, unless the proxy specifically directs him to vote in that way.".

[15.301]

7.12 Resolutions

(1) Subject to any contrary provision in the Act or the Rules, at any meeting of creditors, contributories or members of a company, a resolution is passed when a majority in value of those voting, in person or by proxy, have voted in favour of it.

(2) . . .

(3) In a liquidation, in the case of a resolution for the appointment of a liquidator—

- (a) if, on any vote, there are two nominees for appointment, the person for whom a majority in value has voted shall be appointed;
- (b) if there are three or more nominees, and one of them has a clear majority over both or all the others together, that one is appointed; and
- (c) in any other case, the chairman of the meeting shall continue to take votes (disregarding at each vote any nominee who has withdrawn and, if no nominee has withdrawn, the nominee who obtained the least support last time), until a clear majority is obtained for any one nominee.

The chairman may, at any time, put to the meeting a resolution for the joint appointment of any two or more nominees.

(4) Where a resolution is proposed which affects a person in respect of his remuneration or conduct as a responsible insolvency practitioner, the vote of that person, or of his firm or of any partner or employee of his shall not be reckoned in the majority required for passing the resolution. This paragraph applies with respect to a vote given by a person [(whether personally or on his behalf by a proxy-holder),] either as creditor or contributory or member or as [proxy-holder] for a creditor, contributory, or member.

NOTES

Para (2): revoked by the Insolvency (Scotland) Amendment Rules 2010, SI 2010/688, r 3, Sch 1, para 110, subject to transitional provisions in r 4 thereof at **[2.80]**, and previously read as follows:

> "(2) In a voluntary arrangement, at a creditors' meeting for any resolution to pass approving any proposal or modification, there must be at least three quarters in value of the creditors present or represented and voting, in person or by proxy, in favour of the resolution.".

Para (4): words in first pair of square brackets inserted and words in second pair of square brackets substituted by the Insolvency (Scotland) Amendment Rules 1987, SI 1987/1921, r 3(1), Schedule, Pt I, para 41.

[15.302]

7.13 Report of meeting

(1) The chairman at any meeting shall cause a report to be made of the proceedings at the meeting which shall be signed by him.

(2) The report of the meeting shall include—

- (a) a list of all the creditors or, as the case may be, contributories who attended the meeting, either in person or by proxy;
- (b) a copy of every resolution passed; and
- (c) if the meeting established a creditors' committee or a liquidation committee, as the case may be, a list of the names and addresses of those elected to be members of the committee.

(3) The chairman shall keep a copy of the report of the meeting as part of the sederunt book in the insolvency proceedings.

[CHAPTER 1A PRESCRIBED PART

[15.303]
7.13A Application under section 176A(5) to disapply section 176A

An application under section 176A(5) shall include averments as to—
- (a) the type of insolvency proceedings in which the application arises,
- (b) the financial position of the company,
- (c) the basis of the applicant's view that the cost of making a distribution to unsecured creditors would be disproportionate to the benefits, and
- (d) whether any other insolvency practitioner is acting in relation to the company and, if so, his address.]

NOTES

Inserted, together with preceding Chapter heading and r 7.13B, by the Enterprise Act 2002 (Consequential Amendments) (Prescribed Part) (Scotland) Order 2003, SI 2003/2108, art 7, as from 15 September 2003.

[15.304]
[7.13B Notice of order under section 176A(5)

(1) Where the court makes an order under section 176A(5) the applicant shall, as soon as reasonably practicable after the making of the order—
- (a) send to the company a copy of the order certified by the clerk of court,
- (b) send to the registrar of companies and, where a receiver or liquidator has been appointed, to the Accountant in Bankruptcy a copy of the order together with the form required by Rule 7.30 and Schedule 5, and
- (c) give notice of the order to each creditor of whose claim and address he is aware.

(2) The court may direct that the requirement of paragraph (1)(c) of this Rule be met by the publication of a notice in a newspaper calculated to come to the attention of the unsecured creditors stating that the court has made an order disapplying the requirement to set aside the prescribed part.]

[(3) In an administration, paragraph (2) does not apply and the court may direct that the requirement of paragraph (1)(c) of this Rule be met by the publication of a notice containing the standard content and stating that the Court has made an order disapplying the requirement to set aside the prescribed part.

(4) The notice referred to in paragraph (3) must be published as soon as reasonably practicable in the Edinburgh Gazette and may be advertised in such other manner as the administrator thinks fit.]

NOTES

Inserted as noted to r 7.13A at **[15.303]**.

Paras (3), (4): added by the Insolvency (Scotland) Amendment Rules 2010, SI 2010/688, r 3, Sch 1, para 111, subject to transitional provisions in r 4 thereof at **[2.80]**.

Para (1): see Sch 5, Form 4.31 (Scot) at **[15.349]**, and the notes to that Schedule.

CHAPTER 2 PROXIES AND COMPANY REPRESENTATION

[15.305]
7.14 Definition of "proxy"

(1) For the purposes of the Rules, a person ("the principal") may authorise another person ("the proxy-holder") to attend, speak and vote as his representative at meetings of creditors or contributories or of the company in insolvency proceedings, and any such authority is referred to as a proxy.

(2) A proxy may be given either generally for all meetings in insolvency proceedings or specifically for any meeting or class of meetings.

(3) Only one proxy may be given by the principal for any one meeting; and it may only be given to one person, being an individual aged 18 or over. The principal may nevertheless nominate one or more other such persons to be proxy-holder in the alternative in the order in which they are named in the proxy.

(4) Without prejudice to the generality of paragraph (3), a proxy, for a particular meeting may be given to whoever is to be the chairman of the meeting [and any person to whom such a proxy is given cannot decline to be the proxy-holder in relation to that proxy].

(5) A proxy may require the holder to vote on behalf of the principal on matters arising for determination at any meeting, or to abstain, either as directed or in accordance with the holder's own discretion; and it may authorise or require the holder to propose, in the principal's name, a resolution to be voted on by the meeting.

NOTES

Para (4): words in square brackets added by the Insolvency (Scotland) Amendment Rules 1987, SI 1987/1921, r 3(1), Schedule, Pt I, para 42.

[15.306]
7.15 Form of proxy

(1) With every notice summoning a meeting of creditors or contributories or of the company in insolvency proceedings there shall be sent out forms of proxy.

(2) A form of proxy shall not be sent out with the name or description of any person inserted in it.

(3) A proxy shall be in the form sent out with the notice summoning the meeting or in a form substantially to the same effect.

(4) A form of proxy shall be filled out and signed by the principal, or by some person acting under his authority and, where it is signed by someone other than the principal, the nature of his authority shall be stated on the form.

NOTES

See Sch 5, Form 4.29 (Scot) at **[15.349]**, and the notes to that Schedule.

[15.307]
7.16 Use of proxy at meeting

(1) A proxy given for a particular meeting may be used at any adjournment of that meeting.

(2) A proxy may be lodged at or before the meeting at which it is to be used.

(3) Where the responsible insolvency practitioner holds proxies to be used by him as chairman of the meeting, and some other person acts as chairman, the other person may use the insolvency practitioner's proxies as if he were himself proxy-holder.

[(4) Where a proxy directs a proxy-holder to vote for or against a resolution for the nomination or appointment of a person to be the responsible insolvency practitioner, the proxy-holder may, unless the proxy states otherwise, vote for or against (as he thinks fit) any resolution for the nomination or appointment of that person jointly with another or others.

(5) A proxy-holder may propose any resolution which, if proposed by another, would be a resolution in favour of which he would be entitled to vote by virtue of the proxy.

(6) Where a proxy gives specific directions as to voting, this does not, unless the proxy states otherwise, preclude the proxy-holder from voting at his discretion on resolutions put to the meeting which are not dealt with in the proxy.]

NOTES

Paras (4)–(6): added by the Insolvency (Scotland) Amendment Rules 1987, SI 1987/1921, r 3(1), Schedule, Pt I, para 43.

[15.308]
7.17 Retention of proxies

(1) Proxies used for voting at any meeting shall be retained by the chairman of the meeting.

(2) The chairman shall deliver the proxies forthwith after the meeting to the responsible insolvency practitioner (where he was not the chairman).

(3) The responsible insolvency practitioner shall retain all proxies in the sederunt book.

[15.309]
7.18 Right of inspection

(1) The responsible insolvency practitioner shall, so long as proxies lodged with him are in his hands, allow them to be inspected at all reasonable times on any business day, by—

- (a) the creditors, in the case of proxies used at a meeting of creditors,
- (b) a company's members or contributories, in the case of proxies used at a meeting of the company or of its contributories.

(2) The reference in paragraph (1) to creditors is—

- (a) in the case of a company in liquidation, those creditors whose claims have been accepted in whole or in part, and
- (b) in any other case, persons who have submitted in writing a claim to be creditors of the company concerned,

but in neither case does it include a person whose claim has been wholly rejected for purposes of voting, dividend or otherwise.

(3) The right of inspection given by this Rule is also exercisable, in the case of an insolvent company, by its directors.

(4) Any person attending a meeting in insolvency proceedings is entitled immediately before or in the course of the meeting, to inspect proxies and associated documents [(including claims)—

- (a) to be used in connection with that meeting, or
- (b) sent or given to the chairman of that meeting or to any other person by a creditor, member or contributory for the purpose of that meeting, whether or not they are to be used at it.]

NOTES

Para (4): words in square brackets substituted by the Insolvency (Scotland) Amendment Rules 1987, SI 1987/1921, r 3(1), Schedule, Pt I, para 44.

[15.310]
7.19 Proxy-holder with financial interest

(1) A proxy-holder shall not vote in favour of any resolution which would directly or indirectly place him, or any associate of his, in a position to receive any remuneration out of the insolvent estate, unless the proxy specifically directs him to vote in that way.

[(1A) Where a proxy-holder has signed the proxy as being authorised to do so by his principal and the proxy specifically directs him to vote in the way mentioned in paragraph (1), he shall nevertheless not vote in that way unless he produces to the chairman of the meeting written authorisation from his principal sufficient to show that the proxy-holder was entitled so to sign the proxy.]

(2) This Rule applies also to any person acting as chairman of a meeting and using proxies in that capacity [in accordance with Rule 7.16(3)]; and [in the application of this Rule to any such person], the proxy-holder is deemed an associate of his.

NOTES

Para (1A): inserted by the Insolvency (Scotland) Amendment Rules 1987, SI 1987/1921, r 3(1), Schedule, Pt I, para 45(1).

Para (2): words in first pair of square brackets inserted and words in second pair of square brackets substituted by SI 1987/1921, r 3(1), Schedule, Pt I, para 45(2).

[15.311]

7.20 Representation of corporations

(1) Where a person is authorised under section 375 of the Companies Act to represent a corporation at a meeting of creditors or contributories, he shall produce to the chairman of the meeting a copy of the resolution from which he derives his authority.

(2) The copy resolution must be executed in accordance with the provisions of section 36(3) of the Companies Act, or certified by the secretary or a director of the corporation to be a true copy.

[(3) Nothing in this Rule requires the authority of a person to sign a proxy on behalf of a principal which is a corporation to be in the form of a resolution of that corporation.]

NOTES

Para (3): added by the Insolvency (Scotland) Amendment Rules 1987, SI 1987/1921, r 3(1), Schedule, Pt I, para 46.

[15.312]

[7.20A Interpretation of creditor

(1) This Rule applies where a member State liquidator has been appointed in relation to a person subject to insolvency proceedings.

(2) For the purposes of the Rule 7.18(1) (right of inspection of proxies) a member State liquidator appointed in main proceedings is deemed to be a creditor.

(3) Paragraph (2) is without prejudice to the generality of the right to participate referred to in paragraph 3 of [Article 45 of the EU Regulation] (exercise of creditors' rights).]

NOTES

Inserted by the Insolvency (Scotland) Regulations 2003, SI 2003/2109, regs 23, 28(1), as from 8 September 2003, subject to the saving that anything done under or for the purposes of any provision of these Rules before 8 September 2003 has effect as if done under or for the purposes of the provision as amended.

Para (3): words in square brackets substituted for original words "Article 32 of the EC Regulation" by the Insolvency Amendment (EU 2015/848) Regulations 2017, SI 2017/702, regs 2, 3, Schedule, Pt 5, paras 61, 89, as from 26 June 2017, except in relation to proceedings opened before that date.

[CHAPTER 2A THE EU REGULATION

[15.313]

7.20B Main proceedings in Scotland: undertaking by office-holder in respect of assets in another member State (Article 36 of the EU Regulation)

(1) This rule applies where an office-holder in main proceedings proposes to give an undertaking under Article 36 of the EU Regulation in respect of assets located in another member State.

(2) The following requirements apply in respect of the proposed undertaking.

(3) In addition to the requirements as to form and content set out in Article 36 the undertaking must contain—

- (a) the heading "Proposed Undertaking under Article 36 of the EU Insolvency Regulation (2015/848)";
- (b) identification details for the company and for the main proceedings;
- (c) identification and contact details for the office-holder; and
- (d) a description of the effect of the undertaking if approved.

(4) The proposed undertaking must be delivered to all the local creditors in the member State concerned of whose address the office-holder is aware.

(5) Where the undertaking is rejected the office-holder must inform all the creditors of the company of the rejection of the undertaking as soon as reasonably practicable.

(6) Where the undertaking is approved the office-holder must as soon as reasonably practicable—

- (a) send a copy of the undertaking to all the creditors with a notice informing them of the approval of the undertaking and of its effect (so far as they have not already been given this information under paragraph (3)(d));
- (b) where the insolvency proceedings relate to a registered company deliver a copy of the undertaking to the registrar of companies.

(7) The office-holder may advertise details of the undertaking in the other member State in such manner as the office-holder thinks fit.]

NOTES

Commencement: 26 June 2017 (except in relation to proceedings opened before that date).

Inserted, together with Chapter heading and rr 7.20C–7.20J, by the Insolvency Amendment (EU 2015/848) Regulations 2017, SI 2017/702, regs 2, 3, Schedule, Pt 5, paras 61, 90, as from 26 June 2017, except in relation to proceedings opened before that date.

[15.314]

[7.20C Main proceedings in another member State: approval of undertaking offered by the member State liquidator to local creditors in the UK

(1) This rule applies where a member State liquidator proposes an undertaking under Article 36 and the secondary proceedings which the undertaking is intended to avoid would be insolvency proceedings to which these Rules apply.

(2) A decision by the local creditors whether to approve the undertaking shall be taken as if it were a decision taken by a company's creditors to approve a proposed company voluntary arrangement under section 4A of the Act.

(3) Without prejudice to the generality of paragraph (2), Rules 1.14 to 1.16E apply to that decision.

(4) Where the main proceedings relate to a registered company the member State liquidator must deliver a copy of the approved undertaking to the registrar of companies.]

NOTES

Commencement: 26 June 2017 (except in relation to proceedings opened before that date).

Inserted as noted to r 7.20B at **[15.313]**.

[15.315]

[7.20D Powers of an office-holder or member State liquidator in proceedings concerning members of a group of companies (Article 60 of the EU Regulation)

Where an office-holder or a member State liquidator makes an application in accordance with paragraph (1)(b) of Article 60 of the EU Regulation the application must state with reasons why the applicant thinks the matters set out in (i) to (iv) of that paragraph apply.]

NOTES

Commencement: 26 June 2017 (except in relation to proceedings opened before that date).

Inserted as noted to r 7.20B at **[15.313]**.

[15.316]

[7.20E Group coordination proceedings (Section 2 of Chapter 5 of the EU Regulation)

(1) An application to open group coordination proceedings must be headed "Application under Article 61 of Regulation (EU) 2015/848 to open group coordination proceedings" and must, in addition to the requirements in Article 61 contain—

- (a) identification and contact details for the office-holder making the application;
- (b) identification details for the company and the insolvency proceedings by virtue of which the office-holder is making the application;
- (c) identification details for the company and the insolvency proceedings in respect of each company which is a member of the group;
- (d) contact details for the office-holders and member State liquidators appointed in those proceedings;
- (e) identification details for any insolvency proceedings in respect of a member of the group which are not to be subject to the coordination because of an objection to being included; and
- (f) if relevant, a copy of any such agreement as is mentioned in Article 66 of the EU Regulation.

(2) "office-holder" in this rule includes as the context requires a person holding office in insolvency proceedings in relation to the company in [England and Wales] or Northern Ireland and a member State liquidator.]

NOTES

Commencement: 26 June 2017 (except in relation to proceedings opened before that date).

Inserted as noted to r 7.20B at **[15.313]**.

Para (2): words in square brackets substituted by the Insolvency (England and Wales) and Insolvency (Scotland) (Miscellaneous and Consequential Amendments) Rules 2017, SI 2017/1115, rr 18, 19.

[15.317]

[7.20F Group coordination order (Article 68 EU Regulation)

(1) An order opening group coordination proceedings must also contain—

- (a) identification details for the insolvency proceedings by virtue of which the office-holder is making the application;
- (b) identification and contact details for the office-holder making the application;
- (c) identification details for the insolvency proceedings which are subject to the coordination; and
- (d) identification details for any insolvency proceedings for a member of the group which is not subject to the coordination because of an objection to being included.

(2) The office-holder making the application must deliver a copy of the order to the coordinator and to any person who is, in respect of proceedings subject to the coordination,—

(a) an office-holder,
(b) a person holding office in insolvency proceedings in relation to the company in England and Wales or Northern Ireland, and
(c) a member State liquidator.]

NOTES

Commencement: 26 June 2017 (except in relation to proceedings opened before that date).
Inserted as noted to r 7.20B at **[15.313]**.

[15.318]
[7.20G Delivery of group coordination order to registrar of companies

An office-holder in respect of insolvency proceedings subject to coordination must deliver a copy of the group coordination order to the registrar of companies.]

NOTES

Commencement: 26 June 2017 (except in relation to proceedings opened before that date).
Inserted as noted to r 7.20B at **[15.313]**.

[15.319]
[7.20H Office holder's report

Where, under the second paragraph of Article 70(2) of the EU Regulation, an office-holder is required to give reasons for not following the coordinator's recommendations or the group coordination plan those reasons must be given as soon as reasonably practicable by a notice to all the creditors.]

NOTES

Commencement: 26 June 2017 (except in relation to proceedings opened before that date).
Inserted as noted to r 7.20B at **[15.313]**.

[15.320]
[7.20I Publication of opening of proceedings by a member State liquidator

(1) This rule applies where—
(a) a company subject to insolvency proceedings has an establishment in Scotland; and
(b) a member State liquidator is required or authorised under Article 28 of the EU Regulation to publish a notice.

(2) The notice must be published in the Edinburgh Gazette.]

NOTES

Commencement: 26 June 2017 (except in relation to proceedings opened before that date).
Inserted as noted to r 7.20B at **[15.313]**.

[15.321]
[7.20J Statement by member State liquidator that insolvency proceedings in another member State are closed etc

A statement by a member State liquidator under any of sections 201, 204, 205 or paragraph 84 of Schedule B1 informing the registrar of companies that the insolvency proceedings in another member State are closed or that the member State liquidator consents to the dissolution must contain—
(a) identification details for the company; and
(b) identification details for the member State liquidator.]

NOTES

Commencement: 26 June 2017 (except in relation to proceedings opened before that date).
Inserted as noted to r 7.20B at **[15.313]**.

CHAPTER 3 MISCELLANEOUS

[15.322]
7.21 Giving of notices, etc

(1) All notices required or authorised by or under the Act or the Rules to be given, sent or delivered must be in writing, unless it is otherwise provided, or the court allows the notice to be sent or given in some other way.

[(1A) In Parts 1 [to 6] where electronic delivery is permitted a notice or other document in electronic form is treated as being in writing if a copy of it is capable of being produced in a legible form.]

(2) Any reference in the [Act or the] Rules to giving, sending or delivering a notice or any such document means, without prejudice to any other way and unless it is otherwise provided, that the notice or document may be sent by post, and that, subject to Rule 7.22, any form of post may be used. Personal service of the notice or document is permissible in all cases.

(3) Where under the Act or the Rules a notice or other document is required or authorised to be given, sent or delivered by a person ("the sender") to another ("the recipient"), it may be given, sent or delivered by any person duly authorised by the sender to do so to any person duly authorised by the recipient to receive or accept it.

(4) Where two or more persons are acting jointly as the responsible insolvency practitioner in any proceedings, the giving, sending or delivering of a notice or document to one of them is to be treated as the giving, sending or delivering of a notice or document to each or all.

NOTES

Para (1A): inserted by the Insolvency (Scotland) Amendment Rules 2010, SI 2010/688, r 3, Sch 1, para 112, subject to transitional provisions in r 4 thereof at **[2.80]**; words in square brackets substituted for original words "and 2", by the Insolvency (Scotland) Amendment Rules 2014, SSI 2014/114, rr 2, 26(4), subject to savings in r 29 thereof as noted to r 0.2 at **[15.2]**.

Para (2): words in square brackets inserted by the Insolvency (Scotland) Amendment Rules 1987, SI 1987/1921, r 3(1), Schedule, Pt I, para 47.

[15.323]

[7.21A Contents of notices . . . to be published in the Edinburgh Gazette under the Act or Rules

(1) [Subject to paragraph (1A), where under Parts I to IV of the Act or Parts 1, 2, 4, 5 and 6] of the Rules a notice must be published or advertised in the Edinburgh Gazette, in addition to any content specifically required by the Act or any other provision of the Rules, the content of such a notice must be as set out in this Rule.

[(1A) This rule does not apply to a notice to be published or advertised under—

(a) section 59(2);

(b) Rule 4.2(2); or

(c) Rule 4.80(2)(b).]

(2) All notices published must specify insofar as it is applicable in relation to the particular notice—

(a) the name and postal address of the office-holder acting in the proceedings to which the notice relates;

(b) the capacity in which the office holder is acting and the date of appointment;

(c) either an e-mail address, or a telephone number, through which the office holder may be contacted;

(d) the name of any person other than the office-holder (if any) who may be contacted regarding the proceedings;

(e) the number assigned to the office-holder by the Secretary of State; and

(f) the court name and any number assigned to the proceedings by the court.

(3) All notices published must specify as regards the company to which the notice relates—

(a) the registered name of the company;

(b) its registered number;

(c) its registered office, or if an unregistered company, the postal address of its principal place of business;

(d) any principal trading address if this is different from its registered office;

(e) any name under which it was registered in the 12 months prior to the date of the commencement of the proceedings which are the subject of the notice in the Edinburgh Gazette; and

(f) any name or style (other than its registered name) under which—

(i) the company carried on business; and

(ii) any debt owed to a creditor was incurred.]

NOTES

Inserted, together with rr 7.21B–7.21D, by the Insolvency (Scotland) Amendment Rules 2010, SI 2010/688, r 3, Sch 1, para 113, subject to transitional provisions in r 4 thereof at **[2.80]**.

Rule heading: words "in Parts 1 and 2" (omitted) revoked by the Insolvency (Scotland) Amendment Rules 2014, SSI 2014/114, rr 2, 27(2), subject to savings in r 29 thereof as noted to r 0.2 at **[15.2]**.

Para (1): words in square brackets substituted for original words "Where under Parts I and II of the Act or Parts 1 and 2", by SSI 2014/114, rr 2, 27(1)(a), subject to savings in r 29 thereof as noted to r 0.2 at **[15.2]**.

Para (1A): inserted by SSI 2014/114, rr 2, 27(1)(b), subject to savings in r 29 thereof as noted to r 0.2 at **[15.2]**.

[15.324]

[7.21B Notices otherwise advertised under the Act or Rules

(1) [Subject to paragraph (1A), where under Parts I to IV of the Act or Parts 1, 2, 4, 5 and 6] of the Rules a notice may be advertised otherwise than in the Edinburgh Gazette, in addition to any content specifically required by the Act or any other provision of the Rules, the content of such a notice must be as set out in this Rule.

[(1A) This rule does not apply to a notice to be advertised under—

(a) section 59(2); or

(b) Rule 4.2(2).]

(2) All notices published must specify insofar as it is applicable in relation to the particular notice—

(a) the name and postal address of the office-holder acting in the proceedings to which the notice relates; and

(b) either an e-mail address, or a telephone number, through which the office holder may be contacted.

(3) All notices published must specify as regards the company to which the notice relates—

(a) the registered name of the company;

(b) its registered number;

(c) any name under which it was registered in the 12 months prior to the date of the commencement of the proceedings which are the subject of the Edinburgh Gazette notice; and
(d) any name or style (other than its registered name) under which—
(i) the company carried on business; and
(ii) any debt owed to a creditor was incurred.]

NOTES

Inserted as noted to r 7.21A at **[15.323]**.

Para (1): words in square brackets substituted for original words "Where under Parts I and II of the Act or Parts 1 and 2", by the Insolvency (Scotland) Amendment Rules 2014, SSI 2014/114, rr 2, 27(3)(a), subject to savings in r 29 thereof as noted to r 0.2 at **[15.2]**.

Para (1A): inserted by SSI 2014/114, rr 2, 27(3)(b), subject to savings in r 29 thereof as noted to r 0.2 at **[15.2]**.

[15.325]
[7.21C Notices otherwise advertised—other additional provision

The information required to be contained in a notice to which Rule 7.21B applies must be included in the advertisement of that notice in a manner that is reasonably likely to ensure, in relation to the form of the advertising used, that a person reading, hearing or seeing the advertisement, will be able to read, hear or see that information.]

NOTES

Inserted as noted to r 7.21A at **[15.323]**.

[15.326]
[7.21D Omission of unobtainable information

Information required by Rules 7.21A and 7.21B to be included in a notice may be omitted if it is not reasonably practicable to obtain it.]

NOTES

Inserted as noted to r 7.21A at **[15.323]**.

[15.327]
7.22 Sending by post

(1) For a document to be properly sent by post, it must be contained in an envelope addressed to the person to whom it is to be sent, and pre-paid for either first or second class post.

[(1A) Any document to be sent by post may be sent to the last known address of the person to whom the document is to be sent.]

(2) Where first class post is used, the document is to be deemed to be received on the second business day after the date of posting, unless the contrary is shown.

(3) Where second class post is used, the document is to be deemed to be received on the fourth business day after the date of posting, unless the contrary is shown.

NOTES

Para (1A): inserted by the Insolvency (Scotland) Amendment Rules 1987, SI 1987/1921, r 3(1), Schedule, Pt I, para 48.

[15.328]
7.23 Certificate of giving notice, etc

(1) Where in any proceedings a notice or document is required to be given, sent or delivered by the responsible insolvency practitioner, the date of giving, sending or delivery of it may be proved by means of a certificate signed by him or on his behalf by his solicitor, or a partner or an employee of either of them, that the notice or document was duly given, posted or otherwise sent, or delivered on the date stated in the certificate.

(2) In the case of a notice or document to be given, sent or delivered by a person other than the responsible insolvency practitioner, the date of giving, sending or delivery of it may be proved by means of a certificate by that person that he gave, posted or otherwise sent or delivered the notice or document on the date stated in the certificate, or that he instructed another person (naming him) to do so.

(3) A certificate under this Rule may be endorsed on a copy of the notice to which it relates.

(4) A certificate purporting to be signed by or on behalf of the responsible insolvency practitioner, or by the person mentioned in paragraph (2), shall be deemed, unless the contrary is shown, to be sufficient evidence of the matters stated therein.

[15.329]
7.24 Validity of proceedings

Where in accordance with the Act or the Rules a meeting of creditors or other persons is summoned by notice, the meeting is presumed to have been duly summoned and held, notwithstanding that not all those to whom the notice is to be given have received it.

[15.330]
7.25 Evidence of proceedings at meetings

A report of proceedings at a meeting of the company or of the company's creditors or contributories in any insolvency proceedings, which is signed by a person describing himself as the chairman of that meeting, shall be deemed, unless the contrary is shown, to be sufficient evidence of the matters contained in that report.

[15.331]
7.26 Right to list of creditors and copy documents

(1) Paragraph (2) applies to—

(a) proceedings under Part II of the Act (company administration), and

(b) proceedings in a creditors' voluntary winding up, or a winding up by the court.

(2) Subject to Rule 7.27, in any such proceedings, a creditor who has the right to inspect documents also has the right to require the responsible insolvency practitioner to furnish him with a list of the company's creditors and the amounts of their respective debts.

[(2A) For the purpose of this Rule a member State liquidator appointed in main proceedings in relation to a person is deemed to be a creditor.]

[(2A) Where the responsible insolvency practitioner is requested by a creditor, member, contributory or by a member of a liquidation committee or of a creditors' committee to supply a copy of any document, he is entitled to require payment of the appropriate fee in respect of the supply of that copy.]

(3) Subject to Rule 7.27, where a person has the right to inspect documents, the right includes that of taking copies of those documents, on payment of the appropriate fee.

(4) In this Rule, the appropriate fee means 15 pence per A4 or A5 page and 30 pence per A3 page.

NOTES

First para (2A): inserted by the Insolvency (Scotland) Regulations 2003, SI 2003/2109, regs 23, 28(2), subject to the saving that anything done under or for the purposes of any provision of these Rules before 8 September 2003 has effect as if done under or for the purposes of the provision as amended.

Second para (2A): inserted by the Insolvency (Scotland) Amendment Rules 1987, SI 1987/1921, r 3(1), Schedule, Pt I, para 49.

[15.332]
7.27 Confidentiality of documents

(1) Where, in any insolvency proceedings, the responsible insolvency practitioner considers, in the case of a document forming part of the records of those proceedings—

(a) that it should be treated as confidential, or

(b) that it is of such a nature that its disclosure would be calculated to be injurious to the interests of the company's creditors or, in the case of the winding up of a company, its members or the contributories in its winding up,

he may decline to allow it to be inspected by a person who would otherwise be entitled to inspect it.

(2) The persons who may be refused the right to inspect documents under this Rule by the responsible insolvency practitioner include the members of a creditors' committee in administration or in receivership, or of a liquidation committee.

(3) Where under this Rule the responsible insolvency practitioner refuses inspection of a document, the person who made that request may apply to the court for an order to overrule the refusal and the court may either overrule it altogether, or sustain it, either unconditionally or subject to such conditions, if any, as it thinks fit to impose.

[(4) Nothing in this Rule entitles the responsible insolvency practitioner to decline to allow inspection of any claim or proxy.]

NOTES

Para (4): added by the Insolvency (Scotland) Amendment Rules 1987, SI 1987/1921, r 3(1), Schedule, Pt I, para 50.

[15.333]
7.28 Insolvency practitioner's caution

(1) Wherever under the Rules any person has to appoint, or certify the appointment of, an insolvency practitioner to any office, he is under a duty to satisfy himself that the person appointed or to be appointed has caution for the proper performance of his functions.

(2) It is the duty—

(a) of the creditors' committee in administration or in receivership,

(b) of the liquidation committee in companies winding up, and

(c) of any committee of creditors established for the purposes of a voluntary arrangement under Part I of the Act,

to review from time to time the adequacy of the responsible insolvency practitioner's caution.

(3) In any insolvency proceedings the cost of the responsible insolvency practitioner's caution shall be paid as an expense of the proceedings.

[15.334]
7.29 Punishment of offences

(1) Schedule 4 has effect with respect to the way in which contraventions of the Rules are punishable on conviction.

(2) In that Schedule—

(a) the first column specifies the provision of the Rules which creates an offence;

(b) in relation to each such offence, the second column describes the general nature of the offence;

(c) the third column indicates its mode of trial, that is to say whether the offence is punishable on conviction on indictment, or on summary conviction, or either in the one way or the other;

(d) the fourth column shows the maximum punishment by way of fine or imprisonment which may be imposed on a person convicted of the offence in the mode of trial specified in relation to it in the third column (that is to say, on indictment or summarily), a reference to a period of years or months being to a maximum term of imprisonment of that duration; and

(e) the fifth column shows (in relation to an offence for which there is an entry in that column) that a person convicted of the offence after continued contravention is liable to a daily default fine; that is to say, he is liable on a second or subsequent conviction of the offence to the fine specified in that column for each day on which the contravention is continued (instead of the penalty specified for the offence in the fourth column of that Schedule).

(3) Section 431 (summary proceedings), as it applies to Scotland, has effect in relation to offences under the Rules as to offences under the Act.

[15.335]
7.30 Forms for use in insolvency proceedings

The forms contained in Schedule 5, with such variations as circumstances require, are the forms to be used for the purposes of the provisions of the Act or the Rules which are referred to in those forms.

[15.336]
[7.30A Electronic submission of information instead of submission of forms to the Secretary of State, office-holders, and of copies to the registrar of companies

(1) This Rule applies in any case where information in a prescribed form is required by [Parts 1 to 6] of these Rules to be sent by any person to the Secretary of State, or an office-holder, or a copy of a prescribed form is to be sent to the registrar of companies.

(2) A requirement of the kind mentioned in paragraph (1) is treated as having been satisfied where—

(a) the information is submitted electronically with the agreement of the person to whom the information is sent;

(b) the form in which the electronic submission is made satisfies the requirements of the person to whom the information is sent (which may include a requirement that the information supplied can be reproduced in the format of the prescribed form);

(c) that all the information required to be given in the prescribed form is provided in the electronic submission; and

(d) the person to whom the information is sent can produce in legible form the information so submitted.

(3) Where information in a prescribed form is permitted to be sent electronically under paragraph (2), any requirement in the prescribed form that the prescribed form be accompanied by a signature is taken to be satisfied—

(a) if the identity of the person who is supplying the information in the prescribed form and whose signature is required is confirmed in a manner specified by the recipient; or

(b) where no such manner has been specified by the recipient, if the communication contains or is accompanied by a statement of the identity of the person who is providing the information in the prescribed form, and the recipient has no reason to doubt the truth of that statement.

(4) Where information required in prescribed form has been supplied to a person, whether or not it has been supplied electronically in accordance with paragraph (2), and a copy of that information is required to be supplied to another person falling within paragraph (1), the requirements contained in paragraph (2) apply in respect of the supply of the copy to that other person as they apply in respect of the original.]

NOTES

Inserted, together with r 7.30B, by the Insolvency (Scotland) Amendment Rules 2010, SI 2010/688, r 3, Sch 1, para 114, subject to transitional provisions in rr 4, 5 thereof at **[2.80]**, **[2.81]**.

Para (1): words in square brackets substituted for original words "Part 1 or 2", by the Insolvency (Scotland) Amendment Rules 2014, SSI 2014/114, rr 2, 26(5), subject to savings in r 29 thereof as noted to r 0.2 at **[15.2]**.

[15.337]
[7.30B Electronic submission of information instead of submission of forms in all other cases

(1) This Rule applies in any case where Rule 7.30A does not apply, where information in a prescribed form is required by [Parts 1 to 6] of these Rules to be sent by any person.

(2) A requirement of the kind mentioned in paragraph (1) is treated as having been satisfied where—

(a) the person to whom the information is sent has agreed—

(i) to receiving the information electronically and to the form in which it is to be sent; and

(ii) to the specified manner in which paragraph (3) is to be satisfied.

(b) all the information required to be given in the prescribed form is provided in the electronic submission; and

(c) the person to whom the information is sent can produce in legible form the information so sent.

(3) Any requirement in a prescribed form that it be accompanied by a signature is taken to be satisfied if the identity of the person who is supplying the information and whose signature is required, is confirmed in the specified manner.

(4) Where information required in prescribed form has been supplied to a person, whether or not it has been supplied electronically in accordance with paragraph (2), and a copy of that information is required to be supplied to another person falling within paragraph (1), the requirements contained in paragraph (2) apply in respect of the supply of the copy to that other person, as they apply in respect of the original.]

NOTES

Inserted as noted to r 7.30A at **[15.336]**.

Para (1): words in square brackets substituted for original words "Part 1 or 2", by the Insolvency (Scotland) Amendment Rules 2014, SSI 2014/114, rr 2, 26(5), subject to savings in r 29 thereof as noted to r 0.2 at **[15.2]**.

[15.338]

[7.30C Electronic submission: exceptions

(1) Rule 7.30A does not apply to a form to be sent—

(a) under section 204(6) and Rule 4.77 or section 205(6) and Rule 4.77; or

(b) to or by a provisional liquidator appointed under section 135.

(2) Rule 7.30B does not apply—

(a) to a Form to be sent under Rule 4.80;

(b) to a form to be sent to or by a provisional liquidator appointed under section 135; or

(c) in respect of a statutory demand.]

NOTES

Commencement: 30 May 2014.

Inserted, by the Insolvency (Scotland) Amendment Rules 2014, SSI 2014/114, rr 2, 26(6), subject to savings in r 29 thereof as noted to r 0.2 at **[15.2]**.

[15.339]

7.31 Fees, expenses, etc

All fees, costs, charges and other expenses incurred in the course of insolvency proceedings are to be regarded as expenses of those proceedings[, with the exception of the fees, costs, charges and other expenses associated with the prescribed part, which shall be met out of the prescribed part].

NOTES

Words in square brackets inserted by the Enterprise Act 2002 (Consequential Amendments) (Prescribed Part) (Scotland) Order 2003, SI 2003/2108, art 8.

[15.340]

[7.32 Power of court to cure defects in procedure

(1) The court may, on the application of any person having an interest—

(a) if there has been a failure to comply with any requirement of the Act or the Rules, make an order waiving any such failure and, so far as practicable, restoring any person prejudiced by the failure to the position that person would have been in but for the failure;

(b) if for any reason anything required or authorised to be done in, or in connection with, the insolvency proceedings cannot be done, make such order as may be necessary to enable that thing to be done.

(2) The court, in an order under paragraph (1) above, may impose such conditions, including conditions as to expenses, as the court thinks fit and may—

(a) authorise or dispense with the performance of any act in the insolvency proceedings;

(b) appoint as responsible insolvency practitioner on the company's estate a person who would be eligible to act as a responsible insolvency practitioner, whether or not in place of an existing insolvency practitioner;

(c) extend or waive any time limit specified in or under the Act or the Rules.

(3) An application under paragraph (1) above which is made to the sheriff—

(a) may at any time be remitted by the sheriff to the Court of Session;

(b) shall be so remitted if the Court of Session so directs on an application by any such person,

if the sheriff or the Court of Session, as the case may be, considers that the remit is desirable because of the importance or complexity of the matters raised by the application.

(4) The responsible insolvency practitioner shall record in the sederunt book the decision of the sheriff or the Court of Session under this Rule.]

NOTES

Commencement: 30 May 2014.

Substituted by the Insolvency (Scotland) Amendment Rules 2014, SSI 2014/114, rr 2, 22, subject to savings in r 29 thereof as noted to r 0.2 at **[15.2]**. This rule previously read as follows—

"**7.32 Power of court to cure defects in procedure**

(1) Section 63 of the Bankruptcy Act (power of court to cure defects in procedure) shall apply in relation to any insolvency proceedings as it applies in relation to sequestration, subject to the modifications specified in paragraph (2) and to any other necessary modifications.

(2) For any reference in the said section 63 to any expression in column 1 below, there shall be substituted a reference to the expression in column 2 opposite thereto—

Column 1	*Column 2*
This Act or any regulations made under it	The Act or the Rules

Part 15 Insolvency (Scotland) Rules 1986

Column 1	*Column 2*
Permanent trustee	Responsible insolvency practitioner
Sequestration process	Insolvency proceedings
Debtor	Company
Sheriff	The court
Person who would be eligible to be elected under section 24 of this Act	Person who would be eligible to act as a responsible insolvency practitioner".

[15.341]

7.33 Sederunt book

(1) The responsible insolvency practitioner shall maintain a sederunt book during his term of office for the purpose of providing an accurate record of the administration of each insolvency proceedings.

(2) Without prejudice to the generality of the above paragraph, there shall be inserted in the sederunt book a copy of anything required to be recorded in it by any provision of the Act or of the Rules.

(3) The responsible insolvency practitioner shall make the sederunt book available for inspection at all reasonable hours by any interested person.

(4) Any entry in the sederunt book shall be sufficient evidence of the facts stated therein, except where it is founded on by the responsible insolvency practitioner in his own interest.

[(5) Without prejudice to paragraph (3), the responsible insolvency practitioner shall retain, or shall make arrangements for retention of, the sederunt book for a period of ten years from the relevant date.

(6) Where the sederunt book is maintained in non-documentary form it shall be capable of reproduction in legible form.

(7) In this Rule "the relevant date" has the following meanings—

(a) in the case of a company voluntary arrangement under Part I of the Act, the date of final completion of the voluntary arrangement;

(b) in the case of an administration . . . under Part II of the Act, the date on which the administration [ends in accordance with that Part];

(c) in the case of a receivership under Part III of the Act, the date on which the receiver resigns and the receivership terminates without a further receiver being appointed; and

(d) in the case of a winding-up, the date of dissolution of the company.]

NOTES

Paras (5), (6): added together with para (7) by the Insolvency (Scotland) Amendment Rules 1987, SI 1987/1921, r 3(1), Schedule, Pt I, para 51.

Para (7): added together with paras (5), (6) by SI 1987/1921, r 3(1), Schedule, Pt I, para 51; word "order" omitted revoked, and words in square brackets substituted for words "order is discharged" by the Insolvency (Scotland) Amendment Rules 2003, SI 2003/2111, r 6, Sch 2, para 10, subject to savings in r 7 thereof at **[2.34]**.

[15.342]

[7.34 Disposal of company's books, papers and other records

(1) Where a company has been the subject of insolvency proceedings ("the original proceedings") which have terminated and other insolvency proceedings ("the subsequent proceedings") have commenced in relation to that company, the responsible insolvency practitioner appointed in relation to the original proceedings, shall, before the expiry of the later of—

(a) the period of 30 days following a request to him to do so by the responsible insolvency practitioner appointed in relation to the subsequent proceedings, or

(b) the period of 6 months after the relevant date (within the meaning of Rule 7.33),

deliver to the responsible insolvency practitioner appointed in relation to the subsequent proceedings the books, papers and other records of the company.

(2) In the case of insolvency proceedings, other than winding up [or administration], where—

(a) the original proceedings have terminated, and

(b) no subsequent proceedings have commenced within the period of 6 months after the relevant date in relation to the original proceedings,

the responsible insolvency practitioner appointed in relation to the original proceedings may dispose of the books, papers and records of the company after the expiry of the period of 6 months referred to in sub-paragraph (b), but only in accordance with directions given by—

(i) . . .

(ii) the members of the company by extraordinary resolution, or

(iii) the court.

(3) Where a company is being wound up the liquidator shall dispose of the books, papers and records of the company either in accordance with—

(a) in the case of a winding up by the court, directions of the liquidation committee, or, if there is no such committee, directions of the court;

(b) in the case of a members' voluntary winding up, directions of the members by extraordinary resolution; and

(c) in the case of a creditors' voluntary winding up, directions of the liquidation committee, or, if there is no such committee, of the creditors given at or before the final meeting under section 106, or, if, by the date which is 12 months after the dissolution of the company, no such directions have been given, he may do so after that date in such a way as he deems appropriate.

[(4) In the case of administration proceedings, the administrator shall dispose of the books, papers and records of the company either in accordance with—

(a) the directions of the creditors' committee (if any); or

(b) where there is no such committee, the court,

or, if by the date which is 12 months after dissolution of the company, no such directions have been given, he may do so after that date in such a way as he deems appropriate.

(5) An administrator or former administrator shall within 14 days of a request by the Secretary of State give the Secretary of State particulars of any money in his hands or under his control representing unclaimed or undistributed assets of the company or dividends or other sums due to any person as a member or former member of the company.]]

NOTES

Inserted by the Insolvency (Scotland) Amendment Rules 1987, SI 1987/1921, r 3(1), Schedule, Pt I, para 52.

Para (2): words in square brackets inserted and sub-para (i) revoked, by the Insolvency (Scotland) Amendment Rules 2006, SI 2006/734, r 14(a), (b), subject to transitional provisions in r 2(2) thereof at **[2.43]**, and sub-para (i) originally read as follows:

"(i) the creditors' committee (if any) appointed in the original proceedings,".

Paras (4), (5): added by SI 2006/734, r 14(c), subject to transitional provisions in r 2(2) thereof at **[2.43]**.

[15.343]

[7.35 Information about time spent on a case—administration and company voluntary arrangements

(1) Subject as set out in this Rule, a person ("the relevant person") who has acted or is acting as—

(a) a nominee in respect of a proposed voluntary arrangements;

(b) a supervisor in respect of a voluntary arrangement; or

(c) an administrator,

must, on request in writing by any person mentioned in paragraph (2), supply free of charge to that person a statement of the kind described in paragraph (3).

(2) The persons referred to in paragraph (1) are—

(a) any director of the company, or

(b) where the proposed voluntary arrangement has been approved, or where the company is in administration, any creditor or member of the company.

(3) The statement referred to in paragraph (1)—

(a) must comprise the following details—

(i) the total number of hours spent on all or any of the proposal, the voluntary arrangement and administration by the relevant person, and any staff assigned to the case during that period;

(ii) for each grade of individual so engaged, the average hourly rate at which any work carried out by individuals in that grade is charged; and

(iii) the number of hours spent by each grade of staff during the period covered by the statement; and

(b) must cover the period beginning with the date of the appointment of the relevant person as nominee, supervisor or administrator (whichever is the earlier), as the case may be, and ending—

(i) with the date next before the date of making the request on which the relevant person has completed any period as nominee, supervisor or administrator, which is a multiple of 6 months, or

(ii) where the relevant person has ceased to act in any capacity in relation to the proposal, the voluntary arrangement or administration, the date upon which the person so ceased.

(4) No request pursuant to this Rule may be made where more than 2 years has elapsed since the relevant person ceased to act in any capacity in relation to the proposal, any voluntary arrangement arising out of the approval of the proposal or administration.

(5) Any statement required to be provided to any person under this Rule must be supplied within 28 days of the date of the receipt of the request by the person required to supply it.]

NOTES

Inserted by the Insolvency (Scotland) Amendment Rules 2006, SI 2006/734, r 15, subject to transitional provisions in r 2(3) thereof at **[2.43]**.

Substituted by the Insolvency (Scotland) Amendment Rules 2010, SI 2010/688, r 3, Sch 1, para 115, subject to transitional provisions in r 4 thereof at **[2.80]**, and previously read as follows:

"**7.35 Information about time spent on a case—administration and company voluntary arrangements**

(1) Subject as set out in this Rule, in respect of any administration or company voluntary arrangement in which he acts, an insolvency practitioner shall on request in writing made by any person mentioned in paragraph (2), supply free of charge to that person a statement of the kind described in paragraph (3).

(2) The persons referred to in paragraph (1) are—

(a) any creditor in the case; and

(b) any director or contributory of the company.

(3) The statement referred to in paragraph (1) shall comprise in relation to the period beginning with the date of the insolvency practitioner's appointment and ending with the relevant date the following details—

(a) the total number of hours spent on the case by the insolvency practitioner and any staff assigned to the case during that period;
(b) for each grade of individual so engaged, the average hourly rate at which any work carried out by individuals in that grade is charged; and
(c) the number of hours spent by each grade of staff during that period.

(4) In relation to paragraph (3) the "relevant date" means the date next before the date of the making of the request on which the insolvency practitioner has completed any period in office which is a multiple of six months or, where the insolvency practitioner has vacated office, the date that he vacated office.

(5) Where an insolvency practitioner has vacated office, an obligation to provide information under this Rule shall only arise in relation to a request that is made within 2 years of the date he vacates office.

(6) Any statement required to be provided to any person under this Rule shall be supplied within 28 days of the date of the receipt of the request by the insolvency practitioner.".

[15.344]
[7.36 Information about time spent on a case

(1) Subject as set out in this Rule, in respect of any liquidation or receivership in which an insolvency practitioner acts, the insolvency practitioner shall on request in writing made by any person mentioned in paragraph (2), supply free of charge to that person a statement of the kind described in paragraph (3).

(2) The persons referred to in paragraph (1) are—
(a) any creditor in the case; and
(b) where the case relates to a company, any director or contributory of that company.

(3) The statement referred to in paragraph (1) shall comprise in relation to the period beginning with the date of the insolvency practitioner's appointment and ending with the relevant date the following details—
(a) the total number of hours spent on the case by the insolvency practitioner and any staff assigned to the case during that period;
(b) for each grade of individual so engaged, the average hourly rate at which any work carried out by individuals in that grade is charged; and
(c) the number of hours spent by each grade of staff during that period.

(4) In relation to paragraph (3) the "relevant date" means the date next before the date of the making of the request on which the insolvency practitioner has completed any period in office which is a multiple of six months or, where the insolvency practitioner has vacated office, the date that the insolvency practitioner vacated office.

(5) Where an insolvency practitioner has vacated office, an obligation to provide information under this Rule shall only arise in relation to a request that is made within 2 years of the date the insolvency practitioner vacates office.

(6) Any statement required to be provided to any person under this Rule shall be supplied within 28 days of the date of the receipt of the request by the insolvency practitioner.]

NOTES

Inserted by the Insolvency (Scotland) Rules 1986 Amendment Rules 2008, SSI 2008/393, rr 2, 5, 7(2), except where a provisional liquidator, liquidator or receiver is appointed before 20 December 2008.

SCHEDULES

SCHEDULE 1

MODIFICATIONS OF PART 4 IN RELATION TO CREDITORS' VOLUNTARY WINDING UP

Rule 5

[15.345]
1. The following paragraphs describe the modifications to be made to the provisions of Part 4 in their application by Rule 5 to a creditors' voluntary winding up of a company.

General

2. Any reference, in any provision in Part 4, which is applied to a creditors' voluntary winding up, to any other Rule is a reference to that Rule as so applied.

Chapter 1
(Provisional liquidator)

3. This Chapter shall not apply.

Chapter 2
(Statement of affairs)

Rules 4.7 and 4.8

4. For these Rules, there shall be substituted the following—

"**4.7.** (1) This Rule applies with respect to the statement of affairs made out by the liquidator under section 95(3) (or as the case may be) by the directors under section 99(1).

(2) The statement of affairs shall be in the form required by Rule 7.30 and Schedule 5.
(3) Where the statement of affairs is made out by the directors under section 99(1), it shall be sent by them to the liquidator, when appointed.
[(3A) Where a liquidator is nominated by the company at a general meeting held on a day prior to that on which the creditors' meeting summoned under section 98 is held, the directors shall forthwith after his nomination or the making of the statement of affairs, whichever is the later, deliver to him a copy of the statement of affairs.]
(4) [Subject to Rule 4.8A,] the liquidator shall insert a copy of the statement of affairs made out under this Rule in the sederunt book.
[(5) The statement of affairs under section 99(1) shall be made up to the nearest practicable date before the date of the meeting of creditors under section 98 or to a date not more than 14 days before that on which the resolution for voluntary winding up is passed by the company, whichever is the later.
(6) At any meeting held under section 98 where the statement of affairs laid before the meeting does not state the company's affairs as at the date of the meeting, the directors of the company shall cause to be made to the meeting, either by the director presiding at the meeting or by another person with knowledge of the relevant matters, a report (written or oral) on any material transactions relating to the company occurring between the date of the making of the statement of affairs and that of the meeting and any such report shall be recorded in the report of the meeting kept under Rule 7.13.]".

[Rule 4.8A

4A. After paragraph (6) there shall be inserted the following—

"(7) This Rule does not apply so far as section 95, 98 or 99 does not permit limited disclosure."]

Rule 4.9

5. For this Rule, there shall substituted—

"4.9 Expenses of statement of affairs
(1) Payment may be made as an expense of the liquidation, either before or after the commencement of the winding up, of any reasonable and necessary expenses of preparing the statement of affairs under section 99.
(2) Where such a payment is made before the commencement of the winding up, the director presiding at the creditors' meeting held under section 98 shall inform the meeting of the amount of the payment and the identity of the person to whom it was made.
(3) The liquidator appointed under section 100 may make such a payment (subject to the next paragraph); but if there is a liquidation committee, he must give the committee at least 7 days' notice of his intention to make it.
(4) Such a payment shall not be made by the liquidator to himself, or to any associate of his, otherwise than with the approval of the liquidation committee, the creditors, or the court.
(5) This Rule is without prejudice to the powers of the court under Rule 4.67(2) (voluntary winding up succeeded by winding up by the court).".

Chapter 3
(Information)

Rule 4.10

6. For this Rule, there shall be substituted the following—

"4.10 Information to creditors and contributories
[(1)] The liquidator shall, within 28 days of a meeting held under section 95 or 98, send to creditors and contributories of the company—
(a) a copy or summary of the statement of affairs, and
(b) a report of the proceedings at the meeting.
[(2) The report under paragraph 1(b) shall include—
(a) to the best of the liquidator's knowledge and belief—
(i) an estimate of the value of the prescribed part (whether or not he proposes to make an application to the court under section 176A(5) or section 176A(3) applies), and
(ii) an estimate of the value of the company's net property,
provided that such estimates shall not be required to include any information the disclosure of which could seriously prejudice the commercial interests of the company, but if such information is excluded the estimates shall be accompanied by a statement to that effect; and
(b) whether, and, if so, why, the liquidator proposes to make an application to the court under section 176A(5).]".

Chapter 4
(Meetings of creditors and contributories)

Rule 4.12

7. This Rule shall not apply.

Rule 4.14

8. After this Rule, there shall be inserted the following—

"4.14A Expenses of meeting under section 98

(1) Payment may be made out of the company's assets as an expense of the liquidation, either before or after the commencement of the winding up, of any reasonable and necessary expenses incurred in connection with the summoning, advertisement and holding of a creditors' meeting under section 98.

(2) Where any such payments are made before the commencement of the winding up, the director presiding at the creditors' meeting shall inform the meeting of their amount and the identity of the persons to whom they were made.

(3) The liquidator appointed under section 100 may make such a payment (subject to the next paragraph); but if there is a liquidation committee, he must give the committee at least 7 days' notice of his intention to make the payment.

(4) Such a payment shall not be made by the liquidator to himself, or to any associate of his, otherwise than with the approval of the liquidation committee, the creditors, or the court.

(5) This Rule is without prejudice to the powers of the court under Rule 4.67(2) (voluntary winding up succeeded by winding up by the court).".

Rule 4.15

9. [(1)] In paragraph (5), for the reference to section 129, there shall be substituted a reference to section 86.

[(2) In paragraph (6) there shall be inserted at the end the following—

"and to the director who presides over any meeting of creditors as provided by section 99(1)".]

[Rules 4.16E and 4.16G

10. In Rules 4.16E and 4.16G, for the references to section 129, there shall be substituted a reference to section 86.]

Chapter 6
(The liquidator)

Rule 4.18

11. (1) For paragraph (1), there shall be substituted the following—

"(1) This Rule applies where the liquidator is appointed by the court under section 100(3) or 108.".

(2) Paragraphs 4(a) and 5 shall be deleted.

Rule 4.19

12. (1) For paragraphs (1) to (3) there shall be substituted the following—

"(1) This Rule applies where a person is nominated for appointment as liquidator under section 100(1) either by a meeting of the creditors or by a meeting of the company.

(2) Subject as follows, the chairman of the meeting shall certify the appointment, but not unless and until the person to be appointed has provided him with a written statement to the effect that he is an insolvency practitioner, duly qualified under the Act to be the liquidator and that he consents so to act. The liquidator's appointment [takes effect on the passing of the resolution for his appointment].

(3) The chairman shall forthwith send the certificate to the liquidator, who shall keep it in the sederunt book.".

(2) Paragraphs 4(a) and (5) shall not apply.

(3) In paragraph (6), for the reference to paragraphs (4) and (5), there shall be substituted a reference to paragraphs (3) and (4).

[(4) After paragraph 6 there shall be inserted the following paragraph—

"(7) Where a vacancy in the office of liquidator occurs in the manner mentioned in section 104, a meeting of creditors to fill the vacancy may be convened by any creditor or, if there were more liquidators than one, by any continuing liquidator".]

Rule 4.23

13. (1) In paragraph (1), for the references to section 172(2) and (3), there shall be substituted a reference to section 171(2) and (3).

(2) In paragraph (2), for the references to section 172(2) and 174(4)(a) or (b), there shall be substituted a reference to section 171(2) and 173(2)(a) or (b).

Rule 4.24

14. In this Rule the references to the court shall be deleted.

Rule 4.25

15. In paragraph (1), for the reference to section 174(4)(a), there shall be substituted a reference to section 173(2)(a), and the reference to the court shall be deleted.

Rule 4.28

16. (1) In paragraph (1), for the reference to section 172(6), there shall be substituted a reference to section 171(5).

(2) In paragraph (2), for the reference to section 174(4)(c), there shall be substituted a reference to section 173(2)(c).

Rule 4.29

17. In this Rule for paragraph (3) there shall be substituted the following—

"(3) The liquidator, whose resignation is accepted, shall forthwith after the meeting give notice of his resignation to [the Accountant in Bankruptcy] as required by section 171(5).".

Rule 4.31

18. For this Rule, substitute the following—

"4.31 Final Meeting

(1) The liquidator shall give at least 28 days' notice of the final meeting of creditors to be held under section 106. The notice shall be sent to all creditors whose claims in the liquidation have been accepted.

(2) At the final meeting, the creditors may question the liquidator with respect to any matter contained in the account required under that section and may resolve against the liquidator having his release.

(3) The liquidator shall, within 7 days of the meeting, give notice to [the Accountant in Bankruptcy] under section 171(6) that the final meeting has been held. The notice shall state whether or not he has been released.

(4) If the creditors at the final meeting have not resolved against the liquidator having his release, he is released in terms of section 173(2)(e)(ii) when he vacates office under section 171(6). If they have so resolved, he must obtain his release from the Accountant of Court and Rule 4.25(2) and (3) shall apply accordingly [subject to the modifications that in Rule 4.25(3) sub-paragraph (a) shall apply with the word "new" replaced by the word "former" and sub-paragraph (b) shall not apply]".

Rule 4.36

19. For the reference to the court there shall be substituted a reference to the liquidation committee (if any) or a member of that committee.

Rule 4.37

20. (1) In paragraph (2), the reference to the court shall be omitted.

(2) At the end of this Rule, there shall be inserted the following—

"4.37A Vacation of office on making of winding up order

Where the liquidator vacates office in consequence of the court making a winding up order against the company, Rule 4.25(2) and (3) apply as regards the liquidator obtaining his release, as if he had been removed by the court.".

Chapter 7
(The Liquidation Committee)

Rule 4.40

21. This Rule shall not apply.

Rule 4.41

22. For paragraph (1) there shall be substituted the following—

"(1) The committee must have at least 3 members before it can be established.".

Rule 4.43

23. This Rule shall not apply.

Rule 4.47

24. For this Rule, there shall be substituted the following—

"4.47 Quorum
A meeting of the committee is duly constituted if due notice of it has been given to all the members and at least 2 members are present or represented.".

Rule 4.53

25. After paragraph (4) there shall be inserted the following—

"(4A) Where the contributories made an appointment under paragraph (4), the creditor members of the committee may, if they think fit, resolve that the person appointed ought not to be a member of the committee; and—

(a) that person is not then, unless the court otherwise directs, qualified to act as a member of the committee, and

(b) on any application to the court for a direction under this paragraph the court may, if it thinks fit, appoint another person (being a contributory) to fill the vacancy on the committee.".

Rule 4.54

26. Paragraphs (2) and (3) shall not apply.

Rule 4.55

27. In paragraphs (3) and (4), the word "creditor" shall be omitted.

Chapter 8

(The liquidation committee where winding up follows immediately on administration)

28. This Chapter shall not apply.

Chapter 9

(Distribution of company's assets by liquidator)

Rule 4.66

29. (1) At the beginning of paragraph (1), insert the following—
"Subject to the provision of section 107,".

(2) In paragraph (1)(b), for the reference to section 129, there shall be substituted a reference to section 86.

[Rule 4.68

29A. In Rule 4.68, for the reference to section 129, there shall be substituted a reference to section 86.]

Chapter 10

(Special manager)

Rule 4.70

30. For paragraph (5), there shall be substituted the following—

"(5) The cost of finding caution shall be paid in the first instance by the special manager; but he is entitled to be reimbursed out of the assets as an expense of the liquidation.".

Rule 4.71

31. Paragraph (1) shall not apply.

Chapter 11

(Public examination of company officers and others)

32. This Chapter shall not apply.

[Rule 4.75A

32A. After Rule 4.75A(2)(d) there shall be inserted the following—

"(da) a notice or other document to be given, delivered or sent under section 84(2A) or (2B)(b);".]

Chapter 12

(Miscellaneous)

Rule 4.77

33. This Rule shall not apply.

NOTES

Para 4: in the substituted r 4.7, paras (3A), (5), (6) inserted by the Insolvency (Scotland) Amendment Rules 1987, SI 1987/1921, r 3(1), Schedule, Pt I, para 53; words in square brackets in the substituted r 4.7, para (4) inserted by the Insolvency (Scotland) Amendment Rules 2014, SSI 2014/114, rr 2, 25(4)(a), subject to savings in r 29 thereof as noted to r 0.2 at **[15.2]**.

Para 4A: inserted by SSI 2014/114, rr 2, 25(4)(b), subject to savings in r 29 thereof as noted to r 0.2 at **[15.2]**.

Para 6: in the substituted r 4.10, para (1) numbered as such, and para (2) inserted, by the Enterprise Act 2002 (Consequential Amendments) (Prescribed Part) (Scotland) Order 2003, SI 2003/2108, art 9(1).

Para 9: sub-para (1) numbered as such and sub-para (2) added by SI 1987/1921, r 3(1), Schedule, Pt I, para 54.

Para 10: substituted by SSI 2014/114, rr 2, 23(a), (b), subject to savings in r 29 thereof as noted to r 0.2 at **[15.2]**, and previously read as follows—

> **"Rule 4.16**
>
> **10.** In paragraph (2), for the reference to section 129, there shall be substituted a reference to section 86.".

Para 12: in sub-para (1) words in square brackets in the substituted r 4.19(2) substituted, and sub-para (4) added, by SI 1987/1921, r 3(1), Schedule, Pt I, para 55.

Para 17: in the substituted r 4.29(3) words in square brackets substituted by the Scotland Act 1998 (Consequential Modifications) (No 2) Order 1999, SI 1999/1820, art 4, Sch 1, Pt II, para 141(1), (20).

Para 18: in the substituted r 4.31(3), words in square brackets substituted for original words "the registrar of companies" by the Insolvency (Scotland) Rules 1986 Amendment Rules 2008, SSI 2008/393, rr 2, 6, 7(1), except where a company commenced liquidation before 20 December 2008; in the substituted r 4.31(4) words in square brackets added by SI 1987/1921, r 3(1), Schedule, Pt I, para 56. Note that SI 2003/2108, art 9(2), inserts in the substituted r 4.31(2) the words "and a statement as to the amount paid to unsecured creditors by virtue of the application of section 176A (prescribed part)" after the word "payments", which does not appear in that substituted subsection.

Para 29A: inserted by SSI 2014/114, rr 2, 23(c), subject to savings in r 29 thereof as noted to r 0.2 at **[15.2]**.

Para 32A: inserted by SSI 2014/114, rr 2, 26(7), subject to savings in r 29 thereof as noted to r 0.2 at **[15.2]**.

SCHEDULE 2
APPLICATION OF PART 4 IN RELATION TO MEMBERS' VOLUNTARY WINDING UP

Rule 6

[15.346]

1. The following paragraphs describe the provisions of Part 4 which, subject to the modifications set out in those paragraphs and any other necessary modifications, apply to a members' voluntary winding up.

General

2. Any reference in any provision of Part 4, which is applied to a members' voluntary winding up, to any other Rule is a reference to that Rule as so applied.

Chapter 3
(Information)

Rule 4.11

3. This Rule shall apply [subject to the modifications that for the words "accounting period" where they occur, there shall be substituted the words "period of twenty six weeks"].

Chapter 6
(The liquidator)

Rule 4.18

4. (1) This Rule shall apply subject to the following modifications.

(2) For paragraph (1), there shall be substituted the following—

> "(1) This Rule applies where the liquidator is appointed by the court under section 108.".

(3) Paragraphs 4 and 5 shall be deleted.

Rule 4.19

5. (1) This Rule shall apply subject to the following modifications.

(2) For paragraphs (1) to (3) there shall be substituted the following—

> "(1) This Rule applies where the liquidator is appointed by a meeting of the company.
> (2) Subject as follows, the chairman of the meeting shall certify the appointment, but not unless and until the person to be appointed has provided him with a written statement to the effect that he is an insolvency practitioner, duly qualified under the Act to be the liquidator and that he consents so to act. The liquidator's appointment [takes effect on the passing of the resolution for his appointment].
> (3) The chairman shall forthwith send the certificate to the liquidator, who shall keep it in the sederunt book.".

(3) Paragraphs 4(a), (5) and (6) shall be deleted.

[Rules 4.20 to 4.22A]

6. These Rules shall apply.

Rule 4.26

7. This Rule shall apply except that in paragraph (1) for the reference to "creditors" there shall be substituted the words "the company".

[Rules 4.26A to 4.26C

7A. Thes Rules shall apply.]

Rule 4.27

8. This Rule shall apply.

Rule 4.28

9. (1) This Rule shall apply subject to the following modifications.

(2) In paragraph (1)—

(a) for the reference to section 172(6), there shall be substituted a reference to section 171(5), and

(b) for the reference to a meeting of creditors, there shall be substituted a reference to a meeting of the company.

(3) In paragraph (2)—

(a) for reference to section 174(4)(c) there shall be substituted a reference to section 173(2)(c), and

(b) for the reference to Rule 4.29(4), there shall be substituted a reference to Rule 4.28A.

(4) After paragraph (4) there shall be inserted the following paragraphs—

"(5) The notice of the liquidator's resignation required by section 171(5) shall be given by him to [the Accountant in Bankruptcy] forthwith after the meeting.

(6) Where a new liquidator is appointed in place of the one who has resigned, the former shall, in giving notice of his appointment, state that his predecessor has resigned and whether he has been released.

[(7) If there is no quorum present at the meeting summoned to receive the liquidator's resignation the meeting is deemed to have been held.]".

(5) After this Rule, there shall be inserted the following Rule—

"4.28A Release of resigning or removed liquidator

(1) Where the liquidator resigns, he has his release from the date on which he gives notice of his resignation to [the Accountant in Bankruptcy].

(2) Where the liquidator is removed by a meeting of the company, he shall forthwith give notice to [the Accountant in Bankruptcy] of his ceasing to act.

(3) Where the liquidator is removed by the court, he must apply to the Accountant of Court for his release.

(4) Where the Accountant of Court gives the release, he shall certify it accordingly, and send the certificate to [the Accountant in Bankruptcy].

(5) A copy of the certificate shall be sent by the Accountant of Court to the former liquidator, whose release is effective from the date of the certificate.".

Rule 4.36

10. This Rule shall apply, except that for any reference to the court, there shall be substituted a reference to the directors of the company or any one of them.

Rule 4.37

11. (1) This Rule shall apply subject to the following modifications.

(2) In paragraph (2), the reference to the court shall be omitted.

(3) For paragraph (3), there shall be substituted the following—

"(3) Rule 4.28A applies as regards the liquidator obtaining his release, as if he had been removed by the court.".

(4) At the end of this Rule, there shall be inserted the following—

"4.37A Vacation of office on making of winding up order

Where the liquidator vacates office in consequence of the court making a winding up order against the company, Rule 4.28A applies as regards the liquidator obtaining his release, as if he had been removed by the court.".

Rule 4.38

12. This Rule shall apply.

Rule 4.39

13. This Rule shall apply.

Chapter 10
(Special manager)

14. (1) This Chapter shall apply subject to the following modifications.
(2) In Rule 4.70 for paragraph (5), there shall be substituted the following—

"(5) The cost of finding caution shall be paid in the first instance by the special manager; but he is entitled to be reimbursed out of the assets as an expense of the liquidation.".

(3) In Rule 4.71, paragraph (1) shall not apply.

[Rules 4.75A to 4.75C

15. These Rules shall apply subject to the modification that after Rule 4.75A(2)(d) there shall be inserted the following—

"(da) a notice or other document to be given, delivered or sent under section 84(2A) or (2B)(b);".]

NOTES

Para 3: words in square brackets added by the Insolvency (Scotland) Amendment Rules 1987, SI 1987/1921, r 3(1), Schedule, Pt I, para 57.

Para 5: in the substituted r 4.19(2) words in square brackets substituted by SI 1987/1921, r 3(1), Schedule, Pt I, para 58.

Para 6: words in square brackets in the title substituted for original words "Rules 4.20 to 4.22", by the Insolvency (Scotland) Amendment Rules 2014, SSI 2014/114, rr 2, 10(2), subject to savings in r 29 thereof as noted to r 0.2 at **[15.2]**.

Para 7A: inserted by SSI 2014/114, rr 2, 11(2), subject to savings in r 29 thereof as noted to r 0.2 at **[15.2]**.

Para 9: in sub-para (4) the words in square brackets in the inserted r 4.28(5) were substituted, and in sub-para (5) the words in square brackets in the inserted r 4.38A were also substituted by the Scotland Act 1998 (Consequential Modifications) (No 2) Order 1999, SI 1999/1820, art 4, Sch 1, Pt II, para 141(1), (21), (22); in sub-para (4) the inserted r 4.28(7) was added by SI 1987/1921, r 3(1), Schedule, Pt I, para 59.

Para 15: added by SSI 2014/114, rr 2, 26(8), subject to savings in r 29 thereof as noted to r 0.2 at **[15.2]**.

SCHEDULE 3
DEPOSIT PROTECTION BOARD'S VOTING RIGHTS

Rule 7.4(6)

[15.347]
1. This Schedule applies where Rule 7.4 does.

2. In relation to any meeting at which the Deposit Protection Board is under Rule 7.4 entitled to be represented, the Board may submit in the liquidation, instead of a claim, a written statement of voting rights ("the statement").

3. The statement shall contain details of—
(a) the names of creditors of the company in respect of whom an obligation of the Board has arisen or may reasonably be expected to arise as a result of the liquidation or proposed liquidation;
(b) the amount of the obligation so arising; and
(c) the total amount of all such obligations specified in the statement.

4. The Board's statement shall, for the purpose of voting at a meeting (but for no other purpose), be treated in all respects as if it were a claim.

5. Any voting rights which a creditor might otherwise exercise at a meeting in respect of a claim against the company are reduced by a sum equal to the amount of that claim in relation to which the Board, by virtue of its having submitted a statement, is entitled to exercise voting rights at that meeting.

6. The Board may from time to time submit a further statement, and, if it does so, that statement supersedes any statement previously submitted.

SCHEDULE 4
PUNISHMENT OF OFFENCES UNDER THE RULES

Rule 7.29

[15.348]
Note: In the fourth and fifth columns of this Schedule, "the statutory maximum" means the prescribed sum under section 289B(6) of the Criminal Procedure (Scotland) Act 1975 (c 21).

Rule creating offence	*General nature of offence*	*Mode of prosecution*	*Punishment*	*Daily default fine (where applicable)*
. . .	. . .	. . .	. . .	
In Part 2, [Rule 2.38(6)]	Administrator failing to send notification as to progress of administration	Summary	One-fifth of the statutory maximum	One-fiftieth of the statutory maximum

Rule creating offence	*General nature of offence*	*Mode of prosecution*	*Punishment*	*Daily default fine (where applicable)*
[In Part 2, Rule 2.43(3)]	[Administrator failing to lodge notice of automatic end of administration]	[Summary]	[One-fifth of the statutory maximum]	[One-fiftieth of the statutory maximum]
In Part 3, Rule 3.9(5)	Receiver failing to send notification as to progress of receivership	Summary	One-fifth of the statutory maximum	One-fiftieth of the statutory maximum

NOTES

Entry relating to r 1.24 revoked by the Insolvency (Scotland) Amendment Rules 2002, SI 2002/2709, r 5, and originally read as follows:

In Part 1, Rule 1.24	False representation or fraud for purpose of obtaining members' or creditors' consent to proposal for voluntary arrangement	1. On indictment 2. Summary	7 years or a fine, or both 6 months or the statutory maximum, or both	

Words in square brackets in entry relating to r 2.38(6) substituted for words "Rule 2.17(4)" by the Insolvency (Scotland) Amendment Rules 2003, SI 2003/2111, r 6, Sch 2, para 11, subject to savings in r 7 thereof at **[2.34]**.

Entry relating to r 2.43(3) inserted by SI 2003/2111, r 4, subject to savings in r 7 thereof at **[2.34]**.

SCHEDULE 5
FORMS

Rule 7.30

[15.349]

NOTES

The forms themselves are not reproduced in this work, but their numbers and descriptions are listed below.

FORM NO	**TITLE**
PART 1: COMPANY VOLUNTARY ARRANGEMENTS	
[1.1 (Scot)	Notice to registrar of companies of voluntary arrangement taking effect]
[1.2 (Scot)	Notice to registrar of companies of order of revocation or suspension of voluntary arrangement]
[1.3 (Scot)	Notice to registrar of companies of supervisor's abstract of receipts and payments]
[1.4 (Scot)	Notice to registrar of companies of completion or termination of voluntary arrangement]
[1.5 (Scot)	Nominee's statement of opinion pursuant to paragraph 6(2) of Schedule A1 to the Insolvency Act 1986]
[1.6 (Scot)	Statement of affairs]
[1.7 (Scot)	Statement of eligibility for a moratorium pursuant to paragraph 7(1)(c) of Schedule A1 to the Insolvency Act 1986]
[1.8 (Scot)	Statement of consent to act by nominee]
[1.9 (Scot)	Documents to be submitted to court to obtain moratorium]
[1.10 (Scot)	Advertisement of coming into force or ending of moratorium (Edinburgh Gazette and other advertising)]
[1.11(Scot)	Notice to registrar of companies of commencement of moratorium]
[1.12 (Scot)	Notice to registrar of companies of extension or further extension or renewal or continuation of moratorium]
[1.13 (Scot)	Notice to court of extension or further extension of moratorium]
[1.14 (Scot)	Notice to registrar of companies of ending of moratorium]
[1.15 (Scot)	Nominee's notice to court of end of moratorium]
[1.16 Scot)	Notice to registrar of companies of withdrawal of nominee's consent to act]
[1.17 (Scot)	Notice to court by nominee of withdrawal of consent to act]
[1.18 (Scot)	Notice to registrar of companies of appointment of a replacement nominee]
[1.19 (Scot)	Notice to court of appointment of replacement nominee]

FORM NO	TITLE
PART 2: ADMINISTRATION PROCEDURE	
[2.1B (Scot)	Statement of proposed administrator]
[2.2B (Scot)	Notice of petition for administration order]
[2.3B (Scot)	Notice of dismissal of petition for administration order]
[2.4B (Scot)	Notice of intention to appoint an administrator by holder of qualifying floating charge]
[2.5B (Scot)	Notice of appointment of an administrator by holder of qualifying floating charge]
[2.6B (Scot)	Notice of appointment of an administrator by holder of qualifying floating charge]
[2.7B (Scot)	Notice of appointment of an administrator by holder of qualifying floating charge]
[2.8B (Scot)	Notice of appointment of an administrator by company or director(s)]
[2.9 (Scot)	Notice of appointment of an administrator by company or director(s)]
[2.10B (Scot)	Notification of appointment of administrator (for Edinburgh Gazette and other advertising)]
[2.11B (Scot))	Notice of administrator's appointment]
[2.12B (Scot)	Notice requiring submission of a statement of affairs]
[2.13B (Scot)	Statement of affairs]
[2.14B (Scot)	Statement of concurrence]
[2.15B (Scot)	Notice of statement of affairs]
[2.16B (Scot)	Statement of administrator's proposals]
[2.16ZB (Scot)	Notice of deemed approval of proposals]
[2.17B (Scot)	Statement of administrator's revised proposals]
[2.18B (Scot)	Notice of result of meeting of creditors]
[2.19B (Scot)	Notice of order to deal with secured property]
[2.20B (Scot)	Administrator's progress report]
[2.21B (Scot)	Notice of automatic end of administration]
[2.22B (Scot)	Notice of extension of period of administration]
[2.23B (Scot)	Notice of end of administration]
[2.24B (Scot)	Notice of court order ending administration]
[2.25B (Scot)	Notice of move from administration to creditors' voluntary liquidation]
[2.26B (Scot)	Notice of move from administration to dissolution]
[2.27B (Scot)	Notice to registrar of companies in respect of date of dissolution]
[2.28B (Scot)	Notice to intention to resign as administrator]
[2.29B (Scot)	Notice of resignation by administrator]
[2.30B (Scot)	Notice of vacation of office by administrator]
[2.31B (Scot)	Notice of appointment of replacement/additional administrator]
[2.32B (Scot)	Notice of insufficient property for distribution to unsecured creditors other than by virtue of s 176A(2)(a).]
PART 3: RECEIVERS	
3.1 (Scot)	Notice requiring submission of receivership statement of affairs
3.2 (Scot)	Receiver's abstract of receipts and payments
3.3 (Scot)	Notice of receiver's death
3.4 (Scot)	Notice of authorisation to dispose of secured property
3.5 (Scot)	Notice of receiver's report
PART 4: WINDING UP	
[4.1 (Scot)	Statutory demand for payment of debt]
4.2 (Scot)	Notice of winding up order
4.3 (Scot)	Notice requiring submission of statement of affairs in a liquidation
4.4 (Scot)	Statement of affairs
4.5 (Scot)	Liquidator's statement of receipts and payments
4.6 (Scot)	Notice of liquidator's statement of receipts and payments

FORM NO	TITLE
[4.7 (Scot)	Statement of claim by creditor]
4.8 (Scot)	Certificate of appointment of liquidator
[4.9 (Scot)	Notice of appointment of liquidator]
4.10 (Scot)	Certificate of removal of liquidator
4.11 (Scot)	Notice of removal of liquidator
4.12 (Scot)	Application by liquidator to the Accountant of Court for his release
4.13 (Scot)	Certificate by the Accountant of Court of release of the liquidator
4.14 (Scot)	Notice of certificate of release of liquidator
4.15 (Scot)	Notice to court of resignation of liquidator
4.16 (Scot)	Notice of resignation of liquidator
4.17 (Scot)	Notice of final meeting of creditors
4.18 (Scot)	Notice of death of liquidator
4.19 (Scot)	Notice of vacation of office of liquidator
4.20 (Scot)	Certificate of constitution of creditors'/liquidation committee
4.21 (Scot)	Liquidator's certificate of continuance of liquidation committee
4.22 (Scot)	Notice of constitution/continuance of liquidation/creditors' committee
4.23 (Scot)	Liquidator's certificate that creditors paid in full
[4.24 (Scot)	Notice of certificate that creditors have been paid in full]
4.25 (Scot)	Declaration of solvency
4.26 (Scot)	Return of final meeting in a voluntary winding up
4.27 (Scot)	Notice of court's order sisting proceedings in winding up by the court
4.28 (Scot)	Notice under section 204(6) or 205(6)
[4.29 (Scot)	Proxy]
[4.30 (Scot)	Confirmation by court of creditor's voluntary winding up application and order]
[4.31 (Scot)	Notice in respect of order under section 176A]
[4.32 (Scot)	Notice to the creditors of an insolvent company of the re-use of a prohibited name]

NOTES

Forms 1.1 (Scot)–1.19 (Scot) substituted for original forms 1.1 (Scot)–1.4 (Scot) by the Insolvency (Scotland) Amendment Rules 2002, SI 2002/2709, r 6(1), Schedule, Part 3, subject to transitional provisions in r 6(2) of those Rules, which provides:

"(2) Forms 1.1 (Scot) to 1.19 (Scot) are for use in relation to any voluntary arrangement under Part I of the Act other than any of the cases mentioned in paragraph (2) of Rule 4 to these Rules and in those cases Forms 1.1 (Scot) to 1.4 (Scot) in Schedule 5 to the principal Rules, instead of those substituted by Part 3 of the Schedule to these Rules, shall continue to be used.".

For r 4(2) of SI 2002/2709, see the note to r 1.1 at **[15.4]**.

The original forms 1.1 (Scot)–1.4 (Scot) were named as follows:

"1.1 (Scot)	Notice of report of a meeting approving voluntary arrangement
1.2 (Scot)	Notice of order of revocation or suspension of voluntary arrangement
1.3 (Scot)	Notice of voluntary arrangement supervisor's abstract of receipts and payments
1.4 (Scot)	Notice of completion of voluntary arrangement".

Form 1.10 (Scot) further substituted by the Insolvency (Scotland) Amendment Rules 2009, SI 2009/662, r 2, Schedule, para 14, subject to transitional provisions in r 3 thereof as noted to r 1.4 at **[15.10]**, and previously read as follows:

"[1.10 (Scot)	Advertisement of coming into force or ending of moratorium (for newspaper or Edinburgh Gazette)]".

Forms 2.1B (Scot)–2.32B (Scot) substituted for forms 2.1 (Scot)–2.13 (Scot) by the Insolvency (Scotland) Amendment Rules 2003, SI 2003/2111, r 5, Sch 1, Pt 2, subject to savings in r 7 thereof at **[2.34]**.

Forms 2.1–2.13, as amended by SI 1987/1921, were previously named as follows:

"2.1 (Scot)	Notice of petition for administration order
2.2 (Scot)	Notice of administration order
2.3 (Scot)	Notice of dismissal of petition for administration order
2.4 (Scot)	Notice of discharge of administration order
2.5 (Scot)	Notice requiring submission of administration statement of affairs
2.6 (Scot)	Statement of affairs

2.7 (Scot)	Notice of statement of administrator's proposals
2.8 (Scot)	Notice of result of meeting of creditors
2.9 (Scot)	Administrator's abstract of receipts and payments
2.10 (Scot)	Statement of administrator's proposed revisions and notice of meeting to consider them
2.11 (Scot)	Notice of order to deal with secured property
2.12 (Scot)	Notice of variation of administration order
2.13 (Scot)	Notice to court of resignation of administrator".

Forms 2.4B (Scot)–2.10B (Scot), 2.12B (Scot) further substituted and Form 2.13B (Scot) amended by the Insolvency (Scotland) Amendment Rules 2006, SI 2006/734, r 4, Schedule.

Form 2.10B (Scot) further substituted by SI 2009/662, r 2, Schedule, para 15, subject to transitional provisions in r 3 thereof as noted to r 1.4 at **[15.10]**, and previously read as follows:

"[2.10B (Scot) Notification of appointment of administrator (for newspaper or Edinburgh Gazette)]".

Forms 2.2B (Scot), 2.3B (Scot), 2.11B (Scot), 2.15B (Scot)–2.27B (Scot), 2.29B (Scot), 2.31B (Scot), 2.32B (Scot), 4.31 (Scot) amended and Form 2.30B substituted by the Insolvency (Scotland) Amendment (No 2) Rules 2009, SI 2009/2375, r 2, Schs 1, 2.

Form 2.16ZB (Scot) inserted and Forms 2.25B (Scot), 2.30B (Scot) amended by the Insolvency (Scotland) Amendment Rules 2010, SI 2010/688, r 3, Sch 1, paras 116–118, Sch 2, subject to transitional provisions in r 4 thereof at **[2.80]**.

Forms 3.4 (Scot), 4.2 (Scot), 4.5 (Scot), 4.6 (Scot), 4.11 (Scot), 4.14 (Scot), 4.16 (Scot)– 4.19 (Scot), 4.22 (Scot), 4.25 (Scot)–4.27 (Scot) amended by the Scotland Act 1998 (Consequential Modifications) (No 2) Order 1999, SI 1999/1820, art 4, Sch 1, Pt II, para 141(1), (23).

Forms 4.1 (Scot), 4.9 (Scot) substituted, and Form 4.29 (Scot) added, by the Insolvency (Scotland) Amendment Rules 1987, SI 1987/1921, r 3(1), Schedule, Pt I, para 60, Pt II.

Form 4.4 (Scot) amended by the Enterprise Act 2002 (Consequential Amendments) (Prescribed Part) (Scotland) Order 2003, SI 2003/2108, art 10(2), Schedule, Pt 2.

Forms 4.4 (Scot), 5 (Scot) amended by the Insolvency (Scotland) Amendment Order 2006, SI 2006/735, art 2, Schedule.

Form 4.7 (Scot) substituted (for Form 4.7 (Scot): Statement of claim by creditor, as earlier substituted by SI 2003/2109) by SI 2003/2111, r 6, Sch 2, para 12, subject to savings in r 7 thereof at **[2.34]**.

Forms 4.7, 4.30 amended by the Insolvency Amendment (EU 2015/848) Regulations 2017, SI 2017/702, regs 2, 3, Schedule, Pt 5, paras 61, 91, as from 26 June 2017, except in relation to proceedings opened before that date.

Forms 4.9 (Scot), 4.24 (Scot) substituted by the Insolvency (Scotland) Amendment Rules 2014, SSI 2014/114, rr 2, 28, Schedule, subject to savings in r 29 thereof as noted to r 0.2 at **[15.2]**.

Form 4.30 (Scot) added by the Insolvency (Scotland) Regulations 2003, SI 2003/2109, regs 23, 29, subject to the saving that anything done under or for the purposes of any provision of these Rules before 8 September 2003 has effect as if done under or for the purposes of the provision as amended.

Form 4.31 (Scot) added by SI 2003/2108, art 10(1), Schedule, Pt 1.

Form 4.32 (Scot) added by the Insolvency (Scotland) Amendment Rules 2007, SI 2007/2537, r 3(1), (3), Schedule.

PART 16
OTHER STATUTORY INSTRUMENTS—SCOTLAND

RECEIVERS (SCOTLAND) REGULATIONS 1986

(SI 1986/1917 (S 141))

NOTES

Made: 10 November 1986.
Authority: Insolvency Act 1986, ss 53(1), (6), 54(3), 62(1), (5), 65(1)(a), 66(1), 67(2)(b), 70(1), 71.
Commencement: 29 December 1986.

ARRANGEMENT OF REGULATIONS

1 Citation and commencement . . . . . [16.1]
2 Interpretation . . . . . [16.2]
3 Forms . . . . . [16.3]
4 Instrument of appointment . . . . . [16.4]
5 Joint receivers . . . . . [16.5]
6 Resignation . . . . . [16.6]
7 Report to creditors . . . . . [16.7]

SCHEDULES

Schedule—Forms . . . . . [16.8]

[16.1]
1 Citation and commencement
These regulations may be cited as the Receivers (Scotland) Regulations 1986 and shall come into operation on 29th December 1986.

[16.2]
2 Interpretation
In these regulations, "the Act" means the Insolvency Act 1986.

[16.3]
3 Forms
The forms set out in the Schedule to these regulations, with such variations as circumstances require, are the forms prescribed for the purposes of the provisions of the Act which are referred to in these forms.

[16.4]
4 Instrument of appointment
The certified copy instrument of appointment of a receiver which is required to be submitted to the registrar of companies [and the Accountant in Bankruptcy] by or on behalf of the person making the appointment under section 53(1) of the Act shall be certified to be a correct copy by or on behalf of that person.

NOTES

Words in square brackets inserted by the Scotland Act 1998 (Consequential Modifications) (No 2) Order 1999, SI 1999/1820, art 4, Sch 2, Pt II, para 142(1), (2).

[16.5]
5 Joint receivers
Where two or more persons are appointed joint receivers by the holder of a floating charge under section 53 of the Act, subsection (6) of that section shall apply subject to the following modifications—

(a) the appointment of any of the joint receivers shall be of no effect unless the appointment is accepted by all of them in accordance with paragraph (a) of that subsection and Rule 3.1 of the Insolvency (Scotland) Rules 1986; and

(b) their appointment as joint receivers shall be deemed to be made on the day on and at the time at which the instrument of appointment is received by the last of them, as evidenced by the written docquet required by paragraph (b) of that subsection.

[16.6]
6 Resignation
For the purposes of section 62(1) of the Act, a receiver, who wishes to resign his office, shall give at least 7 days' notice of his resignation to—

(a) the holder of the floating charge by virtue of which he was appointed;
(b) the holder of any other floating charge and any receiver appointed by him;
(c) the members of any committee of creditors established under section 68 of the Act; and
(d) the company, or if it is then in liquidation, its liquidator,

and the notice shall specify the date on which the resignation takes effect.

[16.7]
7 Report to creditors

[(1)] Where the receiver determines to publish a notice under paragraph (b) of section 67(2) of the Act, the notice shall be published in a newspaper circulating in the area where the company has its principal place of business or in such other newspaper as he thinks most appropriate for ensuring that it comes to the notice of the unsecured creditors of the company.

[(2) The receiver's report under section 67(1) shall state, to the best of his knowledge and belief—

(a) an estimate of the value of the prescribed part (whether or not he proposes to make an application under section 176A(5) or whether section 176A(3) applies), and

(b) an estimate of the value of the company's net property,

provided that such estimates shall not be required to include any information the disclosure of which could seriously prejudice the commercial interests of the company, but if such information is excluded the estimates shall be accompanied by a statement to that effect.

(3) The report shall also state whether, and, if so, why, the receiver proposes to make an application to the court under section 176A(5).]

NOTES

Para (1): numbered as such by the Enterprise Act 2002 (Consequential Amendments) (Prescribed Part) (Scotland) Order 2003, SI 2003/2108, art 11(1).

Paras (2), (3): added by SI 2003/2108, art 11(1).

SCHEDULE
FORMS

Regulation 3

[16.8]

NOTES

The forms themselves are not reproduced in this work, but their numbers and descriptions are listed below.

FORM NO	TITLE
1 (Scot)	Notice of appointment of a receiver by the holder of a floating charge
2 (Scot)	Notice of appointment of a receiver by the court
3 (Scot)	Notice of the receiver ceasing to act or of his removal
4 (Scot)	Notice of appointment of receiver
5 (Scot)	Statement of affairs

NOTES

Forms 1 (Scot)–3 (Scot): amended by the Scotland Act 1998 (Consequential Modifications) (No 2) Order 1999, SI 1999/1820, art 4, Sch 2, Pt II, para 142(1), (3).

Form 5 (Scot): amended by the Enterprise Act 2002 (Consequential Amendments) (Prescribed Part) (Scotland) Order 2003, SI 2003/2108, art 11(2), Schedule, Pt 2.

ACT OF SEDERUNT (COMPANY DIRECTORS DISQUALIFICATION) 1986

(SI 1986/2296 (S 168))

NOTES

Made: 19 December 1986.

Commencement: 29 December 1986.

[16.9]
1 Citation, commencement and interpretation

(1) This Act of Sederunt may be cited as the Act of Sederunt (Company Directors Disqualification) 1986 and shall come into operation on 29th December 1986.

(2) This Act of Sederunt shall be inserted in the Books of Sederunt.

(3) In this Act of Sederunt—

"disqualification order" shall have the meaning assigned to it by section 1(1) of the Company Directors Disqualification Act 1986.

2 (*Revokes the Act of Sederunt (Disqualification of Directors etc) 1986, SI 1986/692.*)

[16.10]
3 Applications for disqualification orders

(1) An application to the sheriff for a disqualification order or for leave of the court under the Company Directors Disqualification Act 1986 shall be made by summary application.

(2) In an application under sub-paragraph (1) which proceeds as unopposed, evidence submitted by way of affidavit shall be admissible in place of parole evidence.

(3) For the purposes of this paragraph—
(a) "affidavit" includes affirmation and statutory declaration; and
(b) an affidavit shall be treated as admissible if it is duly emitted before a notary public or any other competent authority.

[16.11]

4 Orders to furnish information or for inspection

(1) Subject to sub-paragraph (2), an application for an order of the court under rule 4(2) of the Insolvent Companies (Reports on Conduct of Directors) (No 2) (Scotland) Rules 1986 (order to furnish information, etc) shall be made by summary application.

(2) Where an application has been made under the Company Directors Disqualification Act 1986 for a disqualification order, an application under this paragraph may be made by minute in the proceedings in which the disqualification order is sought.

NOTES

The Insolvent Companies (Reports on Conduct of Directors) (No 2) (Scotland) Rules 1986, SI 1986/1916: revoked (subject to savings) and replaced by the Insolvent Companies (Reports on Conduct of Directors) (Scotland) Rules 1996, SI 1996/1910 at **[16.126]** et seq.

ACT OF SEDERUNT (SHERIFF COURT COMPANY INSOLVENCY RULES) 1986

(SI 1986/2297 (S 169))

NOTES

Made: 19 December 1986.
Commencement: 29 December 1986.

ARRANGEMENT OF RULES

1 Citation and commencement . . . [16.12]
3 Interpretation . . . [16.13]
3A Representation . . . [16.14]
3B Expenses . . . [16.15]

PART I
COMPANY VOLUNTARY ARRANGEMENTS

4 Lodging of nominee's report (Part 1, Chapter 2 of the Insolvency Rules) . . . [16.16]
5 Lodging of nominee's report (Part 1, Chapter 4 of the Insolvency Rules) . . . [16.17]
6 Applications to replace nominee . . . [16.18]
7 Report of meetings to approve arrangement . . . [16.19]
8 Abstracts of supervisor's receipts and payments and notices of completion of arrangement . . . [16.20]
9 Form of certain applications . . . [16.21]

PART II
ADMINISTRATION PROCEDURE

10 Petitions for administration orders . . . [16.22]
11 Notice of petition . . . [16.23]
12 Applications during an administration . . . [16.24]
13 Report of administrator's proposals . . . [16.25]
14 Report of administrator's proposals: Schedule B1 to the Act of 1986 . . . [16.26]
14A Time and date of lodging in an administration . . . [16.27]

PART III
RECEIVERS

15 Petitions to appoint receivers . . . [16.28]
16 Intimation, service and advertisement . . . [16.29]
17 Form of certain applications where receiver appointed . . . [16.30]

PART IV
WINDING UP BY THE COURT OF COMPANIES REGISTERED UNDER THE COMPANIES ACTS AND OF UNREGISTERED COMPANIES

18 Petitions to wind up a company . . . [16.31]
19 Intimation, service and advertisement . . . [16.32]
20 Lodging of caveats . . . [16.33]
21 Substitution of creditor or contributory for petitioner . . . [16.34]

22 Advertisement of appointment of liquidator .... [16.35]
23 Provisional liquidators .... [16.36]
24 Applications and appeals in relation to a statement of affairs .... [16.37]
25 Appeals against adjudication of claims .... [16.38]
26 Appointment of liquidator by the court .... [16.39]
27 Removal of liquidator .... [16.40]
28 Applications in relation to remuneration of liquidator .... [16.41]
29 Application to appoint a special manager .... [16.42]
30 Other applications .... [16.43]

PART V
GENERAL PROVISIONS

31 Application .... [16.44]
31A Applications under section 176A of the Act of 1986 .... [16.45]
31AA Limited disclosure of statement of affairs .... [16.46]
31B UNCITRAL Model Law on Cross-Border Insolvency .... [16.47]
32 Intimation, service and advertisement of notes and appeals .... [16.48]
33 Affidavits .... [16.49]
34 Notices, reports and other documents sent to the court .... [16.50]
35 Failure to comply with rules .... [16.51]
35A Vulnerable witnesses .... [16.52]

PART VI
APPEALS

36 Appeals to the Court of Session .... [16.53]
36A Appeals to the Sheriff Appeal Court .... [16.54]

[16.12]
1 Citation and commencement

(1) This Act of Sederunt may be cited as the Act of Sederunt (Sheriff Court Company Insolvency Rules) 1986 and shall come into operation on 29th December 1986.

(2) This Act of Sederunt shall be inserted in the Books of Sederunt.

2 (*Revokes the Act of Sederunt (Sheriff Court Liquidations) 1930 in relation to proceedings commenced on or after 29 December 1986.*)

[16.13]
3 Interpretation

(1) In these rules—

"the Act of 1986" means the Insolvency Act 1986;

["the Act of 2004" means the Energy Act 2004;

"the Act of 2011" means the Energy Act 2011;

"administration" shall include an energy administration under the Act of 2004 or the Energy Administration Rules and an energy supply company administration under the Act of 2011 or the Energy Supply Company Administration Rules and "administration order" and "administrator" shall be construed accordingly;]

["Council Regulation" means Regulation (EU) 2015/848 of the European Parliament and of the Council of 20th May 2015 on insolvency proceedings, as amended from time to time;]

["the Energy Administration Rules" means the Energy Administration (Scotland) Rules 2006;

"the Energy Supply Company Administration Rules" means the Energy Supply Company Administration (Scotland) Rules 2013;]

"the Insolvency Rules" means the Insolvency (Scotland) Rules 1986;

["the Model Law" means the Model Law on Cross-Border Insolvency as set out in Schedule 1 to the Cross-Border Insolvency Regulations 2006.]

["non GB company" for the purposes of an energy administration shall have the meaning assigned in section 171 of the Act of 2004 and for the purposes of an energy supply company administration shall have the meaning assigned in section 102 of the 2011 Act;]

"registered office" means—

(a) the place specified, in the statement of the company delivered to the registrar of companies under section 10 of the Companies Act 1985, as the intended place of its registered office on incorporation; or

(b) where notice has been given by the company to the registrar of companies under section 287 of the Companies Act 1985 of a change of registered office, the place specified in the last such notice;

"sheriff-clerk" has the meaning assigned to it in section 3(f) of the Sheriff Courts (Scotland) Act 1907.

(2) Unless the context otherwise requires, words and expressions used in these rules which are also used in the Act of 1986[, the Act of 2004, the Act of 2011, the Energy Administration Rules, the Energy Supply Company Administration Rules] or the Insolvency Rules have the same meaning as in [those Acts] or those Rules.

NOTES

Para (1): definitions "the Act of 2004", "the Act of 2011", "administration", "the Energy Administration Rules", "the Energy Supply Company Administration Rules" and "non GB company" inserted by the Act of Sederunt (Sheriff Court Rules) (Miscellaneous Amendments) (No 3) 2013, SSI 2013/171, rr 3(1), (2)(a), 6(2), except in respect of any action raised but not yet determined by 7 June 2013; definition "the Model Law" inserted by the Act of Sederunt (Sheriff Court Company Insolvency Rules 1986) Amendment (UNCITRAL Model Law on Cross-Border Insolvency) 2006, SSI 2006/200, r 2(1), (2); definition "Council Regulation" substituted by the Act of Sederunt (Rules of the Court of Session 1994 and Sheriff Court Rules Amendment) (Regulation (EU) 2015/848) 2017, SSI 2017/202, rr 5, 6, except in relation to proceedings which are subject to Regulation (EC) 1346/2000 of 29th May 2000 on insolvency proceedings. The definition "the Council Regulation" (as inserted by the Act of Sederunt (Sheriff Court Rules) (Miscellaneous Amendments) 2008, SSI 2008/223, r 10(1), (2)) originally read as follows:

> "["the Council Regulation" means Council Regulation (EC) 1346/2000 of 29th May 2000 on insolvency proceedings as it may be amended from time to time;]".

Para (2): words in first pair of square brackets inserted and words in second pair of square brackets substituted for original words "that Act", by SSI 2013/171, rr 3(1), (2)(b), 6(2), except in respect of any action raised but not yet determined by 7 June 2013.

[16.14]

[3A Representation

(1) A party may be represented by any person authorised under any enactment to conduct proceedings in the sheriff court in accordance with the terms of that enactment.

(2) The person referred to in paragraph (1) may do everything for the preparation and conduct of the proceedings as may have been done by an individual conducting his own action.

(3) For the purposes of this rule, "enactment" includes an enactment comprised in, or in an instrument made under, an Act of . . . the Scottish Parliament.]

NOTES

Inserted, together with r 3B, by the Act of Sederunt (Sheriff Court Rules) (Miscellaneous Amendments) 2008, SSI 2008/223, r 12.

Para (3): words omitted revoked by the Act of Sederunt (Sheriff Court Rules) (Miscellaneous Amendments) (No 3) 2013, SSI 2013/171, r 3(1), (3). This amendment is made to correct a drafting error in this rule (as inserted by SSI 2008/223) where the words "the Scottish" appeared twice.

[16.15]

[3B Expenses

A party who—

(a) is or has been represented by a person authorised under any enactment to conduct proceedings in the sheriff court; and

(b) would have been found entitled to expenses if he had been represented by a solicitor or an advocate,

may be awarded expenses or outlays to which a party litigant may be found entitled under the Litigants in Person (Cost and Expenses) Act 1975 or under any enactment under that Act.]

NOTES

Inserted as noted to r 3A at **[16.14]**.

PART I
COMPANY VOLUNTARY ARRANGEMENTS

[16.16]

4 Lodging of nominee's report (Part 1, Chapter 2 of the Insolvency Rules)

(1) This rule applies where the company is not being wound up, is not in liquidation and [is not in administration].

(2) A report of a nominee, sent to the court under section 2(2) of the Act of 1986, shall be accompanied by a covering letter, lodged in the offices of the court and marked by the sheriff-clerk with the date on which it is received.

(3) The report shall be placed before the sheriff for consideration of any direction which he may make under section 3(1) of the Act of 1986.

(4) An application by a nominee to extend the time within which he may lodge his report under section 2(2) of the Act of 1986 shall be made by letter addressed to the sheriff-clerk, who shall place the matter before the sheriff for determination.

(5) The letter of application under paragraph (4) and a copy of the reply by the court shall be placed by the sheriff-clerk with the nominee's report when it is subsequently lodged.

(6) A person who states in writing that he is a creditor, member or director of the company may, by himself or his agent, on payment of the appropriate fee, inspect the nominee's report lodged under paragraph (2).

NOTES

Para (1): words in square brackets substituted by the Act of Sederunt (Sheriff Court Company Insolvency Rules 1986) Amendment 2003, SSI 2003/388, r 4, Schedule, paras 1, 2.

[16.17]

5 Lodging of nominee's report (Part 1, Chapter 4 of the Insolvency Rules)

(1) This rule applies where the company is being wound up, is in liquidation or [is in administration].

(2) Where a report of a nominee is sent to the court under section 2(2) of the Act of 1986, it shall be lodged in the process of the petition to wind up the company or the petition for [any petition in respect of an administration] which is in force in respect of it, as the case may be.

(3) Where the nominee is not the liquidator or administrator, the report shall be placed before the sheriff for consideration of any direction which he may make under section 3(1) of the Act of 1986.

(4) An application by a nominee to extend the time within which he may lodge his report under section 2(2) of the Act of 1986 shall be made by letter addressed to the sheriff-clerk, who shall place the matter before the sheriff for determination.

(5) The letter of application under paragraph (4) and a copy of the reply by the court shall be placed by the sheriff-clerk in the process of the petition to wind up the company or [any petition in respect of an administration] which is in force in respect of it, as the case may be.

(6) A person who states in writing that he is a creditor, member or director of the company may, by himself or his agent, on payment of the appropriate fee, inspect the nominee's report lodged under paragraph (2).

NOTES

Para (1): words in square brackets substituted by the Act of Sederunt (Sheriff Court Company Insolvency Rules 1986) Amendment 2003, SSI 2003/388, r 4, Schedule, paras 1, 3(a).

Para (2): words in square brackets substituted by SSI 2003/388, r 4, Schedule, paras 1, 3(b).

Para (5): words in square brackets substituted by SSI 2003/388, r 4, Schedule, paras 1, 3(c).

[16.18]

6 Applications to replace nominee

An application under section 2(4) of the Act of 1986 to replace a nominee who has failed to lodge a report under section 2(2) of the Act of 1986, shall be made—

- (a) by petition where the company is not being wound up, is not in liquidation and [there is no order in respect of an administration]; or
- (b) by note in the process of the petition to wind up the company or the petition [in respect of an administration] which is in force in respect of it, as the case may be,

and shall be intimated and served as the court shall direct.

NOTES

Para (a): words in square brackets substituted by the Act of Sederunt (Sheriff Court Company Insolvency Rules 1986) Amendment 2003, SSI 2003/388, r 4, Schedule, paras 1, 4(a).

Para (b): words in square brackets substituted by SSI 2003/388, r 4, Schedule, paras 1, 4(b).

[16.19]

7 Report of meetings to approve arrangement

The report of the result of a meeting to be sent to the court under section 4(6) of the Act of 1986 shall be sent to the sheriff-clerk who shall cause it to be lodged—

- (a) in a case to which rule 4 applies, with the nominee's report lodged under that rule; or
- (b) in a case to which rule 5 applies, in the process of the petition to wind up the company or the petition for [an order in respect of an administration] which is in force in respect of it, as the case may be.

NOTES

Para (b): words in square brackets substituted by the Act of Sederunt (Sheriff Court Company Insolvency Rules 1986) Amendment 2003, SSI 2003/388, r 4, Schedule, paras 1, 5.

[16.20]

8 Abstracts of supervisor's receipts and payments and notices of completion of arrangement

An abstract of receipts and payments prepared by a supervisor to be sent to the court under rule 1.21(2) of the Insolvency Rules or a notice of completion of the arrangement (together with a copy of the supervisor's report) to be sent to the court under rule 1.23(3) of those Rules shall be sent to the sheriff-clerk, who shall cause it to be lodged—

- (a) in a case to which rule 4 applies, with the nominee's report lodged under that rule; or
- (b) in a case to which rule 5 applies, in the process of the petition to wind up the company or the petition for [an order in respect of an administration] which is in force in respect of it, as the case may be.

NOTES

Para (b): words in square brackets substituted by the Act of Sederunt (Sheriff Court Company Insolvency Rules 1986) Amendment 2003, SSI 2003/388, r 4, Schedule, paras 1, 6.

[16.21]
9 Form of certain applications

(1) This rule applies to applications under any of the following provisions of the Act of 1986 and the Insolvency Rules—

(a) section 6 (to challenge a decision in relation to an arrangement);
(b) section 7(3) (to challenge actings of a supervisor);
(c) section 7(4)(a) (by supervisor for directions);
(d) section 7(5) (to appoint a supervisor);
(e) rule 1.21(5) (to dispense with sending abstracts or reports or to vary dates on which obligation to send abstracts or reports arises);
(f) rule 1.23(4) (by supervisor to extend period for sending notice of implementation of arrangement); and
(g) any other provision relating to company voluntary arrangements not specifically mentioned in this Part.

(2) An application shall be made—

(a) in a case to which rule 4 applies, by petition; or
(b) in a case to which rule 5 applies, by note in the process of the petition to wind up the company or the petition for [an order in respect of an administration] which is in force in respect of it, as the case may be.

NOTES

Para (2): words in square brackets in sub-para (b) substituted by the Act of Sederunt (Sheriff Court Company Insolvency Rules 1986) Amendment 2003, SSI 2003/388, r 4, Schedule, paras 1, 7.

PART II
ADMINISTRATION [PROCEDURE]

[16.22]
10 Petitions for administration orders

(1) A petition for an administration order [or any other order in an administration] shall include averments in relation to—

(a) the petitioner and the capacity in which he presents the petition, if other than the company;
(b) whether it is believed that the company is, or is likely to become, unable to pay its debts and the grounds of that belief;
[(c) [in the case of a petition under the Act of 1986,] how the making of that order will achieve—
 (i) any of the purposes specified in section 8(3) of the Act of 1986; or
 (ii) an objective specified in paragraph 3 of Schedule B1 to the Act of 1986;]
(d) the company's financial position, specifying (so far as known) assets and liabilities, including contingent and prospective liabilities;
(e) any security known or believed to be held by creditors of the company, whether in any case the security confers power on the holder to appoint a receiver, and whether a receiver has been appointed;
(f) so far as known to the petitioner, whether any steps have been taken for the winding up of the company, giving details of them;
(g) other matters which, in the opinion of the petitioner, will assist the court in deciding whether to grant [that] order;
[(h) [in the case of a petition under the Act of 1986,] jurisdiction under the Council Regulation, in particular stating, so far as known to the petitioner—
 (i) where the centre of main interests of the company is and whether the company has any other establishments in another member State;
 (ii) whether there are insolvency proceedings elsewhere in respect of the company and whether those proceedings are main or territorial proceedings; . . .]
[(i) the name and address of the person proposed to be appointed, and his or her qualification to act, as administrator;
(j) whether the Secretary of State has certified the case as one in which he or she considers it would be appropriate for him or her to petition under section 124A of the Act of 1986 (petition for winding up on grounds of public interest);
(k) so far as is known to the petitioner in a petition for an energy administration order or an energy supply company administration order, whether any steps have been taken for an administration order under Schedule B1 to the Act of 1986; and
(l) whether a protected energy company in a petition for an energy administration order, or an energy supply company in a petition for an energy supply company administration order, is a non GB company.]

(2) There shall be produced with the petition—

(a) any document instructing the facts relied on, or otherwise founded on, by the petitioner; and
(b) . . .

NOTES

Word in square brackets in Part heading preceding this rule substituted by the Act of Sederunt (Sheriff Court Company Insolvency Rules 1986) Amendment 2003, SSI 2003/388, r 2(1), (2).

Para (1): words in first pair of square brackets inserted, sub-para (c) substituted, and word in square brackets in sub-para (g) substituted, by SSI 2003/388, r 2(1), (3)(a)–(c); sub-para (h) substituted by the Act of Sederunt (Sheriff Court Rules)

(Miscellaneous Amendments) 2008, SSI 2008/223, r 10(1), (3); words in square brackets in sub-para (c) inserted, word "and" omitted from sub-para (h) revoked, and sub-paras (i)–(l) substituted for original sub-para (i), by the Act of Sederunt (Sheriff Court Rules) (Miscellaneous Amendments) (No 3) 2013, SSI 2013/171, rr 3(1), (4), 6(2), except in respect of any action raised but not yet determined by 7 June 2013. Sub-para (i) originally read as follows:

> "(i) the person proposed to be appointed as administrator, giving his name and address and that he is qualified to act as an insolvency practitioner in relation to the company.".

Para (2): sub-para (b) revoked by SSI 2003/388, r 2(1), (3)(e).

[16.23]
11 Notice of petition

Notice of the petition on the persons to whom notice is to be given under rule [2.3] of the Insolvency Rules[, section 156(2)(a) to (c) of the 2004 Act, rule 5(1) of the Energy Administration Rules or rule 6(1) of the Energy Supply Company Administration Rules,] shall be made in such manner as the court shall direct.

NOTES

Rule reference in square brackets substituted by the Act of Sederunt (Sheriff Court Company Insolvency Rules 1986) Amendment 2003, SSI 2003/388, r 2(1), (4); words in second pair of square brackets inserted by the Act of Sederunt (Sheriff Court Rules) (Miscellaneous Amendments) (No 3) 2013, SSI 2013/171, rr 3(1), (5), 6(2), except in respect of any action raised but not yet determined by 7 June 2013.

[16.24]
[12 Applications during an administration

An application or appeal under any provision of the Act of 1986[, the Insolvency Rules [the Act of 2004, the Energy Administration Rules, the Act of 2011,] or an application to participate under article 12 of the Model Law in an administration] during an administration shall be—

(a) where no previous application or appeal has been made, by petition; or

(b) where a petition for an order in respect of an administration has been made, by note in the process of that petition.]

NOTES

Substituted by the Act of Sederunt (Sheriff Court Company Insolvency Rules 1986) Amendment 2003, SSI 2003/388, r 2(1), (5); words in first (outer) pair of square brackets substituted by the Act of Sederunt (Sheriff Court Company Insolvency Rules 1986) Amendment (UNCITRAL Model Law on Cross-Border Insolvency) 2006, SSI 2006/200, r 2(1), (3); words in second (inner) pair of square brackets inserted by the Act of Sederunt (Sheriff Court Rules) (Miscellaneous Amendments) (No 3) 2013, SSI 2013/171, rr 3(1), (6), 6(2), except in respect of any action raised but not yet determined by 7 June 2013.

[16.25]
13 Report of administrator's proposals

(1) A report of the meeting to approve the administrator's proposals to be sent to the court under section 24(4) of the Act of 1986 shall be sent to the sheriff-clerk, who shall cause it to be lodged in the process of the petition.

(2) Where the report lodged under paragraph (1) discloses that the meeting has declined to approve the administrator's proposals, the court shall appoint a special diet for determination by the sheriff of any order he may make under section 24(5) of the Act of 1986.

[16.26]
[14 Report of administrator's proposals: Schedule B1 to the Act of 1986

(1) Paragraph (2) shall apply where a report under paragraphs 53(2) or 54(6) of Schedule B1 to the Act of 1986 discloses a failure to approve, or to approve a revision of, an administrator's proposals.

(2) The sheriff clerk shall appoint a hearing for determination by the sheriff of any order that may be made under paragraph 55(2) of Schedule B1 to the Act of 1986.]

NOTES

Substituted, together with r 14A, for original r 14, by the Act of Sederunt (Sheriff Court Company Insolvency Rules 1986) Amendment 2003, SSI 2003/388, r 2(1), (6).

[16.27]
[14A Time and date of lodging in an administration

(1) The time and date of lodging of a notice or document relating to an administration . . . shall be noted by the sheriff clerk upon the notice or document.

(2) Subject to any provision of the Insolvency Rules—

(a) where the time of lodging of a notice or document cannot be ascertained by the sheriff clerk, the notice or document shall be deemed to be lodged at 10 a.m. on the date of lodging; and

(b) where a notice or document under paragraph (1) is delivered on any day other than a business day, the date of lodging shall be the first business day after such delivery.]

NOTES

Substituted as noted to r 14 at **[16.26]**.

Sub-s (1): words "under the Act of 1986 or the Insolvency Rules" (omitted) revoked by the Act of Sederunt (Sheriff Court Rules) (Miscellaneous Amendments) (No 3) 2013, SSI 2013/171, rr 3(1), (7), 6(2), except in respect of any action raised but not yet determined by 7 June 2013.

PART III
RECEIVERS

[16.28]
15 Petitions to appoint receivers

(1) A petition to appoint a receiver for a company shall include averments in relation to—

(a) any floating charge and the property over which it is secured;

(b) so far as known to the petitioner whether any petition for [an order in respect of an administration] has been made[, or an administrator has been appointed] in respect of the company, giving details of it;

(c) other matters which, in the opinion of the petitioner, will assist the court in deciding whether to appoint a receiver; and

(d) the person proposed to be appointed as receiver, giving his name and address and that he is qualified to act as a receiver.

(2) There shall be produced with the petition any document instructing the facts relied on, or otherwise founded on, by the petitioner.

NOTES

Para (1): in sub-para (b), words in first pair of square brackets substituted and words in second pair of square brackets inserted, by the Act of Sederunt (Sheriff Court Company Insolvency Rules 1986) Amendment 2003, SSI 2003/388, r 4, Schedule, paras 1, 8.

[16.29]
16 Intimation, service and advertisement

(1) Intimation, service and advertisement of the petition shall be made, in accordance with the following provisions of this rule unless the court otherwise directs.

(2) There shall be included in the order for service, a requirement to serve—

(a) upon the company; . . .

(b) where a petition for [an order in respect of an administration] has been presented, on that petitioner and any respondent to that petition[; and

(c) upon an administrator.]

(3) Subject to paragraph (5), service of a petition on the company shall be effected at its registered office—

(a) by registered or recorded delivery post addressed to the company; or

(b) by sheriff officer—

(i) leaving the citation in the hands of a person who, after due inquiry, he has reasonable grounds for believing to be a director, other officer or responsible employee of the company or authorised to accept service on behalf of the company; or

(ii) if there is no such person as is mentioned in head (i) present, depositing it in the registered office in such a way that it is likely to come to the attention of such a person attending at that office.

(4) Where service is effected in accordance with paragraph (3)(b)(ii), the sheriff officer thereafter shall send a copy of the petition and citation by ordinary first class post to the registered office of the company.

(5) Where service cannot be effected at the registered office of the company or the company has no registered office—

(a) service may be effected at the last known principal place of business of the company in Scotland or at some place in Scotland at which the company carries on business, by leaving the citation in the hands of such a person as is mentioned in paragraph (3)(b)(i) or by depositing it as specified in paragraph (3)(b)(ii); and

(b) where the citation is deposited as is specified in paragraph (3)(b)(ii), the sheriff officer thereafter shall send a copy of the petition and citation by ordinary first class post to such place mentioned in sub-paragraph (a) of this paragraph in which the citation was deposited.

(6) The petition shall be advertised forthwith—

(a) once in the Edinburgh Gazette; and

(b) once in one or more newspapers as the court shall direct for ensuring that it comes to the notice of the creditors of the company.

(7) The advertisement under paragraph (6) shall state—

(a) the name and address of the petitioner;

(b) the name and address of the solicitor for the petitioner;

(c) the date on which the petition was presented;

(d) the precise order sought;

(e) the period of notice; and

(f) that any person who intends to appear in the petition must lodge answers to the petition within the period of notice.

(8) The period of notice within which answers to the petition may be lodged and after which further consideration of the petition may proceed shall be 8 days after such intimation, service and advertisement as the court may have ordered.

NOTES

Para (2): word omitted from sub-para (a) revoked, words in first pair of square brackets in sub-para (b) substituted, and sub-para (c) and word immediately preceding it added, by the Act of Sederunt (Sheriff Court Company Insolvency Rules 1986) Amendment 2003, SSI 2003/388, r 4, Schedule, paras 1, 9.

[16.30]

17 Form of certain applications where receiver appointed

(1) An application under any of the following sections of the Act of 1986 shall be made by petition or, where the receiver was appointed by the court, by note in the process of the petition for appointment of a receiver:—

- (a) section 61(1) (by receiver for authority to dispose of interest in property);
- (b) section 62 (for removal or resignation of receiver);
- (c) section 63(1) (by receiver for directions);
- (d) section 69(1) (to enforce receiver to make returns, etc); and
- (e) any other section relating to receivers not specifically mentioned in this Part.

(2) An application under any of the following provisions of the Act of 1986 or the Insolvency Rules shall be made by motion in the process of the petition:—

- (a) section 67(1) or (2) (by receiver to extend time for sending report); and
- (b) rule 3.9(2) (by receiver to extend time for sending abstract of receipts and payments).

PART IV
WINDING UP BY THE COURT OF COMPANIES REGISTERED UNDER THE COMPANIES ACTS AND OF UNREGISTERED COMPANIES

[16.31]

18 Petitions to wind up a company

(1) A petition to wind up a company under the Act of 1986 shall include—

- (a) particulars of the petitioner, if other than the company;
- [(aa) averments in relation to jurisdiction under the Council Regulation, in particular stating, so far as known to the petitioner—
  - (i) where the centre of main interests of the company is and whether the company has any other establishments in another member State;
  - (ii) whether there are insolvency proceedings elsewhere in respect of the company and whether those proceedings are main or territorial proceedings;]
- (b) in respect of the company—
  - (i) the registered name;
  - (ii) the address of the registered office and any change of that address within the last 6 months so far as known to the petitioner;
  - (iii) a statement of the nature and objects, the amount of its capital (nominal and issued) and indicating what part is called up, paid up or credited as paid, and the amount of the assets of the company so far as known to the petitioner;
- (c) a narrative of the facts on which the petitioner relies and any particulars required to instruct the title of the petitioner to present the petition;
- (d) the name and address of the person to be appointed as interim liquidator and a statement that he is qualified to act as an insolvency practitioner in relation to the company; and
- (e) a crave setting out the orders applied for, including any intimation, service and advertisement and any appointment of an interim liquidator.

(2) There shall be lodged with the petition any document—

- (a) instructing the title of the petitioner; and
- (b) instructing the facts relied on, or otherwise founded on, by the petitioner.

NOTES

Para (1): sub-para (aa) inserted by the Act of Sederunt (Sheriff Court Rules) (Miscellaneous Amendments) 2008, SSI 2008/223, r 10(1), (4).

[16.32]

19 Intimation, service and advertisement

(1) Intimation, service and advertisement shall be in accordance with the following provisions of this rule unless the court—

- (a) summarily dismisses the petition; or
- (b) otherwise directs.

(2) There shall be included in the order for intimation and service, a requirement—

- (a) to intimate on the walls of the court;
- (b) where the petitioner is other than the company, to serve upon the company;
- (c) where the company is being wound up voluntarily and a liquidator has been appointed, to serve upon the liquidator;
- (d) where a receiver has been appointed for the company, to serve upon the receiver;
- [(dd) where a company is in administration, to serve upon the administrator;]

(e) where the company is—
(i) a recognised bank or licensed institution within the meaning of the Banking Act 1979; or
(ii) an institution to which sections 16 and 18 of that Act apply as if it were licensed,
and the petitioner is not the Bank of England, to serve upon the Bank of England.

(3) Subject to paragraph (5), service of a petition on the company shall be executed at its registered office—
(a) by registered or recorded delivery post addressed to the company; or
(b) by sheriff officer—
(i) leaving the citation in the hands of a person who, after due inquiry, he has reasonable grounds for believing to be a director, other officer or responsible employee of the company or authorised to accept service on behalf of the company; or
(ii) if there is no such person as is mentioned in head (i) present, depositing it in the registered office in such a way that it is likely to come to the attention of such a person attending at that office.

(4) Where service is effected in accordance with paragraph (3)(b)(ii), the sheriff officer thereafter shall send a copy of the petition and citation by ordinary first class post to the registered office of the company.

(5) Where service cannot be effected at the registered office or the company has no registered office—
(a) service may be effected at the last known principal place of business of the company in Scotland or at some place in Scotland at which the company carries on business, by leaving the citation in the hands of such a person as is mentioned in paragraph (3)(b)(i) or by depositing it as specified in paragraph (3)(b)(ii); and
(b) where the citation is deposited as is specified in paragraph (3)(b)(ii), the sheriff officer thereafter shall send a copy of the petition and the citation by ordinary first class post to such place mentioned in sub-paragraph (a) of this paragraph in which the citation was deposited.

(6) The petition shall be advertised forthwith—
(a) once in the Edinburgh Gazette; and
(b) once in one or more newspapers as the court shall direct for ensuring that it comes to the notice of the creditors of the company.

(7) The advertisement under paragraph (6) shall state—
(a) the name and address of the petitioner and, where the petitioner is the company, the registered office;
(b) the name and address of the solicitor for the petitioner;
(c) the date on which the petition was presented;
(d) the precise order sought;
(e) where a provisional liquidator has been appointed, his name, address and the date of his appointment;
(f) the period of notice; and
(g) that any person who intends to appear in the petition must lodge answers to the petition within the period of notice.

(8) The period of notice within which answers to the petition may be lodged and after which further consideration of the petition may proceed shall be 8 days after such intimation, service and advertisement as the court may have ordered.

NOTES

Para (2): sub-para (dd) inserted by the Act of Sederunt (Sheriff Court Company Insolvency Rules 1986) Amendment 2003, SSI 2003/388, r 4, Schedule, paras 1, 10.

[16.33]

20 Lodging of caveats

(1) A company, debenture holder, holder of a floating charge, receiver, shareholder of a company or other person claiming an interest, apprehensive that a petition to wind up that company may be presented and wishing to be heard by the court before an order for intimation, service and advertisement is pronounced, may lodge a caveat with the sheriff-clerk.

(2) A caveat shall endure for 12 months on the expiry of which a new caveat may be lodged.

(3) Where a caveat has been lodged and has not expired, no order may be pronounced without the person lodging the caveat having been given an opportunity to be heard by the court.

NOTES

Revoked by the Act of Sederunt (Sheriff Court Caveat Rules) 2006, SSI 2006/198, r 4(1), subject to r 5 thereof, which provides as follows:

"**5 Transitional and savings provision**

(1) Subject to paragraph (2), nothing in this Act of Sederunt shall affect a caveat lodged prior to 28th April 2006.

(2) A caveat lodged prior to 28th April 2006 may not be renewed unless the caveat complies with the requirements of this Act of Sederunt.".

[16.34]

21 Substitution of creditor or contributory for petitioner

(1) This rule applies where a petitioner—
(a) is subsequently found not entitled to present the petition;
(b) fails to make intimation, service and advertisement as directed by the court;

(c) consents to withdraw the petition or to allow it to be dismissed or refused;
(d) fails to appear when the petition is called for hearing; or
(e) appears, but does not move for an order in terms of the prayer of the petition.

(2) The court may, on such terms as it considers just, sist as petitioner in room of the original petitioner any creditor or contributory who, in the opinion of the court, is entitled to present a petition.

(3) An application by a creditor or contributory to be sisted under paragraph (2)—
(a) may be made at any time before the petition is dismissed or refused; and
(b) shall be made by note in the process of the petition, and if necessary the court may continue the cause for a specified period to allow a note to be presented.

[16.35]
22 Advertisement of appointment of liquidator

Where a liquidator is appointed by the court, the court may order that the liquidator shall advertise his appointment once in one or more newspapers as the court shall direct for ensuring that it comes to the notice of creditors of the company.

[16.36]
23 Provisional liquidators

(1) An application to appoint a provisional liquidator under section 135 of the Act of 1986 may be made—
(a) by the petitioner, in the crave of the petition or subsequently by note in the process of the petition; or
(b) by a creditor or contributory of the company, the company, Secretary of State or a person entitled under any enactment to present a petition to wind up the company, in a note in the process of the petition.

(2) The petition or note, as the case may be, shall include averments in relation to—
(a) the grounds on which it is proposed that a provisional liquidator should be appointed;
(b) the name and address of the person to be appointed as provisional liquidator and that he is qualified to act as an insolvency practitioner in relation to the company; and
(c) whether, to the knowledge of the applicant, there is a receiver [or administrator] for the company or a liquidator has been appointed for the voluntary winding up of the company.

(3) Where the court is satisfied that sufficient grounds exist for the appointment of a provisional liquidator, it shall, on making the appointment, specify the functions to be carried out by him in relation to the affairs of the company.

(4) The applicant shall send a certified copy of the interlocutor appointing a provisional liquidator forthwith to the person appointed.

(5) On receiving a certified copy of his appointment on an application by note, the provisional liquidator shall intimate his appointment forthwith—
(a) once in the Edinburgh Gazette; and
(b) once in one or more newspapers as the court shall direct for ensuring that it comes to the notice of creditors of the company.

(6) An application for discharge of a provisional liquidator shall be by note in the process of the petition.

NOTES

Para (2): words in square brackets in sub-para (c) inserted by the Act of Sederunt (Sheriff Court Company Insolvency Rules 1986) Amendment 2003, SSI 2003/388, r 4, Schedule, paras 1, 11.

[16.37]
24 Applications and appeals in relation to a statement of affairs

(1) An application under section 131(5) of the Act of 1986 for—
(a) release from an obligation imposed under section 131(1) or (2) of the Act of 1986; or
(b) an extension of time for the submission of a statement of affairs, shall be made by note in the process of the petition.

(2) A note under paragraph (1) shall be served on the liquidator or provisional liquidator, as the case may be.

(3) The liquidator or provisional liquidator may lodge answers to the note or lodge a report of any matters which he considers should be drawn to the attention of the court.

(4) Where the liquidator or provisional liquidator lodges a report under paragraph (3), he shall send a copy of it to the noter forthwith.

(5) Where the liquidator or provisional liquidator does not appear, a certified copy of the interlocutor pronounced by the court disposing of the note shall be sent by the noter forthwith to him.

(6) An appeal under rule 4.9(6) of the Insolvency Rules against a refusal by the liquidator of an allowance towards the expense of preparing a statement of affairs shall be made by note in the process of the petition.

[16.38]
25 Appeals against adjudication of claims

[(1) An appeal under rule 4.16B(6) of the Insolvency Rules (adjudication of claims) by a creditor or any member or contributory of the company against a decision of the liquidator shall be made by note in the process of the petition.]

(2) A note under paragraph (1) shall be served on the liquidator.

(3) On receipt of the note served on him under this rule, the liquidator forthwith shall send to the court the claim in question and a copy of his adjudication for lodging in process.

(4) After the note has been disposed of, the court shall return the claim and the adjudication to the liquidator together with a copy of the interlocutor.

NOTES

Para (1): substituted by the Act of Sederunt (Rules of the Court of Session and Sheriff Court Company Insolvency Rules Amendment) (Miscellaneous) 2014, SSI 2014/119, r 3(1), (2).

[16.39]
26 Appointment of liquidator by the court

(1) An application to appoint a liquidator under section 139(4) of the Act of 1986 shall be made by note in the process of the petition.

(2) Where the court appoints a liquidator under section 138(5) of the Act of 1986, the sheriff-clerk shall send a certified copy of the interlocutor pronounced by the court to the liquidator forthwith.

[16.40]
27 Removal of liquidator

An application by a creditor of the company for removal of a liquidator or provisional liquidator from office under section 172 of the Act of 1986 or for an order under section 171(3) of the Act of 1986 directing a liquidator to summon a meeting of creditors for the purpose of removing him shall be made by note in the process of the petition.

[16.41]
28 Applications in relation to remuneration of liquidator

(1) An application by a liquidator under rule 4.34 of the Insolvency Rules shall be made by note in the process of the petition.

(2) An application by a creditor of the company under rule 4.35 of the Insolvency Rules shall be made by note in the process of the petition.

(3) A note under paragraph (2) shall be served on the liquidator.

[16.42]
29 Application to appoint a special manager

(1) An application under section 177 of the Act of 1986 by a liquidator or provisional liquidator for the appointment of a special manager shall be made by note in the process of the petition.

(2) The cautioner, for the caution to be found by the special manager within such time as the court shall direct, may be—

- (a) a private person, if approved by the court; or
- (b) a guarantee company, chosen from a list of such companies prepared for this purpose annually by the Accountant of Court and approved by the Lord President of the Court of Session.

(3) A bond of caution certified by the noter under rule 4.70(4) of the Insolvency Rules shall be delivered to the sheriff-clerk by the noter, marked as received by him and transmitted forthwith by him to the Accountant of Court.

(4) On receipt of the bond of caution, the sheriff-clerk shall issue forthwith to the person appointed to be special manager a certified copy of the interlocutor appointing him.

(5) An application by a special manager to extend the time within which to find caution shall be made by motion.

[16.43]
30 Other applications

An application under the Act of 1986 or rules made under that Act in relation to a winding up by the court not specifically mentioned in this Part [or an application to participate under article 12 of the Model Law in a winding up by the court] shall be made by note in the process of the petition.

NOTES

Words in square brackets inserted by the Act of Sederunt (Sheriff Court Company Insolvency Rules 1986) Amendment (UNCITRAL Model Law on Cross-Border Insolvency) 2006, SSI 2006/200, r 2(1), (4).

PART V
GENERAL PROVISIONS

[16.44]
31 Application

This Part applies to Parts I to IV of these rules.

[16.45]
[31A Applications under section 176A of the Act of 1986

(1) An application by a liquidator, administrator or receiver under section 176A of the Act of 1986 shall be—

(a) where there is no existing process in relation to any liquidation, administration or receivership, by petition; or

(b) where a process exists in relation to any liquidation, administration or receivership, by note in that process.

(2) The sheriff clerk shall—

(a) after lodging of any petition or note fix a hearing for the sheriff to consider an application under paragraph (1); and

(b) give notice of the hearing fixed under paragraph (2)(a) to the petitioner or noter.

(3) The petitioner or noter shall not be required to give notice to any person of the hearing fixed under paragraph (2)(a), unless the sheriff directs otherwise.]

NOTES

Inserted by the Act of Sederunt (Sheriff Court Company Insolvency Rules 1986) Amendment 2003, SSI 2003/388, r 3.

[16.46]
[31AA Limited disclosure of statement of affairs

Any application under rules 1.50, 2.22, 3.2A or 4.8A of the Insolvency Rules (orders of limited disclosure etc) shall be made—

(a) where there is no existing process in relation to any liquidation, administration or receivership, by petition; or

(b) where a process exists in relation to any liquidation, administration or receivership, by note in that process.]

NOTES

Commencement: 30 May 2014.

Inserted by the Act of Sederunt (Rules of the Court of Session and Sheriff Court Company Insolvency Rules Amendment) (Miscellaneous) 2014, SSI 2014/119, r 3(1), (3).

[16.47]
[31B UNCITRAL Model Law on Cross-Border Insolvency

On receipt of a certified copy interlocutor of a Lord Ordinary ordering proceedings under these rules to be transferred to the Court of Session under paragraph 11 of Schedule 3 to the Cross-Border Insolvency Regulations 2006, the sheriff clerk shall within four days transmit the process to the deputy principal clerk of session.]

NOTES

Inserted by the Act of Sederunt (Sheriff Court Company Insolvency Rules 1986) Amendment (UNCITRAL Model Law on Cross-Border Insolvency) 2006, SSI 2006/200, r 2(1), (5).

[16.48]
32 Intimation, service and advertisement of notes and appeals

An application by note, or an appeal, to the court under these rules shall be intimated, served and, if necessary, advertised as the court shall direct.

[16.49]
33 Affidavits

The court may accept as evidence an affidavit lodged in support of a petition or note.

[16.50]
34 Notices, reports and other documents sent to the court

Where, under the Act of 1986 or rules made under that Act—

(a) notice of a fact is to be given to the court;

(b) a report is to be made, or sent, to the court; or

(c) some other document is to be sent to the court;

it shall be sent or delivered to the sheriff-clerk of the court, who shall cause it to be lodged in the appropriate process.

[16.51]
35 Failure to comply with rules

(1) The court may, in its discretion, relieve a party from the consequences of any failure to comply with the provisions of a rule shown to be due to mistake, oversight or other cause, which is not wilful non-observance of the rule, on such terms and conditions as the court considers just.

(2) Where the court relieves a party from the consequences of failure to comply with a rule under paragraph 1, the court may pronounce such interlocutor as may be just so as to enable the cause to proceed as if the failure to comply with the rule had not occurred.

[16.52]
[35A Vulnerable witnesses

(1) At any hearing on an application under these rules the sheriff shall ascertain whether there is or is likely to be a vulnerable witness who is to give evidence at or for the purposes of any proof or hearing, consider any child witness notice or vulnerable witness application that has been lodged where no order has been made under section 12(1) or (6) of the Vulnerable Witnesses (Scotland) Act 2004 and consider whether any order under section 12(1) of that Act requires to be made.

(2) Except where the sheriff otherwise directs, where a vulnerable witness is to give evidence at or for the purposes of any proof or hearing in an application under these rules, any application in relation to the vulnerable witness or special measure that may be ordered shall be dealt with in accordance with the rules within Chapter 45 of the Ordinary Cause Rules in the First Schedule to the Sheriff Courts (Scotland) Act 1907.

(3) In this rule, "vulnerable witness" means a witness within the meaning of section 11(1) of the Vulnerable Witnesses (Scotland) Act 2004.]

NOTES

Inserted by the Act of Sederunt (Sheriff Court Company Insolvency Rules 1986) Amendment (Vulnerable Witnesses (Scotland) Act 2004) 2007, SSI 2007/464, r 2.

PART VI
APPEALS

[16.53]
36 [Appeals to the Court of Session]

(1) Where an appeal to . . . the Court of Session is competent, it shall be taken by note of appeal which shall—
- (a) be written by the appellant or his solicitor on—
  - (i) the interlocutor sheet or other written record containing the interlocutor appealed against; or
  - (ii) a separate document lodged with the sheriff-clerk;
- (b) be as nearly as may be in the following terms:—"The (petitioner, noter, respondent or other party) appeals to [the Court of Session]"; and
- (c) be signed by the appellant or his solicitor and bear the date on which it is signed.

(2) Such an appeal shall be marked within 14 days of the date of the interlocutor appealed against.

(3) . . . The note of appeal shall specify the name and address of the solicitor in Edinburgh who will be acting for the appellant.

(4) On an appeal being taken, the sheriff-clerk shall within 4 days—
- [(a) transmit the process to the Deputy Principal Clerk of Session; and]
- (b) send written notice of the appeal to any other party to the cause and certify in the interlocutor sheet, or other written record containing the interlocutor appealed against, that he has done so.

(5) Failure of the sheriff-clerk to give notice under paragraph 4(b) shall not invalidate the appeal.

NOTES

Rule heading: words in square brackets substituted for original words "Appeals to the Sheriff Principal or Court of Session" by the Act of Sederunt (Rules of the Court of Session, Sheriff Appeal Court Rules and Sheriff Court Rules Amendment) (Sheriff Appeal Court) 2015, SSI 2015/419, rr 3(1), (2)(d), 20(1)(a), except for the purposes of an appeal against a decision of the sheriff made before 1 January 2016.

Para (1): words "the Sheriff Principal or" (omitted) revoked and words in square brackets in sub-para (b) substituted for original words "the Sheriff Principal or Court of Session", by SSI 2015/419, rr 3(1), (2)(a), 20(1)(a), except for the purposes of an appeal against a decision of the sheriff made before 1 January 2016.

Para (3): words "Where the appeal is to the Court of Session," (omitted) revoked by SSI 2015/419, rr 3(1), (2)(b), 20(1)(a), except for the purposes of an appeal against a decision of the sheriff made before 1 January 2016.

Para (4): sub-para (a) substituted by SSI 2015/419, rr 3(1), (2)(c), 20(1)(a), except for the purposes of an appeal against a decision of the sheriff made before 1 January 2016, and originally read as follows—

"(a) transmit the process—
  (i) where the appeal is to Sheriff Principal, to him; or
  (ii) where the appeal is to the Court of Session, to the Deputy Principal Clerk of Session; and".

[16.54]
[36A Appeals to the Sheriff Appeal Court

Where an appeal to the Sheriff Appeal Court is competent, it is to be made in accordance with Chapter 6 of the Act of Sederunt (Sheriff Appeal Court Rules) 2015.]

NOTES

Commencement: 1 January 2016.

Inserted by the Act of Sederunt (Rules of the Court of Session, Sheriff Appeal Court Rules and Sheriff Court Rules Amendment) (Sheriff Appeal Court) 2015, SSI 2015/419, rr 3(1), (3), 20(1)(a), except for the purposes of an appeal against a decision of the sheriff made before 1 January 2016.

BANKRUPTCY (SCOTLAND) ACT 1993 COMMENCEMENT AND SAVINGS ORDER 1993

(SI 1993/438 (S 49))

NOTES

Made: 3 March 1993.

Authority: Bankruptcy (Scotland) Act 1993, s 12(4), (5).

[16.55]

1 Citation

This Order may be cited as the Bankruptcy (Scotland) Act 1993 Commencement and Savings Order 1993.

[16.56]

2 Interpretation

In this Order—

"the Act" means the Bankruptcy (Scotland) Act 1993;

"the 1985 Act" means the Bankruptcy (Scotland) Act 1985;

"trust deed" means a voluntary trust deed granted by or on behalf of a debtor, whereby his estate is conveyed to the trustee for the benefit of his creditors generally.

and, unless the context otherwise requires, any expression used in this Order which is also used in the 1985 Act shall have the same meaning as in that Act.

[16.57]

3 Provisions brought into force by this Order

The provisions of the Act not already in force shall come into force on 1st April 1993.

[16.58]

4 Sequestrations; savings

(1) Without prejudice to section 12(6) of the Act, nothing in any provision of the Act brought into force by this Order shall have effect as regards any sequestration in respect of which the petition is presented on or after 1st April 1993 and before 1st October 1993 by a trustee acting under a trust deed granted before 1st April 1993.

(2) Without prejudice to section 12(6) of the Act, paragraph (1) of this article, or to article 5(1) of this Order and notwithstanding the provisions of the Act brought into force by this Order, the 1985 Act as in force immediately before 1st April 1993 shall continue to apply and have effect in relation to any sequestration—

(a) in respect of which the petition is presented before that date; or

(b) as referred to in paragraph (1) of this article.

(3) Without prejudice to paragraph (2) of this article and notwithstanding the provisions of the Act brought into force by this Order, the following provisions of the 1985 Act, as in force immediately before 1st April 1993 relating to the maintenance of the list of interim trustees, namely—

section 1(1)(b),

section 2(2), (3) and (4), and

in section 73(1), the definition of the expression "list of interim trustees"

shall continue to apply and have effect for the purposes of any sequestration referred to in paragraphs (1) and (2) of this article.

[16.59]

5 Trust deeds; savings

(1) Nothing in any provision of the Act brought into force by this Order shall have effect as regards any trust deed granted before 1st April 1993.

(2) Without prejudice in paragraph (1) of this article and notwithstanding the provisions brought into force by this Order, section 59 of and Schedule 5 to the 1985 Act, as in force immediately before 1st April 1993, shall continue to apply and have effect in relation to any trust deed granted before that date.

ACT OF SEDERUNT (RULES OF THE COURT OF SESSION 1994) 1994

(SI 1994/1443 (S 69))

NOTES

Made: 31 May 1994.

Commencement: 5 September 1994.

Only provisions of this Act of Sederunt relevant to this work are reproduced.

ARRANGEMENT OF RULES

SCHEDULE 2

CHAPTER 16

SERVICE, INTIMATION AND DILIGENCE

PART I

SERVICE AND INTIMATION

16.1 Methods and manner of service .....[16.60]
16.4 Service by post .....[16.61]

CHAPTER 18

DEFENCES AND ANSWERS

18.3 Answers .....[16.62]

CHAPTER 62

RECOGNITION, REGISTRATION AND ENFORCEMENT OF FOREIGN JUDGMENTS ETC

PART XIII

UNCITRAL MODEL LAW ON CROSS-BORDER INSOLVENCY

62.90 Application and interpretation of this Part .....[16.63]
62.91 General .....[16.64]
62.92 Recognition application .....[16.65]
62.93 Application for interim remedy .....[16.66]
62.94 Application for remedy .....[16.67]
62.95 Application for confirmation of status of replacement foreign representative .....[16.68]
62.96 Review application .....[16.69]

CHAPTER 74

COMPANIES

PART I

GENERAL PROVISIONS

74.1 Application and interpretation of this Chapter .....[16.70]
74.2 .....[16.71]
74.3 .....[16.72]

PART II

COMPANY VOLUNTARY ARRANGEMENTS

74.4 Lodging of nominee's report (company not in liquidation etc) .....[16.73]
74.5 Lodging of nominee's report (company in liquidation etc) .....[16.74]
74.6 Inspection of nominee's report .....[16.75]
74.7 Report of meetings to approve arrangement .....[16.76]
74.8 Abstracts of supervisor's receipts and payments and notices of completion of arrangement .....[16.77]
74.9 Form of other applications .....[16.78]

PART III

ADMINISTRATION PROCEDURE

74.10 Form of petition in administration procedure .....[16.79]
74.10A Interim orders .....[16.80]
74.11 Notice of petition .....[16.81]
74.12 Report of proposals of administrator .....[16.82]
74.13 Report of administrator's proposals: Schedule B1 to the Act of 1986 .....[16.83]
74.14 Time and date of lodging in administration or energy administration .....[16.84]
74.15 Applications during an administration or energy administration .....[16.85]
74.15A Application for administration by a bank liquidator .....[16.86]

PART IV

RECEIVERS

74.16 Interpretation of this Part .....[16.87]
74.17 Petition to appoint a receiver .....[16.88]
74.18 Intimation, service and advertisement under this Part .....[16.89]
74.19 Form of other applications and appeals .....[16.90]

PART V

WINDING UP OF COMPANIES

74.20 Interpretation of this Part .....[16.91]
74.21 Petition to wind up a company .....[16.92]

74.22 Intimation, service and advertisement under this Part .[16.93]
74.23 Remits from one court to another .[16.94]
74.24 Substitution of creditor or contributory for petitioner .[16.95]
74.25 Provisional liquidator. .[16.96]
74.26 Appointment of a liquidator .[16.97]
74.27 Applications and appeals in relation to a statement of affairs .[16.98]
74.28 Appeals against adjudication of claims .[16.99]
74.29 Removal of liquidator .[16.100]
74.30 Application in relation to remuneration of liquidator .[16.101]
74.30A Applications under section 176A of the Act of 1986 .[16.102]
74.31 Application to appoint a special manager .[16.103]
74.32 Other applications .[16.104]
74.32A Replacement liquidators: block transfer orders .[16.105]
74.32B Approval of the voluntary winding up of a bank or building society .[16.106]

PART VI
DISQUALIFICATION OF COMPANY DIRECTORS
74.33 Applications in relation to disqualification orders .[16.107]
74.34 Intimation, service and advertisement under this Part .[16.108]

PART VII
BANK INSOLVENCY PROCEDURE
74.35 Petition for bank insolvency .[16.109]
74.36 Intimation, service and advertisement under this Part .[16.110]
74.37 Provisional bank liquidator .[16.111]
74.38 Applications and appeals in relation to a statement of affairs .[16.112]
74.40 Removal of bank liquidator .[16.113]
74.41 Application in relation to remuneration of bank liquidator .[16.114]
74.42 Applications under section 176A of the Act of 1986 .[16.115]
74.43 Applications to appoint a special manager .[16.116]
74.44 Other applications .[16.117]

PART VIII
BANK ADMINISTRATION PROCEDURE
74.45 Petition for bank administration .[16.118]
74.46 Hearing of petition .[16.119]
74.47 Provisional bank administrator .[16.120]
74.48 Report of bank administrator's proposals: Schedule B1 to the Act of 1986 .[16.121]
74.49 Time and date of lodging in a bank administration .[16.122]
74.50 Applications during a bank administration .[16.123]

PART IX
BUILDING SOCIETY SPECIAL ADMINISTRATION PROCEDURE
74.51 Application of rules to building society special administration .[16.124]

PART X
BUILDING SOCIETY INSOLVENCY PROCEDURE
74.52 Application of rules to building society insolvency .[16.125]

SCHEDULE 2

CHAPTER 16 SERVICE, INTIMATION AND DILIGENCE

PART I
SERVICE AND INTIMATION

[16.60]
16.1 Methods and manner of service

(1)–(3) (*Outside the scope of this work.*)

(4) In relation to a petition or note, where service has been executed by a petitioner or noter, he shall attach the documents required by paragraph (3)(a) and (b) to a copy of the petition or note, as the case may be, marked "Execution Copy" and certified a true copy.

[16.61]
16.4 Service by post

(1)–(5) (*Outside the scope of this work.*)

(6) The date of execution of service shall be deemed to be the day after the date of the posting.

(7) *(Outside the scope of this work.)*

CHAPTER 18 DEFENCES AND ANSWERS

[16.62]
18.3 Answers

(1) This rule applies to answers, lodged to a petition, counterclaim, minute or note.

(2) Answers shall consist of—

(a) numbered answers corresponding to the paragraphs of the statement of facts in the writ to which they apply; and

(b) appropriate pleas-in-law.

(3) Answers may be lodged at any time within the period of notice specified in the interlocutor calling for answers.

CHAPTER 62 RECOGNITION, REGISTRATION AND ENFORCEMENT OF FOREIGN JUDGMENTS ETC

[PART XIII
UNCITRAL MODEL LAW ON CROSS-BORDER INSOLVENCY

[16.63]
62.90 Application and interpretation of this Part

(1) This Part applies to applications under the Model Law and applications under the Scottish Provisions.

(2) In this Part—

"application for an interim remedy" means an application under article 19 of the Model Law for an interim remedy by a foreign representative;

"former representative" means a foreign representative who has died or who for any other reason has ceased to be the foreign representative in the foreign proceeding in relation to the debtor;

"main proceeding" means proceedings opened in accordance with Article 3(1) of the EC Insolvency Regulation and falling within the definition of insolvency proceedings in Article 2(a) of the EC Insolvency Regulation;

"the Model Law" means the UNCITRAL Model Law on Cross-Border Insolvency as set out in Schedule 1 to the Cross-Border Insolvency Regulations 2006;

"modification or termination order" means an order by the court pursuant to its powers under the Model Law modifying or terminating recognition of a foreign proceeding, the restraint, sist and suspension referred to in article 20(1) of the Model Law or any part of it or any remedy granted under article 19 or 21 of the Model Law;

"recognition application" means an application by a foreign representative in accordance with article 15 of the Model Law for an order recognising the foreign proceeding in which he has been appointed;

"recognition order" means an order by the court recognising a proceeding as a foreign main proceeding or a foreign non-main proceeding, as appropriate;

"review application" means an application to the court for a modification or termination order;

"the Scottish Provisions" are the provisions of Schedule 3 to the Cross-Border Insolvency Regulations 2006; and

words and phrases defined in the Model Law have the same meaning when used in this Part.

(3) References in this Part to a debtor who is of interest to the [Financial Conduct Authority or the Prudential Regulation Authority] are references to a debtor who—

(a) is, or has been, an authorised person within the meaning of section 31 of the Financial Services and Markets Act 2000 (authorised persons);

(b) is, or has been, an appointed representative within the meaning of section 39 (exemption of appointed representatives) of that Act; or

(c) is carrying on, or has carried on, a regulated activity in contravention of the general prohibition.

(4) In paragraph (3) "the general prohibition" has the meaning given by section 19 of the Financial Services and Markets Act 2000 and the reference to "regulated activity" shall be construed in accordance with—

(a) section 22 of that Act (classes of regulated activity and categories of investment);

(b) any relevant order under that section; and

(c) Schedule 2 to that Act (regulated activities).]

NOTES

Pt XIII (rr 62.90–62.96) inserted by the Act of Sederunt (Rules of the Court of Session Amendment No 2) (UNCITRAL Model Law on Cross-Border Insolvency) 2006, SSI 2006/199, r 2(1), (3).

Para (3): words in square brackets substituted by the Financial Services Act 2012 (Consequential Amendments and Transitional Provisions) Order 2013, SI 2013/472, art 3, Sch 2, para 10(a).

[16.64]
[62.91 General

(1) Rule 62.1 (disapplication of certain rules to Chapter 62) shall not apply to an application to which this Part relates.

(2) Unless otherwise specified in this Part, an application under the Model Law or the Scottish Provisions shall be made by petition.

(3) For the purposes of the application of rule 14.5(1) (first order for intimation, service and advertisement) to a petition under this Part, where necessary, the petitioner shall seek an order for service of the petition on:—

(a) the foreign representative;

(b) the debtor;

(c) any British insolvency officeholder acting in relation to the debtor;

(d) any person appointed an administrative receiver of the debtor or as a receiver or manager of the property of the debtor in Scotland;

(e) any member State [insolvency practitioner] who has been appointed in main proceedings in relation to the debtor;

(f) any foreign representative who has been appointed in any other foreign proceeding regarding the debtor;

(g) if there is pending in Scotland a petition for the winding up or sequestration of the debtor, the petitioner in those proceedings;

(h) any person who is or may be entitled to appoint an administrator of the debtor under paragraph 14 of Schedule B1 to the Insolvency Act 1986 ((appointment of administrator by holder of qualifying floating charge); and

(i) the [Financial Conduct Authority or the Prudential Regulation Authority] if the debtor is a debtor who is of interest to that Authority.

(4) On the making of—

(a) a recognition order;

(b) an order granting an interim remedy under article 19 of the Model Law;

(c) an order granting a remedy under article 21 of the Model Law;

(d) an order confirming the status of a replacement foreign representative; or

(e) a modification or termination order,

the Deputy Principal Clerk shall send a certified copy of the interlocutor to the foreign representative.]

NOTES

Inserted as noted to r 62.90 at **[16.63]**.

Para (3): words in square brackets in sub-para (e) substituted for original word "liquidator" by the Act of Sederunt (Rules of the Court of Session 1994 and Sheriff Court Rules Amendment) (Regulation (EU) 2015/848) 2017, SSI 2017/202, rr 3(1), (2), 6, except in relation to proceedings which are subject to Regulation (EC) 1346/2000 of 29th May 2000 on insolvency proceedings.

[16.65]

[62.92 Recognition application

(1) A petition containing a recognition application shall include averments as to—

(a) the name of the applicant and his address for service in Scotland;

(b) the name of the debtor in respect of which the foreign proceeding is taking place;

(c) the name or names in which the debtor carries on business in the country where the foreign proceeding is taking place and in this country, if other than the name given under sub-paragraph (b);

(d) the principal or last known place of business of the debtor in Great Britain (if any) and, in the case of an individual, his last known place of residence in Great Britain, (if any);

(e) any registered number allocated to the debtor under the Companies Act [2006];

(f) the foreign proceeding in respect of which recognition is applied for, including the country in which it is taking place and the nature of the proceeding;

(g) whether the foreign proceeding is a proceeding within the meaning of article 2(i) of the Model Law;

(h) whether the applicant is a foreign representative within the meaning of article 2(j) of the Model Law;

(i) the address of the debtor's centre of main interests and, if different, the address of its registered office or habitual residence as appropriate;

(j) if the debtor does not have its centre of main interests in the country where the foreign proceeding is taking place, whether the debtor has an establishment within the meaning of article 2(e) of the Model Law in that country, and if so, its address.

(3) There shall be lodged with the petition—

(a) an affidavit sworn by the foreign representative as to the matters averred under paragraph (2);

(b) the evidence and statement required under article 15(2) and (3) respectively of the Model Law;

(c) any other evidence which in the opinion of the applicant will assist the court in deciding whether the proceeding in respect of which the application is made is a foreign proceeding within the meaning of article 2(i) of the Model Law and whether the applicant is a foreign representative within the meaning of article 2(j) of the Model Law; and

(d) evidence that the debtor has its centre of main interests or an establishment, as the case may be, within the country where the foreign proceeding is taking place.

(4) The affidavit to be lodged under paragraph (3)(a) shall state whether, in the opinion of the applicant, the EC Insolvency Regulation applies to any of the proceedings identified in accordance with article 15(3) of the Model Law and, if so, whether those proceedings are main proceedings, secondary proceedings or territorial proceedings.

(5) Any subsequent information required to be given to the court by the foreign representative under article 18 of the Model Law shall be given by amendment of the petition.]

NOTES

Inserted as noted to r 62.90 at **[16.63]**.

Para (1): "2006" in square brackets substituted by the Act of Sederunt (Rules of the Court of Session Amendment No 9) (Miscellaneous) 2009, SSI 2009/450, r 4(1), (2).

[16.66]
[62.93 Application for interim remedy

(1) An application for an interim remedy shall be made by note in process.

(2) There shall be lodged with the note an affidavit sworn by the foreign representative stating—

(a) the grounds on which it is proposed that the interim remedy applied for should be granted;

(b) the details of any proceeding under British insolvency law taking place in relation to the debtor;

(c) whether to the foreign representative 213 s knowledge, an administrative receiver or receiver or manager of the debtors property is acting in relation to the debtor;

(d) an estimate of the assets of the debtor in Scotland in respect of which the remedy is applied for;

(e) all other matters that would in the opinion of the foreign representative assist the court in deciding whether or not to grant the remedy applied for, including whether, to the best of the knowledge and belief of the foreign representative, the interests of the debtors creditors (including any secured creditors or parties to hire-purchase agreements) and any other interested parties, including if appropriate the debtor, are adequately protected; and

(f) whether to the best of the foreign representatives knowledge and belief, the grant of any of the remedy applied for would interfere with the administration of the foreign main proceeding.]

NOTES

Inserted as noted to r 62.90 at **[16.63]**.

[16.67]
[62.94 Application for remedy

(1) An application under article 21 of the Model Law for a remedy shall be made by note in process.

(2) There shall be lodged with the note an affidavit sworn by the foreign representative stating—

(a) the grounds on which it is proposed that the remedy applied for should be granted;

(b) an estimate of the value of the assets of the debtor in Scotland in respect of which the remedy is requested;

(c) in the case of an application by a foreign representative who is or believes that he is a representative of a foreign non-main proceeding, the reasons why the applicant believes that the remedy relates to assets that, under the law of Great Britain, should be administered in the foreign non-main proceeding or concerns information required in that proceeding; and

(d) all other matters that would in the opinion of the foreign representative assist the court in deciding whether or not it is appropriate to grant the remedy requested, including whether, to the best of the knowledge and belief of the foreign representative, the interests of the debtors creditors (including any secured creditors or parties to hire-purchase agreements) and any other interested parties, including if appropriate the debtor, are adequately protected.]

NOTES

Inserted as noted to r 62.90 at **[16.63]**.

[16.68]
[62.95 Application for confirmation of status of replacement foreign representative

(1) An application under paragraph 2(3) of the Scottish Provisions for an order confirming the status of a replacement foreign representative shall be made by note in process.

(2) The note shall include averments as to—

(a) the name of the replacement foreign representative and his address for service within Scotland;

(b) the circumstances in which the former foreign representative ceased to be foreign representative in the foreign proceeding in relation to the debtor (including the date on which he ceased to be the foreign representative);

(c) his own appointment as replacement foreign representative in the foreign proceeding (including the date of that appointment).

(3) There shall be lodged with the note—

(a) an affidavit sworn by the foreign representative as to the matters averred under paragraph (2);

(b) a certificate from the foreign court affirming—

(i) the cessation of the appointment of the former foreign representative as foreign representative, and

(ii) the appointment of the applicant as the foreign representative in the foreign proceeding, or

(c) in the absence of such a certificate, any other evidence acceptable to the court of the matters referred to in sub-paragraph (a).]

NOTES

Inserted as noted to r 62.90 at **[16.63]**.

[16.69]
[62.96 Review application

(1) A review application shall be made by note in process.

(2) There shall be lodged with the note an affidavit sworn by the applicant as to—

(a) the grounds on which it is proposed that the remedy applied for should be granted; and

(b) all other matters that would in the opinion of the applicant assist the court in deciding whether or not it is appropriate to grant the remedy requested, including whether, to the best of the knowledge and belief of the applicant, the interests of the debtors creditors (including any secured creditors or parties to hire-purchase agreements) and any other interested parties, including if appropriate the debtor, are adequately protected.]

NOTES

Inserted as noted to r 62.90 at **[16.63]**.

CHAPTER 74 COMPANIES

PART I
General Provisions

[16.70]
74.1 Application and interpretation of this Chapter

(1) This Chapter applies to causes under—

[(a) the Insolvency Act 1986; and]
(b) the Company Directors Disqualification Act 1986[; and
(c) Chapter 3 of Part 3 of the Energy Act 2004][; and
(d) Parts 2 or 3 of the Banking Act 2009];
[(e) Chapter 5 of Part 2 of the Energy Act 2011].

(2) In this Chapter—

"the Act of 1986" means the Insolvency Act 1986;

["the Act of 2004" means the Energy Act 2004;]

["the Act of 2009" means the Banking Act 2009;

["the Act of 2011" means the Energy Act 2011;]

"the Bank Administration Rules" means the Bank Administration (Scotland) Rules 2009;

"the Bank Insolvency Rules" means the Bank Insolvency (Scotland) Rules 2009;]

"the Insolvency Rules" means the Insolvency (Scotland) Rules 1986;

["the Energy Administration Rules" means the Energy Administration (Scotland) Rules 2006;]

["the 2013 Rules" means the Energy Supply Company Administration (Scotland) Rules 2013;]

["Council Regulation" means Regulation (EU) 2015/848 of the European Parliament and of the Council of 20th May 2015 on insolvency proceedings, as amended from time to time;]

["centre of main interests" has the same meaning as in the Council Regulation;

"establishment" has the same meaning as in [Article 2(10)] of the Council Regulation;

["the Investment Bank Regulations" means the Investment Bank Special Administration Regulations 2011;

"the Investment Bank Rules" means the Investment Bank Special Administration (Scotland) Rules 2011;]

"main proceedings" means proceedings opened in accordance with Article 3(1) of the Council Regulation and falling within the definition of insolvency proceedings in [Article 2(4)] of the Council Regulation and—

(a) in relation to England and Wales and Scotland, set out in Annex A to the Council Regulation under the heading "United Kingdom"; and

(b) in relation to another Member State, set out in Annex A to the Council Regulation under the heading relating to that Member State;

"Member State" means a Member State of the European Community that has adopted the Council Regulation;]

["non GB company" shall have the meaning assigned in section 171 of the Act of 2004;]

"registered office" means—

(i) the place specified in the statement of the company delivered to the register of companies under [section 9 of the Companies Act 2006] as the intended place of its registered office on incorporation, or

(ii) where notice has been given by the company to the registrar of companies under [section 87 of the Companies Act 2006] of a change of registered office, the place specified in the last such notice;

["territorial proceedings" means proceedings opened in accordance with Article 3(2) and 3(4) of the Council Regulation and falling within the definition of insolvency proceedings in Article 2(a) of the Council Regulation and—

(a) in relation to England and Wales and Scotland, set out in Annex A to the Council Regulation under the heading "United Kingdom"; and

(b) in relation to another Member State, set out in Annex A to the Council Regulation under the heading relating to that Member State.]

[(3) Unless the context otherwise requires, words and expressions used in this Chapter which are also used in the Act of 1986, Chapter 3 of Part 3 of the Act of 2004, [Parts 2 or 3 of the Act of 2009], [Chapter 5 of Part 2 of the Act of 2011,] the Insolvency Rules[, the Bank Insolvency Rules, the Bank Administration Rules,] . . . the Energy Administration Rules [or the 2013 Rules] have the same meaning as in those Acts or Rules, as the case may be.]

NOTES

Para (1): sub-para (a) substituted by the Act of Sederunt (Rules of the Court of Session Amendment No 3) (Miscellaneous) 1996, SI 1996/1756, r 2(42); sub-para (c) and word immediately preceding it inserted by the Act of Sederunt (Rules of the Court of Session Amendment) (Miscellaneous) 2006, SSI 2006/83, r 2(1), (8)(a); sub-para (d) and word immediately preceding it inserted by the Act of Sederunt (Rules of the Court of Session Amendment) (Miscellaneous) 2009, SSI 2009/63, rr 2, 3(3)(a); sub-para (e) added by the Act of Sederunt (Rules of the Court of Session Amendment No 4) (Miscellaneous) 2013, SSI 2013/162, rr 1(5), 5(1)(a).

Para (2): definitions "the Act of 2004", "the Energy Administration Rules" and "non GB company" inserted by SSI 2006/83, r 2(1), (8)(b); definitions "the Act of 2009", "the Bank Administration Rules" and "the Bank Insolvency Rules" inserted by SSI 2009/63, rr 2, 3(3)(b); definitions "the Act of 2011" and "the 2013 Rules" inserted by SSI 2013/162, rr 1(5), 5(1)(b); definition "the EC Regulation" (as inserted by the Act of Sederunt (Rules of the Court of Session Amendment No 5) (Insolvency Proceedings) 2003, SSI 2003/385, r 2(1), (2)) substituted by new definitions "the Council Regulation", "centre of main interests", "establishment", "main proceedings", "Member State", and definition "territorial proceedings" inserted by the Act of Sederunt (Rules of the Court of Session Amendment No 8) (Miscellaneous) 2007, SSI 2007/449, r 2(1), (8); definitions "the Investment Bank Regulations" and "the Investment Bank Rules" inserted by the Act of Sederunt (Rules of the Court of Session Amendment No 6) (Miscellaneous) 2011, SSI 2011/385, r 3(1), (2); in definition "registered office" words in square brackets substituted by the Act of Sederunt (Rules of the Court of Session Amendment No 9) (Miscellaneous) 2009, SSI 2009/450, r 4(1), (3); definition "Council Regulation" substituted by the Act of Sederunt (Rules of the Court of Session 1994 and Sheriff Court Rules Amendment) (Regulation (EU) 2015/848) 2017, SSI 2017/202, rr 3(1), (3)(a), 6, except in relation to proceedings which are subject to Regulation (EC) 1346/2000 of 29th May 2000 on insolvency proceedings, and originally read as follows:

""the Council Regulation" means Council Regulation (EC) No 1346/2000 of 29th May 2000 on insolvency proceedings as it may be amended from time to time;";

words in square brackets in definitions "establishment" and "main proceedings" substituted for original words "Article 2(h)" and "Article 2(a)" respectively, by SSI 2017/202, rr 3(1), (3)(b), (c), 6, except in relation to proceedings which are subject to Regulation (EC) 1346/2000 of 29th May 2000 on insolvency proceedings.

Para (3): substituted by SSI 2006/83, r 2(1), (8)(c); words in first and third pairs of square brackets inserted by SSI 2009/63, rr 2, 3(3)(c); words in second and final pairs of square brackets inserted and word omitted revoked by SSI 2013/162, rr 1(5), 5(1)(c).

[16.71]

[74.2 All proceedings in the Outer House in a cause under or by virtue of the Act of 1986, the Company Directors Disqualification Act 1986[, Chapter 3 of Part 3 of the Act of 2004 or Parts 2 or 3 of the Act of 2009,] shall be brought before a judge of the court nominated by the Lord President as the insolvency judge or, where the insolvency judge is not available, any other judge of the court (including the vacation judge): and "insolvency judge" shall be construed accordingly.]

NOTES

Substituted by the Act of Sederunt (Rules of the Court of Session Amendment) (Miscellaneous) 2006, SSI 2006/83, r 2(1), (8)(d); words in square brackets substituted by the Act of Sederunt (Rules of the Court of Session Amendment) (Miscellaneous) 2009, SSI 2009/63, rr 2, 3(4).

[16.72]

[74.3 Where, under the Act of 1986, the Act of 2004, [the Act of 2009,] [the Act of 2011,] the Insolvency Rules[, the Bank Insolvency Rules, the Bank Administration Rules,] . . . the Energy Administration Rules [or the 2013 Rules]—

(a) notice of a fact is to be given to the court,
(b) a report is to be made, or sent, to the court, or
(c) any other document is to be sent to the court,

it shall be sent to the Deputy Principal Clerk who shall cause it to be lodged in the process to which it relates.]

NOTES

Substituted by the Act of Sederunt (Rules of the Court of Session Amendment) (Miscellaneous) 2006, SSI 2006/83, r 2(1), (8)(e); words in first and third pairs of square brackets inserted by the Act of Sederunt (Rules of the Court of Session Amendment) (Miscellaneous) 2009, SSI 2009/63, rr 2, 3(5); words in second and final pairs of square brackets inserted and word omitted revoked by the Act of Sederunt (Rules of the Court of Session Amendment No 4) (Miscellaneous) 2013, SSI 2013/162, rr 1(5), 5(2).

PART II
COMPANY VOLUNTARY ARRANGEMENTS

[16.73]

74.4 Lodging of nominee's report (company not in liquidation etc)

(1) This rule applies where the company is not being wound up by the court and [is not in administration].

(2) A report of a nominee submitted to the court under section 2(2) of the Act of 1986 (procedure where nominee is not the liquidator or administrator) shall be—

(a) lodged, with a covering letter, in the Petition Department;
(b) marked by the clerk of session receiving it with the date on which it is received; and
(c) placed before the insolvency judge for consideration of any direction which he may make under section 3(1) of that Act (which relates to the summoning of meetings).

(3) An application by a nominee to extend the time within which he may submit his report under section 2(2) of the Act of 1986 shall be made by letter addressed to the Deputy Principal Clerk who shall—
(a) place the letter before the insolvency judge for determination;
(b) intimate that determination by a written reply; and
(c) attach the letter, and a copy of the reply, to the nominee's report when it is subsequently lodged.

NOTES

Para (1): words in square brackets substituted by the Act of Sederunt (Rules of the Court of Session Amendment No 5) (Insolvency Proceedings) 2003, SSI 2003/385, r 2(1), (3).

[16.74]
74.5 Lodging of nominee's report (company in liquidation etc)

(1) This rule applies where the company is being wound up by the court or [is in administration].

(2) In this rule, "process" means the process of the petition under section 9 (petition for administration order), or section 124 (petition to wind up a company), of the Act of 1986, as the case may be.

(3) A report of a nominee submitted to the court under section 2(2) of the Act of 1986 (procedure where nominee is not the liquidator or administrator) shall be—
(a) lodged in process; and
(b) placed before the insolvency judge for consideration of any direction which he may make under section 3(1) of that Act.

(4) An application by a nominee to extend the time within which he may submit his report under section 2(2) of the Act of 1986 shall be made by letter addressed to the Deputy Principal Clerk who shall—
(a) place the letter before the insolvency judge for determination;
(b) intimate that determination by a written reply; and
(c) lodge the letter, and a copy of the reply, in the process of the petition to which it relates.

NOTES

Para (1): words in square brackets substituted by the Act of Sederunt (Rules of the Court of Session Amendment No 5) (Insolvency Proceedings) 2003, SSI 2003/385, r 2(1), (4).

[16.75]
74.6 Inspection of nominee's report

A person who states in a letter addressed to the Deputy Principal Clerk that he is a creditor, member or director of the company or his agent, may, on payment of the appropriate fee, inspect the nominee's report lodged under rule 74.4(2) (company not in liquidation etc) 74.5(3) (company in liquidation etc), as the case may be.

[16.76]
74.7 Report of meetings to approve arrangement

The report of the result of a meeting to be sent to the court under section 4(6) of the Act of 1986 shall be sent to the Deputy Principal Clerk who shall lodge it—
(a) in a case to which rule 74.4 (lodging of nominee's report (company not in liquidation etc)) applies, with the nominee's report lodged under that rule; or
(b) in a case to which rule 74.5 (lodging of nominee's report (company in liquidation etc)) applies, in process as defined by paragraph (2) of that rule.

[16.77]
74.8 Abstracts of supervisor's receipts and payments and notices of completion of arrangement

An abstract of receipts and payments prepared by a supervisor and sent to the court under rule 1.21(2) of the Insolvency Rules or a notice of completion of the arrangement (and a copy of the supervisor's report) to be sent to the court under rule 1.23(3) of those Rules shall be sent to the Deputy Principal Clerk who shall cause it to be lodged—
(a) in a case to which rule 74.4 (lodging of nominee's report (company not in liquidation etc)) applies, with the nominee's report lodged under that rule; or
(b) in a case to which rule 74.5 (lodging of nominee's report (company in liquidation etc)) applies, in process as defined by paragraph (2) of that rule.

[16.78]
74.9 Form of other applications

(1) An application to which this rule applies shall be made—
(a) where the company is not being wound up by the court and [is not in administration], by petition; or
(b) where the company is being wound up by the court or [is in administration], by note in the process to which it relates.

[(1A) In the case of a bank, an application to which this rule applies shall be made—

(a) where the bank is not subject to a bank insolvency order and is not in bank administration, by petition; or
(b) where the bank is subject to a bank insolvency order by the court or is in bank administration, by note in the process to which it relates.]

(2) This rule applies to an application under—
(a) section 2(4) of the Act of 1986 (for the replacement of a nominee);
(b) section 6 of that Act (to challenge a decision made in relation to an arrangement);
(c) section 7(3) of that Act (to challenge the actings of a supervisor);
(d) section 7(4)(a) of that Act (by a supervisor for directions);
(e) section 7(5) of that Act (for the appointment of a supervisor);
(f) rule 1.21(5) of the Insolvency Rules (to dispense with sending abstracts or reports or to vary the dates on which the obligation to send abstracts or reports arises);
(g) rule 1.23(4) of those Rules (to extend the period for sending a notice of implementation of arrangement or report); or
(h) any other provision in the Act of 1986 or the Insolvency Rules relating to company voluntary arrangements not mentioned in this Part[; or
(i) any provision in the Act of 1986, as applied by the Act of 2009, relating to voluntary arrangements.]

NOTES

Para (1): words in square brackets substituted by the Act of Sederunt (Rules of the Court of Session Amendment No 5) (Insolvency Proceedings) 2003, SSI 2003/385, r 2(1), (5).

Para (1A): inserted by the Act of Sederunt (Rules of the Court of Session Amendment) (Miscellaneous) 2009, SSI 2009/63, rr 2, 3(6)(a).

Para (2): sub-para (i) and word immediately preceding it inserted by SSI 2009/63, rr 2, 3(6)(b).

PART III
ADMINISTRATION [PROCEDURE]

[16.79]
74.10 Form of petition [in administration procedure]

[(1) In this Part, "the petition" means a petition under section 9 of, or section 8 of and Schedule B1 to, the Act of 1986 (petition for administration order), or section 156 of the Act of 2004 (petition for energy administration order).]

(2) The petition shall include averments in relation to—
(a) the petitioner and the capacity in which he presents the petition, if other than the company;
(b) whether it is believed that the company is, or is likely to become, unable to pay its debts and the grounds of that belief;
[(c) [in the case of a petition under the Act of 1986,] how the making of that order will achieve—
(i) any of the purposes specified in section 8(3) of the Act of 1986; or
(ii) an objective specified in paragraph 3 of Schedule B1 to the Act of 1986;]
(d) the company's financial position specifying, so far as known, assets and liabilities, including contingent and prospective liabilities;
(e) any security known or believed to be held by creditors of the company, whether in any case the security confers power on the holder to appoint a receiver [or an administrator], and whether a receiver [or an administrator, as the case may be,] has been appointed;
(f) so far as known to the petitioner, whether any steps have been taken for the winding up [of] the company;
(g) other matters which, in the opinion of the petitioner, will assist the court in deciding whether to grant an [order in respect of an administration] [or an energy administration, as the case may be];
(h) . . .
(i) the name and address of the person proposed to be appointed, and his qualification to act, as administrator [or energy administrator, as the case may be][; and
[(j) in the case of a petition under the Act of 1986, jurisdiction under the Council Regulation, in particular stating, so far as known to the petitioner—
(i) where the centre of main interests of the company is and whether the company has any other establishments in another Member State; and
(ii) whether there are insolvency proceedings elsewhere in respect of the company and whether those proceedings are main or territorial proceedings;]]
[(k) whether the Secretary of State has certified the case as one in which he considers it would be appropriate for him to petition under section 124A of the Act of 1986 (petition for winding up on grounds of public interest);
(l) so far as known to the petitioner in a petition for an energy administration order, whether any steps have been taken for an administration order under Schedule B1 to the Act of 1986;
(m) whether a protected energy company in a petition for an energy administration order is a non GB company.]

(2) Where a report has been prepared under rule 2.1 of the Insolvency Rules, a copy of that report shall be lodged with the petition.

NOTES

Words in square brackets in Part heading and rule heading substituted by the Act of Sederunt (Rules of the Court of Session Amendment No 5) (Insolvency Proceedings) 2003, SSI 2003/385, r 2(1), (6), (7)(a).

Para (1): substituted by the Act of Sederunt (Rules of the Court of Session Amendment) (Miscellaneous) 2006, SSI 2006/83, r 2(1), (9)(a).

Para (2): words in square brackets in sub-paras (c), (e), (i) inserted, words in second pair of square brackets in sub-para (g) inserted, sub-para (h) revoked, and sub-paras (k), (l), (m) added by SSI 2006/83, r 2(1), (9)(b)–(h); sub-para (c) substituted, words in first pair of square brackets in sub-para (g) substituted, and sub-para (j) and word immediately preceding it added, by SSI 2003/385, r 2(1), (7)(b); word in square brackets in sub-para (f) inserted by the Act of Sederunt (Rules of the Court of Session 1994 Amendment No 3) (Miscellaneous) 1994, SI 1994/2901, r 2(20); sub-para (j) substituted by the Act of Sederunt (Rules of the Court of Session Amendment No 8) (Miscellaneous) 2007, SSI 2007/449, r 2(1), (9).

[16.80]
[74.10A Interim orders

(1) On making an interim order under paragraph 13(1)(d) of Schedule B1 to the Act of 1986 [or section 157(1)(d) of the Act of 2004] the Lord Ordinary shall fix a hearing on the By Order Roll for a date after the expiry of the period of notice mentioned in rule 14.6 (period of notice for lodging answers).

(2) At the hearing under paragraph (1) the Lord Ordinary shall make such order as to further procedure as he thinks fit.]

NOTES

Inserted by the Act of Sederunt (Rules of the Court of Session Amendment No 7) (Miscellaneous) 2005, SSI 2005/268, r 2(1), (9).

Para (1): words in square brackets inserted by the Act of Sederunt (Rules of the Court of Session Amendment) (Miscellaneous) 2006, SSI 2006/83, r 2(1), (9)(j).

[16.81]
74.11 Notice of petition

Where—

(a) the petition is to be served on a person mentioned in rule [2.3] of the Insolvency Rules, and
(b) by virtue of paragraph (2) of that rule, notice requires to be given to that person, [or,
(c) the petition and a notice are to be served on a person mentioned in section 156(2)(a) to (c) of the Act of 2004 (notice of application for energy administration order) . . . rule 5(1) of the Energy Administration Rules [or rule 6(1) of the 2013 Rules],]

it shall be sufficient for the petitioner, where such notice and service is to be executed by post, to enclose the statutory notice and a copy of the petition in one envelope and to certify the giving of such notice and the execution of such service by one certificate.

NOTES

Rule reference in square brackets in para (a) substituted by the Act of Sederunt (Rules of the Court of Session Amendment No 5) (Insolvency Proceedings) 2003, SSI 2003/385, r 2(1), (8); para (c) and word immediately preceding it inserted by the Act of Sederunt (Rules of the Court of Session Amendment) (Miscellaneous) 2006, SSI 2006/83, r 2(1), (9)(k), word omitted from para (c) and words in square brackets inserted by the Act of Sederunt (Rules of the Court of Session Amendment No 4) (Miscellaneous) 2013, SSI 2013/162, rr 1(5), 5(3).

[16.82]
74.12 Report of proposals of administrator

(1) A report of the meeting to approve the proposals of the administrator to be sent to the court under section 24(4) of the Act of 1986 shall be sent to the Deputy Principal Clerk of Session, who shall—

(a) cause it to be lodged in the process of the petition to which it relates; and
(b) give written intimation to the parties of the receipt and lodging of the report.

(2) Where a report under section 24(4) of the Act of 1986 discloses that the meeting has declined to approve the proposals of the administrator, the Keeper of the Rolls shall put the cause out on the By Order Roll for determination by the insolvency judge for any order he may make under section 24(5) of that Act.

[16.83]
[74.13 Report of administrator's proposals: Schedule B1 to the Act of 1986

(1) Paragraph (2) shall apply where a report under paragraphs 53(2) or 54(6) of Schedule B1 to the Act of 1986 discloses a failure to approve, or to approve a revision of, an administrator's proposals.

(2) The Deputy Principal Clerk shall fix a hearing for determination by the insolvency judge of any order that may be made under paragraph 55(2) of Schedule B1 to the Act of 1986.]

NOTES

Substituted by the Act of Sederunt (Rules of the Court of Session Amendment No 5) (Insolvency Proceedings) 2003, SSI 2003/385, r 2(1), (9).

[16.84]
[74.14 Time and date of lodging in administration or energy administration

(1) The time and date of lodging of a notice or document relating to an administration under the Act of 1986 or the Insolvency Rules, or an energy administration under the Act of 2004 or the Energy Administration Rules, shall be noted by the Deputy Principal Clerk upon the notice or document.

(2) Subject to any provision in the Insolvency Rules or the Energy Administration Rules, as the case may be—

(a) where the time of lodging of a notice or document cannot be ascertained by the Deputy Principal Clerk, the notice or document shall be deemed to be lodged at 10 am on the date of lodging; and

(b) where a notice or document under paragraph (1) is delivered on any day other than a business day, the date of lodging shall be the first business day after such delivery.]

NOTES

Substituted by the Act of Sederunt (Rules of the Court of Session Amendment) (Miscellaneous) 2006, SSI 2006/83, r 2(1), (9)(l).

[16.85]
[74.15 Applications during an administration or energy administration

An application or appeal under any provision of the Act of 1986, the Insolvency Rules, the Act of 2004 or the Energy Administration Rules during an administration or energy administration, as the case may be, shall be—

(a) where no previous application or appeal has been made, by petition; or

(b) where a petition for an order in respect of an administration, or energy administration, as the case may be, has been lodged, by note in the process of that petition.]

NOTES

Substituted by the Act of Sederunt (Rules of the Court of Session Amendment) (Miscellaneous) 2006, SSI 2006/83, r 2(1), (9)(m).

[16.86]
[74.15A Application for administration by a bank liquidator

An application by a bank liquidator for an administration order under section 114 of the Act of 2009 shall be made by note in the existing process of the bank insolvency petition.]

NOTES

Inserted by the Act of Sederunt (Rules of the Court of Session Amendment) (Miscellaneous) 2009, SSI 2009/63, rr 2, 3(7).

PART IV
RECEIVERS

[16.87]
74.16 Interpretation of this Part

In this Part, "the petition" means a petition under section 54(1) of the Act of 1986 (petition to appoint a receiver).

[16.88]
74.17 Petition to appoint a receiver

The petition shall include averments in relation to—

(a) any floating charge and the property over which it is secured;

(b) so far as known to the petitioner, whether any application for [an order in respect of an administration] has been made[, or an administrator has been appointed] in respect of the company;

(c) other matters which, in the opinion of the petitioner, will assist the court in deciding whether to appoint a receiver; and

(d) the name and address of the person proposed to be appointed, and his qualification to act, as receiver.

NOTES

In para (b), words in first pair of square brackets substituted and words in second pair of square brackets inserted, by the Act of Sederunt (Rules of the Court of Session Amendment No 5) (Insolvency Proceedings) 2003, SSI 2003/385, r 2(1), (10).

[16.89]
74.18 Intimation, service and advertisement under this Part

(1) Unless the court otherwise directs, the order under rule 14.5 (first order in petitions) for intimation, service and advertisement of the petition shall include a requirement—

(a) to serve the petition—

(i) on the company; and

(ii) where an application for an administration order has been presented, on that applicant and any respondent to that application; and

(b) to advertise the petition forthwith—

(i) once in the Edinburgh Gazette; and

(ii) once in one or more of such newspapers as the court shall direct.

(2) Subject to rule 14.6(2) (application to shorten or extend the period of notice), the period of notice for lodging answers to the petition shall be 8 days.

(3) An advertisement under paragraph (1) shall include—
- (a) the name and address of the petitioner;
- (b) the name and address of the agent for the petitioner;
- (c) the date on which the petition was presented;
- (d) the nature of the order sought;
- (e) the period of notice for lodging answers; and
- (f) a statement that any person who intends to appear in the petition must lodge answers within the period of notice.

[16.90]
74.19 Form of other applications and appeals

(1) An application under—
- (a) section 61(1) of the Act of 1986 (by a receiver for authority to dispose of property or an interest in property),
- (b) section 62 of that Act (for removal of a receiver),
- (c) section 63(1) of that Act (by a receiver for directions),
- (d) section 69(1) of that Act (to enforce the receiver's duty to make returns etc), or
- (e) any other provision of the Act of 1986 or the Insolvency Rules relating to receivers not mentioned in this Part,

shall, where the court has appointed the receiver, be made by note or, in any other case, by petition.

(2) An appeal against a decision of a receiver as to expenses of submitting a statement of affairs under rule 3.3(2) of the Insolvency Rules shall, where the receiver was appointed by the court, be made by note or, in any other case, by petition.

(3) An application by a receiver—
- (a) under section 67(1) or (2) of the Act of 1986 (to extend the time for sending a report),
- (b) under rule 3.9(2) of the Insolvency Rules (to extend the time for sending an abstract of his receipts and payments),

shall, where the court has appointed the receiver, be made by motion or, in any other case, by petition.

PART V
WINDING UP OF COMPANIES

[16.91]
74.20 Interpretation of this Part

In this Part, "the petition" means a petition under section 124 of the Act of 1986 (petition to wind up a company).

[16.92]
74.21 Petition to wind up a company

(1) The petition shall include averments in relation to
- (a) the petitioner, if other than the company, and his title to present the petition;
- (b) in respect of the company—
  - (i) its current and any previous registered name;
  - (ii) the address of its registered office, and any previous such address within 6 months immediately before the presentation of the petition so far as known to the petitioner;
  - (iii) a statement of the nature of its business and objects, the amount of its capital (nominal and issued) indicating what part is called up, paid up or credited as paid up, and the amount of the assets of the company so far as known to the petitioner;
  - [(iv) where the centre of main interests of the company is and whether the company has any other establishments in another Member State;]
- (c) whether, to the knowledge of the petitioner, a receiver has been appointed in respect of any part of the property of the company or a liquidator has been appointed for the voluntary winding up of the company;
- (d) the grounds on which the petition proceeds;
- (e) the name and address of the person proposed to be appointed, and his qualification to act, as interim liquidator; and
- [(f) whether there are insolvency proceedings elsewhere in respect of the company and whether those proceedings are main or territorial proceedings.]

NOTES

Sub-paras (b)(iv), (f) inserted by the Act of Sederunt (Rules of the Court of Session Amendment No 8) (Miscellaneous) 2007, SSI 2007/449, r 2(1), (10).

[16.93]
74.22 Intimation, service and advertisement under this Part

(1) Unless the court otherwise directs, the order under rule 14.5 (first order in petitions) for intimation, service and advertisement of the petition shall include a requirement—
- (a) to serve the petition—
  - (i) where the petitioner is not the company, on the company;

(ii) where the company is being wound up voluntarily and a liquidator has been appointed, on the liquidator; and

(iii) where a receiver or administrator has been appointed, on the receiver or administrator, as the case may be;

(b) where the company is an authorised institution or former authorised institution within the meaning assigned in section 106(1) of the Banking Act 1987 and the petitioner is not the Bank of England, to serve the petition on the Bank of England; and

(c) to advertise the petition forthwith—

(i) once in the Edinburgh Gazette; and

(ii) once in one or more of such newspapers as the court shall direct.

(2) Subject to rule 14.6(2) (application to shorten or extend the period of notice), the period of notice for lodging answers to the petition shall be 8 days.

(3) An advertisement under paragraph (1) shall include—

(a) the name and address of the petitioner and, where the petitioner is the company, its registered office;

(b) the name and address of the agent for the petitioner;

(c) the date on which the petition was presented—

(d) the nature of the order sought;

(e) where a provisional liquidator has been appointed by the court, his name, address and the date of his appointment;

(f) the period of notice for lodging answers; and

(g) a statement that any person who intends to appear in the petition must lodge answers within the period of notice.

[16.94]
74.23 Remits from one court to another

(1) An application under section 120(3)(a)(i) of the Act of 1986 (application for remit of petition to a sheriff court) shall be made by motion.

(2) An application under—

(a) section 120(3)(a)(ii) of the Act of 1986 (application for remit of petition from a sheriff court to the court), or

(b) section 120(3)(b) of that Act (application for remit of petition from one sheriff court to another),

shall be made by petition.

[16.95]
74.24 Substitution of creditor or contributory for petitioner

(1) Where a petitioner in the petition—

(a) is subsequently found not entitled to present the petition,

(b) fails to make intimation, service and advertisement as directed by the court,

(c) moves or consents to withdraw the petition or to allow it to be dismissed or refused,

(d) fails to appear when the petition is called for hearing, or

(e) appears, but does not move for an order in terms of the prayer of the petition,

the court may, on such terms as it thinks fit, sist as petitioner in place of the original petitioner any creditor or contributory who, in the opinion of the court, is entitled to present the petition.

[(1A) Where a member State liquidator has been appointed in main proceedings in relation to the company, without prejudice to paragraph (1) the court may, on such terms as it thinks fit, substitute the member State [insolvency practitioner] as petitioner, where he is desirous of prosecuting the petition.]

(2) An application by a creditor or a contributory to be sisted under paragraph (1)—

(a) may be made at any time before the petition is dismissed or refused, and

(b) shall be made by note;

and, if necessary, the court may continue the petition for a specified period to allow a note to be presented.

NOTES

Para (1A): inserted by the Act of Sederunt (Rules of the Court of Session Amendment No 5) (Insolvency Proceedings) 2003, SSI 2003/385, r 2(1), (11); words in square brackets substituted for original word "liquidator" by the Act of Sederunt (Rules of the Court of Session 1994 and Sheriff Court Rules Amendment) (Regulation (EU) 2015/848) 2017, SSI 2017/202, rr 3(1), (4), 6, except in relation to proceedings which are subject to Regulation (EC) 1346/2000 of 29th May 2000 on insolvency proceedings.

[16.96]
74.25 Provisional liquidator

(1) An application to appoint a provisional liquidator under section 135 of the Act of 1986 may be made—

(a) by the petitioner, in the prayer of the petition or, if made after the petition has been presented, by note; or

(b) by a creditor or contributory of the company, the company, the Secretary of State[, a member State [insolvency practitioner] appointed in main proceedings] or a person entitled under any enactment to present a petition, by note.

(2) The application mentioned in paragraph (1) shall include averments in relation to—

(a) the grounds for the appointment of the provisional liquidator;

(b) the name and address of the person proposed to be appointed, and his qualification to act, as provisional liquidator; and

(c) whether, to the knowledge of the applicant, an administrator has been appointed to the company or a receiver has been appointed in respect of any part of its property or a liquidator has been appointed voluntarily to wind it up.

(3) Where the court decides to appoint a provisional liquidator—

(a) it shall pronounce an interlocutor making the appointment and specifying the functions to be carried out by him in relation to the affairs of the company; and

(b) the applicant shall forthwith send a certified copy of such interlocutor to the person appointed.

(4) On receiving a certified copy of an interlocutor pronounced under paragraph (3), the provisional liquidator shall intimate his appointment forthwith—

(a) once in the Edinburgh Gazette; and

(b) once in one or more of such newspapers as the court has directed.

(5) An application for the discharge of a provisional liquidator shall be made by note.

NOTES

Para (1): in sub-para (b), words in first (outer) pair of square brackets inserted by the Act of Sederunt (Rules of the Court of Session Amendment No 5) (Insolvency Proceedings) 2003, SSI 2003/385, r 2(1), (12); words in second (inner) pair of square brackets substituted for original word "liquidator" by the Act of Sederunt (Rules of the Court of Session 1994 and Sheriff Court Rules Amendment) (Regulation (EU) 2015/848) 2017, SSI 2017/202, rr 3(1), (5), 6, except in relation to proceedings which are subject to Regulation (EC) 1346/2000 of 29th May 2000 on insolvency proceedings.

[16.97]

74.26 Appointment of a liquidator

(1) Where the court pronounces an interlocutor appointing a liquidator—

(a) the Deputy Principal Clerk shall send a certified copy of that interlocutor to the liquidator;

(b) the court may, for the purposes of rule 4.18(4) of the Insolvency Rules (liquidator to give notice of appointment), give such direction as it thinks fit as to advertisement of such appointment.

(2) An application to appoint a liquidator under section 139(4) of the Act of 1986 shall be made by note.

[16.98]

74.27 Applications and appeals in relation to a statement of affairs

(1) An application under section 131(5) of the Act of 1986 for—

(a) release from an obligation imposed under section 131(1) or (2) of that Act, or

(b) an extension of time for the submission of a statement of affairs,

shall be made by note.

(2) A note under paragraph (1) shall be served on the liquidator or provisional liquidator, as the case may be, who may lodge—

(a) answers to the note; or

(b) a report on any matters which he considers should be drawn to the attention of the court.

(3) Where the liquidator or provisional liquidator lodges a report under paragraph (2), he shall forthwith send a copy of it to the noter.

(4) Where the liquidator or the provisional liquidator does not appear at any hearing on the note, a certified copy of the interlocutor disposing of the note shall be sent to him forthwith by the noter.

(5) An appeal under rule 4.9(6) of the Insolvency Rules (appeal against refusal by liquidator of allowance towards expenses of preparing statement of affairs) shall be made by note.

[16.99]

74.28 Appeals against adjudication of claims

[(1) An appeal under rule 4.16B(6) of the Insolvency Rules (adjudication of claims) by a creditor or any member or contributory of the company against a decision of the liquidator shall be made by note in process.]

(2) A note under paragraph (1) shall be served on the liquidator.

(3) On such a note being served on him, the liquidator shall send the claim in question, and a copy of his adjudication, forthwith to the Deputy Principal Clerk who shall cause them to be lodged in process.

(4) After the note has been disposed of, the Deputy Principal Clerk shall return the claim and the adjudication to the liquidator with a copy of the interlocutor disposing of the note.

NOTES

Para (1): substituted by the Act of Sederunt (Rules of the Court of Session and Sheriff Court Company Insolvency Rules Amendment) (Miscellaneous) 2014, SSI 2014/119, r 2(1), (2).

[16.100]

74.29 Removal of liquidator

An application by a creditor of the company for an order—

(a) under section 171(3) of the Act of 1986 (order directing a liquidator to summon a meeting of creditors for the purpose of removing him), or

(b) under section 172 of that Act (order for removal of a liquidator),

shall be made by note.

[16.101]
74.30 Application in relation to remuneration of liquidator

(1) An application—

(a) by a liquidator under rule 4.34 of the Insolvency Rules (application to increase remuneration), or

(b) by a creditor of the company under rule 4.35 of those Rules (application to reduce liquidator's remuneration),

shall be made by note.

(2) A note under paragraph (1)(b) shall be served on the liquidator.

[16.102]
[74.30A Applications under section 176A of the Act of 1986

(1) An application by a liquidator, administrator or receiver under section 176A of the Act of 1986 shall be—

(a) where there is no existing process in relation to any liquidation, administration or receivership, by petition; or

(b) where a process exists in relation to any liquidation, administration or receivership, by note in that process.

(2) The Deputy Principal Clerk shall—

(a) after the lodging of any petition or note fix a hearing for the insolvency judge to consider an application under paragraph (1); and

(b) give notice of the hearing fixed under paragraph (2)(a) to the petitioner or noter.

(3) The petitioner or noter shall not be required to give notice to any person of the hearing fixed under paragraph (2)(a), unless the insolvency judge directs otherwise.]

NOTES

Inserted by the Act of Sederunt (Rules of the Court of Session Amendment No 5) (Insolvency Proceedings) 2003, SSI 2003/385, r 2(1), (13).

[16.103]
74.31 Application to appoint a special manager

(1) An application under section 177 of the Act of 1986 (application for the appointment of a special manager) shall be made by note.

(2) A bond of caution certified by the noter under rule 4.70(4) of the Insolvency Rules shall be sent to the Petition Department by the noter.

(3) After the Deputy Principal Clerk has satisfied himself as to the sufficiency of caution under rule 33.7(1) of these Rules, the clerk of session shall issue to the person appointed to be special manager a certified copy of the interlocutor appointing him.

(4) A special manager may, before the expiry of the period for finding caution, apply to the insolvency judge for an extension of that period.

[16.104]
74.32 Other applications

(1) An application under the Act of 1986 or any subordinate legislation made under that Act, or Part VII of the Companies Act 1989, in relation to a winding up by the court not mentioned in this Part shall—

(a) if made by a party to the petition, be made by motion; or

(b) in any other case, be made by note.

(2) At the hearing of a motion under paragraph (1)(a), the court may order that the application be made by note; and, in such a case, shall make an order for the lodging of answers to the note in process within such period as it thinks fit.

[16.105]
[74.32A Replacement liquidators: block transfer orders

(1) This rule applies to an application under rule 4.26B(1) of the Insolvency Rules (application for block transfer order).

(2) An application mentioned in paragraph (1) shall be made by petition.

(3) Paragraph (4) applies where an application includes the name of one or more sheriff court petition.

(4) The Deputy Principal Clerk shall notify the sheriff clerk of every sheriff court listed in the application that an application has been made.

(5) Where the court grants an application, it may order the replacement liquidator to be appointed in any or all of the cases listed in the application.

(6) Where the court pronounces an interlocutor granting a block transfer order—

(a) the Deputy Principal Clerk shall send a certified copy of that interlocutor to the replacement liquidator;

(b) the court may direct that a copy of the interlocutor is—

(i) to be put in the process of every Court of Session petition where the replacement liquidator has been appointed;

(ii) to be sent to the sheriff clerk to be put in the process of every sheriff court petition where the replacement liquidator has been appointed; and

(c) the court may make such orders as it thinks fit for the intimation and advertisement of the appointment of the replacement liquidator.]

NOTES

Commencement: 30 May 2014.

Inserted by the Act of Sederunt (Rules of the Court of Session Amendment) (Miscellaneous) 2006, SSI 2006/83, r 2(1), (10); substituted by the Act of Sederunt (Rules of the Court of Session and Sheriff Court Company Insolvency Rules Amendment) (Miscellaneous) 2014, SSI 2014/119, r 2(1), (3).

[16.106]
[74.32B [Approval of the voluntary winding up of a bank or building society]

(1) An application for the prior approval of a resolution for voluntary winding up of a bank under section 84 of the Act of 1986 [or voluntary winding up of a building society under section 88 of the Building Societies Act 1986] shall be made to the Deputy Principal Clerk by letter.

(2) An application under paragraph (1) shall be marked as having been made on the date on which the letter is received by the court.

(3) The letter shall be placed before the insolvency judge forthwith for consideration.

(4) The court shall approve such a resolution by pronouncing an interlocutor to that effect.]

NOTES

Inserted by the Act of Sederunt (Rules of the Court of Session Amendment) (Miscellaneous) 2009, SSI 2009/63, rr 2, 3(8).

Rule heading: words in square brackets substituted by the Act of Sederunt (Rules of the Court of Session Amendment No 6) (Building Society Special Administration etc) 2009, SSI 2009/135, r 2(1), (3).

Para (1): words in square brackets inserted by SSI 2009/135, r 2(1), (2).

PART VI
DISQUALIFICATION OF COMPANY DIRECTORS

[16.107]
74.33 Applications in relation to disqualification orders [or undertakings]

An application—

(a) under section 3(2) of the Company Directors Disqualification Act 1986 (for disqualification for persistent breaches of companies legislation);
(b) under section 6(1) of that Act (to disqualify unfit directors of insolvent companies);
(c) under section 8 of that Act (for disqualification of unfit director after investigation of a company);
[(ca) under section 8A of that Act (variation or cessation of disqualification undertaking)]
(d) under section 11(1) of that Act (for leave by an undischarged bankrupt to be concerned in a company),
(e) for leave under that Act; or
(f) by the Secretary of State under rule 4(2) of the Insolvent Companies (Reports on Conduct of Directors (No 2) (Scotland) Rules 1986 (application for direction to comply with requirements to furnish information etc),

shall be made by petition.

NOTES

Words in square brackets in rule heading, and para (ca) inserted by the Act of Sederunt (Rules of the Court of Session Amendment No 8) (Miscellaneous) 2005, SSI 2005/521, r 2(1), (4)(a).

The Insolvent Companies (Reports on Conduct of Directors) (No 2) (Scotland) Rules 1986, SI 1986/1916: revoked (subject to savings) and replaced by the Insolvent Companies (Reports on Conduct of Directors) (Scotland) Rules 1996, SI 1996/1910 at **[16.126]** et seq.

[16.108]
74.34 Intimation, service and advertisement under this Part

(1) Rule 74.22, except paragraphs (1)(c) and (2) of that rule, shall apply to the intimation, service and advertisement of a petition referred to in rule 74.33 (applications in relation to disqualification orders) as it applies to a petition under that rule.

[(2) A petition presented under rule 74.33 shall be intimated—

[(a) to the Secretary of State for Business, Enterprise and Regulatory Reform; or]
(b) where a petition is presented under rule 74.33(ca) and the disqualification undertaking was given under section 9B of the Company Directors Disqualification Act 1986 (competition undertaking), to the Office of Fair Trading or any specified regulator which has accepted the undertaking, as the case may be;

unless the petition is presented by that person or body.]

NOTES

Para (2): substituted by the Act of Sederunt (Rules of the Court of Session Amendment No 8) (Miscellaneous) 2005, SSI 2005/521, r 2(1), (4)(b); sub-para (a) substituted by the Act of Sederunt (Rules of the Court of Session Amendment No 8) (Miscellaneous) 2007, SSI 2007/449, r 2(1), (11).

[PART VII
BANK INSOLVENCY PROCEDURE

[16.109]
74.35 Petition for bank insolvency

(1) An application for a bank insolvency order under section 95 of the Act of 2009 shall be made by petition.

(2) A petition under paragraph (1) shall include averments in relation to—
(a) the name and address of the person to be appointed as the bank liquidator, and his qualification to act;
(b) the current name and any other trading names of the bank;
(c) the address of the bank's registered office, and any previous such address within six months immediately before the presentation of the petition so far as known to the petitioner;
(d) a home address for each director of the bank;
(e) a statement of the amount of the bank's capital (nominal and issued) indicating what part is called up, paid up or credited as paid up, and the amount of the assets of the bank so far as known to the petitioner;
(f) whether, to the knowledge of the petitioner, a bank administrator has been appointed in respect of the bank or a supervisor has been appointed in respect of the bank under a voluntary arrangement under Part 1 of the Act of 1986; and
(g) the grounds on which the petition proceeds.]

NOTES
Parts VII and VIII (rr 74.35–74.50) inserted, together with preceding Part headings, by the Act of Sederunt (Rules of the Court of Session Amendment) (Miscellaneous) 2009, SSI 2009/63, rr 2, 3(9).

[16.110]
[74.36 Intimation, service and advertisement under this Part

(1) Unless the court otherwise directs, the order under rule 14.5 (first order in petitions) for intimation, service and advertisement of a petition referred to in rule 74.35 shall include—
(a) a requirement to serve two copies of the petition—
(i) on the bank and each director of the bank;
(ii) on the Bank of England, if it is not the petitioner;
(iii) on the [Financial Conduct Authority], if it is not the petitioner;
[(iiia) the Prudential Regulation Authority, if it is not the petitioner;]
(iv) on the Secretary of State, if he is not the petitioner;
(v) on the proposed bank liquidator;
(vi) on the Financial Services Compensation Scheme;
(vii) on any person who has given notice to the [Financial Conduct Authority or the Prudential Regulation Authority] in respect of the bank under section 120 of the Act of 2009;
(viii) if there is in force for the bank a voluntary arrangement under Part 1 of the Act of 1986, the supervisor of that arrangement; and
(ix) where a bank administrator has been appointed in relation to the bank, on that bank administrator;
(b) a requirement to advertise the petition forthwith—
(i) once in the Edinburgh Gazette; and
(ii) once in one or more of such newspapers as the court shall direct; and
(c) the time and date fixed by the court for the hearing of the petition.

(2) In fixing the time and date for the hearing of the petition mentioned in paragraph (1)(c), the court shall ensure that the date and time is as soon as reasonably practicable, having regard to the need to give the directors of the bank a reasonable opportunity to attend.

(3) Unless the court otherwise directs, where the petition is served under paragraph (1), one copy of the petition shall be sent electronically as soon as practicable to each of the persons named in the order and the other copy shall be served on those persons in accordance with Chapter 16 of these Rules.

(4) Any answers to the petition must be lodged 24 hours before the date fixed by the court under this rule and a copy of the answers must be served on the petitioner before that date.

(5) An advertisement under paragraph (1) shall include—
(a) the identity of the petitioner;
(b) the name and address of the agent for the petitioner;
(c) the date on which the petition was presented;
(d) where a provisional bank liquidator has been appointed by the court, his name, address and the date of his appointment; and
(e) a statement that any person who intends to appear in the petition must lodge answers no later than 24 hours prior to the date set down for a hearing in terms of paragraph (1)(c).]

NOTES
Inserted as noted to r 74.35 at **[16.109]**.
Para (1)(a): sub-para (iiia) inserted and words in square brackets in sub-paras (iii), (vii) substituted by the Financial Services Act 2012 (Consequential Amendments and Transitional Provisions) Order 2013, SI 2013/472, art 3, Sch 2, para 10(b)–(d).

[16.111]
[74.37 Provisional bank liquidator

(1) An application to appoint a provisional bank liquidator under section 135 of the Act of 1986, as that provision is applied and modified by section 103 of the Act of 2009, may be made—

(a) by the petitioner, in the prayer of the petition or, if made after the petition has been presented, by note; or

(b) by any other person entitled to make an application under section 95 of the Act of 2009, by note.

(2) The application mentioned in paragraph (1) shall include averments in relation to—

(a) the grounds for appointment of the provisional bank liquidator;

(b) the name and address of the person proposed to be appointed, and his qualification to act, as provisional bank liquidator; and

(c) confirmation that the person to be appointed has consented to act as provisional bank liquidator.

(3) Where the court decides to appoint a provisional bank liquidator—

(a) it shall pronounce an interlocutor making the appointment and specifying the functions to be carried out by him in relation to the affairs of the bank; and

(b) the applicant shall forthwith send a certified copy of such interlocutor to the person appointed and to such other persons as are specified under rule 12 of the Bank Insolvency Rules (order of appointment of provisional bank liquidator).

(4) On receiving a certified copy of an interlocutor pronounced under paragraph (3), the provisional bank liquidator shall intimate his appointment forthwith—

(a) once in the Edinburgh Gazette; and

(b) once in one or more such newspapers as the court has directed.

(5) An application for the discharge of a provisional bank liquidator shall be made by note.]

NOTES

Inserted as noted to r 74.35 at **[16.109]**.

[16.112]
[74.38 Applications and appeals in relation to a statement of affairs

(1) An application under section 131(5) of the Act of 1986, as applied and modified by section 103 of the Act of 2009, for—

(a) release from an obligation imposed under section 131(1) or (2) of the Act of 1986, as so applied and modified; or

(b) an extension of time for the submission of a statement of affairs,

shall be made by note.

(2) A note under paragraph (1) shall be served on the bank liquidator or provisional bank liquidator, as the case may be, who may lodge—

(a) answers to the note; or

(b) a report on any matters which he considers should be drawn to the attention of the court.

(3) Where the bank liquidator or provisional bank liquidator lodges a report under paragraph (2), he shall forthwith send a copy of it to the noter.

(4) Where the bank liquidator or provisional bank liquidator does not appear at any hearing on the note, a certified copy of the interlocutor disposing of the note shall be sent to him forthwith by the noter.

(5) Where a certified copy of the interlocutor is sent to the bank liquidator or provisional bank liquidator in accordance with paragraph (4), the noter shall forthwith provide notice of that fact to the court.

(6) An appeal under rule 4.9(6) of the Insolvency Rules (appeal against refusal by liquidator of allowance towards expenses of preparing statement of affairs), as applied by rule 19 of the Bank Insolvency Rules, shall be made by note.]

NOTES

Inserted as noted to r 74.35 at **[16.109]**.

74.39 (*Inserted as noted to r 74.35 at* **[16.109]**; *revoked by the Act of Sederunt (Rules of the Court of Session, Sheriff Appeal Court Rules and Sheriff Court Rules Amendment) (Bankruptcy (Scotland) Act 2016) 2016, SSI 2016/312, r 2(1), (5).*)

[16.113]
[74.40 Removal of bank liquidator

An application for an order under section 108 of the Act of 2009 (removal of bank liquidator by the court) shall be made by note.]

NOTES

Inserted as noted to r 74.35 at **[16.109]**.

[16.114]
[74.41 Application in relation to remuneration of bank liquidator

(1) An application—

(a) by a bank liquidator under rule 4.34 of the Insolvency Rules (application to increase remuneration), as that rule is applied by rule 47 of the Bank Insolvency Rules; or

(b) by a creditor of the bank under rule 4.35 of the Insolvency Rules (application to reduce liquidator's remuneration), as that rule is applied by rule 48 of the Bank Insolvency Rules,

shall be made by note.]

NOTES

Inserted as noted to r 74.35 at **[16.109]**.

[16.115]

[74.42 Applications under section 176A of the Act of 1986

(1) An application by a bank liquidator or bank administrator under section 176A of the Act of 1986 (share of assets for unsecured creditors), as applied and modified by section 103 of the Act of 2009, shall be made by note in the existing bank liquidation or bank administration process.

(2) The Deputy Principal Clerk shall—

(a) after the lodging of any note fix a hearing for the insolvency judge to consider an application under paragraph (1); and

(b) give notice of the hearing fixed under paragraph (2)(a) to the noter.

(3) The noter shall not be required to give notice to any person of the hearing fixed under paragraph (2)(a), unless the insolvency judge directs otherwise.]

NOTES

Inserted as noted to r 74.35 at **[16.109]**.

[16.116]

[74.43 Applications to appoint a special manager

(1) An application under section 177 of the Act of 1986 (application for the appointment of a special manager), as applied and modified by section 103 of the Act of 2009, shall be made by note.

(2) A bond of caution certified by the noter under rule 4.70(4) of the Insolvency Rules, as that rule is applied by rule 82 of the Bank Insolvency Rules, shall be sent to the Petition Department by the noter.

(3) After the Deputy Principal Clerk has satisfied himself as to the sufficiency of caution under rule 33.7(1) of these Rules, the clerk of session shall issue to the person appointed to be special manager a certified copy of the interlocutor appointing him.

(4) A special manager may, before the expiry of the period for finding caution, apply to the insolvency judge for an extension of that period.]

NOTES

Inserted as noted to r 74.35 at **[16.109]**.

[16.117]

[74.44 Other applications

(1) An application under the Act of 1986 as applied by the Act of 2009, under the Act of 2009 or under any subordinate legislation made under those Acts, in relation to a bank insolvency not mentioned in this Part shall—

(a) if made by a party to the petition, be made by motion; or

(b) in any other case, be made by note.

(2) At the hearing of a motion under paragraph (1)(a), the court may order that the application be made by note; and, in such a case, shall make an order for the lodging of answers to the note in process within such period as it thinks fit.]

NOTES

Inserted as noted to r 74.35 at **[16.109]**.

[PART VIII

BANK ADMINISTRATION PROCEDURE

[16.118]

74.45 Petition for bank administration

(1) An application by the Bank of England for a bank administration order under section 142 of the Act of 2009 shall be made by petition.

(2) A petition under paragraph (1) shall include averments on the following matters—

(a) the name and address of the person to be appointed as the bank administrator, and his qualification to act;

(b) confirmation that the conditions for applying for a bank administration order, set out in section 143 of the Act of 2009, are met in respect of the bank;

(c) the bank's current financial position to the best of the Bank of England's knowledge and belief, including actual, contingent and prospective assets and liabilities;

(d) any security which the Bank of England knows or believes to be held by the creditors of the bank;

(e) whether any security confers power to appoint an administrator under paragraph 14 of Schedule B1 to the Act of 1986 (holder of qualifying floating charge) or a receiver of the whole (or substantially the whole) of the bank's property, and whether such an administrator or receiver has been appointed;
(f) any insolvency proceedings which have been instituted in respect of the bank, including any process notified to the [Financial Conduct Authority or the Prudential Regulation Authority] under section 120 of the Act of 2009;
(g) details of any property transfer instrument which the Bank of England has made or intends to make under section 11(2)(b) or 12(2) of the Act of 2009 in respect of the bank;
(h) where the property transfer instrument has not yet been made, an explanation of what effect it is likely to have on the bank's financial position;
(i) how the making of a bank administration order will achieve the objectives specified in section 137 of the Act of 2009;
(j) how functions are to be apportioned where more than one person is to be appointed as bank administrator and, in particular, whether functions are to be exercisable jointly or individually; and
(k) other matters which the Bank of England considers will assist the court in deciding whether to grant a bank administration order.]

NOTES

Inserted as noted to r 74.35 at **[16.109]**.

Para (2): words in square brackets substituted by the Financial Services Act 2012 (Consequential Amendments and Transitional Provisions) Order 2013, SI 2013/472, art 3, Sch 2, para 10(d).

[16.119]
[74.46 Hearing of petition

(1) Where a petition is lodged under rule 74.45, the court shall fix a time and date for the hearing of the petition and in doing so shall ensure that the date and time is as soon as is reasonably practicable, having regard to the need to give the directors of the bank a reasonable opportunity to attend.

(2) At the hearing of a petition, each of the following may appear or be represented—
(a) the Bank of England;
[(b) the Financial Conduct Authority;
(ba) the Prudential Regulation Authority;]
(c) the bank;
(d) any director of the bank;
(e) any person nominated for appointment as bank administrator of the bank;
(f) any person who holds a qualifying floating charge for the purposes of paragraph 14 of Schedule B1 to the Act of 1986; and
(g) with the permission of the court, any other person who appears to have an interest.]

NOTES

Inserted as noted to r 74.35 at **[16.109]**.

Para (2): paras (b), (ba) substituted for original para (b) by the Financial Services Act 2012 (Consequential Amendments and Transitional Provisions) Order 2013, SI 2013/472, art 3, Sch 2, para 10(e).

[16.120]
[74.47 Provisional bank administrator

(1) An application to appoint a provisional bank administrator under section 135 of the Act of 1986, as that provision is applied and modified by section 145 of the Act of 2009, may be made by the Bank of England in the prayer of the petition or, if made after the petition has been presented, by note.

(2) The application mentioned in paragraph (1) shall include averments on the following matters—
(a) the grounds for appointment of the provisional bank administrator;
(b) the name and address of the person proposed to be appointed, and his qualification to act, as provisional bank administrator;
(c) confirmation that the person to be appointed has consented to act as provisional bank administrator; and
(d) the Bank of England's estimate of the value of the assets in respect of which the provisional bank administrator is entitled to be appointed.

(3) An order appointing any provisional bank administrator shall specify the functions to be carried out in relation to the bank's affairs and how those functions are to be apportioned where more than one person is to be appointed as provisional bank administrator and, in particular, shall specify whether functions are to be exercisable jointly or individually.

(4) Where the court decides to appoint a provisional bank administrator—
(a) it shall pronounce an interlocutor making the appointment and specifying the functions to be carried out by him in relation to the affairs of the bank; and
(b) it shall forthwith send a certified copy of the interlocutor to the person appointed . . . (appointment of provisional bank administrator).

(5) On receiving a certified copy of an interlocutor pronounced under paragraph (4)(a), the provisional bank administrator shall intimate his appointment forthwith—
(a) once in the Edinburgh Gazette; and
(b) once in one or more such newspapers as the court has directed.

(6) An application for the discharge of a provisional bank administrator shall be made by note.]

NOTES

Inserted as noted to r 74.35 at **[16.109]**.

Para (4): words omitted revoked by the Act of Sederunt (Rules of the Court of Session Amendment No 5) (Miscellaneous) 2010, SSI 2010/417, r 4(1), (4).

[16.121]
[74.48 Report of bank administrator's proposals: Schedule B1 to the Act of 1986

(1) Paragraph (2) shall apply where a report under paragraphs 53(2) or 54(6) of Schedule B1 to the Act of 1986 (report at conclusion of creditors' meeting), as those provisions are applied and modified by section 145 of the Act of 2009, discloses a failure to approve, or to approve a revision of, a bank administrator's proposals.

(2) The Deputy Principal Clerk shall fix a hearing for determination by the insolvency judge of any order that may be made under paragraph 55(2) of Schedule B1 to the Act of 1986, as that provision is applied and modified by section 145 of the Act of 2009.]

NOTES

Inserted as noted to r 74.35 at **[16.109]**.

[16.122]
[74.49 Time and date of lodging in a bank administration

(1) The time and date of lodging of a notice or document relating to a bank administration under—

(a) the Act of 2009;
(b) the Act of 1986, as applied by the Act of 2009;
(c) the Bank Administration Rules; or
(d) the Insolvency Rules, as applied by the Bank Administration Rules,

shall be noted by the Deputy Principal Clerk upon the notice or document.

(2) Subject to any provision of the Bank Administration Rules, or the Insolvency Rules as applied by the Bank Administration Rules—

(a) where the time of lodging of a notice or document cannot be ascertained by the Deputy Principal Clerk, the notice or document shall be deemed to have been lodged at 10 am on the date of lodging; and
(b) where a notice or document under paragraph (1) is delivered on any day other than a business day [but is not lodged on that day], the date of lodging shall be the first business day after such delivery.]

NOTES

Inserted as noted to r 74.35 at **[16.109]**.

Para (2): words in square brackets inserted by the Act of Sederunt (Rules of the Court of Session Amendment No 6) (Building Society Special Administration etc) 2009, SSI 2009/135, r 2(1), (4).

[16.123]
[74.50 Applications during a bank administration

An application or appeal under any provision of the Act of 1986 as applied by the Act of 2009, the Insolvency Rules as applied by the Bank Administration Rules, the Act of 2009 or the Bank Administration Rules, during a bank administration shall be—

(a) where no previous application or appeal has been made, by petition; or
(b) where a petition for an order in respect of a bank administration has been lodged, by note in the process of that petition.]

NOTES

Inserted as noted to r 74.35 at **[16.109]**.

[PART IX
BUILDING SOCIETY SPECIAL ADMINISTRATION PROCEDURE

[16.124]
74.51 Application of rules to building society special administration

(1) Subject to paragraph (3), Part VIII of this Chapter applies to an application mentioned in paragraph (2) as it applies to an application for a bank administration order.

(2) An application referred to in paragraph (1) is an application for a building society special administration order under the Act of 2009, as that Act is applied and modified by section 90C of the Building Societies Act 1986 and the Building Societies (Insolvency and Special Administration) Order 2009.

(3) In the application of Part VIII of this Chapter under paragraph (1)—

(a) references to the Bank Administration Rules shall be read as references to the Building Society Special Administration (Scotland) Rules 2009;
(b) references to a rule in the Bank Administration Rules shall be read as references to the corresponding rule in the Building Society Special Administration (Scotland) Rules 2009;

(c) references to the Act of 2009 shall be read as references to the Act of 2009, as applied and modified by [sections 84 and 90C] of the Building Societies Act 1986 and the Building Societies (Insolvency and Special Administration) Order 2009; and references to specific provisions in the Act of 2009 shall be read accordingly;
(d) references to "bank" shall be read as references to "building society";
(e) references to "bank administration" shall be read as references to "building society special administration";
(f) references to "bank administration order" shall be read as references to "building society special administration order";
(g) references to "bank administrator" shall be read as references to "building society special administrator";
(h) in rule 74.45(2)(e) (averments on power to appoint administrator or receiver), the words "an administrator under paragraph 14 of Schedule B1 to the Act of 1986 (holder of qualifying floating charge) or" and "an administrator or" shall be omitted;
(i) in rule 74.45(2)(f) (averments on insolvency proceedings), for "section 120 of the Act of 2009" substitute "section 90D of the Building Societies Act 1986"; and
(j) in rule 74.46(2) (representation at hearing of petition), subparagraph (f) shall be omitted.

(4) The following rules shall, with the necessary modifications, apply in relation to building society special administration procedure as they apply in relation to bank administration procedure—

. . .

. . .

rule 74.1 (application and interpretation of Chapter 74),
rule 74.2 (proceedings before insolvency judge),
rule 74.3 (notices and reports etc sent to the court),
rule 74.9 (form of applications).]

NOTES

Inserted, together with preceding Part heading by the Act of Sederunt (Rules of the Court of Session Amendment No 6) (Building Society Special Administration etc) 2009, SSI 2009/135, r 2(1), (5).

Para (3): in sub-para (c) words in square brackets substituted by the Act of Sederunt (Rules of the Court of Session Amendment No 5) (Miscellaneous) 2010, SSI 2010/417, r 4(1), (5)(a).

Para (4): words omitted revoked by SSI 2010/417, r 4(1), (5)(b).

[PART X
BUILDING SOCIETY INSOLVENCY PROCEDURE

[16.125]
74.52 Application of rules to building society insolvency

(1) Subject to paragraph (3), Part VII of this Chapter applies to an application mentioned in paragraph (2) as it applies to an application for a bank insolvency order.

(2) An application referred to in paragraph (1) is an application for a building society insolvency order under the Act of 2009, as that Act is applied and modified by section 90C of the Building Societies Act 1986 and the Building Societies (Insolvency and Special Administration) Order 2009.

(3) In the application of Part VII of this Chapter under paragraph (1)—
(a) references to the Bank Insolvency Rules shall be read as references to the Building Society Insolvency (Scotland) Rules 2010;
(b) references to a rule in the Bank Insolvency Rules shall be read as references to the corresponding rule in the Building Society Insolvency (Scotland) Rules 2010;
(c) references to the Act of 2009 shall be read as references to the Act of 2009, as applied and modified by section 90C of the Building Societies Act 1986 and the Building Societies (Insolvency and Special Administration) Order 2009; and references to specific provisions in the Act of 2009 shall be read accordingly;
(d) references to any Part or provision of the Act of 1986 that is not applied by Part 2 of the Act of 2009 shall be read as references to that Part or provision as applied and modified by section 90A of, and Schedule 15A to, the Building Societies Act 1986;
(e) references to "bank" shall be read as references to "building society";
(f) references to "bank administration" shall be read as references to "building society special administration";
(g) references to "bank administrator" shall be read as references to "building society special administrator";
(h) references to "bank insolvency order" shall be read as references to "building society insolvency order";
(i) references to "bank liquidator" shall be read as references to "building society liquidator";
(j) rule 74.36(1)(a)(iv) (intimation, service and advertisement) shall be disregarded; and
(k) in rule 74.36(1)(a)(vii), the reference to "section 120 of the Act of 2009" shall be read as a reference to "section 90D of the Building Societies Act 1986".

(4) The following rules shall, with the necessary modifications, apply in relation to building society insolvency procedure as they apply in relation to bank insolvency procedure:—
rule 74.1 (application and interpretation of Chapter 74),
rule 74.2 (proceedings before insolvency judge),
rule 74.3 (notices and reports etc. sent to the court).]

NOTES

Inserted, together with preceding Part heading, by the Act of Sederunt (Rules of the Court of Session Amendment No 5) (Miscellaneous) 2010, SSI 2010/417, r 4(1), (6).

[PART XI

INVESTMENT BANK SPECIAL ADMINISTRATION PROCEDURE

74.53–74.61 *(Inserted by the Act of Sederunt (Rules of the Court of Session Amendment No 6) (Miscellaneous) 2011, SSI 2011/385, r 3(1), (3); contain specialised procedural rules.)*]

INSOLVENT COMPANIES (REPORTS ON CONDUCT OF DIRECTORS) (SCOTLAND) RULES 1996

(SI 1996/1910 (S 154))

NOTES

Made: 22 July 1996.

Authority: Insolvency Act 1986, s 411, Company Directors Disqualification Act 1986, s 21(2).

Commencement: 30 September 1996.

Revocation: these Rules are revoked by the Insolvent Companies (Reports on Conduct of Directors) (Scotland) Rules 2016, SI 2016/185, art 2(a), as from 6 April 2016, subject to transitional and savings provisions in r 10 thereof at **[16.294]**.

Application: these Rules are applied to limited liability partnerships with such modifications as the context requires for the purpose of giving effect to the provisions of the Insolvency Act 1986, by the Limited Liability Partnerships Regulations 2001, SI 2001/1090, reg 10, Sch 6, Pt III at **[10.38]**, **[10.44]**.

ARRANGEMENT OF RULES

1 Citation, commencement and interpretation . . . . . [16.126]
3 Reports required under section 7(3) of the Act . . . . . [16.127]
4 Return by office-holder . . . . . [16.128]
5 Forms . . . . . [16.129]
6 Enforcement of section 7(4) . . . . . [16.130]
7 Transitional and saving provisions . . . . . [16.131]

SCHEDULES

Schedule—Forms . . . . . [16.132]

[16.126]

1 Citation, commencement and interpretation

(1) These Rules may be cited as the Insolvent Companies (Reports on Conduct of Directors) (Scotland) Rules 1996.

(2) These Rules shall come into force on 30th September 1996.

(3) In these Rules—

"the Act" means the Company Directors Disqualification Act 1986;

"the former Rules" means the Insolvent Companies (Reports on Conduct of Directors) (No 2) (Scotland) Rules 1986;

"the commencement date" means 30th September 1996; and

"a company" means a company which the courts in Scotland have jurisdiction to wind up.

NOTES

Revoked as noted at the beginning of these Rules.

2 *(Revoked as noted at the beginning of these Rules. Revokes (subject to r 7 below) the Insolvent Companies (Reports on Conduct of Directors) (No 2) (Scotland) Rules 1986, SI 1986/1916.)*

[16.127]

3 Reports required under section 7(3) of the Act

(1) This rule applies to any report made to the Secretary of State under section 7(3) of the Act by:—

(a) the liquidator of a company which is being wound up by an order of the court made on or after the commencement date;

(b) the liquidator of a company which passes a resolution for voluntary winding up on or after that date;

(c) a receiver of a company appointed under section 51 of the Insolvency Act 1986 (power to appoint receiver under the law of Scotland) on or after that date, who is an administrative receiver; or

(d) the administrator of a company in relation to which the court makes an administration order on or after that date.

(2) Such a report shall be made in the Form Dl (Scot) set out in the Schedule hereto, or in a form which is substantially similar, and in the manner and to the extent required by the Form Dl (Scot).

NOTES

Revoked as noted at the beginning of these Rules.

[16.128]

4 Return by office-holder

(1) This rule applies where it appears to a liquidator of a company as mentioned in rule 3(1)(a) or (b), to an administrative receiver as mentioned in rule 3(1)(c), or to an administrator as mentioned in rule 3(1)(d) (each of whom is referred to hereinafter as "an office-holder") that the company has at any time become insolvent within the meaning of section 6(2) of the Act.

(2) Subject as follows there may be furnished to the Secretary of State by an office-holder at any time during the period of 6 months from the relevant date (defined in paragraph (4) below) a return with respect to every person who:—

- *(a) was, on the relevant date, a director or shadow director of the company, or*
- *(b) had been a director or shadow director of the company at any time in the 3 years immediately preceding that date.*

(3) The return shall be made in the Form D2 (Scot) set out in the Schedule hereto, or in a form which is substantially similar, and in the manner and to the extent required by the Form D2 (Scot).

(4) For the purposes of this rule, "the relevant date" means:—

- *(a) in the case of a company in liquidation (except in the case mentioned in paragraph (4)(b) below), the date on which the company goes into liquidation within the meaning of section 247(2) of the Insolvency Act 1986,*
- *(b) in the case of a company in members' voluntary winding up, the date on which the liquidator forms the opinion that, at the time when the company went into liquidation, its assets were insufficient for the payment of its debts and other liabilities and the expenses of winding up,*
- *(c) in the case of the administrative receiver, the date of his appointment,*
- *(d) in the case of the administrator, the date of the administration order made in relation to the company,*

and for the purposes of sub-paragraph (c) above the only appointment of an administrative receiver to be taken into account in determining the relevant date shall be that appointment which is not that of a successor in office to an administrative receiver who has vacated office either by death or pursuant to section 62 of the Insolvency Act 1986.

(5) Subject to paragraph (6) below, it shall be the duty of an office-holder to furnish a return complying with the provisions of paragraphs (3) and (4) of this rule to the Secretary of State:—

- *(a) where he is in office in relation to the company on the day one week before the expiry of the period of 6 months from the relevant date, not later than the expiry of such period;*
- *(b) where he vacates office (otherwise than by death) before the day one week before the expiry of the period of 6 months from the relevant date, within 14 days after his vacation of office except where he has furnished such a return on or prior to the day one week before the expiry of such period.*

(6) A return need not be provided under this rule by an office-holder if he has, whilst holding that office in relation to the company, since the relevant date, made a report under rule 3 with respect to all persons falling within paragraph (2) of this rule and (apart from this paragraph) required to be the subject of a return.

(7) If an office-holder without reasonable excuse fails to comply with the duty imposed by paragraph (5) of this rule, he is guilty of an offence and—

- *(a) on summary conviction of the offence, is liable to a fine not exceeding level 3 on the standard scale, and*
- *(b) after continued contravention, is liable to a daily default fine; that is to say, he is liable on a second or subsequent summary conviction of the offence to a fine of one-tenth of level 3 on the standard scale for each day on which the contravention is continued (instead of the penalty specified in sub-paragraph (a)).*

(8) Section 431 of the Insolvency Act 1986 (summary proceedings), as it applies to Scotland, has effect in relation to an offence under this rule as to offences under Parts I to VII of that Act.

NOTES

Revoked as noted at the beginning of these Rules.

[16.129]

5 Forms

The forms referred to in rule 3(2) and rule 4(3) shall be used with such variations, if any, as the circumstances may require.

NOTES

Revoked as noted at the beginning of these Rules.

[16.130]

6 Enforcement of section 7(4)

(1) This rule applies where under section 7(4) of the Act (power to call on liquidators, former liquidators and others to provide information) the Secretary of State requires or has required a person—

(a) to furnish him with information with respect to a person's conduct as director or shadow director of a company, and

(b) to produce and permit inspection of relevant books, papers and other records.

(2) On the application of the Secretary of State, the court may make an order directing compliance within such period as may be specified.

(3) The court's order may provide that all expenses of and incidental to the application shall be borne by the person to whom the order is directed.

NOTES

Revoked as noted at the beginning of these Rules.

[16.131]

7 Transitional and saving provisions

(1) Subject to paragraph (2) below, rules 2 and 3 of the former Rules shall continue to apply as if the former Rules had not been revoked when any of the events mentioned in sub-paragraphs (a), (b), (c) or (d) of rule 2(1) of the former Rules (order of the court for winding up, passing of resolution for voluntary winding up, appointment of administrative receiver, making of administration order) occurred on or after 29th December 1986 but before the commencement date.

(2) Until 31st December 1996—

(a) the forms contained in the Schedule to the former Rules which were required to be used for the purpose of complying with those Rules, or

(b) the Form Dl (Scot) or D2 (Scot) as set out in the Schedule to these Rules, as appropriate, or a form which is substantially similar thereto, with such variations, if any, as the circumstances may require,

may be used for the purpose of complying with rules 2 and 3 of the former Rules as applied by paragraph (1) above; but after that date the forms mentioned in sub-paragraph (b) of this paragraph shall be used for that purpose.

(3) When a period referred to in rule 4(2) of the former Rules is current immediately before the commencement date, these Rules have effect as if rule 6(2) of these Rules had been in force when the period began and the period is deemed to expire whenever it would have expired if these Rules had not been made and any right, obligation or power dependent on the beginning, duration or end of such period shall be under rule 6(2) of these Rules as it was or would have been under the said rule 4(2).

(4) The provisions of this rule are to be without prejudice to the operation of section 16 of the Interpretation Act 1978 (saving from repeals) as it is applied by section 23 of that Act.

NOTES

Revoked as noted at the beginning of these Rules.

SCHEDULE
FORMS

Rules 3(2), 4(3) and 7(2)

[16.132]

NOTES

The forms themselves are not reproduced in this work, but their numbers and descriptions are listed below.

FORM NO	*PURPOSE*
[D1 (Scot)	*Report under Section 7(3) of the Company Directors Disqualification Act 1986]*
D2 (Scot)	*Return by Office-Holder under Rule 4 of the Insolvent Companies (Reports on Conduct of Directors) (Scotland) Rules 1996.*

NOTES

Revoked as noted at the beginning of these Rules.

Form D1: substituted by the Insolvent Companies (Reports on Conduct of Directors) (Scotland) (Amendment) Rules 2001, SI 2001/768, r 2, Schedule.

LIMITED LIABILITY PARTNERSHIPS (SCOTLAND) REGULATIONS 2001

(SSI 2001/128)

NOTES

Made: 28 March 2001.
Authority: Limited Liability Partnerships Act 2000, ss 14–17.
Commencement: 6 April 2001.

ARRANGEMENT OF REGULATIONS

PART I
CITATION, COMMENCEMENT, EXTENT AND INTERPRETATION

1 Citation, commencement and extent . . . . . [16.133]
2 Interpretation . . . . . [16.134]

PART II
COMPANIES ACT

3 Application of the 1985 Act to limited liability partnerships . . . . . [16.135]

PART III
WINDING UP AND INSOLVENCY

4 Application of the 1986 Act to limited liability partnerships . . . . . [16.136]

PART IV
MISCELLANEOUS

6 Application of subordinate legislation . . . . . [16.137]

SCHEDULES

Schedule 1—Modifications to provisions of the 1985 Act . . . . . [16.138]
Schedule 2—Provisions of the 1986 Act . . . . . [16.139]
Schedule 3—Modifications to provisions of the 1986 Act . . . . . [16.140]

PART I
CITATION, COMMENCEMENT EXTENT AND INTERPRETATION

[16.133]
1 Citation, commencement and extent

(1) These Regulations may be cited as the Limited Liability Partnerships (Scotland) Regulations 2001 and shall come into force on 6th April 2001.

(2) These Regulations extend to Scotland only.

[16.134]
2 Interpretation

In these Regulations—

"the 1985 Act" means the Companies Act 1985;

"the 1986 Act" means the Insolvency Act 1986;

"limited liability partnership agreement", in relation to a limited liability partnership, means any agreement, express or implied, made between the members of the limited liability partnership or between the limited liability partnership and the members of the limited liability partnership which determines the mutual rights and duties of the members, and their rights and duties in relation to the limited liability partnership;

"the principal Act" means the Limited Liability Partnerships Act 2000; and

"shadow member", in relation to a limited liability partnership, means a person in accordance with whose directions or instructions the members of the limited liability partnership are accustomed to act (but so that a person is not deemed a shadow member by reason only that the members of the limited liability partnership act on advice given by that person in a professional capacity).

PART II
COMPANIES ACT

[16.135]
3 Application of the 1985 Act to limited liability partnerships

The provisions of the 1985 Act specified in the first column of Schedule 1 to these Regulations shall apply to limited liability partnerships, with the following modifications—

(a) references to a company shall include references to a limited liability partnership;

(b) references to the Companies Acts shall include references to the principal Act and any regulations made thereunder;

(c) references to the 1986 Act shall include references to that Act as it applies to limited liability partnerships by virtue of Part III of these Regulations;
(d) references in a provision of the 1985 Act to other provisions of that Act shall include references to those other provisions as they apply to limited liability partnerships by virtue of these Regulations; and
(e) the modifications, if any, specified in the second column of Schedule 1 of the provision specified opposite them in the first column.

PART III
WINDING UP AND INSOLVENCY

[16.136]
4 Application of the 1986 Act to limited liability partnerships

(1) Subject to paragraph (2), the provisions of the 1986 Act listed in Schedule 2 shall apply in relation to limited liability partnerships as they apply in relation to companies.

(2) The provisions of the 1986 Act referred to in paragraph (1) shall so apply, with the following modifications—
(a) references to a company shall include references to a limited liability partnership;
(b) references to a director or to an officer of a company shall include references to a member of a limited liability partnership;
(c) references to a shadow director shall include references to a shadow member;
(d) references to the 1985 Act, the Company Directors Disqualification Act 1986, the Companies Act 1989 or to any provisions of those Acts or to any provisions of the 1986 Act shall include references to those Acts or provisions as they apply to limited liability partnerships by virtue of the principal Act or these Regulations; and
(e) the modifications set out in Schedule 3 to these Regulations.

PART IV
MISCELLANEOUS

5 (*Introduces Sch 4 to these Regulations.*)

[16.137]
6 Application of subordinate legislation

(1) The Insolvency (Scotland) Rules 1986 shall apply to limited liability partnerships with such modifications as the context requires for the purpose of giving effect to the provisions of the Insolvency Act 1986 which are applied by these Regulations.

(2) In the case of any conflict between any provision of the subordinate legislation applied by paragraph (1) and any provision of these Regulations, the latter shall prevail.

SCHEDULES

SCHEDULE 1
MODIFICATIONS TO PROVISIONS OF THE 1985 ACT

Regulation 3

[16.138]

Formalities of Carrying on Business	
36B (execution of documents by companies)	
Floating Charges and Receivers (Scotland)	
462 (power of incorporated company to create floating charge)	In subsection (1), for the words "an incorporated company (whether a company within the meaning of this Act or not)," substitute "a limited liability partnership", and the words "(including uncalled capital)" are omitted.
463 (effect of floating charge on winding up)	
466 (alteration of floating charges) Subsections (1), (2), (3) and (6)	
486 (interpretation for Part XVIII generally)	For the definition of "company" substitute ""company" means a limited liability partnership;"
487 (extent of Part XVIII)	

SCHEDULE 2
PROVISIONS OF THE 1986 ACT

Regulation 4(1)

[16.139]
The relevant provisions of the 1986 Act are as follows:

Sections 50 to 52;
Section 53(1) and (2), to the extent that those subsections do not relate to the requirement for a copy of the instrument and notice being delivered to the registrar of companies; Section 53(4), (6) and (7);
Section 54(1), (2), (3) (to the extent that that subsection does not relate to the requirement for a copy of the interlocutor to be delivered to the registrar of companies), and subsections (5), (6) and (7);
Sections 55 to 58;
Section 60, other than subsection (1);
Section 61, including subsections (6) and (7) to the extent that those subsections do not relate to anything to be done or which may be sent to the registrar of companies;
Section 62, including subsection (5) to the extent that that subsection does not relate to anything to be done or which may be sent to the registrar of companies;
Sections 63 to 66;
Section 67, including subsections (1) and (8) to the extent that those subsections do not relate to anything to be sent to the registrar of companies;
Section 68;
Section 69, including subsections (1) and (2) to the extent that those subsections do not relate to anything to be done or which may be done by the registrar of companies;
Sections 70 and 71;
Subsection 84(3) to the extent that it does not concern the copy of the resolution being forwarded to the registrar of companies within 15 days;
Sections 91 to [92A];
Section 94, including subsections (3) and (4) to the extent that those subsections do not relate to the liquidator being required to send to the registrar of companies a copy of the account and a return of the final meeting;
Section 95;
Section 97;
Sections 100 to 102;
Sections 104 to [104A];
Section 106, including subsections [(3) to (7)] to the extent that those subsections do not relate to the liquidator being required to send to the registrar of companies a copy of the account of winding up and a return of the final meeting/quorum [or a statement about a member State liquidator];
Sections 109 to 111;
Section 112, including subsection (3) to the extent that that subsection does not relate to the liquidator being required to send to the registrar of companies a copy of the order made by the court;
Sections 113 to 115;
Sections 126 to 128;
Section 130(1) to the extent that that subsection does not relate to a copy of the order being forwarded by the court to the registrar of companies;
Section 131;
Sections 133 to 135;
Sections 138 to 140;
Sections 142 to 146;
Section 147, including subsection (3) to the extent that that subsection does not relate to a copy of the order being forwarded by the company to the registrar of companies;
Section 162 to the extent that the section concerns the matters set out in Section C 2 of Schedule 5 to the Scotland Act 1998 as being exceptions to the reservation of insolvency;
Sections 163 to 167;
Section 169;
Section 170, including subsection (2) to the extent that that subsection does not relate to an application being made by the registrar to make good the default;
Section 171;
Section 172, including [subsections (8)–(10) to the extent that those subsections do] not relate to the liquidator being required to give notice to the registrar of companies [or a statement about a member State liquidator];
Sections 173 and 174;
Section 177;
Sections 185 to 189;
Sections 191 to 194;
Section 196;
Section 199;
Section 200;
Sections 206 to 215;
Section 218 subsections (1), (2),(4) and (6);
Sections 231 to 232 to the extent that the sections apply to administrative receivers, liquidators and provisional liquidators;
Section 233 to the extent that that section applies in the case of the appointment of an administrative receiver, of a voluntary arrangement taking effect, of a company going into liquidation or where a provisional liquidator is appointed;
[Section 233A to the extent that that section applies in the case of a voluntary arrangement taking effect;]

Section 234 to the extent that that section applies to situations other than those where an administration [has been entered into];
Section 235 to the extent that that section applies to situations other than those where an administration [has been entered into];
Sections 236 to 237 to the extent that those sections apply to situations other than [administrations entered into] and winding up;
Sections 242 to 243;
Section 244 to the extent that that section applies in circumstances other than a company which [has entered into administration];
Section 245;
Section 251;
Section 416(1) and (4) to the extent that those subsections apply to section 206(1)(a) and (b) in connection with the offence provision relating to the winding up of a limited liability partnership;
Section 430;
Section 436;
Schedule 2;
Schedule 3;
Schedule 4;
Schedule 8 to the extent that that Schedule does not apply to voluntary arrangements or administrations within the meaning of Parts I and II of the 1986 Act;
Schedule 10 to the extent that it refers to any of the sections referred to above.

NOTES

Figure "92A" in square brackets substituted (for original figure "93"), and figure "104A" in square brackets substituted (for original figure "105"), by the Public Services Reform (Insolvency) (Scotland) Order 2016, SSI 2016/141, art 7(2)(a) (for savings, see the note to the Insolvency Act 1986, s 66 at **[1.52]**).

In entries relating to ss 106 and 172, words in first pair of square brackets substituted and words in second pair of square brackets inserted by the Insolvency (Miscellaneous Amendments) Regulations 2017, SI 2017/1119, reg 2, Sch 1, Pt 3, para 57.

Entry relating to section 233A inserted by the Insolvency (Protection of Essential Supplies) Order 2015, SI 2015/989, art 6, Schedule, para 3.

Other words in square brackets substituted by the Limited Liability Partnerships (Scotland) Amendment Regulations 2009, SSI 2009/310, reg 3, Sch 1.

SCHEDULE 3
MODIFICATIONS TO PROVISIONS OF THE 1986 ACT

Regulation 4(2)

[16.140]

Provisions	*Modifications*
Section 84 (circumstances in which company may be wound up voluntarily)	
Subsection (3)	For subsection (3) substitute the following— "(3) Within 15 days after a limited liability partnership has determined that it be wound up there shall be forwarded to the registrar of companies either a printed copy or a copy in some other form approved by the registrar of the determination."
Subsection [(3A)]	After subsection (3) insert a new subsection— "[(3A)] If a limited liability partnership fails to comply with this regulation the limited liability partnership and every designated member of it who is in default is liable on summary conviction to a fine not exceeding level 3 on the standard scale."
Section 91 (appointment of liquidator)	
Subsection (1)	Delete "in general meeting".
Subsection (2)	For subsection (2) substitute the following— "(2) On the appointment of a liquidator the powers of the members of the limited liability partnership shall cease except to the extent that a meeting of the members of the limited liability partnership summoned for the purpose or the liquidator sanctions their continuance." After subsection (2) insert— "(3) Subsections (3) and (4) of section 92 shall apply for the purposes of this section as they apply for the purposes of that section."
Section 92 (power to fill vacancy in office of liquidator)	

Provisions	*Modifications*
Subsection (1)	For "the company in general meeting" substitute "a meeting of the members of the limited liability partnership summoned for the purpose".
Subsection (2)	For "a general meeting" substitute "a meeting of the members of the limited liability partnership".
Subsection (3)	In subsection (3), for "articles" substitute "limited liability partnership agreement".
new subsection (4)	Add a new subsection (4) as follows—
	"(4) The quorum required for a meeting of the members of the limited liability partnership shall be any quorum required by the limited liability partnership agreement for meetings of the members of the limited liability partnership and if no requirement for a quorum has been agreed upon the quorum shall be 2 members."
Section 93 (general company meeting at each year's end)	
subsection (1)	*For "a general meeting of the company" substitute "a meeting of the members of the limited liability partnership".*
new subsection (4)	*Add a new subsection (4) as follows—*
	"(4) Subsections (3) and (4) of section 92 shall apply for the purposes of this section as they apply for the purposes of that section."
Section 94 (final meeting prior to dissolution)	
subsection (1)	For "a general meeting of the company" substitute "a meeting of the members of the limited liability partnership".
new subsection (5A)	Add a new subsection (5A) as follows—
	"(5A) Subsections (3) and (4) of section 92 shall apply for the purposes of this section as they apply for the purposes of that section."
subsection (6)	For "a general meeting of the company" substitute "a meeting of the members of the limited liability partnership".
Section 95 (effect of company's insolvency)	
subsection (1)	For "directors'" substitute "designated members'".
subsection (7)	For subsection (7) substitute the following—
	"(7) In this section 'the relevant period' means the period of 6 months immediately preceding the date on which the limited liability partnership determined that it be wound up voluntarily."
Section 100 (appointment of liquidator)	
subsection (1)	For "The creditors and the company at their respective meetings mentioned in section 98" substitute "The creditors at their meeting mentioned in section 98 and the limited liability partnership".
subsection (3)	Delete "director,".
Section 101 (appointment of liquidation committee)	
subsection (2)	For subsection (2) substitute the following—
	"(2) If such a committee is appointed, the limited liability partnership may, when it determines that it be wound up voluntarily or at any time thereafter, appoint such number of persons as they think fit to act as members of the committee, not exceeding 5."
Section 105 (meetings of company and creditors at each year's end)	
subsection (1)	*For "a general meeting of the company" substitute "a meeting of the members of the limited liability partnership".*
new subsection (5)	*Add a new subsection (5) as follows—*

Provisions	***Modifications***
	"(5) Subsections (3) and (4) of section 92 shall apply for the purposes of this section as they apply for the purposes of that section."
Section 106 (final meeting prior to dissolution)	
subsection (1)	For "a general meeting of the company" substitute "a meeting of the members of the limited liability partnership".
new subsection (5A)	After subsection (5) insert a new subsection (5A) as follows— "(5A) Subsections (3) and (4) of section 92 shall apply for the purposes of this section as they apply for the purposes of that section."
subsection (6)	For "a general meeting of the company" substitute "a meeting of the members of the limited liability partnership".
Sections 110 (acceptance of shares, etc, as consideration for sale of company property)	
	For the existing section substitute the following: "(1) This section applies, in the case of a limited liability partnership proposed to be, or being, wound up voluntarily, where the whole or part of the limited liability partnership's business or property is proposed to be transferred or sold to another company whether or not it is a company within the meaning of the Companies Act ("the transferee company") or to a limited liability partnership ("the transferee limited liability partnership"). (2) With the requisite sanction, the liquidator of the limited liability partnership being, or proposed to be, wound up ("the transferor limited liability partnership") may receive, in compensation or part compensation for the transfer or sale, shares, policies or other like interests in the transferee company or the transferee limited liability partnership for distribution among the members of the transferor limited liability partnership. (3) The sanction required under subsection (2) is— (a) in the case of a members' voluntary winding up, that of a determination of the limited liability partnership at a meeting of the members of the limited liability partnership conferring either a general authority on the liquidator or an authority in respect of any particular arrangement, (subsections (3) and (4) of section 92 to apply for this purpose as they apply for the purposes of that section), and (b) in the case of a creditor's voluntary winding up, that of either court or the liquidation committee. (4) Alternatively to subsection (2), the liquidator may (with the sanction) enter into any other arrangement whereby the members of the transferor limited liability partnership may, in lieu of receiving cash, shares, policies or other like interests (or in addition thereto), participate in the profits, or receive any other benefit from the transferee company or the transferee limited liability partnership. (5) A sale or arrangement in pursuance of this section is binding on members of the transferor limited liability partnership.

Provisions	***Modifications***
	(6) A determination by the limited liability partnership is not invalid for the purposes of this section by reason that it is made before or concurrently with a determination by the limited liability partnership that it be wound up voluntarily or for appointing liquidators; but, if an order is made within a year for winding up the limited liability partnership by the court, the determination by the limited liability partnership is not valid unless sanctioned by the court."
Section 111 (dissent from arrangement under section 110)	
subsections (1)–(3)	For subsections (1)–(3) substitute the following— "(1) This section applies in the case of a voluntary winding up where, for the purposes of section 110(2) or (4), a determination of the limited liability partnership has provided the sanction requisite for the liquidator under that section. (2) If a member of the transferor limited liability partnership who did not vote in favour of providing the sanction required for the liquidator under section 110 expresses his dissent from it in writing addressed to the liquidator and left at the registered office of the limited liability partnership within 7 days after the date on which that sanction was given, he may require the liquidator either to abstain from carrying the arrangement so sanctioned into effect or to purchase his interest at a price to be determined by agreement or arbitration under this section. (3) If the liquidator elects to purchase the member's interest, the purchase money must be paid before the limited liability partnership is dissolved and be raised by the liquidator in such manner as may be determined by the limited liability partnership."
subsection (4)	Omit subsection (4).
Section 126 (power to stay or restrain proceedings against company)	
subsection (2)	Delete subsection (2).
Section 127 (avoidance of property dispositions, etc)	
	For "any transfer of shares" substitute "any transfer by a member of the limited liability partnership of his interest in the property of the limited liability partnership".
Section 165 (voluntary winding up)	
subsection (2)	In paragraph (a) for "an extraordinary resolution of the company" substitute "a determination by a meeting of the members of the limited liability partnership".
subsection (4)	For paragraph (c) substitute the following— "(c) summon meetings of the members of the limited liability partnership for the purpose of obtaining their sanction or for any other purpose he may think fit."
new subsection (4A)	Insert a new subsection (4A) as follows— "(4A) Subsections (3) and (4) of section 92 shall apply for the purposes of this section as they apply for the purposes of that section."
Section 166 (creditors' voluntary winding up)	
subsection (5)	In paragraph (b) for "directors" substitute "designated members".
Section 171 (removal, etc (voluntary winding up))	
subsection (2)	For paragraph (a) substitute the following— "(a) in the case of a members' voluntary winding up, by a meeting of the members of the limited liability partnership summoned specially for that purpose, or".

Provisions	*Modifications*
subsection (6)	In paragraph (a) for "final meeting of the company" substitute "final meeting of the members of the limited liability partnership" and in paragraph (b) for "final meetings of the company" substitute "final meetings of the members of the limited liability partnership".
new subsection (7)	Insert a new subsection (7) as follows— "(7) Subsections (3) and (4) of section 92 apply for the purposes of this section as they apply for the purposes of that section."
Section 173 (release (voluntary winding up))	
subsection (2)	In paragraph (a) for "a general meeting of the company" substitute "a meeting of the members of the limited liability partnership".
Section 187 (power to make over assets to employees)	
	Delete section 187.
Section 194 (resolutions passed at adjourned meetings)	
	After "contributories" insert "or of the members of a limited liability partnership".
Section 206 (fraud, etc in anticipation of winding up)	
subsection (1)	For "passes a resolution for voluntary winding up" substitute "makes a determination that it be wound up voluntarily".
Section 207 (transactions in fraud of creditors)	
subsection (1)	For "passes a resolution for voluntary winding up" substitute "makes a determination that it be wound up voluntarily".
Section 210 (material omissions from statement relating to company's affairs)	
subsection (2)	For "passed a resolution for voluntary winding up" substitute "made a determination that it be wound up voluntarily".
Section 214 (wrongful trading)	
subsection (2)	Delete from "but the court shall not" to the end of the subsection.
After section 214	Insert the following new section 214A:

"214A Adjustment of withdrawals

(1) This section has effect in relation to a person who is or has been a member of a limited liability partnership where, in the course of the winding up of that limited liability partnership, it appears that subsection (2) of this section applies in relation to that person.

(2) This subsection applies in relation to a person if—

(a) within the period of two years ending with the commencement of the winding up, he was a member of the limited liability partnership who withdrew property of the limited liability partnership, whether in the form of a share of profits, salary, repayment of or payment of interest on a loan to the limited liability partnership or any other withdrawal of property, and

(b) it is proved by the liquidator to the satisfaction of the court that at the time of the withdrawal he knew or had reasonable grounds for believing that the limited liability partnership—

(i) was at the time of the withdrawal unable to pay its debts within the meaning of section 123 of the Act, or

Part 16 Other SIs: Scotland

Provisions	*Modifications*
	(ii) would become so unable to pay its debts after the assets of the limited liability partnership had been depleted by that withdrawal taken together with all other withdrawals (if any) made by any members contemporaneously with that withdrawal or in contemplation when that withdrawal was made. (3) Where this section has effect in relation to any person the court, on the application of the liquidator, may declare that that person is to be liable to make such contribution (if any) to the limited liability partnership's assets as the court thinks proper. (4) The court shall not make a declaration in relation to any person the amount of which exceeds the aggregate of the amounts or values of all the withdrawals referred to in subsection (2) made by that person within the period of 2 years referred to in that subsection. (5) The court shall not make a declaration under this section with respect to any person unless that person knew or ought to have concluded that after each withdrawal referred to in subsection (2) there was no reasonable prospect that the limited liability partnership would avoid going into insolvent liquidation. (6) For the purposes of subsection (5) the facts which a member ought to know or ascertain, the conclusions which he ought to reach and the steps which he ought to have taken are those which would be known or ascertained, or reached or taken, by a reasonably diligent person having both: (a) the general knowledge, skill and experience that may reasonably be expected of a person carrying out the same functions as are carried out by that member in relation to the limited liability partnership, and (b) the general knowledge, skill and experience that that member has. (7) For the purposes of this section a limited liability partnership goes into insolvent liquidation if it goes into liquidation at a time when its assets are insufficient for the payment of its debts and other liabilities and the expenses of the winding up. (8) In this section "member" includes a shadow member. (9) This section is without prejudice to section 214."
Section 215 (proceedings under ss 213, 214)	
subsection (1)	Omit the word "or" between the words "213" and "214" and insert after "214" "or 214A".
subsection (2)	For "either section" substitute "any of those sections".
subsection (4)	For "either section" substitute "any of those sections".
subsection (5)	For "Sections 213 and 214" substitute "Sections 213, 214 or 214A".
Section 218 (prosecution of delinquent officers and members of company)	
subsection (1)	For "officer, or any member, of the company" substitute "member of the limited liability partnership".
subsections (4) and (6)	For "officer of the company, or any member of it," substitute "officer or member of the limited liability partnership".
. . .	
Section 251 (expressions used generally)	
	Delete the word "and" appearing after the definition of "the rules" and insert the word "and" after the definition of "shadow director".

Provisions	***Modifications***
	After the definition of "shadow director" insert the following— ""shadow member", in relation to a limited liability partnership, means a person in accordance with whose directions or instructions the members of the limited liability partnership are accustomed to act (but so that a person is not deemed a shadow member by reason only that the members of the limited liability partnership act on advice given by him in a professional capacity);".
Section 416 (monetary limits (companies winding up))	
subsection (1)	In subsection (1), omit the words "section 117(2) (amount of company's share capital determining whether county court has jurisdiction to wind it up);" and the words "section 120(3) (the equivalent as respects sheriff court jurisdiction in Scotland);".
Section 436 (expressions used generally)	
	The following expressions and definitions shall be added to the section— "designated member" has the same meaning as it has in the Limited Liability Partnerships Act 2000; "limited liability partnership" means a limited liability partnership formed and registered under the Limited Liability Partnership Act 2000; "limited liability partnership agreement", in relation to a limited liability partnership, means any agreement, express or implied, made between the members of the limited liability partnership or between the limited liability partnership and the members of the limited liability partnership which determines the mutual rights and duties of the members, and their rights and duties in relation to the limited liability partnership.
Schedule 2	
Paragraph 17	For paragraph 17 substitute the following— "**17** Power to enforce any rights the limited liability partnership has against the members under the terms of the limited liability partnership agreement".
Schedule 10(a)	
Section 93(3)	In the entry relating to section 93(3) for "general meeting of the company" substitute "meeting of members of the limited liability partnership".
Section 105(3)	In the entry relating to section 105(3) for "company general meeting" substitute "meeting of the members of the limited liability partnership".
Section 106(6)	In the entry relating to section 106(6) for "company" substitute "the members of the limited liability partnership".

NOTES

Figures in square brackets in the entry relating to section 84 substituted, and entry relating to section 233 (omitted) revoked, by the Limited Liability Partnerships (Scotland) Amendment Regulations 2009, SSI 2009/310, reg 4, Sch 2.

Entries relating to ss 93 and 105 repealed by the Public Services Reform (Insolvency) (Scotland) Order 2016, SSI 2016/141, art 7(2)(b) (for savings, see the note to the Insolvency Act 1986, s 66 at **[1.52]**).

SCHEDULE 4

(*Sch 4 amends the Insolvency Act 1986, s 110 at* **[1.108]** *and contains other amendments which are outside the scope of this work.*)

BANKRUPTCY (FINANCIAL SERVICES AND MARKETS ACT 2000) (SCOTLAND) RULES 2001

(SI 2001/3591 (S 19))

NOTES

Made: 5 November 2001.
Authority: Financial Services and Markets Act 2000, ss 372, 428.
Commencement: 1 December 2001 (in accordance with r 1).

ARRANGEMENT OF RULES

1 Citation and commencement .... [16.141]
2 Interpretation .... [16.142]
3 Form of a demand .... [16.143]
4 Service of a demand .... [16.144]
5 Application to set aside a demand .... [16.145]
6 Setting aside a demand .... [16.146]

[16.141]
1 Citation and commencement

These Rules may be cited as the Bankruptcy (Financial Services and Markets Act 2000) (Scotland) Rules 2001 and come into force on the day on which section 19 of the Act comes into force.

[16.142]
2 Interpretation

In these Rules—

"the Act" means the Financial Services and Markets Act 2000;

"the court" means the sheriff court in the sheriffdom where the individual had an established place of business, or was habitually resident, at any time in the year immediately preceding the date of presentation of the application under rule 5;

"debt" means the sum referred to in section 372(4)(a) of the Act;

"demand" means a demand made under section 372(4)(a) of the Act;

"individual" has the meaning given by section 372(7) of the Act.

["the regulator" in relation to an individual means—

(a) if the individual is a PRA-authorised person, or was carrying on a PRA-regulated activity in contravention of the general prohibition, the FCA or the PRA,

(b) in any other case, the FCA,

and terms used in this definition which are defined in the Act have the meaning given in the Act.]

NOTES

Definition "the regulator" inserted by the Financial Services Act 2012 (Consequential Amendments and Transitional Provisions) Order 2013, SI 2013/472, art 3, Sch 2, para 61(a).

[16.143]
3 Form of a demand

A demand must—

(a) be dated and signed by a member of the [regulator's] staff authorised by it for that purpose;

(b) specify that it is made under section 372(4)(a) of the Act;

(c) state the amount of the debt, to whom it is owed and the way in which it arises;

(d) state the grounds on which it is alleged that the individual appears to have no reasonable prospect of paying the debt;

(e) specify the name, address and telephone number of one or more persons with whom the individual may enter into communication with a view to establishing to the [regulator's] satisfaction that there is a reasonable prospect that the debt will be paid when it falls due or (as the case may be) that the debt will be secured or compounded; and

(f) include an explanation to the individual of the following matters:

(i) the purpose of the demand and the fact that, if the individual does not comply with the demand, the [regulator] may petition under section 5 of the Bankruptcy (Scotland) Act 1985 for the sequestration of his estate;

(ii) the time within which the demand must be complied with, if that consequence is to be avoided;

(iii) the methods of compliance which are open to the individual; and

(iv) the individual's right to apply to the court for the demand to be set aside.

NOTES

Words in square brackets substituted by the Financial Services Act 2012 (Consequential Amendments and Transitional Provisions) Order 2013, SI 2013/472, art 3, Sch 2, para 61(b).

[16.144]
4 Service of a demand

The demand must be served on the individual by leaving it at his usual or last known address or by sending it by first class recorded delivery post to that address.

[16.145]
5 Application to set aside a demand

(1) An individual may, within 18 days from the date of service on him of a demand, apply to the court by way of summary application for an order setting aside the demand.

(2) The [regulator] must be cited as a defender to the summary application.

NOTES

Para (2): word in square brackets substituted by the Financial Services Act 2012 (Consequential Amendments and Transitional Provisions) Order 2013, SI 2013/472, art 3, Sch 2, para 61(c).

[16.146]
6 Setting aside a demand

(1) The court must order the demand to be set aside if—

(a) the individual appears to have a counterclaim or set-off which equals or exceeds the amount of the debt or debts specified in the demand;

(b) the debt is disputed on grounds which appear to the court to be substantial;

(c) it appears that the creditor holds some security in respect of the debt claimed by the demand and the court is satisfied that the value of the security equals or exceeds the full amount of the debt; or

(d) the court is satisfied, on other grounds, that the demand ought to be set aside.

(2) The decision of the court on such an application is final.

INSURERS (WINDING UP) (SCOTLAND) RULES 2001

(SI 2001/4040 (S 21))

NOTES

Made: 20 December 2001.

Authority: Insolvency Act 1986, s 411, Financial Services and Markets Act 2000, s 379.

Commencement: 18 January 2002.

ARRANGEMENT OF RULES

1 Citation, commencement and revocation . . . . [16.147]
2 Interpretation . . . . [16.148]
3 Application . . . . [16.149]
4 Financial Services Compensation Scheme . . . . [16.150]
5 Maintenance of separate financial records for long-term and other business in winding up . . . . [16.151]
6 Valuation of general business policies . . . . [16.152]
7 Valuation of long-term policies . . . . [16.153]
8 Valuation of long-term policies: stop order made . . . . [16.154]
9 Attribution of liabilities to company's long-term business . . . . [16.155]
10 Attribution of assets to company's long-term business . . . . [16.156]
11 Excess of long-term business assets . . . . [16.157]
12 Actuarial advice . . . . [16.158]
13 Utilisation of excess of assets . . . . [16.159]
14 Custody of assets . . . . [16.160]
15 Maintenance of accounting, valuation and other records . . . . [16.161]
16 Additional powers in relation to long-term business . . . . [16.162]
17 Accounts and audit . . . . [16.163]
18 Caution for long-term and other business . . . . [16.164]
19 Claims . . . . [16.165]
20 Failure to pay premiums . . . . [16.166]
21 Notice of valuation of policy . . . . [16.167]
22 Dividends to creditors . . . . [16.168]
23 Meetings of creditors . . . . [16.169]
24 Apportionment of expenses of liquidation . . . . [16.170]
25 Notice of stop order . . . . [16.171]

SCHEDULES

Schedule 1—Rules for Valuing General Business Policies . . . . . [16.172]
Schedule 2—Rules for Valuing Non-Linked Life Policies, Non-Linked Deferred Annuity Policies, Non-Linked Annuities in Payment, Unitised Non-Linked Policies and Capital Redemption Policies . . . . . [16.173]
Schedule 3—Rules for Valuing Life Policies and Deferred Annuity Policies which are Linked Policies. . . . . [16.174]
Schedule 4—Rules for Valuing Long-Term Policies which are not Dealt with in Schedules 2 or 3. . . . . [16.175]
Schedule 5—Rules for Valuing Long-Term Policies where a Stop Order has been Made . . . . [16.176]
Schedule 6—Form. . . . . [16.177]

[16.147]
1 Citation, commencement and revocation

(1) These Rules may be cited as the Insurers (Winding Up) (Scotland) Rules 2001 and shall come into force on 18th January 2002.

(2) The Insurance Companies (Winding Up) (Scotland) Rules 1986 are revoked.

[16.148]
2 Interpretation

(1) In these Rules, unless the context otherwise requires—

"the 1923 Act" means the Industrial Assurance Act 1923;

"the 1985 Act" means the Companies Act 1985;

"the 1986 Act" means the Insolvency Act 1986;

"the 2000 Act" means the Financial Services and Markets Act 2000;

"the Authority" means the [Financial Conduct Authority or the Prudential Regulation Authority];

"company" means an insurer which is being wound up;

"contract of general insurance" and "contract of long-term insurance" have the meaning given by article 3(1) of the Financial Services and Markets Act 2000 (Regulated Activities) Order 2001;

"excess of the long-term business assets" means the amount, if any, by which the value of the assets representing the fund or funds maintained by the company in respect of its long-term business as at the liquidation date exceeds the value as at that date of the liabilities of the company attributable to that business;

"excess of the other business assets" means the amount, if any, by which the value of the assets of the company which do not represent the fund or funds maintained by the company in respect of its long-term business as at the liquidation date exceeds the value as at that date of the liabilities of the company (other than liabilities in respect of share capital) which are not attributable to that business;

"Financial Services Compensation Scheme" means the scheme established under section 213 of the 2000 Act;

"general business" means the business of effecting or carrying out a contract of general insurance;

"the Industrial Assurance Acts" means the 1923 Act and the Industrial Assurance and Friendly Societies Act 1948;

"insurer" has the meaning given by article 2 of the Financial Services and Markets Act 2000 (Insolvency) (Definition of "Insurer") Order 2001;

"linked liability" means any liability under a policy the effecting of which constitutes the carrying on of long-term business the amount of which is determined by reference to—

(a) the value of property of any description (whether or not specified in the policy),
(b) fluctuations in the value of such property,
(c) income from any such property, or
(d) fluctuations in an index of the value of such property;

"linked policy" means a policy which provides for linked liabilities, and a policy which when made provided for linked liabilities is deemed to be a linked policy even if the policy holder has elected to convert his rights under the policy so that at the liquidation date there are no longer linked liabilities under the policy;

"liquidation date" means the date of the winding-up order or the date on which a resolution for the winding up of the company is passed by the members of the company (or the policyholders in the case of a mutual insurance company) and, if both a winding-up order and a winding-up resolution have been made, the earlier date;

"long-term business" means the business of effecting or carrying out any contract of long-term insurance;

"non-linked policy" means a policy which is not a linked policy;

"other business", in relation to a company carrying on long-term business, means such of the business of the company as is not long-term business; "the principal rules" means the Insolvency (Scotland) Rules 1986;

"stop order", in relation to a company, means an order of the court, made under section 376(2) of the 2000 Act, ordering the liquidator to stop carrying on the long-term business of the company;

"unit" in relation to a policy means any unit (whether or not described as a unit in the policy) by reference to the numbers and the value of which the amount of the liabilities under the policy at any time is measured.

(2) Unless the context otherwise requires, words or expressions contained in these Rules bear the same meaning as in the principal rules, the 1986 Act, the 2000 Act or any statutory modification thereof respectively.

NOTES

Para (1): words in square brackets in definition "the Authority" substituted by the Financial Services Act 2012 (Consequential Amendments and Transitional Provisions) Order 2013, SI 2013/472, art 3, Sch 2, para 74.

Industrial Assurance Act 1923: repealed with savings by the Financial Services and Markets Act 2000, ss 416(1)(a), 432(3), Sch 22.

Industrial Assurance and Friendly Societies Act 1948: repealed with savings by the Financial Services and Markets Act 2000, ss 416(1)(a), 432(3), Sch 22.

[16.149]
3 Application

(1) These Rules apply in relation to an insurer which the courts in Scotland have jurisdiction to wind up.

(2) These Rules apply to proceedings for the winding up of such an insurer which commence on or after the date on which these Rules come into force.

(3) These Rules supplement the principal rules which also apply to the proceedings in the winding up of such an insurer under the 1986 Act as they apply to proceedings in the winding up of any company under that Act; but in the event of a conflict between these Rules and the principal rules these Rules prevail.

[16.150]
4 Financial Services Compensation Scheme

In any proceedings for the appointment of a liquidator by the court under—

(a) section 139(4) of the 1986 Act (appointment of liquidator where conflict between creditors and contributories), or

(b) section 140 of that Act (appointment of liquidator following administration or voluntary arrangement),

the manager of the Financial Services Compensation Scheme shall be entitled to appear and make representations as to the person to be appointed.

[16.151]
[5 Maintenance of separate financial records for long-term and other business in winding up

(1) This rule applies in the case of a company carrying on long-term business in whose case no stop order has been made.

(2) The liquidator shall prepare and keep separate financial records in respect of the long-term business and the other business of the company.

(3) Paragraphs (4) and (5) apply in the case of a company to which this rule applies which also carries on permitted general business ('a hybrid insurer').

(4) Where, before the liquidation date, a hybrid insurer has, or should properly have, apportioned the assets and liabilities attributable to its permitted general business to its long term business for the purposes of any accounts, those assets and liabilities must be apportioned to its long term business for the purposes of complying with paragraph (2) of this rule.

(5) Where, before the liquidation date, a hybrid insurer has, or should properly have, apportioned the assets and liabilities attributable to its permitted general business other than to its long term business for the purposes of any accounts, those assets and liabilities must be apportioned to its other business for the purposes of complying with paragraph (2) of this rule.

(6) Regulation 10 of the general regulations (financial records) applies only in relation to the company's other business.

(7) In relation to the long-term business, the liquidator shall, with a view to the long-term business of the company being transferred to another insurer, maintain such accounting, valuation and other records as will enable such other insurer upon the transfer being effected to comply with the requirements of any rules made by the Authority under [Part 9A] of the 2000 Act relating to accounts and statements of insurers.

(8) In paragraphs (4) and (5)—

(a) "accounts" means any accounts or statements maintained by the company in compliance with a requirement under the Companies Act 1985 or any rules made by the Authority under [Part 9A] of the 2000 Act;

(b) "permitted general business" means the business of effecting or carrying out a contract of general insurance where the risk insured against relates to either accident or sickness.]

NOTES

Substituted by the Insurers (Reorganisation and Winding Up) Regulations 2003, SI 2003/1102, regs 52, 53(2).

Paras (7), (8): words in square brackets substituted by the Financial Services Act 2012 (Consequential Amendments and Transitional Provisions) Order 2013, SI 2013/472, art 5.

[16.152]
6 Valuation of general business policies

Except in relation to amounts which have fallen due for payment before the liquidation date and liabilities referred to in paragraph 2(1)(b) of Schedule 1, the holder of a general business policy shall be accepted as a creditor in relation to his policy, without submitting or lodging a claim, for an amount equal to the value of the policy and for this purpose the value of a policy shall be determined in accordance with Schedule 1.

[16.153]
7 Valuation of long-term policies

(1) This rule applies in relation to a company's long-term business where no stop order has been made.

(2) In relation to a claim under a policy which has fallen due for payment before the liquidation date, a policy holder shall be accepted as a creditor, without submitting or lodging a claim, for such amount as appears from the records of the company to be due in respect of that claim.

(3) In all other respects a policy holder shall be accepted as a creditor in relation to his policy, without submitting or lodging a claim, for an amount equal to the value of the policy and for this purpose the value of a policy of any class shall be determined in the manner applicable to policies of that class provided by Schedules 2, 3 and 4.

(4) This rule applies in relation to a person entitled to apply for a free paid-up policy under section 24 of the 1923 Act (provisions as to forfeited policies) and to whom no such policy has been issued before the liquidation date (whether or not it was applied for) as if such a policy had been issued immediately before the liquidation date—

(a) for the minimum amount determined in accordance with section 24(2) of the 1923 Act, or

(b) if the liquidator is satisfied that it was the practice of the company during the five years immediately before the liquidation date to issue policies under that section in excess of the minimum amounts so determined, for the amount determined in accordance with that practice.

[16.154]
8 Valuation of long-term policies: stop order made

(1) This rule applies in relation to a company's long-term business where a stop order has been made.

(2) In relation to a claim under a policy which has fallen due for payment on or after the liquidation date and before the date of the stop order, a policy holder shall be accepted as a creditor, without submitting or lodging a claim, for such amount as appears from the records of the company and of the liquidator to be due in respect of that claim.

(3) In all other respects a policy holder shall be accepted as a creditor in relation to his policy, without submitting or lodging a claim, for an amount equal to the value of the policy and for this purpose the value of a policy of any class shall be determined in the manner applicable to the policies of that class provided by Schedule 5.

(4) Paragraph (4) of rule 7 applies for the purposes of this rule as if references to the liquidation date (other than that in sub-paragraph (b) of that paragraph) were references to the date of the stop order.

[16.155]
9 Attribution of liabilities to company's long-term business

(1) This rule applies in the case of a company carrying on long-term business if at the liquidation date there are liabilities of the company in respect of which it is not clear from the accounting and other records of the company whether they are or are not attributable to the company's long-term business.

(2) The liquidator shall, in such manner and according to such accounting principles as he shall determine, identify the liabilities referred to in paragraph (1) as attributable or not attributable to a company's long-term business and those liabilities shall for the purposes of the winding up be deemed as at the liquidation date to be so attributable or not as the case may be.

(3) For the purposes of paragraph (2) the liquidator may—

(a) determine that some liabilities are attributable to the company's long-term business and that others are not (the first method); or

(b) determine that a part of a liability shall be attributable to the company's long-term business and that the remainder of the liability is not (the second method),

and he may use the first method for some of the liabilities and the second method for the remainder of them.

(4) Notwithstanding anything in the preceding paragraphs of this rule, the court may order that the determination of which (if any) of the liabilities referred to in paragraph (1) are attributable to the company's long-term business and which (if any) are not shall be made in such manner and by such methods as the court may direct or the court may itself make the determination.

[16.156]
10 Attribution of assets to company's long-term business

(1) This rule applies in the case of a company carrying on long-term business if at the liquidation date there are assets of the company in respect of which—

(a) it is not clear from the accounting and other records of the company whether they do or do not represent the fund or funds maintained by the company in respect of its long-term business, and

(b) it cannot be inferred from the source of the income out of which those assets were provided whether they do or do not represent those funds.

(2) Subject to paragraph (6) the liquidator shall determine which (if any) of the assets referred to in paragraph (1) are attributable to those funds and which (if any) are not and those assets shall, for the purposes of the winding up, be deemed as at the liquidation date to represent those funds or not in accordance with the liquidator's determination.

(3) For the purposes of paragraph (2) the liquidator may—

(a) determine that some of those assets shall be attributable to those funds and that others of them shall not (the first method); or

(b) determine that a part of the value of one of those assets shall be attributable to those funds and that the remainder of that value shall not (the second method),

and he may use the first method for some of those assets and the second method for others of them.

(4)

(a) In making the attribution the liquidator's objective shall in the first instance be so far as possible to reduce any deficit that may exist, at the liquidation date and before any attribution is made, either in the company's long-term business or in its other business.

(b) If there is a deficit in both the company's long-term business and its other business the attribution shall be in the ratio that the amount of the one deficit bears to the amount of the other until the deficits are eliminated.

(c) Thereafter the attribution shall be in the ratio which the aggregate amount of the liabilities attributable to the company's long-term business bears to the aggregate amount of the liabilities not so attributable.

(5) For the purposes of paragraph (4) the value of a liability of the company shall, if it falls to be valued under rule 6 or 7, have the same value as it has under that rule but otherwise it shall have such value as would have been included in relation to it in a balance sheet of the company prepared in accordance with the 1985 Act as at the liquidation date; and, for the purpose of determining the ratio referred to in paragraph (4) but not for the purpose of determining the amount of any deficit therein referred to, the net balance of the shareholders' funds shall be included in the liabilities not attributable to the company's long-term business.

(6) Notwithstanding anything in the preceding paragraphs of this rule, the court may order that the determination of which (if any) of the assets referred to in paragraph (1) are attributable to the fund or funds maintained by the company in respect of its long-term business and which (if any) are not shall be made in such manner and by such methods as the court may direct or the court may itself make the determination.

[16.157]
11 Excess of long-term business assets

(1) Where the company is one carrying on long-term business [and in whose case no stop order has been made], for the purpose of determining the amount, if any, of the excess of the long-term business assets, there shall be included amongst the liabilities of the company attributable to its long-term business an amount determined by the liquidator in respect of liabilities and expenses likely to be incurred in connection with the transfer of the company's long-term business as a going concern to another insurance company being liabilities not included in the valuation of the long-term policies made in pursuance of rule 7.

(2) Where the liquidator is carrying on the long-term business of an insurer with a view to that business being transferred as a going concern to a person or persons ("the transferee") who may lawfully carry out those contracts (or substitute policies being issued by another insurer), the liquidator may, in addition to any amounts paid by the Financial Services Compensation Scheme for the benefit of the transferee to secure such a transfer or to procure substitute policies being issued, pay to the transferee or other insurer all or part of such funds or assets as are attributable to the long-term business being transferred or substituted.

NOTES

Para (1): words in square brackets inserted by the Insurers (Reorganisation and Winding Up) Regulations 2003, SI 2003/1102, regs 52, 54.

[16.158]
12 Actuarial advice

(1) Before—

(a) determining the value of a policy in accordance with Schedules 1 to 5 (other than paragraph 3 of Schedule 1);

(b) identifying long-term liabilities and assets in accordance with rules 9 and 10;

(c) determining the amount (if any) of the excess of the long-term business assets in accordance with rule 11;

(d) determining the terms on which he will accept payment of overdue premiums under rule 20(1) or the amount and nature of any recompense under rule 20(2);

the liquidator shall obtain and consider advice thereon (including an estimate of any value or amount required to be determined) from an actuary.

(2) Before seeking, for the purpose of valuing a policy, the direction of the court as to the assumption of a particular rate of interest or the employment of any rates of mortality or disability, the liquidator shall obtain and consider advice thereon from an actuary.

[16.159]
13 Utilisation of excess of assets

(1) Except at the direction of the court, no distribution may be made out of and no transfer to another insurer may be made of—

(a) any part of the excess of the long-term business assets which has been transferred to the other business; or

(b) any part of the excess of the other business assets, which has been transferred to the long-term business.

(2) Before giving a direction under paragraph (1) the court may require the liquidator to advertise the proposal to make a distribution or a transfer in such manner as the court shall direct.

[16.160]
14 Custody of assets

(1) The Secretary of State may, in the case of a company carrying on long-term business in whose case no stop order has been made, require that the whole or a specified proportion of the assets representing the fund or funds maintained by the company in respect of its long-term business shall be held by a person approved by him for the purpose as trustee for the company.

(2) No assets held by a person as trustee for a company in compliance with a requirement imposed under this rule shall, so long as the requirement is in force, be released except with the consent of the Secretary of State but they may be transposed by the trustee into other assets by any transaction or series of transactions on the written instructions of the liquidator.

(3) The liquidator may not, except with the consent of the Secretary of State, grant any security over assets which are held by a person as trustee for the company in compliance with a requirement imposed under this rule.

[16.161]
15 Maintenance of accounting, valuation and other records

The liquidator of a company carrying on long-term business in whose case no stop order has been made shall, with a view to the long-term business of the company being transferred to another insurance company, maintain such accounting, valuation and other records as will enable such other insurer upon the transfer being effected to comply with the requirements of any rules made by the Authority under [Part 9A] of the 2000 Act relating to accounts and statements of insurers.

NOTES

Words in square brackets substituted by the Financial Services Act 2012 (Consequential Amendments and Transitional Provisions) Order 2013, SI 2013/472, art 5.

[16.162]
16 Additional powers in relation to long-term business

The liquidator of a company carrying on long-term business shall, so long as no stop order has been made, have power to do all such things as may be necessary to the performance of his duties under section 376(2) of the 2000 Act (continuation of contracts of long-term insurance where insurer in liquidation) but the Secretary of State may require him—

(a) not to make investments of a specified class or description,

(b) to realise, before the expiration of a specified period, the whole or a specified proportion of investments of a specified class or description held by the liquidator.

[16.163]
17 Accounts and audit

(1) The liquidator of a company carrying on long-term business in whose case no stop order has been made shall supply the Secretary of State, at such times or intervals as he may specify, with such accounts as he may specify and audited in such manner as he may require and with such information about specified matters and verified in such specified manner as he may require.

(2) The liquidator of such a company shall, if required to do so by the Secretary of State, instruct an actuary to investigate the financial condition of the company's long-term business and to report thereon in such manner as the Secretary of State may specify.

[16.164]
18 Caution for long-term and other business

Where a company carries on long-term business and—

(a) no stop order has been made; and

(b) a special manager has been appointed,

rule 4.70 of the principal rules (caution) applies separately to the company's long-term business and to its other business.

[16.165]
19 Claims

(1) This rule applies to a company carrying on long-term business [in whose case no stop order has been made].

(2) The liquidator may, in relation to the long-term business of the company and to its other business, fix different days on or before which the creditors of the company, who are required to submit or lodge claims, are to do so and he may fix one of those days without at the same time fixing the other.

(3) In submitting or lodging a claim, a creditor may claim the whole or part of such claim as attributable to the long-term business of the company or to its other business or he may make no such attribution.

(4) When he accepts any claim, in whole or in part, the liquidator shall state in writing how much of what he accepts is attributable to the long-term business of the company and how much to the other business of the company.

NOTES

Para (1): words in square brackets inserted by the Insurers (Reorganisation and Winding Up) Regulations 2003, SI 2003/1102, regs 52, 55.

[16.166]
20 Failure to pay premiums

(1) The liquidator may in the course of carrying on the company's long-term business and on such terms as he thinks fit accept payment of a premium even though the payment is tendered after the date on which under the terms of the policy it was finally due to be paid.

(2) The liquidator may in the course of carrying on the company's long-term business, and having regard to the general practice of insurers, compensate a policy holder whose policy has lapsed in consequence of a failure to pay any premium by issuing a free paid-up policy for reduced benefits or otherwise as the liquidator thinks fit.

[16.167]
21 Notice of valuation of policy

(1) Before paying a dividend in respect of claims other than under contracts of long-term insurance, the liquidator shall give notice of the value of each general business policy, as determined by him in accordance with rule 6, to the persons appearing from the records of the company or otherwise to be entitled to an interest in that policy and he shall do so in such manner as the court may direct.

(2) Before paying a dividend in respect of claims under contracts of long-term insurance and where a stop order has not been made in relation to the company, the liquidator shall give notice to the persons appearing from the records of the company or otherwise to be entitled to a payment under or to an interest in a long-term policy of the amount of that payment or the value of that policy as determined by him in accordance with rule 7(2) or (3), as the case may be.

(3) If a stop order is made in relation to the company, the liquidator shall give notice to all the persons appearing from the records of the company or otherwise to be entitled to a payment under or to an interest in a long-term policy of the amount of that payment or the value of that policy as determined by him in accordance with rule 8(2) or (3), as the case may be, and he shall give that notice in such manner as the court may direct.

(4) Any person to whom notice is so given shall be bound by the value so determined unless and until the court otherwise orders.

(5) Paragraphs (2) and (3) of this rule have effect as though references therein to persons appearing to be entitled to an interest in a long-term policy and to the value of that policy included, respectively, references to persons appearing to be entitled to apply for a free paid-up policy under section 24 of the 1923 Act and to the value of that entitlement under rule 7 (in the case of paragraph (2) of this rule) or under rule 8 (in the case of paragraph (3) of this rule).

(6) Where the liquidator summons a meeting of creditors in respect of liabilities of the company [attributable to either or both] attributable either to its long-term business or other business, he may adopt any valuation carried out in accordance with rules 6, 7 or 8 as the case may be or, if no such valuation has been carried out by the time of the meeting, he may conduct the meeting using such estimates of the value of policies as he thinks fit.

NOTES

Para (6): words in square brackets substituted by the Insurers (Reorganisation and Winding Up) Regulations 2003, SI 2003/1102, regs 52, 56.

[16.168]
22 Dividends to creditors

(1) This rule applies in the case of a company carrying on long-term business.

(2) The procedure for payment of dividends to creditors under Chapter 9 of Part 4 of the principal rules (distribution of company's assets by liquidator) applies separately in relation to the two separate companies assumed for the purposes of rule 5 above.

(3) The court may, at any time before the making of a stop order, permit a dividend to be declared and paid on such terms as it thinks fit in respect only of debts which fell due for payment before the liquidation date or, in the case of claims under long-term policies, which have fallen due for payment on or after the liquidation date.

[16.169]
23 Meetings of creditors

[(1) In the case of a company carrying on long-term business in whose case no stop order has been made, the creditors entitled to participate in creditors' meetings may be—

(a) in relation to the long-term business assets of the company, only those who are creditors in respect of liabilities attributable to the long-term business of the company; and

(b) in relation to the other business assets of the company, only those who are creditors in respect of liabilities attributable to the other business of the company.

(1A) In a case where separate general meetings of the creditors are summoned by the liquidator pursuant to—

(a) paragraph (1) above; or

(b) [regulation 28 of the Insurers (Reorganisation and Winding Up) Regulations 2004] (composite insurers: general meetings of creditors),

chapter 4 (meetings of creditors) and rule 4.31 (final meeting) of Part 4 and Chapters 1 and 2 of Part 7 (meetings and proxies and company representation) of the principal rules apply to each such separate meeting.]

(2) In relation to any such separate meeting—

(a) rule 7.6(6) of the principal rules (meetings requisitioned) has effect as if the reference therein to assets of the company was a reference to the assets available under the above-mentioned Regulations for meeting the liabilities of the company owed to the creditors summoned to the meeting, and

(b) rule 7.12 of the principal rules (resolutions) applies as if the reference therein to value in relation to a creditor who is not, by virtue of rule 6, 7 or 8, required to submit or lodge a claim, was a reference to the value most recently notified to him under rule 21 above or, if the court has determined a different value in accordance with rule 21(4), as if it were a reference to that different value.

[(3) In paragraph (1)—

"long-term business assets" means the assets representing the fund or funds maintained by the company in respect of its long-term business;

"other business assets" means any assets of the company which are not long-term business assets.]

NOTES

Para (1): substituted, together with para (1A), for original para (1), by the Insurers (Reorganisation and Winding Up) Regulations 2003, SI 2003/1102, regs 52, 57(4), (5).

Para (1A): substituted as noted to para (1); words in square brackets substituted by the Insurers (Reorganisation and Winding Up) Regulations 2004, SI 2004/353, reg 51(1), (3).

Para (3): inserted by SI 2003/1102, regs 52, 57(4), (6).

[16.170]
24 Apportionment of expenses of liquidation

(1) [Where no stop order has been made in relation to a company, Rule 4.67] of the principal rules (appointment and remuneration) applies separately to the assets of the long-term business of the company and to the assets of the other business of the company.

(2) Where any fee, expense, cost, charge, outlay or remuneration does not relate exclusively to the assets of the company's long-term business or to the assets of the company's other business, the liquidator shall apportion it amongst those assets in such manner as he shall determine.

NOTES

Para (1): words in square brackets substituted by the Insurers (Reorganisation and Winding Up) Regulations 2003, SI 2003/1102, regs 52, 58(2).

[16.171]
25 Notice of stop order

(1) When a stop order has been made in relation to the company, the clerk of court shall, on the same day, send—

(a) to the liquidator,

(b) to the registrar of companies for Scotland, and

(c) to such other person as the court may direct,

a certified copy of the stop order.

(2) The liquidator shall forthwith after receiving a certified copy give notice of the order in the Form in Schedule 6—

(a) in the Edinburgh Gazette, and

(b) in the newspaper in which the winding-up order was advertised.

SCHEDULES

SCHEDULE 1
RULES FOR VALUING GENERAL BUSINESS POLICIES

Rule 6

[16.172]

1. (1) This paragraph applies in relation to periodic payments under a general business policy which fall due for payment after the liquidation date where the event giving rise to the liability to make the payments occurred before the liquidation date.

(2) The value to be attributed to such periodic payments shall be determined on such actuarial principles and assumptions in regard to all relevant factors as the court shall direct.

2. (1) This paragraph applies in relation to liabilities under a general business policy which arise from events which occurred before the liquidation date but which have not—

(a) fallen due for payment before the liquidation date; or

(b) been notified to the company before the liquidation date.

(2) The value to be attributed to such liabilities shall be determined on such actuarial principles and assumptions in regard to all relevant factors as the court shall direct.

3. (1) This paragraph applies in relation to liabilities under a general business policy not dealt with by paragraphs 1 or 2.

(2) The value to be attributed to those liabilities shall—

(a) if the terms of the policy provide for a repayment of premium upon the early termination of the policy or the policy is expressed to run from one definite date to another or the policy may be terminated by any of the parties with effect from a definite date, be the greater of the following two amounts:

(i) the amount (if any) which under the terms of the policy would have been repayable on early termination of the policy had the policy terminated on the liquidation date, and

(ii) where the policy is expressed to run from one definite date to another or may be terminated by any of the parties with effect from a definite date, such proportion of the last premium paid as is proportionate to the unexpired portion of the period in respect of which that premium was paid; and

(b) in any other case, be a just estimate of that value.

SCHEDULE 2
RULES FOR VALUING NON-LINKED LIFE POLICIES, NON-LINKED DEFERRED ANNUITY POLICIES, NON-LINKED ANNUITIES IN PAYMENT, UNITISED NON-LINKED POLICIES AND CAPITAL REDEMPTION POLICIES

Rule 7

[16.173]

1 General

In valuing a policy—

(a) where it is necessary to calculate the present value of future payments by or to the company, interest shall be assumed at such fair and reasonable rate or rates as the court may direct;

(b) where relevant, the rates of mortality and the rates of disability to be employed shall be such rates as the court considers appropriate after taking into account:

(i) relevant published tables of rates of mortality and rates of disability, and

(ii) the rates of mortality and the rates of disability experienced in connection with similar policies issued by the company;

(c) there shall be determined:

(i) the present value of the ordinary benefits,

(ii) the present value of additional benefits;

(iii the present value of options, and

(iv) if further premiums fall due to be paid under the policy on or after the liquidation date, the present value of the premiums;

and for the purposes of this Schedule if the ordinary benefits only take into account premiums paid to date, the present value of future premiums shall be taken as nil.

2 Present value of the ordinary benefits

(1) Ordinary benefits are the benefits which will become payable to the policy holder on or after the liquidation date without his having to exercise any option under the policy (including any bonus or addition to the sum assured or the amount of annuity declared before the liquidation date) and for this purpose "option" includes a right to surrender the policy.

(2) Subject to sub-paragraph (3), the present value of the ordinary benefits shall be the value at the liquidation date of the reversion in the ordinary benefits according to the contingency upon which those benefits are payable calculated on the basis of the rates of interest, mortality and disability referred to in paragraph 1.

(3) For accumulating with profits policies—

(a) where the benefits are not expressed in the form of units in a with-profits fund, the value of the ordinary benefits is the amount that would have been payable, excluding any discretionary additions, if the policyholder had been able to exercise a right to terminate the policy at the liquidation date; and

(b) where the benefits are expressed in the form of units in a with-profits fund, the value of the ordinary benefits is the number of units held by the policy holder at the liquidation date valued at the unit price in force at that time or, if that price is not calculated on a daily basis, such price as the court may determine having regard to the last published unit price and any change in the value of assets attributable to the fund since the date of the last published unit price.

(4) Where—

(a) sub-paragraph (3) applies, and

(b) paragraph 3(1) of Schedule 3 applies to the calculation of the unit price (or as the case may be) the fund value,

the value shall be adjusted on the basis set out in paragraph 3(3) to (5) of Schedule 3.

(5) Where sub-paragraph (3) applies, the value may be further adjusted by reference to the value of the assets underlying the unit price (or as the case may be) the value of the fund, if the liquidator considers such an adjustment to be necessary.

3 Present value of additional benefits

(1) Where under the terms of the policy or on the basis of the company's established practice the policy holder has a right to receive or an expectation of receiving benefits additional to the minimum benefits guaranteed under those terms, the court shall determine rates of interest, bonus (whether reversionary, terminal or any other type of bonus used by the company), mortality and disability to provide for the present value (if any) of that right or expectation.

(2) In determining what (if any) value to attribute to any such expectations the court shall have regard to the premium payable in relation to the minimum guaranteed benefits and the amount (if any) an insurer is required to provide in respect of those expectations in any rules made by the Authority under [Part 9A] of the 2000 Act.

4 Present value of options

The amount of the present value of options shall be the amount which, in the opinion of the liquidator, is necessary to be provided at the liquidation date (in addition to the amount of the present value of the ordinary benefits) to cover the additional liabilities likely to arise upon the exercise on or after that date by the policy holder of any option conferred upon him by the terms of the policy or, in the case of an industrial assurance policy, by the Industrial Assurance Acts other than an option whereby the policy holder can secure a guaranteed cash payment within the period of 12 months beginning with that date.

5 Present value of premiums

The present value of the premiums shall be the value at the liquidation date of the premiums which fall due to be paid by the policy holder after the liquidation date calculated on the basis of the rates of interest, mortality and disability referred to in paragraph 1.

6 Value of the policy

(1) Subject to sub-paragraph (2)—

(a) if no further premiums fall due to be paid under the policy on or after the liquidation date, the value of the policy shall be the aggregate of:

(i) the present value of the ordinary benefits;

(ii) the present value of options; and

(iii) the present value of additional benefits;

(b) if further premiums fall due to be so paid and the aggregate value referred to in sub-paragraph (a) exceeds the present value of the premiums, the value of the policy shall be the amount of that excess; and

(c) if further premiums fall due to be so paid and that aggregate does not exceed the present value of the premiums, the policy shall have no value.

(2) Where the policy holder has a right conferred upon him by the terms of the policy or by the Industrial Assurance Acts whereby the policy holder can secure a guaranteed cash payment within the period of 12 months beginning with the liquidation date, the liquidator shall determine the amount which in his opinion it is necessary to provide at that date to cover the liabilities which will accrue when that option is exercised (on the assumption that it will be exercised) and the value of the policy shall be that amount if it exceeds the value of the policy (if any) determined in accordance with sub-paragraph (1).

NOTES

Para 3: words in square brackets substituted by the Financial Services Act 2012 (Consequential Amendments and Transitional Provisions) Order 2013, SI 2013/472, art 5.

SCHEDULE 3
RULES FOR VALUING LIFE POLICIES AND DEFERRED ANNUITY POLICIES WHICH ARE LINKED POLICIES

Rule 7

[16.174]

1. (1) Subject to sub-paragraph (2) the value of the policy shall be the aggregate of the value of the linked liabilities (calculated in accordance with paragraphs 2 or 4) and the value of other than linked liabilities (calculated in accordance with paragraph 5) except where that aggregate is a negative amount in which case the policy shall have no value.

(2) Where the terms of the policy include a right whereby the policy holder can secure a guaranteed cash payment within the period of 12 months beginning with the liquidation date then, if the amount which in the opinion of the liquidator is necessary to be provided at that date to cover any liabilities which will accrue when that option is exercised (on the assumption that it will be exercised) is greater than the value determined under sub-paragraph (1) of this paragraph, the value of the policy shall be that greater amount.

2. (1) Where the linked liabilities are expressed in terms of units the value of those liabilities shall, subject to paragraph 3, be the amount arrived at by taking the product of the number of units of each class of units allocated to the policy on the liquidation date and the value of each such unit on that date and then adding those products.

(2) For the purposes of sub-paragraph (1)—

(a) where under the terms of the policy the value of a unit at any time falls to be determined by reference to the value at that time of the assets of a particular fund maintained by the company in relation to that and other policies, the value of a unit on the liquidation date shall be determined by reference to the net realisable value of the assets credited to that fund on that date (after taking account of disposal costs, any tax liabilities resulting from the disposal of assets insofar as they have not already been provided for by the company and any other amounts which under the terms of those policies are chargeable to the fund), and

(b) in any other case, the value of a unit on the liquidation date shall be the value which would have been ascribed to each unit credited to the policy holder, after any deductions which may be made under the terms of the policy, for the purpose of determining the benefits payable under the policy on the liquidation date had the policy matured on that date.

3. (1) This paragraph applies where—

(a) paragraph 2(2)(a) applies and the company has a right under the terms of the policy either to make periodic withdrawals from the fund referred to in that paragraph or to retain any part of the income accruing in respect of the assets of that fund,

(b) paragraph 2(2)(b) applies and the company has a right under the terms of the policy to receive the whole or any part of any distributions made in respect of the units referred to in that paragraph, or

(c) paragraph 2(2)(a) or paragraph 2(2)(b) applies and the company has a right under the terms of the policy to make periodic cancellations of a proportion of the number of units credited to the policy.

(2) Where this paragraph applies, the value of the linked liabilities calculated in accordance with paragraph 2(1) shall be reduced by an amount calculated in accordance with sub-paragraph (3) of this paragraph.

(3) The said amount is—

(a) where this paragraph applies by virtue of head (a) or (b) of sub-paragraph (1), the value as at the liquidation date, calculated on actuarial principles, of the future income of the company in respect of the units in question arising from the rights referred to in head (a) or (b) of sub-paragraph (1) as the case may be, or

(b) where this paragraph applies by virtue of head (c) of sub-paragraph (1), the value as at the liquidation date, calculated on actuarial principles, of the liabilities of the company in respect of the units which fall to be cancelled in the future under the right referred to in head (c) of sub-paragraph (1).

(4) In calculating any amount in accordance with sub-paragraph (3) there shall be disregarded—

(a) such part of the rights referred to in the relevant head of sub-paragraph (1) which in the opinion of the liquidator constitutes appropriate provision for future expenses and mortality risks, and

(b) such part of those rights (if any) which the court considers to constitute appropriate provision for any right or expectation of the policy holder to receive benefits additional to the benefits guaranteed under the terms of the policy.

(5) In determining the said amount—

(a) interest shall be assumed at such rate or rates as the court may direct, and

(b) where relevant, the rates of mortality and the rates of disability to be employed shall be such rates as the court considers appropriate after taking into account:

(i) relevant published tables of rates of mortality and rates of disability, and

(ii) the rates of mortality and the rates of disability experienced in connection with similar policies issued by the company.

4. Where the linked liabilities are not expressed in terms of units the value of those liabilities shall be the value (subject to adjustment for any amounts which would have been deducted for taxation) which would have been ascribed to those liabilities had the policy matured on the liquidation date.

5. (1) The value of any liabilities other than linked liabilities including reserves for future expenses, options and guarantees shall he determined on actuarial principles and appropriate assumptions in regard to all relevant factors including the assumption of such rate or rates of interest, mortality and disability as the court may direct.

(2) In valuing liabilities under this paragraph credit shall be taken for those parts of future premiums which do not fall to be applied in the allocation of further units to the policy and for any rights of the company which have been disregarded under paragraph 3(4)(a) in valuing the linked liabilities.

SCHEDULE 4
RULES FOR VALUING LONG-TERM POLICIES WHICH ARE NOT DEALT WITH IN SCHEDULES 2 OR 3

Rule 7

[16.175]
The value of a long-term policy not covered by Schedule 2 or 3 shall be the value of the benefits due to the policy holder determined on such actuarial principles and assumptions in regard to all relevant factors as the court shall determine.

SCHEDULE 5
RULES FOR VALUING LONG-TERM POLICIES WHERE A STOP ORDER HAS BEEN MADE

Rule 8

[16.176]
1. Subject to paragraphs 2 and 3, in valuing a policy Schedules 2, 3 or 4 shall apply according to the class of that policy as if those Schedules were herein repeated but with a view to a fresh valuation of each policy on appropriate assumptions in regard to all relevant factors and subject to the following modifications—

(a) references to the stop order shall be substituted for references to the liquidation date,

(b) in paragraph 4 of Schedule 2 for the words "whereby the policy holder can secure a guaranteed cash payment within the period of 12 months beginning with that date" there shall be substituted the words "to surrender the policy which can be exercised on that date",

(c) paragraph 6(2) of Schedule 2 shall be deleted, and

(d) paragraph 1(2) of Schedule 3 shall be deleted.

2. (1) This paragraph applies where the policy holder has a right conferred upon him under the terms of the policy or by the Industrial Assurance Acts to surrender the policy and that right is exercisable on the date of the stop order.

(2) Where this paragraph applies and the amount required at the date of the stop order to provide for the benefits payable upon surrender of the policy (on the assumption that the policy is surrendered on the date of the stop order) is greater than the value of the policy determined in accordance with paragraph 1, the value of the policy shall, subject to paragraph 3, be the said amount so required.

(3) Where any part of the surrender value is payable after the date of the stop order, sub-paragraph (2) shall apply but the value therein referred to shall be discounted at such rate of interest as the court may direct.

3. (1) This paragraph applies in the case of a linked policy where—

(a) the terms of the policy include a guarantee that the amount assured will on maturity of the policy be worth a minimum amount calculable in money terms, or

(b) the terms of the policy include a right on the part of the policy holder to surrender the policy and a guarantee that the payment on surrender will be worth a minimum amount calculable in money terms and that right is exercisable on or after the date of the stop order.

(2) Where this paragraph applies the value of the policy shall be the greater of the following two amounts—

(a) the value the policy would have had at the date of the stop order had the policy been a non-linked policy, that is to say, had the linked liabilities provided by the policy not been so provided but the policy had otherwise been on the same terms, and

(b) the value the policy would have had at the date of the stop order had the policy not included any guarantees of payments on maturity or surrender worth a minimum amount calculable in money terms.

SCHEDULE 6
FORM

Rule 25

FORM

[16.177]
Notice of order made under section 376(2) of the Financial Services and Markets Act 2000 for cessation of long-term business

Name of Company . . . . Address of Registered Office

On . . . ., the Court . . . ., under section 376(2) of the Financial Services and Markets Act 2000, ordered the cessation of the long-term business of the above company.

Date

Signed . . . .

Liquidator

ENERGY ADMINISTRATION (SCOTLAND) RULES 2006

(SI 2006/772 (S 8))

NOTES

Made: 13 March 2006.
Authority: Insolvency Act 1986, s 411; Energy Act 2004, s 159.
Commencement: 6 April 2006.

ARRANGEMENT OF RULES

PART 1
CONSTRUCTION AND INTERPRETATION

1 Citation and commencement . . . . [16.178]
2 Construction and interpretation . . . . [16.179]
3 Application . . . . [16.180]

PART 2
APPOINTMENT OF ENERGY ADMINISTRATOR BY COURT

4 Form of application . . . . [16.181]
5 Service of petition . . . . [16.182]
6 Expenses . . . . [16.183]
7 Notice of dismissal of application for an energy administration order . . . . [16.184]

PART 3
PROCESS OF ENERGY ADMINISTRATION

8 Notification and advertisement of energy administrator's appointment . . . . [16.185]
9 Notice requiring statement of affairs . . . . [16.186]
10 Statements of affairs and statements of concurrence . . . . [16.187]
11 Limited disclosure . . . . [16.188]
12 Release from duty to submit statement of affairs; extension of time . . . . [16.189]
13 Expenses of statement of affairs . . . . [16.190]
14 Energy administrator's proposals . . . . [16.191]

PART 4
MEETINGS AND REPORTS

15 Meetings generally and notice . . . . [16.192]
16 Adjournment . . . . [16.193]
17 The chairman at meetings . . . . [16.194]
18 Quorum at meeting of creditors . . . . [16.195]
19 Chairman of meeting as proxy holder . . . . [16.196]
20 Meeting following nomination of alternative liquidator . . . . [16.197]
21 Entitlement to vote (creditors and members) . . . . [16.198]
22 Hire-purchase, conditional sale and hiring agreements . . . . [16.199]
23 Disposal of secured property . . . . [16.200]
24 Resolutions . . . . [16.201]
25 Report of Meeting . . . . [16.202]
26 Revision of the energy administrator's proposals . . . . [16.203]
27 Reports to creditors . . . . [16.204]

PART 5
CLAIMS IN ENERGY ADMINISTRATION

28 Submission of claims . . . . [16.205]
29 Secured debts . . . . [16.206]
30 Entitlement to vote and draw dividend . . . . [16.207]
31 Adjudication of claims . . . . [16.208]
32 Evidence in relation to claims . . . . [16.209]
33 Criminal offences in relation to false claims or evidence . . . . [16.210]
34 Amount which may be claimed generally . . . . [16.211]

35 Debts depending on contingency . . . [16.212]
36 Liabilities and rights of co-obligants . . . [16.213]
37 Claims in foreign currency . . . [16.214]

PART 6
DISTRIBUTION TO CREDITORS

38 Application of Part and general . . . [16.215]
39 Order of priority in distribution . . . [16.216]
40 Expenses of the energy administration . . . [16.217]
41 Assets to be distributed . . . [16.218]
42 Procedure after accounting period . . . [16.219]
43 Unclaimed Dividends. . . . [16.220]

PART 7
ENDING ENERGY ADMINISTRATION

44 Final progress reports . . . [16.221]
45 Application to court . . . [16.222]
46 Notification by energy administrator of court order . . . [16.223]
47 Moving from energy administration to creditors' voluntary liquidation . . . [16.224]
48 Moving from energy administration to dissolution . . . [16.225]
49 Provision of information to the Secretary of State . . . [16.226]

PART 8
REPLACING ENERGY ADMINISTRATOR

50 Grounds for resignation . . . [16.227]
51 Notice of intention to resign. . . . [16.228]
52 Notice of resignation . . . [16.229]
53 Application to court to remove energy administrator from office . . . [16.230]
54 Incapacity to act, through death or otherwise . . . [16.231]
55 Application to replace . . . [16.232]
56 Joint or concurrent appointments . . . [16.233]
57 Notification and advertisement of appointment of replacement energy administrator . . . [16.234]
58 Hand-over of assets to successor energy administrator. . . . [16.235]

PART 9
PRESCRIBED PART

59 Application under section 176A(5) of the 1986 Act to disapply section 176A of the 1986 Act . . . [16.236]
60 Notice of order under section 176A(5) of the 1986 Act . . . [16.237]

PART 10
PROXIES AND COMPANY REPRESENTATION

61 Definition of "proxy". . . . [16.238]
62 Form of proxy. . . . [16.239]
63 Use of proxy at meeting . . . [16.240]
64 Retention of proxies . . . [16.241]
65 Right of inspection . . . [16.242]
66 Proxy-holder with financial interest . . . [16.243]
67 Representation of corporations . . . [16.244]

PART 11
MISCELLANEOUS AND GENERAL

68 Giving of notices, etc . . . [16.245]
69 Sending by post. . . . [16.246]
70 Certificate of giving notice, etc . . . [16.247]
71 Validity of proceedings. . . . [16.248]
72 Evidence of proceedings at meetings. . . . [16.249]
73 Right to list of creditors and copy documents. . . . [16.250]
74 Confidentiality of documents . . . [16.251]
75 Energy administrator's caution . . . [16.252]
76 Punishment of offences . . . [16.253]
77 Forms for use in energy administration proceedings . . . [16.254]
78 Fees, expenses, etc . . . [16.255]
79 Power of court to cure defects in procedure. . . . [16.256]
80 Sederunt book. . . . [16.257]
81 Disposal of protected energy company's books, papers and other records. . . . [16.258]
82 Information about time spent on a case . . . [16.259]

SCHEDULES

Schedule—Forms . . . .[16.260]

PART 1
CONSTRUCTION AND INTERPRETATION

[16.178]

1 Citation and commencement

These Rules may be cited as the Energy Administration (Scotland) Rules 2006 and shall come into force on 6th April 2006.

[16.179]

2 Construction and interpretation

(1) In these Rules—

"the 1986 Act" means the Insolvency Act 1986;

"the 2004 Act" means the Energy Act 2004;

"administrative receiver" has the same meaning as in section 156(4) of the 2004 Act;

"the Companies Act" means the Companies Act 1985;

"GEMA" means the Gas and Electricity Markets Authority;

"insolvency proceedings" has the same meaning as in the Insolvency Rules;

"the Insolvency Rules" means the Insolvency (Scotland) Rules 1986;

"qualifying floating charge" has the same meaning as in paragraph 14(2) of Schedule B1 to the 1986 Act, without the modifications made by Schedule 20 to the 2004 Act;

"responsible insolvency practitioner" means, in relation to any insolvency proceedings, the person acting as supervisor of a voluntary arrangement under Part I of the 1986 Act, or as receiver, liquidator or provisional liquidator;

"the Rules" means the Energy Administration (Scotland) Rules 2006; and

"venue" means, in respect of any proceedings or meetings, the time, date and place for the proceedings or meeting.

(2) References to provisions of Schedule B1 to the 1986 Act are references to those provisions as modified and applied by Schedule 20 to the 2004 Act unless otherwise stated.

(3) References to other provisions of the 1986 Act are, where those provisions have been modified by Schedule 20 to the 2004 Act, references to those provisions as so modified.

(4) Where the protected energy company is a non GB company within the meaning of section 171 of the 2004 Act, references in these Rules to the affairs, business and property of the company are references only to its affairs and business so far as carried on in Great Britain and to its property in Great Britain unless otherwise stated.

(5) Where the protected energy company is an unregistered company, any requirement to send information to the registrar of companies applies only if the company is subject to a requirement imposed by virtue of section 691(1) or 718 of the Companies Act.

[16.180]

3 Application

The Rules apply in relation to protected energy companies which the courts in Scotland have jurisdiction to wind up.

PART 2
APPOINTMENT OF ENERGY ADMINISTRATOR BY COURT

[16.181]

4 Form of application

(1) Where an application is made by way of petition for an energy administration order to be made in relation to a protected energy company, there shall be lodged together with the petition a Statement of the Proposed Energy Administrator.

(2) In this Part, references to a Statement of the Proposed Energy Administrator are to a statement by each of the persons proposed to be energy administrator of a protected energy company, in the form required by Form EA1(S) stating—

(a) that he consents to accept appointment as energy administrator of that protected energy company; and

(b) details of any prior professional relationship that he has had with that company.

(3) Where an application is made by GEMA, it shall also state that it is made with the consent of the Secretary of State.

[16.182]

5 Service of petition

(1) In addition to those persons referred to in section 156(2)(a) to (c) of the 2004 Act, notice of a petition shall be given by the petitioner in Form EA2(S) to—

(a) an administrative receiver, if appointed;

(b) if there is pending an administration application under Schedule B1 to the 1986 Act, without the modifications made by Schedule 20 to the 2004 Act, the applicant;
(c) if a petition for the winding up of the protected energy company has been presented but no order for winding up has yet been made, the petitioner under that petition;
(d) any creditor who has served notice in accordance with section 164 of the 2004 Act of his intention to enforce his security over property of the protected energy company;
(e) a provisional liquidator, if appointed;
(f) the person proposed in the petition to be the energy administrator;
(g) if the applicant is the Secretary of State, GEMA;
(h) if the applicant is GEMA, the Secretary of State;
(i) the protected energy company;
(j) the registrar of companies;
(k) the Keeper of the Register of Inhibitions and Adjudications for recording in that register; and
(l) the supervisor of a voluntary arrangement under Part I of the 1986 Act, if such has been appointed.

(2) Notice of the petition shall also be given to the persons upon whom the court orders that the petition be served.

[16.183]
6 Expenses

If the court makes an energy administration order, the expenses of the petitioner, and of any other party whose expenses are allowed by the court, shall be regarded as expenses of the energy administration.

[16.184]
7 Notice of dismissal of application for an energy administration order

If the court dismisses the petition the petitioner shall as soon as reasonably practicable send notice of the court's order dismissing the petition to all those to whom the petition was notified under Rule 5 in Form EA3(S).

PART 3
PROCESS OF ENERGY ADMINISTRATION

[16.185]
8 Notification and advertisement of energy administrator's appointment

(1) As soon as is reasonably practicable, the energy administrator shall advertise his appointment, in Form EA4(S), once in the Edinburgh Gazette and once in a newspaper circulating in the area where the protected energy company has its principal place of business or in such newspaper as he thinks appropriate for ensuring that the order comes to the notice of the protected energy company's creditors.

(2) The energy administrator shall at the same time give notice of his appointment to the following persons—
(a) if the application for the energy administration order was made by the Secretary of State, to GEMA;
(b) if the application for the energy administration order was made by GEMA, to the Secretary of State;
(c) a receiver or an administrative receiver, if appointed;
(d) a petitioner in a petition for the winding up of the protected energy company, if that petition is pending;
(e) any provisional liquidator of the protected energy company, if appointed;
(f) any person who has applied to the court for an administration order under Schedule B1 to the 1986 Act, without the modifications made by Schedule 20 to the 2004 Act, in relation to the protected energy company;
(g) any supervisor of a voluntary arrangement under Part 1 of the 1986 Act;
(h) any holder of a qualifying floating charge who, to the energy administrator's knowledge, has served notice in accordance with section 163 of the 2004 Act that he is seeking to appoint an administrator;
(i) any creditor who, to the energy administrator's knowledge, has served notice in accordance with section 164 of the 2004 Act of his intention to enforce his security over property of the protected energy company; and
(j) the Keeper of the Register of Inhibitions and Adjudications for recording in that register.

(3) Where, under a provision of Schedule B1 to the 1986 Act or these Rules, the energy administrator is required to send a notice of his appointment to any person, he shall do so in Form EA5(S).

[16.186]
9 Notice requiring statement of affairs

(1) In this Part "relevant person" has the meaning given to it in paragraph 47(3) of Schedule B1 to the 1986 Act.

(2) The energy administrator shall send a notice in Form EA6(S) to each relevant person whom he determines appropriate requiring him to prepare and submit a statement of the protected energy company's affairs.

(3) The notice shall inform each of the relevant persons—
(a) of the names and addresses of all others (if any) to whom the same notice has been sent;

(b) of the time within which the statement must be delivered;
(c) of the effect of paragraph 48(4) of Schedule B1 to the 1986 Act (penalty for non compliance); and
(d) of the application to him, and to each other relevant person, of section 235 of the 1986 Act (duty to co-operate with office-holder).

(4) The energy administrator shall furnish each relevant person upon whom he has sent notice in Form EA6(S) with the forms required for the preparation of the statement of affairs.

[16.187]
10 Statements of affairs and statements of concurrence

(1) The statement of the protected energy company's affairs shall be in Form EA7(S), contain all the particulars required by that form and shall be a statutory declaration.

(2) Where more than one relevant person is required to submit a statement of affairs the energy administrator may require one or more such persons to submit, in place of a statement of affairs, a statement of concurrence in Form EA8(S); and where the energy administrator does so, he shall inform the person making the statement of affairs of that fact.

(3) The person making the statutory declaration in support of a statement of affairs shall send the statement, together with one copy thereof, to the energy administrator, and a copy of the statement to each of those persons whom the energy administrator has required to submit a statement of concurrence.

(4) A person required to submit a statement of concurrence shall deliver to the energy administrator the statement of concurrence, together with one copy thereof, before the end of the period of 5 business days (or such other period as the energy administrator may agree) beginning with the day on which the statement of affairs being concurred with is received by him.

(5) A statement of concurrence may be qualified in respect of matters dealt with in the statement of affairs, where the maker of the statement of concurrence is not in agreement with the statement of affairs, he considers that statement to be erroneous or misleading, or he is without the direct knowledge necessary for concurring with it.

(6) A statement of concurrence shall be a statutory declaration.

(7) Subject to Rule 11, the energy administrator shall—
(a) as soon as is reasonably practicable, file a copy of the statement of affairs and any statement of concurrence with the registrar of companies in Form EA9(S), and
(b) insert any statement of affairs submitted to him, together with any statement of concurrence, in the sederunt book.

[16.188]
11 Limited disclosure

(1) Where the energy administrator thinks that it would prejudice the conduct of the energy administration for the whole or part of the statement of the protected energy company's affairs to be disclosed, he may apply to the court for an order of limited disclosure in respect of the statement, or any specified part of it.

(2) The court may order that the statement or, as the case may be, the specified part of it, shall not be filed with the registrar of companies or entered in the sederunt book.

(3) The energy administrator shall as soon as reasonably practicable file a copy of that order with the registrar of companies, and shall place a copy of the order in the sederunt book.

(4) If a creditor seeks disclosure of the statement of affairs or a specified part of it in relation to which an order has been made under this Rule, he may apply to the court for an order that the energy administrator disclose it or a specified part of it.

(5) The court may attach to an order for disclosure any conditions as to confidentiality, duration and scope of the order in any material change of circumstances, and other matters as it sees fit.

(6) If there is a material change in circumstances rendering the limit on disclosure unnecessary, the energy administrator shall, as soon as reasonably practicable after the change, apply to the court for the order to be discharged or varied; and upon the discharge or variation of the order the energy administrator shall, as soon as reasonably practicable—
(a) file a copy of the full statement of affairs (or so much of the statement of affairs as is no longer subject to the order) with the registrar of companies;
(b) where he has previously sent a copy of his proposals to the creditors in accordance with paragraph 49 of Schedule B1 to the 1986 Act, provide the creditors with a copy of the full statement of affairs (or so much of the statement as is no longer subject to the order) or a summary thereof; and
(c) place a copy of the full statement of affairs (or so much of the statement as is no longer subject to the order) in the sederunt book.

[16.189]
12 Release from duty to submit statement of affairs; extension of time

(1) The power of the energy administrator under paragraph 48(2) of Schedule B1 to the 1986 Act to revoke a requirement under paragraph 47(1) of Schedule B1 to the 1986 Act, or to grant an extension of time, may be exercised at the energy administrator's own instance, or at the request of any relevant person.

(2) A relevant person whose request under this Rule has been refused by the energy administrator may apply to the court for a release or extension of time.

(3) An applicant under this Rule shall bear his own expenses in the application and, unless the court otherwise orders, no allowance towards such expenses shall be made out of the assets of the protected energy company.

[16.190]
13 Expenses of statement of affairs

(1) A relevant person who provides to the energy administrator a statement of the protected energy company's affairs or statement of concurrence shall be allowed, and paid by the energy administrator out of his receipts, any expenses incurred by the relevant person in so doing which the energy administrator considers reasonable.

(2) Any decision by the energy administrator under this Rule is subject to appeal to the court.

(3) Nothing in this Rule relieves a relevant person from any obligation to provide a statement of affairs or statement of concurrence, or to provide information to the energy administrator.

[16.191]
14 Energy administrator's proposals

(1) The statement required to be made by the energy administrator under paragraph 49 of Schedule B1 to the 1986 Act shall include, in addition to the matters set out in that paragraph—

(a) details of the court which granted the energy administration order and the relevant court reference number (if any);

(b) the full name, registered address, registered number and any other trading names of the protected energy company;

(c) details relating to his appointment as energy administrator, including the date of appointment and whether the application was made by the Secretary of State or GEMA and, where there are joint energy administrators, details of the matters set out in section 158(5) of the 2004 Act;

(d) the names of the directors and secretary of the protected energy company and details of any shareholdings which they have in the protected energy company;

(e) an account of the circumstances giving rise to the appointment of the energy administrator;

(f) if a statement of the protected energy company's affairs has been submitted, a copy or summary of it, with the energy administrator's comments, if any;

(g) if an order limiting the disclosure of the statement of affairs has been made, a statement of that fact, as well as—

(i) details of who provided the statement of affairs;

(ii) the date of the order of limited disclosure; and

(iii) the details or a summary of the details that are not subject to that order;

(h) if a full statement of affairs is not provided, the names and addresses of the creditors, and details of the debts owed to, and security held by, each of them;

(i) if no statement of affairs has been submitted—

(i) details of the financial position of the protected energy company at the latest practicable date (which must, unless the court otherwise orders, be a date not earlier than that on which the protected energy company entered energy administration);

(ii) the names and addresses of the creditors, and details of the debts owed to, and security held by, each of them; and

(iii) an explanation as to why there is no statement of affairs;

(j) except where the energy administrator proposes a voluntary arrangement in relation to the protected energy company—

(i) to the best of the energy administrator's knowledge and belief—

(aa) an estimate of the value of the prescribed part (whether or not he proposes to make an application to the court under section 176A(5) of the 1986 Act and whether or not section 176A(3) of the 1986 Act applies); and

(bb) an estimate of the value of the protected energy company's net property,

provided that such estimates shall not be required to include any information the disclosure of which could seriously prejudice the commercial interests of the protected energy company, but if such information is excluded the estimates shall be accompanied by a statement to that effect; and

(ii) whether and, if so, why the energy administrator proposes to make an application to the court under section 176A(5) of the 1986 Act;

(k) how it is envisaged the objective of the energy administration will be achieved and how it is proposed that the energy administration shall end;

(l) where a creditors' voluntary liquidation is proposed—

(i) details of the proposed liquidator; and

(ii) a statement that, in accordance with paragraph 83(7) of Schedule B1 to the 1986 Act and Rule 47(3), creditors may nominate a different person to act as liquidator, provided that the nomination is made at a meeting of creditors called for that purpose;

(m) where it is proposed to make distributions to creditors in accordance with Part 6, the classes of creditors to whom it is proposed that distributions be made and whether or not the energy administrator intends to make an application to the court under paragraph 65(3) of Schedule B1 to the 1986 Act;

(n) the manner in which the affairs and business of the protected energy company—

(i) have, since the date of the energy administrator's appointment, been managed and financed, including, where any assets have been disposed of, the reasons for such disposals and the terms upon which such disposals were made; and

(ii) will continue to be managed and financed; and

(o) such other information (if any) as the energy administrator thinks necessary.

(2) A copy of the energy administrator's statement of his proposals shall be sent to the registrar of companies together with a notice in Form EA10(S).

(3) Where the court orders, upon an application by the energy administrator under paragraph 107 of the Schedule B1 to the 1986 Act, an extension of the period of time in paragraph 49(5) of Schedule B1 to the 1986 Act, the energy administrator shall notify in Form EA11(S) all the persons set out in paragraph 49(4) of Schedule B1 to the 1986 Act as soon as reasonably practicable after the making of the order.

(4) Where the energy administrator wishes to publish a notice under paragraph 49(6) of Schedule B1 to the 1986 Act he shall publish the notice once in the Edinburgh Gazette and once in the newspaper in which the energy administrator's appointment was advertised. The notice shall—

(a) state the full name of the protected energy company;

(b) state the full name and address of the energy administrator;

(c) give details of the energy administrator's appointment; and

(d) specify an address to which any member of the protected energy company may apply in writing for a copy of the statement of proposals to be provided free of charge.

(5) This notice must be published as soon as reasonably practicable after the energy administrator sends his statement of proposals to the protected energy company's creditors and in any case no later than 8 weeks (or such other period as may be ordered by the court) from the date that the protected energy company entered energy administration.

PART 4
MEETINGS AND REPORTS

[16.192]

15 Meetings generally and notice

(1) This Rule and Rule 16 apply to any meetings summoned by the energy administrator under paragraph 62 of Schedule B1 to the 1986 Act.

(2) In fixing the venue for a meeting, the energy administrator shall have regard to the convenience of the persons who are to attend and the meeting shall be summoned for commencement between 10.00 and 16.00 hours on a business day, unless the court otherwise directs.

(3) Subject to Rule 20, the energy administrator shall give not less than 21 days' notice of the venue for the meeting to every person known to him as being entitled to attend the meeting.

(4) The energy administrator may also publish notice of the venue of the meeting in a newspaper circulating in the areas of the principal place of business of the protected energy company or in such other newspaper as he thinks most appropriate for ensuring that it comes to the notice of the persons who are entitled to attend the meeting.

(5) Any notice published under paragraph (4) shall be published not less than 21 days before the meeting.

(6) Any notice under this Rule shall state—

(a) the purpose of the meeting;

(b) the persons who are entitled to attend and vote at the meeting;

(c) the effects of Rule 21 and of the relevant provisions of Rule 24; and

(d) in the case of a meeting of creditors—

(i) that proxies may be lodged at or before the meeting and the place where they may be lodged; and

(ii) that claims may be lodged by those who have not already done so at or before the meeting and the place where they may be lodged.

(7) With the notice given under paragraph (1), the energy administrator shall also send out a proxy form.

(8) In the case of any meeting of creditors, the court may order that notice of the meeting be given by public advertisement in such form as may be specified in the order and not by individual notice to the persons concerned. In considering whether to make such an order, the court shall have regard to the cost of the public advertisement, to the amount of the assets available and to the extent of the interest of creditors or any particular class of them.

[16.193]

16 Adjournment

(1) This Rule applies to meetings of creditors.

(2) If, within a period of 30 minutes from the time appointed for the commencement of a meeting, a quorum is not present, then, unless the chairman otherwise decides, the meeting shall be adjourned to the same time and place in the following week or, if that is not a business day, to the business day immediately following.

(3) In the course of any meeting, the chairman may, in his discretion, and shall, if the meeting so resolves, adjourn it to such venue as seems to him to be appropriate in the circumstances.

(4) An adjournment under paragraph (2) or (3) shall not be for a period of more than 21 days and notice of the adjourned meeting may be given by the chairman.

(5) Where a meeting is adjourned, any proxies given for the original meeting may be used at the adjourned meeting.

[16.194]
17 The chairman at meetings

(1) At any meeting of creditors summoned by the energy administrator, either he shall be chairman, or a person nominated by him in writing to act in his place.

(2) A person so nominated must be either—
- (a) one who is qualified to act as an insolvency practitioner in relation to the protected energy company; or
- (b) an employee of the energy administrator or his firm who is experienced in insolvency matters.

[16.195]
18 Quorum at meeting of creditors

(1) Any meeting of creditors in energy administration proceedings is competent to act if a quorum is present.

(2) Subject to paragraph (3), a quorum is at least one creditor entitled to vote.

(3) For the purposes of this Rule, the reference to the creditor necessary to constitute a quorum is to those persons present or represented by proxy by any person (including the chairman) and includes persons duly represented under section 375 of the Companies Act.

(4) Where at any meeting of creditors—
- (a) the provisions of this Rule as to a quorum being present are satisfied by the attendance of—
  - (i) the chairman alone, or
  - (ii) one other person in addition to the chairman; and
- (b) the chairman is aware, by virtue of claims and proxies received or otherwise, that one or more additional persons would, if attending, be entitled to vote,

the meeting shall not commence until at least the expiry of 15 minutes after the time appointed for its commencement.

[16.196]
19 Chairman of meeting as proxy holder

Where the chairman at a meeting of creditors holds a proxy which requires him to vote for a particular resolution and no other person proposes that resolution—
- (a) he shall propose it himself, unless he considers that there is good reason for not doing so, and
- (b) if he does not propose it, he shall forthwith after the meeting notify the person who granted him the proxy of the reason why he did not do so.

[16.197]
20 Meeting following nomination of alternative liquidator

(1) Where under Rules 14(1)(k), (1)(l) or 26(2)(h), the energy administrator has proposed that the protected energy company enter creditors' voluntary liquidation once the energy administration has ended, the energy administrator shall, in the circumstances detailed in paragraph (2), summon a meeting of creditors for the purpose of nominating a person other than the person named as proposed liquidator in the energy administrator's proposals or revised proposals.

(2) The energy administrator shall summon a meeting of creditors where such a meeting is requested by creditors of the protected energy company whose debts amount to at least 25 per cent of the total debts of the protected energy company.

(3) A request for such a meeting shall be made within 21 days of the date on which the energy administrator's statement of proposals is sent out, or where revised proposals have been sent out and a proposed revision relates to the ending of the energy administration by a creditors' voluntary liquidation, within 21 days from the date on which the revised statement of proposals is sent out.

(4) A request under this Rule shall include—
- (a) a list of creditors concurring with the request, showing the amounts of their respective debts in the energy administration; and
- (b) from each creditor concurring, written confirmation of his concurrence,

but sub-paragraph (a) does not apply if the requesting creditor's debt is alone sufficient without the concurrence of other creditors.

(5) A meeting requested under this Rule shall be held within 21 days of the energy administrator's receipt of the notice requesting the meeting.

[16.198]
21 Entitlement to vote (creditors and members)

(1) Except Rule 29(2) and (3), Part 5 (claims in energy administration) applies for the purpose of determining a creditor's entitlement to vote at any creditors' meeting in an energy administration.

(2) Members of a protected energy company at their meetings shall vote according to their rights attaching to their shares in accordance with the articles of association.

(3) The reference in paragraph (2) to a member's share shall include any other interests which he may have as a member of the protected energy company.

[16.199]

22 Hire-purchase, conditional sale and hiring agreements

(1) Subject as follows, an owner of goods under a hire-purchase agreement or under an agreement for the hire of goods for more than 3 months, or a seller of goods under a conditional sale agreement, is entitled to vote in respect of the amount of the debt due and payable to him by the protected energy company on the date that the protected energy company entered energy administration.

(2) In calculating the amount of any debt for this purpose, no account shall be taken of any amount attributable to the exercise of any right under the relevant agreement, so far as the right has become exercisable solely by virtue of the making of an energy administration application or any matter arising as a consequence, or of the protected energy company entering energy administration.

[16.200]

23 Disposal of secured property

(1) The following applies where the energy administrator applies to the court under paragraphs 71 or 72 of Schedule B1 to the 1986 Act for authority to dispose of property of the protected energy company which is subject to a security (other than a floating charge), or goods in the possession of the protected energy company under a hire purchase agreement.

(2) If an order is made under paragraphs 71 or 72 of Schedule B1 to the 1986 Act, the energy administrator shall as soon as reasonably practicable send a copy of it certified by the clerk of court to the person who is the holder of the security or owner under the agreement.

(3) The energy administrator shall send to the registrar of companies a copy of the order, certified by the clerk of court, together with Form EA12(S), and shall place a copy of the order in the sederunt book.

[16.201]

24 Resolutions

(1) Subject to paragraph (2) and (3), at a creditors' or members' meeting in energy administration proceedings, a resolution is passed when a majority (in value) of those present and voting, in person or by proxy, have voted in favour of it.

(2) Any resolution is invalid if those voting against it include more than half in value of the creditors to whom notice of the meeting was sent and who are not, to the best of the chairman's belief, persons connected with the protected energy company.

(3) In this Rule, "connected with the protected energy company" has the same meaning as the phrase "connected with a company" in section 249 of the 1986 Act.

[16.202]

25 Report of Meeting

(1) The chairman of the meeting shall cause a report to be made of the proceedings at the meeting which shall be signed by him.

(2) The report shall include—

- (a) a list of all the creditors who attended the meeting, either in person or by proxy; and
- (b) a copy of every resolution passed.

(3) The chairman shall keep a copy of the report of the meeting as part of the sederunt book in the energy administration.

[16.203]

26 Revision of the energy administrator's proposals

(1) Where the energy administrator revises his proposals under paragraph 54 of Schedule B1 to the 1986 Act, he shall send a statement of the revised proposals in Form EA13(S) as soon as reasonably practicable to all those to whom he is required to do so.

(2) The statement of revised proposals shall include—

- (a) details of the court which granted the energy administration order and the relevant court reference number (if any);
- (b) the full name, registered address, registered number and any other trading names of the protected energy company;
- (c) details relating to the appointment of the energy administrator, including the date of appointment and whether the energy administration application was made by the Secretary of State or by GEMA;
- (d) the names of the directors and secretary of the protected energy company and details of any shareholdings which they have in the protected energy company;
- (e) a summary of the initial proposals and the reason(s) for proposing a revision;
- (f) details of the proposed revision including details of the energy administrator's assessment of the likely impact of the proposed revision upon creditors generally or upon each class of creditors (as the case may be);
- (g) where it is proposed, by virtue of the revision, to make distributions to creditors in accordance with Part 6, the classes of creditors to whom it is proposed that distributions be made and whether or not the energy administrator intends to make an application to the court under paragraph 65(3) of Schedule B1 to the 1986 Act;
- (h) where the revision includes a proposal to move from energy administration to a creditors' voluntary liquidation—
  - (i) details of the proposed liquidator; and

(ii) a statement that, in accordance with paragraph 83(7) of Schedule B1 to the 1986 Act and Rule 47(3), creditors may nominate another person to act as liquidator, provided that the nomination is made at a meeting of creditors called for that purpose; and

(i) any other information that the energy administrator thinks necessary to enable creditors to decide whether or not to vote for the proposed revisions.

(3) Subject to paragraph 54(4) of Schedule B1 to the 1986 Act, within 5 days of sending out the statement in paragraph (1) above, the energy administrator shall send a copy of the statement to every member of the protected energy company.

(4) A notice under paragraph 54(4) of Schedule B1 to the 1986 Act shall be published once in the Edinburgh Gazette and once in the newspaper in which the energy administrator's appointment was advertised, and shall—

(a) state the full name of the protected energy company;
(b) state the name and address of the energy administrator;
(c) specify an address to which members can write for a copy of the statement, to be provided free of charge; and
(d) be published as soon as reasonably practicable after the energy administrator sends the statement to creditors.

[16.204]
27 Reports to creditors

(1) The energy administrator shall—

(a) within six weeks after the end of each accounting period; and
(b) within six weeks after he ceases to act as energy administrator,

send to the court, the registrar of companies, each creditor, the Secretary of State and GEMA, a progress report attached to Form EA14(S).

(2) For the purposes of this Part, "accounting period", in relation to an energy administration, shall be construed in accordance with Rule 41.

(3) For the purposes of this Part, "progress report" means a report which includes—

(a) the name of the court which granted the energy administration order, and the court reference number (if any);
(b) details of the protected energy company's name, address and registration number;
(c) details of the energy administrator's name and address, date of appointment and name and address of the applicant for the energy administration order, including any changes in office-holder, and, in the case of joint energy administrators, their functions as set out in the statement made for the purposes of section 158(5) of the 2004 Act;
(d) details of progress to date, including a receipts and payments account which states what assets of the protected energy company have been realised, for what value, and what payments have been made to creditors;
(e) details of what assets remain to be realised;
(f) where a distribution is to be made in accordance with Part 7 in respect of an accounting period, the scheme of division; and
(g) any other relevant information for the creditors.

(4) For the purposes of paragraph (3)(d), the account shall be in the form of an abstract showing—

(a) receipts and payments during the relevant accounting period; or
(b) where the energy administrator has ceased to act, receipts and payments during the period from the end of the last accounting period to the time when he so ceased (or, where he has made no previous progress report, receipts and payments in the period since his appointment as energy administrator).

(5) In a receipts and payments account falling within paragraph (4)(b), the energy administrator shall include a statement as to the amount paid to unsecured creditors by virtue of the application of section 176A of the 1986 Act (prescribed part).

(6) The court may, on the application of the energy administrator, extend the period of six weeks referred to in paragraph (1) of this Rule.

(7) If the energy administrator makes default in complying with this Rule without reasonable excuse, he shall be guilty of an offence.

(8) An energy administrator convicted of an offence under paragraph (7) shall be liable—

(a) on summary conviction to a fine not exceeding one-fifth of the statutory maximum; or
(b) in relation to a second or subsequent conviction of the offence, to a daily default fine of one-fiftieth of the statutory maximum in respect of each day on which the contravention is continued.

(9) This Rule is without prejudice to the requirements of Part 6 (distribution to creditors).

PART 5
CLAIMS IN ENERGY ADMINISTRATION

[16.205]
28 Submission of claims

(1) A creditor, in order to obtain an adjudication as to his entitlement to vote at any meeting of the creditors in the energy administration or to a dividend (so far as funds are available) out of the assets of the protected energy company in respect of any accounting period, shall submit his claim to the energy administrator—

(a) at or before the meeting; or,

(b) not later than 8 weeks before the end of the accounting period.

(2) A creditor shall submit his claim by producing to the energy administrator—

(a) a statement of claim in the Form EA15(S); and

(b) an account or voucher (according to the nature of the debt claimed) which constitutes prima facie evidence of the debt,

but the energy administrator may dispense with any requirement of this paragraph in respect of any debt or any class of debt.

(3) A claim submitted by a creditor, which has been accepted in whole or in part by the energy administrator for the purpose of voting at a meeting or of drawing a dividend in respect of any accounting period, shall be deemed to have been resubmitted for the purpose of obtaining an adjudication as to his entitlement both to vote at any subsequent meeting and (so far as funds are available) to a dividend in respect of an accounting period or, as the case may be, any subsequent accounting period.

(4) A creditor, who has submitted a claim, may at any time submit a further claim specifying a different amount for his claim;

Provided that a secured creditor shall not be entitled to produce a further claim specifying a different value for the security at any time after the energy administrator has required the creditor to discharge, or convey or assign, the security under Rule 29(2).

[16.206]

29 Secured debts

(1) In calculating the amount of his claim, a secured creditor shall deduct the value of any security as estimated by him;

Provided that if he surrenders, or undertakes in writing to surrender, a security for the benefit of the protected energy company's assets, he shall not be required to make a deduction of the value of that security.

(2) The energy administrator may, at any time after the expiry of 12 weeks from the date on which the protected energy company enters energy administration, require a secured creditor to discharge the security or convey or assign it to the energy administrator on payment to the creditor of the value specified by the creditor (the expense of such discharge, conveyance or assignation being met from the assets of the protected energy company); and the amount in respect of which the creditor shall then be entitled to claim shall be any balance of his debt remaining after receipt of such payment.

(3) In calculating the amount of his claim, a creditor whose security has been realised shall deduct the amount (less the expenses of realisation) which he has received, or is entitled to receive, from the realisation.

[16.207]

30 Entitlement to vote and draw dividend

(1) A creditor who has had his claim accepted in whole or in part by the energy administrator or on appeal under paragraph (5) of Rule 31 shall be entitled—

(a) in a case where the acceptance is under (or on appeal arising from) paragraph (1) of Rule 31, to vote on any matter at the meeting of creditors for the purpose of voting at which the claim is accepted; and

(b) in a case where the acceptance is under (or on appeal arising from) paragraph (2) of Rule 31, to payment out of the assets of the protected energy company of a dividend in respect of the distribution for the purposes of which the claim is accepted; but such entitlement to payment shall arise only in so far as the protected energy company has funds available to make that payment, having regard to Rule 39, and payment would be consistent with the power and duties of the energy administrator.

(2) Votes are calculated according to the amount of a creditor's debt as at the date on which the protected energy company entered energy administration, deducting any amount paid in respect of that debt after that date.

(3) No vote shall be cast by virtue of a debt more than once on any resolution put to the meeting.

(4) Any reference in this Rule and Rules 28 to 36 to the energy administrator includes, where applicable, a reference to the chairman of the meeting.

[16.208]

31 Adjudication of claims

(1) At the commencement of every meeting of creditors, the energy administrator shall, for the purposes of Rule 30 so far as it relates to voting at that meeting, accept or reject the claim of each creditor.

(2) Where funds are available for payment of a dividend out of the assets of the protected energy company in respect of an accounting period, the energy administrator for the purpose of determining who is entitled to such a dividend shall, not later than 4 weeks before the end of the period, accept or reject every claim submitted or deemed to have been re-submitted to him under these Rules; and shall at the same time make a decision on any matter requiring to be specified under sub-paragraph (a) or (b) of paragraph (4).

(3) Where the energy administrator rejects a claim, he shall forthwith notify the creditor giving reasons for the rejection.

(4) Where the energy administrator accepts or rejects a claim, he shall record in the sederunt book his decision on the claim specifying—

(a) the amount of the claim accepted by him;

(b) the category of debt, and the value of any security, as decided by him, and

(c) if he is rejecting the claim, his reasons therefor.

(5) Any member or creditor may, if dissatisfied with the acceptance or rejection of any claim (or, in relation to such acceptance or rejection, with a decision in respect of any matter requiring to be specified under paragraph (4)(a) or (b) above), appeal therefrom to the court—

(a) if the acceptance or rejection is under paragraph (1) above, within 2 weeks of that acceptance or rejection;

(b) if the acceptance or rejection is under paragraph (2) above, not later than 2 weeks before the end of the accounting period,

and the energy administrator shall record the court's decision in the sederunt book.

(6) Any reference in this Rule to the acceptance or rejection of a claim shall be construed as a reference to the acceptance or rejection of the claim in whole or in part.

[16.209]
32 Evidence in relation to claims

(1) The energy administrator, for the purpose of satisfying himself as to the validity or amount of a claim submitted by a creditor may require—

(a) the creditor to produce further evidence; or

(b) any other person who he believes can produce relevant evidence, to produce such evidence,

and, if the creditor or other person refuses or delays to do so, the energy administrator may apply to the court for an order requiring the creditor or other person to attend for his private examination before the court.

(2) On an application being made in accordance with paragraph (1), the court may make an order requiring the creditor or other person to attend for private examination before it on a date (being not earlier than 8 days nor later than 16 days after the date of the order) and at a time specified in the order.

(3) A person who fails without reasonable excuse to comply with an order made under paragraph (2) shall be guilty of an offence and liable on summary conviction to a fine not exceeding level 5 on the standard scale or to imprisonment for a term not exceeding three months or to both.

(4) The examination shall be taken on oath.

(5) At any private examination, a solicitor or counsel may act on behalf of the energy administrator or he may appear himself.

[16.210]
33 Criminal offences in relation to false claims or evidence

(1) If a creditor produces under Rule 28 a statement of claim, account, voucher or other evidence which is false, the creditor shall be guilty of an offence unless he shows that he neither knew nor had reason to believe that the statement of claim, account, voucher or other evidence was false.

(2) A person convicted of an offence under paragraph (1) shall be liable—

(a) on summary conviction to a fine not exceeding the statutory maximum or—

(i) to imprisonment for a term not exceeding three months; or

(ii) if he has previously been convicted of an offence inferring dishonest appropriation of property or an attempt at such appropriation, to imprisonment for a term not exceeding six months, or (in the case of either sub-paragraph) to both such fine and such imprisonment; or

(b) on conviction on indictment to a fine or to imprisonment for a term not exceeding two years or to both.

[16.211]
34 Amount which may be claimed generally

(1) Subject to Rules 29 and 35, the amount in respect of which a creditor shall be entitled to claim shall be the accumulated sum of principal and any interest which is due on the debt as at the date upon which the protected energy company entered energy administration.

(2) If a debt does not depend on a contingency but would not be payable but for the energy administration until after the date upon which the protected energy company entered energy administration, the amount of the claim shall be calculated as if the debt were payable on the date when the protected energy company entered energy administration but subject to the deduction of interest at the rate specified in section 17 of the Judgments Act 1838 on the date when the protected energy company entered energy administration from the said date until the date for payment of the debt.

(3) In calculating the amount of his claim, a creditor shall deduct any discount (other than any discount for payment in cash) which is allowable by contract or course of dealing between the creditor and the protected energy company or by the usage of trade.

[16.212]
35 Debts depending on contingency

(1) Subject to paragraph (2), the amount which a creditor shall be entitled to claim shall not include a debt in so far as its existence or amount depends upon a contingency.

(2) On an application by the creditor to the energy administrator, the energy administrator shall put a value on the debt in so far as it is contingent, and the amount in respect of which the creditor shall then be entitled to claim shall be that value but no more; and, where the contingent debt is an annuity, a cautioner may not then be sued for more than that value.

[16.213]
36 Liabilities and rights of co-obligants

(1) Where a creditor has an obligant (in this Rule referred to as the "co-obligant") bound to him along with the protected energy company for the whole or part of the debt, the co-obligant shall not be freed or discharged from his liability for the debt by reason of the dissolution of the protected energy company or by virtue of the creditor's voting or drawing a dividend.

(2) Where—

(a) a creditor has had a claim accepted in whole or in part; and

(b) a co-obligant holds a security over any part of the assets of the protected energy company,

the co-obligant shall account to the energy administrator so as to put the protected energy company in the same position as if the co-obligant had paid the debt to the creditor and thereafter had had his claim accepted in whole or in part in the energy administration after deduction of the value of the security.

(3) Without prejudice to any right under any rule of law of a co-obligant who has paid the debt, the co-obligant may require and obtain at his own expense from the creditor an assignation of the debt on payment of the amount thereof, and thereafter may in respect of that debt submit a claim, and vote and draw a dividend, if otherwise legally entitled to do so.

(4) In this Rule a "co-obligant" includes a cautioner.

[16.214]
37 Claims in foreign currency

(1) A creditor may state the amount of his claim in currency other than sterling where—

(a) his claim is constituted by decree or other order made by a court ordering the protected energy company to pay the creditor a sum expressed in a currency other than sterling, or

(b) where it is not so constituted, his claim arises from a contract or bill of exchange in terms of which payment is or may be required to be made by the protected energy company to the creditor in a currency other than sterling.

(2) Where a claim is stated in currency other than sterling for the purposes of the preceding paragraph, it shall be converted into sterling at the official exchange rate prevailing on the date when the protected energy company entered energy administration.

PART 6
DISTRIBUTION TO CREDITORS

[16.215]
38 Application of Part and general

(1) This Part applies where the energy administrator makes, or proposes to make, a distribution to creditors or any class of them.

(2) Where the distribution is to a particular class of creditors, references in this Part (except in rule 41(5)(c)) to creditors shall, in so far as the context requires, be a reference to that class of creditors only.

(3) This Part and Part 5 apply with regard to a dividend out of the assets of the protected energy company in energy administration.

[16.216]
39 Order of priority in distribution

(1) If the funds of the protected energy company's assets are to be distributed then they shall be distributed by the energy administrator to meet the following expenses and debts in the order in which they are mentioned—

(a) the expenses of the energy administration;

(b) any preferential debts within the meaning of section 386 of the 1986 Act (excluding any interest which has been accrued thereon to the date on which the protected energy company entered energy administration);

(c) ordinary debt, that is to say a debt which is neither a secured debt nor a debt mentioned in any other sub-paragraph of this paragraph;

(d) interest at the official rate on—

(i) the preferential debts, and

(ii) the ordinary debts,

between the said date on which the protected energy company entered energy administration and the date of payment of the debt; and

(e) any postponed debt.

(2) In the above paragraph—

(a) "postponed debt" means a creditor's right to any alienation which has been reduced or restored to the protected energy company's assets under section 242 of the 1986 Act or to the proceeds of sale of such an alienation; and

(b) "official rate" shall be construed in accordance with subsection (4) of section 189 of the 1986 Act and, for the purposes of paragraph (a) of that subsection, as applied to Scotland by subsection (5), the rate specified in the Rules shall be 15 per centum per annum.

(3) The expenses of the energy administration mentioned in sub-paragraph (a) of paragraph (1) above are payable in the order of priority mentioned in Rule 40.

(4) Subject to the provisions of paragraph (5), any debt falling within any of sub-paragraphs (b) to (e) of paragraph (1) shall have the same priority as any other debt falling within the same sub paragraph and, where the funds of the protected energy company's assets are inadequate to enable the debts mentioned in this paragraph to be paid in full, they shall abate in equal proportions.

(5) So far as the assets of the protected energy company available for payment of general creditors are insufficient to meet them, preferential debts have priority over the claims of holders of debentures secured by, or holders of, any floating charge created by the protected energy company, and shall be paid accordingly out of any property comprised in or subject to that charge.

(6) Any surplus remaining, after all expenses and debts mentioned in paragraph (1) have been paid in full, shall (unless the articles of the protected energy company otherwise provide) be distributed among the members according to their rights and interests in the company.

(7) Nothing in this Rule shall affect—

(a) the right of a secured creditor which is preferable to the rights of the energy administrator; or

(b) any preference of the holder of a lien over a title deed or other document which has been delivered to the energy administrator.

[16.217]
40 Expenses of the energy administration

(1) The expenses of the energy administration are payable out of the assets in the following order of priority—

(a) expenses properly incurred by the energy administrator in performing his functions in the energy administration of the protected energy company;

(b) the cost of any caution provided by the energy administrator in accordance with the 1986 Act or the Rules;

(c) where an energy administration order was made, the expenses of the applicant and any person appearing on the hearing of the application whose expenses are allowed by the court;

(d) any amount payable to a person employed or authorised, under Part 3 of the Rules, to assist in the preparation of a statement of affairs or statement of concurrence;

(e) any allowance made, by order of the court, towards expenses on an application for release from the obligation to submit a statement of affairs or statement of concurrence;

(f) any necessary disbursements by the energy administrator in the course of the energy administration (but not including any payment of corporation tax in circumstances referred to in sub-paragraph (i) below);

(g) the remuneration or emoluments of any person who has been employed by the energy administrator to perform any services for the protected energy company, as required or authorised under the 1986 Act or 2004 Act, Schedule B1 to the 1986 Act or the Rules;

(h) the remuneration of the energy administrator agreed under Part 6 of the Rules;

(i) the amount of any corporation tax on chargeable gains accruing on the realisation of any asset of the protected energy company (without regard to whether the realisation is effected by the energy administrator, a secured creditor, or otherwise).

(2) Nothing in this Rule applies to or affects the power of any court in proceedings by or against the protected energy company, to order expenses to be paid by the protected energy company or the energy administrator, nor does it affect the rights of any person to whom such expenses are ordered to be paid.

(3) The priorities laid down by paragraph (1) of this Rule are subject to the power of the court to make orders under paragraph (4) of this Rule where the assets are insufficient to satisfy the liabilities.

(4) The court may, in the event of the assets being insufficient to satisfy the liabilities, make an order as to the payment out of the assets of the expense incurred in the energy administration in such order of priority as the court thinks just.

[16.218]
41 Assets to be distributed

(1) The energy administrator shall make up accounts of his intromissions with the protected energy company's assets in respect of each accounting period.

(2) In this Rule "accounting period" shall be construed as follows—

(a) the first accounting period shall be the period of six months beginning with the date on which the protected energy company entered energy administration; and

(b) any subsequent accounting period shall be the period of six months beginning with the end of the last accounting period; except that in a case where the energy administrator determines that the accounting period shall be such other period beginning with the end of the last accounting period as may be determined, it shall be that other period.

(3) A determination in paragraph (2)(b)—

(a) may be made in respect of one or more than one accounting period;

(b) may be made before the beginning of the accounting period in relation to which it has effect and, in any event, shall not have effect unless made before the day on which such accounting period would, but for the determination, have ended;

(c) may provide for different accounting periods to be of different durations,

and shall be recorded in the sederunt book by the energy administrator.

(4) Subject to the following paragraphs, the energy administrator may, if the funds of the protected energy company are sufficient and after making allowance for future contingencies, pay under Rule 42(7) a dividend out of the assets of the protected energy company to the creditors in respect of each accounting period.

(5) The energy administrator may make a distribution to secured or preferential creditors or, where he has the permission of the court, to unsecured creditors only if—

(a) he has sufficient funds for the purpose;

(b) he does not intend to give notice pursuant to paragraph 83 of Schedule B1 to the 1986 Act;

(c) his statement of proposals contains a proposal to make a distribution to the class of creditors in question; and

(d) the payment of a dividend is consistent with the powers and duties of the energy administrator and any proposals made by him or which he intends to make.

(6) The energy administrator may pay—

(a) the expenses of the energy administration mentioned in Rule 40(1)(a), other than his own remuneration, at any time;

(b) the preferential debts at any time.

(7) If the energy administrator—

(a) is not ready to pay a dividend in respect of an accounting period; or

(b) considers it would be inappropriate to pay such a dividend because the expense of doing so would be disproportionate to the amount of the dividend,

he may postpone such payment to a date not later than the time for payment of a dividend in respect of the next accounting period.

(8) Where an appeal is taken under Rule 31(5) against the acceptance or rejection of a creditor's claim, the energy administrator shall, at the time of payment of dividends and until the appeal is determined, set aside an amount which would be sufficient, if the determination in the appeal were to provide for the claim being accepted in full, to pay a dividend in respect of that claim.

(9) Where a creditor—

(a) has failed to produce evidence in support of his claim earlier than eight weeks before the end of an accounting period on being required by the energy administrator to do so under Rule 32(1); and

(b) has given a reason for such failure which is acceptable to the energy administrator,

the energy administrator shall set aside, for such time as is reasonable to enable him to produce that evidence or any other evidence that will enable the energy administrator to be satisfied under that Rule, an amount which would be sufficient, if the claim were accepted in full, to pay a dividend in respect of that claim.

(10) Where a creditor submits a claim to the energy administrator later than eight weeks before the end of an accounting period but more than eight weeks before the end of a subsequent accounting period in respect of which, after making allowance for contingencies, funds are available for the payment of a dividend, the energy administrator shall, if he accepts the claim in whole or in part, pay to the creditor—

(a) the same dividend or dividends as has or have already been paid to creditors of the same class in respect of any accounting period or periods; and

(b) whatever dividend may be payable to him in respect of the said subsequent accounting period,

provided that sub-paragraph (a) above shall be without prejudice to any dividend which has already been paid.

(11) In the declaration of and payment of a dividend, no payments shall be made more than once by virtue of the same debt.

(12) If a person entitled to a dividend gives notice to the energy administrator that he wishes the dividend to be paid to another person, or that he has assigned his entitlement to another person, the energy administrator shall pay the dividend to that other accordingly, provided that such notice specifies the name and address of that other.

[16.219]

42 Procedure after accounting period

(1) Within two weeks after the end of an accounting period, the energy administrator shall in respect of that period submit to the court—

(a) his accounts of his intromissions with the assets of the protected energy company for audit and, where funds are available after making allowance for contingencies, a scheme of division of the divisible funds; and

(b) a claim for the outlays reasonably incurred by him and for his remuneration.

(2) The energy administrator may, at any time before the end of an accounting period, submit to the court an interim claim in respect of that period for the outlays reasonably incurred by him and for his remuneration and the court may make an interim determination in relation to the amount of the outlays and remuneration payable to the energy administrator and, where it does so, it shall take into account that interim determination when making its determination under paragraph (3)(a)(ii).

(3) Within six weeks after the end of an accounting period—

(a) the court—

(i) may audit the accounts; and

(ii) shall issue a determination fixing the amount of the outlays and the remuneration payable to the energy administrator; and

(b) the energy administrator shall make the audited accounts, scheme of division and the said determination available for inspection by the members and the creditors.

(4) The basis for fixing the amount of the remuneration payable to the energy administrator shall take into account—

(a) the work which, having regard to that value, was reasonably undertaken by him; and

(b) the extent of his responsibilities in administering the protected energy company's assets.

(5) In fixing the amount of such remuneration in respect of any accounting period, the court may take into account any adjustment which it may wish to make in the amount of the remuneration and outlays fixed in respect of any earlier accounting period.

(6) Not later than eight weeks after the end of an accounting period, the energy administrator, the protected energy company or any creditor may appeal against a determination issued under paragraph (2) or (3)(a)(ii) above and the decision of the court on such appeal shall be final.

(7) On the expiry of the period within which an appeal may be taken under paragraph (5) above or, if an appeal is so taken, on the final determination of the last such appeal, the energy administrator shall pay to the creditors their dividends in accordance with the scheme of division.

(8) Any dividend—

(a) allocated to a creditor which is not cashed or uplifted; or

(b) dependent on a claim in respect of which an amount has been set aside under paragraphs (8) or (9) of Rule 41,

shall be deposited by the energy administrator in an appropriate bank or institution.

(9) If a creditor's claim is revalued, the energy administrator may—

(a) in paying any dividend to that creditor, make such adjustment to it as he considers necessary to take account of that revaluation; or

(b) require the creditor to repay him the whole or part of a dividend already paid to him.

(10) The energy administrator shall insert in the sederunt book the audited accounts, the scheme of division and final determination in relation to the energy administrator's outlays and remuneration.

(11) For the purposes of paragraph 99(3) of Schedule B1 to the 1986 Act, the former energy administrator's remuneration and expenses shall comprise all those items set out in Rule 40.

(12) Where there are joint energy administrators—

(a) it is for them to agree between themselves as to how the remuneration payable should be apportioned,

(b) if they cannot agree as to how the remuneration payable should be apportioned, any one of them may refer the issue for determination by the court.

[16.220]
43 Unclaimed Dividends

(1) Any person, producing evidence of his right, may apply to the court to receive a dividend deposited under Rule 42, if the application is made not later than seven years after the date of such deposit.

(2) If the court is satisfied of the applicant's right to the dividend, it shall authorise the appropriate bank or institution to pay to the applicant the amount of that dividend and of any interest which accrued thereon.

(3) The court shall, at the expiry of seven years from the date of deposit of any unclaimed dividend or unapplied balance under Rule 42, hand over the deposit receipt or other voucher relating to such dividend or balance to the Secretary of State, who shall thereupon be entitled to payment of the amount due, principal and interest, from the bank or institution in which the deposit was made.

PART 7
ENDING ENERGY ADMINISTRATION

[16.221]
44 Final progress reports

(1) In this Part reference to a progress report is to a report in the form specified in Rule 27.

(2) The final progress report means a progress report which includes a summary of—

(a) the energy administrator's original proposals;

(b) any major amendments to, or deviations from, those proposals;

(c) the steps taken during the energy administration; and

(d) the outcome.

[16.222]
45 Application to court

(1) An application under paragraph 79 of Schedule B1 to the 1986 Act for an order providing for the appointment of an energy administrator of the protected energy company to cease to have effect shall be accompanied by a progress report for the period since the last such report (if any) and a statement indicating what the applicant thinks should be the next steps for the protected energy company (if applicable).

(2) Subject to paragraph (3), where the applicant applies to the court he shall give to—

(a) the applicant for the energy administration order (unless the applicant in both cases is the same); and

(b) the creditors of the protected energy company,

at least 7 days' written notice of his intention so to apply.

(3) Where an applicant other than the energy administrator applies to the court—

(a) the applicant shall give to the energy administrator at least 7 days' written notice of his intention so to apply; and

(b) upon receipt of such written notice the energy administrator shall, before the end of the 7 day notice period, provide the applicant with a progress report for the period since the last progress report (if any) or the date the protected energy company entered energy administration.

(4) Where the application is made other than by the Secretary of State, it shall also state that it is made with the consent of the Secretary of State.

(5) Where the energy administrator applies to court under paragraph 79 of Schedule B1 to the 1986 Act in conjunction with a petition under section 124 of the 1986 Act for an order to wind up the protected energy company, he shall, in addition to the requirements of paragraphs (2) and (4), notify the creditors of whether he intends to seek appointment as liquidator.

[16.223]

46 Notification by energy administrator of court order

(1) Where the court makes an order to end the energy administration, the energy administrator shall notify the registrar of companies in Form EA16(S), attaching a copy of the court order and a copy of the final progress report.

(2) Where the court makes an order to end the energy administration and the applicant was not the energy administrator then that applicant shall give a copy of the order to the energy administrator.

[16.224]

47 Moving from energy administration to creditors' voluntary liquidation

(1) A notice pursuant to paragraph 83(3) of Schedule B1 to the 1986 Act shall be in Form EA17(S) and shall be accompanied by a final progress report which includes details of the assets to be dealt with in the liquidation.

(2) As soon as reasonably practicable, the energy administrator shall send a copy of the notice and accompanying documents to—

(a) all those who received notice of the energy administrator's appointment;

(b) where the Secretary of State did not receive notice of the energy administrator's appointment, to the Secretary of State; and

(c) where GEMA did not receive notice of the energy administrator's appointment, to GEMA.

(3) For the purposes of paragraph 83(7) of Schedule B1 to the 1986 Act, a person shall be nominated as liquidator in accordance with the provisions of Rule 14(1)(l) or Rule 26(2)(h) and his appointment takes effect—

(a) by virtue of the energy administrator's proposals or revised proposals; or

(b) where a creditors' meeting is held in accordance with Rule 20, as a consequence of such a meeting.

(4) GEMA must notify the Secretary of State before consenting to the energy administrator sending a notice of moving from energy administration to creditors' voluntary liquidation to the registrar of companies.

[16.225]

48 Moving from energy administration to dissolution

(1) The notice required by paragraph 84(1) of Schedule B1 to the 1986 Act shall be in Form EA18(S) and shall be accompanied by a final progress report.

(2) As soon as reasonably practicable a copy of the notice and accompanying documents shall be sent to—

(a) all those who received notice of the energy administrator's appointment;

(b) where the Secretary of State did not receive notice of the energy administrator's appointment, the Secretary of State; and

(c) where GEMA did not receive notice of the energy administrator's appointment, to GEMA.

(3) Where the court makes an order under paragraph 84(7) of Schedule B1 to the 1986 Act it shall, where the applicant is not the energy administrator, give a copy of the order to the energy administrator.

(4) The notice required by paragraph 84(8) of Schedule B1 to the 1986 Act shall be in Form EA19(S).

(5) GEMA must notify the Secretary of State before directing the energy administrator to send a notice of moving from energy administration to dissolution to the registrar of companies.

[16.226]

49 Provision of information to the Secretary of State

Where the energy administration ends pursuant to paragraphs 79, 83 or 84 of Schedule B1 to the 1986 Act, the energy administrator shall, within 5 business days from the date of the end of the energy administration, provide the Secretary of State with the following information—

(a) a breakdown of the relevant debts (within the meaning of section 169(4) of the 2004 Act) of the protected energy company, which remain outstanding; and

(b) details of any shortfall (within the meaning of section 169(3)(a) of the 2004 Act) in the property of the protected energy company available for meeting those relevant debts.

PART 8
REPLACING ENERGY ADMINISTRATOR

[16.227]
50 Grounds for resignation

(1) The energy administrator may give notice of his resignation on grounds of ill health or because—

(a) he intends ceasing to be in practice as an insolvency practitioner; or

(b) there is some conflict of interest, or change of personal circumstances, which precludes or makes impracticable the further discharge by him of the duties of energy administrator.

(2) The energy administrator may, with the leave of the court, give notice of his resignation on grounds other than those specified in paragraph (1).

[16.228]
51 Notice of intention to resign

The energy administrator must give to the persons specified below at least 7 days' notice in Form EA20(S) of his intention to resign, or to apply for the court's leave to do so—

(a) the Secretary of State;

(b) GEMA;

(c) if there is a continuing energy administrator of the protected energy company, to him; and

(d) if there is no such energy administrator, to the protected energy company and its creditors.

[16.229]
52 Notice of resignation

The notice of resignation shall be in Form EA21(S), lodged in court and a copy sent to the registrar of companies. A copy of the notice of resignation shall be sent, not more than 5 business days after it has been lodged in court, to all those to whom notice of intention to resign was sent.

[16.230]
53 Application to court to remove energy administrator from office

(1) An application to the court to remove an energy administrator from office shall be served upon—

(a) the energy administrator;

(b) the Secretary of State;

(c) GEMA;

(d) the joint energy administrator (if any); and

(e) the protected energy company and all the creditors, including any floating charge holders, where there is no joint energy administrator.

(2) An applicant under this Rule shall, within 5 business days of the order being made, send a copy of the order to—

(a) all those to whom notice of the application was sent; and

(b) the registrar of companies in Form EA22(S).

[16.231]
54 Incapacity to act, through death or otherwise

(1) Subject to paragraph (2), where the energy administrator has died, it is the duty of his executors or, where the deceased energy administrator was a partner in a firm, of a partner of that firm to give notice of that fact to the court and to the registrar of companies, specifying the date of death, in Form EA22(S).

(2) Notice of the death may also be given by any person.

(3) Where an energy administrator who has ceased to be qualified to act as an insolvency practitioner in relation to the protected energy company gives notice in accordance with paragraph 89(2) of Schedule B1 to the 1986 Act, he shall also give notice to the registrar of companies.

[16.232]
55 Application to replace

(1) Where an application is made to the court under paragraph 91 of Schedule B1 to the 1986 Act to appoint a replacement energy administrator, the application shall be accompanied by a Statement of the Proposed Administrator in Form EA1(S).

(2) A copy of the application shall be served, in addition to those persons listed in section 156(2) of the 2004 Act and Rule 5, on the person who made the application for the energy administration order.

(3) Where the court makes an order filling a vacancy in the office of energy administrator, the same provisions shall apply, subject to such modification as may be necessary, in respect of giving notice of, and advertising, the appointment as in the case of the original appointment of an energy administrator.

[16.233]
56 Joint or concurrent appointments

(1) Where, after an initial appointment has been made, an additional person or persons are to be appointed as joint energy administrator the same rules shall apply in respect of giving notice of and advertising the appointment as in the case of the initial appointment, subject to paragraph (2).

(2) The replacement or additional energy administrator shall send notice of the appointment in Form EA23(S) to the registrar of companies.

[16.234]

57 Notification and advertisement of appointment of replacement energy administrator

(1) This Rule applies where any person has appointed an energy administrator in accordance with these Rules and a replacement energy administrator is appointed.

(2) The same provisions apply in respect of giving notice of, and advertising, the replacement appointment as in the case of an initial appointment, and all statements, consents and other documents as required shall also be required in this case.

[16.235]

58 Hand-over of assets to successor energy administrator

(1) This Rule applies where a person appointed as energy administrator ("the succeeding energy administrator") succeeds a previous energy administrator ("the former energy administrator").

(2) When the succeeding energy administrator's appointment takes effect, the former energy administrator shall forthwith do all that is required for putting the succeeding energy administrator into possession of the protected energy company's assets.

(3) The former energy administrator shall give to the succeeding energy administrator all such information, relating to the affairs of the protected energy company and the course of the energy administration, as the succeeding energy administrator considers to be reasonably required for the effective discharge by him of his duties as such and shall hand over all books, accounts, statements of affairs, statements of claim and other records and documents in his possession relating to the affairs of the protected energy company and its energy administration.

PART 9
PRESCRIBED PART

[16.236]

59 Application under section 176A(5) of the 1986 Act to disapply section 176A of the 1986 Act

An application under section 176A(5) of the 1986 Act shall include averments as to—

(a) the fact that the application arises in the course of an energy administration;
(b) the financial position of the protected energy company;
(c) the basis of the energy administrator's view that the cost of making a distribution to unsecured creditors would be disproportionate to the benefits; and
(d) whether any other insolvency practitioner is acting in relation to the protected energy company and, if so, his address.

[16.237]

60 Notice of order under section 176A(5) of the 1986 Act

(1) Where the court makes an order under section 176A(5) of the 1986 Act the energy administrator shall, as soon as reasonably practicable after the making of the order—

(a) send to the protected energy company a copy of the order certified by the clerk of court;
(b) send to the registrar of companies a copy of the order together with Form EA24(S); and
(c) give notice of the order to each creditor of whose claim and address he is aware.

(2) The court may direct that the requirement of paragraph (1)(c) of this Rule be met by the publication of a notice in a newspaper calculated to come to the attention of the unsecured creditors stating that the court has made an order disapplying the requirement to set aside the prescribed part.

PART 10
PROXIES AND COMPANY REPRESENTATION

[16.238]

61 Definition of "proxy"

(1) For the purposes of these Rules, a person ("the principal") may authorise another person ("the proxy-holder") to attend, speak and vote as his representative at meetings of creditors or of the protected energy company in energy administration proceedings, and such authority is referred to as a proxy.

(2) A proxy may be given either generally for all meetings in energy administration proceedings or specifically for any meeting or class of meetings.

(3) Only one proxy may be given by the principal for any one meeting; and it may only be given to one person, being an individual aged 18 or over. The principal may nevertheless nominate one or more other such persons to be proxy-holder in the alternative in the order in which they are named in the proxy.

(4) Without prejudice to the generality of paragraph (3), a proxy for a particular meeting may be given to whoever is to be the chairman of the meeting and any person to whom such a proxy is given cannot decline to be a proxy-holder in relation to that proxy.

(5) A proxy may require the holder to vote on behalf of the principal on matters arising for determination at any meeting, or to abstain, either as directed or in accordance with the holder's own discretion; and it may authorise or require the holder to propose, in the principal's name, a resolution to be voted on by the meeting.

[16.239]
62 Form of proxy

(1) With every notice summoning a meeting of creditors or of the protected energy company in energy administration proceedings there shall be sent out forms of proxy in Form EA25(S).

(2) A form of proxy shall not be sent out with the name or description of any person inserted in it.

(3) A proxy shall be in the form sent out with the notice summoning the meeting or in a form substantially to the same effect.

(4) A form of proxy shall be filled out and signed by the principal, or by some person acting under his authority and, where it is signed by someone other than the principal, the nature of his authority shall be stated on the form.

[16.240]
63 Use of proxy at meeting

(1) A proxy given for a particular meeting may be used at any adjournment of that meeting.

(2) A proxy may be lodged at or before the meeting at which it is to be used.

(3) Where the energy administrator holds proxies to be used by him as chairman of the meeting, and some other person acts as chairman, the other person may use the energy administrator's proxies as if he were himself proxy-holder.

(4) Where a proxy directs a proxy-holder to vote for or against a resolution for the appointment of a person other than the energy administrator as proposed liquidator of the protected energy company, the proxy-holder may, unless the proxy states otherwise, vote for or against (as he thinks fit) any resolution for the appointment of that person jointly with another or others.

(5) A proxy-holder may propose any resolution which, if proposed by another, would be a resolution in favour of which he would be entitled to vote by virtue of the proxy.

(6) Where a proxy gives specific directions as to voting, this does not, unless the proxy states otherwise, preclude the proxy-holder from voting at his discretion on resolutions put to the meeting which are not dealt with in the proxy.

[16.241]
64 Retention of proxies

(1) Proxies used for voting at any meeting shall be retained by the chairman of the meeting.

(2) The chairman shall deliver the proxies forthwith after the meeting to the energy administrator (where that is someone other than himself).

(3) The energy administrator shall retain all proxies in the sederunt book.

[16.242]
65 Right of inspection

(1) The energy administrator shall, so long as proxies lodged with him are in his hands, allow them to be inspected at all reasonable times on any business day, by—

(a) the creditors, in the case of proxies used at a meeting of creditors; and

(b) a protected energy company's members, in the case of proxies used at a meeting of the protected energy company.

(2) The reference in paragraph (1) to creditors is a reference to those persons who have submitted in writing a claim to be creditors of the protected energy company but does not include a person whose claim has been wholly rejected for purposes of voting, dividend or otherwise.

(3) The right of inspection given by this Rule is also exercisable by the directors of the protected energy company.

(4) Any person attending a meeting in energy administration proceedings is entitled, immediately before or in the course of the meeting, to inspect proxies and associated documents (including claims)—

(a) to be used in connection with that meeting; or

(b) sent or given to the chairman of that meeting or to any other person by a creditor or member for the purpose of that meeting, whether or not they are to be used at it.

[16.243]
66 Proxy-holder with financial interest

(1) A proxy-holder shall not vote in favour of any resolution which would directly or indirectly place him, or any associate of his, in a position to receive any remuneration of the assets of the protected energy company, unless the proxy specifically directs him to vote that way.

(2) Where a proxy-holder has signed the proxy as being authorised to do so by his principal and the proxy specifically directs him to vote in the way mentioned in paragraph (1), he shall nevertheless not vote in that way unless he produces to the chairman of the meeting written authorisation from his principal sufficient to show the proxy-holder was entitled so to sign the proxy.

(3) This Rule applies also to any person acting as chairman of a meeting and using proxies in that capacity in accordance with Rule 63(3); and in the application of this Rule to any such person, the proxy-holder is deemed an associate of his.

[16.244]
67 Representation of corporations

(1) Where a person is authorised under section 375 of the Companies Act to represent a corporation at a meeting of creditors or of the protected energy company, he shall produce to the chairman of the meeting a copy of the resolution from which he derives his authority.

(2) The copy resolution must be executed in accordance with the provisions of section 36B(2) of the Companies Act, or certified by the secretary or a director of the corporation to be a true copy.

(3) Nothing in this Rule requires the authority of a person to sign a proxy on behalf of a principal which is a corporation to be in the form of a resolution of that corporation.

PART 11
MISCELLANEOUS AND GENERAL

[16.245]
68 Giving of notices, etc

(1) All notices required or authorised by or under the 1986 Act, Schedule B1 to the 1986 Act, the 2004 Act or the Rules to be given, sent or delivered must be in writing, unless it is otherwise provided, or the court allows the notice to be sent or given in some other way.

(2) Any reference in the 1986 Act, Schedule B1 to the 1986 Act, the 2004 Act or the Rules to giving, sending or delivering a notice or any such document means, without prejudice to any other way and unless it is otherwise provided, that the notice or document may be sent by post, and that, subject to Rule 69, any form of post may be used. Personal service of the notice or document is permissible in all cases.

(3) Where under the 1986 Act, Schedule B1 to the 1986 Act, the 2004 Act or the Rules a notice or other document is required or authorised to be given, sent or delivered by a person ("the sender") to another ("the recipient"), it may be given, sent or delivered by any person duly authorised by the sender to do so to any person duly authorised by the recipient to receive or accept it.

(4) Where two or more persons are acting jointly as the energy administrator in energy administration proceedings, the giving, sending or delivering of a notice or document to one of them is to be treated as the giving, sending or delivering of a notice or document to each or all.

[16.246]
69 Sending by post

(1) For a document to be properly sent by post, it must be contained in an envelope addressed to the person to whom it is to be sent, and pre-paid for either first or second class post.

(2) Any document to be sent by post may be sent to the last known address of the person to whom the document is to be sent.

(3) Where first class post is used, the document is to be deemed to be received on the second business day after the date of posting, unless the contrary is shown.

(4) Where second class post is used, the document is to be deemed to be received on the fourth business day after the date of posting, unless the contrary is shown.

[16.247]
70 Certificate of giving notice, etc

(1) Where in any proceedings a notice or document is required to be given, sent or delivered by the energy administrator, the date of giving, sending or delivery of it may be proved by means of a certificate signed by him or on his behalf by his solicitor, or a partner or an employee of either of them, that the notice or document was duly given, posted or otherwise sent, or delivered on the date stated in the certificate.

(2) In the case of a notice or document to be given, sent or delivered by a person other than the energy administrator, the date of giving, sending or delivery of it may be proved by means of a certificate by that person that he gave, posted or otherwise sent or delivered the notice or document on the date stated in the certificate, or that he instructed another person (naming him) to do so.

(3) A certificate under this Rule may be endorsed on a copy of the notice to which it relates.

(4) A certificate purporting to be signed by or on behalf of the energy administrator, or by the person mentioned in paragraph (2), shall be deemed, unless the contrary is shown, to be sufficient evidence of the matters stated therein.

[16.248]
71 Validity of proceedings

Where in accordance with the 1986 Act, Schedule B1 to the 1986 Act or the Rules a meeting of creditors or other persons is summoned by notice, the meeting is presumed to have been duly summoned and held, notwithstanding that not all those to whom the notice is to be given have received it.

[16.249]
72 Evidence of proceedings at meetings

A report of proceedings at a meeting of the protected energy company or of the creditors in an energy administration, which is signed by a person describing himself as the chairman of that meeting, shall be deemed, unless the contrary is shown, to be sufficient evidence of the matters contained that report.

[16.250]
73 Right to list of creditors and copy documents

(1) Subject to Rule 74, in any energy administration proceedings, a creditor who has the right to inspect documents also has the right to require the energy administrator to furnish him with a list of the protected energy company's creditors and the amounts of their respective debts.

(2) Where the energy administrator is requested by the Secretary of State, GEMA, a creditor or member to supply a copy of any document, he is entitled to require payment of the appropriate fee in respect of the supply of that copy.

(3) Subject to Rule 74, where a person has the right to inspect documents, the right includes that of taking copies of those documents, on payment of the appropriate fee.

(4) In this Rule, the appropriate fee means 15 pence per A4 or A5 page and 30 pence per A3 page.

[16.251]
74 Confidentiality of documents

(1) Where the energy administrator considers, in the case of a document forming part of the records of those proceedings—

(a) that it should be treated as confidential; or

(b) that it is of such nature that its disclosure would be calculated to be injurious to the interest of the creditors or the members,

he may decline to allow it to be inspected by a person who would otherwise be entitled to inspect it.

(2) Where under this Rule the energy administrator refuses inspection of a document, the person who made that request may apply to the court for an order to overrule the refusal and the court may either overrule it altogether, or sustain it, either unconditionally or subject to such conditions, if any, as it thinks fit to impose.

(3) Nothing in this Rule entitles the energy administrator to decline to allow inspection of any claim or proxy.

[16.252]
75 Energy administrator's caution

(1) Wherever under the Rules any person has to appoint a person to the office of energy administrator, he is under a duty to satisfy himself that the person appointed or to be appointed has caution for the proper performance of his functions.

(2) In any energy administration proceedings the cost of the energy administrator's caution shall be paid as an expense of the energy administration.

[16.253]
76 Punishment of offences

Section 431 (summary proceedings), as it applies to Scotland, has effect in relation to offences under the Rules as to offences under the 1986 Act.

[16.254]
77 Forms for use in energy administration proceedings

(1) The forms contained in the Schedule to the Rules shall be used in, and in connection with, energy administration proceedings.

(2) The forms shall be used with such variations, if any, as the circumstances may require.

[16.255]
78 Fees, expenses, etc

(1) All fees, costs, charges and other expenses incurred in the course of the energy administration are to be regarded as expenses of the energy administration.

(2) The expenses associated with the prescribed part shall be paid out of the prescribed part.

[16.256]
79 Power of court to cure defects in procedure

(1) The court may, on the application of any person having an interest—

(a) if there has been a failure to comply with any requirement of the 1986 Act, Schedule B1 to the 1986 Act, the 2004 Act or the Rules, make an order waiving any such failure and, so far as practicable, restoring any person prejudiced by the failure to the position he would have been in but for the failure;

(b) if for any reason anything required or authorised to be done in, or in connection with, the energy administration proceedings cannot be done, make such order as may be necessary to enable that thing to be done.

(2) The court, in an order under paragraph (1), may impose such conditions, including conditions as to expenses, as it thinks fit and may—

(a) authorise or dispense with the performance of any act in the energy administration proceedings;

(b) extend or waive any time limit specified in the 1986 Act, Schedule B1 to the 1986 Act, the 2004 Act or the Rules.

(3) An application under paragraph (1)—

(a) may at any time be remitted by the sheriff to the Court of Session, of his own accord or on an application by any person having an interest;

(b) shall be so remitted, if the Court of Session so directs on an application by any such person, if the sheriff or the Court of Session, as the case may be, considers that the remit is desirable because of the importance or complexity of the matters raised by the application.

(4) The energy administrator shall record in the sederunt book the decision of the court.

[16.257]

80 Sederunt book

(1) The energy administrator shall maintain a sederunt book during his term of office for the purpose of providing an accurate record of the administration of the energy administration.

(2) Without prejudice to the generality of the above paragraph, there shall be inserted in the sederunt book a copy of anything required to be recorded in it by any provision of the 1986 Act or of the Rules.

(3) The energy administrator shall make the sederunt book available for inspection at all reasonable hours by any interested person.

(4) Any entry in the sederunt book shall be sufficient evidence of the facts stated therein, except where it is founded on by the energy administrator in his own interest.

(5) Without prejudice to paragraph (3), the energy administrator shall retain, or shall make arrangements for retention of, the sederunt book for a period of ten years from the date on which the energy administration ends.

(6) Where the sederunt book is maintained in non-documentary form it shall be capable of reproduction in legible form.

[16.258]

81 Disposal of protected energy company's books, papers and other records

(1) Where a protected energy company has been the subject of energy administration proceedings ("the original proceedings") which have terminated and other insolvency proceedings ("the subsequent proceedings") have commenced in relation to that protected energy company, the energy administrator appointed in relation to the original proceedings, shall, before the expiry of the later of—

(a) the period of 30 days following a request to him to do so by the responsible insolvency practitioner appointed in relation to the subsequent proceedings; or

(b) the period of 6 months after the protected energy company entered energy administration,

deliver to the responsible insolvency practitioner appointed in relation to the subsequent proceedings the books, papers and other records of the protected energy company.

(2) The energy administrator shall dispose of the books, papers and records of the protected energy company in accordance with the directions of the court or, if by the date which is 12 months after dissolution of the protected energy company no such directions have been given, he may do so after that date in such a way as he deems appropriate.

(3) The energy administrator or former energy administrator shall within 14 days of a request by the Secretary of State give the Secretary of State particulars of any money in his hands or under his control representing unclaimed or undistributed assets of the protected energy company or dividends or other sums due to any person as a member or former member of the protected energy company.

[16.259]

82 Information about time spent on a case

(1) Subject as set out in this Rule, in respect of any energy administration in which he acts, the energy administrator shall on request in writing made by any person mentioned in paragraph (2), supply free of charge to that person a statement of the kind described in paragraph (3).

(2) The persons referred to in paragraph (1) are—

(a) any creditor in the case; and

(b) any director of the protected energy company.

(3) The statement referred to in paragraph (1) shall comprise in relation to the period beginning with the date of the energy administrator's appointment and ending with the relevant date the following details—

(a) the total number of hours spent on the case by the energy administrator and any staff assigned to the case during that period;

(b) for each grade of individual so engaged, the average hourly rate at which any work carried out by individuals in that grade is charged; and

(c) the number of hours spent by each grade of staff during that period.

(4) In relation to paragraph (3) the "relevant date" means the date next before the date of the making of the request on which the energy administrator has completed any period in office which is a multiple of six months or, where the energy administrator has vacated office, the date that he vacated office.

(5) Where the energy administrator has vacated office, an obligation to provide information under this Rule shall only arise in relation to a request that is made within 2 years of the date he vacates office.

(6) Any statement required to be provided to any person under this Rule shall be supplied within 28 days of the date of the receipt of the request by the energy administrator.

SCHEDULE
FORMS

Rule 77(1)

[16.260]

NOTES

The forms themselves are not reproduced in this work, but their numbers and descriptions are listed below.

Number	*Title*
Form EA1(S)	Statement of the Proposed Energy Administrator
Form EA2(S)	Notice of Petition for Energy Administration Order
Form EA3(S)	Notice of Dismissal of Petition for Energy Administration Order
Form EA4(S)	Notification of Appointment of Administrator (for Newspaper or Edinburgh Gazette)
Form EA5(S)	Notice of Energy Administrator's Appointment
Form EA6(S)	Notice Requiring Submission of a Statement of Affairs
Form EA7(S)	Statement of Affairs
Form EA8(S)	Statement of Concurrence
Form EA9(S)	Notice of Statement of Affairs
Form EA10(S)	Statement of Energy Administrator's Proposals
Form EA11(S)	Notice of Extension of Time Period
Form EA12(S)	Notice of Order to Deal with Secured Property
Form EA13(S)	Statement of Energy Administrator's Revised Proposals
Form EA14(S)	Energy Administrator's Progress Report
Form EA15(S)	Statement of Claim by Creditor
Form EA16(S)	Notice of Court Order Ending Administration
Form EA17(S)	Notice of Move from Energy Administration to Creditor's Voluntary Liquidation
Form EA18(S)	Notice of Move from Energy Administration to Dissolution
Form EA19(S)	Notice to Registrar of Companies in Respect of Date of Dissolution
Form EA20(S)	Notice of Intention to Resign as Energy Administrator
Form EA21(S)	Notice of Resignation by Energy Administrator
Form EA22(S)	Notice of Vacation of Office by Energy Administrator
Form EA23(S)	Notice of Appointment of Replacement/Additional Energy Administrator
Form EA24(S)	Notice in Respect of Order under Section 176A of the Insolvency Act 1986 (Energy Administration)
Form EA25(S)	Proxy—Energy Administration
Form B1/115	Notice of Insufficient Property for Distribution to Unsecured Creditors other than by virtue of s 176A(2)(a) of Insolvency Act 1986

BANKRUPTCY (SCOTLAND) ACT 1985 (LOW INCOME, LOW ASSET DEBTORS ETC) REGULATIONS 2008 (NOTE)

(SSI 2008/81)

[16.261]

NOTES

Made: 4 March 2008.

Authority: Bankruptcy (Scotland) Act 1985, ss 5A, 39A(4)(a).

Commencement: 1 April 2008.

Revocation: these Regulations are revoked by the Bankruptcy (Money Advice and Deduction from Income etc) (Scotland) Regulations 2014, SSI 2014/296, reg 10, subject to reg 11 thereof which provides that regs 1–3 continue to apply to debtor applications made before 1 April 2015. They have been omitted for reasons of space and can be found in the 18th edition of this Handbook.

BANKRUPTCY (SCOTLAND) REGULATIONS 2008 (NOTE)

(SSI 2008/82)

[16.262]

NOTES

Made: 4 March 2008.

Authority: Bankruptcy (Scotland) Act 1985, ss 5(4C), 6(7), 7(1)(d), 8(2), 11(1), 15(6), 19(1), 22(2)(a), (6), 23(1)(a), 25(6)(b), 45(3)(a), 48(7), 49(3), 51(7)(a), 54(2), 67(8), 69, 73, 74; Bankruptcy and Diligence (Scotland) Act 2007, s 225(1).

Commencement: 1 April 2008.

Revocation: these Regulations are largely revoked by the Bankruptcy (Scotland) Regulations 2014, SSI 2014/225, regs 23(a), 24, subject to savings in relation to sequestration before 1 April 2015. They have been omitted for reasons of space and can be found in the 18th edition of this Handbook.

ACT OF SEDERUNT (SHERIFF COURT BANKRUPTCY RULES) 2008 (NOTE)

(SSI 2008/119)

[16.263]

NOTES

Made: 13 March 2008.

Authority: Sheriff Courts (Scotland) Act 1971, s 32; Bankruptcy (Scotland) Act 1985, ss 1A(1)(b),14(4), 62(2), Sch 5, para 2; European Communities Act 1972, Sch 2, para 1A.

Commencement: 1 April 2008.

Revocation: these Rules are revoked by the Act of Sederunt (Rules of the Court of Session, Sheriff Appeal Court Rules and Sheriff Court Rules Amendment) (Bankruptcy (Scotland) Act 2016) 2016, SSI 2016/312, r 6, as from 30 November 2016, subject to savings in r 8(4), (5) thereof (as amended by SSI 2016/367) which provides as follows:

"(4) Paragraph 6 has no effect in relation to—

(a) sequestrations as regards to which the petition is presented, or the debtor application is made before 30th November 2016; or

(b) the application of the provisions mentioned in subparagraph (5) to trust deeds executed before 30th November 2016.

(5) The provisions are, in the schedule of the Act of Sederunt (Sheriff Court Bankruptcy Rules) 2008—

(a) rule 1(3), so far as relating to Forms 8 and 9 in appendix 1 of the schedule;

(b) rule 9(2) and (3); and

(c) Forms 8 and 9 in appendix 1 of the schedule.".

See now the Act of Sederunt (Sheriff Court Bankruptcy Rules) 2016, SSI 2016/313 at **[16.322]**. The 2008 Rules have been omitted for reasons of space and can be found in the 18th edition of this Handbook.

BANKRUPTCY (CERTIFICATE FOR SEQUESTRATION) (SCOTLAND) REGULATIONS 2010 (NOTE)

(SSI 2010/397)

[16.264]

NOTES

Made: 11 November 2010.

Authority: Bankruptcy (Scotland) Act 1985, ss 5(2B)(c)(ib), 5B(5)(a), (b), (c).

Commencement: 15 November 2010.

Revocation: these Regulations are revoked by the Bankruptcy (Scotland) Regulations 2016, SSI 2016/397, reg 32, Sch 3, as from 30 November 2016, subject to savings in reg 33 thereof at **[16.433]**. They have been omitted for reasons of space and can be found in the 18th edition of this Handbook.

INVESTMENT BANK SPECIAL ADMINISTRATION (SCOTLAND) RULES 2011 (NOTE)

(SI 2011/2262)

[16.265]

NOTES

Made: 12 September 2011.

Authority: Insolvency Act 1986, s 411(1A)(b), (2), (2C), (3), as applied by the Investment Bank Special Administration Regulations 2011.

Commencement: 14 November 2011.

These Rules set out the procedure in Scotland for the investment bank special administration process under the Investment Bank Special Administration Regulations 2011 (SI 2011/245). The main features of investment bank special administration are that:

(a) the investment bank enters the procedure by court order;
(b) the order appoints an administrator;
(c) the administrator is to pursue the special administration objectives in accordance with the statement of proposals approved by the meeting of creditors and clients and, in certain circumstances, the FCA and the PRA;
(d) in other respects the procedure is similar to administration under the Insolvency Act 1986, Sch B1.

Where the investment bank is also a deposit-taking bank, the Rules also apply in relation to the special administration (bank insolvency) and special administration (bank administration) processes under Schs 1 and 2 to SI 2011/245.

PROTECTED TRUST DEEDS (SCOTLAND) REGULATIONS 2013 (NOTE)

(SSI 2013/318)

[16.266]

NOTES

Made: 6 November 2013.
Authority: Bankruptcy (Scotland) Act 1985, ss 69A, 72(1), Sch 5, para 5.
Commencement: 28 November 2013.
Revocation: these Regulations are revoked by the Bankruptcy (Scotland) Act 2016, s 234(2), Sch 9, Pt 2, as from 30 November 2016 and subject to transitional provisions and savings in s 234(3)–(8) thereof at **[5.432]**. They have been omitted for reasons of space and can be found in the 18th edition of this Handbook.

BANKRUPTCY (SCOTLAND) REGULATIONS 2014 (NOTE)

(SSI 2014/225)

[16.267]

NOTES

Made: 20 August 2014.
Authority: Bankruptcy (Scotland) Act 1985, ss 1A(1)(b), (5), 2(8), 5(2ZA)(a)(ii), (2D), (6A), 6(7), 7(1)(d), 11(1), 19(2), 22(2)(a), (6), 23(1)(a), 32(9A), 40(3B), 43A(2), 43B(1), 45(3)(a), 49(3), 51(7)(a), 54(2), 54A(2), 54C(2), 54D(2)(a), (c), 54E(2), (5), 69, 71C, 72(1A), 73(1), Sch 3, paras 5(1), 6.
Commencement: 1 April 2015.
Revocation: these Regulations are largely revoked by the Bankruptcy (Scotland) Regulations 2016, SSI 2016/397, reg 32, Sch 3, as from 30 November 2016, subject to savings in reg 33 thereof at **[16.433]**. They have been omitted for reasons of space and can be found in the 18th edition of this Handbook.

BANKRUPTCY (APPLICATIONS AND DECISIONS) (SCOTLAND) REGULATIONS 2014 (NOTE)

(SSI 2014/226)

[16.268]

NOTES

Made: 20 August 2014.
Authority: Bankruptcy (Scotland) Act 1985, ss 71C, 72(1A), 72A.
Commencement: 1 April 2015.
Revocation: these Regulations are revoked by the Bankruptcy (Applications and Decisions) (Scotland) Regulations 2016, SSI 2016/295, reg 25, as from 30 November 2016, subject to savings in reg 26 thereof at **[16.320]**. They have been omitted for reasons of space and can be found in the 18th edition of this Handbook.

BANKRUPTCY FEES (SCOTLAND) REGULATIONS 2014

(SSI 2014/227)

NOTES

Made: 20 August 2014.
Authority: Bankruptcy (Scotland) Act 1985, ss 69A, 72(1A).
Commencement: 1 April 2015.

[16.269]

1 Citation and commencement

(1) These Regulations may be cited as the Bankruptcy Fees (Scotland) Regulations 2014.
(2) They come into force on 1st April 2015.

NOTES

Commencement: 1 April 2015.

[16.270]

2 Interpretation

In these Regulations—

"the 1985 Act" means the Bankruptcy (Scotland) Act 1985;

"bankruptcy restrictions order" means an order made under section 56A of the 1985 Act;

"debtor who has few assets" means a debtor to whom section 5(2ZA) of the 1985 Act applies;

"debtor's contribution" has the meaning given by section 5D(1) of the 1985 Act;

"expenses of realisation" means any outlays incurred by the trustee in realising the debtor's estate which in the course of normal business practice are deducted from the price payable to the trustee;

"member State liquidator" has the meaning given by section 73(1) of the 1985 Act;

["member State insolvency practitioner" has the meaning given by section 228(1) of the Bankruptcy (Scotland) Act 2016;]

"table of fees" means the Table of Fees in the Schedule;

"statutory fee" means any fee payable under an enactment;

"the statutory meeting" has the meaning given by section 20A of the 1985 Act;

"trading expenses" means any outlays incurred by the trustee in the carrying on of any business of the debtor;

"trust deed", where granted before 1st April 1993, means a voluntary trust deed granted by or on behalf of a debtor, whereby the debtor's estate is conveyed to the trustee for the benefit of the creditors of that debtor generally and, where granted on or after that date, has the meaning assigned by section 5(4A) of the 1985 Act; and

"trustee vote" is to be construed in accordance with section 24(1) of the 1985 Act.

NOTES

Commencement: 1 April 2015.

Definition "member State insolvency practitioner" inserted by the Insolvency (Regulation (EU) 2015/848) (Miscellaneous Amendments) (Scotland) Regulations 2017, SSI 2017/210, regs 5(1), (2), 9, as from 26 June 2017, except in relation to proceedings opened before that date.

[16.271]

3 Fees and outlays as interim trustee or trustee

The fees payable to the Accountant in Bankruptcy in respect of the exercise by, or on behalf of, that office of its functions as interim trustee or trustee in a sequestration, which are specified in column 1 of Part 1 of the table of fees are the fees specified in relation to those functions in column 2 of the table of fees.

NOTES

Commencement: 1 April 2015.

[16.272]

4

The outlays payable to the Accountant in Bankruptcy in respect of the exercise by, or on behalf of, that office of its functions as interim trustee or trustee in a sequestration are those outlays actually, necessarily and reasonably incurred in respect of the exercise of any of those functions and include, but are not limited to, outlays so incurred in respect of—

(a) the making of searches in any public register;
(b) the valuation of property;
(c) legal services and related expenses;
(d) estate agency services;
(e) the services of auctioneers and valuers;
(f) services related to taxation matters; and
(g) travel and subsistence expenses.

NOTES

Commencement: 1 April 2015.

[16.273]

5

Any fees and outlays payable to the Accountant in Bankruptcy in respect of the exercise by, or on behalf of, that office of its functions as interim trustee or trustee in a sequestration are due for payment from the sequestrated estate where—

(a) the Accountant in Bankruptcy has made a determination of its fees and outlays calculated in accordance with these Regulations, under and in accordance with, as appropriate, one of these provisions of the 1985 Act—
  (i) section 26A(3)(b) (determination of fees and outlays where Accountant in Bankruptcy was interim trustee and some other person becomes trustee);
  (ii) section 53(1), as modified by section 53A(2) (determination of fees and outlays at end of each accounting period where Accountant in Bankruptcy is trustee);

(iii) section 58A(4)(a) (determination of fees and outlays on discharge of Accountant in Bankruptcy as trustee); and

(b) the period within which an appeal against such a determination may be taken to the sheriff has expired or, if an appeal is so taken, that appeal has been determined, under, as appropriate, one of these provisions of the 1985 Act—

(i) section 26A(5) and (6);

(ii) section 53(4), as modified by section 53A(2);

(iii) section 58A(5) and (6).

NOTES

Commencement: 1 April 2015.

[16.274]

6 Other fees

The fees payable to the Accountant in Bankruptcy in respect of the exercise of that office's functions, other than as interim trustee or trustee in a sequestration, specified in column 1 of Part 2 of the table of fees are the fees specified in relation to those functions in column 2 of the table of fees.

NOTES

Commencement: 1 April 2015.

[16.275]

7

A fee payable under regulation 6 is payable even although it is payable by or on behalf of the Accountant in Bankruptcy in the exercise of that office's functions as interim trustee or trustee in a sequestration.

NOTES

Commencement: 1 April 2015.

[16.276]

8 Manner of payment

A fee payable to the Accountant in Bankruptcy for a function specified in Part 2 of the table of fees is due for payment—

(a) on the application for these services being made to the Accountant in Bankruptcy, in respect of—

(i) item 14 (removal of trustee and trustee not acting);

(ii) item 15 (declaration of office of trustee as vacant);

(iii) item 16 (replacement of trustee acting in more than one sequestration);

(iv) item 17 (appointment or reappointment of trustee where newly identified estate);

(v) item 18 (application by trustee for a direction);

(vi) item 19 (curing defects in procedure);

(vii) item 21 (conversion of trust deed into sequestration);

(b) in respect of the functions specified in item 2 (supervision of sequestration proceedings)—

(i) at the end of each 12 month period of supervision; or

(ii) if the trustee is discharged during a 12 month period, in advance of the granting of a certificate of discharge under section 57(3) of the 1985 Act;

(c) in respect of the functions specified in item 8(c) (protected trust deed supervision)—

(i) at the end of each 12 month period of supervision; or

(ii) if the trustee is discharged during a 12 month period, in advance of the date of discharge of the trustee under regulation 25 of the Protected Trust Deeds (Scotland) Regulations 2013;

(d) in respect of the functions specified in item 12 (election of replacement trustee by trustee vote), on the submission of the relevant report to the Accountant in Bankruptcy;

(e) in respect of the functions specified in item 22 (determination of debtor applications)—

(i) on the application being made to the Accountant in Bankruptcy; and

(ii) if paragraph 1 of Schedule A1 to the 1985 Act ceases to apply to the debtor, on receiving a request from the Accountant in Bankruptcy for the fee due under item 22(b) taking account of the fee already paid under item 22(a);

(f) in respect of any other such function, on performance by the Accountant in Bankruptcy of that function.

NOTES

Commencement: 1 April 2015.

[16.277]

9

A fee payable to the Accountant in Bankruptcy in respect of the functions specified in item 22 (determination of debtor applications) of Part 2 of the table of fees is payable whether or not it is subsequently determined in favour of the applicant.

NOTES

Commencement: 1 April 2015.

[16.278]

10

A fee payable to the Accountant in Bankruptcy in respect of a function specified in Part 2 of the table of fees by an interim trustee, trustee in a sequestration or trustee under a protected trust deed is payable by the trustee whether or not there are subsequently funds available for distribution from the debtor's estate to meet that fee.

NOTES

Commencement: 1 April 2015.

[16.279]

11 Waiver of fees not permissible

(1) Subject to paragraphs (2) and (3), the fees in Part 2 of the table of fees payable to the Accountant in Bankruptcy may not be waived by the Accountant in Bankruptcy in whole or in part.

(2) For the purposes of regulation 8(c)(ii), the Accountant in Bankruptcy may waive the balance due, if the debtor who granted the protected trust deed failed to meet the debtor's obligations for the purposes of regulation 24(2)(a) of the Protected Trust Deeds (Scotland) Regulations 2013.

(3) For the purposes of regulation 8(e)(ii), the Accountant in Bankruptcy may waive the balance due, unless the debtor provided false or misleading information in the debtor application.

NOTES

Commencement: 1 April 2015.

[16.280]

12 Repayment of fees – refusal of bankruptcy restrictions order

(1) Where the Accountant in Bankruptcy or a sheriff does not grant an application for a bankruptcy restrictions order under section 56A(1) of the 1985 Act, the Accountant in Bankruptcy or the sheriff may hold that in the circumstances of the case it was not reasonable to make the application.

(2) In that event, any fee charged by the Accountant in Bankruptcy under item 23 of Part 2 of the table of fees must be repaid.

NOTES

Commencement: 1 April 2015.

[16.281]

13 Sequestrations and trust deeds before 1st April 2015

(1) Except as mentioned in paragraph (4), nothing in these Regulations has effect as regards any sequestration in respect of which—

(a) the petition is presented before 1st April 2015; or

(b) a debtor application [is] made before that date.

(2) Except as mentioned in paragraph (4), nothing in these Regulations has effect as regards any trust deed which was granted before 1st April 2015.

(3) The Bankruptcy Fees etc (Scotland) Regulations 2012, continue to apply and have effect in relation to any such sequestration or trust deed.

[(4) This regulation does not apply in respect of—

(a) items 18, 20 and 21 in Part 2 in the table of fees; or

(b) the revocation of items 10, 11, 12 and 13 in Part 2 of the Table of Fees in Schedule 1 to the Bankruptcy Fees etc (Scotland) Regulations 2012.]

NOTES

Commencement: 1 April 2015.

Para (1): word in square brackets in sub-para (b) substituted by the Bankruptcy (Miscellaneous Amendments) (Scotland) Regulations 2015, SSI 2015/80, reg 4(a).

Para (4): substituted by SSI 2015/80, reg 4(b).

14 (*Revokes the Bankruptcy Fees etc (Scotland) Regulations 2012, SSI 2012/118, subject to reg 13 above.*)

SCHEDULE
TABLE OF FEES

Regulations 3 and 6

PART 1
FEES FOR ACCOUNTANT IN BANKRUPTCY AS INTERIM TRUSTEE OR TRUSTEE IN SEQUESTRATION

[16.282]

Column 1 (Functions)	*Column 2 (Fee Payable)*	*Column 3 (Former Rates)*
1 In respect of the exercise by the Accountant in Bankruptcy of that office's functions as interim trustee in a sequestration where the Accountant in Bankruptcy is not appointed as trustee in that sequestration.	£200.00	£100 per hour for each hour of work done
2 In respect of the exercise by the Accountant in Bankruptcy of that office's functions as interim trustee or trustee in a sequestration, other than in respect of—	£1,100.00	£100 per hour for each hour of work done
(a) the realisation of assets in the sequestrated estate;		
(b) ingathering debtor's contributions; and		
(c) payment of dividends to creditors.		
3 In respect of the exercise by the Accountant in Bankruptcy of that office's functions as trustee in a sequestration in relation to the realisation of assets in the sequestrated estate—		
(a) in respect of the total price paid in a transaction by the purchaser of heritable property, including any interest paid thereon, but after the deduction of any sums paid to secured creditors in respect of their securities over that property—		
(i) on the first £10,000 or fraction of that sum;	15% of that amount	*(No change)*
(ii) on the next £10,000 or fraction of that sum;	5% of that amount	*(No change)*
(iii) on all further sums;	2% of that amount	*(No change)*
(b) in respect of the proceeds of the sale of moveable property, after the deduction of the expenses of sale and any sums paid to secured creditors in respect of their securities over that property—		
(i) on the first £10,000 or fraction of that sum;	15% of that amount	*(No change)*
(ii) on the next £10,000 or fraction of that sum;	5% of that amount	*(No change)*
(iii) on all further sums;	2% of that amount	*(No change)*

Column 1 *(Functions)*	*Column 2* *(Fee Payable)*	*Column 3* *(Former Rates)*
4 In respect of the exercise by the Accountant in Bankruptcy of that office's functions as interim trustee or trustee in a sequestration in ingathering debtor's contributions.	25% of funds ingathered	*(No change to fee; function formerly in respect of ingathering debtor's estate)*
5 In respect of the exercise by the Accountant in Bankruptcy of that office's functions as trustee in relation to the payment of dividends to creditors—		
(a) on the first £10,000 or fraction of that sum;	10% of that amount	*(No change)*
(b) on the next £10,000 or fraction of that sum;	5% of that amount	*(No change)*
(c) on all further sums.	1% of that amount	2% of that amount

NOTES

Commencement: 1 April 2015.

PART 2
FEES FOR OTHER FUNCTIONS OF THE ACCOUNTANT IN BANKRUPTCY

[16.283]

Column 1 *(Functions)*	*Column 2* *(Fee Payable)*	*Column 3* *(Fee Formerly Payable)*
1 For administration of—		
(a) any petition by a creditor or trustee under a protected trust deed;	£100.00	*(No change to fee, but petition by executor of a deceased debtor is now administered by debtor application—see item 22(b))*
(b) any such petition where following award of sequestration the Accountant in Bankruptcy is the trustee.	£200.00	*(No change)*
2 For supervising proceedings in sequestration—		
(a) where commissioners have been elected;	(a) £70.00 per 12 month period of supervision beginning on the date of appointment of the trustee and ending on discharge of the trustee (or part of such period) for the first 12 month period (or part of such period); and (b) thereafter £50.00 per 12 month period of supervision throughout which commissioners are in post (or part of such period).	Where applicable— (a) £139.00 for supervising proceedings; (b) £20.00 for registering award of sequestration; (c) £69.00 for any special report to the court; (d) £36.00 for examination of the sederunt book and related work, in connection with the discharge of a trustee; (e) £36.00 for granting a certificate of discharge to an interim trustee.
(b) where no commissioners have been elected;	£70.00 per 12 month period of supervision beginning on the date of appointment of the trustee and ending on discharge of the trustee (or part of such period).	Where applicable— (a) £210.00 for supervision of trustee; (b) £20.00 for registering award of sequestration;

Column 1 (Functions)	Column 2 (Fee Payable)	Column 3 (Fee Formerly Payable)
		(c) £69.00 for supervising payment of dividend to creditors where no commissioners have been elected; (d) £69.00 for any special report to court; (e) £36.00 for examination of the sederunt book and related work, in connection with the discharge of a trustee; (f) £36.00 for granting a certificate of discharge to an interim trustee.
3 For considering and issuing a determination in an appeal against a determination of commissioners as to the outlays and remuneration payable to a trustee.	5% of the sum remaining on deduction from the sum of outlays and remuneration determined by the Accountant in Bankruptcy of any outlays incurred by way of statutory fees, trading expenses or expenses of realisation.	*(No change)*
4 For issuing a determination fixing the outlays and remuneration payable to— (a) an interim trustee; or (b) a trustee.	17.5% of the sum remaining on deduction from the sum of outlays and remuneration determined of any outlays incurred by way of statutory fees, trading expenses or expenses of realisation.	*(No change)*
5 For attendance at any meeting of creditors—fee per hour or part thereof, including travelling time.	£69.00	*(No change)*
6 For calling any meeting of creditors.	£36.00	*(No change)*
7 For attendance at any examination of the debtor—fee per hour or part thereof, including travelling time.	£69.00	*(No change)*
8 In respect of protected trust deeds— (a) for publishing a notice in the register of insolvencies where—		
(i) the notice is sent by the trustee using the electronic service provided by the Accountant in Bankruptcy;	£35.00	*(No change)*
(ii) the notice is sent by the trustee by any other method;	£90.00	*(No change)*
(b) for registering a protected trust deed;	£36.00	*(No change)*
(c) for supervision of a trustee under a protected trust deed.	£100.00 per 12 month period of supervision beginning on the date of registration of the protected trust deed and ending on the discharge of the trustee (or part of such period).	*(No change)*

Column 1 *(Functions)*	*Column 2* *(Fee Payable)*	*Column 3* *(Fee Formerly Payable)*
9 For auditing the accounts of a trustee under a protected trust deed and fixing the trustee's remuneration.	5% of the sum remaining on deduction from the sum of outlays and remuneration determined of any outlays incurred by way of statutory fees, trading expenses or expenses of realisation.	*(No change)*
10 For lodging any unclaimed dividend in an appropriate bank or institution set aside for payment to a creditor or creditors, in respect of each creditor on consignation.	£26.00	*(No change)*
11 For uplifting any unclaimed dividend consigned in an appropriate bank or institution, in respect of each creditor.	£26.00	*(No change)*
12 For receiving a report of proceedings at the statutory meeting to elect a replacement trustee, other than following the death of a trustee acting in only one sequestration.	£50.00	None
13 For appointing a replacement trustee where the original trustee has resigned and no new trustee is elected by trustee vote.	£50.00	None
14 For considering and making an order in relation to an application for removal of a trustee by commissioners or a person representing at least one quarter in value of the creditors.	£50.00	None
15 For considering and making a declaration and any necessary order in relation to an application for declaration of the office of trustee as vacant by commissioners, a debtor or a creditor.	£50.00	None
16 For making a determination or appointment on receipt of an application by a person with an interest for the replacement of a trustee acting in more than one sequestration.	£50.00	None
17 For appointing a trustee where newly identified estate is discovered after the trustee's discharge, on receipt of an application by the trustee who was discharged.	£50.00	None
18 For giving a direction on receipt of an application by a trustee in relation to a particular matter arising in the sequestration.	£50.00	None

Column 1 (Functions)	Column 2 (Fee Payable)	Column 3 (Fee Formerly Payable)
19 For issuing an order curing defects in procedure on receipt of an application by any person having an interest.	£50.00	None
20 For determination of an application for recall of sequestration (except on direction of a sheriff).	£100.00	None
21 For considering and making any order in relation to an application by a member State liquidator [or member State insolvency practitioner] for conversion of a trust deed into sequestration.	£50.00	None
22 For determination of a debtor application in relation to—		
(a) a debtor who has few assets;	£90.00	£200
(b) any other debtor.	£200.00	*(No change to fee, but fee now applicable to executor of deceased debtor)*
23 For an application to the court or the Accountant in Bankruptcy for a bankruptcy restrictions order.	£250.00	*(No change)*
24 For registering a court order appointing a replacement trustee.	£19.00	*(No change)*

NOTES

Commencement: 1 April 2015.

Words in square brackets in item 21 inserted by the Insolvency (Regulation (EU) 2015/848) (Miscellaneous Amendments) (Scotland) Regulations 2017, SSI 2017/210, regs 5(1), (3), 9, as from 26 June 2017, except in relation to proceedings opened before that date.

BANKRUPTCY (MONEY ADVICE AND DEDUCTION FROM INCOME ETC) (SCOTLAND) REGULATIONS 2014 (NOTE)

(SSI 2014/296)

[16.284]

NOTES

Made: 5 November 2014.

Authority: Bankruptcy (Scotland) Act 1985, ss 5A, 5B(5)(b), 5C(1)(d), (2)(b), 32E(7), 39A(4)(a), 71C, 72(1A).

Commencement: 1 April 2015.

Revocation: these Regulations are revoked by the Bankruptcy (Scotland) Regulations 2016, SSI 2016/397, reg 32, Sch 3, as from 30 November 2016, subject to savings in reg 33 thereof at **[16.433]**. They have been omitted for reasons of space and can be found in the 18th edition of this Handbook.

INSOLVENT COMPANIES (REPORTS ON CONDUCT OF DIRECTORS) (SCOTLAND) RULES 2016

(SI 2016/185)

NOTES

Made: 7 February 2016.

Authority: Insolvency Act 1986, s 411(1)(b); Company Directors Disqualification Act 1986, s 21(2).

Commencement: 6 April 2016.

ARRANGEMENT OF RULES

1 Citation, extent commencement and interpretation . . . [16.285]
2 Revocation . . . [16.286]
3 Enforcement of section 7(4) of the Act . . . [16.287]
4 Conduct reports required to be sent under section 7A(4) of the Act . . . [16.288]
5 Applications for a longer period under section 7A(4)(b) of the Act . . . [16.289]
6 New information required to be sent under section 7A(5) of the Act . . . [16.290]
7 Unavailability of the portal . . . [16.291]
8 Enforcement of rules 4 to 6 . . . [16.292]
9 Review . . . [16.293]
10 Transitional and savings provisions . . . [16.294]

[16.285]

1 Citation, extent commencement and interpretation

(1) These Rules may be cited as the Insolvent Companies (Reports on Conduct of Directors) (Scotland) Rules 2016, and extend to Scotland only.

(2) These Rules come into force on 6th April 2016.

(3) In these Rules—

"by electronic means" means sent initially and received at its destination by means of electronic equipment for the processing (which expression includes digital compression) or storage of data, and entirely transmitted, conveyed and received by wire, by radio, by optical means or by other electromagnetic means;

"the Act" means the Company Directors Disqualification Act 1986;

"the former Rules" means the Insolvent Companies (Reports on Conduct of Directors) (Scotland) Rules 1996; and

"the portal" means a digital service provided by the Secretary of State for the functions of both the sending and acknowledgement of receipt, by electronic means, of reports, applications, information and notifications in accordance with these Rules.

NOTES

Commencement: 6 April 2016.

[16.286]

2 Revocation

Subject to rule 10 the following are revoked—

(a) the former Rules,

(b) the Insolvent Companies (Reports on Conduct of Directors) (Scotland) (Amendment) Rules 2001.

NOTES

Commencement: 6 April 2016.

[16.287]

3 Enforcement of section 7(4) of the Act

(1) This rule applies where, for the purpose of determining whether to exercise any function under section 7 of the Act (disqualification orders under section 6: applications and acceptance of undertakings), the Secretary of State requires or has required a person to—

(a) furnish the Secretary of State with information under section 7(4)(a), or

(b) produce and permit inspection of books, papers and other records in accordance with section 7(4)(b).

(2) On the application of the Secretary of State the court may make an order directing compliance within such period as may be specified.

(3) The court's order may provide that all expenses of and incidental to the application are to be borne by the person to whom the order is directed.

NOTES

Commencement: 6 April 2016.

[16.288]

4 Conduct reports required to be sent under section 7A(4) of the Act

(1) This rule is subject to rule 7.

(2) A conduct report required to be sent under section 7A(4) of the Act must be sent by the office-holder to the Secretary of State by electronic means via the portal.

(3) The Secretary of State must as soon as reasonably practicable acknowledge receipt, by electronic means via the portal, of a conduct report sent in accordance with this rule.

Part 16 Other SIs: Scotland

NOTES

Commencement: 6 April 2016.

[16.289]

5 Applications for a longer period under section 7A(4)(b) of the Act

(1) This rule is subject to rule 7.

(2) This rule applies where the particular circumstances of a case may require a period longer than that provided for by section 7A(4)(a) of the Act for the sending of a conduct report to the Secretary of State.

(3) The office-holder may apply to the Secretary of State for a longer period in which to send the report.

(4) The application must be sent by electronic means via the portal before the expiry of the period specified in section 7A(4)(a) of the Act.

(5) The application must explain the particular circumstances for the making of the application.

(6) The Secretary of State must as soon as reasonably practicable acknowledge receipt, by electronic means via the portal, of an application sent in accordance with this rule.

(7) The Secretary of State must, as soon as is reasonably practicable, notify the office-holder, by electronic means via the portal,—

(a) of the outcome of the application; and

(b) if the application is successful, of the longer period considered appropriate in the particular circumstances for the sending of the report to the Secretary of State under section 7A(4)(b) of the Act.

NOTES

Commencement: 6 April 2016.

[16.290]

6 New information required to be sent under section 7A(5) of the Act

(1) This rule is subject to rule 7.

(2) New information required to be sent under section 7A(5) of the Act must be sent by the office-holder to the Secretary of State by electronic means via the portal.

(3) The Secretary of State must as soon as reasonably practicable acknowledge receipt, by electronic means via the portal, of new information sent in accordance with this rule.

NOTES

Commencement: 6 April 2016.

[16.291]

7 Unavailability of the portal

(1) The Secretary of State—

(a) may at any time when the portal is unable to carry out one or more of its functions, and

(b) must, where the portal has been unable to carry out one or more of its functions for a period of 7 business days,

provide alternative means for complying with a requirement under rules 4, 5 or 6.

(2) The Secretary of State must give notice to office-holders specifying the means provided for the purposes of paragraph (1) and the period of time for which those means are made available.

(3) The Secretary of State may by notice vary the means provided under paragraph (1) or the period of time for which those means are made available.

(4) A notice under paragraph (3) must give office-holders at least 1 business day's notice before any variation takes effect.

(5) The time within which an office-holder must comply with rules 4, 5 or 6 does not include any day the whole or part of which forms part of a suspension period.

(6) For the purpose of paragraph (5) a suspension period is a period of time during which—

(a) the portal is unable to receive reports, applications or information;

(b) no notice under paragraph (2) or (3) is in force; and

(c) the office-holder has attempted to and been prevented from sending a report, application or information at least once during that period on the basis of sub-paragraph (a).

(7) In this rule "business day" means any day other than a Saturday, a Sunday, Christmas Day, Good Friday or a day which is a bank holiday in any part of Great Britain.

NOTES

Commencement: 6 April 2016.

[16.292]

8 Enforcement of rules 4 to 6

(1) An office-holder who without reasonable excuse fails to comply with any of the obligations imposed by section 7A(4) or 7A(5) of the Act is guilty of an offence and—

(a) on summary conviction of the offence, is liable to a fine not exceeding level 3 on the standard scale, and

(b) for continued contravention, is liable to a daily default fine; that is to say, the office-holder is liable on a second or subsequent summary conviction of the offence to a fine not exceeding one-tenth of level 3 on the standard scale for each day on which the contravention is continued (instead of the penalty specified in sub-paragraph (a)).

(2) Section 431 of the Insolvency Act 1986 (summary proceedings), as it applies to Scotland, has effect in relation to an offence under this rule as to offences under Parts 1 to 7 of that Act.

NOTES

Commencement: 6 April 2016.

[16.293]
9 Review

(1) The Secretary of State must from time to time—
- (a) carry out a review of these Rules,
- (b) set out the conclusions of the review in a report, and
- (c) publish the report.

(2) The report must in particular—
- (a) set out the objectives intended to be achieved by the regulatory system established by these Rules,
- (b) assess the extent to which those objectives are achieved, and
- (c) assess whether those objectives remain appropriate and, if so, the extent to which they could be achieved with a system that imposes less regulation.

(3) The first report under this rule must be published before the end of the period of 5 years beginning on 6th April 2016.

(4) Reports under this rule are afterwards to be published at intervals not exceeding 5 years.

NOTES

Commencement: 6 April 2016.

[16.294]
10 Transitional and savings provisions

(1) Rule 6 of the former Rules continues to apply when a period referred to in rule 6(2) of the former Rules has not expired by 6th April 2016.

(2) Until 6th October 2016 rules 3 to 5 of the former Rules continue to apply as if the former Rules had not been revoked when the relevant date for the purposes of rule 4 of the former Rules occurred before 6th April 2016.

(3) Until 6th October 2016 the forms contained in the Schedule to the former Rules must be used for the purpose of complying with rules 3 to 5 of the former Rules.

NOTES

Commencement: 6 April 2016.

BANKRUPTCY (APPLICATIONS AND DECISIONS) (SCOTLAND) REGULATIONS 2016

(SSI 2016/295)

NOTES

Made: 15 September 2016.
Authority: Bankruptcy (Scotland) Act 2016, ss 224, 225(2), 227.
Commencement: 30 November 2016.

ARRANGEMENT OF REGULATIONS

PART 1
INTRODUCTORY

1 Citation and commencement . . . . . [16.295]
2 Interpretation . . . . . [16.296]
3 Dispensing power . . . . . [16.297]

PART 2
APPLICATIONS: GENERAL

4 Applications . . . . . [16.298]
5 Application form: first instance applications to the Accountant in Bankruptcy . . . . . [16.299]
6 Application procedure: first instance applications to the Accountant in Bankruptcy . . . . . [16.300]
7 Inquiries . . . . . [16.301]
8 Further evidence . . . . . [16.302]

PART 3
SPECIFIC APPLICATIONS

9 Recall of sequestration by Accountant in Bankruptcy . . . [16.303]
10 Application for direction by trustee . . . [16.304]
11 Appointment of replacement trustee . . . [16.305]
12 Replacement trustee acting in more than one sequestration . . . [16.306]
13 Removal of trustee and trustee not acting . . . [16.307]
14 Contractual powers of trustee . . . [16.308]
15 Bankruptcy restrictions orders: proposal to make an order . . . [16.309]
16 Bankruptcy restrictions orders: revocation or variation . . . [16.310]
17 Conversion of protected trust deed into bankruptcy . . . [16.311]
18 Power to cure defects . . . [16.312]
19 Debts depending on contingency . . . [16.313]

PART 4
REFERENCE TO COURT AND REVIEW BY ACCOUNTANT IN BANKRUPTCY

20 Reference to court: time limits . . . [16.314]
21 Review applications . . . [16.315]
22 Review proceedings: staff of the Accountant in Bankruptcy . . . [16.316]
23 Review proceedings: persons assisting the Accountant in Bankruptcy . . . [16.317]
24 Review decision . . . [16.318]

PART 5
REVOCATIONS AND SAVING

25 Revocations . . . [16.319]
26 Sequestrations and trust deeds before 30th November 2016 . . . [16.320]

SCHEDULES

Schedule—Forms . . . [16.321]

PART 1
INTRODUCTORY

[16.295]

1 Citation and commencement

(1) These Regulations may be cited as the Bankruptcy (Applications and Decisions) (Scotland) Regulations 2016.

(2) They come into force on 30th November 2016.

NOTES

Commencement: 30 November 2016.

[16.296]

2 Interpretation

(1) In these Regulations—

"the Act" means the Bankruptcy (Scotland) Act 2016;

"the Accountant in Bankruptcy" (or "AiB") is to be construed in accordance with section 199 of the Act; and

"review application" has the meaning given by regulation 21(1).

(2) Any reference in these Regulations—

(a) to a form is to be construed as a reference to the form so numbered in the schedule;

(b) to a time when an application is made is to be construed as a reference to the time when the application is received by AiB.

NOTES

Commencement: 30 November 2016.

[16.297]

3 Dispensing power

AiB may relieve any person from the consequences of any failure to comply with a provision of these Regulations that is shown to be due to mistake, oversight or other reasonable cause.

NOTES

Commencement: 30 November 2016.

PART 2
APPLICATIONS: GENERAL

[16.298]
4 Applications

(1) Any application to AiB for which a form is prescribed by these Regulations (including a review application) may be made—
- (a) by personal delivery;
- (b) by being sent to the address of AiB at 1 Pennyburn Road, Kilwinning, Ayrshire, KA13 6SA—
  - (i) by a registered post service (as defined in section 125(1) of the Postal Services Act 2000); or
  - (ii) by a postal service which provides for the delivery of the document to be recorded;
- (c) by email or using the computer system provided by AiB for that purpose; or
- (d) by such other means as AiB may agree to.

(2) Such an application must specify the name and address of the applicant, and (where relevant) the details of the applicant's representative.

NOTES

Commencement: 30 November 2016.

[16.299]
5 Application form: first instance applications to the Accountant in Bankruptcy

(1) An application to AiB under the following provisions of the Act must be made in writing in Form 1 (application to the Accountant in Bankruptcy: general)—
- (a) section 31(1) (recall of sequestration: where the only ground is that the debtor has paid or is able to pay debts in full);
- (b) section 60(3)(a) (objection to election of replacement trustee);
- (c) section 66(7)(a) (trustee replacement in more than one sequestration);
- (d) section 70(2)(a) (removal of trustee);
- (e) section 72(3)(a) (declaration of office of trustee as vacant);
- (f) section 110(4)(b) (contractual powers of trustee);
- (g) section 159(3) (revocation or variation of bankruptcy restrictions order);
- (h) section 212(2)(a) (power of Accountant in Bankruptcy to cure defects in procedure); and
- (i) paragraph 3(3)(b) of schedule 2 (valuing contingent debts).

(2) Form 1 must also be used (where AiB is the applicant or trustee) for—
- (a) representations under section 66(10) of the Act (trustee replacement in more than one sequestration); and
- (b) representations under section 212(5) of the Act (curing defect in procedure).

NOTES

Commencement: 30 November 2016.

[16.300]
6 Application procedure: first instance applications to the Accountant in Bankruptcy

(1) This regulation applies to any application under the Act for which a form is prescribed by these Regulations (except a review application).

(2) A copy of such an application must, before the application is made, be sent by the applicant—
- (a) to any person specified in the Act as a person—
  - (i) to be notified of the application;
  - (ii) able to make representations in relation to the application; or
  - (iii) able to seek review of or to appeal the decision on that application; and
- (b) to any other interested person.

(3) Under paragraph (2), the application must be sent to the proper address of the person—
- (a) by a registered post service (as defined in section 125(1) of the Postal Services Act 2000); or
- (b) by a postal service which provides for the delivery of the document to be recorded.

(4) An applicant required to send an application under paragraph (2), or ordered to serve an application by AiB under the Act or paragraph (6), must inform the recipient in writing that the person has the right to make representations to AiB in relation to the application within any period provided for in the Act or paragraph (10).

(5) The applicant must, if requested to do so by AiB, provide AiB with evidence of delivery of that application to the persons to whom it has been delivered.

(6) AiB may require the application to be sent by the applicant to such persons as AiB deems appropriate.

(7) Where an application is incomplete it may be rejected by AiB.

(8) Where an application is unopposed it must be granted without the attendance of parties, unless AiB directs otherwise.

(9) Any representations made under the Act by any person in relation to an application must be made in writing by any means by which an application may be made (see regulation 4(1)).

(10) Where no time limit for such representations is specified in the Act or these Regulations, the representations must be made within 14 days beginning with the day on which the application was made.

(11) Paragraphs (2) to (4) and (9) do not apply to the extent that equivalent provision is made in the Act or these Regulations, or service is ordered by AiB under a provision of the Act.

(12) In paragraph (3) the "proper address" of a person means—

(a) in the case of a body corporate, the address of the registered or principal office of the body;

(b) in the case of a partnership, the address of any place of business of the partnership where it appears to the applicant service will be effective;

(c) in any other case, the last known address of the person.

NOTES

Commencement: 30 November 2016.

[16.301]

7 Inquiries

(1) This regulation applies where in relation to any application required to be on a form under these Regulations (including a review application) or any representation under the Act AiB considers that—

(a) further information is required in relation to the application or representation; or

(b) further evidence is required to substantiate any fact relevant to the application or representation.

(2) AiB may before any date set out in the Act for the decision of AiB specify by notice in writing—

(a) any further information which is to be provided; and

(b) any further evidence which is to be provided,

within 21 days from the date of sending that notice or such shorter period as may be specified in the notice.

(3) Where a notice is given under paragraph (2)—

(a) any time limit set out in the Act for the decision of AiB is extended by the period specified in the notice; and

(b) if the information or evidence specified is provided to AiB, the period allowed for the decision of AiB after the date on which it is provided is the greater of—

(i) the unexpired days before the original time limit would have elapsed (ignoring its extension) after the date on which that notice was given; or

(ii) 7 days.

(4) AiB may refuse to consider an application if, after the expiry of the period specified under paragraph (2), AiB considers that the applicant has provided insufficient information or evidence specified under that paragraph.

(5) Where AiB has set any time limit for the giving of written evidence under these Regulations, AiB must not consider any written evidence which is not given in accordance with those time limits unless satisfied that there is good reason to do so.

NOTES

Commencement: 30 November 2016.

[16.302]

8 Further evidence

(1) In respect of an application for which a form is required under these Regulations (other than a review application) AiB may require in writing any person making an application or representations—

(a) to attend a hearing, at such time and place as AiB may specify, for the purposes of giving evidence;

(b) to give AiB, by such day as AiB may specify, such documents or information as AiB may reasonably require.

(2) Paragraph (1) does not apply unless AiB is satisfied there is a good reason to impose such a requirement following written representations, or evidence or information in response to an inquiry.

(3) Paragraph (1) does not authorise AiB to require any person to answer any question or to disclose anything which the person would be entitled to refuse to answer or disclose on grounds of confidentiality in civil proceedings in the Court of Session.

(4) AiB may determine such further procedure in relation to the hearing as AiB considers appropriate.

(5) Where a person is required to attend or give documents or information under paragraph (1)—

(a) any time limit set out in the Act for the decision of AiB is extended until the date of the hearing or the day specified, as the case may be; and

(b) following the date of the hearing or the day specified, as the case may be, the period allowed for the decision of AiB is the greater of—

(i) the unexpired days before that time limit would have elapsed (ignoring its extension) after the date on which the person was required by AiB to attend the hearing or give documents or information under paragraph (1); or

(ii) 7 days.

NOTES

Commencement: 30 November 2016.

PART 3
SPECIFIC APPLICATIONS

[16.303]

9 Recall of sequestration by Accountant in Bankruptcy

(1) Where the statement of the debtor's affairs is not submitted in accordance with section 32(3)(a) of the Act (recall where the only ground is that the debtor has paid or is able to pay debts in full), the application is not to be considered by AiB until it is submitted.

(2) Where paragraph (1) applies AiB may make inquiries under regulation 7.

(3) AiB must send to the persons listed in section 31(2) of the Act a copy of AiB's decision under section 34(1) or 35(6) of the Act.

(4) AiB must send with any notification under section 35(2) of the Act (recall where the only ground is that debtor has paid or is able to pay the debtor's debts in full: AiB acting as trustee)—

(a) a statement of the debtor's affairs; and
(b) a copy of the application for recall,

and advise the recipients of the period for making representations under section 35(5)(a) of the Act.

(5) Where AiB gives notification under section 35(2) of the Act, AiB must also notify any other interested person, informing the recipient that the person has the right to make representations to AiB in relation to the application within 21 days beginning with the day on which the notice is given.

(6) Where recall is under consideration (including on a review application), and sequestration is recalled by AiB, AiB must at that time consider whether to revoke under section 161(4) of the Act any bankruptcy restrictions order (or interim order) in effect in relation to the debtor.

(7) Where an original recall decision is amended or revoked on review, AiB must send a certified copy of the revised decision to the Keeper of the Register of Inhibitions for recording in that register.

NOTES

Commencement: 30 November 2016.

[16.304]

10 Application for direction by trustee

(1) An application to AiB under section 52(2) of the Act (application for direction) must be made in writing in Form 2.

(2) Where an application is made under that subsection, AiB must before the expiry of 28 days beginning with the day on which the application is made—

(a) give a direction; or
(b) refer the matter to the sheriff under section 52(3) of the Act.

NOTES

Commencement: 30 November 2016.

[16.305]

11 Appointment of replacement trustee

(1) A report to AiB under section 60(2)(a) of the Act of a statutory meeting appointing a replacement trustee must be made in writing in Form 4.

(2) If AiB declares an elected person to be trustee under section 60(5) of the Act, AiB must send a copy of the decision to the original trustee and the replacement trustee.

(3) Where AiB gives an opportunity to make representations under section 61(2) of the Act (on receiving an objection), AiB must—

(a) notify the original and replacement trustees, the objector and any other interested person; and
(b) advise those persons that written submissions under section 61(2) must be made within 14 days beginning with the date on which the notification was given.

(4) AiB must notify the original and replacement trustees, the objector and any other interested person of any declaration or order under section 61(3) of the Act (and in the case of such an order must do so without delay).

NOTES

Commencement: 30 November 2016.

[16.306]

12 Replacement trustee acting in more than one sequestration

A determination or appointment under section 66 of the Act (replacement of trustee acting in more than one sequestration) must be made by AiB within 14 days following the expiry of the period mentioned in section 66(10) of the Act.

NOTES

Commencement: 30 November 2016.

[16.307]

13 Removal of trustee and trustee not acting

(1) An order under section 70(1)(b) of the Act (removal of trustee from office by AiB) must be made in writing in Form 5.

(2) Where the trustee has the opportunity to make representations under section 70(4)(c) of the Act, AiB must allow 21 days beginning with the date on which the copy application was sent under section 70(4)(a) of the Act for those representations.

(3) AiB must within 14 days beginning after the expiry of that period of 21 days—

- (a) decide whether to remove or refuse to remove the trustee (or make any other order) under section 70(1)(b) or (5) of the Act; or
- (b) refer the matter to the sheriff under section 71(7)(a) of the Act.

(4) Before making any declaration or order under section 72(1) of the Act, AiB must give the trustee an opportunity to make representations.

(5) In the case of an application under section 72(3)(a) of the Act, AiB must within 14 days beginning after the expiry of the period for representations under regulation 6(10)—

- (a) decide whether to make any declaration (or any other order) under section 72(1) of the Act; or
- (b) refer the matter to the sheriff under section 71(7)(a) of the Act.

(6) The Accountant must notify the trustee, the debtor, commissioners or any creditor of any order or decision under section 70(1)(b) or (5) or section 72(1) of the Act.

(7) Where a review application is made under sections 71 or 73, AiB must notify any commissioners required to call a meeting under sections 71(6) or 73(1) of the Act.

(8) The requirement to hold that meeting under sections 71(6) or 73(1) within 28 days—

- (a) is extended until the date of the review decision (or any appeal from that decision); and
- (b) on that decision (or any appeal from that decision) the period allowed for holding the meeting is the greater of—
  - (i) the unexpired days before the period specified in sections 71(6) or 73(1) of the Act would have elapsed (ignoring its extension) after the date on which the review application was made; or
  - (ii) 28 days.

(9) Where a review decision is made under sections 71 or 73 of the Act, AiB must notify any commissioners required to call a meeting under sections 71(6) or 73(1) of the Act.

NOTES

Commencement: 30 November 2016.

[16.308]

14 Contractual powers of trustee

(1) Where an application is made under section 110(4)(b) of the Act (to extend the 28 days for a trustee to adopt or refuse to adopt a contract), AiB must within 14 days beginning with the day on which the application is made—

- (a) decide whether to extend the 28 days; or
- (b) refer the matter to the sheriff under section 110(8) of the Act.

(2) AiB must notify all interested persons—

- (a) of any decision of AiB on such an application; and
- (b) of any direction of the sheriff within 7 days of receipt of that direction.

(3) For the avoidance of doubt, the time limit in paragraph (1) does not apply to any review application.

NOTES

Commencement: 30 November 2016.

[16.309]

15 Bankruptcy restrictions orders: proposal to make an order

(1) AiB must allow 14 days beginning with the day on which notice is given under section 155(2) of the Act (proposal to make bankruptcy restrictions order) for representations by the debtor.

(2) Those representations must be made in writing by any means by which an application may be made (see regulation 4(1)).

(3) Notice under section 155(2) informing the debtor under section 155(3) of the Act must also inform the debtor—

- (a) of the reasons for proposing to make the order;
- (b) of any grounds for proposing an interim bankruptcy restrictions order;
- (c) that the representations must be made—
  - (i) in writing (including by email or using the computer system); and
  - (ii) within 14 days beginning with the date on which the notice was given (or in the case of any proposed interim bankruptcy restrictions order, within 2 days beginning with the date on which the notice was given).

(4) AiB must make or decide not to make the bankruptcy restrictions order within 21 days beginning with the date on which the notice was given.

NOTES

Commencement: 30 November 2016.

[16.310]

16 Bankruptcy restrictions orders: revocation or variation

(1) Where an application is made to AiB under section 159(3) of the Act (to revoke or vary a bankruptcy restrictions order), AiB must notify all interested persons that those persons have the right to make representations to AiB in relation to the application within 21 days beginning with the day on which the application is made.

(2) Those representations must be made in writing by any means by which an application may be made (see regulation 4(1)).

(3) Where following recall of sequestration AiB refuses under section 161(4) of the Act to revoke a bankruptcy restrictions order, AiB must inform the debtor that the debtor has the right to apply to AiB for review of that decision within 14 days beginning with the day on which the award of sequestration was recalled.

NOTES

Commencement: 30 November 2016.

[16.311]

17 Conversion of protected trust deed into bankruptcy

(1) An application to AiB under section 190(1) and (2) of the Act (conversion of protected trust deed into sequestration) must be made in writing in Form 6.

(2) An award under section 192(1) of the Act (power of Accountant in Bankruptcy: conversion of protected trust deed into sequestration) must be made in writing in Form 7.

(3) Where AiB makes, or refuses to make, an order for conversion into sequestration, AiB must inform the member State [insolvency practitioner], the debtor, the trustee and any other person who has been served with a copy of the application and the affidavit.

NOTES

Commencement: 30 November 2016.

Para (3): words in square brackets substituted for original word "liquidator" by the Insolvency (Regulation (EU) 2015/848) (Miscellaneous Amendments) (Scotland) Regulations 2017, SSI 2017/210, regs 8(1), (2), 9, as from 26 June 2017, except in relation to proceedings opened before that date.

[16.312]

18 Power to cure defects

Where AiB makes, or refuses to make, under section 212 of the Act (curing defects in procedure) a corrective order or to waive a time limit, AiB must notify all interested persons.

NOTES

Commencement: 30 November 2016.

[16.313]

19 Debts depending on contingency

Where AiB puts a value on a debt under paragraph 3(3) of schedule 2 of the Act (debts depending on a contingency), AiB must notify the creditor and all other interested persons.

NOTES

Commencement: 30 November 2016.

PART 4
REFERENCE TO COURT AND REVIEW BY ACCOUNTANT IN BANKRUPTCY

[16.314]

20 Reference to court: time limits

Where AiB has applied to refer or remit a matter to the court under the Act—

(a) if the court (or a court on appeal from that court) makes any disposal which requires AiB to make an order, declaration or decision, the period allowed for the decision of AiB is the greater of—
  (i) the unexpired days before the time limit set out in the Act for that decision would have elapsed (ignoring its reference or remit) after the date on which the reference or remit was made; or
  (ii) 7 days;

(b) if the court's disposal has no such requirement, that time limit does not apply.

NOTES

Commencement: 30 November 2016.

[16.315]
21 Review applications

(1) An application for a review by AiB under the following provisions of the Act must be made in writing in Form 3—

(a) section 27(5) (refusal of sequestration on debtor application);
(b) section 37(1) (recall: only ground that debtor has paid or is able to pay debts in full);
(c) section 39(5) (interim preservation);
(d) section 52(4) (power of direction of trustee);
(e) section 57(5) (interim trustee termination);
(f) section 59(1) (Accountant in Bankruptcy interim trustee termination);
(g) section 61(5) (appointment of replacement trustee);
(h) section 64(5) (Accountant in Bankruptcy to account for intromissions);
(i) section 65(4) (discharge of original trustee);
(j) section 68(1) (trustee replacement in more than one sequestration);
(k) section 71(1) (removal of trustee);
(l) section 73(2) (removal—declaring vacancy);
(m) section 92(1) (debtor contribution order);
(n) section 97(1) (variation and payment break);
(o) section 110(5) (contractual powers of trustee);
(p) section 127(1) (adjudication of claims);
(q) section 139(1) (discharge);
(r) section 144(1) (discharge—subsequent contact);
(s) section 149(1) (discharge of trustee);
(t) section 151(4) (Accountant in Bankruptcy discharge as trustee);
(u) section 161(5) (refusal to revoke bankruptcy restrictions order);
(v) section 213(1) (curing defects); and
(w) paragraph 3(6) of schedule 2 (valuing contingent debts).

(2) A review application must specify—

(a) the decision to be reviewed and its date;
(b) the change sought to the decision; and
(c) the reasons for seeking that change.

(3) When a review application is made to AiB, AiB must—

(a) without delay send a copy to any person specified in the provision of the Act which provides for the review as a person to be notified, able to make representations or appeal against the review decision; and
(b) advise those persons that they have the period of 21 days beginning with the date specified in the Act to make representations to AiB.

(4) Those representations must be made in writing by any means by which an application may be made (see regulation 4(1)).

(5) On making a review decision under the relevant provision of the Act, AiB must notify the persons mentioned in paragraph (3)(a) of AiB's decision.

(6) Paragraphs (3) to (5) do not apply to the extent that equivalent provision is made in the Act.

NOTES

Commencement: 30 November 2016.

[16.316]
22 Review proceedings: staff of the Accountant in Bankruptcy

(1) No member of the staff of AiB who was involved in a decision under review may be involved in the review decision.

(2) If the Accountant in Bankruptcy herself or himself was involved in a decision under review, he or she must not be involved in any review decision (and is accordingly unable to exercise those functions in which case the Depute Accountant in Bankruptcy may act in accordance with section 199(2) of the Act).

NOTES

Commencement: 30 November 2016.

[16.317]
23 Review proceedings: persons assisting the Accountant in Bankruptcy

(1) In relation to a review application AiB may take account of the views of any independent person whom AiB appoints for that purpose.

(2) AiB may disclose information held about review applications to persons appointed under paragraph (1) to be used only for the purpose specified in that paragraph.

NOTES

Commencement: 30 November 2016.

[16.318]
24 Review decision

The decision of AiB and a statement of reasons on the review application will be made publicly available.

NOTES

Commencement: 30 November 2016.

PART 5
REVOCATIONS AND SAVING

[16.319]

25 Revocations

The Bankruptcy (Applications and Decisions) (Scotland) Regulations 2014 and regulation 3 of the Bankruptcy (Miscellaneous Amendments) (Scotland) Regulations 2015 are revoked, subject to regulation 26.

NOTES

Commencement: 30 November 2016.

The Bankruptcy (Applications and Decisions) (Scotland) Regulations 2014, SSI 2014/226 are noted at **[16.268]**. The full text of the Regulations can be found in the 18th edition of this Handbook.

[16.320]

26 Sequestrations and trust deeds before 30th November 2016

These Regulations have no effect in relation to—

(a) sequestrations as regards which the petition was presented or the debtor application was made before; or

(b) trust deeds executed before,

30th November 2016.

NOTES

Commencement: 30 November 2016.

SCHEDULE
FORMS

Regulations 2(2)(a), 5, 10(1),11(1), 13(1), 17(1) and (2) and 21(1)

[16.321]

NOTES

The forms themselves are not reproduced in this work, but their numbers and descriptions are listed below.

Form	*Purpose*	*Relevant provision of the Regulations*
1	Application to the Accountant in Bankruptcy: general	Regulation 5
2	Application for direction under section 52(2)	Regulation 10(1)
3	Application for review by the Accountant in Bankruptcy: general	Regulation 21(1)
4	Report of statutory meeting appointing replacement trustee: section 60(2)(a)	Regulation 11(1)
5	Grant of removal of trustee: section 70(1)(b)	Regulation 13(1)
6	Conversion of protected trust deed into bankruptcy: section 190 application	Regulation 17(1)
7	Conversion of protected trust deed into bankruptcy: section 192 award	Regulation 17(2)

NOTES

Commencement: 30 November 2016.

Forms 6, 7 are amended by the Insolvency (Regulation (EU) 2015/848) (Miscellaneous Amendments) (Scotland) Regulations 2017, SSI 2017/210, regs 8(1), (3), 9, as from 26 June 2017, except in relation to proceedings opened before that date.

ACT OF SEDERUNT (SHERIFF COURT BANKRUPTCY RULES) 2016

(SSI 2016/313)

NOTES

Made: 6 October 2016.

Authority: European Communities Act 1972, Sch 2, para 1A, Courts Reform (Scotland) Act 2014, s 104(1), Bankruptcy (Scotland) Act 2016, s 26(6), (8), Sch 4, para 3.

Commencement: 30 November 2016.

ARRANGEMENT OF SECTIONS

CHAPTER 1
CITATION, COMMENCEMENT AND INTERPRETATION ETC

1.1 Citation, commencement and application, etc . . . [16.322]
1.2 Interpretation . . . [16.323]
1.3 Computation of periods of time . . . [16.324]
1.4 Forms . . . [16.325]
1.5 Sequestration process . . . [16.326]

CHAPTER 2
RELIEF FOR FAILURE TO COMPLY

2.1 Relief for failure to comply with rules . . . [16.327]

CHAPTER 3
SANCTIONS FOR FAILURE TO COMPLY

3.1 Circumstances where a party is in default . . . [16.328]
3.2 Sanctions where a party is in default . . . [16.329]

CHAPTER 4
REPRESENTATION AND SUPPORT

4.1 Representation and support . . . [16.330]
4.2 Legal representation . . . [16.331]
4.3 Representation by authorised person . . . [16.332]
4.4 Lay representation . . . [16.333]
4.5 Expenses . . . [16.334]
4.6 Lay support . . . [16.335]

CHAPTER 5
INTIMATION AND LODGING

5.1 Interpretation of this Chapter . . . [16.336]
5.2 Intimation . . . [16.337]
5.3 Methods of intimation . . . [16.338]
5.4 Methods of intimation: intimation by recorded delivery . . . [16.339]
5.5 Methods of intimation: intimation by sheriff officer . . . [16.340]
5.6 Additional methods of intimation where receiving party represented by solicitor . . . [16.341]
5.7 Form of certificate of intimation . . . [16.342]
5.8 Lodging . . . [16.343]

CHAPTER 6
PETITIONS FOR SEQUESTRATION

6.1 Form of petition for sequestration . . . [16.344]
6.2 Debt payment programmes and moratorium on diligence . . . [16.345]
6.2A Warrant for citation . . . [16.346]
6.3 Citation of debtor . . . [16.347]
6.4 Service by sheriff officer . . . [16.348]
6.5 Service furth of Scotland . . . [16.349]
6.6 Authority to serve by other means . . . [16.350]
6.7 Intimation of appointment of trustee . . . [16.351]

CHAPTER 7
APPLICATIONS ETC UNDER THE BANKRUPTCY (SCOTLAND) ACT 2016

7.1 Form of applications . . . [16.352]
7.1A Warrant to enter premises and warrant to apprehend . . . [16.353]
7.2 Form of remit by AiB . . . [16.354]
7.3 Applications and remits relating to AiB sequestration . . . [16.355]
7.4 Determination of applications and remits . . . [16.356]
7.5 Form of report by original trustee . . . [16.357]

CHAPTER 8
APPLICATIONS UNDER THE UNCITRAL MODEL LAW ON CROSS-BORDER INSOLVENCY

8.1 Form of applications . . . [16.358]
8.2 Transfer of proceedings to Court of Session . . . [16.359]

CHAPTER 9
APPEALS TO THE SHERIFF UNDER THE BANKRUPTCY (SCOTLAND) ACT 2016

9.1 Form of appeal . . . [16.360]
9.2 Appeals relating to AiB sequestration . . . [16.361]
9.3 Determination of appeal . . . [16.362]

CHAPTER 10
APPEALS TO THE SHERIFF APPEAL COURT

10.1 Appeals to the Sheriff Appeal Court . . . . [16.363]

CHAPTER 11
MOTIONS

11.1 Interpretation . . . . [16.364]
11.2 Making of motions . . . . [16.365]
11.3 Written motions . . . . [16.366]
11.4 Intimation of written motions . . . . [16.367]
11.5 Opposition to written motions . . . . [16.368]
11.6 Consent to written motions . . . . [16.369]
11.7 Lodging of written motions . . . . [16.370]
11.8 Joint written motions . . . . [16.371]
11.9 Determination of unopposed written motions . . . . [16.372]
11.10 Hearing of opposed written motions . . . . [16.373]

CHAPTER 12
WITHDRAWAL OF SOLICITORS

12.1 Interpretation of this Chapter . . . . [16.374]
12.2 Giving notice of withdrawal . . . . [16.375]
12.3 Arrangements for peremptory hearing . . . . [16.376]
12.4 Peremptory hearing . . . . [16.377]

CHAPTER 13
EXPENSES

13.1 Taxation of expenses . . . . [16.378]
13.2 Procedure for taxation of expenses . . . . [16.379]
13.3 Objections to taxed account . . . . [16.380]
13.4 Decree for expenses in name of solicitor . . . . [16.381]

CHAPTER 14
VULNERABLE WITNESSES

14.1 Interpretation and application of this Chapter . . . . [16.382]
14.2 Form of notices and applications . . . . [16.383]
14.3 Determination of notices and applications . . . . [16.384]
14.4 Determination of notices and applications: supplementary orders . . . . [16.385]
14.5 Intimation of orders . . . . [16.386]
14.6 Taking of evidence by commissioner: preparatory steps . . . . [16.387]
14.7 Taking of evidence by commissioner: interrogatories . . . . [16.388]
14.8 Taking of evidence by commissioner: conduct of commission . . . . [16.389]
14.9 Taking of evidence by commissioner: lodging and custody of video record and documents . . [16.390]

CHAPTER 15
LIVE LINKS

15.1 Interpretation . . . . [16.391]
15.2 Application for use of live link . . . . [16.392]

CHAPTER 16
REPORTING RESTRICTIONS

16.1 Interpretation and application of this Chapter . . . . [16.393]
16.2 Interim orders: notification to interested persons . . . . [16.394]
16.3 Interim orders: representations . . . . [16.395]
16.4 Notification of reporting restrictions . . . . [16.396]
16.5 Applications for variation or revocation . . . . [16.397]

SCHEDULES

Schedule 1—Forms . . . . [16.398]
Schedule 2—Forms for Use in Register of Inhibitions . . . . [16.399]
Schedule 3—Service of Documents Furth of Scotland . . . . [16.400]

CHAPTER 1
CITATION, COMMENCEMENT AND INTERPRETATION ETC

[16.322]
1.1 Citation, commencement and application, etc

(1) This Act of Sederunt may be cited as the Act of Sederunt (Sheriff Court Bankruptcy Rules) 2016.

(2) It comes into force on 30th November 2016.

(3) It applies to sequestrations as regards which the petition is presented, or the debtor application is made, on or after that date.

(4) A certified copy is to be inserted in the Books of Sederunt.

NOTES

Commencement: 30 November 2016.

[16.323]

1.2 Interpretation

(1) In this Act of Sederunt—

"the 2016 Act" means the Bankruptcy (Scotland) Act 2016;

"AiB sequestration" means the sequestration of a debtor's estate by AiB following a debtor application made under the following provisions of the 2016 Act—

(a) section 2(1)(a);
(b) section 5(a);
(c) section 6(3)(a);
(d) section 6(4)(a);
(e) section 6(4)(b); or
(f) section 6(7)(a);

["Council Regulation" means Regulation (EU) 2015/848 of the European Parliament and of the Council of 20th May 2015 on insolvency proceedings, as amended from time to time;]

"Model Law on Cross-Border Insolvency" means the Model Law on cross-border insolvency as adopted by the United Nations Commission on International Trade Law on 30th May 1997 as set out in schedule 1 of the Cross-Border Insolvency Regulations 2006;

"Register of Inhibitions" means the register mentioned in section 44(1) of the Conveyancing (Scotland) Act 1924.

(2) In this Act of Sederunt, the following expressions have the meaning given by section 228(1) of the 2016 Act—

"AiB";
"debtor application";
"establishment";
"main proceedings";
"member State [insolvency practitioner]";
"temporary administrator".

NOTES

Commencement: 30 November 2016.

Para (1): definition "Council Regulation" substituted by the Act of Sederunt (Rules of the Court of Session 1994 and Sheriff Court Rules Amendment) (Regulation (EU) 2015/848) 2017, SSI 2017/202, rr 2(1), (2)(a), 6, except in relation to proceedings which are subject to Regulation (EC) 1346/2000 of 29th May 2000 on insolvency proceedings, and originally read as follows:

""Council Regulation" means Council Regulation (EC) No 1346/2000 of 29th May 2000 on insolvency proceedings as amended from time to time;".

Para (2): words in square brackets substituted for original word "liquidator" by SSI 2017/202, rr 2(1), (2)(b), 6, except in relation to proceedings which are subject to Regulation (EC) 1346/2000 of 29th May 2000 on insolvency proceedings.

[16.324]

1.3 Computation of periods of time

If any period of time specified in these Rules expires on a Saturday, Sunday or public or court holiday, it is extended to expire on the next day that the sheriff clerk's office is open for civil business.

NOTES

Commencement: 30 November 2016.

[16.325]

1.4 Forms

(1) Where there is a reference in these Rules to a form, it is a reference to that form in schedule 1.

(2) Schedule 2 makes provision about forms relating to the Register of Inhibitions.

(3) Where these Rules require a form to be used, that form may be varied where the circumstances require it.

NOTES

Commencement: 30 November 2016.

[16.326]

1.5 Sequestration process

(1) The sheriff clerk must prepare a sequestration process when an initiating document mentioned in paragraph (2) is lodged.

(2) The initiating documents are—

(a) a petition for sequestration;

(b) a petition for recall of sequestration;
(c) an application or remit under the 2016 Act;
(d) an appeal under the 2016 Act.

(3) Any other document lodged with the sheriff clerk is to be placed in the sequestration process.

(4) Where a further initiating document relating to a sequestration is lodged—
(a) paragraph (1) does not apply;
(b) that document is to be placed in the existing sequestration process.

NOTES

Commencement: 30 November 2016.

CHAPTER 2
RELIEF FOR FAILURE TO COMPLY

[16.327]

2.1 Relief for failure to comply with rules

(1) The sheriff may relieve a party from the consequences of a failure to comply with a provision in these Rules.

(2) The sheriff may do so only where the party shows that the failure is due to—
(a) mistake;
(b) oversight;
(c) any other excusable cause.

(3) Where relief is granted, the sheriff may—
(a) impose conditions that must be satisfied before relief is granted;
(b) make an order to enable the proceedings to proceed as if the failure had not occurred.

NOTES

Commencement: 30 November 2016.

CHAPTER 3
SANCTIONS FOR FAILURE TO COMPLY

[16.328]

3.1 Circumstances where a party is in default

A party is in default if that party fails—
(a) to implement an order made by the sheriff within the period specified in the order;
(b) to appear or be represented at any hearing; or
(c) otherwise to comply with any requirement imposed on that party by these Rules.

NOTES

Commencement: 30 November 2016.

[16.329]

3.2 Sanctions where a party is in default

(1) This rule—
(a) applies where a party is in default; but
(b) does not apply where a party is in default because the party has failed to comply with rule 12.4(1) (peremptory hearing).

(2) The sheriff may make any order to secure the expeditious disposal of the proceedings.

(3) In particular, the sheriff may—
(a) refuse the appeal, application or petition, if the party in default is the appellant, applicant or petitioner;
(b) allow the appeal, application or petition, if the condition in paragraph (4) is satisfied, where—
(i) the party in default is the sole respondent; or
(ii) every respondent is in default.

(4) The condition is that the appellant, applicant or petitioner must show cause why the appeal, application or petition should be allowed.

NOTES

Commencement: 30 November 2016.

CHAPTER 4
REPRESENTATION AND SUPPORT

[16.330]

4.1 Representation and support

(1) A natural person who is a party to proceedings may appear and act on the party's own behalf.

(2) A party who appears and acts on the party's own behalf is to be known as a party litigant.

(3) A party may be represented in any proceedings by—
(a) a legal representative (see rule 4.2); or

(b) an authorised person (see rule 4.3).

(4) A party who is a natural person may also be represented by a lay representative (see rule 4.4).

(5) A lay supporter (see rule 4.6) may assist a party litigant with the conduct of any proceedings.

NOTES

Commencement: 30 November 2016.

[16.331]

4.2 Legal representation

A party is represented by a legal representative if that party is represented by an advocate or a solicitor.

NOTES

Commencement: 30 November 2016.

[16.332]

4.3 Representation by authorised person

(1) This rule applies where an enactment authorises a person to conduct proceedings in the sheriff court.

(2) A party is represented by an authorised person if that party is represented by a person who is authorised in accordance with such an enactment.

(3) An authorised person may do everything for the preparation and conduct of the proceedings that a party litigant may do, unless the enactment provides otherwise.

NOTES

Commencement: 30 November 2016.

[16.333]

4.4 Lay representation

(1) A party may apply to the sheriff for permission to be represented by a person who is not a legal representative or an authorised person, and such a person is to be known as a lay representative.

(2) The sheriff may grant an application only if the sheriff considers that it would assist the sheriff's consideration of the case to grant it.

(3) If the sheriff no longer considers that it would assist the sheriff's consideration of the case for a party to be represented by a lay representative, the sheriff may withdraw permission.

(4) A lay representative may represent a party at a specified hearing for the purpose of making oral submissions on behalf of the party.

(5) The party must appear along with the lay representative at any hearing where the lay representative is to make oral submissions.

(6) A party may show any document (including a court document) or communicate any information about the proceedings to that party's lay representative without contravening any prohibition or restriction on disclosure of the document or information.

(7) Where a document or information is disclosed under paragraph (6), the lay representative is subject to any prohibition or restriction on disclosure in the same way as the party is.

(8) A lay representative must not receive directly or indirectly from the party any remuneration or other reward for assisting the party.

NOTES

Commencement: 30 November 2016.

[16.334]

4.5 Expenses

(1) This rule applies where a party is represented by an authorised person or a lay representative.

(2) Despite that representation, the sheriff may award the party any expenses or outlays that the party would be entitled to by virtue of the Litigants in Person (Costs and Expenses) Act 1975.

NOTES

Commencement: 30 November 2016.

[16.335]

4.6 Lay support

(1) A party litigant may apply to the sheriff for permission for a named person to assist the party litigant in the conduct of proceedings, and such a person is to be known as a lay supporter.

(2) The sheriff may refuse an application only if the sheriff is of the opinion that—

(a) the named person is an unsuitable person to act as a lay supporter; or

(b) it would be contrary to the efficient administration of justice to grant it.

(3) The sheriff, if satisfied that it would be contrary to the efficient administration of justice for permission to continue, may withdraw permission.

(4) A lay supporter may assist a party by accompanying the party at hearings.

(5) A lay supporter may, if authorised by the party, assist the party by—
- (a) providing moral support;
- (b) helping to manage court documents and other papers;
- (c) taking notes of the proceedings;
- (d) quietly advising on—
  - (i) points of law and procedure;
  - (ii) issues which the party litigant might want to raise with the court.

(6) A party may show any document (including a court document) or communicate any information about the proceedings to that party's lay supporter without contravening any prohibition or restriction on disclosure of the document or information.

(7) Where a document or information is disclosed under paragraph (6), the lay supporter is subject to any prohibition or restriction on disclosure in the same way as the party is.

(8) A lay supporter must not receive directly or indirectly from the party any remuneration or other reward for assisting the party.

NOTES

Commencement: 30 November 2016.

CHAPTER 5
INTIMATION AND LODGING

[16.336]
5.1 Interpretation of this Chapter

In this Chapter—

"first class post" means a postal service which seeks to deliver documents or other things by post no later than the next working day in all or the majority of cases;

"intimating party" means any party who has to give intimation in accordance with rule 5.2;

"receiving party" means any party to whom intimation is to be given in accordance with rule 5.2;

"recorded delivery" means a postal service which provides for the delivery of the document or other thing by post to be recorded.

NOTES

Commencement: 30 November 2016.

[16.337]
5.2 Intimation

Unless the sheriff orders otherwise, where—
- (a) any provision in these Rules requires a party to—
  - (i) take any procedural step;
  - (ii) lodge any document;
  - (iii) intimate any other matter; or
- (b) the sheriff orders a party to intimate something,

intimation is to be given to every other party.

NOTES

Commencement: 30 November 2016.

[16.338]
5.3 Methods of intimation

(1) Intimation may be given to a receiving party by any of the methods specified in rules 5.4 and 5.5.

(2) Where the receiving party is represented by a solicitor, intimation may also be given by any of the methods specified in rule 5.6.

NOTES

Commencement: 30 November 2016.

[16.339]
5.4 Methods of intimation: intimation by recorded delivery

An intimating party may give intimation by recorded delivery to the receiving party.

NOTES

Commencement: 30 November 2016.

[16.340]
5.5 Methods of intimation: intimation by sheriff officer

(1) A sheriff officer may give intimation on behalf of an intimating party by—
- (a) delivering the intimation personally to the receiving party; or
- (b) leaving the intimation in the hands of—
  - (i) a resident at the receiving party's dwelling place; or
  - (ii) an employee, agent or representative at the receiving party's place of business.

(2) Where a sheriff officer has been unsuccessful in intimation in accordance with paragraph (1), the sheriff officer may give intimation by—

(a) depositing it in the receiving party's dwelling place or place of business; or
(b) leaving it at the receiving party's dwelling place or place of business in such a way that it is likely to come to the attention of that party.

NOTES

Commencement: 30 November 2016.

[16.341]
5.6 Additional methods of intimation where receiving party represented by solicitor

(1) An intimating party may give intimation to the solicitor for the receiving party by—

(a) delivering it personally to the solicitor;
(b) delivering it to a document exchange of which the solicitor is a member;
(c) first class post;
(d) fax.

(2) Where intimation is given by the method in paragraph (1)(a) or (d) not later than 1700 hours on any day, the date of intimation is that day.

(3) Where intimation is given by the method in—

(a) paragraph (1)(b) or (c); or
(b) paragraph (1)(a) or (d) after 1700 hours on any day,

the date of intimation is the next day.

NOTES

Commencement: 30 November 2016.

[16.342]
5.7 Form of certificate of intimation

A certificate of intimation is to be in Form 5.7.

NOTES

Commencement: 30 November 2016.

[16.343]
5.8 Lodging

(1) Where any provision in these Rules requires a party to lodge a document, it is to be lodged with the sheriff clerk.

(2) A document may be lodged by—

(a) delivering it personally to the sheriff clerk's office;
(b) delivering it to a document exchange of which the sheriff clerk is a member;
(c) first class post;
(d) fax.

NOTES

Commencement: 30 November 2016.

CHAPTER 6
PETITIONS FOR SEQUESTRATION

[16.344]
6.1 Form of petition for sequestration

(1) A petition for sequestration is to be made in Form 6.1–A.

(2) An undertaking for the purposes of section 51(1) or (6) of the 2016 Act is to be in Form 6.1–B.

NOTES

Commencement: 30 November 2016.

[16.345]
6.2 Debt payment programmes and moratorium on diligence

(1) This rule applies where a creditor is petitioning for sequestration on the ground of the debtor's apparent insolvency.

(2) The petitioner must, when lodging the sequestration petition, lodge a statement in Form 6.2.

NOTES

Commencement: 30 November 2016.

[16.346]
[6.2A Warrant for citation

A warrant for citation under section 22(3) of the 2016 Act may be authenticated electronically.]

NOTES

Commencement: 15 December 2016.

Inserted by the Act of Sederunt (Sheriff Court Rules Amendment) (Electronic Authentication) 2016, SSI 2016/415, r 3(1), (2).

[16.347]

6.3 Citation of debtor

(1) A debtor is cited for the purposes of section 22(3) of the 2016 Act by serving the documents mentioned in paragraph (2) in accordance with rules 6.4 to 6.6.

(2) Those documents are—

(a) a citation in Form 6.3–A;

(b) a copy of the petition for sequestration;

(c) a copy of the warrant of citation.

(3) The petitioner must lodge a certificate of citation in Form 6.3–B no later than 2 days before the date on which the debtor has been cited to appear.

NOTES

Commencement: 30 November 2016.

[16.348]

6.4 Service by sheriff officer

(1) Where the debtor is of a type mentioned in the first column of the following table, a sheriff officer may effect service of the documents referred to in rule 6.3(2) by the method specified in the second column—

Debtor	*Method of service*
Living individual	Giving the document personally to the individual
Deceased individual	Giving the document personally to an executor or a person entitled to be appointed as executor
Trust	Giving the document personally to the individual trustees (if known)
Partnership or limited partnership	(a) Giving the document personally to the individual partners (if known); and (b) leaving the document in the hands of an employee, agent or representative at the place of business of the partnership
Dissolved partnership or dissolved limited partnership	Giving the document personally to the individual partners (if known)
Body corporate or unincorporated body	(a) Giving the document personally to a senior official (if known); and (b) leaving the document in the hands of an employee, agent or representative at the place of business of the entity

(2) The sheriff officer is to be accompanied by a witness.

(3) Section 3 of the Citation Amendment (Scotland) Act 1882 does not apply to a document that is to be served in accordance with this rule.

NOTES

Commencement: 30 November 2016.

[16.349]

6.5 Service furth of Scotland

Where a person mentioned in the second column of the table in rule 6.4(1) is furth of Scotland, service on that person is to be effected in accordance with schedule 3.

NOTES

Commencement: 30 November 2016.

[16.350]

6.6 Authority to serve by other means

(1) A petitioner may apply to the sheriff for authority to serve a document by a method other than those specified in rule 6.4 or 6.5.

(2) That application is to be made—

(a) by crave in the petition, where authority is sought at the time of lodging the petition; or

(b) by motion, where authority is sought at any other time.

(3) Where the sheriff grants the application, the sheriff may authorise the petitioner to effect service by any method that the sheriff thinks fit.

NOTES

Commencement: 30 November 2016.

[16.351]

6.7 Intimation of appointment of trustee

(1) This rule applies where the sheriff appoints a person to be—

(a) the trustee in a sequestration under section 51 of the 2016 Act;
(b) an interim trustee under section 54 of the 2016 Act;
(c) a new interim trustee under section 55 of the 2016 Act.

(2) The sheriff clerk must, without delay, intimate that appointment to—

(a) the person appointed; and
(b) AiB, unless AiB is the person appointed.

NOTES

Commencement: 30 November 2016.

CHAPTER 7
APPLICATIONS ETC UNDER THE BANKRUPTCY (SCOTLAND) ACT 2016

[16.352]

7.1 Form of applications

(1) An application under the 2016 Act is to be made in Form 7.1–A unless these Rules provide otherwise.

(2) An application by AiB for a direction under the following provisions of the 2016 Act is to be in Form 7.1–B—

(a) section 50(6) (AiB application for directions);
(b) section 52(3) (referral of trustee application for direction);
(c) section 68(5) (replacement of trustee acting in more than one sequestration);
(d) section 71(7) (removal of trustee other than where unable to act etc);
(e) section 73(6) (removal of trustee where unable to act etc);
(f) section 110(8) (contractual powers of trustee);
(g) paragraph 3(10) of schedule 2 (debts depending on contingency).

NOTES

Commencement: 30 November 2016.

[16.353]

[7.1A Warrant to enter premises and warrant to apprehend

A warrant under section 39(4) of the 2016 Act or a warrant under section 120(1) of the 2016 Act may be authenticated electronically.]

NOTES

Commencement: 15 December 2016.

Inserted by the Act of Sederunt (Sheriff Court Rules Amendment) (Electronic Authentication) 2016, SSI 2016/415, r 3(1), (3).

[16.354]

7.2 Form of remit by AiB

A remit by AiB under section 36(1) or (2) of the 2016 Act is to be made in Form 7.2.

NOTES

Commencement: 30 November 2016.

[16.355]

7.3 Applications and remits relating to AiB sequestration

(1) This rule applies where an application or a remit relates to an AiB sequestration.

(2) When the application or remit is lodged, the applicant must also lodge a copy of the debtor application.

NOTES

Commencement: 30 November 2016.

[16.356]

7.4 Determination of applications and remits

(1) When an application or a remit is lodged, the sheriff is to make—

(a) an order for intimation to any person who appears to the sheriff to have an interest in it;
(b) an order specifying how it is to be determined.

(2) A certificate of intimation in Form 5.7 must be lodged within 14 days after the date of intimation by—

(a) in the case of an application, the applicant;
(b) in the case of a remit, AiB.

(3) Without prejudice to the generality of paragraph (1), where—

(a) an application, or a remitted application, is unopposed, the sheriff is to dispose of it in chambers without the appearance of parties, unless the sheriff otherwise determines;
(b) the sheriff requires to hear parties on an application or remit, the sheriff clerk is to fix a hearing and intimate the date and time of the hearing to the parties.

(4) Where an order is granted disposing of an application or a remit in accordance with paragraph (3)(a), the sheriff clerk is to intimate the order to the parties.

NOTES

Commencement: 30 November 2016.

[16.357]
7.5 Form of report by original trustee

A report to the sheriff by the original trustee under section 49(8) or (9) of the 2016 Act is to be in Form 7.5.

NOTES

Commencement: 30 November 2016.

CHAPTER 8
APPLICATIONS UNDER THE UNCITRAL MODEL LAW ON CROSS-BORDER INSOLVENCY

[16.358]
8.1 Form of applications

An application under article 12 of the Model Law on Cross-Border Insolvency is to be made by application in accordance with Chapter 7.

NOTES

Commencement: 30 November 2016.

[16.359]
8.2 Transfer of proceedings to Court of Session

(1) This rule applies where the Lord Ordinary orders proceedings under these Rules to be transferred to the Court of Session under paragraph 11 of schedule 3 of the Cross-Border Insolvency Regulations 2006.

(2) Within 4 days after receipt of a certified copy interlocutor containing that order, the sheriff clerk must transmit the sequestration process to the Deputy Principal Clerk of Session.

NOTES

Commencement: 30 November 2016.

CHAPTER 9
APPEALS TO THE SHERIFF UNDER THE BANKRUPTCY (SCOTLAND) ACT 2016

[16.360]
9.1 Form of appeal

An appeal to the sheriff under the 2016 Act is to be made in Form 9.1.

NOTES

Commencement: 30 November 2016.

[16.361]
9.2 Appeals relating to AiB sequestration

(1) This rule applies where an appeal relates to an AiB sequestration.

(2) When the appeal is lodged, the appellant must also lodge a copy of the debtor application.

NOTES

Commencement: 30 November 2016.

[16.362]
9.3 Determination of appeal

(1) When an appeal is lodged, the sheriff is to make—

(a) an order for intimation to any person who appears to the sheriff to have an interest in it;
(b) an order specifying the procedure to be followed in the appeal.

(2) The appellant must lodge a certificate of intimation in Form 5.7 within 14 days after the date of intimation.

(3) Where an appeal is disposed of in chambers without the appearance of parties, the sheriff clerk is to intimate the order disposing of the appeal to every party on whom intimation was ordered in accordance with paragraph (1)(a).

NOTES

Commencement: 30 November 2016.

CHAPTER 10
APPEALS TO THE SHERIFF APPEAL COURT

[16.363]

10.1 Appeals to the Sheriff Appeal Court

(1) This rule applies to an appeal to the Sheriff Appeal Court under the following provisions of the 2016 Act—

- (a) section 27(3) (appeal against transfer of sequestration);
- (b) section 27(4) (appeal against refusal to award sequestration);
- (c) section 77(11) (appeal against removal of commissioner);
- (d) section 161(2) (appeal against refusal to revoke bankruptcy restrictions order).

(2) An appeal is to be made in accordance with Chapter 6 of the Sheriff Appeal Court Rules.

(3) Within 4 days after a note of appeal is lodged under rule 6.2(1) (form of appeal) of the Sheriff Appeal Court Rules, the Clerk must—

- (a) give written notice of the appeal in accordance with paragraph (4); and
- (b) certify that subparagraph (a) has been complied with.

(4) In relation to an appeal made under a provision of the 2016 Act specified in the first column of the following table, the persons to whom notice is to be given are the persons specified in the second column, unless that person is the appellant—

Type of appeal	*Persons to whom notice is to be given*
Section 27(3)	The trustee
	The petitioner
	Any concurring creditor
	AiB
Section 27(4)	The debtor
	Any concurring creditor
Section 77(11)	The trustee
	AiB
	Any commissioner
	Any creditor who lodged answers to, or was otherwise heard in relation to, the application to the sheriff
Section 161(2)	The trustee
	AiB

(5) Where the Clerk fails to comply with paragraph (3)—

- (a) that failure does not affect the validity of the appeal;
- (b) the procedural Appeal Sheriff may make an order to enable the appeal to proceed as if the failure had not occurred.

(6) In this rule—

- (a) "the Sheriff Appeal Court Rules" means the Act of Sederunt (Sheriff Appeal Court Rules) 2015;
- (b) "the Clerk" and "the procedural Appeal Sheriff" have the meanings given in rule 1.2 of the Sheriff Appeal Court Rules.

NOTES

Commencement: 30 November 2016.

CHAPTER 11
MOTIONS

[16.364]

11.1 Interpretation

In this Chapter—

"lodging party" means the party lodging the motion;

"receiving party" means a party receiving the intimation of the motion from the lodging party.

NOTES

Commencement: 30 November 2016.

[16.365]
11.2 Making of motions

A motion may be made—
(a) orally; or
(b) in writing, in accordance with rule 11.3.

NOTES
Commencement: 30 November 2016.

[16.366]
11.3 Written motions

(1) A motion in writing is made by lodging it with the sheriff clerk in accordance with rule 11.7(1).

(2) A motion in writing must specify the grounds on which it is made.

NOTES
Commencement: 30 November 2016.

[16.367]
11.4 Intimation of written motions

(1) The lodging party must give intimation of his or her intention to lodge the motion, and of the terms of the motion, to every other party in Form 11.4.

(2) That intimation must be accompanied by a copy of any document referred to in the motion.

NOTES
Commencement: 30 November 2016.

[16.368]
11.5 Opposition to written motions

(1) A receiving party may oppose a motion by lodging a notice of opposition in Form 11.5.

(2) Any notice of opposition must be lodged within 7 days after the date of intimation of the motion.

(3) The sheriff may, on the application of the lodging party—
(a) vary the period of 7 days mentioned in paragraph (2); or
(b) dispense with intimation on any party.

(4) An application mentioned in paragraph (3) must—
(a) be included in the motion;
(b) give reasons for varying the period or dispensing with intimation, as the case may be.

(5) The sheriff may allow a notice of opposition to be lodged late, on cause shown.

NOTES
Commencement: 30 November 2016.

[16.369]
11.6 Consent to written motions

Where a receiving party seeks to consent to a motion, that party may do so by lodging a notice to that effect.

NOTES
Commencement: 30 November 2016.

[16.370]
11.7 Lodging of written motions

(1) The motion must be lodged by the lodging party within 5 days after the date of intimation of the motion, unless paragraph (3) applies.

(2) The lodging party must also lodge—
(a) a certificate of intimation in Form 5.7;
(b) so far as practicable, any document referred to in the motion that has not already been lodged.

(3) Where the sheriff varies the period for lodging a notice of opposition to a period of 5 days or less, the motion must be lodged no later than the day on which that period expires.

NOTES
Commencement: 30 November 2016.

[16.371]
11.8 Joint written motions

(1) A joint motion by all parties need not be intimated.

(2) Such a motion is to be lodged by any of the parties.

NOTES
Commencement: 30 November 2016.

[16.372]
11.9 Determination of unopposed written motions

(1) The sheriff clerk may determine any unopposed motion in writing other than a motion which seeks a final interlocutor.

(2) Where the sheriff clerk considers that such a motion should not be granted, the sheriff clerk must refer the motion to the sheriff.

(3) The sheriff is to determine—
(a) a motion referred under paragraph (2);
(b) an unopposed motion which seeks a final interlocutor,
in chambers without the appearance of parties, unless the sheriff otherwise determines.

(4) The sheriff clerk must intimate to every party an interlocutor determining a joint written motion or an unopposed written motion.

NOTES
Commencement: 30 November 2016.

[16.373]
11.10 Hearing of opposed written motions

(1) Where a notice of opposition in Form 11.5 is lodged, the motion is to be heard by the sheriff on the first suitable court day after the lodging of the notice of opposition.

(2) The sheriff clerk must intimate the date and time of the hearing to the parties.

NOTES
Commencement: 30 November 2016.

CHAPTER 12
WITHDRAWAL OF SOLICITORS

[16.374]
12.1 Interpretation of this Chapter

In this Chapter, "peremptory hearing" means a hearing at which a party whose solicitor has withdrawn from acting must appear or be represented in order to state whether or not the party intends to proceed.

NOTES
Commencement: 30 November 2016.

[16.375]
12.2 Giving notice of withdrawal

(1) Where a solicitor withdraws from acting on behalf of a party, the solicitor must give notice in writing to the sheriff clerk and to every other party.

(2) Paragraph (1) does not apply if the solicitor withdraws from acting at a hearing in the presence of the other parties or their representatives.

(3) Paragraph (4) applies if a solicitor who withdraws from acting is aware that the address of the party for whom the solicitor acted has changed from that specified in the instance of the appeal, application, petition or answers.

(4) The solicitor must disclose to the sheriff clerk and every other party the last known address of the party for whom the solicitor acted.

NOTES
Commencement: 30 November 2016.

[16.376]
12.3 Arrangements for peremptory hearing

(1) On notice being given under rule 12.2(1), the sheriff is to make an order—
(a) ordaining the party whose solicitor has withdrawn from acting to appear or be represented at a peremptory hearing;
(b) fixing a date and time for the peremptory hearing;
(c) appointing any other party to the proceedings to intimate the order and a notice in Form 12.3 to that party within 7 days after the date of the order.

(2) A peremptory hearing is to be fixed no sooner than 14 days after the date on which an order is made under paragraph (1).

(3) The sheriff may vary the period of 7 days mentioned in paragraph (1) or the period of 14 days mentioned in paragraph (2)—
(a) of the sheriff's own accord; or
(b) on cause shown, on the application of any other party to the proceedings.

(4) Where any previously fixed hearing is to occur within 14 days after the date on which the sheriff clerk is given notice under rule 12.2(1), the sheriff may continue consideration of the withdrawal to that previously fixed hearing instead of making an order under paragraph (1).

(5) Where an order and a notice in Form 12.3 are intimated under this rule, the party appointed to intimate them must lodge a certificate of intimation in Form 5.7—

(a) within 14 days from the date of intimation; or

(b) before the peremptory hearing,

whichever is sooner.

NOTES

Commencement: 30 November 2016.

[16.377]

12.4 Peremptory hearing

(1) At a peremptory hearing, the party whose solicitor has withdrawn from acting must appear or be represented in order to state whether the party intends to proceed.

(2) Where the party fails to comply with paragraph (1), the sheriff may make an order mentioned in paragraph (3) only if the sheriff is satisfied that the order and notice in Form 12.3 have been intimated to that party.

(3) The orders are—

(a) if the party is the appellant, applicant or petitioner, an order refusing the appeal, application or petition; or

(b) if the party is the respondent and the condition in paragraph (4) is satisfied, an order allowing the appeal, application or petition.

(4) The condition is that the appellant, applicant or petitioner must show cause why the appeal, application or petition should be allowed.

(5) If the sheriff is not satisfied that the order and notice in Form 12.3 have been intimated to that party, the sheriff may make—

(a) an order fixing a further peremptory hearing;

(b) any other order that the sheriff considers appropriate to secure the expeditious disposal of the proceedings.

NOTES

Commencement: 30 November 2016.

CHAPTER 13
EXPENSES

[16.378]

13.1 Taxation of expenses

(1) Where the sheriff makes an order allowing expenses in any proceedings, those expenses must be taxed before decree is granted for them

(2) This rule does not apply where the sheriff modifies those expenses to a fixed sum.

NOTES

Commencement: 30 November 2016.

[16.379]

13.2 Procedure for taxation of expenses

(1) Where an account of expenses is lodged for taxation, the sheriff clerk must transmit the account and the process to the auditor of court.

(2) The auditor must—

(a) fix a taxation hearing no sooner than 7 days after the auditor receives the account;

(b) intimate the date, time and place of the taxation hearing to every party.

(3) If the auditor reserves consideration of the account at the taxation hearing, the auditor must intimate the auditor's decision to the parties who attended the hearing.

(4) After the account has been taxed, the auditor must transmit the account and the process, together with the auditor's report, to the sheriff clerk.

(5) Where no objections are lodged under rule 13.3, the sheriff may grant decree for the expenses as taxed.

NOTES

Commencement: 30 November 2016.

[16.380]

13.3 Objections to taxed account

(1) A party may lodge a note of objections to an account as taxed only where the party attended the taxation hearing.

(2) A note of objections must be lodged within 7 days after—

(a) the taxation hearing; or

(b) where the auditor reserves consideration of the account, the date on which the auditor intimates the auditor's decision to the parties.

(3) The sheriff is to dispose of the note of objections in a summary manner.

NOTES

Commencement: 30 November 2016.

[16.381]

13.4 Decree for expenses in name of solicitor

The sheriff may allow a decree for expenses to be extracted in the name of the solicitor who conducted the proceedings.

NOTES

Commencement: 30 November 2016.

CHAPTER 14
VULNERABLE WITNESSES

[16.382]

14.1 Interpretation and application of this Chapter

(1) This Chapter applies where the evidence of a witness is to be taken in proceedings.

(2) In this Chapter—

"2004 Act" means the Vulnerable Witnesses (Scotland) Act 2004;

"child witness notice" has the meaning given by section 12(2) of the 2004 Act;

"review application" means an application under section 13 of the 2004 Act;

"vulnerable witness application" has the meaning given by section 12(6) of the 2004 Act.

NOTES

Commencement: 30 November 2016.

[16.383]

14.2 Form of notices and applications

(1) A child witness notice is to be made in Form 14.2–A.

(2) A vulnerable witness application is to be made in Form 14.2–B.

(3) A review application is to be made—

(a) in Form 14.2–C; or

(b) orally, with the leave of the sheriff.

NOTES

Commencement: 30 November 2016.

[16.384]

14.3 Determination of notices and applications

(1) When a notice or application under this Chapter is lodged, the sheriff may require any of the parties to provide further information before determining the notice or application.

(2) The sheriff may—

(a) determine the notice or application by making an order under section 12(1) or (6) or 13(2) of the 2004 Act without holding a hearing;

(b) fix a hearing at which parties are to be heard on the notice or application before determining it.

(3) The sheriff may make an order altering the date of any hearing at which evidence is to be taken in order that the notice or application may be determined.

NOTES

Commencement: 30 November 2016.

[16.385]

14.4 Determination of notices and applications: supplementary orders

Where the sheriff determines a notice or application under this Chapter and makes an order under section 12(1) or (6) or 13(2) of the 2004 Act, the sheriff may make further orders to secure the expeditious disposal of the proceedings.

NOTES

Commencement: 30 November 2016.

[16.386]

14.5 Intimation of orders

(1) Where the sheriff makes an order—

(a) fixing a hearing under rule 14.3(2)(b);

(b) altering the date of a hearing under rule 14.3(3); or

(c) under section 12(1) or (6) or 13(2) of the 2004 Act,

the sheriff clerk is to intimate the order in accordance with this rule.

(2) Intimation is to be given to—

(a) every party to the proceedings; and
(b) any other person named in the order.

(3) Intimation is to be given—
(a) on the day that the hearing is fixed or the order is made;
(b) in the manner ordered by the sheriff.

NOTES

Commencement: 30 November 2016.

[16.387]

14.6 Taking of evidence by commissioner: preparatory steps

(1) This rule applies where the sheriff authorises the special measure of taking evidence by a commissioner under section 19(1) of the 2004 Act.

(2) The commission is to proceed without interrogatories unless the sheriff otherwise orders.

(3) The order of the sheriff authorising the special measure is sufficient authority for citing the vulnerable witness to appear before the commissioner.

(4) The party who cited the vulnerable witness—
(a) must give the commissioner—
(i) a certified copy of the order of the sheriff appointing the commissioner;
(ii) a copy of the pleadings;
(iii) where rule 14.7 applies, the approved interrogatories and cross-interrogatories;
(b) must instruct the clerk to the commission;
(c) is responsible in the first instance for the fee of the commissioner and the clerk.

(5) The commissioner is to fix a hearing at which the commission will be carried out.

(6) The commissioner must consult the parties before fixing the hearing.

(7) An application by a party for leave to be present in the room where the commission is carried out is to be made by motion.

NOTES

Commencement: 30 November 2016.

[16.388]

14.7 Taking of evidence by commissioner: interrogatories

(1) This rule applies where the sheriff—
(a) authorises the special measure of taking evidence by a commissioner under section 19(1) of the 2004 Act; and
(b) orders that interrogatories are to be prepared.

(2) When the sheriff makes an order for interrogatories to be prepared, the sheriff is to specify the periods within which parties must comply with the steps in this rule.

(3) The party who cited the vulnerable witness must lodge draft interrogatories in process.

(4) Any other party may lodge cross-interrogatories.

(5) The parties may adjust their interrogatories and cross-interrogatories.

(6) At the expiry of the adjustment period, the parties must lodge the interrogatories and cross-interrogatories as adjusted in process.

(7) The sheriff is to resolve any dispute as to the content of the interrogatories and cross-interrogatories, and approve them.

NOTES

Commencement: 30 November 2016.

[16.389]

14.8 Taking of evidence by commissioner: conduct of commission

(1) The commissioner is to administer the oath de *fideli administratione* to the clerk.

(2) The commissioner is to administer the oath to the vulnerable witness in Form 14.8–A unless the witness elects to affirm.

(3) Where the witness elects to affirm, the commissioner is to administer the affirmation in Form 14.8–B.

NOTES

Commencement: 30 November 2016.

[16.390]

14.9 Taking of evidence by commissioner: lodging and custody of video record and documents

(1) The commissioner is to lodge the video record of the commission and any relevant documents with the sheriff clerk.

(2) When the video record and any relevant document are lodged, the sheriff clerk is to notify every party—
(a) that the video record has been lodged;

(b) whether any relevant documents have been lodged;
(c) of the date on which they were lodged.

(3) The video record and any relevant documents are to be kept by the sheriff clerk.

(4) Where the video record has been lodged—
(a) the name and address of the vulnerable witness and the record of the witness's evidence are to be treated as being in the knowledge of the parties;
(b) the parties need not include—
(i) the name of the witness in any list of witnesses; or
(ii) the record of evidence in any list of productions.

NOTES
Commencement: 30 November 2016.

CHAPTER 15
LIVE LINKS

[16.391]
15.1 Interpretation

In this Chapter—
"evidence" means the evidence of—
(a) a party; or
(b) a person who has been or may be cited to appear before the court as a witness
"live link" means—
(c) a live television link; or
(d) where the sheriff gives permission in accordance with rule 15.2(4), an alternative arrangement;
"submission" means any oral submission which would otherwise be made to the sheriff by a party or that party's representative, including an oral submission in support of a motion.

NOTES
Commencement: 30 November 2016.

[16.392]
15.2 Application for use of live link

(1) A party may apply to the sheriff to use a live link to make a submission or to give evidence.

(2) An application to use a live link is to be made by motion.

(3) Where a party seeks to use a live link other than a live television link, the motion must specify the proposed arrangement.

(4) The sheriff must not grant a motion to use a live link other than a live television link unless the person using the live link is able to—
(a) be heard in the courtroom; and
(b) hear the proceedings in the courtroom.

NOTES
Commencement: 30 November 2016.

CHAPTER 16
REPORTING RESTRICTIONS

[16.393]
16.1 Interpretation and application of this Chapter

(1) This Chapter applies to orders which restrict the reporting of proceedings.

(2) In this Chapter, "interested person" means a person—
(a) who has asked to see any order made by the sheriff which restricts the reporting of proceedings, including an interim order; and
(b) whose name is included on a list kept by the Lord President for the purposes of this Chapter.

NOTES
Commencement: 30 November 2016.

[16.394]
16.2 Interim orders: notification to interested persons

(1) Where the sheriff is considering making an order, the sheriff may make an interim order.

(2) Where the sheriff makes an interim order, the sheriff clerk must immediately send a copy of the interim order to any interested person.

(3) The sheriff is to specify in the interim order why the sheriff is considering making an order.

NOTES
Commencement: 30 November 2016.

[16.395]
16.3 Interim orders: representations

(1) Paragraph (2) applies where the sheriff has made an interim order.

(2) An interested person who would be directly affected by the making of an order is to be given an opportunity to make representations to the sheriff before the order is made.

(3) Representations are to—
- (a) be made in Form 16.3;
- (b) include reasons why an urgent hearing is necessary, if an urgent hearing is sought;
- (c) be lodged no later than 2 days after the interim order is sent to interested persons in accordance with rule 16.2(2).

(4) If representations are made—
- (a) the sheriff is to appoint a date and time for a hearing—
  - (i) on the first suitable court day; or
  - (ii) where the sheriff considers that an urgent hearing is necessary, at an earlier date and time;
- (b) the sheriff clerk must—
  - (i) notify the date and time of the hearing to the parties to the proceedings and any person who has made representations; and
  - (ii) send a copy of the representations to the parties.

(5) Where no interested person makes representations in accordance with paragraph (3), the sheriff clerk is to put the interim order before the sheriff in chambers in order that the sheriff may resume consideration of whether to make an order.

(6) Where the sheriff, having resumed consideration, makes no order, the sheriff must recall the interim order.

(7) Where the sheriff recalls an interim order, the sheriff clerk must immediately notify any interested person.

NOTES
Commencement: 30 November 2016.

[16.396]
16.4 Notification of reporting restrictions

(1) Where the sheriff makes an order, the sheriff clerk must immediately—
- (a) send a copy of the order to any interested person;
- (b) arrange for the publication of the making of the order on the Scottish Courts and Tribunals Service website.

NOTES
Commencement: 30 November 2016.

[16.397]
16.5 Applications for variation or revocation

(1) A person aggrieved by an order may apply to the sheriff for its variation or revocation.

(2) An application is to be made in Form 16.5.

(3) When an application is made—
- (a) the sheriff is to appoint a date and time for a hearing;
- (b) the sheriff clerk must—
  - (i) notify the date and time of the hearing to the parties to the proceedings and the applicant; and
  - (ii) send a copy of the application to the parties.

(4) The hearing is, so far as reasonably practicable, to be before the sheriff who made the order.

NOTES
Commencement: 30 November 2016.

SCHEDULE 1
FORMS

Rule 1.4(1)

[16.398]

NOTES
The forms themselves are not reproduced in this work, but their numbers and descriptions are listed below.

FORM NO	TITLE
5.7	Certificate of intimation
6.1—A	Form of petition for sequestration
6.1—B	Form of undertaking by prospective trustee
6.2	Form of debt payment programme and moratorium on diligence statement
6.3—A	Form of citation

FORM NO	TITLE
6.3—B	Form of certificate of citation
7.1—A	Form of application under Bankruptcy (Scotland) Act 2016
7.1—B	Form of application for direction under Bankruptcy (Scotland) Act 2016
7.2	Form of remit by Accountant in Bankruptcy
7.5	Form of report by the original trustee
9.1	Form of note of appeal to sheriff
11.4	Form of motion
11.5	Form of opposition to motion
12.3	Notice of peremptory hearing
14.2—A	Child witness notice
14.2—B	Vulnerable witness application
14.2—C	Application for review of arrangements for vulnerable witness
14.8—A	Form of oath for witness
14.8—B	Form of affirmation for witness
16.3	Representations about a proposed order restricting the reporting of proceedings
16.5	Application for variation or revocation of an order restricting the reporting of proceedings

NOTES

Commencement: 30 November 2016.

Form 6.1—A: amended by the Act of Sederunt (Sheriff Court Rules Amendment) (Miscellaneous) 2016, SSI 2016/367, r 7(1), (2) and the Act of Sederunt (Rules of the Court of Session 1994 and Sheriff Court Rules Amendment) (Regulation (EU) 2015/848) 2017, SSI 2017/202, rr 2(1), (3), 6, except in relation to proceedings which are subject to Regulation (EC) 1346/2000 of 29th May 2000 on insolvency proceedings.

SCHEDULE 2
FORMS FOR USE IN REGISTER OF INHIBITIONS

Rule 1.4(2)

[16.399]

NOTES

The forms themselves are not reproduced in this work, but their numbers and descriptions are listed below.

FORM	TITLE
A	Form of memorandum by trustee under section 26(6) of the Bankruptcy (Scotland) Act 2016
B	Form of memorandum by trustee under section 26(8) of the Bankruptcy (Scotland) Act 2016
C	Form of notice of inhibition by trustee under paragraph 3(1) of schedule 4 to the Bankruptcy (Scotland) Act 2016
D	Form of notice of recall of inhibition by trustee under paragraph 3(3) of schedule 4 of the Bankruptcy (Scotland) Act 2016

NOTES

Commencement: 30 November 2016.

SCHEDULE 3
SERVICE OF DOCUMENTS FURTH OF SCOTLAND

Rule 6.5

[16.400]

1 Interpretation of this Schedule

In this Schedule—

"consular service" is to be construed in accordance with paragraph 8;

"EU member state" means a state which is a member of the European Union, within the meaning of Part II of schedule 1 of the European Communities Act 1972;

"Hague Convention country" means a country in respect of which the Convention of 15 November 1965 on the Service Abroad of Judicial and Extrajudicial Documents in Civil or Commercial Matters is in force, other than an EU member state;

"personal service" is to be construed in accordance with paragraph 9;

"postal service" is to be construed in accordance with paragraph 10;

"Service Regulation" means Regulation (E.C.) No 1393/2007 of the European Parliament and of the Council of 13th November 2007 on the service in the Member States of judicial and extrajudicial documents in civil or commercial matters (service of documents), and repealing Council Regulation (E.C.) No 1348/2000, as amended from time to time.

2 Service furth of Scotland

(1) Service of a document furth of Scotland is to be effected in accordance with this paragraph.

(2) If the person's known residence or place of business is in England and Wales, Northern Ireland, the Isle of Man or the Channel Islands, see paragraph 3.

(3) If the person's known residence or place of business is in an EU member state (including Denmark), see paragraph 4.

(4) If the person's known residence or place of business is in a Hague Convention country (other than an EU member state), see paragraph 5.

(5) If the person's known residence or place of business in a country with which the United Kingdom has a convention about how to serve court documents (such as Algeria, Libya and the United Arab Emirates), see paragraph 6.

(6) If none of the above applies, see paragraph 7.

3 Service in England and Wales etc

(1) A document may be served in England and Wales, Northern Ireland, the Isle of Man or the Channel Islands by—

(a) postal service; or
(b) personal service.

(2) Personal service may be effected by a person who is authorised to do so under the domestic law of the place where the document is to be served.

4 Service in an EU member state

(1) A document may be served in an EU member state (including Denmark) under the Service Regulation by—

(a) postal service;
(b) service by transmitting agency;
(c) direct service, where the law of the member state permits it;
(d) consular service.

(2) Service by transmitting agency may be effected by sending the document to a messenger-at-arms and instructing them to arrange for it to be served.

(3) Direct service may be effected by sending the document to a person who is entitled to serve court documents in that member state and asking them to arrange for it to be served.

(4) Where service is to be effected by transmitting agency, the party must give the messenger-at-arms a translation of the document into a language which the recipient understands or an official language of the member state where the document is to be served.

5 Service in a Hague Convention country

(1) A document may be served in a Hague Convention country (other than an EU member state) by—

(a) postal service, where the law of the country permits it;
(b) service via central authority;
(c) consular service;
(d) service by competent person, where the law of the country permits it.

(2) Service via central authority may be effected by sending the document to the Scottish Ministers and asking them to arrange for it to be served.

(3) Service by competent person may be effected by sending the document to a person who is entitled to serve court documents in that country and asking them to arrange for it to be served.

(4) Any document must be accompanied by a translation into an official language of the country where it is to be served, unless English is an official language of that country.

6 Service in a country with which the United Kingdom has a convention about how to serve court documents

A document may be served in a country with which the United Kingdom has a convention about how to serve court documents by any method that is permitted by the convention.

7 Service in any other country

(1) Where none of paragraphs 3 to 6 apply, a document may be served by—

(a) postal service;
(b) personal service.

(2) Where service is effected by personal service, the party executing service must lodge a certificate stating that the method of service employed is in accordance with the law of the country where service was executed.

(3) That certificate is to be given by a person who—

(a) practises or has practised law in that country; or
(b) is an accredited representative of that country's government, conversant with the law of that country.

8 Consular service

(1) Consular service is service by a British consular authority.

(2) Consular service may be effected only if—

(a) the law of the . . . state where the document is to be served permits it; or

(b) the document is being served on a British national.

(3) Consular service may be effected by sending the document to the Secretary of State for Foreign and Commonwealth Affairs and asking the Secretary of State to arrange for it to be served by a British consular authority.

9 Personal service

(1) Personal service is service using the rules for personal service under the domestic law of the place where the document is to be served.

(2) Personal service may be effected by a person who is authorised to do so under the domestic law of the place where the document is to be served.

10 Postal service

(1) Postal service is service by posting the document to the person's home or business address using a postal service which records delivery.

(2) Postal service may be effected by a solicitor or a sheriff officer.

(3) Where postal service is used, the envelope containing the document must have the following label printed or written on it—

THIS ENVELOPE CONTAINS A (*name of document*) FROM (*name of sheriff court*), SCOTLAND

IF DELIVERY CANNOT BE MADE, THE LETTER MUST BE RETURNED TO THE SHERIFF CLERK AT (*full address of sheriff court*)

(4) That label must be translated into an official language of the country where the document is to be served, unless English is an official language of that country.

11 Certification of translations

(1) This paragraph applies where this schedule requires a document to be translated into a language other than English.

(2) The party executing service must lodge a certificate stating that the translation is correct.

(3) That certificate—

(a) is to be given by the person who made the translation;

(b) must include the full name, address and qualifications of the translator.

NOTES

Commencement: 30 November 2016.

Para 8: in sub-para (2)(a) word omitted revoked by the Act of Sederunt (Sheriff Court Rules Amendment) (Miscellaneous) 2016, SSI 2016/367, r 7(1), (3).

BANKRUPTCY (SCOTLAND) REGULATIONS 2016

(SSI 2016/397)

NOTES

Made: 24 November 2016.

Authority: Debt Arrangement and Attachment (Scotland) Act 2002, s 7(2)(bd); Bankruptcy (Scotland) Act 2016, ss 2(2)(a)(ii), (f), 3(1), 4(1)(d), (2)(b), 6(8), 8(3)(a), 9(4)(b), 19(1), 46(2)(a), (6), 48(1)(a), 51(14), 54(4), 87(8), 89, 94(7), 113(5), 116(2), 117(1), 119(6)(a), 126(5), 129(10)(a), 137(2), 138(2), 140(2) 141(2)(a), (c), 142(2), (5), 200(1)(c), (8), 221, 224(1), 225(2), 228(1), 234(3)(b), Sch 1, para 2(5)(a).

Commencement: 30 November 2016.

ARRANGEMENT OF SECTIONS

1 Citation and commencement . . . [16.401]
2 Interpretation . . . [16.402]
3 Forms . . . [16.403]

PART 1
MONEY ADVISERS

4 Approved categories of money advisers . . . [16.404]
5 Persons who may not be approved money advisers . . . [16.405]
6 Other matters on which a debtor must obtain advice . . . [16.406]
7 Money advice on debtor applications: procedure on evidence and information . . . [16.407]
8 Certificate for sequestration: form and manner . . . [16.408]
9 Certificate for sequestration: fee . . . [16.409]
10 Certificate for sequestration: prescribed period . . . [16.410]

PART 2
SEQUESTRATION PROCESS

11 Debt advice and information package . . . . . [16.411]
12 Debtor applications . . . . . [16.412]
13 "Minimal Asset Process" debtors to whom section 2(2) of Act applies: prescribed payments . . [16.413]
14 "Minimal Asset Process" debtors to whom section 2(2) of Act applies: total assets . . . . . [16.414]

PART 3
DEBTOR'S CONTRIBUTION

15 Common financial tool . . . . . [16.415]
16 Common financial tool: contingency allowance. . . . . [16.416]
17 Common financial tool: supporting statements and evidence . . . . . [16.417]
18 Money Advice Trust licence requirements: report . . . . . [16.418]
19 Debtor contribution orders. . . . . [16.419]
20 Deduction from debtor's earnings and other income . . . . . [16.420]

PART 4
ADMINISTRATION OF SEQUESTRATION

21 Claims in foreign currency . . . . . [16.421]
22 Conversion of foreign currency claims. . . . . [16.422]
23 Trustee resignation application . . . . . [16.423]
24 Abandonment of heritable property by trustee . . . . . [16.424]
25 Financial education . . . . . [16.425]
26 Interest on claims in sequestration . . . . . [16.426]
27 Certificate of deferral of debtor's discharge . . . . . [16.427]
28 Premium of bond of caution. . . . . [16.428]

PART 5
MORATORIUM ON DILIGENCE

29 Moratorium on diligence: notice of intention to apply . . . . . [16.429]

PART 6
REGISTER OF INSOLVENCIES

30 Register of Insolvencies . . . . . [16.430]

PART 7
LIMITED PARTNERSHIPS

31 Application of Bankruptcy (Scotland) Act 2016 to limited partnerships . . . . . [16.431]

PART 8
REVOCATIONS AND SEQUESTRATIONS AND TRUST DEEDS
BEFORE 30TH NOVEMBER 2016

32 Revocations . . . . . [16.432]
33 Sequestrations and trust deeds before 30th November 2016. . . . . [16.433]
34 Moratorium on diligence: notice of intention to apply under Bankruptcy (Scotland) Act 2016. . [16.434]

SCHEDULES

Schedule 1—Forms . . . . . [16.435]
Schedule 2—Register of Insolvencies . . . . . [16.436]
Schedule 3—Revocations. . . . . [16.437]

[16.401]

1 Citation and commencement

These Regulations may be cited as the Bankruptcy (Scotland) Regulations 2016 and come into force on 30th November 2016.

NOTES

Commencement: 30 November 2016.

[16.402]

2 Interpretation

(1) In these Regulations—

"the Act" means the Bankruptcy (Scotland) Act 2016;

"AiB" means the Accountant in Bankruptcy (with the meaning given by section 199 of the Act);

"Common Financial Statement" means the style and format for income and expenditure categories under that title (and, where relevant, related spread sheets, budget sheets, trigger figures, guidance materials and notes) published by the Money Advice Trust;

"common financial tool" has the meaning given by section 89(1) of the Act (see regulations 15 to 17);

"debtor's contribution" has the meaning given by section 89(1) of the Act; and

"the Keeper" means the Keeper of the Registers of Scotland.

(2) Any reference in these Regulations, except regulation 20, to anything done in writing or produced in written form includes a reference to an electronic communication, as defined in section 15(1) of the Electronic Communications Act 2000, which has been recorded and is consequently capable of being reproduced.

NOTES

Commencement: 30 November 2016.

[16.403]

3 Forms

(1) The forms set out in schedule 1 are the forms referred to in regulations 8, 12, 19, 20, 23, 24, 27 and 29, failing which they are prescribed for the purposes of the provisions of the Act referred to in the form.

(2) Any signature required as shown on a form set out in schedule 1 must be provided either by—
- (a) a manuscript signature; or
- (b) except in Forms 19 to 21, an image of a manuscript signature sent electronically.

NOTES

Commencement: 30 November 2016.

PART 1
MONEY ADVISERS

[16.404]

4 Approved categories of money advisers

Subject to regulation 5, the following classes of persons are prescribed for the purposes of section 4(2)(b) of the Act as money advisers—
- (a) persons who—
  - (i) are qualified to act as insolvency practitioners in accordance with sections 390 of the Insolvency Act 1986 who are fully authorised, or partially authorised so to act in relation to individuals, within the meaning of 390A of that Act; or
  - (ii) work for such an insolvency practitioner, who have been given authority by that insolvency practitioner to act on his or her behalf in providing money advice under the Act; and
- (b) persons who—
  - (i) work as money advisers for organisations which have been awarded accreditation at Type 2 level or above against the Scottish National Standards for Information and Advice Provision; or
  - (ii) are approved for the purposes of the Debt Arrangement Scheme; or
  - (iii) work as money advisers for a citizens advice bureau which is a full member of the Scottish Association of Citizens Advice Bureaux—Citizens Advice Scotland; or
  - (iv) work as money advisers for a local authority.

NOTES

Commencement: 30 November 2016.

[16.405]

5 Persons who may not be approved money advisers

(1) The following persons may not be a money adviser—
- (a) a sheriff officer or messenger-at-arms, or an employee of such a person;
- (b) a person or body providing financial services, or financial advice other than money advice, in the course of a business or otherwise for profit, or an employee of such a person, unless the person is a—
  - (i) solicitor;
  - (ii) chartered or certified accountant;
  - (iii) a credit union registered under the Co-operative and Community Benefit Societies Act 2014 or the Industrial and Provident Societies Act 1965 by virtue of section 1 of the Credit Unions Act 1979;
- (c) a person providing debt collection services, or an employee of such a person;
- (d) a person convicted of an offence involving theft, fraud or other dishonesty;
- (e) a person subject to a bankruptcy restrictions order (including an interim order) under section 155 or 160 of the Act or subject to a bankruptcy restrictions order, or bound by a bankruptcy restrictions undertaking, under schedule 4A of the Insolvency Act 1986;
- (f) a person in respect of whom a court has made a disqualification order under section 1, or who has had a disqualification undertaking accepted under section 1A, of the Company Directors Disqualification Act 1986;
- (g) persons without a licence from the Money Advice Trust to use the Common Financial Statement; or
- (h) persons whose approval is revoked or suspended under paragraph (2).

(2) AiB may revoke or suspend the approval of a money adviser who fails without good cause—
- (a) to apply the common financial tool in accordance with Part 3; or
- (b) to comply with regulation 7.

(3) AiB must provide written notice of the revocation or suspension to the money adviser (together with reasons for the decision to revoke or suspend).

(4) AiB must provide written notice of the revocation or suspension to any debtor where it is known to AiB that the money adviser is acting as money adviser to that debtor.

NOTES

Commencement: 30 November 2016.

[16.406]

6 Other matters on which a debtor must obtain advice

The following are prescribed for the purposes of section 4(1)(d) of the Act as matters on which the debtor must obtain advice from a money adviser—

- (a) the income and expenditure of the debtor in accordance with the common financial tool;
- (b) the evidence required to confirm the debts of the debtor in making the debtor application;
- (c) the debt advice and information package;
- (d) the options of a voluntary repayment plan, debt payment programme under the Debt Arrangement Scheme or a trust deed;
- (e) the consequences of sequestration and that an award of sequestration, if granted, is recorded in a public register and may result in one or more of—
  - (i) the debtor being refused credit, or being offered credit at a higher rate, whether before or after the date of the debtor being discharged;
  - (ii) the debtor not being able to remain in his or her current place of residence;
  - (iii) the debtor being required to relinquish property which the debtor owns;
  - (iv) the debtor requiring to make contributions from income for the benefit of creditors;
  - (v) damage to the debtor's business interests and employment prospects;
  - (vi) the debtor still being liable for some debts;
  - (vii) the debtor's past financial transactions being investigated; and
  - (viii) other restrictions or requirements imposed on the debtor as a result of the debtor's own circumstances and actions.

NOTES

Commencement: 30 November 2016.

[16.407]

7 Money advice on debtor applications: procedure on evidence and information

(1) In advising under section 4 of the Act on a debtor application, a money adviser must obtain evidence of the debtor's income and expenditure.

(2) A money adviser must retain records in relation to the advice given to the debtor (including the evidence obtained under paragraph (1)) in making a debtor application, for 2 years from the date on which the advice was given.

(3) A money adviser must provide as required by AiB, information about a debtor's application (including evidence obtained under paragraph (1) or the debtor's consent to the application).

NOTES

Commencement: 30 November 2016.

[16.408]

8 Certificate for sequestration: form and manner

(1) A certificate for sequestration granted in accordance with section 9 of the Act must be in Form 2.

(2) The certificate must be signed and dated to the effect provided in that form—

- (a) by the money adviser; and
- (b) by the debtor.

(3) The certificate must be printed on the headed notepaper—

- (a) where the money adviser belongs to an organisation, of the organisation to which the money adviser belongs, or
- (b) in other cases, of the money adviser.

NOTES

Commencement: 30 November 2016.

[16.409]

9 Certificate for sequestration: fee

No fee is chargeable for granting a certificate for sequestration.

NOTES

Commencement: 30 November 2016.

[16.410]

10 Certificate for sequestration: prescribed period

The time period prescribed for a granted certificate for sequestration for the purposes of section 2(2)(f) or (8)(e)(ii) of the Act is 30 days.

NOTES

Commencement: 30 November 2016.

PART 2
SEQUESTRATION PROCESS

[16.411]

11 Debt advice and information package

(1) Subject to paragraph (2), the time prescribed for the purposes of section 3(1) of the Act is not less than 14 days before the presentation of the petition and not more than 12 weeks before the presentation of the petition.

(2) Paragraph (1) (and so the requirement to provide the debtor with a debt advice and information package in that section) does not apply where it is averred that the address of the debtor is not known.

NOTES

Commencement: 30 November 2016.

[16.412]

12 Debtor applications

(1) A debtor application to AiB—

(a) in the case of an application by a living debtor, or by the executor (or a person entitled to be appointed executor) on the estate of a deceased debtor, must be in Form 1;

(b) in the case of an application by an entity referred to in section 6(1) of the Act, must be in Form 3 accompanied by a statement of assets and liabilities in Form 4.

(2) Where in a debtor application the debtor nominates an insolvency practitioner to act as the trustee in the sequestration and the insolvency practitioner agrees to act, the application must be accompanied by the insolvency practitioner's written undertaking to act as the trustee in Form 12.

(3) The Accountant in Bankruptcy or Depute Accountant in Bankruptcy must daily sign a Schedule in Form 7 listing those debtors whose estates have been sequestrated that day, and must enter the Schedule into the register of insolvencies.

(4) AiB must notify in writing debtors in respect of whom an award of sequestration has been made without delay after the award of sequestration.

(5) Where AiB refuses to award sequestration, the Accountant in Bankruptcy or Depute Accountant in Bankruptcy must complete and sign a Form 8 in respect of the debtor and without delay send a copy to the applicant, or applicants, in the debtor application.

(6) Where AiB awards sequestration the certified notice of the determination to be sent by AiB to the Keeper for recording in terms of section 26(2) of the Act must be in Form 9 and the certification is to be by the Accountant in Bankruptcy, Depute Accountant in Bankruptcy or any other person authorised by the Accountant in Bankruptcy to certify the notice of the determination on behalf of the Accountant in Bankruptcy.

(7) A certified notice containing an electronic signature, in a form to be agreed between AiB and the Keeper, of a determination referred to in paragraph (6) may be sent by AiB to the Keeper electronically.

NOTES

Commencement: 30 November 2016.

[16.413]

13 "Minimal Asset Process" debtors to whom section 2(2) of Act applies: prescribed payments

(1) The payments specified in paragraph (2) are prescribed for the purposes of section 2(2)(a)(ii) of the Act (criteria for sequestration where debtor has minimal assets).

(2) Where the debtor has no other income (than from any of these payments) at the date of making his or her debtor application—

(a) universal credit under Part 1 of the Welfare Reform Act 2012;

(b) another income-related benefit (as defined in section 191 of the Social Security Administration Act 1992);

(c) an income-based jobseeker's allowance, as defined by section 1(4) of the Jobseekers Act 1995;

(d) state pension credit under the State Pension Credit Act 2002;

(e) child tax credit under the Tax Credits Act 2002; or

(f) an income-related allowance under Part 1 of the Welfare Reform Act 2007 (employment and support).

NOTES

Commencement: 30 November 2016.

[16.414]

14 "Minimal Asset Process" debtors to whom section 2(2) of Act applies: total assets

The amount of £2,000 is prescribed for the purposes of paragraph 2(5)(a) of schedule 1 of the Act (total value of debtor's assets after date of debtor application for AiB duty to consider whether paragraph 1 of that schedule should cease to have effect).

NOTES

Commencement: 30 November 2016.

PART 3
DEBTOR'S CONTRIBUTION

[16.415]

15 Common financial tool

(1) The specified method to be used to assess the debtor's contribution in accordance with paragraphs (2) to (11) and regulations 16 and 17 ("the common financial tool") is the Common Financial Statement.

(2) Subject to paragraphs (3) and (7), the debtor's contribution is to be the debtor's whole surplus income (assessed for instance weekly, fortnightly or monthly in accordance with the Common Financial Statement) in excess of the lower of—

- (a) the trigger figures for a reasonable amount of the debtor's expenditure published from time to time as part of the Common Financial Statement; or
- (b) the debtor's expenditure over that period (for each relevant Common Financial Statement category of expenditure).

(3) AiB, the trustee on variation or removal under section 95 of the Act, the court, or the trustee acting under a protected trust deed—

- (a) may allow an amount of expenditure to the debtor which exceeds those trigger figures if satisfied that the expenditure is reasonable; and
- (b) must allow the debtor to decide to retain an additional amount of income in accordance with regulation 16 towards contingencies which may arise.

(4) In determining what is reasonable under paragraph (3)(a), evidence of why the expenditure is reasonable must be provided, or supplied by the debtor on request, to satisfy AiB, the trustee or court with regard to that evidence and any explanation provided.

(5) Insofar as the income and expenditure of any other person may be taken into account in the Common Financial Statement, if either income or expenditure is so taken into account, both the income and the expenditure of that person must be taken into account.

(6) In calculating the debtor's income where she or he is paid regularly by a period other than a week, fortnight or month, the debtor's income shall be the income for that period times such multiplier as converts the period into a year divided by 52, 26 or 12 as the case may be.

(7) If the debtor has income solely from social security benefits and tax credits, no contribution is due.

(8) If the expenditure amount so determined is less than the total amount of any income received by the debtor by way of guaranteed minimum pension (within the meaning of the Pension Schemes Act 1993) that income amount shall be allowed instead.

(9) The expenditure amount determined under paragraph (3)(a) must be sufficient to allow for—

- (a) aliment for the debtor;
- (b) any obligation of aliment owed by the debtor ("obligation of aliment" having the same meaning as in the Family Law (Scotland) Act 1985);
- (c) any obligation of the debtor to make a periodical allowance to a former spouse or former civil partner; and
- (d) any obligation of the debtor to pay child support maintenance under the Child Support Act 1991.

(10) The amount referred to in paragraph (9)(b) and (c) need not be sufficient for compliance with a subsisting order or agreement as regards the aliment or periodical allowance.

(11) Any person applying the common financial tool must have regard to guidance issued by AiB on—

- (a) the treatment of types of income and expenditure under paragraph (3);
- (b) how income and expenditure are to be verified by the money adviser and the trustee; and
- (c) the conduct of money advisers in carrying out their functions under the Act in relation to the common financial tool.

NOTES

Commencement: 30 November 2016.

[16.416]

16 Common financial tool: contingency allowance

(1) The amount of income which the debtor may decide to retain towards contingencies under regulation 15(3)(b) is—

- (a) up to 10% of the weekly, fortnightly or monthly (or the equivalent amount for another period) debtor's contribution assessed under regulation 15, before any calculation is made under this regulation for the purposes of regulation 15(3)(b);
- (b) subject to a maximum amount of £4.62 per week, £9.23 per fortnight, £20 per month or the equivalent maximum for such other period, as the case may be.

(2) The amount to be retained under paragraph (1) must be treated as an item of expenditure for the purposes of the relevant form setting out the debtor's expenditure in applying the common financial tool.

NOTES

Commencement: 30 November 2016.

[16.417]

17 Common financial tool: supporting statements and evidence

(1) Any debtor application, initial proposals under section 90(2) of the Act, or application for review or appeal of the debtor's contribution under section 92 or 97 of the Act must contain or be accompanied by a statement—

(a) that the money adviser or trustee, as the case may be, assessed the debtor's expenditure against the Common Financial Statement; and

(b) explaining any instance in which those trigger figures are exceeded.

(2) Any such statement setting out expenditure in excess of the trigger figures must be accompanied by evidence of why any expenditure allowed that exceeds the trigger figures is reasonable.

(3) Paragraphs (1) and (2) do not apply to an application for review or appeal mentioned in paragraph (1) by an interested person other than the debtor or the trustee.

(4) Any statement for the purposes of assessment by the common financial tool that there has been a change in the debtor's financial circumstances must be accompanied by evidence that the debtor's circumstances were not as they were when last assessed for those purposes.

NOTES

Commencement: 30 November 2016.

[16.418]

18 Money Advice Trust licence requirements: report

Where it appears to AiB that in using the Common Financial Statement to advise on completion of a debtor application a money adviser has contravened a licence requirement imposed by the Money Advice Trust, AiB may notify the Trust of that matter.

NOTES

Commencement: 30 November 2016.

[16.419]

19 Debtor contribution orders

(1) A debtor contribution order under section 90(1)(a) of the Act must be in Form 17.

(2) A debtor contribution order under section 90(1)(b) of the Act must be in Form 18.

NOTES

Commencement: 30 November 2016.

[16.420]

20 Deduction from debtor's earnings and other income

(1) This regulation applies where an instruction to make deductions of specified amounts from the debtor's earnings or other income and payments to the trustee of the amounts so deducted is given by a debtor or trustee under section 94(2) or (4) of the Act.

(2) Except in the case of a subsequent variation under paragraph (7)—

(a) an instruction given by the debtor under section 94(2) must be in Form 19; and

(b) an instruction given by the trustee under section 94(4) must be in Form 20.

(3) On delivery of the instruction and while the instruction is in effect, the—

(a) person by whom the debtor is employed; or

(b) third person required to pay to the trustee money otherwise due to the debtor by way of income ("third person"),

must deduct the sum specified in the instruction on every pay day or day on which a payment is to be made to the debtor, as the case may be, and pay the sum deducted to the trustee as soon as it is reasonably practicable to do so.

(4) Where an employer or third person fails without good cause to make a payment due under an instruction, the employer or third person is—

(a) liable to pay on demand by a trustee the amount that should have been paid; and

(b) not entitled to recover from a debtor the amount paid to the debtor in breach of the instruction.

(5) An employer or third person may on making a payment due under an instruction charge a fee equivalent to the fee chargeable for the time being under section 71 of the Debtors (Scotland) Act 1987 (employer's fee for operating diligence against earnings) and deduct that fee from the balance due to the debtor.

(6) The trustee must, without delay after the end of the payment period for the debtor under section 91 of the Act, notify in writing any person who has received an instruction in accordance with paragraph (2) (or varied in accordance with paragraph (7)) that the instruction has been recalled.

(7) Following any change to the debtor's contribution, the debtor or trustee may give a variation instruction under section 94(2) or (4) of the Act in accordance with that change to the instruction mentioned in paragraph (2) in Form 21 to the employer or third person.

NOTES

Commencement: 30 November 2016.

PART 4
ADMINISTRATION OF SEQUESTRATION

[16.421]

21 Claims in foreign currency

A creditor may state the amount of that creditor's claim in a foreign currency for the purposes of section 46(6) or 125(1) of the Act—

(a) where the claim is constituted by decree or other order made by a court ordering the debtor to pay to the creditor a sum expressed in a foreign currency; or

(b) where the claim is not so constituted, it arises from a contract or bill of exchange in terms of which payment is or may be required to be made by the debtor to the creditor in a foreign currency.

NOTES

Commencement: 30 November 2016.

[16.422]

[22 Conversion of foreign currency claims

For the purposes of sections 48(1)(a) and 126(5) of the Act, the manner of conversion into sterling of the amount of a claim stated in foreign currency is to be at a single exchange rate for that currency determined by the trustee with reference to the exchange rates prevailing at the close of business on the date of sequestration.]

NOTES

Commencement: 1 May 2017.

Substituted by the Bankruptcy and Protected Trust Deeds (Miscellaneous Amendments) (Scotland) Regulations 2017, SSI 2017/136, reg 2(1), (2).

[16.423]

23 Trustee resignation application

An application under section 69(1) of the Act by a trustee for authority to resign must be in Form 14.

NOTES

Commencement: 30 November 2016.

[16.424]

24 Abandonment of heritable property by trustee

(1) Where a trustee in sequestration has abandoned to the debtor any heritable property, notice of abandonment for the purposes of section 87(8) of the Act must be—

(a) where the trustee is not AiB, in Form 15; or

(b) where AiB is the trustee, in Form 16.

(2) Where AiB records a certified copy notice of abandonment under section 87(9) of the Act, it may be sent electronically to the Keeper containing an electronic signature in a form to be agreed between AiB and the Keeper.

(3) The Accountant in Bankruptcy, Depute Accountant in Bankruptcy or any other person authorised by the Accountant in Bankruptcy must certify such a copy on behalf of AiB.

NOTES

Commencement: 30 November 2016.

[16.425]

25 Financial education

The course of financial education prescribed for the purposes of section 117(1) of the Act is—

(a) the Scottish Financial Education Module learning materials divided into sections and published under that title by Money Advice Scotland; or

(b) all of the sections of that Module except for any section where the debtor's circumstances indicate the debtor does not require financial education on the topic of that section, in relation to any of the following topics—

- (i) budgeting and financial planning;
- (ii) saving;
- (iii) borrowing;
- (iv) insurance;
- (v) tax;
- (vi) financial life stages (financial considerations in relation to renting or buying a home, having a baby and loss of employment);
- (vii) welfare benefits.

NOTES

Commencement: 30 November 2016.

[16.426]

26 Interest on claims in sequestration

The prescribed rate of interest for the purposes of section 129(10)(a) of the Act (interest on preferred debts and ordinary debts between the date of sequestration and the date of payment of the debt) is 8 per cent per annum.

NOTES

Commencement: 30 November 2016.

[16.427]

27 Certificate of deferral of debtor's discharge

A certificate deferring indefinitely the discharge of the debtor under section 141(4)(b) or (6)(b) of the Act (where the debtor cannot be traced) must be in Form 30.

NOTES

Commencement: 30 November 2016.

[16.428]

28 Premium of bond of caution

Any premium (or a proportionate part of any premium) of any bond of caution or other security required to be given by an insolvency practitioner in respect of the practitioner's actings as interim trustee or trustee in any sequestration in which the practitioner is elected or appointed may be taken into account as part of that practitioner's outlays in that sequestration.

NOTES

Commencement: 30 November 2016.

PART 5
MORATORIUM ON DILIGENCE

[16.429]

29 Moratorium on diligence: notice of intention to apply

(1) A notice given by a person for the purposes of section 195(1) of the Act (notice of intention to make debtor application, protect trust deed or apply to the Debt Arrangement Scheme) must be in Form 33.

(2) A notice given by a person for the purposes of section 196(1) of the Act (notice of intention to apply: sequestration of estate under section 6) must be in Form 34.

NOTES

Commencement: 30 November 2016.

PART 6
REGISTER OF INSOLVENCIES

[16.430]

30 Register of Insolvencies

(1) The register of insolvencies maintained by AiB under section 200(1)(c) of the Act is to be in the form specified in schedule 2.

(2) Information need not be included in the register of insolvencies where AiB is of the opinion that inclusion of the information would be likely to put any person at risk of violence or otherwise jeopardise the safety or welfare of any person.

NOTES

Commencement: 30 November 2016.

PART 7
LIMITED PARTNERSHIPS

[16.431]

31 Application of Bankruptcy (Scotland) Act 2016 to limited partnerships

(1) The application of the Act to the sequestration of the estate of a limited partnership is subject to the modifications specified in this regulation.

(2) Any reference in the Act or in legislation made under it (unless the context suggests otherwise) to a partnership (other than in section 6(1)) or to a firm shall be construed as including a reference to a limited partnership.

(3) In the application of section 15 of the Act (jurisdiction) to limited partnerships—

(a) AiB has jurisdiction if a limited partnership is registered in Scotland and has a place of business in Scotland; and
(b) the sheriff has jurisdiction if a limited partnership is registered in Scotland and has a place of business within the sheriff's sheriffdom.

(4) Without prejudice to the provisions of sections 26(1), 27(11) and 30(9) of the Act, the sheriff clerk must send a copy of every court order mentioned in those sections to the Registrar of Limited Partnerships in Scotland.

(5) In the case of a debtor application by a limited partnership, AiB must send a copy of the determination to the Registrar of Limited Partnerships in Scotland.

NOTES

Commencement: 30 November 2016.

PART 8
REVOCATIONS AND SEQUESTRATIONS AND TRUST DEEDS BEFORE 30TH NOVEMBER 2016

[16.432]

32 Revocations

The Regulations specified in schedule 3 are revoked to the extent mentioned in the second column of that schedule, subject to regulation 33.

NOTES

Commencement: 30 November 2016.

[16.433]

33 Sequestrations and trust deeds before 30th November 2016

These Regulations have no effect in relation to—
(a) sequestrations as regards which the petition was presented or the debtor application was made before, or
(b) trust deeds executed before,
30th November 2016.

NOTES

Commencement: 30 November 2016.

[16.434]

34 Moratorium on diligence: notice of intention to apply under Bankruptcy (Scotland) Act 2016

For the avoidance of doubt, notice given under section 4A or 4B of the Bankruptcy (Scotland) Act 1985 before 30th November 2016 is treated as validly given after that date notwithstanding that it refers to an application for sequestration under the Bankruptcy (Scotland) Act 2016 rather than under that Act of 1985.

NOTES

Commencement: 30 November 2016.

SCHEDULE 1
FORMS

Regulation 3

[16.435]

NOTES

The forms themselves are not reproduced in this work, but their numbers and descriptions are listed below.

LIST OF FORMS TO BE USED

Form	*Purpose*	*Relevant provisions of the Act*	*Relevant provision of the Regulations*	*Form consolidated*
1	Debtor Application	Sections 2(1)(a), 5(a), 8(3)(a), 224(3)(c) and 228(1)	Regulation 12(1)(a)	*Form 14*
2	Certificate for sequestration	Section 9	Regulation 8(1)	*SSI 2010/397, amended by SSI 2014/296.*

Part 16 Other SIs: Scotland

Form	Purpose	Relevant provisions of the Act	Relevant provision of the Regulations	Form consolidated
3	Debtor Application (Trust, Partnership etc)	Sections 6(3)(a), (4)(b) and (7)(a) and 8(3)(a) and 228(1)	Regulation 12(1)(b)	*Form 15*
4	Statement of Assets and Liabilities (Trusts, Partnerships etc)	Sections 6(9), 8(3)(a) and 228(1)	Regulation 12(1)(b)	*Form 16*
5	Statutory Demand for Payment of Debt	Section 16(1)(i)	Regulation 3	*Form 2*
6	Oath By Creditor	Section 19(1)	Regulation 3	*Form 3*
7	Form of Schedule of Award of Sequestration on Application by Debtor or Executor	Section 22(1) and (2)	Regulation 12(3)	*Form 18*
8	Form of Refusal of Award of Sequestration	Section 22	Regulation 12(5)	*Form 19*
9	Notice of Award of Sequestration to the Keeper	Section 26(2)	Regulation 12(6)	*Form 20*
10	Statement of Assets and Liabilities Petition by creditor or trustee under a trust deed	Section 41(2) and 228(1)	Regulation 3	*Form 4*
11	Statement of Claim by Creditor	Sections 46(2)(a) and 122(9)(a)	Regulation 3	*Form 5*
12	Form of Undertaking to act as Trustee in Sequestration on the Application of a Debtor	Section 51(8) and (9)	Regulation 12(2)	*Form 17*
13	Statement of Undertakings	Sections 8(3)(b), 51(14), 54(4) and 228(1)	Regulation 3	*Form 1*
14	Trustee Application for Authority to Resign Office as Trustee in Sequestration	Section 69(1)	Regulation 23	*Form 21*
15	Notice of Abandonment of Heritable Property by Trustee in Sequestration where Accountant in Bankruptcy not the Trustee	Section 87(8)	Regulation 24	*Form 22*
16	Notice of Abandonment of Heritable Property where the Accountant in Bankruptcy is the Trustee	Section 87(8)	Regulation 24	*Form 23*
17	Debtor Contribution Order (Debtor Application)	Section 90(1)(a)	Regulation 19	*Form 24*
18	Debtor Contribution Order (Petition for Sequestration)	Section 90(1)(b)	Regulation 19	*Form 25*
19	Deduction from Income—Debtor's payment instruction to employer or third person	Section 94(2) and (7)(a)	Regulation 20(2)(a)	*SSI 2014/296, Form 1*
20	Deduction from Income—Trustee's payment instruction to employer or third person	Section 94(4) and (7)(a)	Regulation 20(2)(b)	*SSI 2014/296, Form 2*
21	Deduction from Income—Payment variation instruction to employer or third person	Section 94(2), (4) and (7)(a)	Regulation 20(7)	*SSI 2014/296, Form 3*
22	Notice of Proceedings by Trustee to Obtain Authority in Relation to Debtor's Family Home	Section 113(4) and (5)	Regulation 3	*Form 26*
23	Debtor's Account of Current State of Affairs	Section 116(2)	Regulation 3	*Form 27*

Form	***Purpose***	***Relevant provisions of the Act***	***Relevant provision of the Regulations***	***Form consolidated***
24	Notice by Trustee: Public Examination of the Debtor or a Relevant Person	Section 119(6)(a)	Regulation 3	*Form 6*
25	Debtor Certificate of Discharge (where Accountant in Bankruptcy not the trustee)	Section 137(2)	Regulation 3	*Form 7*
26	Debtor Certificate of Discharge (where Accountant in Bankruptcy is the trustee)	Section 138(2)	Regulation 3	*Form 8*
27	Debtor Certificate of Discharge (debtor to whom section 2(2) applies)	Section 140(2)	Regulation 3	*Form 9*
28	Deferral Notice	Section 141(2)(a)	Regulation 3	*Form 10*
29	Application for Deferral	Section 141(2)(c)	Regulation 3	*Form 11*
30	Certificate of Deferral of Discharge	Section 141(4)(b) or (6)(b)	Regulation 27	*Form 28*
31	Trustee Application for Authority to Resign Office: debtor not traced	Section 142(2)	Regulation 3	*Form 12*
32	Notice granting Trustee Authority to Resign Office	Section 142(5)	Regulation 3	*Form 13*
33	Moratorium—Notice of Intention to Apply	Section 195(1)	Regulation 29	*Form 29*
34	Moratorium—Notice of Intention to Apply (Trust, Partnership, etc)	Section 196(1)	Regulation 29	*Form 30*

NOTES

Commencement: 30 November 2016.

Forms 1, 13, 26, 27 are amended by the Bankruptcy and Protected Trust Deeds (Miscellaneous Amendments) (Scotland) Regulations 2017, SSI 2017/136, reg 2(1), (3).

Form 11 is amended by the Insolvency (Regulation (EU) 2015/848) (Miscellaneous Amendments) (Scotland) Regulations 2017, SSI 2017/210, regs 7(1), (2), 9, as from 26 June 2017, except in relation to proceedings opened before that date.

SCHEDULE 2
REGISTER OF INSOLVENCIES

Regulation 30

[16.436]

A Sequestrations

Name of debtor
Debtor's date of birth (where known)
Debtor's residence and any former residence within the past 5 years and principal place of business (if any) at date of sequestration or date of death
Date of death in case of deceased debtor
Occupation of debtor
Whether sequestration awarded by sheriff or by AiB
Date of any order converting protected trust deed to sequestration
Whether sequestration under paragraph 1 of schedule 1 of the Act (the Minimal Asset Process ("MAP"))
Name and address of petitioner for sequestration (where applicable)
Court by which sequestration awarded (where applicable)
Date of presentation of petition (where applicable)
Date of first order (where applicable)
Date of award of sequestration
Particulars of petition for recall of sequestration (where applicable)
Date of recall of sequestration (where applicable)
Name and address of trustee and date of appointment
Level of debt when trustee's statement of debtor's affairs is produced
Level of assets when trustee's statement of debtor's affairs is produced
Name and address of trustee (or replacement trustee) and date of confirmation of appointment
Particulars of notice of public examination of debtor or relevant person (where applicable)

If the MAP ceases to apply
Issue of certificate deferring debtor's discharge indefinitely (where applicable)
Particulars of any application for removal of trustee and any order removing trustee or declaring office vacant
Date of debtor's discharge and whether on composition or by operation of law
Date of trustee's discharge and of any decision to grant or refuse certificate of discharge
Period of any MAP bankruptcy credit restriction following discharge

B Protected trust deeds for creditors
Name and address of granter of trust deed
Granter's date of birth (where known)
Address of the centre of main interests and all establishments, within the meaning of the [Regulation (EU) 2015/848], of the granter of the trust deed, unless the granter of the trust deed is an undertaking as described in Article 1(2) of the said [EU] Regulation
Whether the protected trust deed is considered to be main or territorial proceedings within the meaning of the said [EU] Regulation
The location and nature of any other insolvency proceedings
Name and address of trustee under deed
Date (or dates) of execution of deed
Date on which copy deed and certificate of accession was registered
Date of registration of statement indicating how the estate was realised and distributed and certificate to the effect that the distribution was in accordance with the trust deed
Date of trustee's discharge
Date of registration of copy of order of court that non-acceding creditor is not bound by trustee's discharge

C Bankruptcy Restrictions Orders, Interim Bankruptcy Restrictions Orders and Bankruptcy Restrictions Undertakings
Name of debtor
Debtor's date of birth (where known)
Date of sequestration
Date of making of bankruptcy restrictions order or interim bankruptcy restrictions order
Date of acceptance of bankruptcy restrictions undertaking
Date of order varying bankruptcy restrictions order or bankruptcy restrictions undertaking (where applicable)
Date of annulment or revocation of bankruptcy restrictions order or bankruptcy restrictions undertaking (where applicable)
Date of discharge of bankruptcy restrictions undertaking (where applicable)
Date bankruptcy restrictions order, interim bankruptcy restrictions order or bankruptcy restrictions undertaking ceased to have effect

D Moratorium
Notice of intention to apply—moratorium on diligence (where applicable)

E Winding up and receivership of business associations
Company number
Company name
Type of proceedings
Name of office holder(s)
Date of appointment of office holder(s)
Date of termination of appointment of office holder(s)
Date of winding-up order (for compulsory liquidations)
Court by which company wound up

NOTES

Commencement: 30 November 2016.

In section B words in first pair of square brackets substituted for original words "Council Regulation (EC) No 1346/2000" and word in second and third pairs of square brackets substituted for original word "Council" by the Insolvency (Regulation (EU) 2015/848) (Miscellaneous Amendments) (Scotland) Regulations 2017, SSI 2017/210, regs 7(1), (3), 9, as from 26 June 2017, except in relation to proceedings opened before that date.

SCHEDULE 3
REVOCATIONS

Regulation 32

[16.437]

Regulations revoked	*Extent of revocation*	*References*
The Bankruptcy (Certificate for Sequestration) (Scotland) Regulations 2010	The whole instrument.	SSI 2010/397, amended by SSI 2014/296.
The Bankruptcy (Scotland) Regulations 2014	Regulations 2(2) to 20, 22 to 24 and the schedules.	SSI 2014/225, amended by SSI 2015/80.

The Bankruptcy (Miscellaneous Amendments) (Scotland) Regulations 2015	Regulation 2.	SSI 2015/80
The Common Financial Tool etc (Scotland) Regulations 2014	Regulations 1 to 5 and 11.	SSI 2014/290 amended by SSI 2015/149.
The Common Financial Tool etc (Scotland) Amendment Regulations 2015	The whole instrument.	SSI 2015/149
The Bankruptcy (Money Advice and Deduction from Income etc) (Scotland) Regulations 2014	The whole instrument.	SSI 2014/296.

NOTES

Commencement: 30 November 2016.

PROTECTED TRUST DEEDS (FORMS) (SCOTLAND) REGULATIONS 2016

(SSI 2016/398)

NOTES

Made: 24 November 2016.

Authority: Bankruptcy (Scotland) Act 2016, ss 166(2)(b), (c), 169, 170(1)(b), (e), 174(2), (3), 175(1), 181(2), 183(1)(a), (b), 184(1)(b), (2)(a), 186(3), (9), 194(1), (3), 225(2).

Commencement: 30 November 2016.

[16.438]

1 Citation, commencement and interpretation

(1) These Regulations may be cited as the Protected Trust Deeds (Forms) (Scotland) Regulations 2016 and come into force on 30th November 2016.

(2) In these Regulations "the Act" means the Bankruptcy (Scotland) Act 2016.

NOTES

Commencement: 30 November 2016.

[16.439]

2 Forms

(1) The forms set out in the schedule are prescribed for the purposes of the provisions of the Act referred to in the third column of the table in the schedule.

(2)–(4) . . .

NOTES

Commencement: 30 November 2016.

Paras (2)–(4): amend the Bankruptcy (Scotland) Act 2016, ss 170, 171, 193 at **[5.367]**, **[5.368]**, **[5.391]**.

SCHEDULE
LIST OF FORMS TO BE USED IN CONNECTION WITH PROTECTED TRUST DEEDS

Regulation 2(1)

[16.440]

NOTES

The forms themselves are not reproduced in this work, but their numbers and descriptions are listed below.

Form	*Purpose*	*Relevant provision of the Act*
1	Notice in the register of insolvencies by trustee under a trust deed for the benefit of creditor	Section 169
1A	Consents required for exclusion of a secured creditor from a protected trust deed	Section 166(2)(b) and (c)
1B	Agreement in respect of heritable property	Section 175
2	Statement of claim by creditors in a trust deed	Section 170(1)(b)
2A	Income and Expenditure	Section 170(1)(d)(ii)

Part 16 Other SIs: Scotland

3	Trust deed protection proposal and trustee's application	Sections 170(1)(e), 171(1)(i) and section 183(1)(a) and (b)
4	Trustee's annual statement report on protected trust deed management	Section 181(2)
4A	Employee's payment instruction to employer	Section 174(2)
4B	Trustee's payment instruction to employer	Section 174(3)
4C	Payment variation instruction to employer	Section 174(2) and (4)
5	Application for discharge of debtor	Section 184(1)(b) and (2)(a)
6	Application to creditors for discharge of the trustee of a protected trust deed	Section 186(2) and (3)
7	Trustee statement of realisation and distribution of estate under a protected trust deed	Section 186(8) and (9)

NOTES

Commencement: 30 November 2016.

Forms 1B, 2, 3 are amended by the Bankruptcy and Protected Trust Deeds (Miscellaneous Amendments) (Scotland) Regulations 2017, SSI 2017/136, reg 3.

DISQUALIFIED DIRECTORS COMPENSATION ORDERS (FEES) (SCOTLAND) ORDER 2016

(SI 2016/1048)

NOTES

Made: 1 November 2016.
Authority: Insolvency Act 1986, s 414(1)(b).
Commencement: 30 November 2016.

[16.441]
1 Citation, commencement and interpretation

(1) This Order may be cited as the Disqualified Directors Compensation Orders (Fees) (Scotland) Order 2016 and comes into force on 30th November 2016.

(2) In this Order—

"compensation order" means a court order under section 15A(1) of the Company Directors Disqualification Act 1986; and

"compensation undertaking" means an undertaking accepted by the Secretary of State under section 15A(2) of the Company Directors Disqualification Act 1986.

NOTES

Commencement: 30 November 2016.

[16.442]
2 Application

This Order applies in relation to—

(a) compensation orders made by the courts in Scotland; and
(b) compensation undertakings accepted in cases where the courts in Scotland would have had jurisdiction to make a compensation order.

NOTES

Commencement: 30 November 2016.

[16.443]
3 Fees payable in connection with compensation orders and compensation undertakings

(1) The Secretary of State is to be paid a fee for performing the function of distributing to a creditor an amount received by the Secretary of State in respect of a compensation order or a compensation undertaking to which this Order applies.

(2) The fee is to be paid out of the amount received before such a distribution is made to a creditor.

(3) The fee means the aggregate of—

(a) the time spent by the appropriate officials carrying out the Secretary of State's function under paragraph (1) in relation to all creditors specified in a compensation order or a compensation undertaking, multiplied by the hourly rate in accordance with the table in the Schedule; and

(b) any necessary disbursements or expenses properly incurred in carrying out that function, divided equally between the total number of creditors specified in the compensation order or the compensation undertaking.

NOTES

Commencement: 30 November 2016.

[16.444]

4 Value Added Tax

Where Value Added Tax is chargeable in respect of the provision of a service for which a fee is payable by virtue of this Order, the amount of the Value Added Tax must be paid in addition to the fee.

NOTES

Commencement: 30 November 2016.

SCHEDULE

Article 3

Hourly rates for Secretary of State's fee

[16.445]

Grade according to the Insolvency Service grading structure	Total hourly rate £
D2/Section Head	69
C2/Deputy Section Head	58
C1/Senior Examiner	52
L3/Examiner	46
L2/Examiner	40
B2/Administrator	43
L1/Examiner	38
B1/Administrator	42
A2/Administrator	36
A1/Administrator	31

NOTES

Commencement: 30 November 2016.

SCOTLAND ACT 1998 (INSOLVENCY FUNCTIONS) ORDER 2018

(SI 2018/174)

NOTES

Made: 8 February 2018.
Authority: Scotland Act 1998, ss 63(1)(b), (3), 108(1)(b), (3), 113(3), (4), 124(2).
Commencement: 9 February 2018.

[16.446]

1 Citation, commencement, extent and interpretation

(1) This Order may be cited as the Scotland Act 1998 (Insolvency Functions) Order 2018 and comes into force on the day after the day on which it is made.

(2) This Order does not extend to Northern Ireland.

(3) In this Order—

"the 1986 Act" means the Insolvency Act 1986;
"the 1992 Act" means the Friendly Societies Act 1992;
"the 1998 Act" means the Scotland Act 1998;
"the 2000 Act" means the Limited Liability Partnerships Act 2000;
"the 2010 Act" means the Interpretation and Legislative Reform (Scotland) Act 2010;
"incorporated friendly society" has the same meaning as in section 116 of the 1992 Act;
"limited liability partnership" has the same meaning as section 1(2) of the 2000 Act;
"oversea limited liability partnership" has the same meaning as in section 14(3) of the 2000 Act;
"the EU Regulation" has the same meaning as in section 436(1) of the 1986 Act; and
"winding up" in relation to companies, incorporated friendly societies and limited liability partnerships, includes winding up of solvent, as well as insolvent companies, incorporated friendly societies and limited liability partnerships.

NOTES

Commencement: 9 February 2018.

[16.447]

2 Reserved functions shared by a Minister of the Crown and the Scottish Ministers

(1) Subject to paragraph (2), the functions described in paragraph (3) are exercisable by the Scottish Ministers concurrently with a Minister of the Crown, so far as they are exercisable by the Minister of the Crown in or as regards Scotland.

(2) The Scottish Ministers may exercise a function under paragraph (1) only with the agreement of a Minister of the Crown.

(3) The functions are those conferred by—

(a) section 411(1)(b) and (2) of the 1986 Act (company insolvency rules) for the purpose of making rules which give effect to any provision about winding up in the Parts of the 1986 Act described in paragraph (4) or the EU Regulation;

(b) section 411(1)(b) and (2) of the 1986 Act as applied by section 23, paragraph 69(1)(a) of Schedule 10 to the 1992 Act (insolvency rules and fees) for the purpose of making rules, in relation to incorporated friendly societies, which give effect to any provision about winding up in the Parts of the 1986 Act described in paragraph (5);

(c) sections 14(2)(a), 16 and 17(1), (2) and (3) of the 2000 Act (insolvency and winding up) for the purpose of making provision by regulations about the winding up of—

(i) limited liability partnerships; and

(ii) oversea limited liability partnerships,

by applying or incorporating, with such modifications as appear appropriate, rules made under section 411(1)(b) and (2) of the 1986 Act which give effect to any provision about winding up in the Parts of the 1986 Act described in paragraph (5) or the EU Regulation.

(4) The Parts of the 1986 Act are—

(a) Part 4 (winding up of companies registered under the Companies Acts);

(b) Part 5 (winding up of unregistered companies);

(c) Part 6 (miscellaneous provisions applying to companies which are insolvent or in liquidation); and

(d) Part 7 (interpretation for First Group of Parts), so far as it relates to Parts 4, 5 or 6.

(5) The Parts of the 1986 Act are—

(a) Part 4 (winding up of companies registered under the Companies Acts);

(b) Part 6 (miscellaneous provisions applying to companies which are insolvent or in liquidation); and

(c) Part 7 (interpretation for First Group of Parts), so far as it relates to Part 4 or Part 6.

NOTES

Commencement: 9 February 2018.

[16.448]

3 General modifications of enactments

(1) Section 117 of the 1998 Act (general modification of enactments: Ministers of the Crown) applies in relation to the exercise of functions by the Scottish Ministers by virtue of article 2 as it applies in relation to the exercise of functions by the Scottish Ministers within devolved competence.

(2) In the application of that section by virtue of this article, the reference in it to any pre-commencement enactment is to be read as if it were a reference to any enactment.

NOTES

Commencement: 9 February 2018.

[16.449]

4 Rules and regulations made by the Scottish Ministers

(1) Section 411(4) of the 1986 Act does not apply in relation to rules made by the Scottish Ministers by virtue of article 2(3)(a) or (b).

(2) Rules made by the Scottish Ministers by virtue of article 2(3)(a) or (b) are subject to the negative procedure (see section 28 of the 2010 Act).

(3) Section 411(5) of the 1986 Act does not apply in relation to regulations made under rules made by the Scottish Ministers by virtue of paragraph 27 of Schedule 8 to the 1986 Act and article 2(3)(a) or (b) (but see section 30(2) of the 2010 Act).

(4) Section 17(1), (4) and (6) of the 2000 Act do not apply in relation to regulations made by the Scottish Ministers by virtue of article 2(3)(c).

(5) Subject to paragraph (6), regulations made by the Scottish Ministers by virtue of article 2(3)(c) are subject to the negative procedure (see section 28 of the 2010 Act).

(6) Regulations made by the Scottish Ministers under section 14(2)(a) and 16 of the 2000 Act in the circumstances set out in section 17(5) of that 2000 Act are subject to the affirmative procedure (see section 29 of the 2010 Act).

NOTES

Commencement: 9 February 2018.

[16.450]

5 Devolved functions shared by the Scottish Ministers and a Minister of the Crown

(1) Subject to paragraph (2), the functions of the Scottish Ministers described in paragraph (3) are exercisable by a Minister of the Crown concurrently with the Scottish Ministers.

(2) A Minister of the Crown may exercise a function mentioned in paragraph (1) only with the agreement of the Scottish Ministers.

(3) The functions are those conferred by—

(a) section 411(1)(b) and (2) of the 1986 Act (company insolvency rules) for the purpose of making rules which give effect to any provision about winding up in the Parts of the 1986 Act described in paragraph (4) or the EU Regulation;

(b) section 411(1)(b) and (2) of the 1986 Act as applied by section 23, paragraph 69(1)(a) of Schedule 10 to the 1992 Act (insolvency rules and fees) for the purpose of making rules, in relation to incorporated friendly societies, which give effect to any provision about winding up in the Parts of the 1986 Act described in paragraph (5);

(c) sections 14(2)(a), 16 and 17(1), (2) and (3) of the 2000 Act (insolvency and winding up) for the purpose of making provision by regulations about the winding up of—

(i) limited liability partnerships; and

(ii) oversea limited liability partnerships,

by applying or incorporating, with such modifications as appear appropriate, rules made under section 411(1)(b) and (2) of the 1986 Act which give effect to any provision about winding up in the Parts of the 1986 Act described in paragraph (5) or the EU Regulation.

(4) The Parts of the 1986 Act are—

(a) Part 4 (winding up of companies registered under the Companies Acts);

(b) Part 5 (winding up of unregistered companies);

(c) Part 6 (miscellaneous provisions applying to companies which are insolvent or in liquidation); and

(d) Part 7 (interpretation for First Group of Parts), so far as it relates to Parts 4, 5 or 6.

(5) The Parts of the 1986 Act are—

(a) Part 4 (winding up of companies registered under the Companies Acts);

(b) Part 6 (miscellaneous provisions applying to companies which are insolvent or in liquidation); and

(c) Part 7 (interpretation for First Group of Parts), so far as it relates to Part 4 or Part 6.

NOTES

Commencement: 9 February 2018.

[16.451]

6 Transitional provision for functions conferred on a Minister of the Crown and the Scottish Ministers

(1) Anything done (or having effect as if done) by or in relation to a Minister of the Crown for the purposes of or in connection with the functions conferred on the Scottish Ministers by virtue of article 2, if in force at the time when that conferral takes effect, is to have effect as if done by or in relation to the Scottish Ministers (as well as the Minister of the Crown) in so far as that is required for continuing its effect after that time.

(2) Anything done (or having effect as if done) by or in relation to the Scottish Ministers for the purposes of or in connection with the functions conferred on a Minister of the Crown by virtue of article 5, if in force at the time when that conferral takes effect, is to have effect as if done by or in relation to a Minister of the Crown (as well as the Scottish Ministers) in so far as that is required for continuing its effect after that time.

NOTES

Commencement: 9 February 2018.

PART 17
MISCELLANEOUS ACTS

LAW OF PROPERTY ACT 1925

(1925 c 20)

ARRANGEMENT OF SECTIONS

PART III
MORTGAGES, RENTCHARGES AND POWERS OF ATTORNEY

Mortgages

101 Powers incident to estate or interest of mortgagee . . . . . . [17.1]
103 Regulation of exercise of power of sale . . . . . . [17.2]
104 Conveyance on sale . . . . . . [17.3]
105 Application of proceeds of sale . . . . . . [17.4]
106 Provisions as to exercise of power of sale . . . . . . [17.5]
109 Appointment, powers, remuneration and duties of receiver . . . . . . [17.6]
110 Effect of bankruptcy of the mortgagor on the power to sell or appoint a receiver . . . . . . [17.7]

PART XII
CONSTRUCTION, JURISDICTION AND GENERAL PROVISIONS

209 Short title, commencement, extent . . . . . . [17.8]

An Act to consolidate the enactments relating to Conveyancing and the Law of Property in England and Wales

[9 April 1925]

1–84 *((Pts I, II) outside the scope of this work.)*

PART III
MORTGAGES, RENTCHARGES AND POWERS OF ATTORNEY

Mortgages

85–100 *(Outside the scope of this work.)*

[17.1]

101 Powers incident to estate or interest of mortgagee

(1) A mortgagee, where the mortgage is made by deed, shall, by virtue of this Act, have the following powers, to the like extent as if they had been in terms conferred by the mortgage deed, but not further (namely)—

(i) A power, when the mortgage money has become due, to sell, or to concur with any other person in selling, the mortgaged property, or any part thereof, either subject to prior charges or not, and either together or in lots, by public auction or by private contract, subject to such conditions respecting title, or evidence of title, or other matter, as the mortgagee thinks fit, with power to vary any contract for sale, and to buy in at an auction, or to rescind any contract for sale, and to re-sell, without being answerable for any loss occasioned thereby; and

(ii) A power, at any time after the date of the mortgage deed, to insure and keep insured against loss or damage by fire any building, or any effects or property of an insurable nature, whether affixed to the freehold or not, being or forming part of the property which or an estate or interest wherein is mortgaged, and the premiums paid for any such insurance shall be a charge on the mortgaged property or estate or interest, in addition to the mortgage money, and with the same priority, and with interest at the same rate, as the mortgage money; and

(iii) A power, when the mortgage money has become due, to appoint a receiver of the income of the mortgaged property, or any part thereof; or, if the mortgaged property consists of an interest in income, or of a rentcharge or an annual or other periodical sum, a receiver of that property or any part thereof; and

(iv) A power, while the mortgagee is in possession, to cut and sell timber and other trees ripe for cutting, and not planted or left standing for shelter or ornament, or to contract for any such cutting and sale, to be completed within any time not exceeding twelve months from the making of the contract.

[(1A) Subsection (1)(i) is subject to section 21 of the Commonhold and Leasehold Reform Act 2002 (no disposition of part-units).]

(2) Where the mortgage deed is executed after the thirty-first day of December, nineteen hundred and eleven, the power of sale aforesaid includes the following powers as incident thereto (namely):—

(i) A power to impose or reserve or make binding, as far as the law permits, by covenant, condition, or otherwise, on the unsold part of the mortgaged property or any part thereof, or on the purchaser and any property sold, any restriction or reservation with respect to building on or other user of land, or with respect to mines and minerals, or for the purpose of the more beneficial working thereof, or with respect to any other thing:

(ii) A power to sell the mortgaged property, or any part thereof, or all or any mines and minerals apart from the surface—

(a) With or without a grant or reservation of rights of way, rights of water, easements, rights, and privileges for or connected with building or other purposes in relation to the property remaining in mortgage or any part thereof, or to any property sold: and

(b) With or without an exception or reservation of all or any of the mines and minerals in or under the mortgaged property, and with or without a grant or reservation of powers of working, wayleaves, or rights of way, rights of water and drainage and other powers, easements, rights, and privileges for or connected with mining purposes in relation to the property remaining unsold or any part thereof, or to any property sold: and

(c) With or without covenants by the purchaser to expend money on the land sold.

(3) The provisions of this Act relating to the foregoing powers, comprised either in this section, or in any other section regulating the exercise of those powers, may be varied or extended by the mortgage deed, and, as so varied or extended, shall, as far as may be, operate in the like manner and with all the like incidents, effects, and consequences, as if such variations or extensions were contained in this Act.

(4) This section applies only if and as far as a contrary intention is not expressed in the mortgage deed, and has effect subject to the terms of the mortgage deed and to the provisions therein contained.

(5) Save as otherwise provided, this section applies where the mortgage deed is executed after the thirty-first day of December, eighteen hundred and eighty-one.

(6) The power of sale conferred by this section includes such power of selling the estate in fee simple or any leasehold reversion as is conferred by the provisions of this Act relating to the realisation of mortgages.

NOTES

Sub-s (1A): inserted by the Commonhold and Leasehold Reform Act 2002, s 68, Sch 5, para 2.

102 (*Outside the scope of this work.*)

[17.2]

103 Regulation of exercise of power of sale

A mortgagee shall not exercise the power of sale conferred by this Act unless and until—

(i) Notice requiring payment of the mortgage money has been served on the mortgagor or one of two or more mortgagors, and default has been made in payment of the mortgage money, or of part thereof, for three months after such service; or

(ii) Some interest under the mortgage is in arrear and unpaid for two months after becoming due; or

(iii) There has been a breach of some provision contained in the mortgage deed or in this Act, or in an enactment replaced by this Act, and on the part of the mortgagor, or of some person concurring in making the mortgage, to be observed or performed, other than and besides a covenant for payment of the mortgage money or interest thereon.

[17.3]

104 Conveyance on sale

(1) A mortgagee exercising the power of sale conferred by this Act shall have power, by deed, to convey the property sold, for such estate and interest therein as he is by this Act authorised to sell or convey or may be the subject of the mortgage, freed from all estates, interests, and rights to which the mortgage has priority, but subject to all estates, interests, and rights which have priority to the mortgage.

(2) Where a conveyance is made in exercise of the power of sale conferred by this Act, or any enactment replaced by this Act, the title of the purchaser shall not be impeachable on the ground—

(a) that no case had arisen to authorise the sale; or

(b) that due notice was not given; or

(c) where the mortgage is made after the commencement of this Act, that leave of the court, when so required, was not obtained; or

(d) whether the mortgage was made before or after such commencement, that the power was otherwise improperly or irregularly exercised;

and a purchaser is not, either before or on conveyance, concerned to see or inquire whether a case has arisen to authorise the sale, or due notice has been given, or the power is otherwise properly and regularly exercised; but any person damnified by an unauthorised, or improper, or irregular exercise of the power shall have his remedy in damages against the person exercising the power.

(3) A conveyance on sale by a mortgagee, made after the commencement of this Act, shall be deemed to have been made in exercise of the power of sale conferred by this Act unless a contrary intention appears.

[17.4]

105 Application of proceeds of sale

The money which is received by the mortgagee, arising from the sale, after discharge of prior incumbrances to which the sale is not made subject, if any, or after payment into court under this Act of a sum to meet any prior incumbrance, shall be held by him in trust to be applied by him, first, in payment of all costs, charges, and expenses properly incurred by him as incident to the sale or any attempted sale, or otherwise; and secondly, in discharge of the mortgage money, interest, and costs, and other money, if any, due under the mortgage; and the residue of the money so received shall be paid to the person entitled to the mortgaged property, or authorised to give receipts for the proceeds of the sale thereof.

[17.5]

106 Provisions as to exercise of power of sale

(1) The power of sale conferred by this Act may be exercised by any person for the time being entitled to receive and give a discharge for the mortgage money.

(2) The power of sale conferred by this Act does not affect the right of foreclosure.
(3) The mortgagee shall not be answerable for any involuntary loss happening in or about the exercise or execution of the power of sale conferred by this Act, or of any trust connected therewith, or, where the mortgage is executed after the thirty-first day of December, nineteen hundred and eleven, of any power or provision contained in the mortgage deed.
(4) At any time after the power of sale conferred by this Act has become exercisable, the person entitled to exercise the power may demand and recover from any person, other than a person having in the mortgaged property an estate, interest, or right in priority to the mortgage, all the deeds and documents relating to the property, or to the title thereto, which a purchaser under the power of sale would be entitled to demand and recover from him.

107, 108 (*Outside the scope of this work.*)

[17.6]
109 Appointment, powers, remuneration and duties of receiver
(1) A mortgagee entitled to appoint a receiver under the power in that behalf conferred by this Act shall not appoint a receiver until he has become entitled to exercise the power of sale conferred by this Act, but may then, by writing under his hand, appoint such person as he thinks fit to be receiver.
(2) A receiver appointed under the powers conferred by this Act, or any enactment replaced by this Act, shall be deemed to be the agent of the mortgagor; and the mortgagor shall be solely responsible for the receiver's acts or defaults unless the mortgage deed otherwise provides.
(3) The receiver shall have power to demand and recover all the income of which he is appointed receiver, by action, [or under section 72(1) of the Tribunals, Courts and Enforcement Act 2007 (commercial rent arrears recovery)], or otherwise, in the name either of the mortgagor or of the mortgagee, to the full extent of the estate or interest which the mortgagor could dispose of, and to give effectual receipts accordingly for the same, and to exercise any powers which may have been delegated to him by the mortgagee pursuant to this Act.
(4) A person paying money to the receiver shall not be concerned to inquire whether any case has happened to authorise the receiver to act.
(5) The receiver may be removed, and a new receiver may be appointed, from time to time by the mortgagee by writing under his hand.
(6) The receiver shall be entitled to retain out of any money received by him, for his remuneration, and in satisfaction of all costs, charges, and expenses incurred by him as receiver, a commission at such rate, not exceeding five per centum on the gross amount of all money received, as is specified in his appointment, and if no rate is so specified, then at the rate of five per centum on that gross amount, or at such other rate as the court thinks fit to allow, on application made by him for that purpose.
(7) The receiver shall, if so directed in writing by the mortgagee, insure to the extent, if any, to which the mortgagee might have insured and keep insured against loss or damage by fire, out of the money received by him, any building, effects, or property comprised in the mortgage, whether affixed to the freehold or not, being of an insurable nature.
(8) Subject to the provisions of this Act as to the application of insurance money, the receiver shall apply all money received by him as follows, namely—
- (i) In discharge of all rents, taxes, rates, and outgoings whatever affecting the mortgaged property; and
- (ii) In keeping down all annual sums or other payments, and the interest on all principal sums, having priority to the mortgage in right whereof he is receiver; and
- (iii) In payment of his commission, and of the premiums on fire, life, or other insurances, if any, properly payable under the mortgage deed or under this Act, and the cost of executing necessary or proper repairs directed in writing by the mortgagee; and
- (iv) In payment of the interest accruing due in respect of any principal money due under the mortgage; and
- (v) In or towards discharge of the principal money if so directed in writing by the mortgagee;

and shall pay the residue, if any, of the money received by him to the person who, but for the possession of the receiver, would have been entitled to receive the income of which he is appointed receiver, or who is otherwise entitled to the mortgaged property.

NOTES
Sub-s (3): words in square brackets substituted by the Tribunals, Courts and Enforcement Act 2007, s 86, Sch 14, paras 21, 22.

[17.7]
110 Effect of bankruptcy of the mortgagor on the power to sell or appoint a receiver
(1) Where the statutory or express power for a mortgagee either to sell or to appoint a receiver is made exercisable by reason of the mortgagor . . . being adjudged a bankrupt, such power shall not be exercised only on account of the . . . adjudication, without the leave of the court.
(2) This section applies only where the mortgage deed is executed after the commencement of this Act . . .

NOTES
Sub-ss (1), (2): words omitted repealed by the Insolvency Act 1985, s 235(3), Sch 10, Pt III.

111–200 (*Ss 111–129, ss 130–200 (Pts IV–XI) outside the scope of this work.*)

PART XII
CONSTRUCTION, JURISDICTION, AND GENERAL PROVISIONS

201–208 (*Outside the scope of this work.*)

[17.8]
209 Short title, commencement, extent
(1) This Act may be cited as the Law of Property Act 1925.
(2) . . .
(3) This Act extends to England and Wales only.

NOTES
Sub-s (2): repealed by the Statute Law Revision Act 1950.

SCHEDULES 1–7

(*Schs 1–7 outside the scope of this work.*)

THIRD PARTIES (RIGHTS AGAINST INSURERS) ACT 1930

(1930 c 25)

NOTES
This Act is repealed by the Third Parties (Rights against Insurers) Act 2010, s 20(3), Sch 4, as from 1 August 2016, subject to transitional provisions in s 20(2) of, and Sch 3, para 3 to, the 2010 Act at **[17.425]**, **[17.429]**.

An Act to confer on third parties rights against insurers of third-party risks in the event of the insured becoming insolvent, and in certain other events

[10 July 1930]

[17.9]
1 Rights of third parties against insurers on bankruptcy, etc, of the insured
(1) Where under any contract of insurance a person (hereinafter referred to as the insured) is insured against liabilities to third parties which he may incur, then—
- *(a) in the event of the insured becoming bankrupt or making a composition or arrangement with his creditors; or*
- *(b) in the case of the insured being a company, in the event of a winding-up order [. . .] being made, or a resolution for a voluntary winding-up being passed, with respect to the company [or of the company entering administration], or of a receiver or manager of the company's business or undertaking being duly appointed, or of possession being taken, by or on behalf of the holders of any debentures secured by a floating charge, of any property comprised in or subject to the charge [or of [a voluntary arrangement proposed for the purposes of Part I of the Insolvency Act 1986 being approved under that Part]];*

if, either before or after that event, any such liability as aforesaid is incurred by the insured, his rights against the insurer under the contract in respect of the liability shall, notwithstanding anything in any Act or rule of law to the contrary, be transferred to and vest in the third party to whom the liability was so incurred.

(2) Where [the estate of any person falls to be administered in accordance with an order under section [421 of the Insolvency Act 1986]], then, if any debt provable in bankruptcy [(in Scotland, any claim accepted in the sequestration)] is owing by the deceased in respect of a liability against which he was insured under a contract of insurance as being a liability to a third party, the deceased debtor's rights against the insurer under the contract in respect of that liability shall, notwithstanding anything in [any such order], be transferred to and vest in the person to whom the debt is owing.

(3) In so far as any contract of insurance made after the commencement of this Act in respect of any liability of the insured to third parties purports, whether directly or indirectly, to avoid the contract or to alter the rights of the parties thereunder upon the happening to the insured of any of the events specified in paragraph (a) or paragraph (b) of subsection (1) of this section or upon the [estate of any person falling to be administered in accordance with an order under section [421 of the Insolvency Act 1986]], the contract shall be of no effect.

(4) Upon a transfer under subsection (1) or subsection (2) of this section, the insurer shall, subject to the provisions of section three of this Act, be under the same liability to the third party as he would have been under to the insured, but—
- *(a) if the liability of the insurer to the insured exceeds the liability of the insured to the third party, nothing in this Act shall affect the rights of the insured against the insurer in respect of the excess; and*
- *(b) if the liability of the insurer to the insured is less than the liability of the insured to the third party, nothing in this Act shall affect the rights of the third party against the insured in respect of the balance.*

(5) For the purposes of this Act, the expression "liabilities to third parties", in relation to a person insured under any contract of insurance, shall not include any liability of that person in the capacity of insurer under some other contract of insurance.

(6) This Act shall not apply—

(a) where a company is wound up voluntarily merely for the purposes of reconstruction or of amalgamation with another company; or

(b) to any case to which subsections (1) and (2) of section seven of the Workmen's Compensation Act 1925 applies.

NOTES

Repealed as noted at the beginning of this Act.

Sub-s (1): words "or an administration order" (omitted) repealed (originally inserted by the Insolvency Act 1985, s 235(1), Sch 8, para 7(2)(a)), and second words in square brackets inserted, by the Enterprise Act 2002 (Insolvency) Order 2003, SI 2003/2096, arts 4, 6, Schedule, paras 1, 2, except in any case where a petition for an administration order was presented before 15 September 2003; third (outer) words in square brackets inserted by the Insolvency Act 1985, s 235(1), Sch 8, para 7(2)(a); fourth (inner) words in square brackets substituted by the Insolvency Act 1986, s 439(2), Sch 14.

Sub-s (2): first (outer) and fourth words in square brackets substituted by the Insolvency Act 1985, s 235(1), Sch 8, para 7(2)(b); second (inner) words in square brackets substituted by the Insolvency Act 1986, s 439(2), Sch 14; third words in square brackets inserted by the Bankruptcy (Scotland) Act 1985, s 75(1), Sch 7, Pt I, para 6(1).

Sub-s (3): first (outer) words in square brackets inserted by the Insolvency Act 1985, s 235(1), Sch 8, para 7(2)(c); second (inner) words in square brackets substituted by the Insolvency Act 1986, s 439(2), Sch 14.

Workmen's Compensation Act 1925: repealed subject to savings by the National Insurance (Industrial Injuries) Act 1946, s 89, Sch 9, now itself repealed by the Social Security Act 1973, ss 100, 101, Sch 26, Sch 28, Pt I, and the Social Security (Consequential Provisions) Act 1975, s 1(2), (5), Sch 1, Pt I.

[17.10]

2 Duty to give necessary information to third parties

(1) In the event of any person becoming bankrupt or making a composition or arrangement with his creditors, or in the event of [the estate of any person falling to be administered in accordance with an order under section [421 of the Insolvency Act 1986]], or in the event of a winding-up order [. . .] being made, or a resolution for a voluntary winding-up being passed, with respect to any company [or of the company entering administration] or of a receiver or manager of the company's business or undertaking being duly appointed or of possession being taken by or on behalf of the holders of any debentures secured by a floating charge of any property comprised in or subject to the charge it shall be the duty of the bankrupt, debtor, personal representative of the deceased debtor or company, and, as the case may be, of the trustee in bankruptcy, trustee, liquidator, [administrator,] receiver, or manager, or person in possession of the property to give at the request of any person claiming that the bankrupt, debtor, deceased debtor, or company is under a liability to him such information as may reasonably be required by him for the purpose of ascertaining whether any rights have been transferred to and vested in him by this Act and for the purpose of enforcing such rights, if any, and any contract of insurance, in so far as it purports, whether directly or indirectly, to avoid the contract or to alter the rights of the parties thereunder upon the giving of any such information in the events aforesaid or otherwise to prohibit or prevent the giving thereof in the said events shall be of no effect.

[(1A) The reference in subsection (1) of this section to a trustee includes a reference to the supervisor of a [voluntary arrangement proposed for the purposes of, and approved under, Part I or Part VIII of the Insolvency Act 1986].]

(2) If the information given to any person in pursuance of subsection (1) of this section discloses reasonable ground for supposing that there have or may have been transferred to him under this Act rights against any particular insurer, that insurer shall be subject to the same duty as is imposed by the said subsection on the persons therein mentioned.

(3) The duty to give information imposed by this section shall include a duty to allow all contracts of insurance, receipts for premiums, and other relevant documents in the possession or power of the person on whom the duty is so imposed to be inspected and copies thereof to be taken.

NOTES

Repealed as noted at the beginning of this Act.

Sub-s (1): first (outer) words in square brackets substituted and fifth words in square brackets inserted by the Insolvency Act 1985, s 235(1), Sch 8, para 7(3)(a); second (inner) words in square brackets substituted by the Insolvency Act 1986, s 439(2), Sch 14; words "or an administration order" omitted repealed (originally inserted by the Insolvency Act 1985, s 235(1), Sch 8, para 7(3)(a)), and fourth words in square brackets inserted, by the Enterprise Act 2002 (Insolvency) Order 2003, SI 2003/2096, arts 4, 6, Schedule, paras 1, 2, except in any case where a petition for an administration order was presented before 15 September 2003.

Sub-s (1A): inserted by the Insolvency Act 1985, s 235(1), Sch 8, para 7(3)(b); words in square brackets substituted by the Insolvency Act 1986, s 439(2), Sch 14.

[17.11]

3 Settlement between insurers and insured persons

Where the insured has become bankrupt or where in the case of the insured being a company, a winding-up order [or an administration order] has been made or a resolution for a voluntary winding-up has been passed, with respect to the company, no agreement made between the insurer and the insured after liability has been incurred to a third party and after the commencement of the bankruptcy or winding-up [or the day of the making of the administration order], as the case may be, nor any waiver, assignment, or other disposition made by, or payment made to the insured after the commencement [or day] aforesaid shall be effective to defeat or affect the rights transferred to the third party under this Act, but those rights shall be the same as if no such agreement, waiver, assignment, disposition or payment had been made.

NOTES
Repealed as noted at the beginning of this Act.
Words in square brackets inserted by the Insolvency Act 1985, s 235(1), Sch 8, para 7(4).

[17.12]
[3A Application to limited liability partnerships
(1) This Act applies to limited liability partnerships as it applies to companies.
(2) In its application to limited liability partnerships, references to a resolution for a voluntary winding-up being passed are references to a determination for a voluntary winding-up being made.]

NOTES
Repealed as noted at the beginning of this Act.
Inserted by the Limited Liability Partnerships Regulations 2001, SI 2001/1090, reg 9(1), Sch 5, para 2.

[17.13]
4 Application to Scotland
In the application of this Act to Scotland—
(a) . . .
(b) any reference to [an estate falling to be administered in accordance with an order under section [421 of the Insolvency Act 1986]], shall be deemed to include a reference to an award of sequestration of the estate of a deceased debtor, and a reference to an appointment of a judicial factor, under section [11A of the Judicial Factors (Scotland) Act 1889], on the insolvent estate of a deceased person.

NOTES
Repealed as noted at the beginning of this Act.
Para (a): repealed by the Bankruptcy (Scotland) Act 1985, s 75(1), (2), Sch 7, para 6(2)(a), Sch 8.
Para (b): first (outer) words in square brackets substituted by the Insolvency Act 1985, s 235(1), Sch 8, para 7(1), (5); second (inner) words in square brackets substituted by the Insolvency Act 1986, s 439(2), Sch 14; third words in square brackets substituted by the Bankruptcy (Scotland) Act 1985, s 75(1), Sch 7, para 6(2)(b).

[17.14]
5 Short title
This Act may be cited as the Third Parties (Rights Against Insurers) Act 1930.

NOTES
Repealed as noted at the beginning of this Act.

MATRIMONIAL CAUSES ACT 1973

(1973 c 18)

An Act to consolidate certain enactments relating to matrimonial proceedings, maintenance agreements, and declarations of legitimacy, validity of marriage and British nationality, with amendments to give effect to recommendations of the Law Commission

[23 May 1973]

1–20 *((Pt I) outside the scope of this work.)*

PART II
FINANCIAL RELIEF FOR PARTIES TO MARRIAGE AND CHILDREN OF FAMILY

21–36 *(Outside the scope of this work.)*

Miscellaneous and Supplemental

37, 38 *(Outside the scope of this work.)*

[17.15]
39 Settlement, etc, made in compliance with a property adjustment order may be avoided on bankruptcy of settlor
The fact that a settlement or transfer of property had to be made in order to comply with a property adjustment order shall not prevent that settlement or transfer from being [a transaction in respect of which an order may be made under [section 339 or 340 of the Insolvency Act 1986] (transactions at an undervalue and preferences)].

NOTES
Words in first (outer) pair of square brackets substituted by the Insolvency Act 1985, s 235(1), Sch 8, para 23; words in second (inner) pair of square brackets substituted by the Insolvency Act 1986, s 439(2), Sch 14.

40–44 *(Ss 40–40B, ss 41–44 (Pt III) in so far as unrepealed, outside the scope of this work.)*

PART IV
MISCELLANEOUS AND SUPPLEMENTAL

45–54 (*In so far as unrepealed, outside the scope of this work.*)

[17.16]
55 Citation, commencement and extent
(1) This Act may be cited as the Matrimonial Causes Act 1973.
(2) This Act shall come into force on such day as the Lord Chancellor may appoint by order made by statutory instrument.
(3) Subject to the provisions of paragraphs 3(2) . . . of Schedule 2 below, this Act does not extend to Scotland or Northern Ireland.

NOTES
Sub-s (3): words omitted repealed by the Statute Law (Repeals) Act 1977.
Orders: the Matrimonial Causes Act 1973 (Commencement) Order 1973, SI 1973/1972.

SCHEDULES 1–3

(*Schs 1, 2 outside the scope of this work; Sch 3 repealed by the Statute Law (Repeals) Act 1977.*)

LAND COMPENSATION ACT 1973

(1973 c 26)

An Act to confer a new right to compensation for depreciation of the value of interests in land caused by the use of highways, aerodromes and other public works; to confer powers for mitigating the injurious effect of such works on their surroundings; to make new provision for the benefit of persons displaced from land by public authorities; to amend the law relating to compulsory purchase and planning blight; to amend section 35 of the Roads (Scotland) Act 1970; and for purposes connected with those matters

[23 May 1973]

1–28 (*(Pts I, II) outside the scope of this work.*)

PART III
PROVISIONS FOR BENEFIT OF PERSONS DISPLACED FROM LAND

29–33E (*Outside the scope of this work.*)

[17.17]
[33F Insolvency
(1) This section applies if a person is entitled to a payment under section 33A, 33B or 33C but before a claim is made under section 33E insolvency proceedings are started in relation to the person.
(2) Any of the following may make a claim instead of the person mentioned in subsection (1)—
  (a) a receiver, trustee in bankruptcy or the official receiver in the case of an individual;
  (b) an administrator, administrative receiver, liquidator or provisional liquidator or the official receiver in the case of a company or a partnership.
(3) Insolvency proceedings are—
  (a) proceedings in bankruptcy;
  (b) proceedings under the Insolvency Act 1986 for the winding up of a company or an unregistered company (including voluntary winding up of a company under Part 4 of that Act);
  (c) proceedings for the winding up of a partnership.]

NOTES
Inserted by the Planning and Compulsory Purchase Act 2004, s 109.

33G–83 (*Ss 33G–43, ss 44–83 (Pts IV, V) in so far as unrepealed, outside the scope of this work.*)

PART VI
SUPPLEMENTARY PROVISIONS

84–88 (*Outside the scope of this work.*)

[17.18]
89 Short title, commencement and extent
(1) This Act may be cited as the Land Compensation Act 1973.
(2), (3) . . .
(4) This Act, except section 88, does not extend to Northern Ireland [and, except section 86 and Schedule 3, does not extend to Scotland].

NOTES
Sub-ss (2), (3): outside the scope of this work.

Sub-s (4): words in square brackets substituted by the Land Compensation (Scotland) Act 1973, s 81(1), Sch 2, Part I.

SCHEDULES 1–3

(Schs 1, 2 repealed by the Land Compensation (Scotland) Act 1973, s 81(1), Sch 2, Pt I; Sch 3 outside the scope of this work.)

COUNTY COURTS ACT 1984

(1984 c 28)

ARRANGEMENT OF SECTIONS

PART 6
ADMINISTRATION ORDERS

Administration orders

112A Administration orders .[17.19]
112B Power to make order .[17.20]

Scheduling debts

112C Scheduling declared debts .[17.21]
112D Scheduling new debts .[17.22]

Requirements imposed by order

112E Repayment requirement .[17.23]
112F Presentation of bankruptcy petition .[17.24]
112G Remedies other than bankruptcy .[17.25]
112H Charging of interest etc .[17.26]
112I Stopping supplies of gas or electricity .[17.27]

Making an order

112J Application for an order .[17.28]
112K Duration .[17.29]

Effects of order

112L Effect on other debt management arrangements .[17.30]
112M Duty to provide information .[17.31]
112N Offence if information not provided .[17.32]
112O Existing county court proceedings to be stayed .[17.33]
112P Appropriation of money paid .[17.34]
112Q Discharge from debts .[17.35]

Variation

112R Variation .[17.36]
112S Variation of duration .[17.37]
112T De-scheduling debts .[17.38]

Revocation

112U Duty to revoke order .[17.39]
112V Power to revoke order .[17.40]
112W Effect of revocation .[17.41]

Notification of certain events

112X Notice when order made, varied, revoked etc .[17.42]

Total amount of qualifying debts not properly calculated

112Y Failure to take account of all qualifying debts .[17.43]

Interpretation

112Z Introduction .[17.44]
112AA Main definitions .[17.45]
112AB Expressions relating to debts .[17.46]
112AC Inability to pay debts .[17.47]
112AD Calculating the debtor's qualifying debts .[17.48]
112AE Calculating the debtor's surplus income .[17.49]
112AF Debts becoming due .[17.50]
112AG Scheduling and de-scheduling debts .[17.51]

112AH The AO, voluntary arrangement and bankruptcy exclusions . . . . [17.52]

Regulations

112AI Regulations under this Part . . . . [17.53]

An Act to consolidate certain enactments relating to county courts

[26 June 1984]

A1–111 *((Pts I–V) outside the scope of this work.)*

[PART 6
ADMINISTRATION ORDERS

Administration orders

[17.19]
112A Administration orders

An administration order is an order—

(a) to which certain debts are scheduled in accordance with section 112C, 112D or 112Y(3) or (4),
(b) which imposes the requirement specified in section 112E on the debtor, and
(c) which imposes the requirements specified in sections 112F to 112I on certain creditors.]

NOTES

Commencement: to be appointed.

Pt 6 (this section and ss 112B–112AI) substituted for original Pt 6 (s 112, ss 112A, 112B (as inserted by the Courts and Legal Services Act 1990, s 13(5)), ss 113–117) by the Tribunals, Courts and Enforcement Act 2007, s 106(1), (3), as from a day to be appointed, except in relation to any case in which an administration order was made, or an application for such an order was made, before the day on which this substitution comes into force.

[17.20]
[112B Power to make order

(1) [The county court] may make an administration order if the conditions in subsections (2) to (7) are met.

(2) The order must be made in respect of an individual who is a debtor under two or more qualifying debts.

(3) That individual ("the debtor") must not be a debtor under any business debts.

(4) The debtor must not be excluded under any of the following—

(a) the AO exclusion;
(b) the voluntary arrangement exclusion;
(c) the bankruptcy exclusion.

(5) The debtor must be unable to pay one or more of his qualifying debts.

(6) The total amount of the debtor's qualifying debts must be less than, or the same as, the prescribed maximum.

(7) The debtor's surplus income must be more than the prescribed minimum.

(8) Before making an administration order, the county court must have regard to any representations made—

(a) by any person about why the order should not be made, or
(b) by a creditor under a debt about why the debt should not be taken into account in calculating the total amount of the debtor's qualifying debts.]

NOTES

Commencement: to be appointed.

Substituted as noted to s 112A at **[17.19]**.

Sub-s (1): words in square brackets substituted by the Crime and Courts Act 2013, s 17(5), Sch 9, Pt 1, paras 1, 10(1)(a).

[Scheduling debts

[17.21]
112C Scheduling declared debts

(1) This section applies to a qualifying debt ("the declared debt") if—

(a) an administration order is made, and
(b) when the order is made, the debt is taken into account in calculating the total amount of the debtor's qualifying debts for the purposes of section 112B(6).

(2) If the declared debt is already due at the time the administration order is made, the . . . county court must schedule the debt to the order when the order is made.

(3) If the declared debt becomes due after the administration order is made, the . . . county court must schedule the debt to the order if the debtor, or the creditor under the debt, applies to the court for the debt to be scheduled.

(4) This section is subject to section 112AG(5).]

NOTES

Commencement: to be appointed.

Substituted as noted to s 112A at **[17.19]**.

Sub-ss (2), (3): words omitted repealed by the Crime and Courts Act 2013, s 17(5), Sch 9, Pt 1, paras 1, 10(52)(a).

[17.22]

[112D Scheduling new debts

(1) This section applies to a qualifying debt ("the new debt") if the debt—

(a) arises after an administration order is made, and

(b) becomes due during the currency of the order.

(2) The . . . county court may schedule the new debt to the administration order if these conditions are met—

(a) the debtor, or the creditor under the new debt, applies to the court for the debt to be scheduled;

(b) the total amount of the debtor's qualifying debts (including the new debt) is less than, or the same as, the prescribed maximum.]

NOTES

Commencement: to be appointed.

Substituted as noted to s 112A at **[17.19]**.

Sub-s (2): word omitted repealed by the Crime and Courts Act 2013, s 17(5), Sch 9, Pt 1, paras 1, 10(52)(a).

[Requirements imposed by order

[17.23]

112E Repayment requirement

(1) An administration order must, during the currency of the order, impose a repayment requirement on the debtor.

(2) A repayment requirement is a requirement for the debtor to repay the scheduled debts.

(3) The repayment requirement may provide for the debtor to repay a particular scheduled debt in full or to some other extent.

(4) The repayment requirement may provide for the debtor to repay different scheduled debts to different extents.

(5) In the case of a new debt scheduled to the order in accordance with section 112D, the repayment requirement may provide that no due repayment in respect of the new debt is to be made until the debtor has made all due repayments in respect of declared debts.

(6) The repayment requirement must provide that the due repayments are to be made by instalments.

(7) It is for the . . . county court to decide when the instalments are to be made.

(8) But the . . . county court is to determine the amount of the instalments in accordance with repayment regulations.

(9) Repayment regulations are regulations which make provision for instalments to be determined by reference to the debtor's surplus income.

(10) The repayment requirement may provide that the due repayments are to be made by other means (including by one or more lump sums) in addition to the instalments required in accordance with subsection (6).

(11) The repayment requirement may include provision in addition to any that is required or permitted by this section.

(12) In this section—

"declared debt" has the same meaning as in section 112C (and for this purpose it does not matter whether a declared debt is scheduled to the administration order when it is made, or afterwards);

"due repayments" means repayments which the repayment requirement requires the debtor to make;

"new debt" has the same meaning as in section 112D.]

NOTES

Commencement: to be appointed.

Substituted as noted to s 112A at **[17.19]**.

Sub-ss (7), (8): words omitted repealed by the Crime and Courts Act 2013, s 17(5), Sch 9, Pt 1, paras 1, 10(52)(a).

[17.24]

[112F Presentation of bankruptcy petition

(1) An administration order must, during the currency of the order, impose the following requirement.

(2) The requirement is that no qualifying creditor of the debtor is to present a bankruptcy petition against the debtor in respect of a qualifying debt, unless the creditor has the permission of the . . . county court.

(3) The . . . county court may give permission for the purposes of subsection (2) subject to such conditions as it thinks fit.]

NOTES

Commencement: to be appointed.

Substituted as noted to s 112A at **[17.19]**.

Sub-ss (2), (3): words omitted repealed by the Crime and Courts Act 2013, s 17(5), Sch 9, Pt 1, paras 1, 10(52)(a).

[17.25]

[112G Remedies other than bankruptcy

(1) An administration order must, during the currency of the order, impose the following requirement.

(2) The requirement is that no qualifying creditor of the debtor is to pursue any remedy for the recovery of a qualifying debt unless—

(a) regulations under subsection (3) provide otherwise, or

(b) the creditor has the permission of the proper county court.

(3) Regulations may specify classes of debt which are exempted (or exempted for specified purposes) from the restriction imposed by subsection (2).
(4) The . . . county court may give permission for the purposes of subsection (2)(b) subject to such conditions as it thinks fit.
(5) This section does not have any effect in relation to bankruptcy proceedings.]

NOTES
Commencement: to be appointed.
Substituted as noted to s 112A at **[17.19]**.
Sub-s (4): word omitted repealed by the Crime and Courts Act 2013, s 17(5), Sch 9, Pt 1, paras 1, 10(52)(a).

[17.26]
[112H Charging of interest etc
(1) An administration order must, during the currency of the order, impose the following requirement.
(2) The requirement is that no creditor under a scheduled debt is to charge any sum by way of interest, fee or other charge in respect of that debt.]

NOTES
Commencement: to be appointed.
Substituted as noted to s 112A at **[17.19]**.

[17.27]
[112I Stopping supplies of gas or electricity
(1) An administration order must, during the currency of the order, impose the requirement in subsection (3).
(2) In relation to that requirement, a domestic utility creditor is any person who—
(a) provides the debtor with a supply of mains gas or mains electricity for the debtor's own domestic purposes, and
(b) is a creditor under a qualifying debt that relates to the provision of that supply.
(3) The requirement is that no domestic utility creditor is to stop the supply of gas or electricity, or the supply of any associated services, except in the cases in subsections (4) to (6).
(4) The first case is where the reason for stopping a supply relates to the non-payment by the debtor of charges incurred in connection with that supply after the making of the administration order.
(5) The second case is where the reason for stopping a supply is unconnected with the non-payment by the debtor of any charges incurred in connection with—
(a) that supply, or
(b) any other supply of mains gas or mains electricity, or of associated services, that is provided by the domestic utility creditor.
(6) The third case is where the . . . county court gives permission to stop a supply.
(7) The . . . county court may give permission for the purposes of subsection (6) subject to such conditions as it thinks fit.
(8) A supply of mains gas is a supply of the kind mentioned in section 5(1)(b) of the Gas Act 1986.
(9) A supply of mains electricity is a supply of the kind mentioned in section 4(1)(c) of the Electricity Act 1989.]

NOTES
Commencement: to be appointed.
Substituted as noted to s 112A at **[17.19]**.
Sub-ss (6), (7): words omitted repealed by the Crime and Courts Act 2013, s 17(5), Sch 9, Pt 1, paras 1, 10(52)(a).

[Making an order

[17.28]
112J Application for an order
(1) [The county court] may make an administration order only on the application of the debtor.
(2) The debtor may make an application for an administration order whether or not a judgment has been obtained against him in respect of any of his debts.]

NOTES
Commencement: to be appointed.
Substituted as noted to s 112A at **[17.19]**.
Sub-s (1): words in square brackets substituted by the Crime and Courts Act 2013, s 17(5), Sch 9, Pt 1, paras 1, 10(1)(a).

[17.29]
[112K Duration
(1) [The county court] may, at the time it makes an administration order, specify a day on which the order will cease to have effect.
(2) The court may not specify a day which falls after the last day of the maximum permitted period.
(3) If the court specifies a day under this section, the order ceases to have effect on that day.
(4) If the court does not specify a day under this section, the order ceases to have effect at the end of the maximum permitted period.
(5) The maximum permitted period is the period of five years beginning with the day on which the order is made.
(6) This section is subject to—

(a) section 112S (variation of duration);
(b) section 112W (effect of revocation).

(7) This section is also subject to the following (effect of enforcement restriction order or debt relief order on administration order)—
(a) section 117I of this Act;
(b) section 251F of the Insolvency Act 1986.]

NOTES

Commencement: to be appointed.
Substituted as noted to s 112A at **[17.19]**.
Sub-s (1): words in square brackets substituted by the Crime and Courts Act 2013, s 17(5), Sch 9, Pt 1, paras 1, 10(1)(a).

[Effects of order

[17.30]
112L Effect on other debt management arrangements

(1) This section applies if—
(a) an administration order is made, and
(b) immediately before the order is made, other debt management arrangements are in force in respect of the debtor.

(2) The other debt management arrangements cease to be in force when the administration order is made.

(3) If the . . . county court is aware of the other debt management arrangements, the court must give the relevant authority notice that the order has been made.

(4) In a case where the . . . county court is aware of other debt management arrangements at the time it makes the order, it must give the notice as soon as practicable after making the order.

(5) In a case where the . . . county court becomes aware of those arrangements after it makes the order, it must give the notice as soon as practicable after becoming aware of them.

(6) "Other debt management arrangements" means any of the following—
(a) an enforcement restriction order under Part 6A of this Act;
(b) a debt relief order under Part 7A of the Insolvency Act 1986;
(c) a debt repayment plan arranged in accordance with a debt management scheme that is approved under Chapter 4 of Part 5 of the Tribunals, Courts and Enforcement Act 2007.

(7) "The relevant authority" means—
(a) in relation to an enforcement restriction order: the . . . county court . . . ;
(b) in relation to a debt relief order: the official receiver;
(c) in relation to a debt repayment plan: the operator of the debt management scheme in accordance with which the plan is arranged.

(8) For the purposes of this section a debt relief order is "in force" if the moratorium applicable to the order under section 251H of the Insolvency Act 1986 has not yet ended.]

NOTES

Commencement: to be appointed.
Substituted as noted to s 112A at **[17.19]**.
Sub-ss (3)–(5): words omitted repealed by the Crime and Courts Act 2013, s 17(5), Sch 9, Pt 1, paras 1, 10(52)(a).
Sub-s (7): words omitted repealed by the Crime and Courts Act 2013, s 17(5), Sch 9, Pt 1, paras 1, 10(52)(a), (b).

[17.31]
[112M Duty to provide information

(1) This section applies if, and for as long as, an administration order has effect in respect of a debtor.

(2) The debtor must, at the prescribed times, provide the . . . county court with particulars of his—
(a) earnings,
(b) income,
(c) assets, and
(d) outgoings.

(3) The debtor must provide particulars of those matters—
(a) as the matters are at the time the particulars are provided, and
(b) as the debtor expects the matters to be at such times in the future as are prescribed.

(4) If the debtor intends to dispose of any of his property he must, within the prescribed period, provide the . . . county court with particulars of the following matters—
(a) the property he intends to dispose of;
(b) the consideration (if any) he expects will be given for the disposal;
(c) such other matters as may be prescribed;
(d) such other matters as the court may specify.

(5) But subsection (4) does not apply if the disposal is of—
(a) goods that are exempt goods for the purposes of Schedule 12 to the Tribunals, Courts and Enforcement Act 2007,
(b) goods that are protected under any other enactment from being taken control of under that Schedule, or
(c) prescribed property.

(6) The duty under subsection (4) to provide the . . . county court with particulars of a proposed disposal of property applies whether the debtor is the sole owner, or one of several owners, of the property.

(7) In any provision of this section "prescribed" means prescribed in regulations for the purposes of that provision.]

NOTES

Commencement: to be appointed.
Substituted as noted to s 112A at **[17.19]**.
Sub-ss (2), (4), (6): words omitted repealed by the Crime and Courts Act 2013, s 17(5), Sch 9, Pt 1, paras 1, 10(52)(a).

[17.32]
[112N Offence if information not provided

(1) A person commits an offence if he fails to comply with—
(a) section 112M(2) and (3), or
(b) section 112M(4).
(2) A person who commits an offence under subsection (1) may be ordered by a judge of the . . . county court to pay a fine of not more than £250 or to be imprisoned for not more than 14 days.
(3) Where under subsection (2) a person is ordered to be imprisoned by a judge of the . . . county court, the judge may at any time—
(a) revoke the order, and
(b) if the person is already in custody, order his discharge.
(4) Section 129 of this Act (enforcement of fines) applies to payment of a fine imposed under subsection (2).
(5) For the purposes of section 13 of the Administration of Justice Act 1960 (appeal in cases of contempt of court), subsection (2) is to be treated as an enactment enabling [the county court] to deal with an offence under subsection (1) as if it were a contempt of court.
(6) . . .]

NOTES

Commencement: to be appointed.
Substituted as noted to s 112A at **[17.19]**.
Sub-ss (2), (3): words omitted repealed by the Crime and Courts Act 2013, s 17(5), Sch 9, Pt 1, paras 1, 10(52)(a).
Sub-s (5): words in square brackets substituted by the Crime and Courts Act 2013, s 17(5), Sch 9, Pt 1, paras 1, 10(1)(b).
Sub-s (6): repealed by the Crime and Courts Act 2013, s 17(5), Sch 9, Pt 1, paras 1, 10(52)(d).

[17.33]
[112O Existing county court proceedings to be stayed

(1) This section applies if these conditions are met—
(a) an administration order is made;
(b) proceedings in [the county court] (other than bankruptcy proceedings) are pending against the debtor in respect of a qualifying debt;
(c) by virtue of a requirement included in the order by virtue of section 112G, the creditor under the qualifying debt is not entitled to continue the proceedings in respect of the debt;
(d) the county court receives notice of the administration order.
(2) The county court must stay the proceedings.
(3) The court may allow costs already incurred by the creditor.
(4) If the court allows such costs, it may on application or of its motion add them—
(a) to the debt, or
(b) if the debt is a scheduled debt, to the amount scheduled to the order in respect of the debt.
(5) But the court may not add the costs under subsection (4)(b) if the court is under a duty under section 112U(6)(b) to revoke the order because the total amount of the debtor's qualifying debts (including the costs) is more than the prescribed maximum.]

NOTES

Commencement: to be appointed.
Substituted as noted to s 112A at **[17.19]**.
Sub-s (1): words in square brackets substituted by the Crime and Courts Act 2013, s 17(5), Sch 9, Pt 1, paras 1, 10(1)(b).

[17.34]
[112P Appropriation of money paid

(1) Money paid into court under an administration order is to be appropriated—
(a) first in satisfaction of any relevant court fees, and
(b) then in liquidation of debts.
(2) Relevant court fees are any fees under an order made under section 92 of the Courts Act 2003 which are payable by the debtor in respect of the administration order.]

NOTES

Commencement: to be appointed.
Substituted as noted to s 112A at **[17.19]**.

[17.35]
[112Q Discharge from debts

(1) If the debtor repays a scheduled debt to the extent provided for by the administration order, the . . . county court must—
(a) order that the debtor is discharged from the debt, and

(b) de-schedule the debt.

(2) If the debtor repays all of the scheduled debts to the extent provided for by the administration order, the . . . county court must revoke the order.

(3) Subsections (1) and (2) apply to all scheduled debts, including any which, under the administration order, are to be repaid other than to their full extent.]

NOTES

Commencement: to be appointed.
Substituted as noted to s 112A at **[17.19]**.
Sub-ss (1), (2): words omitted repealed by the Crime and Courts Act 2013, s 17(5), Sch 9, Pt 1, paras 1, 10(52)(a).

[Variation

[17.36]

112R Variation

(1) The . . . county court may vary an administration order.

(2) The power under this section is exercisable—

(a) on the application of the debtor;
(b) on the application of a qualifying creditor;
(c) of the court's own motion.]

NOTES

Commencement: to be appointed.
Substituted as noted to s 112A at **[17.19]**.
Sub-s (1): word omitted repealed by the Crime and Courts Act 2013, s 17(5), Sch 9, Pt 1, paras 1, 10(52)(a).

[17.37]

[112S Variation of duration

(1) The power under section 112R includes power to vary an administration order so as to specify a day, or (if a day has already been specified under section 112K or this subsection) a different day, on which the order will cease to have effect.

(2) But the new termination day must fall on or before the last day of the maximum permitted period.

(3) If the . . . county court varies an administration under subsection (1), the order ceases to have effect on the new termination day.

(4) In this section—

(a) "new termination day" means the day on which the order will cease to have effect in accordance with the variation under subsection (1);
(b) "maximum permitted period" means the period of five years beginning with the day on which the order was originally made.

(5) This section is subject to section 112W (effect of revocation).]

NOTES

Commencement: to be appointed.
Substituted as noted to s 112A at **[17.19]**.
Sub-s (3): word omitted repealed by the Crime and Courts Act 2013, s 17(5), Sch 9, Pt 1, paras 1, 10(52)(a).

[17.38]

[112T De-scheduling debts

(1) The power under section 112R includes power to vary an administration order by de-scheduling a debt.

(2) But the debt may be de-scheduled only if it appears to the . . . county court that it is just and equitable to do so.]

NOTES

Commencement: to be appointed.
Substituted as noted to s 112A at **[17.19]**.
Sub-s (2): word omitted repealed by the Crime and Courts Act 2013, s 17(5), Sch 9, Pt 1, paras 1, 10(52)(a).

[Revocation

[17.39]

112U Duty to revoke order

(1) The . . . county court must revoke an administration order in either of these cases—

(a) where it becomes apparent that, at the time the order was made, the condition in subsection 112B(2) was not met (debtor in fact did not have two or more qualifying debts);
(b) where the debtor is no longer a debtor under any qualifying debts.

(2) The . . . county court must revoke an administration order in either of these cases—

(a) where it becomes apparent that, at the time the order was made, the condition in subsection 112B(3) was not met (debtor in fact had business debt), and he is still a debtor under the business debt, or any of the business debts, in question;
(b) where the debtor subsequently becomes a debtor under a business debt, and he is still a debtor under that debt.

(3) The . . . county court must revoke an administration order where it becomes apparent that, at the time the order was made, the condition in section 112B(4) was not met (debtor in fact excluded under AO, voluntary arrangement or bankruptcy exclusion).

(4) The . . . county court must revoke an administration order where, after the order is made—
(a) the debtor becomes excluded under the voluntary arrangement exclusion, or
(b) a bankruptcy order is made against the debtor, and is still in force.
(5) The . . . county court must revoke an administration order in either of these cases—
(a) where it becomes apparent that, at the time the order was made, the condition in section 112B(5) was not met (debtor in fact able to pay qualifying debts);
(b) where the debtor is now able to pay all of his qualifying debts.
(6) The . . . county court must revoke an administration order in either of these cases—
(a) where it becomes apparent that, at the time the order was made, the condition in section 112B(6) was not met (debtor's qualifying debts in fact more than prescribed maximum);
(b) where the total amount of the debtor's qualifying debts is now more than the prescribed maximum.
(7) The . . . county court must revoke an administration order in either of these cases—
(a) where it becomes apparent that, at the time the order was made, the condition in section 112B(7) was not met (debtor's surplus income in fact less than, or the same as, the prescribed minimum);
(b) where the debtor's surplus income is now less than, or the same as, the prescribed minimum.]

NOTES
Commencement: to be appointed.
Substituted as noted to s 112A at **[17.19]**.
Words omitted repealed by the Crime and Courts Act 2013, s 17(5), Sch 9, Pt 1, paras 1, 10(52)(a).

[17.40]
[112V Power to revoke order
(1) The . . . county court may revoke an administration order in any case where there is no duty under this Part to revoke it.
(2) The power of revocation under this section may, in particular, be exercised in any of the following cases—
(a) where the debtor has failed to make two payments (whether consecutive or not) required by the order;
(b) where the debtor has failed to provide the . . . county court with the particulars required by—
(i) section 112M(2) and (3), or
(ii) section 112M(4).
(3) The power of revocation under this section is exercisable—
(a) on the application of the debtor;
(b) on the application of a qualifying creditor;
(c) of the court's own motion.]

NOTES
Commencement: to be appointed.
Substituted as noted to s 112A at **[17.19]**.
Sub-ss (1), (2): word omitted repealed by the Crime and Courts Act 2013, s 17(5), Sch 9, Pt 1, paras 1, 10(52)(a).

[17.41]
[112W Effect of revocation
(1) This section applies if, under any duty or power in this Part, the . . . county court revokes an administration order.
(2) The order ceases to have effect in accordance with the terms of the revocation.]

NOTES
Commencement: to be appointed.
Substituted as noted to s 112A at **[17.19]**.
Sub-s (1): word omitted repealed by the Crime and Courts Act 2013, s 17(5), Sch 9, Pt 1, paras 1, 10(52)(a).

[Notification of certain events

[17.42]
112X Notice when order made, varied, revoked etc
(1) If a notifiable event occurs in relation to an administration order, the . . . county court must send notice of the event to the creditor under every scheduled debt.
(2) There is a notifiable event in any of the following cases—
(a) when the administration order is made;
(b) when a debt is scheduled to the administration order at any time after the making of the order;
(c) when the administration order is varied;
(d) when the administration order is revoked;
(e) when the . . . county court is given notice under any of the provisions listed in section 112K(7) (effect of enforcement restriction order or debt relief order on administration order).]

NOTES
Commencement: to be appointed.
Substituted as noted to s 112A at **[17.19]**.
Words omitted repealed by the Crime and Courts Act 2013, s 17(5), Sch 9, Pt 1, paras 1, 10(52)(a).

[Total amount of qualifying debts not properly calculated

[17.43]
112Y Failure to take account of all qualifying debts

(1) This section applies if—

(a) an administration order has been made, but
(b) it becomes apparent that the total amount of the debtor's qualifying debts was not properly calculated for the purposes of section 112B(6), because of an undeclared debt.

(2) A debt is undeclared if it ought to have been, but was not, taken into account in the calculation for the purposes of section 112B(6).

(3) If these conditions are met—

(a) the undeclared debt is due (whether it became due before or after the making of the order);
(b) the total debt is less than, or the same as, the prescribed maximum;

the . . . county court must schedule the undeclared debt to the order.

(4) If these conditions are met—

(a) the undeclared debt is not due;
(b) the total debt is less than, or the same as, the prescribed maximum;

the . . . county court must schedule the undeclared debt to the order when the debt becomes due.

(5) If the total debt is more than the prescribed maximum, the . . . county court must revoke the administration order (whether or not the undeclared debt is due).

(6) In this section "total debt" means the total amount of the debtor's qualifying debts (including the undeclared debt).

(7) Subsections (3) and (4) are subject to section 112AG(5).]

NOTES

Commencement: to be appointed.
Substituted as noted to s 112A at **[17.19]**.
Sub-ss (3)–(5): words omitted repealed by the Crime and Courts Act 2013, s 17(5), Sch 9, Pt 1, paras 1, 10(52)(a).

[Interpretation

[17.44]
112Z Introduction

Sections 112AA to 112AH apply for the purposes of this Part.]

NOTES

Commencement: to be appointed.
Substituted as noted to s 112A at **[17.19]**.

[17.45]
[112AA Main definitions

(1) In this Part—

"administration order" has the meaning given by section 112A;
"debtor" has the meaning given by section 112B;
"prescribed maximum" means the amount prescribed in regulations for the purposes of section 112B(6);
"prescribed minimum" means the amount prescribed in regulations for the purposes of section 112B(7);
"qualifying creditor" means a creditor under a qualifying debt.

(2) References to the currency of an administration order are references to the period which—

(a) begins when the order first has effect, and
(b) ends when the order ceases to have effect.

(3) . . .
(4) . . .]

NOTES

Commencement: to be appointed.
Substituted as noted to s 112A at **[17.19]**.
Sub-ss (3), (4): repealed by the Crime and Courts Act 2013, s 17(5), Sch 9, Pt 1, paras 1, 10(52)(e).

[17.46]
[112AB Expressions relating to debts

(1) All debts are qualifying debts, except for the following—

(a) any debt secured against an asset;
(b) any debt of a description specified in regulations.

(2) A business debt is any debt (whether or not a qualifying debt) which is incurred by a person in the course of a business.

(3) Only debts that have already arisen are included in references to debts; and accordingly such references do not include any debt that will arise only on the happening of some future contingency.]

NOTES

Commencement: to be appointed.
Substituted as noted to s 112A at **[17.19]**.

[17.47]
[112AC Inability to pay debts
(1) In a case where an individual is the debtor under a debt that is repayable by a single payment, the debtor is to be regarded as unable to pay the debt only if—
(a) the debt has become due,
(b) the debtor has failed to make the single payment, and
(c) the debtor is unable to make that payment.
(2) In a case where an individual is the debtor under a debt that is repayable by a number of payments, the debtor is to be regarded as unable to pay the debt only if—
(a) the debt has become due,
(b) the debtor has failed to make one or more of the payments, and
(c) the debtor is unable to make all of the missed payments.]

NOTES
Commencement: to be appointed.
Substituted as noted to s 112A at **[17.19]**.

[17.48]
[112AD Calculating the debtor's qualifying debts
(1) The total amount of a debtor's qualifying debts is to be calculated in accordance with subsections (2) and (3).
(2) All of the debtor's qualifying debts which have arisen before the calculation must be taken into account (whether or not the debts are already due at the time of the calculation).
(3) Regulations must make further provision about how the total amount of a debtor's qualifying debts is to be calculated.
(4) Regulations may make provision about how the amount of any particular qualifying debt is to be calculated.
(5) That includes the calculation of the amount of a debt for these purposes—
(a) calculating the total amount of the debtor's qualifying debts;
(b) scheduling the debt to an administration order.]

NOTES
Commencement: to be appointed.
Substituted as noted to s 112A at **[17.19]**.

[17.49]
[112AE Calculating the debtor's surplus income
(1) The debtor's surplus income is to be calculated in accordance with regulations.
(2) Regulations under this section must, in particular, make the following provision—
(a) provision about what is surplus income;
(b) provision about the period by reference to which the debtor's surplus income is to be calculated.
(3) Regulations under this section may, in particular, provide for the debtor's assets to be taken account of when calculating his surplus income.]

NOTES
Commencement: to be appointed.
Substituted as noted to s 112A at **[17.19]**.

[17.50]
[112AF Debts becoming due
(1) A debt that is repayable by a single payment becomes due when the time for making that payment is reached.
(2) A debt that is repayable by a number of payments becomes due when the time for making the first of the payments is reached.]

NOTES
Commencement: to be appointed.
Substituted as noted to s 112A at **[17.19]**.

[17.51]
[112AG Scheduling and de-scheduling debts
(1) A debt is scheduled to an administration order if the relevant information is included in a schedule to the order.
(2) A debt is de-scheduled if the relevant information is removed from a schedule in which it was included as mentioned in subsection (1).
(3) In relation to a debt, the relevant information is—
(a) the amount of the debt, and
(b) the name of the creditor under the debt.
(4) A scheduled debt is a debt that is scheduled to an administration order.
(5) The . . . county court must not schedule a debt to an administration order unless the court has had regard to any representations made by any person about why the debt should not be scheduled.
(6) But subsection (5) does not apply to any representations which are made by the debtor in relation to the scheduling of a debt under section 112Y.

(7) The . . . county court must not de-schedule a debt unless the court has had regard to any representations made by any person about why the debt should not be de-scheduled.
(8) But subsection (7) does not apply in relation to the de-scheduling of a debt under section 112Q.
(9) A court must not schedule a debt to an administration order, or de-schedule a debt, except in accordance with the provisions of this Part.]

NOTES

Commencement: to be appointed.
Substituted as noted to s 112A at **[17.19]**.
Sub-ss (5), (7): word omitted repealed by the Crime and Courts Act 2013, s 17(5), Sch 9, Pt 1, paras 1, 10(52)(a).

[17.52]
[112AH The AO, voluntary arrangement and bankruptcy exclusions
(1) The debtor is excluded under the AO exclusion if—
 (a) an administration order currently has effect in respect of him, or
 (b) an administration order has previously had effect in respect of him, and the period of 12 months—beginning with the day when that order ceased to have effect—has yet to finish.
(2) But in a case that falls within subsection (1)(b), the debtor is not excluded under the AO exclusion if the previous administration order—
 (a) ceased to have effect in accordance with any of the provisions listed in section 112K(7) (effect of enforcement restriction order or debt relief order on administration order), or
 (b) was revoked in accordance with section 112U(1)(b) (debtor no longer has any qualifying debts).
(3) The debtor is excluded under the voluntary arrangement exclusion if—
 (a) an interim order under section 252 of the Insolvency Act 1986 has effect in respect of him (interim order where debtor intends to make proposal for voluntary arrangement), or
 (b) he is bound by a voluntary arrangement approved under Part 8 of the Insolvency Act 1986.
(4) The debtor is excluded under the bankruptcy exclusion if—
 (a) a petition for a bankruptcy order to be made against him has been presented but not decided, or
 (b) he is an undischarged bankrupt.]

NOTES

Commencement: to be appointed.
Substituted as noted to s 112A at **[17.19]**.

[Regulations

[17.53]
112AI Regulations under this Part
(1) It is for the Lord Chancellor to make regulations under this Part.
(2) Any power to make regulations under this Part is exercisable by statutory instrument.
(3) A statutory instrument containing regulations under this Part is subject to annulment in pursuance of a resolution of either House of Parliament.]

NOTES

Commencement: to be appointed.
Substituted as noted to s 112A at **[17.19]**.

117A–151 *((Pts 6A–IX) outside the scope of this work.)*

SCHEDULES 1–4

(Schs 1–4 outside the scope of this work.)

COMPANIES ACT 1985

(1985 c 6)

An Act to consolidate the greater part of the Companies Acts

[11 March 1985]

1–457 *((Pts I–XV) outside the scope of this work.)*

PART XVI
FRAUDULENT TRADING BY A COMPANY

[17.54]
458 Punishment for fraudulent trading
If any business of a company is carried on with intent to defraud creditors of the company or creditors of any other person, or for any fraudulent purpose, every person who was knowingly a party to the carrying on of the business in that manner is liable to imprisonment or a fine, or both.
This applies whether or not the company has been, or is in the course of being, wound up.

NOTES

This section derived from the Companies Act 1948, s 332(3), the Companies Act 1980, s 80, Sch 2, and the Companies Act 1981, s 96.

Repealed by the Companies Act 2006, s 1295, Sch 16, as from 1 October 2007, except in relation to offences completed before that date.

459–744A *((Pts XVII–XXVI) outside the scope of this work.)*

PART XXVII
FINAL PROVISIONS

745, 745A *(Outside the scope of this work.)*

[17.55]

746 Commencement

. . . *this Act comes into force on 1st July 1985.*

NOTES

Repealed by the Companies Act 2006, s 1295, Sch 16, as from a day to be appointed.

Words omitted repealed by the Companies Act 1989, s 212, Sch 24.

[17.56]

747 Citation

This Act may be cited as the Companies Act 1985.

SCHEDULES 1–25

(Schs 1–25 outside the scope of this work.)

COMPANIES ACT 1989

(1989 c 40)

ARRANGEMENT OF SECTIONS

PART VII
FINANCIAL MARKETS AND INSOLVENCY

Introduction

154 Introduction . . . [17.57]

Recognised bodies

155 Market contracts . . . [17.58]
155A Qualifying collateral arrangements and qualifying property transfers . . . [17.59]
157 Change in default rules . . . [17.60]
158 Modifications of the law of insolvency . . . [17.61]
159 Proceedings of recognised bodies take precedence over insolvency procedures . . . [17.62]
160 Duty to give assistance for purposes of default proceedings . . . [17.63]
161 Supplementary provisions as to default proceedings . . . [17.64]
162 Duty to report on completion of default proceedings . . . [17.65]
163 Net sum payable on completion of default proceedings . . . [17.66]
164 Disclaimer of property, rescission of contracts, &c . . . [17.67]
165 Adjustment of prior transactions . . . [17.68]
166 Powers to give directions . . . [17.69]
167 Application to determine whether default proceedings to be taken . . . [17.70]
169 Supplementary provisions . . . [17.71]

Other exchanges and clearing houses

170 Certain overseas exchanges and clearing houses . . . [17.72]
170A EEA central counterparties and third country central counterparties . . . [17.73]
170B EEA central counterparties and third country central counterparties: procedure . . . [17.74]
170C EEA CSDs and third country CSDs . . . [17.74A]
172 Settlement arrangements provided by the Bank of England . . . [17.75]

Market charges

173 Market charges . . . [17.76]
174 Modifications of the law of insolvency . . . [17.77]
175 Administration orders, &c . . . [17.78]

176 Power to make provision about certain other charges . . . [17.79]

Market property

177 Application of margin or default fund contribution not affected by certain other interests . . . [17.80]
178 Priority of floating market charge over subsequent charges . . . [17.81]
179 Priority of market charge over unpaid vendor's lien . . . [17.82]
180 Proceedings against market property by unsecured creditors . . . [17.83]
181 Power to apply provisions to other cases . . . [17.84]

Supplementary provisions

182 Powers of court in relation to certain proceedings begun before commencement . . . [17.85]
182A Recognised central counterparties: disapplication of provisions on mutual credit and set-off . . [17.86]
183 Insolvency proceedings in other jurisdictions . . . [17.87]
184 Indemnity for certain acts, &c . . . [17.88]
185 Power to make further provision by regulations . . . [17.89]
186 Supplementary provisions as to regulations . . . [17.90]
187 Construction of references to parties to market contracts . . . [17.91]
188 Meaning of "default rules" and related expressions . . . [17.92]
189 Meaning of "relevant office-holder" . . . [17.93]
189A Meaning of "transfer" . . . [17.94]
190 Minor definitions . . . [17.95]
191 Index of defined expressions . . . [17.96]

PART X
MISCELLANEOUS AND GENERAL PROVISIONS

215 Commencement and transitional provisions . . . [17.97]
216 Short title . . . [17.98]

An Act to amend the law relating to company accounts; to make new provision with respect to the persons eligible for appointment as company auditors; to amend the Companies Act 1985 and certain other enactments with respect to investigations and powers to obtain information and to confer new powers exercisable to assist overseas regulatory authorities; to make new provision with respect to the registration of company charges and otherwise to amend the law relating to companies; to amend the Fair Trading Act 1973; to enable provision to be made for the payment of fees in connection with the exercise by the Secretary of State, the Director General of Fair Trading and the Monopolies and Mergers Commission of their functions under Part V of that Act; to make provision for safeguarding the operation of certain financial markets; to amend the Financial Services Act 1986; to enable provision to be made for the recording and transfer of title to securities without a written instrument; to amend the Company Directors Disqualification Act 1986, the Company Securities (Insider Dealing) Act 1985, the Policyholders Protection Act 1975 and the law relating to building societies; and for connected purposes

[16 November 1989]

1–153 *((Pts I–VI) in so far as unrepealed, outside the scope of this work.)*

PART VII
FINANCIAL MARKETS AND INSOLVENCY

NOTES

Transfer of functions: by the Transfer of Functions (Financial Services) Order 1992, SI 1992/1315, art 2(1)(c), the functions of the Secretary of State under this Part of this Act are transferred to the Treasury. However, by art 4 of, and Sch 2, para 7 to, that Order, the functions of the Secretary of State under (i) ss 158(4), (5), 160(5), 170 (other than the function under s 170(1) of approving an overseas investment exchange), 171–174, 176, 181, 185, and (ii) so much of his functions under s 186 which relate to any function under the sections listed in (i) above, are exercisable jointly by the Secretary of State and the Treasury.

Application: the Secretary of State and the Treasury, acting jointly, may by regulations provide for this Part of this Act to apply to relevant contracts (as defined) as it applies to contracts connected with a recognised investment exchange or recognised clearing house; see the Financial Services and Markets Act 2000, s 301.

Modification: this Act is applied, with modifications, in so far as it relates to bank insolvency or administration under the Banking Act 2009, Pts 2, 3, by the Banking Act 2009 (Parts 2 and 3 Consequential Amendments) Order 2009, SI 2009/317, art 3, Schedule at **[7.86]**, **[7.92]**.

Introduction

[17.57]
154 Introduction

This Part has effect for the purposes of safeguarding the operation of certain financial markets by provisions with respect to—

(a) the insolvency, winding up or default of a person party to transactions in the market (sections 155 to 172),
(b) the effectiveness or enforcement of certain charges given to secure obligations in connection with such transactions (sections 173 to 176), and

(c) rights and remedies in relation to certain property provided as cover for margin in relation to such transactions [or as default fund contribution,] or subject to such a charge (sections 177 to 181).

NOTES

Words in square brackets in para (c) inserted by the Financial Markets and Insolvency Regulations 2009, SI 2009/853, reg 2(1), (2).

[Recognised bodies]

[17.58]

155 Market contracts

[(1) In this Part—

(a) "clearing member client contract" means a contract between a recognised central counterparty and one or more of the parties mentioned in subsection (1A) which is recorded in the accounts of the recognised central counterparty as a position held for the account of a client, an indirect client or a group of clients or indirect clients;

(b) "clearing member house contract" means a contract between a recognised central counterparty and a clearing member recorded in the accounts of the recognised central counterparty as a position held for the account of a clearing member;

(c) "client trade" means a contract between two or more of the parties mentioned in subsection (1A) which corresponds to a clearing member client contract;

(d) "market contracts" means the contracts to which this Part applies by virtue of subsections (2) to [(3ZA)].]

[(1A) The parties referred to in subsections (1)(a) and (c) are—

(a) a clearing member;

(b) a client; and

(c) an indirect client.]

[(2) Except as provided in subsection (2A), in relation to a recognised investment exchange this Part applies to—

(a) contracts entered into by a member or designated non-member of the exchange [with a person other than the exchange] which are either

(i) contracts made on the exchange or an exchange to whose undertaking the exchange has succeeded whether by amalgamation, merger or otherwise; or

(ii) contracts in the making of which the member or designated non-member was subject to the rules of the exchange or of an exchange to whose undertaking the exchange has succeeded whether by amalgamation, merger or otherwise;

[(b) contracts entered into by the exchange, in its capacity as such, with a member of the exchange or with a recognised clearing house [or with a recognised CSD] or with another recognised investment exchange for the purpose of enabling the rights and liabilities of that member [or recognised body] under a transaction to be settled; and

(c) contracts entered into by the exchange with a member of the exchange or with a recognised clearing house [or with a recognised CSD] or with another recognised investment exchange for the purpose of providing central counterparty clearing services to that member [or recognised body].]

A "designated non-member" means a person in respect of whom action may be taken under the default rules of the exchange but who is not a member of the exchange.

[(2A) Where the exchange in question is a recognised overseas investment exchange, this Part does not apply to a contract that falls within paragraph (a) of subsection (2) (unless it also falls within subsection (3)).]

[(2B) In relation to transactions which are cleared through a recognised central counterparty, this Part applies to—

(a) clearing member house contracts;

(b) clearing member client contracts;

(c) client trades, other than client trades excluded by subsection (2C) [or (2D)]; and

(d) contracts entered into by the recognised central counterparty with a recognised investment exchange [or with a recognised CSD] or a recognised clearing house for the purpose of providing central counterparty clearing services to [that recognised body].

(2C) A client trade is excluded by this subsection from subsection (2B)(c) if—

(a) the clearing member which is a party to the clearing member client contract corresponding to the client trade defaults; and

(b) the clearing member client contract is not transferred to another clearing member within the period specified for this purpose in the default rules of the recognised central counterparty.]]

[(2D) A client trade is also excluded by this subsection from subsection (2B)(c) if—

(a) the client trade was entered into by a client in the course of providing indirect clearing services to an indirect client;

(b) the client defaults; and

(c) the clearing member client contract corresponding to the client trade is not transferred within—

(i) the period specified for this purpose in the default rules of the recognised central counterparty; or

(ii) if no such period is specified in the default rules of the recognised central counterparty, a period of 14 days beginning with the day on which proceedings in respect of the client's insolvency are begun.]

[(3) In relation to a recognised clearing house [which is not a recognised central counterparty,] this Part applies to—

(a) contracts entered into by the clearing house, in its capacity as such, with a member of the clearing house or with a recognised investment exchange [or with a recognised CSD] or with another recognised clearing house for the purpose of enabling the rights and liabilities of that member [or recognised body] under a transaction to be settled; and

(b) contracts entered into by the clearing house with a member of the clearing house or with a recognised investment exchange [or with a recognised CSD] or with another recognised clearing house for the purpose of providing central counterparty clearing services to that member [or recognised body].]

[(3ZA) In relation to a recognised CSD, this Part applies to contracts entered into by the central securities depository with a member of the central securities depository or with a recognised investment exchange or with a recognised clearing house or with another recognised CSD for the purpose of providing authorised central securities depository services to that member or recognised body.]

[(3A) In this section "central counterparty clearing services" means—

(a) the services provided by a recognised investment exchange or a recognised clearing house to the parties to a transaction in connection with contracts between each of the parties and the investment exchange or clearing house (in place of, or as an alternative to, a contract directly between the parties),

(b) the services provided by a recognised clearing house to [a recognised body] in connection with contracts between them, or

(c) the services provided by a recognised investment exchange to [a recognised body] in connection with contracts between them.]

[(3B) The reference in subsection (2D)(c)(ii) to the beginning of insolvency proceedings is to—

(a) [the making of a bankruptcy application or] the presentation of a bankruptcy petition or a petition for sequestration of a client's estate, or

(b) the application for an administration order or the presentation of a winding-up petition or the passing of a resolution for voluntary winding up, or

(c) the appointment of an administrative receiver.

(3C) In subsection (3B)(b) the reference to an application for an administration order is to be taken to include a reference to—

(a) in a case where an administrator is appointed under paragraph 14 or 22 of Schedule B1 to the Insolvency Act 1986 (appointment by floating charge holder, company or directors) following filing with the court of a copy of a notice of intention to appoint under that paragraph, the filing of the copy of the notice, and

(b) in a case where an administrator is appointed under either of those paragraphs without a copy of a notice of intention to appoint having been filed with the court, the appointment of the administrator.]

[(3D) In this Part "authorised central securities depository services" means, in relation to a recognised CSD—

(a) the core services listed in Section A of the Annex to the CSD regulation which that central securities depository is authorised to provide pursuant to Article 16 or 19(1)(a) or (c) of the CSD regulation;

(b) the non-banking-type ancillary services listed in or permitted under Section B of that Annex which that central securities depository is authorised to provide, including services notified under Article 19 of the CSD regulation; and

(c) the banking-type ancillary services listed in or permitted under Section C of that Annex which that central securities depository is authorised to provide pursuant to Article 54(2)(a) of the CSD regulation.]

(4) The Secretary of State may by regulations make further provision as to the contracts to be treated as "market contracts", for the purposes of this Part, in relation to [a recognised body].

(5) The regulations may add to, amend or repeal the provisions of subsections [(2), (3), (3ZA) and (3D)] above.

NOTES

The heading preceding this section was substituted by the Central Securities Depositories Regulations 2017, SI 2017/1064, reg 3(1), (2) (for transitional provisions and savings see regs 6–9 thereof).

Sub-s (1): substituted by the Financial Services and Markets Act 2000 (Over the Counter Derivatives, Central Counterparties and Trade Repositories) Regulations 2013, SI 2013/504, reg 4(1), (2)(a). Figure "(3ZA)" in square brackets substituted by SI 2017/1064, reg 3(1), (3)(a) (for transitional provisions and savings see regs 6–9 thereof).

Sub-ss (1A), (2B), (2C): inserted by SI 2013/504, reg 4(1), (2)(b), (c). Words in square brackets in sub-s (2B)(c) inserted by the Financial Services and Markets Act 2000 (Over the Counter Derivatives, Central Counterparties and Trade Repositories) (No 2) Regulations 2013, SI 2013/1908, reg 2(1), (2)(a). Words in first pair of square brackets in sub-s (2B)(d) inserted, and words in second pair of square brackets substituted, by SI 2017/1064, reg 3(1), (3)(c) (for transitional provisions and savings see regs 6–9 thereof).

Sub-s (2) is amended as follows:

Substituted, together with sub-s (2A), for the original sub-s (2) by the Financial Markets and Insolvency Regulations 1991, SI 1991/880, reg 3.

Words in square brackets in para (a) inserted by the Financial Markets and Insolvency Regulations 1998, SI 1998/1748, reg 3.

Word omitted from para (a) repealed, and paras (b), (c) substituted (for the original para (b)) by the Financial Markets and Insolvency Regulations 2009, SI 2009/853, reg 2(1), (3)(a).

Words in first pair of square brackets in paras (b) and (c) inserted, and words in second pair of square brackets substituted, by SI 2017/1064, reg 3(1), (3)(b) (for transitional provisions and savings see regs 6–9 thereof).

Sub-s (2A): substituted as noted above; further substituted by SI 2009/853, reg 2(1), (3)(b).

Sub-ss (2D), (3B), (3C): inserted by SI 2013/1908, reg 2(1), (2)(b), (c). Words in square brackets in sub-s (3B) inserted by the Enterprise and Regulatory Reform Act 2013 (Consequential Amendments) (Bankruptcy) and the Small Business, Enterprise and Employment Act 2015 (Consequential Amendments) Regulations 2016, SI 2016/481, reg 2(1), Sch 1, para 9(1), (2).

Sub-s (3): substituted by SI 2009/853, reg 2(1), (3)(c). Words in first pair of square brackets substituted by SI 2013/504, reg 4(1), (2)(d). Words in first pair of square brackets in paras (a) and (b) inserted, and words in second pair of square brackets substituted, by SI 2017/1064, reg 3(1), (3)(d) (for transitional provisions and savings see regs 6–9 thereof).

Sub-ss (3ZA), (3D): inserted by SI 2017/1064, reg 3(1), (3)(e), (g) (for transitional provisions and savings see regs 6–9 thereof).

Sub-s (3A): inserted by SI 2009/853, reg 2(1), (3)(d). Words in square brackets substituted by SI 2017/1064, reg 3(1), (3)(f) (for transitional provisions and savings see regs 6–9 thereof).

Sub-ss (4), (5): words in square brackets substituted by SI 2017/1064, reg 3(1), (3)(h), (i) (for transitional provisions and savings see regs 6–9 thereof).

Regulations: the Financial Markets and Insolvency Regulations 1991, SI 1991/880 at **[9.1]**; the Financial Markets and Insolvency Regulations 1998, SI 1998/1748; the Financial Markets and Insolvency Regulations 2009, SI 2009/853; the Financial Services and Markets Act 2000 (Over the Counter Derivatives, Central Counterparties and Trade Repositories) Regulations 2013, SI 2013/504; the Financial Services and Markets Act 2000 (Over the Counter Derivatives, Central Counterparties and Trade Repositories) (No 2) Regulations 2013, SI 2013/1908.

[17.59]

[155A Qualifying collateral arrangements and qualifying property transfers

(1) In this Part—

(a) "qualifying collateral arrangements" means the contracts and contractual obligations to which this Part applies by virtue of subsection (2); and

(b) "qualifying property transfers" means the property transfers to which this Part applies by virtue of subsection (4).

(2) In relation to transactions which are cleared through a recognised central counterparty, this Part applies to any contracts or contractual obligations for, or arising out of, the provision of property as margin where—

(a) the margin is provided to a recognised central counterparty and is recorded in the accounts of the recognised central counterparty as an asset held for the account of a client, an indirect client, or a group of clients or indirect clients; or

(b) the margin is provided to a client or clearing member for the purpose of providing cover for exposures arising out of present or future client trades.

(3) In subsection (2)—

(a) "property" has the meaning given by section 436(1) of the Insolvency Act 1986 and

(b) the reference to a contract or contractual obligation for, or arising out of, the provision of property as margin in circumstances falling within paragraph (a) or (b) of that subsection includes a reference to a contract or contractual obligation of that kind which has been amended to reflect the transfer of a clearing member client contract or client trade.

(4) In relation to transactions which are cleared through a recognised central counterparty, this Part applies to—

(a) transfers of property made in accordance with Article 48(7) of the EMIR Level 1 Regulation;

[(aa) transfers of property made in accordance with Article 4(6) and (7) of the EMIR Level 2 Regulation or Article 4(6) and (7) of the MIFIR Level 2 Regulation;]

(b) transfers of property to the extent that they—

(i) are made by a recognised central counterparty to a non-defaulting clearing member instead of, or in place of, a defaulting clearing member;

(ii) represent the termination or close out value of a clearing member client contract which is transferred from a defaulting clearing member to a non-defaulting clearing member; and

(iii) are determined in accordance with the default rules of the recognised central counterparty;

[(c) transfers of property to the extent that they—

(i) are made by a clearing member to a non-defaulting client or another clearing member instead of, or in place of, a defaulting client;

(ii) represent the termination or close out value of a client trade which is transferred from a defaulting client to another clearing member or a non-defaulting client; and

(iii) do not exceed the termination or close out value of the clearing member client contract corresponding to that client trade, as determined in accordance with the default rules of the recognised central counterparty.]]

NOTES

Inserted by the Financial Services and Markets Act 2000 (Over the Counter Derivatives, Central Counterparties and Trade Repositories) Regulations 2013, SI 2013/504, reg 4(1), (3).

Sub-s (4): paras (aa), (c) inserted by the Financial Services and Markets Act 2000 (Over the Counter Derivatives, Central Counterparties and Trade Repositories) (No 2) Regulations 2013, SI 2013/1908, reg 2(1), (3); para (aa) substituted by the Companies Act 1989 (Financial Markets and Insolvency) (Amendment) Regulations 2017, SI 2017/1247, reg 2(1), (2).

156 (*Repealed by the Financial Services and Markets Act 2000 (Consequential Amendments and Repeals) Order 2001, SI 2001/3649, art 75(e).*)

[17.60]

157 Change in default rules

(1) [A recognised body] shall give the [appropriate regulator] at least [three months] notice of any proposal to amend, revoke or add to its default rules; and the [regulator] may within [three months] from receipt of the notice direct [the recognised body] not to proceed with the proposal, in whole or in part.

[(1A) The appropriate regulator may, if it considers it appropriate to do so, agree a shorter period of notice and, in a case where it does so, any direction under this section must be given by it within that shorter period.]
(2) A direction under this section may be varied or revoked.
(3) Any amendment or revocation of, or addition to, the default rules of [a recognised body] in breach of a direction under this section is ineffective.
[(4) "The appropriate regulator"—
(a) in relation to a recognised UK investment exchange, means the FCA, and
(b) in relation to a [recognised clearing house] [or a recognised CSD], means the Bank of England.]

NOTES

Sub-s (1) is amended as follows:

Words "A recognised body" and "the recognised body" in square brackets substituted by the Central Securities Depositories Regulations 2017, SI 2017/1064, reg 3(1), (4)(a) (for transitional provisions and savings see regs 6–9 thereof).

Words "appropriate regulator" and "regulator" in square brackets substituted by the Financial Services Act 2012, s 114(1), Sch 18, Pt 2, paras 62, 65(1), (2).

Words "three months" in square brackets (in both places they occur) substituted by the Financial Services and Markets Act 2000 (Over the Counter Derivatives, Central Counterparties and Trade Repositories) Regulations 2013, SI 2013/504, reg 4(1), (4)(a)(ii).

Sub-s (1A): inserted by SI 2013/504, reg 4(1), (4)(b).

Sub-s (3): words in square brackets substituted by SI 2017/1064, reg 3(1), (4)(b) (for transitional provisions and savings see regs 6–9 thereof).

Sub-s (4): added by the Financial Services Act 2012, s 114(1), Sch 18, Pt 2, paras 62, 65(1), (3). Words "recognised clearing house" in square brackets in para (b) substituted by SI 2013/504, reg 4(1), (4)(c). Words "or a recognised CSD" in square brackets in para (b) substituted by SI 2017/1064, reg 3(1), (4)(c) (for transitional provisions and savings see regs 6–9 thereof).

Transitional provisions: see further the Financial Services Act 2012 (Transitional Provisions) (Miscellaneous Provisions) Order 2013, SI 2013/442, art 65 at **[18.284]**.

[17.61]
158 Modifications of the law of insolvency

[(1) The general law of insolvency has effect in relation to—
(a) market contracts,
(b) action taken under the rules of [a recognised body other than a recognised central counterparty], with respect to market contracts,
(c) action taken under the rules of a recognised central counterparty to transfer clearing member client contracts, or settle clearing member client contracts or clearing member house contracts, in accordance with the default rules of the recognised central counterparty,
(d) where clearing member [or client] client contracts transferred in accordance with the default rules of a recognised central counterparty were entered into by the clearing member as a principal, action taken to transfer . . . client trades, or groups of client trades, corresponding to those clearing member client contracts,
(e) action taken to transfer qualifying collateral arrangements in conjunction with a transfer of clearing member client contracts as mentioned in paragraph (c) or a transfer of client trades as mentioned in paragraph (d), and
(f) qualifying property transfers,
subject to the provisions of sections 159 to 165.]
(2) So far as those provisions relate to insolvency proceedings in respect of a person other than a defaulter, they apply in relation to—
[(a) proceedings in respect of a recognised investment exchange or a member or designated non-member of a recognised investment exchange,
(aa) proceedings in respect of a recognised clearing house or a member of a recognised clearing house, . . .]
[(ab) proceedings in respect of a recognised CSD or a member of a recognised CSD, and]
(b) proceedings in respect of a party to a market contract [other than a client trade which are] begun after [a recognised body] has taken action under its default rules in relation to a person party to the contract as principal,
but not in relation to any other insolvency proceedings, notwithstanding that rights or liabilities arising from market contracts fall to be dealt with in the proceedings.
(3) The reference in subsection (2)(b) to the beginning of insolvency proceedings is to—
(a) [the making of a bankruptcy application or] the presentation of a bankruptcy petition or a petition for sequestration of a person's estate, or
[(b) the application for an administration order or the presentation of a winding-up petition or the passing of a resolution for voluntary winding up,] or
(c) the appointment of an administrative receiver.
[(3A) In subsection (3)(b) the reference to an application for an administration order shall be taken to include a reference to—
(a) in a case where an administrator is appointed under paragraph 14 or 22 of Schedule B1 to the Insolvency Act 1986 (appointment by floating charge holder, company or directors) following filing with the court of a copy of a notice of intention to appoint under that paragraph, the filing of the copy of the notice, and
(b) in a case where an administrator is appointed under either of those paragraphs without a copy of a notice of intention to appoint having been filed with the court, the appointment of the administrator.]

(4) The Secretary of State may make further provision by regulations modifying the law of insolvency in relation to the matters mentioned in [paragraphs (a) to (d) of] subsection (1).

(5) The regulations may add to, amend or repeal the provisions mentioned in subsection (1), and any other provision of this Part as it applies for the purposes of those provisions, or provide that those provisions have effect subject to such additions, exceptions or adaptations as are specified in the regulations.

NOTES

Sub-s (1): substituted by the Financial Services and Markets Act 2000 (Over the Counter Derivatives, Central Counterparties and Trade Repositories) Regulations 2013, SI 2013/504, reg 4(1), (5)(a). Words in square brackets in para (b) substituted by the Central Securities Depositories Regulations 2017, SI 2017/1064, reg 3(1), (5)(a) (for transitional provisions and savings see regs 6–9 thereof). Words in square brackets in para (d) inserted, and the word omitted from that paragraph repealed, by the Financial Services and Markets Act 2000 (Over the Counter Derivatives, Central Counterparties and Trade Repositories) (No 2) Regulations 2013, SI 2013/1908, reg 2(1), (4).

Sub-s (2): paras (a), (aa) substituted for original para (a) by the Financial Markets and Insolvency Regulations 2009, SI 2009/853, reg 2(1), (4), with effect in relation to specified insolvency events taking place on or after 15 June 2009, as provided in reg 1(2), (3) thereof, which reads as follows:

"(2) Regulation 2 paragraphs (4), (5), (6), (7), (8), (9), (10) and (12) apply to insolvency proceedings which relate to any of the insolvency events set out in paragraph (3) which take place on or after the date on which these Regulations come into force.

(3) The insolvency events are—

(a) an application for an administration order;
(b) an application for a bank administration order under Part 3 of the Banking Act 2009;
(c) the filing of a notice of intention to appoint an administrator for an appointment under paragraph 14 or 22 of Schedule B1 to the Insolvency Act 1986;
(d) where no notice of intention to appoint is filed, the appointment of an administrator under paragraph 14 or 22 of Schedule B1 to the Insolvency Act 1986;
(e) the presentation of a bankruptcy petition;
(f) the presentation of a petition for sequestration of a person's estate;
(g) the presentation of a winding up petition;
(h) an application for a bank insolvency order under Part 2 of the Banking Act 2009;
(i) the passing of a resolution for voluntary winding up;
(j) the appointment of an administrative receiver;
(k) the making of an order appointing an interim receiver.".

Sub-s (2)(a) originally read as follows:

"(a) proceedings in respect of a member or designated non-member of a recognised investment exchange or a member of a recognised clearing house, and";

Word omitted from para (aa) repealed, para (ab) inserted, and words in second pair of square brackets in para (b) substituted, by SI 2017/1064, reg 3(1), (5)(a) (for transitional provisions and savings see regs 6–9 thereof). Words in first pair of square brackets in para (b) inserted by SI 2013/504, reg 4(1), (5)(b).

Sub-s (3): para (b) substituted by the Enterprise Act 2002, s 248(3), Sch 17, paras 43, 44(a), subject to savings and transitional provisions (i) in a case where a petition for an administration order has been presented before 15 September 2003 (see the Enterprise Act 2002 (Commencement No 4 and Transitional Provisions and Savings) Order 2003, SI 2003/2093, art 3 at **[2.26]**), and (ii) in relation to special administration regimes (see s 249 of the 2002 Act at **[2.10]**); the original para (b) read as follows:

"(b) the presentation of a petition for an administration order or a winding-up petition or the passing of a resolution for voluntary winding up, or".

Sub-s (3A): inserted by the Enterprise Act 2002, s 248(3), Sch 17, paras 43, 44(b), subject to savings and transitional provisions as noted to sub-s (3) above.

Sub-s (4): words in square brackets inserted by SI 2013/504, reg 4(1), (5)(c).

Regulations: the Financial Markets and Insolvency Regulations 1991, SI 1991/880 at **[9.1]**; the Financial Markets and Insolvency Regulations 2009, SI 2009/853; the Financial Services and Markets Act 2000 (Over the Counter Derivatives, Central Counterparties and Trade Repositories) Regulations 2013, SI 2013/504; the Financial Services and Markets Act 2000 (Over the Counter Derivatives, Central Counterparties and Trade Repositories) (No 2) Regulations 2013, SI 2013/1908.

[17.62]

159 [Proceedings of recognised bodies take precedence over insolvency procedures]

(1) None of the following shall be regarded as to any extent invalid at law on the ground of inconsistency with the law relating to the distribution of the assets of a person on bankruptcy, winding up or sequestration, or [in the administration of a company or other body or] in the administration of an insolvent estate—

(a) a market contract,
(b) the default rules of a [a recognised body],
(c) the rules of [a recognised body other than a recognised central counterparty] as to the settlement of market contracts not dealt with [under its default rules,]
[(d) the rules of a recognised central counterparty on which the recognised central counterparty relies to give effect to the transfer of a clearing member client contract, or the settlement of a clearing member client contract or clearing member house contract, in accordance with its default rules,
(e) a transfer of a clearing member client contract, or the settlement of a clearing member client contract or a clearing member house contract, in accordance with the default rules of a recognised central counterparty,

(f) where a clearing member client contract transferred in accordance with the default rules of a recognised central counterparty was entered into by the clearing member [or client] as principal, a transfer of [a client trade] or group of client trades corresponding to that clearing member client contract,

(g) a transfer of a qualifying collateral arrangement in conjunction with the transfer of clearing member client contract as mentioned in paragraph (e) or of a client trade as mentioned in paragraph (f), or

(h) a qualifying property transfer.]

(2) The powers of a relevant office-holder in his capacity as such, and the powers of the court under the Insolvency Act 1986[, the Bankruptcy (Scotland) Act [2016], Part 10 of the Building Societies Act 1986, Parts 2 and 3 of the Banking Act 2009 or under regulations made under section 233 of that Act,] shall not be exercised in such a way as to prevent or interfere with—

(a) the settlement in accordance with the rules of [a recognised body other than a recognised central counterparty] of a market contract not dealt with under its default rules,

(b) any action taken under the default rules of [a recognised body other than a recognised central counterparty]

[(c) the transfer of a clearing member client contract, or the settlement of a clearing member client contract or a clearing member house contract, in accordance with the default rules of a recognised central counterparty,

(d) where a clearing member client contract transferred in accordance with the default rules of a recognised central counterparty was entered into by the clearing member [or client] as principal, the transfer of [a client trade] or group of client trades corresponding to that clearing member contract,

(e) the transfer of a qualifying collateral arrangement in conjunction with a transfer of a clearing member client contract as mentioned in paragraph (c), or a transfer of a client trade as mentioned in paragraph (d),

(f) any action taken to give effect to any of the matters mentioned in paragraphs (c) to (e), or

(g) any action taken to give effect to a qualifying property transfer.]

This does not prevent a relevant office-holder from afterwards seeking to recover any amount under section 163(4) or 164(4) or prevent the court from afterwards making any such order or decree as is mentioned in section 165(1) or (2) (but subject to subsections (3) and (4) of that section).

(3) Nothing in the following provisions of this Part shall be construed as affecting the generality of the above provisions.

(4) A debt or other liability arising out of a market contract which is the subject of default proceedings may not be proved in a winding up or bankruptcy [or in the administration of a company or other body], or in Scotland claimed in a winding up or sequestration [or in the administration of a company or other body], until the completion of the default proceedings.

A debt or other liability which by virtue of this subsection may not be proved or claimed shall not be taken into account for the purposes of any set-off until the completion of the default proceedings.

[(4A) However, prior to the completion of default proceedings—

(a) where it appears [to the convener] that a sum will be certified under section 162(1) to be payable, subsection (4) shall not prevent any proof or claim including or consisting of an estimate of that sum which has been lodged or, in Scotland, submitted, from being admitted or, in Scotland, accepted, for the purpose only of determining the entitlement of a creditor to vote [in a decision procedure]; and

(b) a creditor whose claim or proof has been lodged and admitted or, in Scotland, submitted and accepted, for the purpose of determining the entitlement of a creditor to vote [in a decision procedure] and which has not been subsequently wholly withdrawn, disallowed or rejected, is eligible as a creditor to be a member of a liquidation committee or, in bankruptcy proceedings in England and Wales, [or in the administration of a company or other body] a creditors' committee.]

(5) For the purposes of [subsections (4) and (4A)] the default proceedings shall be taken to be completed in relation to a person when a report is made under section 162 stating the sum (if any) certified to be due to or from him.

NOTES

Section heading substituted by the Central Securities Depositories Regulations 2017, SI 2017/1064, reg 3(1), (6)(a) (for transitional provisions and savings see regs 6–9 thereof).

Sub-s (1) is amended as follows:

Words in first pair of square brackets inserted by the Financial Markets and Insolvency Regulations 2009, SI 2009/853, reg 2(1), (5)(a), with effect in relation to specified insolvency events taking place on or after 15 June 2009, as noted to s 158 at **[17.61]**.

Words in square brackets in para (b) substituted SI 2017/1064, reg 3(1), (6)(b) (for transitional provisions and savings see regs 6–9 thereof).

Words "a recognised body other than a recognised central counterparty" in para (c) substituted SI 2017/1064, reg 3(1), (6)(c) (for transitional provisions and savings see regs 6–9 thereof).

Words "under its default rules," in para (c) substituted by the Financial Services and Markets Act 2000 (Over the Counter Derivatives, Central Counterparties and Trade Repositories) Regulations 2013, SI 2013/504, reg 4(1), (6)(a)(ii).

Paras (d)–(h) inserted by SI 2013/504, reg 4(1), (6)(b).

Words in first pair of square brackets in para (f) inserted, and words in second pair of square brackets substituted, by the Financial Services and Markets Act 2000 (Over the Counter Derivatives, Central Counterparties and Trade Repositories) (No 2) Regulations 2013, SI 2013/1908, reg 2(1), (5)(a).

Sub-s (2): the year "2016" in square brackets was substituted for the year "1985" by the Bankruptcy (Scotland) Act 2016 (Consequential Provisions and Modifications) Order 2016, SI 2016/1034, art 7(1), (3), Sch 1, para 6(1), (2), as from

30 November 2016 (except in relation to (i) a sequestration as regards which the petition is presented, or the debtor application is made before that date; or (ii) a trust deed executed before that date). Words in square brackets in paras (a) and (b) substituted by SI 2017/1064, reg 3(1), (6)(d), (e) (for transitional provisions and savings see regs 6–9 thereof). Words in first pair of square brackets in para (d) inserted, and words in second pair of square brackets substituted, by SI 2013/1908, reg 2(1), (5)(b). Paras (c)–(g) inserted, other words in square brackets substituted, and words omitted repealed, by SI 2013/504, reg 4(1), (6)(c)–(f).

Sub-s (4): words in square brackets inserted by the Financial Markets and Insolvency Regulations 2009, SI 2009/853, reg 2(1), (5)(b), with effect in relation to specified insolvency events taking place on or after 15 June 2009, as noted to s 158 at **[17.61]**.

Sub-s (4A): inserted by the Financial Markets and Insolvency Regulations 1991, SI 1991/880, reg 4(1), (2); words in square brackets in para (a) substituted, and words in first pair of square brackets in para (b) substituted, by the Deregulation Act 2015 and Small Business, Enterprise and Employment Act 2015 (Consequential Amendments) (Savings) Regulations 2017, SI 2017/540, reg 2, Sch 1, para 2(1), (2); words in second pair of square brackets in para (b) inserted by SI 2009/853, reg 2(1), (5)(c), with effect in relation to specified insolvency events taking place on or after 15 June 2009, as noted to s 158 at **[17.61]**.

Sub-s (5): words in square brackets substituted by SI 1991/880, reg 4(1), (3).

[17.63]

160 Duty to give assistance for purposes of default proceedings

(1) It is the duty of—

(a) any person who has or had control of any assets of a defaulter, and

(b) any person who has or had control of any documents of or relating to a defaulter,

to give [a recognised body] such assistance as it may reasonably require for the purposes of its default proceedings.

This applies notwithstanding any duty of that person under the enactments relating to insolvency.

(2) A person shall not under this section be required to provide any information or produce any document which he would be entitled to refuse to provide or produce on grounds of legal professional privilege in proceedings in the High Court or on grounds of confidentiality as between client and professional legal adviser in proceedings in the Court of Session.

(3) Where original documents are supplied in pursuance of this section, [the recognised body] shall return them forthwith after the completion of the relevant default proceedings, and shall in the meantime allow reasonable access to them to the person by whom they were supplied and to any person who would be entitled to have access to them if they were still in the control of the person by whom they were supplied.

(4) The expenses of a relevant office-holder in giving assistance under this section are recoverable as part of the expenses incurred by him in the discharge of his duties; and he shall not be required under this section to take any action which involves expenses which cannot be so recovered, unless [the recognised body] undertakes to meet them.

There shall be treated as expenses of his such reasonable sums as he may determine in respect of time spent in giving the assistance [and for the purpose of determining the priority in which his expenses are payable out of the assets, sums in respect of time spent shall be treated as his remuneration and other sums shall be treated as his disbursements or, in Scotland, outlays].

(5) The Secretary of State may by regulations make further provision as to the duties of persons to give assistance to [a recognised body] for the purposes of its default proceedings, and the duties of [the recognised body] with respect to information supplied to it.

The regulations may add to, amend or repeal the provisions of subsections (1) to (4) above.

(6) In this section "document" includes information recorded in any form.

NOTES

Words "and for the purpose of determining the priority in which his expenses are payable out of the assets, sums in respect of time spent shall be treated as his remuneration and other sums shall be treated as his disbursements or, in Scotland, outlays" in square brackets in sub-s (4) added by the Financial Markets and Insolvency Regulations 1991, SI 1991/880, reg 5.

All other words in square brackets in this section were substituted by the Central Securities Depositories Regulations 2017, SI 2017/1064, reg 3(1), (7) (for transitional provisions and savings see regs 6–9 thereof).

Regulations: the Financial Markets and Insolvency Regulations 1991, SI 1991/880 at **[9.1]**.

[17.64]

161 Supplementary provisions as to default proceedings

(1) If the court is satisfied on an application by a relevant office-holder that a party to a market contract with a defaulter intends to dissipate or apply his assets so as to prevent the officer-holder recovering such sums as may become due upon the completion of the default proceedings, the court may grant such interlocutory relief (in Scotland, such interim order) as it thinks fit.

(2) A liquidator[, administrator] or trustee of a defaulter or, in Scotland, a [trustee in the sequestration of the] estate of the defaulter shall not—

(a) declare or pay any dividend to the creditors, or

(b) return any capital to contributories,

unless he has retained what he reasonably considers to be an adequate reserve in respect of any claims arising as a result of the default proceedings of [the recognised body] concerned.

(3) The court may on an application by a relevant office-holder make such order as it thinks fit altering or dispensing from compliance with such of the duties of his office as are affected by the fact that default proceedings are pending or could be taken, or have been or could have been taken.

(4) Nothing in [section 126, 128, 130, 185 or 285 of, or paragraph [40, 41,] 42 or 43 ([including those paragraphs as applied by paragraph 44]) of Schedule B1 to, the Insolvency Act 1986] (which restrict the taking of certain legal proceedings and other steps), and nothing in any rule of law in Scotland to the like

effect as the said section 285, in the Bankruptcy (Scotland) Act [2016] or in the Debtors (Scotland) Act 1987 as to the effect of sequestration, shall affect any action taken by [a recognised body] for the purpose of its default proceedings.

NOTES

Sub-s (2): word in first pair of square brackets inserted by the Financial Markets and Insolvency Regulations 2009, SI 2009/853, reg 2(1), (6)(a), with effect in relation to specified insolvency events taking place on or after 15 June 2009, as noted to s 158 at **[17.61]**; words in second pair of square brackets substituted for the original words "permanent trustee on the sequestrated" by the Bankruptcy (Scotland) Act 2016 (Consequential Provisions and Modifications) Order 2016, SI 2016/1034, art 7(1), (3), Sch 1, para 6(1), (3)(a), as from 30 November 2016 (except in relation to (i) a sequestration as regards which the petition is presented, or the debtor application is made before that date; or (ii) a trust deed executed before that date). Words in final pair of square brackets substituted by the Central Securities Depositories Regulations 2017, SI 2017/1064, reg 3(1), (8)(a) (for transitional provisions and savings see regs 6–9 thereof).

Sub-s (4): words in first (outer) pair of square brackets substituted for original words "sections 10(1)(c), 11(3), 126, 128, 130, 185 or 285 of the Insolvency Act 1986" by the Enterprise Act 2002, s 248(3), Sch 17, paras 43, 45, subject to savings and transitional provisions (i) in a case where a petition for an administration order has been presented before 15 September 2003 (see the Enterprise Act 2002 (Commencement No 4 and Transitional Provisions and Savings) Order 2003, SI 2003/2093, art 3 at **[2.26]**), and (ii) in relation to special administration regimes (see s 249 of the 2002 Act at **[2.10]**). (Note SI 2009/853, reg 2(1), (6)(c) provides for the amendment of sub-s (4) as it has effect, by virtue of section 249(1) of the Enterprise Act 2002, without the amendments made by Sch 17, para 45 to that Act, by substituting "10, 11" for previous words "10(1)(c), 11(3)", with effect in relation to specified insolvency events taking place on or after 15 June 2009, as noted to s 158 at **[17.61]**; figures in second (inner) pair of square brackets inserted and words in third (inner) pair of square brackets substituted for words "including paragraph 43(6) as applied by paragraph 44" by SI 2009/853, reg 2(1), (6)(b), with effect in relation to specified insolvency events taking place on or after 15 June 2009, as noted to s 158 at **[17.61]**; year "2016" in square brackets substituted for the original year "1985" by SI 2016/1034, art 7(1), (3), Sch 1, para 6(1), (3)(b), as from 30 November 2016 (except in relation to (i) a sequestration as regards which the petition is presented, or the debtor application is made before that date; or (ii) a trust deed executed before that date). Words in final pair of square brackets substituted by SI 2017/1064, reg 3(1), (8)(b) (for transitional provisions and savings see regs 6–9 thereof).

[17.65]

162 Duty to report on completion of default proceedings

(1) [Subject to subsection (1A),] [a recognised body] house shall, on the completion of proceedings under its default rules, report to the [appropriate regulator] on its proceedings stating in respect of each creditor or debtor the sum [or sums] certified by them to be payable from or to the defaulter or, as the case may be, the fact that no sum is payable.

[(1A) A recognised overseas investment exchange or recognised overseas clearing house shall not be subject to the obligation under subsection (1) unless it has been notified by the [appropriate regulator] that a report is required for the purpose of insolvency proceedings in any part of the United Kingdom.]

[(1B) The report under subsection (1) need not deal with a clearing member client contract which has been transferred in accordance with the default rules of a recognised central counterparty.]

(2) [The recognised body] may make a single report or may make reports from time to time as proceedings are completed with respect to the transactions affecting particular persons.

(3) [The recognised body] shall supply a copy of every report under this section to the defaulter and to any relevant office-holder acting in relation to him or his estate.

(4) When a report under this section is received by the [[appropriate regulator], it] shall publish notice of that fact in such manner as [it] thinks appropriate for bringing [the report] to the attention of creditors and debtors of the defaulter.

(5) [A recognised body] shall make available for inspection by a creditor or debtor of the defaulter so much of any report by it under this section as relates to the sum (if any) certified to be due to or from him or to the method by which that sum was determined.

(6) Any such person may require [the recognised body], on payment of such reasonable fee as [the recognised body] may determine, to provide him with a copy of any part of a report which he is entitled to inspect.

[(7) "The appropriate regulator"—

(a) in relation to a recognised investment exchange or a recognised overseas investment exchange, means the FCA, and

(b) in relation to a [recognised CSD, a] recognised clearing house or a recognised overseas clearing house, means the Bank of England.]

NOTES

Sub-s (1): words in first pair of square brackets inserted by the Financial Markets and Insolvency Regulations 1991, SI 1991/880, reg 6(1), (2). Words in second pair of square brackets substituted by the Central Securities Depositories Regulations 2017, SI 2017/1064, reg 3(1), (9)(a) (for transitional provisions and savings see regs 6–9 thereof). Words in third pair of square brackets substituted by the Financial Services Act 2012, s 114(1), Sch 18, Pt 2, paras 62, 66(1), (2). Words in final pair of square brackets inserted by the Financial Services and Markets Act 2000 (Over the Counter Derivatives, Central Counterparties and Trade Repositories) Regulations 2013, SI 2013/504, reg 4(1), (7)(a).

Sub-s (1A): inserted by SI 1991/880, reg 6(1), (3); words in square brackets substituted by the Financial Services Act 2012, s 114(1), Sch 18, Pt 2, paras 62, 66(1), (2).

Sub-s (1B): inserted by SI 2013/504, reg 4(1), (7)(b).

Sub-ss (2), (3), (5), (6): words in square brackets substituted by SI 2017/1064, reg 3(1), (9)(b)–(d) (for transitional provisions and savings see regs 6–9 thereof).

Sub-s (4): words in first (outer), third and fourth pairs of square brackets substituted by SI 2001/3649, art 80(1), (4); words in second (inner) pair of square brackets substituted by the Financial Services Act 2012, s 114(1), Sch 18, Pt 2, paras 62, 66(1), (3).

Sub-s (7): added by the Financial Services Act 2012, s 114(1), Sch 18, Pt 2, paras 62, 66(1), (4). Words in square brackets substituted by SI 2017/1064, reg 3(1), (9)(e) (for transitional provisions and savings see regs 6–9 thereof).

Transitional provisions: see further the Financial Services Act 2012 (Transitional Provisions) (Miscellaneous Provisions) Order 2013, SI 2013/442, art 66 at **[18.285]**.

[17.66]
163 Net sum payable on completion of default proceedings

[(1) The following provisions apply with respect to a net sum certified by [a recognised body] under its default rules to be payable by or to a defaulter.]

(2) If, in England and Wales, a bankruptcy[, winding-up or administration order has been made], or a resolution for voluntary winding up has been passed, the debt—

(a) is provable in the bankruptcy[, winding up or administration] or, as the case may be, is payable to the relevant officer-holder, and

(b) shall be taken into account, where appropriate, under section 323 of the Insolvency Act 1986 (mutual dealings and set-off) or the corresponding provision applicable in the case of winding up [or administration],

in the same way as a debt due before the commencement of the bankruptcy, the date on which the body corporate goes into liquidation (within the meaning of section 247 of the Insolvency Act 1986)[, or enters administration] or, in the case of a partnership, the date of the winding-up order [or the date on which the partnership enters administration].

(3) If, in Scotland, an award of sequestration or a winding-up [or administration] order has been made, or a resolution for voluntary winding up has been passed, the debt—

(a) may be claimed in the sequestration[, winding up or administration] or, as the case may be, is payable to the relevant office-holder, and

(b) shall be taken into account for the purposes of any rule of law relating to set-off applicable in sequestration[, winding up or administration],

in the same way as a debt due before the date of sequestration (within the meaning of section [22(7) of the Bankruptcy (Scotland) Act 2016]) or the commencement of the winding up (within the meaning of section 129 of the Insolvency Act 1986) [or the date on which the body corporate enters administration].

[(3A) In subsections (2) and (3), a reference to the making of an administration order shall be taken to include a reference to the appointment of an administrator under—

(a) paragraph 14 of Schedule B1 to the Insolvency Act 1986 (appointment by holder of qualifying floating charge); or

(b) paragraph 22 of that Schedule (appointment by company or directors).]

(4) However, where (or to the extent that) a sum is taken into account by virtue of subsection (2)(b) or (3)(b) which arises from a contract entered into at a time when the creditor had notice—

(a) that [a bankruptcy application or] a bankruptcy petition or, in Scotland, a petition for sequestration was pending, . . .

(b) that [a statement as to the affairs of the company had been made out and sent under section 99] of the Insolvency Act 1986 or that a winding-up petition was pending, [or]

[(c) that an application for an administration order was pending or that any person had given notice of intention to appoint an administrator,]

the value of any profit to him arising from the sum being so taken into account (or being so taken into account to that extent) is recoverable from him by the relevant office-holder unless the court directs otherwise.

(5) Subsection (4) does not apply in relation to a sum arising from a contract effected under the default rules of [a recognised body].

(6) Any sum recoverable by virtue of subsection (4) ranks for priority, in the event of the insolvency of the person from whom it is due, immediately before preferential or, in Scotland, preferred debts.

NOTES

Sub-s (1): substituted by the Financial Services and Markets Act 2000 (Over the Counter Derivatives, Central Counterparties and Trade Repositories) Regulations 2013, SI 2013/504, reg 4(1), (8). Words in square brackets substituted by the Central Securities Depositories Regulations 2017, SI 2017/1064, reg 3(1), (10) (for transitional provisions and savings see regs 6–9 thereof).

Sub-s (2): words in first pair of square brackets substituted for original words "or winding-up order has been made", words in square brackets in para (a) substituted for original words "or winding up", words in square brackets in para (b) and words in final pairs of square brackets inserted by the Financial Markets and Insolvency Regulations 2009, SI 2009/853, reg 2(1), (7)(a), with effect in relation to specified insolvency events taking place on or after 15 June 2009, as noted to s 158 at **[17.61]**.

Sub-s (3): words "22(7) of the Bankruptcy (Scotland) Act 2016" in square brackets substituted for the original words "73(1) of the Bankruptcy (Scotland) Act 1985" by the Bankruptcy (Scotland) Act 2016 (Consequential Provisions and Modifications) Order 2016, SI 2016/1034, art 7(1), (3), Sch 1, para 6(1), (4), as from 30 November 2016 (except in relation to (i) a sequestration as regards which the petition is presented, or the debtor application is made before that date; or (ii) a trust deed executed before that date); words ", winding up or administration" (in both places that they occur) substituted and other words in square brackets inserted by SI 2009/853, reg 2(1), (7)(b), with effect in relation to specified insolvency events taking place on or after 15 June 2009, as noted to s 158 at **[17.61]**.

Sub-s (3A): inserted by SI 2009/853, reg 2(1), (7)(c), with effect in relation to specified insolvency events taking place on or after 15 June 2009, as noted to s 158 at **[17.61]**.

Sub-s (4): words in square brackets in para (a) inserted by the Enterprise and Regulatory Reform Act 2013 (Consequential Amendments) (Bankruptcy) and the Small Business, Enterprise and Employment Act 2015 (Consequential Amendments) Regulations 2016, SI 2016/481, reg 2(1), Sch 1, para 9(1), (4); the word omitted from the end of para (a) was repealed, and the word "or" at the end of para (b) was inserted together with para (c), by SI 2009/853, reg 2(1), (7)(d), with effect in relation to specified insolvency events taking place on or after 15 June 2009, as noted to s 158 at **[17.61]**; the first words in square brackets in para (b) were substituted by the Deregulation Act 2015 and Small Business, Enterprise and Employment Act 2015 (Consequential Amendments) (Savings) Regulations 2017, SI 2017/540, reg 2, Sch 1, para 2(1), (3).

Sub-s (5): words in square brackets substituted by SI 2017/1064, reg 3(1), (10) (for transitional provisions and savings see regs 6–9 thereof).

[17.67]

164 Disclaimer of property, rescission of contracts, &c

(1) Sections 178, 186, 315 and 345 of the Insolvency Act 1986 (power to disclaim onerous property and court's power to order rescission of contracts, &c) do not apply in relation to—

(a) a market contract, . . .

[(aa) a qualifying collateral arrangement,

(ab) a transfer of a clearing member client contract, a client trade or a qualifying collateral arrangement, as mentioned in paragraphs (c) to (e) of section 158(1),

(ac) a qualifying property transfer, or]

(b) a contract effected by [the recognised body] for the purpose of realising property provided as margin in relation to market contracts [or as default fund contribution].

In the application of this subsection in Scotland, the reference to sections 178, 315 and 345 shall be construed as a reference to any rule of law having the like effect as those sections.

(2) In Scotland, a [trustee in the sequestration of the] estate of a defaulter or a liquidator is bound by any market contract to which that defaulter is a party and by any contract as is mentioned in subsection (1)(b) above notwithstanding section [110 of the Bankruptcy (Scotland) Act 2016] or any rule of law to the like effect applying in liquidations.

(3) Sections 127 and 284 of the Insolvency Act 1986 (avoidance of property dispositions effected after commencement of winding up[, submission of bankruptcy application] or presentation of bankruptcy petition), and section [87(4) of the Bankruptcy (Scotland) Act 2016] (effect of dealing with debtor relating to estate vested in *permanent* trustee) do not apply to—

(a) a market contract, or any disposition of property in pursuance of such a contract,

(b) the provision of margin in relation to market contracts,

[(ba) the provision of default fund contribution to [the recognised body],]

[(bb) a qualifying collateral arrangement,

(bc) a transfer of a clearing member client contract, a client trade or a qualifying collateral arrangement, as mentioned in paragraphs (c) to (e) of section 158(1),

(bd) a qualifying property transfer]

(c) a contract effected by [the recognised body] for the purpose of realising property provided as margin in relation to a market contract [or as default fund contribution], or any disposition of property in pursuance of such a contract, or

(d) any disposition of property in accordance with the rules of [the recognised body] as to the application of property provided as margin [or as default fund contribution].

(4) However, where—

(a) a market contract is entered into by a person who has notice that [a bankruptcy application has been submitted or] a petition has been presented for the winding up or bankruptcy or sequestration of the estate of the other party to the contract, or

(b) margin in relation to a market contract [or default fund contribution] is accepted by a person who has notice that [such an application has been made or petition presented] in relation to the person by whom or on whose behalf the margin [or default fund contribution] is provided,

the value of any profit to him arising from the contract or, as the case may be, the amount or value of the margin [or default fund contribution] is recoverable from him by the relevant office-holder unless the court directs otherwise.

[(5) Subsection (4)(a) does not apply where the person entering into the contract is [a recognised body] acting in accordance with its rules, or where the contract is effected under the default rules of such [a recognised body]; but subsection (4)(b) applies in relation to the provision of—

(a) margin in relation to any such contract, unless the contract has been transferred in accordance with the default rules of the central counterparty, or

(b) default fund contribution.]

(6) Any sum recoverable by virtue of subsection (4) ranks for priority, in the event of the insolvency of the person from whom it is due, immediately before preferential or, in Scotland, preferred debts.

NOTES

The word omitted from para (a) of sub-s (1) was repealed, paras (aa)–(ac) of that subsection were inserted, paras (bb)–(bd) of sub-s (3) were inserted, and sub-s (5) was substituted, by the Financial Services and Markets Act 2000 (Over the Counter Derivatives, Central Counterparties and Trade Repositories) Regulations 2013, SI 2013/504, reg 4(1), (9).

The words "the recognised body" in square brackets in sub-s (1)(b) were substituted by the Central Securities Depositories Regulations 2017, SI 2017/1064, reg 3(1), (11)(a) (for transitional provisions and savings see regs 6–9 thereof).

The words "trustee in the sequestration of the" and "42 of the Bankruptcy (Scotland) Act 1985" in square brackets in sub-s (2) were substituted for the original words "permanent trustee on the sequestrated" and "42 of the Bankruptcy (Scotland) Act 1985" respectively, the words "87(4) of the Bankruptcy (Scotland) Act 2016" in square brackets in sub-s (3) were substituted for the original words "32(8) of the Bankruptcy (Scotland) Act 1985", and the word "permanent" in italics was repealed, by the Bankruptcy (Scotland) Act 2016 (Consequential Provisions and Modifications) Order 2016, SI 2016/1034, art 7(1), (3), Sch 1, para 6(1), (5), as from 30 November 2016 (except in relation to (i) a sequestration as regards which the petition is presented, or the debtor application is made before that date; or (ii) a trust deed executed before that date).

The words ", submission of bankruptcy application" in sub-s (3), and the words "a bankruptcy application has been submitted or" in sub-s (4)(a) were inserted, and the words "such an application has been made or petition presented" in subs-s (4)(b) were substituted, by the Enterprise and Regulatory Reform Act 2013 (Consequential Amendments) (Bankruptcy) and the Small Business, Enterprise and Employment Act 2015 (Consequential Amendments) Regulations 2016, SI 2016/481, reg 2(1), Sch 1, para 9(1), (5).

The words "the recognised body" in square brackets in sub-s (3) (in each place they occur) were substituted by SI 2017/1064, reg 3(1), (11)(b) (for transitional provisions and savings see regs 6–9 thereof).

The words "a recognised body" in square brackets in sub-s (5) (in both places they occur) were substituted by SI 2017/1064, reg 3(1), (11)(c) (for transitional provisions and savings see regs 6–9 thereof).

All other words in square brackets were inserted by the Financial Markets and Insolvency Regulations 2009, SI 2009/853, reg 2(1), (8), with effect in relation to specified insolvency events taking place on or after 15 June 2009, as noted to s 158 at **[17.61]**.

[17.68]

165 Adjustment of prior transactions

(1) No order shall be made in relation to a transaction to which this section applies under—

(a) section 238 or 339 of the Insolvency Act 1986 (transactions at an undervalue),

(b) section 239 or 340 of that Act (preferences), or

(c) section 423 of that Act (transactions defrauding creditors).

(2) As respects Scotland, no decree shall be granted in relation to any such transaction—

(a) under section [98 or 99 of the Bankruptcy (Scotland) Act 2016] or section 242 or 243 of the Insolvency Act 1986 (gratuitous alienations and unfair preferences), or

(b) at common law on grounds of gratuitous alienations or fraudulent preferences.

(3) This section applies to—

(a) a market contract to which a [recognised body] is a party or which is entered into under its default rules, . . .

[(ab) a market contract to which this Part applies by virtue of section 155(2B), and

(b) a disposition of property in pursuance of a market contract referred to in paragraph (a) or (ab).]

(4) Where margin is provided in relation to a market contract and (by virtue of subsection (3)(a)[, (3)(ab)] or otherwise) no such order or decree as is mentioned in subsection (1) or (2) has been, or could be, made in relation to that contract, this section applies to—

(a) the provision of the margin,

[(ab) a qualifying collateral arrangement,]

(b) any contract effected by [the recognised body] in question for the purpose of realising the property provided as margin, and

(c) any disposition of property in accordance with the rules of [the recognised body] [in question] as to the application of property provided as margin.

[(5) This section also applies to—

(a) the provision of default fund contribution to a [recognised body],

(b) any contract effected by a [recognised body] for the purpose of realising the property provided as default fund contribution, . . .

(c) any disposition of property in accordance with the rules of the [recognised body] as to the application of property provided as default fund [contribution,]

[(d) a transfer of a clearing member client contract, a client trade or a qualifying collateral arrangement as mentioned in paragraphs (c) to (e) of section 158(1), and

(e) a qualifying property transfer.]]

NOTES

Sub-s (2): words in square brackets substituted for the original words "34 or 36 of the Bankruptcy (Scotland) Act 1985" by the Bankruptcy (Scotland) Act 2016 (Consequential Provisions and Modifications) Order 2016, SI 2016/1034, art 7(1), (3), Sch 1, para 6(1), (6), as from 30 November 2016 (except in relation to (i) a sequestration as regards which the petition is presented, or the debtor application is made before that date; or (ii) a trust deed executed before that date).

Sub-s (3): word omitted from para (a) repealed, and paras (ab), (b) substituted (for the original para (b)), by the Financial Services and Markets Act 2000 (Over the Counter Derivatives, Central Counterparties and Trade Repositories) Regulations 2013, SI 2013/504, reg 4(1), (10)(a), (b). Words "recognised body" in square brackets in para (a) substituted by the Central Securities Depositories Regulations 2017, SI 2017/1064, reg 3(1), (12)(a) (for transitional provisions and savings see regs 6–9 thereof).

Sub-s (4): words in first pair of square brackets inserted, and para (ab) inserted, by SI 2013/504, reg 4(1), (10)(c), (d). Words in square brackets in para (b) and words in first pair of square brackets in para (c) substituted by SI 2017/1064, reg 3(1), (12)(b) (for transitional provisions and savings see regs 6–9 thereof). Words in second pair of square brackets in para (c) inserted by the Financial Markets and Insolvency Regulations 2009, SI 2009/853, reg 2(1), (9)(a), with effect in relation to specified insolvency events taking place on or after 15 June 2009, as noted to s 158 at **[17.61]**.

Sub-s (5): added by SI 2009/853, reg 2(1), (9)(b), with effect in relation to specified insolvency events taking place on or after 15 June 2009, as noted to s 158 at **[17.61]**. Words "recognised body" in square brackets in paras (a)–(c) substituted by SI 2017/1064, reg 3(1), (12)(a) (for transitional provisions and savings see regs 6–9 thereof). Word omitted from para (b) repealed, word "contribution" in square brackets in para (c) substituted, and paras (d), (e) added by SI 2013/504, reg 4(1), (10)(e)–(g).

[17.69]

166 Powers . . . to give directions

(1) The powers conferred by this section are exercisable in relation to a recognised UK investment exchange or [recognised clearing house] [or recognised CSD].

(2) Where in any case [a recognised body] has not taken action under its default rules—

(a) if it appears to the [appropriate regulator] that it could take action, [the [regulator]] may direct it to do so, and

(b) if it appears to the [appropriate regulator] that it is proposing to take or may take action, [the [regulator]] may direct it not to do so.

(3) Before giving such a direction the [appropriate regulator] shall consult the [recognised body] house in question; and [it] shall not give a direction unless [it] is satisfied, in the light of that consultation—

(a) in the case of a direction to take action, that failure to take action would involve undue risk to investors or other participants in the market, . . .

(b) in the case of a direction not to take action, that the taking of action would be premature or otherwise undesirable in the interests of investors or other participants in the market,

[(c) in either case, that the direction is necessary having regard to the public interest in the stability of the financial system of the United Kingdom, or

(d) in either case, that the direction is necessary—

(i) to facilitate a proposed or possible use of a power under Part 1 of the Banking Act 2009 (special resolution regime), or

(ii) in connection with a particular exercise of a power under that Part.]

[(3A) The appropriate regulator may give a direction to a relevant office-holder appointed in respect of a defaulting clearing member to take any action, or refrain from taking any action, if the direction is given for the purposes of facilitating—

(a) the transfer of a clearing member client contract, a client trade or a qualifying collateral arrangement, or

(b) a qualifying property transfer.

(3B) The relevant office-holder to whom a direction is given under subsection (3A)—

(a) must comply with the direction notwithstanding any duty on the relevant office-holder under any enactment relating to insolvency, but

(b) is not required to comply with the direction given if the value of the clearing member's estate is unlikely to be sufficient to meet the office-holder's reasonable expenses of complying.

(3C) The expenses of the relevant office-holder in complying with a direction of the regulator under subsection (3A) are recoverable as part of the expenses incurred in the discharge of the office-holder's duties.]

(4) A direction shall specify the grounds on which it is given.

(5) A direction not to take action may be expressed to have effect until the giving of a further direction (which may be a direction to take action or simply revoking the earlier direction).

(6) No direction shall be given not to take action if, in relation to the person in question—

(a) a bankruptcy order or an award of sequestration of his estate has been made, or an interim receiver or interim trustee has been appointed, or

(b) a winding up order has been made, a resolution for voluntary winding up has been passed or an administrator, administrative receiver or provisional liquidator has been appointed;

and any previous direction not to take action shall cease to have effect on the making or passing of any such order, award or appointment.

(7) Where [a recognised body] has taken or been directed to take action under its default rules, the [appropriate regulator] may direct it to do or not to do such things (being things which it has power to do under its default rules) as are specified in the direction.

. . .

[(7A) Where the [recognised body] is acting in accordance with a direction under subsection (2)(a) that was given only by virtue of paragraph (a) of subsection (3), the appropriate regulator shall not give a direction under subsection (7) unless it is satisfied that the direction under that subsection will not impede or frustrate the proper and efficient conduct of the default proceedings.

(7B) Where the [recognised body] has taken action under its default rules without being directed to do so, the appropriate regulator shall not give a direction under subsection (7) unless—

(a) it is satisfied that the direction under that subsection will not impede or frustrate the proper and efficient conduct of the default proceedings, or

(b) it is satisfied that the direction is necessary—

(i) having regard to the public interest in the stability of the financial system of the United Kingdom,

(ii) to facilitate a proposed or possible use of a power under Part 1 of the Banking Act 2009 (special resolution regime), or

(iii) in connection with a particular exercise of a power under that Part.]

(8) A direction under this section is enforceable, on the application of the [regulator which gave the direction], by injunction or, in Scotland, by an order under section 45 of the Court of Session Act 1988; and where [a recognised body] [or a relevant office-holder] has not complied with a direction, the court may make such order as it thinks fit for restoring the position to what it would have been if the direction had been complied with.

[(9) "The appropriate regulator"—

(a) in relation to a recognised UK investment exchange, means the FCA, and

(b) in relation to a [recognised CSD, a] [recognised clearing house] [or a defaulting clearing member], means the Bank of England.]

NOTES

Section heading: words omitted repealed by the Financial Services Act 2012, s 111(1), (9).

Sub-s (1): words in first pair of square brackets substituted by the Financial Services and Markets Act 2000 (Over the Counter Derivatives, Central Counterparties and Trade Repositories) Regulations 2013, SI 2013/504, reg 4(1), (11)(a). Words in second pair of square brackets inserted by the Central Securities Depositories Regulations 2017, SI 2017/1064, reg 3(1), (13)(a) (for transitional provisions and savings see regs 6–9 thereof).

Sub-s (2): words "a recognised body" in square brackets substituted by SI 2017/1064, reg 3(1), (13)(b) (for transitional provisions and savings see regs 6–9 thereof). In each of paras (a), (b), words in first and third (inner) pairs of square brackets substituted by the Financial Services Act 2012, s 111(1)–(3), and words in second (outer) pair of square brackets substituted by the Financial Services and Markets Act 2000 (Consequential Amendments and Repeals) Order 2001, SI 2001/3649, art 81(1), (2).

Sub-s (3): words in first pair of square brackets substituted, word omitted from para (a) repealed and paras (c), (d) inserted by the Financial Services Act 2012, s 111(1), (4). Words in second pair of square brackets substituted by SI 2017/1064, reg 3(1), (13)(c) (for transitional provisions and savings see regs 6–9 thereof). Words in third and fourth pairs of square brackets substituted by the Financial Services and Markets Act 2000 (Consequential Amendments and Repeals) Order 2001, SI 2001/3649, art 81(1), (3).

Sub-ss (3A)–(3C): inserted by SI 2013/504, reg 4(1), (11)(b).

Sub-s (7): words "a recognised body" in square brackets substituted by SI 2017/1064, reg 3(1), (13)(b) (for transitional provisions and savings see regs 6–9 thereof). Other words in square brackets substituted, and words omitted repealed, by the Financial Services Act 2012, s 111(1), (5).

Sub-ss (7A), (7B): inserted by the Financial Services Act 2012, s 111(1), (6). Words in square brackets substituted by SI 2017/1064, reg 3(1), (13)(c) (for transitional provisions and savings see regs 6–9 thereof).

Sub-s (8): words in first pair of square brackets substituted by the Financial Services Act 2012, s 111(1), (7). Words in second pair of square brackets substituted by SI 2017/1064, reg 3(1), (13)(d) (for transitional provisions and savings see regs 6–9 thereof). Words in final pair of square brackets substituted by virtue of SI 2013/504, reg 4(1), (11)(c).

Sub-s (9): added by the Financial Services Act 2012, s 111(1), (8). Words in first pair of square brackets substituted by SI 2017/1064, reg 3(1), (13)(c) (for transitional provisions and savings see regs 6–9 thereof). Words in second pair of square brackets inserted by SI 2013/504, reg 4(1), (11)(e). Words in final pair of square brackets inserted by the Financial Services and Markets Act 2000 (Over the Counter Derivatives, Central Counterparties and Trade Repositories) (No 2) Regulations 2013, SI 2013/1908, reg 2(1), (6).

Transitional provisions: see further the Financial Services Act 2012 (Transitional Provisions) (Miscellaneous Provisions) Order 2013, SI 2013/442, art 67 at **[18.286]**.

[17.70]
167 Application to determine whether default proceedings to be taken

[(1) This section applies where a relevant insolvency event has occurred in the case of—

(a) a recognised investment exchange or a member or designated non-member of a recognised investment exchange, . . .

(b) a recognised clearing house or a member of a recognised clearing house[; . . .

[(ba) a recognised CSD or a member of a recognised CSD, or]

(c) a client which is providing indirect clearing services to an indirect client.]

[The person referred to in paragraphs (a) to (c)] in whose case a relevant insolvency event has occurred is referred to below as "the person in default".

(1A) For the purposes of this section a "relevant insolvency event" occurs where—

(a) a bankruptcy order is made,

(b) an award of sequestration is made,

(c) an order appointing an interim receiver is made,

(d) an administration or winding up order is made,

(e) an administrator is appointed under paragraph 14 of Schedule B1 to the Insolvency Act 1986 (appointment by holder of qualifying floating charge) or under paragraph 22 of that Schedule (appointment by company or directors),

(f) a resolution for voluntary winding up is passed, or

(g) an order appointing a provisional liquidator is made.

(1B) Where in relation to a person in default [a recognised body] ("[the responsible recognised body]")—

(a) has power under its default rules to take action in consequence of the relevant insolvency event or the matters giving rise to it, but

(b) has not done so,

a relevant office-holder appointed in connection with or in consequence of the relevant insolvency event may apply to the [appropriate regulator].]

(2) The application shall specify [the responsible recognised body] and the grounds on which it is made.

(3) On receipt of the application the [appropriate regulator] shall notify [the responsible recognised body], and unless within three business days after the day on which the notice is received [the responsible recognised body]—

(a) takes action under its default rules, or

(b) notifies the [appropriate regulator] that it proposes to do so forthwith,

then, subject as follows, the provisions of sections 158 to 165 above do not apply in relation to market contracts to which [the person in default] is a party or to anything done by [the responsible recognised body] for the purposes of, or in connection with, the settlement of any such contract.

For this purpose a "business day" means any day which is not a Saturday or Sunday, Christmas Day, Good Friday or a bank holiday in any part of the United Kingdom under the Banking and Financial Dealings Act 1971.

(4) The provisions of sections 158 to 165 are not disapplied if before the end of the period mentioned in subsection (3) the [appropriate regulator] gives [the responsible recognised body] a direction under section 166(2)(a) (direction to take action under default rules).

No such direction may be given after the end of that period.

(5) If [the responsible recognised body] notifies the [appropriate regulator] that it proposes to take action under its default rules forthwith, it shall do so; and that duty is enforceable, on the application of the [appropriate regulator], by injunction or, in Scotland, by an order under section 45 of the Court of Session Act 1988.

[(6) "The appropriate regulator"—

(a) in relation to a recognised investment exchange, means the FCA, and

(b) in relation to a recognised clearing house or recognised CSD, means the Bank of England.]

NOTES

Sub-ss (1), (1A), (1B): substituted for sub-ss (1), (1A), by the Financial Markets and Insolvency Regulations 2009, SI 2009/853, reg 2(1), (10)(a), with effect in relation to specified insolvency events taking place on or after 15 June 2009, as noted to s 158 at **[17.61]**.

Sub-s (1): word omitted from para (a) repealed, para (c) and word immediately preceding it inserted and words in final pair of square brackets substituted, by the Financial Services and Markets Act 2000 (Over the Counter Derivatives, Central Counterparties and Trade Repositories) (No 2) Regulations 2013, SI 2013/1908, reg 2(1), (7). Word omitted from para (b) repealed, para (ba) inserted, and words "The person referred to in paragraphs (a) to (c)" in square brackets substituted, by the Central Securities Depositories Regulations 2017, SI 2017/1064, reg 3(1), (14)(a) (for transitional provisions and savings see regs 6–9 thereof).

Sub-s (1A): substituted as noted to sub-s (1) above.

Sub-s (1B): substituted as noted to sub-s (1) above. Words in first and second pairs of square brackets substituted by SI 2017/1064, reg 3(1), (14)(b), (c) (for transitional provisions and savings see regs 6–9 thereof). Words in final pair of square brackets substituted by the Financial Services Act 2012, s 114(1), Sch 18, Pt 2, paras 62, 67(1), (2).

Sub-s (2): words in square brackets substituted by SI 2017/1064, reg 3(1), (14)(c) (for transitional provisions and savings see regs 6–9 thereof).

Sub-ss (3)–(5): words "appropriate regulator" in square brackets (in each place they occur) substituted by the Financial Services Act 2012, s 114(1), Sch 18, Pt 2, paras 62, 67(1), (2). Words "the responsible recognised body" in square brackets (in each place they occur) substituted by 2017/1064, reg 3(1), (14)(c) (for transitional provisions and savings see regs 6–9 thereof). Other words in square brackets substituted by SI 2009/853, reg 2(1), (10)(c), (d), with effect in relation to specified insolvency events taking place on or after 15 June 2009, as noted to s 158 at **[17.61]**.

Sub-s (6): added by the Financial Services Act 2012, s 114(1), Sch 18, Pt 2, paras 62, 67(1), (3). Substituted by SI 2017/1064, reg 3(1), (14)(d) (for transitional provisions and savings see regs 6–9 thereof).

Transitional provisions: see further the Financial Services Act 2012 (Transitional Provisions) (Miscellaneous Provisions) Order 2013, SI 2013/442, arts 67, 68 at **[18.284]**, **[18.285]**.

168 (*Repealed by the Financial Services and Markets Act 2000 (Consequential Amendments and Repeals) Order 2001, SI 2001/3649, art 75(f).*)

[17.71]

169 Supplementary provisions

(1) . . .

(2) [Sections 296 and 297 of the Financial Services and Markets Act 2000 apply] in relation to a failure by a recognised investment exchange or recognised clearing house to comply with an obligation under this Part as to a failure to comply with an obligation under that Act.

[(2A) Section 296 of the Financial Services and Markets Act 2000 applies in relation to a failure by a recognised CSD to comply with an obligation under this Part as to a failure to comply with an obligation under that Act.]

(3) Where the recognition of [an investment exchange, clearing house or central securities depository] is revoked under the [Financial Services and Markets Act 2000, the appropriate authority] may, before or after the revocation order, give such directions as [it] thinks fit with respect to the continued application of the provisions of this Part, with such exceptions, additions and adaptations as may be specified in the direction, in relation to cases where a relevant event of any description specified in the directions occurred before the revocation order takes effect.

[(3A) "The appropriate authority" means—

(a) in the case of an overseas investment exchange or clearing house, the Treasury;

[(b) in the case of a UK investment exchange, the FCA, . . .

(c) in the case of a UK clearing house, the Bank of England];[and

(d) in the case of a central securities depository, the Bank of England].]

(4) . . .

(5) [Regulations under section 414 of the Financial Services and Markets Act 2000 (service of notices) may make provision] in relation to a notice, direction or other document required or authorised by or under this Part to be given to or served on any person other than the [Treasury[, the FCA or the Bank of England]].

NOTES

Sub-s (1): repealed by the Financial Services and Markets Act 2000 (Consequential Amendments and Repeals) Order 2001, SI 2001/3649, art 75(g).

Sub-s (2): words in square brackets substituted by SI 2001/3649, art 83(1)–(3).

Sub-s (2A): inserted by the Central Securities Depositories Regulations 2017, SI 2017/1064, reg 3(1), (15)(a) (for transitional provisions and savings see regs 6–9 thereof).

Sub-s (3): words "an investment exchange, clearing house or central securities depository" in square brackets substituted by SI 2017/1064, reg 3(1), (15)(b), (for transitional provisions and savings see regs 6–9 thereof). Other words in square brackets substituted by SI 2001/3649, art 83(1)–(3).

Sub-s (3A): inserted by SI 2001/3649, art 83(1), (4). Paras (b), (c) substituted (for the original para (b) and the word immediately preceding it) by the Financial Services Act 2012, s 114(1), Sch 18, Pt 2, paras 62, 68(1), (2). Word omitted from para (b) repealed, and para (d) (and the preceding word) inserted by SI 2017/1064, reg 3(1), (15)(c) (for transitional provisions and savings see regs 6–9 thereof).

Sub-s (4): repealed (without having been brought into force) by SI 2001/3649, art 75(g).

Sub-s (5): words in first and second (outer) pair of square brackets substituted by SI 2001/3649, art 83(1), (5); words in second (inner) pair of square brackets substituted by the Financial Services Act 2012, s 114(1), Sch 18, Pt 2, paras 62, 68(1), (3).

Other exchanges and clearing houses

[17.72]

170 Certain overseas exchanges and clearing houses

[(1) The Secretary of State and the Treasury may by regulations provide that this Part applies in relation to contracts connected with an overseas investment exchange or overseas clearing house which—

(a) is not a recognised investment exchange or recognised clearing house, but

(b) is approved by the Treasury in accordance with such requirements as may be so specified,

as it applies in relation to contracts connected with a recognised investment exchange or recognised clearing house.]

(2) The [Treasury] shall not approve an overseas investment exchange or clearing house unless [they are] satisfied—

(a) that the rules and practices of the body, together with the law of the country in which the body's head office is situated, provide adequate procedures for dealing with the default of persons party to contracts connected with the body, and

(b) that it is otherwise appropriate to approve the body.

(3) The reference in subsection (2)(a) to default is to a person being unable to meet his obligations.

(4) The regulations may apply in relation to the approval of a body under this section such of the provisions of the [Financial Services and Markets Act 2000] as the Secretary of State considers appropriate.

(5) The Secretary of State may make regulations which, in relation to a body which is so approved—

(a) apply such of the provisions of the [Financial Services and Markets Act 2000] as the Secretary of State considers appropriate, and

(b) provide that the provisions of this Part apply with such exceptions, additions and adaptations as appear to the Secretary of State to be necessary or expedient;

and different provision may be made with respect to different bodies or descriptions of body.

(6) Where the regulations apply any provisions of the [Financial Services and Markets Act 2000], they may provide that those provisions apply with such exceptions, additions and adaptations as appear to the Secretary of State to be necessary or expedient.

NOTES

Commencement: Pt VII (ss 154–191, Schs 21, 22) came into force on 25 March 1991 in so far as is necessary to enable regulations to be made under ss 155(4), (5), 158(4), (5), 160(5), 173(4), (5), 174(2)–(4), 185, 186, 187(3), Sch 21, para 2(3); no order has subsequently been made bringing this section into force.

Sub-s (1): substituted by the Financial Markets and Insolvency Regulations 2009, SI 2009/853, reg 2(1), (11).

Sub-ss (2), (4)–(6): words in square brackets substituted by the Financial Services and Markets Act 2000 (Consequential Amendments and Repeals) Order 2001, SI 2001/3649, art 84(1), (3), (4).

[17.73]

[170A EEA central counterparties and third country central counterparties

(1) In this section and section 170B—

(a) "assets" has the meaning given by Article 39(10) of the EMIR Level 1 Regulation;

(b) "EBA" means the European Banking Authority established by Regulation 1093/2010/EU of 24 November 2010 establishing a European Supervisory Authority (European Banking Authority);

(c) "ESMA" means the European Securities and Markets Authority established by Regulation 1095/2010/EU of 24 November 2010 establishing a European Supervisory Authority (European Securities and Markets Authority);

(d) "overseas competent authority" means a competent authority responsible for the authorisation or supervision of clearing houses or central counterparties in a country or territory other than the United Kingdom;

(e) "relevant provisions" means any provisions of the default rules of an EEA central counterparty or third country central counterparty which—

(i) provide for the transfer of the positions or assets of a defaulting clearing member;

(ii) are not necessary for the purposes of complying with the minimum requirements of Articles 48(5) and (6) of the EMIR Level 1 Regulation; and

(iii) may be relevant to a question falling to be determined in accordance with the law of a part of the United Kingdom;

(f) "relevant requirements" means the requirements specified in paragraph 34(2) (portability of accounts: default rules going beyond requirements of EMIR) of Part 6 of the Schedule to the Financial Services and Markets Act 2000 (Recognition Requirements for Investment Exchanges[, Clearing Houses and Central Securities Depositories]) Regulations 2001;

(g) "UK clearing member" means a clearing member to which the law of a part of the United Kingdom will apply for the purposes of an insolvent reorganisation or winding up[, and

(h) "UK client" means a client—

(i) which offers indirect clearing services, and
(ii) to which the law of a part of the United Kingdom will apply for the purposes of an insolvent re-organisation or winding up].

(2) This Part applies to transactions cleared through an EEA central counterparty or a third country central counterparty by a UK clearing member [or a UK client] as it applies to transactions cleared through a recognised central counterparty, but subject to the modifications in subsections (3) to (5).

(3) For section 157 there is to be substituted—

> **"157 Change in default rules**
>
> (1) An EEA central counterparty or a third country central counterparty in respect of which an order under section 170B(4) has been made and not revoked must give the Bank of England at least three months' notice of any proposal to amend, revoke or add to its default rules.
>
> (2) The Bank of England may, if it considers it appropriate to do so, agree a shorter period of notice.
>
> (3) Where notice is given to the Bank of England under subsection (1) an EEA central counterparty or third country central counterparty must provide the Bank of England with such information, documents and reports as the Bank of England may require.
>
> (4) Information, documents and reports required under subsection (3) must be provided in English and be given at such times, in such form and at such place, and verified in such a manner, as the Bank of England may direct."

(4) Section 162 does not apply to an EEA central counterparty or a third country central counterparty unless it has been notified by the Bank of England that a report under that section is required for the purposes of insolvency proceedings in any part of the United Kingdom.

(5) In relation to an EEA central counterparty or third country central counterparty, references in this Part to the "rules" or "default rules" of the central counterparty are to be taken not to include references to any relevant provisions unless—

(a) the relevant provisions satisfy the relevant requirements; or
(b) the Bank of England has made an order under section 170B(4) recognising that the relevant provisions of its default rules satisfy the relevant requirements and the order has not been revoked.]

NOTES

Inserted, together with s 170B at **[17.74]**, by the Financial Services and Markets Act 2000 (Over the Counter Derivatives, Central Counterparties and Trade Repositories) Regulations 2013, SI 2013/504, reg 4(1), (12).

Words in square brackets in sub-s (1)(f) inserted by the Central Securities Depositories Regulations 2017, SI 2017/1064, reg 3(1), (16) (for transitional provisions and savings see regs 6–9 thereof).

Sub-s (1): para (h) and word immediately preceding it inserted by the Financial Services and Markets Act 2000 (Over the Counter Derivatives, Central Counterparties and Trade Repositories) (No 2) Regulations 2013, SI 2013/1908, reg 2(1), (8)(a).

Sub-s (2): words in square brackets inserted by SI 2013/1908, reg 2(1), (8)(b).

[17.74]

[170B EEA central counterparties and third country central counterparties: procedure

(1) An EEA central counterparty or third country central counterparty may apply to the Bank of England for an order recognising that the relevant provisions of its default rules satisfy the relevant requirements.

(2) The application must be made in such manner, and must be accompanied by such information, documents and reports, as the Bank of England may direct.

(3) Information, documents and reports required under subsection (2) must be provided in English and be given at such times, in such form and at such place, and verified in such manner, as the Bank of England may direct.

(4) The Bank of England may make an order recognising that the relevant provisions of the default rules satisfy the relevant requirements.

(5) The Bank of England may by order revoke an order made under subsection (4) if—

(a) the EEA central counterparty or third country central counterparty consents;
(b) the EEA central counterparty or third country central counterparty has failed to pay a fee which is owing to the Bank of England under paragraph 36 of Schedule 17A to the Financial Services and Markets Act 2000;
(c) the EEA central counterparty or third country central counterparty is failing or has failed to comply with a requirement of or imposed under section 157 (as modified by section 170A(3)); or
(d) it appears to the Bank of England that the relevant provisions no longer satisfy the relevant requirements.

(6) An order made under subsection (4) or (5) must state the time and date when it is to have effect.

(7) An order made under subsection (5) may contain such transitional provision as the Bank of England considers appropriate.

(8) The Bank of England must—

(a) maintain a register of orders made under subsection (4) which are in force; and
(b) publish the register in such manner as it appears to the Bank of England to be appropriate.

(9) Section 298 of the Financial Services and Markets Act 2000 applies to a refusal to make an order under subsection (4) or the making of a revocation order under subsection (5)(b), (c) or (d) as it applies to the making of a revocation order under section 297(2) of the Financial Services and Markets Act 2000, but with the following modifications—

(a) for "appropriate regulator" substitute "the Bank of England";
(b) for "recognised body" substitute "EEA central counterparty or third country central counterparty"; and
(c) in subsection (7), for "give a direction under section 296" substitute "make an order under paragraph (b), (c) or (d) of section 170B(5) of the Companies Act 1989".

(10) If the Bank of England refuses to make an order under subsection (4) or makes an order under subsection (5)(b), (c) or (d), the EEA central counterparty or third country central counterparty may refer the matter to the Upper Tribunal.

(11) The Bank of England may rely on information or advice from an overseas competent authority, the EBA or ESMA in its determination of an application under subsection (1) or the making of a revocation order under subsection (5)(d).]

NOTES

Inserted as noted to s 170A at **[17.73]**.

[17.74A]

[170C EEA CSDs and third country CSDs

(1) This Part applies to transactions settled through an EEA CSD or a third country CSD by a UK member of the central securities depository as it applies to transactions settled through a recognised CSD, but subject to subsections (2), (3) and (4).

(2) The definition of "authorised central securities depository services" in section 155(3D) applies to third country CSDs as if it read—

""authorised central securities depository services" means, in relation to a third country CSD, those services which that central securities depository is authorised to provide that are equivalent to the services listed in the Annex to the CSD regulation.".

(3) Section 157 does not apply to an EEA CSD or a third country CSD.

(4) Section 162 does not apply to an EEA CSD or a third country CSD unless it has been notified by the Bank of England that a report under that section is required for the purposes of insolvency proceedings in any part of the United Kingdom. Where an EEA CSD or a third country CSD has been so notified, the appropriate regulator for the purposes of section 162 shall be the Bank of England.

(5) In this section "UK member" means a member of an EEA CSD or a third country CSD to which the law of a part of the United Kingdom will apply for the purposes of an insolvent reorganisation or winding up.]

NOTES

Commencement: 28 November 2017.

Inserted by the Central Securities Depositories Regulations 2017, SI 2017/1064, reg 3(1), (17) (for transitional provisions and savings see regs 6–9 thereof).

171 (*Repealed by the Financial Services and Markets Act 2000 (Consequential Amendments and Repeals) Order 2001, SI 2001/3649, art 75(h), subject to a saving in the Financial Services and Markets Act 2000 (Miscellaneous Provisions) Order 2001, SI 2001/3650, art 24(1), (2), that s 171(6A) shall continue to have effect in relation to things done or omitted to be done before 1 December 2001, and in relation to anything done on or after that date for the purposes of or in connection with any proceedings arising from anything done or omitted to be done before 1 December 2001.*)

[17.75]

172 Settlement arrangements provided by the Bank of England

(1) The Secretary of State may by regulations provide that this Part applies to contracts of any specified description in relation to which settlement arrangements are provided by the Bank of England, as it applies to contracts connected with [a recognised body].

(2) Regulations under this section may provide that the provisions of this Part apply with such exceptions, additions and adaptations as appear to the Secretary of State to be necessary or expedient.

(3) Before making any regulations under this section, the Secretary of State [and the Treasury shall consult] the Bank of England.

NOTES

Commencement: Pt VII (ss 154–191, Schs 21, 22) came into force on 25 March 1991 in so far as is necessary to enable regulations to be made under ss 155(4), (5), 158(4), (5), 160(5), 173(4), (5), 174(2)–(4), 185, 186, 187(3), Sch 21, para 2(3); no order has subsequently been made bringing this section into force.

Sub-s (1): words in square brackets substituted by the Central Securities Depositories Regulations 2017, SI 2017/1064, reg 3(1), (18) (for transitional provisions and savings see regs 6–9 thereof).

Sub-s (3): words in square brackets substituted by the Transfer of Functions (Financial Services) Order 1992, SI 1992/1315, art 10(1), Sch 4, para 13.

Market charges

[17.76]

173 Market charges

(1) In this Part "market charge" means a charge whether fixed or floating, granted—

(a) in favour of a recognised investment exchange, for the purpose of securing debts or liabilities arising in connection with the settlement of market contracts,

[(aa) in favour of The Stock Exchange, for the purpose of securing debts or liabilities arising in connection with short term certificates;]

(b) in favour of a recognised clearing house, for the purpose of securing debts or liabilities arising in connection with their ensuring the performance of market contracts, . . .

[(ba) in favour of a recognised CSD, for the purpose of securing debts or liabilities arising in connection with their ensuring the performance of market contracts, or]

(c) in favour of a person who agrees to make payments as a result of the transfer [or allotment] of specified securities made through the medium of a computer-based system established by the Bank of England and The Stock Exchange, for the purpose of securing debts or liabilities of the transferee [or allottee] arising in connection therewith.

(2) Where a charge is granted partly for purposes specified in subsection (1)(a), [(aa),] (b)[, (ba)] or (c) and partly for other purposes, it is a "market charge" so far as it has effect for the specified purposes.

(3) [In subsection (1)—

"short term certificate" means an instrument issued by The Stock Exchange undertaking to procure the transfer of property of a value and description specified in the instrument to or to the order of the person to whom the instrument is issued or his endorsee or to a person acting on behalf of either of them and also undertaking to make appropriate payments in cash, in the event that the obligation to procure the transfer of property cannot be discharged in whole or in part;]

"specified securities" means securities for the time being specified in the list in Schedule 1 to the Stock Transfer Act 1982, and includes any right to such securities; and

"transfer", in relation to any such securities or right, means a transfer of the beneficial interest.

(4) The Secretary of State may by regulations make further provision as to the charges granted in favour of any such person as is mentioned in subsection (1)(a), (b)[, (ba)] or (c) which are to be treated as "market charges" for the purposes of this Part; and the regulations may add to, amend or repeal the provisions of subsections (1) to (3) above.

(5) The regulations may provide that a charge shall or shall not be treated as a market charge if or to the extent that it secures obligations of a specified description, is a charge over property of a specified description or contains provisions of a specified description.

(6) Before making regulations under this section in relation to charges granted in favour of a person within subsection (1)(c), the Secretary of State [and the Treasury shall consult] the Bank of England.

NOTES

Sub-s (1): para (aa) and the words in square brackets in para (c) inserted by the Financial Markets and Insolvency Regulations 1991, SI 1991/880, reg 9(a), (b). Word omitted from para (b) repealed, and para (ba) inserted, by the Central Securities Depositories Regulations 2017, SI 2017/1064, reg 3(1), (19)(a) (for transitional provisions and savings see regs 6–9 thereof).

Sub-s (2): reference to "(aa)" in square brackets inserted by SI 1991/880, reg 9(c). Reference ", (ba)" in square brackets inserted by SI 2017/1064, reg 3(1), (19)(b) (for transitional provisions and savings see regs 6–9 thereof).

Sub-s (3): words in square brackets substituted by SI 1991/880, reg 9(d).

Sub-s (4): reference ", (ba)" in square brackets inserted by SI 2017/1064, reg 3(1), (19)(b) (for transitional provisions and savings see regs 6–9 thereof).

Sub-s (6): words in square brackets substituted by the Transfer of Functions (Financial Services) Order 1992, SI 1992/1315, art 10(1), Sch 4, para 13.

Regulations: the Financial Markets and Insolvency Regulations 1991, SI 1991/880 at **[9.1]**; the Financial Markets and Insolvency (CGO Service) Regulations 1999, SI 1999/1209.

[17.77]

174 Modifications of the law of insolvency

(1) The general law of insolvency has effect in relation to market charges and action taken in enforcing them subject to the provisions of section 175.

(2) The Secretary of State may by regulations make further provision modifying the law of insolvency in relation to the matters mentioned in subsection (1).

(3) The regulations may add to, amend or repeal the provisions mentioned in subsection (1), and any other provision of this Part as it applies for the purposes of those provisions, or provide that those provisions have effect with such exceptions, additions or adaptations as are specified in the regulations.

(4) The regulations may make different provision for cases defined by reference to the nature of the charge, the nature of the property subject to it, the circumstances, nature or extent of the obligations secured by it or any other relevant factor.

(5) Before making regulations under this section in relation to charges granted in favour of a person within section 173(1)(c), the Secretary of State [and the Treasury shall consult] the Bank of England.

NOTES

Sub-s (5): words in square brackets substituted by the Transfer of Functions (Financial Services) Order 1992, SI 1992/1315, art 10(1), Sch 4, para 13.

Regulations: the Financial Markets and Insolvency Regulations 1991, SI 1991/880 at **[9.1]**; the Financial Markets and Insolvency (CGO Service) Regulations 1999, SI 1999/1209; the Financial Services and Markets Act 2000 (Over the Counter Derivatives, Central Counterparties and Trade Repositories) Regulations 2013, SI 2013/504.

[17.78]

175 Administration orders, &c

[(1) The following provisions of Schedule B1 to the Insolvency Act 1986 (administration) do not apply in relation to a market charge—

(a) paragraph 43(2) and (3) (restriction on enforcement of security or repossession of goods) (including that provision as applied by paragraph 44 (interim moratorium)), and

(b) paragraphs 70, 71 and 72 (power of administrator to deal with charged or hire-purchase property).

(1A) Paragraph 41(2) of that Schedule (receiver to vacate office at request of administrator) does not apply to a receiver appointed under a market charge.]

(2) However, where a market charge falls to be enforced after [the occurrence of an event to which subsection (2A) applies], and there exists another charge over some or all of the same property ranking in priority to or *pari passu* with the market charge, [on the application of any person interested] the court may order that there shall be taken after enforcement of the market charge such steps as the court may direct for the purpose of ensuring that the chargee under the other charge is not prejudiced by the enforcement of the market charge.

[(2A) This subsection applies to—

(a) making an administration application under paragraph 12 of Schedule B1 to the Insolvency Act 1986,

(b) appointing an administrator under paragraph 14 or 22 of that Schedule (appointment by floating charge holder, company or directors),

(c) filing with the court a copy of notice of intention to appoint an administrator under either of those paragraphs.]

(3) The following provisions of the Insolvency Act 1986 (which relate to the powers of receivers) do not apply in relation to a market charge—

(a) section 43 (power of administrative receiver to dispose of charged property), and

(b) section 61 (power of receiver in Scotland to dispose of an interest in property).

(4) Sections 127 and 284 of the Insolvency Act 1986 (avoidance of property dispositions effected after commencement of winding up[, making of bankruptcy application] or presentation of bankruptcy petition), and section [87(4) of the Bankruptcy (Scotland) Act 2016] (effect of dealing with debtor relating to estate vested in . . . trustee), do not apply to a disposition of property as a result of which the property becomes subject to a market charge or any transaction pursuant to which that disposition is made.

[(5) However, if a person who is party to a disposition mentioned in subsection (4) has notice at the time of the disposition that a petition has been presented for the winding up or bankruptcy or sequestration of the estate of the party making the disposition, the value of any profit to him arising from the disposition is recoverable from him by the relevant office-holder unless—

(a) the person is a chargee under the market charge,

(b) the disposition is made in accordance with the default rules of a recognised central counterparty for the purposes of transferring a position or asset of a clearing member in default, or

(c) the court directs otherwise.]

[(5A) In subsection (5)(b), "asset" has the meaning given by Article 39(10) of the EMIR Level 1 Regulation.]

(6) Any sum recoverable by virtue of subsection (5) ranks for priority, in the event of the insolvency of the person from whom it is due, immediately before preferential or, in Scotland, preferred debts.

(7) In a case falling within both subsection (4) above (as a disposition of property as a result of which the property becomes subject to a market charge) and section 164(3) (as the provision of margin in relation to a market contract), section 164(4) applies with respect to the recovery of the amount or value of the margin and subsection (5) above does not apply.

NOTES

Sub-ss (1), (1A): substituted for original sub-s (1) by the Enterprise Act 2002, s 248(3), Sch 17, paras 43, 47(1), (2), subject to savings and transitional provisions (i) in a case where a petition for an administration order has been presented before 15 September 2003 (see the Enterprise Act 2002 (Commencement No 4 and Transitional Provisions and Savings) Order 2003, SI 2003/2093, art 3 at **[2.26]**), and (ii) in relation to special administration regimes (see s 249 of the 2002 Act at **[2.10]**).

Note that the original sub-s (1) (as it continues to apply to special administration regimes by virtue of the Enterprise Act 2002, s 249(1)) is further substituted by the Financial Markets and Insolvency Regulations 2009, SI 2009/853, reg 2(1), (12) with effect in relation to specified insolvency events taking place on or after 15 June 2009, as noted to s 158 at **[17.61]**, as follows:

"(1) The following provisions of the Insolvency Act 1986 (which relate to administration orders and administrators) do not apply in relation to a market charge—

(a) sections 10 and 11 (effect of application for administration order and of an administration order), and

(b) section 15(1), (2) and (3) (power of administrator to deal with charged property).".

Sub-s (2): words in first pair of square brackets substituted for original words "an administration order has been made or a petition for an administration order has been presented" by the Enterprise Act 2002, s 248(3), Sch 17, paras 43, 47(1), (3), subject to savings and transitional provisions as noted to sub-ss (1), (1A) above; words in second pair of square brackets inserted by the Financial Markets and Insolvency Regulations 1991, SI 1991/880, reg 18.

Sub-s (2A): inserted by the Enterprise Act 2002, s 248(3), Sch 17, paras 43, 47(1), (4), subject to savings and transitional provisions as noted to sub-ss (1), (1A) above.

Sub-s (4): words in first pair of square brackets inserted by the Enterprise and Regulatory Reform Act 2013 (Consequential Amendments) (Bankruptcy) and the Small Business, Enterprise and Employment Act 2015 (Consequential Amendments) Regulations 2016, SI 2016/481, reg 2(1), Sch 1, para 9(1), (6)(a); words in second pair of square brackets substituted for the original words "32(8) of the Bankruptcy (Scotland) Act 1985", and word "permanent" (omitted) repealed, by the Bankruptcy (Scotland) Act 2016 (Consequential Provisions and Modifications) Order 2016, SI 2016/1034, art 7(1), (3), Sch 1, para 6(1), (7), as from 30 November 2016 (except in relation to (i) a sequestration as regards which the petition is presented, or the debtor application is made before that date; or (ii) a trust deed executed before that date).

Sub-s (5): substituted by the Financial Services and Markets Act 2000 (Over the Counter Derivatives, Central Counterparties and Trade Repositories) Regulations 2013, SI 2013/504, reg 4(1), (13).

Sub-s (5A): inserted by SI 2013/504, reg 4(1), (14).

[17.79]

176 Power to make provision about certain other charges

(1) The Secretary of State may by regulations provide that the general law of insolvency has effect in relation to charges of such descriptions as may be specified in the regulations, and action taken in enforcing them, subject to such provisions as may be specified in the regulations.

(2) The regulations may specify any description of charge granted in favour of—

(a) a body approved under section 170 (certain overseas exchanges and clearing houses),

[(aa) an EEA CSD or a third country CSD,]

(b) a person included in the list maintained by the [. . . [Bank of England]] for the purposes of [section 301 of the Financial Services and Markets Act 2000] (certain money market institutions),

(c) the Bank of England,

[(d) a person who has permission under [Part 4A] of the Financial Services and Markets Act 2000 to carry on a relevant regulated activity, or

(e) an international securities self-regulating organisation approved for the purposes of an order made under section 22 of the Financial Services and Markets Act 2000,]

for the purpose of securing debts or liabilities arising in connection with or as a result of the settlement of contracts or the transfer of assets, rights or interests on a financial market.

(3) The regulations may specify any description of charge granted for that purpose in favour of any other person in connection with exchange facilities or clearing services [or settlement arrangements] provided by a recognised investment exchange or recognised clearing house or by any such body, person, authority or organisation as is mentioned in subsection (2)[, or in connection with authorised central securities depository services (see section 155(3D)) provided by a recognised CSD].

(4) Where a charge is granted partly for the purpose specified in subsection (2) and partly for other purposes, the power conferred by this section is exercisable in relation to the charge so far as it has effect for that purpose.

(5) The regulations may—

(a) make the same or similar provision in relation to the charges to which they apply as is made by or under sections 174 and 175 in relation to market charges, or

(b) apply any of those provisions with such exceptions, additions or adaptations as are specified in the regulations.

[(6) Before making regulations under this section relating to a description of charges defined by reference to their being granted in favour of a person included in the list maintained by the . . . [Bank of England] for the purposes of [section 301 of the Financial Services and Markets Act 2000], or in connection with exchange facilities or clearing services [or settlement arrangements] provided by a person included in that list, the Secretary of State and the Treasury shall consult the [FCA] and the Bank of England.

(6A) Before making regulations under this section relating to a description of charges defined by reference to their being granted in favour of the Bank of England, or in connection with settlement arrangements provided by the Bank, the Secretary of State and the Treasury shall consult the Bank.]

(7) Regulations under this section may provide that they apply or do not apply to a charge if or to the extent that it secures obligations of a specified description, is a charge over property of a specified description or contains provisions of a specified description.

[(8) For the purposes of subsection (2)(d), "relevant regulated activity" means—

(a) dealing in investments as principal or as agent;

(b) arranging deals in investments;

[(ba) operating a multilateral trading facility;]

[(bb) operating an organised trading facility;]

(c) managing investments;

(d) safeguarding and administering investments;

(e) sending dematerialised instructions; . . .

[(ea) managing a UCITS;

(eb) acting as trustee or depositary of a UCITS;

(ec) managing an AIF;

(ed) acting as trustee or depositary of an AIF; or]

(f) establishing etc a collective investment scheme.

(9) Subsection (8) must be read with—

(a) section 22 of the Financial Services and Markets Act 2000;

(b) any relevant order under that section; and

(c) Schedule 2 to that Act.]

NOTES

Sub-s (2) is amended as follows:

Para (aa) inserted by the Central Securities Depositories Regulations 2017, SI 2017/1064, reg 3(1), (20)(a) (for transitional provisions and savings see regs 6–9 thereof).

Words in first (outer) pair of square brackets in para (b) substituted by the Bank of England Act 1998, s 23(1), Sch 5, Pt III, paras 46, 48(1), (2).

Words in second (inner) pair of square brackets in para (b) substituted, and words in square brackets in para (d) substituted, by the Financial Services Act 2012, s 114(1), Sch 18, Pt 2, paras 62, 69(1), (2).

Words omitted from para (b) repealed, and words in third pair of square brackets substituted, by the Financial Services and Markets Act 2000 (Consequential Amendments and Repeals) Order 2001, SI 2001/3649, art 85(1), (2). Note that the section heading of the Financial Services and Markets Act 2000, s 301 is "supervision of certain contracts" and not "certain money market institutions" as stated in sub-s (2)(b) above, therefore it is thought that the words "certain money market institutions" should be deleted from the text of this subsection.

Paras (d), (e) substituted by SI 2001/3649, art 85(1), (3).

Sub-s (3): words in square brackets inserted by SI 2017/1064, reg 3(1), (20)(b) (for transitional provisions and savings see regs 6–9 thereof).

Sub-s (6): substituted, together with sub-s (6A) (for the original sub-s (6)), by the Bank of England Act 1998, s 23(1), Sch 5, Pt III, paras 46, 48(1), (3). Words omitted repealed, and words in second pair of square brackets substituted, by SI 2001/3649, art 85(1), (4). Words in first and final pairs of square brackets substituted by the Financial Services Act 2012, s 114(1), Sch 18, Pt 2, paras 62, 69(1), (3). Words in third pair of square brackets inserted by SI 2017/1064, reg 3(1), (20)(c) (for transitional provisions and savings see regs 6–9 thereof).

Sub-s (6A): substituted as noted above.

Sub-s (8): added, together with sub-s (9), by SI 2001/3649, art 85(1), (5); para (ba) inserted by the Financial Services and Markets Act 2000 (Regulated Activities) (Amendment No 3) Order 2006, SI 2006/3384, art 32; para (bb) inserted by the Financial Services and Markets Act 2000 (Regulated Activities) (Amendment) Order 2017, SI 2017/488, art 14, Schedule, para 2; word omitted from para (e) repealed, and paras (ea)–(ed) inserted by the Alternative Investment Fund Managers Regulations 2013, SI 2013/1773, reg 80, Sch 1, Pt 2, para 39.

Sub-s (9): added as noted above.

Market property

[17.80]

177 Application of margin [or default fund contribution] not affected by certain other interests

(1) The following provisions have effect with respect to the application by [a recognised body] of property (other than land) held by [the recognised body] as margin in relation to a market contract [or as default fund contribution].

(2) So far as necessary to enable the property to be applied in accordance with the rules of [the recognised body], it may be so applied notwithstanding any prior equitable interest or right, or any right or remedy arising from a breach of fiduciary duty, unless [the recognised body] had notice of the interest, right or breach of duty at the time the property was provided as margin [or as default fund contribution].

(3) No right or remedy arising subsequently to the property being provided as margin [or as default fund contribution] may be enforced so as to prevent or interfere with the application of the property by [the recognised body] in accordance with its rules.

(4) Where [a recognised body] has power by virtue of the above provisions to apply property notwithstanding an interest, right or remedy, a person to whom [the recognised body] disposes of the property in accordance with its rules takes free from that interest, right or remedy.

NOTES

Words "a recognised body" and "the recognised body" in square brackets (in each place they occur) substituted by the Central Securities Depositories Regulations 2017, SI 2017/1064, reg 3(1), (21) (for transitional provisions and savings see regs 6–9 thereof).

Other words in square brackets inserted by the Financial Markets and Insolvency Regulations 2009, SI 2009/853, reg 2(1), (13).

[17.81]

178 Priority of floating market charge over subsequent charges

(1) The Secretary of State may by regulations provide that a market charge which is a floating charge has priority over a charge subsequently created or arising, including a fixed charge.

(2) The regulations may make different provision for cases defined, as regards the market charge or the subsequent charge, by reference to the description of charge, its terms, the circumstances in which it is created or arises, the nature of the charge, the person in favour of whom it is granted or arises or any other relevant factor.

NOTES

Commencement: Pt VII (ss 154–191, Schs 21, 22) came into force on 25 March 1991 in so far as is necessary to enable regulations to be made under ss 155(4), (5), 158(4), (5), 160(5), 173(4), (5), 174(2)–(4), 185, 186, 187(3), Sch 21, para 2(3); no order has subsequently been made bringing this section into force.

[17.82]

179 Priority of market charge over unpaid vendor's lien

Where property subject to an unpaid vendor's lien becomes subject to a market charge, the charge has priority over the lien unless the chargee had actual notice of the lien at the time the property became subject to the charge.

[17.83]

180 Proceedings against market property by unsecured creditors

(1) Where property (other than land) is held by [a recognised body] as margin in relation to market contracts [or as default fund contribution,] or is subject to a market charge, no execution or other legal process for the enforcement of a judgment or order may be commenced or continued, and no distress may be levied, [and no power to use the procedure in Schedule 12 to the Tribunals, Courts and Enforcement Act 2007 (taking control of goods) may be exercised,] against the property by a person not seeking to enforce any interest in or security over the property, except with the consent of—

- (a) in the case of property provided as cover for margin [or as default fund contribution], [the recognised body] in question, or
- (b) in the case of property subject to a market charge, the person in whose favour the charge was granted.

(2) Where consent is given the proceedings may be commenced or continued notwithstanding any provision of the Insolvency Act 1986 or the Bankruptcy (Scotland) Act [2016].

(3) Where by virtue of this section a person would not be entitled to enforce a judgment or order against any property, any injunction or other remedy granted with a view to facilitating the enforcement of any such judgment or order shall not extend to that property.
(4) In the application of this section to Scotland, the reference to execution being commenced or continued includes a reference to diligence being carried out or continued, and the reference to distress being levied shall be omitted.

NOTES

Sub-s (1): words "a recognised body" and "the recognised body" in square brackets substituted by the Central Securities Depositories Regulations 2017, SI 2017/1064, reg 3(1), (22) (for transitional provisions and savings see regs 6–9 thereof). Words "or as default fund contribution," in square brackets (in both places they occur) inserted by the Financial Markets and Insolvency Regulations 2009, SI 2009/853, reg 2(1), (14). Words in third pair of square brackets inserted by the Tribunals, Courts and Enforcement Act 2007, s 62(3), Sch 13, para 91.

Sub-s (2): year "2016" in square brackets substituted for the original year "1985" by the Bankruptcy (Scotland) Act 2016 (Consequential Provisions and Modifications) Order 2016, SI 2016/1034, art 7(1), (3), Sch 1, para 6(1), (8), as from 30 November 2016 (except in relation to (i) a sequestration as regards which the petition is presented, or the debtor application is made before that date; or (ii) a trust deed executed before that date).

[17.84]

181 Power to apply provisions to other cases

(1) [A power to which this subsection applies includes the] power to apply sections 177 to 180 to any description of property provided as cover for margin in relation to contracts in relation to which the power is exercised or, as the case may be, property subject to charges in relation to which the power is exercised.
(2) The regulations may provide that those sections apply with such exceptions, additions and adaptations as may be specified in the regulations.
[(3) Subsection (1) applies to the powers of the Secretary of State and the Treasury to act jointly under—
 (a) sections 170, 172 and 176 of this Act; and
 (b) section 301 of the Financial Services and Markets Act 2000 (supervision of certain contracts).]

NOTES

Sub-s (1): words in square brackets substituted by the Financial Services and Markets Act 2000 (Consequential Amendments and Repeals) Order 2001, SI 2001/3649, art 86(1), (2).

Sub-s (3): added by SI 2001/3649, art 86(1), (3).

Supplementary provisions

[17.85]

182 Powers of court in relation to certain proceedings begun before commencement

(1) The powers conferred by this section are exercisable by the court where insolvency proceedings in respect of—
 (a) a member of a recognised investment exchange or a recognised clearing house, or
 (b) a person by whom a market charge has been granted,
are begun on or after 22nd December 1988 and before the commencement of this section.
That person is referred to in this section as "the relevant person".
(2) For the purposes of this section "insolvency proceedings" means proceedings under Part II, IV, V or IX of the Insolvency Act 1986 (administration, winding up and bankruptcy) or under the Bankruptcy (Scotland) Act [2016]; and references in this section to the beginning of such proceedings are to—
 [(za) the making of a bankruptcy application on which a bankruptcy order is made,]
 (a) the presentation of a petition on which an administration order, winding-up order, bankruptcy order or award of sequestration is made, or
 (b) the passing of a resolution for voluntary winding up.
(3) This section applies in relation to—
 (a) in England and Wales, the administration of the insolvent estate of a deceased person, and
 (b) in Scotland, the administration by a judicial factor appointed under section 11A of the Judicial Factors (Scotland) Act 1889 of the insolvent estate of a deceased person,
as it applies in relation to insolvency proceedings.
In such a case references to the beginning of the proceedings shall be construed as references to the death of the relevant person.
(4) The court may on an application made, within three months after the commencement of this section, by—
 (a) a recognised investment exchange or recognised clearing house, or
 (b) a person in whose favour a market charge has been granted,
make such order as it thinks fit for achieving, except so far as assets of the relevant person have been distributed before the making of the application, the same result as if the provisions of Schedule 22 had come into force on 22nd December 1988.
(5) The provisions of that Schedule ("the relevant provisions") reproduce the effect of certain provisions of this Part as they appeared in the Bill for this Act as introduced into the House of Lords and published on that date.
(6) The court may in particular—
 (a) require the relevant person or a relevant office-holder—

(i) to return property provided as cover for margin or which was subject to a market charge, or to pay to the applicant or any other person the proceeds of realisation of such property, or

(ii) to pay to the applicant or any other person such amount as the court estimates would have been payable to that person if the relevant provisions had come into force on 22nd December 1988 and market contracts had been settled in accordance with the rules of the recognised investment exchange or recognised clearing house, or a proportion of that amount if the property of the relevant person or relevant office-holder is not sufficient to meet the amount in full;

(b) provide that contracts, rules and dispositions shall be treated as not having been void;

(c) modify the functions of a relevant office-holder, or the duties of the applicant or any other person, in relation to the insolvency proceedings, or indemnify any such person in respect of acts or omissions which would have been proper if the relevant provisions had been in force;

(d) provide that conduct which constituted an offence be treated as not having done so;

(e) dismiss proceedings which could not have been brought if the relevant provisions had come into force on 22nd December 1988, and reverse the effect of any order of a court which could not, or would not, have been made if those provisions had come into force on that date.

(7) An order under this section shall not be made against a relevant office-holder if the effect would be that his remuneration, costs and expenses could not be met.

NOTES

Sub-s (2): year "2016" in square brackets substituted for the original year "1985" by the Bankruptcy (Scotland) Act 2016 (Consequential Provisions and Modifications) Order 2016, SI 2016/1034, art 7(1), (3), Sch 1, para 6(1), (8), as from 30 November 2016 (except in relation to (i) a sequestration as regards which the petition is presented, or the debtor application is made before that date; or (ii) a trust deed executed before that date); para (za) inserted by the Enterprise and Regulatory Reform Act 2013 (Consequential Amendments) (Bankruptcy) and the Small Business, Enterprise and Employment Act 2015 (Consequential Amendments) Regulations 2016, SI 2016/481, reg 2(1), Sch 1, para 9(1), (7).

[17.86]

[182A Recognised central counterparties: disapplication of provisions on mutual credit and set-off

(1) Nothing in the law of insolvency shall enable the setting off against each other of—

(a) positions and assets recorded in an account at a recognised central counterparty and held for the account of a client, an indirect client or a group of clients or indirect clients in accordance with Article 39 of the EMIR Level 1 Regulation[, Article 3(1) of the EMIR Level 2 Regulation or Article 3(1) of the MIFIR Level 2 Regulation]; and

(b) positions and assets recorded in any other account at the recognised central counterparty.

[(2) Nothing in the law of insolvency shall enable the setting off against each other of—

(a) positions and assets recorded in an account at a clearing member and held for the account of an indirect client or a group of indirect clients in accordance with [Article 4(2) of the EMIR Level 2 Regulation or Article 4(2) of the MIFIR Level 2 Regulation]; and

(b) positions and assets recorded in any other account at the clearing member.]

NOTES

Commencement: 1 April 2013 (sub-s (1)); 26 August 2013 (sub-s (2)).

Inserted by the Financial Services and Markets Act 2000 (Over the Counter Derivatives, Central Counterparties and Trade Repositories) Regulations 2013, SI 2013/504, reg 4(1), (15).

Sub-s (1): words in square brackets substituted by the Companies Act 1989 (Financial Markets and Insolvency) (Amendment) Regulations 2017, SI 2017/1247, reg 2(1), (3)(a).

Sub-s (2): added by the Financial Services and Markets Act 2000 (Over the Counter Derivatives, Central Counterparties and Trade Repositories) (No 2) Regulations 2013, SI 2013/1908, reg 2(1), (9); words in square brackets substituted by SI 2017/1247, reg 2(1), (3)(b).

[17.87]

183 Insolvency proceedings in other jurisdictions

(1) The references to insolvency law in section 426 of the Insolvency Act 1986 (co-operation with courts exercising insolvency jurisdiction in other jurisdictions) include, in relation to a part of the United Kingdom, the provisions made by or under this Part and, in relation to a relevant country or territory within the meaning of that section, so much of the law of that country or territory as corresponds to any provisions made by or under this Part.

(2) A court shall not, in pursuance of that section or any other enactment or rule of law, recognise or give effect to—

(a) any order of a court exercising jurisdiction in relation to insolvency law in a country or territory outside the United Kingdom, or

(b) any act of a person appointed in such a country or territory to discharge any functions under insolvency law,

in so far as the making of the order or the doing of the act would be prohibited in the case of a court in the United Kingdom or a relevant office-holder by provisions made by or under this Part.

(3) Subsection (2) does not affect the recognition or enforcement of a judgment required to be recognised or enforced under or by virtue of the Civil Jurisdiction and Judgments Act 1982 [or] [Regulation (EU) No 1215/2012 of the European Parliament and of the Council of 12 December 2012 on jurisdiction and the recognition and enforcement of judgments in civil and commercial matters (recast),

as amended from time to time and as applied by virtue of the Agreement made on 19 October 2005 between the European Community and the Kingdom of Denmark on jurisdiction and the recognition and enforcement of judgments in civil and commercial matters (OJ No L299, 16.11.2005, p 62; OJ No L79, 21.3.2013, p 4)].

NOTES

Sub-s (3) is amended as follows:

Word in first pair of square brackets added by virtue of the Civil Jurisdiction and Judgments Order 2001, SI 2001/3929, art 5, Sch 3, para 21.

Words in second pair of square brackets substituted by the Civil Jurisdiction and Judgments (Amendment) Regulations 2014, SI 2014/2947, reg 5, Sch 4, para 2. Note that for the purposes of proceedings, judgments and authentic instruments and court settlements to which, by virtue of Article 66(2) of Regulation 1215/2012/EU (transitional provisions), Regulation 44/2001/EC continues to apply (a) the amendments made by the 2014 Regulations do not apply; and (b) the enactments amended by the 2014 Regulations continue to have effect as if those amendments had not been made); the original text (as amended by SI 2001/3929, art 5, Sch 3, para 21 and the Civil Jurisdiction and Judgments Regulations 2007, SI 2007/1655, reg 5, Schedule, Pt 1, para 15) read as follows—

> "Council Regulation (EC) No 44/2001 of 22nd December 2000 on jurisdiction and the recognition and enforcement of judgments in civil and commercial matters][, as amended from time to time and as applied by the Agreement made on 19th October 2005 between the European Community and the Kingdom of Denmark on jurisdiction and the recognition and enforcement of judgments in civil and commercial matters (OJ No L299 16.11.2005 at p 62)".

[17.88]
184 Indemnity for certain acts, &c

(1) Where a relevant office-holder takes any action in relation to property of a defaulter which is liable to be dealt with in accordance with the default rules of a [recognised body], and believes and has reasonable grounds for believing that he is entitled to take that action, he is not liable to any person in respect of any loss or damage resulting from his action except in so far as the loss or damage is caused by the office-holder's own negligence.

(2) Any failure by a [recognised body] to comply with its own rules in respect of any matter shall not prevent that matter being treated for the purposes of this Part as done in accordance with those rules so long as the failure does not substantially affect the rights of any person entitled to require compliance with the rules.

(3) No [recognised body], nor any officer or servant or member of the governing body of a [recognised body], shall be liable in damages for anything done or omitted in the discharge or purported discharge of any functions to which this subsection applies unless the act or omission is shown to have been in bad faith.

(4) The functions to which subsection (3) applies are the functions of [the recognised body] so far as relating to, or to matters arising out of—

(a) its default rules, or

(b) any obligations to which it is subject by virtue of this Part.

(5) No person [to whom the exercise of any function of a [recognised body] is delegated under its default rules], nor any officer or servant of such a person, shall be liable in damages for anything done or omitted in the discharge or purported discharge of those functions unless the act or omission is shown to have been in bad faith.

NOTES

Words "recognised body" and "the recognised body" in square brackets substituted by the Central Securities Depositories Regulations 2017, SI 2017/1064, reg 3(1), (23) (for transitional provisions and savings see regs 6–9 thereof).

Other words in square brackets in sub-s (5): substituted by the Financial Services and Markets Act 2000 (Consequential Amendments and Repeals) Order 2001, SI 2001/3649, art 87.

[17.89]
185 Power to make further provision by regulations

(1) The Secretary of State may by regulations make such further provision as appears to him necessary or expedient for the purposes of this Part.

(2) Provision may, in particular, be made—

(a) for integrating the provisions of this Part with the general law of insolvency, and

(b) for adapting the provisions of this Part in their application to overseas investment exchanges and clearing houses.

(3) Regulations under this section may add to, amend or repeal any of the provisions of this Part or provide that those provisions have effect subject to such additions, exceptions or adaptations as are specified in the regulations.

[(4) References in this section to the provisions of this Part include any provision made under section 301 of the Financial Services and Markets Act 2000.]

NOTES

Sub-s (4): added by the Financial Services and Markets Act 2000 (Consequential Amendments and Repeals) Order 2001, SI 2001/3649, art 88.

Regulations: the Financial Markets and Insolvency Regulations 1991, SI 1991/880 at **[9.1]**; the Financial Markets and Insolvency Regulations 1996, SI 1996/1469 at **[9.14]**; the Financial Markets and Insolvency Regulations 1998, SI 1998/1748; the Financial Markets and Insolvency (CGO Service) Regulations 1999, SI 1999/1209; the Financial Markets and Insolvency Regulations 2009, SI 2009/853; the Financial Services and Markets Act 2000 (Over the Counter Derivatives,

Central Counterparties and Trade Repositories) Regulations 2013, SI 2013/504; the Financial Services and Markets Act 2000 (Over the Counter Derivatives, Central Counterparties and Trade Repositories) (No 2) Regulations 2013, SI 2013/1908.

[17.90]
186 Supplementary provisions as to regulations
(1) Regulations under this Part may make different provision for different cases and may contain such incidental, transitional and other supplementary provisions as appear to the Secretary of State to be necessary or expedient.
(2) Regulations under this Part shall be made by statutory instrument which shall be subject to annulment in pursuance of a resolution of either House of Parliament.

NOTES
Regulations: the Financial Markets and Insolvency (CGO Service) Regulations 1999, SI 1999/1209; the Financial Services and Markets Act 2000 (Over the Counter Derivatives, Central Counterparties and Trade Repositories) (No 2) Regulations 2013, SI 2013/1908.

[17.91]
187 Construction of references to parties to market contracts
(1) Where a person enters into market contracts in more than one capacity, the provisions of this Part apply (subject as follows) as if the contracts entered into in each different capacity were entered into by different persons.
(2) References in this Part to a market contract to which a person is a party include (subject as follows, and unless the context otherwise requires) contracts to which he is party as agent.
[(2A) Subsections (1) and (2) do not apply to market contracts to which this Part applies by virtue of section 155(2B).]
(3) The Secretary of State may by regulations—
(a) modify or exclude the operation of subsections (1) and (2), and
(b) make provision as to the circumstances in which a person is to be regarded for the purposes of those provisions as acting in different capacities.

NOTES
Sub-s (2A): inserted by the Financial Services and Markets Act 2000 (Over the Counter Derivatives, Central Counterparties and Trade Repositories) Regulations 2013, SI 2013/504, reg 4(1), (16).
Regulations: the Financial Markets and Insolvency Regulations 1991, SI 1991/880 at **[9.1]**; the Financial Markets and Insolvency (Amendment) Regulations 1992, SI 1992/716; the Financial Markets and Insolvency Regulations 2009, SI 2009/853; the Financial Services and Markets Act 2000 (Over the Counter Derivatives, Central Counterparties and Trade Repositories) Regulations 2013, SI 2013/504; the Financial Services and Markets Act 2000 (Over the Counter Derivatives, Central Counterparties and Trade Repositories) (No 2) Regulations 2013, SI 2013/1908.

[17.92]
188 Meaning of "default rules" and related expressions
(1) In this Part "default rules" means rules of a [recognised body] which provide for the taking of action in the event of a person [(including another [recognised body]] appearing to be unable, or likely to become unable, to meet his obligations in respect of one or more market contracts [connected with [the recognised body] . . . .]
[(1A) In the case of a recognised central counterparty, "default rules" includes—
(a) the default procedures referred to in Article 48 of the EMIR Level 1 Regulation; and
(b) any rules of the recognised central counterparty which provide for the taking of action in accordance with a request or instruction from a clearing member under the default procedures referred to in [Article 4(6) and (7) of the EMIR Level 2 Regulation or Article 4(6) and (7) of the MIFIR Level 2 Regulation] in respect of assets or positions held by the recognised central counterparty for the account of an indirect client or group of indirect clients.]
[(1B) In the case of a recognised CSD, "default rules" includes the default rules and procedures referred to in Article 41 of the CSD regulation.]
(2) References in this Part to a "defaulter" are to a person in respect of whom action has been taken by [a recognised body] under its default rules, whether by declaring him to be a defaulter or otherwise; and references in this Part to "default"[, "defaulting" and "non-defaulting"] shall be construed accordingly.
[(2A) For the purposes of subsection (2), where a recognised central counterparty takes action under the rules referred to in subsection (1A)(b), the action is to be treated as taken in respect of the client providing the indirect clearing services.]
(3) In this Part "default proceedings" means proceedings taken by [a recognised body] under its default rules.
[(3A) In this Part "default fund contribution" means—
(a) contribution by a member or designated non-member of a recognised investment exchange to a fund which—
(i) is maintained by that exchange for the purpose of covering losses arising in connection with defaults by any of the members of the exchange, or defaults by any of the members or designated non-members of the exchange, and
(ii) may be applied for that purpose under the default rules of the exchange;
(b) contribution by a member of a recognised clearing house to a fund which—
(i) is maintained by that clearing house for the purpose of covering losses arising in connection with defaults by any of the members of the clearing house, and
(ii) may be applied for that purpose under the default rules of the clearing house;

(c) contribution by a recognised clearing house to a fund which—
[(i) is maintained by another recognised body (A) for the purpose of covering losses arising in connection with defaults by recognised bodies other than A or by any of their members, and]
(ii) may be applied for that purpose under A's default rules; . . .
(d) contribution by a recognised investment exchange to a fund which—
[(i) is maintained by another recognised body (A) for the purpose of covering losses arising in connection with defaults by recognised bodies other than A or by any of their members, and]
(ii) may be applied for that purpose under A's default rules];
[(e) contribution by a member of a recognised CSD to a fund which—
(i) is maintained by that central securities depository for the purpose of covering losses arising in connection with defaults by any of the members of the central securities depository, and
(ii) may be applied for that purpose under the default rules of the central securities depository; or
(f) contribution by a recognised CSD to a fund which—
(i) is maintained by another recognised body (A) for the purpose of covering losses arising in connection with defaults by recognised bodies other than A or by any of their members, and
(ii) may be applied for that purpose under A's default rules].

(4) If [a recognised body] takes action under its default rules in respect of a person, all subsequent proceedings under its rules for the purposes of or in connection with the settlement of market contracts to which the defaulter is a party shall be treated as done under its default rules.

NOTES

Sub-s (1): words "recognised body" and "the recognised body" in square brackets substituted by the Central Securities Depositories Regulations 2017, SI 2017/1064, reg 3(1), (24)(a) (for transitional provisions and savings see regs 6–9 thereof). Words in second (outer) pair of square brackets inserted by the Financial Markets and Insolvency Regulations 2009, SI 2009/853, reg 2(1), (15)(a). Words in fourth (outer) of square brackets substituted by the Financial Services and Markets Act 2000 (Over the Counter Derivatives, Central Counterparties and Trade Repositories) Regulations 2013, SI 2013/504, reg 4(1), (17)(a). Words omitted repealed by the Financial Services and Markets Act 2000 (Over the Counter Derivatives, Central Counterparties and Trade Repositories) (No 2) Regulations 2013, SI 2013/1908, reg 2(1), (10)(a).

Sub-ss (1A), (2A): inserted by SI 2013/1908, reg 2(1), (10)(b), (c). Words in square brackets in sub-s (1A)(b) substituted by the Companies Act 1989 (Financial Markets and Insolvency) (Amendment) Regulations 2017, SI 2017/1247, reg 2(1), (4).

Sub-s (1B): inserted by SI 2017/1064, reg 3(1), (24)(b) (for transitional provisions and savings see regs 6–9 thereof).

Sub-s (2): words in first pair of square brackets substituted by SI 2017/1064, reg 3(1), (24)(c) (for transitional provisions and savings see regs 6–9 thereof). Words in second pair of square brackets inserted by SI 2013/504, reg 4(1), (17)(b).

Sub-ss (3), (4): words in square brackets substituted by SI 2017/1064, reg 3(1), (24)(c), (e) (for transitional provisions and savings see regs 6–9 thereof).

Sub-s (3A): inserted by SI 2009/853, reg 2(1), (15)(b). Words in square brackets substituted or inserted, and words omitted repealed, by SI 2017/1064, reg 3(1), (24)(d) (for transitional provisions and savings see regs 6–9 thereof).

[17.93]

189 Meaning of "relevant office-holder"

(1) The following are relevant office-holders for the purposes of this Part—
(a) the official receiver,
(b) any person acting in relation to a company as its liquidator, provisional liquidator, administrator or administrative receiver,
(c) any person acting in relation to an individual (or, in Scotland, any debtor within the meaning of the Bankruptcy (Scotland) Act [2016]) as his trustee in bankruptcy or interim receiver of his property or as [trustee] or interim trustee in the sequestration of his estate,
(d) any person acting as administrator of an insolvent estate of a deceased person.

(2) In subsection (1)(b) "company" means any company, society, association, partnership or other body which may be wound up under the Insolvency Act 1986.

NOTES

Sub-s (1): year "2016" in square brackets substituted for the original year "1985", and word "trustee" in square brackets substituted for the original word "permanent", by the Bankruptcy (Scotland) Act 2016 (Consequential Provisions and Modifications) Order 2016, SI 2016/1034, art 7(1), (3), Sch 1, para 6(1), (10), as from 30 November 2016 (except in relation to (i) a sequestration as regards which the petition is presented, or the debtor application is made before that date; or (ii) a trust deed executed before that date).

[17.94]

[189A Meaning of "transfer

(1) In this Part, a reference to a transfer of a clearing member client contract, a client trade or a qualifying collateral arrangement shall be interpreted in accordance with this section.

(2) A transfer of a clearing member client contract or client trade includes—
(a) an assignment;
(b) a novation; and
(c) terminating or closing out the clearing member client contract or client trade and establishing an equivalent position between different parties.

(3) Where a clearing member client contract is recorded in the accounts of a recognised central counterparty as a position held for the account of an indirect client or group of indirect clients, the clearing member client contract is to be treated as having been transferred if the position is transferred to a different account at the recognised central counterparty.

(4) A reference to a transfer of a qualifying collateral arrangement includes an assignment or a novation.]

NOTES

Commencement: 26 August 2013.

Inserted by the Financial Services and Markets Act 2000 (Over the Counter Derivatives, Central Counterparties and Trade Repositories) (No 2) Regulations 2013, SI 2013/1908, reg 2(1), (11).

[17.95]

190 Minor definitions

(1) In this Part—

"administrative receiver" has the meaning given by section 251 of the Insolvency Act 1986;

[. . .]

"charge" means any form of security, including a mortgage and, in Scotland, a heritable security;

["clearing member", in relation to a recognised central counterparty, has the meaning given by Article 2(14) of the EMIR Level 1 Regulation;]

["client" has the meaning given by Article 2(15) of the EMIR Level 1 Regulation;]

["CSD regulation" means Regulation (EU) No 909/2014 of the European Parliament and of the Council of 23 July 2014 on improving securities settlement in the European Union and on central securities depositories;]

["EEA CSD", "recognised central counterparty", "recognised CSD", "recognised clearing house", "recognised investment exchange" and "third country CSD" have the same meaning as in the Financial Services and Markets Act 2000 (see section 285 of that Act);]

["EMIR Level 1 Regulation" means Regulation (EU) No 648/2012 of the European Parliament and of the Council of 4 July 2012 on OTC derivatives, central counterparties and trade repositories;]

["EMIR Level 2 Regulation" means Commission Delegated Regulation (EU) No 149/2013 of 19 December 2012 supplementing Regulation (EU) No 648/2012 of the European Parliament and of the Council of 4 July 2012 with regard to regulatory technical standards on indirect clearing arrangements, the clearing obligation, the public register, access to a trading venue, non-financial counterparties, risk mitigation for OTC derivatives contracts not cleared by a CCP [as amended by Commission Delegated Regulation (EU) 2017/2155 of 22 September 2017];]

["the FCA" means the Financial Conduct Authority;]

["indirect clearing services" has the same meaning as in the EMIR Level 2 Regulation;]

["indirect client" has the meaning given by Article 1(a) of the EMIR Level 2 Regulation;]

["interim trustee" has the same meaning as in the Bankruptcy (Scotland) Act 2016;]

. . .

["member", in relation to a central securities depository, means a participant of that central securities depository as defined in Article 2(1)(19) of the CSD regulation;]

["member of a clearing house" includes a clearing member of a recognised central counterparty;]

[MIFIR Level 2 Regulation" means Commission Delegated Regulation (EU) 2017/2154 of 22 September 2017 supplementing Regulation (EU) No 600/2014 of the European Parliament and of the Council with regard to regulatory technical standards on indirect clearing arrangements;]

"overseas", in relation to an investment exchange or clearing house [or central securities depository], means having its head office outside the United Kingdom;

["position" has the same meaning as in the EMIR Level 1 Regulation;]

["the PRA" means the Prudential Regulation Authority;]

["recognised body" has the same meaning as in section 313 of the Financial Services and Markets Act 2000;]

["sequestration" means sequestration under the Bankruptcy (Scotland) Act 2016;]

. . .

"set-off", in relation to Scotland, includes compensation;

["The Stock Exchange" means the London Stock Exchange Limited;]

["UK", in relation to an investment exchange, means having its head office in the United Kingdom].

[(2) References in this Part to settlement—

(a) mean, in relation to a market contract, the discharge of the rights and liabilities of the parties to the contract, whether by performance, compromise or otherwise;

(b) include, in relation to a clearing member client contract or a clearing member house contract, a reference to its liquidation for the purposes of Article 48 of the EMIR Level 1 Regulation.]

(3) In this Part the expressions "margin" and "cover for margin" have the same meaning.

[(3A)], (4) . . .

(5) For the purposes of this Part a person shall be taken to have notice of a matter if he deliberately failed to make enquiries as to that matter in circumstances in which a reasonable and honest person would have done so.

This does not apply for the purposes of a provision requiring "actual notice".

[(6) References in this Part to the law of insolvency—

(a) include references to every provision made by or under the Insolvency Act 1986 or the Bankruptcy (Scotland) Act [2016]; and in relation to a building society references to insolvency law or to any provision of the Insolvency Act 1986 are to that law or provision as modified by the Building Societies Act 1986;

(b) are also to be interpreted in accordance with the modifications made by the enactments mentioned in subsection (6B).

(6A) For the avoidance of doubt, references in this Part to administration, administrator, liquidator and winding up are to be interpreted in accordance with the modifications made by the enactments mentioned in subsection (6B).

(6B) The enactments referred to in subsections (6)(b) and (6A) are—

(a) article 3 of, and the Schedule to, the Banking Act 2009 (Parts 2 and 3 Consequential Amendments) Order 2009;

(b) article 18 of, and paragraphs 1(a), (2) and (3) of Schedule 2 to, the Building Societies (Insolvency and Special Administration) Order 2009; and

(c) regulation 27 of, and Schedule 6 to, the Investment Bank Special Administration Regulations 2011.]

(7) In relation to Scotland, references in this Part—

(a) to sequestration include references to the administration by a judicial factor of the insolvent estate of a deceased person, and

(b) to an interim [trustee or to a trustee in the sequestration of an estate] include references to a judicial factor on the insolvent estate of a deceased person,

unless the context otherwise requires.

NOTES

Sub-s (1) is amended as follows:

Definition "the Authority" (omitted) originally inserted by the Financial Services and Markets Act 2000 (Consequential Amendments and Repeals) Order 2001, SI 2001/3649, art 89(1), (2); repealed by the Financial Services Act 2012, s 114(1), Sch 18, Pt 2, paras 62, 70(1), (2).

Definitions "clearing house", "investment and investment exchange" and "recognised" (omitted) repealed by SI 2001/3649, art 89(1), (3).

Definitions "clearing member", "client", "EMIR Level 1 Regulation", "EMIR Level 2 Regulation", "indirect client", "member of a clearing house", and "position" inserted by the Financial Services and Markets Act 2000 (Over the Counter Derivatives, Central Counterparties and Trade Repositories) Regulations 2013, SI 2013/504, reg 4(1), (18)(a).

Definitions "CSD regulation", "member" and "recognised body" inserted, by the Central Securities Depositories Regulations 2017, SI 2017/1064, reg 3(1), (25)(a) (for transitional provisions and savings see regs 6–9 thereof).

Definitions "EEA CSD", "recognised central counterparty", "recognised CSD", "recognised clearing house" and "recognised investment exchange" substituted (for the original definitions "recognised central counterparty", "recognised clearing house" and "recognised investment exchange" by SI 2017/1064, reg 3(1), (25)(c) (for transitional provisions and savings see regs 6–9 thereof).

Words in square brackets in the definition "EMIR Level 2 Regulation" inserted, and definition "MIFIR Level 2 Regulation" inserted, by the Companies Act 1989 (Financial Markets and Insolvency) (Amendment) Regulations 2017, SI 2017/1247, reg 2(1), (5).

Definitions "the FCA" and "the PRA" inserted by the Financial Services Act 2012, s 114(1), Sch 18, Pt 2, paras 62, 70(1), (3), (4).

Definition "indirect clearing services" inserted by the Financial Services and Markets Act 2000 (Over the Counter Derivatives, Central Counterparties and Trade Repositories) (No 2) Regulations 2013, SI 2013/1908, reg 2(1), (12)(a).

Definition "interim trustee" substituted (for the original definitions "interim trustee" and "permanent trustee") by the Bankruptcy (Scotland) Act 2016 (Consequential Provisions and Modifications) Order 2016, SI 2016/1034, art 7(1), (3), Sch 1, para 6(1), (11)(a)(i), as from 30 November 2016 (except in relation to (i) a sequestration as regards which the petition is presented, or the debtor application is made before that date; or (ii) a trust deed executed before that date). The original definitions read as follows—

"interim trustee" and "permanent trustee" have the same meaning as in the Bankruptcy (Scotland) Act 1985;".

Words in square brackets in the definition "overseas" inserted by SI 2017/1064, reg 3(1), (25)(b) (for transitional provisions and savings see regs 6–9 thereof).

Definition "sequestration" inserted by SI 2016/1034, art 7(1), (3), Sch 1, para 6(1), (11)(a)(ii), as from 30 November 2016 (except in relation to (i) a sequestration as regards which the petition is presented, or the debtor application is made before that date; or (ii) a trust deed executed before that date).

Definition "The Stock Exchange" substituted by SI 2001/3649, art 89(1), (5).

Definition "UK" substituted by SI 2013/504, reg 4(1), (18)(b)(ii).

Sub-s (2): substituted by SI 2013/504, reg 4(1), (18)(c).

Sub-s (3A): inserted by SI 2013/504, reg 4(1), (18)(d), and repealed by SI 2013/1908, reg 2(1), (12)(b).

Sub-s (4): repealed by SI 2001/3649, art 89(1), (6).

Sub-ss (6), (6A)–(6C): substituted (for the original sub-s (6)) by SI 2013/504, reg 4(1), (18)(e). Year "2016" in square brackets in sub-s (6)(a) substituted for the original year "1985" by SI 2016/1034, art 7(1), (3), Sch 1, para 6(1), (11)(b), as from 30 November 2016 (except in relation to (i) a sequestration as regards which the petition is presented, or the debtor application is made before that date; or (ii) a trust deed executed before that date).

Sub-s (7): words in square brackets substituted for the original words "or permanent trustee" by SI 2016/1034, art 7(1), (3), Sch 1, para 6(1), (11)(c), as from 30 November 2016 (except in relation to (i) a sequestration as regards which the petition is presented, or the debtor application is made before that date; or (ii) a trust deed executed before that date).

[17.96]

191 Index of defined expressions

The following Table shows provisions defining or otherwise explaining expressions used in this Part (other than provisions defining or explaining an expression used only in the same section or paragraph)—

[Defined Expression	Section
administration	Sections 190(6A) and (6B)
administrator	Sections 190(6A) and (6B)
administrative receiver	Section 190(1)
[authorised central securities depository services	Section 155(3D)]
charge	Section 190(1)
clearing member	Section 190(1)
clearing member client contract	Section 155(1)(a)
clearing member house contract	Section 155(1)(b)
client	Section 190(1)
client trade	Section 155(1)(c)
cover for margin	Section 190(3)
[CSD regulation	Section 190(1)]
default fund contribution	Section 188(3A)
default rules (and related expressions)	Section 188
designated non-member	Section 155(2)
[EEA CSD	Section 190(1)]
EMIR Level 1 Regulation	Section 190(1)
EMIR Level 2 Regulation	Section 190(1)
the FCA	Section 190(1)
[indirect clearing services	Section 190(1)]
indirect client	Section 190(1)
insolvency law (and similar expressions)	Sections 190(6) and (6B)
interim trustee	Sections 190(1) and 190(7)(b)
liquidator	Sections 190(6A) and (6B)
margin	Section 190(3)
market charge	Section 173
market contract	Section 155
[member (in relation to a central securities depository)	Section 190(1)]
member of a clearing house	Section 190(1)
[MIFIR Level 2 Regulation	Section 190(1)]
notice	Section 190(5)
overseas (in relation to investment exchanges[, clearing houses and central securities depositories]	Section 190(1)
party (in relation to a market contract)	Section 187
permanent trustee	*Sections 190(1) and 190(7)(b)*
the PRA	Section 190(1)
qualifying collateral arrangement	Section 155A(1)(a)
qualifying property transfers	Section 155A(1)(b)
[recognised body	Section 190(1)]
recognised central counterparty	Section 190(1)
recognised clearing house	Section 190(1)
[recognised CSD	Section 190(1)]
recognised investment exchange	Section 190(1)
relevant office-holder	Section 189
sequestration	Section 190(7)(a)
set off (in relation to Scotland)	Section 190(1)
settlement and related expressions (in relation to a market contract)	Section 190 (2)
The Stock Exchange	Section 190(1)
[third country CSD	Section 190(1)]

[Defined Expression	Section
[transfer	Section 189A]
[interim trustee and trustee in the sequestration of an estate (in relation to Scotland)	section 190(1) and (7)(b)]
UK (in relation to investment exchanges)	Section 190(1)
winding up	Sections 190(6A) and (6B)]

NOTES

Table substituted by the Financial Services and Markets Act 2000 (Over the Counter Derivatives, Central Counterparties and Trade Repositories) Regulations 2013, SI 2013/504, reg 4(1), (19), Schedule.

Entries "authorised central securities depository services", "CSD regulation", "EEA CSD", "member (in relation to a central securities depository), "recognised body", "recognised CSD", and "third country CSD" inserted, and words in square brackets in the entry "overseas" inserted, by the Central Securities Depositories Regulations 2017, SI 2017/1064, reg 3(1), (26) (for transitional provisions and savings see regs 6–9 thereof).

Entries "indirect clearing services" and "transfer" inserted by the Financial Services and Markets Act 2000 (Over the Counter Derivatives, Central Counterparties and Trade Repositories) (No 2) Regulations 2013, SI 2013/1908, reg 2(1), (13).

Entry "MIFIR Level 2 Regulation" inserted by the Companies Act 1989 (Financial Markets and Insolvency) (Amendment) Regulations 2017, SI 2017/1247, reg 2(1), (6).

Entry "permanent trustee" in italics repealed, and final entry in square brackets substituted, by the Bankruptcy (Scotland) Act 2016 (Consequential Provisions and Modifications) Order 2016, SI 2016/1034, art 7(1), (3), Sch 1, para 6(1), (12), as from 30 November 2016 (except in relation to (i) a sequestration as regards which the petition is presented, or the debtor application is made before that date; or (ii) a trust deed executed before that date). The original entry read as follows—

"trustee, interim or permanent (in relation to Scotland) Section 190(7)(b)".

192–207 *((Pts VIII, IX) in so far as unrepealed, outside the scope of this work.)*

PART X
MISCELLANEOUS AND GENERAL PROVISIONS

208–211 *(Ss 208, 210, 211 outside the scope of this work; s 209 repealed by the Criminal Justice Act 1993, s 79(14), Sch 6, Pt I.)*

General

212–214 *(Ss 212, 213 outside the scope of this work; s 214 repealed by the Financial Services and Markets Act 2000 (Consequential Amendments and Repeals) Order 2001, SI 2001/3649, art 75(m).)*

[17.97]
215 Commencement and transitional provisions

(1) *(Outside the scope of this work.)*

(2) The other provisions of this Act come into force on such day as the Secretary of State may appoint by order made by statutory instrument; and different days may be appointed for different provisions and different purposes.

(3) An order bringing into force any provision may contain such transitional provisions and savings as appear to the Secretary of State to be necessary or expedient.

(4) *(Outside the scope of this work.)*

NOTES

Orders: at present, 18 Commencement orders have been made under this section. The ones relevant to the provisions of the Act printed in this work are the Companies Act 1989 (Commencement No 9 and Saving and Transitional Provisions) Order 1991, SI 1991/488, the Companies Act 1989 (Commencement No 10 and Saving Provisions) Order 1991, SI 1991/878, the Companies Act 1989 (Commencement No 16) Order 1995, SI 1995/1591, and the Companies Act 1989 (Commencement No 17) Order 1998, SI 1998/1747.

[17.98]
216 Short title

This Act may be cited as the Companies Act 1989.

SCHEDULES

SCHEDULES 1–24

(Schs 1–24, in so far as unrepealed, outside the scope of this work.)

ENVIRONMENTAL PROTECTION ACT 1990

(1990 c 43)

An Act to make provision for the improved control of pollution arising from certain industrial and other processes; to re-enact the provisions of the Control of Pollution Act 1974 relating to waste on land with modifications as respects the functions of the regulatory and other authorities concerned in the collection and disposal of waste and to make further provision in relation to such waste; to restate the law defining statutory nuisances and improve the summary procedures for dealing with them, to provide for the termination of the existing controls over offensive trades or businesses and to provide for the extension of the Clean Air Acts to prescribed gases; to amend the law relating to litter and make further provision imposing or conferring powers to impose duties to keep public places clear of litter and clean; to make provision conferring powers in relation to trolleys abandoned on land in the open air; to amend the Radioactive Substances Act 1960; to make provision for the control of genetically modified organisms; to make provision for the abolition of the Nature Conservancy Council and for the creation of councils to replace it and discharge the functions of that Council and, as respects Wales, of the Countryside Commission; to make further provision for the control of the importation, exportation, use, supply or storage of prescribed substances and articles and the importation or exportation of prescribed descriptions of waste; to confer powers to obtain information about potentially hazardous substances; to amend the law relating to the control of hazardous substances on, over or under land; to amend section 107(6) of the Water Act 1989 and sections 31(7)(a), 31A(c)(i) and 32(7)(a) of the Control of Pollution Act 1974; to amend the provisions of the Food and Environment Protection Act 1985 as regards the dumping of waste at sea; to make further provision as respects the prevention of oil pollution from ships; to make provision for and in connection with the identification and control of dogs; to confer powers to control the burning of crop residues; to make provision in relation to financial or other assistance for purposes connected with the environment; to make provision as respects superannuation of employees of the Groundwork Foundation and for remunerating the chairman of the Inland Waterways Amenity Advisory Council; and for purposes connected with those purposes

[1 November 1990]

1–78 *((Pts I, II) outside the scope of this work.)*

[PART IIA
CONTAMINATED LAND]

78A–78W *(Outside the scope of this work.)*

[17.99]

[78X Supplementary provisions

(1), (2) *(Outside the scope of this work.)*

(3) A person acting in a relevant capacity—

(a) shall not thereby be personally liable, under this Part, to bear the whole or any part of the cost of doing any thing by way of remediation, unless that thing is to any extent referable to substances whose presence in, on or under the contaminated land in question is a result of any act done or omission made by him which it was unreasonable for a person acting in that capacity to do or make; and

(b) shall not thereby be guilty of an offence under or by virtue of section 78M above unless the requirement which has not been complied with is a requirement to do some particular thing for which he is personally liable to bear the whole or any part of the cost.

(4) In subsection (3) above, "person acting in a relevant capacity" means—

(a) a person acting as an insolvency practitioner, within the meaning of section 388 of the Insolvency Act 1986 (including that section as it applies in relation to an insolvent partnership by virtue of any order made under section 421 of that Act);

(b) the official receiver acting in a capacity in which he would be regarded as acting as an insolvency practitioner within the meaning of section 388 of the Insolvency Act 1986 if subsection (5) of that section were disregarded;

(c) the official receiver acting as receiver or manager;

(d) a person acting as a special manager under section 177 or 370 of the Insolvency Act 1986;

(e) the Accountant in Bankruptcy acting as [trustee] or interim trustee in a sequestration (within the meaning of the Bankruptcy (Scotland) Act [2016]);

(f) a person acting as a receiver or receiver and manager—

(i) under or by virtue of any enactment; or

(ii) by virtue of his appointment as such by an order of a court or by any other instrument.

[(g) in relation to property and rights that have vested as bona vacantia in the Crown, or that have fallen to the Crown as ultimus haeres, the Queen's and Lord Treasurer's Remembrancer.]

[(4A) In subsection (4)(f)(i) above, "enactment" includes an enactment comprised in, or in an instrument made under, an Act of the Scottish Parliament.]

(5) *(Outside the scope of this work.)*]

NOTES

Inserted, together with ss 78A–78W, 78Y, 78YA–78YC (Pt IIA), by the Environment Act 1995, s 57.

Sub-s (4): in para (e) word and year in square brackets substituted for original word "permanent" and original year "1985" respectively, by the Bankruptcy (Scotland) Act 2016 (Consequential Provisions and Modifications) Order 2016, SI 2016/1034, art 7(1), (3), Sch 1, para 7, as from 30 November 2016 (except in relation to (i) a sequestration as regards which the petition is presented, or the debtor application is made before that date; or (ii) a trust deed executed before that date); para (g) inserted, in relation to Scotland, by the Regulatory Reform (Scotland) Act 2014, s 45(1), (5).

Sub-s (4A): inserted, in relation to Scotland, by the Regulatory Reform (Scotland) Act 2014, s 57, Sch 3, Pt 6, para 40(1), (6).

78Y–155 (*Ss 78Y–78YC, ss 79–155 (Pts III–VIII) outside the scope of this work.*)

PART IX
GENERAL

156–163A (*Outside the scope of this work.*)

[17.100]
164 Short title, commencement and extent
(1) This Act may be cited as the Environmental Protection Act 1990.
(2)–(5) (*Outside the scope of this work.*)

SCHEDULES 1–16

(*Schs 1–16 outside the scope of this work.*)

PENSION SCHEMES ACT 1993

(1993 c 48)

ARRANGEMENT OF SECTIONS

PART VII
INSOLVENCY OF EMPLOYERS

CHAPTER II
PAYMENT BY SECRETARY OF STATE OF UNPAID SCHEME CONTRIBUTIONS

123 Interpretation of Chapter II. . . . . [17.101]
124 Duty of Secretary of State to pay unpaid contributions to schemes. . . . . [17.102]
125 Certification of amounts payable under s 124 by insolvency officers . . . . . [17.103]
126 Complaint to employment tribunal . . . . . [17.104]
127 Transfer to Secretary of State of rights and remedies. . . . . [17.105]
128 Priority in bankruptcy etc . . . . . [17.106]

PART XI
GENERAL AND MISCELLANEOUS PROVISIONS

Avoidance of certain transactions and provisions

159A No forfeiture on bankruptcy of rights under personal pension schemes . . . . . [17.107]

PART XII
SUPPLEMENTARY PROVISIONS

Interpretation

181 General interpretation. . . . . [17.108]

Supplemental provisions

193 Short title and commencement. . . . . [17.109]

SCHEDULES

Schedule 4—Priority in Bankruptcy etc. . . . . [17.110]

An Act to consolidate certain enactments relating to pension schemes with amendments to give effect to recommendations of the Law Commission and the Scottish Law Commission

[5 November 1993]

1–118 (*(Pts I–VI) in so far as unrepealed, outside the scope of this work.*)

PART VII
INSOLVENCY OF EMPLOYERS

NOTES

Modification: this Act is applied, with modifications, in so far as it relates to bank insolvency or administration under the Banking Act 2009, Pts 2, 3, by the Banking Act 2009 (Parts 2 and 3 Consequential Amendments) Order 2009, SI 2009/317, art 3, Schedule at **[7.86]**, **[7.92]**.

119–122 (*(Ch I) repealed by the Pensions Act 1995, ss 122, 177, Sch 3, paras 22, 30, Sch 7, Pt I.*)

CHAPTER II PAYMENT BY SECRETARY OF STATE OF UNPAID SCHEME CONTRIBUTIONS

[17.101]
123 Interpretation of Chapter II

(1) For the purposes of this Chapter, an employer shall be taken to be insolvent if, but only if, in England and Wales—
- (a) he has been [made] bankrupt or has made a composition or arrangement with his creditors;
- (b) he has died and his estate falls to be administered in accordance with an order under section 421 of the Insolvency Act 1986; . . .
- (c) where the employer is a company—
  - (i) a winding-up order . . . is made or a resolution for voluntary winding up is passed with respect to it [or the company enters administration],
  - (ii) a receiver or manager of its undertaking is duly appointed,
  - (iii) possession is taken, by or on behalf of the holders of any debentures secured by a floating charge, of any property of the company comprised in or subject to the charge, or
  - (iv) a voluntary arrangement proposed for the purpose of Part I of the Insolvency Act 1986 is approved under that Part[, or
- (d) where subsection (2A) is satisfied.]

(2) For the purposes of this Chapter, an employer shall be taken to be insolvent if, but only if, in Scotland—
- (a) sequestration of his estate is awarded or he executes a trust deed for his creditors or enters into a composition contract;
- (b) he has died and a judicial factor appointed under section 11A of the Judicial Factors (Scotland) Act 1889 is required by that section to divide his insolvent estate among his creditors; or
- (c) where the employer is a company—
  - (i) a winding-up order . . . is made or a resolution for voluntary winding up is passed with respect to it [or the company enters administration],
  - (ii) a receiver of its undertaking is duly appointed, or
  - (iii) a voluntary arrangement proposed for the purpose of Part I of the Insolvency Act 1986 is approved under that Part.

[(2A) This subsection is satisfied if—
- (a) a request has been made for the first opening of collective proceedings—
  - (i) based on the insolvency of the employer, as provided for under the laws, regulations and administrative provisions of a member State; and
  - (ii) involving the partial or total divestment of the employer's assets and the appointment of a liquidator or a person performing a similar task; and
- (b) the competent authority has—
  - (i) decided to open the proceedings; or
  - (ii) established that the employer's undertaking or business has been definitively closed down and the available assets of the employer are insufficient to warrant the opening of the proceedings.

(2B) For the purposes of subsection (2A)—
- (a) "liquidator or person performing a similar task" includes the official receiver or an administrator, trustee in bankruptcy, judicial factor, supervisor of a voluntary arrangement, or person performing a similar task,
- (b) "competent authority" includes—
  - (i) a court,
  - (ii) a meeting of creditors,
  - (iii) a creditors' committee,
  - (iv) the creditors by a decision procedure, and
  - (v) an authority of a member State empowered to open insolvency proceedings, to confirm the opening of such proceedings or to take decisions in the course of such proceedings.

(2C) An application under section 124 may only be made in respect of a worker who worked or habitually worked in Great Britain in that employment to which the application relates.]

(3) In this Chapter—

["employer", "employment", "worker" and "worker's contract" and other expressions which are defined in the Employment Rights Act 1996 have the same meaning as in that Act (see further subsections (3A) and (3B));]

"holiday pay" means—
- (a) pay in respect of holiday actually taken; or
- (b) any accrued holiday pay which under [the worker's contract] would in the ordinary course have become payable to him in respect of the period of a holiday if his employment with the employer had continued until he became entitled to a holiday;

. . .

[(3A) Section 89 of the Pensions Act 2008 (agency workers) applies for the purposes of this Chapter as it applies for the purposes of Part 1 of that Act.

(3B) References in this Chapter to a worker include references to an individual to whom Part 1 of the Pensions Act 2008 applies as if the individual were a worker because of regulations made under section 98 of that Act; and related expressions are to be read accordingly.]

(4) . . .

(5) Any reference in this Chapter to the resources of a scheme is a reference to the funds out of which the benefits provided by the scheme are from time to time payable.

NOTES

Sub-s (1): word in square brackets in para (a) substituted by the Enterprise and Regulatory Reform Act 2013 (Consequential Amendments) (Bankruptcy) and the Small Business, Enterprise and Employment Act 2015 (Consequential Amendments) Regulations 2016, SI 2016/481, reg 2(1), Sch 1, Pt 2, para 18; word omitted from para (b) repealed and para (d) inserted together with word preceding it, by the Employment Rights Act 1996 and Pension Schemes Act 1993 (Amendment) Regulations 2017, SI 2017/1205, reg 3(1), (2)(a); in sub-para (c)(i), words "or an administration order" (omitted) repealed, and words in square brackets added, by the Enterprise Act 2002 (Insolvency) Order 2003, SI 2003/2096, arts 4, 6, Schedule, para 22(a), except in any case where a petition for an administration order was presented before 15 September 2003.

Sub-s (2): in sub-para (c)(i), words "or an administration order" (omitted) repealed, and words in square brackets added, by the Enterprise Act 2002 (Insolvency) Order 2003, SI 2003/2096, arts 4, 6, Schedule, para 22(b), except in any case where a petition for an administration order was presented before 15 September 2003.

Sub-ss (2A)–(2C): inserted by SI 2017/1205, reg 3(1), (2)(b).

Sub-s (3): definition ""employer", "employment", "worker" and "worker's contract"" substituted, for definition ""contract of employment", "employee", "employer" and "employment"", as originally enacted, and in definition "holiday pay" in para (b) words in square brackets substituted, by the Pensions Act 2014, s 42(1), (2)(a), (b); definition "occupational pension scheme" (omitted) repealed by the Pensions Act 2004, ss 319(1), 320, Sch 12, paras 9, 19(a), Sch 13, Pt I.

Sub-ss (3A), (3B): inserted by the Pensions Act 2014, s 42(1), (2)(c).

Sub-s (4): repealed by the Pensions Act 2004, ss 319(1), 320, Sch 12, paras 9, 19(b), Sch 13, Pt I.

[17.102]

124 Duty of Secretary of State to pay unpaid contributions to schemes

(1) If, on an application made to him in writing by the persons competent to act in respect of an occupational pension scheme or a personal pension scheme, the Secretary of State is satisfied—

- (a) that an employer has become insolvent; and
- (b) that at the time he did so there remained unpaid relevant contributions falling to be paid by him to the scheme,

then, subject to the provisions of this section and section 125, the Secretary of State shall pay into the resources of the scheme the sum which in his opinion is payable in respect of the unpaid relevant contributions.

(2) In this section and section 125 "relevant contributions" means contributions falling to be paid by an employer to an occupational pension scheme or a personal pension scheme, either on his own account or on behalf of [a worker]; and for the purposes of this section a contribution shall not be treated as falling to be paid on behalf of [a worker] unless a sum equal to that amount has been deducted from the pay of [the worker] by way of a contribution from him.

(3) [Subject to subsection (3A),] the sum payable under this section in respect of unpaid contributions of an employer on his own account to an occupational pension scheme or a personal pension scheme shall be the least of the following amounts—

- (a) the balance of relevant contributions remaining unpaid on the date when he became insolvent and payable by the employer on his own account to the scheme in respect of the 12 months immediately preceding that date;
- (b) the amount certified by an actuary to be necessary for the purpose of meeting the liability of the scheme on dissolution to pay the benefits provided by the scheme to or in respect of the [workers] of the employer;
- (c) an amount equal to 10 per cent of the total amount of remuneration paid or payable to those [workers] in respect of the 12 months immediately preceding the date on which the employer became insolvent.

[(3A) Where the scheme in question is a money purchase scheme, the sum payable under this section by virtue of subsection (3) shall be the lesser of the amounts mentioned in paragraphs (a) and (c) of that subsection.]

(4) For the purposes of subsection (3)(c), "remuneration" includes holiday pay, statutory sick pay, statutory maternity pay under Part V of the Social Security Act 1986 or Part XII of the Social Security Contributions and Benefits Act 1992 [and any payment such as is referred to in section 184(2) of the Employment Rights Act 1996].

(5) Any sum payable under this section in respect of unpaid contributions on behalf of [a worker] shall not exceed the amount deducted from the pay of [the worker] in respect of [the workers's] contributions to the scheme during the 12 months immediately preceding the date on which the employer became insolvent.

[(6) In this section "on his own account", in relation to an employer, means on his own account but to fund benefits for, or in respect of, one or more [workers].]

NOTES

Sub-ss (2), (5): words in square brackets substituted by the Pensions Act 2014, s 42(1), (3)(a)–(c).

Sub-s (3): first words in square brackets inserted by the Pensions Act 1995, s 90; in para (b) word in square brackets substituted by the Pensions Act 2014, s 42(1), (3)(d).

Sub-s (3A): inserted by the Pensions Act 1995, s 90; substituted by the Pension Schemes Act 2015, s 46, Sch 2, paras 1, 4, as from a day to be appointed, as follows—

"(3A) The sum payable under this section by virtue of subsection (3) shall be the lesser of the amounts mentioned in paragraphs (a) and (c) of that subsection in any case where the scheme is—

- (a) a defined contributions scheme,
- (b) a shared risk scheme under which all the benefits that may be provided are money purchase benefits, or
- (c) a shared risk scheme under which all the benefits that may be provided are money purchase benefits or collective benefits.".

Sub-s (4): words in square brackets substituted by the Employment Rights Act 1996, s 240, Sch 1, para 61(1), (3).
Sub-s (6): added by the Pensions Act 2004, s 319(1), Sch 12, paras 9, 20; word in square brackets substituted by the Pensions Act 2014, s 42(1), (3)(d).
Social Security Act 1986, Pt V: repealed by the Social Security (Consequential Provisions) Act 1992, s 3, Sch 1.

[17.103]
125 Certification of amounts payable under s 124 by insolvency officers
(1) This section applies where one of the officers mentioned in subsection (2) ("the relevant officer") has been or is required to be appointed in connection with an employer's insolvency.
(2) The officers referred to in subsection (1) are—
(a) a trustee in bankruptcy;
(b) a liquidator;
(c) an administrator;
(d) a receiver or manager; or
(e) a trustee under a composition or arrangement between the employer and his creditors or under a trust deed for his creditors executed by the employer;
and in this subsection "trustee", in relation to a composition or arrangement, includes the supervisor of a voluntary arrangement proposed for the purposes of and approved under Part I or VIII of the Insolvency Act 1986.
(3) Subject to subsection (5), where this section applies the Secretary of State shall not make any payment under section 124 in respect of unpaid relevant contributions until he has received a statement from the relevant officer of the amount of relevant contributions which appear to have been unpaid on the date on which the employer became insolvent and to remain unpaid; and the relevant officer shall on request by the Secretary of State provide him as soon as reasonably practicable with such a statement.
(4) Subject to subsection (5), an amount shall be taken to be payable, paid or deducted as mentioned in subsection (3)(a) or (c) or (5) of section 124 only if it is so certified by the relevant officer.
(5) If the Secretary of State is satisfied—
(a) that he does not require a statement under subsection (3) in order to determine the amount of relevant contributions that was unpaid on the date on which the employer became insolvent and remains unpaid, or
(b) that he does not require a certificate under subsection (4) in order to determine the amounts payable, paid or deducted as mentioned in subsection (3)(a) or (c) or (5) of section 124,
he may make a payment under that section in respect of the contributions in question without having received such a statement or, as the case may be, such a certificate.

[17.104]
126 Complaint to [employment tribunal]
(1) Any persons who are competent to act in respect of an occupational pension scheme or a personal pension scheme and who have applied for a payment to be made under section 124 into the resources of the scheme may present a complaint to an [employment tribunal] that—
(a) the Secretary of State has failed to make any such payment; or
(b) any such payment made by him is less than the amount which should have been paid.
(2) Such a complaint must be presented within the period of three months beginning with the date on which the decision of the Secretary of State on that application was communicated to the persons presenting it or, if that is not reasonably practicable, within such further period as is reasonable.
(3) Where an [employment tribunal] finds that the Secretary of State ought to make a payment under section 124, it shall make a declaration to that effect and shall also declare the amount of any such payment which it finds that the Secretary of State ought to make.

NOTES
Words in square brackets substituted by the Employment Rights (Dispute Resolution) Act 1998, s 1(2)(a).

[17.105]
127 Transfer to Secretary of State of rights and remedies
(1) Where in pursuance of section 124 the Secretary of State makes any payment into the resources of an occupational pension scheme or a personal pension scheme in respect of any contributions to the scheme, any rights and remedies in respect of those contributions belonging to the persons competent to act in respect of the scheme shall, on the making of the payment, become rights and remedies of the Secretary of State.
(2) Where the Secretary of State makes any such payment as is mentioned in subsection (1) and the sum (or any part of the sum) falling to be paid by the employer on account of the contributions in respect of which the payment is made constitutes—
(a) a preferential debt within the meaning of the Insolvency Act 1986 for the purposes of any provision of that Act (including any such provision as applied by an order made under that Act) or any provision of [the Companies Acts (as defined in section 2(1) of the Companies Act 2006)]; or
(b) a preferred debt within the meaning of the Bankruptcy (Scotland) Act [2016] for the purposes of any provision of that Act (including any such provision as applied by section 11A of the Judicial Factors (Scotland) Act 1889),
then, without prejudice to the generality of subsection (1), there shall be included among the rights and remedies which become rights and remedies of the Secretary of State in accordance with that subsection any right arising under any such provision by reason of the status of that sum (or that part of it) as a preferential or preferred debt.

(3) In computing for the purposes of any provision referred to in subsection (2)(a) or (b) the aggregate amount payable in priority to other creditors of the employer in respect of—

(a) any claim of the Secretary of State to be so paid by virtue of subsection (2); and

(b) any claim by the persons competent to act in respect of the scheme,

any claim falling within paragraph (a) shall be treated as if it were a claim of those persons; but the Secretary of State shall be entitled, as against those persons, to be so paid in respect of any such claim of his (up to the full amount of the claim) before any payment is made to them in respect of any claim falling within paragraph (b).

NOTES

Sub-s (2): words in square brackets in para (a) substituted by the Companies Act 2006 (Consequential Amendments, Transitional Provisions and Savings) Order 2009, SI 2009/1941, art 2(1), Sch 1, para 144(1), (2); year in square brackets in para (b) substituted for original year "1985", by the Bankruptcy (Scotland) Act 2016 (Consequential Provisions and Modifications) Order 2016, SI 2016/1034, art 7(1), (3), Sch 1, para 11(1), (3), as from 30 November 2016 (except in relation to (i) a sequestration as regards which the petition is presented, or the debtor application is made before that date; or (ii) a trust deed executed before that date).

CHAPTER III PRIORITY IN BANKRUPTCY

[17.106]

128 Priority in bankruptcy etc

Schedule 4 shall have effect for the purposes of paragraph 8 of Schedule 6 to the Insolvency Act 1986 and paragraph [1 of Schedule 3 to the Bankruptcy (Scotland) Act 2016] (by virtue of which sums to which Schedule 4 to this Act applies are preferential or, as the case may be, preferred debts in cases of insolvency).

NOTES

Words in square brackets substituted for original words "4 of Schedule 3 to the Bankruptcy (Scotland) Act 1985" by the Bankruptcy (Scotland) Act 2016 (Consequential Provisions and Modifications) Order 2016, SI 2016/1034, art 7(1), (3), Sch 1, para 11(1), (4), as from 30 November 2016 (except in relation to (i) a sequestration as regards which the petition is presented, or the debtor application is made before that date; or (ii) a trust deed executed before that date).

129–152 *((Pts VIII–X) in so far as unrepealed, outside the scope of this work.)*

PART XI
GENERAL AND MISCELLANEOUS PROVISIONS

153–158A *(Outside the scope of this work.)*

Avoidance of certain transactions and provisions

159 *(Outside the scope of this work.)*

[17.107]

[159A No forfeiture on bankruptcy of rights under personal pension schemes

(1) A person's rights under a personal pension scheme cannot be forfeited by reference to his bankruptcy.

(2) For the purposes of this section—

(a) a person shall be treated as having a right under a personal pension scheme where—

(i) he is entitled to a credit under section 29(1)(b) of the Welfare Reform and Pensions Act 1999 (sharing of rights on divorce etc [or on dissolution etc of a civil partnership]),

(ii) he is so entitled as against the person responsible for the scheme (within the meaning of Chapter I of Part IV of that Act), and

(iii) the person so responsible has not discharged his liability in respect of the credit; and

(b) forfeiture shall be taken to include any manner of deprivation or suspension.]

NOTES

Inserted by the Welfare Reform and Pensions Act 1999, s 14(1).

Sub-s (2): words in square brackets inserted by the Civil Partnership (Pensions and Benefit Payments) (Consequential, etc Provisions) Order 2005, SI 2005/2053, art 2, Schedule, Pt 3, para 17.

160–177 *(Outside the scope of this work.)*

PART XII
SUPPLEMENTARY PROVISIONS

Interpretation

178–180A *(Outside the scope of this work.)*

[17.108]

181 General interpretation

(1) In this Act, unless the context otherwise requires—

. . .

"contracted-out employment" shall be construed in accordance with section 8;

. . .

"contributions equivalent premium" [means a premium that was paid under] [section 55(2)];

. . .

["defined contributions scheme" has the meaning given by section 4 of the Pension Schemes Act 2015;]

. . .

"earner" and "earnings" shall be construed in accordance with [section 8(1B) of this Act and] sections 3, 4 and 112 of the Social Security Contributions and Benefits Act 1992;

. . .

"employer" means—

(a) in the case of an employed earner employed under a contract of service, his employer;

(b) in the case of an employed earner employed in an office with emoluments—

(i) such person as may be prescribed in relation to that office; or

(ii) if no person is prescribed, the government department, public authority or body of persons responsible for paying the emoluments of the office;

"[employment tribunal]" means a tribunal established or having effect as if established under [section 1(1) of [the Employment Tribunals Act 1996]];

. . .

"linked qualifying service" has the meaning given in section 179;

. . .

"lower earnings limit" and "upper earnings limit" shall be construed in accordance with section 5 of the Social Security Contributions and Benefits Act 1992 and "current", in relation to those limits, means for the time being in force;

. . .

["money purchase contracted-out scheme" is to be construed in accordance with [section 7B];]

"money purchase scheme" means a pension scheme under which all the benefits that may be provided are money purchase benefits;

. . .

"occupational pension scheme" has the meaning given in section 1;

"personal pension scheme" has the meaning given in section 1;

["salary related contracted-out scheme" is to be construed in accordance with section 7B;]

["shared risk scheme" has the meaning given by section 3 of the Pension Schemes Act 2015;]

. . .

(2)–(7) (*Outside the scope of this work.*)

NOTES

Sub-s (1): definitions omitted outside the scope of this work;

in definition "contributions equivalent premium" words in first pair of square brackets substituted by the Pensions Act 2014, s 24(1), Sch 13, Pt 1, paras 1, 43(1), (6), and words in second pair of square brackets substituted by the Pensions Act 1995, s 151, Sch 5, para 77(a); in definition ""earner" and "earnings"" words in square brackets inserted, and definition "salary related contracted-out scheme" inserted, by the Pensions Act 2014, s 24(1), Sch 13, Pt 1, paras 1, 43(1), (2), (7); definitions "defined contributions scheme" and "shared risk scheme" inserted, and definition "money purchase scheme" repealed, by the Pension Schemes Act 2015, s 46, Sch 2, paras 1, 5, as from a day to be appointed; in definition "employment tribunal" words in first and third (inner) pairs of square brackets substituted by the Employment Rights (Dispute Resolution) Act 1998, s 1(2)(c), words in second (outer) pair of square brackets substituted by the Employment Tribunals Act 1996, s 43, Sch 1, para 11; definition "money purchase contracted-out scheme" substituted by the Pensions Act 2007, s 15(3), Sch 4, Pt 1, paras 1, 34(1), (2)(d) and words in square brackets therein substituted by the Pensions Act 2014, s 24(1), Sch 13, Pt 1, paras 1, 43(1), (8).

181A–187 (*Ss 181A–186 outside the scope of this work; s 187 repealed by the Northern Ireland Act 1998, s 100(2), Sch 15.*)

Supplemental provisions

188–192 (*Outside the scope of this work.*)

[17.109]

193 Short title and commencement

(1) This Act may be cited as the Pension Schemes Act 1993.

(2) Subject to the provisions of Schedule 9, this Act shall come into force on such day as the Secretary of State may by order appoint

(3) (*Outside the scope of this work.*)

NOTES

Orders: the Pension Schemes Act 1993 (Commencement No 1) Order 1994, SI 1994/86.

SCHEDULES

SCHEDULES 1–3

(*Sch 1 repealed by the Pensions Act 1995, ss 151, 177, Sch 5, paras 18, 83, Sch 7, Pt III; Schs 2, 3 outside the scope of this work.*)

SCHEDULE 4
PRIORITY IN BANKRUPTCY ETC

Section 128

Earner's contributions to occupational pension scheme

[17.110]

1. This Schedule applies to any sum owed on account of an earner's contributions to an occupational pension scheme being contributions deducted from earnings paid in the period of four months immediately preceding the relevant date or otherwise due in respect of earnings paid or payable in that period.

Employer's contributions to occupational pension scheme

2. [(1) This Schedule applies to any sum owed on account of an employer's contributions to a [Northern Ireland] salary related contracted-out scheme which were payable in the period of 12 months immediately preceding the relevant date.

(1A) The amount of the debt having priority by virtue of sub-paragraph (1) shall be taken to be an amount equal to the appropriate amount.

(2) . . .

(3) . . .

(3A) In sub-paragraph (1A) . . . "the appropriate amount" means the aggregate of—

(a) the percentage for non-contributing earners of the total reckonable earnings paid or payable, in the period of 12 months referred to in sub-paragraph (1) . . . , to or for the benefit of non-contributing earners; and

(b) the percentage for contributing earners of the total reckonable earnings paid or payable, in that period, to or for the benefit of contributing earners.]

(4) For the purposes of [sub-paragraph (3A)]—

(a) the earnings to be taken into account as reckonable earnings are those paid or payable to or for the benefit of earners in employment which is contracted-out by reference to the scheme in the whole or any part of the period of 12 months there mentioned; and

(b) earners are to be identified as contributing or non-contributing in relation to service of theirs in employment which is contracted-out by reference to the scheme according to whether or not in the period in question they were liable under the terms of the scheme to contribute in respect of that service towards the provision of pensions under the scheme.

(5) In this paragraph—

[. . .]

"employer" shall be construed in accordance with regulations made under section 181(2);

["the percentage for contributing earners" means . . . 3 per cent, . . .

"the percentage for non-contributing earners" means . . . 4.8 per cent, . . .] and

["Northern Ireland salary related contracted-out scheme" means a salary related contracted-out scheme within the meaning of the Pension Schemes (Northern Ireland) Act 1993 (and references to employment that is contracted-out by reference to a scheme are to be read accordingly);]

"reckonable earnings", in relation to any employment, means the earner's earnings from that employment so far as those earnings—

(a) were comprised in any payment of earnings made to him or for his benefit at a time when the employment was contracted-out employment; and

(b) exceeded the current lower earnings limit but not [the upper accrual point].

[(6) . . .]

[Contributions equivalent premiums]

3. (1) This Schedule applies to any sum owed on account of a [Northern Ireland] [contributions equivalent premium] payable at any time before, or in consequence of, a person going into liquidation or being [made] bankrupt, or in Scotland, the sequestration of a debtor's estate, or (in the case of a company not in liquidation)—

(a) the appointment of a receiver as mentioned in section 40 of the Insolvency Act 1986 (debenture-holders secured by floating charge), or

(b) the appointment of a receiver under section 53(6) or 54(5) of that Act (Scottish company with property subject to floating charge), or

(c) the taking of possession by debenture-holders (so secured) as mentioned in [section 754 of the Companies Act 2006].

(2) Where any such premium is payable in respect of a period of service of more than 12 months (taking into account any previous linked qualifying service), the amount to be paid in priority by virtue of this paragraph shall be limited to the amount of the premium that would have been payable if the service had been confined to the last 12 months taken into account in fixing the actual amount of the premium.

(3) Where—

(a) by virtue of this paragraph the whole or part of a premium is required to be paid in priority to other debts of the debtor or his estate; and

(b) the person liable for the payment would be entitled to recover the whole or part of any sum paid on account of it from another person either under section 61 or under any provision made by the relevant scheme for the purposes of that section or otherwise, then, subject to sub-paragraph (4), that other person shall be liable for any part of the premium for the time being unpaid.

(4) No person shall be liable by virtue of sub-paragraph (3) for an amount in excess of the sum which might be so recovered from him if the premium had been paid in full by the person liable for it, after deducting from that sum any amount which has been or may be recovered from him in respect of any part of that payment paid otherwise than under that sub-paragraph.

(5) The payment under sub-paragraph (3) of any amount in respect of a premium shall have the same effect on the rights and liabilities of the person making it (other than his liabilities under that sub-paragraph) as if it had been a payment of that amount on account of the sum recoverable from him in respect of a premium as mentioned in sub-paragraph (3)(b).

[(6) In this paragraph "Northern Ireland contributions equivalent premium" means a contributions equivalent premium within the meaning of the Pension Schemes (Northern Ireland) Act 1993.]

Interpretation

4. (1) In this Schedule—

(a) in its application in England and Wales, [section 754(3) of the Companies Act 2006] and section 387 of the Insolvency Act 1986 apply as regards the meaning of the expression "the relevant date"; and

(b) in its application in Scotland, that expression has the same meaning as in [Part 1] of Schedule 3 to the Bankruptcy (Scotland) Act [2016].

(2) . . .

NOTES

Para 2: sub-paras (1)–(3A) substituted for original sub-paras (1)–(3), and words in square brackets in sub-para (4) substituted by the Welfare Reform and Pensions Act 1999, s 18, Sch 2, para 8; in sub-para (1) words in square brackets, and in sub-para (5) definition "Northern Ireland salary related contracted-out scheme", inserted by the Pensions Act 2014, s 24(1), Sch 13, Pt 1, paras 1, 47(1), (2); sub-paras (2), (3) and words omitted from sub-para (3A) repealed by the Pensions Act 2007, ss 15(3)(a), 27(2), Sch 4, Pt 2, para 46(1), (2), Sch 7, Pt 7; in sub-para (5), definition "appropriate flat-rate percentage" (omitted) inserted by the Pensions Act 1995, s 137(7) and repealed by the Pensions Act 2007, ss 15(3)(a), 27(2), Sch 4, Pt 2, paras 46, 60(1), (4)(a), Sch 7, Pt 7; in sub-para (5), definitions "the percentage for contributing earners" and "the percentage for non-contributing earners" inserted by the Pensions Act 1995, s 137(7) and words omitted from those definitions repealed by the Pensions Act 2007, s 15(3)(a), Sch 4, Pt 2, paras 46, 60(1), (4)(b), (c) (as amended by the Pensions Act 2011, s 27); words in square brackets in definition "reckonable earnings" in sub-para (5) substituted and sub-para (6) (as originally added by the Pensions Act 2007, s 12(4), Sch 1, Pt 7, para 39(b)) repealed by the National Insurance Contributions Act 2008, s 4, Sch 1, paras 7, 13, Sch 2, in relation to payments made in a tax week falling in 2009–10 or any subsequent tax year.

Para 3: in sub-para (1) second words in square brackets substituted, and heading substituted by virtue of, the Pensions Act 1995, s 151, Sch 5, para 85; in sub-para (1) first words in square brackets, and sub-para (6), inserted by the Pensions Act 2014, s 24(1), Sch 13, Pt 1, paras 1, 47(1), (3); words in square brackets in sub-para (1)(c) substituted for original words "section 196 of the Companies Act 1985" by the Companies Act 2006 (Consequential Amendments etc) Order 2008, SI 2008/948, art 3(1)(b), Sch 1, Pt 2, para 194(1), (3)(a), subject to transitional provisions and savings in arts 6, 11, 12 thereof; word in third pair of square brackets in sub-para (1) substituted by the Enterprise and Regulatory Reform Act 2013 (Consequential Amendments) (Bankruptcy) and the Small Business, Enterprise and Employment Act 2015 (Consequential Amendments) Regulations 2016, SI 2016/481, reg 2(1), Sch 1, Pt 2, para 18.

Para 4: in sub-para (1)(a) words in square brackets substituted, for original words "section 196(3) of the Companies Act 1985", by SI 2008/948, art 3(1)(b), Sch 1, Pt 2, para 194(1), (3)(b), subject to transitional provisions and savings in arts 6, 11, 12 thereof; in sub-para (1)(b), words and year in square brackets substituted for original "Part I" and "1985" respectively, by the Bankruptcy (Scotland) Act 2016 (Consequential Provisions and Modifications) Order 2016, SI 2016/1034, art 7(1), (3), Sch 1, para 11(1), (6), as from 30 November 2016 (except in relation to (i) a sequestration as regards which the petition is presented, or the debtor application is made before that date; or (ii) a trust deed executed before that date); sub-para (2) repealed by the Pensions Act 2014, s 24(1), Sch 13, Pt 1, paras 1, 47(1), (4).

See further, in relation to the application of this Schedule, with modifications, in respect of bank insolvency and administration: the Banking Act 2009, ss 103(3), (4), Table, 145(3), (4), Table 2.

SCHEDULES 5–9

(Schs 5–9 outside the scope of this work.)

COAL INDUSTRY ACT 1994

(1994 c 21)

An Act to provide for the establishment and functions of a body to be known as the Coal Authority; to provide for the restructuring of the coal industry, for transfers of the property, rights and liabilities of the British Coal Corporation and its wholly-owned subsidiaries to other persons and for the dissolution of that Corporation; to abolish the Domestic Coal Consumers' Council; to make provision for the licensing of coal-mining operations and provision otherwise in relation to the carrying on of such operations; to amend the Coal Mining Subsidence Act 1991 and the Opencast Coal Act 1958; and for connected purposes

[5 July 1994]

1–24 *((Pt I) outside the scope of this work.)*

PART II
LICENSING OF COAL-MINING OPERATIONS

25 (*Outside the scope of this work.*)

Licences under Part II

26–28 (*Outside the scope of this work.*)

[17.111]

29 Conditions for the provision of security

(1) Conditions included in a licence under this Part may include provision requiring the holder of the licence, on or before the coming into force of the authorisation contained in the licence and at such subsequent times as may be determined by or under the conditions—

(a) to provide such security as may be so determined for his performance of any of the obligations to which he is or may become subject, either in accordance with the licence itself or otherwise by virtue of his being at any time the holder of that licence; and

(b) for the purposes of that security and in relation to any property or rights in which it consists, to take such steps for or in connection with the establishment and maintenance of any trust or other arrangements as may be so determined.

(2) Where—

(a) any security for the performance of any person's obligations has been provided in accordance with any condition included by virtue of subsection (1) above in a licence under this Part, and

(b) any trust or other arrangements which have, in pursuance of that condition, been established and maintained for the purposes of that security are for the time being registered under section 35(1)(f) below,

the manner in which, and the purposes for which, that security and any property or rights in which it consists are to be applied and enforceable (whether in the event of that person's insolvency or otherwise) shall be determined in accordance with the trust or other arrangements and without regard to so much of the Insolvency Act 1986 or any other enactment or rule of law as, in its operation in relation to that person or any conduct of his, would prevent or restrict their being applied in accordance with the trust or other arrangements or would prevent or restrict their enforcement for the purpose of being so applied.

30–34 (*Outside the scope of this work.*)

Supplemental

35 (*Outside the scope of this work.*)

[17.112]

36 Insolvency of licensed operators etc

(1) A licence under this Part and the obligations arising out of, or incidental to, such a licence shall not be treated as property for any of the purposes of the Insolvency Act 1986 ("the 1986 Act"); but this subsection shall be without prejudice to so much of any licence as, by virtue of section 27(4) or (5) above, authorises the official receiver or any person who is for the time being acting as an insolvency practitioner in relation to the holder of the licence to carry on any of the coal-mining operations to which the licence relates or to transfer the rights and obligations of the holder of the licence to another person.

(2) Where, in the case of the winding up of a company which is or has been a licensed operator, the liquidator or official receiver sends to the registrar of companies—

(a) any such account or return as is mentioned in section 94(3) or 106(3) of the 1986 Act (account of the winding up and return of final meeting or meetings),

(b) any notice for the purposes of section 172(8) of that Act (notice of final meeting and of its decisions),

(c) an application under section 202(2) of that Act (applications for early dissolution),

(d) a copy of such an order for dissolution of the company as is mentioned in section 204(4) of that Act (order for early dissolution in Scotland), or

(e) such a notice as is mentioned in section 205(1)(b) of that Act (notice that winding up complete),

the liquidator or official receiver, on sending it to the registrar of companies, shall also send a copy to the Authority.

[(2A) Where the administrator of a company which is or has been a licensed operator files a notice with the registrar of companies under paragraph 84(1) of Schedule B1 to the Insolvency Act 1986 (c 45) (administration: moving to dissolution), he shall at the same time send a copy to the Authority.]

(3) A liquidator [or administrator] who contravenes subsection (2) [or 2A] above shall be guilty of an offence and liable, on summary conviction, to a fine not exceeding level 3 on the standard scale.

(4) In any proceedings against any person for an offence under subsection (3) above it shall be a defence for that person to show that at the time of the contravention he did not know and had no grounds for suspecting that the company in question had ever been a licensed operator.

(5) In the case of any company which is either—

(a) the holder of a licence under this Part, or

(b) a licensed operator by virtue of section 25(3) above,

the Authority shall be included in the persons who are entitled to make an application under [section 1029 of the Companies Act 2006 (application to court for restoration to the register)] or under section 201(3), 202(5), 204(5) or 205(3) or (5) of the 1986 Act (applications in the case of a winding up for the deferment of a company's dissolution).

(6) . . .

(7) In this section "registrar of companies" has the same meaning as in [the Companies Acts (see section 1060 of the Companies Act 2006)]; and the reference in subsection (1) above to a person's acting as an insolvency practitioner shall be construed in accordance with section 388 of the 1986 Act.

NOTES

Sub-s (2A): inserted by the Enterprise Act 2002, s 248(3), Sch 17, para 48(1), (2), subject to savings and transitional provisions (i) in a case where a petition for an administration order has been presented before 15 September 2003 (see the Enterprise Act 2002 (Commencement No 4 and Transitional Provisions and Savings) Order 2003, SI 2003/2093, art 3 at **[2.26]**), and (ii) in relation to special administration regimes (see s 249 of the 2002 Act at **[2.10]**).

Sub-s (3): words in square brackets inserted by the Enterprise Act 2002, s 248(3), Sch 17, para 48(1), (3), subject to savings and transitional provisions as noted to sub-s (2A) above.

Sub-s (5): words in square brackets substituted by the Companies Act 2006 (Consequential Amendments, Transitional Provisions and Savings) Order 2009, SI 2009/1941, art 2(1), Sch 1, para 147(1), (2)(a).

Sub-s (6): repealed by SI 2009/1941, art 2(1), Sch 1, para 147(1), (2)(b).

Sub-s (7): words in square brackets substituted by SI 2009/1941, art 2(1), Sch 1, para 147(1), (2)(c).

37–56 *((Pt III) outside the scope of this work.)*

PART IV
GENERAL AND SUPPLEMENTAL

Information provisions

57, 58 (*Outside the scope of this work.*)

[17.113]

59 Information to be kept confidential by the Authority

(1) Subject to the following provisions of this section, it shall be the duty of the Authority to establish and maintain such arrangements as it considers best calculated to secure that information which—

(a) is in the Authority's possession in consequence of either the carrying out of any of its functions or the transfer to the Authority, in accordance with a restructuring scheme, of any records, and

(b) relates to the affairs of any individual or to any particular business,

is not, during the lifetime of that individual or so long as that business continues to be carried on, disclosed to any person without the consent of that individual or, as the case may be, of the person for the time being carrying on that business.

(2) Nothing in subsection (1) above shall authorise or require the making of arrangements which prevent the disclosure of information—

(a) for the purpose of facilitating the carrying out by the Secretary of State, the Treasury or the Authority of any of his, their or, as the case may be, its functions under this Act;

(b) in pursuance of arrangements made under section 57 above;

(c) for the purpose of facilitating the carrying out by any relevant authority of any of the functions in relation to which it is such an authority;

(d) in connection with the investigation of any criminal offence or for the purposes of criminal proceedings;

(e) for the purposes of any civil proceedings brought under this Act or any relevant enactment, of any proceedings before the [Upper Tribunal or] the Lands Tribunal for Scotland under the 1991 Act or of any arbitration for which provision is made by regulations under section 47(2) above; or

(f) in pursuance of any [EU] obligation.

(3) For the purposes of this section—

(a) every Minister of the Crown and local weights and measures authority in Great Britain is a relevant authority in relation to his or, as the case may be, their functions under any relevant enactment;

[(b) the Secretary of State, the Treasury[, the Financial Conduct Authority and the Prudential Regulation Authority] are relevant authorities in relation to their functions under the Financial Services and Markets Act 2000[, the Consumer Credit Act 1974] and the enactments relating to companies and insolvency;]

(c) an inspector appointed under the enactments relating to companies, an official receiver and any recognised professional body for the purposes of section 391 of the Insolvency Act 1986 are relevant authorities in relation to their functions as such;

(d) every enforcing authority, within the meaning of Part I of the Health and Safety at Work etc Act 1974, is a relevant authority in relation to its functions under any relevant statutory provision, within the meaning of that Act; and

[(dd) the Civil Aviation Authority is a relevant authority in relation to its functions under Part I of the Transport Act 2000;] and

(e) the following are relevant authorities in relation to all of their functions, that is to say—

(i) the Comptroller and Auditor General;

(ii) the Health and Safety Executive . . . ;

[(iia) the Office for Nuclear Regulation;]

(iii) the [Environment Agency];

(iv) . . .

(v) [the Competition and Markets Authority] and [the Gas and Electricity Markets Authority];

[(vi) the Scottish Environment Protection Agency.]

[(f) the Natural Resources Body for Wales is a relevant authority in relation to its relevant transferred functions (within the meaning of article 11 of the Natural Resources Body for Wales (Establishment) Order 2012 (SI 2012/1903)).]

(4) In subsections (2) and (3) above "relevant enactment" means any of the following, that is to say—

(a) the Trade Descriptions Act 1968;
(b) the Fair Trading Act 1973;
(c) the Consumer Credit Act 1974;
(d) Part II of the Control of Pollution Act 1974;
(e), (f) . . .
(g) the Estate Agents Act 1979;
(h) the Competition Act 1980;
(i) the Consumer Protection Act 1987;
(j) the Electricity Act 1989;
(k) the Water Resources Act 1991;
(l) the Land Drainage Act 1991;
(m) . . .
[(n) the Competition Act 1998];
[(o) the Enterprise Act 2002];
[(p) the Water Act 2003];
[(q) any subordinate legislation made for the purpose of securing compliance with Directive 2005/29/EC of the European Parliament and of the Council of 11 May 2005 concerning unfair business-to-consumer commercial practices in the internal market;
(r) any subordinate legislation made for the purpose of securing compliance with Directive 2006/114/EC of the European Parliament and of the Council of 12 December 2006 concerning misleading and comparative advertising];
[(s) Parts 3 and 4 of the Enterprise and Regulatory Reform Act 2013];
[(t) the Water Act 2014.]

(5) Nothing in any arrangements under this section shall—

(a) limit the matters which may be contained in a report under section 60 below or section 49 of the 1991 Act (report on operation of that Act); or
(b) restrict or prohibit the disclosure of any information which has already been made public—
   (i) as part of such a report;
   (ii) in pursuance of any arrangements under section 57 above;
   (iii) under any provision of section 31 or 32 above or Part III of this Act requiring the publication of any notice or other matter; or
   (iv) in the exercise of any power or the performance of any duty which is conferred or imposed on any person apart from this Act.

(6) The Secretary of State may by order made by statutory instrument modify subsections (2) to (5) above so as to add to or restrict the descriptions of disclosures which are to be excluded from any prohibition contained in arrangements under subsection (1) above; and the power to make an order under this subsection shall be exercisable by statutory instrument subject to annulment in pursuance of a resolution of either House of Parliament.

(7) Subject to subsection (8) below, where any licence under Part II of this Act or any such undertaking as is mentioned in section 57(4)(b) above contains provision for any information furnished to the Authority to be treated as subject to such an obligation of confidence as restricts the disclosure or use of that information without the consent of the person to whom that obligation is to be owed—

(a) the requirement to comply with that obligation shall be a duty owed by the Authority to that person; and
(b) any such disclosure or use, in contravention of that provision, of any information as causes the person to whom it is owed to sustain loss or damage shall be actionable against the Authority at the suit or instance of that person.

(8) Subsection (7) above shall not apply, except in so far as the provisions of the licence or undertaking contain express provision to the contrary, to any disclosure of information which is for the time being excluded by virtue of subsections (2) to (5) above from the prohibition contained in arrangements under subsection (1) above.

(9) In this section "records" has the same meaning as in section 57 above.

NOTES

Sub-s (2): words in square brackets in para (e) substituted for original words "Lands Tribunal or" by the Transfer of Tribunal Functions (Lands Tribunal and Miscellaneous Amendments) Order 2009, SI 2009/1307, art 5(1), (2), Sch 1, paras 255, 257, subject to transitional provisions and savings in art 5(6), Sch 5 thereto; reference in square brackets in para (f) substituted by the Treaty of Lisbon (Changes in Terminology) Order 2011, SI 2011/1043, art 6(1)(e).

Sub-s (3): para (b) substituted by the Financial Services and Markets Act 2000 (Consequential Amendments) Order 2002, SI 2002/1555, art 23, words in first pair of square brackets substituted by the Financial Services Act 2012, s 114(2), Sch 18, Pt 2, para 80, and words in second pair of square brackets inserted by the Financial Services Act 2012 (Consumer Credit) Order 2013, SI 2013/1882, art 10(2); para (dd) inserted by the Transport Act 2000 (Consequential Amendments) Order 2001, SI 2001/4050, art 2, Schedule, Pt IV, para 24; words omitted from para (e)(ii) repealed by the Legislative Reform (Health and Safety Executive) Order 2008, SI 2008/960, art 22, Sch 3; para (e)(iia) inserted by the Energy Act 2013, s 116(1), Sch 12, Pt 5, para 70; words in square brackets in para (e)(iii) substituted by the Environment Act 1995 (Consequential Amendments) Regulations 1996, SI 1996/593, reg 2, Sch 1; para (e)(iv) repealed and words in first pair of square brackets in para (e)(v) substituted by the Enterprise and Regulatory Reform Act 2013 (Competition) (Consequential, Transitional and Saving Provisions) Order 2014, SI 2014/892, art 2, Sch 1, Pt 2, para 113(a); words in second pair of square brackets in para (e)(v) substituted by virtue of the Utilities Act 2000, s 3(2); para (e)(vi) substituted by the Environment Act 1995 (Consequential and

Transitional Provisions) (Scotland) Regulations 1996, SI 1996/973, reg 2, Schedule, para 16; para (f) inserted by the Natural Resources Body for Wales (Functions) Order 2013, SI 2013/755, art 4(1), Sch 2, Pt 1, para 360.

Sub-s (4): paras (e), (f) repealed and para (n) inserted by the Competition Act 1998, s 74(1), (3), Sch 12, para 18(a), (b), Sch 14, Pt I; para (m) repealed and paras (q), (r) inserted by the Consumer Protection from Unfair Trading Regulations 2008, SI 2008/1277, reg 30(1), (3), Sch 2, Pt 1, para 57, Sch 4, Pt 1; para (o) inserted by the Enterprise Act 2002, s 278, Sch 25, para 32(1), (2)(b); para (p) inserted by the Water Act 2003, s 101(1), Sch 7, Pt 2, para 31; para (s) inserted by SI 2014/892, art 2, Sch 1, Pt 2, para 113(b); para (t) inserted by the Water Act 2014 (Consequential Amendments etc) Order 2017, SI 2017/506, art 9.

60, 61 *(Outside the scope of this work.)*

Supplemental

62–64 *(Outside the scope of this work.)*

[17.114]

65 Interpretation

(1) In this Act, except in so far as the context otherwise requires—

. . .

"the 1991 Act" means the Coal Mining Subsidence Act 1991;

"the Authority" means the Coal Authority;

"business" includes any trade or profession;

. . .

"coal-mining operations" includes—

(a) searching for coal and boring for it,

(b) winning, working and getting it (whether underground or in the course of opencast operations),

(c) bringing underground coal to the surface, treating coal and rendering it saleable,

(d) treating coal in the strata for the purpose of winning any product of coal and winning, working or getting any product of coal resulting from such treatment, and

(e) depositing spoil from any activities carried on in the course of any coal-mining operations and draining coal mines,

and an operation carried on in relation to minerals other than coal is a coal-mining operation in so far as it is carried on in relation to those minerals as part of, or is ancillary to, operations carried on in relation to coal;

"company" [has the meaning given by section 1(1) of the Companies Act 2006];

"contravention" includes a failure to comply, and cognate expressions shall be construed accordingly;

. . .

"holder", in relation to a licence under Part II of this Act, means the following person (whether or not the authorisation contained in the licence remains in force), that is to say—

(a) in a case where there has been no such transfer in relation to that licence as is mentioned in section 27(5) above, the person to whom the licence was granted, and

(b) in any other case, the person to whom the rights and obligations of the holder of that licence were last transferred;

. . .

"licensed operator" means any person who is for the time being either—

(a) authorised by a licence under Part II of this Act to carry on coal-mining operations to which section 25 above applies, or

(b) authorised by virtue of subsection (3) of that section to carry on any such operations;

. . .

"restructuring scheme" means a scheme under section 12 above;

. . .

"subordinate legislation" has the same meaning as in the Interpretation Act 1978;

. . .

(2)–(4) *(Outside the scope of this work.)*

NOTES

Sub-s (1): definitions omitted outside the scope of this work; words in square brackets in definition "company" substituted by the Companies Act 2006 (Consequential Amendments, Transitional Provisions and Savings) Order 2009, SI 2009/1941, art 2(1), Sch 1, para 147(1), (3)(a).

65A–67 *(Outside the scope of this work.)*

[17.115]

68 Short title, commencement and extent

(1) This Act may be cited as the Coal Industry Act 1994.

(2), (3) *(Outside the scope of this work.)*

(4) Apart from the provisions to which subsections (2) and (3) above apply and the provisions specified in subsection (6) below (which come into force on the passing of this Act), this Act shall come into force on such day as the Secretary of State may by order made by statutory instrument appoint.

(5) An order under subsection (4) above may—

(a) appoint different days for different provisions and for different purposes; and

(b) make any such transitional provision (including provision modifying for transitional purposes any of the provisions of this Act or of any enactment amended or repealed by this Act) as the Secretary of State considers appropriate in connection with the bringing into force of any provision of this Act;

but, where an order under that subsection makes any such provision as is mentioned in paragraph (b) above, the statutory instrument containing the order shall be subject to annulment in pursuance of a resolution of either House of Parliament.

(6) The provisions of this Act mentioned in subsection (4) above are this section and—

(a)–(c) (*outside the scope of this work*);

(d) sections 62 to 66;

(e), (f) (*outside the scope of this work.*)

(7) The following provisions of this Act do not extend to Scotland, that is to say—

[(za)] (*outside the scope of this work*);

(a) sections 49 and 50 and Schedule 7; and

(b) so much of Schedules 9 and 11 as relates to enactments extending to England and Wales only.

[(7A)], (8), (9) (*Outside the scope of this work.*)

NOTES

Orders: at present 8 commencement orders have been made under this section. The order relevant to the provisions of this Act reproduced here is the Coal Industry Act 1994 (Commencement No 2 and Transitional Provision) Order 1994, SI 1994/2552. S 36 of this Act was brought into force by virtue of the Coal Industry (Restructuring Date) Order 1994, SI 1994/2553.

SCHEDULES 1–11

(*Schs 1–11 outside the scope of this work.*)

PENSIONS ACT 1995

(1995 c 26)

ARRANGEMENT OF SECTIONS

PART I
OCCUPATIONAL PENSIONS

Independent trustees

22 Circumstances in which following provisions apply . . . . . [17.116]
23 Requirement for independent trustee . . . . . [17.117]
25 Appointment and powers of independent trustees: further provisions . . . . . [17.118]
26 Insolvency practitioner or official receiver to give information to trustees . . . . . [17.119]

Modification of schemes

71A Modification by Authority to secure winding-up . . . . . [17.120]

Winding up

73 Preferential liabilities on winding up . . . . . [17.121]
73A Operation of scheme during winding up period . . . . . [17.122]
73B Sections 73 and 73A: supplementary . . . . . [17.123]
75 Deficiencies in the assets . . . . . [17.124]
75A Deficiencies in the assets: multi-employer schemes . . . . . [17.125]

Assignment, forfeiture, bankruptcy etc

91 Inalienability of occupational pension . . . . . [17.126]
92 Forfeiture, etc . . . . . [17.127]
93 Forfeiture by reference to obligation to employer . . . . . [17.128]

General

124 Interpretation of Part I . . . . . [17.129]
125 Section 124: supplementary . . . . . [17.130]

PART IV
MISCELLANEOUS AND GENERAL

General

180 Commencement . . . . . [17.131]
181 Short title . . . . . [17.132]

An Act to amend the law about pensions and for connected purposes

[19 July 1995]

PART I
OCCUPATIONAL PENSIONS

NOTES

Modification: this Act is applied, with modifications, in so far as it relates to bank insolvency or administration under the Banking Act 2009, Pts 2, 3, by the Banking Act 2009 (Parts 2 and 3 Consequential Amendments) Order 2009, SI 2009/317, art 3, Schedule at **[7.86]**, **[7.92]**.

1–21 (*In so far as unrepealed, outside the scope of this work.*)

Independent trustees

[17.116]

22 Circumstances in which following provisions apply

(1) This section applies in relation to a trust scheme—

(a) if a person (referred to in this section and sections 23 [to 26] as "the practitioner") begins to act as an insolvency practitioner in relation to a company which, or an individual who, is the employer in relation to the scheme, or

(b) if the official receiver becomes—

(i) the liquidator or provisional liquidator of a company which is the employer in relation to the scheme, . . .

[(ia) the interim receiver of the property of a person who is the employer in relation to the scheme, or]

(ii) the receiver and the manager, or the trustee, of the estate of a bankrupt who is the employer in relation to the scheme.

(2) Where this section applies in relation to a scheme [by virtue of subsection (1)], it ceases to do so—

(a) if some person other than the employer mentioned in subsection (1) becomes the employer, or

(b) if at any time neither the practitioner nor the official receiver is acting in relation to the employer;

but this subsection does not affect the application of this section in relation to the scheme on any subsequent occasion when the conditions specified in subsection (1)(a) or (b) are satisfied in relation to it.

[(2A) To the extent that it does not already apply by virtue of subsection (1), this section also applies in relation to a trust scheme—

(a) at any time during an assessment period (within the meaning of section 132 of the Pensions Act 2004) in relation to the scheme, and

(b) at any time, not within paragraph (a), when the scheme is authorised under section 153 of that Act (closed schemes) to continue as a closed scheme.

(2B) The responsible person must, as soon as reasonably practicable, give notice of an event within subsection (2C) to—

(a) the Authority,

(b) the Board of the Pension Protection Fund, and

(c) the trustees of the scheme.

(2C) The events are—

(a) the practitioner beginning to act as mentioned in subsection (1)(a), if immediately before he does so this section does not apply in relation to the scheme;

(b) the practitioner ceasing to so act, if immediately after he does so this section does not apply in relation to the scheme;

(c) the official receiver beginning to act in a capacity mentioned in subsection (1)(b)(i), (ia) or (ii), if immediately before he does so this section does not apply in relation to the scheme;

(d) the official receiver ceasing to act in such a capacity, if immediately after he does so this section does not apply in relation to the scheme.

(2D) For the purposes of subsection (2B) "the responsible person" means—

(a) in the case of an event within subsection (2C)(a) or (b) the practitioner, and

(b) in the case of an event within subsection (2C)(c) or (d), the official receiver.

(2E) Regulations may require prescribed persons in prescribed circumstances where this section begins or ceases to apply in relation to a trust scheme by virtue of subsection (2A) to give a notice to that effect to—

(a) the Authority,

(b) the Board of the Pension Protection Fund, and

(c) the trustees of the scheme.

(2F) A notice under subsection (2B), or regulations under subsection (2E), must be in writing and contain such information as may be prescribed.]

(3) In this section and sections 23 [to 26]—

"acting as an insolvency practitioner" and "official receiver" shall be construed in accordance with sections 388 and 399 of the Insolvency Act 1986,

"bankrupt" has the meaning given by section 381 of the Insolvency Act 1986,

"company" means a company [as defined in section 1(1) of the Companies Act 2006] or a company which may be wound up under Part V of the Insolvency Act 1986 (unregistered companies), *and "interim trustee" and "permanent trustee" have the same meanings as they have in the Bankruptcy (Scotland) Act 1985.*

NOTES

Sub-s (1): words in square brackets in para (a) substituted, and in para (b) word omitted repealed and words in square brackets inserted by the Pensions Act 2004, ss 36(1), (2)(a), 319(1), 320, Sch 12, paras 34, 40, Sch 13, Pt I, subject to transitional provisions in SI 2005/695, arts 3, 5.

Sub-s (2): words in square brackets inserted by the Pensions Act 2004, s 36(1), (2)(b).

Sub-ss (2A)–(2F): inserted by the Pensions Act 2004, s 36(1), (2)(c), (d).

Sub-s (3): words in first pair of square brackets substituted by the Pensions Act 2004, s 319(1), Sch 12, paras 34, 40, subject to transitional provisions in SI 2005/695, arts 3, 5; words in square brackets in definition "company" substituted by the Companies Act 2006 (Consequential Amendments, Transitional Provisions and Savings) Order 2009, SI 2009/1941, art 2(1), Sch 1, para 155(1), (3); definitions "interim trustee" and "permanent trustee" repealed, together with preceding word "and", by the Bankruptcy (Scotland) Act 2016 (Consequential Provisions and Modifications) Order 2016, SI 2016/1034, art 7(1), (3), Sch 1, para 13(1), (2), as from 30 November 2016 (except in relation to (i) a sequestration as regards which the petition is presented, or the debtor application is made before that date; or (ii) a trust deed executed before that date).

Regulations: the Occupational Pension Schemes (Independent Trustee) Regulations 2005, SI 2005/703.

[17.117]

[23 Power to appoint independent trustees

(1) While section 22 applies in relation to a trust scheme, the Authority may by order appoint as a trustee of the scheme a person who—

(a) is an independent person in relation to the scheme, *and*

(b) is registered in the register maintained by the Authority in accordance with regulations under subsection (4).

(2) In relation to a particular trust scheme, no more than one trustee may at any time be an independent trustee appointed under subsection (1).

(3) For the purposes of this section a person is independent in relation to a trust scheme only if—

(a) he has no interest in the assets of the employer or of the scheme otherwise than as trustee of the scheme,

(b) he is neither connected with, nor an associate of—

(i) the employer,

(ii) any person for the time being acting as an insolvency practitioner in relation to the employer, or

(iii) the official receiver acting in any of the capacities mentioned in section 22(1)(b) in relation to the employer, and

(c) he satisfies any prescribed requirements;

and any reference in this Part to an independent trustee is to be construed accordingly.

(4) Regulations must provide for the Authority to compile and maintain a register of persons who satisfy the prescribed conditions for registration.

(5) Regulations under subsection (4) may provide—

(a) for copies of the register or of extracts from it to be provided to prescribed persons in prescribed circumstances;

(b) for the inspection of the register by prescribed persons in prescribed circumstances.

(6) The circumstances which may be prescribed under subsection (5)(a) or (b) include the payment by the person to whom the copy is to be provided, or by whom the register is to be inspected, of such reasonable fee as may be determined by the Authority.

(7) This section is without prejudice to the powers conferred by section 7.]

NOTES

Substituted, for original ss 23, 24, by the Pensions Act 2004, s 36(1), (3).

Sub-s (1): para (b) and word immediately preceding it repealed by the Pension Schemes Act 2015, s 44(1), (2), as from a day to be appointed.

Sub-ss (4)–(6): repealed by the Pension Schemes Act 2015, s 44(1), (3), as from a day to be appointed.

Regulations: the Personal and Occupational Pension Schemes (Miscellaneous Amendments) (No 2) Regulations 1997, SI 1997/3038; the Occupational Pension Schemes (Winding Up Notices and Reports etc) Regulations 2002, SI 2002/459 at **[9.67]**; the Occupational Pension Schemes (Independent Trustee) Regulations 2005, SI 2005/703.

24 *(Substituted, together with original s 23, by a new s 23 by the Pensions Act 2004, s 36(1), (3).)*

[17.118]

25 Appointment and powers of independent trustees: further provisions

(1) If, immediately before the appointment of an independent trustee under [section 23(1)], there is no trustee of the scheme other than the employer, the employer shall cease to be a trustee upon the appointment of the independent trustee.

(2) While section 22 applies in relation to a scheme [and there is an independent trustee of the scheme appointed under section 23(1)]—

(a) any power vested in the trustees of the scheme and exercisable at their discretion may be exercised only by the independent trustee, and

(b) any power—

(i) which the scheme confers on the employer (otherwise than as trustee of the scheme), and

(ii) which is exercisable by him at his discretion but only as trustee of the power,

may be exercised only by the independent trustee,

. . .

(3) While section 22 applies in relation to a scheme [and there is an independent trustee of the scheme appointed under section 23(1), the independent trustee may not] be removed from being a trustee by virtue only of any provision of the scheme.

(4) If a trustee appointed under [section 23(1)] ceases to be an independent person [(within the meaning of section 23(3))], then—

[(a) he must as soon as reasonably practicable give written notice of that fact to the Authority, and]

(b) subject to subsection (5), he shall cease to be a trustee of the scheme.

(5) If, in a case where subsection (4) applies, there is no other trustee of the scheme than the former independent trustee, he shall not cease by virtue of that subsection to be a trustee until such time as another trustee is appointed.

[(5A) Section 10 applies to any person who, without reasonable excuse, fails to comply with subsection (4)(a).]

[(6) An order under section 23(1) may provide for any fees and expenses of the trustee appointed under the order to be paid—

(a) by the employer,

(b) out of the resources of the scheme, or

(c) partly by the employer and partly out of those resources.

(7) Such an order may also provide that an amount equal to the amount (if any) paid out of the resources of the scheme by virtue of subsection (6)(b) or (c) is to be treated for all purposes as a debt due from the employer to the trustees of the scheme.

(8) Where, by virtue of subsection (6)(b) or (c), an order makes provision for any fees or expenses of the trustee appointed under the order to be paid out of the resources of the scheme, the trustee is entitled to be so paid in priority to all other claims falling to be met out of the scheme's resources.]

NOTES

Sub-s (1): words in square brackets substituted by the Pensions Act 2004, s 319(1), Sch 12, paras 34, 41(a), subject to transitional provisions in SI 2005/695, arts 3, 5.

Sub-s (2): words in square brackets inserted and words omitted repealed by the Pensions Act 2004, ss 319(1), 320, Sch 12, paras 34, 41(b), Sch 13, Pt I, subject to transitional provisions in SI 2005/695, arts 3, 5.

Sub-s (3): words in square brackets substituted by the Pensions Act 2004, s 319(1), Sch 12, paras 34, 41(c), subject to transitional provisions in SI 2005/695, arts 3, 5.

Sub-s (4): words in first pair of square brackets substituted, words in second pair of square brackets inserted, and para (a) substituted by the Pensions Act 2004, ss 36(1), (4)(a), 319(1), Sch 12, paras 34, 41(d), subject to transitional provisions in SI 2005/695, arts 3, 5.

Sub-s (5A): inserted by the Pensions Act 2004, s 36(1), (4)(b).

Sub-ss (6)–(8): substituted, for original sub-s (6), by the Pensions Act 2004, s 36(1), (4)(c).

[17.119]

26 Insolvency practitioner or official receiver to give information to trustees

(1) Notwithstanding anything in section 155 of the Insolvency Act 1986 (court orders for inspection etc), while section 22 applies in relation to a scheme [by virtue of subsection (1) of that section], the practitioner or official receiver must provide the trustees of the scheme, as soon as practicable after the receipt of a request, with any information which the trustees may reasonably require for the purposes of the scheme.

(2) Any expenses incurred by the practitioner or official receiver in complying with a request under subsection (1) are recoverable by him as part of the expenses incurred by him in discharge of his duties.

(3) The practitioner or official receiver is not required under subsection (1) to take any action which involves expenses that cannot be so recovered, unless the trustees of the scheme undertake to meet them.

NOTES

Sub-s (1): words in square brackets inserted by the Pensions Act 2004, s 319(1), Sch 12, paras 34, 42, subject to transitional provisions in SI 2005/695, arts 3, 5.

26A–66A *(In so far as unrepealed, outside the scope of this work.)*

Modification of schemes

67–71 *(Outside the scope of this work.)*

[17.120]

[71A Modification by Authority to secure winding-up

(1) The Authority may at any time while—

(a) an occupational pension scheme is being wound up, and

(b) the employer in relation to the scheme is subject to an insolvency procedure,

make an order modifying that scheme with a view to ensuring that it is properly wound up.

(2) The Authority shall not make such an order except on an application made to them, at a time such as is mentioned in subsection (1), by the trustees or managers of the scheme.

(3) Except in so far as regulations otherwise provide, an application for the purposes of this section must be made in writing.

(4) Regulations may make provision—

(a) for the form and manner in which an application for the purposes of this section is to be made to the Authority;

(b) for the matters which are to be contained in such an application;

(c) for the documents which must be attached to an application for the purposes of this section or which must otherwise be delivered to the Authority with or in connection with any such application;
(d) for persons to be required, [before an application is made for the purposes of this section], to give such notifications of the making of [the application] as may be prescribed;
(e) for the matters which are to be contained in a notification of such an application;
(f), (g) . . .

(5) The power of the Authority to make an order under this section—
(a) shall be limited to what they consider to be the minimum modification necessary to enable the scheme to be properly wound up; and
(b) shall not include power to make any modification that would have a significant adverse effect on—
(i) the accrued rights of any member of the scheme; or
(ii) any person's entitlement under the scheme to receive any benefit.

(6) A modification of an occupational pension scheme by an order of the Authority under this section shall be as effective in law as if—
(a) it had been made under powers conferred by or under the scheme;
(b) the modification made by the order were capable of being made in exercise of such powers notwithstanding any enactment, rule of law or rule of the scheme that would have prevented their exercise for the making of that modification; and
(c) the exercise of such powers for the making of that modification would not have been subject to any enactment, rule of law or rule of the scheme requiring the implementation of any procedure or the obtaining of any consent in connection with the making of a modification.

(7) Regulations may provide that, in prescribed circumstances, this section—
(a) does not apply in the case of occupational pension schemes of a prescribed class or description; or
(b) in the case of occupational pension schemes of a prescribed class or description applies with prescribed modifications.

(8) The times when an employer in relation to an occupational pension scheme shall be taken for the purposes of this section to be subject to an insolvency procedure are—
(a) in the case of a trust scheme, while section 22 applies in relation to the scheme; and
(b) in the case of a scheme that is not a trust scheme, while section 22 would apply in relation to the scheme if it were a trust scheme;

and for the purposes of this subsection no account shall be taken of modifications or exclusions contained in any regulations under section 118.

(9) The Authority shall not be entitled to make an order under this section in relation to a public service pension scheme.]

NOTES

Inserted by the Child Support, Pensions and Social Security Act 2000, s 48.

Sub-s (4): words in square brackets in para (d) substituted, and paras (f), (g) repealed by the Pensions Act 2004, ss 319(1), 320, Sch 12, paras 34, 58, Sch 13, Pt I.

Regulations: the Occupational Pension Schemes (Winding Up Notices and Reports etc) Regulations 2002, SI 2002/459 at **[9.67]**.

72–72C (*Outside the scope of this work.*)

Winding up

[17.121]

[73 Preferential liabilities on winding up

(1) This section applies where an occupational pension scheme to which this section applies is being wound up to determine the order in which the assets of the scheme are to be applied towards satisfying the liabilities of the scheme in respect of pensions and other benefits.

(2) This section applies to an occupational pension scheme other than a scheme which is—
(a) a money purchase scheme, or
(b) a prescribed scheme or a scheme of a prescribed description.

(3) The assets of the scheme must be applied first towards satisfying the amounts of the liabilities mentioned in subsection (4) and, if the assets are insufficient to satisfy those amounts in full, then—
(a) the assets must be applied first towards satisfying the amounts of the liabilities mentioned in earlier paragraphs of subsection (4) before the amounts of the liabilities mentioned in later paragraphs, and
(b) where the amounts of the liabilities mentioned in one of those paragraphs cannot be satisfied in full, those amounts must be satisfied in the same proportions.

(4) The liabilities referred to in subsection (3) are—
(a) where—
(i) the trustees or managers of the scheme are entitled to benefits under a relevant pre-1997 contract of insurance entered into in relation to the scheme, and
(ii) either that contract may not be surrendered or the amount payable on surrender does not exceed the liability secured by the contract,

the liability so secured;
(b) any liability for pensions or other benefits to the extent that the amount of the liability does not exceed the corresponding PPF liability, other than a liability within paragraph (a);

(c) any liability for pensions or other benefits which, in the opinion of the trustees or managers, are derived from the payment by any member of voluntary contributions, other than a liability within paragraph (a) or (b);

(d) any other liability in respect of pensions or other benefits.

(5) For the purposes of subsection (4)—

"corresponding PPF liability" in relation to any liability for pensions or other benefits means—

(a) where the liability is to a member of the scheme, the cost of securing benefits for or in respect of the member corresponding to the compensation which would be payable to or in respect of the member in accordance with the pension compensation provisions if the Board of the Pension Protection Fund assumed responsibility for the scheme in accordance with Chapter 3 of Part 2 of the Pensions Act 2004 (pension protection), and

(b) where the liability is to another person in respect of a member of the scheme, the cost of securing benefits for that person corresponding to the compensation which would be payable to that person in respect of the member in accordance with the pension compensation provisions if the Board assumed responsibility for the scheme in accordance with that Chapter;

"relevant pre-1997 contract of insurance" means a contract of insurance which was entered into before 6th April 1997 with a view to securing the whole or part of the scheme's liability for—

(a) any pension or other benefit payable to or in respect of one particular person whose entitlement to payment of a pension or other benefit has arisen, and

(b) any benefit which will be payable in respect of that person on his death.

(6) For the purposes of this section, when determining the corresponding PPF liability in relation to any liability of a scheme to, or in respect of, a member for pensions or other benefits, the pension compensation provisions apply with such modifications as may be prescribed.

(7) Regulations may modify subsection (4).

(8) For the purposes of that subsection—

(a) regulations may prescribe how it is to be determined whether a liability for pensions or other benefits which, in the opinion of the trustees or managers of the scheme, are derived from the payment by any member of voluntary contributions falls within paragraph (a) or (b) of that subsection;

(b) no pension or other benefit which is attributable (directly or indirectly) to a pension credit is to be regarded for the purposes of paragraph (c) of that subsection as derived from the payment of voluntary contributions.

(9) Where, on the commencement of the winding up period, a member becomes a person to whom [Chapter 2 of Part 4ZA] of the Pension Schemes Act 1993 (early leavers: cash transfer sums and contribution refunds) applies, that Chapter applies in relation to him with such modifications as may be prescribed.

(10) For the purposes of this section—

"assets" of a scheme to which this section applies do not include any assets representing the value of any rights in respect of money purchase benefits under the scheme rules;

"liabilities" of such a scheme do not include any liabilities in respect of money purchase benefits under the scheme rules;

"the pension compensation provisions" has the same meaning as in Part 2 of the Pensions Act 2004 (see section 162 of that Act);

"scheme rules" has the same meaning as in the Pensions Act 2004 (see section 318 of that Act);

"winding up period", in relation to an occupational pension scheme to which this section applies, means the period which—

(a) begins with the day on which the time immediately after the beginning of the winding up of the scheme falls, and

(b) ends when the winding up of the scheme is completed.]

NOTES

Substituted, together with ss 73A, 73B, for original s 73, by the Pensions Act 2004, s 270(1), except in relation to certain specified schemes immediately before 6 April 2005 (see SI 2005/275, art 2(3), (8), (9), Schedule, Pt 3).

Prior to this substitution, s 73 and the notes relating to it read as follows:

"73 Preferential liabilities on winding up

(1) This section applies, where a salary related occupational pension scheme to which section 56 applies is being wound up, to determine the order in which the assets of the scheme are to be applied towards satisfying the liabilities in respect of pensions and other benefits (including increases in pensions).

(2) The assets of the scheme must be applied first towards satisfying the amounts of the liabilities mentioned in subsection (3) and, if the assets are insufficient to satisfy those amounts in full, then—

(a) the assets must be applied first towards satisfying the amounts of the liabilities mentioned in earlier paragraphs of subsection (3) before the amounts of the liabilities mentioned in later paragraphs, and

(b) where the amounts of the liabilities mentioned in one of those paragraphs cannot be satisfied in full, those amounts must be satisfied in the same proportions.

(3) The liabilities referred to in subsection (2) are—

(a) any liability for pensions or other benefits which, in the opinion of the trustees, are derived from the payment by any member of the scheme of voluntary contributions,

[(aa) where—

(i) the trustees or managers of the scheme are entitled to benefits under a contract of insurance which was entered into before 6th April 1997 with a view to securing the whole or part of the scheme's liability for any pension or other benefit payable in respect of one particular person whose entitlement to payment of a pension or other benefit has arisen and for any benefit which will be payable in respect of that person on his death, and

(ii) either that contract may not be surrendered or the amount payable on surrender does not exceed the liability secured by the contract (but excluding liability for increases to pensions),

the liability so secured.]

(b) [in a case not falling within paragraph (aa),] where a person's entitlement to payment of pension or other benefit has arisen, liability for that pension or benefit and for any pension or other benefit which will be payable [in respect] of that person on his death (but excluding increases to pensions),

(c) any liability for—

(i) pensions or other benefits which have accrued to or in respect of any members of the scheme (but excluding increases to pensions),

[(ia) future pensions, or other future benefits, attributable (directly or indirectly) to pension credits (but excluding increases to pensions),] or

(ii) (in respect of members with less than two years pensionable service) the return of contributions,

(d) any liability for increases to pensions referred to in paragraphs (b) and (c);

and, for the purposes of subsection (2), the amounts of the liabilities mentioned in paragraphs (b) to (d) are to be taken to be the amounts calculated and verified in the prescribed manner.

[(3A) No pension or other benefit which is attributable (directly or indirectly) to a pension credit may be regarded for the purposes of subsection (3)(a) as derived from the payment of voluntary contributions.]

(4) To the extent that any liabilities, as calculated in accordance with the rules of the scheme, have not been satisfied under subsection (2), any remaining assets of the scheme must then be applied towards satisfying those liabilities (as so calculated) in the order provided for in the rules of the scheme.

(5) If the scheme confers power on any person other than the trustees or managers to apply the assets of the scheme in respect of pensions or other benefits (including increases in pensions), it cannot be exercised by that person but may be exercised instead by the trustees or managers.

(6) If this section is not complied with—

(a) section 3 applies to any trustee who has failed to take all such steps as are reasonable to secure compliance, and

(b) section 10 applies to any trustee or manager who has failed to take all such steps.

(7) Regulations may modify subsection (3).

(8) This section does not apply to an occupational pension scheme falling within a prescribed class or description.

(9) This section shall have effect with prescribed modifications in cases where part of a salary related occupational pension scheme to which section 56 applies is being wound up.

NOTES

Sub-s (3): para (aa) and words in first pair of square brackets in para (b) inserted, and words in second pair of square brackets in para (b) substituted by the Occupational Pension Schemes (Winding Up) Regulations 1996, SI 1996/3126, reg 3(1)(a), (3), (4); para (c)(ia) inserted by the Welfare Reform and Pensions Act 1999, s 38(1).

Sub-s (3A): inserted by the Welfare Reform and Pensions Act 1999, s 84(1), Sch 12, Pt I, paras 43, 55.

Sub-s (6): para (a) repealed by the Pensions Act 2004, ss 319(1), 320, Sch 12, paras 34, 61, Sch 13, Pt I, as from a day to be appointed.

Modifications: in addition to the amendments made by the Occupational Pension Schemes (Winding Up) Regulations 1996, SI 1996/3126, reg 3(1)(a), (3), (4) as noted above, this section is modified by reg 3(1)(b), (c), (5)–(7) of those Regulations (as amended by SI 1999/3198, reg 11, SI 2000/2691, reg 3(1), (3), SI 2004/1140, regs 2, 3 and SI 2005/706, reg 14, Schedule, Pt 1, para 2(d)) in cases where a scheme is wound up before, or after, the expiry of the "transitional period" as defined in reg 3(2) thereof.".

Sub-s (2): substituted as follows by the Pension Schemes Act 2015, s 46, Sch 2, paras 6, 11, as from a day to be appointed:

"(2) This section applies to a pension scheme that is—

(a) an occupational defined benefits scheme,

(b) an occupational shared risk scheme, or

(c) an occupational defined contributions scheme,

unless subsection (2A) provides for the scheme to be exempt.

(2A) A scheme is exempt from this section if it is—

(a) a scheme under which all the benefits that may be provided are money purchase benefits, or

(b) a prescribed scheme or a scheme of a prescribed description.".

Sub-s (9): words in square brackets substituted by the Pension Schemes Act 2015, s 67, Sch 4, Pt 1, paras 28, 30.

Disapplication: as to the disapplication of this section to schemes which have begun to be wound up after 6 April 2005, see the Occupational Pension Schemes (Winding up etc) Regulations 2005, SI 2005/706, reg 3.

Modifications: in relation to the application of the pension compensation provisions (as defined in the Pensions Act 2004, s 162), this section is applied, with modifications, for the purposes of determining the corresponding PPF liability in relation to any liability of a scheme to or in respect of a member for pensions or other benefits under this section, by the Occupational Pension Schemes (Winding up etc) Regulations 2005, SI 2005/706, reg 4 (as amended by SI 2005/2159, reg 3(1), (2)). In relation to multi-employer schemes, this section is applied, with modifications, by the Occupational Pension Schemes (Winding Up) (Modification for Multi-employer Schemes and Miscellaneous Amendments) Regulations 2005, SI 2005/2159, reg 2.

Regulations: the Occupational Pension Schemes (Winding Up) Regulations 1996, SI 1996/3126; the Personal and Occupational Pension Schemes (Miscellaneous Amendments) Regulations 1999, SI 1999/3198; the Pension Sharing (Consequential and Miscellaneous Amendments) Regulations 2000, SI 2000/2691; the Occupational Pension Schemes (Minimum Funding Requirement and Miscellaneous Amendments) Regulations 2002, SI 2002/380; the Occupational Pension Schemes (Winding Up and Deficiency on Winding Up etc) (Amendment) Regulations 2004, SI 2004/403; the Occupational Pension Schemes (Winding Up) (Amendment) Regulations 2004, SI 2004/1140; the Occupational Pension Schemes (Winding Up, Deficiency on Winding Up and Transfer Values) (Amendment) Regulations 2005, SI 2005/72; the Occupational Pension Schemes (Winding up etc) Regulations 2005, SI 2005/706; the Occupational Pension Schemes (Winding Up) (Modification for Multi-employer Schemes and Miscellaneous Amendments) Regulations 2005, SI 2005/2159; the Occupational Pension Schemes (Republic of Ireland Schemes Exemption (Revocation) and Tax Exempt Schemes (Miscellaneous Amendments)) Regulations 2006, SI 2006/467; the Occupational and Personal Pension Schemes (Miscellaneous Amendments) Regulations 2007, SI

2007/814; the Occupational Pension Schemes (Scottish Parliamentary Pensions Act 2009) Regulations 2009, SI 2009/1906; the Pensions Act 2011 (Transitional, Consequential and Supplementary Provisions) Regulations 2014, SI 2014/1711.

[17.122]

[73A Operation of scheme during winding up period

(1) This section applies where an occupational pension scheme to which section 73 applies is being wound up.

(2) During the winding up period, the trustees or managers of the scheme—

- (a) must secure that any pensions or other benefits (other than money purchase benefits) paid to or in respect of a member are reduced, so far as necessary, to reflect the liabilities of the scheme to or in respect of the member which will be satisfied in accordance with section 73, and
- (b) may, for the purposes of paragraph (a), take such steps as they consider appropriate (including steps adjusting future payments) to recover any overpayment or pay any shortfall.

(3) During the winding up period—

- (a) no benefits may accrue under the scheme rules to, or in respect of, members of the scheme, and
- (b) no new members of any class may be admitted to the scheme.

(4) Subsection (3) does not prevent any increase, in a benefit, which would otherwise accrue in accordance with the scheme or any enactment.

(5) Subsection (3) does not prevent the accrual of money purchase benefits to the extent that they are derived from income or capital gains arising from the investment of payments which are made by, or in respect of, a member of the scheme.

(6) Where a person is entitled to a pension credit derived from another person's shareable rights under the scheme, subsection (3) does not prevent the trustees or managers of the scheme discharging their liability in respect of the credit under Chapter 1 of Part 4 of the Welfare Reform and Pensions Act 1999 (sharing of rights under pension arrangements) by conferring appropriate rights under the scheme on that person.

[(6A) During the winding up period no right or entitlement of any member, or of any other person in respect of a member, to a benefit that is not a money purchase benefit is to be converted into, or replaced with, a right or entitlement to a money purchase benefit under the scheme rules.]

(7) Regulations may require the trustees or managers of the scheme, in prescribed circumstances—

- (a) to adjust the entitlement of a person to a pension or other benefit under the scheme rules where the entitlement arises as a result of a discretionary award which takes effect during the winding up period;
- (b) to adjust the entitlement of a person ("the survivor") to a pension or other benefit under the scheme rules where—
  - (i) a member of the scheme, or a person who was (or might have become) entitled to a pension or other benefit in respect of a member, dies during the winding up period, and
  - (ii) the survivor's entitlement is to a pension or other benefit in respect of the member (whether arising on the date of that death or subsequently).

(8) Regulations under subsection (7) may, in particular—

- (a) prescribe how the required adjustments to entitlement are to be determined and the manner in which they are to be made;
- (b) in a case where the commencement of the winding up of the scheme is backdated (whether in accordance with section 154 of the Pensions Act 2004 (requirement to wind up schemes with sufficient assets to meet protected liabilities) or otherwise), require any adjustment to a person's entitlement to be made with effect from the time the award takes effect;
- (c) without prejudice to sections 10(3) to (9), 73B(2) and 116, make provision about the consequences of breaching the requirements of the regulations.

(9) If the scheme confers power on any person other than the trustees or managers of the scheme to apply the assets of the scheme in respect of pensions or other benefits (including increases in pensions or benefits), it cannot be exercised by that person but may, subject to the provisions made by or by virtue of this section and sections 73 and 73B, be exercised instead by the trustees or managers.

(10) For the purposes of this section—

"appropriate rights" has the same meaning as in paragraph 5 of Schedule 5 to the Welfare Reform and Pensions Act 1999 (pension credits: mode of discharge);

"discretionary award" means an award of a prescribed description;

"shareable rights" has the same meaning as in Chapter 1 of Part 4 of the Welfare Reform and Pensions Act 1999 (sharing of rights under pension arrangements);

and subsection (10) of section 73 applies as it applies for the purposes of that section.]

NOTES

Substituted as noted to s 73 at **[17.121]**.

Sub-s (6A): inserted by the Pension Schemes Act 2015, s 58(1).

Modification: in relation to multi-employer schemes, this section is applied, with modifications, by the Occupational Pension Schemes (Winding Up) (Modification for Multi-employer Schemes and Miscellaneous Amendments) Regulations 2005, SI 2005/2159, reg 2.

Regulations: the Occupational Pension Schemes (Winding up etc) Regulations 2005, SI 2005/706.

[17.123]

[73B Sections 73 and 73A: supplementary

(1) Any action taken in contravention of section 73A(3) [or (6A)] is void.

(2) If any provision made by or by virtue of the winding up provisions is not complied with in relation to a scheme to which section 73 applies, section 10 applies to any trustee or manager of the scheme who has failed to take all reasonable steps to secure compliance.

(3) For the purposes of subsection (2), when determining whether section 73A(3) [or (6A)] has been complied with subsection (1) of this section is to be disregarded.

(4) Regulations may—

(a) prescribe how, for the purposes of the winding up provisions—

(i) the assets and liabilities of a scheme to which section 73 applies, and

(ii) their value or amount,

are to be determined, calculated and verified;

(b) modify any of the winding up provisions as it applies—

(i) to prescribed schemes or prescribed descriptions of schemes;

(ii) in relation to a scheme where only part of the scheme is being wound up;

(iii) in relation to a case where any liability of the scheme in respect of a member has been discharged by virtue of regulations under section 135(4) of the Pensions Act 2004 (power to make regulations permitting discharge of scheme's liabilities during an assessment period).

(5) Without prejudice to the generality of subsection (4), regulations under paragraph (b)(i) of that subsection may, in particular, modify any of the winding up provisions as it applies in relation to a scheme in relation to which there is more than one employer.

(6) The winding up provisions do not apply—

(a) in relation to any liability for an amount by way of pensions or other benefits which a person became entitled to payment of, under the scheme rules, before commencement of the winding up period,

(b) in prescribed circumstances, in relation to any liability in respect of rights of a prescribed description to which a member of the scheme became entitled under the scheme rules by reason of his pensionable service under the scheme terminating before the commencement of the winding up period,

(c) in relation to any liability in respect of rights of prescribed descriptions to which a member of the scheme had become entitled under the scheme rules before the commencement of the winding up period, or

(d) in relation to any liability the discharge of which is validated under section 136 of the Pensions Act 2004 (power to validate actions taken during an assessment period to discharge liabilities of a scheme).

(7) But nothing in subsection (6) prevents the winding up provisions applying in relation to a liability under [Chapter 1 of Part 4ZA] of the Pension Schemes Act 1993 (transfer values) which—

(a) arose before the commencement of the winding up of the scheme, and

(b) was not discharged before the commencement of the winding up period.

(8) Regulations may provide that, in prescribed circumstances, where—

(a) an occupational pension scheme to which section 73 applies is being wound up,

(b) a member of the scheme died before the winding up began, and

(c) during the winding up period a person becomes entitled under the scheme rules to a benefit of a prescribed description in respect of the member,

his entitlement to payment of all or part of the benefit is, for the purposes of subsection (6), to be treated as having arisen immediately before the commencement of the winding up period.

(9) If, immediately before the winding up period in relation to an occupational pension scheme to which section 73 applies, a person is entitled to an amount but has postponed payment of it, he is not, for the purposes of subsection (6), to be regarded as having become entitled to payment of the amount before that period.

(10) For the purposes of this section—

(a) "winding up provisions" means this section and sections 73, 73A and 74, and

(b) subsection (10) of section 73 applies as it applies for the purposes of that section.]

NOTES

Substituted as noted to s 73 at **[17.121]**.

Sub-ss (1), (3): words in square brackets inserted by the Pension Schemes Act 2015, s 58(2).

Sub-s (7): words in square brackets substituted by the Pension Schemes Act 2015, s 67, Sch 4, Pt 1, paras 28, 31.

Modification: in relation to multi-employer schemes, this section is applied, with modifications, by the Occupational Pension Schemes (Winding Up) (Modification for Multi-employer Schemes and Miscellaneous Amendments) Regulations 2005, SI 2005/2159, reg 2.

Regulations: the Occupational Pension Schemes (Winding up etc) Regulations 2005, SI 2005/706.

74 (*Outside the scope of this work.*)

[17.124]

75 Deficiencies in the assets

[(1) This section applies in relation to an occupational pension scheme other than a scheme which is—

(a) a money purchase scheme, or

(b) a prescribed scheme or a scheme of a prescribed description.

(2) If—

(a) at any time which falls—

(i) when a scheme is being wound up, but

(ii) before any relevant event in relation to the employer which occurs while the scheme is being wound up,

the value of the assets of the scheme is less than the amount at that time of the liabilities of the scheme, and

(b) the trustees or managers of the scheme designate that time for the purposes of this subsection (before the occurrence of an event within paragraph (a)(ii)),

an amount equal to the difference shall be treated as a debt due from the employer to the trustees or managers of the scheme.

This is subject to subsection (3).

(3) Subsection (2) applies only if—

(a) either—

(i) no relevant event within subsection (6A)(a) or (b) occurred in relation to the employer during the period beginning with the appointed day and ending with the commencement of the winding up of the scheme, or

(ii) during the period—

(a) beginning with the occurrence of the last such relevant event which occurred during the period mentioned in sub-paragraph (i), and

(b) ending with the commencement of the winding up of the scheme,

a cessation notice was issued in relation to the scheme and became binding, and

(b) no relevant event within subsection (6A)(c) has occurred in relation to the employer during the period mentioned in paragraph (a)(i).

(4) Where—

(a) immediately before a relevant event ("the current event") occurs in relation to the employer the value of the assets of the scheme is less than the amount at that time of the liabilities of the scheme,

(b) the current event—

(i) occurred on or after the appointed day, and

(ii) did not occur in prescribed circumstances,

(c) if the scheme was being wound up immediately before that event, subsection (2) has not applied in relation to the scheme to treat an amount as a debt due from the employer to the trustees or managers of the scheme,

(d) if the current event is within subsection (6A)(a) or (b), either—

(i) no relevant event within subsection (6A)(a) or (b) occurred in relation to the employer during the period beginning with the appointed day and ending immediately before the current event, or

(ii) a cessation event has occurred in relation to the scheme in respect of a cessation notice issued during the period—

(a) beginning with the occurrence of the last such relevant event which occurred during the period mentioned in sub-paragraph (i), and

(b) ending immediately before the current event, and

(e) no relevant event within subsection (6A)(c) has occurred in relation to the employer during the period mentioned in paragraph (d)(i),

an amount equal to the difference shall be treated as a debt due from the employer to the trustees or managers of the scheme.

(4A) Where the current event is within subsection (6A)(a) or (b), the debt under subsection (4) is to be taken, for the purposes of the law relating to insolvency as it applies to the employer, to arise immediately before the occurrence of the current event.

(4B) Subsection (4C) applies if, in a case within subsection (4)—

(a) the current event is within subsection (6A)(a) or (b), and

(b) the scheme was not being wound up immediately before that event.

(4C) Where this subsection applies, the debt due from the employer under subsection (4) is contingent upon—

(a) a scheme failure notice being issued in relation to the scheme after the current event and the following conditions being satisfied—

(i) the scheme failure notice is binding,

(ii) no relevant event within subsection (6A)(c) has occurred in relation to the employer before the scheme failure notice became binding, and

(iii) a cessation event has not occurred in relation to the scheme in respect of a cessation notice issued during the period—

(a) beginning with the occurrence of the current event, and

(b) ending immediately before the issuing of the scheme failure notice,

and the occurrence of such a cessation event in respect of a cessation notice issued during that period is not a possibility, or

(b) the commencement of the winding up of the scheme before—

(i) any scheme failure notice or cessation notice issued in relation to the scheme becomes binding, or

(ii) any relevant event within subsection (6A)(c) occurs in relation to the employer.]

(5) For the purposes of [subsections (2) and (4)], the liabilities and assets to be taken into account, and their amount or value, must be determined, calculated and verified by a prescribed person and in the prescribed manner.

(6) In calculating the value of any liabilities for those purposes, a provision of the scheme [rules] which limits the amount of its liabilities by reference to the amount of its assets is to be disregarded.

[In this subsection "scheme rules" has the same meaning as in the Pensions Act 2004 ("the 2004 Act") (see section 318 of that Act).]

[(6A) For the purposes of this section, a relevant event occurs in relation to the employer in relation to an occupational pension scheme if and when—

(a) an insolvency event occurs in relation to the employer,

(b) the trustees or managers of the scheme make an application under subsection (1) of section 129 of the 2004 Act or receive a notice from the Board of the Pension Protection Fund under subsection (5)(a) of that section, or

(c) a resolution is passed for a voluntary winding up of the employer in a case where a declaration of solvency has been made under section 89 of the Insolvency Act 1986 (members' voluntary winding up).

(6B) For the purposes of this section—

(a) a "cessation notice", in the case of a relevant event within subsection (6A)(a), means—

(i) a withdrawal notice issued under section 122(2)(b) of the 2004 Act (scheme rescue has occurred),

(ii) a withdrawal notice issued under section 148 of that Act (no insolvency event has occurred or is likely to occur),

(iii) a notice issued under section 122(4) of that Act (inability to confirm status of scheme) in a case where the notice has become binding and section 148 of that Act does not apply,

(b) a "cessation notice" in the case of a relevant event within subsection (6A)(b), means a withdrawal notice issued under section 130(3) of the 2004 Act (scheme rescue has occurred),

(c) a cessation event occurs in relation to a scheme when a cessation notice in relation to the scheme becomes binding,

(d) the occurrence of a cessation event in relation to a scheme in respect of a cessation notice issued during a particular period ("the specified period") is a possibility until each of the following are no longer reviewable—

(i) any cessation notice which has been issued in relation to the scheme during the specified period,

(ii) any failure to issue such a cessation notice during the specified period,

(iii) any notice which has been issued by the Board under Chapter 2 or 3 of Part 2 of the 2004 Act which is relevant to the issue of a cessation notice in relation to the scheme during the specified period or to such a cessation notice which has been issued during that period becoming binding,

(iv) any failure to issue such a notice as is mentioned in sub-paragraph (iii),

(e) the issue or failure to issue a notice is to be regarded as reviewable—

(i) during the period within which it may be reviewed by virtue of Chapter 6 of Part 2 of the 2004 Act, and

(ii) if the matter is so reviewed, until—

(a) the review and any reconsideration,

(b) any reference to the Ombudsman for the Board of the Pension Protection Fund in respect of the matter, and

(c) any appeal against his determination or directions,

has been finally disposed of, and

(f) a "scheme failure notice" means a scheme failure notice issued under section 122(2)(a) or 130(2) of the 2004 Act (scheme rescue not possible).

(6C) For the purposes of this section—

(a) section 121 of the 2004 Act applies for the purposes of determining if and when an insolvency event has occurred in relation to the employer,

(b) "appointed day" means the day appointed under section 126(2) of the 2004 Act (no pension protection under Chapter 3 of Part 2 of that Act if the scheme begins winding up before the day appointed by the Secretary of State),

(c) references to a relevant event in relation to an employer do not include a relevant event which occurred in relation to him before he became the employer in relation to the scheme,

(d) references to a cessation notice becoming binding are to the notice in question mentioned in subsection (6B)(a) or (b) and issued under Part 2 of the 2004 Act becoming binding within the meaning given by that Part of that Act, and

(e) references to a scheme failure notice becoming binding are to the notice in question mentioned in subsection (6B)(f) and issued under Part 2 of the 2004 Act becoming binding within the meaning given by that Part of that Act.

(6D) Where—

(a) a resolution is passed for a voluntary winding up of the employer in a case where a declaration of solvency has been made under section 89 of the Insolvency Act 1986 (members' voluntary winding up), and

[(b) the voluntary winding up of the employer—

(i) is stayed other than in prescribed circumstances, or

(ii) becomes a creditors' voluntary winding up under section 96 of that Act (conversion to creditors' voluntary winding up),]

this section has effect as if that resolution had never been passed and any debt which arose under this section by virtue of the passing of that resolution shall be treated as if it had never arisen.]

(7) This section does not prejudice any other right or remedy which the trustees or managers may have in respect of a deficiency in the scheme's assets.

(8) A debt due by virtue only of this section shall not be regarded—

(a) as a preferential debt for the purposes of the Insolvency Act 1986, or

(b) as a preferred debt for the purposes of the Bankruptcy (Scotland) Act [2016].

(9) . . .

(10) Regulations may modify this section as it applies in prescribed circumstances.

NOTES

Sub-ss (1)–(4), (4A)–(4C): substituted for original sub-ss (1)–(4), by the Pensions Act 2004, s 271(1), (2), except in relation to certain specified schemes immediately before 6 April 2005 (see SI 2005/275, art 2(3), (10), (11), Schedule, Pt 3).

Sub-s (1): substituted as follows by the Pension Schemes Act 2015, s 46, Sch 2, paras 6, 12, as from a day to be appointed:

"(1) This section applies in relation to a pension scheme that is—

(a) an occupational defined benefits scheme,

(b) an occupational shared risk scheme, or

(c) an occupational defined contributions scheme,

unless subsection (1A) provides for the scheme to be exempt.

(1A) A scheme is exempt from this section if it is—

(a) a scheme under which all the benefits that may be provided are money purchase benefits,

(b) a scheme under which all the benefits that may be provided are collective benefits,

(c) a scheme under which all the benefits that may be provided are money purchase benefits or collective benefits, or

(d) a prescribed scheme or a scheme of a prescribed description.

(1B) Where—

(a) some of the benefits that may be provided under a scheme are collective benefits and some are not, and

(b) the scheme does not fall within paragraph (c) or (d) of subsection (1A),

the scheme is to be treated for the purposes of this Part as two separate schemes, one relating to the collective benefits and the other relating to the other benefits.".

Sub-s (5): words in square brackets substituted for original words "subsection (1)" by the Pensions Act 2004, s 271(1), (3), except in relation to certain specified schemes immediately before 6 April 2005 (see SI 2005/275, art 2(3), (10), (11), Schedule, Pt 3).

Sub-s (6): words in square brackets inserted by the Pensions Act 2004, s 271(1), (4), except in relation to certain specified schemes immediately before 6 April 2005 (see SI 2005/275, art 2(3), (10), (11), Schedule, Pt 3).

Sub-ss (6A)–(6D): inserted by the Pensions Act 2004, s 271(1), (5), except in relation to certain specified schemes immediately before 6 April 2005 (see SI 2005/275, art 2(3), (10), (11), Schedule, Pt 3); in sub-s (6D), para (b) substituted by the Deregulation Act 2015 and Small Business, Enterprise and Employment Act 2015 (Consequential Amendments) (Savings) Regulations 2017, SI 2017/540, reg 2, Sch 1, para 3.

Sub-s (8): in para (b) year in square brackets substituted for original year "1985" by the Bankruptcy (Scotland) Act 2016 (Consequential Provisions and Modifications) Order 2016, SI 2016/1034, art 7(1), (3), Sch 1, para 13(1), (3), as from 30 November 2016 (except in relation to (i) a sequestration as regards which the petition is presented, or the debtor application is made before that date; or (ii) a trust deed executed before that date).

Sub-s (9): repealed by the Pensions Act 2004, ss 271(1), (6), 320, Sch 13, Pt I, except in relation to certain specified schemes immediately before 6 April 2005 (see SI 2005/275, art 2(3), (10), (11), Schedule, Pt 3 and SI 2005/695, arts 2(7), 5, Sch 1). Sub-s (9) originally read as follows:

"(9) This section does not apply to an occupational pension scheme falling within a prescribed class or description.".

Modifications: this section is modified in relation to multi-employer schemes and money purchase schemes, by the Occupational Pension Schemes (Deficiency on Winding Up etc) Regulations 1996, SI 1996/3128, regs 4, 7, 8, and in relation to money purchase schemes, by the Occupational and Personal Pension Schemes (Levy) Regulations 1997, SI 1997/666, reg 11.

Regulations: the Occupational Pension Schemes (Minimum Funding Requirement and Actuarial Valuations) Regulations 1996, SI 1996/1536 (revoked by SI 2005/3377); the Occupational Pension Schemes (Deficiency on Winding Up etc) Regulations 1996, SI 1996/3128; the Personal and Occupational Pension Schemes (Miscellaneous Amendments) (No 2) Regulations 1997, SI 1997/3038; the Personal and Occupational Pension Schemes (Miscellaneous Amendments) Regulations 1999, SI 1999/3198; the Occupational Pension Schemes (Minimum Funding Requirement and Miscellaneous Amendments) Regulations 2002, SI 2002/380; the Occupational Pension Schemes (Winding Up and Deficiency on Winding Up etc) (Amendment) Regulations 2004, SI 2004/403; the Occupational Pension Schemes (Winding Up, Deficiency on Winding Up and Transfer Values) (Amendment) Regulations 2005, SI 2005/72; the Occupational Pension Schemes (Employer Debt) Regulations 2005, SI 2005/678 at **[18.103]**; the Occupational Pension Schemes (Employer Debt etc) (Amendment) Regulations 2005, SI 2005/2224; the Occupational Pension Schemes (Republic of Ireland Schemes Exemption (Revocation) and Tax Exempt Schemes (Miscellaneous Amendments)) Regulations 2006, SI 2006/467; the Occupational Pension Schemes (Fraud Compensation Levy) Regulations 2006, SI 2006/558; the Occupational and Personal Pension Schemes (Prescribed Bodies) Regulations 2007, SI 2007/60; the Occupational Pension Schemes (Employer Debt and Miscellaneous Amendments) Regulations 2008, SI 2008/731; the Occupational Pension Schemes (Employer Debt—Apportionment Arrangements) (Amendment) Regulations 2008, SI 2008/1068; the Occupational Pension Schemes (Scottish Parliamentary Pensions Act 2009) Regulations 2009, SI 2009/1906, the Occupational Pension Schemes (Employer Debt and Miscellaneous Amendments) Regulations 2010, SI 2010/725; the Occupational Pension Schemes (Employer Debt and Miscellaneous Amendments) Regulations 2011, SI 2011/2973; the Occupational and Personal Pension Schemes (Prescribed Bodies) Regulations 2012, SI 2012/1817; the Pensions Act 2011 (Transitional, Consequential and Supplementary Provisions) Regulations 2014, SI 2014/1711; the Pensions (Institute and Faculty of Actuaries and Consultation by Employers—Amendment) Regulations 2012, SI 2012/692; the Occupational Pension Schemes (Employer Debt and Miscellaneous Amendments) Regulations 2018, SI 2018/237.

[17.125]

[75A Deficiencies in the assets: multi-employer schemes

(1) Regulations may modify section 75 (deficiencies in the assets) as it applies in relation to multi-employer schemes.

(2) The regulations may in particular provide for the circumstances in which a debt is to be treated as due under section 75 from an employer in relation to a multi-employer scheme (a "multi-employer debt").

(3) Those circumstances may include circumstances other than those in which the scheme is being wound up or a relevant event occurs (within the meaning of section 75).

(4) For the purposes of regulations under this section, regulations under section 75(5) may prescribe alternative manners for determining, calculating and verifying—

(a) the liabilities and assets of the scheme to be taken into account, and

(b) their amount or value.

(5) The regulations under this section may in particular—

(a) provide for the application of each of the prescribed alternative manners under section 75(5) to depend upon whether prescribed requirements are met;

(b) provide that, where in a particular case a prescribed alternative manner under section 75(5) is applied, the Authority may in prescribed circumstances issue a direction—

(i) that any resulting multi-employer debt is to be unenforceable for such a period as the Authority may specify, and

(ii) that the amount of the debt is to be re-calculated applying a different prescribed manner under section 75(5) if prescribed requirements are met within that period.

(6) The prescribed requirements mentioned in subsection (5) may include a requirement that a prescribed arrangement, the details of which are approved in a notice issued by the Authority, is in place.

(7) The regulations may provide that the Authority may not approve the details of such an arrangement unless prescribed conditions are met.

(8) Those prescribed conditions may include a requirement that—

(a) the arrangement identifies one or more persons to whom the Authority may issue a contribution notice under the regulations, and

(b) the Authority are satisfied of prescribed matters in respect of each of those persons.

(9) For the purposes of subsection (8) a "contribution notice" is a notice stating that the person to whom it is issued is under a liability to pay the sum specified in the notice—

(a) to the trustees of the multi-employer scheme in question, or

(b) where the Board of the Pension Protection Fund has assumed responsibility for the scheme in accordance with Chapter 3 of Part 2 of the Pensions Act 2004 (pension protection), to the Board.

(10) The regulations may provide for the Authority to have power to issue a contribution notice to a person identified in an arrangement as mentioned in subsection (8) if—

(a) the arrangement ceases to be in place or the Authority consider that the arrangement is no longer appropriate, and

(b) the Authority are of the opinion that it is reasonable to impose liability on the person to pay the sum specified in the notice.

(11) Where a contribution notice is issued to a person under the regulations as mentioned in subsection (8), the sum specified in the notice is to be treated as a debt due from that person to the person to whom it is to be paid as specified in the notice.

(12) Where the regulations provide for the issuing of a contribution notice by the Authority as mentioned in subsection (8)—

(a) the regulations must—

(i) provide for how the sum specified by the Authority in a contribution notice is to be determined,

(ii) provide for the circumstances (if any) in which a person to whom a contribution notice is issued is jointly and severally liable for the debt,

(iii) provide for the matters which the notice must contain, and

(iv) provide for who may exercise the powers to recover the debt due by virtue of the contribution notice, and

(b) the regulations may apply with or without modifications some or all of the provisions of sections 47 to 51 of the Pensions Act 2004 (contribution notices where non-compliance with financial support direction) in relation to contribution notices issued under the regulations.

(13) In this section "multi-employer scheme" means a trust scheme which applies to earners in employments under different employers.

(14) This section is without prejudice to the powers conferred by—

section 75(5) (power to prescribe the manner of determining, calculating and verifying assets and liabilities etc),

section 75(10) (power to modify section 75 as it applies in prescribed circumstances),

section 118(1)(a) (power to modify any provisions of this Part in their application to multi-employer trust schemes), and

section 125(3) (power to extend for the purposes of this Part the meaning of "employer").]

NOTES

Inserted by the Pensions Act 2004, s 272.

Regulations: the Occupational Pension Schemes (Employer Debt) Regulations 2005, SI 2005/678 at **[18.103]**; the Occupational Pension Schemes (Employer Debt etc) (Amendment) Regulations 2005, SI 2005/2224; the Occupational Pension Schemes (Republic of Ireland Schemes Exemption (Revocation) and Tax Exempt Schemes (Miscellaneous Amendments)) Regulations 2006, SI 2006/467; the Occupational Pension Schemes (Employer Debt and Miscellaneous Amendments) Regulations 2008, SI 2008/731; the Occupational Pension Schemes (Employer Debt—Apportionment Arrangements) (Amendment) Regulations 2008, SI 2008/1068; the Occupational Pension Schemes (Employer Debt and Miscellaneous Amendments) Regulations 2010, SI 2010/725; the Occupational Pension Schemes (Employer Debt and Miscellaneous Amendments) Regulations 2011, SI 2011/2973; the Occupational and Personal Pension Schemes (Prescribed Bodies) Regulations 2012, SI 2012/1817; the Pension Protection Fund, Occupational and Personal Pension Schemes (Miscellaneous

Amendments) Regulations 2013, SI 2013/627; the Occupational Pension Schemes (Employer Debt and Miscellaneous Amendments) Regulations 2018, SI 2018/237.

76–90 *(Ss 76–80, 84–90 outside the scope of this work; ss 81–83 repealed by the Pensions Act 2004, s 320, Sch 13, Pt I, as from 1 September 2005, subject to transitional provisions and savings in relation to the Pensions Compensation Board: see SI 2005/1720, arts 3–5.)*

Assignment, forfeiture, bankruptcy etc

[17.126]

91 Inalienability of occupational pension

(1) Subject to subsection (5), where a person is entitled [to a pension under an occupational pension scheme or has a right to a future pension under such a scheme]—

(a) the entitlement or right cannot be assigned, commuted or surrendered,

(b) the entitlement or right cannot be charged or a lien exercised in respect of it, and

(c) no set-off can be exercised in respect of it,

and an agreement to effect any of those things is unenforceable.

(2) Where by virtue of this section a person's entitlement [to a pension under an occupational pension scheme, or right to a future pension under such a scheme,] cannot, apart from subsection (5), be assigned, no order can be made by any court the effect of which would be that he would be restrained from receiving that pension.

(3) . . .

(4) Subsection (2) does not prevent the making of—

(a) an attachment of earnings order under the Attachment of Earnings Act 1971, or

(b) an income payments order under the Insolvency Act 1986.

(5) In the case of a person ("the person in question") who is entitled [to a pension under an occupational pension scheme, or has a right to a future pension under such a scheme], subsection (1) does not apply to any of the following, or any agreement to effect any of the following—

(a) an assignment in favour of the person in question's widow, widower[, surviving civil partner] or dependant,

(b) a surrender, at the option of the person in question, for the purpose of—

(i) providing benefits for that person's widow, widower[, surviving civil partner] or dependant, or

(ii) acquiring for the person in question entitlement to further benefits under the scheme,

(c) a commutation—

(i) of the person in question's benefit on or after retirement or in exceptional circumstances of serious ill health,

(ii) in prescribed circumstances, of any benefit for that person's widow, widower[, surviving civil partner] or dependant, or

(iii) in other prescribed circumstances,

(d) subject to subsection (6), a charge or lien on, or set-off against, the person in question's entitlement, or [right,] (except to the extent that it includes transfer credits other than prescribed transfer credits) for the purpose of enabling the employer to obtain the discharge by him of some monetary obligation due to the employer and arising out of a criminal, negligent or fraudulent act or omission by him,

(e) subject to subsection (6), except in prescribed circumstances a charge or lien on, or set-off against, the person in question's entitlement, or [right], for the purpose of discharging some monetary obligation due from the person in question to the scheme and—

(i) arising out of a criminal, negligent or fraudulent act or omission by him, or

(ii) in the case of a trust scheme of which the person in question is a trustee, arising out of a breach of trust by him.

[(f) subject to subsection (6), a charge or lien on, or set-off against, the person in question's entitlement, or right, for the purpose of discharging some monetary obligation due from the person in question to the scheme arising out of a payment made in error in respect of the pension].

(6) Where a charge, lien or set-off is exercisable by virtue of subsection (5)(d)[, (e) or (f)]—

(a) its amount must not exceed the amount of the monetary obligation in question, or (if less) the value (determined in the prescribed manner) of the person in question's entitlement or accrued right, and

(b) the person in question must be given a certificate showing the amount of the charge, lien or set-off and its effect on his benefits under the scheme,

and where there is a dispute as to its amount, the charge, lien or set-off must not be exercised unless the obligation in question has become enforceable under an order of a competent court or in consequence of an award of an arbitrator or, in Scotland, an arbiter to be appointed (failing agreement between the parties) by the sheriff.

(7) This section is subject to section 159 of the Pension Schemes Act 1993 (inalienability of guaranteed minimum pension . . .).

NOTES

Sub-ss (1), (2): words in square brackets substituted by the Welfare Reform and Pensions Act 1999, s 84(1), Sch 12, Pt I, paras 43, 57(1)–(3).

Sub-s (3): repealed by the Welfare Reform and Pensions Act 1999, s 88, Sch 13, Pt I.

Sub-s (5): words in first pair of square brackets and words in square brackets in paras (d), (e) substituted by the Welfare Reform and Pensions Act 1999, s 84(1), Sch 12, Pt I, paras 43, 57(1), (4); words in square brackets in paras (a)–(c) inserted by the Civil Partnership (Pensions and Benefit Payments) (Consequential, etc Provisions) Order 2005, SI 2005/2053, art 2, Schedule, Pt 4, para 23; para (f) inserted by the Pensions Act 2004, s 266(1), (2).

Sub-s (6): words in square brackets substituted by the Pensions Act 2004, s 266(1), (3).

Sub-s (7): words omitted repealed by the Pensions Act 2008 (Abolition of Protected Rights) (Consequential Amendments) (No 2) Order 2011, SI 2011/1730, art 6(2A).

Disapplication: this section is disapplied in relation to a court making a recovery order by virtue of the Proceeds of Crime Act 2002 (External Requests and Orders) Order 2005, SI 2005/3181, art 184(2).

Modifications: this section is modified, in relation to public service pension schemes and the Armed Forces Pension Scheme, by the Occupational Pension Schemes (Assignment, Forfeiture, Bankruptcy etc) Regulations 1997, SI 1997/785, reg 7. This section is applied, with modifications, to European members of occupational pension schemes which carry out cross-border activity, by the Occupational Pension Schemes (Cross-border Activities) Regulations 2005, SI 2005/3381, reg 14, Sch 2, paras 1, 3.

Regulations: the Occupational Pension Schemes (Assignment, Forfeiture, Bankruptcy etc) Regulations 1997, SI 1997/785; the Stakeholder Pension Schemes Regulations 2000, SI 2000/1403; the Occupational Pension Schemes (Winding up etc) Regulations 2005, SI 2005/706.

[17.127]

92 Forfeiture, etc

(1) Subject to the provisions of this section and section 93, an entitlement [to a pension under an occupational pension scheme or a right to a future pension under such a scheme] cannot be forfeited.

(2) Subsection (1) does not prevent forfeiture by reference to—

(a) a transaction or purported transaction which under section 91 is of no effect, . . .

(b) . . .

whether or not that event occurred before or after the pension became payable.

(3) Where such forfeiture as is mentioned in subsection (2) occurs, any pension which was, or would but for the forfeiture have become, payable may, if the trustees or managers of the scheme so determine, be paid to all or any of the following—

(a) the member of the scheme to or in respect of whom the pension was, or would have become, payable,

[(b) the spouse, civil partner, widow, widower or surviving civil partner of the member,]

(c) any dependant of the member, and

(d) any other person falling within a prescribed class.

(4) Subsection (1) does not prevent forfeiture by reference to the [pensioner, or prospective pensioner], having been convicted of one or more offences—

(a) which are committed before the pension becomes payable, and

(b) which are—

(i) offences of treason,

(ii) offences under the Official Secrets Acts 1911 to 1989 for which the person has been sentenced on the same occasion to a term of imprisonment of, or to two or more consecutive terms amounting in the aggregate to, at least 10 years, or

(iii) prescribed offences.

(5) Subsection (1) does not prevent forfeiture by reference to a failure by any person to make a claim for pension—

(a) where the forfeiture is in reliance on any enactment relating to the limitation of actions, or

(b) where the claim is not made within six years of the date on which the pension becomes due.

(6) Subsection (1) does not prevent forfeiture in prescribed circumstances.

(7) In this section and section 93, references to forfeiture include any manner of deprivation or suspension.

NOTES

Sub-s (1): words in square brackets substituted by the Welfare Reform and Pensions Act 1999, s 84(1), Sch 12, Pt I, paras 43, 58(1), (2).

Sub-s (2): para (b) and word "or" immediately preceding it repealed by the Welfare Reform and Pensions Act 1999, ss 14(3), 88, Sch 13, Pt I.

Sub-s (3): para (b) substituted by the Civil Partnership (Pensions and Benefit Payments) (Consequential, etc Provisions) Order 2005, SI 2005/2053, art 2, Schedule, Pt 4, para 24.

Sub-s (4): words in square brackets substituted by the Welfare Reform and Pensions Act 1999, s 84(1), Sch 12, Pt I, paras 43, 58(1), (3).

Modifications: this section is applied, with modifications, to European members of occupational pension schemes which carry out cross-border activity, by the Occupational Pension Schemes (Cross-border Activities) Regulations 2005, SI 2005/3381, reg 14, Sch 2, paras 1, 3.

Regulations: the Occupational Pension Schemes (Assignment, Forfeiture, Bankruptcy etc) Regulations 1997, SI 1997/785; the Stakeholder Pension Schemes Regulations 2000, SI 2000/1403; the Occupational and Personal Pension Schemes (Contracting-out) (Miscellaneous Amendments) Regulations 2002, SI 2002/681.

[17.128]

93 Forfeiture by reference to obligation to employer

(1) Subject to subsection (2), section 92(1) does not prevent forfeiture of a person's entitlement [to a pension under an occupational pension scheme or right to a future pension under such a scheme] by reference to the person having incurred some monetary obligation due to the employer and arising out of a criminal, negligent or fraudulent act or omission by the person.

(2) A person's entitlement or [right] may be forfeited by reason of subsection (1) to the extent only that it does not exceed the amount of the monetary obligation in question, or (if less) the value (determined in the prescribed manner) of the person's entitlement or [right].

(3) Such forfeiture as is mentioned in subsection (1) must not take effect where there is a dispute as to the amount of the monetary obligation in question, unless the obligation has become enforceable under an order of a competent court or in consequence of an award of an arbitrator or, in Scotland, an arbiter to be appointed (failing agreement between the parties) by the sheriff.
(4) Where a person's entitlement or [right] is forfeited by reason of subsection (1), the person must be given a certificate showing the amount forfeited and the effect of the forfeiture on his benefits under the scheme.
(5) Where such forfeiture as is mentioned in subsection (1) occurs, an amount not exceeding the amount forfeited may, if the trustees or managers of the scheme so determine, be paid to the employer.

NOTES

Sub-ss (1), (2), (4): words in square brackets substituted by the Welfare Reform and Pensions Act 1999, s 84(1), Sch 12, Pt I, paras 43, 59.

Modifications: this section is applied, with modifications, to European members of occupational pension schemes which carry out cross-border activity, by the Occupational Pension Schemes (Cross-border Activities) Regulations 2005, SI 2005/3381, reg 14, Sch 2, paras 1, 3.

94–114 *(In so far as unrepealed, outside the scope of this work.)*

General

115–123 *(Outside the scope of this work.)*

[17.129]

124 Interpretation of Part I

(1) In this Part—

"active member", in relation to an occupational pension scheme, means a person who is in pensionable service under the scheme,

"the actuary" and "the auditor", in relation to an occupational pension scheme, have the meanings given by section 47,

["the Authority" means the Pensions Regulator,]

[. . .]

"the Compensation Board" has the meaning given by section 78(1),

"the compensation provisions" has the meaning given by section 81(3),

"contravention" includes failure to comply,

"deferred member", in relation to an occupational pension scheme, means a person (other than an active or pensioner member) who has accrued rights under the scheme,

"employer", in relation to an occupational pension scheme, means the employer of persons in the description *or category* of employment to which the scheme in question relates (but see section 125(3)),

"equal treatment rule" has the meaning given by section 62,

"firm" means a body corporate or a partnership,

"fund manager", in relation to an occupational pension scheme, means a person who manages the investments held for the purposes of the scheme, "independent trustee" has the meaning given by section 23(3),

"managers", in relation to an occupational pension scheme other than a trust scheme, means the persons responsible for the management of the scheme,

"member", in relation to an occupational pension scheme, means any active, deferred[, pensioner or pension credit] member (but see section 125(4)),

. . .

. . .

"normal pension age" has the meaning given by section 180 of the Pension Schemes Act 1993,

"payment schedule" has the meaning given by section 87(2),

["pension credit" means a credit under section 29(1)(b) of the Welfare Reform and Pensions Act 1999 or under corresponding Northern Ireland legislation,

"pension credit member", in relation to an occupational pension scheme, means a person who has rights under the scheme which are attributable (directly or indirectly) to a pension credit,

"pension credit rights", in relation to an occupational pension scheme, means rights to future benefits under the scheme which are attributable (directly or indirectly) to a pension credit,]

"pensionable service", in relation to a member of an occupational pension scheme, means service in any description *or category* of employment to which the scheme relates which qualifies the member (on the assumption that it continues for the appropriate period) for pension or other benefits under the scheme,

"pensioner member", in relation to an occupational pension scheme, means a person who in respect of his pensionable service under the scheme or by reason of transfer credits, is entitled to the present payment of pension or other benefits [. . .],

"prescribed" means prescribed by regulations,

"professional adviser", in relation to a scheme, has the meaning given by section 47,

"public service pension scheme" has the meaning given by section 1 of the Pension Schemes Act 1993,

"regulations" means regulations made by the Secretary of State,

"resources", in relation to an occupational pension scheme, means the funds out of which the benefits provided by the scheme are payable from time to time, including the proceeds of any policy of insurance taken out, or annuity contract entered into, for the purposes of the scheme,

"Scottish partnership" means a partnership constituted under the law of Scotland,
"the Taxes Act 1988" means the Income and Corporation Taxes Act 1988,
"transfer credits" means rights allowed to a member under the rules of an occupational pension scheme by reference to[—
(a) a transfer to the scheme of, or transfer payment to the trustees or managers of the scheme in respect of, any of his rights (including transfer credits allowed) under another occupational pension scheme or a personal pension scheme, other than pension credit rights, or
(b) a cash transfer sum paid under Chapter 5 of Part 4 of the Pension Schemes Act 1993 (early leavers) in respect of him, to the trustees or managers of the scheme],
"trustees or managers", in relation to an occupational pension scheme, means—
(a) in the case of a trust scheme, the trustees of the scheme, and
(b) in any other case, the managers of the scheme,
"trust scheme" means an occupational pension scheme established under a trust.

(2) For the purposes of this Part—
(a) the accrued rights of a member of an occupational pension scheme at any time are the rights which have accrued to or in respect of him at that time to future benefits under the scheme, and
(b) at any time when the pensionable service of a member of an occupational pension scheme is continuing, his accrued rights are to be determined as if he had opted, immediately before that time, to terminate that service;

and references to accrued pension or accrued benefits are to be interpreted accordingly.

[(2A) In subsection (2)(a), the reference to rights which have accrued to or in respect of the member does not include any rights which are pension credit rights.]

(3) In determining what is "pensionable service" for the purposes of this Part—
(a) service notionally attributable for any purpose of the scheme is to be disregarded, and
(b) no account is to be taken of any rules of the scheme by which a period of service can be treated for any purpose as being longer or shorter than it actually is

[but, in its application for the purposes of section 51, paragraph (b) does not affect the operation of any rules of the scheme by virtue of which a period of service is to be rounded up or down by a period of less than a month].

[(3A) In a case of the winding-up of an occupational pension scheme in pursuance of an order of the Authority under section 11 or of an order of a court, the winding-up shall (subject to subsection (3E) [and to sections 28, 154 and 219 of the Pensions Act 2004]) be taken for the purposes of this Part to begin—
(a) if the order provides for a time to be the time when the winding-up begins, at that time; and
(b) in any other case, at the time when the order comes into force.

(3B) In a case of the winding-up of an occupational pension scheme in accordance with a requirement or power contained in the rules of the scheme, the winding-up shall (subject to subsections (3C) to (3E) [and to sections 154 and 219 of the Pensions Act 2004]) be taken for the purposes of this Part to begin—
(a) at the time (if any) which under those rules is the time when the winding-up begins; and
(b) if paragraph (a) does not apply, at the earliest time which is a time fixed by the trustees or managers as the time from which steps for the purposes of the winding-up are to be taken.

(3C) Subsection (3B) shall not require a winding-up of a scheme to be treated as having begun at any time before the end of any period during which effect is being given—
(a) to a determination under section 38 that the scheme is not for the time being to be wound up; or
(b) to a determination in accordance with the rules of the scheme to postpone the commencement of a winding-up.

(3D) In subsection (3B)(b) the reference to the trustees or managers of the scheme shall have effect in relation to any scheme the rules of which provide for a determination that the scheme is to be wound up to be made by persons other than the trustees or managers as including a reference to those other persons.

(3E) Subsections (3A) to (3D) above do not apply for such purposes as may be prescribed.]

(4) In the application of this Part to Scotland, in relation to conviction on indictment, references to imprisonment are to be read as references to imprisonment for a term not exceeding two years.

(5) Subject to the provisions of this Act, expressions used in this Act and in the Pension Schemes Act 1993 have the same meaning in this Act as in that.

NOTES

Sub-s (1): definition "the Authority" substituted by the Pensions Act 2004, s 7(2)(b); definition "civil partnership status" (omitted) inserted by the Civil Partnership (Pensions and Benefit Payments) (Consequential, etc Provisions) Order 2005, SI 2005/2053, art 2, Schedule, Pt 4, para 25, repealed in relation to England and Wales by the Marriage (Same Sex Couples) Act 2013 (Consequential and Contrary Provisions and Scotland) Order 2014, SI 2014/560, art 2, Sch 1, para 27 and in relation to Scotland by the Marriage and Civil Partnership (Scotland) Act 2014 and Civil Partnership Act 2004 (Consequential Provisions and Modifications) Order 2014, SI 2014/3229, art 29, Sch 5, para 13; words in italics in definitions "employer" and "pensionable service" repealed by the Pensions Act 2004, s 320, Sch 13, Pt I, as from a day to be appointed; words in square brackets in definition "member" substituted and definitions "pension credit", "pension credit member" and "pension credit rights" inserted by the Welfare Reform and Pensions Act 1999, s 84(1), Sch 12, Pt I, paras 43, 61(1)–(3); definitions "member-nominated director", "member-nominated trustee" and "the minimum funding requirement" (all omitted) repealed by the Pensions Act 2004, s 320, Sch 13, Pt I; in definition "pensioner member" words omitted from square brackets (originally inserted by the Child Support, Pensions and Social Security Act 2000, s 56, Sch 5, Pt I, para 8(3)) repealed by the Taxation of Pension Schemes (Consequential Amendments) Order 2006, SI 2006/745, art 10(1), (7); words in square brackets in definition "transfer credits" substituted by the Pensions Act 2004, s 319(1), Sch 12, paras 34, 69(1), (2).

Sub-s (2A): inserted by the Welfare Reform and Pensions Act 1999, s 84(1), Sch 12, Pt I, paras 43, 61(1), (4).

Sub-s (3): words in square brackets inserted by the Welfare Reform and Pensions Act 1999, s 18, Sch 2, para 18.

Sub-s (3A): inserted by the Child Support, Pensions and Social Security Act 2000, s 49(2); words in square brackets inserted by the Pensions Act 2004, s 319(1), Sch 12, paras 34, 69(1), (3).

Sub-s (3B): inserted by the Child Support, Pensions and Social Security Act 2000, s 49(2); words in square brackets inserted by the Pensions Act 2004, s 319(1), Sch 12, paras 34, 69(1), (4).

Sub-ss (3C)–(3E): inserted by the Child Support, Pensions and Social Security Act 2000, s 49(2).

Disapplication: in relation to the disapplication of sub-ss (3A)–(3D) of this section, see the Occupational Pension Schemes (Winding Up Notices and Reports etc) Regulations 2002, SI 2002/459, reg 12 at **[9.75]**.

Regulations: the Occupational Pension Schemes (Winding Up Notices and Reports etc) Regulations 2002, SI 2002/459 at **[9.67]**; the Occupational Pension Schemes (Employer Debt) Regulations 2005, SI 2005/678 at **[18.103]**; the Occupational Pension Schemes (Independent Trustee) Regulations 2005, SI 2005/703; the Occupational Pension Schemes (Winding up etc) Regulations 2005, SI 2005/706; the Occupational and Personal Pension Schemes (Automatic Enrolment) Regulations 2010, SI 2010/772; the Public Service Pensions (Record Keeping and Miscellaneous Amendments) Regulations 2014, SI 2014/3138; the Occupational Pension Schemes (Charges and Governance) Regulations 2015, SI 2015/879.

[17.130]

125 Section 124: supplementary

(1) For the purposes of this Part, an occupational pension scheme is salary related if—

(a) the scheme is not a money purchase scheme, and

(b) the scheme does not fall within a prescribed class or description,

and "salary related trust scheme" is to be read accordingly.

(2) Regulations may apply this Part with prescribed modifications to occupational pension schemes—

(a) which are not money purchase schemes, but

(b) where some of the benefits that may be provided are money purchase benefits.

(3) Regulations may, in relation to occupational pension schemes, extend for the purposes of this Part the meaning of "employer" to include[—

(a)] persons who have been the employer in relation to the scheme[;

(b) such other persons as may be prescribed].

(4) For any of the purposes of this Part, regulations may in relation to occupational pension schemes—

(a) extend or restrict the meaning of "member",

(b) determine who is to be treated as a prospective member, and

(c) determine the times at which a person is to be treated as becoming, or as ceasing to be, a member or prospective member.

NOTES

Sub-s (1): in para (a) words in italics substituted as follows by the Pension Schemes Act 2015, s 46, Sch 2, paras 6, 18(1), (2), as from a day to be appointed:

"(a) the scheme is not a scheme under which all the benefits that may be provided are money purchase benefits,".

Sub-s (2): paras (a), (b) substituted by the words "under which some but not all of the benefits that may be provided are money purchase benefits" by the Pension Schemes Act 2015, s 46, Sch 2, paras 6, 18(1), (3), as from a day to be appointed.

Sub-s (3): words in square brackets inserted by the Pensions Act 2004, s 240(1), as from a day to be appointed.

Regulations: the Occupational Pension Schemes (Minimum Funding Requirement and Actuarial Valuations) Regulations 1996, SI 1996/1536; the Occupational Pension Schemes (Winding Up) Regulations 1996, SI 1996/3126; the Occupational Pension Schemes (Deficiency on Winding Up etc) Regulations 1996, SI 1996/3128; the Occupational Pension Schemes (Minimum Funding Requirement and Miscellaneous Amendments) Regulations 2002, SI 2002/380; the Occupational Pension Schemes (Employer Debt) Regulations 2005, SI 2005/678 at **[18.103]**; the Occupational Pension Schemes (Independent Trustee) Regulations 2005, SI 2005/703; the Occupational Pension Schemes (Investment) Regulations 2005, SI 2005/3378; the Occupational Pension Schemes (Payments to Employer) Regulations 2006, SI 2006/802.

126–151 *((Pts II, III) outside the scope of this work.)*

PART IV
MISCELLANEOUS AND GENERAL

152–175 *(Outside the scope of this work.)*

General

176–179 *(Outside the scope of this work.)*

[17.131]

180 Commencement

(1) Subject to the following provisions, this Act shall come into force on such day as the Secretary of State may by order made by statutory instrument appoint and different days may be appointed for different purposes.

(2), (3) *(Outside the scope of this work.)*

(4) Without prejudice to section 174(3), the power to make an order under this section includes power—

(a) to make transitional adaptations or modifications—

(i) of the provisions brought into force by the order, or

(ii) in connection with those provisions, of any provisions of this Act, or the Pension Schemes Act 1993, then in force, or

(b) to save the effect of any of the repealed provisions of that Act, or those provisions as adapted or modified by the order,

as it appears to the Secretary of State expedient, including different adaptations or modifications for different periods.

NOTES

Orders: at present, 10 commencement orders have been made under this section. The orders relevant to the provisions of this Act reproduced here are the Pensions Act 1995 (Commencement No 2) Order 1995, SI 1995/3104; the Pensions Act 1995 (Commencement No 3) Order 1996, SI 1996/778; the Pensions Act 1995 (Commencement No 4) Order 1996, SI 1996/1412; the Pensions Act 1995 (Commencement No 8) Order 1996, SI 1996/2637; the Pensions Act 1995 (Commencement No 10) Order 1997, SI 1997/664. In addition, the Occupational Pension Schemes (Reference Scheme and Miscellaneous Amendments) Regulations 1997, SI 1997/819 are made under this section.

[17.132]
181 Short title

This Act may be cited as the Pensions Act 1995.

SCHEDULES 1–7

(*Schs 1–7 outside the scope of this work.*)

LANDLORD AND TENANT (COVENANTS) ACT 1995

(1995 c 30)

An Act to make provision for persons bound by covenants of a tenancy to be released from such covenants on the assignment of the tenancy, and to make other provision with respect to rights and liabilities arising under such covenants; to restrict in certain circumstances the operation of rights of re-entry, forfeiture and disclaimer; and for connected purposes

[19 July 1995]

1–20 (*Outside the scope of this work.*)

Forfeiture and disclaimer

[17.133]
21 Forfeiture or disclaimer limited to part only of demised premises

(1) Where—

(a) as a result of one or more assignments a person is the tenant of part only of the premises demised by a tenancy, and

(b) under a proviso or stipulation in the tenancy there is a right of re-entry or forfeiture for a breach of a tenant covenant of the tenancy, and

(c) the right is (apart from this subsection) exercisable in relation to that part and other land demised by the tenancy,

the right shall nevertheless, in connection with a breach of any such covenant by that person, be taken to be a right exercisable only in relation to that part.

(2) Where—

(a) a company which is being wound up, or a trustee in bankruptcy, is as a result of one or more assignments the tenant of part only of the premises demised by a tenancy, and

(b) the liquidator of the company exercises his power under section 178 of the Insolvency Act 1986, or the trustee in bankruptcy exercises his power under section 315 of that Act, to disclaim property demised by the tenancy,

the power is exercisable only in relation to the part of the premises referred to in paragraph (a).

22 (*Outside the scope of this work.*)

Supplemental

23–30 (*Outside the scope of this work.*)

[17.134]
31 Commencement

(1) The provisions of this Act come into force on such day as the Lord Chancellor may appoint by order made by statutory instrument.

(2) An order under this section may contain such transitional provisions and savings (whether or not involving the modification of any enactment) as appear to the Lord Chancellor necessary or expedient in connection with the provisions brought into force by the order.

NOTES

Orders: the Landlord and Tenant (Covenants) Act 1995 (Commencement) Order 1995, SI 1995/2963.

[17.135]
32 Short title and extent

(1) This Act may be cited as the Landlord and Tenant (Covenants) Act 1995.

(2) This Act extends to England and Wales only.

SCHEDULES 1 AND 2

(Schs 1, 2 outside the scope of this work.)

EMPLOYMENT RIGHTS ACT 1996

(1996 c 18)

ARRANGEMENT OF SECTIONS

PART XI
REDUNDANCY PAYMENTS ETC

CHAPTER VI
PAYMENTS BY SECRETARY OF STATE

166 Applications for payments . . . . . [17.136]
167 Making of payments . . . . . [17.137]

PART XII
INSOLVENCY OF EMPLOYERS

182 Employee's rights on insolvency of employer . . . . . [17.138]
183 Insolvency . . . . . [17.139]
184 Debts to which Part applies . . . . . [17.140]
185 The appropriate date . . . . . [17.141]
186 Limit on amount payable under section 182 . . . . . [17.142]
187 Role of relevant officer . . . . . [17.143]
188 Complaints to employment tribunals . . . . . [17.144]
189 Transfer to Secretary of State of rights and remedies . . . . . [17.145]

PART XV
GENERAL AND SUPPLEMENTARY

Final provisions

243 Commencement . . . . . [17.146]
244 Extent . . . . . [17.147]
245 Short title . . . . . [17.148]

An Act to consolidate enactments relating to employment rights

[22 May 1996]

NOTES

Modification: this Act is applied, with modifications, in so far as it relates to bank insolvency or administration under the Banking Act 2009, Pts 2, 3, by the Banking Act 2009 (Parts 2 and 3 Consequential Amendments) Order 2009, SI 2009/317, art 3, Schedule at **[7.86]**, **[7.92]**.

1–134A *((Pts I–X) outside the scope of this work.)*

PART XI
REDUNDANCY PAYMENTS ETC

135–165 *((Chs I–V) outside the scope of this work.)*

CHAPTER VI PAYMENTS BY SECRETARY OF STATE

[17.136]
166 Applications for payments

(1) Where an employee claims that his employer is liable to pay to him an employer's payment and either—

(a) that the employee has taken all reasonable steps, other than legal proceedings, to recover the payment from the employer and the employer has refused or failed to pay it, or has paid part of it and has refused or failed to pay the balance, or

(b) that the employer is insolvent and the whole or part of the payment remains unpaid,

the employee may apply to the Secretary of State for a payment under this section.

(2) In this Part "employer's payment", in relation to an employee, means—

(a) a redundancy payment which his employer is liable to pay to him under this Part, . . .

[(aa) a payment which his employer is liable to make to him under an agreement to refrain from instituting or continuing proceedings for a contravention or alleged contravention of section 135 which has effect by virtue of section 203(2)(e) or (f), or]

(b) a payment which his employer is, under an agreement in respect of which an order is in force under section 157, liable to make to him on the termination of his contract of employment.

(3) In relation to any case where (in accordance with any provision of this Part) an [employment tribunal] determines that an employer is liable to pay part (but not the whole) of a redundancy payment the reference in subsection (2)(a) to a redundancy payment is to the part of the redundancy payment.

(4) In subsection (1)(a) "legal proceedings"—

(a) does not include any proceedings before an [employment tribunal], but

(b) includes any proceedings to enforce a decision or award of an [employment tribunal].

(5) An employer is insolvent for the purposes of subsection (1)(b)—

(a) where the employer is an individual, if (but only if) subsection (6) [or (8A)] is satisfied, . . .

(b) where the employer is a company, if (but only if) subsection (7) [or (8A)] is satisfied[, . . .

(c) where the employer is a limited liability partnership, if (but only if) subsection (8) [or (8A)] is satisfied][; and

(d) where the employer is not any of the above, if (but only if) subsection (8A) is satisfied.]

(6) This subsection is satisfied in the case of an employer who is an individual—

(a) in England and Wales if—

(i) he has been adjudged bankrupt or has made a composition or arrangement with his creditors, or

(ii) he has died and his estate falls to be administered in accordance with an order under section 421 of the Insolvency Act 1986, and

(b) in Scotland if—

(i) sequestration of his estate has been awarded or he has executed a trust deed for his creditors or has entered into a composition contract, or

(ii) he has died and a judicial factor appointed under section 11A of the Judicial Factors (Scotland) Act 1889 is required by that section to divide his insolvent estate among his creditors.

(7) This subsection is satisfied in the case of an employer which is a company—

(a) if a winding up order . . . has been made, or a resolution for voluntary winding up has been passed, with respect to the company,

[(aa) if the company is in administration for the purposes of the Insolvency Act 1986,]

(b) if a receiver or (in England and Wales only) a manager of the company's undertaking has been duly appointed, or (in England and Wales only) possession has been taken, by or on behalf of the holders of any debentures secured by a floating charge, of any property of the company comprised in or subject to the charge, or

(c) if a voluntary arrangement proposed in the case of the company for the purposes of Part I of the Insolvency Act 1986 has been approved under that Part of that Act.

[(8) This subsection is satisfied in the case of an employer which is a limited liability partnership—

(a) if a winding-up order, an administration order or a determination for a voluntary winding-up has been made with respect to the limited liability partnership,

(b) if a receiver or (in England and Wales only) a manager of the undertaking of the limited liability partnership has been duly appointed, or (in England and Wales only) possession has been taken, by or on behalf of the holders of any debentures secured by a floating charge, of any property of the limited liability partnership comprised in or subject to the charge, or

(c) if a voluntary arrangement proposed in the case of the limited liability partnership for the purpose of Part I of the Insolvency Act 1986 has been approved under that Part of that Act.]

[(8A) This subsection is satisfied in the case of an employer if—

(a) a request has been made for the first opening of collective proceedings—

(i) based on the insolvency of the employer, as provided for under the laws, regulations and administrative provisions of a member State, and

(ii) involving the partial or total divestment of the employer's assets and the appointment of a liquidator or a person performing a similar task, and

(b) the competent authority has—

(i) decided to open the proceedings, or

(ii) established that the employer's undertaking or business has been definitively closed down and the available assets of the employer are insufficient to warrant the opening of the proceedings.

(8B) For the purposes of subsection (8A)—

(a) "liquidator or person performing a similar task" includes the official receiver or an administrator, trustee in bankruptcy, judicial factor, supervisor of a voluntary arrangement, or person performing a similar task,

(b) "competent authority" includes—

(i) a court,

(ii) a meeting of creditors,

(iii) a creditors' committee,

(iv) the creditors by a decision procedure, and

(v) an authority of a member State empowered to open insolvency proceedings, to confirm the opening of such proceedings or to take decisions in the course of such proceedings.

(8C) An employee may apply under this section only if he or she worked or habitually worked in Great Britain in that employment to which the application relates.]

[(9) In this section—

(a) references to a company are to be read as including references to a charitable incorporated organisation, and

(b) any reference to the Insolvency Act 1986 in relation to a company is to be read as including a reference to that Act as it applies to charitable incorporated organisations.]

NOTES

Sub-s (2): word omitted from para (a) repealed and para (aa) inserted by the Employment Rights (Dispute Resolution) Act 1998, ss 11(2), 15, Sch 2, except in relation to dismissals where the relevant date (within the meaning of s 145 of this Act) falls before 1 October 1998.

Sub-ss (3), (4): words in brackets substituted by the Employment Rights (Dispute Resolution) Act 1998, s 1(2)(a).

Sub-s (5): word omitted from para (a) repealed and para (c) added, together with word preceding it, by the Limited Liability Partnerships Regulations 2001, SI 2001/1090, reg 9(1), Sch 5, para 18(1), (2); words in square brackets in paras (a), (b), (c) inserted, word omitted from para (b) repealed and para (d) added together with word preceding it, by the Employment Rights Act 1996 and Pension Schemes Act 1993 (Amendment) Regulations 2017, SI 2017/1205, reg 2(1), (2)(a).

Sub-s (7): in para (a) words "or an administration order" (omitted) repealed, and para (aa) inserted, by the Enterprise Act 2002, ss 248(3), 278(2), Sch 17, para 49(1), (2), Sch 26, subject to savings and transitional provisions (i) in a case where a petition for an administration order has been presented before 15 September 2003 (see the Enterprise Act 2002 (Commencement No 4 and Transitional Provisions and Savings) Order 2003, SI 2003/2093, art 3 at **[2.26]**), and (ii) in relation to special administration regimes (see s 249 of the 2002 Act at **[2.10]**).

Sub-s (8): added by SI 2001/1090, reg 9(1), Sch 5, para 18(1), (3).

Sub-ss (8A)–(8C): inserted by SI 2017/1205, reg 2(1), (2)(b).

Sub-s (9): added by the Charitable Incorporated Organisations (Consequential Amendments) Order 2012, SI 2012/3014, art 3.

[17.137]

167 Making of payments

(1) Where, on an application under section 166 by an employee in relation to an employer's payment, the Secretary of State is satisfied that the requirements specified in subsection (2) are met, he shall pay to the employee out of the National Insurance Fund a sum calculated in accordance with section 168 but reduced by so much (if any) of the employer's payment as has already been paid.

(2) The requirements referred to in subsection (1) are—

(a) that the employee is entitled to the employer's payment, and

(b) that one of the conditions specified in paragraphs (a) and (b) of subsection (1) of section 166 is fulfilled,

and, in a case where the employer's payment is a payment such as is mentioned in subsection (2)(b) of that section, that the employee's right to the payment arises by virtue of a period of continuous employment (computed in accordance with the provisions of the agreement in question) which is not less than two years.

(3) Where under this section the Secretary of State pays a sum to an employee in respect of an employer's payment—

(a) all rights and remedies of the employee with respect to the employer's payment, or (if the Secretary of State has paid only part of it) all the rights and remedies of the employee with respect to that part of the employer's payment, are transferred to and vest in the Secretary of State, and

(b) any decision of an [employment tribunal] requiring the employer's payment to be paid to the employee has effect as if it required that payment, or that part of it which the Secretary of State has paid, to be paid to the Secretary of State.

(4) Any money recovered by the Secretary of State by virtue of subsection (3) shall be paid into the National Insurance Fund.

NOTES

Sub-s (3): words in brackets substituted by the Employment Rights (Dispute Resolution) Act 1998, s 1(2)(a).

168–181 *(Ss 168–170, ss 171–181 (Ch VII) outside the scope of this work.)*

PART XII
INSOLVENCY OF EMPLOYERS

[17.138]

182 Employee's rights on insolvency of employer

If, on an application made to him in writing by an employee, the Secretary of State is satisfied that—

(a) the employee's employer has become insolvent,

(b) the employee's employment has been terminated, and

(c) on the appropriate date the employee was entitled to be paid the whole or part of any debt to which this Part applies,

the Secretary of State shall, subject to section 186, pay the employee out of the National Insurance Fund the amount to which, in the opinion of the Secretary of State, the employee is entitled in respect of the debt.

[17.139]

183 Insolvency

(1) An employer has become insolvent for the purposes of this Part—

(a) where the employer is an individual, if (but only if) subsection (2) [or (4A)] is satisfied, . . .

(b) where the employer is a company, if (but only if) subsection (3) [or (4A)] is satisfied[, . . .

(c) where the employer is a limited liability partnership, if (but only if) subsection (4) [or (4A)] is satisfied][; and

(d) where the employer is not any of the above, if (but only if) subsection (4A) is satisfied.]

(2) This subsection is satisfied in the case of an employer who is an individual—

(a) in England and Wales if—
[(ai) a moratorium period under a debt relief order applies in relation to him,]
(i) he has been [made] bankrupt or has made a composition or arrangement with his creditors, or
(ii) he has died and his estate falls to be administered in accordance with an order under section 421 of the Insolvency Act 1986, and
(b) in Scotland if—
(i) sequestration of his estate has been awarded or he has executed a trust deed for his creditors or has entered into a composition contract, or
(ii) he has died and a judicial factor appointed under section 11A of the Judicial Factors (Scotland) Act 1889 is required by that section to divide his insolvent estate among his creditors.

(3) This subsection is satisfied in the case of an employer which is a company—
(a) if a winding up order . . . has been made, or a resolution for voluntary winding up has been passed, with respect to the company,
[(aa) if the company is in administration for the purposes of the Insolvency Act 1986,]
(b) if a receiver or (in England and Wales only) a manager of the company's undertaking has been duly appointed, or (in England and Wales only) possession has been taken, by or on behalf of the holders of any debentures secured by a floating charge, of any property of the company comprised in or subject to the charge, or
(c) if a voluntary arrangement proposed in the case of the company for the purposes of Part I of the Insolvency Act 1986 has been approved under that Part of that Act.

[(4) This subsection is satisfied in the case of an employer which is a limited liability partnership—
(a) if a winding-up order, an administration order or a determination for a voluntary winding-up has been made with respect to the limited liability partnership,
(b) if a receiver or (in England and Wales only) a manager of the undertaking of the limited liability partnership has been duly appointed, or (in England and Wales only) possession has been taken, by or on behalf of the holders of any debentures secured by a floating charge, of any property of the limited liability partnership comprised in or subject to the charge, or
(c) if a voluntary arrangement proposed in the case of the limited liability partnership for the purposes of Part I of the Insolvency Act 1986 has been approved under that Part of that Act.]

[(4A) This subsection is satisfied in the case of an employer if—
(a) a request has been made for the first opening of collective proceedings—
(i) based on the insolvency of the employer, as provided for under the laws, regulations and administrative provisions of a member State, and
(ii) involving the partial or total divestment of the employer's assets and the appointment of a liquidator or a person performing a similar task, and
(b) the competent authority has—
(i) decided to open the proceedings, or
(ii) established that the employer's undertaking or business has been definitively closed down and the available assets of the employer are insufficient to warrant the opening of the proceedings.

(4B) For the purposes of subsection (4A)—
(a) "liquidator or person performing a similar task" includes the official receiver or an administrator, trustee in bankruptcy, judicial factor, supervisor of a voluntary arrangement, or person performing a similar task,
(b) "competent authority" includes—
(i) a court,
(ii) a meeting of creditors,
(iii) a creditors' committee,
(iv) the creditors by a decision procedure, and
(v) an authority of a member State empowered to open insolvency proceedings, to confirm the opening of such proceedings or to take decisions in the course of such proceedings.

(4C) An employee may apply under section 182 (employee's rights on insolvency of employer) only if he or she worked or habitually worked in England, Wales or Scotland in that employment to which the application relates.]

[(5) In this section—
(a) references to a company are to be read as including references to a charitable incorporated organisation, and
(b) any reference to the Insolvency Act 1986 in relation to a company is to be read as including a reference to that Act as it applies to charitable incorporated organisations.]

NOTES

Sub-s (1): word omitted from para (a) repealed and para (c) added, together with word preceding it, by the Limited Liability Partnerships Regulations 2001, SI 2001/1090, reg 9(1), Sch 5, para 19(1), (2); words in square brackets in paras (a), (b), (c) inserted, word omitted from para (b) repealed and para (d) added together with word preceding it, by the Employment Rights Act 1996 and Pension Schemes Act 1993 (Amendment) Regulations 2017, SI 2017/1205, reg 2(1), (3)(a).

Sub-s (2): para (a)(ai) inserted by the Tribunals, Courts and Enforcement Act 2007, s 108(3), Sch 20, Pt 2, para 17; in para (a)(i) word in square brackets substituted by the Enterprise and Regulatory Reform Act 2013 (Consequential Amendments) (Bankruptcy) and the Small Business, Enterprise and Employment Act 2015 (Consequential Amendments) Regulations 2016, SI 2016/481, reg 2(1), Sch 1, Pt 2, para 18.

Sub-s (3): in para (a) words "or an administration order" (omitted) repealed, and para (aa) inserted, by the Enterprise Act 2002, ss 248(3), 278(2), Sch 17, para 49(1), (3), Sch 26, subject to savings and transitional provisions (i) in a case where a petition for an administration order has been presented before 15 September 2003 (see the Enterprise Act 2002 (Commencement No 4 and Transitional Provisions and Savings) Order 2003, SI 2003/2093, art 3 at **[2.26]**), and (ii) in relation to special administration regimes (see s 249 of the 2002 Act at **[2.10]**).

Sub-s (4): added by SI 2001/1090, reg 9(1), Sch 5, para 19(1), (3).

Sub-ss (4A)–(4C): inserted by SI 2017/1205, reg 2(1), (3)(b).

Sub-s (5): added by the Charitable Incorporated Organisations (Consequential Amendments) Order 2012, SI 2012/3014, art 4.

[17.140]

184 Debts to which Part applies

(1) This Part applies to the following debts—

(a) any arrears of pay in respect of one or more (but not more than eight) weeks,

(b) any amount which the employer is liable to pay the employee for the period of notice required by section 86(1) or (2) or for any failure of the employer to give the period of notice required by section 86(1),

(c) any holiday pay—

(i) in respect of a period or periods of holiday not exceeding six weeks in all, and

(ii) to which the employee became entitled during the twelve months ending with the appropriate date,

(d) any basic award of compensation for unfair dismissal [or so much of an award under a designated dismissal procedures agreement as does not exceed any basic award of compensation for unfair dismissal to which the employee would be entitled but for the agreement], and

(e) any reasonable sum by way of reimbursement of the whole or part of any fee or premium paid by an apprentice or articled clerk.

(2) For the purposes of subsection (1)(a) the following amounts shall be treated as arrears of pay—

(a) a guarantee payment,

(b) any payment for time off under Part VI of this Act or section 169 of the Trade Union and Labour Relations (Consolidation) Act 1992 (payment for time off for carrying out trade union duties etc),

(c) remuneration on suspension on medical grounds under section 64 of this Act and remuneration on suspension on maternity grounds under section 68 of this Act, and

(d) remuneration under a protective award under section 189 of the Trade Union and Labour Relations (Consolidation) Act 1992.

(3) In subsection (1)(c) "holiday pay", in relation to an employee, means—

(a) pay in respect of a holiday actually taken by the employee, or

(b) any accrued holiday pay which, under the employee's contract of employment, would in the ordinary course have become payable to him in respect of the period of a holiday if his employment with the employer had continued until he became entitled to a holiday.

(4) A sum shall be taken to be reasonable for the purposes of subsection (1)(e) in a case where a trustee in bankruptcy, or (in Scotland) a [trustee or interim trustee in the sequestration of an estate under the Bankruptcy (Scotland) Act 2016], or liquidator has been or is required to be appointed—

(a) as respects England and Wales, if it is admitted to be reasonable by the trustee in bankruptcy or liquidator under section 348 of the Insolvency Act 1986 (effect of bankruptcy on apprenticeships etc), whether as originally enacted or as applied to the winding up of a company by rules under section 411 of that Act, and

(b) as respects Scotland, if it is accepted by the [trustee] or interim trustee or liquidator for the purposes of the sequestration or winding up.

NOTES

Sub-s (1): words in square brackets substituted by the Employment Rights (Dispute Resolution) Act 1998, s 12(4).

Sub-s (4): words in first pair of square brackets substituted for original words "permanent or interim trustee (within the meaning of the Bankruptcy (Scotland) Act 1985)" and word in square brackets in para (b) substituted for original word "permanent" by the Bankruptcy (Scotland) Act 2016 (Consequential Provisions and Modifications) Order 2016, SI 2016/1034, art 7(1), (3), Sch 1, para 16(1), (2), as from 30 November 2016 (except in relation to (i) a sequestration as regards which the petition is presented, or the debtor application is made before that date; or (ii) a trust deed executed before that date).

[17.141]

185 The appropriate date

In this Part "the appropriate date"—

(a) in relation to arrears of pay (not being remuneration under a protective award made under section 189 of the Trade Union and Labour Relations (Consolidation) Act 1992) and to holiday pay, means the date on which the employer became insolvent,

(b) in relation to a basic award of compensation for unfair dismissal and to remuneration under a protective award so made, means whichever is the latest of—

(i) the date on which the employer became insolvent,

(ii) the date of the termination of the employee's employment, and

(iii) the date on which the award was made, and

(c) in relation to any other debt to which this Part applies, means whichever is the later of—

(i) the date on which the employer became insolvent, and

(ii) the date of the termination of the employee's employment.

[17.142]

186 Limit on amount payable under section 182

(1) The total amount payable to an employee in respect of any debt to which this Part applies, where the amount of the debt is referable to a period of time, shall not exceed—

(a) [£508] in respect of any one week, or

(b) in respect of a shorter period, an amount bearing the same proportion to [£508] as that shorter period bears to a week.

(2) . . .

NOTES

Sub-s (1): sums in square brackets substituted (for the sum of £489, as previously substituted by SI 2017/175) by the Employment Rights (Increase of Limits) Order 2018, SI 2018/194, art 3, Schedule, except in relation to cases where the event giving rise to entitlement to compensation or other payments occurred before 6 April 2018.

Sub-s (2): repealed by the Employment Relations Act 1999, ss 36(1)(a), (3), 44, Sch 9, Table 10, except in relation to any increase effected under this subsection before s 34 of the 1999 Act comes into force.

[17.143]

187 Role of relevant officer

(1) Where a relevant officer has been, or is required to be, appointed in connection with an employer's insolvency, the Secretary of State shall not make a payment under section 182 in respect of a debt until he has received a statement from the relevant officer of the amount of that debt which appears to have been owed to the employee on the appropriate date and to remain unpaid.

(2) If the Secretary of State is satisfied that he does not require a statement under subsection (1) in order to determine the amount of a debt which was owed to the employee on the appropriate date and remains unpaid, he may make a payment under section 182 in respect of the debt without having received such a statement.

(3) A relevant officer shall, on request by the Secretary of State, provide him with a statement for the purposes of subsection (1) as soon as is reasonably practicable.

(4) The following are relevant officers for the purposes of this section—

(a) a trustee in bankruptcy or a [trustee] or interim trustee (within the meaning of the Bankruptcy (Scotland) Act [2016]),

(b) a liquidator,

(c) an administrator,

(d) a receiver or manager,

(e) a trustee under a composition or arrangement between the employer and his creditors, and

(f) a trustee under a trust deed for his creditors executed by the employer.

(5) In subsection (4)(e) "trustee" includes the supervisor of a voluntary arrangement proposed for the purposes of, and approved under, Part I or VIII of the Insolvency Act 1986.

NOTES

Sub-s (4): in para (a) word and year in square brackets substituted for original word "permanent" and year "1985" respectively, by the Bankruptcy (Scotland) Act 2016 (Consequential Provisions and Modifications) Order 2016, SI 2016/1034, art 7(1), (3), Sch 1, para 16(1), (3), as from 30 November 2016 (except in relation to (i) a sequestration as regards which the petition is presented, or the debtor application is made before that date; or (ii) a trust deed executed before that date).

[17.144]

188 Complaints to [employment tribunals]

(1) A person who has applied for a payment under section 182 may present a complaint to an [employment tribunal]—

(a) that the Secretary of State has failed to make any such payment, or

(b) that any such payment made by him is less than the amount which should have been paid.

(2) An [employment tribunal] shall not consider a complaint under subsection (1) unless it is presented—

(a) before the end of the period of three months beginning with the date on which the decision of the Secretary of State on the application was communicated to the applicant, or

(b) within such further period as the tribunal considers reasonable in a case where it is not reasonably practicable for the complaint to be presented before the end of that period of three months.

(3) Where an [employment tribunal] finds that the Secretary of State ought to make a payment under section 182, the tribunal shall—

(a) make a declaration to that effect, and

(b) declare the amount of any such payment which it finds the Secretary of State ought to make.

NOTES

Words in square brackets substituted by the Employment Rights (Dispute Resolution) Act 1998, s 1(2)(a), (b).

[17.145]

189 Transfer to Secretary of State of rights and remedies

(1) Where, in pursuance of section 182, the Secretary of State makes a payment to an employee in respect of a debt to which this Part applies—

(a) on the making of the payment any rights and remedies of the employee in respect of the debt (or, if the Secretary of State has paid only part of it, in respect of that part) become rights and remedies of the Secretary of State, and

(b) any decision of an [employment tribunal] requiring an employer to pay that debt to the employee has the effect that the debt (or the part of it which the Secretary of State has paid) is to be paid to the Secretary of State.

(2) Where a debt (or any part of a debt) in respect of which the Secretary of State has made a payment in pursuance of section 182 constitutes—

(a) a preferential debt within the meaning of the Insolvency Act 1986 for the purposes of any provision of that Act (including any such provision as applied by any order made under that Act) or any provision of [the Companies Act 2006], or

(b) a preferred debt within the meaning of the Bankruptcy (Scotland) Act [2016] for the purposes of any provision of that Act (including any such provision as applied by section 11A of the Judicial Factors (Scotland) Act 1889),

the rights which become rights of the Secretary of State in accordance with subsection (1) include any right arising under any such provision by reason of the status of the debt (or that part of it) as a preferential or preferred debt.

(3) In computing for the purposes of any provision mentioned in subsection (2)(a) or (b) the aggregate amount payable in priority to other creditors of the employer in respect of—

(a) any claim of the Secretary of State to be paid in priority to other creditors of the employer by virtue of subsection (2), and

(b) any claim by the employee to be so paid made in his own right,

any claim of the Secretary of State to be so paid by virtue of subsection (2) shall be treated as if it were a claim of the employee.

(4) . . .

(5) Any sum recovered by the Secretary of State in exercising any right, or pursuing any remedy, which is his by virtue of this section shall be paid into the National Insurance Fund.

NOTES

Sub-s (1): words in square brackets substituted by the Employment Rights (Dispute Resolution) Act 1998, s 1(2)(a).

Sub-s (2): words in square brackets in para (a) substituted for original words "the Companies Act 1985" by the Companies Act 2006 (Consequential Amendments etc) Order 2008, SI 2008/948, art 3(1)(b), Sch 1, Pt 2, para 201, subject to transitional provisions and savings in arts 6, 11, 12 thereof; year in square brackets in para (b) substituted for original year "1985" by the Bankruptcy (Scotland) Act 2016 (Consequential Provisions and Modifications) Order 2016, SI 2016/1034, art 7(1), (3), Sch 1, para 16(1), (4), as from 30 November 2016 (except in relation to (i) a sequestration as regards which the petition is presented, or the debtor application is made before that date; or (ii) a trust deed executed before that date).

Sub-s (4): repealed by the Enterprise Act 2002, ss 248(3), 278(2), Sch 17, para 49(1), (4), Sch 26, subject to savings and transitional provisions (i) in a case where a petition for an administration order has been presented before 15 September 2003 (see the Enterprise Act 2002 (Commencement No 4 and Transitional Provisions and Savings) Order 2003, SI 2003/2093, art 3 at **[2.26]**), and (ii) in relation to special administration regimes (see s 249 of the 2002 Act at **[2.10]**). Sub-s (4) originally read as follows:

> "(4) But the Secretary of State shall be entitled, as against the employee, to be so paid in respect of any such claim of his (up to the full amount of the claim) before any payment is made to the employee in respect of any claim by the employee to be so paid made in his own right.".

190–235 *(S 190, ss 191–235 (Pts XIII, XIV) outside the scope of this work.)*

PART XV
GENERAL AND SUPPLEMENTARY

236–239 *(Outside the scope of this work.)*

Final provisions

240–242 *(Outside the scope of this work.)*

[17.146]
243 Commencement

This Act shall come into force at the end of the period of three months beginning with the day on which it is passed.

[17.147]
244 Extent

(1) Subject to the following provisions, this Act extends to England and Wales and Scotland but not to Northern Ireland.

(2) [Sections 36(2) and (4), 37(1) and (5), 38 and 39] extend to England and Wales only.

(3), (4) *(Outside the scope of this work.)*

NOTES

Sub-s (2): words in square brackets substituted by the Sunday Working (Scotland) Act 2003, s 1(1), (5).

[17.148]
245 Short title

This Act may be cited as the Employment Rights Act 1996.

SCHEDULES 1–3

(*Schs 1–3 outside the scope of this work.*)

HOUSING ACT 1996

(1996 c 52)

ARRANGEMENT OF SECTIONS

PART I
SOCIAL RENTED SECTOR REGULATED BY THE WELSH MINISTERS

CHAPTER IV
GENERAL POWERS OF THE WELSH MINISTERS

39 Insolvency, &c of registered social landlord: scheme of provisions . . . [17.149]
40 Initial notice to be given to the Welsh Ministers . . . [17.150]
41 Further notice to be given to the Welsh Ministers . . . [17.151]
42 Moratorium on disposal of land, &c . . . [17.152]
43 Period of moratorium . . . [17.153]
43A Appointment of interim manager . . . [17.154]
44 Proposals as to ownership and management of landlord's land . . . [17.155]
45 Effect of agreed proposals . . . [17.156]
46 Appointment of manager to implement agreed proposals . . . [17.157]
47 Powers of the manager . . . [17.158]
48 Powers of the manager: transfer of engagements . . . [17.159]
49 Assistance by the Welsh Ministers . . . [17.160]
50 Application to court to secure compliance with agreed proposals . . . [17.161]

PART VIII
MISCELLANEOUS AND GENERAL PROVISIONS

Final provisions

231 Extent . . . [17.162]
232 Commencement . . . [17.163]
233 Short title . . . [17.164]

An Act to make provision about housing, including provision about the social rented sector, houses in multiple occupation, landlord and tenant matters, the administration of housing benefit, the conduct of tenants, the allocation of housing accommodation by local housing authorities and homelessness; and for connected purposes

[24 July 1996]

PART I
[SOCIAL RENTED SECTOR] [REGULATED BY THE WELSH MINISTERS]

NOTES

Part heading: first words in square brackets substituted by the Housing and Regeneration Act 2008, s 61(1); second words in square brackets substituted by the Housing (Wales) Measure 2011, s 88, Schedule, paras 1, 2.

A1–29 ((*Chs I–III) outside the scope of this work.*)

CHAPTER IV GENERAL POWERS OF [THE WELSH MINISTERS]

NOTES

Chapter heading: words in square brackets substituted by the Housing and Regeneration Act 2008, s 61(1), (7).

30–38 (*Outside the scope of this work.*)

Insolvency, &c of registered social landlord

[17.149]
39 Insolvency, &c of registered social landlord: scheme of provisions

(1) The following sections make provision—
(a) for notice to be given to [the Welsh Ministers] of any proposal to take certain steps in relation to a registered social landlord (section 40), and for further notice to be given when any such step is taken (section 41),
(b) for a moratorium on the disposal of land, and certain other assets, held by the registered social landlord (sections 42 and 43),
[(ba) for the appointment of an interim manager during a moratorium (section 43A),]

(c) for proposals by [the Welsh Ministers] as to the future ownership and management of the land held by the landlord (section 44), which are binding if agreed (section 45),
(d) for the appointment of a manager to implement agreed proposals (section 46) and as to the powers of such a manager (sections 47 and 48),
(e) for the giving of assistance by [the Welsh Ministers] (section 49), and
(f) for application to the court to secure compliance with the agreed proposals (section 50).

(2) In those sections—

"disposal" means sale, lease, mortgage, charge or any other disposition, and includes the grant of an option;

"secured creditor" means a creditor who holds a mortgage or charge (including a floating charge) over land held by the landlord or any existing or future interest of the landlord in rents or other receipts from land; and

"security" means any mortgage, charge or other security.

(3) The [Welsh Ministers] may make provision by order defining for the purposes of those sections what is meant by a step to enforce security over land.

Any such order shall be made by statutory instrument which shall be subject to annulment in pursuance of a resolution of [the National Assembly for Wales].

NOTES

Sub-s (1): words in square brackets in paras (a), (c), (e) substituted by the Housing and Regeneration Act 2008, s 61(1), (7); para (ba) inserted by the Housing (Wales) Measure 2011, s 88, Schedule, paras 1, 9.

Sub-s (3): words in square brackets substituted by the Housing and Regeneration Act 2008, ss 62(a), 63.

[17.150]

40 Initial notice to be given to [the Welsh Ministers]

(1) Notice must be given to [the Welsh Ministers] before any of the steps mentioned below is taken in relation to a registered social landlord.

The person by whom the notice must be given is indicated in the second column.

(2) Where the registered social landlord is [a registered society], the steps and the person by whom notice must be given are—

Any step to enforce any security over land held by the landlord.	The person proposing to take the step.
Presenting a petition for the winding up of the landlord.	The petitioner.
Passing a resolution for the winding up of the landlord.	The landlord.

(3) Where the registered social landlord is [a company] (including a registered charity), the steps and the person by whom notice must be given are—

Any step to enforce any security over land held by the landlord	The person proposing to take the step.
Applying for an administration order	The applicant.
Presenting a petition for the winding up of the landlord	The petitioner.
Passing a resolution for the winding up of the landlord.	The landlord.

(4) Where the registered social landlord is a registered charity (other than [a company]), the steps and the person by whom notice must be given are—

Any step to enforce any security over land held by the landlord.	The person proposing to take the step.

(5) Notice need not be given under this section in relation to a resolution for voluntary winding up where the consent of [the Welsh Ministers] is required (see paragraphs 12(4) and 13(6) of Schedule 1).

(6) Any step purportedly taken without the requisite notice being given under this section is ineffective.

[(7) Subsections (8) and (9) apply in relation to the reference in subsection (3) to applying for an administration order.

(8) In a case where an administrator is appointed under paragraph 14 or 22 of Schedule B1 to the Insolvency Act 1986 (appointment by floating charge holder, company or directors)—
(a) the reference includes a reference to appointing an administrator under that paragraph, and
(b) in respect of an appointment under either of those paragraphs the reference to the applicant shall be taken as a reference to the person making the appointment.

(9) In a case where a copy of a notice of intention to appoint an administrator under either of those paragraphs is filed with the court—
(a) the reference shall be taken to include a reference to the filing of the copy of the notice, and
(b) in respect of the filing of a copy of a notice of intention to appoint under either of those paragraphs the reference to the applicant shall be taken as a reference to the person giving the notice.]

NOTES

Section heading, sub-ss (1), (5): words in square brackets substituted by the Housing and Regeneration Act 2008, s 61(1), (7).

Sub-s (2): words in square brackets substituted by the Co-operative and Community Benefit Societies Act 2014, s 151(1), Sch 4, Pt 2, paras 55, 56.

Sub-ss (3), (4): words in square brackets substituted by the Companies Act 2006 (Consequential Amendments, Transitional Provisions and Savings) Order 2009, SI 2009/1941, art 2(1), Sch 1, para 161(1), (2)(b).

Sub-ss (7)–(9): added by the Enterprise Act 2002, s 248(3), Sch 17, paras 50, 51, subject to savings and transitional provisions (i) in a case where a petition for an administration order has been presented before 15 September 2003 (see the Enterprise Act 2002 (Commencement No 4 and Transitional Provisions and Savings) Order 2003, SI 2003/2093, art 3 at **[2.26]**), and (ii) in relation to special administration regimes (see s 249 of the 2002 Act at **[2.10]**).

[17.151]

41 Further notice to be given to [the Welsh Ministers]

(1) Notice must be given to [the Welsh Ministers] as soon as may be after any of the steps mentioned below is taken in relation to a registered social landlord.

The person by whom the notice must be given is indicated in the second column.

(2) Where the registered social landlord is [a registered society], the steps and the person by whom notice must be given are—

The taking of a step to enforce any security over land held by the landlord	The person taking the step.
The making of an order for the winding up of the landlord.	The petitioner.
The passing of a resolution for the winding up of the landlord.	The landlord.

(3) Where the registered social landlord is [a company] (including a registered charity), the steps and the person by whom notice must be given are—

The taking of a step to enforce any security over land held by the landlord.	The making of an administration order.
The making of an order for the winding up of the landlord.	The passing of a resolution for the winding up of the landlord.

(4) Where the registered social landlord is a registered charity (other than [a company]), the steps and the person by whom notice must be given are—

The taking of a step to enforce any security over land held by the landlord.	The person taking the step.
The making of an administration order	The person who applied for the order.
The making of an order for the winding up of the landlord.	The petitioner.
The passing of a resolution for the winding up of the landlord.	The landlord.

(5) Failure to give notice under this section does not affect the validity of any step taken; but the period of 28 days mentioned in section 43(1) (period after which moratorium on disposal of land, &c ends) does not begin to run until any requisite notice has been given under this section.

[(6) In subsection (3)—

(a) the reference to the making of an administration order includes a reference to appointing an administrator under paragraph 14 or 22 of Schedule B1 to the Insolvency Act 1986 (administration), and

(b) in respect of an appointment under either of those paragraphs the reference to the applicant shall be taken as a reference to the person making the appointment.]

NOTES

Section heading, sub-s (1): words in square brackets substituted by the Housing and Regeneration Act 2008, s 61(1), (7).

Sub-s (2): words in square brackets substituted by the Co-operative and Community Benefit Societies Act 2014, s 151(1), Sch 4, Pt 2, paras 55, 56.

Sub-ss (3), (4): words in square brackets substituted by the Companies Act 2006 (Consequential Amendments, Transitional Provisions and Savings) Order 2009, SI 2009/1941, art 2(1), Sch 1, para 161(1), (2)(b).

Sub-s (6): added by the Enterprise Act 2002, s 248(3), Sch 17, paras 50, 52, subject to savings and transitional provisions (i) in a case where a petition for an administration order has been presented before 15 September 2003 (see the Enterprise Act 2002 (Commencement No 4 and Transitional Provisions and Savings) Order 2003, SI 2003/2093, art 3 at **[2.26]**), and (ii) in relation to special administration regimes (see s 249 of the 2002 Act at **[2.10]**).

[17.152]

42 Moratorium on disposal of land, &c

(1) Where any of the steps mentioned in section 41 is taken in relation to a registered social landlord, there is a moratorium on the disposal of land held by the landlord.

(2) During the moratorium the consent of [the Welsh Ministers] under this section is required (except as mentioned below) for any disposal of land held by the landlord, whether by the landlord itself or any person having a power of disposal in relation to the land.

Consent under this section may be given in advance and may be given subject to conditions.

(3) Consent is not required under this section for any such disposal as is mentioned in section 10(1), (2) or (3) (lettings and other disposals not requiring consent under section 9).

(4) A disposal made without the consent required by this section is void.

(5) Nothing in this section prevents a liquidator from disclaiming any land held by the landlord as onerous property.

(6) The provisions of this section apply in relation to any existing or future interest of the landlord in rent or other receipts arising from land as they apply to an interest in land.

NOTES

Sub-s (2): words in square brackets substituted by the Housing and Regeneration Act 2008, s 61(1), (7).

[17.153]

43 Period of moratorium

(1) The moratorium in consequence of the taking of any step as mentioned in section 41—

(a) begins when the step is taken, and

(b) ends at the end of the period of 28 days beginning with the day on which notice of its having been taken was given to [the Welsh Ministers] under that section,

subject to the following provisions.

(2) The taking of any further step as mentioned in section 41 at a time when a moratorium is already in force does not start a further moratorium or affect the duration of the existing one.

(3) A moratorium may be extended from time to time with the consent of all the landlord's secured creditors.

Notice of any such extension shall be given by [the Welsh Ministers] to—

(a) the landlord, and

(b) any liquidator, administrative receiver, receiver or administrator appointed in respect of the landlord or any land held by it.

(4) If during a moratorium [the Welsh Ministers] [consider] that the proper management of the landlord's land can be secured without making proposals under section 44 (proposals as to ownership and management of landlord's land), [the Welsh Ministers] may direct that the moratorium shall cease to have effect.

Before making any such direction [the Welsh Ministers] shall consult the person who took the step which brought about the moratorium.

(5) When a moratorium comes to an end, or ceases to have effect under subsection (4), [the Welsh Ministers] shall give notice of that fact to the landlord and the landlord's secured creditors.

(6) When a moratorium comes to an end (but not when it ceases to have effect under subsection (4)), the following provisions of this section apply.

[The Welsh Ministers'] notice shall, in such a case, inform the landlord and the landlord's secured creditors of the effect of those provisions.

(7) If any further step as mentioned in section 41 is taken within the period of three years after the end of the original period of the moratorium, the moratorium may be renewed with the consent of all the landlord's secured creditors (which may be given before or after the step is taken).

Notice of any such renewal shall be given by [the Welsh Ministers] to the persons to whom notice of an extension is required to be given under subsection (3).

(8) If a moratorium ends without any proposals being agreed, then, for a period of three years the taking of any further step as mentioned in section 41 does not start a further moratorium except with the consent of the landlord's secured creditors as mentioned in subsection (7) above.

NOTES

Sub-ss (1), (3)–(7): words in square brackets substituted by the Housing and Regeneration Act 2008, s 61(1), (7).

[17.154]

[43A Appointment of interim manager

(1) During a moratorium the Welsh Ministers may appoint an interim manager of the registered social landlord.

(2) An appointment may relate to the registered social landlord's affairs generally or to affairs specified in the appointment.

(3) But an appointment may not relate to affairs relating only to the provision of housing in England.

(4) Appointment is to be on terms and conditions (including as to remuneration and expenses) specified in, or determined in accordance with, the appointment.

(5) An interim manager has—

(a) any power specified in the appointment, and

(b) any other power in relation to the registered social landlord's affairs required by the manager for the purposes specified in the appointment (including the power to enter into agreements and take other action on behalf of the landlord).

(6) But an interim manager may not—

(a) dispose of land, or

(b) grant security over land.

(7) The Welsh Ministers may give the interim manager general or specific directions.

(8) The Welsh Ministers may revoke or amend any directions given.

(9) An appointment under this section comes to an end with the earliest of the following—
(a) the end of the moratorium,
(b) the agreement of proposals made under section 44, or
(c) a date specified in the appointment.
(10) If a person ceases to be an interim manager before the appointment has come to an end, the Welsh Ministers may appoint a new interim manager in place of that person.]

NOTES

Inserted by the Housing (Wales) Measure 2011, s 83.

[17.155]

44 Proposals as to ownership and management of landlord's land

(1) During the moratorium (see sections 42 and 43) [the Welsh Ministers] may make proposals as to the future ownership and management of the land held by the registered social landlord, designed to secure the continued proper management of the landlord's land by a registered social landlord.
(2) In drawing up [their] proposals [the Welsh Ministers]—
(a) shall consult the landlord and, so far as is practicable, its tenants, and
(b) shall have regard to the interests of all the landlord's creditors, both secured and unsecured.
(3) [The Welsh Ministers] shall also consult—
(a) where the landlord is [a registered society], the appropriate registrar, and
(b) where the landlord is a registered charity, the [Charity Commission].
(4) No proposals shall be made under which—
(a) a preferential debt of the landlord is to be paid otherwise than in priority to debts which are not preferential debts, . . .
[(aa) an ordinary preferential debt of the landlord is to be paid otherwise than in priority to any secondary preferential debts that the landlord may have,]
(b) a preferential creditor is to be paid a smaller proportion of [an ordinary preferential debt] than another preferential creditor, except with the concurrence of the creditor concerned [or
(c) a preferential creditor is to be paid a smaller proportion of a secondary preferential debt than another preferential creditor, except with the concurrence of the creditor concerned.]
In this subsection references to preferential debts[, ordinary preferential debts, secondary preferential debts] and preferential creditors have the same meaning as in the Insolvency Act 1986.
(5) So far as practicable no proposals shall be made which have the effect that unsecured creditors of the landlord are in a worse position than they would otherwise be.
(6) Where the landlord is a charity the proposals shall not require the landlord to act outside the terms of its trusts, and any disposal of housing accommodation occupied under a tenancy or licence from the landlord must be to another charity whose objects appear to [the Welsh Ministers] to be, as nearly as practicable, akin to those of the landlord.
(7) [The Welsh Ministers] shall serve a copy of its proposals on—
(a) the landlord and its officers,
(b) the secured creditors of the landlord, and
(c) any liquidator, administrator, administrative receiver or receiver appointed in respect of the landlord or its land;
and [they] shall make such arrangements as [they consider] appropriate to see that the members, tenants and unsecured creditors of the landlord are informed of the proposals.

NOTES

Sub-ss (1), (2), (6), (7): words in square brackets substituted by the Housing and Regeneration Act 2008, s 61(1), (7).
Sub-s (3): first words in square brackets substituted by the Housing and Regeneration Act 2008, s 61(1), (7); second words in square brackets substituted by the Co-operative and Community Benefit Societies Act 2014, s 151(1), Sch 4, Pt 2, paras 55, 56; third words in square brackets substituted by the Charities Act 2006, s 75(1), Sch 8, paras 183, 187.
Sub-s (4): word omitted from para (a) repealed, para (aa), and para (c) and word immediately preceding it inserted, and final words in square brackets inserted, by the Banks and Building Societies (Depositor Preference and Priorities) Order 2014, SI 2014/3486, art 29.

[17.156]

45 Effect of agreed proposals

(1) The following provisions apply if proposals made by [the Welsh Ministers] under section 44 are agreed, with or without modifications, by all the secured creditors of the registered social landlord.
(2) Once agreed the proposals are binding on [the Welsh Ministers], the landlord, all the landlord's creditors (whether secured or unsecured) and any liquidator, administrator, administrative receiver or receiver appointed in respect of the landlord or its land.
(3) It is the duty of—
(a) the members of the committee where the landlord is [a registered society],
(b) the directors where the landlord is [a company (including a company that is a registered charity)], and
(c) the trustees where the landlord is a charitable trust,
to co-operate in the implementation of the proposals.
This does not mean that they have to do anything contrary to any fiduciary or other duty owed by them.
(4) [The Welsh Ministers] shall serve a copy of the agreed proposals on—
(a) the landlord and its officers,
(b) the secured creditors of the landlord, and

(c) any liquidator, administrator, administrative receiver or receiver appointed in respect of the landlord or its land, and

(d) where the landlord is [a registered society] or registered charity, the [Financial Conduct Authority] or the [Charity Commission], as the case may be;

and [they] shall make such arrangements as [they consider] appropriate to see that the members, tenants and unsecured creditors of the landlord are informed of the proposals.

(5) The proposals may subsequently be amended with the consent of [the Welsh Ministers] and all the landlord's secured creditors.

Section 44(2) to (7) and subsections (2) to (4) above apply in relation to the amended proposals as in relation to the original proposals.

NOTES

Sub-ss (1), (2), (5): words in square brackets substituted by the Housing and Regeneration Act 2008, s 61(1), (7).

Sub-s (3): in para (a) words in square brackets substituted by the Co-operative and Community Benefit Societies Act 2014, s 151(1), Sch 4, Pt 2, paras 55, 56; in para (b) words in square brackets substituted by the Companies Act 2006 (Consequential Amendments, Transitional Provisions and Savings) Order 2009, SI 2009/1941, art 2(1), Sch 1, para 161(1), (4).

Sub-s (4): first, fifth and final words in square brackets substituted by the Housing and Regeneration Act 2008, s 61(1), (7); in para (d) first words in square brackets substituted by the Co-operative and Community Benefit Societies Act 2014, s 151(1), Sch 4, Pt 2, paras 55, 56, second words in square brackets substituted by the Financial Services Act 2012 (Mutual Societies) Order 2013, SI 2013/496, art 2(c), Sch 11, para 5(1), (2)(d), and third words in square brackets substituted by the Charities Act 2006, s 75(1), Sch 8, paras 183, 188.

[17.157]

46 Appointment of manager to implement agreed proposals

(1) Where proposals agreed as mentioned in section 45 so provide, [the Welsh Ministers] may by order . . . appoint a manager to implement the proposals or such of them as are specified in the order.

(2) If the landlord is a registered charity, [the Welsh Ministers] shall give notice to the [Charity Commission] of the appointment.

(3) Where proposals make provision for the appointment of a manager, they shall also provide for the payment of his reasonable remuneration and expenses.

(4) [The Welsh Ministers] may give the manager directions in relation to the carrying out of his functions.

[(4A) The Welsh Ministers may amend or revoke any directions given by them.]

(5) The manager may apply to the High Court for directions in relation to any particular matter arising in connection with the carrying out of his functions.

A direction of the court supersedes any direction of [the Welsh Ministers] in respect of the same matter.

(6) If a vacancy occurs by death, resignation or otherwise in the office of manager, [the Welsh Ministers] may by further order . . . fill the vacancy.

[(7) [An order made by] the [Welsh Ministers] [under this section], shall be made in writing.]

NOTES

Sub-s (1): words in square brackets substituted by the Housing and Regeneration Act 2008, s 61(1), (7); words omitted repealed by the Government of Wales Act 1998, ss 140, 152, Sch 16, paras 81, 88(1), (2), Sch 18, Pt VI.

Sub-s (2): words in first pair of square brackets substituted by the Housing and Regeneration Act 2008, s 61(1), (7); words in second pair of square brackets substituted by the Charities Act 2006, s 75(1), Sch 8, paras 183, 189.

Sub-ss (4), (5): words in square brackets substituted by the Housing and Regeneration Act 2008, s 61(1), (7).

Sub-s (4A): inserted by the Housing (Wales) Measure 2011, s 88, Schedule, paras 1, 10.

Sub-s (6): words in square brackets substituted by the Housing and Regeneration Act 2008, s 61(1), (7); words omitted repealed by the Government of Wales Act 1998, ss 140, 152, Sch 16, paras 81, 88(1), (2), Sch 18, Pt VI.

Sub-s (7): added by the Government of Wales Act 1998, ss 140, 141, Sch 16, paras 81, 88(1), (3); words in first pair of square brackets substituted and words in third pair of square brackets inserted by the Housing and Regeneration Act 2008 (Consequential Provisions) Order 2010, SI 2010/866, art 5, Sch 2, Pt 2, paras 81, 91, subject to transitional provisions in art 6 of, and Sch 3, paras 1, 3, 4 to, that Order; words in second pair of square brackets substituted by the Housing and Regeneration Act 2008, s 62(a).

[17.158]

47 Powers of the manager

(1) An order under section 46(1) shall confer on the manager power generally to do all such things as are necessary for carrying out his functions.

(2) The order may include the following specific powers—

1 Power to take possession of the land held by the landlord and for that purpose to take any legal proceedings which seem to him expedient.

2 Power to sell or otherwise dispose of the land by public auction or private contract.

3 Power to raise or borrow money and for that purpose to grant security over the land.

4 Power to appoint a solicitor or accountant or other professionally qualified person to assist him in the performance of his functions.

5 Power to bring or defend legal proceedings relating to the land in the name and on behalf of the landlord.

6 Power to refer to arbitration any question affecting the land.

7 Power to effect and maintain insurance in respect of the land.

8 Power where the landlord is a body corporate to use the seal of the body corporate for purposes relating to the land.

9 Power to do all acts and to execute in the name and on behalf of the landlord any deed, receipt or other document relating to the land.

10 Power to appoint an agent to do anything which he is unable to do for himself or which can more conveniently be done by an agent, and power to employ and dismiss any employees.
11 Power to do all such things (including the carrying out of works) as may be necessary in connection with the management or transfer of the land.
12 Power to make any payment which is necessary or incidental to the performance of his functions.
13 Power to carry on the business of the landlord so far as relating to the management or transfer of the land.
14 Power to grant or accept a surrender of a lease or tenancy of any of the land, and to take a lease or tenancy of any property required or convenient for the landlord's housing activities.
15 Power to make any arrangement or compromise on behalf of the landlord in relation to the management or transfer of the land.
16 Power to do all other things incidental to the exercise of any of the above powers.

(3) In carrying out his functions the manager acts as the landlord's agent and he is not personally liable on a contract which he enters into as manager.
(4) A person dealing with the manager in good faith and for value is not concerned to inquire whether the manager is acting within his powers.
(5) The manager shall, so far as practicable, consult the landlord's tenants about any exercise of his powers which is likely to affect them and inform them about any such exercise of his powers.

NOTES

Modification in relation to solicitors: sub-s (2) is applied with modifications in relation to a "licensed body", by the Legal Services Act 2007 (Designation as a Licensing Authority) (No 2) Order 2011, SI 2011/2866, art 8, Sch 2.

[17.159]
48 Powers of the manager: transfer of engagements
(1) An order under section 46(1) may, where the landlord is [a registered society], give the manager power to make and execute on behalf of the society an instrument transferring the engagements of the society.
(2) Any such instrument has the same effect as a transfer of engagements under [section 110 or 112 of the Co-operative and Community Benefit Societies Act 2014] (transfer of engagements by special resolution to another society or a company).
[In particular, it does not prejudice any right of a creditor of the society.]
(3) A copy of the instrument, signed by the manager, shall be sent to the [[Financial Conduct Authority] and registered by it]; and until that copy is so registered the instrument shall not take effect.
(4) It is the duty of the manager to send a copy for registration within 14 days from the day on which the instrument is executed; but this does not invalidate registration after that time.

NOTES

Sub-ss (1), (2): words in square brackets substituted by the Co-operative and Community Benefit Societies Act 2014, s 151(1), Sch 4, Pt 2, paras 55, 56, 59.
Sub-s (3): first (outer) words in square brackets substituted by the Financial Services and Markets Act 2000 (Consequential Amendments and Repeals) Order 2001, SI 2001/3649, art 355; second (inner) words in square brackets substituted by the Financial Services Act 2012 (Mutual Societies) Order 2013, SI 2013/496, art 2(c), Sch 11, para 5(1), (2)(e).

[17.160]
49 Assistance by [the Welsh Ministers]
(1) [The Welsh Ministers] may give such assistance as [they think] fit—
(a) to the landlord, for the purpose of preserving the position pending the making of and agreement to proposals;
(b) to the landlord or a manager appointed under section 46, for the purpose of carrying out any agreed proposals.
(2) [The Welsh Ministers] may, in particular—
(a) lend staff;
(b) pay or secure payment of the manager's reasonable remuneration and expenses;
(c) give such financial assistance as appears to [the Welsh Ministers] to be appropriate.
(3) . . .

NOTES

Section heading, sub-ss (1), (2): words in square brackets substituted by the Housing and Regeneration Act 2008, s 61(1), (7).
Sub-s (3): repealed by the Housing and Regeneration Act 2008 (Consequential Provisions) Order 2010, SI 2010/866, arts 5, 7, Sch 2, Pt 2, paras 81, 92, Sch 4, subject to transitional provisions in art 6 of, and Sch 3, paras 1, 3, 4 to, that Order.

[17.161]
50 Application to court to secure compliance with agreed proposals
(1) The landlord or any creditor of the landlord may apply to the High Court on the ground that an action of the manager appointed under section 46 is not in accordance with the agreed proposals.
On such an application the court may confirm, reverse or modify any act or decision of the manager, give him directions or make such other order as it thinks fit.
(2) [The Welsh Ministers] or any other person bound by agreed proposals may apply to the High Court on the ground that any action, or proposed action, by another person bound by the proposals is not in accordance with those proposals. On such an application the court may—
(a) declare any such action to be ineffective, and

(b) grant such relief by way of injunction, damages or otherwise as appears to the court appropriate.

NOTES

Sub-s (2): words in square brackets substituted by the Housing and Regeneration Act 2008, s 61(1), (7).

50A–218 *(Ss 50A–64 (Chs 4A, V), ss 65–218 (Pts II–VII) outside the scope of this work.)*

PART VIII
MISCELLANEOUS AND GENERAL PROVISIONS

218A–230 *(Outside the scope of this work.)*

Final provisions

[17.162]
231 Extent

(1) The provisions of this Act extend to England and Wales, and only to England and Wales, subject as follows.

(2)–(5) *(Outside the scope of this work.)*

[17.163]
232 Commencement

(1) The following provisions of this Act come into force on Royal Assent—

. . .

sections 223 to 226 and 228 to 233 (general provisions).

(2) *(Outside the scope of this work.)*

(3) The other provisions of this Act come into force on a day appointed by order of the Secretary of State, and different days may be appointed for different areas and different purposes.

(4) An order under subsection (3) shall be made by statutory instrument and may contain such transitional provisions and savings as appear to the Secretary of State to be appropriate.

NOTES

Sub-s (1): words omitted outside the scope of this work.

Orders: at present, 13 commencement orders have been made under this section. The order relevant to the provisions of this Act reproduced here is the Housing Act 1996 (Commencement No 3 and Transitional Provisions) Order 1996, SI 1996/2402, bringing, inter alia, ss 39–50 into force on 1 October 1996.

[17.164]
233 Short title

This Act may be cited as the Housing Act 1996.

SCHEDULES 1–19

(Schs 1–19 outside the scope of this work.)

PETROLEUM ACT 1998

(1998 c 17)

An Act to consolidate certain enactments about petroleum, offshore installations and submarine pipelines.

[11 June 1998]

1–28 *((Pts I–III) outside the scope of this work.)*

PART IV
ABANDONMENT OF OFFSHORE INSTALLATIONS

29–38 *(Outside the scope of this work.)*

[17.165]
[38A Protection of funds set aside for the purposes of abandonment programme

(1) This section applies where any security for the performance of obligations under an approved abandonment programme has been provided by a person ("the security provider") by way of a trust or other arrangements.

(2) Subsection (1) applies whether the security is provided before or after the programme is approved.

(3) In this section a reference to "the protected assets" is a reference to the security and any property or rights in which it consists.

(4) In this section "security" includes—

(a) a charge over a bank account or any other asset;
(b) a deposit of money;
(c) a performance bond or guarantee;
(d) an insurance policy;
(e) a letter of credit.

(5) The manner in which, and purposes for which, the protected assets are to be applied and enforceable (whether in the event of the security provider's insolvency or otherwise) is to be determined in accordance with the trust or other arrangements.
(6) For the purposes of subsection (5), no regard is to be had to so much of the Insolvency Act 1986, the Insolvency (Northern Ireland) Order 1989 or any other enactment or rule of law as, in its operation in relation to the security provider or any conduct of the security provider, would—
(a) prevent or restrict the protected assets from being applied in accordance with the trust or other arrangement, or
(b) prevent or restrict their enforcement for the purposes of being so applied.
(7) In subsection (6) "enactment" includes an enactment comprised in, or in an instrument made under, an Act of the Scottish Parliament or Northern Ireland legislation.]

NOTES

Inserted, together with s 38B, by the Energy Act 2008, s 74(1), subject to s 74(2) thereof which provides that this insertion has effect in relation to a trust or other arrangements established on or after 1 December 2007.

[17.166]
[38B Directions to provide information about protected assets
(1) The Secretary of State may direct a security provider to publish specified information about the protected assets.
(2) A direction under this section may specify—
(a) the time when the information must be published, and
(b) the manner of publication.
(3) If a security provider fails to comply with a direction, the Secretary of State, or a creditor of the security provider, may make an application to the court under this section.
(4) If, on an application under this section, the court decides that the security provider has failed to comply with the direction, it may order the security provider to take such steps as the court directs for securing that the direction is complied with.
(5) In this section—
"court"—
(a) in relation to an application in England and Wales or Northern Ireland, means the High Court, and
(b) in relation to an application in Scotland, means the Court of Session;
"security provider" means a person who has provided security in relation to which section 38A applies;
"the protected assets", in relation to a security provider, means the security, and any property or rights in which it consists.]

NOTES

Inserted, together with s 38A, by the Energy Act 2008, s 74(1), subject to s 74(2) thereof which provides that this insertion has effect in relation to a trust or other arrangements established on or after 1 December 2007.

39–45 (*Outside the scope of this work.*)

PART V
MISCELLANEOUS AND GENERAL

45A–51 (*Outside the scope of this work.*)

[17.167]
52 Commencement
(1)–(3) (*Outside the scope of this work.*)
(4) Subject to subsections (1) and (2), this Act shall come into force on such day as the Secretary of State may by order appoint.
(5) Orders under this section shall be made by statutory instrument.

NOTES

Orders: the Petroleum Act 1998 (Commencement No 1) Order 1999, SI 1999/161.

[17.168]
53 Short title and extent
(1) This Act may be cited as the Petroleum Act 1998.
(2) This Act, except for sections 7 and 8, extends to Northern Ireland.

SCHEDULES 1–5

(*Schs 1–5 outside the scope of this work.*)

WELFARE REFORM AND PENSIONS ACT 1999

(1999 c 30)

ARRANGEMENT OF SECTIONS

PART II
PENSIONS: GENERAL

Pensions and bankruptcy

11 Effect of bankruptcy on pension rights: approved arrangements . . . . [17.169]
12 Effect of bankruptcy on pension rights: unapproved arrangements . . . . [17.170]
13 Sections 11 and 12: application to Scotland . . . . [17.171]

PART VI
GENERAL

Supplementary

89 Commencement . . . . [17.172]
90 Extent . . . . [17.173]
91 Short title, general interpretation and Scottish devolution . . . . [17.174]

An Act to make provision about pensions and social security; to make provision for reducing under-occupation of dwellings by housing benefit claimants; to authorise certain expenditure by the Secretary of State having responsibility for social security; and for connected purposes

[11 November 1999]

1–8 (*(Pt I) outside the scope of this work.*)

PART II
PENSIONS: GENERAL

9, 10 (*Outside the scope of this work.*)

Pensions and bankruptcy

[17.169]

11 Effect of bankruptcy on pension rights: approved arrangements

(1) Where a bankruptcy order is made against a person on a [bankruptcy application made or] petition presented after the coming into force of this section, any rights of his under an approved pension arrangement are excluded from his estate.

(2) In this section "approved pension arrangement" means—

[(a) a pension scheme registered under section 153 of the Finance Act 2004;]

(b) . . .

(c) [an occupational pension scheme] set up by a government outside the United Kingdom for the benefit, or primarily for the benefit, of its employees;

(d)–(f) . . .

[(g) an annuity purchased for the purpose of giving effect to rights under a scheme falling within paragraph (a), including an annuity in payment before 6th April 2006, giving effect to rights under any scheme approved—

(i) before that date under Chapters 1, 3 or 4 of Part 14 of the Taxes Act; or

(ii) any relevant statutory scheme, as defined in section 611 of that Act;]

(h) any pension arrangements of any description which may be prescribed by regulations made by the Secretary of State.

(3) . . .

[(4) Subsection (5) applies if—

(a) at the time when a bankruptcy order is made against a person, an appeal against a decision not to register a pension scheme has been made under section 156 of the Finance Act 2004, and

(b) the decision of the [tribunal] (see section 156(3) of that Act) is to uphold the decision of Her Majesty's Revenue and Customs not to register the scheme.]

(5) Any rights of that person under the scheme shall (without any conveyance, assignment or transfer) vest in his trustee in bankruptcy, as part of his estate, immediately on—

(a) the [tribunal's] decision being made, or

(b) (if later) the trustee's appointment taking effect or, in the case of the official receiver, his becoming trustee.

[(6) Subsection (7) applies if, at any time after a bankruptcy order is made against a person Her Majesty's Revenue and Customs—

(a) give notice withdrawing registration of the pension scheme under section 157 of the Finance Act 2004, and

(b) the date specified as being that from which de-registration occurs under sub-section (4) of that section ("the de-registration date") is the date from which the scheme ceases to be a registered pension scheme.]

(7) Any rights of that person under the scheme or arising by virtue of the arrangements, and any rights of his under any related annuity, shall (without any conveyance, assignment or transfer) vest in his trustee in bankruptcy, as part of his estate, immediately on—

(a) the giving of the notice, or

(b) (if later) the trustee's appointment taking effect or, in the case of the official receiver, his becoming trustee.

(8) In subsection (7) "related annuity" means an annuity purchased on or after the [de-registration date] for the purpose of giving effect to rights under the scheme or (as the case may be) to rights arising by virtue of the arrangements.

(9) Where under subsection (5) or (7) any rights vest in a person's trustee in bankruptcy, the trustee's title to them has relation back to the commencement of the person's bankruptcy; but where any transaction is entered into by the trustees or managers of the scheme in question—

(a) in good faith, and

(b) without notice of the making of the decision mentioned in subsection (4)(b) or (as the case may be) the giving of the notice mentioned in subsection (6),

the trustee in bankruptcy is not in respect of that transaction entitled by virtue of this subsection to any remedy against them or any person whose title to any property derives from them.

(10) Without prejudice to section 83, regulations under subsection (2)(h) may, in the case of any description of arrangements prescribed by the regulations, make provision corresponding to any provision made by subsections (4) to (9).

(11) In this section—

[(a) "occupational pension scheme" has the meaning given in section 150(5) of the Finance Act 2004;

(b) "pension scheme" has the meaning given in section 150(1) of the Finance Act 2004 and "registered pension scheme" means a pension scheme registered under section 153 of the Finance Act 2004;]

(c) "estate", in relation to a person against whom a bankruptcy order is made, means his estate for the purposes of Parts VIII to XI of the Insolvency Act 1986;

(d) "the Taxes Act" means the Income and Corporation Taxes Act 1988.

(12) For the purposes of this section a person shall be treated as having a right under an approved pension arrangement where—

(a) he is entitled to a credit under section 29(1)(b) as against the person responsible for the arrangement (within the meaning of Chapter I of Part IV), and

(b) the person so responsible has not discharged his liability in respect of the credit.

NOTES

Sub-s (1): words in square brackets inserted by the Enterprise and Regulatory Reform Act 2013 (Consequential Amendments) (Bankruptcy) and the Small Business, Enterprise and Employment Act 2015 (Consequential Amendments) Regulations 2016, SI 2016/481, reg 2(1), Sch 1, Pt 1, para 12.

Sub-s (2): paras (a), (g), and words in square brackets in para (c) substituted and paras (b), (d)–(f) repealed by the Taxation of Pension Schemes (Consequential Amendments) Order 2006, SI 2006/745, art 15(1), (3)(a).

Sub-s (3): repealed by SI 2006/745, art 15(1), (3)(b).

Sub-s (4): substituted by SI 2006/745, art 15(1), (3)(c); word in square brackets in para (b) substituted for original words "General or Special Commissioners" by the Transfer of Tribunal Functions and Revenue and Customs Appeals Order 2009, SI 2009/56, art 3(1), Sch 1, para 284(1), (2), subject to transitional provisions and savings in Sch 3, paras 1, 6–8, 12, 13 thereto.

Sub-s (5): word in square brackets in para (a) substituted for original words "General or Special Commissioners" by SI 2009/56, art 3(1), Sch 1, para 284(1), (3), subject to transitional provisions and savings in Sch 3, paras 1, 6–8, 12, 13 thereto.

Sub-s (6): substituted by SI 2006/745, art 15(1), (3)(e).

Sub-ss (8), (11): words in square brackets substituted by SI 2006/745, art 15(1), (3)(f), (g).

Regulations: the Occupational and Personal Pension Schemes (Bankruptcy) (No 2) Regulations 2002, SI 2002/836 at **[11.24]**.

[17.170]

12 Effect of bankruptcy on pension rights: unapproved arrangements

(1) The Secretary of State may by regulations make provision for or in connection with enabling rights of a person under an unapproved pension arrangement to be excluded, in the event of a bankruptcy order being made against that person, from his estate for the purposes of Parts VIII to XI of the Insolvency Act 1986.

(2) Regulations under this section may, in particular, make provision—

(a) for rights under an unapproved pension arrangement to be excluded from a person's estate—

(i) by an order made on his application by a prescribed court, or

(ii) in accordance with a qualifying agreement made between him and his trustee in bankruptcy;

(b) for the court's decision whether to make such an order in relation to a person to be made by reference to—

(i) future likely needs of him and his family, and

(ii) whether any benefits (by way of a pension or otherwise) are likely to be received by virtue of rights of his under other pension arrangements and (if so) the extent to which they appear likely to be adequate for meeting any such needs;

(c) for the prescribed persons in the case of any pension arrangement to provide a person or his trustee in bankruptcy on request with information reasonably required by that person or trustee for or in connection with the making of such applications and agreements as are mentioned in paragraph (a).

(3) In this section—

"prescribed" means prescribed by regulations under this section;

"qualifying agreement" means an agreement entered into in such circumstances, and satisfying such requirements, as may be prescribed;

"unapproved pension arrangement" means a pension arrangement which—

(a) is not an approved pension arrangement within the meaning of section 11, and

(b) is of a prescribed description.

(4) For the purposes of this section a person shall be treated as having a right under an unapproved pension arrangement where—

(a) he is entitled to a credit under section 29(1)(b) as against the person responsible for the arrangement (within the meaning of Chapter I of Part IV), and

(b) the person so responsible has not discharged his liability in respect of the credit.

NOTES

Regulations: the Occupational and Personal Pension Schemes (Bankruptcy) (No 2) Regulations 2002, SI 2002/836 at **[11.24]**.

[17.171]

13 Sections 11 and 12: application to Scotland

(1) This section shall have effect for the purposes of the application of sections 11 and 12 to Scotland.

(2) A reference to—

(a) the making of a bankruptcy order against a person is a reference to the award of sequestration on his estate or the making of the appointment on his estate of a judicial factor under section 41 of the Solicitors (Scotland) Act 1980;

(b) the estate of a person is a reference to his estate for the purposes of the Bankruptcy (Scotland) Act [2016] or of the Solicitors (Scotland) Act 1980, as the case may be;

(c) assignment is a reference to assignation;

(d) a person's trustee in bankruptcy is a reference to his [trustee or interim trustee in a sequestration under the Bankruptcy (Scotland) Act 2016] or judicial factor, as the case may be;

(e) the commencement of a person's bankruptcy is a reference to the date of sequestration (within the meaning of section [22(7) of the Bankruptcy (Scotland) Act 2016]) or of the judicial factor's appointment taking effect, as the case may be.

(3) For paragraph (b) of each of subsections (5) and (7) of section 11 there shall be substituted—

"(b) if later, the date of sequestration (within the meaning of section [22(7) of the Bankruptcy (Scotland) Act 2016]) or of the judicial factor's appointment taking effect, as the case may be."

NOTES

Sub-s (2): year in square brackets in para (b) substituted for original year "1985", words in square brackets in para (d) substituted for original words "permanent trustee" and words in square brackets in para (e) substituted for original words "12(4) of the Bankruptcy (Scotland) Act 1985", by the Bankruptcy (Scotland) Act 2016 (Consequential Provisions and Modifications) Order 2016, SI 2016/1034, art 7(1), (3), Sch 1, para 19(1), (2), as from 30 November 2016 (except in relation to (i) a sequestration as regards which the petition is presented, or the debtor application is made before that date; or (ii) a trust deed executed before that date).

Sub-s (3): words in square brackets substituted for original words "12(4) of the Bankruptcy (Scotland) Act 1985" by SI 2016/1034, art 7(1), (3), Sch 1, para 19(1), (3), as from 30 November 2016 (except in relation to (i) a sequestration as regards which the petition is presented, or the debtor application is made before that date; or (ii) a trust deed executed before that date).

14–80 *(Ss 14–18, ss 19–80 (Pts III–V) outside the scope of this work.)*

PART VI
GENERAL

81, 82 (*Outside the scope of this work.*)

Supplementary

83–88 (*Outside the scope of this work.*)

[17.172]

89 Commencement

(1) Subject to the provisions of this section, the provisions of this Act shall not come into force until such day as the Secretary of State may by order appoint.

(2), (3) (*Outside the scope of this work.*)

(4) The following provisions come into force on the day on which this Act is passed—

(a)–(g) (*outside the scope of this work*);

(h) sections 86 and 87, this section and sections 90 and 91.

(5) The following provisions come into force on the day on which this Act is passed, but for the purpose only of the exercise of any power to make regulations—

(a) Parts I to IV;

(b), (c) (*outside the scope of this work.*)

(6) Without prejudice to section 83, an order under this section may appoint different days for different purposes or different areas.

NOTES

Orders: at present, 16 commencement orders have been made under this section. The orders relevant to the provisions of the Act reproduced here are the Welfare Reform and Pensions Act 1999 (Commencement No 7) Order 2000, SI 2000/1382 and the Welfare Reform and Pensions Act 1999 (Commencement No 13) Order 2002, SI 2002/153.

[17.173]
90 Extent

(1) (*Outside the scope of this work.*)

(2) The following provisions extend to Scotland only—
  (a) sections 13 and 16;
  (b)–(e) (*Outside the scope of this work.*)

(3) The following provisions extend to England and Wales and Scotland only—
  (a) (*Outside the scope of this work*);
  (b) sections 9 to 12, 14 and 17;
  (c)–(k) (*Outside the scope of this work.*)

(4)–(6) (*Outside the scope of this work.*)

[17.174]
91 Short title, general interpretation and Scottish devolution

(1) This Act may be cited as the Welfare Reform and Pensions Act 1999.

(2)–(4) (*Outside the scope of this work.*)

SCHEDULES 1–13

(*Schs 1–13 outside the scope of this work.*)

FINANCIAL SERVICES AND MARKETS ACT 2000

(2000 c 8)

ARRANGEMENT OF SECTIONS

PART 1A
THE REGULATORS

CHAPTER 2
THE PRUDENTIAL REGULATION AUTHORITY

2A The Prudential Regulation Authority . . . . [17.175]
2AB Functions of the PRA . . . . [17.176]

PART 9A
RULES AND GUIDANCE

CHAPTER I
RULE-MAKING POWERS

General rule-making powers of the FCA and the PRA

137J Rules about recovery plans: duty to consult . . . . [17.177]
137K Rules about resolution packs: duty to consult . . . . [17.178]
137L Interpretation of sections 137J and 137K . . . . [17.179]
137N Recovery plans and resolution packs: restriction on duty of confidence . . . . [17.180]

PART XV
THE FINANCIAL SERVICES COMPENSATION SCHEME

Provisions of the scheme

215 Rights of the scheme in insolvency . . . . [17.181]

Miscellaneous

224 Scheme manager's power to inspect documents held by Official Receiver etc . . . . [17.182]
224ZA Discharge of functions . . . . [17.183]
224A Functions under the Banking Act 2009 . . . . [17.184]

PART XXIV
INSOLVENCY

Interpretation

355 Interpretation of this Part . . . . [17.185]

Voluntary arrangements

356 Powers of FCA and PRA to participate in proceedings: company voluntary arrangements . . [17.186]

357 Powers of FCA and PRA to participate in proceedings: individual voluntary arrangements . . .[17.187]
358 Powers of FCA and PRA to participate in proceedings: trust deeds for creditors in Scotland . .[17.188]

Administration orders

359 Administration order . . . .[17.189]
360 Insurers . . . .[17.190]
361 Administrator's duty to report to FCA and PRA . . . .[17.191]
362 Powers of FCA and PRA to participate in proceedings. . . . .[17.192]
362A Administrator appointed by company or directors . . . .[17.193]

Receivership

363 Powers of FCA and PRA to participate in proceedings. . . . .[17.194]
364 Receiver's duty to report to FCA and PRA . . . .[17.195]

Voluntary winding up

365 Powers of FCA and PRA to participate in proceedings. . . . .[17.196]
366 Insurers effecting or carrying out long-term contracts or insurance . . . .[17.197]

Winding up by the court

367 Winding-up petitions . . . .[17.198]
368 Winding-up petitions: EEA and Treaty firms. . . . .[17.199]
369 Insurers: service of petition etc on FCA and PRA . . . .[17.200]
369A Reclaim funds: service of petition etc on FCA and PRA. . . . .[17.201]
370 Liquidator's duty to report to FCA and PRA . . . .[17.202]
371 Powers of FCA and PRA to participate in proceedings. . . . .[17.203]

Bankruptcy

372 Petitions . . . .[17.204]
373 Insolvency practitioner's duty to report to FCA and PRA . . . .[17.205]
374 Powers of FCA or PRA powers to participate in proceedings . . . .[17.206]

Provisions against debt avoidance

375 Right of FCA and PRA to apply for an order . . . .[17.207]

Supplemental provisions concerning insurers

376 Continuation of contracts of long-term insurance where insurer in liquidation . . . .[17.208]
377 Reducing the value of contracts instead of winding up. . . . .[17.209]
378 Treatment of assets on winding up . . . .[17.210]
379 Winding-up rules . . . .[17.211]

PART XXIX
INTERPRETATION

417 Definitions . . . .[17.212]

PART XXX
SUPPLEMENTAL

426 Consequential and supplementary provision . . . .[17.213]
428 Regulations and orders . . . .[17.214]
430 Extent. . . . .[17.215]
431 Commencement . . . .[17.216]
433 Short title. . . . .[17.217]

An Act to make provision about the regulation of financial services and markets; to provide for the transfer of certain statutory functions relating to building societies, friendly societies, industrial and provident societies and certain other mutual societies; and for connected purposes

[14 June 2000]

NOTES

Application to bank insolvency and administration: as to the application of this Act to bank insolvency and administration, see the Banking Act 2009 (Parts 2 and 3 Consequential Amendments) Order 2009, SI 2009/317 at **[7.84]** et seq and the Investment Bank Special Administration Regulations 2011, SI 2011/245 at **[7.1661]** et seq.

[PART 1A
THE REGULATORS

1A–1T *((Chapter 1) Outside the scope of this work.)*

CHAPTER 2 THE PRUDENTIAL REGULATION AUTHORITY

The Prudential Regulation Authority

[17.175]

[2A The Prudential Regulation Authority

(1) The "Prudential Regulation Authority" is the Bank of England.

(2) The Bank's functions as the Prudential Regulation Authority—

(a) are to be exercised by the Bank acting through its Prudential Regulation Committee (see Part 3A of the Bank of England Act 1998), and

(b) are not exercisable by the Bank in any other way.

(3) References in this Act or any other enactment to the Prudential Regulation Authority do not include the Bank of England acting otherwise than in its capacity as the Prudential Regulation Authority.

(4) References in this Act to the Bank of England do not (unless otherwise provided) include the Bank acting in its capacity as the Prudential Regulation Authority.

(5) Subsections (3) and (4) do not apply to this section.

(6) Subsection (4) does not apply for the interpretation of references to the court of directors of the Bank of England, or to a Deputy Governor or committee of the Bank.

(7) The Prudential Regulation Authority is referred to in this Act as the PRA.]

NOTES

Commencement: 1 March 2017.

Part 1A (ie, ss 1A–1T, 2A–2O, 3A–3S) was substituted for the original Part I (ss 1–18)) by the Financial Services Act 2012, s 6(1) (for transitional provisions and savings in relation to the transfer of the FSA's functions, property, rights and liabilities, see s 119 of, and Schs 20, 21 to, the 2012 Act).

This section was further substituted (by new ss 2A, 2AB), by the Bank of England and Financial Services Act 2016, s 12.

[17.176]

[2AB Functions of the PRA

(1) The PRA is to have the functions conferred on it by or under this Act.

(2) Schedule 1ZB makes provision about functions of the PRA.

(3) References in this Act or any other enactment to functions conferred on the PRA by or under this Act include references to functions conferred on the PRA by or under—

(a) the Insolvency Act 1986,

(b) the Banking Act 2009,

(c) the Financial Services Act 2012, or

(d) a qualifying EU provision that is specified, or of a description specified, for the purposes of this subsection by the Treasury by order.]

NOTES

Commencement: 1 March 2017.

Substituted as noted to s 2A at **[17.175]**.

2B–137 *(2B–2P, 3A–3S (Pt 1A, Ch 3), 19–137 (Pts II–IX) outside the scope of this work.)*

[PART 9A
RULES AND GUIDANCE

NOTES

Part 9A (ss 137A–137T, 138A–138O, 139A, 139B, 140A–140H, 141A) is substituted for the original Part X (ss 138–164) by the Financial Services Act 2012, s 24(1); see further the note to s 137J at **[17.177]**.

CHAPTER 1 RULE-MAKING POWERS

General rule-making powers of the FCA and the PRA

137A–137I (*Outside the scope of this work.*)

[17.177]

137J Rules about recovery plans: duty to consult

(1) Before either regulator prepares a draft of any general rules that require [a] relevant person (or [a] relevant person of a specified description) to prepare a recovery plan, the regulator must consult [the Treasury].

[(1A) The FCA must also consult the Bank of England.]

[(2) "Relevant person" means—

(a) an institution authorised in the UK; or

(b) a qualifying parent undertaking within the meaning given by section 192B.

(3) A "recovery plan" is a document which provides for measures to be taken—

(a) by an institution authorised in the UK which is not part of a group, following a significant deterioration of the financial position of the institution, in order to restore its financial position; or

(b) in relation to a group, to achieve the stabilisation of the group as a whole, or of any institution within the group, where the group or institution is in a situation of financial stress, in order to address or remove the causes of the financial stress and restore the financial position of the group or institution.

(4) For the purposes of subsection (3)(a) the definition of "group" in section 421 applies with the omission of subsection (1)(e) and (f) of that section.]

(6) In this section—

"authorised person", in relation to the PRA, means PRA-authorised person;

["institution" means—

(a) a credit institution within the meaning given by Article 2.1(2) of Directive 2014/59/EU of the European Parliament and of the Council of 15th May 2014 establishing a framework for the recovery and resolution of credit institutions and investment firms; or

(b) an investment firm within the meaning given by Article 2.1(3) of that directive;

"institution authorised in the UK" means an institution which is an authorised person and—

(a) a bank within the meaning given by section 2 of the Banking Act 2009;

(b) a building society within the meaning given in section 119 of the Building Societies Act 1986; or

(c) an investment firm within the meaning given by section 258A of the Banking Act 2009;]

"specified" means specified in the rules.]

NOTES

This section is substituted (together with the rest of Part 9A (ie, ss 137A–137I, 137K–137T, 138A–138O, 139A, 139B, 140A–140H, 141A) for the original Part X (ss 138–164)) by the Financial Services Act 2012, s 24(1).

The words in the first and second pairs of square brackets in sub-s (1) were substituted, sub-ss (2)–(4) were substituted (for the original sub-ss (2)–(5)), and the definitions "institution" and "institution authorised in the UK" in sub-s (6) were inserted, by the Bank Recovery and Resolution (No 2) Order 2014, SI 2014/3348, art 226, Sch 3, Pt 1, paras 1, 2.

The words in the third pair of square brackets in sub-s (1) were substituted, and sub-s (1A) was inserted, by the Bank of England and Financial Services Act 2016, s 16, Sch 2, Pt 2, paras 26, 33.

[17.178]

[137K [Rules about resolution packs: duty to consult]

(1) Before [either regulator] prepares a draft of any general rules that require [a] relevant person (or [a] relevant person of a specified description) to prepare a [resolution pack], [the regulator] must consult [the Treasury].

[(1A) The FCA must also consult the Bank of England.]

[(2) "Relevant person" has the same meaning as in section 137J(2).]

(3) A "[resolution pack]" is a document containing information within subsection (4) or (5).

(4) Information is within this subsection if it relates to action to be taken in the event of—

(a) circumstances arising in which it is likely that the business (or any part of the business) of an authorised person will fail, or

(b) the failure of the business (or any part of the business) of an authorised person.

(5) Information is within this subsection if it would facilitate anything falling to be done by any person in consequence of that failure.

(6) An example of information within subsection (5) is information that, in the event of that failure, would facilitate—

(a) planning by the Treasury in relation to the possible exercise of any of its powers under Part 1 of the Banking Act 2009, or

(b) planning by the Bank of England in relation to the possible exercise of any of its powers under Part 1, 2 or 3 of that Act.]

[(7) In this section "authorised person", in relation to the PRA, means PRA-authorised person.]

NOTES

Substituted as noted to s 137A at **[17.177]**.

The section heading was substituted, the words in the first to fifth pairs of square brackets in sub-s (1) and the words in square brackets in sub-s (3) were substituted, sub-s (2) was substituted, and sub-s (7) was added, by the Bank Recovery and Resolution (No 2) Order 2014, SI 2014/3348, art 226, Sch 3, Pt 1, paras 1, 3.

The words in the final pair of square brackets were substituted and sub-s (1A) was inserted, by the Bank of England and Financial Services Act 2016, s 16, Sch 2, Pt 2, paras 26, 34.

[17.179]

[137L Interpretation of sections 137J and 137K

(1) This section has effect for the interpretation of sections 137J and 137K.

(2) References to the taking of action include the taking of action by—

(a) the authorised person,

(b) any other person in the same group as the authorised person, or

(c) a partnership of which the authorised person is a member.

(3) In subsection (2)(b) the definition of "group" in section 421 applies with the omission of subsection (1)(e) and (f) of that section.

(4) References to the business of an authorised person include the business of—

(a) any person in the same group as the authorised person, and

(b) a partnership of which the authorised person is a member.

(5) For the purposes of section 137K the cases in which the business (or any part of the business) of the authorised person ("A") is to be regarded as having failed include those where—

(a) A enters insolvency,

(b) any of the stabilisation options in Part 1 of the Banking Act 2009 is achieved in relation to A, or

(c) A falls to be taken for the purposes of the compensation scheme to be unable, or likely to be unable, to satisfy claims against A.

(6) In subsection (5)(a) "insolvency" includes—
(a) bankruptcy,
(b) liquidation,
(c) bank insolvency,
(d) administration,
(e) bank administration,
(f) receivership,
(g) a composition between A and A's creditors, and
(h) a scheme of arrangement of A's affairs.]

NOTES

Substituted as noted to s 137A at **[17.177]**.

137M (*Repealed by the Bank Recovery and Resolution (No 2) Order 2014, SI 2014/3348, art 226, Sch 3, Pt 1, paras 1, 4.*).

[17.180]

[137N Recovery plans and [resolution packs]: restriction on duty of confidence

(1) A contractual or other requirement imposed on a person ("P") to keep information in confidence does not apply if—
(a) the information is or may be relevant to anything required to be done as a result of a requirement imposed by general rules made by either regulator to prepare a recovery plan or a [resolution pack],
(b) an authorised person or a skilled person requests or requires P to provide the information for the purpose of securing that those things are done, and
(c) the regulator in question has approved the making of the request or the imposition of the requirement before it is made or imposed.

(2) An authorised person [or a qualifying parent undertaking] may provide information (whether received under subsection (1) or otherwise) that would otherwise be subject to a contractual or other requirement to keep it in confidence if it is provided for the purposes of anything required to be done as a result of a requirement imposed by general rules to prepare a recovery plan or a [resolution pack].

(3) In this section, references to preparing a recovery plan or a [resolution pack] include—
(a) keeping [that plan or pack] up to date, and
(b) collecting specified information for the purposes of [that plan or pack].

(4) In this section, references to a skilled person are to a person appointed in accordance with section 166A.

(5) In this section—
"authorised person", in relation to rules of the PRA, means a PRA-authorised person;
["qualifying parent undertaking" means—
(a) a qualifying parent undertaking within the meaning given by section 192B; or
(b) an undertaking which—
(i) is a parent undertaking of an institution (within the meaning given in section 137J(6)) authorised in another EEA State; and
(ii) would be a qualifying parent undertaking within the meaning given by section 192B if the institution were a qualifying authorised person within the meaning given by section 192A(1).]
"specified" means specified in the rules.]

NOTES

Substituted as noted to s 137A at **[17.177]**.

All words in square brackets (including those in the section heading) were substituted or inserted by the Bank Recovery and Resolution (No 2) Order 2014, SI 2014/3348, art 226, Sch 3, Pt 1, paras 1, 5.

137O–211 (*Ss 137O–141A, ss 142A–211 (Pts 9B–XIV) outside the scope of this work.*)

PART XV
THE FINANCIAL SERVICES COMPENSATION SCHEME

212, 213 (*Outside the scope of this work.*)

Provisions of the scheme

214–214D (*Outside the scope of this work.*)

[17.181]

215 [Rights of the scheme in insolvency]

[(1) The compensation scheme may make provision—
(a) about the effect of a payment of compensation under the scheme on rights or obligations arising out of matters in connection with which the compensation was paid;
(b) giving the scheme manager a right of recovery in respect of those rights or obligations.]

(2) Such a right of recovery conferred by the scheme does not, in the event of [a person's insolvency], exceed such right (if any) as the claimant would have had in that event.

[(2A) Any payment made by the scheme manager under section 214B(2) in connection with the exercise of a stabilisation power in respect of a bank, building society or credit union is to be treated as a debt due to the scheme manager from that bank, building society or (as the case may be) credit union.

(2B) In subsection (2)—
"bank" has the meaning given in section 2 of the Banking Act 2009;
"building society" has the meaning given in the Building Societies Act 1986;
"credit union" means a credit union within the meaning of—
(a) the Credit Unions Act 1979; or
(b) article 2 of the Credit Unions (Northern Ireland) Order 1985.]

(3) If a person other than the scheme manager [makes an administration application under Schedule B1 to the 1986 Act or [Schedule B1 to] the 1989 Order] in relation to[—
(a) a company or partnership which is a relevant person; or
(b) a body corporate or unincorporated association which is a relevant exchange;
the scheme manager has the same rights as are conferred on the regulators by section 362.]

[(3A) In subsection (3) the reference to making an administration application includes a reference to—
(a) appointing an administrator under paragraph 14 or 22 of Schedule B1 to the 1986 Act [or paragraph 15 or 23 of Schedule B1 to the 1989 Order], or
(b) filing with the court a copy of notice of intention to appoint an administrator under [any] of those paragraphs.]

(4) If a person other than the scheme manager presents a petition for the winding up of a body which is a relevant person [or relevant exchange], the scheme manager has the same rights as are conferred on the [regulators] by section 371.

(5) If a person other than the scheme manager presents a bankruptcy petition to the court in relation to an individual who, or an entity which, is a relevant person, the scheme manager has the same rights as are conferred on the [regulators] by section 374.

(6) Insolvency rules may be made for the purpose of integrating any procedure for which provision is made as a result of subsection (1) into the general procedure on the administration of a company or partnership or on a winding-up, bankruptcy or sequestration.

(7) "Bankruptcy petition" means a petition to the court—
(a) under section 264 of the 1986 Act or Article 238 of the 1989 Order for a bankruptcy order to be made against an individual;
(b) under section [2 or 5 of the 2016] Act for the sequestration of the estate of an individual; or
(c) under section 6 of the [2016] Act for the sequestration of the estate belonging to or held for or jointly by the members of an entity mentioned in subsection (1) of that section.

(8) "Insolvency rules" are—
(a) for England and Wales, rules made under sections 411 and 412 of the 1986 Act;
(b) for Scotland, rules made by order by the Treasury, after consultation with the Scottish Ministers, for the purposes of this section; and
(c) for Northern Ireland, rules made under Article 359 of the 1989 Order and section 55 of the Judicature (Northern Ireland) Act 1978.

(9) *"The 1985 Act"*, "the 1986 Act", "the 1989 Order"[, "the 2016 Act"] and "court" have the same meaning as in Part XXIV.

NOTES

Section heading: words in square brackets substituted by the Banking Act 2009, s 175(1), (4).

Sub-s (1): substituted by the Banking Act 2009, s 175(1), (2).

Sub-s (2): words in square brackets substituted by the Banking Act 2009, s 175(1), (3).

Sub-ss (2A), (2B): inserted by the Deposit Guarantee Scheme Regulations 2015, SI 2015/486, reg 13(1), (3).

Sub-s (3): words in first (outer) pair of square brackets substituted for words "presents a petition under section 9 of the 1986 Act or Article 22 of the 1989 Order" by the Enterprise Act 2002, s 248(3), Sch 17, paras 53, 54(1), (2), subject to savings and transitional provisions (i) in a case where a petition for an administration order has been presented before 15 September 2003 (see the Enterprise Act 2002 (Commencement No 4 and Transitional Provisions and Savings) Order 2003, SI 2003/2093, art 3 at **[2.26]**), and (ii) in relation to special administration regimes (see s 249 of the 2002 Act at **[2.10]**); words in second (inner) pair of square brackets substituted by the Insolvency (Northern Ireland) Order 2005, SI 2005/1455, art 3(3), Sch 2, paras 56, 57(1), (2); words in third pair of square brackets substituted by the Financial Services and Markets Act 2000 (Markets in Financial Instruments) Regulations 2017, SI 2017/701, reg 50(1), Sch 2, paras 1, 25(1), (2).

Sub-s (3A): inserted by the Enterprise Act 2002, s 248(3), Sch 17, paras 53, 54(1), (3), subject to savings and transitional provisions as noted to sub-s (3) above; words in square brackets in para (a) inserted and word in square brackets in para (b) substituted by SI 2005/1455, art 3(3), Sch 2, paras 56, 57(1), (3).

Sub-s (4): words in first pair of square brackets inserted by SI 2017/701, reg 50(1), Sch 2, paras 1, 25(1), (3); word in second pair of square brackets substituted by the Financial Services Act 2012, s 38(1), Sch 10, Pt 1, paras 1, 5.

Sub-s (5): words in square brackets substituted by the Financial Services Act 2012, s 38(1), Sch 10, paras 1, 5.

Sub-s (7): words in first pair of square brackets substituted for the original words "5 of the 1985", and year "2016" in square brackets substituted for the original year "1985", by the Bankruptcy (Scotland) Act 2016 (Consequential Provisions and Modifications) Order 2016, SI 2016/1034, art 7(1), (3), Sch 1, para 20(1), (2), as from 30 November 2016 (except in relation to (i) a sequestration as regards which the petition is presented, or the debtor application is made before that date; or (ii) a trust deed executed before that date).

Sub-s (9): words in italics repealed, and words in square brackets inserted, by SI 2016/1034, art 7(1), (3), Sch 1, para 20(1), (3), as from 30 November 2016 (except in relation to (i) a sequestration as regards which the petition is presented, or the debtor application is made before that date; or (ii) a trust deed executed before that date).

216–221 *(Outside the scope of this work.)*

Miscellaneous

221A–223C *(Outside the scope of this work.)*

[17.182]
224 Scheme manager's power to inspect documents held by Official Receiver etc
(1) If, as a result of the insolvency or bankruptcy of a relevant person [or relevant exchange], [or a successor falling within section 213(1)(b),] any documents have come into the possession of a person to whom this section applies, he must permit any person authorised by the scheme manager to inspect the documents for the purpose of establishing—
(a) the identity of persons to whom the scheme manager may be liable to make a payment in accordance with the compensation scheme; or
(b) the amount of any payment which the scheme manager may be liable to make.
(2) A person inspecting a document under this section may take copies or extracts from the document.
(3) In this section "relevant person" means a person who was—
(a) an authorised person at the time the act or omission which may give rise to the liability mentioned in subsection (1)(a) took place; or
(b) an appointed representative at that time.
(4) But a person who, at that time—
(a) qualified for authorisation under Schedule 3, and
(b) fell within a prescribed category,
is not to be regarded as a relevant person for the purposes of this section in relation to any activities for which he had permission as a result of any provision of, or made under, that Schedule unless he had elected to participate in the scheme in relation to those activities at that time.
[(4A) In this section "relevant exchange" means a body corporate or unincorporated association carrying on a regulated activity relating to a trading facility at the time the act or omission which may give rise to the liability mentioned in subsection (1)(a) took place.]
(5) This section applies to—
(a) the Official Receiver;
(b) the Official Receiver for Northern Ireland; and
(c) the Accountant in Bankruptcy.

NOTES
Sub-s (1): words in first pair of square brackets inserted by the Financial Services and Markets Act 2000 (Markets in Financial Instruments) Regulations 2017, SI 2017/701, reg 50(1), Sch 2, paras 1, 28(1), (2); words in second pair of square brackets inserted by the Financial Services Act 2012, s 38(1), Sch 10, Pt 1, paras 1, 15.
Sub-s (4A): inserted by SI 2017/701, reg 50(1), Sch 2, paras 1, 28(1), (3).
Regulations: the Financial Services and Markets Act 2000 (Compensation Scheme: Electing Participants) Regulations 2001, SI 2001/1783; the Collective Investment Schemes (Miscellaneous Amendments) Regulations 2003, SI 2003/2066; the Alternative Investment Fund Managers Regulations 2013, SI 2013/1773; the European Long-term Investment Funds Regulations 2015, SI 2015/1882; the Financial Services and Markets (Disclosure of Information to the European Securities and Markets Authority etc and Other Provisions) Regulations 2016, SI 2016/1095.

[17.183]
[224ZA Discharge of functions
(1) In discharging its functions the scheme manager must have regard to—
(a) the need to ensure efficiency and effectiveness in the discharge of those functions, and
(b) the need to minimise public expenditure attributable to loans made or other financial assistance given to the scheme manager for the purposes of the scheme.
(2) In subsection (1)(b) "financial assistance" includes the giving of guarantees and indemnities and any other kind of financial assistance (actual or contingent).]

NOTES
Commencement: 1 March 2014.
Inserted by the Financial Services (Banking Reform) Act 2013, s 14.

[17.184]
[224A Functions under the Banking Act 2009
[(1)] A reference in this Part to functions of the scheme manager (including a reference to functions conferred by or under this Part) includes a reference to functions conferred by or under the Banking Act 2009.
[(2) Any payment required to be made by the scheme manager by virtue of section 61 of that Act (special resolution regime: compensation) is to be treated for the purposes of this Part as an expense under the compensation scheme.]]

NOTES
Inserted by the Banking Act 2009, s 180.
Sub-s (1): numbered as such by the Financial Services Act 2010, s 24(1), (2), Sch 2, Pt 1, paras 1, 25(1), (2).
Sub-s (2): added by the Financial Services Act 2010, s 24(1), (2), Sch 2, Pt 1, paras 1, 25(1), (3).

224B–354 *((Pts 15A–XXIII) outside the scope of this work.)*

PART XXIV
INSOLVENCY

NOTES
Transitional provisions etc in connection with the commencement of the Financial Services Act 2012: For transitional provisions in relation to this Part, see Part 10 of the Financial Services Act 2012 (Transitional Provisions) (Miscellaneous

Provisions) Order 2013, SI 2013/442 at **[18.268]** et seq. Article 45 concerns the powers of the FCA and the PRA to participate in proceedings under s 358 (trust deeds for creditors in Scotland). Article 46 contains transitional provisions for cases where an administrator made a report to the FSA in accordance with s 361(2) before 1 April 2013. Article 47 contains transitional provisions in relation to cases where a notice or other document was sent to the FSA in accordance with s 362(3) (powers to participate in proceedings) before that date. Article 48 deals with cases where the FSA had consented for the purposes of s 362A(2) to the appointment of an administrator. Article 49 contains transitional provisions in relation to reports sent to the FSA in accordance with s 363(4). Article 50 concerns reports made to the FSA by a receiver in accordance with s 364. Article 51 concerns notices or other documents sent to the FSA in accordance with s 365(4). Article 52 contains transitional provisions in relation to the voluntary winding-up of an insurer. Article 53 concerns petitions served on the FSA in accordance with s 369(1) (insurers: service of petition etc). Article 54 concerns petitions served on the FSA in accordance with s 369A(1) (reclaim funds: service of petition etc) and applications served in accordance with s 369(2). Article 55 deals with a liquidator's report served on the FSA in accordance with s 370. Article 56 concerns notices or other documents sent to the FSA in accordance with s 371(3). Article 57 contains transitional provisions in relation to reports made to the FSA by an insolvency practitioner in accordance with s 373(1). Article 58 concerns reports sent to the FSA in accordance with s 374(3). Article 59 provides that in s 375(1A) (right to apply for an order), the reference to a PRA-regulated activity includes an activity which would have been a PRA-regulated activity if it had been carried on on 1 April 2013. Article 60 contains transitional provisions in relation to cases where the court appointed an independent actuary for the purposes of s 376(10) (continuation of contracts of long-term insurance where insurer in liquidation) on the application of the FSA.

Interpretation

[17.185]

355 Interpretation of this Part

(1) In this Part—

"the 1985 Act" means the Bankruptcy (Scotland) Act 1985; "the 1986 Act" means the Insolvency Act 1986;

["the 2016 Act" means the Bankruptcy (Scotland) Act 2016;]

"the 1989 Order" means the Insolvency (Northern Ireland) Order 1989;

"body" means a body of persons—

(a) over which the court has jurisdiction under any provision of, or made under, the 1986 Act (or the 1989 Order); but

(b) which is not a building society, a friendly society or [a registered society]; and

"court" means—

(a) the court having jurisdiction for the purposes of the 1985 Act or the 1986 Act; or

(b) in Northern Ireland, the High Court.

["creditors' decision procedure" has the meaning given by section 379ZA(11) of the 1986 Act;]

["PRA-regulated person" means a person who—

(a) is or has been a PRA-authorised person,

(b) is or has been an appointed representative whose principal (or one of whose principals) is, or was, a PRA-authorised person, or

(c) is carrying on or has carried on a PRA-regulated activity in contravention of the general prohibition.]

["qualifying decision procedure" has the meaning given by section 246ZE(11) of the 1986 Act].

(2) In this Part "insurer" has such meaning as may be specified in an order made by the Treasury.

NOTES

Sub-s (1): definition "the 1985 Act" repealed, and definition "the 2016 Act" inserted, by the Bankruptcy (Scotland) Act 2016 (Consequential Provisions and Modifications) Order 2016, SI 2016/1034, art 7(1), (3), Sch 1, para 20(1), (4), as from 30 November 2016 (except in relation to (i) a sequestration as regards which the petition is presented, or the debtor application is made before that date; or (ii) a trust deed executed before that date); in definition "body" words in square brackets substituted by the Co-operative and Community Benefit Societies Act 2014, s 151, Sch 4, Pt 2, paras 68, 70; definitions "creditors' decision procedure" and "qualifying decision procedure" inserted by the Small Business, Enterprise and Employment Act 2015 (Consequential Amendments, Savings and Transitional Provisions) Regulations 2018, SI 2018/208, reg 4(1), (2); definition "PRA-regulated person" added by the Financial Services Act 2012, s 44, Sch 14, paras 1, 2.

Orders: the Financial Services and Markets Act 2000 (Insolvency) (Definition of "Insurer") Order 2001, SI 2001/2634; the Financial Services and Markets Act 2000 (Administration Orders Relating to Insurers) Order 2002, SI 2002/1242 (revoked by SI 2010/3023 and reproduced for reference at **[7.1565]**).

Voluntary arrangements

[17.186]

356 [Powers of FCA and PRA] to participate in proceedings: company voluntary arrangements

[(1) Where a voluntary arrangement has effect under Part I of the 1986 Act in respect of a company or insolvent partnership which is an authorised person, [or recognised investment exchange, the appropriate regulator] may apply to the court under section 6 or 7 of that Act.

(2) Where a voluntary arrangement has been approved under Part II of the 1989 Order in respect of a company or insolvent partnership which is an authorised person, [or recognised investment exchange, the appropriate regulator] may apply to the court under Article 19 or 20 of that Order.]

(3) If a person other than [a regulator] makes an application to the court in relation to the company or insolvent partnership under [any] of those provisions, [the appropriate regulator] is entitled to be heard at any hearing relating to the application.

[(4) The appropriate regulator" means—

(a) in the case of a PRA-authorised person—

(i) for the purposes of subsections (1) and (2), the FCA or the PRA, and

(ii) for the purposes of subsection (3), each of the FCA and the PRA;

(b) in any other case, the FCA.

(5) If either regulator makes an application to the court under any of those provisions in relation to a PRA-authorised person, the other regulator is entitled to be heard at any hearing relating to the application.]

NOTES

Section heading: words in square brackets substituted by the Financial Services Act 2012, s 44, Sch 14, paras 1, 3(1), (5).

Sub-ss (1), (2): substituted by the Insolvency Act 2000, s 15(3)(a), (b); words in square brackets substituted by the Financial Services Act 2012, s 44, Sch 14, paras 1, 3(1), (2).

Sub-s (3): words in first and final pairs of square brackets substituted by the Financial Services Act 2012, s 44, Sch 14, paras 1, 3(1), (3); word in second pair of square brackets substituted by the Insolvency Act 2000, s 15(3)(c).

Sub-ss (4), (5): added by the Financial Services Act 2012, s 44, Sch 14, paras 1, 3(1), (4).

[17.187]

357 [Powers of FCA and PRA] to participate in proceedings: individual voluntary arrangements

(1) The [appropriate regulator] is entitled to be heard on an application by an individual who is an authorised person under section 253 of the 1986 Act (or Article 227 of the 1989 Order).

(2) Subsections [(2A)] to (6) apply if such an order is made on the application of such a person.

[(2A) Where under section 257 of the 1986 Act the individual's creditors are asked to decide whether to approve the proposed voluntary arrangement—

(a) notice of the creditors' decision procedure must be given to the appropriate regulator; and

(b) the appropriate regulator or a person appointed by the appropriate regulator is entitled to participate in (but not vote in) the creditors' decision procedure by which the decision is made.

(2B) Notice of the decision made by the creditors' decision procedure is to be given to the appropriate regulator by the nominee or the nominee's replacement under section 256(3) or 256A(4) of the 1986 Act.]

(3) A person appointed for the purpose by the [appropriate regulator] is entitled to attend any meeting of creditors of the debtor summoned under [Article 231 of the 1989 Order].

(4) Notice of the result of a meeting so summoned is to be given to the [appropriate regulator] by the chairman of the meeting.

(5) The [appropriate regulator] may apply to the court—

(a) under section 262 of the 1986 Act (or Article 236 of the 1989 Order); or

(b) under section 263 of the 1986 Act (or Article 237 of the 1989 Order).

(6) If a person other than [a regulator] makes an application to the court under any provision mentioned in subsection (5), [the appropriate regulator] is entitled to be heard at any hearing relating to the application.

[(7) The appropriate regulator" means—

[(a) in the case of a PRA-authorised person, each of the FCA and the PRA, except that the references in subsections (2A)(b) and (3) to a person appointed by the appropriate regulator are to be read as references to a person appointed by either the FCA or the PRA;]

(b) in any other case, the FCA.

(8) If either regulator makes an application to the court under any of the provisions mentioned in subsection (5) in relation to a PRA-authorised person, the other regulator is entitled to be heard at any hearing relating to the application.]

NOTES

The words in square brackets in the section heading and in sub-ss (1), (4)–(6) were substituted, the words in the first pair of square brackets in sub-s (3) were substituted, and sub-ss (7), (8) were added, by the Financial Services Act 2012, s 44, Sch 14, paras 1, 4.

The figure "(2A)" in square brackets in sub-s (2) was substituted (for the original figure "(3)"), sub-ss (2A) and (2B) were inserted, the words in the second pair of square brackets on sub-s (3) were substituted (for the original words "section 257 of the 1986 Act (or Article 231 of the 1989 Order)"), and sub-s (7)(a) was substituted, by the Small Business, Enterprise and Employment Act 2015 (Consequential Amendments, Savings and Transitional Provisions) Regulations 2018, SI 2018/208, reg 4(1), (3) (subject to transitional provisions as noted below). Note that the original sub-s (7)(a) read as follows—

"(a) in the case of a PRA-authorised person—

(i) for the purposes of subsections (1) and (4) to (6), each of the FCA and the PRA, and

(ii) for the purposes of subsection (3), the FCA or the PRA;".

Transitional provisions: the Small Business, Enterprise and Employment Act 2015 (Consequential Amendments, Savings and Transitional Provisions) Regulations 2018, SI 2018/208, regs 16, 17 provide as follows:

"16 Interpretation of Part 4

In this Part—

"the 1986 Act" means the Insolvency Act 1986;

"the 2000 Act" means the Financial Services and Markets Act 2000;

"the 2009 Act" means the Banking Act 2009; and

"relevant meeting" means a meeting of creditors which is to be held on or after the date on which Parts 2 and 3 of these Regulations come into force, and was—

(a) called, summoned or otherwise required before 6th April 2017 under a provision of the 1986 Act or the Insolvency Rules 1986;

(b) requisitioned by a creditor before 6th April 2017 under a provision of the 1986 Act or the Insolvency Rules 1986; or

(c) called or summoned under section 106, 146 or 331 of the 1986 Act as a result of—

(i) a final report to creditors sent before 6th April 2017 under rule 4.49D of the Insolvency Rules 1986 (final report to creditors in liquidation);

(ii) a final report to creditors and bankrupt sent before that date under rule 6.78B of those Rules (final report to creditors and bankrupt).

17 Transitional provisions for regulation 4

Where a relevant meeting is to be held in proceedings relating to an application by an individual who is an authorised person under section 253 of the 1986 Act (application for interim order where insolvent debtor intends to make a proposal for a voluntary arrangement), section 357 of the 2000 Act applies in relation to the meeting without the amendments made by regulation 4(3).".

[17.188]

358 [Powers of FCA and PRA] to participate in proceedings: trust deeds for creditors in Scotland

(1) This section applies where a trust deed has been granted by or on behalf of a debtor who is an authorised person [or recognised investment exchange].

(2) The trustee must, as soon as practicable after he becomes aware that the debtor is an authorised person [or recognised investment exchange], send to the [appropriate regulator]—

(a) in every case, a copy of the trust deed;

(b) where any other document or information is sent to every creditor known to the trustee in pursuance of [section 170 of the 2016] Act, a copy of such document or information.

(3) Paragraph 7 of that Schedule applies to the [appropriate regulator] as if it were a qualified creditor who has not been sent a copy of the notice as mentioned in paragraph 5(1)(c) of the Schedule.

(4) The [appropriate regulator] must be given the same notice as the creditors of any meeting of creditors held in relation to the trust deed.

(5) A person appointed for the purpose by [appropriate regulator] is entitled to attend and participate in (but not to vote at) any such meeting of creditors as if [that regulator] were a creditor under the deed.

(6) This section does not affect any right [a regulator] has as a creditor of a debtor who is an authorised person [or recognised investment exchange].

[(6A) The appropriate regulator" means—

(a) in the case of a PRA-authorised person—

(i) for the purposes of subsections (2), *(3)* and (4), each of the FCA and the PRA, and

(ii) for the purposes of subsection (5), the FCA or the PRA;

(b) in any other case, the FCA.]

(7) Expressions used in this section and in the [2016] Act have the same meaning in this section as in that Act.

NOTES

The words "section 170 of the 2016" in square brackets in sub-s (2)(b) were substituted for the original words "paragraph 5(1)(c) of Schedule 5 to the 1985", sub-s (3) was repealed, the figure ", (3)" in sub-s (6A)(a)(i) was repealed, and the year "2016" in square brackets in sub-s (7) was substituted (for the original year "1985"), by the Bankruptcy (Scotland) Act 2016 (Consequential Provisions and Modifications) Order 2016, SI 2016/1034, art 7(1), (3), Sch 1, para 20(1), (5), as from 30 November 2016 (except in relation to (i) a sequestration as regards which the petition is presented, or the debtor application is made before that date; or (ii) a trust deed executed before that date).

The words "or recognised investment exchange" in square brackets in sub-ss (1), (2), (6) were inserted, sub-s (6A) was inserted, and all other words in square brackets in this section were substituted, by the Financial Services Act 2012, s 44, Sch 14, paras 1, 5.

Administration orders

[17.189]

[359 Administration order

(1) The [FCA] may make an administration application under Schedule B1 to the 1986 Act [or Schedule B1 to the 1989 Order] in relation to a company or insolvent partnership which—

(a) is or has been an authorised person [or recognised investment exchange],

(b) is or has been an appointed representative, or

(c) is carrying on or has carried on a regulated activity in contravention of the general prohibition.

[(1A) The PRA may make an administration application under Schedule B1 to the 1986 Act or Schedule B1 to the 1989 Order in relation to a company or insolvent partnership which is a PRA-regulated person.]

(2) Subsection (3) applies in relation to an administration application made (or a petition presented) by [a regulator] by virtue of this section.

(3) Any of the following shall be treated for the purpose of paragraph 11(a) of Schedule B1 to the 1986 Act [or paragraph 12(a) of Schedule B1 to the 1989 Order] as unable to pay its debts—

(a) a company or partnership in default on an obligation to pay a sum due and payable under an agreement, . . .

(b) an authorised deposit taker in default on an obligation to pay a sum due and payable in respect of a relevant deposit[, and

(c) an authorised reclaim fund in default on an obligation to pay a sum payable as a result of a claim made by virtue of section 1(2)(b) or 2(2)(b) of the Dormant Bank and Building Society Accounts Act 2008].

(4) In this section—

"agreement" means an agreement the making or performance of which constitutes or is part of a regulated activity carried on by the company or partnership,

"authorised deposit taker" means a person with a [Part 4A] permission to accept deposits (but not a person who has a [Part 4A] permission to accept deposits only for the purpose of carrying on another regulated activity in accordance with that permission), ["authorised reclaim fund" means a reclaim fund within the meaning given by section 5(1) of the Dormant Bank and Building Society Accounts Act 2008 that is authorised for the purposes of this Act,]

"company" means a company—

(a) in respect of which an administrator may be appointed under Schedule B1 to the 1986 Act, or

[(b) in respect of which an administrator may be appointed under Schedule B1 to the 1989 Order,] and

"relevant deposit" shall, ignoring any restriction on the meaning of deposit arising from the identity of the person making the deposit, be construed in accordance with—

(a) section 22,

(b) any relevant order under that section, and

(c) Schedule 2.

(5) The definition of "authorised deposit taker" in subsection (4) shall be construed in accordance with—

(a) section 22,

(b) any relevant order under that section, and

(c) Schedule 2.]

NOTES

Substituted by the Enterprise Act 2002, s 248(3), Sch 17, paras 53, 55, subject to savings and transitional provisions (i) in a case where a petition for an administration order has been presented before 15 September 2003 (see the Enterprise Act 2002 (Commencement No 4 and Transitional Provisions and Savings) Order 2003, SI 2003/2093, art 3 at **[2.26]**), and (ii) in relation to special administration regimes (see s 249 of the 2002 Act at **[2.10]**); the original wording read as follows:

"359 Petitions

(1) The Authority may present a petition to the court under section 9 of the 1986 Act (or Article 22 of the 1989 Order) in relation to a company or insolvent partnership which—

(a) is, or has been, an authorised person;

(b) is, or has been, an appointed representative; or

(c) is carrying on, or has carried on, a regulated activity in contravention of the general prohibition.

(2) Subsection (3) applies in relation to a petition presented by the Authority by virtue of this section.

(3) If the company or partnership is in default on an obligation to pay a sum due and payable under an agreement, it is to be treated for the purpose of section 8(1)(a) of the 1986 Act (or Article 21(1)(a) of the 1989 Order) as unable to pay its debts.

(4) "Agreement" means an agreement the making or performance of which constitutes or is part of a regulated activity carried on by the company or partnership.

(5) "Company" means—

(a) a company to which section 8 of the 1986 Act applies; or

(b) in relation to Northern Ireland, a company to which Article 21 of the 1989 Order applies.".

Sub-s (1): word in first pair of square brackets substituted and words in square brackets in para (a) inserted by the Financial Services Act 2012, s 44, Sch 14, paras 1, 6(1), (2); words in second pair of square brackets substituted by the Insolvency (Northern Ireland) Order 2005, SI 2005/1455, art 3(3), Sch 2, paras 56, 58(1), (2).

Sub-s (1A): inserted by the Financial Services Act 2012, s 44, Sch 14, paras 1, 6(1), (3).

Sub-s (2): words in square brackets substituted by the Financial Services Act 2012, s 44, Sch 14, paras 1, 6(1), (4).

Sub-s (3): words in square brackets substituted by the Insolvency (Northern Ireland) Order 2005, SI 2005/1455, art 3(3), Sch 2, paras 56, 58(1), (3); word omitted from para (a) repealed and para (c) inserted together with word immediately preceding it, by the Dormant Bank and Building Society Accounts Act 2008, s 15, Sch 2, para 6(1), (2).

Sub-s (4): in definition "authorised deposit taker" words in square brackets substituted by the Financial Services Act 2012, s 44, Sch 14, paras 1, 6(1), (5); definition "authorised reclaim fund" inserted by the Dormant Bank and Building Society Accounts Act 2008, s 15, Sch 2, para 6(1), (3); words in square brackets in definition "company" substituted by the Insolvency (Northern Ireland) Order 2005, SI 2005/1455, art 3(3), Sch 2, paras 56, 58(1), (4).

[17.190]

360 Insurers

(1) The Treasury may by order provide that such provisions of Part II of the 1986 Act (or Part III of the 1989 Order) as may be specified are to apply in relation to insurers with such modifications as may be specified.

(2) An order under this section—

(a) may provide that such provisions of this Part as may be specified are to apply in relation to the administration of insurers in accordance with the order with such modifications as may be specified; and

(b) requires the consent of the Secretary of State.

(3) "Specified" means specified in the order.

NOTES

Orders: the Financial Services and Markets Act 2000 (Administration Orders Relating to Insurers) Order 2002, SI 2002/1242 (revoked by SI 2010/3023 and reproduced for reference at **[7.1565]**); the Financial Services and Markets Act 2000 (Administration Orders Relating to Insurers) (Amendment) Order 2003, SI 2003/2134 (which is largely revoked by SI 2010/3023); the Financial Services and Markets Act 2000 (Transitional Provisions, Repeals and Savings) (Financial Services Compensation Scheme) (Amendment) Order 2004, SI 2004/952; the Financial Services and Markets Act 2000 (Administration Orders Relating to Insurers) (Northern Ireland) Order 2007, SI 2007/846; the Financial Services and Markets Act 2000 (Administration Orders Relating to Insurers) Order 2010, SI 2010/3023 at **[7.1618]**.

[17.191]

[361 Administrator's duty to report to [FCA and PRA]

(1) This section applies where a company or partnership is—

(a) in administration within the meaning of Schedule B1 to the 1986 Act, or

[(b) in administration within the meaning of Schedule B1 to the 1989 Order].

[(2) If the administrator thinks that the company or partnership is carrying on, or has carried on—

(a) a regulated activity in contravention of the general prohibition, or

(b) a credit-related regulated activity in contravention of section 20,

the administrator must report the matter to the appropriate regulator without delay.]

[(2A) The appropriate regulator" means—

(a) where the regulated activity is a PRA-regulated activity, the FCA and the PRA;

(b) in any other case, the FCA.]

[(3) Subsection (2) does not apply where—

(a) the administration arises out of an administration order made on an application made or petition presented by a regulator, and

(b) the regulator's application or petition depended on a contravention by the company or partnership of the general prohibition.]]

NOTES

Substituted by the Enterprise Act 2002, s 248(3), Sch 17, paras 53, 56, subject to savings and transitional provisions (i) in a case where a petition for an administration order has been presented before 15 September 2003 (see the Enterprise Act 2002 (Commencement No 4 and Transitional Provisions and Savings) Order 2003, SI 2003/2093, art 3 at **[2.26]**), and (ii) in relation to special administration regimes (see s 249 of the 2002 Act at **[2.10]**); the original wording read as follows:

> **"361 Administrator's duty to report to Authority**
>
> (1) If—
>
> (a) an administration order is in force in relation to a company or partnership by virtue of a petition presented by a person other than the Authority, and
>
> (b) it appears to the administrator that the company or partnership is carrying on, or has carried on, a regulated activity in contravention of the general prohibition,
>
> the administrator must report the matter to the Authority without delay.
>
> (2) "An administration order" means an administration order under Part II of the 1986 Act (or Part III of the 1989 Order).".

Section heading: words in square brackets substituted by the Financial Services Act 2012, s 44, Sch 14, paras 1, 7(1), (5).
Sub-s (1): para (b) substituted by the Insolvency (Northern Ireland) Order 2005, SI 2005/1455, art 3(3), Sch 2, paras 56, 59.
Sub-ss (2), (3): substituted by the Financial Services Act 2012, s 44, Sch 14, paras 1, 7(1), (2), (4).
Sub-s (2A): inserted by the Financial Services Act 2012, s 44, Sch 14, paras 1, 7(1), (3).

[17.192]

362 [Powers of FCA and PRA] to participate in proceedings

(1) This section applies if a person . . . [makes an administration application under Schedule B1 to the 1986 Act [or Schedule B1 to the 1989 Order]] in relation to a company or partnership which—

(a) is, or has been, an authorised person [or recognised investment exchange];

(b) is, or has been, an appointed representative; or

(c) is carrying on, or has carried on, a regulated activity in contravention of the general prohibition.

[(1A) This section also applies in relation to—

(a) the appointment under paragraph 14 or 22 of Schedule B1 to the 1986 Act [or paragraph 15 or 23 of Schedule B1 to the 1989 Order] of an administrator of a company of a kind described in subsection (1)(a) to (c), or

(b) the filing with the court of a copy of notice of intention to appoint an administrator under [any] of those paragraphs.]

[(1B) This section also applies in relation to—

(a) the appointment under paragraph 22 of Schedule B1 to the 1986 Act (as applied by order under section 420 of the 1986 Act), or under paragraph 23 of Schedule B1 to the 1989 Order (as applied by order under Article 364 of the 1989 Order), of an administrator of a partnership of a kind described in subsection (1)(a) to (c), or

(b) the filing with the court of a copy of notice of intention to appoint an administrator under either of those paragraphs (as so applied).]

(2) The [appropriate regulator] is entitled to be heard—

(a) at the hearing of the [administration application . . .]; and

(b) at any other hearing of the court in relation to the company or partnership under Part II of the 1986 Act (or Part III of the 1989 Order).

(3) Any notice or other document required to be sent to a creditor of the company or partnership must also be sent to the [appropriate regulator].

[(4) The [appropriate regulator] may apply to the court under paragraph 74 of Schedule B1 to the 1986 Act [or paragraph 75 of Schedule B1 to the 1989 Order].

(4A) In respect of an application under subsection (4)—

(a) paragraph 74(1)(a) and (b) shall have effect as if for the words "harm the interests of the applicant (whether alone or in common with some or all other members or creditors)" there were substituted the words "harm the interests of some or all members or creditors", and [(b) paragraph 75(1)(a) and (b) of Schedule B1 to the 1989 Order shall have effect as if for the words "harm the interests of the applicant (whether alone or in common with some or all other members or creditors)" there were substituted the words "harm the interests of some or all members or creditors"].]

(5) A person appointed for the purpose by the [appropriate regulator] is entitled—

(a) to attend any meeting of creditors of the company or partnership summoned under any enactment;

(b) to attend any meeting of a committee established under [paragraph 57 of Schedule B1 to the 1986 Act] [or paragraph 58 of Schedule B1 to the 1989 Order]; and

(c) to make representations as to any matter for decision at such a meeting.

[(5A) The appropriate regulator or a person appointed by the appropriate regulator is entitled to participate in (but not vote in) a qualifying decision procedure by which a decision about any matter is sought from the creditors of the company or partnership.]

(6) If, during the course of the administration of a company, a compromise or arrangement is proposed between the company and its creditors, or any class of them, the [appropriate regulator] may apply to the court under [section 896 or 899 of the Companies Act 2006].

[[(7) "The appropriate regulator" means—

(a) where the company or partnership is a PRA-regulated person, each of the FCA and the PRA, except that the references in subsections (5) and (5A) to a person appointed by the appropriate regulator are to be read as references to a person appointed by either the FCA or the PRA;

(b) in any other case, the FCA.]

(8) But where the administration application was made by a regulator "the appropriate regulator" does not include that regulator.]

NOTES

Section heading: words in square brackets substituted by the Financial Services Act 2012, s 44, Sch 14, paras 1, 8(1), (6).

Sub-s (1): words omitted repealed and words in square brackets in para (a) added by the Financial Services Act 2012, s 44, Sch 14, paras 1, 8(1), (2); words in first (outer) pair of square brackets substituted for words "presents a petition to the court under section 9 of the 1986 Act (or Article 22 of the 1989 Order)" by the Enterprise Act 2002, s 248(3), Sch 17, paras 53, 57(a), subject to savings and transitional provisions (i) in a case where a petition for an administration order has been presented before 15 September 2003 (see the Enterprise Act 2002 (Commencement No 4 and Transitional Provisions and Savings) Order 2003, SI 2003/2093, art 3 at **[2.26]**), and (ii) in relation to special administration regimes (see s 249 of the 2002 Act at **[2.10]**); words in second (inner) pair of square brackets substituted by the Insolvency (Northern Ireland) Order 2005, SI 2005/1455, art 3(3), Sch 2, paras 56, 60(1), (2).

Sub-s (1A): inserted by the Enterprise Act 2002, s 248(3), Sch 17, paras 53, 57(b), subject to savings and transitional provisions as noted to sub-s (1) above; words in first pair of square brackets inserted and words in second pair of square brackets substituted by SI 2005/1455, art 3(3), Sch 2, paras 56, 60(1), (3).

Sub-s (1B): inserted by the Financial Services Act 2012, s 44, Sch 14, paras 1, 8(1), (3).

Sub-s (2): words in first pair of square brackets substituted by the Financial Services Act 2012, s 44, Sch 14, paras 1, 8(1), (4); in para (a), words in square brackets substituted for word "petition" by the Enterprise Act 2002, s 248(3), Sch 17, paras 53, 57(c), subject to savings and transitional provisions as noted to sub-s (1) above; words omitted repealed by SI 2005/1455, arts 3(3), 31, Sch 2, paras 56, 60(1), (4), Sch 9.

Sub-s (3): words in square brackets substituted by the Financial Services Act 2012, s 44, Sch 14, paras 1, 8(1), (4).

Sub-s (4): substituted, together with sub-s (4A), for original sub-s (4) by the Enterprise Act 2002, s 248(3), Sch 17, paras 53, 57(d), subject to savings and transitional provisions as noted to sub-s (1) above. The original sub-s (4) read as follows:

> "(4) The Authority may apply to the court under section 27 of the 1986 Act (or Article 39 of the 1989 Order); and on such an application, section 27(1)(a) (or Article 39(1)(a)) has effect with the omission of the words "(including at least himself)".";

words in first pair of square brackets substituted by the Financial Services Act 2012, s 44, Sch 14, paras 1, 8(1), (4); words in second pair of square brackets substituted by SI 2005/1455, art 3(3), Sch 2, paras 56, 60(1), (5).

Sub-s (4A): substituted as noted to sub-s (4) above; para (b) substituted by SI 2005/1455, art 3(3), Sch 2, paras 56, 60(1), (6).

Sub-s (5): words in first pair of square brackets substituted by the Financial Services Act 2012, s 44, Sch 14, paras 1, 8(1), (4); in para (b), words in first pair of square brackets substituted for words "section 26 of the 1986 Act" by the Enterprise Act 2002, s 248(3), Sch 17, paras 53, 57(e), subject to savings and transitional provisions as noted to sub-s (1) above, and words in second pair of square brackets substituted by SI 2005/1455, art 3(3), Sch 2, paras 56, 60(1), (7).

Sub-s (5A): inserted by the Small Business, Enterprise and Employment Act 2015 (Consequential Amendments, Savings and Transitional Provisions) Regulations 2018, SI 2018/208, reg 4(1), (4)(a).

Sub-s (6): words in first pair of square brackets substituted by the Financial Services Act 2012, s 44, Sch 14, paras 1, 8(1), (4); words in second pair of square brackets substituted for original words "section 425 of the Companies Act 1985 (or Article 418 of the Companies (Northern Ireland) Order 1986)" by the Companies Act 2006 (Consequential Amendments etc) Order 2008, SI 2008/948, art 3(1)(b), Sch 1, Pt 2, para 211(4), subject to transitional provisions and savings in arts 6, 11, 12 thereof.

Sub-s (7): originally added by the Financial Services Act 2012, s 44, Sch 14, paras 1, 8(1), (5). Subsequently substituted by SI 2018/208, reg 4(1), (4)(b).

Sub-s (8): inserted by the Financial Services Act 2012, s 44, Sch 14, paras 1, 8(1), (5).

[17.193]

[362A Administrator appointed by company or directors

(1) This section applies in relation to a company [or partnership] of a kind described in section 362(1)(a) to (c).

[(2) An administrator of the company or partnership may not be appointed under a provision specified in subsection (2A) without the consent of the appropriate regulator.

(2A) Those provisions are—

(a) paragraph 22 of Schedule B1 to the 1986 Act (including that paragraph as applied in relation to partnerships by order under section 420 of that Act);
(b) paragraph 23 of Schedule B1 to the 1989 Order (including that paragraph as applied in relation to partnerships by order under article 364 of that Order).

(2B) "The appropriate regulator" means—
(a) where the company or partnership is a PRA-regulated person, the PRA, and
(b) in any other case, the FCA.]

(3) Consent under subsection (2)—
(a) must be in writing, and
(b) must be filed with the court along with the notice of intention to appoint under paragraph 27 of [Schedule B1 to the 1986 Act or paragraph 28 of Schedule B1 to the 1989 Order].

(4) In a case where no notice of intention to appoint is required—
(a) subsection (3)(b) shall not apply, but
(b) consent under subsection (2) must accompany the notice of appointment filed under paragraph 29 of [Schedule B1 to the 1986 Act or paragraph 30 of Schedule B1 to the 1989 Order].]

NOTES

Inserted by the Enterprise Act 2002, s 248(3), Sch 17, paras 53, 58, subject to savings and transitional provisions (i) in a case where a petition for an administration order has been presented before 15 September 2003 (see the Enterprise Act 2002 (Commencement No 4 and Transitional Provisions and Savings) Order 2003, SI 2003/2093, art 3 at **[2.26]**), and (ii) in relation to special administration regimes (see s 249 of the 2002 Act at **[2.10]**).

Sub-s (1): words in square brackets inserted by the Financial Services Act 2012, s 44, Sch 14, paras 1, 9(1), (2)

Sub-ss (2)–(2B): substituted, for original sub-s (2), by the Financial Services Act 2012, s 44, Sch 14, paras 1, 9(1), (3).

Sub-ss (3), (4): words in square brackets substituted by SI 2005/1455, art 3(3), Sch 2, paras 56, 61(1), (3), (4).

Receivership

[17.194]

363 [Powers of FCA and PRA] to participate in proceedings

(1) This section applies if a receiver has been appointed in relation to a company which—
(a) is, or has been, an authorised person [or recognised investment exchange];
(b) is, or has been, an appointed representative; or
(c) is carrying on, or has carried on, a regulated activity in contravention of the general prohibition.

(2) The [appropriate regulator] is entitled to be heard on an application made under section 35 or 63 of the 1986 Act (or Article 45 of the 1989 Order).

(3) The [appropriate regulator] is entitled to make an application under section 41(1)(a) or 69(1)(a) of the 1986 Act (or Article 51(1)(a) of the 1989 Order).

(4) A report under section 48(1) or 67(1) of the 1986 Act (or Article 58(1) of the 1989 Order) must be sent by the person making it to the [appropriate regulator].

(5) A person appointed for the purpose by the [appropriate regulator] is entitled—
(a) to attend any meeting of creditors of the company summoned under any enactment;
(b) to attend any meeting of a committee established under section 49 or 68 of the 1986 Act (or Article 59 of the 1989 Order); and
(c) to make representations as to any matter for decision at such a meeting.

[(6) The appropriate regulator" means—
(a) for the purposes of subsections (2) to (4)—
(i) where the company is a PRA-regulated person, each of the FCA and the PRA, and
(ii) in any other case, the FCA;
(b) for the purposes of subsection (5)—
(i) where the company is a PRA-regulated person, the FCA or the PRA, and
(ii) in any other case, the FCA.]

NOTES

Section heading, sub-ss (2)–(5): words in square brackets substituted by the Financial Services Act 2012, s 44, Sch 14, paras 1, 10(1), (3), (5).

Sub-s (1): words in square brackets in para (a) inserted by the Financial Services Act 2012, s 44, Sch 14, paras 1, 10(1), (2).

Sub-s (6): added by the Financial Services Act 2012, s 44, Sch 14, paras 1, 10(1), (4).

[17.195]

364 Receiver's duty to report to [FCA and PRA]

If—
(a) a receiver has been appointed in relation to a company, and
(b) it appears to the receiver that the company is carrying on, or has carried on, a regulated activity in contravention of the general prohibition [or a credit-related regulated activity in contravention of section 20],

the receiver must report the matter [without delay to the FCA and, if the regulated activity concerned is a PRA-regulated activity, to the PRA].

NOTES

Section heading: words in square brackets substituted by the Financial Services Act 2012, s 44, Sch 14, paras 1, 11(1)(c).

Words in first pair of square brackets inserted and words in second pair of square brackets substituted by the Financial Services Act 2012, s 44, Sch 14, paras 1, 11(1)(a), (b).

Voluntary winding up

[17.196]

365 [Powers of FCA and PRA] to participate in proceedings

(1) This section applies in relation to a company which—

(a) is being wound up voluntarily;

(b) is an authorised person [or recognised investment exchange]; and

(c) is not an insurer effecting or carrying out contracts of long-term insurance.

(2) The [appropriate regulator] may apply to the court under section 112 of the 1986 Act (or Article 98 of the 1989 Order) in respect of the company.

(3) The [appropriate regulator] is entitled to be heard at any hearing of the court in relation to the voluntary winding up of the company.

(4) Any notice or other document required to be sent to a creditor of the company must also be sent to the [appropriate regulator].

(5) A person appointed for the purpose by the [appropriate regulator] is entitled—

(a) to attend any meeting of creditors of the company summoned under any enactment;

(b) to attend any meeting of a committee established under section 101 of the 1986 Act (or Article 87 of the 1989 Order); and

(c) to make representations as to any matter for decision at such a meeting.

[(5A) The appropriate regulator or a person appointed by the appropriate regulator is entitled to participate in (but not vote in) a qualifying decision procedure by which a decision about any matter is sought from the creditors of the company.]

(6) The voluntary winding up of the company does not bar the right of the [appropriate regulator] to have it wound up by the court.

(7) If, during the course of the winding up of the company, a compromise or arrangement is proposed between the company and its creditors, or any class of them, the [appropriate regulator] may apply to the court under [section 896 or 899 of the Companies Act 2006].

[(8) "The appropriate regulator" means—

(a) where the company is a PRA-authorised person, each of the FCA and the PRA, except that the references in subsections (5) and (5A) to a person appointed by the appropriate regulator are to be read as references to a person appointed by either the FCA or the PRA;

(b) in any other case, the FCA.]

NOTES

Section heading, sub-ss (2)–(6): words in square brackets substituted by the Financial Services Act 2012, s 44, Sch 14, paras 1, 12(1), (3), (5).

Sub-s (1): words in square brackets in para (b) inserted by the Financial Services Act 2012, s 44, Sch 14, paras 1, 12(1), (2).

Sub-s (5A): inserted by the Small Business, Enterprise and Employment Act 2015 (Consequential Amendments, Savings and Transitional Provisions) Regulations 2018, SI 2018/208, reg 4(1), (5)(a).

Sub-s (7): words in first pair of square brackets substituted by the Financial Services Act 2012, s 44, Sch 14, paras 1, 12(1), (3); words in second pair of square brackets substituted for original words "section 425 of the Companies Act 1985 (or Article 418 of the Companies (Northern Ireland) Order 1986)" by the Companies Act 2006 (Consequential Amendments etc) Order 2008, SI 2008/948, art 3(1)(b), Sch 1, Pt 2, para 211(4), subject to transitional provisions and savings in arts 6, 11, 12 thereof.

Sub-s (8): added by the Financial Services Act 2012, s 44, Sch 14, paras 1, 12(1), (4) and substituted by SI 2018/208, reg 4(1), (5)(b).

[17.197]

366 Insurers effecting or carrying out long-term contracts or insurance

(1) An insurer effecting or carrying out contracts of long-term insurance may not be wound up voluntarily without the consent of the [PRA].

(2) If notice of a general meeting of such an insurer is given, specifying the intention to propose a resolution for voluntary winding up of the insurer, a director of the insurer must notify the [PRA] as soon as practicable after he becomes aware of it.

(3) A person who fails to comply with subsection (2) is guilty of an offence and liable on summary conviction to a fine not exceeding level 5 on the standard scale.

[(4) A winding up resolution may not be passed—

(a) as a written resolution (in accordance with Chapter 2 of Part 13 of the Companies Act 2006), or

(b) at a meeting called in accordance with section 307(4) to (6) or 337(2) of that Act (agreement of members to calling of meeting at short notice).]

(5) A copy of a winding-up resolution forwarded to the registrar of companies in accordance with [section 30 of the Companies Act 2006] must be accompanied by a certificate issued by the [PRA] stating that it consents to the voluntary winding up of the insurer.

(6) If subsection (5) is complied with, the voluntary winding up is to be treated as having commenced at the time the resolution was passed.

(7) If subsection (5) is not complied with, the resolution has no effect.

(8) "Winding-up resolution" means a resolution for voluntary winding up of an insurer effecting or carrying out contracts of long-term insurance.

[(9) Before giving or refusing consent under subsection (1), the PRA must consult the FCA.

(10) In the event that the activity of effecting or carrying out long-term contracts of insurance as principal is not to any extent a PRA-regulated activity—

(a) references to the PRA in subsections (1), (2) and (5) are to be read as references to the FCA, and

(b) subsection (9) does not apply.]

NOTES

Sub-ss (1), (2): words in square brackets substituted by the Financial Services Act 2012, s 44, Sch 14, paras 1, 13(1), (2).

Sub-s (4): substituted by the Companies Act 2006 (Commencement No 3, Consequential Amendments, Transitional Provisions and Savings) Order 2007, SI 2007/2194, art 10(1), (2), Sch 4, Pt 3, para 93(1), (2), subject to savings in art 12 thereof.

Sub-s (5): words in first pair of square brackets substituted by SI 2007/2194, art 10(1), (2), Sch 4, Pt 3, para 93(1), (3), subject to savings in art 12 thereof; word in second pair of square brackets substituted by the Financial Services Act 2012, s 44, Sch 14, paras 1, 13(1), (2).

Sub-ss (9), (10): added by the Financial Services Act 2012, s 44, Sch 14, paras 1, 13(1), (3).

Winding up by the court

[17.198]

367 Winding-up petitions

(1) The [FCA] may present a petition to the court for the winding up of a body which—

(a) is, or has been, an authorised person [or recognised investment exchange];

(b) is, or has been, an appointed representative; or

(c) is carrying on, or has carried on, a regulated activity in contravention of the general prohibition.

[(1A) The PRA may present a petition to the court for the winding up of a body which is a PRA-regulated person.]

(2) In [subsections (1) and (1A)] "body" includes any partnership.

(3) On such a petition, the court may wind up the body if—

[(za) in the case of an insurance undertaking or reinsurance undertaking, the PRA has cancelled the body's Part 4A permission pursuant to section 55J(7C);]

(a) the body is unable to pay its debts within the meaning of section 123 or 221 of the 1986 Act (or Article 103 or 185 of the 1989 Order); or

(b) the court is of the opinion that it is just and equitable that it should be wound up.

(4) If a body is in default on an obligation to pay a sum due and payable under an agreement, it is to be treated for the purpose of subsection (3)(a) as unable to pay its debts.

(5) "Agreement" means an agreement the making or performance of which constitutes or is part of a regulated activity carried on by the body concerned.

(6) Subsection (7) applies if a petition is presented under subsection (1) [or (1A)] for the winding up of a partnership—

(a) on the ground mentioned in subsection (3)(b); or

(b) in Scotland, on a ground mentioned in subsection (3)(a) or (b).

(7) The court has jurisdiction, and the 1986 Act (or the 1989 Order) has effect, as if the partnership were an unregistered company as defined by section 220 of that Act (or Article 184 of that Order).

NOTES

Sub-s (1): word in first pair of square brackets substituted and words in square brackets in para (a) inserted by the Financial Services Act 2012, s 44, Sch 14, paras 1, 14(1), (2).

Sub-s (1A): inserted by the Financial Services Act 2012, s 44, Sch 14, paras 1, 14(1), (3).

Sub-s (2): words in square brackets substituted by the Financial Services Act 2012, s 44, Sch 14, paras 1, 14(1), (4).

Sub-s (3): para (za) inserted by the Solvency 2 Regulations 2015, SI 2015/575, reg 59, Sch 1, Pt 1, paras 1, 13.

Sub-s (6): words in square brackets inserted by the Financial Services Act 2012, s 44, Sch 14, paras 1, 14(1), (5).

[17.199]

368 Winding-up petitions: EEA and Treaty firms

[(1)] [A regulator] may not present a petition to the court under section 367 for the winding up of—

(a) an EEA firm which qualifies for authorisation under Schedule 3, or

(b) a Treaty firm which qualifies for authorisation under Schedule 4, unless it [or the other regulator] has been asked to do so by the home state regulator of the firm concerned.

[(2) If a regulator receives from the home state regulator of a body falling within subsection (1)(a) or (b) a request to present a petition to the court under section 367 for the winding up of the body, it must—

(a) notify the other regulator of the request, and

(b) provide the other regulator with such information relating to the request as it thinks fit.]

NOTES

Sub-s (1): numbered as such, words in first pair of square brackets substituted, and words in square brackets in para (b) inserted, by the Financial Services Act 2012, s 44, Sch 14, paras 1, 15(1)–(3).

Sub-s (2): inserted by the Financial Services Act 2012, s 44, Sch 14, paras 1, 15(1), (4).

[17.200]

369 Insurers: service of petition etc on [FCA and PRA]

(1) If a person other than [a regulator] presents a petition for the winding up of an authorised person with permission to effect or carry out contracts of insurance, the petitioner must serve a copy of the petition [on the appropriate regulator].

(2) If a person other than [a regulator] applies to have a provisional liquidator appointed under section 135 of the 1986 Act (or Article 115 of the 1989 Order) in respect of an authorised person with permission to effect or carry out contracts of insurance, the applicant must serve a copy of the application [on the appropriate regulator].

[(3) The appropriate regulator" means—

(a) in relation to a PRA-authorised person, the FCA and the PRA, and

(b) in any other case, the FCA.

(4) If either regulator—

(a) presents a petition for the winding up of a PRA-authorised person with permission to effect or carry out contracts of insurance, or

(b) applies to have a provisional liquidator appointed under section 135 of the 1986 Act (or Article 115 of the 1989 Order) in respect of a PRA-authorised person with permission to effect or carry out contracts of insurance,

that regulator must serve a copy of the petition or application (as the case requires) on the other regulator.]

NOTES

Section heading, sub-ss (1), (2): words in square brackets substituted by the Financial Services Act 2012, s 44, Sch 14, paras 1, 16(1)–(3), (5).

Sub-ss (3), (4): added by the Financial Services Act 2012, s 44, Sch 14, paras 1, 16(1), (4).

[17.201]

[369A Reclaim funds: service of petition etc on [FCA and PRA]

(1) If a person [other than a regulator] presents a petition for the winding up of an authorised reclaim fund, the petitioner must serve a copy of the petition [on the appropriate regulator].

(2) If a person [other than a regulator] applies to have a provisional liquidator appointed under section 135 of the 1986 Act (or Article 115 of the 1989 Order) in respect of an authorised reclaim fund, the applicant must serve a copy of the application [on the appropriate regulator].

(3) In this section "authorised reclaim fund" means a reclaim fund within the meaning given by section 5(1) of the Dormant Bank and Building Society Accounts Act 2008 that is authorised for the purposes of this Act.

[(4) The appropriate regulator" means—

(a) in relation to an authorised reclaim fund that is a PRA-authorised person, the FCA and the PRA, and

(b) in relation to any other authorised reclaim fund, the FCA.

(5) If either regulator—

(a) presents a petition for the winding up of an authorised reclaim fund that is a PRA-authorised person, or

(b) applies to have a provisional liquidator appointed under section 135 of the 1986 Act (or Article 115 of the 1989 Order) in respect of an authorised reclaim fund that is a PRA-authorised person,

that regulator must serve a copy of the petition or application (as the case requires) on the other regulator.]]

NOTES

Inserted by the Dormant Bank and Building Society Accounts Act 2008, s 15, Sch 2, para 7.

Section heading, sub-ss (1), (2): words in square brackets substituted by the Financial Services Act 2012, s 44, Sch 14, paras 1, 17(1)–(3), (5).

Sub-ss (4), (5): added by the Financial Services Act 2012, s 44, Sch 14, paras 1, 17(1), (4).

[17.202]

[370 Liquidator's duty to report to FCA and PRA

(1) If—

(a) a company is being wound up voluntarily or a body is being wound up on a petition presented by any person, and

(b) it appears to the liquidator that the company or body is carrying on, or has carried on—

(i) a regulated activity in contravention of the general prohibition, or

(ii) a credit-related regulated activity in contravention of section 20,

the liquidator must report the matter without delay to the FCA and, if the regulated activity concerned is a PRA-regulated activity, to the PRA.

(2) Subsection (1) does not apply where—

(a) a body is being wound up on a petition presented by a regulator, and

(b) the regulator's petition depended on a contravention by the body of the general prohibition.]

NOTES

Substituted by the Financial Services Act 2012, s 44, Sch 14, paras 1, 18.

[17.203]

371 [Powers of FCA and PRA] to participate in proceedings

(1) This section applies if a person . . . presents a petition for the winding up of a body which—

(a) is, or has been, an authorised person [or recognised investment exchange];

(b) is, or has been, an appointed representative; or

(c) is carrying on, or has carried on, a regulated activity in contravention of the general prohibition.

(2) The [appropriate regulator] is entitled to be heard—

(a) at the hearing of the petition; and

(b) at any other hearing of the court in relation to the body under or by virtue of Part IV or V of the 1986 Act (or Part V or VI of the 1989 Order).

(3) Any notice or other document required to be sent to a creditor of the body must also be sent to the [appropriate regulator].

(4) A person appointed for the purpose by the [appropriate regulator] is entitled—

(a) to attend any meeting of creditors of the body;
(b) to attend any meeting of a committee established for the purposes of Part IV or V of the 1986 Act under section 101 of that Act or under section 141 or 142 of that Act;
(c) to attend any meeting of a committee established for the purposes of Part V or VI of the 1989 Order under Article 87 of that Order or under Article 120 of that Order; and
(d) to make representations as to any matter for decision at such a meeting.

[(4A) The appropriate regulator or a person appointed by the appropriate regulator is entitled to participate in (but not vote in) a qualifying decision procedure by which a decision about any matter is sought from the creditors of the body.]

(5) If, during the course of the winding up of a company, a compromise or arrangement is proposed between the company and its creditors, or any class of them, the [appropriate regulator] may apply to the court under [section 896 or 899 of the Companies Act 2006].

[[(6) "The appropriate regulator" means—
(a) where the body is a PRA-regulated person, each of the FCA and the PRA, except that the references in subsections (4) and (4A) to a person appointed by the appropriate regulator are to be read as references to a person appointed by either the FCA or the PRA;
(b) in any other case, the FCA.]

(7) But where the petition was presented by a regulator "the appropriate regulator" does not include the regulator which presented the petition.]

NOTES

Section heading, sub-ss (2)–(4): words in square brackets substituted by the Financial Services Act 2012, s 44, Sch 14, paras 1, 19(1), (3), (5).

Sub-s (1): words omitted repealed and words in square brackets in para (a) inserted by the Financial Services Act 2012, s 44, Sch 14, paras 1, 19(1), (2).

Sub-s (4A): inserted by the Small Business, Enterprise and Employment Act 2015 (Consequential Amendments, Savings and Transitional Provisions) Regulations 2018, SI 2018/208, reg 4(1), (6)(a).

Sub-s (5): words in first pair of square brackets substituted by the Financial Services Act 2012, s 44, Sch 14, paras 1, 19(1), (3); words in second pair of square brackets substituted for original words "section 425 of the Companies Act 1985 (or Article 418 of the Companies (Northern Ireland) Order 1986)" by the Companies Act 2006 (Consequential Amendments etc) Order 2008, SI 2008/948, art 3(1)(b), Sch 1, Pt 2, para 211(4), subject to transitional provisions and savings in arts 6, 11, 12 thereof.

Sub-ss (6), (7): added by the Financial Services Act 2012, s 44, Sch 14, paras 1, 19(1), (4), and sub-s (6) subsequently substituted by SI 2018/208, reg 4(1), (6)(b).

Bankruptcy

[17.204]

372 Petitions

(1) The [FCA] may present a petition to the court—
(a) under section 264 of the 1986 Act (or Article 238 of the 1989 Order) for a bankruptcy order to be made against an individual; or
(b) under section [2 or 5 of the 2016] Act for the sequestration of the estate of an individual.

[(1A) The PRA may present a petition to the court—
(a) under section 264 of the 1986 Act (or Article 238 of the 1989 Order) for a bankruptcy order to be made against an individual who is a PRA-regulated person;
(b) under section [2 or 5 of the 2016] Act for the sequestration of the estate of an individual who is a PRA-regulated person.]

(2) But [a petition may be presented by virtue of subsection (1) or (1A)] only on the ground that—
(a) the individual appears to be unable to pay a regulated activity debt; or
(b) the individual appears to have no reasonable prospect of being able to pay a regulated activity debt.

(3) An individual appears to be unable to pay a regulated activity debt if he is in default on an obligation to pay a sum due and payable under an agreement.

(4) An individual appears to have no reasonable prospect of being able to pay a regulated activity debt if—
(a) [a regulator] has served on him a demand requiring him to establish to the satisfaction of [that regulator] that there is a reasonable prospect that he will be able to pay a sum payable under an agreement when it falls due;
(b) at least three weeks have elapsed since the demand was served; and
(c) the demand has been neither complied with nor set aside in accordance with rules.

(5) A demand made under subsection (4)(a) is to be treated for the purposes of the 1986 Act (or the 1989 Order) as if it were a statutory demand under section 268 of that Act (or Article 242 of that Order).

(6) For the purposes of a petition presented in accordance with subsection (1)(b) [or (1A)(b)]—
(a) [the regulator by which the petition is presented] is to be treated as a qualified creditor; and
(b) a ground mentioned in subsection (2) constitutes apparent insolvency.

(7) "Individual" means an individual—
(a) who is, or has been, an authorised person; or
(b) who is carrying on, or has carried on, a regulated activity in contravention of the general prohibition.

(8) "Agreement" means an agreement the making or performance of which constitutes or is part of a regulated activity carried on by the individual concerned.

(9) "Rules" means—
(a) in England and Wales, rules made under section 412 of the 1986 Act;

(b) in Scotland, rules made by order by the Treasury, after consultation with the Scottish Ministers, for the purposes of this section; and
(c) in Northern Ireland, rules made under Article 359 of the 1989 Order.

NOTES

Sub-s (1): word in first pair of square brackets substituted by the Financial Services Act 2012, s 44, Sch 14, paras 1, 20(1), (2); words in square brackets in para (b) substituted for original words "5 of the 1985", by the Bankruptcy (Scotland) Act 2016 (Consequential Provisions and Modifications) Order 2016, SI 2016/1034, art 7(1), (3), Sch 1, para 20(1), (6), as from 30 November 2016 (except in relation to (i) a sequestration as regards which the petition is presented, or the debtor application is made before that date; or (ii) a trust deed executed before that date).

Sub-s (1A): inserted by the Financial Services Act 2012, s 44, Sch 14, paras 1, 20(1), (3); words in square brackets in para (b) substituted for original words "5 of the 1985", by SI 2016/1034, art 7(1), (3), Sch 1, para 20(1), (6), as from 30 November 2016 (except in relation to (i) a sequestration as regards which the petition is presented, or the debtor application is made before that date; or (ii) a trust deed executed before that date).

Sub-ss (2), (4): words in square brackets substituted by the Financial Services Act 2012, s 44, Sch 14, paras 1, 20(1), (4), (5).

Sub-s (6): words in first pair of square brackets inserted, and words in second pair of square brackets substituted, by the Financial Services Act 2012, s 44, Sch 14, paras 1, 20(1), (6).

Rules: the Bankruptcy (Financial Services and Markets Act 2000) (Scotland) Rules 2001, SI 2001/3591 at **[16.141]**.

[17.205]

373 Insolvency practitioner's duty to report [to FCA and PRA]

(1) If—
(a) a bankruptcy order or sequestration award is in force in relation to an individual . . . , and
(b) it appears to the insolvency practitioner that the individual is carrying on, or has [carried on—
(i) a regulated activity in contravention of the general prohibition, or
(ii) a credit-related regulated activity in contravention of section 20,]

the insolvency practitioner must report the matter [without delay to the FCA and, if the regulated activity concerned is a PRA-regulated activity, to the PRA].

[(1A) Subsection (1) does not apply where—
(a) the bankruptcy order or sequestration award is in force by virtue of a petition presented by a regulator, and
(b) the regulator's petition depended on a contravention by the individual of the general prohibition.]

(2) "Bankruptcy order" means a bankruptcy order under Part IX of the 1986 Act (or Part IX of the 1989 Order).

(3) "Sequestration award" means an award of sequestration under section [22 of the 2016] Act.

(4) "Individual" includes an entity mentioned in section 374(1)(c).

NOTES

Section heading: words in square brackets substituted by the Financial Services Act 2012, s 44, Sch 14, paras 1, 21(1), (4).

Sub-s (1): words omitted repealed, and words in square brackets substituted, by the Financial Services Act 2012, s 44, Sch 14, paras 1, 21(1), (2).

Sub-s (1A): inserted by the Financial Services Act 2012, s 44, Sch 14, paras 1, 21(1), (3).

Sub-s (3): words in square brackets substituted for original words "12 of the 1985" by the Bankruptcy (Scotland) Act 2016 (Consequential Provisions and Modifications) Order 2016, SI 2016/1034, art 7(1), (3), Sch 1, para 20(1), (7), as from 30 November 2016 (except in relation to (i) a sequestration as regards which the petition is presented, or the debtor application is made before that date; or (ii) a trust deed executed before that date).

[17.206]

374 [Powers of FCA or PRA] to participate in proceedings

(1) This section applies if a person . . . presents a petition to the court—
(a) under section 264 of the 1986 Act (or Article 238 of the 1989 Order) for a bankruptcy order to be made against an individual;
(b) under section [2 or 5 of the 2016] Act for the sequestration of the estate of an individual; or
(c) under section 6 of the [2016] Act for the sequestration of the estate belonging to or held for or jointly by the members of an entity mentioned in subsection (1) of that section.

(2) The [appropriate regulator] is entitled to be heard—
(a) at the hearing of the petition; and
(b) at any other hearing in relation to the individual or entity under—
(i) Part IX of the 1986 Act;
(ii) Part IX of the 1989 Order; or
(iii) the [2016] Act.

(3) [In the case of a petition presented under Article 238 of the 1989 Order, a copy of the report prepared under Article 248 of that Order] must also be sent to the [appropriate regulator].

(4) A person appointed for the purpose by the [appropriate regulator] is entitled—
(a) to attend any meeting of creditors of the individual or entity;
(b) to attend any meeting of a committee established under section 301 of the 1986 Act (or Article 274 of the 1989 Order);
(c) to attend any meeting of commissioners held under paragraph [26 or 27 of Schedule 6 to the 2016] Act; and
(d) to make representations as to any matter for decision at such a meeting.

[(4A) The appropriate regulator or a person appointed by the appropriate regulator is entitled to participate in (but not vote in) a creditors' decision procedure by which a decision about any matter is sought from the creditors of the individual or entity.]

(5) "Individual" means an individual who—
(a) is, or has been, an authorised person; or
(b) is carrying on, or has carried on, a regulated activity in contravention of the general prohibition.
(6) "Entity" means an entity which—
(a) is, or has been, an authorised person; or
(b) is carrying on, or has carried on, a regulated activity in contravention of the general prohibition.
[[(7) "The appropriate regulator" means—
(a) where the individual or entity is a PRA-regulated person, each of the FCA and the PRA, except that the references in subsections (4) and (4A) to a person appointed by the appropriate regulator are to be read as references to a person appointed by either the FCA or the PRA;
(b) in any other case, the FCA.]
(8) But where the petition was presented by a regulator "the appropriate regulator" does not include the regulator which presented the petition.]

NOTES

The words "2 or 5 of the 2016" in square brackets in sub-s (1)(b) were substituted (for the original words "5 of the 1985"), the year "2016" in square brackets in sub-s (1)(c) and sub-s (2)(b)(iii) was substituted (for the original year "1985"), and the words "26 or 27 of Schedule 6 to the 2016" in square brackets in sub-s (4)(c) were substituted (for the original words "17 or 18 of Schedule 6 to the 1985"), by the Bankruptcy (Scotland) Act 2016 (Consequential Provisions and Modifications) Order 2016, SI 2016/1034, art 7(1), (3), Sch 1, para 20(1), (8), as from 30 November 2016 (except in relation to (i) a sequestration as regards which the petition is presented, or the debtor application is made before that date; or (ii) a trust deed executed before that date).

Words in first pair of square brackets in sub-s (3) inserted by the Enterprise and Regulatory Reform Act 2013 (Consequential Amendments) (Bankruptcy) and the Small Business, Enterprise and Employment Act 2015 (Consequential Amendments) Regulations 2016, SI 2016/481, reg 2(1), Sch 1, para 13.

Sub-s (4A) was inserted, and sub-s (7) was substituted, by the Small Business, Enterprise and Employment Act 2015 (Consequential Amendments, Savings and Transitional Provisions) Regulations 2018, SI 2018/208, reg 4(1), (7). Note that sub-s (7) was originally added by the Financial Services Act 2012, s 44, Sch 14, paras 1, 22.

Words omitted from sub-s (1) repealed, sub-s, (8) added, and all other words in square brackets in this section substituted, by the Financial Services Act 2012, s 44, Sch 14, paras 1, 22.

Provisions against debt avoidance

[17.207]

375 [Right of FCA and PRA] to apply for an order

(1) The [FCA] may apply for an order under section 423 of the 1986 Act (or Article 367 of the 1989 Order) in relation to a debtor if—
(a) at the time the transaction at an undervalue was entered into, the debtor was carrying on a regulated activity (whether or not in contravention of the general prohibition); and
(b) a victim of the transaction is or was party to an agreement entered into with the debtor, the making or performance of which constituted or was part of a regulated activity carried on by the debtor.
[(1A) The PRA may apply for an order under section 423 of the 1986 Act (or Article 367 of the 1989 Order) in relation to a debtor if—
(a) at the time the transaction at an undervalue was entered into, the debtor was carrying on a PRA-regulated activity (whether or not in contravention of the general prohibition); and
(b) a victim of the transaction is or was party to an agreement entered into with the debtor, the making or performance of which constituted or was part of a PRA-regulated activity carried on by the debtor.]
(2) An application made under this section is to be treated as made on behalf of every victim of the transaction to whom subsection (1)(b) [or subsection (1A)(b) (as the case may be)] applies.
(3) Expressions which are given a meaning in Part XVI of the 1986 Act (or Article 367, 368 or 369 of the 1989 Order) have the same meaning when used in this section.

NOTES

Section heading, sub-s (1): words in square brackets substituted by the Financial Services Act 2012, s 44, Sch 14, paras 1, 23(1), (2), (5).

Sub-s (1A): inserted by the Financial Services Act 2012, s 44, Sch 14, paras 1, 23(1), (3).

Sub-s (2): words in square brackets inserted by the Financial Services Act 2012, s 44, Sch 14, paras 1, 23(1), (4).

Supplemental provisions concerning insurers

[17.208]

376 Continuation of contracts of long-term insurance where insurer in liquidation

(1) This section applies in relation to the winding up of an insurer which effects or carries out contracts of long-term insurance.
(2) Unless the court otherwise orders, the liquidator must carry on the insurer's business so far as it consists of carrying out the insurer's contracts of long-term insurance with a view to its being transferred as a going concern to a person who may lawfully carry out those contracts.
(3) In carrying on the business, the liquidator—
(a) may agree to the variation of any contracts of insurance in existence when the winding up order is made; but
(b) must not effect any new contracts of insurance.

(4) If the liquidator is satisfied that the interests of the creditors in respect of liabilities of the insurer attributable to contracts of long-term insurance effected by it require the appointment of a special manager, he may apply to the court.
(5) On such an application, the court may appoint a special manager to act during such time as the court may direct.
(6) The special manager is to have such powers, including any of the powers of a receiver or manager, as the court may direct.
(7) Section 177(5) of the 1986 Act (or Article 151(5) of the 1989 Order) applies to a special manager appointed under subsection (5) as it applies to a special manager appointed under section 177 of the 1986 Act (or Article 151 of the 1989 Order).
(8) If the court thinks fit, it may reduce the value of one or more of the contracts of long-term insurance effected by the insurer.
(9) Any reduction is to be on such terms and subject to such conditions (if any) as the court thinks fit.
(10) The court may, on the application of an official, appoint an independent actuary to investigate the insurer's business so far as it consists of carrying out its contracts of long-term insurance and to report to the official—
(a) on the desirability or otherwise of that part of the insurer's business being continued; and
(b) on any reduction in the contracts of long-term insurance effected by the insurer that may be necessary for successful continuation of that part of the insurer's business.
(11) "Official" means—
(a) the liquidator;
(b) a special manager appointed under subsection (5); or
(c) the [PRA].
[(11A) The PRA must—
(a) consult the FCA before making an application under subsection (10), and
(b) provide the FCA with a copy of any actuary's report made to the PRA under that subsection.
(11B) In the event that the activity of effecting or carrying out long-term contracts of insurance as principal is not to any extent a [PRA-regulated] activity—
(a) the reference in subsection (11)(c) to the PRA is to be read as a reference to the FCA, and
(b) subsection (11A) does not apply.]
(12) The liquidator may make an application in the name of the insurer and on its behalf under Part VII without obtaining the permission that would otherwise be required by [Article 142 of, and Schedule 2 to, the 1989 Order].

NOTES

Sub-s (11): word in square brackets substituted by the Financial Services Act 2012, s 44, Sch 14, paras 1, 24(1), (2).
Sub-s (11A): inserted, together with sub-s (11B), by the Financial Services Act 2012, s 44, Sch 14, paras 1, 24(1), (3); words in square brackets substituted by the Financial Services (Banking Reform) Act 2013, s 141, Sch 10, para 2.
Sub-s (11B): inserted as noted to sub-s (11A) above.
Sub-s (12): words in square brackets substituted by the Deregulation Act 2015, the Small Business, Enterprise and Employment Act 2015 and the Insolvency (Amendment) Act (Northern Ireland) 2016 (Consequential Amendments and Transitional Provisions) Regulations 2017, SI 2017/400, reg 4.

[17.209]
377 Reducing the value of contracts instead of winding up
(1) This section applies in relation to an insurer which has been proved to be unable to pay its debts.
(2) If the court thinks fit, it may reduce the value of one or more of the insurer's contracts instead of making a winding up order.
(3) Any reduction is to be on such terms and subject to such conditions (if any) as the court thinks fit.

NOTES

See further, in relation to the disapplication of this section in relation to an EEA insurer: the Insurers (Reorganisation and Winding Up) Regulations 2004, SI 2004/353, regs 2, 4(7) at **[3.125]**, **[3.127]**.

[17.210]
378 Treatment of assets on winding up
(1) The Treasury may by regulations provide for the treatment of the assets of an insurer on its winding up.
(2) The regulations may, in particular, provide for—
(a) assets representing a particular part of the insurer's business to be available only for meeting liabilities attributable to that part of the insurer's business;
(b) separate general meetings of the creditors to be held in respect of liabilities attributable to a particular part of the insurer's business.

NOTES

Regulations: the Financial Services and Markets Act 2000 (Treatment of Assets of Insurers on Winding Up) Regulations 2001, SI 2001/2968 (revoked by SI 2003/1102 and reproduced for reference at **[7.1528]**).

[17.211]
379 Winding-up rules
(1) Winding-up rules may include provision—
(a) for determining the amount of the liabilities of an insurer to policyholders of any class or description for the purpose of proof in a winding up; and

(b) generally for carrying into effect the provisions of this Part with respect to the winding up of insurers.

(2) Winding-up rules may, in particular, make provision for all or any of the following matters—

(a) the identification of assets and liabilities;

(b) the apportionment, between assets of different classes or descriptions, of—

(i) the costs, charges and expenses of the winding up; and

(ii) any debts of the insurer of a specified class or description;

(c) the determination of the amount of liabilities of a specified description;

(d) the application of assets for meeting liabilities of a specified description;

(e) the application of assets representing any excess of a specified description.

(3) "Specified" means specified in winding-up rules.

(4) "Winding-up rules" means rules made under section 411 of the 1986 Act (or Article 359 of the 1989 Order).

(5) Nothing in this section affects the power to make winding-up rules under the 1986 Act or the 1989 Order.

NOTES

Rules: the Insurers (Winding Up) Rules 2001, SI 2001/3635 at **[7.1532]**; the Insurers (Winding Up) (Scotland) Rules 2001, SI 2001/4040 at **[16.147]**.

380–416 *((Pts XXV–XXVIII) outside the scope of this work.)*

PART XXIX
INTERPRETATION

[17.212]

417 Definitions

(1) In this Act—

. . .

. . .

. . .

["Bank of England" is to be read in accordance with section 2A(4) to (6);]

"the compensation scheme" has the meaning given in section 213(2);

. . .

"director", in relation to a body corporate, includes—

(a) a person occupying in relation to it the position of a director (by whatever name called); and

(b) a person in accordance with whose directions or instructions (not being advice given in a professional capacity) the directors of that body are accustomed to act;

"documents" includes information recorded in any form and, in relation to information recorded otherwise than in legible form, references to its production include references to producing a copy of the information in legible form[, or in a form from which it can readily be produced in visible and legible form];

. . .

"friendly society" means an incorporated or registered friendly society;

"general prohibition" has the meaning given in section 19(2);

. . .

"partnership" includes a partnership constituted under the law of a country or territory outside the United Kingdom;

"prescribed" (where not otherwise defined) means prescribed in regulations made by the Treasury;

. . .

["registered society" (except where otherwise indicated) means—

(a) a registered society within the meaning of the Co-operative and Community Benefit Societies Act 2014, or

(b) a society registered or deemed to be registered under the Industrial and Provident Societies Act (Northern Ireland) 1969;]

. . .

"rule" means a rule made by the Authority under this Act;

. . .

"the scheme manager" has the meaning given in section 212(1);

. . .

(2) In the application of this Act to Scotland, references to a matter being actionable at the suit of a person are to be read as references to the matter being actionable at the instance of that person.

(3), [(4)] *(Outside the scope of this work.)*

NOTES

Sub-s (1): definition "the Authority"(omitted) repealed by the Financial Services Act 2012, s 48(1)(a); definition "Bank of England" inserted by the Bank of England and Financial Services Act 2016, s 16, Sch 2, Pt 2, paras 26, 49; in definition "documents" words in square brackets added by the Criminal Justice and Police Act 2001, s 70, Sch 2, Pt 2, para 16(1), (2)(f); definition "industrial and provident society" (omitted) repealed, and definition "registered society" inserted, by the Co-operative and Community Benefit Societies Act 2014, s 151, Sch 4, Pt 2, paras 68, 71; all other definitions omitted are outside the scope of this work.

General prohibition: s 19(1) provides that no person may carry on a regulated activity in the UK, or purport to do so, unless he is either an authorised person, or an exempt person. Section 19(2) provides that this prohibition is referred to in this Act as the general prohibition.

418–425B (*Outside the scope of this work.*)

PART XXX
SUPPLEMENTAL

[17.213]
426 Consequential and supplementary provision
(1) A Minister of the Crown may by order make such incidental, consequential, transitional or supplemental provision as he considers necessary or expedient for the general purposes, or any particular purpose, of this Act or in consequence of any provision made by or under this Act or for giving full effect to this Act or any such provision.
(2)–(4) (*Outside the scope of this work.*)

427 (*Outside the scope of this work.*)

[17.214]
428 Regulations and orders
(1) Any power to make an order which is conferred on a Minister of the Crown by this Act and any power to make regulations which is conferred by this Act is exercisable by statutory instrument.
(2) The Lord Chancellor's power to make rules under section 132 is exercisable by statutory instrument.
(3) Any statutory instrument made under this Act may—
(a) contain such incidental, supplemental, consequential and transitional provision as the person making it considers appropriate; and
(b) make different provision for different cases.

429 (*Outside the scope of this work.*)

[17.215]
430 Extent
(1) This Act, except Chapter IV of Part XVII, extends to Northern Ireland.
(2) Except where Her Majesty by Order in Council provides otherwise, the extent of any amendment or repeal made by or under this Act is the same as the extent of the provision amended or repealed.
(3) Her Majesty may by Order in Council provide for any provision of or made under this Act relating to a matter which is the subject of other legislation which extends to any of the Channel Islands or the Isle of Man to extend there with such modifications (if any) as may be specified in the Order.

[17.216]
431 Commencement
(1) The following provisions come into force on the passing of this Act—
(a) this section;
(b) sections 428, 430 and 433;
(c) (*outside the scope of this work.*)
(2) The other provisions of this Act come into force on such day as the Treasury may by order appoint; and different days may be appointed for different purposes.

NOTES

Orders: at present 7 commencement orders have been made under this section. The ones relevant to the provisions of this Act reproduced here are the Financial Services and Markets Act 2000 (Commencement No 1) Order 2001, SI 2001/516; the Financial Services and Markets Act 2000 (Commencement No 3) Order 2001, SI 2001/1820; the Financial Services and Markets Act 2000 (Commencement No 5) Order 2001, SI 2001/2632; the Financial Services and Markets Act 2000 (Commencement No 7) Order 2001, SI 2001/3538.

432 (*Outside the scope of this work.*)

[17.217]
433 Short title
This Act may be cited as the Financial Services and Markets Act 2000.

SCHEDULES 1–22

(*Schs 1–22 outside the scope of this work.*)

LIMITED LIABILITY PARTNERSHIPS ACT 2000

(2000 c 12)

An Act to make provision for limited liability partnerships

[20 July 2000]

1–13 (*Outside the scope of this work.*)

Regulations

[17.218]
14 Insolvency and winding up
(1) Regulations shall make provision about the insolvency and winding up of limited liability partnerships by applying or incorporating, with such modifications as appear appropriate[—
(a) in relation to a limited liability partnership registered in Great Britain, Parts 1 to 4, 6 and 7 of the Insolvency Act 1986;
(b) in relation to a limited liability partnership registered in Northern Ireland, Parts 2 to 5 and 7 of the Insolvency (Northern Ireland) Order 1989, and so much of Part 1 of that Order as applies for the purposes of those Parts.]
(2) Regulations may make other provision about the insolvency and winding up of limited liability partnerships, and provision about the insolvency and winding up of oversea limited liability partnerships, by—
(a) applying or incorporating, with such modifications as appear appropriate, any law relating to the insolvency or winding up of companies or other corporations which would not otherwise have effect in relation to them, or
(b) providing for any law relating to the insolvency or winding up of companies or other corporations which would otherwise have effect in relation to them not to apply to them or to apply to them with such modifications as appear appropriate.
(3) In this Act "oversea limited liability partnership" means a body incorporated or otherwise established outside [the United Kingdom] and having such connection with [the United Kingdom], and such other features, as regulations may prescribe.

NOTES
Sub-s (1): words in square brackets substituted for original words ", Parts I to IV, VI and VII of the Insolvency Act 1986" by the Limited Liability Partnerships (Application of Companies Act 2006) Regulations 2009, SI 2009/1804, reg 85, Sch 3, Pt 1, paras 6(1), (2), 11, except in relation to an obligation arising before 1 October 2009 to deliver a document to the registrar.
Sub-s (3): words in square brackets substituted for original words "Great Britain" by SI 2009/1804, reg 85, Sch 3, Pt 1, paras 6(1), (3), 11, except in relation to an obligation arising before 1 October 2009 to deliver a document to the registrar.
Regulations: the Limited Liability Partnerships Regulations 2001, SI 2001/1090 at **[10.33]**; the Limited Liability Partnerships (Scotland) Regulations 2001, SSI 2001/128 at **[16.133]**.

15–17 (*Outside the scope of this work.*)

Supplementary

18 (*Outside the scope of this work.*)

[17.219]
19 Commencement, extent and short title
(1) The preceding provisions of this Act shall come into force on such day as the Secretary of State may by order made by statutory instrument appoint; and different days may be appointed for different purposes.
(2) The Secretary of State may by order made by statutory instrument make any transitional provisions and savings which appear appropriate in connection with the coming into force of any provision of this Act.
(3) For the purposes of the Scotland Act 1998 this Act shall be taken to be a pre-commencement enactment within the meaning of that Act.
(4) (*Outside the scope of this work.*)
(5) This Act may be cited as the Limited Liability Partnerships Act 2000.

NOTES
Orders: the Limited Liability Partnerships Act 2000 (Commencement) Order 2000, SI 2000/3316.

SCHEDULE

(*Schedule outside the scope of this work.*)

COMMONHOLD AND LEASEHOLD REFORM ACT 2002

(2002 c 15)

ARRANGEMENT OF SECTIONS

PART 1
COMMONHOLD

Termination: voluntary winding-up

43 Winding-up resolution .... [17.220]
44 100 per cent agreement .... [17.221]
45 80 per cent agreement .... [17.222]
46 Termination application .... [17.223]
47 Termination statement .... [17.224]
48 The liquidator .... [17.225]
49 Termination .... [17.226]

Termination: winding-up by court

50 Introduction .... [17.227]
51 Succession order .... [17.228]
52 Assets and liabilities .... [17.229]
53 Transfer of responsibility .... [17.230]
54 Termination of commonhold .... [17.231]

Termination: miscellaneous

55 Termination by court .... [17.232]

PART 3
SUPPLEMENTARY

181 Commencement etc .... [17.233]
182 Extent .... [17.234]
183 Short title .... [17.235]

An Act to make provision about commonhold land and to amend the law about leasehold property

[1 May 2002]

PART 1
COMMONHOLD

1–42 (*Outside the scope of this work.*)

Termination: voluntary winding-up

[17.220]
43 Winding-up resolution

(1) A winding-up resolution in respect of a commonhold association shall be of no effect unless—
- (a) the resolution is preceded by a declaration of solvency,
- (b) the commonhold association passes a termination-statement resolution before it passes the winding-up resolution, and
- (c) each resolution is passed with at least 80 per cent of the members of the association voting in favour.

(2) In this Part—

"declaration of solvency" means a directors' statutory declaration made in accordance with section 89 of the Insolvency Act 1986 (c 45),

"termination-statement resolution" means a resolution approving the terms of a termination statement (within the meaning of section 47), and

"winding-up resolution" means a resolution for voluntary winding-up within the meaning of section 84 of that Act.

[17.221]
44 100 per cent agreement

(1) This section applies where a commonhold association—
- (a) has passed a winding-up resolution and a termination-statement resolution with 100 per cent of the members of the association voting in favour, and
- (b) has appointed a liquidator under section 91 of the Insolvency Act 1986 (c 45).

(2) The liquidator shall make a termination application within the period of six months beginning with the day on which the winding-up resolution is passed.

(3) If the liquidator fails to make a termination application within the period specified in subsection (2) a termination application may be made by—
- (a) a unit-holder, or
- (b) a person falling within a class prescribed for the purposes of this subsection.

[17.222]

45 80 per cent agreement

(1) This section applies where a commonhold association—

(a) has passed a winding-up resolution and a termination-statement resolution with at least 80 per cent of the members of the association voting in favour, and

(b) has appointed a liquidator under section 91 of the Insolvency Act 1986.

(2) The liquidator shall within the prescribed period apply to the court for an order determining—

(a) the terms and conditions on which a termination application may be made, and

(b) the terms of the termination statement to accompany a termination application.

(3) The liquidator shall make a termination application within the period of three months starting with the date on which an order under subsection (2) is made.

(4) If the liquidator fails to make an application under subsection (2) or (3) within the period specified in that subsection an application of the same kind may be made by—

(a) a unit-holder, or

(b) a person falling within a class prescribed for the purposes of this subsection.

NOTES

Regulations: the Commonhold Regulations 2004, SI 2004/1829.

[17.223]

46 Termination application

(1) A "termination application" is an application to the Registrar that all the land in relation to which a particular commonhold association exercises functions should cease to be commonhold land.

(2) A termination application must be accompanied by a termination statement.

(3) On receipt of a termination application the Registrar shall note it in the register.

[17.224]

47 Termination statement

(1) A termination statement must specify—

(a) the commonhold association's proposals for the transfer of the commonhold land following acquisition of the freehold estate in accordance with section 49(3), and

(b) how the assets of the commonhold association will be distributed.

(2) A commonhold community statement may make provision requiring any termination statement to make arrangements—

(a) of a specified kind, or

(b) determined in a specified manner,

about the rights of unit-holders in the event of all the land to which the statement relates ceasing to be commonhold land.

(3) A termination statement must comply with a provision made by the commonhold community statement in reliance on subsection (2).

(4) Subsection (3) may be disapplied by an order of the court—

(a) generally,

(b) in respect of specified matters, or

(c) for a specified purpose.

(5) An application for an order under subsection (4) may be made by any member of the commonhold association.

[17.225]

48 The liquidator

(1) This section applies where a termination application has been made in respect of particular commonhold land.

(2) The liquidator shall notify the Registrar of his appointment.

(3) In the case of a termination application made under section 44 the liquidator shall either—

(a) notify the Registrar that the liquidator is content with the termination statement submitted with the termination application, or

(b) apply to the court under section 112 of the Insolvency Act 1986 (c 45) to determine the terms of the termination statement.

(4) The liquidator shall send to the Registrar a copy of a determination made by virtue of subsection (3)(b).

(5) Subsection (4) is in addition to any requirement under section 112(3) of the Insolvency Act 1986.

(6) A duty imposed on the liquidator by this section is to be performed as soon as possible.

(7) In this section a reference to the liquidator is a reference—

(a) to the person who is appointed as liquidator under section 91 of the Insolvency Act 1986, or

(b) in the case of a members' voluntary winding up which becomes a creditors' voluntary winding up by virtue of sections 95 and 96 of that Act, to the person acting as liquidator in accordance with section 100 of that Act.

[17.226]

49 Termination

(1) This section applies where a termination application is made under section 44 and—

(a) a liquidator notifies the Registrar under section 48(3)(a) that he is content with a termination statement, or

(b) a determination is made under section 112 of the Insolvency Act 1986 (c 45) by virtue of section 48(3)(b).

(2) This section also applies where a termination application is made under section 45.

(3) The commonhold association shall by virtue of this subsection be entitled to be registered as the proprietor of the freehold estate in each commonhold unit.

(4) The Registrar shall take such action as appears to him to be appropriate for the purpose of giving effect to the termination statement.

Termination: winding-up by court

[17.227]

50 Introduction

(1) Section 51 applies where a petition is presented under section 124 of the Insolvency Act 1986 for the winding up of a commonhold association by the court.

(2) For the purposes of this Part—

(a) an "insolvent commonhold association" is one in relation to which a winding-up petition has been presented under section 124 of the Insolvency Act 1986,

(b) a commonhold association is the "successor commonhold association" to an insolvent commonhold association if the land specified for the purpose of section 34(1)(a) is the same for both associations, and

(c) a "winding-up order" is an order under section 125 of the Insolvency Act 1986 for the winding up of a commonhold association.

[17.228]

51 Succession order

(1) At the hearing of the winding-up petition an application may be made to the court for an order under this section (a "succession order") in relation to the insolvent commonhold association.

(2) An application under subsection (1) may be made only by—

(a) the insolvent commonhold association,

(b) one or more members of the insolvent commonhold association, or

(c) a provisional liquidator for the insolvent commonhold association appointed under section 135 of the Insolvency Act 1986.

(3) An application under subsection (1) must be accompanied by—

(a) prescribed evidence of the formation of a successor commonhold association, and

(b) a certificate given by the directors of the successor commonhold association that its [articles of association] comply with regulations under paragraph 2(1) of Schedule 3.

(4) The court shall grant an application under subsection (1) unless it thinks that the circumstances of the insolvent commonhold association make a succession order inappropriate.

NOTES

Sub-s (3): words in square brackets substituted by the Companies Act 2006 (Consequential Amendments, Transitional Provisions and Savings) Order 2009, SI 2009/1941, art 2(1), Sch 1, para 194(1), (11).

Regulations: the Commonhold Regulations 2004, SI 2004/1829.

[17.229]

52 Assets and liabilities

(1) Where a succession order is made in relation to an insolvent commonhold association this section applies on the making of a winding-up order in respect of the association.

(2) The successor commonhold association shall be entitled to be registered as the proprietor of the freehold estate in the common parts.

(3) The insolvent commonhold association shall for all purposes cease to be treated as the proprietor of the freehold estate in the common parts.

(4) The succession order—

(a) shall make provision as to the treatment of any charge over all or any part of the common parts;

(b) may require the Registrar to take action of a specified kind;

(c) may enable the liquidator to require the Registrar to take action of a specified kind;

(d) may make supplemental or incidental provision.

[17.230]

53 Transfer of responsibility

(1) Where a succession order is made in relation to an insolvent commonhold association this section applies on the making of a winding-up order in respect of the association.

(2) The successor commonhold association shall be treated as the commonhold association for the commonhold in respect of any matter which relates to a time after the making of the winding-up order.

(3) On the making of the winding-up order the court may make an order requiring the liquidator to make available to the successor commonhold association specified—

(a) records;

(b) copies of records;

(c) information.

(4) An order under subsection (3) may include terms as to—

(a) timing;

(b) payment.

[17.231]

54 Termination of commonhold

(1) This section applies where the court—

(a) makes a winding-up order in respect of a commonhold association, and

(b) has not made a succession order in respect of the commonhold association.

(2) The liquidator of a commonhold association shall as soon as possible notify the Registrar of—

(a) the fact that this section applies,

(b) any directions given under section 168 of the Insolvency Act 1986 (c 45) (liquidator: supplementary powers),

(c) any notice given to the court and the registrar of companies in accordance with section 172(8) of that Act (liquidator vacating office after final meeting),

(d) any notice given to the Secretary of State under section 174(3) of that Act (completion of winding-up),

(e) any application made to the registrar of companies under section 202(2) of that Act (insufficient assets: early dissolution),

(f) any notice given to the registrar of companies under section 205(1)(b) of that Act (completion of winding-up), and

(g) any other matter which in the liquidator's opinion is relevant to the Registrar.

(3) Notification under subsection (2)(b) to (f) must be accompanied by a copy of the directions, notice or application concerned.

(4) The Registrar shall—

(a) make such arrangements as appear to him to be appropriate for ensuring that the freehold estate in land in respect of which a commonhold association exercises functions ceases to be registered as a freehold estate in commonhold land as soon as is reasonably practicable after he receives notification under subsection (2)(c) to (f), and

(b) take such action as appears to him to be appropriate for the purpose of giving effect to a determination made by the liquidator in the exercise of his functions.

Termination: miscellaneous

[17.232]

55 Termination by court

(1) This section applies where the court makes an order by virtue of section 6(6)(c) or 40(3)(d) for all the land in relation to which a commonhold association exercises functions to cease to be commonhold land.

(2) The court shall have the powers which it would have if it were making a winding-up order in respect of the commonhold association.

(3) A person appointed as liquidator by virtue of subsection (2) shall have the powers and duties of a liquidator following the making of a winding-up order by the court in respect of a commonhold association.

(4) But the order of the court by virtue of section 6(6)(c) or 40(3)(d) may—

(a) require the liquidator to exercise his functions in a particular way;

(b) impose additional rights or duties on the liquidator;

(c) modify or remove a right or duty of the liquidator.

56–179 *(Ss 56–70, ss 71–179 (Pt 2) outside the scope of this work.)*

PART 3
SUPPLEMENTARY

180 *(Outside the scope of this work.)*

[17.233]

181 Commencement etc

(1) Apart from section 104 and sections 177 to 179, the preceding provisions (and the Schedules) come into force in accordance with provision made by order made by the appropriate authority.

(2) The appropriate authority may by order make any transitional provisions or savings in connection with the coming into force of any provision in accordance with an order under subsection (1).

(3) The power to make orders under subsections (1) and (2) is exercisable by statutory instrument.

(4) In this section "the appropriate authority" means—

(a) in relation to any provision of Part 1 or section 180 and Schedule 14 so far as relating to section 104, the Lord Chancellor, and

(b) in relation to any provision of Part 2 or section 180 and Schedule 14 so far as otherwise relating, the Secretary of State (as respects England) and the National Assembly for Wales (as respects Wales).

NOTES

Orders: at present, 10 commencement orders have been made under this section. The order relevant to the provisions of this Act printed in this work is the Commonhold and Leasehold Reform Act 2002 (Commencement No 4) Order 2004, SI 2004/1832.

[17.234]

182 Extent

This Act extends to England and Wales only.

[17.235]
183 Short title

This Act may be cited as the Commonhold and Leasehold Reform Act 2002.

SCHEDULES 1–14

(Schs 1–14 outside the scope of this work.)

PROCEEDS OF CRIME ACT 2002

(2002 c 29)

ARRANGEMENT OF SECTIONS

PART 9
INSOLVENCY ETC

Bankruptcy in England and Wales

417 Modifications of the 1986 Act . . . [17.236]
418 Restriction of powers . . . [17.237]
419 Tainted gifts . . . [17.238]

Sequestration in Scotland

420 Modifications of the 2016 Act . . . [17.239]
421 Restriction of powers . . . [17.240]
422 Tainted gifts . . . [17.241]

Winding up in England and Wales and Scotland

426 Winding up under the 1986 Act . . . [17.242]
427 Tainted gifts . . . [17.243]

Floating charges

430 Floating charges . . . [17.244]

Limited liability partnerships

431 Limited liability partnerships . . . [17.245]

Insolvency practitioners

432 Insolvency practitioners . . . [17.246]
433 Meaning of insolvency practitioner . . . [17.247]

Interpretation

434 Interpretation . . . [17.248]

PART 12
MISCELLANEOUS AND GENERAL

General

458 Commencement . . . [17.249]
462 Short title . . . [17.250]

An Act to establish the Assets Recovery Agency and make provision about the appointment of its Director and his functions (including Revenue functions), to provide for confiscation orders in relation to persons who benefit from criminal conduct and for restraint orders to prohibit dealing with property, to allow the recovery of property which is or represents property obtained through unlawful conduct or which is intended to be used in unlawful conduct, to make provision about money laundering, to make provision about investigations relating to benefit from criminal conduct or to property which is or represents property obtained through unlawful conduct or to money laundering, to make provision to give effect to overseas requests and orders made where property is found or believed to be obtained through criminal conduct, and for connected purposes.

[24 July 2002]

NOTES

Modification: this Act is applied, with modifications, in so far as it relates to bank insolvency or administration under the Banking Act 2009, Pts 2, 3, by the Banking Act 2009 (Parts 2 and 3 Consequential Amendments) Order 2009, SI 2009/317, art 3, Schedule at **[7.86]**, **[7.92]**.

1–416 (*(Pts 1–8) outside the scope of this work.*)

PART 9
INSOLVENCY ETC

Bankruptcy in England and Wales

[17.236]

417 Modifications of the 1986 Act

(1) This section applies if a person is [made] bankrupt in England and Wales.

[(2) The following property is excluded from the person's estate for the purposes of Part 9 of the 1986 Act—

(a) property for the time being subject to a restraint order which was made under section 41, 120 or 190 before the order adjudging the person bankrupt;

(b) property for the time being detained under or by virtue of section 44A, 47J, 47K, 47M, 47P, 122A, 127J, 127K, 127M, 127P, 193A, 195J, 195K, 195M or 195P;

(c) property in respect of which an order under section 50, 128(3) or 198 is in force;

(d) property in respect of which an order under section 67A, 131A or 215A is in force.]

(3) Subsection (2)(a) applies to heritable property in Scotland only if the restraint order is recorded in the General Register of Sasines or registered in the Land Register of Scotland before the order adjudging the person bankrupt.

(4) If in the case of a debtor an interim receiver stands at any time appointed under section 286 of the 1986 Act and any property of the debtor is then subject to a restraint order made under section 41, 120 or 190 the powers conferred on the receiver by virtue of that Act do not apply to property then subject to the restraint order.

NOTES

Sub-s (1): word in square brackets substituted by the Enterprise and Regulatory Reform Act 2013 (Consequential Amendments) (Bankruptcy) and the Small Business, Enterprise and Employment Act 2015 (Consequential Amendments) Regulations 2016, SI 2016/481, reg 2(1), Sch 1, Pt 2, para 18.

Sub-s (2): substituted by the Policing and Crime Act 2009, s 112(1), Sch 7, Pt 6, paras 66, 79.

[17.237]

418 Restriction of powers

(1) If a person is [made] bankrupt in England and Wales the powers referred to in subsection (2) must not be exercised in relation to the property referred to in subsection (3).

(2) These are the powers—

(a) the powers conferred on a court by sections 41 to [67B, the powers conferred on an appropriate officer by section 47C] and the powers of a receiver appointed under section 48 [or 50];

(b) the powers conferred on a court by sections 120 to 136 and Schedule 3[, the powers conferred on an appropriate officer by section 127C] and the powers of an administrator appointed under section 125 or 128(3);

(c) the powers conferred on a court by sections 190 to [215B, the powers conferred on an appropriate officer by section 195C] and the powers of a receiver appointed under section 196 [or 198].

(3) This is the property—

(a) property which is for the time being comprised in the bankrupt's estate for the purposes of Part 9 of the 1986 Act;

(b) property in respect of which his trustee in bankruptcy may (without leave of the court) serve a notice under section 307, 308 or 308A of the 1986 Act (after-acquired property, tools, tenancies etc);

(c) property which is to be applied for the benefit of creditors of the bankrupt by virtue of a condition imposed under section 280(2)(c) of the 1986 Act;

(d) in a case where a confiscation order has been made under section 6 or 156 of this Act, any sums remaining in the hands of a receiver appointed under section 50 [or 198] of this Act after the amount required to be paid under the confiscation order has been fully paid;

(e) in a case where a confiscation order has been made under section 92 of this Act, any sums remaining in the hands of an administrator appointed under section 128 of this Act after the amount required to be paid under the confiscation order has been fully paid;

[(f) in a case where a confiscation order has been made under section 6, 92 or 156 of this Act, any sums remaining in the hands of an appropriate officer after the amount required to be paid under the confiscation order has been fully paid under section 67D(2)(c), 131D(2)(c) or 215D(2)(c).]

(4) But nothing in the 1986 Act must be taken to restrict (or enable the restriction of) the powers referred to in subsection (2).

(5) In a case where a petition in bankruptcy was presented or a receiving order or adjudication in bankruptcy was made before 29 December 1986 (when the 1986 Act came into force) this section has effect with these modifications—

(a) for the reference in subsection (3)(a) to the bankrupt's estate for the purposes of Part 9 of that Act substitute a reference to the property of the bankrupt for the purposes of the 1914 Act;

(b) omit subsection (3)(b);

(c) for the reference in subsection (3)(c) to section 280(2)(c) of the 1986 Act substitute a reference to section 26(2) of the 1914 Act;

(d) for the reference in subsection (4) to the 1986 Act substitute a reference to the 1914 Act.

NOTES

Sub-s (1): word in square brackets substituted by the Enterprise and Regulatory Reform Act 2013 (Consequential Amendments) (Bankruptcy) and the Small Business, Enterprise and Employment Act 2015 (Consequential Amendments) Regulations 2016, SI 2016/481, reg 2(1), Sch 1, Pt 2, para 18.

Sub-s (2): first words in square brackets in para (a) substituted, and words in square brackets in para (b) inserted, by the Policing and Crime Act 2009, s 112(1), Sch 7, Pt 6, paras 66, 80(1), (2)(a), (b); second words in square brackets in para (a), and words in second pair of square brackets in para (c), substituted for original words ", 50 or 52" and ", 198 or 200" respectively by the Serious Crime Act 2007, s 74(2)(a), Sch 8, Pt 1, paras 1, 70(1), (2), subject to transitional provisions and savings in SI 2008/755, arts 3, 4; words in first pair of square brackets in para (c) substituted by the Policing and Crime Act 2009, s 112(1), Sch 7, Pt 6, paras 66, 80(1), (2)(c).

Sub-s (3): words in square brackets in para (d) substituted for original words ", 52, 198 or 200" by the Serious Crime Act 2007, s 74(2)(a), Sch 8, Pt 1, paras 1, 70(1), (3), subject to transitional provisions and savings in SI 2008/755, arts 3, 4; para (f) added by the Policing and Crime Act 2009, s 112(1), Sch 7, Pt 6, paras 66, 80(1), (3).

[17.238]
419 Tainted gifts

(1) This section applies if a person who is [made] bankrupt in England and Wales has made a tainted gift (whether directly or indirectly).

(2) No order may be made under section 339, 340 or 423 of the 1986 Act (avoidance of certain transactions) in respect of the making of the gift at any time when—

(a) any property of the recipient of the tainted gift is subject to a restraint order under section 41, 120 or 190, . . .

[(aa) such property is detained under or by virtue of section 44A, 47J, 47K, 47M, 47P, 122A, 127J, 127K, 127M, 127P, 193A, 195J, 195K, 195M or 195P,]

(b) there is in force in respect of such property an order under section 50, . . . 128(3) [or 198][, or

(c) there is in force in respect of such property an order under section 67A, 131A or 215A.]

(3) Any order made under section 339, 340 or 423 of the 1986 Act after an order mentioned in [subsection (2)(a), (b) or (c)] is discharged must take into account any realisation under Part 2, 3 or 4 of this Act of property held by the recipient of the tainted gift.

(4) A person makes a tainted gift for the purposes of this section if he makes a tainted gift within the meaning of Part 2, 3 or 4.

(5) In a case where a petition in bankruptcy was presented or a receiving order or adjudication in bankruptcy was made before 29 December 1986 (when the 1986 Act came into force) this section has effect with the substitution for a reference to section 339, 340 or 423 of the 1986 Act of a reference to section 27, 42 or 44 of the 1914 Act.

NOTES

Sub-s (1): word in square brackets substituted by the Enterprise and Regulatory Reform Act 2013 (Consequential Amendments) (Bankruptcy) and the Small Business, Enterprise and Employment Act 2015 (Consequential Amendments) Regulations 2016, SI 2016/481, reg 2(1), Sch 1, Pt 2, para 18.

Sub-s (2): word omitted from para (a) repealed, para (aa) inserted, and para (c) and word ", or" immediately preceding it added, by the Policing and Crime Act 2009, s 112(1), (2), Sch 7, Pt 6, paras 66, 81(1), (2), Sch 8, Pt 4; in para (b), figure "52," (omitted) repealed and words in square brackets substituted for original words ", 198 or 200" by the Serious Crime Act 2007, ss 74(2)(a), 92, Sch 8, Pt 1, paras 1, 71, Sch 14, subject to transitional provisions and savings in SI 2008/755, arts 3, 4.

Sub-s (3): words in square brackets substituted by the Policing and Crime Act 2009, s 112(1), Sch 7, Pt 6, paras 66, 81(1), (3).

Sequestration in Scotland

[17.239]
420 [Modifications of the 2016 Act]

(1) This section applies if an award of sequestration is made in Scotland.

[(2) The following property is excluded from the debtor's estate for the purposes of the [2016] Act—

(a) property for the time being subject to a restraint order which was made under section 41, 120 or 190 before the award of sequestration;

(b) property for the time being detained under or by virtue of section 44A, 47J, 47K, 47M, 47P, 122A, 127J, 127K, 127M, 127P, 193A, 195J, 195K, 195M or 195P;

(c) property in respect of which an order under section 50, 128(3) or 198 is in force;

(d) property in respect of which an order under section 67A, 131A or 215A is in force.]

(3) Subsection (2)(a) applies to heritable property in Scotland only if the restraint order is recorded in the General Register of Sasines or registered in the Land Register of Scotland before the award of sequestration.

(4) It shall not be competent to submit a claim in relation to a confiscation order to the [trustee in the sequestration] in accordance with section [122 of the 2016] Act; and the reference here to a confiscation order is to any confiscation order that has been or may be made against the debtor under Part 2, 3 or 4 of this Act.

(5) If at any time in the period before the award of sequestration is made an interim trustee stands appointed under section [54(1) of the 2016] Act and any property in the debtor's estate is at that time subject to a restraint order made under section 41, 120 or 190, the powers conferred on the trustee by virtue of that Act do not apply to property then subject to the restraint order.

NOTES

Section heading: words in square brackets substituted for original words "Modifications of the 1985 Act" by the Bankruptcy (Scotland) Act 2016 (Consequential Provisions and Modifications) Order 2016, SI 2016/1034, art 7(1), (3), Sch 1, para 25(1), (8), as from 30 November 2016 (except in relation to (i) a sequestration as regards which the petition is presented, or the debtor application is made before that date; or (ii) a trust deed executed before that date).

Sub-s (2): substituted by the Policing and Crime Act 2009, s 112(1), Sch 7, Pt 6, paras 66, 82; year in square brackets substituted for original year "1985" by SI 2016/1034, art 7(1), (3), Sch 1, para 25(1), (7)(a), as from 30 November 2016 (except in relation to (i) a sequestration as regards which the petition is presented, or the debtor application is made before that date; or (ii) a trust deed executed before that date).

Sub-s (4): words in first and second pairs of square brackets substituted for original words "permanent trustee" and "48 of the 1985" respectively, by SI 2016/1034, art 7(1), (3), Sch 1, para 25(1), (7)(b), as from 30 November 2016 (except in relation to (i) a sequestration as regards which the petition is presented, or the debtor application is made before that date; or (ii) a trust deed executed before that date).

Sub-s (5): words in square brackets substituted for original words "2(5) of the 1985" by SI 2016/1034, art 7(1), (3), Sch 1, para 25(1), (7)(c), as from 30 November 2016 (except in relation to (i) a sequestration as regards which the petition is presented, or the debtor application is made before that date; or (ii) a trust deed executed before that date).

[17.240]

421 Restriction of powers

(1) If an award of sequestration is made in Scotland the powers referred to in subsection (2) must not be exercised in relation to the property referred to in subsection (3).

(2) These are the powers—

- (a) the powers conferred on a court by sections 41 to [67B, the powers conferred on an appropriate officer by section 47C] and the powers of a receiver appointed under section 48 [or 50];
- (b) the powers conferred on a court by sections 120 to 136 and Schedule 3[, the powers conferred on an appropriate officer by section 127C] and the powers of an administrator appointed under section 125 or 128(3);
- (c) the powers conferred on a court by sections 190 to [215B, the powers conferred on an appropriate officer by section 195C] and the powers of a receiver appointed under section 196 [or 198].

(3) This is the property—

- (a) property which is for the time being comprised in the whole estate of the debtor within the meaning of section [79 of the 2016] Act;
- (b) any income of the debtor which has been ordered under section [90 or 95] of that Act to be paid to the [trustee in the sequestration];
- (c) any estate which under section [79(4) or 86(4) and (5)] of that Act vests in the [trustee in the sequestration];
- (d) in a case where a confiscation order has been made under section 6 or 156 of this Act, any sums remaining in the hands of a receiver appointed under section 50 [or 198] of this Act after the amount required to be paid under the confiscation order has been fully paid;
- (e) in a case where a confiscation order has been made under section 92 of this Act, any sums remaining in the hands of an administrator appointed under section 128 of this Act after the amount required to be paid under the confiscation order has been fully paid;
- [(f) in a case where a confiscation order has been made under section 6, 92 or 156 of this Act, any sums remaining in the hands of an appropriate officer after the amount required to be paid under the confiscation order has been fully paid under section 67D(2)(c), 131D(2)(c) or 215D(2)(c).]

(4) But nothing in the [2016] Act must be taken to restrict (or enable the restriction of) the powers referred to in subsection (2).

(5) In a case where (despite the coming into force of the 1985 Act) the 1913 Act applies to a sequestration, subsection (3) above has effect as if for paragraphs (a) to (c) there were substituted—

"(a) property which is for the time being comprised in the whole property of the debtor which vests in the trustee under section 97 of the 1913 Act;

(b) any income of the bankrupt which has been ordered under section 98(2) of that Act to be paid to the trustee;

(c) any estate which under section 98(1) of that Act vests in the trustee."

(6) In a case where subsection (5) applies, subsection (4) has effect as if for the reference to the 1985 Act there were substituted a reference to the 1913 Act.

NOTES

Sub-s (2): first words in square brackets in para (a) substituted, and words in square brackets in para (b) inserted, by the Policing and Crime Act 2009, s 112(1), Sch 7, Pt 6, paras 66, 83(1), (2)(a), (b); second words in square brackets in para (a), and words in second pair of square brackets in para (c), substituted for original words ", 50 or 52" and ", 198 or 200" respectively by the Serious Crime Act 2007, s 74(2)(a), Sch 8, Pt 1, paras 1, 73(1), (2), subject to transitional provisions and savings in SI 2008/755, arts 3, 4; words in first pair of square brackets in para (c) substituted by the Policing and Crime Act 2009, s 112(1), Sch 7, Pt 6, paras 66, 83(1), (2).

Sub-s (3): amended by the Bankruptcy (Scotland) Act 2016 (Consequential Provisions and Modifications) Order 2016, SI 2016/1034, art 7(1), (3), Sch 1, para 25(1), (9)(a)–(c), as from 30 November 2016 (except in relation to (i) a sequestration as regards which the petition is presented, or the debtor application is made before that date; or (ii) a trust deed executed before that date), as follows:

words in square brackets in para (a) substituted for original words "31(8) of the 1985";

words in first and second pairs of square brackets in para (b) substituted for original number "32(2)" and words "permanent

trustee" respectively; and
words in first and second pairs of square brackets in para (c) substituted for original words "31(10) or 32(6)" and "permanent trustee" respectively.

Words in square brackets in para (d) substituted for original words ", 52, 198 or 200" by the Serious Crime Act 2007, s 74(2)(a), Sch 8, Pt 1, paras 1, 73(1), (3), subject to transitional provisions and savings in SI 2008/755, arts 3, 4.

Para (f) added by the Policing and Crime Act 2009, s 112(1), Sch 7, Pt 6, paras 66, 83(1), (3).

Sub-s (4): year in square brackets substituted for original year "1985" by SI 2016/1034, art 7(1), (3), Sch 1, para 25(1), (9)(d), as from 30 November 2016 (except in relation to (i) a sequestration as regards which the petition is presented, or the debtor application is made before that date; or (ii) a trust deed executed before that date).

Sub-ss (5), (6): repealed by SI 2016/1034, art 7(1), (3), Sch 1, para 25(1), (9)(e), as from 30 November 2016 (except in relation to (i) a sequestration as regards which the petition is presented, or the debtor application is made before that date; or (ii) a trust deed executed before that date).

[17.241]
422 Tainted gifts

(1) This section applies if a person whose estate is sequestrated in Scotland has made a tainted gift (whether directly or indirectly).

(2) No decree may be granted under the Bankruptcy Act 1621 (c 18) or section [98 or 99 of the 2016] Act (gratuitous alienations and unfair preferences), or otherwise, in respect of the making of the gift at any time when—

(a) any property of the recipient of the tainted gift is subject to a restraint order under section 41, 120 or 190, . . .

[(aa) such property is detained under or by virtue of section 44A, 47J, 47K, 47M, 47P, 122A, 127J, 127K, 127M, 127P, 193A, 195J, 195K, 195M or 195P,]

(b) there is in force in respect of such property an order under section 50, . . . 128(3) [or 198][, or

(c) there is in force in respect of such property an order under section 67A, 131A or 215A.]

(3) Any decree made under the Bankruptcy Act 1621 (c 18) or section [98 or 99 of the 2016] Act, or otherwise, after an order mentioned in [subsection (2)(a), (b) or (c)] is discharged must take into account any realisation under Part 2, 3 or 4 of this Act of property held by the recipient of the tainted gift.

(4) A person makes a tainted gift for the purposes of this section if he makes a tainted gift within the meaning of Part 2, 3 or 4.

NOTES

Sub-s (2): words in first pair of square brackets substituted for original words "34 or 36 of the 1985" by the Bankruptcy (Scotland) Act 2016 (Consequential Provisions and Modifications) Order 2016, SI 2016/1034, art 7(1), (3), Sch 1, para 25(1), (10), as from 30 November 2016 (except in relation to (i) a sequestration as regards which the petition is presented, or the debtor application is made before that date; or (ii) a trust deed executed before that date); word omitted from para (a) repealed, para (aa) inserted, and para (c) and word ", or" immediately preceding it added, by the Policing and Crime Act 2009, s 112(1), (2), Sch 7, Pt 6, paras 66, 84(1), (2), Sch 8, Pt 4; in para (b), figure "52," (omitted) repealed and words in square brackets substituted for original words ", 198 or 200" by the Serious Crime Act 2007, ss 74(2)(a), 92, Sch 8, Pt 1, paras 1, 74, Sch 14, subject to transitional provisions and savings in SI 2008/755, arts 3, 4.

Sub-s (3): words in first pair of square brackets substituted for original words "34 or 36 of the 1985" by SI 2016/1034, art 7(1), (3), Sch 1, para 25(1), (10), as from 30 November 2016 (except in relation to (i) a sequestration as regards which the petition is presented, or the debtor application is made before that date; or (ii) a trust deed executed before that date); words in second pair of square brackets substituted by the Policing and Crime Act 2009, s 112(1), Sch 7, Pt 6, paras 66, 84(1), (3).

423–425 (*Outside the scope of this work.*)

Winding up in England and Wales and Scotland

[17.242]
426 Winding up under the 1986 Act

(1) In this section "company" means any company which may be wound up under the 1986 Act.

[(2) If an order for the winding up of a company is made or it passes a resolution for its voluntary winding up, the functions of the liquidator (or any provisional liquidator) are not exercisable in relation to the following property—

(a) property for the time being subject to a restraint order which was made under section 41, 120 or 190 before the relevant time;

(b) property for the time being detained under or by virtue of section 44A, 47J, 47K, 47M, 47P, 122A, 127J, 127K, 127M, 127P, 193A, 195J, 195K, 195M or 195P;

(c) property in respect of which an order under section 50, 128(3) or 198 is in force;

(d) property in respect of which an order under section 67A, 131A or 215A is in force.]

(3) Subsection (2)(a) applies to heritable property in Scotland only if the restraint order is recorded in the General Register of Sasines or registered in the Land Register of Scotland before the relevant time.

(4) If an order for the winding up of a company is made or it passes a resolution for its voluntary winding up the powers referred to in subsection (5) must not be exercised in the way mentioned in subsection (6) in relation to any property—

(a) which is held by the company, and

(b) in relation to which the functions of the liquidator are exercisable.

(5) These are the powers—

(a) the powers conferred on a court by sections 41 to [67B, the powers conferred on an appropriate officer by section 47C] and the powers of a receiver appointed under section 48 [or 50];

(b) the powers conferred on a court by sections 120 to 136 and Schedule 3[, the powers conferred on an appropriate officer by section 127C] and the powers of an administrator appointed under section 125 or 128(3);

(c) the powers conferred on a court by sections 190 to [215B, the powers conferred on an appropriate officer by section 195C] and the powers of a receiver appointed under section 196 [or 198].

(6) The powers must not be exercised—

(a) so as to inhibit the liquidator from exercising his functions for the purpose of distributing property to the company's creditors;

(b) so as to prevent the payment out of any property of expenses (including the remuneration of the liquidator or any provisional liquidator) properly incurred in the winding up in respect of the property.

(7) But nothing in the 1986 Act must be taken to restrict (or enable the restriction of) the exercise of the powers referred to in subsection (5).

(8) For the purposes of the application of Parts 4 and 5 of the 1986 Act (winding up) to a company which the Court of Session has jurisdiction to wind up, a person is not a creditor in so far as any sum due to him by the company is due in respect of a confiscation order made under section 6, 92 or 156.

(9) The relevant time is—

(a) if no order for the winding up of the company has been made, the time of the passing of the resolution for voluntary winding up;

(b) if such an order has been made, but before the presentation of the petition for the winding up of the company by the court such a resolution has been passed by the company, the time of the passing of the resolution;

(c) if such an order has been made, but paragraph (b) does not apply, the time of the making of the order.

(10) In a case where a winding up of a company commenced or is treated as having commenced before 29 December 1986, this section has effect with the following modifications—

(a) in subsections (1) and (7) for "the 1986 Act" substitute "the Companies Act 1985";

(b) in subsection (8) for "Parts 4 and 5 of the 1986 Act" substitute "Parts 20 and 21 of the Companies Act 1985".

NOTES

Sub-s (2): substituted by the Policing and Crime Act 2009, s 112(1), Sch 7, Pt 6, paras 66, 88(1), (2).

Sub-s (5): first words in square brackets in para (a) substituted, and words in square brackets in para (b) inserted, by the Policing and Crime Act 2009, s 112(1), Sch 7, Pt 6, paras 66, 88(1), (3)(a), (b); second words in square brackets in para (a), and words in second pair of square brackets in para (c), substituted for original words ", 50 or 52" and ", 198 or 200" respectively by the Serious Crime Act 2007, s 74(2)(a), Sch 8, Pt 1, paras 1, 78(1), (3), subject to transitional provisions and savings in SI 2008/755, arts 3, 4; words in first pair of square brackets in para (c) substituted by the Policing and Crime Act 2009, s 112(1), Sch 7, Pt 6, paras 66, 88(1), (3)(c).

[17.243]

427 Tainted gifts

(1) In this section "company" means any company which may be wound up under the 1986 Act.

(2) This section applies if—

(a) an order for the winding up of a company is made or it passes a resolution for its voluntary winding up, and

(b) it has made a tainted gift (whether directly or indirectly).

(3) No order may be made under section 238, 239 or 423 of the 1986 Act (avoidance of certain transactions) and no decree may be granted under section 242 or 243 of that Act (gratuitous alienations and unfair preferences), or otherwise, in respect of the making of the gift at any time when—

(a) any property of the recipient of the tainted gift is subject to a restraint order under section 41, 120 or 190, . . .

[(aa) such property is detained under or by virtue of section 44A, 47J, 47K, 47M, 47P, 122A, 127J, 127K, 127M, 127P, 193A, 195J, 195K, 195M or 195P,]

(b) there is in force in respect of such property an order under section 50, . . . 128(3) [or 198][, or

(c) there is in force in respect of such property an order under section 67A, 131A or 215A.]

(4) Any order made under section 238, 239 or 423 of the 1986 Act or decree granted under section 242 or 243 of that Act, or otherwise, after an order mentioned in [subsection (3)(a), (b) or (c)] is discharged must take into account any realisation under Part 2, 3 or 4 of this Act of property held by the recipient of the tainted gift.

(5) A person makes a tainted gift for the purposes of this section if he makes a tainted gift within the meaning of Part 2, 3 or 4.

(6) In a case where the winding up of a company commenced or is treated as having commenced before 29 December 1986 this section has effect with the substitution—

(a) for references to section 239 of the 1986 Act of references to section 615 of the Companies Act 1985 (c 6);

(b) for references to section 242 of the 1986 Act of references to section 615A of the Companies Act 1985;

(c) for references to section 243 of the 1986 Act of references to section 615B of the Companies Act 1985.

NOTES

Sub-s (3): word omitted from para (a) repealed, para (aa) inserted, and para (c) and word ", or" immediately preceding it added, by the Policing and Crime Act 2009, s 112(1), (2), Sch 7, Pt 6, paras 66, 89(1), (2), Sch 8, Pt 4; in para (b), figure "52," (omitted) repealed and words in square brackets substituted for original words ", 198 or 200" by the Serious Crime Act 2007, ss 74(2)(a), 92, Sch 8, Pt 1, paras 1, 79, Sch 14, subject to transitional provisions and savings in SI 2008/755, arts 3, 4.

Sub-s (4): words in square brackets substituted by the Policing and Crime Act 2009, s 112(1), Sch 7, Pt 6, paras 66, 89(1), (3).

428, 429 (*Outside the scope of this work.*)

Floating charges

[17.244]

430 Floating charges

(1) In this section "company" means a company which may be wound up under

(a) the 1986 Act, or

(b) the 1989 Order.

[(2) If a company holds property which is subject to a floating charge, and a receiver has been appointed by or on the application of the holder of the charge, the functions of the receiver are not exercisable in relation to the following property—

(a) property for the time being subject to a restraint order which was made under section 41, 120 or 190 before the relevant time;

(b) property for the time being detained under or by virtue of section 44A, 47J, 47K, 47M, 47P, 122A, 127J, 127K, 127M, 127P, 193A, 195J, 195K, 195M or 195P;

(c) property in respect of which an order under section 50, 128(3) or 198 is in force;

(d) property in respect of which an order under section 67A, 131A or 215A is in force.]

(3) Subsection (2)(a) applies to heritable property in Scotland only if the restraint order is recorded in the General Register of Sasines or registered in the Land Register of Scotland before the appointment of the receiver.

(4) If a company holds property which is subject to a floating charge, and a receiver has been appointed by or on the application of the holder of the charge, the powers referred to in subsection (5) must not be exercised in the way mentioned in subsection (6) in relation to any property—

(a) which is held by the company, and

(b) in relation to which the functions of the receiver are exercisable.

(5) These are the powers—

(a) the powers conferred on a court by sections 41 to [67B, the powers conferred on an appropriate officer by section 47C] and the powers of a receiver appointed under section 48 [or 50];

(b) the powers conferred on a court by sections 120 to 136 and Schedule 3[, the powers conferred on an appropriate officer by section 127C] and the powers of an administrator appointed under section 125 or 128(3);

(c) the powers conferred on a court by sections 190 to [215B, the powers conferred on an appropriate officer by section 195C] and the powers of a receiver appointed under section 196 [or 198].

(6) The powers must not be exercised—

(a) so as to inhibit the receiver from exercising his functions for the purpose of distributing property to the company's creditors;

(b) so as to prevent the payment out of any property of expenses (including the remuneration of the receiver) properly incurred in the exercise of his functions in respect of the property.

(7) But nothing in the 1986 Act or the 1989 Order must be taken to restrict (or enable the restriction of) the exercise of the powers referred to in subsection (5).

(8) In this section "floating charge" includes a floating charge within the meaning of section 462 of the Companies Act 1985 (c 6).

NOTES

Sub-s (2): substituted by the Policing and Crime Act 2009, s 112(1), Sch 7, Pt 6, paras 66, 92(1), (2).

Sub-s (5): first words in square brackets in para (a) substituted, and words in square brackets in para (b) inserted, by the Policing and Crime Act 2009, s 112(1), Sch 7, Pt 6, paras 66, 92(1), (3)(a), (b); second words in square brackets in para (a), and words in second pair of square brackets in para (c), substituted for original words ", 50 or 52" and ", 198 or 200" respectively by the Serious Crime Act 2007, s 74(2)(a), Sch 8, Pt 1, paras 1, 82(1), (3), subject to transitional provisions and savings in SI 2008/755, arts 3, 4; words in first pair of square brackets in para (c) substituted by the Policing and Crime Act 2009, s 112(1), Sch 7, Pt 6, paras 66, 92(1), (3).

Limited liability partnerships

[17.245]

431 Limited liability partnerships

(1) In sections 426, 427 and 430 "company" includes a limited liability partnership which may be wound up under the 1986 Act.

(2) A reference in those sections to a company passing a resolution for its voluntary winding up is to be construed in relation to a limited liability partnership as a reference to the partnership making a determination for its voluntary winding up.

Insolvency practitioners

[17.246]

432 Insolvency practitioners

(1) Subsections (2) and (3) apply if a person acting as an insolvency practitioner seizes or disposes of any property in relation to which his functions are not exercisable because—

(a) it is for the time being subject to a restraint order made under section 41, 120 or 190, or

(b) it is for the time being subject to [a property freezing order made under section 245A, an interim receiving order made under section 246, a prohibitory property order made under section 255A] or an interim administration order made under section 256,

and at the time of the seizure or disposal he believes on reasonable grounds that he is entitled (whether in pursuance of an order of a court or otherwise) to seize or dispose of the property.

(2) He is not liable to any person in respect of any loss or damage resulting from the seizure or disposal, except so far as the loss or damage is caused by his negligence.

(3) He has a lien on the property or the proceeds of its sale—

(a) for such of his expenses as were incurred in connection with the liquidation, bankruptcy, sequestration or other proceedings in relation to which he purported to make the seizure or disposal, and

(b) for so much of his remuneration as may reasonably be assigned to his acting in connection with those proceedings.

(4) Subsection (2) does not prejudice the generality of any provision of . . . the 1986 Act, the 1989 Order[, the 2016 Act] or any other Act or Order which confers protection from liability on him.

(5) Subsection (7) applies if—

(a) property is subject to a restraint order made under section 41, 120 or 190,

(b) a person acting as an insolvency practitioner incurs expenses in respect of property subject to the restraint order, and

(c) he does not know (and has no reasonable grounds to believe) that the property is subject to the restraint order.

(6) Subsection (7) also applies if—

(a) property is subject to a restraint order made under section 41, 120 or 190,

(b) a person acting as an insolvency practitioner incurs expenses which are not ones in respect of property subject to the restraint order, and

(c) the expenses are ones which (but for the effect of the restraint order) might have been met by taking possession of and realising property subject to it.

[(6A) Subsection (7) also applies if—

(a) property is detained under or by virtue of section 44A, 47J, 47K, 47M, 47P, 122A, 127J, 127K, 127M, 127P, 193A, 195J, 195K, 195M or 195P,

(b) a person acting as an insolvency practitioner incurs expenses which are not ones in respect of the detained property, and

(c) the expenses are ones which (but for the effect of the detention of the property) might have been met by taking possession of and realising the property.]

[(7) Whether or not the insolvency practitioner has seized or disposed of any property, the insolvency practitioner is entitled to payment of the expenses under—

(a) section 54(2), 55(3) or 67D(2) if the restraint order was made under section 41 or (as the case may be) the property was detained under or by virtue of section 44A, 47J, 47K, 47M or 47P,

(b) section 130(3), 131(3) or 131D(2) if the restraint order was made under section 120 or (as the case may be) the property was detained under or by virtue of section 122A, 127J, 127K, 127M or 127P, and

(c) section 202(2), 203(3) or 215D(2) if the restraint order was made under section 190 or (as the case may be) the property was detained under or by virtue of section 193A, 195J, 195K, 195M or 195P.]

(8) Subsection (10) applies if—

(a) property is subject to [a property freezing order made under section 245A, an interim receiving order made under section 246, a prohibitory property order made under section 255A] or an interim administration order made under section 256,

(b) a person acting as an insolvency practitioner incurs expenses in respect of property subject to the order, and

(c) he does not know (and has no reasonable grounds to believe) that the property is subject to the order.

(9) Subsection (10) also applies if—

(a) property is subject to [a property freezing order made under section 245A, an interim receiving order made under section 246, a prohibitory property order made under section 255A] or an interim administration order made under section 256,

(b) a person acting as an insolvency practitioner incurs expenses which are not ones in respect of property subject to the order, and

(c) the expenses are ones which (but for the effect of the order) might have been met by taking possession of and realising property subject to it.

(10) Whether or not he has seized or disposed of any property, he is entitled to payment of the expenses under section 280.

NOTES

Sub-ss (1), (8), (9): words in square brackets substituted by the Serious Organised Crime and Police Act 2005, s 109, Sch 6, paras 4, 23.

Sub-s (4): words "the 1985 Act," (omitted) repealed and words in square brackets inserted by the Bankruptcy (Scotland) Act 2016 (Consequential Provisions and Modifications) Order 2016, SI 2016/1034, art 7(1), (3), Sch 1, para 25(1), (11), as from 30 November 2016 (except in relation to (i) a sequestration as regards which the petition is presented, or the debtor application is made before that date; or (ii) a trust deed executed before that date).

Sub-s (6A): inserted by the Policing and Crime Act 2009, s 112(1), Sch 7, Pt 6, paras 66, 93(1), (2).

Sub-s (7): substituted by the Policing and Crime Act 2009, s 112(1), Sch 7, Pt 6, paras 66, 93(1), (3).

[17.247]
433 Meaning of insolvency practitioner

(1) This section applies for the purposes of section 432.

(2) A person acts as an insolvency practitioner if he so acts within the meaning given by section 388 of the 1986 Act or Article 3 of the 1989 Order; but this is subject to subsections (3) to (5).

(3) The expression "person acting as an insolvency practitioner" includes the official receiver acting as receiver or manager of the property concerned.

(4) In applying section 388 of the 1986 Act under subsection (2) above—

(a) the reference in section 388(2)(a) to a permanent or interim trustee in sequestration must be taken to include a reference to a trustee in sequestration;

(b) section 388(5) (which includes provision that nothing in the section applies to anything done by the official receiver or the Accountant in Bankruptcy) must be ignored.

(5) In applying Article 3 of the 1989 Order under subsection (2) above, paragraph (5) (which includes provision that nothing in the Article applies to anything done by the official receiver) must be ignored.

Interpretation

[17.248]
434 Interpretation

(1) The following paragraphs apply to references to Acts or Orders—

(a) the 1913 Act is the Bankruptcy (Scotland) Act 1913 (c 20);

(b) the 1914 Act is the Bankruptcy Act 1914 (c 59);

(c) the 1985 Act is the Bankruptcy (Scotland) Act 1985 (c 66);

(d) the 1986 Act is the Insolvency Act 1986 (c 45);

(e) the 1989 Order is the Insolvency (Northern Ireland) Order 1989 (SI 1989/2405 (NI 19));

[(f) the 2016 Act is the Bankruptcy (Scotland) Act 2016;]

(2) An award of sequestration is made on the date of sequestration within the meaning of section [22(7) of the 2016] Act.

(3) This section applies for the purposes of this Part.

NOTES

Sub-s (1): paras (a)–(c) repealed and para (f) inserted by the Bankruptcy (Scotland) Act 2016 (Consequential Provisions and Modifications) Order 2016, SI 2016/1034, art 7(1), (3), Sch 1, para 25(1), (12)(a), as from 30 November 2016 (except in relation to (i) a sequestration as regards which the petition is presented, or the debtor application is made before that date; or (ii) a trust deed executed before that date).

Sub-s (2): words in square brackets substituted for original words "12(4) of the 1985" by SI 2016/1034, art 7(1), (3), Sch 1, para 25(1), (12)(b), as from 30 November 2016 (except in relation to (i) a sequestration as regards which the petition is presented, or the debtor application is made before that date; or (ii) a trust deed executed before that date).

435–447 (*(Pts 10, 11) outside the scope of this work.*)

PART 12
MISCELLANEOUS AND GENERAL

448–455 (*Outside the scope of this work.*)

General

456, 457 (*Outside the scope of this work.*)

[17.249]
458 Commencement

(1) The preceding provisions of this Act (except the provisions specified in subsection (3) [or (4)]) come into force in accordance with provision made by the Secretary of State by order.

(2)–(4) (*Outside the scope of this work.*)

NOTES

Sub-s (1): words in square brackets inserted by the Northern Ireland Act 1998 (Devolution of Policing and Justice Functions) Order 2010, SI 2010/976, art 12, Sch 14, paras 47, 73(a).

Orders: at present 6 commencement orders have been made under this section. The order relevant to the provisions of this Act reproduced here is the Proceeds of Crime Act 2002 (Commencement No 5, Transitional Provisions, Savings and Amendment) Order 2003, SI 2003/333, as amended by SI 2003/531.

459–461 (*Outside the scope of this work.*)

[17.250]
462 Short title

This Act may be cited as the Proceeds of Crime Act 2002.

SCHEDULES 1–12

(Schs 1–12 outside the scope of this work.)

COMMUNICATIONS ACT 2003

(2003 c 21)

An Act to confer functions on the Office of Communications; to make provision about the regulation of the provision of electronic communications networks and services and of the use of the electro-magnetic spectrum; to make provision about the regulation of broadcasting and of the provision of television and radio services; to make provision about mergers involving newspaper and other media enterprises and, in that connection, to amend the Enterprise Act 2002; and for connected purposes

[17 July 2003]

1–31 *((Pt 1) outside the scope of this work.)*

PART 2
NETWORK, SERVICES AND THE RADIO SPECTRUM

CHAPTER 1 ELECTRONIC COMMUNICATIONS NETWORKS AND SERVICES

32–124N *(Outside the scope of this work.)*

Powers in relation to internet domain registries

124O *(Outside the scope of this work.)*

[17.251]
[124P Appointment of manager of internet domain registry

(1) This section applies where—
- (a) the Secretary of State has given a notification under section 124O to a qualifying internet domain registry specifying a failure,
- (b) the period allowed for making representations has expired, and
- (c) the Secretary of State is satisfied that the registry has not taken the steps that the Secretary of State considers appropriate for remedying the failure.

(2) The Secretary of State may by order appoint a manager in respect of the property and affairs of the internet domain registry for the purpose of securing that the registry takes the steps described in subsection (1)(c).

(3) The person appointed may be anyone whom the Secretary of State thinks appropriate.

(4) The appointment of the manager does not affect—
- (a) a right of a person to appoint a receiver of the registry's property, or
- (b) the rights of a receiver appointed by a person other than the Secretary of State.

(5) The Secretary of State must—
- (a) keep the order under review, and
- (b) if appropriate, discharge all or part of the order.

(6) The Secretary of State must discharge the order on the appointment of a person to act as administrative receiver, administrator, provisional liquidator or liquidator of the registry.

(7) The Secretary of State must discharge the order before the end of the period of 2 years beginning with the day on which it was made (but this does not prevent the Secretary of State from making a further order in the same or similar terms).

(8) When discharging an order under this section, the Secretary of State may make savings and transitional provision.

(9) The Secretary of State must send a copy of an order made under this section to the registry as soon as practicable after it is made.

(10) In subsection (4), "receiver" includes a manager (other than a manager appointed by the registry) and a person who is appointed as both receiver and manager.

(11) In subsection (6)—

"administrative receiver" means an administrative receiver within the meaning of section 251 of the Insolvency Act 1986 or Article 5(1) of the Insolvency (Northern Ireland) Order 1989 (SI 1989/2405 (NI 19));

"administrator" means a person appointed to manage the affairs, business and property of the registry under Schedule B1 to that Act or Schedule B1 to that Order.]

NOTES

Commencement: to be appointed.
Inserted, together with s 124Q, by the Digital Economy Act 2010, s 20(1), as from a day to be appointed.

[17.252]
[124Q Functions of manager etc

(1) An order under section 124P may make provision about the functions to be exercised by, and the powers of, the manager.

(2) The order may, in particular—

(a) provide for the manager to have such of the functions of the registry's directors as are specified in the order (including functions exercisable only by a particular director or class of directors), and

(b) provide for one or more of the registry's directors to be prevented from exercising any of those functions.

(3) The order may make provision about the remuneration of the manager, including in particular—

(a) provision for the amount of the remuneration to be determined by the Secretary of State, and

(b) provision for the remuneration to be payable from the property of the registry.

(4) In carrying out the functions conferred by the order, the manager acts as the registry's agent.

(5) The Secretary of State may apply to the court for directions in relation to any matter arising in connection with the functions or powers of the manager (and the costs of the application are to be paid by the registry).

(6) On an application under subsection (5) the court may give such directions or make such orders as it thinks fit.

(7) In this section "the court" means—

(a) in England and Wales, the High Court or [the county court],

(b) in Scotland, the Court of Session or the sheriff, and

(c) in Northern Ireland, the High Court.

(8) Where the registry is a limited liability partnership, this section applies as if references to a director of the registry were references to a member of the limited liability partnership.]

NOTES

Commencement: to be appointed.

Inserted as noted to s 124P at **[17.251]**.

Sub-s (7): words in square brackets in para (a) substituted by the Crime and Courts Act 2013, s 17(5), Sch 9, Pt 3, para 52(1)(b), (2).

124R–389 (*Ss 124R–197, ss 198–389 (Pts 3–5) outside the scope of this work.*)

PART 6
MISCELLANEOUS AND SUPPLEMENTAL

390–398 (*Outside the scope of this work.*)

Supplemental

399–410 (*Outside the scope of this work.*)

[17.253]

411 Short title, commencement and extent

(1) This Act may be cited as the Communications Act 2003.

(2)–(4) (*Outside the scope of this work.*)

(5) This Act extends to Northern Ireland.

(6) Subject to subsection (7), Her Majesty may by Order in Council extend the provisions of this Act, with such modifications as appear to Her Majesty in Council to be appropriate, to any of the Channel Islands or to the Isle of Man.

(7) Subsection (6) does not authorise the extension to any place of a provision of this Act so far as it gives effect to an amendment of an enactment that is not itself capable of being extended there in exercise of a power conferred on Her Majesty in Council.

(8) (*Outside the scope of this work.*)

NOTES

Orders: the Communications (Bailiwick of Guernsey) (No 2) Order 2004, SI 2004/715; the Broadcasting and Communications (Jersey) (No 2) Order 2004, SI 2004/716; the Broadcasting and Communications (Isle of Man) (No 2) Order 2004, SI 2004/718; the Broadcasting and Communications (Jersey) (No 3) Order 2004, SI 2004/1114; the Broadcasting and Communications (Isle of Man) (No 3) Order 2004, SI 2004/1115; the Communications (Bailiwick of Guernsey) (No 3) Order 2004, SI 2004/1116; the Communications (Jersey) (Amendment) Order 2005, SI 2005/855; the Communications (Bailiwick of Guernsey) (Amendment) Order 2005, SI 2005/856; the Wireless Telegraphy (Jersey) Order 2006, SI 2006/3324; the Wireless Telegraphy (Guernsey) Order 2006, SI 2006/3325; the Wireless Telegraphy (Isle of Man) Order 2007, SI 2007/278; the Communications (Bailiwick of Guernsey) (Amendment) Order 2012, SI 2012/2688; the Communications Act 2003 (Commencement No 5) Order 2017, SI 2017/1063.

SCHEDULES 1–19

(*Schs 1–19 outside the scope of this work.*)

CHILD TRUST FUNDS ACT 2004

(2004 c 6)

An Act to make provision about child trust funds and for connected purposes

[13 May 2004]

Introductory

[17.254]
1 Child trust funds

(1) This Act makes provision about child trust funds and related matters.
(2) In this Act "child trust fund" means an account which—
 (a) is held by a child who is or has been an eligible child (see section 2),
 (b) satisfies the requirements imposed by and by virtue of this Act (see section 3), and
 (c) has been opened in accordance with this Act (see sections 5 and 6).
(3) The matters dealt with by and under this Act are to be under the care and management of the Inland Revenue.

2, 3 (*Outside the scope of this work.*)

[17.255]
4 Inalienability

(1) Any assignment of, or agreement to assign, investments under a child trust fund, and any charge on or agreement to charge any such investments, is void.
(2) On the bankruptcy of a child by whom a child trust fund is held, the entitlement to investments under it does not pass to any trustee or other person acting on behalf of the child's creditors.
(3) "Assignment" includes assignation; and "assign" is to be construed accordingly.
(4) "Charge on or agreement to charge" includes a right in security over or an agreement to create a right in security over.
(5) "Bankruptcy", in relation to a child, includes the sequestration of the child's estate.

5–24 (*Outside the scope of this work.*)

Supplementary

25, 26 (*Outside the scope of this work.*)

[17.256]
27 Commencement

This Act (apart from sections 25 and 26, this section and sections 28 to 31) comes into force in accordance with provision made by order.

NOTES

Orders: the Child Trust Funds Act 2004 (Commencement No 1) Order 2004, SI 2004/2422; the Child Trust Funds Act 2004 (Commencement No 2) Order 2004, SI 2004/3369.

28, 29 (*Outside the scope of this work.*)

[17.257]
30 Extent

This Act extends to Northern Ireland (as well as to England and Wales and Scotland).

[17.258]
31 Short title

This Act may be cited as the Child Trust Funds Act 2004.

COMPANIES (AUDIT, INVESTIGATIONS AND COMMUNITY ENTERPRISE) ACT 2004

(2004 c 27)

ARRANGEMENT OF SECTIONS

PART 2
COMMUNITY INTEREST COMPANIES

Supervision by Regulator

47 Appointment of manager . . . [17.259]
48 Property . . . [17.260]
49 Transfer of shares etc . . . [17.261]
50 Petition for winding up . . . [17.262]

PART 3
SUPPLEMENTARY

65 Commencement etc. . . . [17.263]
66 Extent . . . [17.264]
67 Short title . . . [17.265]

An Act to amend the law relating to company auditors and accounts, to the provision that may be made in respect of certain liabilities incurred by a company's officers, and to company investigations; to make provision for community interest companies; and for connected purposes

[28 October 2004]

1–25 (*(Pt 1) in so far as unrepealed, outside the scope of this work.*)

PART 2
COMMUNITY INTEREST COMPANIES

26–40A (*Outside the scope of this work.*)

Supervision by Regulator

41–46 (*Outside the scope of this work.*)

[17.259]
47 Appointment of manager
(1) The Regulator may by order appoint a manager in respect of the property and affairs of a community interest company.
(2) The person appointed may be anyone whom the Regulator thinks appropriate, other than a member of the Regulator's staff.
(3) An order under subsection (1) may make provision as to the functions to be exercised by, and the powers of, the manager.
(4) The order may in particular provide—
(a) for the manager to have such of the functions of the company's directors as are specified in the order, and
(b) for the company's directors to be prevented from exercising any of those functions.
(5) In carrying out his functions the manager acts as the company's agent; and a person dealing with the manager in good faith and for value need not inquire whether the manager is acting within his powers.
(6) The appointment of the manager does not affect—
(a) any right of any person to appoint a receiver or manager of the company's property (including any right under section 51 of the Insolvency Act 1986 (c 45) [(power to appoint receiver under law of Scotland)]), or
(b) the rights of a receiver or manager appointed by a person other than the Regulator.
(7) The manager's functions are to be discharged by him under the supervision of the Regulator; and the Regulator must from time to time review the order by which the manager is appointed and, if it is appropriate to do so, discharge it in whole or in part.
(8) In particular, the Regulator must discharge the order on the appointment of a person to act as administrative receiver, administrator, provisional liquidator or liquidator of the company.
(9) The Regulator may apply to the court for directions in relation to any matter arising in connection with the manager's functions or powers.
(10) On an application under subsection (9) the court may give such directions or make such orders as it thinks fit.
(11) The costs of any application under subsection (9) are to be paid by the company.
(12) Regulations may authorise the Regulator—
(a) to require a manager to make reports,
(b) to require a manager to give security (or, in Scotland, to find caution) for the due exercise of the manager's functions, and
(c) to remove a manager in circumstances prescribed by the regulations.
(13) Regulations may—
(a) provide for a manager's remuneration to be payable from the property of the company, and
(b) authorise the Regulator to determine the amount of a manager's remuneration and to disallow any amount of remuneration in circumstances prescribed by the regulations.
(14) The company may appeal to the Appeal Officer against an order under this section.

NOTES
Sub-s (6): words in square brackets inserted by the Companies Act 2006 (Commencement No 2, Consequential Amendments, Transitional Provisions and Savings) Order 2007, SI 2007/1093, art 6(2), (3)(a), Sch 4, Pt 1, para 15.
Regulations: the Community Interest Company Regulations 2005, SI 2005/1788 at **[18.137]**.

[17.260]
48 Property
(1) The Regulator may by order—
(a) vest in the Official Property Holder any property held by or in trust for a community interest company, or
(b) require persons in whom such property is vested to transfer it to the Official Property Holder.
(2) The Regulator—

(a) may order a person who holds property on behalf of a community interest company, or on behalf of a trustee of a community interest company, not to part with the property without the Regulator's consent, and
(b) may order any debtor of a community interest company not to make any payment in respect of the debtor's liability to the company without the Regulator's consent.

(3) The Regulator may by order restrict—
(a) the transactions which may be entered into by a community interest company, or
(b) the nature or amount of the payments that a community interest company may make,

and the order may in particular provide that transactions may not be entered into or payments made without the Regulator's consent.

(4) The vesting or transfer of property under subsection (1) does not constitute a breach of a covenant or condition against alienation, and no right listed in subsection (5) operates or becomes exercisable as a result of the vesting or transfer.

(5) The rights are—
(a) a right of reverter (or, in Scotland, the right of the fiar on the termination of a liferent),
(b) a right of pre-emption,
(c) a right of forfeiture,
(d) a right of re-entry,
(e) a right of irritancy,
(f) an option, and
(g) any right similar to those listed in paragraphs (a) to (f).

(6) The Regulator must from time to time review any order under this section and, if it is appropriate to do so, discharge the order in whole or in part.

(7) On discharging an order under subsection (1) the Regulator may make any order as to the vesting or transfer of the property, and give any directions, which he considers appropriate.

(8) If a person fails to comply with an order under subsection (1)(b), the Regulator may certify that fact in writing to the court.

(9) If, after hearing—
(a) any witnesses who may be produced against or on behalf of the alleged offender, and
(b) any statement which may be offered in defence,

the court is satisfied that the offender failed without reasonable excuse to comply with the order, it may deal with him as if he had been guilty of contempt of the court.

(10) A person who contravenes an order under subsection (2) or (3) commits an offence, but a prosecution may be instituted[—
(a) in England and Wales, only with the consent of the Regulator or the Director of Public Prosecutions;
(b) in Northern Ireland, only with the consent of the Regulator or the Director of Public Prosecutions for Northern Ireland].

(11) A person guilty of an offence under subsection (10) is liable on summary conviction to a fine not exceeding level 5 on the standard scale.

(12) Subsections (8) to (10) do not prevent the bringing of civil proceedings in respect of a contravention of an order under subsection (1)(b), (2) or (3).

(13) The company and any person to whom the order is directed may appeal to the Appeal Officer against an order under subsection (1) or (2).

(14) The company may appeal to the Appeal Officer against an order under subsection (3).

NOTES

Sub-s (10): words in square brackets substituted by the Companies Act 2006 (Commencement No 2, Consequential Amendments, Transitional Provisions and Savings) Order 2007, SI 2007/1093, art 6(2), (3)(a), Sch 4, Pt 1, para 16.

[17.261]

49 Transfer of shares etc

(1) If a community interest company has a share capital, the Regulator may by order transfer specified shares in the company to specified persons.

(2) If a community interest company is a company limited by guarantee, the Regulator may by order—
(a) extinguish the interests in the company of specified members of the company (otherwise than as shareholders), and
(b) appoint a new member in place of each member whose interest has been extinguished.

(3) An order under subsection (1) may not transfer any shares in respect of which—
(a) a dividend may be paid, or
(b) a distribution of the company's assets may be made if the company is wound up.

(4) An order under this section in relation to a company—
(a) may only transfer shares to, and appoint as new members, persons who have consented to the transfer or appointment, and
(b) may be made irrespective of any provision made by the [articles] of the company or a resolution of the company in general meeting.

(5) The company and any person from whom shares are transferred by the order may appeal to the Appeal Officer against an order under subsection (1).

(6) The company and any person whose interest is extinguished by the order may appeal to the Appeal Officer against an order under subsection (2).

(7) "Specified", in relation to an order, means specified in the order.

NOTES

Sub-s (4): word in square brackets substituted by the Companies Act 2006 (Consequential Amendments, Transitional Provisions and Savings) Order 2009, SI 2009/1941, art 2(1), Sch 1, para 233.

[17.262]

50 Petition for winding up

(1) The Regulator may present a petition for a community interest company to be wound up if the court is of the opinion that it is just and equitable that the company should be wound up.

(2) Subsection (1) does not apply if the company is already being wound up by the court.

(3) (*Amends the Insolvency Act 1986, 124 at* **[1.122]**.)

51–63 (*Outside the scope of this work.*)

PART 3
SUPPLEMENTARY

64 (*Outside the scope of this work.*)

[17.263]

65 Commencement etc

(1) This Act (apart from this section and sections 66 and 67) does not come into force until such day as the Secretary of State may by order made by statutory instrument appoint; and different days may be appointed for different provisions or otherwise for different purposes.

(2) The Secretary of State may by order made by statutory instrument make any transitional provisions or savings which appear appropriate in connection with the commencement of any provision of this Act.

NOTES

Orders: the Companies (Audit, Investigations and Community Enterprise) Act 2004 (Commencement) and Companies Act 1989 (Commencement No 18) Order 2004, SI 2004/3322.

[17.264]

66 Extent

(1) Any amendment made by this Act has the same extent as the provision to which it relates.

(2) Sections 14, 15(1)(b), (3) and (7) and [16 to [18A]] [and Part 2] extend to Northern Ireland.

(3) Subject to that, this Act (apart from section 65, this section and section 67) does not extend to Northern Ireland.

NOTES

Sub-s (2): words in first (outer) pair of square brackets substituted by the Companies Act 2006, s 1276(5); figure in second (inner) pair of square brackets substituted by the Small Business, Enterprise and Employment Act 2015, s 38(3); words in third pair of square brackets inserted by the Companies Act 2006 (Commencement No 2, Consequential Amendments, Transitional Provisions and Savings) Order 2007, SI 2007/1093, art 6(2), (3)(a), Sch 4, Pt 1, para 25.

[17.265]

67 Short title

This Act may be cited as the Companies (Audit, Investigations and Community Enterprise) Act 2004.

SCHEDULES 1–8

(*Schs 1–8 outside the scope of this work.*)

PENSIONS ACT 2004

(2004 c 35)

ARRANGEMENT OF SECTIONS

PART 1
THE PENSIONS REGULATOR

Contribution notices where avoidance of employer debt

38 Contribution notices where avoidance of employer debt . . . . . [17.266]
38A Section 38 contribution notice: meaning of "material detriment test" . . . . . [17.267]
38B Section 38 contribution notice issued by reference to material detriment test: defence . . . . . [17.268]
39 The sum specified in a section 38 contribution notice . . . . . [17.269]
39A Section 38 contribution notice: transfer of members of the scheme . . . . . [17.270]
39B Section 39A: supplemental . . . . . [17.271]
40 Content and effect of a section 38 contribution notice . . . . . [17.272]
41 Section 38 contribution notice: relationship with employer debt . . . . . [17.273]

42 Section 38 contribution notice: clearance statements . . . . . [17.274]

Financial support directions

43 Financial support directions . . . . . [17.275]
43A Financial support directions: transfer of members of the scheme . . . . . [17.276]
43B Section 43A: supplemental . . . . . [17.277]
44 Meaning of "service company" and "insufficiently resourced" . . . . . [17.278]
45 Meaning of "financial support" . . . . . [17.279]
46 Financial support directions: clearance statements . . . . . [17.280]
47 Contribution notices where non-compliance with financial support direction . . . . . [17.281]
48 The sum specified in a section 47 contribution notice . . . . . [17.282]
49 Content and effect of a section 47 contribution notice . . . . . [17.283]
50 Section 47 contribution notice: relationship with employer debt . . . . . [17.284]
51 Sections 43 to 50: interpretation . . . . . [17.285]

Transactions at an undervalue

52 Restoration orders where transactions at an undervalue . . . . . [17.286]
53 Restoration orders: supplementary . . . . . [17.287]
54 Content and effect of a restoration order . . . . . [17.288]
55 Contribution notice where failure to comply with restoration order . . . . . [17.289]
56 Content and effect of a section 55 contribution notice . . . . . [17.290]

Sections 38 to 56: partnerships and limited liability partnerships

57 Sections 38 to 56: partnerships and limited liability partnerships . . . . . [17.291]

Applications under the Insolvency Act 1986

58 Regulator's right to apply under section 423 of Insolvency Act 1986 . . . . . [17.292]

PART 2
THE BOARD OF THE PENSION PROTECTION FUND

CHAPTER 2
INFORMATION RELATING TO EMPLOYER'S INSOLVENCY ETC

Insolvency events

120 Duty to notify insolvency events in respect of employers . . . . . [17.293]
121 Insolvency event, insolvency date and insolvency practitioner . . . . . [17.294]

Status of scheme

122 Insolvency practitioner's duty to issue notices confirming status of scheme . . . . . [17.295]
123 Approval of notices issued under section 122 . . . . . [17.296]

Board's duties

124 Board's duty where there is a failure to comply with section 122 . . . . . [17.297]
125 Binding notices confirming status of scheme . . . . . [17.298]

CHAPTER 3
PENSION PROTECTION

Circumstances in which Board assumes responsibility for eligible schemes

127 Duty to assume responsibility for schemes following insolvency event . . . . . [17.299]
128 Duty to assume responsibility for schemes following application or notification . . . . . [17.300]
129 Applications and notifications for the purposes of section 128 . . . . . [17.301]
130 Board's duty where application or notification received under section 129 . . . . . [17.302]
131 Protected liabilities . . . . . [17.303]

Restrictions on schemes during the assessment period

132 Assessment periods . . . . . [17.304]
133 Admission of new members, payment of contributions etc . . . . . [17.305]
134 Directions . . . . . [17.306]
135 Restrictions on winding up, discharge of liabilities etc . . . . . [17.307]
136 Power to validate contraventions of section 135 . . . . . [17.308]
137 Board to act as creditor of the employer . . . . . [17.309]
138 Payment of scheme benefits . . . . . [17.310]
139 Loans to pay scheme benefits . . . . . [17.311]

Valuation of assets and liabilities

143 Board's obligation to obtain valuation of assets and protected liabilities . . . . . [17.312]
143A Determinations under section 143 . . . . . [17.313]
144 Approval of valuation . . . . . [17.314]

145 Binding valuations . . . [17.315]

CHAPTER 5
GATHERING INFORMATION

191 Notices requiring provision of information. . . . [17.316]
192 Entry of premises . . . [17.317]
193 Penalties relating to sections 191 and 192 . . . [17.318]
194 Warrants . . . [17.319]

Provision of false or misleading information

195 Offence of providing false or misleading information to the Board. . . . [17.320]

PART 9
MISCELLANEOUS AND SUPPLEMENTARY

Miscellaneous and supplementary

322 Commencement . . . [17.321]
323 Extent. . . . [17.322]
325 Short title. . . . [17.323]

An Act to make provision relating to pensions and financial planning for retirement and provision relating to entitlement to bereavement payments, and for connected purposes

[18 November 2004]

NOTES

Modification: this Act is applied, with modifications, in so far as it relates to bank insolvency or administration under the Banking Act 2009, Pts 2, 3, by the Banking Act 2009 (Parts 2 and 3 Consequential Amendments) Order 2009, SI 2009/317, art 3, Schedule at **[7.86]**, **[7.92]**.

PART 1
THE PENSIONS REGULATOR

1–37 (*Outside the scope of this work.*)

Contribution notices where avoidance of employer debt

[17.266]

38 Contribution notices where avoidance of employer debt

(1) This section applies in relation to an occupational pension scheme other than—

(a) a money purchase scheme, or

(b) a prescribed scheme or a scheme of a prescribed description.

(2) The Regulator may issue a notice to a person stating that the person is under a liability to pay the sum specified in the notice (a "contribution notice")—

(a) to the trustees or managers of the scheme, or

(b) where the Board of the Pension Protection Fund has assumed responsibility for the scheme in accordance with Chapter 3 of Part 2 (pension protection), to the Board.

(3) The Regulator may issue a contribution notice to a person only if—

(a) the Regulator is of the opinion that the person was a party to an act or a deliberate failure to act which falls within subsection (5),

(b) the person was at any time in the relevant period—

(i) the employer in relation to the scheme, or

(ii) a person connected with, or an associate of, the employer,

(c) the Regulator is of the opinion that the person, in being a party to the act or failure, was not acting in accordance with his functions as an insolvency practitioner in relation to another person, and

[(d) the Regulator is of the opinion that it is reasonable to impose liability on the person to pay the sum specified in the notice, having regard to—

(i) the extent to which, in all the circumstances of the case, it was reasonable for the person to act, or fail to act, in the way that the person did, and

(ii) such other matters as the Regulator considers relevant, including (where relevant) the matters falling within subsection (7).]

(4) But the Regulator may not issue a contribution notice, in such circumstances as may be prescribed, to a person of a prescribed description.

(5) An act or a failure to act falls within this subsection if—

(a) the Regulator is of the opinion that [the material detriment test is met in relation to the act or failure (see section 38A) or that] the main purpose or one of the main purposes of the act or failure was—

(i) to prevent the recovery of the whole or any part of a debt which was, or might become, due from the employer in relation to the scheme under section 75 of the Pensions Act 1995 (c 26) (deficiencies in the scheme assets), or

(ii) . . . to prevent such a debt becoming due, to compromise or otherwise settle such a debt, or to reduce the amount of such a debt which would otherwise become due,

(b) it is an act which occurred, or a failure to act which first occurred—

(i) on or after 27th April 2004, and

(ii) before any assumption of responsibility for the scheme by the Board in accordance with Chapter 3 of Part 2, and

(c) it is either—

(i) an act which occurred during the period of six years ending with the [giving of a warning notice in respect of] the contribution notice in question, or

(ii) a failure which first occurred during, or continued for the whole or part of, that period.

(6) For the purposes of subsection (3)—

(a) the parties to an act or a deliberate failure include those persons who knowingly assist in the act or failure, and

(b) "the relevant period" means the period which—

(i) begins with the time when the act falling within subsection (5) occurs or the failure to act falling within that subsection first occurs, and

(ii) ends with the [giving of a warning notice in respect of] the contribution notice in question.

(7) [The matters within this subsection are—]

(a) the degree of involvement of the person in the act or failure to act which falls within subsection (5),

(b) the relationship which the person has or has had with the employer (including, where the employer is a company within the meaning of subsection (11) of section 435 of the Insolvency Act 1986 (c 45), whether the person has or has had control of the employer within the meaning of subsection (10) of that section),

(c) any connection or involvement which the person has or has had with the scheme,

(d) if the act or failure to act was a notifiable event for the purposes of section 69 (duty to notify the Regulator of certain events), any failure by the person to comply with any obligation imposed on the person by subsection (1) of that section to give the Regulator notice of the event,

(e) all the purposes of the act or failure to act (including whether a purpose of the act or failure was to prevent or limit loss of employment),

[(ea) the value of any benefits which directly or indirectly the person receives, or is entitled to receive, from the employer or under the scheme;

(eb) the likelihood of relevant creditors being paid and the extent to which they are likely to be paid;]

(f) the financial circumstances of the person, and

(g) such other matters as may be prescribed.

[(7A) In subsection (7)(eb) "relevant creditors" means—

(a) creditors of the employer, and

(b) creditors of any other person who has incurred a liability or other obligation (including one that is contingent or otherwise might fall due) to make a payment, or transfer an asset, to the scheme.]

(8) For the purposes of this section references to a debt due under section 75 of the Pensions Act 1995 (c 26) include a contingent debt under that section.

(9) Accordingly, in the case of such a contingent debt, the reference in subsection (5)(a)(ii) to preventing a debt becoming due is to be read as including a reference to preventing the occurrence of any of the events specified in section 75(4C)(a) or (b) of that Act upon which the debt is contingent.

(10) For the purposes of this section—

(a) section 249 of the Insolvency Act 1986 (connected persons) applies as it applies for the purposes of any provision of the first Group of Parts of that Act,

(b) section 435 of that Act (associated persons) applies as it applies for the purposes of that Act, and

(c) section [229 of the Bankruptcy (Scotland) Act 2016] (associated persons) applies as it applies for the purposes of that Act.

(11) For the purposes of this section "insolvency practitioner", in relation to a person, means—

(a) a person acting as an insolvency practitioner, in relation to that person, in accordance with section 388 of the Insolvency Act 1986, or

(b) an insolvency practitioner within the meaning of section 121(9)(b) (persons of a prescribed description).

[(12) Subsection (13) applies if the Regulator is of the opinion that—

(a) a person was a party to a series of acts or failures to act,

(b) each of the acts or failures in the series falls within subsection (5)(b) and (c), and

(c) the material detriment test is met in relation to the series, or the main purpose or one of the main purposes of the series was as mentioned in subsection (5)(a)(i) or (ii).

(13) The series of acts or failures to act is to be regarded as an act or failure to act falling within subsection (5) (and, accordingly, the reference in subsection (6)(b)(i) to the act or failure to act falling with subsection (5) is to the first of the acts or failures to act in the series).]

[(14) In this section "a warning notice" means a notice given as mentioned in section 96(2)(a).]

NOTES

Commencement: 10 February 2005 (sub-s (1)(b) (for the purpose of making regulations, orders or rules)); 6 April 2005 (sub-ss (1)(a), (1)(b) (for remaining purposes), (2), (3), (5), (6), (7)(a)–(f), (8)–(11)); to be appointed (sub-ss (4), (7)(g)).

Sub-s (1): substituted as follows by the Pension Schemes Act 2015, s 46, Sch 2, paras 23, 27, as from a day to be appointed:

"(1) This section applies in relation to a pension scheme that is—

(a) an occupational defined benefits scheme,

(b) an occupational shared risk scheme, or

(c) an occupational defined contributions scheme,

unless subsection (1A) provides for the scheme to be exempt.

(1A) A scheme is exempt from this section if it is—

(a) a scheme under benefits that may be provided are money purchase benefits,

(b) a scheme under which all the benefits that may be provided are collective benefits,
(c) a scheme under which all the benefits that may be provided are money purchase benefits or collective benefits, or
(d) a prescribed scheme or a scheme of a prescribed description.
(1B) Where—
(a) some of the benefits that may be provided under a scheme are collective benefits and some are not, and
(b) the scheme does not fall within paragraph (c) or (d) of subsection (1A),
the scheme is to be treated for the purposes of this section and sections 38A to 42 as two separate schemes, one relating to the collective benefits and the other relating to the other benefits.".

Sub-s (3): para (d) substituted by the Pensions Act 2008, s 126, Sch 9, paras 1, 7(1), (2), 15(1), with effect in relation to any act occurring, or any failure to act first occurring, on or after 14 April 2008, and originally read as follows:

"(d) the Regulator is of the opinion that it is reasonable to impose liability on the person to pay the sum specified in the notice.".

Sub-s (5): words in square brackets in para (a) inserted and words "otherwise than in good faith," (omitted from para (a)(ii)) repealed by the Pensions Act 2008, ss 126, 148, Sch 9, paras 1, 2(1), 6, 15(1), Sch 11, Pt 6, with effect in relation to any act occurring, or any failure to act first occurring, on or after 14 April 2008; words in square brackets in para (c) substituted by the Pensions Act 2011, s 26(1), (2).

Sub-s (6): words in square brackets in para (b) substituted by the Pensions Act 2011, s 26(1), (2).

Sub-s (7): words in square brackets substituted for the following original words:

"The Regulator, when deciding for the purposes of subsection (3)(d) whether it is reasonable to impose liability on a particular person to pay the sum specified in the notice, must have regard to such matters as the Regulator considers relevant including, where relevant, the following matters—";

and paras (ea), (eb) inserted by the Pensions Act 2008, s 126, Sch 9, paras 1, 7(1), (3), 15(1), with effect in relation to any act occurring, or any failure to act first occurring, on or after 14 April 2008.

Sub-s (7A): inserted by the Pensions Act 2008, s 126, Sch 9, paras 1, 7(1), (4), 15(1), with effect in relation to any act occurring, or any failure to act first occurring, on or after 14 April 2008.

Sub-s (10): words in square brackets in para (c) substituted for original words "74 of the Bankruptcy (Scotland) Act 1985 (c 66)" by the Bankruptcy (Scotland) Act 2016 (Consequential Provisions and Modifications) Order 2016, SI 2016/1034, art 7(1), (3), Sch 1, para 26(1), (2), as from 30 November 2016 (except in relation to (i) a sequestration as regards which the petition is presented, or the debtor application is made before that date; or (ii) a trust deed executed before that date).

Sub-ss (12), (13): inserted by the Pensions Act 2008, s 126, Sch 9, paras 1, 8(1), 15(2), with effect for the purposes of the material detriment test, where at least one of the acts or failures to act occurs or first occurs on or after 14 April 2008, and for all other purposes, where at least one of the acts or failures to act occurs or first occurs on or after 26 November 2008.

Sub-s (14): added by the Pensions Act 2011, s 26(1), (3).

Modification: this section and ss 39–56 are applied, with modifications, in relation to an occupational pension scheme which is a multi-employer scheme by the Pensions Regulator (Financial Support Directions etc) Regulations 2005, SI 2005/2188, reg 16.

Regulations: the Pensions Regulator (Contribution Notices and Restoration Orders) Regulations 2005, SI 2005/931; the Occupational Pension Schemes and Pension Protection Fund (Amendment) Regulations 2005, SI 2005/993; the Occupational Pension Schemes (Republic of Ireland Schemes Exemption (Revocation) and Tax Exempt Schemes (Miscellaneous Amendments)) Regulations 2006, SI 2006/467; the Occupational Pension Schemes (Scottish Parliamentary Pensions Act 2009) Regulations 2009, SI 2009/1906.

[17.267]

[38A Section 38 contribution notice: meaning of "material detriment test"

(1) For the purposes of section 38 the material detriment test is met in relation to an act or failure if the Regulator is of the opinion that the act or failure has detrimentally affected in a material way the likelihood of accrued scheme benefits being received (whether the benefits are to be received as benefits under the scheme or otherwise).

(2) In this section any reference to accrued scheme benefits being received is a reference to benefits the rights to which have accrued by the relevant time being received by, or in respect of, the persons who were members of the scheme before that time.

(3) In this section "the relevant time" means—
(a) in the case of an act, the time of the act, or
(b) in the case of a failure—
(i) the time when the failure occurred, or
(ii) where the failure continued for a period of time, the time which the Regulator determines and which falls within that period;
and, in the case of acts or failures to act forming part of a series, any reference in this subsection to an act or failure is a reference to the last of the acts or failures in that series.

(4) In deciding for the purposes of section 38 whether the material detriment test is met in relation to an act or failure, the Regulator must have regard to such matters as it considers relevant, including (where relevant)—
(a) the value of the assets or liabilities of the scheme or of any relevant transferee scheme,
(b) the effect of the act or failure on the value of those assets or liabilities,
(c) the scheme obligations of any person,
(d) the effect of the act or failure on any of those obligations (including whether the act or failure causes the country or territory in which any of those obligations would fall to be enforced to be different),
(e) the extent to which any person is likely to be able to discharge any scheme obligation in any circumstances (including in the event of insolvency or bankruptcy),
(f) the extent to which the act or failure has affected, or might affect, the extent to which any person is likely to be able to do as mentioned in paragraph (e), and

(g) such other matters as may be prescribed.

(5) In subsection (4) "scheme obligation" means a liability or other obligation (including one that is contingent or otherwise might fall due) to make a payment, or transfer an asset, to—

(a) the scheme, or

(b) any relevant transferee scheme in respect of any persons who were members of the scheme before the relevant time.

(6) In this section—

(a) "relevant transferee scheme" means any work-based pension scheme to which any accrued rights to benefits under the scheme are transferred;

(b) any reference to the assets or liabilities of any relevant transferee scheme is a reference to those assets or liabilities so far as relating to persons who were members of the scheme before the relevant time.

(7) For the purposes of subsection (6)(a) the reference to the transfer of accrued rights of members of a pension scheme to another pension scheme includes a reference to the extinguishing of those accrued rights in consequence of the obligation to make a payment, or transfer an asset, to that other scheme.

(8) In this section—

(a) "work-based pension scheme" has the meaning given by section 5(3);

(b) any reference to rights which have accrued is to be read in accordance with section 67A(6) and (7) of the Pensions Act 1995 (reading any reference in those subsections to a subsisting right as a reference to a right which has accrued).

(9) In deciding for the purposes of this section whether an act or failure has detrimentally affected in a material way the likelihood of accrued scheme benefits being received, the following provisions of this Act are to be disregarded—

(a) Chapter 3 of Part 2 (the Board of the Pension Protection Fund: pension protection), and

(b) section 286 (the financial assistance scheme for members of certain pension schemes).

(10) Regulations may amend any provision of subsections (4) to (8).]

NOTES

Inserted, together with s 38B, by the Pensions Act 2008, s 126, Sch 9, paras 1, 2(2), 15(1).

[17.268]

[38B Section 38 contribution notice issued by reference to material detriment test: defence

(1) This section applies where—

(a) a warning notice is given to any person ("P") in respect of a contribution notice under section 38, and

(b) the contribution notice under consideration would be issued wholly or partly by reference to the Regulator's opinion that the material detriment test is met in relation to an act or deliberate failure to act to which P was a party.

(2) If the Regulator is satisfied that P has shown that—

(a) conditions A and C are met, and

(b) where applicable, condition B is met,

the Regulator must not issue the contribution notice by reference to its being of the opinion mentioned in subsection (1)(b).

(3) Condition A is that, before becoming a party to the act or failure, P gave due consideration to the extent to which the act or failure might detrimentally affect in a material way the likelihood of accrued scheme benefits being received.

(4) Condition B is that, in any case where as a result of that consideration P considered that the act or failure might have such an effect, P took all reasonable steps to eliminate or minimise the potential detrimental effects that the act or failure might have on the likelihood of accrued scheme benefits being received.

(5) Condition C is that, having regard to all relevant circumstances prevailing at the relevant time, it was reasonable for P to conclude that the act or failure would not detrimentally affect in a material way the likelihood of accrued scheme benefits being received.

(6) P is to be regarded as giving the consideration mentioned in condition A only if P has made the enquiries, and done the other acts, that a reasonably diligent person would have made or done in the circumstances.

(7) For the purposes of condition C—

(a) "the relevant time" means the time at which the act occurred or the failure to act first occurred;

(b) the reference to the circumstances mentioned in that condition is a reference to those circumstances of which P was aware, or ought reasonably to have been aware, at that time (including acts or failures to act which have occurred before that time and P's expectation at that time of other acts or failures to act occurring).

(8) In the case of acts or failures to act forming part of a series, P is to be regarded as having shown the matters mentioned in subsection (2) if P shows in the case of each of the acts or failures in the series that—

(a) conditions A and C are met, and (where applicable) condition B is met, in relation to the act or failure, or

(b) the act or failure was one of a number of acts or failures (a "group" of acts or failures) selected by P in relation to which the following matters are shown.

(9) The matters to be shown are that—

(a) before becoming a party to the first of the acts or failures in the group, condition A is met in relation to the effect of the acts or failures in the group taken together,

(b) condition B is (where applicable) met in relation to that effect, and

(c) condition C is then met in relation to each of the acts or failures in the group (determined at the time at which each act or failure concerned occurred or first occurred).

(10) If at any time P considers that condition C will not be met in relation to any particular act or failure in the group—

(a) the previous acts or failures in the group are to be regarded as a separate group for the purposes of subsection (8), and

(b) P may then select another group consisting of the particular act or failure concerned, and any subsequent act or failure, in relation to which P shows the matters mentioned in subsection (9).

Nothing in paragraph (b) is to be read as preventing P from showing the matters mentioned in subsection (8)(a).

(11) If—

(a) P is unable to show in the case of each of the acts or failures in the series that the matters set out in subsection (8)(a) or (b) are met, but

(b) does show in the case of some of them that those matters are met,

the acts or failures within paragraph (b) are not to count for the purposes of section 38A as acts or failures to act in the series.

(12) In this section—

(a) "a warning notice" means a notice given as mentioned in section 96(2)(a);

(b) any reference to an act or failure to which a person is a party has the same meaning as in section 38(6)(a);

(c) any reference to the accrued scheme benefits being received has the same meaning as in section 38A;

and subsection (9) of section 38A applies for the purposes of conditions A to C as it applies for the purposes of that section.

(13) Regulations may amend this section.]

NOTES

Inserted as noted to s 38A at **[17.267]**.

[17.269]

39 The sum specified in a section 38 contribution notice

(1) The sum specified by the Regulator in a contribution notice under section 38 may be either the whole or a specified part of the shortfall sum in relation to the scheme.

(2) Subject to subsection (3), the shortfall sum in relation to a scheme is—

(a) in a case where, at the relevant time, a debt was due from the employer to the trustees or managers of the scheme under section 75 of the Pensions Act 1995 (c 26) ("the 1995 Act") (deficiencies in the scheme assets), the amount which the Regulator estimates to be the amount of that debt at that time, and

(b) in a case where, at the relevant time, no such debt was due, the amount which the Regulator estimates to be the amount of the debt under section 75 of the 1995 Act which would become due if—

(i) subsection (2) of that section applied, and

(ii) the time designated by the trustees or managers of the scheme for the purposes of that subsection were the relevant time.

(3) Where the Regulator is satisfied that the act or failure to act falling within section 38(5) resulted—

(a) in a case falling within paragraph (a) of subsection (2), in the amount of the debt which became due under section 75 of the 1995 Act being less than it would otherwise have been, or

(b) in a case falling within paragraph (b) of subsection (2), in the amount of any such debt calculated for the purposes of that paragraph being less than it would otherwise have been,

the Regulator may increase the amounts calculated under subsection (2)(a) or (b) by such amount as the Regulator considers appropriate.

(4) For the purposes of this section "the relevant time" means [(subject to subsection (4A)]—

(a) in the case of an act falling within subsection (5) of section 38, the time of the act, or

(b) in the case of a failure to act falling within that subsection—

(i) the time when the failure occurred, or

(ii) where the failure continued for a period of time, the time which the Regulator determines and which falls within that period.

[(4A) In the case of a series of acts or failures to act, "the relevant time" is determined by reference to whichever of the acts or failures in the series is, in the Regulator's opinion, most appropriate.]

(5) For the purposes of this section—

(a) references to a debt due under section 75 of the 1995 Act include a contingent debt under that section, and

(b) references to the amount of such a debt include the amount of such a contingent debt.

NOTES

Sub-s (4): words in square brackets inserted by the Pensions Act 2008, s 126, Sch 9, paras 1, 8(2)(a), 15(2), with effect for the purposes of the material detriment test, where at least one of the acts or failures to act occurs or first occurs on or after 14 April 2008, and for all other purposes, where at least one of the acts or failures to act occurs or first occurs on or after 26 November 2008.

Sub-s (4A): inserted by the Pensions Act 2008, s 126, Sch 9, paras 1, 8(2)(b), 15(2), with effect as noted to sub-s (4) above.

Modification: see the note to s 38 at **[17.266]**.

[17.270]
[39A Section 38 contribution notice: transfer of members of the scheme
(1) This section applies where—
(a) the Regulator is of the opinion that in relation to a scheme ("the initial scheme") in relation to which section 38 applies—
(i) an act or failure to act falling within subsection (5) of that section has occurred (or first occurred) at any time, and
(ii) the other conditions in that section for issuing a contribution notice are met in relation to the initial scheme (or, but for any transfer falling within paragraph (b), would be met), and
(b) the accrued rights of at least two persons who were members of the initial scheme are transferred at that or any subsequent time to one or more work-based pension schemes (whether by virtue of the act or otherwise).
(2) The Regulator may issue a contribution notice under section 38 in relation to any transferee scheme (and, accordingly, any reference in section 40 or 41 to the scheme is to the transferee scheme).
(3) In the case of any contribution notice issued by virtue of subsection (2) to any transferee scheme which is not within subsection (5)(a) or (b), section 39 has effect as if any reference in that section to the scheme were a reference to whichever of—
(a) the initial scheme, and
(b) the transferee scheme,
the Regulator determines to be more appropriate in the circumstances.
(4) In any case where section 39 has effect in relation to the transferee scheme by virtue of subsection (3), any reference in that section to a debt under section 75 of the 1995 Act is a reference to so much of that debt as, in the Regulator's opinion, is attributable to those members of the transferee scheme who were members of the initial scheme.
(5) In the case of any contribution notice issued by virtue of subsection (2) to any transferee scheme which is—
(a) a scheme to which section 75 of the 1995 Act does not apply, or
(b) a scheme to which that section does apply in a case where the liabilities of the scheme that would be taken into account for the purposes of that section do not relate to the members of the initial scheme,
the sum specified by the Regulator in the notice is determined in accordance with regulations (and not in accordance with section 39).
(6) The Regulator may also issue a direction to the trustees or managers of any transferee scheme requiring them to take specified steps to secure that the sum payable under the notice is applied for the benefit of the members of the transferee scheme who were members of the initial scheme.
(7) If the trustees or managers fail to comply with a direction issued to them under subsection (6), section 10 of the 1995 Act (civil penalties) applies to any trustee or manager who has failed to take all reasonable steps to secure compliance.]

NOTES
Inserted, together with s 39B, by the Pensions Act 2008, s 126, Sch 9, paras 1, 9, 15(3).
Regulations: the Pensions Regulator (Contribution Notices) (Sum Specified following Transfer) Regulations 2010, SI 2010/1929.

[17.271]
[39B Section 39A: supplemental
(1) In section 39A a "transferee scheme", in relation to any time, means any work-based pension scheme—
(a) to which the accrued rights of at least two persons who were members of the initial scheme have been transferred, and
(b) of which any of those persons are members at that time.
(2) For the purposes of section 39A(1) and subsection (1) above it does not matter whether any rights are transferred to a work-based pension scheme directly from the initial scheme or following one or more other transfers to other work-based pension schemes.
(3) For the purposes of section 39A and this section references to the transfer of accrued rights of members of a pension scheme to another pension scheme include references to the extinguishing of those accrued rights in consequence of the obligation to make a payment, or transfer an asset, to that other scheme.
(4) In section 39A and this section—
(a) "the 1995 Act" means the Pensions Act 1995;
(b) "work-based pension scheme" has the meaning given by section 5(3);
(c) any reference to rights which have accrued is to be read in accordance with section 67A(6) and (7) of the 1995 Act (reading any reference in those subsections to a subsisting right as a reference to a right which has accrued).
(5) Section 39A applies even if the initial scheme—
(a) is wound up as a result of any transfer falling within subsection (1)(b) of that section, or
(b) otherwise ceases to exist at the time of the transfer or at any subsequent time.
(6) Accordingly, in any such case, in subsection (1) of that section—
(a) the reference to a scheme to which section 38 applies is a reference to a scheme which was such a scheme before the transfer;
(b) the reference to any conditions in section 38 being met is a reference to any conditions in that section that, but for the transfer, would have been met in relation to the scheme.

(7) Nothing in section 39A or this section is to be read as preventing the Regulator from issuing a contribution notice in relation to the initial scheme.

(8) Regulations may make provision applying, with or without modifications, any provision made by or under section 39A or this section in relation to any scheme or other arrangement in any case where the accrued rights of persons who were members of the initial scheme are transferred or extinguished directly or indirectly in consequence of or otherwise in connection with—

(a) the making of any payment at any time to or for the benefit of the scheme or other arrangement,
(b) the transfer of any asset at any time to or for the benefit of the scheme or other arrangement,
(c) the discharge (wholly or partly) at any time of any liability incurred by or on behalf of the scheme or other arrangement, or
(d) the incurring at any time of any obligation to do any act falling within paragraph (a) to (c).

(9) Any reference in subsection (8)(a) to (d) to the doing of an act of any description at any time in relation to the scheme or other arrangement includes a reference to the doing of an act of that description at any previous time in relation to any other scheme or other arrangement.

(10) Regulations under subsection (8) may—

(a) make provision having effect in relation to any case where rights are transferred or extinguished on or after the date on which the Secretary of State publishes a statement of the intention to make the regulations; and
(b) without prejudice to section 315(5), make consequential provision applying with modifications any provision of this Act which relates to contribution notices under section 38.]

NOTES

Inserted as noted to s 39A at **[17.270]**.

[17.272]

40 Content and effect of a section 38 contribution notice

(1) This section applies where a contribution notice is issued to a person under section 38.

(2) The contribution notice must—

(a) contain a statement of the matters which it is asserted constitute the act or failure to act which falls within subsection (5) of section 38,
(b) specify the sum which the person is stated to be under a liability to pay, and
(c) identify any other persons to whom contribution notices have been or are issued as a result of the act or failure to act in question and the sums specified in each of those notices.

(3) Where the contribution notice states that the person is under a liability to pay the sum specified in the notice to the trustees or managers of the scheme, the sum is to be treated as a debt due from the person to the trustees or managers of the scheme.

(4) In such a case, the Regulator may, on behalf of the trustees or managers of the scheme, exercise such powers as the trustees or managers have to recover the debt.

(5) But during any assessment period (within the meaning of section 132) in relation to the scheme, the rights and powers of the trustees or managers of the scheme in relation to any debt due to them by virtue of a contribution notice are exercisable by the Board of the Pension Protection Fund to the exclusion of the trustees or managers and the Regulator.

(6) Where, by virtue of subsection (5), any amount is paid to the Board in respect of a debt due by virtue of a contribution notice, the Board must pay the amount to the trustees or managers of the scheme.

(7) Where the contribution notice states that the person is under a liability to pay the sum specified in the notice to the Board, the sum is to be treated as a debt due from the person to the Board.

(8) Where the contribution notice so specifies, the person to whom the notice is issued ("P") is to be treated as jointly and severally liable for the debt with any persons specified in the notice who are persons to whom corresponding contribution notices are issued.

(9) For the purposes of subsection (8), a corresponding contribution notice is a notice which—

(a) is issued as a result of the same act or failure to act falling within subsection (5) of section 38 as the act or failure as a result of which P's contribution notice is issued,
(b) specifies the same sum as is specified in P's contribution notice, and
(c) specifies that the person to whom the contribution notice is issued is jointly and severally liable with P, or with P and other persons, for the debt in respect of that sum.

(10) A debt due by virtue of a contribution notice is not to be taken into account for the purposes of section 75(2) and (4) of the Pensions Act 1995 (c 26) (deficiencies in the scheme assets) when ascertaining the amount or value of the assets or liabilities of a scheme.

NOTES

Modification: see the note to s 38 at **[17.266]**.

[17.273]

41 Section 38 contribution notice: relationship with employer debt

(1) This section applies where a contribution notice is issued to a person ("P") under section 38 and condition A or B is met.

(2) Condition A is met if, at the time at which the contribution notice is issued, there is a debt due under section 75 of the Pensions Act 1995 ("the 1995 Act") (deficiencies in the scheme assets) from the employer—

(a) to the trustees or managers of the scheme, or
(b) where the Board of the Pension Protection Fund has assumed responsibility for the scheme in accordance with Chapter 3 of Part 2 (pension protection), to the Board.

(3) Condition B is met if, after the contribution notice is issued but before the whole of the debt due by virtue of the notice is recovered, a debt becomes due from the employer to the trustees or managers of the scheme under section 75 of the 1995 Act.
(4) The Regulator may issue a direction to the trustees or managers of the scheme not to take any or any further steps to recover the debt due to them under section 75 of the 1995 Act pending the recovery of all or a specified part of the debt due to them by virtue of the contribution notice.
(5) If the trustees or managers fail to comply with a direction issued to them under subsection (4), section 10 of the 1995 Act (civil penalties) applies to any trustee or manager who has failed to take all reasonable steps to secure compliance.
(6) Any sums paid—
 (a) to the trustees or managers of the scheme in respect of any debt due to them by virtue of the contribution notice, or
 (b) to the Board in respect of any debt due to it by virtue of the contribution notice,
are to be treated as reducing the amount of the debt due to the trustees or managers or, as the case may be, to the Board under section 75 of the 1995 Act.
(7) Where a sum is paid to the trustees or managers of the scheme or, as the case may be, to the Board in respect of the debt due under section 75 of the 1995 Act, P may make an application under this subsection to the Regulator for a reduction in the amount of the sum specified in P's contribution notice.
(8) An application under subsection (7) must be made as soon as reasonably practicable after the sum is paid to the trustees or managers or, as the case may be, to the Board in respect of the debt due under section 75 of the 1995 Act.
(9) Where such an application is made to the Regulator, the Regulator may, if it is of the opinion that it is appropriate to do so—
 (a) reduce the amount of the sum specified in P's contribution notice by an amount which it considers reasonable, and
 (b) issue a revised contribution notice specifying the revised sum.
(10) For the purposes of subsection (9), the Regulator must have regard to such matters as the Regulator considers relevant including, where relevant, the following matters—
 (a) the amount paid in respect of the debt due under section 75 of the 1995 Act since the contribution notice was issued,
 (b) any amounts paid in respect of the debt due by virtue of that contribution notice,
 (c) whether contribution notices have been issued to other persons as a result of the same act or failure to act falling within subsection (5) of section 38 as the act or failure as a result of which P's contribution notice was issued,
 (d) where such contribution notices have been issued, the sums specified in each of those notices and any amounts paid in respect of the debt due by virtue of those notices,
 (e) whether P's contribution notice specifies that P is jointly and severally liable for the debt with other persons, and
 (f) such other matters as may be prescribed.
(11) Where—
 (a) P's contribution notice specifies that P is jointly and severally liable for the debt with other persons, and
 (b) a revised contribution notice is issued to P under subsection (9) specifying a revised sum,
the Regulator must also issue revised contribution notices to those other persons specifying the revised sum and their joint and several liability with P for the debt in respect of that sum.
(12) For the purposes of this section—
 (a) references to a debt due under section 75 of the 1995 Act include a contingent debt under that section, and
 (b) references to the amount of such a debt include the amount of such a contingent debt.

NOTES

Commencement: 6 April 2005 (sub-ss (1)–(9), (10)(a)–(e), (11), (12)); to be appointed (sub-s (10)(f)).
Modification: see the note to s 38 at **[17.266]**.

[17.274]
42 Section 38 contribution notice: clearance statements
(1) An application may be made to the Regulator under this section for the issue of a clearance statement within paragraph (a), (b) or (c) of subsection (2) in relation to circumstances described in the application.
(2) A clearance statement is a statement, made by the Regulator, that in its opinion in the circumstances described in the application—
 (a) the applicant would not be, for the purposes of subsection (3)(a) of section 38, a party to an act or a deliberate failure to act falling within subsection (5)(a) of that section,
 (b) it would not be reasonable to impose any liability on the applicant under a contribution notice issued under section 38, or
 (c) such requirements of that section as may be prescribed would not be satisfied in relation to the applicant.
(3) Where an application is made under this section, the Regulator—
 (a) may request further information from the applicant;
 (b) may invite the applicant to amend the application to modify the circumstances described.
(4) Where an application is made under this section, the Regulator must as soon as reasonably practicable—
 (a) determine whether to issue the clearance statement, and

(b) where it determines to do so, issue the statement.

(5) A clearance statement issued under this section binds the Regulator in relation to the exercise of the power to issue a contribution notice under section 38 to the applicant unless—

(a) the circumstances in relation to which the exercise of the power under that section arises are not the same as the circumstances described in the application, and

(b) the difference in those circumstances is material to the exercise of the power.

NOTES

Commencement: 6 April 2005 (sub-ss (1), (2)(a), (b), (3)–(5)); to be appointed (sub-s (2)(c)).
Modification: see the note to s 38 at **[17.266]**.

Financial support directions

[17.275]

43 Financial support directions

(1) This section applies in relation to an occupational pension scheme other than—

(a) a money purchase scheme, or

(b) a prescribed scheme or a scheme of a prescribed description.

(2) The Regulator may issue a financial support direction under this section in relation to *such a scheme* if the Regulator is of the opinion that the employer in relation to the scheme—

(a) is a service company, or

(b) is insufficiently resourced,

at a time determined by the Regulator which falls within subsection (9) ("the relevant time").

(3) A financial support direction in relation to a scheme is a direction which requires the person or persons to whom it is issued to secure—

(a) that financial support for the scheme is put in place within the period specified in the direction,

(b) that thereafter that financial support or other financial support remains in place while the scheme is in existence, and

(c) that the Regulator is notified in writing of prescribed events in respect of the financial support as soon as reasonably practicable after the event occurs.

(4) A financial support direction in relation to a scheme may be issued to one or more persons.

(5) But the Regulator may issue such a direction to a person only if—

(a) the person is at the relevant time a person falling within subsection (6), and

(b) the Regulator is of the opinion that it is reasonable to impose the requirements of the direction on that person.

(6) A person falls within this subsection if the person is—

(a) the employer in relation to the scheme,

(b) an individual who—

(i) is an associate of an individual who is the employer, but

(ii) is not an associate of that individual by reason only of being employed by him, or

(c) a person, other than an individual, who is connected with or an associate of the employer.

(7) The Regulator, when deciding for the purposes of subsection (5)(b) whether it is reasonable to impose the requirements of a financial support direction on a particular person, must have regard to such matters as the Regulator considers relevant including, where relevant, the following matters—

(a) the relationship which the person has or has had with the employer (including, where the employer is a company within the meaning of subsection (11) of section 435 of the Insolvency Act 1986 (c 45), whether the person has or has had control of the employer within the meaning of subsection (10) of that section),

(b) in the case of a person falling within subsection (6)(b) or (c), the value of any benefits received directly or indirectly by that person from the employer,

(c) any connection or involvement which the person has or has had with the scheme,

(d) the financial circumstances of the person, and

(e) such other matters as may be prescribed.

(8) A financial support direction must identify all the persons to whom the direction is issued.

(9) A time falls within this subsection if it is a time which falls within a prescribed period which ends with the [giving of a warning notice in respect of] the financial support direction in question.

(10) For the purposes of subsection (3), a scheme is in existence until it is wound up.

(11) No duty to which a person is subject is to be regarded as contravened merely because of any information or opinion contained in a notice given by virtue of subsection (3)(c).

This is subject to section 311 (protected items).

[(12) In this section "a warning notice" means a notice given as mentioned in section 96(2)(a).]

NOTES

Commencement: 10 February 2005 (sub-ss (1)(b), (3)(c), (9) (for the purpose of making regulations, orders or rules)); 6 April 2005 (sub-ss (1)(a), (1)(b) (for remaining purposes), (2), (3)(a), (b), (c) (for remaining purposes), (4)–(6), (7)(a)–(d), (8), (9) (for remaining purposes), (10), (11)); to be appointed (sub-s (7)(e)).

Sub-s (1): substituted as follows by the Pension Schemes Act 2015, s 46, Sch 2, paras 23, 28(1), (2), as from a day to be appointed:

"(1) This section applies in relation to a pension scheme that is—

(a) an occupational defined benefits scheme,

(b) an occupational shared risk scheme, or

(c) an occupational defined contributions scheme,

unless subsection (1A) provides for the scheme to be exempt.

(1A) A scheme is exempt from this section if it is—

(a) a scheme under which all the benefits that may be provided are money purchase benefits,
(b) a scheme under which all the benefits that may be provided are collective benefits,
(c) a scheme under which all the benefits that may be provided are money purchase benefits or collective benefits, or
(d) a prescribed scheme or a scheme of a prescribed description.

(1B) Where—
(a) some of the benefits that may be provided under a scheme are collective benefits and some are not, and
(b) the scheme does not fall within paragraph (c) or (d) of subsection (1A),

the scheme is to be treated for the purposes of this section and sections 43A to 51 as two separate schemes, one relating to the collective benefits and the other relating to the other benefits.".

Sub-s (2): for the words in italics there are substituted the words "a scheme to which this section applies" by the Pension Schemes Act 2015, s 46, Sch 2, paras 23, 28(1), (3), as from a day to be appointed.

Sub-s (9): words in square brackets substituted by the Pensions Act 2011, s 26(4), (5).

Sub-s (12): added by the Pensions Act 2011, s 26(4), (6).

Modification: see the note to s 38 at **[17.266]**.

Regulations: the Pensions Regulator (Financial Support Directions etc) Regulations 2005, SI 2005/2188; the Pensions Regulator (Miscellaneous Amendment) Regulations 2009, SI 2009/617.

[17.276]

[43A Financial support directions: transfer of members of the scheme

(1) This section applies where—
(a) the Regulator is of the opinion by reference to any time that the conditions in section 43 for issuing a financial support direction are met in relation to a scheme ("the initial scheme") in relation to which that section applies (or, but for any transfer falling within paragraph (b), would be met), and
(b) the accrued rights of at least two persons who were members of the initial scheme are transferred at any subsequent time to one or more work-based pension schemes.

(2) The Regulator may issue a financial support direction under that section in relation to any transferee scheme (and, accordingly, any reference in section 45 or any of sections 47 to 50 to the scheme is to the transferee scheme).

(3) The Regulator may also issue a direction to the trustees or managers of any transferee scheme requiring them to take specified steps to secure that the financial support is put in place for the benefit of the members of the transferee scheme who were members of the initial scheme.

(4) If the trustees or managers fail to comply with a direction issued to them under subsection (3), section 10 of the 1995 Act (civil penalties) applies to any trustee or manager who has failed to take all reasonable steps to secure compliance.]

NOTES

Inserted, together with s 43B, by the Pensions Act 2008, s 126, Sch 9, paras 1, 10, 15(3).

[17.277]

[43B Section 43A: supplemental

(1) In section 43A a "transferee scheme", in relation to any time, means any work-based pension scheme—
(a) to which the accrued rights of at least two persons who were members of the initial scheme have been transferred, and
(b) of which any of those persons are members at that time.

(2) For the purposes of section 43A(1) and subsection (1) above it does not matter whether any rights are transferred to a work-based pension scheme directly from the initial scheme or following one or more other transfers to other work-based pension schemes.

(3) For the purposes of section 43A and this section references to the transfer of accrued rights of members of a pension scheme to another pension scheme include references to the extinguishing of those accrued rights in consequence of the obligation to make a payment, or transfer an asset, to that other scheme.

(4) In section 43A and this section—
(a) "the 1995 Act" means the Pensions Act 1995;
(b) "work-based pension scheme" has the meaning given by section 5(3);
(c) any reference to rights which have accrued is to be read in accordance with section 67A(6) and (7) of the 1995 Act (reading any reference in those subsections to a subsisting right as a reference to a right which has accrued).

(5) Section 43A applies even if the initial scheme—
(a) is wound up as a result of any transfer falling within subsection (1)(b) of that section, or
(b) otherwise ceases to exist at the time of the transfer or at any subsequent time.

(6) Accordingly, in any such case, in subsection (1) of that section—
(a) the reference to a scheme to which section 43 applies is a reference to a scheme which was such a scheme before the transfer;
(b) the reference to any conditions in section 43 being met is a reference to any conditions in that section that, but for the transfer, would have been met in relation to the scheme.

(7) Nothing in section 43A or this section is to be read as preventing the Regulator from issuing a financial support direction in relation to the initial scheme.

(8) Regulations may make provision applying, with or without modifications, any provision made by section 43A or this section in relation to any scheme or other arrangement in any case where the accrued rights of persons who were members of the initial scheme are transferred or extinguished directly or indirectly in consequence of or otherwise in connection with—

(a) the making of any payment at any time to or for the benefit of the scheme or other arrangement,
(b) the transfer of any asset at any time to or for the benefit of the scheme or other arrangement,
(c) the discharge (wholly or partly) at any time of any liability incurred by or on behalf of the scheme or other arrangement, or
(d) the incurring at any time of any obligation to do any act falling within paragraph (a) to (c).

(9) Any reference in subsection (8)(a) to (d) to the doing of an act of any description at any time in relation to the scheme or other arrangement includes a reference to the doing of an act of that description at any previous time in relation to any other scheme or other arrangement.

(10) Regulations under subsection (8) may—
(a) make provision having effect in relation to any case where rights are transferred or extinguished on or after the date on which the Secretary of State publishes a statement of the intention to make the regulations; and
(b) without prejudice to section 315(5), make consequential provision applying with modifications any provision of this Act which relates to financial support directions under section 43.]

NOTES

Inserted as noted to s 43A at **[17.276]**.

[17.278]
44 Meaning of "service company" and "insufficiently resourced"

(1) This section applies for the purposes of section 43 (financial support directions).

(2) An employer ("E") is a "service company" at the relevant time if—
(a) E is a company [as defined in section 1(1) of the Companies Act 2006],
(b) E is a member of a group of companies, and
(c) E's turnover, as shown in the latest available [individual accounts] for E prepared in accordance with [Part 15 of that Act], is solely or principally derived from amounts charged for the provision of the services of employees of E to other members of that group.

(3) The employer in relation to a scheme is insufficiently resourced at the relevant time if—
(a) at that time the value of the resources of the employer is less than the amount which is a prescribed percentage of the estimated section 75 debt in relation to the scheme, and
[(b) condition A or B is met.]

[(3A) Condition A is met if—
(a) there is at that time a person who falls within section 43(6)(b) or (c), and
(b) the value at that time of that person's resources is not less than the relevant deficit, that is to say the amount which is the difference between—
(i) the value of the resources of the employer, and
(ii) the amount which is the prescribed percentage of the estimated section 75 debt.

(3B) Condition B is met if—
(a) there are at that time two or more persons who—
(i) fall within section 43(6)(b) or (c), and
(ii) are connected with, or associates of, each other, and
(b) the aggregate value at that time of the resources of the persons who fall within paragraph (a) (or any of them) is not less than the relevant deficit.]

(4) For the purposes of [subsections (3) to (3B)]—
(a) what constitutes the resources of a person is to be determined in accordance with regulations, and
(b) the value of a person's resources is to be determined, calculated and verified in a prescribed manner.

(5) In this section the "estimated section 75 debt", in relation to a scheme, means the amount which the Regulator estimates to be the amount of the debt which would become due from the employer to the trustees or managers of the scheme under section 75 of the Pensions Act 1995 (c 26) (deficiencies in the scheme assets) if—
(a) subsection (2) of that section applied, and
(b) the time designated by the trustees or managers of the scheme for the purposes of that subsection were the relevant time.

(6) When calculating the estimated section 75 debt in relation to a scheme under subsection (5), the amount of any debt due at the relevant time from the employer under section 75 of the Pensions Act 1995 (c 26) is to be disregarded.

(7) In this section "the relevant time" has the same meaning as in section 43.

NOTES

Sub-s (2): words in square brackets substituted by the Companies Act 2006 (Consequential Amendments, Transitional Provisions and Savings) Order 2009, SI 2009/1941, art 2(1), Sch 1, para 243(1), (2).

Sub-s (3): para (b) substituted by the Pensions Act 2008, s 126, Sch 9, paras 1, 14(1), 15(4), with effect so as to enable the Pensions Regulator to issue a financial support direction under s 43 of this Act by reference to any time falling on or after 14 April 2008, and originally read as follows:

"(b) there is at that time a person who falls within subsection (6)(b) or (c) of section 43 and the value at that time of that person's resources is not less than the amount which is the difference between—
(i) the value of the resources of the employer, and
(ii) the amount which is the prescribed percentage of the estimated section 75 debt.".

Sub-ss (3A), (3B): inserted by the Pensions Act 2008, s 126, Sch 9, paras 1, 14(2), 15(4), with effect so as to enable the Pensions Regulator to issue a financial support direction under s 43 of this Act by reference to any time falling on or after 14 April 2008.

Sub-s (4): words in square brackets substituted for original words "subsection (3)" by the Pensions Act 2008, s 126, Sch 9, paras 1, 14(3), 15(4), with effect so as to enable the Pensions Regulator to issue a financial support direction under s 43 of this Act by reference to any time falling on or after 14 April 2008.

Modification: see the note to s 38 at **[17.266]**.

Regulations: the Pensions Regulator (Financial Support Directions etc) Regulations 2005, SI 2005/2188.

[17.279]

45 Meaning of "financial support"

(1) For the purposes of section 43 (financial support directions), "financial support" for a scheme means one or more of the arrangements falling within subsection (2) the details of which are approved in a notice issued by the Regulator.

(2) The arrangements falling within this subsection are—

- (a) an arrangement whereby, at any time when the employer is a member of a group of companies, all the members of the group are jointly and severally liable for the whole or part of the employer's pension liabilities in relation to the scheme;
- (b) an arrangement whereby, at any time when the employer is a member of a group of companies, a company ([within the meaning of section 1159 of the Companies Act 2006]) which meets prescribed requirements and is the holding company of the group is liable for the whole or part of the employer's pension liabilities in relation to the scheme;
- (c) an arrangement which meets prescribed requirements and whereby additional financial resources are provided to the scheme;
- (d) such other arrangements as may be prescribed.

(3) The Regulator may not issue a notice under subsection (1) approving the details of one or more arrangements falling within subsection (2) unless it is satisfied that the arrangement is, or the arrangements are, reasonable in the circumstances.

(4) In subsection (2), "the employer's pension liabilities" in relation to a scheme means—

- (a) the liabilities for any amounts payable by or on behalf of the employer towards the scheme (whether on his own account or otherwise) in accordance with a schedule of contributions under section 227, and
- (b) the liabilities for any debt which is or may become due to the trustees or managers of the scheme from the employer whether by virtue of section 75 of the Pensions Act 1995 (deficiencies in the scheme assets) or otherwise.

NOTES

Sub-s (2): words in square brackets substituted by the Companies Act 2006 (Consequential Amendments, Transitional Provisions and Savings) Order 2009, SI 2009/1941, art 2(1), Sch 1, para 243(1), (3).

Modification: see the note to s 38 at **[17.266]**.

Regulations: the Pensions Regulator (Financial Support Directions etc) Regulations 2005, SI 2005/2188.

[17.280]

46 Financial support directions: clearance statements

(1) An application may be made to the Regulator under this section for the issue of a clearance statement within paragraph (a), (b) or (c) of subsection (2) in relation to circumstances described in the application and relating to an occupational pension scheme.

(2) A clearance statement is a statement, made by the Regulator, that in its opinion in the circumstances described in the application—

- (a) the employer in relation to the scheme would not be a service company for the purposes of section 43,
- (b) the employer in relation to the scheme would not be insufficiently resourced for the purposes of that section, or
- (c) it would not be reasonable to impose the requirements of a financial support direction, in relation to the scheme, on the applicant.

(3) Where an application is made under this section, the Regulator—

- (a) may request further information from the applicant;
- (b) may invite the applicant to amend the application to modify the circumstances described.

(4) Where an application is made under this section, the Regulator must as soon as reasonably practicable—

- (a) determine whether to issue the clearance statement, and
- (b) where it determines to do so, issue the statement.

(5) A clearance statement issued under this section binds the Regulator in relation to the exercise of the power to issue a financial support direction under section 43 in relation to the scheme to the applicant unless—

- (a) the circumstances in relation to which the exercise of the power under that section arises are not the same as the circumstances described in the application, and
- (b) the difference in those circumstances is material to the exercise of the power.

NOTES

Modification: see the note to s 38 at **[17.266]**.

[17.281]

47 Contribution notices where non-compliance with financial support direction

(1) This section applies where there is non-compliance with a financial support direction issued in relation to a scheme under section 43.

(2) The Regulator may issue a notice to any one or more of the persons to whom the direction was issued stating that the person is under a liability to pay to the trustees or managers of the scheme the sum specified in the notice (a "contribution notice").
(3) The Regulator may issue a contribution notice to a person only if the Regulator is of the opinion that it is reasonable to impose liability on the person to pay the sum specified in the notice.
(4) The Regulator, when deciding for the purposes of subsection (3) whether it is reasonable to impose liability on a particular person to pay the sum specified in the notice, must have regard to such matters as the Regulator considers relevant including, where relevant, the following matters—
 (a) whether the person has taken reasonable steps to secure compliance with the financial support direction,
 (b) the relationship which the person has or has had with the employer (including, where the employer is a company within the meaning of subsection (11) of section 435 of the Insolvency Act 1986 (c 45), whether the person has or has had control of the employer within the meaning of subsection (10) of that section),
 (c) in the case of a person to whom the financial support direction was issued as a person falling within section 43(6)(b) or (c), the value of any benefits received directly or indirectly by that person from the employer,
 (d) the relationship which the person has or has had with the parties to any arrangements put in place in accordance with the direction (including, where any of those parties is a company within the meaning of subsection (11) of section 435 of the Insolvency Act 1986, whether the person has or has had control of that company within the meaning of subsection (10) of that section),
 (e) any connection or involvement which the person has or has had with the scheme,
 (f) the financial circumstances of the person, and
 (g) such other matters as may be prescribed.
(5) A contribution notice may not be issued under this section in respect of non-compliance with a financial support direction in relation to a scheme where the Board of the Pension Protection Fund has assumed responsibility for the scheme in accordance with Chapter 3 of Part 2 (pension protection).

NOTES
Commencement: 6 April 2005 (sub-ss (1)–(3), (4)(a)–(f), (5)); to be appointed (sub-s (4)(g)).
Modification: see the note to s 38 at **[17.266]**.

[17.282]
48 The sum specified in a section 47 contribution notice
(1) The sum specified by the Regulator in a contribution notice under section 47 may be either the whole or a specified part of the shortfall sum in relation to the scheme.
(2) The shortfall sum in relation to a scheme is—
 (a) in a case where, at the time of non-compliance, a debt was due from the employer to the trustees or managers of the scheme under section 75 of the Pensions Act 1995 (c 26) ("the 1995 Act") (deficiencies in the scheme assets), the amount which the Regulator estimates to be the amount of that debt at that time, and
 (b) in a case where, at the time of non-compliance, no such debt was due, the amount which the Regulator estimates to be the amount of the debt under section 75 of the 1995 Act which would become due if—
  (i) subsection (2) of that section applied, and
  (ii) the time designated by the trustees or managers of the scheme for the purposes of that subsection were the time of non-compliance.
(3) For the purposes of this section "the time of non-compliance" means—
 (a) in the case of non-compliance with paragraph (a) of subsection (3) of section 43 (financial support directions), the time immediately after the expiry of the period specified in the financial support direction for putting in place the financial support,
 (b) in the case of non-compliance with paragraph (b) of that subsection, the time when financial support for the scheme ceased to be in place,
 (c) in the case of non-compliance with paragraph (c) of that subsection, the time when the prescribed event occurred in relation to which there was the failure to notify the Regulator, or
 (d) where more than one of paragraphs (a) to (c) above apply, whichever of the times specified in the applicable paragraphs the Regulator determines.

NOTES
Modification: see the note to s 38 at **[17.266]**.

[17.283]
49 Content and effect of a section 47 contribution notice
(1) This section applies where a contribution notice is issued to a person under section 47.
(2) The contribution notice must—
 (a) contain a statement of the matters which it is asserted constitute the non-compliance with the financial support direction in respect of which the notice is issued, and
 (b) specify the sum which the person is stated to be under a liability to pay.
(3) The sum specified in the notice is to be treated as a debt due from the person to the trustees or managers of the scheme.
(4) The Regulator may, on behalf of the trustees or managers of the scheme, exercise such powers as the trustees or managers have to recover the debt.

(5) But during any assessment period (within the meaning of section 132) in relation to the scheme, the rights and powers of the trustees or managers of the scheme in relation to any debt due to them by virtue of a contribution notice, are exercisable by the Board of the Pension Protection Fund to the exclusion of the trustees or managers and the Regulator.
(6) Where, by virtue of subsection (5), any amount is paid to the Board in respect of a debt due by virtue of a contribution notice, the Board must pay the amount to the trustees or managers of the scheme.
(7) The contribution notice must identify any other persons to whom contribution notices have been or are issued in respect of the non-compliance in question and the sums specified in each of those notices.
(8) Where the contribution notice so specifies, the person to whom the notice is issued ("P") is to be treated as jointly and severally liable for the debt with any persons specified in the notice who are persons to whom corresponding contribution notices are issued.
(9) For the purposes of subsection (8), a corresponding contribution notice is a notice which—
- (a) is issued in respect of the same non-compliance with the financial support direction as the non-compliance in respect of which P's contribution notice is issued,
- (b) specifies the same sum as is specified in P's contribution notice, and
- (c) specifies that the person to whom the contribution notice is issued is jointly and severally liable with P, or with P and other persons, for the debt in respect of that sum.

(10) A debt due by virtue of a contribution notice is not to be taken into account for the purposes of section 75(2) and (4) of the Pensions Act 1995 (c 26) (deficiencies in the scheme assets) when ascertaining the amount or value of the assets or liabilities of a scheme.

NOTES

Modification: see the note to s 38 at **[17.266]**.

[17.284]

50 Section 47 contribution notice: relationship with employer debt

(1) This section applies where a contribution notice is issued to a person ("P") under section 47 and condition A or B is met.
(2) Condition A is met if, at the time at which the contribution notice is issued, there is a debt due from the employer to the trustees or managers of the scheme under section 75 of the Pensions Act 1995 ("the 1995 Act") (deficiencies in the scheme assets).
(3) Condition B is met if, after the contribution notice is issued but before the whole of the debt due by virtue of the notice is recovered, a debt becomes due from the employer to the trustees or managers of the scheme under section 75 of the 1995 Act.
(4) The Regulator may issue a direction to the trustees or managers of the scheme not to take any or any further steps to recover the debt due to them under section 75 of the 1995 Act pending the recovery of all or a specified part of the debt due to them by virtue of the contribution notice.
(5) If the trustees or managers fail to comply with a direction issued to them under subsection (4), section 10 of the 1995 Act (civil penalties) applies to any trustee or manager who has failed to take all reasonable steps to secure compliance.
(6) Any sums paid—
- (a) to the trustees or managers of the scheme in respect of any debt due to them by virtue of the contribution notice, or
- (b) to the Board of the Pension Protection Fund in respect of any debt due to it by virtue of the contribution notice (where it has assumed responsibility for the scheme in accordance with Chapter 3 of Part 2 (pension protection)),

are to be treated as reducing the amount of the debt due to the trustees or managers or, as the case may be, to the Board under section 75 of the 1995 Act.
(7) Where a sum is paid to the trustees or managers of the scheme or, as the case may be, to the Board in respect of the debt due under section 75 of the 1995 Act, P may make an application under this subsection to the Regulator for a reduction in the amount of the sum specified in P's contribution notice.
(8) An application under subsection (7) must be made as soon as reasonably practicable after the sum is paid to the trustees or managers or, as the case may be, to the Board in respect of the debt due under section 75 of the 1995 Act.
(9) Where such an application is made to the Regulator, the Regulator may, if it is of the opinion that it is appropriate to do so—
- (a) reduce the amount of the sum specified in P's contribution notice by an amount which it considers reasonable, and
- (b) issue a revised contribution notice specifying the revised sum.

(10) For the purposes of subsection (9), the Regulator must have regard to such matters as the Regulator considers relevant including, where relevant, the following matters—
- (a) the amount paid in respect of the debt due under section 75 of the 1995 Act since the contribution notice was issued,
- (b) any amounts paid in respect of the debt due by virtue of that contribution notice,
- (c) whether contribution notices have been issued to other persons in respect of the same non-compliance with the financial support direction in question as the non-compliance in respect of which P's contribution notice was issued,
- (d) where such contribution notices have been issued, the sums specified in each of those notices and any amounts paid in respect of the debt due by virtue of those notices,
- (e) whether P's contribution notice specifies that P is jointly and severally liable for the debt with other persons, and
- (f) such other matters as may be prescribed.

(11) Where—

(a) P's contribution notice specifies that P is jointly and severally liable for the debt with other persons, and
(b) a revised contribution notice is issued to P under subsection (9) specifying a revised sum,
the Regulator must also issue revised contribution notices to those other persons specifying the revised sum and their joint and several liability with P for the debt in respect of that sum.

NOTES

Commencement: 6 April 2005 (sub-ss (1)–(9), (10)(a)–(e), (11)); to be appointed (sub-s (10)(f)).
Modification: see the note to s 38 at **[17.266]**.

[17.285]
51 Sections 43 to 50: interpretation
[(1) In sections 43 to 50—
"group of companies" means a holding company and its subsidiaries (and references to a member of a group of companies are to be read accordingly); and
"holding company" and "subsidiary" have the meaning given by section 1159 of the Companies Act 2006.]
(2) For the purposes of those sections—
(a) references to a debt due under section 75 of the Pensions Act 1995 (c 26) include a contingent debt under that section, and
(b) references to the amount of such a debt include the amount of such a contingent debt.
(3) For the purposes of those sections—
(a) section 249 of the Insolvency Act 1986 (c 45) (connected persons) applies as it applies for the purposes of any provision of the first Group of Parts of that Act,
(b) section 435 of that Act (associated persons) applies as it applies for the purposes of that Act, and
(c) section [229 of the Bankruptcy (Scotland) Act 2016] (associated persons) applies as it applies for the purposes of that Act.

NOTES

Sub-s (1): substituted by the Companies Act 2006 (Consequential Amendments, Transitional Provisions and Savings) Order 2009, SI 2009/1941, art 2(1), Sch 1, para 243(1), (4).
Sub-s (3): words in square brackets in para (c) substituted for original words "74 of the Bankruptcy (Scotland) Act 1985 (c 66)" by the Bankruptcy (Scotland) Act 2016 (Consequential Provisions and Modifications) Order 2016, SI 2016/1034, art 7(1), (3), Sch 1, para 26(1), (3), as from 30 November 2016 (except in relation to (i) a sequestration as regards which the petition is presented, or the debtor application is made before that date; or (ii) a trust deed executed before that date).
Modification: see the note to s 38 at **[17.266]**.

Transactions at an undervalue

[17.286]
52 Restoration orders where transactions at an undervalue
(1) This section applies in relation to an occupational pension scheme other than—
(a) a money purchase scheme, or
(b) a prescribed scheme or a scheme of a prescribed description.
(2) The Regulator may make a restoration order in respect of a transaction involving assets of the scheme if—
(a) a relevant event has occurred in relation to the employer in relation to the scheme, and
(b) the transaction is a transaction at an undervalue entered into with a person at a time which—
(i) is on or after 27th April 2004, but
(ii) is not more than two years before the occurrence of the relevant event in relation to the employer.
(3) A restoration order in respect of a transaction involving assets of a scheme is such an order as the Regulator thinks fit for restoring the position to what it would have been if the transaction had not been entered into.
(4) For the purposes of this section a relevant event occurs in relation to the employer in relation to a scheme if and when on or after the appointed day—
(a) an insolvency event occurs in relation to the employer, or
(b) the trustees or managers of the scheme make an application under subsection (1) of section 129 or receive a notice from the Board of the Pension Protection Fund under subsection (5)(a) of that section (applications and notifications prior to the Board assuming responsibility for a scheme).
(5) For the purposes of subsection (4)—
(a) the "appointed day" means the day appointed under section 126(2) (no pension protection under Chapter 3 of Part 2 if the scheme begins winding up before the day appointed by the Secretary of State),
(b) section 121 (meaning of "insolvency event") applies for the purposes of determining if and when an insolvency event has occurred in relation to the employer, and
(c) the reference to an insolvency event in relation to the employer does not include an insolvency event which occurred in relation to him before he became the employer in relation to the scheme.
(6) For the purposes of this section and section 53, a transaction involving assets of a scheme is a transaction at an undervalue entered into with a person ("P") if the trustees or managers of the scheme or appropriate persons in relation to the scheme—
(a) make a gift to P or otherwise enter into a transaction with P on terms that provide for no consideration to be provided towards the scheme, or

(b) enter into a transaction with P for a consideration the value of which, in money or money's worth, is significantly less than the value, in money or money's worth, of the consideration provided by or on behalf of the trustees or managers of the scheme.

(7) In subsection (6) "appropriate persons" in relation to a scheme means a person who, or several persons each of whom is a person who, at the time at which the transaction in question is entered into, is—

(a) a person of a prescribed description, and
(b) entitled to exercise powers in relation to the scheme.

(8) For the purposes of this section and section 53—

"assets" includes future assets;

"transaction" includes a gift, agreement or arrangement and references to entering into a transaction are to be construed accordingly.

(9) The provisions of this section apply without prejudice to the availability of any other remedy, even in relation to a transaction where the trustees or managers of the scheme or appropriate persons in question had no power to enter into the transaction.

NOTES

Sub-s (1): substituted as follows by the Pension Schemes Act 2015, s 46, Sch 2, paras 23, 29, as from a day to be appointed:

"(1) This section applies in relation to a pension scheme that is—

(a) an occupational defined benefits scheme,
(b) an occupational shared risk scheme, or
(c) an occupational defined contributions scheme,

unless subsection (1A) provides for the scheme to be exempt.

(1A) A scheme is exempt from this section if it is—

(a) a scheme under which all the benefits that may be provided are money purchase benefits,
(b) a scheme under which all the benefits that may be provided are collective benefits,
(c) a scheme under which all the benefits that may be provided are money purchase benefits or collective benefits, or
(d) a prescribed scheme or a scheme of a prescribed description.

(1B) Where—

(a) some of the benefits that may be provided under a scheme are collective benefits and some are not, and
(b) the scheme does not fall within paragraph (c) or (d) of subsection (1A),

the scheme is to be treated for the purposes of this section and sections 53 to 56 as two separate schemes, one relating to the collective benefits and the other relating to the other benefits.".

Modification: see the note to s 38 at **[17.266]**.

Regulations: the Pensions Regulator (Contribution Notices and Restoration Orders) Regulations 2005, SI 2005/931; the Occupational Pension Schemes and Pension Protection Fund (Amendment) Regulations 2005, SI 2005/993; the Occupational Pension Schemes (Republic of Ireland Schemes Exemption (Revocation) and Tax Exempt Schemes (Miscellaneous Amendments)) Regulations 2006, SI 2006/467; the Occupational Pension Schemes (Scottish Parliamentary Pensions Act 2009) Regulations 2009, SI 2009/1906.

[17.287]

53 Restoration orders: supplementary

(1) This section applies in relation to a restoration order under section 52 in respect of a transaction involving assets of a scheme ("the transaction").

(2) The restoration order may in particular—

(a) require any assets of the scheme (whether money or other property) which were transferred as part of the transaction to be transferred back—
   (i) to the trustees or managers of the scheme, or
   (ii) where the Board of the Pension Protection Fund has assumed responsibility for the scheme, to the Board;
(b) require any property to be transferred to the trustees or managers of the scheme or, where the Board has assumed responsibility for the scheme, to the Board if it represents in any person's hands—
   (i) any of the assets of the scheme which were transferred as part of the transaction, or
   (ii) property derived from any such assets so transferred;
(c) require such property as the Regulator may specify in the order, in respect of any consideration for the transaction received by the trustees or managers of the scheme, to be transferred—
   (i) by the trustees or managers of the scheme, or
   (ii) where the Board has assumed responsibility for the scheme, by the Board,

   to such persons as the Regulator may specify in the order;
(d) require any person to pay, in respect of benefits received by him as a result of the transaction, such sums (not exceeding the value of the benefits received by him) as the Regulator may specify in the order—
   (i) to the trustees or managers of the scheme, or
   (ii) where the Board has assumed responsibility for the scheme, to the Board.

(3) A restoration order is of no effect to the extent that it prejudices any interest in property which was acquired in good faith and for value or any interest deriving from such an interest.

(4) Nothing in subsection (3) prevents a restoration order requiring a person to pay a sum of money if the person received a benefit as a result of the transaction otherwise than in good faith and for value.

(5) Where a person has acquired an interest in property from a person or has received a benefit as a result of the transaction and—

(a) he is one of the trustees or managers or appropriate persons who entered into the transaction as mentioned in subsection (6) of section 52, or

(b) at the time of the acquisition or receipt—
   (i) he has notice of the fact that the transaction was a transaction at an undervalue,
   (ii) he is a trustee or manager, or the employer, in relation to the scheme, or
   (iii) he is connected with, or an associate of, any of the persons mentioned in paragraph (a) or (b)(ii),

then, unless the contrary is shown, it is to be presumed for the purposes of subsections (3) and (4) that the interest was acquired or the benefit was received otherwise than in good faith.

(6) For the purposes of this section—
(a) section 249 of the Insolvency Act 1986 (c 45) (connected persons) applies as it applies for the purposes of any provision of the first Group of Parts of that Act,
(b) section 435 of that Act (associated persons) applies as it applies for the purposes of that Act, and
(c) section [229 of the Bankruptcy (Scotland) Act 2016] (associated persons) applies as it applies for the purposes of that Act.

(7) For the purposes of this section "property" includes—
(a) money, goods, things in action, land and every description of property wherever situated, and
(b) obligations and every description of interest, whether present or future or vested or contingent, arising out of, or incidental to, property.

(8) References in this section to where the Board has assumed responsibility for a scheme are to where the Board has assumed responsibility for the scheme in accordance with Chapter 3 of Part 2 (pension protection).

NOTES

Sub-s (6): words in square brackets in para (c) substituted for original words "74 of the Bankruptcy (Scotland) Act 1985 (c 66)" by the Bankruptcy (Scotland) Act 2016 (Consequential Provisions and Modifications) Order 2016, SI 2016/1034, art 7(1), (3), Sch 1, para 26(1), (4), as from 30 November 2016 (except in relation to (i) a sequestration as regards which the petition is presented, or the debtor application is made before that date; or (ii) a trust deed executed before that date).

Modification: see the note to s 38 at **[17.266]**.

[17.288]

54 Content and effect of a restoration order

(1) This section applies where a restoration order is made under section 52 in respect of a transaction involving assets of a scheme.

(2) Where the restoration order imposes an obligation on a person to do something, the order must specify the period within which the obligation must be complied with.

(3) Where the restoration order imposes an obligation on a person ("A") to transfer or pay a sum of money to a person specified in the order ("B"), the sum is to be treated as a debt due from A to B.

(4) Where the trustees or managers of the scheme are the persons to whom the debt is due, the Regulator may on their behalf, exercise such powers as the trustees or managers have to recover the debt.

(5) But during any assessment period (within the meaning of section 132) in relation to the scheme, the rights and powers of the trustees or managers of the scheme in relation to any debt due to them by virtue of a restoration order are exercisable by the Board of the Pension Protection Fund to the exclusion of the trustees or managers and the Regulator.

(6) Where, by virtue of subsection (5), any amount is transferred or paid to the Board in respect of a debt due by virtue of a restoration order, the Board must pay the amount to the trustees or managers of the scheme.

NOTES

Modification: see the note to s 38 at **[17.266]**.

[17.289]

55 Contribution notice where failure to comply with restoration order

(1) This section applies where—
(a) a restoration order is made under section 52 in respect of a transaction involving assets of a scheme ("the transaction"), and
(b) a person fails to comply with an obligation imposed on him by the order which is not an obligation to transfer or pay a sum of money.

(2) The Regulator may issue a notice to the person stating that the person is under a liability to pay the sum specified in the notice (a "contribution notice")—
(a) to the trustees or managers of the scheme, or
(b) where the Board of the Pension Protection Fund has assumed responsibility for the scheme in accordance with Chapter 3 of Part 2 (pension protection), to the Board.

(3) The sum specified by the Regulator in a contribution notice may be either the whole or a specified part of the shortfall sum in relation to the scheme.

(4) The shortfall sum in relation to the scheme is the amount which the Regulator estimates to be the amount of the decrease in the value of the assets of the scheme as a result of the transaction having been entered into.

NOTES

Modification: see the note to s 38 at **[17.266]**.

[17.290]

56 Content and effect of a section 55 contribution notice

(1) This section applies where a contribution notice is issued to a person under section 55.

(2) The contribution notice must—

(a) contain a statement of the matters which it is asserted constitute the failure to comply with the restoration order under section 52 in respect of which the notice is issued, and

(b) specify the sum which the person is stated to be under a liability to pay.

(3) Where the contribution notice states that the person is under a liability to pay the sum specified in the notice to the trustees or managers of the scheme, the sum is to be treated as a debt due from the person to the trustees or managers of the scheme.

(4) In such a case, the Regulator may, on behalf of the trustees or managers of the scheme, exercise such powers as the trustees or managers have to recover the debt.

(5) But during any assessment period (within the meaning of section 132) in relation to the scheme, the rights and powers of the trustees or managers of the scheme in relation to any debt due to them by virtue of a contribution notice, are exercisable by the Board of the Pension Protection Fund to the exclusion of the trustees or managers and the Regulator.

(6) Where, by virtue of subsection (5), any amount is paid to the Board in respect of a debt due by virtue of a contribution notice, the Board must pay the amount to the trustees or managers of the scheme.

(7) Where the contribution notice states that the person is under a liability to pay the sum specified in the notice to the Board, the sum is to be treated as a debt due from the person to the Board.

NOTES

Modification: see the note to s 38 at **[17.266]**.

Sections 38 to 56: partnerships and limited liability partnerships

[17.291]

57 Sections 38 to 56: partnerships and limited liability partnerships

(1) For the purposes of any of sections 38 to 56, regulations may modify any of the definitions mentioned in subsection (2) (as applied by any of those sections) in relation to—

(a) a partnership or a partner in a partnership;

(b) a limited liability partnership or a member of such a partnership.

(2) The definitions mentioned in subsection (1) are—

(a) section 249 of the Insolvency Act 1986 (c 45) (connected persons),

(b) section 435 of that Act (associated persons),

(c) section [229 of the Bankruptcy (Scotland) Act 2016] (associated persons), and

(d) [section 1159 of the Companies Act 2006] (meaning of "subsidiary" and "holding company" etc).

(3) Regulations may also provide that any provision of sections 38 to 51 applies with such modifications as may be prescribed in relation to—

(a) any case where a partnership is or was—

(i) the employer in relation to an occupational pension scheme, or

(ii) for the purposes of any of those sections, connected with or an associate of the employer;

(b) any case where a limited liability partnership is—

(i) the employer in relation to an occupational pension scheme, or

(ii) for the purposes of any of those sections, connected with or an associate of the employer.

(4) Regulations may also provide that any provision of sections 52 to 56 applies with such modifications as may be prescribed in relation to a partnership or a limited liability partnership.

(5) For the purposes of this section—

(a) "partnership" includes a firm or entity of a similar character formed under the law of a country or territory outside the United Kingdom, and

(b) references to a partner are to be construed accordingly.

(6) For the purposes of this section, "limited liability partnership" means—

[(a) a limited liability partnership registered under the Limited Liability Partnerships Act 2000, or]

(b) an entity which is of a similar character to such a limited liability partnership and which is formed under the law of a country or territory outside the United Kingdom,

and references to a member of a limited liability partnership are to be construed accordingly.

(7) This section is without prejudice to—

(a) section 307 (power to modify this Act in relation to certain categories of scheme), and

(b) section 318(4) (power to extend the meaning of "employer").

NOTES

Sub-s (2): words in square brackets in para (c) substituted for original words "74 of the Bankruptcy (Scotland) Act 1985 (c 66)" by the Bankruptcy (Scotland) Act 2016 (Consequential Provisions and Modifications) Order 2016, SI 2016/1034, art 7(1), (3), Sch 1, para 26(1), (5), as from 30 November 2016 (except in relation to (i) a sequestration as regards which the petition is presented, or the debtor application is made before that date; or (ii) a trust deed executed before that date); words in square brackets in para (d) substituted by the Companies Act 2006 (Consequential Amendments, Transitional Provisions and Savings) Order 2009, SI 2009/1941, art 2(1), Sch 1, para 243(1), (5)(a).

Sub-s (6): para (a) substituted by SI 2009/1941, art 2(1), Sch 1, para 243(1), (5)(b).

Applications under the Insolvency Act 1986

[17.292]

58 Regulator's right to apply under section 423 of Insolvency Act 1986

(1) In this section "section 423" means section 423 of the Insolvency Act 1986 (transactions defrauding creditors).

(2) The Regulator may apply for an order under section 423 in relation to a debtor if—

(a) the debtor is the employer in relation to an occupational pension scheme, and

(b) condition A or condition B is met in relation to the scheme.

(3) Condition A is that [a determination made, or actuarial valuation obtained, in respect of the scheme by the Board of the Pension Protection Fund under section 143(2)] indicates that the value of the assets of the scheme at the relevant time, as defined by [section 143], was less than the amount of the protected liabilities, as defined by section 131, at that time.

(4) Condition B is that an actuarial valuation, as defined by section 224(2), obtained by the trustees or managers of the scheme indicates that the statutory funding objective in section 222 is not met.

(5) In a case where the debtor—

(a) has been [made] bankrupt,

(b) is a body corporate which is being wound up or is in administration, or

(c) is a partnership which is being wound up or is in administration,

subsection (2) does not enable an application to be made under section 423 except with the permission of the court.

(6) An application made under this section is to be treated as made on behalf of every victim of the transaction who is—

(a) a trustee or member of the scheme, or

(b) the Board.

(7) This section does not apply where the valuation mentioned in subsection (3) or (4) is made by reference to a date that falls before the commencement of this section.

(8) Expressions which are defined by section 423 for the purposes of that section have the same meaning when used in this section.

NOTES

Sub-s (3): words in square brackets substituted by the Pensions Act 2011, s 22, Sch 4, paras 1, 2.

Sub-s (5): word in square brackets in para (a) substituted by the Enterprise and Regulatory Reform Act 2013 (Consequential Amendments) (Bankruptcy) and the Small Business, Enterprise and Employment Act 2015 (Consequential Amendments) Regulations 2016, SI 2016/481, reg 2(1), Sch 1, Pt 2, para 18.

59–106 (*Outside the scope of this work.*)

PART 2
THE BOARD OF THE PENSION PROTECTION FUND

NOTES

This Part is applied, with extensive modifications, in relation to multi-employer schemes by the Pension Protection Fund (Multi-employer Schemes) (Modification) Regulations 2005, SI 2005/441 at **[18.15]** et seq.

107–119 (*(Ch 1) Outside the scope of this work.*)

CHAPTER 2 INFORMATION RELATING TO EMPLOYER'S INSOLVENCY ETC

Insolvency events

[17.293]

120 Duty to notify insolvency events in respect of employers

(1) This section applies where, in the case of an occupational pension scheme, an insolvency event occurs in relation to the employer.

(2) The insolvency practitioner in relation to the employer must give a notice to that effect within the notification period to—

(a) the Board,

(b) the Regulator, and

(c) the trustees or managers of the scheme.

(3) For the purposes of subsection (2) the "notification period" is the prescribed period beginning with the later of—

(a) the insolvency date, and

(b) the date the insolvency practitioner becomes aware of the existence of the scheme.

(4) A notice under this section must be in such form and contain such information as may be prescribed.

NOTES

Regulations: the Pension Protection Fund (Entry Rules) Regulations 2005, SI 2005/590; the Pension Protection Fund (Entry Rules) Amendment Regulations 2005, SI 2005/2153; the Pension Protection Fund (Insolvent Partnerships) (Amendment of Insolvency Events) Order 2005, SI 2005/2893; the Pension Protection Fund (Entry Rules) (Amendment) Regulations 2014, SI 2014/1664.

[17.294]

121 Insolvency event, insolvency date and insolvency practitioner

(1) In this Part each of the following expressions has the meaning given to it by this section—

"insolvency event"

"insolvency date"

"insolvency practitioner".

(2) An insolvency event occurs in relation to an individual where—

(a) he is [made] bankrupt or sequestration of his estate has been awarded;

(b) the nominee in relation to a proposal for a voluntary arrangement under Part 8 of the Insolvency Act 1986 (c 45) submits a report to the court under section 256(1) or 256A(3) of that Act which states that in his opinion [the individual's creditors should] consider the debtor's proposal;

(c) . . .

(d) he executes a trust deed for his creditors or enters into a composition contract;

(e) he has died and—

(i) an insolvency administration order is made in respect of his estate in accordance with an order under section 421 of the Insolvency Act 1986, or

(ii) a judicial factor appointed under section 11A of the Judicial Factors (Scotland) Act 1889 (c 39) is required by that section to divide the individual's estate among his creditors.

(3) An insolvency event occurs in relation to a company where—

(a) the nominee in relation to a proposal for a voluntary arrangement under Part 1 of the Insolvency Act 1986 submits a report to the court under section 2 of that Act (procedure where nominee is not the liquidator or administrator) which states that in his opinion [the proposal should be considered by a meeting of the company and by the company's creditors;]

(b) the directors of the company file (or in Scotland lodge) with the court documents and statements in accordance with paragraph 7(1) of Schedule A1 to that Act (moratorium where directors propose voluntary arrangement);

(c) an administrative receiver within the meaning of section 251 of that Act is appointed in relation to the company;

(d) the company enters administration within the meaning of paragraph 1(2)(b) of Schedule B1 to that Act;

(e) a resolution is passed for a voluntary winding up of the company without a declaration of solvency under section 89 of that Act;

[(f) a winding up becomes a creditors' voluntary winding up under section 96 of that Act (conversion to creditors' voluntary winding up);]

(g) an order for the winding up of the company is made by the court under Part 4 or 5 of that Act.

(4) An insolvency event occurs in relation to a partnership where—

(a) an order for the winding up of the partnership is made by the court under any provision of the Insolvency Act 1986 (c 45) (as applied by an order under section 420 of that Act (insolvent partnerships));

(b) sequestration is awarded on the estate of the partnership under section [22 of the Bankruptcy (Scotland) Act 2016] or the partnership grants a trust deed for its creditors;

(c) the nominee in relation to a proposal for a voluntary arrangement under Part 1 of the Insolvency Act 1986 (as applied by an order under section 420 of that Act) submits a report to the court under section 2 of that Act (procedure where nominee is not the liquidator or administrator) which states that in his opinion [the proposal should be considered by a meeting of the members of the partnership and by the partnership's creditors;]

(d) the members of the partnership file with the court documents and statements in accordance with paragraph 7(1) of Schedule A1 to that Act (moratorium where directors propose voluntary arrangement) (as applied by an order under section 420 of that Act);

[(e) the partnership enters administration within the meaning of paragraph 1(2)(b) of Schedule B1 to that Act (as applied by an order under section 420 of that Act).]

(5) An insolvency event also occurs in relation to a person where an event occurs which is a prescribed event in relation to such a person.

(6) Except as provided by subsections (2) to (5), for the purposes of this Part an event is not to be regarded as an insolvency event in relation to a person.

(7) The Secretary of State may by order amend subsection (4)(e) to make provision consequential upon any order under section 420 of the Insolvency Act 1986 (insolvent partnerships) applying the provisions of Part 2 of that Act (administration) as amended by the Enterprise Act 2002 (c 40).

(8) "Insolvency date", in relation to an insolvency event, means the date on which the event occurs.

(9) "Insolvency practitioner", in relation to a person, means—

(a) a person acting as an insolvency practitioner, in relation to that person, in accordance with section 388 of the Insolvency Act 1986;

(b) in such circumstances as may be prescribed, a person of a prescribed description.

(10) In this section—

"company" means a company [as defined in section 1(1) of the Companies Act 2006] or a company which may be wound up under Part 5 of the Insolvency Act 1986 (c 45) (unregistered companies);

"person acting as an insolvency practitioner", in relation to a person, includes the official receiver acting as receiver or manager of any property of that person.

(11) In applying section 388 of the Insolvency Act 1986 under subsection (9) above—

(a) the reference in section 388(2)(a) to a permanent or interim trustee in sequestration must be taken to include a reference to a trustee in sequestration, and

(b) section 388(5) (which includes provision that nothing in the section applies to anything done by the official receiver or the Accountant in Bankruptcy) must be ignored.

NOTES

Commencement: 10 February 2005 (sub-s (5) (for the purpose of making regulations, orders or rules)); 6 April 2005 (sub-ss (1)–(4), (5) (for remaining purposes), (6), (8), (9)(a), (10), (11)); 30 June 2005 (sub-s (7)); 25 June 2014 (sub-s (9)(b)).

Sub-s (2): word in square brackets in para (a) substituted by the Enterprise and Regulatory Reform Act 2013 (Consequential Amendments) (Bankruptcy) and the Small Business, Enterprise and Employment Act 2015 (Consequential Amendments) Regulations 2016, SI 2016/481, reg 2(1), Sch 1, Pt 2, para 18; words in square brackets in para (b) substituted by the Deregulation Act 2015 and Small Business, Enterprise and Employment Act 2015 (Consequential Amendments) (Savings) Regulations 2017, SI 2017/540, reg 2, Sch 1, para 4(1), (2); para (c) repealed by the Deregulation Act 2015, s 19, Sch 6, Pt 1, para 2(1), (18).

Sub-s (3): words in square brackets in para (a), and para (f) substituted by SI 2017/540, reg 2, Sch 1, para 4(1), (3), (4).

Sub-s (4): words in square brackets in para (b) substituted for original words "12 of the Bankruptcy (Scotland) Act 1985 (c 66)" by the Bankruptcy (Scotland) Act 2016 (Consequential Provisions and Modifications) Order 2016, SI 2016/1034, art 7(1), (3), Sch 1, para 26(1), (6)(a), as from 30 November 2016 (except in relation to (i) a sequestration as regards which the petition is presented, or the debtor application is made before that date; or (ii) a trust deed executed before that date); words in square brackets in para (c) substituted by SI 2017/540, reg 2, Sch 1, para 4(1), (5); para (e) substituted by the Pension Protection Fund (Insolvent Partnerships) (Amendment of Insolvency Events) Order 2005, SI 2005/2893, art 2.

Sub-s (10): words in square brackets substituted by the Companies Act 2006 (Consequential Amendments, Transitional Provisions and Savings) Order 2009, SI 2009/1941, art 2(1), Sch 1, para 243(1), (7).

Sub-s (11): para (a) repealed by SI 2016/1034, art 7(1), (3), Sch 1, para 26(1), (6)(b), as from 30 November 2016 (except in relation to (i) a sequestration as regards which the petition is presented, or the debtor application is made before that date; or (ii) a trust deed executed before that date).

Regulations: the Pension Protection Fund (Entry Rules) Regulations 2005, SI 2005/590; the Pension Protection Fund (Entry Rules) Amendment Regulations 2005, SI 2005/2153; the Pension Protection Fund (Insolvent Partnerships) (Amendment of Insolvency Events) Order 2005, SI 2005/2893; the Pension Protection Fund (Entry Rules) (Amendment) Regulations 2014, SI 2014/1664.

Status of scheme

[17.295]

122 Insolvency practitioner's duty to issue notices confirming status of scheme

(1) This section applies where an insolvency event has occurred in relation to the employer in relation to an occupational pension scheme.

(2) An insolvency practitioner in relation to the employer must—

(a) if he is able to confirm that a scheme rescue is not possible, issue a notice to that effect (a "scheme failure notice"), or

(b) if he is able to confirm that a scheme rescue has occurred, issue a notice to that effect (a "withdrawal notice").

(3) Subsection (4) applies where—

(a) in prescribed circumstances, insolvency proceedings in relation to the employer are stayed or come to an end, or

(b) a prescribed event occurs.

(4) If a person who was acting as an insolvency practitioner in relation to the employer immediately before this subsection applies has not been able to confirm in relation to the scheme—

(a) that a scheme rescue is not possible, or

(b) that a scheme rescue has occurred,

he must issue a notice to that effect.

(5) For the purposes of this section—

(a) a person is able to confirm that a scheme rescue has occurred in relation to an occupational pension scheme if, and only if, he is able to confirm such matters as are prescribed for the purposes of this paragraph, and

(b) a person is able to confirm that a scheme rescue is not possible, in relation to such a scheme if, and only if, he is able to confirm such matters as are prescribed for the purposes of this paragraph.

(6) Where an insolvency practitioner or former insolvency practitioner in relation to the employer issues a notice under this section, he must give a copy of that notice to—

(a) the Board,

(b) the Regulator, and

(c) the trustees or managers of the scheme.

(7) A person must comply with an obligation imposed on him by subsection (2), (4) or (6) as soon as reasonably practicable.

(8) Regulations may require notices issued under this section—

(a) to be in a prescribed form;

(b) to contain prescribed information.

NOTES

Regulations: the Pension Protection Fund (Entry Rules) Regulations 2005, SI 2005/590.

[17.296]

123 Approval of notices issued under section 122

(1) This section applies where the Board receives a notice under section 122(6) ("the section 122 notice").

(2) The Board must determine whether to approve the section 122 notice.

(3) The Board must approve the section 122 notice if, and only if, it is satisfied—

(a) that the insolvency practitioner or former insolvency practitioner who issued the notice was required to issue it under that section, and

(b) that the notice complies with any requirements imposed by virtue of subsection (8) of that section.

(4) Where the Board makes a determination for the purposes of subsection (2), it must issue a determination notice and give a copy of that notice to—

(a) the Regulator,

(b) the trustees or managers of the scheme,

(c) the insolvency practitioner or the former insolvency practitioner who issued the section 122 notice,

(d) any insolvency practitioner in relation to the employer (who does not fall within paragraph (c)), and

(e) if there is no insolvency practitioner in relation to the employer, the employer.

(5) In subsection (4) "determination notice" means a notice which is in the prescribed form and contains such information about the determination as may be prescribed.

NOTES

Regulations: the Pension Protection Fund (Entry Rules) Regulations 2005, SI 2005/590.

Board's duties

[17.297]

124 Board's duty where there is a failure to comply with section 122

(1) This section applies where in relation to an occupational pension scheme—

(a) the Board determines under section 123 not to approve a notice issued under section 122 by an insolvency practitioner or former insolvency practitioner in relation to the employer, or

(b) an insolvency practitioner or former insolvency practitioner in relation to the employer fails to issue a notice under section 122 and the Board is satisfied that such a notice ought to have been issued under that section.

(2) The obligations on the insolvency practitioner or former insolvency practitioner imposed by subsections (2) and (4) of section 122 are to be treated as obligations imposed on the Board and the Board must accordingly issue a notice as required under that section.

(3) Subject to subsections (4) and (5), where a notice is issued under section 122 by the Board by virtue of this section, it has effect as if it were a notice issued under section 122 by an insolvency practitioner or, as the case may be, former insolvency practitioner in relation to the employer.

(4) Where a notice is issued under section 122 by virtue of this section, section 122(6) does not apply and the Board must, as soon as reasonably practicable, give a copy of the notice to—

(a) the Regulator,

(b) the trustees or managers of the scheme,

(c) the insolvency practitioner or former insolvency practitioner mentioned in subsection (1),

(d) any insolvency practitioner in relation to the employer (who does not fall within paragraph (c)), and

(e) if there is no insolvency practitioner in relation to the employer, the employer.

(5) Where the Board—

(a) is required to issue a notice under section 122 by virtue of this section, and

(b) is satisfied that the notice ought to have been issued at an earlier time,

it must specify that time in the notice and the notice is to have effect as if it had been issued at that time.

[17.298]

125 Binding notices confirming status of scheme

(1) Subject to subsection (2), for the purposes of this Part, a notice issued under section 122 is not binding until—

(a) the Board issues a determination notice under section 123 approving the notice,

(b) the period within which the issue of the determination notice under that section may be reviewed by virtue of Chapter 6 has expired, and

(c) if the issue of the determination notice is so reviewed—

(i) the review and any reconsideration,

(ii) any reference to the PPF Ombudsman in respect of the issue of the notice, and

(iii) any appeal against his determination or directions,

has been finally disposed of and the determination notice has not been revoked, varied or substituted.

(2) Where a notice is issued under section 122 by the Board by virtue of section 124, the notice is not binding until—

(a) the period within which the issue of the notice may be reviewed by virtue of Chapter 6 has expired, and

(b) if the issue of the notice is so reviewed—

(i) the review and any reconsideration,

(ii) any reference to the PPF Ombudsman in respect of the issue of the notice, and

(iii) any appeal against his determination or directions,

has been finally disposed of and the notice has not been revoked, varied or substituted.

(3) Where a notice issued under section 122 becomes binding, the Board must as soon as reasonably practicable give a notice to that effect together with a copy of the binding notice to—

(a) the Regulator,
(b) the trustees or managers of the scheme,
(c) the insolvency practitioner or former insolvency practitioner who issued the notice under section 122 or, where that notice was issued by the Board by virtue of section 124, the insolvency practitioner or former insolvency practitioner mentioned in subsection (1) of that section,
(d) any insolvency practitioner in relation to the employer (who does not fall within paragraph (c)), and
(e) if there is no insolvency practitioner in relation to the employer, the employer.

(4) A notice under subsection (3)—
(a) must be in the prescribed form and contain such information as may be prescribed, and
(b) where it is given in relation to a withdrawal notice issued under section 122(2)(b) which has become binding, must state the time from which the Board ceases to be involved with the scheme (see section 149).

CHAPTER 3 PENSION PROTECTION

126 (*Outside the scope of this work.*)

Circumstances in which Board assumes responsibility for eligible schemes

[17.299]
127 Duty to assume responsibility for schemes following insolvency event

(1) This section applies where a qualifying insolvency event has occurred in relation to the employer in relation to an eligible scheme.

(2) The Board must assume responsibility for the scheme in accordance with this Chapter if—
(a) the value of the assets of the scheme at the relevant time was less than the amount of the protected liabilities at that time (see sections 131 and 143),
(b) after the relevant time a scheme failure notice is issued under section 122(2)(a) in relation to the scheme and that notice becomes binding, and
(c) a withdrawal event has not occurred in relation to the scheme in respect of a withdrawal notice which has been issued during the period—
(i) beginning with the occurrence of the qualifying insolvency event, and
(ii) ending immediately before the issuing of the scheme failure notice under section 122(2)(a),
and the occurrence of such a withdrawal event in respect of a withdrawal notice issued during that period is not a possibility (see section 149).

(3) For the purposes of this section, in relation to an eligible scheme an insolvency event ("the current event") in relation to the employer is a qualifying insolvency event if—
(a) it occurs on or after the day appointed under section 126(2), and
(b) it—
(i) is the first insolvency event to occur in relation to the employer on or after that day, or
(ii) does not occur within an assessment period (see section 132) in relation to the scheme which began before the occurrence of the current event.

(4) For the purposes of this section—
(a) the reference in subsection (2)(a) to the assets of the scheme is a reference to those assets excluding any assets representing the value of any rights in respect of money purchase benefits under the scheme rules, and
(b) "the relevant time" means the time immediately before the qualifying insolvency event occurs.

(5) This section is subject to sections 146 and 147 (cases where Board must refuse to assume responsibility for a scheme).

NOTES

Modification: this section is applied, with modifications, to partially guaranteed schemes by the Pension Protection Fund (Partially Guaranteed Schemes) (Modification) Regulations 2005, SI 2005/277, regs 1(2), 2, 3(1)(a), 4(1).

[17.300]
128 Duty to assume responsibility for schemes following application or notification

(1) This section applies where, in relation to an eligible scheme, the trustees or managers of the scheme—
(a) make an application under subsection (1) of section 129 (a "section 129 application"), or
(b) receive a notice from the Board under subsection (5)(a) of that section (a "section 129 notification").

(2) The Board must assume responsibility for the scheme in accordance with this Chapter if—
(a) the value of the assets of the scheme at the relevant time was less than the amount of the protected liabilities at that time (see sections 131 and 143),
(b) after the relevant time the Board issues a scheme failure notice under section 130(2) in relation to the scheme and that notice becomes binding, and
(c) a withdrawal event has not occurred in relation to the scheme in respect of a withdrawal notice which has been issued during the period—
(i) beginning with the making of the section 129 application or, as the case may be, the receipt of the section 129 notification, and
(ii) ending immediately before the issuing of the scheme failure notice under section 130(2),
and the occurrence of such a withdrawal event in respect of a withdrawal notice issued during

that period is not a possibility (see section 149).

(3) In subsection (2)—

(a) the reference in paragraph (a) to the assets of the scheme is a reference to those assets excluding any assets representing the value of any rights in respect of money purchase benefits under the scheme rules, and

(b) "the relevant time" means the time immediately before the section 129 application was made or, as the case may be, the section 129 notification was received.

(4) An application under section 129(1) or notification under section 129(5)(a) is to be disregarded for the purposes of subsection (1) if it is made or given during an assessment period (see section 132) in relation to the scheme which began before the application was made or notification was given.

(5) This section is subject to sections 146 and 147 (cases where Board must refuse to assume responsibility for a scheme).

NOTES

Modification: this section is applied, with modifications, to partially guaranteed schemes by the Pension Protection Fund (Partially Guaranteed Schemes) (Modification) Regulations 2005, SI 2005/277, regs 1(2), 2, 3(1)(b), 4(1).

[17.301]

129 Applications and notifications for the purposes of section 128

(1) Where the trustees or managers of an eligible scheme become aware that—

(a) the employer in relation to the scheme is unlikely to continue as a going concern, and

(b) the prescribed requirements are met in relation to the employer,

they must make an application to the Board for it to assume responsibility for the scheme under section 128.

(2) Where the Board receives an application under subsection (1), it must give a copy of the application to—

(a) the Regulator, and

(b) the employer.

(3) An application under subsection (1) must—

(a) be in the prescribed form and contain the prescribed information, and

(b) be made within the prescribed period.

(4) Where the Regulator becomes aware that—

(a) the employer in relation to an eligible scheme is unlikely to continue as a going concern, and

(b) the requirements mentioned in subsection (1)(b) are met in relation to the employer,

it must give the Board a notice to that effect.

(5) Where the Board receives a notice under subsection (4), it must—

(a) give the trustees or managers of the scheme a notice to that effect, and

(b) give the employer a copy of that notice.

(6) The duty imposed by subsection (1) does not apply where the trustees or managers of an eligible scheme become aware as mentioned in that subsection by reason of a notice given to them under subsection (5).

(7) The duty imposed by subsection (4) does not apply where the Regulator becomes aware as mentioned in that subsection by reason of a copy of an application made by the trustees or managers of the eligible scheme in question given to the Regulator under subsection (2).

(8) Regulations may require notices under this section to be in the prescribed form and contain the prescribed information.

NOTES

Modification: this section is applied, with modifications, to partially guaranteed schemes by the Pension Protection Fund (Partially Guaranteed Schemes) (Modification) Regulations 2005, SI 2005/277, regs 1(2), 2, 4(2).

Regulations: the Pension Protection Fund (Entry Rules) Regulations 2005, SI 2005/590; the Occupational Pension Schemes and Pension Protection Fund (Amendment) Regulations 2005, SI 2005/993; the Pension Protection Fund (Entry Rules) Amendment Regulations 2005, SI 2005/2153; the Pension Protection Fund (Miscellaneous Amendments) Regulations 2009, SI 2009/451.

[17.302]

130 Board's duty where application or notification received under section 129

(1) This section applies where the Board—

(a) receives an application under subsection (1) of section 129 and is satisfied that paragraphs (a) and (b) of that subsection are satisfied in relation to the application, or

(b) is notified by the Regulator under section 129(4).

(2) If the Board is able to confirm that a scheme rescue is not possible, it must as soon as reasonably practicable issue a notice to that effect (a "scheme failure notice").

(3) If the Board is able to confirm that a scheme rescue has occurred, it must as soon as reasonably practicable issue a notice to that effect (a "withdrawal notice").

(4) The Board must, as soon as reasonably practicable, give a copy of any notice issued under subsection (2) or (3) to—

(a) the Regulator,

(b) the trustees or managers of the scheme, and

(c) the employer.

(5) For the purposes of this section—

(a) the Board is able to confirm that a scheme rescue has occurred in relation to an occupational pension scheme if, and only if, it is able to confirm such matters as are prescribed for the purposes of this paragraph, and
(b) the Board is able to confirm that a scheme rescue is not possible in relation to such a scheme if, and only if, it is able to confirm such matters as are prescribed for the purposes of this paragraph.

(6) For the purposes of this Part a notice issued under subsection (2) or (3) is not binding until—
(a) the period within which the issue of the notice may be reviewed by virtue of Chapter 6 has expired, and
(b) if the issue of the notice is so reviewed—
(i) the review and any reconsideration,
(ii) any reference to the PPF Ombudsman in respect of the issue of the notice, and
(iii) any appeal against his determination or directions,
has been finally disposed of and the notice has not been revoked, varied or substituted.

(7) Where a notice issued under subsection (2) or (3) becomes binding, the Board must as soon as reasonably practicable give a notice to that effect together with a copy of the binding notice to—
(a) the Regulator,
(b) the trustees or managers of the scheme, and
(c) the employer.

(8) Notices under this section must be in the prescribed form and contain such information as may be prescribed.

(9) A notice given under subsection (7) in relation to a withdrawal notice under subsection (3) which has become binding must state the time from which the Board ceases to be involved with the scheme (see section 149).

NOTES

Regulations: the Pension Protection Fund (Entry Rules) Regulations 2005, SI 2005/590; the Pension Protection Fund (Miscellaneous Amendments) Regulations 2009, SI 2009/451.

[17.303]
131 Protected liabilities

(1) For the purposes of this Chapter the protected liabilities, in relation to an eligible scheme, at a particular time ("the relevant time") are—
(a) the cost of securing benefits for and in respect of members of the scheme which correspond to the compensation which would be payable, in relation to the scheme, in accordance with the pension compensation provisions (see section 162) if the Board assumed responsibility for the scheme in accordance with this Chapter,
(b) liabilities of the scheme which are not liabilities to, or in respect of, its members, and
(c) the estimated cost of winding up the scheme.

(2) For the purposes of determining the cost of securing benefits within subsection (1)(a), references in sections 140 to 142 and Schedule 7 (pension compensation provisions) to the assessment date are to be read as references to the date on which the time immediately after the relevant time falls.

NOTES

Modification: this section is applied, with modifications, to partially guaranteed schemes by the Pension Protection Fund (Partially Guaranteed Schemes) (Modification) Regulations 2005, SI 2005/277, regs 1(2), 2, 3(2)(a), (4)(a).

Restrictions on schemes during the assessment period

[17.304]
132 Assessment periods

(1) In this Part references to an assessment period are to be construed in accordance with this section.

(2) Where, in relation to an eligible scheme, a qualifying insolvency event occurs in relation to the employer, an assessment period—
(a) begins with the occurrence of that event, and
(b) ends when—
(i) the Board ceases to be involved with the scheme (see section 149),
(ii) the trustees or managers of the scheme receive a transfer notice under section 160, or
(iii) the conditions in section 154(2) (no scheme rescue but sufficient assets to meet protected liabilities etc) are satisfied in relation to the scheme,
whichever first occurs.

(3) In subsection (2) "qualifying insolvency event" has the meaning given by section 127(3).

(4) Where, in relation to an eligible scheme, an application is made under section 129(1) or a notification is received under section 129(5)(a), an assessment period—
(a) begins when the application is made or the notification is received, and
(b) ends when—
(i) the Board ceases to be involved with the scheme (see section 149),
(ii) the trustees or managers of the scheme receive a transfer notice under section 160, or
(iii) the conditions in section 154(2) (no scheme rescue but sufficient assets to meet protected liabilities etc) are satisfied in relation to the scheme,
whichever first occurs.

(5) For the purposes of subsection (4) an application under section 129(1) or notification under section 129(5)(a) is to be disregarded if it is made or given during an assessment period in relation to the scheme which began before the application was made or notification was given.

(6) This section is subject to section 159 (which provides for further assessment periods to begin in certain circumstances where schemes are required to wind up or continue winding up under section 154).

[17.305]

133 Admission of new members, payment of contributions etc

(1) This section applies where there is an assessment period in relation to an eligible scheme.

(2) No new members of any class may be admitted to the scheme during the assessment period.

(3) Except in prescribed circumstances and subject to prescribed conditions, no further contributions (other than those due to be paid before the beginning of the assessment period) may be paid towards the scheme during the assessment period.

(4) Any obligation to pay contributions towards the scheme during the assessment period (including any obligation under section 49(8) of the Pensions Act 1995 (c 26) to pay amounts deducted corresponding to such contributions) is to be read subject to subsection (3) and section 150 (obligation to pay contributions when assessment period ends).

(5) No benefits may accrue under the scheme rules to, or in respect of, members of the scheme during the assessment period.

(6) Subsection (5) does not prevent any increase, in a benefit, which would otherwise accrue in accordance with the scheme or any enactment. This subsection is subject to section 138 (which limits the scheme benefits payable during an assessment period).

(7) Subsection (5) does not prevent the accrual of money purchase benefits to the extent that they are derived from income or capital gains arising from the investment of payments which are made by, or in respect of, a member of the scheme.

(8) Where a person is entitled to a pension credit derived from another person's shareable rights under the scheme, nothing in this section prevents the trustees or managers of the scheme discharging their liability in respect of the credit under Chapter 1 of Part 4 of the Welfare Reform and Pensions Act 1999 (c 30) (sharing of rights under pension arrangements) by conferring appropriate rights under the scheme on that person.

(9) In subsection (8)—

"appropriate rights" has the same meaning as in paragraph 5 of Schedule 5 to that Act (pension credits: mode of discharge);

"shareable rights" has the same meaning as in Chapter 1 of Part 4 of that Act (sharing of rights under pension arrangements).

(10) Any action taken in contravention of this section is void.

(11) Disregarding subsection (10), section 10 of the Pensions Act 1995 (civil penalties) applies to any trustee or manager of a scheme who fails to take all reasonable steps to secure compliance with this section.

NOTES

Regulations: the Pension Protection Fund (Entry Rules) Regulations 2005, SI 2005/590.

[17.306]

134 Directions

(1) This section applies where there is an assessment period in relation to an eligible scheme.

(2) With a view to ensuring that the scheme's protected liabilities do not exceed its assets or, if they do exceed its assets, that the excess is kept to a minimum, the Board may give a relevant person in relation to the scheme directions regarding the exercise during that period of his powers in respect of—

(a) the investment of the scheme's assets,
(b) the incurring of expenditure,
(c) the instigation or conduct of legal proceedings, and
(d) such other matters as may be prescribed.

(3) In subsection (2)—

(a) "relevant person" in relation to a scheme means—
  (i) the trustees or managers of the scheme,
  (ii) the employer in relation to the scheme, or
  (iii) such other persons as may be prescribed, and
(b) the reference to the assets of the scheme is a reference to those assets excluding any assets representing the value of any rights in respect of money purchase benefits under the scheme rules.

(4) The Board may revoke or vary any direction under this section.

(5) Where a direction under this section given to the trustees or managers of a scheme is not complied with, section 10 of the Pensions Act 1995 (c 26) (civil penalties) applies to any such trustee or manager who has failed to take all reasonable steps to secure compliance with the direction.

(6) That section also applies to any other person who, without reasonable excuse, fails to comply with a direction given to him under this section.

NOTES

Modifications: this section is applied, with modifications, to partially guaranteed schemes by the Pension Protection Fund (Partially Guaranteed Schemes) (Modification) Regulations 2005, SI 2005/277, regs 1(2), 2, 5(1), and in relation to hybrid schemes, by the Pension Protection Fund (Hybrid Schemes) (Modification) Regulations 2005, SI 2005/449, reg 3(1).

Regulations: the Pension Protection Fund (Entry Rules) Regulations 2005, SI 2005/590; the Pension Protection Fund (Entry Rules) (Amendment) Regulations 2009, SI 2009/1552.

[17.307]
135 Restrictions on winding up, discharge of liabilities etc
(1) This section applies where there is an assessment period in relation to an eligible scheme.
(2) Subject to subsection (3), the winding up of the scheme must not begin during the assessment period.
(3) Subsection (2) does not apply to the winding up of the scheme in pursuance of an order by the Regulator under section 11(3A) of the Pensions Act 1995 (Regulator's powers to wind up occupational pension schemes to protect Pension Protection Fund) directing the scheme to be wound up (and section 219 makes provision for the backdating of the winding up).
(4) During the assessment period, except in prescribed circumstances and subject to prescribed conditions—
[(za) no right or entitlement of any member, or of any other person in respect of a member, to a benefit that is not a money purchase benefit is to be converted into, or replaced with, a right or entitlement to a money purchase benefit under the scheme rules,]
(a) no transfers of, or transfer payments in respect of, any member's rights under the scheme rules are to be made from the scheme, and
(b) no other steps may be taken to discharge any liability of the scheme to or in respect of a member of the scheme in respect of—
(i) pensions or other benefits, or
(ii) such other liabilities as may be prescribed.
(5) Subsection (4)—
(a) is subject to section 138, and
(b) applies whether or not the scheme was being wound up immediately before the assessment period or began winding up by virtue of subsection (3).
(6) Subsection (7) applies where, on the commencement of the assessment period—
(a) a member's pensionable service terminates, and
(b) he becomes a person to whom [Chapter 2 of Part 4ZA] of the Pension Schemes Act 1993 (c 48) (early leavers: cash transfer sums and contribution refunds) applies.
Section 150(5) (retrospective accrual of benefits in certain circumstances) is to be disregarded for the purposes of determining whether a member falls within paragraph (a) or (b).
(7) Where this subsection applies, during the assessment period—
(a) no right or power conferred by that Chapter may be exercised, and
(b) no duty imposed by that Chapter may be discharged.
(8) Where a person is entitled to a pension credit derived from another person's shareable rights (within the meaning of Chapter 1 of Part 4 under of the Welfare Reform and Pensions Act 1999 (c 30) (sharing of rights under pension arrangements)) under the scheme, nothing in subsection (4) prevents the trustees or managers of the scheme discharging their liability in respect of the credit in accordance with that Chapter.
(9) Any action taken in contravention of this section is void, except to the extent that the Board validates the action (see section 136).
(10) Disregarding subsection (9), where there is a contravention of this section, section 10 of the Pensions Act 1995 (c 26) (civil penalties) applies to any trustee or manager who has failed to take all reasonable steps to secure compliance with this section.
(11) The Regulator may not make a freezing order (see section 23) in relation to the scheme during the assessment period.

NOTES
Sub-s (4): para (za) inserted by the Pension Schemes Act 2015, s 58(3).
Sub-s (6): in para (b) words in square brackets substituted by the Pension Schemes Act 2015, Sch 4, s 67, Pt 1, paras 34, 39.
Regulations: the Pension Protection Fund (Hybrid Schemes) (Modification) Regulations 2005, SI 2005/449; the Pension Protection Fund (Entry Rules) Regulations 2005, SI 2005/590; the Occupational Pension Schemes and Pension Protection Fund (Amendment) Regulations 2005, SI 2005/993; the Occupational Pension Schemes (Employer Debt etc) (Amendment) Regulations 2005, SI 2005/2224; the Pension Protection Fund (Contributions Equivalent Premium) Regulations 2007, SI 2007/834; the Pensions Act 2011 (Transitional, Consequential and Supplementary Provisions) Regulations 2014, SI 2014/1711.

[17.308]
136 Power to validate contraventions of section 135
(1) The Board may validate an action for the purposes of section 135(9) only if it is satisfied that to do so is consistent with the objective of ensuring that the scheme's protected liabilities do not exceed its assets or, if they do exceed its assets, that the excess is kept to a minimum.
(2) Where the Board determines to validate, or not to validate, any action of the trustees or managers for those purposes, it must issue a notice to that effect and give a copy of that notice to—
(a) the Regulator,
(b) the trustees or managers of the scheme,
(c) any insolvency practitioner in relation to the employer or, if there is no such insolvency practitioner, the employer, and
(d) any other person who appears to the Board to be directly affected by the determination.
(3) A notice under subsection (2) must contain a statement of the Board's reasons for the determination.
(4) The validation of an action does not take effect—

(a) until—
(i) the Board has issued a notice under subsection (2) relating to the determination, and
(ii) the period within which the issue of that notice may be reviewed by virtue of Chapter 6 has expired, and
(b) if the issue of the notice is so reviewed, until—
(i) the review and any reconsideration,
(ii) any reference to the PPF Ombudsman in respect of the issue of the notice, and
(iii) any appeal against his determination or directions,
has been finally disposed of.

(5) In subsection (1) the reference to the assets of the scheme is a reference to those assets excluding any assets representing the value of any rights in respect of money purchase benefits under the scheme rules.

NOTES

Modification: this section is applied, with modifications, to partially guaranteed schemes by the Pension Protection Fund (Partially Guaranteed Schemes) (Modification) Regulations 2005, SI 2005/277, regs 1(2), 2, 3(1)(c), 5(2).

[17.309]
137 Board to act as creditor of the employer

(1) Subsection (2) applies where there is an assessment period in relation to an eligible scheme.
(2) During the assessment period, the rights and powers of the trustees or managers of the scheme in relation to any debt (including any contingent debt) due to them by the employer, whether by virtue of section 75 of the Pensions Act 1995 (c 26) (deficiencies in the scheme assets) or otherwise, are exercisable by the Board to the exclusion of the trustees or managers.
(3) Where, by virtue of subsection (2), any amount is paid to the Board in respect of such a debt, the Board must pay that amount to the trustees or managers of the scheme.

[17.310]
138 Payment of scheme benefits

(1) Subsections (2)[, (2A)] and (3) apply where there is an assessment period in relation to an eligible scheme.
(2) The benefits payable to or in respect of any member under the scheme rules during the assessment period must be reduced to the extent necessary to ensure that they do not exceed the compensation which would be payable to or in respect of the member in accordance with this Chapter if—
(a) the Board assumed responsibility for the scheme in accordance with this Chapter, and
(b) the assessment date referred to in Schedule 7 were the date on which the assessment period began.

[(2A) Benefits in the form of a lump sum may be paid to or in respect of a member under the scheme rules during the assessment period only in the circumstances in which, and to the extent to which, lump sum compensation would be payable to or in respect of the member in accordance with this Chapter if—
(a) the Board assumed responsibility for the scheme in accordance with this Chapter, and
(b) the assessment date referred to in Schedule 7 were the date on which the assessment period began.]

(3) . . . where, on the commencement of the assessment period—
(a) a member's pensionable service terminates, and
(b) he becomes a person to whom [Chapter 2 of Part 4ZA] of the Pension Schemes Act 1993 (c 48) (early leavers: cash transfer sums and contribution refunds) applies,
no benefits are payable to or in respect of him under the scheme during the assessment period.

(4) Section 150(5) (retrospective accrual of benefits in certain circumstances) is to be disregarded for the purposes of determining whether a member falls within paragraph (a) or (b) of subsection (3).
(5) Nothing in subsection (3) prevents the payment of benefits attributable (directly or indirectly) to a pension credit, during the assessment period, in accordance with [subsections (2) and (2A)].
(6) Where at any time during the assessment period the scheme is being wound up, subject to any reduction required under subsection (2) and to [subsections (2A) and (3)], the benefits payable to or in respect of any member under the scheme rules during that period are the benefits that would have been so payable in the absence of the winding up of the scheme.
(7) Subsections (2), [(2A),] (3) and (6) are subject to sections 150(1) to (3) and 154(13) (which provide for the adjustment of amounts paid during an assessment period when that period ends other than as a result of the Board assuming responsibility for the scheme).
(8) For the purposes of subsections (2)[, (2A)] and (3) the trustees or managers of the scheme may take such steps as they consider appropriate (including steps adjusting future payments under the scheme rules) to recover any overpayment or pay any shortfall.
(9) Section 10 of the Pensions Act 1995 (c 26) (civil penalties) applies to a trustee or manager of a scheme who fails to take all reasonable steps to secure compliance with [subsections (2) to (3)].
[(9A) Regulations may make provision as to circumstances in which benefits in the form of a lump sum are to be treated for the purposes of subsection (2A) as being paid in the circumstances in which lump sum compensation would be payable in accordance with this Chapter.
(9B) Regulations may create exceptions to subsection (2A).]
(10) Regulations may provide that, where there is an assessment period in relation to an eligible scheme—
(a) in such circumstances as may be prescribed subsection (2) does not operate to require the reduction of benefits payable to or in respect of any member;

(b) the commencement of a member's pension or payment of a member's lump sum or other benefits is, in such circumstances and on such terms and conditions as may be prescribed, to be postponed for the whole or any part of the assessment period for which he continues in employment after attaining normal pension age.

(11) For the purposes of subsection (10)—

(a) "normal pension age", in relation to an eligible scheme and any pension or other benefit under it, means the age specified in the scheme rules as the earliest age at which the pension or other benefit becomes payable without actuarial adjustment (disregarding any scheme rule making special provision as to early payment on the grounds of ill health), and

(b) where different ages are so specified in relation to different parts of a pension or other benefit—

(i) subsection (10) has effect as if those parts were separate pensions or, as the case may be, benefits, and

(ii) in relation to a part of a pension or other benefit, the reference in that subsection to normal pension age is to be read as a reference to the age specified in the scheme rules as the earliest age at which that part becomes so payable.

(12) Regulations may provide that, in prescribed circumstances, where—

(a) a member of the scheme died before the commencement of the assessment period, and

(b) during the assessment period, a person becomes entitled under the scheme rules to a benefit of a prescribed description in respect of the member,

the benefit, or any part of it, is, for the purposes of [subsections (2) and (2A)], to be treated as having become payable before the commencement of the assessment period.

(13) Nothing in subsection (2)[, (2A)] or (3) applies to money purchase benefits.

NOTES

Commencement: 10 February 2005 (sub-ss (10)(b), (12) (for the purpose of making regulations, orders or rules)); 6 April 2005 (sub-ss (1)–(9), (10)(b) (for remaining purposes), (11), (12) (for remaining purposes), (13)); 25 June 2014 (sub-s (10)(a)).

Sub-ss (1), (7), (8), (13): references in square brackets inserted by the Pension Schemes Act 2015, s 59(1), (2), (7), (8), (12).

Sub-ss (2A), (9A), (9B): inserted by the Pension Schemes Act 2015, s 59(1), (3), (10).

Sub-s (3): word omitted repealed and words in square brackets substituted by the Pension Schemes Act 2015, ss 59(1), (4), 67, Sch 4, Pt 1, paras 34, 40.

Sub-ss (5), (6), (9), (12): words in square brackets substituted by the Pension Schemes Act 2015, s 59(1), (5), (6), (9), (11).

Modification: this section is applied, with modifications, to partially guaranteed schemes by the Pension Protection Fund (Partially Guaranteed Schemes) (Modification) Regulations 2005, SI 2005/277, regs 1(2), 2, 3(4)(b), 5(3).

Regulations: the Pension Protection Fund (Entry Rules) Regulations 2005, SI 2005/590; the Pension Protection Fund (Miscellaneous Amendments) Regulations 2009, SI 2009/451; the Pensions Act 2011 (Transitional, Consequential and Supplementary Provisions) Regulations 2014, SI 2014/1711.

[17.311]

139 Loans to pay scheme benefits

(1) Subsection (2) applies where section 138(2) applies in relation to an eligible scheme.

(2) Where the Board is satisfied that the trustees or managers of the scheme are not able to pay benefits under the scheme rules (reduced in accordance with section 138(2)) as they fall due, it may, on an application by the trustees or managers, lend to them such amounts as the Board considers appropriate for the purpose of enabling them to pay those benefits.

(3) Where an amount lent to the trustees or managers of a scheme under subsection (2) is outstanding at—

(a) the time the Board ceases to be involved with the scheme, or

(b) if earlier—

(i) the time during the assessment period when an order is made under section 11(3A) of the Pensions Act 1995 (c 26) directing the winding up of the scheme, or

(ii) where no such order is made during that period, the time when the assessment period ends because the conditions in section 154(2) or (5) are satisfied,

that amount, together with the appropriate interest on it, falls to be repaid by the trustees or managers of the scheme to the Board at that time.

(4) No loan may be made under subsection (2) after the time mentioned in subsection (3)(b)(i).

(5) In subsection (2) the reference to "benefits" does not include money purchase benefits.

(6) In subsection (3) "the appropriate interest" on an amount lent under subsection (2) means interest at the prescribed rate from the time the amount was so lent until repayment.

(7) Subject to this section, the Board may make a loan under subsection (2) on such terms as it thinks fit.

NOTES

Modification: this section is applied, with modifications, to partially guaranteed schemes by the Pension Protection Fund (Partially Guaranteed Schemes) (Modification) Regulations 2005, SI 2005/277, regs 1(2), 2, 5(4).

Regulations: the Pension Protection Fund (Entry Rules) Regulations 2005, SI 2005/590; the Occupational Pension Schemes and Pension Protection Fund (Amendment) Regulations 2005, SI 2005/993.

140–142 (*Outside the scope of this work.*)

Valuation of assets and liabilities

[17.312]

143 Board's obligation to obtain valuation of assets and protected liabilities

(1) This section applies in a case within subsection (1) of section 127 or 128.

[(2) The Board must, as soon as reasonably practicable—

(a) determine whether the condition in subsection (2)(a) of the section in question is satisfied, or
(b) for the purposes of determining whether that condition is satisfied, obtain an actuarial valuation of the scheme as at the relevant time.

(2A) Before doing so, it must give a notice stating whether it will make a determination under subsection (2)(a) or obtain an actuarial valuation under subsection (2)(b) to—
(a) the trustees or managers of the scheme, and
(b) any insolvency practitioner in relation to the employer or, if there is no such insolvency practitioner, the employer.]

(3) For [a determination made under subsection (2)(a) or an actuarial valuation obtained under subsection (2)(b)], regulations may provide that any of the following are to be regarded as assets or protected liabilities of the scheme at the relevant time if prescribed requirements are met—
(a) a debt due to the trustees or managers of the scheme by virtue of a contribution notice issued under section 38, 47 or 55 during the pre-approval period;
(b) an obligation arising under financial support for the scheme (within the meaning of section 45) put in place during the pre-approval period in accordance with a financial support direction issued under section 43;
(c) an obligation imposed by a restoration order made under section 52 during the pre-approval period in respect of a transaction involving assets of the scheme.

(4) For the purposes of [a determination made under subsection (2)(a) or an actuarial valuation obtained under subsection (2)(b)], regulations may prescribe how—
(a) the assets and the protected liabilities of eligible schemes, and
(b) their amount or value,
are to be determined, calculated and verified.

(5) Regulations under subsection (4) may provide, in particular, that when calculating the amount or value of assets or protected liabilities of an eligible scheme at the relevant time which consist of any of the following—
(a) a debt (including any contingent debt) due to the trustees or managers of the scheme from the employer under section 75 of the Pensions Act 1995 (c 26) (deficiencies in the scheme assets),
(b) a debt due to the trustees or managers of the scheme by virtue of a contribution notice issued under section 38, 47 or 55,
(c) an obligation arising under financial support for the scheme (within the meaning of section 45) put in place in accordance with a financial support direction issued under section 43, or
(d) an obligation imposed by a restoration order made under section 52 in respect of a transaction involving assets of the scheme,
account must be taken in the prescribed manner of prescribed events which occur during the pre-approval period.

[(5A) Subsection (5B) applies if—
(a) during the pre-approval period any liability to provide pensions or other benefits to or in respect of any member or members under the scheme is discharged by virtue of regulations under section 135(4) or the Board validating any action mentioned in section 135(9), and
(b) at the relevant time the protected liabilities of the scheme include any cost within section 131(1)(a) relating to compensation in respect of those pensions or other benefits.

(5B) If this subsection applies, for the purposes [of this section]—
(a) in determining that cost the effect of the discharge on the compensation payable in respect of those pensions or other benefits under paragraph 23A of Schedule 7 must be taken into account,
(b) in a case where assets of the scheme at the relevant time were transferred from the scheme during the pre-approval period in consideration for the discharge, those assets are not to be regarded as assets of the scheme at the relevant time, and
(c) in a case where assets that were not assets of the scheme at that time ("later-acquired assets") were so transferred, the value of the assets of the scheme at that time is to be reduced by the value of the later-acquired assets at the time of the discharge.]

[(5C) The Board must issue a statement setting out how (subject to any provision made under subsection (4)) it will make determinations under subsection (2)(a).]

(6) Subject to any provision made under subsection (4), [for the purposes of an actuarial valuation obtained under subsection (2)(b)] the matters mentioned in [subsection (4)(a) and (b)] are to be determined, calculated and verified in accordance with guidance issued by the Board.

(7) In calculating the amount of any liabilities for the purposes of this section, a provision of the scheme rules which limits the amount of the scheme's liabilities by reference to the value of its assets is to be disregarded.

(8) The duty imposed by subsection (2) ceases to apply if and when the Board ceases to be involved with the scheme.

(9) Nothing in subsection (2) [requires a determination to be made, or an] actuarial valuation to be obtained during any period when the Board considers that an event may occur which, by virtue of regulations under subsection (3) or (4) [or by virtue of subsection (5B)], may affect the value of the assets or the amount of the protected liabilities of the scheme for the purposes of [the determination or] the valuation.

(10) In a case where there are one or more reviewable ill health pensions (within the meaning of section 140), nothing in subsection (2) [requires a determination to be made, or an] actuarial valuation to be obtained during the period mentioned in section 141(5)(b) (period during which Board may exercise its power to make a decision following a review) relating to any such pension.

(11) For the purposes of this section—
(a) "actuarial valuation", in relation to the scheme, means a written valuation of the assets and protected liabilities of the scheme which—

(i) is in the prescribed form and contains the prescribed information, and
(ii) is prepared and signed by—
(a) a person with prescribed qualifications or experience, or
(b) a person approved by the Secretary of State,
(b) "the pre-approval period", in relation to the scheme, means the period which—
(i) begins immediately after the relevant time, and
(ii) ends immediately before the time the Board first [makes a determination under subsection (2)(a) or] approves a valuation of the scheme under section 144 after the relevant time,
(c) "the relevant time"—
(i) in a case within subsection (1) of section 127, has the meaning given in subsection (4)(b) of that section, and
(ii) in a case within subsection (1) of section 128, has the meaning given in subsection (3)(b) of that section, and
(d) references to "assets" do not include assets representing the value of any rights in respect of money purchase benefits under the scheme rules.

NOTES

Sub-ss (2), (2A): substituted for original sub-s (2) by the Pensions Act 2011, s 22, Sch 4, paras 1, 5(1), (2).
Sub-s (3): words in square brackets substituted by the Pensions Act 2011, s 22, Sch 4, paras 1, 5(1), (3).
Sub-s (4): words in square brackets substituted by the Pensions Act 2011, s 22, Sch 4, paras 1, 5(1), (4).
Sub-s (5A): inserted, together with sub-s (5B), by the Occupational Pension Schemes (Modification of Pension Protection Provisions) Regulations 2005, SI 2005/705, reg 2(1), (2).
Sub-s (5B): inserted as noted to sub-s (5A) above; words in square brackets substituted by the Pensions Act 2011, s 22, Sch 4, paras 1, 5(1), (5).
Sub-s (5C): inserted by the Pensions Act 2011, s 22, Sch 4, paras 1, 5(1), (6).
Sub-s (6): words in first pair of square brackets inserted and words in second pair of square brackets substituted by the Pensions Act 2011, s 22, Sch 4, paras 1, 5(1), (7).
Sub-s (9): words in first pair of square brackets substituted and words in third pair of square brackets inserted by the Pensions Act 2011, s 22, Sch 4, paras 1, 5(1), (8); words in second pair of square brackets inserted by SI 2005/705, reg 2(1), (3).
Sub-s (10): words in square brackets substituted by the Pensions Act 2011, s 22, Sch 4, paras 1, 5(1), (9).
Sub-s (11): words in square brackets inserted by the Pensions Act 2011, s 22, Sch 4, paras 1, 5(1), (10).
Modification: this section is applied, with modifications, to partially guaranteed schemes by the Pension Protection Fund (Partially Guaranteed Schemes) (Modification) Regulations 2005, SI 2005/277, regs 1(2), 2, 3(4)(f).
Regulations: the Pension Protection Fund (Valuation) Regulations 2005, SI 2005/672; the Occupational Pension Schemes and Pension Protection Fund (Amendment) Regulations 2005, SI 2005/993; the Pension Protection Fund (Miscellaneous Amendments) Regulations 2007, SI 2007/782; the Pension Protection Fund (Miscellaneous Amendments) Regulations 2009, SI 2009/451; the Pensions (Institute and Faculty of Actuaries and Consultation by Employers—Amendment) Regulations 2012, SI 2012/692; the Pension Protection Fund (Miscellaneous Amendments) (No 2) Regulations 2012, SI 2012/3083; the Pension Protection Fund, Occupational and Personal Pension Schemes (Miscellaneous Amendments) Regulations 2013, SI 2013/627.

[17.313]
[143A Determinations under section 143

(1) Where the Board makes a determination under section 143(2)(a) it must give a copy of the determination to—
(a) the Regulator,
(b) the trustees or managers of the scheme, and
(c) any insolvency practitioner in relation to the employer or, if there is no such insolvency practitioner, the employer.
(2) For the purposes of this Chapter a determination under section 143(2)(a) is not binding until—
(a) the period within which the determination may be reviewed by virtue of Chapter 6 has expired, and
(b) if the determination is so reviewed—
(i) the review and any reconsideration,
(ii) any reference to the PPF Ombudsman in respect of the determination, and
(iii) any appeal against the PPF Ombudsman's determination or directions,
has been finally disposed of.
(3) For the purposes of determining whether or not the condition in section 127(2)(a) or, as the case may be, section 128(2)(a) (condition that scheme assets are less than protected liabilities) is satisfied in relation to a scheme, a binding determination under section 143(2)(a) is conclusive.
This subsection is subject to section 172(3) and (4) (treatment of fraud compensation payments).
(4) Where a determination under section 143(2)(a) becomes binding under this section the Board must as soon as reasonably practicable give a notice to that effect together with a copy of the binding determination to—
(a) the Regulator,
(b) the trustees or managers of the scheme, and
(c) any insolvency practitioner in relation to the employer or, if there is no such insolvency practitioner, the employer.
(5) A notice under subsection (4) must be in the prescribed form and contain the prescribed information.]

NOTES

Inserted by the Pensions Act 2011, s 22, Sch 4, paras 1, 6.

Regulations: the Pension Protection Fund (Miscellaneous Amendments) Regulations 2012, SI 2012/1688; the Pension Protection Fund (Miscellaneous Amendments) (No 2) Regulations 2012, SI 2012/3083; the Pension Protection Fund, Occupational and Personal Pension Schemes (Miscellaneous Amendments) Regulations 2013, SI 2013/627.

[17.314]

144 Approval of valuation

(1) This section applies where the Board obtains a valuation in respect of a scheme under section [143(2)(b)].

(2) Where the Board is satisfied that the valuation has been prepared in accordance with [section 143], it must—

- (a) approve the valuation, and
- (b) give a copy of the valuation to—
  - (i) the Regulator,
  - (ii) the trustees or managers of the scheme, and
  - (iii) any insolvency practitioner in relation to the employer or, if there is no such insolvency practitioner, the employer.

(3) Where the Board is not so satisfied, it must obtain another valuation under that section.

NOTES

Sub-s (1): figure in square brackets substituted by the Pensions Act 2011, s 22, Sch 4, paras 1, 7(1), (2).

Sub-s (2): words in square brackets substituted by the Pensions Act 2011, s 22, Sch 4, paras 1, 7(1), (3).

Modification: this section is applied, with modifications, to partially guaranteed schemes by the Pension Protection Fund (Partially Guaranteed Schemes) (Modification) Regulations 2005, SI 2005/277, regs 1(2), 2, 3(3)(b).

[17.315]

145 Binding valuations

(1) For the purposes of this Chapter a valuation obtained under section [143(2)(b)] is not binding until—

- (a) it is approved under section 144,
- (b) the period within which the approval may be reviewed by virtue of Chapter 6 has expired, and
- (c) if the approval is so reviewed—
  - (i) the review and any reconsideration,
  - (ii) any reference to the PPF Ombudsman in respect of the approval, and
  - (iii) any appeal against his determination or directions,

  has been finally disposed of.

(2) For the purposes of determining whether or not the condition in section 127(2)(a) or, as the case may be, section 128(2)(a) (condition that scheme assets are less than protected liabilities) is satisfied in relation to a scheme, a binding valuation is conclusive. This subsection is subject to section 172(3) and (4) (treatment of fraud compensation payments).

(3) Where a valuation becomes binding under this section the Board must as soon as reasonably practicable give a notice to that effect together with a copy of the binding valuation to—

- (a) the Regulator,
- (b) the trustees or managers of the scheme, and
- (c) any insolvency practitioner in relation to the employer or, if there is no such insolvency practitioner, the employer.

(4) A notice under subsection (3) must be in the prescribed form and contain the prescribed information.

NOTES

Sub-s (1): figure in square brackets substituted by the Pensions Act 2011, s 22, Sch 4, paras 1, 8.

Modification: this section is applied, with modifications, to partially guaranteed schemes by the Pension Protection Fund (Partially Guaranteed Schemes) (Modification) Regulations 2005, SI 2005/277, regs 1(2), 2, 3(3)(c).

Regulations: the Pension Protection Fund (Valuation) Regulations 2005, SI 2005/672.

146–189A (*Outside the scope of this work.*)

CHAPTER 5 GATHERING INFORMATION

190 (*Outside the scope of this work.*)

[17.316]

191 Notices requiring provision of information

(1) Any person to whom subsection (3) applies may be required by a notice in writing to produce any document, or provide any other information, which is—

- (a) of a description specified in the notice, and
- (b) relevant to the exercise of the Board's functions in relation to an occupational pension scheme.

(2) A notice under subsection (1) may be given by—

- (a) the Board, or
- (b) a person authorised by the Board for the purposes of this section in relation to the scheme.

(3) This subsection applies to—

- (a) a trustee or manager of the scheme,
- (b) a professional adviser in relation to the scheme,
- (c) the employer in relation to the scheme,

(d) an insolvency practitioner in relation to the employer, and
(e) any other person appearing to the Board, or person giving the notice, to be a person who holds, or is likely to hold, information relevant to the discharge of the Board's functions in relation to the scheme.

(4) Where the production of a document, or the provision of information, is required by a notice given under subsection (1), the document must be produced, or information must be provided, in such a manner, at such a place and within such a period as may be specified in the notice.

NOTES

Modification: this section is applied, with modifications, for the purposes of the Financial Assistance Scheme Regulations 2005, SI 2005/1986, by reg 4(1), (2)(d), (3), (5) of, and Sch 1, para 6 to, those Regulations.

[17.317]

192 Entry of premises

(1) An appointed person may, for the purpose of enabling or facilitating the performance of any function of the Board in relation to an occupational pension scheme, at any reasonable time enter scheme premises and, while there—

(a) may make such examination and inquiry as may be necessary for such purpose,
(b) may require any person on the premises to produce, or secure the production of, any document relevant to that purpose for inspection by the appointed person,
(c) may take copies of any such document,
(d) may take possession of any document appearing to be such a document or take in relation to any such document any other steps which appear necessary for preserving it or preventing interference with it,
(e) may, in the case of any such document which consists of information which is stored in electronic form and is on, or accessible from, the premises, require the information to be produced in a form—
    (i) in which it can be taken away, and
    (ii) in which it is legible or from which it can readily be produced in a legible form, and
(f) may, as to any matter relevant to the exercise of the Board's functions in relation to the scheme, examine, or require to be examined, either alone or in the presence of another person, any person on the premises whom he has reasonable cause to believe to be able to give information relevant to that matter.

(2) Premises are scheme premises for the purposes of subsection (1) if the appointed person has reasonable grounds to believe that—

(a) they are being used for the business of the employer,
(b) an insolvency practitioner in relation to the employer is acting there in that capacity,
(c) documents relevant to—
    (i) the administration of the scheme, or
    (ii) the employer,
    are being kept there, or
(d) the administration of the scheme, or work connected with the administration of the scheme, is being carried out there,

unless the premises are a private dwelling-house not used by, or by permission of, the occupier for the purposes of a trade or business.

(3) An appointed person applying for admission to any premises for the purposes of this section must, if so required, produce his certificate of appointment.

(4) When exercising a power under this section an appointed person may be accompanied by such persons as he considers appropriate.

(5) Any document of which possession is taken under this section may be retained until the end of the period comprising—

(a) the period of 12 months beginning with the date on which possession was taken of the document, and
(b) any extension of that period under subsection (6).

(6) The Board may before the end of the period mentioned in subsection (5) (including any extension of it under this subsection) extend it by such period not exceeding 12 months as the Board considers appropriate.

(7) In this section "appointed person" means a person appointed by the Board for the purposes of this section in relation to the scheme.

NOTES

Modification: this section is applied, with modifications, for the purposes of the Financial Assistance Scheme Regulations 2005, SI 2005/1986, by reg 4(1), (2)(d), (3), (5) of, and Sch 1, para 7 to, those Regulations.

[17.318]

193 Penalties relating to sections 191 and 192

(1) A person who, without reasonable excuse, neglects or refuses to provide information or produce a document when required to do so under section 191 is guilty of an offence.

(2) A person who without reasonable excuse—

(a) intentionally delays or obstructs an appointed person exercising any power under section 192,
(b) neglects or refuses to produce, or secure the production of, any document when required to do so under that section, or
(c) neglects or refuses to answer a question or to provide information when so required,

is guilty of an offence.

(3) In subsection (2)(a) "appointed person" has the same meaning as it has in section 192.

(4) A person guilty of an offence under subsection (1) or (2) is liable on summary conviction to a fine not exceeding level 5 on the standard scale.

(5) An offence under subsection (1) or (2)(b) or (c) may be charged by reference to any day or longer period of time; and a person may be convicted of a second or subsequent offence by reference to any period of time following the preceding conviction of the offence.

(6) Any person who intentionally and without reasonable excuse alters, suppresses, conceals or destroys any document which he is or is liable to be required to produce under section 191 or 192 is guilty of an offence.

(7) Any person guilty of an offence under subsection (6) is liable—

- (a) on summary conviction, to a fine not exceeding the statutory maximum;
- (b) on conviction on indictment, to a fine or imprisonment for a term not exceeding two years, or both.

NOTES

Modification: this section is applied, with modifications, for the purposes of the Financial Assistance Scheme Regulations 2005, SI 2005/1986, by reg 4(1), (2)(d), (3), (5) of, and Sch 1 to, those Regulations.

[17.319]

194 Warrants

(1) A justice of the peace may issue a warrant under this section if satisfied on information on oath given by or on behalf of the Board that there are reasonable grounds for believing—

- (a) that there is on, or accessible from, any premises any document—
  - (i) whose production has been required under section 191 or 192, or any corresponding provision in force in Northern Ireland, and
  - (ii) which has not been produced in compliance with that requirement,
- (b) that there is on, or accessible from, any premises any document relevant to the exercise of the Board's functions in relation to an occupational pension scheme whose production could be so required and, if its production were so required, the document—
  - (i) would not be produced, but
  - (ii) would be removed, or made inaccessible, from the premises, hidden, tampered with or destroyed, or
- (c) that a person will do any act which constitutes a misuse or misappropriation of the assets of an occupational pension scheme and that there is on, or accessible from, any premises any document—
  - (i) which relates to whether the act will be done, and
  - (ii) whose production could be required under section 191 or 192, or any corresponding provision in force in Northern Ireland.

(2) A warrant under this section shall authorise an inspector—

- (a) to enter the premises specified in the information, using such force as is reasonably necessary for the purpose,
- (b) to search the premises and—
  - (i) take possession of any document appearing to be such a document as is mentioned in subsection (1), or
  - (ii) take in relation to such a document any other steps which appear necessary for preserving it or preventing interference with it,
- (c) to take copies of any such document,
- (d) to require any person named in the warrant to provide an explanation of any such document or to state where it may be found or how access to it may be obtained, and
- (e) in the case of any such document which consists of information which is stored in electronic form and is on, or accessible from, the premises, to require the information to be produced in a form—
  - (i) in which it can be taken away, and
  - (ii) in which it is legible or from which it can readily be produced in a legible form.

(3) When executing a warrant under this section, an inspector may be accompanied by such persons as he considers appropriate.

(4) A warrant under this section continues in force until the end of the period of one month beginning with the day on which it is issued.

(5) Any document of which possession is taken under this section may be retained until the end of the period comprising—

- (a) the period of 12 months beginning with the date on which possession was taken of the document, and
- (b) any extension of that period under subsection (6).

(6) The Board may before the end of the period mentioned in subsection (5) (including any extension of it under this subsection) extend it by such period not exceeding 12 months as the Board considers appropriate.

(7) In this section "inspector" means a person appointed by the Board as an inspector.

(8) In the application of this section in Scotland—

- (a) the reference to a justice of the peace is to be read as a reference to the sheriff, and
- (b) the references in subsections (1) and (2)(a) to information are to be read as references to evidence.

NOTES

Modification: this section is applied, with modifications, for the purposes of the Financial Assistance Scheme Regulations 2005, SI 2005/1986, by reg 4(1), (2)(d), (3), (5) of, and Sch 1, para 8 to, those Regulations.

Provision of false or misleading information

[17.320]

195 Offence of providing false or misleading information to the Board

(1) Any person who knowingly or recklessly provides information which is false or misleading in a material particular is guilty of an offence if the information—

(a) is provided in purported compliance with a requirement under—

(i) section 190 (information to be provided to the Board etc),

(ii) section 191 (notices requiring provision of information), or

(iii) section 192 (entry of premises), or

(b) is provided otherwise than as mentioned in paragraph (a) but in circumstances in which the person providing the information intends, or could reasonably be expected to know, that it would be used by the Board for the purposes of exercising its functions under this Act.

(2) Any person guilty of an offence under subsection (1) is liable—

(a) on summary conviction, to a fine not exceeding the statutory maximum;

(b) on conviction on indictment, to a fine or imprisonment for a term not exceeding two years, or both.

NOTES

Modification: this section is applied, with modifications, for the purposes of the Financial Assistance Scheme Regulations 2005, SI 2005/1986, by reg 4(1), (2)(d), (3), (5) of, and Sch 1, para 9 to, those Regulations.

196–299 (*Ss 196–220, ss 221–299 (Pts 3–8) outside the scope of this work.*)

PART 9

MISCELLANEOUS AND SUPPLEMENTARY

300–318 (*Outside the scope of this work.*)

Miscellaneous and supplementary

319–321 (*Outside the scope of this work.*)

[17.321]

322 Commencement

(1) Subject to subsections (2) to (4), the provisions of this Act come into force in accordance with provision made by the Secretary of State by order.

(2) The following provisions come into force on the day this Act is passed—

(a)–(c) (*outside the scope of this work.*)

(d) in this Part (miscellaneous and general)—

(i) (*outside the scope of this work.*)

(ii) this section and sections 313, 315 (other than subsection (6)), 316, 317, 318 (other than subsections (4) and (5)) and 323 to 325;

(e) (*outside the scope of this work.*)

(3), (4) . . .

(5) Without prejudice to section 315(5), the power to make an order under this section includes power—

(a) to make transitional adaptations or modifications—

(i) of the provisions brought into force by the order, or

(ii) in connection with those provisions, of any provisions of Parts 1 to 7 of this Act or of the Pension Schemes Act 1993 (c 48), the Pensions Act 1995, Parts 1, 2 or 4 of the Welfare Reform and Pensions Act 1999 (c 30) or Chapter 2 of Part 2 of the Child Support, Pensions and Social Security Act 2000 (c 19), or

(b) to save the effect of any of the repealed provisions of those Acts, or those provisions as adapted or modified by the order,

as it appears to the Secretary of State expedient, including different adaptations or modifications for different periods.

NOTES

Sub-ss (3), (4): outside the scope of this work.

Orders: at present, 15 commencement orders have been made under this section. The orders relevant to the provisions of this Act printed in this work are the Pensions Act 2004 (Commencement No 1 and Consequential and Transitional Provisions) Order 2004, SI 2004/3350, the Pensions Act 2004 (Commencement No 2, Transitional Provisions and Consequential Amendments) Order 2005, SI 2005/275, the Pensions Act 2004 (Commencement No 6, Transitional Provisions and Savings) Order 2005, SI 2005/1720, the Pensions Act 2004 (Commencement No 10 and Saving Provision) Order 2006, SI 2006/2272, and the Pensions Act 2004 (Commencement No 13) Order 2009, SI 2009/1542; the Pensions Act 2004 (Commencement No 15) Order 2014, SI 2014/1636.

[17.322]

323 Extent

(1) Subject to the following provisions, this Act extends to England, Wales and Scotland.

(2) The following provisions of this Act also extend to Northern Ireland—

(a)–(f) *(outside the scope of this work.)*

(g) in this Part—

(i), (ii) *(outside the scope of this work.)*

(iii) this section and sections 319(2), 321, 322, 324 and 325.

(3) . . .

(4) An amendment or repeal contained in this Act has the same extent as the enactment to which it relates . . .

NOTES

Sub-s (3): outside the scope of this work.

Sub-s (4): words omitted outside the scope of this work.

324 *(Outside the scope of this work.)*

[17.323]

325 Short title

This Act may be cited as the Pensions Act 2004.

SCHEDULES 1–13

(Schs 1–13 outside the scope of this work.)

GAMBLING ACT 2005

(2005 c 19)

An Act to make provision about gambling

[7 April 2005]

1–64 *((Pts 1–4) outside the scope of this work.)*

PART 5
OPERATING LICENCES

65–109 *(Outside the scope of this work.)*

Duration

110–113 *(Outside the scope of this work.)*

[17.324]

114 Lapse

(1) In the case of an operating licence issued to an individual, the licence shall lapse if—

(a) the licensee dies,

(b) the licensee becomes, in the opinion of the Commission as notified to the licensee, incapable of carrying on the licensed activities by reason of mental or physical incapacity,

(c) the licensee becomes bankrupt (within the meaning of section 381 of the Insolvency Act 1986 (c 45)), [or a debt relief order is made in respect of the licensee (under Part 7A of the Insolvency Act 1986),] or

(d) sequestration of the licensee's estate is awarded under section [22(1) of the Bankruptcy (Scotland) Act 2016].

(2) In any other case an operating licence shall lapse if the licensee—

(a) ceases to exist, or

(b) goes into liquidation (within the meaning of section 247(2) of the Insolvency Act 1986).

NOTES

Sub-s (1): words in square brackets in para (c) inserted by the Tribunals, Courts and Enforcement Act 2007 (Consequential Amendments) Order 2012, SI 2012/2404, art 3(2), Sch 2, para 55(1), (2); words in square brackets in para (d) substituted for original words "12(1) of the Bankruptcy (Scotland) Act 1985 (c 66)" by the Bankruptcy (Scotland) Act 2016 (Consequential Provisions and Modifications) Order 2016, SI 2016/1034, art 7(1), (3), Sch 1, para 28(1), (2), as from 30 November 2016 (except in relation to (i) a sequestration as regards which the petition is presented, or the debtor application is made before that date; or (ii) a trust deed executed before that date).

Modification: this section is modified in relation to personal licences by the Gambling (Personal Licences) (Modification of Part 5 of the Gambling Act 2005) Regulations 2006, SI 2006/3267, art 2(2), Schedule, Table 2.

115–149 *(Ss 115–126, ss 127–149 (Pts 6, 7) outside the scope of this work.)*

PART 8
PREMISES LICENCES

150–190 (*Outside the scope of this work.*)

Duration

191–193 (*Outside the scope of this work.*)

[17.325]
194 Lapse

(1) In the case of a premises licence issued to an individual, the licence shall lapse if—
- (a) the licensee dies,
- (b) the licensee becomes, in the opinion of the licensing authority as notified to the licensee, incapable of carrying on the licensed activities by reason of mental or physical incapacity,
- (c) the licensee becomes bankrupt (within the meaning of section 381 of the Insolvency Act 1986 (c 45)), [or a debt relief order is made in respect of the licensee (under Part 7A of the Insolvency Act 1986),] or
- (d) sequestration of the licensee's estate is awarded under section [22(1) of the Bankruptcy (Scotland) Act 2016].

(2) In any other case a premises licence shall lapse if the licensee—
- (a) ceases to exist, or
- (b) goes into liquidation (within the meaning of section 247(2) of the Insolvency Act 1986).

(3) If a licensing authority become aware that a premises licence issued by them has lapsed, they shall as soon as is reasonably practicable notify—
- (a) the Commission,
- (b) either—
  - (i) in England and Wales, the chief officer of police for any area in which the premises are wholly or partly situated, or
  - (ii) in Scotland, the chief constable of the police force maintained for a police area in which the premises are wholly or partly situated, and
- (c) Her Majesty's Commissioners of Customs and Excise.

NOTES

Sub-s (1): words in square brackets in para (c) inserted by the Tribunals, Courts and Enforcement Act 2007 (Consequential Amendments) Order 2012, SI 2012/2404, art 3(2), Sch 2, para 55(1), (3); words in square brackets in para (d) substituted for original words "12(1) of the Bankruptcy (Scotland) Act 1985 (c 66)" by the Bankruptcy (Scotland) Act 2016 (Consequential Provisions and Modifications) Order 2016, SI 2016/1034, art 7(1), (3), Sch 1, para 28(1), (3), as from 30 November 2016 (except in relation to (i) a sequestration as regards which the petition is presented, or the debtor application is made before that date; or (ii) a trust deed executed before that date).

195–362 (*Ss 195–213, ss 214–362 (Pts 9–18) outside the scope of this work.*)

SCHEDULES 1–9

(*Schs 1–9 outside the scope of this work.*)

SCHEDULE 10
FAMILY ENTERTAINMENT CENTRE GAMING MACHINE PERMITS

Section 247

[17.326]
1–11 . . .

Duration

12–14 . . .

15 (1) A permit held by an individual shall lapse if—
- (a) he dies,
- (b) he becomes, in the opinion of the licensing authority as notified to him, incapable of carrying on the activities authorised by the permit by reason of mental or physical incapacity,
- (c) he becomes bankrupt (within the meaning of section 381 of the Insolvency Act 1986 (c 45)), [or a debt relief order is made in respect of him (under Part 7A of the Insolvency Act 1986)] or
- (d) sequestration of his estate is awarded under section [22(1) of the Bankruptcy (Scotland) Act 2016].

(2) In any other case a permit shall lapse if the holder—
- (a) ceases to exist, or
- (b) goes into liquidation (within the meaning of section 247(2) of the Insolvency Act 1986).

(3) During the period of six months beginning with the date on which a permit lapses under this paragraph the following may rely on it as if it had effect and were issued to them—
- (a) the personal representatives of the holder (in the case of an individual holder who dies),
- (b) the trustee of the bankrupt's estate (in the case of an individual holder who becomes bankrupt), and
- (c) the liquidator of the company (in the case of a company holder that goes into liquidation).

16–24 . . .

NOTES

Paras 1–14, 16–24: outside the scope of this work.

Para 15: in sub-para (1)(c) words in square brackets inserted by the Tribunals, Courts and Enforcement Act 2007 (Consequential Amendments) Order 2012, SI 2012/2404, art 3(2), Sch 2, para 55(1), (4); words in square brackets in sub-para (1)(d) substituted for original words "12(1) of the Bankruptcy (Scotland) Act 1985 (c 66)" by the Bankruptcy (Scotland) Act 2016 (Consequential Provisions and Modifications) Order 2016, SI 2016/1034, art 7(1), (3), Sch 1, para 28(1), (4), as from 30 November 2016 (except in relation to (i) a sequestration as regards which the petition is presented, or the debtor application is made before that date; or (ii) a trust deed executed before that date).

SCHEDULES 11–13

(Schs 11–13 outside the scope of this work.)

SCHEDULE 14
PRIZE GAMING PERMITS

Section 289

[17.327]

1–12 . . .

Duration

13, 14 . . .

15 (1) A permit held by an individual shall lapse if—

(a) he dies,

(b) he becomes, in the opinion of the licensing authority as notified to the individual, incapable of carrying on the activities authorised by the permit by reason of mental or physical incapacity,

(c) he becomes bankrupt (within the meaning of section 381 of the Insolvency Act 1986 (c 45)), [or a debt relief order is made in respect of him, (under Part 7A of the Insolvency Act 1986)] or

(d) sequestration of his estate is awarded under section [22(1) of the Bankruptcy (Scotland) Act 2016].

(2) In any other case a permit shall lapse if the holder—

(a) ceases to exist, or

(b) goes into liquidation (within the meaning of section 247(2) of that Act).

(3) During the period of six months beginning with the date on which a permit lapses under this paragraph the following may rely on it as if it had effect and were issued to them—

(a) the personal representatives of the holder (in the case of an individual holder who dies),

(b) the trustee of the bankrupt's estate (in the case of an individual holder who becomes bankrupt),

(c) the holder's interim or permanent trustee (in the case of an individual holder whose estate is sequestrated), and

(d) the liquidator of the company (in the case of a company holder that goes into liquidation).

(4) In relation to premises in Scotland—

(a) sub-paragraph (2)(a) shall have effect as if it referred to a sheriff within whose sheriffdom the premises are wholly or partly situated,

(b) sub-paragraph (2)(b) shall not have effect,

(c) the reference in sub-paragraph (3) to a magistrate's court shall have effect as a reference to the sheriff, and

(d) the reference in sub-paragraph (3)(d) to costs shall have effect as a reference to expenses.

16–24 . . .

NOTES

Paras 1–14, 16–24: outside the scope of this work.

Para 15: in sub-para (1)(c) words in square brackets inserted by the Tribunals, Courts and Enforcement Act 2007 (Consequential Amendments) Order 2012, SI 2012/2404, art 3(2), Sch 2, para 55(1), (5); words in square brackets in sub-para (1)(d) substituted for original words "12(1) of the Bankruptcy (Scotland) Act 1985 (c 66)" by the Bankruptcy (Scotland) Act 2016 (Consequential Provisions and Modifications) Order 2016, SI 2016/1034, art 7(1), (3), Sch 1, para 28(1), (5), as from 30 November 2016 (except in relation to (i) a sequestration as regards which the petition is presented, or the debtor application is made before that date; or (ii) a trust deed executed before that date).

SCHEDULES 15–18

(Schs 15–18 outside the scope of this work.)

COMPANIES ACT 2006

(2006 c 46)

ARRANGEMENT OF SECTIONS

PART 10
A COMPANY'S DIRECTORS

CHAPTER 4
TRANSACTIONS WITH DIRECTORS REQUIRING APPROVAL OF MEMBERS

193 Exception in case of company in winding up or administration . . . . . [17.328]

PART 15
ACCOUNTS AND REPORTS

CHAPTER 3
A COMPANY'S FINANCIAL YEAR

392 Alteration of accounting reference date . . . . . [17.329]

PART 19
DEBENTURES

Supplementary provisions

754 Priorities where debentures secured by floating charge . . . . . [17.330]

PART 29
FRAUDULENT TRADING

993 Offence of fraudulent trading . . . . . [17.331]

PART 47
FINAL PROVISIONS

1298 Short title . . . . . [17.332]
1299 Extent . . . . . [17.333]
1300 Commencement . . . . . [17.334]

An Act to reform company law and restate the greater part of the enactments relating to companies; to make other provision relating to companies and other forms of business organisation; to make provision about directors' disqualification, business names, auditors and actuaries; to amend Part 9 of the Enterprise Act 2002; and for connected purposes.

[8 November 2006]

1–153 ((*Pts 1–9) outside the scope of this work.*)

PART 10
A COMPANY'S DIRECTORS

154–187 ((*Chs 1–3) outside the scope of this work.*)

CHAPTER 4 TRANSACTIONS WITH DIRECTORS REQUIRING APPROVAL OF MEMBERS

188, 189 (*Outside the scope of this work.*)

Substantial property transactions

190–192 (*Outside the scope of this work.*)

[17.328]
193 Exception in case of company in winding up or administration

(1) This section applies to a company—
(a) that is being wound up (unless the winding up is a members' voluntary winding up), or
(b) that is in administration within the meaning of Schedule B1 to the Insolvency Act 1986 (c 45) or the Insolvency (Northern Ireland) Order 1989 (SI 1989/2405 (NI 19)).

(2) Approval is not required under section 190 (requirement of members' approval for substantial property transactions)—
(a) on the part of the members of a company to which this section applies, or
(b) for an arrangement entered into by a company to which this section applies.

NOTES

Modification: this section is applied, with modifications, in so far as it relates to bank insolvency or administration under the Banking Act 2009, Pts 2, 3, by the Banking Act 2009 (Parts 2 and 3 Consequential Amendments) Order 2009, SI 2009/317, art 3, Schedule at **[7.86]**, **[7.92]**.

Disapplication: this section is disapplied in respect of certain specified persons while Northern Rock is wholly owned by the Treasury, by the Northern Rock plc Transfer Order 2008, SI 2008/432, art 17, Schedule, para 2(h); in respect of certain specified persons while Bradford & Bingley is wholly owned by the Treasury, by the Bradford & Bingley plc Transfer of Securities and Property etc Order 2008, SI 2008/2546, art 13(1), Schedule, para 2(h); and in respect of certain specified persons while Deposits

Management (Heritable) is wholly owned by the Treasury, by the Heritable Bank plc Transfer of Certain Rights and Liabilities Order 2008, SI 2008/2644, art 26, Sch 2, para 2(h).

194–379 *(Ss 194–226, ss 227–259 (Chs 5–9), ss 260–379 (Pts 11–14) outside the scope of this work.)*

PART 15
ACCOUNTS AND REPORTS

380–389 *((Chs 1, 2) outside the scope of this work.)*

CHAPTER 3 A COMPANY'S FINANCIAL YEAR

390, 391 *(Outside the scope of this work.)*

[17.329]
392 Alteration of accounting reference date

(1), (2) . . .

(3) A notice extending a company's current or previous accounting reference period is not effective if given less than five years after the end of an earlier accounting reference period of the company that was extended under this section.

This does not apply—

(a) . . .

(b) where the company is in administration under Part 2 of the Insolvency Act 1986 (c 45) or Part 3 of the Insolvency (Northern Ireland) Order 1989 (SI 1989/2405 (NI 19)), or

(c) . . .

(4)–(6) . . .

NOTES

Sub-ss (1), (2), (4)–(6): outside the scope of this work.

Sub-s (3): paras (a), (c) outside the scope of this work.

Modifications: this section is applied, with modifications, to limited liability partnership accounts for financial years beginning on or after 1 October 2008, by the Limited Liability Partnerships (Accounts and Audit) (Application of Companies Act 2006) Regulations 2008, SI 2008/1911, regs 2(1), 7; in so far as it relates to bank insolvency or administration under the Banking Act 2009, Pts 2, 3, by the Banking Act 2009 (Parts 2 and 3 Consequential Amendments) Orders 2009, SI 2009/317, art 3, Schedule at **[7.86]**, **[7.92]**; in so far as it relates to certain overseas companies that have an establishment in the UK and are not credit or financial institutions or companies whose constitution does not limit the liability of its members, by the Overseas Companies Regulations 2009, SI 2009/1801, regs 36, 37, 80, Sch 8, Pt 2; and in so far as it relates to certain credit or financial institutions that have branches in the UK, by the Overseas Companies Regulations 2009, SI 2009/1801, regs 51, 52, 80, Sch 8, Pt 2.

Disapplication: this section is disapplied, with regards to the preparation of accounts of qualifying banks for financial years beginning on or after 6 April 2008 and auditors appointed in respect of those financial years, by the Bank Accounts Directive (Miscellaneous Banks) Regulations 2008, SI 2008/567, reg 4, Schedule, para 3.

393–737 *(Ss 393–474 (Chs 4–12), ss 475–737 (Pts 16–18) outside the scope of this work.)*

PART 19
DEBENTURES

738–748 *(Outside the scope of this work.)*

Supplementary provisions

749–753 *(Outside the scope of this work.)*

[17.330]
754 Priorities where debentures secured by floating charge

(1) This section applies where debentures of a company registered in England and Wales or Northern Ireland are secured by a charge that, as created, was a floating charge.

(2) If possession is taken, by or on behalf of the holders of the debentures, of any property comprised in or subject to the charge, and the company is not at that time in the course of being wound up, the company's preferential debts shall be paid out of assets coming to the hands of the persons taking possession in priority to any claims for principal or interest in respect of the debentures.

(3) "Preferential debts" means the categories of debts listed in Schedule 6 to the Insolvency Act 1986 (c 45) or Schedule 4 to the Insolvency (Northern Ireland) Order 1989 (SI 1989/2405 (NI 19)).

For the purposes of those Schedules "the relevant date" is the date of possession being taken as mentioned in subsection (2).

(4) Payments under this section shall be recouped, as far as may be, out of the assets of the company available for payment of general creditors.

NOTES

Modification: this section is applied, with modifications, in so far as it relates to bank insolvency or administration under the Banking Act 2009, Pts 2, 3, by the Banking Act 2009 (Parts 2 and 3 Consequential Amendments) Order 2009, SI 2009/317, art 3, Schedule at **[7.86]**, **[7.92]**, and in so far as it relates to limited liability partnerships by the Limited Liability Partnerships (Application of Companies Act 2006) Regulations 2009, SI 2009/1804, reg 23.

755–992 *((Pts 20–28) outside the scope of this work.)*

PART 29
FRAUDULENT TRADING

[17.331]
993 Offence of fraudulent trading

(1) If any business of a company is carried on with intent to defraud creditors of the company or creditors of any other person, or for any fraudulent purpose, every person who is knowingly a party to the carrying on of the business in that manner commits an offence.

(2) This applies whether or not the company has been, or is in the course of being, wound up.

(3) A person guilty of an offence under this section is liable—

(a) on conviction on indictment, to imprisonment for a term not exceeding ten years or a fine (or both);

(b) on summary conviction—

(i) in England and Wales, to imprisonment for a term not exceeding twelve months or a fine not exceeding the statutory maximum (or both);

(ii) in Scotland or Northern Ireland, to imprisonment for a term not exceeding six months or a fine not exceeding the statutory maximum (or both).

NOTES

Application: this section is applied to unregistered companies by the Unregistered Companies Regulations 2009, SI 2009/2436, regs 3–5, 7, Sch 1, paras 15, 21.

Modification: in relation to an offence committed after the commencement of s 1131 of this Act but before the commencement of the Criminal Justice Act 2003, s 154(1), the reference in sub-s (3)(b)(i) to "twelve months" shall be read as a reference to "six months". This section is also applied, with modifications, in so far as it relates to bank insolvency or administration under the Banking Act 2009, Pts 2, 3, by the Banking Act 2009 (Parts 2 and 3 Consequential Amendments) Order 2009, SI 2009/317, art 3, Schedule at **[7.86]**, **[7.92]**.

Deferred Prosecution Agreements: as to the application of Deferred Prosecution Agreements to an offence under this section (ie, an agreement between a designated prosecutor and a person accused of a crime (P) whereby proceedings against P in respect of the alleged offence are automatically suspended as soon as they are instituted if P agrees to comply with certain requirements), see the Crime and Courts Act 2013, s 45, Sch 17, Pt 1, Pt 2, para 24.

994–1297 (*(Pts 30–46) outside the scope of this work.*)

PART 47
FINAL PROVISIONS

[17.332]
1298 Short title

The short title of this Act is the Companies Act 2006.

[17.333]
1299 Extent

Except as otherwise provided (or the context otherwise requires), the provisions of this Act extend to the whole of the United Kingdom.

[17.334]
1300 Commencement

(1) The following provisions come into force on the day this Act is passed—

(a)–(c) (*outside the scope of this work.*)

(d) this Part.

(2) The other provisions of this Act come into force on such day as may be appointed by order of the Secretary of State or the Treasury.

NOTES

Orders: at present, 8 commencement orders have been made under this section. The orders relevant to the provisions of this Act printed in this work are the Companies Act 2006 (Commencement No 3, Consequential Amendments, Transitional Provisions and Savings) Order 2007, SI 2007/2194 and the Companies Act 2006 (Commencement No 5, Transitional Provisions and Savings) Order 2007, SI 2007/3495.

SCHEDULES 1–16

(*Schs 1–16 outside the scope of this work.*)

BANKING (SPECIAL PROVISIONS) ACT 2008

(2008 c 2)

ARRANGEMENT OF SECTIONS

Introduction

1 Meaning of "authorised UK deposit-taker" . . . . [17.335]
2 Cases where Treasury's powers are exercisable . . . . [17.336]

Transfer of securities

3 Transfer of securities. . . . .[17.337]
4 Extinguishment of subscription rights . . . .[17.338]
5 Compensation etc for securities transferred etc. . . . .[17.339]

Transfer of property etc

6 Transfer of property, rights and liabilities . . . .[17.340]
7 Compensation etc for property etc transferred . . . .[17.341]

Further transfers

8 Further transfers following transfer to public sector . . . .[17.342]

Supplementary

9 Supplementary provision about compensation schemes etc . . . .[17.343]
10 Tax consequences. . . . .[17.344]

Building societies

11 Modification of legislation applying in relation to building societies. . . . .[17.345]

General

12 Consequential and supplementary provision. . . . .[17.346]
13 Orders and regulations: general . . . .[17.347]
14 Orders and regulations: retrospective provisions . . . .[17.348]
15 Interpretation . . . .[17.349]
16 Financial provision . . . .[17.350]
17 Short title, commencement and extent . . . .[17.351]

SCHEDULES

Schedule 1—Transfer Orders under Section 3 . . . .[17.352]
Schedule 2—Transfer Orders under Section 6 . . . .[17.353]

An Act to make provision to enable the Treasury in certain circumstances to make an order relating to the transfer of securities issued by, or of property, rights or liabilities belonging to, an authorised deposit-taker; to make further provision in relation to building societies; and for connected purposes

[21 February 2008]

Introduction

[17.335]

1 Meaning of "authorised UK deposit-taker"

(1) In this Act "authorised UK deposit-taker" means a UK undertaking that under Part 4 of FSMA 2000 has permission to accept deposits.

(2) That expression does not, however, include such an undertaking with permission to accept deposits only for the purposes of, or in the course of, an activity other than accepting deposits.

[17.336]

2 Cases where Treasury's powers are exercisable

(1) The power of the Treasury to make an order under—

(a) section 3 (transfer of securities issued by an authorised UK deposit-taker), or

(b) section 6 (transfer of property, rights and liabilities of an authorised UK deposit-taker),

is exercisable in relation to an authorised UK deposit-taker if (and only if) it appears to the Treasury to be desirable to make the order for either or both of the following purposes.

This is subject to subsection (7).

(2) The purposes are—

(a) maintaining the stability of the UK financial system in circumstances where the Treasury consider that there would be a serious threat to its stability if the order were not made;

(b) protecting the public interest in circumstances where financial assistance has been provided by the Treasury to the deposit-taker for the purpose of maintaining the stability of the UK financial system.

(3) The reference in subsection (2)(b) to the provision of financial assistance by the Treasury to the deposit-taker includes—

(a) any case where the Bank of England has provided financial assistance to the deposit-taker and—

(i) the Treasury have assumed a liability in respect of the assistance,

(ii) the liability is of a kind of which the Treasury are expected to give relevant notice, and

(iii) the Treasury have given relevant notice of the liability;

(b) any case where the Chancellor of the Exchequer has announced that the Treasury (whether acting alone or with the Bank of England) would, if necessary, put in place relevant guarantee arrangements in relation to the deposit-taker (as well as any case where any such arrangements have been put in place, whether or not following such an announcement).

(4) For the purposes of subsection (3) the Treasury give "relevant notice" of a liability if—

(a) they lay a Minute before the House of Commons containing information about the liability, or

(b) they give written notice containing such information to the person who chairs the House of Commons Committee of Public Accounts and the person who chairs the House of Commons Treasury Committee.

(5) It is immaterial whether the notice or announcement mentioned in subsection (3) is given or made before or after the passing of this Act.

(6) In this Act "relevant guarantee arrangements", in relation to any authorised UK deposit-taker, means any guarantee arrangements for protecting some or all of the depositors or other creditors of the deposit-taker.

(7) Where an order has been made under section 3 or 6 in relation to any authorised UK deposit-taker, subsection (1) does not apply in relation to any subsequent exercise of the power to make an order under either of those sections in relation to that deposit-taker.

(8) The power of the Treasury to make an order under section 3 or 6 in relation to an authorised UK deposit-taker may not be exercised after the end of the period of one year beginning with the day on which this Act is passed.

(9) Subsection (8) does not affect the continuation in force or effect of any order made or other thing done by virtue of either of those sections before the end of that period.

(10) In this section "the UK financial system" means the financial system in the United Kingdom.

(11) Section 13 of the National Audit Act 1983 (c 44) (interpretation of references to Committee of Public Accounts) applies for the purposes of this section, but as if—

(a) the references in that section to that Act were to this Act, and

(b) the references in that section to the House of Commons Committee of Public Accounts included the House of Commons Treasury Committee.

Transfer of securities

[17.337]

3 Transfer of securities

(1) The Treasury may, in relation to all or any securities of a specified description that have been issued by an authorised UK deposit-taker, by order make provision for or in connection with, or in consequence of, the transfer of the securities to any of the following—

(a) the Bank of England;

(b) a nominee of the Treasury;

(c) a company wholly owned by the Bank of England or the Treasury;

(d) any body corporate not within paragraph (c).

(2) Schedule 1 specifies particular kinds of provisions that may be included in an order under this section.

(3) Where an order providing for the transfer of any securities has been made under this section, the power to make an order under this section may be subsequently exercised so as to make provision in connection with, or in consequence of, the transfer (including provision of a kind specified in Schedule 1) even though the order does not itself provide for the transfer of any securities.

(4) Where an order under this section or section 6 ("the initial order") has been made in relation to an authorised UK deposit-taker, the power to make an order under this section may be subsequently exercised in relation to that deposit-taker whether or not any transfer of securities provided for by the order is to the person to whom any transfer was made by or under the initial order.

(5) For the purposes of this section any provision made by an order under this section in relation to any transaction or event taking place while securities transferred by such an order are held by a person within subsection (1)(a), (b) or (c) is to be regarded as provision made in consequence of the transfer.

NOTES

Note that the power of the Treasury to make orders under this section may not be exercised after 21 February 2009; see s 2(8), (9) at **[17.336]**.

Orders: the Northern Rock plc Transfer Order 2008, SI 2008/432; the Bradford & Bingley plc Transfer of Securities and Property etc Order 2008, SI 2008/2546; the Bradford & Bingley plc Transfer of Securities and Property etc (Amendment) Order 2009, SI 2009/320.

[17.338]

4 Extinguishment of subscription rights

(1) This section applies where the Treasury make, or have made, an order under section 3 providing for the transfer of securities issued by an authorised UK deposit-taker.

(2) The Treasury may by order make provision for or in connection with, or in consequence of, the extinguishment of rights of any specified description to subscribe for, or otherwise acquire, securities of—

(a) the deposit-taker, or

(b) any of its subsidiary undertakings.

(3) Subsection (2) applies whether the rights have been granted by the deposit-taker or otherwise.

(4) Where an order providing for the extinguishment of any rights has been made under this section, the power to make an order under this section may be subsequently exercised so as to make provision in connection with, or in consequence of, the extinguishment of those rights even though the order does not itself provide for any rights to be extinguished.

NOTES

Orders: the Northern Rock plc Transfer Order 2008, SI 2008/432; the Bradford & Bingley plc Transfer of Securities and Property etc Order 2008, SI 2008/2546.

[17.339]

5 Compensation etc for securities transferred etc

(1) The Treasury must by order—

(a) in relation to an order under section 3 that transfers securities only to the public sector, make a scheme for determining the amount of any compensation payable by the Treasury to persons who held the securities immediately before they were so transferred;

(b) in relation to an order under section 3 that transfers securities only to a private sector body, make provision for determining the amount of any consideration payable by the body to persons who held the securities immediately before they were so transferred;

(c) in relation to an order under section 3 that transfers securities both to the public sector and a private sector body, make provision for determining—

(i) the amount of any compensation payable by the Treasury, and

(ii) the amount of any consideration payable by the private sector body concerned,

to persons who held the securities immediately before they were so transferred.

(2) The Treasury must by order make provision for determining the amount of any compensation payable to persons whose rights are extinguished by virtue of an order under section 4 (a "section 4 order") and—

(a) in any case where the section 4 order is made in consequence of an order under section 3 that transfers securities only to the public sector, the order must provide for any compensation to be payable by the Treasury;

(b) in any case where the section 4 order is made in consequence of an order under section 3 that transfers securities only to a private sector body, the order must provide for any compensation to be payable by the private sector body concerned;

(c) in any case where the section 4 order is made in consequence of an order under section 3 that transfers securities both to the public sector and a private sector body, the order must make provision for determining the amount of any compensation payable by the Treasury or the private sector body concerned (or both).

(3) An order under this section may also make provision for extending provisions of the order, in any specified circumstances, to persons otherwise affected by any provision made in an order under section 3 or 4.

(4) In determining the amount of any compensation payable by the Treasury by virtue of any provision in an order under this section, it must be assumed—

(a) that all financial assistance provided by the Bank of England or the Treasury to the deposit-taker in question has been withdrawn (whether by the making of a demand for repayment or otherwise), and

(b) that no financial assistance would in future be provided by the Bank of England or the Treasury to the deposit-taker in question (apart from ordinary market assistance offered by the Bank of England subject to its usual terms).

(5) For the purposes of subsection (4)—

(a) the references to the provision of financial assistance by the Treasury to the deposit-taker include any case where the Chancellor of the Exchequer announces that the Treasury (whether acting alone or with the Bank of England) would, if necessary, put in place relevant guarantee arrangements in relation to the deposit-taker (as well as any case where any such arrangements are put in place, whether or not following such an announcement);

(b) "ordinary market assistance" means assistance provided as part of the Bank's standing facilities in the sterling money markets or as part of the Bank's open market operations in those markets.

(6) It is immaterial whether the announcement mentioned in subsection (5)(a) is made before or after the passing of this Act.

(7) In this section—

(a) any reference to any transfer of securities to the public sector is a reference to the transfer of any securities to any person within paragraphs (a) to (c) of subsection (1) of section 3;

(b) any reference to any transfer of securities to a private sector body is a reference to the transfer of any securities to any body corporate within paragraph (d) of that subsection.

(8) An order under subsection (1) or (2) must be made within the period of 3 months beginning with—

(a) the day on which the order under section 3 is made (in the case of an order under subsection (1)), or

(b) the day on which the order under section 4 is made (in the case of an order under subsection (2)).

(9) But nothing in subsection (8) prevents the making, at any time after the end of that period, of a second or subsequent order under this section in relation to the order under section 3 or 4.

NOTES

Orders: the Northern Rock plc Compensation Scheme Order 2008, SI 2008/718; the Bradford & Bingley plc Compensation Scheme Order 2008, SI 2008/3249; the Bradford & Bingley plc Compensation Scheme (Amendment) Order 2009, SI 2009/790; the Northern Rock plc Compensation Scheme (Amendment) Order 2009, SI 2009/791.

Transfer of property etc

[17.340]

6 Transfer of property, rights and liabilities

(1) The Treasury may by order make provision for or in connection with, or in consequence of, the transfer of property, rights and liabilities of an authorised UK deposit-taker to either (or each) of the following—

(a) a company wholly owned by the Bank of England or the Treasury;

(b) a body corporate not within paragraph (a).

(2) An order under this section may define the property, rights and liabilities to be transferred in one or more of the following ways—

(a) by specifying or describing the property, rights and liabilities in question;

(b) by referring to all the property, rights and liabilities comprised in the whole or a specified part of the deposit-taker's business;

(c) by identifying the manner in which the property, rights and liabilities to be transferred are to be determined.

(3) Schedule 2 specifies particular kinds of provisions that may be included in an order under this section.

(4) Where an order providing for the transfer of any property, rights or liabilities has been made under this section, the power to make an order under this section may be subsequently exercised so as to make provision in connection with, or in consequence of, the transfer (including provision of a kind specified in Schedule 2) even though the order does not itself provide for the transfer of any property, rights or liabilities.

(5) Where an order under this section or section 3 ("the initial order") has been made in relation to an authorised UK deposit-taker, the power to make an order under this section may be subsequently exercised in relation to that deposit-taker whether or not any transfer of property, rights or liabilities provided for by the order is to the person to whom any transfer was made by or under the initial order.

(6) A second or subsequent order made under this section in relation to an authorised UK deposit-taker may make provision for any of the property, rights or liabilities transferred by or under a previous order under this section to be transferred back to the deposit-taker.

(7) The provisions of this section and Schedule 2 apply for the purposes of subsection (6) with any necessary modifications.

(8) For the purposes of this section any provision made by an order under this section in relation to any transaction or event taking place while property, rights or liabilities transferred by or under such an order are held by a company within subsection (1)(a) is to be regarded as provision made in consequence of the transfer.

NOTES

Note that the power of the Treasury to make orders under this section may not be exercised after 21 February 2009; see s 2(8), (9) at **[17.336]**.

Orders: the Heritable Bank plc Transfer of Certain Rights and Liabilities Order 2008, SI 2008/2644; the Transfer of Rights and Liabilities to ING Order 2008, SI 2008/2666; the Kaupthing Singer & Friedlander Limited Transfer of Certain Rights and Liabilities Order 2008, SI 2008/2674; the Kaupthing Singer & Friedlander Limited Transfer of Certain Rights and Liabilities (Amendment) Order 2009, SI 2009/308; the Heritable Bank plc Transfer of Certain Rights and Liabilities (Amendment) Order 2009, SI 2009/310; the Bradford & Bingley plc Transfer of Securities and Property etc (Amendment) Order 2009, SI 2009/320.

[17.341]

7 Compensation etc for property etc transferred

(1) The Treasury must by order make provision—

(a) in relation to an order under section 6 providing for the transfer of property, rights or liabilities to a company within subsection (1)(a) of that section, for determining the amount of any compensation payable by the Treasury to the authorised UK deposit-taker concerned;

(b) in relation to an order under section 6 providing for the transfer of property, rights or liabilities to any other body, for determining the amount of any consideration payable by the transferee to the authorised UK deposit-taker concerned.

(2) An order under this section may also make provision for extending provisions of the order, in any specified circumstances, to persons otherwise affected by any provision made in an order under section 6.

(3) In determining the amount of any compensation payable by the Treasury by virtue of any provision in an order under this section, it must be assumed—

(a) that all financial assistance provided by the Bank of England or the Treasury to the deposit-taker in question has been withdrawn (whether by the making of a demand for repayment or otherwise), and

(b) that no financial assistance would in future be provided by the Bank of England or the Treasury to the deposit-taker in question (apart from ordinary market assistance offered by the Bank of England subject to its usual terms).

(4) For the purposes of subsection (3)—

(a) the references to the provision of financial assistance by the Treasury to the deposit-taker include any case where the Chancellor of the Exchequer announces that the Treasury (whether acting alone or with the Bank of England) would, if necessary, put in place relevant guarantee arrangements in relation to the deposit-taker (as well as any case where any such arrangements are put in place, whether or not following such an announcement);

(b) "ordinary market assistance" means assistance provided as part of the Bank's standing facilities in the sterling money markets or as part of the Bank's open market operations in those markets.

(5) It is immaterial whether the announcement mentioned in subsection (4)(a) is made before or after the passing of this Act.

(6) An order under this section must be made within the period of 3 months beginning with the day on which the order under section 6 is made.

(7) But nothing in subsection (6) prevents the making, at any time after the end of that period, of a second or subsequent order under this section in relation to the order under section 6.

NOTES

Orders: the Kaupthing Singer & Friedlander Limited (Determination of Compensation) Order 2008, SI 2008/3250; the Heritable Bank plc (Determination of Compensation) Order 2008, SI 2008/3251.

Further transfers

[17.342]

8 Further transfers following transfer to public sector

(1) Subsection (2) applies where any securities issued by an authorised UK deposit-taker have been transferred to a person within section 3(1)(a) to (c) by an order under section 3.

(2) In such a case the Treasury may by order make provision for or in connection with, or in consequence of, the transfer to a specified person of any of the following—

(a) any of the securities transferred as mentioned in subsection (1);

(b) any securities issued by the deposit-taker at any time after the transfer mentioned in that subsection;

(c) any of the property, rights and liabilities of the deposit-taker;

(d) any of the property, rights and liabilities of any UK undertaking which is a subsidiary undertaking of the deposit-taker;

(e) where the securities so transferred were transferred to a company within section 3(1)(c)—

(i) any securities issued by the company;

(ii) any property, rights and liabilities of the company.

(3) Subsection (4) applies where any property, rights or liabilities have been transferred to a company within section 6(1)(a) ("the company") by or under an order under section 6.

(4) In such a case the Treasury may by order make provision for or in connection with, or in consequence of, the transfer to a specified person of any of the following—

(a) any property, rights and liabilities of the company;

(b) any property, rights and liabilities of any UK undertaking which is a subsidiary undertaking of the company;

(c) any securities issued by the company.

(5) The following provisions apply in relation to an order under subsection (2) or (4) with any necessary modifications—

(a) sections 3(2) to (4) and 4, together with Schedule 1, so apply in relation to an order making provision for or in connection with, or in consequence of, the transfer of any securities;

(b) section 6(2) to (5), together with Schedule 2, so apply in relation to an order making provision for or in connection with, or in consequence of, the transfer of any property, rights or liabilities.

(6) The Treasury may by order make provision, in relation to any description of order under subsection (2) or (4), for determining the amount of any consideration payable by the transferee in respect of any securities, or any property, rights and liabilities, transferred by or under any such order under that subsection.

(7) A person to whom anything is transferred by or under an order under section 3 or 6 is not to be regarded as precluded by subsection (2) or (4) from making any contractual or other disposition of, or relating to, anything falling within those subsections.

NOTES

Orders: the Bradford & Bingley plc Transfer of Securities and Property etc Order 2008, SI 2008/2546; the Transfer of Rights and Liabilities to ING Order 2008, SI 2008/2666; the Kaupthing Singer & Friedlander Limited Transfer of Certain Rights and Liabilities Order 2008, SI 2008/2674; the Kaupthing Singer & Friedlander Limited Transfer of Certain Rights and Liabilities (Amendment) Order 2009, SI 2009/308; the Bradford & Bingley plc Transfer of Securities and Property etc (Amendment) Order 2009, SI 2009/320; the Northern Rock plc Transfer Order 2009, SI 2009/3226; the NRAM plc (formerly Northern Rock plc) Consequential and Supplementary Provisions Order 2016, SI 2016/114.

Supplementary

[17.343]

9 Supplementary provision about compensation schemes etc

(1) An order under section 5, 7 or 8(6) may in particular make provision—

(a) for the manner in which any compensation or consideration is to be assessed, including provision as to methods of calculation, valuation dates and matters to be taken into, or left out of, account in making valuations;

(b) for the assessment to be made by an independent valuer appointed by the Treasury;

(c) as to the procedure in relation to the assessment of any compensation or consideration, including provision enabling any such valuer to make rules as to that procedure;

(d) for decisions relating to the assessment of any compensation or consideration to be reconsidered by the person who made those decisions (including any such provision as to procedure as is mentioned in paragraph (c));

(e) for enabling persons to apply for decisions relating to the assessment of any compensation or consideration to be reviewed by the [Upper Tribunal] or a tribunal appointed by the Treasury for the purposes of the order;

(f) as to the powers of a relevant tribunal (that is to say, the [Upper Tribunal] or a tribunal appointed by the Treasury for the purposes of the order);

(g) as to the procedure for applying for any review to a [tribunal appointed by the Treasury for the purposes of the order], including provision enabling the tribunal to make rules as to that procedure;

(h) as to remuneration and expenses of any independent valuer, or of any tribunal, appointed by the Treasury for the purposes of the order;
(i) as to the appointment of any staff of any such valuer (including provision as to their terms and conditions of employment and as to their pensions, allowances or gratuities).

(2) The provision that may be made by virtue of subsection (1)(a) includes the making of assumptions as to any matter, including in particular the making of one or more of the following assumptions about the authorised UK deposit-taker in question—
(a) that it is unable to continue as a going concern;
(b) that it is in administration;
(c) that it is being wound up.

(3) Subsection (1)(a) is subject to sections 5(4) and 7(3), but those subsections do not—
(a) prevent the inclusion of provision requiring the making of the assumptions mentioned in those subsections in any case where they are not required to be made by either of those subsections; or
(b) otherwise restrict the provision that may be made by virtue of subsection (1)(a).

(4) In subsection (1)(a) the reference to valuation dates includes—
(a) valuation dates falling before the day on which this Act is passed; and
(b) valuation dates falling before the day on which the relevant event takes place.

(5) In subsection (1)(e)—
(a) the reference to persons includes the Treasury; and
(b) the reference to decisions relating to the assessment of any compensation or consideration includes decisions following any such reconsideration as is mentioned in subsection (1)(d).

(6) The provision that may be made by virtue of subsection (1)(f)—
(a) includes provision enabling a relevant tribunal, where satisfied that the decision in question was not a reasonable decision, to send the matter back to the person who made the decision for reconsideration in accordance with such directions (if any) as it considers appropriate; but
(b) does not include provision enabling a relevant tribunal to substitute its own decision for that of the person who made the decision.

(7) The power of any valuer or tribunal to make provision as to procedure by virtue of subsection (1)(c), (d) or (g) includes power to make different provision for different cases or circumstances.

(8) In this section "the relevant event" means the transfer or (as the case may be) extinguishment of rights made by or under the order to which the order mentioned in subsection (1) relates.

NOTES

Sub-s (1): words in square brackets in paras (e), (f) substituted for original words "Financial Services and Markets Tribunal" and words in square brackets in para (g) substituted for original words "relevant tribunal" by the Transfer of Tribunal Functions Order 2010, SI 2010/22, art 5(1), Sch 2, para 144, subject to transitional provisions and savings in art 5(4) of, and Sch 5 to, that Order.

Orders: the Northern Rock plc Compensation Scheme Order 2008, SI 2008/718; the Bradford & Bingley plc Compensation Scheme Order 2008, SI 2008/3249; the Bradford & Bingley plc Compensation Scheme (Amendment) Order 2009, SI 2009/790; the Northern Rock plc Compensation Scheme (Amendment) Order 2009, SI 2009/791.

[17.344]

10 Tax consequences

(1) The Treasury may by regulations make provision for or in connection with varying the way in which any relevant tax would, apart from the regulations, have effect in relation to, or in connection with, any of the following—
(a) anything done for the purpose of, in relation to, or by or under or in consequence of, a relevant order;
(b) any securities, or any property, rights or liabilities, which are transferred, extinguished or otherwise affected by any provision made by or under a relevant order;
(c) any securities issued by, or any property, rights or liabilities of, any transferee which have not been transferred by or under a relevant order;
(d) any securities issued by, or any property, rights or liabilities of, any relevant institution which have not been so transferred.

(2) The provision that may be made by the regulations includes provision for or in connection with any of the following—
(a) a tax provision not to apply, or to apply with modifications, in prescribed cases or circumstances;
(b) anything done to have or not to have a specified consequence for the purposes of a tax provision in prescribed cases or circumstances;
(c) any securities, or any property, rights or liabilities, to be treated in a specified way for the purposes of a tax provision in prescribed cases or circumstances (whether or not affected by any provision made by or under a relevant order);
(d) the withdrawal of relief (whether or not granted by virtue of the regulations), and the charging of any relevant tax, in prescribed cases or circumstances;
(e) requiring or enabling the Treasury to determine, or to specify the method to be used for determining, anything (including amounts or values, or times or periods of time) which needs to be determined for the purposes of any tax provision (whether or not modified by the regulations) as it applies in relation to, or in connection with, any of the matters mentioned in subsection (1)(a) to (d).

(3) In this section—

"prescribed" means prescribed by or determined in accordance with regulations under this section;

"relevant institution" means any body in relation to which a relevant order is made;
"relevant order" means an order under section 3, 4, 6 or 8;
"relevant tax" means corporation tax, income tax, capital gains tax, stamp duty, stamp duty reserve tax and stamp duty land tax;
"tax provision" means any enactment relating to any relevant tax;
"transferee" means any person to whom any securities, or any property, rights or liabilities, are transferred by or under a relevant order.

NOTES
Regulations: the Northern Rock plc (Tax Consequences) Regulations 2009, SI 2009/3227.

Building societies

[17.345]
11 Modification of legislation applying in relation to building societies
(1) The Treasury may by order make such modifications of the Building Societies Act 1986 (c 53) as they consider appropriate for or in connection with facilitating the provision of relevant financial assistance by the Bank of England to building societies.
(2) In this section "relevant financial assistance" means any financial assistance provided for the purpose of maintaining the stability of the financial system in the United Kingdom.
(3) An order under this section may in particular make provision for or in connection with modifying the operation of any of the following—
(a) sections 5, 6 and 7 of, and Schedule 2 to, the Building Societies Act 1986 (c 53) (establishment, constitution and powers, the lending limit and the funding limit);
(b) any other provision of that Act which might otherwise prevent any relevant financial assistance from being provided by the Bank of England to building societies or affect the amount of any such assistance;
[(c) sections 8 and 9A of the Building Societies Act 1986 (restrictions on raising funds and borrowing and on transactions involving derivative instruments etc);]
(d) any other provision of that Act which might otherwise prevent building societies from entering into any transaction in connection with the provision of financial assistance by the Bank of England to building societies;
(e) sections 90 and 90A of, and Schedules 15 and 15A to, that Act (application of companies winding up legislation and other companies insolvency legislation to building societies).
(4) An order under this section may in particular disapply (to such extent as is specified) any specified statutory provision.
(5) In this section "building society" means a building society incorporated (or deemed to be incorporated) under the Building Societies Act 1986.

NOTES
Sub-s (3): para (c) substituted by the Financial Services (Banking Reform) Act 2013, s 138, Sch 9, para 4(3)(c).
Orders: the Building Societies (Financial Assistance) Order 2010, SI 2010/1188 at **[18.217]**.

General

[17.346]
12 Consequential and supplementary provision
(1) The Treasury may by order make—
(a) such supplementary, incidental or consequential provision, or
(b) such transitory, transitional or saving provision,
as they consider appropriate for the general purposes, or any particular purposes, of this Act or in consequence of any provision made by or under this Act, or for giving full effect to this Act or any such provision.
(2) An order under this section may in particular—
(a) disapply (to such extent as is specified) any specified statutory provision or rule of law;
(b) provide for any specified statutory provision to apply (whether or not it would otherwise apply) with specified modifications;
(c) make provision for or in connection with any of the matters mentioned in subsection (3).
(3) Those matters are—
(a) imposing a moratorium on the commencement or continuation of proceedings or other legal processes of any specified description in relation to any body or property of any such description;
(b) providing exceptions from any provision made in pursuance of paragraph (a), whether framed by reference to—
(i) the leave of the court or the consent of the Treasury or the Bank of England, or
(ii) instruments or transactions of specified descriptions,
or otherwise;
(c) the dissolution of any relevant deposit-taker or of any UK undertaking which is a subsidiary undertaking of any relevant deposit-taker;
(d) exempting directors of any relevant deposit-taker, or of any group undertaking of any relevant deposit-taker, from liability in connection with acts or omissions in relation to the deposit-taker or undertaking;
(e) the payment of any compensation by the Treasury to persons affected by an order under this section.

(4) An order under this section may, in connection with the payment of any such compensation, make provision for any matter for which provision is or may be made by or under section 5, 7 or 9.
(5) In this section "relevant deposit-taker" means any authorised UK deposit-taker in relation to which an order is being, or has been, made under section 3 or 6.

NOTES

Orders: the Northern Rock plc Transfer Order 2008, SI 2008/432; the Northern Rock plc Compensation Scheme Order 2008, SI 2008/718; the Building Societies (Financial Assistance) Order 2008, SI 2008/1427; the Bradford & Bingley plc Transfer of Securities and Property etc Order 2008, SI 2008/2546; the Heritable Bank plc Transfer of Certain Rights and Liabilities Order 2008, SI 2008/2644; the Transfer of Rights and Liabilities to ING Order 2008, SI 2008/2666; the Kaupthing Singer & Friedlander Limited Transfer of Certain Rights and Liabilities Order 2008, SI 2008/2674; the Bradford & Bingley plc Compensation Scheme Order 2008, SI 2008/3249; the Kaupthing Singer & Friedlander Limited Transfer of Certain Rights and Liabilities (Amendment) Order 2009, SI 2009/308; the Heritable Bank plc Transfer of Certain Rights and Liabilities (Amendment) Order 2009, SI 2009/310; the Bradford & Bingley plc Transfer of Securities and Property etc (Amendment) Order 2009, SI 2009/320; the Bradford & Bingley plc Compensation Scheme (Amendment) Order 2009, SI 2009/790; the Northern Rock plc Compensation Scheme (Amendment) Order 2009, SI 2009/791; the Northern Rock plc Transfer Order 2009, SI 2009/3226.

[17.347]
13 Orders and regulations: general

(1) Orders and regulations under this Act are to be made by statutory instrument.
(2) Such orders and regulations—
 (a) may make different provision for different cases or circumstances;
 (b) may make such supplementary, incidental, consequential, transitory, transitional or saving provision as the Treasury consider appropriate.
(3) A statutory instrument which contains an order under section 5, 7, 8(6) or 11 (whether alone or with other provision) may not be made unless a draft of the instrument has been laid before, and approved by a resolution of, each House of Parliament.
(4) If a statutory instrument to which subsection (3) applies would, apart from this subsection, be treated as a hybrid instrument for the purposes of the Standing Orders of either House of Parliament, it is to proceed in that House as if it were not such an instrument.
(5) A statutory instrument containing an order under this Act to which subsection (3) does not apply is subject to annulment in pursuance of a resolution of either House of Parliament.
(6) A statutory instrument containing regulations under section 10 is subject to annulment in pursuance of a resolution of the House of Commons.
(7) Nothing in any provision of this Act that authorises the making of any order or regulations, or the making of any particular kind of provision by any order or regulations, affects the generality of any other such provision of this Act.

[17.348]
14 Orders and regulations: retrospective provisions

(1) Subsections (2) and (3) apply to any order made under section 3, 4, 6 or 12 (a "relevant order").
(2) A relevant order may—
 (a) provide for any provision made by the order to have retrospective effect as from any appropriate time or any specified later time;
 (b) make provision for or in connection with, or in consequence of, nullifying the effect of transactions or events taking place after the time in question.
(3) "Appropriate time", in relation to a relevant order, means—
 (a) the specified time on the date of a statement published by the Treasury of their intention to make an order that would have the same general effect as the relevant order;
 (b) the specified time on the date on which any transfer was effected by or under a previous relevant order.
(4) It is immaterial whether the statement mentioned in subsection (3)(a) is published before or after the passing of this Act.
(5) Regulations under section 10 may provide for any of their provisions to have retrospective effect as from any time which is not earlier than 3 months before the day on which this Act is passed.

[17.349]
15 Interpretation

(1) In this Act—
"authorised UK deposit-taker" has the meaning given by section 1;
"body corporate" includes a body incorporated outside the United Kingdom, but does not include the Bank of England;
"company" means a company within the meaning of section 1 of the Companies Act 2006 (c 46);
"director", in relation to a body corporate whose affairs are managed by its members, means a member of the body corporate;
"enactment" includes—
 (a) an enactment comprised in subordinate legislation within the meaning of the Interpretation Act 1978 (c 30),
 (b) an enactment contained in, or in an instrument made under, an Act of the Scottish Parliament, and
 (c) an enactment contained in, or in an instrument made under, Northern Ireland legislation within the meaning of the Interpretation Act 1978;
"financial assistance", in relation to any person, includes—

(a) assistance provided by way of loan, guarantee or indemnity,
(b) assistance provided by way of any transaction which equates, in substance, to a transaction for lending money at interest (such as a transaction involving the sale and repurchase of securities or other assets), and
(c) assistance falling within paragraph (a) or (b) provided indirectly to or otherwise for the benefit of the person (including the provision of assistance within paragraph (a) or (b) to any group undertaking of that person),

whether provided in pursuance of an agreement or otherwise and whether provided before or after the passing of this Act;

"FSMA 2000" means the Financial Services and Markets Act 2000 (c 8);

"group undertaking" has the meaning given by section 1161 of the Companies Act 2006;

"indemnity" includes any undertaking or other arrangement entered into for the purpose of indemnifying any person or for any similar purpose;

"liabilities" includes obligations;

"modifications" includes omissions, additions and alterations, and "modify" has a corresponding meaning;

"pension scheme" means a scheme or other arrangements for the provision of benefits to or in respect of people—

(a) on retirement,
(b) on death,
(c) on having reached a particular age,
(d) on the onset of any serious ill-health or incapacity, or
(e) in similar circumstances;

"relevant guarantee arrangements", in relation to any authorised UK deposit-taker, has the meaning given by section 2(6);

"securities" includes—

(a) shares and stock,
(b) debentures, including debenture stock, loan stock, bonds, certificates of deposit and other instruments creating or acknowledging indebtedness, and
(c) warrants or other instruments entitling the holder to subscribe for, or otherwise acquire, securities falling within paragraph (a) or (b),

and see also subsection (2);

"specified", in relation to any order or regulations under this Act, means specified in the order or regulations;

"statutory provision" means any provision made by or under an enactment (whenever passed or made);

"subsidiary undertaking" has the meaning given by section 1162 of the Companies Act 2006 (c 46);

"UK undertaking" means an undertaking which is incorporated in, or formed under the law of any part of, the United Kingdom;

"undertaking" has the meaning given by section 1161 of the Companies Act 2006 (except in the definition of "indemnity");

"wholly owned", in relation to the Bank of England or the Treasury, is to be construed in accordance with subsection (6);

"wholly-owned subsidiary" has the meaning given by section 1159 of the Companies Act 2006.

(2) In this Act any reference (however expressed) to securities issued by any authorised UK deposit-taker includes a reference to rights granted by the deposit-taker which form part of its own funds for the purposes of [Title 1 of Part Two of Regulation (EU) No 575/2013 of the European Parliament and of the Council] (and which would not otherwise be securities by virtue of subsection (1)).

(3) . . .

(4) For the purposes of this Act any undertaking that was an authorised UK deposit-taker immediately before the making of the first order under section 3 or 6 in relation to the undertaking is to be regarded as continuing to be an authorised UK deposit-taker, whether or not it would be one apart from this subsection.

(5) For the purposes of this Act any reference (however expressed) to an undertaking which is—

(a) a group undertaking of an authorised UK deposit-taker, or
(b) a subsidiary undertaking of an authorised UK deposit-taker,

includes, in relation to any time after the making of the first order under section 3 or 6 in relation to the deposit-taker ("the relevant time"), a reference to an undertaking which was a group or subsidiary undertaking of the deposit-taker immediately before the making of that order but is not one at the relevant time.

(6) For the purposes of this Act—

(a) a company is to be regarded as wholly owned by the Bank of England at any time if at that time—
 (i) it is a company of which no person other than the Bank or a nominee of the Bank is a member, or
 (ii) it is a wholly-owned subsidiary of a company within sub-paragraph (i); and
(b) a company is to be regarded as wholly owned by the Treasury at any time if at that time—
 (i) it is a company of which no person other than a nominee of the Treasury is a member, or
 (ii) it is a wholly-owned subsidiary of a company within sub-paragraph (i).

(7) This subsection makes transitional provision for the purposes of this Act in relation to expressions defined by subsection (1) by reference to provisions of the Companies Act 2006 (c 46) ("the 2006 Act")—

(a) in relation to any time before the commencement of section 1 of the 2006 Act, "company" means a company within the meaning of the Companies Act 1985 (c 6) ("the 1985 Act") or the Companies (Northern Ireland) Order 1986 (SI 1986/1032 (NI 6)) ("the 1986 Order");
(b) in relation to any time before the commencement of section 1159 of the 2006 Act, "wholly-owned subsidiary" has the meaning given by section 736 of the 1985 Act or Article 4 of the 1986 Order;
(c) in relation to any time before the commencement of sections 1161 and 1162 of the 2006 Act, "group undertaking", "subsidiary undertaking" and "undertaking" have the meanings given by sections 258 and 259 of the 1985 Act or Articles 266 and 267 of the 1986 Order.

NOTES

Sub-s (2): words in square brackets substituted by the Capital Requirements Regulations 2013, SI 2013/3115, reg 46(1), Sch 2, Pt 2, para 43(1), (2).

Sub-s (3): repealed by SI 2013/3115, reg 46(1), Sch 2, Pt 2, para 43(1), (3).

[17.350]
16 Financial provision

(1) There is to be paid out of money provided by Parliament—
(a) any expenditure incurred by the Treasury in connection with the provision of financial assistance to any authorised UK deposit-taker in relation to which an order is made under section 3 or 6;
(b) any expenditure incurred by the Treasury in connection with the provision of financial assistance to any person to whom any transfer is made under this Act;
(c) any expenditure incurred by the Treasury in connection with the giving of any relevant indemnity or the putting in place of relevant guarantee arrangements in relation to any particular authorised UK deposit-taker; and
(d) any other expenditure incurred by the Treasury by virtue of this Act.
(2) In subsection (1)(c) "relevant indemnity" means any indemnity given to—
(a) directors of any authorised UK deposit-taker in relation to which an order is made under section 3 or 6,
(b) directors of any body to which any transfer is made under this Act,
(c) directors of any body which is a group undertaking of any body to which any transfer is made under this Act,
(d) the Bank of England in respect of, or in connection with, any financial assistance provided by it to any body within any of paragraphs (a) to (c), or
(e) any person appointed by the Treasury as an independent valuer for the purposes of any order made under this Act.
(3) It is immaterial whether the indemnity or arrangements mentioned in subsection (1) are given or put in place before or after the passing of this Act.

[17.351]
17 Short title, commencement and extent

(1) This Act may be cited as the Banking (Special Provisions) Act 2008.
(2) This Act comes into force on the day on which it is passed.
(3) This Act extends to England and Wales, Scotland and Northern Ireland.

SCHEDULES

SCHEDULE 1
TRANSFER ORDERS UNDER SECTION 3

Section 3

[17.352]
1 Provisions relating to securities transferred: general

(1) An order under section 3 may make provision—
(a) for securities to be transferred free from all trusts, liabilities and incumbrances;
(b) for any transfer of securities to take effect despite—
(i) the absence of any required consent or concurrence to or with the transfer,
(ii) any other restriction relating to the transfer of the securities, or
(iii) the absence of the delivery of any instrument representing securities transferable by delivery (a "bearer instrument");
(c) for the delivery of any such instruments to a specified person, and the issue to the transferee of instruments representing such securities;
(d) for the transferee to be entitled to be entered in any register of securities without the need for delivery of any instrument of transfer;
(e) for requiring the person maintaining any such register to register the transferee in the register;
(f) for the transferee to be, as from the transfer date, entitled, or subject, to rights, privileges, advantages and liabilities arising from or relating to transferred securities, whether or not the transferee has been so registered or any bearer instrument representing the transferred securities has been delivered to the transferee;
(g) for deeming the transferee for any specified purposes to be the holder of the transferred securities at a time when the transferee has yet to be so registered or any such instrument has yet to be so delivered;

(h) for securing that rights of holders of securities, and rights relating to securities that are held by persons other than—
(i) the holders of the securities, or
(ii) the transferee,
cease to be exercisable by the holders of the securities or (as the case may be) such other persons;
(i) for requiring distributions or other relevant amounts payable by the relevant deposit-taker on or after the transfer date to be paid into the Consolidated Fund.

(2) Sub-paragraph (1)(h) applies to—
(a) securities issued by the relevant deposit-taker (whether or not transferred by an order under section 3), or
(b) securities issued by any of its group undertakings;
and, in relation to any transferred securities, any references in that provision to holders of securities are to former holders of them.

2 Conversion of form in which securities held etc

(1) An order under section 3 may make provision—
(a) for securities held in one form to be converted, in the specified manner, from that form into another specified form;
(b) for converting a specified class of securities into securities of another specified class;
(c) for matters consequential on any such conversion as is mentioned in paragraph (a) or (b).

(2) Sub-paragraph (1) applies to securities issued by the relevant deposit-taker, whether or not transferred by an order under section 3.

3 Delisting of securities

(1) An order under section 3 may make provision for discontinuing the listing of securities issued by the relevant deposit-taker (whether or not the securities have been transferred by such an order).

(2) In this paragraph "listing" has the meaning given by section 74(5) of FSMA 2000.

4 Alteration of terms of securities or contracts etc

(1) An order under section 3 may make provision for varying or nullifying the terms, or the effect of terms, of—
(a) securities issued by the relevant deposit-taker (whether or not transferred by such an order),
(b) securities issued by any of its group undertakings, or
(c) other relevant instruments.

(2) The provision that may be made by virtue of sub-paragraph (1) includes provision—
(a) for securing that transactions or events of any specified description have or do not have (directly or indirectly) such consequences as are specified, or are to be treated in the specified manner for any specified purposes;
(b) for discharging persons from further performance of obligations under relevant instruments, and for dealing with the consequences of persons being so discharged.

(3) In this paragraph "relevant instrument" means any agreement, licence or other instrument to or by which any of the following is a party or bound—
(a) the relevant deposit-taker,
(b) any of its group undertakings, or
(c) any person having a specified connection with the relevant deposit-taker or any of its group undertakings (whether framed by reference to a sale of assets by one to the other, or otherwise).

5 Creation of new rights etc

An order under section 3 may make provision for the creation of new rights and liabilities as between the relevant deposit-taker and any of its group undertakings.

6 Rights etc under pension schemes

(1) An order under section 3 may make provision—
(a) as to the consequences of any transfer, by such an order, in relation to any pension scheme;
(b) in relation to any property, rights and liabilities of any relevant occupational pension scheme.

(2) Such an order may—
(a) modify any such rights and liabilities;
(b) apportion any such rights and liabilities between different persons;
(c) provide for property of, or accrued rights in, any relevant occupational pension scheme to be transferred to another occupational pension scheme without the consent of any person.

(3) Provision made in pursuance of this paragraph may be made by means of modifications of a relevant occupational pension scheme or otherwise.

(4) In this paragraph—
"occupational pension scheme" has the meaning given by section 150(5) of the Finance Act 2004 (c 12);
"relevant occupational pension scheme" means an occupational pension scheme in relation to which—
(a) the relevant deposit-taker, or
(b) any of its group undertakings,
is or has been an employer.

7 Provisions relating to directors of relevant deposit-taker etc

(1) An order under section 3 may make provision enabling the Treasury—

(a) to remove or appoint directors of the relevant deposit-taker or any of its group undertakings;

(b) to determine, by agreement with persons so appointed by the Treasury, their remuneration and the other terms and conditions of their service contracts;

(c) to terminate, or vary the terms and conditions of, the service contracts of persons who (however appointed) are directors of the relevant deposit-taker or any of its group undertakings.

(2) An order under section 3 may provide for anything done by the Treasury in accordance with provision made by virtue of sub-paragraph (1) to be treated as done by the relevant deposit-taker.

(3) In this paragraph "service contract" has the meaning given by section 227 of the Companies Act 2006 (c 46).

8 Supplementary provisions

(1) An order under section 3 may make provision—

(a) for agreements made or other things done by or in relation to former holders of transferred securities to be treated as made or done by or in relation to the transferee;

(b) for references to such persons in instruments or documents to have effect with specified modifications;

(c) for anything that relates to anything transferred by an order under section 3, and is in the process of being done by or in relation to any such person immediately before it is transferred, to be continued by or in relation to the transferee.

(2) An order under section 3 may require former holders of transferred securities to provide the transferee with such information and other assistance as is specified.

(3) An order under section 3 may make provision for disputes as to specified matters arising under or by virtue of an order under that section to be determined in the specified manner.

9 Interpretation

(1) In this Schedule—

"distributions or other relevant amounts" includes dividends, payments of interest, principal or capital, premiums and other payments arising in connection with securities transferred by an order under section 3;

"former holder", in relation to transferred securities, means a person holding the securities before the transfer date;

"the relevant deposit-taker", in relation to an order under section 3, means the authorised UK deposit-taker in relation to which the order is made;

"remuneration" includes any benefit in kind;

"register of securities" means a register of members or any other register of the holders of securities;

"specified purposes" include the purposes of any specified statutory provision;

"the transferee" means the person to whom securities are transferred by an order under section 3;

"the transfer date" means (subject to sub-paragraph (2)) the date on which such a transfer takes place.

(2) If an order under section 3 provides for any transfer to take place at a particular time on a particular date, then in relation to that transfer, references to the transfer date are to that time on that date.

NOTES

Note that the power of the Treasury to make orders under s 3 may not be exercised after 21 February 2009; see s 2(8), (9) at **[17.336]**.

Orders: the Bradford & Bingley plc Transfer of Securities and Property etc Order 2008, SI 2008/2546; the NRAM plc (formerly Northern Rock plc) Consequential and Supplementary Provisions Order 2016, SI 2016/114.

SCHEDULE 2
TRANSFER ORDERS UNDER SECTION 6

Section 6

[17.353]

1 Property, rights and liabilities that may be transferred by or under order

The property, rights and liabilities that may be transferred by or under an order under section 6 include—

(a) property, rights and liabilities that would not be capable of being assigned or otherwise transferred by the relevant deposit-taker;

(b) property, rights and liabilities acquired or incurred in the period between the making of the order and the transfer date;

(c) rights and liabilities arising on or after the transfer date in respect of matters occurring before that date;

(d) rights and liabilities under any pension scheme or under any other arrangement for the payment of pensions, allowances and gratuities;

(e) property situated outside the United Kingdom and rights and liabilities under the law of a place outside the United Kingdom;

(f) rights and liabilities under an enactment or Community instrument.

2 Provisions relating to property, rights and liabilities transferred

(1) An order under section 6 may make provision—

(a) for any transfer of any interests or rights to take effect despite the absence of any required consent or concurrence to or with the transfer;

(b) for any transfer of any interests or rights to take effect as if—
(i) no associated liability existed in respect of any failure to comply with any other requirement, and
(ii) there were no associated interference with the interests or rights;
(c) for securing that in any specified circumstances—
(i) a person is not entitled to terminate, modify, acquire or claim an interest or right (or to treat an interest or right as terminated or modified) until it is transferred by or under the order, and
(ii) the entitlement is subsequently either not enforceable or enforceable only to the specified extent;
(d) for rights and liabilities—
(i) to be transferred so as to be enforceable by or against both the transferee and the transferor, and
(ii) where they are so enforceable, to be enforceable in different or modified respects by or against each of those persons;
(e) for interests, rights or liabilities of third parties in relation to anything to which an order under section 6 relates to be modified in the specified manner, including provision—
(i) for securing that transactions or events of any specified description do or do not have (directly or indirectly) such consequences as are specified, or are to be treated in the specified manner for any specified purposes;
(ii) for persons to be discharged from the further performance of contracts and for dealing with the consequences of persons being so discharged;
(f) for the manner in which—
(i) any property held in trust by the relevant deposit-taker before the transfer date (whether as sole or joint trustee) is to be held on or after that date, and
(ii) any powers, provisions and liabilities relating to any such property are to be exercisable or to have effect on or after that date;
(g) for excluding from the transfer specified property, rights and liabilities comprised in the relevant deposit-taker's business or a specified part of it;
(h) for the creation of rights, liabilities or interests in relation to property, rights or liabilities transferred from or retained by the relevant deposit-taker;
(i) for dealing with cases where securities of a subsidiary undertaking are transferred by or under the order;
(j) for enabling the relevant deposit-taker and the transferee (in accordance with the order) to agree on any modification of the order, so long as the order could originally have been made with that modification in accordance with the relevant provisions of this Act;
(k) for apportioning liabilities in respect of any tax or duty (in the United Kingdom or elsewhere) between the relevant deposit-taker and the transferee.

(2) In sub-paragraph (1)(b) "associated liability" and "associated interference" mean respectively any liability or interference that would otherwise exist by virtue of any provision (of an enactment or agreement or otherwise) having effect in relation to the terms on which the relevant deposit-taker is entitled, or subject, to anything to which the transfer relates.

(3) In sub-paragraph (1)(e) "third parties" means persons other than the relevant deposit-taker or the transferee under an order under section 6.

3 Creation of new rights etc

An order under section 6 may make provision for the creation of new rights and liabilities as between the relevant deposit-taker and any of its group undertakings.

4 Rights etc under pension schemes

(1) An order under section 6 may make provision—
(a) as to the consequences of any transfer, by or under such an order, in relation to any pension scheme;
(b) in relation to any property, rights and liabilities of any relevant occupational pension scheme.

(2) Such an order may—
(a) modify any such rights and liabilities;
(b) apportion any such rights and liabilities between different persons;
(c) provide for property of, or accrued rights in, any relevant occupational pension scheme to be transferred to another occupational pension scheme without the consent of any person.

(3) Provision made in pursuance of this paragraph may be made by means of modifications of a relevant occupational pension scheme or otherwise.

(4) In this paragraph—
"occupational pension scheme" has the meaning given by section 150(5) of the Finance Act 2004 (c 12);
"relevant occupational pension scheme" means an occupational pension scheme in relation to which—
(a) the relevant deposit-taker, or
(b) any of its group undertakings,
is or has been an employer.

5 Foreign property etc

(1) An order under section 6 may make provision—

(a) for requiring or authorising the relevant deposit-taker or the transferee to take any specified steps—
 (i) for securing the vesting in the transferee under the relevant foreign law of foreign property or foreign rights or liabilities, or
 (ii) pending any such vesting of such property, rights or liabilities, or
 (iii) otherwise in relation to such property, rights or liabilities;
(b) for the payment by a specified person of expenses incurred in connection with such property, rights or liabilities.

(2) In this paragraph—
(a) "foreign law" means the law of a place outside the United Kingdom; and
(b) "foreign property" and "foreign rights or liabilities" mean respectively property and rights and liabilities as respects which an issue arising in any proceedings would be determined (in accordance with the rules of private international law) by reference to foreign law.

6 Authorisations and permissions etc

(1) An order under section 6 may make provision for securing that, if on the transfer date the transferee satisfies the specified conditions, it is to be treated for the specified period—
(a) as an authorised person in relation to any specified regulated activities carried on by the relevant deposit-taker before that date, or
(b) as an authorised person who has a Part IV permission granted by the Financial Services Authority to carry on any such activities.

(2) Where an order makes provision in accordance with sub-paragraph (1)(b), it may provide that any decision by the Financial Services Authority of a specified description is to have the effect of varying or cancelling (to any specified extent) the Part IV permission which the transferee is to be treated as having by virtue of that provision.

(3) An order under section 6 may make provision—
(a) for securing that licences, permissions or approvals—
 (i) relating to anything transferred by or under the order, and
 (ii) in force or effective immediately before the transfer date,
 are to continue in force or in effect as from that date;
(b) for apportioning (by means of making modifications of the instruments concerned or otherwise) responsibility between the relevant deposit-taker and the transferee as regards compliance with requirements of licences, permissions or approvals.

(4) In this paragraph "authorised person", "Part IV permission" and "regulated activities" have the same meanings as in FSMA 2000.

7 Supplementary provisions

(1) An order under section 6 may make provision—
(a) for the transferee to be treated for any purpose connected with the transfer as the same person in law as the relevant deposit-taker;
(b) for agreements made or other things done by or in relation to any relevant deposit-taker to be treated as made or done by or in relation to the transferee;
(c) for references in instruments or documents to the relevant deposit-taker, to any combination of bodies that includes that deposit-taker, or to any officer or employee of that deposit-taker, to have effect with specified modifications;
(d) for securing continuity of employment in the case of contracts of employment transferred by or under the order;
(e) for anything (including legal proceedings) that relates to anything transferred by or under the order, and is in the process of being done by or in relation to the relevant deposit-taker immediately before it is transferred, to be continued by or in relation to the transferee.

(2) In sub-paragraph (1)(b), (c) and (e) any reference to the relevant deposit-taker includes a reference to any of its group undertakings.

(3) An order under section 6 may require the relevant deposit-taker to provide the transferee with such information and other assistance as is specified.

(4) An order under section 6 may make provision for disputes as to specified matters arising under or by virtue of an order under that section to be determined in the specified manner.

8 Interpretation

(1) In this Schedule—

"the relevant deposit-taker", in relation to an order under section 6, means the authorised UK deposit-taker in relation to which the order is made;

"specified purposes" include the purposes of any specified statutory provision;

"the transferee" means the person to whom property, rights or liabilities are transferred by or under an order under section 6;

"the transfer date" means (subject to sub-paragraph (2)) the date on which such a transfer takes place.

(2) If provision is made by or under an order under section 6 for any transfer to take place at a particular time on a particular date, then in relation to that transfer—
(a) references to the transfer date are to that time on that date; and
(b) references to things occurring before or on or after the transfer date are references to things occurring before or at or after that time on that date.

(3) In this Schedule any reference to anything transferred by or under a particular order under section 6 includes a reference to anything transferred by or under any other order under that section.

NOTES

Note that the power of the Treasury to make orders under s 6 may not be exercised after 21 February 2009; see s 2(8), (9) at **[17.336]**.

Orders: the Heritable Bank plc Transfer of Certain Rights and Liabilities Order 2008, SI 2008/2644; the Kaupthing Singer & Friedlander Limited Transfer of Certain Rights and Liabilities Order 2008, SI 2008/2674; the Northern Rock plc Transfer Order 2009, SI 2009/3226.

HOUSING AND REGENERATION ACT 2008

(2008 c 17)

ARRANGEMENT OF SECTIONS

PART 2
REGULATION OF SOCIAL HOUSING

CHAPTER 4
REGISTERED PROVIDERS

Insolvency etc

143A Application of rules about insolvency . . . [17.354]
144 Preparatory steps: notice . . . [17.355]
145 Moratorium. . . . [17.356]
146 Duration of moratorium . . . [17.357]
147 Further moratorium . . . [17.358]
148 Effect of moratorium . . . [17.359]
149 Exempted disposals . . . [17.360]
150 Disposals without consent . . . [17.361]
151 Interim manager . . . [17.362]
152 Proposals . . . [17.363]
153 Proposals: procedure . . . [17.364]
154 Proposals: effect . . . [17.365]
155 Manager: appointment . . . [17.366]
156 Manager: powers . . . [17.367]
157 Manager of registered society: extra powers . . . [17.368]
158 Assistance by regulator . . . [17.369]
159 Applications to court . . . [17.370]

Restructuring and dissolution

159A Application of rules about restructuring and dissolution . . . [17.371]
160 Company: arrangements and reconstructions . . . [17.372]
161 Company: conversion into registered society . . . [17.373]
162 Company: winding up . . . [17.374]
163 Registered society: restructuring . . . [17.375]
164 Registered society: winding up . . . [17.376]
165 Registered society: dissolution . . . [17.377]
167 Transfer of property . . . [17.378]
168 Section 167: supplemental . . . [17.379]
169 Extension of sections 167 and 168 . . . [17.380]

PART 4
SUPPLEMENTARY AND FINAL PROVISIONS

324 Extent . . . [17.381]
325 Commencement . . . [17.382]
326 Short title . . . [17.383]

An Act to establish the Homes and Communities Agency and make provision about it; to abolish the Urban Regeneration Agency and the Commission for the New Towns and make provision in connection with their abolition; to regulate social housing; to enable the abolition of the Housing Corporation; to make provision about sustainability certificates, landlord and tenant matters, building regulations and mobile homes; to make further provision about housing; and for connected purposes.

[22 July 2008]

1–58 *((Pt 1) outside the scope of this work.)*

PART 2
REGULATION OF SOCIAL HOUSING

59–121 *((Chs 1–3) outside the scope of this work.)*

CHAPTER 4 REGISTERED PROVIDERS

122–143 *(Outside the scope of this work.)*

Insolvency etc

[17.354]
[143A Application of rules about insolvency
This group of sections does not apply to local authorities.]

NOTES
Inserted by the Housing and Regeneration Act 2008 (Registration of Local Authorities) Order 2010, SI 2010/844, art 5, Sch 1, para 27.

[17.355]
144 Preparatory steps: notice
A step specified in the Table has effect only if the person specified has given the regulator notice.

Step	*Person to give notice*
Any step, of a kind prescribed for the purposes of this section by the Secretary of State by order, to enforce a security over land held by a [private registered provider]	*The person taking the step*
Presenting a petition for the winding up of a registered provider which is— (a) a registered company, or (b) [a registered society] But not the presenting of a petition by the regulator under section 166	*The petitioner*
Passing a resolution for the winding up of a registered provider which is— (a) a registered company, or (b) [a registered society] But not the passing of a resolution for winding-up where the regulator's consent is required under section 162 or 164	*The registered provider*
Making an administration application in accordance with paragraph 12 of Schedule B1 to the Insolvency Act 1986 in respect of a registered provider which is a registered company	*The applicant*
Appointing an administrator under paragraph 14 or 22 of that Schedule in respect of a registered provider which is a registered company	*The person making the appointment*
Filing with the court a copy of a notice of intention to appoint a person under either of those paragraphs in respect of a registered provider which is a registered company	*The person filing the notice*

NOTES
Repealed by the Housing and Planning Act 2016, s 115, Sch 6, paras 1, 2, as from a day to be appointed.
Table: in first entry in column 1 words in square brackets substituted by the Housing and Regeneration Act 2008 (Registration of Local Authorities) Order 2010, SI 2010/844, art 5, Sch 1, para 28; in second and third entries in column 1 words in square brackets substituted by the Co-operative and Community Benefit Societies Act 2014, s 151(1), Sch 4, Pt 2, paras 121, 122.
Orders: the Housing and Regeneration Act 2008 (Moratorium) (Prescribed Steps) Order 2010, SI 2010/660.

[17.356]
145 Moratorium
(1) If a step specified in the Table below is taken in respect of a [private registered provider], a moratorium on the disposal of land by the provider begins.
(2) Where a step specified in the Table is taken in respect of a [private registered provider], the person specified must give the regulator notice as soon as is reasonably practicable.

(3) If the notice is not given the step is not invalidated (but the end of the moratorium depends on the notice being given—see section 146(2)).

(4) . . .

[(5) Where the private registered provider owns land in Greater London, the regulator shall give the Greater London Authority a copy of any notice received under this section.]

Step	*Person*
Any step, of a kind prescribed for the purposes of this section by the Secretary of State by order, to enforce a security over land held by a [private registered provider]	*The person taking the step*
The presenting of a petition for winding up a registered provider which is— *(a) a registered company, or* *(b) [a registered society]* *But not the presenting of a petition by the directors or other governing body of the registered provider or by the regulator under section 166*	*The petitioner*
The passing of a resolution for the winding up of a registered provider which is— *(a) a registered company, or* *(b) [a registered society]*	*The registered provider*
A decision by the directors or other governing body of a registered provider to present a petition for winding up where the registered provider is— *(a) a registered company, or* *(b) [a registered society]*	*The directors or governing body*
The making of an administration order in accordance with paragraph 13 of Schedule B1 to the Insolvency Act 1986 in respect of a registered provider which is a registered company	*The person who applied for the order*
The appointment of an administrator under paragraph 14 or 22 of that Schedule in respect of a registered provider which is a registered company	*The person making the appointment*

NOTES

Substituted by the Housing and Planning Act 2016, s 115, Sch 6, paras 1, 3, as from a day to be appointed, as follows—

"145 Moratorium

A moratorium on the disposal of land by a private registered provider begins if a notice is given to the regulator under any of the following provisions of the Housing and Planning Act 2016—

(a) section 104(2)(a) (notice of winding up petition);
(b) section 105(4)(a) (notice of application for permission to pass a resolution for voluntary winding up);
(c) section 106(3)(a) (notice of ordinary administration application);
(d) section 107(4)(a) (notice of appointment of ordinary administrator);
(e) section 108(2)(a) (notice of intention to enforce security).".

Sub-ss (1), (2): words in square brackets substituted by the Housing and Regeneration Act 2008 (Registration of Local Authorities) Order 2010, SI 2010/844, art 5, Sch 1, para 29(a).

Sub-s (4): repealed by the Localism Act 2011, ss 178(1), 237, Sch 16, Pt 1, paras 1, 38, Sch 25, Pt 26.

Sub-s (5): added by the Localism Act 2011, s 195(1), Sch 19, paras 46, 49.

Table: in first entry in column 1 words in square brackets substituted by SI 2010/844, art 5, Sch 1, para 29(b); in second, third and fourth entries in column 1 words in square brackets substituted by the Co-operative and Community Benefit Societies Act 2014, s 151(1), Sch 4, Pt 2, paras 121, 122.

[17.357]

146 Duration of moratorium

(1) The moratorium begins when the step specified in section 145 is taken.

(2) The moratorium ends (unless extended or cancelled) with the period of 28 working days beginning with the day on which the regulator receives notice under section 145(2).

(3) During a moratorium the regulator may extend it (or further extend it) for a specified period, with the consent of each secured creditor of the registered provider whom the regulator is able to locate after making reasonable enquiries.

(4) If the regulator extends a moratorium it shall notify—

(a) the registered provider, [and]

(b) any liquidator, administrator, administrative receiver or receiver appointed in respect of the registered provider or its land, . . .

(c) . . .

[(4A) If the regulator extends a moratorium in respect of a private registered provider who owns land in Greater London, the regulator shall also notify the Greater London Authority.]

(5) During a moratorium the regulator may cancel it if satisfied that it is unnecessary to make proposals under section 152.

(6) Before cancelling a moratorium the regulator must consult the person who took the step that triggered it.

(7) When a moratorium ends the regulator shall give notice, and (except in the case of cancellation) an explanation of section 147, to—

(a) the registered provider, and

(b) such of its secured creditors as the regulator is able to locate after making reasonable enquiries.

(8) . . .

[(8A) When a moratorium in respect of a private registered provider who owns land in Greater London ends, the regulator shall also give notice to the Greater London Authority.]

(9) Taking a further step during a moratorium does not—

(a) start a new moratorium, or

(b) alter the existing moratorium's duration.

NOTES

Sub-ss (1), (2): substituted, by new sub-ss (1), (2), (2A), by the Housing and Planning Act 2016, s 92, Sch 6, paras 1, 4(1), (2), as from a day to be appointed, as follows—

"(1) The moratorium begins when the notice mentioned in section 145 is given.

(2) The moratorium ends when one of the following occurs—

(a) the expiry of the relevant period,

(b) the making of a housing administration order under Chapter 5 of Part 4 of the Housing and Planning Act 2016 in relation to the registered provider, or

(c) the cancellation of the moratorium (see subsection (5)).

(2A) The "relevant period" is—

(a) the period of 28 days beginning with the day on which the notice mentioned in section 145 is given, plus

(b) any period by which that period is extended under subsection (3).".

Sub-s (4): word in square brackets in para (a) inserted, and para (c) and the word immediately preceding it repealed by the Localism Act 2011, ss 178(1), 237, Sch 16, Pt 1, paras 1, 39(1), (2), Sch 25, Pt 26.

Sub-s (4A): inserted by the Localism Act 2011, s 195(1), Sch 19, paras 46, 50(1), (2).

Sub-s (6): repealed by the Housing and Planning Act 2016, s 115, Sch 6, paras 1, 4(1), (3), as from a day to be appointed.

Sub-s (8): repealed by the Localism Act 2011, ss 178(1), 237, Sch 16, Pt 1, paras 1, 39(1), (3), Sch 25, Pt 26.

Sub-s (8A): inserted by the Localism Act 2011, s 195(1), Sch 19, paras 46, 50(1), (3).

Sub-s (9): substituted by the Housing and Planning Act 2016, s 92, Sch 6, paras 1, 4(1), (4), as from a day to be appointed, as follows—

"(9) If a notice mentioned in section 145 is given during a moratorium, that does not—

(a) start a new moratorium, or

(b) alter the existing moratorium's duration.".

[17.358]

147 Further moratorium

(1) This section applies if—

(a) a moratorium in respect of a [private registered provider] ends otherwise than by cancellation, and

(b) a further *step specified in section 145 is taken* in relation to the provider within the period of 3 years beginning with the end of the moratorium.

(2) The further *step* does not automatically trigger a further moratorium.

(3) But the regulator may impose a further moratorium for a specified period, if each secured creditor of the registered provider whom the regulator is able to locate after making reasonable enquiries consents.

(4) If the regulator imposes a new moratorium it shall notify—

(a) the registered provider, [and]

(b) any liquidator, administrator, administrative receiver or receiver appointed in respect of the registered provider or any of its land, . . .

(c) . . .

[(4A) If the regulator imposes a new moratorium in respect of a private registered provider who owns land in Greater London, the regulator shall also notify the Greater London Authority.]

(5) This group of sections applies to a further moratorium as to a first moratorium (except for section 146(2)).

NOTES

Sub-s (1): words in square brackets in para (a) substituted by the Housing and Regeneration Act 2008 (Registration of Local Authorities) Order 2010, SI 2010/844, art 5, Sch 1, para 30; for the words in italics in para (b) there are substituted the words "notice mentioned in section 145 is given", by the Housing and Planning Act 2016, s 115, Sch 6, paras 1, 5(1), (2), as from a day to be appointed.

Sub-s (2): for the word in italics there is substituted the word "notice", by the Housing and Planning Act 2016, s 115, Sch 6, paras 1, 5(1), (3), as from a day to be appointed.

Sub-s (4): word in square brackets in para (a) inserted, and para (c) and the word immediately preceding it repealed by the Localism Act 2011, ss 178(1), 237, Sch 16, Pt 1, paras 1, 40, Sch 25, Pt 26.

Sub-s (4A): inserted by the Localism Act 2011, s 195(1), Sch 19, paras 46, 51.

[17.359]

148 Effect of moratorium

(1) During a moratorium [neither] the HCA[, nor the Greater London Authority, may]—

(a) . . . give the registered provider a direction under section 32(4), [or]

(b) . . . take steps to enforce such a direction against the registered provider.

(2) During a moratorium a disposal of the registered provider's land requires the regulator's prior consent.

(3) Section 149 sets out exceptions to subsection (2).

(4) Consent—

(a) may be given before the moratorium begins, and

(b) may be subject to conditions.

(5) This section does not prevent a liquidator from disclaiming land as onerous property during a moratorium.

(6) In this section "land" includes a present or future interest in rent or other receipts arising from land.

NOTES

Sub-s (1): words in first and second pair of square brackets inserted, words omitted repealed, and word in third pair of square brackets substituted, by the Localism Act 2011, ss 195(1), 237, Sch 19, paras 46, 52, Sch 25, Pt 31.

[17.360]

149 Exempted disposals

(1) The regulator's consent is not required under section 148 for the following exceptions.

(2) Exception 1 is a letting under—

(a) an assured tenancy, or

(b) an assured agricultural occupancy.

(3) Exception 2 is a letting under what would be an assured tenancy or an assured agricultural occupancy but for any of paragraphs 4 to 8, 12(1)(h) and 12ZA to 12B of Schedule 1 to the Housing Act 1988 (c 50) (tenancies which cannot be assured tenancies).

(4) Exception 3 is a letting under a secure tenancy.

(5) Exception 4 is a letting under what would be a secure tenancy but for any of paragraphs 2 to 12 of Schedule 1 to the Housing Act 1985 (c 68) (tenancies which are not secure tenancies).

(6) . . .

(7) Exception [5] is a disposal under Part V of the Housing Act 1985 (right to buy).

(8) Exception [6] is a disposal under the right conferred by—

(a) section 180, *or*

(b) *section 16 of the Housing Act 1996 (c 52) (tenant's right to acquire social housing in Wales).*

NOTES

Sub-s (6): repealed by the Housing and Planning Act 2016, s 92, Sch 4, Pt 1, paras 7, 12(a).

Sub-s (7): reference in square brackets substituted by the Housing and Planning Act 2016, s 92, Sch 4, Pt 1, paras 7, 12(b).

Sub-s (8): reference in square brackets substituted by the Housing and Planning Act 2016, s 92, Sch 4, Pt 1, paras 7, 12(c); para (b) repealed (together with word in italics in para (a)) by the Abolition of the Right to Buy and Associated Rights (Wales) Act 2018, s 6(3), Sch 1, para 6(1), (4), as from 26 January 2019.

[17.361]

150 Disposals without consent

(1) A purported disposal by a registered provider is void if—

(a) it requires the regulator's consent under section 148, and

(b) the regulator has not given consent.

(2) But subsection (1) does not apply to a disposal by a non-profit registered provider to one or more individuals ("the buyer") if—

(a) the disposal is of a single dwelling, and

(b) the registered provider reasonably believes at the time of the disposal that the buyer intends to use the property as the buyer's principal residence.

[17.362]

151 Interim manager

(1) During a moratorium the regulator may appoint an interim manager of the registered provider.

(2) An appointment may relate to the registered provider's affairs generally or to affairs specified in the appointment.

(3) Appointment shall be on terms and conditions (including as to remuneration) specified in, or determined in accordance with, the appointment.

(4) An appointment under this section shall come to an end with the earliest of the following—

(a) the end of the moratorium,

(b) the agreement of proposals under section 152, or

(c) a date specified in the appointment.

(5) An interim manager shall have—

(a) any power specified in the appointment, and

(b) any other power in relation to the registered provider's affairs required by the manager for the purposes specified in the appointment (including the power to enter into agreements and take other action on behalf of the registered provider).

(6) But an interim manager may not—

(a) dispose of land, or

(b) grant security over land.

[17.363]

152 Proposals

(1) During a moratorium the regulator may make proposals about the future ownership and management of the registered provider's land, with a view to ensuring that the property will be properly managed by a registered provider.

(2) In making proposals the regulator shall—

(a) have regard to the interests of the registered provider's creditors as a whole, and

(b) so far as is reasonably practicable avoid worsening the position of unsecured creditors.

(3) Proposals may provide for the appointment of a manager in accordance with section 155 to implement all or part of the proposals.

(4) Proposals may not include anything which would result in—

(a) a preferential debt being paid otherwise than in priority to a non-preferential debt, . . .

[(aa) an ordinary preferential debt being paid otherwise than in priority to a secondary preferential debt,]

(b) a preferential creditor (PC1) being paid a smaller proportion of [an ordinary preferential debt] than another preferential creditor (PC2) (unless PC1 consents) [or

(c) a preferential creditor (PC1) being paid a smaller proportion of a secondary preferential debt than another preferential creditor (PC2) (unless PC2 consents).]

(5) Proposals relating to a registered provider which is a charity (C1)—

(a) may not require it to act outside the terms of its trusts, and

(b) may provide for the disposal of accommodation only to another charity whose objects the regulator thinks are similar to those of C1.

NOTES

Sub-s (4): word omitted from para (a) repealed, para (aa) inserted, in para (b) words in square brackets substituted, and para (c) and word immediately preceding it added, by the Banks and Building Societies (Depositor Preference and Priorities) Order 2014, SI 2014/3486, art 30(1), (2).

[17.364]

153 Proposals: procedure

(1) Before making proposals the regulator shall consult—

(a) the registered provider,

(b) its tenants (so far as is reasonably practicable),

(c) if the registered provider is [a registered society], the [Financial Conduct Authority], and

(d) if the registered provider is a registered charity, the Charity Commission.

(2) The regulator shall send a copy of proposals to—

(a) the registered provider and its officers,

(b) such of its secured creditors as the regulator is able to locate after making reasonable enquiries, and

(c) any liquidator, administrator, administrative receiver or receiver appointed in respect of the registered provider or any of its land.

(3) The regulator shall also make arrangements for bringing proposals to the attention of—

(a) the registered provider's members,

(b) its tenants, and

(c) its unsecured creditors.

(4) If each secured creditor to whom proposals were sent agrees to the proposals by notice to the regulator, the proposals have effect.

(5) Proposals may be agreed with modifications if—

(a) each secured creditor to whom the proposals were sent consents by notice to the regulator, and

(b) the regulator consents.

(6) The regulator shall send a copy of agreed proposals to—

(a) the registered provider and its officers,

(b) its secured creditors to whom the original proposals were sent,

(c) any liquidator, administrator, administrative receiver or receiver appointed in respect of the registered provider or any of its land,

(d) if the registered provider is [a registered society], the [Financial Conduct Authority], and

(e) if the registered provider is a registered charity, the Charity Commission.

(7) The regulator shall also make arrangements for bringing agreed proposals to the attention of—

(a) the registered provider's members,

(b) its tenants, and

(c) its unsecured creditors.

(8) Proposals may be amended by agreement between the secured creditors to whom the original proposals were sent and the regulator; and this section and section 152 apply to an amendment as to the original proposals.

NOTES

Sub-s (1): in para (c) first words in square brackets substituted by the Co-operative and Community Benefit Societies Act 2014, s 151(1), Sch 4, Pt 2, paras 121, 122; second words in square brackets substituted by the Financial Services Act 2012 (Mutual Societies) Order 2013, SI 2013/496, art 2(c), Sch 11, para 8(1), (3)(b).

Sub-s (6): in para (d) first words in square brackets substituted by the Co-operative and Community Benefit Societies Act 2014, s 151(1), Sch 4, Pt 2, paras 121, 122; second words in square brackets substituted by SI 2013/496, art 2(c), Sch 11, para 8(1), (3)(b).

[17.365]

154 Proposals: effect

(1) The following are obliged to implement agreed proposals—
- (a) the regulator,
- (b) the registered provider,
- (c) its creditors, and
- (d) any liquidator, administrator, administrative receiver or receiver appointed in respect of the registered provider or any of its land.

(2) The following shall co-operate with implementation of agreed proposals—
- (a) in the case of a charitable trust, its trustees,
- [(aa) in the case of a charitable incorporated organisation, its charity trustees (as defined by section 177 of the Charities Act 2011),]
- (b) in the case of [a registered society], its committee members, and
- (c) in the case of a registered company, its directors.

(3) Subsection (2) does not require or permit a breach of a fiduciary or other duty.

NOTES

Sub-s (2): para (aa) inserted by the Housing and Planning Act 2016, s 115, Sch 6, paras 1, 6, as from a day to be appointed; in para (b) words in square brackets substituted by the Co-operative and Community Benefit Societies Act 2014, s 151(1), Sch 4, Pt 2, paras 121, 122.

[17.366]

155 Manager: appointment

(1) This section applies where agreed proposals provide for the appointment of a manager.

(2) The proposals must provide for the manager to be paid reasonable remuneration and expenses.

(3) The regulator shall appoint a manager.

(4) The regulator may give the manager directions (general or specific).

(5) The manager may apply to the High Court for directions (and directions of the regulator are subject to directions of the High Court).

(6) If the registered provider is a charity, the regulator must notify the Charity Commission that a manager has been appointed.

(7) The regulator may appoint a new manager in place of a person who ceases to be manager (in accordance with terms of appointment specified in the proposals or determined by the regulator).

[17.367]

156 Manager: powers

(1) A manager—
- (a) may do anything necessary for the purpose of the appointment,
- (b) acts as the registered provider's agent (and is not personally liable on a contract), and
- (c) has ostensible authority to act for the registered provider (so that a person dealing with the manager in good faith and for value need not inquire into the manager's powers).

(2) In particular, the terms of a manager's appointment may confer power—
- (a) to sell or otherwise dispose of land by public auction or private contract;
- (b) to raise or borrow money;
- (c) to grant security over land;
- (d) to grant or accept surrender of a lease;
- (e) to take a lease;
- (f) to take possession of property;
- (g) to appoint a solicitor, accountant or other professional to assist the manager;
- (h) to appoint agents and staff (and to dismiss them);
- (i) to make payments;
- (j) to bring or defend legal proceedings;
- (k) to refer a question to arbitration;
- (l) to make any arrangement or compromise;
- (m) to carry on the business of the registered provider;
- (n) to carry out works and do other things in connection with the management or transfer of land;
- (o) to take out insurance;
- (p) to use the registered body's seal;
- (q) to execute in the name and on behalf of the registered provider any deed, receipt or other document;
- (r) to do anything incidental to a power in paragraphs (a) to (q).

(3) A manager shall so far as is reasonably practicable consult and inform the registered provider's tenants about an exercise of powers likely to affect them.

[17.368]

157 Manager of [registered society]: extra powers

(1) This section applies to a manager appointed to implement proposals relating to [a registered society].

(2) The appointment may confer on the manager power to make and execute on behalf of the society—

(a) an instrument providing for the amalgamation of the society with another [registered society], or

(b) an instrument transferring its engagements.

(3) An instrument providing for the amalgamation of a society ("S1") with another has the same effect as a resolution by S1 under [section 109 of the Co-operative and Community Benefit Societies Act 2014] (amalgamation of societies by special resolution).

(4) An instrument transferring engagements has the same effect as a transfer of engagements under [section 110 or 112 of the Co-operative and Community Benefit Societies Act 2014] (transfer by special resolution to another society or company).

(5) A copy of the instrument shall be sent to and registered by the [Financial Conduct Authority].

(6) An instrument does not take effect until the copy is registered.

(7) The copy must be sent for registration during the period of 14 days beginning with the date of execution; but a copy registered after that period is valid.

NOTES

Section heading, sub-ss (1), (2), (4): words in square brackets substituted by the Co-operative and Community Benefit Societies Act 2014, s 151(1), Sch 4, Pt 2, paras 121–123, 126(1), (3).

Sub-s (3): words in square brackets substituted by the Co-operative and Community Benefit Societies Act 2014, s 151(1), Sch 4, Pt 2, paras 121, 126(1), (2). Note: original text included a reference to "(c 12)" which was not specifically substituted; this chapter number belongs to the title of the Act which was substituted, therefore it is assumed this a drafting error, and the chapter number has been omitted accordingly.

Sub-s (5): words in square brackets substituted by the Financial Services Act 2012 (Mutual Societies) Order 2013, SI 2013/496, art 2(c), Sch 11, para 8(1), (3)(c).

[17.369]

158 Assistance by regulator

(1) The regulator may give financial or other assistance to [the registered provider] for the purpose of preserving its position pending the agreement of proposals.

(2) The regulator may give financial or other assistance to [the registered provider], or a manager appointed under section 155, to facilitate the implementation of agreed proposals.

(3) In particular, the regulator may—

(a) lend staff;

(b) arrange payment of the manager's remuneration and expenses.

(4) The regulator may do the following only with the Secretary of State's consent—

(a) make grants,

(b) make loans,

(c) indemnify a manager,

(d) make payments in connection with secured loans, and

(e) guarantee payments in connection with secured loans.

NOTES

Sub-ss (1), (2): words in square brackets substituted by the Housing and Regeneration Act 2008 (Registration of Local Authorities) Order 2010, SI 2010/844, art 5, Sch 1, para 31.

[17.370]

159 Applications to court

(1) [A private registered provider] may apply to the High Court where the registered provider thinks that action taken by a manager is not in accordance with the agreed proposals.

(2) A creditor of [a private registered provider] may apply to the High Court where the creditor thinks that action taken by a manager is not in accordance with the agreed proposals.

(3) The High Court may—

(a) confirm, annul or modify an act of the manager;

(b) give the manager directions;

(c) make any other order.

(4) If a person bound by agreed proposals (P1) thinks that action by another person (P2) breaches section 154, P1 may apply to the High Court.

(5) The High Court may—

(a) confirm, annul or modify the action;

(b) grant relief by way of injunction, damages or otherwise.

NOTES

Sub-ss (1), (2): words in square brackets substituted by the Housing and Regeneration Act 2008 (Registration of Local Authorities) Order 2010, SI 2010/844, art 5, Sch 1, para 32.

Restructuring and dissolution

[17.371]

[159A Application of rules about restructuring and dissolution

This group of sections does not apply to local authorities.]

NOTES

Inserted by the Housing and Regeneration Act 2008 (Registration of Local Authorities) Order 2010, SI 2010/844, art 5, Sch 1, para 33.

[17.372]

[160 Company: arrangements and reconstructions

(1) This section applies to a non-profit registered provider which is a registered company.
(2) The registered provider must notify the regulator of any voluntary arrangement under Part 1 of the Insolvency Act 1986.
(3) The registered provider must notify the regulator of any order under section 899 of the Companies Act 2006 (court sanction for compromise or arrangement).
(4) An order under section 899 of Companies Act 2006 does not take effect until the registered provider has confirmed to the registrar of companies that the regulator has been notified.
(5) The registered provider must notify the regulator of any order under section 900 of the Companies Act 2006 (powers of court to facilitate reconstruction or amalgamation).
(6) The requirement in section 900(6) of the Companies Act 2006 (sending copy of order to registrar) is satisfied only if the copy is accompanied by confirmation that the regulator has been notified.]

NOTES

Commencement: 6 April 2017.
Substituted by the Housing and Planning Act 2016, s 92, Sch 4, Pt 2, paras 22, 24.

[17.373]

[161 Company: conversion into registered society

(1) This section applies to a non-profit registered provider which is a registered company.
(2) The registered provider must notify the regulator of any resolution under section 115 of the Co-operative and Community Benefit Societies Act 2014 for converting the registered provider into a registered society.
(3) The registrar of companies may register a resolution under that section only if the registered provider has confirmed to the registrar that the regulator has been notified.
(4) The regulator must decide whether the new body is eligible for registration under section 112.
(5) If the new body is eligible for registration, the regulator must register it and designate it as a non-profit organisation.
(6) If the new body is not eligible for registration, the regulator must notify it of that fact.
(7) Pending registration, or notification that it is not eligible for registration, the new body is to be treated as if it were registered and designated as a non-profit organisation.]

NOTES

Commencement: 6 April 2017.
Substituted by the Housing and Planning Act 2016, s 92, Sch 4, Pt 2, paras 22, 25.

[17.374]

162 Company: winding up

(1) This section applies to a non-profit registered provider which is a registered company.
(2) A special resolution for the voluntary winding-up of the company under the Insolvency Act 1986 (c 45) is effective only if the regulator has first consented.
(3) The requirement under section 30 of the Companies Act 2006 (c 46) (sending copy of resolution to registrar) is satisfied only if the copy is accompanied by a copy of the regulator's consent.

NOTES

Repealed by the Housing and Planning Act 2016, s 115, Sch 6, paras 1, 7, as from a day to be appointed.

[17.375]

[163 Registered society: restructuring

(1) This section applies to a non-profit registered provider which is a registered society.
(2) The registered provider must notify the regulator of any resolution passed by the society for the purposes of the restructuring provisions listed in subsection (4).
(3) The Financial Conduct Authority may register the resolution only if the registered provider has confirmed to the Financial Conduct Authority that the regulator has been notified.
(4) The following provisions of the Co-operative and Community Benefit Societies Act 2014 are the restructuring provisions—
- (a) section 109 (amalgamation of societies);
- (b) section 110 (transfer of engagements between societies);
- (c) section 112 (conversion of society into a company etc).

(5) The regulator must decide whether the body created or to whom engagements are transferred ("the new body") is eligible for registration under section 112.
(6) If the new body is eligible for registration, the regulator must register it and designate it as a non-profit organisation.
(7) If the new body is not eligible for registration, the regulator must notify it of that fact.
(8) Pending registration, or notification that it is not eligible for registration, the new body is to be treated as if it were registered and designated as a non-profit organisation.]

NOTES

Commencement: 6 April 2017.

Substituted by the Housing and Planning Act 2016, s 92, Sch 4, Pt 2, paras 22, 26.

[17.376]

164 [Registered society]: winding up

(1) This section applies to a non-profit registered provider which is [a registered society].

(2) A resolution for the voluntary winding-up of the society under the Insolvency Act 1986 is effective only if the regulator has first consented.

(3) The requirement in section 30 of the Companies Act 2006 (c 46) (as applied by [section 123 of the Co-operative and Community Benefit Societies Act 2014] and section 84(3) of the Insolvency Act 1986) (sending copy of resolution to [Financial Conduct Authority]) is satisfied only if the copy is accompanied by a copy of the regulator's consent.

NOTES

Repealed by the Housing and Planning Act 2016, s 115, Sch 6, paras 1, 8, as from a day to be appointed.

Section heading, sub-s (1): words in square brackets substituted by the Co-operative and Community Benefit Societies Act 2014, s 151(1), Sch 4, Pt 2, paras 121–123.

Sub-s (3): first words in square brackets substituted by the Co-operative and Community Benefit Societies Act 2014, s 151(1), Sch 4, Pt 2, paras 121, 129; second words in square brackets substituted by the Financial Services Act 2012 (Mutual Societies) Order 2013, SI 2013/496, art 2(c), Sch 11, para 8(1), (4).

[17.377]

165 [Registered society]: dissolution

(1) This section applies to a non-profit registered provider which is—

(a) [a registered society], and

(b) to be dissolved by instrument of dissolution in accordance with [section 119 of the Co-operative and Community Benefit Societies Act 2014].

[(2) The registered provider must notify the regulator.

(3) The Financial Conduct Authority may register the instrument under section 121 of that Act, or cause notice of the dissolution to be advertised under section 122 of that Act, only if the registered provider has confirmed to the Financial Conduct Authority that the regulator has been notified.]

NOTES

Section heading, sub-s (1): words in square brackets substituted by the Co-operative and Community Benefit Societies Act 2014, s 151(1), Sch 4, Pt 2, paras 121–123, 130(1), (2).

Sub-ss (2), (3): substituted for original sub-s (2) by the Housing and Planning Act 2016, s 92, Sch 4, Pt 2, paras 22, 27.

166 (*Repealed by the Housing and Planning Act 2016, s 92, Sch 4, Pt 2, paras 22, 28.*)

[17.378]

167 Transfer of property

(1) This section applies—

(a) where a non-profit registered provider which is [a registered society] is dissolved in accordance with [section 119 or 123 of the Co-operative and Community Benefit Societies Act 2014], and

(b) where a non-profit registered provider which is a registered company is wound up under the Insolvency Act 1986.

(2) Any surplus property that is available after satisfying the registered provider's liabilities shall be transferred—

(a) to the regulator, or

(b) if the regulator directs, to a specified non-profit registered provider.

(3) If land belonging to the registered provider needs to be sold to satisfy its liabilities, the regulator may discharge those liabilities so as to ensure that the land is instead transferred in accordance with subsection (2).

(4) Where the registered provider dissolved or wound up is a charity, a registered provider may be specified under subsection (2)(b) only if it is a charity whose objects the regulator thinks are similar to those of the original charity.

(5) This section has effect despite anything in—

(a) . . .

(b) the Insolvency Act 1986,

(c) the Companies Act 2006 (c 46),

[(ca) the Co-operative and Community Benefit Societies Act 2014,] or

(d) the constitution of a registered provider.

NOTES

Sub-s (1): words in square brackets substituted by the Co-operative and Community Benefit Societies Act 2014, s 151(1), Sch 4, Pt 2, paras 121, 122, 131(1), (2). Note: original text included a reference to "(c 12)" which was not specifically substituted; this chapter number belongs to the title of the Act which was substituted, therefore it is assumed this a drafting error, and the chapter number has been omitted accordingly.

Sub-s (5): para (a) repealed and para (ca) inserted by the Co-operative and Community Benefit Societies Act 2014, s 151(1), Sch 4, Pt 2, paras 121, 131(1), (3).

[17.379]
168 Section 167: supplemental
(1) This section applies to property transferred to the regulator in accordance with section 167(2)(a).
(2) The regulator may dispose of the property only to a non-profit registered provider.
(3) Where the registered provider wound up or dissolved was a charity, the regulator may dispose of the property only to a registered provider—
(a) which is a charity, and
(b) whose objects the regulator thinks are similar to those of the original charity.
(4) If the property includes land subject to a mortgage or charge, the regulator may dispose of the land—
(a) subject to that mortgage or charge, or
(b) subject to a new mortgage or charge in favour of the regulator.

[17.380]
169 Extension of sections 167 and 168
The Secretary of State may by regulations provide for sections 167 and 168 to apply in relation to a registered provider which is a charity but not a registered company—
(a) in specified circumstances, and
(b) with specified modifications.

170–319 *(Ss 169A–169D, 170–278A (Pt 2, Chs 5–8), ss 279–319 (Pt 3) outside the scope of this work.)*

PART 4
SUPPLEMENTARY AND FINAL PROVISIONS

320–323 (*Outside the scope of this work.*)

[17.381]
324 Extent
(1) Subject as follows, Parts 1 to 3 (including Schedules 1 to 15) and Schedule 16 extend to England and Wales only.
(2) Any amendment, repeal or revocation made by this Act, other than one falling within subsection (3), has the same extent as the provision to which it relates.
(3) (*Outside the scope of this work.*)

[17.382]
325 Commencement
(1) Subject as follows, this Act comes into force on such day as the Secretary of State may by order appoint; and different days may be appointed for different purposes or different areas.
(2)–(5) (*Outside the scope of this work.*)
(6) Subsection (1) does not apply to sections 320, 321(2) to (4), 322, 323 and 324, this section and section 326.

NOTES
Orders: at present, 12 orders have been made under this section. The orders relevant to provisions reproduced in this work are the Housing and Regeneration Act 2008 (Commencement No 4 and Transitory Provisions) Order 2009, SI 2009/803 and the Housing and Regeneration Act 2008 (Commencement No 7 and Transitional and Saving Provisions) Order 2010, SI 2010/862.

[17.383]
326 Short title
This Act may be cited as the Housing and Regeneration Act 2008.

SCHEDULES 1–16

(*Schs 1–16 outside the scope of this work.*)

DORMANT BANK AND BUILDING SOCIETY ACCOUNTS ACT 2008

(2008 c 31)

ARRANGEMENT OF SECTIONS

PART 1
TRANSFER OF BALANCES IN DORMANT ACCOUNTS

The general scheme
1 Transfer of balances to reclaim fund . . . . . [17.384]
Alternative scheme for smaller institutions
2 Transfer of balances to charities, with proportion to reclaim fund . . . . . [17.385]
3 The assets-limit condition . . . . . [17.386]

Shareholding members of building societies
4 Effect of balance transfer on membership rights . . . . [17.387]
Reclaim funds
5 Functions etc of a reclaim fund . . . . [17.388]
Interpretation etc
6 Interpretation of Part 1 . . . . [17.389]
7 "Bank" . . . . [17.390]
8 "Balance" . . . . [17.391]
9 "Account" . . . . [17.392]
10 "Dormant" . . . . [17.393]
Supplemental
11 Customer's rights preserved on insolvency etc of bank or building society . . . . [17.394]
PART 3
FINAL PROVISIONS
30 Extent . . . . [17.395]
31 Commencement . . . . [17.396]
32 Short title . . . . [17.397]

An Act to make provision for, and in connection with, using money from dormant bank and building society accounts for social or environmental purposes.

[26 November 2008]

NOTES

Modification: this Act is applied, with modifications, in so far as it relates to bank insolvency or administration under the Banking Act 2009, Pts 2, 3, by the Banking Act 2009 (Parts 2 and 3 Consequential Amendments) Order 2009, SI 2009/317, art 3, Schedule at **[7.86]**, **[7.92]**.

PART 1
TRANSFER OF BALANCES IN DORMANT ACCOUNTS

The general scheme

[17.384]

1 Transfer of balances to reclaim fund

(1) This section applies where—

(a) a bank or building society transfers to an authorised reclaim fund the balance of a dormant account that a person ("the customer") holds with it, and

(b) the reclaim fund consents to the transfer.

(2) After the transfer—

(a) the customer no longer has any right against the bank or building society to payment of the balance, but

(b) the customer has against the reclaim fund whatever right to payment of the balance the customer would have against the bank or building society if the transfer had not happened.

(3) The reference in subsection (1) to an account that a person holds is to be read as including an account held by a deceased individual immediately before his or her death.

In such a case, a reference in subsection (2) to the customer is to be read as a reference to the person to whom the right to payment of the balance has passed.

Alternative scheme for smaller institutions

[17.385]

2 Transfer of balances to charities, with proportion to reclaim fund

(1) This section applies where—

(a) a smaller bank or building society transfers to an authorised reclaim fund an agreed proportion of the balance of a dormant account that a person ("the customer") holds with it,

(b) the bank or building society transfers the remainder of that balance to one or more charities,

(c) the charity, or each of the charities, either—

(i) is a charity that the bank or building society considers to have a special connection with it, or

(ii) undertakes to apply the money in question for the benefit of members of communities that are local to the branches of the bank or building society,

(d) the reclaim fund consents to the transfer to it, and

(e) the charity, or each of the charities, consents to the transfer to it.

(2) After the transfers—

(a) the customer no longer has any right against the bank or building society to payment of the balance, but

(b) the customer has against the reclaim fund whatever right to payment of the balance the customer would have against the bank or building society if the transfers had not happened.

(3) The reference in subsection (1) to an account that a person holds is to be read as including an account held by a deceased individual immediately before his or her death.

In such a case, a reference in subsection (2) to the customer is to be read as a reference to the person to whom the right to payment of the balance has passed.

(4) In subsection (1) "agreed proportion" means a proportion agreed between the bank or building society and the reclaim fund.

In agreeing that proportion, the reclaim fund must take account of the need for the fund to have access at any given time to enough money to enable it to meet whatever repayment claims it is prudent to anticipate.

(5) For the purposes of this section—

- (a) "repayment claim" means a claim made by virtue of subsection (2)(b);
- (b) a "smaller" bank or building society is one that meets the assets-limit condition (see section 3);
- (c) a charity has a "special connection" with a bank if (and only if) the purpose, or any of the main purposes, of the charity is to benefit members of communities that are local to the branches of the bank;
- (d) a charity has a "special connection" with a building society if (and only if) the purpose, or any of the main purposes, of the charity—
  - (i) is to benefit members of communities that are local to the branches of the building society, or
  - (ii) is especially consonant with any particular purposes that the building society has.

(6) The reference in subsection (5)(d)(ii) to particular purposes does not include the purpose mentioned in section 5(1)(a) of the Building Societies Act 1986 (c 53) (making loans that are secured on residential property and substantially funded by members).

[17.386]

3 The assets-limit condition

(1) A bank or building society meets the assets-limit condition if the aggregate of the amounts shown in its balance sheet as assets on the last day of the latest financial year for which it has prepared accounts is less than £7,000 million.

(2) In relation to a bank or building society that was a member of a group on the day referred to in subsection (1), that subsection has effect as if the aggregate of the amounts shown in its balance sheet as assets on that day also included the aggregate of the amounts shown in each group member's balance sheet as assets—

- (a) on that day, or
- (b) (in the case of a group member whose financial year did not end on that day) on the last day of its latest financial year to end before that day.

(3) Where a balance sheet for a particular day shows amounts in a currency other than sterling, for the purposes of this section the amounts are to be converted into sterling at the London closing exchange rate for that currency and that day.

(4) The Treasury may by order amend the figure in subsection (1).

(5) An order under this section is subject to annulment in pursuance of a resolution of either House of Parliament.

Shareholding members of building societies

[17.387]

4 Effect of balance transfer on membership rights

(1) This section applies where a person ("the member") holds a share in a building society represented by an account with the society, and either—

- (a) a transfer is made to a reclaim fund with the result that section 1 applies in relation to the account, or
- (b) transfers are made to a reclaim fund and one or more charities with the result that section 2 applies in relation to the account.

(2) After the transfer or transfers the member is to be treated as having whatever share in the building society the member would have if the transfer or transfers had not happened (and accordingly as having whatever rights, including distribution rights, a holder of that share would have as such).

(3) In subsection (2) "distribution rights" means rights to any distribution arising as mentioned in section 96 (amalgamation or transfer of engagements) or 100 (transfer of business) of the Building Societies Act 1986.

(4) Subsection (2) ceases to apply where the balance of the account is paid out following a claim made by virtue of section 1(2)(b) or 2(2)(b).

(5) But where the balance of the account is paid out following such a claim and, as soon as reasonably practical, the money is—

- (a) paid back into the account, or
- (b) paid into another share account with the building society in the member's name,

subsection (2) continues to apply until the account is credited with the money.

(6) Where, after the transfer or transfers referred to in subsection (1), the building society is succeeded by another building society as a result of an amalgamation or transfer of engagements, a reference in subsection (2) or (5) to the building society is to be read, in relation to any time after the amalgamation or transfer of engagements, as a reference to the successor building society (or to the successor building society of the successor, in relation to any time after a subsequent amalgamation or transfer; and so on).

Reclaim funds

[17.388]

5 Functions etc of a reclaim fund

(1) A "reclaim fund" is a company the objects of which are restricted by its articles of association to the following—

(a) the meeting of repayment claims;

(b) the management of dormant account funds in such a way as to enable the company to meet whatever repayment claims it is prudent to anticipate;

(c) the transfer of money to the body or bodies for the time being specified in section 16(1), subject to the need for the company—

(i) to have access at any given time to enough money to meet whatever repayment claims it is prudent to anticipate,

(ii) to comply with any requirement with regard to its financial resources that is imposed on it by or under any enactment, and

(iii) to defray its expenses;

(d) objects that are incidental or conducive to, or otherwise connected with, any of the above (including in particular the prudent investment of dormant account funds).

(2) Schedule 1 makes further provision about provision that must be made in the articles of association of a reclaim fund.

(3) An alteration by a reclaim fund of its articles of association is ineffective if it would result in—

(a) the company ceasing to have objects restricted to those mentioned in subsection (1);

(b) the company's articles of association not containing any provision that they are required to make under Schedule 1.

(4) The Treasury may give a direction to a reclaim fund requiring it—

(a) to give effect to any specified object that it has, or

(b) to comply with any specified obligation or prohibition imposed on it by a provision that its articles of association are required to make under Schedule 1.

"Specified" means specified in the direction.

(5) The Treasury shall lay before Parliament a copy of any direction given under subsection (4).

(6) In this section—

"company" has the meaning given by section 1(1) of the Companies Act 2006 (c 46);

"dormant account funds" means money paid to a reclaim fund by banks and by building societies in respect of dormant accounts;

"repayment claims" means claims made by virtue of section 1(2)(b) or 2(2)(b).

Interpretation etc

[17.389]

6 Interpretation of Part 1

In this Part—

"account" has the meaning given by section 9;

"authorised", in relation to a reclaim fund, means authorised for the purposes of the Financial Services and Markets Act 2000 (c 8);

"balance" has the meaning given by section 8;

"bank" has the meaning given by section 7;

"building society" means a building society incorporated (or deemed to be incorporated) under the Building Societies Act 1986 (c 53);

"charity" means a body, or the trustees of a trust, established for charitable purposes only;

"dormant" has the meaning given by section 10;

"financial year"—

(a) in relation to a company (other than a building society) within the meaning of the Companies Act 2006, has the meaning given in section 390(1) to (3) of that Act;

(b) in relation to an undertaking that is not a company within the meaning of that Act (and is not a building society), has the meaning given in section 390(4) of that Act;

(c) in relation to a building society, has the meaning given in section 117 of the Building Societies Act 1986;

"group" means a parent undertaking and its subsidiary undertakings;

"parent undertaking" and "subsidiary undertaking" have the same meaning as in the Companies Act 2006 (see section 1162 of that Act);

"reclaim fund" has the meaning given by section 5(1).

[17.390]

7 "Bank"

(1) Subject to subsection (4), "bank" means an authorised deposit-taker that has its head office, or one or more branches, in the United Kingdom.

(2) In subsection (1) "authorised deposit-taker" means—

(a) a person who under [Part 4A] of FSMA 2000 has permission to accept deposits;

(b) an EEA firm of the kind mentioned in paragraph 5(b) of Schedule 3 to FSMA 2000 that has permission under paragraph 15 of that Schedule (as a result of qualifying for authorisation under paragraph 12(1) of that Schedule) to accept deposits.

(3) A reference in subsection (2) to a person or firm with permission to accept deposits does not include a person or firm with permission to do so only for the purposes of, or in the course of, an activity other than accepting deposits.

(4) "Bank" does not include—
(a) a building society;
(b) a person who is specified, or is within a class of persons specified, by an order under section 38 of FSMA 2000 (exemption orders);
(c) a credit union;
(d) a friendly society.

(5) In this section—

["credit union" means a credit union within the meaning of section 31(1) of the Credit Unions Act 1979 or a credit union within the meaning of Article 2(2) of the Credit Unions (Northern Ireland) Order 1985;]

"friendly society" has the same meaning as in the Friendly Societies Act 1992 (c 40) (see section 116 of that Act);

"FSMA 2000" means the Financial Services and Markets Act 2000 (c 8).

NOTES

Sub-s (2): words in square brackets substituted by the Financial Services Act 2012, s 114(1), Sch 18, Pt 2, para 128.

Sub-s (5): definition "credit union" substituted by the Financial Services and Markets Act 2000 (Permissions, Transitional Provisions and Consequential Amendments) (Northern Ireland Credit Unions) Order 2011, SI 2011/2832, art 12(1).

[17.391]
8 "Balance"

(1) The balance of a person's account at any particular time is the amount owing to the person in respect of the account at that time, after the appropriate adjustments have been made for such things as interest due and fees and charges payable.

(2) In relation to a time after a transfer has been made as mentioned in section 1(1) or transfers have been made as mentioned in section 2(1), the adjustments referred to in subsection (1) above include those that would fall to be made but for the transfer or transfers.

[17.392]
9 "Account"

(1) "Account" means an account that has at all times consisted only of money.

(2) A reference in this Part to an account held with a bank or building society is to an account provided by the bank or building society as part of its activity of accepting deposits.

(3) In relation to a building society, "account" includes an account representing shares in the society, other than—
(a) preferential shares, or
(b) deferred shares within the meaning given in section 119(1) of the Building Societies Act 1986 (c 53).

[17.393]
10 "Dormant"

(1) An account is "dormant" at a particular time if—
(a) the account has been open throughout the period of 15 years ending at that time, but
(b) during that period no transactions have been carried out in relation to the account by or on the instructions of the holder of the account.

(2) But an account is to be treated as not dormant if at any time during that period—
(a) the bank or building society in question was under instructions from the holder of the account not to communicate with that person about the account, or
(b) under the terms of the account—
(i) withdrawals were prevented, or
(ii) there was a penalty or other disincentive for making withdrawals in all circumstances.

(3) For the purposes of subsection (1) an account is to be treated as remaining open where it is closed otherwise than on the instructions of the holder of the account.

(4) For the purposes of subsection (2)(b)(i) withdrawals are prevented if they are prevented except as permitted by provision made under subsection (4)(d) of section 3 of the Child Trust Funds Act 2004 (c 6) (requirements to be satisfied by child trust funds).

(5) The Treasury may by order amend the figure in subsection (1)(a).

(6) An order under this section may not be made unless a draft of the statutory instrument containing it has been laid before, and approved by a resolution of, each House of Parliament.

Supplemental

[17.394]
11 Customer's rights preserved on insolvency etc of bank or building society

(1) Where after a person has acquired a right to payment under section 1(2)(b) or 2(2)(b)—
(a) the bank or building society in question is dissolved or wound up, or
(b) for any other reason the liability that the bank or building society would have to the person (but for the transfer referred to in section 1(1) or the transfers referred to in section 2(1)) is extinguished or reduced,

the dissolution, winding-up, extinguishment or reduction is to be disregarded for the purposes of section 1(2)(b) or 2(2)(b).

(2) Subsection (1)(b) does not apply to an extinguishment of liability by prescription under the law of Scotland.

12–27 *(Ss 12–15, 16–27 (Pt 2) outside the scope of this work.)*

PART 3
FINAL PROVISIONS

28, 29 (*Outside the scope of this work.*)

[17.395]

30 Extent

This Act extends to England and Wales, Scotland and Northern Ireland.

[17.396]

31 Commencement

(1) Parts 1 and 2 come into force in accordance with provision made by order of the Treasury.

(2) An order under this section—

(a) may make different provision for different purposes;

(b) may make transitional or saving provision.

NOTES

Orders: the Dormant Bank and Building Society Accounts Act 2008 (Commencement and Transitional Provisions) Order 2009, SI 2009/490.

[17.397]

32 Short title

This Act may be cited as the Dormant Bank and Building Society Accounts Act 2008.

SCHEDULES 1–3

(*Schs 1–3 outside the scope of this work.*)

ENERGY ACT 2008

(2008 c 32)

An Act to make provision relating to gas importation and storage; to make provision in relation to electricity generated from renewable sources; to make provision relating to electricity transmission; to make provision about payments to small-scale generators of low-carbon electricity; to make provision about the decommissioning of energy installations and wells; to make provision about the management and disposal of waste produced during the operation of nuclear installations; to make provision relating to petroleum licences; to make provision about third party access to oil and gas infrastructure and modifications of pipelines; to make provision about reports relating to energy matters; to make provision about the duties of the Gas and Electricity Markets Authority; to make provision about payments in respect of the renewable generation of heat; to make provision relating to gas meters and electricity meters and provision relating to electricity safety; to make provision about the security of equipment, software and information relating to nuclear matters; and for connected purposes.

[26 November 2008]

1–44 ((*Pts 1, 2*) *outside the scope of this work.*)

PART 3
DECOMMISSIONING OF ENERGY INSTALLATIONS

CHAPTER 1 NUCLEAR SITES: DECOMMISSIONING AND CLEAN-UP

45–55 (*Outside the scope of this work.*)

Protection of decommissioning funds

[17.398]

56 Protection of security under approved programme

(1) This section applies where, in relation to a site to which section 45 applies, any security for the performance of obligations relating to the designated technical matters has been provided by a person ("the security provider") by way of a trust or other arrangements, in accordance with an approved funded decommissioning programme.

(2) In this section a reference to "the protected assets" is a reference to the security and any property or rights in which it consists.

(3) In this section "security" includes—

(a) a charge over a bank account or any other asset;

(b) a deposit of money;

(c) a performance bond or guarantee;

(d) an insurance policy;

(e) a letter of credit.

(4) The manner in which, and purposes for which, the protected assets are to be applied and enforceable (whether in the event of the security provider's insolvency or otherwise) is to be determined in accordance with the trust or other arrangements.

(5) For the purposes of subsection (4), no regard is to be had to so much of the Insolvency Act 1986 (c 45), the Insolvency (Northern Ireland) Order 1989 (SI 1989/2405 (NI 19)) or any other enactment or rule of law as, in its operation in relation to the security provider or any conduct of the security provider, would—

(a) prevent or restrict the protected assets from being applied in accordance with the trust or other arrangement, or

(b) prevent or restrict their enforcement for the purposes of being so applied.

57–102 *(Ss 57–69, 70(2), 71–73, 75, ss 76–102 (Pts 4–5) outside the scope of this work; s 70(1) inserts the Energy Act 2004, ss 110A, 110B at* **[7.847]**, **[7.848]**; *s 74 inserts the Petroleum Act 1998, ss 38A, 38B at* **[17.165]**, **[17.166]**.)

PART 6
GENERAL

103–109 *(Outside the scope of this work.)*

[17.399]
110 Commencement

(1) The following provisions come into force on the day on which this Act is passed—

(a)–(c) *(outside the scope of this work.)*

(d) this section and sections 106, 111, 112 and 113;

(e) *(outside the scope of this work.)*

(2) Subject to that, the provisions of this Act come into force on such day as may be appointed by order of the Secretary of State.

(3) An order under this section may—

(a) include incidental, supplementary and consequential provision;

(b) make transitory or transitional provisions or savings;

(c) make different provision for different cases or circumstances or for different purposes.

NOTES

At present 6 commencement orders have been made under this section. The order relevant to the provisions reproduced in this work is the Energy Act 2008 (Commencement No 1 and Savings) Order 2009, SI 2009/45.

111 *(Outside the scope of this work.)*

[17.400]
112 Extent

(1) Subject to subsections (2) to (5), this Act extends to England and Wales, Scotland and Northern Ireland.

(2) *(Outside the scope of this work.)*

(3) Chapter 1 of Part 3 . . . (nuclear decommissioning) extends to England and Wales and Northern Ireland only.

(4) *(Outside the scope of this work.)*

(5) An amendment or repeal contained in this Act has the same extent as the enactment or relevant part of the enactment to which the amendment or repeal relates.

NOTES

Sub-s (3): words omitted repealed by the Energy Act 2013, s 116, Sch 12, Pt 2, para 30.

[17.401]
113 Short title

This Act may be cited as the Energy Act 2008.

SCHEDULES 1–6

(Schs 1–6 outside the scope of this work.)

LOCAL DEMOCRACY, ECONOMIC DEVELOPMENT AND CONSTRUCTION ACT 2009

(2009 c 20)

An Act to make provision for the purposes of promoting public involvement in relation to local authorities and other public authorities; to make provision about bodies representing the interests of tenants; to make provision about local freedoms and honorary titles; to make provision about the procedures of local authorities, their powers relating to insurance and the audit of entities connected with them; to establish the Local Government Boundary Commission for England and to make provision relating to local government boundary and electoral change; to make provision about local and regional development; to amend the law relating to construction contracts; and for connected purposes.

[12 November 2009]

NOTES

Note: only the provisions of this Act relevant to this work are reproduced; the remainder is not annotated.

SCHEDULE 1
LOCAL GOVERNMENT BOUNDARY COMMISSION FOR ENGLAND

Section 55

Members

[17.402]

1 (1) The Local Government Boundary Commission for England ("the Commission") is to consist of—

(a) the chair of the Commission, and

(b) at least four and no more than eleven other members ("ordinary members").

(2) The ordinary members are to be appointed by Her Majesty on the recommendation of the Secretary of State.

(3)–(7) . . .

(8) An ordinary member may, on the recommendation of the Secretary of State, be removed from office by Her Majesty on any of the following grounds—

(a) failure to discharge the functions of membership for a continuous period of at least three months;

(b) failure to comply with the terms of appointment;

(c) conviction of a criminal offence;

(d) being an undischarged bankrupt or having their estate sequestrated in Scotland and not being discharged;

(e) making an arrangement or composition contract with, or granting a trust deed for, their creditors;

(f) otherwise being unfit to hold office or unable to carry out the functions of membership.

(9), (10) . . .

Chair

2 (1) The chair of the Commission is to be appointed by Her Majesty on an Address from the House of Commons.

(2)–(7) . . .

(8) The chair may be removed from office by Her Majesty on an Address from the House of Commons.

(9) No motion may be made for such an Address unless the Speaker's Committee have presented a report to the House of Commons stating that the Speaker's Committee are satisfied that one or more of the following grounds is made out in relation to the chair—

(a) failure to discharge the functions of their office for a continuous period of at least three months;

(b) failure to comply with the terms of appointment as chair;

(c) conviction of a criminal offence;

(d) being an undischarged bankrupt or having their estate sequestrated in Scotland and not being discharged;

(e) making an arrangement or composition contract with, or granting a trust deed for, their creditors;

(f) otherwise being unfit to hold office as chair or unable to carry out the functions of that office.

(10)–(12) . . .

3–24 . . .

NOTES

Provisions omitted are outside the scope of this work.

[SCHEDULE 5B
MAYORS FOR COMBINED AUTHORITY AREAS: FURTHER PROVISION ABOUT ELECTIONS

Interpretation

[17.403]

1 In this Schedule references to a mayor are references to a mayor for the area of a combined authority.

2–8 . . .

9 (1) A person is disqualified for being elected or holding office as the mayor for the area of a combined authority if the person—

(a) holds any paid office or employment (other than the office of mayor or deputy mayor) appointments or elections to which are or may be made by or on behalf of the combined authority or any of the constituent councils;

(b) is the subject of—

(i) a debt relief restrictions order or an interim debt relief restrictions order under Schedule 4ZB to the Insolvency Act 1986, or
(ii) a bankruptcy restrictions order or an interim bankruptcy restrictions order under Schedule 4A to the Insolvency Act 1986;

(c) has in the five years before being elected, or at any time since being elected, been convicted in the United Kingdom, the Channel Islands or the Isle of Man of an offence and been sentenced to a period of imprisonment of three months or more without the option of a fine;
(d) is disqualified for being elected or for being a member of a constituent council under Part 3 of the Representation of the People Act 1983 (consequences of corrupt or illegal practices).

(2) For the purposes of sub-paragraph (1)(c), a person is to be treated as having been convicted on—
(a) the expiry of the ordinary period allowed for making an appeal or application with respect to the conviction, or
(b) if an appeal or application is made, the date on which it is finally disposed of or abandoned or fails because it is not prosecuted.

(3) In this paragraph, "constituent council" means—
(a) a county council the whole or any part of whose area is within the area of the combined authority, or
(b) a district council whose area is within the area of the combined authority.

3–12 . . .]

NOTES

Commencement: 28 January 2016 (for the purpose of making orders or regulations); 28 March 2016 (for remaining purposes).
Schedule inserted by the Cities and Local Government Devolution Act 2016, s 2(2), Sch 1.
Provisions omitted are outside the scope of this work.

THIRD PARTIES (RIGHTS AGAINST INSURERS) ACT 2010

(2010 c 10)

ARRANGEMENT OF SECTIONS

Transfer of rights to third parties

1 Rights against insurer of insolvent person etc . . . . [17.404]
2 Establishing liability in England and Wales and Northern Ireland . . . . [17.405]
3 Establishing liability in Scotland . . . . [17.406]

Relevant persons

4 Individuals . . . . [17.407]
5 Individuals who die insolvent . . . . [17.408]
6 Corporate bodies etc . . . . [17.409]
6A Corporate bodies etc that are dissolved. . . . . [17.410]
7 Scottish trusts . . . . [17.411]

Transferred rights: supplemental

8 Limit on rights transferred . . . . [17.412]
9 Conditions affecting transferred rights . . . . [17.413]
10 Insurer's right of set off. . . . . [17.414]

Provision of information etc

11 Information and disclosure for third parties . . . . [17.415]

Enforcement of transferred rights

12 Limitation and prescription . . . . [17.416]
13 Jurisdiction within the United Kingdom . . . . [17.417]

Enforcement of insured's liability

14 Effect of transfer on insured's liability . . . . [17.418]

Application of Act

15 Reinsurance. . . . . [17.419]
16 Voluntarily-incurred liabilities . . . . [17.420]
17 Avoidance. . . . . [17.421]
18 Cases with a foreign element. . . . . [17.422]

Supplemental

19 Power to change the meaning of "relevant person" . . . . [17.423]

19A Interpretation . . . [17.424]
20 Amendments, transitionals, repeals, etc . . . [17.425]
21 Short title, commencement and extent . . . [17.426]

SCHEDULES

Schedule A1—Administration under relevant sectoral legislation. . . . [17.427]
Schedule 1—Information and Disclosure for Third Parties . . . [17.428]
Schedule 3—Transitory, Transitional and Saving Provisions . . . [17.429]

An Act to make provision about the rights of third parties against insurers of liabilities to third parties in the case where the insured is insolvent, and in certain other cases

[25 March 2010]

Transfer of rights to third parties

[17.404]

1 Rights against insurer of insolvent person etc

(1) This section applies if—

(a) a relevant person incurs a liability against which that person is insured under a contract of insurance, or

(b) a person who is subject to such a liability becomes a relevant person.

(2) The rights of the relevant person under the contract against the insurer in respect of the liability are transferred to and vest in the person to whom the liability is or was incurred (the "third party").

(3) The third party may bring proceedings to enforce the rights against the insurer without having established the relevant person's liability; but the third party may not enforce those rights without having established that liability.

(4) For the purposes of this Act, a liability is established only if its existence and amount are established; and, for that purpose, "establish" means establish—

(a) by virtue of a declaration under section 2 or a declarator under section 3,

(b) by a judgment or decree,

(c) by an award in arbitral proceedings or by an arbitration, or

(d) by an enforceable agreement.

(5) In this Act—

(a) references to an "insured" are to a person who incurs or who is subject to a liability to a third party against which that person is insured under a contract of insurance;

(b) references to a "relevant person" are to a person within sections 4 to 7 [(and see also paragraph 1A of Schedule 3)];

(c) references to a "third party" are to be construed in accordance with subsection (2);

(d) references to "transferred rights" are to rights under a contract of insurance which are transferred under this section.

NOTES

Commencement: 1 August 2016.

Sub-s (5): in para (b) words in square brackets added by the Insurance Act 2015, s 20, Sch 2, paras 1, 4.

[17.405]

2 Establishing liability in England and Wales and Northern Ireland

(1) This section applies where a person (P)—

(a) claims to have rights under a contract of insurance by virtue of a transfer under section 1, but

(b) has not yet established the insured's liability which is insured under that contract.

(2) P may bring proceedings against the insurer for either or both of the following—

(a) a declaration as to the insured's liability to P;

(b) a declaration as to the insurer's potential liability to P.

(3) In such proceedings P is entitled, subject to any defence on which the insurer may rely, to a declaration under subsection (2)(a) or (b) on proof of the insured's liability to P or (as the case may be) the insurer's potential liability to P.

(4) Where proceedings are brought under subsection (2)(a) the insurer may rely on any defence on which the insured could rely if those proceedings were proceedings brought against the insured in respect of the insured's liability to P.

(5) Subsection (4) is subject to section 12(1).

(6) Where the court makes a declaration under this section, the effect of which is that the insurer is liable to P, the court may give the appropriate judgment against the insurer.

(7) Where a person applying for a declaration under subsection (2)(b) is entitled or required, by virtue of the contract of insurance, to do so in arbitral proceedings, that person may also apply in the same proceedings for a declaration under subsection (2)(a).

(8) In the application of this section to arbitral proceedings, subsection (6) is to be read as if "tribunal" were substituted for "court" and "make the appropriate award" for "give the appropriate judgment".

(9) When bringing proceedings under subsection (2)(a), P may also make the insured a defendant to those proceedings.

(10) If (but only if) the insured is a defendant to proceedings under this section (whether by virtue of subsection (9) or otherwise), a declaration under subsection (2) binds the insured as well as the insurer.

(11) In this section, references to the insurer's potential liability to P are references to the insurer's liability in respect of the insured's liability to P, if established.

NOTES

Commencement: 1 August 2016.

[17.406]

3 Establishing liability in Scotland

(1) This section applies where a person (P)—

(a) claims to have rights under a contract of insurance by virtue of a transfer under section 1, but

(b) has not yet established the insured's liability which is insured under that contract.

(2) P may bring proceedings against the insurer for either or both of the following—

(a) a declarator as to the insured's liability to P;

(b) a declarator as to the insurer's potential liability to P.

(3) Where proceedings are brought under subsection (2)(a) the insurer may rely on any defence on which the insured could rely if those proceedings were proceedings brought against the insured in respect of the insured's liability to P.

(4) Subsection (3) is subject to section 12(1).

(5) Where the court grants a declarator under this section, the effect of which is that the insurer is liable to P, the court may grant the appropriate decree against the insurer.

(6) Where a person applying for a declarator under subsection (2)(b) is entitled or required, by virtue of the contract of insurance, to do so in an arbitration, that person may also apply in the same arbitration for a declarator under subsection (2)(a).

(7) In the application of this section to an arbitration, subsection (5) is to be read as if "tribunal" were substituted for "court" and "make the appropriate award" for "grant the appropriate decree".

(8) When bringing proceedings under subsection (2)(a), P may also make the insured a defender to those proceedings.

(9) If (but only if) the insured is a defender to proceedings under this section (whether by virtue of subsection (8) or otherwise), a declarator under subsection (2) binds the insured as well as the insurer.

(10) In this section, the reference to the insurer's potential liability to P is a reference to the insurer's liability in respect of the insured's liability to P, if established.

NOTES

Commencement: 1 August 2016.

Relevant persons

[17.407]

4 Individuals

(1) An individual is a relevant person if any of the following is in force in respect of that individual in England and Wales—

(a) . . .

(b) an administration order made under Part 6 of the County Courts Act 1984,

(c) an enforcement restriction order made under Part 6A of that Act,

(d) subject to subsection (4), a debt relief order made under Part 7A of the Insolvency Act 1986,

(e) a voluntary arrangement approved in accordance with Part 8 of that Act, or

(f) a bankruptcy order made under Part 9 of that Act.

(2) An individual is a relevant person if [either] of the following is in force in respect of [the individual's estate] in Scotland—

(a) an award of sequestration made [by virtue of section 2 or 5 of the Bankruptcy (Scotland) Act 2016], [or]

(b) a protected trust deed within the meaning of that Act, *or*

(c) a composition approved in accordance with Schedule 4 to that Act.

(3) An individual is a relevant person if any of the following is in force in respect of that individual in Northern Ireland—

(a) an administration order made under Part 6 of the Judgments Enforcement (Northern Ireland) Order 1981 (SI 1981/226 (NI 6)),

(b) a deed of arrangement registered in accordance with Chapter 1 of Part 8 of the Insolvency (Northern Ireland) Order 1989 (SI 1989/2405 (NI 19)),

[(ba) subject to subsection (4), a debt relief order made under Part 7A of that Order,]

(c) a voluntary arrangement approved under Chapter 2 of Part 8 of that Order, or

(d) a bankruptcy order made under Part 9 of that Order.

(4) If an individual is a relevant person by virtue of subsection (1)(d) [or (3)(ba)], that person is a relevant person for the purposes of section 1(1)(b) only.

(5) Where an award of sequestration made [by virtue of section 2 or 5 of the Bankruptcy (Scotland) Act 2016] is recalled or reduced, any rights which were transferred under section 1 as a result of that award are re-transferred to and vest in the person who became a relevant person as a result of the award.

(6) Where an order discharging an individual from an award of sequestration made under section 5 of the Bankruptcy (Scotland) Act 1985 is recalled or reduced under paragraph 17 or 18 of Schedule 4 to that Act, the order is to be treated for the purposes of this section as never having been made.

NOTES

Commencement: 1 August 2016.

Sub-s (1): para (a) repealed by the Deregulation Act 2015, s 19, Sch 6, Pt 1, para 2(1), (22).

Sub-s (2): words in first and second pairs of square brackets substituted for original words "any" and "that individual (or, in the case of paragraph (a) or (b), that individual's estate)" respectively, words in first pair of square brackets in para (a) substituted for original words "under section 5 of the Bankruptcy (Scotland) Act 1985", word in second pair of square brackets in para (a) inserted, and para (c) repealed together with word preceding it, by the Bankruptcy (Scotland) Act 2016 (Consequential Provisions and Modifications) Order 2016, SI 2016/1034, art 7(1), (3), Sch 1, para 35(1), (2)(a), as from 30 November 2016 (except in relation to (i) a sequestration as regards which the petition is presented, or the debtor application is made before that date; or (ii) a trust deed executed before that date).

Sub-s (3): para (ba) inserted by the Insurance Act 2015, s 20, Sch 2, paras 1, 2(1), (2).

Sub-s (4): words in square brackets inserted by the Insurance Act 2015, s 20, Sch 2, paras 1, 2(1), (3).

Sub-s (5): words in square brackets substituted for original words "under section 5 of the Bankruptcy (Scotland) Act 1985" by SI 2016/1034, art 7(1), (3), Sch 1, para 35(1), (2)(b), as from 30 November 2016 (except in relation to (i) a sequestration as regards which the petition is presented, or the debtor application is made before that date; or (ii) a trust deed executed before that date).

Sub-s (6): repealed by SI 2016/1034, art 7(1), (3), Sch 1, para 35(1), (2)(c), as from 30 November 2016 (except in relation to (i) a sequestration as regards which the petition is presented, or the debtor application is made before that date; or (ii) a trust deed executed before that date).

[17.408]

5 Individuals who die insolvent

(1) An individual who dies insolvent is a relevant person for the purposes of section 1(1)(b) only.

(2) For the purposes of this section an individual (D) is to be regarded as having died insolvent if, following D's death—

(a) D's estate falls to be administered in accordance with an order under section 421 of the Insolvency Act 1986 or Article 365 of the Insolvency (Northern Ireland) Order 1989 (SI 1989/2405 (NI 19)),

(b) an award of sequestration is made [by virtue of section 2 or 5 of the Bankruptcy (Scotland) Act 2016] in respect of D's estate and the award is not recalled or reduced, or

(c) a judicial factor is appointed under section 11A of the Judicial Factors (Scotland) Act 1889 in respect of D's estate and the judicial factor certifies that the estate is absolutely insolvent within the meaning of the Bankruptcy (Scotland) Act [2016].

(3) Where a transfer of rights under section 1 takes place as a result of an insured person being a relevant person by virtue of this section, references in this Act to an insured are, where the context so requires, to be read as references to the insured's estate.

NOTES

Commencement: 1 August 2016.

Sub-s (2): words in square brackets in para (b) substituted for original words "under section 5 of the Bankruptcy (Scotland) Act 1985" and year in square brackets in para (c) substituted for original year "1985", by the Bankruptcy (Scotland) Act 2016 (Consequential Provisions and Modifications) Order 2016, SI 2016/1034, art 7(1), (3), Sch 1, para 35(1), (3), as from 30 November 2016 (except in relation to (i) a sequestration as regards which the petition is presented, or the debtor application is made before that date; or (ii) a trust deed executed before that date).

[17.409]

6 Corporate bodies etc

[(1) A body corporate or unincorporated body is a relevant person if a compromise or arrangement between the body and its creditors (or a class of them) is in force, having been sanctioned in accordance with section 899 of the Companies Act 2006.]

(2) A body corporate or an unincorporated body is a relevant person if, in England and Wales or Scotland—

(a) a voluntary arrangement approved in accordance with Part 1 of the Insolvency Act 1986 is in force in respect of it,

[(b) the body is in administration under Schedule B1 to that Act,]

(c) there is a person appointed in accordance with Part 3 of that Act who is acting as receiver or manager of the body's property (or there would be such a person so acting but for a temporary vacancy),

(d) the body is, or is being, wound up voluntarily in accordance with Chapter 2 of Part 4 of that Act,

(e) there is a person appointed under section 135 of that Act who is acting as provisional liquidator in respect of the body (or there would be such a person so acting but for a temporary vacancy), or

(f) the body is, or is being, wound up by the court following the making of a winding-up order under Chapter 6 of Part 4 of that Act or Part 5 of that Act.

(3) A body corporate or an unincorporated body is a relevant person if, in Scotland—

(a) an award of sequestration has been made [by virtue of section 6 of the Bankruptcy (Scotland) Act 2016] in respect of the body's estate, and the body has not been discharged under that Act,

(b) the body has been dissolved and an award of sequestration has been made [by virtue of] that section in respect of its estate, [or]

(c) a protected trust deed within the meaning of the Bankruptcy (Scotland) Act [2016] is in force in respect of the body's estate, *or*

(d) a composition approved in accordance with Schedule 4 to that Act is in force in respect of the body.

(4) A body corporate or an unincorporated body is a relevant person if, in Northern Ireland—

(a) a voluntary arrangement approved in accordance with Part 2 of the Insolvency (Northern Ireland) Order 1989 (SI 1989/2405 (NI 19)) is in force in respect of the body,

[(b) the body is in administration under Schedule B1 to that Order,]

(c) there is a person appointed in accordance with Part 4 of that Order who is acting as receiver or manager of the body's property (or there would be such a person so acting but for a temporary vacancy),

(d) the body is, or is being, wound up voluntarily in accordance with Chapter 2 of Part 5 of that Order,

(e) there is a person appointed under Article 115 of that Order who is acting as provisional liquidator in respect of the body (or there would be such a person so acting but for a temporary vacancy), or

(f) the body is, or is being, wound up by the court following the making of a winding-up order under Chapter 6 of Part 5 of that Order or Part 6 of that Order.

[(4A) A body corporate or unincorporated body is a relevant person if it is in insolvency under Part 2 of the Banking Act 2009.

(4B) A body corporate or unincorporated body is a relevant person if it is in administration under relevant sectoral legislation as defined in Schedule A1.]

(5) A body within [subsection (1)] is not a relevant person in relation to a liability that is transferred to another body by the order sanctioning the compromise or arrangement.

(6) Where a body is a relevant person by virtue of [subsection (1)], section 1 has effect to transfer rights only to a person on whom the compromise or arrangement is binding.

(7) Where an award of sequestration made [by virtue of section 6 of the Bankruptcy (Scotland) Act 2016] is recalled or reduced, any rights which were transferred under section 1 as a result of that award are re-transferred to and vest in the person who became a relevant person as a result of the award.

(8) Where an order discharging a body from an award of sequestration made under section 6 of the Bankruptcy (Scotland) Act 1985 is recalled or reduced under paragraph 17 or 18 of Schedule 4 to that Act, the order is to be treated for the purposes of this section as never having been made.

(9) In this section—

(a) a reference to a person appointed in accordance with Part 3 of the Insolvency Act 1986 includes a reference to a person appointed under section 101 of the Law of Property Act 1925;

(b) a reference to a receiver or manager of a body's property includes a reference to a receiver or manager of part only of the property and to a receiver only of the income arising from the property or from part of it;

(c) for the purposes of subsection (3) "body corporate or unincorporated body" includes any entity, other than a trust, the estate of which may be sequestrated [by virtue of section 6 of the Bankruptcy (Scotland) Act 2016];

(d) a reference to a person appointed in accordance with Part 4 of the Insolvency (Northern Ireland) Order 1989 (SI 1989/2405 (NI 19)) includes a reference to a person appointed under section 19 of the Conveyancing Act 1881.

NOTES

Commencement: 1 August 2016.

Sub-s (1): substituted by the Third Parties (Rights against Insurers) Regulations 2016, SI 2016/570, reg 7(1)(a).

Sub-s (2): para (b) substituted by the Insurance Act 2015, s 20, Sch 2, paras 1, 3(1), (2).

Sub-s (3): words in square brackets in para (a) substituted for original words "under section 6 of the Bankruptcy (Scotland) Act 1985", in para (b) words in first pair of square brackets substituted for original word "under" and word in second pair of square brackets inserted, year in square brackets in para (c) substituted for original year "1985", and para (d) repealed together with word preceding it, by the Bankruptcy (Scotland) Act 2016 (Consequential Provisions and Modifications) Order 2016, SI 2016/1034, art 7(1), (3), Sch 1, para 35(1), (4)(a), as from 30 November 2016 (except in relation to (i) a sequestration as regards which the petition is presented, or the debtor application is made before that date; or (ii) a trust deed executed before that date).

Sub-s (4): para (b) substituted by the Insurance Act 2015, s 20, Sch 2, paras 1, 3(1), (3).

Sub-ss (4A), (4B): inserted by SI 2016/570, reg 3(1).

Sub-ss (5), (6): words in square brackets substituted by SI 2016/570, reg 7(1)(b).

Sub-s (7): words in square brackets substituted for original words "under section 6 of the Bankruptcy (Scotland) Act 1985" by SI 2016/1034, art 7(1), (3), Sch 1, para 35(1), (4)(b), as from 30 November 2016 (except in relation to (i) a sequestration as regards which the petition is presented, or the debtor application is made before that date; or (ii) a trust deed executed before that date).

Sub-s (8): repealed by SI 2016/1034, art 7(1), (3), Sch 1, para 35(1), (4)(c), as from 30 November 2016 (except in relation to (i) a sequestration as regards which the petition is presented, or the debtor application is made before that date; or (ii) a trust deed executed before that date).

Sub-s (9): words in square brackets in para (c) substituted for original words "under section 6 of the Bankruptcy (Scotland) Act 1985" by SI 2016/1034, art 7(1), (3), Sch 1, para 35(1), (4)(d), as from 30 November 2016 (except in relation to (i) a sequestration as regards which the petition is presented, or the debtor application is made before that date; or (ii) a trust deed executed before that date).

[17.410]

[6A Corporate bodies etc that are dissolved

(1) A body corporate or unincorporated body is a relevant person if the body has been dissolved, subject to the exceptions in subsections (2) and (3).

(2) The body is not a relevant person by virtue of subsection (1) if, since it was dissolved (or, if it has been dissolved more than once, since it was last dissolved), something has happened which has the effect that the body is treated as not having been dissolved or as no longer being dissolved.

(3) Subsection (1) applies to a partnership only if it is a body corporate.

(4) For the purposes of this section, "dissolved" means dissolved under the law of England and Wales, Scotland or Northern Ireland (whether or not by a process referred to as dissolution).]

NOTES

Commencement: 1 August 2016.

Inserted by the Third Parties (Rights against Insurers) Regulations 2016, SI 2016/570, reg 4.

[17.411]

7 Scottish trusts

(1) A trustee of a Scottish trust is, in respect of a liability of that trustee that falls to be met out of the trust estate, a relevant person if—

(a) an award of sequestration has been made [by virtue of section 6 of the Bankruptcy (Scotland) Act 2016] in respect of the trust estate, and the trust has not been discharged under that Act, [or]

(b) a protected trust deed within the meaning of that Act is in force in respect of the trust estate, *or*

(c) a composition approved in accordance with Schedule 4 to that Act is in force in respect of the trust estate.

(2) Where an award of sequestration made [by virtue of section 6 of the Bankruptcy (Scotland) Act 2016] is recalled or reduced any rights which were transferred under section 1 as a result of that award are re-transferred to and vest in the person who became a relevant person as a result of the award.

(3) Where an order discharging an individual, body or trust from an award of sequestration made under section 6 of the Bankruptcy (Scotland) Act 1985 is recalled or reduced under paragraph 17 or 18 of Schedule 4 to that Act, the order is to be treated for the purposes of this section as never having been made.

(4) In this section "Scottish trust" means a trust the estate of which may be sequestrated [by virtue of section 6 of the Bankruptcy (Scotland) Act 2016].

NOTES

Commencement: 1 August 2016.

Sub-s (1): in para (a) words in first pair of square brackets substituted for original words "under section 6 of the Bankruptcy (Scotland) Act 1985" and word in second pair of square brackets inserted, and para (c) repealed together with word preceding it, by the Bankruptcy (Scotland) Act 2016 (Consequential Provisions and Modifications) Order 2016, SI 2016/1034, art 7(1), (3), Sch 1, para 35(1), (5)(a), as from 30 November 2016 (except in relation to (i) a sequestration as regards which the petition is presented, or the debtor application is made before that date; or (ii) a trust deed executed before that date).

Sub-ss (2), (4): words in square brackets substituted for original words "under section 6 of the Bankruptcy (Scotland) Act 1985" by SI 2016/1034, art 7(1), (3), Sch 1, para 35(1), (5)(b), (d), as from 30 November 2016 (except in relation to (i) a sequestration as regards which the petition is presented, or the debtor application is made before that date; or (ii) a trust deed executed before that date).

Sub-s (3): repealed by SI 2016/1034, art 7(1), (3), Sch 1, para 35(1), (5)(c), as from 30 November 2016 (except in relation to (i) a sequestration as regards which the petition is presented, or the debtor application is made before that date; or (ii) a trust deed executed before that date).

Transferred rights: supplemental

[17.412]

8 Limit on rights transferred

Where the liability of an insured to a third party is less than the liability of the insurer to the insured (ignoring the effect of section 1), no rights are transferred under that section in respect of the difference.

NOTES

Commencement: 1 August 2016.

[17.413]

9 Conditions affecting transferred rights

(1) This section applies where transferred rights are subject to a condition (whether under the contract of insurance from which the transferred rights are derived or otherwise) that the insured has to fulfil.

(2) Anything done by the third party which, if done by the insured, would have amounted to or contributed to fulfilment of the condition is to be treated as if done by the insured.

(3) The transferred rights are not subject to a condition requiring the insured to provide information or assistance to the insurer if that condition cannot be fulfilled because the insured is—

(a) an individual who has died, . . .

(b) a body corporate that has been dissolved[, or

(c) an unincorporated body, other than a partnership, that has been dissolved.]

(4) A condition requiring the insured to provide information or assistance to the insurer does not include a condition requiring the insured to notify the insurer of the existence of a claim under the contract of insurance.

(5) The transferred rights are not subject to a condition requiring the prior discharge by the insured of the insured's liability to the third party.

(6) In the case of a contract of marine insurance, subsection (5) applies only to the extent that the liability of the insured is a liability in respect of death or personal injury.

(7) In this section—

"contract of marine insurance" has the meaning given by section 1 of the Marine Insurance Act 1906;

. . .

"personal injury" includes any disease and any impairment of a person's physical or mental condition.

[(8) For the purposes of this section—

(a) "dissolved" means dissolved under the law of England and Wales, Scotland or Northern Ireland (whether or not by a process referred to as dissolution), and

(b) a body has been dissolved even if, since it was dissolved, something has happened which has the effect that (but for this paragraph) the body is treated as not having been dissolved or as no longer being dissolved.]

NOTES

Commencement: 1 August 2016.

Sub-s (3): word omitted from para (a) repealed, and para (c) inserted together with word preceding it, by the Third Parties (Rights against Insurers) Regulations 2016, SI 2016/570, reg 5(1), (2).

Sub-s (7): definition "dissolved" (omitted) repealed by SI 2016/570, reg 5(1), (3).

Sub-s (8): added by SI 2016/570, reg 5(1), (4).

[17.414]

10 Insurer's right of set off

(1) This section applies if—

(a) rights of an insured under a contract of insurance have been transferred to a third party under section 1,

(b) the insured is under a liability to the insurer under the contract ("the insured's liability"), and

(c) if there had been no transfer, the insurer would have been entitled to set off the amount of the insured's liability against the amount of the insurer's own liability to the insured.

(2) The insurer is entitled to set off the amount of the insured's liability against the amount of the insurer's own liability to the third party in relation to the transferred rights.

NOTES

Commencement: 1 August 2016.

Provision of information etc

[17.415]

11 Information and disclosure for third parties

Schedule 1 (information and disclosure for third parties) has effect.

NOTES

Commencement: 1 August 2016.

Enforcement of transferred rights

[17.416]

12 Limitation and prescription

(1) Subsection (2) applies where a person brings proceedings for a declaration under section 2(2)(a), or for a declarator under section 3(2)(a), and the proceedings are started or, in Scotland, commenced—

(a) after the expiry of a period of limitation applicable to an action against the insured to enforce the insured's liability, or of a period of prescription applicable to that liability, but

(b) while such an action is in progress.

(2) The insurer may not rely on the expiry of that period as a defence unless the insured is able to rely on it in the action against the insured.

(3) For the purposes of subsection (1), an action is to be treated as no longer in progress if it has been concluded by a judgment or decree, or by an award, even if there is an appeal or a right of appeal.

(4) Where a person who has already established an insured's liability to that person brings proceedings under this Act against the insurer, nothing in this Act is to be read as meaning—

(a) that, for the purposes of the law of limitation in England and Wales, that person's cause of action against the insurer arose otherwise than at the time when that person established the liability of the insured,

(b) that, for the purposes of the law of prescription in Scotland, the obligation in respect of which the proceedings are brought became enforceable against the insurer otherwise than at that time, or

(c) that, for the purposes of the law of limitation in Northern Ireland, that person's cause of action against the insurer arose otherwise than at the time when that person established the liability of the insured.

NOTES

Commencement: 1 August 2016.

[17.417]

13 Jurisdiction within the United Kingdom

(1) Where a person (P) domiciled in a part of the United Kingdom is entitled to bring proceedings under this Act against an insurer domiciled in another part, P may do so in the part where P is domiciled or in the part where the insurer is domiciled (whatever the contract of insurance may stipulate as to where proceedings are to be brought).

(2) The following provisions of the Civil Jurisdiction and Judgments Act 1982 (relating to determination of domicile) apply for the purposes of subsection (1)—

(a) section 41(2), (3), (5) and (6) (individuals);

(b) section 42(1), (3), (4) and (8) (corporations and associations);

(c) section 45(2) and (3) (trusts);

(d) section 46(1), (3) and (7) (the Crown).

(3) (*Amends the Civil Jurisdiction and Judgments Act 1982, Sch 5.*)

NOTES

Commencement: 1 August 2016.

Enforcement of insured's liability

[17.418]

14 Effect of transfer on insured's liability

(1) Where rights in respect of an insured's liability to a third party are transferred under section 1, the third party may enforce that liability against the insured only to the extent (if any) that it exceeds the amount recoverable from the insurer by virtue of the transfer.

(2) Subsection (3) applies if a transfer of rights under section 1 occurs because the insured person is a relevant person by virtue of—

(a) section 4(1)(a) or (e), (2)(b) or (3)(b) or (c),

(b) section [6(1)], (2)(a), (3)(c) or (4)(a), or

(c) section 7(1)(b).

(3) If the liability is subject to the arrangement, trust deed or compromise by virtue of which the insured is a relevant person, the liability is to be treated as subject to that arrangement, trust deed or compromise only to the extent that the liability exceeds the amount recoverable from the insurer by virtue of the transfer.

(4) . . .

(5) . . .

(6) For the purposes of this section the amount recoverable from the insurer does not include any amount that the third party is unable to recover as a result of—

(a) a shortage of assets on the insurer's part, in a case where the insurer is a relevant person, or

(b) a limit set by the contract of insurance on the fund available to meet claims in respect of a particular description of liability of the insured.

(7) Where a third party is eligible to make a claim in respect of the insurer's liability under or by virtue of rules made under Part 15 of the Financial Services and Markets Act 2000 (the Financial Services Compensation Scheme)—

(a) subsection (6)(a) applies only if the third party has made such a claim, and

(b) the third party is to be treated as being able to recover from the insurer any amount paid to, or due to, the third party as a result of the claim.

NOTES

Commencement: 1 August 2016.

Sub-s (2): figure in square brackets in para (b) substituted by the Third Parties (Rights against Insurers) Regulations 2016, SI 2016/570, reg 7(2).

Sub-ss (4), (5): repealed by the Bankruptcy (Scotland) Act 2016 (Consequential Provisions and Modifications) Order 2016, SI 2016/1034, art 7(1), (3), Sch 1, para 35(1), (6), as from 30 November 2016 (except in relation to (i) a sequestration as regards which the petition is presented, or the debtor application is made before that date; or (ii) a trust deed executed before that date), and originally read as follows—

"(4) Subsection (5) applies if a transfer of rights under section 1 occurs in respect of a liability which, after the transfer, becomes one that is subject to a composition approved in accordance with Schedule 4 to the Bankruptcy (Scotland) Act 1985.

(5) The liability is to be treated as subject to the composition only to the extent that the liability exceeds the amount recoverable from the insurer by virtue of the transfer.".

Application of Act

[17.419]

15 Reinsurance

This Act does not apply to a case where the liability referred to in section 1(1) is itself a liability incurred by an insurer under a contract of insurance.

NOTES

Commencement: 1 August 2016.

[17.420]

16 Voluntarily-incurred liabilities

It is irrelevant for the purposes of section 1 whether or not the liability of the insured is or was incurred voluntarily.

NOTES

Commencement: 1 August 2016.

[17.421]

17 Avoidance

(1) A contract of insurance to which this section applies is of no effect in so far as it purports, whether directly or indirectly, to avoid or terminate the contract or alter the rights of the parties under it in the event of the insured—

(a) becoming a relevant person, or

(b) dying insolvent (within the meaning given by section 5(2)).

(2) A contract of insurance is one to which this section applies if the insured's rights under it are capable of being transferred under section 1.

NOTES

Commencement: 1 August 2016.

[17.422]

18 Cases with a foreign element

Except as expressly provided, the application of this Act does not depend on whether there is a connection with a part of the United Kingdom; and in particular it does not depend on—

(a) whether or not the liability (or the alleged liability) of the insured to the third party was incurred in, or under the law of, England and Wales, Scotland or Northern Ireland;

(b) the place of residence or domicile of any of the parties;

(c) whether or not the contract of insurance (or a part of it) is governed by the law of England and Wales, Scotland or Northern Ireland;

(d) the place where sums due under the contract of insurance are payable.

NOTES

Commencement: 1 August 2016.

Supplemental

[17.423]

[19 Power to change the meaning of "relevant person"

(1) The Secretary of State may by regulations make provision adding or removing circumstances in which a person is a "relevant person" for the purposes of this Act, subject to subsection (2).

(2) Regulations under this section may add circumstances only if, in the Secretary of State's opinion, the additional circumstances—

(a) involve actual or anticipated dissolution of a body corporate or an unincorporated body,

(b) involve actual or anticipated insolvency or other financial difficulties for an individual, a body corporate or an unincorporated body, or

(c) are similar to circumstances for the time being described in sections 4 to 7.

(3) Regulations under this section may make provision about—

(a) the persons to whom, and the extent to which, rights are transferred under section 1 in the circumstances added or removed by the regulations (the "affected circumstances"),

(b) the re-transfer of rights transferred under section 1 where the affected circumstances change, and

(c) the effect of a transfer of rights under section 1 on the liability of the insured in the affected circumstances.

(4) Regulations under this section which add or remove circumstances involving actual or anticipated dissolution of a body corporate or unincorporated body may change the cases in which the following provisions apply so that they include or exclude cases involving that type of dissolution or any other type of dissolution of a body—

(a) section 9(3) (cases in which transferred rights are not subject to a condition requiring the insured to provide information or assistance to the insurer), and

(b) paragraph 3 of Schedule 1 (notices requiring disclosure).

(5) Regulations under this section which add circumstances may provide that section 1 of this Act applies in cases involving those circumstances in which either or both of the following occurred in relation to a person before the day on which the regulations come into force—

(a) the circumstances arose in relation to the person;

(b) a liability against which the person was insured under an insurance contract was incurred.

(6) Regulations under this section which—

(a) add circumstances, and

(b) provide that section 1 of this Act applies in a case involving those circumstances in which both of the events mentioned in subsection (5)(a) and (b) occurred in relation to a person before the day on which the regulations come into force,

must provide that, in such a case, the person is to be treated for the purposes of this Act as not having become a relevant person until that day or a later day specified in the regulations.

(7) Regulations under this section which remove circumstances may provide that section 1 of this Act does not apply in cases involving those circumstances in which one of the events mentioned in subsection (5)(a) and (b) (but not both) occurred in relation to a person before the day on which the regulations come into force.

(8) Regulations under this section may—

(a) include consequential, incidental, supplementary, transitional, transitory or saving provision,

(b) make different provision for different purposes, and

(c) make provision by reference to an enactment as amended, extended or applied from time to time,

(and subsections (3) to (7) are without prejudice to the generality of this subsection).

(9) Regulations under this section may amend an enactment, whenever passed or made, including this Act.

(10) Regulations under this section are to be made by statutory instrument.

(11) Regulations under this section may not be made unless a draft of the statutory instrument containing the regulations has been laid before, and approved by a resolution of, each House of Parliament.]

NOTES

Commencement: 12 April 2015.

Substituted by the Insurance Act 2015, s 19.

[17.424]

[19A Interpretation

(1) The references to enactments in sections 4 to 7 . . . . . . [, Schedule A1 and paragraph 3(2)(b)] of Schedule 1 are to be treated as including references to those enactments as amended, extended or applied by another enactment, whenever passed or made, unless the contrary intention appears.

(2) In this Act, "enactment" means an enactment contained in, or in an instrument made under, any of the following—

(a) an Act;
(b) an Act or Measure of the National Assembly for Wales;
(c) an Act of the Scottish Parliament;
(d) Northern Ireland legislation.]

NOTES

Commencement: 1 August 2016.

Inserted by the Insurance Act 2015, s 20, Sch 2, paras 1, 6.

Sub-s (1): words omitted in the first place repealed and words in square brackets substituted by the Third Parties (Rights against Insurers) Regulations 2016, SI 2016/570, reg 7(3); words "and 14(4)" omitted in the second place repealed by the Bankruptcy (Scotland) Act 2016 (Consequential Provisions and Modifications) Order 2016, SI 2016/1034, art 7(1), (3), Sch 1, para 35(1), (7), as from 30 November 2016 (except in relation to (i) a sequestration as regards which the petition is presented, or the debtor application is made before that date; or (ii) a trust deed executed before that date).

Regulations: the Third Parties (Rights against Insurers) Regulations 2016, SI 2016/570.

[17.425]

20 Amendments, transitionals, repeals, etc

(1) Schedule 2 (amendments) has effect.

(2) Schedule 3 (transitory, transitional and saving provisions) has effect.

(3) Schedule 4 (repeals and revocations) has effect.

NOTES

Commencement: 1 August 2016.

[17.426]

21 Short title, commencement and extent

(1) This Act may be cited as the Third Parties (Rights against Insurers) Act 2010.

(2) This Act comes into force on such day as the Secretary of State may by order made by statutory instrument appoint.

(3) This Act extends to England and Wales, Scotland and Northern Ireland, subject as follows.

(4) Section 2 and paragraphs 3 and 4 of Schedule 1 do not extend to Scotland.

(5) Section 3 extends to Scotland only.

(6) Any amendment, repeal or revocation made by this Act has the same extent as the provision to which it relates.

NOTES

Commencement: 1 August 2016.

Orders: the Third Parties (Rights against Insurers) Act 2010 (Commencement) Order 2016, SI 2016/550.

SCHEDULES

[SCHEDULE A1
ADMINISTRATION UNDER RELEVANT SECTORAL LEGISLATION

Section 6(4B)

[17.427]

For the purposes of section 6(4B)—

(a) a body is in administration under relevant sectoral legislation if the appointment of an administrator of the body under an enactment listed below has effect, and
(b) the body does not cease to be in administration merely because an administrator vacates office (by reason of resignation, death or otherwise) or is removed from office.

List of Enactments

Aviation

Chapter 1 of Part 1 of the Transport Act 2000

Energy

Chapter 3 of Part 3 of the Energy Act 2004

Chapter 5 of Part 2 of the Energy Act 2011

Part 2 of the Energy Act (Northern Ireland) 2011 (c 6 (NI))

Financial Services

Part 2 of the Insolvency Act 1986 (as it has effect by virtue of section 249 of the Enterprise Act 2002), as applied by Schedule 15A to the Building Societies Act 1986

Part 3 of the Insolvency (Northern Ireland) Order 1989 (SI 1989/2405 (NI 19)) (as it has effect by virtue of article 4 of the Insolvency (Northern Ireland) Order 2005 (SI 2005/1455 (NI 10))), as applied by Schedule 15A to the Building Societies Act 1986

Part 3 of the Banking Act 2009

Investment Bank Special Administration Regulations 2011 (SI 2011/245)

Part 6 of the Financial Services (Banking Reform) Act 2013

Postal Services

Part 4 of the Postal Services Act 2011

Railways

Part 1 of the Railways Act 1993

Chapter 7 of Part 4 of the Greater London Authority Act 1999

Water and sewerage

Chapter 2 of Part 2 of the Water Industry Act 1991

Chapter 2 of Part 3 of the Water and Sewerage Services (Northern Ireland) Order 2006 (SI 2006/3336 (NI 21))]

NOTES

Commencement: 1 August 2016.

Inserted by the Third Parties (Rights against Insurers) Regulations 2016, SI 2016/570, reg 3(2).

SCHEDULE 1
INFORMATION AND DISCLOSURE FOR THIRD PARTIES

Section 11

Notices requesting information

[17.428]

1. (1) If a person (A) reasonably believes that—

(a) another person (B) has incurred a liability to A, and

(b) B is a relevant person,

A may, by notice in writing, request from B such information falling within sub-paragraph (3) as the notice specifies.

(2) If a person (A) reasonably believes that—

(a) a liability has been incurred to A,

(b) the person who incurred the liability is insured against it under a contract of insurance,

(c) rights of that person under the contract have been transferred to A under section 1, and

(d) there is a person (C) who is able to provide information falling within sub-paragraph (3),

A may, by notice in writing, request from C such information falling within that sub-paragraph as the notice specifies.

(3) The following is the information that falls within this sub-paragraph—

(a) whether there is a contract of insurance that covers the supposed liability or might reasonably be regarded as covering it;

(b) if there is such a contract—

(i) who the insurer is;

(ii) what the terms of the contract are;

(iii) whether the insured has been informed that the insurer has claimed not to be liable under the contract in respect of the supposed liability;

(iv) whether there are or have been any proceedings between the insurer and the insured in respect of the supposed liability and, if so, relevant details of those proceedings;

(v) in a case where the contract sets a limit on the fund available to meet claims in respect of the supposed liability and other liabilities, how much of it (if any) has been paid out in respect of other liabilities;

(vi) whether there is a fixed charge to which any sums paid out under the contract in respect of the supposed liability would be subject.

(4) For the purpose of sub-paragraph (3)(b)(iv), relevant details of proceedings are—

(a) in the case of court proceedings—

(i) the name of the court;

(ii) the case number;

(iii) the contents of all documents served in the proceedings in accordance with rules of court or orders made in the proceedings, and the contents of any such orders;

(b) in the case of arbitral proceedings or, in Scotland, an arbitration—
 (i) the name of the arbitrator;
 (ii) information corresponding with that mentioned in paragraph (a)(iii).

(5) In sub-paragraph (3)(b)(vi), in its application to Scotland, "fixed charge" means a fixed security within the meaning given by section 47(1) of the Bankruptcy and Diligence etc (Scotland) Act 2007 (asp 3).

(6) A notice given by a person under this paragraph must include particulars of the facts on which that person relies as entitlement to give the notice.

Provision of information where notice given under paragraph 1

2. (1) A person (R) who receives a notice under paragraph 1 must, within the period of 28 days beginning with the day of receipt of the notice—
(a) provide to the person who gave the notice any information specified in it that R is able to provide;
(b) in relation to any such information that R is not able to provide, notify that person why R is not able to provide it.

(2) Where—
(a) a person (R) receives a notice under paragraph 1,
(b) there is information specified in the notice that R is not able to provide because it is contained in a document that is not in R's control,
(c) the document was at one time in R's control, and
(d) R knows or believes that it is now in another person's control,

R must, within the period of 28 days beginning with the day of receipt of the notice, provide the person who gave the notice with whatever particulars R can as to the nature of the information and the identity of that other person.

(3) If R fails to comply with a duty imposed on R by this paragraph, the person who gave R the notice may apply to court for an order requiring R to comply with the duty.

(4) No duty arises by virtue of this paragraph in respect of information as to which a claim to legal professional privilege or, in Scotland, to confidentiality as between client and professional legal adviser could be maintained in legal proceedings.

Notices requiring disclosure: [bodies that have been dissolved]

3. (1) If—
(a) a person (P) has started proceedings under this Act against an insurer in respect of a liability
. . .
[(b) P claims the liability has been incurred to P by—
 (i) a body corporate, or
 (ii) an unincorporated body other than a partnership, and
(c) the body has been dissolved,]

P may by notice in writing require a person to whom sub-paragraph (2) applies to disclose to P any documents that are relevant to that liability.

(2) This sub-paragraph applies to a person if—
(a) immediately before the time of the alleged transfer under section 1, that person was an officer or employee of the body, or
(b) immediately before the body [was dissolved (or, if it has been dissolved more than once, immediately before it was last dissolved)], that person was—
 (i) acting as an insolvency practitioner in relation to the body (within the meaning given by section 388(1) of the Insolvency Act 1986 or Article 3 of the Insolvency (Northern Ireland) Order 1989 (SI 1989/2405 NI 19)), or
 (ii) acting as the official receiver in relation to the winding up of the body.

(3) A notice under this paragraph must be accompanied by—
(a) a copy of the particulars of claim required to be served in connection with the proceedings mentioned in sub-paragraph (1), or
(b) where those proceedings are arbitral proceedings, the particulars of claim that would be required to be so served if they were court proceedings.

(4) . . .

(5) . . .

[(6) For the purposes of this paragraph—
(a) "dissolved" means dissolved under the law of England and Wales, Scotland or Northern Ireland (whether or not by a process referred to as dissolution), and
(b) a body has been dissolved even if, since it was dissolved, something has happened which has the effect that (but for this paragraph) the body is treated as not having been dissolved or as no longer being dissolved.]

Disclosure and inspection where notice given under paragraph 3

4. (1) Subject to the provisions of this paragraph and to any necessary modifications—
(a) the duties of disclosure of a person who receives a notice under paragraph 3, and
(b) the rights of inspection of the person giving the notice,

are the same as the corresponding duties and rights under Civil Procedure Rules of parties to court proceedings in which an order for standard disclosure has been made.

(2) In sub-paragraph (1), in its application to Northern Ireland—
- (a) the reference to Civil Procedure Rules is—
  - (i) in the case of proceedings in the High Court, to be read as a reference to the Rules of the Court of Judicature (Northern Ireland) 1980 (SR 1980 No 346), and
  - (ii) in the case of proceedings in the county court, to be read as a reference to the County Court Rules (Northern Ireland) 1981 (SR 1981 No 225), and
- (b) the reference to an order for standard disclosure is to be read as a reference to an order for discovery.

(3) A person who by virtue of sub-paragraph (1) or (2) has to serve a list of documents must do so within the period of 28 days beginning with the day of receipt of the notice.

(4) A person who has received a notice under paragraph 3 and has served a list of documents in response to it is not under a duty of disclosure by reason of that notice in relation to documents that the person did not have when the list was served.

Avoidance

5. A contract of insurance is of no effect in so far as it purports, whether directly or indirectly—
- (a) to avoid or terminate the contract or alter the rights of the parties under it in the event of a person providing information, or giving disclosure, that the person is required to provide or give by virtue of a notice under paragraph 1 or 3, or
- (b) otherwise to prohibit, prevent or restrict a person from providing such information or giving such disclosure.

Other rights to information etc

6. Rights to information, or to inspection of documents, that a person has by virtue of paragraph 1 or 3 are in addition to any such rights as the person has apart from that paragraph.

Interpretation

7. For the purposes of this Schedule—
- (a) a person is able to provide information only if—
  - (i) that person can obtain it without undue difficulty from a document that is in that person's control, or
  - (ii) where that person is an individual, the information is within that person's knowledge;
- (b) a document is in a person's control if it is in that person's possession or if that person has a right to possession of it or to inspect or take copies of it.

NOTES

Commencement: 1 August 2016.

Para 3: words in square brackets in the heading substituted, in sub-para (1), words omitted from sub-para (a) repealed and sub-paras (b), (c) substituted for sub-para (b), words in square brackets in sub-para (2)(b) substituted, sub-paras (4), (5) repealed and sub-para (6) added, by the Third Parties (Rights against Insurers) Regulations 2016, SI 2016/570, reg 6.

SCHEDULE 2

(*Sch 2 contains amendments only.*)

SCHEDULE 3
TRANSITORY, TRANSITIONAL AND SAVING PROVISIONS

Section 20

[Application of this Act]

[17.429]
1. (1) Section 1(1)(a) applies where the insured became a relevant person before, as well as when the insured becomes such a person on or after, commencement day.

(2) Section 1(1)(b) applies where the liability was incurred before, as well as where it is incurred on or after, commencement day.

[Relevant persons

1A. (1) An individual, company or limited liability partnership not within sections 4 to 7 is to be treated as a relevant person for the purposes of this Act in the following cases.

(2) The first case is where an individual—
- (a) became bankrupt before commencement day, and
- (b) has not been discharged from that bankruptcy.

(3) The second case is where—
- (a) an individual made a composition or arrangement with his or her creditors before commencement day, and
- (b) the composition or arrangement remains in force.

(4) The third case is where—
- (a) a winding-up order was made, or a resolution for a voluntary winding-up was passed, with respect to a company or limited liability partnership before commencement day, and
- (b) the company or partnership is still wound up.

(5) The fourth case is where a company or limited liability partnership—
(a) entered administration before commencement day, and
(b) is still in administration.

(6) The fifth case is where—
(a) a receiver or manager of the business or undertaking of a company or limited liability partnership was appointed before commencement day, and
(b) the appointment remains in force.

(7) In those cases, the person is a relevant person only in relation to liabilities under a contract of insurance under which the person was insured at the time of the event mentioned in sub-paragraph (2)(a), (3)(a), (4)(a), (5)(a) or (6)(a) (as appropriate).]

[Bankruptcy and Diligence etc (Scotland) Act 2007]

2. Until the coming into force of section 47(1) of the Bankruptcy and Diligence etc (Scotland) Act 2007 (asp 3), the reference to that provision in paragraph 1(5) of Schedule 1 is to be read as a reference to section 486(1) of the Companies Act 1985.

[Application of 1930 Acts]

3. Despite its repeal by this Act, the Third Parties (Rights against Insurers) Act 1930 continues to apply in relation to—
(a) cases where the event referred to in subsection (1) of section 1 of that Act and the incurring of the liability referred to in that subsection both happened before commencement day;
(b) cases where the death of the deceased person referred to in subsection (2) of that section happened before that day.

4. Despite its repeal by this Act, the Third Parties (Rights against Insurers) Act (Northern Ireland) 1930 continues to apply in relation to—
(a) cases where the event referred to in subsection (1) of section 1 of that Act and the incurring of the liability referred to in that subsection both happened before commencement day;
(b) cases where the death of the deceased person referred to in subsection (2) of that section happened before that day.

[Interpretation]

5. In this Schedule "commencement day" means the day on which this Act comes into force.

NOTES

Commencement: 1 August 2016.

Paras 1–3, 5: cross-headings inserted by the Insurance Act 2015, s 20, Sch 2, paras 1, 5(1), (2), (4)–(6).

Para 1A: inserted, together with preceding cross-heading, by the Insurance Act 2015, s 20, Sch 2, paras 1, 5(1), (3).

SCHEDULE 4

(*Sch 4 contains repeals and revocations only.*)

CHARITIES ACT 2011

(2011 c 25)

ARRANGEMENT OF SECTIONS

PART 6
CY-PRÈS POWERS AND ASSISTANCE AND SUPERVISION OF CHARITIES BY COURT AND COMMISSION

Legal proceedings relating to charities

113 Petitions for winding up charities under Insolvency Act . . . .[17.430]

PART 9
CHARITY TRUSTEES, TRUSTEES AND AUDITORS ETC

Meaning of "charity trustees"

177 Meaning of "charity trustees" . . . .[17.431]

Disqualification of charity trustees and trustees

178 Persons disqualified from being charity trustees or trustees of a charity . . . .[17.432]
178A Case A: specified offences . . . .[17.433]
179 Disqualification: pre-commencement events etc . . . .[17.434]
180 Disqualification: exceptions in relation to charitable companies. . . . .[17.435]
181 Power to waive disqualification . . . .[17.436]
182 Records of persons removed from office . . . .[17.437]
183 Criminal consequences of acting while disqualified. . . . .[17.438]

184 Civil consequences of acting while disqualified . . . .[17.439]

PART 11
CHARITABLE INCORPORATED ORGANISATIONS (CIOS)

CHAPTER 1
GENERAL

Nature and constitution

204 Meaning of "CIO" . . . .[17.440]

CHAPTER 5
SUPPLEMENTARY

245 Regulations about winding up, insolvency and dissolution. . . . .[17.441]
247 Meaning of "CIO regulations". . . . .[17.442]

PART 18
MISCELLANEOUS AND SUPPLEMENTARY

Interpretation

353 Minor definitions . . . .[17.443]

PART 19
FINAL PROVISIONS

355 Commencement . . . .[17.444]
356 Extent. . . . .[17.445]
358 Short title. . . . .[17.446]

An Act to consolidate the Charities Act 1993 and other enactments which relate to charities.

[14 December 2011]

1–60 *((Pts 1–5) outside the scope of this work.)*

PART 6
CY-PRÈS POWERS AND ASSISTANCE AND SUPERVISION OF CHARITIES BY COURT AND COMMISSION

61–112 *(Outside the scope of this work.)*

Legal proceedings relating to charities

[17.430]
113 Petitions for winding up charities under Insolvency Act

(1) This section applies where a charity may be wound up by the High Court under the Insolvency Act 1986.

(2) A petition for the charity to be wound up under the 1986 Act by any court in England or Wales having jurisdiction may be presented by the Attorney General, as well as by any person authorised by that Act.

(3) Such a petition may also be presented by the Commission if, at any time after it has instituted an inquiry under section 46 with respect to the charity, it is satisfied either as mentioned in section 76(1)(a) (misconduct or mismanagement etc) or as mentioned in section 76(1)(b) (need to protect property etc).

(4) The power exercisable by the Commission by virtue of this section is exercisable—
- (a) by the Commission of its own motion, but
- (b) only with the agreement of the Attorney General on each occasion.

114–176 *(Ss 114–116, ss 117–176 (Pts 7, 8) outside the scope of this work.)*

PART 9
CHARITY TRUSTEES, TRUSTEES AND AUDITORS ETC

Meaning of "charity trustees"

[17.431]
177 Meaning of "charity trustees"

In this Act, except in so far as the context otherwise requires, "charity trustees" means the persons having the general control and management of the administration of a charity.

Disqualification of charity trustees and trustees

[17.432]
178 Persons disqualified from being charity trustees or trustees of a charity

(1) A person ("P") is disqualified from being a charity trustee or trustee for a charity in the following cases—

Case A

P has been convicted *of any offence involving dishonesty or deception.*

Case B

P has been [made] bankrupt or sequestration of P's estate has been awarded and (in either case)—
- (a) P has not been discharged, or

(b) P is the subject of a bankruptcy restrictions order or an interim order.

Case C

P has made a composition or arrangement with, or granted a trust deed for, creditors and has not been discharged in respect of it.

Case D

P has been removed *from the office of charity trustee or trustee for a charity* by an order made—

(a) by the Commission under section [79(4)] or by the Commission or the Commissioners under a relevant earlier enactment (as defined by section 179(5)), or

(b) by the High Court,

on the ground of any misconduct or mismanagement in the administration of the charity for which P was responsible or [which P knew of and failed to take any reasonable step to oppose,] or which P's conduct contributed to or facilitated.

Case E

P has been removed, under section 34(5)(e) of the Charities and Trustee Investment (Scotland) Act 2005 (asp 10) (powers of the Court of Session) or the relevant earlier legislation (as defined by section 179(6)), from being concerned in the management or control of any body.

Case F

P is subject to—

(a) a disqualification order or disqualification undertaking under the Company Directors Disqualification Act 1986 or the Company Directors Disqualification (Northern Ireland) Order 2002 (SI 2002/3150 (NI 4)), or

(b) an order made under section 429(2) of the Insolvency Act 1986 (disabilities on revocation of county court administration order).

[Case G

P is subject to—

(a) a moratorium period under a debt relief order under Part 7A of the Insolvency Act 1986; or

(b) a debt relief restrictions order or interim order under Schedule 4ZB to that Act.]

[Case H

P has been found to be in contempt of court under Civil Procedure Rules for—

(a) making a false disclosure statement, or causing one to be made, or

(b) making a false statement in a document verified by a statement of truth, or causing one to be made.

Case I

P has been found guilty of disobedience to an order or direction of the Commission on an application to the High Court under section 336(1).

Case J

P is a designated person for the purposes of—

(a) Part 1 of the Terrorist Asset-Freezing etc Act 2010, or

(b) the Al-Qaida (Asset-Freezing) Regulations 2011.

Case K

P is subject to the notification requirements of Part 2 of the Sexual Offences Act 2003.]

(2) Subsection (1) is subject to sections 179 to 181.

[(3) While a person is disqualified under this section in relation to a charity, the person is also disqualified from holding an office or employment in the charity with senior management functions.

(4) A function of an office or employment held by a person "(A)" is a senior management function if—

(a) it relates to the management of the charity, and A is not responsible for it to another officer or employee (other than a charity trustee or trustee for the charity), or

(b) it involves control over money and the only officer or employee (other than a charity trustee or trustee for the charity) to whom A is responsible for it is a person with senior management functions other than ones involving control over money.]

NOTES

Sub-s (1) is amended as follows:

Case A: for the words in italics there are substituted the following words by the Charities (Protection and Social Investment) Act 2016, s 9(1), (3), as from 1 August 2018—

"of—

(a) an offence specified in section 178A;

(b) an offence, not specified in section 178A, that involves dishonesty or deception.".

Case B: word in square brackets substituted by the Enterprise and Regulatory Reform Act 2013 (Consequential Amendments) (Bankruptcy) and the Small Business, Enterprise and Employment Act 2015 (Consequential Amendments) Regulations 2016, SI 2016/481, reg 2(1), Sch 1, Pt 1, para 17(1), (3).

Case D: for the words in italics there are substituted the words "as a trustee, charity trustee, officer, agent or employee of a charity" by the Charities (Protection and Social Investment) Act 2016, s 9(1), (4)(a), as from 1 August 2018; figure and words in square brackets substituted by the Charities (Protection and Social Investment) Act 2016, ss 4(1), (5), 9(1), (4)(b).

Case G: words in square brackets added, in relation to a debt relief restrictions order, an interim debt relief restrictions order, a debt relief restrictions undertaking or interim debt relief restrictions undertaking where the order is made, or (as the case may be) the debtor gives the undertaking, after 1 October 2012, by the Tribunals, Courts and Enforcement Act 2007 (Consequential Amendments) Order 2012, SI 2012/2404, arts 3(2), 6, Sch 2, para 62(1), (3).

Cases H–K: inserted by the Charities (Protection and Social Investment) Act 2016, s 9(1), (5), as from 1 August 2018.

Sub-ss (3), (4): inserted by the Charities (Protection and Social Investment) Act 2016, s 9(1), (6), as from 1 August 2018.

[17.433]

[178A Case A: specified offences

(1) The following offences are specified for the purposes of Case A—

1 An offence to which Part 4 of the Counter-Terrorism Act 2008 applies (see sections 41 to 43 of that Act).

2 An offence under section 13 or 19 of the Terrorism Act 2000 (wearing of uniform etc, and failure to disclose information).

3 A money laundering offence within the meaning of section 415 of the Proceeds of Crime Act 2002.

4 An offence under any of the following provisions of the Bribery Act 2010—

(a) section 1 (bribing another person),

(b) section 2 (offences relating to being bribed),

(c) section 6 (bribery of foreign public officials),

(d) section 7 (failure of commercial organisations to prevent bribery).

5 An offence under section 77 of this Act.

6 An offence of—

(a) misconduct in public office,

(b) perjury,

(c) perverting the course of justice.

(2) An offence which has been superseded (directly or indirectly) by an offence specified in subsection (1) is also specified for the purposes of Case A.

(3) In relation to an offence specified in subsection (1) or (2), the following offences are also specified for the purposes of Case A—

(a) an offence of attempt, conspiracy or incitement to commit the offence;

(b) an offence of aiding, abetting, counselling or procuring the commission of the offence;

(c) an offence under Part 2 of the Serious Crime Act 2007 (encouraging or assisting) in relation to the offence.

(4) The [Secretary of State] may amend this section by regulations to add or remove an offence.]

NOTES

Commencement: 1 August 2018.

Inserted by the Charities (Protection and Social Investment) Act 2016, s 9(1), (7).

Sub-s (4): words in square brackets substituted by the Transfer of Functions (Elections, Referendums, Third Sector and Information) Order 2016, SI 2016/997, art 13, Sch 2, para 25(1), (2)(dd).

[17.434]

179 Disqualification: pre-commencement events etc

(1) Case A—

(a) applies whether the conviction occurred before or after the commencement of section 178(1) [or section 178A or any amendment of that section], but

(b) does not apply in relation to any conviction which is a spent conviction for the purposes of the Rehabilitation of Offenders Act 1974.

(2) Case B applies whether the [making bankrupt] or the sequestration or the making of a bankruptcy restrictions order or an interim order occurred before or after the commencement of section 178(1).

(3) Case C applies whether the composition or arrangement was made, or the trust deed was granted, before or after the commencement of section 178(1).

(4) Cases D to F apply in relation to orders made and removals effected before or after the commencement of section 178(1).

(5) In Case D—

(a) "the Commissioners" means the Charity Commissioners for England and Wales, and

(b) "relevant earlier enactment" means—

(i) section 18(2)(i) of the Charities Act 1993 (power to act for protection of charities),

(ii) section 20(1A)(i) of the Charities Act 1960, or

(iii) section 20(1)(i) of the 1960 Act (as in force before the commencement of section 8 of the Charities Act 1992).

(6) In Case E, "the relevant earlier legislation" means section 7 of the Law Reform (Miscellaneous Provisions) (Scotland) Act 1990 (powers of Court of Session to deal with management of charities).

[(7) Case H does not apply in relation to a finding of contempt which, if it had been a conviction for which P was dealt with in the same way, would be a spent conviction for the purposes of the Rehabilitation of Offenders Act 1974.]

NOTES

Sub-s (1): words in square brackets inserted by the Charities (Protection and Social Investment) Act 2016, s 9(1), (8), (9), as from 1 August 2018.

Sub-s (2): words in square brackets substituted by the Enterprise and Regulatory Reform Act 2013 (Consequential Amendments) (Bankruptcy) and the Small Business, Enterprise and Employment Act 2015 (Consequential Amendments) Regulations 2016, SI 2016/481, reg 2(1), Sch 1, Pt 1, para 17(1), (4).

Sub-s (7): added by the Charities (Protection and Social Investment) Act 2016, s 9(1), (8), (10), as from 1 August 2018.

[17.435]

180 Disqualification: exceptions in relation to charitable companies

(1) Where (apart from this subsection) a person ("P") is disqualified under Case B [or G] from being a charity trustee or trustee for a charitable company [or a CIO], P is not so disqualified if leave has been granted under section 11 of the Company Directors Disqualification Act 1986 (undischarged bankrupts) for P to act as director of the company [or charity trustee of the CIO (as the case may be)].

(2) Similarly, a person ("P") is not disqualified under Case F from being a charity trustee or trustee for a charitable company [or a CIO] if, in a case set out in the first column of the table, leave has been granted as mentioned in the second column for P to act as director of the company [or charity trustee of the CIO (as the case may be)]—

P is subject to a disqualification order or disqualification undertaking under the Company Directors Disqualification Act 1986.	Leave has been granted for the purposes of section 1(1)(a) or 1A(1)(a) of the 1986 Act.
P is subject to a disqualification order or disqualification undertaking under the Company Directors Disqualification (Northern Ireland) Order 2002 (SI 2002/3150 (NI 4)).	Leave has been granted by the High Court in Northern Ireland.
P is subject to an order under section 429(2) of the Insolvency Act 1986.	Leave has been granted by the court which made the order.

NOTES

Sub-s (1): first words in square brackets added, in relation to a debt relief restrictions order, an interim debt relief restrictions order, a debt relief restrictions undertaking or interim debt relief restrictions undertaking where the order is made, or (as the case may be) the debtor gives the undertaking, after 1 October 2012, by the Tribunals, Courts and Enforcement Act 2007 (Consequential Amendments) Order 2012, SI 2012/2404, arts 3(2), 6, Sch 2, para 62(1), (4); second and final words in square brackets inserted by the Charitable Incorporated Organisations (Consequential Amendments) Order 2012, SI 2012/3014, art 5(a).

Sub-s (2): words in square brackets inserted by SI 2012/3014, art 5(b).

[17.436]

181 Power to waive disqualification

(1) This section applies where a person ("P") is disqualified under section 178(1).

(2) The Commission may, if P makes an application under this subsection, waive P's disqualification—

(a) generally, or

(b) in relation to a particular charity or a particular class of charities.

[(2A) A waiver under subsection (2)—

(a) may relate to the whole of P's disqualification or only to disqualification under section 178(3);

(b) in relation to disqualification under section 178(3) may relate to a particular office or employment or to any office or employment of a particular description.]

(3) If—

(a) P is disqualified under Case D *or E* and makes an application under subsection (2) 5 years or more after the date on which the disqualification took effect, and

(b) the Commission is not prevented from granting the application by subsection (5),

the Commission must grant the application unless satisfied that, because of any special circumstances, it should be refused.

(4) Any waiver under subsection (2) must be notified in writing to P.

(5) No waiver may be granted under subsection (2) in relation to any charitable company [or CIO] if—

(a) P is for the time being prohibited from acting as director of the company [or charity trustee of the CIO (as the case may be)], by virtue of—

(i) a disqualification order or disqualification undertaking under the Company Directors Disqualification Act 1986, or

(ii) a provision of the 1986 Act mentioned in subsection (6), and

(b) leave has not been granted for P to act as [director of any company or charity trustee of any CIO].

(6) The provisions of the 1986 Act are—

section 11(1) (undischarged bankrupts);

section 12(2) (failure to pay under county court administration order);

section 12A (Northern Irish disqualification orders);

section 12B (Northern Irish disqualification undertakings).

NOTES

Sub-s (2A): inserted by the Charities (Protection and Social Investment) Act 2016, s 9(1), (11), (12), as from 1 August 2018.

Sub-s (3): for the words in italics in para (a) there are substituted the words ", E or I", by the Charities (Protection and Social Investment) Act 2016, s 9(1), (11), (13), as from 1 August 2018.

Sub-s (5): first and second words in square brackets inserted and final words in square brackets substituted by the Charitable Incorporated Organisations (Consequential Amendments) Order 2012, SI 2012/3014, art 6.

181A–181D (*Outside the scope of this work.*)

[17.437]
182 Records of persons removed from office
(1) For the purposes of sections 178 to *181* the Commission must keep, in such manner as it thinks fit, a register of *all persons who have been removed from office as mentioned in Case D—*
(a) *by an order of the Commission or the Commissioners made before or after the commencement of section 178(1), or*
(b) *by an order of the High Court made after the commencement of section 45(1) of the Charities Act 1992;*
and, where any person is so removed from office by an order of the High Court, the court must notify the Commission of the person's removal.
[(1A) The register must include all persons who have been removed from office as mentioned in Case D—
(a) by an order of the Commission or the Commissioners made before or after the commencement of section 178(1), or
(b) by an order of the High Court made after the commencement of section 45(1) of the Charities Act 1992;
and, where any person is so removed from office by an order of the High Court, the court must notify the Commission of the person's removal.
(1B) The register must include all persons who have been disqualified by an order of the Commission under section 181A.
(1C) The register must include all persons who have been removed from office by an order of the Commission under section 79A (removal of disqualified trustee).]
(2) The entries in the register kept under subsection (1) must be available for public inspection in legible form at all reasonable times.
(3) In this section "the Commissioners" means the Charity Commissioners for England and Wales.

NOTES
Sub-s (1): for the figure in italics there is substituted "181A", and for the words in italics there are substituted the words "the following.", by the Charities (Protection and Social Investment) Act 2016, s 11(1), (2), as from 1 August 2018.
Sub-s (1A): inserted by the Charities (Protection and Social Investment) Act 2016, s 11(1), (3), (4), as from 1 August 2018.
Sub-ss (1B), (1C): inserted by the Charities (Protection and Social Investment) Act 2016, s 11(1), (5).

[17.438]
183 Criminal consequences of acting while disqualified
(1) Subject to subsection (2), it is an offence for any person to act as a charity trustee or trustee for a charity [or to hold an office or employment] while disqualified from being such a trustee [or from holding that office or employment] by virtue of section 178 [or an order under section 181A].
(2) Subsection (1) does not apply if—
(a) the charity concerned is a company [or a CIO], and
(b) the disqualified person is disqualified by virtue only of Case B[, F or G] [in section 178].
(3) A person guilty of an offence under subsection (1) is liable—
(a) on summary conviction, to imprisonment for a term not exceeding 12 months or to a fine not exceeding the statutory maximum, or both;
(b) on conviction on indictment, to imprisonment for a term not exceeding 2 years or to a fine, or both.

NOTES
Sub-s (1): words in first and second pairs of square brackets inserted (as from 1 August 2018) and words in third pair of square brackets inserted (as from 1 October 2016) by the Charities (Protection and Social Investment) Act 2016, ss 9(1), (14), 10(1), (3)(a).
Sub-s (2): words in square brackets in para (a) inserted by the Charitable Incorporated Organisations (Consequential Amendments) Order 2012, SI 2012/3014, art 7; words in first pair of square brackets in para (b) substituted, in relation to a debt relief restrictions order, an interim debt relief restrictions order, a debt relief restrictions undertaking or interim debt relief restrictions undertaking where the order is made, or (as the case may be) the debtor gives the undertaking, after 1 October 2012, by the Tribunals, Courts and Enforcement Act 2007 (Consequential Amendments) Order 2012, SI 2012/2404, arts 3(2), 6, Sch 2, para 62(5); words in second pair of square brackets in para (b) inserted by the Charities (Protection and Social Investment) Act 2016, s 10(1), (3)(b).

[17.439]
184 Civil consequences of acting while disqualified
(1) Any acts done as charity trustee or trustee for a charity [or as officer or employee of a charity] by a person disqualified from being such a trustee [or from holding that office or employment] by virtue of section 178 [or an order under section 181A] are not invalid merely because of that disqualification.
(2) Subsection (3) applies if the Commission is satisfied that any person—
(a) has acted as charity trustee or trustee for a charity [or as officer or employee of a charity] while disqualified from being such a trustee [or from holding that office or employment] by virtue of section 178 [or an order under section 181A], and
(b) while so acting, has received from the charity any sums by way of remuneration or expenses, or any benefit in kind, in connection with acting as charity trustee or trustee for the charity [or holding the office or employment].
(3) The Commission may by order direct the person—
(a) to repay to the charity the whole or part of any such sums, or
(b) (as the case may be) to pay to the charity the whole or part of the monetary value (as determined by the Commission) of any such benefit.

(4) Subsection (3) does not apply to any sums received by way of remuneration or expenses in respect of any time when the person concerned was not disqualified from being a charity trustee or trustee for the charity.

NOTES

Sub-s (1): words in first and second pairs of square brackets inserted (as from 1 August 2018) and words in third pair of square brackets inserted (as from 1 October 2016) by the Charities (Protection and Social Investment) Act 2016, ss 9(1), (15), (16), 10(1), (4)(a).

Sub-s (2): words in first and second pairs of square brackets in para (a) and words in square brackets in para (b) inserted (as from 1 August 2018), and words in third pair of square brackets in para (a) inserted (as from 1 October 2016), by the Charities (Protection and Social Investment) Act 2016, ss 9(1), (15)–(17), 10(1), (4)(b).

184A–203 *(Ss 184A–192, ss 193–203 (Pt 10) outside the scope of this work.)*

PART 11
CHARITABLE INCORPORATED ORGANISATIONS (CIOS)

CHAPTER 1 GENERAL

Nature and constitution

[17.440]
204 Meaning of "CIO"
In this Act "CIO" means charitable incorporated organisation.

205–244 *(Ss 205–215, ss 216–244 (Chs 2–4) outside the scope of this work.)*

CHAPTER 5 SUPPLEMENTARY

[17.441]
245 Regulations about winding up, insolvency and dissolution
(1) CIO regulations may make provision about—
- (a) the winding up of CIOs,
- (b) their insolvency,
- (c) their dissolution, and
- (d) their revival and restoration to the register following dissolution.

(2) The regulations may, in particular, make provision—
- (a) about the transfer on the dissolution of a CIO of its property and rights (including property and rights held on trust for the CIO) to the official custodian or another person or body;
- (b) requiring any person in whose name any stocks, funds or securities are standing in trust for a CIO to transfer them into the name of the official custodian or another person or body;
- (c) about the disclaiming, by the official custodian or other transferee of a CIO's property, of title to any of that property;
- (d) about the application of a CIO's property cy-près;
- (e) about circumstances in which charity trustees may be personally liable for contributions to the assets of a CIO or for its debts;
- (f) about the reversal on a CIO's revival of anything done on its dissolution.

(3) The regulations may—
- (a) apply any enactment which would not otherwise apply, either without modification or with modifications specified in the regulations,
- (b) disapply, or modify (in ways specified in the regulations) the application of, any enactment which would otherwise apply.

(4) In subsection (3), "enactment" includes a provision of subordinate legislation within the meaning of the Interpretation Act 1978.

NOTES

Regulations: the Charitable Incorporated Organisations (Insolvency and Dissolution) Regulations 2012, SI 2012/3013 at **[18.221]**.

246 *(Outside the scope of this work.)*

[17.442]
247 Meaning of "CIO regulations"
In this Part "CIO regulations" means regulations made by the [Secretary of State].

NOTES

Words in square brackets substituted by the Transfer of Functions (Elections, Referendums, Third Sector and Information) Order 2016, SI 2016/997, art 13, Sch 2, para 25(1), (2)(gg).

248–331 *(Ss 248–250, ss 251–331 (Pts 12–17) outside the scope of this work.)*

PART 18
MISCELLANEOUS AND SUPPLEMENTARY

332–349 *(Outside the scope of this work.)*

Interpretation

350–352 (*Outside the scope of this work.*)

[17.443]
353 Minor definitions

(1) In this Act, except in so far as the context otherwise requires—

"company" means a company registered under the Companies Act 2006 in England and Wales or Scotland;

"the court" means—

(a) the High Court, and

(b) within the limits of its jurisdiction, any other court in England and Wales having a jurisdiction in respect of charities concurrent (within any limit of area or amount) with that of the High Court,

and includes any judge or officer of the court exercising the jurisdiction of the court;

"ecclesiastical charity" has the same meaning as in the Local Government Act 1894;

"financial year"—

(a) in relation to a charitable company, is to be construed in accordance with section 390 of the Companies Act 2006, and

(b) in relation to any other charity, is to be construed in accordance with regulations made by virtue of section 132(3);

but this is subject to any provision of regulations made by virtue of section 142(3) (financial years of subsidiary undertakings);

"gross income", in relation to a charity, means its gross recorded income from all sources including special trusts;

"independent examiner", in relation to a charity, means such a person as is mentioned in section 145(1)(a);

"members", in relation to a charity with a body of members distinct from the charity trustees, means any of those members;

. . .

"trusts"—

(a) in relation to a charity, means the provisions establishing it as a charity and regulating its purposes and administration, whether those provisions take effect by way of trust or not, and

(b) in relation to other institutions has a corresponding meaning.

(2) In this Act, except in so far as the context otherwise requires, "document" includes information recorded in any form, and, in relation to information recorded otherwise than in legible form—

(a) any reference to its production is to be read as a reference to the provision of a copy of it in legible form, and

(b) any reference to the provision of a copy of, or extract from, it is accordingly to be read as a reference to the provision of a copy of, or extract from, it in legible form.

(3) A charity is to be treated for the purposes of this Act as having a permanent endowment unless all property held for the purposes of the charity may be expended for those purposes without distinction between—

(a) capital, and

(b) income;

and in this Act "permanent endowment" means, in relation to any charity, property held subject to a restriction on its being expended for the purposes of the charity.

NOTES

Sub-s (1): definition "the Minister" (omitted) repealed by the Transfer of Functions (Elections, Referendums, Third Sector and Information) Order 2016, SI 2016/997, art 13, Sch 2, Pt 1, para 25(1), (4).

PART 19
FINAL PROVISIONS

354 (*Outside the scope of this work.*)

[17.444]
355 Commencement

This Act comes into force at the end of the period of 3 months beginning with the day on which it is passed.

[17.445]
356 Extent

(1) Subject to subsections (2) to (7), this Act extends to England and Wales only.

(2)–(7) . . .

NOTES

Sub-ss (2)–(7): outside the scope of this work.

357 (*Outside the scope of this work.*)

[17.446]
358 Short title
This Act may be cited as the Charities Act 2011.

SCHEDULES 1–11

(*Schs 1–11 outside the scope of this work.*)

PENSION SCHEMES ACT 2015

(2015 c 8)

ARRANGEMENT OF SECTIONS

PART 2
COLLECTIVE BENEFITS

Winding up

26 Winding up . . . . . [17.447]
27 Requirement to wind up scheme in specified circumstances . . . . . [17.448]
28 Policies about winding up . . . . . [17.449]

Interpretation of Part 2

35 Interpretation of Part 2 . . . . . [17.450]

PART 6
GENERAL

84 Regulations . . . . . [17.451]
86 Regulations: supplementary . . . . . [17.452]
88 Extent . . . . . [17.453]
89 Commencement . . . . . [17.454]
90 Short title . . . . . [17.455]

An Act to make provision about pension schemes, including provision designed to encourage arrangements that offer people different levels of certainty in retirement or that involve different ways of sharing or pooling risk and provision designed to give people greater flexibility in accessing benefits and to help them make informed decisions about what to do with benefits

[3 March 2015]

1–7 (*Outside the scope of this work.*)

PART 2
COLLECTIVE BENEFITS

8–25 (*Outside the scope of this work.*)

Winding up

[17.447]
26 Winding up
(1) Regulations may make provision about the winding up of a pension scheme under which collective benefits may be provided or part of such a scheme.
(2) The regulations may, in particular, make provision about—
(a) the distribution of assets (including any order of priority);
(b) the operation of the scheme during winding up;
(c) the discharge of liabilities;
(d) excess assets on winding up.
(3) The regulations may, in particular—
(a) disapply or amend or otherwise modify the application of any of sections 38, 73, 73A, 73B, 74 and 76 of the Pensions Act 1995 (winding up);
(b) make provision corresponding or similar to any provision made by those sections.

NOTES
Commencement: to be appointed.

[17.448]
27 Requirement to wind up scheme in specified circumstances
(1) Regulations may require the trustees or managers of a pension scheme under which collective benefits may be provided to wind up the whole or part of the scheme in specified circumstances.
(2) The regulations may, in particular—
(a) provide for the winding up of the scheme or part to be as effective in law as if it had been made under powers conferred by or under the scheme;

(b) require the scheme or part to be wound up in spite of any legislative provision, rule of law or provision of a scheme, which would otherwise operate to prevent the winding up;
(c) require the scheme or part to be wound up without regard to any legislative provision, rule of law or provision of a scheme that would otherwise require, or might otherwise be taken to require, the implementation of any procedure or the obtaining of any consent with a view to the winding up.

NOTES

Commencement: to be appointed.

[17.449]
28 Policies about winding up

(1) Regulations may require the trustees or managers of a pension scheme under which collective benefits may be provided—
(a) to have a policy about the winding up of the scheme or part of it;
(b) to follow that policy.
(2) The regulations may, in particular—
(a) require the trustees or managers to consult about the policy;
(b) make provision about the content of the policy;
(c) set out matters that the trustees or managers must take into account, or principles they must follow, in formulating the policy;
(d) make provision about reviewing and revising the policy.
(3) The regulations may, in particular, require the policy—
(a) to contain an explanation of the circumstances in which the trustees or managers are permitted or required to wind up the scheme or part and any requirements about the distribution of assets (including any order of priority);
(b) to contain an explanation of how the trustees or managers intend to use any powers to wind up the scheme or part and how they intend to use any powers in relation to the distribution of assets (including any order of priority);
(c) to contain an explanation of how the costs of winding up are required to be met or how the trustees or managers will use any powers to decide how those costs are to be met.

NOTES

Commencement: to be appointed.

29–34 (*Outside the scope of this work.*)

Interpretation of Part 2

[17.450]
35 Interpretation of Part 2

(1) In this Part—

"collective benefit" has the meaning given by section 8;

. . .

"pension scheme" has the meaning given by section 1(5) of the Pension Schemes Act 1993;
"regulations" means regulations made by the Secretary of State;

. . .

"trustees or managers" means—
(a) in relation to a scheme established under a trust, the trustees, and
(b) in relation to any other scheme, the managers;

. . .

(2) A power conferred by this Part to make provision corresponding or similar to any provision made by a section of another Act includes a power to make provision corresponding or similar to any provision that may be made by regulations under that section.

NOTES

Commencement: to be appointed.
Definitions omitted are outside the scope of this work.

PART 6
GENERAL

83 (*Outside the scope of this work.*)

[17.451]
84 Regulations

(1) Regulations made by the Secretary of State or the Treasury under this Act are to be made by statutory instrument.
(2) (*Outside the scope of this work.*)
(3) Any other statutory instrument containing regulations under this Act is subject to annulment in pursuance of a resolution of either House of Parliament.
(4) Subsection (3) does not apply to a statutory instrument containing regulations under section 89(4) or (6) only.

NOTES

Commencement: 3 March 2015.

85 (*Outside the scope of this work.*)

[17.452]

86 Regulations: supplementary

(1) A power to make regulations under this Act may be used—

(a) to make different provision for different purposes;

(b) in relation to all or only some of the purposes for which it may be used.

(2) Regulations under this Act may include incidental, supplementary, consequential, transitional, transitory or saving provision.

NOTES

Commencement: 3 March 2015.

87 (*Outside the scope of this work.*)

[17.453]

88 Extent

(1) This Act extends to England and Wales and Scotland only, subject to the following provisions of this section.

(2)–(5) (*Outside the scope of this work.*)

NOTES

Commencement: 3 March 2015.

[17.454]

89 Commencement

(1) The following come into force on the day on which this Act is passed—

(a)–(d) *(outside the scope of this work);*

(e) this Part.

(2), (3) (*Outside the scope of this work.*)

(4) The following come into force on such day or days as may be appointed by regulations made by the Secretary of State—

(a) Parts 1 to 3 other than paragraphs 24, 30, 33 and 36 of Schedule 2 (and section 46 so far as relating to those provisions);

(b) *(outside the scope of this work).*

(5) Regulations under subsection (4) may appoint different days for different purposes.

(6) The Secretary of State or the Department for Social Development in Northern Ireland may by regulations make transitional, transitory or saving provision in connection with the coming into force of any provision of this Act.

NOTES

Commencement: 3 March 2015.

Regulations: the Pension Schemes Act 2015 (Commencement No 1) Regulations 2015, SI 2015/1851; the Pensions Act 2014 (Commencement No 11) and the Pension Schemes Act 2015 (Commencement No 2) Regulations 2017, SI 2017/916.

[17.455]

90 Short title

This Act may be cited as the Pension Schemes Act 2015.

NOTES

Commencement: 3 March 2015.

SCHEDULES 1–5

(*Schs 1–5 outside the scope of this work.*)

SMALL BUSINESS, ENTERPRISE AND EMPLOYMENT ACT 2015

(2015 c 26)

ARRANGEMENT OF SECTIONS

PART 10
INSOLVENCY

144 Power to establish single regulator of insolvency practitioners . . . [17.456]
145 Regulations under section 144: designation of existing body . . . [17.457]
146 Regulations under section 144: timing and supplementary . . . [17.458]

PART 12
GENERAL

161 Supplementary provision about regulations . . . .[17.459]
163 Extent. . . . .[17.460]
165 Short title. . . . .[17.461]

SCHEDULES

Schedule 11—Single Regulator of Insolvency Practitioners: Supplementary Provision. . . . .[17.462]

An Act to make provision about improved access to finance for businesses and individuals; to make provision about regulatory provisions relating to business and certain voluntary and community bodies; to make provision about the exercise of procurement functions by certain public authorities; to make provision for the creation of a Pubs Code and Adjudicator for the regulation of dealings by pub-owning businesses with their tied pub tenants; to make provision about the regulation of the provision of childcare; to make provision about information relating to the evaluation of education; to make provision about the regulation of companies; to make provision about company filing requirements; to make provision about the disqualification from appointments relating to companies; to make provision about insolvency; to make provision about the law relating to employment; and for connected purposes

[26 March 2015]

1–116 ((*Pts 1–9*) *outside the scope of this work.*)

PART 10
INSOLVENCY

117–143 (*Outside the scope of this work.*)

Power to Establish Single Regulator of Insolvency Practitioners

[17.456]
144 Power to establish single regulator of insolvency practitioners

(1) The Secretary of State may by regulations designate a body for the purposes of—
(a) authorising persons to act as insolvency practitioners, and
(b) regulating persons acting as such.

(2) The designated body may be either—
(a) a body corporate established by the regulations, or
(b) a body (whether a body corporate or an unincorporated association) already in existence when the regulations are made (an "existing body").

(3) The regulations may, in particular, confer the following functions on the designated body—
(a) establishing criteria for determining whether a person is a fit and proper person to act as an insolvency practitioner;
(b) establishing the requirements as to education, practical training and experience which a person must meet in order to act as an insolvency practitioner;
(c) establishing and maintaining a system for providing full authorisation or partial authorisation to persons who meet those criteria and requirements;
(d) imposing technical standards for persons so authorised and enforcing compliance with those standards;
(e) imposing professional and ethical standards for persons so authorised and enforcing compliance with those standards;
(f) monitoring the performance and conduct of persons so authorised;
(g) investigating complaints made against, and other matters concerning the performance or conduct of, persons so authorised.

(4) The regulations may require the designated body, in discharging regulatory functions, so far as is reasonably practicable, to act in a way—
(a) which is compatible with the regulatory objectives, and
(b) which the body considers most appropriate for the purpose of meeting those objectives.

(5) Provision made under subsection (3)(d) or (3)(e) for the enforcement of the standards concerned may include provision enabling the designated body to impose a financial penalty on a person who is or has been authorised to act as an insolvency practitioner.

(6) The regulations may, in particular, include provision for the purpose of treating a person authorised to act as an insolvency practitioner by virtue of being a member of a professional body recognised under section 391 of the Insolvency Act 1986 immediately before the regulations come into force as authorised to act as an insolvency practitioner by the body designated by the regulations after that time.

(7) Expressions used in this section which are defined for the purposes of Part 13 of the Insolvency Act 1986 have the same meaning in this section as in that Part.

(8) Section 145 makes further provision about regulations under this section which designate an existing body.

(9) Schedule 11 makes supplementary provision in relation to the designation of a body by regulations under this section.

NOTES

Commencement: 1 October 2015.

[17.457]

145 Regulations under section 144: designation of existing body

(1) The Secretary of State may make regulations under section 144 designating an existing body only if it appears to the Secretary of State that—

(a) the body is able and willing to exercise the functions that would be conferred by the regulations, and

(b) the body has arrangements in place relating to the exercise of those functions which are such as to be likely to ensure that the conditions in subsection (2) are met.

(2) The conditions are—

(a) that the functions in question will be exercised effectively, and

(b) where the regulations are to contain any requirements or other provisions prescribed under subsection (3), that those functions will be exercised in accordance with any such requirements or provisions.

(3) Regulations which designate an existing body may contain such requirements or other provisions relating to the exercise of the functions by the designated body as appear to the Secretary of State to be appropriate.

NOTES

Commencement: 1 October 2015.

[17.458]

146 Regulations under section 144: timing and supplementary

(1) Section 144 and, accordingly, section 145 and subsections (3) and (4) below expire at the end of the relevant period unless the power conferred by subsection (1) of section 144 is exercised before the end of that period.

(2) The "relevant period" is the period of 7 years beginning with the day on which section 144 comes into force.

(3) Regulations under section 144 are subject to affirmative resolution procedure.

(4) If a draft of a statutory instrument containing regulations under section 144 would, apart from this subsection, be treated for the purposes of the Standing Orders of either House of Parliament as a hybrid instrument, it is to proceed in that House as if it were not a hybrid instrument.

NOTES

Commencement: 1 October 2015.

147–158 *((Pt 11) outside the scope of this work.)*

PART 12
GENERAL

159, 160 *(Outside the scope of this work.)*

[17.459]

161 Supplementary provision about regulations

(1) Regulations under this Act, other than regulations made by the Scottish Ministers under section 1[, 153A] or 154(1), are to be made by statutory instrument.

(2) Regulations under this Act may make—

(a) different provision for different purposes or cases;

(b) different provision for different areas;

(c) provision generally or for specific cases;

(d) provision subject to exceptions;

(e) incidental, supplementary, consequential, transitional or transitory provision or savings.

(3) Where regulations under this Act are subject to "negative resolution procedure" the statutory instrument containing the regulations is subject to annulment in pursuance of a resolution of either House of Parliament.

(4) Where regulations under this Act are subject to "affirmative resolution procedure" the regulations may not be made unless a draft of the statutory instrument containing them has been laid before Parliament and approved by a resolution of each House of Parliament.

(5) Any provision that may be included in an instrument under this Act for which no Parliamentary procedure is prescribed may be made by regulations subject to negative or affirmative resolution procedure.

(6) Any provision that may be included in an instrument under this Act subject to negative resolution procedure may be made by regulations subject to affirmative resolution procedure.

NOTES

Commencement: 26 March 2015.

Sub-s (1): reference in square brackets inserted by the Enterprise Act 2016, s 41(2), Sch 6, paras 1, 3, as from a day to be appointed.

162 *(Outside the scope of this work.)*

[17.460]
163 Extent
(1) Subject to subsections (2) to (4), this Act extends to England and Wales, Scotland and Northern Ireland.
(2), (3) (*Outside the scope of this work.*)
(4) In Part 10, sections 144 to 146 and Schedule 11 extend to England and Wales and Scotland only.

NOTES
Commencement: 26 March 2015.

164 (*Outside the scope of this work.*)

[17.461]
165 Short title
This Act may be cited as the Small Business, Enterprise and Employment Act 2015.

NOTES
Commencement: 26 March 2015.

SCHEDULES 1–10

(*Schs 1–10 outside the scope of this work.*)

SCHEDULE 11
SINGLE REGULATOR OF INSOLVENCY PRACTITIONERS: SUPPLEMENTARY PROVISION

Section 144

[17.462]

Operation of this Schedule

1 (1) This Schedule has effect in relation to regulations under section 144 designating a body (referred to in this Schedule as "the Regulations") as follows—
(a) paragraphs 2 to 13 have effect where the Regulations establish the body;
(b) paragraphs 6, 7 and 9 to 13 have effect where the Regulations designate an existing body (see section 144(2)(b));
(c) paragraph 14 also has effect where the Regulations designate an existing body that is an unincorporated association.

(2) Provision made in the Regulations by virtue of paragraph 6 or 12, where that paragraph has effect as mentioned in sub-paragraph (1)(b), may only apply in relation to—
(a) things done by or in relation to the body in or in connection with the exercise of functions conferred on it by the Regulations, and
(b) functions of the body which are functions so conferred.

Name, members and chair

2 (1) The Regulations must prescribe the name by which the body is to be known.
(2) The Regulations must provide that the members of the body must be appointed by the Secretary of State after such consultation as the Secretary of State thinks appropriate.
(3) The Regulations must provide that the Secretary of State must appoint one of the members as the chair of the body.
(4) The Regulations may include provision about—
(a) the terms on which the members of the body hold and vacate office;
(b) the terms on which the person appointed as the chair holds and vacates that office.

Remuneration etc

3 (1) The Regulations must provide that the body must pay to its chair and members such remuneration and allowances in respect of expenses properly incurred by them in the exercise of their functions as the Secretary of State may determine.
(2) The Regulations must provide that, as regards any member (including the chair) in whose case the Secretary of State so determines, the body must pay or make provision for the payment of—
(a) such pension, allowance or gratuity to or in respect of that person on retirement or death as the Secretary of State may determine, or
(b) such contributions or other payment towards the provision of such a pension, allowance or gratuity as the Secretary of State may determine.

(3) The Regulations must provide that where—
(a) a person ceases to be a member of the body otherwise than on the expiry of the term of office, and
(b) it appears to the Secretary of State that there are special circumstances which make it right for that person to be compensated,

the body must make a payment to the person by way of compensation of such amount as the Secretary of State may determine.

Staff

4 The Regulations must provide that—
(a) the body may appoint such persons to be its employees as the body considers appropriate, and
(b) the employees are to be appointed on such terms and conditions as the body may determine.

Proceedings

5 (1) The Regulations may make provision about the proceedings of the body.
(2) The Regulations may, in particular—
(a) authorise the body to exercise any function by means of committees consisting wholly or partly of members of the body;
(b) provide that the validity of proceedings of the body, or of any such committee, is not affected by any vacancy among the members or any defect in the appointment of a member.

Fees

6 (1) The Regulations may make provision—
(a) about the setting and charging of fees by the body in connection with the exercise of its functions;
(b) for the retention by the body of any such fees payable to it;
(c) about the application by the body of such fees.
(2) The Regulations may, in particular, make provision—
(a) for the body to be able to set such fees as appear to it to be sufficient to defray the expenses of the body exercising its functions, taking one year with another;
(b) for the setting of fees by the body to be subject to the approval of the Secretary of State.
(3) The expenses referred to in sub-paragraph (2)(a) include any expenses incurred by the body on such staff, accommodation, services and other facilities as appear to it to be necessary or expedient for the proper exercise of its functions.

Consultation

7 The Regulations may make provision as to the circumstances and manner in which the body must consult others before exercising any function conferred on it by the Regulations.

Training and other services

8 (1) The Regulations may make provision authorising the body to provide training or other services to any person.
(2) The Regulations may make provision authorising the body—
(a) to charge for the provision of any such training or other services, and
(b) to calculate any such charge on the basis that it considers to be the appropriate commercial basis.

Report and accounts

9 (1) The Regulations must require the body, at least once in each 12 month period, to report to the Secretary of State on—
(a) the exercise of the functions conferred on it by the Regulations, and
(b) such other matters as may be prescribed in the Regulations.
(2) The Regulations must require the Secretary of State to lay before Parliament a copy of each report received under this paragraph.
(3) Unless section 394 of the Companies Act 2006 applies to the body (duty on every company to prepare individual accounts), the Regulations must provide that the Secretary of State may give directions to the body with respect to the preparation of its accounts.
(4) Unless the body falls within sub-paragraph (5), the Regulations must provide that the Secretary of State may give directions to the body with respect to the audit of its accounts.
(5) The body falls within this sub-paragraph if it is a company whose accounts—
(a) are required to be audited in accordance with Part 16 of the Companies Act 2006 (see section 475 of that Act), or
(b) are exempt from the requirements of that Part under section 482 of that Act (non-profit making companies subject to public sector audit).
(6) The Regulations may provide that, whether or not section 394 of the Companies Act 2006 applies to the body, the Secretary of State may direct that any provisions of that Act specified in the directions are to apply to the body with or without modifications.

Funding

10 The Regulations may provide that the Secretary of State may make grants to the body.

Financial penalties

11 (1) This paragraph applies where the Regulations include provision enabling the body to impose a financial penalty on a person who is, or has been, authorised to act as an insolvency practitioner (see section 144(5)).
(2) The Regulations—
(a) must include provision about how the body is to determine the amount of a penalty, and

(b) may, in particular, prescribe a minimum or maximum amount.

(3) The Regulations must provide that, unless the Secretary of State (with the consent of the Treasury) otherwise directs, income from penalties imposed by the body is to be paid into the Consolidated Fund.

(4) The Regulations may also, in particular—

(a) include provision for a penalty imposed by the body to be enforced as a debt;

(b) prescribe conditions that must be met before any action to enforce a penalty may be taken.

Status etc

12 The Regulations must provide that—

(a) the body is not to be regarded as acting on behalf of the Crown, and

(b) its members, officers and employees are not to be regarded as Crown servants.

Transfer schemes

13 (1) This paragraph applies if the Regulations make provision designating a body (whether one established by the Regulations or one already in existence) in place of a body designated by earlier regulations under section 144; and those bodies are referred to as the "new body" and the "former body" respectively.

(2) The Regulations may make provision authorising the Secretary of State to make a scheme (a "transfer scheme") for the transfer of property, rights and liabilities from the former body to the new body.

(3) The Regulations may provide that a transfer scheme may include provision—

(a) about the transfer of property, rights and liabilities that could not otherwise be transferred;

(b) about the transfer of property acquired, and rights and liabilities arising, after the making of the scheme.

(4) The Regulations may provide that a transfer scheme may make consequential, supplementary, incidental or transitional provision and may in particular—

(a) create rights, or impose liabilities, in relation to property or rights transferred;

(b) make provision about the continuing effect of things done by the former body in respect of anything transferred;

(c) make provision about the continuation of things (including legal proceedings) in the process of being done by, on behalf of or in relation to the former body in respect of anything transferred;

(d) make provision for references to the former body in an instrument or other document in respect of anything transferred to be treated as references to the new body;

(e) make provision for the shared ownership or use of property;

(f) if the TUPE regulations do not apply to in relation to the transfer, make provision which is the same or similar.

(5) The Regulations must provide that, where the former body is an existing body, a transfer scheme may only make provision in relation to—

(a) things done by or in relation to the former body in or in connection with the exercise of functions conferred on it by previous regulations under section 144, and

(b) functions of the body which are functions so conferred.

(6) In sub-paragraph (4)(f), "TUPE regulations" means the Transfer of Undertakings (Protection of Employment) Regulations 2006 (SI 2006/246).

(7) In this paragraph—

(a) references to rights and liabilities include rights and liabilities relating to a contract of employment;

(b) references to the transfer of property include the grant of a lease.

Additional provision where body is unincorporated association

14 (1) This paragraph applies where the body is an unincorporated association.

(2) The Regulations must provide that any relevant proceedings may be brought by or against the body in the name of any body corporate whose constitution provides for the establishment of the body.

(3) In sub-paragraph (2) "relevant proceedings" means proceedings brought in or in connection with the exercise of any function conferred on the body by the Regulations.

NOTES

Commencement: 1 October 2015.

REGULATION AND INSPECTION OF SOCIAL CARE (WALES) ACT 2016

(2016 anaw 2)

An Act of the National Assembly for Wales to make provision for the registration and regulation of persons providing care home services, secure accommodation services, residential family centre services, adoption services, fostering services, adult placement services, advocacy services and domiciliary support services, amending the Social Services and Well-being (Wales) Act 2014 in connection with the regulation of the social services functions of local authorities, for the renaming of the Care Council for Wales as Social Care Wales, for Social Care Wales to provide advice and other assistance to persons providing services involving care and support, for the registration, regulation and training of social care workers, and for connected purposes.

[18 January 2016]

NOTES

Note: only the provision of this Act relevant to this work is reproduced; the remainder is not annotated.

[17.463]

30 Regulations about service providers who are liquidated etc

(1) The Welsh Ministers may by regulations make provision—

(a) requiring an appointed person to notify them of that appointment;

(b) for this Part to apply with prescribed modifications to service providers in relation to whom such a person has been appointed.

(2) In subsection (1) "appointed person" means a person appointed as—

(a) a receiver or administrative receiver of the property of a service provider who is a body corporate or a partnership;

(b) a liquidator, provisional liquidator or administrator of a service provider who is a body corporate or a partnership;

(c) a trustee in bankruptcy of a service provider who is an individual or a partnership.

NOTES

Commencement: 2 April 2018.

Regulations: the Regulated Services (Service Providers and Responsible Individuals) (Wales) Regulations 2017, SI 2017/1264.

PART 18
MISCELLANEOUS STATUTORY INSTRUMENTS

LANDFILL TAX REGULATIONS 1996

(SI 1996/1527)

NOTES

Made: 12 June 1996.

Authority: Finance Act 1996, ss 47(9), 48(1), (2), 49, 51(1)–(6), 52(1)–(3), 53(1)–(4), 58(1), (4)–(6), 61(2), 62(1)–(3), (5), (6), 68(1)–(6), Sch 5, paras 2(1)–(3), 13(1), (6), 14(5), 20(3), 23(1), 42(1)–(5), 43(1)–(5).

Commencement: 1 August 1996.

PART I
PRELIMINARY

[18.1]

1 Citation and commencement

These Regulations may be cited as the Landfill Tax Regulations 1996 and shall come into force on 1st August 1996.

2–44 *(Regs 2, 3, regs 4–44 (Pts II–X) outside the scope of this work.)*

PART XI
SET-OFF OF AMOUNTS

[18.2]

45 Landfill tax amount owed to Commissioners

(1) Subject to regulation 47, this regulation applies where—

(a) a person is under a duty to pay to the Commissioners at any time an amount or amounts in respect of landfill tax; and

(b) the Commissioners are under a duty to pay to that person at the same time an amount or amounts in respect of any tax or taxes under their care and management.

(2) Where the total of the amount or amounts mentioned in paragraph (1)(a) above exceeds the total of the amount or amounts mentioned in paragraph (1)(b) above, the latter shall be set off against the former.

(3) Where the total of the amount or amounts mentioned in paragraph (1)(b) above exceeds the total of the amount or amounts mentioned in paragraph (1)(a) above, the Commissioners may set off the latter in paying the former.

(4) Where the total of the amount or amounts mentioned in paragraph (1)(a) above is the same as the total of the amount or amounts mentioned in paragraph (1)(b) above, no payment need be made in respect of either.

(5) Where this regulation applies and an amount has been set off in accordance with any of paragraphs (2) to (4) above, the duty of both the person and the Commissioners to pay the amount or amounts concerned shall be treated as having been discharged accordingly.

(6) References in paragraph (1) above to an amount in respect of a particular tax include references not only to an amount of tax itself but also to amounts of penalty, surcharge or interest.

(7) In this regulation "tax" includes "duty".

[18.3]

46 Landfill tax amount owed by Commissioners

(1) Subject to regulation 47, this regulation applies where—

(a) a person is under a duty to pay to the Commissioners at any time an amount or amounts in respect of any tax or taxes under their care and management; and

(b) the Commissioners are under a duty to pay to that person at the same time an amount or amounts in respect of landfill tax.

(2) Where the total of the amount or amounts mentioned in paragraph (1)(a) above exceeds the total of the amount or amounts mentioned in paragraph (1)(b) above, the latter shall be set off against the former.

(3) Where the total of the amount or amounts mentioned in paragraph (1)(b) above exceeds the total of the amount or amounts mentioned in paragraph (1)(a) above, the Commissioners may set off the latter in paying the former.

(4) Where the total of the amount or amounts mentioned in paragraph (1)(a) above is the same as the total of the amount or amounts mentioned in paragraph (1)(b) above, no payment need be made in respect of either.

(5) Where this regulation applies and an amount has been set off in accordance with any of paragraphs (2) to (4) above, the duty of both the person and the Commissioners to pay the amount or amounts concerned shall be treated as having been discharged accordingly.

(6) Paragraphs (6) and (7) of regulation 45 shall apply in relation to this regulation as they apply in relation to that regulation.

[18.4]
47 No set-off where insolvency procedure applied

(1) Neither regulation 45 nor 46 shall require any such amount as is mentioned in paragraph (1)(b) of those regulations (in either case, "the credit") to be set against any such sum as is mentioned in paragraph (1)(a) of those regulations (in either case, "the debit") in any case where—

(a) an insolvency procedure has been applied to the person entitled to the credit;
(b) the credit became due after that procedure was so applied;
(c) the liability to pay the debit either arose before that procedure was so applied or (having risen afterwards) relates to, or to matters occurring in the course of—
  (i) the carrying on of any business; or
  (ii) in the case of any sum such as is mentioned in regulation 46(1)(b), the carrying out of taxable activities,

at times before the procedure was so applied.

(2) Subject to paragraph (3) below, the following are the times when an insolvency procedure is to be taken, for the purposes of this regulation, to have been applied to any person, that is to say—

(a) when a bankruptcy order, winding-up order, . . . or award of sequestration is made in relation to that person [or that person enters administration];
(b) when that person is put into administrative receivership;
(c) when that person, being a corporation, passes a resolution for voluntary winding-up;
(d) when any voluntary arrangement approved in accordance with Part I or Part VIII of the Insolvency Act 1986, or Part II or Chapter II of Part VIII of the Insolvency (Northern Ireland) Order 1989, comes into force in relation to that person;
(e) when a deed of arrangement registered in accordance with . . . Chapter I of Part VIII of that Order of 1989 takes effect in relation to that person;
(f) when that person's estate becomes vested in any other person as that person's trustee under a trust deed.

(3) References in this regulation, in relation to any person, to the application of an insolvency procedure to that person shall not include—

(a) the making of a bankruptcy order, winding-up order, . . . or award of sequestration [or that person entering administration] at a time when any such arrangements or deed as is mentioned in paragraph (2)(d) to (f) above is in force in relation to that person;
(b) the making of a winding-up order at any of the following times—
  (i) immediately upon [the appointment of the administrator ceasing to have effect];
  (ii) when that person is being wound-up voluntarily;
  (iii) when that person is in administrative receivership; or
(c) the making of an administration order in relation to that person at any time when that person is in administrative receivership.

(4) For the purposes of this regulation a person shall be regarded as being in administrative receivership throughout any continuous period for which (disregarding any temporary vacancy in the office of receiver) there is an administrative receiver of that person, and the reference in paragraph (2) above to a person being put into administrative receivership shall be construed accordingly.

NOTES

Para (2): in sub-para (a) words omitted revoked, and words in square brackets inserted, by the Enterprise Act 2002 (Insolvency) Order 2003, SI 2003/2096, arts 5, 6, Schedule, para 67(a), except in any case where a petition for an administration order was presented before 15 September 2003; in sub-para (e) words omitted revoked by the Deregulation Act 2015 (Insolvency) (Consequential Amendments and Transitional and Savings Provisions) Order 2015, SI 2015/1641, art 6, Sch 3, para 3(4).

Para (3): in sub-para (a) words omitted revoked, words in square brackets inserted, and in sub-para (b) words in square brackets substituted for words "the discharge of an administration order made in relation to that person", by SI 2003/2096, arts 5, 6, Schedule, para 67(b), except in any case where a petition for an administration order was presented before 15 September 2003.

A48, 48, 49 *((Pt XII) outside the scope of this work.)*

SCHEDULE

(Schedule outside the scope of this work.)

LOCAL AUTHORITIES (CONTRACTING OUT OF TAX BILLING, COLLECTION AND ENFORCEMENT FUNCTIONS) ORDER 1996

(SI 1996/1880)

NOTES

Made: 17 July 1996.
Authority: Deregulation and Contracting Out Act 1994, ss 70(2), (4), 77(1) Sch 16, para 3.
Commencement: 18 July 1996.

PART I
GENERAL

[18.5]
1 Title, commencement and interpretation

(1) This Order may be cited as the Local Authorities (Contracting Out of Tax Billing, Collection and Enforcement Functions) Order 1996 and shall come into force on the day immediately following the day on which it is made.

(2) In this Order, "contractor" means any person to whom an authorisation is given by virtue of Part II, Part IV or Part VI of this Order, and includes the employees of that person.

(3) *(Inserted by the Tribunals, Courts and Enforcement Act 2007 (Consequential, Transitional and Saving Provision) Order 2014, SI 2014/600; outside the scope of this work.)*

2–30 *((Pts II, III) outside the scope of this work.)*

PART IV
COMMUNITY CHARGES: CONTRACTING OUT

31–42 *(Outside the scope of this work.)*

[18.6]
43 Insolvency

Subject to article 70, an authority may authorise a contractor for the purposes of collecting a community charge to present to the court—

(a) in respect of an amount equal to any outstanding sum which is or forms part of the amount for which a liability order has been made against a debtor who is an individual, a petition for a bankruptcy order to be made against the debtor under section 264 of the Insolvency Act 1986 (who may present a bankruptcy petition); and

(b) in respect of an amount equal to any outstanding sum which is or forms part of the amount for which a liability order has been made against a debtor which is a company or an unregistered company, a petition for an order to be made under section 125 of that Act (powers of court on hearing of petition) for the winding up of the company.

44–47 *(Art 44, arts 45–47 (Pt V) outside the scope of this work.)*

PART VI
NON-DOMESTIC RATING: CONTRACTING OUT

48–58 *(Outside the scope of this work.)*

[18.7]
59 Insolvency

Subject to article 70, an authority may authorise a contractor for the purposes of collecting non-domestic rates to present to the court—

(a) in respect of an amount equal to any outstanding sum which is or forms part of the amount for which a liability order has been made against a debtor who is an individual, a petition for a bankruptcy order to be made against the debtor under section 264 of the Insolvency Act 1986 (who may present a bankruptcy petition); and

(b) in respect of an amount equal to any outstanding sum which is or forms part of the amount for which a liability order has been made against a debtor which is a company, a petition for an order to be made under that Act for the winding up of the company.

60–76 *(Art 60, arts 61–76 (Pts VII–IX) outside the scope of this work.)*

COMMONHOLD (LAND REGISTRATION) RULES 2004

(SI 2004/1830)

NOTES

Made: 14 July 2004.
Authority: Commonhold and Leasehold Reform Act 2002, s 65.
Commencement: 27 September 2004 (see r 1 at **[18.8]**).

General

[18.8]
1 Citation and commencement

These rules may be cited as the Commonhold (Land Registration) Rules 2004 and shall come into force on the day that section 2 of the Act comes into force.

NOTES

Section 2 of the Act: brought into force on 27 September 2004 by the Commonhold and Leasehold Reform Act 2002 (Commencement No 4) Order 2004, SI 2004/1832, art 2.

[18.9]
2 Interpretation

(1) In these rules—

"the Act" means Part 1 of the Commonhold and Leasehold Reform Act 2002,

"commonhold entries" means the entries referred to in paragraphs (a) to (c) of rule 28(1) and

"main rules" means the Land Registration Rules 2003.

(2) In these rules except where otherwise stated, a form referred to by letters or numbers means the form so designated in Schedule 1 to these rules.

3 (*Outside the scope of this work.*)

Applications

4–20 (*Outside the scope of this work.*)

[18.10]
21 Termination application following a voluntary winding up

(1) A termination application must be—

(a) made in Form CM5, and

(b) accompanied by the order, appointment by the Secretary of State or resolution under which the liquidator was appointed and such other evidence as the Registrar may require.

(2) Where a termination application is made and the liquidator notifies the Registrar that he is content with the termination statement, or sends to the Registrar a copy of the court's determination of the terms of the termination statement, the Registrar must—

(a) enter the commonhold association as proprietor of the commonhold units, and

(b) cancel the commonhold entries on every registered title affected.

[18.11]
22 Application to terminate a commonhold registration following the winding-up of a commonhold association by the court

(1) An application to terminate a commonhold registration where the court has made a winding-up order in respect of a commonhold association and has not made a succession order must be made in Form CM5.

(2) When the Registrar has received notification under section 54(2)(c) to (f) of the Act, and is otherwise satisfied that the application is in order, he may cancel the commonhold entries on the registered titles affected.

[18.12]
23 Registration of a successor commonhold association

(1) Where a succession order is made, an application must be made to the Registrar to register the successor commonhold association in Form CM6.

(2) Unless the Registrar otherwise directs, the application must be accompanied by—

(a) the succession order,

(b) the [articles of association] of the successor commonhold association, and

(c) the winding up order.

(3) When satisfied that the application is in order, the Registrar must—

(a) cancel the note of the [articles of association] of the insolvent commonhold association in the property register of the registered title to the common parts,

(b) enter a note of the [articles of association] of the successor commonhold association in the property register of the registered title to the common parts, and

(c) give effect to the terms of the succession order in the individual registers of the registered titles affected.

(4) Where a succession order includes provisions falling within section 52(4) of the Act, the successor commonhold association must make an application to give effect in the register to those provisions so far as necessary.

NOTES

Paras (2), (3): words in square brackets substituted by the Commonhold (Land Registration) (Amendment) Rules 2009, SI 2009/2024, r 5.

24–32 (*Outside the scope of this work.*)

SCHEDULES 1 AND 2

(*Schs 1, 2 outside the scope of this work.*)

BUSINESS IMPROVEMENT DISTRICTS (ENGLAND) REGULATIONS 2004

(SI 2004/2443)

NOTES

Made: 16 September 2004.

Authority: Local Government and Housing Act 1989, s 150(1)–(3); Local Government Act 2003, ss 47(4), 48(1), (2), 49(2), 51(2), (3), 52(2), 54(4), (5), 55(1), (2), 56(1), 123(2).

Commencement: 17 September 2004.

[18.13]

1 Application, citation, commencement and interpretation

(1) These Regulations, which apply in England only, may be cited as the Business Improvement Districts (England) Regulations 2004 and shall come into force on the day after the day on which they are made.

(2) In these Regulations—

. . .

"the 1989 Regulations" means the Non-Domestic Rating (Collection and Enforcement) (Local Lists) Regulations 1989 as modified by paragraph 9 of Schedule 4 below;

. . .

"liability order" has the meaning given in regulation 10 of the 1989 Regulations;

. . .

NOTES

Definitions omitted outside the scope of this work.

1A–21 *(Outside the scope of this work.)*

SCHEDULES 1–3

(Schs 1–3 outside the scope of this work.)

SCHEDULE 4
IMPOSITION, ADMINISTRATION, COLLECTION, RECOVERY AND APPLICATION OF THE BID LEVY

Regulation 15

[18.14]

1–12 *(Outside the scope of this work.)*

13 Joint owners and occupiers: enforcement

(1)–(7) *(Outside the scope of this work.)*

(8) Where a liability order has been made against more than one person in respect of an amount, and a warrant of commitment is issued against (or a term of imprisonment is fixed in the case of) one of them under regulation 16(3) of the 1989 Regulations, no steps, or no further steps, may be taken against any of them by way of [the Schedule 12 procedure], bankruptcy or winding up in relation to the amount mentioned in regulation 16(4) of the 1989 Regulations.

(9) Where a liability order has been made against more than one person in respect of an amount—

(a) steps by way of [the Schedule 12 procedure], commitment, bankruptcy or winding up may not be taken against a person in respect of the amount while steps by way of another of those methods are being taken against him in respect of it; and

(b) subject to sub-paragraph (10), steps by way of [the Schedule 12 procedure] may not be taken against a person in respect of an amount whilst steps by way of [the Schedule 12 procedure] are being taken against one of the others in respect of it.

(10)–(14) *(Outside the scope of this work.)*

14 Enforcement in relation to partnerships

(1)–(4) *(Outside the scope of this work.)*

[(5) Where a liability order is made against partners in their firm name, regulation 18(2) of the 1989 Regulations shall have effect as if the reference to a company included a reference to the partnership and the reference to section 221(5)(b) of the Insolvency Act 1986 were—

(a) in a case where article 7 of the Insolvent Partnerships Order 1994 applies, a reference to section 221(7)(b) of that Act as modified by article 7(2) of and Part 1 of Schedule 3 to that Order; or

(b) in a case where article 8 of that Order applies, a reference to section 221(8)(a) of that Act as modified by article 8(2) of and Part 1 of Schedule 4 to that Order.]

(6) Where a liability order is made against partners in their firm name, paragraph 13(9)(a) does not preclude insolvency proceedings being brought against the partnership as well as against members of the partnership, and those proceedings being dealt with in accordance with the Insolvent Partnerships Order 1994.

NOTES

Para 13: sub-paras (8), (9), words in square brackets substituted by the Tribunals, Courts and Enforcement Act 2007 (Consequential, Transitional and Saving Provision) Order 2014, SI 2014/600, art 7, Schedule, Pt 1, para 9(1), (2)(d)(iii).

Para 14: sub-para (5) substituted by the Business Improvement Districts (England) (Amendment) Regulations 2013, SI 2013/2265, regs 2, 7(c).

SCHEDULE 5

(*Outside the scope of this work.*)

PENSION PROTECTION FUND (MULTI-EMPLOYER SCHEMES) (MODIFICATION) REGULATIONS 2005

(SI 2005/441)

NOTES

Made: 2 March 2005.

Authority: Pensions Act 2004, ss 307(1)(b), (2)(b), (e), 315(1), (2), (4), (5), 318(1), (4)(a).

Commencement: see reg 1(1) at **[18.15]**.

ARRANGEMENT OF REGULATIONS

PART 1
PRELIMINARY

1 Citation, commencement and interpretation . . . [18.15]

PART 2
SEGREGATED SCHEMES:

SINGLE EMPLOYER SECTIONS

2 Application and effect . . . [18.16]
3 Notification of insolvency events, confirmation of scheme status etc . . . [18.17]
4 Eligible schemes . . . [18.18]
5 Board's duty where application or notification received under section 129 . . . [18.19]
6 Protected liabilities and assessment periods . . . [18.20]
7 Directions and power to validate contraventions of section 135 . . . [18.21]
8 Valuation of assets . . . [18.22]
9 Refusal to assume responsibility for a scheme . . . [18.23]
10 Reconsideration and duty to assume responsibility for a scheme following reconsideration . . . [18.24]
11 Closed schemes and requirement to wind up schemes with sufficient assets to meet protected liabilities . . . [18.25]
12 Transfer notices and assumption of responsibility . . . [18.26]
13 The pension compensation provisions . . . [18.27]

PART 3
SEGREGATED SCHEMES:

MULTI-EMPLOYER SECTIONS WITHOUT REQUIREMENT FOR PARTIAL WIND UP ON WITHDRAWAL OF A PARTICIPATING EMPLOYER

14 Application and effect . . . [18.28]
15 Notification of insolvency events, confirmation of scheme status etc . . . [18.29]
16 Eligible schemes . . . [18.30]
17 Duty to assume responsibility for schemes . . . [18.31]
18 Board's duty where application or notification received under section 129 . . . [18.32]
19 Protected liabilities . . . [18.33]
20 Assessment periods . . . [18.34]
21 Directions . . . [18.35]
22 Power to validate contraventions of section 135 and Board to act as creditor of the employer . . . [18.36]
23 Valuation of assets . . . [18.37]
24 Refusal to assume responsibility for a scheme . . . [18.38]

25 Reconsideration, closed schemes and requirement to wind up schemes with sufficient assets to meet protected liabilities . . . . [18.39]
26 Transfer notice and assumption of responsibility for a scheme . . . . [18.40]
27 The pension compensation provisions . . . . [18.41]

PART 4
SEGREGATED SCHEMES:

NON-SEGREGATED MULTI-EMPLOYER SECTIONS OF SEGREGATED SCHEMES WITH REQUIREMENT FOR PARTIAL WIND UP ON WITHDRAWAL OF PARTICIPATING EMPLOYER

28 Application and effect . . . . [18.42]
29 Notification of insolvency events, confirmation of scheme status etc . . . . [18.43]
30 Eligible schemes . . . . [18.44]
31 Duty to assume responsibility for schemes . . . . [18.45]
32 Board's duty where application or notification received under section 129 . . . . [18.46]
33 Protected liabilities . . . . [18.47]
34 Assessment periods . . . . [18.48]
35 Directions . . . . [18.49]
36 Restrictions on winding up, discharge of liabilities etc, and power to validate contraventions of section 135 . . . . [18.50]
37 Board to act as creditor of the employer . . . . [18.51]
37A Ill health pensions . . . . [18.52]
38 Valuation of assets . . . . [18.53]
39 Refusal to assume responsibility for a scheme . . . . [18.54]
40 Reconsideration . . . . [18.55]
41 Closed schemes, requirement to wind up schemes with sufficient assets and applications and notifications where closed schemes have insufficient assets . . . . [18.56]
42 Transfer notices and assumption of responsibility for a scheme . . . . [18.57]
43 Further actuarial valuation of segregated parts . . . . [18.58]
44 The pension compensation provisions . . . . [18.59]

PART 5
NON-SEGREGATED SCHEMES:

SCHEMES WITH A REQUIREMENT FOR PARTIAL WIND UP ON THE WITHDRAWAL OF A PARTICIPATING EMPLOYER

45 Application and effect . . . . [18.60]
46 Notification of insolvency events, confirmation of scheme status etc . . . . [18.61]
47 Eligible schemes . . . . [18.62]
48 Duty to assume responsibility for schemes . . . . [18.63]
49 Board's duty where application or notification received under section 129 . . . . [18.64]
50 Protected liabilities and assessment period . . . . [18.65]
51 Directions . . . . [18.66]
52 Restrictions on winding up, discharge of liabilities etc and power to validate contraventions of section 135 . . . . [18.67]
53 Board to act as creditor of the employer . . . . [18.68]
53A Ill health pensions . . . . [18.69]
54 Valuation of assets . . . . [18.70]
55 Refusal to assume responsibility for a scheme . . . . [18.71]
56 Reconsideration . . . . [18.72]
57 Closed schemes, requirement to wind up schemes with sufficient assets and applications and notifications where closed schemes have insufficient assets . . . . [18.73]
58 Transfer notices and assumption of responsibility for a scheme . . . . [18.74]
59 Further actuarial valuation of segregated parts . . . . [18.75]
60 The pension compensation provisions . . . . [18.76]

PART 6
NON-SEGREGATED SCHEMES:

SCHEMES WITHOUT PROVISION FOR PARTIAL WIND UP ON WITHDRAWAL OF A PARTICIPATING EMPLOYER

61 Application and effect . . . . [18.77]
62 Notification of insolvency events, confirmation of scheme status etc . . . . [18.78]
63 Eligible schemes . . . . [18.79]
64 Duty to assume responsibility for schemes . . . . [18.80]
65 Applications and notifications and Board's duty where application or notification received under section 129 . . . . [18.81]

66 Assessment periods . . . . . . [18.82]
67 Power to validate contraventions of section 135 and Board to act as creditor of the employer . . . . . . [18.83]
68 Valuation of assets . . . . . . [18.84]
69 Refusal to assume responsibility . . . . . . [18.85]
70 Transfer notice and the pension compensation provisions. . . . . . . [18.86]

PART 7
NON-SEGREGATED SCHEME WITH AN OPTION TO SEGREGATE ON THE WITHDRAWAL OF A PARTICIPATING EMPLOYER

71 Application and effect . . . . . . [18.87]

PART 8
SEGREGATED SCHEMES:

MULTI-EMPLOYER SECTIONS OF SEGREGATED SCHEMES WITH AN OPTION TO SEGREGATE ON THE WITHDRAWAL OF A PARTICIPATING EMPLOYER

72 Application and effect . . . . . . [18.88]

PART 1
PRELIMINARY

[18.15]

1 Citation, commencement and interpretation

(1) These Regulations may be cited as the Pension Protection Fund (Multi-employer Schemes) (Modification) Regulations 2005 and shall come into force—

(a) for the purposes of this regulation and regulations 2(2)(b), 3(2)(d), 5(2)(d), 9(1)(a) and (2)(a), 14(3)(b), 15(2)(e), 18(c), 24(1)(a) and (2)(a), 28(4)(b), 29(2)(d), 32(d), 38(1)(d)(i), 39(1)(a) and (2)(a), 45(4)(b), 46(2)(d), 49(d), 54(1)(d)(i), 55(1)(a) and (2)(a), 63(1) and 73(3) for the purpose only of the making of regulations on 9th March 2005; and

(b) (*outside the scope of this work.*)

(c) for the purposes of regulations 4, 16, 30, 47, 63(2), 73(2)(b) and 74(2) on 1st April 2005; and

(d) for all other purposes on 6th April 2005.

(2) In these Regulations—

"the Act" means the Pensions Act 2004;

["the assessment date" means the date on which the assessment period in relation to the scheme or section, or (where there has been more than one such assessment period) the last one, began;]

["employer", in relation to a single-employer section of a segregated scheme which has no active members, includes the person who was the employer of persons in the description of employment to which the scheme or section relates immediately before the time at which the scheme or section ceased to have any active members in relation to it;]

"multi-employer section" means a section of a segregated scheme which has at least two employers in relation to that section;

"pensionable service" has the meaning given by section 70(2) of the Pension Schemes Act 1993 (interpretation); and

"segregated scheme" means a multi-employer scheme which is divided into two or more sections where—

(a) any contributions payable to the scheme by an employer in relation to the scheme or by a member are allocated to that employer's or that member's section; and

(b) a specified proportion of the assets of the scheme is attributable to each section of the scheme and cannot be used for the purposes of any other section.

[(3) In the application of Part 2 of the Act, the definition of "multi-employer scheme" in section 307(4) of the Act and of these Regulations, "employer", in relation to a multi-employer scheme that is not a segregated scheme or a multi-employer section of a segregated scheme—

(a) in an assessment period, includes any person who before the assessment date has ceased to be the employer of persons in the description of employment to which the scheme or section relates unless condition A, B, [C, [D, E or F]] is satisfied where—

(i) condition A is that a debt under section 75 of the Pensions Act 1995 (deficiencies in the assets) became due from that employer and the full amount of the debt has been paid before the assessment date;

(ii) condition B is that—

(aa) such a debt became due;

(bb) a legally enforceable agreement has been entered into the effect of which is to reduce the amount which may be recovered in respect of the debt; and

(cc) the reduced amount has been paid in full before the assessment date;

(iii) condition C is that such a debt became due but before the assessment date it is excluded from the value of the assets of the scheme or section because it is unlikely to be recovered without disproportionate costs or within a reasonable time;

(iv) condition D is that at the time at which any such person ceased to be the employer of persons in the description of employment to which the scheme or section relates the value of the assets of the scheme or section was such that no such debt was treated as becoming due;

[(v) condition E is that—

(aa) there is a restructuring within regulation 6ZB or 6ZC of the Occupational Pension Schemes (Employer Debt) Regulations 2005 (employment-cessation events: exemptions);

(bb) in that restructuring, the employer was the exiting employer for the purposes of those Regulations (see the definition of "exiting employer" in regulation 2(3A) of those Regulations (interpretation)); and

(cc) regulation 6ZA(3) or (4) of those Regulations (employment-cessation events: general) does not apply in relation to that restructuring;]

[(vi) condition F is that a flexible apportionment arrangement has taken effect in accordance with regulation 6E of the Occupational Pension Schemes (Employer Debt) Regulations 2005 (flexible apportionment arrangements) where the employer was the leaving employer within the meaning given in paragraph (7) of that regulation;]

(b) in any other case, includes any person who before the assessment date has ceased to be the employer of persons in the description of employment to which the scheme or section relates unless condition A, B, [C, [D, E or F]] is satisfied where—

(i) condition A is that a debt under section 75 of the Pensions Act 1995 became due from that employer and the full amount of the debt has been paid before the assessment date;

(ii) condition B is that—

(aa) such a debt became due;

(bb) a legally enforceable agreement has been entered into the effect of which is to reduce the amount which may be recovered in respect of the debt; and

(cc) the reduced amount has been paid in full before the assessment date;

(iii) condition C is that such a debt became due but before the assessment date it is excluded from the value of the assets of the scheme or section because it is unlikely to be recovered without disproportionate costs or within a reasonable time;

(iv) condition D is that at the time at which any such person ceased to be the employer of persons in the description of employment to which the scheme or section relates the value of the assets of the scheme or section was such that no such debt was treated as becoming due

[(v) condition E is that—

(aa) there is a restructuring within regulation 6ZB or 6ZC of the Occupational Pension Schemes (Employer Debt) Regulations 2005 (employment-cessation events: exemptions);

(bb) in that restructuring, the employer was the exiting employer for the purposes of those Regulations (see the definition of "exiting employer" in regulation 2(3A) of those Regulations (interpretation)); and

(cc) regulation 6ZA(3) or (4) of those Regulations (employment-cessation events: general) does not apply in relation to that restructuring;]

[(vi) condition F is that a flexible apportionment arrangement has taken effect in accordance with regulation 6E of the Occupational Pension Schemes (Employer Debt) Regulations 2005 where the employer was the leaving employer within the meaning given in paragraph (7) of that regulation.]]

NOTES

Para (2): definitions "the assessment date" and "employer" inserted by the Occupational Pension Schemes (Miscellaneous Amendments) Regulations 2005, SI 2005/2113, regs 4(1), (2)(c), 10(1), (2)(a).

Para (3): substituted by SI 2005/2113, reg 10(1), (2)(b); in sub-paras (a), (b) words in first (outer) pairs of square brackets substituted, and sub-paras (a)(v), (b)(v) inserted by the Occupational Pension Schemes (Employer Debt and Miscellaneous Amendments) Regulations 2010, SI 2010/725, reg 2; words in second (inner) pairs of square brackets in sub-paras (a), (b) substituted and sub-paras (a)(vi), (b)(vi) inserted by the Occupational Pension Schemes (Employer Debt and Miscellaneous Amendments) Regulations 2011, SI 2011/2973, reg 2.

PART 2
SEGREGATED SCHEMES:

SINGLE EMPLOYER SECTIONS

[18.16]

2 Application and effect

(1) This regulation applies to a section of a segregated scheme with one employer in relation to that section in circumstances where—

(a) an insolvency event occurs in relation to an employer in relation to that section; or

(b) the trustees or managers of the scheme become aware that the employer in relation to that section is unlikely to continue as a going concern and meets the requirements prescribed under subsection (1)(b) of section 129 of the Act (applications and notifications for the purposes of section 128).

(2) Except as otherwise provided in this Part, in a case to which this regulation applies—

(a) Part 2 of the Act, except Chapter 4, shall be read as if it contained the modifications provided for by this Part; and
(b) references in Part 2 of the Act, except in Chapter 4, to—
(i) "scheme rules" shall be read as if they were references to "scheme rules relating to the section";
(ii) "the scheme" shall be read as if they were references to "the section";
(iii) "the employer" shall be read as if they were references to "the employer in relation to the section"; and
(iv) "trustees or managers of the scheme" shall, in relation to a section of a segregated scheme, be read as if they were references to "trustees or managers with ultimate responsibility for the administration of the section".

(3) Paragraph (2) shall not have effect in relation to section 174 of the Act (initial levy).

[18.17]
3 Notification of insolvency events, confirmation of scheme status etc

(1) Section 120 of the Act (duty to notify insolvency events in respect of employers) shall be modified in its application to a section of a segregated scheme to which regulation 2 applies so that it shall be read as if—
(a) for the words "in the case of an occupational pension scheme, an insolvency event occurs in relation to the employer" in subsection (1), there were substituted the words "in the case of a multi-employer scheme which is divided into two or more sections ("a segregated scheme"), an insolvency event occurs in relation to an employer in relation to a section of the scheme in circumstances where that employer is the only employer in relation to that section"; and
(b) after subsection (2), there were inserted the following subsection—

"(2A) Where the trustees or managers of a section of a segregated scheme receive a notice from an insolvency practitioner under subsection (2), they must send a copy of that notice as soon as practicable to the trustees or managers of each section of the scheme (if different) and to all the employers in relation to the scheme.".

(2) Section 122 of the Act (insolvency practitioner's duty to issue notices confirming status of the scheme) shall be modified in its application to a section of a segregated scheme to which regulation 2 applies so that it shall be read as if—
(a) for the words "employer in relation to an occupational pension scheme" in subsection (1), there were substituted the words "employer in relation to a section of a segregated scheme in circumstances where that employer is the only employer in relation to that section";
(b) in subsection (2)—
(i) after the words "a scheme rescue is not possible" in paragraph (a), there were inserted the words "in relation to the relevant section of the scheme"; and
(ii) after the words "a scheme rescue has occurred" in paragraph (b), there were inserted the words "in relation to the relevant section of the scheme";
(c) for the words "in relation to the scheme" in subsection (4), there were substituted the words "in relation to the relevant section of the scheme";
[(d) in subsection (5)—
(i) in paragraph (a), for the words "in relation to an occupational pension scheme" there were substituted the words "in relation to a section of a segregated scheme"; and
(ii) in paragraph (b), for the words "in relation to such a scheme" there were substituted the words "in relation to such a section"; and]
(e) after subsection (6), there were inserted the following subsection—

"(6A) Where the trustees or managers of a section of a segregated scheme receive a copy of a notice issued by an insolvency practitioner or former insolvency practitioner under subsection (6), they must send a copy of that notice as soon as practicable to the trustees or managers of each section of the scheme (if different) and to all the employers in relation to the scheme.".

(3) Section 123 of the Act (approval of notices issued under section 122) shall be modified in its application to a section of a segregated scheme to which regulation 2 applies so that it shall be read as if, after subsection (4), there were inserted the following subsection—

"(4A) Where the trustees or managers of a section of a segregated scheme receive a copy of a determination notice issued by the Board under subsection (4), they must send a copy of that notice as soon as practicable to the trustees or managers of each section of the scheme (if different) and to all the employers in relation to the scheme.".

(4) Section 124 of the Act (Board's duty where there is a failure to comply with section 122) shall be modified in its application to a section of a segregated scheme to which regulation 2 applies so that it shall be read as if—
(a) for the words "in relation to an occupational pension scheme" in subsection (1), there were substituted the words "in relation to a section of a segregated scheme in circumstances where the employer is the only employer in relation to that section"; and
(b) after subsection (4), there were inserted the following subsection—

"(4A) Where the trustees or managers of a section of a segregated scheme receive a copy of a notice issued by the Board under section 122 by virtue of this section, they must send a copy of that notice as soon as practicable to the trustees or managers of each section of the scheme (if different) and to all the employers in relation to the scheme.".

(5) Section 125 of the Act (binding notices confirming status of scheme) shall be modified in its application to a section of a segregated scheme to which regulation 2 applies so that it shall be read as if—

(a) after subsection (3), there were inserted the following subsection—

"(3A) Where the trustees or managers of a section of a segregated scheme receive a notice from the Board under subsection (3) together with a copy of the binding notice, they must send a copy of the notice and the binding notice as soon as practicable to the trustees or managers of each section of the scheme (if different) and to all the employers in relation to the scheme."; and

(b) for the words "ceases to be involved with the scheme" in paragraph (b) of subsection (4), there were substituted the words "ceases to be involved with the relevant section of the scheme".

NOTES

Para (2): sub-para (d) substituted by the Occupational Pension Schemes and Pension Protection Fund (Amendment) Regulations 2005, SI 2005/993, regs 1(2), 5(1), (3)(a).

[18.18]
4 Eligible schemes

(1) Except as otherwise provided in this Part, for the purposes of Part 2 of the Act, except Chapter 4, as it applies in the case of a section of a segregated scheme to which regulation 2 applies, references to "an eligible scheme" shall be read as if they were references to a section of a segregated scheme in circumstances where that section, if it were a scheme, would not be—

(a) a money purchase scheme; or

(b) a scheme which is a prescribed scheme or a scheme of a prescribed description under section 126(1)(b) of the Act (eligible schemes).

(2) Paragraph (1) above shall not apply for the purposes of sections 174 to 181 of the Act (the levies).

[18.19]
5 Board's duty where application or notification received under section 129

(1) Section 129 of the Act (applications and notifications for the purposes of section 128) shall be modified in its application to a section of a segregated scheme to which regulation 2 applies so that it shall be read as if—

(a) after subsection (1), there were inserted the following subsection—

"(1A) Where the trustees or managers of a section of a segregated scheme make an application to the Board under subsection (1), they must issue a notice to that effect as soon as practicable to the trustees or managers of each section of the scheme (if different) and to all the employers in relation to the scheme."; and

(b) after subsection (5), there were inserted the following subsection—

"(5A) Where the trustees or managers of a section of a segregated scheme receive a notice from the Board under subsection (5), they must send a copy of that notice as soon as practicable to the trustees or managers of each section of the scheme (if different) and to all the employers in relation to the scheme.".

(2) Section 130 of the Act (Board's duty where application or notification received under section 129) shall be modified in its application to a section of a segregated scheme to which regulation 2 applies so that it shall be read as if—

(a) after the words "a scheme rescue is not possible" in subsection (2), there were inserted the words "in relation to the relevant section of a segregated scheme";

(b) after the words "a scheme rescue has occurred" in subsection (3), there were inserted the words "in relation to that section";

(c) after subsection (4), there were inserted the following subsection—

"(4A) Where the trustees or managers of a section of a segregated scheme receive a copy of a notice from the Board under subsection (4), they must send a copy of that notice as soon as practicable to the trustees or managers of each section of the scheme (if different) and to all the employers in relation to the scheme.";

[(d) in subsection (5)—

(i) in paragraph (a), for the words "in relation to an occupational pension scheme" there were substituted the words "in relation to a section of a segregated scheme"; and

(ii) in paragraph (b), for the words "in relation to such a scheme" there were substituted the words "in relation to such a section"; and]

(e) after subsection (7), there were inserted the following subsection—

Part 18 Miscellaneous SIs

"(7A) Where the trustees or managers of a section of a segregated scheme receive a notice from the Board under subsection (7) together with a copy of the binding notice, they must send a copy of the notice and the binding notice as soon as practicable to the trustees or managers of each section of the scheme (if different) and to all the employers in relation to the scheme.".

NOTES

Para (2): sub-para (d) substituted by the Occupational Pension Schemes and Pension Protection Fund (Amendment) Regulations 2005, SI 2005/993, regs 1(2), 5(1), (3)(b).

[18.20]

6 Protected liabilities and assessment periods

(1) Section 131 of the Act (protected liabilities) shall be modified in its application to a section of a segregated scheme to which regulation 2 applies so that it shall be read as if, for subsection (1), there were substituted the following subsection—

"(1) For the purposes of this Chapter the protected liabilities, in relation to a section of a segregated scheme which is, for the purposes of this Part, an eligible scheme, at a particular time ("the relevant time"), are—

(a) the cost of securing benefits for and in respect of members of the section which correspond to the compensation which would be payable, in relation to the section, in accordance with the pension compensation provisions (see section 162) if the Board assumed responsibility for the section in accordance with this Chapter,

(b) a proportion of the liabilities of the scheme as a whole [as determined by the Board or as calculated in the Board's valuation of the relevant section of the scheme under section 143] which are not liabilities to, or in respect of, members,

(c) the estimated cost of winding up the section.".

(2) Section 132 of the Act (assessment periods) shall be modified in its application to a section of a segregated scheme to which regulation 2 applies so that it shall be read as if, after the words "an assessment period" in subsections (2) and (4), there were inserted the words "in relation to a section of a segregated scheme".

NOTES

Para (1): words in square brackets in s 131(1)(b) (as set out) substituted by the Pension Protection Fund (Miscellaneous Amendments) (No 2) Regulations 2012, SI 2012/3083, reg 2(1), (2); for a transitional provision see reg 10 thereof.

[18.21]

7 Directions and power to validate contraventions of section 135

(1) Section 134 of the Act (directions) shall be modified in its application to a section of a segregated scheme to which regulation 2 applies so that it shall be read as if—

(a) in subsection (2)—

(i) for the words "the scheme's protected liabilities do not exceed its assets", there were substituted the words "the protected liabilities of the section do not exceed its assets"; and

(ii) for the words "in relation to the scheme", there were substituted the words "in relation to the segregated scheme in question"; and

(b) for the words "the trustees or managers" in paragraph (a)(i) of subsection (3), there were substituted the words "any trustees or managers".

(2) Section 136 of the Act (power to validate contraventions of section 135) shall be modified in its application to a section of a segregated scheme to which regulation 2 applies so that it shall be read as if, after subsection (2), there were inserted the following subsection—

"(2A) Where the trustees or managers of a section of a segregated scheme receive a copy of a notice from the Board under subsection (2), they must send a copy of that notice as soon as practicable to the trustees or managers of each section of the scheme (if different) and to all the employers in relation to the scheme.".

[18.22]

8 Valuation of assets

[(1) Section 143 of the Act (Board's obligation to obtain valuation of assets and protected liabilities) shall be modified in its application to a section of a segregated scheme to which regulation 2 applies so that it shall be read as if—

(a) for the words "the scheme" in subsection (2)(b), there were substituted the words "the relevant section of the scheme"; and

(b) after subsection (2A), there were inserted the following subsection—

"(2B) Where the trustees or managers of a segregated scheme receive a copy of a notice under subsection (2A), they must send a copy of that notice as soon as practicable to the trustees or managers of each section of the scheme (if different) and to all the employers in relation to the scheme."]

[(1A) Section 143A of the Act (determinations under section 143) shall be modified in its application to a section of a segregated scheme to which regulation 2 applies so that it shall be read as if—

(a) after subsection (1), there were inserted the following subsection—

"(1A) Where the trustees or managers of a segregated scheme receive a copy of a determination under subsection (1), they must send a copy of that determination as soon as practicable to the trustees or managers of each section of the scheme (if different) and to all the employers in relation to the scheme."; and

(b) for the words "a scheme" in subsection (3), there were substituted the words "the relevant section of a scheme".]

(2) Section 144 of the Act (approval of valuation) shall be modified in its application to a section of a segregated scheme to which regulation 2 applies so that it shall be read as if—

(a) for the words "obtains a valuation in respect of a scheme" in subsection (1), there were substituted the words "obtains a valuation in respect of the relevant section of the scheme"; and

(b) after subsection (2), there were inserted the following subsection—

"(2A) Where the trustees or managers of a segregated scheme receive a copy of a valuation of the relevant section of the scheme under subsection (2), they must send a copy of that valuation as soon as practicable to the trustees or managers of each section of the scheme (if different) and to all the employers in relation to the scheme.".

(3) Section 145 of the Act (binding valuations) shall be modified in its application to a section of a segregated scheme to which regulation 2 applies so that it shall be read as if—

(a) for the words "in relation to a scheme" in subsection (2), there were substituted the words "in relation to the relevant section of the scheme"; and

(b) after subsection (3), there were inserted the following subsection—

"(3A) Where the trustees or managers of a section of a segregated scheme receive a notice from the Board under subsection (3) together with a copy of the binding valuation, they must send a copy of the notice and the binding valuation as soon as practicable to the trustees or managers of each section of the scheme (if different) and to all the employers in relation to the scheme.".

NOTES

Para (1): substituted by the Pension Protection Fund (Miscellaneous Amendments) (No 2) Regulations 2012, SI 2012/3083, reg 2(1), (3)(a); for a transitional provision see reg 10 thereof.

Para (1A): inserted by SI 2012/3083, reg 2(1), 3(b); for a transitional provision see reg 10 thereof.

[18.23]

9 Refusal to assume responsibility for a scheme

(1) Section 146 of the Act (schemes which become eligible schemes) shall be modified in its application to a section of a segregated scheme to which regulation 2 applies so that it shall be read as if—

(a) for subsection (1), there were substituted the following subsection—

"(1) Regulations may provide that where the Board is satisfied that any section of a segregated scheme is not, for the purposes of this Part, an eligible scheme throughout such period as may be prescribed, the Board must refuse to assume responsibility for that section under this Chapter.";

(b) for the words "a scheme" in subsection (2), there were substituted the words "a section of the scheme";

(c) after subsection (2), there were inserted the following subsection—

"(2A) Where the trustees or managers of a section of a segregated scheme receive a copy of a withdrawal notice from the Board under subsection (2), they must send a copy of that notice as soon as practicable to the trustees or managers of each section of the scheme (if different) and to all the employers in relation to the scheme."; and

(d) after subsection (4), there were inserted the following subsection—

"(4A) Where the trustees or managers of a section of a segregated scheme receive a notice from the Board under subsection (4) together with a copy of the binding notice, they must send a copy of the notice and the binding notice as soon as practicable to the trustees or managers of each section of the scheme (if different) and to all the employers in relation to the scheme.".

(2) Section 147 of the Act (new schemes created to replace existing schemes) shall be modified in its application to a new section of a segregated scheme or a section of a new segregated scheme to which regulation 2 applies so that it shall be read as if—

(a) for subsection (1), there were substituted the following subsection—

"(1) The Board must refuse to assume responsibility for a new section of a segregated scheme or a section of a new segregated scheme ("the new section") under this Chapter where it is satisfied that—

(a) the new section was established during such period as may be prescribed,

(b) the employer in relation to the new section was, at the date of establishment of that section, also an employer in relation to another scheme ("the old scheme") or another section of the scheme ("the old section") established before the new section,

(c) a transfer or transfers of, or a transfer payment or transfer payments in respect of, any rights of members under the old scheme or the old section has or have been made to the new section, and

Part 18 Miscellaneous SIs

(d) the main purpose or one of the main purposes of establishing the new section and making the transfer or transfers, or transfer payment or transfer payments, was to enable those members to receive compensation under the pension compensation provisions in respect of their rights under the new section in circumstances where, in the absence of the transfer or transfers, regulations under section 146 would have operated to prevent such payments in respect of their rights under the old scheme or the old section.";

(b) after subsection (2), there were inserted the following subsection—

"(2A) Where the trustees or managers of a section of a segregated scheme receive a copy of a withdrawal notice from the Board under subsection (2), they must send a copy of that notice as soon as practicable to the trustees or managers of each section of the scheme (if different) and to all the employers in relation to the scheme."; and

(c) after subsection (4), there were inserted the following subsection—

"(4A) Where the trustees or managers of a section of a segregated scheme receive a notice from the Board under subsection (4) together with a copy of the binding notice, they must send a copy of the notice and the binding notice as soon as practicable to the trustees or managers of each section of the scheme (if different) and to all the employers in relation to the scheme.".

(3) Section 148 of the Act (withdrawal following issue of section 122(4) notice) shall be modified in its application to a section of a segregated scheme to which regulation 2 applies so that it shall be read as if—

(a) after subsection (5), there were inserted the following subsection—

"(5A) Where the trustees or managers of a section of a segregated scheme receive a copy of a withdrawal notice issued by the Board under this section, they must send a copy of that notice as soon as practicable to the trustees or managers of each section of the scheme (if different) and to all the employers in relation to the scheme."; and

(b) after subsection (7), there were inserted the following subsection—

"(7A) Where the trustees or managers of a section of a segregated scheme receive a notice from the Board under subsection (7) together with a copy of the binding notice, they must send a copy of the notice and the binding notice as soon as practicable to the trustees or managers of each section of the scheme (if different) and to all the employers in relation to the scheme.".

[18.24]

10 Reconsideration and duty to assume responsibility for a scheme following reconsideration

(1) Section 151 of the Act (application for reconsideration) shall be modified in its application to a section of a segregated scheme to which regulation 2 applies so that it shall be read as if, in the definition of "protected benefits quotation" in subsection (8), for the words from ""protected benefits quotation" in relation to a scheme means" to the words "from the reconsideration time" there were substituted the following words—

""protected benefits quotation", in relation to a section of a segregated scheme, means a quotation for one or more annuities from one or more insurers, being companies willing to accept payment in respect of the members of the section from the trustees or managers of the scheme, which would provide in respect of each member of the section from the reconsideration time—".

(2) Section 152 of the Act (duty to assume responsibility following reconsideration) shall be modified in its application to a section of a segregated scheme to which regulation 2 applies so that it shall be read as if—

(a) for subsection (2), there were substituted the following subsection—

"(2) The Board must assume responsibility in accordance with this Chapter for a section of a segregated scheme if it is satisfied that the value of the assets of the section at the reconsideration time is less than the aggregate of—

(a) the amount quoted in the protected benefits quotation accompanying the application;

(b) a proportion of the amount of liabilities of the scheme as a whole at that time, [as determined by the Board or calculated in the valuation of the relevant section of the scheme] referred to in [subsection (2) or (3) of section 151], which are not liabilities to, or in respect of, members of the scheme;

(c) the estimated cost of winding up the section at that time.";

(b) after subsection (3), there were inserted the following subsection—

"(3A) Where the trustees or managers of a section of a segregated scheme receive a copy of a determination notice from the Board under subsection (3), they must send a copy of that notice as soon as practicable to the trustees or managers of each section of the scheme (if different) and to all the employers in relation to the scheme."; and

(c) after subsection (7), there were inserted the following subsection—

"(7A) Where the trustees or managers of a section of a segregated scheme receive a notice from the Board under subsection (7) together with a copy of the binding notice, they must send a copy of the notice and the binding notice as soon as practicable to the trustees or managers of each section of the scheme (if different) and to all the employers in relation to the scheme.".

NOTES

Para (2): in sub-para (a), in s 152(2)(b) (as set out) words in first pair of square brackets substituted by the Pension Protection Fund (Miscellaneous Amendments) (No 2) Regulations 2012, SI 2012/3083, reg 2(1), (4); for a transitional provision see reg 10 thereof; words in second pair of square brackets substituted by the Occupational Pension Schemes and Pension Protection Fund (Amendment) Regulations 2005, SI 2005/993, regs 1(2), 5(1), (3)(c).

[18.25]

11 Closed schemes and requirement to wind up schemes with sufficient assets to meet protected liabilities

(1) Section 153 of the Act (closed schemes) shall be modified in its application to a section of a segregated scheme to which regulation 2 applies so that it shall be read as if—

(a) for the words "a closed scheme" in subsection (2), there were substituted the words "a closed section of a scheme";

(b) for the words "a closed scheme" in subsection (5), there were substituted the words "a closed section of a scheme"; and

(c) after subsection (6), there were inserted the following subsection—

"(6A) Where the trustees or managers of a section of a segregated scheme receive a copy of a determination notice from the Board under subsection (6), they must send a copy of that notice as soon as practicable to the trustees or managers of each section of the scheme (if different) and to all the employers in relation to the scheme.".

(2) Section 154 of the Act (requirement to wind up schemes with sufficient assets to meet protected liabilities) shall be modified in its application to a section of a segregated scheme to which regulation 2 applies so that it shall be read as if—

(a) for the words "(scheme rescue not possible but scheme has sufficient assets to meet the protected liabilities)" in paragraph (a) of subsection (2), there were substituted the words "(scheme rescue not possible in relation to a section of a segregated scheme but section has sufficient assets to meet the protected liabilities)";

(b) for the words "a scheme is wound up" in subsection (6), there were substituted the words "a section of a segregated scheme is wound up";

(c) for the words "winding up of a scheme" in subsection (11), there were substituted the words "winding up of a section of a segregated scheme"; and

(d) for the words "in relation to a scheme" in subsection (12), there were substituted the words "in relation to a section of a segregated scheme".

(3) Section 155 of the Act (treatment of closed schemes) shall be modified in its application to a section of a segregated scheme to which regulation 2 applies so that it shall be read as if, for subsection (1), there were substituted the following subsection—

"(1) In this section "closed scheme" means a section of a segregated scheme which is, for the purposes of this Part, an eligible scheme which is authorised under section 153 to continue as a closed section of the scheme.".

(4) Section 157 of the Act (applications and notifications where closed schemes have insufficient assets) shall be modified in its application to a section of a segregated scheme to which regulation 2 applies so that it shall be read as if, after subsection (4), there were inserted the following subsection—

"(4A) Where the trustees or managers of a section of a segregated scheme receive a notice from the Board under subsection (4), they must send a copy of that notice as soon as practicable to the trustees or managers of each section of the scheme (if different) and to all the employers in relation to the scheme.".

[(5) Section 158 of the Act (duty to assume responsibility for closed schemes) shall be modified in its application to a section of a segregated scheme to which regulation 2 applies so that it shall be read as if, after subsection (3A), there were inserted the following subsection—

"(3B) Where the trustees or managers of a section of a segregated scheme receive a notice from the Board under subsection (3A), they must send a copy of that notice as soon as practicable to the trustees or managers of each section of the scheme (if different) and to all the employers in relation to the scheme.".]

NOTES

Para (5): added by the Pension Protection Fund (Miscellaneous Amendments) (No 2) Regulations 2012, SI 2012/3083, reg 2(1), (5); for a transitional provision see reg 10 thereof.

[18.26]

12 Transfer notices and assumption of responsibility

(1) Section 160 of the Act (transfer notice) shall be modified in its application to a section of a segregated scheme to which regulation 2 applies so that it shall be read as if—

Part 18 Miscellaneous SIs

(a) for the words "required to assume responsibility for a scheme" in subsection (1), there were substituted the words "required to assume responsibility for a section of a segregated scheme";
(b) after subsection (2), there were inserted the following subsection—

"(2A) Where the trustees or managers of a section of a segregated scheme receive a transfer notice from the Board under subsection (2), they must send a copy of that notice as soon as practicable to the trustees or managers of each section of the scheme (if different) and to all the employers in relation to the scheme."; and

(c) for subsection (6), there were substituted the following subsection—

"(6) The Board must give a copy of the transfer notice under subsection (2) to—
(a) the Regulator, and
(b) an insolvency practitioner acting in relation to the employer in relation to the section of the scheme in respect of which the transfer notice is issued.".

(2) Section 161 of the Act (effect of Board assuming responsibility for a scheme) shall be modified in its application to a section of a segregated scheme to which regulation 2 applies so that it shall be read as if—
(a) after the word "obligations" in paragraph (b) of subsection (2), there were inserted the words "to or in respect of members of that section"; and
(b) after the words "to or in respect of persons" in paragraph (a) of subsection (4), there were inserted the words "who are or were members of that section".

(3) Paragraph 1 of Schedule 6 to the Act (transfer of rights and liabilities to the Board) shall be modified in its application to a section of a segregated scheme to which regulation 2 applies so that it shall be read as if, for the words "an occupational pension scheme", there were substituted the words "a section of a segregated multi-employer scheme".

[18.27]
13 The pension compensation provisions

(1) Section 162 of the Act (the pension compensation provisions) shall be modified in its application to a section of a segregated scheme to which regulation 2 applies so that it shall be read as if, in subsection (1)—
(a) for the words "in relation to a scheme", there were substituted the words "in relation to a section of a segregated scheme";
(b) after the word "members" in paragraphs (a) and (b), there were added the words "of that section";
(c) after the word "payable" in paragraph (c), there were added the words "to or in respect of members of that section"; and
(d) at the end of paragraph (d), there were added the words "payable to or in respect of members of that section".

(2) Section 163 of the Act (adjustments to be made where the Board assumes responsibility for a scheme) shall be modified in its application to a section of a segregated scheme to which regulation 2 applies so that it shall be read as if, after the words "to any member" in paragraph (a) of subsection (2), there were inserted the words "of that section".

(3) Section 166 of the Act (duty to pay scheme benefits unpaid at assessment date etc) shall be modified in its application to a section of a segregated scheme to which regulation 2 applies so that it shall be read as if, for the words "assumes responsibility for a scheme" in subsection (1), there were substituted the words "assumes responsibility for a section of a segregated scheme with only one employer in relation to that section of the scheme".

[PART 3
SEGREGATED SCHEMES:

MULTI-EMPLOYER SECTIONS WITHOUT REQUIREMENT FOR PARTIAL WIND UP ON WITHDRAWAL OF A PARTICIPATING EMPLOYER

[18.28]
14 Application and effect

(1) This regulation applies to a multi-employer section of a segregated scheme the rules of which do not provide for the partial winding up of the section when an employer in relation to the section ceases to participate in the scheme.

(2) Except as otherwise provided in this Part, in the case of a section of a scheme to which this regulation applies—
(a) Part 2 of the Act, except Chapter 4 (fraud compensation), shall be read as if it contained the modifications provided for by this Part; and
(b) references in Part 2 of the Act, except in Chapter 4, to—
(i) "scheme rules" shall be read as if they were references to "scheme rules relating to the section";
(ii) "the scheme" shall be read as if they were references to "the section";
(iii) "the employer" shall be read as if they were references to "an employer in relation to the section"; and

(iv) "trustees or managers of the scheme" shall, in relation to a multi-employer section of a segregated scheme, be read as if they were references to "trustees or managers with ultimate responsibility for the administration of the section".

(3) Paragraph (2) shall not have effect in relation to section 174 of the Act (initial levy).]

NOTES

Part 3 (regs 14–27) substituted by the Occupational Pension Schemes (Miscellaneous Amendments) Regulations 2005, SI 2005/2113, reg 10(1), (3).

[18.29]

[15 Notification of insolvency events, confirmation of scheme status etc

(1) Section 120 of the Act (duty to notify insolvency events in respect of employers) shall be modified in its application to a section of a scheme to which regulation 14 applies so that it shall be read as if—

(a) for subsection (1), there were substituted the following subsection—

"(1) This section applies where, in the case of a section of a multi-employer scheme which is divided into two or more sections ("a segregated scheme") with at least two employers in relation to that section of the scheme ("a multi-employer section"), an insolvency event occurs in relation to any employer in relation to that section."; and

(b) after subsection (2), there were inserted the following subsection—

"(2A) Where the trustees or managers of a multi-employer section of a segregated scheme receive a notice from an insolvency practitioner under subsection (2), they must send a copy of that notice as soon as practicable to all the employers in relation to that section of the scheme and to the trustees or managers of each section of the scheme (if different).".

(2) Section 122 of the Act (insolvency practitioner's duty to issue notices confirming status of scheme) shall be modified in its application to a section of a scheme to which regulation 14 applies so that it shall be read as if—

(a) for subsection (1), there were substituted the following subsection—

"(1) This section applies where an insolvency event has occurred in relation to any employer in relation to a multi-employer section of a segregated scheme.";

(b) in subsection (2)—

(i) for the words "the employer", there were substituted the words "an employer";

(ii) in paragraph (a), after the words "a scheme rescue is not possible", there were inserted the words "in relation to the relevant section of the scheme"; and

(iii) in paragraph (b), after the words "a scheme rescue has occurred", there were inserted the words "in relation to the relevant section of the scheme";

(c) in paragraph (a) of subsection (3), for the words "the employer", there were substituted the words "an employer";

(d) in subsection (4)—

(i) for the words "the employer", there were substituted the words "an employer"; and

(ii) for the words "in relation to the scheme", there were substituted the words "in relation to the section";

(e) in subsection (5)—

(i) in paragraph (a), for the words "in relation to an occupational pension scheme", there were substituted the words "in relation to a multi-employer section of a segregated scheme"; and

(ii) in paragraph (b), for the words "in relation to such a scheme", there were substituted the words "in relation to such a section";

(f) in subsection (6), for the words "the employer", there were substituted the words "an employer"; and

(g) after subsection (6), there were inserted the following subsection—

"(6A) Where the trustees or managers of a multi-employer section of a segregated scheme receive a notice issued by an insolvency practitioner or former insolvency practitioner under subsection (6), they must send a copy of that notice as soon as practicable to all the employers in relation to that section of the scheme and to the trustees or managers of each section of the scheme (if different).".

(3) Section 123 of the Act (approval of notices issued under section 122) shall be modified in its application to a section of a scheme to which regulation 14 applies so that it shall be read as if—

(a) . . .

(b) for subsection (2), there were substituted the following subsection—

"(2) The Board must determine whether to approve the section 122 notice received in relation to that employer."; and

(c) after subsection (4), there were inserted the following subsection—

"(4A) Where the trustees or managers of a multi-employer section of a segregated scheme receive a copy of a determination notice issued by the Board under subsection (4), they must send a copy of that notice as soon as practicable to all the employers in relation to that section of the scheme and to the trustees or managers of each section of the scheme (if different).".

(4) Section 124 of the Act (Board's duty where there is a failure to comply with section 122) shall be modified in its application to a section of a scheme to which regulation 14 applies so that it shall be read as if—

(a) in subsection (1)—

(i) for the words "This section applies where in relation to an occupational pension scheme", there were substituted the words "This section applies where in relation to a multi-employer section of a segregated scheme"; and

(ii) in paragraphs (a) and (b), for the words "the employer", there were substituted the words "an employer";

(b) in subsection (4)—

(i) in paragraph (d), for the words "the employer", there were substituted the words "an employer"; and

(ii) in paragraph (e), for the words "in relation to the employer, the employer", there were substituted the words "in relation to an employer, that employer"; and

(c) after subsection (4), there were inserted the following subsection—

"(4A) Where the trustees or managers of a multi-employer section of a segregated scheme receive a copy of a notice issued by the Board under section 122 by virtue of this section, they must send a copy of that notice as soon as practicable to all the employers in relation to that section of the scheme and to the trustees or managers of each section of the scheme (if different).".

(5) Section 125 of the Act (binding notices confirming status of scheme) shall be modified in its application to a section of a scheme to which regulation 14 applies so that it shall be read as if, after subsection (3), there were inserted the following subsection—

"(3A) Where the trustees or managers of a multi-employer section of a segregated scheme receive a notice from the Board under subsection (3) together with a copy of the binding notice, they must send a copy of the notice and the binding notice as soon as practicable to all the employers in relation to that section of the scheme and to the trustees or managers of each section of the scheme (if different).".]

NOTES

Substituted as noted to reg 14 at **[18.28]**.

Para (3): sub-para (a) revoked by the Occupational Pension Schemes (Employer Debt and Miscellaneous Amendments) Regulations 2008, SI 2008/731, reg 17.

[18.30]
[16 Eligible schemes

(1) Except as otherwise provided in this Part, for the purposes of Part 2 of the Act, except Chapter 4, as it applies to a section of a scheme to which regulation 14 applies, references to "an eligible scheme" shall be read as if they were references to a multi-employer section of a segregated scheme where that section, if it were a scheme, would not be—

(a) a money purchase scheme; or

(b) a scheme which is a prescribed scheme or a scheme of a prescribed description under section 126(1)(b) of the Act.

(2) Paragraph (1) shall not apply for the purposes of sections 174 to 181 of the Act (the levies).]

NOTES

Substituted as noted to reg 14 at **[18.28]**.

[18.31]
[17 Duty to assume responsibility for schemes

(1) Section 127 of the Act (duty to assume responsibility for schemes following insolvency event) shall have effect in relation to a section of a scheme to which regulation 14 applies and, for this purpose, shall be modified so that it shall be read as if—

(a) for subsection (1), there were substituted the following subsection—

"(1) This section applies where a qualifying insolvency event has occurred in relation to an employer in relation to a multi-employer section of a segregated scheme.";

(b) for subsection (3), there were substituted the following subsection—

"(3) For the purposes of this section, an insolvency event ("the current event") in relation to an employer in relation to a multi-employer section of a segregated scheme which is, for the purposes of this Part, an eligible scheme, is a qualifying insolvency event if—

(a) it occurs—

(i) simultaneously in relation to more than one of the employers in relation to that section of the scheme at a time when those employers are the only employers in relation to that section, or

(ii) in relation to an employer in relation to that section of the scheme at a time when all other employers in relation to that section have either had—

(aa) an insolvency event occur in relation to them and an insolvency practitioner is still required by law to be appointed to act in relation to them, or (bb) a notice given in respect of them by the trustees or managers of the section under section 129(1A) or a notice given by the Board in respect of them under section 129(5) by virtue of a notice given by the Regulator under section 129(4)(a),

(b) it occurs on or after the day appointed under section 126(2), and

(c) it—

(i) is the first insolvency event to occur in relation to that employer on or after that day, or

(ii) does not occur within an assessment period (see section 132) in relation to the section which began before the occurrence of the current event.".

(2) Section 128 of the Act (duty to assume responsibility for schemes following application or notification) shall be modified in its application to a section of a scheme to which regulation 14 applies so that it shall be read as if, for subsection (1), there were substituted the following subsection—

"(1) This section applies where, in relation to a multi-employer section of a segregated scheme which is, for the purposes of this Part, an eligible scheme—

(a) the trustees or managers make an application under subsection (1)(a) or (b) of section 129 (a "section 129 application"), or

(b) the Board receives a notice given by the Regulator under subsection (4)(b) of that section.".

(3) Section 129 of the Act (applications and notifications for the purposes of section 128) shall be modified in its application to a section of a scheme to which regulation 14 applies so that it shall be read as if—

(a) for subsection (1), there were substituted the following subsection—

"(1) Where the trustees or managers of a multi-employer section of a segregated scheme which is, for the purposes of this Part, an eligible scheme—

(a) have—

(i) notified the Board in accordance with subsection (1A) that an employer in relation to the section is unlikely to continue as a going concern at a time when all other employers in relation to that section have either had—

(aa) an insolvency event occur in relation to them and an insolvency practitioner is still required by law to be appointed to act in relation to them, or

(bb) a notice given in respect of them by the trustees or managers of the section under subsection (1A) or a notice given by the Board in respect of them under subsection (5) by virtue of a notice given by the Regulator under subsection (4)(a), or

(ii) received a notice given by the Board under subsection (5) by virtue of a notice given by the Regulator under subsection (4)(a) in respect of an employer in relation to the section at a time when all other employers in relation to that section have either had—

(aa) an insolvency event occur in relation to them and an insolvency practitioner is still required by law to be appointed to act in relation to them, or

(bb) a notice given in respect of them by the trustees or managers of the section under subsection (1A) or a notice given by the Board in respect of them under subsection (5) by virtue of a notice given by the Regulator under subsection (4)(a), or

(b) are aware that a person is no longer an employer, or that persons are no longer employers, in relation to the section at a time when—

(i) all other employers in relation to that section have either had—

(aa) an insolvency event occur in relation to them and an insolvency practitioner is still required by law to be appointed to act in relation to them, or

(bb) a notice given in respect of them by the trustees or managers of the section under subsection (1A) or a notice given by the Board in respect of them under subsection (5) by virtue of a notice given by the Regulator under subsection (4)(a), and

(ii) at least one such insolvency event occurred, or at least one such notice was given under subsection (1A) or (5) by virtue of a notice given by the Regulator under subsection (4)(a), on or after 6th April 2005 in relation to an employer in relation to that section,

they must, except where an assessment period has already begun in relation to that section of the scheme, make an application to the Board for it to assume responsibility for the section under section 128.";

(b) after subsection (1), there were inserted the following subsections—

"(1A) Where the trustees or managers of a multi-employer section of a segregated scheme which is, for the purposes of this Part, an eligible scheme become aware that an employer in relation to that section—

(a) is unlikely to continue as a going concern, and
(b) the prescribed requirements are met in relation to that employer,

they must give the Board a notice to that effect.

(1B) The notice which must be given to the Board in accordance with subsection (1A) must be in writing and must contain the following information—

(a) a description of the type or purpose of the notice,
(b) the name of the employer in relation to the section of the scheme in respect of which the notice is given,
(c) a statement by the trustees or managers of the section that the employer in respect of which the notice is given is unlikely to continue as a going concern and that the requirements prescribed under subsection (1A)(b) have been met in relation to that employer,
(d) the date on which the trustees or managers of the section became aware that the employer in respect of which the notice is given is unlikely to continue as a going concern, and
(e) the date on which the notice was sent to the Board by the trustees or managers of the scheme.

(1C) Where the trustees or managers of a multi-employer section of a segregated scheme which is, for the purposes of this Part, an eligible scheme make an application to the Board under subsection (1)(a) or (b), they must as soon as practicable notify that fact to all the employers in relation to that section of the scheme and to the trustees or managers of each section of the scheme (if different).";

(c) for subsection (4), there were substituted the following subsection—

"(4) Where, in relation to a multi-employer section of a segregated scheme which is, for the purposes of this Part, an eligible scheme, the Regulator—

(a) becomes aware that an employer in relation to that section of the scheme—
(i) is unlikely to continue as a going concern, and
(ii) meets the requirements prescribed under subsection (1A)(b), or
(b) is aware that a person is no longer an employer, or that persons are no longer employers, in relation to that section of the scheme at a time when—
(i) all other employers in relation to that section of the scheme have either had—
(aa) an insolvency event occur in relation to them and an insolvency practitioner is still required by law to be appointed to act in relation to them, or
(bb) a notice given in respect of them by the trustees or managers of the section under subsection (1A) or a notice given by the Board in respect of them under subsection (5) by virtue of a notice given by the Regulator under subsection (4)(a), and
(ii) at least one such insolvency event occurred, or at least one such notice was given under subsection (1A) or (5) by virtue of a notice given by the Regulator under subsection (4)(a), on or after 6th April 2005 in relation to an employer in relation to that section of the scheme,

it must, except where an assessment period has already begun in relation to that section of the scheme, give the Board a notice to that effect."; and

(d) after subsection (5), there were inserted the following subsection—

"(5A) Where the trustees or managers of a multi-employer section of a segregated scheme receive a notice from the Board under subsection (5), they must send a copy of that notice as soon as practicable to all the employers in relation to that section of the scheme and to the trustees or managers of each section of the scheme (if different).".]

NOTES

Substituted as noted to reg 14 at **[18.28]**.

[18.32]

[18 Board's duty where application or notification received under section 129

Section 130 of the Act (Board's duty where application or notification received under section 129) shall be modified in its application to a section of a scheme to which regulation 14 applies so that it shall be read as if—

(a) for subsection (1), there were substituted the following subsection—

"(1) This section applies where the Board—

(a) receives an application under subsection (1) of section 129 and is satisfied that either paragraph (a) or (b) of that subsection is satisfied in relation to the application, or
(b) is notified by the Regulator under section 129(4)(b).";

(b) in subsection (2), after the words "a scheme rescue is not possible", there were inserted the words "in relation to a multi-employer section of a segregated scheme";
(c) in subsection (3), after the words "a scheme rescue has occurred", there were inserted the words "in relation to that section";
(d) after subsection (4), there were inserted the following subsection—

"(4A) Where the trustees or managers of a multi-employer section of a segregated scheme receive a copy of a notice from the Board under subsection (4), they must send a copy of that notice as soon as practicable to all the employers in relation to that section of the scheme and to the trustees or managers of each section of the scheme (if different).";

(e) in subsection (5)—
(i) in paragraph (a), for the words "in relation to an occupational pension scheme", there were substituted the words "in relation to a multi-employer section of a segregated scheme"; and
(ii) in paragraph (b), for the words "in relation to such a scheme", there were substituted the words "in relation to such a section"; and

(f) after subsection (7), there were inserted the following subsection—

"(7A) Where the trustees or managers of a multi-employer section of a segregated scheme receive a notice from the Board under subsection (7) together with a copy of the binding notice, they must send a copy of the notice and the binding notice as soon as practicable to all the employers in relation to that section of the scheme and to the trustees or managers of each section of the scheme (if different).".]

NOTES

Substituted as noted to reg 14 at **[18.28]**.

[18.33]

[19 Protected liabilities

Section 131 of the Act (protected liabilities) shall be modified in its application to a section of a scheme to which regulation 14 applies so that it shall be read as if, for subsection (1), there were substituted the following subsection—

"(1) For the purposes of this Chapter the protected liabilities, in relation to a multi-employer section of a segregated scheme which is, for the purposes of this Part, an eligible scheme, at a particular time ("the relevant time") are—
(a) the cost of securing benefits for and in respect of members of the section which correspond to the compensation which would be payable, in relation to the section, in accordance with the pension compensation provisions (see section 162) if the Board assumed responsibility for the section in accordance with this Chapter,
(b) the liabilities of the scheme as a whole which are reasonably attributable to the section and which are not liabilities to, or in respect of, its members, and
(c) the estimated cost of winding up the section.".]

NOTES

Substituted as noted to reg 14 at **[18.28]**.

[18.34]

[20 Assessment periods

Section 132 of the Act (assessment periods) shall be modified in its application to a section of a scheme to which regulation 14 applies so that it shall be read as if—

(a) in subsection (2)—
(i) for the words "in relation to an eligible scheme", there were substituted the words "in relation to a multi-employer section of a segregated scheme which is, for the purposes of this Part, an eligible scheme";
(ii) for the words "the employer", there were substituted the words "an employer in relation to that section"; and
(iii) after the words "an assessment period", there were inserted the words "in relation to the section";

(b) in subsection (4), for the words "in relation to an eligible scheme, an application is made under section 129(1) or a notification is received under section 129(5)(a), an assessment period", there were substituted the words "in relation to a multi-employer section of a segregated scheme which is, for the purposes of this Part, an eligible scheme, an application is made under section 129(1)(a) or (b) or a notification is received under section 129(4)(b), an assessment period in relation to that section of the scheme"; and

(c) in subsection (5), for the words "section 129(5)(a)", there were substituted the words "section 129(4)(b)".]

NOTES

Substituted as noted to reg 14 at **[18.28]**.

[18.35]

[21 Directions

Section 134 of the Act (directions) shall be modified in its application to a section of a scheme to which regulation 14 applies so that it shall be read as if—

(a) in subsection (2)—
(i) for the words "the scheme's protected liabilities do not exceed its assets", there were substituted the words "the protected liabilities of the section do not exceed its assets"; and

(ii) for the words "in relation to the scheme", there were substituted the words "in relation to the segregated scheme in question"; and

(b) in paragraph (a)(i) of subsection (3), for the words "the trustees or managers" there were substituted the words "any trustees or managers".]

NOTES

Substituted as noted to reg 14 at **[18.28]**.

[18.36]

[22 Power to validate contraventions of section 135 and Board to act as creditor of the employer

(1) Section 136 of the Act (power to validate contraventions of section 135) shall be modified in its application to a section of a scheme to which regulation 14 applies so that it shall be read as if—

(a) in paragraph (c) of subsection (2), for the words "in relation to the employer, or if there is no such insolvency practitioner, the employer", there were substituted the words "in relation to an employer, or if there is no such insolvency practitioner, that employer"; and

(b) after subsection (2), there were inserted the following subsection—

"(2A) Where the trustees or managers of a multi-employer section of a segregated scheme receive a copy of a notice from the Board under subsection (2), they must send a copy of that notice as soon as practicable to all the employers in relation to that section of the scheme and to the trustees or managers of each section of the scheme (if different).".

(2) Section 137(2) of the Act (Board to act as creditor of the employer) shall be modified in its application to a section of a scheme to which regulation 14 applies so that it shall be read as if, for the words "the employer", there were substituted the words "an employer".]

NOTES

Substituted as noted to reg 14 at **[18.28]**.

[18.37]

[23 Valuation of assets

[(1) Section 143 of the Act (Board's obligation to obtain valuation of assets and protected liabilities) shall be modified in its application to a section of a scheme to which regulation 14 applies so that it shall be read as if—

(a) for the words "the scheme" in subsection (2)(b), there were substituted the words "the relevant section of the scheme"; and

(b) after subsection (2A), there were inserted the following subsection—

"(2B) Where the trustees or managers of a multi-employer section of a segregated scheme receive a copy of a notice under subsection (2A), they must send a copy of that notice as soon as practicable to all the employers in relation to that section of the scheme and to the trustees or managers of each section of the scheme (if different).".]

[(1A) Section 143A of the Act (determinations under section 143) shall be modified in its application to a section of a scheme to which regulation 14 applies so that it shall be read as if—

(a) after subsection (1), there were inserted the following subsection—

"(1A) Where the trustees or managers of a multi-employer section of a segregated scheme receive a copy of a determination under subsection (1), they must send a copy of that determination as soon as practicable to all the employers in relation to that section of the scheme and to the trustees or managers of each section of the scheme (if different)."; and

(b) for the words "a scheme" in subsection (3), there were substituted the words "the relevant section of a scheme".]

(2) Section 144 of the Act (approval of valuation) shall be modified in its application to a section of a scheme to which regulation 14 applies so that it shall be read as if—

(a) in subsection (1), for the words "obtains a valuation in respect of a scheme", there were substituted the words "obtains a valuation in respect of the relevant section of the scheme";

(b) in paragraph (b)(iii) of subsection (2), for the words "in relation to the employer or, if there is no such insolvency practitioner, the employer", there were substituted the words "in relation to an employer or, if there is no such insolvency practitioner, that employer"; and

(c) after subsection (2), there were inserted the following subsection—

"(2A) Where the trustees or managers of a multi-employer section of a segregated scheme receive a copy of a valuation from the Board under subsection (2), they must send a copy of that valuation as soon as practicable to all the employers in relation to that section of the scheme and to the trustees or managers of each section of the scheme (if different).".

(3) Section 145 of the Act (binding valuations) shall be modified in its application to a section of a scheme to which regulation 14 applies so that it shall be read as if—

(a) in subsection (2), for the words "in relation to a scheme", there were substituted the words "in relation to the relevant section of the scheme";

(b) in paragraph (c) of subsection (3), for the words "in relation to the employer or, if there is no such insolvency practitioner, the employer", there were substituted the words "in relation to an employer or, if there is no such insolvency practitioner, that employer"; and

(c) after subsection (3), there were inserted the following subsection—

"(3A) Where the trustees or managers of a multi-employer section of a segregated scheme receive a notice from the Board under subsection (3) together with a copy of a binding valuation, they must send a copy of the notice and the binding valuation as soon as practicable to all the employers in relation to that section of the scheme and to the trustees or managers of each section of the scheme (if different).".]

NOTES

Substituted as noted to reg 14 at **[18.28]**.

Para (1): substituted by the Pension Protection Fund (Miscellaneous Amendments) (No 2) Regulations 2012, SI 2012/3083, reg 2(1), (6)(a); for a transitional provision see reg 10 thereof.

Para (1A): inserted by SI 2012/3083, reg 2(1), (6)(b); for a transitional provision see reg 10 thereof.

[18.38]

[24 Refusal to assume responsibility for a scheme

(1) Section 146 of the Act (schemes which become eligible schemes) shall be modified in its application to a section of a scheme to which regulation 14 applies so that it shall be read as if—

(a) for subsection (1), there were substituted the following subsection—

"(1) Regulations may provide that where the Board is satisfied that any multi-employer section of a segregated scheme is not, for the purposes of this Part, an eligible scheme throughout such a period as may be prescribed, the Board must refuse to assume responsibility for that section under this Chapter.";

(b) in subsection (2)—

(i) for the words "a scheme", there were substituted the words "a section of the scheme"; and

(ii) in paragraph (b)(iii), for the words "in relation to the employer or, if there is no such insolvency practitioner, the employer", there were substituted the words "in relation to an employer or, if there is no such insolvency practitioner, that employer";

(c) after subsection (2), there were inserted the following subsection—

"(2A) Where the trustees or managers of a multi-employer section of a segregated scheme receive a copy of a withdrawal notice from the Board under subsection (2), they must send a copy of that notice as soon as practicable to all the employers in relation to that section of the scheme and to the trustees or managers of each section of the scheme (if different).";

(d) in paragraph (c) of subsection (4), for the words "in relation to the employer or, if there is no such insolvency practitioner, the employer", there were substituted the words "in relation to an employer or, if there is no such insolvency practitioner, that employer"; and

(e) after subsection (4), there were inserted the following subsection—

"(4A) Where the trustees or managers of a multi-employer section of a segregated scheme receive a notice from the Board under subsection (4) together with a copy of the binding notice, they must send a copy of the notice and the binding notice as soon as practicable to all the employers in relation to that section of the scheme and to the trustees or managers of each section of the scheme (if different).".

(2) Section 147 of the Act (new schemes created to replace existing schemes) shall be modified in its application to a section of a scheme to which regulation 14 applies so that it shall be read as if—

(a) for subsection (1), there were substituted the following subsection—

"(1) The Board must refuse to assume responsibility for a new multi-employer section of a segregated scheme ("the new section") under this Chapter where it is satisfied that—

(a) the new section was established during such period as may be prescribed,

(b) an employer in relation to the new section was, at the date of establishment of that section, also the employer in relation to another scheme ("the old scheme") or another section of the scheme ("the old section") established before the new section,

(c) a transfer or transfers of, or a transfer payment or transfer payments in respect of, any rights of members under the old scheme or the old section has or have been made to the new section, and

(d) the main purpose or one of the main purposes of establishing the new section and making the transfer or transfers, or transfer payment or transfer payments, was to enable those members to receive compensation under the pension compensation provisions in respect of their rights under the new section in circumstances where, in the absence of the transfer or transfers, regulations under section 146 would have operated to prevent such payments in respect of their rights under the old scheme or the old section.";

(b) in paragraph (b)(iii) of subsection (2), for the words "in relation to the employer or, if there is no such insolvency practitioner, the employer", there were substituted the words "in relation to an employer or, if there is no such insolvency practitioner, that employer";

(c) after subsection (2), there were inserted the following subsection—

"(2A) Where the trustees or managers of a multi-employer section of a segregated scheme receive a copy of a withdrawal notice from the Board under subsection (2), they must send a copy of that notice as soon as practicable to all the employers in relation to that section of the scheme and to the trustees or managers of each section of the scheme (if different).";

(d) in paragraph (c) of subsection (4), for the words "in relation to the employer or, if there is no such insolvency practitioner, the employer", there were substituted the words "in relation to an employer or, if there is no such insolvency practitioner, that employer"; and

(e) after subsection (4), there were inserted the following subsection—

"(4A) Where the trustees or managers of a multi-employer section of a segregated scheme receive a notice from the Board under subsection (4) together with a copy of the binding notice, they must send a copy of the notice as soon as practicable to all the employers in relation to that section of the scheme and to the trustees or managers of each section of the scheme (if different).".

(3) Section 148 of the Act (withdrawal following issue of section 122(4) notice) shall be modified in its application to a section of a scheme to which regulation 14 applies so that it shall be read as if—

(a) in paragraph (c) of subsection (5), for the words "the employer", there were substituted the words "any employer";

(b) after subsection (5), there were inserted the following subsection—

"(5A) Where the trustees or managers of a multi-employer section of a segregated scheme receive a copy of a withdrawal notice issued by the Board under this section, they must send a copy of that notice as soon as practicable to all the employers in relation to that section of the scheme and to the trustees or managers of each section of the scheme (if different).";

(c) in paragraph (c) of subsection (7), for the words "the employer", there were substituted the words "any employer"; and

(d) after subsection (7), there were inserted the following subsection—

"(7A) Where the trustees or managers of a multi-employer section of a segregated scheme receive a notice from the Board under subsection (7) together with a copy of the binding notice, they must send a copy of the notice and the binding notice as soon as practicable to all the employers in relation to that section of the scheme and to the trustees or managers of each section of the scheme (if different).".]

NOTES

Substituted as noted to reg 14 at **[18.28]**.

[18.39]

[25 Reconsideration, closed schemes and requirement to wind up schemes with sufficient assets to meet protected liabilities

(1) Section 151(8) of the Act (application for reconsideration) shall be modified in its application to a section of a scheme to which regulation 14 applies so that it shall be read as if, in the definition of "protected benefits quotation", for the words from ""protected benefits quotation", in relation to a scheme, means" to the words "from the reconsideration time—", there were substituted the following words—

""protected benefits quotation", in relation to a section of a segregated scheme, means a quotation for one or more annuities from one or more insurers, being companies willing to accept payment in respect of the members of the section from the trustees or managers of the scheme, which would provide in respect of each member of the section from the reconsideration time—".

(2) Section 152 of the Act (duty to assume responsibility following reconsideration) shall be modified in its application to a section of a scheme to which regulation 14 applies so that it shall be read as if—

(a) for subsection (2), there were substituted the following subsection—

"(2) The Board must assume responsibility in accordance with this Chapter for a multi-employer section of a segregated scheme if it is satisfied that the value of the assets of the section at the reconsideration time is less than the aggregate of—

(a) the amount quoted in the protected benefits quotation accompanying the application,

(b) the liabilities of the scheme as a whole at that time which are reasonably attributable to the section and which are not liabilities to, or in respect of, members of the scheme, and

(c) the estimated cost of winding up the section at that time.";

(b) after subsection (3), there were inserted the following subsection—

"(3A) Where the trustees or managers of a multi-employer section of a segregated scheme receive a copy of a determination notice from the Board under subsection (3), they must send a copy of that notice as soon as practicable to all the employers in relation to that section of the scheme and to the trustees or managers of each section of the scheme (if different)."; and

(c) after subsection (7), there were inserted the following subsection—

"(7A) Where the trustees or managers of a multi-employer section of a segregated scheme receive a notice from the Board under subsection (7), they must send a copy of that notice as soon as practicable to all the employers in relation to that section of the scheme and to the trustees or managers of each section of the scheme (if different).".

(3) Section 153 of the Act (closed schemes) shall be modified in its application to a section of a scheme to which regulation 14 applies so that it shall be read as if—

(a) in subsections (2) and (5), for the words "a closed scheme", there were substituted the words "a closed section of the scheme"; and

(b) after subsection (6), there were inserted the following subsection—

"(6A) Where the trustees or managers of a multi-employer section of a segregated scheme receive a copy of a determination notice from the Board under subsection (6), they must send a copy of that notice as soon as practicable to all the employers in relation to that section of the scheme and to the trustees or managers of each section of the scheme (if different).".

(4) Section 154 of the Act (requirement to wind up schemes with sufficient assets to meet protected liabilities) shall be modified in its application to a section of a scheme to which regulation 14 applies so that it shall be read as if—

(a) in paragraph (a) of subsection (2), for the words "(scheme rescue not possible but scheme has sufficient assets to meet the protected liabilities)", there were substituted the words "(scheme rescue not possible in relation to a multi-employer section of a segregated scheme but section has sufficient assets to meet the protected liabilities)";

(b) in subsection (6), for the words "a scheme is wound up", there were substituted the words "a multi-employer section of a segregated scheme is wound up";

(c) in subsection (11), for the words "winding up of a scheme", there were substituted the words "winding up of a multi-employer section of a segregated scheme"; and

(d) in subsection (12), for the words "in relation to a scheme", there were substituted the words "in relation to a multi-employer section of a segregated scheme".

(5) Section 155 of the Act (treatment of closed schemes) shall be modified in its application to a section of a scheme to which regulation 14 applies so that it shall be read as if, for subsection (1), there were substituted the following subsection—

"(1) In this section "closed scheme" means a multi-employer section of a segregated scheme which is, for the purposes of this Part, an eligible scheme which is authorised under section 153 to continue as a closed section of the scheme.".

(6) Section 157 of the Act (applications and notifications where closed schemes have insufficient assets) shall be modified in its application to a section of a scheme to which regulation 14 applies so that it shall be read as if, after subsection (4), there were inserted the following subsection—

"(4A) Where the trustees or managers of a multi-employer section of a segregated scheme receive a notice from the Board under subsection (4), they must send a copy of that notice as soon as practicable to all the employers in relation to that section of the scheme and to the trustees or managers of each section of the scheme (if different).".]

[(7) Section 158 of the Act (duty to assume responsibility for closed schemes) shall be modified in its application to a section of a scheme to which regulation 14 applies so that it shall be read as if, after subsection (3A), there were inserted the following subsection—

"(3B) Where the trustees or managers of a multi-employer section of a segregated scheme receive a notice from the Board under subsection (3A), they must send a copy of that notice as soon as practicable to all the employers in relation to that section of the scheme and to the trustees or managers of each section of the scheme (if different).".]

NOTES

Substituted as noted to reg 14 at **[18.28]**.

Para (7): added by the Pension Protection Fund (Miscellaneous Amendments) (No 2) Regulations 2012, SI 2012/3083, reg 2(1), (7); for a transitional provision see reg 10 thereof.

[18.40]

[26 Transfer notice and assumption of responsibility for a scheme

(1) Section 160 of the Act (transfer notice) shall be modified in its application to a section of a scheme to which regulation 14 applies so that it shall be read as if—

(a) in subsection (1), for the words "required to assume responsibility for a scheme", there were substituted the words "required to assume responsibility for a multi-employer section of a segregated scheme";

(b) after subsection (2), there were inserted the following subsection—

"(2A) Where the trustees or managers of a multi-employer section of a segregated scheme receive a transfer notice from the Board under subsection (2), they must send a copy of that notice as soon as practicable to all the employers in relation to that section of the scheme and to the trustees or managers of each section of the scheme (if different)."; and

(c) for subsection (6), there were substituted the following subsection—

"(6) The Board must give a copy of the transfer notice given under subsection (2) to—

(a) the Regulator, and
(b) an insolvency practitioner acting in relation to every employer in relation to the section of the scheme in respect of which the transfer notice is given.".

(2) Section 161 of the Act (effect of Board assuming responsibility for a scheme) shall be modified in its application to a section of a scheme to which regulation 14 applies so that it shall be read as if—
(a) in paragraph (b) of subsection (2), after the word "obligations", there were inserted the words "to or in respect of members of that section"; and
(b) in paragraph (a) of subsection (4), after the words "to or in respect of persons", there were inserted the words "who are or were members of that section".

(3) Schedule 6 to the Act (transfer of property, rights and liabilities to the Board) shall be modified in its application to a section of a scheme to which regulation 14 applies so that it shall be read as if, in paragraph 1, for the words "an occupational pension scheme", there were substituted the words "a multi-employer section of a segregated multi-employer scheme".]

NOTES

Substituted as noted to reg 14 at **[18.28]**.

[18.41]
[27 The pension compensation provisions

(1) Section 162(1) of the Act (the pension compensation provisions) shall be modified in its application to a section of a scheme to which regulation 14 applies so that it shall be read as if—
(a) for the words "in relation to a scheme", there were substituted the words "in relation to a multi-employer section of a segregated scheme";
(b) in paragraphs (a) and (b), after the word "members", there were added the words "of that section";
(c) in paragraph (c), after the word "payable", there were added the words "to or in respect of members of that section"; and
(d) at the end of paragraph (d), there were added the words "payable to or in respect of members of that section".

(2) Section 163(2) of the Act (adjustments to be made where the Board assumes responsibility for a scheme) shall be modified in its application to a section of a scheme to which regulation 14 applies so that it shall be read as if, in paragraph (a), after the words "to any member", there were inserted the words "of that section".

(3) Section 166(1) of the Act (duty to pay scheme benefits unpaid at assessment date etc) shall be modified in its application to a section of a scheme to which regulation 14 applies so that it shall be read as if, for the words "assumes responsibility for a scheme", there were substituted the words "assumes responsibility for a multi-employer section of a segregated scheme".]

NOTES

Substituted as noted to reg 14 at **[18.28]**.

PART 4
SEGREGATED SCHEMES:

NON-SEGREGATED MULTI-EMPLOYER SECTIONS OF SEGREGATED SCHEMES WITH REQUIREMENT FOR PARTIAL WIND UP ON WITHDRAWAL OF PARTICIPATING EMPLOYER

[18.42]
28 Application and effect

(1) This regulation applies to a non-segregated multi-employer section of a segregated scheme in circumstances where—
(a) an insolvency event occurs in relation to an employer in relation to that section; or
(b) the trustees or managers of the scheme become aware that an employer in relation to that section is unlikely to continue as a going concern and meets the requirements prescribed under subsection (1)(b) of section 129 of the Act (applications and notifications for the purposes of section 128).

(2) Where—
(a) in relation to an employer in relation to a section of a scheme to which this regulation applies, an event described in paragraph (1)(a) or (b) of this regulation occurs; and
(b) the requirement in the scheme rules relating to that section for the trustees or managers of the scheme to segregate such part of the assets of the section as is attributable to the liabilities of the section to provide pensions or other benefits to or in respect of the pensionable service of some or all of the members of the section by reference to an employer in relation to the section ("the segregation requirement") would be triggered when an employer in relation to the section ceases to participate in the scheme,

the segregation requirement shall, in relation to the employer referred to in sub-paragraph (a) of this paragraph, be deemed to have been triggered immediately after the occurrence of the event described in paragraph (1)(a) or (b) and a segregated part of the section shall be deemed to have been created for and in respect of any period after the occurrence of that event where a withdrawal event within the meaning of section 149(2) of the Act has not occurred in relation to the segregated part.

(3) In this Part—

"non-segregated multi-employer section" means a multi-employer section of a segregated scheme where, under the scheme rules relating to that section, the trustees or managers of the scheme are required, in circumstances where an employer in relation to that section ceases to participate in the scheme, to segregate such part of the assets of the section as are attributable to the liabilities of the section to provide pensions or other benefits to or in respect of the pensionable service of some or all of the members of the section by reference to that employer; and

"segregated part" means a section of a non-segregated multi-employer section which is created when a segregation requirement in the scheme rules relating to that multi-employer section of the scheme has been triggered.

(4) Except as otherwise provided in this Part, in a case where this regulation applies—

(a) Part 2 of the Act, except Chapter 4, shall be read as if it contained the modifications provided for by this Part; and

(b) references in Part 2 of the Act, except in Chapter 4, to—

(i) "scheme rules" shall be read as if they were references to "rules of the scheme which apply to the segregated part";

(ii) "the scheme" shall be read as if they were references to "the segregated part";

(iii) "the employer" shall be read as if they were references to "the employer in relation to the segregated part"; and

(iv) "trustees or managers of the scheme" shall, in relation to a non-segregated multi-employer section of a segregated scheme, be read as if they were references to "trustees or managers with ultimate responsibility for the administration of the section"[; and

(c) Part 2 of the Act shall be read as if section 143A were omitted.]

(5) Paragraph (4) shall not have effect in relation to section 174 of the Act (initial levy).

NOTES

Para (4): sub-para (c) and word immediately preceding it added by the Pension Protection Fund (Miscellaneous Amendments) (No 2) Regulations 2012, SI 2012/3083, reg 2(1), (8); for a transitional provision see reg 10 thereof.

[18.43]

29 Notification of insolvency events, confirmation of scheme status etc

(1) Section 120 of the Act (duty to notify insolvency events in respect of employers) shall be modified in its application to a segregated part to which regulation 28 applies so that it shall be read as if—

(a) for subsection (1), there were substituted the following subsection—

"(1) This section applies where an insolvency event occurs in relation to an employer in relation to a section of a multi-employer scheme which is divided into two or more sections ("a segregated scheme") with at least two employers in relation to that section of the scheme ("a multi-employer section") under the rules of which the trustees or managers are required, in circumstances where an employer in relation to that section of the scheme ceases to participate in the scheme, to segregate such part of the assets of the section as is attributable to the liabilities of the section to provide pensions or other benefits to or in respect of the pensionable service of some or all of the members of the section by reference to that employer ("the segregated part")."; and

(b) after subsection (2) there were inserted the following subsection—

"(2A) Where the trustees or managers of a segregated part of a multi-employer section of a segregated scheme to which this section applies receive a notice from an insolvency practitioner under subsection (2), they must send a copy of that notice as soon as practicable to the trustees or managers of each section of the scheme (if different) and to all the employers in relation to the scheme.".

(2) Section 122 of the Act (insolvency practitioner's duty to issue notices confirming status of scheme) shall be modified in its application to a segregated part to which regulation 28 applies so that it shall be read as if—

(a) for subsection (1), there were substituted the following subsection—

"(1) This section applies where an insolvency event has occurred in relation to an employer in relation to a multi-employer section of a segregated scheme and a segregated part of the section is created."; and

(b) in subsection (2)—

(i) after the words "a scheme rescue is not possible" in paragraph (a), there were inserted the words "in relation to the relevant segregated part of a multi-employer section of the scheme"; and

(ii) after the words "a scheme rescue has occurred" in paragraph (b), there were inserted the words "in relation to the relevant segregated part of a multi-employer section of the scheme";

(c) in subsection (4)—

(i) after the words "a scheme rescue is not possible" in paragraph (a), there were inserted the words "in relation to the relevant segregated part"; and

(ii) after the words "a scheme rescue has occurred" in paragraph (b), there were inserted the words "in relation to the relevant segregated part";

[(d) in subsection (5)—

(i) in paragraph (a), for the words "in relation to an occupational pension scheme" there were substituted the words "in relation to a segregated part of a multi-employer section of a segregated scheme"; and

(ii) in paragraph (b), for the words "in relation to such a scheme" there were substituted the words "in relation to such a segregated part"; and]

(e) after subsection (6), there were inserted the following subsection—

"(6A) Where the trustees or managers of a segregated part of a multi-employer section of a segregated scheme receive a copy of a notice from an insolvency practitioner or former insolvency practitioner under subsection (6), they must send a copy of that notice as soon as practicable to the trustees or managers of each section of the scheme (if different) and to all the employers in relation to the scheme.".

(3) Section 123 of the Act (approval of notices issued under section 122) shall be modified in its application to a segregated part to which regulation 28 applies so that it shall be read as if—

(a) for subsection (1), there were substituted the following subsection—

"(1) This section applies where the Board receives a notice under section 122(6) ("the section 122 notice") in relation to an employer in relation to a segregated part of a multi-employer section of a segregated scheme."; and

(b) after subsection (4) there were inserted the following subsection—

"(4A) Where the trustees or managers of a segregated part of a multi-employer section of a segregated scheme receive a copy of a determination notice issued by the Board under subsection (4), they must send a copy of that notice as soon as practicable to the trustees or managers of each section of the scheme (if different) and to all the employers in relation to the scheme.".

(4) Section 124 of the Act (Board's duty where there is a failure to comply with section 122) shall be modified in its application to a segregated part to which regulation 28 applies so that it shall be read as if—

(a) for the words "in relation to an occupational pension scheme" in subsection (1), there were substituted the words "in relation to a segregated part of a multi-employer section of a segregated scheme"; and

(b) after subsection (4), there were inserted the following subsection—

"(4A) Where the trustees or managers of a segregated part of a multi-employer section of a segregated scheme receive a copy of a notice issued by the Board under section 122 by virtue of this section, they must send a copy of that notice as soon as practicable to the trustees or managers of each section of the scheme (if different) and to all the employers in relation to the scheme.".

(5) Section 125 of the Act (binding notices confirming status of scheme) shall be modified in its application to a segregated part to which regulation 28 applies so that it shall be read as if, after subsection (3), there were inserted the following subsection—

"(3A) Where the trustees or managers of a segregated part of a multi-employer section of a segregated scheme receive a notice from the Board under subsection (3) together with a copy of the binding notice, they must send a copy of the notice and the binding notice as soon as practicable to the trustees or managers of each section of the scheme (if different) and to all the employers in relation to the scheme.".

NOTES

Para (2): sub-para (d) substituted by the Occupational Pension Schemes and Pension Protection Fund (Amendment) Regulations 2005, SI 2005/993, regs 1(2), 5(1), (5)(a).

[18.44]

30 Eligible schemes

(1) Except as otherwise provided in this Part, for the purposes of Part 2 of the Act, except Chapter 4, as it applies in the case of a segregated part to which regulation 28 applies, references to an "eligible scheme" shall be read as if they were references to a segregated part of a multi-employer section of a segregated scheme in circumstances where that segregated part, if it were a scheme, would not be—

(a) a money purchase scheme; or

(b) a scheme which is a prescribed scheme or a scheme of a prescribed description under section 126(1)(b) of the Act.

(2) Paragraph (1) shall not apply for the purposes of sections 174 to 181 of the Act (the levies).

[18.45]

31 Duty to assume responsibility for schemes

(1) Section 127 of the Act (duty to assume responsibility for schemes following insolvency event) shall be modified in its application to a segregated part to which regulation 28 applies so that it shall be read as if, after the words "at the relevant time" in paragraph (a) of subsection (2), there were inserted the words "as determined by the Board's valuation of the section as a whole under section 143".

(2) Section 128 of the Act (duty to assume responsibility for schemes following application or notification) shall be modified in its application to a segregated part to which regulation 28 applies so that it shall be read as if, after the words . . . "at the relevant time" in paragraph (a) of subsection (2), there were inserted the words "as determined by the Board's valuation of the section as a whole under section 143".

(3) Section 129 of the Act (applications and notifications for the purposes of section 128) shall be modified in its application to a segregated part to which regulation 28 applies so that it shall be read as if—

(a) after subsection (1), there were inserted the following subsection—

"(1A) Where the trustees or managers of a segregated part of a multi-employer section of a segregated scheme make an application to the Board under subsection (1), they must issue a notice to that effect as soon as practicable to the trustees or managers of each section of the scheme (if different) and to all the employers in relation to the scheme."; and

(b) after subsection (5), there were inserted the following subsection—

"(5A) Where the trustees or managers of a segregated part of a multi-employer section of a segregated scheme receive a notice from the Board under subsection (5), they must send a copy of that notice as soon as practicable to the trustees or managers of each section of the scheme (if different) and to all the employers in relation to the scheme.".

NOTES

Para (2): word omitted revoked by the Occupational Pension Schemes and Pension Protection Fund (Amendment) Regulations 2005, SI 2005/993, regs 1(2), 5(1), (5)(b).

[18.46]

32 Board's duty where application or notification received under section 129

Section 130 of the Act (Board's duty where application or notification received under section 129) shall be modified in its application to a segregated part to which regulation 28 applies so that it shall be read as if—

(a) after the words "a scheme rescue is not possible" in subsection (2), there were inserted the words "in relation to a segregated part of a multi-employer section of a segregated scheme";

(b) after the words "a scheme rescue has occurred" in subsection (3), there were inserted the words "in relation to that segregated part";

(c) after subsection (4), there were inserted the following subsection—

"(4A) Where the trustees or managers of a segregated part of a multi-employer section of a segregated scheme receive a copy of a notice from the Board under subsection (4), they must send a copy of that notice as soon as practicable to the trustees or managers of each section of the scheme (if different) and to all the employers in relation to the scheme.";

[(d) in subsection (5)—

(i) in paragraph (a), for the words "in relation to an occupational pension scheme" there were substituted the words "in relation to a segregated part of a multi-employer section of a segregated scheme"; and

(ii) in paragraph (b), for the words "in relation to such a scheme" there were substituted the words "in relation to such a segregated part"; and]

(e) after subsection (7), there were inserted the following subsection—

"(7A) Where the trustees or managers of a segregated part of a multi-employer section of a segregated scheme receive a notice from the Board under subsection (7) together with a copy of the binding notice, they must send a copy of the notice and the binding notice as soon as practicable to the trustees or managers of each section of the scheme (if different) and to all the employers in relation to the scheme.".

NOTES

Para (d): substituted by the Occupational Pension Schemes and Pension Protection Fund (Amendment) Regulations 2005, SI 2005/993, regs 1(2), 5(1), (5)(c).

[18.47]

33 Protected liabilities

Section 131 of the Act (protected liabilities) shall be modified in its application to a segregated part to which regulation 28 applies so that it shall be read as if, for subsection (1), there were substituted the following subsection—

"(1) Except as otherwise provided, for the purposes of this Chapter the protected liabilities, in relation to a segregated part which is, for the purposes of this Part, an eligible scheme, at a particular time ("the relevant time") are—

(a) the cost of securing benefits for and in respect of members of the segregated part of a multi-employer section of a segregated scheme which correspond to the compensation which would be payable, in relation to the segregated part, in accordance with the pension compensation provisions (see section 162) if the Board assumed responsibility for the segregated part in accordance with this Chapter,

(b) a proportion of the liabilities of the scheme as a whole as calculated in the Board's valuation under section 143, which are not liabilities to, or in respect of, members, and

(c) the estimated cost of winding up the segregated part.".

[18.48]
34 Assessment periods

Section 132 of the Act (assessment periods) shall be modified in its application to a segregated part to which regulation 28 applies so that it shall be read as if, after the words "an assessment period" in subsection (2), there were inserted the words "in relation to a segregated part of a multi-employer section of a segregated scheme".

[18.49]
35 Directions

Section 134 of the Act (directions) shall be modified in its application to a non-segregated multi-employer section to which regulation 28 applies so that it shall be read as if—

(a) in subsection (2)—

(i) for the words "the scheme's protected liabilities do not exceed its assets", there were substituted the words ["the protected liabilities of the segregated part do not exceed its assets"]; and

(ii) for the words "in relation to the scheme", there were substituted the words "in relation to the segregated scheme in question";

(iii) for the words "the investment of the scheme's assets" in paragraph (a), there were substituted the words "the investment of the assets of the section"; and

(b) for sub-paragraph (i) of paragraph (a) of subsection (3), there were substituted the following sub-paragraph—

"(i) any trustees or managers of the scheme in relation to which the segregated part relates,".

NOTES

Words in square brackets substituted by the Occupational Pension Schemes and Pension Protection Fund (Amendment) Regulations 2005, SI 2005/993, regs 1(2), 5(1), (5)(d).

[18.50]
36 Restrictions on winding up, discharge of liabilities etc, and power to validate contraventions of section 135

(1) Section 135 of the Act (restrictions on winding up, discharge of liabilities etc) shall be modified in its application to a segregated part to which regulation 28 applies so that it shall be read as if—

(a) after the words "the winding up of the scheme" in subsection (2), there were inserted the words "under or by virtue of the scheme rules"; and

(b) after subsection (4), there were inserted the following subsection—

"(4A) Where an assessment period has begun in relation to a segregated part of a multi-employer section of a segregated scheme, the trustees or managers of the scheme shall not, without the prior approval of the Board, take any action to discharge or transfer any of the assets in that part or any assets that may be assigned to that part.".

(2) Section 136 of the Act (power to validate contraventions of section 135) shall be modified in its application to a segregated part to which regulation 28 applies so that it shall be read as if, after subsection (2), there were inserted the following subsection—

"(2A) Where the trustees or managers of a segregated part of a multi-employer section of a segregated scheme receive a copy of a notice from the Board under subsection (2), they must send a copy of that notice as soon as practicable to the trustees or managers of each section of the scheme (if different) and to all employers in relation to the scheme.".

[18.51]
37 Board to act as creditor of the employer

Section 137 of the Act (Board to act as creditor of the employer) shall be modified in its application to a segregated part to which regulation 28 applies so that it shall be read as if—

(a) after the words "due to them by the employer" in subsection (2), there were inserted the words "in respect of the protected liabilities that are included in the segregated part"; and

(b) after subsection (3), there were added the following subsection—

"(3A) Where an amount is paid to the trustees or managers of a multi-employer scheme in respect of any debt owed to the scheme by the employer in relation to a segregated part of a multi-employer section of the scheme which does not relate to the employer's liabilities to or in respect of members of the scheme who are not designated to that segregated part, that amount shall be applied by the trustees or managers of the scheme towards the liabilities of the scheme as a whole.".

[18.52]
[37A Ill health pensions

(1) Section 141 of the Act (effect of a review) shall be modified in its application to a segregated part to which regulation 28 applies so that it shall be read as if—

(a) in subsection (4) the words "a determination under section 143(2)(a) or" were omitted; and
(b) in subsection (5)(a) the words "makes a determination under section 143(2)(a) or" were omitted.

(2) Section 142(1) of the Act (sections 140 and 141: interpretation) shall be modified in its application to a segregated part to which regulation 28 applies so that it shall be read as if, for the words "143(2)(b)" in the definition of "scheme valuation" there were substituted the word "143".]

NOTES

Inserted by the Pension Protection Fund (Miscellaneous Amendments) (No 2) Regulations 2012, SI 2012/3083, reg 2(1), (9); for a transitional provision see reg 10 thereof.

[18.53]

38 Valuation of assets

(1) Section 143 of the Act (Board's obligation to obtain valuation of assets and protected liabilities) shall be modified in its application to a segregated part to which regulation 28 applies, so that it shall be read as if—

(a) for subsection (1), there were substituted the following subsection—

"(1) This section applies in a case within subsection (1) of section 127 or 128 which relates to a segregated part of a multi-employer section of a segregated scheme.";

[(b) for subsection (2), there were substituted the following subsection—

"(2) For the purposes of determining whether the condition in subsection (2)(a) of the section in question is satisfied, the Board must, as soon as reasonably practicable, obtain an actuarial valuation of the section as a whole and of the segregated part as at the relevant time."]

[(ba) subsection (2A) were omitted;
(bb) for the words "a determination made under subsection (2)(a) or an actuarial valuation obtained under subsection (2)(b)" in subsection (4), there were substituted the words "this section";
(bc) subsection (5C) were omitted;
(bd) in subsection (6), the words "for the purposes of an actuarial valuation obtained under subsection (2)(b)" were omitted;"]
(c) for the words "the scheme's liabilities" in subsection (7), there were substituted the words "the liabilities of the scheme or the segregated part"; . . .
[(ca) in subsection (9)—
(i) for the words "requires a determination to be made, or an", there were substituted the words "requires the", and
(ii) the words "the determination or" were omitted;
(cb) for the words "requires a determination to be made, or an" in subsection (10), there were substituted the words "requires the";]
(d) in subsection (11)—
(i) for the words ""actuarial valuation", in relation to the scheme, means a written valuation of the assets and protected liabilities of the scheme" in paragraph (a), there were substituted the words ""actuarial valuation", in relation to the section as a whole and the segregated part, means a written valuation of the assets and protected liabilities of the section as a whole and the segregated part";
[(ia) the words "makes a determination under subsection (2)(a) or" in paragraph (b)(ii) were omitted; and]
(ii) the word "and" at the end of paragraph (c)(ii) were omitted; and
(iii) after paragraph (d), there were inserted the following paragraph—

"(e) "protected liabilities" means, in relation to a multi-employer section of a segregated scheme, the cost of securing benefits for and in respect of members of the section which correspond to the compensation which would be payable, in relation to the section, in accordance with the pension compensation provisions (see section 162) if the Board assumed responsibility for the section in accordance with this Chapter.".

(2) Section 144 of the Act (approval of valuation) shall be modified in its application to a segregated part to which regulation 28 applies so that it shall be read as if—

[(a) for the words "obtains a valuation in respect of a scheme under section 143(2)(b)" in subsection (1), there were substituted the words "obtains a valuation or a further valuation in respect of the section as a whole and of the segregated part under section 143"; and]
(b) after subsection (2), there were inserted the following subsection—

"(2A) Where the trustees or managers of a segregated part of a multi-employer section of a segregated scheme receive a copy of a valuation from the Board under subsection (2), they must send a further copy of that valuation as soon as practicable to the trustees or managers of each section of the scheme (if different) and to all the employers in relation to the scheme.".

(3) Section 145 of the Act (binding valuations) shall be modified in its application to a segregated part to which regulation 28 applies so that it shall be read as if—

[(a) for the words "a valuation obtained under section 143(2)(b) is not binding" in subsection (1), there were substituted the words "a valuation or a further valuation obtained under section 143 of the section as a whole and of the segregated part is not binding".]

(b) for the words "in relation to a scheme" in subsection (2), there were substituted the words "in relation to a multi-employer section of a segregated scheme in relation to which there is a segregated part"; and
(c) after subsection (3), there were inserted the following subsection—

"(3A) Where the trustees or managers of a segregated part of a multi-employer section of a segregated scheme receive a notice from the Board under subsection (3) together with a copy of the binding valuation, they must send a copy of the notice and the binding valuation as soon as practicable to the trustees or managers of each section of the scheme (if different) and to all the employers in relation to the scheme.".

NOTES

Para (1): sub-para (b) substituted, sub-paras (ba)–(bd), (ca), (cb), (d)(ia) inserted, and word omitted from sub-para (c) revoked, by the Pension Protection Fund (Miscellaneous Amendments) (No 2) Regulations 2012, SI 2012/3083, reg 2(1), (10)(a)–(e); for a transitional provision see reg 10 thereof.

Para (2): sub-para (a) substituted by SI 2012/3083, reg 2(1), (10)(f); for a transitional provision see reg 10 thereof.

Para (3): sub-para (a) substituted by SI 2012/3083, reg 2(1), (10)(g); for a transitional provision see reg 10 thereof.

[18.54]

39 Refusal to assume responsibility for a scheme

(1) Section 146 of the Act (schemes which become eligible schemes) shall be modified in its application to a segregated part to which regulation 28 applies so that it shall be read as if—
(a) for subsection (1), there were substituted the following subsection—

"(1) Regulations may provide that where the Board is satisfied that a multi-employer section of a segregated scheme, or a segregated part of such a section, is not, for the purposes of this Part, an eligible scheme throughout such period as may be prescribed, the Board must refuse to assume responsibility for that section under this Chapter.";

(b) for the words "a scheme" in subsection (2), there were substituted the words "a section of the scheme";
(c) after subsection (2), there were inserted the following subsection—

"(2A) Where the trustees or managers of a segregated part of a multi-employer section of a segregated scheme receive a copy of a withdrawal notice from the Board under subsection (2), they must send a copy of that notice as soon as practicable to the trustees or managers of each section of the scheme (if different) and to all the employers in relation to the scheme."; and

(d) after subsection (4), there were inserted the following subsection—

"(4A) Where the trustees or managers of a segregated part of a multi-employer section of a segregated scheme receive a notice from the Board under subsection (4) together with a copy of the binding notice, they must send a copy of the notice and the binding notice as soon as practicable to the trustees or managers of each section of the scheme (if different) and to all the employers in relation to the scheme.".

(2) Section 147 of the Act (new schemes created to replace existing schemes) shall be modified in its application to a segregated part to which regulation 28 applies so that it shall be read as if—
(a) for subsection (1), there were substituted the following subsection—

"(1) The Board must refuse to assume responsibility for a segregated part of a multi-employer section of a segregated scheme ("the new scheme") under this Chapter where it is satisfied that—
(a) the new scheme was established during such a period as may be prescribed,
(b) the employer in relation to the segregated part was, at the date of establishment of the new scheme, also the employer in relation to another scheme ("the old scheme") or another section of the scheme ("the old section") established before the new scheme,
(c) the assignment of scheme assets made to the new scheme has been made in respect of any rights of members under the old scheme, and
(d) the main purpose or one of the main purposes of establishing the new scheme and making the transfer or transfers, or transfer payment or transfer payments, was to enable those members to receive compensation under the pension compensation provisions in respect of their rights under the new section in circumstances where, in the absence of the transfer or transfers, regulations under section 146 would have operated to prevent such payments in respect of their rights under the old scheme or the old section.";

(b) after subsection (2), there were inserted the following subsection—

"(2A) Where the trustees or managers of a segregated part of a multi-employer section of a segregated scheme receive a copy of a withdrawal notice from the Board under subsection (2), they must send a copy of that notice as soon as practicable to the trustees or managers of each section of the scheme (if different) and to all the employers in relation to the scheme."; and

(c) after subsection (4), there were inserted the following subsection—

"(4A) Where the trustees or managers of a segregated part of a multi-employer section of a segregated scheme receive a notice from the Board under subsection (4) together with a copy of the binding . . . notice, they must send a copy of the notice and the binding notice as soon as practicable to the trustees or managers of each section of the scheme (if different) and to all the employers in relation to the scheme.".

(3) Section 148 of the Act (withdrawal following issue of section 122(4) notice) shall be modified in its application to a segregated part to which regulation 28 applies so that it shall be read as if—

(a) after subsection (5), there were inserted the following subsection—

"(5A) Where the trustees or managers of a segregated part of a multi-employer section of a segregated scheme receive a copy of a withdrawal notice from the Board under subsection (5), they must send a copy of that notice as soon as practicable to the trustees or managers of each section of the scheme (if different) and to all the employers in relation to the scheme."; and

(b) after subsection (7), there were inserted the following subsection—

"(7A) Where the trustees or managers of a segregated part of a multi-employer section of a segregated scheme receive a notice from the Board under subsection (7) together with a copy of the binding notice, they must send a copy of the notice and the binding notice as soon as practicable to the trustees or managers of each section of the scheme (if different) and to all the employers in relation to the scheme.".

NOTES

Para (2): in sub-para (c), in s 147(4A) (as set out above) word omitted revoked by the Occupational Pension Schemes and Pension Protection Fund (Amendment) Regulations 2005, SI 2005/993, regs 1(2), 5(1), (5)(f).

[18.55]

40 Reconsideration

[(1) Section 151 of the Act (application for reconsideration) shall be modified in its application to a segregated part to which regulation 28 applies, so that it shall be read as if—

(a) for the words "the determination made by the Board or valuation obtained by the Board in respect of the scheme under section 143(2)" in subsections (2)(b) and (3)(b) there were substituted the words "the valuation obtained by the Board under section 143 in respect of the segregated part";

(b) the words "determination or" in paragraphs (a)(ii) and (b)(ii) of subsection (6) were omitted;

(c) in the definition of "protected benefits quotation" in subsection (8), from the words "in relation to a scheme" to "the reconsideration time" there were substituted—

"in relation to a segregated part of a multi-employer section of a segregated scheme, means a quotation for one or more annuities from one or more insurers, being companies willing to accept payment in respect of the members of the segregated part from the trustees or managers of the scheme, which would provide in respect of each member of the segregated part from the reconsideration time"; and

(d) for the words "under section 143(2)(b)" in subsection (10), there were substituted the words "under that section".]

(2) Section 152 of the Act (duty to assume responsibility following reconsideration) shall be modified in its application to a segregated part to which regulation 28 applies so that it shall be read as if—

(a) for subsection (1), there were substituted the following subsection—

"(1) This section applies where an application is made in respect of a segregated part of a multi-employer section of a segregated scheme in accordance with section 151.";

(b) for subsection (2), there were substituted the following subsection—

"(2) The Board must assume responsibility in accordance with this Chapter for a segregated part of a multi-employer section of a segregated scheme if it is satisfied that the value of the assets of the segregated part at the reconsideration time is less than the aggregate of—

(a) the amount quoted in the protected benefits quotation accompanying the application;

(b) a proportion of the amount of the liabilities of the scheme as a whole at that time, as calculated in the Board's valuation referred to in [subsection (2) or (3) of section 151], which are not liabilities to, or in respect of, members of the scheme;

(c) the estimated costs of winding up the segregated part at that time.";

(c) after subsection (3), there were inserted the following subsection—

"(3A) Where the trustees or managers of a segregated part of a multi-employer section of a segregated scheme receive a copy of a determination notice from the Board under subsection (3), they must send a copy of that notice as soon as practicable to the trustees or managers of each section of the scheme (if different) and to all the employers in relation to the scheme."; and

(d) after subsection (7), there were inserted the following subsection—

"(7A) Where the trustees or managers of a segregated part of a multi-employer section of a segregated scheme receive a notice from the Board under subsection (7) together with a copy of the binding determination notice, they must send a copy of the notice and the binding notice as soon as practicable to the trustees or managers of each section of the scheme (if different) and to all the employers in relation to the scheme.".

NOTES

Para (1): substituted by the Pension Protection Fund (Miscellaneous Amendments) (No 2) Regulations 2012, SI 2012/3083, reg 2(1), (11); for a transitional provision see reg 10 thereof.

Para (2): in sub-para (b), in s 152(2)(b) (as set out above) words in square brackets substituted by SI 2005/993, reg 5(1), (5)(g)(ii).

[18.56]

[41 Closed schemes, requirement to wind up schemes with sufficient assets and applications and notifications where closed schemes have insufficient assets]

(1) Section 153 of the Act (closed schemes) shall be modified in its application to a segregated part to which regulation 28 applies so that it shall be read as if—

(a) for the words "(scheme rescue not possible but scheme has sufficient assets to meet the protected liabilities)" in subsection (1), there were substituted the words "(scheme rescue not possible in relation to a segregated part of a multi-employer section of a segregated scheme but segregated part has sufficient assets to meet the protected liabilities)";

(b) for the words "a closed scheme" in subsection (2), there were substituted the words "a closed section of a scheme";

(c) for the words "a closed scheme" in subsection (5), there were substituted the words "a closed section of a scheme";

(d) after subsection (6), there were inserted the following subsection—

"(6A) Where the trustees or managers of a segregated part of a multi-employer section of a segregated scheme receive a notice from the Board under subsection (6), they must send a copy of that notice as soon as practicable to the trustees or managers of each section of the scheme (if different) and to all the employers in relation to the scheme."; and

(e) for the definition of "full buy-out quotation" in subsection (7), there were substituted the following definition—

""full buy-out quotation", in relation to a segregated part of a multi-employer section of a segregated scheme, means a quotation for one or more annuities from one or more insurers (being companies willing to accept payment in respect of members of the segregated part from the trustees or managers of the scheme) which would provide in respect of each of those members, from a relevant date, benefits in accordance with the member's entitlement or accrued rights, including pension credit rights, under the scheme rules (other than entitlement or rights in respect of money purchase benefits).".

(2) Section 154 of the Act (requirement to wind up schemes with sufficient assets to meet protected liabilities) shall be modified in its application to a segregated part to which regulation 28 applies so that it shall be read as if—

(a) for the words "(scheme rescue not possible but scheme has sufficient assets to meet the protected liabilities)" in paragraph (a) of subsection (2), there were substituted the words "(scheme rescue not possible in relation to a segregated part of a multi-employer section of a segregated scheme but segregated part has sufficient assets to meet the protected liabilities)";

[(aa) the words "determination made by the Board or" in subsection (5)(b), were omitted;]

(b) for the words "a scheme is wound up" in subsection (6), there were substituted the words "a segregated part of a multi-employer section of a segregated scheme is wound up";

(c) for the words "winding up of a scheme" in subsection (11), there were substituted the words "winding up of a segregated part of a multi-employer section of a segregated scheme"; and

(d) for the words "in relation to a scheme" in subsection (12), there were substituted the words "in relation to a segregated part of a multi-employer section of a segregated scheme".

(3) Section 155 of the Act (treatment of closed schemes) shall be modified in its application to a segregated part to which regulation 28 applies so that it shall be read as if—

(a) for subsection (1), there were substituted the following subsection—

"(1) In this section "closed scheme" means a segregated part of a multi-employer section of a segregated scheme which is, for the purposes of this Part, an eligible scheme which is authorised under section 153 to continue as a closed section of the scheme."; and

(b) after the words "The provisions mentioned in subsection (3)" in subsection (2), there were inserted the words "as they apply to a segregated part of a multi-employer section of a segregated scheme".

(4) Section 156 of the Act (valuations of closed schemes) shall be modified in its application to a segregated part to which regulation 28 applies so that it shall be read as if—

(a) for the words "closed schemes" in subsection (1) and paragraph (a) of subsection (2), there were substituted the words "a closed segregated part of a multi-employer section of a segregated scheme"; and

(b) for the words "a closed scheme" in subsection (5), there were substituted the words "a closed segregated part of a multi-employer section of a segregated scheme".

(5) Section 157 of the Act [(applications and notifications where closed schemes have insufficient assets)] shall be modified in its application to a segregated part to which regulation 28 applies so that it shall be read as if, after subsection (4), there were inserted the following subsection—

"(4A) Where the trustees or managers of a segregated part of a multi-employer section of a segregated scheme receive a notice from the Board under subsection (4), they must send a copy of that notice as soon as practicable to the trustees or managers of each section of the scheme (if different) and to all the employers in relation to the scheme.".

[(6) Section 158 of the Act (duty to assume responsibility for closed schemes) shall be modified in its application to a segregated part to which regulation 28 applies so that it shall be read as if—

(a) for subsection (3), there were substituted the following subsection—

"(3) For the purposes of determining whether the condition in subsection (1) is satisfied, the Board must, as soon as reasonably practicable, obtain an actuarial valuation (within the meaning of section 143) of the segregated part as at the relevant time.";

(b) subsection (3A) were omitted;

(c) in subsection (5)—

(i) for the words "a determination made under subsection (3)(a) and a valuation obtained under subsection (3)(b)" there were substituted the words "a valuation obtained under subsection (3)";

(ii) for the words "a determination made under section 143(2)(a) and a valuation obtained under section 143(2)(b)" there were substituted the words "a valuation obtained under section 143"; and

(iii) paragraph (aa) were omitted; and

(d) in subsection (6)—

(i) ", 143A" were omitted; and

(ii) paragraph (aa) were omitted.]

NOTES

Regulation heading: substituted by the Occupational Pension Schemes and Pension Protection Fund (Amendment) Regulations 2005, SI 2005/993, regs 1(2), 5(1), (5)(h)(i).

Para (2): sub-para (aa) inserted by the Pension Protection Fund (Miscellaneous Amendments) (No 2) Regulations 2012, SI 2012/3083, reg 2(1), (12)(a); for a transitional provision see reg 10 thereof.

Para (5): words in square brackets substituted by SI 2005/993, regs 1(2), 5(1), (5)(h)(ii).

Para (6): added by SI 2012/3083, reg 2(1), (12)(b); for a transitional provision see reg 10 thereof.

[18.57]

42 Transfer notices and assumption of responsibility for a scheme

(1) Section 160 of the Act (transfer notice) shall be modified in its application to a segregated part to which regulation 28 applies so that it shall be read as if—

(a) after subsection (1), there were inserted the following section—

"(1A) This section also applies where the Board is required to assume responsibility for a segregated part of a multi-employer section of a segregated scheme.";

(b) after subsection (2) there were inserted the following subsection—

"(2A) Where the trustees or managers of a segregated part of a multi-employer section of a segregated scheme receive a transfer notice from the Board under subsection (2), they must send a copy of that notice as soon as practicable to the trustees or managers of each section of the scheme (if different) and to all the employers in relation to the scheme.";

[(ba) for the words "determination made or valuation obtained under section 143(2)" in subsection (3), there were substituted the words "valuation obtained under section 143";

(bb) in subsection (4) the words "determination made or" were omitted;]

(c) after subsection (4), there were inserted the following subsection—

"(4B) In a case where the Board is required to assume responsibility for a segregated part of a multi-employer section of a segregated scheme under section 127, 128, 152 or 158, a transfer notice may not be given until the Board has obtained a further actuarial valuation of the assets and protected liabilities of the section as a whole and of the segregated part under section 160A as at the date on which it is required to assume responsibility for the segregated part and that valuation has been approved by the Board and become binding."; and

(d) for subsection (6) there were substituted the following subsection—

"(6) The Board must give a copy of the transfer notice under subsection (2) to—

(a) the Regulator, and

(b) an insolvency practitioner acting in relation to the employer in relation to the segregated part of the multi-employer section of the segregated scheme in respect of which the transfer notice is issued.".

(2) Section 161 of the Act (effect of Board assuming responsibility for a scheme) shall be modified in its application to a segregated part to which regulation 28 applies so that it shall be read as if—

(a) after the word "obligations" in paragraph (b) of subsection (2), there were inserted the words "to or in respect of members of the segregated part"; and

(b) after the words "to or in respect of persons" in paragraph (a) of subsection (4), there were inserted the words "who are or were members of the segregated part".

(3) Paragraph 1 of Schedule 6 to the Act (transfer of property, rights and liabilities to the Board) shall be modified in its application to a segregated part to which regulation 28 applies so that it shall be read as if, for the words "an occupational pension scheme", there were substituted the words "a segregated part of a multi-employer section of a segregated multi-employer scheme".

NOTES

Para (1): sub-paras (ba), (bc) inserted by the Pension Protection Fund (Miscellaneous Amendments) (No 2) Regulations 2012, SI 2012/3083, reg 2(1), (13); for a transitional provision see reg 10 thereof.

[18.58]

43 Further actuarial valuation of segregated parts

Part 2 of the Act shall be modified in its application to a segregated part to which regulation 28 applies so that it shall be read as if, after section 160 (transfer notice), there were inserted the following section—

"160A Further actuarial valuations of segregated parts

(1) This section applies in any case where the Board is required to obtain a further actuarial valuation under section 160(4B).

(2) The Board must obtain a further actuarial valuation of the assets and protected liabilities of the section as a whole and of the segregated part as at the date on which the Board is required to assume responsibility for the segregated part.

(3) A valuation obtained by the Board under this section shall have effect as if it were a valuation obtained by the Board under section 143 of the Act (Board's obligation to obtain valuation of assets and protected liabilities).

(4) For the purposes of this section, subsections (3), (4), (6) to (8) and (11)(a) of section 143 shall apply in relation to a valuation obtained under this section as they apply in relation to a valuation of the section as a whole and of the segregated part obtained under section 143.

(5) In the application of section 143 by virtue of this section—

(a) subsections (5) and (11)(b) of that section shall apply as if the references to "the relevant time" were to the date on which the Board is required to assume responsibility for the segregated part; and

(b) references to "assets" do not include assets representing the value of any rights in respect of money purchase benefits under the scheme rules which apply to the segregated part.".

[18.59]

44 The pension compensation provisions

(1) Section 162 of the Act (the pension compensation provisions) shall be modified in its application to a segregated part to which regulation 28 applies so that subsection (1) shall be read as if—

(a) for the words "in relation to a scheme", there were substituted the words "in relation to a segregated part of a multi-employer section of a segregated scheme";

(b) after the word "members" in paragraphs (a) and (b), there were added the words "of that segregated part";

(c) after the word "payable" in paragraph (c), there were inserted the words "to or in respect of members of that segregated part"; and

(d) at the end of paragraph (d), there were added the words "payable to or in respect of members of that segregated part".

(2) Section 163 of the Act (adjustments to be made where the Board assumes responsibility for a scheme) shall be modified in its application to a segregated part to which regulation 28 applies so that it shall be read as if, after the words "to any member" in paragraph (a) of subsection (2), there were inserted the words "of that segregated part".

(3) Section 166 of the Act (duty to pay scheme benefits unpaid at assessment date etc) shall be modified in its application to a segregated part to which regulation 28 applies so that it shall be read as if, for the words "assumes responsibility for a scheme" in subsection (1), there were substituted the words "assumes responsibility for a segregated part of a multi-employer section of a segregated scheme".

PART 5
NON-SEGREGATED SCHEMES:

SCHEMES WITH A REQUIREMENT FOR PARTIAL WIND UP ON THE WITHDRAWAL OF A PARTICIPATING EMPLOYER

[18.60]

45 Application and effect

(1) This regulation applies to a non-segregated scheme in circumstances where—

(a) an insolvency event occurs in relation to an employer in relation to the scheme; or

(b) the trustees or managers of the scheme become aware that an employer in relation to the scheme is unlikely to continue as a going concern and meets the requirements prescribed under subsection (1)(b) of section 129 of the Act (applications and notifications for the purposes of section 128).

(2) Where—

(a) in relation to an employer in relation to a non-segregated scheme, an event described in paragraph (1)(a) or (b) occurs; and

(b) the requirement in the scheme rules for the trustees or managers of the scheme to segregate such part of the assets of the scheme as is attributable to the scheme's liabilities to provide pensions or other benefits to or in respect of the pensionable service of some or all of the members by reference to an employer in relation to the scheme ("the segregation requirement") would be triggered when an employer in relation to the scheme ceases to participate in the scheme,

the segregation requirement shall, in relation to the employer referred to in sub-paragraph (a) of this paragraph, be deemed to have been triggered immediately after the occurrence of the event described in paragraph (1)(a) or (b) and a segregated part of the scheme shall be deemed to have been created for and in respect of any period after the occurrence of that event where a withdrawal event within the meaning of section 149(2) of the Act has not occurred in relation to the segregated part.

(3) In this Part—

"non-segregated scheme" means a multi-employer scheme which is not divided into two or more sections under the rules of which the trustees or managers are required, in circumstances where an employer in relation to the scheme ceases to participate in the scheme, to segregate such part of the assets of the scheme as is attributable to the scheme's liabilities to provide pensions or other benefits to or in respect of the pensionable service of some or all of the members by reference to that employer; and

"segregated part" means a section of a non-segregated scheme which is created when a segregation requirement in the scheme rules has been triggered.

(4) Except as otherwise provided in this Part of these Regulations, in a case where this regulation applies—

(a) Part 2 of the Act, except Chapter 4, shall be read as if it contained the modifications provided for by this Part; and

(b) references in Part 2 of the Act, except in Chapter 4, to—

(i) "scheme rules" shall be read as if they were references to "rules of the scheme which apply to the segregated part";

(ii) "the scheme" shall be read as if they were references to "the segregated part";

(iii) "the employer" shall be read as if they were references to "the employer in relation to the segregated part"; and

(iv) "trustees or managers of the scheme" shall, in relation to a segregated part of a non-segregated scheme, be read as if they were references to "trustees or managers with ultimate responsibility for the administration of the segregated part"[; and

(c) Part 2 of the Act shall be read as if section 143A were omitted].

(5) Paragraph (4) shall not have effect in relation to section 174 of the Act (initial levy).

NOTES

Para (4): sub-para (c) and word immediately preceding it inserted by the Pension Protection Fund (Miscellaneous Amendments) (No 2) Regulations 2012, SI 2012/3083, reg 2(1), (14); for a transitional provision see reg 10 thereof.

[18.61]

46 Notification of insolvency events, confirmation of scheme status etc

(1) Section 120 of the Act (duty to notify insolvency events in respect of employers) shall be modified in its application to a segregated part to which regulation 45 applies so that it shall be read as if—

(a) for subsection (1), there were substituted the following subsection—

"(1) This section applies where an insolvency event occurs in relation to an employer in relation to a multi-employer scheme which is not divided into two or more sections ("a non-segregated scheme") under the rules of which the trustees or managers of the scheme are required, in circumstances where an employer in relation to the scheme ceases to participate in the scheme, to segregate such part of the assets of the scheme as is attributable to the scheme's liabilities to provide pensions or other benefits to or in respect of the pensionable service of some or all of the members of the scheme by reference to that employer ("the segregated part")."; and

(b) after subsection (2), there were inserted the following subsection—

"(2A) Where the trustees or managers of a segregated part of a non-segregated scheme receive a notice from an insolvency practitioner under subsection (2), they must send a copy of that notice as soon as practicable to all the employers in relation to the scheme.".

(2) Section 122 of the Act (insolvency practitioner's duty to issue notices confirming status of scheme) shall be modified in its application to a segregated part to which regulation 45 applies so that it shall be read as if—

(a) for subsection (1), there were substituted the following subsection—

"(1) This section applies where an insolvency event has occurred in relation to an employer in relation to a non-segregated scheme and a segregated part of the scheme is created.";

(b) in subsection (2)—

(i) after the words "a scheme rescue is not possible" in paragraph (a), there were inserted the words "in relation to a segregated part"; and

(ii) after the words "a scheme rescue has occurred" in paragraph (b), there were inserted the words "in relation to a segregated part";

(c) in subsection (4)—
(i) after the words "a scheme rescue is not possible" in paragraph (a), there were inserted the words "in relation to the relevant segregated part"; and
(ii) after the words "a scheme rescue has occurred" there were inserted the words "in relation to the relevant segregated part";
[(d) in subsection (5)—
(i) in paragraph (a), for the words "in relation to an occupational pension scheme" there were substituted the words "in relation to a segregated part of a non-segregated scheme"; and
(ii) in paragraph (b), for the words "in relation to such a scheme" there were substituted the words "in relation to such a segregated part"; and]
(e) after subsection (6), there were inserted the following subsection—

"(6A) Where the trustees or managers of a segregated part of a non-segregated scheme receive a notice issued by an insolvency practitioner or former insolvency practitioner under subsection (6), they must send a copy of that notice as soon as practicable to all the employers in relation to the scheme.".

(3) Section 123 of the Act (approval of notices issued under section 122) shall be modified in its application to a segregated part to which regulation 45 applies so that it shall be read as if—
(a) for subsection (1), there were substituted the following subsection—

"(1) This section applies where the Board receives a notice under section 122(6) ("the section 122 notice") in relation to a segregated part of a non-segregated scheme."; and

(b) after subsection (4), there were inserted the following subsection—

"(4A) Where the trustees or managers of a segregated part of a non-segregated scheme receive a copy of a determination notice from the Board under subsection (4), they must send a copy of that notice as soon as practicable to all the employers in relation to the scheme.".

(4) Section 124 of the Act (Board's duty where there is a failure to comply with section 122) shall be modified in its application to a segregated part to which regulation 45 applies so that it shall be read as if—
(a) for the words "This section applies where, in relation to an occupational pension scheme" in subsection (1), there were substituted the words "This section applies where, in relation to a segregated part of a non-segregated scheme"; and
(b) after subsection (4), there were inserted the following subsection—

"(4A) Where the trustees or managers of a segregated part of a non-segregated scheme receive a copy of a notice issued by the Board under [section 122] by virtue of this section, they must send a copy of that notice as soon as practicable to all the employers in relation to the scheme.".

(5) Section 125 of the Act (binding notices confirming status of the scheme) shall be modified in its application to a segregated part to which regulation 45 applies so that [it shall be read as if] after subsection (3), there were inserted the following subsection—

"(3A) Where the trustees or managers of a segregated part of a non-segregated scheme receive a notice from the Board under subsection (3) together with a copy of the binding notice, they must send a copy of the notice and the binding notice as soon as practicable to all the employers in relation to the scheme.".

NOTES

Para (2): sub-para (d) substituted by the Occupational Pension Schemes and Pension Protection Fund (Amendment) Regulations 2005, SI 2005/993, regs 1(2), 5(1), (6)(a)(i).

Para (4): in sub-para (b), in s 124(4A) (as set out above) words in square brackets substituted by SI 2005/993, regs 1(2), 5(1), (6)(a)(ii).

Para (5): words in square brackets inserted by SI 2005/993, regs 1(2), 5(1), (6)(a)(iii).

[18.62]

47 Eligible schemes

(1) Except as otherwise provided in this Part, for the purposes of Part 2 of the Act, except Chapter 4, as it applies in the case of a segregated part to which regulation 45 applies, references to "an eligible scheme" shall be read as if they were references to a segregated part of the scheme in circumstances where that segregated part, if it were a scheme, would not be—
(a) a money purchase scheme; or
(b) a scheme which is a prescribed scheme or a scheme of a prescribed description under section 126(1)(b) of the Act.

(2) Paragraph (1) above shall not apply for the purposes of sections 174 to 181 of the Act (the levies).

[18.63]

48 Duty to assume responsibility for schemes

(1) Section 127 of the Act (duty to assume responsibility for schemes following insolvency event) shall be modified in its application to a segregated part to which regulation 45 applies so that it shall be read as if, after the words "at the relevant time" in paragraph (a) of subsection (2), there were inserted the words "as determined by the Board's valuation of the scheme under section 143, was less than the amount of the protected liabilities of that part as determined by that valuation".

(2) Section 128 of the Act (duty to assume responsibility for schemes following application or notification) shall be modified in its application to a segregated part to which regulation 45 applies so that it shall be read as if, after the words . . . "at the relevant time" in paragraph (a) of subsection (2), there were inserted the words "as determined by the Board's valuation of the scheme under section 143, was less than the amount of the protected liabilities of that part as determined by that valuation".

(3) Section 129 of the Act (applications and notifications for the purposes of section 128) shall be modified in its application to a segregated part to which regulation 45 applies so that it shall be read as if—

(a) after subsection (1), there were inserted the following subsection—

"(1A) Where the trustees or managers of a segregated part of a non-segregated scheme make an application to the Board under subsection (1), they must issue a notice to that effect as soon as practicable to all the employers in relation to the scheme."; and

(b) after subsection (5), there were inserted the following subsection—

"(5A) Where the trustees or managers of a segregated part of a non-segregated scheme receive a notice from the Board under subsection (5), they must send a copy of that notice as soon as practicable to all the employers in relation to the scheme.".

NOTES

Para (2): word omitted revoked by the Occupational Pension Schemes and Pension Protection Fund (Amendment) Regulations 2005, SI 2005/993, regs 1(2), 5(1), (6)(b).

[18.64]

49 Board's duty where application or notification received under section 129

Section 130 of the Act (Board's duty where application or notification received under section 129) shall be modified in its application to a segregated part to which regulation 45 applies so that it shall be read as if—

(a) after the words "a scheme rescue is not possible" in subsection (2), there were inserted the words "in relation to a segregated part of a non-segregated scheme";

(b) after the words "a scheme rescue has occurred" in subsection (3), there were inserted the words "in relation to a segregated part";

(c) after subsection (4), there were inserted the following subsection—

"(4A) Where the trustees or managers of a segregated part of a non-segregated scheme receive a copy of a notice from the Board under subsection (4), they must send a copy of that notice as soon as practicable to all the employers in relation to the scheme.";

[(d) in subsection (5)—

(i) in paragraph (a), for the words "in relation to an occupational pension scheme" there were substituted the words "in relation to a segregated part of a non-segregated scheme"; and

(ii) in paragraph (b), for the words "in relation to such a scheme" there were substituted the words "in relation to such a segregated part"; and]

(e) after subsection (7), there were inserted the following subsection—

"(7A) Where the trustees or managers of a segregated part of a non-segregated scheme receive a notice from the Board under subsection (7) together with a copy of the binding notice, they must send a copy of the notice and the binding notice as soon as practicable to all the employers in relation to the scheme.".

NOTES

Para (d): substituted by the Occupational Pension Schemes and Pension Protection Fund (Amendment) Regulations 2005, SI 2005/993, regs 1(2), 5(1), (6)(c).

[18.65]

50 Protected liabilities and assessment period

(1) Section 131 of the Act (protected liabilities) shall be modified in its application to a segregated part to which regulation 45 applies so that it shall be read as if, for subsection (1), there were substituted the following subsection—

"(1) Except as otherwise provided, for the purposes of this Chapter the protected liabilities, in relation to a segregated part of a non-segregated scheme which is, for the purposes of this Part, an eligible scheme, at a particular time ("the relevant time") are—

(a) the cost of securing benefits for and in respect of members of the segregated part which correspond to the compensation which would be payable, in relation to members of that part in accordance with the pension compensation provisions (see section 162) if the Board assumed responsibility for the segregated part in accordance with this Chapter,

(b) a proportion of the liabilities of the scheme as a whole, as calculated in the Board's valuation under section 143, which are not liabilities to, or in respect of, members,

(c) the estimated cost of winding up the segregated part.".

Part 18 Miscellaneous SIs

(2) Section 132 of the Act (assessment periods) shall be modified in its application to a segregated part to which regulation 45 applies so that it shall be read as if, after the words "an assessment period" in subsection (2), there were inserted the words "in relation to a segregated part of a non-segregated scheme".

[18.66]
51 Directions

Section 134 of the Act (directions) shall be modified in its application to a segregated part to which regulation 45 applies so that it shall be read as if—

(a) in subsection (2)—

(i) for the words "the scheme's protected liabilities do not exceed its assets", there were substituted the words "the protected liabilities of the segregated part do not exceed its assets";

(ii) for the words "in relation to the scheme" there were substituted the words "in relation to the non-segregated scheme in question";

(iii) for the words "the investment of the scheme's assets" in paragraph (a), there were substituted the words "the investment of the assets of the segregated part"; and

(b) for subparagraph (i) of paragraph (a) of subsection (3), there were substituted the following paragraph—

"(i) any trustees or managers of the scheme in relation to which the segregated part relates,".

[18.67]
52 Restrictions on winding up, discharge of liabilities etc and power to validate contraventions of section 135

(1) Section 135 of the Act (restrictions on winding up, discharge of liabilities etc) shall be modified in its application to a segregated part to which regulation 45 applies so that it shall be read as if—

(a) after the words "the winding up of the scheme" in subsection (2), there were inserted the words "under or by virtue of the scheme rules"; and

(b) after subsection (4), there were inserted the following subsection—

"(4A) Where an assessment period has begun in relation to a segregated part of a non-segregated scheme, the trustees or managers shall not, without the prior approval of the Board, take any action to discharge or transfer any of the assets in that part or any assets that may be assigned to that part.".

(2) Section 136 of the Act (power to validate contraventions of section 135) shall be modified in its application to a segregated part to which regulation 45 of these Regulations applies so that it shall be read as if, after subsection (2), there were inserted the following subsection—

"(2A) Where the trustees or managers of a segregated part of a non-segregated scheme receive a notice from the Board under subsection (2), they must send a copy of that notice as soon as practicable to all the employers in relation to the scheme.".

[18.68]
53 Board to act as creditor of the employer

Section 137 of the Act (Board to act as creditor of the employer) shall be modified in its application to a segregated part to which regulation 45 applies so that it shall be read as if—

(a) after the words "due to them by the employer" in subsection (2), there were inserted the words "in respect of the protected liabilities that are included in the segregated part"; and

(b) after subsection (3), there were added the following subsection—

"(3A) Where an amount is paid to the trustees or managers of a non-segregated multi-employer scheme in respect of any debt owed to the scheme by the employer in relation to a segregated part of the scheme which does not relate to the employer's liabilities to or in respect of members of the scheme who are not designated to that segregated part, that amount shall be applied by the trustees or managers of the scheme towards the liabilities of the scheme as a whole.".

[18.69]
[53A Ill health pensions

(1) Section 141 of the Act (effect of a review) shall be modified in its application to a segregated part to which regulation 45 applies so that it shall be read as if—

(a) in subsection (4) the words "a determination under section 143(2)(a) or" were omitted; and

(b) in subsection (5)(a) the words "makes a determination under section 143(2)(a) or" were omitted.

(2) Section 142(1) of the Act (sections 140 and 141: interpretation) shall be modified in its application to a segregated part to which regulation 45 applies, so that it shall be read as if for the words "143(2)(b)" in the definition of "scheme valuation" there were substituted the word "143".]

NOTES

Inserted by the Pension Protection Fund (Miscellaneous Amendments) (No 2) Regulations 2012, SI 2012/3083, reg 2(1), (15); for a transitional provision see reg 10 thereof.

[18.70]
54 Valuation of assets

(1) Section 143 of the Act (Board's obligation to obtain valuation of assets and protected liabilities) shall be modified in its application to a segregated part to which regulation 45 applies, so that it shall be read as if—

(a) for subsection (1), there were substituted the following subsection—

"(1) This section applies in a case within subsection (1) of section 127 or 128 which relates to a non-segregated scheme."; and

[(b) for subsection (2) there were substituted the following subsection—

"(2) For the purposes of determining whether the condition in subsection (2)(a) of the section in question is satisfied, the Board must, as soon as reasonably practicable, obtain an actuarial valuation of the section as a whole and of the segregated part as at the relevant time.";]

[(ba) subsection (2A) were omitted;

(bb) for the words "a determination made under subsection (2)(a) or an actuarial valuation obtained under subsection (2)(b)" in subsection (4), there were substituted the words "this section";

(bc) subsection (5C) were omitted;

(bd) in subsection (6), the words "for the purposes of an actuarial valuation obtained under subsection (2)(b)" were omitted;]

(c) for the words "the scheme's liabilities" in subsection (7), there were substituted the words "the liabilities of the scheme or the segregated part"; . . .

[(ca) in subsection (9)—

(i) for the words "requires a determination to be made, or an", there were substituted the words "requires the"; and

(ii) the words "the determination or" were omitted;

(cb) for the words "requires a determination to be made, or an" in subsection (10), there were substituted the words "requires the";]

(d) in subsection (11)—

(i) for the words ""actuarial valuation", in relation to the scheme, means a written valuation of the assets and protected liabilities of the scheme" in paragraph (a), there were substituted the words ""actuarial valuation", in relation to the scheme as a whole and the segregated part, means a written valuation of the assets and protected liabilities of the scheme as a whole and the segregated part";

[(ia) the words "makes a determination under subsection (2)(a) or" in paragraph (b)(ii) were omitted; and]

(ii) the word "and" at the end of paragraph (c)(ii) were omitted; and

(iii) after paragraph (d), there were added the following paragraph—

"(e) "protected liabilities" means, in relation to a non-segregated scheme, the cost of securing benefits for and in respect of members of the scheme which correspond to the compensation which would be payable, in relation to the scheme, in accordance with the pension compensation provisions (see section 162) if the Board assumed responsibility for the scheme in accordance with this Chapter.".

(2) Section 144 of the Act (approval of valuation) shall be modified in its application to a segregated part to which regulation 45 applies so that it shall be read as if—

[(a) for the words "obtains a valuation in respect of a scheme under section 143(2)(b)" in subsection (1), there were substituted the words "obtains a valuation or a further valuation in respect of the section as a whole and of the segregated part under section 143"; and]

(b) after subsection (2), there were inserted the following subsection—

"(2A) Where the trustees or managers of a segregated part of a non-segregated scheme receive a copy of a valuation from the Board under subsection (2), they must send a copy of that valuation as soon as practicable to all the employers in relation to the scheme.".

(3) Section 145 of the Act (binding valuations) shall be modified in its application to a segregated part to which regulation 45 applies so that it shall be read as if—

[(a) for the words "a valuation obtained under section 143(2)(b) is not binding" in subsection (1), there were substituted the words "a valuation or a further valuation obtained under section 143 of the section as a whole and of the segregated part is not binding";]

(b) for the words "in relation to a scheme" in subsection (2), there were substituted the words "in relation to a non-segregated scheme in relation to which there is a segregated part"; and

(c) after subsection (3), there were inserted the following subsection—

"(3A) Where the trustees or managers of a segregated part of a non-segregated scheme receive a notice from the Board under subsection (3) together with a copy of the binding valuation, they must send a copy of that notice and the binding valuation as soon as practicable to all the employers in relation to the scheme.".

NOTES

Para (1): sub-para (b) substituted, sub-paras (ba)–(bd), (ca), (cb), (d)(ia) inserted and word omitted from sub-para (c) revoked by the Pension Protection Fund (Miscellaneous Amendments) (No 2) Regulations 2012, SI 2012/3083, reg 2(1), (16)(a)–(e); for a transitional provision see reg 10 thereof.

Para (2): sub-para (a) substituted by SI 2012/3083, reg 2(1), (16)(f); for a transitional provision see reg 10 thereof.

Para (3): sub-para (a) substituted by SI 2012/3083, reg 2(1), (16)(g); for a transitional provision see reg 10 thereof.

[18.71]
55 Refusal to assume responsibility for a scheme

(1) Section 146 of the Act (schemes which become eligible schemes) shall be modified in its application to a segregated part to which regulation 45 applies, so that it shall be read as if—

(a) for subsection (1), there were substituted the following subsection—

"(1) Regulations may provide that where the Board is satisfied that a non-segregated scheme, or a segregated part of such a scheme, is not, for the purposes of this Part, an eligible scheme throughout such period as may be prescribed, the Board must refuse to assume responsibility for that part of the scheme under this Chapter.";

(b) for the words "a scheme" in subsection (2), there were substituted the words "a segregated part of a non-segregated scheme";

(c) after subsection (2), there were inserted the following subsection—

"(2A) Where the trustees or managers of a segregated part of a non-segregated scheme receive a copy of a withdrawal notice from the Board under subsection (2), they must send a copy of that notice as soon as practicable to all the employers in relation to the scheme."; and

(d) after subsection (4), there were inserted the following subsection—

"(4A) Where the trustees or managers of a segregated part of a non-segregated scheme receive a notice from the Board under subsection (4) together with a copy of the binding notice, they must send a copy of the notice and the binding notice as soon as practicable to all the employers in relation to the scheme.".

(2) Section 147 of the Act (new schemes created to replace existing schemes) shall be modified in its application to a segregated part to which regulation 45 applies, so that it shall be read as if—

(a) for subsection (1), there were substituted the following subsection—

"(1) The Board must refuse to assume responsibility for a segregated part of a non-segregated scheme ("the new scheme") under this Chapter where it is satisfied that—

(a) the new scheme was established during such period as may be prescribed,

(b) the employer in relation to the segregated part was, at the date of establishment of the new scheme, also an employer in relation to another scheme ("the old scheme") established before the new scheme,

(c) the assignment of scheme assets made to the new scheme has been made in respect of any rights of members under the old scheme, and

(d) the main purpose or one of the main purposes of establishing the new scheme and making the transfer or transfers or transfer payment or transfer payments was to enable those members to receive compensation under the pension compensation provisions in respect of their rights under the new section in circumstances where, in the absence of the assignment, regulations under section 146 would have operated to prevent such payments in respect of their rights under the old scheme.";

(b) after subsection (2), there were inserted the following subsection—

"(2A) Where the trustees or managers of a segregated part of a non-segregated scheme receive a copy of a withdrawal notice from the Board under subsection (2), they must send a copy of that notice as soon as practicable to all the employers in relation to the scheme."; and

(c) after subsection (4), there were inserted the following subsection—

"(4A) Where the trustees or managers of a segregated part of a non-segregated scheme receive a notice from the Board under subsection (4) together with a copy of the binding notice, they must send a copy of the notice and the binding notice as soon as practicable to all the employers in relation to the scheme.".

(3) Section 148 of the Act (withdrawal following issue of section 122(4) notice) shall be modified in its application to a segregated part to which regulation 45 applies so that it shall be read as if—

(a) after subsection (5), there were inserted the following subsection—

"(5A) Where the trustees or managers of a segregated part of a non-segregated scheme receive a notice from the Board under this section, they must send a copy of that notice as soon as practicable to all the employers in relation to the scheme."; and

(b) after subsection (7), there were inserted the following subsection—

"(7A) Where the trustees or managers of a segregated part of a non-segregated scheme receive a notice from the Board under subsection (7) together with a copy of the binding notice, they must send a copy of the notice and the binding notice as soon as practicable to all the employers in relation to the scheme.".

[18.72]
56 Reconsideration

[(1) Section 151 of the Act (application for reconsideration) shall be modified in its application to a segregated part to which regulation 45 applies so that it shall be read as if—

(a) for the words "the determination made by the Board or the valuation obtained by the Board in respect of the scheme under section 143(2)" in subsections (2)(b) and (3)(b), there were substituted the words "the valuation obtained by the Board under section 143 in respect of the segregated part";

(b) the words "determination or" in paragraphs (a)(ii) and (b)(ii) of subsection (6) were omitted;

(c) in the definition of "protected benefits quotation" in subsection (8), from the words "in relation to a scheme" to "the reconsideration time" there were substituted—

"in relation to a segregated part of a non-segregated scheme, means a quotation for one or more annuities from one or more insurers, being companies willing to accept payment in respect of the members of the segregated part from the trustees or managers of the scheme, which would provide in respect of each member of the segregated part from the reconsideration time"; and

(d) for the words "under section 143(2)(b)" in subsection (10), there were substituted "under that section".]

(2) Section 152 of the Act (duty to assume responsibility following reconsideration) shall be modified in its application to a segregated part to which regulation 45 applies so that it shall be read as if—

(a) for subsection (1), there were substituted the following subsection—

"(1) This section applies where an application is made in respect of a segregated part of a non-segregated scheme in accordance with section 151.";

(b) for subsection (2), there were substituted the following subsection—

"(2) The Board must assume responsibility in accordance with this Chapter for a segregated part of a non-segregated scheme if it is satisfied that the value of the assets of the segregated part at the reconsideration time is less than the aggregate of—

(a) the amount quoted in the protected benefits quotation accompanying the application;

(b) a proportion of the amount of the liabilities of the scheme as a whole at that time, as calculated in the Board's valuation of the segregated part referred to in [subsection (2) or (3) of section 151], which are not liabilities to, or in respect of, members of the scheme;

(c) the estimated costs of winding up the segregated part at that time.";

(c) after subsection (3), there were inserted the following subsection—

"(3A) Where the trustees or managers of a segregated part of a non-segregated scheme receive a copy of a determination notice from the Board under subsection (3), they must send a copy of that notice as soon as practicable to all the employers in relation to the scheme.";

(d) after subsection (7), there were inserted the following subsection—

"(7A) Where the trustees or managers of a segregated part of a non-segregated scheme receive a notice from the Board under subsection (7) together with a copy of the binding notice, they must send a copy of the notice and the binding notice as soon as practicable to all the employers in relation to the scheme.".

NOTES

Para (1): substituted by the Pension Protection Fund (Miscellaneous Amendments) (No 2) Regulations 2012, SI 2012/3083, reg 2(1), (17); for a transitional provision see reg 10 thereof.

Para (2): in sub-para (b), in s 152(2)(b) (as set out) words in square brackets substituted by the Occupational Pension Schemes and Pension Protection Fund (Amendment) Regulations 2005, SI 2005/993, regs 1(2), 5(1), (6)(d).

[18.73]

[57 Closed schemes, requirement to wind up schemes with sufficient assets and applications and notifications where closed schemes have insufficient assets]

(1) Section 153 of the Act (closed schemes) shall be modified in its application to a segregated part to which regulation 45 applies so that it shall be read as if—

(a) for the words "(scheme rescue not possible but scheme has sufficient assets to meet the protected liabilities)" in subsection (1), there were substituted the words "(scheme rescue not possible in relation to segregated part of a non-segregated scheme but segregated part has sufficient assets to meet the protected liabilities)";

(b) for the words "a closed scheme" in subsection (2), there were substituted the words "a closed section of a scheme";

(c) for the words "a closed scheme" in subsection (5), there were substituted the words "a closed section of a scheme";

(d) after subsection (6), there were inserted the following subsection—

"(6A) Where the trustees or managers of a segregated part of a non-segregated scheme receive a copy of a determination notice from the Board under subsection (6), they must send a copy of that notice as soon as practicable to all the employers in relation to the scheme."; and

(e) for the definition of "full buy-out quotation" in subsection (7), there were substituted the following definition—

""full buy-out quotation", in relation to a segregated part of a non-segregated scheme, means a quotation for one or more annuities from one or more insurers (being companies willing to accept payment in respect of members of the segregated part from the trustees

Part 18 Miscellaneous SIs

or managers of the scheme) which would provide in respect of each of those members, from a relevant date, benefits in accordance with the member's entitlement or accrued rights, including pension credit rights, under the scheme rules (other than entitlement or rights in respect of money purchase benefits),".

(2) Section 154 of the Act (requirement to wind up schemes with sufficient assets to meet protected liabilities) shall be modified in its application to a segregated part to which regulation 45 applies so that it shall be read as if—

(a) for the words "(scheme rescue not possible but scheme has sufficient assets to meet the protected liabilities)" in subsection (2), there were substituted the words "(scheme rescue not possible in relation to a segregated part of a non-segregated scheme but segregated part has sufficient assets to meet the protected liabilities)";

[(aa) the words "determination made by the Board or" in subsection (5)(b), were omitted;]

(b) for the words "a scheme is wound up" in subsection (6), there were substituted the words "a segregated part of a non-segregated scheme is wound up";

(c) for the words "winding up of a scheme" in subsection (11), there were substituted the words "winding up of a segregated part of a non-segregated scheme"; and

(d) for the words "in relation to a scheme" in subsection (12), there were substituted the words "in relation to a segregated part of a non-segregated scheme".

(3) Section 155 of the Act (treatment of closed schemes) shall be modified in its application to a segregated part to which regulation 45 applies, so that it shall be read as if—

(a) for subsection (1) there were substituted the following subsection—

"(1) In this section "closed scheme" means a segregated part of a non-segregated scheme which is, for the purpose of this Part, an eligible scheme which is authorised under section 153 to continue as a closed section of the scheme."; and

(b) after the words "The provisions mentioned in subsection (3)" in subsection (2), there were inserted the words "as they apply to a segregated part of a non-segregated scheme".

(4) Section 156 of the Act (valuations of closed schemes) shall be modified in its application to a segregated part to which regulation 45 applies, so that it shall be read as if—

(a) for the words "closed schemes" in subsection (1) and paragraph (a) of subsection (2), there were substituted the words "a closed segregated part of a non-segregated scheme which is authorised under section 153 to continue as a closed section of a scheme"; and

(b) for the words "closed scheme" in subsection (5), there were substituted the words "closed segregated part of a non-segregated scheme which is authorised under section 153 to continue as a closed section of a scheme".

(5) Section 157 of the Act (applications and notifications where closed schemes have sufficient assets) shall be modified in its application to a segregated part to which regulation 45 applies so that it shall be read as if, after subsection (4), there were inserted the following subsection—

"(4A) Where the trustees or managers of a segregated part of a non-segregated scheme receive a notice from the Board under subsection (4), they must send a copy of that notice as soon as practicable to all the employers in relation to the scheme.".

[(6) Section 158 of the Act (duty to assume responsibility for closed schemes) shall be modified in its application to a segregated part to which regulation 45 applies so that it shall be read as if—

(a) for subsection (3), there were inserted the following subsection—

"(3) For the purposes of determining whether the condition in subsection (1) is satisfied the Board must, as soon as reasonably practicable, obtain an actuarial valuation (within the meaning of section 143) of the segregated part as at the relevant time.";

(b) subsection (3A) were omitted;

(c) in subsection (5)—

(i) for the words "a determination made under subsection (3)(a) and a valuation obtained under subsection (3)(b)" there were substituted the words "a valuation obtained under subsection (3)";

(ii) for the words "a determination made under section 143(2)(a) and a valuation obtained under section 143(2)(b)" there were substituted the words "a valuation obtained under section 143"; and

(iii) paragraph (aa) were omitted; and

(d) in subsection (6)—

(i) ", 143A" were omitted; and

(ii) paragraph (aa) were omitted.]

NOTES

Regulation heading: substituted by the Occupational Pension Schemes and Pension Protection Fund (Amendment) Regulations 2005, SI 2005/993, regs 1(2), 5(1), (6)(e).

Para (2): sub-para (aa) inserted by the Pension Protection Fund (Miscellaneous Amendments) (No 2) Regulations 2012, SI 2012/3083, reg 2(1), (18)(a); for a transitional provision see reg 10 thereof.

Para (6): added by SI 2012/3083, reg 2(1), (18)(b); for a transitional provision see reg 10 thereof.

[18.74]

58 Transfer notices and assumption of responsibility for a scheme

(1) Section 160 of the Act (transfer notice) shall be modified in its application to a segregated part to which regulation 45 applies, so that it shall be read as if—

(a) after subsection (1), there were inserted the following subsection—

"(1A) This section also applies where the Board is required to assume responsibility for a segregated part of a non-segregated scheme.".

(b) after subsection (2), there were inserted the following subsection—

"(2A) Where the trustees or managers of a segregated part of a non-segregated scheme receive a transfer notice from the Board under subsection (2), they must send a copy of that notice as soon as practicable to all the employers in relation to the scheme.";

[(ba) for the words "determination made or valuation obtained under section 143(2)" in subsection (3), there were substituted the words "valuation obtained under section 143";

(bb) in subsection (4) the words "determination made or" were omitted;]

(c) after subsection (4), there were inserted the following subsections—

"(4B) In a case where the Board is required to assume responsibility for a segregated part of a non-segregated scheme under section 127, 128, 152 or 158, a transfer notice may not be given until the Board has obtained a further actuarial valuation of the assets and protected liabilities of the scheme as a whole and of the segregated part under section 160A as at the date on which it is required to assume responsibility for the segregated part and that valuation has been approved by the Board and become binding."; and

(d) for subsection (6), there were substituted the following subsection—

"(6) The Board must give a copy of the transfer notice under subsection (2) to—

(a) the Regulator, and

(b) an insolvency practitioner acting in relation to the employer in relation to the segregated part of the multi-employer scheme in respect of which the transfer notice is issued.".

(2) Section 161 of the Act (effect of Board assuming responsibility for a scheme) shall be modified in its application to a segregated part to which regulation 45 applies, so that it shall be read as if—

(a) after the word "obligations" in paragraph (b) of subsection (2), there were inserted the words "to or in respect of members of the segregated part"; and

(b) after the words "to or in respect of persons" in paragraph (a) of subsection (4), there were inserted the words "who are or were members of that segregated part".

(3) Paragraph 1 of Schedule 6 to the Act (transfer of property, rights and liabilities) shall be modified in its application to a segregated part to which regulation 45 applies so that it shall be read as if, for the words "an occupational pension scheme", there were substituted the words to "a segregated part of a non-segregated multi-employer scheme".

NOTES

Para (1): sub-paras (ba), (bb) inserted by the Pension Protection Fund (Miscellaneous Amendments) (No 2) Regulations 2012, SI 2012/3083, reg 2(1), (19); for a transitional provision see reg 10 thereof.

[18.75]

59 Further actuarial valuation of segregated parts

Part 2 of the Act shall be modified in its application to a segregated part to which regulation 45 applies so that it shall be read as if, after section 160 (transfer notice), there were inserted the following section—

"160A Further actuarial valuations of segregated parts

(1) This section applies in any case where the Board is required to obtain a further actuarial valuation under section 160(4B).

(2) The Board must obtain a further actuarial valuation of the assets and protected liabilities of the scheme as a whole and of the segregated part as at the date on which the Board is required to assume responsibility for that section.

(3) A valuation obtained by the Board under this section shall have effect as if it were a valuation obtained by the Board under section 143 (Board's obligation to obtain valuation of assets and protected liabilities).

(4) For the purposes of this section, subsections (3), (4), (6) to (8) and (11)(a) of section 143 shall apply in relation to a valuation of the scheme as a whole and of the segregated part obtained under this section as they apply in relation to a valuation obtained under section 143.

(5) In the application of section 143 by virtue of this section—

(a) subsections (5) and (11)(b) of that section shall apply as if the references to "the relevant time" were to the date on which the Board is required to assume responsibility for the segregated part; and

(b) references to "assets" do not include assets representing the value of any money purchase benefits under the scheme rules which apply to the segregated part.".

Part 18 Miscellaneous SIs

[18.76]

60 The pension compensation provisions

(1) Section 162 of the Act (the pension compensation provisions) shall be modified in its application to a segregated part to which regulation 45 applies so that it shall be read as if, in subsection (1)—

(a) for the words "in relation to a scheme", there were substituted the words "in relation to a segregated part of a non-segregated scheme";

(b) after the word "members" in paragraphs (a) and (b), there were added the words "of that segregated part";

(c) after the word "payable" in paragraph (c), there were inserted the words "to or in respect of members of that part"; and

(d) at the end of paragraph (d), there were added the words "payable to or in respect of members of that segregated part".

(2) Section 163 of the Act (adjustments to be made where the Board assumes responsibility for a scheme) shall be modified in its application to a segregated part to which regulation 45 applies so that it shall be read as if, after the words "to any member" in paragraph (a) of subsection (2), there were inserted the words "of that part".

(3) Section 166 of the Act (duty to pay benefits unpaid at assessment date) shall be modified in its application to a segregated part to which regulation 45 applies so that it shall be read as if, for the words "assumes responsibility for a scheme" in subsection (1), there were substituted the words "assumes responsibility for a segregated part of a non-segregated scheme".

[PART 6
NON-SEGREGATED SCHEMES:

SCHEMES WITHOUT PROVISION FOR PARTIAL WIND UP ON WITHDRAWAL OF A PARTICIPATING EMPLOYER

[18.77]

61 Application and effect

This regulation applies to a multi-employer scheme which is not divided into two or more sections (a "non-segregated scheme") the rules of which do not provide for the partial winding up of the scheme when an employer in relation to the scheme ceases to participate in the scheme.]

NOTES

Part 6 (regs 61–70) substituted by the Occupational Pension Schemes (Miscellaneous Amendments) Regulations 2005, SI 2005/2113, reg 10(1), (4).

[18.78]

[62 Notification of insolvency events, confirmation of scheme status etc

(1) Section 120 of the Act (duty to notify insolvency events in respect of employers) shall be modified in its application to a scheme to which regulation 61 applies so that it shall be read as if—

(a) for subsection (1), there were substituted the following subsection—

"(1) This section applies where, in the case of a multi-employer scheme which is not divided into two or more sections (a "non-segregated scheme"), an insolvency event occurs in relation to an employer in relation to the scheme."; and

(b) after subsection (2), there were inserted the following subsection—

"(2A) Where the trustees or managers of a non-segregated scheme receive a notice from an insolvency practitioner under subsection (2), they must send a copy of that notice as soon as practicable to all the employers in relation to the scheme.".

(2) Section 122 of the Act (insolvency practitioner's duty to issue notices confirming status of the scheme) shall be modified in its application to a scheme to which regulation 61 applies so that it shall be read as if—

(a) for subsection (1), there were substituted the following subsection—

"(1) This section applies where an insolvency event has occurred in relation to any employer in relation to a non-segregated scheme.";

(b) in subsections (2), (3)(a), (4) and (6), for the words "the employer", there were substituted the words "an employer"; and

(c) after subsection (6), there were inserted the following subsection—

"(6A) Where the trustees or managers of a non-segregated scheme receive a notice issued by an insolvency practitioner or a former insolvency practitioner under subsection (6), they must send a copy of that notice as soon as practicable to all the employers in relation to the scheme.".

(3) Section 123 of the Act (approval of notices issued under section 122) shall be modified in its application to a scheme to which regulation 61 applies so that it shall be read as if—

(a) . . .

(b) for subsection (2), there were substituted the following subsection—

"(2) The Board must determine whether to approve the section 122 notice received in relation to that employer.";

(c) in paragraph (e) of subsection (4), for the words "in relation to the employer, the employer", there were substituted the words "in relation to an employer, that employer"; and

(d) after subsection (4), there were inserted the following subsection—

"(4A) Where the trustees or managers of a non-segregated scheme receive a copy of a determination notice issued by the Board under subsection (4), they must send a copy of that notice as soon as practicable to all the employers in relation to the scheme.".

(4) Section 124 of the Act (Board's duty where there is a failure to comply with section 122) shall be modified in its application to a scheme to which regulation 61 applies so that it shall be read as if—

(a) in subsection (1)—

(i) for the words "This section applies where in relation to an occupational pension scheme", there were substituted the words "This section applies where in relation to a non-segregated scheme"; and

(ii) in paragraphs (a) and (b) of subsection (1), for the words "the employer", there were substituted the words "an employer";

(b) in subsection (4)—

(i) in paragraph (d), for the words "the employer", there were substituted the words "an employer"; and

(ii) in paragraph (e), for the words "in relation to the employer, the employer", there were substituted the words "in relation to an employer, that employer"; and

(c) after subsection (4), there were inserted the following subsection—

"(4A) Where the trustees or managers of a non-segregated scheme receive a copy of a notice issued by the Board under section 122 by virtue of this section, they must send a copy of that notice as soon as practicable to all the employers in relation to the scheme.".

(5) Section 125 of the Act (binding notices confirming status of scheme) shall be modified in its application to a scheme to which regulation 61 applies so that it shall be read as if—

(a) in subsection (3)—

(i) in paragraph (d), for the words "the employer", there were substituted the words "an employer"; and

(ii) in paragraph (e), for the words "in relation to the employer, the employer", there were substituted the words "in relation to an employer, that employer"; and

(b) after subsection (3), there were inserted the following subsection—

"(3A) Where the trustees or managers of a non-segregated scheme receive a notice from the Board under subsection (3) together with a copy of the binding notice, they must send a copy of the notice and the binding notice as soon as practicable to all the employers in relation to the scheme.".]

NOTES

Substituted as noted to reg 61 at **[18.77]**.

Para (3): sub-para (a) revoked by the Occupational Pension Schemes (Employer Debt and Miscellaneous Amendments) Regulations 2008, SI 2008/731, reg 17.

[18.79]

[63 Eligible schemes

(1) Section 126(1) of the Act (eligible schemes) shall be modified in its application to a scheme to which regulation 61 applies so that it shall be read as if, for the words "an occupational pension scheme", there were substituted the words "a non-segregated scheme".

(2) Paragraph (1) shall not have effect in relation to sections 174 to 181 of the Act (the levies).]

NOTES

Substituted as noted to reg 61 at **[18.77]**.

[18.80]

[64 Duty to assume responsibility for schemes

(1) Section 127 of the Act (duty to assume responsibility for schemes following insolvency event) shall have effect in relation to a scheme to which regulation 61 applies and, for this purpose, shall be modified so that it shall be read as if—

(a) for subsection (1), there were substituted the following subsection—

"(1) This section applies where a qualifying insolvency event has occurred in relation to an employer in relation to a non-segregated scheme."; and

(b) for subsection (3), there were substituted the following subsection—

"(3) For the purposes of this section, an insolvency event ("the current event") in relation to an employer in relation to an eligible scheme is a qualifying insolvency event if—

(a) it occurs—

(i) simultaneously in relation to more than one of the employers in relation to the scheme at a time when those employers are the only employers in relation to the scheme, or

(ii) in relation to an employer in relation to the scheme at a time when all other employers in relation to the scheme have either had—

(aa) an insolvency event occur in relation to them and an insolvency practitioner is still required by law to be appointed to act in relation to them, or

(bb) a notice given in respect of them by the trustees or managers of the section under section 129(1A) or a notice given by the Board in respect of them under section 129(5) by virtue of a notice given by the Regulator under section 129(4)(a),

(b) it occurs on or after the day appointed under section 126(2), and

(c) it—

(i) is the first insolvency event to occur in relation to that employer on or after that day, or

(ii) does not occur within an assessment period (see section 132) in relation to the scheme which began before the occurrence of the current event.".

(2) Section 128 of the Act (duty to assume responsibility for schemes following application or notification) shall be modified in its application to a scheme to which regulation 61 applies so that it shall be read as if, for subsection (1), there were substituted the following subsection—

"(1) This section applies where, in relation to a non-segregated scheme which is, for the purposes of this Part, an eligible scheme—

(a) the trustees or managers of the scheme make an application under subsection (1)(a) or (b) of section 129 (a "section 129 application"), or

(b) the Board receives a notice given by the Regulator under subsection (4)(b) of that section.".]

NOTES

Substituted as noted to reg 61 at **[18.77]**.

[18.81]

[65 Applications and notifications and Board's duty where application or notification received under section 129

(1) Section 129 of the Act (applications and notifications for the purposes of section 128) shall be modified in its application to a scheme to which regulation 61 applies so that it shall be read as if—

(a) for subsection (1), there were substituted the following subsection—

"(1) Where the trustees or managers of a non-segregated scheme which is, for the purposes of this Part, an eligible scheme—

(a) have—

(i) notified the Board in accordance with subsection (1A) that an employer in relation to the scheme is unlikely to continue as a going concern at a time when all other employers in relation to the scheme have either had—

(aa) an insolvency event occur in relation to them and an insolvency practitioner is still required by law to be appointed to act in relation to them, or

(bb) a notice given in respect of them by the trustees or managers of the scheme under subsection (1A) or a notice given by the Board in respect of them under subsection (5) by virtue of a notice given by the Regulator under subsection (4)(a), or

(ii) received a notice given by the Board under subsection (5) by virtue of a notice given by the Regulator under subsection (4)(a) in respect of an employer in relation to the scheme at a time when all other employers in relation to the scheme have either had—

(aa) an insolvency event occur in relation to them and an insolvency practitioner is still required by law to be appointed to act in relation to them, or

(bb) a notice given in respect of them by the trustees or managers of the scheme under subsection (1A) or a notice given by the Board in respect of them under subsection (5) by virtue of a notice given by the Regulator under subsection (4)(a), or

(b) are aware that a person is no longer an employer, or that persons are no longer employers, in relation to the scheme at a time when—

(i) all other employers in relation to the scheme have either had—

(aa) an insolvency event occur in relation to them and an insolvency practitioner is still required by law to be appointed to act in relation to them, or

(bb) a notice given in respect of them by the trustees or managers of the scheme under subsection (1A) or a notice given by the Board in respect of them under subsection (5) by virtue of a notice given by the Regulator under subsection (4)(a), and

(ii) at least one such insolvency event occurred, or at least one such notice was given under subsection (1A) or (5) by virtue of a notice given by the Regulator under subsection (4)(a), on or after 6th April 2005 in relation to an employer in relation to that scheme,

they must, except where an assessment period has already begun in relation to that scheme, make an application to the Board for it to assume responsibility for the scheme under section 128."; and

(b) after subsection (1), there were inserted the following subsections—

"(1A) Where the trustees or managers of a non-segregated scheme which is, for the purposes of this Part, an eligible scheme become aware that an employer in relation to the scheme—

(a) is unlikely to continue as a going concern, and

(b) the prescribed requirements are met in relation to that employer,

they must give the Board a notice to that effect.

(1B) The notice which must be given to the Board in accordance with subsection (1A) must be in writing and must contain the following information—

(a) a description of the type or purpose of the notice,

(b) the name of the employer in relation to the scheme in respect of which the notice is given,

(c) a statement by the trustees or managers of the scheme that the employer in respect of which the notice is given is unlikely to continue as a going concern and that the requirements prescribed under subsection (1A)(b) have been met in relation to that employer,

(d) the date on which the trustees or managers of the scheme became aware that the employer in respect of which the notice is given is unlikely to continue as a going concern, and

(e) the date on which the notice was sent to the Board by the trustees or managers of the scheme.

(1C) Where the trustees or managers of a non-segregated scheme which is, for the purposes of this Part, an eligible scheme make an application to the Board under subsection (1)(a) or (b), they must as soon as practicable notify that fact to all the employers in relation to the scheme.";

(c) for subsection (4), there were substituted the following subsection—

"(4) Where, in relation to a non-segregated scheme which is, for the purposes of this Part, an eligible scheme, the Regulator—

(a) becomes aware that an employer in relation to the scheme—

(i) is unlikely to continue as a going concern, and

(ii) meets the requirements prescribed under subsection (1A)(b), or

(b) is aware that a person is no longer an employer, or that persons are no longer employers, in relation to the scheme at a time when—

(i) all other employers in relation to the scheme have either had—

(aa) an insolvency event occur in relation to them and an insolvency practitioner is still required by law to be appointed to act in relation to them, or

(bb) a notice given in respect of them by the trustees or managers of the scheme under subsection (1A) or a notice given by the Board in respect of them under subsection (5) by virtue of a notice given by the Regulator under subsection (4)(a), and

(ii) at least one such insolvency event occurred, or at least one such notice was given under subsection (1A) or (5) by virtue of a notice given by the Regulator under subsection (4)(a), on or after 6th April 2005 in relation to an employer in relation to that scheme,

it must, except where an assessment period has already begun in relation to the scheme, give the Board a notice to that effect."; and

(d) after subsection (5), there were inserted the following subsection—

"(5A) Where the trustees or managers of a non-segregated scheme receive a copy of a notice from the Board under subsection (5), they must send a copy of that notice as soon as practicable to all the employers in relation to the scheme.".

(2) Section 130 of the Act (Board's duty where application or notification received under section 129) shall be modified in its application to a scheme to which regulation 61 applies so that it shall be read as if—

(a) for subsection (1), there were substituted the following subsection—

"(1) This section applies where the Board—

(a) receives an application under subsection (1) of section 129 and is satisfied that either paragraph (a) or (b) of that subsection is satisfied in relation to the application, or

(b) is notified by the Regulator under section 129(4)(b).";

(b) after subsection (4), there were inserted the following subsection—

"(4A) Where the trustees or managers of a non-segregated scheme receive a copy of a notice from the Board under subsection (4), they must send a copy of that notice as soon as practicable to all the employers in relation to the scheme."; and

(c) after subsection (7), there were inserted the following subsection—

"(7A) Where the trustees or managers of a non-segregated scheme receive a notice from the Board under subsection (7) together with a copy of the binding notice, they must send a copy of the notice and the binding notice as soon as practicable to all the employers in relation to the scheme.".]

NOTES

Substituted as noted to reg 61 at **[18.77]**.

[18.82]

[66 Assessment periods

Section 132 of the Act (assessment periods) shall be modified in its application to a scheme to which regulation 61 applies so that it shall be read as if—

(a) in subsection (2)—

(i) for the words "in relation to an eligible scheme", there were substituted the words "in relation to a non-segregated scheme which is, for the purposes of this Part, an eligible scheme";

(ii) for the words "the employer,", there were substituted the words "an employer in relation to the scheme"; and

(iii) after the words "an assessment period", there were inserted the words "in relation to the scheme";

(b) in subsection (4), for the words "in relation to an eligible scheme, an application is made under section 129(1) or a notification is received under section 129(5)(a), an assessment period", there were substituted the words "in relation to a non-segregated scheme which is, for the purposes of this Part, an eligible scheme, an application is made under section 129(1)(a) or (b) or a notification is received under section 129(4)(b), an assessment period in relation to the scheme"; and

(c) in subsection (5), for the words "section 129(5)(a)", there were substituted the words "section 129(4)(b)".]

NOTES

Substituted as noted to reg 61 at **[18.77]**.

[18.83]

[67 Power to validate contraventions of section 135 and Board to act as creditor of the employer

(1) Section 136(2)(of the Act (power to validate contraventions of section 135) shall be modified in its application to a scheme to which regulation 61 applies so that it shall be read as if, for the words "in relation to the employer, or if there is no such insolvency practitioner, the employer", there were substituted the words "in relation to an employer or, if there is no such insolvency practitioner, that employer".

(2) Section 137(2) of the Act (Board to act as creditor of the employer) shall be modified in its application to a scheme to which regulation 61 applies so that it shall be read as if, for the words "the employer", there were substituted the words "an employer".]

NOTES

Substituted as noted to reg 61 at **[18.77]**.

[18.84]

[68 Valuation of assets

Sections [143A(4)(c) (Determinations under section 143),] 144(2)(b)(iii) (approval of valuation) and 145(3)(c) (binding valuations) of the Act shall be modified in their application to a scheme to which regulation 61 applies so that they shall be read as if, for the words "in relation to the employer or, if there is no such insolvency practitioner, the employer", there were substituted the words "in relation to an employer or, if there is no such insolvency practitioner, that employer".]

NOTES

Substituted as noted to reg 61 at **[18.77]**.

Words in square brackets inserted by the Pension Protection Fund (Miscellaneous Amendments) (No 2) Regulations 2012, SI 2012/3083, reg 2(1), (20); for a transitional provision see reg 10 thereof.

[18.85]

[69 Refusal to assume responsibility

(1) The provisions of the Act specified in paragraph (2) shall be modified in their application to a scheme to which regulation 61 applies so that they shall be read as if, for the words "in relation to the employer or, if there is no such insolvency practitioner, the employer", there were substituted the words "in relation to an employer or, if there is no such insolvency practitioner, that employer".

(2) The provisions specified in this paragraph are—

(a) section 146(2)(b)(iii) and (4)(c) (schemes which become eligible schemes); and

(b) section 147(2)(b)(iii) and (4)(c) (new schemes created to replace existing schemes).

(3) Section 148(5)(c) and (7)(c) of the Act (withdrawal following issue of section 122(4) notice) shall be modified in its application to a scheme to which regulation 61 applies so that it shall be read as if, for the words "the employer", there were substituted the words "any employer".]

NOTES

Substituted as noted to reg 61 at **[18.77]**.

[18.86]

[70 Transfer notice and the pension compensation provisions

(1) Section 160 of the Act (transfer notice) shall be modified in its application to a scheme to which regulation 61 applies so that it shall be read as if—

(a) in subsection (1), for the words "where the Board is required to assume responsibility for a scheme", there were substituted the words "where the Board is required to assume responsibility for a non-segregated scheme";

(b) after subsection (2), there were inserted the following subsection—

"(2A) Where the trustees or managers of a non-segregated scheme receive a transfer notice from the Board under subsection (2), they must send a copy of that notice as soon as practicable to all the employers in relation to the scheme."; and

(c) for subsection (6), there were substituted the following subsection—

"(6) The Board must give a copy of the transfer notice given under subsection (2) to—

(a) the Regulator, and

(b) an insolvency practitioner acting in relation to every employer in relation to the scheme in respect of which the transfer notice is given.".

(2) Schedule 6 to the Act (transfer of property, rights and liabilities to the Board) shall be modified in its application to a scheme to which regulation 61 applies so that it shall be read as if, in paragraph 1, for the words "an occupational pension scheme", there were substituted the words "a non-segregated multi-employer scheme".

(3) Schedule 7 to the Act (pension compensation provisions) shall be modified in its application to a scheme to which regulation 61 applies so that it shall be read as if, in paragraph 1, for the words "an eligible scheme", there were substituted the words "a non-segregated multi-employer scheme which is, for the purposes of Part 2, an eligible scheme".]

NOTES

Substituted as noted to reg 61 at **[18.77]**.

PART 7
NON-SEGREGATED SCHEME WITH AN OPTION TO SEGREGATE ON THE WITHDRAWAL OF A PARTICIPATING EMPLOYER

[18.87]

71 Application and effect

(1) This regulation applies to a non-segregated multi-employer scheme in circumstances—

(a) where—

(i) an insolvency event occurs in relation to an employer in relation to the scheme; or

(ii) the trustees or managers of the scheme become aware that an employer in relation to the scheme is unlikely to continue as a going concern and meets the requirements prescribed under subsection (1)(b) of section 129 of the Act (applications and notifications for the purposes of section 128); and

(b) where, under the rules of the scheme, the trustees or managers have an option, in circumstances where an employer in relation to the scheme ceases to participate in the scheme, to segregate such part of the assets of the scheme as is attributable to the scheme's liabilities to provide pensions or other benefits to or in respect of the pensionable service of some or all of the members by reference to that employer.

(2) In the case of a scheme to which this regulation applies—

(a) the trustees or managers of the scheme shall be deemed to have exercised the option to segregate under the scheme rules so as to create a segregated part of the scheme unless and until they decide not to exercise that option and have given the Board a notice to this effect as required by section 120(3A) or 129(1B) of the Act as modified by this Part; and

(b) except as otherwise provided for in paragraph (3) below, Part 2 of the Act shall be read in relation to the scheme as if it contained the modifications provided for in Part 5 of these Regulations.

(3) The exceptions referred to in paragraph (2) above are that—

(a) section 120 of the Act (duty to notify insolvency events in respect of employers) shall be modified so that it shall be read as if—

(i) for subsection (1), there were substituted the following subsection—

"(1) This section applies where an insolvency event occurs in relation to an employer in relation to a multi-employer scheme which is not divided into two or more sections ("a non-segregated scheme") under the rules of which the trustees or managers of the scheme have an option, in

Part 18 Miscellaneous SIs

circumstances where an employer in relation to the scheme ceases to participate in the scheme, to segregate such part of the assets of the scheme as is attributable to the scheme's liabilities to provide pensions or other benefits to or in respect of the pensionable service of some or all of the members of the scheme by reference to that employer ("the segregated part")."; and

(ii) after subsection (3), there were inserted the following subsection—

"(3A) If, where this section applies to a non-segregated scheme, the trustees or managers [of] the scheme decide not to exercise the option to segregate under the scheme rules so as to create a segregated part of the scheme they must, as soon as practicable—

(a) give a notice to the Board to that effect (a "non-segregation notice"); and

(b) send a copy of that notice to—

(i) an insolvency practitioner acting in relation to the employer, and

(ii) the Regulator.";

(b) section 122 of the Act (insolvency practitioner's duty to issue notices confirming status of scheme) shall be modified so that it shall be read as if, after subsection (2), there were inserted the following subsection—

"(2A) Where an insolvency practitioner acting in relation to an employer in relation to a non-segregated scheme receives a non-segregation notice under subsection (3A) of section 120 from the trustees or managers of the scheme, he must as soon as practicable issue a notice under subsection (2)(b) (a "withdrawal notice") [in relation to the scheme]."; and

(c) section 129 of the Act (applications and notifications for the purposes of section 128) shall be modified so that it shall be read as if—

(i) for subsection (1), there were substituted the following subsection—

"(1) The trustees or managers of a non-segregated scheme which is, for the purposes of this Part, an eligible scheme must make an application to the Board for it to assume responsibility for a segregated part of the scheme under section 128 where they become aware that—

(a) an employer in relation to the scheme is unlikely to continue as a going concern, and

(b) the prescribed requirements are met in relation to that employer, and where the rules of the scheme contain an option, in circumstances where an employer in relation to the scheme ceases to participate in the scheme, for the trustees or managers to segregate such part of the assets of the scheme as is attributable to the scheme's liabilities to provide pensions or other benefits to or in respect of the pensionable service of some or all of the members by reference to that employer."; and

(ii) after subsection (1A), there were inserted the following subsections—

"(1B) If, where subsection (1) applies to a non-segregated scheme, the trustees or managers of the scheme decide not to exercise the option to segregate under the scheme rules so as to create a segregated part of the scheme they must, as soon as practicable—

(a) give a notice to the Board to that effect (a "non-segregation notice"); and

(b) send a copy of that notice to the Regulator."; and

"(1C) Where the Board receives a non-segregation notice from the trustees or managers of a non-segregated scheme under paragraph (a) of subsection (1B), it must as soon as practicable issue a notice under subsection (3) of section 130 (a "withdrawal notice") in relation to the scheme.".

NOTES

Para (3): in sub-para (a)(ii), in s 120(3A) (as set out above) word in square brackets inserted, and in sub-para (b), in s 122(2A) (as set out above) words in square brackets substituted by the Occupational Pension Schemes and Pension Protection Fund (Amendment) Regulations 2005, SI 2005/993, regs 1(2), 5(1), (8).

PART 8
SEGREGATED SCHEMES:

MULTI-EMPLOYER SECTIONS OF SEGREGATED SCHEMES WITH AN OPTION TO SEGREGATE ON THE WITHDRAWAL OF A PARTICIPATING EMPLOYER

[18.88]

72 Application and effect

(1) This regulation applies to a multi-employer section of a segregated scheme in circumstances—

(a) where—

(i) an insolvency event occurs in relation to an employer in relation to that section; or

(ii) the trustees or managers of the scheme become aware that an employer in relation to that section is unlikely to continue as a going concern and meets the requirements prescribed under subsection (1)(b) of section 129 of the Act (applications and notifications for the purposes of section 128); and

(b) where, under the rules of the scheme, the trustees or managers have an option, in circumstances where an employer in relation to the section ceases to participate in the scheme, to segregate such part of the assets of the scheme as is attributable to the liabilities of the section to provide pensions or other benefits to or in respect of the pensionable service of some or all of the members by reference to that employer.

(2) In the case of a multi-employer section of a segregated scheme to which this regulation applies—

(a) the trustees or managers of that section shall be deemed to have exercised the option to segregate under the scheme rules so as to create a segregated part of the section unless and until they decide not to exercise that option and have given the Board a notice to this effect as required by section 120(3A) or 129(1B) of the Act as modified by this Part; and

(b) except as otherwise provided for in paragraph (3) below, Part 2 of the Act shall be read in relation to that section as if it contained the modifications provided for in Part 4 of these Regulations.

(3) The exceptions referred to in paragraph (2) above are that—

(a) section 120 of the Act (duty to notify insolvency events in respect of employers) shall be modified so that it shall be read as if—

(i) for subsection (1), there were substituted the following subsection—

"(1) This section applies where an insolvency event occurs in relation to an employer in relation to a section of a multi-employer scheme which is divided into two or more sections ("a segregated scheme") with at least two employers in relation to that section of the scheme ("a multi-employer section") under the rules of which the trustees or managers of that section have an option, in circumstances where an employer in relation to that section of the scheme ceases to participate in the scheme, to segregate such part of the assets of the section as is attributable to the liabilities of the section to provide pensions or other benefits to or in respect of the pensionable service of some or all of the members of that section by reference to that employer ("the segregated part").";

(ii) after subsection (3), there were inserted the following subsection—

"(3A) If, where this section applies to a multi-employer section of a segregated scheme, the trustees or managers of the section decide not to exercise the option to segregate under the scheme rules so as to create a segregated part of that section they must, as soon as practicable—

(a) give a notice to the Board to that effect (a "non-segregation notice"); and

(b) send a copy of that notice to—

(i) an insolvency practitioner acting in relation to the employer, and

(ii) the Regulator.";

(b) section 122 of the Act (insolvency practitioner's duty to issue notices confirming status of scheme) shall be modified so that it shall be read as if, after subsection (2), there were inserted the following subsection—

"(2A) Where an insolvency practitioner acting in relation to an employer in relation to a multi-employer section of a segregated scheme receives a non-segregation notice under subsection (3A) of section 120 from the trustees or managers of that section, he must as soon as practicable issue a notice under subsection (2)(b) (a "withdrawal notice") in relation to that section."; and

(c) section 129 of the Act (applications and notifications for the purposes of section 128) shall be modified so that it shall be read as if—

(i) for subsection (1), there were substituted the following subsection—

"(1) The trustees or managers of a multi-employer section of a segregated scheme which is, for the purposes of this Part, an eligible scheme must make an application to the Board for it to assume responsibility for a segregated part of the section under section 128 where they become aware that—

(a) an employer in relation to the section is unlikely to continue as a going concern, and

(b) the prescribed requirements are met in relation to that employer, and where the rules of the scheme contain an option, in circumstances where an employer in relation to a section of the scheme ceases to participate in the scheme, for the trustees or managers to segregate such part of the assets of the section as is attributable to the liabilities of the section to provide pensions or other benefits to or in respect of the pensionable service of some or all of the members by reference to that employer."; and

(ii) after subsection (1A), there were [inserted] the following subsections—

"(1B) If, where subsection (1) applies to a multi-employer section of a segregated scheme, the trustees or managers of the section decide not to exercise the option to segregate under the scheme rules so as to create a segregated part of that section they must, as soon as practicable—

(a) give a notice to the Board to that effect (a "non-segregation notice"); and

(b) send a copy of the notice to the Regulator."; and

"(1C) Where the Board receives a non-segregation notice from the trustees or managers of a multi-employer section of a segregated scheme under paragraph (a) of subsection (1B), it must as soon as practicable issue a notice under subsection (3) of section 130 (a "withdrawal notice") in relation to that section.".

NOTES

Para (3): word in square brackets in sub-para (c)(ii) substituted by the Occupational Pension Schemes and Pension Protection Fund (Amendment) Regulations 2005, SI 2005/993, regs 1(2), 5(1), (9).

73–76 *((Pts 9, 10) outside the scope of this work.)*

Part 18 Miscellaneous SIs

PENSION PROTECTION FUND (ENTRY RULES) REGULATIONS 2005

(SI 2005/590)

NOTES

Made: 10 March 2005.

Authority: Pensions Act 2004, ss 120(3), (4), 121(5), 122(3), (5), (8), 123(5), 126(1)(b), (3), (5), 129(1)(b), (3), (8), 130(5), (8), 133(3), 134(3)(a)(iii), 135(4), 138(10)(b), (12), 139(6), 146(1), (5), 147(1)(a), (5), 148(8), 150(5), (6)(a)–(c), 151(4), (6), (8), (9)(b), 315(2), (4), (5), 318(1), (4)(a).

Commencement: 1 April 2005 (in part) and 6 April 2005 (remainder); see reg 1(2).

Modification: these Regulations are applied with modifications in relation to a society registered under the Co-operative and Community Benefit Societies Act 2014, by the Co-operative and Community Benefit Societies and Credit Unions (Arrangements, Reconstructions and Administration) Order 2014, SI 2014/229, art 12, Sch 5, at **[7.1437]**, **[7.1450]**.

[18.89]

1 Citation, commencement and interpretation

(1) These Regulations may be cited as the Pension Protection Fund (Entry Rules) Regulations 2005.

(2) These Regulations shall come into force—

(a) for the purposes of regulation 1 (except paragraphs (4) and (5)) and regulation 2, on 1st April 2005; and

(b) for all other purposes on 6th April 2005.

(3) In these Regulations—

"the Act" means the Pensions Act 2004;

"the 1986 Act" means the Insolvency Act 1986;

"the 1988 Act" means the Income and Corporation Taxes Act 1988;

"the 1993 Act" means the Pension Schemes Act 1993;

"the 1995 Act" means the Pensions Act 1995;

["the appointed day" is the day appointed for the coming into force of section 29 of the Pensions Act 2011 (definition of money purchase benefits);]

["the assessment date" means the date on which the assessment period in relation to the scheme or section, or (where there has been more than one such assessment period) the last one, began;]

"the FSMA" means the Financial Services and Markets Act 2000;

"the Authority" has the meaning given in section 124(1) of the 1995 Act (interpretation);

["cash balance benefits" has the meaning given by regulation 2 of the Pensions Act 2011 (Transitional, Consequential and Supplementary Provisions) Regulations 2014;]

["EEA credit institution" means a credit institution, authorised under Directive 2006/48/EC of the European Parliament and of the Council dated 14th June 2006 relating to the taking up and pursuit of the business of credit institutions, [as last amended [on 24th November 2010 by Directives 2010/76/EU and 2010/78/EU] of the European Parliament and of the Council,] which has its relevant office in an EEA state other than the United Kingdom;

"EEA insurer" means an undertaking, other than a UK insurer, pursuing the activity of direct insurance [(within the meaning of Article 2 of the Solvency 2 Directive) which has received authorisation under Article 14 of the Solvency 2 Directive from its home state regulator;]

"EEA regulator" [means a supervisory authority (within the meaning of Article 13(10) of the Solvency 2 Directive) of an EEA state];

["establishment"[, except in regulation 5A,] has the meaning given in Article 2 of the Insolvency Regulation;]

. . .

"home state regulator" means the relevant EEA regulator in the EEA state where its head office is located;]

["the Insolvency Regulation" means Regulation (EU) 2015/848 of the European Parliament and of the Council of 20 May 2015 on insolvency proceedings,]

. . .

[. . .]

["the Multi-employer Regulations" means the Pension Protection Fund (Multi-employer Schemes) (Modification) Regulations 2005;]

"multi-employer scheme" has the meaning given in section 307(4) of the Act (modification of the Act in relation to certain categories of pension scheme);

"multi-employer section" means a section of a segregated scheme which has at least two employers in relation to that section;

"non-segregated scheme" means a multi-employer scheme which is not a segregated scheme;

"normal pension age" has the meaning given in section 138(11) of the Act (payment of scheme benefits);

"pensionable service" has the meaning given in section 70(2) of the 1993 Act (interpretation);

"public body" means a government department or any non-departmental public body established by an Act of Parliament or by a statutory instrument made under an Act of Parliament to perform functions conferred on it under or by virtue of that Act or instrument or any other Act or instrument;

["relevant office" means—

(a) in relation to a body corporate, its registered office or, if it has no registered office, its head office;

(b) in relation to a person other than a body corporate, the person's head office;]

"relevant public authority" has the meaning given in section 307(4) of the Act;

"restricted information" has the meaning given in section 197(4) of the Act (restricted information);

"segregated scheme" means a multi-employer scheme which is divided into two or more sections where—

(a) any contributions payable to the scheme by an employer in relation to the scheme or by a member are allocated to that employer's or that member's section; and

(b) a specified proportion of the assets of the scheme is attributable to each section of the scheme and cannot be used for the purposes of any other section;

"segregated part"—

(a) in relation to a non-segregated scheme, means a part of the scheme which is created when the rules of the scheme require the trustees or managers, in circumstances where an employer in relation to the scheme ceases to participate in the scheme, to segregate such part of the assets of the scheme as is attributable to the liabilities of the scheme to provide pensions or other benefits to or in respect of the pensionable service of members of the scheme by reference to that employer; and

(b) in relation to a multi-employer section of a segregated scheme, means a part of the section which is created when the rules of the scheme relating to that section require the trustees or managers of the section, in circumstances where an employer in relation to the section ceases to participate in the scheme, to segregate such part of the assets of the section as is attributable to the liabilities of the section to provide pensions or other benefits to or in respect of the pensionable service of members of the section by reference to that employer; and

["the Solvency 2 Directive" means Directive 2009/138/EC of the European Parliament and of the Council of 25 November 2009 on the taking-up and pursuit of the business of Insurance and Reinsurance (Solvency II);]

["tax registered scheme" means a pension scheme which is registered under Chapter 2 of Part 4 of the Finance Act 2004 (registration of pension schemes)];

[. . .

"UK insurer" means a person who has permission under Part 4 of the FSMA to effect or carry out contracts of insurance, but does not include a person who, in accordance with that permission, carries on that activity exclusively in relation to reinsurance contracts].

[(4) In Part 2 of the Act and these Regulations, "employer", in relation to—

(a) an occupational pension scheme which is not a multi-employer scheme; or

(b) a single-employer section of a segregated scheme,

which has no active members, includes the person who was the employer of persons in the description of employment to which the scheme or section relates immediately before the time at which the scheme or section ceased to have any active members in relation to it.]

[(5) In these Regulations, "employer", in relation to a non-segregated scheme or a multi-employer section of a segregated scheme—

(a) in an assessment period, includes any person who before the assessment date has ceased to be the employer of persons in the description of employment to which the scheme or section relates unless condition A, B, [C,] [D, E or F] is satisfied where—

(i) condition A is that a debt under section 75 of the 1995 Act became due from that employer and the full amount of the debt has been paid before the assessment date;

(ii) condition B is that—

(aa) such a debt became due;

(bb) a legally enforceable agreement has been entered into the effect of which is to reduce the amount which may be recovered in respect of the debt; and

(cc) the reduced amount has been paid in full before the assessment date;

(iii) condition C is that such a debt became due but before the assessment date it is excluded from the value of the assets of the scheme or section because it is unlikely to be recovered without disproportionate costs or within a reasonable time;

(iv) condition D is that at the time at which any such person ceased to be the employer of persons in the description of employment to which the scheme or section relates the value of the assets of the scheme or section was such that no such debt was treated as becoming due;

[(v) condition E is that—

(aa) there is a restructuring within regulation 6ZB or 6ZC of the Occupational Pension Schemes (Employer Debt) Regulations 2005 (employment-cessation events: exemptions);

(bb) in that restructuring, the employer was the exiting employer for the purposes of those Regulations (see the definition of "exiting employer" in regulation 2(3A) of those Regulations (interpretation)); and

(cc) regulation 6ZA(3) or (4) of those Regulations (employment-cessation events: general) does not apply in relation to that restructuring;]

[(vi) condition F is that a flexible apportionment arrangement has taken effect in accordance with regulation 6E of the Occupational Pension Schemes (Employer Debt) Regulations 2005 (flexible apportionment arrangements) where the employer was the leaving employer within the meaning given in paragraph (7) of that regulation;]

(b) in any other case, includes any person who has ceased to be the employer of persons in the description of employment to which the scheme or section relates unless condition A, B, [C,] [D, E or F] is satisfied where—
(i) condition A is that a debt under section 75 of the 1995 Act became due from that employer and the full amount of the debt has been paid;
(ii) condition B is that—
(aa) such a debt became due;
(bb) a legally enforceable agreement has been entered into the effect of which is to reduce the amount which may be recovered in respect of the debt; and
(cc) the reduced amount has been paid in full;
(iii) condition C is that such a debt became due but it is excluded from the value of the assets of the scheme or section because it is unlikely to be recovered without disproportionate costs or within a reasonable time;
(iv) condition D is that at the time at which any such person ceased to be the employer of persons in the description of employment to which the scheme or section relates the value of the assets of the scheme or section was such that no such debt was treated as becoming due;
[(v) condition E is that—
(aa) there is a restructuring within regulation 6ZB or 6ZC of the Occupational Pension Schemes (Employer Debt) Regulations 2005 (employment-cessation events: exemptions);
(bb) in that restructuring, the employer was the exiting employer for the purposes of those Regulations (see the definition of "exiting employer" in regulation 2(3A) of those Regulations (interpretation)); and
(cc) regulation 6ZA(3) or (4) of those Regulations (employment-cessation events: general) does not apply in relation to that restructuring];
[(vi) condition F is that a flexible apportionment arrangement has taken effect in accordance with regulation 6E of the Occupational Pension Schemes (Employer Debt) Regulations 2005 where the employer was the leaving employer within the meaning given in paragraph (7) of that regulation].]

[(6) Until 30th April 2011, amendments made to Directive 2006/48/EC of the European Parliament and of the Council by Directive 2009/110/EC of the European Parliament and of the Council shall be disregarded for the purposes of the definition of "EEA credit institution" in paragraph (3).]

[(7) In these Regulations, references to the centre of a person's main interests are to be construed in accordance with Article 3 of the Insolvency Regulation.]

NOTES

Para (3) is amended as follows:

definition "the assessment date" inserted by the Occupational Pension Schemes (Miscellaneous Amendments) Regulations 2005, SI 2005/2113, reg 4(1), (2)(b);

definitions "the appointed day" and "cash balance benefits" inserted by the Pensions Act 2011 (Transitional, Consequential and Supplementary Provisions) Regulations 2014, SI 2014/1711, reg 58(1), (2);

definition "EEA credit institution" inserted by the Pension Protection Fund (Miscellaneous Amendments) Regulations 2009, SI 2009/451, reg 2(1), (2)(a); words in first (outer) pair of square brackets inserted by SI 2010/2628, reg 14, Sch 2, para 7; words in second (inner) pair of square brackets substituted by SI 2012/917, reg 16, Sch 2, para 5;

definitions "EEA insurer" and "EEA regulator" inserted by SI 2009/451, reg 2(1), (2)(a); words in square brackets substituted by SI 2015/575, reg 60, Sch 2, para 22(1), (2)(c), (d);

definitions "establishment" and "the Insolvency Regulation" inserted by the Pension Protection Fund and Occupational and Personal Pension Schemes (Miscellaneous Amendments) Regulations 2016, SI 2016/294, reg 5(1), (2)(a);

words in square brackets in definition "establishment" substituted and definition "the Insolvency Regulation" substituted, by the Insolvency Amendment (EU 2015/848) Regulations 2017, SI 2017/702, regs 2, 3, Schedule, Pt 6, para 93(1), (2), except in relation to proceedings opened before 26 June 2017. The definition "the Insolvency Regulation" (as inserted by SI 2016/294 as noted above) previously read a follows:

"["the Insolvency Regulation" means Council Regulation (EC) No 1346/2000 of 29th May 2000 on insolvency proceedings;]";

definitions "the first non-life insurance directive", "the life insurance directive" and "the third non-life insurance directive" (omitted) inserted by SI 2009/451, reg 2(1), (2)(b) and revoked by SI 2015/575, reg 60, Sch 2, para 22(1), (2)(a);

definitions "home state regulator" and "relevant office" inserted by SI 2009/451, reg 2(1), (2)(a), (c);

definition "the Insolvency Rules" (omitted) revoked by the Insolvency (England and Wales) Rules 2016 (Consequential Amendments and Savings) Rules 2017, SI 2017/369, r 2(2), Sch 2, para 7(1), (2);

definition "the Multi-employer Regulations" inserted by the Pension Protection Fund (Entry Rules) Amendment Regulations 2005, SI 2005/2153, reg 2(1), (2);

definition "the Solvency 2 Directive" inserted by SI 2015/575, reg 60, Sch 2, para 22(1), (2)(b);

definition "tax registered scheme" substituted, for definition "tax approved scheme" as originally enacted, by SI 2006/580, reg 21(1), (2).

Para (4): substituted by SI 2005/2113, reg 5(3).

Para (5): substituted by SI 2005/2113, reg 6(3); in sub-para (a) words in square brackets beginning with the reference to "C," substituted by SI 2010/725, reg 3(1), (2)(a); in sub-para (a) words "D, E or F" in square brackets substituted by SI 2011/2973, reg 3(1), (2)(a); sub-para (a)(v) inserted by SI 2010/725, reg 3(1), (2)(b); sub-para (a)(vi) inserted by SI 2011/2973, reg 3(1), (2)(b); in sub-para (b) words in square brackets beginning with the reference to "C," substituted by SI 2010/725, reg 3(1), (2)(a); in sub-para (b) words "D, E or F" in square brackets substituted by SI 2011/2973, reg 3(1), (2)(a); sub-para (b)(v) inserted by SI 2010/725, reg 3(1), (2)(c); sub-para (b)(vi) inserted by SI 2011/2973, reg 3(1), (2)(c).

Para (6): inserted by SI 2011/99, reg 79, Sch 4, Pt 2, para 18.

Para (7): inserted by SI 2016/294, reg 5(1), (2)(b).

2, 3 (*Outside the scope of this work.*)

[18.90]

4 Notification of insolvency events in respect of employers

(1) The "notification period" in section 120(3) of the Act (duty to notify insolvency events in respect of employers) shall be the period of 14 days beginning on whichever date is the later of—

(a) the insolvency date; and

(b) the date on which the insolvency practitioner becomes aware of the existence of the scheme.

(2) A notice issued by an insolvency practitioner under section 120(2) of the Act shall be in writing and shall contain the following information—

(a) the name or type of the notice issued;

(b) the date on which the notice is issued;

(c) the name, address and pension scheme registration number of the scheme in respect of which the notice is issued;

(d) the name of the employer in relation to the scheme in respect of which the notice is issued;

(e) the nature of the insolvency event which has occurred and the date of the occurrence of that event;

(f) the name of the insolvency practitioner in relation to the employer in relation to the scheme;

(g) the date on which the insolvency practitioner in relation to the employer in relation to the scheme was appointed to act or consented to act in relation to that employer or, in any case where the insolvency practitioner is the official receiver, the date on which the official receiver began to act in relation to that employer;

(h) the address for communications at which the insolvency practitioner may be contacted by the Board in connection with the issue of the notice; and

(i) whether the notice issued contains any commercially sensitive information.

[18.91]

5 Prescribed insolvency events

(1) An insolvency event occurs—

[(a) in relation to a company, where—

(i) an administration order is made by the court in respect of the company by virtue of any enactment which applies Part 2 of the 1986 Act (administration orders) (with or without modification);

(ii) a notice from an administrator under paragraph 83(3) of Schedule B1 to the 1986 Act (moving from administration to creditors' voluntary liquidation) in relation to the company is registered by the registrar of companies;

(iii) the company moves from administration to winding up pursuant to an order of the court under [rule 21.3 of the Insolvency (England and Wales) Rules 2016 (conversion into winding up proceedings or bankruptcy: court order)]; or

(iv) an administrator or liquidator of the company, being the nominee in relation to a proposal for a voluntary arrangement under Part 1 of the 1986 Act (company voluntary arrangements), summons meetings of the company and of its creditors, to consider the proposal, in accordance with section 3(2) of the 1986 Act (summoning of meetings);]

[(aa) in relation to a partnership, where—

(i) the partnership moves from administration to winding up pursuant to an order of the court under Rule 2.61 of the [Insolvency Rules 1986] (conversion of administration to winding up—power of court) (as applied by an order under section 420 of the 1986 Act (insolvent partnerships)) as that Rule stood before the coming into force of the Insolvency (Amendment) Rules 2003; or

(ii) an administrator, liquidator or trustee of the partnership, being the nominee in relation to a proposal for a voluntary arrangement under Part 1 of the 1986 Act (as applied by an order under section 420 of the 1986 Act), summons meetings of the members of the partnership and of the partnership's creditors, to consider the proposal, in accordance with section 3(2) of the 1986 Act (as applied by an order under section 420 of the 1986 Act);]

(b) in relation to a relevant body, where—

(i) any of the events referred to in section 121(3) of the Act (insolvency events) occurs in relation to that body by virtue of the application (with or without modification) of any provision of the 1986 Act by or under any other enactment; or

(ii) an administration order is made by the court in respect of the relevant body by virtue of any enactment which applies Part 2 of the 1986 Act (with or without modification);

(c) in relation to a building society, where there is dissolution by consent of the members under section 87 of the Building Societies Act 1986 (dissolution by consent)[, where a building society insolvency order is made under Part 2 of the Banking Act 2009 (bank insolvency) (as applied in relation to building societies by an order under section 130 of the Banking Act 2009) or where a building society special administration order is made under Part 3 of that Act (bank administration) (as applied in relation to building societies by an order made under section 158 of the Banking Act 2009)];

(d) in relation to a friendly society, where there is dissolution by consent of the members under section 20 of the Friendly Societies Act 1992 (dissolution by consent); and

Part 18 Miscellaneous SIs

[(e) in relation to a co-operative or community benefit society, where there is dissolution by consent of the members under section 119 of the Co-operative and Community Benefit Societies Act 2014 (dissolution of society by an instrument of dissolution)].

(2) In this regulation—

"administration order" means an order whereby the management of the company or relevant body, as the case may be, is placed in the hands of a person appointed by the court;

["co-operative or community benefit society" means a registered society within the meaning given by section 1(1) of the Co-operative and Community Benefit Societies Act 2014 (meaning of "registered society"), other than a society registered as a credit union;]

"relevant body" means—

(a) a credit union within the meaning given in section 31(1) of the Credit Unions Act 1979 (interpretation);

(b) a limited liability partnership within the meaning given in section 57(6) of the Act (sections 38 to 56: partnerships and limited liability partnerships);

(c) a building society within the meaning given in section 119 of the Building Societies Act 1986 (interpretation);

(d) a person who has permission to act under Part 4 of the FSMA (permission to carry out regulated activities);

(e) the society of Lloyd's and Lloyd's members who have permission under Part 19 of the FSMA (Lloyd's);

(f) a friendly society within the meaning given in the Friendly Societies Act 1992; or

[(g) a co-operative or community benefit society].

(3) In this regulation, a reference to Part 2 of the 1986 Act (administration orders) shall, insofar as it relates to a company or society listed in section 249(1) of the Enterprise Act 2002 (special administration regimes), have effect as if it referred to Part 2 of the 1986 Act as it had effect immediately before the coming into force of section 248 of the Enterprise Act 2002 (replacement of Part 2 of the Insolvency Act 1986).

NOTES

Para (1): sub-para (a) substituted and sub-para (aa) inserted by the Pension Protection Fund (Entry Rules) Amendment Regulations 2005, SI 2005/2153, reg 2(1), (4); words in square brackets in sub-paras (a)(iii), (aa)(i) substituted by the Insolvency (England and Wales) Rules 2016 (Consequential Amendments and Savings) Rules 2017, SI 2017/369, r 2(2), Sch 2, para 7(1), (3), (4); words in square brackets in sub-para (c) inserted by the Building Societies (Insolvency and Special Administration) (Amendment) Order 2010, SI 2010/1189, art 3(1), (2); sub-para (e) substituted by the Co-operative and Community Benefit Societies and Credit Unions Act 2010 (Consequential Amendments) Regulations 2014, SI 2014/1815, reg 2, Schedule, para 14(a).

Para (2): definition "co-operative or community benefit society" inserted and in definition "relevant body" sub-para (g) substituted, by SI 2014/1815, reg 2, Schedule, para 14(b).

[18.92]

[5A European insolvency event

(1) An insolvency event occurs in relation to an employer on the fifth anniversary of the date that the insolvency proceedings mentioned in paragraph (2)(a) were commenced.

(2) The insolvency proceedings are proceedings which—

(a) on 20th July 2014—

(i) relate to an employer which has the centre of its main interests in the territory of a Member State of the European Economic Area other than the United Kingdom;

(ii) have been commenced in that Member State; and

(iii) have not come to an end;

(b) relate to an employer in relation to which a winding up order as mentioned in section 121(3)(g) of the Act (insolvency events) was granted and which was later set aside by the court on the basis that the court did not have jurisdiction to grant the order because the employer did not have an establishment in the United Kingdom; and

(c) relate to an employer in relation to an occupational pension scheme in respect of which an assessment period would have begun as a result of the grant of the winding up order mentioned in sub-paragraph (b) had that order not been set aside.

(3) The insolvency practitioner is the liquidator in relation to the insolvency proceedings mentioned in paragraph (2)(a)(i).

(4) . . .]

[(5) In this regulation "insolvency proceedings", "establishment" and "liquidator" each has the meaning given by Article 2 of Council Regulation (EC) No 1346/2000 of 29th May 2000 on insolvency proceedings.]

NOTES

Commencement: 21 July 2014.

Inserted by the Pension Protection Fund (Entry Rules) Amendment Regulations, SI 2014/1664, reg 2(1), (2). Note however that SI 2014/1664, reg 1(2) provides that SI 2014/1664 and the amendments it makes cease to have effect on 21 July 2017.

Para (4): revoked by the Pension Protection Fund and Occupational and Personal Pension Schemes (Miscellaneous Amendments) Regulations 2016, SI 2016/294, reg 5(1), (3)(a).

Para (5): substituted by the Insolvency Amendment (EU 2015/848) Regulations 2017, SI 2017/702, regs 2, 3, Schedule, Pt 6, para 93(1), (3), except in relation to proceedings opened before 26 June 2017. Para (5) (as substituted by SI 2016/294, reg 5(1), (3)(b)) previously read a follows:

"[(5) In this regulation "insolvency proceedings" and "liquidator" each has the meaning given by Article 2 of the Insolvency Regulation.]".

[18.93]

6 Circumstances in which insolvency proceedings in relation to the employer are stayed or come to an end

(1) *[Subject to paragraph (1A),]* the prescribed circumstances referred to in section 122(3)(a) of the Act (insolvency practitioner's duty to issue notices confirming status of scheme) in which insolvency proceedings in relation to an employer in relation to an occupational pension scheme are stayed or come to an end are—

(a) in a case where the employer is a company, where—

(i) the nominee in relation to a proposal for a voluntary arrangement under Part 1 of the 1986 Act (company voluntary arrangements) has submitted a report to the court under section 2 of that Act (procedure where nominee is not the liquidator or administrator) which states that in his opinion meetings of the company and its creditors should be summoned to consider the proposal, but no voluntary arrangement has effect or, where a voluntary arrangement has effect, it later ceases to have effect as the result of a court order under section 6 of the 1986 Act (challenge of decisions);

(ii) the directors of the company have filed (or in Scotland, lodged) documents and statements in accordance with paragraph 7(1) (documents to be submitted to court) of Schedule A1 (moratorium where directors propose voluntary arrangement) to the 1986 Act but—

(aa) the resulting moratorium comes to an end without a voluntary arrangement taking effect, or

(bb) where a voluntary arrangement has effect, it later ceases to have effect as a result of a court order under paragraph 38 (challenge of decisions) of Schedule A1 to the 1986 Act;

(iii) the appointment of an administrator in respect of the company ceases to have effect except where—

(aa) the company moves from administration into winding up pursuant to paragraph 83 (moving from administration to creditor's voluntary liquidation) of Schedule B1 (administration) to the 1986 Act or pursuant to an order of the court under [rule 21.3 of the Insolvency (England and Wales) Rules 2016 (conversion into winding up proceedings or bankruptcy: court order)], or

(bb) a winding up order is made by the court immediately upon the appointment of the administrator ceasing to have effect;

(iv) an administrative receiver within the meaning of section 251 of the 1986 Act (interpretation) appointed in relation to the company vacates office under section 45 of that Act (vacation of office); or

(v) all proceedings in the winding up of a company are stayed altogether or an order for the winding up of the company is rescinded or discharged except in circumstances where the court has made an administration order in accordance with paragraph 37 or 38 (application where company in liquidation) of Schedule B1 to the 1986 Act;

[(vi) where the company is a bank (as defined in section 91 of the Banking Act 2009), the bank insolvency procedure is stayed under section 130 of the Insolvency Act 1986 (as applied by section 103 of the Banking Act 2009), or the bank insolvency order is rescinded or discharged, except in circumstances where the court has made an administration order in accordance with section 114 of the Banking Act 2009.]

(b) in a case where the employer is an individual, where—

(i) the nominee in relation to a proposal for a voluntary arrangement under Part 8 of the 1986 Act (individual voluntary arrangements) has submitted a report to the court under section 256(1) (nominee's report on debtor's proposal) or 256A(3) (debtor's proposal and nominee's report) of that Act which states that in his opinion a meeting of the individual's creditors should be summoned to consider the proposal but no voluntary arrangement takes effect or, where a voluntary arrangement takes effect, it later ceases to have effect as a result of a court order under section 262 of the 1986 Act (challenge of meeting's decision);

(ii) a bankruptcy order against the individual is annulled or rescinded; or

(iii) an insolvency administration order in respect of the estate of the individual made in accordance with an order under section 421 of the 1986 Act (insolvent estates of deceased persons) is annulled or rescinded;

(c) in a case where the employer is a partnership, where—

(i) the nominee in relation to a proposal for a voluntary arrangement under Part 1 of the 1986 Act (company voluntary arrangements) (as applied by an order under section 420 of that Act (insolvent partnerships)) has submitted a report to the court under section 2 of that Act (procedure where nominee is not the liquidator or administrator) which states that in his opinion meetings of the partnership and its creditors should be summoned to consider the proposal, but no voluntary arrangement has effect or, where a voluntary arrangement has effect, it later ceases to have effect as a result of a court order under section 6 of the 1986 Act (challenge of decisions) (as applied by an order under section 420 of that Act);

(ii) the members of the partnership have filed documents and statements in accordance with paragraph 7(1) (documents to be submitted to the court) of Schedule A1 (moratorium where directors propose voluntary arrangement) to the 1986 Act (as applied by an order under section 420 of that Act) but—

(aa) the resulting moratorium comes to an end without a voluntary arrangement taking effect, or

(bb) where a voluntary arrangement has effect, it later ceases to have effect as a result of a court order under paragraph 38 (application where company in liquidation) of Schedule A1 to the 1986 Act (as applied by an order under section 420 of that Act);

(iii) an administration order in relation to a partnership under Part 2 of the 1986 Act (administration orders) is discharged except where—

(aa) a winding up order is made by a court immediately upon the discharge of the administration order, or

(bb) the discharge is pursuant to an order of the court for the administration to be converted into winding up under Rule 2.61(1) of [the Insolvency Rules 1986] (conversion of administration into winding up – power of court) as those rules stood before the coming into force of the Insolvency (Amendment) Rules 2003; or

(iv) all proceedings in a winding up of the partnership are stayed altogether or an order for the winding up of the partnership is rescinded or discharged;

[(d) in a case where the employer is a building society, where—

(i) the appointment of a building society special administrator under Part 3 of the Banking Act 2009 (bank administration) (as applied in relation to building societies by an order under section 158 of that Act) in respect of the building society ceases to have effect; or

(ii) the building society insolvency procedure is stayed under section 130 of the 1986 Act (as applied by section 103 of the Banking Act 2009 and an order made under section 130 of that Act), or the building society insolvency order is rescinded or discharged, except in circumstances where the court has made an administration order in accordance with section 114 of the Banking Act 2009 (as applied by an order made under section 130 of that Act)].

[(1A) This regulation does not apply in relation to an insolvency event under regulation 5A.]

(2) . . .

NOTES

Para (1): words in first pair of square brackets inserted by the Pension Protection Fund (Entry Rules) Amendment Regulations, SI 2014/1664, reg 2(1), (3)(a) (note however that SI 2014/1664, reg 1(2) provides that SI 2014/1664 and the amendments it makes cease to have effect on 21 July 2017); words in square brackets in sub-paras (a)(iii), (c)(iii) substituted by the Insolvency (England and Wales) Rules 2016 (Consequential Amendments and Savings) Rules 2017, SI 2017/369, r 2(2), Sch 2, para 7(1), (5), (6); sub-para (a)(vi) inserted by the Banking Act 2009 (Parts 2 and 3 Consequential Amendments) Order 2009, SI 2009/317, art 8; sub-para (d) inserted by the Building Societies (Insolvency and Special Administration) (Amendment) Order 2010, SI 2010/1189, art 3(1), (3).

Para (1A): inserted by SI 2014/1664, reg 2(1), (3)(b), with effect until 21 July 2017, as noted to para (1) above.

Para (2): revoked by the Deregulation Act 2015 (Insolvency) (Consequential Amendments and Transitional and Savings Provisions) Order 2015, SI 2015/1641, art 6, Sch 3, para 3(7).

[18.94]

[7 Applications and notifications to the Board

(1) Except in a case to which regulation 7A applies, the prescribed requirement for the purposes of section 129(1)(b) and (4)(b) of the Act (applications and notifications for the purposes of section 128) is that at least one of paragraphs (2), (4) and (5) applies to the employer.

(2) This paragraph applies to an employer if it is not—

(a) an individual;

(b) a company as defined in section 1(1) of the Companies Act 2006;

(c) a company which may be wound up under Part 5 of the Insolvency Act 1986 (unregistered companies);

(d) a partnership; or

(e) a relevant body as defined in regulation 5(2).

(3) For the purposes of paragraph (2)(c), an employer which is a company incorporated outside the United Kingdom is to be regarded as a company which may be wound up under Part 5 of the Insolvency Act 1986.

(4) This paragraph applies to an employer if it is an EEA insurer or an EEA credit institution.

(5) This paragraph applies to an employer if—

(a) the centre of the employer's main interests is situated within the territory of a member State other than the United Kingdom;

(b) insolvency proceedings have been opened against the employer in a member State in accordance with Article 3 of the Insolvency Regulation; and

(c) the employer does not have an establishment in the United Kingdom.

(6) In this regulation references to a member State do not include Denmark.]

NOTES

Commencement: 6 April 2016.

Substituted by the Pension Protection Fund and Occupational and Personal Pension Schemes (Miscellaneous Amendments) Regulations 2016, SI 2016/294, reg 5(1), (4).

[18.95]

[7A Applications and notifications to the Board—multi-employer schemes

(1) This regulation applies to—

(a) a multi-employer section to which Part 3 of the Multi-employer Regulations (segregated schemes: multi-employer sections without requirement for partial wind up on withdrawal of a participating employer) applies which is, for the purposes of Part 2 of the Act, an eligible scheme; and

(b) a non-segregated scheme to which Part 6 of the Multi-employer Regulations (non-segregated schemes: schemes without provision for partial wind up on withdrawal of a participating employer) applies which is, for the purposes of Part 2 of the Act, an eligible scheme.

[(2) In the case of a scheme, or a section of a scheme, to which this regulation applies, the prescribed requirement for the purposes of section 129(1A)(b) and (4)(a)(ii) of the Act (applications and notifications for the purposes of section 128) is that at least one of paragraphs (3), (5) and (6) applies to the employer.

(3) This paragraph applies to an employer if it is not—

(a) an individual;

(b) a company as defined in section 1(1) of the Companies Act 2006;

(c) a company which may be wound up under Part 5 of the Insolvency Act 1986;

(d) a partnership; or

(e) a relevant body as defined in regulation 5(2).

(4) For the purposes of paragraph (3)(c), an employer which is a company incorporated outside the United Kingdom is to be regarded as a company which may be wound up under Part 5 of the Insolvency Act 1986.

(5) This paragraph applies to an employer if it is an EEA insurer or an EEA credit institution.

(6) This paragraph applies to an employer if—

(a) the centre of the employer's main interests is situated within the territory of a member State other than the United Kingdom;

(b) insolvency proceedings have been opened against the employer in a member State in accordance with Article 3 of the Insolvency Regulation; and

(c) the employer does not have an establishment in the United Kingdom.

(7) In this regulation references to a member State do not include Denmark.]]

NOTES

Inserted by the Pension Protection Fund (Entry Rules) Amendment Regulations 2005, SI 2005/2153, reg 2(1), (6).

Paras (2)–(7): substituted, for original para (2), by the Pension Protection Fund and Occupational and Personal Pension Schemes (Miscellaneous Amendments) Regulations 2016, SI 2016/294, reg 5(1), (5).

[18.96]

8 Applications and notifications to the Board—further provision

[(1) Except in a case to which regulation 8A applies, the prescribed period for making an application to the Board under section 129(1) of the Act (applications and notifications for the purposes of section 128) shall be the period of—

(a) 28 days; or

(b) such longer period of not more than three months as the Board may determine is reasonable in the circumstances of a particular case,

beginning with the date on which the trustees or managers of an eligible scheme become aware that the employer in relation to the scheme is unlikely to continue as a going concern.]

(2) Applications to the Board for the purposes of section 128 of the Act shall be in writing and shall contain the following information—

(a) a description of the type or purpose of the application;

(b) the name, address and pension scheme registration number of the scheme in respect of which the application is made;

(c) the name of the employer in relation to the scheme in respect of which the application is made;

(d) a statement by the trustees or managers of the scheme that the employer in relation to the scheme is unlikely to continue as a going concern and that the requirements prescribed under section 129(1)(b) of the Act have been met in relation to that employer;

(e) the date on which the trustees or managers of the scheme became aware that the employer in relation to the scheme is unlikely to continue as a going concern; . . .

(f) the date on which the application was sent to the Board by the trustees or managers of the scheme[; and

(g) if the application was not sent to the Board within the period specified in paragraph (1)(a) of this regulation, the reasons for this].

(3) Where the Regulator becomes aware that the employer in relation to an eligible scheme is unlikely to continue as a going concern and that the requirements prescribed under section 129(1)(b) of the Act are met in relation to that employer, the prescribed information to be contained in the notice referred to in section 129(4) of the Act which the Regulator must give to the Board is as follows—

(a) the name or type of notice issued;

(b) the date on which the notice is issued;

(c) the name, address and pension scheme registration number of the scheme in respect of which the [notice is issued;]

(d) the name of the employer in relation to the scheme in respect of which the notice is issued;

(e) a statement by the Regulator that the employer in relation to the scheme is unlikely to continue as a going concern and that the requirements prescribed under section 129(1)(b) of the Act are met in relation to that employer; and

(f) the date on which the Regulator became aware that the employer in relation to the scheme is unlikely to continue as a going concern.

(4) Where the Board receives a notice from the Regulator to which paragraph (3) applies, the prescribed information that must be contained in the notice referred to in section 129(5) of the Act which the Board must give to the trustees or managers of the scheme concerned and copy to the employer in relation to that scheme is as follows—

(a) the name or type of notice issued;

(b) the date on which the notice is issued;

(c) the name, address and pension scheme registration number of the scheme in respect of which the notice is issued;

(d) the name of the employer in relation to the scheme in respect of which the notice is issued;

(e) a statement that the Board received a notice from the Regulator under section 129(4) of the Act and the date on which that notice was received by the Board;

(f) the date on which the Regulator became aware that the employer in relation to the scheme is unlikely to continue as a going concern;

(g) the address for communications at which the Board may be contacted in respect of the issue of the notice; and

(h) whether the notice issued by the Board contains any restricted information and, if so, the nature of the restrictions.

NOTES

Para (1): substituted by the Pension Protection Fund and Occupational and Personal Pension Schemes (Miscellaneous Amendments) Regulations 2016, SI 2016/294, reg 5(1), (6)(a).

Para (2): word omitted from sub-para (e) revoked, and sub-para (g) and word immediately preceding it inserted, by SI 2016/294, reg 5(1), (6)(b).

Para (3): words in square brackets in sub-para (c) substituted by the Occupational Pension Schemes and Pension Protection Fund (Amendment) Regulations 2005, SI 2005/993, regs 1(2), 4(b).

[18.97]

[8A Applications and notifications to the Board—further provision for multi-employer schemes]

[(1) This regulation applies to—

(a) a multi-employer section to which Part 3 of the Multi-employer Regulations (segregated schemes: multi-employer sections without requirement for partial wind up on withdrawal of a participating employer) applies which is, for the purposes of Part 2 of the Act, an eligible scheme; and

(b) a non-segregated scheme to which Part 6 of the Multi-employer Regulations (non-segregated schemes: schemes without provision for partial wind up on withdrawal of a participating employer) applies which is, for the purposes of Part 2 of the Act, an eligible scheme.

(2) The prescribed period for making an application to the Board under section 129(1)(a) or (b) of the Act (applications and notifications for the purposes of section 128) shall be—

(a) where the application is under section 129(1)(a) of the Act, the period of 28 days beginning with the date on which the trustees or managers of a scheme, or a section of a scheme, become aware that the conditions for making an application to the Board under that section of the Act are met in relation to that scheme or section; or

(b) where the application is under section 129(1)(b) of the Act, the period of 28 days beginning with—

(i) 24th August 2005 if the trustees or managers of a scheme, or a section of a scheme, are aware on that date that the conditions for making an application to the Board under that section of the Act were met in relation to that scheme or section between 6th April 2005 and that date; or

(ii) the date on which the trustees or managers of a scheme, or a section of a scheme, become aware after 24th August 2005 that the conditions for making an application to the Board under that section of the Act are met in relation to that scheme or section.

(3) Applications to the Board for the purposes of section 128 of the Act (duty to assume responsibility for schemes following application or notification) shall, where the application is made under section 129(1)(a) of the Act, be in writing and shall contain the following information—

(a) a description of the type or purpose of the application;

(b) the name, address and pension scheme registration number of the scheme, or section of the scheme, in respect of which the application is made;

(c) the name of the employer in relation to the scheme, or section of the scheme, in respect of which the application is made;
(d) a statement by the trustees or managers of the scheme, or section of the scheme, that the conditions for making an application to the Board under section 129(1)(a) of the Act have been met;
(e) the date on which the trustees or managers of the scheme, or section of the scheme, became aware that the conditions for making an application to the Board under section 129(1)(a) of the Act were met; and
(f) the date on which the application was sent to the Board by the trustees or managers of the scheme or section of the scheme.

(4) Applications to the Board for the purposes of section 128 of the Act shall, where the application is made under section 129(1)(b) of the Act, be in writing and shall contain the following information—
(a) a description of the type or purpose of the application;
(b) the name, address and pension scheme registration number of the scheme, or section of the scheme, in respect of which the application is made;
(c) the name of each employer in relation to the scheme, or section of the scheme, in respect of which the application is made;
(d) the name of the person who is no longer an employer or the persons who are no longer employers in relation to the scheme, or section of the scheme, at the time referred to in section 129(4)(b) of the Act;
(e) a statement by the trustees or managers of the scheme, or section of the scheme, that the conditions for making an application to the Board under section 129(1)(b) of the Act have been met;
(f) the date on which the trustees or managers of the scheme, or section of the scheme, became aware that the conditions for making an application to the Board under section 129(1)(b) of the Act were met; and
(g) the date on which the application was sent to the Board by the trustees or managers of the scheme or section of the scheme.

(5) Where the Regulator becomes aware that the conditions for making a notification to the Board under section 129(4)(a) of the Act are met in relation to a scheme, or a section of a scheme, which is, for the purposes of Part 2 of the Act, an eligible scheme, the notice which the Regulator must give to the Board under that section of the Act shall be in writing and shall contain the following information—
(a) the name or type of notice given;
(b) the date on which the notice is given;
(c) the name, address and pension scheme registration number of the scheme, or section of the scheme, in respect of which the notice is given;
(d) the name of the employer in relation to the scheme, or section of the scheme, in respect of which the notice is given;
(e) a statement by the Regulator that the employer referred to in sub-paragraph (d) is unlikely to continue as a going concern and meets the requirements specified in regulation 7A(2); and
(f) the date on which the Regulator became aware of the matter in respect of which the statement is provided by it under sub-paragraph (e).

(6) Where the Regulator is aware that the conditions for making an application to the Board under section 129(4)(b) of the Act are met in relation to a scheme, or a section of a scheme, which is, for the purposes of Part 2 of the Act, an eligible scheme, the notice which the Regulator must give to the Board under that section of the Act shall be in writing and shall contain the following information—
(a) the name or type of notice given;
(b) the date on which the notice is given;
(c) the name, address and pension scheme registration number of the scheme, or section of the scheme, in respect of which the notice is given;
(d) the name of each employer in relation to the scheme, or section of the scheme, in respect of which the notice is given;
(e) the name of the person who is no longer an employer or the persons who are no longer employers in relation to the scheme, or section of the scheme, at the time referred to in section 129(4)(b) of the Act;
(f) a statement by the Regulator that the person or persons referred to in sub-paragraph (e) is no longer an employer or are no longer employers in relation to the scheme, or section of the scheme, at the time referred to in section 129(4)(b) of the Act; and
(g) the date on which the Regulator became aware of the matter in respect of which the statement is provided by it under sub-paragraph (f).

(7) Where the Board receives a notice from the Regulator to which paragraph (5) or (6) applies, the notice referred to in section 129(5) of the Act which the Board must give to the trustees or managers of the scheme, or section of the scheme, concerned and copy to any employer in relation to that scheme, or section, shall be in writing and shall contain the following information—
(a) the name or type of the notice given;
(b) the date on which the notice is given;
(c) the name, address and pension scheme registration number of the scheme, or section of the scheme, in respect of which the notice is given;
(d) a statement that the Board received the notice from the Regulator under section 129(4)(a) or (b) of the Act and the date on which the notice was received by the Board;

(e) where the notice referred to in sub-paragraph (d) is a notice under section 129(4)(a) of the Act, the date on which the Regulator became aware that the employer in relation to the scheme, or section of the scheme, is unlikely to continue as a going concern;

(f) where the notice referred to in sub-paragraph (d) is a notice under section 129(4)(b) of the Act, the date on which the Regulator became aware that the person or persons referred to in paragraph (6)(e) is no longer an employer or are no longer employers in relation to the scheme, or section of the scheme, at the time referred to in section 129(4)(b) of the Act;

(g) the address for communications at which the Board may be contacted in respect of the giving of the notice; and

(h) whether the notice given by the Board contains any restricted information and, if so, the nature of the restrictions.]

NOTES

Inserted by the Pension Protection Fund (Entry Rules) Amendment Regulations 2005, SI 2005/2153, reg 2(1), (8).

[18.98]

9 Confirmation of scheme status by insolvency practitioner

(1) The prescribed matters referred to in section 122(5)(a) of the Act (insolvency practitioner's duty to issue notices confirming status of scheme) which the insolvency practitioner in relation to the employer in relation to [an occupational pension scheme] must be able to confirm are—

(a) in circumstances where the employer is [not an individual or a partnership], that—

(i) [the employer] has been rescued as a going concern and the employer—

(aa) retains responsibility for meeting the pension liabilities under the scheme, and

(bb) has not entered into an agreement to which paragraph (3)(c) of regulation 2 applies; or

(ii) another person or other persons has or have assumed responsibility for meeting the employer's pension liabilities under the scheme;

(b) in circumstances where the employer is an individual, that—

(i) [there has been] a rescue of all or part of the employer's business as a going concern and the employer—

(aa) retains responsibility for meeting the pension liabilities under the scheme, and

(bb) has not entered into an agreement to which paragraph (3)(c) of regulation 2 applies; or

(ii) another person or other persons has or have assumed responsibility for meeting the employer's pension liabilities under the scheme;

(c) in circumstances where the employer is a partnership, that—

(i) there has been a rescue of all or part of the employer's business and the employer—

(aa) retains responsibility for meeting the pension liabilities under the scheme, and

(bb) has not entered into an agreement to which paragraph (3)(c) of regulation 2 applies; or

(ii) another person or other persons has or have assumed responsibility for meeting the employer's pension liabilities under the scheme.

(2) The prescribed matters referred to in section 122(5)(b) of the Act which the insolvency practitioner must be able to confirm are—

(a) in circumstances where the employer is [not an individual or a partnership]—

(i) that employer has entered into an agreement to which paragraph (3)(c) of regulation 2 applies; or

(ii) that employer is not continuing as a going concern and—

(aa) no other person or other persons has or have assumed responsibility for meeting the employer's pension liabilities under the scheme, and

(bb) the insolvency practitioner is of the opinion that the employer's pension liabilities under the scheme will not be assumed by another person;

(b) in circumstances where the employer is an individual—

(i) that employer has entered into an agreement to which paragraph (3)(c) of regulation 2 applies; or

(ii) no part of that employer's business is being continued by that employer as a going concern and—

(aa) no other person or other persons has or have assumed responsibility for meeting the employer's pension liabilities under the scheme, and

(bb) the insolvency practitioner is of the opinion that the employer's pension liabilities under the scheme will not be assumed by another person;

(c) in circumstances where the employer is a partnership—

(i) that employer has entered into an agreement to which paragraph (3)(c) of regulation 2 applies; or

(ii) no part of the employer's business is being continued by one or more of the partners as a going concern and—

(aa) no other person or other persons has or have assumed responsibility for meeting the employer's pension liabilities under the scheme, and

(bb) the insolvency practitioner is of the opinion that the employer's pension liabilities under the scheme will not be assumed by another person.

(3) A notice issued by an insolvency practitioner under section 122(2)(a) or (b) of the Act or by a former insolvency practitioner under section 122(4) of the Act shall be in writing and shall contain the following information—

(a) the name or type of notice issued;

(b) the date on which the notice is issued;

(c) the name, address and pension scheme registration number of the scheme in respect of which the notice is issued;

(d) the name of the employer in relation to the scheme in respect of which the notice is issued;

(e) the name of the insolvency practitioner or former insolvency practitioner and the address at which that insolvency practitioner may be contacted by the Board in connection with the issue of the notice;

(f) a statement by the insolvency practitioner or former insolvency practitioner that, as the case may be, a scheme rescue has occurred or a scheme rescue is not possible or that he has been unable to confirm that a scheme rescue has occurred or that a scheme rescue is not possible;

(g) if a scheme rescue has occurred, the date or the approximate date of the scheme rescue and, if there is a new employer in relation to the scheme, the name and address of that employer in relation to the scheme;

(h) if a scheme rescue is not possible, a statement from the insolvency practitioner or former insolvency practitioner as to why, in his opinion, that is not possible;

(i) if section 122(4) of the Act applies and the former insolvency practitioner has not been able to confirm in relation to the scheme that a scheme rescue is not possible, a statement from that insolvency practitioner as to why, in his opinion, that is the case;

(j) a statement that the notice issued will not become binding until it has been approved by the Board; and

(k) whether, in the opinion of the insolvency practitioner or former insolvency practitioner, the notice issued contains any commercially sensitive information.

NOTES

Para (1): words in first pair of square brackets and words in square brackets in sub-para (b)(i) substituted by the Occupational Pension Schemes and Pension Protection Fund (Amendment) Regulations 2005, SI 2005/993, regs 1(2), 4(c); in sub-para (a) words in first pair of square brackets and words in square brackets in sub-para (a)(i) substituted by the Pension Protection Fund and Occupational and Personal Pension Schemes (Miscellaneous Amendments) Regulations 2016, SI 2016/294, reg 5(1), (7)(a).

Para (2): in sub-para (a) words in square brackets substituted by SI 2016/294, reg 5(1), (7)(b).

[18.99]

10 Confirmation of scheme status by Board

(1) This regulation applies in a case where section 129 of the Act (applications and notifications for the purposes of section 128) applies and where the requirements prescribed in regulation 7 [or 7A] have been met in relation to the employer in relation to an eligible scheme.

(2) The prescribed matters referred to in section 130(5)(a) of the Act (Board's duty where application or notification received under section 129) which the Board must be able to confirm are that—

(a) all or part of the employer's business has been rescued as a going concern and the employer—

(i) retains responsibility for meeting the pension liabilities under the scheme, and

(ii) has not entered into an agreement to which paragraph (3)(c) of regulation 2 applies; or

(b) the Board is satisfied that another person or other persons has or have assumed responsibility for meeting the employer's pension liabilities under the scheme.

(3) The prescribed matters referred to in section 130(5)(b) of the Act which the Board must confirm are that—

(a) in circumstances where [the employer is not an individual or a partnership]—

(i) that employer has entered into an agreement to which paragraph (3)(c) of regulation 2 applies; or

(ii) that employer is not continuing as a going concern and—

(aa) no other person or other persons has or have assumed responsibility for meeting the employer's pension liabilities under the scheme, and

(bb) the Board is of the opinion that the employer's pension liabilities under the scheme will not be assumed by another person;

(b) in circumstances where the employer is an individual—

(i) that employer has entered into an agreement to which paragraph (3)(c) of regulation 2 applies; or

(ii) no part of the employer's business is being continued by that employer as a going concern and—

(aa) no other person or other persons has or have assumed responsibility for meeting the employer's pension liabilities under the scheme, and

(bb) the Board is of the opinion that the employer's pension liabilities under the scheme will not be assumed by another person;

(c) in circumstances where the employer is a partnership [. . .]—

(i) that employer has entered into an agreement to which paragraph (3)(c) of regulation 2 applies; or

(ii) no part of the employer's business is being continued by one or more of the partners as a going concern and—

(aa) no other person or other persons has or have assumed responsibility for meeting the employer's pension liabilities under the scheme, and (bb) the Board is of the opinion that the employer's pension liabilities under the scheme will not be assumed by another person.

(4) A notice issued by the Board under section 130(2) or (3) of the Act shall be in writing and shall contain the following information—

(a) the name or type of notice issued;
(b) the date on which the notice is issued;
(c) the name, address and pension scheme registration number of the scheme in respect of which the notice is issued;
(d) the name of the employer in relation to the scheme in respect of which the notice is issued;
(e) a statement by the Board that a scheme rescue has occurred or that a scheme rescue is not possible;
(f) if a scheme rescue has occurred, the date or the approximate date of the scheme rescue and, if there is a new employer in relation to the scheme, the name and address of that employer;
(g) if a scheme rescue is not possible, a statement by the Board to that effect;
(h) the address for communications at which the Board may be contacted in connection with the issue of the notice;
(i) whether the issue of the notice by the Board is a reviewable matter and, if so, the time limit for applying for a review of or appeal against the issue of the notice;
(j) the date on which the notice issued will become binding; and
(k) whether the notice issued contains any restricted information and, if so, the nature of the restrictions.

NOTES

Para (1): words in square brackets inserted by the Pension Protection Fund (Miscellaneous Amendments) Regulations 2009, SI 2009/451, reg 2(1), (4)(a).

Para (3): in sub-para (a) words in square brackets substituted by the Pension Protection Fund and Occupational and Personal Pension Schemes (Miscellaneous Amendments) Regulations 2016, SI 2016/294, reg 5(1), (8)(a); words omitted from square brackets in sub-para (c) inserted by SI 2009/451, reg 2(1), (4)(c) and revoked by SI 2016/294, reg 5(1), (8)(b).

[18.100]

11 Confirmation of scheme status by insolvency practitioner—multi-employer schemes

(1) This regulation applies to—

(a) a section of a segregated scheme with only one employer in relation to that section;
(b) a multi-employer section of a segregated scheme; or
(c) a non-segregated scheme,

where the scheme rules contain a provision for the partial winding up of the scheme, or the section, in circumstances where an employer in relation to the scheme, or the section, ceases to participate in the scheme.

(2) Where, by virtue of section 122 of the Act (insolvency practitioner's duty to issue notices confirming status of scheme), an insolvency practitioner is required to issue a notice under subsection (2)(a) (a "scheme failure notice") or (2)(b) (a "scheme rescue notice") of that section in relation to—

(a) a section of a segregated scheme;
(b) a segregated part of a multi-employer section of a segregated scheme; or
(c) a segregated part of a non-segregated scheme,

to which this regulation applies, regulation 9 shall have effect and shall be read as if, for the words "the scheme" in each place where they appear in that regulation, there were substituted the words "the section" or, as the case may be, "the segregated part".

(3) Where, by virtue of section 120(3A) or, as the case may be, 129(1B) of the Act, the trustees or managers of a scheme or a section of a scheme to which this regulation applies are required to give a non-segregation notice to the Board, the notice shall be in writing and shall contain the following information—

(a) the name or type of the notice issued;
(b) the date on which the notice is issued;
(c) the name, address and pension scheme registration number of the scheme in respect of which the notice is issued;
(d) the name of the employer in relation to the scheme in respect of which the notice is issued; and
(e) a statement that the trustees or managers have decided not to exercise the option to segregate under the scheme.

(4) Where, under section 130 of the Act (Board's duty where application or notification received under section 129), the Board is required to issue a notice under subsection (2) (a "scheme failure notice") or (3) (a "scheme rescue notice") of that section in relation to—

(a) a section of a segregated scheme;
(b) a segregated part of a multi-employer section of a segregated scheme; or
(c) a segregated part of a non-segregated scheme,

to which this regulation applies, regulation 10 shall have effect and shall be read as if, for the words "the scheme" in each place where they appear in that regulation, there were substituted the words "the section" or, as the case may be, "the segregated part".

[18.101]

12 Confirmation of scheme status by Board—multi-employer schemes

(1) This regulation applies to—

(a) a non-segregated scheme; or

(b) a multi-employer section of a segregated scheme,

the rules of which do not contain a provision for the partial winding up of the scheme, or the section, in circumstances where an employer in relation to the scheme, or the section, ceases to participate in the scheme.

(2) Where, under section 122(2)(a) of the Act (insolvency practitioner's duty to issue notices confirming status of scheme), an insolvency practitioner is required to issue a scheme failure notice in relation to a multi-employer section of a segregated scheme or a non-segregated scheme to which this regulation applies, regulation 9(2) shall have effect and shall be read as if—

(a) in the case of a multi-employer section of a segregated scheme—

(i) for the words "no other person or other persons has or have assumed responsibility for meeting the employer's pension liabilities under the scheme" in sub-paragraph (a)(ii)(aa), there were substituted the words "no other person or other persons has or have assumed responsibility for meeting all of the pension liabilities under the section"; and

(ii) for the words "the insolvency practitioner is of the opinion that the employer's pension liabilities under the scheme will not be assumed by another person" in sub-paragraph (a)(ii)(bb), there were substituted the words "the insolvency practitioner is of the opinion that all of the pension liabilities under the section will not be assumed by another person"; and

(b) in the case of a non-segregated scheme—

(i) for the words "no other person or other persons has or have assumed responsibility for meeting the employer's pension liabilities under the scheme" in sub-paragraph (a)(ii)(aa), there were substituted the words "no other person or other persons has or have assumed responsibility for meeting all of the pension liabilities under the scheme"; and

(ii) for the words "the insolvency practitioner is of the opinion that the employer's pension liabilities under the scheme will not be assumed by another person" in sub-paragraph (a)(ii)(bb), there were substituted the words "the insolvency practitioner is of the opinion that all of the pension liabilities under the scheme will not be assumed by another person".

(3) Where, under section 122(2)(b) of the Act (insolvency practitioner's duty to issue notices confirming status of scheme), an insolvency practitioner is required to issue a scheme rescue notice in relation to a multi-employer section of a segregated scheme or a non-segregated scheme to which this regulation applies, regulation 9(1) shall have effect and shall be read as if—

(a) in the case of a multi-employer section of a segregated scheme—

(i) for the words "retains responsibility for meeting the pension liabilities under the scheme" in each place where they appear, there were substituted the words "assumes responsibility for meeting all of the pension liabilities under the section"; and

(ii) for the words "another person or other persons has or have assumed responsibility for meeting the employer's pension liabilities under the scheme" in each place where they appear, there were substituted the words "another person or other persons has or have assumed responsibility for meeting all of the pension liabilities under the section"; and

(b) in the case of a non-segregated scheme—

(i) for the words "retains responsibility for meeting the pension liabilities under the scheme" in each place where they appear, there were substituted the words "assumes responsibility for meeting all of the pension liabilities under the scheme"; and

(ii) for the words "another person or other persons has or have assumed responsibility for meeting the employer's pension liabilities under the scheme" in each place where they appear, there were substituted the words "another person or other persons has or have assumed responsibility for meeting all of the pension liabilities under the scheme".

(4) Where, under section 130(2) of the Act (Board's duty to issue notices confirming status of scheme), the Board is required to issue a scheme failure notice in relation to a multi-employer section of a segregated scheme or a non-segregated scheme to which this regulation applies, regulation 10(3) shall have effect and shall be read as if—

(a) in the case of a multi-employer section of a segregated scheme—

(i) for the words "no other person or other persons has or have assumed responsibility for meeting the employer's pension liabilities under the scheme" in sub-paragraph (a)(ii)(aa), there were substituted the words "no other person or other persons has or have assumed responsibility for meeting all of the pension liabilities under the section"; and

(ii) for the words "the Board is of the opinion that the employer's pension liabilities under the scheme will not be assumed by another person" in sub-paragraph (a)(ii)(bb), there were substituted the words "the Board is of the opinion that all of the pension liabilities under the section will not be assumed by another person"; and

(b) in the case of a non-segregated scheme—

(i) for the words "no other person or other persons has or have assumed responsibility for meeting the employer's pension liabilities under the scheme" in sub-paragraph (a)(ii)(aa), there were substituted the words "no other person or other persons has or have assumed responsibility for meeting all of the pension liabilities under the scheme"; and

(ii) for the words "the Board is of the opinion that the employer's pension liabilities under the scheme will not be assumed by another person" in sub-paragraph (a)(ii)(bb), there were substituted the words "the Board is of the opinion that all of the pension liabilities under the scheme will not be assumed by another person".

(5) Where, under section 130(3) of the Act (Board's duty to issue notices confirming status of scheme), the Board is required to issue a scheme rescue notice in relation to a multi-employer section of a segregated scheme or a non-segregated scheme to which this regulation applies, regulation 10(2) shall have effect and shall be read as if—

(a) in the case of a multi-employer section of a segregated scheme—

(i) for the words "retains responsibility for meeting the pension liabilities under the scheme" in sub-paragraph (a)(i), there were substituted the words "assumes responsibility for meeting all of the pension liabilities under the section"; and

(ii) for the words "the Board is satisfied that another person or other persons has or have assumed responsibility for meeting the employer's pension liabilities under the scheme" in sub-paragraph (b), there were substituted the words "the Board is satisfied that another person or other persons has or have assumed responsibility for meeting all of the pension liabilities under the section"; and

(b) in the case of a non-segregated scheme—

(i) for the words "retains responsibility for meeting the pension liabilities under the scheme" in sub-paragraph (a)(i), there were substituted the words "assumes responsibility for meeting all of the pension liabilities under the scheme"; and

(ii) for the words "the Board is satisfied that another person or other persons has or have assumed responsibility for meeting the employer's pension liabilities under the scheme" in sub-paragraph (b), there were substituted the words "the Board is satisfied that another person or other persons has or have assumed responsibility for meeting all of the pension liabilities under the scheme".

[18.102]

13 Confirmation of scheme status—binding notices

(1) Where the Board determines to approve or not to approve a notice issued by an insolvency practitioner or former insolvency practitioner in relation to an employer in relation to [an occupational pension scheme] under section 122 of the Act [(insolvency practitioner's duty to issue notices confirming status of scheme)], the determination notice which the Board must issue under section 122(4) of the Act to that effect shall be in writing and shall contain the following information—

(a) the name or type of notice issued;

(b) the date on which the notice is issued;

(c) the name, address and pension scheme registration number of the scheme in respect of which the notice is issued;

(d) the name of the employer in relation to the scheme in respect of which the notice is issued;

(e) a statement that the Board received a notice from the insolvency practitioner, or former insolvency practitioner, under section 122 of the Act, the effect of that notice and the date on which it was issued by the insolvency practitioner;

(f) the name of the insolvency practitioner, or former insolvency practitioner;

(g) a statement of whether or not the Board has determined to approve the notice issued by the insolvency practitioner or former insolvency practitioner under section 122 of the Act;

(h) the address for communications at which the Board may be contacted in connection with the issue of the notice; and

(i) whether the notice issued by the Board contains any restricted information and, if so, the nature of the restriction.

[(1A) Where a notice issued under section 122 of the Act becomes binding, the notice which the Board must give under section 125(3) of the Act (binding notices confirming status of scheme) shall be in writing.]

(2) Where a notice issued under section 130(2) or (3) of the Act becomes binding, the notice which the Board must issue under section 130(7) of the Act to that effect shall be in writing and shall contain the following information—

(a) the name or type of notice issued;

(b) the date on which the notice is issued;

(c) the name, address and pension scheme registration number of the scheme in respect of which the notice is issued;

(d) the name of the employer in relation to the scheme in respect of which the notice is issued;

(e) a statement that the notice issued under section 130(2) or (3) of the Act has become binding;

(f) the date on which the notice under section 130(2) or (3) of the Act was issued; and

(g) whether the notice issued by the Board contains any restricted information and, if so, the nature of the restriction.

NOTES

Para (1): words in square brackets substituted by the Occupational Pension Schemes and Pension Protection Fund (Amendment) Regulations 2005, SI 2005/993, regs 1(2), 4(d).

Para (1A): inserted by the Pension Protection Fund (Entry Rules) Amendment Regulations 2005, SI 2005/2153, reg 2(1), (9).

14–25 (*Outside the scope of this work.*)

SCHEDULE

(*Outside the scope of this work.*)

OCCUPATIONAL PENSION SCHEMES (EMPLOYER DEBT) REGULATIONS 2005

(SI 2005/678)

NOTES

Made: 11 March 2005.

Authority: Pensions Act 1995, ss 40(1), (2), 49(2), (3), 57(2), (4), 60(2), 68(2)(e), 75(1)(b), (5), (6D)(b)(i), (10), 75A(1)–(4), 89(2), 118(1), 119, 124(1), 125(3), 174(2), (3).

Commencement: 6 April 2005.

ARRANGEMENT OF REGULATIONS

Preliminary

1 Citation, commencement, application and extent . . . [18.103]
2 Interpretation . . . [18.104]
3 Disapplication of the 1996 Regulations . . . [18.105]
4 Schemes to which section 75 of the 1995 Act does not apply . . . [18.106]

Valuations

5 Calculation of the amount of scheme liabilities and value of scheme assets . . . [18.107]

Multi-employer schemes

6 Multi-employer schemes: general . . . [18.108]
6ZA Employment-cessation events: general . . . [18.109]
6ZB–6ZD Employment-cessation events: exemptions . . . [18.110]–[18.112]
6A Employment-cessation events: periods of grace . . . [18.113]
6B Scheme apportionment arrangements . . . [18.114]
6C Withdrawal Arrangements . . . [18.115]
6D Notifiable events . . . [18.116]
6E Flexible apportionment arrangements . . . [18.117]
6F Deferred debt arrangement . . . [18.118]
7 Approved withdrawal arrangements . . . [18.119]
7A Regulated apportionment arrangements . . . [18.120]
8 Single employer sections, multi-employer sections, etc . . . [18.121]

Former employers

9 Frozen schemes and former employers . . . [18.122]

Money purchase schemes

10 Money purchase schemes: fraud and levy deficiencies etc . . . [18.123]
11 Money purchase schemes: valuations etc . . . [18.124]
12 Multi-employer money purchase schemes . . . [18.125]
13 Former employers of money purchase schemes . . . [18.126]

Other schemes treated as more than one scheme

14 Schemes covering United Kingdom and foreign employment . . . [18.127]
15 Schemes with partial government guarantee . . . [18.128]

Supplementary

16 Modification of schemes: apportionment of section 75 debts . . . [18.129]
17 Disregard of staying of voluntary winding up of employer for purposes of section 75 of the 1995 Act . . . [18.130]
19 Review . . . [18.131]

SCHEDULES

Schedule 1—Actuary's Certificate of Total Difference Between Scheme Assets and Liabilities and Liability Share Debt of Employer in a Multi-Employer Scheme . . . [18.132]
Schedule 1A—Withdrawal Arrangements and Approved Withdrawal Arrangements . . . [18.133]
Schedule 1B—Notifiable Events . . . [18.134]
Schedule 1C—Actuary's Certificate for Withdrawal Arrangement Share or Approved Withdrawal Arrangement Share in Multi-Employer Scheme . . . [18.135]
Schedule 1D—Actuary's Certificate for Amount B under a Withdrawal Arrangement or an Approved Withdrawal Arrangement in a Multi-Employer Scheme . . . [18.136]

Part 18 Miscellaneous SIs

Preliminary

[18.103]

1 Citation, commencement, application and extent

(1) These Regulations may be cited as the Occupational Pension Schemes (Employer Debt) Regulations 2005.

(2) These Regulations come into force on 6th April 2005.

(3) These Regulations do not apply to—

[(a) any employer in relation to any debt which has arisen under section 75(1) of the 1995 Act to the trustees or managers of the scheme before that date;]

(b) any scheme which immediately before that date was regarded by virtue of regulation 2 of the Occupational Pension Schemes (Winding Up) Regulations 1996 as having begun to be wound up before that date for the purposes of those Regulations; or

(c) any scheme which according to the rules in section 124(3A) to (3E) of the 1995 Act began to wind up before that date.

(4) These Regulations extend to England and Wales and Scotland.

NOTES

Para (3): sub-para (a) substituted by the Occupational Pension Schemes (Employer Debt and Miscellaneous Amendments) Regulations 2008, SI 2008/731, regs 3, 4(1), subject to transitional provisions in reg 2(2)–(10) thereof, as noted below.

Transitional provisions: SI 2008/731, reg 2 (as amended by the Occupational Pension Schemes (Employer Debt and Miscellaneous Amendments) Regulations 2010, SI 2010/725, reg 22) provides as follows:

"2 Commencement and transitional provisions

(1) Subject to the transitional provisions in paragraphs (3) to (8), these Regulations shall come into force on 6th April 2008 ("the commencement date").

(2) Notwithstanding those provisions, regulation 5(12) of the Employer Debt Regulations, as substituted by these Regulations, shall apply when the amount of a debt arising under section 75(2) or (4) of the 1995 Act falls to be calculated after the commencement date.

(3) Paragraph (4) shall apply where before the commencement date—

(a) a person ceased to employ at least one active member in relation to a scheme at a time when at least one other person continued to employ persons in the description of employment to which the scheme related, and

(b) that event was not an employment-cessation event, under regulation 6(4) of the old Regulations, in relation to the scheme[; and

(c) the scheme had not ceased to have active members].

(4) The definition of "employment-cessation event" [referred to in paragraph (4A)], shall continue to apply after the commencement date, in the case of a person to whom paragraph (3) applies, until—

(a) immediately after such time as that person has ceased to employ persons in the description of employment to which the scheme relates at a time when at least one other person continues to employ such persons, or

(b) such time as that person employs an active member.

[(4A) The definition referred to in this paragraph is the definition of "employment-cessation event" as it appeared in regulation 6(4) of the old Regulations but with "who is not a defined contribution employer" inserted after "when at least one other person".]

(5) The old Regulations shall continue to apply on and after the commencement date in relation to a debt arising under section 75(2) or (4) of the 1995 Act where—

(a) the applicable time, in relation to the debt arising under section 75(2) or (4) of the Pensions Act 1995, is before the commencement date, or

(b) the employment-cessation event occurred before the commencement date.

(6) The old Regulations shall continue to apply on and after the commencement date where a scheme commenced winding-up before the commencement date.

(7) Paragraph (8) shall apply where—

(a) an agreement is entered into before, on or within 12 months after the commencement date on the basis that a scheme's apportionment rule will apply after the commencement date in relation to a specific employment-cessation event, or in relation to a debt arising as a result of the commencement of winding-up of the scheme;

(b) the scheme's apportionment rule was in force before the date on which these Regulations were laid before Parliament; and

(c) the transaction to which the agreement related was considered before that date by the managing body of at least one of the parties to the agreement or of a connected or associated person of such a party.

(8) The old Regulations shall continue to apply on and after the commencement date in relation to that employment-cessation event, or in relation to the winding-up of the scheme, where the employment-cessation event, or the commencement of winding-up, takes place during the period of 12 months beginning on the commencement date.

(9) In paragraph (7)—

(a) a "scheme's apportionment rule" means a scheme rule for the purposes of regulation 6(2)(b) of the old Regulations, which makes provision for the difference between the value of a scheme's assets and the amount of its liabilities to be apportioned among the employers in different proportions from those which would otherwise arise;

(b) "managing body" means—

(i) in relation to a company or other corporate body, its board of directors or governing body;

(ii) in relation to a partnership, its partners;

(iii) in relation to an individual, that individual.

(c) "connected or associated person" has the meaning given by section 123 of the Pensions Act 1995 ("connected" and "associated" persons).

(10) In this regulation, references to "the old Regulations" are to the Employer Debt Regulations as they existed before the commencement date.".

[18.104]

2 Interpretation

(1) In these Regulations—

"the 1993 Act" means the Pension Schemes Act 1993;

"the 1995 Act" means the Pensions Act 1995;

"the 2004 Act" means the Pensions Act 2004;

"the 1996 Regulations" means the Occupational Pension Schemes (Deficiency on Winding Up etc) Regulations 1996;

["actuarial valuation" has the same meaning as in Part 3 of the 2004 Act;]

"the actuary" means the actuary appointed for the scheme in pursuance of subsection (1)(b) of section 47 of the 1995 Act or, in the case of a scheme to which that provision does not apply by virtue of regulations made under subsection (5) of that section, an actuary otherwise authorised by the trustees or managers to provide such valuations or certifications as may be required under these Regulations;

["amount A" means the amount calculated in accordance with paragraph 4 of Schedule 1A;]

["amount B" means the amount calculated in accordance with either sub-paragraph (2) or (3) of paragraph 5 of Schedule 1A;]

"the applicable time" means the time as at which the value of the assets of a scheme and the amount of its liabilities are to be determined, calculated and verified for the purposes of section 75 of the 1995 Act;

["approved withdrawal arrangement" means an arrangement that meets the funding test and is approved by the Authority under regulation 7;]

["approved withdrawal arrangement share" means an amount that is—

(a) a cessation employer's share of the difference,

(b) less than amount A, and

(c) payable by a cessation employer pursuant to an approved withdrawal arrangement;]

["assessment period" has the meaning given in section 132 of the 2004 Act (assessment periods);]

[. . .]

["the Board of the PPF" means the Board of the Pension Protection Fund;]

["cessation employer" means an employer in relation to the scheme in respect of whom an employment-cessation event has occurred;]

["cessation expenses" are all expenses which, in the opinion of the trustees or managers of a scheme, are likely to be incurred by the scheme in connection with an employment-cessation event occurring to an employer in relation to the scheme;]

["the corresponding assets" means the assets transferred in connection with the transfer from the scheme in respect of any relevant transfer liabilities;]

["deferred debt arrangement" means an arrangement that takes effect in accordance with regulation 6F;]

["defined benefits", in relation to a member of an occupational pension scheme, means benefits which are not money purchase benefits (but the rate or amount of which is calculated by reference to earnings or service of the member or any other factor other than an amount available for their provision);]

["defined contribution employer" means an employer all the liabilities attributable to whom in relation to a scheme are liabilities in respect of money purchase benefits as defined in section 181(1) of the 1993 Act or in respect of supplementary benefits provided on an ancillary basis in the form of payments on death;]

["departing employer" means—

(a) a cessation employer; or

(b) an employer in respect of whom an insolvency event has occurred;]

"employer" has the same meaning as in section 75 of the 1995 Act (but see paragraph (2) and regulations [6,][6A, 6F,] 9 and 13);

["employment-cessation event" has the meaning given in regulation 6ZA;]

["flexible apportionment arrangement" means an arrangement that takes effect in accordance with regulation 6E;]

["frozen scheme" means a scheme which has ceased to have active members;]

["guarantors" means such one or more of the parties to a withdrawal arrangement or an approved withdrawal arrangement as are specified in the arrangement as the persons who have given guarantees in relation to amount B for the purposes of the arrangement;]

["the FSD Regulations" means the Pensions Regulator (Financial Support Directions etc) Regulations 2005;]

["the guarantee time" means the earliest time when an event specified in paragraph 3 of Schedule 1A occurs;]

["liability proportion" means "[K divided by L]" where—

(a) "K" equals the amount of a scheme's liabilities attributable to an employer in accordance with paragraph (4) of regulation 6; and

(b) "L" equals the total amount of the scheme's liabilities attributable to employment with the employers;]

["liability share" means an amount equal to the liability proportion [multiplied by the total] difference between the value of the assets and the amount of the liabilities of the scheme;]

"the MFR Regulations" means the Occupational Pension Schemes (Minimum Funding Requirement and Actuarial Valuations) Regulations 1996;

"money purchase scheme" means an occupational pension scheme under which all the benefits that may be provided other than death benefits are money purchase benefits;

["multi-employer scheme" means a scheme (or a section of a scheme treated pursuant to regulation 8 as a separate scheme) in relation to which there is more than one employer;]

[. . .]

["the PPF Valuation Regulations" means the Pension Protection Fund (Valuation) Regulations 2005;]

["protected liabilities" has the same meaning as for the purposes of a valuation under section 179 of the 2004 Act (valuations to determine scheme under funding);]

["recovery plan" means a recovery plan that complies with the requirements in section 226 of the 2004 Act and the Scheme Funding Regulations;]

["regulated apportionment arrangement" is an arrangement under the scheme rules that—

- (a) provides for the amount that would have been the employer's liability share to be changed;
- (b) where the employer's liability share is reduced, apportions all or part of the amount that would have been the employer's liability share to one or more of the remaining employers and may provide for when the amount apportioned is to be paid;
- (c) may provide for when the amount apportioned is to be paid;
- (d) is entered into before, on or after the applicable time;
- (e) sets out the amount of an employer's regulated apportionment arrangement share; and
- (f) meets the conditions in regulation 7A;]

["regulated apportionment arrangement share" means the amount under a regulated apportionment arrangement that is an employer's share of the difference;]

["relevant accounts" means the audited accounts for the scheme that comply with the requirements imposed under section 41 of the 1995 Act (provision of documents to members);]

["the relevant transfer deduction" means the amount of the relevant transfer liabilities less the value of the corresponding assets;]

["the relevant transfer liabilities" means the liabilities attributable to a departing employer that are transferred after the applicable time to an occupational or personal pension scheme or are otherwise secured;]

["schedule of contributions" means the most recent schedule of contributions that is adopted in relation to the scheme for the purposes of Part 3 of the 2004 Act;]

["scheme apportionment arrangement" means an arrangement under the scheme rules that—

- (a) provides for the employer to pay a scheme apportionment arrangement share instead of the employer's liability share;
- (b) where that amount is less than the employer's liability share, apportions all or part of the amount that would have been the employer's liability share to one or more of the remaining employers;
- (c) may provide for when the amount apportioned is to be paid;
- (d) is entered into before, on or after the applicable time;
- (e) sets out the amount of an employer's scheme apportionment arrangement share;
- [(f) each of the following persons consents to—
  - (i) the trustees or managers, and either
  - (ii) (where the circumstances referred to in paragraph (b) apply) any remaining employer to whom all or part of the amount that would have been the employer's liability share is being apportioned, or
  - (iii) (where the circumstances referred to in paragraph (b) do not apply) the employer; and]
- (g) meets the funding test;]

["scheme apportionment arrangement share" means the amount under a scheme apportionment arrangement that is an employer's share of the difference;]

["scheme's apportionment rule" means a scheme rule which makes provision for the difference between the value of a scheme's assets and the amount of its liabilities to be apportioned among the employers in different proportions from those which would otherwise arise;]

["the Scheme Funding Regulations" means the Occupational Pension Schemes (Scheme Funding) Regulations 2005;]

["share of the difference" means the amount calculated as at the applicable time that is an employer's share of the total difference between the value of the assets and the amount of the liabilities of a scheme;]

[. . .]

"the tax condition", in relation to a scheme, means—

- (a) that the scheme has been approved by the Commissioners of the Board of Inland Revenue for the purposes of section 590 or 591 of the Taxes Act at any time before 6th April 2006; or
- (b) that the scheme is registered under section 153 of the Finance Act 2004;

"the Taxes Act" means the Income and Corporation Taxes Act 1988;

["technical provisions" has the meaning given by section 222(2) of the 2004 Act;]

[. . .]

["updated asset assessment" means an update (whether or not audited) of the value of the assets of the scheme identified in the most recent relevant accounts received by the trustees or managers which—

- (a) is prepared by the trustees or managers, and

(b) estimates where they consider appropriate any alteration in the value of the assets of the scheme between the date by reference to which those accounts are prepared and the applicable time;]

["updated liabilities assessment" means the actuary's assessment of any changes in the liabilities of the scheme in respect of pensions and other benefits between—

(a) the effective date of the actuary's estimate of the solvency of the scheme (as defined in regulation 7(6) of the Scheme Funding Regulations) included in the most recent actuarial valuation of the scheme received by the trustees or managers—

(i) under section 224 of the 2004 Act (actuarial valuations and reports); or

(ii) where the trustees or managers have not received an actuarial valuation under section 224, which the actuary thinks it is appropriate to use, and

(b) the applicable time;]

["withdrawal arrangement" means an arrangement that meets the conditions specified in paragraph 1 of Schedule 1A and meets the funding test];

["withdrawal arrangement share" means an amount that is—

(a) a cessation employer's share of the difference,

(b) equal to or, where the employer agrees, greater than amount A, and

(c) payable by a cessation employer pursuant to a withdrawal arrangement].

(2) In these Regulations "scheme" must be read in appropriate cases in accordance with the modifications of section 75 of the 1995 Act made by regulation 8, 14 or 15, as the case may be; and "employer" and "member" must be read accordingly.

[(3) References in these Regulations to FRC standards are to actuarial standards on winding up and scheme asset deficiency adopted or prepared, and from time to time revised, by the Financial Reporting Council Limited.]

[(3A) For the purposes of a restructuring within regulations 6ZB or 6ZC—

"exiting employer" means an employer—

(a) in relation to a multi-employer scheme,

(b) who employs at least one active member of the scheme in respect of whom defined benefits are accruing, and

(c) in respect of whom a relevant event has not occurred; and

"receiving employer" means an employer who, on the date on which there is a restructuring within regulation 6ZB or 6ZC, is—

(a) an employer in relation to the same multi-employer scheme as the exiting employer,

(b) either—

(i) associated (within the meaning in section 435 of the Insolvency Act 1986 or section 74 of the Bankruptcy (Scotland) Act 1985) with the exiting employer, or

[(ii) not associated but falls within paragraph (3B),]

(c) employing at least one active member of the scheme in respect of whom defined benefits are accruing, and

(d) an employer in respect of whom a relevant event has not occurred.]

[(3B) An employer falls within this paragraph where it is—

(a) a limited company, limited partnership or limited liability partnership;

(b) a charitable company; or

(c) a CIO.

(3C) For the purposes of paragraph (3B)—

(a) "charitable company"—

(i) in relation to England and Wales, has the meaning given by section 193 of the Charities Act 2011("the 2011 Act"); and

(ii) in relation to Scotland, has the meaning given by section 112 of the Companies Act 1989;

(b) "CIO"—

(i) in relation to England and Wales, means a charitable incorporated organisation within the meaning of Part 11 of the 2011 Act; and

(ii) in relation to Scotland, means a Scottish charitable incorporated organisation within the meaning of section 49 of the Charities and Trustee Investment (Scotland) Act 2005;

(c) "limited company" has the meaning given by section 3(1) of the Companies Act 2006Act;

(d) "limited liability partnership" has the meaning given by section 1(2) of the Limited Liability Partnerships Act 2000; and

(e) "limited partnership" has the meaning given by section 4 of the Limited Partnerships Act 1907.

(3D) Where regulation 6F(6)(f) applies, the definitions of "exiting employer" and "receiving employer" in paragraph (3A) shall be deemed to include deferred employers.]

(4) . . .

[(4A) For the purposes of regulations 6B, 6C[, 6E] and 7, an arrangement relating to a scheme meets the funding test where the trustees or managers are reasonably satisfied that—

(a) when the arrangement takes effect, the remaining employers will be reasonably likely to be able to fund the scheme so that after the applicable time [(or, in the case of a flexible apportionment arrangement, after the time that arrangement takes effect)] it will have sufficient and appropriate assets to cover its technical provisions, taking account of any change in those provisions which will in the opinion of the trustees or managers be necessary as a result of the arrangement, and

(b) in the case of a scheme apportionment arrangement under regulation 6B [or a flexible apportionment arrangement under regulation 6E], the effect of the arrangement will not be to adversely affect the security of members' benefits as a result of any—
   (i) material change in legal, demographic or economic circumstances, as described in regulation 5(4)(d) of the Scheme Funding Regulations, that would justify a change to the method or assumptions used on the last occasion on which the scheme's technical provisions were calculated, or
   (ii) material revision to any existing recovery plan made in accordance with section 226 of the 2004 Act.

(4B) For the purposes of paragraph (4A), where at the applicable time [(or, in the case of a flexible apportionment arrangement, at the time that arrangement takes effect)] the trustees or managers of the scheme have not received its first actuarial valuation under Part 3 of the 2004 Act, that paragraph shall apply as if for that paragraph there were substituted—

> "(4A) For the purposes of regulations 6B, 6C[, 6E] and 7, an arrangement relating to a scheme meets the funding test where the trustees or managers are reasonably satisfied that, after taking account of the financial resources of the remaining employers, the arrangement is unlikely to adversely affect the security of the members' benefits under the scheme.".

(4C) The trustees or managers may consider that the test in paragraph (4A)(a) is met if in their opinion the remaining employers are able to meet the relevant payments as they fall due under the schedule of contributions for the purposes of section 227 of the 2004 Act, taking into account any revision of that schedule that they think will be necessary when the arrangement takes effect.

(4D) In paragraphs (4A) and (4C), references to "remaining employers" may in relevant circumstances be read as referring only to the employer or employers to whom all or part of the liability share is apportioned under the scheme rules.]

[(4E) For the purposes of these Regulations "deferred employer" in relation to a multi-employer scheme means a person—
(a) who formerly employed at least one active member of the scheme in respect of whom defined benefits were accruing;
(b) in respect of whom a relevant event has not occurred; and
(c) who—
   (i) has proposed to the trustees or managers of the scheme to enter into a deferred debt arrangement; and
   (ii) having made that proposal, is participating in a deferred debt arrangement.]

(5) Subject to the previous provisions of this regulation, expressions used in these Regulations have the same meaning as in Part 1 of the 1995 Act (see section 124).

NOTES

Para (1): definitions "actuarial valuation", "amount A", "amount B", "approved withdrawal arrangement", "approved withdrawal arrangement share", "assessment period", "cessation employer", "cessation expenses", "the corresponding assets", "defined contribution employer", "departing employer", "frozen scheme", "guarantors", "the guarantee time", "liability proportion", "liability share", "the PPF Valuation Regulations", "protected liabilities", "recovery plan", "regulated apportionment arrangement", "regulated apportionment arrangement share", "relevant accounts", "the relevant transfer deduction", "the relevant transfer liabilities", "schedule of contributions", "scheme apportionment arrangement", "scheme apportionment arrangement share", "scheme's apportionment rule", "the Scheme Funding Regulations", "share of the difference", "updated asset assessment", "withdrawal arrangement share" inserted, definitions "employment-cessation event", and "multi-employer scheme" substituted, definition "withdrawal arrangement" substituted (for definition ""withdrawal arrangement" and "approved withdrawal arrangement"" as inserted by SI 2005/2224, reg 2(1)), and figure in first pair of square brackets in definition "employer" inserted by the Occupational Pension Schemes (Employer Debt and Miscellaneous Amendments) Regulations 2008, SI 2008/731, regs 3, 4(2), subject to transitional provisions as noted to reg 1 at **[18.103]**; definition "the Board for Actuarial Standards" inserted by the Occupational and Personal Pension Schemes (Prescribed Bodies) Regulations 2007, SI 2007/60, reg 2, Schedule, para 14(a)(i), revoked by the Occupational and Personal Pension Schemes (Prescribed Bodies) Regulations 2012, SI 2012/1817, reg 2, Schedule, para 7(a)(i); definition "flexible apportionment arrangement" inserted, and words in square brackets in definitions "liability proportion" and "liability share" substituted by the Occupational Pension Schemes (Employer Debt and Miscellaneous Amendments) Regulations 2011, SI 2011/2973, reg 4(1), (2); in definition "scheme apportionment arrangement" para (f) substituted by the Occupational Pension Schemes (Employer Debt–Apportionment Arrangements) (Amendment) Regulations 2008, SI 2008/1068, reg 2(1), (2); definitions "the Board of the PPF", "defined benefits", "technical provisions", "updated liabilities assessment" inserted, definition "employment-cessation event" substituted and definitions "PPF", "statutory funding objective", "updated actuarial assessment" (as inserted by SI 2008/731 and now omitted) revoked by the Occupational Pension Schemes (Employer Debt and Miscellaneous Amendments) Regulations 2010, SI 2010/725, reg 4(1), (2); definitions "deferred debt arrangement" and "the FSD Regulations" inserted and figures in second pair of square brackets in definition "employer" inserted, by the Occupational Pension Schemes (Employer Debt and Miscellaneous Amendments) Regulations 2018, SI 2018/237, reg 3(1), (2).

Para (3): substituted by SI 2012/1817, reg 2, Schedule, para 7(a)(ii).

Para (3A): inserted by SI 2010/725, reg 4(1), (3); in definition "receiving employer" sub-para (b)(ii) substituted by SI 2018/237, reg 3(1), (3).

Paras (3B)–(3D): inserted by SI 2018/237, reg 3(1), (4).

Para (4): revoked by SI 2008/731, regs 3, 4(4), subject to transitional provisions as noted to reg 1 at **[18.103]**.

Para (4A): inserted, together with paras (4B)–(4D), by SI 2008/731, regs 3, 4(4), subject to transitional provisions as noted to reg 1 at **[18.103]**; figure and words in square brackets inserted by SI 2011/2973, reg 4(1), (3).

Para (4B): inserted as noted to para (4A) above; words in square brackets inserted by SI 2011/2973, reg 4(1), (4).

Paras (4C), (4D): inserted as noted to para (4A) above.

Para (4E): inserted by SI 2018/237, reg 3(1), (5).

[18.105]

3 Disapplication of the 1996 Regulations

The 1996 Regulations do not apply in any case where these Regulations apply (and accordingly they only apply to a scheme as respects which regulation 1(3)(a), (b) or (c) applies).

[18.106]

4 Schemes to which section 75 of the 1995 Act does not apply

(1) Section 75 of the 1995 Act does not apply to any scheme which is—

(a) a public service pension scheme under the provisions of which there is no requirement for assets related to the intended rate or amount of benefit under the scheme to be set aside in advance (disregarding requirements relating to additional voluntary contributions);

(b) a scheme which is made under section 7 of the Superannuation Act 1972 (superannuation of persons employed in local government etc) and provides pensions to local government employees;

(c) a scheme which is made under section 2 of the Parliamentary and Other Pensions Act 1987 (power to provide for pensions for Members of the House of Commons etc);

[(ca) a scheme, provision for which is made by virtue of section 81(3) of the Scotland Act 1998 (remuneration of members of the Parliament and Executive);]

(d) a scheme in respect of which a relevant public authority, as defined in section 307(4) of the 2004 Act, has given a guarantee or made any other arrangements for the purposes of securing that the assets of the scheme are sufficient to meet its liabilities;

(e) a scheme which does not meet the tax condition;

(f) a scheme which—

(i) has been categorised by the Commissioners of the Board of Inland Revenue for the purposes of its approval as a centralised scheme for non-associated employers;

(ii) which [was not contracted-out at any time before the second abolition date]; and

(iii) under the provisions of which the only benefits that may be provided on or after retirement (other than money purchase benefits derived from the payment of voluntary contributions by any person) are lump sum benefits which are not calculated by reference to a member's salary;

[(g) a scheme—

(i) which has such a superannuation fund as is mentioned in section 615(6) of the Taxes Act (exemption from tax in respect of certain pensions); and

(ii) in relation to which the trustees or managers are not—

(aa) authorised under section 288 of the 2004 Act (general authorisation to accept contributions from European employer); or

(bb) approved under section 289 of the 2004 Act (approval in relation to particular European employer) in relation to a European employer);]

(h) a scheme with fewer than two members;

(i) a scheme with fewer than twelve members where all the members are trustees of the scheme and either—

(i) the rules of the scheme provide that all decisions are made only by the trustees who are members of the scheme by unanimous agreement; or

(ii) the scheme has a trustee who is independent in relation to the scheme for the purposes of section 23 of the 1995 Act (power to appoint independent trustees) (see subsection (3) of that section) and is registered in the register maintained by the Authority in accordance with regulations made under subsection (4) of that section;

(j) a scheme with fewer than twelve members where all the members are directors of a company which is the sole trustee of the scheme and either—

(i) the rules of the scheme provide that all decisions are made only by the members of the scheme by unanimous agreement, or

(ii) one of the directors of the company is independent in relation to the scheme for the purposes of section 23 of the 1995 Act and is registered in the register maintained by the Authority in accordance with regulations made under subsection (4) of that section;

(k) the Chatsworth Settlement Estate Pension Scheme; or

(l) . . .

(2) Before 6th April 2006 paragraph (1)(e) applies with the addition at the end of the words "and is not a relevant statutory scheme providing relevant benefits"; and for the purposes of that paragraph "relevant statutory scheme" and "relevant benefits" have the same meaning as in Chapter 1 of Part 14 of the Taxes Act (see sections 611A and 612(1) of that Act).

[(3) In this regulation—

"contracted-out" is to be construed in accordance with section 7B(2) (meaning of "contracted-out scheme" etc) of the Pension Schemes Act 1993; and

"the second abolition date" has the meaning given in section 181(1) (general interpretation) of the Pension Schemes Act 1993.]

NOTES

Para (1): sub-para (ca) inserted by the Occupational Pension Schemes (Scottish Parliamentary Pensions Act 2009) Regulations 2009, SI 2009/1906, reg 2, Schedule, para 3; in sub-para (f)(ii) words in square brackets substituted by the Pensions Act 2014 (Abolition of Contracting-out for Salary Related Pension Schemes) (Consequential Amendments and Savings) Order 2016, SI 2016/200, art 22(a); sub-para (g) substituted by the Occupational Pension Schemes (Republic of Ireland Schemes

Exemption (Revocation) and Tax Exempt Schemes (Miscellaneous Amendments)) Regulations 2006, SI 2006/467, reg 6; sub-para (l) revoked by the Occupational Pension Schemes (Employer Debt etc) (Amendment) Regulations 2005, SI 2005/2224, reg 4(1).

Para (3): added by SI 2016/200, art 22(b).

Valuations

[18.107]

[5 Calculation of the amount of scheme liabilities and value of scheme assets

(1) The value of the assets which are to be taken into account for the purposes of section 75(2) and (4) of the 1995 Act shall be determined, calculated and verified by the trustees or managers.

(2) The liabilities which are to be taken into account for the purposes of section 75(2) and (4) of the 1995 Act shall be determined by the trustees or managers and the amount of those liabilities shall be calculated and verified by the actuary.

[(3) The assets of the scheme are to be valued, the liabilities of the scheme are to be determined and the amounts of those liabilities are to be calculated by reference to the same date.]

(4) Subject to paragraph (15), the assets of a scheme to be taken into account by the trustees or managers are the assets attributable to the scheme in the relevant accounts, excluding—

(a) any resources invested (or treated as invested by or under section 40 of the 1995 Act) in contravention of section 40(1) of the 1995 Act (employer-related investments);

[(b) any amounts which are—

(i) treated as a debt due to the trustees or managers under—

(aa) section 75(2) or (4) of the 1995 Act (deficiencies in assets);

(bb) section 228(3) of the 2004 Act (amounts due in accordance with a schedule of contributions);

(cc) sections 59(2) (determination of contributions: supplementary) or 60(5) (serious underprovision) of the 1995 Act as they were in force before 30th December 2005;

(dd) section 75(1) of the 1995 Act as it was in force before 6th April 2005; or

(ee) section 144(1) of the 1993 Act (deficiencies in the assets of a scheme on winding up) as it was in force before 6th April 1997, and

(ii) unlikely to be recovered without disproportionate cost or within a reasonable time;]

(c) where it appears to the actuary that the circumstances are such that it is appropriate to exclude them, any rights under an insurance policy; and

(d) assets representing the value of any rights to money purchase benefits under the scheme; and

where arrangements are being made by the scheme for the transfer to or from it of any accrued rights and any pension credit rights, until such time as the trustees or managers of the scheme to which the transfer is being made ("the receiving scheme") have received the assets of the full amount agreed by them as consideration for the transfer, it shall be assumed that any assets transferred in respect of the transfer of those rights are assets of the scheme making the transfer and not assets of the receiving scheme.

(5) An updated asset assessment may be used for the purposes of paragraph (4) if—

(a) the trustees or managers, after consulting the cessation employer and other scheme employers, so decide; and

(b) section 75(4) of the 1995 Act applies by virtue of an employment-cessation event.

(6) The value to be given to the assets of a scheme by the trustees or managers is—

(a) the value given to those assets in the relevant accounts or in the updated asset assessment less, in either case, the amount of the external liabilities;

(b) in the case of any rights under an insurance policy taken into account notwithstanding paragraph (4)(c), the value the actuary considers appropriate in the circumstances of the case.

[(7) For the purposes of paragraph (6)—

(a) "external liabilities" means such liabilities of the scheme as are shown in—

(i) the net assets statement in the relevant accounts; or

(ii) an estimate used for the purposes of an updated asset statement,

except that the liabilities in paragraph (8) are to be disregarded; and

(b) the amount of the external liabilities is—

(i) where sub-paragraph (a)(i) applies, the amount shown in the statement referred to in that sub-paragraph in respect of the external liabilities; or

(ii) where sub-paragraph (a)(ii) applies, the amount shown in the estimate referred to in that sub-paragraph in respect of the external liabilities.]

(8) Subject to paragraphs (9), (13) and [(14)], the liabilities of a scheme to be taken into account by the trustees or managers are any liabilities—

(a) in relation to a member of the scheme by virtue of—

(i) any right that has accrued to or in respect of him to future benefits under the scheme rules,

(ii) any entitlement to the present payment of a pension or other benefit which he has under the scheme rules, and

(b) in relation to the survivor of a member of the scheme, by virtue of any entitlement to benefits, or right to future benefits which he has under the scheme rules in respect of the member.

(9) The liabilities of a scheme to be excluded from paragraph (8) are—

(a) liabilities secured by an insurance policy the rights under which are excluded under paragraph (4)(a)(iii); and

(b) liabilities representing the value of any rights to money purchase benefits under the scheme.

(10) For the purposes of paragraph (8)—

(a) where arrangements are being made by the scheme for the transfer to or from it of accrued rights and any pension credit rights, until such time as the trustees or managers of the scheme to which the transfer is being made . . . have received the assets of the full amount agreed by them as consideration for the transfer, it shall be assumed that the rights have not been transferred;

(b) it shall be assumed that all pensionable service under the scheme ceased before the applicable time; and

(c) the following definitions shall apply—

"right" includes a pension credit right; and

"the survivor" of a member is a person who has survived the member and has any entitlement to benefit, or right to future benefits, under the scheme on account of the member.

(11) The amount of the liabilities in respect of pensions and other benefits are to be calculated and verified by the actuary on the assumption that they will be discharged by the purchase of annuities of the kind described in section 74(3)(c) of the 1995 Act (discharge of liabilities; annuity purchase) and for this purpose the actuary must estimate the cost of purchasing annuities.

(12) [For the purposes of paragraph (11),] the actuary must estimate the cost of purchasing the annuities—

(a) on terms the actuary considers consistent with those in the available market and which he considers would be sufficient to satisfy the scheme's liabilities in respect of pensions and other benefits, or

(b) where the actuary considers that it is not practicable to make an estimate in accordance with sub-paragraph (a), in such manner as the actuary considers appropriate in the circumstances of the case.

(13) The liabilities shall include all expenses (except the cost of the annuities) which, in the opinion of the trustees or managers of the scheme, are likely to be incurred in connection with the winding-up of the scheme.

(14) An [updated liabilities assessment] may be prepared by the actuary for the purposes of paragraph (8) if—

(a) the trustees or managers, after consulting the actuary and the cessation employer, so decide; and

(b) section 75(4) of the 1995 Act applies by virtue of an employment-cessation event.

[(15) An amount B is an asset of the scheme to be taken into account by the trustees or managers only if—

(a) the scheme has not commenced winding-up at the applicable time;

(b) the amount B is part of a withdrawal arrangement or an approved withdrawal arrangement which is in force before the applicable time; and

(c) the trustees or managers are reasonably satisfied that the guarantors have sufficient financial resources at the applicable time to be likely to pay the amount B.]

(16) For the purposes of paragraph (15), amount B shall be determined by the trustees or managers and calculated by the actuary as if it had become due at the applicable time.

(17) Where in these Regulations there is a reference to—

(a) the amount of any liability being calculated or verified in accordance with the opinion of the actuary or as he thinks appropriate, or

(b) the actuary preparing an [updated liabilities assessment],

he must apply any relevant [FRC standards] in making that calculation or verification, or preparing that update.

(18) The amount of the liabilities of a scheme which are to be taken into account for the purposes of section 75(2) and (4) of the 1995 Act must be certified by the actuary in the form set out in Schedule 1 to these Regulations.

(19) This regulation is subject to regulation 6 (multi-employer schemes: general), regulation 6C (withdrawal arrangements) and regulation 7 (approved withdrawal arrangements).]

NOTES

Substituted by the Occupational Pension Schemes (Employer Debt and Miscellaneous Amendments) Regulations 2008, SI 2008/731, regs 3, 5; subject to transitional provisions as noted to reg 1 at **[18.103]**.

Para (3): substituted by the Occupational Pension Schemes (Employer Debt and Miscellaneous Amendments) Regulations 2011, SI 2011/2973, reg 5(1), (2).

Para (4): sub-para (b) substituted by the Occupational Pension Schemes (Employer Debt and Miscellaneous Amendments) Regulations 2010, SI 2010/725, reg 5(1), (2).

Para (7): substituted by SI 2010/725, reg 5(1), (3).

Para (8): figure in square brackets substituted by SI 2011/2973, reg 5(1), (3).

Para (10): words omitted revoked by SI 2010/725, reg 5(1), (4).

Para (12): words in square brackets inserted by SI 2010/725, reg 5(1), (5).

Para (14): words in square brackets substituted by SI 2010/725, reg 5(1), (6).

Para (15): substituted by SI 2011/2973, reg 5(1), (4).

Para (17): words in first pair of square brackets substituted by SI 2010/725, reg 5(1), (6); words in second pair of square brackets substituted by the Occupational and Personal Pension Schemes (Prescribed Bodies) Regulations 2012, SI 2012/1817, reg 2, Schedule, para 7(b).

[18.108]

6 Multi-employer schemes: general

(1) In its application to a multi-employer scheme, section 75 of the 1995 Act has effect in relation to each employer as if—

(a) the reference in section 75(2)(a) to a time which falls before any relevant event in relation to the employer which occurs while the scheme is being wound up were a reference to a time which falls before relevant events have occurred in relation to all the employers;

(b) the reference in section 75(2) to an amount equal to the difference being treated as a debt due from the employer were a reference to an amount equal to that employer's share of the difference being treated as a debt due from that employer;

(c) the references in section 75(3)(a)(i) and (b) to no relevant event of the kind there mentioned occurring in relation to the employer were references to no event of that kind occurring in relation to all the employers;

(d) the reference in section 75(4)(a) to a relevant event ("the current event") occurring in relation to the employer were a reference to a relevant event or an employment-cessation event occurring only in relation to that employer;

(e) the reference in section 75(4) to an amount equal to the difference being treated as a debt due from the employer were—

(i) in a case where the difference is ascertained immediately before a relevant event occurs in relation to the employer, a reference to an amount equal to [the sum of any unpaid expenses which were incurred by the scheme in connection with a previous employment-cessation event occurring to the employer and] the employer's share of the difference being treated as a debt due from the employer; and

(ii) in a case where the difference is ascertained immediately before an employment cessation event occurs in relation to the employer, a reference to an amount equal to the sum of the cessation expenses attributable to the employer and the employer's share of the difference being treated as a debt due from the employer; and

(f) section 75(4)(d) and (e) were omitted.

[(2) For the purposes of paragraph (1), an employer's share of the difference is the liability share unless the conditions are met for it being one of the following—

(a) the scheme apportionment arrangement share;

(b) the regulated apportionment arrangement share;

(c) the withdrawal arrangement share; or

(d) the approved withdrawal arrangement share.

(3) Where—

(a) the withdrawal arrangement share applies, the modification in regulation 6C(2) of section 75(4) of the 1995 Act shall apply when the withdrawal arrangement comes into force;

(b) the approved withdrawal arrangement share applies, the modification in regulation 7(6) of section 75(4) of the 1995 Act shall apply when the approved withdrawal arrangement comes into force.

(4) For the purposes of calculating the liability proportion for the purposes of the liability share, the liabilities attributable to employment with any employer ("Employer A") shall be determined by the trustees or managers, after consulting the actuary and Employer A, as follows—

(a) where a scheme apportionment arrangement (or before 6th April 2008, an exercise of a scheme apportionment rule) or a regulated apportionment arrangement has required certain liabilities to be apportioned to one or more employer in a particular way, those liabilities shall be so attributed;

[(aa) where there is a restructuring within regulation 6ZB or 6ZC and regulation 6ZA(3) or (4) does not apply in relation to that restructuring, all of the liabilities in relation to the scheme which were attributable to the exiting employer shall be attributed to the receiving employer;]

[(ab) where a flexible apportionment arrangement has taken effect, the liabilities to be attributed to Employer A must include the liabilities for which Employer A—

(i) has taken over responsibility under that arrangement; or

(ii) is treated for all purposes as being responsible under that arrangement;]

[(b) subject to sub-paragraph (c), the liabilities to or in respect of any member which arose during or as a result of pensionable service with Employer A (including any liabilities attributable to a transfer in respect of that member received by the scheme during that period or periods of pensionable service) are attributable to Employer A; and]

(c) where any of the circumstances in paragraph (5) applies in respect of certain liabilities in respect of any member, those liabilities shall be attributable in accordance with the following sub-paragraphs applied in sequence—

(i) either—

(aa) if Employer A is the last employer of any member and the liabilities in respect of that member cannot be attributed to any employer, all of the liabilities to or in respect of any such member shall be attributable to Employer A, or

(bb) the liabilities in respect of any member which cannot be attributed to any employer shall be attributable in a reasonable manner to one or more employer (which may or may not include Employer A), or

(ii) if the trustees or managers are unable to determine whether or not Employer A is the last employer of any member and the liabilities in respect of that member cannot be attributed to any employer, the liabilities attributable to any such member shall not be attributable to any employer.

(5) The circumstances referred to in paragraph 4(c) are—

(a) where the trustees or managers are unable to determine to whom liabilities in respect of any member should be attributed in accordance with paragraph (4) (b), paragraph (4)(c) shall apply in relation to those liabilities which cannot be attributed to any employer under paragraph (4)(b); or

(b) where the trustees or managers are able to determine to whom liabilities in respect of any member should be attributed in accordance with paragraph (4)(b), but to do so they expect disproportionate costs will be incurred by the scheme, paragraph (4)(c) shall apply in relation to those liabilities which cannot be attributed to any employer under paragraph (4)(b) except at disproportionate costs.

(6) Where an employer notifies the trustees that a relevant transfer deduction shall apply to a departing employer's liabilities—

(a) the departing employer's liability share shall be reduced by the amount of the relevant transfer deduction, provided the relevant transfer liabilities and corresponding assets are transferred out during the period commencing with the applicable time and ending on the day that is 12 months later ("transfer out period"); and

(b) the liability share shall be calculated after the end of the transfer out period or if all transfers are completed on a date before the end of that period, after that date.

(7) For the purposes of paragraph (6), the relevant transfer deduction shall be determined by calculating the relevant transfer liabilities and the corresponding assets in accordance with regulation 5.

(8) The amount of the liabilities attributable to an employer under paragraph (4), the liability proportion, and the amount of the liability share shall be calculated and verified by the actuary in accordance with any relevant [FRC standards] and shall be certified by him in the form set out in Schedule 1 to these Regulations.]

NOTES

Para (1): words in square brackets inserted by the Occupational Pension Schemes (Employer Debt and Miscellaneous Amendments) Regulations 2010, SI 2010/725, reg 6(1), (2).

Paras (2), (3), (5)–(7): substituted, together with paras (4), (8), for original paras (2)–(5), by the Occupational Pension Schemes (Employer Debt and Miscellaneous Amendments) Regulations 2008, SI 2008/731, regs 3, 6, subject to transitional provisions as noted to reg 1 at **[18.103]**.

Para (4): substituted as noted to para (2) above; sub-para (aa) substituted by SI 2010/725, reg 6(1), (3); sub-para (ab) inserted and sub-para (b) substituted by the Occupational Pension Schemes (Employer Debt and Miscellaneous Amendments) Regulations 2011, SI 2011/2973, reg 6.

Para (8): substituted as noted to para (2) above; words in square brackets substituted by the Occupational and Personal Pension Schemes (Prescribed Bodies) Regulations 2012, SI 2012/1817, reg 2, Schedule, para 7(c).

[18.109]

[6ZA Employment-cessation events: general

(1) In these regulations, "employment-cessation event" means, subject to [paragraphs (2) to (7)], an event which—

(a) occurs in relation to a multi-employer scheme,

(b) is not a relevant event, and

(c) subject to [regulations 6A and 6F], occurs on the date on which—

(i) an employer has ceased to employ at least one person who is an active member of the scheme, and

(ii) at least one other employer who is not a defined contribution employer continues to employ at least one active member of the scheme.

(2) Subject to paragraphs (3) and (4), an employment-cessation event does not occur where there is a restructuring within regulation 6ZB or 6ZC.

(3) An employment-cessation event occurs where there is a restructuring within regulation 6ZB and within six years of that, it becomes apparent that—

(a) the exiting employer or receiving employer provided the trustees or managers with—

(i) incorrect information, or

(ii) incomplete information,

and the trustees or managers are satisfied that they would have made a different decision in step 4 in regulation 6ZB(9) if they had had the correct or complete information,

(b) step 6 has not been completed in accordance with regulation 6ZB(13) and (14), or

(c) step 7 has not been completed in accordance with regulation 6ZB(15) and (16).

(4) An employment-cessation event occurs where there is a restructuring within regulation 6ZC and within six years of that, it becomes apparent that—

(a) step 4 has not been completed in accordance with regulation 6ZC(9) and (10), or

(b) step 5 has not been completed in accordance with regulation 6ZC(11) and (12).

(5) An employment-cessation event does not occur where—

(a) there is a restructuring within regulation 6ZB or 6ZC,

(b) at any time after that, it becomes apparent that any step has not been completed in accordance with regulation 6ZB or 6ZC, and

(c) paragraphs (3) and (4) of this regulation do not apply.

(6) Where an employment-cessation event occurs in accordance with paragraph (3) or (4)—

(a) section 75(4) of the 1995 Act applies as if the amount of the debt due from the exiting employer is treated as a debt due from the exiting employer and the receiving employer jointly and severally,

(b) the date on which the employment-cessation event occurs is the date referred to in paragraph (1)(c), and

(c) for the purposes of calculating the exiting employer's liability proportion for the purposes of the exiting employer's liability share, the liabilities attributable to employment with the exiting employer shall be determined as if nothing had been done in relation to carrying out any of the steps in regulations 6ZB or 6ZC.

[(7) An employment-cessation event does not occur in respect of the leaving employer within the meaning given in regulation 6E(7) where—

(a) the conditions in regulation 6E(2) are met, and

(b) before the end of the period of 28 days beginning with the day on which those conditions were met, an event occurs in relation to that employer which meets the requirements of sub-paragraphs (a) to (c) of paragraph (1) of this regulation.]]

NOTES

Inserted, together with regs 6ZB–6ZD, by the Occupational Pension Schemes (Employer Debt and Miscellaneous Amendments) Regulations 2010, SI 2010/725, reg 7.

Para (1): words in first pair of square brackets substituted by the Occupational Pension Schemes (Employer Debt and Miscellaneous Amendments) Regulations 2011, SI 2011/2973, reg 7(1), (2); words in square brackets in sub-para (c) substituted by the Occupational Pension Schemes (Employer Debt and Miscellaneous Amendments) Regulations 2018, SI 2018/237, reg 4.

Para (7): added by SI 2011/2973, reg 7(1), (3).

[18.110]

[6ZB Employment-cessation events: exemptions

(1) There is a restructuring within this regulation if each of steps 1 to 6 in the following paragraphs are completed and the date on which there is a restructuring within this regulation is the date on which step 6 has been completed.

(2) Each of steps 2 to 7 can only be carried out if the previous step has been completed.

(3) Step 1 is for the exiting employer to write to the trustees or managers asking them to make a decision for the purposes of this regulation.

(4) The exiting employer decides whether and when to carry out step 1.

(5) Step 2 is for the exiting employer and receiving employer (unless the receiving employer has not yet been created) to provide any information which the trustees or managers—

(a) may request, and

(b) are satisfied is necessary to complete step 4.

(6) The trustees or managers must request any information, and the exiting employer and receiving employer must provide any information, for the purposes of completing step 2 without undue delay.

(7) Step 3 is for the trustees or managers to consult—

(a) the exiting employer about the decision to be made in step 4, and

(b) the receiving employer about the decision to be made in step 4, unless the receiving employer has not yet been created.

(8) The trustees or managers must complete step 3 without undue delay.

(9) Step 4 is for the trustees or managers to decide whether they are satisfied that the receiving employer will be at least as likely—

(a) as the exiting employer to meet all the exiting employer's liabilities in relation to the scheme, and

(b) to meet any liabilities in relation to the scheme which the receiving employer has immediately before step 6 is carried out.

(10) The trustees or managers must—

(a) complete step 4 without undue delay, and

(b) consider, when carrying out step 4, factors including, but not limited to, any material change in legal, demographic or economic circumstances, as described in regulation 5(4)(d) of the Scheme Funding Regulations, that would justify a change to the method or assumptions used on the last occasion on which the scheme's technical provisions were calculated.

(11) Step 5 is for the trustees or managers to send—

(a) the exiting employer, and

(b) the receiving employer, unless the receiving employer has not yet been created,

their decision in step 4, and the reasons for that decision, in writing.

(12) The trustees or managers must complete step 5 without undue delay.

(13) Step 6 is for—

(a) the receiving employer to take over responsibility, under a legally enforceable agreement, for all of the exiting employer's—

(i) assets,

(ii) employees, and

(iii) scheme members, and

(b) all of the exiting employer's liabilities in relation to the scheme to be—
(i) taken over by the receiving employer under a legally enforceable agreement so that the receiving employer is responsible for them, or
(ii) where it is impossible for the receiving employer to take over the exiting employer's liabilities in relation to the scheme under a legally enforceable agreement, treated for all purposes as being the responsibility of the receiving employer.

(14) The receiving employer decides whether to carry out step 6, but the receiving employer can only carry out step 6—
(a) where the trustees or managers decided in step 4 that they are satisfied,
(b) where the trustees or managers are satisfied that there has been no change which would alter that decision in step 4, and
(c) within the 18 weeks, or such longer period up to a total of 36 weeks as the trustees or managers may choose, after the date of the written decision in step 5.

(15) Step 7 is for the receiving employer and exiting employer to send the trustees or managers written confirmation—
(a) that step 6 has been completed, and
(b) of the date on which step 6 was completed.

(16) The receiving employer and exiting employer must complete step 7 without undue delay.

(17) In this regulation, liabilities in relation to the scheme means all such liabilities including, but not limited to, any—
(a) liabilities which—
(i) have accrued to or in respect of scheme members, and
(ii) are attributable to the employer under regulation 6(4),
(b) amounts treated as a debt due to the trustees or managers of the scheme, including such debts due in accordance with section 75 of the 1995 Act,
(c) liabilities or amounts which have been apportioned to the employer in—
(i) a scheme apportionment arrangement,
(ii) an exercise of a scheme apportionment rule before 6th April 2008, or
(iii) a regulated apportionment arrangement,
(d) liabilities which were attributed to the employer as part of a previous restructuring within this regulation or regulation 6ZC,
(e) amount for which the employer is a guarantor under a withdrawal arrangement or an approved withdrawal arrangement,
(f) payments which are due to be made by the employer under—
(i) the schedule of contributions, or
(ii) any recovery plan, . . .
(g) liability share of the employer;
[(h) liabilities for which the employer—
(i) has taken over responsibility under a flexible apportionment arrangement, or
(ii) is treated for all purposes as being responsible under such an arrangement, and
(i) actual and contingent liabilities.]]

NOTES

Inserted as noted to reg 6ZA at **[18.109]**.

Para (17): word omitted from sub-para (f) revoked and sub-paras (h), (i) added by the Occupational Pension Schemes (Employer Debt and Miscellaneous Amendments) Regulations 2011, SI 2011/2973, reg 8.

[18.111]
[6ZC

(1) There is a restructuring within this regulation if each of steps 1 to 4 in the following paragraphs are completed and the date on which there is a restructuring within this regulation is the date on which step 4 has been completed.

(2) Each of steps 2 to 5 can only be carried out if the previous step has been completed.

(3) Step 1 is for the exiting employer to write to the trustees or managers asking them to make a decision for the purposes of this regulation.

(4) The exiting employer decides whether and when to carry out step 1.

(5) Step 2 is for the trustees or managers to decide whether they are satisfied that the following four conditions are met—
(a) the assets of the scheme are at least equal to the protected liabilities of the scheme,
(b) either—
(i) there are only one or two relevant members, or
(ii) no more than 3% of the total number of scheme members in respect of whom defined benefits have accrued are relevant members,
(c) the annual amount of accrued pension in respect of the relevant members does not exceed the maximum amount where—
(i) the annual amount of accrued pension includes pensions in payment and pensions not in payment,
(ii) the annual amount of accrued pensions in payment means the most recent payment of pension to each relevant member multiplied to produce an estimated annual amount,
(iii) the annual amount of accrued pensions not in payment means the annual amount of pension to which each relevant member has accrued rights, and

(iv) the maximum amount means—
(aa) in the year commencing on 6th April 2010, £20,000, and
(bb) in any subsequent year, £20,000 plus £500 for each year after the year commencing on 6th April 2010, and
(d) if any restructurings within this regulation in relation to the scheme have occurred in the three years before step 4 is completed, those restructurings and the restructuring which occurs when step 4 is completed involve a combined total of—
(i) no more than—
(aa) five scheme members in respect of whom defined benefits have accrued, or
(bb) 7.5% of the total number of scheme members in respect of whom defined benefits have accrued,
whichever is the higher, and
(ii) no more than £50,000 of the annual amount of accrued pension as calculated for the purposes of sub-paragraph (c).

(6) The trustees or managers must complete step 2—
(a) without undue delay, and
(b) using the figures contained in the most recent—
(i) actuarial valuation under section 179 of the 2004 Act (valuations to determine scheme underfunding) for the assets and protected liabilities of the scheme, and
(ii) scheme return within the meaning in section 65(2) of the 2004 Act (scheme returns: supplementary) for the number of members of the scheme.

(7) Step 3 is for the trustees or managers to send—
(a) the exiting employer, and
(b) the receiving employer, unless the receiving employer has not yet been created,
their decision in step 2 in writing.

(8) The trustees or managers must complete step 3 without undue delay.

(9) Step 4 is for—
(a) the receiving employer to take over responsibility, under a legally enforceable agreement, for all of the exiting employer's—
(i) assets,
(ii) employees, and
(iii) scheme members, and
(b) all of the exiting employer's liabilities in relation to the scheme (as defined in regulation 6ZB(17)) to be—
(i) taken over by the receiving employer under a legally enforceable agreement so that the receiving employer is responsible for them, or
(ii) where it is impossible for the receiving employer to take over the exiting employer's liabilities in relation to the scheme under a legally enforceable agreement, treated for all purposes as being the responsibility of the receiving employer.

(10) The receiving employer decides whether to carry out step 4, but the receiving employer can only carry out step 4—
(a) where the trustees or managers decided in step 2 that they are satisfied, and
(b) within the 18 weeks, or such longer period up to a total of 36 weeks as the trustees or managers may choose, of the date of the written decision in step 3.

(11) Step 5 is for the receiving employer and exiting employer to send the trustees or managers written confirmation—
(a) that step 4 has been completed, and
(b) of the date on which step 4 was completed.

(12) The receiving employer and exiting employer must complete step 5 without undue delay.

(13) In this regulation, "relevant members" means scheme members in respect of whom defined benefits accrued as a result of pensionable service with the exiting employer.]

NOTES

Inserted as noted to reg 6ZA at **[18.109]**.

[18.112]
[6ZD

(1) The trustees or managers may decide that any costs incurred by them as a result of the steps in regulation 6ZB or 6ZC are to be met by the exiting employer, the receiving employer or both.

(2) The trustees or managers may make a decision under paragraph (1)—
(a) at any time during the steps in regulation 6ZB or 6ZC, or
(b) within one month after the final step in either of those regulations is completed.

(3) Where the trustees or managers make such a decision—
(a) they must write to the exiting employer, the receiving employer or both (as the case may be) with details of their costs, and
(b) the exiting employer, the receiving employer or both (as the case may be) must pay those costs.]

NOTES

Inserted as noted to reg 6ZA at **[18.109]**.

[18.113]
[6A Employment-cessation events: periods of grace

(1) Where but for this regulation an employment-cessation event would have occurred in relation to an employer ("A") and before, on, or [within [3 months]] after, the cessation date A gives the trustees or managers of a relevant scheme ("the scheme") a period of grace notice, A will be treated for a period of grace as if he employed a person who is an active member of the scheme, but—

(a) if by the last day of the period of grace A does not employ a person who is an active member of the scheme [or enters into a deferred debt arrangement], A will be treated as if the period of grace had not applied;

[(b) if at any time during the period of grace A—

(i) no longer intends to employ any person who will be an active member of the scheme; or

(ii) does not intend to enter into a deferred debt arrangement by the last day of the period of grace,

A must notify the trustees or managers of the scheme and A must be treated as if the period of grace had not applied;]

(c) if any time during the period of grace A employs an active member (whether before or after giving the period of grace notice), A will be treated as if an employment-cessation event had not occurred in relation to him on the cessation date which applied to the period of grace notice; or

(d) if during the period of grace an insolvency event occurs in relation to A, A will be treated as if the period of grace had not applied.

(2) Where in accordance with paragraph (1) an employer is treated for the period of grace as if he employed at least one person who is an active member of the scheme, he will for the purposes of these Regulations [and regulation 16 of the FSD Regulations (multi-employer schemes)] be treated during that period as if he were an employer in relation to the scheme.

(3) For the purposes of this regulation, the following definitions shall apply—

"cessation date" means the date on which the employer ceases to employ at least one person who is an active member of the scheme and at least one other person who is not a defined contribution employer continues to employ at least one person who is an active member of the scheme;

"relevant scheme" means a scheme in relation to which A is not aware of any intention for it to become a frozen scheme during the period of grace;

"period of grace" means a period commencing on the cessation date and ending on the earlier of—

[(a) the day referred to in paragraph (4), or]

(b) the day on which the employer employs a person who is an active member of the scheme;

"period of grace notice" means a notice in writing that an employer intends during the period of grace to employ at least one person who will be an active member of the scheme.

[(4) The day mentioned in paragraph (a) of the definition of "period of grace" in paragraph (3) is—

(a) the day which is 12 months after the cessation date; or

(b) a day which—

(i) is more than 12 months after the cessation date;

(ii) is less than 36 months after the cessation date; and

(iii) the trustees or managers of the scheme choose to nominate in accordance with paragraph (5).

(5) A nomination mentioned in paragraph (4)(b)(iii) may only be made—

(a) in writing; and

(b) before—

(i) the end of 12 months after the cessation date, where no day has previously been nominated under paragraph (4)(b)(iii); or

(ii) the day previously nominated under paragraph (4)(b)(iii).]]

NOTES

Inserted, together with regs 6B–6D, by the Occupational Pension Schemes (Employer Debt and Miscellaneous Amendments) Regulations 2008, SI 2008/731, regs 3, 7, subject to transitional provisions as noted to reg 1 at **[18.103]**.

Para (1): words in first (outer) pair of square brackets substituted by the Occupational Pension Schemes (Employer Debt and Miscellaneous Amendments) Regulations 2011, SI 2011/2973, reg 9(1), (2); words in second (inner) pair of square brackets substituted, words in square brackets in sub-para (a) inserted and sub-para (b) substituted by the Occupational Pension Schemes (Employer Debt and Miscellaneous Amendments) Regulations 2018, SI 2018/237, reg 5(1), (2).

Para (2): words in square brackets inserted by SI 2018/237, reg 5(1), (3).

Para (3): words in square brackets in definition "period of grace" substituted by SI 2011/2973, reg 9(1), (3).

Paras (4), (5): added by SI 2011/2973, reg 9(1), (4).

[18.114]
[6B Scheme apportionment arrangements

(1) Before the trustees or managers of the scheme enter into a scheme apportionment arrangement, the funding test must be met in relation to it.

[(2) Paragraph (1) does not apply where paragraph (3) or (4) applies.]

[(3) This paragraph applies where—

(a) the employer's scheme apportionment arrangement share will be higher than the liability share, and

(b) the trustees or managers are satisfied that the employer is able to pay the scheme apportionment arrangement share.

(4) This paragraph applies where—

Part 18 Miscellaneous SIs

(a) the scheme has commenced winding-up by the date the scheme apportionment arrangement is entered into,
(b) the employer's scheme apportionment arrangement share will be lower than that employer's liability share,
(c) the trustees or managers are satisfied that it is likely that the employer—
 (i) will be able to pay the scheme apportionment arrangement share, and
 (ii) would have been unable to pay the liability share if it applied,
(d) the trustees or managers are satisfied that it is likely that any of the employers who—
 (i) are remaining in the scheme, and
 (ii) are not defined contribution employers,
will be able to pay any amount by which the employer's scheme apportionment arrangement share will be less than the employer's liability share,
(e) the scheme is not in an assessment period, and
(f) the trustees or managers are satisfied that an assessment period is unlikely to begin in relation to the scheme within the following 12 months.]

NOTES

Inserted as noted to reg 6A at **[18.113]**.

Para (2): substituted by the Occupational Pension Schemes (Employer Debt and Miscellaneous Amendments) Regulations 2010, SI 2010/725, reg 8(1), (2).

Paras (3), (4): added by SI 2010/725, reg 8(1), (3).

[18.115]
[6C Withdrawal Arrangements

(1) The trustees or managers may enter into a withdrawal arrangement, before, on or after the applicable time (which applies to an employment-cessation event), provided that—
(a) the funding test is met, and
(b) they are satisfied that at the date of the agreement, the guarantors have sufficient financial resources to be likely to be able to pay amount B that would arise on that date (or pay the likely amount B).

(2) [Where a] withdrawal arrangement comes into force—
(a) the cessation employer's share of the difference shall for the purposes of regulation 6(2) be the withdrawal arrangement share, and
[(b) section 75(4) of the 1995 Act shall apply as if amount B is treated as a debt due from the guarantors at the guarantee time for which (if there is more than one guarantor) they are jointly liable or, if the withdrawal arrangement so provides, jointly and severally liable.]

(3) A relevant transfer deduction will apply to a withdrawal arrangement share provided any transfer or transfers of the cessation employer's relevant transfer liabilities and corresponding assets are completed on or before the date which is twelve months after the employment-cessation event.

(4) Schedule 1A makes further provision in relation to withdrawal arrangements.]

NOTES

Inserted as noted to reg 6A at **[18.113]**.

Para (2): words in square brackets substituted by the Occupational Pension Schemes (Employer Debt and Miscellaneous Amendments) Regulations 2010, SI 2010/725, reg 9.

[18.116]
[6D Notifiable events

Schedule 1B applies for the purposes of section 69(2)(a) and (3)(a) of the 2004 Act so as to require notice of the events prescribed in that Schedule to be given to the Authority by the persons prescribed in relation to those events, unless the Authority directs otherwise.]

NOTES

Inserted as noted to reg 6A at **[18.113]**.

[18.117]
[6E Flexible apportionment arrangements

(1) [Except in the case of a frozen scheme, a flexible] apportionment arrangement takes effect on the date on which both—
(a) the conditions in paragraph (2) are met; and
(b) an employment-cessation event—
 (i) has occurred in relation to the leaving employer before the date on which the conditions in paragraph (2) are met; [or]
 (ii) would have occurred in relation to the leaving employer if regulation 6ZA(7) had not [applied.]
 (iii) . . .

[(1A) Where the scheme is a frozen scheme, the flexible apportionment arrangement takes effect on the date on which the conditions in paragraph (2) are met.]

(2) The conditions are that—
(a) subject to paragraph (4), the funding test is met;
(b) one or more replacement employers—

(i) take over responsibility under a legally enforceable agreement for all the liabilities in relation to the scheme (within the meaning given in regulation 6ZB(17)) of the leaving employer as those liabilities stand immediately before the flexible apportionment arrangement takes effect, taking into account any reduction mentioned in paragraph (5)(c); or

(ii) where it is impossible for the replacement employer(s) to take over responsibility for those liabilities under a legally enforceable agreement, are treated for all purposes as being responsible for those liabilities;

(c) the following persons consent in writing—

(i) the trustees or managers of the scheme;

(ii) the leaving employer; and

(iii) all the replacement employers referred to in sub-paragraph (b);

(d) the leaving employer is not in a period of grace in accordance with regulation 6A;

(e) the requirements set out in paragraph (5) are met for any payment of any part of a debt—

(i) due as a result of the employment-cessation event referred to in paragraph (1)(b)(i); or

(ii) that would have been due as a result of the employment-cessation event referred to in paragraph (1)(b)(ii) that would have occurred if regulation 6ZA(7) had not applied;

(f) the scheme is not—

(i) in an assessment period; or

(ii) being wound up; and

(g) the trustees or managers of the scheme are satisfied that an assessment period is unlikely to begin in relation to the scheme within the period of 12 months beginning with the date on which a flexible apportionment arrangement takes effect.

(3) Where a flexible apportionment arrangement takes effect in accordance with paragraph (1)(b)(i), section 75(4) of the 1995 Act is modified so that no amount is to be treated as a debt due to the trustees or managers of the scheme as a result of the employment-cessation event.

(4) The funding test does not have to be met where—

(a) the funding test is met for a different flexible apportionment arrangement;

(b) the time when the flexible apportionment arrangement takes effect is or will be, in the opinion of the trustees or managers of the scheme, the same as or similar to the time when the different flexible apportionment arrangement takes effect; and

(c) the trustees or managers of the scheme are satisfied that the funding test would be met if it was carried out again.

(5) The requirements referred to in paragraph (2)(e) are—

(a) the payment (which in this paragraph means the payment referred to in paragraph (2)(e)) is made to the trustees or managers of the scheme by or on behalf of the leaving employer;

(b) the payment is in addition to any amount that is required to be paid under the schedule of contributions;

(c) the trustees or managers of the scheme decide to make a reduction of the liabilities in relation to the scheme (within the meaning given in regulation 6ZB(17)) of the leaving employer as a result of the payment; and

(d) the reduction of those liabilities relates to the amount of the payment.

(6) The trustees or managers of the scheme may require the leaving employer or the replacement employers (or both) to pay all or part of the costs which the trustees or managers of the scheme have incurred by virtue of this regulation.

(7) In this regulation—

"the leaving employer" means an employer—

(a) in relation to a multi-employer scheme;

(b) in respect of whom a relevant event has not occurred; and

(c) who—

(i) employs at least one active member of the scheme in respect of whom defined benefits are accruing; or

(ii) used to employ at least one such active member;

"replacement employer" means an employer who, on the date on which the flexible apportionment arrangement takes effect—

(a) is an employer in relation to the same multi-employer scheme as the leaving employer;

(b) either—

(i) is employing at least one active member of the scheme in respect of whom defined benefits are accruing; or

(ii) used to employ at least one such active member and no amount was treated as a debt due to the trustees or managers of the scheme when the last such active member ceased to be employed; and

(c) is an employer in respect of whom a relevant event has not occurred.]

NOTES

Inserted by the Occupational Pension Schemes (Employer Debt and Miscellaneous Amendments) Regulations 2011, SI 2011/2973, reg 10.

Para (1): first words in square brackets substituted, word in square brackets in sub-para (b)(i) inserted, word in square brackets in sub-para (b)(ii) substituted and sub-para (b)(iii) revoked, by the Occupational Pension Schemes (Employer Debt and Miscellaneous Amendments) Regulations 2018, SI 2018/237, reg 6.

Para (1A): inserted by SI 2018/237, reg 6(1), (4).

[18.118]

[6F Deferred debt arrangement

(1) A deferred debt arrangement takes effect on the date on which the trustees or managers of the scheme, being satisfied that the conditions in paragraphs (2) and (3) are met, consent in writing to the arrangement.

(2) The condition in this paragraph is that an employment-cessation event—

(a) has occurred in relation to the deferred employer before the date on which the conditions in paragraph (3) are met; or

(b) would have occurred in relation to the deferred employer if the deferred employer had not entered into and remained in a period of grace in accordance with regulation 6A until immediately before the date on which the deferred debt arrangement is to take effect.

(3) The conditions in this paragraph are—

(a) the scheme is not in an assessment period within the meaning of Part 2 of the 2004 Act (the Board of the Pension Protection Fund) or being wound up; and

(b) the trustees or managers of the scheme are satisfied that—

(i) an assessment period is unlikely to begin in relation to the scheme within the period of 12 months beginning with the date on which the trustees or managers expect the deferred debt arrangement to take effect; and

(ii) the deferred employer's covenant with the scheme is not likely to weaken materially within the period of 12 months beginning with the date on which the trustees or managers expect the deferred debt arrangement to take effect.

(4) A deferred employer must be treated during the period that the deferred debt arrangement is in place—

(a) as if employing at least one person who is an active member of the scheme; and

(b) for the purposes of these Regulations and regulation 16 of the FSD Regulations (multi-employer schemes), as an employer in relation to the scheme.

(5) Where a deferred debt arrangement is in place the deferred employer must be treated as if the employment-cessation event in paragraph (2) had not, or would not have, occurred.

(6) The deferred debt arrangement terminates on the first date on which one of the following events occurs—

(a) the deferred employer commences employing a person who is an active member of the scheme;

(b) the deferred employer and the trustees or managers of the scheme agree that an employment-cessation event shall be treated as having occurred for the purposes of bringing the deferred debt arrangement to an end in relation to the deferred employer;

(c) a relevant event occurs in relation to the deferred employer;

(d) all the employers in the scheme have experienced a relevant event or have become deferred employers;

(e) the scheme commences winding up;

(f) the deferred employer restructures, unless—

(i) the restructuring falls within either regulation 6ZB (employment-cessation events: exemptions) or regulation 6ZC; and

(ii) where the receiving employer is a deferred employer, the trustees or managers of the scheme are satisfied that the conditions in paragraph (3) are met;

(g) a freezing event as defined in regulation 9(2)(b)(frozen schemes and former employers) occurs in relation to the scheme;

(h) the trustees or managers of the scheme serve a notice on the deferred employer stating that the deferred debt arrangement has come to an end on the grounds that the trustees or managers of the scheme are reasonably satisfied that—

(i) the deferred employer has failed to comply materially with its duties under the Scheme Funding Regulations;

(ii) the deferred employer's covenant with the scheme is likely to weaken materially in the next 12 months; or

(iii) the deferred employer has failed to comply materially with its duties under regulation 6 (duty to disclose information) of the Occupational Pension Schemes (Scheme Administration) Regulations 1996.

(7) For the purposes of these Regulations where—

(a) an event referred to in paragraph (6)(a) or (e) of this regulation occurs, the deferred employer must be treated as if the employment-cessation event in paragraph (2) had not, or would not have, occurred;

(b) an event referred to in paragraph (6)(b), (c), (d) or (h) of this regulation occurs, the date of that event must be treated as the date of the employment-cessation event in relation to the deferred employer;

(c) the deferred employer restructures in circumstances where—

(i) paragraph (6)(f) of this regulation does not apply, the date of the restructuring must be treated as the date of the employment-cessation event in relation to the deferred employer;

(ii) paragraph (6)(f) of this regulation applies—

(aa) if the receiving employer is not a deferred employer, paragraph (6)(a) of this regulation applies to the receiving employer; and

(bb) if the receiving employer is a deferred employer, the deferred debt arrangement must continue;

(d) a freezing event referred to in paragraph (6)(g) of this regulation occurs, the deferred employer—
   (i) becomes a former employer in relation to the scheme for the purposes of regulation 9 (frozen schemes and former employers); and
   (ii) must be treated as if the employment-cessation event referred to in paragraph (2)(a) had not, or would not have, occurred and the deferred debt arrangement had never taken effect.]

NOTES

Commencement: 6 April 2018.

Inserted by the Occupational Pension Schemes (Employer Debt and Miscellaneous Amendments) Regulations 2018, SI 2018/237, reg 7.

[18.119]

[7 Approved withdrawal arrangements

(1) If a cessation employer notifies the Authority in writing that he proposes to enter into an arrangement under this regulation and proposes to seek the Authority's approval of the arrangement, the Authority may issue directions that—
   (a) a debt which may be treated as due under section 75(4) of the 1995 Act is to be unenforceable for such period ("suspension period") as the Authority may specify in the direction;
   (b) the suspension period is to be extended by such further periods as it specifies; and
   (c) if an approved withdrawal arrangement comes into force before the end of the suspension period, section 75(4) of the 1995 Act is to apply with the modifications in paragraph (6).

(2) The Authority may not approve an arrangement under this regulation unless—
   (a) the amount the cessation employer proposes to pay as its approved withdrawal arrangement share is less than amount A,
   (b) the trustees have notified the Authority that the funding test is met, and
   (c) the Authority is satisfied that it is reasonable to do so having regard to such matters as the Authority considers relevant, which may include the following—
      (i) the potential effect of the employment-cessation event on the method or assumptions used to calculate the scheme's technical provisions;
      (ii) the financial circumstances of the proposed guarantors;
      (iii) the amount of the cessation employer's share of the difference under the liability share;
      (iv) the amount the cessation employer proposes to pay as its approved withdrawal arrangement share (and, where there is likely to be a relevant transfer deduction, an estimate of the amount that the cessation employer will pay if the transfer is completed); and
      (v) the effect of the proposed arrangement on the security of members' benefits under the scheme.

(3) Approval by the Authority of an arrangement—
   (a) may be given subject to such conditions as the Authority considers appropriate; and
   (b) is to be given in a notice issued by the Authority.

(4) An arrangement may be approved by the Authority in advance of an employment-cessation event occurring (see paragraph 6 of Schedule 1A) or following the occurrence of such an event.

(5) An arrangement may be approved by the Authority where a departing employer notifies the trustees that a relevant transfer deduction shall apply to the proposed approved withdrawal arrangement share, but such approval will cease to be effective if the transfer or transfers of the cessation employer's liabilities are not completed on or before the date which is twelve months after the employment-cessation event or within such a longer period as the Authority approves.

(6) If the Authority issues the directions referred to in paragraph (1) and an approved withdrawal arrangement comes into force before the end of the suspension period (referred to in that paragraph)—
   (a) the cessation employer's share of the difference shall for the purposes of regulation 6(2) be the approved withdrawal arrangement share, and
   (b) section 75(4) of the 1995 Act shall apply as if amount B is treated as a debt due from the guarantors at the guarantee time for which (if there is more than one guarantor) they are jointly, of if the approved withdrawal arrangement provides, jointly and severally liable.

(7) The Authority may issue a direction that amount B under an approved withdrawal arrangement is not to be treated as a debt due from the guarantors under section 75(4) of the 1995 Act and any such direction must be issued—
   (a) before the guarantee time, and
   (b) if the Authority considers that the approved withdrawal arrangement is no longer required.

(8) The Authority may issue a notice that it considers amount B (or the balance remaining) under an approved withdrawal arrangement should be paid but it may not issue such a notice unless it considers that it is reasonable for the guarantors to be required to pay that amount at that time.

(9) In forming an opinion for the purposes of paragraph (8), the Authority must have regard to such matters as the Authority considers relevant including—
   (a) whether the guarantors have taken reasonable steps to comply with the approved withdrawal arrangement;
   (b) whether the guarantors have complied with their obligations under Schedule 1B (notifiable events); and
   (c) the guarantors' financial circumstances.

Part 18 Miscellaneous SIs

(10) Where the Authority considers that an arrangement no longer requires to be continued in force, it may issue a notice to the parties to that effect.

(11) Schedule 1A makes further provision in relation to approved withdrawal arrangements.]

NOTES

Substituted, together with reg 7A, for original regs 7, 7A, 7B, by the Occupational Pension Schemes (Employer Debt and Miscellaneous Amendments) Regulations 2008, SI 2008/731, regs 3, 8, subject to transitional provisions as noted to reg 1 at **[18.103]**.

[18.120]

[7A Regulated apportionment arrangements

(1) The conditions which apply to a regulated apportionment arrangement are as follows—

(a) the arrangement applies to a trust scheme where—

(i) the trustees are of the opinion that there is a reasonable likelihood of an assessment period commencing in relation to the scheme within the following twelve months; or

(ii) an assessment period has already commenced in relation to the scheme and has not come to an end;

[(b) where an assessment period has not already commenced, each of the following persons agrees to the arrangement—

(i) the trustees of the scheme, and either

(ii) where the employer's liability share is increased, the employer, or

(iii) where the employer's liability share is reduced, any remaining employer to whom all or part of the amount that would have been the employer's liability share is being apportioned;]

(c) the arrangement and any amendments to the arrangement are approved by the Authority by a notice of approval; and

(d) the Board of the PPF do not object to the arrangement.

(2) A notice of approval is a confirmation, issued by the Authority, that in its opinion in the circumstances described in the application it would be reasonable to issue a notice of approval.]

NOTES

Substituted as noted to reg 7 at **[18.119]**.

Para (1): sub-para (b) substituted by the Occupational Pension Schemes (Employer Debt–Apportionment Arrangements) (Amendment) Regulations 2008, SI 2008/1068, reg 2(1), (3).

[18.121]

[8 Single employer sections, multi-employer sections, etc

(1) Where section 75 of the 1995 Act and these Regulations (apart from this regulation) apply to a scheme in relation to which there is more than one employer they shall apply to each of the following sections or parts of that scheme as if the section or part were a separate scheme—

(a) a section of a segregated scheme with one employer in relation to the section;

(b) a section of a segregated scheme with more than one employer in relation to the section;

(c) a death benefits section of a segregated scheme;

(d) a frozen section of a segregated scheme.

(2) For the purposes of paragraph (1)—

(a) subject to sub-paragraph (b), a "segregated scheme" means a scheme in relation to which there is more than one employer and which is divided into two or more sections where—

[(i) any contributions payable to the scheme by an employer in relation to the scheme, or by a member in employment under that employer, are allocated to that employer's section, or if more than one section applies to that employer, to the section which is appropriate in respect of the employment in question; and]

(ii) a specified proportion of the assets of the scheme is attributable to each section of the scheme and cannot be used for the purposes of any other section;

(b) when determining whether a scheme is a segregated scheme there shall (for that purpose) be disregarded any provisions of the scheme which—

(i) permit contributions or transfers of assets to be used to provide death benefits;

(ii) permit any assets of a section of a scheme to be used for the purpose of another section in the event of the winding-up of the scheme or a section;

(c) a "death benefits section of a segregated scheme" shall mean a section—

(i) which provides death benefits only; and

(ii) to which contributions or transfers of assets may only be made for the purpose of providing death benefits;

(d) a "frozen section of a segregated scheme" shall mean a section—

(i) which applies only to members who are no longer in pensionable service in relation to the section (and a period of grace notice has not been given under regulation 6A and a period of grace under that regulation is not in progress); and

(ii) where the scheme rules have not been amended to prevent the scheme from otherwise being a segregated scheme.]

NOTES

Substituted by the Occupational Pension Schemes (Employer Debt and Miscellaneous Amendments) Regulations 2008, SI 2008/731, regs 3, 9, subject to transitional provisions as noted to reg 1 at **[18.103]**.

Para (2): words in square brackets substituted by the Occupational Pension Schemes (Employer Debt and Miscellaneous Amendments) Regulations 2018, SI 2018/237, reg 8.

Former employers

[18.122]

[9 Frozen schemes and former employers

(1) In the application of section 75 of the 1995 Act to a scheme, subject to paragraph (3), references to employers include former employers.

(2) For the purposes of this regulation—

(a) a "former employer" means any person who employed persons in the description of employment to which the scheme relates [and, in the case of a frozen scheme includes any person who employed persons in the description of employment to which the scheme relates immediately before the relevant time,] but at the relevant time has ceased to do so;

(b) in relation to a frozen scheme, "freezing event" means the event in consequence of which the scheme became a frozen scheme (this is subject to regulation 6A);

(c) "relevant time" means in relation to a scheme which is not a frozen scheme, the applicable time, and in relation to a frozen scheme, the time of occurrence of the freezing event.

(3) A person shall not be included as a former employer if—

(a) he is a defined contribution employer;

(b) before 19th December 1996, he ceased to be a person employing persons in the description or category of employment to which the scheme related and was not regarded as a "former participator" for the purposes of the 1996 Regulations by virtue of regulation 6 of those Regulations (ceasing to participate: transitional provision);

(c) at a time before the relevant time, when the scheme had not commenced winding-up and the scheme continued to have active members, he—

(i) on or after 19th December 1996 and before 6th April 1997, ceased to be a person employing persons in the description or category of employment to which the scheme related and was not regarded as a "former participator" for the purposes of the 1996 Regulations by virtue of regulation 6 of those Regulations (ceasing to participate: transitional provision);

(ii) on or after 6th April 1997 and before 6th April 2008, ceased to be a person employing persons in the description or category of employment to which the scheme related and one of conditions A to I is met;

(iii) on or after 6th April 2008 and before the applicable time, ceased to be a person employing persons in the description or category of employment to which the scheme related or an employment-cessation event or insolvency event occurs in respect of him and one of conditions [A to K is met;]

(d) in relation to a frozen scheme, at a time on or after 6th April 2008, after the freezing event, when the scheme had not commenced winding-up and before the applicable time, he ceased to be a person employing persons in the description or category of employment to which the scheme related, or an employment-cessation event or insolvency event occurred in respect of him and one of conditions [A to J] is met[; or

(e) in relation to a frozen scheme, the person is the leaving employer within the meaning given in regulation 6E(7) in a flexible apportionment arrangement which has taken effect in accordance with regulation 6E.]

[(3A) Where a scheme which has one or more deferred employers experiences a freezing event as defined in paragraph (2)(b), the deferred employers must all be treated as if they have ceased to employ persons in the description of employment to which the scheme relates immediately before the relevant time.]

(4) In the application of regulation 6 to a frozen scheme which was a multi-employer scheme before the event as a result of which the scheme became a frozen scheme, in relation to a person who before the applicable time was a former employer under this regulation, an employment-cessation event shall be treated as having occurred where notice is given to the trustees or manager by such a person for the purposes of this paragraph.

(5) A notice given for the purposes of paragraph (4) must specify the date on which the employment-cessation event is to be treated as having occurred, being a date not earlier than 3 months before the date on which the notice is given, and not more than 3 months after that date.

(6) Condition A is that as a result of the employment-cessation event, insolvency event or assumption of his liabilities by another person, no debt arose under section 75(2) or (4) of the 1995 Act (or, before 6th April 2005, under section 75(1) of that Act).

(7) Condition B is that no debt was treated as becoming due from him under section 75(2) or (4) of the 1995 Act (or, before 6th April 2005, under section 75(1) of that Act).

(8) Condition C is that a debt was treated as becoming due from him under section 75(2) or (4) of the 1995 Act (or, before 6th April 2005, under section 75(1) of that Act) and has been paid by him before the applicable time.

(9) Condition D is that in accordance with a withdrawal arrangement a debt that was treated as becoming due from him under section 75(4) of the 1995 Act and has been paid by him before the applicable time.

(10) Condition E is that in accordance with an approved withdrawal arrangement a debt was treated as becoming due from him under section 75(4) of the 1995 Act and has been paid by him before the applicable time.

(11) Condition F is that in accordance with a scheme apportionment arrangement a debt was treated as becoming due from him under section 75(2) or (4) of the 1995 Act and has been paid by him before the applicable time.

(12) Condition G is that in accordance with a regulated apportionment arrangement a debt was treated as becoming due from him under section 75(2) or (4) of the 1995 Act and has been paid by him before the applicable time.

(13) Condition H is that a debt was treated as becoming due from him [under section 75(2) or (4) of the 1995 Act] and has not been paid solely because he was not notified of the debt, and of the amount of it, sufficiently in advance of the applicable time for it to be paid before that time.

(14) Condition I is that a debt was treated as becoming due from him under section 75(2) or (4) of the 1995 Act but at the applicable time it is excluded from the value of the assets of the scheme because it is unlikely to be recovered without disproportionate cost or within a reasonable time.

[(14A) Condition J is that—

(a) as a result of a restructuring occurring within regulation 6ZB or 6ZC, no debt was treated as becoming due from the person under section 75(2) or (4) of the 1995 Act, and

(b) regulation 6ZA(3) or (4) does not apply in relation to that restructuring.]

[(14B) Condition K is that a flexible apportionment arrangement took effect in accordance with regulation 6E—

(a) with the result that no debt was treated as due from the person under section 75(4) of the 1995 Act, or

(b) with the result that no debt arose in respect of the person because regulation 6ZA(7) applied.]

(15) For the purposes of paragraph (6), an "employment-cessation event" shall include circumstances where before 6th April 2005—

(a) section 75(1) of the 1995 Act applied when a scheme was not being wound-up, and

(b) an employer ceased to be a person employing persons in the description or category of employment to which the scheme related at a time when at least one other person continued to employ such persons.]

NOTES

Substituted by the Occupational Pension Schemes (Employer Debt and Miscellaneous Amendments) Regulations 2008, SI 2008/731, regs 3, 10, subject to transitional provisions as noted to reg 1 at **[18.103]**.

Para (2): words in square brackets inserted by the Occupational Pension Schemes (Employer Debt and Miscellaneous Amendments) Regulations 2018, SI 2018/237, reg 9(1), (2).

Para (3): words in square brackets in sub-para (c) substituted and sub-para (e) inserted together with word immediately preceding it, by the Occupational Pension Schemes (Employer Debt and Miscellaneous Amendments) Regulations 2011, SI 2011/2973, reg 11(1), (2); words in square brackets in sub-para (d) substituted by the Occupational Pension Schemes (Employer Debt and Miscellaneous Amendments) Regulations 2010, SI 2010/725, reg 10(1), (2).

Para (3A): inserted by SI 2018/237, reg 9(1), (3).

Para (13): words in square brackets inserted by SI 2010/725, reg 10(1), (3).

Para (14A): inserted by SI 2010/725, reg 10(1), (4).

Para (14B): inserted by SI 2011/2973, reg 11(1), (3).

Money purchase schemes

[18.123]

10 Money purchase schemes: fraud and levy deficiencies etc

(1) Notwithstanding subsection (1)(a) of section 75 of the 1995 Act, that section applies to money purchase schemes as if—

(a) subsection (2)—

(i) provided that if the levy deficit condition is met the levy deficit is to be treated as a debt due from the employer to the trustees or managers of the scheme; and

(ii) was not subject to subsection (3) of that section;

(b) subsection (4) provided that where the criminal reduction conditions are met the criminal deficit is to be treated as a debt due from the employer to the trustees or managers of the scheme; and

(c) subsections (4A) to (4C) and (6) were omitted.

(2) The levy deficit condition is that an amount payable by way of general levy [or fraud compensation levy] in respect of any money purchase scheme exceeds the value of the unallocated assets of the scheme either—

(a) at the time when the amount first becomes payable to the Secretary of State; or

(b) at a later time designated by the trustees or managers of the scheme for the purposes of this paragraph.

(3) The criminal reduction conditions are that—

(a) a reduction in the aggregate value of the allocated assets of the scheme occurs;

(b) the reduction is attributable to an act or omission which—

(i) constitutes an offence prescribed for the purposes of [section 182(1)(b) of the 2004 Act]; or

(ii) in the case of an act or omission which occurred outside England and Wales or Scotland, would constitute such an offence if it occurred in England and Wales or in Scotland; and

(c) immediately after the act or omission or, if that time cannot be determined, at the earliest time when the auditor of the scheme knows that the reduction has occurred, the amount of that reduction exceeds the value of the unallocated assets of the scheme.

(4) [In this regulation]—

"allocated assets", in relation to a scheme, means assets which have been specifically allocated for the provision of benefits to or in respect of members (whether generally or individually) or for the payment of the scheme's expenses (and "unallocated" is to be read accordingly);

"the criminal deficit" means the amount of the excess mentioned in paragraph (3)(c);

["the fraud compensation levy" means the levy imposed in accordance with section 189 of the 2004 Act;]

"the levy deficit" means the amount of the excess mentioned in paragraph (2);

"the general levy" means the levy imposed under section 175 of the 1993 Act by regulation 3(1) or (2) of the Occupational and Personal Pension Schemes (General Levy) Regulations 2005.

NOTES

Para (2): words in square brackets inserted by the Occupational Pension Schemes (Fraud Compensation Levy) Regulations 2006, SI 2006/558, reg 12(a).

Para (3): in sub-para (b) words in square brackets substituted by the Occupational Pension Schemes (Miscellaneous Amendments) Regulations 2014, SI 2014/540, reg 5.

Para (4): words in first pair of square brackets substituted and definition "the fraud compensation levy" inserted by SI 2006/558, reg 12(b).

[18.124]

11 Money purchase schemes: valuations etc

(1) For the purposes of section 75 of the 1995 Act as applied by regulation 10, this regulation applies instead of regulation 5 . . .

(2) In the case of a scheme other than an ear-marked scheme—

(a) the value at any time of the unallocated assets of the scheme is to be taken to be the value of those assets as certified in a statement by the scheme's auditor; and

(b) the amount of the criminal reduction in the aggregate value of the allocated assets of the scheme at any time is to be calculated by subtracting the actual aggregate value of those assets at that time from the notional aggregate value of those assets.

(3) The notional aggregate value mentioned in paragraph (2)(b) is to be taken to be the sum of the values of the assets—

(a) as stated in the audited accounts which most immediately precede the relevant act or omission; or

(b) if there are none, as certified in a statement by the scheme's auditor,

adjusted appropriately to take account of any alteration in their values (other than any alteration attributable to that act or omission) between the date as at which those accounts are prepared or, as the case may be, as at which that statement is given and the time in question.

(4) The actual aggregate value mentioned in paragraph (2)(b) is to be calculated in the same manner as it was calculated for the purposes of the accounts mentioned in paragraph (3)(a) or, as the case may be, the statement mentioned in paragraph (3)(b).

(5) In the case of an ear-marked scheme—

(a) the value at any time of the unallocated assets of the scheme; and

(b) the amount of the criminal reduction in the aggregate value of the allocated assets of the scheme,

are the amounts certified in a statement by the relevant insurer.

(6) In this regulation—

"ear-marked scheme" means a scheme under which all the benefits are secured by one or more policies of insurance or annuity contracts, being policies or contracts specifically allocated to the provision of benefits for individual members or any other person who has a right to benefits under the scheme; and

"the relevant insurer", in relation to such a scheme, is the insurer with whom the insurance contract or annuity contract is made.

NOTES

Para (1): words omitted revoked by the Occupational Pension Schemes (Employer Debt and Miscellaneous Amendments) Regulations 2008, SI 2008/731, regs 3, 11(1), subject to transitional provisions as noted to reg 1 at **[18.103]**.

[18.125]

12 Multi-employer money purchase schemes

(1) In its application to a money purchase scheme that is a multi-employer scheme regulation 10 applies with the substitution for paragraph (1) of the following paragraphs—

"(1) Notwithstanding subsection (1)(a) of section 75 of the 1995 Act, that section applies to money purchase schemes as if—

(a) subsection (2)—

(i) provided that if the levy deficit condition is met each employer's share of the levy deficit is to be treated as a debt due from that employer to the trustees or managers of the scheme; and

(ii) was not subject to subsection (3) of that section;

(b) subsection (4) provided that where the criminal reduction conditions are met each employer's share of the criminal deficit is to be treated as a debt due from the employer to the trustees or managers of the scheme; and

(c) subsections (4A) to (4C) and (6) were omitted.

(1A) For the purposes of paragraph (1), an employer's share of the levy deficit or the criminal deficit is—

(a) such proportion of that total deficit as, in the opinion of [the trustees or managers], the amount of the scheme's liabilities attributable to employment with that employer bears to the total amount of the scheme's liabilities attributable to employment with the employers; or

(b) . . .

(1B) For the purposes of paragraph (1A)—

(a) the total amount of the scheme's liabilities which are attributable to employment with the employers; and

(b) . . .

are such amounts as are determined, calculated and verified by the actuary . . . ".

(2) Regulation 6 does not apply to a money purchase scheme that is a multi-employer scheme.

NOTES

Para (1): in reg 10(1A)(a) (as set out) words in square brackets substituted by virtue of the Occupational Pension Schemes (Employer Debt etc) (Amendment) Regulations 2005, SI 2005/2224, reg 4(2); in reg 10(1A), (1B) (as set out) sub-para (b) revoked by the Occupational Pension Schemes (Employer Debt and Miscellaneous Amendments) Regulations 2008, SI 2008/731, regs 3, 11(2), subject to transitional provisions as noted to reg 1 at **[18.103]**; in reg 10(1B) (as set out) words omitted in the second place revoked by the Occupational Pension Schemes (Employer Debt and Miscellaneous Amendments) Regulations 2010, SI 2010/725, reg 11.

[18.126]
13 Former employers of money purchase schemes

Regulation 9 does not apply to a money purchase scheme, but in the application of section 75 of the 1995 Act and these Regulations to such a scheme which has no active members references to employers include every person who employed persons in the description of employment to which the scheme relates immediately before the occurrence of the event after which the scheme ceased to have any active members.

Other schemes treated as more than one scheme

[18.127]
14 Schemes covering United Kingdom and foreign employment

(1) Paragraph (2) applies where a scheme which applies to members in employment in the United Kingdom and members in employment outside the United Kingdom is divided into two or more sections and the provisions of the scheme are such that—

(a) different sections of the scheme apply to members in employment in the United Kingdom and to members in employment outside the United Kingdom ("the United Kingdom section" and "the foreign section");

(b) contributions payable to the scheme in respect of a member are allocated to the section applying to that member's employment;

(c) a specified part or proportion of the assets of the scheme is attributable to each section and cannot be used for the purposes of any other section; and

(d) the United Kingdom section meets the tax condition and the foreign section does not do so.

(2) If this paragraph applies—

(a) section 75 of the 1995 Act and these Regulations (apart from this regulation) apply as if each section of the scheme were a separate scheme; and

(b) the reference to the scheme in the [forms set out in Schedules 1, 1C and 1D] may be modified appropriately.

(3) Paragraph (4) applies where—

(a) a scheme applies to members in employment in the United Kingdom and members in employment outside the United Kingdom;

(b) paragraph (2) does not apply to the scheme; and

(c) part of the scheme meets paragraph (b) of the tax condition by virtue of that part having been treated as a separate scheme under section 611(3) of the Taxes Act that is treated as becoming a registered pension scheme under paragraph 1(1) of Schedule 36 to the Finance Act 2004 by virtue of paragraph 1(2) of that Schedule.

(4) If this paragraph applies—

(a) section 75 of the 1995 Act and these Regulations (apart from this regulation) apply as if the [registered and unregistered] parts of the scheme were separate schemes; and

(b) the reference to the scheme in the [forms set out in Schedules 1, 1C and 1D] may be modified appropriately.

(5) Paragraph (6) applies where—

(a) a scheme has been such a scheme as is mentioned in paragraph (1) or (3),

(b) the scheme is divided into two or more sections, some or all of which apply only to members who are not in pensionable service under the section;

(c) the provisions of the scheme have not been amended so as to prevent the conditions in paragraph (1) or, as the case may be, paragraph (3) being met in relation to two or more sections; and

(d) in relation to one or more sections of the scheme those conditions have ceased to be met at any time by reason only of there being no members in pensionable service under the section and, in the case of paragraph (1), no contributions which are to be allocated to it.

(6) If this paragraph applies—

(a) section 75 of the 1995 Act and these Regulations (apart from this regulation) apply as if any section in relation to which those conditions have ceased to be met were a separate scheme; and

(b) the reference to the scheme in the [forms set out in Schedules 1, 1C and 1D] may be modified appropriately.

(7) Before 6th April 2006 paragraph (3) applies with the substitution for sub-paragraph (c) of the following paragraph—

"(c) part of the scheme meets paragraph (a) of the tax condition by virtue of section 611(3) of the Taxes Act."

NOTES

Paras (2), (4), (6): words in square brackets substituted by the Occupational Pension Schemes (Employer Debt and Miscellaneous Amendments) Regulations 2010, SI 2010/725, reg 12.

[18.128]

15 Schemes with partial government guarantee

(1) This regulation applies if a relevant public authority has—

(a) given a guarantee in relation to any part of a scheme, any benefits payable under the scheme or any member of the scheme; or

(b) made any other arrangements for the purposes of securing that the assets of the scheme are sufficient to meet any part of its liabilities.

(2) Where this regulation applies—

(a) section 75 of the 1995 Act and these Regulations (apart from this regulation) apply as if the guaranteed part of the scheme and the other part of the scheme were separate schemes; and

(b) the reference to the scheme in the [forms set out in Schedules 1, 1C and 1D] may be modified appropriately.

(3) In this regulation—

"the guaranteed part of the scheme" means the part of the scheme—

(a) in relation to which the guarantee has been given;

(b) which relates to benefits payable under the scheme in relation to which the guarantee has been given; or

(c) which relates to benefits payable under the scheme in relation to the liabilities for which those other arrangements have been made; and

"relevant public authority" has the meaning given in section 307(4) of the 2004 Act.

NOTES

Para (2): words in square brackets substituted by the Occupational Pension Schemes (Employer Debt and Miscellaneous Amendments) Regulations 2010, SI 2010/725, reg 13.

Supplementary

[18.129]

[16 Modification of schemes: apportionment of section 75 debts

(1) This regulation prescribes a purpose for which the trustees of a trust scheme (whether or not a money purchase scheme) may by resolution modify the scheme under section 68 of the 1995 Act (power of trustees to modify schemes by resolution).

(2) The purpose is to enable—

(a) a scheme apportionment arrangement, or

(b) a regulated apportionment arrangement,

to be entered into.

(3) No modification may be made for the purpose in paragraph (2) unless the trustees have consulted such employers in relation to the scheme as they think appropriate.]

NOTES

Substituted by the Occupational Pension Schemes (Employer Debt and Miscellaneous Amendments) Regulations 2010, SI 2010/725, reg 14.

[18.130]

17 Disregard of staying of voluntary winding up of employer for purposes of section 75 of the 1995 Act

(1) This regulation applies for the purposes of [section 75(6D)(b)(i)] of the 1995 Act (by virtue of which where a members' voluntary winding up of an employer is stayed section 75 of the 1995 Act has effect as if the resolution for the winding up had never been passed and any debt which arose under that section by virtue of the passing of the resolution had never arisen, except where the winding up is stayed in prescribed circumstances).

(2) The circumstances that are prescribed are where the stay is granted for a limited period.

NOTES

Para (1): words in square brackets substituted by the Occupational Pension Schemes (Employer Debt and Miscellaneous Amendments) Regulations 2010, SI 2010/725, reg 15.

18 (*Introduces Sch 2 to the Regulations.*)

[18.131]
[19 Review

(1) The Secretary of State must from time to time—

(a) carry out a review of the regulatory provision contained in regulation 6F of these Regulations; and

(b) publish a report setting out the conclusions of the review.

(2) The first report must be published before 6th April 2023.

(3) Subsequent reports must be published at intervals not exceeding five years.

(4) Section 30(4) of the Small Business, Enterprise and Employment Act 2015 requires that a report published under this regulation must, in particular—

(a) set out the objectives intended to be achieved by the regulatory provision referred to in paragraph (1)(a);

(b) assess the extent to which those objectives are achieved;

(c) assess whether those objectives remain appropriate; and

(d) if those objectives remain appropriate, assess the extent to which they could be achieved in another way which involves less onerous regulatory provision.

(5) In this regulation, "regulatory provision" has the same meaning as in sections 28 to 32 of the Small Business, Enterprise and Employment Act 2015 (see section 32 of that Act).]

NOTES

Commencement: 6 April 2018.

Inserted by the Occupational Pension Schemes (Employer Debt and Miscellaneous Amendments) Regulations 2018, SI 2018/237, reg 11.

[SCHEDULE 1
ACTUARY'S CERTIFICATE OF TOTAL DIFFERENCE BETWEEN SCHEME ASSETS AND LIABILITIES AND LIABILITY SHARE DEBT OF EMPLOYER IN A MULTI-EMPLOYER SCHEME [DELETE AS APPROPRIATE]

Regulation 5(18) and 6(8)

[18.132]

Given for the purposes of regulation 5(18) and regulation 6(8) of the Occupational Pension Schemes (Employer Debt) Regulations 2005 ("the Employer Debt Regulations")

This Certificate is subject to the Notes below

Name of scheme

Date used as the applicable time for purposes of calculations

1 Comparison of value of scheme assets with amount of scheme liabilities

In my opinion, at the applicable time, the value of the assets of the scheme was less than the amount of the liabilities of the scheme.

The amount of the total liabilities was [ ]

The amount of the total difference between the value of the [assets of the scheme] and the amount of the liabilities of the scheme was [approximately]

2 Multi-Employer Schemes: Employer's share of the difference on the liability share basis

[name of Employer]'s debt was calculated on the liability share basis, where—

Amount K was [£x];

Amount L was [£y]; and

[Employer's] debt (that is, Employer's liability share [after the relevant transfer deduction] [delete as appropriate]) was [£d].

3 Valuation principles

The scheme's assets and liabilities are valued in accordance with section 75(5) of the Pensions Act 1995, regulations 56 and 6 of the Employer Debt Regulations and any relevant [FRC standards].

[4 Approximations

With the agreement of the trustees or managers of the scheme, approximate calculations were used in arriving at the amount of the liabilities at [ ] [specify] above.] [Delete as appropriate]

Signature

Date

Name

Qualification
Address
Name of employer
(if applicable)

Notes:

The references to—

"applicable time" means the time as at which the value of the assets of a scheme and the amount of the liabilities are to be determined, calculated and verified for the purposes of section 75 of the Pensions Act 1995;

"liability proportion" means "[K divided by L]" where—

(a) "K" equals the amount of a scheme's liabilities attributable to an employer in accordance with paragraph (4) of regulation 6 of the Employer Debt Regulations; and

(b) "L" equals the total amount of the scheme's liabilities attributable to employment with the employers;

"liability share" means an amount equal to the liability proportion [multiplied by the total] difference between the value of the assets and the amount of the liabilities of the scheme;

"multi-employer scheme" means a scheme (or a section of a scheme treated pursuant to regulation 8 of the Employer Debt Regulations as a separate scheme) in relation to which there is more than one employer;

"relevant transfer deduction" means the amount of the relevant transfer liabilities less the value of the corresponding assets, by which the liability share is to be reduced by virtue of regulation 6(6)(a) of the Employer Debt Regulations;

"share of the difference" means the amount calculated as at the applicable time that is an employer's share of the total difference between the value of the assets and the amount of the liabilities of the scheme.

The valuation of the amount of the liabilities of the scheme may not reflect the actual cost of securing those liabilities by the purchase of annuities [if the scheme were to have been wound-up on the date as at which the valuation is made] [delete if scheme had commenced winding-up on the applicable date].

. . .

The value of the assets was provided by the trustees or managers of the scheme by relying on an updated asset assessment, that they decided to use in accordance with the conditions in regulation 5(5) of the Employer Debt Regulations [delete as appropriate].

The liabilities were calculated and verified by relying on an [updated liabilities assessment] which the trustees or managers of the scheme decided to use in accordance with the conditions in regulation 5(11) of the Employer Debt Regulations [delete as appropriate].

Where approximate calculations are used in arriving at the amount of liabilities, the amount calculated on a more accurate basis may be significantly different.

[The total amount of the employer's debt will be the amount stated in paragraph 2 of the certificate plus any cessation expenses (as defined in regulation 2(1) of the Employer Debt Regulations). See regulation 6(1)(e)(ii) of the Employer Debt Regulations.]

In the case of multi-employer schemes:

The amount of the liabilities attributed to each of the employers was determined by the trustees or managers of the scheme in accordance with regulation 6(4) of the Employer Debt Regulations.

The liability share amount was reduced to reflect a relevant transfer deduction under regulation 6(5) of the Employer Debt Regulations [delete as appropriate].]

NOTES

Substituted by the Occupational Pension Schemes (Employer Debt and Miscellaneous Amendments) Regulations 2008, SI 2008/731, regs 3, 13, Sch 1, subject to transitional provisions as noted to reg 1 at **[18.103]**.

In the Certificate, words "assets of the scheme" in square brackets in the first para substituted, and in the Notes, the third para revoked, the words "updated liabilities assessment" in square brackets substituted, and the seventh para inserted by the Occupational Pension Schemes (Employer Debt and Miscellaneous Amendments) Regulations 2010, SI 2010/725, reg 16; words "FRC standards" in square brackets substituted by the Occupational and Personal Pension Schemes (Prescribed Bodies) Regulations 2012, SI 2012/1817, reg 2, Schedule, para 7(d).

In the Notes, words in square brackets in the definitions "liability proportion" and "liability share" substituted by the Occupational Pension Schemes (Employer Debt and Miscellaneous Amendments) Regulations 2011, SI 2011/2973, reg 12.

[SCHEDULE 1A
WITHDRAWAL ARRANGEMENTS AND APPROVED WITHDRAWAL ARRANGEMENTS

Regulation 6C(4) and 7(11)

[18.133]

1. Conditions for withdrawal arrangements and approved withdrawal arrangements

The conditions a withdrawal arrangement, or a withdrawal arrangement after it has been approved by the Authority, must comply with are—

(a) the trustees or managers, the cessation employer and the guarantor are parties;

(b) it provides the date on which it is to come into force;

(c) it provides that at or before the time specified the cessation employer will pay—

(i) in the case of a withdrawal arrangement, the withdrawal arrangement share; or

Part 18 Miscellaneous SIs

(ii) in the case of an approved withdrawal arrangement, the approved withdrawal arrangement share;

(d) where the withdrawal arrangement share or approved withdrawal arrangement share will be paid in instalments, the dates for payment of such instalments;

(e) it provides that the guarantors will pay an amount or amounts equal to amount B;

(f) it provides that if an event specified in paragraph 3 of this Schedule occurs before amount B has been paid and while the agreement is still in force, the guarantors will pay amount B;

(g) it specifies whether amount B is calculated under either sub-paragraph (2) or (3) of paragraph 5 of this Schedule;

(h) specifies where there is more than one guarantor, whether the guarantors are jointly or jointly and severally liable;

(i) provides details of any relevant transfer deduction which may apply, the anticipated relevant transfer liabilities, the anticipated corresponding assets and the anticipated time scale for finalisation of the relevant transfer deduction;

(j) it provides that amounts payable under the withdrawal arrangement or approved withdrawal arrangement are payable to the trustees or managers of the scheme;

(k) it provides that one or more parties to the withdrawal arrangement or approved withdrawal arrangement are to meet any expenses incurred by the parties in connection with one or both of the following—

(i) the making of the arrangement;

(ii) the making of any calculations by the actuary for the purpose of the arrangement;

(l) the arrangement will continue in force until—

(i) the winding up of the scheme is completed;

(ii) in the case of an approved withdrawal arrangement, the Authority issues a notice to the parties to the arrangement stating that the Authority considers that the arrangement is no longer required; or

(iii) the arrangement is replaced by another arrangement that is in the case of an approved withdrawal arrangement approved by the Authority as an approved withdrawal arrangement,

whichever occurs first.

2. Actuarial certificates

The amount of the liabilities of a scheme which are to be taken into account—

(a) for the purposes of a withdrawal arrangement share or an approved withdrawal arrangement share must be certified by the actuary in the form set out in Schedule 1C to these Regulations;

(b) to determine amount B under sub-paragraph (3) of paragraph 5 of this Schedule must be certified by the actuary in the form set out in Schedule 1D to these Regulations;

(c) to determine amount B under sub-paragraph (2) of paragraph 5 of this Schedule must be certified by the actuary after the guarantee time in the form set out in Schedule 1D to these Regulations.

3. Events for payment of amount B

The events where amount B must be paid are—

(a) the scheme commences winding-up;

(b) a relevant event occurs in relation to the last remaining employer in relation to the scheme (where the last remaining employer is the only employer remaining who has not had a relevant event);

(c) in the case of an approved withdrawal arrangement, the Authority issues a notice to the parties to the arrangement stating that it considers that amount B (or the balance remaining) should be paid; or

(d) a date on which the guarantors agree to pay and the trustees or managers agree to receive payment of amount B.

4. Calculation of amount A

(1) Amount A shall be equal to either of the following amounts—

(a) where a relevant transfer deduction does not apply to a withdrawal arrangement share or an approved withdrawal arrangement share, the liability proportion of the scheme shortfall amount; or

(b) where a relevant transfer deduction applies to a withdrawal arrangement share or an approved withdrawal arrangement share, the liability proportion of the scheme shortfall amount minus the relevant transfer deduction.

(2) For the purposes of sub-paragraph 1(b), the relevant transfer deduction shall be determined by calculating the relevant transfer liabilities and the corresponding assets in accordance with regulation 5.

(3) The scheme shortfall amount is the amount of the difference as at the applicable time between the value of the assets and the amount of the liabilities of the scheme determined, calculated and verified in accordance with paragraph (3).

(4) The scheme shortfall amount and, for the purposes of this paragraph, the relevant transfer deduction shall be determined, calculated and verified as follows—

(a) where at the applicable time the trustees or managers of the scheme have received its first actuarial valuation under Part 3 of the 2004 Act, in accordance with regulation 5, but that regulation shall apply as if—

(i) paragraph (11) provided the following—

"(11) The amount of the liabilities in respect of pensions and other benefits are to be calculated and verified by the actuary using the same methods and assumptions as were set out in the most recent statement of funding principles under Part 3 of the 2004 Act.", and

(ii) paragraph (12) were omitted.

(b) where at the applicable time the trustees or managers of the scheme have not received its first actuarial valuation under Part 3 of the 2004 Act, in accordance with paragraph (4).

(5) Where sub-paragraph (b) of paragraph (3) applies, the amounts or value of the assets and liabilities of a scheme and, for the purposes of this paragraph the relevant transfer deduction, must be determined, calculated and verified by the trustees or managers of the scheme and the Actuary at the application time in accordance with—

(a) regulation 3 (excluded assets), regulation 4 (contribution notices etc), regulation 5 (valuation of assets), regulation 6 (valuation of protected liabilities) and regulation 7 (alternative valuation of assets and protected liabilities in specific cases) of the PPF Valuation Regulations; and

(b) guidance issued by the Board of the PPF;

(6) For the purposes of paragraph (4), in the PPF Valuation Regulations—

(i) references to *"section 143 valuations" and provisions which relate to section 143 valuations* shall be disregarded;

(ii) references to "relevant time" shall be read as if they were references to "applicable time"; and

(ii) references to "section 179 valuations" shall be read as if they were references to a valuation for the purposes of section 75(4) of the 1995 Act.

5. Calculation of amount B

(1) Amount B must be calculated in accordance with either sub-paragraph (2) or (3).

(2) Where a withdrawal arrangement or approved withdrawal arrangement provides that amount B is to be calculated in accordance with this paragraph, amount B is equal to the amount (if any) that would be the amount of the liability share due from the cessation employer under section 75(4) of the 1995 Act if—

(a) the employment-cessation event had occurred at the guarantee time; and

(b) the cessation employer had not entered into a withdrawal arrangement or an approved withdrawal arrangement.

(3) When the withdrawal arrangement or approved withdrawal arrangement provides that amount B is to be calculated in accordance with this paragraph, amount B is equal to the amount of the liability share that would have been treated as due from the cessation employer under section 75(4) of the 1995 Act if the cessation employer had not entered into a withdrawal arrangement or approved withdrawal arrangement, less the sum of—

(a) in the case of a withdrawal arrangement, the withdrawal arrangement share or in the case of an approved withdrawal arrangement, the approved withdrawal arrangement share;

(b) in the case of a withdrawal arrangement, if the amount that the withdrawal arrangement provides for the cessation employer to pay exceeds the withdrawal arrangement share, an amount equal to that excess.

6. Approval of withdrawal arrangements in advance

(1) A withdrawal arrangement may be approved by the Authority in advance of an employment-cessation event occurring in relation to an employer and for the purposes of approving a withdrawal arrangement prior to an employment-cessation event occurring in relation to an employer, references in this Schedule and regulations 7 to "cessation employer", "approved withdrawal arrangement share", "amount B", "amount A", "cessation expenses", "guarantors" and "relevant transfer deduction" shall be read accordingly.

(2) Where an approved withdrawal arrangement has been approved prior to an employment-cessation event regulation 7 shall apply as if—

(a) following an employment-cessation event occurring in relation to the employer who is party to the approved withdrawal arrangement, the employer gave the notice required under regulation 7(1);

(b) the Authority issued the directions under regulation 7(1);

(c) at the time when the approved withdrawal arrangement comes into force regulation 7(6) applies and the approved withdrawal arrangement share and amount B are treated as debts due.

7. Replacement withdrawal arrangements

(1) Where a withdrawal arrangement is replaced with an amended withdrawal arrangement or an amended approved withdrawal arrangement, paragraph 1, regulation 6B and regulation 7 shall apply to the amended withdrawal arrangement or amended approved withdrawal arrangement as they applied to the original arrangement.]

NOTES

Inserted by the Occupational Pension Schemes (Employer Debt etc) (Amendment) Regulations 2005, SI 2005/2224, reg 2(5), Schedule; substituted by the Occupational Pension Schemes (Employer Debt and Miscellaneous Amendments) Regulations 2008, SI 2008/731, regs 3, 14, Sch 2, subject to transitional provisions as noted to reg 1 at **[18.103]**; for the words in italics in para 4(6)(i) there are substituted the words ""section 143 valuations" and "section 143 determinations" and provisions which relate to section 143 valuations and section 143 determinations" by the Pension Protection Fund, Occupational and Personal Pension Schemes (Miscellaneous Amendments) Regulations 2013, SI 2013/627, reg 9, as from 30 April 2013.

[SCHEDULE 1B
NOTIFIABLE EVENTS

Regulation 6D

[18.134]

1. (1) Where a withdrawal arrangement or an approved withdrawal arrangement is in force in relation to a scheme, each of the guarantors must give notice to the Authority if such an event as is mentioned in sub-paragraph (2) occurs in relation to that person.

(2) The events referred to in sub-paragraph (1) are—

(a) any decision by the relevant person to take action which will, or is intended to, result in a debt which is or may become due—

(i) to the trustees of the scheme, or

(ii) if the Board of the PPF has assumed responsibility for the scheme in accordance with Chapter 3 of Part 2 of the 2004 Act, to the Board,

not being paid in full;

(b) a decision by the relevant person to cease to carry on business (including any trade or profession) in the United Kingdom or, if the relevant person ceases to carry on such business without taking such a decision, his doing so;

(c) where applicable, receipt by the relevant person of advice that the person is trading wrongfully within the meaning of section 214 of the Insolvency Act 1986 (wrongful trading), or circumstances occurring in which a director or former director of the company knows that there is no reasonable prospect that the company will avoid going into insolvent liquidation within the meaning of that section, and for this purpose section 214(4) of that Act applies;

(d) any breach by the relevant person of a covenant in an agreement between the relevant person and a bank or other institution providing banking services, other than where the bank or other institution agrees with the relevant person not to enforce the covenant;

(e) . . .

(f) where the relevant person is a company, a decision by a controlling company to relinquish control of the relevant person or, if the controlling company relinquishes such control without taking such a decision, its doing so;

(g) . . .

(h) where the relevant person is a company or partnership, the conviction of an individual, in any jurisdiction, for an offence involving dishonesty, if the offence was committed while the individual was a director or partner of the relevant person;

(i) an insolvency event occurring in relation to the relevant person for the purposes of Part 2 of the 2004 Act (see section 121 of that Act: insolvency event, insolvency date and insolvency practitioner).

(3) A notice under sub-paragraph (1) must be given in writing as soon as reasonably practicable after the relevant person becomes aware of the event.

(4) In this paragraph—

"control" has the meaning given in section 435(10) of the Insolvency Act 1986 (meaning of "associate" meaning of "control") and "controlling company" is to be read accordingly;

"director" has the meaning given in section 741(1) of the Companies Act 1985 (meaning of "director" and "shadow director");

"key relevant person posts" means the Chief Executive and any director or partner responsible in whole or in part for the financial affairs of the relevant person.

2. (1) The trustees or managers of a scheme must give notice to the Authority of any decision by them to take action which will, or is intended to, result in[—

(a)] any entering into a scheme apportionment arrangement on or after the applicable time[; or

(b) a flexible apportionment arrangement taking [effect; or]]

[(c) a deferred debt arrangement taking effect; or

(d) any event which terminates a deferred debt arrangement in accordance with regulation 6F(6).]

(2) A notice under sub-paragraph (1) must be given in writing as soon as reasonably practicable after [the trustees or managers of the scheme make the decision or become aware of the event.].

3. (1) No duty to which a person is subject . . . is to be regarded as contravened merely because of any information or opinion contained in a notice under paragraph 1 or 2.

(2) But sub-paragraph (1) does not require any person to disclose protected items within the meaning of section 311 of the 2004 Act (protected items).

(3) Section 10 of the 1995 Act (civil penalties) applies to any person who without reasonable excuse fails to comply with an obligation imposed on him under paragraph 1 or 2.]

NOTES

Inserted by the Occupational Pension Schemes (Employer Debt etc) (Amendment) Regulations 2005, SI 2005/2224, reg 2(5), Schedule; substituted, together with Schs 1C, 1D, by the Occupational Pension Schemes (Employer Debt and Miscellaneous Amendments) Regulations 2008, SI 2008/731, regs 3, 15, Sch 3, subject to transitional provisions as noted to reg 1 at **[18.103]**.

Paras 1, 3: words omitted revoked by the Occupational Pension Schemes (Employer Debt and Miscellaneous Amendments) Regulations 2010, SI 2010/725, reg 17.

Para 2: sub-para (1)(a) numbered as such and sub-para (1)(b) inserted by the Occupational Pension Schemes (Employer Debt and Miscellaneous Amendments) Regulations 2011, SI 2011/2973, reg 13; words in square brackets in sub-paras (1)(b), (2) substituted, sub-para (1)(c), (d) inserted by the Occupational Pension Schemes (Employer Debt and Miscellaneous Amendments) Regulations 2018, SI 2018/237, reg 10.

[SCHEDULE 1C
ACTUARY'S CERTIFICATE FOR WITHDRAWAL ARRANGEMENT SHARE OR APPROVED WITHDRAWAL ARRANGEMENT SHARE IN MULTI-EMPLOYER SCHEME

paragraph 2(a) of Schedule 1A

[18.135]

Given for the purposes of paragraph 2(a) of Schedule 1A to the Occupational Pension Schemes (Employer Debt) Regulations 2005 ("the Employer Debt Regulations")

Name of scheme

Date used as the applicable time for purposes of calculations

1 Comparison of value of scheme assets with amount of scheme liabilities

In my opinion, at the applicable time, the value of the assets of the scheme was less than the amount of the liabilities of the scheme.

The amount of the total liabilities was [approximately]

2 Employer's withdrawal arrangement share or approved withdrawal arrangement share

[name of Employer]'s [approved] withdrawal arrangement share [after the relevant transfer reduction] [delete as appropriate] was

In the case of an approved withdrawal arrangement share, the amount A which applied for the purposes of determining [name of Employer]'s approved withdrawal arrangement share was

[3 Valuation principles

The scheme's assets and liabilities are valued in accordance with—

(a) section 75(5) of the Pensions Act 1995, and

(b) regulations 5, 6[, 6C(3) and 7(5)] [delete as appropriate] of the Employer Debt Regulations.]

[4 Approximations

With the agreement of the trustees or managers of the scheme, approximate calculations were used in arriving at the amount of the liabilities at [ ] [specify] above. [delete as appropriate]

Signature

Date

Name

Qualification

Address

Name of employer

(if applicable)

Notes:

The references to—

"amount A" means the amount calculated in accordance with paragraph 4 of Schedule 1A to the Employer Debt Regulations;

"applicable time" means the time as at which the value of the assets of a scheme and the amount of the liabilities are to be determined, calculated and verified for the purposes of section 75 of the Pensions Act 1995;

"approved withdrawal arrangement share" means an amount that is—

(a) a cessation employer's share of the difference,

(b) less than amount A, and

(c) payable by a cessation employer pursuant to an approved withdrawal arrangement;

"multi-employer scheme" means a scheme (or a section of a scheme treated pursuant to regulation 8 of the Employer Debt Regulations as a separate scheme) in relation to which there is more than one employer;

["relevant transfer deduction" means the amount of the relevant transfer liabilities less the value of the corresponding assets;]

"share of the difference" means the amount calculated as at the applicable time that is an employer's share of the total difference between the value of the assets and the amount of the liabilities of the scheme;

"withdrawal arrangement share" means an amount that is—

(a) a cessation employer's share of the difference,

(b) equal to or greater than amount A, and

(c) payable by a cessation employer pursuant to a withdrawal arrangement.

. . .

The value of the assets was provided by the trustees or managers of the scheme by relying on an [updated liabilities assessment], that they decided to use in accordance with the conditions in regulation 5(5) of the Employer Debt Regulations [delete as appropriate].

The liabilities were calculated and verified by relying on an [updated liabilities assessment] which the trustees or managers of the scheme decided to use in accordance with the conditions in regulation 5(11) of the Employer Debt Regulations.

Where approximate calculations are used in arriving at the amount of liabilities, the amount calculated on a more accurate basis may be significantly different.

The withdrawal arrangement share amount was reduced to reflect a relevant transfer deduction under regulation 6C(3) of the Employer Debt Regulations [delete as appropriate].

The approved withdrawal arrangement share was calculated by reference to an amount A which was reduced to reflect where the Authority permitted, under regulation 7(5) of the Employer Debt Regulations, a relevant transfer deduction to apply [delete as appropriate].]

[The total amount of the employer's debt will be the amount of the (approved) withdrawal arrangement share stated in paragraph 2 of the certificate plus any cessation expenses (as defined in regulation 2(1) of the Employer Debt Regulations). See regulation 6(1)(e)(ii) of the Employer Debt Regulations.]

NOTES

Substituted as noted to Sch 1B at **[18.134]**.

In the certificate, the third para substituted, and in the Notes, definition "relevant transfer deduction" substituted, second para revoked, words "updated liabilities assessment" in square brackets substituted and final para added by the Occupational Pension Schemes (Employer Debt and Miscellaneous Amendments) Regulations 2010, SI 2010/725, reg 18.

[SCHEDULE 1D
ACTUARY'S CERTIFICATE FOR AMOUNT B UNDER A WITHDRAWAL ARRANGEMENT OR AN APPROVED WITHDRAWAL ARRANGEMENT IN A MULTI-EMPLOYER SCHEME

paragraph 2(b) and (c) of Schedule 1A

[18.136]

Given for the purposes of sub-paragraph (b) or (c) of paragraph 2 of Schedule 1A to the Occupational Pension Schemes (Employer Debt) Regulations 2005 ("the Employer Debt Regulations")

This certificate is subject to the Notes below

Name of multi-employer scheme

Date used for purposes of calculations

1 Amount B

For the purposes of [sub-paragraph (2)] [sub-paragraph (3)] [delete as appropriate] of paragraph 5 of Schedule 1A t the Employer Debt Regulations, the guarantors' amount B for the purposes of a withdrawal arrangement or an approved withdrawal arrangement was

2 Valuation principles

The value of the scheme's assets and the amount of the liabilities are valued in accordance with section 75(5) of the Pensions Act 1995, regulation 5 of, and paragraph 5(2) or (3) of Schedule 1A to, the [Employer Debt Regulations] and with relevant [FRC standards].

Signature

Date

Name

Qualification

Address

Name of employer

(if applicable)

Notes:

The references to—

"amount B" means the amount calculated in accordance with sub-paragraph (2) or (3) of paragraph 5 of Schedule 1A to the Employer Debt Regulations;

"approved withdrawal arrangement" means an arrangement that meets the conditions in paragraph 1 of Schedule 1A to the Employer Debt Regulations and is approved by the Authority under regulation 7 of those Regulations;

"guarantors" means such one or more of the parties to a withdrawal arrangement or an approved withdrawal arrangement who are specified in the arrangement as the persons who have given guarantees in relation to amount B for the purposes of the arrangement;

"withdrawal arrangement" means an arrangement that meets the conditions specified in paragraph 1 of Schedule 1A to the Employer Debt Regulations and meets the test in paragraph (1) of regulation 6C of those Regulations;

The valuation of the amount of the liabilities of the scheme may not reflect the actual cost of securing those liabilities by the purchase of annuities [if the scheme were to have been wound-up on the date as at which the valuation is made] [delete if scheme had not commenced winding-up on the applicable date].

. . .

The value of the assets was provided by the trustees or managers of the scheme by relying on an updated asset assessment, that they decided to use in accordance with the conditions in regulation 5(5) of the Employer Debt Regulations [delete as appropriate].

The liabilities were calculated and verified by relying on an [updated liabilities assessment] which the trustees or managers of the scheme decided to use in accordance with the conditions in regulation 5(11) of the Employer Debt Regulations.

A relevant transfer deduction (as defined in regulation 2(1) of the Employer Debt Regulations) applied [delete as appropriate].]

NOTES

Substituted as noted to Sch 1B at **[18.134]**.

In the certificate, words "Employer Debt Regulations" substituted, and in the Notes, third para revoked and words "updated liabilities assessment" in square brackets substituted by the Occupational Pension Schemes (Employer Debt and Miscellaneous Amendments) Regulations 2010, SI 2010/725, reg 19; words "FRC standards" in square brackets substituted by the Occupational and Personal Pension Schemes (Prescribed Bodies) Regulations 2012, SI 2012/1817, reg 2, Schedule, para 7(d).

SCHEDULE 2

(Sch 2 contains consequential amendments outside the scope of this work.)

COMMUNITY INTEREST COMPANY REGULATIONS 2005

(SI 2005/1788)

NOTES

Made: 30 June 2005.

Authority: Companies (Audit, Investigations and Community Enterprise) Act 2004, ss 30(1)–(4), 30(7), 31, 32(3), (4), (6), 34(3), 35(4)–(6), 36(2), 37(7), 47(12), (13), 57(1), (2), 58, 59(1), 62(2), (3), Sch 4, para 4.

Commencement: 1 July 2005.

1–16 *((Pts 1–5) outside the scope of this work.)*

PART 6
RESTRICTIONS ON DISTRIBUTIONS AND INTEREST

17–22 *(Outside the scope of this work.)*

[18.137]

23 Distribution of assets on a winding up

(1) This regulation applies where—

(a) a community interest company is wound up under the Insolvency Act 1986 [or the Insolvency (Northern Ireland) Order 1989]; and

(b) some property of the company (the "residual assets") remains after satisfaction of the company's liabilities.

(2) Subject to paragraph (3), the residual assets shall be distributed to those members of the community interest company (if any) who are entitled to share in any distribution of assets on the winding up of the company according to their rights and interests in the company.

(3) No member shall receive under paragraph (2) an amount which exceeds the paid up value of the shares which he holds in the company.

(4) If any residual assets remain after any distribution to members under paragraph (2) (the "remaining residual assets"), they shall be distributed in accordance with paragraphs (5) and (6).

(5) If the . . . articles of the company specify an asset-locked body to which any remaining residual assets of the company should be distributed, then, unless either of the conditions specified in sub-paragraphs (b) and (c) of paragraph (6) is satisfied, the remaining residual assets shall be distributed to that asset-locked body in such proportions or amounts as the Regulator shall direct.

(6) If—

(a) the . . . articles of the company do not specify an asset-locked body to which any remaining residual assets of the company should be distributed;

(b) the Regulator is aware that the asset-locked body to which the . . . articles of the company specify that the remaining residual assets of the company should be distributed is itself in the process of being wound up; or

(c) the Regulator—

(i) has received representations from a member or director of the company stating, with reasons, that the asset-locked body to which the . . . articles of the company specify that the remaining residual assets of the company should be distributed is not an appropriate recipient of the company's remaining residual assets; and

(ii) has agreed with those representations,

then the remaining residual assets shall be distributed to such asset-locked bodies, and in such proportions or amounts, as the Regulator shall direct.

Part 18 Miscellaneous SIs

(7) In considering any direction to be made under this regulation, the Regulator must—
(a) consult the directors and members of the company, to the extent that he considers it practicable and appropriate to do so; and
(b) have regard to the desirability of distributing assets in accordance with any relevant provisions of the company's . . . articles.

(8) The Regulator must give notice of any direction under this regulation to the company and the liquidator.

(9) This regulation has effect notwithstanding anything in the Insolvency Act 1986 [or the Insolvency (Northern Ireland) Order 1989].

(10) This regulation has effect subject to the provisions of the Housing Act 1996[, Part 2 of the Housing and Regeneration Act 2008] and the Housing (Scotland) Act 2001.

(11) Any member or director of the company may appeal to the Appeal Officer against a direction of the Regulator made under this regulation.

NOTES

Paras (1), (9): words in square brackets inserted by the Companies Act 2006 (Commencement No 2, Consequential Amendments, Transitional Provisions and Savings) Order 2007, SI 2007/1093, art 6(2), (3)(b), Sch 4, Pt 2, para 36, subject to savings in art 8 of, Sch 6, para 4 to, the 2007 order.

Paras (5)–(7): words omitted revoked by the Community Interest Company (Amendment) Regulations 2009, SI 2009/1942, reg 15.

Para (10): words in square brackets inserted by the Housing and Regeneration Act 2008 (Consequential Provisions) (No 2) Order 2010, SI 2010/671, art 4, Sch 1, para 42, subject to transitional and savings provisions in art 5 of, and Sch 2, paras 1, 2, 6 to, the 2010 Order.

24–33 *(Regs 24, 25, regs 26–33 (Pts 7, 8) outside the scope of this work.)*

PART 9
THE REGISTRAR OF COMPANIES

34 *(Outside the scope of this work.)*

[18.138]
35 Documents

(1) The registrar of companies shall, on receiving any notice under section 109(1) of the Insolvency Act 1986 [or Article 95 of the Insolvency (Northern Ireland) Order 1989] (notice by liquidator of his appointment) in relation to a community interest company, provide a copy of that notice to the Regulator.

(2) The registrar of companies shall, on receiving any copy of a winding-up order forwarded under section 130(1) of the Insolvency Act 1986 [or Article 110 of the Insolvency (Northern Ireland) Order 1989] (consequences of a winding-up order) in relation to a community interest company, provide the Regulator with a copy of that winding-up order.

NOTES

Words in square brackets inserted by the Companies Act 2006 (Commencement No 2, Consequential Amendments, Transitional Provisions and Savings) Order 2007, SI 2007/1093, art 6(2), (3)(b), Sch 4, Pt 2, para 40, subject to savings in art 8 of, Sch 6, para 4 to, the 2007 order.

36–42 *((Pts 10, 11) outside the scope of this work.)*

SCHEDULES 1–5

(Schs 1–5 outside the scope of this work.)

TRANSFER OF UNDERTAKINGS (PROTECTION OF EMPLOYMENT) REGULATIONS 2006

(SI 2006/246)

NOTES

Made: 6 February 2006.
Authority: European Communities Act 1972, s 2(2); Employment Relations Act 1999, s 38.
Commencement: 6 April 2006.

ARRANGEMENT OF REGULATIONS

1 Citation, commencement and extent . . . . . [18.139]
2 Interpretation . . . . . [18.140]
3 A relevant transfer . . . . . [18.141]
4 Effect of relevant transfer on contracts of employment . . . . . [18.142]
4A Effect of relevant transfer on contracts of employment which incorporate provisions of collective agreements . . . . . [18.143]

5 Effect of relevant transfer on collective agreements . . . . . [18.144]
6 Effect of relevant transfer on trade union recognition . . . . . [18.145]
7 Dismissal of employee because of relevant transfer . . . . . [18.146]
8 Insolvency. . . . . [18.147]
9 Variations of contract where transferors are subject to relevant insolvency proceedings . . . . . [18.148]
10 Pensions . . . . . [18.149]
11 Notification of Employee Liability Information. . . . . [18.150]
12 Remedy for failure to notify employee liability information . . . . . [18.151]
13 Duty to inform and consult representatives . . . . . [18.152]
13A Duty to inform and consult Micro-business's duty to inform and consult where no appropriate representatives . . . . . [18.153]
14 Election of employee representatives. . . . . [18.154]
15 Failure to inform or consult . . . . . [18.155]
16 Failure to inform or consult: supplemental . . . . . [18.156]
16A Extension of time limit to facilitate conciliation before institution of proceedings. . . . . [18.157]
17 Employers' Liability Compulsory Insurance. . . . . [18.158]
18 Restriction on contracting out. . . . . [18.159]
20 Repeals, revocations and amendments . . . . . [18.160]
21 Transitional provisions and savings. . . . . [18.161]

[18.139]
1 Citation, commencement and extent

(1) These Regulations may be cited as the Transfer of Undertakings (Protection of Employment) Regulations 2006.

(2) These Regulations shall come into force on 6 April 2006.

(3) These Regulations shall extend to Northern Ireland, except where otherwise provided.

[18.140]
2 Interpretation

(1) In these Regulations—

"assigned" means assigned other than on a temporary basis;

"collective agreement", "collective bargaining" and "trade union" have the same meanings respectively as in the 1992 Act;

"contract of employment" means any agreement between an employee and his employer determining the terms and conditions of his employment;

references to "contractor" in regulation 3 shall include a sub-contractor;

"employee" means any individual who works for another person whether under a contract of service or apprenticeship or otherwise but does not include anyone who provides services under a contract for services and references to a person's employer shall be construed accordingly;

"insolvency practitioner" has the meaning given to the expression by Part XIII of the Insolvency Act 1986;

references to "organised grouping of employees" shall include a single employee;

"recognised" has the meaning given to the expression by section 178(3) of the 1992 Act;

"relevant transfer" means a transfer or a service provision change to which these Regulations apply in accordance with regulation 3 and "transferor" and "transferee" shall be construed accordingly and in the case of a service provision change falling within regulation 3(1)(b), "the transferor" means the person who carried out the activities prior to the service provision change and "the transferee" means the person who carries out the activities as a result of the service provision change;

"the 1992 Act" means the Trade Union and Labour Relations (Consolidation) Act 1992;

"the 1996 Act" means the Employment Rights Act 1996;

"the 1996 Tribunals Act" means the Employment Tribunals Act 1996;

"the 1981 Regulations" means the Transfer of Undertakings (Protection of Employment) Regulations 1981.

(2) For the purposes of these Regulations the representative of a trade union recognised by an employer is an official or other person authorised to carry on collective bargaining with that employer by that trade union.

(3) In the application of these Regulations to Northern Ireland the Regulations shall have effect as set out in Schedule 1.

[18.141]
3 A relevant transfer

(1) These Regulations apply to—

(a) a transfer of an undertaking, business or part of an undertaking or business situated immediately before the transfer in the United Kingdom to another person where there is a transfer of an economic entity which retains its identity;

(b) a service provision change, that is a situation in which—

Part 18 Miscellaneous SIs

(i) activities cease to be carried out by a person ("a client") on his own behalf and are carried out instead by another person on the client's behalf ("a contractor");
(ii) activities cease to be carried out by a contractor on a client's behalf (whether or not those activities had previously been carried out by the client on his own behalf) and are carried out instead by another person ("a subsequent contractor") on the client's behalf; or
(iii) activities cease to be carried out by a contractor or a subsequent contractor on a client's behalf (whether or not those activities had previously been carried out by the client on his own behalf) and are carried out instead by the client on his own behalf,

and in which the conditions set out in paragraph (3) are satisfied.

(2) In this regulation "economic entity" means an organised grouping of resources which has the objective of pursuing an economic activity, whether or not that activity is central or ancillary.

[(2A) References in paragraph (1)(b) to activities being carried out instead by another person (including the client) are to activities which are fundamentally the same as the activities carried out by the person who has ceased to carry them out.]

(3) The conditions referred to in paragraph (1)(b) are that—
(a) immediately before the service provision change—
(i) there is an organised grouping of employees situated in Great Britain which has as its principal purpose the carrying out of the activities concerned on behalf of the client;
(ii) the client intends that the activities will, following the service provision change, be carried out by the transferee other than in connection with a single specific event or task of short-term duration; and
(b) the activities concerned do not consist wholly or mainly of the supply of goods for the client's use.

(4) Subject to paragraph (1), these Regulations apply to—
(a) public and private undertakings engaged in economic activities whether or not they are operating for gain;
(b) a transfer or service provision change howsoever effected notwithstanding—
(i) that the transfer of an undertaking, business or part of an undertaking or business is governed or effected by the law of a country or territory outside the United Kingdom or that the service provision change is governed or effected by the law of a country or territory outside Great Britain;
(ii) that the employment of persons employed in the undertaking, business or part transferred or, in the case of a service provision change, persons employed in the organised grouping of employees, is governed by any such law;
(c) a transfer of an undertaking, business or part of an undertaking or business (which may also be a service provision change) where persons employed in the undertaking, business or part transferred ordinarily work outside the United Kingdom.

(5) An administrative reorganisation of public administrative authorities or the transfer of administrative functions between public administrative authorities is not a relevant transfer.

(6) A relevant transfer—
(a) may be effected by a series of two or more transactions; and
(b) may take place whether or not any property is transferred to the transferee by the transferor.

(7) Where, in consequence (whether directly or indirectly) of the transfer of an undertaking, business or part of an undertaking or business which was situated immediately before the transfer in the United Kingdom, a ship within the meaning of the Merchant Shipping Act 1995 registered in the United Kingdom ceases to be so registered, these Regulations shall not affect the right conferred by section 29 of that Act (right of seamen to be discharged when ship ceases to be registered in the United Kingdom) on a seaman employed in the ship.

NOTES

Para (2A): inserted by the Collective Redundancies and Transfer of Undertakings (Protection of Employment) (Amendment) Regulations 2014, SI 2014/16, regs 4, 5, in relation to a TUPE transfer which takes place on or after 31 January 2014.

[18.142]

4 Effect of relevant transfer on contracts of employment

(1) Except where objection is made under paragraph (7), a relevant transfer shall not operate so as to terminate the contract of employment of any person employed by the transferor and assigned to the organised grouping of resources or employees that is subject to the relevant transfer, which would otherwise be terminated by the transfer, but any such contract shall have effect after the transfer as if originally made between the person so employed and the transferee.

(2) Without prejudice to paragraph (1), but subject to paragraph (6), and regulations 8 and 15(9), on the completion of a relevant transfer—
(a) all the transferor's rights, powers, duties and liabilities under or in connection with any such contract shall be transferred by virtue of this regulation to the transferee; and
(b) any act or omission before the transfer is completed, of or in relation to the transferor in respect of that contract or a person assigned to that organised grouping of resources or employees, shall be deemed to have been an act or omission of or in relation to the transferee.

(3) Any reference in paragraph (1) to a person employed by the transferor and assigned to the organised grouping of resources or employees that is subject to a relevant transfer, is a reference to a person so employed immediately before the transfer, or who would have been so employed if he had not been

dismissed in the circumstances described in regulation 7(1), including, where the transfer is effected by a series of two or more transactions, a person so employed and assigned or who would have been so employed and assigned immediately before any of those transactions.

[(4) Subject to regulation 9, any purported variation of a contract of employment that is, or will be, transferred by paragraph (1), is void if the sole or principal reason for the variation is the transfer.

(5) Paragraph (4) does not prevent a variation of the contract of employment if—

(a) the sole or principal reason for the variation is an economic, technical, or organisational reason entailing changes in the workforce, provided that the employer and employee agree that variation; or

(b) the terms of that contract permit the employer to make such a variation.

(5A) In paragraph (5), the expression "changes in the workforce" includes a change to the place where employees are employed by the employer to carry on the business of the employer or to carry out work of a particular kind for the employer (and the reference to such a place has the same meaning as in section 139 of the 1996 Act).

(5B) Paragraph (4) does not apply in respect of a variation of the contract of employment in so far as it varies a term or condition incorporated from a collective agreement, provided that—

(a) the variation of the contract takes effect on a date more than one year after the date of the transfer; and

(b) following that variation, the rights and obligations in the employee's contract, when considered together, are no less favourable to the employee than those which applied immediately before the variation.

(5C) Paragraphs (5) and (5B) do not affect any rule of law as to whether a contract of employment is effectively varied.]

(6) Paragraph (2) shall not transfer or otherwise affect the liability of any person to be prosecuted for, convicted of and sentenced for any offence.

(7) Paragraphs (1) and (2) shall not operate to transfer the contract of employment and the rights, powers, duties and liabilities under or in connection with it of an employee who informs the transferor or the transferee that he objects to becoming employed by the transferee.

(8) Subject to paragraphs (9) and (11), where an employee so objects, the relevant transfer shall operate so as to terminate his contract of employment with the transferor but he shall not be treated, for any purpose, as having been dismissed by the transferor.

(9) Subject to regulation 9, where a relevant transfer involves or would involve a substantial change in working conditions to the material detriment of a person whose contract of employment is or would be transferred under paragraph (1), such an employee may treat the contract of employment as having been terminated, and the employee shall be treated for any purpose as having been dismissed by the employer.

(10) No damages shall be payable by an employer as a result of a dismissal falling within paragraph (9) in respect of any failure by the employer to pay wages to an employee in respect of a notice period which the employee has failed to work.

(11) Paragraphs (1), (7), (8) and (9) are without prejudice to any right of an employee arising apart from these Regulations to terminate his contract of employment without notice in acceptance of a repudiatory breach of contract by his employer.

NOTES

Paras (4), (5), (5A)–(5C): substituted for original paras (4), (5) by SI 2014/16, regs 4, 6, in relation to any purported variation of a contract of employment that is transferred by a TUPE transfer if the transfer takes place on or after 31 January 2014, and that purported variation is agreed on or after that date, or, in a case where the variation is not agreed, it starts to have effect on or after that date. The original paras (4), (5) read as follows—

"(4) Subject to regulation 9, in respect of a contract of employment that is, or will be, transferred by paragraph (1), any purported variation of the contract shall be void if the sole or principal reason for the variation is—

(a) the transfer itself; or

(b) a reason connected with the transfer that is not an economic, technical or organisational reason entailing changes in the workforce.

(5) Paragraph (4) shall not prevent the employer and his employee, whose contract of employment is, or will be, transferred by paragraph (1), from agreeing a variation of that contract if the sole or principal reason for the variation is—

(a) a reason connected with the transfer that is an economic, technical or organisational reason entailing changes in the workforce; or

(b) a reason unconnected with the transfer.".

[18.143]

[4A Effect of relevant transfer on contracts of employment which incorporate provisions of collective agreements

(1) Where a contract of employment, which is transferred by regulation 4(1), incorporates provisions of collective agreements as may be agreed from time to time, regulation 4(2) does not transfer any rights, powers, duties and liabilities in relation to any provision of a collective agreement if the following conditions are met—

(a) the provision of the collective agreement is agreed after the date of the transfer; and

(b) the transferee is not a participant in the collective bargaining for that provision.

(2) For the purposes of regulation 4(1), the contract of employment has effect after the transfer as if it does not incorporate provisions of a collective agreement which meet the conditions in paragraph (1).]

NOTES

Commencement: 31 January 2014.

Inserted by the Collective Redundancies and Transfer of Undertakings (Protection of Employment) (Amendment) Regulations 2014, SI 2014/16, regs 4, 7, in relation to a TUPE transfer which takes place on or after 31 January 2014.

[18.144]

5 Effect of relevant transfer on collective agreements

Where at the time of a relevant transfer there exists a collective agreement made by or on behalf of the transferor with a trade union recognised by the transferor in respect of any employee whose contract of employment is preserved by regulation 4(1) above, then—

(a) without prejudice to sections 179 and 180 of the 1992 Act (collective agreements presumed to be unenforceable in specified circumstances) that agreement, in its application in relation to the employee, shall, after the transfer, have effect as if made by or on behalf of the transferee with that trade union, and accordingly anything done under or in connection with it, in its application in relation to the employee, by or in relation to the transferor before the transfer, shall, after the transfer, be deemed to have been done by or in relation to the transferee; and

(b) any order made in respect of that agreement, in its application in relation to the employee, shall, after the transfer, have effect as if the transferee were a party to the agreement.

[18.145]

6 Effect of relevant transfer on trade union recognition

(1) This regulation applies where after a relevant transfer the transferred organised grouping of resources or employees maintains an identity distinct from the remainder of the transferee's undertaking.

(2) Where before such a transfer an independent trade union is recognised to any extent by the transferor in respect of employees of any description who in consequence of the transfer become employees of the transferee, then, after the transfer—

(a) the trade union shall be deemed to have been recognised by the transferee to the same extent in respect of employees of that description so employed; and

(b) any agreement for recognition may be varied or rescinded accordingly.

[18.146]

7 Dismissal of employee because of relevant transfer

[(1) Where either before or after a relevant transfer, any employee of the transferor or transferee is dismissed, that employee is to be treated for the purposes of Part 10 of the 1996 Act (unfair dismissal) as unfairly dismissed if the sole or principal reason for the dismissal is the transfer.

(2) Where either before or after a relevant transfer, any employee of the transferor or transferee is dismissed, that employee is to be treated for the purposes of Part 10 of the 1996 Act (unfair dismissal) as unfairly dismissed if the sole or principal reason for the dismissal is the transfer.

(3) Where paragraph (2) applies—

(a) paragraph (1) does not apply;

(b) without prejudice to the application of section 98(4) of the 1996 Act (test of fair dismissal), for the purposes of sections 98(1) and 135 of that Act (reason for dismissal)—

(i) the dismissal is regarded as having been for redundancy where section 98(2)(c) of that Act applies; or

(ii) in any other case, the dismissal is regarded as having been for a substantial reason of a kind such as to justify the dismissal of an employee holding the position which that employee held.

(3A) In paragraph (2), the expression "changes in the workforce" includes a change to the place where employees are employed by the employer to carry on the business of the employer or to carry out work of a particular kind for the employer (and the reference to such a place has the same meaning as in section 139 of the 1996 Act).]

(4) The provisions of this regulation apply irrespective of whether the employee in question is assigned to the organised grouping of resources or employees that is, or will be, transferred.

(5) Paragraph (1) shall not apply in relation to the dismissal of any employee which was required by reason of the application of section 5 of the Aliens Restriction (Amendment) Act 1919 to his employment.

(6) Paragraph (1) shall not apply in relation to a dismissal of an employee if the application of section 94 of the 1996 Act to the dismissal of the employee is excluded by or under any provision of the 1996 Act, the 1996 Tribunals Act or the 1992 Act.

NOTES

Paras (1)–(3A): substituted for original paras (1)–(3) by the Collective Redundancies and Transfer of Undertakings (Protection of Employment) (Amendment) Regulations 2014, SI 2014/16, regs 4, 8, in relation to any case where a TUPE transfer takes place on or after 31 January 2014, and the date when any notice of termination is given by an employer or an employee in respect of any dismissal is that date or later, or, in a case where no notice is given, the date on which the termination takes effect is that date or later. The original paras (1)–(3) read as follows—

"(1) Where either before or after a relevant transfer, any employee of the transferor or transferee is dismissed, that employee shall be treated for the purposes of Part X of the 1996 Act (unfair dismissal) as unfairly dismissed if the sole or principal reason for his dismissal is—

(a) the transfer itself; or

(b) a reason connected with the transfer that is not an economic, technical or organisational reason entailing changes in the workforce.

(2) This paragraph applies where the sole or principal reason for the dismissal is a reason connected with the transfer that is an economic, technical or organisational reason entailing changes in the workforce of either the transferor or the transferee before or after a relevant transfer.

(3) Where paragraph (2) applies—

(a) paragraph (1) shall not apply;

(b) without prejudice to the application of section 98(4) of the 1996 Act (test of fair dismissal), the dismissal shall, for the purposes of sections 98(1) and 135 of that Act (reason for dismissal), be regarded as having been for redundancy where section 98(2)(c) of that Act applies, or otherwise for a substantial reason of a kind such as to justify the dismissal of an employee holding the position which that employee held.".

[18.147]

8 Insolvency

(1) If at the time of a relevant transfer the transferor is subject to relevant insolvency proceedings paragraphs (2) to (6) apply.

(2) In this regulation "relevant employee" means an employee of the transferor—

(a) whose contract of employment transfers to the transferee by virtue of the operation of these Regulations; or

(b) whose employment with the transferor is terminated before the time of the relevant transfer in the circumstances described in regulation 7(1).

(3) The relevant statutory scheme specified in paragraph (4)(b) (including that sub-paragraph as applied by paragraph 5 of Schedule 1) shall apply in the case of a relevant employee irrespective of the fact that the qualifying requirement that the employee's employment has been terminated is not met and for those purposes the date of the transfer shall be treated as the date of the termination and the transferor shall be treated as the employer.

(4) In this regulation the "relevant statutory schemes" are—

(a) Chapter VI of Part XI of the 1996 Act;

(b) Part XII of the 1996 Act.

(5) Regulation 4 shall not operate to transfer liability for the sums payable to the relevant employee under the relevant statutory schemes.

(6) In this regulation "relevant insolvency proceedings" means insolvency proceedings which have been opened in relation to the transferor not with a view to the liquidation of the assets of the transferor and which are under the supervision of an insolvency practitioner.

(7) Regulations 4 and 7 do not apply to any relevant transfer where the transferor is the subject of bankruptcy proceedings or any analogous insolvency proceedings which have been instituted with a view to the liquidation of the assets of the transferor and are under the supervision of an insolvency practitioner.

[18.148]

9 Variations of contract where transferors are subject to relevant insolvency proceedings

(1) If at the time of a relevant transfer the transferor is subject to relevant insolvency proceedings these Regulations shall not prevent the transferor or transferee (or an insolvency practitioner) and appropriate representatives of assigned employees agreeing to permitted variations.

(2) For the purposes of this regulation "appropriate representatives" are—

(a) if the employees are of a description in respect of which an independent trade union is recognised by their employer, representatives of the trade union; or

(b) in any other case, whichever of the following employee representatives the employer chooses—

(i) employee representatives appointed or elected by the assigned employees (whether they make the appointment or election alone or with others) otherwise than for the purposes of this regulation, who (having regard to the purposes for, and the method by which they were appointed or elected) have authority from those employees to agree permitted variations to contracts of employment on their behalf;

(ii) employee representatives elected by assigned employees (whether they make the appointment or election alone or with others) for these particular purposes, in an election satisfying requirements identical to those contained in regulation 14 except those in regulation 14(1)(d).

(3) An individual may be an appropriate representative for the purposes of both this regulation and regulation 13 provided that where the representative is not a trade union representative he is either elected by or has authority from assigned employees (within the meaning of this regulation) and affected employees (as described in regulation 13(1)).

(4) (*Amends the Trade Union and Labour Relations (Consolidation) Act 1992, s 168.*)

(5) Where assigned employees are represented by non-trade union representatives—

(a) the agreement recording a permitted variation must be in writing and signed by each of the representatives who have made it or, where that is not reasonably practicable, by a duly authorised agent of that representative; and

(b) the employer must, before the agreement is made available for signature, provide all employees to whom it is intended to apply on the date on which it is to come into effect with copies of the text of the agreement and such guidance as those employees might reasonably require in order to understand it fully.

(6) A permitted variation shall take effect as a term or condition of the assigned employee's contract of employment in place, where relevant, of any term or condition which it varies.

(7) In this regulation—

"assigned employees" means those employees assigned to the organised grouping of resources or employees that is the subject of a relevant transfer;

"permitted variation" is a variation to the contract of employment of an assigned employee where—

[(a) the sole or principal reason for the variation is the transfer and not a reason referred to in regulation 4(5)(a); and]

(b) it is designed to safeguard employment opportunities by ensuring the survival of the undertaking, business or part of the undertaking or business that is the subject of the relevant transfer;

"relevant insolvency proceedings" has the meaning given to the expression by regulation 8(6).

NOTES

Para (7): sub-para (a) substituted by the Collective Redundancies and Transfer of Undertakings (Protection of Employment) (Amendment) Regulations 2014, SI 2014/16, regs 4, 9, in relation to any case where the TUPE transfer takes place on or after 31 January 2014, and the permitted variation is agreed on or after 31st January 2014. The original sub-para (a) read as follows—

"(a) the sole or principal reason for it is the transfer itself or a reason connected with the transfer that is not an economic, technical or organisational reason entailing changes in the workforce; and".

[18.149]
10 Pensions

(1) Regulations 4 and 5 shall not apply—

(a) to so much of a contract of employment or collective agreement as relates to an occupational pension scheme within the meaning of the Pension Schemes Act 1993; or

(b) to any rights, powers, duties or liabilities under or in connection with any such contract or subsisting by virtue of any such agreement and relating to such a scheme or otherwise arising in connection with that person's employment and relating to such a scheme.

(2) For the purposes of paragraphs (1) and (3), any provisions of an occupational pension scheme which do not relate to benefits for old age, invalidity or survivors shall not be treated as being part of the scheme.

(3) An employee whose contract of employment is transferred in the circumstances described in regulation 4(1) shall not be entitled to bring a claim against the transferor for—

(a) breach of contract; or

(b) constructive unfair dismissal under section 95(1)(c) of the 1996 Act,

arising out of a loss or reduction in his rights under an occupational pension scheme in consequence of the transfer, save insofar as the alleged breach of contract or dismissal (as the case may be) occurred prior to the date on which these Regulations took effect.

[18.150]
11 Notification of Employee Liability Information

(1) The transferor shall notify to the transferee the employee liability information of any person employed by him who is assigned to the organised grouping of resources or employees that is the subject of a relevant transfer—

(a) in writing; or

(b) by making it available to him in a readily accessible form.

(2) In this regulation and in regulation 12 "employee liability information" means—

(a) the identity and age of the employee;

(b) those particulars of employment that an employer is obliged to give to an employee pursuant to section 1 of the 1996 Act;

(c) information of any—

(i) disciplinary procedure taken against an employee;

(ii) grievance procedure taken by an employee,

within the previous two years, in circumstances where [a Code of Practice issued under Part IV of the Trade Union and Labour Relations (Consolidation) Act 1992 which relates exclusively or primarily to the resolution of disputes applies];

(d) information of any court or tribunal case, claim or action—

(i) brought by an employee against the transferor, within the previous two years;

(ii) that the transferor has reasonable grounds to believe that an employee may bring against the transferee, arising out of the employee's employment with the transferor; and

(e) information of any collective agreement which will have effect after the transfer, in its application in relation to the employee, pursuant to regulation 5(a).

(3) Employee liability information shall contain information as at a specified date not more than fourteen days before the date on which the information is notified to the transferee.

(4) The duty to provide employee liability information in paragraph (1) shall include a duty to provide employee liability information of any person who would have been employed by the transferor and assigned to the organised grouping of resources or employees that is the subject of a relevant transfer immediately before the transfer if he had not been dismissed in the circumstances described in regulation 7(1), including, where the transfer is effected by a series of two or more transactions, a person so employed and assigned or who would have been so employed and assigned immediately before any of those transactions.

(5) Following notification of the employee liability information in accordance with this regulation, the transferor shall notify the transferee in writing of any change in the employee liability information.

(6) A notification under this regulation shall be given not less than [28 days] before the relevant transfer or, if special circumstances make this not reasonably practicable, as soon as reasonably practicable thereafter.

(7) A notification under this regulation may be given—

(a) in more than one instalment;

(b) indirectly, through a third party.

NOTES

Para (2): words in square brackets in sub-para (c) substituted by the Transfer of Undertakings (Protection of Employment) (Amendment) Regulations 2009, SI 2009/592, reg 2(1), (2).

Para (6): words in square brackets substituted for original words "fourteen days" by the Collective Redundancies and Transfer of Undertakings (Protection of Employment) (Amendment) Regulations 2014, SI 2014/16, regs 4, 10, in relation to a TUPE transfer which takes place on or after 1 May 2014.

[18.151]

12 Remedy for failure to notify employee liability information

(1) On or after a relevant transfer, the transferee may present a complaint to an employment tribunal that the transferor has failed to comply with any provision of regulation 11.

(2) An employment tribunal shall not consider a complaint under this regulation unless it is presented—

(a) before the end of the period of three months beginning with the date of the relevant transfer;

(b) within such further period as the tribunal considers reasonable in a case where it is satisfied that it was not reasonably practicable for the complaint to be presented before the end of that period of three months.

[(2A) Regulation 16A (extension of time limits to facilitate conciliation before institution of proceedings) applies for the purposes of paragraph (2).]

(3) Where an employment tribunal finds a complaint under paragraph (1) well-founded, the tribunal—

(a) shall make a declaration to that effect; and

(b) may make an award of compensation to be paid by the transferor to the transferee.

(4) The amount of the compensation shall be such as the tribunal considers just and equitable in all the circumstances, subject to paragraph (5), having particular regard to—

(a) any loss sustained by the transferee which is attributable to the matters complained of; and

(b) the terms of any contract between the transferor and the transferee relating to the transfer under which the transferor may be liable to pay any sum to the transferee in respect of a failure to notify the transferee of employee liability information.

(5) Subject to paragraph (6), the amount of compensation awarded under paragraph (3) shall be not less than £500 per employee in respect of whom the transferor has failed to comply with a provision of regulation 11, unless the tribunal considers it just and equitable, in all the circumstances, to award a lesser sum.

(6) In ascertaining the loss referred to in paragraph (4)(a) the tribunal shall apply the same rule concerning the duty of a person to mitigate his loss as applies to any damages recoverable under the common law of England and Wales, Northern Ireland or Scotland, as applicable.

(7) [Sections 18A to 18C] of the 1996 Tribunals Act (conciliation) shall apply to the right conferred by this regulation and to proceedings under this regulation as it applies to the rights conferred by that Act and the employment tribunal proceedings mentioned in that Act.

NOTES

Para (2A): inserted by the Enterprise and Regulatory Reform Act 2013 (Consequential Amendments) (Employment) (No 2) Order 2014, SI 2014/853, arts 2(1), (2), 3, with effect in any case where the worker concerned complies with the requirement in the Employment Tribunals Act 1996, s 18A(1) on or after 20 April 2014.

Para (7): words in square brackets substituted by the Enterprise and Regulatory Reform Act 2013 (Consequential Amendments) (Employment) Order 2014, SI 2014/386, art 2, Schedule, paras 36, 37.

[18.152]

13 Duty to inform and consult representatives

(1) In this regulation and regulations [13A] 14 and 15 references to affected employees, in relation to a relevant transfer, are to any employees of the transferor or the transferee (whether or not assigned to the organised grouping of resources or employees that is the subject of a relevant transfer) who may be affected by the transfer or may be affected by measures taken in connection with it; and references to the employer shall be construed accordingly.

(2) Long enough before a relevant transfer to enable the employer of any affected employees to consult the appropriate representatives of any affected employees, the employer shall inform those representatives of—

(a) the fact that the transfer is to take place, the date or proposed date of the transfer and the reasons for it;

(b) the legal, economic and social implications of the transfer for any affected employees;

(c) the measures which he envisages he will, in connection with the transfer, take in relation to any affected employees or, if he envisages that no measures will be so taken, that fact; and

(d) if the employer is the transferor, the measures, in connection with the transfer, which he envisages the transferee will take in relation to any affected employees who will become employees of the transferee after the transfer by virtue of regulation 4 or, if he envisages that no measures will be so taken, that fact.

[(2A) Where information is to be supplied under paragraph (2) by an employer—

(a) this must include suitable information relating to the use of agency workers (if any) by that employer; and.

(b) "suitable information relating to the use of agency workers" means—

(i) the number of agency workers working temporarily for and under the supervision and direction of the employer;.

(ii) the parts of the employer's undertaking in which those agency workers are working; and.

(iii) the type of work those agency workers are carrying out.]

(3) For the purposes of this regulation the appropriate representatives of any affected employees are—

(a) if the employees are of a description in respect of which an independent trade union is recognised by their employer, representatives of the trade union; or

(b) in any other case, whichever of the following employee representatives the employer chooses—

(i) employee representatives appointed or elected by the affected employees otherwise than for the purposes of this regulation, who (having regard to the purposes for, and the method by which they were appointed or elected) have authority from those employees to receive information and to be consulted about the transfer on their behalf;

(ii) employee representatives elected by any affected employees, for the purposes of this regulation, in an election satisfying the requirements of regulation 14(1).

(4) The transferee shall give the transferor such information at such a time as will enable the transferor to perform the duty imposed on him by virtue of paragraph (2)(d).

(5) The information which is to be given to the appropriate representatives shall be given to each of them by being delivered to them, or sent by post to an address notified by them to the employer, or (in the case of representatives of a trade union) sent by post to the trade union at the address of its head or main office.

(6) An employer of an affected employee who envisages that he will take measures in relation to an affected employee, in connection with the relevant transfer, shall consult the appropriate representatives of that employee with a view to seeking their agreement to the intended measures.

(7) In the course of those consultations the employer shall—

(a) consider any representations made by the appropriate representatives; and

(b) reply to those representations and, if he rejects any of those representations, state his reasons.

(8) The employer shall allow the appropriate representatives access to any affected employees and shall afford to those representatives such accommodation and other facilities as may be appropriate.

(9) If in any case there are special circumstances which render it not reasonably practicable for an employer to perform a duty imposed on him by any of paragraphs (2) to (7), he shall take all such steps towards performing that duty as are reasonably practicable in the circumstances.

(10) Where—

(a) the employer has invited any of the affected employee to elect employee representatives; and

(b) the invitation was issued long enough before the time when the employer is required to give information under paragraph (2) to allow them to elect representatives by that time,

the employer shall be treated as complying with the requirements of this regulation in relation to those employees if he complies with those requirements as soon as is reasonably practicable after the election of the representatives.

(11) If, after the employer has invited any affected employees to elect representatives, they fail to do so within a reasonable time, he shall give to any affected employees the information set out in paragraph (2).

(12) The duties imposed on an employer by this regulation shall apply irrespective of whether the decision resulting in the relevant transfer is taken by the employer or a person controlling the employer.

NOTES

Para (1): figure in square brackets inserted by the Collective Redundancies and Transfer of Undertakings (Protection of Employment) (Amendment) Regulations 2014, SI 2014/16, regs 4, 10(1), (5), in relation to a TUPE transfer which takes place on or after 31 July 2014.

Para (2A): inserted by the Agency Workers Regulations 2010, SI 2010/93, reg 25, Sch 2, Pt 2, paras 28, 29.

[18.153]

[13A Micro-business's duty to inform and consult where no appropriate representatives

(1) This regulation applies if, at the time when the employer is required to give information under regulation 13(2)—

(a) the employer employs fewer than 10 employees;

(b) there are no appropriate representatives within the meaning of regulation 13(3); and

(c) the employer has not invited any of the affected employees to elect employee representatives.

(2) The employer may comply with regulation 13 by performing any duty which relates to appropriate representatives as if each of the affected employees were an appropriate representative.]

NOTES

Commencement: 31 July 2014.

Inserted by the Collective Redundancies and Transfer of Undertakings (Protection of Employment) (Amendment) Regulations 2014, SI 2014/16, regs 4, 11(2), (5), in relation to a TUPE transfer which takes place on or after 31 July 2014.

[18.154]

14 Election of employee representatives

(1) The requirements for the election of employee representatives under regulation 13(3) are that—

(a) the employer shall make such arrangements as are reasonably practicable to ensure that the election is fair;

(b) the employer shall determine the number of representatives to be elected so that there are sufficient representatives to represent the interests of all affected employees having regard to the number and classes of those employees;

(c) the employer shall determine whether the affected employees should be represented either by representatives of all the affected employees or by representatives of particular classes of those employees;

(d) before the election the employer shall determine the term of office as employee representatives so that it is of sufficient length to enable information to be given and consultations under regulation 13 to be completed;

(e) the candidates for election as employee representatives are affected employees on the date of the election;

(f) no affected employee is unreasonably excluded from standing for election;

(g) all affected employees on the date of the election are entitled to vote for employee representatives;

(h) the employees entitled to vote may vote for as many candidates as there are representatives to be elected to represent them or, if there are to be representatives for particular classes of employees, may vote for as many candidates as there are representatives to be elected to represent their particular class of employee;

(i) the election is conducted so as to secure that—

(i) so far as is reasonably practicable, those voting do so in secret; and

(ii) the votes given at the election are accurately counted.

(2) Where, after an election of employee representatives satisfying the requirements of paragraph (1) has been held, one of those elected ceases to act as an employee representative and as a result any affected employees are no longer represented, those employees shall elect another representative by an election satisfying the requirements of paragraph (1)(a), (e), (f) and (i).

[18.155]

15 Failure to inform or consult

(1) Where an employer has failed to comply with a requirement of regulation 13 or regulation 14, a complaint may be presented to an employment tribunal on that ground—

(a) in the case of a failure relating to the election of employee representatives, by any of his employees who are affected employees;

(b) in the case of any other failure relating to employee representatives, by any of the employee representatives to whom the failure related;

(c) in the case of failure relating to representatives of a trade union, by the trade union; and

(d) in any other case, by any of his employees who are affected employees.

(2) If on a complaint under paragraph (1) a question arises whether or not it was reasonably practicable for an employer to perform a particular duty or as to what steps he took towards performing it, it shall be for him to show—

(a) that there were special circumstances which rendered it not reasonably practicable for him to perform the duty; and

(b) that he took all such steps towards its performance as were reasonably practicable in those circumstances.

(3) If on a complaint under paragraph (1) a question arises as to whether or not an employee representative was an appropriate representative for the purposes of regulation 13, it shall be for the employer to show that the employee representative had the necessary authority to represent the affected employees [except where the question is whether or not regulation 13A applied].

[(3A) If on a complaint under paragraph (1), a question arises as to whether or not regulation 13A applied, it is for the employer to show that the conditions in sub-paragraphs (a) and (b) of regulation 13A(1) applied at the time referred to in regulation 13A(1).]

(4) On a complaint under paragraph (1)(a) it shall be for the employer to show that the requirements in regulation 14 have been satisfied.

(5) On a complaint against a transferor that he had failed to perform the duty imposed upon him by virtue of regulation 13(2)(d) or, so far as relating thereto, regulation 13(9), he may not show that it was not reasonably practicable for him to perform the duty in question for the reason that the transferee had failed to give him the requisite information at the requisite time in accordance with regulation 13(4) unless he gives the transferee notice of his intention to show that fact; and the giving of the notice shall make the transferee a party to the proceedings.

(6) In relation to any complaint under paragraph (1), a failure on the part of a person controlling (directly or indirectly) the employer to provide information to the employer shall not constitute special circumstances rendering it not reasonably practicable for the employer to comply with such a requirement.

(7) Where the tribunal finds a complaint against a transferee under paragraph (1) well-founded it shall make a declaration to that effect and may order the transferee to pay appropriate compensation to such descriptions of affected employees as may be specified in the award.

(8) Where the tribunal finds a complaint against a transferor under paragraph (1) well-founded it shall make a declaration to that effect and may—

(a) order the transferor, subject to paragraph (9), to pay appropriate compensation to such descriptions of affected employees as may be specified in the award; or

(b) if the complaint is that the transferor did not perform the duty mentioned in paragraph (5) and the transferor (after giving due notice) shows the facts so mentioned, order the transferee to pay appropriate compensation to such descriptions of affected employees as may be specified in the award.

(9) The transferee shall be jointly and severally liable with the transferor in respect of compensation payable under sub-paragraph (8)(a) or paragraph (11).

(10) An employee may present a complaint to an employment tribunal on the ground that he is an employee of a description to which an order under paragraph (7) or (8) relates and that—

(a) in respect of an order under paragraph (7), the transferee has failed, wholly or in part, to pay him compensation in pursuance of the order;

(b) in respect of an order under paragraph (8), the transferor or transferee, as applicable, has failed, wholly or in part, to pay him compensation in pursuance of the order.

(11) Where the tribunal finds a complaint under paragraph (10) well-founded it shall order the transferor or transferee as applicable to pay the complainant the amount of compensation which it finds is due to him.

(12) An employment tribunal shall not consider a complaint under paragraph (1) or (10) unless it is presented to the tribunal before the end of the period of three months beginning with—

(a) in respect of a complaint under paragraph (1), the date on which the relevant transfer is completed; or

(b) in respect of a complaint under paragraph (10), the date of the tribunal's order under paragraph (7) or (8),

or within such further period as the tribunal considers reasonable in a case where it is satisfied that it was not reasonably practicable for the complaint to be presented before the end of the period of three months.

[(13) Regulation 16A (extension of time limits to facilitate conciliation before institution of proceedings) applies for the purposes of paragraph (12).]

NOTES

Para (3): words in square brackets inserted by the Collective Redundancies and Transfer of Undertakings (Protection of Employment) (Amendment) Regulations 2014, SI 2014/16, regs 4, 11(3), (5), in relation to a TUPE transfer which takes place on or after 31 July 2014.

Para (3A): inserted by SI 2014/16, regs 4, 11(4), (5), in relation to a TUPE transfer which takes place on or after 31 July 2014.

Para (13): added by the Enterprise and Regulatory Reform Act 2013 (Consequential Amendments) (Employment) (No 2) Order 2014, SI 2014/853, arts 2(1), (3), 3, with effect in any case where the worker concerned complies with the requirement in the Employment Tribunals Act 1996, s 18A(1) on or after 20 April 2014.

[18.156]

16 Failure to inform or consult: supplemental

(1) Section 205(1) of the 1996 Act (complaint to be sole remedy for breach of relevant rights) and [sections 18A to 18C] of the 1996 Tribunals Act (conciliation) shall apply to the rights conferred by regulation 15 and to proceedings under this regulation as they apply to the rights conferred by those Acts and the employment tribunal proceedings mentioned in those Acts.

(2) An appeal shall lie and shall lie only to the Employment Appeal Tribunal on a question of law arising from any decision of, or arising in any proceedings before, an employment tribunal under or by virtue of these Regulations; and section 11(1) of the Tribunals and Inquiries Act 1992 (appeals from certain tribunals to the High Court) shall not apply in relation to any such proceedings.

(3) "Appropriate compensation" in regulation 15 means such sum not exceeding thirteen weeks' pay for the employee in question as the tribunal considers just and equitable having regard to the seriousness of the failure of the employer to comply with his duty.

(4) Sections 220 to 228 of the 1996 Act shall apply for calculating the amount of a week's pay for any employee for the purposes of paragraph (3) and, for the purposes of that calculation, the calculation date shall be—

(a) in the case of an employee who is dismissed by reason of redundancy (within the meaning of sections 139 and 155 of the 1996 Act) the date which is the calculation date for the purposes of any entitlement of his to a redundancy payment (within the meaning of those sections) or which would be that calculation date if he were so entitled;

(b) in the case of an employee who is dismissed for any other reason, the effective date of termination (within the meaning of sections 95(1) and (2) and 97 of the 1996 Act) of his contract of employment;

(c) in any other case, the date of the relevant transfer.

NOTES

Para (1): words in square brackets substituted by the Enterprise and Regulatory Reform Act 2013 (Consequential Amendments) (Employment) Order 2014, SI 2014/386, art 2, Schedule, paras 36, 38.

[18.157]

[16A Extension of time limit to facilitate conciliation before institution of proceedings

(1) This regulation applies where these Regulations provide for it to apply for the purposes of a provision in these Regulations ("a relevant provision").

(2) In this regulation—

(a) Day A is the day on which the worker concerned complies with the requirement in subsection (1) of section 18A of the Employment Tribunals Act 1996 (requirement to contact ACAS before instituting proceedings) in relation to the matter in respect of which the proceedings are brought, and

(b) Day B is the day on which the worker concerned receives or, if earlier, is treated as receiving (by virtue of regulations made under subsection (11) of that section) the certificate issued under subsection (4) of that section.

(3) In working out when the time limit set by a relevant provision expires the period beginning with the day after Day A and ending with Day B is not to be counted.

(4) If the time limit set by a relevant provision would (if not extended by this paragraph) expire during the period beginning with Day A and ending one month after Day B, the time limit expires instead at the end of that period.

(5) Where an employment tribunal has power under these Regulations to extend the time limit set by a relevant provision, the power is exercisable in relation to that time limit as extended by this regulation.]

NOTES

Commencement: 20 April 2014.

Inserted by the Enterprise and Regulatory Reform Act 2013 (Consequential Amendments) (Employment) (No 2) Order 2014, SI 2014/853, arts 2(1), (4), 3, with effect in any case where the worker concerned complies with the requirement in the Employment Tribunals Act 1996, s 18A(1) on or after 20 April 2014.

[18.158]

17 Employers' Liability Compulsory Insurance

(1) Paragraph (2) applies where—

(a) by virtue of section 3(1)(a) or (b) of the Employers' Liability (Compulsory Insurance) Act 1969 ("the 1969 Act"), the transferor is not required by that Act to effect any insurance; or

(b) by virtue of section 3(1)(c) of the 1969 Act, the transferor is exempted from the requirement of that Act to effect insurance.

(2) Where this paragraph applies, on completion of a relevant transfer the transferor and the transferee shall be jointly and severally liable in respect of any liability referred to in section 1(1) of the 1969 Act, in so far as such liability relates to the employee's employment with the transferor.

[18.159]

18 Restriction on contracting out

Section 203 of the 1996 Act (restrictions on contracting out) shall apply in relation to these Regulations as if they were contained in that Act, save for that section shall not apply in so far as these Regulations provide for an agreement (whether a contract of employment or not) to exclude or limit the operation of these Regulations.

19 (*Amends the Employment Rights Act 1996, s 104.*)

[18.160]

20 Repeals, revocations and amendments

(1) Subject to regulation 21, the 1981 Regulations are revoked.

(2) Section 33 of, and paragraph 4 of Schedule 9 to, the Trade Union Reform and Employment Rights Act 1993 are repealed.

(3) Schedule 2 (consequential amendments) shall have effect.

[18.161]

21 Transitional provisions and savings

(1) These Regulations shall apply in relation to—

(a) a relevant transfer that takes place on or after 6 April 2006;

(b) a transfer or service provision change, not falling within sub-paragraph (a), that takes place on or after 6 April 2006 and is regarded by virtue of any enactment as a relevant transfer.

(2) The 1981 Regulations shall continue to apply in relation to—

(a) a relevant transfer (within the meaning of the 1981 Regulations) that took place before 6 April 2006;

(b) a transfer, not falling within sub-paragraph (a), that took place before 6 April 2006 and is regarded by virtue of any enactment as a relevant transfer (within the meaning of the 1981 Regulations).

(3) In respect of a relevant transfer that takes place on or after 6 April 2006, any action taken by a transferor or transferee to discharge a duty that applied to them under regulation 10 or 10A of the 1981 Regulations shall be deemed to satisfy the corresponding obligation imposed by regulations 13 and 14 of these Regulations, insofar as that action would have discharged those obligations had the action taken place on or after 6 April 2006.

(4) The duty on a transferor to provide a transferee with employee liability information shall not apply in the case of a relevant transfer that takes place on or before 19 April 2006.

(5) Regulations 13, 14, 15 and 16 shall not apply in the case of a service provision change that is not also a transfer of an undertaking, business or part of an undertaking or business that takes place on or before 4 May 2006.

(6) The repeal of paragraph 4 of Schedule 9 to the Trade Union Reform and Employment Rights Act 1993 does not affect the continued operation of that paragraph so far as it remains capable of having effect.

SCHEDULES 1 AND 2

(*Sch 1 applies to Northern Ireland only; Sch 2 contains consequential amendments, outside the scope of this work.*)

OCCUPATIONAL PENSION SCHEMES (FRAUD COMPENSATION LEVY) REGULATIONS 2006

(SI 2006/558)

NOTES

Made: 1 March 2006

Authority: Pensions Act 1995, ss 10(3), 75(10), 89(2), 124(1); Pensions Act 2004, ss 189(1), (4), (6), (11), 315(2), (5), 318(1).

Commencement: 1 April 2006.

[18.162]

1 Citation and commencement

These Regulations may be cited as the Occupational Pension Schemes (Fraud Compensation Levy) Regulations 2006 and shall come into force on 1st April 2006.

[18.163]

2 Interpretation

In these Regulations—

"the Act" means the Pensions Act 2004;

. . .

"scheme" means an occupational pension scheme to which Chapter 4 of Part 2 of the Act (fraud compensation) applies;

. . .

"stakeholder pension scheme" means a stakeholder pension scheme within the meaning of section 1 of the Welfare Reform and Pensions Act 1999 (meaning of stakeholder pension scheme) which is established under a trust;

. . .

NOTES

Definitions omitted outside the scope of this work.

3–6 (*Outside the scope of this work.*)

[18.164]

7 Waiver

(1) Where any fraud compensation levy is payable, the Board shall waive payment of an amount payable by way of such levy if the trustees or managers of the scheme confirm in writing to the Board—

(a) that—

(i) there is no employer in relation to the scheme, or

(ii) the employer is insolvent; and

(b) in the case of a scheme in which all the benefits that may be provided (other than death benefits) are money purchase benefits, there are insufficient unallocated assets in the scheme to meet its liabilities in respect of the payment of the levy in full.

(2) For the purposes of paragraph (1), an employer is insolvent if an insolvency event, within the meaning of section 121 of the Act (insolvency events), has occurred in relation to him.

(3) Paragraph (1) shall not apply in the case of a stakeholder pension scheme.

8–12 (*Regs 8–11 outside the scope of this work; reg 12 amends the Employer Debt Regulations 2005, SI 2005/678, reg 10 at* **[18.123]**.)

PRODUCER RESPONSIBILITY OBLIGATIONS (PACKAGING WASTE) REGULATIONS 2007

(SI 2007/871)

NOTES

Made: 15 March 2007.
Authority: European Communities Act 1972, s 2(2); Environment Act 1995, ss 93–95.
Commencement: 16 March 2007.

PART I
GENERAL

[18.165]
1 Citation, commencement and extent

(1) These Regulations may be cited as the Producer Responsibility Obligations (Packaging Waste) Regulations 2007 and shall come into force on the day after the day on which they are made.

(2) These Regulations extend to Great Britain.

2–19 *(Regs 2, 3, 4–19 (Pts II, III) outside the scope of this work.)*

PART IV
RECORDS, RETURNS AND CERTIFICATE

20–22 *(Outside the scope of this work.)*

[18.166]
[22A Notification of winding-up, receivership, administration, etc

(1) This regulation applies to—
- (a) the operator of a scheme;
- (b) a producer; or
- (c) a reprocessor or an exporter accredited in accordance with Part 5 (accreditation of reprocessors and exporters).

(2) A company or limited liability partnership to which this regulation applies shall inform the appropriate Agency as soon as is practicable upon becoming aware that one or more relevant circumstances apply or are about to apply to them.

(3) The operator of a scheme must inform the appropriate Agency as soon as is practicable upon becoming aware that one or more relevant circumstances apply or are about to apply to the scheme it operates.

(4) For the purposes of this regulation "relevant circumstances" are—
- (a) a winding-up order has been made or a resolution for voluntary winding-up has been passed;
- (b) a determination for a voluntary winding-up has been made;
- (c) a receiver or a manager of the company or limited liability partnership's undertaking has been duly appointed;
- (d) its undertaking has entered administration;
- (e) a voluntary arrangement proposed for the purposes of Part 1 of the Insolvency Act 1986 has been approved under that Part of the Act.]

NOTES

Inserted by the Producer Responsibility Obligations (Packaging Waste) (Amendment) Regulations 2010, SI 2010/2849, regs 2, 11.

23–41 *((Pts V–X) Outside the scope of this work.)*

SCHEDULES 1–10

(Outside the scope of this work.)

REGULATED COVERED BONDS REGULATIONS 2008

(SI 2008/346)

NOTES

Made: 13 February 2008.
Authority: European Communities Act 1972, s 2(2).
Commencement: 6 March 2008.
Modification: these Regulations are applied, with modifications, in so far as they relate to bank insolvency or administration under the Banking Act 2009, Pts 2, 3, by the Banking Act 2009 (Parts 2 and 3 Consequential Amendments) Order 2009, SI 2009/317, art 3, Schedule at **[7.86]**, **[7.92]**.

ARRANGEMENT OF REGULATIONS

PART 1
INTRODUCTION

1 Citation, commencement and interpretation . . . [18.167]
2 Eligible property . . . [18.168]
3 Asset Pool . . . [18.169]
4 Owner . . . [18.170]
5 Connected person . . . [18.171]

PART 4
ISSUERS

17 General requirements . . . [18.172]
17A Asset pool monitor . . . [18.173]

PART 5
OWNERS

24 . . . [18.174]

PART 6
PRIORITY OF PAYMENT

27 Priority in a winding up . . . [18.175]
28 Realisation of a charge . . . [18.176]
29 . . . [18.177]

PART 9
MISCELLANEOUS

46 Modifications of primary and secondary legislation . . . [18.178]

SCHEDULES

Schedule—Modifications to Primary and Secondary Legislation
Part 1—Primary Legislation . . . [18.179]
Part 2—Secondary Legislation . . . [18.180]

PART 1
INTRODUCTION

[18.167]

1 Citation, commencement and interpretation

(1) These Regulations may be cited as the Regulated Covered Bonds Regulations 2008 and come into force on 6th March 2008.

(2) In these Regulations—

"the 1986 Act" means the Insolvency Act 1986;

"the 2006 Act" means the Companies Act 2006;

"the 1989 Order" means the Insolvency (Northern Ireland) Order 1989;

"the Act" means the Financial Services and Markets Act 2000;

"asset" means any property, right, entitlement or interest;

"asset pool" has the meaning given by regulation 3;

"the Authority" means the [Financial Conduct Authority];

. . .

["building society" means a building society incorporated (or deemed to be incorporated) under the Building Societies Act 1986;]

["capital requirements regulation" means Regulation (EU) 575/2013 of the European Parliament and of the Council of 26 June 2013 on prudential requirements for credit institutions and investment firms and amending Regulation (EU) No 648/2012;]

"centre of main interests" has the same meaning as in Article 3(1) of [Regulation (EU) 2015/848 of the European Parliament and of the Council of 20 May 2015 on insolvency proceedings];

"connected person" has the meaning given by regulation 5;

"covered bond" means a bond in relation to which the claims attaching to that bond are guaranteed to be paid by an owner from an asset pool it owns;

["deposit" has the meaning given in article 5(2) of the Financial Services and Markets Act 2000 (Regulated Activities) Order 2001;]

"eligible property" has the meaning given by regulation 2;

["government stock" means stock or bonds of any of the descriptions included in Part 1 of Schedule 11 to the Finance Act 1942;]

"hedging agreement" means an agreement entered into or asset held as protection against possible financial loss;

"issuer" means a person which issues a covered bond;

["liquid assets" means—

(a) government stock or treasury bills issued by Her Majesty's Government in the United Kingdom and other specified government securities which comply with [Article 129(1)(a) or (b) of the capital requirements regulation];

(b) deposits in sterling or another specified currency in an account held in the name of the owner with the issuer or with a specified credit institution which comply with the requirements set out in [Article 129(1)(c) of the capital requirements regulation],

and "specified" for the purposes of this definition means specified by the Authority in guidance issued under regulation 42;]

["mixed asset class bond" means a mixed asset class regulated covered bond included in Part one of the register of regulated covered bonds;]

"owner" has the meaning given by regulation 4;

"programme" means issues, or series of issues, of covered bonds which have substantially similar terms and are subject to a framework contract or contracts;

["reference rate" means a rate used to set the interest rates charged to borrowers in relation to a loan included in the asset pool;]

["registered office" in relation to a building society means its principal office;]

"register of issuers" means the register maintained under regulation 7(1)(a);

"register of regulated covered bonds" means the register maintained under regulation 7(1)(b);

"regulated covered bond" means a covered bond or a programme of covered bonds, as the case may be, which is admitted to the register of regulated covered bonds;

"relevant asset pool" in relation to a regulated covered bond means the asset pool from which the claims attaching to that bond are guaranteed to be paid by the owner of that pool in the event of the failure of the issuer;

["the relevant date" is the date on which the Regulated Covered Bonds (Amendment) Regulations 2011 come into force;]

"relevant persons" has the meaning given by regulation 27(2).

["single asset class bond" means a single asset class regulated covered bond included in Part 2 of the register of regulated covered bonds;]

["total principal amounts outstanding" means—

(a) in relation to loans, the sum of the original amounts advanced on the loan and any further advances, less any repayments of principal made on the loan;

(b) in relation to other assets, the total amount of principal which remains due to be repaid in relation to the asset;]

. . .

(3) Unless otherwise defined, any expression used in these Regulations and in Article 22(4) of directive 85/611/EEC of the Council of 20 December 1985 relating to undertakings for collective investment in transferable securities has the same meaning as in that Article of that Directive.

NOTES

Para (2): words in square brackets in definition "the Authority" substituted by the Financial Services Act 2012 (Consequential Amendments and Transitional Provisions) Order 2013, SI 2013/472, art 3, Sch 2, para 134(a); first definition omitted revoked, and definition "capital requirements regulation" inserted by the Capital Requirements Regulations 2013, SI 2013/3115, reg 46(1), Sch 2, Pt 3, para 69(1), (2); definition "building society" inserted and definition "registered office" substituted by the Regulated Covered Bonds (Amendment) Regulations 2008, SI 2008/1714, reg 2(1), (2); in definition "centre of main interests" words in square brackets substituted by the Insolvency (Miscellaneous Amendments) Regulations 2017, SI 2017/1119, reg 2, Sch 5, para 2; definitions "deposit", "government stock", "mixed asset class bond", "reference rate", "the relevant date", "single asset class bond" and "total principal amounts outstanding" inserted by the Regulated Covered Bonds (Amendment) Regulations 2011, SI 2011/2859, reg 2(1), (2); definition "liquid assets" inserted by SI 2011/2859, reg 2(1), (2), words in square brackets substituted, by SI 2013/3115, reg 46(1), Sch 2, Pt 3, para 69(1), (2); definition "the Tribunal" (omitted) revoked by the Transfer of Tribunal Functions Order 2010, SI 2010/22, art 5(2), Sch 3, paras 148, 149, subject to transitional provisions and savings in art 5(4) of, and Sch 5 to, the 2010 Order.

[18.168]

2 Eligible property

(1) [In these Regulations, "eligible property" in relation to a mixed asset class bond or programme means any interest in—]

[(a) subject to paragraph (1B), eligible assets specified in and compliant with the requirements contained in [Article 129 of the capital requirements regulation];]

(b) loans to a registered social landlord or, in Northern Ireland, to a registered housing association where the loans are secured—

(i) over housing accommodation; or

(ii) by rental income from housing accommodation;

(c) loans to a person ("A") which provides loans directly to a registered social landlord or, in Northern Ireland, to a registered housing association, where the loans to A are secured directly or indirectly—

(i) over housing accommodation; or

(ii) by rental income from housing accommodation;

(d) loans to a project company of a project which is a public-private partnership project where the loans are secured by payments made by a public body with step-in rights;

(e) loans to a person ("B") which provides loans directly to a project company of a project which is a public-private partnership project where the loans to B are secured directly or indirectly by payments made by a public body with step-in rights;

[(f) other liquid assets].

Part 18 Miscellaneous SIs

[(1A) In these Regulations, "eligible property" in relation to a single asset class bond or programme means, subject to paragraph (1B), any interest in eligible assets specified in and compliant with the requirements of one (and only one) of the following classes—

(a) class 1 (public sector assets): eligible assets referred to in subparagraph (a) and (b) of [Article 129(1) of the capital requirements regulation], assets referred to in sub-paragraph (b), (c), (d) and (e) of paragraph (1) above and other liquid assets;

(b) class 2 (residential mortgage assets): eligible assets referred to in [sub-paragraph (d) and (e) of Article 129(1) of the capital requirements regulation], and liquid assets;

(c) class 3 (commercial mortgage assets): eligible assets referred to in [sub-paragraph (f) of Article 129(1) of the capital requirements regulation] and liquid assets.

(1B) Assets in the following categories—

(a) exposures to a body which does not qualify for credit quality step 1 on the credit quality assessment scale set out in [Part Three, Title II, Chapter 2 of the capital requirements regulations]; and

(b) senior units, issued by [French Fonds Communs de Titrisation] or equivalent securitisation entities governed by the laws of the United Kingdom or an EEA State, securitising residential real estate or commercial real estate exposures;

shall not be eligible property for the purposes of paragraph (1)(a) or (1A).]

(2) Eligible property (and any relevant security) must be situated in an EEA state, Switzerland, the United States of America, Japan, Canada, Australia, New Zealand, the Channel Islands or the Isle of Man.

(3) In this regulation—

"the 1996 Act" means the Housing Act 1996;

"the 2001 Act" means the Housing (Scotland) Act 2001;

"housing accommodation"—

(a) in England and Wales, has the meaning given by section 63 of the 1996 Act (minor modifications: Part 1);

(b) in Scotland, has the meaning given by section 111 of the 2001 Act (interpretation); and

(c) in Northern Ireland, has the meaning given by Article 2 of the Housing (Northern Ireland) Order 1981;

"project company" has the meaning given by paragraph 4H of Schedule A1 to the 1986 Act or, in Northern Ireland, paragraph 12 of Schedule A1 to the 1989 Order;

"public body" means a body which exercises public functions;

"public-private partnership project" has the meaning given by paragraph 4I of Schedule A1 to the 1986 Act or, in Northern Ireland, paragraph 13 of Schedule A1 to the 1989 Order;

"registered housing association" means a body registered as a housing association under Chapter II of Part II of the Housing (Northern Ireland) Order 1992;

"registered social landlord"—

(a) in England and Wales, means [a private registered provider of social housing or] a body registered as a social landlord under Part 1 of the 1996 Act; and

(b) in Scotland, means a body registered as a social landlord under [Part 2 of the Housing (Scotland) Act 2010];

"step-in rights" has the meaning given by paragraph 4J of Schedule A1 to the 1986 Act or, in Northern Ireland, paragraph 14 of Schedule A1 to the 1989 Order.

(4) Unless otherwise defined, any expression used in this regulation and the [capital requirements regulation has the same meaning as in that regulation].

NOTES

Para (1): words in first pair of square brackets and whole of sub-para (a) substituted, sub-para (f) added, by the Regulated Covered Bonds (Amendment) Regulations 2011, SI 2011/2859, reg 2(1), (3)(a); words in square brackets in sub-para (a) substituted by the Capital Requirements Regulations 2013, SI 2013/3115, reg 46(1), Sch 2, Pt 3, para 69(1), (3)(a).

Paras (1A), (1B): inserted by SI 2011/2859, reg 2(1), (3)(b); words in square brackets substituted by SI 2013/3115, reg 46(1), Sch 2, Pt 3, para 69(1), (3)(b)–(f).

Para (3): in definition "registered social landlord" words in first pair of square brackets inserted by the Housing and Regeneration Act 2008 (Consequential Provisions) (No 2) Order 2010, SI 2010/671, art 4, Sch 1, para 68, subject to transitional and savings provisions in art 5 of, and Sch 2, paras 1, 2, 5, 6 to, the 2010 Order; words in second pair of square brackets substituted by the Housing (Scotland) Act 2010 (Consequential Provisions and Modifications) Order 2012, SI 2012/700, art 4, Schedule, Pt 2, para 18.

Para (4): words in square brackets substituted by SI 2013/3115, reg 46(1), Sch 2, Pt 3, para 69(1), (3)(g).

[18.169]

3 Asset Pool

(1) Subject to paragraph (2), in these Regulations an "asset pool" comprises the following assets—

(a) sums derived from the issue of regulated covered bonds and lent to the owner in accordance with regulation 16;

(b) eligible property which is acquired by the owner using sums lent to it in accordance with regulation 22;

(c) eligible property transferred to the asset pool by the issuer or a connected person to enable the issuer or owner, as the case may be, to comply with—

(i) the requirements specified in regulation 17(2);

(ii) a direction of the Authority under regulation 30; or

(iii) an order of the court under regulation 33;

(d) eligible property transferred to the asset pool by the issuer or a connected person for the purpose of over collateralisation;
(e) contracts relating to the asset pool or to a regulated covered bond;
(f) eligible property acquired by the owner using sums derived from any of the assets referred to in sub-paragraph (b), (c), (d) or (e);
(g) sums derived from any of the assets referred to in sub-paragraph (b), (c), (d), (e) or (f); and
(h) sums lent by persons (other than the issuer) to the owner to enable it to comply with the requirements specified in regulation 24(1)(a).

(2) Any of the assets referred to in sub-paragraphs (a) to (f) and (h) of paragraph (1) may only form part of an asset pool at any time if they are recorded at that time, pursuant to arrangements made in accordance with regulation 17, 23 or 24, as being in that pool.

(3) In paragraph (1), "over collateralisation" means the provision of additional assets that assist the payment from the relevant asset pool of claims attaching to a regulated covered bond in the event of the failure of the issuer.

[18.170]
4 Owner

In these Regulations "owner" means a person which—
(a) owns an asset pool; and
(b) issues a guarantee to pay from that asset pool claims attaching to a regulated covered bond in the event of a failure of the issuer of that bond.

[18.171]
5 Connected person

(1) In these Regulations "connected person" in relation to an issuer means a person which—
(a) is—
(i) a parent undertaking of the issuer;
(ii) a subsidiary undertaking of the issuer; or
(iii) a subsidiary undertaking of a parent undertaking of the issuer;
(b) has its registered office in the United Kingdom; and
(c) either—
(i) has its centre of main interests in the United Kingdom; or
(ii) is authorised under Part 4 of the Act (permission to carry on regulated activities) to carry on the regulated activity referred to in article 5 (accepting deposits) of the Financial Services and Markets Act 2000 (Regulated Activities) Order 2001.

(2) In paragraph (1) "parent undertaking" and "subsidiary undertaking" have the meanings given by section 1162 of the 2006 Act (parent and subsidiary undertakings).

6–14 *((Pts 2, 3) outside the scope of this work.)*

PART 4
ISSUERS

15, 16 *(Outside the scope of this work.)*

[18.172]
17 General requirements

(1) An issuer of a regulated covered bond must enter into arrangements with the owner of the relevant asset pool for the maintenance and administration of that pool.

(2) The arrangements must provide for the following requirements—
(a) a record is kept of each asset in the asset pool;
(b) the asset pool is, during the whole period of validity of the regulated covered bond, capable of covering—
(i) claims attaching to the bond; and
(ii) sums required for the maintenance, administration and winding up of the asset pool;
(c) there is timely payment of claims attaching to the bond to the regulated covered bond holder;
(d) the asset pool is of sufficient quality to give investors confidence that in the event of the failure of the issuer there will be a low risk of default in the timely payment by the owner of claims attaching to the bond;
[(e) the eligible property in the asset pool of a single asset class bond consists only of eligible property of the same class as the eligible property included in the asset pool of the regulated covered bond when it was registered;
(f) the total principal amounts outstanding in respect of eligible property in the asset pool is more than 108% of the total principal amounts outstanding in relation to the bonds to which the asset pool relates; and
(g) the total amount of interest payable in the period of twelve months following any given date in respect of eligible property in the asset pool is not less than the interest which would be payable in relation to the regulated covered bonds issued under the programme in that period, assuming that the reference rates applicable on the given date do not change in that period.]

[(2A) In determining whether the requirements in subparagraphs (e) and (f) of paragraph (2) are satisfied, no account shall be taken of eligible property which is liquid assets.

Part 18 Miscellaneous SIs

(2B) In ensuring that the arrangements satisfy the requirements in subparagraphs (f) and (g) of paragraph (2), the issuer may take account of any hedging agreements which it has entered into in relation to the assets in the asset pool and the regulated covered bonds.

(2C) Nothing in this regulation shall prevent the Authority directing an issuer to observe additional requirements in relation to its asset pool.]

(3) This regulation does not apply in the event of the insolvency of the issuer.

NOTES

Para (2): word omitted from sub-para (c) revoked and sub-paras (e)–(g) inserted, by the Regulated Covered Bonds (Amendment) Regulations 2011, SI 2011/2859, reg 2(1), (9)(a), (b).

Paras (2A)–(2C): inserted by SI 2011/2859, reg 2(1), (9)(c).

[18.173]

[17A Asset pool monitor

(1) An issuer of a regulated covered bond must appoint an asset pool monitor for each asset pool maintained for the regulated covered bonds it has issued.

(2) The person appointed as asset pool monitor must—

(a) be eligible for appointment as a statutory auditor of the issuer under Part 42 of the Companies Act 2006; and

(b) not be disqualified from acting as a statutory auditor of the issuer by section 1214 of that Act (independence requirement).

(3) The asset pool monitor shall—

(a) inspect the compliance of the issuer with the requirements in regulations 16 and 17, and in particular—

(i) the extent to which the asset pool satisfies the conditions set out in regulation 17(2); and

(ii) the accuracy of the records kept in relation to each asset in the asset pool,

once every twelve months; and

(b) prepare an annual report in accordance with guidance issued by the Authority on the steps the issuer has taken to comply with regulations 16 and 17, and on the quality of the assets in the asset pool.

(4) Guidance issued to the asset pool monitor of an individual issuer under paragraph (3)(b) may identify particular issues to be addressed in the report for that issuer.

(5) A copy of the report prepared by the asset pool monitor shall be delivered to the Authority at such time as the Authority may direct.

(6) If it appears to the asset pool monitor that the issuer has failed to comply with the requirements set out in regulation 17, or that the issuer has not provided the monitor with all the information and explanations to which the monitor is entitled under this regulation, the asset pool monitor shall report in writing on that fact to the Authority as soon as possible.

(7) The asset pool monitor—

(a) has a right of access at all times to all books, accounts and vouchers of the issuer and of the owner of the relevant asset pool which are related to that asset pool, in whatever form they are held, and

(b) may require any of the persons referred to in paragraph (8) to provide such information and explanations as the asset pool monitor thinks necessary for the performance of the monitor's duties under this regulation.

(8) The persons referred to in paragraph (7)(b) are—

(a) any officer or employee of the issuer or the owner;

(b) any person holding or accountable for any of the books, accounts or vouchers of the issuer or the owner;

(c) any person who fell within either sub-paragraph (a) or (b) at a time to which the information or explanations required by the asset pool monitor relates or relate.

(9) A statement made by a person in response to a requirement under this regulation may not be used in evidence against him in criminal proceedings, except proceedings for an offence under section 398 of the Act in connection with the giving of information pursuant to requirements imposed by or under these Regulations.

(10) On the insolvency of the issuer of a regulated covered bond—

(a) the asset pool monitor appointed by the issuer shall continue to act as asset pool monitor for the owner of the relevant asset pool;

(b) any subsequent appointment of an asset pool monitor required under paragraph (1) of this regulation shall be made by the owner of the relevant asset pool;

(c) references in paragraphs (2), (3), (4) and (6) to the issuer shall be understood as references to the owner of the relevant asset pool; and

(d) references in paragraph (3) to regulations 16 and 17 shall be understood as references to regulation 24.]

NOTES

Inserted by the Regulated Covered Bonds (Amendment) Regulations 2011, SI 2011/2859, reg 2(1), (10).

18–20 (*Outside the scope of this work.*)

PART 5
OWNERS

21–23 (*Outside the scope of this work.*)

[18.174]
24

(1) On the insolvency of the issuer of a regulated covered bond, the owner of the relevant asset pool must—

(a) make arrangements for the maintenance and administration of the asset pool which provide for the following requirements—
  (i) a record is kept of each asset in the asset pool;
  (ii) the asset pool is capable of covering—
    (aa) claims attaching to the bond; and
    (bb) sums required for the maintenance, administration and winding up of the asset pool;
  (iii) there is timely payment of claims attaching to the bond to the regulated covered bond holder;
  [(iv) the asset pool of a single asset class bond consists only of eligible property of the same class as the assets included in the asset pool of the regulated covered bond when it was registered;]

(b) give the Authority such information in respect of—
  (i) the composition of the asset pool; and
  (ii) the steps it has taken to comply with sub-paragraph (a);
as the Authority may direct; and

(c) inform the Authority if at any time any of the requirements set out in sub-paragraph (a)(ii) or (iii) are not, or are not likely to be, satisfied.

(2) The information required under paragraph (1)(b) and (c) must be given at such times, in such form and verified in such manner, as the Authority may direct.

[(2A) In determining whether the requirement in paragraph (1)(a)(iv) is satisfied, no account shall be taken of eligible property which is liquid assets.

(2B) Nothing in this regulation shall prevent the Authority directing the owner to observe additional requirements in relation to its asset pool.]

NOTES

Para (1): sub-para (a)(iv) inserted by the Regulated Covered Bonds (Amendment) Regulations 2011, SI 2011/2859, reg 2(1), (13)(a).

Paras (2A), (2B): added by SI 2011/2859, reg 2(1), (13)(b).

25, 26 (*Outside the scope of this work.*)

PART 6
PRIORITY OF PAYMENT

[18.175]
27 Priority in a winding up

(1) Subject to—
(a) section 115 of the 1986 Act (expenses of voluntary winding up) or, in Northern Ireland, article 100 of the 1989 Order (expenses of voluntary winding up); and
(b) the priority of the expenses of the winding up in a compulsory liquidation;
where an owner is wound up, the claims of relevant persons shall be paid from the relevant asset pool in priority to all other creditors.

(2) "Relevant persons" are—
(a) regulated covered bond holders;
(b) persons providing services for the benefit of those bond holders;
(c) the counter-parties to hedging instruments which are incidental to the maintenance and administration of the asset pool or to the terms of the regulated covered bond; and
(d) persons (other than the issuer) providing a loan to the owner to enable it to satisfy the claims of the persons mentioned in sub-paragraph (a), (b) or (c).

(3) The claims of the persons mentioned in paragraph (2)(b), (c) and (d) may rank equally with, but not in priority to, the claims of the persons mentioned in paragraph (2)(a).

[18.176]
28 Realisation of a charge

(1) Subject to regulation 29, if—
(a) any asset comprised in the asset pool is charged as security for claims in priority to any charge over that asset granted to secure the claims of relevant persons; and
(b) the charge which has priority is realised at any time when the owner is not in the course of being wound up;
the proceeds of the realisation of that charge must, after payment of the expenses referred to in regulation 29 and any other expenses relating to that charge, be first applied to satisfy the claims of relevant persons at such time as those claims fall due for payment.

(2) Subject to regulation 29, if—

(a) any asset comprised in the asset pool is charged as security for several claims;

(b) any agreement between the creditors of that charge gives priority to the claims of any person above the claims of the relevant persons; and

(c) that charge is realised at any time when the owner is not in the course of being wound up;

the proceeds of the realisation of that charge must, after payment of the expenses referred to in regulation 29 and any other expenses relating to that charge, be first applied to satisfy the claims of the relevant persons at such time as those claims fall due for payment.

[(3) For the purposes of paragraphs (1) and (2) the claims of the persons mentioned in regulation 27(2)(b), (c) and (d) may rank equally with, but not in priority to, the claims of the persons mentioned in regulation 27(2)(a).]

NOTES

Para (3): added by the Regulated Covered Bonds (Amendment) Regulations 2008, SI 2008/1714, reg 2(1), (5).

[18.177]
[29

(1) Disbursements made by a liquidator, provisional liquidator, administrator, administrative receiver, receiver or manager of the owner in respect of costs which—

(a) are incurred after the commencement of any winding up, administration, administrative receivership or receivership; and

(b) relate to any of the persons mentioned in paragraph (2);

shall be expenses of the winding up, administration, administrative receivership or receivership, as the case may be, and shall rank equally among themselves in priority to all other expenses.

(2) The persons referred to in paragraph (1)(b) are—

(a) persons providing services for the benefit of regulated covered bond holders;

(b) the counter-parties to hedging instruments which are incidental to the maintenance and administration of the asset pool or to the terms of the regulated covered bonds; and

(c) persons (other than the issuer) providing a loan to the owner to enable it to meet the claims of regulated covered bond holders or pay costs which relate to persons falling within sub-paragraph (a) or (b).]

NOTES

Substituted by the Regulated Covered Bonds (Amendment) Regulations 2008, SI 2008/1714, reg 2(1), (6).

30–40 (*(Pts 7, 8) outside the scope of this work.*)

PART 9
MISCELLANEOUS

41–45 (*Outside the scope of this work.*)

[18.178]
46 Modifications of primary and secondary legislation

The Schedule (which modifies primary and secondary legislation) has effect.

SCHEDULE
MODIFICATIONS TO PRIMARY AND SECONDARY LEGISLATION

Regulation 46

PART 1
PRIMARY LEGISLATION

[18.179]
1. Modification of the Companies Act 1985

Section 196 (payment of debts out of assets subject to floating charge (England and Wales)) of the Companies Act 1985 shall not apply to an owner.

2. Modifications of the 1986 Act

(1) Sections 40 (payment of debts out of assets subject to floating charge) and 43 (power to dispose of charged property) of the 1986 Act shall not apply to an owner.

(2) Section 107 of the 1986 Act (distribution of company's property) shall apply only after payment has been made of the claims of relevant persons.

(3) Section 156 of the 1986 Act (payment of expenses of winding up) shall apply only after payment has been made of the expenses referred to in regulation 29.

(4) Section 175 (preferential debts (general provision)) and 176A (share of assets for unsecured creditors) of the 1986 Act shall not apply to an owner.

(5) Paragraphs 65(1) and 66 of Schedule B1 (distributions) to the 1986 Act shall apply only after payment has been made of the claims of relevant persons.

3–5. . . .

6. Modification of the 2006 Act

Where an owner is wound up, section 754 of the 2006 Act (priorities where debentures secured by floating charge) shall apply only after payment has been made of the claims of relevant persons.

NOTES

Paras 3–5: outside the scope of this work.

PART 2
SECONDARY LEGISLATION

[18.180]

7. Modifications of the Insolvency Rules 1986

(1) Rule 4.181(1) of the Insolvency Rules 1986 (debts of insolvent company to rank equally) shall apply only after payment has been made of the claims of relevant persons.

(2) Rules 2.67, 4.218 and 4.219 of the Insolvency Rules 1986 (priority of expenses) shall apply to an owner subject to the provisions of regulation 29.

[8. Modification to the Insolvency (Scotland) Rules 1986

Rules 2.39B (expenses of the administration) and 4.67 (order of priority of expenses of liquidation) of the Insolvency (Scotland) Rules 1986 shall apply to an owner subject to the provisions of regulation 29.]

9, 10. . . .

11. Modification of the Cross-Border Insolvency Regulations 2006

The Cross-Border Insolvency Regulations 2006 shall not apply to an owner.

12. . . .

NOTES

Para 8: substituted by the Regulated Covered Bonds (Amendment) Regulations 2008, SI 2008/1714, reg 2(1), (7)(a).
Paras 9, 10, 12: outside the scope of this work.

NON-DOMESTIC RATING (UNOCCUPIED PROPERTY) (ENGLAND) REGULATIONS 2008

(SI 2008/386)

NOTES

Made: 18 February 2008.
Authority: Local Government Finance Act 1988, ss 45(1)(d), (9), (10), 143(2), 146(6).
Commencement: 1 April 2008.

[18.181]

1 Citation, application and commencement

These Regulations, which apply in relation to England only, may be cited as the Non-Domestic Rating (Unoccupied Property) (England) Regulations 2008 and shall come into force on 1st April 2008.

2, 3 (*Outside the scope of this work.*)

[18.182]

4 Hereditaments not prescribed for the purposes of section 45(1)(d) of the Act

The relevant non-domestic hereditaments described in this regulation are any hereditament—

(a)–(h) (*outside the scope of this work*);
(i) where, in respect of the owner's estate, there subsists a bankruptcy order within the meaning of section 381(2) of the Insolvency Act 1986;
(j) . . .
(k) whose owner is a company which is subject to a winding-up order made under the Insolvency Act 1986 or which is being wound up voluntarily under that Act;
(l) whose owner is a company in administration within the meaning of paragraph 1 of Schedule B1 to the Insolvency Act 1986 or is subject to an administration order made under the former administration provisions within the meaning of article 3 of the Enterprise Act 2002 (Commencement No 4 and Transitional Provisions and Savings) Order 2003;
(m) whose owner is entitled to possession of the hereditament in his capacity as liquidator by virtue of an order made under section 112 or section 145 of the Insolvency Act 1986.

NOTES

Para (j) revoked by the Deregulation Act 2015 (Insolvency) (Consequential Amendments and Transitional and Savings Provisions) Order 2015, SI 2015/1641, art 6, Sch 3, para 3(8).

5–7 (*Outside the scope of this work.*)

GENERAL OPHTHALMIC SERVICES CONTRACTS REGULATIONS 2008

(SI 2008/1185)

NOTES

Made: 28 April 2008.

Authority: National Health Service Act 1977, ss 28WB, 28WC, 28WE, 28WF, 126(4); National Health Service Act 2006, s 9(8).

Commencement: 1 August 2008.

PART 1
GENERAL

[18.183]

1 Citation, commencement and application

(1) These Regulations may be cited as the General Ophthalmic Services Contracts Regulations 2008 and shall come into force on 1st August 2008.

(2) These Regulations apply in relation to England.

2 (*Outside the scope of this work.*)

PART 2
CONTRACTORS

3 (*Outside the scope of this work.*)

[18.184]

4 Persons eligible to enter into GOS contracts

(1) For the purposes of section 118 (persons eligible to enter into GOS contracts) it is a prescribed condition that a person must not fall within paragraph (3).

(2) The reference to a person in paragraph (1) includes any director, chief executive or secretary of a corporate body.

(3) A person falls within this paragraph if—

(a)–(h) (*outside the scope of this work.*)

(i) it has—

(i) been adjudged bankrupt or had sequestration of his estate awarded unless (in either case) he has been discharged or the bankruptcy order has been annulled;

(ii) been made the subject of a bankruptcy restrictions order or an interim bankruptcy restrictions order under Schedule 4A to the Insolvency Act 1986 unless that order has ceased to have effect or has been annulled; or

(iii) made a composition or arrangement with, or granted a trust deed for, its creditors unless he or it has been discharged in respect of it;

(j) an administrator, administrative receiver or receiver is appointed in respect of it;

(k)–(m) (*outside the scope of this work.*)

(n) he is subject to a disqualification order under the Company Directors Disqualification Act 1986, the Companies (Northern Ireland) Order 1986 or to an order made under section 429(2)(b) of the Insolvency Act 1986 (failure to pay under county court administration order).

(4)–(7) . . .

NOTES

Paras (4)–(7): outside the scope of this work.

5–20 (*Regs 5, 6, 7–20 (Pts 3–6) outside the scope of this work.*)

SCHEDULES 1–4

(*Schs 1–4 outside the scope of this work.*)

DEBT RELIEF ORDERS (DESIGNATION OF COMPETENT AUTHORITIES) REGULATIONS 2009

(SI 2009/457)

NOTES

Made: 2 March 2009.

Authority: Insolvency Act 1986, s 251U(4).

Commencement: 6 April 2009.

ARRANGEMENT OF REGULATIONS

1 Citation, commencement and interpretation . . . . [18.185]
2 . . . . [18.186]

PART I
COMPETENT AUTHORITIES

3 Designated competent authorities . . . . [18.187]
4 Application for designation as a competent authority . . . . [18.188]
5 Fit and proper body . . . . [18.189]
6 Extent of designation . . . . [18.190]
7 Withdrawal of designation as competent authority . . . . [18.191]

PART II
APPROVAL OF INTERMEDIARIES

8 Approval by competent authority . . . . [18.192]
9 Ineligibility . . . . [18.193]
10 Applications to a competent authority for approval to act as intermediary . . . . [18.194]
11 Procedure for withdrawal of approval to act as intermediary . . . . [18.195]

[18.185]
1 Citation, commencement and interpretation

These Regulations may be cited as the Debt Relief Orders (Designation of Competent Authorities) Regulations and come into force on 6th April 2009.

[18.186]
2

"The Act" means the Insolvency Act 1986.

PART I
COMPETENT AUTHORITIES

[18.187]
3 Designated competent authorities

(1) The Secretary of State may designate a body which appears to him to fall within paragraph (2) to be a competent authority for the purposes of granting approvals under section 251U of the Act.

(2) A body may be designated by the Secretary of State if—
- (a) it makes an application to the Secretary of State to be designated as a competent authority in accordance with the Act and these Regulations;
- (b) it provides or ensures—
  - (i) the provision of debt management or debt counselling services through intermediaries, and
  - (ii) the provision to those intermediaries of education, training and development (including continuing education, training and development) in debt management or debt counselling services, and
- (c) it appears to the Secretary of State that it is a fit and proper body to approve individuals to act as intermediaries between a person wishing to make an application for a debt relief order and the official receiver.

[18.188]
4 Application for designation as a competent authority

(1) An application by a body ("the applicant body") for designation as a competent authority for the purposes of granting approvals under section 251U of the Act ("the application") shall be made to the Secretary of State in writing and contain—
- (a) the applicant body's full name;
- (b) the address of its registered office or, if it has no registered office, the address of its centre of administration or principal place of business;
- (c) its registered number (if any);
- (d) if registered outside the United Kingdom, the state in which it is registered and the place where the register is maintained;
- (e) if not registered, the nature of the applicant body;
- (f) a copy of its constitution;
- (g) if a charitable body, the objects or purposes of the charity (if not set out in the constitution) and—
  - (i) if registered as a charity, its registered number as such and (if registered outside the United Kingdom) the state in which it is registered and the place where the register is maintained, or,
  - (ii) if not registered as a charity, reasons why it is not so registered;
- (h) a description of the applicant body's current occupation or activities;
- (i) reasons why the applicant body should be considered for designation;
- (j) a copy of its most recent—

(i) audited accounts and balance sheet, and
(ii) other statutorily required report,
if any;

(k) a statement of the sources of the applicant body's income over the past 24 months and of its assets and liabilities not earlier than 12 months before the day on which the application is made;

(l) details of the nature of the applicant body's connection with the provision of debt management or debt counselling services to the public;

(m) details of existing or proposed education, training and development programmes which are, or which are to be, made available to individuals who are to be approved as, or who are acting as, approved intermediaries;

(n) a description and explanation of—
(i) the procedure which the applicant body proposes to adopt for the approval of individuals to act as intermediaries;
(ii) the manner in which the applicant body will ensure that individuals meet the conditions set out in these Regulations subject to compliance with which an intermediary may be approved;
(iii) any additional criteria which the applicant body proposes to adopt against which it will assess the competence of individuals to act as intermediaries;

(o) an undertaking on the part of the applicant body that—
(i) it will not grant approval to individuals to act as intermediaries except as provided in these Regulations;
(ii) it will withdraw approvals of individuals to act as intermediaries as provided in these Regulations; and
(iii) it will adopt an accessible, effective, fair and transparent procedure for dealing with complaints about its functions as a competent authority, including complaints about—
(aa) any intermediary approved by it, or
(bb) the activities of any such intermediary;

(p) details of the procedures referred to in subparagraph (o)(iii) and how and to what extent they are or will be published;

(q) a statement that such procedures will include the giving of notice to any complainant to the applicant body under subparagraph (o)(iii) that, if dissatisfied with the applicant body's response to the complaint, the complainant may refer the complaint and the response to the Secretary of State;

(r) details of any consumer credit licence and public liability or indemnity insurance which the applicant body holds;

(s) if the applicant body holds a consumer credit licence, whether it provides cover for persons approved by it to act as, and in the course of acting as such intermediaries.

(2) The application may be accompanied by further information in support of the application; and the Secretary of State may request the applicant body to supply further information or evidence.

[18.189]
5 Fit and proper body

(1) A body may not be designated a competent authority unless it is a fit and proper body to act as such.

(2) Without prejudice to the generality of paragraph (1), a body is not a fit and proper body qualified to act as a competent authority if it—

(a) has committed any offence under any enactment contained in insolvency legislation;

(b) has engaged in any deceitful or oppressive or otherwise unfair or improper practices, whether unlawful or not, or any practices which otherwise cast doubt upon the probity of the body; or

(c) has not carried on its activities with integrity and the skills appropriate to the proper performance of the duties of—
(i) a body which purports to ensure the provision of, or to provide, debt management or debt counselling services to the public, or
(ii) a competent authority; or

(d) has entered into a company voluntary arrangement under Part 1 of the Act.

[18.190]
6 Extent of designation

The Secretary of State shall designate a competent authority by sending to the applicant body a letter of designation which shall contain—

(a) a statement that the applicant body as competent authority is designated to approve persons of any description ("unlimited designation"), or

(b) a statement that the applicant body as competent authority is designated to approve persons only of a particular description ("limited designation") and the description of person to which the designation is limited.

[18.191]
7 Withdrawal of designation as competent authority

(1) The Secretary of State may at any time—

(a) modify or withdraw an existing designation where a competent authority so requests or with its consent, or

(b) withdraw an existing designation where it appears to the Secretary of State that a body—
(i) is not or is no longer a fit and proper body to act as a competent authority;

(ii) has failed to comply with any provision of Part 7A of the Act or any rules, regulations or order made under it, including any failure to approve an intermediary, or failure to withdraw approval of an intermediary, in accordance with these regulations;

(iii) has furnished the Secretary of State with any false, inaccurate or misleading information.

(2) The Secretary of State may from time to time request a competent authority to supply such information or evidence about—

(a) itself and its activities as a competent authority, or

(b) any intermediary appointed by it or the activities of any such intermediary,

as may be required by him or her for the purpose of ensuring that the requirements of these regulations are being met.

PART II
APPROVAL OF INTERMEDIARIES

[18.192]

8 Approval by competent authority

(1) A competent authority may approve an individual to act as an intermediary between a person wishing to make an application for a debt relief order and the official receiver subject as follows.

(2) An individual may be approved—

(a) if the individual makes an application to a competent authority to be approved as an intermediary in accordance with the Act and these regulations; and

(b) it appears to the competent authority that the individual is a fit and proper person to act as intermediary between a person wishing to make an application for a debt relief order and the official receiver.

[18.193]

9 Ineligibility

Individuals of any of the following descriptions are ineligible to be approved by a competent authority to act as intermediaries—

(a) individuals convicted of any offence involving fraud or other dishonesty or violence whose convictions are not spent;

(b) individuals who have committed any offence in any enactment contained in insolvency legislation;

(c) individuals who, in the course of carrying on any trade, profession or vocation or in the course of the discharge of any functions relating to any office or employment have engaged in any deceitful or oppressive or otherwise unfair or improper practices, whether unlawful or not, or which otherwise cast doubt upon their probity;

(d) individuals who have no experience, education or other training in the provision of debt management or debt counselling services;

(e) individuals who have not acted with the independence, integrity and the skills appropriate to the proper performance of the duties of a provider of debt management or debt counselling services or of an approved intermediary;

(f) undischarged bankrupts;

(g) individuals in respect of whom there is or has been in force a bankruptcy restrictions order or undertaking or an interim bankruptcy restrictions order or undertaking or any bankruptcy restrictions order or undertaking made under the Insolvency (Northern Ireland) Order 1989 or the Bankruptcy (Scotland) Act 1985

(h) individuals to whom a moratorium period applies or in respect of whom a debt relief order or application for a debt relief order, has been made;

(i) individuals in respect of whom there is or has been in force a debt relief restrictions order or undertaking or an interim debt relief restrictions order or undertaking;

(j) individuals who are or have been subject to a disqualification order or undertaking accepted under the Company Directors Disqualification Act 1986 or to a disqualification order made under Part 11 of the Companies (Northern Ireland) Order 1989 or to a disqualification undertaking accepted under the Company Directors Disqualification (Northern Ireland) Order 2002

(k) individuals who are patients within meaning of section 329(1) of the Mental Health (Care and Treatment) (Scotland) Act 2003 or have had a guardian appointed to them under the Adults with Incapacity (Scotland) Act 2000;

(l) individuals who lack capacity within the meaning of the Mental Health Capacity Act 2005 to act as intermediaries between a person wishing to make an application for a debt relief order and the official receiver;

(m) individuals who, subject to any exemption from the requirement to possess or be covered by a relevant consumer credit licence which would otherwise apply to or in relation to them, neither possess nor are validly covered by such a licence; and

(n) individuals who are not covered, either individually or by way of a group policy, by public liability or personal indemnity insurance.

[18.194]

10 Applications to a competent authority for approval to act as intermediary

(1) Applications to a competent authority by an individual for approval to act as an intermediary shall be in writing and contain—

(a) the individual's full name and address, date of birth and gender;
(b) any name or names used by the applicant for any purpose, if different from the above;
(c) a description of the individual's current occupation or activities;
(d) a description giving reasons why the individual should be considered suitable for approval;
(e) whether the individual is a member of a relevant body and if so which;
(f) the individual's educational and professional qualifications;
(g) the source of the individual's income and the individual's current financial status;
(h) details of the individual's expertise in the provision of debt management or debt counselling services including details of any education, training and development which the individual has undergone and any qualifications the individual has acquired in connection with the provision of debt management or debt counselling services;
(i) details of any consumer credit licence which the individual has in place or of any exemption claimed by him or her from the requirement to possess or be covered by such a licence (as the case may be), or, if none, how the individual proposes to secure that he or she has in place, or is validly covered by, a consumer credit licence;
(j) details of any public liability or personal indemnity insurance which the individual has in place, or, if none, how the individual proposes to secure that he or she has in place, or is validly covered by, appropriate public liability or personal indemnity insurance;
(k) copies of—
 (i) documents confirming the individual's name, address and date of birth;
 (ii) material relating to the educational, training and development experience referred to in sub-paragraph (h);
 (iii) material relating to the individual's professional or other qualifications.

(2) In this regulation, "relevant body" means a body concerned with the regulation of persons who provide or ensure the provision of debt management or debt counselling services.

(3) The application may be accompanied by further information in support of the application; [and the competent authority may request the individual to supply further information or evidence].

NOTES

Para (3): words in square brackets substituted by the Debt Relief Orders (Designation of Competent Authorities) (Amendment) Regulations 2009, SI 2009/1553, reg 2.

[18.195]

11 Procedure for withdrawal of approval to act as intermediary

A competent authority shall withdraw an approval to act as intermediary from any individual—
(a) where the individual so requests or with the individual's consent;
(b) where it becomes clear to the competent authority after approval that the individual—
 (i) was ineligible at the time of approval, or
 (ii) has become ineligible for approval;
 (iii) is at any time not or no longer a fit and proper person to act as intermediary;
 (iv) has failed to comply with any provision of Part 7A of the Act or any rule, regulations or orders made under it, including these regulations;
 (v) has furnished the competent authority with any false, inaccurate or misleading information.

(2) The competent authority may from time to time request an approved intermediary to supply such information or evidence about that intermediary or his or her activities as may be required by that authority for the purpose of ensuring that the requirements of these Regulations are being met.

OVERSEAS COMPANIES REGULATIONS 2009

(SI 2009/1801)

NOTES

Made: 8 July 2009.

Authority: Companies Act 2006, ss 1046(1), (2), (4)–(6), 1047(1), 1049(1)–(3), 1050(3)–(5), 1051(1)–(3), 1053(2)–(5), 1054(1), (2), 1055, 1056, 1058(1)–(3), 1078(5), 1105(1), (2), 1140(2), 1292(1), (4), 1294.

Commencement: 1 October 2009.

ARRANGEMENT OF REGULATIONS

PART 1
INTRODUCTION

1 Citation and commencement . . . [18.196]
2 Interpretation . . . [18.197]

PART 7
TRADING DISCLOSURES

63 Particulars to appear in business letters, order forms and websites . . . [18.198]
66 Civil consequences of failure to make a required disclosure . . . [18.199]
67 Penalty for non-compliance . . . [18.200]

PART 8
RETURNS IN CASE OF WINDING UP ETC

68 Application of Part . . . . . [18.201]
69 Return in case of winding up . . . . . [18.202]
70 Returns to be made by liquidator . . . . . [18.203]
71 Return in case of insolvency proceedings etc (other than winding up) . . . . . [18.204]
72 Penalties for non-compliance . . . . . [18.205]
73 Notice of appointment of judicial factor . . . . . [18.206]
74 Offence of failure to give notice . . . . . [18.207]

PART 1
INTRODUCTION

[18.196]

1 Citation and commencement

(1) These Regulations may be cited as the Overseas Companies Regulations 2009.

(2) These Regulations come into force on 1st October 2009.

[18.197]

2 Interpretation

In these Regulations—

"accounting documents"—

(a) in relation to an overseas company to which Chapter 2 of Part 5 applies (companies required to prepare and disclose accounts under parent law), has the meaning given by regulation 31(2), and

(b) in relation to a credit or financial institution to which Chapter 2 of Part 6 applies (institutions required to prepare accounts under parent law), has the meaning given by regulation 44(2);

"certified copy" means a copy certified as a correct copy;

"constitution", in relation to an overseas company, means the charter, statutes, memorandum and articles of association or other instrument constituting or defining the company's constitution;

"credit or financial institution" means a credit or financial institution to which section 1050 of the Companies Act 2006 applies;

"disclosure", in relation to a credit or financial institution to which Chapter 2 of Part 6 applies, has the meaning given by regulation 44(2);

"establishment" means—

(a) a branch within the meaning of the Eleventh Company Law Directive (89/666/EEC), or

(b) a place of business that is not such a branch,

and "UK establishment" means an establishment in the United Kingdom;

"financial period"—

(a) in relation to an overseas company to which Chapter 2 of Part 5 applies (companies required to prepare and disclose accounts under parent law), has the meaning given by regulation 31(2), and

(b) in relation to a credit or financial institution to which Chapter 2 of Part 6 applies (institutions required to prepare accounts under parent law), has the meaning given by regulation 44(2);

"First Company Law Directive" means the First Council Directive on co-ordination of safeguards which, for the protection of the interests of members and others, are required by Member States of companies within the meaning of the second paragraph of Article 58 of the Treaty, with a view to making such safeguards equivalent throughout the Community (68/151/EEC);

"former name", in the case of an individual, means a name by which the individual was formerly known for business purposes;

"name", in the case of an individual, means the person's Christian name (or other forename) and surname, except that in the case of—

(a) a peer, or

(b) an individual usually known by a title,

the title may be stated instead of the individual's Christian name (or other forename) and surname or in addition to either or both of them; and

"parent law"—

(a) in relation to an overseas company to which Chapter 2 of Part 5 applies (companies required to prepare and disclose accounts under parent law), has the meaning given by regulation 31(2), and

(b) in relation to a credit or financial institution to which Chapter 2 of Part 6 applies (institutions required to prepare accounts under parent law), has the meaning given by regulation 44(2).

3–57 *((Pts 2–6) outside the scope of this work.)*

Part 18 Miscellaneous SIs

PART 7
TRADING DISCLOSURES

58–62 (*Outside the scope of this work.*)

[18.198]
63 Particulars to appear in business letters, order forms and websites

(1), (2) (*Outside the scope of this work.*)

(3) An overseas company which is not incorporated in an EEA State must state the particulars required by paragraph (4) on all—

(a) its business letters,
(b) its order forms, and
(c) its websites,

that are used in carrying on business in the United Kingdom.

(4) The particulars are—

(a) the company's country of incorporation,
(b) the identity of the registry, if any, in which the company is registered in its country of incorporation,
(c) if applicable, the number with which the company is registered in that registry,
(d) the location of its head office,
(e) the legal form of the company,
(f) if the liability of the members of the company is limited, the fact that it is a limited company, and
(g) if applicable, the fact that the company is being wound up, or is subject to other insolvency proceedings or an arrangement or composition or any analogous proceedings.

(5) (*Outside the scope of this work.*)

(6) Paragraph (4)(g) does not apply to a company required to make disclosures under—

(a) section 39(1) or 188(a) of, or paragraph 16(1) of Schedule A1 or paragraph 45 of Schedule B1 to, the Insolvency Act 1986, or
(b) (*outside the scope of this work.*)

64, 65 (*Outside the scope of this work.*)

[18.199]
66 Civil consequences of failure to make a required disclosure

(1) This regulation applies to any legal proceedings brought by a company to which this Part applies to enforce a right arising out of a contract made in the course of a business in respect of which, at the time the contract was made, there was a failure to comply with the requirements of this Part.

(2) The proceedings must be dismissed if it is shown that the defendant (in Scotland, the defender)—

(a) has a claim against the claimant (pursuer) arising out of the contract and has been unable to pursue that claim by reason of the latter's failure to comply with the requirements of this Part, or
(b) has suffered some financial loss in connection with the contract by reason of the claimant's (pursuer's) failure to comply with those requirements,

unless the court before which the proceedings are brought is satisfied that it is just and equitable to permit the proceedings to continue.

(3) This regulation does not affect the right of any person to enforce such rights as the person may have against another in any proceedings brought by the other.

[18.200]
67 Penalty for non-compliance

(1) Where a company fails, without reasonable excuse, to comply with any requirement of this Part, an offence is committed by—

(a) the company, and
(b) every officer of the company who is in default.

(2) A person guilty of an offence under paragraph (1) is liable on summary conviction to—

(a) a fine not exceeding level 3 on the standard scale, and
(b) for continued contravention, a daily default fine not exceeding one-tenth of level 3 on the standard scale.

(3) For the purposes of this regulation a shadow director is to be treated as an officer of the company.

PART 8
RETURNS IN CASE OF WINDING UP ETC

[18.201]
68 Application of Part

This Part applies to an overseas company that has one or more UK establishments.

[18.202]
69 Return in case of winding up

(1) Where a company to which this Part applies is being wound up, it must deliver to the registrar a return containing the following particulars—

(a) the company's name;
(b) whether the company is being wound up by an order of a court and if so, the name and address of the court and the date of the order;
(c) if the company is not being so wound up, as a result of what action the winding up has commenced;
(d) whether the winding up has been instigated by—
  (i) the company's members,
  (ii) the company's creditors, or
  (iii) some other person (stating the person's identity); and
(e) the date on which the winding up became or will become effective.

(2) The return must be delivered not later than—

(a) if the winding up began before the company had a UK establishment, one month after the company first opens a UK establishment;
(b) if the winding up begins when the company has a UK establishment, 14 days after the date on which the winding up begins.

(3) Where the company has more than one UK establishment the obligation to deliver a return under this regulation applies in respect of each of them, but a return giving the registered numbers of more than one UK establishment is regarded as a return in respect of each establishment whose number is given.

(4) No return is required under this regulation in respect of winding up under the Insolvency Act 1986 or the Insolvency (Northern Ireland) Order 1989.

[18.203]
70 Returns to be made by liquidator

(1) A person appointed to be the liquidator of a company to which this Part applies must deliver to the registrar a return containing the following particulars—

(a) their name and address,
(b) date of the appointment, and
(c) a description of such of the person's powers, if any, as are derived otherwise than from the general law or the company's constitution.

(2) The period allowed for delivery of the return required by paragraph (1) is—

(a) if the liquidator was appointed before the company had a UK establishment (and continues in office at the date of the opening), one month after the company first opens a UK establishment;
(b) if the liquidator is appointed when the company has a UK establishment, 14 days after the date of the appointment.

(3) The liquidator of a company to which this Part applies must—

(a) on the termination of the winding up of the company, deliver a return to the registrar stating the name of the company and the date on which the winding up terminated;
(b) on the company ceasing to be registered in circumstances where ceasing to be registered is an event of legal significance, deliver a return to the registrar stating the name of the company and the date on which it ceased to be registered.

(4) The period allowed for delivery of the return required by paragraph (3)(a) or (b) is 14 days from the date of the event.

(5) Where the company has more than one UK establishment the obligation to deliver a return under this regulation applies in respect of each of them, but a return giving the registered numbers of more than one UK establishment is regarded as a return in respect of each establishment whose number is given.

(6) No return is required under this regulation in respect of a liquidator appointed under the Insolvency Act 1986 or the Insolvency (Northern Ireland) Order 1989.

[18.204]
71 Return in case of insolvency proceedings etc (other than winding up)

(1) Where a company to which this Part applies becomes subject to insolvency proceedings or an arrangement or composition or any analogous proceedings (other than proceedings for winding up of the company), it must deliver to the registrar a return containing the following particulars—

(a) the company's name;
(b) whether the proceedings are by an order of a court and if so, the name and address of the court and the date of the order;
(c) if the proceedings are not by an order of a court, as a result of what action the proceedings have been commenced;
(d) whether the proceedings have been commenced by—
  (i) the company's members,
  (ii) the company's creditors, or
  (iii) some other person (giving the person's identity);
(e) the date on which the proceedings became or will become effective.

(2) The period allowed for delivery of the return required by paragraph (1) is—

(a) if the company became subject to the proceedings before it had a UK establishment, one month after the company first opens a UK establishment;

(b) if the company becomes subject to the proceedings when it has a UK establishment, 14 days from the date on which it becomes subject to the proceedings.

(3) Where a company to which this Part applies ceases to be subject to any of the proceedings referred to in paragraph (1) it must deliver to the registrar a return stating—

(a) the company's name, and

(b) the date on which it ceased to be subject to the proceedings.

(4) The period allowed for delivery of the return required by paragraph (3) is 14 days from the date on which it ceases to be subject to the proceedings.

(5) Where the company has more than one UK establishment the obligation to deliver a return under this regulation applies in respect of each of them, but a return giving the registered numbers of more than one UK establishment is regarded as a return in respect of each establishment whose number is given.

(6) No return is required under this regulation in respect of—

(a) a company's becoming or ceasing to be subject to a voluntary arrangement under Part 1 of the Insolvency Act 1986 or Part 2 of the Insolvency (Northern Ireland) Order 1989, or

(b) a company's entering administration under Part 2 and Schedule B1 of that Act or becoming or ceasing to be subject to an administration order under Part 3 of that Order.

[18.205]

72 Penalties for non-compliance

(1) If a company fails to comply with regulation 69(1) or 71(1) or (3) within the period allowed for compliance, an offence is committed by—

(a) the company, and

(b) every person who immediately before the end of that period was a director of the company.

(2) A liquidator who fails to comply with regulation 70(1) or (3)(a) or (b) within the period allowed for compliance commits an offence.

(3) A person who takes all reasonable steps to secure compliance with the requirements concerned does not commit an offence under this regulation.

(4) A person guilty of an offence under this regulation is liable—

(a) on conviction on indictment, to a fine;

(b) on summary conviction to a fine not exceeding the statutory maximum and, for continued contravention, a daily default fine not exceeding [one-fiftieth of the greater of £5,000 or the amount corresponding to level 4 on the standard scale for summary offences].

NOTES

Sub-s (4): words in square brackets substituted (for the original words "one-fiftieth of the statutory maximum") by the Legal Aid, Sentencing and Punishment of Offenders Act 2012 (Fines on Summary Conviction) Regulations 2015, SI 2015/664, regs 3, 5, Sch 3, Pt 1, para 13(1), (5), in relation to England and Wales only (except in relation to (a) fines for offences committed before 12 March 2015, (b) the operation of restrictions on fines that may be imposed on a person aged under 18, or (c) fines that may be imposed on a person convicted by a magistrates' court who is to be sentenced as if convicted on indictment).

[18.206]

73 Notice of appointment of judicial factor

(1) Notice must be given to the registrar of the appointment in relation to a company to which this Part applies of a judicial factor (in Scotland).

(2) The notice must be given by the judicial factor.

(3) The notice must specify an address at which service of documents (including legal process) may be effected on the judicial factor.

(4) Notice of a change in the address for service may be given to the registrar by the judicial factor.

(5) A judicial factor who has notified the registrar of the appointment must also notify the registrar of the termination of the appointment.

[18.207]

74 Offence of failure to give notice

(1) A judicial factor who fails to give notice of the appointment in accordance with regulation 73 within the period of 14 days after the appointment commits an offence.

(2) A person guilty of an offence under this regulation is liable on summary conviction to—

(a) a fine not exceeding level 5 on the standard scale, and

(b) for continued contravention, a daily default fine not exceeding [one-tenth of the greater of £5,000 or level 4 on the standard scale].

NOTES

Sub-s (2): words in square brackets substituted (for the original words "one-tenth of level 5 on the standard scale") by the Legal Aid, Sentencing and Punishment of Offenders Act 2012 (Fines on Summary Conviction) Regulations 2015, SI 2015/664, regs 3, 5, Sch 3, Pt 1, para 13(1), (6), in relation to England and Wales only (except in relation to (a) fines for offences committed before 12 March 2015, (b) the operation of restrictions on fines that may be imposed on a person aged under 18, or (c) fines that may be imposed on a person convicted by a magistrates' court who is to be sentenced as if convicted on indictment).

75–80 (*(Pts 9, 10) outside the scope of this work.*)

SCHEDULES 1–8

(Schs 1–8 outside the scope of this work.)

BUILDING SOCIETIES (FINANCIAL ASSISTANCE) ORDER 2010

(SI 2010/1188)

NOTES

Made: 6 April 2010.

Authority: Banking Act 2009, ss 251(1), (2), (3), (5), (8), 259(1); Banking (Special Provisions) Act 2008, s 11.

Commencement: 7 April 2010.

ARRANGEMENT OF ARTICLES

1 Citation and commencement . . . . [18.208]
2 Interpretation . . . . [18.209]
3 Purpose or principal purpose of building societies . . . . [18.210]
4 The lending limit . . . . [18.211]
5 The funding limit . . . . [18.212]
6 Raising funds and borrowing . . . . [18.213]
8 Memorandum and rules . . . . [18.214]
9 Application of companies winding up legislation to building societies . . . . [18.215]
10, 11 Application of other companies insolvency legislation to building societies . . . . [18.216], [18.217]

[18.208]

1 Citation and commencement

(1) This Order may be cited as the Building Societies (Financial Assistance) Order 2010.

(2) It comes into force on the day after the day on which it is made.

[18.209]

2 Interpretation

(1) In this Order—

"the 1986 Act" means the Building Societies Act 1986;

. . .

"qualifying institution" means the Treasury, the Bank of England, another central bank of a Member State of the European Economic Area or the European Central Bank;

"relevant building society" means any building society which—

(a) receives financial assistance from a qualifying institution,

(b) has entered into an agreement with a qualifying institution under which it may receive financial assistance from that institution, or

(c) has received an offer of such an agreement, or of financial assistance, from a qualifying institution;

. . .

(2) References in this Order to a qualifying institution include—

(a) any person acting for or on behalf of that qualifying institution;

(b) any person providing, offering, or entering into an agreement for the provision of, financial assistance to a building society, who does so on the basis of financial assistance that person receives from the qualifying institution in question for that purpose.

NOTES

Para (1): definitions omitted revoked by the Financial Services Act 2012 (Mutual Societies) Order 2013, SI 2013/496, art 2(c), Sch 11, para 18(1), (2).

[18.210]

3 Purpose or principal purpose of building societies

(1) Section 5 of the 1986 Act (establishment, constitution and powers) applies in relation to a relevant building society with the following modification.

(2) No relevant building society shall be regarded as failing to comply with section 5(1)(a) (purpose or principal purpose) by virtue of any financial assistance it receives from a qualifying institution.

(3) The powers conferred . . . by sections 36 and 37 of the 1986 Act (power to direct restructuring of business etc and powers to petition for winding up etc) shall not become exercisable in relation to a building society which receives financial assistance if, but for the financial assistance, they would not have become exercisable.

(4) Sections 5(4A), 36(1) and 37(1) shall be construed accordingly.

[(5) A building society to which paragraph (3) applies is to be disregarded for the purposes of section 1(1)(a) and (1A)(a) of the 1986 Act.]

NOTES

Para (3): words omitted revoked by the Financial Services Act 2012 (Mutual Societies) Order 2013, SI 2013/496, art 2(c), Sch 11, para 18(1), (3)(a).

Para (5): substituted by SI 2013/496, art 2(c), Sch 11, para 18(1), (3)(b).

[18.211]

4 The lending limit

(1) Section 6(1) of the 1986 Act (the lending limit) shall not apply in relation to a relevant building society for the relevant period where—

- (a) the society receives financial assistance from a qualifying institution,
- (b) as a consequence of the financial assistance, the society transfers, assigns or otherwise disposes of any of its assets, and
- (c) that transfer, assignment or other disposal would, apart from this article, put the society in breach of section 6(1).

(2) No building society within paragraph (1) shall be regarded as failing to comply with section 5(1)(a) of the 1986 Act in the relevant period by virtue of the matters referred to in paragraph (1).

(3) The powers conferred . . . by sections 36 and 37 of the 1986 Act shall not become exercisable in relation to a building society within paragraph (1) in respect of the relevant period.

(4) Sections 5(4A), 36(1) and 37(1) shall be construed accordingly.

[(5) A building society to which paragraph (3) applies is to be disregarded for the purposes of section 1(1)(a) and (1A)(a) of the 1986 Act.]

(6) In this article "the relevant period" is the period commencing on the date on which paragraph (1) is first satisfied in relation to the society and ending—

- (a) one year after that date, or
- (b) if later, on the date on which the financial assistance referred to in paragraph (1) is no longer provided.

NOTES

Para (3): words omitted revoked by the Financial Services Act 2012 (Mutual Societies) Order 2013, SI 2013/496, art 2(c), Sch 11, para 18(1), (4)(a).

Para (5): substituted by SI 2013/496, art 2(c), Sch 11, para 18(1), (4)(b).

[18.212]

5 The funding limit

(1) Section 7 of the 1986 Act (the funding limit) applies to a relevant building society with the following modification.

(2) There shall be disregarded for the purposes of section 7(2) any financial assistance the society receives from a qualifying institution.

[18.213]

6 Raising funds and borrowing

Section 8(1)(c) of the 1986 Act (raising funds and borrowing) shall not apply to a relevant building society in relation to any financial assistance the society receives from, or is offered by, a qualifying institution.

7 (*Revoked by the Financial Services (Banking Reform) Act 2013 (Commencement (No 8) and Consequential Provisions) Order 2015, SI 2015/428, art 3(a).*)

[18.214]

8 Memorandum and rules

(1) Schedule 2 to the 1986 Act (establishment, incorporation and constitution of building societies) applies in relation to a relevant building society with the following modifications.

(2) Paragraph 2 (the memorandum) shall have effect as if, after sub-paragraph (4), there were inserted—

"(4A) However, no provision of the memorandum of a building society shall be binding on any member or officer of the society, or on any person claiming on account of a member or under the rules, to the extent that it would prevent the society (whether acting through its officers or otherwise) from—

- (a) receiving any financial assistance from a qualifying institution, or
- (b) entering into any transaction connected with the receipt of such financial assistance,

and sub-paragraph (4) shall be construed accordingly.

(4B) In sub-paragraph (4A)—

- (a) "financial assistance" has the same meaning as in section 251 of the Banking Act 2009 and "qualifying institution" means the Treasury, the Bank of England, another central bank of a Member State of the European Economic Area or the European Central Bank; and
- (b) references to a qualifying institution include—
  - (i) any person acting for or on behalf of that institution, and

(ii) any person providing, offering, or entering into an agreement for the provision of, financial assistance to a building society, who does so on the basis of financial assistance that person receives from the qualifying institution for that purpose.".

(3) Paragraph 3 (the rules) shall have effect as if, after sub-paragraph (2), there were inserted—

"(2A) However, nothing in the rules of a building society shall be binding on any member or officer of the society, or on any person claiming on account of a member or under the rules, to the extent that it would prevent the society (whether acting through its officers or otherwise) from—

(a) receiving any financial assistance from a qualifying institution, or

(b) entering into any transaction connected with the receipt of such financial assistance,

and sub-paragraph (2) shall be construed accordingly.

(2B) In sub-paragraph (2A)—

(a) "financial assistance" and "qualifying institution" have the same meanings as in paragraph 2(4A) (see paragraph 2(4B)); and

(b) references to a qualifying institution include—

(i) any person acting for or on behalf of that institution, and

(ii) any person providing, offering, or entering into an agreement for the provision of, financial assistance to a building society, who does so on the basis of financial assistance that person receives from the qualifying institution for that purpose.".

(4) No member of a building society may bring proceedings under paragraph 16(2) (capacity of society not limited by its memorandum) to restrain the doing of any act by a building society for or in connection with the receipt of financial assistance from a qualifying institution.

(5) Paragraph 16(3) shall not operate so as to—

(a) require the directors to observe any limitations on their powers flowing from the society's memorandum which would, apart from this article, prevent them entering into any transaction for or in connection with the receipt of financial assistance by the society from a qualifying institution, or

(b) require any such action by the directors which, but for paragraph 16(1), would be beyond the society's capacity, to be ratified by the society by special resolution.

[18.215]

9 Application of companies winding up legislation to building societies

(1) Schedule 15 to the 1986 Act (application of companies winding up legislation to building societies) applies in relation to a relevant building society with the following modifications.

(2) In paragraph 3(2), omit paragraph (b).

(3) In paragraph 33, for "subsections (2) and (4) to (6)" substitute "subsections (2), (5) and (6)".

(4) In paragraph 55E, for "paragraphs (2) and (4) to (6)" substitute "paragraphs (2), (5) and (6)".

[18.216]

10 Application of other companies insolvency legislation to building societies

Section 90A of the 1986 Act (application of other companies insolvency legislation to building societies) applies in relation to a relevant building society as if [for "or receivers," in paragraph (c) there were substituted "receivers or administrative receivers"].

NOTES

Words in square brackets substituted for the following original words, by the Building Societies (Floating Charges and Other Provisions) Order 2016, SI 2016/679, art 5(1), (2), in relation to a floating charge created by a building society on or after 28 June 2016—

"—

(a) after "England and Wales" in paragraph (c) there were inserted ", Scotland";

(b) after "receivers and managers" in that paragraph there were inserted ", receivers or administrative receivers".".

[18.217]

11

(1) Schedule 15A to the 1986 Act (application of other companies insolvency legislation to building societies) applies in relation to a relevant building society with the following modifications.

[(2) In paragraph 1(2)(a), for ", II, III," substitute "and II, Chapters I, II and III of Part III, Parts".

(2A) In paragraph 1(2)(b), for "Parts III, IV" substitute "Part III, Part IV (except Articles 59A to 59J)".]

(3) In paragraph 2(2), omit paragraph (b).

(4) In paragraph 11—

(a) in sub-paragraph (2), for "is a reference to the [FCA or the PRA]" substitute "includes a reference to the [FCA or the PRA]";

(b) omit sub-paragraph (3).

(5) Omit paragraphs [12 and 13].

[(6) For paragraph 27A substitute—

27A

In Chapters I and II of Part III of the Act, as applied to a building society, the following provisions have effect as if a reference to the creditors or unsecured creditors of the society included a reference to the holders of shares in the society—

(a) subsection (1) of section 46 of the Act (information to be given by administrative receiver);
(b) subsection (2) of section 47 of the Act (statement of affairs to be submitted);
(c) subsection (2)(a) and (b) of section 48 of the Act (report by administrative receiver);
(d) subsection (1) of section 65 of the Act (information to be given by receiver);
(e) subsection (2) of section 66 of the Act (building society's statement of affairs); and
(f) subsection (2)(a) and (b) of section 67 of the Act (report by receiver).

27AA

Subsection (1) of section 48 of the Act, as applied to a building society, has effect as if—

(a) the reference to the Financial Conduct Authority included a reference to the scheme manager; and
(b) in paragraph (d) the reference to other creditors included a reference to shareholding members of the society in respect of deposits which are not relevant deposits.

27AB

Sections 49 and 68 of the Act (committee of creditors), as applied to a building society, have effect as if the reference to the society's unsecured creditors included a reference to the holders of shares in the society.".

(6A) Until the coming into force of paragraph 12(3)(b) of Schedule 9 to the Small Business, Enterprise and Employment Act 2015 ("the 2015 Act"), paragraph 27AA (treated as substituted by paragraph (6) above) is to be read as also providing that subsection (2) of section 48 of the Insolvency Act 1986, as applied to a building society, has effect as if the reference to a meeting of the society's unsecured creditors included a reference to a meeting of holders of shares in the society.

(6B) Until the coming into force of paragraph 13 of Schedule 9 to the 2015 Act, paragraph 27AB (treated as substituted by paragraph (6) above) is to be read as providing that section 49 of the Insolvency Act 1986, as applied to a building society, has effect as if the reference to a meeting of creditors included a reference to a meeting of holders of shares in the society.

(6C) Until the coming into force of paragraph 15 of Schedule 9 to the 2015 Act, paragraph 27AB (treated as substituted by paragraph (6) above) is to be read as providing that section 68 of the Insolvency Act 1986, as applied to a building society, has effect as if the reference to a meeting of creditors included a reference to a meeting of holders of shares in the society.

(6D) Until the coming into force of paragraph 14(3)(b) of Schedule 9 to the 2015 Act, paragraph 27D has effect as if the existing provision became sub-paragraph (1) and after that sub-paragraph there were inserted—

"(2) Subsection (2) of that section, as so applied, has effect as if the reference to a meeting of the society's unsecured creditors included a reference to a meeting of the holders of shares in the society.".

(6E) Omit paragraph 27F.".]

(7) In paragraph 33—

(a) in sub-paragraph (2), for "is a reference to the [FCA or, as the case may be, the PRA]" substitute "includes a reference to the [FCA or, as the case may be, the PRA]";
(b) omit sub-paragraph (3).

(8) Omit paragraphs [34 and 35].

[(9) For paragraph 50 substitute—

50

In Part 4 of the Order, as applied to a building society, the following provisions have effect as if a reference to the creditors or unsecured creditors of the society included a reference to the holders of shares in the society—

(a) paragraph (1) of Article 56 of the Order (information to be given by administrative receiver);
(b) paragraph (2) of Article 57 of the Order (statement of affairs to be submitted); and
(c) paragraph (2)(a) and (b) of Article 58 of the Order (report by administrative receiver).

50A

Article 58 of the Order, as applied to a building society, has effect as if—

(a) in paragraph (1)—
   (i) the reference to the Financial Conduct Authority included a reference to the scheme manager; and
   (ii) in sub-paragraph (d) the reference to other creditors included a reference to shareholding members of the society in respect of deposits which are not relevant deposits; and
(b) in paragraph (2) the reference to a meeting of the society's unsecured creditors included a reference to a meeting of holders of shares in the society.

50AA
Article 59 of the Order (committee of creditors), as applied to a building society, has effect as if the reference to a meeting of creditors included a reference to a meeting of holders of shares in the society.".

(10) Omit paragraphs 51 and 52.]

NOTES

Paras (2), (2A): substituted for original para (2) by the Building Societies (Floating Charges and Other Provisions) Order 2016, SI 2016/679, art 5(1), (3)(a), in relation to a floating charge created by a building society on or after 28 June 2016. Para (2) originally read as follows—

"(2) In paragraph 1(2)(a), for "Chapter I of Part III" substitute "Chapters I, II and III of Part III".".

Paras (4), (7): words in square brackets substituted by the Financial Services Act 2012 (Mutual Societies) Order 2013, SI 2013/496, art 2(c), Sch 11, para 18(1), (5).

Paras (5), (8): words in square brackets substituted by the Financial Services (Banking Reform) Act 2013 (Commencement (No 8) and Consequential Provisions) Order 2015, SI 2015/428, art 3(a).

Paras (6), (6A)–(6E): substituted for original para (6) by SI 2016/679, art 5(1), (3)(b), in relation to a floating charge created by a building society on or after 28 June 2016. Para (6) (as amended by SI 2013/496, art 2(c), Sch 11, para 18(1), (5)) previously read as follows—

"(6) For paragraph 27, substitute—

"**27** (1) Subsection (3) of section 40 of the Act (payment of debts out of assets subject to floating charge) as applied to a building society has effect as if the reference to general creditors included a reference to holders of shares in the society.

(2) Subsection (3) of section 59 of the Act (priority of debts) as applied to a building society has effect as if the reference to ordinary creditors included a reference to holders of shares in the society.

27A Subsection (1) of section 46 of the Act (information to be given by administrative receiver) or subsection (1) of 65 of the Act (information to be given by receiver) as applied to a building society has effect as if the reference to all the creditors of the society included a reference to all the holders of shares in the society.

27B Subsection (2) of section 47 of the Act (statement of affairs to be submitted) or subsection (2) of section 66 of the Act (building society's statement of affairs) as applied to a building society has effect as if the reference to its creditors included a reference to all holders of shares in the society.

27C Section 48 of the Act (report by administrative receiver) or section 67 of the Act (report by receiver) as applied to a building society has effect as if—

(a) the reference in subsection (1) to the [Financial Conduct Authority] included a reference to the scheme manager;
(b) the reference in subsection (1)(d) to other creditors included a reference to holders of shares in the society;
(c) the references in paragraphs (a) and (b) of subsection (2) to unsecured creditors of the society included references to holders of shares in the society; and
(d) the reference in subsection (2) to a meeting of the society's unsecured creditors included a reference to a meeting of holders of shares in the society.

27D Subsection (1) of section 49 or 68 of the Act (committee of creditors) as applied to a building society has effect as if the reference to a meeting of creditors included a reference to a meeting of holders of shares in the society.".".

Paras (9), (10): substituted for original para (9) by SI 2016/679, art 5(1), (3)(c), in relation to a floating charge created by a building society on or after 28 June 2016. Para (9) (as amended by SI 2013/496, art 2(c), Sch 11, para 18(1), (5)) previously read as follows—

"(9) For paragraph 49, substitute—

"**49** Paragraph (3) of Article 50 of the Order (payment of debts out of assets subject to floating charge) as applied to a building society has effect as if the reference to general creditors included a reference to holders of shares in the society.

49A Paragraph (1) of Article 56 of the Order (information to be given by administrative receiver) as applied to a building society has effect as if the reference to all the creditors of a society included a reference to all the holders of shares in the society.

49B Paragraph (2) of Article 57 of the Order (statement of affairs to be submitted) as applied to a building society has effect as if the reference to its creditors included a reference to all holders of shares in the society.

49C Article 58 of the Order (report by administrative receiver) as applied to a building society has effect as if—

(a) the reference in paragraph (1) to the [Financial Conduct Authority] included a reference to the scheme manager;
(b) the reference in paragraph (1)(d) to other creditors included a reference to holders of shares in the society;
(c) the references in sub-paragraphs (a) and (b) of paragraph (2) to unsecured creditors of the society included references to holders of shares in the society; and
(d) the reference in paragraph (2) to a meeting of the society's unsecured creditors included a reference to a meeting of holders of shares in the society.

49D Paragraph (1) of article 59 of the Order (committee of creditors) as applied to a building society has effect as if the reference to a meeting of creditors included a reference to a meeting of holders of shares in the society.".".

12 (*Revokes the Building Societies (Financial Assistance) Order 2008, SI 2008/1427.*)

ELECTRONIC MONEY REGULATIONS 2011

(SI 2011/99)

NOTES

Made: 18 January 2011.
Authority: European Communities Act 1972, s 2(2).
Commencement: see reg 1(2).

PART 1
INTRODUCTORY PROVISIONS

[18.218]

1 Citation and commencement

(1) These Regulations may be cited as the Electronic Money Regulations 2011.

(2) These Regulations come into force on—

(a) 9th February 2011 for the purposes of—

(i) enabling applications to become an authorised electronic money institution and for the variation of an authorisation to be made under regulation 5 and the Authority to determine such applications in accordance with regulations 6 to 9;

(ii) enabling applications for registration as a small electronic money institution and the variation of a registration to be made under regulation 12 and the Authority to determine such applications in accordance with regulation 13 and regulations 7 to 9 (as applied by regulation 15);

(iii) enabling applications for an agent to be included on the register under regulation 34 and the Authority to determine such applications in accordance with that regulation;

(iv) enabling the Authority to give directions as to the manner in which an application under regulation 5(1) or (2), 12(1) or (2) or 34(3) is to be made and enabling the Authority to require the applicant to provide further information in accordance with regulation 5(4), 12(4) or 34(3)(a)(iv), as the case may be;

(v) enabling the Authority to cancel an authorisation or registration or vary an authorisation or registration on its own initiative in accordance with regulation 10 or 11 (as applied, in the case of registration, by regulation 15);

(vi) requiring a person who has made an application under regulation 5(1) or (2) or 12(1) or (2) to provide information to the Authority in accordance with regulation 17 and enabling the Authority to give directions under that regulation;

(vii) enabling a person to make a reference to the Upper Tribunal under regulation 9(8), 10(6), 11(5), 29(4) or 34(11);

(viii) enabling an applicant for authorisation as an electronic money institution to give the Authority a notice of intention under regulation 28(2) and the Authority to give directions as to the manner in which such a notice is to be given and to inform the host state competent authority in accordance with regulation 28(3);

(ix) enabling the Authority to decide whether to register an EEA branch or to cancel such a registration under regulation 29(1);

(x) enabling the Authority to give directions under regulation 49 to a person whose application under regulation 5(1) or 12(1) has been granted before 30th April 2011 in respect of—

(aa) its provision as from that date of electronic money issuance or payment services; and

(bb) its compliance as from that date with requirements imposed by or under Parts 2 to 5 of these Regulations;

(xi) enabling the Authority to give directions under paragraph 8, 10, 13(a), 15 or 16 of Schedule 2 to a person whose application under regulation 5(1) or 12(1) has been granted before 30th April 2011;

(xii) requiring a person whose application under regulation 5(1), 12(1) or 34(3) has been granted before 30th April 2011 to provide information to the Authority in accordance with regulation 37 and enabling the Authority to give directions under that regulation;

(xiii) regulations 30, 47, 59 to 61, 66 to 71, 74 and 78;

(xiv) regulation 62 in respect of paragraphs 2, 6 and 8 to 11 of Schedule 3;

(xv) regulation 79 in respect of paragraphs 2, 18 and 19(g) of Schedule 4; and

(b) 30th April 2011 for all other purposes.

2–19 (*Outside the scope of this work.*)

PART 3
PRUDENTIAL SUPERVISION AND PASSPORTING

Safeguarding

20, 21 (*Outside the scope of this work.*)

[18.219]
22 Safeguarding option 2

(1) An electronic money institution must ensure that—
  (a) any relevant funds are covered by—
    (i) an insurance policy with an authorised insurer;
    (ii) a [comparable] guarantee from an authorised insurer; or
    (iii) a [comparable] guarantee from an authorised credit institution; and
  (b) the proceeds of any such insurance policy or guarantee are payable upon an insolvency event into a separate account held by the electronic money institution which must—
    (i) be designated in such a way as to show that it is an account which is held for the purpose of safeguarding relevant funds in accordance with this regulation; and
    (ii) be used only for holding such proceeds[, or for holding those proceeds together with funds or assets held in accordance with regulation 21(3)].

(2) No person other than the electronic money institution may have any interest or right over the proceeds placed in an account in accordance with paragraph (1)(b) except as provided by this regulation.

(3) In this regulation—

"authorised credit institution" has the same meaning as in regulation 21;

"authorised insurer" means a person authorised for the purposes of the 2000 Act to effect and carry out a contract of general insurance as principal or otherwise authorised in accordance with [Article 14 of Directive 2009/138/EC of the European Parliament and of the Council of 25 November 2009 on the taking-up and pursuit of the business of Insurance and Reinsurance (Solvency II) to carry out non-life insurance activities within the meaning of Article 2(2) of that Directive], other than a person in the same group as the electronic money institution;

"insolvency event" means any of the following procedures in relation to an electronic money institution—
  (a) the making of a winding-up order;
  (b) the passing of a resolution for voluntary winding-up;
  (c) the entry of the institution into administration;
  (d) the appointment of a receiver or manager of the institution's property;
  (e) the approval of a proposed voluntary arrangement (being a composition in satisfaction of debts or a scheme of arrangement);
  (f) the making of a bankruptcy order;
  (g) in Scotland, the award of sequestration;
  (h) the making of any deed of arrangement for the benefit of creditors or, in Scotland, the execution of a trust deed for creditors;
  (i) the conclusion of any composition contract with creditors;
  (j) the making of an insolvency administration order or, in Scotland, the execution of a trust deed for creditors;
  (k) the conclusion of any composition contract with creditors; or
  (l) the making of an insolvency administration order or, in Scotland, sequestration, in respect of the estate of a deceased person.

NOTES

Para (1): words in square brackets in sub-para (a) inserted by the Payment Services Regulations 2017, SI 2017/752, reg 156, Sch 8, Pt 2, para 5(1), (15); words in square brackets in sub-para (b) inserted by the Payment Systems and Services and Electronic Money (Miscellaneous Amendments) Regulations 2017, SI 2017/1173, reg 5(b).

Para (3): words in square brackets definition "authorised insurer" substituted by the Solvency 2 Regulations 2015, SI 2015/575, reg 60, Sch 2, para 34.

23 (*Outside the scope of this work.*)

[18.220]
24 Insolvency events

(1) Subject to paragraph (2), where there is an insolvency event—
  (a) the claims of electronic money holders are to be paid from the asset pool in priority to all other creditors; and
  (b) until all the claims of electronic money holders have been paid, no right of set-off or security right may be exercised in respect of the asset pool except to the extent that the right of set-off relates to fees and expenses in relation to operating an account held in accordance with regulation 21(2)(a) or (b) [or (4A),] or 22(1)(b).

(2) The claims referred to in paragraph (1)(a) shall not be subject to the priority of expenses of an insolvency proceeding except in respect of the costs of distributing the asset pool.

(3) An electronic money institution must maintain organisational arrangements sufficient to minimise the risk of the loss or diminution of relevant funds or relevant assets through fraud, misuse, negligence or poor administration.

(4) In this regulation—

"asset pool" means—
  (a) any relevant funds segregated in accordance with regulation 21(1);
  (b) any relevant funds held in an account accordance with regulation 21(2)(a);

[(ba) where regulation 21(4A) applies, any funds that are received into the account held at the Bank of England upon settlement in respect of transfer orders that have been entered into the designated system on behalf of electronic money holders, whether settlement occurs before or after the insolvency event;]
(c) any relevant assets held in an account in accordance with regulation 21(2)(b);
(d) any proceeds of an insurance policy or guarantee held in an account in accordance with regulation 22(1)(b);

"insolvency event" has the same meaning as in regulation 22;
"insolvency proceeding" means—
(a) winding-up, administration, receivership, bankruptcy or, in Scotland, sequestration;
(b) a voluntary arrangement, deed of arrangement or trust deed for the benefit of creditors; or
(c) the administration of the insolvent estate of a deceased person;

"security right" means—
(a) security for a debt owed by an electronic money institution and includes any charge, lien, mortgage or other security over the asset pool or any part of the asset pool; and
(b) any charge arising in respect of the expenses of a voluntary arrangement.

[(5) In paragraph (4) "designated system", "settlement" and "transfer order" have the same meanings as in the Financial Markets and Insolvency (Settlement Finality) Regulations 1999.]

NOTES

Words in square brackets in para (1) inserted, sub-para (ba) of the definition "asset pool" in para (4) inserted, and para (5) added, by the Payment Services Regulations 2017, SI 2017/752, reg 156, Sch 8, Pt 2, para 5(1), (16).

25–80 (*Outside the scope of this work.*)

SCHEDULES 1–5

(*Schs 1–5 outside the scope of this work.*)

CHARITABLE INCORPORATED ORGANISATIONS (INSOLVENCY AND DISSOLUTION) REGULATIONS 2012

(SI 2012/3013)

NOTES

Made: 5 December 2012.
Authority: Charities Act 2011, ss 245, 347(3).
Commencement: 2 January 2013.

Note: the Insolvency Rules 1986, SI 1986/1925 are revoked and replaced (as from 6 April 2017 and subject to transitional provisions) by the Insolvency (England and Wales) Rules 2016, SI 2016/1024 at **[6.2]**, however, the Insolvency (England and Wales) Rules 2016 (Consequential Amendments and Savings) Rules 2017, SI 2017/369, r 3(h) at **[6.947]** provides that the Insolvency Rules 1986 as they had effect immediately before 6 April 2017 and insofar as they apply to proceedings under the Charitable Incorporated Organisations (Insolvency and Dissolution) Regulations 2012, continue to have effect for the purposes of the application of the 2012 Regulations.

See also the Deregulation Act 2015 and Small Business, Enterprise and Employment Act 2015 (Consequential Amendments) (Savings) Regulations 2017, SI 2017/540, reg 4(1), (2)(h) and the Insolvency Amendment (EU 2015/848) Regulations 2017, SI 2017/702, reg 4 at **[2.103]**, for savings in relation to the Insolvency Act 1986 in so far as it applies to proceedings under these Regulations.

ARRANGEMENT OF REGULATIONS

PART 1
GENERAL

1 Citation and commencement .... [18.221]
2 Interpretation: general .... [18.222]

PART 2
APPLICATION OF THE INSOLVENCY ACT 1986

3 Application of the Insolvency Act 1986 to CIOs .... [18.223]

PART 3
DISSOLUTION OTHERWISE THAN UNDER THE INSOLVENCY ACT 1986

4 Dissolution by Commission on application of CIO .... [18.224]
5 Application for dissolution .... [18.225]
6 Dissolution resolution .... [18.226]
7 Notice to be given before dissolution .... [18.227]
8 Application not to be made if CIO procedures not completed .... [18.228]
9 Application not to be made if other procedures not completed .... [18.229]
10 Restrictions following application for dissolution .... [18.230]
11 Property received after making application for dissolution .... [18.231]

12 Trustees to give notice of application for dissolution . . . . . [18.232]
13 Notice of application for dissolution: how to be given . . . . . [18.233]
14 Circumstances in which application must be withdrawn . . . . . [18.234]
15 Offences under the Companies Acts . . . . . [18.235]
16 Dissolution of CIO which is not in operation . . . . . [18.236]
17 Dissolution of CIO which is no longer a charity . . . . . [18.237]
18 Dissolution of CIO which is being wound up . . . . . [18.238]
19 Procedure for dissolution: delivery of letters and notices . . . . . [18.239]
20 Date of dissolution . . . . . [18.240]
21 Notice to be given of dissolution . . . . . [18.241]
22 Liabilities and powers unaffected by dissolution . . . . . [18.242]

PART 4
APPLICATION OF PROPERTY ON DISSOLUTION UNDER PART 3

23 Vesting of property to official custodian on dissolution . . . . . [18.243]
24 Disposal of property vested in official custodian . . . . . [18.244]
25 Power of Commission to specify charitable purposes etc . . . . . [18.245]
26 Power of Commission to make vesting order . . . . . [18.246]
27 Disclaimer of property by official custodian . . . . . [18.247]
28 Effect of a disclaimer by official custodian . . . . . [18.248]
29 Disclaimer of leaseholds . . . . . [18.249]
30 Power of court to make vesting order . . . . . [18.250]
31 Protection of persons holding under a lease . . . . . [18.251]
32 Land subject to rentcharge . . . . . [18.252]

PART 5
RESTORATION OF A CIO TO THE REGISTER

33 Restoration by Commission . . . . . [18.253]
34 Restoration by the court . . . . . [18.254]
35 Time limit for applying to court . . . . . [18.255]
36 Court order with directions . . . . . [18.256]
37 CIO's name on restoration . . . . . [18.257]
38 Notification of restoration to the register . . . . . [18.258]
39 Effect of restoration . . . . . [18.259]
40 Property to vest in restored CIO . . . . . [18.260]
41 Accounts, reports and returns of restored CIO . . . . . [18.261]

SCHEDULES

Schedule—Application of the Insolvency Act 1986 to CIOs . . . . . [18.262]

PART 1
GENERAL

[18.221]
1 Citation and commencement

These Regulations may be cited as the Charitable Incorporated Organisations (Insolvency and Dissolution) Regulations 2012 and come into force on the twenty eighth day after the day on which they are made.

[18.222]
2 Interpretation: general

(1) In these Regulations—

"the 1986 Act" means the Insolvency Act 1986;

"the 2011 Act" means the Charities Act 2011;

"constitutional directions" means the directions included in the CIO's constitution in accordance with section 206(2)(c) of the 2011 Act.

(2) For the purposes of these Regulations "body corporate" includes a body incorporated outside the United Kingdom but does not include—

(a) a corporation sole; or

(b) a partnership that, whether or not a legal person, is not regarded as a body corporate under the law by which it is governed.

Part 18 Miscellaneous SIs

PART 2
APPLICATION OF THE INSOLVENCY ACT 1986

[18.223]

3 Application of the Insolvency Act 1986 to CIOs

The Schedule (which makes provision concerning the application to CIOs of the 1986 Act and subordinate legislation made under that Act) has effect.

PART 3
DISSOLUTION OTHERWISE THAN UNDER THE INSOLVENCY ACT 1986

[18.224]

4 Dissolution by Commission on application of CIO

(1) The Commission may, on the application of a CIO, dissolve the CIO by removing it from the register.

(2) Such an application is referred to in this Part as an application for dissolution and must be made in accordance with regulation 5.

[18.225]

5 Application for dissolution

An application for dissolution—

(a) must be made on the CIO's behalf by the charity trustees or by a majority of them; and

(b) must contain—

(i) a copy of the resolution passed in accordance with the procedure prescribed in regulation 6;

(ii) a declaration, made by or on behalf of the charity trustees of the CIO, that any debts and other liabilities of the CIO have been settled or otherwise provided for in full; and

(iii) a statement, made by or on behalf of the charity trustees of the CIO, setting out the way in which any property vested in, or held on trust for, the CIO has been or is to be applied on dissolution in accordance with its constitutional directions.

[18.226]

6 Dissolution resolution

(1) The resolution to make an application for dissolution ("a dissolution resolution") must be passed by the members—

(a) at a general meeting of the CIO—

(i) by a 75% majority of those voting (including those voting by proxy or by post, if voting that way is permitted); or

(ii) where the CIO's constitution permits the members to make decisions otherwise than by voting, by a decision taken without a vote and without any expression of dissent in response to the question put to the meeting; or

(b) unanimously, otherwise than at a general meeting.

(2) Subject to paragraph (4), where a dissolution resolution is to be proposed at a general meeting of a CIO the person calling the meeting must give notice of not less than 14 days to—

(a) all members of the CIO entitled to vote at the meeting or, where the CIO's constitution permits the members to make decisions otherwise than by voting, all members entitled to take part in the decision to be made as to whether to pass the resolution at the meeting; and

(b) any charity trustee of the CIO who is not also a member of the CIO entitled to vote at the meeting or, where the CIO's constitution permits the members to make decisions otherwise than by voting, who is not also a member entitled to take part in the decision to be made as to whether to pass the resolution at that meeting;

and the notice must contain particulars of the dissolution resolution that is to be proposed.

(3) For the purpose of calculating the period of notice to be given under paragraph (2) the following are to be excluded—

(a) the day of the meeting; and

(b) the day on which notice is given.

(4) If a qualifying majority agrees, a dissolution resolution which is to be proposed at a general meeting may be passed without the notice provisions in paragraph (2) being satisfied.

(5) Where a dissolution resolution is passed otherwise than at a general meeting it is treated as having been passed on the date on which the last member agreed to it, unless the CIO's constitution provides that it is to be treated as having been passed on a later date.

(6) In this regulation—

"qualifying majority" means—

(a) in relation to a CIO whose members take decisions by voting, a majority in number of the members having a right to attend and vote at the meeting, who together represent not less than the requisite percentage of the total voting rights at that meeting of all the members;

(b) in relation to a CIO where the CIO's constitution permits the members to make decisions otherwise than by voting, all of the members having the right to attend the meeting and take part in the decisions to be made at the meeting;

"requisite percentage" means 90% or such higher percentage (not exceeding 95%) as may be specified in the CIO's constitution for the purposes of this regulation.

[18.227]

7 Notice to be given before dissolution

(1) The Commission must not dissolve a CIO under regulation 4 until 3 months after the publication by the Commission, in such manner as it thinks fit, of a notice stating that it has received an application for dissolution from the CIO.

(2) The Commission must not dissolve the CIO if, within the period mentioned in sub-paragraph (1), any person has shown cause why the Commission should not dissolve the CIO.

[18.228]

8 Application not to be made if CIO procedures not completed

(1) The charity trustees must not make an application for dissolution if—

(a) the CIO has any debts or other liabilities which have not been settled or otherwise provided for in full; or

(b) any decision which must be taken for the purpose of giving effect to the constitutional directions has not been taken.

(2) Subsections (5) to (7) of section 1004 of the Companies Act 2006 (offence of applying for a company to be struck off in contravention of requirements of that section) apply in relation to an application by a charity trustee in contravention of paragraph (1) as they apply in relation to an application in contravention of that section.

(3) Section 1004(6) of that Act, in its application by virtue of paragraph (2), has effect as if for "that he did not know, and could not reasonably have known, of the existence of the facts that led to the contravention" there were substituted—

"(a) if the CIO had outstanding debts or other liabilities at the time the application was made, that the accused reasonably believed all of the CIO's debts or other liabilities had been settled in full or otherwise provided for;

(b) if a decision required to be taken for the purpose of the constitutional directions had not been taken, that the accused reasonably believed the necessary decision had been properly taken.".

[18.229]

9 Application not to be made if other procedures not completed

(1) The charity trustees must not make an application for dissolution if—

(a) a voluntary arrangement in relation to the CIO has been proposed under Part 1 of the 1986 Act and the matter has not been finally concluded;

(b) the CIO is in administration under Part 2 of that Act;

(c) an interim moratorium is in effect in relation to the CIO under paragraph 44 of Schedule B1 to that Act;

(d) the CIO is being wound up under Part 4 of that Act, whether voluntarily or by the court, or a petition under that Part for the winding up of the CIO by the court has been presented and not been finally dealt with or withdrawn;

(e) a receiver, manager or interim manager of the CIO's property has been appointed.

(2) For the purposes of paragraph (1)(a), the matter is finally concluded if—

(a) no meetings are to be summoned under section 3 of the 1986 Act;

(b) meetings summoned under that section fail to approve the arrangement;

(c) an arrangement approved by meetings summoned under that section, or in consequence of a direction under section 6(4)(b) of that Act, has been fully implemented; or

(d) the court makes an order under section 6(5) of that Act revoking approval given at previous meetings and, if the court gives any directions under section 6(6) of that Act, the CIO has done whatever it is required to do under those directions.

(3) Subsections (4) to (6) of section 1005 of the Companies Act 2006 (offence of applying for a company to be struck off in contravention of requirements of that section) apply in relation to an application by a charity trustee in contravention of paragraph (1) as they apply in relation to an application in contravention of that section.

[18.230]

10 Restrictions following application for dissolution

In any case where an application for dissolution has been made, the CIO must not—

(a) engage in any activity except one which is necessary or expedient for the purposes of—

(i) proceeding with the application;

(ii) giving effect to any decision made under the constitutional directions; or

(iii) complying with any statutory requirement; or

(b) otherwise incur any debts or other liabilities.

[18.231]

11 Property received after making application for dissolution

If property is received by the CIO after the date on which the application for dissolution was made, the charity trustees must give notice to the Commission and either—

(a) withdraw the application; or

(b) send to the Commission a statement, made by or on behalf of the charity trustees of the CIO, setting out the way in which the property has been or is to be applied on dissolution in accordance with its constitutional directions.

[18.232]
12 Trustees to give notice of application for dissolution

(1) The charity trustees who make an application for dissolution on behalf of a CIO must secure that, within 7 days beginning with the day on which the application is made, notice of it is given to every person who at any time on that day is—

(a) a member of the CIO;
(b) an employee of the CIO; or
(c) a charity trustee of the CIO.

(2) Paragraph (1) does not require notice to be given to any charity trustee who is party to the application.

(3) The notice must state—

(a) the date on which the application for dissolution is made;
(b) the names of the charity trustees making the application.

(4) The duty imposed by this regulation ceases to apply if the application is withdrawn before the end of the period for giving notice.

(5) Subsections (4) to (7) of section 1006 of the Companies Act 2006 (offence of failing to comply with duty to provide copy of striking off application in respect of a company to members, employees etc) apply in relation to a failure by a charity trustee to perform the duty imposed by paragraph (1) as they apply in relation to a failure to perform the duty imposed by that section.

(6) Section 1006(7) of that Act, in its application by virtue of paragraph (5), has effect as if paragraph (b)(ii) were omitted.

[18.233]
13 Notice of application for dissolution: how to be given

(1) The following provisions have effect for the purposes of regulation 12.

(2) Notice of an application for dissolution is treated as being given to a person ("P") if it is—

(a) delivered to P;
(b) left at P's proper address; or
(c) sent by post to P at that address.

(3) For the purposes of paragraph (2) above and section 7 (service of documents by post) of the Interpretation Act 1978 as it applies in relation to that paragraph, the proper address of a person is—

(a) in the case of a body corporate incorporated in the United Kingdom, its registered or principal office;
(b) in the case of a body corporate incorporated outside the United Kingdom—
 (i) if it has a place of business in the United Kingdom, its principal office in the United Kingdom; or
 (ii) if it does not have a place of business in the United Kingdom, its registered or principal office;
(c) in the case of an individual, that individual's last known address.

[18.234]
14 Circumstances in which application must be withdrawn

(1) This regulation applies if an application for dissolution has been made and before it is finally dealt with or withdrawn—

(a) an application to the court for an administration order in respect of the CIO is made under paragraph 12 of Schedule B1 to the 1986 Act;
(b) an administrator is appointed in respect of the CIO under paragraph 14 or 22 of Schedule B1 to that Act or a copy of notice of intention to appoint an administrator of the CIO under either of those provisions is filed with the court;
(c) there arise any of the circumstances in which, under section 84(1) of that Act, the CIO may be voluntarily wound up;
(d) a petition is presented for the winding up of the CIO by the court under Part 4 of that Act;
(e) a receiver, manager or interim manager of the CIO's property is appointed; or
(f) the CIO incurs any liability contrary to regulation 10.

(2) A person who, at the end of the day on which any of the events mentioned in paragraph (1) occurs, is a charity trustee of the CIO must immediately notify the Commission that the event has occurred and withdraw the CIO's application.

(3) Subsections (5) to (7) of section 1009 of the Companies Act 2006 (offence of failing to withdraw striking off application in respect of a company) apply in relation to a failure by a charity trustee to perform the duty imposed by paragraph (2) as they apply in relation to a failure to perform the duty imposed by that section.

(4) Section 1009(6) of that Act, in its application by virtue of paragraph (3), has effect as if for "the company had made an application under section 1003" there were substituted "an application for the dissolution of the CIO had been made under regulation 5 of the Charitable Incorporated Organisations (Insolvency and Dissolution) Regulations 2012".

[18.235]

15 Offences under the Companies Acts

(1) The following provisions of Part 36 of the Companies Act 2006 (offences under the Companies Act) apply to an offence under that Act committed by virtue of regulation 8, 9, 12 or 14 as they apply to an offence under the Companies Acts—

(a) section 1127 (summary proceedings: venue);

(b) section 1128 (summary proceedings: time limit for proceedings);

(c) section 1129 (legal professional privilege);

(d) section 1131 (imprisonment on summary conviction in England and Wales: transitory provision); and

(e) section 1132 (production and inspection of documents where offence suspected).

(2) In their application to CIOs those sections have effect as if—

(a) for references to a company there were substituted references to a CIO;

(b) for references to an officer of a company there were substituted references to a charity trustee of a CIO;

(c) provisions relating only to Scotland or Northern Ireland were omitted;

(d) references to the Secretary of State were omitted.

(3) In its application to CIOs section 1132(3)(b) has effect as if for "the secretary of the company, or such other officer of it" there were substituted "such charity trustee of the CIO".

[18.236]

16 Dissolution of CIO which is not in operation

(1) If the Commission has reasonable cause to believe that a CIO is not in operation it must send the CIO a letter inquiring whether the CIO is in operation.

(2) If it does not receive an answer within 1 month after the date of the letter the Commission must, no later than 2 months after the date of the letter, send the CIO a second letter inquiring whether the CIO is in operation.

(3) The second letter must refer to the first letter and state that, if an answer is not received to either letter within 1 month after the date of the second letter, the Commission will publish notice of its intention to dissolve the CIO.

(4) If the Commission—

(a) receives an answer to either letter to the effect that the CIO is not in operation; or

(b) has, after 1 month beginning with the date of the second letter, not received any answer to either letter,

the Commission must publish, in such manner as it thinks fit, notice of its intention to dissolve the CIO after 3 months from the date of the notice unless it is shown that the CIO is in operation or will be in operation within a reasonable period of time.

(5) The Commission must send the CIO a copy of the notice published under paragraph (4).

(6) No earlier than 3 months after the publication of the notice of intention the Commission must dissolve the CIO by removing it from the register, unless it is satisfied that—

(a) the CIO is in operation; or

(b) the CIO will be in operation within a reasonable period of time.

(7) In this regulation the date of a letter is the date on which it is sent.

[18.237]

17 Dissolution of CIO which is no longer a charity

(1) If the Commission no longer considers a CIO to be a charity it must publish, in such manner as it thinks fit, notice of its intention to dissolve the CIO after 3 months beginning with the date of the notice unless cause is shown to the contrary.

(2) The Commission must send the CIO a copy of the notice published under paragraph (1).

(3) No earlier than 3 months after the publication of the notice of intention the Commission must, unless cause has been shown to the contrary, dissolve the CIO by removing it from the register.

[18.238]

18 Dissolution of CIO which is being wound up

(1) If a CIO is being wound up and—

(a) the Commission has reasonable cause to believe that no liquidator is acting or that the affairs of the CIO are fully wound up; and

(b) the returns required to be made by the liquidator have not been made for a period of 6 consecutive months,

the Commission must publish, in such manner as it thinks fit, notice of its intention to dissolve the CIO after 3 months beginning with the date of the notice unless cause is shown to the contrary.

(2) The Commission must send the CIO and the liquidator (if any) a copy of the notice published under paragraph (1).

(3) No earlier than 3 months after the publication of the notice of intention the Commission must, unless cause has been shown to the contrary, dissolve the CIO by removing it from the register.

[18.239]
19 Procedure for dissolution: delivery of letters and notices

(1) This regulation applies for the purpose of determining the manner of delivery of letters and notices to be sent under regulation 16, 17 or 18.

(2) The letter or notice must be sent to the CIO at its principal office as it appears on the register of charities.

(3) If the Commission has reasonable grounds to believe that sending the letter or notice to the CIO's principal office as it appears on the register of charities is unlikely to bring it to the attention of the charity trustees, the Commission must also send it to any other address the Commission has for the CIO.

(4) If the Commission has reasonable grounds to believe that sending the letter or notice to any other address it has for the CIO is unlikely to bring it to the attention of the charity trustees, the Commission must also send it to each charity trustee of the CIO for whom the Commission has an address.

(5) If there are no charity trustees for whom the Commission has an address, the Commission must also send the letter or notice to any member of the CIO for whom the Commission has an address.

(6) A notice to be sent to a liquidator may be addressed to the liquidator at the liquidator's last known place of business.

(7) The Commission may send a letter (other than a letter under regulation 16(3)) or notice by electronic means to an electronic address if the intended recipient has agreed that the Commission may send documents or other information by electronic means to that address.

(8) In this regulation "electronic means" has the meaning given by regulation 4 of the Charitable Incorporated Organisations (General) Regulations 2012.

[18.240]
20 Date of dissolution

If the Commission removes a CIO from the register under this Part, it is dissolved on the date on which it is removed.

[18.241]
21 Notice to be given of dissolution

(1) If the Commission dissolves a CIO under this Part the Commission must publish a notice stating the date on which the CIO was dissolved.

(2) The notice under paragraph (1) must be published by the Commission in the same manner as any notice published in relation to the CIO under regulation 7, 16, 17 or 18 (as the case may be).

[18.242]
22 Liabilities and powers unaffected by dissolution

Despite the dissolution of a CIO under this Part—

(a) the liability (if any) of every charity trustee and member of the CIO continues and may be enforced as if the CIO had not been dissolved; and

(b) the court continues to have the power to wind up the CIO.

PART 4
APPLICATION OF PROPERTY ON DISSOLUTION UNDER PART 3

[18.243]
23 Vesting of property to official custodian on dissolution

(1) On the dissolution of a CIO under Part 3, all relevant property vests in the official custodian.

(2) For the purposes of this regulation "relevant property" includes any property and rights whatsoever (including leasehold property) vested in or held on trust for the CIO immediately before its dissolution.

(3) But "relevant property" does not include—

(a) any property held by the CIO on trust for any other person;

(b) any property held by the CIO on trust for any special purposes of the CIO;

(c) any property vested in or held on trust for the CIO if—

(i) the CIO, or the charity trustees (as the case may be) had, before its dissolution, complied with the constitutional directions in respect of that property; but

(ii) in accordance with those directions, the transfer or other disposition of that property would only take effect on the dissolution of the CIO.

(4) Subject to regulation 25, any property which vests in the official custodian under this regulation is held by the official custodian on trust for the charitable purposes of the CIO immediately before its dissolution.

[18.244]
24 Disposal of property vested in official custodian

The official custodian may not dispose of any property which vests in him under regulation 23 otherwise than—

(a) in accordance with an order of the Commission under regulation 26; or

(b) by disclaiming title to it under regulation 27.

[18.245]
25 Power of Commission to specify charitable purposes etc

(1) The Commission may by order specify the charitable purposes, charity or charities (as the case may be) for which the official custodian holds the property of a CIO on trust.

(2) In determining what charitable purposes, charity or charities to specify the Commission must have regard to—

(a) the constitutional directions included in the CIO's constitution immediately before its dissolution;
(b) the desirability of securing that the property of the CIO is applied for charitable purposes which are close to the charitable purposes of the CIO immediately before its dissolution; and
(c) the need for the property to be applied for charitable purposes which are suitable and effective in the light of current social and economic circumstances.

(3) The Commission may not make an order under this regulation until 3 months after the date on which the CIO was dissolved.

(4) Section 88 of the 2011 Act (publicity relating to schemes) applies to an order under this regulation as it applies to an order under that Act to establish a scheme for the administration of a charity.

(5) The Commission may determine that either or both of the publicity requirements in section 88(2) of the 2011 Act is or are not to apply if it is satisfied that compliance with the requirement or requirements is unnecessary in a particular case.

[18.246]
26 Power of Commission to make vesting order

(1) Where property is held by the official custodian in accordance with an order made under regulation 25, the Commission may by order make provision for the vesting of all or any of that property—

(a) in a charity or, in such shares as it considers appropriate, in any two or more of the charities specified in the order made under regulation 25; or
(b) in a charity or, in such shares as it considers appropriate, in any two or more charities which, in the Commission's view, further the charitable purposes specified in the order made under regulation 25.

(2) An order under this regulation may be made at the same time as an order under regulation 25.

(3) Any order made under paragraph (1) may give such directions as the Commission thinks necessary or expedient in consequence of the provision made by the order.

(4) A person acting in conformity with an order made under this regulation, or giving effect to anything done in pursuance of such an order, is not liable for any loss occasioned by so acting.

(5) A person is not excused from acting in conformity with an order made under this regulation by reason of the order having been in any respect improperly obtained.

[18.247]
27 Disclaimer of property by official custodian

(1) Where property vests in the official custodian under regulation 23 the official custodian may by notice disclaim title to any or all of that property.

(2) A notice for the purposes of this regulation—

(a) may be in such form as the official custodian thinks fit; but
(b) must be signed by, or on behalf of, the official custodian.

(3) The official custodian may disclaim property under this regulation whether or not the Commission has made an order under regulation 25.

(4) The right to disclaim property under this regulation may be waived by or on behalf of the official custodian by an express waiver or by the official custodian taking possession of the property.

(5) A notice of disclaimer is not effective unless it is signed within 3 years after—

(a) the date on which the fact that the property may have vested in the official custodian under regulation 23 first comes to the notice of the official custodian; or
(b) if ownership of the property is not established at that date, the end of the period reasonably necessary for the official custodian to establish ownership of the property.

(6) If an application in writing is made to the official custodian by a person interested in the property requiring the official custodian to decide whether or not to disclaim, a notice of disclaimer is not effective unless it is signed within 12 months after the application is made or such further period as may be allowed by the court.

(7) The official custodian must within 14 days after signing a notice of disclaimer—

(a) send a copy of it to—
  (i) the Commission; and
  (ii) any person who has given notice to the official custodian claiming to be interested in the property; and
(b) publish it in such manner as the official custodian thinks fit having regard in particular to the manner in which the Commission published any notice relating to the CIO under any provision of Part 3 of these Regulations.

[18.248]
28 Effect of a disclaimer by official custodian

(1) Where any property is disclaimed, it is treated as not having vested in the official custodian under regulation 23.

(2) A disclaimer operates so as to terminate, from the date the notice of disclaimer is signed, the rights, interests and liabilities of the CIO in or in respect of the disclaimed property.

(3) A disclaimer does not, except so far as is necessary for the purpose of releasing the CIO from any liability, affect the rights or liabilities of any other person.

[18.249]
29 Disclaimer of leaseholds

(1) A disclaimer of property of a leasehold character does not take effect unless a copy of the notice under regulation 27 has been served (so far as the official custodian is aware of their addresses) on every person claiming under the CIO as underlessee or mortgagee and either—

(a) no application under regulation 30 is made with respect to that property within 14 days of the day on which the copy of the notice was served; or

(b) where such an application has been made, the court directs that the disclaimer shall take effect.

(2) If the court directs that the disclaimer shall take effect, it may make such order as it thinks fit with respect to fixtures, tenant's improvements and other matters arising out of the lease.

[18.250]
30 Power of court to make vesting order

(1) The court may make an order under paragraph (2), on such terms as it thinks fit, on the application of a person who—

(a) claims an interest in the disclaimed property; or

(b) is under a liability in respect of the disclaimed property that is not discharged by the disclaimer.

(2) An order under this paragraph is an order to vest the disclaimed property in, or require its delivery to—

(a) a person entitled to it (or a trustee for such a person); or

(b) a person subject to a liability as is mentioned in paragraph (1)(b) (or a trustee for such a person).

(3) An order under paragraph (2)(b) may only be made where it appears to the court that it would be just to do so for the purpose of compensating the person subject to the liability in respect of the disclaimed property.

(4) On an order being made, the property comprised in it vests in the person named in the order without conveyance, assignment or transfer.

[18.251]
31 Protection of persons holding under a lease

(1) The court must not make an order under regulation 30 vesting property of a leasehold nature in a person ("P") claiming under the CIO as underlessee or mortgagee except on terms making P—

(a) subject to the same liabilities and obligations as those to which the CIO was subject under the lease; or

(b) if the court thinks fit, subject to the same liabilities and obligations as if the lease had been assigned to P.

(2) Where the order relates to only part of the property comprised in the lease, paragraph (1) applies as if the lease had comprised only the property comprised in the order.

(3) A person claiming under the CIO as underlessee or mortgagee who declines to accept a vesting order on such terms is excluded from all interest in the property.

(4) If there is no person claiming under the CIO as underlessee or mortgagee who is willing to accept an order on such terms, the court may vest the CIO's estate or interest in the property in any person who is liable (whether personally or in a representative character, and whether alone or jointly with the CIO) to perform the lessee's covenants in the lease.

(5) The court may vest that estate and interest in such person freed and discharged from all estates, incumbrances and interests created by the CIO.

[18.252]
32 Land subject to rentcharge

Where, in consequence of the disclaimer, land that is subject to a rentcharge vests in any person ("P"), neither P nor P's successors in title are subject to any personal liability in respect of sums becoming due under the rentcharge, except sums becoming due after P, or some person claiming under or through P, has taken possession or control of the land or has entered into occupation of it.

PART 5
RESTORATION OF A CIO TO THE REGISTER

[18.253]
33 Restoration by Commission

(1) The Commission may restore to the register any CIO which it removed from the register under regulation 16 or 18.

(2) The Commission may restore a CIO under this regulation of its own motion or on the application of any person who was a charity trustee of the CIO immediately before its dissolution.

(3) Where the Commission has made an order under regulation 26 vesting in a charity or charities all of the property which is or was held on trust by the official custodian under regulation 23, the Commission must not restore the CIO to the register unless—

(a) all appeal rights in connection with that order have been exhausted;

(b) any appeal brought in connection with that order has been discontinued before it was finally determined; or

(c) the period within which any appeal, or any subsequent appeal, may have been made has expired.

(4) The Commission must not restore the CIO to the register after the end of the period of 6 years from the date of dissolution.

[18.254]

34 Restoration by the court

(1) On an application under this regulation the court may, if it considers it just to do so, order that a CIO is restored to the register.

(2) An application may be made to restore a CIO—

(a) that has been dissolved under Chapter 9 of Part 4 of the 1986 Act, as it applies to CIOs; or

(b) that is treated as having been dissolved under paragraph 84(6) of Schedule B1 to that Act, as it applies to CIOs.

(3) An application may be made by—

(a) the Commission;

(b) any person who was a charity trustee of the CIO immediately prior to its dissolution;

(c) any person having an interest in land in which the CIO had a superior or derivative interest;

(d) any person having an interest in land or other property—

(i) that was subject to rights vested in the CIO; or

(ii) that was benefitted by obligations owed by the CIO;

(e) any person who but for the CIO's dissolution would have had a contractual relationship with it;

(f) any person who has a potential legal claim against the CIO;

(g) any manager or trustee of a pension fund established for the benefit of employees of the CIO;

(h) any person who was a member of the CIO immediately prior to its dissolution (or the personal representatives of such a person);

(i) any person who was a creditor of the CIO at the time of its dissolution;

(j) any former liquidator of the CIO; or

(k) any other person appearing to the court to have an interest in the matter.

(4) If the court orders that the CIO is restored to the register—

(a) the Commission must restore the CIO to the register; and

(b) the CIO is treated as restored to the register on delivery to the Commission of a copy of the court order.

[18.255]

35 Time limit for applying to court

(1) Subject to paragraph (2), an application to the court to restore a CIO to the register may not be made after the end of the period of 6 years from the date of dissolution.

(2) An application may be made at any time for the purpose of bringing proceedings against the CIO for damages for personal injury.

(3) The court must refuse an application under paragraph (2) if it appears to the court that the proceedings would fail by virtue of any enactment as to the time within which proceedings must be brought.

(4) In making that decision the court must have regard to its power under regulation 36 to direct that the period between the dissolution of the CIO and the making of the order is not to count for the purposes of any such enactment.

(5) For the purposes of this regulation—

(a) "personal injury" includes any disease and any impairment of a person's physical or mental condition; and

(b) references to damages for personal injury include any sum claimed by virtue of section 1(2)(c) of the Law Reform (Miscellaneous Provisions) Act 1934.

[18.256]

36 Court order with directions

(1) Where a court orders the restoration of a CIO to the register, it may give such directions and make such provision as seems just for placing the CIO and all other persons in the same position (as nearly as may be) as if the CIO had not been dissolved.

(2) Despite paragraph (1) the court may not give any directions or make any provision in relation to the matters covered by regulation 41.

[18.257]

37 CIO's name on restoration

(1) Subject to paragraphs (2) and (3), a CIO is to be restored to the register with the name it had immediately before it was dissolved.

(2) Where—
(a) the CIO is to be restored to the register following an application to the court; and
(b) the order made by the court specifies a new name for the CIO on restoration,
the CIO must be restored to the register with that name.
(3) Where—
(a) the CIO is to be restored to the register otherwise than following an application to the court; and
(b) the Commission is satisfied that it would, were an application being made for the registration of the CIO with the name it had immediately prior to its dissolution, refuse to register the CIO on the grounds specified in section 208(2)(a) of the 2011 Act,
the CIO must be restored to the register with a new name specified by the Commission.
(4) Where—
(a) the CIO is restored to the register with a new name specified by the court, and
(b) the Commission is satisfied that it could, were an application being made for the registration of the CIO with the new name, refuse to register the CIO on the grounds specified in section 208(2)(a) of the 2011 Act,
the Commission may give a direction to the charity trustees of the CIO requiring the name of the CIO to be changed, within such period as is specified in the direction, to such other name as the charity trustees of the CIO may determine with the approval of the Commission.
(5) The Commission may not give a direction under paragraph (4) after 12 months from the date of the CIO's restoration to the register.
(6) Sections 43 and 44 of the 2011 Act apply to a direction made under paragraph (4) as they apply to a direction made under section 42(1) of that Act.

[18.258]
38 Notification of restoration to the register
(1) Where a CIO is restored to the register the Commission must publish notice of the restoration in such manner as it thinks fit.
(2) A notice published by the Commission under paragraph (1) must state—
(a) the name of the CIO; and
(b) the date on which the restoration took effect.
(3) Where a CIO is to be restored to the register with a name other than the name it had immediately before it was dissolved, the notice published by the Commission must include—
(a) the name with which the CIO is restored to the register; and
(b) the name the CIO had immediately prior to its dissolution.

[18.259]
39 Effect of restoration
(1) A CIO which is restored to the register is treated for all purposes as having continued in existence as if it had not been dissolved.
(2) Paragraph (1) does not affect the validity of anything done by the charity trustees of the restored CIO before its restoration in reliance on consent given by the Commission in accordance with section 131(3) of the 2011 Act (preservation of accounting records) or section 134(3) of that Act (preservation of statement of accounts or account and statement).

[18.260]
40 Property to vest in restored CIO
On the date of restoration any property of the CIO which is vested in the official custodian vests in the restored CIO.

[18.261]
41 Accounts, reports and returns of restored CIO
(1) In its application to a relevant financial year of a restored CIO, Part 8 of the 2011 Act (charity accounts, reports and returns) is to be read subject to the provisions of this regulation.
(2) The following provisions do not apply unless the Commission requests that the accounts, annual report or annual return (as the case may be) for that year are prepared—
(a) section 132(1) (requirement to prepare statement of accounts);
(b) section 138(2) (requirement to prepare group accounts);
(c) section 162(1) (requirement to prepare annual report);
(d) section 169(1) (requirement to prepare annual return).
(3) The charity trustees must transmit to the Commission, within 10 months from the date of any request under paragraph (2), the accounts, annual report or annual return (as the case may be). The following provisions are modified accordingly—
(a) section 163(1) (requirement to transmit annual report to Commission); and
(b) section 169(3) (requirement to transmit annual return to Commission).
(4) Where the Commission requests that accounts are prepared, but not an annual report, a copy of the relevant auditor's or examiner's report must be transmitted to the Commission with the accounts as if section 164 (documents to be transmitted with annual report) applied.
(5) The Commission's power in the following provisions applies only where the accounts have not been audited within 10 months from the date of the Commission's request—
(a) section 146(1)(a) (power to require accounts to be audited);

(b) section 153(1)(a) (power to require group accounts to be audited).

(6) In the following provisions the requirement is to preserve for at least 6 years from the date of the Commission's request—

(a) section 134(1) (preservation of statement of accounts or account and statement);

(b) section 140(1) (preservation of group accounts).

(7) The charity trustees are not guilty of an offence under section 173 (offences of failing to supply certain documents) in relation to a failure to transmit an annual report or annual return unless the Commission has requested that the annual report or annual return (as the case may be) is prepared for that year.

(8) For the purposes of this regulation "relevant financial year" means a year other than—

(a) a financial year of the CIO in relation to which the period for transmission to the Commission, under section 163 (transmission of annual reports to Commission in certain cases), of the annual report for that year ended before the dissolution of the CIO;

(b) a financial year of the CIO which began after restoration of the CIO.

SCHEDULE
APPLICATION OF THE INSOLVENCY ACT 1986 TO CIOS

Regulation 3

[18.262]

Application to CIOs of the 1986 Act

1 (1) The provisions of the 1986 Act specified in sub-paragraph (2) apply in relation to CIOs as they apply in relation to companies registered in England and Wales with—

(a) the general modifications set out in sub-paragraph (3);

(b) the substitution of the provision specified in sub-paragraph (4) for section 84 of that Act;

(c) the substitution of the provision specified in sub-paragraph (5) for section 122 of that Act;

(d) the substitution of the provision specified in sub-paragraph (6) for section 154 of that Act;

(e) the further modifications specified in the Table in sub-paragraph (7); and

(f) any other necessary modification.

(2) The specified provisions of the 1986 Act are—

(a) Parts 1 to 4 other than—

(i) section 28;

(ii) Chapters 2 and 3 of Part 3;

(iii) sections 72B to 72F, 72GA, 76 to 78, 83, 93, 105, 111, 113, 120, 121, 124A to 124C, 138, 142, 157, 161, 162, 169, 185, 193, 198, 199 and 204;

(iv) paragraphs 3, 4A to 5, 21, 23 and 44 of Schedule A1;

(v) paragraphs 9, 111A to 116 of Schedule B1;

(vi) paragraph 19 of Schedule 1;

(vii) paragraph 3 of Schedule 4;

(b) Parts 6 and 7 other than section 242, 243 and 250;

(c) the Third Group of Parts (miscellaneous matters bearing on both company and individual insolvency; general interpretation; final provisions) other than sections 389B, 402, 412, 415, 417, 418, 420, 421, 421A, 422, 426, 426A, 426B, 426C, 427, 428, 429, 434E, 437, 438, 439, 440, 441 and 442.

(3) The general modifications are—

(a) any reference to a company or a company registered under the Companies Act 2006 in England and Wales, is to be read as a reference to a CIO;

(b) any reference to a company being wound up by the court in England and Wales is to be read as a reference to a CIO being wound by the court;

(c) any reference to a company being wound up in England and Wales is to be read as a reference to a CIO being wound up;

(d) any reference to a winding up in England and Wales is to be read as a reference to the winding up of a CIO;

(e) any reference to the registrar of companies is to be read as a reference to the Charity Commission;

(f) in any provision which requires an original document to be sent to the Charity Commission, any reference to an original document is to be read as a reference to a copy of that document;

(g) any reference to the registered office of a company is to be read as a reference to the principal office of a CIO;

(h) any reference to a general meeting of a company is to be read as a general meeting of a CIO;

(i) any reference to a director of a company is to be read as a reference to a charity trustee of a CIO;

(j) any reference to an officer of a company is to be read as a reference to a charity trustee of a CIO;

(k) any reference to a shadow director is to be treated as omitted;

(l) in any enactment of the 1986 Act which makes provision (for any purpose) for "officer" to include a shadow director, any such provision is to be treated as omitted;

(m) any reference to a company's articles of association is to be read as a reference to a CIO's constitution;

(n) any reference to the interests of a member is to be read as a reference to the interests of the relevant CIO;

(o) any reference to the business of a company is to be read as a reference to the activities the CIO undertakes in furtherance of its charitable purposes;

in each case, unless the context otherwise requires.

Part 18 Miscellaneous SIs

(4) The provision to be substituted for section 84 of the 1986 Act is—

"Circumstances in which CIO may be wound up voluntarily

84 (1) A CIO may be wound up voluntarily if its members pass a resolution that it be wound up voluntarily.

(2) A resolution under subsection (1) must be passed—

(a) at a general meeting of the CIO—

(i) by a 75% majority of those voting (including those voting by proxy or by post, if voting that way is permitted); or

(ii) where the CIO's constitution permits the members to make decisions otherwise than by voting, by a decision taken without a vote and without any expression of dissent in response to the question put to the meeting; or

(b) unanimously, otherwise than at a general meeting.

(3) In this Act "a resolution for voluntary winding up" means a resolution passed under subsection (1).

(4) Before the members of a CIO pass a resolution for voluntary winding up, they must give written notice of the resolution to the holder of any qualifying floating charge to which section 72A applies.

(5) Where notice is given under subsection (4), a resolution for voluntary winding-up may be passed only—

(a) after the end of the period of five business days beginning with the day on which the notice was given; or

(b) if the person to whom the notice was given has consented in writing to the passing of the resolution.

(6) If a resolution for voluntary winding up is to be proposed at a general meeting of a CIO, the person calling the meeting must give notice of not less than 14 days to—

(a) all members of the CIO entitled to vote at the meeting or, where the CIO's constitution permits the members to make decisions otherwise than by voting, all members entitled to take part in the decision to be made as to whether to pass the resolution at the meeting; and

(b) any charity trustee of the CIO who is not also a member of the CIO entitled to vote at the meeting or, where the CIO's constitution permits the members to make decisions otherwise than by voting, who is not also a member entitled to take part in the decision to be made as to whether to pass the resolution at the meeting;

and the notice must contain particulars of the resolution that is to be proposed.

(7) For the purpose of calculating the period of notice to be given under subsection (6) the following are to be excluded—

(a) the day of the meeting; and

(b) the day on which notice is given.

(8) If a qualifying majority agrees, a resolution for voluntary winding up which is to be proposed at a general meeting may be passed without the notice provisions in subsection (6) being satisfied.

(9) Where a resolution for voluntary winding up is passed otherwise than at a general meeting it is treated as having been passed on the date on which the last member agreed to it, unless the CIO's constitution provides that it is to be treated as having been passed on a later date.

(10) A copy of every resolution for voluntary winding up or (in the case of a resolution that is not in writing) a written memorandum setting out its terms must be sent to the Charity Commission within 15 days of the date on which it is passed.

(11) If a CIO fails to comply with subsection (10) an offence is committed by the liquidator and by every charity trustee of the CIO who is in default.

(12) In this section—

"qualifying majority" means—

(a) in relation to a CIO whose members take decisions by voting, a majority in number of the members having a right to attend and vote at the meeting, who together represent not less than the requisite percentage of the total voting rights at that meeting of all the members;

(b) in relation to a CIO whose members take decisions otherwise than by voting, all of the members having the right to attend the meeting and to take part in the decisions to be made at that meeting;

"requisite percentage" means 90% or such higher percentage (not exceeding 95%) as may be specified in the CIO's constitution for the purposes of this section.".

(5) The provision to be substituted for section 122 of the 1986 Act is—

"Circumstances in which CIO may be wound up by the court

122 (1) A CIO may be wound up by the court if—

(a) the members of the CIO have passed a resolution that the CIO be wound up by the court ("resolution for court winding up");

(b) the CIO does not commence its business within a year of its registration in the register of charities or suspends its business for a whole year;

(c) the CIO is unable to pay its debts;

(d) at the time when a moratorium for the CIO under section 1A comes to an end, no voluntary arrangement approved under Part 1 has effect in relation to the CIO;

(e) it is just and equitable in the opinion of the court that the CIO should be wound up.

(2) The resolution for court winding up must be passed by the members of the CIO in accordance with section 84(2).
(3) Subsections (6) to (12) of section 84 apply in relation to a resolution for court winding up as they apply to a resolution for voluntary winding up.".

(6) The provision to be substituted for section 154 of the 1986 Act is—

"Application of surplus

154 The court shall make such directions as it considers necessary to secure the application of the surplus in accordance with the directions contained in the CIO's constitution pursuant to section 206(2)(c) of the Charities Act 2011.".

(7) The Table of further modifications is as follows—

TABLE OF FURTHER MODIFICATIONS TO PROVISIONS OF THE 1986 ACT APPLIED TO CIOS

Provision of the 1986 Act	*Modification(s)*
FIRST GROUP OF PARTS (Company insolvency; companies winding up)	
Section 1 (Those who may propose an arrangement)	Omit subsections (4) to (6).
Section 4A (Approval of arrangement)	Omit subsection (5).
Section 5 (Effect of approval)	
Subsection (3)	In paragraph (a) omit "or sist".
Subsections (5) and (6)	Omit subsections (5) and (6).
Section 6 (Challenge of decisions)	
Subsection (1)	In paragraph (a) omit ", member".
Subsection (2A)	Omit subsection (2A).
Subsection (4)	Omit "or in the case of an application under subsection (2A), as to the ground mentioned in that subsection".
Subsection (8)	Omit subsection (8).
Section 7A (Prosecution of delinquent officers of CIO)	
Subsection (2)	In the full out words omit paragraph (ii).
Subsection (3)	After "1985" substitute "to investigate the CIO's affairs as if the CIO were a company".
Subsection (7)	Omit paragraph (b).
Subsection (8)	Omit the reference to "the Lord Advocate".
Section 30 (Disqualification of body corporate from acting as receiver)	Any reference to a body corporate is to be read as a reference to a body corporate other than a body corporate appointed as an interim manager under section 76(3)(g) of the Charities Act 2011.
Section 38 (Receivership accounts to be delivered to Charity Commission)	In subsection (1) omit "for registration".
Section 47 (Statement of affairs to be submitted)	For subsection (3)(d) substitute: "those who are or have been within that year officers of, or in the employment of, a company or a CIO which is, or within that year was, a charity trustee of the CIO.".
Section 72A (Floating charge holder not to appoint an administrative receiver)	
Subsection (2)	Omit subsection (2).
Subsection (3)	For "subsections (1) and (2)" substitute "subsection (1)".
Subsection (6)	For "sections 72B to 72GA" substitute "section 72G".
Section 72G (Sixth exception: registered social landlords)	Omit "or under Part 3 of the Housing (Scotland) Act 2001 (asp 10)".
Section 72H (Sections 72A to 72G: supplementary)	

Provision of the 1986 Act	*Modification(s)*
Subsection (1)	For "sections 72B to 72G" substitute "section 72G".
Subsection (2)	In paragraph (d) for "sections 72B to 72G" substitute "section 72G".
Subsection (5)	Omit paragraph (b).
Section 73 (Scheme of this Part)	Omit "or Scotland".
Section 74 (Liability as contributories of present and past members)	
Subsection (1)	For subsection (1) substitute: "(1) When— (a) a CIO is wound up; and (b) its constitution states that its members are liable to contribute to its assets if it is wound up, every present and past member of the CIO is liable to contribute to its assets to any amount sufficient for the payment of its debts and liabilities, and the expenses of winding up, and for the adjustment of the rights of the contributories amongst themselves.".
Subsection (2)	Omit paragraphs (d) and (f); in paragraph (e) for "the Companies Acts" substitute "the Charities Act 2011".
Subsection (3)	For subsection (3) substitute: "(3) No contribution is required from any member of a CIO exceeding the amount specified in the CIO's constitution under section 206(1)(d) of the Charities Act 2011 as the amount to be contributed by that member in the event of the CIO being wound up.".
Section 79 (Meaning of contributory)	Omit subsection (3).
Section 81 (Contributories in case of death of a member)	
Subsection (1)	Omit the words from ", and the heirs and legatees" to "in Scotland,".
Subsection (2)	Omit subsection (2).
Subsection (3)	Omit the words "in England and Wales".
Section 88 (Avoidance of share transfers, etc after winding-up resolution)	Omit the words from "Any transfer" to "liquidator, and".
Section 95 (Effect of a CIO's insolvency)	Omit subsections (2), (4A)(b) and (5) to (7).
Section 98 (Meeting of creditors)	
Subsection (1)	Omit subsection (1).
Subsections (3) to (5)	Omit subsections (3) to (5).
Subsection (6)	For "(1), (1A) or (2)" substitute "(1A) or (2)".
Section 99 (Charity trustees to lay statement of affairs before creditors)	Omit subsection (2A)(b).
Section 101 (Appointment of liquidation committee)	Omit subsection (4).
Section 107 (Distribution of CIO's property)	For "shall (unless the articles otherwise provide) be distributed among the members according to their rights and interests in the company" substitute "shall be applied in accordance with the directions contained in the CIO's constitution pursuant to section 206(2)(c) of the Charities Act 2011; and for this purpose the liquidator may require the charity trustees of the CIO to take any necessary action to secure that application.".
Section 109 (Notice by liquidator of his appointment)	In subsection (1) omit "for registration".

Provision of the 1986 Act	***Modification(s)***
Section 110 (Acceptance of shares, etc, as consideration for sale of CIO property)	
Subsection (1)	For paragraph (a) substitute: "to a company ("the transferee company"), whether or not the latter is a company registered under the Companies Act 2006, or".
Subsection (2)	In paragraphs (a) and (b) for "distribution among members of the transferor company" substitute "to be applied in accordance with the directions contained in the CIO's constitution pursuant to section 206(2)(c) of the Charities Act 2011".
Subsection (3)	In paragraph (a) for "company" substitute "members of the CIO".
Subsection (4)	Omit subsection (4).
New subsections (7) to (11)	After subsection (6) insert: "(7) For the purposes of this section, a resolution of the members of a CIO is to be treated as a special resolution if it is passed— (a) at a general meeting of the CIO— (i) by a 75% majority of those voting (including those voting by proxy or by post, if voting that way is permitted); or (ii) where the CIO's constitution permits the members to make decisions otherwise than by voting, by a decision taken without a vote and without any expression of dissent in response to the question put to the meeting; or (b) unanimously, otherwise than at a general meeting. (8) Subject to subsection (10), if a resolution under subsection (3)(a) is to be proposed at a general meeting of a CIO, the person calling the meeting must give notice of not less than 14 days to— (a) all members of the CIO entitled to vote at the meeting or take part in the decision to be made as to whether to pass the resolution at the meeting; and (b) any charity trustee of the CIO who is not also a member of the CIO entitled to vote at the meeting or, where the CIO's constitution permits the members to make decisions otherwise than by voting, who is not also a member entitled to take part in the decision to be made as to whether to pass the resolution at the meeting; and the notice must contain particulars of the resolution that is to be proposed. (9) For the purpose of calculating the period of notice to be given under subsection (8) the following are to be excluded— (a) the day of the meeting; and (b) the day on which notice is given. (10) If a qualifying majority agrees, a resolution under subsection (3)(a) which is to be proposed at a general meeting of a CIO may be passed without the notice provisions in subsection (8) being satisfied. (11) In this section "qualifying majority" has the meaning given by section 84.".
Section 117 (High Court and county court jurisdiction)	
Subsection (2)	Omit the words from "Where the amount" to "(subject to this section)".

Provision of the 1986 Act	*Modification(s)*
Subsection (3)	Omit subsection (3).
Subsection (7)	Omit subsection (7).
Section 123 (Definition of inability to pay debts)	Omit subsection (1)(c) and (d).
Section 124 (Application for winding up)	
Subsection (1)	Omit the words from "or by the designated officer" to "fines imposed on companies)".
Subsections (2) and (3)	Omit subsections (2) and (3).
Subsection (3A)	For "section 122(1)(fa)" substitute "section 122(1)(d)".
Subsections (4) to (4A)	Omit subsections (4) to (4A).
Section 126 (Power to stay or restrain proceedings against company)	
Subsection (1)	In paragraph (a) omit "or Northern Ireland"; and in the full out words omit "sist".
Subsection (2)	Omit subsection (2).
Section 127 (Avoidance of property dispositions, etc)	In subsection (1) omit the words from "and any transfer" to "the company's members,".
Section 128 (Avoidance of attachments etc)	Omit subsection (2).
Section 130 (Consequences of a winding up order)	Omit subsection (3).
Section 131 (CIO's statement of affairs)	
Subsection (2A)	Omit paragraph (b).
Subsection (3)	For paragraph (d) substitute: "those who are or have been within that year officers of, or in the employment of, a company or a CIO which is, or within that year was, a charity trustee of the CIO.".
Subsection (8)	Omit subsection (8).
Section 133 (Public examination of officers)	
Subsection (1)	In the opening words omit "or in Scotland, the liquidator"; in paragraph (b) omit "or, in Scotland, receiver of its property".
Subsection (2)	Omit "or, in Scotland, the liquidator".
Subsection (4)(d)	Omit "or, in Scotland, submitted a claim".
Section 135 (Appointment and powers of provisional liquidator)	Omit subsection (3).
Section 143 (General functions in winding up the court)	In subsection (1) for "to the persons entitled to it" substitute "applied in accordance with the directions contained in the CIO's constitution pursuant to section 206(2)(c) of the Charities Act 2011".
Section 144 (Custody of CIO's property)	Omit subsection (2).
Section 147 (Power to stay winding up)	Omit all references to the sisting of proceedings.
Section 149 (Debts due from contributory to company)	
Subsection (2)	Omit subsection (2).
Subsection (3)	Omit "whether limited or unlimited".
Section 152 (Order on contributory to be conclusive evidence)	In subsection (2) omit from "except proceedings in Scotland" to the end.
Section 165 (Voluntary winding up)	
Subsection (2)	In paragraph (a) for "company" substitute "members of the CIO".

Provision of the 1986 Act	*Modification(s)*
New subsections (7) to (11)	After subsection (6) insert: "(7) For the purposes of this section, a resolution of the members of a CIO is to be treated as a special resolution if it is passed— (a) at a general meeting of the CIO— (i) by a 75% majority of those voting (including those voting by proxy or by post, if voting that way is permitted); or (ii) where the CIO's constitution permits the members to make decisions otherwise than by voting, by a decision taken without a vote and without any expression of dissent in response to the question put to the meeting; or (b) unanimously, otherwise than at a general meeting. (8) Subject to subsection (10), if a resolution under subsection (2)(a) is to be proposed at a general meeting of a CIO, the person calling the meeting must give notice of not less than 14 days to— (a) all members of the CIO entitled to vote at the meeting or take part in the decision to be made as to whether to pass the resolution at the meeting; and (b) any charity trustee of the CIO who is not also a member of the CIO entitled to vote at the meeting or, where the CIO's constitution permits the members to make decisions otherwise than by voting, who is not also a member entitled to take part in the decision to be made as to whether to pass the resolution at the meeting; and the notice must contain particulars of the resolution that is to be proposed. (9) For the purpose of calculating the period of notice to be given under subsection (8) the following are to be excluded— (a) the day of the meeting; and (b) the day on which notice is given. (10) If a qualifying majority agrees, a resolution under subsection (2)(a) which is to be proposed at a general meeting of a CIO may be passed without the notice provisions of subsection (8) being satisfied. (11) In this section "qualifying majority" has the meaning given by section 84.".
Section 172 (Removal, etc (winding up by the court))	Omit subsection (7).
Section 173 (Release (voluntary winding up))	Omit subsection (3).
Section 174 (Release (winding up by court))	Omit subsection (7).
Section 176A (Share of assets for unsecured creditors)	Omit subsection (4)(b).
Section 177 (Power to appoint special manager)	
Subsection (2)	Omit "or members generally".
Subsection (5)(a)	Omit "or, in Scotland, caution".
Section 184 (Duties of officers charges with execution of writs and other processes (England and Wales))	Omit subsection (8).
Section 187 (Power to make over assets to employees)	

Part 18 Miscellaneous SIs

Provision of the 1986 Act	*Modification(s)*
Subsection (1)	In subsection (1) for the words from "payment" to "business)" substitute "ex-gratia payment authorised, before the commencement of the winding up, by the Charity Commission under section 106 of the Charities Act 2011 or the Attorney General".
Subsection (2)	For subsection (2) substitute: "(2) The liquidator may, after the winding up has commenced, make any relevant payment if the CIO's liabilities have been fully satisfied and provision has been made for the expenses of the winding up. (2A) For the purposes of subsection (2) a payment is a relevant payment if it is an ex-gratia payment authorised, after the commencement of the winding-up, by the Charity Commission under section 106 of the Charities Act 2011 or the Attorney General.".
Subsection (3)	For "the members on winding up" substitute "be applied in accordance with the directions contained in the CIO's constitution in compliance with section 206(2)(c) of the Charities Act 2011.".
Section 189 (Interest on debts)	Omit subsection (5).
Section 190 (Documents exempt from stamp duty)	
Subsection (2)	Omit "If the company is registered in England and Wales".
Subsection (3)	Omit subsection (3).
Section 196 (Judicial notice of court documents)	Omit references to the Court of Session, sheriff court and High Court in Northern Ireland; in paragraph (b) omit "or the Companies Acts".
Section 197 (Commission for receiving evidence)	
Subsection (1)	In the opening words omit "in England and Wales or in Scotland"; omit paragraphs (b) and (c).
Subsections (2) and (3)	Omit references to the sheriff principal.
Subsection (5)	Omit subsection (5).
Section 201 (Dissolution (voluntary winding up)	
Subsection (2)	For subsection (2), substitute: "(2) The Charity Commission must remove the CIO from the register of charities on the expiration of 3 months from the date on which it received the account and return and the CIO is dissolved on the date on which it is removed from the register.".
Subsection (4)	Omit "for registration".
New subsections (5) and (6)	After subsection (4) insert: "(5) Where the Charity Commission removes a CIO from the register of charities in accordance with this section, it must publish a notice, in such manner as it thinks fit, stating— (a) that the CIO has been removed from the register of charities; and (b) the date on which the CIO was so removed.

Provision of the 1986 Act	*Modification(s)*
	(6) In determining the manner in which to publish a notice under subsection (5) the Charity Commission must have regard in particular to— (a) the location of the CIO's principal office; (b) the area in which the CIO operated; and (c) the charitable purposes of the CIO.".
Section 202 (Early Dissolution (England and Wales))	For subsection (5), substitute: "(5) The Charity Commission must remove the CIO from the register of charities on the expiration of 3 months from the date on which it received the official receiver's application under subsection (2) and the CIO is dissolved on the date on which it is removed from the register. However the Secretary of State may, on the application of the official receiver or any other person who appears to the Secretary of State to be interested, give directions under section 203 at any time before the end of that period. (6) Where the Charity Commission removes a CIO from the register of charities in accordance with this section, it must publish a notice, in such manner as it thinks fit, stating— (a) that the CIO has been removed from the register of charities; and (b) the date on which the CIO was so removed. (7) In determining the manner in which to publish a notice under subsection (6), the Charity Commission must have regard in particular to— (a) the location of the CIO's principal office; (c) the area in which the CIO operated; and (c) the charitable purposes of the CIO.".
Section 203 (Consequence of notice under s 202)	In subsection (5) omit "for registration".
Section 205 (Dissolution otherwise than under ss 202–204)	
Subsection (2)	For subsection (2), substitute: "(2) The Charity Commission must remove the CIO from the register of charities on the expiration of 3 months from the date on which it received the notice and the CIO is dissolved on the date on which it is removed from the register.".
Subsection (5)	Omit subsection (5).
Subsection (6)	Omit paragraph (c); and in the full out words omit "for registration".
New subsections (8) and (9)	After subsection (7), insert: "(8) Where the Charity Commission removes a CIO from the register of charities in accordance with this section, it must publish a notice, in such manner as it thinks fit, stating— (a) that the CIO has been removed from the register of charities; and (b) the date on which the CIO was so removed. (9) In determining the manner in which to publish a notice under subsection (8), the Charity Commission must have regard in particular to— (a) the location of the CIO's principal office; (b) the area in which the CIO operated; and (c) the charitable purposes of the CIO.".

Provision of the 1986 Act	*Modification(s)*
Section 216 (Restriction on re-use of company names)	Omit subsection (8).
Section 217 (Personal liability for debts, following contravention of s 216)	Omit subsection (6).
Section 218 (Prosecution of delinquent officers and members of CIO)	
Subsection (1)	Omit paragraph (b).
Subsection (4)	Omit paragraph (b); and in the full out words omit "or (as the case may be) the Lord Advocate" in both places it occurs.
Subsection (5)	After "1985" substitute "to investigate the CIO's affairs as if the CIO were a company".
Section 219 (Obligations arising under s 218)	
Subsection (2B)	Omit paragraph (b)
Subsection (3)	Omit the references to the "Lord Advocate" and "defender".
Subsection (4)	Omit the reference to the "Lord Advocate".
Section 233 (Supplies of gas, water, electricity, etc)	In subsection (3)(c) omit the reference to Scottish Water.
Section 235 (Duty to co-operate with office-holder)	For subsection (3)(d) substitute: "those who are, or have within that year been, officers of or in the employment (including employment under a contract for services) of a company or a CIO which is, or within that year was, a charity trustee of the CIO in question".
Section 236 (Inquiry into CIO's dealings, etc)	In subsection (3A) omit from "(in England and Wales)" to the end.
Section 244 (Extortionate credit transactions)	In subsection (5) omit "or under section 242 (gratuitous alienations in Scotland)".
Section 245 (Avoidance of certain floating charges)	In subsection (1) omit "but applies to Scotland as well as to England and Wales".
Section 246A (Remote attendance at meetings)	Omit subsection (2).
Section 246B (Use of websites)	Omit subsection (2).
Section 248 ("Secured creditor" etc)	Omit paragraph (b)(ii).
Section 251 (Expressions used generally)	
Definition of administrative receiver	Omit paragraph (b).
Definition of "chattel leasing agreement"	Omit "or, in Scotland, the hiring".
Definition of "floating charge"	Omit the words from "and includes" to "(Scottish floating charges)".
Definition of "the Gazette"	Omit paragraph (b).
Definition of "receiver"	Omit the definition.
Section 387 ("The relevant date")	Omit subsections (4)(b), (5) and (6).
Section 388 (Meaning of "to act as an insolvency practitioner")	
Subsection (2)	Omit subsection (2).
Subsection (2A)	Omit subsection (2A).
Subsection (3)	Omit subsection (3).
Subsection (4)	Omit the definitions of "company", "interim trustee" and "permanent trustee".
Subsection (5)	Omit paragraph (b).
Section 389 (Acting without qualification an offence)	In subsection (2) omit the words from "or the Accountant" to "Act 1985".
Section 389A (Authorisation of nominees and supervisors)	
Subsection (1)	Omit "or Part 8".

Provision of the 1986 Act	*Modification(s)*
Subsection (2)(b)	Omit "(in Scotland, caution)"; and "or caution".
Section 390 (Persons not qualified to act as insolvency practitioners)	
Subsection (3)	In paragraph (a) omit "or, in Scotland, caution"; in paragraph (b) omit "or caution".
New subsection (6)	After subsection (5) insert: "(6) This section does not apply to a body corporate appointed as an interim manager under section 76(3)(g) of the Charities Act 2011.".
Section 399 (Appointment, etc of official receivers)	
Subsections (1) and (4)	Omit each reference to bankruptcy; individual voluntary arrangement; debt relief order or application for such an order.
Section 411 (CIO insolvency rules)	
Subsection (1)	Omit paragraph (b).
Subsections (1A) and (1B)	Omit subsections (1A) and (1B).
Subsection (2)	Omit the reference to subsections (1A) and (1B) and to the Treasury.
Subsections (2C) and (2D)	Omit subsections (2C) and (2D).
Subsection (3)	Omit "bank liquidator or administrator" and the references to the Banking Act 2009.
Subsection (3A)	Omit subsection (3A).
Section 413 (Insolvency Rules Committee)	In subsection (2) omit the reference to section 412.
Section 414 (Fees orders (CIO insolvency proceedings)	
Subsection (2)	Omit paragraph (b).
Subsection (5)	Omit the reference to the Secretary of State.
Subsection (8A) to (8C)	Omit subsections (8A) to (8C).
Subsection (9)	Omit the words from "and the application of" to the end.
Section 415A (Fees orders (general))	Omit subsection (A1).
Section 416 (Monetary limits (companies winding up))	
Subsection (1)	Omit the entries relating to sections 117(2) and 120(3).
Subsection (3)	Omit "117(2), 120(3) or".
Section 423 (Transactions defrauding creditors)	For subsection (4) substitute: "(4) In this section "the court" means— (a) the High Court; or (b) any county court having jurisdiction to wind up the CIO.".
Section 424 (Those who may apply for an order under s 423) Subsection (1)	For paragraph (a) substitute: "(a) in a case where the debtor is being wound up or is in administration, by the official receiver, by the liquidator or administrator or (with the leave of the court) by a victim of the transaction;".
Section 431 (Summary proceedings)	
Subsection (3)	Omit subsection (3).
Subsection (4)	Omit the reference to the Lord Advocate.
Section 432 (Offences by bodies corporate)	
Subsection (2)	The reference to any director, manager, secretary or other similar officer of a body corporate is to be read as including a reference to a charity trustee of a CIO.

Provision of the 1986 Act	***Modification(s)***
Subsection (4)	Omit the words "51, 53, 54, 62, 64, 66," and "and 23(1)(a)".
Section 433 (Admissibility in evidence of statements of affairs, etc)	
Subsection (1)	Omit paragraphs (aa) and (ab).
Subsection (3)	In paragraph (a) omit the words "66(6), 67(8)," and from ", 353(1)" to "(2)(a) or (b)"; omit paragraph (e).
Section 434A (Introductory)	For "416 and 417" substitute "416".
Section 434D (Enforcement of a CIO's filing obligations)	In subsection (4) omit "(in Scotland, expenses)".
Section 436 (Expressions used generally)	In subsection (2) in the opening words after "Companies Acts" insert: "with the substitution, in relation to CIOs, of references to charity trustees for references to directors; omit the entries relating to: "articles", "the Joint Stock Companies Acts", "overseas company", "paid up", "private company", "public company" and "registrar of companies".
Section 436B (References to things in writing)	In subsection (2) ignore paragraphs (a), (b), (c) (e), (h) and (i).
SCHEDULE A1 (Moratorium where directors propose voluntary arrangements)	
Paragraph 1	Omit the definitions of "market contract", "market charge", "settlement finality regulations" and "system-charge".
Paragraph 2	For paragraph 2 substitute: "**2** A CIO is eligible for a moratorium unless it is excluded from being eligible by virtue of paragraph 4.".
Paragraph 7	
Sub-paragraph (1)	Omit "(in Scotland, lodge)".
Sub-paragraph (4)	Omit "(in Scotland, lodged)".
Paragraph 12	
Sub-paragraph (3)	Omit sub-paragraph (3).
Sub-paragraph (5)	For sub-paragraph (5) substitute: "(5) For the purposes of this paragraph "excepted petition" means a petition presented by the Attorney General or the Charity Commission under section 113 of the Charities Act 2011.".
Paragraph 17	In sub-paragraph (2) omit "(in Scotland, hired)".
Paragraph 22	In sub-paragraph (1)(c) omit the reference to paragraph 21.
Paragraph 38	In sub-paragraph (1)(a) omit ", member".
Paragraph 40	In sub-paragraph (2) omit references to a "member" or "members".
Paragraph 45	
Sub-paragraph (4)	Omit the words "(except regulations under paragraph 5)".
Sub-paragraph (5)	Omit sub-paragraph (5).
SCHEDULE B1 (Administration)	
Paragraph 14	Omit sub-paragraph (2)(d).
Paragraph 15	Omit sub-paragraph (3).
Paragraph 39	In sub-paragraph (1)(d) omit "or under any rule of the law of Scotland".

Provision of the 1986 Act	*Modification(s)*
Paragraph 40	For sub-paragraph (2) substitute: "(2) Sub-paragraph (1)(b) does not apply to a petition presented by the Attorney General or the Charity Commission under section 113 of the Charities Act 2011".
Paragraph 42	For sub-paragraph (4) substitute: "(4) Sub-paragraph (3) does not apply to a petition presented by the Attorney General or the Charity Commission under section 113 of the Charities Act 2011.".
Paragraph 43	Omit sub-paragraph (5).
Paragraph 47	
Sub-paragraph (3)	For sub-paragraph (3)(d) substitute: "a person who is or has been during that period an officer or employee of a company or a CIO which is or has been during that year a charity trustee of the CIO."
Sub-paragraph (5)	Omit sub-paragraph (5).
Paragraph 49	Omit sub-paragraph (3)(b).
Paragraph 73	Omit sub-paragraph (2)(c) and (d).
Paragraph 74	
The whole paragraph	Omit all references to a "member" or "members".
Sub-paragraph (6)	Omit sub-paragraphs (b) and (ba).
Paragraph 82	For sub-paragraph (1) substitute: "(1) This paragraph applies where a winding-up order is made for the winding up of a CIO in administration on a petition presented by the Attorney General or the Charity Commission under section 113 of the Charities Act 2011.".
Paragraph 83	
Sub-paragraph (2)	Omit sub-paragraph (2).
Sub-paragraph (4)	For sub-paragraph (4) substitute: "(4) On receipt of a notice under sub-paragraph (3), the Charity Commission must publish it in such manner as it thinks fit. (4A) In determining the manner in which to publish the notice under sub-paragraph (3) the Charity Commission must have regard in particular to— (a) the location of the principal office of the CIO; (b) the area in which the CIO operates; and (c) the charitable purposes of the CIO.".
Sub-paragraph (6)	For "registration" substitute "publication" and for "registered" substitute "published".
Paragraph 84	
Sub-paragraph (3)	For sub-paragraph (3) substitute: "(3) On receipt of a notice under sub-paragraph (1), the Charity Commission must publish it in such manner as it thinks fit. (3A) In determining the manner in which to publish the notice under sub-paragraph (1) the Charity Commission must have regard in particular to— (a) the location of the principal office of the CIO; (b) the area in which the CIO operates; and (c) the charitable purposes of the CIO.".
Sub-paragraph (4)	For "registration" substitute "publication".
Sub-paragraph (6)	For "registration" substitute "publication".

Part 18 Miscellaneous SIs

Provision of the 1986 Act	*Modification(s)*
Paragraph 96	Omit sub-paragraph (4).
Paragraph 111	Omit sub-paragraphs (1A) and (1B).
SCHEDULE 1 (Powers of administrator or administrative receiver)	
Paragraph 2	Omit the words from "or, in Scotland," to "private bargain".
SCHEDULE 4 (Powers of liquidator in a winding up)	
Paragraph 3	Omit the paragraph.
Paragraph 3A	Omit ", 242, 243".
SCHEDULE 6 (The categories of preferential debts)	
Paragraph 14	Omit sub-paragraphs (1)(b) and (c).
SCHEDULE 8 (Provisions capable of inclusion in CIO insolvency rules)	
Paragraph 14	Omit the words "or in the Bankruptcy (Scotland) Act 1985".
Paragraph 29	Omit ", 66".
SCHEDULE 10 (Punishment of offences under this Act)	In the table, after the entry relating to section 67(8) insert:

"84(11)	Failing to comply with requirement to send resolution to Charity Commission.	Summary.	One-fifth of the statutory maximum.	One-fiftieth of the statutory maximum."

Application to CIOs of subordinate legislation made under the 1986 Act

2 (1) The legislation made under the 1986 Act specified in sub-paragraph (3) applies to CIOs with any necessary modifications for the purpose of giving effect to the provisions of the 1986 Act which are applied to CIOs by paragraph 1 above.

(2) Where there is a conflict between a provision of the subordinate legislation applied by sub-paragraph (1) and any provision of these Regulations, the latter prevails.

(3) The specified legislation is—

(a) the Insolvency Rules 1986;
(b) the Insolvency Practitioners (Recognised Professional Bodies) Order 1986;
(c) the Insolvency Proceedings (Monetary Limits) Order 1986;
(d) the Insolvency Practitioners Tribunal (Conduct of Investigations) Rules 1986;
(e) the Insolvency Regulations 1994;
(f) the Insolvency Act 1986 (Prescribed Part) Order 2003;
(g) the Insolvency Proceedings (Fees) Order 2004;
(h) the Insolvency Practitioners Regulations 2005; and
(i) the Civil Proceedings Fees Order 2008.

LEGAL AID, SENTENCING AND PUNISHMENT OF OFFENDERS ACT 2012 (COMMENCEMENT NO 5 AND SAVING PROVISION) ORDER 2013

(SI 2013/77)

NOTES

Made: 18 January 2013.

Authority: Legal Aid, Sentencing and Punishment of Offenders Act 2012, s 151(1), (5).

This Order brings into force specified provisions of the Legal Aid, Sentencing and Punishments of Offenders Act 2012, all of which are beyond the scope of this work. However, this Order is included because of the saving provisions contained within art 4 at **[18.266]** in relation to certain proceedings brought by officeholders in insolvency proceedings.

[18.263]
1 Citation and interpretation

(1) This Order may be cited as the Legal Aid, Sentencing and Punishment of Offenders Act 2012 (Commencement No 5 and Saving Provision) Order 2013.

(2) In this Order—

"the 1986 Act" means the Insolvency Act 1986;

"the 2012 Act" means the Legal Aid, Sentencing and Punishment of Offenders Act 2012;

"company" means a company within the meaning of section 1 of the Companies Act 2006 or a company which may be wound up under Part V of the 1986 Act;

"diffuse mesothelioma" has the same meaning as in section 48(2) of the 2012 Act;

"news publisher" means a person who publishes a newspaper, magazine or website containing news or information about or comment on current affairs;

"proceedings" has the same meaning as in section 58A(4) of the Courts and Legal Services Act 1990;

"publication and privacy proceedings" means proceedings for—

(a) defamation;
(b) malicious falsehood;
(c) breach of confidence involving publication to the general public;
(d) misuse of private information; or
(e) harassment, where the defendant is a news publisher.

[18.264]
2 Provisions coming into force on 19th January 2013

(1) Subject to article 4, the following provisions of the 2012 Act come into force on 19th January 2013 for the purpose only of exercising any power to make orders, regulations or rules of court—

(a) section 44 (conditional fee agreements: success fees);
(b) section 45 (damages-based agreements), in so far as it is not already in force for that purpose; and
(c) section 46 (recovery of insurance premiums).

(2) Section 48 (sections 44 and 46 and diffuse mesothelioma proceedings) of the 2012 Act comes into force on 19th January 2013.

[18.265]
3 Provisions coming into force on 1st April 2013

Subject to article 4, the following provisions come into force, in so far as they are not already in force, on 1st April 2013—

(a) section 44;
(b) section 45;
(c) section 46; and
(d) section 47 (recovery where a body undertakes to meet costs liabilities).

[18.266]
4 Saving provision

Article 2(1)(a) and (c) and article 3(a) and (c) do not apply to—

(a) proceedings relating to a claim for damages in respect of diffuse mesothelioma;
(b) publication and privacy proceedings;
(c) proceedings in England and Wales brought by a person acting in the capacity of—
    (i) a liquidator of a company which is being wound up in England and Wales or Scotland under Parts IV or V of the 1986 Act; or
    (ii) a trustee of a bankrupt's estate under Part IX of the 1986 Act;
(d) proceedings brought by a person acting in the capacity of an administrator appointed pursuant to the provisions of Part II of the 1986 Act;
(e) proceedings in England and Wales brought by a company which is being wound up in England and Wales or Scotland under Parts IV or V of the 1986 Act; or
(f) proceedings brought by a company which has entered administration under Part II of the 1986 Act.

FINANCIAL SERVICES ACT 2012 (TRANSITIONAL PROVISIONS) (MISCELLANEOUS PROVISIONS) ORDER 2013

(SI 2013/442)

NOTES

Made: 27 February 2013.
Authority: Financial Services Act 2012, ss 115(2), 119(3)–(5).
Commencement: 25 March 2013 (art 1); 1 April 2013 (remainder).

ARRANGEMENT OF ARTICLES

PART 1
INTRODUCTORY

1 Citation, commencement and interpretation . . . [18.267]

PART 10
INSOLVENCY

45 Powers of FCA and PRA to participate in proceedings: trust deeds for creditors in Scotland . . [18.268]
46 Administrator's duty to report to FCA and PRA . . . [18.269]
47 Powers of FCA and PRA to participate in proceedings: administration . . . [18.270]
48 Administrator appointed by company or directors . . . [18.271]
49 Powers of FCA and PRA to participate in proceedings (receivership) . . . [18.272]
50 Receiver's duty to report to FCA and PRA . . . [18.273]
51 Powers of FCA and PRA to participate in proceedings (voluntary winding up) . . . [18.274]
52 Insurers effecting or carrying out long-term contracts of insurance . . . [18.275]
53 Insurers: service of petition etc . . . [18.276]
54 Reclaim funds: service of petition etc . . . [18.277]
55 Liquidator's duty to report to FCA and PRA . . . [18.278]
56 Powers of FCA and PRA to participate in proceedings: liquidation . . . [18.279]
57 Insolvency practitioner's duty to report to FCA and PRA . . . [18.280]
58 Powers of FCA and PRA to participate in proceedings: insolvency . . . [18.281]
59 Right of PRA to apply for an order . . . [18.282]
60 Continuation of contracts of long-term insurance where insurer in liquidation . . . [18.283]

PART 12
COMPANIES ACT 1989

65 Change in default rules . . . [18.284]
66 Duty to report on completion of default proceedings . . . [18.285]
67 Powers to give directions . . . [18.286]
68 Application to determine whether default proceedings to be taken . . . [18.287]

PART 1
INTRODUCTORY

[18.267]
1 Citation, commencement and interpretation

(1) This Order may be cited as the Financial Services Act 2012 (Transitional Provisions) (Miscellaneous Provisions) Order 2013.

(2) This article and article 70 come into force on 25th March 2013.

(3) The rest of this Order comes into force on 1st April 2013.

(4) In this Order—

"the 2012 Act" means the Financial Services Act 2012;
"the Authority" means the Financial Services Authority;
"the commencement date" means 1st April 2013.

(5) A reference in this Order to a provision of an Act is a reference to a provision of FSMA 2000, except where indicated otherwise.

(6) A term used in this Order which is defined in FSMA 2000 has the same meaning as in that Act.

2–44 *((Pts 2–9) Outside the scope of this work.)*

PART 10
INSOLVENCY

[18.268]
45 Powers of FCA and PRA to participate in proceedings: trust deeds for creditors in Scotland

(1) Paragraph (2) applies if, before the commencement date—
- (a) a trust deed had been granted by or on behalf of a debtor who is, on the commencement date, a PRA-authorised person;
- (b) the trustee had sent to the Authority—
  - (i) a copy of the trust deed, or any other document or information in accordance with section 358(2) (powers of FCA and PRA to participate in proceedings: trust deeds for creditors in Scotland), or
  - (ii) notice of a meeting of creditors in accordance with section 358(4); and
- (c) the trust deed had not ceased to have effect.

(2) The copy of the trust deed, other document, information or notice is to be treated as if it had been sent to the PRA (as well as to the FCA).

[18.269]

46 Administrator's duty to report to FCA and PRA

(1) Paragraph (2) applies if, before the commencement date—

(a) an administrator made a report to the Authority in accordance with section 361(2) (administrator's duty to report); and

(b) the administration had not ended.

(2) If the report relates to a regulated activity which is, on the commencement date, a PRA-regulated activity, the report is to be treated as if it had been made to the PRA (as well as to the FCA).

[18.270]

47 Powers of FCA and PRA to participate in proceedings: administration

(1) Paragraph (2) applies if, before the commencement date—

(a) a notice or other document was sent to the Authority in accordance with section 362(3) (powers to participate in proceedings); and

(b) the administration had not ended.

(2) If the notice or other document relates to a person who is, on the commencement date, a PRA-regulated person within the meaning of section 355 (interpretation of Part 24), the notice or other document is to be treated as if it had been sent to the PRA (as well as to the FCA).

[18.271]

48 Administrator appointed by company or directors

(1) Paragraph (2) applies if, before the commencement date—

(a) the Authority had consented for the purposes of section 362A(2) (requirement for consent to the appointment of an administrator) to the appointment of an administrator; and

(b) an administrator had not been appointed.

(2) If the appointment relates to the administration of a company or partnership which is, on the commencement date, a PRA-regulated person within the meaning of section 355, the consent is to be treated as if it had been given by the PRA.

[18.272]

49 Powers of FCA and PRA to participate in proceedings (receivership)

(1) Paragraph (2) applies if, before the commencement date—

(a) a report was sent to the Authority in accordance with section 363(4) (powers to participate in proceedings); and

(b) the receivership had not ended.

(2) If the report relates to person who is, on the commencement date, a PRA-regulated person within the meaning of section 355, the report is to be treated as if it had been sent to the PRA (as well as to the FCA).

[18.273]

50 Receiver's duty to report to FCA and PRA

(1) Paragraph (2) applies if, before the commencement date—

(a) a receiver made a report to the Authority in accordance with section 364 (receiver's duty to report); and

(b) the receivership had not ended.

(2) If the report relates to a regulated activity which is, on the commencement date, a PRA-regulated activity, the report is to be treated as if it had been made to the PRA (as well as to the FCA).

[18.274]

51 Powers of FCA and PRA to participate in proceedings (voluntary winding up)

(1) Paragraph (2) applies if, before the commencement date—

(a) a notice or other document was sent to the Authority in accordance with section 365(4) (powers to participate in proceedings); and

(b) the company had not been wound up.

(2) If the notice or other document relates to a person who is, on the commencement date, a PRA-authorised person, the notice or other document is to be treated as if it had been sent to the PRA (as well as to the FCA).

[18.275]

52 Insurers effecting or carrying out long-term contracts of insurance

(1) Paragraph (2) applies if, before the commencement date—

(a) the Authority gave consent to the voluntary winding-up of an insurer for the purposes of section 366(1) (insurers effecting or carrying out long-term contracts of insurance); and

(b) the insurer had not been wound up.

(2) The consent is to be treated as if it had been given by the PRA.

(3) Paragraph (4) applies where, before the commencement date—

(a) the Authority had been notified under section 366(2) that notice had been given of a general meeting of an insurer specifying the intention to propose a resolution for voluntary winding up of the insurer; and

(b) the insurer had not been wound up.

(4) The notice is to be treated as if it had been received by the PRA.

(5) Paragraph (6) applies where, before the commencement date—

(a) a copy of a winding-up resolution was forwarded to the registrar of companies in accordance with section 30 of the Companies Act 2006 (copies of resolutions or agreements to be forwarded to registrar) accompanied by a certificate issued by the Authority stating that it consents to the voluntary winding up of the insurer, in accordance with section 366(5); and

(b) the registrar had not recorded the information contained in the resolution.

(6) The certificate is to be treated as if it had been issued by the PRA.

(7) This article does not apply in the event that the activity of effecting or carrying out long-term contracts of insurance as principal is not to any extent a PRA-regulated activity.

[18.276]

53 Insurers: service of petition etc

(1) Paragraph (2) applies if, before the commencement date—

(a) a copy of—

(i) a petition was served on the Authority in accordance with section 369(1) (insurers: service of petition etc), or

(ii) an application was served on the Authority in accordance with section 369(2); and

(b) the petition or application had not been heard.

(2) If the petition or application relates to a person who is, on the commencement date, a PRA-authorised person, the copy is to be treated as if it had been served on the PRA (as well as on the FCA).

[18.277]

54 Reclaim funds: service of petition etc

(1) Paragraph (2) applies if, before the commencement date—

(a) a copy of—

(i) a petition was served on the Authority in accordance with section 369A(1) (reclaim funds: service of petition etc), or

(ii) an application was served on the Authority in accordance with section 369(2); and

(b) the petition or application had not been heard.

(2) If the petition or application relates to a person who is, on the commencement date, a PRA-authorised person, the copy is to be treated as if it had been served on the PRA (as well as on the FCA).

[18.278]

55 Liquidator's duty to report to FCA and PRA

(1) Paragraph (2) applies if, before the commencement date—

(a) a liquidator made a report to the Authority in accordance with section 370 (liquidator's duty to report); and

(b) the liquidation had not ended.

(2) If the report relates to a regulated activity which is, on the commencement date, a PRA-regulated activity, the report is to be treated as if it had been made to the PRA (as well as to the FCA).

[18.279]

56 Powers of FCA and PRA to participate in proceedings: liquidation

(1) Paragraph (2) applies if, before the commencement date—

(a) a notice or other document was sent to the Authority in accordance with section 371(3) (powers of FCA and PRA to participate in proceedings); and

(b) the body had not been liquidated.

(2) If the notice or other document relates to a person who is, on the commencement date, a PRA-regulated person within the meaning of section 355, the notice or other document is to be treated as if it had been sent to the PRA (as well as to the FCA).

[18.280]

57 Insolvency practitioner's duty to report to FCA and PRA

(1) Paragraph (2) applies if, before the commencement date—

(a) an insolvency practitioner made a report to the Authority in accordance with section 373(1) (insolvency practitioner's duty to report); and

(b) the insolvency had not ended.

(2) If the report relates to a regulated activity which is, on the commencement date, a PRA-regulated activity, the report is to be treated as if it had been made to the PRA (as well as to the FCA).

[18.281]

58 Powers of FCA and PRA to participate in proceedings: insolvency

(1) Paragraph (2) applies if, before the commencement date—

(a) a report was sent to the Authority in accordance with section 374(3) (powers to participate in proceedings); and

(b) the insolvency had not ended.

(2) If the report relates to person who is, on the commencement date, a PRA-authorised person, the report is to be treated as if it had been sent to the PRA (as well as to the FCA).

[18.282]
59 Right of PRA to apply for an order

In section 375(1A) (right to apply for an order), the reference to a PRA-regulated activity includes an activity which would have been a PRA-regulated activity if it had been carried on on the commencement date.

[18.283]
60 Continuation of contracts of long-term insurance where insurer in liquidation

(1) Paragraph (2) applies if, before the commencement date—

(a) the court appointed an independent actuary for the purposes of subsection (10) of section 376 (continuation of contracts of long-term insurance where insurer in liquidation) on the application of the Authority; and

(b) the actuary had not reported to the Authority for the purposes of that subsection.

(2) The actuary is to report to the PRA.

(3) This article does not apply in the event that the activity of effecting or carrying out long-term contracts of insurance as principal is not to any extent a PRA-regulated activity.

61–63 *((Pt 11) Outside the scope of this work.)*

PART 12
COMPANIES ACT 1989

64 (*Outside the scope of this work.*)

[18.284]
65 Change in default rules

(1) This article applies if a recognised UK clearing house has given the Authority notice under section 157(1) of the Companies Act 1989 (change in default rules) on a day which is 14 days or less before the commencement date.

(2) If the Authority gave a direction under that provision before the commencement date, the direction is to be treated as if it had been given by the Bank of England.

(3) If the Authority did not give a direction under that provision before the commencement date, the notice is to be treated as if it had been given to the Bank of England.

[18.285]
66 Duty to report on completion of default proceedings

(1) Paragraph (2) applies if, before the commencement date—

(a) the Authority gave notice to a recognised overseas clearing house under section 162(1A) of the Companies Act 1989 (duty to report on completion of default proceedings); and

(b) a report in respect of a proceeding was not provided to the Authority in accordance with section 162(1) of that Act.

(2) The report is to be provided to the Bank of England.

(3) Paragraph (4) applies if, before the commencement date—

(a) a recognised clearing house was under an obligation to report on a proceeding to the Authority in accordance with section 162 of the Companies Act 1989, and

(b) the recognised clearing house did not report to the Authority on the proceeding.

(4) The recognised clearing house must report to the Bank of England on the proceeding.

(5) Paragraph (6) applies if, before the commencement date, the Authority—

(a) received a report from a recognised clearing house in accordance with section 162 of the Companies Act 1989; and

(b) had not published notice of that fact in accordance with subsection (4) of that section.

(6) The Bank of England must publish notice of that fact in accordance with that subsection (4).

[18.286]
67 Powers to give directions

(1) This article applies in any case where, before the commencement date, a clearing house has not taken action under its default rules.

(2) Paragraph (3) applies if, before the commencement date, the Authority—

(a) had consulted the clearing house for the purposes of section 166(3) of the Companies Act 1989 (powers to give directions); and

(b) had not given a direction for the purposes of section 166(2) of the Companies Act 1989.

(3) The Bank of England is to be treated as if it had consulted the clearing house for the purposes of section 166(3) of the Companies Act 1989.

(4) A direction given, before the commencement date, by the Authority for the purposes of section 166 of the Companies Act 1989 is to be treated for the purposes of sections 166 and 167 (application to determine whether default proceedings to be taken) of that Act as if it had been given by the Bank of England.

(5) In this article, "default rules" has the meaning given in section 188(1) of the Companies Act 1989 (meaning of "default rules" and related expressions).

[18.287]
68 Application to determine whether default proceedings to be taken

(1) Paragraph (2) applies if, before the commencement date, the Authority—
(a) had received an application made under section 167(1B) of the Companies Act 1989 and in accordance with section 167(2) of that Act; and
(b) had not—
(i) notified the clearing house; or
(ii) given a direction under section 166(2)(a) of that Act.

(2) The application is to be treated as if it had been made to the Bank of England.

(3) Paragraph (4) applies if, before the commencement date, a clearing house—
(a) notified the Authority that it proposed to take action under its default rules; and
(b) had not taken such action.

(4) The duty to take action is enforceable, on the application of the Bank of England, by injunction or, in Scotland, by an order under section 45 of the Court of Session Act 1988.

69, 70 *((Pt 13) Outside the scope of this work.)*

CONDITIONAL FEE AGREEMENTS ORDER 2013

(SI 2013/689)

NOTES
Made: 19 March 2013.
Authority: Courts and Legal Services Act 1990, ss 58(4)(a), (c), (4A)(b), (4B)(c), (d), 120(3).
Commencement: 1 April 2013.

[18.288]
1 Citation, commencement, interpretation and application

(1) This Order may be cited as the Conditional Fee Agreements Order 2013 and will come into force on 1st April 2013.

(2) In this Order—
"the 1986 Act" means the Insolvency Act 1986;
"the 1990 Act" means the Courts and Legal Services Act 1990;
"claim for personal injuries" has the same meaning as in Rule 2.3 of the Civil Procedure Rules 1998;
"company" means a company within the meaning of section 1 of the Companies Act 2006 or a company which may be wound up under Part V of the 1986 Act;
"diffuse mesothelioma" has the same meaning as in section 48(2) of the Legal Aid, Sentencing and Punishment of Offenders Act 2012;
"news publisher" means a person who publishes a newspaper, magazine or website containing news or information about or comment on current affairs;
"publication and privacy proceedings" means proceedings for—
(a) defamation;
(b) malicious falsehood;
(c) breach of confidence involving publication to the general public;
(d) misuse of private information; or
(e) harassment, where the defendant is a news publisher.
"representative" means the person or persons providing the advocacy services or litigation services to which the conditional fee agreement relates.

[18.289]
2 Agreements providing for a success fee

All proceedings which, under section 58 of the Act, can be the subject of an enforceable conditional fee agreement, except proceedings under section 82 of the Environmental Protection Act 1990, are proceedings specified for the purpose of section 58(4)(a) of the Act.

[18.290]
3 Amount of success fee

In relation to all proceedings specified in article 2, the percentage specified for the purposes of section 58(4)(c) of the Act is 100%.

[18.291]
4 Specified proceedings

A claim for personal injuries shall be proceedings specified for the purpose of section 58(4A)(b) of the Act.

[18.292]
5 Amount of success fee in specified proceedings

(1) In relation to the proceedings specified in article 4, the percentage prescribed for the purposes of section 58(4B)(c) of the Act is—
(a) in proceedings at first instance, 25%; and

(b) in all other proceedings, 100%.

(2) The descriptions of damages specified for the purposes of section 58(4B)(d) of the Act are—

(a) general damages for pain, suffering, and loss of amenity; and

(b) damages for pecuniary loss, other than future pecuniary loss,

net of any sums recoverable by the Compensation Recovery Unit of the Department for Work and Pensions.

[18.293]

6 Transitional and saving provisions

(1) Articles 4 and 5 do not apply to a conditional fee agreement which is entered into before the date upon which this Order comes into force if—

(a) the agreement was entered into specifically for the purposes of the provision to a person ("P") of advocacy or litigation services in connection with the matter which is the subject of the proceedings; or

(b) advocacy or litigation services were provided to P under the agreement in connection with those proceedings before that date.

(2) Articles 4 and 5 do not apply to any conditional fee agreement entered into in relation to—

(a) proceedings relating to a claim for damages in respect of diffuse mesothelioma;

(b) publication and privacy proceedings;

(c) proceedings in England and Wales brought by a person acting in the capacity of—

(i) a liquidator of a company which is being wound up in England and Wales or Scotland under Parts IV or V of the 1986 Act; or

(ii) a trustee of a bankrupt's estate under Part IX of the 1986 Act;

(d) proceedings brought by a person acting in the capacity of an administrator appointed pursuant to the provisions of Part II of the 1986 Act;

(e) proceedings in England and Wales brought by a company which is being wound up in England and Wales or Scotland under Parts IV or V of the 1986 Act; or

(f) proceedings brought by a company which has entered administration under Part II of the 1986 Act.

7 (*Revokes the Conditional Fee Agreements Order 2000, SI 2000/823.*)

NATIONAL COLLEGE FOR HIGH SPEED RAIL (GOVERNMENT) REGULATIONS 2015

(SI 2015/1458)

NOTES

Made: 2 July 2015.

Authority: Further and Higher Education Act 1992, ss 20(2), 21(1), Sch 4.

Commencement: 30 July 2015.

[18.294]

1

These Regulations may be cited as the National College for High Speed Rail (Government) Regulations 2015 and come into force on 30th July 2015.

NOTES

Commencement: 30 July 2015.

[18.295]

2

The instrument of government and the articles of government of the further education corporation called "the National College for High Speed Rail" are set out in Schedules 1 and 2 to these Regulations respectively.

NOTES

Commencement: 30 July 2015.

SCHEDULE 1
INSTRUMENT OF GOVERNMENT

Regulation 2

[18.296]

1 . . .

2 Composition of the Corporation

(1) The Corporation shall consist of—

(a) up to fourteen members who appear to the Corporation to have the necessary skills to ensure that the Corporation carries out its functions under article 3 of the Articles of Government;

(b) the Principal of the institution, unless the Principal chooses not to be a member;

(c) at least one and not more than three members who are members of the institution's staff and have a contract of employment with the institution and who have been nominated and elected as set out in paragraphs (3), (4) or (5) ("staff member"); and

(d) at least one and not more than three members who are students at the institution and have been nominated and elected by their fellow students, or if the Corporation so decides, by a recognised association representing such students ("student member").

(2) A person who is not for the time being enrolled as a student at the institution, shall nevertheless be treated as a student during any period of authorised absence from the institution for study, travel or for carrying out the duties of any office held by that person in the institution's students' union.

(3) Where the Corporation has decided or decides that there is to be one staff member, the member may be a member of the academic staff or the non-academic staff and shall be nominated and elected by all staff.

(4) Where the Corporation has decided or decides that there are to be two staff members—

(a) one may be a member of the academic staff, nominated and elected only by academic staff, and the other may be a member of the non-academic staff, nominated and elected only by non-academic staff, or

(b) each may be a member of the academic or non-academic staff, nominated and elected by all staff.

(5) Where the Corporation has decided that there are to be three staff members—

(a) all may be members of the academic or non-academic staff, nominated and elected by all staff,

(b) one may be a member of the academic or the non-academic staff, nominated and elected by all staff, one may be a member of the academic staff, nominated and elected by academic staff only, and one may be a member of the non-academic staff nominated and elected by non-academic staff only,

(c) two may be members of the academic staff, nominated and elected by academic staff only, and one may be a member of the non-academic staff, nominated and elected by non-academic staff only, or

(d) one may be a member of the academic staff, nominated and elected by academic staff only, and two may be members of the non-academic staff, nominated and elected by non-academic staff only.

(6) The appointing authority, as set out in clause 4, will decide whether a person is eligible for nomination, election and appointment as a member of the Corporation under paragraph (1).

3–6 . . .

7 Persons who are ineligible to be members

(1)–(4) . . .

(5) Subject to paragraphs (6) and (7), a person shall be disqualified from holding, or from continuing to hold, office as a member, if that person has been [made] bankrupt or is the subject of a bankruptcy restrictions order, an interim bankruptcy restrictions order or a bankruptcy restrictions undertaking within the meaning of the Insolvency Act 1986, or if that person has made a composition or arrangement with creditors, including an individual voluntary arrangement.

(6) Where a person is disqualified by reason of having been [made] bankrupt or by reason of being the subject of a bankruptcy restrictions order, an interim bankruptcy restrictions order or a bankruptcy restrictions undertaking, that disqualification shall cease—

(a) on that person's discharge from bankruptcy, unless the bankruptcy order has before then been annulled; or

(b) if the bankruptcy order is annulled, at the date of that annulment; or

(c) if the bankruptcy restrictions order is rescinded as a result of an application under section 375(1) of the Insolvency Act 1986, on the date so ordered by the court; or

(d) if the interim bankruptcy restrictions order is discharged by the court, on the date of that discharge; or

(e) if the bankruptcy restrictions undertaking is annulled, at the date of that annulment.

(7) Where a person is disqualified by reason of having made a composition or arrangement with creditors, including an individual voluntary arrangement, and then pays the debts in full, the disqualification shall cease on the date on which the payment is completed and in any other case it shall cease on the expiration of three years from the date on which the terms of the deed of composition, arrangement or individual voluntary arrangement are fulfilled.

(8)–(10) . . .

8–19 . . .

NOTES

Commencement: 30 July 2015.

Paras 1, 3–6, 7(1)–(4), (8)–(10), 8–19: outside the scope of this work.

Para 7: in sub-paras (5), (6), word in square brackets substituted by the Enterprise and Regulatory Reform Act 2013 (Consequential Amendments) (Bankruptcy) and the Small Business, Enterprise and Employment Act 2015 (Consequential Amendments) Regulations 2016, SI 2016/481, reg 2(2), Sch 2, Pt 2, para 13.

SCHEDULE 2

(Sch 2 outside the scope of this work.)

CARE QUALITY COMMISSION (MEMBERSHIP) REGULATIONS 2015

(SI 2015/1479)

NOTES

Made: 7 July 2015.
Authority: Health and Social Care Act 2008, s 161(3), (4), Sch 1, para 3(3)–(5).
Commencement: 1 September 2015.

[18.297]

1 Citation, commencement and interpretation

(1) These Regulations may be cited as the Care Quality Commission (Membership) Regulations 2015 and come into force on 1st September 2015.

(2) In these Regulations—

"NHS Act 2006" means the National Health Service Act 2006;

"NHS Body" means—

(a) an English NHS body;
(b) the NHS Business Services Authority (Awdurdod Gwasanaethau Busnes y GIG);
(c) Monitor;
(d) the Wales Centre for Health;
(e) a Local Health Board established under section 11 of the National Health Service (Wales) Act 2006;
(f) a National Health Service trust established under section 18 of the National Health Service (Wales) Act 2006;
(g) a Special Health Authority established under section 22 of the National Health Service (Wales) Act 2006;
(h) a Health Board or Special Health Board constituted under section 2 of the National Health Service (Scotland) Act 1978;
(i) the Scottish Dental Practice Board constituted under section 4 of the National Health Service (Scotland) Act 1978;
(j) the Common Services Agency for the Scottish Health Service constituted under section 10 of the National Health Service (Scotland) Act 1978;
(k) Healthcare Improvement Scotland constituted under section 10A of the National Health Service (Scotland) Act 1978;
(l) a National Health Service trust constituted under section 12A of the National Health Service (Scotland) Act 1978;
(m) a special health and social care agency established under article 3 of the Health and Personal Social Services (Special Agencies) (Northern Ireland) Order 1990;
(n) a Health and Social Care trust established under article 10 of the Health and Personal Social Services (Northern Ireland) Order 1991;
(o) the Health and Social Care Regulation and Quality Improvement Authority established under article 3 of the Health and Personal Social Services (Quality, Improvement and Regulation) (Northern Ireland) Order 2003;
(p) the Regional Health and Social Care Board established by section 7 of the Health and Social Care (Reform) Act (Northern Ireland) 2009;
(q) the Regional Agency for Public Health and Social Well-Being established by section 12 of the Health and Social Care (Reform) Act (Northern Ireland) 2009;
(r) the Regional Business Services Organisation established under section 14 of the Health and Social Care (Reform) Act (Northern Ireland) 2009;

"performers list" means a list published in accordance with the Performers Lists Regulations;

"Performers Lists Regulations" means the National Health Service (Performers Lists) (England) Regulations 2013;

"pharmaceutical list" means a list published in accordance with regulations made under section 129(2)(a) of the NHS Act 2006.

NOTES

Commencement: 1 September 2015.

[18.298]

2 Members

The Commission must have no fewer than 6 and no more than 14 members in addition to the chair.

NOTES

Commencement: 1 September 2015.

[18.299]

3 Tenure of office of non-executive members

(1) Subject to regulation 6, the term of office of a non-executive member is such period, not exceeding four years, as is specified by the Secretary of State at the time of the appointment.

(2) A non-executive member who has ceased to hold office may be reappointed

NOTES

Commencement: 1 September 2015.

[18.300]

4 Disqualification for appointment or from holding office

Subject to regulation 5, a person is disqualified from appointment or from holding office as a non-executive member where that person falls within one or more paragraphs of the Schedule.

NOTES

Commencement: 1 September 2015.

[18.301]

5 Cessation of disqualification

(1) A person who is disqualified under paragraph 6 or 15 of the Schedule may, after the expiry of the period of two years beginning with the date of the dismissal or removal, apply in writing to the Secretary of State to remove the disqualification, and the Secretary of State may direct that the disqualification ceases to have effect.

(2) Where the Secretary of State refuses an application to remove a disqualification, no further application may be made by that person until the expiry of the period of two years beginning with the date of the application, and this paragraph applies to any subsequent application.

(3) Where a person is disqualified under paragraphs 16 to 21 of the Schedule, the disqualification ceases on the expiry of—

(a) the period of two years beginning with the date of the termination or cessation of, or removal or disqualification from, office referred to in those paragraphs; or

(b) such longer period as the Secretary of State specifies when terminating that person's period of office,

but, where application is made to the Secretary of State by that person, the Secretary of State may reduce the period of disqualification.

NOTES

Commencement: 1 September 2015.

6–8 (*Outside the scope of this work.*)

SCHEDULE
GROUNDS FOR DISQUALIFICATION

Regulation 4

[18.302]

1 . . .

2 The person is an undisclosed bankrupt or a person whose estate has had sequestration awarded in respect of it and who has not been discharged.

3 The person is the subject of a bankruptcy restrictions order or an interim bankruptcy restrictions order or an order to like effect made in Scotland or Northern Ireland.

4 The person is a person to whom a moratorium period under a debt relief order applies under Part 7A of the Insolvency Act 1986 (debt relief orders).

5 The person has made a composition or arrangement with, or granted a trust deed for, creditors and not been discharged in respect of it.

6–13 . . .

14 The person is subject to—

(a) a disqualification order or disqualification undertaking under the Company Directors Disqualification Act 1986;

(b) a disqualification order or disqualification undertaking under the Company Directors Disqualification (Northern Ireland Order) 2002; or

(c) an order made under section 429(2)(b) of the Insolvency Act 1986 (disabilities on revocation of administration order against an individual).

15–29 . . .

NOTES

Commencement: 1 September 2015.

Paras 1, 6–13, 15–29: outside the scope of this work.

NATIONAL HEALTH SERVICE (GENERAL MEDICAL SERVICES CONTRACTS) REGULATIONS 2015

(SI 2015/1862)

NOTES

Made: 6 November 2015.

Authority: National Health Service Act 2006, ss 9(8), 83(3), (6), 85(1), 86(1), (4), 89(1), (1A)(a), (b), (3), (4), 90(1), (3), 91(1), 97(6), (8), 187, 272(7), (8).

Commencement: 7 December 2015.

PART 1
GENERAL

[18.303]

1 Citation and commencement

(1) These Regulations may be cited as the National Health Service (General Medical Services Contracts) Regulations 2015.

(2) They come into force on 7th December 2015.

NOTES

Commencement: 7 December 2015.

[18.304]

2 Application

These Regulations apply to a contract—

(a) to which the National Health Service (General Medical Services Contracts) Regulations 2004 applied immediately before the date on which these Regulations come into force; or

(b) which is entered into between a contractor and the Board on or after that date.

NOTES

Commencement: 7 December 2015.

3 *(Outside the scope of this work.)*

PART 2
CONTRACTORS: CONDITIONS AND ELIGIBILITY

4, 5 *(Outside the scope of this work.)*

[18.305]

6 General condition relating to all contracts

(1) The Board must not enter into a contract with—

(a) a medical practitioner to whom paragraph (2) applies; or

(b) two or more persons practising in partnership, where paragraph (2) applies to any person who is a partner in the partnership; or

(c) a company limited by shares where paragraph (2) applies to—

(i) the company,

(ii) any person both legally and beneficially owning a share in the company, or

(iii) any director or secretary of the company.

(2) This paragraph applies if—

(a)–(k) . . .

(l) the contractor—

(i) has been [made] bankrupt and has not been discharged from the bankruptcy or the bankruptcy order has not been annulled, or

(ii) has had sequestration of the contractor's estate awarded and has not been discharged from the sequestration;

(m) the contractor is the subject of a bankruptcy restrictions order or an interim bankruptcy restrictions order under Schedule 4A to the Insolvency Act 1986 (bankruptcy restrictions order and undertaking), Schedule 2A to the Insolvency (Northern Ireland) Order 1989 (bankruptcy restrictions order and undertaking), or sections 56A to 56K of the Bankruptcy (Scotland) Act 1985 (bankruptcy restrictions order, interim bankruptcy restrictions order and bankruptcy restrictions undertaking), unless the contractor has been discharged from that order or that order has been annulled;

(n) the contractor—

(i) is subject to moratorium period under a debt relief order under Part VIIA of the Insolvency Act 1986 (debt relief orders), or

(ii) is the subject of a debt relief restrictions order or an interim debt relief restrictions order under Schedule 4ZB to that Act (debt relief restrictions orders and undertakings);

(o) the contractor has made a composition agreement or arrangement with, or granted a trust deed for, the contractor's creditors and the contractor has not been discharged in respect of it;

Part 18 Miscellaneous SIs

(p) the contractor is subject to—

(i) a disqualification order under section 1 of the Company Directors Disqualification Act 1986 (disqualification orders: general) or a disqualification undertaking under section 1A of that Act (disqualification undertakings: general),

(ii) a disqualification order or disqualification undertaking under article 3 (disqualification orders: general) or article 4 (disqualification undertakings: general) of the Company Directors Disqualification (Northern Ireland) Order 2002, or

(iii) a disqualification order under section 429(2) of the Insolvency Act 1986 (disabilities on revocation of an administration order against an individual);

(q) the contractor has had an administrator, administrative receiver or receiver appointed in respect of the contractor;

(r) the contractor has had an administration order made in respect of the contractor under Schedule B1 to the Insolvency Act 1986 (administration); or

(s) . . .

(3)–(5) . . .

NOTES

Commencement: 7 December 2015.

Paras (2)(a)–(k), (s), (3)–(5): outside the scope of this work.

Para (2): in sub-para (l)(i) word in square brackets substituted by the Enterprise and Regulatory Reform Act 2013 (Consequential Amendments) (Bankruptcy) and the Small Business, Enterprise and Employment Act 2015 (Consequential Amendments) Regulations 2016, SI 2016/481, reg 2(2), Sch 2, Pt 2, para 13.

7–13 (*Regs 7, 8, regs 9–13 (Pts 3, 4) outside the scope of this work.*)

PART 5
CONTRACTS: REQUIRED TERMS

13–31 (*Outside the scope of this work.*)

[18.306]
32 Other contractual terms

(1) Subject to paragraph (2), a contract must also contain provisions which are equivalent in their effect to the provisions set out in Parts 6 to 14 of, and Schedules 1 to 3 to, these Regulations, unless the contract is of a type or nature to which a particular provision does not apply.

(2) . . .

NOTES

Commencement: 7 December 2015.

Para (2): outside the scope of this work.

33–98 (*(Pts 6–15) Outside the scope of this work.*)

SCHEDULES 1 AND 2

(*Schs 1, 2 outside the scope of this work.*)

SCHEDULE 3
OTHER CONTRACTUAL TERMS

Regulation 32

PART 7
NOTICE REQUIREMENTS AND RIGHTS OF ENTRY

Notice provisions specific to a contract with a company limited by shares

[18.307]

50 (1) Where a contractor is a company limited by shares, the contractor must give notice in writing to the Board as soon as—

(a)–(e) . . .

(f) the company is unable to pay its debts within the meaning of section 123 of the Insolvency Act 1986 (definition of inability to pay debts).

(2), (3) . . .

NOTES

Commencement: 7 December 2015.

Note: only the relevant provision of Sch 3 is reproduced; the remainder is not annotated.

SCHEDULES 4 AND 5

(*Schs 4, 5 outside the scope of this work.*)

NATIONAL HEALTH SERVICE (PERSONAL MEDICAL SERVICES AGREEMENTS) REGULATIONS 2015

(SI 2015/1879)

NOTES

Made: 6 November 2015.

Authority: National Health Service Act 2006, ss 93(2), 94(1), (2) (3), (3A)(a),(6)–(9), 272(7), (8).

Commencement: 7 December 2015.

PART 1
GENERAL

[18.308]

1 Citation and commencement

(1) These Regulations may be cited as the National Health Service (Personal Medical Services Agreements) Regulations 2015.

(2) They come into force on 7th December 2015.

NOTES

Commencement: 7 December 2015.

[18.309]

2 Application

These Regulations apply to an agreement—

(a) to which the National Health Service (Personal Medical Services Agreements) Regulations 2004 applied immediately before the date on which these Regulations come into force; or

(b) which is entered into between a contractor and the Board on or after that date.

NOTES

Commencement: 7 December 2015.

3 (*Outside the scope of this work.*)

PART 2
AGREEMENTS

4 (*Outside the scope of this work.*)

[18.310]

5 General condition relating to all agreements

(1) The Board must not enter into an agreement with—

(a) a person falling within section 93(1)(b) to (d) of the Act (persons with whom agreements may be made under section 92), to whom paragraph (2) applies;

(b) a qualifying body if paragraph (2) applies to—

(i) the qualifying body,

(ii) any person both legally and beneficially owning a share in the qualifying body, and

(iii) any director or secretary of the qualifying body.

(2) This paragraph applies if—

(a)–(k) . . .

(l) the contractor—

(i) has been [made] bankrupt and has not been discharged from the bankruptcy or the bankruptcy order has not been annulled, or

(ii) has had sequestration of the contractor's estate awarded and has not been discharged from the sequestration;

(m) the contractor is the subject of a bankruptcy restrictions order or an interim bankruptcy restrictions order under Schedule 4A to the Insolvency Act 1986 (bankruptcy restrictions order and undertaking), or Schedule 2A to the Insolvency (Northern Ireland) Order 1989 (bankruptcy restrictions order and undertaking), or sections 56A to 56K of the Bankruptcy (Scotland) Act 1985 (bankruptcy restrictions order, interim bankruptcy restrictions order and bankruptcy restrictions undertaking), unless the contractor has been discharged from that order or that order has been annulled;

(n) the contractor—

(i) is subject to a moratorium period under a debt relief order under Part VIIA of the Insolvency Act 1986 (debt relief orders), or

(ii) is the subject of a debt relief restrictions order or an interim debt relief restrictions order under Schedule 4ZB to that Act (debt relief restrictions orders and undertakings);

(o) the contractor has made a composition agreement or arrangement with, or granted a trust deed for, the contractor's creditors and the contractor has not been discharged in respect of it;

(p) the contractor is subject to—

(i) a disqualification order under section 1 of the Company Directors Disqualification Act 1986 (disqualification orders: general) or a disqualification undertaking under section 1A of that Act (disqualification undertakings: general),

(ii) a disqualification order or disqualification undertaking under article 3 (disqualification orders: general) or article 4 (disqualification undertakings: general) of the Company Directors Disqualification (Northern Ireland) Order 2002, or

(iii) a disqualification order under section 429(2) of the Insolvency Act 1986 (disabilities on revocation of an administration order against an individual);

(q) the contractor has had an administrator, administrative receiver or receiver appointed in respect of the contractor; or

(r) the contractor has had an administration order made in respect of the contractor under Schedule B1 to the Insolvency Act 1986 (administration).

(3)–(5) . . .

NOTES

Commencement: 7 December 2015.

Paras (2)(a)–(k), (3)–(5): outside the scope of this work.

Para (2): in sub-para (l)(i) word in square brackets substituted by the Small Business, Enterprise and Employment Act 2015 (Consequential Amendments) Regulations 2016, SI 2016/481, reg 2(2), Sch 2, Pt 2, para 13.

6–11 *(Regs 6, 7, regs 8–11 (Pts 3, 4) outside the scope of this work.)*

PART 5
AGREEMENTS: REQUIRED TERMS

12–26 *(Outside the scope of this work.)*

[18.311]
27 Other required terms

(1) Subject to paragraph (2), an agreement must also contain provisions which are equivalent in their effect to the provisions set out in Parts 6 to 14 of, and Schedules 1 and 2 to, these Regulations, unless the agreement is of a type or nature to which a particular provision does not apply.

(2) . . .

NOTES

Commencement: 7 December 2015.

Para (2): outside the scope of this work.

28–90 *((Pts 6–15) outside the scope of this work.)*

SCHEDULE 1

(Sch 1 outside the scope of this work.)

SCHEDULE 2
OTHER REQUIRED TERMS

Regulation 27

PART 7
NOTICE REQUIREMENTS AND RIGHTS OF ENTRY

Notice provisions specific to an agreement with a qualifying body

[18.312]

46 (1) Where a qualifying body is a party to the agreement, the contractor must give notice in writing to the Board as soon as—

(a)–(e) . . .

(f) the qualifying body is unable to pay its debts within the meaning of section 123 of the Insolvency Act 1986 (definition of inability to pay debts).

(2), (3) . . .

NOTES

Commencement: 7 December 2015.

Note: only the relevant provision of Sch 2 is reproduced; the remainder is not annotated.

SCHEDULES 3 AND 4

(Schs 3, 4 outside the scope of this work.)

GENERAL MEDICAL COUNCIL (CONSTITUTION OF THE MEDICAL PRACTITIONERS TRIBUNAL SERVICE) RULES ORDER OF COUNCIL 2015

(SI 2015/1967)

NOTES

Made: 1 December 2015.
Authority: Medical Act 1983, Sch 1, para 19F.
Commencement: 31 December 2015.

[18.313]
1 Citation and commencement

This Order may be cited as the General Medical Council (Constitution of the Medical Practitioners Tribunal Service) Rules Order of Council 2015 and comes into force on 31st December 2015.

NOTES

Commencement: 31 December 2015.

2 (*Outside the scope of this work.*)

SCHEDULE
THE GENERAL MEDICAL COUNCIL (CONSTITUTION OF THE MEDICAL PRACTITIONERS TRIBUNAL SERVICE) RULES 2015

Article 2

[18.314]
6 Disqualification from appointment as a member

(1) A person (P) is disqualified from appointment as a member of the MPTS if any of the following paragraphs apply.

(2)–(6) . . .

(7) If P has at any time been adjudged bankrupt or sequestration of P's estate has been awarded, and—
 (a) P has not been discharged; or
 (b) P is the subject of a bankruptcy restrictions order or an interim bankruptcy restrictions order under Schedule 4A to the Insolvency Act 1986 (bankruptcy restrictions order and undertaking).

(8) If P has at any time made a composition or arrangement with, or granted a trust deed for, P's creditors and P has not been discharged in respect of it.

(9) If P is subject to any of the following—
 (a) a disqualification order or disqualification undertaking under the Company Directors Disqualification Act 1986;
 (b) a disqualification order or disqualification undertaking under the Company Directors Disqualification (Northern Ireland) Order 2002;
 (c) an order made under section 429(2) of the Insolvency Act 1986 (disabilities on revocation of a county court administration order).

(10)–(16) . . .

NOTES

Commencement: 31 December 2015.
Note: only the relevant provision of the Schedule is reproduced; the remainder is not annotated.

LEGAL AID, SENTENCING AND PUNISHMENT OF OFFENDERS ACT 2012 (COMMENCEMENT NO 12) ORDER 2016

(SI 2016/345)

NOTES

Made: 10 March 2016.
Authority: Legal Aid, Sentencing and Punishment of Offenders Act 2012, s 151(1).

[18.315]
1 Citation and interpretation

(1) This Order may be cited as the Legal Aid, Sentencing and Punishment of Offenders Act 2012 (Commencement No 12) Order 2016.

(2) In this Order—
"the 1986 Act" means the Insolvency Act 1986;
"the 2012 Act" means the Legal Aid, Sentencing and Punishment of Offenders Act 2012;

"company" means a company within the meaning of section 1 of the Companies Act 2006 or a company which may be wound up under Part V of the 1986 Act; and

"proceedings" has the same meaning as in section 58A(4) of the Courts and Legal Services Act 1990.

[18.316]

2 Provisions coming into force on 6th April 2016

Section 44 (conditional fee agreements: success fees) and section 46 (recovery of insurance premiums) of the 2012 Act come into force on 6th April 2016 in relation to—

(a) proceedings in England and Wales brought by a person acting in the capacity of—

  (i) a liquidator of a company which is being wound up in England and Wales or Scotland under Parts IV or V of the 1986 Act; or

  (ii) a trustee of a bankrupt's estate under Part IX of the 1986 Act;

(b) proceedings brought by a person acting in the capacity of an administrator appointed pursuant to the provisions of Part II of the 1986 Act;

(c) proceedings in England and Wales brought by a company which is being wound up in England and Wales or Scotland under Parts IV or V of the 1986 Act; and

(d) proceedings brought by a company which has entered administration under Part II of the 1986 Act.

PART 19
PRACTICE DIRECTIONS

PRACTICE DIRECTION: INSOLVENCY PROCEEDINGS (2014)

NOTES

This Practice Direction is up to date to 6 April 2018. The text and details of any further amendments can be found at www.justice.gov.uk.

PART ONE: GENERAL PROVISIONS

1. DEFINITIONS

[19.1]

1.1 In this Practice Direction:

(1) 'The Act' means the Insolvency Act 1986 and includes the Act as applied to limited liability partnerships by the Limited Liability Partnerships Regulations 2001 or to any other person or body by virtue of the Act or any other legislation;

(2) 'The Insolvency Rules' means the rules for the time being in force and made under s 411 and s 412 of the Act in relation to insolvency proceedings, and, save where otherwise provided, any reference to a rule is to a rule in the Insolvency Rules;

(3) 'CPR' means the Civil Procedure Rules and 'CPR' followed by a Part or rule identified by number means the Part or rule with that number in those Rules;

(4) 'EC Regulation on Insolvency Proceedings' means Council Regulation (EC) No 1346/2000 of 29 May 2000 on Insolvency Proceedings;

(5) 'Service Regulation' means Council Regulation (EC) No. 1393/2007 of 13 November 2007 on the service in the Member States of judicial and extrajudicial documents in civil and commercial matters (service of documents);

(6) 'Insolvency proceedings' means:

(a) any proceedings under the Act, the Insolvency Rules, the Administration of Insolvent Estates of Deceased Persons Order 1986 (SI 1986 No 1999), the Insolvent Partnerships Order 1994 (SI 1994 No 2421) or the Limited Liability Partnerships Regulations 2001;

(b) any proceedings under the EC Regulation on Insolvency Proceedings or the Cross-Border Insolvency Regulations 2006 (SI 2006/1030);

(7) References to a 'company' include a limited liability partnership and references to a 'contributory' include a member of a limited liability partnership;

(8) References to a 'Registrar' are to a Registrar in Bankruptcy of the High Court and (save in cases where it is clear from the context that a particular provision applies only to the Royal Courts of Justice) include a District Judge in a District Registry of the High Court and in any county court hearing centre having relevant insolvency jurisdiction;

(9) 'Court' means the High Court or any county court hearing centre having relevant insolvency jurisdiction;

(10) 'Royal Courts of Justice' means the Royal Courts of Justice, 7 Rolls Buildings, Fetter Lane, London EC4A 1NL or such other place in London where the Registrars sit;

(11) In Part Six of this Practice Direction:

(a) "appointee" means:

(i) a provisional liquidator appointed under section 135 of the Act;

(ii) a special manager appointed under section 177 or section 370 of the Act;

(iii) a liquidator appointed by the members of a company or partnership or by the creditors of a company or partnership or by the Secretary of State pursuant to section 137 of the Act, or by the court pursuant to section 140 of the Act;

(iv) an administrator of a company appointed to manage the property, business and affairs of that company under the Act or other enactment and to which the provisions of the Act are applicable;

(v) a trustee in bankruptcy (other than the Official Receiver) appointed under the Act;

(vi) a nominee or supervisor of a voluntary arrangement under Part I or Part VIII of the Act;

(vii) a licensed insolvency practitioner appointed by the court pursuant to section 273 of the Act;

(viii) an interim receiver appointed by the court pursuant to section 286 of the Act;

(b) "assessor" means a person appointed in accordance with CPR 35.15;

(c) "remuneration application" means any application to fix, approve or challenge the remuneration or expenses of an appointee or the basis of remuneration;

(d) "remuneration" includes expenses (where the Act or the Insolvency Rules give the court jurisdiction in relation thereto) and, in the case of an administrator, any pre-appointment administration costs or remuneration.

2. COMING INTO FORCE

[19.2]

2.1 This Practice Direction shall come into force on 29 July 2014 and shall replace all previous Practice Directions, Practice Statements and Practice Notes relating to insolvency proceedings. For the avoidance of doubt, this Practice Direction does not affect the Practice Direction relating to contributories' winding up petitions (Practice Direction 49B – Order under section 127 Insolvency Act 1986).

3. DISTRIBUTION OF BUSINESS

[19.3]

3.1 As a general rule all petitions and applications (except those listed in paragraphs 3.2 and 3.3 below) should be listed for initial hearing before a Registrar in accordance with rule 7.6A(2) and (3).

3.2 The following applications relating to insolvent companies should always be listed before a Judge:

(1) applications for committal for contempt;

(2) applications for an administration order;

(3) applications for an injunction pursuant to the Court's inherent jurisdiction (e.g. to restrain the presentation or advertisement of a winding up petition) or pursuant to section 37 of the Senior Courts Act 1981 or section 38 of the County Courts Act 1984 but not applications for any order to be made pursuant to the Act or the Rules;

(4) applications for the appointment of a provisional liquidator;

(5) interim applications and applications for directions or case management after any proceedings have been referred or adjourned to the Judge (except where liberty to apply to the Registrar has been given).

3.3 The following applications relating to insolvent individuals should always be listed before a Judge:

(1) applications for committal for contempt;

(2) applications for an injunction pursuant to the Court's inherent jurisdiction (e.g. to restrain the presentation of a bankruptcy petition) or pursuant to section 37 of the Senior Courts Act 1981 or section 38 of the County Courts Act 1984 but not applications for any order to be made pursuant to the Act or the Rules;

(3) interim applications and applications for directions or case management after any proceedings have been referred or adjourned to the Judge (except where liberty to apply to the Registrar has been given).

3.4 When deciding whether to hear proceedings or to refer or adjourn them to the Judge, the Registrar should have regard to the following factors:

(1) the complexity of the proceedings;

(2) whether the proceedings raise new or controversial points of law;

(3) the likely date and length of the hearing;

(4) public interest in the proceedings.

4. COURT DOCUMENTS

[19.4]

4.1 All insolvency proceedings should be commenced and applications in proceedings should be made using the forms prescribed by the Act, the Insolvency Rules or other legislation under which the same is or are brought or made and/or should contain the information prescribed by the Act, the Insolvency Rules or other legislation.

4.2 Every court document in insolvency proceedings under Parts I to VII of the Act shall be headed:

IN THE HIGH COURT OF JUSTICE

CHANCERY DIVISION

[DISTRICT REGISTRY] or in the Royal Courts of Justice [COMPANIES COURT]

or

IN THE COUNTY COURT AT [ ]

followed by

IN THE MATTER OF [name of company]

AND IN THE MATTER OF THE INSOLVENCY ACT 1986

4.3 Every court document in insolvency proceedings under Parts IX to XI of the Act shall be headed:

IN THE [HIGH COURT OF JUSTICE] or COUNTY COURT AT [ ]]

IN BANKRUPTCY

IN THE MATTER OF [name of bankrupt]

or

RE: [name of bankrupt].

Every application should also be headed:

AND IN THE MATTER OF THE INSOLVENCY ACT 1986

4.4 Every court document in proceedings to which the Act applies by virtue of other legislation should also be headed:

IN THE MATTER OF [THE FINANCIAL SERVICES AND MARKETS ACT 2000 or as the case may be]

AND IN THE MATTER OF THE INSOLVENCY ACT 1986

5. EVIDENCE

[19.5]
5.1 Subject to the provisions of rule 7.9 or any other provisions or directions as to the form in which evidence should be given, written evidence in insolvency proceedings must be given by witness statement.

6. SERVICE OF COURT DOCUMENTS IN INSOLVENCY PROCEEDINGS

[19.6]
6.1 Except where the Insolvency Rules otherwise provide (and, in this regard, the attention of practitioners is particularly drawn to rule 12A.16(2)), CPR Part 6 applies to the service of court documents both within and out of the jurisdiction as modified by this Practice Direction or as the court may otherwise direct.

6.2 Except where the Insolvency Rules otherwise provide or as may be required under the Service Regulation, service of documents in insolvency proceedings will be the responsibility of the parties and will not be undertaken by the court.

6.3 A document which, pursuant to rule 12A.16(3)(b), is treated as a claim form, is deemed to have been served on the date specified in CPR Part 6.14, and any other document (including any document which is treated as a claim form pursuant to rule 12A.16(3)(a) but which is not a document of a type specified in rule 12A.16(2)) is deemed to have been served on the date specified in CPR Part 6.26, unless the court otherwise directs. (Pursuant to rule 12A.16(2), the provisions of CPR Part 6 do not apply to the service of any of the following documents within the jurisdiction: (a) a winding-up petition; (b) a bankruptcy petition; (c) any document relating to such a petition; or (d) any administration, winding-up or bankruptcy order.)

6.4 Except as provided below, service out of the jurisdiction of an application which is to be treated as a claim form under rule 12A.16(3) requires the permission of the court.

6.5 An application which is to be treated as a claim form under rule 12A.16(3) may be served out of the jurisdiction without the permission of the court if:

(1) the application is by an office-holder appointed in insolvency proceedings in respect of a company with its centre of main interests within the jurisdiction exercising a statutory power under the Act, and the person to be served is to be served within the EU; or

(2) it is a copy of an application, being served on a Member State liquidator (as defined by Article 2 of the EC Regulation on Insolvency Proceedings).

6.6 An application for permission to serve out of the jurisdiction must be supported by a witness statement setting out:

(1) the nature of the claim or application and the relief sought;

(2) that the applicant believes that the claim has a reasonable prospect of success; and

(3) the address of the person to be served or, if not known, in what place or country that person is, or is likely, to be found.

6.7 CPR 6.36 and 6.37(1) and (2) do not apply in insolvency proceedings.

7. JURISDICTION

[19.7]
7.1 Where CPR 2.4 provides for the court to perform any act, that act may be performed by a Registrar.

8. DRAWING UP OF ORDERS

[19.8]
8.1 The court will draw up all orders except orders on the application of the Official Receiver or for which the Treasury Solicitor is responsible or where the court otherwise directs.

9. URGENT APPLICATIONS

[19.9]
9.1 In the Royal Courts of Justice the Registrars (and in other courts exercising insolvency jurisdiction

the District Judges) operate urgent applications lists for urgent and time-critical applications and may be available to hear urgent applications at other times. Parties asking for an application to be dealt with in the urgent applications lists or urgently at any other time must complete the certificate below:

No:

Heading of action

I estimate that this matter is likely to occupy the court for . . . . mins/hours.

I certify that it is urgent for the following reasons:

. . . .

[name of representative]

. . . .

[telephone number]

Counsel/Solicitor for the . . . .

WARNING. If, in the opinion of the Registrar/District Judge, the application is not urgent then such sanction will be applied as is thought appropriate in all the circumstances.

PART TWO: COMPANY INSOLVENCY

10. ADMINISTRATIONS

[19.10]

10.1 In the absence of special circumstances, an application for the extension of an administration should be made not less than one month before the end of the administration. The evidence in support of any later application must explain why the application is being made late. The court will consider whether any part of the costs should be disallowed where an application is made less than one month before the end of the administration.

11. WINDING-UP PETITIONS

[19.11]

11.1 Before presenting a winding-up petition the creditor must conduct a search to ensure that no petition is already pending. Save in exceptional circumstances a second winding up petition should not be presented whilst a prior petition is pending. A petitioner who presents his own petition while another petition is pending does so at risk as to costs.

11.2 Save where by reason of the nature of the company or its place of incorporation the information cannot be stated (in which case as much similar information as is available should be given), every creditor's winding-up petition must (in the case of a company) contain the following—

(1) the full name and address of the petitioner;

(2) the name and any registered number/s of the company in respect of which a winding up order is sought

(3) the date of incorporation of the company and the legislation under which it was incorporated;

(4) the address of the company's registered office and, in the case of any overseas company, the address of any establishment registered under the Companies Act or Acts;

(5) (a) In the case of companies incorporated under any of the Companies Acts prior to the Companies Act 2006, a statement of the nominal capital of the company, the manner in which its shares are divided up and the amount of the capital paid up or credited as paid up; or (b) In the case of any other companies, a statement of the known issued share capital of the company, the manner in which its shares are divided up and the amount of the capital paid up or credited as paid up.

(6) (a) In the case of companies incorporated under any of the Companies Acts prior to the Companies Act 2006, brief details of the principal objects for which the company was established followed, where appropriate, by the words "and other objects stated in the memorandum of association of the company"; or (b) In the case of companies incorporated under the Companies Act 2006, either: (i) a statement confirming that its objects are unrestricted pursuant to section 31(1) of the Companies Act 2006, or alternatively (ii) a statement confirming that its objects are restricted by its Articles of Association and brief details of such restrictions;

(7) details of the basis on which it is contended that the company is insolvent including, where a debt is relied on, sufficient particulars of the debt (the amount, nature and approximate date(s) on which it was incurred) to enable the company and the court to identify the debt;

(8) a statement that the company is insolvent and unable to pay its debts;
(9) a statement that for the reasons set out in the evidence verifying the petition the EC Regulation on Insolvency Proceedings either applies or does not and if the former whether the proceedings will be main, territorial or secondary proceedings;
(10) the statement that, "In the circumstances it is just and equitable that the company be wound up under the provisions of the Insolvency Act 1986";
(11) a prayer that the company be wound up, for such other order as the court thinks fit and any other specific relief sought.

Similar information (so far as is appropriate) should be given where the petition is presented against a partnership.

11.3 The statement of truth verifying the petition in accordance with rule 4.12 should be made no more than ten business days before the date of issue of the petition.

11.4 Where the company to be wound up has been struck off the register, the petition should state that fact and include as part of the relief sought an order that it be restored to the register. Save where the petition has been presented by a Minister of the Crown or a government department, evidence of service on the Treasury Solicitor or the Solicitor for the affairs of the Duchy of Lancaster or the Solicitor to the Duchy of Cornwall (as appropriate) should be filed exhibiting the bona vacantia waiver letter.

11.5 Gazetting of the petition

11.5.1 Rule 4.11 must be complied with (unless waived by the court): it is designed to ensure that the class remedy of winding up by the court is made available to all creditors, and is not used as a means of putting improper pressure on the company to pay the petitioner's debt or costs. Failure to comply with the rule, without good reason accepted by the court, may lead to the summary dismissal of the petition on the return date (rule 4.11(6)) or to the court depriving the petitioner of the costs of the hearing. If the court, in its discretion, grants an adjournment, this will usually be on terms that notice of the petition is gazetted or otherwise given in accordance with the rule in due time for the adjourned hearing. No further adjournment for the purpose of gazetting will normally be granted.

11.5.2 Copies of every notice gazetted in connection with a winding up petition, or where this is not practicable a description of the form and content of the notice, must be lodged with the court as soon as possible after publication and in any event not later than five business days before the hearing of the petition. This direction applies even if the notice is defective in any way (e.g. is published on a date not in accordance with the Insolvency Rules, or omits or misprints some important words) or if the petitioner decides not to pursue the petition (e.g. on receiving payment).

11.6 Errors in petitions

11.6.1 Applications for permission to amend errors in petitions which are discovered after a winding up order has been made should be made to the member of court staff in charge of the winding up list in the Royal Courts of Justice or to a District Judge in any other court.

11.6.2 Where the error is an error in the name of the company, the member of court staff in charge of the winding up list in the Royal Courts of Justice or a District Judge in any other court may make any necessary amendments to ensure that the winding up order is drawn up with the correct name of the company inserted. If there is any doubt, e.g. where there might be another company in existence which could be confused with the company to be wound up, the member of court staff in charge of the winding up list will refer the application to a Registrar at the Royal Courts of Justice and a District Judge may refer it to a Judge.

11.6.3 Where it is discovered that the company has been struck off the Register of Companies prior to the winding up order being made, the matter must be restored to the list as soon as possible to enable an order for the restoration of the name to be made as well as the order to wind up and, save where the petition has been presented by a Minister of the Crown or a government department, evidence of service on the Treasury Solicitor or the Solicitor for the Affairs of the Duchy of Lancaster or the Solicitor to the Duchy of Cornwall (as appropriate) should be filed exhibiting the bona vacantia waiver letter.

11.7 Rescission of a winding up order

11.7.1 An application to rescind a winding up order must be made by application.

11.7.2 The application should normally be made within five business days after the date on which the order was made (rule 7.47(4)) failing which it should include an application to extend time. Notice of any such application must be given to the petitioning creditor, any supporting or opposing creditor and the Official Receiver.

11.7.3 Applications will only be entertained if made (a) by a creditor, or (b) by a contributory, or (c) by the company jointly with a creditor or with a contributory. The application must be supported by a witness statement which should include details of assets and liabilities and (where appropriate) reasons for any failure to apply within five business days.

11.7.4 In the case of an unsuccessful application the costs of the petitioning creditor, any supporting creditors and of the Official Receiver will normally be ordered to be paid by the creditor or the contributory making or joining in the application. The reason for this is that if the costs of an unsuccessful application are made payable by the company, they fall unfairly on the general body of creditors.

11.8 Validation orders

11.8.1 A company against which a winding up petition has been presented may apply to the court after presentation of the petition for relief from the effects of section 127(1) of the Act by seeking an order that a disposition or dispositions of its property, including payments out of its bank account (whether such account is in credit or overdrawn), shall not be void in the event of a winding up order being made on the hearing of the petition (a validation order).

11.8.2 An application for a validation order should generally be made to the Registrar. An application should be made to the Judge only if: (a) it is urgent and no Registrar is available to hear it; or (b) it is complex or raises new or controversial points of law; or (c) it is estimated to last longer than 30 minutes.

11.8.3 Save in exceptional circumstances, notice of the making of the application should be given to: (a) the petitioning creditor; (b) any person entitled to receive a copy of the petition pursuant to rule 4.10; (c) any creditor who has given notice to the petitioner of his intention to appear on the hearing of the petition pursuant to rule 4.16; and (d) any creditor who has been substituted as petitioner pursuant to rule 4.19.

11.8.4 The application should be supported by a witness statement which, save in exceptional circumstances, should be made by a director or officer of the company who is intimately acquainted with the company's affairs and financial circumstances. If appropriate, supporting evidence in the form of a witness statement from the company's accountant should also be produced.

11.8.5 The extent and contents of the evidence will vary according to the circumstances and the nature of the relief sought, but in the majority of cases it should include, as a minimum, the following information:

(1) when and to whom notice has been given in accordance with paragraph 11.8.3 above;
(2) the company's registered office;
(3) the company's nominal and paid up capital;
(4) brief details of the circumstances leading to presentation of the petition;
(5) how the company became aware of presentation of the petition;
(6) whether the petition debt is admitted or disputed and, if the latter, brief details of the basis on which the debt is disputed;
(7) full details of the company's financial position including details of its assets (including details of any security and the amount(s) secured) and liabilities, which should be supported, as far as possible, by documentary evidence, e.g. the latest filed accounts, any draft audited accounts, management accounts or estimated statement of affairs;
(8) a cash flow forecast and profit and loss projection for the period for which the order is sought;
(9) details of the dispositions or payments in respect of which an order is sought;
(10) the reasons relied on in support of the need for such dispositions or payments to be made;
(11) any other information relevant to the exercise of the court's discretion;
(12) details of any consents obtained from the persons mentioned in paragraph 11.8.3 above (supported by documentary evidence where appropriate);
(13) details of any relevant bank account, including its number and the address and sort code of the bank at which such account is held and the amount of the credit or debit balance on such account at the time of making the application.

11.8.6 Where an application is made urgently to enable payments to be made which are essential to continued trading (e.g. wages) and it is not possible to assemble all the evidence listed above, the court may consider granting limited relief for a short period, but there should be sufficient evidence to satisfy the court that the interests of creditors are unlikely to be prejudiced.

11.8.7 Where the application involves a disposition of property the court will need details of the property (including its title number if the property is land) and to be satisfied that any proposed disposal will be at a proper value. Accordingly, an independent valuation should be obtained and exhibited to the evidence.

11.8.8 The court will need to be satisfied by credible evidence either that the company is solvent and able to pay its debts as they fall due or that a particular transaction or series of transactions in respect of which the order is sought will be beneficial to or will not prejudice the interests of all the unsecured creditors as a class (Denney v John Hudson & Co Ltd [1992] BCLC 901; Re Fairway Graphics Ltd [1991] BCLC 468).

11.8.9 A draft of the order sought should be attached to the application.

11.8.10 Similar considerations to those set out above are likely to apply to applications seeking ratification of a transaction or payment after the making of a winding-up order.

12. APPLICATIONS

[19.12]

12.1 In accordance with rule 13.2(2), in the Royal Courts of Justice the member of court staff in charge of the winding up list has been authorised to deal with applications:

(1) to extend or abridge time prescribed by the Insolvency Rules in connection with winding up (rule 4.3);
(2) for permission to withdraw a winding up petition (rule 4.15);
(3) for the substitution of a petitioner (rule 4.19);
(4) by the Official Receiver for limited disclosure of a statement of affairs (rule 4.35);
(5) by the Official Receiver for relief from duties imposed upon him by the Insolvency Rules (rule 4.47);
(6) by the Official Receiver for permission to give notice of a meeting by advertisement only (rule 4.59);
(7) to transfer proceedings from the High Court (Royal Courts of Justice) to a county court hearing centre (in which proceedings to wind up companies may be commenced under the Act) after the making of a winding-up order (rule 7.11).

12.2 In District Registries or the County Court such applications must be made to a District Judge.

PART THREE: PERSONAL INSOLVENCY

13. STATUTORY DEMANDS

[19.13]
13.1 Service abroad of statutory demands

13.1.1 A statutory demand is not a document issued by the court. Permission to serve out of the jurisdiction is not, therefore, required.

13.1.2 Rule 6.3(2) ('Requirements as to service') applies to service of the statutory demand whether within or out of the jurisdiction.

13.1.3 A creditor wishing to serve a statutory demand out of the jurisdiction in a foreign country with which a civil procedure convention has been made (including the Hague Convention) may and, if the assistance of a British Consul is desired, must adopt the procedure prescribed by CPR Part 6.42 and 6.43. In the case of any doubt whether the country is a 'convention country', enquiries should be made of the Queen's Bench Masters' Secretary Department, Royal Courts of Justice, Strand, London WC2A 2LL.

13.1.4 In all other cases, service of the demand must be effected by private arrangement in accordance with rule 6.3(2) and local foreign law.

13.1.5 When a statutory demand is to be served out of the jurisdiction, the time limits of 21 days and 18 days respectively referred to in the demand must be amended as provided in the next paragraph. For this purpose reference should be made to the table set out in the practice direction supplementing Section IV of CPR Part 6.

13.1.6 A creditor should amend the statutory demand as follows:
(1) for any reference to 18 days there must be substituted the appropriate number of days set out in the table plus 4 days;
(2) for any reference to 21 days there must be substituted the appropriate number of days in the table plus 7 days.

13.1.7 Attention is drawn to the fact that in all forms of the statutory demand the figure 18 and the figure 21 occur in more than one place.

13.2 Substituted service of statutory demands

13.2.1 The creditor is under an obligation to do all that is reasonable to bring the statutory demand to the debtor's attention and, if practicable, to cause personal service to be effected (rule 6.3(2)).

13.2.2 In the circumstances set out in rule 6.3(3) the demand may instead be advertised. As there is no statutory form of advertisement, the court will accept an advertisement in the following form:

STATUTORY DEMAND

(Debt for liquidated sum payable immediately following a judgment or order of the court)

To (Block letters)

of

TAKE NOTICE that a statutory demand has been issued by:

Name of Creditor:

Address:

The creditor demands payment of £ the amount now due on a judgment or order of the (High Court of Justice Division) (County Court at . . . .) dated the [day] of [month] 20[ ].

The statutory demand is an important document and it is deemed to have been served on you on the date of the first appearance of this advertisement. You must deal with this demand within 21 days of the service upon you or you could be made bankrupt and your property and goods taken away from you. If you are in any doubt as to your position, you should seek advice immediately from a solicitor or your nearest

Citizens' Advice Bureau. The statutory demand can be obtained or is available for inspection and collection from:

Name:

Address:

(Solicitor for) the creditor

Tel. No. Reference:

You have only 21 days from the date of the first appearance of this advertisement before the creditor may present a bankruptcy petition. You have only 18 days from the date of the first appearance of this advertisement within which to apply to the court to set aside the demand.

13.2.3 Where personal service is not effected or the demand is not advertised in the limited circumstances permitted by rule 6.3(3), substituted service is permitted, but the creditor must have taken all those steps which would justify the court making an order for substituted service of a petition. The steps to be taken to obtain an order for substituted service of a petition are set out below. Failure to comply with these requirements may result in the court declining to issue the petition (rule 6.11(9)) or dismissing it.

13.2.4 In most cases, evidence of the following steps will suffice to justify acceptance for presentation of a petition where the statutory demand has been served by substituted service (or to justify making an order for substituted service of a petition):

(1) One personal call at the residence and place of business of the debtor where both are known or at either of such places as is known. Where it is known that the debtor has more than one residential or business address, personal calls should be made at all the addresses.

(2) Should the creditor fail to effect personal service, a first class prepaid letter should be written to the debtor referring to the call(s), the purpose of the same and the failure to meet the debtor, adding that a further call will be made for the same purpose on the [day] of [month] 20[ ] at [ ] hours at [place]. Such letter may be sent by first class prepaid post or left at or delivered to the debtor's address in such a way as it is reasonably likely to come to the debtor's attention. At least two business days' notice should be given of the appointment and copies of the letter sent to or left at all known addresses of the debtor. The appointment letter should also state that:

    (a) in the event of the time and place not being convenient, the debtor should propose some other time and place reasonably convenient for the purpose;

    (b) (In the case of a statutory demand) if the debtor fails to keep the appointment the creditor proposes to serve the debtor by [advertisement] [post] [insertion through a letter box] or as the case may be, and that, in the event of a bankruptcy petition being presented, the court will be asked to treat such service as service of the demand on the debtor;

    (c) (In the case of a petition) if the debtor fails to keep the appointment, application will be made to the Court for an order for substituted service either by advertisement, or in such other manner as the court may think fit.

(3) When attending any appointment made by letter, inquiry should be made as to whether the debtor has received all letters left for him. If the debtor is away, inquiry should also be made as to whether or not letters are being forwarded to an address within the jurisdiction (England and Wales) or elsewhere.

(4) If the debtor is represented by a solicitor, an attempt should be made to arrange an appointment for personal service through such solicitor. The Insolvency Rules enable a solicitor to accept service of a statutory demand on behalf of his client but there is no similar provision in respect of service of a bankruptcy petition.

(5) The certificate of service of a statutory demand filed pursuant to rule 6.11 should deal with all the above matters including all relevant facts as to the debtor's whereabouts and whether the appointment letter(s) have been returned. It should also set out the reasons for the belief that the debtor resides at the relevant address or works at the relevant place of business and whether, so far as is known, the debtor is represented by a solicitor.

13.3 Setting aside a statutory demand

13.3.1 The application (Form 6.4) and witness statement in support (Form 6.5) exhibiting a copy of the statutory demand must be filed in court within 18 days of service of the statutory demand on the debtor. Where service is effected by advertisement the period of 18 days is calculated from the date of the first appearance of the advertisement. Three copies of each document must be lodged with the application to enable the court to serve notice of the hearing date on the applicant, the creditor and the person named in Part B of the statutory demand.

13.3.2 Where copies of the documents are not lodged with the application, any order of the Registrar fixing a venue is conditional upon copies of the documents being lodged on the next business day after the Registrar's order otherwise the application will be deemed to have been dismissed.

13.3.3 Where the debt claimed in the statutory demand is based on a judgment, order, liability order, costs certificate, tax assessment or decision of a tribunal, the court will not at this stage inquire into the validity of the debt nor, as a general rule, will it adjourn the application to await the result of an application to set aside the judgment, order decision, costs certificate or any appeal.

13.3.4 Where the debtor (a) claims to have a counterclaim, set-off or cross demand (whether or not he could have raised it in the action in which the judgment or order was obtained) which equals or exceeds the amount of the debt or debts specified in the statutory demand or (b) disputes the debt (not being a debt subject to a judgment, order, liability order, costs certificate or tax assessment) the court will normally set aside the statutory demand if, in its opinion, on the evidence there is a genuine triable issue.

13.3.5 A debtor who wishes to apply to set aside a statutory demand after the expiration of 18 days from the date of service of the statutory demand must apply for an extension of time within which to apply. If the applicant wishes to apply for an injunction to restrain presentation of a petition the application must be made to the Judge. Paragraphs 1 and 2 of Form 6.5 (witness statement in support of application to set aside statutory demand) should be used in support of the application for an extension of time with the following additional paragraphs:

> "(3) To the best of my knowledge and belief the creditor(s) named in the demand has/have not presented a petition against me.
> (4) The reasons for my failure to apply to set aside the demand within 18 days after service are as follows: . . . "

If application is made to restrain presentation of a bankruptcy petition the following additional paragraph should be added:

> "(5) Unless restrained by injunction the creditor(s) may present a bankruptcy petition against me".

14. BANKRUPTCY PETITIONS

[19.14]

14.1 Listing of petitions

14.1.1 All petitions presented will be listed under the name of the debtor unless the court directs otherwise.

14.2 Content of petitions

14.2.1 The attention of practitioners is drawn to the following points:

(1) A creditor's petition does not require dating, signing or witnessing but must be verified in accordance with rule 6.12.

(2) In the heading it is only necessary to recite the debtor's name e.g. Re John William Smith or Re J W Smith (Male). Any alias or trading name will appear in the body of the petition.

14.2.2 Where the petition is based solely on a statutory demand, only the debt claimed in the demand may be included in the petition.

14.2.3 The attention of practitioners is also drawn to rules 6.7 and 6.8, and in particular to rule 6.8(1) where the 'aggregate sum' is made up of a number of debts.

14.2.4 The date of service of the statutory demand should be recited as follows:

(1) In the case of personal service, the date of service as set out in the certificate of service should be recited and whether service is effected before/after 16.00 hours on Monday to Friday or before/after 12.00 hours on a Saturday.

(2) In the case of substituted service (other than by advertisement), the date alleged in the certificate of service should be recited.

(3) In the strictly limited case of service by advertisement under rule 6.3, the date to be alleged is the date of the advertisement's appearance or, as the case may be, its first appearance (see rules 6.3(3) and 6.11(8)).

14.3 Searches

14.3.1 The petitioning creditor shall, before presenting a petition, conduct an Official Search with the Chief Land Registrar in the register of pending actions for pending petitions presented against the debtor and shall include the following certificate at the end of the petition:

"I/we certify that within 7 days ending today I/we have conducted a search for pending petitions presented against the debtor and that to the best of my/our knowledge information and belief [no prior petitions have been presented which are still pending] [a prior petition (No [ ]) has been presented and is/may be pending in the [Court] and I/we am/are issuing this petition at risk as to costs].

Signed. . . . . Dated. . . . . ".

14.4 Deposit

14.4.1 The deposit will be taken by the court and forwarded to the Official Receiver. In the Royal Courts of Justice the petition fee and deposit should be paid in the Fee Room, which will record the receipt and will impress two entries on the original petition, one in respect of the court fee and the other in respect of the deposit. In a District Registry or a county court hearing centre, the petition fee and deposit should be handed to the duly authorised officer of the court's staff who will record its receipt.

14.4.2 In all cases cheque(s) for the whole amount should be made payable to 'HM Courts and Tribunals Service' or 'HMCTS'.

14.5 Certificates of continuing debt and of notice of adjournment

14.5.1 On the hearing of a petition where a bankruptcy order is sought, in order to satisfy the court that the debt on which the petition is founded has not been paid or secured or compounded for the court will normally accept as sufficient a certificate signed by the person representing the petitioning creditor in the following form:

"I certify that I have/my firm has made enquiries of the petitioning creditor(s) within the last business day prior to the hearing/adjourned hearing and to the best of my knowledge and belief the debt on which the petition is founded is still due and owing and has not been paid or secured or compounded for save as to . . .

Signed . . . . Dated . . . . "

14.5.2 For convenience, in the Royal Courts of Justice this certificate is incorporated in the attendance sheet for the parties to complete when they come to court and which is filed after the hearing. A fresh certificate will be required on each adjourned hearing.

14.5.3 On any adjourned hearing of a petition where a bankruptcy order is sought, in order to satisfy the court that the petitioner has complied with rule 6.29, the petitioner will be required to file evidence of the date on which, manner in which and address to which notice of the making of the order of adjournment and of the venue for the adjourned hearing has been sent to:

(1) the debtor, and
(2) any creditor who has given notice under rule 6.23 but was not present at the hearing when the order for adjournment was made or was present at the hearing but the date of the adjourned hearing was not fixed at that hearing. For convenience, in the Royal Courts of Justice this certificate is incorporated in the attendance sheet for the parties to complete when they come to court and which is filed after the hearing and is as follows:

"I certify that the petitioner has complied with rule 6.29 by sending notice of adjournment to the debtor [supporting/opposing creditor(s)] on [date] at [address]".

A fresh certificate will be required on each adjourned hearing.

14.6 Extension of hearing date of petition

14.6.1 Late applications for extension of hearing dates under rule 6.28, and failure to attend on the listed hearing of a petition, will be dealt with as follows:

(1) If an application is submitted less than two clear working days before the hearing date (for example, later than Monday for Thursday, or Wednesday for Monday) the costs of the application will not be allowed under rule 6.28(3).
(2) If the petition has not been served and no extension has been granted by the time fixed for the hearing of the petition, and if no one attends for the hearing, the petition may be dismissed or re-listed for hearing about 21 days later. The court will notify the petitioning creditor's solicitors (or the petitioning creditor in person), and any known supporting or opposing creditors or their solicitors, of the new date and times. Written evidence should then be filed on behalf of the petitioning creditor explaining fully the reasons for the failure to apply for an extension or to appear at the hearing, and (if appropriate) giving reasons why the petition should not be dismissed.
(3) On the re-listed hearing the court may dismiss the petition if not satisfied it should be adjourned or a further extension granted.

14.6.2 All applications for an extension should include a statement of the date fixed for the hearing of the petition.

14.6.3 The petitioning creditor should contact the court (by solicitors or in person) on or before the hearing date to ascertain whether the application has reached the file and been dealt with. It should not be assumed that an extension will be granted.

14.7 Substituted service of bankruptcy petitions

14.7.1 In most cases evidence that the steps set out in paragraph 13.3.4 have been taken will suffice to justify an order for substituted service of a bankruptcy petition.

14.8 Validation orders

14.8.1 A person against whom a bankruptcy petition has been presented ('the debtor') may apply to the court after presentation of the petition for relief from the effects of section 284(1) – (3) of the Act by seeking an order that any disposition of his assets or payment made out of his funds, including any bank account (whether it is in credit or overdrawn) shall not be void in the event of a bankruptcy order being made on the petition (a 'validation order').

14.8.2 Save in exceptional circumstances, notice of the making of the application should be given to (a) the petitioning creditor(s) or other petitioner, (b) any creditor who has given notice to the petitioner of his intention to appear on the hearing of the petition pursuant to rule 6.23 1986, (c) any creditor who has been substituted as petitioner pursuant to rule 6.30 Insolvency Rules 1986 and (d) any creditor who has carriage of the petition pursuant to rule 6.31 Insolvency Rules 1986.

14.8.3 The application should be supported by a witness statement which, save in exceptional circumstances, should be made by the debtor. If appropriate, supporting evidence in the form of a witness statement from the debtor's accountant should also be produced.

14.8.4 The extent and contents of the evidence will vary according to the circumstances and the nature of the relief sought, but in a case where the debtor is trading or carrying on business it should include, as a minimum, the following information:

(1) when and to whom notice has been given in accordance with paragraph 14.8.2 above;
(2) brief details of the circumstances leading to presentation of the petition;
(3) how the debtor became aware of the presentation of the petition;
(4) whether the petition debt is admitted or disputed and, if the latter, brief details of the basis on which the debt is disputed;
(5) full details of the debtor's financial position including details of his assets (including details of any security and the amount(s) secured) and liabilities, which should be supported, as far as possible, by documentary evidence, e.g. accounts, draft accounts, management accounts or estimated statement of affairs;
(6) a cash flow forecast and profit and loss projection for the period for which the order is sought;
(7) details of the dispositions or payments in respect of which an order is sought;
(8) the reasons relied on in support of the need for such dispositions or payments to be made;
(9) any other information relevant to the exercise of the court's discretion;
(10) details of any consents obtained from the persons mentioned in paragraph 14.8.2 above (supported by documentary evidence where appropriate);
(11) details of any relevant bank account, including its number and the address and sort code of the bank at which such account is held and the amount of the credit or debit balance on such account at the time of making the application.

14.8.5 Where an application is made urgently to enable payments to be made which are essential to continued trading (e.g. wages) and it is not possible to assemble all the evidence listed above, the court may consider granting limited relief for a short period, but there must be sufficient evidence to satisfy the court that the interests of creditors are unlikely to be prejudiced.

14.8.6 Where the debtor is not trading or carrying on business and the application relates only to a proposed sale, mortgage or re-mortgage of the debtor's home evidence of the following will generally suffice:

(1) when and to whom notice has been given in accordance with 14.8.2 above;
(2) whether the petition debt is admitted or disputed and, if the latter, brief details of the basis on which the debt is disputed;
(3) details of the property to be sold, mortgaged or re-mortgaged (including its title number);
(4) the value of the property and the proposed sale price, or details of the mortgage or re-mortgage;
(5) details of any existing mortgages or charges on the property and redemption figures;
(6) the costs of sale (e.g. solicitors' or agents' costs);
(7) how and by whom any net proceeds of sale (or sums coming into the debtor's hands as a result of any mortgage or re-mortgage) are to be held pending the final hearing of the petition;
(8) any other information relevant to the exercise of the court's discretion;
(9) details of any consents obtained from the persons mentioned in 14.8.2 above (supported by documentary evidence where appropriate).

14.8.7 Whether or not the debtor is trading or carrying on business, where the application involves a disposition of property the court will need to be satisfied that any proposed disposal will be at a proper value. Accordingly an independent valuation should be obtained and exhibited to the evidence.

14.8.8 The court will need to be satisfied by credible evidence that the debtor is solvent and able to pay his debts as they fall due or that a particular transaction or series of transactions in respect of which the order is sought will be beneficial to or will not prejudice the interests of all the unsecured creditors as a class (Denney v John Hudson & Co Ltd [1992] BCLC 901, [1992] BCC 503, CA; Re Fairway Graphics Ltd [1991] BCLC 468).

14.8.9 A draft of the order sought should be attached to the application.

14.8.10 Similar considerations to those set out above are likely to apply to applications seeking ratification of a transaction or payment after the making of a bankruptcy order.

15. APPLICATIONS

[19.15]

15.1 In accordance with rule 13.2(2), in the Royal Courts of Justice the member of court staff in charge of the winding up list has been authorised to deal with applications:

(1) by petitioning creditors to extend the time for hearing petitions (rule 6.28);
(2) by the Official Receiver:

(a) to transfer proceedings from the High Court to a county court hearing centre (rule 7.13);
(b) to amend the title of the proceedings (rules 6.35 and 6.47).

15.2 In District Registries or the County Court such applications must be made to the District Judge.

16. ORDERS WITHOUT ATTENDANCE

[19.16]

16.1 In suitable cases the court will normally be prepared to make orders under Part VIII of the Act (Individual Voluntary Arrangements), without the attendance of the parties, provided there is no bankruptcy order in existence and (so far as is known) no pending petition. The orders are:

(1) A 14 day interim order adjourning the application for 14 days for consideration of the nominee's report, where the papers are in order, and the nominee's signed consent to act includes a waiver of notice of the application or the consent by the nominee to the making of an interim order without attendance.

(2) A standard order on consideration of the nominee's report, extending the interim order to a date seven weeks after the date of the proposed meeting, directing the meeting to be summoned and adjourning to a date about three weeks after the meeting. Such an order may be made without attendance if the nominee's report has been delivered to the court and complies with section 256(1) of the Act and rule 5.11(2) and (3) and proposes a date for the meeting not less than 14 days from that on which the nominee's report is filed in court under rule 5.11 nor more than 28 days from that on which that report is considered by the court under rule 5.13.

(3) A 'concertina' order, combining orders as under (1) and (2) above. Such an order may be made without attendance if the initial application for an interim order is accompanied by a report of the nominee and the conditions set out in (1) and (2) above are satisfied.

(4) A final order on consideration of the chairman's report. Such an order may be made without attendance if the chairman's report has been filed and complies with rule 5.27(1). The order will record the effect of the chairman's report and may discharge the interim order.

16.2 Provided that the conditions under sub-paragraphs (2) and (4) above are satisfied and that the appropriate report has been lodged with the court in due time the parties need not attend or be represented on the adjourned hearing for consideration of the nominee's report or of the chairman's report (as the case may be) unless they are notified by the court that attendance is required. Sealed copies of the order made (in all four cases as above) will be posted by the court to the applicant or his solicitor and to the nominee.

16.3 In suitable cases the court may also make consent orders without attendance by the parties. The written consent of the parties will be required. Examples of such orders are as follows:

(1) on applications to set aside a statutory demand, orders:
   (a) dismissing the application, with or without an order for costs as may be agreed (permission will be given to present a petition on or after the seventh day after the date of the order, unless a different date is agreed);
   (b) setting aside the demand, with or without an order for costs as may be agreed; or

(2) On petitions where there is a negative list of supporting or opposing creditors in Form 6.21, or a statement signed by or on behalf of the petitioning creditor that no notices have been received from supporting or opposing creditors, orders:
   (a) dismissing the petition, with or without an order for costs as may be agreed; or
   (b) if the petition has not been served, giving permission to withdraw the petition (with no order for costs).

(3) On other applications, orders:
   (a) for sale of property, possession of property, disposal of proceeds of sale;
   (b) giving interim directions;
   (c) dismissing the application, with or without an order for costs as may be agreed;
   (d) giving permission to withdraw the application, with or without an order for costs as may be agreed.

16.4 If, as may often be the case with orders under subparagraphs 3(a) or (b) above, an adjournment is required, whether generally with liberty to restore or to a fixed date, the order by consent may include an order for the adjournment. If adjournment to a date is requested, a time estimate should be given and the court will fix the first available date and time on or after the date requested.

16.5 The above lists should not be regarded as exhaustive, nor should it be assumed that an order will be made without attendance as requested.

16.6 Applications for consent orders without attendance should be lodged at least two clear working days (and preferably longer) before any hearing date.

16.7 Whenever a document is lodged or a letter sent, the correct case number should be quoted. A note should also be given of the date and time of the next hearing (if any).

17. BANKRUPTCY RESTRICTIONS UNDERTAKINGS

[19.17]

17.1 Where a bankrupt has given a bankruptcy restrictions undertaking, the Secretary of State or official receiver must file a copy in court and send a copy to the bankrupt as soon as reasonably practicable (rule 6.250). In addition the Secretary of State must notify the court immediately that the bankrupt has given such an undertaking in order that any hearing date can be vacated.

18. PERSONS AT RISK OF VIOLENCE

[19.18]

18.1 Where an application is made pursuant to rule 5.67, 5.68, 5A 18, or 6.235B or otherwise to limit disclosure of information as to a person's current address by reason of the possibility of violence, the relevant application should be accompanied by a witness statement which includes the following:

(1) The grounds upon which it is contended that disclosure of the current address as defined by the Insolvency Rules might reasonably be expected to lead to violence against the debtor or a person who normally resides with him or her as a member of his or her family or where appropriate any other person.

(2) Where the application is made in respect of the address of the debtor, the debtor's proposals with regard to information which may safely be given to potential creditors in order that they can recognise that the debtor is a person who may be indebted to them, in particular the address at which the debtor previously resided or carried on business and the nature of such business.

(3) The terms of the order sought by the applicant by reference to the court's particular powers as set out in the rule under which the application is made and, unless impracticable, a draft of the order sought.

(4) Where the application is made by the debtor in respect of whom a nominee or supervisor has been appointed or against whom a bankruptcy order has been made, evidence of the consent of the nominee/supervisor, or, in the case of bankruptcy, the trustee in bankruptcy, if one has been appointed, and the official receiver if a trustee in bankruptcy has not been appointed. Where such consent is not available the statement must indicate whether such consent has been refused. The application shall in any event make such person a respondent to the application.

18.2 The application shall be referred to the Registrar who will consider it without a hearing in the first instance but without prejudice to the right of the court to list it for hearing if:

(1) the court is minded to refuse the application;
(2) the consent of any respondent is not attached;
(3) the court is of the view that there is another reason why listing is appropriate.

PART FOUR: FINANCIAL MARKETS AND INSOLVENCY (SETTLEMENT FINALITY) REGULATIONS 1999 – REQUIRED INFORMATION

[19.19]

19.1 In any case in which the court is asked to make an order to which regulation 22(1) of the Financial Markets and Insolvency (Settlement Finality) Regulations 1999 (SI 1999/2979) applies, the party applying for the order must include in the petition or application a statement to that effect, identifying the system operator of the relevant designated system, the relevant designating authority, and the email or other addresses to which the court will be required to send notice pursuant to regulation 22(1) if an order is made.

19.2 At the date of this Practice Direction, the Regulations apply where, in respect of "a participant in a designated system" (as those terms are defined in the Regulations), an order is made for administration, winding-up, bankruptcy, sequestration, bank insolvency, bank administration, building society insolvency, building society special administration or investment bank special administration. Applicants must before making the application check for any amendments to the Regulations.

PART FIVE: APPEALS

20. APPEALS

[19.20]

20.1 An appeal from a decision of the County Court (whether made by a District Judge, a Recorder or a Circuit Judge) or of a Registrar in insolvency proceedings lies to a Judge of the High Court.

20.2 An appeal from a decision of a Judge of the High Court, whether at first instance or on appeal, lies to the Court of Appeal.

20.3 A first appeal, whether under 20.1 or 20.2 above, is subject to the permission requirements of CPR Part 52, rule 3.

20.4 An appeal from a decision of a Judge of the High Court which was made on a first appeal requires the permission of the Court of Appeal.

20.5 Filing Appeals

20.5.1 An appeal from a decision of a Registrar must be filed at the Royal Courts of Justice in London.

20.5.2 An appeal from a decision of a District Judge sitting in a district registry of the High Court may be filed:

(1) at the Royal Courts of Justice in London; or
(2) in that district registry.

20.6 The court centres at which appeals from decisions of the County Court at hearing centres on any particular Circuit must be filed, managed and heard (unless the appeal court otherwise orders) are as follows:

Midland Circuit: Birmingham

North Eastern Circuit: Leeds or Newcastle upon Tyne

Northern Circuit: Manchester or Liverpool

Wales Circuit: Cardiff, Caernarfon or Mold

Western Circuit: Bristol

South Eastern Circuit: Royal Courts of Justice.

20.7 Where the lower court is the County Court:

(1) an appeal or application for permission to appeal from a decision of a District Judge will be heard or considered by a High Court Judge or by any person authorised under section 9 of the Senior Courts Act 1981 to act as a judge of the High Court in the Chancery Division;

(2) an appeal or application for permission to appeal from a decision of a Recorder or a Circuit Judge will be heard or considered by a High Court Judge or by a person authorised under paragraphs (1), (2) or (4) of the table in section 9(1) of the Senior Courts Act 1981 to act as a judge of the High Court in the Chancery Division;

(3) other applications in any appeal or application for permission to appeal may be heard or considered and directions may be given by a High Court Judge or by any person authorised under section 9 of the Senior Courts Act 1981 to act as a judge of the High Court in the Chancery Division.

20.8 In the case of appeals from decisions of Registrars or District Judges in the High Court, appeals, applications for permission to appeal and other applications may be heard or considered and directions may be given by a High Court Judge or by any person authorised under section 9 of the Senior Courts Act 1981 to act as a judge of the High Court in the Chancery Division.

20.9.1 CPR Part 52 and Practice Directions 52A, 52B and 52C and its Forms shall, as appropriate, apply to appeals in insolvency proceedings, save as provided in paragraph 20.9.2 below.

20.9.2 Paragraphs 4.3 to 4.5 of Practice Direction 52A and Section 2 and Tables A and B of Practice Direction 52B shall not apply.

20.10 For the avoidance of any doubt, references in this Part to the County Court include, in respect of decisions made before 22 April 2014, a county court.

PART SIX: APPLICATIONS RELATING TO THE REMUNERATION OF APPOINTEES

21. REMUNERATION OF APPOINTEES

[19.21]

21.1. Introduction

21.1.1 This Part of the Practice Direction applies to any remuneration application made under the Act or the Insolvency Rules.

21.2 The objective and guiding principles

21.2.1 The objective of this Part of the Practice Direction is to ensure that the remuneration of an appointee which is fixed and approved by the court is fair, reasonable and commensurate with the nature and extent of the work properly undertaken by the appointee in any given case and is fixed and approved by a process which is consistent and predictable.

21.2.2 Set out below are the guiding principles by reference to which remuneration applications are to be considered both by applicants, in the preparation and presentation of their application, and by the court determining such applications.

21.2.3 The guiding principles are as follows:

(1) "Justification"

It is for the appointee who seeks to be remunerated at a particular level and / or in a particular manner to justify his claim and in order to do so the appointee should be prepared to provide full particulars of the basis for and the nature of his claim for remuneration.

(2) "The benefit of the doubt"

The corollary of guiding principle (1) is that on any remuneration application, if after considering the evidence before it and after having regard to the guiding principles (in particular guiding principle (3)), the matters contained in paragraph 21.4.2 (in particular paragraph 21.4.2 (10)) and the matters referred to in paragraph 21.4.3 (as appropriate) there remains any element of doubt as to the appropriateness, fairness or reasonableness of the remuneration sought or to be fixed (whether arising from a lack of particularity as to the basis for and the nature of the appointee's claim to remuneration or otherwise) such element of doubt should be resolved by the court against the appointee.

(3) "Professional integrity"

The court should (where this is the case) give weight to the fact that the appointee is a member of a regulated profession and as such is subject to rules and guidance as to professional conduct and the fact that (where this is the case) the appointee is an officer of the court.

(4) "The value of the service rendered"

The remuneration of an appointee should reflect the value of the service rendered by the appointee, not simply reimburse the appointee in respect of time expended and cost incurred.

(5) "Fair and reasonable"

The amount of the appointee's remuneration should represent fair and reasonable remuneration for the work properly undertaken or to be undertaken.

(6) "Proportionality"

(a) "Proportionality of information"

In considering the nature and extent of the information which should be provided by an appointee in respect of a remuneration application the court, the appointee and any other parties to the application shall have regard to what is proportionate by reference to the amount of remuneration to be fixed, the nature, complexity and extent of the work to be completed (where the application relates to future remuneration) or that has been completed by the appointee and the value and nature of the assets and liabilities with which the appointee will have to deal or has had to deal.

(b) "Proportionality of remuneration"
The amount of remuneration to be fixed by the court should be proportionate to the nature, complexity and extent of the work to be completed (where the application relates to future remuneration) or that has been completed by the appointee and the value and nature of the assets and/or potential assets and the liabilities and/or potential liabilities with which the appointee will have to deal or has had to deal, the nature and degree of the responsibility to which the appointee has been subject in any given case, the nature and extent of the risk (if any) assumed by the appointee and the efficiency (in respect of both time and cost) with which the appointee has completed the work undertaken.

(7) "Professional guidance"
In respect of an application for the fixing and approval of the remuneration of an appointee, the appointee may have regard to the relevant and current statements of practice promulgated by any relevant regulatory and professional bodies in relation to the fixing of the remuneration of an appointee. In considering a remuneration application, the court may also have regard to such statements of practice and the extent of compliance with such statements of practice by the appointee.

(8) "Timing of application"
The court will take into account whether any application should have been made earlier and if so the reasons for any delay in making it.

21.3 Hearing of remuneration applications

21.3.1 On the hearing of the application the court shall consider the evidence then available to it and may either summarily determine the application or adjourn it giving such directions as it thinks appropriate.

21.3.2 Whilst the application will normally be determined summarily by a Registrar sitting alone, where it is sufficiently complex, the court may direct that:

(1) an assessor or a Costs Judge prepare a report to the court in respect of the remuneration which is sought to be fixed and approved; and/or

(2) the application be heard by the Registrar sitting with or without an assessor or a Costs Judge or by a Judge sitting with or without an assessor or a Costs Judge.

21.4 Relevant criteria and procedure

21.4.1 When considering a remuneration application the court shall have regard to the objective, the guiding principles and all relevant circumstances including the matters referred to in paragraph 21.4.2 and where appropriate paragraph 21.4.3, each of which should be addressed in the evidence placed before the court.

21.4.2 On any remuneration application, the appointee should:

(1) Provide a narrative description and explanation of:

(a) the background to, the relevant circumstances of and the reasons for the appointment;

(b) the work undertaken or to be undertaken in respect of the appointment; the description should be divided, insofar as possible, into individual tasks or categories of task (general descriptions of work, tasks, or categories of task should (insofar as possible) be avoided);

(c) the reasons why it is or was considered reasonable and/or necessary and/or beneficial for such work to be done, giving details of why particular tasks or categories of task were undertaken and why such tasks or categories of task are to be undertaken or have been undertaken by particular individuals and in a particular manner;

(d) the amount of time to be spent or that has been spent in respect of work to be completed or that has been completed and why it is considered to be fair, reasonable and proportionate;

(e) what is likely to be and has been achieved, the benefits that are likely to and have accrued as a consequence of the work that is to be or has been completed, the manner in which the work required in respect of the appointment is progressing and what, in the opinion of the appointee, remains to be achieved.

(2) Provide details sufficient for the court to determine the application by reference to the criteria which are required to be taken into account by reference to the Insolvency Rules and any other applicable enactments or rules relevant to the fixing of the remuneration.

(3) Provide a statement of the total number of hours of work undertaken or to be undertaken in respect of which the remuneration is sought, together with a breakdown of such hours by individual member of staff and individual tasks or categories of tasks to be performed or that have been performed. Where appropriate, a proportionate level of detail should also be given of:

(a) the tasks or categories of tasks to be undertaken as a proportion of the total amount of work to be undertaken in respect of which the remuneration is sought and the tasks or categories of tasks that have been undertaken as a proportion of the total amount of work that has been undertaken in respect of which the remuneration is sought; and

(b) the tasks or categories of task to be completed by individual members of staff or grade of personnel including the appointee as a proportion of the total amount of work to be completed by all members of staff including the appointee in respect of which the remuneration is sought, or the tasks or categories of task that have been completed by individual members of staff or grade of personnel as a proportion of the total amount of work that has been completed by all members of staff including the appointee in respect of which the remuneration is sought.

(4) Provide a statement of the total amount to be charged for the work to be undertaken or that has been undertaken in respect of which the remuneration is sought which should include:

(a) a breakdown of such amounts by individual member of staff and individual task or categories of task performed or to be performed;

(b) details of the time expended or to be expended and the remuneration charged or to be charged in respect of each individual task or category of task as a proportion (respectively) of the total time expended or to be expended and the total remuneration charged or to be charged. In respect of an application pursuant to which some or all of the amount of the appointee's remuneration is to be fixed on a basis other than time properly spent, the appointee shall provide (for the purposes of comparison) the same details as are required by this paragraph (4), but on the basis of what would have been charged had he been seeking remuneration on the basis of the time properly spent by him and his staff.

(5) Provide details of each individual to be engaged or who has been engaged in work in respect of the appointment and in respect of which the remuneration is sought, including details of their relevant experience, training, qualifications and the level of their seniority.

(6) Provide an explanation of:

(a) the steps, if any, to be taken or that have been taken by the appointee to avoid duplication of effort and cost in respect of the work to be completed or that has been completed in respect of which the remuneration is sought;

(b) the steps to be taken or that have been taken to ensure that the work to be completed or that has been completed is to be or was undertaken by individuals of appropriate experience and seniority relative to the nature of the work to be or that has been undertaken.

(7) Provide details of the individual rates charged by the appointee and members of his staff in respect of the work to be completed or that has been completed and in respect of which the remuneration is sought. Such details should include:

(a) a general explanation of the policy adopted in relation to the fixing or calculation of such rates and the recording of time spent;

(b) where, exceptionally, the appointee seeks remuneration in respect of time spent by secretaries, cashiers or other administrative staff whose work would otherwise be regarded as an overhead cost forming a component part of the rates charged by the appointee and members of his staff, a detailed explanation as to why such costs should be allowed should be provided.

(8) Where the remuneration application is in respect of a period of time during which the charge-out rates of the appointee and/or members of his staff engaged in work in respect of the appointment have increased, provide an explanation of the nature, extent and reason for such increase and the date when such increase took effect. This paragraph (8) does not apply to applications to which paragraph 21.4.3 applies.

(9) Provide details of any remuneration previously fixed or approved in relation to the appointment (whether by the court or otherwise) including in particular the amounts that were previously sought to be fixed or approved and the amounts that were in fact fixed or approved and the basis upon which such amounts were fixed or approved.

(10) In order that the court may be able to consider the views of any persons who the appointee considers have an interest in the assets that are under his control, provide details of:

(a) what (if any) consultation has taken place between the appointee and those persons and if no such consultation has taken place an explanation as to the reason why;

(b) the number and value of the interests of the persons consulted including details of the proportion (by number and by value) of the interests of such persons by reference to the entirety of those persons having an interest in the assets under the control of the appointee.

(11) Provide such other relevant information as the appointee considers, in the circumstances, ought to be provided to the court.

21.4.3 This paragraph applies to applications where some or all of the remuneration of the appointee is to be fixed and approved on a basis other than time properly spent. On such applications in addition to the matters referred to in paragraph 21.4.2 (as applicable) the appointee shall:

(1) Provide a full description of the reasons for remuneration being sought by reference to the basis contended for.

(2) Where the remuneration is sought to be fixed by reference to a percentage of the value of the assets which are realised or distributed, provide a full explanation of the basis upon which any percentage rates to be applied to the values of the assets realised and/or distributed have been chosen.

(3) Provide a statement that to the best of the appointee's belief the percentage rates or other bases by reference to which some or all of the remuneration is to be fixed are similar to the percentage rates or other bases that are applied or have been applied in respect of other appointments of a similar nature.

(4) Provide a comparison of the amount to be charged by reference to the basis contended for and the amount that would otherwise have been charged by reference to the other available bases of remuneration, including the scale of fees in Schedule 6 to the Insolvency Rules.

21.4.4 If and insofar as any of the matters referred to in paragraph 21.4.2 or 21.4.3 (as appropriate) are not addressed in the evidence, an explanation for why this is the case should be included in such evidence.

21.4.5 For the avoidance of doubt and where appropriate and proportionate, paragraphs 21.4.2 to 21.4.4 (inclusive) are applicable to applications for the apportionment of remuneration as between a new appointee and a former appointee in circumstances where some or all of the former appointee's remuneration was based upon a set amount under the Insolvency Rules and the former appointee has ceased (for whatever reason) to hold office before the time has elapsed or the work has been completed in respect of which the set amount of remuneration was fixed.

21.4.6 The evidence placed before the court by the appointee in respect of any remuneration application should include the following documents:

(1) a copy of the most recent receipts and payments account;

(2) copies of any reports by the appointee to the persons having an interest in the assets under his control relevant to the period for which the remuneration sought to be fixed and approved relates;
(3) any schedules or such other documents providing the information referred to in paragraphs 21.4.2 and 21.4.3 where these are likely to be of assistance to the court in considering the application;
(4) evidence of any consultation with those persons having an interest in the assets under the control of appointee in relation to the remuneration of the appointee.

21.4.7 On any remuneration application the court may make an order allowing payments of remuneration to be made on account subject to final approval whether by the court or otherwise.

21.4.8 Unless otherwise ordered by the court (or as may otherwise be provided for in any enactment or rules of procedure) the costs of and occasioned by an application for the fixing and/or approval of the remuneration of an appointee, including those of any assessor, shall be paid out of the assets under the control of the appointee.

PRACTICE DIRECTION: DIRECTORS DISQUALIFICATION PROCEEDINGS

NOTES

This Practice Direction is up to date to 6 April 2018. The text and details of any further amendments can be found at www.justice.gov.uk.

PART ONE GENERAL

1 APPLICATION AND INTERPRETATION

[19.22]

1.1 In this practice direction—
(1) "the Act" means the Company Directors Disqualification Act 1986 (as amended);
(2) "the Disqualification Rules" means the rules for the time being in force made under section 411 of the Insolvency Act 1986 in relation to disqualification proceedings;[1]
(3) "the Insolvency Rules" means the rules for the time being in force made under sections 411 and 412 of the Insolvency Act 1986 in relation to insolvency proceedings;
(4) "CPR" means the Civil Procedure Rules 1998 and "CPR" followed by "Part" or "Rule" and a number means the part or Rule with that number in those Rules;
(5) "disqualification proceedings" has the meaning set out in paragraph 1.3 below;
(6) "a disqualification application" is an application under the Act for the making of a disqualification order;
(7) References to a 'Registrar' are to a Registrar in Bankruptcy of the High Court and (save in cases where it is clear from the context that a particular provision applies only to the High Court in London) include a District Judge in a District Registry of the High Court and in County Court having insolvency jurisdiction;
(8) except where the context otherwise requires references to—
   (a) "company" or "companies" shall include references to "partnership" or "partnerships" and to "limited liability partnership" and "limited liability partnerships"
   (b) "director" shall include references to an "officer" of a partnership and to a "member" of a limited liability partnership
   (c) "shadow director" shall include references to a "shadow member" of a limited liability partnership

   and, in appropriate cases, the forms annexed to this practice direction shall be varied accordingly.
(9) Where the Act applies to other entities as it applies to companies, references in this practice direction to director or officer of a company and to other terms in the Act as provided for by legislation shall also apply for the purposes of this practice direction.

1.2 This practice direction shall come into effect on 9 December 2014, and shall replace the practice direction which came into effect on 26 April 1999 (as subsequently amended). Steps taken prior to 9 December 2014, and steps taken on or after that date in accordance with an obligation which arose before that date or a court direction made before that date, shall not thereby be invalidated.

1.3 This practice direction applies to all proceedings brought under the Act and/or the Disqualification Rules ("disqualification proceedings").[2]

2 MULTI-TRACK

2.1 All disqualification proceedings are allocated to the multi-track. The CPR relating to allocation questionnaires and track allocation shall not apply.

3 RIGHTS OF AUDIENCE

3.1 Official receivers and deputy official receivers have right of audience in any proceedings to which this Practice Direction applies, including cases where a disqualification application is made by the Secretary of State or by the official receiver at his direction.[3]

[1] The current rules are the Insolvent Companies (Disqualification of Unfit Directors) Proceedings Rules 1987, as amended ("the 1987 Rules"). For convenience, relevant references to the 1987 Rules, which apply to disqualification applications

under sections 7, 8 and 9A of the Act (see rule 1(3)), are set out in footnotes to this Practice Direction. This Practice Direction applies certain provisions contained in the 1987 Rules to disqualification proceedings other than applications under sections 7, 8 and 9A of the Act.

[2] This includes any applications under the Act to the extent provided for by subordinate legislation.

[3] Rule 10 of the 1987 Rules.

PART TWO
DISQUALIFICATION APPLICATIONS

4 COMMENCEMENT

[19.23]

4.1 A disqualification application must be commenced by a claim form in the form annexed hereto.

4.2 The procedure set out in CPR Part 8,[4] as modified by this practice direction and (where the application is made under sections 7, 8 or 9A of the Act) the Disqualification Rules shall apply to all disqualification applications. CPR rule 8.2 (contents of the claim form) shall not apply. CPR rule 8.1(3) (power of the Court to order the application to continue as if the claimant had not used the Part 8 Procedure) shall not apply.

4.3 When the claim form is issued, the claimant will be given a date for the first hearing of the disqualification application. This date is to be not less than eight weeks from the date of issue of the claim form.[5] The first hearing will be before a registrar.

5 HEADINGS

5.1 Every court document in disqualification applications shall be headed:

IN THE HIGH COURT OF JUSTICE

CHANCERY DIVISION

[DISTRICT REGISTRY] or [COMPANIES COURT] if in the Royal Courts of Justice

or

IN THE COUNTY COURT SITTING AT [ ]

followed by

IN THE MATTER OF [name of company]

AND IN THE MATTER OF THE COMPANY DIRECTORS DISQUALIFICATION ACT 1986

6 SERVICE OF THE CLAIM FORM

6.1 Service of claim forms in disqualification proceedings will be the responsibility of the claimant and will not be undertaken by the court.

6.2 If serving by first class post on the defendant's last known address, the day of service shall, unless the contrary is shown, be deemed to be the 7th day next following that on which the claim form was posted.[6] Otherwise, Sections I and II of CPR Part 6 apply. Attention is drawn to CPR 16.17 regarding a certificate of service of the claim form.

6.3 The claim form served on the defendant shall be accompanied by an acknowledgment of service.

6.4 Section IV of CPR Part 6 shall not apply. In any disqualification proceedings where a claim form or order of the court or other document is required to be served on any person who is not in England and Wales, the court may order service on him to be effected within such time and in such manner as it thinks fit,[7] may require such proof of service as it thinks fit, and may give such directions as to acknowledgment of service as it thinks fit.

7 ACKNOWLEDGEMENT OF SERVICE

7.1 The form of acknowledgment of service annexed to this Practice Direction shall be used in disqualification proceedings. CPR rule 8.3(2) and 8.3(3)(a) shall not apply.

7.2 The defendant shall—

(1) (subject to any directions to the contrary given under paragraph 6.4 above) file an acknowledgment of service in the prescribed form not more than 14 days after service of the claim form; and

(2) serve a copy of the acknowledgment of service on the claimant and any other party.

7.3 Where the defendant has failed to file an acknowledgment of service and the time period for doing so has expired, the defendant may attend the hearing of the application but (unless the court orders otherwise) may not take part in the hearing unless the court gives permission and the defendant undertakes to file and serve an acknowledgment of service.

8 EVIDENCE

8.1 Evidence in disqualification applications shall be by affidavit, except where the official receiver is a party, in which case his evidence may be in the form of a written report (with or without affidavits by other persons) which shall be treated as if it had been verified by affidavit by him and shall be prima facie evidence of any matter contained in it.[8]

8.2 The affidavits or the official receiver's report in support of the application shall include a statement of the matters by reference to which it is alleged that a disqualification order should be made against the defendant.[9]

8.3 When the claim form is issued—

(1) the affidavit or report in support of the disqualification application must be filed in court; and

(2) except where the court requires otherwise, exhibits must be lodged with the court where they shall be retained until the conclusion of the proceedings; and

(3) copies of the affidavit/report and exhibits shall be served with the claim form on the defendant.[10]

(4) If, as a result of the court's requirement, exhibits are not lodged in accordance with 8.3(2), the exhibits should be available at the trial and any other hearing at which reference to them may be made.

8.4 The defendant shall, within 28 days from the date of service of the claim form—[11]

(1) file in court any affidavit evidence in opposition to the disqualification application that he or she wishes the court to take into consideration; and

(2) except where the court requires otherwise, lodge the exhibits with the court where they shall be retained until the conclusion of the proceedings; and

(3) at the same time, serve upon the claimant a copy of the affidavits and exhibits.

If, as a result of the court's requirement, exhibits are not lodged in accordance with 8.4(2), the exhibits should be available at the trial and any other hearing at which reference to them may be made.

8.5 In cases where there is more than one defendant, each defendant is required to serve his evidence on the other defendants at the same time as service on the claimant unless the court otherwise orders.

8.6 The claimant shall, within 14 days from receiving the copy of the defendant's evidence—[12]

(1) file in court any further affidavit or report in reply he wishes the court to take into consideration; and

(2) except where the court requires otherwise, lodge the exhibits with the court where they shall be retained until the conclusion of the proceedings; and

(3) at the same time serve a copy of the affidavits/reports and exhibits upon the defendant.

If, as a result of the court's requirement, exhibits are not lodged in accordance with 8.6(2), the exhibits should be available at the trial and any other hearing at which reference to them may be made.

8.7 Prior to the first hearing of the disqualification application, the time for serving evidence may be extended by written agreement between the parties. After the first hearing, any extension of time for serving evidence is governed by CPR rules 2.11 and 29.5.

8.8 So far as is possible all evidence should be filed before the first hearing of the disqualification application.

9 THE FIRST HEARING OF THE DISQUALIFICATION APPLICATION

9.1 The registrar shall either determine the case at the first hearing or give directions and adjourn it.[13]

9.2 All directions should insofar as possible be sought at the first hearing of the disqualification application so that the disqualification application can be determined at the earliest possible date. The parties should take all possible steps to avoid successive directions hearings.

10 THE TRIAL

10.1 Trial bundles containing copies of—

(1) the claim form;

(2) the acknowledgement of service;

(3) all evidence filed by or on behalf of each of the parties to the proceedings, together with the exhibits thereto;

(4) all relevant correspondence; and

(5) such other documents as the parties consider necessary;

shall be lodged with the court, in accordance with the time limits and guidelines specified in the Chancery Guide.

10.2 Skeleton arguments should be prepared by all parties, whether the case is to be heard by a registrar or a judge. They should comply with all relevant guidelines, in particular the Chancery Guide.

10.3 Where appropriate the advocate for the claimant should also provide: (a) a chronology; and (b) a list of persons involved in the facts of the case.

10.4 The documents mentioned in paragraph 10.1–10.3 above must be delivered to the appropriate court office.

10.5 Copies of documents delivered to the court must, so far as possible, be provided to each of the other parties to the disqualification application.

10.6 The provisions in paragraphs 10.1 to 10.5 above are subject to any order of the court making different provision.

11 UNCONTESTED DISPOSALS

11.1 If the defendant fails to file evidence within the time set out in paragraph 9.4 above and/or within any extension of time granted by the court, the court may make an order that unless the defendant files evidence by a specified date he shall be debarred from filing evidence without the permission of the court. If the defendant then fails to file evidence within the time specified by the debarring order and subject to any further court order, the disqualification application will be determined by way of an uncontested disposal hearing.

11.2 Not less than 3 days prior to an uncontested disposal hearing, bundles containing copies of—
(1) the claim form;
(2) the acknowledgment of service;
(3) all evidence filed by the claimant together with the exhibits thereto;
(4) any relevant correspondence;
shall be lodged with the court.

11.3 The claimant should in all cases prepare a skeleton argument, which shall be lodged no later than 2 days before the hearing.

11.4 The provisions in paragraphs 11.1 to 11.3 above are subject to any order of the court making different provision.

12 *CARECRAFT* PROCEDURE

12.1 The parties may invite the court to deal with the disqualification application under the procedure adopted in *Re Carecraft Construction Co Ltd* [1994] 1 WLR 172, as clarified by the decision of the Court of Appeal in Secretary of *State for Trade and Industry v Rogers* [1996] 4 All ER 854. The claimant must submit a written statement of agreed or undisputed facts, and an agreed period of disqualification or an agreed range of years (eg 2 to 5 years; 6 to 10 years; 11 to 15 years).

12.2 Unless the Court otherwise orders, a hearing under the *Carecraft* procedure will be held in private.

12.3 If the Court is minded to make a disqualification order having heard the parties' representations, it will usually give judgment and make the disqualification order in public. Unless the Court otherwise orders, the written statement referred to in paragraph 12.1 shall be annexed to the disqualification order.

13 MAKING AND SETTING ASIDE OF DISQUALIFICATION ORDER

13.1 The court may make a disqualification order against the defendant, whether or not the defendant appears, and whether or not he has completed and returned the acknowledgment of service of the claim form, or filed evidence.[14]

13.2 Any disqualification order made in the absence of the defendant may be set aside or varied by the court on such terms as it thinks just.[15]

14 SERVICE OF ORDERS

14.1 Service of orders (including any disqualification order) will be the responsibility of the claimant.

---

4 Rule 2(2) of the 1987 Rules.

5 Rule 7(1) of the 1987 Rules.

6 Rule 5(1) of the 1987 Rules.

7 Rule 5(2) of the 1987 Rules.

8 Rule 3(2) of the 1987 Rules. Section 441 of the Companies Act 1985 makes provision for the admissibility in legal proceedings of a certified copy of a report of inspectors appointed under Part XIV of the Companies Act 1985.

9 Rule 3(3) of the 1987 Rules.

10 Rule 3(1) of the 1987 Rules.

11 Rule 6(1) of the 1987 Rules.

12 Rule 6(2) of the 1987 Rules.

13 Rule 7(3) of the 1987 Rules.

14 Rule 8(1) of the 1987 Rules.

15 Rule 8(2) of the 1987 Rules.

PART THREE
APPLICATIONS UNDER SECTIONS 7(2) AND 7(4) OF THE ACT

15 PROVISIONS APPLICABLE TO APPLICATIONS UNDER SECTION 7(2) OF THE ACT TO MAKE A DISQUALIFICATION APPLICATION AFTER THE END OF THE 2 YEAR PERIOD SPECIFIED

[19.24]

15.1 Applications under section 7(2) of the Act shall be made by Practice Form N208 under CPR Part 8 save where it is sought to join a director or former director to existing proceedings, in which case such application shall be made by application notice under CPR Part 23, and Practice Direction 23A shall apply save as modified below.

15.2 Service of claim forms and application notices seeking orders under section 7(2) of the Act will be the responsibility of the applicant and will not be undertaken by the court.

15.3 Every claim form and application notice by which such an application is begun and all witness statements, affidavits, notices and other documents in relation thereto must be entitled in the matter of the company or companies in question and in the matter of the Act.

16 APPLICATIONS FOR EXTRA INFORMATION MADE UNDER SECTION 7(4) OF THE ACT

16.1 Such applications may be made—

(1) by Practice Form N.208 under CPR Part 8;

(2) by application notice in existing disqualification proceedings; or

(3) by application under the Insolvency Rules in the relevant insolvency, if the insolvency practitioner against whom the application is made remains the officeholder.

16.2 Service of claim forms and application notices seeking orders under section 7(4) of the Act will be the responsibility of the applicant and will not be undertaken by the court.

16.3 Every claim form and application notice by which such an application is begun and all witness statements, affidavits, notices and other documents in relation thereto must be entitled in the matter of the company or companies in question and in the matter of the Act.

PART FOUR
APPLICATIONS FOR PERMISSION TO ACT

17 COMMENCING AN APPLICATION FOR PERMISSION TO ACT

[19.25]

17.1 This Practice Direction governs applications for permission to act made under—

(1) section 17 of the Act for the purposes of any of sections 1(1)(a), 1A(1)(a) or 9B(4); and

(2) section 12(2) of the Act.

17.2 Sections 12 and 17 of the Act identify the courts which have jurisdiction to deal with applications for permission to act. Subject to these sections, such applications may be made—

(1) by Practice Form N.208 under CPR Part 8; or

(2) by application notice in an existing disqualification application.

17.3 In the case of a person subject to disqualification under section 12A or 12B of the Act (by reason of being disqualified in Northern Ireland), permission to act notwithstanding disqualification can only be granted by the High Court of Northern Ireland.

18 HEADINGS

18.1 Every claim form by which an application for permission to act is begun, and all affidavits, notices and other documents in the application must be entitled in the matter of the company or companies in question and in the matter of the Act.

18.2 Every application notice by which an application for permission to act is made and all affidavits, notices and other documents in the application shall be entitled in the same manner as the heading of the claim form in the existing disqualification application.

19 EVIDENCE

19.1 Evidence in support of an application for permission to act shall be by affidavit.

20 SERVICE

20.1 Where a disqualification application has been made under section 9A of the Act or a disqualification undertaking has been accepted under section 9B of the Act, the claim form or application notice for permission to act (as appropriate), together with the evidence in support thereof, must be served on the Office of Fair Trading or specified regulator which made the relevant disqualification application or accepted the disqualification undertaking (as the case may be).

20.2 In all other cases, the claim form or application notice (as appropriate), together with the evidence in support thereof, must be served on the Secretary of State.

20.3 Addresses for service on government departments are set out in the List of Authorised Government Departments issued by the Cabinet Office under section 17 of the Crown Proceedings Act 1947, which is annexed to the Practice Direction supplementing Part 66.

PART FIVE
APPLICATIONS IN THE COURSE OF PROCEEDINGS

21 FORM OF APPLICATION

[19.26]

21.1 CPR Part 23 and Practice Direction 23A shall apply in relation to applications governed by this Practice Direction save as modified below.

22 HEADINGS

22.1 Every notice and all witness statements and affidavits in relation thereto must be entitled in the same manner as the Claim Form in the proceedings in which the application is made.

23 SERVICE

23.1 Service of an application notice in disqualification proceedings will be the responsibility of the party making such application and will not be undertaken by the court.

23.2 Where any application notice or order of the court or other document is required in any application to be served on any person who is not in England and Wales, the court may order service on him to be effected within such time and in such manner as it thinks fit, and may also require such proof of service as it thinks fit. Section IV of CPR Part 6 does not apply.

PART SIX
DISQUALIFICATION PROCEEDINGS OTHER THAN IN THE ROYAL COURTS OF JUSTICE

24 MODIFICATIONS

[19.27]
24.1 Where a disqualification application or a section 8A application is made by a claim form issued other than in the Royal Courts of Justice this Practice Direction shall apply with the following modifications.

(1) Upon the issue of the claim form the court shall endorse it with the date and time for the first hearing before a district judge. The powers exercisable by a registrar under this Practice Direction shall be exercised by a district judge.

(2) If the district judge (either at the first hearing or at any adjourned hearing before him) directs that the disqualification claim or section 8A application is to be heard by a High Court judge or by an authorised circuit judge he will direct that the case be entered forthwith in the list for hearing by that judge and the court will allocate (i) a date for the hearing of the trial by that judge and (ii) unless the district judge directs otherwise a date for the hearing of a Pre Trial Review by the trial judge.

PART SEVEN
DISQUALIFICATION UNDERTAKINGS

25 COSTS

[19.28]
25.1 The general rule is that where an undertaking is given after a disqualification application has been commenced the court will order the defendant to pay the costs where the claimant has accepted a disqualification undertaking.

25.2 The general rule will not apply where the court considers that the circumstances are such that it should make another order.

PART EIGHT
APPLICATIONS UNDER SECTION 8A OF THE ACT TO REDUCE THE PERIOD FOR WHICH A DISQUALIFICATION UNDERTAKING IS IN FORCE OR TO PROVIDE FOR IT TO CEASE TO BE IN FORCE

26 HEADINGS

[19.29]
26.1 Every claim form by which a section 8A application is begun and all affidavits, notices and other documents in the proceedings must be entitled in the matter of a disqualification undertaking and its date and in the matter of the Act.

27 COMMENCEMENT: THE CLAIM FORM

27.1 Section 8A(3) of the Act identifies the courts which have jurisdiction to deal with section 8A applications.

27.2 A section 8A application shall be commenced by a claim form in the form annexed hereto issued—

(1) in the case of a disqualification undertaking given under section 9B of the Act, in the High Court out of the office of the companies court at the Royal Courts of Justice;

(2) in any other case,

  (a) in the High Court out of the office of the companies court or a chancery district registry which has jurisdiction under the Act; and

  (b) in the County Court which has jurisdiction under the Act, out of the appropriate county court office.

27.3 In section 8A applications the procedure set out in CPR Part 8, as modified by the Disqualification Rules and this Practice Direction shall apply. CPR rule 8.2 (contents of the claim form) shall not apply. CPR rule 8.1 (3) (power of the Court to order the application to continue as if the claimant had not used the Part 8 procedure) shall not apply.

27.4 In the case of a disqualification undertaking given under section 9B of the Act, the defendant to the section 8A application shall be the Office of Fair Trading or specified regulator which accepted the undertaking. In all other cases, the Secretary of State shall be made the defendant to the section 8A application.

27.5 Service of claim forms in section 8A applications will be the responsibility of the claimant and will not be undertaken by the court. If serving by first class post on the defendant's last known address the day of service shall, unless the contrary is shown, be deemed to be the 7th day next following that on which the claim form was posted. Otherwise, Sections I and II of CPR Part 6 apply. Attention is drawn to CPR r 6.14(2) regarding a certificate of service of the claim form.

27.6 Section IV of CPR Part 6 shall not apply. In any disqualification proceedings where a claim form or other document is required to be served on any person who is not in England and Wales, the court may order service on him to be effected within such time and in such manner as it thinks fit, may require such proof of service as it thinks fit, and may give such directions as to acknowledgment of service as it thinks fit.

27.7 The claim form served on the defendant shall be accompanied by an acknowledgment of service in the form annexed hereto.

28 ACKNOWLEDGEMENT OF SERVICE

28.1 The defendant shall—

(1) file an acknowledgement of service in the relevant practice form not more than 14 days after service of the claim form; and

(2) serve a copy of the acknowledgement of service on the claimant and any other party.

28.2 Where the defendant has failed to file an acknowledgment of service and the time period for doing so has expired, the defendant may nevertheless attend the hearing of the application and take part in the hearing as provided for by section 8A(2) or (2A) of the Act. However, this is without prejudice to the Court's case management powers and its powers to make costs orders.

29 EVIDENCE

29.1 Evidence in section 8A applications shall be by affidavit. The undertaking (or a copy) shall be exhibited to the affidavit.

29.2 When the claim form is issued—

(1) the affidavit in support of the section 8A application must be filed in court;

(2) except where the court requires otherwise, exhibits must be lodged with the court where they shall be retained until the conclusion of the proceedings; and

(3) copies of the affidavit and exhibits shall be served with the claim form on the defendant.

(4) If, as a result of the court's requirement, exhibits are not lodged in accordance with 28.2(2), the exhibits should be available at the trial and any other hearing at which reference to them may be made.

29.3 The defendant shall, within 28 days from the date of service of the claim form—

(1) file in court any affidavit evidence that he wishes the court to take into consideration on the application; and

(2) except where the court requires otherwise, lodge the exhibits with the court where they shall be retained until the conclusion of the proceedings; and

(3) at the same time, serve upon the claimant a copy of the affidavits and exhibits.

If, as a result of the court's requirement, exhibits are not lodged in accordance with 28.3(2), the exhibits should be available at the trial and any other hearing at which reference to them may be made.

29.4 The claimant shall, within 14 days from receiving the copy of the defendant's evidence—

(1) file in court any further affidavit evidence in reply he wishes the court to take into consideration; and

(2) except where the court requires otherwise, lodge the exhibits with the court where they shall be retained until the conclusion of the proceedings; and

(3) at the same time serve a copy of the affidavits and exhibits upon the defendant.

If, as a result of the court's requirement, exhibits are not lodged in accordance with 28.4(2), the exhibits should be available at the trial and any other hearing at which reference to them may be made.

29.5 Prior to the first hearing of the section 8A application, the time for serving evidence may be extended by written agreement between the parties. After the first hearing, the extension of time for serving evidence is governed by CPR rules 2.11 and 29.5.

29.6 So far as is possible all evidence should be filed before the first hearing of the section 8A application.

30 HEARINGS

30.1 Insofar as is relevant the provisions of paragraph 9 in Part Two above concerning hearings shall apply in respect of section 8A applications as they do in respect of disqualification applications.

31 THE TRIAL

31.1 Insofar as is relevant the provisions of paragraph 10 in Part Two above concerning trials shall apply in respect of section 8A applications as they do in respect of disqualification applications.

PART NINE
APPEALS

32 APPEALS

[19.30]

32.1 Rules 7.47 and 7.49A of the Insolvency Rules, as supplemented by Part Four of the Insolvency Proceedings Practice Direction, apply to an appeal from, or review of, a decision made by the court in the course of—

(1) disqualification proceedings under any of sections 6 to 8A or 9A of the Act;

(2) an application made under section 17 of the Act for the purposes of any of sections 1(1)(a), 1A(1)(a) or 9B(4), for permission to act notwithstanding a disqualification order made, or a disqualification undertaking accepted, under any of sections 6 to 10.

Any such decision, and any appeal from it, constitutes 'insolvency proceedings' for the purposes of the Insolvency Proceedings Practice Direction.

32.2 An appeal from a decision made by the court in the course of disqualification proceedings under any of sections 2(2)(a), 3 or 4 of the Act or on an application for permission to act notwithstanding a disqualification order made under any of those sections is governed by CPR Part 52 and Practice Direction 52.

NOTE ON LISTING AND CRITERIA FOR THE TRANSFER OF WORK FROM THE REGISTRARS TO THE COUNTY COURT SITTING IN CENTRAL LONDON

NOTES

The Chancellor of the High Court issued the following note in March 2015.

[19.31]

1. All winding up petitions must be issued and listed for initial hearing in the Royal Courts of Justice sitting in the Rolls Building.

2. All bankruptcy petitions must be listed and allocated in accordance with rule 6.9A Insolvency Rules 1986.

3. Save as provided above, all High Court proceedings which are to be listed before a registrar in accordance with the Practice Direction – Insolvency Proceedings will continue to be issued and listed in the Royal Courts of Justice sitting in the Rolls Building. In each case consideration will be given by a registrar at an appropriate stage to whether the proceedings should remain in the High Court or be transferred to the County Court sitting in Central London.

4. When deciding whether proceedings which have been issued in the High Court should be transferred to the County Court sitting in Central London, the registrar should have regard to the following factors:

(a) the complexity of the proceedings;

(b) whether the proceedings raise new or controversial points of law;

(c) the likely date and length of the hearing;

(d) public interest in the proceedings;

(e) (where it is ascertainable) the amount in issue in the proceedings.

5. As a general rule, and subject to 4 (a)–(d) above, where the amount in issue in the proceedings is £100,000 or less, the proceedings should be transferred to the County Court sitting in Central London.

6. Subject to paragraph 4 (a)–(e), the following will be transferred to be heard in the County Court sitting in Central London:

(a) private examinations ordered to take place under ss 236 or 366 Insolvency Act 1986 (but not necessarily the application for the private examination);

(b) applications to extend the term of office of an administrator (para 76 Sch B1 Insolvency Act 1986);

(c) applications for permission to distribute the prescribed part (para 65(3) Sch B1 Insolvency Act 1986);

(d) applications to disqualify a director and applications for a bankruptcy restrictions order where it appears likely that an order will be made for a period not exceeding five years.

7. With effect from 6 April 2015 the following proceedings will be issued and heard in the County Court sitting in Central London:

(a) applications for the restoration of a company to the register (s 1029 ff. Companies Act 2006);

(b) applications to extend the period allowed for the delivery of particulars relating to a charge (s 859F Companies Act 2006);

(c) applications to rectify the register by reason of omission or mis-statement in any statement or notice delivered to the registrar of companies (s 859M Companies Act 2006) or to replace an instrument or debenture delivered to the registrar of companies (s 859N Companies Act 2006).

PRACTICE DIRECTION 51P: PILOT FOR INSOLVENCY EXPRESS TRIALS

NOTES

This Practice Direction is up to date to 6 April 2018. The text and details of any further amendments can be found at www.justice.gov.uk.

GENERAL

[19.32]

1.1

(1) This Practice Direction is made under rule 51.2. It provides for a pilot scheme ("IET") to operate—
- (a) from 1 April 2016 for two years;
- (b) in the Bankruptcy and Companies Courts of the Chancery Division of the High Court;
- (c) in relation to proceedings before the Bankruptcy Registrars.

(2) IET is designed to deal with simple applications made to a Bankruptcy Registrar:
- (a) which can be disposed of in no more than two days;
- (b) which require limited directions (as opposed to case management) and disclosure of documents; and
- (c) where the costs of each party will not exceed £75,000 (excluding VAT and court fees but including any conditional fee agreement uplift).

1.2

(1) IET works within and is subject to the—
- (a) Insolvency Act 1986;
- (b) Insolvency Rules 1986;
- (c) Practice Direction – Insolvency Proceedings (Chancery Division, 29 July 2014, [2014] B.C.C. 502; [2014] B.P.I.R. 1286);
- (d) Cross-Border Insolvency Regulations 2006 (SI 2006/1030);
- (e) Administration of Insolvent Estates of Deceased Persons Order 1986 (SI 1986/1999);
- (f) Limited Liability Partnerships Regulations 2001, EC Regulation on Insolvency Proceedings no 1346/2000 of 29 May 2000.

(2) Parties will also need to give careful consideration to the Chancery Guide.

COMMENCEMENT OF IET PROCEEDINGS

[19.33]

2.1 IET proceedings must be commenced by application (Form 7.1A in schedule 4 Insolvency Rules 1986). The application must—
- (a) be marked "IET" clearly in bold on the first page of the application;
- (b) include a statement at the end of the application that the case is suitable for the IET list; and
- (c) include a statement at the end of the application that the respondent is entitled to object to the use of the IET procedure (see paragraph 2.6 for the procedure if the respondent objects).

2.2 The application should include the following—
- (a) a statement of the relief sought;
- (b) a description of the nature of the dispute;
- (c) a summary of the issues likely to arise in the application;
- (d) the applicant's contentions, including material facts upon which the applicant intends to rely (which must be stated with adequate particularity); and
- (e) the legal grounds for the relief sought.

2.3 The applicant must file evidence in support of the application at the time the application is issued. The evidence in support and any subsequent evidence filed should exhibit all the documents relied on (so that any further disclosure can be limited as far as possible) but should not exhibit correspondence between the parties or the parties' solicitors save where it is relevant to the issues in the application.

2.4 The application should be no longer than 15 pages of A4 with a 12-point font and 1.5-minimum spacing between lines.

2.5 On issue, the court will endorse the application with a date for the directions hearing which will be no more than 45 days from the date of issue with a time estimate of 30 minutes.

2.6

(1) In the event that the respondent objects, the respondent must file and serve brief reasons for such objection no later than 14 working days before the directions hearing.

(2) The applicant may file and serve a reply to the respondent's objection no later than 7 working days before the directions hearing.

(3) The objection and any reply should be no longer than two sides of A4 paper with a 12-point font and 1.5-minimum spacing between lines (including the heading of the action as it appears on the application).

DIRECTIONS HEARING

[19.34]

3.1

(1) At the directions hearing (which should, where possible, be attended by the advocates who will conduct the final hearing), the Bankruptcy Registrar will give binding directions and fix the final hearing, which will be between 3 and 6 months from the date of the directions hearing with an agreed time estimate.

(2) When fixing the date of the final hearing, the Bankruptcy Registrar will generally take into account dates the parties have specified are to be avoided, but may refuse to consider the availability of counsel as a factor in determining the date.

3.2

(1) The court will deal with any objection to the use of the IET procedure at the directions hearing, and decide whether or not the application should continue under the IET procedure.

(2) The court may of its own initiative disapply the IET procedure if it sees fit.

3.3 Directions will normally be given for—

(a) the service of evidence in answer and reply;

(b) disclosure by lists of documents or by other means (e.g. informal disclosure by inspection of documents held by an insolvency office-holder or reliance on documents exhibited to the evidence);

(c) witnesses to attend for cross-examination, where appropriate;

(d) a date to be fixed for trial/hearing of the substantive application, subject to the provisions of paragraphs 3.1(1) and (2);

(e) the applicant to file and serve a bundle in accordance with the Chancery Guide;

(f) the parties to file and exchange skeleton arguments in accordance with the Chancery Guide.

3.4 A costs cap of £75,000 (excluding VAT and court fees but including conditional fee agreement uplift) will be imposed. The costs cap is not intended to act as a costs target. The provisions for costs management contained in the Civil Procedure Rules 1998 will not apply.

TRIAL

[19.35]

4.1 The trial date may not be vacated by consent, and an adjournment will only be granted in exceptional circumstances.

4.2 At the end of trial or when judgment is handed down, the court may assess costs summarily or order detailed assessment.

JUDGMENT

[19.36]

5 The court will generally give judgment at trial, provided that sufficient time has been allowed in the time estimate to enable it to do so, or, if judgment has to be reserved, within 4 weeks of the end of the trial.

NOTE ON BANKRUPTCY PETITIONS – HEARINGS IN MULTIPLE LISTS IN THE ROLLS BUILDING

NOTES

The Chief Bankruptcy Registrar issued the following note in October 2016.

[19.37]

On 17 September 2015 I sent out a note entitled Electronic Filing in the Bankruptcy & Companies Court (Rolls Building) to provide some guidance to practitioners pending the coming into force of a Practice Direction. It has now been superseded by the Practice Direction 51O – The Electronic Working Pilot Scheme.

As frequent users will have experienced, the use of C-File in court for multiple bankruptcy petition lists is not satisfactory. Accordingly the registrars have decided that bankruptcy hearings in the multiple lists should be dealt with in line with Practice Direction 51O – The Electronic Working Pilot Scheme.

First hearings

Three working days before the first hearing of any bankruptcy petition the petitioning creditor should lodge a bundle containing:

(a) the statutory demand and evidence of service;

(b) the petition and evidence of service (including any order for substituted service and any extension order served).

An attendance sheet (incorporating the certificate of continuing debt) and list of supporting/opposing creditors should be handed to the registrar at the hearing along with any relevant documents received late.

The court will retain the bundle for any adjourned hearing until the petition is either dismissed or a bankruptcy order is made.

Subsequent hearings

If the papers were in order at the first hearing it will be unnecessary to file a further bundle. Any papers not filed for the first hearing should, however, be filed to complete the bundle. Otherwise, completion of the attendance sheet (including the certificate of continuing debt and of service of the adjournment notice) will generally suffice.

All hearings

Whilst the foregoing will suffice for the majority of hearings, practitioners should also file any other documents which the court needs to consider (eg any notice of or evidence in opposition from the debtor).

The procedure outlined above will take effect on 1 November 2016.

PRACTICE DIRECTION – INSOLVENCY PROCEEDINGS (APRIL 2018)

[19.38]

NOTES

Practice Direction made by order of the Chancellor of the High Court, Sir Geoffrey Vos, with the approval of the Lord Chancellor, the Right Honourable David Gauke MP, Secretary of State for Justice, on 25 April 2018

PART ONE: GENERAL PROVISIONS

1. Definitions

1.1 In this Practice Direction, which shall be referred to as the "IPD", the following definitions will apply:

(1) The "Act" means the Insolvency Act 1986 and includes the Act as applied to limited liability partnerships by the Limited Liability Partnerships Regulations 2001 or as applied to any other person or body by virtue of the Act or any other legislation;

(2) The "Insolvency Rules" means the rules for the time being in force and made under s.411 and s.412 of the Act in relation to Insolvency Proceedings (currently The Insolvency (England and Wales) Rules 2016, as amended), and, save where otherwise provided, any reference to a 'rule' is to a rule in the Insolvency Rules;

(3) "CPR" means the Civil Procedure Rules and "CPRPD" means a Civil Procedure Rules Practice Direction;

(4) "EU Regulation on Insolvency Proceedings" means either the Council Regulation (EC) No 1346/2000 of 29 May 2000 on Insolvency Proceedings or the Regulation (EU) 2015/848 of the European Parliament and of the Council of 20 May 2015 on Insolvency Proceedings (known as the "Recast" EU Insolvency Regulation), as applicable

(5) "Service Regulation" means Council Regulation (EC) No. 1393/2007 or such successor regulation as may come into force replacing Council Regulation (EC) No. 1393/2007 concerning the service in the Member States of judicial and extrajudicial documents in civil and commercial matters;

(6) "Insolvency proceedings" means:

(a) any proceedings under Parts 1 to 11 of the Act, the Insolvency Rules, the Administration of Insolvent Estates of Deceased Persons Order 1986 (S.I. 1986 No.1999), the Insolvent Partnerships Order 1994 (S.I. 1994 No. 2421) or the Limited Liability Partnerships Regulations 2001;

(b) any proceedings under the EU Regulation on Insolvency Proceedings or the Cross-Border Insolvency Regulations 2006 (SI 2006/1030); and

(c) in an insolvency context an application made pursuant to s.423 of the Act.

(7) References to a 'company' include a limited liability partnership and references to a 'contributory' include a member of a limited liability partnership;

(8) The following judicial definitions apply:

(a) "District Judge" means a person appointed a District Judge under s.6(1) of the County Courts Act 1984;

(b) "District Judge Sitting in a District Registry" means a District Judge sitting in an assigned District Registry having insolvency jurisdiction as a District Judge of the High Court under s.100 of the Senior Courts Act 1981;

(c) "Circuit Judge" means a judge sitting pursuant to s.5(1)(a) of the County Courts Act 1984;

Part 19 Practice Directions

(d) "ICC Judge" means a person appointed to the office of Insolvency and Companies Court Judge (previously, Registrar in Bankruptcy) under s.89(1) of the Senior Courts Act 1981;

(e) "High Court Judge" means a High Court Judge listed in s.4(1) of the Senior Courts Act 1981.

(9) The definitions in paragraph 1.1(8) include Deputies unless otherwise specified and Deputies are defined as meaning, for each definition above respectively, a deputy District judge appointed under s.8 of the County Courts Act 1984, a deputy District Judge of the High Court appointed under s.102 of the Senior Courts Act 1981, a deputy Circuit Judge appointed under s.24 of the Courts Act 1971, a deputy ICC Judge appointed under s.91 of the Senior Courts Act 1981, and a judicial office holder acting as a judge of the High Court under s.9(1) of the Senior Courts Act 1981 or a deputy judge of the High Court appointed under s.9(4) of the Senior Courts Act 1981;

(10) "Court" means the High Court or any County Court hearing centre having insolvency jurisdiction;

(11) "Royal Courts of Justice" means the Business and Property Courts of England and Wales at the Rolls Building, 7 Rolls Buildings, Fetter Lane, London EC4A 1NL.

(12) In part six of this IPD "assessor" means a person appointed [see CPR 35.15/s.70 of the Senior Courts Act 1981 or s.63 of the County Courts Act 1984] as an assessor.

2. Coming into force

2.1 This IPD shall come into force on 25 April 2018 and shall replace all previous Practice Directions, Practice Statements and Practice Notes relating to insolvency proceedings. This IPD does not affect the CPRPD or Pilot concerning Insolvency Express Trials, and for the avoidance of doubt, does not affect the PD for Directors Disqualification Proceedings.

3. Distribution of business

3.1 In the High Court, all petitions and applications, save where paragraph 3.3 below provides otherwise, should be listed for an initial hearing before an ICC Judge in the Royal Courts of Justice, or a District Judge Sitting in a District Registry.

3.2 In the County Court, petitions and applications that may be heard by a District Judge are set out in the Business and Property Courts Practice Direction at paragraph 4.2(d).

3.3 The following applications relating to insolvent companies or insolvent individuals must be listed before a High Court Judge:

(1) applications for committal for contempt; and

(2) applications for a search order (CPR 25.1(1)(h)), a freezing order (CPR 25.1(1)(f)) and an ancillary order under CPR 25.1(1)(g).

3.4 The following applications relating to insolvent companies or insolvent individuals may be listed only before a High Court Judge or ICC Judge but, subject to paragraph 3.5 below, not before a District Judge Sitting in a District Registry or a District Judge:

(1) applications for an administration order;

(2) applications for an injunction pursuant to the Court's inherent jurisdiction (e.g. to restrain the presentation or advertisement of a winding up petition);

(3) interim applications and applications for directions or case management after any proceedings have been referred or adjourned to the Judge;

(4) applications for the appointment of a provisional liquidator; and

(5) applications for an injunction (other than those referred to in paragraph 3.3(2) above) pursuant to s.37 of the Senior Courts Act 1981 or s.38 of the County Courts Act 1984.

3.5 The following applications relating to insolvent companies or insolvent individuals may be listed before a District Judge Sitting in a District Registry only with the consent of the Supervising Judge for the circuit in which the District Judge is sitting, or with the consent of the Supervising Judge's nominee:

(1) applications pursuant to the Court's inherent jurisdiction (e.g. to restrain the presentation or advertisement of a winding up petition);

(2) interim applications and applications for directions or case management after any proceedings have been referred or adjourned to a High Court Judge.

3.6 When deciding whether to hear and determine proceedings or to refer or adjourn them to a different level of judge, regard must be had to the following factors:

(1) whether the proceedings raise new or controversial points of law or have wide public interest implications;

(2) which venue can provide the earliest date for the hearing;

(3) the likely length of the hearing; and/or

(4) whether the petition or application includes or is likely to include matters that must be heard by a High Court Judge under paragraph 3.3 above.

3.7 Where insolvency proceedings are commenced or an insolvency application is made in a County Court hearing centre having insolvency jurisdiction, such proceedings or application shall be transferred to a County Court hearing centre located at a District Registry having insolvency jurisdiction in the same circuit, or to the Royal Courts of Justice if the proceedings were commenced in a County Court hearing centre located in the South-East circuit, unless it is Local Business.

3.8 For the purpose of paragraph 3.7, Local Business means (i) applications to set aside statutory demands; (ii) unopposed creditors' winding up petitions and (iii) unopposed bankruptcy petitions.

4. Court documents

4.1 All insolvency proceedings should be commenced and applications in insolvency proceedings should be made using the information prescribed by the Act, Insolvency Rules, the Business and Property Courts Practice Direction and/or other legislation under which the same is or are brought or made. Some forms relating to insolvency proceedings may be found at http://hmctsformfinder.justice.gov.uk/HMCTS/GetForms.do?court_forms_category=Bankruptcy%20and%20Insolvency.

5. Service of Court documents in insolvency proceedings

5.1 Schedule 4 to the Insolvency Rules prescribes the requirements for service where a Court document is required to be served pursuant to the Act or the Insolvency Rules. Pursuant to Schedule 4, CPR Part 6 applies except where Schedule 4 provides otherwise, or the court otherwise approves or directs.

5.2 Subject to the Court approving or directing otherwise, CPR Part 6 applies to the service of Court documents both within and out of the jurisdiction.

5.3 Attention is drawn to paragraph 6 of Schedule 4 to the Insolvency Rules which provides that where the Court has directed that service be effected in a particular manner, the certificate of service must be accompanied by a sealed copy of the order directing such manner of service.

5.4 The provisions of CPR Part 6 are modified by Schedule 4 to the Insolvency Rules in respect of certain documents. Reference should be made to the "Table of requirements for service" in Schedule 4. Notable modifications relate to the service of: (a) a winding up petition; and (b) an application for an administration order.

5.5 A statutory demand is not a Court document.

6. Drawing up of orders

6.1 The parties are responsible for drawing up all orders, unless the Court directs otherwise. Attention is drawn to CPRPD 40B 1.2 and the Chancery Guide. All applications should be accompanied by draft orders.

7. Urgent applications

7.1 In the Royal Courts of Justice the ICC Judges and the High Court Judges (and in other Courts exercising insolvency jurisdiction the High Court Judges, District Judges Sitting in a District Registry and District Judges) will hear urgent applications and time-critical applications as soon as reasonably practicable. This may involve delaying the hearing of another matter. Accordingly, parties asking for an application to be dealt with urgently must be able to justify the urgency with reasons.

PART TWO: COMPANY INSOLVENCY

8. Administrations

8.1 Attention is drawn to paragraph 2.1 of the Electronic Practice Direction 51O -The Electronic Working Pilot Scheme, or to any subsequent Electronic Practice Direction made after the date of this IPD, where an application is made, or intention to appoint an administrator is made using the electronic filing system. For the avoidance of doubt, and notwithstanding the restriction in sub-paragraph (c) to notices of appointment made by qualifying floating charge holders, paragraph 2.1 of the Electronic Practice Direction 51O shall not apply to any filing of a notice of appointment of an administrator outside Court opening hours, and the provisions of Insolvency Rules 3.20 to 3.22 shall in those circumstances continue to apply.

8.2 Paragraph 5.4 of the Electronic Practice Direction 510 provides that 'the date and time of payment' will be the filing date and time and 'it will also be the date and time of issue for all claim forms and other originating processes submitted using Electronic Working'.

8.3 In the absence of special circumstances, an application for the extension of an administration should be made not less than one month before the end of the administration. The evidence in support of any later application must explain why the application is being made late. The Court will consider whether any part of the costs should be disallowed where an application is made less than one month before the end of the administration.

9. Winding up petitions

9.1. Where a winding up petition is presented following service of a statutory demand, the statutory demand must contain the information set out in rule 7.3 of the Insolvency Rules and should, as far as possible, follow the form which appears at https://www.gov.uk/government/publications/demand-immediate-payment-of-adebt-from-a-limited-company-form-sd1.

9.2 Before presenting a winding up petition, the creditor must conduct a search to ensure that no petition is pending. Save in exceptional circumstances a second winding up petition should not be presented whilst a prior petition is pending. A petitioner who presents a petition while another petition is pending does so at risk as to costs.

9.3 Payment of the fee and deposit

9.3.1 Unless the petition is one in respect of which rule 7.7(2)(b) of the Insolvency Rules applies, a winding up petition will not be treated as having been presented until the Court fee and official receiver's deposit have been paid.

9.3.2 A petition filed electronically without payment of the deposit will be marked "private" and will not be available for inspection until the deposit has been paid. The date of presentation of the petition will accord with the date on which the deposit has been paid. If the official receiver's deposit is not paid within 7 calendar days after filing the petition, the petition will not be accepted, in accordance with paragraph 5.3 of the Electronic Practice Direction 510 - The Electronic Working Pilot Scheme. If a petition is not accepted, a new petition will have to be filed if the petitioner wishes to wind up a company.

9.3.3 The deposit will be taken by the Court and forwarded to the official receiver. In the Royal Courts of Justice the petition fee and deposit should be paid by cheque, or by debit or credit card over the phone. The Court will record the receipt and will impress two entries on the original petition, one in respect of the Court fee and the other in respect of the deposit. In a District Registry or a County Court hearing centre, the petition fee and deposit should be paid to the staff of the duly authorised officer of the Court, who will record its receipt.

9.3.4 If payment is made by cheque, it should be made payable to 'HM Courts and Tribunals Service' or 'HMCTS'. For the purposes of paragraph 9.3 of this IPD, the deposit will be treated as paid when the cheque is received by the Court.

9.4 Save where by reason of the nature of the company or its place of incorporation the information cannot be stated (in which case as much similar information as is available should be given), every creditor's winding up petition must (in the case of a company) contain the information set out in rule 7.5. Similar information (so far as is appropriate) should be given where the petition is presented against a partnership.

9.5 Where the petitioning creditor relies on failure to pay a debt, details of the debt relied on should be given in the petition (whether or not they have been given in any statutory demand served in respect of the debt), including the amount of the debt, its nature and the date or dates on or between which it was incurred.

9.6 The statement of truth verifying the petition in accordance with rule 7.6 should be made no more than ten business days before the date of issue of the petition.

9.7 Where the company to be wound up has been struck off the register, the petition should state that fact and include as part of the relief sought an order that it be restored to the register. Save where the petition has been presented by a Minister of the Crown or a government department, evidence of service on the Government Legal Department or the Solicitor for the Affairs of the Duchy of Lancaster or the Solicitor to the Duchy of Cornwall (as appropriate) should be filed exhibiting the bona vacantia waiver letter.

9.8 Notice of the petition

9.8.1 The provisions contained in Chapter 4 of Part 1 and in particular rule 7.10 must be followed (unless waived by the Court). These provisions are designed to preserve the sanctity of the class remedy in any given winding up by the Court. Failure to comply with rule 7.10 may lead to summary dismissal of the petition on the return date. If the Court, in its discretion, grants an adjournment, this will usually be on terms that notice of the petition is gazetted or otherwise given in accordance with the Insolvency Rules in due time for the adjourned hearing. No further adjournment to comply with rule 7.10 will normally be given.

9.8.2 Copies of every notice gazetted in connection with a winding up petition, or where this is not practicable a description of the form and content of the notice, must be lodged with the Court as soon as possible after publication and in any event not later than five business days before the hearing of the petition. This direction applies even if the notice is defective in any way (e.g. is published on a date not in accordance with the Insolvency Rules, or omits or misprints some important words) or if the petitioner decides not to pursue the petition (e.g. on receiving payment).

9.8.3 Attention is drawn to the requirement to give notice of the dismissal of a petition under rule 7.23(1). The Court will usually, on request, dispense with the requirement where (a) presentation of the petition has not previously been gazetted or (b) the company has become the subject of some supervening insolvency process, or (c) the company consents.

9.9 Errors in petitions

9.9.1 Applications for permission to amend errors in petitions which are discovered after a winding up order has been made should be made to the member of Court staff in charge of the winding up list in the Royal Courts of Justice or to a District Judge Sitting in a District Registry or District Judge.

9.9.2 Where the error is an error in the name of the company, the member of Court staff in charge of the winding up list in the Royal Courts of Justice or a District Judge Sitting in a District Registry or District Judge may make any necessary amendments to ensure that the winding up order is drawn up with the correct name of the company inserted. If there is any doubt, e.g. where there might be another company in existence which could be confused with the company to be wound up, the member of Court staff in charge of the winding up list will refer the application to an ICC Judge at the Royal Courts of Justice. A District Judge Sitting in a District Registry or District Judge may refer the matter to a High Court Judge.

9.9.3 Where it is discovered that the company has been struck off the Register of Companies prior to the winding up order being made, the petition must be restored to the list as soon as possible to enable an order for the restoration of the name to be made as well as the order to wind up and, save where the petition has been presented by a Minister of the Crown or a government department, evidence of service on the Government Legal Department or the Solicitor for the Affairs of the Duchy of Lancaster or the Solicitor to the Duchy of Cornwall (as appropriate) should be filed exhibiting the bona vacantia waiver letter.

9.10 Rescission of a winding up order

9.10.1 A request to rescind a winding up order must be made by application.

9.10.2 The application must be made within five business days after the date on which the order was made, failing which it should include an application to extend time pursuant to Schedule 5 to the Insolvency Rules. Notice of any such application must be given to the petitioning creditor, any supporting or opposing creditor, any incumbent insolvency practitioner and the official receiver.

9.10.3 An application to rescind will only be entertained if made by a (a) creditor, or (b) contributory, or (c) by the company jointly with a creditor or with a contributory. The application must be supported by a witness statement which should include details of assets and liabilities and (where appropriate) reasons for any failure to apply within five business days.

9.10.4 In the case of an unsuccessful application, the costs of the petitioning creditor, any supporting or opposing creditor, any incumbent insolvency practitioner and the official receiver will normally be ordered to be paid by the creditor or the contributory making or joining in the application. The reason for this is that if the costs of an unsuccessful application are made payable by the company, those costs will inevitably fall on the general body of creditors.

9.11 Validation orders

9.11.1 A company against which a winding up petition has been presented may apply to the Court after the presentation of a petition for relief from the effects of s.127(1) of the Act, by seeking an order that a certain disposition or dispositions of its property, including payments out of its bank account (whether such account is in credit or overdrawn), shall not be void in the event of a winding up order being made at the hearing of the petition (a validation order).

9.11.2 Save in exceptional circumstances, notice of the making of the application should be given to: (a) the petitioning creditor; (b) any person entitled to receive a copy of the petition pursuant to rule 7.9; (c) any creditor who has given notice to the petitioner of their intention to appear on the hearing of the petition pursuant to rule 7.14; and (d) any creditor who has been substituted as petitioner pursuant to rule 7.17. Failure to do so is likely to lead to an adjournment of the application or dismissal.

9.11.3 The application should be supported by a witness statement which should be made by a director or officer of the company who is intimately acquainted with the company's affairs and financial circumstances. If appropriate, supporting evidence in the form of a witness statement from the company's accountant should also be produced.

9.11.4 The extent and content of the evidence will vary according to the circumstances and the nature of the relief sought, but in the majority of cases it should include, as a minimum, the following information:

(1) when and to whom notice has been given in accordance with paragraph 9.11.2 above;

(2) the company's registered office;

(3) the company's capital;

(4) brief details of the circumstances leading to presentation of the petition;

(5) how the company became aware of presentation of the petition;

(6) whether the petition debt is admitted or disputed and, if the latter, brief details of the basis on which the debt is disputed;

(7) full details of the company's financial position including details of its assets (and including details of any security and the amount(s) secured) and liabilities, which should be supported, as far as possible, by documentary evidence, e.g. the latest filed accounts, any draft audited accounts, management accounts or estimated statement of affairs;

(8) a cash flow forecast and profit and loss projection for the period for which the order is sought;

(9) details of the dispositions or payments in respect of which an order is sought;

(10) the reasons relied on in support of the need for such dispositions or payments to be made prior to the hearing of the petition;

(11) any other information relevant to the exercise of the Court's discretion;

(12) details of any consents obtained from the persons mentioned in paragraph 9.11.2 above (supported by documentary evidence where appropriate);

(13) details of any relevant bank account, including its number and the address and sort code of the bank at which such account is held, and the amount of the credit or debit balance on such account at the time of making the application.

9.11.5 Where an application is made urgently to enable payments to be made which are essential to continued trading (e.g. wages) and it is not possible to assemble all the evidence listed above, the Court may consider granting limited relief for a short period, but there should be sufficient evidence to satisfy the Court that the interests of creditors are unlikely to be prejudiced by the grant of limited relief.

9.11.6 Where the application involves a disposition of property, the Court will need details of the property (including its title number if the property is land) and to be satisfied that any proposed disposal will be at a proper value. Accordingly, an independent valuation should be obtained and exhibited to the evidence.

9.11.7 The Court will need to be satisfied by credible evidence either that the company is solvent and able to pay its debts as they fall due or that a particular transaction or series of transactions in respect of which the order is sought will be beneficial to or will not prejudice the interests of all the unsecured creditors as a class.

9.11.8 A draft of the order sought should be attached to the application.

9.11.9 Similar considerations to those set out above are likely to apply to applications seeking ratification of a transaction or payment after the making of a winding up order.

10. Applications

10.1 In accordance with rule 12.2(2), in the Royal Courts of Justice an officer acting on behalf of the operations manager or chief clerk has been authorised to deal with applications:

(1) to extend or abridge time prescribed by the Insolvency Rules in connection with winding up;

(2) for permission to withdraw a winding up petition (rule 7.134);

(3) made by the official receiver for a public examination (s.133(1)(c) of the Act), where no penal notice is endorsed and no unless order is made;

(4) made by the official receiver to transfer proceedings from the High Court to a specified hearing centre within the meaning of rule 12.30;

(5) to list a hearing for directions with a time estimate of 30 minutes or less in circumstances where both parties are represented without reference to an ICC Judge;

(6) for a first extension of time to serve a bankruptcy petition.

10.2 Outside of the Royal Courts of Justice, applications listed in paragraph 10.1 must be made to a District Judge Sitting in a District Registry or in the County Court to a District Judge.

10.3 Where an application is made by an official receiver in respect of the matters listed in paragraph 10.1(4) above, the official receiver must comply with rule 12.32 and give any incumbent office-holder 14 days' written notice of the application.

PART THREE: PERSONAL INSOLVENCY

11. Statutory demands

11.1 Rule 10.1 prescribes the contents of a statutory demand. An example of a statutory demand may be found at:
http://hmctsformfinder.justice.gov.uk/HMCTS/GetForms.do?court_forms_category=Bankruptcy%20and%20 Insolvency.

11.2 Rule 10.2 applies to service of a statutory demand whether within or out of the jurisdiction. If personal service is not practicable in the particular circumstances, a creditor must do all that is reasonable to bring the statutory demand to the debtor's attention. This could include taking those steps set out at paragraph 12.7 below which justify the Court making an order for service of a bankruptcy petition other than by personal service. It may also include any other form of physical or electronic communication which will bring the statutory demand to the notice of the debtor.

11.3 A creditor wishing to serve a statutory demand out of the jurisdiction in a foreign country with an applicable civil procedure convention (including the Hague Convention) may and, if the assistance of a

British Consul is desired, must adopt the procedure prescribed by CPR rule 6.42 and CPR rule 6.43. In the case of any doubt whether the country is a 'convention country', enquiries should be made of the Foreign Process Section of the Queen's Bench Division, Room E16, Royal Courts of Justice, Strand, London WC2A 2LL.

11.4 Setting aside a statutory demand

11.4.1 The application and witness statement in support of setting aside a statutory demand, exhibiting a copy of the statutory demand, must be filed in Court within 18 days of service of the statutory demand on the debtor. The time limits are different if the statutory demand has been served out of the jurisdiction: see rule 10.1(10).

11.4.2 A debtor who wishes to apply to set aside a statutory demand after the expiration of 18 days, or if service is out of the jurisdiction, after the expiration of the time limit specified by rule 10.1(10)(a) from the date of service of the statutory demand, must apply for an extension of time within which to apply to set aside the statutory demand. The witness statement in support of the application to set aside statutory demand should also contain evidence in support of the application for an extension of time and should state that to the best of the debtor's knowledge and belief the creditor(s) named in the statutory demand has/have not presented a bankruptcy petition.

11.4.3 Unless the Court to which the application to set aside is made operates Electronic Filing and Electronic Practice Direction 51O applies, the following applies:

(1) Three copies of each document must be lodged with the application, to enable the Court to serve notice of the hearing date on the applicant, the creditor and the person named under rule 10.1(3).

(2) Where copies of the documents are not lodged with the application, any order of the Court fixing a venue is conditional upon copies of the documents being lodged on the next business day after the Court's order, otherwise the application will be deemed to have been dismissed.

11.4.4 Where the debt claimed in the statutory demand is based on a judgment, order, liability order, costs certificate, tax assessment or decision of a tribunal, the Court will not at this stage inquire into the validity of the debt nor, as a general rule, will it adjourn the application to await the result of an application to set aside the judgment, order, decision, costs certificate or any appeal.

11.4.5 The Court will determine an application to set aside a statutory demand in accordance with rule 10.5.

11.4.6 Attention is drawn to the power of the Court to decline to file a petition if there has been a failure to comply with the requirement of rule 10.2: see rule 10.9(4).

12. Bankruptcy petitions

12.1 All petitions presented will be listed under the name of the debtor unless the Court directs otherwise.

12.2 Content of petitions

12.2.1 The attention of Court users is drawn to the following points:

(1) A creditor's petition does not require dating, signing or witnessing, but must be verified in accordance with rule 10.10.

(2) In the heading, it is only necessary to recite the debtor's name e.g. Re John William Smith or Re J W Smith (Male). Any alias or trading name will appear in the body of the petition.

12.2.2 Where the petition is based solely on a statutory demand, only the debt claimed in the demand may be included in the petition.

12.2.3 The attention of Court users is also drawn to rules 10.8 and 10.9, where the 'aggregate sum' is made up of a number of debts.

12.2.4 The date of service of the statutory demand should be recited as follows:

(1) Where the demand has been served personally, the date of service as set out in the certificate of service.

(2) Where the demand has been served other than personally, the date as set out in the certificate of service filed in compliance with rule 10.3.

12.3 Searches

12.3.1 The petitioning creditor shall, before presenting a petition, conduct an Official Search with the Chief Land Registrar in the register of pending actions for pending petitions presented against the debtor and shall include the following certificate at the end of the petition:

"I/we certify that within 7 days ending today, I/we have conducted a search for pending petitions presented against the debtor and that to the best of my/our knowledge, information, and belief [no prior petitions have been presented which are still pending] [a prior petition (No [ ]) has been presented and is/may be pending in the [Court] and I/we am/are issuing this petition at risk as to costs].
Signed........................ Dated........................"

Part 19 Practice Directions

12.4 The deposit

12.4.1 A bankruptcy petition will not be treated as having been presented until the Court fee and official receiver's deposit have been paid. A petition filed electronically without payment of the deposit will be marked "private" and will not be available for inspection until the deposit has been paid. The date of presentation of the petition will accord with the date on which the deposit has been paid. If the official receiver's deposit is not paid within 7 calendar days after filing the petition, the petition will not be accepted, in accordance with paragraph 5.3 of the Electronic Practice Direction 51O - The Electronic Working Pilot Scheme.

12.4.2 The deposit will be taken by the Court and forwarded to the official receiver. In the Royal Courts of Justice the petition fee and deposit should be paid by cheque, or by debit or credit card over the phone. In a District Registry or a County Court hearing centre, the petition fee and deposit should be handed to the staff of the duly authorised officer of the Court who will record its receipt. For the purposes of paragraph 12.4.1 above, the deposit will be treated as paid when received by the Court.

12.4.3 If payment is made by cheque, it should be made payable to 'HM Courts and Tribunals Service' or 'HMCTS'. For the purposes of paragraph 12.4 of this IPD, the deposit will be treated as paid when the cheque is received by the Court

12.5 Certificates of continuing debt and of notice of adjournment

12.5.1 At the final hearing of a petition, the Court will need to be satisfied that the debt on which the petition is founded has not been paid or secured or compounded. The Court will normally accept as sufficient evidence a certificate signed by the person representing the petitioning creditor in the following form:

"I certify that I have/my firm has made enquiries of the petitioning creditor(s) within the last business day prior to the hearing/adjourned hearing and to the best of my knowledge and belief the debt on which the petition is founded is still due and owing and has not been paid or secured or compounded for save as to ....

Signed...................... Dated.......................".

12.5.2 For convenience, in the Royal Courts of Justice this certificate is incorporated in the attendance sheet for the parties to complete when they come to Court and is to be filed after the hearing. A fresh certificate will be required on each adjourned hearing.

12.5.3 On any adjourned hearing of a petition, in order to satisfy the Court that the petitioner has complied with rule 10.23, the petitioner will be required to file evidence of when (the date), how (the manner), and where (the address), notice of the adjournment order and notification of the venue for the adjourned hearing was sent to:

(1) the debtor, and

(2) any creditor who has given notice under rule 10.19 but was not present at the hearing when the order for adjournment was made or was present at the hearing but the date of the adjourned hearing was not fixed at that hearing. For convenience, in the Royal Courts of Justice this certificate is incorporated in the attendance sheet for the parties to complete when they come to Court and is to be filed after the hearing. It is as follows:

"I certify that the petitioner has complied with rule 10.23 of the Insolvency Rules 2016 by sending notice of adjournment to the debtor [supporting/opposing creditor(s)] on [date] at [address]".

A fresh certificate will be required on each adjourned hearing.

12.6 Extension of hearing date of petition

12.6.1 Late applications for extension of hearing dates under rule 10.22, and failure to attend on the listed hearing of a petition, will be dealt with as follows:

(1) If an application is submitted less than two clear working days before the hearing date (for example, later than Monday for Thursday, or Wednesday for Monday), the costs of the application will not be allowed under rule 10.22.

(2) If the petition has not been served and no extension has been granted by the time fixed for the hearing of the petition, and if no one attends for the hearing, the petition may be dismissed or re-listed for hearing about 21 days later. The Court will notify the petitioning creditor's solicitors (or the petitioning creditor in person), and any known supporting or opposing creditors or their solicitors, of the new date and time. A witness statement should then be filed on behalf of the petitioning creditor explaining fully the reasons for the failure to apply for an extension or to appear at the hearing, and (if appropriate) giving reasons why the petition should not be dismissed.

(3) On the re-listed hearing the Court may dismiss the petition if not satisfied it should be adjourned or a further extension granted.

12.6.2 All applications for an extension should include a statement of the date fixed for the hearing of the petition.

12.6.3 The petitioning creditor should contact the Court (by solicitors or in person) on or before the hearing date to ascertain whether the application has reached the file and been dealt with. It should not be assumed that an extension will be granted.

12.7 Service of bankruptcy petitions other than by personal service

12.7.1 Where personal service of the bankruptcy petition is not practicable, service by other means may be permitted. In most cases, evidence that the steps set out in the following paragraphs have been taken will suffice to justify an order for service of a bankruptcy petition other than by personal service:

(1) One personal call at the residence and place of business of the debtor. Where it is known that the debtor has more than one residential or business addresses, personal calls should be made at all the addresses.

(2) Should the creditor fail to effect personal service, a letter should be written to the debtor referring to the call(s), the purpose of the same, and the failure to meet the debtor, adding that a further call will be made for the same purpose on the [day] of [month] 20[ ] at [ ] hours at [place]. Such letter may be sent by first class prepaid post or left at or delivered to the debtor's address in such a way as it is reasonably likely to come to the debtor's attention. At least two business days' notice should be given of the appointment and copies of the letter sent to or left at all known addresses of the debtor. The appointment letter should also state that:

(a) in the event of the time and place not being convenient, the debtor should propose some other time and place reasonably convenient for the purpose;

(b) in the case of a statutory demand as suggested in paragraph 11.2 above, reference is being made to this paragraph for the purpose of service of a statutory demand, the appointment letter should state that if the debtor fails to keep the appointment the creditor proposes to serve the demand by advertisement/ post/ insertion through a letter box as the case may be, and that, in the event of a bankruptcy petition being presented, the Court will be asked to treat such service as service of the demand on the debtor;

(c) (in the case of a petition) if the debtor fails to keep the appointment, an application will be made to the Court for an order that service be effected either by advertisement or in such other manner as the Court may think fit.

(d) when attending any appointment made by letter, inquiry should be made as to whether the debtor is still resident at the address or still frequents the address, and/or other enquiries should be made to ascertain receipt of all letters left for them. If the debtor is away, inquiry should also be made as to when they are returning and whether the letters are being forwarded to an address within the jurisdiction (England and Wales) or elsewhere.

(4) If the debtor is represented by a solicitor, an attempt should be made to arrange an appointment for personal service through such solicitor. The Insolvency Rules permit a solicitor to accept service of a statutory demand on behalf of their client but not the service of a bankruptcy petition.

12.8 Validation orders

12.8.1 A person against whom a bankruptcy petition has been presented may apply to the Court after presentation of the petition for relief from the effects of s.284(1) – (3) of the Act by seeking an order that a certain disposition or dispositions of that person's property, including payments out of their bank account (whether such account is in credit or overdrawn), shall not be void in the event of a bankruptcy order being made at the hearing of the petition (a validation order).

12.8.2 Save in exceptional circumstances, notice of the making of the application should be given to (a) the petitioning creditor(s) or other petitioner, (b) any creditor who has given notice to the petitioner of their intention to appear on the hearing of the petition pursuant to rule 10.19, (c) any creditor who has been substituted as petitioner pursuant to rule 10.27 and (d) any creditor who has carriage of the petition pursuant to rule 10.29.

12.8.3 The application should be supported by a witness statement which, save in exceptional circumstances, should be made by the debtor. If appropriate, supporting evidence in the form of a witness statement from the debtor's accountant should also be produced.

12.8.4 The extent and contents of the evidence will vary according to the circumstances and the nature of the relief sought, but in a case where the debtor is trading or carrying on business it should include, as a minimum, the following information:

(1) when and to whom notice has been given in accordance with paragraph 12.8.2 above;

(2) brief details of the circumstances leading to presentation of the petition;

(3) how the debtor became aware of the presentation of the petition;

(4) whether the petition debt is admitted or disputed and, if the latter, brief details of the basis on which the debt is disputed;

(5) full details of the debtor's financial position including details of their assets (including details of any security and the amount(s) secured) and liabilities, which should be supported, as far as possible, by documentary evidence, e.g. accounts, draft accounts, management accounts or estimated statement of affairs;

(6) a cash flow forecast and profit and loss projection for the period for which the order is sought;

(7) details of the dispositions or payments in respect of which an order is sought;

(8) the reasons relied on in support of the need for such dispositions or payments to be made;

(9) any other information relevant to the exercise of the Court's discretion;

(10) details of any consents obtained from the persons mentioned in paragraph 12.8.2 above (supported by documentary evidence where appropriate);

(11) details of any relevant bank account, including its number and the address and sort code of the bank at which such account is held and the amount of the credit or debit balance on such account at the time of making the application.

12.8.5 Where an application is made urgently to enable payments to be made which are essential to continued trading (e.g. wages) and it is not possible to assemble all the evidence listed above, the Court may consider granting limited relief for a short period, but there must be sufficient evidence to satisfy the Court that the interests of creditors are unlikely to be prejudiced.

12.8.6 Where the debtor is not trading or carrying on business and the application relates only to a proposed sale, mortgage or re-mortgage of the debtor's home, evidence of the following will generally suffice:

(1) when and to whom notice has been given in accordance with 12.8.2 above;

(2) whether the petition debt is admitted or disputed and, if the latter, brief details of the basis on which the debt is disputed;

(3) details of the property to be sold, mortgaged or re-mortgaged (including its title number);

(4) the value of the property and the proposed sale price, or details of the mortgage or re-mortgage;

(5) details of any existing mortgages or charges on the property and redemption figures;

(6) the costs of sale (e.g. solicitors' or agents' costs);

(7) how and by whom any net proceeds of sale (or sums coming into the debtor's hands as a result of any mortgage or re-mortgage) are to be held pending the final hearing of the petition;

(8) any other information relevant to the exercise of the Court's discretion;

(9) details of any consents obtained from the persons mentioned in 12.8.2 above (supported by documentary evidence where appropriate).

12.8.7 Whether or not the debtor is trading or carrying on business, where the application involves a disposition of property the Court will need to be satisfied that any proposed disposal will be at a proper value. An independent valuation should be obtained for this purpose and exhibited to the evidence.

12.8.8 The Court will need to be satisfied by credible evidence that the debtor is solvent and able to pay their debts as they fall due or that a particular transaction or series of transactions in respect of which the order is sought will be beneficial to or will not prejudice the interests of all the unsecured creditors as a class.

12.8.9 A draft of the order should accompany the application.

12.8.10 Similar considerations to those set out above are likely to apply to applications seeking ratification of a transaction or payment after the making of a bankruptcy order.

13. Applications

13.1 In accordance with rule 12.2(2), in the Royal Courts of Justice an officer acting on behalf of the Operations Manager or chief clerk has been authorised to deal with applications:

(1) by petitioning creditors to extend the time for hearing petitions (rule 10.22);

(2) by the official receiver:

(a) to transfer proceedings from the High Court to a specified hearing centre within the meaning of rule 12.30.

(b) to amend the title of the proceedings (rule 10.165).

13.2 Outside of the Royal Courts of Justice, applications listed in paragraph 13.1 must be made to a District Judge Sitting in a District Registry or in the County Court to a District Judge.

13.3 Where an application is to be made under 13.1(2)(a) above, the official receiver must comply with rule 12.32, and give any incumbent office-holder 14 days' written notice of the application.

14. Orders without attendance

14.1 In suitable cases the Court will normally be prepared to make orders under Part VIII of the Act (Individual Voluntary Arrangements), without the attendance of the parties, provided there is no bankruptcy order in existence and (so far as is known) no pending petition. The orders are:

(1) A 14 day interim order adjourning the application for 14 days for consideration of the nominee's report, where the papers are in order, and the nominee's signed consent to act includes a waiver of notice of the application or the consent by the nominee to the making of an interim order without attendance.

(2) A standard order on consideration of the nominee's report, extending the interim order to a date seven weeks after the proposed decision date, directing the implementation of the decision procedure and adjourning to a date about three weeks after the decision date. Such an order may be made without attendance if the nominee's report has been delivered to the Court and complies with s.256(1) of the Act, and proposes a decision date not less than 14 days from that on which the nominee's report is filed in Court under rule 8.15, nor more than 28 days from that on which that report is considered by the Court under rule 8.18.

(3) A 'concertina' order, combining orders as under (1) and (2) above. Such an order may be made without attendance if the initial application for an interim order is accompanied by a report of the nominee and the conditions set out in (1) and (2) above are satisfied.

(4) A final order on consideration of the report of the creditors' consideration of the proposal. Such an order may be made without attendance if the report has been filed and complies with rule 8.24. The order will record the effect of the report and may discharge the interim order.

14.2 Provided that the conditions under sub-paragraphs 14.1(2) and 14.1 (4) above are satisfied and that the appropriate report has been lodged with the Court in due time the parties need not attend or be represented on the adjourned hearing for consideration of the nominee's report or of the report of the creditors' giving consideration of the proposal (as the case may be), unless they are notified by the Court that attendance is required. Sealed copies of the order made (in all four cases paragraph 14.1 above) will be posted by the Court to the applicant or their solicitor and to the nominee.

14.3 In suitable cases the Court may make consent orders without attendance by the parties. The written consent of the parties endorsed on the consent order will be required. Examples of such orders are as follows:

(1) on applications to set aside a statutory demand, orders:

(a) dismissing the application, with or without an order for costs as may be agreed (permission will be given to present a petition on or after the seventh day after the date of the order, unless a different date is agreed);

(b) setting aside the demand, with or without an order for costs as may be agreed.

(2) On petitions where there are no supporting or opposing creditors (see rule 10.19), and there is a statement signed by or on behalf of the petitioning creditor confirming that no notices have been received from supporting or opposing creditors, orders:

(a) dismissing the petition, with or without an order for costs as may be agreed; or

(b) if the petition has not been served, giving permission to withdraw the petition (with no order for costs).

(3) On other applications or orders:

(a) for sale of property, possession of property, disposal of proceeds of sale;

(b) giving interim directions;

(c) dismissing the application, with or without an order for costs as may be agreed;

(d) giving permission to withdraw the application, with or without an order for costs as may be agreed.

14.4 If, as may often be the case with orders under sub-paragraphs 3(a) or (b) above, an adjournment is required, whether generally with liberty to restore or to a fixed date, the order by consent may include an order for the adjournment. If adjournment to a date is requested, a time estimate should be given and the Court will fix the first available date and time on or after the date requested.

14.5 The above lists should not be regarded as exhaustive, nor should it be assumed that an order will be made without attendance as requested.

14.6 Applications for consent orders without attendance should be lodged at least two clear working days (and preferably longer) before any hearing date.

14.7 Whenever a document is lodged or a letter sent, the correct case number should be quoted. A note should also be given of the date and time of the next hearing (if any).

15. Bankruptcy restrictions undertakings

15.1 Where a bankrupt has given a bankruptcy restrictions undertaking, the Secretary of State or official receiver must file a copy in Court and send a copy to the bankrupt as soon as reasonably practicable (rule 11.11). In addition the Secretary of State must notify the Court immediately that the bankrupt has given such an undertaking in order that any hearing date can be vacated.

16. Persons at risk of violence

16.1 Where an application is made pursuant to rules 8.6, 20.2, 20.3, 20.4, 20.5, 20.6 or otherwise to limit disclosure of information as to a person's current address by reason of the possibility of violence, the relevant application should be accompanied by a witness statement which includes the following:

(1) The grounds upon which it is contended that disclosure of the current address as defined by rule 20.1 might reasonably be expected to lead to violence against the debtor or a person who normally resides with them as a member of their family or where appropriate any other person.

(2) Where the application is made in respect of the address of the debtor, the debtor's proposals with regard to information which may safely be given to potential creditors in order that they can recognise that the debtor is a person who may be indebted to them, in particular the address at which the debtor previously resided or carried on business and the nature of such business.

(3) The terms of the order sought by the applicant by reference to the Court's particular powers as set out in the rule under which the application is made and, unless impracticable, a draft of the order sought.

(4) Where the application is made by the debtor in respect of whom a nominee or supervisor has been appointed or against whom a bankruptcy order has been made, evidence of the consent of the nominee/supervisor, or, in the case of bankruptcy, the official receiver or any other person appointed as trustee in bankruptcy. Where such consent is not available the statement must indicate whether such consent has been refused.

16.2 Any person listed in 16.1(4) shall be made a respondent to the application.

16.3 The application shall be referred to a District Judge Sitting in a District Registry, ICC Judge, or High Court Judge where it will be considered without a hearing in the first instance but without prejudice to the right of the Court to list it for hearing if:

(1) the Court is not persuaded by the written evidence, and consequently may refuse the application;

(2) the consent of any respondent is not attached; or(3) the Court is of the view that there is another reason why listing is appropriate.

PART FOUR: APPEALS

17. Appeals

17.1 CPR Part 52 and its attendant practice directions apply to insolvency appeals unless dis-applied or inconsistent with the Act or the Insolvency Rules. This IPD provides greater detail on the routes of appeal as applied to insolvency proceedings under the Act, the Insolvency Rules and CPR Part 52.

17.2 Appeals in Personal Insolvency Matters

17.2(1) Paragraph 17.2 applies to all permissions to appeal and appeals from decisions made in personal insolvency matters, save those that arise from s.263N of the Act relating to bankruptcy applications to an adjudicator.

17.2(2) An application for permission to appeal relating to a decision made in a personal insolvency matter by a District Judge lies to a High Court Judge.

17.2(3) An application for permission to appeal relating to a decision made in a personal insolvency matter by a District Judge Sitting in a District Registry, a Circuit Judge, or an ICC Judge lies to a High Court Judge, but not to a Deputy.

17.2(4) An appeal from a decision in a personal insolvency matter made by a District Judge lies to a High Court Judge.

17.2(5) An appeal from a decision in a personal insolvency matter made by a District Judge Sitting in a District Registry, a Recorder, a Circuit Judge, or an ICC Judge lies to a High Court Judge, but not to a Deputy. Supervising Judges for the Business and Property Courts may, in circumstances they consider to be appropriate, allow for an appeal from a decision in a personal insolvency matter made by a District Judge Sitting in a District Registry to be handled by a Circuit Judge acting as a judge of the High Court under s.9(1) of the Senior Courts Act 1981.

17.3 Appeals from Decisions of Adjudicators

17.3(1) An application under s.263N(5) of the Act appealing the decision of an adjudicator to refuse to make a bankruptcy order is made to the Court, in accordance with the provisions in rule 10.48.

17.3(2) No prior application for permission to appeal is required.

17.3(3) An application under s.263N(5) of the Act will be treated as the first hearing of the matter.

17.4(4) It is the responsibility of the applicant to obtain from the adjudicator a copy (digital or otherwise) of the original application reviewed by the adjudicator (including the adjudicator's notice of refusal to make a bankruptcy order and notice confirming that refusal) and a record of (a) the verification checks undertaken under rule 10.38 by the adjudicator and (b) any additional information provided under rule 10.39(3) and available to the adjudicator at the date when the adjudicator refused to make a bankruptcy order.

17.4(5) Prior to making a final decision the Court may:

(a) direct that notice of the application be given to any interested person;

(b) give permission to any interested person and the petitioner to file evidence;

(c) make any case management order to assist in determining whether to dismiss the application or make a bankruptcy order.

NOTES

Editorial note: the above paragraph is reproduced as per the original version. Ie, the numbering in the paragraph goes from "17.3(3)" to "17.4(4)".

17.5 Appeals in Corporate Insolvency Matters

17.5(1) Routes of appeal for appeals from decisions in corporate insolvency matters under Parts 1 to 7 of the Act (and the corresponding Insolvency Rules) are specified in rule 12.59.

17.5(2) An application for permission to appeal relating to a decision made in a corporate insolvency matter by a District Judge lies to a High Court Judge or an ICC Judge but not to a Deputy ICC Judge. Whether it lies to a High Court Judge or an ICC Judge depends on the location from which the decision being appealed originates, in conformity with Schedule 10 of the Insolvency Rules.

17.5(3) An application for permission to appeal relating to a decision made in a corporate insolvency matter by a District Judge Sitting in a District Registry or a Circuit Judge lies to a High Court Judge, but not to a Deputy.

17.5(4) An application for permission to appeal relating to a decision made at first instance in a corporate insolvency matter by an ICC Judge lies to a High Court Judge, but not to a Deputy.

17.5(5) An application for permission to appeal relating to a decision made by an ICC Judge on appeal from a District Judge in a corporate insolvency matter lies to the Civil Division of the Court of Appeal.

17.5(6) An appeal from a decision in a corporate insolvency matter made by a District Judge lies to a High Court Judge or to an ICC Judge, depending on the location from which the decision being appealed originates, in accordance with Schedule 10 of the Insolvency Rules.

17.5(7) An appeal from a decision in a corporate insolvency matter made by a District Judge Sitting in a District Registry lies to a High Court Judge but not to a Deputy. Supervising Judges for the Business and Property Courts may, in circumstances they consider to be appropriate, allow for an appeal from a decision in a corporate insolvency matter made by a District Judge Sitting in a District Registry to be handled by a Circuit Judge acting as a judge of the High Court under s.9(1) of the Senior Courts Act 1981.

17.5(8) An appeal from a decision in a corporate insolvency matter made by a Recorder or a Circuit Judge lies to a High Court Judge, but not to a Deputy.

17.5(9) An appeal from a decision in a corporate insolvency matter made at first instance by an ICC Judge lies to a High Court Judge, but not to a Deputy.

17.5(10) An appeal from a decision in a corporate insolvency matter made by an ICC Judge on appeal from a District Judge in a corporate insolvency matter lies to the Civil Division of the Court of Appeal.

18.1 Permission to Appeal

18.2 A first appeal is subject to the permission requirements of CPR Part 52, rule 3.

18.3 An appeal from a decision of the High Court by either a High Court Judge or an ICC Judge which was made at first instance requires the permission of the Court of Appeal.

NOTES

Editorial note: the above paragraph is reproduced as per the original version. It is assumed that the heading should be "Paragraph 18" rather than "Paragraph 18.1".

19 Filing Appeals

19.1 An application for permission to appeal or an appeal from a decision of an ICC Judge which lies to a High Court Judge must be filed at the Royal Courts of Justice.

19.2 An application for permission to appeal or an appeal from a decision of a District Judge Sitting in a District Registry must be filed in that District Registry.

19.3 An application for permission to appeal or an appeal from a decision of a District Judge must be filed in its corresponding appeal centre, as identified in the table in Schedule 10 of the Insolvency Rules.

PART FIVE: FINANCIAL MARKETS AND INSOLVENCY (SETTLEMENT FINALITY) REGULATIONS 1999 – REQUIRED INFORMATION

20 In any case in which the Court is asked to make an order to which regulation 22(1) of the Financial Markets and Insolvency (Settlement Finality) Regulations 1999 (SI 1999/2979) applies, the party applying for the order must include in the petition or application a statement to that effect, identifying the system operator of the relevant designated system, the relevant designating authority, and the email or other addresses to which the Court will be required to send notice pursuant to regulation 22(1) if an order is made.

20.1 At the date of this IPD, the Regulations apply where, in respect of "a participant in a designated system" (as those terms are defined in the Regulations), an order is made for administration, winding-up, bankruptcy, sequestration, bank insolvency, bank administration, building society insolvency, building society special administration or investment bank special administration. Applicants must, before making the application, check for any amendments to the Regulations.

PART SIX: APPLICATIONS RELATING TO THE REMUNERATION OF OFFICE-HOLDERS

21 This IPD sets out the governing principles and court practice. Reference should also be made to the Act and the Insolvency Rules.

21.1 The objective in any remuneration application is to ensure that the amount and/or basis of any remuneration fixed by the Court is fair, reasonable and commensurate with the nature and extent of the work properly undertaken or to be undertaken by the office-holder in any given case and is fixed and approved by a process which is consistent and predictable.

21.2 The guiding principles which follow are intended to assist in achieving the objective:

(1) "Justification". It is for the office-holder who seeks to be remunerated at a particular level and / or in a particular manner to justify their claim. They are responsible for preparing and providing full particulars of the basis for, and the nature of, their claim for remuneration.

(2) "The benefit of the doubt". The corollary of the "justification" principle is that if after having regard to the evidence and guiding principles there remains any doubt as to the appropriateness, fairness or reasonableness of the remuneration sought or to be fixed (whether arising from a lack of particularity as to the basis for and the nature of the office-holder's claim to remuneration or otherwise), such element of doubt should be resolved by the Court against the office-holder.

(3) "Professional integrity". The Court should (where this is the case) give weight to the fact that the officeholder is a member of a regulated profession and as such is subject to rules and guidance as to professional conduct and the fact that (where this is the case) the office-holder is an officer of the Court.

(4) "The value of the service rendered". The remuneration of an office-holder should reflect the value of the service rendered by the office-holder, not simply reimburse the office-holder in respect of time expended and cost incurred.

(5) "Fair and reasonable". The amount and basis of the office-holder's remuneration should represent fair and reasonable remuneration for the work properly undertaken or to be undertaken.

(6) "Proportionality of information". In considering the nature and extent of the information which should be provided by an office-holder in respect of a remuneration application to the Court, the office-holder and any other parties to the application shall have regard to what is proportionate by reference to the amount of remuneration to be fixed, the nature, complexity and extent of the work to be completed (where the application relates to future remuneration) or that has been completed by the office-holder and the value and nature of the assets and liabilities with which the office-holder will have to deal or has had to deal.

(7) "Proportionality of remuneration". The amount and basis of remuneration to be fixed by the Court should be proportionate to the nature, complexity and extent of the work to be completed (where the application relates to future remuneration) or that has been completed by the office-holder and the value and nature of the assets and/or potential assets and the liabilities and/or potential liabilities with which the office-holder will have to deal or has had to deal, the nature and degree of the responsibility to which the office-holder has been subject in any given case, the nature and extent of the risk (if any) assumed by the office-holder and the efficiency (in respect of both time and cost) with which the office-holder has completed the work undertaken.

(8) "Professional guidance". In respect of an application for the fixing and approval of the amount and/or basis of the remuneration, the office-holder may have regard to the relevant and current statements of practice promulgated by any relevant regulatory and professional bodies in relation to the fixing of the remuneration of an office-holder. In considering a remuneration application, the Court may also have regard to such statements of practice and the extent of compliance with such statements of practice by the officeholder.

(9) "Timing of application". The Court will take into account whether any application should have been made earlier and if so the reasons for any delay.

21.3 Hearing of a remuneration application. The general rule applies for the listing of hearings as set out in paragraph 3 of this IPD. The judge hearing the application may summarily determine the application or adjourn with directions including (but not confined to) directions as to (i) whether an assessor or costs judge should prepare a report to the Court in respect of the remuneration (ii) or whether the application should be heard by a judge and an assessor or a costs judge.

21.4 On any remuneration application, the office-holder should provide the information and evidence referred to in paragraphs 21.4.1 to 21.4.12 below.

21.4.1 A narrative description and explanation of:

(a) the background to, the relevant circumstances of, and the reasons for their appointment;

(b) the work undertaken or to be undertaken in respect of the appointment; the description should be divided, insofar as possible, into individual tasks or categories of task (general descriptions of work, tasks, or categories of task should (insofar as possible) be avoided);

(c) the reasons why it is or was considered reasonable and/or necessary and/or beneficial for such work to be done, giving details of why particular tasks or categories of task were undertaken and why such tasks or categories of task are to be undertaken or have been undertaken by particular individuals and in a particular manner;

(d) the amount of time to be spent or that has been spent in respect of work to be completed or that has been completed and why it is considered to be fair, reasonable and proportionate;

(e) what is likely to be and has been achieved, the benefits that are likely to and have accrued as a consequence of the work that is to be or has been completed, the manner in which the work required in respect of the appointment is progressing and what, in the opinion of the office-holder, remains to be achieved.

21.4.2 Details sufficient for the Court to determine the application by reference to the criteria which are required to be taken into account by reference to the Insolvency Rules and any other applicable enactments or rules relevant to the fixing of the remuneration.

21.4.3 A statement of the total number of hours of work undertaken or to be undertaken in respect of which the remuneration is sought, together with a breakdown of such hours by individual member of staff and individual tasks or categories of tasks to be performed or that have been performed. Where appropriate, a proportionate level of detail should also be given of:

(a) the tasks or categories of tasks to be undertaken as a proportion of the total amount of work to be undertaken in respect of which the remuneration is sought and the tasks or categories of tasks that have been undertaken as a proportion of the total amount of work that has been undertaken in respect of which the remuneration is sought; and

(b) the tasks or categories of task to be completed by individual members of staff or grade of personnel including the office-holder as a proportion of the total amount of work to be completed by all members of staff including the office-holder in respect of which the remuneration is sought and the tasks or categories of task that have been completed by individual members of staff or grade of personnel as a proportion of the total amount of work that has been completed by all members of staff including the office-holder in respect of which the remuneration is sought.

21.4.4 A statement of the total amount to be or likely to be charged for the work to be undertaken or that has been undertaken in respect of which the remuneration is sought which should include:

(a) a breakdown of such amounts by individual member of staff and individual task or categories of task performed or to be performed;

(b) details of the time expended or to be expended and the remuneration charged or to be charged in respect of each individual task or category of task as a proportion (respectively) of the total time expended or to be expended and the total remuneration charged or to be charged.

In respect of an application pursuant to which some or all of the amount of the office-holder's remuneration is to be fixed on a basis other than time properly spent, the office-holder shall provide (for the purposes of comparison) the same details as are required by this paragraph 19.4.4, but on the basis of what would have been charged had they been seeking remuneration on the basis of the time properly spent by the officeholder and their staff.

21.4.5 Details of each individual to be engaged or who has been engaged in work in respect of the appointment and in respect of which the remuneration is sought, including details of their relevant experience, training, qualifications and the level of their seniority.

21.4.6 An explanation of:

(a) the steps, if any, to be taken or that have been taken by the office-holder to avoid duplication of effort and cost in respect of the work to be completed or that has been completed in respect of which the remuneration is sought;

(b) the steps to be taken or that have been taken to ensure that the work to be completed or that has been completed is to be or was undertaken by individuals of appropriate experience and seniority relative to the nature of the work to be or that has been undertaken.

21.4.7 Details of the individual rates charged by the office-holder and members of their staff in respect of the work to be completed or that has been completed and in respect of which the remuneration is sought. Such details should include:

(a) a general explanation of the policy adopted in relation to the fixing or calculation of such rates and the recording of time spent;

(b) where, exceptionally, the office-holder seeks remuneration in respect of time spent by secretaries, cashiers or other administrative staff whose work would otherwise be regarded as an overhead cost forming a component part of the rates charged by the office-holder and members of their staff, a detailed explanation as to why such costs should be allowed or should be provided.

21.4.8 Where the remuneration application is in respect of a period of time during which the charge-out rates of the office-holder and/or members of their staff engaged in work in respect of the appointment have increased, an explanation of the nature, extent and reason for such increase and the date when such increase took effect.

21.4.9 Details of any basis or amount of remuneration previously fixed or approved in relation to the appointment (whether by the Court or otherwise) including in particular the bases or amounts that were previously sought to be fixed or approved and the bases or amounts that were in fact fixed or approved and the method by which such amounts were fixed or approved.

21.4.10 Where the application is for approval to draw remuneration in excess of the total amount set out in the fees estimate, their evidence must exhibit a copy of the fees estimate and address the matters listed in rule 18.30(3).

21.4.11 In order that the Court may be able to consider the views of any persons who the office-holder considers have an interest in the assets that are under their control and of any other persons who are required by the Insolvency Rules to be notified of the hearing of the application, the office-holder must provide details of:

(a) the names and contact details for all such persons;

(b) what (if any) consultation has taken place between the office-holder and those persons and if no such consultation has taken place, an explanation as to the reason why;

(c) the number and value of the interests of the persons consulted including details of the proportion (by number and by value) of the interests of such persons by reference to the entirety of those persons having an interest in the assets under the control of the office-holder.

21.4.12 Such other relevant information as the office-holder considers, in the circumstances, ought to be provided to the Court.

21.5 This paragraph applies to applications where some or all of the remuneration of the office-holder is to be fixed and/or approved on a basis other than time properly spent. On such applications in addition to the matters referred to in paragraph 21.4, the office-holder shall:

(a) Provide a full description of the reasons for remuneration being sought by reference to the basis contended for.

(b) Where the remuneration is sought to be fixed by reference to a percentage of the value of the property with which the office-holder has to deal or of the assets which are realised or distributed, provide a full explanation of the basis upon which any percentage rates to be applied to the values of such property or the assets realised and/or distributed have been chosen.

(c) Provide a statement that to the best of the office-holder's belief the percentage rates or other bases by reference to which some or all of the remuneration is to be fixed are similar to the percentage rates or other bases that are applied or have been applied in respect of other appointments of a similar nature.

(d) Provide a comparison of the amount to be charged by reference to the basis contended for and the amount that would otherwise have been charged by reference to the other available bases of remuneration, including by reference to rule 18.22 and Schedule 11 to the Insolvency Rules (scale of fees).

21.6 The witness evidence may exclude matters set out in paragraph 21.4 above but an explanation as to why a decision to exclude such material should be included in the witness evidence.

21.7 The evidence placed before the Court by the office-holder in respect of any remuneration application should also include the following documents:

(a) a copy of the most recent receipts and payments account;

(b) copies of any reports by the office-holder to the persons having an interest in the assets under their control relevant to the period for which the remuneration sought to be fixed and approved relates;

(c) any fees estimate, details of anticipated expenses or other relevant information given or required to be given to the creditors in relation to remuneration by the office-holder pursuant to the Insolvency Rules;

(d) any other schedules or such other documents providing the information referred to in paragraphs 19.4 above, where these are likely to be of assistance to the Court in considering the application;

(e) evidence of any consultation or copies of any relevant communications with those persons having an interest in the assets under the control of office-holder in relation to the remuneration of the office-holder.

21.8 On any remuneration application the Court may make an order allowing payments of remuneration to be made on account subject to final approval whether by the Court or otherwise.

21.9 Unless otherwise ordered by the Court (or as may otherwise be provided for in any enactment or rules of procedure), the costs of and occasioned by an application for the fixing and/or approval of the remuneration of an office-holder, including those of any assessor, shall be paid out of the assets under the control of the office-holder.

PART SEVEN: UNFAIR PREJUDICE PETITIONS, WINDING UP AND VALIDATION ORDERS

22. Unfair Prejudice Petitions

22.1 Attention is drawn to the undesirability of asking as a matter of course for a winding up order as an alternative to an order under s.994 of the 2006 Act. The petition should not ask for a winding up order unless that is the remedy which the petitioner prefers, or it is thought that it may be the only remedy to which the petitioner is entitled.

22.2 Whenever a winding up order is asked for in a contributory's petition, the petition must state whether the petitioner consents or objects to a validation order under s.127 of the Insolvency Act 1986 in the standard form. If the petitioner objects, the written evidence in support must contain a short statement of the petitioner's reasons.

22.3 If the petitioner objects to a validation order in the standard form but consents to such an order in a modified form, the petition must set out the form of order to which the petitioner consents, and the written evidence in support must contain a short statement of the petitioner's reasons for seeking the modification.

22.4 If the petition contains a statement that the petitioner consents to a validation order, whether in the standard or a modified form, but the petitioner changes their mind before the first hearing of the petition, the petitioner must notify the respondents and may apply on notice to the court for an order directing that no validation order or a modified order only (as the case may be) shall be made by the Court, but validating dispositions made without notice of the order made by the Court.

22.5 If the petition contains a statement that the petitioner consents to validation order, whether in the standard or a modified form, the Court shall without further enquiry make such an order at the first hearing unless an order to the contrary has been made by the Court in the meantime.

22.6 If the petition contains a statement that the petitioner objects to a validation order in the standard form, the company may apply (in the case of urgency, without notice) to the Court for an order.

Index

A

ABSCONDING
bankruptcy, offence, [1.437]
contributories, power to arrest, [1.159]
ACCOUNTS
administrative receivership, abstract of receipts and payments to be sent to registrar of companies, [6.198]
Insolvency Services Account, [1.514], [12.29]
insurance company, winding up
audit, [7.1501]
records, maintenance, [7.1499]
Investment Account, [1.515]–[1.517]. *See also* INVESTMENT ACCOUNT
liquidator, [8.38]
special manager, [6.225]
trustee in bankruptcy
audit, [8.53]
provision, [8.53]
separate, if carrying on business, [8.51]
ADJOURNMENT
creditors and contributories, meetings of, [7.144], [7.598]
creditors' meeting, of. *See* CREDITORS' MEETING
hearings, of
bank insolvency, [7.291]
building society insolvency, [7.738]
cross-border insolvency, principal applications, [3.316], [3.319]
public-private partnership application in proceedings, [7.2357]
water administration, special administration, [7.2704]
investment bank, special administration meetings, [7.1790]–[7.1792]
Scotland. *See* SCOTLAND
winding-up. *See* WINDING UP
ADMINISTRATION
administrative receiver appointed, circumstances in which petition dismissed, [1.13], [1.575]
administrator. *See* ADMINISTRATOR
air traffic, [1.13], [7.5], [7.12]
applicable law, [1.13]
application
administrative receivership existing, dismissal of administration application, [1.575]
contents, [6.114]
ADMINISTRATION – *cont.*
application – *cont.*
directors, by, [6.115]
effect, [1.13]
filing, [6.118]
hearing, [6.123]
holder of floating charge, by, [1.575], [6.122]
notice of other insolvency proceedings, [6.121]
notice to enforcement agents, [6.120]
petition, eligible petitioners, [1.13]
service, [6.119]
supervisor of CVA, by, [6.116]
witness statement supporting, [6.117]
application for order
court, powers, [1.575]
procedure, [1.575]
banks, former authorised institutions, Banking Act 1987, [1.13], [7.18], [7.20]
books, papers, records, property etc to which company may be entitled, delivery/surrender etc to office-holder, [1.239]
building societies, [1.13], [7.455], [7.468]
cessation, [1.575]
charged property
disposal, [6.160]
floating charge, subject to, [1.250], [1.575], [2.10], [2.26], [3.290]
See also floating charge, *below*
non-floating charge, [1.575], [6.160]
claim, quantification
discounts, [6.744]
foreign currency, debt in, [6.745]
interest provable, [6.747]
mutual credits and set-off, [6.748]
payments of periodical nature, [6.746]
secured creditors
realisation/surrender of security, [6.743]
redemption, [6.741]
test of security's value, [6.742]
surrender for non-disclosure, [6.740]
See also distributions to creditors: proving a debt, *below*
clearing houses, [1.13], [17.85]
company records, disposal of, [8.25]
compensation scheme, Financial Services and Markets Act 2000
administrator
appointment by company/directors, [17.193]

ADMINISTRATION – *cont.*
compensation scheme, Financial Services and Markets Act 2000 – *cont.*
administrator – *cont.*
report to Authority, [17.191]
Authority, powers, [17.189], [17.192]
court, power to make, [1.13]
creditors' claims, [6.726]–[6.749]
creditors' committee, [1.13], [1.575], [6.824]–[6.852]. *See also* CREDITORS' COMMITTEE
creditors' meeting, [1.13], [1.575], [6.789]–[6.807]. *See also* CREDITORS' MEETING
creditors' voluntary liquidation, moving from administration to, [1.575], [6.171]
debt, proving, [6.726]–[6.735]. *See also* distributions to creditors, *below*
deceased person's estate, [11.1]–[11.10]. *See also* DECEASED PERSON
decisions, procedures for, [6.771]–[6.776]
meetings. See meetings, generally, *below*
notices, [6.777], [6.780]–[6.784]
remuneration, [6.785]
requisitioned decisions, [6.787], [6.788]
venue, [6.779]
voting, [6.778]
discharge where administration ends, [1.13], [1.575]
dissolution, company, after, [1.575]
distributions to creditors
debts, insolvent company to act equally, [6.736]
generally, [6.750]–[6.769]
proving debt
admission for dividend, [6.731]
appeal against decision on, [6.732]
costs, [6.729]
exclusion by court, [6.735]
inspection, proofs, [6.730]
proof, submission, [6.727]
rejection for dividend, [6.731]
requirements, [6.728]
withdrawal, [6.734]
dividend
assignment, right to, [6.767]
cancellation, [6.757]
declaration, [6.758]
disqualification from, [6.766]
non payment, [6.769]
notice of declaration, [6.759]
postponement, [6.757]
sole or final, [6.762]
unclaimed, payment of, [8.26]
EU Regulation, conversion into winding up, [6.911], [6.912]
effect, [1.13], [1.575]
ending, [6.164]–[6.172]
automatic, [1.575], [6.166]
court, by
administrator, application, [1.575]
creditor, application, [1.575]
notice to
Registrar, [1.575], [6.166], [6.167]

ADMINISTRATION – *cont.*
energy administration order. *See* ENERGY ADMINISTRATION ORDER
Enterprise Act 2002
special administration regimes, [2.10], [2.21]
enters administration, meaning, [1.576]
exclusions from court's power to make, [1.13]
expenses, [6.161]–[6.163]
extension, application for, [6.165]
extortionate credit transactions, prior adjustment, [1.249], [2.10]
FCA and PRA, participation in proceedings, [18.270]
floating charge prior to
administrator, powers to deal, charged property as if no charge, [1.575]
avoidance, conditions, [1.250], [2.10], [2.26], [3.290]
fraudulent trading, [1.252]
proceedings, [1.254]
gas, water, electricity etc supplies, management, [1.237], [1.238]
hire-purchase property, [1.575]
in administration, meaning, [1.575]
insurers, [1.13], [7.1565]–[7.1569]
intervention by floating chargeholder, [1.575]
investment bank. *See* INVESTMENT BANK
investment exchanges, [1.13], [17.85]
lien on books etc, unenforceable against office-holder, [1.251], [2.10], [2.26]
market charges
enforcement, [17.78]
persons to whom granted, [1.13], [17.85]
meetings, generally
adjournment
absence of chair, [6.794]
chair, by, [6.792]
proofs in, [6.795]
removal of liquidator/trustee, [6.793]
chair, [6.790], [6.791]
exclusions from, [6.805]–[6.807]
quorum, [6.789]
records, [6.809]
remote attendance, [6.811]
suspension, [6.796]
voting, [6.797]–[6.804]
creditors' rights, [6.797]
contributories' rights, [6.808]
requisite majorities, [6.803], [6.808]
scheme manager's rights, [6.798]
moratorium, insolvency proceedings, [1.575]
nature, [1.575]
non-company, applicable to under Enterprise Act 2002, [2.12]
notice
order, of, [6.126]
petition, of, to whom required, [1.13]
statement of affairs, requiring, [6.140]
notification, [1.13]
offences, penalties, [1.575]
order, contents, [6.124]
pending winding up petition, dismissal, [1.575]
petition presented before 15 September 2003, [1.13], [2.26]

ADMINISTRATION – *cont.*
postal. *See* POSTAL ADMINISTRATION
pre-administration costs, [6.163]
preferences, prior, application for adjustment by office-holder, [1.244], [1.245], [1.246]
preferential creditor, protection, [1.575]
procedure generally, rules, [6.112]–[6.181]
process, [1.575]
property excluded from bankrupt's estate, vesting by trustee in bankruptcy, [1.372]
protection, interests, creditors/members, [1.13]
proving debt, [6.726]–[6.735]. *See also* distributions to creditors, *above*
public private partnerships, [1.13], [7.2300], [7.2307]
purposes, [1.13], [1.575]
railway companies, [1.13], [7.2437], [7.2448]
Secretary of State, information to, [8.25]
secured creditor, protection, [1.575]
special administration regimes, [1.13], [2.10]
statement of company's affairs
contents, [6.141]
disclosure, limited, [6.155]–[6.159]
expenses of, [6.145]
filing, [6.143]
notice of, [6.140]
release from duty to submit, [6.144]
requirement, [1.575], [6.140]
verification, [6.142]
time limits, extension, [1.575]
transitional provisions/savings, [1.596], [2.26]
unclaimed dividends or other money, payment of, [8.26]
undervalue, prior transaction at, application for adjustment by office-holder, [1.243], [1.245], [1.246], [2.10], [2.26]
variation, [1.13]
water or sewerage undertakers, [1.13], [7.2619]–[7.2621], [7.2625]
winding up
by court on discharge, appointment of liquidator by court, [1.141]
conversion into, EU Regulation, [6.911], [6.912]
public interest, [1.575]
withdrawal, petition, [1.13]
wrongful trading, [1.253]
proceedings, [1.254]
bank. *See* BANK ADMINISTRATION
county court, in
application for, [17.28]
bankruptcy petition, presentation of, [17.24]
debt management arrangements, effect on, [17.30]
debts becoming due, [17.50]
duration, [17.29]
variation of, [17.37]
exclusions, [17.52]
existing county court proceedings, stay of, [17.33]
gas or electricity supply, requirement not to stop, [17.27]
inability to pay debts, meaning, [17.47]

ADMINISTRATION – *cont.*
county court, in – *cont.*
information, duty of debtor to provide, [17.31]
failure to comply, offence of, [17.32]
interest requirement, [17.26]
interpretation, [17.45]
meaning, [17.19]
money paid into court, appropriation of, [17.34]
notifiable events, [17.42]
power to make, [17.20]
qualifying debts
calculation of, [17.48]
failure to take account of all of, [17.43]
interpretation, [17.46]
regulations, [17.53]
remedies other than bankruptcy, requirement as to, [17.25]
repayment, requirement, [17.23]
revocation
duty of court, [17.39]
effect of, [17.41]
power of, [17.40]
scheduling debts
declared, [17.21]
de-scheduling, [17.38]
new, [17.22]
repayment, discharge on, [17.35]
scheduling and de-scheduling, [17.51]
surplus income, calculation of, [17.49]
variation of, [17.36]
insurers, relating to
Insolvency Act 1986, application of, [7.1619], [7.1623]
Insolvency Rules 1986, application of, [7.1620]
Insolvency (Scotland) Rules 1986, application of, [7.1621]
meaning, [1.574]
revocation against individual with disabilities, [1.546]

ADMINISTRATIVE RECEIVER
abstract of receipts and payments sent to registrar of companies, [6.198]
administration order, petition after appointment, [1.13], [1.575]
agent of company, as, [1.30]
appointment
acceptance, [6.182]
confirmation of acceptance, [6.182]
notice and advertisement of, [6.186]
books, papers, records, property etc to which company may be entitled, delivery or surrender etc to office-holder, [1.239]
capital market arrangement, appointment, [1.60]
contracts, liability, [1.30]
creditors' committee
chairman, [6.838]
establishment, formalities, [6.828]
formal defects, [6.850]
functions, [6.825]
information, [6.845], [6.846]
invitation to form, [6.196]
meetings, [6.837]–[6.844]

ADMINISTRATIVE RECEIVER – *cont.*
creditors' committee – *cont.*
member
eligibility, [6.827]
expenses, [6.847]
numbers, [6.826]
removal, [6.835]
resignation, [6.833]
membership
changes, [6.830]
vacancies, [6.831], [6.832]
quorum, [6.839]
death, [6.200]
definition, [1.15], [1.267]
disposal of charged property, [6.197]
exceptions to prohibition, appointment
capital market arrangement, [1.60], [1.578]
capital market investment, [1.578]
financial market
collateral security charge, [1.65]
market charge, [1.65]
system-charge, [1.65]
project finance, [1.64]
public private partnership, [1.61]
railway companies, protected, [1.67]
Secretary of State, powers to create, [1.68]
social landlord, registered, [1.66]
urban regeneration project, [1.63]
utility project with step-in rights, [1.62]
water industry company, [1.67]
financial market, appointment, conditions, [1.65]
gas, water, electricity etc supplies, management, [1.237]
indemnity
contracts, liability, [1.30]
from company assets, [1.13]
information to be given by, when appointed, [1.32]
powers
disposal, charged property etc, [1.29]
general, [1.28], [1.576]
prohibition, appointment
administration order in force, [1.13]
floating charge holder not to appoint
exceptions, [1.60]–[1.68]. *See also* exceptions to prohibition, appointment, *above*
principle, [1.59]
project finance, appointment, [1.64]
public-private partnership, appointment, [1.61]
qualified insolvency practitioner, requirement, [1.234]
railway companies, protected, appointment, [1.67]
remuneration/expenses, [6.886]–[6.890]
charge on company property, [1.13]
vacation, office, [1.31]
report to creditors
administrative receiver, [6.194], [6.195]
receiver other than administrative receiver, prescribed part
powers to deal with, [6.205]
value, [6.204]
report to registrar
administrative receiver, [6.194]

ADMINISTRATIVE RECEIVER – *cont.*
report to registrar – *cont.*
contents, [1.34]
copies, to whom required, [1.34]
creditors' committee, attendance before, [1.35]
disclosure restrictions, [1.34]
non-compliance, penalties, [1.34]
time limit, [1.34]
resignation, [1.32], [6.199]
security
requirements, [6.185]
social landlord, registered, appointment, [1.66]
statement of affairs submitted to
contents, [6.188]
delivery, [6.188]
disclosure, limited, [6.193]
expenses of, [6.192]
extension, time to submit, [6.191]
notice requiring, [6.187]
persons required, [1.33], [6.187]
retention, [6.190]
statement of concurrence, [6.189]
verification, [6.190]
unclaimed dividends or other money, payment of, [8.27]
urban regeneration project with step-in rights, [1.63]
utility project with step-in rights, appointment, [1.62]
vacation of office
administration order, after, [1.13]
ceasing to be qualified, [6.201]
notice, to whom required, [6.201], [6.202]
removal, court order, [1.31]
resignation, notice, [1.31], [6.199]
validity, acts of, [1.236]
VAT bad debt relief, certificate of insolvency
water industry company, appointment, [1.67]

ADMINISTRATOR
agent of company, as, [1.575]
appointment
advertisement or announcement of, [1.575], [6.138]
commencement, [1.575]
company, by, [1.575], [6.134]–[6.137]
court, by, [1.575], [6.114]–[6.126]
directors, by, [1.575], [6.134]–[6.137]
generally, [1.13], [1.575]
holder of floating charge, by, [1.575], [6.127]–[6.133]
invalid, indemnity, [1.575]
notice of, [1.575], [6.127]–[6.129]
restrictions, power to appoint, [1.575]
ceasing to be qualified, [1.575], [6.177]
company or directors, appointment by, [18.271]
company voluntary arrangement, proposal for company in administration, [1.1]. *See also* COMPANY VOLUNTARY ARRANGEMENT
conduct of company, challenge to, [1.575]
consent to act, [6.113]
death, [6.178]
distribution to creditor, [1.575]
duties, general, [1.13], [1.575]

ADMINISTRATOR – *cont.*
information to be given by, [1.13]
liabilities on vacation, office, [1.575]
meaning, [1.575]
misfeasance, [1.575]
powers
general, [1.13], [1.575], [1.576]
to deal with charged property etc, [1.13]
progress reports, [6.854]–[6.865]
proposals, [6.146]–[6.154]
approval, [6.149]
consideration, creditors' meeting, [1.13]
creditors' committee, power to require attendance, [1.13]. *See also* CREDITORS' COMMITTEE
revision, [6.153]
statement, [1.13]
substantial revisions, approval, creditors, [1.13]
proposals to registrar of companies, [1.575]
release, time, [1.13]
removal from office
application to court, [6.176]
grounds, [1.575]
remuneration, [6.867]–[6.890]
replacement
application to replace, [6.179]
appointment, notification and advertisement, [6.180]
generally, [1.575], [6.173]–[6.181]
resignation
generally, [1.575]
grounds for, [6.173]
notice of, [6.175]
notice of intention, [6.174]
rights of action, power to assign, [1.255]
Scotland. *See* SCOTLAND
statement, [1.13]
statement of affairs to be submitted to, [1.13]
status, [1.575]
substitution, competing floating charge holder, [1.575]
vacation, office, [1.13], [1.575], [6.177], [6.181]
validity of acts, presumption, [1.575]

AFFIDAVITS/WITNESS STATEMENT
cross-border insolvency, application
foreign proceedings, recognition, [3.312]
foreign representative, replacement, [3.314]
review, court order, [3.315]
UNCITRAL model law, relief under, [3.313]
energy administration application, [7.877], [7.879]
railway administration order, to support petition, [7.2455], [7.2457], [7.2530]
statement of affairs, verification
creditors voluntary winding up, directors, [1.96]
submitted to administrative receiver, [1.33]
winding up by court, persons required, [1.132]
winding up proceedings
statement of affairs, [1.132]
swearing, UK/overseas, [1.204]

AFTER-ACQUIRED PROPERTY
bankruptcy, [6.584], [6.585]

AFTER-ACQUIRED PROPERTY – *cont.*
claim for bankrupt's estate by trustee in bankruptcy, notice in writing, [1.375], [1.378]

AGENT
administrative receiver, of company, as, [1.30]
administrator, of company, as, [1.575]

AGRICULTURAL MARKETING BOARD
winding up by agricultural marketing scheme, [1.224]–[1.233]

AIR TRAFFIC SERVICES
air traffic administration orders
duty to make, [7.2]
generally, [1.13], [7.1]–[7.15]
government help, [7.6]
guarantee re government help, [7.7]
licence companies, protection, [7.1]
Northern Ireland. *See* NORTHERN IRELAND
petitions etc, [7.5]
power to make, [7.3]
schemes, [7.14]

AIRCRAFT
credit institution, reorganisation/winding up, effect of EC Directive, [3.196]
debtor, rights subject to registration in, EC Regulation, [3.47]
insurance undertakings, reorganisation or winding up, effect of EC Directive, [3.107]

ANNULMENT
bankruptcy. *See* BANKRUPTCY
individual voluntary arrangement, order on default
advertisement, [6.430]
application
bankrupt, [6.426]
official receiver, [6.427]
final account, trustee, [6.431]
generally, [6.426]–[6.431]
notice, [6.429]

APPEALS
cross-border insolvency, [3.321]
energy administration order, [7.1000], [7.1001]
individual insolvency, from courts exercising insolvency jurisdiction, [1.455]
jurisdiction, [6.712]–[6.716]
winding up by court, Scotland. *See* SCOTLAND

APPRENTICESHIPS ETC
bankruptcy of person to whom apprenticed, powers of trustee in bankruptcy
termination, [1.426]
transfer, [1.426]

ARBITRATION AGREEMENT
bankruptcy of party, powers of court, [1.428]

ARTICLED CLERK.
See APPRENTICESHIPS ETC

ASSIGNMENT
book debts, of, prior to bankruptcy, [1.422]

ASSOCIATE
meaning, [1.265], [1.557]
person 'connected' with a company, [1.265]

ATTACHMENT ORDER
bankruptcy
enforcement procedures, [1.424]

ATTACHMENT ORDER – *cont.*
bankruptcy – *cont.*
income payments
agreement, effect, [1.380]
court order, effect, [1.379]
winding up, registered company
by court, avoidance after commencement, [1.129]
effect, [1.187]

B

BAD DEBT RELIEF
Scotland. *See* SCOTLAND: receiver
BANK ADMINISTRATION
administration order
application for
application of rules, [7.393]
Bank of England witness statement, [7.397]
contents of, [7.394], [7.395]
filing, [7.398], [7.399]
generally, [7.71]
grounds for, [7.72]
hearing, [7.407]
notification of, [7.405]
service of, [7.400]–[7.404]
venue for hearing, [7.406]
costs, [7.411]
grounds for making, [7.73]
making of, [7.408]
meaning, [7.70]
notice of, [7.409], [7.410]
application of provisions, [7.412]
applied provisions, table of, [7.74]
bank administrator
additional joint, appointment of, [7.433]
Objective 1 Stage, [7.413]
Objective 2 Stage, [7.414]–[7.420]
eligibility for appointment, [7.70]
nomination of, [7.71]
powers and duties of, [7.74]
proposed, statement of, [7.396]
provisional, appointment of, [7.426]–[7.432]
removal, Objective 1 Stage, [7.425]
reports to creditors, [7.421]–[7.424]
bridge bank
supporting, objective of, [7.67]
duration, [7.68]
court procedure and practice
application of provisions, [7.437]
file, right to inspect, [7.439]–[7.444]
title of proceedings, [7.438]
effect of, [7.74]
end of
dissolution on, [7.436]
successful rescue, [7.435]
features of, [7.65]
forms, [7.392]
Insolvency Rules, application of, [7.445]–[7.448]
interpretation, [7.389], [7.390]

BANK ADMINISTRATION – *cont.*
objectives
bridge bank, supporting, [7.67]
duration, [7.68]
generally, [7.66]
normal administration, [7.69]
private sector purchaser, supporting, [7.67]
duration, [7.68]
overview, [7.391], [7.65]
private sector purchaser
supporting, objective of, [7.67]
duration, [7.68]
procedure, [7.65]
protected deposits, disapplication of set-off for, [7.434]
provisions applying, [4.41]
modifications to legislation
Companies Act 2006, [7.89]
Dormant Bank and Building Society Accounts Act 2008, [7.90]
Finance (No 2) Act 1992, [7.87]
FSMA 2000, [7.88]
general, legislation subject to, [7.86]
Pension Protection Fund (Entry Rules) Regulations 2005, [7.91]
Scotland. *See* SCOTLAND
BANK INSOLVENCY
administration order
application, conditions for determining, [7.57]
liquidator, application by, [7.51]
administrator, conditions for appointment, [7.57]
appeals, [7.315]–[7.317]
application of rules, [7.95]
applications to court
adjournment of hearings, [7.291]
application of rules, [7.280]
application to disapply provisions, [7.283]
evidence, use of, [7.288]
filing and service, [7.284]
form and content of, [7.282]
hearing, [7.287]
hearings without notice, [7.286]
interpretation, [7.281]
notice of, [7.285]
reports, use of, [7.290]
witness statements, filing and service, [7.289]
applied provisions, table of, [7.40]
attendance, rights of, [7.319]
bank liquidator
accounts, submission of, [7.124]
administration order, application for, [7.51]
appointment
advertisement, [7.178]
authentication of, [7.177]
registration, [7.178]
authentication of appointment, [7.109]
calls, [7.253]–[7.256]
collection and distribution of assets
debts of insolvent company, ranking, [7.231]
dividend, supplementary provision as to, [7.232]
enforced delivery up of property, [7.235]
final distribution, [7.236]

BANK INSOLVENCY – *cont.*
bank liquidator – *cont.*
collection and distribution of assets – *cont.*
general duties, [7.228]
general powers, [7.234]
general qualification on powers, [7.229]
manner of distributing, [7.230]
unsold assets, division of, [7.233]
company voluntary arrangements, proposal for, [7.50]
completion of winding up, release on, [7.188], [7.189]
court, removal by, [7.45]
creditors, removal by, [7.46]
deceased, [7.199]
disclaimer, [7.237]–[7.244]
disqualification, [7.47]
duties on vacation of office, [7.203]
eligibility for appointment, [7.31]
intention to vacate office, notice of, [7.202]
liquidation committee, obligations to, [7.210]
list of contributories, settlement of, [7.245]–[7.252]
loss of qualification, [7.200]
objectives, [7.36]
officer of the court, as, [7.42]
powers, [7.41]
powers and duties, [7.40]
release, [7.48]
removal
advertisement, [7.185]
court, by, [7.186]
meeting of creditors, [7.182]
power of court to regulate meetings, [7.183]
procedure, [7.184]
release on, [7.187]
remuneration
court, recourse to, [7.195]
creditors' meeting, recourse to, [7.194]
entitlement to, [7.191]
excessive, creditors' claiming, [7.196]
fixing, [7.190]
generally, [7.175]
matters affecting, [7.193]
Objective 1, primacy of, [7.197]
realisation of assets on behalf of chargeholder, on, [7.192]
replacement, [7.198], [7.49]
replacement by creditors, [7.176]
report by, [7.126]
reports to liquidation committee, [7.222]
resignation
action following acceptance of, [7.180]
advertisement, [7.181]
creditors' meeting, notification, [7.179]
generally, [7.201], [7.44]
release on, [7.187]
term of appointment, [7.43]
winding up, application for, [7.52]
witness statement, [7.108]
bank, meaning, [7.95], [7.28]
bank with prohibited name, leave to act as director, etc, of, [7.273]–[7.279]

BANK INSOLVENCY – *cont.*
banks not regulated by PRA, [7.63]
capital, return of, [7.269], [7.270]
company representation, [7.331]
company voluntary arrangements, proposal for, [7.50]
conclusion of, [7.271], [7.272]
concurrent proceedings and remedies, restriction on, [7.320]
confidentiality of documents, [7.363]
copy documents, [7.365], [7.366]
costs and expenses
application for, [7.308]
application of rules, [7.302]
detailed procedure, requirement to assess by, [7.303], [7.304]
final certificate, [7.310]
generally, [7.352]
officers, of, [7.305]
paid otherwise than from insolvent estate, [7.306]
responsible insolvency practitioner, award against, [7.307]
witnesses, of, [7.309]
court
co-operation between, [7.62]
meaning, [7.29]
records and returns, [7.298]–[7.301]
rules and practice applying, [7.318]
creditors and contributories, information to
bank liquidator, report by, [7.126]
creditors, meaning, [7.127]
reporting, general rule, [7.130]
statement of affairs dispensed with, where, [7.129]
statement of affairs lodged, where, [7.128]
declaration and payment of dividend, [7.338]–[7.350]
directors, disqualification, [7.59]
dissolution
date, deferment of, [7.53]
liquidator, application by, [7.52]
effect of, [7.40]
enforcement procedures, [7.294]–[7.297]
examination of persons involved in, [7.332]–[7.337]
false claim of status as creditor, [7.369]
features of, [7.27]
forms, [7.97]
further disclosure, [7.125]
further information and disclosure, [7.323]
insolvency law, application of, [7.60]
insolvency practitioner, security, [7.358]
Insolvency Services Account, payments into, [7.61]
interpretation, [7.95], [7.374]–[7.383], [7.30]
judgment creditor, insolvency of, [7.370]
limited disclosure, order for, [7.121]
liquidation committee
application of rules, [7.206]
chair, [7.212]
composition where creditors paid in full, [7.225]
contributories, established by, [7.209]

BANK INSOLVENCY – *cont.*
liquidation committee – *cont.*
dealings by, [7.224]
establishment of, [7.37]
expenses, [7.223]
final meeting, [7.52]
formal defects, [7.227]
formalities of establishment, [7.208]
functions of, [7.37]
initial duties of, [7.110]
liquidator's report, [7.222]
meetings, [7.211]–[7.214], [7.38]
members of, [7.207], [7.37]
objectives, recommendation of, [7.39]
obligations of liquidator to, [7.210]
removal, [7.217]
resignation, [7.215]
resolutions by post, [7.221]
Secretary of State, functions vested in, [7.226]
termination of membership, [7.216]
vacancy in, [7.218], [7.219]
voting rights and resolutions, [7.220]
list of creditors, right to, [7.368]
meetings of creditors and contributories
admission and rejection of proof, [7.147]
attendance by bank's personnel, [7.138]
chair, [7.135], [7.143]
entitlement to vote, [7.145], [7.146]
evidence at, [7.356]
expenses, [7.141]
first
business at, [7.133]
summoning, [7.132]
general power to call, [7.134]
notice by advertisement, [7.139]
quorum, [7.355]
record of proceedings, [7.148]
requisitioned, [7.136], [7.137]
resolutions, [7.142]
suspension and adjournment, [7.144]
venue, [7.140]
non-receipt of notice of meeting, [7.367]
notices, [7.354]
offences, [7.372]
office copies of documents, [7.324]
order
advertisement, [7.108]
alternative to winding up or administration, as, [7.54]
application for
certificate of compliance, [7.105]
filing, [7.99]
grounds for, [7.33]
leave to withdraw, [7.106]
person making, [7.32]
persons to receive, [7.102], [7.104]
service of, [7.100], [7.101]
verification of, [7.103]
witness statement in opposition, [7.107]
commencement, [7.35]
grounds for making, [7.34]
making of, [7.108]
meaning, [7.31]

BANK INSOLVENCY – *cont.*
order – *cont.*
other procedures, exclusion of, [7.56]
transmission, [7.108]
overview, [7.96], [7.27]
provisions applying, [4.40], [7.86]
payment into court, [7.322]
payment of costs out of assets, order of, [7.262]–[7.268]
persons incapable of managing own affairs, [7.311]–[7.314]
procedure, [7.27]
proof of debts
admission and rejection of proofs for dividend, [7.156]
appeals, [7.157]
claim established by witness statement, [7.152]
contents of, [7.151]
cost of proving, [7.153]
debts payable at future time, [7.169]
discounts, [7.163]
eligible depositors, disapplication of set off, [7.165]
expunging by court, [7.159]
foreign currency debts, [7.166]
forms, [7.150]
inspection of, liquidator allowing, [7.154]
interest, [7.168]
meaning, [7.149]
mutual credits and set-off, [7.164]
negotiable instruments, [7.161]
new bank liquidator appointed, where, [7.155]
periodical nature, payments of, [7.167]
quantum, estimation of, [7.160]
secured creditors, [7.162]
withdrawal or variation, [7.158]
provable debts, [7.353]
provisional bank liquidator
appointment of, [7.112]
notice of, [7.113]
order of, [7.114]
termination, [7.118]
remuneration, [7.117]
security, [7.115], [7.116]
proxies, [7.325]–[7.330]
regulation of matters, [7.351]
Scotland. *See* SCOTLAND
Secretary of State, documents issuing from, [7.357]
secured creditors
non-disclosure, surrender for, [7.171]
proof of debts, [7.162]
realisation of security, [7.174]
redemption by liquidator, [7.172]
test of security's value, [7.173]
value of security, [7.170]
security in court, [7.321]
service of documents, [7.360]–[7.362]
shorthand writers, [7.292], [7.293]
solicitation, rule against, [7.205]
special manager
accounting, [7.260]
appointment, [7.257]

BANK INSOLVENCY – *cont.*
special manager – *cont.*
remuneration, [7.257]
security, [7.258], [7.259]
termination of appointment, [7.261]
special resolution regime, [7.25], [7.26]
statement of affairs
expenses of, [7.123]
extension of time for, [7.122]
notice requiring, [7.119]
release from duty to submit, [7.122]
verification and filing, [7.120]
staying of, [7.131]
time limits, [7.98], [7.359]
transactions, power of court to set aside, [7.204]
voluntary arrangement, expenses of, [7.111]
voluntary winding up, resolution for
approval of court for, [7.55]
conditions for, [7.57]
winding up
liquidator, application by, [7.52]
notice to regulators, [7.58]
petition, conditions for determining, [7.57]
Scotland. *See* SCOTLAND
BANK OF ENGLAND
building society, modification of provisions to facilitate financial assistance to, [17.345]
partial property transfer, third party compensation for
application of regulations, [9.85]
creditors, valuations provided by, [9.92]
independent valuer, appointment of, [9.87]
insolvency process, choice of, [9.89]
insolvency treatment, assessment of, [9.87]
interim payments, [9.91]
interpretation, [9.84]
third party compensation order, requirement to include, [9.85]
valuation principles, [9.90], [9.93]
BANKRUPT
bankruptcy debt, meaning, [1.468]
detention, property released from, [1.371]
director, permission to act as, [6.586]–[6.590]
disclosure, state of affairs
creditor's petition, [6.513]–[6.519]
debtor's petition, [6.520]–[6.523]
dispositions, property, restrictions, [1.346]
disqualification from office, [1.541]–[1.543], [2.15], [2.16]
distribution, estate, [1.393]–[1.403], [1.405]. *See also* TRUSTEE IN BANKRUPTCY
dwelling-house occupied by bankrupt/spouse/former/civil partner/former
charge, application by trustee for, [1.383]
disclaimer, onerous property, trustee in bankruptcy, [1.389]
Enterprise Act 2002 provisions, [2.14]
home rights
bankrupt, [1.409]
former spouse or civil partner
charge, as, [1.408]
nothing occurring during initial period of bankruptcy given rise, [1.408]

BANKRUPT – *cont.*
dwelling-house occupied by bankrupt/spouse/former/civil partner/former – *cont.*
low-value home, powers of court on application by trustee, [1.384]
notice to bankrupt by trustee, property falling within definition, [6.627]
payments, premises occupied by bankrupt, [1.410]
sole/principal residence, protection, [1.345]
vesting, interest in
application in registered land, [6.628]
bankrupt's interest in unregistered land, [6.629]
estate, protection
dwelling-house as sole or principal residence of bankrupt or spouse, [1.345]
estate, definition, [1.344]
excluded property, [1.344]
interim receiver, power of court to appoint, [1.348]
receivership pending appointment, trustee, [1.349]
stay, proceedings/action, [1.347]
income payments
agreement
acceptance, [6.575]
approval, [6.574]
attachment order, effect, [1.380]
meaning, [1.380]
variation, [1.380], [6.576]
orders, court
action to follow making, [6.569]
application, conditions, [1.379], [6.567]
attachment order, effect, [1.379]
contents, [1.379]
duration, [1.379]
order for, [6.568]
payer of income, to, administration, [6.571]
review, [6.572]
variation, [6.570]
manager/receiver, acting as
disqualification, [1.17]
undischarged bankrupt, acting on behalf of, [1.17]
meaning, [1.467]
membership of Parliament, disqualification, [1.541], [1.543], [2.15]
monetary limits, [1.531], [8.1]
official receiver
bankrupt, duties re, [1.353]
investigatory duties, [1.351]
public examination, bankruptcy, [1.352], [6.557]–[6.563]
statement of affairs by bankrupt to, time limit, [1.350]
party to arbitration agreement, of, powers of court, [1.428]
party to contract, powers of court, [1.423]
pensions. *See* PENSIONS
public examination, [6.557]–[6.563]
adjournment, [6.562]
expenses, [6.563]

BANKRUPT – *cont.*
public examination, – *cont.*
notice, [6.558]
procedure, [6.561]
unfit, for, [6.560]
statement of affairs submitted to official receiver, time limit, [1.350]
trustee in bankruptcy
bankrupt's duties re, [1.404]
generally. *See* TRUSTEE IN BANKRUPTCY
undischarged
director, disqualification, [4.24]
individual voluntary arrangement, approval, [1.302]
manager/receiver, acting as
appointed by court, [1.17]
criminal offence, if acting on behalf, debenture holders, [1.14]

BANKRUPTCY
accounts. *See* ACCOUNTS
adjudicator
application to
conditions applying to, [1.317]
determination of, [1.318]
false representations and omissions, [1.322]
further information, requests for, [1.319]
individual, by, [1.315]
appointment, [1.509]
order, making, [1.315]
debtors, orders made against, [1.316]
refusal to make order, [1.321]
adjustments between earlier/later bankruptcy estates, [1.406]
after-acquired property, [6.584], [6.585]
annulment of order, powers of court, [1.343], [6.591]–[6.600]
apprenticeships etc, effect, [1.426]. *See also* APPRENTICESHIPS ETC
assignment of existing or future book debts, avoidance, [1.422]
attachment. *See* ATTACHMENT ORDER
bankruptcy order
annulment, [1.343], [6.591]–[6.600]
Chief Land Registrar, notice to, [6.491]
contents, [6.489]
delivery and notice, [6.490]
meaning, [1.467]
charging order, [6.631]
commencement date, [1.338]
compensation scheme, Financial Services and Markets Act 2000
Authority, power to participate, proceedings, [17.206]
insolvency practitioner, report to Authority, [17.205]
petition, [17.204]
contributory, winding up, registered company, [1.78]
costs, priority on payment out of estate, [6.607], [6.608
court, powers
arrest, [1.443]
enforcement, [1.446]
general control, [1.442]

BANKRUPTCY – *cont.*
court, powers – *cont.*
inland revenue to produce documents, [1.448]
inquiry, bankrupt's dealings/property, [1.445], [1.447]
re-direction, bankrupt's letters etc, [1.450]
seizure, bankrupt's property, [1.444]
special manager, appointment, [1.449]
creditors' claims, [6.726]–[6.749]
creditors' committee
chairman, [6.838]
establishment, formalities, [6.828]
formal defects, [6.850]
functions, [6.825]
information, [6.845], [6.846]
invitation to form, [6.196]
meetings, [6.837]–[6.844]
member
eligibility, [6.827]
expenses, [6.847]
numbers, [6.826]
removal, [6.835]
resignation, [6.833]
membership
changes, [6.830]
vacancies, [6.831], [6.832]
quorum, [6.839]
creditor's petition
amendment, [6.475]
amendment, title of proceedings, [6.625]
amount, debt, [1.326]
carriage of, change, [6.488]
Chief Land Registrar, notice to, [6.472]
content, [6.466]
court in which presented, [6.470]
criteria, court order, [1.330]
disclosure, [6.513]–[6.519]
dismissal, [1.330]
expedited, [1.329]
filing, [6.471]
generally, [6.465]–[6.491]
grounds, [1.326]
hearing, [6.480]
adjournment, [6.482]
decision, [6.483]
postponement, [6.481]
identification
debt, [6.468]
debtor, [6.467]
inability to pay, meaning, [1.327]
liquidated sum, [1.326]
list of appearances, [6.479]
meaning, [1.472]
non-appearance, creditor, [6.485]
opposition, debtor, [6.477]
persons intending to appear, notice, [6.478]
presentation, [6.471]
reasonable prospect, repayment, assessment, [1.330]
secured debt, [1.328]
security for costs, [6.476]
service
death of debtor before, [6.474]

BANKRUPTCY – *cont.*
creditor's petition – *cont.*
service – *cont.*
method, [6.473]
statutory demand
generally, [1.327], [6.460]–[6.464]
See also statutory demand, *below*
substitution, petitioner, [6.486], [6.487]
unsecured debt, [1.328]
vacating registration on dismissal, [6.484]
verification, [6.469]
criminal bankruptcy
criminal bankruptcy order, meaning, [1.472]
discharge, debtor's application, [6.617]
inapplicable rules, [6.618]
interim receivership, [6.616]
Official Petitioner, status and functions, [6.615]
order made
annulment, [6.619]
bankruptcy order, requirements, [1.337]
dismissal, petition, [1.325]
distribution, estate, [1.398]
notice of, [6.617]
proof of debts, [6.617]
who may present petition, [1.323]
petition, contents, [6.614]
proof, bankruptcy debts, [6.617]
report, [6.621]
debtor's application for, [6.492]–[6.506]
action following order, [6.503]
bankruptcy file, [6.505]
Chief Land Registrar, notice to, [6.495]
contents, [6.493], [6.499]
court in which made, [6.506]
determination, [6.497], [6.498]
disclosure, [6.520]–[6.523]
procedure, [6.494]
refusal
appeals, [6.502]
notice, [6.500]
review, [6.501]
settlement, [6.499]
verification checks, [6.496]
debtor's petition
amount, debt, [1.332]
debt relief order, debtor meeting conditions for, [1.334]
grounds, [1.331]
insolvency practitioner
court, appointment, [1.332]
report, action on, [1.333]
interim order, [1.333]
meaning, [1.472]
meeting, creditors, summoning, [1.333]
small bankruptcies level, meaning, [1.332]
summary administration
certificate, [1.335], [2.31]
debts, proof
admission for dividend, [6.731]
appeal against decision, [6.732]
claim, quantification
discounts, [6.744]
interest payable, [6.747]

BANKRUPTCY – *cont.*
debts, proof – *cont.*
claim, quantification – *cont.*
periodical payments, [6.746]
cost of proving, [6.729]
exclusion by court, [6.735]
inspection, proofs, [6.730]
rejection for dividend, [6.731]
requirements, [6.728]
submission of proof, [6.727]
variation, [6.734]
withdrawal, [6.734]
decisions, procedures for, [6.771]–[6.776]
meetings. See meetings, generally, *below*
notices, [6.777], [6.780]–[6.784]
remuneration, [6.785]
requisitioned decisions, [6.787], [6.788]
venue, [6.779]
voting, [6.778]
director, permission to act as, [6.586]–[6.590]
discharge
certificate, [6.603], [6.604]
costs, [6.606]
court order, by, [1.340]
date, [1.339], [2.13], [2.22]
debts from which released/not released, [1.341], [6.605]
effect, [1.341]
suspension
application for, [6.601]
lifting, [6.602]
disclaimer, [6.891]–[6.901]
distress. *See* DISTRESS
distribution, estate, [1.393]–[1.403], [1.405]
distribution to creditors, generally, [6.750]–[6.769]
See also TRUSTEE IN BANKRUPTCY
dividends, payment, creditors, [8.47], [8.48]
domicile, debtor, [1.324]
duration, [1.338], [1.339], [2.13], [2.22]
execution. *See* EXECUTION
extortionate credit transactions, [1.421]
fees, [8.21]
final accounts, [6.866]
Financial Services and Markets Act 2000, [11.16]–[11.23]
generally, [1.323]–[1.450]
HMRC, order to
application, [6.577]
making, [6.578]
production/custody, documents, [1.448], [6.579]
individual. *See* INDIVIDUAL INSOLVENCY
individual voluntary arrangement
conversion, arrangement into
EU Regulation, [6.911], [6.912]
order on default
application for annulment
bankrupt, [6.426]
official receiver, [6.427]
conditions for making, [1.336]
generally, [6.426]–[6.431]

BANKRUPTCY – *cont.*
Insolvency Services Account, payment into/out of, [8.44]
interim receiver appointed
application for appointment, [6.507]
court, powers, inquiries re bankrupt's dealings/ property, [1.447]
deposit, [6.508]
failure to give/keep security, [6.510]
order of appointment, [6.509]
remuneration, [6.511]
security, [6.510]
termination, appointment, [6.512]
liens on books etc unenforceable, [1.427]
Lloyd's member
reorganisation controller
petition, [7.1596]
powers, [7.1596]
meetings, generally
adjournment
absence of chair, [6.794]
chair, by, [6.792]
proofs in, [6.795]
removal of liquidator/trustee, [6.793]
chair, [6.790], [6.791]
exclusions from, [6.805]–[6.807]
quorum, [6.789]
records, [6.809]
remote attendance, [6.811]
suspension, [6.796]
voting, [6.797]–[6.804]
creditors' rights, [6.797]
contributories' rights, [6.808]
requisite majorities, [6.803], [6.808]
scheme manager's rights, [6.798]
mortgaged property
mortgagee of land, claim, [6.581]
sale
court, power to order, [6.582]
proceeds, [6.583]
offences, [1.429]–[1.441]. *See also* OFFENCES
official receiver
bankrupt, duties re, [1.353]
investigatory duties, [1.351]
public examination, bankruptcy, [1.352]
statement of affairs by bankrupt to, time limit, [1.350]
old summary cases, transitional provisions, [2.31]
pensions, bankrupt person. *See* PENSIONS
persons at risk of violence, non-disclosure [6.905]
petition
creditor's. *See* creditor's petition, *above*
debtor's. *See* debtor's petition, *above*
generally
conditions generally, [1.325]
debtor, qualifying conditions, [1.324]
dismissal, [1.325]
who may present, [1.323]
withdrawal, leave of court, [1.325]
meaning, [1.467]
post-discharge restrictions, [1.342]
preferences, adjustment of prior transaction, [1.412]

BANKRUPTCY – *cont.*
re-direction of bankrupt's documents, application for, [6.626]
register of
bankruptcy restrictions, [6.644]
replacement, exempt property, [6.564], [6.565]
residence, debtor, [1.324]
Scotland. *See* SCOTLAND
second
distribution, stay in case, second bankruptcy, [1.405]
existing trustee
expenses, [6.612]
general duty, [6.610]
generally, [6.609]–[6.612]
later trustee, delivery up to, [6.611]
secured creditor
security
realisation or surrender, [6.743]
redemption, [6.741]
surrender for non-disclosure, [6.740]
test of value, [6.742]
value, [6.739]
special manager
accounts, [6.555]
appointment, [6.552]
security
failure to give/keep, [6.554]
undertaking etc, [6.553]
termination, appointment, [6.556]
statutory demand
content, [6.460]
creditors' petition, generally, [1.327], [6.460]–[6.464]
form, [6.460]
service, [6.461]
set aside, application, [6.463], [6.464]
stay, proceedings/action, [1.347]
trustee in bankruptcy, [1.355]–[1.406], [6.525]–[6.551]. *See also* TRUSTEE IN BANKRUPTCY
trusts of land, rights under, [1.407]
undervalue, transactions at, adjustment, [1.411]–[1.414], [1.537], [17.15], [17.248]

BANKRUPTCY RESTRICTIONS ORDER
annulment, effect of bankruptcy order, [1.587]
application, [6.633]
timing, [1.587]
duration, [1.587]
evidence, bankrupt or debtor, [6.635]
grounds, [1.587], [2.30]
interim, [1.587], [6.637]–[6.640]
making, [6.636]
registration, [1.587], [6.651], [6.652]
Secretary of State, reference to, [6.632]
service, notice of application, [6.634]

BANKRUPTCY RESTRICTIONS UNDERTAKING
acceptance, [6.641]
annulment, [6.643]
notification to court, [6.642]
registration, [1.587], [6.651], [6.652]
terms, [1.587]

BANKS
administration, *See* BANK ADMINISTRATION
compulsory liquidation, [7.87]
dormant accounts
account, meaning, [17.392]
assets-limit conditions, [17.386]
balance, meaning, [17.391]
bank, meaning, [17.390]
charities, transfer of balances to with proportion to reclaim fund, [17.385]
dormant, meaning, [17.393]
insolvency, customer's rights preserved on, [17.394]
interpretation, [17.389]
reclaim fund
functions of, [17.388]
transfer of balances to, [17.384], [17.385]
former authorised institutions
administration order, [1.13], [7.16]–[7.20]
modified provisions, [7.23], [7.24]
Secretary of State, powers to make orders, [1.536], [7.16]
insolvency. *See* BANK INSOLVENCY
BODY CORPORATE
disqualification, acting as receiver, [1.16]
offences, [1.549], [4.28]
BOOK DEBTS
existing or future, avoidance of assignment prior to bankruptcy, [1.422]
BUILDING SOCIETY INSOLVENCY
appeals, [7.762]–[7.764]
application of rules, [7.548]
applications to court
adjournment of hearings, [7.738]
application of rules, [7.727]
application to disapply provisions, [7.730]
evidence, use of, [7.735]
filing and service, [7.731]
form and content of, [7.729]
hearing, [7.734]
hearings without notice, [7.733]
interpretation, [7.728]
notice of, [7.732]
reports, use of, [7.737]
witness statements, filing and service, [7.736]
attendance, rights of, [7.766]
bank insolvency provisions application of, [7.471]
building society liquidator
accounts, submission of, [7.577]
appointment
advertisement, [7.632]
authentication of, [7.631]
registration, [7.632]
authentication of appointment, [7.562]
calls, [7.707]–[7.710]
collection and distribution of assets
debts of insolvent company, ranking, [7.685]
dividend, supplementary provision as to, [7.686]
enforced delivery up of property, [7.689]
final distribution, [7.690]
general duties, [7.682]
general powers, [7.688]

BUILDING SOCIETY INSOLVENCY – *cont.*
building society liquidator – *cont.*
collection and distribution of assets – *cont.*
general qualification on powers, [7.683]
manner of distributing, [7.684]
unsold assets, division of, [7.687]
completion of winding up, release on, [7.642], [7.643]
deceased, [7.653]
disclaimer, [7.691]–[7.698]
duties on vacation of office, [7.657]
intention to vacate office, notice of, [7.656]
liquidation committee, obligations to, [7.664]
list of contributories, settlement of, [7.699]–[7.706]
loss of qualification, [7.654]
removal
advertisement, [7.639]
court, by, [7.640]
meeting of creditors, [7.636]
power of court to regulate meetings, [7.637]
procedure, [7.638]
release on, [7.641]
remuneration
court, recourse to, [7.649]
creditors' meeting, recourse to, [7.648]
entitlement to, [7.645]
excessive, creditors' claiming, [7.650]
fixing, [7.644]
generally, [7.629]
matters affecting, [7.647]
Objective 1, primacy of, [7.651]
realisation of assets on behalf of chargeholder, on, [7.646]
replacement, [7.652]
replacement by creditors, [7.630]
report by, [7.579]
reports to liquidation committee, [7.676]
resignation
action following acceptance of, [7.634]
advertisement, [7.635]
creditors' meeting, notification, [7.633]
generally, [7.655]
release on, [7.641]
witness statement, [7.561]
capital, return of, [7.723], [7.724]
conclusion of, [7.725], [7.726]
concurrent proceedings and remedies, restriction on, [7.767]
confidentiality of documents, [7.809]
copy documents, [7.811], [7.812]
costs and expenses
application for, [7.755]
application of rules, [7.749]
detailed procedure, requirement to assess by, [7.750], [7.751]
final certificate, [7.757]
generally, [7.798]
officers, of, [7.752]
paid otherwise than from insolvent estate, [7.753]
responsible insolvency practitioner, award against, [7.754]
witnesses, of, [7.756]

BUILDING SOCIETY INSOLVENCY – *cont.*
court
records and returns, [7.745]–[7.748]
rules and practice applying, [7.765]
creditors and contributories, information to
building society liquidator, report by, [7.579]
creditors, meaning, [7.580]
reporting, general rule, [7.583]
statement of affairs dispensed with, where, [7.582]
statement of affairs lodged, where, [7.581]
declaration and payment of dividend, [7.784]–[7.796]
enforcement procedures, [7.741]–[7.744]
examination of persons involved in, [7.778]–[7.783]
false claim of status as creditor, [7.815]
forms, [7.550]
further disclosure, [7.578]
further information and disclosure, [7.770]
insolvency practitioner, security, [7.804]
interpretation, [7.548], [7.820]–[7.829]
judgment creditor, insolvency of, [7.816]
limited disclosure, order for, [7.574]
liquidation committee
application of rules, [7.660]
chair, [7.666]
composition where creditors paid in full, [7.679]
contributories, established by, [7.663]
dealings by, [7.678]
expenses, [7.677]
formal defects, [7.681]
formalities of establishment, [7.662]
initial duties of, [7.563]
liquidator's report, [7.676]
meetings, [7.665]–[7.668]
members of, [7.661]
obligations of liquidator to, [7.664]
removal, [7.671]
resignation, [7.669]
resolutions by post, [7.675]
Secretary of State, functions vested in, [7.680]
termination of membership, [7.670]
vacancy in, [7.672], [7.673]
voting rights and resolutions, [7.674]
list of creditors, right to, [7.814]
meetings of creditors and contributories
admission and rejection of proof, [7.601]
attendance by bank's personnel, [7.592]
chair, [7.589], [7.597]
entitlement to vote, [7.599], [7.600]
evidence at, [7.802]
expenses, [7.595]
first
business at, [7.587]
summoning, [7.587]
general power to call, [7.588]
notice by advertisement, [7.593]
quorum, [7.801]
record of proceedings, [7.602]
requisitioned, [7.590], [7.591]
resolutions, [7.596]

BUILDING SOCIETY INSOLVENCY – *cont.*
meetings of creditors and contributories – *cont.*
suspension and adjournment, [7.598]
venue, [7.594]
non-receipt of notice of meeting, [7.813]
notices, [7.800]
offences, [7.818]
office copies of documents, [7.771]
order
advertisement, [7.561]
application for
certificate of compliance, [7.558]
filing, [7.552]
leave to withdraw, [7.559]
persons to receive, [7.555], [7.557]
service of, [7.553], [7.554]
verification of, [7.556]
witness statement in opposition, [7.560]
making of, [7.561]
transmission, [7.561]
overview, [7.549]
payment into court, [7.769]
payment of costs out of assets, order of, [7.716]–[7.722]
persons incapable of managing own affairs, [7.758]–[7.761]
proof of debts
admission and rejection of proofs for dividend, [7.610]
appeals, [7.611]
claim established by witness statement, [7.606]
contents of, [7.605]
cost of proving, [7.607]
debts payable at future time, [7.623]
discounts, [7.617]
eligible depositors, disapplication of set off, [7.619]
expunging by court, [7.613]
foreign currency debts, [7.620]
forms, [7.604]
inspection of, liquidator allowing, [7.608]
interest, [7.622]
meaning, [7.603]
mutual credits and set-off, [7.618]
negotiable instruments, [7.615]
new building society liquidator appointed, where, [7.609]
periodical nature, payments of, [7.621]
quantum, estimation of, [7.614]
secured creditors, [7.616]
withdrawal or variation, [7.612]
provable debts, [7.799]
provisional building society liquidator
appointment of, [7.565]
notice of, [7.566]
order of, [7.567]
termination, [7.571]
remuneration, [7.570]
security, [7.568], [7.569]
provisions applying, [4.42]
Banking Act provisions applied, [7.479]–[7.481]
Northern Ireland, [7.477]
subordinate legislation, [7.478], [7.482]

BUILDING SOCIETY INSOLVENCY – *cont.*
proxies, [7.772]–[7.777]
regulation of matters, [7.797]
Scotland. *See* SCOTLAND
Secretary of State, documents issuing from, [7.803]
secured creditors
non-disclosure, surrender for, [7.625]
proof of debts, [7.616]
realisation of security, [7.628]
redemption by liquidator, [7.626]
test of security's value, [7.627]
value of security, [7.624]
security in court, [7.768]
service of documents, [7.806]–[7.808]
shorthand writers, [7.739], [7.740]
solicitation, rule against, [7.659]
special manager
accounting, [7.714]
appointment, [7.711]
remuneration, [7.711]
security, [7.712], [7.713]
termination of appointment, [7.715]
statement of affairs
expenses of, [7.576]
extension of time for, [7.575]
notice requiring, [7.572]
release from duty to submit, [7.575]
verification and filing, [7.573]
staying of, [7.584]
time limits, [7.551], [7.805]
transactions, power of court to set aside, [7.658]
voluntary arrangement, expenses of, [7.564]
BUILDING SOCIETIES
administration
applicable legislation, [1.13], [7.455], [7.468]
bank administration provisions, application of, [7.472]
preliminary steps, notice to Authority, [7.458]
special. *See* special administration, *below*
bank insolvency and administration legislation, application of, [7.457]
companies insolvency legislation, application of, [18.216], [18.217]
companies winding up legislation, application of, [18.215]
company voluntary arrangement, [1.1], [7.455], [7.468]. *See also* COMPANY VOLUNTARY ARRANGEMENT
disqualification of directors, [4.44], [7.459]. *See also* DISQUALIFICATION OF DIRECTORS
dissolution
priorities, alteration of, [7.456]
process, [7.449], [7.450]
void, power of court to declare, [7.461]
dormant accounts
account, meaning, [17.392]
assets-limit conditions, [17.386]
balance, meaning, [17.391]
charities, transfer of balances to with proportion to reclaim fund, [17.385]
dormant, meaning, [17.393]

BUILDING SOCIETIES – *cont.*
dormant accounts – *cont.*
insolvency, customer's rights preserved on, [17.394]
interpretation, [17.389]
membership rights, effect of balance transfer on, [17.387]
reclaim fund
functions of, [17.388]
transfer of balances to, [17.384], [17.385]
financial assistance
funding limit, application of provisions, [18.212]
interpretation, [18.209]
lending limit, application of provisions, [18.211]
memorandum and rules, effect of, [18.214]
modification of provisions to facilitate, [17.345]
purpose or principal purpose, effect on, [18.210]
raising funds and borrowing, application of provisions, [18.213]
insolvency. *See* BUILDING SOCIETY INSOLVENCY
preferential debts, [1.473], [1.474], [7.454], [7.455], [7.464], [7.468]
receiver/manager, appointment, [1.14], [7.455], [7.468]
special administration
court procedure and practice, [7.534]–[7.541]
end of
dissolution, [7.533]
successful rescue, [7.532]
forms, [7.489]
Insolvency Rules, application of, [7.542]–[7.545]
interpretation, [7.486], [7.487]
order
application for, [7.490]–[7.508]
Bank of England witness statement, [7.494]
costs, [7.508]
form of, [7.505]
hearing, [7.504]
notice of, [7.506], [7.507]
overview, [7.488]
process, [7.509]–[7.533]
protected deposits, disapplication of set-off for, [7.531]
provisions applying, [4.42]
right to inspect file, [7.536]–[7.541]
title of proceedings, [7.535]
special administrator
additional joint, [7.530]
proposals
Objective 1 Stage, [7.510]
Objective 2 Stage, [7.511]–[7.517]
proposed, statement of, [7.493]
provisional, appointment of, [7.523]–[7.529]
removal of, Objective 1 Stage, [7.522]
reports to creditors, [7.518]–[7.521]
winding up, registered company
applicable law, [7.454], [7.455], [7.464], [7.465], [7.468], [7.469]

BUILDING SOCIETIES – *cont.*
winding up, registered company – *cont.*
court, by, [7.452], [7.465]
insolvency as alterative order, [7.453]
monetary limits to determine jurisdiction, powers of Secretary of State, [1.528], [8.1], [7.454], [7.455], [7.464], [7.468]
preliminary steps, notice to Authority, [7.458]
provisions generally, [1.149], [1.234]–[1.251], [1.522], [7.454], [7.455], [7.464], [7.465]
voluntary, [7.451], [7.465]
See also WINDING UP, REGISTERED COMPANY
BUSINESS DAY
meaning, [1.267]
BUSINESS DOCUMENT
See also INVOICES, LETTERS ETC
meaning, [1.575]
BUSINESS IMPROVEMENT DISTRICT
interpretation, [18.13]
liability order
joint owners and occupiers, against, [18.14]
partners, against, [18.14]

C

CALLS
enforcement, [6.365]
leave to make, application to court, [6.363]
liquidator, by, [6.361]
making, [6.365]
order, [6.364]
payment, [6.366]
sanctions, [6.362]
Scotland. *See* SCOTLAND
winding up by court, on contributories in, [1.152]
CAPITAL MARKET ARRANGEMENT
administrative receiver, appointment permitted, [1.60], [1.578]
meaning, [1.60]
moratorium
company party, exclusion, [1.569]
debt, amount, [1.569]
interpretation, [1.569]
CAPITAL MARKET INVESTMENT
administrative receiver, appointment permitted, [1.60], [1.578]
meaning, [1.60]
moratorium, interpretation, [1.569]
CARE QUALITY COMMISSION
membership, [18.297]–[18.302]
CHANNEL ISLANDS
Insolvency Act 1986, extent applicable, [1.566]
CHARGE
administration, charged property
disposal, [6.160]
effect, [1.575]
administrative receiver, disposal of charged property, [6.197]
bankruptcy, charging order, [6.631]
energy administration order, disposal of charged property, [7.907]
CHARGE – *cont.*
floating. *See* FLOATING CHARGE
market. *See* FINANCIAL MARKETS
preferential. *See* PREFERENTIAL CHARGE
CHARITABLE INCORPORATED ORGANISATION
disqualification of directors, [4.48]. *See also* DISQUALIFICATION OF DIRECTORS
winding up, insolvency and dissolution
dissolution other than under Insolvency Act
application for, [18.225]
application of CIO, on, [18.224]
charity, CIO no longer being, [18.237]
CIO not in operation, where, [18.236]
CIO procedures not completed, where, [18.228]
date of, [18.240]
letters and notices, delivery of, [18.239]
liability and powers unaffected, [18.242]
notice before, [18.227]
notice to be given of, [18.241]
offences under Companies Act, [18.235]
official custodian
disclaimer of property by, [18.247]–[18.252]
property vesting in, [18.243]–[18.246]
other procedures not completed, where, [18.229]
procedure for, [18.239]
property, application of, [18.243]–[18.252]
property received after making application, [18.231]
resolution, [18.226]
restrictions following application, [18.230]
trustees to give notice of application, [18.232], [18.233]
withdrawal of application, [18.234]
wound up, CIO being, [18.238]
Insolvency Act 1986, application of, [18.223], [18.262]
interpretation, [18.222]
regulations, [17.441], [18.221]–[18.262]
restoration to register
accounts, reports and returns, [18.261]
Commission, by, [18.253]
court, by, [18.254]
court order with directions, [18.256]
effect of, [18.259]
name of CIO on, [18.257]
notification of, [18.258]
property vesting in, [18.260]
time limit for applying to court, [18.255]
CHARITY TRUSTEES
disqualification
acting during
civil consequences of, [17.439]
criminal consequences of, [17.438]
cases of, [17.432]
charitable companies, exceptions relating to, [17.435]
power to waive, [17.436]
pre-commencement events, [17.434]
meaning, [17.431]
removal of, records, [17.437]

CHIEF LAND REGISTRAR
bankruptcy, notice to
creditor's petition, [6.495]
cross-border insolvency
application to, following court orders, [3.317]
CHILD TRUST FUND
generally, [17.254]–[17.258]
inalienability, [17.255]
meaning, [17.254]
CIVIL PARTNERSHIP
associate, meaning, [1.557]. *See also* ASSOCIATE
home rights, effect of bankruptcy. *See* DWELLING-HOUSE; HOME RIGHTS
property adjustment orders, settlements, [1.411], [1.413], [1.414], [17.15]
Scotland. *See* SCOTLAND
transaction in consideration of formation of, transaction at undervalue in bankruptcy, [1.411], [1.413], [1.414], [1.537]–[1.539]
CLEARING HOUSES
administration order, [1.13], [17.85]
charge in favour as market charge, [9.6]
default
proceedings
application to determine whether should be taken, [17.70], [18.287]
completion
duty to report, [17.65], [18.285]
net sum payable, [17.66]
duty, assistance for, [17.63], [17.64]
rules
change, [17.60], [18.284]
directions under, [18.286]
meaning, [17.92]
disclaimer, property, [17.67]
EEA central counterparties, [17.73], [17.74]
generally, [17.57]–[17.98]
market charges, [9.6], [17.76]–[17.79]
market contracts, [17.58]
market property, [17.80]–[17.84]
modification, insolvency law, [17.61]
overseas, [17.72]
prior transactions, adjustment, [17.68]
proceedings of, precedence over insolvency proceedings, [17.62]
qualifying collateral arrangements and qualifying property transfers, [17.59]
recognised central counterparties, disapplication of provisions on mutual credit and set-off, [17.86]
rescission, contracts, [17.67]
Secretary of State, directions, [17.69]
settlement arrangements, Bank of England, [17.75]
third country central counterparties, [17.73], [17.74]
transfer, meaning, [17.94]
winding up, registered company, [1.69]–[1.223], [1.224]–[1.233], [17.85]
COAL INDUSTRY
Coal Authority, confidential information, [17.113]
coal-mining operations
insolvency of licensed operators, [17.112]
COAL INDUSTRY – *cont.*
coal-mining operations – *cont.*
licensing, provision of security, [17.111]
COLLATERAL
collateral taker or provider, winding up
disapplication of disclaimer of onerous property, [1.182], [3.290]
property dispositions etc, avoidance after commencement, [1.128], [3.290]
financial collateral arrangement
EC Directive, financial collateral arrangements
close-out netting provisions, recognition, [3.275]
conflict of laws, [3.277]
enforcement, [3.272]
formal requirements, [3.271]
implementation, [3.280]
insolvency provisions which are disapplied, [3.276]
report on application, Directive, [3.279]
right of use
under security financial collateral arrangements, [3.273]
text, [3.268]–[3.282]
title transfer, recognition, [3.274]
Northern Ireland. *See* NORTHERN IRELAND
regulations
applicable legislation, [3.285]
appropriation, [3.298], [3.299]
close-out netting provisions, [3.292]
conflict of laws, [3.301]
contracts, avoidance
inapplicable legislation, [3.290], [3.291]
enforceable arrangements, [3.293]
enforcement, restrictions, [3.300]
inapplicable, [3.288]
floating charges
inapplicable legislation, [3.290], [3.291]
generally, [3.283]–[3.301]
other jurisdictions, insolvency proceedings in, [3.296]
right of use, [3.297]
valuation of collateral, [3.299]
Scotland. *See* SCOTLAND
floating charge, share for unsecured creditors, provisions inapplicable, [1.180], [3.290]
security charge
administrative receiver, appointment permitted, [1.65]
settlement finality, [9.57], [9.58]
COLLECTIVE INVESTMENT SCHEME
contractual, meaning, [7.832]
co-ownership
insolvent
insolvency rules, application of, [7.841]–[7.846]
statutory provisions, application of, [7.840]–[7.840]
winding up, [7.835]
partnership
insolvent, liability of general partner, [7.836]
COMMONHOLD
interpretation, [18.9]
successor association, registration of, [18.12]

COMMONHOLD – *cont.*
termination
application following, [18.10], [18.11]
voluntary winding up
80 per cent agreement, [17.222]
100 per cent agreement, [17.221]
liquidator, [17.225]
resolution, [17.220]
termination application etc, [17.223], [17.226]
winding up by court
assets, [17.229]
liabilities, [17.229]
petition, [17.227]
succession order, [17.228]
termination, court order, [17.232]
termination of commonhold, [17.231]
transfer, responsibility, [17.230]
COMMUNITY CHARGE
bankruptcy petition against debtor, [18.6]
COMMUNITY INTEREST COMPANY
liquidator's appointment, notice of, [18.138]
supervision, Regulator
manager, appointment, [17.259]
property, [17.260]
shares, transfer, [17.261]
winding up petition, [17.262]
winding up, distribution of assets on, [18.137]
COMPANY VOLUNTARY ARRANGEMENT
accounts
production to Secretary of State, [6.108]
supervisor, [6.107]
administrator, proposal, company in administration, [1.1]
approval
conditions, [1.5]
effect, [1.6], [1.7]
effective as if made at creditors' meeting, [1.6]
false representations etc to obtain, [1.9]
persons bound by, [1.6]
procedure, [1.6]
charges, [6.109]
company, meaning, [1.1]
compensation scheme under FSMA 2000, Authority's power to participate in proceedings, [17.186], [17.196]
completion, [6.110]
conversion to winding up
EU Regulation, [6.911], [6.912]
costs, [6.109]
decisions, challenge, [1.8]
delinquent company officers, prosecution, [1.11]
directors, who may propose, [1.1]. *See also* proposal, *below*
EU Regulation
conversion to winding up, [6.911], [6.912]
expenses, [6.109]
false representations etc to obtain approval, [1.9]
fees, [6.109]
gas, water, electricity etc supplies, management, [1.237]
hand-over of property to supervisor, [6.105]
liquidator, proposal, company being wound up, [1.1]
COMPANY VOLUNTARY ARRANGEMENT – *cont.*
moratorium
approval, proposal, [1.573]
beginning
advertisement, [6.81]
notice, [6.81]
challenge, decisions, [1.573]
directors, procedure, [1.2]
end
advertisement, [6.85]
notice, [6.85]
extension, notice of, [1.573]
implementation, [1.573]
meetings
conduct, [1.573]
summoning, [1.573]
moratorium committee, [1.573]
nominee
replacement
by court, [6.88]
statement, [6.79]
withdrawal, consent to act, [6.87]
proposal, approval, [1.573]
transitional provisions, [2.70]
non-company, applicable to under Enterprise Act 2002, [2.12]
prematurely ending, [1.12]
procedure, generally, [6.460]–[6.631]
proposal
amendment to, [6.68]
consideration by creditors/members, [6.91]–[6.104]
contents, [6.69]
general principles, [6.68]
implementation, [1.10]
meetings
decisions, [1.5]
summoning, [1.4]
moratorium, [1.2]
nominee
disclosure to, [6.74]
not liquidator/administrator, [1.3], [6.70]
replacement, [6.76]
report, [6.75]
official receiver, information for, [6.71]
statement of affairs, [6.72]
information, omission of, [6.73]
those who may propose, [1.1]
records, production to Secretary of State, [6.108]
revocation, [6.106]
Scotland. *See* SCOTLAND
supervisor
accounts, [6.107]
hand-over of property to, [6.105]
reports, [6.107]
suspension, [6.106]
termination, [6.110]
COMPENSATION
depreciation, value, interests in land, [17.17], [17.18]

COMPENSATION – *cont.*
Financial Services and Markets Act 2000
administration order
administrator
appointment by company/directors, [17.193]
report to Authority, [17.191]
Authority, powers, [17.189], [17.192]
bankruptcy
Authority, power to participate, proceedings, [17.206]
insolvency practitioner, report to Authority, [17.205]
petition, [17.204]
company voluntary arrangement
Authority's power to participate, proceedings, [17.186], [17.196]
debt avoidance, provisions against
Authority, right to apply for order, [17.207]
generally, [17.181]–[17.217]
individual voluntary arrangement
Authority's power to participate, proceedings, [17.187], [17.196]
inspection, documents held by Official Receiver
scheme manager, power, [17.182], [17.183], [17.184]
insurers
assets on winding up, treatment, [17.210]
continuation, long-term contracts
insurer in liquidation, [17.197], [17.208]
receivership
Authority, power to participate, proceedings, [17.194]
receiver, report to Authority, [17.195]
reduction, value, contracts
alternative to winding up, [17.209]
rights of scheme, relevant person's insolvency, [17.181]
Scotland. *See* SCOTLAND
voluntary winding up generally
Authority's powers to participate, proceedings, [17.186], [17.187], [17.196]
insurers effecting/carrying out long-term contracts etc, [17.197]
winding up by court
Authority, power to participate, proceedings, [17.203]
EEA/Treaty firms, [17.199]
insurers
rules, [17.211]
service of petition on Authority, [17.200]
liquidator, report to Authority, [17.202]
petition, [17.198]
reclaim funds, service of petition on Authority, [17.201]
COMPETITION LAW
infringement, disqualification, director
co-ordination, functions re, [4.21]
investigation, [4.20]
order, [4.18]
specified regulator, meaning, [4.22]
undertaking, [4.19]
CONDITIONAL FEES
success fee
agreements providing for, [18.289]
amount of, [18.290], [18.292]
specified proceedings, in, [18.291], [18.292]
transitional proceedings, [18.293]
CONFISCATION ORDER
bankruptcy, property subject
discharge, effect, [1.341], [1.374]
exclusion from bankrupt's estate
vesting by trustee in bankruptcy, [1.372]
quashed, effect, [1.374]
drug trafficking
Scotland. *See* SCOTLAND
Scotland. *See* SCOTLAND: sequestrated estate
CONFLICT OF LAWS
financial collateral arrangements
EC Directive, [3.277]
Regulation, [3.301]
CONNECTED WITH A COMPANY
meaning, [1.265]
CONSOLIDATED FUND
payment from Investment Account, [1.516], [1.519]
payment to Insolvency Services Account, from, [1.518], [1.519]
recourse to, [1.519]
CONTEMPT OF COURT
winding up by court, failure to attend public examination, [1.135]
CONTRACTS
administrative receiver, liability, [1.30]
bankrupt as party to, powers of court, [1.423]
employment. *See* EMPLOYMENT
immovable property, EC Regulation, [3.44]
rescission, application on winding up of registered company, [1.190]
CONTRIBUTORIES
decisions, qualifying procedure, [1.256], [1.460]
deemed consent procedure, [1.257], [1.461]
liability, nature of, [2.72]
list, settlement of
costs, [6.360]
court's duty, delegation to liquidator, [6.354]
form of list, [6.356]
generally, [6.354]–[6.360]
liquidator, duty, [6.355]
procedure, [6.357]
variation, list
application, court, [6.358]
liquidator, power, [6.359]
meaning, [1.75]
winding up of registered company, liability
bankruptcy of contributory, effect, [1.78]
company registered under Companies Act, Pt XXII, Ch 8, [1.79]
contributory, meaning, [1.75]
death of member, in case of, [1.77]
directors etc with unlimited liability, [1.71]
falsification, company's books, [1.213]
limited company formerly unlimited, [1.73]
nature, [1.76]
past and present members, as, [1.70]

CONTRIBUTORIES – *cont.*
winding up of registered company, liability – *cont.*
past directors, [1.72]
past shareholders, [1.72]
unlimited company formerly limited, [1.74]
CONTROLLED/CONTROLLING UNDERTAKING
transnational information, consultation of employees, [12.8], [12.9]
CO-OPERATION BETWEEN COURTS
insolvency jurisdiction, exercise, [1.540]
CO-OPERATIVE AND COMMUNITY BENEFITS SOCIETY
administration
dissolution following, [7.1414]
administrative receiver, restrictions on appointment, [7.1405]
arrangements, reconstructions and administration, application of provisions, [7.1425]–[7.1450]
certificate obtained prior to dissolution, [7.1415]
company law, application to, [7.1416], [7.1417]
dissolution by instrument of dissolution, [7.1408]
advertisement, [7.1411]
notification to FCA, [7.1410]
setting aside, [7.1411]
special resolutions, [7.1409]
property, duty to account, [7.1406]
voluntary arrangements, [7.1407]
winding up
dissolution of society, [7.1412]
liability of existing and former members, [7.1413]
COSTS
applications for, [6.702]
bankruptcy
payment out of estate, priority, [6.607], [6.608]
company voluntary arrangement
generally, [6.109]
Scotland. *See* SCOTLAND
CPR applicable, [6.695]
cross-border insolvency proceedings, detailed assessment, [3.320]
detailed assessment
cross-border insolvency proceedings, [3.320]
procedure, [6.697]
requirement, [6.696], [7.989], [7.990]
EC Regulation
registration, judgment, public register, Member State, [3.59]
secondary insolvency proceedings, advance payment, [3.66]
energy administration order. *See* ENERGY ADMINISTRATION ORDER
execution of writs or other process, enforcement officer etc, [6.698]
final costs certificate, [6.704]
insurance company, winding up, apportionment of costs payable out of assets, [7.1509]
liquidation
payment out of assets, priority, [6.269], [6.270]
litigation expenses, [6.271]–[6.275]
paid otherwise than out of insolvent estate, [6.700]

COSTS – *cont.*
petitions by insolvents, [6.699]
railway administration order
application for, [7.2517]
award against special railway administrator, [7.2516]
CPR applicable, [7.2512]
detailed assessment
procedure, [7.2514]
requirement, [7.2513]
final costs certificate, [7.2519]
payment otherwise than from assets, protected railway company, [7.2515]
witnesses, [7.2518]
witnesses, [6.703]
COUNCIL FOR HEALTHCARE REGULATORY EXCELLENCE
appointments, [11.46], [11.47]
COURT PROCEDURE AND PRACTICE
appeals. *See* APPEALS
applications
adjournment of hearing, [6.667]
affidavit. *See* AFFIDAVITS
distribution to unsecured creditors, [6.668]–[6.670]
filing, [6.661]
generally, [6.660]–[6.667]
hearing, urgent cases, [6.664]
private examination, [6.671]–[6.676]
service, [6.663]
commencement of proceedings, [6.657]–[6.659]
costs. *See* COSTS
CPR applicable, [6.655]
court file, [6.693]–[6.694]
court orders, [6.717]
disclosure. *See* DISCLOSURE
dividend. *See* DIVIDEND
enforcement procedures
court orders, [6.705]
energy administration order, [7.979]–[7.981]
orders enforcing compliance with Rules, [6.706]
railway administration order, [7.2503]–[7.2505]
warrants
debtor/bankrupt, arrest, [6.708]
general provisions, [6.707]
inquiry into dealings, insolvent company/bankrupt, [6.709]
search of premises not belonging to bankrupt, [6.710]
examination, persons, company/individual insolvency, [6.671]–[6.676]
formal defects, [6.718]
information and evidence, [6.681]–[6.683]
official receiver. *See* OFFICIAL RECEIVER
persons lacking capacity to manage own affairs, [6.677]–[6.680]. *See also* INCAPACITY
proxies, [6.816]–[6.823]. *See also* PROXIES
railway administration order, [7.2492]–[7.2534]
shorthand writers, [6.719], [7.2502]
transfer of proceedings between courts
application, [6.686]
commenced in wrong court, [6.685]

COURT PROCEDURE AND PRACTICE – *cont.*
transfer of proceedings between courts – *cont.*
consequential transfer, other proceedings, [6.688]
general power, [6.684]
order
procedure following, [6.687]
CREDIT INSTITUTION
consolidated supervision, [3.34], [3.35]
EC Directive, reorganisation/winding up
credit institution, head office outside Community
reorganisation of branches, third-country institutions, [3.184]
winding up of branches, third-country institutions, [3.195]
credit institution, head office within Community
reorganisation
applicable law, [3.179]
competent authorities, host Member State, information, [3.180]
creditors, right to lodge claims, [3.183]
known creditors, information, [3.183]
publication, decisions, [3.182]
supervisory authorities, home Member State, information, [3.181]
winding up
applicable law, [3.186]
creditor, right to lodge claims, [3.192]
honouring obligations, [3.191]
known creditors, information, [3.190], [3.193], [3.194]
opening, information, other competent authorities, [3.185]
publication, decisions, [3.189], [3.193]
voluntary, consultation, competent authorities before, [3.187]
withdrawal, authorisation, institution, [3.188]
detrimental acts, [3.206]
employment contract, effects, [3.196]
immovable property, contracts, effect, [3.196]
lex rei sitae, [3.200]
liquidator, appointment, proof, [3.204]
netting agreements, [3.201]
pending lawsuits, [3.208]
professional secrecy, [3.209]
registration, public register, [3.205]
regulated markets, [3.203]
repurchase agreements, [3.202]
reservation of title, [3.198]
set-off, [3.199]
text, [3.176]–[3.264]
third parties
protection, [3.207]
rights in re, [3.197]
EU Directive, recovery and resolution
appeals, [3.503], [3.504]
capital instruments, write down, [3.445]–[3.448]
confidentiality, [3.502]
cross-border group resolution, [3.505]–[3.510]

CREDIT INSTITUTION – *cont.*
EU Directive, recovery and resolution – *cont.*
designation of authorities responsible for resolution, [3.421]
early intervention measures, [3.445]–[3.448]
failure of institution, notification, [3.499]
financing arrangements, [3.517]–[3.527]
group financial support agreement, [3.437]
approval, [3.439]
conditions, [3.441]
decision to provide support, [3.442]
disclosure, [3.444]
opposition, right of, [3.443]
review, [3.438]
transmission to resolution authorities, [3.440]
penalties, [3.528]–[3.531]
recovery plans, [3.423]
assessment, [3.424]
group recovery plans, [3.425], [3.426]
indicators, [3.427]
resolution
conditions, [3.450], [3.451]
objectives, [3.449]
powers, [3.481]–[3.490]
special management, [3.453]
tools for
asset separation tool, [3.460]
bail-in tool, [3.461]–[3.476]
bridge institution tool, [3.458], [3.459]
general principles, [3.455]
sale of business tool, [3.456], [3.457]
valuation, [3.454]
resolution authority
decisions, [3.500]
procedural obligations, [3.501]
resolution plans, [3.428]
cooperation from institution, [3.429]
group resolution plans, [3.430], [3.431]
transmission to competent authorities, [3.432]
resolvability
assessment, [3.433], [3.434]
impediments to, [3.435], [3.436]
safeguards, [3.491]–[3.498]
simplified obligations for certain institutions, [3.422]
third countries agreements, recognition etc, [3.511]–[3.516]
group companies, [3.256]–[3.259]
investment firms, [3.251]–[3.255]
Regulations, reorganisation/winding up
creditors
notification, winding up proceedings, [3.226]
reports to, [3.228]
EEA credit institution
measures effective, UK, [3.217]
prohibition against winding up in UK, [3.215]
schemes of arrangement, [3.216]
EEA creditors, submission of claims, submission, [3.227]

CREDIT INSTITUTION – *cont.*
Regulations, reorganisation/winding up – *cont.*
EEA regulators
disclosure, confidential information from, [3.230]
notification, decisions to, [3.222]
EEA rights, recognition, [3.231]–[3.247]
FCA
consultation before resolution to wind up, [3.220]
notification, relevant decision to, [3.221]
generally, [3.213]–[3.250]
lex rei sitae, [3.245]
Northern Ireland. *See* NORTHERN IRELAND
obligations, relevant to be honoured, [3.225]
pending lawsuits, [3.244]
PRA
consultation before resolution to wind up, [3.220]
notification, relevant decision to, [3.221]
publication of qualifying decisions re voluntary arrangement etc, [3.224]
service of notices and documents, [3.229]
voluntary arrangement
publication, [3.224]
withdrawal, authorisation, [3.223]
third country institutions, [3.248]–[3.250]
CREDIT UNION
arrangements, reconstructions and administration, application of provisions, [7.1425]–[7.1450]
CREDITORS
administration order
distribution to, administrator, powers, [1.575]
protection, interests, [1.13], [1.575]
creditor's petition, bankruptcy. *See* BANKRUPTCY
decisions, qualifying procedure, [1.256], [1.460]
deemed consent procedure, [1.257], [1.461]
EC Regulation
information for, [3.76]
languages, [3.78]
lodgement, claim, content, [3.77]
right to lodge claims, [3.75]
satisfaction, claim, EU Member State, [3.56]
secondary insolvency proceedings, EU Member State
rights, exercise, [3.68]
energy administration order
false claim, status as, [7.1045]
list of creditors, right, [7.1044]
false claim, status as, [7.2565], [7.1045]
false representation to in winding up, [1.215]
fraud against, winding up transactions, [1.211], [1.537]–[1.539]
list, right to have, [7.2564], [7.1044]
meaning, in relation to bankrupt, [1.469]
notices, opting out of receipt, [1.261], [1.465]
preferential, protection in administration, [1.575]
railway administration order
false claim to be, [7.2566]
list, right, [7.2564]
satisfaction of claim, EU Member State requirements, [3.56]

CREDITORS – *cont.*
secondary insolvency proceedings, exercise of rights in EU Member State, [3.68]
secured
administration
protection, [1.13], [1.575]
debtor, discharge from bankruptcy, not releasing from secured debt, [1.341]
liquidation
security
realisation or surrender, [6.743]
redemption, [6.741]
surrender for non-disclosure, [6.740]
test of value, [6.742]
value, [6.739]
meaning, [1.263]
unsecured
meaning, [1.263]
winding up etc
floating charge, property subject, [1.180], [7.1539]
voluntary winding up
administration moving to, [1.575]
credit institution, notification, [3.226]
generally. *See* WINDING UP, VOLUNTARY, REGISTERED COMPANY
members' voluntary winding up
conversion from, [1.93]
distinguished, [1.86]
CREDITORS' COMMITTEE
administration
administrator's proposals approved, attendance at creditor's, [1.13], [1.575]
invitation to form, [6.150]
administrative receiver's report to registrar, power to require attendance, [1.35]
general provisions
chairman, [6.838]
establishment, formalities, [6.828]
formal defects, [6.850]
functions, [6.825]
information, [6.845], [6.846]
invitation to form, [6.196]
meetings, [6.837]–[6.844]
member
eligibility, [6.827]
expenses, [6.847]
numbers, [6.826]
removal, [6.835]
resignation, [6.833]
membership
changes, [6.830]
vacancies, [6.831], [6.832]
quorum, [6.839]
Scotland. *See* SCOTLAND
CREDITORS' MEETING
administration
administrator's proposals
consideration, [1.13], [1.575]
failure to obtain approval, [1.575]
revision, [1.575]
further, [1.575]
initial, [1.575]
corporation, representation of, [1.553]

CREDITORS' MEETING – *cont.*
energy administration order. *See* ENERGY ADMINISTRATION ORDER
generally
adjournment
absence of chair, [6.794]
chair, by, [6.792]
proofs in, [6.795]
removal of liquidator/trustee, [6.793]
chair, [6.790], [6.791]
exclusions from, [6.805]–[6.807]
quorum, [6.789]
records, [6.809]
remote attendance, [6.811]
suspension, [6.796]
voting, [6.797]–[6.804]
creditors' rights, [6.797]
contributories' rights, [6.808]
requisite majorities, [6.803], [6.808]
scheme manager's rights, [6.798]
individual voluntary arrangement
approval, proposal, [1.301], [1.302], [2.7]
challenge, decision, [1.303], [2.7]
decision re approval
modifications to which may be subject, [1.299]
report to court, [1.300]
nominee to summon, [1.298], [2.7]
persons to be summoned, [1.298], [2.7]
insurance company, winding up, [7.1507]
winding up, registered company
CVL
notice, [1.95]
procedure, [1.95]
winding up converted under s 96, [1.99]
CRIMINAL MATTERS
See also OFFENCES
criminal bankruptcy
criminal bankruptcy order, meaning, [1.472]
inapplicable rules, [6.618]
order made
bankruptcy order
court, requirements, [1.337]
dismissal, petition, [1.325]
distribution, estate, [1.398]
who may present petition, [1.323]
insolvency practitioner, criminal investigation
Proceeds of Crime Act 2002, external orders/ requests
application of sums by enforcement receivers, [12.53]
generally, [12.49]–[12.59]
Northern Ireland. *See* NORTHERN IRELAND
Scotland. *See* SCOTLAND
sums received by relevant Director, [12.54]
vesting/realisation, recoverable property
applying realised proceeds, [12.59]
Proceeds of Crime Act 2002
bankruptcy
applicable law, [17.236]
restriction, powers of bankrupt, [17.237]
tainted gifts, [17.238]
CRIMINAL MATTERS – *cont.*
Proceeds of Crime Act 2002 – *cont.*
detention, property released from, [1.371]
floating charges, [17.244]
insolvency practitioner, external orders/requests
application of sums by
enforcement receivers, [12.53]
generally, [12.49]–[12.59], [17.246], [17.247]
Northern Ireland. *See* NORTHERN IRELAND
Scotland. *See* SCOTLAND
sums received by relevant Director, [12.54]
vesting/realisation, recoverable property
applying realised proceeds, [12.59]
partnerships, limited liability, [17.245]
realisation order, property subject to, [1.373]
Scotland. *See* SCOTLAND
winding up
order, [17.242]
tainted gifts, [17.243]
CROSS-BORDER INSOLVENCY
appeals, [3.321]
applications, principal
adjournment of hearing, [3.316], [3.319]
court procedure, [3.316]
filing, [3.316], [3.319]
form, [3.316], [3.319]
hearing, [3.316]
service, [3.316], [3.319]
urgent, [3.316]
applications to Chief Land Registrar, [3.317]
co-operation, courts exercising jurisdiction, [3.308], [13.1]–[13.3], [13.19]–[13.23]
costs, detailed assessment, [3.320]
cross-border insolvency regulations 2006 [3.302]–[3.328]
court records, [3.319]
foreign representative
misfeasance, [3.318]
replacement, confirmation of status of
affidavit, [3.314]
application, [3.314]
hearing, [3.314]
Guernsey, provisions, [13.16]–[13.18]
modification of British insolvency law, [3.304]
notices to registrar etc, [3.307], [3.322], [3.327].
See also REGISTRAR OF COMPANIES
orders, notification and advertisement of, [3.316]
procedural matters, [3.305], [3.311]–[3.322]
recognition of foreign proceedings, application to court
affidavit, [3.312], [3.319]
content, [3.312], [3.319]
form, [3.312], [3.319]
hearing, [3.312]
notification, subsequent information, [3.312]
review of court orders
affidavit, [3.315]
application, [3.315]
court making order of own motion, [3.315]
hearing, [3.315]
Scotland. *See* SCOTLAND

CROSS-BORDER INSOLVENCY – *cont.*
transfer of proceedings
detriment to creditors, to avoid, [3.319]
within High Court, [3.319]
UNCITRAL model law
application, scope, [3.2]
authorisation, person administering reorganisation/liquidation, [3.6]
competent court/authority, [3.5]
concurrent proceedings, [3.29]–[3.33]
force of law, having, [3.303], [3.310]
foreign court
co-operation, court in this State, [3.26]–[3.28]
foreign creditors
access to courts in this State, [3.10]–[3.15]
foreign proceedings, recognition
application, [3.16]
decision to recognise, [3.18]
detriment to creditors
actions to avoid, [3.24]
foreign main proceeding
effect, [3.21]
relief that may be granted, [3.22]
information subsequent to application, [3.19]
presumptions, [3.17]
protection, creditors/other interested persons, [3.23]
relief, grant, [3.20]
foreign representatives
access to courts in this State, [3.10]–[3.15]
co-operation, court in this State, [3.26]–[3.28]
intervention, proceedings in this State, [3.25]
giving effect to, [3.87]
international obligations, this State, conflicts, [3.4]
public policy exception, [3.7]
relief under, application
affidavit, [3.313]
hearing, [3.313]
interim relief, [3.313]
service, interim relief not required, [3.313]
text, [3.2]–[3.33], [3.310]
CROWN
Crown preference, abolition, [2.27]
legislation binding, [1.551]
Scotland. *See* SCOTLAND: bankruptcy
CUSTOMS AND EXCISE
debts to, preferential, [1.473], [1.591]

D

DEATH
administrative receiver, [6.200]
individual voluntary arrangement, modification for deceased person, [1.292], [11.3], [11.5], [11.6], [11.9]
liquidator, [1.88], [1.101], [6.216], [6.248], [6.256]
trustee in bankruptcy, [6.542]
DEATH – *cont.*
winding up of registered company
liquidator, power to fill vacancy, [1.88], [1.101]
member as contributory, effect of liability, [1.77]
DECEASED PERSON
administration, insolvent estate
death of debtor, after presentation of bankruptcy petition, [11.9]
generally, [11.1]–[11.10]
individual voluntary arrangement, modification of provisions, [1.292], [11.3], [11.5], [11.6], [11.9]
employer, estate, [1.534]
insolvent estate, [1.534]
joint tenancies, [1.535]
DEBENTURE HOLDERS
bankrupt, undischarged, receiver/manager, property of
criminal offence, [1.17]
DEBT AVOIDANCE
compensation scheme, Financial Services and Markets Act 2000
debt avoidance, provisions against
Authority, right to apply for order, [17.207]
transactions defrauding creditors, [1.537]–[1.539], [4.55]
DEBT RELIEF ORDER
amendment, [6.450]
application for
approved intermediary, by, [6.437]
court to which made, [6.453], [6.454]
delivery, [6.436]
false representations and omissions, making, [1.282]
information in, [6.435]
making of, [1.269]
official receiver, consideration and determination by, [1.270]
presumptions applicable to determination, [1.271]
refusal of, [6.445]
approved intermediary
meaning, [1.288]
competent authorities, designation of
application for, [18.188]
extent of, [18.190]
fit and proper body, as, [18.189]
purposes of, [18.187]
withdrawal of, [18.191]
conditions for making, [1.584], [1.585]
contents, [6.442]
creditor
meaning, [6.446]
objection by, [6.447]
response to, [6.448]
prescribed information to, [6.444]
request for revocation, [6.449]
debtor
dealings and property, inquiry into, [1.281]
family, meaning, [6.433]
matters notified to official receiver, [6.451]
monthly surplus income, determination of, [6.439]

DEBT RELIEF ORDER – *cont.*
debtor – *cont.*
property, determination of value of, [6.440], [6.441]
provision of assistance to official receiver, [1.277]
verification checks against, [6.438]
debtor's bankruptcy petition, made on, [1.334]
disqualification of directors, application for leave, [6.457]–[6.459]
excluded debts, [1.268], [6.434]
fees, [8.82]–[8.89]
individual insolvency rules, inclusion of provisions, [1.594]
insolvency rules, [6.433]–[6.459]
intermediary, approval of
application for, [18.194]
generally, [18.192]
ineligibility, [18.193]
withdrawal, [18.195]
interpretation, [1.291]
making of, [1.272]
moratorium period
death of debtor, during, [6.452]
extension, [6.456]
objections and investigations, [1.278]
offences
business, engaging in, [1.286]
concealment or falsification of documents, [1.283]
credit, obtaining, [1.286]
false representations and omissions, making, [1.282]
fraudulent disposal of property, [1.284]
penalties, [1.287]
proceedings, institution of, [1.287]
property obtained on credit, fraudulent dealing with, [1.285]
official receiver
revocation or amendment of order, [1.279]
other debt arrangement orders, effect on, [1.273]
person subject to acting as manager or receiver, disqualification, [1.17]
persons at risk of violence, [6.905]
powers of court, [1.280]
prescribed verification checks, [6.438]
qualifying debt
discharge from, [1.276]
meaning, [1.268]
moratorium, [1.274], [1.275]
register of, [1.290]
restrictions order and undertakings, [1.586]
revocation or amendment, power of official receiver, [1.279], [6.450]
DEBT RELIEF RESTRICTIONS ORDER
application, [6.633]
evidence, bankrupt or debtor, [6.635]
interim, [6.637]–[6.640]
making, [6.636]
registration, [6.651], [6.652]
Secretary of State, reference to, [6.632]
service, notice of application, [6.634]
DEBT RELIEF RESTRICTIONS UNDERTAKING
acceptance, [6.641]
annulment, [6.643]
notification to court, [6.642]
registration, [6.651], [6.652]
DEBTS, PROOF OF
admission, dividend, for, [6.731]
appeal, [6.732]
costs, [6.729]
energy administration order. *See* ENERGY ADMINISTRATION ORDER
inspection, [6.730]
provable, meaning, [6.726]
rejection, dividend, for, [6.731]
requirements, [6.728]
submission of, [6.727]
variation, [6.734]
withdrawal, [6.734]
DEPOSIT PROTECTION BOARD
Scotland. *See* SCOTLAND: winding up
DEPOSIT PROTECTION SCHEME. *SEE* BANKS
DEPOSIT TAKER
authorised UK
meaning, [17.335]
property, rights and liabilities, transfer of
compensation for, [17.341], [17.343]
interpretation, [17.349]
order for, [17.340], [17.353]
orders and regulations, [17.347], [17.348]
tax consequences of, [17.344]
transfer to public sector, further transfers following, [17.342]
Treasury powers, exercise of, [17.336]
securities issued by, transfer of
compensation for, [17.339], [17.343]
interpretation, [17.349]
order for, [17.337], [17.352]
orders and regulations, [17.347], [17.348]
subscription rights, extinguishment of, [17.338]
tax consequences of, [17.344]
transfer to public sector, further transfers following, [17.342]
Treasury powers, exercise of, [17.336]
DIRECTORS
administrator, appointment, [1.575]
bankrupt, permission to act as director, [6.586]–[6.590]
company voluntary arrangement, proposal, [1.1]
company with prohibited name, leave to act as director of, [6.927]–[6.933]. *See also* NAME, COMPANY
connected with a company, as person, [1.265]
contributory, liability on winding up of registered company
directors etc with unlimited liability, [1.71]
past directors, [1.72]
creditors' voluntary winding up
cesser of powers on appointment of liquidator, exception, [1.87], [1.100]
statement of affairs to creditors
contents, [1.96]

DIRECTORS – *cont.*
creditors' voluntary winding up – *cont.*
statement of affairs to creditors – *cont.*
non-compliance, [1.96]
disqualification. *See* DISQUALIFICATION OF DIRECTORS
meaning, [1.267]
offences
creditors' voluntary winding up, non-compliance with statement of affairs, [1.96]
re-use of company name, restricted period, [1.220]
personal liability for debts following contravention of restriction on re-use of company name after insolvent liquidation, [1.221]
shadow director
'connected' with a company, as person, [1.265]
meaning, [1.267]
winding up
false representation to creditor, [1.215]
fraud in anticipation, [1.210]
misconduct during, [1.211]
unfitness, debt avoidance provisions, [1.537]–[1.539], [4.55]. *See also* DISQUALIFICATION OF DIRECTORS
unlimited liability, saving for, [2.71]
winding up, summary remedy against delinquent director, [1.216]

DISCLAIMER
covenant as to part of tenancy, demised premises limited to, [17.133]
trustee in bankruptcy, by
dwelling house, conditions, [1.389]
generally, [6.891]–[6.901]
leaseholds, [1.388], [1.392]. *See also* LEASEHOLDS
market contracts, [1.386]
notice, [1.386], [1.387]
onerous property, [1.386]–[1.392]
operation, [1.182], [1.386], [17.133]
rentcharge, land subject, [1.390]
tenancies, [1.386]
winding up, registered company
court, powers, [1.185], [1.186], [6.901]
interested party, application under, s 178(5), [6.899]
land subject to rentcharge, [1.182], [1.184]
leaseholds, [1.183], [1.186]
liquidator
onerous property, power, [1.182], [1.185]
notices, [6.891]–[6.896]
onerous property
liquidator, power, [1.182], [1.185]

DISCLOSURE
administrative receiver's report to registrar, [1.34]
bankrupt, state of affairs
creditor's petition, [6.513]–[6.519]
debtor's application, [6.520]–[6.523]
court practice, [6.681]
energy administration order
confidentiality, documents, [7.1011], [7.1039]
statement of affairs, [7.890]

DISCLOSURE – *cont.*
financial markets, [12.13]–[12.22]
railway administration order, [7.2533]
winding up by court
statement of affairs, limited, [6.318]

DISQUALIFICATION OF DIRECTORS
administration order, county court
failure to pay under, [4.25]
administrative receiver, statement of affairs, submission to
non-compliance, [1.33]
applications, practice direction, [19.23]–[19.26]
bankrupt, undischarged, [4.24]
body corporate, offences, [4.28]
building society, [4.44], [7.459]
charitable incorporated organisations, [4.48]
Company Directors Disqualification Act, [4.1]–[4.59]
compensation orders, [14.51]–[14.59]
applications, [14.52]
form and content, [14.53]
hearing, [14.58]
claim form
acknowledgement of service, [14.56]
evidence, [14.57]
information of, [14.55]
claimant's case, [14.54]
fees, [14.60]–[14.64]
making of by court, [14.59]
setting aside of, [14.59]
competition infringements
co-ordination, functions re, [4.21]
investigation, [4.20]
order, [4.18]
specified regulator, meaning, [4.22]
undertaking, [4.19]
conduct of director, reports, [4.10], [14.41]–[14.50]
enforcement, requirements, [14.22]
forms, [14.21], [14.24]
generally, [14.18]–[14.24]
requirements, [14.19]
return by office-holder, [14.20]
conviction
foreign offence, [4.7]
indictable offence, [4.3]
criminal penalties, [4.27]
European grouping of territorial cooperation, provisions applying [3.545]
evidence, admissibility of statements, [4.37]
legal professional privilege, [4.38]
fraud etc, winding up, [4.5]
friendly society, incorporated, [4.45]
further education bodies, [4.49]
NHS foundation trust, [4.46]
industrial and provident societies, [4.47]
interpretation, [14.34]
investigation of company, after
unfit director, [4.11]
investment bank, of, [7.1699]
officers of court, particulars to be furnished by, [14.37]–[14.39]

DISQUALIFICATION OF DIRECTORS – *cont.*
orders
application, [4.33]
application for leave under, [4.34]
compensation orders, [4.30]
amount payable under, [4.31]
variation and revocation, [4.32]
competition infringements, [4.18]
content, [4.1]
court, powers/duties, [4.1]
grounds other than criminal convictions, [4.1]
Northern Ireland, [14.36], [14.40]
person already subject, order/undertaking, [4.1]
register, [4.35]
unfit director, [4.9], [4.12], [4.13]
particulars to be furnished by officers of the court
requirements, [14.25]–[14.32]
revoked legislation, [14.2]–[14.6]
partnership, insolvent, applicable to, [10.15]
persistent breaches, companies legislation, [4.4]
personal liability, company's debts
acting while disqualified, [4.29]
practice direction
application of, [19.22]
applications, [19.23]–[19.26]
interpretation, [19.22]
proceedings other than in Royal Courts of Justice, [19.27], [19.31]
undertakings, [19.28]
protected cell companies, [4.50]
receiver/manager, failure in duty to file returns, subsequent, [1.27], [4.4], [4.6]
Scotland. *See* SCOTLAND
summary conviction, [4.6]
transitional provisions, [14.35]
undertaking
application for leave under, [4.34]
compensation undertakings, [4.30]
amount payable under, [4.31]
variation and revocation, [4.32]
competition infringement, [4.19]
content, [4.2]
criteria, acceptance, [4.2]
duration, maximum, [4.2]
person already subject, order/undertaking, [4.2]
practice direction, [19.28]
register, [4.35]
Secretary of State, power to accept, [4.2]
unfit director, [4.9], [4.14], [4.16], [4.17]
variation etc undertaking
unfitness
application for order on grounds of
acknowledgement, [14.12]
application of rules, [14.7], [14.9]
content, [14.8]
endorsement on claim form, [14.11]
form, [14.8]
hearing, [14.14]
service, [14.12]
audience, right of, [14.16]
court, duty to disqualify unfit director, insolvent company, [4.8]
determination, criteria, [4.26], [4.55], [14.10]

DISQUALIFICATION OF DIRECTORS – *cont.*
unfitness – *cont.*
evidence, [14.13]
investigation, company, disqualification after, [4.11]
order, [4.9], [4.12], [4.13], [14.15]
reporting provisions, [4.9]
revocations, [14.17]
setting aside order, [14.15]
undertaking, [4.9], [4.14], [4.16]
variation etc, of undertaking, [4.17]
unfit director, [4.17]
winding up by court
property dispositions etc after commencement, [1.128], [1.522], [1.537], [4.39]
wrongful trading, [4.23]

DISSOLUTION OF COMPANY
administration, after, [1.575]
investment company, open-ended, [7.2053], [7.2054]
winding up, after
early, [1.206]
investment company, open-ended, [7.2053]
notice under s 202, [1.207]
other than under ss 202–204, [1.209]
Scotland. *See* SCOTLAND
voluntary winding up, [1.205]

DISTRESS
See also EXECUTION
landlord etc, by, for rent, enforcement procedure, [1.425]

DISTRIBUTIONS
administration, to creditors
debts, insolvent company to act equally, [6.736]
generally, [6.750]–[6.769]
proving a debt
admission for dividend, [6.731]
appeal against decision on, [6.732]
costs, [6.729]
exclusion by court, [6.735]
inspection, proofs, [6.730]
proof, submission, [6.727]
rejection for dividend, [6.731]
requirements, [6.728]
variation, [6.734]
withdrawal, [6.734]
liquidator, by
creditors, to, [6.750]–[6.769]
debts, insolvent company to rank equally, [6.736]
declaration, [6.751]
general duties, collection/distribution, [6.351]
members' voluntary winding up, in, [1.105]

DIVIDEND
bankruptcy, payment of creditor, [8.47], [8.48]
creditors' claims, generally, [6.750]–[6.769]
distribution, bankrupt's estate by, [1.395]
energy administration order
assignment, right, [7.945]
declaration, [7.938]
disqualification from, [7.944]
distribution, [7.911]
no dividend, notice, [7.941]

DIVIDEND – *cont.*
energy administration order – *cont.*
no further dividend, notice, [7.941]
notice of declaration, [7.939]
payment etc, [7.940]
proofs, admission/rejection for, [7.918]
insurance company, winding up, [7.1506]
unclaimed
after discharge, permanent trustee, [1.197], [5.140], [5.194]
Consolidated Fund, [1.518], [1.519]
liquidator, payment, [8.42]
trustee in bankruptcy, payment, [8.56]
voluntary winding up, payment to creditor, [8.32]
winding up by court, payment to creditor, [8.32]
DOMICILE
bankruptcy of debtor, [1.324]
DRUG TRAFFICKING
bankrupt's estate, property not part, [1.344]
confiscation orders
Scotland. *See* SCOTLAND
DWELLING-HOUSE
meaning, [1.472]
occupied by bankrupt/spouse/former/civil partner/former
charge, application by trustee for, [1.383]
disclaimer, onerous property, trustee in bankruptcy, [1.389]
home rights
bankrupt, [1.409]
spouse/former/civil partner/former
charge, as, [1.408]
nothing occurring during initial period of bankruptcy given rise, [1.408]
low-value home, powers of court on application by trustee, [1.384]
notice to bankrupt by trustee, property falling within definition, [6.627]
payments, premises occupied by bankrupt, [1.410]
sole/principal residence, protection, [1.345]
vesting of interest in
application re registered land, [6.628]
bankrupt's interest in unregistered land, [6.629]
substituted period, [6.630]

E

ECCLESIASTICAL BENEFICE
vacant, right to nomination to not part of, bankrupt's estate, [1.344]
EC DIRECTIVES
credit institution. *See* CREDIT INSTITUTION
financial collateral arrangements
close-out netting provisions, recognition, [3.275]
conflict of laws, [3.277]
enforcement, [3.272]
formal requirements, [3.271]
implementation, [3.280]
EC DIRECTIVES – *cont.*
financial collateral arrangements – *cont.*
insolvency provisions which are disapplied, [3.276]
report on application, Directive, [3.279]
right of use under security financial collateral arrangements, [3.273]
text, [3.268]–[3.282]
title transfer, recognition, [3.274]
insurance undertakings on reorganisation and winding up. *See* INSURANCE COMPANY/ UNDERTAKING
EU REGULATION
administration, conversion to winding up application, [6.911], [6.912]
applications to court under, standard contents, [6.910]
company voluntary arrangement
conversion to winding up, [6.911], [6.912]
member State liquidator, notice to, [6.916]
creditor's voluntary winding up, confirmation by court, [6.913]–[6.915]
individual voluntary arrangement, conversion into bankruptcy, [6.911], [6.912]
insolvency proceedings
applicable law, [3.40]
Conventions, relationship to, [3.80]
creditors
information for, [3.76]
languages, [3.78]
lodgement, claim, content, [3.77]
right to lodge claims, [3.75]
employment contracts, [3.46]
entry into force, [3.83]
financial markets, [3.45]
group coordination proceedings, [6.921]–[6.924]
immovable property
contract, [3.44]
debtor, rights subject to registration, [3.47]
insolvency proceedings referred to, [3.84]
international jurisdiction, [3.39]
liquidator
appointment, proof, [3.55]
Member State, of
closing of proceedings, statement, [6.926]
opening of proceedings, publication, [6.925]
undertakings, [6.919]
powers, [3.54]
publication, notice of judgment, [3.57]
reference to, [3.86]
return by creditor to
satisfaction, claim, Member State, [3.56]
patents/trade marks, [3.48]
payments systems, [3.45]
pending lawsuits, [3.51]
proceedings to which applicable, [3.37]
recognition, proceedings in Member State
effect, [3.53]
enforceability etc, other judgments, [3.61]
honouring obligation to debtor, [3.60]
liquidator, [3.54]–[3.57]. *See also* liquidator, *above*

EU REGULATION – *cont.*
insolvency proceedings – *cont.*
recognition, proceedings in Member State – *cont.*
principle, [3.52]
public policy, [3.62]
registration, judgment, public register, [3.58], [3.59]
reports on application, frequency, [3.82]
reservation of title, [3.43]
rights subject to registration, [3.47]
set-off, [3.42]
text, [3.36]–[3.86]
third parties
purchasers, protection, [3.50]
rights in rem, [3.41]
winding-up proceedings referred to, [3.85]
meaning, [1.558]
property, meaning, [1.559]
Scotland. *See* SCOTLAND
secondary insolvency proceedings
applicable law, [3.64]
assets remaining after, [3.71]
costs and expenses, advance payment, [3.66]
creditors' rights, exercise, [3.68]
earlier proceedings, conversion, [3.73]
ending, [3.70]
information, co-operation/communication, [3.67]
opening, [3.63]
preservation measures, [3.74]
right to request opening, [3.65]
stay, liquidation, [3.69]
subsequent opening, main proceedings, [3.72]
statute for a European company (SE). *See* EUROPEAN COMPANY
EDUCATION
teachers. *See* TEACHERS
Wales. *See* WALES
EDUCATION ADMINISTRATION
conduct of, [7.2602]
education administrator
appointment, [7.2598]
functions, [7.2601]
status, [7.2600]
transfer schemes, power to make, [7.2602]
objective, [7.2593]
order for, [7.2594]
applications for, [7.2595]
court powers, [7.2597]
grounds for making, [7.2596]
grants or loans made, [7.2604]
guarantees, [7.2607], [7.2608]
indemnities, [7.2605], [7.2606]
ordinary administration order, duty to dismiss, [7.2599]
rules, power to make, [7.2609]
EEA STATE
company incorporated in EEA State other than UK, company voluntary arrangement, [1.1]
company not incorporated in EEA State, company voluntary arrangement, [1.1]
EEA STATE – *cont.*
compensation scheme under Financial Services and Markets Act 2000, winding up by court of EEA/Treaty firms, [17.199]
credit institutions
creditors, submission of claims, [3.227]
measures effective, UK, [3.217]
prohibition against winding up in UK, [3.215]
regulators
disclosure, confidential information from, [3.230]
notification, decisions to, [3.222]
rights, recognition, [3.231]–[3.247]
schemes of arrangement, [3.216]
insurers
creditors, submission of, [3.136]
employment contracts, effect, [3.162]
insurers
prohibition against winding up, UK, [3.127]
reorganisation measures effective, UK, [3.129]
schemes of arrangement, [3.128]
regulators, notification of reorganisation decisions to, [3.133]
rights, recognition on UK reorganisation/winding up, [3.158]–[3.171]
Lloyd's market reorganisation
creditor, submission of claims, [7.1606]
rights, recognition, [7.1614]
meaning, [1.558]
SCE, registered office in GB, petition for winding up by court, [1.125]
SE, registered office in GB, petition for winding up by court, [1.124]
ELECTRONIC FORM
documents in, [1.560]
ELECTRONIC MONEY
insolvency events, [18.220]
regulations, [18.218]–[18.220]
safeguarding, [18.219]
EMPLOYMENT
associate, meaning, [1.557]. *See also* ASSOCIATE
contract
administrative receiver, qualifying liability arising, [1.30]
EC Directive
credit institution, reorganisation/winding up, [3.196]
insurance undertakings, reorganisation/winding up, [3.107]
EC Regulation, insolvency, [3.46]
EEA State
credit institution, reorganisation/winding up, UK, effect, [3.235]
insurers, reorganisation/winding up, UK, effect, [3.162]
Scotland. *See* SCOTLAND
employee
company wound up by court/voluntarily power to make assets over to, [1.191]
consultation, transnational information, [12.8], [12.9]

EMPLOYMENT – *cont.*
employee – *cont.*
redundancy payments by Secretary of State
application, [17.136]
making, [17.137]
remuneration as preferential debt, [1.473], [1.591]
rights on insolvency of employer, [17.138]–[17.145], [3.341]–[3.360]
employer, insolvent
deceased estate, [1.534]
pensions, unpaid contributions
priority in bankruptcy, [17.110]
Secretary of State, payment, [17.101]–[17.106]
transfer of rights etc to preferential charge on goods distrained to Secretary of State, [1.177], [1.399]
pensions generally. *See* PENSIONS
ENERGY ACT 2004
energy administration order. *See* ENERGY ADMINISTRATION ORDER; ENERGY SUPPLY COMPANY ADMINISTRATION
protected energy company
administrator appointment by creditors, restriction, [7.858]
enforcement, security, restriction, [7.859]
ordinary administration order, restriction, [7.857]
voluntary winding up, restriction, [7.856]
winding up, restriction, [7.855]
ENERGY ADMINISTRATION ORDER
See also ENERGY ACT 2004
appeals, [7.1000], [7.1001]
applications, procedure, [7.965]–[7.976], [7.851]
attendance, rights of, [7.1004], [7.1005]
audience, rights of, [7.1003]
claim, quantification, [7.922]–[7.946]. *See also* debt, proof, *below*
company meeting
conduct, [7.906]
venue, [7.906]
company representation, [7.1019]
concurrent proceedings/remedies, restriction, [7.1007]
copy documents, [7.1041], [7.1042]
costs
application for, [7.993]
award against energy administrator, [7.992]
CPR applicable, [7.988]
detailed assessment, requirement, [7.989], [7.990]
expenses, [7.1027]
final costs certificate, [7.995]
otherwise than from assets, protected energy company, [7.991]
witnesses, [7.994]
court, powers, [7.852]
creditor
false claim, status as, [7.1045]
list of creditors, right, [7.1044]
creditors' meetings
admission or rejection of claims, [7.898]
alternative liquidator, nomination, [7.896]
ENERGY ADMINISTRATION ORDER – *cont.*
creditors' meetings – *cont.*
chairman, [7.895]
conditional sale and chattel leasing agreements, owner or seller under, [7.901]
evidence of proceedings, [7.1031]
hire-purchase, owner of goods, [7.901]
minutes, [7.903]
negotiable instruments, holders of, [7.900]
notice of, non-receipt, [7.1043]
quorum, [7.1030]
reports to creditors, [7.905]
resolutions, [7.902]
revision of energy administrator's proposals, [7.904]
secured creditors, [7.899]
summoning, [7.894]
voting entitlement, [7.897]
debt, proof of
admission for dividend, [7.1018]
affidavit to establish claim, [7.914]
alteration after payment, dividend, [7.942]
appeal against decision, [7.919]
claims, quantification
admission/rejection, proofs, [7.937]
discounts, [7.925]
dividend. *See* dividend, *below*
estimate, quantum, [7.922]
foreign currency, [7.927]
future payment, debt, [7.930], [7.946]
interest payable, [7.929]
mutual credits, [7.926]
negotiable instruments etc, [7.923]
periodical payments, [7.928]
proposed distribution, notice, [7.936]
redemption by energy administrator, [7.933]
secured creditors, [7.924], [7.943]
security
realisation by creditor, [7.935]
test of value, [7.934]
value, [7.931]
set-off, [7.926]
surrender for non-disclosure, [7.932]
costs, [7.915]
expunging by court, [7.921]
inspection of proofs, energy administrator to allow, [7.916]
method, [7.913]
new energy administrator appointed, [7.917]
provable debts, [7.1028]
rejection for dividend, [7.918]
variation, [7.920]
withdrawal, [7.920]
disclosure, [7.1011], [7.1039]
disposal, charged property
authority, [7.907]
distribution
creditors, to, generally, [7.909]
debts, insolvent company to rank equally, [7.910]
proposed, notice of, [7.936]
unsold assets, division, [7.912]

ENERGY ADMINISTRATION ORDER – *cont.*
dividend
assignment, right, [7.945]
declaration, [7.938]
disqualification from, [7.944]
distribution, [7.911]
no dividend, notice, [7.941]
no further dividend, notice, [7.941]
notice of declaration, [7.939]
payment etc, [7.940]
proofs, admission/rejection for, [7.918]
ending
application to court, [7.949]
court order, notification by energy administrator, [7.950]
creditors' voluntary winding up, moving to, [7.951]
dissolution, moving to, [7.952]
final progress reports, [7.948]
Secretary of State, information to, [7.953]
energy administrator
appointment
by court, [7.877]–[7.886]
notification/advertisement, [7.887]
costs award against, [7.992]
meaning, [7.853]
proposals, [7.893]
remuneration, [7.947]
replacement, [7.954]–[7.964]
security, [7.1034]
energy supply company. *See* ENERGY SUPPLY COMPANY ADMINISTRATION
enforcement procedures, [7.979]–[7.981]
Enterprise Act 2002 provisions, [7.865]
modification, [7.1068]
examination, persons, [7.1020]–[7.1025]
expenses
costs, as, [7.1027]
priority, [7.908]
financial support, company, [7.860]–[7.862]
formal defects, [7.1006]
forms, [7.1061]
generally, [7.874]–[7.1062], [7.849]–[7.854], [7.860]–[7.862], [7.863]–[7.873]
incapacity of person incapable of managing own affairs, appointment of another person to act, [7.996]–[7.999]
insolvency legislation, modification of, [7.1069]
licence modification
conditions to secure funding, energy administration, [7.864]
particular or standard conditions, discretion of Secretary of State, [7.863]
meaning, [7.849]
notices, [7.886], [7.1029], [7.1040], [7.1046], [7.1048], [7.1052], [7.1053]
objective, [7.850]
offences, [7.1047], [7.1062]
particular or standard conditions, modification of, [7.1066]
proxies, [7.1013]–[7.1018]
records, court
file, court proceedings, [7.985]
Gazette notices etc, [7.987]

ENERGY ADMINISTRATION ORDER – *cont.*
records, court – *cont.*
inspection, [7.984], [7.986]
requirement to keep, [7.983]
Scotland. *See* SCOTLAND
Secretary of State
documents, [7.1032]
powers, [7.1026]
security in court, [7.1009]
shorthand writers, [7.977], [7.978]
statement of affairs
disclosure, limited, [7.890]
expenses, [7.892]
extension, time for submission, [7.891]
filing, [7.889]
notice requiring, [7.888]
release from duty, submission, [7.891]
verification, [7.889]
time limits, [7.1035]
transfer schemes, [7.854]

ENERGY SUPPLY COMPANY ADMINISTRATION
appeals, [7.1197], [7.1198]
applications to court
court file, [7.1184]
disapplication of s 176A, for, [7.1170]
filing and service, [7.1171]
form and contents of, [7.1169]
further information and disclosure, for, [7.1204]
hearings
adjournment, [7.1178]
generally, [7.1174]
without notice, [7.1173]
office copies of documents, provision of, [7.1205]
reports, use of, [7.1177]
s 176A(5), under, [7.1172]
shorthand writers, [7.1179], [7.1180]
witness statements, [7.1175], [7.1176]
company meetings
energy supply company representative at, [7.1212]
notice
advertisement of, [7.1229]
non-delivery of, [7.1227]
proxies
definition, [7.1206]
financial interest, holder with, [7.1211]
inspection, right of, [7.1210]
issue and use of forms, [7.1207]
retention of, [7.1209]
use of, [7.1208]
venue and conduct of, [7.1107]
costs
administrator, awarded against, [7.1189]
application for, [7.1190]
application of rules, [7.1185]
detailed assessment, [7.1186], [7.1187]
examination of persons in proceedings, of, [7.1218]
final certificate, [7.1192]
paid otherwise than from energy supply company assets, [7.1188]

ENERGY SUPPLY COMPANY ADMINISTRATION – *cont.*
costs – *cont.*
witnesses, of, [7.1191]
creditors' meetings
admission and rejection of claims, [7.1099]
alternative liquidator, for nomination of, [7.1097]
chair, [7.1096]
energy supply company representative at, [7.1212]
entitlement to vote, [7.1098]
excluded persons, [7.1247]–[7.1249]
generally, [7.1095]
hire-purchase, conditional sale and chattel leasing agreements, voting by owners under, [7.1102]
holders of negotiable instruments, voting by, [7.1101]
minutes, [7.1104]
notice
advertisement of, [7.1229]
non-delivery of, [7.1227]
proxies
definition, [7.1206]
financial interest, holder with, [7.1211]
inspection, right of, [7.1210]
issue and use of forms, [7.1207]
retention of, [7.1209]
use of, [7.1208]
quorum, [7.1245]
remote attendance at, [7.1246]
resolutions, [7.1103]
revision of proposals by, [7.1105]
secured creditors, voting by, [7.1100]
debt, proof of
admission and rejection of, [7.1119], [7.1138]
alteration after payment of dividend, [7.1144]
appeal against decisions on, [7.1120]
claim, making, [7.1115]
costs of, [7.1116]
debt payable at future time, [7.1131]
discounts, [7.1126]
estimate of quantum of claim, [7.1123]
expunging by court, [7.1122]
foreign currency debts, [7.1128]
inspection of, [7.1117]
interest, [7.1130]
mutual credits and set-off, [7.1127]
negotiable instruments, in respect of, [7.1124]
new energy administrator, transmission to, [7.1118]
periodical nature, payments of, [7.1129]
secured creditors, of, [7.1125]
security
non-disclosure, surrender for, [7.1133]
realisation by creditor, [7.1136]
redemption, [7.1134]
test of value, [7.1135]
value of, [7.1132]
withdrawal or variation of, [7.1121]
distribution to creditors
dividend
adjustment where paid before time, [7.1148]

ENERGY SUPPLY COMPANY ADMINISTRATION – *cont.*
distribution to creditors – *cont.*
dividend – *cont.*
alteration of proof after payment, [7.1144]
assignment of right to, [7.1147]
calculation and distribution of, [7.1113]
declaration of, [7.1140]
disqualification from, [7.1146]
no, or no further, notice of, [7.1143]
notice of declaration, [7.1141]
payments, [7.1142]
postponement or cancellation of, [7.1139]
equal ranking of debts, [7.1112]
generally, [7.1111]
proposed, notice of, [7.1137]
secured creditors, revaluation of security, [7.1145]
unsold assets, division of, [7.1114]
documents
copies of, [7.1268], [7.1269]
court, service of, [7.1240]–[7.1244]
inspection of, [7.1270]–[7.1270]
personal delivery of, [7.1225]
postal delivery of, [7.1226]
electronic delivery of proceedings, [7.1239]
ending of
application to court, [7.1152]
court order, notification of, [7.1153]
creditors' voluntary liquidation, move to, [7.1154]
dissolution, move to, [7.1155]
final progress reports, [7.1151]
Secretary of State, provision of information to, [7.1156]
Energy Act 2004, application of provisions, [7.1065]
energy administrator
appointment, notification and advertisement of, [7.1087]
authority to dispose of property, [7.1108]
award of costs against, [7.1189]
ceasing to be qualified to act, notice of vacation of office, [7.1161]
court order ending administration, notification of, [7.1153]
death of, [7.1162]
duties on vacating office, [7.1167]
limited disclosure, order for, [7.1094]
notices and documents
authorisation, [7.1234]
electronic delivery, [7.1235], [7.1236]
form of, [7.1232]
joint administrators, notice to, [7.1231]
orders under s 176A(5), notice of, [7.1273]
proof of sending, [7.1233]
progress reports by, [7.1106], [7.1151]
proposals
revision of, [7.1105]
statement of, [7.1093]
removal from office, application for, [7.1160]
remuneration
fixing, [7.1149]
new administrator, of, [7.1150]

ENERGY SUPPLY COMPANY ADMINISTRATION – *cont.*
energy administrator – *cont.*
replacement of
application for, [7.1163]
notification and advertisement of appointment, [7.1164], [7.1165]
registrar of companies, notification to, [7.1166]
resignation
grounds for, [7.1157]
notice of, [7.1159]
notice of intention, [7.1158]
security, [7.1272]
websites, use of, [7.1237], [7.1238]
enforcement of orders
compliance with rules, as to, [7.1182]
generally, [7.1181]
warrants, [7.1183]
examination of persons in
application for, form and contents of, [7.1214]
application of rules, [7.1213]
costs, [7.1218]
order for, [7.1215]
procedure, [7.1216]
record of, [7.1217]
expenses
costs pre-administration, [7.1110]
energy supply company, of, [7.1220]
priority of, [7.1109]
false claim of status as creditor, [7.1222]
forms, [7.1250]–[7.1252], [7.1282]
formal defects in proceedings, [7.1201]
funding, licence conditions to secure, [7.1067]
Gazette notices, [7.1253]–[7.1255]
interpretation, [7.1070], [7.1075], [7.1275]–[7.1280]
list of creditors, right to, [7.1270]
meaning, [7.1063]
notices other than in Gazette, [7.1256], [7.1257]
objective, [7.1064]
offences, punishment of, [7.1223], [7.1283]
order
appeals, [7.1197], [7.1198]
application for
contents, [7.1079]
filing, [7.1080]
form of, [7.1078]
hearing, [7.1085]
notice to officers, [7.1082]
service, [7.1084]–[7.1084]
notice of, [7.1086]
witness statement, [7.1077], [7.1079]
order staying proceedings, service of, [7.1202]
payments into court, [7.1203]
persons lacking capacity to manage affairs
application of rules, [7.1193]
appointment of person to act for, [7.1194]–[7.1196]
principal court rules and practice, application of, [7.1199]
provable debts, [7.1221]

ENERGY SUPPLY COMPANY ADMINISTRATION – *cont.*
registrar of companies, notifications to
application of rules, [7.1258]
court orders, relating to, [7.1262]
documents, relating to, [7.1261]
information in, [7.1259]
more than one nature, of, [7.1265]
office of administrator, relating to, [7.1260]
other events as to, [7.1264]
other persons at same time, to, [7.1266]
returns or reports of meetings, [7.1263]
rights of audience, [7.1200]
Secretary of State, powers of, [7.1219]
solicitors, notice etc to, [7.1228]
statement of affairs
expenses, [7.1092]
extension of time for, [7.1091]
limited disclosure, [7.1090]
notice requiring, [7.1088]
release from duty to submit, [7.1091]
verification and filing, [7.1089]
time limits, [7.1271]
ENFORCEMENT PROCEDURES. *SEE* COURT PROCEDURE AND PRACTICE
ENTERPRISE ACT 2002
bankruptcy
disqualification from office, [2.15], [2.16]
duration, [2.13], [2.22]
home of bankrupt, [2.14]
energy administration order, applicable provisions, [7.865]
fees, [2.17]
foreign company, applicable law, [2.11]
generally, [2.9]–[2.22]
non-company
company arrangement/administration, applicable law, [2.12], [2.21]
special administration regimes, [2.10]
ENVIRONMENTAL PROTECTION
contaminated land, remedial measures, [17.99]
EUROPEAN COMMUNITY/IES
See EUROPEAN UNION
EUROPEAN COMPANY
cessation of payments in winding up, liquidation or insolvency, [3.264]–[3.267]
public limited company, treated as, [3.263]
registered office, [3.262]
Statute for, [3.262]–[3.267]
EUROPEAN ECONOMIC INTEREST GROUPING
cessation of membership, [13.6]
Companies Act provisions, application of, [13.9], [13.14], [13.15]
competent authority, [13.7]
Council Regulation, [13.13]
disqualification of directors, [13.11]
insolvency legislation, application of, [13.10]
interpretation, [13.5]
liquidation, conclusion of, [13.8]
winding up, [13.8]
EUROPEAN GROUPING OF TERRITORIAL COOPERATION
applicable law, [3.331]

EUROPEAN GROUPING OF TERRITORIAL COOPERATION – *cont.*
competent authority and court, [3.543]
composition, [3.332]
disqualification of directors, [3.545]
dissolution, [3.336]
EU Regulation, text of, [3.329]–[3.339]
interpretation, [3.542]
jurisdiction, [3.337]
liquidation, insolvency, cessation of payments and liability, [3.334]
nature of, [3.330]
public interest activities, [3.335]
regulations, text of, [3.541]–[3.545]
winding up, [3.544]
EUROPEAN UNION
professional qualifications, recognition, [12.60]–[12.65]
EVIDENCE
disqualification of director, admissibility of statements, [4.37]
statements of affairs etc, admissibility, [1.550]
winding up of registered company
commission for receiving, power of court to refer, [1.201]
company's books as, [1.195]
EXECUTION
See also DISTRESS
bankruptcy, enforcement procedures against goods and land, [1.424]
effect of insolvency on, [6.711]
winding up of registered company
by court, avoidance after commencement, [1.129]
effect, [1.187]
officers charged with (writs etc), duties, [1.188]
EXTORTIONATE CREDIT TRANSACTIONS
administration/liquidation, prior adjustment, application by office-holder, [1.249], [2.10]
bankruptcy, prior adjustment, application by trustee in bankruptcy, [1.421]
extortionate, meaning, [1.249]
Scotland. *See* SCOTLAND: bankruptcy

F

FALSE OR MISLEADING INFORMATION
Pension Protection Fund Board, to, [17.320]
FALSE REPRESENTATION
company voluntary arrangement, to obtain approval, [1.9]
individual voluntary arrangement, to obtain approval, [1.304], [2.7]
winding up by court, to creditors in, [1.215]
FALSE STATEMENT
bankrupt, offence, [1.435]
FALSIFICATION, BOOKS
bankrupt, by, [1.434]
winding up, in, by officer or contributory, [1.213]
FEES ORDERS
company insolvency proceedings, [1.525]
company voluntary arrangement, [6.109]
FEES ORDERS – *cont.*
Enterprise Act 2002, [2.17]
general, [1.527], [8.7]–[8.21], [8.71]–[8.81]
individual insolvency proceedings, [1.526]
insolvency practitioners, [8.19], [12.24], [12.25]
insolvency proceedings, [2.37]–[2.39], [2.46], [8.76], [8.77], [8.81]
Insolvency Services Account, [12.24], [12.25], [12.29]
limits, [8.11]
Secretary of State, powers, [1.527]
transitional provisions, [2.48], [2.67], [2.85]
FILING OBLIGATIONS
enforcement, [1.555]
overseas companies, of, [1.556]
FINANCIAL MARKETS
administrative receiver, appointment in permitted circumstances, [1.65]
bankruptcy
disclaimer, onerous property by trustee, [1.386]
EC Regulation, [3.45]
transactions at undervalue, [1.411], [1.537], [17.68]
disclosure, [12.13]–[12.22]
Financial Services and Markets Act 2000
administration order, insurers, [7.1565]–[7.1569]
compensation scheme, [17.181]–[17.217]. *See also* COMPENSATION
disclosure, [12.13]–[12.22]
regulated activities, exemptions, [12.10], [12.12]
indemnity, [17.88]
infrastructure administration, [7.1452]–[7.1472], [7.1473]
administrator
appointment, [7.1456]
directions to, [7.1460]
management by, [7.1458]
status of, [7.1458]
companies in, support for, [7.1465], [7.1466]
conduct of, [7.1461], [7.1472]
continuity of supply, [7.1459]
interpretation, [7.1452], [7.1453], [7.1467], [7.1469]
Northern Ireland, provision for, [7.1468]
objective of, [7.1455]
orders
application for, [7.1456]
meaning, [7.1454]
powers of court, [7.1457]
other insolvency provisions, restrictions on, [7.1462]–[7.1464]
transfer schemes, [7.1473]
jurisdiction, [9.13]
market charge
administration orders etc, [17.78]
administrative receiver, appointment permitted, [1.65]
CGO service charge, [9.8]–[9.11]
charges not treated as, [9.4]
meaning, [17.76]
modifications, insolvency law, [17.77]
moratorium, [1.569], [9.10]

FINANCIAL MARKETS – *cont.*
market charge – *cont.*
persons to whom granted
administration order, [1.13], [17.85]
winding up, registered company, [1.128], [1.224]–[1.233], [17.67], [17.78], [17.85]
recognised clearing house, charge in favour, [9.6]
recognised CSD, charge in favour, [9.7]
recognised investment exchange, charge in favour, [9.5]
Secretary of State, powers, [17.79]
Talisman charge, [9.11]
market contract
moratorium
entry into during, [1.571]
meaning, [1.569]
parties, [9.12], [17.91]
market property
floating, priority over subsequent charges, [17.81]
generally, [17.80]–[17.84]
margin, application of not affected by other interests, [17.80]
priority over unpaid vendor's lien, [17.82]
unsecured creditors, proceedings against, [17.83]
proceedings in other jurisdictions, [17.87]
recognised investment exchanges/clearing house, [17.58]–[17.71]
regulated activities, exemptions, FSMA 2000, [12.10], [12.12]
settlement finality
designated systems, [9.42]–[9.51]
generally, [9.40]–[9.66]
transfer orders
effected through
collateral security charges, [9.57], [9.58]
designated system, [9.52]–[9.56]
system-charges
administrative receiver, appointment permitted, [1.65]
generally, [9.14]–[9.21]
winding up, registered company
disclaimer, onerous property by liquidator disapplication, [1.182]
generally, [1.69]–[1.223], [17.85]

FINANCIAL CONDUCT AUTHORITY (FCA)
administration
participation in proceedings, [18.270]
report by administrator, [18.269]
bankruptcy
insolvency practitioner, report of, [18.280]
participation in proceedings, [18.281]
credit institution, reorganisation/winding up
consultation before resolution to wind up, [3.220]
notification, relevant decision to, [3.221]
creditors in Scotland, trust deeds for, [18.268]
friendly societies, functions relating to, [7.1284]
insolvency, participation in proceedings, [18.281]

FINANCIAL CONDUCT AUTHORITY (FCA) – *cont.*
insurers
effecting or carrying out long-term contract of insurance, consents, [18.275]
petition, service of, [18.276]
reorganisation or winding up, notification of relevant decisions to, [3.132]
liquidation, participation in proceedings, [18.280]
liquidator, duty to report by, [18.278]
receivership
participation in proceedings, [18.272]
receiver, report by, [18.273]
reclaim funds, service of petition, [18.277]
voluntary winding up
insurers, of, [18.275], [18.276]
participation in proceedings, [18.274]

FLOATING CHARGE
debentures secured by, priorities, [17.330]
holder
administration
application, [1.575]
intervention, [1.575]
administrative receiver, prohibition, appointment by holder, [1.59]
administrator
appointment by, [1.575], [6.130]
replacement by, [1.575]
meaning, [1.180], [1.267]
prior to administration/winding up
administrator, powers to deal, charged property as if no charge, [1.575]
avoidance, conditions, [1.250], [2.10], [2.26], [3.290]
Proceeds of Crime Act 2002, [17.244]
Proceeds of office-holder claims, [1.179]
property subject to, priority of expenses of winding up, [1.178], [6.386]–[6.391]
receivership, payment, debts from assets subject, [1.26]
Scotland. *See* SCOTLAND
winding up etc, of property subject to, unsecured creditors' share of assets, [1.180], [8.68]

FOREIGN COMPANY
Enterprise Act 2002, application to insolvency law, [2.11]

FOREIGN CURRENCY
debt, quantification, claim
administration, [6.745]
bankruptcy, [6.745]
energy administration order, [7.927]
liquidation, [6.745]
Scotland. *See* SCOTLAND: winding up by court

FORFEITURE
pensions, occupational scheme
by reference to obligation to employer, [17.128]
general prohibition, [17.127]
tenancy, covenant limited to part of demised premises, [17.133]

FRAUD
bankrupt
not released from debt incurred by fraud, [1.341]

FRAUD – *cont.*
bankrupt – *cont.*
fraudulent dealing, property obtained on credit, [1.438]
fraudulent disposal, property, [1.436]
creditor, against, [1.211], [1.537]–[1.539], [17.243]
debt avoidance provisions, transactions defrauding creditors, [1.537]–[1.539], [17.243]
winding up by court/voluntary, in anticipation creditors, of, transactions, [1.211], [1.537]–[1.539], [17.243]
director, disqualification, [4.5]
officer of company/shadow director, by acts constituting, [1.210]
defences, [1.210]
FRAUDULENT TRADING
punishment, [17.54]
winding up, registered company, during, [1.217], [1.219]
FRIENDLY SOCIETIES
administration, applicable legislation, [1.13]
company voluntary arrangement, [2.12]. *See also* COMPANY VOLUNTARY ARRANGEMENT
disqualification of director, [4.45]. *See also* DISQUALIFICATION, DIRECTOR
dissolution
consent, by, [7.1286]
modes of, [7.1285]
registration, cancellation of, [7.1292]
void, power to declare, [7.1291]
Financial Services Authority, functions of, [7.1284]
winding up
court, by, [7.1288]
incorporated societies, [7.1289], [7.1294]–[7.1297]
long term business, continuation of, [7.1290]
modes of, [7.1285]
registered company, [1.69]–[1.224]–[1.233], [1.234]–[1.251]
voluntary, [7.1287]
FURTHER EDUCATION BODIES
insolvency
administrator, appointment by creditors, [7.2587]
application of IA 1986, [7.2583], [7.2584]
definitions, [7.2582], [7.2591]
education administration, [7.2592]–[7.2612]
meaning, [7.2581]
ordinary administration orders, making of, [7.2586]
overview, [7.2580]
records, [7.2585]
security, enforcement of, [7.2590]
sixth form college corporations, trust property, [7.2613]
voluntary winding up, [7.2589]
winding up order, [7.2588]

G

GAMBLING
family entertainment centre gaming machine permits, duration, [17.326]
operating licences, lapse, [17.324]
premises licences, lapse, [17.325]
prize gaming permits, duration, [17.327]
GAS, WATER, ELECTRICITY ETC SUPPLIES. *SEE* ENERGY ACT 2004; ENERGY ADMINISTRATION ORDER; UTILITIES, SUPPLIES
GAZETTE
Edinburgh. *See* SCOTLAND
notice in
energy administration order, [7.987], [7.1046]
railway administration order, [7.2511]
GENERAL MEDICAL COUNCIL
medical practitioners tribunal service, [18.313], [18.314]
GENERAL OPHTHALMIC SERVICES
contract, persons eligible to enter into, [18.184]
GIFT
bankruptcy
'tainted gift' by bankrupt, [1.411]–[1.414], [1.537]–[1.539], [17.238], [17.243]
transaction at undervalue, [1.411], [1.413], [1.414]
GUERNSEY
cross-border insolvency, provisions, [13.16]–[13.18]

H

HEALTH CARE PROVIDERS
continuation of provision of services
at risk, notification of commissioners, [7.1355]
licence conditions, [7.1354]
licence
appeals, [7.1348]
application for, [7.1341]
continuation of provision of services, conditions, [7.1354]
grant or refusal of, [7.1343]
modification of conditions, limits on Monitor's functions, [7.1352]
NHS foundation trust, treatment of, [7.1344]
notice of decision, [7.1347]
register of holders, [7.1349]
representations, right to make, [7.1346]
revocation, [7.1345]
special conditions, [7.1351], [7.1353]
standard conditions, [7.1350], [7.1353]
modification, [7.1356]
licensing
criteria, [7.1342]
deemed breach of requirement, [7.1338]
exemption regulations, [7.1339], [7.1340]
requirement of, [7.1337]

HEALTH SPECIAL ADMINISTRATION
administrator
appointment, [7.1305], [7.1307]
consultation plan, [7.1310]
consultation requirements, [7.1311]
draft report, [7.1309]
final report
provision of, [7.1312]
rejection, action following, [7.1317]
resubmitted, response to, [7.1318]
generally, [7.1357]
replacement of, [7.1321]
dissolution of trust, [7.1320]
extension of time, [7.1313]
financial assistance
application for, [7.1365]
establishment of mechanism for, [7.1363]
fund, establishment of, [7.1364]
grants and loans, [7.1366]
guidance, [7.1322]
indemnities, [7.1361]
interpretation, [7.1323]
modification of provisions, [7.1362]
objective, [7.1358], [7.1308]
order
application for, [7.1357]
meaning, [7.1357]
regulations, [7.1359]
regulator, decision of, [7.1315]
Secretary of State, response by, [7.1316]
transfer schemes, [7.1360]
trusts coming out of, [7.1319]
HER MAJESTY'S REVENUE AND CUSTOMS
bankruptcy
order to
application, [6.577]
making, [6.578]
production/custody, documents, [1.448], [6.579]
debts to, preferential, [1.473], [1.591]
Investment Account, taxation, [1.517]
HIRE-PURCHASE PROPERTY
administration
effect, [1.575]
energy administration order, [7.901]
moratorium, effect, [1.569]
Scotland. *See* SCOTLAND: administration
HOME RIGHTS
See also DWELLING-HOUSE
bankruptcy, dwelling-house occupied by bankrupt or spouse
bankrupt, [1.409]
payments, [1.410]
spouse or former spouse or civil partner
charge, as, [1.408]
nothing occurring during initial period of bankruptcy given rise, [1.408]
Scotland. *See* SCOTLAND
HOUSING
landlord. *See* LANDLORD
social housing, administration
conduct of, [7.1381], [7.1399]–[7.1401]
HOUSING – *cont.*
social housing, administration – *cont.*
housing administration order, [7.1374]
applications, [7.1378]
grants and loans, [7.1388]
guarantees, [7.1391], [7.1392]
indemnities, [7.1389], [7.1390]
ordinary order, making of, [7.1385]
powers of court, [7.1379]
housing administrator, [7.1380]
appointment, creditors by, [7.1386]
sale of land free from planning obligations, [7.1382]
security, enforcement of, [7.1387]
objectives of administration, [7.1375]–[7.1377]
voluntary winding up, [7.1384]
winding up orders, [7.1383]
social rented sector
Corporation, general powers, [17.149]–[17.164]
social landlord. *See* LANDLORD
tenancy. *See* TENANCY

I

IMMOVABLE PROPERTY
contract as to
EC Directive
credit institution, reorganisation/winding up, [3.196]
insurance undertakings, reorganisation/winding up, effect, [3.107]
EC Regulation, insolvency, [3.44]
insurers, reorganisation/winding up, UK, effect, [3.163]
debtor, rights subject to registration
EC Regulation, [3.47]
INCAPACITY
persons incapable, management, own affairs
energy administration order, appointment of another person to act, [7.996]–[7.999]
railway administration order
appointment of another person to act
affidavit supporting application, [7.2522]
service, notices following, [7.2523]
generally, [7.2520]–[7.2523]
INDEMNITY
administrator, invalid appointment, [1.575]
INDEPENDENT REGULATOR OF NHS FOUNDATION TRUSTS. *SEE* NATIONAL HEALTH SERVICE
INDIVIDUAL INSOLVENCY
appeals etc exercising insolvency jurisdiction, [1.455]
examination of persons involved, [6.671]–[6.676]
fees, [8.9]
formal defects, [1.457]
gas, water, electricity supplies etc
conditions, generally, [1.451], [1.452]
personal guarantee, payment, office-holder may be required, [1.451]
insolvency districts, [1.454]

INDIVIDUAL INSOLVENCY – *cont.*
jurisdiction, [1.453]
meetings, remote attendance at, [1.463]
preferential debts, [1.473], [1.474]. *See also* PREFERENTIAL DEBTS
register, [6.644], [6.645]–[6.650]
Secretary of State, annual report re operation of legislation, [1.459]
stamp duty, documents, exemption, [1.458]
time-limits, [1.456]
transitional provisions/savings, [1.597]

INDIVIDUAL VOLUNTARY ARRANGEMENT
accounts etc
Secretary of State, production to, [6.423]
supervisor, [6.422]
approval, effect, [1.301], [1.302], [2.7]
bankruptcy
conversion, arrangement into
EC Regulation, [6.911], [6.912]
order on default
annulment, [6.426]–[6.431]
conditions for making, [1.336]
challenge, decision to approve
applicant, eligible, [1.303], [2.7]
grounds, [1.303], [2.7]
compensation scheme, Financial Services and Markets Act 2000
Authority's power to participate, proceedings, [17.187], [17.196]
creditors' meeting
approval, proposal, [1.301], [1.302], [2.7]
challenge, decision, [1.303], [2.7]
decision re approval
modifications to which may be subject, [1.299]
report to court, [1.300]
nominee to summon, [1.298], [2.7]
persons to be summoned, [1.298], [2.7]
debtor, delinquent after approval
criminal liability, [1.304], [1.305], [2.7]
nominee/supervisor
report to Secretary of State, [1.304], [1.305], [2.7]
debtor, proposal
consideration by creditors, [6.416]–[6.418]
contents, [6.397]
disclosure to assist nominee, [6.401]
nominee's consent, notice, [6.398]
preparation, [6.396]
statement of affairs, [6.399], [6.400]
deceased person, modification of provisions, [1.292], [11.3], [11.5], [11.6], [11.9]
false representation to obtain approval, [1.304], [2.7]
fast-track
approval, [1.311]
availability, [1.308]
implementation, [1.312]
offences, [1.314]
official receiver
decision, [1.309]
report, results of decision, [1.310]
procedure, [1.309]
revocation, [1.313]

INDIVIDUAL VOLUNTARY ARRANGEMENT – *cont.*
fees, [6.424], [8.82]–[8.89]
generally, [6.395]–[6.432]
hand-over of property to supervisor, [6.419]
implementation, [1.307], [2.7]
interim order, court
action to follow, [6.407]
application, [6.402]
conditions, [1.293]
court to which made, [6.403]
effect, [1.294], [2.7]
hearing, [6.405]
cases in which may be made, [1.295], [2.7]
content, [6.406]
effect, [1.292], [2.7]
extension of, [6.410]
nominee
replacement, [6.411]
report, [6.409], [6.412]
no interim order
court
application, [6.414]
debtor's proposal, [1.297], [2.7]
nominee
replacement, [6.415]
report, [1.297], [2.7], [6.413]
nominee
creditors' meeting
to summon, [1.298], [2.7]
debtor's proposal
report, [1.296], [1.297], [2.7]
delinquent debtor, duties, [1.305]
interim order
replacement, nominee, [6.411]
report, [6.409], [6.412]
no interim order, report, [1.297], [2.7], [6.413]
time spent on case, information as to, [6.432]
persons at risk of violence, limitation of disclosure, [6.903], [6.904]
prematurely ended, [1.306]
revocation, [6.421]
Secretary of State
delinquent debtor, powers re, [1.305]
reports to, [6.420]
supervision, [1.307], [2.7]
suspension, [6.421]
termination, [6.425]
undischarged bankrupt
approval, effect, [1.302]

INDUSTRIAL AND PROVIDENT SOCIETIES
administration, applicable legislation, [1.13]
company voluntary arrangement, [2.12]. *See also* COMPANY VOLUNTARY ARRANGEMENT
disqualification of directors, [4.47]. *See also* DISQUALIFICATION OF DIRECTORS
winding up of registered company, [1.69]–[1.223]

INSOLVENCY
individual. *See* INDIVIDUAL INSOLVENCY
meaning, [1.262]

INSOLVENCY EXPRESS TRIALS
practice direction, [19.32]–[19.36]

INSOLVENCY PRACTITIONER
acting as, meaning, [1.475], [2.8], [3.309], [10.4]
authorisation, [1.479], [1.480]
competent authority, [1.502], [12.30], [12.34]–[12.41]
fit and proper applicant, criteria, [12.35]
grant, [1.503], [12.30]
maximum period, [12.40]
notice of, to whom required, [1.504]
proposed refusal/withdrawal
without reference to Tribunal, [1.508]
refusal, [1.503], [12.30]
withdrawal, [1.503], [12.30]
bankruptcy, debtor's petition
court, appointment, [1.332]
report, action on, [1.333]
competent authority, authorisation by, [1.502], [12.30], [12.34]–[12.41]
continuing professional development, records of, [12.39]
costs, award against, [6.701]
criminal investigation
Proceeds of Crime Act 2002, external orders/ requests
application of sums by enforcement receivers, [12.53]
generally, [12.49]–[12.59], [17.246], [17.247]
Northern Ireland. *See* NORTHERN IRELAND
Scotland. *See* SCOTLAND
sums received by relevant Director, [12.54]
vesting/realisation, recoverable property
applying realised proceeds, [12.59]
death of, block transfer of cases, [6.689]–[6.692]
education, training and experience, [12.36]–[12.38], [12.60]–[12.65]
fees, [8.19], [12.24], [12.25]
holders of office required to be qualified as, [1.234]
Lloyd's market, conduct, challenge by reorganisation controller, [7.1613]
not qualified to act as, persons, list, [1.478]
notice of authorisation
representations re, [1.505]
to whom required, [1.504]
offence
acting without qualification, [1.476]
office held in initial and subsequent capacity, [12.32]
official receiver as nominee/supervisor, [1.477]
recognised professional bodies, [1.481], [10.38], [10.43], [12.2], [12.3], [12.24], [12.25]
application for recognition, [1.482]
oversight of, [1.485]–[1.492]
revocation of recognition, [1.493]–[1.499]
records
inspection, [12.45]–[12.48]
maintenance, [12.43]
whereabouts, notification, [12.44]
regulator, establishment of, [17.456], [17.462]
regulatory objectives, [1.483], [1.484]
returns authorised by Secretary of State, [12.41]
revoked provisions, [12.33]

INSOLVENCY PRACTITIONER – *cont.*
Scotland. *See* SCOTLAND
Secretary of State, regulatory powers, [1.532], [12.30], [12.41]
security or caution
requirements, [12.42], [12.48]
time spent on case, statement by persons who may be supplied, [8.62]
transitional provisions, [1.599], [7.1896], [12.33]
trustee in bankruptcy
loss, qualification, [6.543]
required qualification as, [1.355]
two or more persons, appointment, [1.235]

INSOLVENCY PRACTITIONERS TRIBUNAL
action on reference, [1.507]
members
panels, [1.592]
remuneration, [1.592]
procedure, [1.592]
reference to, [1.506]
Scotland. *See* SCOTLAND
sittings, [1.592]

INSOLVENCY PROCEEDINGS
contravention
offences, [6.7]
decision procedures, [6.771]–[6.776]
defined terms, [6.10]
documents
contents, [6.27]–[6.35]
delivery
authorised recipient, [6.48]
creditors, [6.45]
document exchange, by, [6.51]
electronic, [6.53]–[6.56]
joint office-holder, [6.49]
opting out, [6.46], [6.47]
personal, [6.52]
post, by, [6.50]
proof, [6.60], [6.61]
form of, [6.12]
inspection and copies, [6.62]–[6.66]
requirement, [6.12]
websites, use of, [6.57]–[6.59]
EU Regulation
amendments to national legislation, [2.100]–[2.103]
applicable law, [3.551]
arbitral proceedings, [3.562]
Community trade marks, [3.558]
companies, group of, [3.600]–[3.621]
creditors, lodging of claims, [3.597]–[3.599]
data protection, [3.622]–[3.627]
employment, contracts of, [3.557]
European patents, [3.558]
financial markets, [3.556]
immovable property, contracts, [3.555]
insolvency practitioner
cooperation, [3.585]
powers, [3.565]
proof of appointment, [3.566]
insolvency register
establishment, [3.568]
interconnection of, [3.569]–[3.571]

INSOLVENCY PROCEEDINGS – *cont.*
EU Regulation – *cont.*
judicial review, [3.583]
jurisdiction, [3.548]–[3.550]
recognition, [3.563]–[3.576]
reservation of title, [3.554]
scope and definitions, [3.546], [3.547]
secondary proceedings, [3.578]–[3.596]
applicable law, [3.579]
cooperation with main proceedings, [3.585]–[3.588]
opening, [3.578], [3.581]–[3.583]
closure, [3.592]
conversion, [3.595]
set-off, [3.553]
text, [3.546]–[3.640]
third party
protection, [3.561]
rights in rem, [3.552]
further education bodies
administrator, appointment by creditors, [7.2587]
application of IA 1986, [7.2583], [7.2584]
definitions, [7.2582], [7.2591]
education administration, [7.2592]–[7.2612]
meaning, [7.2581]
ordinary administration orders, making of, [7.2586]
overview, [7.2580]
records, [7.2585]
security, enforcement of, [7.2590]
sixth form college corporations, trust property, [7.2613]
voluntary winding up, [7.2589]
winding up order, [7.2588]
Insolvency and Companies Court Judge, [8.90]–[8.92]
Insolvency Rules 1986
court procedure and practice, [6.1]
general note, [6.1]
savings, special insolvency rules, for, [6.946], [6.947]
transitional provisions, [6.935]
meetings, [6.789]–[6.807]
voting, [6.797]–[6.804]
notices
advertised other than in Gazette, [6.23]–[6.26]
delivery, [6.36]–[6.42]
Gazette, [6.20]–[6.22]
standard contents, [6.19]
practice directions
appeals, [19.20]
appointees, remuneration, [19.21]
companies
administration, [19.10]
applications, [19.12]
winding up provisions, [19.11]
court documents, [19.4]
definition, [19.1]
distribution of business, [19.3]
evidence, [19.5]
jurisdiction, [19.7]
orders, drawing up, [19.8]

INSOLVENCY PROCEEDINGS – *cont.*
practice directions – *cont.*
personal insolvency
applications, [19.15]
bankruptcy petitions, [19.14]
bankruptcy restrictions undertakings, [19.17]
orders without attendance, [19.16]
persons at risk of violence, [19.18]
statutory demands, [19.13]
urgent applications, [19.9]
registered providers of social housing, [7.1374]–[7.1401]
Registrar in Bankruptcy of the High Court
change of name, [8.90]–[8.92]
remuneration of officer-holders, [6.867]–[6.890]
time, computation of, [6.11]

INSOLVENCY RULES
amendment, [2.23], [2.32]–[2.34], [2.35], [2.36], [2.44], [2.58], [2.63], [2.74], [2.77], [2.86], [2.87]
company, general rules, [1.522], [1.593]
individual, general rules, [1.523], [1.594]

INSOLVENCY RULES COMMITTEE
function, [1.524]

INSOLVENCY SERVICES ACCOUNT
claim, money paid in, [8.57]
fees, [12.24], [12.25], [12.29]
payments into/out of, [8.29]–[8.31], [8.44]–[8.46]
purpose, [1.514]

INSURANCE COMPANY/UNDERTAKING
See also LLOYD'S OF LONDON
administration order, insurers, [1.13], [7.1565]–[7.1569]
compensation scheme, Financial Services and Markets Act 2000
assets on winding up, treatment, [17.210]
continuation, long-term contracts
insurer in liquidation, [17.197], [17.208]
EU Directive on taking-up and pursuit of direct insurance and reinsurance
contracts of branches in winding-up, treatment of, [3.382], [3.383]
co-insurance contracts, treatment in winding up, [3.384]
definitions, [3.373]
difficulty or irregular situation, undertakings in, [3.374]–[3.381]
exclusions from scope
life, [3.369], [3.370]
non-life, [3.365]–[3.368]
reinsurance, [3.371], [3.372]
size, due to, [3.364]
statutory systems, [3.363]
general rules, [3.361]–[3.383]
EU Directives, reorganisation and winding up provisions
administrator, appointment, [3.115], [3.411]
branches of third country insurance undertakings, treatment of, [3.118], [3.414]
contracts and rights, effects on, [3.403]
detrimental acts, [3.112], [3.408]
employment contracts, effect, [3.107]
immovable property, contract re, effect, [3.107]

INSURANCE COMPANY/UNDERTAKING – *cont.*
EU Directives, reorganisation and winding up provisions – *cont.*
liquidator, appointment, [3.115], [3.411]
pending lawsuits, [3.114], [3.410]
professional secrecy, [3.117], [3.413]
registration in public register, [3.116], [3.413]
regulated markets, [3.111], [3.407]
reorganisation
applicable law, [3.92]
information to
known creditors, right, claims, [3.95]
supervisory authorities, [3.93]
measures, [3.387]–[3.390]
publication, decisions, [3.94]
reservation of title, [3.109], [3.405]
scope and definitions, [3.385], [3.386]
set-off, [3.110], [3.406]
text, [3.88]–[3.122], [3.385]–[3.413]
third parties
purchasers, protection, [3.113], [3.409]
rights in rem, [3.108], [3.404]
winding up
applicable law, [3.97], [3.392]
authorisation, withdrawal, [3.101], [3.397]
creditors
information to, [3.103], [3.105], [3.106], [3.399], [3.401]
right to lodge claims, [3.104], [3.400]
insurance claims, treatment, [3.97], [3.122], [3.393]
opening
information to supervisory authorities, [3.96], [3.391]
payment, [8.33]
preferential claims, representation by assets, [3.100], [3.396]
proceedings, [3.391]–[3.402]
publication of decisions, [3.102], [3.398]
special register, [3.394]
subrogation to guarantee scheme, [3.99], [3.395]
See also EEA State, *below*
EEA State
EEA creditors, submission of claims, [3.136]
EEA insurers
prohibition against winding up, UK, [3.127]
reorganisation measures effective, UK, [3.129]
schemes of arrangement, [3.128]
EEA regulators
notification, reorganisation decisions to, [3.133]
EEA rights
recognition on UK reorganisation/winding up, [3.158]–[3.171]
Insurance Companies Act 1982
insurance business, meaning, [7.1481]
reduction, contracts as alternative to winding up, [7.1479]
winding up
Companies Acts provisions, [7.1474]

INSURANCE COMPANY/UNDERTAKING – *cont.*
Insurance Companies Act 1982 – *cont.*
winding up – *cont.*
long-term business, company with conditions, [7.1476]
continuation in liquidation, [7.1477]
petition, Treasury, [7.1475]
rules, [7.1480]
subsidiary company, [7.1478]
insurer
assets, treatment on winding up, [7.1528]–[7.1531]
meaning, [7.1526], [7.1527]
priority, payment, claims on winding up, [3.140]–[3.157]
reorganisation and winding up regulations
EEA creditors
claims, submission, [3.136]
EEA insurers
prohibition against winding up, UK, [3.127]
reorganisation measures effective, UK, [3.129]
schemes of arrangement, [3.128]
EEA regulators
notification, reorganisation decisions to, [3.133]
EEA rights
recognition on UK reorganisation/winding up, [3.158]–[3.171]
generally, [3.123], [3.124]–[3.175]
notification, decisions
EEA regulators, to, [3.133]
FSA, to, [3.132]
generally, [3.131]–[3.139]
priority, payment, claims on winding up, [3.140]–[3.157]
publication, decisions, [3.131]–[3.139]
third country insurers
reorganisation/winding up, [3.172]–[3.174]
third party rights against insurers
avoidance of provisions, ineffective, [17.421]
England and Wales, establishing liability in, [17.405]
foreign element, cases with, [17.422]
information and disclosure, [17.428]
insolvency person, of, [17.404]
insured's liability, enforcement of, [17.418]
Northern Ireland, establishing liability in, [17.405]
reinsurance, [17.419]
relevant persons
corporate bodies, [17.409]
individuals, [17.407], [17.408]
Scottish trusts, [17.411]
Scotland, establishing liability in, [17.406]
transferred rights
conditions affecting, [17.416]
enforcement, [17.415], [17.417]
insurer's right of set-off, [17.414]
limit on, [17.412]
voluntarily-incurred liabilities, [17.420]

INSURANCE COMPANY/UNDERTAKING – *cont.*
winding up rules
accounts
audit, [7.1501], [7.1549]
records, maintenance, [7.1499], [7.1547]
actuarial advice, [7.1495], [7.1543]
costs payable out of assets
apportionment, [7.1509], [7.1557]
creditors' meetings, [7.1507], [7.1555]
deferred annuity policies, linked, valuation, [7.1513], [7.1561]
dividends to creditors, [7.1506]
forms, [7.1564]
general business policies
periodic payments, [7.1511]
valuation, [7.1489], [7.1537], [7.1559]
generally, [1.522], [7.1484]–[7.1516]
life policies, valuation, [7.1513], [7.1561]
liquidator
appointment, [7.1487], [7.1535]
powers, [7.1500], [7.1548]
remuneration
carrying on long-term business, [7.1508], [7.1556]
security, [7.1502], [7.1550]
long-term business
accounts, [7.1499], [7.1501]
actuarial advice, [7.1495], [7.1543]
additional powers, liquidator, [7.1500]
attribution, assets/liabilities to, [7.1492], [7.1493], [7.1540], [7.1541]
continuation of contract, [18.283]
custody of assets, [7.1498], [7.1546]
dividends to creditors, [7.1506], [7.1554]
excess of assets
determination, [7.1494], [7.1542]
utilisation, [7.1496], [7.1544], [7.1545]
policies
notice of valuation, [7.1505], [7.1553]
stop order made, valuation, [7.1515], [7.1563]
valuation, [7.1490], [7.1491], [7.1514], [7.1515], [7.1538], [7.1562]
premiums, failure to pay, [7.1504], [7.1552]
proof, debts, [7.1503], [7.1551]
records, maintenance, [7.1499], [7.1536], [7.1547]
separation, other business, [7.1488], [7.1536]
special bank account, [7.1497]
non-linked annuities in payment/capital redemption policies, valuation, [7.1512], [7.1560]
non-linked deferred annuity policies, valuation, [7.1512], [7.1560]
non-linked life policies, valuation, [7.1512], [7.1560]
special manager, security, [7.1502], [7.1550]
stop order
long-term policies where made
valuation, [7.1515], [7.1563]
notice, [7.1510], [7.1558]
valuation records, maintenance, [7.1499]

INSURANCE LINKED SECURITIES
protected cell companies
administration, disapplication of, [7.1632]
assets, [7.1631], [7.1633], [7.1634]
dissolution, [7.1643]–[7.1645]
formation, [7.1628]
group of cells, meaning, [7.1626]
insolvency, [7.1639]–[7.1641]
modification of legislation, [7.1651], [7.1652]
liabilities and obligations, [7.1631]–[7.1633]
overview, [7.1627]
records, [7.1633], [7.1634]
restoration
applications for, [7.1646]–[7.1648]
court order, effect of, [7.1650]
decision, [7.1649]
security interests, creation, [7.1638]
segregation, [7.1635]
structure, [7.1629]–[7.1637]
voluntary arrangement, disapplication of, [7.1632]

INTEREST PAYABLE
administration, quantification of claim, [6.747]
bankruptcy, quantification of claim, [6.747]
energy administration order, quantification of claim, [7.929]
liquidation, quantification of claim, interest provable, [6.747]
winding up, registered company debts, [1.193]

INTERNET DOMAIN REGISTRY
manager
appointment of, [17.251]
functions, [17.252]

INVESTMENT ACCOUNT
adjustment, balances, [1.516]
application, income in, [1.516]
interest on money received by liquidators/trustees in bankruptcy invested, [1.517]
moneys, investment by National Debt Commissioners, [1.515]
Treasury, directions, [1.515]

INVESTMENT BANK
client assets, meaning, [7.1660]
insolvency regulations, [7.77]–[7.80]
meaning, [7.76]
amendment, [7.2047]
special administration
appeals, [7.1984]–[7.1987]
application of rules, [7.1715]
applications to court, [7.1949]–[7.1955]
appropriate fee, meaning, [7.2042]
bank administration order
administrator
additional joint, [7.1927]
application to replace, [7.1924]
provisional, [7.1759], [7.1760]
remuneration, [7.1758]
application for
Bank of England witness statement, [7.1749]
contents of, [7.1747]
filing, [7.1750]
hearing, [7.1754]

INVESTMENT BANK – *cont.*
special administration – *cont.*
bank administration order – *cont.*
application for – *cont.*
other notification, [7.1752]
proposed administrator, statement of, [7.1748]
service, [7.1751]
venue, [7.1753]
contents of, [7.1755]
costs, [7.1756]
notice of, [7.1757]
bank insolvency order
administrator
application to replace, [7.1923]
authentication of appointment, [7.1738]
advertisement, [7.1736]
application for
certificate of compliance, [7.1733]
filing, [7.1727]
leave to withdraw, [7.1734]
persons to receive copy, [7.1730], [7.1732]
service, [7.1728], [7.1719]
verification, [7.1731]
witness statement in opposition, [7.1735]
contents of, [7.1737]
making of, [7.1736]
Objective A committee, duties of, [7.1739]
provisional liquidator
appointment of, [7.1740]–[7.1742]
remuneration, [7.1745]
security, [7.1743], [7.1744]
termination of appointment, [7.1746]
transmission, [7.1736]
charged property, disposal of, [7.1841], [7.1842]
company representation, [7.1840]
continuity of supply, [7.1689]
costs, [7.1971]–[7.1979], [7.1993]
court
file, [7.1937]
leave of, [7.2044]
meaning, [7.2039]
office copies of documents, [7.1938]
procedure and practice, application of, [7.1935]
shorthand writer, [7.1936]
creditors' committee
administrator, information from, [7.1828]
chair, [7.1817]
committee members' representatives, [7.1819]
constitution, [7.1814]
expenses of members, [7.1829]
formal defects, [7.1831]
formalities of establishment, [7.1815]
functions and meetings, [7.1816]
members dealing with investment bank, [7.1830]
postal resolutions, [7.1827]
procedure, [7.1824]
quorum, [7.1818]
remote attendance at, [7.1825]

INVESTMENT BANK – *cont.*
special administration – *cont.*
creditors' committee – *cont.*
removal of members, [7.1822]
request that place be specified, [7.1826]
resignation from, [7.1820]
termination of membership, [7.1821]
vacancies, [7.1823]
debt, meaning, [7.2043]
deposit-taking bank, investment bank being, [7.1669], [7.1704], [7.1705]
disqualification of directors, [7.1699]
dissolution or voluntary arrangement, [7.1697]
distribution to creditors
admission or rejection of proof, [7.1886]
application of provisions, [7.1858]
debts payable at future time, [7.1879], [7.1896]
debts ranking equally, [7.1859]
discounts, [7.1873]
dividend
alteration of proof after payment, [7.1892]
assignment of right to, [7.1895]
calculation and distribution of, [7.1860]
declaration of, [7.1888], [7.1889]
disqualification from, [7.1894]
no, notice of, [7.1891]
payment, [7.1890]
postponement or cancellation, [7.1887]
estimate of quantum, [7.1870]
foreign currency debts, [7.1876]
interest, [7.1878]
mutual credit and set-off, [7.1874], [7.1875]
negotiable instruments, [7.1871]
notice of proposed distribution, [7.1885]
periodical payments, [7.1877]
proof of debts, [7.1862]–[7.1869]
quantification of claims, [7.1870]–[7.1896]
realisation of security by creditor, [7.1884]
redemption by administrator, [7.1882]
secured creditors, [7.1872], [7.1893]
surrender for non-disclosure, [7.1881]
unsold assets, division of, [7.1861]
value of security, [7.1880], [7.1883]
documents
charges for copies, [7.2032]
confidentiality, [7.2030]
right to copy, [7.2022]
supply of, [7.1997]–[7.2000]
administrator, to or by, [7.2001]–[7.2021]
end of
administrator, application to court by, [7.1931]
creditor, application to court by, [7.1932]
dissolution, moving to, [7.1934]
final progress report, [7.1930]
notification of court order, [7.1933]
enforcement procedures, [7.1980]–[7.1983]
expenses, [7.1843]–[7.1847], [7.1993]
false claim of status as creditor, [7.1995]
formal defects, [7.1970]

INVESTMENT BANK – *cont.*
special administration – *cont.*
information and evidence, obtaining, [7.1940]–[7.1943]
insolvent estate, meaning, [7.2041]
interpretation, [7.1662], [7.1714], [7.2038]–[7.2043]
liability, meaning, [7.2043]
limited liability partnership, provisions applying to, [7.1700], [7.1706]
list of creditors, right to, [7.2033]
meetings
adjournment, [7.1790]–[7.1792]
chair, [7.1789]
company, venue and control of, [7.1794]
correspondence instead of, [7.1807]
excluded persons, [7.1809]–[7.1811]
gazetting and advertisement, [7.1784]
generally, [7.1778]
initial, to consider proposals, [7.1771]–[7.1777]
minutes, [7.1812]
non-receipt of notice, [7.1750]
notice of, [7.1780]–[7.1783]
quorum, [7.1788]
requisition, [7.1786], [7.1787]
remote attendance at, [7.1808]
returns or reports, [7.1813]
suspension, [7.1793]
venue, [7.1779]
voting, [7.1795]–[7.1806]
modified and amended enactments, [7.1709], [7.1710]
Northern Irish equivalent enactments, [7.1702], [7.1708]
notice, giving, [7.1997]–[7.2000]
administrator, to or by, [7.2001]–[7.2021]
Objective 1
bar date, setting, [7.1848]–[7.1852]
distribution plan, [7.1854]–[7.1857]
further notification, [7.1853]
objectives, [7.1670]–[7.1688]
administrator's duty, [7.1671]
bar date notices, [7.1686]
distribution of client assets, [7.1680]
distribution of client money, [7.1682]
partial property transfers, restrictions, [7.1673]–[7.1677]
transfer of client assets, [7.1672]
offences, punishment of, [7.1996], [7.2045]
order
alternative order, as, [7.1698]
application for, [7.1665]
contents of, [7.1716]
filing, [7.1719]
further notification, [7.1722]
hearing, [7.1713]
proposed administrator, statement of, [7.1717]
service, [7.1720], [7.1721]
witness statement in support, [7.1718]
contents of, [7.1724]
costs, [7.1725]
grounds for applying, [7.1666]

INVESTMENT BANK – *cont.*
special administration – *cont.*
order – *cont.*
meaning, [7.1664]
notice of, [7.1726]
notification of, [7.1933]
overview, [7.1663]
partnership, provisions applying to, [7.1701], [7.1707]
payments into court, [7.1939]
persons lacking capacity to manage affairs, [7.1966]–[7.1969]
powers of court, [7.1667]
preliminary steps to other insolvency proceedings, notice to appropriate regulator, [7.1668]
progress reports
contents of, [7.1832]
final, [7.1930]
meaning, [7.1832]
sending, [7.1833]
prohibited names, [7.1988]–[7.1992]
provable debts, [7.1994]
proxies, [7.1834]–[7.1839]
registrar, meaning, [7.2039]
registrar of companies, notifications to, [7.2022]–[7.2029]
Scotland, procedure in, [16.265]
service of court documents, [7.1944]–[7.1948]
share of assets for unsecured creditors, applications for order, [7.1960]–[7.1965]
successful rescue, [7.1696]
time limits, [7.2034]
transfer of proceedings, [7.2036], [7.2037]
venue, meaning, [7.2040]
witness statements, [7.1941]–[7.1943]
special administrator
accounts submitted to, [7.1768]
additional notices, [7.1900]
application to court to remove from office, [7.1919]
application to replace, [7.1922]–[7.1924]
appointment, notification and advertisement of, [7.1761]
appropriate regulator directions to, [7.1691]
withdrawal of, [7.1694]
general powers, duties and effect, [7.1690]
ceasing to be qualified, notice of vacation of office, [7.1920]
charged property, disposal of, [7.1841], [7.1842]
court order, notification of, [7.1933]
creditors' committee, information to, [7.1828]
deceased, [7.1921]
disclaimer, [7.1898], [7.1899], [7.1904]
duties on vacating office, [7.1929]
electronic submission of information, [7.2013], [7.2014]
end of administration, application to court, [7.1931]
exercise of court's powers, application for, [7.1905]
interest in property, declaration of, [7.1903]

INVESTMENT BANK – *cont.*
special administrator – *cont.*
interested party, application by, [7.1902]
joint
notification and advertisement of appointment, [7.1926]
notice to, [7.2010]
new, notification of, [7.1928]
notice and supply of documents to or by, [7.2001]–[7.2021]
powers of, [7.1897]–[7.1905]
proposals, [7.1692], [7.1693]
progress reports, [7.1832], [7.1833]
final, [7.1930]
records, [7.1901]
remuneration, fixing, [7.1906]–[7.1915]
replacement, notification and advertisement of appointment of, [7.1925]
resignation, [7.1916]–[7.1918]
security, [7.2035]
statement of affairs
client assets, details of, [7.1763]
expenses of, [7.1767]
limited disclosure, [7.1765]
notice requiring, [7.1762]
release from duty to submit, [7.1766]
verification and filing, [7.1764]
statement of proposals, [7.1769], [7.1770]

INVESTMENT COMPANY
open-ended
collective investment, carrying on, [7.2049]
dissolution, [7.2053], [7.2054]
generally, [7.2050]–[7.2054]
master UCITS
merger or division of, [7.2056]
winding up, [7.2055]
sub-funds winding up, [7.2057]
winding up by court, [1.224]–[1.233], [7.2052]

INVESTMENT EXCHANGES
administration order, [1.13], [17.85]
charge in favour
market charge, as, [9.5]
default
proceedings
application to determine whether should be taken, [17.70]
completion
duty to report, [17.65]
net sum payable, [17.66]
duty, assistance for, [17.63], [17.64]
rules
change, [17.60]
meaning, [17.92]
disclaimer, property, [17.67]
EEA central counterparties, [17.73], [17.74]
generally, [17.57]–[17.98]
market charges, [9.6], [17.76]–[17.79]
market contracts, [17.58]
market property, [17.80]–[17.84]
modification, insolvency law, [17.61]
overseas, [17.72]
prior transactions, adjustment, [17.68]

INVESTMENT EXCHANGES – *cont.*
proceedings of, precedence over insolvency proceedings, [17.62]
qualifying collateral arrangements and qualifying property transfers, [17.59]
recognised central counterparties, disapplication of provisions on mutual credit and set-off, [17.86]
rescission, contracts, [17.67]
Secretary of State, directions, [17.69]
settlement arrangements, Bank of England, [17.75]
third country central counterparties, [17.73], [17.74]
winding up, registered company, [1.69]–[1.233], [17.85]

INVOICES, LETTERS ETC
administration order, effect, [1.575]
moratorium, effect, [1.571]

L

LANDFILL TAX
set-off, [18.2]–[18.4]

LANDLORD
distress for rent against bankrupt, [1.425]
registered social, appointment of administrative receiver, [1.66]
social, insolvency of
administrative receiver, appointment permitted, [1.66]
disposal of land, moratorium
duration, [17.153]
reasons, [17.152]
further notice to Relevant Authority, [17.151]
initial notice to Relevant Authority, [17.150]
manager
appointment to implement proposals, [17.157]
interim, appointment of, [17.154]
powers, [17.158]
transfer, engagements, [17.159]
proposals as to ownership and management of landlord's land
compliance, application to court, [17.161]
during moratorium, [17.155]
effect, [17.156]
scheme of provisions, [17.149]
See also HOUSING

LEASEHOLDS
bankruptcy
disclaimed property, vesting, trustee, conditions, [1.392]
disclaimer, onerous property, trustee, [1.388]
winding up of registered company, disclaimer, [1.183], [1.186]

LIEN
books etc
administration/liquidation, unenforceable against office-holder, [1.251], [2.10], [2.26]
bankruptcy, unenforceable against official receiver/trustee in bankruptcy, [1.427]

LIEN – *cont.*
financial markets, priority of market charge over vendor's lien, [17.82]
insolvency practitioner, criminal investigation, [12.51]
LIMITED COMPANY
formerly unlimited, contributory in winding up of registered company, [1.73]
LIMITED LIABILITY PARTNERSHIP
provisions applying to, [10.33]–[10.44]
Scotland. *See* SCOTLAND
LIQUIDATION COMMITTEE
appointment, [1.98]
general provisions
chairman, [6.838]
establishment, formalities, [6.828]
formal defects, [6.850]
functions, [6.825]
information, [6.845], [6.846]
invitation to form, [6.196]
meetings, [6.837]–[6.844]
member
eligibility, [6.827]
expenses, [6.847]
numbers, [6.826]
removal, [6.835]
resignation, [6.833]
membership
changes, [6.830]
vacancies, [6.831], [6.832]
quorum, [6.839]
Scotland. *See* SCOTLAND
winding up by court, [1.142], [1.143]
LIQUIDATION, COMPANY GOING INTO
books, papers, records, property etc to which company may be entitled, delivery/surrender etc to office-holder, [1.239]
debt, proof, [6.726]–[6.735]. *See also* DEBT, PROOF
extortionate credit transactions, prior adjustment, application of office-holder, [1.249], [2.10]
floating charge prior to, avoidance, [1.250], [2.10], [2.26], [3.290]
gas, water, electricity etc supplies, management, [1.237]
lien on books etc, unenforceable against office-holder, [1.251], [2.10], [2.26]
meaning, [1.262]
preferences, prior adjustment, application by office-holder, [1.244]–[1.246]
provisional liquidator, appointment
books, papers, records, property etc to which company may be entitled, delivery/surrender etc to office-holder, [1.239]
gas, water, electricity etc supplies, management, [1.237]
lien on books unenforceable, [1.251], [2.10], [2.26]
secured creditor
security
realisation by creditor, [6.743]
redemption by liquidator, [6.741]
surrender for non-disclosure, [6.740]
test of value, [6.742]
LIQUIDATION, COMPANY GOING INTO – *cont.*
secured creditor – *cont.*
security – *cont.*
value, [6.739]
undervalue, prior transaction at
adjustment, application by office-holder, [1.243], [1.245], [1.246], [2.10], [2.26]
LIQUIDATOR
accounts/audit, [8.38]
appointment
advertisement, [6.250], [6.334]
contributories, by, [6.328]
court, by, [6.331]
creditors, by, [6.328]
creditors' voluntary winding up
court, by, [1.106], [6.249]
nomination, creditors/company, [1.97], [6.247]
notice by liquidator of, [1.107]
members' voluntary winding up
company, by, [6.207]
registration, [6.250]
assets, hand-over, [6.335]
bankruptcy petition, [1.323]. *See also* BANKRUPTCY
carrying on business, [8.36]
collection, company's assets, [6.351]–[6.353]. *See also* DISTRIBUTIONS
company books and papers, disposal, [8.40]
company voluntary arrangement, proposal for company being wound up, [1.1]. *See also* COMPANY VOLUNTARY ARRANGEMENT
creditors' voluntary winding up, registered company
account, final, [6.255]
meeting, [1.104]
appointment
court, by, [1.106], [6.249]
nomination, creditors/company, [1.97], [3.221]
notice by liquidator of, [1.107]
death, [6.256]
general meeting, requirement to summon annually, [1.103]
information to Secretary of State, [8.41]
none appointed or nominated by company, [1.112]
powers, [6.263]
progress report by, [1.102]
release on
Secretary of State, by, [6.260]
removal
ceasing to be qualified, [6.257]
court, powers, [1.106], [6.254]
creditors' by, [6.253]
resignation, [6.252]
vacancy by death etc
creditors, power to fill, [1.101], [6.248]
vacation of office on making winding up order, [6.258]
death, [1.88], [1.101], [6.216], [6.248], [6.256], [6.342]

LIQUIDATOR – *cont.*
disclaimer
onerous property, power, [1.182], [1.185]
distribution, company's assets, [6.351]–[6.353]. *See also* DISTRIBUTIONS
duty to report to FCA and PRA, [18.278]
EC Regulation, recognition of insolvency proceedings by Member States
appointment, proof, [3.55]
powers, [3.54]
information, provision by, [8.35]
insolvency practitioner, qualification
loss, [6.217]
requirement, [1.234]
members' voluntary winding up, registered company
account, final, [6.214], [6.215]
meeting, [1.104]
appointment
court, by, [1.106], [6.209]
general meeting, at, [1.87]
notice by liquidator of, [1.107]
death, [6.216]
final meeting prior to dissolution, [1.91]
general meeting
requirement to summon, [1.90]
vacancy, power to fill, [1.88]
information to Secretary of State, [8.41]
insolvency practitioner, loss of qualification as, [6.217]
none appointed or nominated by company, [1.112]
progress report by, [1.89]
release
Secretary of State, by, [6.219], [6.260]
removal
company meeting, by, [6.213]
court, by, [1.106], [6.212]
remuneration, [6.867]–[6.890]
resignation
grounds, [6.211]
notice, [6.211]
security
cost of, [6.210]
statement when company unable to pay debts
duty, [1.92]
procedure, [1.92], [3.221]
vacancy by death etc
creditors, power to fill, [1.101], [6.248]
official receiver as. *See* OFFICIAL RECEIVER
progress reports, [6.854]–[6.865]
provisional
qualified insolvency practitioner, requirement, [1.234]
validity, acts of, [1.236]
winding up by court/voluntary (except CVL)
appointment
deposit before order, [6.309]
eligible applicants, [6.308]
notice, [6.311]
order, [6.310]
termination, [6.314]
remuneration, [6.313]
security, [6.312]

LIQUIDATOR – *cont.*
See also LIQUIDATION, COMPANY GOING INTO
records, financial
delivery, [8.37]
disposal, [8.40]
duty, [8.34]
inspection, [8.39]
production, [8.39]
retention, [8.37]
removal
advertisement, [6.334]
court, by, [6.340]
creditors' by, [6.338], [6.339]
Secretary of State, [6.341]
remuneration, [6.867]–[6.890]
resignation, [6.336]
return of capital, authorisation
application, court, [6.392]
procedure, [6.393]
rights of action, power to assign, [1.255]
unclaimed/undistributed assets/dividends etc, payment, [8.42]
vacation, office
ceasing to be qualified, [6.343]
duties, [6.259], [6.348]
notice, [6.337]
validity, acts of, [1.236]

LLOYD'S OF LONDON
individual voluntary arrangement
creditors' meeting, modifications applicable, [1.299], [3.156], [3.157], [7.1601], [7.1609]
Lloyd's Market Reorganisation Order
administrator, appointment re member, [7.1588]
application, [7.1575]
bankruptcy, member
reorganisation controller
petition, [7.1596]
powers, [7.1596]
condition for making, [7.1573]
court, powers, [7.1576]
interim trustee, appointment re member, [7.1588]
market reorganisation plan, [7.1580]
meaning, [7.1572]
members
revocations re, [7.1583]
treatment, [7.1582]
moratorium, [7.1577]
objective, [7.1574]
payments from central funds, [7.1600]
receiver, appointment re member, [7.1588]
reorganisation controller
appointment, announcement, [7.1579]
consent to voluntary winding up of members, [7.1592]
officer of the court, [7.1578]
petition by
bankruptcy, member, [7.1596]
winding up of member by, [7.1594]
winding up of the Society, [7.1598]

LLOYD'S OF LONDON – *cont.*
Lloyd's Market Reorganisation Order – *cont.*
reorganisation controller – *cont.*
powers
administration order re member, [7.1589]
bankruptcy, member, [7.1597]
compromise/arrangement, [7.1587]
individual voluntary arrangements re members, [7.1585]
receivership re member, [7.1590]
Scotland. *See* SCOTLAND
voluntary arrangements re member, [7.1584]
voluntary winding up, member, [7.1593]
winding up, member, [7.1595]
remuneration, [7.1581]
syndicate set-off, [7.1591]
voluntary winding up, members, reorganisation controller
consent, [7.1592]
powers, [7.1593]
winding up of member, reorganisation controller
petition, [7.1594]
powers, [7.1595]
winding up of the Society, reorganisation controller
petition, [7.1598]
service of petition on, [7.1599]
reorganisation/winding up regulations
assets undistributed, members, [7.1611]
dispositions before Lloyd's market reorganisation order in force, [7.1616]
EEA creditor, submission of claims, [7.1606]
EEA rights, recognition, [7.1614]
generally, [7.1570]–[7.1617]
insolvency practitioner, conduct
challenge by reorganisation controller, [7.1613]
non-EEA countries, [7.1617]
notifications required
creditors, to, winding up re members, [7.1605]
EEA Regulators, to, [7.1603]
PRA, to, [7.1602]
priority, insurance claims, [7.1609]
publication requirements, [7.1604]
reinsurance, contract subject to, liabilities re closure, [7.1610]
reports to creditors, [7.1607]
service, notices/documents, [7.1608]
settlements, protection, [7.1612]
winding up, unregistered company, [1.225]
LONDON INSOLVENCY DISTRICT
allocation of proceedings to, [6.659]
areas within, [11.52]
LOCAL GOVERNMENT BOUNDARY COMMISSION FOR ENGLAND
members, [17.402]

M

MANAGER
appointment out of court
application for directions, [1.21]
invalid, liability, [1.20]
receivership accounts, delivery to registrar, [1.24]
remuneration, power of court to fix, [1.22]
time from which effective, [1.19]
bankrupt, disqualification from acting as, [1.17]
building society, appointment, [1.14], [7.455], [7.468]
definition, [1.15]
notification of appointment, method, [1.25]
person subject to debt relief order, disqualification from acting as, [1.17]
returns, enforcement of duty to file etc, [1.27]
special
winding up proceedings
accounting, [6.225], [6.267], [6.371]
appointment
court, [1.181], [6.222], [6.264], [6.368]
termination, [6.226], [6.268], [6.372]
remuneration, [6.368]
security
failure to give/keep up, [6.224], [6.266], [6.370]
undertaking, [6.223], [6.265], [6.369]
transitional provisions/savings, [1.596]
undischarged bankrupt acting on behalf of debenture holders, criminal offence, [1.17]
MARKET CHARGES. *SEE* FINANCIAL MARKETS
MARKET CONTRACTS. *SEE* FINANCIAL MARKETS
MARRIAGE
associate, meaning, [1.557]. *See also* ASSOCIATE
home rights, effect of bankruptcy. *See* DWELLING-HOUSE; HOME RIGHTS
property adjustment orders, settlements, [1.411], [1.413], [1.414], [17.15]
transaction in consideration of at undervalue, [1.411], [1.413], [1.414], [1.537]–[1.539]
MATRIMONIAL CAUSES
financial relief for parties and children of the family, [17.15], [17.16]
MAYOR
bankrupt, disqualification from acting as, [17.403]
MEETINGS
company voluntary arrangement proposal
decisions, [1.5]
summoning, procedure, [1.4]
creditors. *See* CREDITORS' MEETING
remote attendance at, [1.463]
MEMBERS
administration order, protection of interests, [1.13]
liability, nature of, [2.72]
meaning, [1.266]

MEMBERS – *cont.*
winding up
creditors' voluntary winding up
conversion to, [1.93], [1.103]
distinguished, [1.86]
members' voluntary winding up generally. *See* WINDING UP, VOLUNTARY, REGISTERED COMPANY
prosecution, delinquent member, [1.222], [1.223]

MISCONDUCT
winding up, during, of officer or shadow director, [1.212]

MONETARY LIMITS
insolvency proceedings, [8.1]–[8.6]

MORATORIUM
administration order, matters on which effective as moratorium, [1.575]
beginning
meaning, [1.569]
notification, [1.570]
capital market arrangement
company party, exclusion, [1.569]
debt, amount, [1.569]
interpretation, [1.569]
capital market investment
interpretation, [1.569]
company, effects on, [1.571]
company voluntary arrangement
approval, proposal, [1.573]
challenge, decisions, [1.573]
continuation
notice, [6.82]
directors, procedure, [1.2]
disposal of charged property during, [6.86]
documents
submission to court to obtain, [6.80]
extension, notice, [1.573], [6.83], [6.84]
implementation, [1.573]
meetings
conduct, [1.573]
summoning, [1.573]
moratorium committee, [1.573]
nominee
applications to court, notice of, [6.90]
replacement
court, by, [6.88]
time-recording information, [6.111]
withdrawal of consent to act, [6.87]
proposal
approval, [1.573]
consideration, [6.91]–[6.104]
statement of affairs, [6.77]
omission of information from, [6.77]
credit
maximum amount permitted to obtain without disclosure, [1.530], [1.571]
creditors, effects on, [1.571]
criminal liability, company officer
minimum value, property
concealed/fraudulently removed affecting, [1.530]
date of filing, meaning, [1.569]
directors' actions, challenge, [1.574]

MORATORIUM – *cont.*
disposal
charged property, [1.571]
company property during, [1.571]
duration, [1.570]
eligible companies, [1.569]
end, notification, [1.570]
excluded companies, [1.569]
Financial Services Authority, functions, [1.574]
floating charge documents, void provisions, [1.574]
gas, water, electricity etc supplies
management, office-holder
supplier, conditions, [1.237]
hire-purchase agreement, meaning, [1.569]
individual voluntary arrangement, insolvent debtor, [1.292]–[1.296]. *See also* INDIVIDUAL VOLUNTARY ARRANGEMENT
interim, administration order effective as, [1.575]
invoices etc, effects, [1.571]
Lloyd's market reorganisation, [7.1577]
market charge, meaning, [1.569]
market contract
entry into during, [1.571]
meaning, [1.569]
meaning, [1.569]
nominee
challenge, actions of, [1.572]
meaning, [1.569]
monitoring, company's affairs, [1.572]
replacement by court, [1.572]
statement, [1.570]
withdrawal, consent to act, [1.572]
obtaining
documents, submission, court, [1.570]
nominee, statement, [1.570]
offences, [1.574]
project company
interpretation, [1.569]
public-private partnership
exclusion, [1.569]
meaning, [1.569]
step-in rights, [1.569]
settlement finality regulations, meaning, [1.569]
system-charge, meaning, [1.569]
winding up by court
no voluntary arrangement approved by end, [1.120]

MORTGAGE
bankruptcy, mortgaged property
mortgagee of land, claim, [6.581]
sale
court, power to order, [6.582], [17.7]
proceeds, [6.583], [17.7]
mortgagee
conveyance on sale, [17.3]
power of sale, [17.2], [17.5]
powers incident to estate/interest, [17.1]
mortgagor, bankruptcy, effect
power of sale, [17.7]
receiver, appointment, [17.7]
proceeds of sale, application of, [17.4]

MORTGAGE – *cont.*
receiver, appointment by mortgagee
bankruptcy, mortgagor, effect, [17.7]
duties, [17.6]
powers, [17.6]
remuneration, [17.6]

N

NAME, COMPANY
administration order in force, requirements re use, [1.575]
prohibited, leave to act as director, [6.927]–[6.933]
re-use, restriction
director/shadow director, company in insolvent liquidation
penalty for contravention, [1.220]
personal liability, debts
contravention of restrictions, [1.221]
time limits, [1.220]
NATIONAL COLLEGE FOR HIGH SPEED RAIL
instrument of government, [18.294]–[18.296]
NATIONAL DEBT COMMISSIONERS
annual financial statement and audit, [1.516], [1.520]
Consolidated Fund, adjusted balances/unclaimed dividends etc, [1.518], [1.519]
Insolvency Services Account, excess, notification, [1.514]
interest on money received by liquidators/trustees in bankruptcy and invested, certification of sum payable etc to Commissioners, [1.517]
Investment Account, moneys which may be invested by Commissioners, [1.515]
unclaimed dividends/undistributed balances, [1.518]
NATIONAL HEALTH SERVICE
foundation trust
application to become, [7.1299]
authorisation, [7.1300], [7.1301]
constitution, amendments, [7.1302]
disqualification of director, [4.46]. *See also* DISQUALIFICATION OF DIRECTORS
general medical services
contracts, [18.303]–[18.312]
licence, application for, [7.1344]
Monitor
adult social care services, power to confer functions as to, [7.1330]
conflict between functions, [7.1332]
continuation of, [7.1326]
exercise of functions, matters to have regard to, [7.1331]
failure to perform functions, directions of Secretary of State, [7.1336]
general duties of, [7.1327]–[7.1329]
health care providers, licensing. *See* HEALTH CARE PROVIDERS
impact assessments, duty to carry out, [7.1334]
information, use and provision of, [7.1335]

NATIONAL HEALTH SERVICE – *cont.*
foundation trust – *cont.*
Monitor – *cont.*
regulatory burden, duty to review, [7.1333]
special administration. *See* HEALTH SPECIAL ADMINISTRATION
register of, [7.1303]
special administrator, appointment of, [7.1307]
NHS trusts
directors, suspension of, [7.1306]
establishment of, [7.1298]
Secretary of State, decision of, [7.1314]
special administrator, appointment of, [7.1305]
pension scheme, additional voluntary contributions, [11.11], [11.12]
premature retirement, compensation, [11.43], [11.44]
NETTING
close-out provisions
financial collateral arrangements
EC Directive, [3.275]
Regulation, [3.292]
credit institutions, arrangements for reorganisation/winding up, EC Directive, [3.201]
NOMINEE
company voluntary arrangement proposal, procedure when not liquidator/administrator, [1.3]
individual voluntary arrangement
creditors' meeting
to summon, [1.298], [2.7]
debtor's proposal
report, [1.296], [1.297], [2.7]
delinquent debtor, duties, [1.305]
no interim order, report, [1.297], [2.7]
moratorium
challenge, actions of, [1.572]
meaning, [1.569]
monitoring, company's affairs, [1.572]
replacement by court, [1.572]
statement, [1.570]
withdrawal, consent to act, [1.572]
NON-DOMESTIC RATING
bankruptcy petition against debtor, [18.7]
unoccupied property, [18.182]
NORTHERN IRELAND
air traffic administration order, [7.8], [7.15]
bankrupt
membership, Northern Ireland Assembly, [1.542]–[1.544], [2.15]
offence, England and Wales, before discharge, [1.439]
building society
dissolution on winding up, [7.467]
insolvency provisions applying, [7.477]
winding up etc, [7.466], [7.470]
co-operation, UK courts exercising insolvency jurisdiction, [1.540]
creditors' voluntary winding up, confirmation by UK court
credit institution, [3.218]
insurers, [3.130]

NORTHERN IRELAND – *cont.*
disqualification of directors, orders, [14.36], [14.40]
financial collateral arrangements, applicable law, [3.287], [3.289], [3.291], [3.294]
Insolvency Act 1986, extent applicable, [1.565]
insolvency practitioner
Proceeds of Crime Act 2002, external orders or requests under
enforcement receivers, application of sums by, [12.57]
sums received by appropriate chief clerk, [12.58]
insolvency services, exemption from Restrictive Trade Practices Act, [1.545]
postal administration provisions applying, [7.2077]
principal place of business, company incorporated outside UK, company, [1.1]
urban regeneration projects, exclusion from provisions as to appointment of administrative receiver, [1.63]
winding up of unregistered company, jurisdiction, [1.225]
NUCLEAR SITES
decommissioning funds, protection of security, [7.27]

O

OCCUPATION RIGHTS. *SEE* HOME RIGHTS
OCCUPATIONAL PENSION SCHEME
employer debt
actuary's certificates, [18.132], [18.136]
deferred debt arrangements, [18.118]
employment-cessation events, [18.109]–[18.113]
deferred debt arrangements, [18.118]
review, [18.131]
flexible apportionment arrangements, [18.117]
interpretation, [18.104]
liabilities and assets, calculation of amount of, [18.107]
modification of schemes, apportionment of debt on, [18.129]
money purchase schemes, [18.123]–[18.126]
multi-employer schemes, [18.108]
regulated apportionment arrangements, [18.120]
scheme apportionment arrangements, [18.114]
schemes to which provisions not applying, [18.106]
schemes treated as more than one scheme, [18.127], [18.128]
single or multi-employer sections, [18.121]
staying of voluntary winding up, disregard of, [18.130]
withdrawal arrangements, [18.115]–[18.119], [18.133]–[18.136]
fraud compensation levy
interpretation, [18.162]
waiver of payment, [18.163]
OFFENCES
administration, [1.575]
bankruptcy
absconding, [1.437]
concealment
books/papers, [1.434]
property, [1.433]
defence of innocent intention, [1.431]
engaging in business in name other than which adjudged bankrupt, [1.439]
failure to keep proper business accounts, [1.440]
false statements, [1.435]
falsification, documents etc, [1.434]
fraudulent dealing, property obtained on credit, [1.438]
fraudulent disposal, property, [1.436]
gambling by bankrupt, [1.441]
generally, [1.429]–[1.441]
institution, proceedings, [1.429]
non-disclosure by bankrupt before/after, [1.432]
obtaining credit without giving relevant information, [1.439]
bodies corporate, [1.549], [4.28]
energy administration order, [7.1047], [7.1062]
legal professional privilege, [1.554]
punishments, schedule, [1.547], [1.595], [7.1047]
sentencing and punishment of offenders, [18.263]–[18.266]
summary proceedings, [1.548]
OFFICE-HOLDER, INSOLVENCY
meaning, [6.10]
remuneration, [6.867]–[6.890]
reporting requirements, [6.854]–[6.865]
OFFICERS OF COMPANY
company voluntary arrangement, approval or moratorium, prosecution of delinquent officer, [1.11]
fraud in anticipation, winding up, [1.210]
winding up
false representation to creditor, [1.215]
falsification, company's books, [1.213]
fraud in anticipation, [1.210]
misconduct during, [1.212]
prosecution, delinquent officer, [1.222], [1.223]
public examination, winding up by court, [1.134], [6.373]–[6.382]
summary remedy against delinquent officer, [1.216]
OFFICIAL PETITIONER
function/status, [1.513]
OFFICIAL RECEIVER
appointment, [1.510], [6.720]
bankruptcy
bankrupt, duties re, [1.353]
investigatory duties, [1.351]
public examination, bankruptcy, [1.352]
statement of affairs by bankrupt to, time limit, [1.350]
bankrupt's estate, protection etc
bankrupt, duties re, [1.353]
investigatory duties, [1.351]
public examination, bankruptcy, [1.352]

OFFICIAL RECEIVER – *cont.*
bankrupt's estate, protection etc – *cont.*
statement of affairs by bankrupt to, time limit, [1.350]
contracting out functions, [12.4]–[12.7]
court, power to appoint, [1.18]
deputy, appointment, [1.512]
directions application, [6.722]
expenses, [6.723]
functions, [1.511]
individual voluntary arrangement, fast-track decision, [1.309]
report, results of decision, [1.310]
insolvency practitioner, as, authorisation to act as nominee/supervisor, [1.477]
inspection of documents held by, power of Financial Services Compensation scheme manager, [17.182], [17.184]
liquidator
not appointed, as, [6.724]
meaning, [1.510]
person entitled to act on behalf, [6.721]
provisional liquidator as, qualifications, [1.234]
remuneration, [8.58]–[8.61], [8.64]
rights of audience, [6.720]
Secretary of State, powers re, [1.510]
staff, appointment, [1.512]
status, [1.511]
trustee in bankruptcy
as, [1.360], [1.361]
first trustee in bankruptcy, [1.354]
criminal bankruptcy, bankruptcy order on, [1.360]
not appointed, as, [6.724]
release, [1.362]
winding up by court
EU proceedings
duty to notify registrar, [1.148]
investigative duty, [1.133]
report to creditors/contributories, [6.237]–[6.246]

OFFSHORE INSTALLATIONS
abandonment programme, protection of funds set aside for, [17.165]
decommissioning, [7.847], [7.848]
protected assets, directions to provide information about, [17.166]

OVERSEAS COMPANY
filing obligations, application of, [1.556]
insolvency proceedings, returns, [18.204], [18.205]
interpretation, [18.197]
judicial factor, notice of appointment, [18.206], [18.207]
trading disclosures
business letters, etc, particulars to appear on, [18.198]
failure to make, civil consequences of, [18.199]
non-compliance, penalty for, [18.200]
unregistered, winding up although dissolved, [1.229]
winding up
application of provisions, [18.201]

OVERSEAS COMPANY – *cont.*
winding up – *cont.*
returns, [18.202], [18.203]
penalties for non-compliance, [18.205]

P

PACKAGING WASTE
producers, notification of winding-up, receivership etc, [18.166]

PARTNERSHIPS, INSOLVENT
administration, [10.6], [10.21]
creditors' etc winding up petitions, [10.7], [10.8], [10.22]–[10.25]
deposit on petitions, [10.14]
decision procedure, insolvency proceedings in, [10.12], [10.29]
disqualification, Company Directors' Disqualification Act 1986, [10.15], [10.30]
forms, [10.16], [10.31]
generally, [10.1]–[10.32]
limited liability partnerships
applicable legislation, [10.36], [10.37], [10.39]–[10.41]
generally, [10.33]–[10.44], [17.218], [17.219]
pensions, powers of Pension Regulator, [17.291]
Proceeds of Crime Act 2002 provisions, [17.245]
Scotland. *See* SCOTLAND
subordinate legislation, [10.38]
members' petitions, [10.9]–[10.11], [10.26], [10.27]
order-making powers re, [1.533]
pensions, powers of Pension Regulator, [17.291]
subordinate legislation, application, [10.17], [10.32]
transitional provisions, [2.40], [2.41], [10.8], [10.10], [10.18], [10.21]–[10.27], [10.31], [10.45]
unregistered company as member of insolvent partnership, winding up, [10.13], [10.28]
voluntary arrangements, [10.4], [10.5], [10.19], [10.20]

PATENTS AND TRADE MARKS
inclusion in insolvency proceedings, EC Regulation, [3.48]

PAYMENT SYSTEMS
EC Regulation, [3.45]

PENSION PROTECTION FUND
entry rules, [18.89]–[18.102]
multi-employer schemes
interpretation, [18.15]
non-segregated
option to segregate on withdrawal of participating employer, with, [18.87]
requirement for partial wind up on withdrawal of participating employer, with, [18.60]–[18.76]
without requirement for partial wind up on withdrawal of participating employer, [18.77]–[18.86]

PENSION PROTECTION FUND – *cont.*
multi-employer schemes – *cont.*
segregated
multi-employer sections with option to segregate on withdrawal of participating employer, [18.88]
multi-employer sections without requirement for partial wind up on withdrawal of participating employer, [18.28]–[18.41]
non-segregate multi-employer sections with requirement for partial wind up on withdrawal of participating employer, [18.42]–[18.59]
single employer sections, [18.16]–[18.27]

PENSION PROTECTION FUND BOARD
duties
binding notices confirming status, scheme, [17.298]
failure, insolvency practitioner to issue notices confirming status of scheme, [17.297]
responsibility, schemes following
application/notification, [17.300]–[17.302]
insolvency event, [17.299]
protected liabilities, [17.303]
false or misleading information, provision to, [17.320]
information, gathering
entry, premises, [17.317], [17.318]
notices requiring provision, information, [17.316], [17.318]
warrants, [17.319]
occupational scheme, insolvent employer
information re employer's insolvency
insolvency date, meaning, [17.294]
insolvency event
insolvency practitioner, notification, Board, [17.293]
meaning, [17.294]
status of scheme
insolvency practitioner, notices confirming
approval, [17.296]
duty to issue, [17.295]
restrictions, schemes during assessment period
assessment period, meaning, [17.304]
Board as creditor of employer, [17.309]
contributions, payment, [17.305]
directions, [17.306]
new members, admission, [17.305]
scheme benefits
loans to pay, [17.311]
payment, [17.310]
winding up
contravention of restriction, power to validate, [17.308]
restriction, [17.307]
valuation of assets and protected liabilities
approval, [17.314]
binding, [17.315]
determinations, [17.313]
obligation to obtain, [17.312]

PENSIONS
bankrupt
income payments order
adjustments between earlier/later bankruptcies, [1.406]
pension payments to which applicable, [1.379]
personal pension scheme, no forfeiture of rights, [17.107]
recovery of excessive contributions
approved/unapproved pension arrangement, [1.415]–[1.417]
pension-sharing cases, [1.418]–[1.420]
bankruptcy, effect on rights, [17.169]–[17.174]
NHS, additional voluntary contributions, [11.11], [11.12]
occupational schemes
bankruptcy, contributions as preferential debts, [1.473], [1.591]
deficiency on winding up, [9.22]–[9.39], [17.124], [17.125]
destination arrangements
calculation, rights, [11.32]
verification, rights, [11.32]
exclusion orders, [11.28]
forfeiture, [17.127], [17.128]
generally, [17.116]–[17.132]
inalienability, [17.126]
independent trustees, [17.116]–[17.119]
information request, time for compliance, [11.33]
multi-employer schemes, deficiencies in assets on winding up, [17.125]
Pensions Regulator
notification by insolvency practitioner
employer insolvency, [17.293]
power to modify
winding up, to secure, [17.120]
prescribed pension arrangements
calculation, rights under, [11.30]
meaning, [11.25]
verification, rights under, [11.30]
qualifying agreements, [11.29]
restoration order, time for compliance, [11.31]
Scotland. *See* SCOTLAND
unapproved pension arrangements
exclusion, rights under, [11.27]
meaning, [11.26]
unpaid contributions on insolvency of employer
priority in bankruptcy, [17.110]
Secretary of State, payment, [17.101]–[17.106]
winding up
deficiencies, assets
multi-employer schemes, [17.125]
schemes to which applicable, [9.22]–[9.39], [17.124]
notices, [9.67]–[9.77]
operation, scheme during winding up period, [17.122], [17.123]

PENSIONS – *cont.*
occupational schemes – *cont.*
winding up – *cont.*
Pensions Regulator, power to modify scheme for, [17.120]
preferential liabilities, [17.121], [17.123]
reports, [9.67]–[9.77]
Pensions Regulator
contribution notices where avoidance, employer debt
clearance statements, [17.274]
content, [17.272]
effect, [17.272]
generally, [17.266]–[17.274]
material detriment test, [17.267], [17.268]
relationship, notice and debt, [17.273]
sum specified, [17.269]
transfer of members of scheme, [17.270], [17.271]
financial support directions
clearance statements, [17.280]
financial support, meaning, [17.279]
generally, [17.275]–[17.285]
insufficiently resourced, meaning, [17.278]
non-compliance
contribution notices
content, [17.283]
effect, [17.281], [17.283]
relationship, employer debt, [17.284]
sum specified, [17.282]
service company, meaning, [17.278]
transfer of members of scheme, [17.276], [17.277]
Insolvency Act 1986, right to apply, [17.292]
occupational pension
insolvency practitioner, notification, insolvent employee, [17.293]
winding up
scheme, power to modify, [17.120]
partnerships/limited liability partnerships, [17.291]
undervalue, transactions at
restoration order
content, [17.288]
effect, [17.288]
non-compliance
contribution order, [17.289], [17.290]
when applicable, [17.286], [17.287]
personal schemes
bankrupt, no forfeiture of rights, [17.107]
destination arrangements
calculation, rights, [11.32]
verification, rights, [11.32]
exclusion orders, [11.28]
information request, time for compliance, [11.33]
prescribed pension arrangements
calculation, rights under, [11.30]
meaning, [11.25]
verification, rights under, [11.30]
qualifying agreements, [11.29]
restoration order, time for compliance, [11.31]
Scotland. *See* SCOTLAND

PENSIONS – *cont.*
personal schemes – *cont.*
unapproved pension arrangements
exclusion, rights under, [11.27]
meaning, [11.26]
protection generally. *See* PENSION PROTECTION FUND BOARD
rights, effect of bankruptcy, [17.169]–[17.174]
Scotland. *See* SCOTLAND
teachers, [11.50]

PETROLEUM EXPLORATION LICENSING
seaward/landward, [9.78]–[9.83]

POSTAL ADMINISTRATION
administrators, [7.2062]
appeals, [7.2213], [7.2214]
applications to court
court file, [7.2200]
disapplication of s 176A, for, [7.2182]
filing and service, [7.2183]
form and contents of, [7.2181]
further information and disclosure, for, [7.2220]
hearings
adjournment, [7.2190]
generally, [7.2186]
without notice, [7.2185]
office copies of documents, provision of, [7.2221]
reports, use of, [7.2189]
s 176A(5), under, [7.2184]
shorthand writers, [7.2195], [7.2196]
transfer of proceedings, [7.2191]–[7.2194]
witness statements, [7.2187], [7.2188]
wrong court, proceedings commenced in, [7.2192]
companies in
grants and loans for, [7.2069]
guarantees, [7.2071]
indemnities, [7.2070]
company meetings
company representative at, [7.2228]
notice
advertisement of, [7.2110]
non-delivery of, [7.2243]
proxies
definition, [7.2222]
financial interest, holder with, [7.2227]
inspection, right of, [7.2226]
issue and use of forms, [7.2223]
retention of, [7.1209]
use of, [7.2224]
venue and conduct of, [7.2120]
conduct of, [7.2063]
costs
administrator, awarded against, [7.2205]
application for, [7.2206]
application of rules, [7.2201]
detailed assessment, [7.2202], [7.2203]
examination of persons in proceedings, of, [7.2234]
final certificate, [7.2208]
paid otherwise than from energy supply company assets, [7.2204]
witnesses, of, [7.2207]

POSTAL ADMINISTRATION – *cont.*
creditors' meetings
admission and rejection of claims, [7.2112]
alternative liquidator, for nomination of, [7.2109]
chair, [7.2108]
company representative at, [7.2228]
entitlement to vote, [7.2111]
excluded persons, [7.2260]–[7.2262]
generally, [7.2107]
hire-purchase, conditional sale and chattel leasing agreements, voting by owners under, [7.2115]
holders of negotiable instruments, voting by, [7.2114]
minutes, [7.2117]
notice
advertisement of, [7.2110]
non-delivery of, [7.2243]
proxies
definition, [7.2222]
financial interest, holder with, [7.2227]
inspection, right of, [7.2226]
issue and use of forms, [7.2223]
retention of, [7.2225]
use of, [7.2224]
quorum, [7.2258]
remote attendance at, [7.2259]
resolutions, [7.2116]
revision of proposals by, [7.2118]
secured creditors, voting by, [7.2113]
debt, proof of
admission and rejection of, [7.2132], [7.2151]
alteration after payment of dividend, [7.2157]
appeal against decisions on, [7.2133]
claim, making, [7.2128]
costs of, [7.2129]
debt payable at future time, [7.2144], [7.2161]
discounts, [7.2139]
estimate of quantum of claim, [7.2136]
expunging by court, [7.2135]
foreign currency debts, [7.2141]
inspection of, [7.2130]
interest, [7.2143]
mutual credits and set-off, [7.2140]
negotiable instruments, in respect of, [7.2137]
new postal administrator, transmission to, [7.2131]
periodical nature, payments of, [7.2142]
secured creditors, of, [7.2138]
security
non-disclosure, surrender for, [7.2146]
realisation by creditor, [7.2149]
redemption, [7.2147]
test of value, [7.2148]
value of, [7.2145]
withdrawal or variation of, [7.2134]
distribution to creditors
dividend
adjustment where paid before time, [7.2161]
alteration of proof after payment, [7.2157]
assignment of right to, [7.2160]
calculation and distribution of, [7.2126]

POSTAL ADMINISTRATION – *cont.*
distribution to creditors – *cont.*
dividend – *cont.*
declaration of, [7.2153]
disqualification from, [7.2159]
no, or no further, notice of, [7.2156]
notice of declaration, [7.2154]
payments, [7.2155]
postponement or cancellation of, [7.2152]
equal ranking of debts, [7.2125]
generally, [7.2124]
proposed, notice of, [7.2150]
secured creditors, revaluation of security, [7.2158]
unsold assets, division of, [7.2127]
documents
copies of, [7.2281], [7.2282]
court, service of, [7.2255]–[7.2257]
inspection of, [7.2280]–[7.2283]
personal delivery of, [7.2241]
postal delivery of, [7.2242]
electronic delivery of proceedings, [7.2253]
ending of
application to court, [7.2164]
court order, notification of, [7.2165]
creditors' voluntary liquidation, move to, [7.2166]
dissolution, move to, [7.2167]
final progress reports, [7.2163]
Secretary of State, provision of information to, [7.2168]
enforcement of orders
compliance with rules, as to, [7.2198]
generally, [7.2197]
warrants, [7.2199]
examination of persons in
application for, form and contents of, [7.2230]
application of rules, [7.2229]
costs, [7.2234]
order for, [7.2231]
procedure, [7.2232]
record of, [7.2233]
expenses
costs pre-administration, [7.2123]
payment of, [7.2236]
priority of, [7.2122]
false claim of status as creditor, [7.2238]
forms, [7.2263]–[7.2265], [7.2297]
formal defects in proceedings, [7.2217]
Gazette notices, [7.2266]–[7.2268]
interpretation, [7.2075], [7.2087], [7.2288]–[7.2294]
list of creditors, right to, [7.2283]
modification of Enterprise Act provisions, [7.2074]
modification of Insolvency Act provisions, [7.2082], [7.2084]
foreign companies, [7.2083]
Northern Ireland, provisions applying, [7.2077]
notices other than in Gazette, [7.2269], [7.2270]
objective of, [7.2059]
offences, punishment of, [7.2239], [7.2298]
order
appeals, [7.2213], [7.2214]

POSTAL ADMINISTRATION – *cont.*
order – *cont.*
application for
applicant, [7.2060]
contents, [7.2091]
filing, [7.2092]
form of, [7.2090]
hearing, [7.2097]
notice to officers, [7.2094]
service, [7.2093]–[7.2096]
meaning, [7.2058]
notice of, [7.2098]
powers of court, [7.2061]
regulatory conditions to secure funding of, [7.2073]
witness statement, [7.2089], [7.2091]
order staying proceedings, service of, [7.2218]
other insolvency procedures, restrictions on, [7.2064]–[7.2068]
payments into court, [7.2219]
persons lacking capacity to manage affairs
application of rules, [7.2209]
appointment of person to act for, [7.2210]–[7.2212]
partnerships, in case of, [7.2076]
postal administrator
appointment, notification and advertisement of, [7.2099]
authority to dispose of property, [7.2121]
award of costs against, [7.2205]
ceasing to be qualified to act, notice of vacation of office, [7.2173]
court order ending administration, notification of, [7.2165]
death of, [7.2174]
duties on vacating office, [7.2179]
limited disclosure, order for, [7.2106]
notices and documents
authorisation, [7.2248]
electronic delivery, [7.2249], [7.2250]
form of, [7.2246]
joint administrators, notice to, [7.2254]
orders under s 176A(5), notice of, [7.2286]
proof of sending, [7.2247]
progress reports by, [7.2119], [7.2163]
proposals
revision of, [7.2118]
statement of, [7.2105]
removal from office, application for, [7.2172]
remuneration
fixing, [7.2162]
replacement of
application for, [7.2175]
notification and advertisement of appointment, [7.2176], [7.2177]
registrar of companies, notification to, [7.2178]
resignation
grounds for, [7.2169]
notice of, [7.2171]
notice of intention, [7.2170]
security, [7.2285]
websites, use of, [7.2251], [7.2252]
postal transfer schemes, [7.2085]

POSTAL ADMINISTRATION – *cont.*
principal court rules and practice, application of, [7.2215]
provable debts, [7.2237]
provider
creditors, appointment of administrator by, [7.2067]
enforcement of security over assets of, [7.2067]
ordinary administration orders in relation to, [7.2066]
voluntary winding up, [7.2065]
winding up, [7.2064]
registrar of companies, notifications to
application of rules, [7.2271]
court orders, relating to, [7.2275]
documents, relating to, [7.2274]
information in, [7.2272]
more than one nature, of, [7.2278]
office of administrator, relating to, [7.2273]
other events as to, [7.2277]
other persons at same time, to, [7.2279]
returns or reports of meetings, [7.2276]
regulatory powers exercisable during, [7.2072]
review of provisions, [7.2078]
rights of audience, [7.2216]
Secretary of State, powers of, [7.2235]
solicitors, notice etc to, [7.2244]
statement of affairs
expenses, [7.2104]
extension of time for, [7.2103]
limited disclosure, [7.2102]
notice requiring, [7.2100]
release from duty to submit, [7.2103]
verification and filing, [7.2101]
time limits, [7.2284]
PREFERENCES
administration and liquidation, adjustment of prior transaction, [1.244], [1.245]
bankruptcy, adjustment of prior transaction, [1.412]–[1.414]
PREFERENTIAL CHARGE
goods distrained, on, [1.177]
insolvent employer, transfer of right to Secretary of State, [1.177]
PREFERENTIAL DEBTS
building societies, [1.473], [1.474], [7.454], [7.455], [7.464], [7.468]
categories, [1.473], [1.591]
debentures secured by floating charge, payment from, [17.330]
priority, winding up, [1.176]
relevant date, determination, existence/amount, [1.474]
Scotland. *See* SCOTLAND: bankruptcy
PRIORITY
bankruptcy
costs, payment out of estate, [6.607], [6.608
distribution of bankrupt's estate, priority of debts, [1.399]
costs, payment out of assets, [6.269], [6.270], [6.383]–[6.385]
energy administration order, expenses, [7.908]
floating charge, debentures secured by, [17.330]

PRIORITY – *cont.*
insurance claims on winding up, priority of payment of claims on winding up, [3.140]–[3.157]
Lloyd's market, insurance claims, [7.1609]
preferential debts, winding up, [1.176]
Scotland. *See* SCOTLAND
PRIVATE HIRE VEHICLES
operators' licences, [11.13]–[11.15]
PROCEEDS OF CRIME ACT 2002. *SEE* CRIMINAL MATTERS
PROJECT FINANCE
moratorium for project company, interpretation, [1.569]
step-in rights, with, appointment of administrative receiver, [1.64], [1.578]
PROOF OF DEBT. *SEE* DEBT, PROOF OF
PROXIES
blank, [6.818]
continuing, [6.817]
definition, [6.816]
energy administration order, [7.1013]–[7.1018]
financial interest, proxy-holder with, [7.1018]
generally, [6.816]–[6.823]
proxy-holder, [6.822]
railway administration order, [7.2535]–[7.2541]
retention, [6.821]
specific, [6.817]
use at meetings, [6.819], [6.820]
PRUDENTIAL REGULATION AUTHORITY (PRA)
administration
participation in proceedings, [18.270]
report by administrator, [18.269]
bankruptcy
insolvency practitioner, report of, [18.280]
participation in proceedings, [18.281]
credit institution, reorganisation/winding up
consultation before resolution to wind up, [3.220]
notification, relevant decision to, [3.221]
creditors in Scotland, trust deeds for, [18.268]
friendly societies, functions relating to, [7.1284]
functions, [17.175], [17.176]
insolvency, participation in proceedings, [18.281]
insurers
effecting or carrying out long-term contract of insurance, consents, [18.275]
long-term insurance, continuation where in liquidation, [18.283]
petition, service of, [18.276]
reorganisation or winding up, notification of relevant decisions to, [3.132]
liquidation, participation in proceedings, [18.280]
liquidator, duty to report by, [18.278]
Lloyd's market, notification of relevant decision to, [7.1602]
order, right to apply for, [18.282]
receivership
participation in proceedings, [18.272]
receiver, report by, [18.273]
reclaim funds, service of petition, [18.277]
rules
recovery plans, [17.177], [17.179], [17.180]
PRUDENTIAL REGULATION AUTHORITY (PRA) – *cont.*
rules – *cont.*
resolution packs, [17.178]–[17.180]
voluntary winding up
insurers, of, [18.275], [18.276]
participation in proceedings, [18.274]
rules
recovery plans, [17.177], [17.179], [17.180]
resolution plans, [17.178]–[17.180]
PUBLIC INTEREST
winding up by court, [1.123], [1.575]
PUBLIC POLICY
cross-border insolvency, model law, UNCITRAL, [3.7]
EC Regulation, recognition, insolvency proceedings, other Member State, [3.62]
PUBLIC-PRIVATE PARTNERSHIP
administration order
advertisement, [7.2323]
affidavits
evidence by, use of, [7.2354]
filing, [7.2355]
practice and procedure, [7.2387]
service, [7.2355]
appeals, [7.2380], [7.2381]
application in proceedings
adjournment of hearing, directions for, [7.2357]
affidavit evidence by, use of, [7.2354], [7.2355]
application of provisions, [7.2349]
filing, [7.2351]
form and content of, [7.2350]
hearing, [7.2353]
notice, hearing without, [7.2352]
reports, use of, [7.2356]
service, [7.2351]
application of rules, [7.2435]
appropriate fee, meaning, [7.2433]
confidentiality of documents, [7.2416]
costs
application for, [7.2373]
Civil Procedure Rules, application of, [7.2368]
detailed procedure, assessment by, [7.2369], [7.2370]
examination of persons in proceedings, of, [7.2404]
final certificate, [7.2375]
payment otherwise than from assets of PPP company, [7.2371]
security for, [7.2388], [7.2389]
special PPP administrator, against, [7.2372]
witnesses, of, [7.2374]
court, meaning, [7.2426]
court records, [7.2363]
inspection of, [7.2364]
court rules and practice applying, [7.2382]
creditor or member, false claim to status, [7.2422]
creditors' meetings
adjournment, [7.2332]
chairman, [7.2333]

PUBLIC-PRIVATE PARTNERSHIP – *cont.*
administration order – *cont.*
creditors' meetings – *cont.*
claims, admission and rejection of, [7.2335]
company representation, [7.2398]
entitlement to vote, [7.2334]
evidence of proceedings at, [7.2408]
hire-purchase etc agreement, entitlement of owner of goods to vote, [7.2339]
minutes, [7.2340]
negotiable instrument holders, voting by, [7.2337]
non-receipt of notice, [7.2420]
notice of, [7.2332]
proxy forms, [7.2332]
quorum, [7.2407]
resolutions, [7.2340]
retention of title creditors, voting by, [7.2338]
secured creditors, voting by, [7.2336]
time of, [7.2332]
venue, [7.2332]
discharge of, [7.2324]
documents
charge for copies, [7.2419]
right to copy, [7.2418]
same person, sent simultaneously to, [7.2417]
enforcement
compliance with rules, of, [7.2360]
manner of, [7.2359]
warrants, [7.2361]
examination of persons in proceedings
application, form and contents of, [7.2400]
application of rules, [7.2399]
books, papers and records, order for production of, [7.2401]
costs of, [7.2404]
order for, [7.2401]
procedure, [7.2402]
record of, [7.2403]
extent of rules, [7.2313]
file of proceedings
maintenance of, [7.2365]
right to inspect, [7.2366]
formal defects in proceedings, [7.2386]
forms, [7.2436]
forms of use in proceedings, [7.2410]
further information and disclosure, order for, [7.2390]
Gazette as evidence of facts in notice, [7.2423]
Gazette notices and advertisements, filing, [7.2367]
giving notice, meaning, [7.2427]
Greater London Authority Act 1999, [1.13], [7.2300], [7.2301], [7.2307], [7.2310]
interpretation, [7.2312]
members' meetings
chairman, [7.2342]
conduct of, [7.2342]
evidence of proceedings at, [7.2408]
venue, [7.2342]
notice of, [7.2323], [7.2406]
offences, punishment of, [7.2424]

PUBLIC-PRIVATE PARTNERSHIP – *cont.*
administration order – *cont.*
office copies of documents, [7.2391]
persons incapable of managing affairs, representative of, [7.2376]–[7.2379]
petition
affidavit to support, [7.2314], [7.2315]
enforcement officer, notice to, [7.2319]
filing, [7.2317]
form of, [7.2316]
hearing, [7.2322]
manner in which service effected, [7.2320]
meaning, [7.2430]
proof of service, [7.2321]
service of, [7.2318]
proceedings, meaning, [7.2432]
proposals to creditors
members, notice to, [7.2331]
statement of affairs annexed to, [7.2330]
proxies
definition, [7.2392]
financial interest, holder with, [7.2397]
forms, issue and use of, [7.2393]
inspection, right of, [7.2396]
meetings, use at, [7.2394]
retention of, [7.2395]
registrar, acts before, [7.2426]
review of, [7.2380]
rights of attendance in proceedings, [7.2384]
rights of audience, [7.2383]
Secretary of State
documents issuing from, [7.2409]
regulations by, [7.2405]
service of documents
outside the jurisdiction, [7.2415]
post, by, [7.2413]
rules applying, [7.2414]
shorthand writers, appointment and remuneration of, [7.2358]
solicitors, notice to, [7.2428]
special PPP administrator
award of costs against, [7.2372]
charged property, disposal of, [7.2344]
death of, [7.2347]
joint, notice to, [7.2429]
list of creditors, supply of, [7.2421]
receipts and payments, abstract of, [7.2345]
remuneration, fixing, [7.2343]
report to creditors, [7.2341]
resignation, [7.2346]
security for performance of functions, [7.2411]
solicitor, attendance by, [7.2385]
vacancy in office, filling, [7.2348]
statement of affairs
expenses of, [7.2329]
extension of time for, [7.2328]
filing, [7.2326]
limited disclosure of, [7.2327]
notice requiring, [7.2325]
proposals, annexed to, [7.2330]
release from duty to submit, [7.2328]
verification, [7.2326]

PUBLIC-PRIVATE PARTNERSHIP – *cont.*
administration order – *cont.*
time-limits, [7.2412]
title of proceedings, [7.2362]
transitional provisions, [7.2435]
venue for proceedings, [7.2431]
witnesses, costs and expenses of, [7.2374]
administrative receiver, appointment permitted, [1.61], [1.578]
Greater London Authority
administration order
effect, [7.2300]
generally, [1.13], [7.2300], [7.2301], [7.2307], [7.2310]
meaning, [7.2300]
special petition, [7.2301]
transfer, relevant activities, [7.2310]
agreement, meaning, [7.2299]
company, meaning, [7.2304]
foreign companies, [7.2304], [7.2308]
unregistered etc companies, [7.2304]
voluntary winding up, restriction, [7.2303]
winding up order, restriction, [7.2302]
moratorium
exclusion, [1.569]
meaning, [1.569]
step-in rights, [1.569]

R

RAILWAY COMPANIES
company, meaning, [7.2444]
foreign companies, applicable law, [7.2444], [7.2449]
government financial assistance
railway administration order made, [7.2441]
protected, Railways Act 1993
administrative receiver, appointment, [1.67]
guarantees, [7.2442]
insolvency proceedings, restriction, [7.2440]
voluntary winding up order, restriction, [7.2440]
winding up order, restriction, [7.2439]
railway administration order
affidavit to support petition, [7.2455], [7.2457], [7.2530]
applicable law, [7.2448]
applications, [7.2492]–[7.2501]
attendance at hearings, right, [7.2526], [7.2527]
audience, right of, [7.2525]
company representation, [7.2541]
concurrent proceedings/remedies, restriction, [7.2529]
costs, [7.2512]–[7.2519]. *See also* COSTS
creditors
false claim to be, [7.2566]
list, right, [7.2564]
disclosure, [7.2533]
enforcement procedures, [7.2503]–[7.2505]
examination, persons in proceedings, [7.2542]–[7.2547]
formal defects, [7.2528]

RAILWAY COMPANIES – *cont.*
railway administration order – *cont.*
forms, [7.2553]
further information, [7.2533]
generally, [1.13], [1.522], [7.2452]–[7.2579], [7.2437], [7.2448]
incapacity, persons incapable, management, own affairs, [7.2520]–[7.2523]. *See also* INCAPACITY
independent report, company's affairs, [7.2456]
meaning, [7.2437]
meetings, [7.2473]–[7.2483], [7.2550], [7.2551]
notice/advertisement of, [7.2465], [7.2549]
offences, punishment, [7.2567]
payment into court, [7.2532]
petition
filing, [7.2459]
form, [7.2458]
hearing, [7.2464]
notice of filing, to whom required, [7.2461]
service, [7.2460], [7.2462], [7.2463], [7.2556], [7.2557]
special, [7.2438]
proposals to creditors, [7.2471], [7.2472]
proxies etc, [7.2535]–[7.2541]
records/returns, court, [7.2506]–[7.2511]
Secretary of State
documents, [7.2552]
powers, [7.2548]
security in court, [7.2531]
shorthand writers, [7.2502]
special railway administrator
costs award against, [7.2516]
functions, [7.2484]–[7.2491]
security, [7.2554]
statement of affairs, [7.2466]–[7.2471]
transfer, relevant activities, [7.2451]
unregistered companies, applicable law, [7.2444]
RECEIVER
accounts, receivership
appointment out of court
delivery to registrar, [1.24]
appointment out of court
application for directions, [1.21]
invalid, liability, [1.20]
receivership accounts, delivery to registrar, [1.24]
remuneration, power of court to fix, [1.22]
time from which effective, [1.19]
bankrupt, disqualification from acting as, [1.17]
bankrupt estate, protection
interim receiver, appointment, [1.348]
receivership pending appointment, trustee, [1.349]
body corporate, disqualification, acting as, [1.16]
building society, appointment, [1.14], [7.455], [7.468]
cross-border operation, receivership provisions, [1.58]
debts, payment from assets subject to floating charge, [1.26]
definition, [1.15], [1.267]
FCA and PRA, report to, [18.273]
notification of appointment, method, [1.25]

RECEIVER – *cont.*
official. *See* OFFICIAL RECEIVER
part of company's property, vacation of office after administration order if administrator required, [1.13]
person subject to debt relief order, disqualification from acting as, [1.17]
remuneration on appointment out of court, power of court to fix, [1.22]
returns, enforcement of duty to file etc, [1.27]
Scotland. *See* SCOTLAND
transitional provisions/savings, [1.596]
undischarged bankrupt, acting on behalf, debenture holders, criminal offence, [1.17]

RECEIVERSHIP
FCA and PRA, participation by, [18.272]

RECEIVERSHIP ORDER
compensation scheme, Financial Services and Markets Act 2000
Authority, power to participate, proceedings, [17.194]
receiver, report to Authority, [17.195]
property subject, exclusion from bankrupt's estate vesting by trustee in bankruptcy, [1.372]

REGISTERED COMPANY
winding up. *See* WINDING UP BY COURT, REGISTERED COMPANY; WINDING UP, REGISTERED COMPANY; WINDING UP, VOLUNTARY, REGISTERED COMPANY

REGISTERED OFFICE, COMPANY
SCE, in GB, petition for winding up by court, [1.125]
SE, in GB, petition for winding up by court, [1.124]
winding up petition, [1.115]

REGISTRAR
Chief Land Registrar. *See* CHIEF LAND REGISTRAR
companies. *See* REGISTRAR OF COMPANIES

REGISTRAR OF COMPANIES
administration, notice of end to, [1.575]
administrative receiver
accounts, receipts/payments to, [6.198]
report to
contents, [1.34]
copies, to whom required, [1.34]
creditors' committee, attendance before, [1.35]
disclosure restrictions, [1.34]
non-compliance, penalties, [1.34]
time limit, [1.34]
administrator, proposals to, [1.575]
cross-border insolvency
notices, delivery to
foreign representative's duty to give to enforcement, [3.327]
methods, [3.327]
procedure, [3.307], [3.327]
rectification, register, [3.327]
receivership accounts, delivery by manager to registrar, [1.24]
Scotland. *See* SCOTLAND: winding up by court
winding up of registered company, order to copy, [1.131]

REGULATED BUSINESS
administrative receiver, appointment permitted, [1.61], [1.578]
credit institution, reorganisation/winding up
EC Directive, [3.199]
Regulation, [3.241]
insurance undertaking, reorganisation/winding up
EC Directive, [3.111]
Regulation, [3.168]
meaning, [1.578]

REGULATED COVERED BONDS
asset pool
meaning, [18.169]
owner, [18.170]
charge, realisation of, [18.176]
eligible property, [18.168]
interpretation, [18.167]
issuer
asset pool monitor, appointment and functions of, [18.173]
connected persons, [18.171]
general requirements, [18.172]
insolvency of, [18.174]
primary and secondary legislation, modifications of, [18.179], [18.180]
winding up, etc, expenses of, [18.177]
winding up, priority in, [18.175]

RENTCHARGE
disclaimer of onerous property by trustee
bankruptcy, [1.390]
winding up, [1.182], [1.184]

REPURCHASE AGREEMENTS
credit institution, reorganisation/winding up
EC Directive, [3.202]
Regulation, [3.247]

RESERVATION OF TITLE
credit institution, reorganisation/winding up
EC Directive, [3.198]
Regulation, [3.239]
insolvency proceedings, opening, effect of EC Regulation, [3.43]
insurance undertaking, reorganisation/winding up
EC Directive, [3.109]
Regulation, [3.166]

RESIDENCE
debtor in bankruptcy, of, [1.324]

RESTRAINT ORDER
property subject
exclusion from bankrupt's estate, [1.370]

S

SCOTLAND
administration
administrator. *See* administrator, *below*
applicable Schedules, [1.575], [1.576]
bank liquidator, application by, [16.86]
company in liquidation
order when, [15.76]
conversion to winding up, application, [15.162]–[15.164]
Court of Session rules, [16.79]–[16.86]

SCOTLAND – *cont.*
administration – *cont.*
creditors' committee
administrator, information from, [15.135]
company, dealings with, [15.136]
constitution, [15.118]
establishment, formalities of, [15.120]
expenses of members, [15.133]
formal defects, [15.134]
functions etc, [15.119]
meetings, [15.121]
chairman, [15.124]
members' representative, [15.126]
place, request to specify, [15.123]
quorum, [15.125]
voting rights and resolution, [15.131]
remote attendance at, [15.122]
removal of member, [15.129]
resignation of member, [15.127]
resolutions other than at meetings, [15.132]
termination of membership, [15.128]
vacancies on, [15.130]
distributions to creditors, [15.143]–[15.145]
dividends, payment, [15.145]
EC Regulation
conversion to winding up, application, [15.162]–[15.164]
member State, liquidator, [15.165]
ending
automatic, notice of, [15.148]
court, application to, [15.151]
final progress reports, [15.147]
moving from administration
creditors' voluntary liquidation, to, [15.152]
dissolution, [15.153]
notice of, [15.150]
expenses of, [15.141]
extension of, application, [15.149]
floating charge prior to, conditions for avoidance, [1.250], [2.10], [2.26], [3.290]
generally, [15.70]–[15.165]
gratuitous alienations, [1.247], [2.10], [2.26], [17.243]
meetings
administrator's proposals
consideration, [15.104]
revision, [15.113]
applicable law, [15.107]
creditors' meeting
correspondence instead of, [15.106]
requisition, [15.109]
entitlement to vote and draw dividend, [15.103]
excluded persons, [15.115]–[15.117]
general provisions, [15.100]
hire-purchase/conditional sale/hiring agreements, owner
voting entitlement, [15.112]
member State liquidators
voting entitlement, [15.108]
notice, advertisement of, [15.111], [15.119]
notices to creditors, [15.114]
remote attendance at, [15.102]

SCOTLAND – *cont.*
administration – *cont.*
meetings – *cont.*
suspension and adjournment, [15.105]
notices and documents
application of provisions, [15.96]
electronic delivery, [15.97]
websites, use of, [15.98], [15.99]
order
company in liquidation, [15.76]
dismissal of application, [15.77]
pre-administration costs, [15.142]
process
administrator's proposals, [15.94]
disclosure, limited, [15.91]
limited disclosure of para 49 statement, [15.95]
notification/advertisement
administrator's appointment, [15.88]
statement of affairs
expenses, [15.93]
extension, time, [15.92]
form, [15.90]
notice requiring, [15.89]
release, duty to submit, [15.92]
statement of concurrence, [15.90]
sheriff court insolvency rules, [16.22]–[16.27]
time spent on a case, information, [15.343], [15.344]
unfair preferences, [1.248], [2.10], [2.26], [17.243]
vesting, estate in permanent trustee, [5.70], [5.72]
administrator
appointment by company or directors
no notice, intention to appoint given, [15.86]
notice
administrator, to, [15.87]
appointment, of, [15.85]
intention to appoint, [15.82]
resolution or decision, [15.84]
statutory declaration, timing, [15.83]
appointment by court
application, form, [15.71]
company in liquidation, [15.74]
expenses, [15.75]
service, petition, [15.72]
specified person, application by qualifying floating chargeholder, [15.73]
appointment by floating charge holder
notice
administrator, to, [15.80]
appointment, of, [15.79]
intention to appoint, [15.78]
taking place out of court business hours, [15.81]
disposal, secured property etc, [15.137]
new, appointment of, [15.146]
outlays, determination, [15.139]
power to deal with charged property etc, [1.13], [1.576]
progress reports, [15.138]
remuneration
appeal against fixing, [15.140]

SCOTLAND – *cont.*
administrator – *cont.*
remuneration – *cont.*
determination, [15.139]
replacement
application, [15.158]
death, administrator, [15.157]
joint/concurrent appointments, [15.160]
removal, application to court, [15.161]
resignation
grounds, [15.154]
intention, notice, [15.155]
notice of, [15.156]
bank administration
applications, [16.123]
bank administrator
proposals, report of, [16.121]
provisional, [16.120]
petition for, [16.118]
hearing, [16.119]
time and date of lodging, [16.122]
bank insolvency
bank liquidator
provisional, [16.111]
removal of, [16.113]
remuneration, applications in relations to, [16.114]
share of assets for unsecured creditors, applications, [16.115]
petition for, [16.109]
intimation, service and advertisement of, [16.110]
special manager, application to appoint, [16.116]
statement of affairs, applications and appeals, [16.112]
statutory provisions, applications under, [16.117]
bankrupt, disqualification from membership of Scottish Parliament, [1.542]–[1.544], [2.15]
bankruptcy
Accountant in Bankruptcy
appointment, [5.1], [5.194]
delegation, functions to authorised staff, [5.3], [5.194]
decisions, review of, grounds of appeal, [5.157]
discharge, [5.141], [5.194]
fees, [5.164]
functions, civil proceedings relating to, [5.5]
interim trustee
as, [5.6]
intromissions, period, permanent trustee confirmed in office, [5.61], [5.194]
notices received, to whom copied, [5.167]
procedure after end of accounting period, [5.115]
review by, [16.315]–[16.318]
Secretary of State, directions re functions, powers
exercise after consultation, Lord President, Court of Session, [5.4], [5.194]
supervisory functions, [5.2], [5.194]

SCOTLAND – *cont.*
bankruptcy – *cont.*
Accountant in Bankruptcy – *cont.*
trustee, application for directions, [5.8]
administration of estate by permanent trustee
account of state of affairs, requirement of debtor to give, [5.103]
contractual powers, [5.101]
debtor's family home
civil partner, protection, rights, against arrangements intended to defeat, [5.100]
financial education, course of, undertaken by debtor [5.104]
permanent trustee administering estate, powers, [5.98]
sequestrated estate, ceasing to form part of, [5.97]
spouse, protection, rights, against arrangements intended to defeat, [5.99]
generally, [5.95]–[5.102]
management, [5.94], [5.96]
money received by, [5.102]
realisation, [5.94], [5.96]
taking possession by permanent trustee, [5.95]
administration order, property
vesting, estate in permanent trustee, [5.70], [5.72]
applications and decisions, [16.295]–[16.321]
bankruptcy restrictions orders, [16.309]–[16.311]
evidence, [16.302]
forms, [16.321]
generally, [16.297]–[16.300]
inquiries, [16.301]
reference to court, [16.314]
review, Accountant in Bankruptcy by, [16.315]–[16.318]
trustees, relation to, [16.304]–[16.308]
arbitration, reference to
permanent trustee, conditions, [5.159]
arrestments, [5.191]
associate, meaning, [5.174], [17.117]
award of sequestration
certificate, [16.264]
criteria, [5.194]
recall, [5.39]–[5.45]
application, [5.39], [5.40]
grant of, [5.42]
outlays, remuneration, determination of, [5.41]
petition for, [5.194]
review/appeal, [5.45]
refusal, procedure after, [5.194]
time, [5.194]
Bankruptcy (Scotland) Act 1985, text, [5.1]–[5.191]
claims
adjudication, [5.110]
submission to permanent trustee, [5.109]

SCOTLAND – *cont.*
bankruptcy – *cont.*
commissioners
election
functions, [5.9]
sequestrations to which applicable, [5.9]
statutory/subsequent meeting, at, [5.67], [5.194]
meetings of, generally, procedure, [5.190]
meetings with creditors (other than statutory), [5.160], [5.188]
removal, [5.67], [5.194]
resignation, [5.67], [5.194]
commencement provisions, [16.55]–[16.59]
compromise, power of permanent trustee, to make, [5.159]
confiscation order discharged or quashed, property vesting in permanent trustee, [1.341], [5.70], [5.74]
co-obligants, liabilities and rights, [5.149]
creditor of insolvent person
claims
adjudication, [5.110]
amount, determination, [5.180]
submission to permanent trustee, [5.109]
dividend, entitlement to draw, [5.111]
interests, safeguard
gratuitous alienations, [5.85]
excessive pension contributions, recovery of, [5.88]–[5.93]
recalling, order, payment, capital sum on divorce, [5.86]
recovery orders, [5.92], [5.93]
unfair preferences, [5.87]
meetings with commissioners (other than statutory), [5.160], [5.188]
voluntary trust deeds
Accountant in Bankruptcy, order by, [5.148]
affidavit, [5.147]
application to convert into sequestration, [5.146]
court, powers, [5.187], [5.194]
effective legislation, [5.145]
voting entitlement, [5.111]
Crown as creditor, [5.177]
debtor
co-operation, permanent trustee, [5.158]
dealings with, after sequestration
aliment for debtor, [5.75]
diligence re obligations (child support etc), [5.75]
obligations, debtor, [5.75]
pension schemes etc, [5.75]
discharge, [5.116]–[5.123]
Accountant in Bankruptcy not trustee, [5.116]
assets discovered after, [5.142]–[5.144]
composition, on, [5.127], [5.186], [5.194]
conditions, [5.125]
debtor not traced, [5.120]–[5.122]
deferral, [5.120]
effect, [5.124]
review and appeal, [5.123]

SCOTLAND – *cont.*
bankruptcy – *cont.*
debtor – *cont.*
discharge, – *cont.*
sanctions, [5.126]
trustee, Accountant in Bankruptcy as, [5.117]
distribution of estate, [5.112]–[5.114]. *See also* distribution of debtor's estate, *below*
examination
conduct of, [5.108]
debtor's spouse etc, information to permanent trustee, [5.105]
permanent trustee, powers, [5.105]
private, [5.105], [5.107]
public, [5.106], [5.107]
family home
civil partner, protection, rights, against arrangements intended to defeat, [5.100]
permanent trustee administering estate, powers, [5.98]
spouse, protection, rights, against arrangements intended to defeat, [5.99]
offences, [5.161]
relevant date, meaning as to debtor or deceased debtor, [5.184]
defects, procedural, cure, [5.154], [5.155], [5.156]
detention, property released from, [5.71]
diligence, effect of sequestration on, [1.189], [5.75], [5.94]
disqualification provisions, orders under, [5.168]
distribution of debtor's estate
accounting period
in respect of, [5.113], [5.194]
procedure after end of, [5.114], [5.115], [5.192], [5.194]
priority, [5.112]
EC Regulation, proceedings under
conversion, earlier proceedings, [5.145]
estate, definition, [5.69]
Member State liquidator
deemed creditor, [5.150]
duties, [5.150], [5.151]
Edinburgh Gazette, copy, to whom supplied, [5.166]
extortionate credit transaction, [5.152]
fees, [5.193], [16.269]–[16.283]
FSMA 2000, demands under
application to set aside, [16.145]
form of, [16.143]
service, [16.144]
setting aside, [16.146]
interim trustee
Accountant in Bankruptcy as
no appointment by court/nomination etc in petition, [5.6]
termination of functions, [5.34]
appointment by court
before sequestration awarded, conditions, [5.6]

SCOTLAND – *cont.*
bankruptcy – *cont.*
interim trustee – *cont.*
appointment by court – *cont.*
new, after removal/resignation, [5.32], [5.194]
nomination etc in petition, [5.6]
notification requirements, [5.6]
death, [5.62]
discharge, [5.62], [5.194]
functions, [5.6], [5.194]
insolvency practitioner, qualification as, [5.6]
outlays, [5.163]
removal by court, [5.32], [5.194]
residence within jurisdiction, Court of Session, [5.6]
resignation, [5.32], [5.194]
termination of functions, [5.33], [5.60], [5.194]
undertaking, [5.6]
limited partnerships. *See* limited partnerships, *below*
low income, low asset debtors, [16.261]
period between award and statutory meeting, creditors
assets/liabilities etc
statement, [5.47], [5.194]
trustees, duty on receipt, list, [5.48], [5.194]
interim preservation, estate, [5.46], [5.194]
moratorium on diligence, [5.10]–[5.13]
permanent trustee
administration, estate by, [5.95]–[5.102]
See also administration, estate, permanent trustee, *above*
advice, commissioners, requirement to regard, [5.7]
appeals and applications, sheriff to, [5.59]
applications Accountant in Bankruptcy to, [5.58]
claims, submission to, [5.109], [5.110]
confirmation of election, [5.57], [5.194]
death, [5.63], [5.181], [5.194]
directions, sheriff, application, [5.7]
discharge, [5.139], [5.194]
dissatisfied debtor, creditor or interested person, application to sheriff, [5.7]
election at statutory meeting, [5.56], [5.194]
functions, [5.7], [5.194]
more than one sequestration, acting in, [5.64]
review, [5.65]
outlays, [5.163]
reasonable grounds for suspicion of commission of offence, report to Accountant in Bankruptcy, [5.7]
removal, [5.66], [5.194]
remuneration, [5.192]
resignation, [5.63], [5.181], [5.194]
summary administration, duties, [5.182], [5.194]
vesting estate in
at date of sequestration, [5.68], [5.69]

SCOTLAND – *cont.*
bankruptcy – *cont.*
permanent trustee – *cont.*
vesting estate in – *cont.*
generally, [5.68]–[5.84]
petitions for sequestration
apparent insolvency, meaning, [5.22]
assessment of debtor's contribution, [5.18]
body corporate, estate, [5.19]
certificate, [5.16]
concurrent proceedings, sequestration/analogous remedy, [5.26], [5.27]
debtor application
incomplete, [5.29]
information, provision of, [5.21]
low income, low asset debtors, [5.15]
provisions applying, [5.24]
refusal, inappropriate application, [5.30]
estates to which inapplicable, [5.19]
information, provision of, [5.20], [5.21]
jurisdiction, Court of Session, [5.25]
limited partnership, estate, [5.19], [5.23]
living or deceased debtor, estate of
copy to Accountant in Bankruptcy, [5.14]
death, debtor after presentation but before award, [5.14]
offences, defence, [5.14]
petitioner, eligible, [5.14], [5.194]
qualified creditor, [5.14]
time, [5.23]
money advice, [5.17]
oath, creditor, [5.28]
partnership, estate, [5.19]
time, presentation, [5.23]
trust in respect of debts incurred by it, estate, [5.19]
unincorporated body, estate, [5.19]
poindings, [5.191]
preferred debts, list, [2.27], [5.183]
realisation order, property subject to, [5.73]
receivership order on property, vesting of estate in permanent trustee, [5.72]
registration, court order, [5.35], [5.194]
restraint order, property subject to, [5.70]
restrictions order
annulment, application for, [5.133]
debtor subject to offences, [5.131]
duration of, [5.133]
grounds for, [5.128]
interim, [5.134]
offer of composition, effect of discharge of approval of, [5.138]
power to make, [5.128]
recall of sequestration, effect of, [5.137]
timing for making order, [5.132]
undertaking, [5.135], [5.136]
sederunt book/other documents, [5.153]
stamp duties etc, exemptions, [5.191]
statutory meeting, creditors
calling
Accountant in Bankruptcy as interim trustee, [5.51], [5.194]
interim trustee, [5.49], [5.194]

SCOTLAND – *cont.*
bankruptcy – *cont.*
statutory meeting, creditors – *cont.*
calling – *cont.*
procedure, [5.50], [5.194]
claims for voting purposes, submission, [5.53]
none called
procedure, [5.51], [5.52], [5.181], [5.194]
procedure, generally, [5.189]
proceedings before election, permanent trustee, [5.54], [5.181], [5.194]
summary administration
application, certificate, [5.55], [5.194]
permanent trustee, duties, [5.182], [5.194]
summary proceedings, [5.162], [5.194]
trustee
directions, application, [5.8]
unclaimed dividends
after discharge, permanent trustee, [1.197], [5.140], [5.194]
utilities, supplies, [5.165]
vesting of estate
permanent trustee, in
administration order made, [5.70], [5.72]
after sequestration, [5.75]
at date, sequestration, [5.68]
confiscation order discharged/quashed, orders where, [1.341], [5.70], [5.74]
dealings with debtor after sequestration, [5.75]
debtor contribution order, [5.76]–[5.83]
EC Regulation, meaning of estate, [5.69]
generally, [5.68]–[5.84]
limitations, [5.84]
receivership order made, [5.70], [5.72]
restraint order, property subject, [5.70]
Bankruptcy and Debt Advice (Scotland) Act 2014, commencement, savings etc, [2.88]–[2.99]
bankruptcy restrictions order
application, [16.309]–[16.311]
building society, dissolution on winding up, [7.467]
building society insolvency procedure, application of rules, [16.125]
building society special administration, application of rules, [16.124]
civil partnership, home rights
bankruptcy, debtor's family home
civil partner, protection, rights, against arrangements intended to defeat, [5.100]
permanent trustee administering estate, powers, [5.98]
company voluntary arrangement
conversion into winding up, EC Regulation
affidavit, [15.66]
application, [15.65]
court, powers, [15.67]
Court of Session rules, [16.73]–[16.78]
creditors' claims, admission for voting purposes, [15.27], [15.28]

SCOTLAND – *cont.*
company voluntary arrangement – *cont.*
EC Regulation
conversion into winding up
affidavit, [15.66]
application, [15.65]
court, powers, [15.67]
member State liquidator, [15.68]
electronic delivery of documents, [15.6]
false representations etc, [15.43]
generally, [15.4]–[15.68]
implementation
accounts of supervisor, [15.39]
completion, [15.42]
costs, [15.41]
fees etc, [15.41]
hand-over, property to supervisor, [15.37]
notice of order, [15.36]
resolutions to follow approval, [15.35]
revocation, [15.38]
suspension, [15.38]
termination, [15.42]
meetings
chairman, [15.22]
company officers, attendance, [15.24]
excluded persons, [15.31]–[15.33]
general provisions, [15.19]
members' entitlement to vote, [15.26]
remote attendance at, [15.21]
report, [15.34]
requisite majority, [15.29], [15.30]
summoning, [15.20]
voting entitlement, creditors, [15.25]
moratorium
false statement etc, officer of company, prosecution, [1.11]
nominees
notice to, applications to court, [15.57]
replacement
by court, [15.55]
notification, appointment, [15.56]
withdrawal, consent to act, [15.54]
obtaining
advertisement of
beginning, [15.49]
end, [15.51]
delivery, documents to intended nominee, [15.45]
documents submitted to court, [15.48]
inspection, court file, [15.52]
nominee's statement, [15.47]
notice of
beginning, [15.49]
end, moratorium, [15.51]
extension, moratorium, [15.50]
preparation, proposal
directors, [15.44]
submission to nominee, [15.44]
statement of affairs, [15.46]
proceedings during, disposal of charged property, [15.53]
proposals, consideration where moratorium obtained

SCOTLAND – *cont.*
company voluntary arrangement – *cont.*
moratorium – *cont.*
proposals, consideration where moratorium obtained – *cont.*
agreement
proceedings to obtain, [15.63]
creditors' claims, admission, voting purposes, [15.61]
general provisions, [15.58]
implementation of arrangement, [15.64]
majorities required, [15.62]
meetings, summoning, [15.59]
voting entitlement, creditors, [15.60]
proposal, administrator/liquidator
where a nominee
meetings, summoning, [15.17]
preparation, [15.16]
where another insolvency practitioner is nominee
notice to nominee, [15.18]
preparation, [15.18]
proposal, directors
contents, [15.9]
disclosure
additional, to assist nominee, [15.12]
meetings, summoning, [15.15]
nominee
intended, notice to, [15.10]
replacement, [15.14]
report, [15.13]
notice to intended nominee, [15.10]
statement of affairs, [15.11], [15.69]
sheriff court insolvency rules, [16.16]–[16.21]
time spent on a case, information, [15.343], [15.344]
websites
expense, account of, [15.8]
use by nominee or supervisor, [15.7]
compensation, Financial Service and Markets Act 2000
trust deeds for creditors, Authority's power to participate in proceedings, [17.188]
confiscation order
bankruptcy, discharge, effect, [1.341], [5.70], [5.74]
co-operation, UK courts exercise, insolvency jurisdiction, [1.540]
Court of Session rules
administration, [16.79]–[16.86]
answers to petition etc, [16.62]
companies
application and interpretation, [16.70]
judge, proceedings before, [16.71]
lodging of documents, [16.72]
voluntary arrangements, [16.73]–[16.78]
winding up, [16.91]–[16.106]
cross-border insolvency, transfer of proceedings, [16.63]–[16.69]
directors, disqualification, [16.107], [16.108]
receivers, [16.87]–[16.90]
service of documents
methods and manner of, [16.60]
post, by, [16.61]

SCOTLAND – *cont.*
cross-border insolvency
court process, right to inspect, [3.325]
foreign representative
misfeasance, [3.324]
replacement, confirmation, status, [3.324]
notices etc, [3.326]
orders
copies, [3.325]
notification/advertisement, [3.325]
registration, [3.325]
procedural matters, [3.306], [3.323]–[3.326]
receivership provisions, [1.58]
review, court orders, [3.325]
transfer, proceedings
detriment to creditors, to avoid, [3.325]
diligence, effect of sequestration, [1.189], [5.75], [5.94]
directors, reports on conduct of, [16.285]–[16.294]
enforcement, [16.130]
forms, [16.129], [16.132]
office-holder, returns by, [16.128]
requirement of, [16.127]
transitional and saving provisions, [16.131]
disqualification of directors
application for order, [16.10]
compensation orders, fees, [16.441]–[16.445]
Court of Session rules, [16.107], [16.108]
information, order for, [16.11]
summary proceedings, [4.39]
EC Regulation, bankruptcy proceedings
conversion, earlier proceedings, [5.145]
estate, definition, [5.69]
Member State liquidator
appointment re debtor, notices to interim/ permanent trustee, [5.150], [5.151]
deemed creditor, [5.150]
Edinburgh Gazette
Accountant in Bankruptcy, copy to, [5.166]
administrator, appointment, [15.88]
company voluntary arrangement, moratorium, [15.49], [15.51]
petition department, Court of Session, copy to, [5.166]
energy administration
administrator
appointment by court, [16.181]–[16.184]
caution, [16.252]
proposals, [16.191]
replacement of, [16.227]–[16.235]
revision of proposals, [16.203]
sederunt book, [16.257]
time spent on case, information as to, [16.259]
application of rules, [16.180]
claims, [16.205]–[16.214]
confidentiality of documents, [16.251]
construction and interpretation, [16.179]
corporation, representation of, [16.244]
defects in procedure, curing, [16.256]
distributions, [16.215]–[16.220]
documents, sending by post, [16.246]
ending, [16.221]–[16.226]

SCOTLAND – *cont.*
energy administration – *cont.*
evidence of proceedings at meetings, [16.249]
fees, expenses, etc, [16.255]
forms, [16.254], [16.260]
list of creditors, right to, [16.250]
meetings, [16.192]–[16.202]
notices, [16.245]–[16.247]
order, dismissal of application, [16.184]
prescribed part, [16.236], [16.237]
process, [16.185]–[16.191]
protected energy company, disposal of books etc, [16.258]
proxies, [16.238]–[16.243]
punishment of offences, [16.253]
reports, [16.202]–[16.204]
validity of proceedings, [16.248]
financial collateral arrangements, applicable law, [3.286], [3.295]
home rights
bankruptcy, debtor's family home
civil partner, protection, rights, against arrangements intended to defeat, [5.100]
permanent trustee administering estate, powers, [5.98]
spouse, protection, rights, against arrangements intended to defeat, [5.99]
inhibitions and arrestment, execution before 22 April 2009, [2.62]
insolvency
EU Regulation, [15.313]–[15.321]
functions, Minister of the Crown/Scottish Ministers of, [16.446]–[16.451]
devolved, [16.450]
reserved, [16.447]
limited liability partnerships, provisions applied to, [16.136], [16.139], [16.140]
sheriff court rules. *See* sheriff court insolvency rules, *below*
Insolvency Act 1986, extent applicable, [1.564]
insolvency practitioner
caution, [15.333]
criminal investigation
Proceeds of Crime Act 2002, external orders/requests
application of sums by enforcement administrator, [12.55]
sums received by clerk of court, [12.56]
person acting without qualification as, offence, [1.476]
Insolvency (Scotland) Rules 1986, [15.1]–[15.349]
rules, [1.522], [15.1]
insurers, winding up
application of rules, [16.149]
Financial Services Compensation Scheme, appearance by manager, [16.150]
general business policies, [16.172]
valuation, [16.152]
interpretation, [16.148]
long term and other business, separate financial records for, [16.151]
long term business
accounts and audit, [16.163]

SCOTLAND – *cont.*
insurers, winding up – *cont.*
long term business – *cont.*
actuarial advice, [16.158]
additional powers, [16.162]
attribution of assets to, [16.156]
attribution of liabilities to, [16.155]
caution, [16.164]
cessation, notice of order, [16.177]
claims, [16.165]
custody of assets, [16.160]
dividends to creditors, [16.168]
excess of assets, [16.157], [16.159]
liquidation expenses, apportionment of, [16.170]
meetings of creditors, [16.169]
premium, failure to pay, [16.166]
records, maintenance of, [16.161]
stop order, notice of, [16.171]
valuation of policy, notice of, [16.167]
long term policies, valuation of
no stop order, where, [16.153]
stop order made, where, [16.154]
rules for valuing policies, [16.173]–[7.1548]
investment bank special administration, procedure, [16.265]
limited liability partnerships
Companies Act, application of, [16.135], [16.138]
insolvency, applicable legislation, [10.42]
interpretation, [16.134]
subordinate legislation, application of, [16.137]
winding up and insolvency, provisions applied, [16.136], [16.139], [16.140]
Lloyd's Market Reorganisation Order
reorganisation controller, powers
trust deeds, creditors in Scotland, [7.1586]
pensions
debtor, bankruptcy
excessive amount, income/protected rights recovery for creditor, [5.88]–[5.90]
sheriff, powers to fix amount to be paid to trustee, [5.75]
pension contributions, excessive, debtor
excess, recovery, [5.88]–[5.90]
recovery orders, [5.92], [5.93]
pension-sharing cases, excessive contributions, debtor
recovery orders, [5.92], [5.93]
transferor's rights, [5.91]
occupational/personal schemes
exclusion orders, [11.37]
information, request
time, compliance, [11.42]
prescribed pension arrangements
calculation, rights under, [11.39]
meaning, [11.34]
verification, rights under, [11.39]
qualifying agreements, [11.38]
restoration order
time, compliance, [11.40]
transferee's rights under pension arrangement derived from pension-sharing transaction

SCOTLAND – *cont.*
pensions – *cont.*
occupational/personal schemes – *cont.*
transferee's rights under pension arrangement derived from pension-sharing transaction – *cont.*
calculation/verification, [11.41]
unapproved pension arrangement
exclusion, rights under, [11.36]
meaning, [11.35]
rights, effect, [17.171]
protected trust deeds
forms, [16.438]–[16.440]
generally, [16.266]
railway companies, protected, financial assistance by Scottish Ministers, [7.2443]
receiver
agent of company, as, [1.43]
appointment
acceptance, [15.166]
cessation, [1.48]
circumstances justifying, [1.38]
court, by, [1.40]
disqualification from, [1.37]
holder of charge, by, [1.39]
information to be given by receiver on, [1.51]
notification, [1.50]
power, [1.37]
contracts, liability, [1.43]
Court of Session rules, [16.87]–[16.90]
creditors' committee
attendance before, [1.54]
constitution, [15.170]
functions, [15.171]
information from receiver, [15.173]
liquidation committee provisions
application to, [15.172]
members' dealings with company, [15.174]
prescribed part, company property
receiver, duty, [15.175]
death of receiver, [15.180]
definitions, [1.56]
directions, court, to
eligible applicants, [1.49]
documents etc, electronic delivery, [15.177]–[15.179]
employment contracts, [1.43]
floating charge, property subject
disposal, interest, [1.47]
generally, [1.36]–[1.57]
payments, abstract of, [15.176]
powers, [1.41], [1.577]
precedence among, [1.42]
priority
debts, [1.45]
distribution, moneys, [1.46]
receipts, abstract of, [15.176]
remuneration, [1.44]
report to registrar, time limits, [1.53]
returns, enforcement of duty to make, [1.55]
sheriff court insolvency rules, [16.28]–[16.30]

SCOTLAND – *cont.*
receiver – *cont.*
statement of company's affairs
limited disclosure, [15.168]
notice, [15.167]
submissions by persons required, [1.52]
transitional provisions/savings, [1.596]
vacation of office by receiver, [15.181]
VAT bad debt relief
certificate of insolvency
issue, [15.182]
preservation with company's records, [15.184]
notice to creditors, [15.183]
receivership order
vesting, estate in permanent trustee, [5.70], [5.72]
Register of Inhibitions, references to, [2.61]
sequestrated estate, person
offence in England and Wales before discharge, [1.439]
sequestration
Accountant in Bankruptcy
appointment, [5.397]
conduct of proceedings, [5.402]
directions, [5.401]
fees, [5.403]
functions, [5.398]–[5.400]
administration, [16.421]–[16.428]
applications, [5.195]–[5.215]
certificate for, [5.203], [16.408]–[16.410]
concurrent applications, [5.213], [5.214]
creditor's oath, [5.215]
death or withdrawal, [5.204]
debt advice, [5.197], [16.411]
deceased debtor, estate of, [5.199]
jurisdiction, [5.211]
living debtor, estate of, [5.196]
money advice, [5.198]
arbitration and compromise, [5.414]
award of, [5.218]–[5.225]
incomplete applications, [5.216], [5.217]
Proceeds of Crime Act 2002, [17.239]–[17.241]
bankruptcy restrictions order, [5.352]–[5.356]
interim, [5.357]
commissioners, [5.273], [5.274]
meetings, [5.445]
creditors
claims,
adjudication, [5.323], [5.324]
amount, [5.438]
submission, [5.319]–[5.322]
entitlement to vote, [5.325]
meetings, [5.443], [5.444]
safeguarding, [5.295]–[5.304]
voluntary deeds for, [5.359]–[5.392], [5.441]
debtor
contribution, [5.286]–[5.294], [16.415]–[16.420]
co-operation, [5.413]
discharge, [5.334]–[5.344]
examination, [5.315]–[5.318]

SCOTLAND – *cont.*
sequestration – *cont.*
debtor – *cont.*
general offences, [5.416]
preferred debts, [5.439], [5.440]
distribution of funds, [5.326]–[5.328]
initial stages, [5.236]–[5.239]
main proceedings
member State, in, [5.210]
Scotland, in, [5.209]
moratorium on diligence, [5.393]–[5.396], [16.429]
procedure, rules for, [16.322]–[16.400]
appeals, [16.360]–[16.363]
cross-border insolvency, [16.358], [16.359]
evidence, use of live link, [16.392]
expenses in proceedings, [16.378]–[16.381]
forms, [16.398], [16.399]
intimation, [16.336]–[16.342]
lodging, [16.343]
motions, [16.364]–[16.373]
petitions, [16.344]–[16.351]
reporting restrictions, [16.393]–[16.397]
representation and support, [16.330]–[16.335]
solicitors, withdrawal, [16.374]–[16.377]
vulnerable witnesses, [16.382]–[16.390]
recall of, [5.226]–[5.235], [5.358]
regulations for, [16.401]–[16.437]
statutory meeting, [5.240]–[5.245]
trustee,
administration of estate by, [5.305]–[5.314]
debtors' home, [5.309], [5.310]
civil partner/spouse, rights of, [5.311], [5.312]
appointment, [5.248], [5.271], [5.272]
assets discovered after discharge of, [5.349]–[5.351]
direction, [5.249]
discharge, [5.345], [5.346]
functions, [5.247]
interim, [5.250]–[5.256]
removal, [5.267]–[5.270]
remuneration, [5.330], [5.331]
replacement, [5.257]–[5.265]
resignation or death, [5.266]
vote, [5.246]
vesting, [5.275]–[5.285]
voluntary trust deed, creditors for, [5.359]
protected status, [5.360]
conditions, [5.361]–[5.367]
effect, [5.369]–[5.376]
registration, [5.368]
Sheriff Appeal Court insolvency rules
appeals, [16.54]
sheriff court insolvency rules
administration, [16.22]–[16.27]
affidavits, [16.49]
appeals, [16.53]
application of, [16.44], [16.45]
company voluntary arrangements, [16.16]–[16.21]
cross-border insolvency, transfer of proceedings, [16.47]

SCOTLAND – *cont.*
sheriff court insolvency rules – *cont.*
expenses, [16.15]
failure to comply with, [16.51]
interpretation, [16.13]
notes and appeals, intimation, service and advertisement of, [16.48]
notices, reports and documents sent to court, [16.50]
receivers, [16.28]–[16.30]
representation, [16.14]
statement of affairs, limited disclosure, [16.46]
vulnerable witnesses, [16.52]
winding up, registered companies, [16.31]–[16.43]
interpretation, [15.43]
social landlord, registered
administrative receiver, permitted appointment, [1.66]
transitional provisions, [2.32]–[2.43]
utilities, supplies
bankruptcy, sequestration order, [5.165]
winding up
insurance company, of. *See* insurance company, winding up, *above*
insurers, of. *See* insurers, winding up, *above*
limited liability partnerships, provisions applied to, [16.136], [16.139], [16.140]
books/papers, company, disposal, [15.342]
confidentiality, documents, [15.332]
court, by
appeal from orders, [1.163]
attendance, officer of company
company meetings, [1.158], [15.199]
claims in liquidation
adjudication, [15.203]
amount, [15.206]
co-obligants, rights and liabilities, [15.205]
dividend, right to draw, [15.204]
evidence, [15.202]
false claims, [15.201]
foreign currency, in, [15.209]
secured debts, [15.208]
submission, [15.200]
voting entitlement, [15.204]
contributories
calls on, court power to order, [1.162]
Court of Session
jurisdiction, [1.118]
power to remit to Lord Ordinary, [1.119]
dissolution after, [15.279]
distribution, company's assets
accounting periods, [15.265]
dividends, [15.266], [15.267]
priority
in distribution, [15.263]
of expenses, liquidation, [15.264]
EC Regulation
creditor, meaning, [15.285]
creditor's voluntary winding up
confirmation by court, [15.286]
member State liquidator
notice to, [15.285], [15.287]

SCOTLAND – *cont.*
winding up – *cont.*
court, by – *cont.*
generally, [15.185]–[15.287]
information to
contributories, [15.195]
creditors, [15.195]
registrar of companies, [15.196]
inspection, books by creditors etc, [1.156]
limitation of actions, [15.278]
liquidation committee
chairman, [15.242]
establishment
contributories, by, [15.239]
formalities, [15.238]
generally, [1.143], [15.236]–[15.256]
liquidator
obligations to committee, [15.240]
reports, [15.252]
meetings, [15.241]
members
composition when creditors paid in full, [15.255]
contributory member, vacancy, [15.249]
creditor member, vacancy, [15.248]
dealings with company by, [15.254]
expenses, [15.253]
formal defect, [15.256]
removal, [15.247]
representation, [15.244]
resignation, [15.245]
termination, membership, [15.246]
vacancy, [15.248], [15.249]
voting rights, [15.250]
membership, composition, [15.237]
quorum, [15.243]
resolutions
by post, [15.251]
record, [15.250]
winding up following immediately on administration
creditors' committee, continuation, [15.258]
generally, [15.257]–[15.262]
liquidator, obligations to committee, [15.261]
liquidator's certificate, [15.260]
membership, [15.259]
liquidator
appointment
authentication, [15.212]
court, [1.139], [15.210]
creditors/contributories, [15.211]
death, [15.232]
distribution, company's assets. *See* distribution, company's assets, *above*
duties, [1.168], [1.170]
former, hand-over of assets to succeeding liquidator, [15.213]
insolvency practitioner, loss of qualification as, [15.233]

SCOTLAND – *cont.*
winding up – *cont.*
court, by – *cont.*
liquidator – *cont.*
liquidation committee
certificate, [15.260]
obligations to, [15.240], [15.261]
reports to, [15.252]
meeting summoned by, [15.198]
outlays, amount, determination, [15.228]
powers, [1.168], [1.170]
provisional. *See* provisional liquidator, *below*
realisation, company's assets, [15.214], [15.215]
release on
completion, winding up, [15.227]
removal, [1.175], [15.218]
removal
advertisement of, [15.223]
block transfer of cases, [15.220]–[15.222]
court, by, [15.219]
meeting summoned for, [15.216]
procedure on, [15.217]
release on, [15.218]
remuneration
determination, [15.228]
excessive, claim by creditors, [15.231]
recourse to court, [15.230]
recourse to creditors' meeting, [15.230]
resignation
action following acceptance, [15.225]
creditors' meeting, requirement, liquidator to call, [15.224]
leave to resign, court, grant, [15.226]
setting aside certain transactions of court, power, [15.234]
solicitation, rule against, [15.235]
taking possession, company's assets, [15.214]
meetings
company's personnel, attendance, [15.199]
creditors/contributories, first meetings, [15.197]
liquidator, summoned by, [15.198]
offences, punishment, [15.334], [15.348]
prohibited name, company with
application for leave, [15.281]
excepted cases, [15.282]–[15.284]
prosecution, delinquent officer/member, [1.222], [1.223]
provisional liquidator
appointment
application, eligible persons, [15.185]
termination, [15.190]
caution
failure to find/maintain, [15.188]
provision, cost, [15.187]
notice of appointment
to whom required, [15.186]
remuneration, [15.189]

SCOTLAND – *cont.*
winding up – *cont.*
court, by – *cont.*
public examination, officers, [1.134], [15.273], [15.274]
sheriff court, jurisdiction, [1.118]
sist, proceedings, court, powers, [1.149]
special manager
accounting, [15.271]
appointment
application by liquidator etc, [15.268]
caution before effective, [15.269]
failure to find/maintain caution, [15.270]
termination, [15.272]
remuneration, [15.268]
statement of affairs
expenses, [15.194]
form, [15.192]
limited disclosure, [15.193]
notice requiring, [15.191]
vacation, orders pronounced in
effective until matter disposed of, Inner House, [1.580]
final, [1.579]
Court of Session rules, [16.91]–[16.106]
creditor
interpretation, [15.312]
list, right to, [15.331]
defects, procedural, power of court to cure, [15.340]
Deposit Protection Board, voting rights, [15.347]
diligence, effect, [1.189]
disclaimer, onerous property, liquidator, [1.182]
dissolution after, early, [1.208]
electronic transmission of information, [15.275]–[15.277], [15.336], [15.337]
exceptions, [15.338]
evidence
commission for receiving, power of court to refer, [1.201]
examination of persons, power of court to order, [1.202]
meetings, proceedings at, [15.330]
fees etc, [15.339]
floating charge prior to, conditions for avoidance, [1.250], [2.10], [2.26], [3.290]
forms, [15.335], [15.349]
gratuitous alienations, [1.247], [2.10], [2.26]
leave to proceed, costs of unopposed application, [1.203]
meetings
adjournment, [15.297]
chairman, [15.294]
evidence of proceedings, [15.330]
general provisions, [15.290]–[15.304]
notice of, [15.292], [15.293]
proxy-holder, chairman as, [15.300]
quorum, [15.296]
report, [15.302]
requisitioned, [15.295]
resolutions, [15.301]
summoning, [15.291]

SCOTLAND – *cont.*
winding up – *cont.*
meetings – *cont.*
voting entitlement
contributories, [15.299]
creditors, [15.298]
members, [15.299]
monetary limits to determine jurisdiction, powers of Secretary of State, [1.528], [8.1]
notices
advertised other than in Gazette, [15.324], [15.325]
certificate of giving, [15.328]
contents of, [15.323]
Edinburgh Gazette, published in, [15.323]
generally, [15.322]
unobtainable information, omission of, [15.326]
office copy, meaning, [1.267]
prescribed part, application/order re, [15.303], [15.304]
Proceeds of Crime Act 2002 provisions, [17.242], [17.243]
proxy
definition, [15.305]
form, [15.306]
inspection of proxies lodged with insolvency practitioner, [15.309]
proxy-holder with financial interest, [15.310]
retention, [15.308]
use at meeting, [15.307]
representation of corporation, [15.311]
sederunt book, [15.341]
sending by post, [15.327]
sheriff court insolvency rules, [16.31]–[16.43]
stamp duty, exempt documents, company registered in Scotland, [1.194]
unclaimed dividends
company wound up, about to be dissolved, [1.197]
unfair preferences, [1.248], [2.10], [2.26], [17.243]
validity, proceedings, [15.329]
voluntary, creditors/members
court, power to control proceedings, [1.111]
liquidator, release, [1.174]
provisions applicable, [15.224], [15.288], [15.289], [15.345]
winding up, unregistered company
inability to pay debts, when deemed, [1.228]
jurisdiction, [1.225]
sist, proceedings, [1.231]

SECONDARY INSOLVENCY PROCEEDINGS
EC Regulation
applicable law, [3.64]
assets remaining after, [3.71]
costs/expenses
advance payment, [3.66]
creditors' rights, exercise, [3.68]
earlier proceedings, conversion, [3.73]
ending, [3.70]
information, co-operation/communication, [3.67]

SECONDARY INSOLVENCY PROCEEDINGS – *cont.*
EC Regulation – *cont.*
opening, [3.63]
preservation measures, [3.74]
right to request opening, [3.65]
stay, liquidation, [3.69]
subsequent opening, main proceedings, [3.72]
SECRETARY OF STATE
administration, provision of information to, [8.25]
administrative receiver, powers to appoint, [1.68]
bankruptcy
restriction order/undertaking, [1.587]
rights etc, transfer to, employer's insolvency, [1.399]
disqualification, director
undertaking, power to accept, [4.2]
energy administration order, powers, [7.1026]
fees, powers re, [1.527]
individual insolvency
annual report re operation, legislation, [1.459]
individual voluntary arrangement
delinquent debtor, powers re, [1.305]
insolvency practitioners, regulation, [1.532], [12.30]
liquidator
information to Secretary of State, [8.41]
monetary limits, powers re
bankruptcy, [1.531], [8.1]
company moratorium, [1.530]
official receiver, powers re, [1.510]
pensions, payment of unpaid contributions for insolvent employer, [17.101]–[17.106]
railway administration order
documents, [7.2552]
powers, [7.2548]
trustee in bankruptcy
appointment, [1.359]
removal, [1.361]
winding up by court
liquidator
appointment, [1.138]
removal, [1.173], [1.175]
preferential charge, goods distrained
rights etc, transfer to, employer's insolvency, [1.177]
prosecution, delinquent officer/member, [1.222], [1.223]
SECURITY
liquidator, [6.210], [6.251]
meaning, in context of bankruptcy, [1.469]
secured creditor generally. *See* CREDITOR: secured
special manager, [6.223], [6.224]
SEQUESTRATION
winding up by court, avoidance after commencement, [1.129]
SERVICE OF PROCESS
cross-border insolvency application
manner, [3.316], [3.319]
notices to registrar etc
general, [3.322]
service out of jurisdiction, [3.322]
proof, [3.316], [3.319]
SERVICE OF PROCESS – *cont.*
energy administration order, [7.881], [7.883], [7.884], [7.999], [7.1036]
incapacity, appointment, court, person to act notices following, [7.2523]
Lloyd's market, notices/documents, [7.1608]
outside jurisdiction, [7.2558]
post, by, [7.2556], [7.1036]
railway administration order, [7.2460], [7.2462], [7.2463], [7.2556]–[7.2558]
SET-OFF
administration, quantification of claims, [6.748]
creditors, rights
credit institution, reorganisation/winding up
EC Directive, [3.198]
Regulation, [3.240]
Insolvency, EC Regulation, [3.42]
insurance undertaking, reorganisation/winding up
EC Directive, [3.110]
Regulation, [3.167]
liquidation, quantification of claims, [6.749]
Lloyd's market reorganisation, syndicate set-off, [7.1591]
SETTLEMENT FINALITY. *SEE* FINANCIAL MARKETS
SHARE TRANSFERS
avoidance after voluntary winding up resolution, [1.84]
community interest company, [17.261]
SHAREHOLDERS
winding up of registered company, contributories and past shareholders, [1.72]
SHARES
transfer. *See* SHARE TRANSFERS
voluntary winding up, creditors/members
consideration for sale of company's property, acceptance, [1.108]
dissent from arrangement, [1.109]
SHIP
credit institution, reorganisation/winding up, effect of EC Directive, [3.196]
debtor, rights subject to registration in, EC Regulation, [3.47]
insurance undertakings, reorganisation/winding up, effect of EC Directive, [3.107]
SOCIAL CARE
service provider, insolvency of, [17.463]
SOCIAL HOUSING
registered provider, insolvency of
assistance by regulator, [17.369]
company
arrangements and reconstructions, [17.372]
registered society, conversion to, [17.373]
winding up, [17.375]
court, applications to, [17.369]
creditor, application to court by, [17.370]
insolvency rules, non-application to local authorities, [17.354]
manager
appointment, [17.366]
interim, [17.362]
powers, [17.367]
registered society, of, [17.368]

SOCIAL HOUSING – *cont.*
registered provider, insolvency of – *cont.*
manager – *cont.*
remuneration and expenses, [17.366]
moratorium
consent to disposal of land, [17.359]
disposal of land, on, [17.356]
disposals without consent, void, [17.361]
duration, [17.357]
effect of, [17.359]
exempted disposals, [17.360]
further, [17.358]
interim manager, appointment of, [17.362]
proposals. *See* proposals, *below*
steps, [17.355]
preliminary steps, notice of, [17.355]
proposals
effect of, [17.365]
procedure for, [17.364]
regulator, by, [17.363]
registered society
company, conversion of, [17.373]
dissolution, [17.377]
restructuring, [17.375]
winding up, [17.376]
restructuring and dissolution rules, non-application to local authorities, [17.371]
winding up
company, [17.374]
industrial and provident society, [17.376]
transfer of property, [17.378]–[17.380]
SOCIAL SECURITY
contributions, preferential debts, [1.473], [1.591]
SOLICITOR
energy administrator, of, right of attendance, [7.1005]
special railway administrator, of, right of attendance, [7.2527]
STAMP DUTY
individual insolvency, exempt documents, [1.458]
winding up, registered company, exempt documents, [1.194]
STUDENT LOANS
bankrupt estate, exclusion from, [11.48]
SUPERVISOR
individual voluntary arrangement
debtor, delinquent after approval
report to Secretary of State by, [1.304], [1.305], [2.7]
SYSTEM-CHARGE. *SEE* FINANCIAL MARKETS

T

TEACHERS
pension schemes, [11.50]
redundancy/premature retirement
compensation, [11.54]
TENANCY
bankrupt's estate
tenancies not part, list, [1.344]
trustee in bankruptcy
disclaimer, onerous property, powers, [1.386], [17.133]
vesting, notice in writing, [1.377], [1.378]
covenants
part only, demised premises
disclaimer limited to, [17.133]
forfeiture limited to, [17.133]
joint
insolvent estate, deceased person, [1.535]
social rented sector. *See* HOUSING
THIRD PARTIES
purchasers, protection
credit institution, reorganisation/winding up
EC Directive, [3.207]
Regulation, [3.243]
insolvency
EC Regulation, insolvency, [3.50]
insurance undertakings, reorganisation/winding up
EC Directive, [3.113]
Regulation, [3.170]
rights reorganisation or winding up of credit institution, EC Directive, [3.197]
in rem, [3.238]
insolvency, [3.41]
insurance undertakings, reorganisation/winding up
EC Directive, [3.108]
Regulation, [3.165]
Third Parties (Rights Against Insurers) Act 1930, [17.9]–[17.14]
TRADE MARKS. *SEE* PATENTS AND TRADE MARKS
TRANSFER OF UNDERTAKINGS
collective agreements, effect on, [18.144]
contract of employment, effect on, [18.142], [18.143]
contracting out, restriction on, [18.159]
dismissal of employee because of, [18.146]
employee liability information, notification of
failure, remedy for, [18.151]
requirement, [18.150]
employer's liability compulsory insurance, [18.158]
insolvency proceedings, transferor subject to
generally, [18.147]
variation of contract, [18.148]
interpretation, [18.140]
micro-business, duty or to inform and consult, [18.153]
occupational pension schemes, effect on, [18.149]
relevant transfer, [18.141]
representatives, duty to inform and consult, [18.152]–[18.157]
trade union recognition, effect on, [18.145]
transitional provisions and savings, [18.160]

TRANSFER, PROCEEDINGS BETWEEN COURTS. *SEE* COURT PROCEDURE AND PRACTICE

TRANSITIONAL PROVISIONS

Enterprise Act 2002 (Commencement No 4 and Transitional Provisions and Savings) Order 2003, [2.24]–[2.31]
Insolvency Act 1986, [1.596]–[1.600]
Insolvency Act 2000 (Commencement No 1 and Transitional Provisions) Order 2001, [2.1]–[2.3]
Insolvency Act 2000 (Commencement No 3 and Transitional Provisions) Order 2002, [2.4]–[2.8]

TREASURY

compensation scheme under FSMA 2000, treatment of assets of insurer on winding up, [17.210]
Insolvency Services Account, directions, [1.519]
insurance company, winding up, petition, [7.1475]
Investment Account
  application of income in, [1.516]
  directions, [1.515], [1.520]
unclaimed dividends/undistributed balances, [1.518]

TRUSTEE IN BANKRUPTCY

accounts
  audit, [8.53]
  provision, [8.53]
  separate, if carrying on business, [8.51]
adjustments between earlier/later bankruptcy estates, [1.406]
administration order, property subject to excluded from bankrupt's estate when vested in trustee, [1.372]
after-acquired property, claim for bankrupt's estate by, notice in writing, [1.375], [1.378]
annulment of bankruptcy order, effect, [1.361]
appointment
  acceptance, [1.355]
  advertisement, [6.532]
  authentication, [6.531]
  certification, [6.526]
  court, by, [6.529]
  creditors' decision, [6.528]
  first trustee, [1.356]–[1.358], [2.31], [6.525]
  See also meeting to appoint, *below*
  power to make, [1.355]
  replacement, [6.535]
  Secretary of State, by, [1.359], [6.530]
  security, costs, [6.527]
  special cases, [1.360]
bankrupt, duties re, [1.404]
books/papers/record
  acquisition, control, [1.381]
  disposal, [8.55]
confiscation order, property subject to
  discharged or quashed order, vesting by trustee, [1.374]
  exclusion from bankrupt's estate when vested in trustee, [1.372]
control by
  books/papers/records, acquisition, [1.381]

TRUSTEE IN BANKRUPTCY – *cont.*

control by – *cont.*
  court
    directions applications, [1.366]
    general powers on application by bankrupt etc, [1.366]
  creditors' committee, [1.364], [1.365]
  surrender to, persons obliged, [1.382]
creditors' committee
  control
    generally, [1.364]
    restrictions, formation when official receiver is trustee, [1.364]
  invitation to form, [6.534]
  Secretary of State, exercise, functions, [1.365]
criminal bankruptcy, bankruptcy order on
  official receiver, [1.360], [1.361]
death, [6.542]
disclaimed property, vesting
  court order, [1.391], [1.392]
disclaimer, onerous property
  dwelling house, conditions, [1.389]
  leaseholds, [1.388], [1.392]. *See also* LEASEHOLDS
  market contracts, [1.386]
  notice, [1.386], [1.387]
  onerous property, meaning, [1.386]
  operation, [1.182], [1.386], [17.133]
  rentcharge, land subject, [1.390]
  tenancies, [1.386]
distribution, bankrupt's estate
  criminal bankruptcy, in, [1.398]
  dividend, by, [1.395]
  dwelling-house occupied by bankrupt/spouse/former/civil partner/former
    saving for, [1.393]
  final, [1.401]
  final meeting, [1.402]
  in specie, [1.397]
  mutual credit and set-off, [1.394], [17.66]
  priority, debts, [1.399]
  proof, debts, [1.393]
  spouse/civil partner, debts to, [1.400]
  stay in case, second bankruptcy, [1.405]
  unsatisfied creditors, claims, [1.396]
dwelling-house occupied by
    bankrupt/spouse/former/civil partner/former
  charge, application by trustee for, [1.383]
  disclaimer, onerous property, conditions, [1.389]
  low-value home
    court, powers on application by trustee, [1.384]
  saving for, at distribution, [1.403]
excess value, items of vesting in trustee, notice in writing, [1.376], [1.378]
functions, general, [1.368]
generally, [1.355]–[1.406]
hand-over, estate to, [6.533]
income payments
  agreement
    attachment order, effect, [1.380]
    meaning, [1.380]
    variation, [1.380]

TRUSTEE IN BANKRUPTCY – *cont.*
income payments – *cont.*
orders, court
adjustments between earlier/later bankruptcies, [1.406]
application, conditions, [1.379]
contents, [1.379]
duration, [1.379]
insolvency practitioner
required qualification as, [1.355]
liability for misapplication etc of money or property, [1.367]
meeting to appoint
creditors, power to requisition, [1.357]
failure to appoint, [1.358]
summoning, [1.356], [2.31]
official receiver
as, [1.360], [1.361]
criminal bankruptcy, bankruptcy order on, [1.360]
release, [1.362]
powers
ancillary, [1.590]
exercisable with sanction, [1.588]
general, [1.385], [1.589], [2.29]
progress reports, [6.854]–[6.865]
qualification as insolvency practitioner, requirement, [1.355]
receivership order, property subject
exclusion from bankrupt's estate when vested in trustee, [1.372]
records, financial
delivery, [8.52]
duty, [8.49]
information re, provision, [8.50]
inspection, [8.54]
production, [8.54]
retention, [8.52]
release
completion of administration, [1.362], [6.544]–[6.551]
resigning/removed trustee, [6.541]
removal
ceasing to be qualified, [6.543]
court
by, [6.538]
creditors' by, [6.536]
notice, [6.540]
procedure on, [6.537]
reasons, [1.361]
Secretary of State, [1.361], [6.539]
remuneration, [6.867]–[6.890]
resignation, [6.535]
notice, [6.540]
restraint order, property subject
exclusion from bankrupt's estate, [1.370]
second bankruptcy
distribution, stay in case, second bankruptcy, [1.405]
generally, [6.609]–[6.612]
setting aside transactions by
court, powers, [6.549]
solicitation, rule against, [6.550]

TRUSTEE IN BANKRUPTCY – *cont.*
tenancies
disclaimer, onerous property, [1.386], [17.133]
vesting, notice in writing, [1.377], [1.378]
two/more, joint trustees, [1.355]
unclaimed/undistributed assets/dividends, payment, [8.56]
vacancy in office of, [1.363]
vesting, bankrupt's estate in, [1.369]

TRUSTEE SAVINGS BANK
winding up, jurisdiction, [1.225]

TRUSTS
associate, meaning, [1.557]. *See also* ASSOCIATE
property held by bankrupt on trust for other person not part of bankrupt's estate, [1.344]

TRUSTS OF LAND
bankruptcy, effect, rights under, [1.407]

U

UNDERVALUE, TRANSACTION AT
administration/liquidation, adjustment of prior transaction, [1.243], [1.245], [1.246], [2.10], [2.26]
bankruptcy, adjustment of prior transaction, [1.411]–[1.414], [1.537]
debt avoidance provisions, [1.537]–[1.539]
meaning, [1.537]
pensions, powers of Pension Regulator
restoration order
content, [17.288]
effect, [17.288]
non-compliance with contribution order, [17.289], [17.290]
when applicable, [17.286], [17.287]

UNITED NATIONS COMMISSION ON INTERNATIONAL TRADE LAW (UNCITRAL)
cross-border insolvency, model law
application, scope, [3.2]
authorisation, person administering reorganisation/liquidation, [3.6]
competent court/authority, [3.5]
concurrent proceedings, [3.29]–[3.33]
foreign court, co-operation with court in this State, [3.26]–[3.28]
foreign creditors, access to courts in this State, [3.10]–[3.15]
foreign proceedings, recognition
application, [3.16]
decision to recognise, [3.18]
detriment to creditors
actions to avoid, [3.24]
foreign main proceeding
effect, [3.21]
relief that may be granted, [3.22]
information subsequent to application, [3.19]
presumptions, [3.17]
protection, creditors/other interested persons, [3.23]
relief, grant, [3.20]

UNITED NATIONS COMMISSION ON INTERNATIONAL TRADE LAW (UNCITRAL) – *cont.*
cross-border insolvency, model law – *cont.*
foreign representatives
access to courts in this State, [3.10]–[3.15]
co-operation, court in this State, [3.26]–[3.28]
intervention, proceedings in this State, [3.25]
giving effect to, [3.87]
international obligations, conflicts with, [3.4]
public policy exception, [3.7]
text, [3.2]–[3.33], [3.310]

UNLIMITED COMPANY
formerly limited, contributory on winding up of registered company, [1.74]

UNREGISTERED COMPANY
meaning, [1.224]
winding up. *See* WINDING UP, UNREGISTERED COMPANY

URBAN REGENERATION PROJECT
meaning, [1.63]
step-in rights, with, appointment of administrative receiver, [1.63], [1.578]

UTILITIES, SUPPLY
See also ENERGY ACT 2004; ENERGY ADMINISTRATION ORDER
administration order, management, [1.237], [1.238]
individual insolvency
conditions, generally, [1.451], [1.452]
personal guarantee, payment, office-holder may be required, [1.451]
liquidation, company going into, management, [1.237], [1.238]
moratorium, management, [1.237]
Scotland. *See* SCOTLAND

UTILITY PROJECT
meaning, [1.62]
step-in rights, with, appointment of administrative receiver, [1.62], [1.578]

V

VAT
insolvency practitioner, professional fees, [12.28]
Scotland. *See* SCOTLAND: receiver

VOLUNTARY ARRANGEMENT
company. *See* COMPANY VOLUNTARY ARRANGEMENT
individual. *See* INDIVIDUAL VOLUNTARY ARRANGEMENT

W

WALES
bankruptcy of member of National Assembly for Wales, [1.542], [2.15]

WARRANTS
debtor/bankrupt, arrest, [6.708]

WARRANTS – *cont.*
general provisions, [6.707]
inquiry into dealings, insolvent company/bankrupt, [6.709]
Pension Protection Fund Board, [17.319]
search, premises not belonging to bankrupt, [6.710]

WATER INDUSTRY
administrative receiver, appointment
company appointed, Water Industry Act 1991, [1.67], [1.522], [7.2619], [7.2620], [7.2626]
special administration
appeals, [7.2724], [7.2725]
application
adjournment of hearing, [7.2704]
filing, [7.2697]
form and contents of, [7.2696]
hearing in private, [7.2699]
hearings without notice, [7.2698]
registrar, exercise of jurisdiction by, [7.2700]
service of, [7.2697]
application of rules, [7.2630]
company representation at meetings, [7.2693]
costs, [7.2713]–[7.2722]
court records, access to, [7.2707]–[7.2712]
court rules and practice applying, [7.2726]
creditor or members, false claim of status as, [7.2668]
creditors' meetings
adjournment, [7.2673]
application of provisions, [7.2669]
chairman, [7.2672]
claims, admission and rejection of, [7.2665]
entitlement to vote, [7.2674]
hire-purchase etc agreements, voting by creditors under, [7.2679]
holders of negotiable instruments, voting by, [7.2677]
minutes, [7.2682]
non-receipt of notice, [7.2671]
notice of, [7.2670]
quorum, [7.2680]
report to creditors, [7.2683]
resolutions, [7.2681]
retention of title creditors, voting by, [7.2678]
secured creditors, voting by, [7.2676]
venue, [7.2670]
documents, right to copy, [7.2666]
Insolvency Rules, application of, [7.2631]
interpretation, [7.2629]
list of creditors, right to, [7.2667]
members' meetings, [7.2684]
offences, punishment of, [7.2754]
order
discharge, notice of, [7.2644]
effect, [7.2619], [7.2625]
enforcement, [7.2705], [7.2706]
form of, [7.2641]
meaning, [7.2619]
notice and advertisement of, [7.2643]
petitioner's costs, [7.2642]

WATER INDUSTRY – *cont.*
special administration – *cont.*
order – *cont.*
special petitions, [7.2621]
petition
affidavit, content of, [7.2634]
enforcement officer, etc, notice to, [7.2636]
filing, [7.2635]
form of, [7.2633]
proof of service, [7.2638]
service of, [7.2637]
proceedings
affidavits, [7.2731]
brought before petition presented, [7.2639]
examination of persons in, [7.2735]–[7.2743]
formal defects, [7.2730]
forms for use in, [7.2632], [7.2756]
further information and particulars, [7.2734]
notices, [7.2748]–[7.2753]
payment into court, [7.2733]
persons lacking capacity, [7.2723]
powers of court and registrar, [7.2755]
right of audience, [7.2728]
security, giving, [7.2732]
service of documents, [7.2748], [7.2749]
time limits, [7.2747]
title, [7.2727]
proceedings at meetings, evidence of, [7.2685]
proposals to creditors
notice to members, [7.2662]
order discharged before statement of, [7.2661]
revised, statement of, [7.2660]
proxies
application of provisions, [7.2686]
definition, [7.2687]
financial interest, holder with, [7.2692]
forms, use of, [7.2688]
grant of, [7.2687]
inspection, right of, [7.2691]
issue of, [7.2688]
meetings, use at, [7.2689]
retention of, [7.2690]
Secretary of State
orders, directions or certificates, evidence of, [7.2746]
regulation of matters by, [7.2745]
statement of affairs
disclosure, limiting, [7.2656]
expenses of, [7.2658]
extension of time for, [7.2657]
filing, [7.2655]
notice requiring, [7.2653]
obligation to submit, release from, [7.2657]
proposals, annexed to, [7.2659]
responsible person, meaning, [7.2652]
verification, [7.2654]
witness statements
filing and service of, [7.2703]
use of, [7.2701]
special administrator
charged property, disposal of, [7.2663]

WATER INDUSTRY – *cont.*
special administrator – *cont.*
death in office, [7.2650]
documents, confidentiality of, [7.2665]
receipts and payments, abstract of, [7.2664]
remuneration, [7.2645]–[7.2648]
resignation, [7.2649]
security, [7.2744]
solicitor, [7.2729]
vacancy in office, order filling, [7.2651]
undertakers, appointment and regulation, [7.2619]–[7.2626]
voluntary winding up, restrictions, [7.2622]

WATER OR SEWERAGE UNDERTAKERS
administration order, [1.13], [7.2619]–[7.2621], [7.2625]

WEBSITE
documents made available on, [1.260]

WINDING UP
administration order
conversion to winding up
court, powers, [6.171]
effect, dismissal of petition, [1.13]
charities, petition as to, [17.430]
expenses, payment of, [1.178]
monetary limits to determine jurisdiction, powers of Secretary of State, [1.528], [8.1]
pension scheme, [17.447]–[17.449]
registered company
court, by. *See* WINDING UP BY COURT, REGISTERED COMPANY
generally. *See* WINDING UP, REGISTERED COMPANY
preferential debts, [1.176]
Scotland. *See* SCOTLAND
voluntary. *See* WINDING UP, VOLUNTARY, REGISTERED COMPANY
unregistered company. *See* WINDING UP, UNREGISTERED COMPANY

WINDING UP BY COURT, REGISTERED COMPANY
See also LIQUIDATION, COMPANY GOING INTO
adjournment of petition, conditionally or unconditionally, [1.126]
administrator acting while petition suspended, [1.128]
application, [1.122]
avoidance, property dispositions etc after commencement, [1.128]
calls on contributories, [1.152]
circumstances, list, [1.120]
commencement, [1.130]
consequences of order, [1.131]
contributories
absconding, power to arrest, [1.159]
adjustment, rights, [1.155]
bankruptcy, contributory, effect, [1.78]
calls on, [1.152]
company registered under Companies Act, Pt XXII, Ch 8, [1.79]
contributory, meaning, [1.75]
death of member, in case of, [1.77]
debts due from, to company, [1.151]

WINDING UP BY COURT, REGISTERED COMPANY – *cont.*
contributories – *cont.*
directors etc with unlimited liability, [1.71]
falsification, company's books, [1.213]
limited company formerly unlimited, [1.73]
list, settlement after order
distinction, contributories in own right/representative/liable, debts, others, [1.150]
when required, [1.150]
nature of liability, [1.76]
order acts in favour of all, [1.131]
past and present members, liability as, [1.70]
past directors, [1.72]
past shareholders, [1.72]
reports to, [6.323]–[6.326]
unlimited company formerly limited, [1.74]
co-operation with office-holder when order made, duty of, [1.240]
copy, order, to registrar, [1.131]
county court jurisdiction
case stated for High Court, [1.117]
concurrent, High Court, share capital not exceeding £120,000, [1.115]
proceedings taken in wrong court not invalid, [1.116]
transfer of work to, criteria, [19.31]
court, general powers
adjustment, rights, contributories, [1.155]
arrest, absconding contributory, [1.159]
assets, contributories, application of, [1.150]
calls on contributories, power to make, [1.152]
cumulative, [1.160]
debts to company due from contributory, [1.151]
delegation to liquidator, [1.161]
exclusion, creditors not proving in time, [1.154]
expenses, re, [1.157]
inspection, books by creditors etc, [1.156]
payment into bank, money due, [1.153]
settlement, list, contributories, [1.150]. *See also* contributories, *above*
stay, proceedings, [1.149]
creditors
committee, invitation to join, [6.330]
false representation to, officer/shadow director, [1.215]
information to, [6.237]–[6.246]
inspection, books, [1.156]
not proving in time, powers of court, [1.154]
order acts in favour, all, [1.131]
reports to, [6.323]–[6.326]
creditors' claims, generally, [6.726]–[6.749]
proving debt
admission for dividend, [6.731]
appeal against decision on, [6.732]
costs, [6.729]
exclusion by court, [6.735]
inspection, proofs, [6.730]
proof, submission, [6.727]
rejection for dividend, [6.731]
requirements, [6.728]

WINDING UP BY COURT, REGISTERED COMPANY – *cont.*
creditors' claims, generally, – *cont.*
proving debt – *cont.*
withdrawal, [6.734]
creditors' meeting. *See also* meetings, generally, *below*
adjournment
absence of chair, [6.794]
chair, by, [6.792]
proofs in, [6.795]
removal of liquidator/trustee, [6.793]
chair, [6.790], [6.791]
exclusions from, [6.805]–[6.807]
quorum, [6.789]
records, [6.809]
remote attendance, [6.811]
suspension, [6.796]
voting, [6.797]–[6.804]
creditors' rights, [6.797]
contributories' rights, [6.808]
requisite majorities, [6.803], [6.808]
scheme manager's rights, [6.798]
debt, proof, [6.726]–[6.735]. *See also* DEBT, PROOF
decisions, procedures for, [6.771]–[6.776]
meetings. See meetings, generally, *below*
notices, [6.777], [6.780]–[6.784]
remuneration, [6.785]
requisitioned decisions, [6.787], [6.788]
venue, [6.779]
voting, [6.778]
dismissal, petition, [1.12]
distribution to creditors, [6.750]–[6.769]
employees, power to make assets over to, [1.191]
expenses of winding up, payment from assets, [1.157]
false representation to, [1.215]
falsification of company's books by officer or contributory, [1.213]
final accounts, [6.866]
final meeting, duty of liquidator to summon, [1.147]
fraud in anticipation
creditors, of, transactions, [1.211]
officer of company/shadow director, by
acts constituting, [1.210]
defences, [1.210]
See also FRAUD
High Court jurisdiction, [1.115]
inability to pay debts, [1.120], [1.121]
inquiry into company's dealings application to court to summon persons to appear before court, [1.241], [1.242]
inspection, books by creditors etc, [1.156]
interim order, [1.126]
investigation procedures
official receiver, [1.133]
public examination, officers, [1.134], [1.135], [6.557]–[6.563]
statement, company's affairs, [1.132]
liquidation committee, [1.142]

WINDING UP BY COURT, REGISTERED COMPANY – *cont.*
liquidator
appointment
choice, meetings, creditors/contributories, [1.140], [6.327], [6.328]
court, by, [6.331]
court following administration/voluntary arrangement, [1.141]
notice, [6.334]
official receiver, functions re office of, [1.137]
provisional liquidator
powers, [1.136]
time, [1.136]
Secretary of State, by, [1.138], [6.332]
assets, hand-over, [6.335]
death, [6.342]
delegation, powers, court to, [1.161]
duties, [1.168], [1.169]
functions
company property, re
custody, [1.145]
vesting in liquidator, [1.146]
final meeting, duty to summon, [1.147]
general, [1.144]
nomination, [6.329]
powers, [1.168], [1.169]
provisional
appointment
deposit before order, [6.309]
eligible applicants, [6.308]
notice, [6.311]
order, [6.310]
termination, [6.314]
remuneration, [6.313]
security, [6.312]
release etc, [1.175], [6.344], [6.345]
removal etc, [1.173], [6.338]–[6.341]
resignation, [6.336]
security, costs, [6.333]
solicitation, rule against, [6.221], [6.262], [6.350]
summary remedy against delinquent liquidator, [1.216]. *See also* LIQUIDATOR
transactions, setting aside, [6.349]
vacation from office, [6.337]
ceasing to be qualified, [6.343]
duties, [6.348]
meetings, generally
adjournment
absence of chair, [6.794]
chair, by, [6.792]
proofs in, [6.795]
removal of liquidator/trustee, [6.793]
chair, [6.790], [6.791]
exclusions from, [6.805]–[6.807]
quorum, [6.789]
records, [6.809]
remote attendance, [6.811]
suspension, [6.796]
voting, [6.797]–[6.804]
creditors' rights, [6.797]

WINDING UP BY COURT, REGISTERED COMPANY – *cont.*
meetings, generally – *cont.*
voting, – *cont.*
contributories' rights, [6.808]
requisite majorities, [6.803], [6.808]
scheme manager's rights, [6.798]
misconduct, officer/shadow director, [1.212]
money due to company
order on contributory conclusive evidence, [1.153]
notification that company in liquidation, [1.192]
official receiver
accounts delivered to, [6.321]
EU proceedings
duty to notify registrar, [1.148]
functions re office of liquidator, [1.137]
investigation, [1.133]
petition
adjournment of hearing, [6.294]
compliance, certificate of, [6.287]
content, [6.280]
contributories, by, [6.300]–[6.307]
contributory, substitution for petitioner, [6.292]
creditor, substitution for petitioner, [6.292]
dismissal, [1.12], [6.298]
filing, [6.282]
injunction to restrain, [6.299]
list of appearances, [6.290]
notice, [6.285], [6.289]
persons to receive copies, [6.284], [6.286]
presentation, [6.282]
company subject to CVA/administration, [6.283]
substitution, order for, [6.293]
verification, [6.281]
winding up order, [6.295]–[6.297]
withdrawal, with permission, [6.288]
witness statement in opposition, [6.291]
preferential charge, goods distrained, [1.177]. *See also* PREFERENTIAL CHARGE
prosecution, delinquent officer/member, [1.222], [1.223]
public examination of officers
application, eligible persons, [1.134]
failure to attend, contempt of court, [1.135]
participants, [1.134]
public interest
grounds, petition, [1.123]
rectification, register of members after order, [1.150]
refusal, order, grounds, [1.126]
restraint, proceedings against company, [1.127]
Scotland. *See* SCOTLAND
SCE, registered office in GB, [1.125]
SE, registered office in GB, [1.124]
stamp duty, exempt documents, [1.194]
statement, company's affairs
accounts delivered to official receiver, [6.321]
contents, [1.132], [6.316]
CVL, [6.77]–[6.79]
disclosure, limited, [6.318]
expenses, [6.320]

WINDING UP BY COURT, REGISTERED COMPANY – *cont.*
statement, company's affairs – *cont.*
further disclosure, [6.322]
material omissions, [1.214]
notice requiring, [6.315]
persons who may be required, [1.132]
release from duty to submit, [6.319]
statement of concurrence, [6.317]
transitional provisions, [1.596]
statutory demand
content, [6.278]
stay, proceedings against company, [1.127], [1.131], [1.149]
surplus, distribution, [1.155]
transitional provisions/savings, [1.596]
WINDING UP, REGISTERED COMPANY
adjourned meetings, resolutions passed, [1.198]
affidavits. *See* AFFIDAVITS
attachment, effect, [1.187]
contracts, rescission, eligible applicants, [1.190]
contributories, liability
bankruptcy of contributory, effect, [1.78]
company registered under Companies Act, Pt XXII, Ch 8, [1.79]
contributory, meaning, [1.75]
death of member, in case of, [1.77]
directors etc with unlimited liability, [1.71]
limited company formerly unlimited, [1.73]
nature, [1.76]
past and present members, as, [1.70]
past directors, [1.72]
past shareholders, [1.72]
unlimited company formerly limited, [1.74]
court, by, specifically. *See* WINDING UP BY COURT, REGISTERED COMPANY
disclaimer
court, powers, [1.185], [1.186]
land subject to rentcharge, [1.182], [1.184]
leaseholds, [1.183], [1.186]
onerous property, [1.182], [1.185]
dissolution after, [1.205]–[1.209]. *See also* DISSOLUTION, COMPANY
distribution to creditors, [6.750]–[6.769]
evidence
commission for receiving, power to refer to refer, [1.201]
company's books as, [1.195]
execution against goods or land
effect, [1.187]
officers charged with (writs etc), duties, [1.188]
fees, [8.9], [8.20]
floating charge, property subject to, share of assets of unsecured creditors, [1.180], [8.68]
fraudulent trading during, [1.217], [1.219]
interest on debts, [1.193]
judicial notice, court documents, [1.200]
liquidators
corrupt inducement affecting appointment, [1.165]
disclaimer, onerous property, [1.182]
powers, [1.581]–[1.583]
returns, duty to make, enforcement, [1.171]
style and title, [1.164]

WINDING UP, REGISTERED COMPANY – *cont.*
pending liquidations, information, winding up not concluded within one year, [1.196]
Proceeds of Crime Act 2002 provisions, [17.242], [17.243]
special manager, powers of appointment of court, [1.181]
voluntary specifically. *See* WINDING UP, VOLUNTARY, REGISTERED COMPANY
wishes of creditors/contributories, court taking into account meetings to ascertain, [1.199]
wrongful trading during, [1.218], [1.219]
WINDING UP, UNREGISTERED COMPANY
circumstances, [1.225]
contributories, [1.230]
cumulative statutory provisions, [1.232]
inability to pay debts
debt unsatisfied after action brought, [1.227]
other cases in which inability deemed, [1.228]
unpaid creditor, £750/more, [1.226], [1.529]
jurisdiction, determination of principal place of business of company, [1.225]
oversea company, winding up though dissolved, [1.229]
restraint, proceedings, court, [1.231]
stay, proceedings
actions stayed on winding up order, [1.232]
court, powers, [1.231]
unregistered company, meaning, [1.224]
voluntary, in accordance with EC Regulation, [1.225]
WINDING UP, VOLUNTARY, REGISTERED COMPANY
See also LIQUIDATION, COMPANY GOING INTO
business of company, effect of resolution, [1.83]
circumstances, [1.80]
commencement, time, [1.82]
contributories, liability
bankruptcy of contributory, effect, [1.78]
company registered under Companies Act, Pt XXII, Ch 8, [1.79]
contributory, meaning, [1.75]
death of member, in case of, [1.77]
directors etc with unlimited liability, [1.71]
limited company formerly unlimited, [1.73]
nature, [1.76]
past and present members, as, [1.70]
past directors, [1.72]
past shareholders, [1.72]
unlimited company formerly limited, [1.74]
creditors' claims, generally
proving debt
admission for dividend, [6.731]
appeal against decision on, [6.732]
costs, [6.729]
exclusion by court, [6.735]
inspection, proofs, [6.730]
proof, submission, [6.727]
rejection for dividend, [6.731]
requirements, [6.728]
withdrawal, [6.734]

WINDING UP, VOLUNTARY, REGISTERED COMPANY – *cont.*
creditors' voluntary winding up
administration moving to, [1.575]
consideration for sale of company's property, shares etc
acceptance, [1.108]
dissent from arrangement, [1.109]
continuing for more than one year, company/creditors meetings at each year's end, [1.103]
court, reference of liquidator/contributory/creditor questions, [1.110]
creditors' meeting
adjournment
absence of chair, [6.794]
chair, by, [6.792]
proofs in, [6.795]
removal of liquidator/trustee, [6.793]
chair, [6.790], [6.791]
exclusions from, [6.805]–[6.807]
quorum, [6.789]
records, [6.809]
remote attendance, [6.811]
suspension, [6.796]
voting, [6.797]–[6.804]
creditors' rights, [6.797]
contributories' rights, [6.808]
requisite majorities, [6.803], [6.808]
scheme manager's rights, [6.798]
directors
cesser of powers on appointment of liquidator, exception, [1.87], [1.100]
powers not to be exercised where no liquidator appointed/nominated, [1.112]
statement of affairs to creditors, [1.96]
distribution, company's property, [1.105]
expenses, [1.113]
generally, [1.94]–[1.114]
final meeting prior to dissolution, [1.104]
liquidation committee, appointment, [1.98]
liquidator
account, final, [6.255]
meeting, [1.104]
appointment
company, by, [6.207]
court, by, [1.106], [6.249]
nomination, creditors/company, [1.97], [3.221], [6.237]–[6.246]
notice by liquidator of, [1.107]
death, [6.256]
general meeting, requirement to summon at each year's end, [1.103]
information to Secretary of State, [8.41]
insolvency practitioner, loss, qualification, [6.217]
none appointed/nominated by company, [1.112]
powers, [6.263]
release on
Secretary of State, by, [6.260]
removal
ceasing to be qualified, [6.257]

WINDING UP, VOLUNTARY, REGISTERED COMPANY – *cont.*
creditors' voluntary winding up – *cont.*
liquidator – *cont.*
removal – *cont.*
court, powers, [1.106], [6.254]
creditors' by, [6.253]
resignation
grounds, [6.252]
notice, [6.252]
setting aside certain transactions by liquidator, powers of court, [6.261]
solicitation, rule against, [6.262]
vacancy by death etc, power of creditors to fill, [1.101], [6.248]
vacation, office
on making winding up order, [6.258]
See also LIQUIDATOR
members' voluntary winding up
account, final, [6.214], [6.215]
conversion from, [1.93], [1.103]
distinguished, [1.86]
shares etc, consideration, sale, company's property, [1.108], [1.109]
stamp duty, exempt documents, [1.194]
statement of affairs
accounts, delivery of, [6.235]
disclosure, limited, [6.233]
expenses, [6.234], [6.236]
liquidator, by, [6.229], [6.230]
requirements, [6.231]
statement of concurrence, [6.232]
debt, proof, [6.726]–[6.735]. *See also* DEBT, PROOF
decisions, procedures for, [6.771]–[6.776]
meetings. See meetings, generally, *below*
notices, [6.777], [6.780]–[6.784]
remuneration, [6.785]
requisitioned decisions, [6.787], [6.788]
venue, [6.779]
voting, [6.778]
dissolution after, [1.205]
distribution to creditors, [6.750]–[6.769]
employees, company
power to make assets over to, [1.191]
extraordinary resolution, [1.80]
false representation to creditor, [1.215]
falsification, company's books
officer/contributory, [1.213]
fraud in anticipation
creditors, of, transactions, [1.211]
director, disqualification, [4.5]
officer of company/shadow director, by
acts constituting, [1.210]
defences, [1.210]
See also FRAUD
FCA and PRA, participation by, [18.274]
insurers, of, [18.275], [18.276]
liquidator
corrupt inducement affecting appointment, [1.165]
creditors' voluntary winding up specifically. *See* creditor's voluntary winding up, *above*

WINDING UP, VOLUNTARY, REGISTERED COMPANY – *cont.*
liquidator – *cont.*
disqualification order, [1.171]
members' voluntary winding up specifically. *See* members' voluntary winding up, *above*
powers/duties, [1.166]
release etc, [1.174]
removal from office, [1.106], [1.172]
returns, enforcement of duty to make, [1.171]
solicitation, rule against, [6.221], [6.262]
style and title, [1.164]
summary remedy against delinquent liquidator, [1.216]. *See also* LIQUIDATOR
members' voluntary winding up
consideration for sale, company's property
shares etc
acceptance, [1.108]
dissent from arrangement, [1.109]
court, reference of questions by liquidator, contributory or creditor, [1.110]
creditors' voluntary winding up
conversion to, [1.93], [6.227]
distinguished, [1.86]
directors' powers not to be exercised where no liquidator appointed or nominated, [1.112]
distribution of company's property, [1.105]
expenses, [1.113]
final meeting prior to dissolution, [1.91]
general meeting, each year's end, [1.90]
generally, [1.87]–[1.93], [1.105]–[1.114]
liquidator
appointment
company, by, [6.207]
court, by, [1.106], [6.209]
general meeting, at, [1.87]
notice by liquidator of, [1.107]
death, [6.216]
final meeting prior to dissolution, [1.91]
general meeting, requirement to summon, [1.90]
insolvency practitioner
loss, qualification as, [6.217]
none appointed/nominated by company, [1.112]
release
Secretary of State, by, [6.219]
removal
company meeting, by, [6.213]
court, by, [1.106], [6.212]
remuneration, [6.867]–[6.890]
resignation
grounds, [6.211]
notice, [6.211]
security
cost of, [6.210]

WINDING UP, VOLUNTARY, REGISTERED COMPANY – *cont.*
members' voluntary winding up – *cont.*
liquidator – *cont.*
setting aside certain transactions by liquidator, powers of court, [6.220]
solicitation, rule against, [6.221]
statement when company unable to pay debts
duty, [1.92]
procedure, [1.92], [3.221]
vacancy, power to fill, [1.88]
vacation of office
duties, [6.218]
See also LIQUIDATOR
shares etc, consideration, sale, company's property, [1.108]
statutory declaration of solvency, [6.206]
meetings, generally
adjournment
absence of chair, [6.794]
chair, by, [6.792]
proofs in, [6.795]
removal of liquidator/trustee, [6.793]
chair, [6.790], [6.791]
exclusions from, [6.805]–[6.807]
quorum, [6.789]
records, [6.809]
remote attendance, [6.811]
suspension, [6.796]
voting, [6.797]–[6.804]
creditors' rights, [6.797]
contributories' rights, [6.808]
requisite majorities, [6.803], [6.808]
scheme manager's rights, [6.798]
misconduct, officer/shadow director, [1.212]
notice of resolution, [1.80], [1.81]
notification that company in liquidation, [1.192]
prosecution, delinquent officer/member, [1.222], [1.223]
resolution, [1.80], [1.262]
Scotland. *See* SCOTLAND
setting aside certain transactions by liquidator
court, powers, [6.220], [6.261]
share transfers, avoidance
after resolution, [1.84]
solvency, statutory declaration, [1.85]
special resolution, [1.80]
statement, company's affairs
CVL, [6.77]–[6.79]
material omissions, [1.214]
status of company, effect of resolution, [1.83]

WRONGFUL TRADING
director, disqualification, [4.23]
winding up of registered company, during, [1.218], [1.219]